2008 Standard Catalog of®

FIREARMS

THE COLLECTOR'S PRICE & REFERENCE GUIDE

18TH EDITION

DAN SHIDELER

Front Cover Photo

Top to bottom: Nylon 66 (AB) "Apache Black" semi-auto, chromed metal parts and black stock, 14-shot tube magazine, 4 lbs., 1962-1984; Nylon 11, Mohawk brown, bolt action, blued metal parts, 6- or 10-shot box magazine, 4-1/2 lbs.,1962-1964; Nylon "Apache 77," bright green stock, spray coated matte black metal parts. Produced exclusively for K-Mart 1987-1989. The known range of serial numbers covers a spread of 146,000+; however, it is not known if these rifles were numbered consecutively throughout production or whether other models shared the number block.

Published by

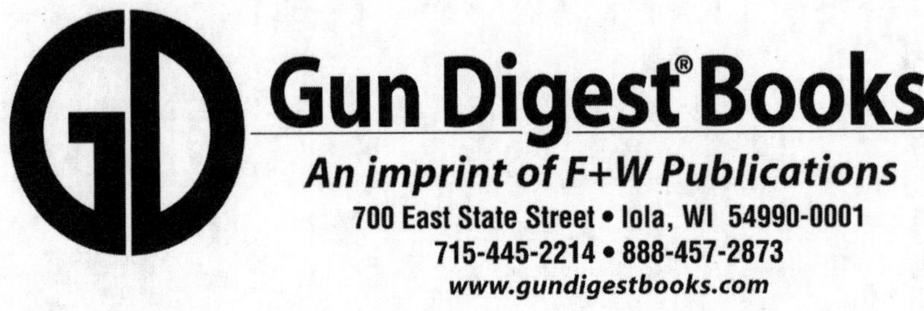

Our toll-free number to place an order
or obtain a free catalog is 800-258-0929.

ISSN 1520-4928

ISBN 13: 978-0-89689-608-6
ISBN 10: 0-89689-608-0

Designed by Patsy Howell and Tom Nelsen
Edited by Dan Shideler

Printed in the United States of America

CONTENTS

Acknowledgments 11
Photo Credits 12
Auction House Credits 12
Contributing Editors 13
Introduction 14
Grading System 14
Pricing 15
Additional Considerations 15
About the Editor 16
Better Than Book: Factors that Add to the Value of a Firearm 17
An Introduction to Firearms Auctions 19
- The AuctionArms.com Perspective 19
- The Rock Island Auctions Perspective 20
- Internet Gun Sales: The Buyer's Perspective 21

Gun Digest® Enters Its Seventh Decade 23
Alphabetical Listings by Manufacturer 24
Firearms Trade Names 1412
Firearms Manufacturers and Importers 1421
Gun Collectors Associations 1424
Bibliography 1425
Manufacturer & Model Index 1427

FIREARMS DIRECTORY

A-SQUARE 23
A. J. ORDNANCE 23
A.A. 23
A.A.A. 23
A & R SALES SOUTH 24
ABADIE 24
ABBEY, F.J. & CO. 24
ABBEY, GEORGE T. 24
ABESSER & MERKEL 24
ACCU-MATCH 25
ACCU-TEK 25
ACHA 27
ACME 27
ACME ARMS 27
ACME HAMMERLESS 27
ACTION 27
ACTION ARMS LTD. 28
ADAMS 28
ADAMY GEBRUDER 28
ADIRONDACK ARMS CO. OR A.S. BABBITT CO. 29
ADLER 29
ADVANCED SMALL ARMS INDUSTRIES 29
ADVANTAGE ARMS U.S.A., INC. 29
AERO 30
AETNA ARMS CO. 30
AFC 30
AFFERBACH, W. A. 31
AGNER (SAXHOJ PRODUCTS INC.) 31
AGUIRRE 31
AGUIRRE Y ARANZABAL (AYA) 31
AIR MATCH 35
AJAX ARMY 35
ALAMO RANGER 35
ALASKA 35
ALDAZABAL 35
ALERT 36
ALEXIA 36
ALFA 36
ALKARTASUNA FABRICA DE ARMAS 36
ALL RIGHT FIREARMS CO. 36
ALLEN, ETHAN 36
ALLEN & THURBER 41
ALLEN & WHEELOCK 41
ALLEN FIREARMS 41
ALPHA ARMS CO. 41
ALSOP, C.R. 41
AMAC 41
AMERICAN ARMS 42
AMERICAN ARMS CO. 42
AMERICAN ARMS, INC. 44
AMERICAN BARLOCK WONDER 48
AMERICAN DERRINGER CORP. 48
AMERICAN FIRE ARMS MFG. CO., INC. 51
AMERICAN FRONTIER FIREARMS 52
AMERICAN GUN CO., NEW YORK 52
AMERICAN HISTORICAL FOUNDATION 52
AMERICAN INDUSTRIES 53
AMERICAN INTERNATIONAL 53
AMERICAN WESTERN ARMS INC. (AWA) 53
AMES, N.P. PISTOLS 53
AMES SWORD CO. 54
AMT 54
ANCION & CIE 58
ANCION MARX 58
ANDERSON 59
ANDRUS & OSBORN 59
ANSCHUTZ 59
ANTI GARROTTER 65
APACHE 65
APALOZO HERMANOS 65
AR-7 INDUSTRIES 66
ARCUS 66
ARIZAGA, G. 66
ARIZMENDI ZULAICA 66
ARIZMENDI, FRANCISCO 66

ARMALITE, INC. 69
ARMAS DE FUEGO 71
ARMERO ESPECIALISTAS 71
ARMES DE CHASSE 72
ARMINEX LTD. 72
ARMINUS 72
ARMITAGE INTERNATIONAL, LTD. . . 72
ARMS CORPORATION OF THE PHILIPPINES 73
ARMSCO FIREARMS CORP. 75
ARMSCORP OF AMERICA 76
ARMY & NAVY CO-OPERATIVE SOCIETY 77
ARNOLD ARMS 77
AROSTEGUI, EULOGIO 78
ARRIETA S.L. 79
ARRIZABALAGA, HIJOS DE C. 81
ARSENAL, INC. 82
ASCASO 82
ASHEVILLE ARMORY 82
ASHTON, PETER & WILLIAM 82
ASTON, H./H. ASTON & CO. PISTOLS 82
ASTRA-UNCETA SA 83
ATCSA 87
ATKIN, HENRY 87
AUBREY, A.J. 87
AUER, B. 87
AUGUSTA MACHINE WORKS 87
AUSTIN & HALLECK, INC. 87
AUSTRALIAN AUTOMATIC ARMS LTD. 88
AUSTRIAN MILITARY FIREARMS . . 88
AUTAUGA ARMS INC. 90
AUTO MAG 90
AUTO ORDNANCE CORP. 91
AUTO POINTER 94
AXTELL RIFLE CO. 94
AZPIRI 94
B.R.F. 95
BABBIT, A. S. 95
BABCOCK, MOSES 95
BACON ARMS CO. 95
BAER CUSTOM, LES 95
BAFORD, ARMS, INC. 103
BAIKAL 103
BAILONS GUNMAKERS, LTD. 104
BAKER GAS SEAL 104
BAKER GUN & FORGING CO. 104
BAKER, M.A. 106
BAKER, THOMAS 106
BAKER, WILLIAM 106
BALL REPEATING CARBINE 106
BALLARD PATENT ARMS 107
BALLARD RIFLE AND CARTRIDGE CO. 109
BALLARD, C. H. 110
BALLESTER—MOLINA 110
BARNETT 110
BARRETT F.A. MFG. CO. 110
BARRETT, J. B. AND A.B. & CO. . . 111
BAR-STO PRECISION MACHINE . . 111
BASCARAN, MARTIN A. 111
BAUER F. A. CORP. 112
BAYARD 112
BAYONNE, MANUFACTURE D'ARMES 112
BEATTIE, J. 115
BEAUMONT 115
BEAUMONT, ADAMS 115
BEAUMONT-VITALI 115
BECKER AND HOLLANDER 115
BEEMAN PRECISION ARMS, INC. . 115
BEERSTECHER, FREDERICK 116
BEESLEY, FREDERICK 116
BEHOLLA 116
BEISTEGUI, HERMANOS 116
BENELLI 116
BENTLEY, DAVID 123
BENTLEY, JOSEPH 123
BENTZ 123
BERETTA, DR. FRANCO 123
BERETTA, PIETRO 124
BERGER, JEAN MARIUS 160
BERGMANN, THEODOR 160
BERN, WAFFENFABRIK 163
BERNARDELLI, VINCENZO 163
BERNARDON MARTIN 168
BERNEDO, VINCENZO 168
BERSA 169
BERTHIER 170
BERTRAND, JULES 171
BERTUZZI 171
BIGHORN ARMS CO. 171
BIGHORN RIFLE CO. 171
BILHARZ, HALL & CO. 172
BILLINGHURST, WILLIAM 172
BILLINGS 172
BINGHAM LTD. 172
BISMARCK 172
BITTERLICH, FRANK J. 172
BITTNER, GUSTAV 173
BLAKE, J. H. 173
BLANCH, JOHN 173
BLAND, THOMAS & SONS 173
BLASER JAGDWAFFEN 173
BLISS & GOODYEAR 175
BLISS, F. D. 175
BLISSETT 175
BLUNT & SYMS 175
BODEO 176
BOLUMBURO, G. 176
BOND 177
BOND ARMS INC. 177
BOOM 178
BORCHARDT 178
BORSIG 178
BOSIS, LUCIANO 178
BOSS & CO. 178
BOSWELL, CHARLES 178
BOSWORTH, B. M. 178
BOWEN CLASSIC ARMS CORP. . . 178
BRAENDLIN ARMOURY 179
BRAND 179
BREDA, ERNESTO 179
BREN 10 180
BRETTON 180
BRIGGS, H. A. 180
BRILEY MANUFACTURING INC. . . 180
BRITISH DOUBLES 181
BRIXIA 185
BRNO ARMS 185
BROLIN ARMS 187
BRONCO 191
BROOKLYN F. A. CO. 191
BROWN CUSTOM, ED 192
BROWN PRODUCTS, INC., ED 192
BROWN MANUFACTURING CO. . . 194
BROWN PRECISION, INC. 194
BROWN, A.A. 195
BROWN, DAVID MCKAY 195
BROWN, E.A. MANUFACTURING CO. 195
BROWNING ARMS CO. 195
BRUCE & DAVIS 239
BRUCHET 239
BRUFF, R.P. 239
BRYCO ARMS 239
BSA GUNS LTD. 239
BUCO 241
BUDISCHOWSKY 241
BUL TRANSMARK LTD. 241
BULLARD REPEATING ARMS CO. . 241
BULLDOG SINGLE-SHOT PISTOL . 242
BURGESS GUN CO. 242
BURGSMULLER, K. 242
BURNSIDE RIFLE CO. 242
BUSHMASTER FIREARMS INC. . . . 243
BUTLER, WM. S. 244
BUTTERFIELD, JESSE 244
CABANAS, INDUSTRIAS S.A. 245
CABELAS, INC. 245
CALICO 245
CAMEX-BLASER USA, INC. 245
CAMPO GIRO 245
CARCANO 246
CARD, S. W. 246
CARLTON, M. 246
CASARTELLI, CARLO 246
CASE WILLARD & CO. 246
CASPIAN ARMS, LTD. 246
CASULL ARMS, INC. 247
CENTURY GUN COMPANY/NEW CENTURY MANFACTURING . . . 247
CENTURY INTERNATIONAL ARMS CO. 247
CETME 248
CHAMELOT-DELVIGNE 248
CHAMPLIN FIREARMS 249
CHAPMAN C. 249
CHAPMAN CHARLES 249
CHAPMAN, G. & J. 249
CHAPUIS ARMES 249

CHARLEVILLE 249
CHARTER 2000, INC. 249
CHARTER ARMS CORP. 250
CHASSEPOT 252
CHEYTAC 252
CHICAGO F. A. CO. 253
CHIPMUNK RIFLES/ROGUE RIFLE CO. 253
CHRISTENSEN ARMS 253
CHURCHILL 254
CHURCHILL, E. J. LTD. 255
CHYLEWSKI, WITOLD 255
CIMARRON F. A. CO. 256
CLAPP, HOFFMAN & CO. CLAPP, GATES & CO. RIFLES 261
CLARK, F. H. 261
CLASSIC DOUBLES 261
CLEMENT, CHAS. 262
CLERKE PRODUCTS 263
COBRA ENTERPRISES, INC. 264
COBRAY INDUSTRIES 265
COCHRAN TURRET 265
CODY, MICHAEL & SONS 265
COFER, T. W. 265
COGSWELL 265
COGSWELL & HARRISON, LTD. .. 266
COLT'S PATENT FIRE ARMS MANUFACTURING COMPANY . 266
COLT REVOLVING LONG GUNS 1837-1847 267
COLT WALKER-DRAGOON MODELS 267
COLT SIDE HAMMER MODELS .. 270
COLT SIDE HAMMER LONG GUNS 271
COLT PERCUSSION REVOLVERS . 272
COLT METALLIC CARTRIDGE CONVERSIONS 274
COLT ANTIQUE LONG ARMS 286
COLT DOUBLE-ACTION REVOLVERS 291
COLT LICENSED AND UNLICENSED FOREIGN-MADE 1911A1 AND VARIATIONS 311
COLT ENHANCED GOVERNMENT MODELS 312
COLT MODEL 1911A1 SEMI-AUTOMATIC PISTOL 312
COLT .22 RIMFIRE SEMI-AUTOMATIC PISTOLS ... 320
COLT WOODSMAN 320
COLT MODERN LONG ARMS 325
COLT CUSTOM SHOP 329
COLT COMMEMORATIVES 331
COLT REPRODUCTION PERCUSSION REVOLVERS 334
COLT BLACKPOWDER ARMS 335
COLTON MANUFACTURING CO. .. 337
COLUMBIA ARMORY 337
COLUMBUS F. A. MFG. CO. 338
COMANCHE (ALSO SEE FIRESTORM) 338
COMBLAIN 338
COMMANDO ARMS 338
COMPETITOR CORP. 338
CONNECTICUT ARMS CO. 339
CONNECTICUT VALLEY ARMS CO. 339
CONSTABLE, R. 342
CONTENTO/VENTUR 342
CONTINENTAL 343
CONTINENTAL ARMS CO. 343
COOK & BROTHER RIFLES AND CARBINES 343
COONAN ARMS CO. 344
COOPER ARMS 345
COOPER, J. M. & CO. 346
COOPERATIVA OBRERA 346
COPELAND, FRANK 346
COSMI, A. & F. 346
COSMOPOLITAN ARMS CO. 346
COWLES & SON 346
CPA RIFLES 346
CRAUSE, CARL PHILLIP MUSKETS AND RIFLES 347
CRESCENT F. A. CO. 347
CRISPIN, SILAS 352
CROSSFIRE 353
CRUCELEGUI, HERMANOS 353
CUMMINGS & WHEELER 353
CUMMINGS, O. S. 353
CUSTOM GUN GUILD 353
CZ 353
CZ 366
D (ANCHOR) C 367
D. W. M. 367
DAEWOO 367
DAISY 368
DAKIN GUN CO. 368
DAKOTA ARMS, INC. 369
DALY, CHARLES 373
DAN ARMS OF AMERICA 381
DANCE & BROTHERS CONFEDERATE REVOLVERS ... 381
DANDOY, C/A LIEGE 381
DANSK REKYLRIFFEL SYNDIKAT . 381
DARDICK CORP. 383
DARLING, B. & B. M. 383
DARNE, S. A. 383
DAUDETEAU 383
DAVENPORT FIREARMS CO. 383
DAVIDSON F. A. 384
DAVIS, A. JR. 384
DAVIS, N.R. & CO. DAVIS, N.R. & SONS 384
DAVIS & BOZEMAN 385
DAVIS INDUSTRIES 385
DAVIS-WARNER ARMS CORPORATION 387
DAW, G. H. 388
DEANE, ADAMS & DEANE 388
DEANE-HARDING 388
DECKER, WILHELM 388
DEFIANCE ANTI-BANDIT GUN ... 388
DEMIRETT, J. 389
DEMRO 389
DERINGER REVOLVER AND PISTOL CO. 389
DERINGER, HENRY RIFLES AND PISTOLS 389
DESENZANI, LABORATORIES ARMI 391
DESERT EAGLE/ISRAELI MILITARY INDUSTRIES 391
DESERT INDUSTRIES 395
DESTROYER CARBINE 395
DETONICS MANUFACTURING CORP. 395
DETONICS USA, LLC 396
DEUTSCHE WERKE 396
DEVISME, F. P. 397
DIAMOND 397
DICKINSON 397
DICKINSON, E. L. & J. 397
DICKSON, JOHN 397
DICKSON, NELSON & CO. 397
DIMICK, H.E. 397
DOMINGO ACHA 397
DOMINO 397
DORMUS 398
DORNHAUS & DIXON 398
DORNHEIM, G.C. 398
DOUBLESTAR, CORP. 398
DOUG TURNBULL RESTORATION, INC. 399
DOWNSIZER CORPORATION 400
DPMS 400
DREYSE 404
DRISCOLL, J.B. 404
DSA, INC. 404
DUBIEL ARMS CO. 406
DUMOULIN 406
DURLOV 408
DUSEK, F. 408
E.M.F. CO., INC. 409
EAGLE ARMS 409
EAGLE ARMS CO. 409
ECHAVE & ARIZMENDI 410
ECHEVERRIA, STAR-BONIFACIO SA 411
ECHEVERRIA 415
ECLIPSE 416
84 GUN CO. 416
EL DORADO ARMS 416
ELGIN CUTLASS 416
ELLS, JOSIAH 417
ENDERS, CARL 417
ENFIELD AMERICAN, INC. 417
ENFIELD ROYAL SMALL ARMS FACTORY 417
ENGLISH MILITARY FIREARMS . 417
ENTREPRISE ARMS, INC. 420

ERA . . . 421
ERICHSON, G. . . . 421
ERMA WERKE WAFFENFABRIK . . . 421
ERQUIAGA . . . 423
ERRASTI, A. . . . 424
ESCODIN, M. . . . 424
ESCORT . . . 424
ESPIRIN, HERMANOS . . . 424
EUROARMS OF AMERICA . . . 425
EUROPEAN AMERICAN ARMORY CORP. . . . 426
EVANS REPEATING RIFLE CO. . . . 432
EVANS, J. E. . . . 433
EVANS, WILLIAM . . . 433
EXCAM . . . 433
EXCEL INDUSTRIES . . . 434
EXEL ARMS OF AMERICA . . . 434
F&T . . . 435
F.A.S. . . . 435
F.I.E. . . . 435
F.L. SELBSTLADER . . . 438
FABARM . . . 438
FABBRI, ARMI . . . 442
FABRIQUE NATIONALE . . . 442
FAIRBANKS, A. B. . . . 446
FALCON FIREARMS . . . 446
FAMARS, A. & S. . . . 446
FARROW ARMS CO. . . . 448
FAYETTEVILLE ARMORY PISTOLS AND RIFLES . . . 449
FEATHER INDUSTRIES, INC. . . . 449
FEDERAL ENGINEERING CORP. . . . 450
FEDERAL ORDNANCE, INC. . . . 450
FEG (FEGYVER ES GAZKESZULEKGYAR) . . . 451
FEINWERKBAU . . . 453
FEMARU . . . 454
FERLACH . . . 454
FERLIB . . . 455
FERRY, ANDREWS & CO. . . . 455
FIALA ARMS COMPANY . . . 455
FINNISH LION . . . 456
FIOCCHI OF AMERICA, INC. . . . 456
FIREARMS INTERNATIONAL . . . 456
FIRESTORM . . . 456
FLETCHER BIDWELL, LLC . . . 457
FLORENCE ARMORY . . . 457
FNH USA, INC. . . . 457
FOEHL & WEEKS . . . 460
FOEHL, C. . . . 461
FOGARTY . . . 461
FOLSOM, H&D ARMS CO. . . . 461
FOLSOM, H. . . . 461
FOREHAND & WADSWORTH . . . 461
FOWLER, B. JR. . . . 462
FOX, A. H. . . . 462
FRANCHI, L. . . . 464
FRANCOTTE, A. . . . 471
FRANKLIN, C. W. . . . 473
FRANKONIAJAGD . . . 474
FRASER F. A. CORP. . . . 474
FRASER, DANIEL & SON . . . 474
FREEDOM ARMS . . . 474
FREEMAN, AUSTIN T. . . . 476
FRENCH MILITARY FIREARMS . . . 476
FRENCH STATE . . . 478
FRIGON . . . 478
FROMMER . . . 478
FRUHWIRTH . . . 478
FUNK, CHRISTOPH . . . 478
FURR ARMS . . . 479
FYRBERG, ANDREW . . . 479
G M . . . 480
GABBET-FAIRFAX, H. . . . 480
GABILONDO Y CIA . . . 480
GABILONDO Y URRESTI . . . 480
GALAND & SOMMERVILLE . . . 482
GALAND, C.F. . . . 482
GALEF . . . 482
GALENA INDUSTRIES INC. . . . 482
GALESI, INDUSTRIA ARMI . . . 484
GALIL . . . 485
GALLAGER . . . 485
GAMBA, RENATO . . . 485
GARAND . . . 488
GARATE, ANITUA . . . 489
GARATE, HERMANOS . . . 490
GARBI . . . 490
GARCIA . . . 491
GARRET, J. & F. CO. . . . 491
GASSER, LEOPOLD . . . 492
GATLING ARMS CO. . . . 492
GAUCHER . . . 492
GAULOIS . . . 492
GAVAGE, A. . . . 492
GAZANAGA, ISIDRO . . . 493
GECO . . . 493
GEHA . . . 493
GEM . . . 493
GENEZ, A. G. . . . 493
GENSCHOW, G. . . . 493
GEORGIA ARMORY . . . 493
GERING, H. M. & CO. . . . 494
GERMAN WWII MILITARY RIFLES 494
GERSTENBERGER & EBERWEIN . . 494
GEVARM . . . 494
GIB . . . 494
GIBBS . . . 494
GIBBS, J. & G. LATER GIBBS, GEORGE . . . 494
GIBBS GUNS, INC. . . . 495
GIBBS RIFLE COMPANY . . . 495
GIBBS TIFFANY & CO. . . . 495
GILLAM & MILLER . . . 495
GILLESPIE . . . 495
GLAZE, W. & CO. . . . 495
GLISENTI . . . 495
GLOCK . . . 496
GODDARD . . . 500
GOLDEN EAGLE . . . 501
GONCZ CO. . . . 501
GOUDRY, J.F. . . . 502
GOVERNOR . . . 502
GRABNER G. . . . 502
GRAND PRECISION, FABRIQUE D'ARMES DE . . . 502
GRANGER, G. . . . 503
GRANT, STEPHEN . . . 503
GRAS . . . 503
GREAT WESTERN ARMS COMPANY . . . 503
GREEN, E. . . . 504
GREENE . . . 504
GREENER, W. W. LTD. . . . 504
GREIFELT & CO. . . . 504
GRENDEL, INC. . . . 505
GRIFFIN & HOWE . . . 506
GRIFFON . . . 506
GRISWOLD & GRIER . . . 506
GRISWOLD & GUNNISON . . . 506
GROSS ARMS CO. . . . 506
GRUBB, J. C. & CO. . . . 506
GRULLA . . . 506
GUEDES-CASTRO . . . 506
GUERINI, CAESAR . . . 507
GUIDE LAMP . . . 508
GUION, T. F. . . . 508
GULIKERS, V./A LIEGE . . . 508
GUNWORKS LTD. . . . 508
GUSTAF, CARL . . . 508
GWYN & CAMPBELL . . . 508
H-S PRECISION, INC. . . . 509
H.J.S. INDUSTRIES, INC. . . . 509
HAENEL, C. G. . . . 510
HAFDASA . . . 510
HAHN, WILLIAM . . . 511
HAKIM . . . 511
HALE & TULLER . . . 511
HALE, H. J. . . . 511
HALL, ALEXANDER . . . 511
HALL-NORTH . . . 511
HAMBUSH, JOSEPH . . . 512
HAMILTON RIFLE COMPANY . . . 512
HAMMERLI, SA . . . 514
HAMMERLI-WALTHER . . . 516
HAMMOND BULLDOG . . . 517
HAMMOND, GRANT MFG. CO. . . . 517
HANKINS, WILLIAM . . . 517
H&R 1871, LLC . . . 517
HANUS, BILL . . . 518
HARPERS FERRY ARMORY MUSKETS AND CARBINES . . . 518
HARRINGTON & RICHARDSON, INC. . . . 520
HARRIS GUNWORKS . . . 533
HARTFORD ARMS & EQUIPMENT CO. . . . 535
HATFIELD RIFLE COMPANY . . . 536
HAVILAND & GUNN . . . 536
HAWES . . . 536
HAWES & WAGGONER . . . 538
HAWKEN . . . 538
HDH, SA. . . . 538

HEAVY EXPRESS INC. 538
HECKLER & KOCH 539
HEINZELMANN, C.E. 548
HEISER, CARL 548
HELFRICHT 548
HELLIS, CHARLES 548
HENRION & DASSY 548
HENRY, ALEXANDER 548
HENRY 548
HENRY REPEATING ARMS COMPANY 549
HERITAGE MANUFACTURING, INC. 550
HEROLD 551
HERTER'S 551
HESSE ARMS 551
HEYM, F. W. 553
HI-POINT FIREARMS 555
HIGGINS, J. C. 556
HIGH STANDARD MANUFACTURING CORPORATION 557
HILL, W.J. 577
HILLIARD, D. H. 577
HINO-KOMURA 577
HODGKINS, D. C. & SONS 577
HOFER, P. 578
HOFFMAN, LOUIS 578
HOLDEN, C. B. 578
HOLECK, EMANUEL 578
HOLLAND & HOLLAND, LTD. 578
HOLLIS & SONS 578
HOLLOWAY ARMS CO. 578
HOLMES FIREARMS 578
HOOD F. A. CO. 579
HOPKINS & ALLEN 579
HORSLEY, THOMAS 579
HOTCHKISS 579
HOWA MACHINE COMPANY 579
HOWARD-WHITNEY 581
HUGLU 581
HUNGARY 583
HUNT 583
HUNTER ARMS CO. 583
HUSQVARNA 583
HYDE & SHATTUCK 584
HY-HUNTER, INC. 584
HYPER 584
I.G.I. 585
IAB 585
IAI-AMERICAN LEGENDS 585
IAR 585
IGA 585
INDIAN ARMS CORP. 586
INDUSTRIA ARMI GALESI 586
INGLIS, JOHN & COMPANY 586
INGRAM 587
INTERARMS 587
INTERDYNAMICS OF AMERICA 588
INTRATEC USA, INC. 589
IRVING, W. 589
IRWINDALE ARMS, INC. 589
ISRAELI MILITARY INDUSTRIES 589
ITHACA GUN CO. 589
IVER JOHNSON ARMS, INC. 602
IXL 606
JACQUESMART, JULES 607
JACQUITH, ELIJAH 607
JAGER WAFFENFABIK 607
JAPANESE STATE MILITARY WEAPONS 607
JEFFERY, W. J. & CO. LTD. 607
JENISON, J. & CO. 608
JENKS CARBINE 608
JENKS-HERKIMER 608
JENKS-MERRILL 608
JENNINGS 608
JENNINGS F. A., INC. 608
JERICHO 609
JIEFFCO 609
JOHNSON AUTOMATIC RIFLE 609
JOHNSON, STAN, BYE & CO. 609
JOSEF JESCHER 609
JOSLYN 609
JOSLYN FIREARMS COMPANY 610
JURRAS, LEE 610
JUSTICE, P. S. 610
K.F.C. 611
KAHR ARMS 611
KASSNAR IMPORTS, INC. 614
KBI, INC. 614
KDF, INC. 614
KEBERST INTERNATIONAL 615
KEL-TEC CNC INDUSTRIES 615
KEMPER, SHRIVER & COMPANY 616
KENDALL, INTERNATIONAL 616
KENDALL, NICANOR 617
KENO 617
KERR 617
KESSLER ARMS CORPORATION 617
KETTNER, EDWARD 617
KIMBALL ARMS COMPANY 617
KIMBER MFG., INC. 617
KIMBER OF AMERICA 638
KIMBER OF OREGON, INC. 638
KING PIN 638
KIRRIKALE, ENDUSTRISI 638
KLIPZIG & COMPANY 638
KNICKERBOCKER 638
KNIGHT RIFLES 638
KNIGHT'S MANUFACTURING CO. 639
KOHOUT & SPOLECNOST 640
KOLB, HENRY M. 641
KOLIBRI 641
KOMMER, THEODOR WAFFENFABRIK 641
KONGSBERG 642
KORRIPHILIA 642
KORTH 642
KRAG JORGENSEN 643
KRAUSER, ALFRED 643
KRICO 643
KRIDER, J. H. 645
KRIEGHOFF, HEINRICH, GUN CO. 645
KRNKA, KAREL 648
KROPATSCHEK 648
KSN INDUSTRIES 648
KUFAHL, G. L. 649
KYNOCH GUN FACTORY 649
LAGRESE 650
LAHTI 650
LAKELANDER 650
LAMB, H. C. & CO. 650
LAMES 650
LANBER ARMAS S.A. 651
LANCASTER, CHARLES 651
LANG, J. 652
LANGENHAN, FRIEDRICH 652
LAR MFG. CO. 653
LASALLE 654
LASERAIM ARMS 654
LAURONA 654
LAW ENFORCEMENT ORDNANCE CORP. 657
LAZZERONI ARMS COMPANY 657
LE FORGERON 658
LE FRANCAIS 658
LE MAT 659
LE PAGE SA. 660
LEBEAU COURALLY 660
LEBEL 660
LEE FIREARMS CO. 660
LEECH & RIGDON 661
LEE-ENFIELD 661
LEE-METFORD 661
LEFAUCHAUX, CASIMER & EUGENE 661
LEFEVER ARMS CO. 661
LEFEVER, D. M., SONS & COMPANY 663
LEMAN, H. E. 663
LEONARD, G. 663
LES, INC. 664
LEWIS, G.E. 664
LIDDLE & KAEDING 664
LIEGEOISE D ARMES 664
LIGNOSE 664
LILLIPUT 665
LINDE A. 665
LINDSAY, JOHN P. 665
LINS, A. F. 666
LITTLE SHARPS RIFLE MFG. CO. 666
LJUNGMAN 666
LJUTIC INDUSTRIES 666
LLAMA 667
LOEWE, LUDWIG & CO. 671
LOHNER, C. 672
LOMBARD, H. C. & CO. 672
LONDON ARMOURY COMPANY 672
LONE STAR RIFLE COMPANY 672
LORCIN ENGINEERING CO., INC. 672
LOWELL ARMS CO. 673
LOWER, J. P. 673

LUGERS 673
LUNA 684
LYMAN 685
M.O.A. CORP. 686
MAB 686
MAC 686
MAS 686
MACNAUGHTON & SON 686
MADSEN 686
MAGNUM RESEARCH, INC. 686
MAKAROV 686
MALIN, F. E. 687
MALTBY, HENLEY AND CO. 687
MANHATTAN FIREARMS COMPANY 687
MANN, FRITZ 688
MANNLICHER PISTOL 688
MANNLICHER SCHOENAUER 688
MANUFRANCE 689
MANURHIN 690
MARATHON PRODUCTS, INC. 691
MARBLE'S ARMS & MFG. CO. 691
MARGOLIN 692
MARIETTE BREVETTE 693
MARLIN FIREARMS CO. 693
MAROCCHI ARMI 726
MARS 727
MARSTON, S.W. 727
MARSTON, W. W. & CO. 727
MASQUELIER S. A. 728
MASSACHUSETTS ARMS CO. 729
MATEBA ARMS 730
MATRA MANURHIN DEFENSE 730
MAUSER WERKE 730
MAVERICK ARMS, INC. 742
MAYNARD/PERRY 742
M. B. ASSOCIATES-GYROJET 742
MCMILLAN, G. & CO. INC. 742
MEAD & ADRIANCE 744
MEIJA 744
MENDENHALL, JONES & GARDNER 744
MENZ, AUGUST 744
MERCURY 744
MERIDEN FIREARMS CO. 744
MERKEL, GEBRUDER 745
MERRILL 755
MERRILL, JAMES H. 755
MERRILL, LATROBE & THOMAS 756
MERRIMACK ARMS 756
MERWIN & BRAY 756
MERWIN HULBERT & CO. 756
METROPOLITAN ARMS CO. 758
MIIDA 758
MILLER ARMS 758
MILTECH 759
MINNEAPOLIS F. A. CO. 759
MIROKU B. C. 759
MITCHELL ARMS, INC. 759
MITCHELL'S MAUSERS 761
MK ARMS, INC. 762
MKE 762
MODESTO SANTOS CIA. 762
MONDRAGON 762
MONTENEGRAN-GASSER 762
MOORE-ENFIELD 762
MOORES PATENT FIREARMS CO. 762
MORGAN & CLAPP 763
MORINI 763
MORRONE 763
MORSE 763
MOSIN-NAGANT 763
MOSSBERG, O. F. & SONS, INC. 763
MOUNTAIN ARMS 788
MOUNTAIN RIFLES, INC. 788
MUGICA, JOSE 789
MURATA 789
MURFEESBORO ARMORY 789
MURPHY & O'CONNEL 789
MURRAY, J. P. 789
MUSGRAVE 789
MUSKETEER RIFLES 789
NAGANT, EMILE & LEON 790
NAMBU 790
NATIONAL ARMS CO. 790
NAVY ARMS COMPANY 790
NEAL, W. 805
NEPPERHAN FIREARMS CO. 805
NESIKA BAY PRECISION, INC. 805
NEW ENGLAND FIREARMS CO. 805
NEWBURY ARMS CO. 807
NEWCOMB, H. G. 807
NEWTON ARMS CO. 807
NICHOLS & CHILDS 808
NIGHTHAWK CUSTOM 808
NOBLE 808
NORINCO 810
NORTH & COUCH 813
NORTH AMERICAN ARMS 811
NORTH AMERICAN ARMS CORP. 813
NORTH AMERICAN SAFARI EXPRESS 813
NORTON ARMS CO. 813
NORWICH PISTOL CO. 813
NOSLER CUSTOM 813
NOWLIN MANUFACTURING COMPANY 813
O.D.I. 814
O.K. 814
O'CONNELL, DAVID 814
O'DELL, STEPHEN 814
OBREGON 814
OHIO ORDNANCE INC. 814
OJANGUREN Y VIDOSA 814
OLD WEST GUN CO. 815
OLYMPIC ARMS, INC. 815
OMEGA 818
OMEGA FIREARMS CO. 819
OPUS SPORTING ARMS, INC. 819
ORBEA & CIA 819
ORTGIES, HEINRICH & CO. 819
ORVIS 819
OSBORN, S. 819
OSGOOD GUN WORKS 819
OVERTON, JOHN 819
OWA 820
P.38 821
P.A.F. 822
P.S.M.G. GUN CO. 822
PAGE-LEWIS ARMS CO. 822
PALMER 823
PANTHER ARMS 823
PAPE, W.R. 823
PARA-ORDNANCE MFG. INC. 823
PARDINI 833
PARKER 833
PARKER BROS. 833
PARKER FIELD & SONS 836
PARKER REPRODUCTIONS 838
PARKER-HALE LTD. 836
PEABODY 838
PEAVY, A. J. 839
PECARE & SMITH 839
PEDERSEN CUSTOM GUNS 839
PEDERSEN, JOHN D. 839
PEDERSOLI, DAVIDE 840
PERAZZI 846
PERRY & GODDARD 850
PERRY PATENT FIREARMS CO. 851
PERUGINI & VISINI 851
PETTINGILL C. S. 851
PFANNL, FRANCOIS 852
PGM PRECISION 852
PHILLIPS & RODGERS INC. 852
PHOENIX 852
PHOENIX ARMS 852
PHOENIX ARMS CO. 853
PICKERT, FRIEDRICH 853
PIEPER, HENRI & NICOLAS 854
PILSEN, ZBROVKA 855
PIOTTI 855
PIRKO 856
PLAINFIELD MACHINE CO. 856
PLAINFIELD ORDNANCE CO. 856
PLANT'S MANUFACTURING CO. 856
POINTER 857
POLY-TECHNOLOGIES, INC. 857
POND, LUCIUS, W. 857
PORTER, P. W. 858
POWELL, W. & SON LTD. 858
PRAGA, ZBROVKA 858
PRAIRIE GUN WORKS 858
PRANDELLI & GASPARINI 858
PRATT, GEORGE 858
PRATT, H. 859
PRECISION SMALL ARMS 859
PREMIER 859
PRESCOTT, E. A. 860
PRETORIA 860
PRINZ 860
PRITCHETT, POTTS & HUNT 860
PROFESSIONAL ORDNANCE, INC. 860
PROTECTION 861

PTK INTERNATIONAL, INC. 861
PULASKI ARMORY 861
PUMA (ROSSI) 861
PURDEY, J. & SONS LTD. 862
PYRENEES 862
QUACKENBUSH 864
QUINABAUG MFG. CO. 864
R. G. INDUSTRIES 865
R.E. 866
RADOM 866
RANDALL FIREARMS CO. 866
RANGER ARMS, INC. 869
RAPTOR ARMS CO. 869
RASHID 869
RAST & GASSER 870
RAU ARMS CORP. 870
RAVELL 870
RAVEN ARMS 870
READ & WATSON 871
RECORD-MATCH ANSCHUTZ 871
REEDER, GARY CUSTOM GUNS .. 871
REFORM 875
REICHS REVOLVER 875
REID, JAMES 875
REISING ARMS CO. 877
REMINGTON ARMS COMPANY, INC. 877
RENETTE, GASTINNE 929
RENWICK ARMS CO. 929
REPUBLIC ARMS, INC. 929
RETOLAZA HERMANOS 929
REUNIES 930
REUTH, F. 930
REXIODE ARMAS 930
RHEINMETALL 931
RHODE ISLAND ARMS CO. 932
RICHLAND ARMS CO. 932
RICHMOND ARMORY 932
RIEDL RIFLE CO. 933
RIFLESMITH INC. 933
RIGBY, JOHN & CO., LTD. 933
RIGDON, ANSLEY & CO. 933
RIPOMANTI, GUY 934
RIVERSIDE ARMS CO. 934
RIZZINI, BATTISTA 934
RIZZINI, FRATELLI 936
ROBAR AND DE KIRKHAVE 937
ROBAR COMPANIES 939
ROBBINS & LAWRENCE 939
ROBERTSON 939
ROBINSON ARMAMENT CO. 939
ROBINSON, ORVIL 940
ROBINSON, S.C. 940
ROCK ISLAND ARMORY (TRADE NAME OF ARMSCOR) . 940
ROCK RIVER ARMS, INC. 940
ROGERS & SPENCER 944
ROGUE RIFLE COMPANY 944
ROGUE RIVER RIFLEWORKS 944
ROHM GMBH 944
ROHRBAUGH 944
ROMERWERKE 945
RONGE, J. B. 945
ROSS RIFLE CO. 945
ROSSI, AMADEO 945
ROTH-SAUER 950
ROTH-STEYR 950
ROTTME, TH. 950
ROTTWEIL 950
ROYAL AMERICAN SHOTGUNS .. 950
RUBY ARMS COMPANY 951
RUGER 951
RUPERTUS, JACOB 951
RWS 951
S.A.C.M. 952
S.A.E. 952
S.E.A.M. 952
S.W.D., INC. 952
SABATTI 952
SACKET, D. D. 952
SAFARI ARMS 952
SAKO 953
SAM, INC. 959
SAMCO GLOBAL ARMS, INC. 959
SARASQUETA, FELIX 959
SARASQUETA, J. J. 960
SARASQUETA, VICTOR 960
SARDIUS 960
SARSILMAZ 961
SAUER, J. P. & SON 961
SAVAGE ARMS CORPORATION .. 971
SAVAGE REVOLVING FIREARMS CO. 997
SAVAGE & NORTH 997
SCATTERGUN TECHNOLOGIES .. 998
SCHALK, G. S. 998
SCHALL & CO. 999
SCHMIDT, E. & COMPANY 999
SCHMIDT, HERBERT 999
SCHMIDT-RUBIN 999
SCHNEIDER & CO. 999
SCHNEIDER & GLASSICK 999
SCHOUBOE 999
SCHUERMAN ARMS, LTD. 999
SCHULER, AUGUST 999
SCHULTZ & LARSEN 1000
SCHWARZLOSE, ANDREAS ... 1000
SEARS, ROEBUCK & CO. BRAND 1000
SEAVER, E.R. 1000
SECURITY INDUSTRIES 1000
SEDCO INDUSTRIES, INC. 1001
SEDERE, TH. 1001
SEDGELY, R. F., INC. 1001
SEECAMP, L. W. CO., INC. 1001
SEMMERLING 1001
SERBU FIREARMS 1001
SHARPS, C. ARMS CO. 1001
SHARPS RIFLE MANUFACTURING COMPANY 1002
SHATTUCK, C. S. 1007
SHAW & LEDOYT 1008
SHAWK & MCLANAHAN 1008
SHERIDEN PRODUCTS, INC. ... 1008
SHILEN RIFLES, INC. 1008
SHILOH RIFLE MFG. CO., INC. .. 1008
SIG 1010
SIG-HAMMERLI 1010
SIGARMS 1011
SILMA 1022
SIMPLEX 1023
SIMPSON, R. J. 1023
SIMSON & COMPANY 1023
SIRKIS INDUSTRIES, LTD. 1024
SKB ARMS COMPANY 1024
SKS 1029
SLOTTER & CO. 1029
SMITH, L. C. 1029
SMITH AMERICAN ARMS COMPANY 1029
SMITH, OTIS 1033
SMITH & WESSON 1033
SNAKE CHARMER 1102
SNEIDER, CHARLES E. 1102
SODIA, FRANZ 1102
SOKOLOVSKY CORP. SPORT ARMS 1102
SPALDING & FISHER 1102
SPANG & WALLACE 1102
SPENCER 1103
SPENCER ARMS CO. 1104
SPENCER REVOLVER 1104
SPHINX 1104
SPIES, A. W. 1106
SPILLER & BURR 1106
SPITFIRE 1106
SPRINGFIELD ARMORY (MODERN) 1107
SPRINGFIELD ARMORY INC. ... 1107
SPRINGFIELD ARMORY 1120
SPRINGFIELD ARMS COMPANY 1122
SQUIBBMAN 1123
SQUIRES BINGHAM MFG. CO., INC. 1123
SSK INDUSTRIES 1123
STAFFORD, T. J. 1123
STALCAP, ALEXANDER T.F.M. .. 1123
STANDARD ARMS CO. 1123
STAR, BONIFACIO ECHEVERRIA 1123
STARR, EBAN T. 1123
STARR ARMS COMPANY 1124
STEEL CITY ARMS, INC. 1125
STENDA WAFFENFABRIK 1125
STERLING ARMAMENT LTD. ... 1125
STERLING ARMS CORPORATION 1125
STEVENS, J. ARMS CO. 1127
STEYR 1141
STEYR HAHN 1151
STEYR MANNLICHER 1151
STI INTERNATIONAL 1151
STOCK, FRANZ 1155
STOCKING & CO. 1156

STOEGER, A. F. 1156
STREET SWEEPER 1158
STURDIVANT, LEWIS G. 1159
STURM, RUGER & CO. 1159
SUNDANCE INDUSTRIES, INC. . . 1187
SUPER SIX LTD. 1187
SUTHERLAND, S. 1187
SYMS, J. G. 1187
TACONIC FIREARMS LTD. 1188
TALLASSEE 1188
TANFOGLIO 1188
TANNER, ANDRE 1188
TARPLEY J. & F. AND E. T. GARRETT & CO. 1189
TAURUS INTERNATIONAL MFG. CO. 1189
TAYLOR'S & CO., INC. 1211
TAYLOR, L.B. 1216
TERRIER ONE 1216
TERRY, J. C. 1216
TEXAS CONTRACT RIFLES 1216
TEXAS GUNFIGHTERS 1216
TEXAS LONGHORN ARMS, INC. . 1216
THAMES ARMS CO. 1217
THIEME & EDELER 1217
THOMPSON 1217
THOMPSON/CENTER ARMS 1217
THUNDER FIVE 1224
TIKKA 1224
TIMBER WOLF 1226
TIPPING & LAWDEN 1226
TIPPMAN ARMS 1226
TISAS (TRABZON GUN INDUSTRY CORP.) 1226
TOBIN ARMS MANUFACTURING CO. 1228
TODD, GEORGE H. 1228
TOKAREV 1228
TOMISKA, ALOIS 1228
TORKELSON ARMS CO. 1228
TRADEWINDS 1228
TRADITIONS 1229
TRANTER, WILLIAM 1231
TRIPLETT & SCOTT/MERIDEN MANUFACTURING COMPANY . 1231
TRISTAR SPORTING ARMS 1232
TROCAOLA 1236
TRYON, EDWARD K. & COMPANY 1236
TUCKER SHERARD & COMPANY 1237
TUFTS & COLLEY 1237
TURBIAUX, JACQUES 1237
TURNER, THOMAS 1237
TYLER ORDNANCE WORKS 1237
U.S. ARMS CO. 1238
U.S. M1 CARBINE 1238
U.S. ORDNANCE 1238
U.S. REPEATING ARMS CO. 1239
UBERTI, ALDO/UBERTI USA 1239
UHLINGER, WILLIAM P. 1247
ULTIMATE 1247
ULTRA LIGHT ARMS, INC. 1248
UNCETA 1248
UNION 1248
UNION FIRE ARMS COMPANY . . 1248
UNIQUE 1249
UNITED SPORTING ARMS, INC. . 1249
UNITED STATES ARMS 1252
UNITED STATES FIRE ARMS MFG. 1252
UNITED STATES HISTORICAL SOCIETY 1252
UNITED STATES REVOLVER ASSOCIATION 1255
UNITED STATES SMALL ARMS CO. 1255
UNIVERSAL FIREARMS 1255
URIZAR, TOMAS 1256
USAS 12 DAEWOO PRECISION IND., LTD. 1257
USELTON ARMS INC. 1257
UZI ISRAELI MILITARY INDUSTRIES 1257
VALKYRIE ARMS, LTD. 1259
VALMET, INC. 1259
VALTION (LAHTI) 1259
VALTRO 1259
VARNER SPORTING ARMS, INC. 1260
VECTOR ARMS, INC 1260
VEKTOR 1260
VENUS WAFFENWERKE 1262
VERNEY-CARRON 1262
VERONA 1263
VETTERLI 1264
VICKERS, LTD. 1264
VICTOR EJECTOR 1264
VICTORY ARMS COT., LTD. 1265
VIRGINIAN 1265
VOERE 1265
VOLCANIC ARMS COMPANY . . . 1266
VOLKSPISTOLE 1266
VOLQUARTSEN CUSTOM 1266
VOLUNTEER ENTERPRISES 1268
VOUZLAUD 1268
WALCH, JOHN 1269
WALDMAN 1269
WALLIS & BIRCH 1269
WALTHER, CARL 1269
WALTHER MANURHIN 1283
WARNANT, L. AND J. 1283
WARNER ARMS CORPORATION . 1283
WARNER, CHAS. 1284
WARNER, JAMES 1284
WATSON BROTHERS 1285
WEATHERBY 1285
WEAVER ARMS 1296
WEBLEY & SCOTT, LTD. 1296
WEIHRAUCH, HANS HERMANN . 1303
WEISBURGER, A. 1304
WESSON, DAN FIREARMS 1304
WESSON FIREARMS CO., INC. . . 1310
WESSON, EDWIN 1316
WESSON, FRANK 1316
WESSON & LEAVITT MASSACHUSETTS ARMS COMPANY 1318
WESTERN ARMS 1318
WESTERN ARMS CORPORATION 1318
WESTERN FIELD 1318
WESTLEY RICHARDS & CO., LTD. 1318
WHEELER, ROBERT 1318
WHITE, ROLLIN 1318
WHITNEY ARMS COMPANY 1319
WHITNEY FIREARMS COMPANY . 1330
WHITWORTH 1331
WICHITA ARMS, INC. 1331
WICKLIFFE RIFLES 1331
WIENER WAFFENFABRIK 1332
WILDEY FIREARMS CO., INC. . . . 1332
WILKES, JOHN 1333
WILKINSON ARMS CO. 1333
WILLIAMSON MOORE FIREARMS COMPANY 1333
WILSON & CO. 1334
WILSON COMBAT 1334
WILSON, J. P. 1334
WINCHESTER REPEATING ARMS COMPANY 1337
WINDSOR 1404
WINSLOW ARMS CO. 1404
WISEMAN, BILL & CO. 1405
WITNESS 1405
WOLF SPORTING PISTOLS 1405
WOODWARD, JAMES & SONS . . 1405
WURFFLEIN, ANDREW & WILLIAM 1405
XL HOPKINS & ALLEN 1406
XPERT HOPKINS & ALLEN 1406
ZANOTTI, FABIO 1407
Z-B RIFLE CO. 1407
ZEHNER, E. WAFFENFABRIK . . . 1407
ZEILINGER 1407
ZEPHYR 1407
ZM WEAPONS 1408
ZOLI USA, ANGELO 1408
ZOLI, ANTONIO 1409
ZULAICA, M. 1410

ACKNOWLEDGMENTS

Standard Catalog of Firearms owes much of its success to many noteworthy contributors, past and present:

Jim Schlender, noted outdoors writer and editor of *Turkey & Turkey Hunting Magazine*, for his work on assembling new shotgun data.

Fred Baumann for his painstaking compilation of our "Value Tracker" sidebars.

Joseph M. Cornell, editor of *Standard Catalog of Winchester Firearms* and proprietor of Accredited Appraisal Services (303-455-1717) for his insights on Colt and Winchester pricing as well as "sleepers."

Tom Caceci of Blacksburg, VA, for his insights on blackpowder revolvers and humane cattle killers.

Jim Stark of Gilbert, SC, for his invaluable review of Remington's "Nylon 66" family of rimfire rifles.

LCDR James Dodd, USN (ret.), for his contributions on Scout rifles and the recent goings-on at Remington.

David Rachwal of Hilliard, OH, for his expertise concerning the elusive MBA Gyrojet.

Robert Hausmann of Barre, VT (www.swiss-guncollectors.com), for his insights on SIGARMS and Swedish weapons in general.

Orvel Reichert is a collector of World War II-era semi-automatic pistols, especially the P38, and has been an invaluable help in sorting out a sometimes-confusing array of pistol variations. He can be reached at P. O. Box 67, Vader, WA 98593, 360-245-3492, email address: mr.p38@localaccess.com.

Bailey Brower, Jr. should be recognized for his knowledgeable input on Remington and Savage auto pistols. Bailey can be reached at P.O. Box 111, Madison, NJ 07940.

David Moore of William Larkin Moore & Co. provided expert information on B. Rizzine, Garbi, F. Rizzine, Piotti, and Lebeau Courally. He can be reached at 8340 E. Raintree Dr. Suite B-7, Scottsdale, AZ, 85260. Phone 480-951- 8913.

The editor would like to acknowledge the kind permision of **Mrs. Gereldene Brophy,** wife of the late **Col. William S. Brophy**, to use her late husband's photos from his outstanding book, *Marlin Firearms.*

John Dougan, Ruger expert, who supplied us with information on the Great Western Arms Co.

Dave Banducci is extremely knowledgelable on Browning High-Power bolt action rifles in all grades. He is a great source for pricing and variations on these complex rifles. He can be reached at 720-272-9914.

Burt O'Neill is an experienced collector of Browning "P" Grades and helped with that pricing. He can be reached at 610-793-3256.

Thanks to Smith & Wesson expert **Roy Jinks**, of Smith & Wesson, who wrote the introduction to that section in this book.

Bud Bugni of Sutter Creek, CA (209-267-5402) for his expertise on the Winchester Model 42.

C.W. Slagle, of Scottsdale, Arizona, for his expertise in antique firearms.

A special thanks to **Simeon Stoddard**, former curator of the Cody Firearms Museum, for his research and contribution on the M-1 Garand rifle.

A special thanks to all the manufacturers and importers who supplied us with information on, and photographs of, their products.

Thanks to the **Lew Horton Distributing Company** for its valuable information on Colt Custom Shop products and Smith & Wesson Performance Center products.

Thanks to **Jerry Cummings** of Manawa, Wisconsin, and **William "Pete" Harvey** of Falmouth, Massachusetts, who contributed photos and research information.

Many thanks to **Harold Hamilton** of Hershey, Pennsylvania, for his invaluable assistance with Hamilton rifles.

Michael McIntosh gave generously of his expert knowledge of A.H. Fox Company and its guns.

Ed Buehlman, a longtime firearms dealer, shared his knowledge of Colt New Frontier models. He can be reached at 847-381-2276.

Special appreciation to **Joe McBride** of McBride's Guns in Austin, Texas, for his expert assistance.

Walter C. Snyder is the "Chronicler of the Ithaca Gun Company" and has devoted a great deal of time and effort to making the Ithaca section the most comprehensive of any price guide on the market.

Tom Turpin is a big help with his invaluable knowledge of F.W. Heym Company and its product line, as well as other European rifles and shotguns.

Horst Held of Midlothian, Texas, provided us with information on interesting and seldom seen antique semi-automatic pistols.

Ted Willems and **Bruce Wolberg** of *Gun List* have been most helpful with information and locating hard-to-find firearms.

We also want to thank the members of the **Ruger Collectors' Association** for their invaluable input.

And a big thank-you to **Summer Sellers** of Goshen, Indiana, for providing such excellent transcriptions of a few of my previously-published pieces. Thanks, Summer!

Thanks to all the readers who have taken the time to contact the editor with corrections, omissions and additional information.

PHOTO CREDITS

Thanks to the **Milwaukee Public Museum**, 800 W. Wells St., Milwaukee, WI 53233; and the **Buffalo Bill Historical Center**, Cody Firearms Museum, P.O. Box 1000, Cody, WY 82414, for supplying us with photographs. We also wish to thank the **Remington Arms Company** for its kind assistance in providing us with photos of out-of-production Remington firearms.

Many thanks to the following who loaned us their firearms to photograph for this book:

Thomas W. Radcliffe
Brook Davis.
Thomas F. Swearengen
Chip Johnson of Direct Firearms, St. Joseph, MO
C. Roy Jones of C. Roy's Gunsmithing, Kaiser, MO
Mike and Wanda Moutray of Mike's Gun Sales, Grant City, MO
Will Parsons of Parsons Gun Shop
Joe Lech of Ironwork Armco, Raytown, MO
Guns of the World, Kansas City, MO
J.M. Stanley of Stan's Gun Shop, Joplin, MO
H.L. Hoeflicker of HLH Enterprises, Shawnee Mission, KS
S.T. Sinclair
Pat Morgan
Steve Comus
William H. Lehman of B & B Guns, Brighton, CO
James D. McKenzie and **Samuel Baum** of Kentucky Rifle, Union City, PA
Dean Parr of Dean's Gun Shop, St. Joseph, MO
E.K. Tryon of Philadelphia, PA
Bob's Gun Rack of Lee's Summit, MO
Pat McWilliams
J.M. Stanley
Ken Waughtal of Merriam, KS
Armond Beetch of Quapaw, OK
Jim Rankin
Eric M. Larson
Jim Taylor of Mt. Vernon, MO
C. Hadley Smith
Walter C. Snyder
Ithaca Gun Company
Tom Turpin
Horst Held
Gary Gelson Photography of Boise, ID
Paul Goodwin Creative Services
Karl Karash
J.B. Wood

AUCTION HOUSES

The following abbreviations are used throughout this edition to identify auction houses that have contributed real-life pricing data to the "Value Tracker" sidebars:

Amos: Amoskeag Auction Company, Inc., 250 Commercial Street #3011, Manchester, NH 03101; www.amoskeag-auction.com

B&B: Bonhams & Butterfields, 220 San Bruno Avenue, San Francisco, CA 94103; www.bonhams.com

GMA: Greg Martin Auctions, 660 Third Street, Suite 100, San Francisco, CA 94107; www.gmartin-auctions.com

JCD: J.C. Devine, Inc., PO Box 413, 20 South Street, Milford, NH 03055; www.jcdevine.com

Julia: James D. Julia, Inc., PO Box 830, Fairfield, ME 04737; www.juliaauctions.com

LJA: Little John's Auction Service, 1740 W. La Venta Ave., Orange, CA 92868; www.littlejohnsauctionservice.com

RIA: Rock Island Auction Co.; 4507 49th Avenue, Moline, IL, 61265-7578; www.rockislandauction.com

CONTRIBUTING EDITORS

INTRODUCTION

Welcome to the 18th edition of *Standard Catalog of Firearms*. This latest and most comprehensive edition contains new features I hope you find useful.

Compiled by Fred Baumann, our "Value Tracker" sidebars establish historical pricing trends for a variety of collectible firearms. Prices in the "Value Tracker" listings are taken from firearms auction firms that publish printed catalogs as well as printed lists of the prices realized. Descriptive commentary displayed in quotation marks is taken from the original auction description (e.g., "Fine"). Where no general description of condition appears in the auction catalog, one is composed by us to summarize the overall condition of the firearm to the best of our ability based on the description given, shown without quotation marks (e.g., about F-VF). Significant flaws are identified wherever possible, though not every minor flaw may be mentioned. As a rule, the "Value Tracker" records only prices for individual firearms that are in good working order or can be easily made so. Exceptionally valuable firearms (such as presentation-cased guns, multi-barrel sets, or lavishly engraved examples) – as well as non-functional firearms (so-called "parts guns") – are deliberately excluded from the listings to avoid skewing the analysis of values up or down.

Throughout this edition, you will see certain models identified as "sleepers": models that are undergoing, or are likely to undergo, an upward shift in value. These entries are identified by the icon shown at the right. In today's volatile market, however, nothing is certain, so we can make no guarantees as to the future appreciation of any model.

We have also expanded our perspective to take into account the growing effect of the internet in establishing collectible firearms pricing. As far as we can tell, internet websites, local gun shops and traditional auction houses can exist quite well side-by-side, and the overall effect of the internet has been to expand the hobby dramatically. We can all profit from its existence: buyers, sellers and window-shoppers alike.

We've also included a few brief feature pieces dealing with specific guns or collecting trends. We hope you enjoy them. These pieces are part of our recent emphasis on what might be called "second-tier" collectibles, an emphasis we plan to continue.

May your collecting always remain safe and enjoyable. Happy hunting!

Dan Shideler
Editor

GRADING SYSTEM

In the opinion of the editor, all grading systems are subjective. It is our task to offer the collector and dealer a measurement that most closely reflects a general consensus on condition. The system we present seems to come closest to describing a firearm in universal terms. We strongly recommend that the reader acquaint himself with this grading system before attempting to determine the correct price for a particular firearm's condition. Remember, in most cases condition determines price.

NIB—New in Box

This category can sometimes be misleading. It means that the firearm is in its original factory carton with all of the appropriate papers. It also means the firearm is new; that it has not been fired and has no wear. This classification brings a substantial premium for both the collector and shooter.

Excellent

Collector quality firearms in this condition are highly desirable. The firearm must be in at least 98 percent condition with respect to blue wear, stock or grip finish, and bore. The firearm must also be in 100 percent original factory condition without refinishing, repair, alterations or additions of any kind. Sights must be factory original as well. This grading classification includes both modern and antique (manufactured prior to 1898) firearms.

Very Good

Firearms in this category are also sought after both by the collector and shooter. Modern firearms must be in working order and retain approximately 92 percent original metal and wood finish. It must be 100 percent factory original, but may have some small repairs, alterations, or non-factory additions. No refinishing is permitted in this category. Antique firearms must have 80 percent original finish with no repairs.

Good

Modern firearms in this category may not be considered to be as collectable as the previous grades, but antique firearms are considered desirable. Modern firearms must retain at least 80 percent metal and wood finish, but may display evidence of old refinishing. Small repairs, alterations, or non-factory additions are sometimes encountered in this class. Factory replacement parts are permitted. The overall working condition of the firearm must be good as well as safe. The bore may exhibit wear or some corrosion, especially in antique arms. Antique firearms may be included in this category if their metal and wood finish is at least 50 percent original factory finish.

Fair

Firearms in this category should be in satisfactory working order and safe to shoot. The overall metal and wood finish on the modern firearm must be at least 30 percent and antique firearms must have at least some original finish or old re-finish remaining. Repairs, alterations, nonfactory additions, and recent refinishing would all place a firearm in this classification. However, the modern firearm must be in working condition, while the antique firearm may not function. In either case the firearm must be considered safe to fire if in a working state.

Poor

Neither collectors nor shooters are likely to exhibit much interest in firearms in this condition. Modern firearms are likely to retain little metal or wood finish. Pitting and rust will be seen in firearms in this category. Modern firearms may not be in working order and may not be safe to shoot. Repairs and refinishing would be necessary to restore the firearm to safe working order. Antique firearms will have no finish and will not function. In the case of modern firearms their principal value lies in spare parts. On the other hand, antique firearms in this condition may be used as "wall hangers" or as an example of an extremely rare variation or have some kind of historical significance.

Pricing Sample Format

NIB	Exc.	V.G.	Good	Fair	Poor
550	450	400	350	300	200

PRICING

The prices given in this book reflect RETAIL values. This is important. You will generally not realize full retail value if you trade a gun in on another or sell it to a dealer. In this situation, your trade-in gun will be valued at wholesale, which is generally substantially below retail value.

Unfortunately for shooters and collectors, there is no central clearinghouse for firearms prices. The prices given in this book are designed as a guide, not as a quote. This is an important distinction because prices for firearms vary with the time of the year, with geographical location, and sometimes for no apparent reason. For example, interest in firearms is at its lowest point in the summer. People are not as interested in shooting and collecting at this time of the year as they are in playing golf or taking a vacation. Therefore, prices are depressed slightly and guns that may sell quickly during the hunting season or the winter months may not sell well at all during this time of year. Geographical location also plays an important part in pricing. Political pundits are often heard to say that all politics is local. Well, the same can be said, in many ways, for the price of firearms. For instance, a Winchester Model 70 in a .264 caliber will bring a higher price in the Western states than along the Eastern seaboard. Smaller gauges and calibers seem to be more popular along both coasts and mid-sections of the United States than in the more open western sections of the country.

It is not practical to list prices in this book with regard to time of year or location. What is given is a reasonable price based on sales at gun shows, auction houses, *Gun List* prices, and information obtained from knowledgeable collectors and dealers. In certain cases there will be no price indicated under a particular condition but rather the notation "N/A" or the symbol "—." This indicates that there is no known price available for that gun in that condition or the sales for that particular model are so few that a reliable price cannot be given. This will usually be encountered only with very rare guns, with newly introduced firearms, or more likely with antique firearms in those conditions most likely to be encountered. Most antique firearms will be seen in the good, fair and poor categories.

As noted above, throughout this edition you will see certain models identified as "sleepers": models that are undergoing, or are likely to undergo, an upward shift in value. These entries are identified by the icon shown at the right. In today's volatile market, however, nothing is certain, so we can make no guarantees as to the future appreciation of any model.

Note that the prices in this book are a GENERAL GUIDE as to what a willing buyer and willing seller might agree on. So how is the reader to use this book? *Standard Catalog of Firearms* can be used as an identification guide and as a source of starting prices for a planned firearms transaction. If you start by valuing a given firearm according to the values shown in this book, you will not be too far off the mark.

In the final analysis, a firearm is worth only what someone is willing to pay for it. New trends arise quickly, and there are many excellent bargains to be found in today's market. With patience and good judgment – and with this book under your arm – you, too, can find them.

ADDITIONAL CONSIDERATIONS

As stated in the pricing section, this publication offers a general guide to prices. There are many factors that may affect the value of a firearm. We have attempted to be as comprehensive as possible, but we cannot cover all possible factors that may influence the worth of any given firearm. Some of these circumstances will be discussed so that the shooter and collector will have a better idea of how certain factors may affect prices.

Firearms have been admired and coveted, not only for their usefulness, but also for their grace and beauty. Since the beginning of the 19th century, firearms makers have adorned their guns with engraving, fine woods, or special order features that set their products apart from the rest. There is no feasible way to give the collector every possible variation of the firearms presented in this book. However, in a general way, certain special factors will significantly influence the price of a firearm.

Perhaps the most recognizable special feature collectors agree affects the price of a firearm is engraving. The artistry, beauty, and intricate nature of engraving draw all collectors toward it. But, firearms engraving is a field unto itself requiring years of experience to determine proper chronological methods and the ability to identify the engraver in question. Factory engraving generally brings more of a premium than after-market engraving. To be able to determine factory work is a difficult task, full of pitfalls. In some cases, factories like Colt and Winchester may have records to verify original factory engraving work. Whereas other manufacturers such as Parker, Remington, or Savage may not have these records. Whenever a firearm purchase is to be made with respect to an engraved gun, it is in the collector's best interest to secure an expert opinion and/or a factory letter prior to the purchase. Engraved firearms are expensive. A mistake could cost the collector thousands of dollars; proceed with caution.

The 18th century was also a time when pistols and rifles were purchased by or given to historically important individuals. Firearms have also been an important part of significant historical events such as the Battle of the Little Bighorn or the Battle of Bull Run or some other meaningful event in our nation's history. Many of these firearms are in museums where the public can enjoy, see and appreciate them. Others are in private collections that seldom, if ever, are offered for sale. If the collector should ever encounter one of these historically important firearms, it cannot be stressed strongly enough to secure an expert determination as to authenticity. Museum curators are perhaps the best source of information for these types of firearms. As with engraved guns, historical firearms are usually expensive, and without documentation their value is questionable.

Special features and variations are also a desirable part of firearms collecting. As with engraving, special order guns can bring a considerable premium. The Colt factory has excellent records regarding its firearms and will provide the collector with a letter of authenticity. Winchester records are not as comprehensive, but rifles made prior to 1908 may have documentation. Other firearm manufacturers either do not have records or do not provide the collector with documentation. This leaves the collector in a difficult position. Special order sights, stocks, barrel lengths, calibers, and so forth must be judged on their own merits. As with other factors, an expert should be consulted prior to purchase. Sometimes this can be difficult. Experienced collectors, researchers, and museums will generally provide the kind of information a collector needs before purchasing a special order or unique firearm.

Perhaps the best advice is for the collector to take his time. Do not be in a hurry, and do not allow yourself to be rushed into making a decision. Learn as much as possible about the firearms you are interested in collecting or shooting. Try to keep current with prices through *Gun List* and this publication. Go to gun shows, not just to buy or sell, but to observe and learn. It is also helpful to join a firearms club or association. These groups have older, experienced collectors who are glad to help the beginner or veteran. Firearms collecting is a rewarding hobby. Firearms are part of our nation's history and represent an opportunity to learn more about their role in that American experience. If done skillfully, firearms collecting can be a profitable hobby as well.

ABOUT THE EDITOR

A lifelong firearms enthusiast, Dan Shideler is the editor of numerous Krause Publications gun-related titles, including *Modern Gun Values* and *Gun Digest® Book of Guns & Prices*. He has been privileged to work with many of the finest firearms authorities of the day, including Layne Simpson, Patrick Sweeney, Richard Nahas, Jim Supica, John Taffin and Ken Ramage, among others. He is a regular contributor to *Gun Digest® Magazine* and various other publications. He and his wife Karen live in northern Indiana.

Better than Book:

Factors that Add to the Value of a Firearm

By Phillip Peterson

In the previous edition of *Standard Catalog of Firearms*, I discussed some of the factors that can dramatically reduce the value of a firearm. Most of these factors concern non-factory alterations: add-on chokes, aftermarket recoil pads, replaced wood, and so on. In virtually every case that I have witnessed, these "improvements" have significantly lowered the value of a given firearm compared to the "book value" of such a firearm in its original factory configuration.

Recently, however, it was suggested to me that there might also be items or features that could add value to a given firearm. So true.

There are many factors that can be used to arrive at a price for a gun. Some reduce the price, some add to it. In fact, almost any of the factors I just mentioned that can lower the price can add to it as well. It really depends on the intended use for the firearm. Certainly, if you repair a broken gun to make it usable again, that will add to the value of that gun. It might hurt the value in the eyes of a collector or investor but not the hunter who wants a functional tool to use in the field. The collector probably would not have wanted that particular firearm anyway. If it was in need of repair it likely was not in good enough condition to appeal to discriminating collectors or investors. Thus it still comes down to the seller and potential buyer agreeing on a price.

Here, the, are just a few of the factors that can add to the value of a firearm:

Scopes & Sights

Many add-on accessories and customizations found on firearms are there to make aiming the piece easier and increase the chance of hitting the target. After all, that is the ultimate use for any firearm. So, the holes that are drilled in the receiver of, say, a Winchester Model 75 bolt action .22 to allow the mounting of a scope might not hurt its value at all. In fact, if a hunter wants that model with a scope he will likely be more interested in it. Yes, it is still reduced in value to a collector, but the hunter's cash is just as spendable. Of course, if a "gunsmith" drilled seven off-center holes in the receiver before he got four to match the mounts he had, the gun just looks bad. You can take a good thing too far.

When a rifle or shotgun is offered with a scope already installed, the value of the scope should be included in the overall value of the gun. How much are used scopes worth? I figure current production optics at about one third to one half of retail price when attached to a gun. That way, if the buyer does not want the particular scope they can negotiate a price reduction with the scope removed. Or they can sell it themselves and buy the scope that suits their needs. Older, out of production scopes have become collectibles in their own right. The long target scopes as made by Unertl, Fecker, Winchester and others can be worth hundreds of dollars. Some firearms manufacturers, such as Marlin and Mossberg, actually used to make their own scopes or had scopes made for them that had their name on it.

Many times I have bought a used Stevens or Mossberg .22 rifle with an old scope on it that is worth more than the gun. I suggest consulting the book *Old Rifle Scopes* by Nick Stroebel when attempting to price older optics. Always check the scope for damage if it is adding to the price of the gun. Make sure the optics are clear, glass lenses have no chips or scratches, crosshairs are intact, and adjusting knobs are working. Getting a broken scope fixed is possible but expensive. Original replacement parts are hard to come by.

In addition to scopes, metallic sights of several configurations will be found. The most popular of these is the tang sight. This is a peep sight that mounts on the tang or back of the receiver of many guns. These were frequently found on Winchester, Sharps, Remington, and other quality sporting rifles. The tang sights made by a gun manufacturer are especially desirable. Winchester-made sights are among the most valuable as collectibles. Other tang sight makers include Marble and Lyman.

Besides tang sights, there are peep sights that mount on the side of a firearm. These were offered by companies like Mossberg, Redfield, Williams, and Lyman. When a firearm is offered that has an older metallic sight, I refer the reader to the book *Old Gunsights*, also by Nick Stroebel. This fine book lists the metallic sights by maker and model number.

Some of the old aftermarket tang or peep sights required the gun to be drilled and tapped to install the sight. This sort of modification usually reduces the price of a firearm. On the other hand, a Winchester Model 1886 that has had its receiver drilled to install a newer Marbles sight might be worth less to some buyers, but if a period, i.e., vintage, sight is present it could add to the value. Depends on the buyer.

All Scratched Up

Fine engraving on a firearm definitely adds to its value. The amount of coverage can range from a fine highlight on the edges all the way to fully engraved hunting scenes complete with gold inlay. If the work is done by a known engraver, pricing the firearm becomes more akin to pricing a piece of art than a useful tool. As with a fine painting or sculpture, when a known engraver dies, examples of his or her work will skyrocket in price. Some gun makers offered engraving as a special order option on their products. The factory engraved Colts and Winchesters done in the late 1800s by artists such as Nimschke and Ulrich will bring several times their book value. Indeed, many books are devoted solely to this subject.

Engraving done by an amateur or unknown craftsman will be judged solely on its attractiveness on a particular firearm. If you are contemplating the purchase of an engraved firearm, look closely at the work. Some engraving I have seen was cut too deep and really did not look pleasing. Or there were errors in the pattern that the engraver tried to blend in. After all, an apprentice engraver had to perfect his craft somewhere. The "practice" pieces frequently were sold to buyers who did not spot the defects.

Sometimes the style of engraving may make a gun more (or less) attractive to a given buyer. For example, Germanic-style engraving, with its deep-cut oak-leaf patterns and dramatic portraiture, may turn off some buyers but attract others.

Got Wood?

Walnut was the primary type of wood used to make factory gunstocks in America through the WW II era. The massive production of rifles for military use reduced the stands of available walnut trees and set the industry on a quest to find acceptable substitutes that cost less. In the 1950s, many of the less expensive firearms began being equipped with birch, ash or particle wood stocks. When a model that was once offered with a walnut stock is then sold with a cheaper kind of wood, the older walnut stocked models can bring a higher price. A good example of this is the Ruger 10-22 semi automatic rifle. When introduced in 1964, it sported a walnut stock. In the early 1980s a birch stock replaced the walnut. So a 10-22 with a walnut stock can be worth as much as $75 more than a recent birch stocked rifle.

The grain structure or pattern in nice walnut stocks can add a lot to the price of a long gun. When walnut stock blanks are sold to gun makers there is a grading system based on the attractiveness of the wood. They use terms like AAA or AA Fancy down to field or utility grade. Very desirable is a striped pattern in the buttstock. This can look like the stripes on a tiger or it might be a pattern of wavy lines of coloration. The finest grade AAA walnut stock blanks can be priced at over $1000 just for an unshaped wood blank. Imagine how much that finished stock would add to the value of a pre 1964 Winchester Model 70. It could quickly make that $750 rifle in to a $4500 rifle.

I have seen many mid-grade stocks on field-grade shotguns and rifles. Mid-grade walnut might have some tiger stripe pattern near the butt end but standard grain in the rest. These are fairly common so they don't attract the high rollers who want the AAA fancy wood. There is no set way to calculate the additional value in stock appearance. It is a very subjective thing, attractiveness of a piece of wood. But it can add to the price of a gun for someone who likes it.

Any discussion of stock materials must also consider synthetics. Some synthetics can add significantly to the value of a gun. A Remington Nylon 66 .22 rifle with Seneca Green stock can bring twice as much as an otherwise identical model in Mohawk Brown.

Get a Grip

Grip materials can also add to the value of a handgun. A S&W First Model .32 Hand Ejector with factory pearl grips can bring 50% more than an otherwise identical gun with hard rubber grips. In fact, in some cases factory pearls are worth more than the gun itself! None-factory aftermarket grips, no matter how nice, do not generally add to the value of a gun. Quite the contrary.

Previous Ownership

Previous ownership of a gun can also add significantly to its value. One of John Wayne's Great Western revolvers, for example, can bring many times as much as a similar model owned by Joe Blow. But such enhanced value depends on the celebrity status of the previous owner. A Colt SAA owned by Mel Torme might not be particularly attractive to a younger buyer ("Mel *Who*?").

Note that previous ownership of a gun always depends on provenance, i.e., the paper trail that proves such ownership. Without provenance, claims of previous ownership are merely talk, and worth about just as much.

Potential Historical Association

Sometimes a gun is worth more merely because it was produced during a historically-relevant era. A Colt SAA whose serial number places it in the range of those used by the U.S. Army at the Battle of Little Big Horn, for example, is automatically more valuable than one outside that range. It doesn't matter if it can't be proven that the gun in question was carried during the battle–although that would be nice. The mere fact that it *might* have been significantly adds to its value.

Wrapping It Up

Another item that will add to the price of an older gun is the original box and paperwork that came with a gun when sold new. On vintage Colts or Smith & Wessons a box and papers could almost double the price of the gun. Of course, the Commemorative guns as made by Colt and Winchester in the 1960s and 70s have to be unfired and have their boxes and literature to be worth full book price. Even utility grade firearms sold as recently as five or 10 years ago can be enhanced by having the box with them.

Finally, there are any number of add-on accessories that might come with a used gun that can add to the value for a prospective buyer: Slings, holsters, extra magazines, boxes of ammunition or brass, scope covers, bi-pods, cases, or any other accessory that was purchased and installed by the owner. All of these cost money. I frequently buy guns, then the owner brings in another $50 or 100 worth of stuff and says "here, these were with that gun." Every little bit helps.

When acquiring or selling firearms, it pays to remember that not everyone wants a museum-quality collectible. Some want hunting guns, some want shooters. Some want guns from a specific period in history. Any factor that caters to any of these interests can add to the value of a gun - sometimes a little, sometimes a lot.

I'M A COLLECTOR

By Joseph Madden Cornell, CMA, ASA, ISA

Editor's Note: Joseph Cornell is the editor of Krause Publications' *Standard Catalog of® Winchester Firearms.*

As the only certified, accredited and designated firearm appraiser in the United States, I am often asked about collecting firearms. It is a subject that is near and dear to my heart, and it is a subject that I have been familiar with for over 50 years. It has also been my life's obsession.

Before I get started with this discussion, I need to clarify one point: there is a difference between collecting and accumulating. Collecting takes place in an organized fashion, usually with specific goals in mind. Accumulating guns means buying particular guns because of specific interest, or, as often occurs, because the opportunity presented itself and the price was right. Some people, including myself, do both: they buy specific guns as part of a collecting plan, and they buy guns because of opportunity and price. Both are worthy pastimes, and both are noble endeavors, but collecting, as far as I'm concerned, is much more interesting and ultimately, much more rewarding. Besides, willy-nilly accumulation of firearms, usually, means that sooner or later you're going to have to build an addition on to your home, and that might not make for marital bliss. In addition, hiding a medium-size collection from one's spouse is much easier than hiding a vast accumulation of miscellaneous firearms.

Another thing I've noticed is that firearm accumulators buy all kinds of guns, e.g., Remingtons, Marlins, Colts, and usually in large numbers. Collectors, on the other hand, tend to have a few other weapons but mostly concentrate on the acquisition of weapons within their collecting purview.

Individual taste in collecting and or accumulating firearms is the most important factor in making good choices - not necessarily choices that will please everyone, but choices that you will be satisfied with long after you have made them. In this way, collecting is a lot like or ordering dinner at a very nice restaurant: everyone doesn't like the same thing. For example, I have in my collection of Winchester Model 62s one weapon that has much less condition than other collectors would like. (I wish it were in better condition, too.) It has a two-digit serial number, and was put together with a 1890 nickeled Expert receiver and other nickeled 1890 Expert parts, but it is numbered as a 62 and it is stamped "Model 62."

Collectors are a breed of human beings unto themselves. It's almost as if they are a subspecies. Some are quiet and methodical as they go about putting together their collections. Others are boisterous, loud and very aggressive. Some work with huge budgets where price isn't a particularly significant issue; others work with very limited budgets, where price is a central issue. Neither is nobler than the other. However, from my experience, I believe that individuals who are working on a limited budget are more careful about their collecting, more circumspect about their purchases. They seem to be more careful about what they buy; certainly they are more careful about what an item costs.

When one decides to become a collector of a specific type of firearm, he is entering a world where, most think, stiff competition is everywhere. This isn't always true; it all depends what guns a person decides to collect. If you're going to collect early Winchester lever actions, for example, competition exists everywhere. If you're going to collect some of the later models, little or moderate competition is what you will find. In addition, Winchester prices have a great deal to do with condition and factory originality, not always rarity. For example, a Winchester Model 255 is quite rare, but no one seems to care. On the other hand, a standard early Winchester Model 1886 is much more common than the model 255, but everyone seems to care about 1886s. An extremely nice 1886, with just a few value-adding features, can cost as much as a brand new sports car. A mint condition Model 255 Winchester usually costs less than a one-night stay at a fancy hotel.

Every serious collector dreams of that moment when the phone rings, and on the line is a neighbor, or someone at work, telling him that a relative has passed away and that they found a Winchester Model 1886 in the closet. They then ask him if he would like to buy the weapon for $1000, because that's what a neighbor told him it was worth. The Winchester collector's heart rate will increase by a minimum of 20 beats a minute then and there. If, upon inspection, the rifle's receiver shows bright case color, the telltale band of a take-down rifle is there, the wood on the rifle is checkered, and the caliber is one of the more rare ones, the collector just might be in danger of having a heart attack.

Such is the collector's dream - except for the heart attack part - and it happens in real life with more regularity than most people might suspect. In the mid-1980s, I purchased seven mint Model 1876 rifles, of which all are different, and all were deluxe models, one being a 1 of 100 model and one being a 1 of a 1000 model. I paid a total of $5000 for the seven rifles. When I think back to those glorious moments, even today, I get excited. I still have these rifles, and they give me great pleasure and satisfaction, and I realize how lucky I was then, and how fortunate I am now.

If you want to become a collector rather than an accumulator, you should begin to develop a "collector's philosophy." You may want to collect a particular model, or you may want to collect a particular "type" of weapon, e.g., US-marked weapons, weapons of a particular caliber or configuration, or a broader category of weapons such as bolt action .22 rimfire rifles. There are so many interesting collections that can be assembled that it would take a whole book to just discuss the possibilities.

To give the reader a little something to think about, I would like to give you a little story about my collecting history. When I first graduated from university, I was mostly broke. I loved guns, and couldn't stay away from other gun people, nor was I able to stay away from the gun shows. But I couldn't afford to buy the guns I really wanted, which were the guns that everyone else wanted: Winchester lever action rifles. Consequently, I looked around for something to buy, and I came up with the idea of collecting High Standard pistols. I did so for seven reasons: 1) they were very inexpensive, 2) there were lots of variations,) there were lots of them around, 4) they were in a caliber, .22 long rifle, that I could afford to shoot, 5) no one seemed to know much about them, 6) they were very well-made, and 7) no one cared about them. In the next few years, I put together a very nice collection of about 50 guns, most of them either in the box or in mint condition, and one that included all of the extremely rare examples.

As my financial situation improved and I found out that I could, for the most part, finance my collecting with buying and selling, I got into collecting Winchesters. As time went on, I became fascinated with almost every Winchester rifle that was hand-fitted and had a machined receiver. However, at one time, I became very interested in the little high-quality .22 bolt action rifles that Winchester made in the 1920s through the 1950s. They are very interesting, and there are a lot of them, and once again, I could accumulate them very inexpensively, because no one else cared. I had a lot of fun with that, and in no way did it interfere with my primary pursuit.

Once, in the late 1970s, I went to a gun show and saw an elderly gentleman selling off his collection of Model 62 and 61 Winchesters. I could not afford to buy them all, but I bought the rarest ones, but only if they were in mint or better condition. Eventually, I was able to fill in the ones I didn't have, but because I had many of the more rare ones, it was easy and it could be done economically.

I share this with you because it demonstrates how a person can begin a collection of particular rifles and in the long run end up with something that provides a lot of pleasure and at the same time is an excellent investment vehicle. At no time, however, did I merely "accumulate" Winchesters. Each of my areas of interest was well-defined. This is one way to get started. It's not difficult, and it doesn't have to be expensive. It can, however, be your obsession.

In short, my collecting philosophy is to buy that which I can afford and need to complete my collection: weapons with condition, originality, and rarity – weapons that, I believe, will, within a reasonable time, undergo accumulation and a resulting increase in value.

That's my collecting philosophy. What's yours?

I'M AN ACCUMULATOR

By Dan Shideler, Editor, Standard Catalog of® Firearms

I'm delighted to have an essay by such a noted authority as Joseph Cornell appear in this edition of *Standard Catalog of® Firearms*. There are very few subjects I'd choose to argue about with Joe, least of all Winchester firearms; but after reading his essay ("I'm A Collector"), I am compelled by honesty to make an admission:

I'm not a collector. I'm an accumulator.

A collector, as Joe quite rightly points out, concentrates with laser-like specificity on a particular make or type of subject: in his case, Winchester Model 62s. Once upon a time, I was indeed a collector, but it didn't have anything to do with guns. Believe it or not, I collected sousaphones.

You know what a sousaphone is: that big snail-shaped tuba you see during football half-time shows. Fifteen years ago, I collected them. In fact, I had 23 of them hanging on my living room walls. My collection included an extremely rare H. N. White 1895 "raincatcher" model and many other scarce types.

I was younger then. Today, I don't even pretend to have the discipline to concentrate single-mindedly on sousaphones or anything else – certainly not firearms. As I write this, I have in my office gunrack the following guns: a Remington Nylon 10-C, a Remington Model 8 in .25 Remington, a Hubertus drilling, a Staggs-Bilt Model 20-30.30, a Smith & Wesson 1st Model Hand Ejector, a Forehand & Wadsworth .32 Double Action, a Taurus Model 63, a Winchester Model 1895, a J. C. Higgins Model 60, a Winchester Model 1910, a Mossberg Model 26-T Targo smoothbore rifle, and a Remington Model 673 Guide Rifle. And those are just the ones in my office.

Is there a trend there, a theme? If so, I don't see it; so I must be what Joe Cornell would call an accumulator. I pick up guns that interest me, frequently for reasons I don't even understand. The 10-C sits in my rack because it's in pristine condition and because when I was a kid, there was nothing cooler than those Remington Nylons. They were the Batmobile of .22 rifles. The Model 8 is there because I like both the .25 Remington cartridge (don't ask me why) as well as the Browning-designed autoloading rifle.

The Hubertus drilling is there because. . .because. . .well, there's got to be a reason. The Staggs-Bilt gets in because it's the ugliest combination gun I've ever seen and the company made only 2000 of them before they got their pants sued off. I give space to the S&W 1st Model Hand Ejector because I think the model is underappreciated. The F&W .32 is there because it my grandfather carried it back in the Dillinger days (he was a banker). The Taurus 63 is there because I was able to buy it new for $189 and Taurus builds quality stuff.

The Winchester Model 1895 is the new model chambered in .405. I like its looks. The J. C. Higgins sits right next to it because it cost me $75 and, besides, it was America's first successful gas-operated shotgun. The Winchester Model 1910 is there simply because I like the name of the cartridge it chambers, the .401 Winchester Self Loading. (I took a Michigan whitetail with it a few years ago, too.) The Mossberg Targo is there because I've always had a fondness for the .22 Shot cartridge and smoothbore .22s. And I give space to the Model 673 in .350 Remington Magnum because it reminds me of the Model 600 Magnum that I was much too young to buy back in 1968.

All of this must sound terribly shabby to serious collectors. I must seem like a ragpicker to them. What's worse, I actually shoot the guns I accumulate. In fact, I shoot them a lot. To me, guns are to be shot, enjoyed, and then passed on to the next guy. I could no more put my guns in a glass case, each bearing a carefully-prepared index tag and a reference number, than I could dump them in Lake Michigan.

If I were a collector – if I had to concentrate on a single type of gun – I think it would be the Winchester Self Loading series: the Models 1903, 1905, 1907, 07, 1910 and 63 semi-auto rifles and the Model 1911 shotgun. There's enough variation there to make a nice little collection. In fact, sometimes I light one of my 300+ pipes (another accumulation) and sit back and contemplate how fine it would be to have a real, bona-fide collection of Winchester Self Loaders.

But then I wonder what would happen if I then stumbled across a nice Winchester Model 12 Duck Gun or a Webley Pug or an H&R Model 999 Deluxe or a Daisy VL rifle? I'd have to buy it, of course, and then, slowly but surely, my collection would degrade into a mere accumulation. Then I'd have nothing to do but take all those wonderful guns out to the range and have myself a shooter's holiday.

And, by gum, that sounds pretty good to me. I like to shoot and, to me, the more variety the better. To concentrate on collecting rather than shooting is a foreign, funny-tasting concept to me. I could no more set my sights on nailing down every known variation of, say, the Winchester Model 1892 than I could go to a Ritz-Carlton buffet and limit myself just to the shrimp cocktail. What about the lobster tail? *The bouef bourgognone*? The cherry torte?

Come to think of it, that's not a bad analogy. I'm a *gourmand*, not a *gourmet*. The world of firearms is a vast smorgasbord, and before I die I intend to sample as much of it as I can. I'll load my plate, empty it, and keep coming back for more. True, I'll never enjoy the deep inner satisfaction that comes from having row after row of museum pieces, but I'll sure be well-rounded.

Have you ever heard of a pair of books titled *Pistols: A Modern Encyclopedia* and *Rifles: A Modern Encyclopedia*? These volumes, which even today sit in my bookshelf, were written around 1960 by a wonderfully chatty old gentleman named Henry M. Stebbins. When I was in my formative years, I devoured these two books. I mean I literally read the covers off them. I read about the Winchester Model 07, the

Colt Police Positive Special, the Remington Model 740 and a host of other guns that were really happening them back then but have since become collectibles. I remember thinking how wonderful it would be to own the guns Stebbins wrote about so enticingly.

Today, thanks to the internet and my local dealer, I can actually go out and buy any of these guns, and doing so satisfies a Stebbins-induced craving that has burned in me for 40 long years. Were I a serious collector, I'd have to forego that pleasure in favor of a more structured, rigidly-defined approach, and that's something I'm just not willing to do.

I sometimes wonder if real collectors aren't just chasing will-o'-the-wisps anyway. Years ago, in another life, I was product manager for the country's largest maker of musical instruments. As such I had an inside view of how instruments are made, and I learned first-hand the futility of collecting any manufactured article in all of its factory variations.

Let's say that on a particular day, we were building trumpets. (Believe it or not, a lot of people collect trumpets.) If we ran out of, say, monel pistons for a particular model of professional-grade trumpet, we'd grab three nickel pistons and use them instead. If we ran out of a No. 1234 tuning slide brace, we'd use a No. 1334 cornet tuning slide brace. If we ran out of a "this" kind of case, we'd use a "that" kind of case. These little substitutions didn't affect the quality of the finished trumpet, but they did constitute that collector's nightmare, the "uncatalogued factory variation."

In the firearms world, one of the most famous uncatalogued factory variations is the Colt 1st Generation Single Action Army "Long Flute" model. This red-headed stepchild came about when Colt decided to use up its inventory of obsolete Model 1878 Frontier Double Action long-fluted cylinders by building Model 1873 Single Action Armies around them. Colt was doing the same thing we did at the instrument factory: using up what we had at hand. Why not? Waste not, want not - and keep those production lines running.

That's just one example. Joe Cornell speaks of another such variation in his collection, a two-digit Winchester that was put together with a Model 1890 nickeled Expert receiver and other nickeled 1890 Expert parts but was numbered and stamped as a Model 62. Can that be the only such factory-put-together variation? Hardly. Yet that's exactly the kind of thing that would drive me crazy if I were a collector: the knowledge that my quest would probably never end.

True collectors are driven by what we might call the organizational impulse: the need to classify, to categorize, to define. They are the accountants of the firearms collecting hobby, the statisticians, the actuarial scientists. I envy their single-mindedness of purpose, and if it weren't for them, we accumulators could not benefit from their admirable research. We owe them an incalculable debt.

Yet for all of that, I think I'll just go on buying whichever guns suit my fancy. Today it might be a Whitney Wolverine; tomorrow, a Stevens Visible Loader or a Bronco .22/.410. And if I should happen to find a really cherry Model 1886 Winchester Express Rifle in .50-110 at a farm auction, of course I'll buy it. I'll take it out back and shoot it, too.

If it's really nice, I might even put it in my office gun rack - right next to my Mossberg Targo.

A

A.A.
Azanza & Arrizabalaga
Eibar, Spain

A.A.
A 6.35mm and 7.65mm caliber semi-automatic pistol with a 6- and 9-shot magazine. Many of these pistols are identifiable by the trademark "AA" on their frames.

Courtesy James Rankin

Exc.	V.G.	Good	Fair	Poor
300	175	150	100	50

Reims
A 6.35mm or 7.65mm caliber semi-automatic pistol with 6- or 8-round magazine capacity. Most of the pistols have their slides marked "1914 Model Automatic Pistol Reims Patent."

Courtesy James Rankin

Exc.	V.G.	Good	Fair	Poor
300	175	150	100	50

A.A.A.
Aldazabal
Eibar, Spain

Modelo 1919
A 7.65mm semi-automatic pistol with 9-round magazine capacity. The trademark of a knight's head over three A's is on the side of the slide and the grips.

Courtesy James Rankin

Exc.	V.G.	Good	Fair	Poor
300	175	150	100	50

A. J. ORDNANCE
A delayed blowback action that is unique in that every shot was double-action. This pistol was chambered for the .45 ACP cartridge and had a 3.5" stainless steel barrel with fixed sights and plastic grips. The detachable magazine held 6 shots, and the standard finish was matte blue. Chrome plating was available and would add approximately 15 percent to the values listed.

NIB	Exc.	V.G.	Good	Fair	Poor
650	550	500	400	250	175

A-SQUARE
Bedford, Kentucky

Hannibal Grade
Using the P-17 Enfield action, with a 22" to 26" barrel, this rifle is chambered for 32 calibers from 7mm Rem. Mag. up to and including the .500 A-Square Mag. and .577 Tyrannosaur. Blued with a checkered walnut pistol-grip stock. Introduced in 1986. Weights range from 9 lbs. to 13.25 lbs. depending on caliber.

NIB	Exc.	V.G.	Good	Fair	Poor
3000	2500	1700	1000	600	350

Caesar Grade
Utilizing a Remington Model 700 action and chambered for the same cartridges as the above, with the exception that A-Square proprietary cartridges are not available. Also made in the left-hand version. Introduced in 1986. Weights are in the 8.5 to 11 lbs. range.

NIB	Exc.	V.G.	Good	Fair	Poor
3000	2500	1700	1000	600	350

Hamilcar Grade

A smaller and lighter version of the Hannibal Grade. It was introduced in 1994. It is designed to be chambered for .30-06 cartridges. Weights are around 8 to 8.5 lbs. Introduced in 1994.

NIB	Exc.	V.G.	Good	Fair	Poor
3000	2500	1700	1000	600	350

Genghis Khan Model

This model is designed for varmint shooting and is fitted with a heavyweight barrel. Offered in .22-250, .243 Win., 6mm Rem., .25-06, .257 Wby., and .264 Win. Barrel length is to customer's specifications, as is length of pull. No iron sights are fitted to this model. Weight is approximately 11 lbs.

NIB	Exc.	V.G.	Good	Fair	Poor
3000	2500	1600	975	550	325

A & R SALES SOUTH

El Monte, California

45 Auto

An alloy-frame version of the Colt Model 1911 semi-automatic pistol.

NIB	Exc.	V.G.	Good	Fair	Poor
450	300	200	150	125	100

Mark IV Sporter

A semi-automatic copy of the M-14 military rifle. Manufactured in .308 cal. (7.65mm NATO) only.

NIB	Exc.	V.G.	Good	Fair	Poor
750	450	300	200	150	100

ABADIE

Liege, Belgium

System Abadie Model 1878

A 9mm double-action revolver with a 6-shot cylinder, octagonal barrel and integral ejector rod.

Exc.	V.G.	Good	Fair	Poor
450	300	175	125	90

System Abadie Model 1886

A heavier version of the above.

Exc.	V.G.	Good	Fair	Poor
500	350	200	125	90

ABBEY, F.J. & CO.

Chicago, Illinois

The Abbey Brothers produced a variety of percussion rifles and shotguns which are all of individual design. The prices listed represent what a plain F.J. Abbey & Company firearm might realize.

Rifle

Exc.	V.G.	Good	Fair	Poor
—	950	500	250	125

Shotgun

Exc.	V.G.	Good	Fair	Poor
—	1250	600	300	150

ABBEY, GEORGE T.

Utica, New York, and Chicago, Illinois

George T. Abbey originally worked in Utica, New York, from 1845 to 1852. He moved to Chicago in 1852 and was in business until 1874. He manufactured a wide variety of percussion and cartridge firearms. The values listed represent those of his most common products.

Single-Barrel .44 Cal.

Exc.	V.G.	Good	Fair	Poor
—	1575	750	400	200

Side-by-Side Double-Barrel .44 Cal.

Exc.	V.G.	Good	Fair	Poor
—	2275	1000	525	250

Over-and-Under Double-Barrel .44 Cal.

Exc.	V.G.	Good	Fair	Poor
—	2525	1000	525	250

ABESSER & MERKEL

Suhl, Germany

Crown Grade

This model is a single-barrel Trap gun with Greener cross bolt-action with two underbolt locks. Offered in 12 gauge with barrel lengths from 28" to 34". Ventilated rib standard. Skip line checkering. Pistol or straight grip stock. Gun weight is between 7 and 7.5 lbs. Engraved receiver with game scenes.

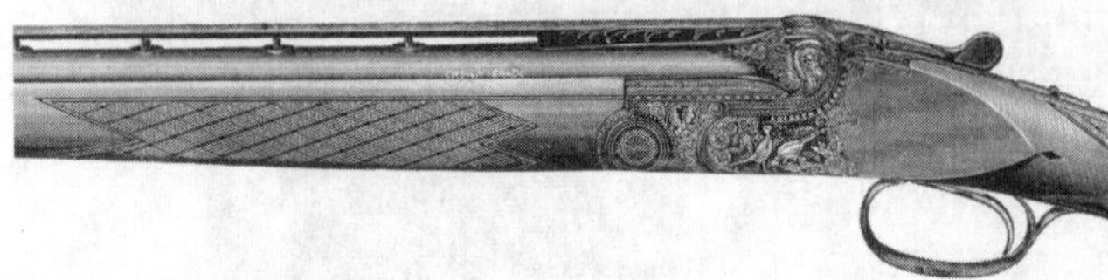

Courtesy Dan Sheil

Exc.	V.G.	Good	Fair	Poor
5550	4525	3525	—	—

Diamond Grade

This model is a side-by-side gun offered in 12, 16, 20, and 28 gauge as well as .410 bore. Auto ejectors. Double triggers. Full coverage engraving with artistic stock carving behind the frame. Skip line checkering. Many extras offered on this grade will affect price. Barrel lengths from 25" to 32". Weights are from 6.5 lbs. to 7 lbs. Prices are for standard gun with no extras.

Courtesy Dan Sheil

Exc.	V.G.	Good	Fair	Poor
10100	8100	7100	—	—

NOTE: Add 50 percent for 20 gauge guns and 100 percent for 28 gauge or .410 bore guns.

Empire Grade

This shotgun is a side-by-side with an Anson-Deeley action. The receiver is fully engraved with game birds and fine scroll. The stock is carved behind the action. Checkering is a fine skip line-style. Auto ejectors. Pistol or straight grip stock. With or without Monte Carlo and cheekpiece. Prices listed are for prewar guns with fluid steel barrels.

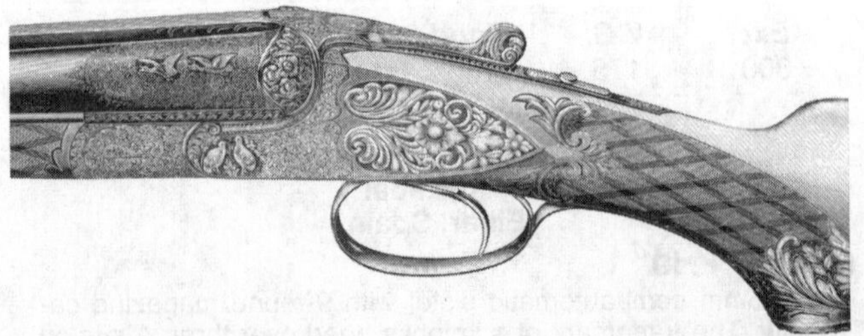

Courtesy Dan Sheil

Exc.	V.G.	Good	Fair	Poor
12200	10150	8200	—	—

NOTE: Add 50 percent for 20 gauge guns and 100 percent for 28 gauge or .410 bore guns.

Excelsior Grade

This side-by-side gun is fitted with engraved side plates. Anson-Deeley action with double triggers. Fine line checkering. Figured walnut stock. All gauges offered from 12 to .410. Barrel lengths from 25" to 32". Many extra cost options available.

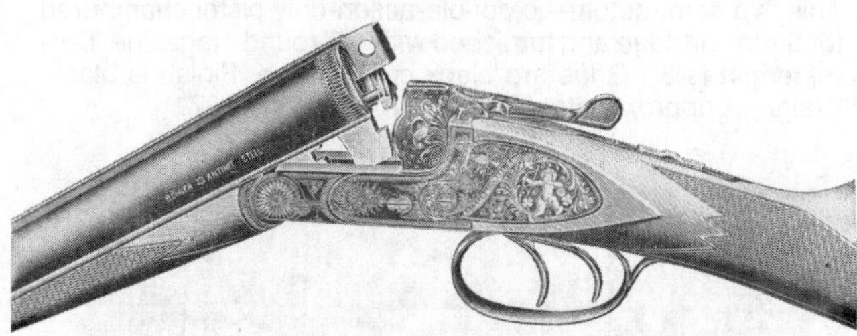

Courtesy Dan Sheil

Exc.	V.G.	Good	Fair	Poor
7700	6700	5200	—	—

NOTE: Add 50 percent for 20 gauge guns and 100 percent for 28 gauge or .410 bore guns.

Diana Grade

This is an over-and-under combination gun with Greener cross bolt-action. Safety is located on the side of the pistol grip. Iron sights. Set trigger for rifle barrel. A wide variety of centerfire calibers offered with barrel lengths from 26" to 30".

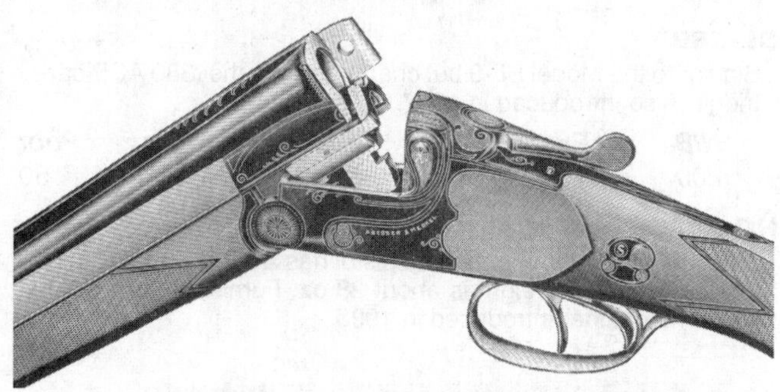

Courtesy Dan Sheil

Exc.	V.G.	Good	Fair	Poor
8250	7250	5250	—	—

Vandalia Grade

This is an over-and-under gun chambered for 4.75" 12 gauge shells. Barrel lengths from 28" to 32". Walnut stock with pistol or straight grip with skip line checkering. Double triggers with extractors. Premium for factory multi-barrel combinations.

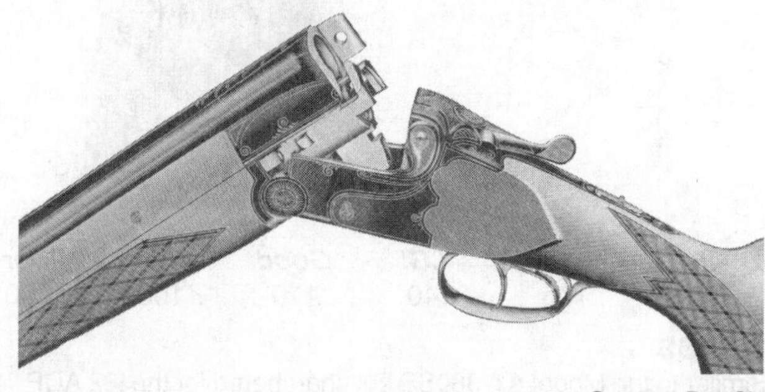

Courtesy Dan Sheil

Exc.	V.G.	Good	Fair	Poor
6000	5000	3500	—	—

Nimrod

This is a drilling with a Greener cross bolt-action and double under bolt. Safety is located on side of grip. Top two barrels may be 12, 16, or 20 gauge. The bottom barrel is offered in a variety of centerfire calibers. Iron sights. Pistol or straight grip stock. Receiver engraved with game scenes. Add 50 percent for 20 gauge.

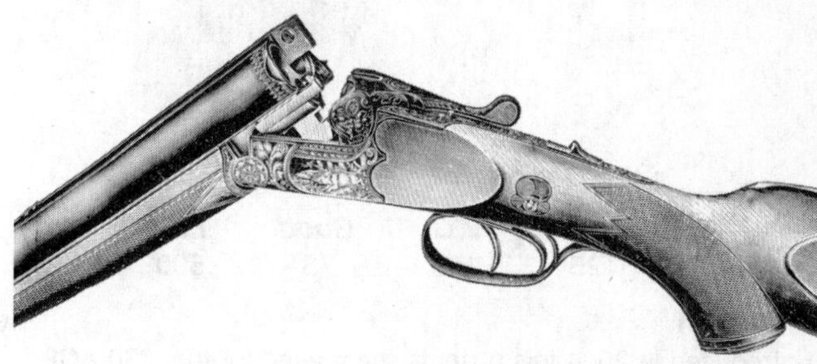

Courtesy Dan Sheil

Exc.	V.G.	Good	Fair	Poor
8750	7250	5250	—	—

Magazine Rifle

A bolt-action rifle offered in a wide variety of calibers. Barrel lengths from 24" to 30". Calibers from 6.5mm to .404 Rimless. This model may have a Zeiss scope or other special order features that will affect price. Add $2000 for Magnum actions.

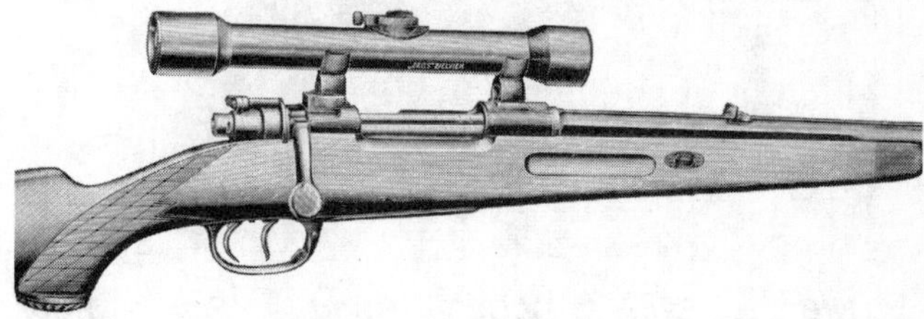

Courtesy Dan Sheil

Exc.	V.G.	Good	Fair	Poor
4250	3250	2750	—	—

ACCU-MATCH

Mesa, Arizona

Accu-Match Custom Pistol

This is a competition pistol built on the Colt 1911 design. Chambered for the .45 ACP it is fitted with a 5-1/2" match grade stainless steel barrel, stainless steel slide and frame with extended slide release and safety. Fitted with a beavertail grip safety and wraparound finger groove rubber grips, this pistol has a threaded three port compensator and dual action recoil spring system with three dot sight system.

NIB	Exc.	V.G.	Good	Fair	Poor
900	700	550	—	—	—

ACCU-TEK

Chino, California

AT-380SS

Introduced in 1991 this semi-automatic pistol is chambered for the .380 ACP cartridge. Fitted with a 2.75" barrel with adjustable for windage rear sight. Black composition grips. Stainless steel construction. Furnished with a 5-round magazine. Weight is about 20 oz.

NIB	Exc.	V.G.	Good	Fair	Poor
200	125	100	75	500	—

AT-380 II

Introduced in 2004 this pistol is chambered for the .380 ACP cartridge. It is fitted with a 2.8" barrel. Magazine capacity is 6 rounds. Stainless steel. Magazine release is on bottom of grip. Weight is about 23 oz.

NIB	Exc.	V.G.	Good	Fair	Poor
215	175	150	125	95	—

CP-9SS

This semi-automatic double-action-only stainless steel pistol is chambered for the 9mm cartridge and is fitted with a 3.2" barrel with adjustable for windage rear sight. Magazine capacity is 8 rounds. Grips are black checkered nylon. Weight is about 28 oz. Introduced in 1992.

NIB	Exc.	V.G.	Good	Fair	Poor
225	175	150	100	75	—

CP-45SS

Similar to the Model CP-9SS but chambered for the .45 ACP cartridge. Furnished with a 6-round magazine. Introduced in 1996.

NIB	Exc.	V.G.	Good	Fair	Poor
250	225	175	150	125	—

CP-40SS

Introduced in 1992 and similar to the CP-9SS but chambered for .40 S&W cartridge. Furnished with a 7-round magazine.

NIB	Exc.	V.G.	Good	Fair	Poor
250	225	165	150	125	—

BL-9

This is a semi-automatic double-action-only pistol chambered for 9mm cartridge and furnished with a 5-round magazine. Barrel length is 3". Grips are black composition. Finish is black. Weight is approximately 22 oz. Introduced in 1997.

NIB	Exc.	V.G.	Good	Fair	Poor
235	150	125	100	75	50

BL-380

Similar to the Model BL-9 but chambered for the .380 ACP cartridge. Also introduced in 1997.

NIB	Exc.	V.G.	Good	Fair	Poor
200	150	120	100	75	50

HC-380SS

This .380 ACP semi-automatic pistol has a 2.75" barrel. Stainless steel finish. Weight is about 28 oz. Furnished with a 10-round magazine. Introduced in 1993.

NIB	Exc.	V.G.	Good	Fair	Poor
225	175	140	110	100	50

AT-32SS

Similar to the Model AT-380SS but chambered for the .32 ACP cartridge. Introduced in 1991.

NIB	Exc.	V.G.	Good	Fair	Poor
200	125	100	75	50	40

ACHA
Domingo Acha
Vizcaya, Spain

Atlas
A 6.35mm caliber semi-automatic pistol manufactured during the 1920s in the style of the Model 1906 Browning. Grips are plain checkered hard rubber. Some grips had the ACHA trademark of the Count's head. The name Atlas appears on the slide. Later models incorporated a grip safety.

Courtesy James Rankin

Exc.	*V.G.*	*Good*	*Fair*	*Poor*
200	150	100	75	50

Looking Glass (Ruby-Style)
This is a 7.65mm semi-automatic pistol in the Ruby-style. These pistols were furnished with a 7-, 9-, or 12-round magazine.

Courtesy James Rankin

Exc.	*V.G.*	*Good*	*Fair*	*Poor*
250	150	100	75	50

Looking Glass
A 6.35mm or 7.65mm caliber semi-automatic pistol. Various markings are seen on these pistols and their grips as they were sold in both France and Spain by different distributors. The pistol pictured has two trademarks: Domingo Acha on the grips and Fabrique D'Arms de Guerre De Grande Presision on the slide.

Courtesy James Rankin

Exc.	*V.G.*	*Good*	*Fair*	*Poor*
250	150	100	75	50

ACME
SEE—Davenport Arms Co., Maltby Henley & Co., and Merwin & Hulbert & Co.

ACME ARMS
New York, New York

A trade name found on .22 and .32 caliber revolvers and 12 gauge shotguns marketed by the Cornwall Hardware Company.

.22 Revolver
A 7-shot single-action revolver.

Exc.	*V.G.*	*Good*	*Fair*	*Poor*
375	275	175	125	75

.32 Revolver
A 5-shot single-action revolver.

Exc.	*V.G.*	*Good*	*Fair*	*Poor*
400	300	200	150	100

Shotgun
A 12 gauge double-barrel shotgun with external hammers.

Exc.	*V.G.*	*Good*	*Fair*	*Poor*
400	275	175	125	75

ACME HAMMERLESS
Made by Hopkins & Allen
Norwich, Connecticut

Acme Hammerless
A .32 or .38 caliber 5-shot revolver with either exposed hammer or enclosed hammer. Sometimes known as the "Forehand 1891."

Exc.	*V.G.*	*Good*	*Fair*	*Poor*
—	300	175	50	25

ACTION
Eibar, Spain
Maker—Modesto Santos

Action
A 6.35mm or 7.65mm semi-automatic pistol marked on the slide "Pistolet Automatique Modele 1920." Often found bearing the trade name "Corrientes" as well as the maker's trademark "MS."

Exc.	*V.G.*	*Good*	*Fair*	*Poor*
250	150	100	80	60

ACTION ARMS LTD.

Philadelphia, Pennsylvania

AT-84, AT-88

This pistol is the Swiss version of of the CZ-75. It is built at ITM, Solothurn, Switzerland. The AT-84 is chambered for the 9mm cartridge. The AT-88 is chambered for the .41 Action Express. Both have a 4.75" barrel. The 9mm pistol has a magazine capacity of 15 rounds while the .41 AE has a capacity of 10 rounds. Finish is either blue or chrome. with walnut grips.

Courtesy James Rankin

NIB	Exc.	V.G.	Good	Fair	Poor
800	600	525	350	300	150

AT-84P, AT-88P

As above, with a 3.7" barrel and smaller frame.

NIB	Exc.	V.G.	Good	Fair	Poor
800	600	525	350	300	150

AT-84H, AT-88H

As above with a 3.4" barrel and smaller frame.

NIB	Exc.	V.G.	Good	Fair	Poor
800	600	525	350	300	150

Timber Wolf Carbine

Introduced in 1989, this slide-action carbine features an 18.5" barrel with adjustable rear sight and blade front sight. Chambered for the .357 Magnum or .38 Special cartridges, it is offered in either blue or hard chrome finish. Weight is approximately 5.5 lbs. Built in Israel by Israel Military Industries.

NIB	Exc.	V.G.	Good	Fair	Poor
500	450	350	300	200	125

Action Arms/IMI Uzi Carbine Models A and B

16-inch-barreled semi-auto version of the Uzi submachine gun chambered in 9mm Parabellum. Add 10 percent for nylon Uzi case and accessories.

NIB	Exc.	V.G.	Good	Fair	Poor
1500	1300	1050	850	600	250

ADAMS

Deane, Adams & Deane
London, England
London Armoury Co. (After 1856)

Revolvers based upon Robert Adams' patents were manufactured by the firm of Deane, Adams & Deane. Although more technically advanced than the pistols produced by Samuel Colt, Adams' revolvers were popular primarily in England and the British Empire.

Adams Model 1851 Self-Cocking Revolver

A .44 caliber double-action percussion revolver with a 7.5" octagonal barrel and 5-shot cylinder. The barrel and frame are blued, the cylinder case hardened and the grips are walnut. The top strap is marked "Deane, Adams and Deane 30 King William St. London Bridge." This revolver does not have a hammer spur and functions only as a double-action.

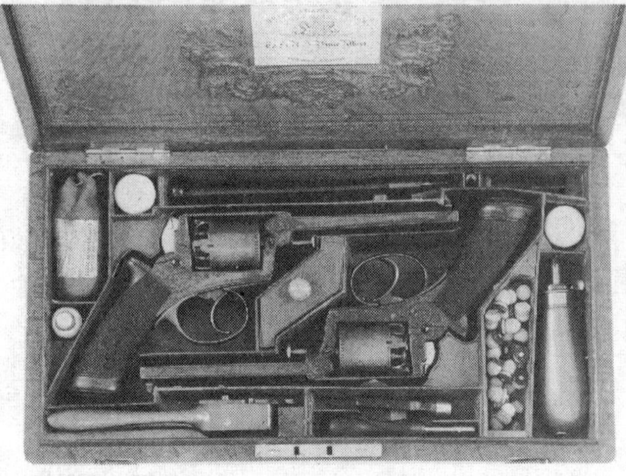

Exc.	V.G.	Good	Fair	Poor
—	2550	1000	700	400

Adams Pocket Revolver

As above, in .31 caliber with a 4.5" barrel.

Exc.	V.G.	Good	Fair	Poor
—	2775	1200	850	400

Beaumont-Adams Revolver

As above, fitted with a Tranter Patent loading lever and the hammer made with a spur.

Exc.	V.G.	Good	Fair	Poor
—	1750	850	625	300

ADAMY GEBRUDER

Suhl, Germany

Over-and-Under Shotgun

A 12 or 16 gauge double-barrel over-and-under shotgun with 26" to 30" barrels, double triggers and a walnut stock.

Exc.	V.G.	Good	Fair	Poor
1950	1500	1100	750	400

This symbol denotes "Sleepers" with rapidly-rising values and/or significant collector potential.

ADIRONDACK ARMS CO. or A.S. BABBITT CO.

Plattsburgh, New York

Orvil M. Robinson Patent Rifle

The Robinson tube-fed repeating rifle was made in New York between 1870 and 1874. The early models, 1870-1872, are marked "A.S. Babbitt"; the later models, 1872-1874, "Adirondack Arms Co." The Company was sold to Winchester in 1874, but they never produced the Robinson after that date. The rifle has been found in two styles: The first with small fingers on the hammer to cock and operate the mechanism; the second with buttons on the receiver to retract the bolt and cock the hammer. The rifle was made in .44 cal. with an octagonal barrel usually found in 26" or 28" length. The frames were predominantly brass; but some iron frames have been noted, and they will bring a premium of approximately 25 percent. The barrel and magazine tube have a blued finish.

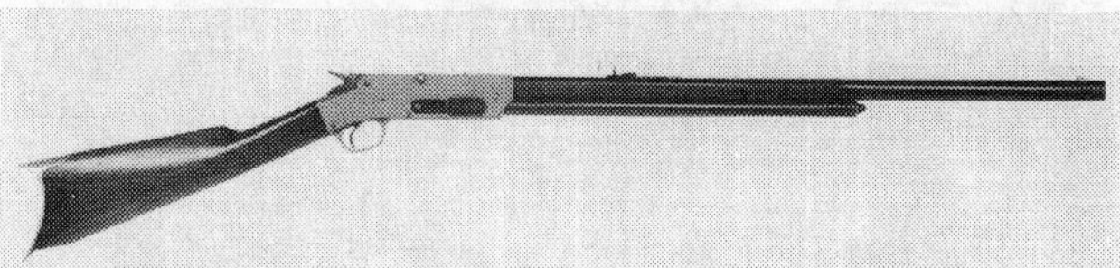

Courtesy Buffalo Bill Historical Center, Cody, Wyoming

First Model

Exc.	*V.G.*	*Good*	*Fair*	*Poor*
—	4500	1750	750	300

Second Model

Exc.	*V.G.*	*Good*	*Fair*	*Poor*
—	4500	1750	750	300

ADLER

Engelbrecht & Wolff
Blasii, Germany

An extremely rare and unusually designed semi-automatic pistol adapted for the 7.25mm Adler cartridge. This is a striker-fired blowback pistol with a 3.4" barrel. Single-column magazine has an 8-round capacity. Weight is approximately 24 oz. Produced in very limited numbers, probably only a few hundred, between 1906 and 1907.

Courtesy James Rankin

Courtesy James Rankin

Exc.	*V.G.*	*Good*	*Fair*	*Poor*
—	6000	3000	1250	700

ADVANCED SMALL ARMS INDUSTRIES

Solothurn, Switzerland

one Pro .45

Introduced in 1997 and built in Switzerland by ASAI this pistol features a 3" barrel chambered for the .45 ACP cartridge. It is based on a short recoil operation and is available in double-action or double-action-only. Also available is a kit (purchased separately) to convert the pistol to .400 Cor-Bon caliber. The pistol weighs about 24 oz. empty. The conversion kit has a retail price of $209.00.

NIB	*Exc.*	*V.G.*	*Good*	*Fair*	*Poor*
650	525	—	—	—	—

ADVANTAGE ARMS U.S.A., INC.

Distributed by Wildfire Sports
St. Paul, Minnesota

Model 422

A .22 or .22 Magnum caliber 4 barrel derringer with 2.5" barrels. Entirely made of an aluminum alloy. Finished in either blue or nickel-plate. Manufactured in 1986 and 1987.

REMINDER

An "N/A" or "—" instead of a price indicates that there is no known price available for that gun in that condition, or the sales for that particular model are so few that a reliable price cannot be given.

NIB	Exc.	V.G.	Good	Fair	Poor
225	125	100	85	65	45

AERO
Manufactura De Armas De Fuego
Guernica, Spain

Model 1914 (Aero)

A 7.65mm caliber semi-automatic pistol with a 3.25" barrel in the Ruby design. The Aero name is on the slide along with an airplane. Magazine capacity is 7 rounds, weight is about 23 oz.

Courtesy James Rankin

Exc.	V.G.	Good	Fair	Poor
350	250	200	125	95

AETNA ARMS CO.
New York

A .22 caliber spur trigger revolver with an octagonal barrel and 7-shot cylinder. The barrel marked "Aetna Arms Co. New York." Manufactured from approximately 1870 to 1880.

Exc.	V.G.	Good	Fair	Poor
—	—	650	350	150

AFC
Auguste Francotte
Liege, Belgium

This was one of the most prolific makers of revolvers in Liege during the last half of the 19th century. It is estimated that over 150 different revolvers were made and marketed by them before they were forced out of business by the German occupation of 1914. Francotte produced many variations from Tranter copies to pinfires, early Smith & Wesson designs to the 11mm M1871 Swedish troopers revolver. They made break-open revolvers and produced only one semi-auto, a 6.35mm blowback design. A good portion of their pistols were produced for the wholesale market and were sold under other names. These particular revolvers will bear the letters "AF" stamped somewhere on the frame. Because of the vast number and variety of pistols produced by this company, cataloging and pricing is beyond the scope of this or any general reference book. It is suggested that any examples encountered be researched on an individual basis.

For more information on Francotte see the information under that listing.

Model 1895

One of the earliest Francotte pistols. Chambered for the 8mm cartridge, it is a lever-operated repeater. Marked "A. Francotte & Co. Makers" on the top of the slide.

Courtesy James Rankin

Exc.	V.G.	Good	Fair	Poor
5250	4250	3250	2000	1500

Trainer

A single-shot target pistol made for competition in .22 caliber short. AFC trademark on the left side of the frame. This model was probably not made by Francotte, but sold by that firm and others.

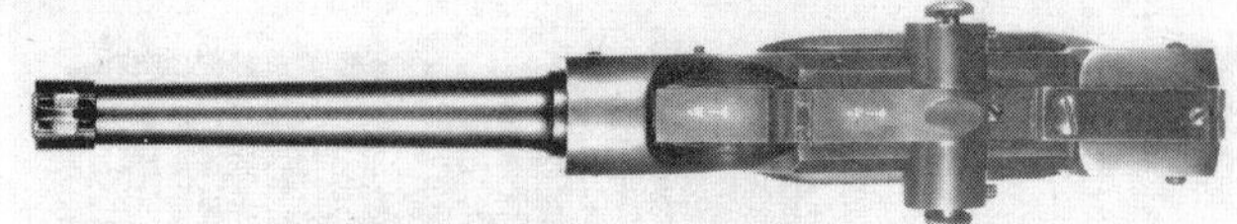

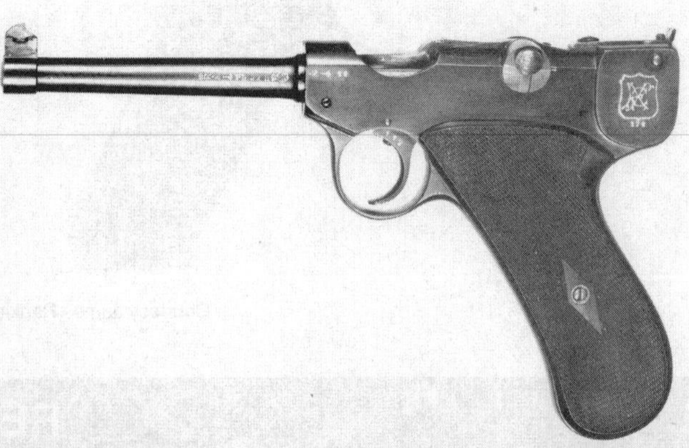

Courtesy James Rankin

Exc.	V.G.	Good	Fair	Poor
3250	2950	2500	2000	1500

Semi-Auto

A 6.35mm, 6-shot detachable magazine pocket pistol with blue finish. This model was marked "A. Francotte A Liege" on the frame.

Courtesy James Rankin

Exc.	V.G.	Good	Fair	Poor
400	275	200	125	90

AFFERBACH, W. A.

Philadelphia, Pennsylvania

This maker is known to have produced copies of Henry Derringer's percussion pocket pistols. Though uncommon, their values would be approximately as listed.

Exc.	V.G.	Good	Fair	Poor
—	—	1750	850	300

AGNER (SAXHOJ PRODUCTS INC.)

Copenhagen, Denmark

Model M 80

A .22 caliber single-shot stainless steel target pistol with a 5.9" barrel, adjustable sights and walnut grips. This pistol is fitted with a dry fire mechanism. Also available in a left-hand version. Imported from 1981 to 1986.

Courtesy James Rankin

Exc.	V.G.	Good	Fair	Poor
1000	700	500	300	150

AGUIRRE

Eibar, Spain

A Spanish manufacturer of pistols prior to World War II.

Basculant

A 6.35mm semi-automatic pistol marked on the slide "Cal. 6.35 Automatic Pistol Basculant."

Exc.	V.G.	Good	Fair	Poor
250	125	100	75	50

LeDragon

As above, with the slide marked "Cal. 6.35 Automatic Pistol Le-Dragon." It is patterend after the Browning Model 1906. A stylized dragon is molded into the grips.

Courtesy James Rankin

Exc.	V.G.	Good	Fair	Poor
250	150	100	75	45

AGUIRRE Y ARANZABAL (AyA)

Eibar, Spain

SIDE-BY-SIDE

Matador Side-by-Side

A 12, 16, 20, 28 or .410 bore boxlock double-barrel shotgun with 26", 28" or 30" barrels, single-selective trigger and automatic ejectors. Blued with a walnut stock. Manufactured from 1955 to 1963.

Exc.	V.G.	Good	Fair	Poor
500	400	350	300	200

NOTE: 28 gauge and .410 add 20 percent.

Matador II Side-by-Side

As above, in 12 or 20 gauge with a ventilated rib.

Exc.	V.G.	Good	Fair	Poor
600	425	375	300	200

Matador III Side-by-Side

As above, with 3" chambers.

NIB	Exc.	V.G.	Good	Fair	Poor
950	750	600	450	350	250

Bolero Side-by-Side

As above, with a non-selective single trigger and extractors. Manufactured until 1984.

Exc.	V.G.	Good	Fair	Poor
500	400	300	250	200

Iberia Side-by-Side

A 12 or 20 gauge Magnum boxlock double-barrel shotgun with 26", 28" or 30" barrels, double triggers and extractors. Blued with a walnut stock.

NIB	Exc.	V.G.	Good	Fair	Poor
600	500	425	325	250	200

Iberia II Side-by-Side

Similar to the above, in 12 or 16 gauge with 28" barrels and 2-3/4" chambers. Still in production.

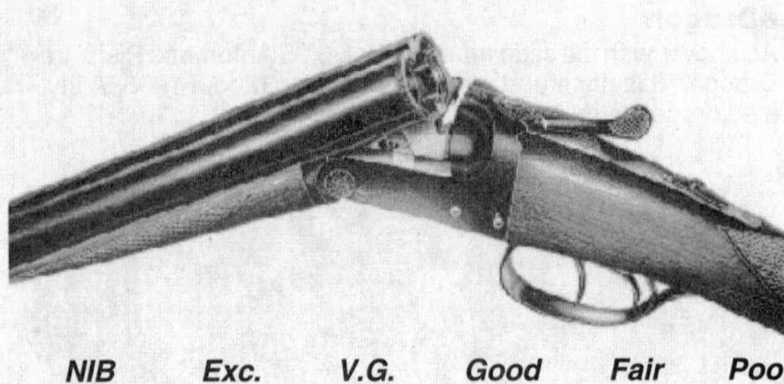

NIB	Exc.	V.G.	Good	Fair	Poor
600	500	425	325	250	200

Model 106 Side-by-Side

A 12, 16, or 20 gauge boxlock double-barrel shotgun with 28" barrels, double triggers and extractors. Blued with a walnut stock. Manufactured until 1985.

NIB	Exc.	V.G.	Good	Fair	Poor
600	500	400	300	250	200

Model 107-LI Side-by-Side

As above, with the receiver lightly engraved and an English-style stock. In 12 or 16 gauge only.

NIB	Exc.	V.G.	Good	Fair	Poor
700	600	525	450	300	250

Model 116 Side-by-Side

A 12, 16 or 20 gauge sidelock double-barrel shotgun with 27" to 30" barrels, double triggers and ejectors. Engraved, blued with a walnut stock. Manufactured until 1985.

NIB	Exc.	V.G.	Good	Fair	Poor
950	800	600	475	350	275

Model 117 Side-by-Side

As above, with 3" chambers.

NIB	Exc.	V.G.	Good	Fair	Poor
850	700	500	425	300	250

Model 117 "Quail Unlimited" Side-by-Side

As above in 12 gauge only with 26" barrels and the receiver engraved "Quail Unlimited of North America." Forty-two were manufactured.

NIB	Exc.	V.G.	Good	Fair	Poor
1500	1200	875	650	425	300

Model 210 Side-by-Side

An exposed hammer, 12 or 16 gauge, boxlock shotgun with 26" to 28" barrels and double triggers. Blued with a walnut stock. Manufactured until 1985.

NIB	Exc.	V.G.	Good	Fair	Poor
800	675	550	400	325	225

Model 711 Boxlock Side-by-Side

A 12 gauge boxlock double-barrel shotgun with 28" or 30" barrels having ventilated ribs, single-selective trigger and automatic ejectors. Manufactured until 1984.

NIB	Exc.	V.G.	Good	Fair	Poor
900	800	700	500	350	250

Model 711 Sidelock Side-by-Side

As above, with sidelocks. Manufactured in 1985 only.

NIB	Exc.	V.G.	Good	Fair	Poor
1000	900	750	500	400	300

Senior Side-by-Side

A custom order 12 gauge double-barrel sidelock shotgun, gold inlaid and engraved. Made strictly to individual customer's specifications.

NIB	Exc.	V.G.	Good	Fair	Poor
15000	12500	9000	7000	4500	2250

OVER-AND-UNDERS

Model 79 "A" Over-and-Under

A 12 gauge boxlock over-and-under double-barrel shotgun with 26", 28" or 30" barrels, single-selective trigger and automatic ejectors. Blued with a walnut stock. Manufactured until 1985.

NIB	Exc.	V.G.	Good	Fair	Poor
1250	1050	925	750	500	300

Model 79 "B" Over-and-Under

As above, with a moderate amount of engraving.

NIB	Exc.	V.G.	Good	Fair	Poor
1350	1150	950	800	575	350

Model 79 "C" Over-and-Under

As above, with extensive engraving.

NIB	Exc.	V.G.	Good	Fair	Poor
2000	1800	1500	1150	675	400

Model 77 Over-and-Under

As above, patterned after the Merkel shotgun.

NIB	Exc.	V.G.	Good	Fair	Poor
3000	2700	2000	1500	1000	500

Coral "A" Over-and-Under

A 12 or 16 gauge over-and-under boxlock double-barrel shotgun with 26" or 28" barrels having ventilated ribs, double triggers and automatic ejectors. Fitted with a Kersten cross bolt. Manufactured until 1985.

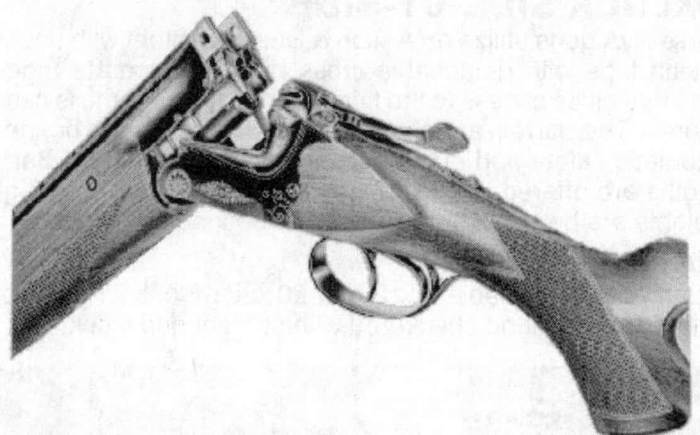

NIB	Exc.	V.G.	Good	Fair	Poor
1250	900	700	500	300	200

Coral "B" Over-and-Under

As above, with an engraved French case hardened receiver.

NIB	Exc.	V.G.	Good	Fair	Poor
1400	1100	750	600	350	250

REMINDER

The prices listed in this book are given to assist the shooter and collector in pursuing their hobby with a better understanding of what is going on in the marketplace.

CURRENTLY IMPORTED SHOTGUNS

SIDELOCK/SIDE-BY-SIDE

AyA sidelock shotguns use the Holland and Holland system. They feature double triggers, articulated front trigger, cocking indicators, bushed firing pins, replaceable firing pins, replaceable hinge pins, and chopper lump barrels. Frame and sidelocks are case-colored. These shotguns weigh between 5 and 7 pounds depending on gauge and barrel length. Barrel lengths are offered in 26", 27", 28", and 29" depending on gauge. All stocks are figured walnut with hand checkering and oil finish. These guns are available with several extra cost options that may affect price. Also influencing price of new guns is the fluctuating dollar in relation to Spanish currency.

Model No. 1

This model is offered in 12 gauge and 20 gauge with special English scroll engraving. Fitted with automatic ejectors and straight grip stock with exhibition quality wood.

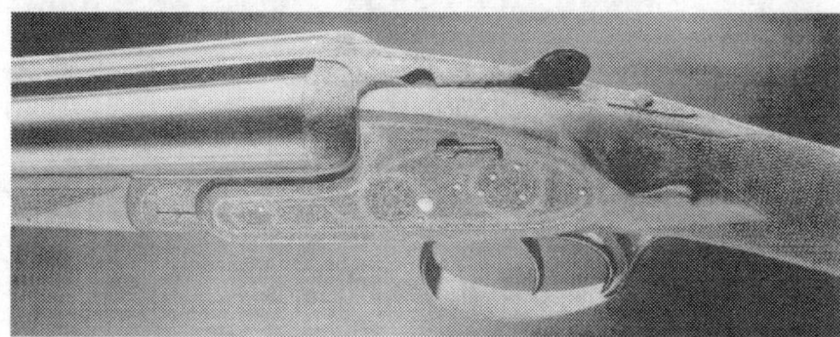

NIB	Exc.	V.G.	Good	Fair	Poor
8200	6500	4750	3500	2000	—

Model No. 1 Deluxe

A deluxe version of the No. 1 with finer wood and engraving.

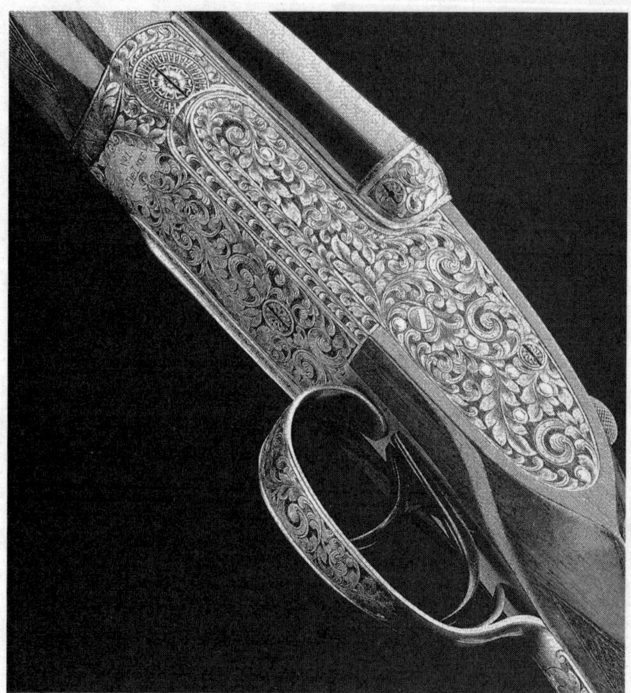

NIB	Exc.	V.G.	Good	Fair	Poor
11000	8500	6500	4750	3000	—

NOTE: For round body deluxe add $350.

Model No. 1 Round Body

As above, but with a round body action.

NIB	Exc.	V.G.	Good	Fair	Poor
8400	6750	5000	2900	1300	—

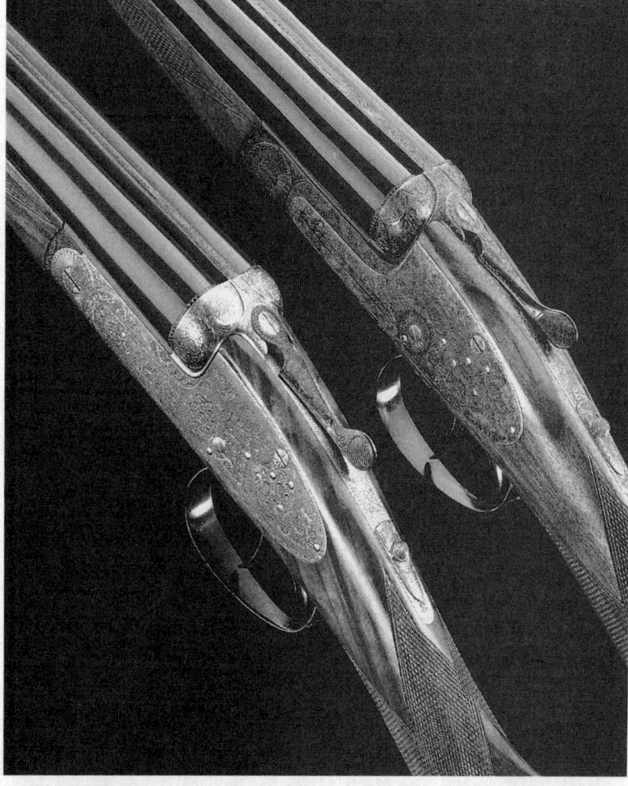

Model No. 2

The Model 2 is offered in 12, 16, 20, and 28 gauge as well as .410 bore. It has automatic ejectors and straight-grip, select walnut stock.

NIB	Exc.	V.G.	Good	Fair	Poor
4000	3000	2500	1850	—	—

Model No. 2 Round Body

As above, but with round body action.

NIB	Exc.	V.G.	Good	Fair	Poor
4200	3250	2750	1950	—	—

Model No. 53

Chambered for 12, 16, and 20 gauge, this model features three locking lugs and side clips. It also has automatic ejectors and straight grip stock.

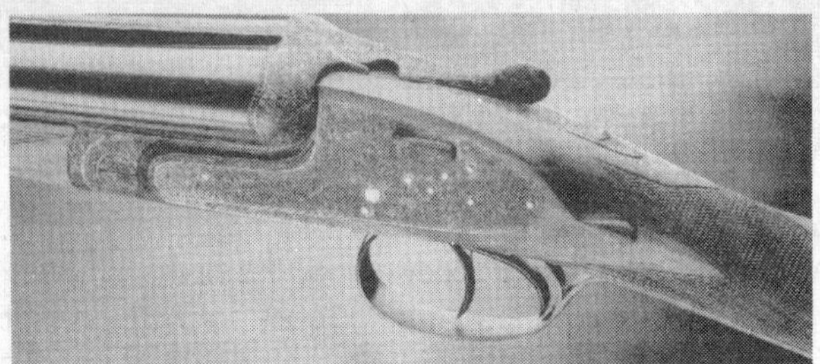

NIB	Exc.	V.G.	Good	Fair	Poor
5400	4000	3250	2650	—	—

Model No. 56

This model is available in 12 gauge only and features three locking lugs, side clips, special wide action body, and raised matted rib. Select walnut, straight-grip stock.

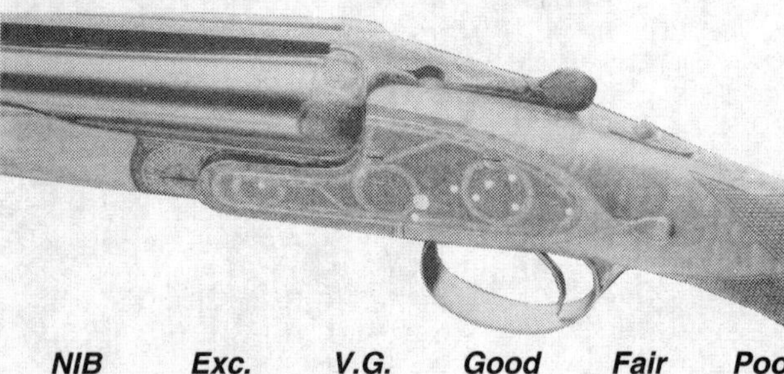

NIB	Exc.	V.G.	Good	Fair	Poor
6500	4000	2500	1200	800	400

Model XXV—Sidelock

Offered in 12 gauge and 20 gauge only this model is fitted with a Churchill-type rib. Automatic ejectors and select straight grip walnut stock are standard.

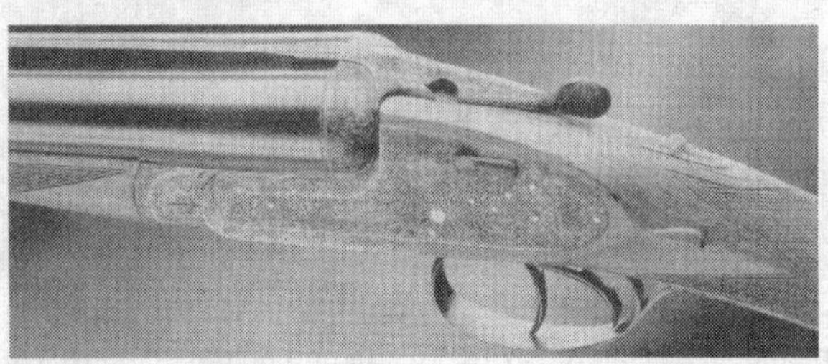

NIB	Exc.	V.G.	Good	Fair	Poor
3250	1750	1200	750	500	300

BOXLOCK SIDE-BY-SIDE

These AyA guns utilize an Anson & Deeley system with double locking lugs with detachable cross pin and separate trigger plate that gives access to the firing mechanism. Frame is case-colored. The barrels are chopper lump, firing pins are bushed, automatic safety and automatic ejectors are standard. Barrel lengths are offered in 26", 27", and 28" depending on gauge. Weights are between 5 and 7 pounds depending on gauge.

Model XXV—Boxlock

This model is available in 12 and 20 gauge only. The select walnut stock is hand checkered with straight grip stock.

NIB	Exc.	V.G.	Good	Fair	Poor
2500	1250	800	600	350	250

Model No. 4

This model is available in 12, 16, 20, and 28 gauge as well as .410 bore. It is fitted with select hand checkered walnut stock with straight grip. Light scroll engraving on this model. Add 75 percent for 28 and .410.

NIB	Exc.	V.G.	Good	Fair	Poor
2000	1650	1250	—	—	—

Model No. 4 Deluxe

Same as above, but with select walnut stock and slightly more engraving coverage. Addf 75 percent for 28 and .410.

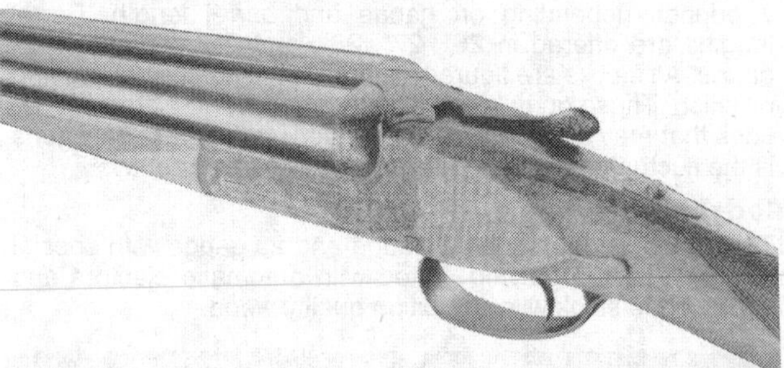

NIB	Exc.	V.G.	Good	Fair	Poor
4000	2995	1500	1000	550	350

OVER-AND-UNDER

These AyA shotguns are similar in design and appearance to the Gebruder Merkel over-and-under sidelocks with three-part forend, Kersten cross bolt, and double under locking lugs.

Model No. 37 Super

This model is available in 12 gauge only with ventilated rib, automatic ejectors, internally gold-plated sidelocks. Offered with three different types of engraving patterns: ducks, scroll, or deep cut engraving. Very few of this model were imported into the U.S.

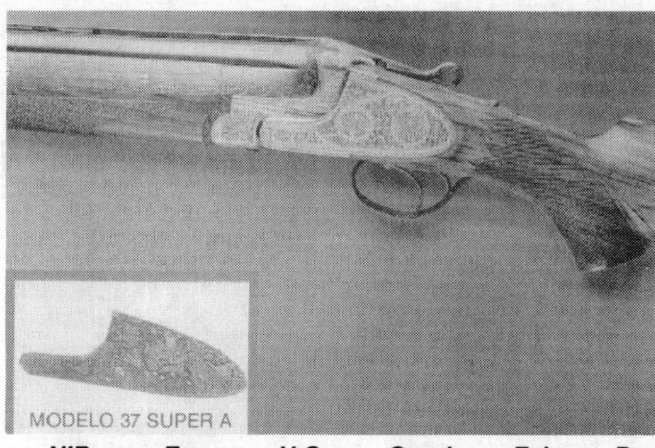

NIB	Exc.	V.G.	Good	Fair	Poor
11000	8500	5000	3500	2000	1000

Model Augusta

This is the top-of-the-line AyA model offered in 12 gauge only. It features presentation wood and deep cut scroll engraving. Very few of this model were imported into the U.S.

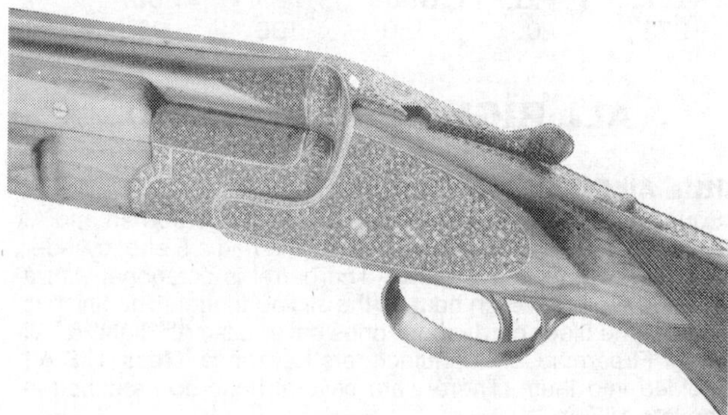

NIB	Exc.	V.G.	Good	Fair	Poor
20000	15000	8000	4500	3500	1500

NOTE: For extra cost options add approximately: Pistol grip–$90; Rubber recoil pad–$190; Left-hand gun–$775; Length of pull longer than 15"–$125; Select wood–$235; Deluxe wood–$550; Single non-selective trigger–$400; Single-selective trigger–$600; Chrome-lined barrels–$140; Churchill rib–$375; Raised rib–$180; Extra set of barrels–$1500.

AIR MATCH
Paris, Kentucky

Air Match 500

A .22 caliber single-shot target pistol with a 10.5" barrel, adjustable sights and adjustable front-mounted counterweights. Blued with walnut grips. Imported from 1984 to 1986.

NIB	Exc.	V.G.	Good	Fair	Poor
700	550	400	300	250	125

AJAX ARMY

Single-Action

A spur-trigger, single-action, solid-frame revolver that was chambered for the .44 rimfire cartridge. It had a 7" barrel and was blued with walnut grips. It was manufactured in the 1880s.

Exc.	V.G.	Good	Fair	Poor
—	400	300	250	200

ALAMO RANGER
Spain

A double-action Spanish copy of the Colt SAA, chambered for the .38 caliber centerfire. The cylinder held 6 shots. The finish was blued; grips were checkered hard rubber. The maker of this pistol is unknown.

Exc.	V.G.	Good	Fair	Poor
200	175	100	75	45

ALASKA
SEE—Hood Firearms Co.
Norwich, Connecticut

ALDAZABAL
Eibar, Spain
Aldazabal, Leturiondo & CIA

Model 1919

A vest pocket semi-automatic pistol copied from the FN Browning Model 1906. Caliber is 6.35mm.

Courtesy James Rankin

Exc.	V.G.	Good	Fair	Poor
250	150	100	75	50

Military Model

A semi-automatic pistol in the Ruby-style. Caliber is 7.65mm with a 9-round magazine.

Courtesy James Rankin

Exc.	V.G.	Good	Fair	Poor
350	250	175	125	75

Aldazabal

Another typical low-quality, "Eibar"-type semi-automatic. It was a Browning blowback copy, chambered for the 7.65mm cartridge. It had a 7-shot detachable magazine and blued finish with checkered wood grips. This company ceased production before the Spanish Civil War.

Exc.	*V.G.*	*Good*	*Fair*	*Poor*
250	125	95	65	40

ALERT

SEE—Hood Firearms Co.
Norwich, Connecticut

ALEXIA

SEE—Hopkins & Allen
Norwich, Connecticut

ALFA

SEE—Armero Especialistas Reunides
Eibar, Spain

ALKARTASUNA FABRICA DE ARMAS

Guernica, Spain

This company began production during World War I to help Gabilondo y Urresti supply sidearms to the French. After the hostilities ceased, they continued to produce firearms under their own name. They produced a number of variations in both 6.35mm and 7.65mm marked "Alkar." Collector interest is very thin. The factory burned down in 1920, and by 1922 business had totally ceased.

Alkar

A 6.35mm semi-automatic pistol with a cartridge counter in the grip plates. One variation of many built in either 6.35mm or 7.65mm.

Courtesy James Rankin

Exc.	*V.G.*	*Good*	*Fair*	*Poor*
275	225	175	125	100

Alkar (Ruby-Style)

A 7.65mm semi-automatic pistol built in the Ruby-style. This pistol was supplied to the French government during World War I.

Courtesy James Rankin

Exc.	*V.G.*	*Good*	*Fair*	*Poor*
275	200	150	100	90

ALL RIGHT FIREARMS CO.

Lawrence, Massachusetts

Little All Right Palm Pistol

Squeezer-type pocket pistol invented by E. Boardman and A. Peavy in 1876, was made in .22 cal. and had a 5-shot cylinder with a 1-5/8" or 2-3/8" barrel. The barrel is octagonal with a tube on top of it which houses the sliding trigger. The finish is nickel. The black hard rubber grips have "Little All Right" & "All Right Firearms Co., Manufacturers Lawrence, Mass. U.S.A." molded into them. There were several hundred produced in the late 1870s.

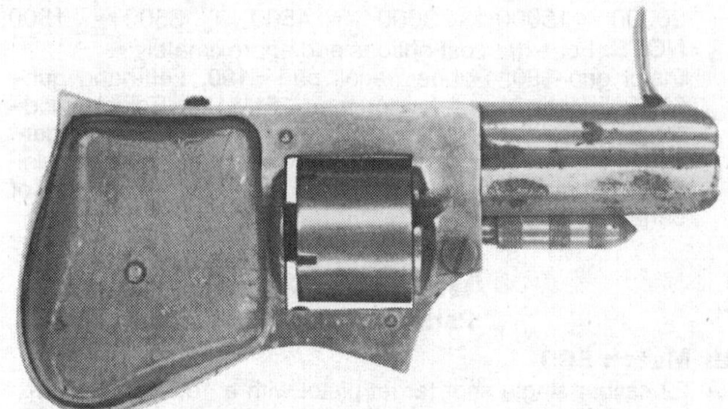

Courtesy Milwaukee Public Museum, Milwaukee, Wisconsin

Exc.	*V.G.*	*Good*	*Fair*	*Poor*
—	2800	2750	950	300

ALLEN, ETHAN

Grafton, Massachusetts

The company was founded by Ethan Allen in the early 1800s. It became a prolific gun-making firm that evolved from Ethan Allen to Allen & Thurber, as well as the Allen & Wheelock Company. It was located in Norwich, Connecticut, and Worchester, Massachusetts, as well as Grafton. It eventually became the Forehand & Wadsworth Company in 1871 after the death of Ethan Allen. There were many and varied firearms produced under all of the headings described above. If one desires to collect Ethan Allen firearms, it would be advisable to educate oneself, as there are a number of fine publications available on the subject. The basic models and their values are listed.

First Model Pocket Rifle

Manufactured by Ethan Allen in Grafton, Massachusetts. It was a bootleg-type, under-hammer, single-shot pistol chambered for .31 percussion. Larger-caliber versions have also been noted. It had barrel lengths from 5" to 9" that were part-octagon in configuration. It had iron mountings and was blued with walnut grips. The barrel was marked, "E. Allen/ Grafton/Mass." as well as "Pocket Rifle/Cast Steel/ Warranted." There were approximately 2,000 manufactured from 1831 to 1842.

Exc.	*V.G.*	*Good*	*Fair*	*Poor*
—	—	1350	550	200

Second Model Pocket Rifle

A rounded-frame, round-grip version of the First Model.

Exc.	*V.G.*	*Good*	*Fair*	*Poor*
—	—	1250	450	200

Bar Hammer Pistol

A double-action pistol with a top-mounted bar hammer. It was chambered for .28 to .36 caliber percussion. The half-octagon barrels were from 2" to 10" in length. They screwed out of the frame so it was possible to breech load them. The finish was blued with rounded walnut grips. They were marked, "Allen & Thurber/Grafton Mass." There were approximately 2,000 manufactured between the early 1830s and 1860.

Exc.	*V.G.*	*Good*	*Fair*	*Poor*
—	—	1350	500	200

Tube Hammer Pistol

This version was similar to the Bar Hammer with a curved hammer without a spur. There were only a few hundred manufactured between the early 1830s and the early 1840s.

Exc.	*V.G.*	*Good*	*Fair*	*Poor*
—	—	2600	1100	400

Side Hammer Pistol

A single-shot, target-type pistol that was chambered for .34, .41, and .45 caliber percussion. It had a part-octagon barrel that was from 6" to 10" in length. There was a wooden ramrod mounted under the barrel. This model had a good quality rear sight that was adjustable. The ornate trigger guard had a graceful spur at its rear. The finish was blued with a rounded walnut grip. The barrel was marked, "Allen & Thurber, Worchester." There were approximately 300 manufactured in the late 1840s and early 1850s.

Exc.	*V.G.*	*Good*	*Fair*	*Poor*
—	—	1100	450	200

Center Hammer Pistol

A single-action chambered for .34, .36, or .44 percussion. It had a half-octagon barrel from 4" to 12" in length. It had a centrally mounted hammer that was offset to the right side to allow for sighting the pistol. The finish was blued with walnut grips. It was marked, "Allen & Thurber, Allen Thurber & Company." Some specimens are marked, "Allen & Wheelock." There were several thousand manufactured between the late 1840s and 1860.

Exc.	*V.G.*	*Good*	*Fair*	*Poor*
—	—	1100	450	200

Double-Barrel Pistol

A SxS, double-barrel pistol with a single trigger. It was chambered for .36 caliber percussion with 3" to 6" round barrels. The finish was blued with walnut grips. Examples with a ramrod mounted under the barrel have been noted. The flute between the barrels was marked, "Allen & Thurber," "Allen Thurber & Company," or "Allen & Wheelock." There were approximately 1,000 manufactured in the 1850s.

Exc.	*V.G.*	*Good*	*Fair*	*Poor*
—	—	950	400	150

Allen & Wheelock Center Hammer Pistol

A single-action pocket pistol chambered for .31 to .38 caliber percussion. It had octagon barrels from 3" to 6" in length. The finish was blued with square butt walnut grips. The barrel was marked, "Allen & Wheelock." There were approximately 500 manufactured between 1858 and 1865.

Exc.	*V.G.*	*Good*	*Fair*	*Poor*
—	—	850	350	100

Allen Thurber & Company Target Pistol

A deluxe, single-action target pistol that was chambered for .31 or .36 caliber percussion. It had a heavy, octagon barrel that was from 11" to 16" in length. There was a wooden ramrod mounted underneath the barrel. The mountings were of German silver, and there was a detachable walnut stock with a deluxe, engraved patchbox. This weapon was engraved, and the barrel was marked, "Allen Thurber & Co./Worchester/Cast Steel." This firearm was furnished in a fitted case with the stock, false muzzle, and various accessories. It was considered to be a very high grade target pistol in its era. The values listed are for a complete-cased outfit. There were very few manufactured in the 1850s.

Exc.	*V.G.*	*Good*	*Fair*	*Poor*
—	—	8600	3500	1000

NOTE: For pistols without attachable stock deduct 75 percent.

Ethan Allen Pepperboxes

During the period from the early 1830s to the 1860s, this company manufactured over 50 different variations of the revolving, pepperbox-type pistol. They were commercially quite successful and actually competed successfully with the Colt revolving handguns for more than a decade. They were widely used throughout the United States, as well as in Mexico, and during our Civil War. They are widely collectible because of the number of variations that exist. The potential collector should avail himself of the information available on the subject. These pepperboxes can be divided into three categories.

No. 1: Manufactured from the 1830s until 1842, at Grafton, Massachusetts.

No. 2: Manufactured from 1842 to 1847, at Norwich, Connecticut.

No. 3: Manufactured from 1847 to 1865, at Worchester, Massachusetts.

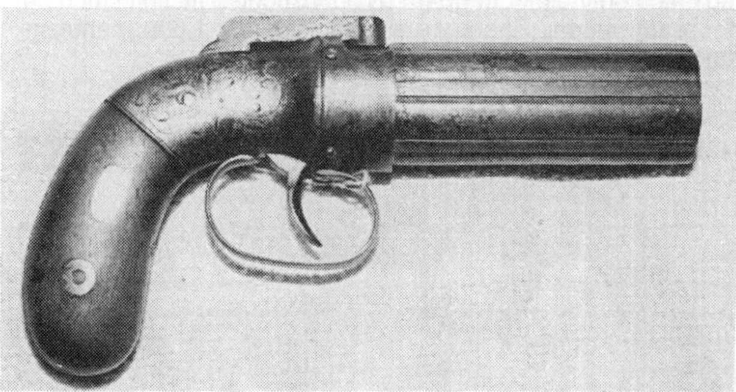

There are a number of subdivisions among these three basic groups that would pertain to trigger type, size, barrel length etc. It would be impossible to cover all 50 of these variations in a text of this type. We strongly suggest that qualified, individual appraisal be secured if contemplating a transaction. The values of these pepperbox pistols in excellent condition would be between $1,500 and $5,000. Most examples will be seen in the fair to good condition and will bring $1,000 to 2,000 depending on variation.

Large Frame Pocket Revolver

A double-action pocket revolver that was chambered for .34 caliber percussion. It had an octagon barrel from 3" to 5" in length. There were no sights. The 5-shot, unfluted cylinder was game scene engraved. The finish was blued with rounded walnut grips. It had a bar-type hammer. This was the first conventional revolver manufactured by this company, and it was directly influenced by the pepperbox pistol for which Ethan Allen had become famous. It was marked, "Allen & Wheelock" as well as "Patented April 16, 1845." There were approximately 1,500 manufactured between 1857 and 1860.

Courtesy Milwaukee Public Museum, Milwaukee, Wisconsin

Exc.	V.G.	Good	Fair	Poor
—	—	1000	400	150

Small Frame Pocket Revolver

This version was similar to the Large Frame Pocket Revolver except chambered for .31 caliber percussion, with a 2" to 3.5" octagon barrel. It was slightly smaller in size, finished and marked the same. There were approximately 1,000 made between 1858 and 1860.

Exc.	V.G.	Good	Fair	Poor
—	—	1000	400	150

Side Hammer Belt Revolver

A single-action revolver chambered for .34 caliber percussion. It had an octagon barrel from 3" to 7.5" in length. It featured a hammer that was mounted on the right side of the frame and a 5-shot, engraved, unfluted cylinder. The cylinder access pin is inserted from the rear of the weapon. The finish is blued with a case-colored hammer and trigger guard and flared butt walnut grips. It is marked, "Allen & Wheelock." There were two basic types. Values for the early model, of which 100 were manufactured between 1858 and 1861, are listed.

Exc.	V.G.	Good	Fair	Poor
—	—	1050	400	200

Standard Model

The second type was the Standard Model, with a spring-loaded catch on the trigger guard as opposed to a friction catch on the early model. There were approximately 1,000 manufactured between 1858 and 1861.

Courtesy Milwaukee Public Museum, Milwaukee, Wisconsin

Exc.	V.G.	Good	Fair	Poor
—	—	900	350	150

Side Hammer Pocket Revolver

This version was chambered for .28 caliber percussion and had a 2" to 5" octagon barrel. The frame was slightly smaller than the belt model.

Courtesy Milwaukee Public Museum, Milwaukee, Wisconsin

Early Production

100 manufactured.

Exc.	V.G.	Good	Fair	Poor
—	—	900	325	150

Standard Production

1,000 manufactured.

Exc.	V.G.	Good	Fair	Poor
—	1600	600	200	100

Side Hammer Navy Revolver

This was a large-frame, military-type revolver that was similar to the Side Hammer Belt Model, chambered for .36 caliber percussion. It features an octagon, 5.5" to 8" barrel with a 6-shot, engraved cylinder. There was an early-production type with a friction catch on the trigger guard. There were approximately 100 manufactured between 1858 and 1861.

Exc.	V.G.	Good	Fair	Poor
—	—	3850	1500	500

Standard Model

1,000 manufactured.

Exc.	V.G.	Good	Fair	Poor
—	—	3350	1250	500

Center Hammer Army Revolver

A large, military-type, single-action revolver that was chambered for .44 caliber percussion. It had a 7.5", half-octagon barrel and a 6-shot, unfluted cylinder. The hammer was mounted in the center of the frame. The finish was blued with a case-colored hammer and trigger guard and walnut grips. The barrel was marked, "Allen & Wheelock. Worchester, Mass. U.S./Allen's Pt's. Jan. 13, 1857. Dec. 15, 1857, Sept. 7, 1858." There were approximately 700 manufactured between 1861 and 1862.

Courtesy Milwaukee Public Museum, Milwaukee, Wisconsin

REMINDER

Perhaps the best advice is for the collector to take his time. Do not be in a hurry, and do not allow yourself to be rushed into making a decision. Learn as much as possible about the firearm you are interested in collecting or shooting.

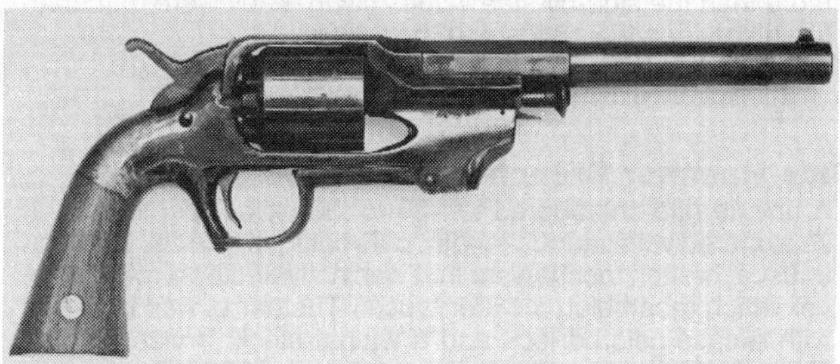

Courtesy Milwaukee Public Museum, Milwaukee, Wisconsin

Exc.	V.G.	Good	Fair	Poor
—	—	3850	1500	500

Center Hammer Navy Revolver

Similar to the Army Revolver except chambered for .36 caliber percussion with a 7.5", full-octagon barrel. Examples have been noted with 5", 6", or 8" barrels. Otherwise, it was similar to the Army model.

Exc.	V.G.	Good	Fair	Poor
—	—	3100	1250	500

Center Hammer Percussion Revolver

A single-action revolver chambered for .36 caliber percussion. It had an octagonal, 3" or 4" barrel with a 6-shot, unfluted cylinder. The finish was blued with walnut grips. This model supposedly was made for the Providence, Rhode Island, Police Department and has become commonly referred to as the "Providence Police Model." There were approximately 700 manufactured between 1858 and 1862.

Exc.	V.G.	Good	Fair	Poor
—	—	1350	500	200

Lipfire Army Revolver

A large, military-type, single-action revolver that was chambered for the .44 lipfire cartridge. It had a 7.5", half-octagon barrel with a 6-shot, unfluted cylinder that had notches at its rear for the cartridge lips. The finish was blued with a case-colored hammer and trigger guard and square butt walnut grips. The barrel was marked, "Allen & Wheelock, Worchester, Mass." It resembled the Center Hammer Percussion Army Revolver. There were two basic variations, with a total of 250 Lipfire Army Revolver manufactured in the early 1860s.

Early Model

Top hinged loading gate.

Exc.	V.G.	Good	Fair	Poor
—	—	3850	1500	500

Late Model

Bottom hinged loading gate.

Exc.	V.G.	Good	Fair	Poor
—	—	3350	1200	400

Lipfire Navy Revolver

Similar to the Army model, except chambered for the .36 lipfire cartridge, with an octagonal, 4", 5", 6", 7.5", or 8" barrel. There were approximately 500 manufactured in the 1860s.

Exc.	V.G.	Good	Fair	Poor
—	—	2600	1000	400

Lipfire Pocket Revolver

A smaller version chambered for the .32 lipfire cartridge, with an octagonal, 4", 5", or 6" barrel. There were approximately 200 manufactured in the early 1860s.

Exc.	V.G.	Good	Fair	Poor
—	—	1600	600	250

.32 Side Hammer Rimfire Revolver

A single-action, spur-trigger, pocket revolver chambered for the .32 caliber rimfire cartridge. It had octagonal barrels from 3" to 5" in length. The finish was blued with flared-butt, walnut grips. It was marked "Allen & Wheelock Worchester, Mass." There were three variations with a total of approximately 1,000 manufactured between 1859 and 1862.

First Model

Rounded top strap.

Exc.	V.G.	Good	Fair	Poor
—	—	900	350	150

Second Model

July 3, 1860 marked on frame.

Exc.	V.G.	Good	Fair	Poor
—	—	800	300	100

Third Model

1858 and 1861 patent dates.

Exc.	V.G.	Good	Fair	Poor
—	—	700	200	100

.22 Side Hammer Rimfire Revolver

A smaller version of the .32 revolver, chambered for the .22 rimfire cartridge. It has octagonal barrels from 2.25" to 4" in length. It has a 7-shot, unfluted cylinder. There were approximately 1,500 manufactured between 1858 and 1862. There were many variations.

Early Model First Issue

Access pin enters from rear.

Exc.	V.G.	Good	Fair	Poor
—	—	900	300	100

Second Issue

Access pin enters from front.

Exc.	V.G.	Good	Fair	Poor
—	—	900	300	100

Third Issue

Separate rear sight.

Exc.	V.G.	Good	Fair	Poor
—	—	1050	400	150

Fourth to Eighth Issue

Very similar, values the same.

Exc.	V.G.	Good	Fair	Poor
—	—	600	200	100

Single-Shot Center Hammer

A single-shot derringer-type pistol that was chambered for the .22 caliber rimfire cartridge. It had part-octagon barrels from 2" to 5.5" in length that swung to the right side for loading. Some had automatic ejectors; others did not. The frame was either brass or iron with bird's-head or squared butt walnut grips. It was marked "Allen & Wheelock" or "E. Allen & Co." There were very few manufactured in the early 1860s.

Early Issue

Full-length, octagon barrel and a round, iron frame. It is rarely encountered.

Exc.	V.G.	Good	Fair	Poor
—	—	950	300	100

Standard Issue

Squared butt or bird's-head.

Exc.	V.G.	Good	Fair	Poor
—	—	700	200	100

.32 Single-Shot Center Hammer

A larger-frame pocket pistol chambered for the .32 rimfire cartridge. It has a part-octagon or full-octagon barrel of 4" or 5" in length. It swung to the right side for loading. Otherwise, this model was similar to the .22-caliber version.

Exc.	V.G.	Good	Fair	Poor
—	—	750	300	100

Vest Pocket Derringer

A small pocket pistol chambered for the .22 rimfire cartridge. It had a 2", part-octagon barrel that swung to the right-hand side for loading. The cartridges were manually extracted. It featured a brass frame with a blued or plated barrel and walnut, bird's-head grips. The barrel was marked "Allen & Co. Makers." This was an extremely small firearm, and there were approximately 200 manufactured between 1869 and 1871.

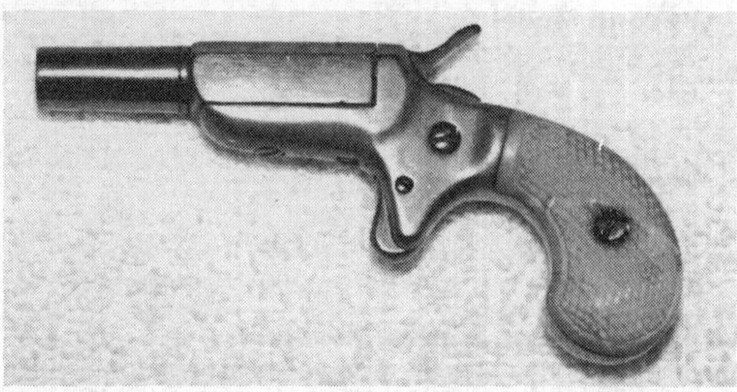

Exc.	V.G.	Good	Fair	Poor
—		800	300	100

.32 Derringer

Similar to the Vest Pocket version, larger in size, and chambered for the .32 rimfire cartridge. It had a part-octagon barrel from 2" to 4" in length that swung to the right for loading. This version featured an automatic extractor. The barrel was marked "E. Allen & Co. Worchester, Mass." This was a very rare firearm, made between 1865 and 1871.

Exc.	V.G.	Good	Fair	Poor
—	—	700	250	100

.41 Derringer

The same size and configuration as the .32 caliber model except it was chambered for the .41 rimfire cartridge with barrel lengths of 2.5" to 2.75" in length. The markings were the same. There were approximately 100 manufactured between 1865 and 1871.

Exc.	V.G.	Good	Fair	Poor
—	—	2100	800	350

Center Hammer Muzzleloading Rifle

A single-shot rifle chambered for .44 caliber percussion. It had a 36" round barrel with an octagonal breech. It had a center-mounted hammer that was offset to the right for sighting. It had iron mountings. The finish was browned with a case-colored lock. There was a ramrod mounted under the barrel. It had a walnut buttstock with a crescent buttplate and no forearm. There were approximately 100 manufactured in the 1850s.

Exc.	V.G.	Good	Fair	Poor
—	—	1700	500	250

Side Hammer Muzzleloading Rifle

Similar to the Center Hammer model, with the hammer mounted on the right side of the lock. It was chambered for .38 caliber percussion, with an octagon barrel from 28" to 32" in length. It is occasionally found with a patchbox. The barrel is browned with a case-colored lock and a walnut stock with crescent buttplate. There were several hundred manufactured from the early 1840s to the 1860s.

Exc.	V.G.	Good	Fair	Poor
—	—	2600	800	350

Combination Gun

Either an Over/Under or side-by-side rifle chambered for 12 gauge and .38 caliber percussion. The barrels were from 28" to 34" in length. It had two hammers and double triggers with a ramrod mounted either beneath or on the right side of the barrels. The finish was browned with a walnut stock. Examples with a patchbox have been noted. Production was very limited, with the Over/Under versions worth approximately 20 percent more than the side-by-side values given. They were manufactured between the 1840s and the 1860s.

Exc.	V.G.	Good	Fair	Poor
—	—	3950	1250	500

Side Hammer Breech-loading Rifle

A unique rifle chambered for .36 to .50 caliber percussion. It was offered with various-length, part-octagon barrels. It had an unusual breech mechanism that was activated by a rotating lever which resembled a water faucet. The barrel was browned with a case-colored lock and a walnut stock. It was marked "Allen & Wheelock/ Allen's Patent July 3, 1855." There were approximately 500 manufactured between 1855 and 1860.

Courtesy Buffalo Bill Historical Center, Cody, Wyoming

Exc.	V.G.	Good	Fair	Poor
—	—	3350	1500	500

Drop Breech Rifle

This single-shot rifle was chambered for the .22 through the .44 rimfire cartridges. It had a part-octagon barrel from 23" to 28" in length. The breech was activated by the combination trigger guard action lever. Opening the breech automatically ejected the empty cartridge. The external hammer was manually cocked, and it featured an adjustable sight. The barrel was blued with a case-colored frame and a walnut stock. It was marked "Allen & Wheelock/ Allen's Pat. Sept. 18, 1860." There were approximately 2,000 manufactured between 1860 and 1871.

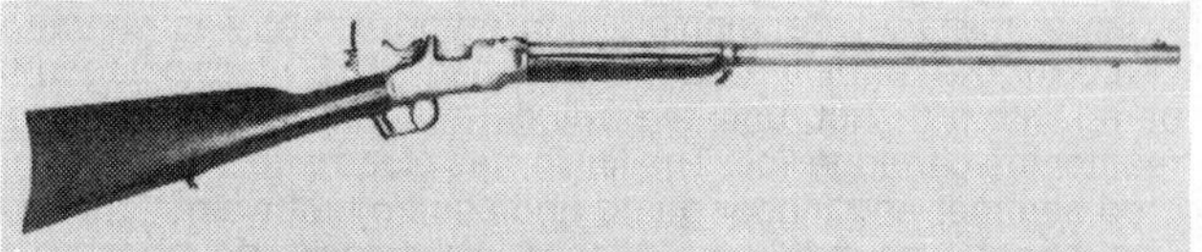

Courtesy Milwaukee Public Museum, Milwaukee, Wisconsin

Exc.	V.G.	Good	Fair	Poor
—	—	1350	500	200

Lipfire Revolving Rifle

A 6-shot, cylinder-type rifle chambered for the .44 caliber lipfire cartridge. It had an unfluted cylinder with slots at its rear to allow for the cartridge lips. The round barrels were 26" to 28" in length with an octagon breech. The finish was blued with a case-colored frame and a walnut buttstock. This model was not marked with the maker's name. There were approximately 100 manufactured between 1861 and 1863.

Courtesy Buffalo Bill Historical Center, Cody, Wyoming

Exc.	V.G.	Good	Fair	Poor
—	—	17800	7000	2000

Double-Barrel Shotgun

A side-by-side gun chambered for 10 or 12 gauge. The barrel length was 28". It was loaded by means of a trapdoor-type breech that had a lever handle. The finish was blued with checkered walnut stock. There were a few hundred manufactured between 1865 and 1871.

Exc.	V.G.	Good	Fair	Poor
—	—	1750	700	250

ALLEN & THURBER

SEE—Ethan Allen

ALLEN & WHEELOCK

SEE—Ethan Allen

ALLEN FIREARMS

Santa Fe, New Mexico

SEE—Aldo Uberti

ALPHA ARMS CO.

Flower Mound, Texas

Alpha Arms Co. produced high-grade bolt-action rifles on a semi-custom basis. It manufactured a number of standard models but offered many options at additional cost. Some of these options were custom sights and finishes and an octagonal barrel. These extra features would add to the value of the models listed. This company operated from 1983 until 1987.

Alpha Jaguar Grade I

Built on a Mauser-type action with barrel lengths from 20" to 24". It was chambered for most calibers between .222 Rem. and .338 Win. Mag. The stock was made from a synthetic laminated material that the company called Alphawood. This model was introduced in 1987 and only produced that year.

NIB	Exc.	V.G.	Good	Fair	Poor
1500	900	650	400	300	200

Jaguar Grade II

Similar to the Grade I with a Douglas Premium barrel.

NIB	Exc.	V.G.	Good	Fair	Poor
1600	975	700	500	400	250

Jaguar Grade III

Has the Douglas barrel plus a hand-honed trigger and action and a three-position safety like the Winchester Model 70.

NIB	Exc.	V.G.	Good	Fair	Poor
1700	1200	1000	700	400	200

Jaguar Grade IV

Has all the features of the Grade III with a specially lightened action and sling-swivel studs.

NIB	Exc.	V.G.	Good	Fair	Poor
1750	1250	1100	900	500	250

Alpha Grand Slam

Features the same high quality as the Jaguar models and is available in a left-hand model. It has a fluted bolt, laminated stock, and a matte blue finish.

NIB	Exc.	V.G.	Good	Fair	Poor
1400	1200	1000	700	450	250

Alpha Custom

Similar to the Grand Slam with a select grade stock.

NIB	Exc.	V.G.	Good	Fair	Poor
1700	1500	1250	750	500	250

Alpha Alaskan

Similar to the Grand Slam but chambered for the .308 Win., .350 Rem. Mag., .358 Win. and the .458 Win. Mag. It features all stainless steel construction. Add 20 percent for .458.

NIB	Exc.	V.G.	Good	Fair	Poor
1700	1500	1250	750	500	250

Alpha Big - Five

Similar to the Jaguar Grade IV chambered for the .300 Win. Mag., .375 H&H Mag. and the .458 Win. Mag. It had a reinforced through-bolt stock to accommodate the recoil of the larger caliber cartridges for which it was chambered. It also had a decelerator recoil pad. This model was manufactured in 1987 only. Add 20 percent for .458.

NIB	Exc.	V.G.	Good	Fair	Poor
1900	1650	1300	850	600	300

ALSOP, C.R.

Middletown, Connecticut

This firearms manufacturer made revolvers during 1862 and 1863. They made two basic models, the Navy and the Pocket model. Some collectors consider the Alsop to be a secondary U.S. martial handgun, but no verifying government contracts are known to exist.

First Model Navy Revolver

A .36 cal. revolver with a 3.5", 4.5", 5.5", or 6.5" barrel length and a 5-shot cylinder. It has a blued finish, wood grips, and a peculiar hump in its backstrap. The first model has a safety device which blocks the spur trigger. This device is found on serial numbers 1-100. Markings are: "C.R. Alsop Middletown, Conn. 1860 & 1861" on the barrel. The cylinder is marked "C.R. Alsop" & "Nov. 26th, 1861"; the side plate, "Patented Jan. 21st, 1862."

Exc.	V.G.	Good	Fair	Poor
—	—	3750	1250	500

Standard Model Navy Revolver

Exactly the same as the First Model without the safety device. They are serial numbered 101 to 300.

Exc.	V.G.	Good	Fair	Poor
—	—	3250	850	300

Pocket Model Revolver

A .31 cal. 5-shot revolver with spur trigger, 4" round barrel, blued finish, and wood grips. It is very similar in appearance to the Navy model but smaller in size. It is marked "C.R. Alsop Middletown, Conn. 1860 & 1861" on the barrel. The cylinder is marked "C.R. Alsop Nov. 26th, 1861." They are serial numbered 1-300.

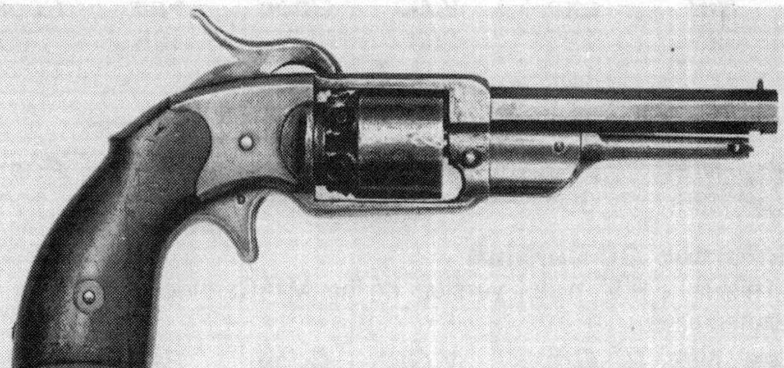

Courtesy Milwaukee Public Museum, Milwaukee, Wisconsin

Exc.	V.G.	Good	Fair	Poor
—	—	1500	600	200

AMAC

American Military Arms Corporation
formerly Iver Johnson
Jacksonville, Arkansas

The Iver Johnson Arms Co. was founded in 1871 in Fitchsburg, Massachusetts. It was one of the oldest and most successful of the old-line arms companies on which our modern era has taken its toll. In 1984 the company moved to Jacksonville, Arkansas; in 1987 it was purchased by the American Military Arms Corporation. This company has released some of the older designs as well as some new models. In 1993 the company went out of business. The original Iver Johnson line is listed under its own heading.

U.S. Carbine .22

This is a semi-automatic, military-style carbine that is patterned after the M1 of WWII fame. It is chambered for the .22 LR cartridge, has an 18.5" barrel and features military-style peep sights and a 15-shot detachable magazine.

NIB	Exc.	V.G.	Good	Fair	Poor
250	150	125	100	75	50

Wagonmaster Lever Action Rifle

This model is chambered for the .22 rimfire cartridge, has an 18.5" barrel and is styled after the Win. 94. The stock has a straight grip; and the forend, a barrel band. There are adjustable sights and a tube magazine that holds 15 LR cartridges.

NIB	Exc.	V.G.	Good	Fair	Poor
250	150	120	100	75	50

Wagonmaster .22 Magnum

This model is the same as the Wagonmaster except that it is chambered for the .22 rimfire magnum.

NIB	Exc.	V.G.	Good	Fair	Poor
300	175	120	100	75	50

Targetmaster Pump-Action Rifle

This model is a slide- or pump-action that is chambered for the .22 rimfire cartridges. It has an 18.5" barrel with adjustable sights and a straight grip stock. It holds 12 LR cartridges.

NIB	Exc.	V.G.	Good	Fair	Poor
300	150	120	100	75	50

Li'L Champ Bolt-Action Rifle

This model is a scaled-down single-shot that is chambered for the .22 rimfire cartridges. It has a 16.25" barrel, adjustable sights, a molded stock, and nickel-plated bolt. This model is 33" overall and is designed to be the ideal first rifle for a young shooter.

NIB	Exc.	V.G.	Good	Fair	Poor
150	75	60	45	35	20

M .30 Cal. Carbine

A military-style carbine styled after the M1 of WWII fame. It is chambered for the .30 Carbine cartridge and has an 18" barrel with military-style sights and hardwood stock. There are detachable 5-, 15-, and 30-round magazines available.

NIB	Exc.	V.G.	Good	Fair	Poor
325	225	200	175	125	90

Paratrooper .30 Carbine

This model is similar to the M1 model with a folding stock.

NIB	Exc.	V.G.	Good	Fair	Poor
425	350	300	250	160	100

Enforcer .30 Carbine

This is a 9.5" pistol version of the M1 Carbine. It has no buttstock.

NIB	Exc.	V.G.	Good	Fair	Poor
500	400	350	250	150	100

Long Range Rifle System

This is a specialized long-range, bolt-action rifle chambered for the .50 Cal. Browning Machine gun cartridge. It has a 33" barrel and a special muzzlebrake system. A custom order version in the .338 or .416 caliber is also available.

NIB	Exc.	V.G.	Good	Fair	Poor
8500	7000	5000	3500	2000	1000

TP-22 and TP-25

This model is a compact, double-action, pocket automatic that was styled after the Walther TP series. Chambered for either the .22 rimfire or the .25 centerfire cartridges, it has a 2.75" barrel, fixed sights and black plastic grips. The detachable magazine holds 7 shots and the finish is either blue or nickel-plated. The nickel-plated version is worth 10 percent more than the blue.

NIB	Exc.	V.G.	Good	Fair	Poor
250	175	150	100	75	50

AMAC 22 Compact or 25 Compact

This is a compact, single-action, semi-automatic pocket pistol that is chambered for the .22 rimfire or the .25 ACP cartridge. It has a 2" barrel, 5-shot magazine, plastic grips and blue or nickel finish. The nickel finish is 10 percent higher in cost than the blue.

NIB	Exc.	V.G.	Good	Fair	Poor
200	125	100	80	55	35

AMERICAN ARMS

Garden Grove, California

Eagle .380

This pistol was a stainless steel copy of the Walther PPKS. It was a semi-auto blowback that was chambered for the .380 ACP. It was double-action and had a 3.25" barrel and a 6-shot detachable magazine. An optional feature was a black Teflon finish that would increase the value by 10 percent. This company ceased production in 1985.

Exc.	V.G.	Good	Fair	Poor
300	225	175	150	100

AMERICAN ARMS CO.

Boston, Massachusetts

The history of American Arms is rather sketchy, but it appears the company was formed in 1853 as the G. H. Fox Co. and then became the American Tool & Machine Co. in 1865. In 1870 they formed a new corporation called American Arms Company with George Fox as the principle stockholder. This corporation was dissolved in 1873; a second American Arms Co. was incorporated in 1877 and a third in 1890. It is unclear if these corporations had essentially the same owners, but George H. Fox appears as a principal owner in two of the three. One could assume that financial problems forced them to bankrupt one corporation and reorganize under another. American Arms manufactured firearms in Boston, Massachusetts, from 1866 until 1893. In 1893 they moved to Bluffton, Alabama and manufactured guns until 1901.

Fox Model "Swing Out" Hammer Double

Manufactured from 1870 to 1884, designed by George H. Fox, not to be confused with A.H. Fox. This model is unusual in that the barrel swings to the right for loading and the barrel release is located on the tang. It comes in 10 and 12 gauge, 26", 28", 30" and 32", with twist, Damascus or laminated barrels. Early production models have conventional soldered together barrels. Later variations after 1878 feature a unique design in that the barrels are dovetailed together. These guns could be ordered with several options and choices of finish; this would add premium value to a particular gun.

Exc.	V.G.	Good	Fair	Poor
—	1600	600	300	150

This symbol denotes "Sleepers" with rapidly-rising values and/or significant collector potential.

Semi-Hammerless Double

Manufactured from 1892 to 1901. This model features a cocking lever that cocks an internal firing pin. It comes in 12 gauge with 30" twist barrels.

Exc.	V.G.	Good	Fair	Poor
—	1100	400	250	150

Whitmore Model Hammerless Double

Manufactured from 1890 to 1901. It comes in 10, 12, and 16 gauge with 28", 30" or 32" twist, laminated or Damascus barrels. It is marked Whitmore's patent.

Courtesy Nick Niles, Paul Goodwin photo

Exc.	V.G.	Good	Fair	Poor
—	1100	500	250	150

Semi-Hammerless Single-Barrel

Manufactured from 1882 to 1901. It comes in 10, 12, and 16 gauge with 28", 30" or 32" twist or Damascus barrel.

Exc.	V.G.	Good	Fair	Poor
—	1100	400	200	100

TOP BREAK REVOLVERS

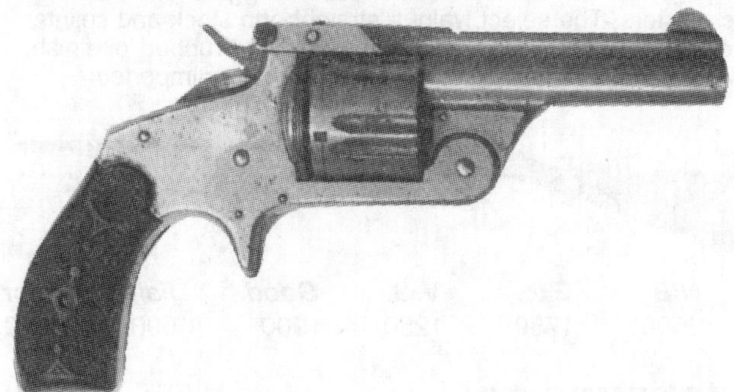

Courtesy Milwaukee Public Museum, Milwaukee, Wisconsin

Spur Trigger—Single-Action Five-Shot Revolver

These revolvers were made between 1883 and 1887 in .38 S&W only. They feature an unusual manual ring extractor and double-fluted cylinder. They are nickel plated with hard rubber grips and are marked "American Arms Company Boston Mass."

Exc.	V.G.	Good	Fair	Poor
—	450	250	100	75

Standard Trigger Double-Action Model 1886 Revolver

This model has a standard trigger and trigger guard, comes in .32 short and .38 S&W with a 3.5" barrel, in blue or nickel finish. The early models are equipped with the ring extractor and double fluted cylinder. Later variations have a standard star extractor and single fluted cylinder.

Exc.	V.G.	Good	Fair	Poor
—	650	250	100	75

Hammerless Model 1890 Double-Action

These guns were manufactured from 1890 to 1901. It has an adjustable single- or double-stage trigger pull and several unusual safety devices. It comes in .32 and .38 S&W with a 3.25" ribbed barrel, fluted cylinder, nickel finish, hard rubber grips with logo and ivory or mother of pearl grips. It is marked "American Arms Co. Boston/Pat. May 25, 1886." The top strap is marked "Pat. Pending" on early models and "Pat's May 25'86/Mar 11'89/June 17'90" on later models.

Exc.	V.G.	Good	Fair	Poor
—	650	250	100	75

Double-Barrel Derringers

American Arms Co. manufactured a two-barrel derringer-style pocket pistol. The barrels were manually rotated to load and fire the weapon. The pistol had a nickel-plated brass frame, blued barrels, and walnut grips. The markings were: "American Arms Co. Boston, Mass." on one barrel and "Pat. Oct. 31, 1865" on the other barrel. There were approximately 2,000-3,000 produced between 1866 and 1878. Beware of fakes!

Combination .22 caliber R.F. and .32 caliber R.F.

A two-caliber combination with 3" barrel, square butt only. The most common variation.

Exc.	V.G.	Good	Fair	Poor
—	—	750	300	100

.32 cal. R.F., Both Barrels

3" barrel with square butt.

Courtesy Milwaukee Public Museum, Milwaukee, Wisconsin

Exc.	V.G.	Good	Fair	Poor
—	—	950	400	100

.32 caliber R.F., Both Barrels

2-5/8" barrel with bird's-head grips.

Exc.	V.G.	Good	Fair	Poor
—	—	995	450	150

.38 caliber R.F., Both Barrels

2-5/8" barrel with bird's-head grips. A rare variation.

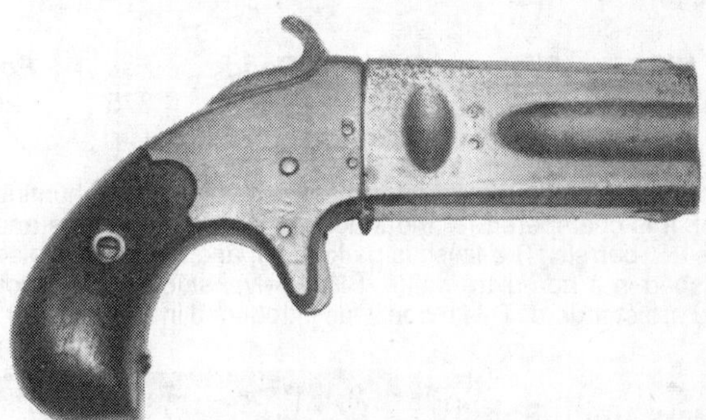

Exc.	V.G.	Good	Fair	Poor
—	—	2350	950	350

.41 caliber R.F., Both Barrels

2-5/8" barrel with square butt only.

Exc.	V.G.	Good	Fair	Poor
—	—	1750	750	200

AMERICAN ARMS, INC.

North Kansas City, Missouri

SHOTGUNS SIDE-BY-SIDE

Gentry-York

These two designations cover the same model. Prior to 1988 this model was called the York. In 1988 the receiver was case-colored and the designation was changed to the Gentry. This model was chambered for 12, 20, 28 gauge and .410. It had chrome-lined barrels from 26" to 30" in length, double triggers, 3" chambers, and automatic ejectors. The boxlock action featured scroll engraving, and the walnut stock was hand checkered. It was introduced in 1986.

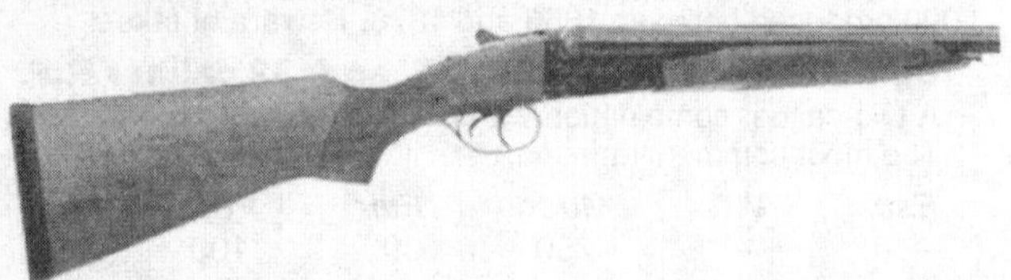

NIB	Exc.	V.G.	Good	Fair	Poor
750	625	450	300	200	150

10 Gauge Magnum Shotgun

A 10 gauge with 3.5" chambers and 32" barrels. It featured a scroll-engraved, chromed boxlock action and double triggers. It was imported from Spain in 1986 only.

NIB	Exc.	V.G.	Good	Fair	Poor
850	750	550	350	250	150

12 Gauge Magnum Shotgun

As above but chambered for 12 gauge 3-1/2" magnum shell.

NIB	Exc.	V.G.	Good	Fair	Poor
800	700	500	300	200	150

Brittany

Chambered for 12 and 20 gauge with 25" or 27" barrels with screw-in choke tubes. It had a solid matted rib and a case-colored, engraved boxlock action. Automatic ejectors and a single-selective trigger were standard on this model, as was a hand checkered, walnut, straight grip stock with semi-beavertail forend. This model was introduced in 1989.

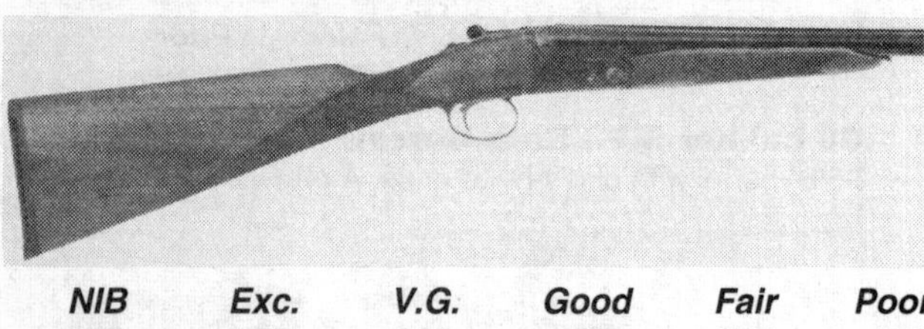

NIB	Exc.	V.G.	Good	Fair	Poor
850	750	600	450	375	200

Turkey Special

A utilitarian model designed to be an effective turkey hunting tool. It is chambered for the Magnum 10 and 12 gauges and has 26" barrels. The finish is parkerized, and the stock is also finished in a non-glare matte. Sling-swivel studs and a recoil pad are standard. This model was introduced in 1987.

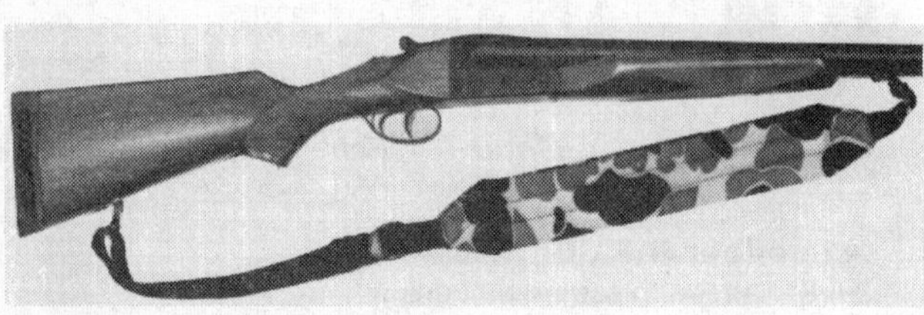

NIB	Exc.	V.G.	Good	Fair	Poor
800	700	450	350	250	150

Waterfowl Special

Similar to the Turkey Special but chambered for the 10 gauge only. It is furnished with a camouflaged sling. Introduced in 1987.

NIB	Exc.	V.G.	Good	Fair	Poor
950	850	550	350	250	150

Specialty Model

Similar to the Turkey Special and offered in 12 gauge 3-1/2" magnum.

NIB	Exc.	V.G.	Good	Fair	Poor
875	750	500	300	200	150

Derby

Chambered for the 12 and 20 gauge. It has 26" or 28" barrels with 3" chambers and automatic ejectors. Either double or single-selective triggers are offered, and the sidelock action is scroll engraved and chromed. The checkered straight grip stock and forearm are oil-finished. This model was introduced in 1986. No longer imported.

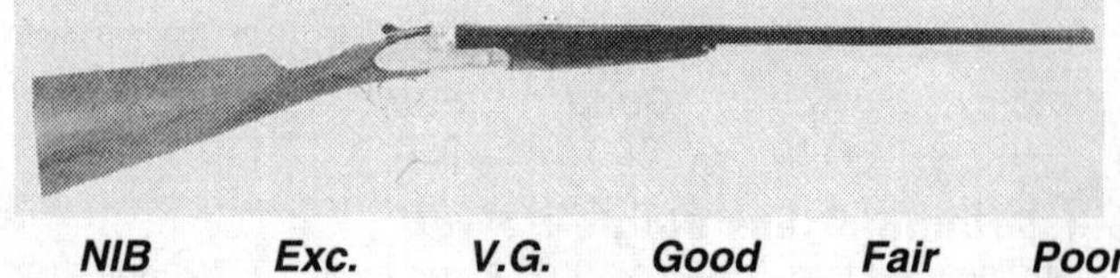

NIB	Exc.	V.G.	Good	Fair	Poor
825	700	600	500	350	200

Grulla #2

Top-of-the-line model chambered for 12, 20 and 28 gauge and .410. The barrels are 26" or 28" with a concave rib. The hand-fitted full sidelock action is extensively engraved and case-colored. There are various chokes, double triggers, and automatic ejectors. The select walnut, straight grip stock and splinter forend is hand checkered and has a hand-rubbed oil finish. This model was introduced in 1989. No longer imported.

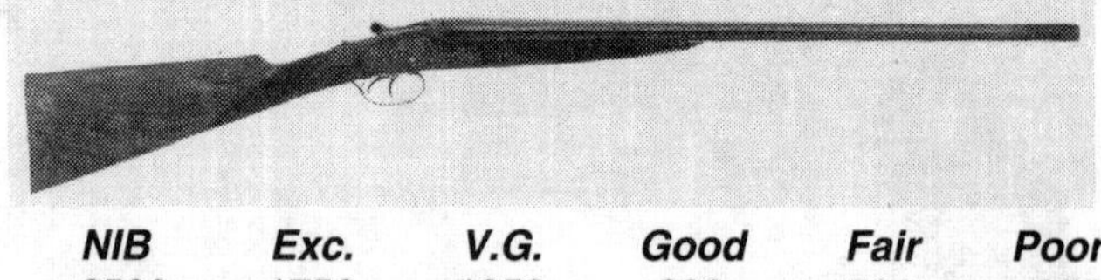

NIB	Exc.	V.G.	Good	Fair	Poor
2500	1750	1250	900	500	250

SHOTGUNS O/U

F.S. 200

A trap or skeet model that was chambered for 12 gauge only. It had 26" Skeet & Skeet barrels or 32" Full choke barrels on the trap model. The barrels were separated and had a vent rib. The boxlock action had a Greener crossbolt and was either black or matte chrome-plated. It featured a single-selective trigger, automatic ejectors, and a checkered walnut pistol grip stock. The F.S. 200 was imported in 1986 and 1987 only.

Exc.	V.G.	Good	Fair	Poor
675	575	465	350	150

F.S. 300

Similar to the F. S. 200 with lightly engraved side plates and a 30" barrel offered in the trap grade. It was imported in 1986 only.

Exc.	V.G.	Good	Fair	Poor
800	675	565	450	250

F.S. 400

Similar to the F.S. 300 with an engraved, matte chrome-plated receiver. It was imported in 1986 only.

Exc.	V.G.	Good	Fair	Poor
1100	950	800	650	350

F.S. 500

Similar to the F.S. 400 with the same general specifications. It was not imported after 1985.

Exc.	V.G.	Good	Fair	Poor
1150	1000	850	700	350

Waterfowl Special

Chambered for the 12 gauge Magnum with 3.5" chambers. It has 28" barrels with screw-in choke tubes. There are automatic ejectors and a single-selective trigger. The finish is parkerized with a matte finished stock, sling swivels, and camouflaged sling and a recoil pad. It was introduced in 1987.

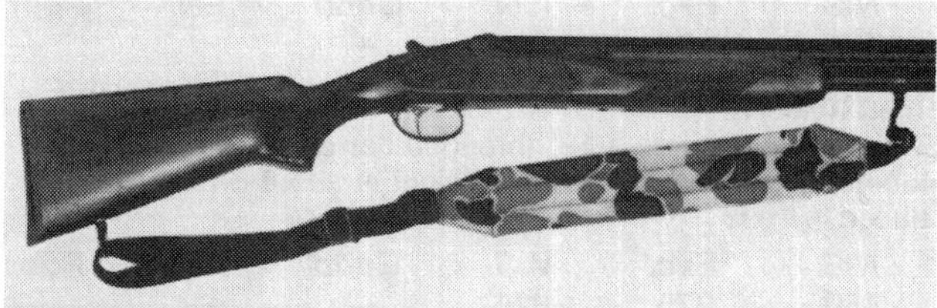

NIB	Exc.	V.G.	Good	Fair	Poor
875	700	500	350	300	150

Waterfowl 10 Gauge

The same as the Waterfowl Special but is chambered for the 10 gauge Magnum with double triggers.

NIB	Exc.	V.G.	Good	Fair	Poor
975	850	600	400	300	200

Turkey Special

Similar to the Waterfowl Special 10 gauge with a 26" barrel with screw-in choke tubes.

NIB	Exc.	V.G.	Good	Fair	Poor
975	850	600	350	300	200

Lince

Chambered for the 12 and 20 gauge and had 26" or 28" barrels with 3" chambers and various chokes. The boxlock action had a Greener crossbolt and was either blued or polished and chrome-plated. The barrels were blued with a ventilated rib. It had a single-selective trigger and automatic ejectors. The Lince was imported in 1986 only.

Exc.	V.G.	Good	Fair	Poor
500	425	350	300	200

Silver Model

Similar to the Lince with a plain, unengraved, brushed-chrome-finished receiver. It was imported in 1986 and 1987.

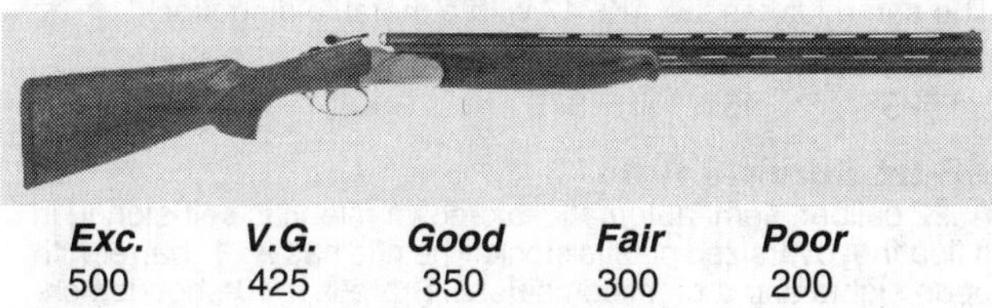

Exc.	V.G.	Good	Fair	Poor
500	425	350	300	200

Silver I

Similar to the Silver but is available in 28 gauge and .410, as well as 12 and 20 gauge. It also has a single-selective trigger, fixed chokes, extractors, and a recoil pad. It was introduced in 1987.

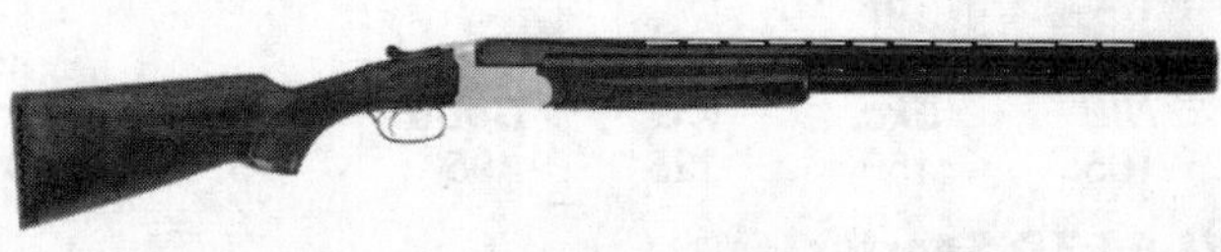

NIB	Exc.	V.G.	Good	Fair	Poor
650	550	325	275	200	175

NOTE: Add $25 for 28 gauge and .410 bore guns.

Silver II

Similar to the Silver I with screw-in choke tubes, automatic ejectors, and select walnut. It was introduced in 1987.

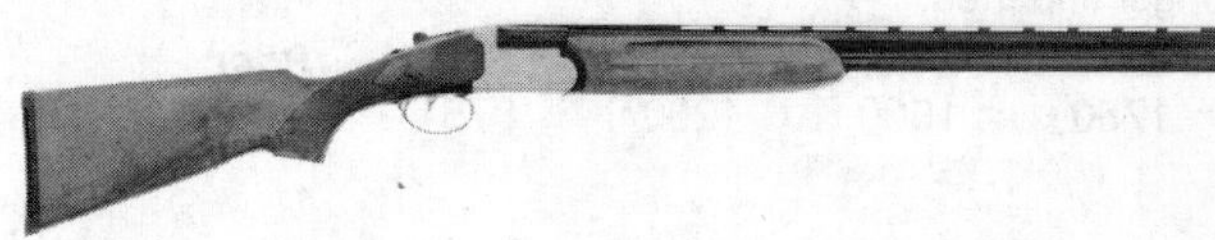

NIB	Exc.	V.G.	Good	Fair	Poor
750	650	450	350	300	150

NOTE: Add $25 for 28 gauge and .410 bore guns.

Silver II Lite

Introduced in 1994 this model is designed as an upland game gun. Offered in 12, 20, and 28 gauge with 26" barrels. Chambered for both 2-3/4" and 3" shells. Frame is made from a lightweight steel alloy. No longer imported.

NIB	Exc.	V.G.	Good	Fair	Poor
875	775	550	400	300	150

Silver Competition/Sporting

Offered in 12 gauge with a choice of 28" or 30" barrels which are made from chrome moly. Barrels have elongated forcing cones, chromed bores and are ported to help reduce recoil. Comes with interchangeable choke tubes. The single-selective trigger is mechanical. Weighs about 7-1/2 pounds. In 1996 a 20 gauge model was added with 28" barrel and 3" chambers.

NIB	Exc.	V.G.	Good	Fair	Poor
950	800	600	400	300	150

Silver Hunter

Introduced in 1999 this model is offered in 12 and 20 gauges with 26" and 28" barrels. Single-selective trigger with extractors. Choke tubes standard. Weight is about 7 lbs.

NIB	Exc.	V.G.	Good	Fair	Poor
625	500	400	—	—	—

Bristol (Sterling)

Chambered for 12 and 20 gauge. It has various barrel lengths with a vent rib and screw-in choke tubes. The chambers are 3", and the chrome-finished action is a boxlock with Greener crossbolt and game scene engraved side plates. There are automatic ejectors and a single-selective trigger. It was introduced in 1986, and in 1989 the designation was changed to the Sterling. No longer imported.

NIB	Exc.	V.G.	Good	Fair	Poor
825	750	675	500	400	200

Sir

Chambered for the 12 and 20 gauge with 3" chambers, various barrel lengths and chokings and a ventilated rib. The chrome-finished sidelock action has a Greener crossbolt and is engraved with a game scene. There are automatic ejectors and a single-selective trigger. This model was imported in 1986. No longer imported.

Exc.	V.G.	Good	Fair	Poor
875	750	625	500	250

Royal

Chambered for the 12 and 20 gauge. It is manufactured in various barrel lengths and chokes with a vent rib and 3" chambers. The chrome-finished sidelock action has a Greener crossbolt and is profusely scroll-engraved. It has automatic ejectors and a single-selective trigger. The select pistol grip walnut stock is hand checkered and oil-finished. This model was imported in 1986 and 1987. No longer imported.

Exc.	V.G.	Good	Fair	Poor
1500	1275	1000	800	400

Excelsior

Similar to the Royal with extensive deep relief engraving and gold inlays. This model was imported in 1986 and 1987. No longer imported.

Exc.	V.G.	Good	Fair	Poor
1750	1500	1200	875	450

SINGLE-BARREL SHOTGUNS

AASB

The standard single-barrel, break-open, hammerless shotgun. It is chambered for 12 and 20 gauge and .410. It has a 26" barrel with various chokes and 3" chambers. It has a pistol grip stock and a matte finish. It was introduced in 1988. No longer imported.

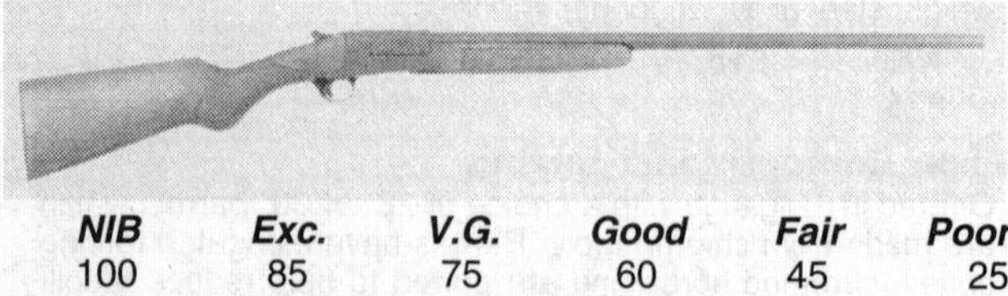

NIB	Exc.	V.G.	Good	Fair	Poor
100	85	75	60	45	25

Campers Special

Similar to the standard model with a 21" barrel and a folding stock. It was introduced in 1988. No longer imported.

NIB	Exc.	V.G.	Good	Fair	Poor
107	95	85	70	50	35

Single-Barrel Shotguns Youth Model

Chambered for the 20 gauge and .410 and has a 12.5" stock with a recoil pad. It was introduced in 1989. No longer imported.

NIB	Exc.	V.G.	Good	Fair	Poor
115	100	80	65	50	35

Slugger

This version has a 24" barrel with rifle sights. It is chambered for the 12 and 20 gauge and has a recoil pad. No longer imported.

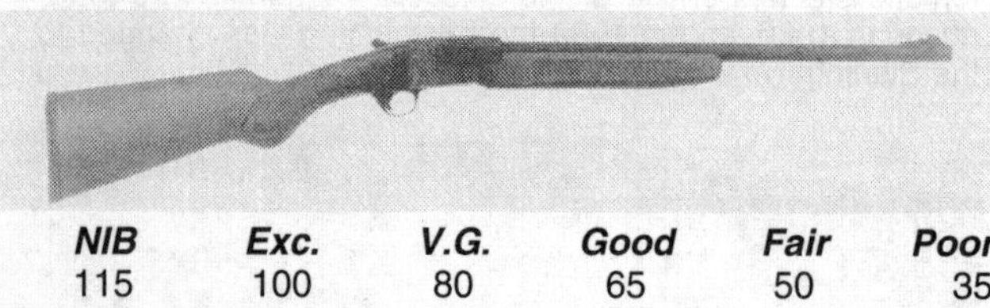

NIB	Exc.	V.G.	Good	Fair	Poor
115	100	80	65	50	35

10 Gauge Model

Chambered for the 10 gauge 3.5" Magnum. It has a 32" full choke barrel and a recoil pad. This model was introduced in 1988. No longer imported.

NIB	Exc.	V.G.	Good	Fair	Poor
150	135	100	85	60	45

Combo Model

Similar in appearance to the other single-barrel models but is offered in an interchangeable-barreled rifle/shotgun combination—the 28" barreled .22 Hornet and the 12 gauge, or the 26" barreled .22 LR and 20 gauge. This model was furnished with a fitted hard case to hold the interchangeable barrels. It was introduced in 1989. No longer imported.

NIB	Exc.	V.G.	Good	Fair	Poor
250	200	175	145	110	75

SEMI-AUTO SHOTGUNS

Phantom Field

Chambered for 12 gauge and fitted with choice of 24", 26", or 28" barrels. Fitted with 3" chamber. Gas operated action. Choke tubes standard. Five-round magazine. Checkered walnut stock. Weight is about 7 lbs. Introduced in 1999.

NIB	Exc.	V.G.	Good	Fair	Poor
425	350	300	—	—	—

Phantom Synthetic

Same as model above but furnished with checkered synthetic stock. Weight is about 6.75 lbs. Introduced in 1999.

NIB	Exc.	V.G.	Good	Fair	Poor
425	350	300	—	—	—

Phantom HP

This model features a 19" threaded barrel for external choke tubes. Five-round magazine. Weight is about 6.75 lbs. Introduced in 1999.

NIB	Exc.	V.G.	Good	Fair	Poor
450	375	325	—	—	—

RIFLES

Model ZCY.308

Essentially the same rifle as the ZCY.223 — only it is chambered for the .308 cartridge. This model was imported in 1988 only.

Exc.	V.G.	Good	Fair	Poor
500	425	350	300	200

AKY39

The semi-automatic version of the Soviet AK-47 as it is manufactured by Yugoslavia. It is offered with folding tritium night sights and a wooden fixed stock. It was imported in 1988.

Exc.	V.G.	Good	Fair	Poor
500	425	350	300	200

AKF39

The same rifle as the AKY39 with a metal folding stock.

Exc.	V.G.	Good	Fair	Poor
525	450	375	300	200

AKC47

Basically the same rifle as the AKY39 without the tritium night sights.

Exc.	V.G.	Good	Fair	Poor
525	450	375	300	200

AKF47

The same rifle as the AKC47 with a metal folding stock.

Exc.	V.G.	Good	Fair	Poor
525	450	375	300	200

EXP-64 Survival Rifle

A .22 caliber, semi-automatic takedown rifle. It is self-storing in a floating, oversized plastic stock. The rifle has a 21" barrel with open sights and a crossbolt safety. There is a 10-shot detachable magazine. Importation by American Arms began in 1989.

NIB	Exc.	V.G.	Good	Fair	Poor
165	150	125	95	75	50

SM-64 TD Sporter

A .22 LR semi-automatic with a takedown 21" barrel. It has adjustable sights and a checkered hardwood stock and forend. Importation commenced in 1989.

NIB	Exc.	V.G.	Good	Fair	Poor
150	135	110	85	65	45

1860 Henry

Replica of lever action Henry rifle. Brass frame. Steel half-octagon barrel with tube magazine. Chambered for .44-40 or .45 Long Colt. Offered in 24" or 18.5" barrels. Weight with 24" barrel is about 9.25 lbs. Built by Uberti.

NIB	Exc.	V.G.	Good	Fair	Poor
950	800	650	—	—	—

1866 Winchester

Replica of Winchester 1866. Offered in .44-40 or .45 Long Colt. Barrel lengths in 24" or 19". Brass frame. Weight is about 8.25 lbs. for 24" barrel model. Built by Uberti.

NIB	Exc.	V.G.	Good	Fair	Poor
725	625	475	—	—	—

1873 Winchester

Replica of Winchester Model 1873. Offered with choice of 24" or 30" barrels. Chambered for .44-40 or .45 Long Colt. Case hardened steel frame. Weight is about 8.25 lbs. for 24" model. Built by Uberti.

NIB	Exc.	V.G.	Good	Fair	Poor
850	700	550	—	—	—

NOTE: Add $80 for 30" barrel.

1885 Single-Shot High Wall

Chambered for .45-70 cartridge this Winchester replica is fitted with a 28" round barrel. Weight is about 8.75 lbs. Built by Uberti.

NIB	Exc.	V.G.	Good	Fair	Poor
800	650	500	—	—	—

Sharps Cavalry Carbine

This Sharps replica is fitted with a 22" round barrel and chambered for the .45-70 cartridge. Adjustable rear sight. Weight is about 8 lbs.

NIB	Exc.	V.G.	Good	Fair	Poor
650	500	350	—	—	—

Sharps Frontier Carbine

Similar to the Cavalry carbine but with a 22" octagonal barrel and double set triggers. Weight is about 7.75 lbs.

NIB	Exc.	V.G.	Good	Fair	Poor
675	525	375	—	—	—

Sharps Sporting Rifle

This model features a 28" octagonal barrel chambered for either the .45-70 or .45-120 cartridge. Double set triggers. Adjustable rear sight. Checkered walnut stock. Weight is about 9 lbs.

NIB	Exc.	V.G.	Good	Fair	Poor
675	525	375	—	—	—

Sharps 1874 Deluxe Sporting Rifle

Similar to the above model but with browned barrels.

NIB	Exc.	V.G.	Good	Fair	Poor
700	550	400	—	—	—

HANDGUNS

Model EP-.380

A high-quality, stainless steel pocket pistol that is chambered for the .380 ACP cartridge. It is a double-action semi-automatic that holds 7 shots and has a 3.5" barrel. The grips are checkered walnut. This pistol has been imported from West Germany since 1988.

NIB	Exc.	V.G.	Good	Fair	Poor
450	400	350	275	225	100

Model PK-22

A domestic semi-automatic that is chambered for the .22 LR. It is a double-action with a 3.5" barrel and an 8-shot finger extension magazine. It is made of stainless steel and has black plastic grips. This model is manufactured in the U.S.A. by American Arms.

NIB	Exc.	V.G.	Good	Fair	Poor
200	175	150	125	100	75

Model CX-22

A compact version of the PK-22 with a 2.75" barrel and a 7-shot magazine. Manufacture began in 1989.

NIB	Exc.	V.G.	Good	Fair	Poor
200	175	150	125	100	75

Model TT Tokarev

The Yugoslavian version of the Soviet Tokarev chambered for 9mm Parabellum and with a safety added to make importation legal. It has a 4.5" barrel, 9-shot magazine and a blued finish with checkered plastic grips. Importation began in 1988.

NIB	*Exc.*	*V.G.*	*Good*	*Fair*	*Poor*
275	225	175	150	125	100

Model ZC-.380

A scaled-down version of the Tokarev that is chambered for the .380 ACP. It has a 3.5" barrel and holds 8 shots. The finish and grips are the same as on the full-sized version. Importation from Yugoslavia began in 1988.

NIB	*Exc.*	*V.G.*	*Good*	*Fair*	*Poor*
275	225	175	150	125	100

Aussie Model

Introduced in 1996, this is an Australian-designed semi-automatic pistol made in Spain. Chambered for the 9mm or .40 S&W cartridge it has a polymer frame with nickeled steel slide. Sold with 10-shot magazine. Barrel length is 4-3/4" and weight is 23 oz.

NIB	*Exc.*	*V.G.*	*Good*	*Fair*	*Poor*
400	350	300	250	200	100

Regulator

Built by Uberti this single-action revolver has a case hardened frame, polished brass trigger guard and backstrap. Barrel and cylinder are blued. One piece walnut grips. Choice of chambers in .44-40, .45 LC, or .357 Magnum. Barrel lengths from 4.75", 5.5", to 7.5". Weight is about 34 oz. with 5.75" barrel.

NIB	*Exc.*	*V.G.*	*Good*	*Fair*	*Poor*
250	225	200	—	—	—

Regulator Deluxe

Same as above but with steel trigger guard and backstrap. Chambered in .45 Long Colt only.

NIB	*Exc.*	*V.G.*	*Good*	*Fair*	*Poor*
295	275	175	—	—	—

AMERICAN BARLOCK WONDER

SEE—Crescent Arms Co.

AMERICAN DERRINGER CORP.

Waco, Texas

Model 1 Derringer

Fashioned after the Remington O/U derringer this is a high quality, rugged pistol. It is built from high tensile strength stainless steel. There are over 60 different rifle and pistol calibers to choose from on special order. The upper barrel can be chambered different from the lower barrel on request. Available in a high polish finish or a satin finish. Offered with rosewood, bacote, walnut, or blackwood grips. Ivory, bonded ivory, stag, or pearl are available at extra cost. Overall length is 4.8", barrel length is 3", width across the frame is .9", width across the grip is 1.2". Typical weight is 15 oz. in .45 caliber. All guns are furnished with French fitted leatherette case. Prices are determined by caliber.

Caliber: .22 Long Rifle through .357 Mag. and .45 ACP

NIB	*Exc.*	*V.G.*	*Good*	*Fair*	*Poor*
350	325	250	125	100	75

Calibers: .41 Mag., .44-40, .44 Special, .44 Mag., .45 Long Colt, .410 Bore, .22 Hornet, .223 Rem., 30-30, and .45-70 Gov't.

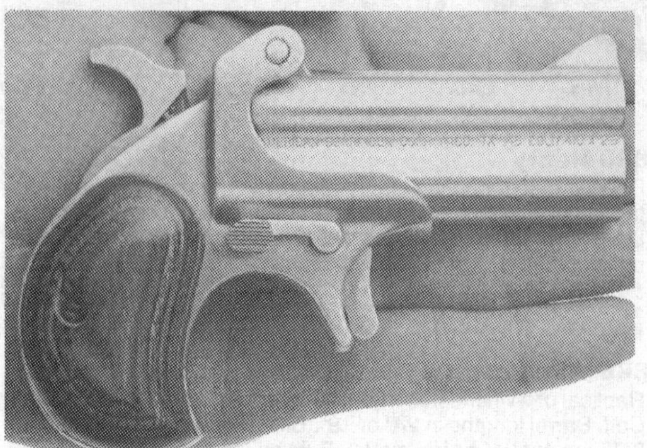

NIB	*Exc.*	*V.G.*	*Good*	*Fair*	*Poor*
375	300	250	200	150	100

NOTE: Premium for rifle cartridges.

Model 1 Lady Derringer

Similar to the Model 1 but chambered for the .38 Special, .32 Magnum, .45 Colt, or .357 Magnum. Offered in two grades.

Deluxe Grade

High polished stainless steel with scrimshawed ivory grips with cameo or rose design.

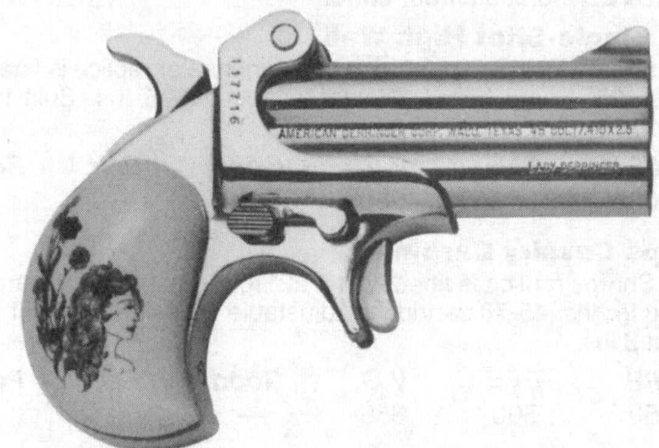

NIB	*Exc.*	*V.G.*	*Good*	*Fair*	*Poor*
325	250	200	150	100	75

Deluxe Engraved Grade

Same as above but hand engraved in 1880s style.

NIB	*Exc.*	*V.G.*	*Good*	*Fair*	*Poor*
650	550	500	450	250	150

NOTE: For .45 Colt and .45/.410 add $75. For .357 magnum add $50.

Model 1 NRA 500 Series

Limited edition of 500. Also available in gold and blue finishes over stainless steel.

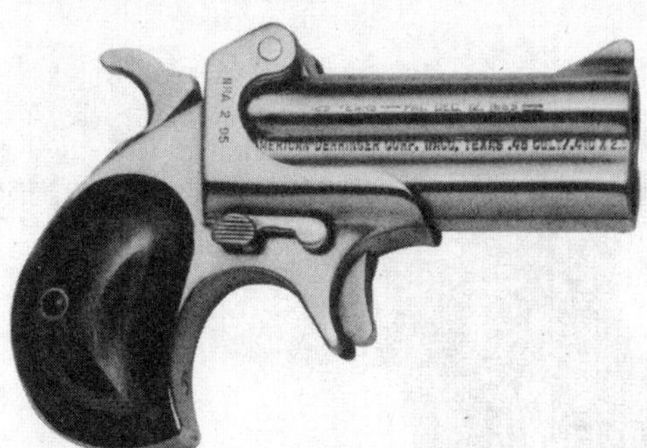

NIB	Exc.	V.G.	Good	Fair	Poor
350	300	250	200	150	100

Model 1 Texas Commemorative

Built with a solid brass frame and stainless steel barrel. Dimensions are same as Model 1. Grips are stag or rosewood and offered in .45 Colt, .44-40, or .38 Special. Barrels marked "Made in the 150th Year of Texas Freedom." Limited to 500 pistols in each caliber.

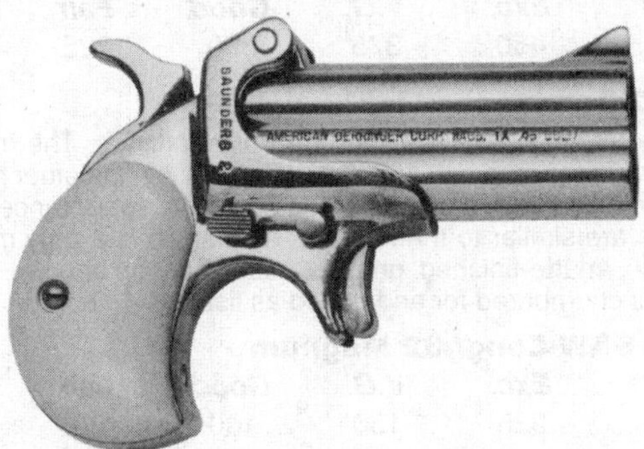

Caliber: .38 Special

NIB	Exc.	V.G.	Good	Fair	Poor
325	250	200	150	100	75

Calibers: .45 Colt and .44-40

NIB	Exc.	V.G.	Good	Fair	Poor
400	325	250	200	125	100

Deluxe Engraved

Special serial number engraved on backstrap.

NIB	Exc.	V.G.	Good	Fair	Poor
900	750	550	350	250	150

Model 1 125th Anniversary Commemorative

Built to commemorate the 125th anniversary of the derringer, 1866 to 1991. Similar to the Model 1 but marked with the patent date December 12, 1865. Brass frame and stainless steel barrel. Chambered for .440-40, .45 Colt, or .38 Special.

NIB	Exc.	V.G.	Good	Fair	Poor
300	250	225	175	125	100

Deluxe Engraved

NIB	Exc.	V.G.	Good	Fair	Poor
650	550	500	450	250	150

Model 2—Pen Pistol

Introduced in 1993 this is a legal pistol that cannot be fired from its pen position but requires that it be pulled apart and bent 80 degrees to fire. Made from stainless steel it is offered in .22 LR, .25 ACP, and .32 ACP. The length in pen form is 5.6" and in pistol form is 4.2". Barrel length is 2". Diameter varies from 1/2" to 5/8". Weight is 5 oz. No longer in production.

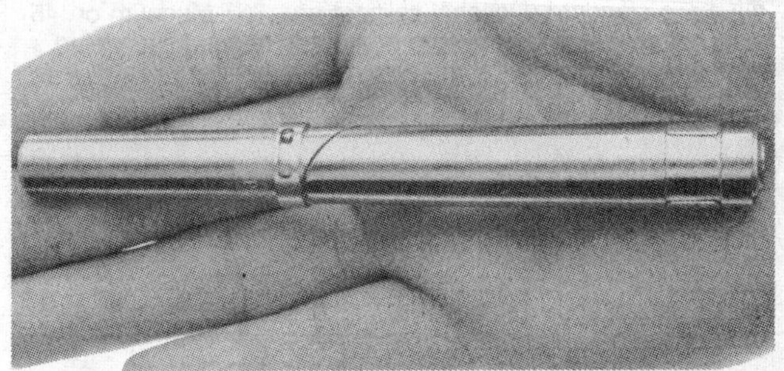

NIB	Exc.	V.G.	Good	Fair	Poor
600	395	300	225	100	85

Model 3

This model is a single-barrel derringer. Barrel length is 2.5" and swing down to load. Frame and barrel are stainless steel. Offered in .38 Special or .32 Magnum. Weighs about 8 oz. Production of this model has been temporary halted.

NIB	Exc.	V.G.	Good	Fair	Poor
150	100	85	75	65	50

Model 4

Similar in appearance to the Model 3 but fitted with a 4.1" barrel. Overall length is 6" and weight is about 16.5 oz. Chambered for 3" .410 bore, .45 Long Colt, .44 Magnum, or .357 Magnum.

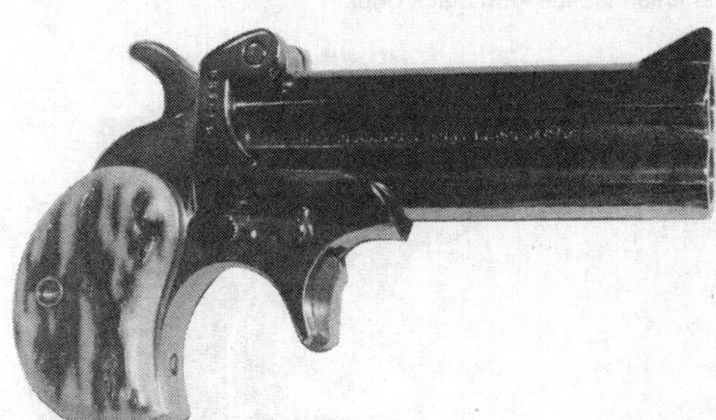

NIB	Exc.	V.G.	Good	Fair	Poor
375	300	275	250	200	125

NOTE: For .45-70 add $150. For .44 magnum add $100.

Model 4—Engraved

NIB	Exc.	V.G.	Good	Fair	Poor
1500	1200	—	—	—	—

Model 4—Alaskan Survival Model

Similar to the Model 4 but with upper barrel chambered for .45-70 and lower barrel for .45 LC or .410. Both barrels can also be chambered for .44 Magnum or .45-70. Comes with oversized rosewood grips.

NIB	Exc.	V.G.	Good	Fair	Poor
425	350	275	200	150	100

Model 6

This double-barrel derringer is fitted with a 6" barrel chambered for the .45 LC or .410 bore. Weighs about 21 oz. Rosewood grips are standard. Optional calibers are .357 Magnum or .45 ACP. Oversize grips are optional and add about $35 to value.

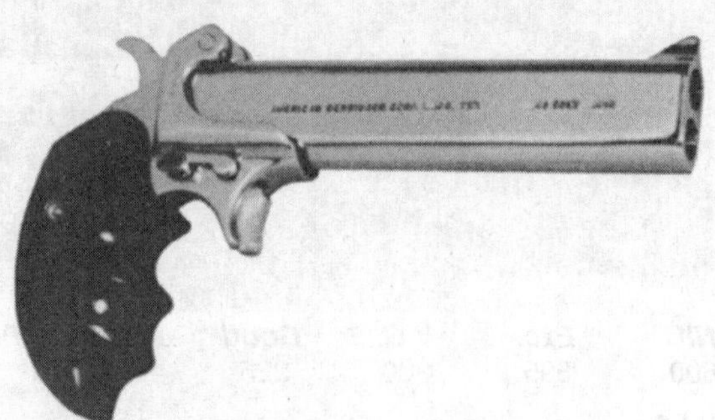

NIB	Exc.	V.G.	Good	Fair	Poor
400	350	250	200	150	100

Model 6—Engraved

NIB	Exc.	V.G.	Good	Fair	Poor
1700	1400	—	—	—	—

Double-Action Derringer

Hi Standard-type double-barrel, double-action derringer is chambered for the .22 LR or .22 Magnum. Its barrel length is 3.5" and overall length is 5.125". Weighs approximately 11 oz. The finish is blue with black grips.

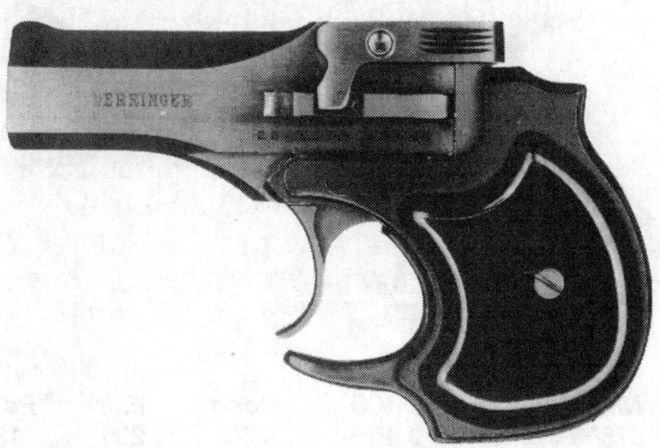

NIB	Exc.	V.G.	Good	Fair	Poor
170	150	125	100	85	75

DA 38 Double-Action Derringer

Similar to above but chambered for .38 Special, .357 Magnum, 9mm Luger, and .40 S&W. Finish is satin stainless. Grip is made from aluminum. Grips are rosewood or walnut.

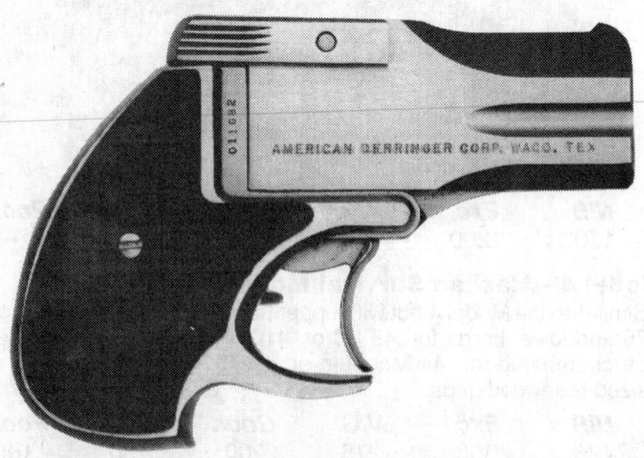

NIB	Exc.	V.G.	Good	Fair	Poor
400	325	250	200	150	100

NOTE: For .40 S&W add $40.

Mini Cop 4-Shot

This is a four-barrel derringer chambered for the .22 Magnum Rimfire cartridge.

NIB	Exc.	V.G.	Good	Fair	Poor
310	285	250	225	175	125

Cop 4-Shot

Same as above but chambered for the .357 Magnum cartridge.

NIB	Exc.	V.G.	Good	Fair	Poor
550	450	375	300	225	150

Model 7 Derringer—Lightweight

Manufactured as a backup gun for police officers. The frame and barrels are made of aircraft aluminum alloy; the other parts are stainless steel. This gun weighs 7.5 oz. Its appearance and function are similar to the Model 1. The finish is a gray matte with thin, matte-finished grips of rosewood or bacote. This model is chambered for and priced as listed.

.32 S&W Long/.32 Magnum

NIB	Exc.	V.G.	Good	Fair	Poor
275	225	150	100	80	50

.38 S&W and .380 ACP

NIB	Exc.	V.G.	Good	Fair	Poor
275	225	150	100	80	50

.22 LR and .38 Special

NIB	Exc.	V.G.	Good	Fair	Poor
275	225	150	100	80	50

.44 Special

NIB	Exc.	V.G.	Good	Fair	Poor
525	450	375	300	250	150

Model 8

This is a single-action two-shot target pistol with a manually operated hammer block safety. Safety automatically disengages when the hammer is cocked. Barrel length is 8". Chambered for the .45 Colt and .410 shotshell. Weight is 24 oz.

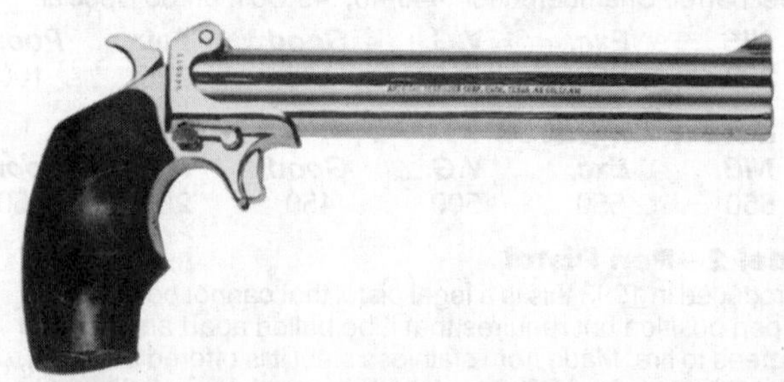

NIB	Exc.	V.G.	Good	Fair	Poor
475	400	325	250	175	100

Model 8—Engraved

NIB	Exc.	V.G.	Good	Fair	Poor
1850	1500	—	—	—	—

Model 10 Derringer

Similar to the Model 1 with a frame of aluminum alloy and all other parts, including the barrels, stainless steel. It has a gray matte finish and thin grips of rosewood or bacote. It weighs 10 oz. and is chambered for the .38 Special, .45 ACP or the .45 Colt.

NIB	Exc.	V.G.	Good	Fair	Poor
250	200	175	140	110	80

NOTE: For .45 Colt add $75.

Model 11 Derringer

A stainless steel barrel and all other parts aluminum. It weighs 11 oz. and is chambered for the .38 Special, .380 Auto, .32 Mag., .22 LR, and .22 Magnum. The grips and finish are the same as on the Model 10.

NIB	Exc.	V.G.	Good	Fair	Poor
275	225	150	125	100	75

Semmerling LM-4

This gun has been in production for approximately 10 years, built by various companies. This latest offering by American Derringer may, with the right marketing and manufacturing approach, be the one that makes a commercial success of this fine firearm concept. The LM-4 was designed as the ultimate police backup/defense weapon. It is a manually operated, 5-shot repeater only 5.2" long, 3.7" high, and 1" wide. It is chambered for the .45 ACP and is undoubtedly the smallest 5-shot .45 ever produced. The LM-4 is made of a special tool steel and is either blued or, at extra cost, hard chrome-plated. A stainless steel version is also available. The LM-4 is not a semi-automatic, although it physically resembles one. The slide is flicked forward and back after each double-action squeeze of the trigger. This weapon is virtually hand-built and features high visibility sights and a smooth trigger. It is an extremely limited production item, and the company produces only two per week. The price and availability may fluctuate, so the company should be contacted for accurate figures. The values for the guns produced before American Derringer's involvement will be found in the section dealing with the Semmerling. These values are for the latest production by American Derringer. Prices listed may change due to supply and demand.

NIB	Exc.	V.G.	Good	Fair	Poor
2500	2000	1500	—	—	—

NOTE: Hard chrome add $200.00. Stainless steel add 35 percent.

LM-5

Built of stainless steel this semi-auto is chambered for the .32 Mag. or .25 Auto. The barrel length is 2.25" and the overall length is 4", height is 3". Wooden grips are standard. Offered in limited quantities. Weight is approximately 15 oz.

NIB	Exc.	V.G.	Good	Fair	Poor
300	250	200	150	100	75

Millennium Series 2000

This model chambered for .38 Special, .45 Colt, or .44-40. Single-action. Fitted with scrimshaw grips with a yellow rose of Texas on the left side and the Lone Star flag on the right side. Weight is about 15 oz. Supplied with red velvet box with silver inlay. Introduced in 1999.

NIB	Exc.	V.G.	Good	Fair	Poor
400	325	—	—	—	—

Gambler Millennium 2000

Similar to the Millennium Series above but fitted with rosewood grips with etched Lone Star of Texas. Supplied with brown leatherette box with copper logo inlay.

NIB	Exc.	V.G.	Good	Fair	Poor
400	325	—	—	—	—

Women of Texas Series

This model has the same features as the Millennium Series 2000. Stamped "Women of Texas Series 2000."

NIB	Exc.	V.G.	Good	Fair	Poor
400	325	—	—	—	—

Cowboy Series 2000

This model has the same features as the Gambler Millennium 200 but with "Cowboy Series 2000" stamped on the barrel.

NIB	Exc.	V.G.	Good	Fair	Poor
400	325	—	—	—	—

AMERICAN FIRE ARMS MFG. CO., INC.

San Antonio, Texas

This company operated between 1972 and 1974, producing a .25 ACP pocket pistol and a stainless steel .38 Special derringer. A .380 auto was produced on an extremely limited basis.

American .38 Special Derringer

A well-made, stainless steel O/U derringer that was similar in appearance and function to the old Remington O/U. It had 3" barrels that pivoted upward for loading. This gun was a single-action that had an automatic selector and a spur trigger. The smooth grips were of walnut. There were approximately 3,500 manufactured between 1972 and 1974.

Exc.	V.G.	Good	Fair	Poor
200	180	150	125	90

American .25 Automatic

A small, blowback, semi-automatic pocket pistol that was chambered for the .25 ACP cartridge. It had a 2" barrel and was made of either stainless steel or blued carbon steel. The grips were of plain uncheckered walnut, and the detachable magazine held 7 shots. It was manufactured until 1974.

Courtesy J.B. Wood

Exc.	V.G.	Good	Fair	Poor
200	150	125	100	75

NOTE: For stainless steel add 20 percent.

American .380 Automatic

Similar to the .25 except larger. The barrel was 3.5", and the gun was made in stainless steel only. The grips were of smooth walnut, and it held 8 shots. There were only 10 of these .380's manufactured between 1972 and 1974. They are extremely rare, but there is little collector base for this company's products, and the value is difficult to estimate.

Exc.	V.G.	Good	Fair	Poor
600	550	475	375	200

AMERICAN FRONTIER FIREARMS

Aguanga, California

1871-72 Open Top Standard Model

Offered in .38 or .44 caliber with non-rebated cylinder. Barrel lengths are 7.5" or 8" in round. Blued finish except silver backstrap and trigger guard. Walnut grips.

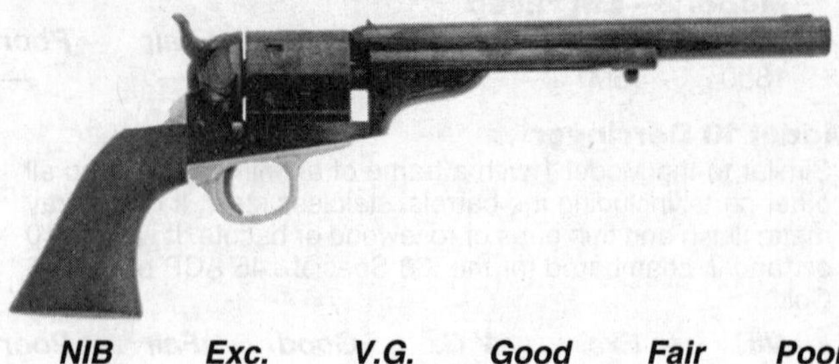

NIB	Exc.	V.G.	Good	Fair	Poor
795	625	500	400	—	—

Richards & Mason Conversion 1851 Navy Standard Model

Offered in .38 and .44 calibers with Mason ejector assembly and non-rebated cylinder with a choice of octagon barrels in 4.75", 5.5", or 7.5". Blued finish with blued backstrap and trigger guard. Walnut grips.

NIB	Exc.	V.G.	Good	Fair	Poor
795	325	500	400	—	—

1860 Richards Army Model

Chambered for .44 Colt and .38 caliber. Rebated cylinder with or without ejector assembly. Barrel length is 7.5". High polish blue finish with silver trigger guard and case hardened frame.

NOTE: Guns shipped without ejector assembly will be supplied with a ramrod and plunger typical of the period.

NIB	Exc.	V.G.	Good	Fair	Poor
795	325	500	400	—	—

AMERICAN GUN CO., NEW YORK

Norwich, Connecticut

Maker—Crescent Firearms Co.

Side-by-Side Shotgun

A typical trade gun made around the turn of the century by the Crescent Firearms Co. to be distributed by H. & D. Folsom. These are sometimes known as "Hardware Store Guns," as that is where many were sold. This particular gun was chambered for 12, 16, and 20 gauges and was produced with or without external hammers. The length of the barrels varied, as did the chokes. Some were produced with Damascus barrels; some, with fluid steel. The latter are worth approximately 25 percent more.

NOTE: For a full listing of most of the variations of the Crescent Arms Co., and shotguns marked with American Gun Co. see "Crescent F.A. Co."

Knickerbocker Pistol

(See Knickerbocker)

AMERICAN HISTORICAL FOUNDATION

Richmond, Virginia

The American Historical Foundation is a private organization that commissions historical commemoratives. Secondary market sales are infrequent and are difficult to confirm. The American Historical Foundation sells only direct and not through dealers or distributors. For information on past and current issues contact the American Historical Foundation at 1142 West Grace Street, Richmond, VA 23220.

AMERICAN INDUSTRIES

Cleveland, Ohio
aka CALICO LIGHT WEAPONS SYSTEMS
Sparks, Nevada

Calico M-100

A semi-automatic carbine that has a 16.1" barrel with a flash suppressor. It is chambered for the .22 LR and features a folding stock, full shrouding hand guards, a 100-round capacity, helical feed, and detachable magazine. It features an ambidextrous safety, pistol grip storage compartment, and a black finished alloy frame and adjustable sights. This model was introduced in 1986.

NIB	Exc.	V.G.	Good	Fair	Poor
600	500	350	250	200	100

Calico M-100P/M-110

Similar to the M-100 .22 rimfire with a 6" barrel with muzzle-brake and no shoulder stock.

NIB	Exc.	V.G.	Good	Fair	Poor
600	500	350	250	200	75

Calico M-100S Sporter/M-105

Similar to the Model 100 with a futuristically styled walnut buttstock and forearm.

NIB	Exc.	V.G.	Good	Fair	Poor
600	500	350	250	200	75

Calico M-101 Solid Stock Carbine

Introduced in 1994 this rifle features a 100-round magazine and a composite buttstock that is removable.

NIB	Exc.	V.G.	Good	Fair	Poor
675	550	400	300	200	75

Calico M-900

A black polymer-stocked rifle that is similar to the M-100S, chambered for the 9mm Parabellum. It has a delayed blowback action and features a stainless steel bolt and alloy receiver. The cocking handle is non-reciprocating, and the rear sight is fixed with an adjustable front. There is a 50-round magazine standard and a 100-round capacity model optional. This model was introduced in 1989.

NIB	Exc.	V.G.	Good	Fair	Poor
700	575	425	350	275	100

Calico M-950 Pistol

Similar to the Model 900 rifle with a 6" barrel and no shoulder stock.

NIB	Exc.	V.G.	Good	Fair	Poor
700	575	425	350	275	100

Calico M-951

The M-951 is a tactical carbine with a sliding buttstock. The barrel is 16" in length. It weighs about 7 pounds.

NIB	Exc.	V.G.	Good	Fair	Poor
700	575	425	350	275	100

Calico M-951S

Same as above but furnished with more conventional buttstock. Referred to as a light tactical carbine. Weighs about 7-1/4 pounds.

NIB	Exc.	V.G.	Good	Fair	Poor
700	575	425	350	275	100

AMERICAN INTERNATIONAL

Salt Lake City, Utah
aka American Research & Development

American 180 Carbine (SAM-180)

This firearm, imported from Austria, is a semi-automatic, 16.5" barreled carbine chambered for the .22 LR. The sights are adjustable, and the stock is made of high-impact plastic. The unique drum magazine holds 177 rounds and is affixed to the top of the receiver. There is a select-fire version available for law enforcement agencies only and an optional laser lock sight system. Later manufactured by Feather Industries in Boulder, Colorado. It is now known as the SAM-180. Deduct 25 percent for U.S. manufacture.

NIB	Exc.	V.G.	Good	Fair	Poor
1200	1000	600	400	200	100

AMERICAN WESTERN ARMS INC. (AWA)

Delray Beach, Florida

AWA Lightning Rifle LE

A copy of the Colt Lightning slide-action rifle chambered for the .32-20, .38 Special, .38-40, .44-40, or the .45 Colt cartridge. Choice of round barrel lengths in 20" or 24". Engraved AWA logo and stage scene on the receiver. Limited edition to 500 guns.

NIB	Exc.	V.G.	Good	Fair	Poor
1200	950	—	—	—	—

AWA Lightning Rifle

This slide action rifle is chambered for those cartridges above with a 24" barrel length with the choice of round or octagon barrel. Blued finish.

NIB	Exc.	V.G.	Good	Fair	Poor
800	675	—	—	—	—

NOTE: Add $40 for octagon barrel.

AWA Lightning Carbine

As above but with 20" barrel in round or octagon.

NIB	Exc.	V.G.	Good	Fair	Poor
800	675	—	—	—	—

NOTE: Add $40 for octagon barrel.

AMES, N.P. PISTOLS

Springfield, Massachusetts

Overall length-11-5/8"; barrel length-6"; caliber-.54. Markings: on lockplate, forward of hammer "N.P. AMES/SPRINGFIELD/MASS," on tail, either "USN" or "USR" over date; on barrel, standard U.S. Navy inspection marks. N. P. Ames of Springfield, Massachusetts received a contract from the U.S. Navy in September 1842 for the delivery of 2,000 single-shot muzzleloading percussion pistols. All are distinguished by having a lock mechanism that lies flush with the right side of the stock. On the first 300 Ames pistols, this lock terminates in a point; the balance produced were made with locks with a rounded tail. This "boxlock" had been devised by Henry Nock in England, and was adapted to the U.S. Navy for the percussion pistols they ordered from Ames and Derringer. In addition to the 2,000 pistols for the Navy, the U.S. Revenue Cutter Service purchased 144 (distinguished by the "U S R" marks) for the forerunner of the U.S. Coast Guard. The latter commands triple the price over the "U S N" marked pistols, while the Navy pistols with pointed tails quadruple the value.

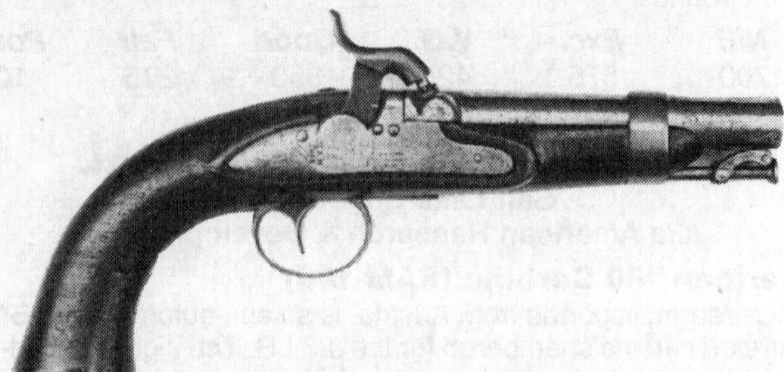

Courtesy Milwaukee Public Museum, Milwaukee, Wisconsin

Courtesy Milwaukee Public Museum, Milwaukee, Wisconsin

Exc.	V.G.	Good	Fair	Poor
—	—	2500	1000	400

AMES SWORD CO.
Chicopee Falls, Massachusetts

Turbiaux Le Protector

Ames Sword Co. became one of three U.S. companies that produced this unique, French palm-squeezer pistol. The design consists of a round disk with a protruding barrel on one side and a lever on the other. The disk contains the cylinder that holds either seven 8mm rimfire or ten 6mm rimfire cartridges. The barrel protrudes between the fingers, and the lever trigger is squeezed to fire the weapon. The design was patented in 1883 and sold successfully in France into the 1890s. In 1892 Peter Finnegan bought the patents and brought them to Ames Sword. He contracted with them to produce 25,000 pistols for the Minneapolis Firearms Company. After approximately 1,500 were delivered, Finnegan declared insolvency, and after litigation, Ames secured the full patent rights. The Ames Company produced Protector Revolvers until at least 1917.

(See Chicago Firearms Co. and Minneapolis Firearms Co.)

Exc.	V.G.	Good	Fair	Poor
—	—	3000	1250	500

REMINDER
In most cases, condition determines price.

AMT
formerly Arcadia Machine and Tool
Irwindale, California
See also—Galena Industries Inc.

In May 1998 Galena Industries Inc. purchased rights to produce most (not all) of the AMT-developed firearms. Galena Industries also purchased the logo and rights to use the trade name "AMT." Galena Industries did not purchase Arcadia Machine and Tool Inc.

NOTE: The firearms listed are for AMT-built guns only. These guns are no longer in production. Also see *Galena Industries*, which is no longer in business.

Lightning

A single-action, semi-automatic .22 caliber pistol. Available with barrel lengths of 5" (Bull only), 6.5", 8.5", 10.5" and 12.5" (either Bull or tapered), and adjustable sights, as well as the trigger. The grips are checkered black rubber. Manufactured between 1984 and 1987.

Courtesy John J. Stimson, Jr.

Exc.	V.G.	Good	Fair	Poor
300	200	175	125	85

Bull's Eye Regulation Target

As above, with a 6.5" vent rib bull barrel, wooden target grips, and an extended rear sight. Manufactured in 1986 only.

Exc.	V.G.	Good	Fair	Poor
400	300	250	200	100

Baby Automag

Similar to the above with an 8.5" ventilated rib barrel, and Millett adjustable sights. Approximately 1,000 were manufactured. No longer in production.

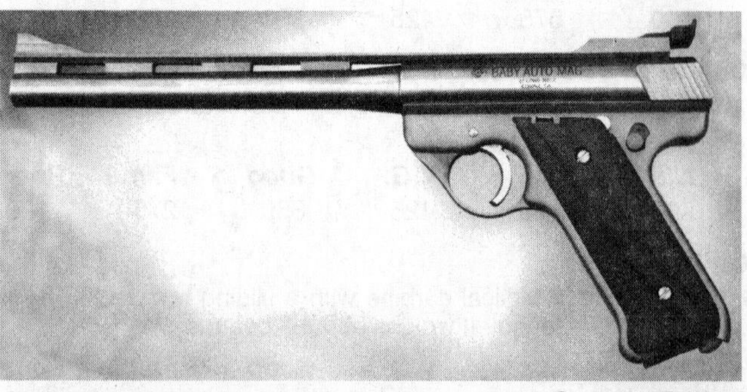

Courtesy J.B. Wood

This symbol denotes "Sleepers" with rapidly-rising values and/or significant collector potential.

Courtesy J.B. Wood

Exc.	V.G.	Good	Fair	Poor
500	350	275	225	150

Automag II

A stainless steel, semi-automatic .22 Magnum pistol. Available with 3-3/8", 4.5", and 6" barrel lengths and Millett adjustable sights, grips of black, grooved, plastic. Was first manufactured in 1987. Still in production.

Courtesy J.B. Wood

NIB	Exc.	V.G.	Good	Fair	Poor
500	400	300	200	100	80

Automag III

This semi-automatic pistol is chambered for the .30 Carbine cartridge and the 9mm Winchester Magnum cartridge. Barrel length is 6.37" and overall length is 10.5". The magazine capacity is 8 rounds. Fitted with Millett adjustable rear sight and carbon fiber grips. Stainless steel finish. Pistol weighs 43 oz.

NIB	Exc.	V.G.	Good	Fair	Poor
650	550	475	275	100	80

Automag IV

Similar in appearance to the Automag III this pistol is chambered for the .45 Winchester Magnum. Magazine capacity is 7 rounds and weight is 46 oz.

NIB	Exc.	V.G.	Good	Fair	Poor
650	600	525	375	225	100

Automag V

Introduced in 1993 this model is similar in appearance to the Automag models but is chambered for the .50 caliber cartridge. A limited production run of 3000 pistols with special serial number from "1 of 3000 to 3000 of 3000." Barrel length is 6.5" and magazine capacity is 5 rounds. Weighs 46 oz. Production stopped in 1995.

Courtesy J.B. Wood

NIB	Exc.	V.G.	Good	Fair	Poor
850	700	600	500	400	150

Javelina

Produced in 1992 this pistol is chambered for the 10mm cartridge and fitted with a 7" barrel with adjustable sights. Rubber wrap-around grips. Adjustable trigger. Magazine is 8 rounds. Weight is about 47 oz.

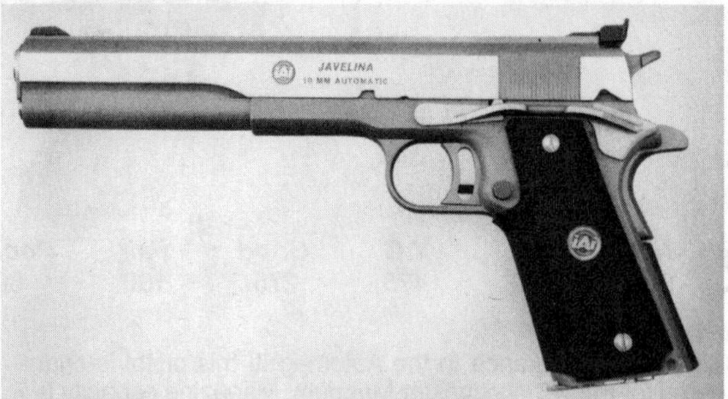

Courtesy J.B. Wood

Courtesy J.B. Wood

NIB	Exc.	V.G.	Good	Fair	Poor
650	525	400	300	200	—

Back Up Pistol

This is a small semi-automatic pocket pistol chambered for the .22 LR and the .380 ACP cartridges. This is fitted with a 2.5" barrel and is offered with either black plastic or walnut grips. The pistol weighs 18 oz. Magazine capacity is 5 rounds. Originally manufactured by TDE, then Irwindale Arms Inc., and then by AMT.

NIB	Exc.	V.G.	Good	Fair	Poor
350	225	175	125	100	85

Back Up .45 ACP, .40 S&W, 9mm

Courtesy J.B. Wood

Courtesy J.B. Wood

NIB	Exc.	V.G.	Good	Fair	Poor
350	250	200	150	100	85

Back Up .38 Super, .357 Sig, .400 CorBon

NIB	Exc.	V.G.	Good	Fair	Poor
400	300	250	200	150	100

.380 Back Up II

Introduced in 1993 this pistol is similar to the Back Up model but with the addition of a double safety, extended finger grip on the magazine, and single-action-only. This was a special order pistol only.

NIB	Exc.	V.G.	Good	Fair	Poor
400	300	250	200	150	100

This symbol denotes "Sleepers" with rapidly-rising values and/or significant collector potential.

Hardballer/Government Model

This model is similar to the Colt Gold Cup .45 ACP. It is offered in two versions. The first has fixed sights and rounded slide top, while the second has adjustable Millett sights and matte rib. Magazine capacity is 7 rounds. Wraparound rubber grips are standard. Long grip safety, beveled magazine well, and adjustable trigger are common to both variations. Weight is 38 oz.

Hardballer

Adjustable sights.

Courtesy J.B. Wood

NIB	Exc.	V.G.	Good	Fair	Poor
495	400	350	275	200	125

Government Model

Fixed sights.

NIB	Exc.	V.G.	Good	Fair	Poor
450	350	300	250	150	100

Hardballer Longslide

Similar to the Hardballer Model but fitted with a 7" barrel. Magazine capacity is 7 rounds. Pistol weighs 46 oz.

NIB	Exc.	V.G.	Good	Fair	Poor
500	400	325	275	200	125

.400 Accelerator

Similar to the models above but chambered for .400 CorBon cartridge and fitted with a 7" barrel. Fully adjustable sights. Introduced in 1997.

NIB	Exc.	V.G.	Good	Fair	Poor
550	450	375	—	—	—

Commando

Built on a Government model-type action and chambered for .40 S&W cartridge. Fitted with a 5" barrel and fully adjustable sights. Introduced in 1997.

NIB	Exc.	V.G.	Good	Fair	Poor
450	350	300	—	—	—

REMINDER

Go to gun shows, not just to buy or sell, but to observe and learn.

On Duty

This semi-automatic pistol features a double-action-only trigger action or double-action with decocker and is chambered for the 9mm, .40 S&W, or .45 ACP calibers. Barrel length is 4.5" and overall length is 7.75". The finish is a black anodized matte. Carbon fiber grips are standard. Furnished with 3-dot sights. Weighs 32 oz.

NIB	Exc.	V.G.	Good	Fair	Poor
450	350	250	200	150	100

Skipper

Identical to the Hardballer with a 1" shorter barrel and slide. Discontinued in 1984.

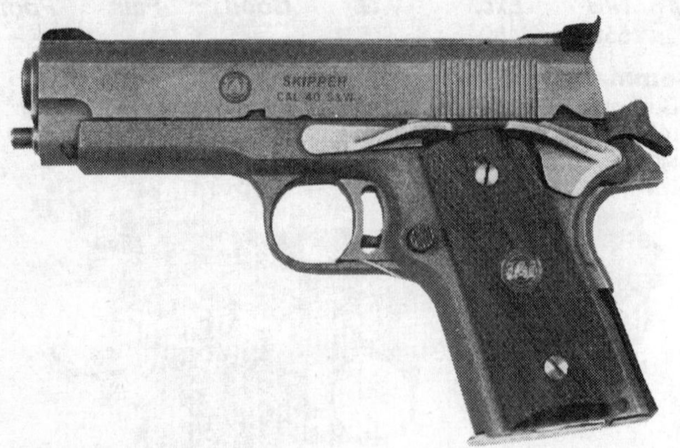

Exc.	V.G.	Good	Fair	Poor
450	325	275	200	125

Combat Skipper

Similar to the Colt Commander. Discontinued in 1984.

Exc.	V.G.	Good	Fair	Poor
400	300	250	200	125

Lightning Rifle

Patterned after the Ruger 10/22, this rifle has a 22" barrel and a 25-round, detachable magazine with a folding stock. Introduced in 1986.

Courtesy J.B. Wood

NIB	Exc.	V.G.	Good	Fair	Poor
300	200	150	125	75	50

Small Game Hunter

As above, with a full stock and 10-round magazine. Introduced in 1986.

NIB	Exc.	V.G.	Good	Fair	Poor
350	225	175	150	125	100

Small Game Hunter II

This semi-automatic rifle is chambered for the .22 LR cartridge. Stock is a checkered black matte nylon and is fitted with a removable recoil pad for ammo, cleaning rod, and knife. Rotary magazine holds 10 rounds. Stainless steel action and barrel. Barrel is a heavyweight target type, 22" long. Weight is 6 lbs.

NIB	Exc.	V.G.	Good	Fair	Poor
350	225	175	150	125	100

Hunter Rifle

This semi-automatic rifle is chambered for the .22 Rimfire Magnum cartridge. Stock is checkered black matte nylon. Other features are similar to the Small Game Hunter II including weight.

NIB	Exc.	V.G.	Good	Fair	Poor
375	250	200	150	125	100

Magnum Hunter

Similar to above but chambered for the .22 Magnum cartridge and fitted with a 22" accurized barrel. Barrel and action are stainless steel. It comes standard with a 5-round magazine and composite stock but a laminated stock was available at an extra cost as is a 10-round magazine.

NIB	Exc.	V.G.	Good	Fair	Poor
525	400	350	250	200	150

Target Model

A semi-automatic rifle chambered for .22 LR cartridge and fitted with a 20" target barrel. Weight is about 7.5 lbs. Choice of Fajen or Hogue stock. For Hogue stock deduct $50.00.

NIB	Exc.	V.G.	Good	Fair	Poor
600	500	450	300	200	—

Challenge Edition

This is a custom ordered .22 caliber semi-automatic rifle built on a Ruger 10/22-like receiver. Offered in either 18" or 22" barrel lengths with all stainless steel construction, McMillan fiberglass stock, and Weaver-style scope mounts.

NIB	Exc.	V.G.	Good	Fair	Poor
1050	800	550	400	300	—

Single-Shot Standard Rifle

Custom-built rifle with choice of barrel length, composite stock, adjustable trigger, post '64 Winchester action, all in stainless and chrome moly steel. Chambered for all standard calibers. First offered in 1996.

NIB	Exc.	V.G.	Good	Fair	Poor
875	675	500	350	200	—

Single-Shot Deluxe Rifle

Custom-built rifle on a Mauser-type action with choice of match grade barrel lengths and custom Kevlar stock. Built from stainless and chrome moly steel. Chambered for all standard calibers. First offered in 1996.

NIB	Exc.	V.G.	Good	Fair	Poor
1800	1400	950	650	400	—

Bolt-Action Repeating Rifle—Standard

Similar in construction and features to the Standard Single-Shot rifle.

NIB	Exc.	V.G.	Good	Fair	Poor
840	675	500	350	200	—

Bolt-Action Repeating Rifle—Deluxe

Similar in construction and features to the Deluxe Single-Shot rifle.

NIB	Exc.	V.G.	Good	Fair	Poor
1800	1400	950	650	400	—

ANCION & CIE

Liege, Belgium

See—French Military Firearms

ANCION MARX

Liege, Belgium

This company began production in the 1860s with a variety of cheaply made pinfire revolvers. They later switched to solid-frame, centerfire, "Velo-Dog"-type revolvers chambered for 5.5mm or 6.35mm. They were marketed in various countries under many different trade names. Some of the names that they will be found under are Cobalt, Extracteur, LeNovo, Lincoln, and Milady. The quality of these revolvers is quite poor; and collector interest, almost non-existent. Values do not usually vary because of trade names.

Exc.	V.G.	Good	Fair	Poor
—	150	125	75	45

ANDERSON

Anderson, Texas

Anderson Under Hammer Pistol

An unmarked, under hammer percussion pistol that was chambered for .45 caliber. It had a 5" half-round/half-octagonal barrel with an all steel, saw handle-shaped frame. There was a flared butt with walnut grips. The finish was blued. There is little information on this pistol, and its origin is strongly suspected but not confirmed.

Exc.	V.G.	Good	Fair	Poor
—	—	900	400	150

ANDRUS & OSBORN

Canton, Connecticut

Andrus & Osborn Under Hammer Pistol

This pistol is of the percussion type and chambered for .25 caliber. The part-round/part-octagonal barrel is 6" long and features small silver star inlays along its length. The barrel is marked "Andrus & Osborn/Canton Conn." with an eagle stamped beside it. It is marked "Cast Steel" near the breech. The grips are of walnut, and the finish is browned. Active 1863 to 1867.

Exc.	V.G.	Good	Fair	Poor
—	—	1400	550	200

ANSCHUTZ

Ulm, Germany

Orginally founded in 1856 by Julius and Lusie Anschutz, the company was called J.G. Anschutz, and manufactured a wide variety of firearms. In 1950, in Ulm, the new company was founded: J.G. Anschutz GmbH. Values for new guns fluctuate according to currency variations.

Mark 10 Target Rifle

A single-shot, bolt-action rifle that is chambered for the .22 LR cartridge. It has a 26" heavy barrel with adjustable target-type sights. The finish was blued, and the walnut target stock had an adjustable palm rest. It was manufactured between 1963 and 1981.

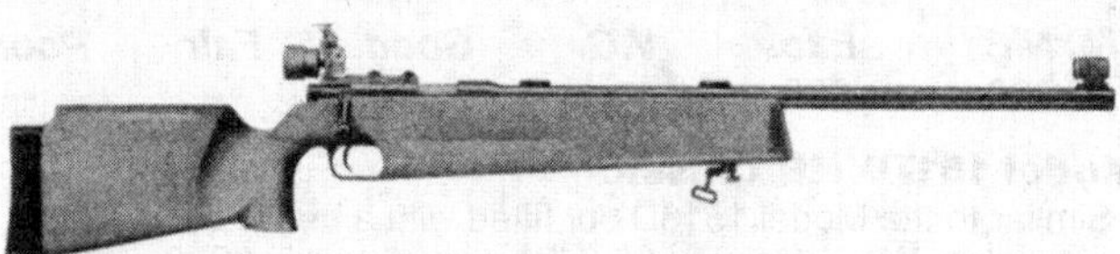

NIB	Exc.	V.G.	Good	Fair	Poor
370	300	250	210	150	100

Model 1403D

A single-shot target rifle chambered for the .22 LR cartridge. It has a 26" barrel and is furnished without sights. It has a fully adjustable trigger and a blued finish with a walnut target-type stock.

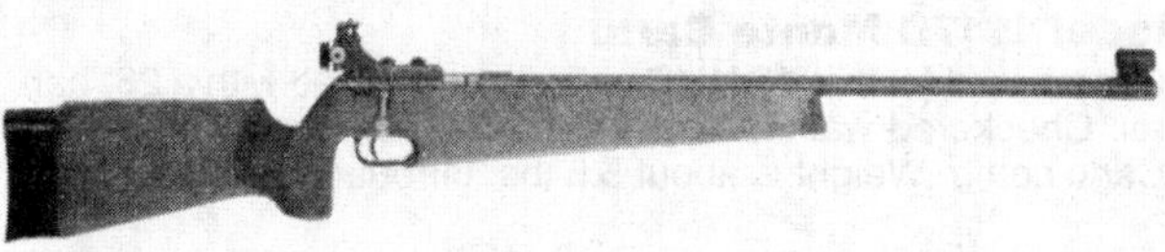

NIB	Exc.	V.G.	Good	Fair	Poor
725	650	575	500	375	250

Model 1407

Similar to the Mark 10 but is furnished without sights. It was known as the "I.S.U." model. It was discontinued in 1981.

NIB	Exc.	V.G.	Good	Fair	Poor
395	325	275	235	175	100

Model 1408

A heavier-barreled version of the Model 1407.

NIB	Exc.	V.G	Good	Fair	Poor
400	330	280	240	180	105

Model 1411

Designed specifically to be fired from the prone position.

NIB	Exc.	V.G.	Good	Fair	Poor
375	300	250	210	150	100

Model 1413 Match

A high-grade, competition version with a heavy target barrel that is furnished without sights; optional sights extra. The walnut stock has an adjustable cheekpiece.

NIB	Exc.	V.G.	Good	Fair	Poor
575	500	450	400	275	150

Model 1416D HB Classic

This model is chambered for the .22 LR cartridge. Magazine capacity is 5 rounds. Fitted with a match grade trigger and target grade barrel. Checkered walnut stock. Built on the 64 action.

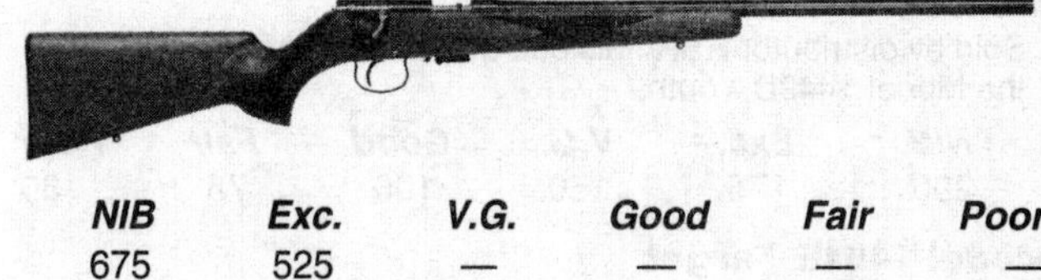

NIB	Exc.	V.G.	Good	Fair	Poor
675	525	—	—	—	—

Model 1416D KL Classic

This sporting rifle is chambered for the .22 LR cartridge and is fitted with an American-style stock of European walnut or hardwood. Built on Anschutz Match 64 action. Left-handed model also offered.

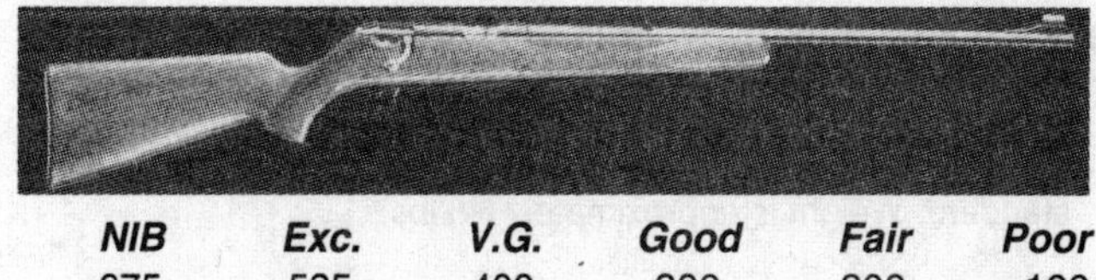

NIB	Exc.	V.G.	Good	Fair	Poor
675	525	400	300	200	100

Model 1416D Custom

Chambered for the .22 LR cartridge, this model features a European-style stock with Monte Carlo cheekpiece, and schnabel forend.

NIB	Exc.	V.G	Good	Fair	Poor
775	550	450	300	200	100

Model 1418D KL Mannlicher

A hunting rifle with a full-length, Mannlicher-type stock made with hand-checkered walnut. Chambered for .22 LR with 5-round magazine. Open iron sights. Weight is about 5.5 lbs.

NIB	Exc.	V.G.	Good	Fair	Poor
1100	850	600	350	200	150

Model 1418/19

A lower-priced sporter model that was formerly imported by Savage Arms.

NIB	Exc.	V.G.	Good	Fair	Poor
300	250	200	150	125	85

Model 1433D

This is a centerfire version of the Model 54 target rifle chambered for the .22 Hornet. It is a special-order item and features a set trigger and a 4-round, detachable magazine. The finish was blued with a full length Mannlicher stock. It was discontinued in 1986.

NIB	Exc.	V.G.	Good	Fair	Poor
1000	850	600	400	200	100

Model 1449D Youth

This bolt-action rifle is chambered for the .22 LR cartridge and fitted with a 16" barrel with adjustable rear sight. Stock is European hardwood with 12.25" length of pull. Magazine capacity is 5 rounds. This model is no longer imported.

NIB	Exc.	V.G.	Good	Fair	Poor
200	175	150	100	75	60

Model Woodchucker

Sold by distributor RSR, this bolt-action .22 caliber is similar to the Model 1449D Youth.

NIB	Exc.	V.G.	Good	Fair	Poor
200	175	150	100	75	60

Model 1451E Target

This is a single-shot .22 caliber target rifle fitted with a 22" barrel. Can be fitted with either micrometer iron sights or telescope sights. Checkered pistol grip, adjustable buttplate. Weight is about 6.25 lbs.

NIB	Exc.	V.G.	Good	Fair	Poor
515	400	—	—	—	—

Model 1451R Sporter Target

This is a bolt-action target rifle chambered for the .22 LR cartridge and fitted with a target-style stock and 22" heavy barrel. Furnished with no open sights. Two-stage target trigger is standard. Weight is approximately 6.5 lbs.

NIB	Exc.	V.G.	Good	Fair	Poor
525	400	300	200	150	100

Model 1451D Custom

Similar to the above model but fitted with a checkered walnut sporting stock with Monte Carlo comb and cheekpiece. Barrel length is 22.75" with open sights. Weight is about 5 lbs.

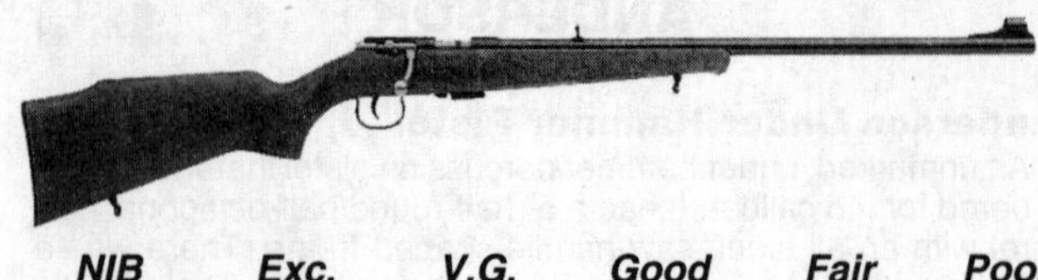

NIB	Exc.	V.G.	Good	Fair	Poor
450	375	300	200	150	100

Model 1451D Classic

Similar to the Model 1451 Custom with the exception of a straight walnut stock. Weight is about 5 lbs.

NIB	Exc.	V.G.	Good	Fair	Poor
350	300	250	200	150	100

Model 1516D KL Classic

Same as above but chambered for .22 Magnum cartridge.

NIB	Exc.	V.G.	Good	Fair	Poor
700	500	400	300	200	100

Model 1516D KL Custom

Same as above but chambered for .22 Magnum cartridge.

NIB	Exc.	V.G.	Good	Fair	Poor
750	550	450	300	200	100

Model 1517D Classic

Based on the 64 action this bolt-action rifle is chambered for the .17 HMR cartridge. Fitted with a 23" barrel. Checkered walnut stock. Magazine capacity is 4 rounds for the .17 HMR. Weight is about 5.5 lbs. Introduced in 2003.

NIB	Exc.	V.G.	Good	Fair	Poor
700	550	—	—	—	—

Model 1517D HB Classic

Similar to the Model 1516D but fitted with a heavy barrel without sights. Weight is about 6.2 lbs. Introduced in 2003.

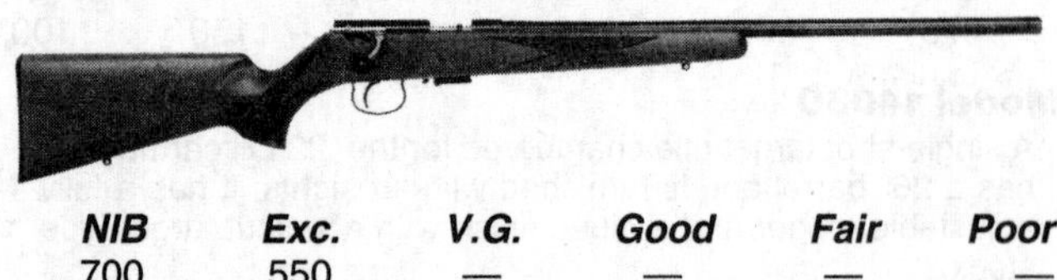

NIB	Exc.	V.G.	Good	Fair	Poor
700	550	—	—	—	—

Model 1517D Monte Carlo

Chambered for the .17 HMR cartridge and fitted with a 23" barrel. Checkered walnut stock with schnabel forend and Monte Carlo comb. Weight is about 5.5 lbs. Introduced in 2003.

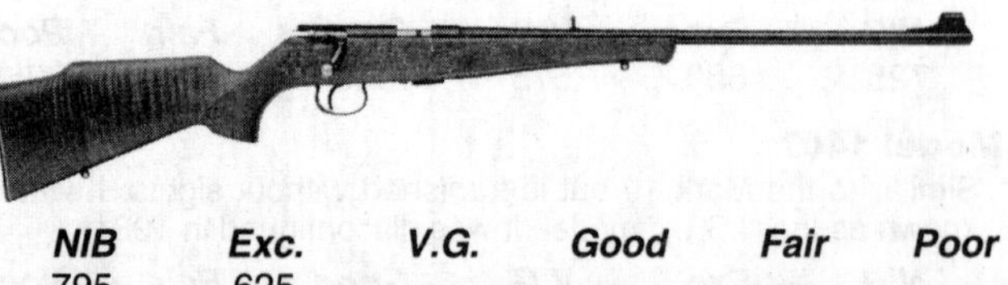

NIB	Exc.	V.G.	Good	Fair	Poor
795	625	—	—	—	—

Model 1517MPR Multi Purpose Rifle

Introduced in 2003 this model features a 25.5" heavy barrel without sights, a two-stage trigger, a hardwood stock with beavertail forend. Chambered for the .17 HMR cartridge. Weight is about 9 lbs.

NOTE: This model is available with a number of extra cost options.

NIB	Exc.	V.G.	Good	Fair	Poor
795	625	—	—	—	—

Model 1518D Mannlicher

Same as above but chambered for the .22 Magnum.

NIB	Exc.	V.G.	Good	Fair	Poor
1100	850	600	350	200	150

Model 184

A high-grade, bolt-action sporting rifle chambered for the .22 LR cartridge. It has a 21.5" barrel with a folding-leaf sight. The finish is blued with a checkered walnut, Monte Carlo stock with a schnabel forend. It was manufactured between 1963 and 1981.

NIB	Exc.	V.G.	Good	Fair	Poor
375	335	280	220	150	100

Model 54 Sporter

A high-grade, bolt-action sporting rifle chambered for the .22 LR cartridge. It has a 24" tapered round barrel and a 5-shot detachable magazine. It features a folding leaf-type rear sight. The finish is blued with a checkered walnut, Monte Carlo stock. It was manufactured between 1963 and 1981.

NIB	Exc.	V.G.	Good	Fair	Poor
650	575	500	350	250	125

Model 54M

This version is chambered for the .22 rimfire Magnum cartridge.

NIB	Exc.	V.G.	Good	Fair	Poor
700	600	525	375	275	125

Model 141

A bolt-action sporter chambered for the .22 LR cartridge. It has a 23" round barrel with a blued finish and walnut Monte Carlo stock. It was manufactured between 1963 and 1981.

NIB	Exc.	V.G.	Good	Fair	Poor
350	300	250	200	150	100

Model 141M

Chambered for the .22 rimfire Magnum cartridge.

NIB	Exc.	V.G.	Good	Fair	Poor
375	325	275	225	175	100

Model 164

This bolt-action rifle is fitted with a 23" round barrel chambered for the .22 LR cartridge. It has a Monte Carlo stock with open sights. Magazine holds 5 rounds.

NIB	Exc.	V.G.	Good	Fair	Poor
400	325	275	225	175	100

Model 164M

Same as model above but chambered for the .22 Win. Magnum cartridge.

NIB	Exc.	V.G.	Good	Fair	Poor
450	350	275	225	175	100

Model 153

A bolt-action sporting rifle chambered for the .222 Remington cartridge. It has a 24" barrel with folding-leaf rear sight. The finish is blued with a checkered French walnut stock featuring a rosewood forend tip and pistol grip cap. It was manufactured between 1963 and 1981.

NIB	Exc.	V.G.	Good	Fair	Poor
575	500	385	300	225	150

Model 153-S

This version was offered with double-set triggers.

NIB	Exc.	V.G.	Good	Fair	Poor
625	550	435	350	275	150

Model 64

A single-shot, bolt-action rifle that is chambered for the .22 LR cartridge. It has a 26" round barrel and is furnished without sights. The finish is blued, and the walnut target-type stock featured a beaver-tail forearm and adjustable buttplate. It was manufactured between 1963 and 1981.

NIB	Exc.	V.G.	Good	Fair	Poor
375	300	250	200	150	100

Model 64MS

This version was designed for silhouette shooting and has a 21.25" barrel, blued finish, and a target-type walnut stock with a stippled pistol grip.

NIB	Exc.	V.G.	Good	Fair	Poor
750	600	525	400	300	200

Model 64 MPR

This is a multi-purpose target repeater. Chambered for the .22 LR cartridge and fitted with a 25.5" heavy barrel. Offered with optional sights and choice of stainless steel barrel with beavertail or beavertail with swivel rail. Weight is about 9 lbs.

NIB	Exc.	V.G.	Good	Fair	Poor
750	600	—	—	—	—

Model 64P

Bolt-action pistol with adjustable trigger. The action is grooved for scope mounts, and the stock is synthetic. Barrel length is 10" and is chambered for .22 LR cartridge. Weight is approximately 3 lb. 8 oz. Introduced in 1998.

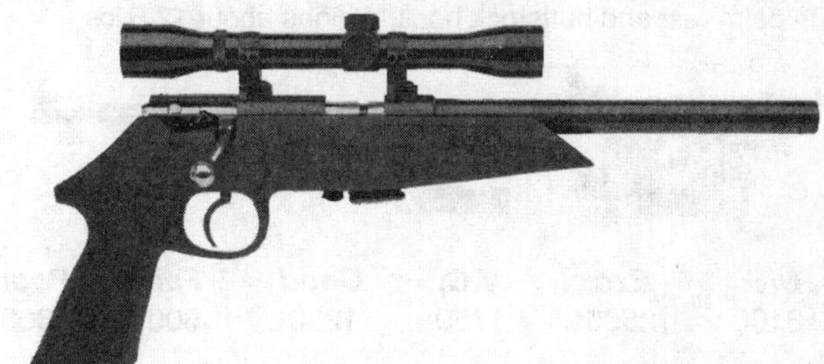

NIB	Exc.	V.G.	Good	Fair	Poor
495	400	350	250	175	75

Model 64P Mag

Same as model above but chambered for .22 WMR cartridge.

NIB	Exc.	V.G.	Good	Fair	Poor
550	425	375	275	175	75

Model 54.18MS

A high-grade silhouette rifle chambered for the .22 LR cartridge. It has a 22" barrel and a match-grade action with fully adjustable trigger. It is furnished without sights. The finish is blued with a target-type walnut stock.

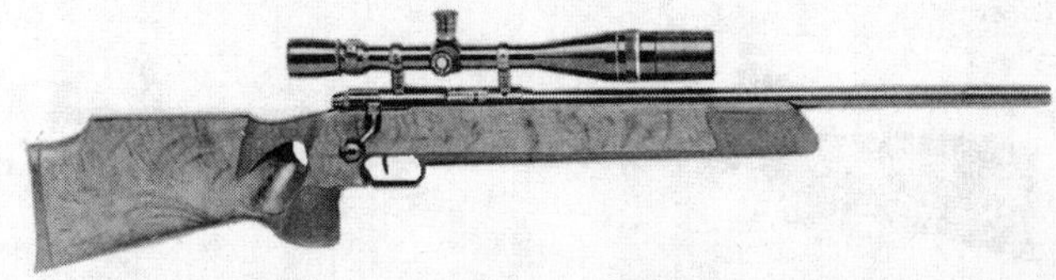

NIB	Exc.	V.G.	Good	Fair	Poor
1250	950	750	500	300	200

Model 54.MS REP

A repeating rifle with a five-shot, detachable magazine and a thumbhole stock with vented forearm.

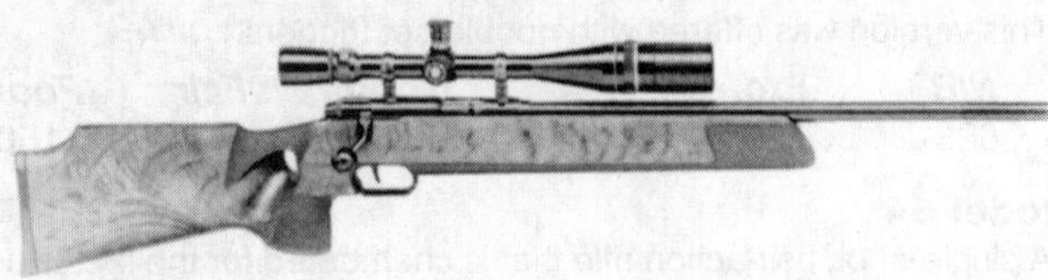

NIB	Exc.	V.G.	Good	Fair	Poor
1650	1350	900	500	300	200

Model 2000 MK

This single-shot rifle was chambered for the .22 LR cartridge. It has a 26" round barrel with target-type sights. The finish was blued and has a checkered walnut stock. It was not imported after 1988.

NIB	Exc.	V.G.	Good	Fair	Poor
350	300	250	200	150	100

Model 2007 Supermatch

Introduced in 1993 this target rifle is chambered for the .22 LR cartridge. It has a 19-3/4" barrel fitted to a Match 54 action. Trigger is a two-stage. The stock is standard ISU configuration with adjustable cheekpiece. Weighs about 10.8 pounds. Offered in left-hand model.

NIB	Exc.	V.G.	Good	Fair	Poor
2250	1750	1250	750	350	200

Model 2013 Supermatch

Similar to the above model but fitted with an International stock with palm rest and buttstock hook. Weighs about 12.5 lbs.

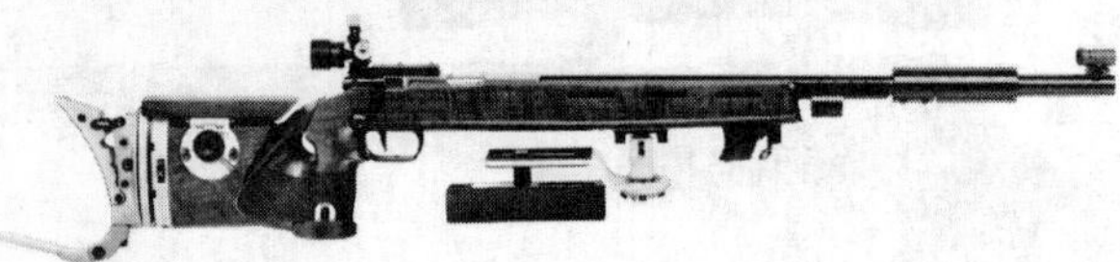

NIB	Exc.	V.G.	Good	Fair	Poor
3100	2500	1750	1250	600	300

Model 1903D

Designed for the advanced junior shooter this target rifle has a 25-1/2" barrel on a Match 64 action with a single stage trigger. The walnut stock is fully adjustable. Weighs about 9.5 pounds and is offered in a left-hand model.

NIB	Exc.	V.G.	Good	Fair	Poor
850	700	600	400	300	200

Model 1803D

A high-grade target rifle chambered for the .22 LR cartridge. It has a 25.5" heavy barrel with adjustable target sights. It features an adjustable trigger. The finish is blued with a light-colored wood stock with dark stippling on the pistol grip and forearm. The stock features an adjustable cheekpiece and buttplate. It was introduced in 1987.

NIB	Exc.	V.G.	Good	Fair	Poor
810	750	675	600	450	200

Model 1808D RT Super

A single-shot, running-boar type rifle that is chambered for the .22 LR cartridge. It has a 32.5" barrel furnished without sights. The finish is blued with a heavy target-type walnut stock with thumbhole. It is furnished with barrel weights. Rifle weighs about 9.4 pounds. Also available in a left-hand version.

NIB	Exc.	V.G.	Good	Fair	Poor
1400	1200	1050	750	450	250

Model 1907ISU Standard Match

Chambered for the .22 LR cartridge this rifle is designed for both prone and position shooting. Weight is 11.2 lbs. Built on a Match 54 action and fitted with a 26" barrel this rifle has a two-stage trigger with a removable cheekpiece and adjustable buttstock.

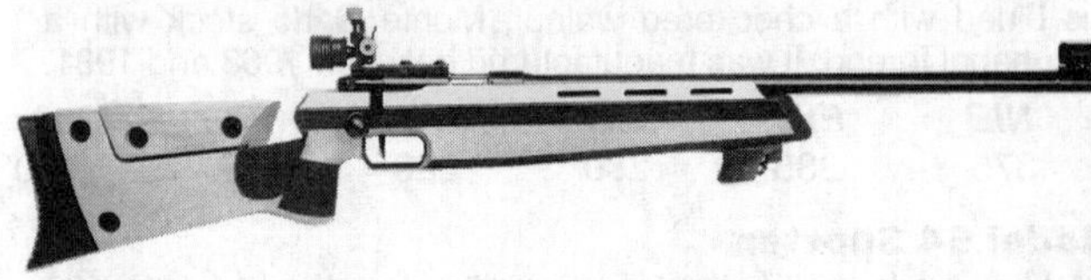

NIB	Exc.	V.G.	Good	Fair	Poor
1500	1250	900	450	300	200

Model 1910 Super Match II

A high-grade, single-shot target rifle chambered for the .22 LR cartridge. It has a 27.25" barrel and is furnished with diopter-type target sights. The finish is blued with a walnut thumbhole stock with adjustable cheekpiece and buttplate. Hand rest and palm rest are not included.

NIB	Exc.	V.G.	Good	Fair	Poor
2200	1750	1300	900	500	250

Model 1911 Prone Match

This version has a stock designed specifically for firing from the prone position.

NIB	Exc.	V.G.	Good	Fair	Poor
1750	1450	950	650	400	250

Model 1913 Super Match

A virtually hand-built, match target rifle. It is chambered for the .22 LR cartridge and features a single-shot action. It has adjustable, diopter-type sights on a 27.25" heavy barrel. This is a custom-made gun that features every target option conceivable. The finish is blued with a fully adjustable walnut stock.

NIB	Exc.	V.G.	Good	Fair	Poor
2600	2000	1500	1000	500	250

Model 1827B Biathlon

A repeating, bolt-action target rifle chambered for the .22 LR cartridge. It is specially designed for the biathlon competition. Production is quite limited and on a custom basis.

NIB	Exc.	V.G.	Good	Fair	Poor
1750	1400	1050	800	400	250

Model 1827BT Biathlon

Similar to the above model but features a straight pull Fortner bolt system. Available in left-hand model.

NIB	Exc.	V.G.	Good	Fair	Poor
2800	2250	1650	1000	500	250

Achiever

Introduced in 1993 this target rifle is chambered for the .22 LR cartridge. Designed for the beginning shooter it is furnished with a 5-shot clip but can be converted to a single-shot with an adaptor. Barrel length is 19-1/2". Action is Mark 2000 with two-stage trigger. Stock pull is adjustable from 12" to 13". Weighs about 5 lbs.

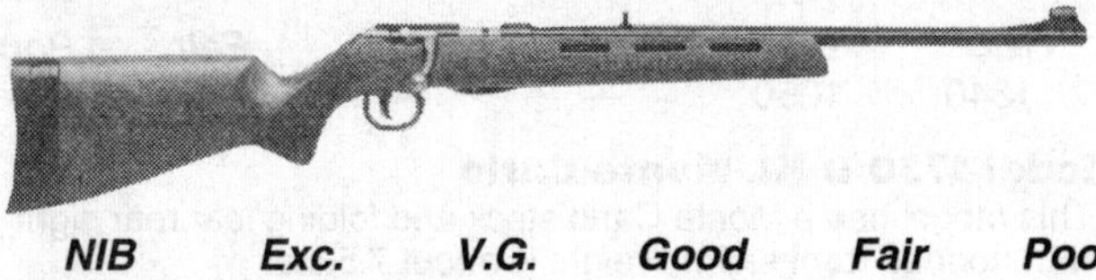

NIB	Exc.	V.G.	Good	Fair	Poor
325	250	200	150	125	100

Achiever Super Target

Designed for the advanced junior shooter this model has a 22" barrel. Weighs about 6.5 lbs.

NIB	Exc.	V.G.	Good	Fair	Poor
400	325	250	175	125	100

Bavarian 1700

A classic-style sporting rifle chambered for the .22 LR, .22 rimfire Magnum, .22 Hornet, and the .222 Remington cartridges. It features a 24" barrel with adjustable sights. It has a detachable magazine and a blued finish with a checkered walnut, European-style Monte Carlo stock with cheekpiece. It was introduced in 1988.

NIB	Exc.	V.G.	Good	Fair	Poor
800	650	500	400	300	200

Classic 1700

Similar in appearance to the Bavarian but furnished with an American-style stock with fluted comb. Furnished in same calibers as Bavarian but weighs 6.75 lbs.

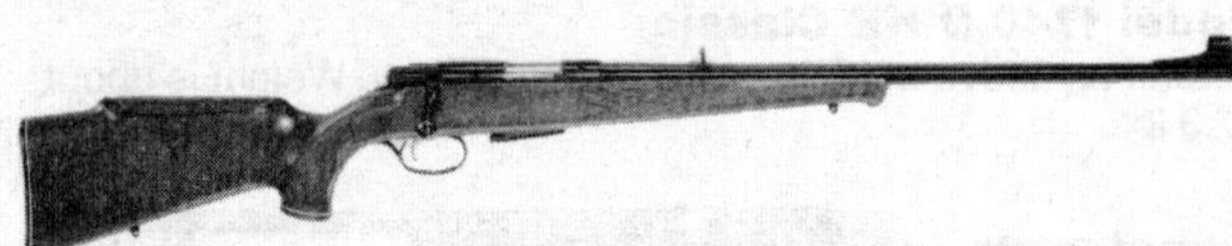

NIB	Exc.	V.G.	Good	Fair	Poor
1200	900	700	400	300	200

NOTE: For fancy wood stocks "Meister Grade" add $175.

Custom 1700

Similar to the Bavarian and Classic in caliber offerings but offered with a fancy European walnut stock with roll-over cheekpiece with Monte Carlo. The pistol grip has a palm swell and is fitted with a white lined rosewood grip cap with a white diamond insert. Forend is schabel type and stock is checkered in ship line pattern.

NIB	Exc.	V.G.	Good	Fair	Poor
1250	950	750	400	300	200

NOTE: For fancy wood stocks "Meister Grade" add $175.

Model 1700 Mannlicher

Similar to the 1700 Classic but fitted with a full-length stock.

NIB	Exc.	V.G.	Good	Fair	Poor
1550	1200	850	550	350	200

NOTE: For fancy wood stocks "Meister Grade" add $175.

Model 1700 FWT

This model has same specifications as the 1700 Custom but is fitted with a McMillan laminated fiberglass stock. Weighs about 6.25 lbs.

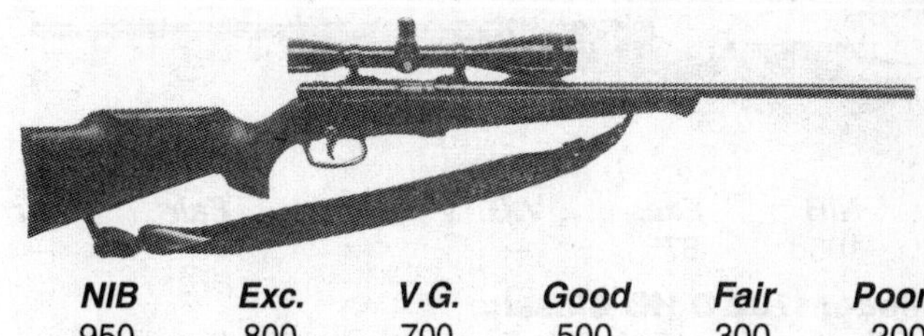

NIB	Exc.	V.G.	Good	Fair	Poor
950	800	700	500	300	200

Model 1700 FWT Deluxe

Same as above but fitted with a laminated wood grain stock.

NIB	Exc.	V.G.	Good	Fair	Poor
1125	900	800	550	300	200

Model 1710 D Classic

Bolt-action .22 caliber rifle with 23.6" barrel with no sights. Walnut stock is checkering. Magazine capacity is 5 rounds. Weight is about 7.3 lbs.

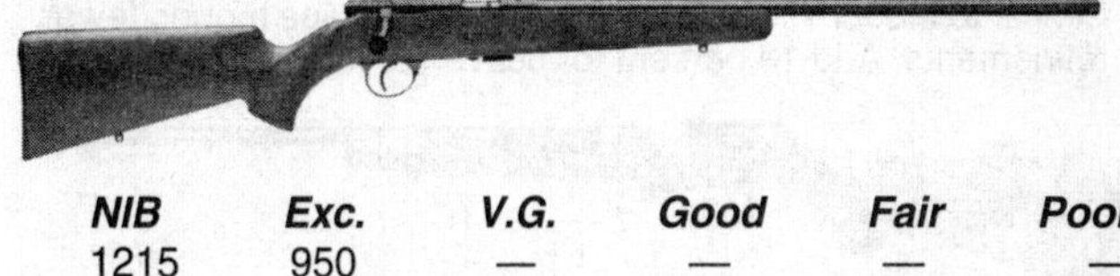

NIB	Exc.	V.G.	Good	Fair	Poor
1215	950	—	—	—	—

Model 1710 D HB Classic

Same as above but with heavy barrel. Weight is about 8 lbs.

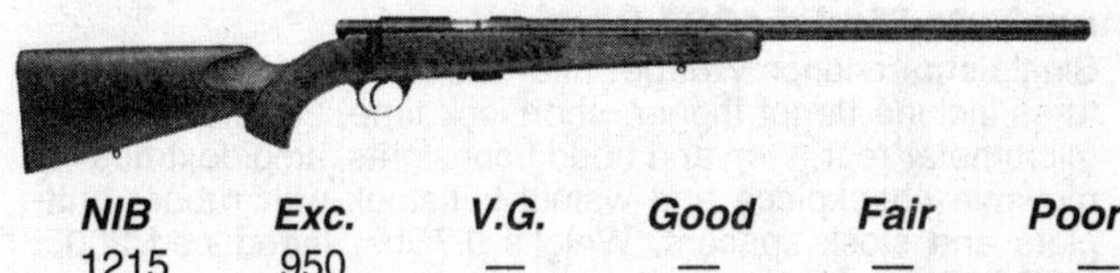

NIB	Exc.	V.G.	Good	Fair	Poor
1215	950	—	—	—	—

Model 1710 D KL Monte Carlo

Same as the Classic but with Monte Carlo stock and folding leaf rear sight with hooded front sight. Weight is about 7.5 lbs.

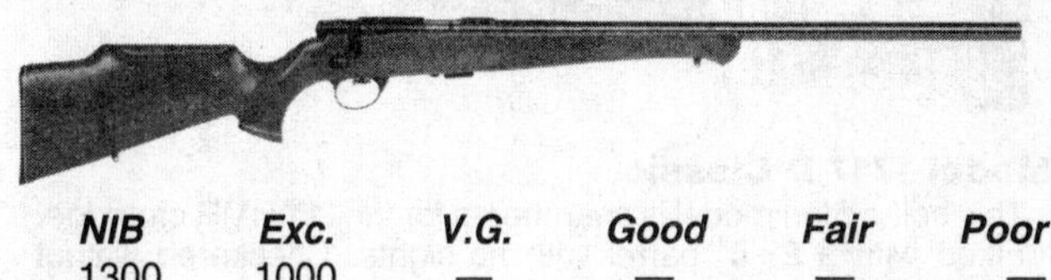

NIB	Exc.	V.G.	Good	Fair	Poor
1300	1000	—	—	—	—

Model 1710 D HB Classic 150 Years Anniversary Version

Similar to Model 1710 D HB Classic but with heavy stainless barrel and stock laser-engraved with 150th anniversary and 1901 "Germania" logos. Introduced in 2007. Only 150 units produced.

NIB	Exc.	V.G.	Good	Fair	Poor
1950	—	—	—	—	—

Model 1712 Silhouette Sporter

Chambered in .22 LR. Features include two-stage trigger, deluxe walnut stock with schnabel, 21.6" blued sightless barrel, 5-shot magazine.

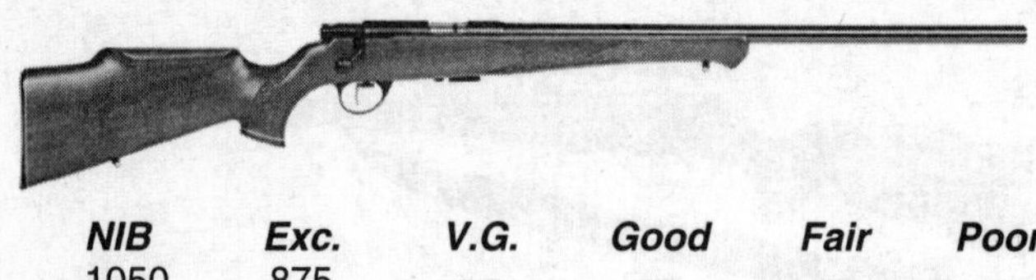

NIB	Exc.	V.G.	Good	Fair	Poor
1050	875	—	—	—	—

Model 1702 D HB Classic

Chambered in .17 Mach 2. Features include finely-tuned double-stage trigger, walnut stock, 23" blued heavy sightless barrel, 5-shot magazine.

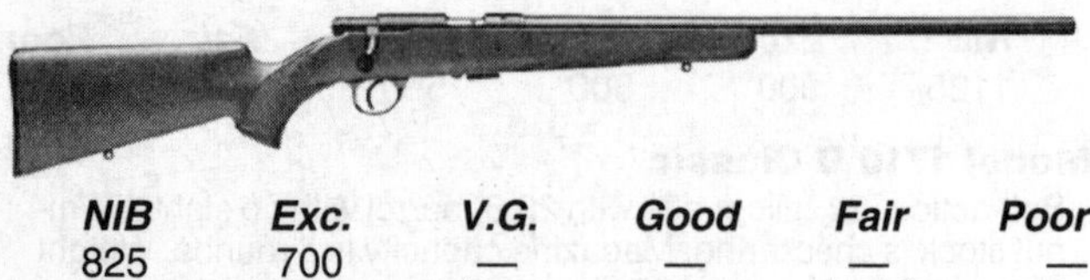

NIB	Exc.	V.G.	Good	Fair	Poor
825	700	—	—	—	—

Model 1502 D HB Classic

Similar to Model 1702 D HB but with single-stage trigger, fewer refinements. Add 10 percent for beavertail forend.

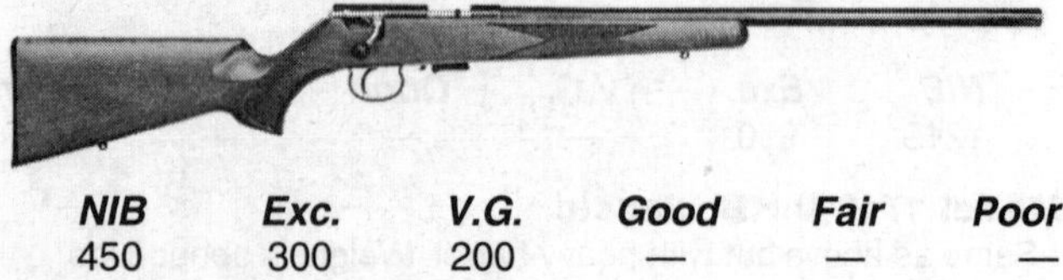

NIB	Exc.	V.G.	Good	Fair	Poor
450	300	200	—	—	—

Anschutz Model 1907 Club

Single-shot economy target rifle chambered in .22 LR. Features include target trigger, short lock time, 26" blued barrel, micrometer rear peep and hood front sights, ambidextrous removable cheekpiece and walnut buttstock with rubber buttplate and stock spacers. Weighs 9.7 lbs. Introduced 2006. MSRP: 1100

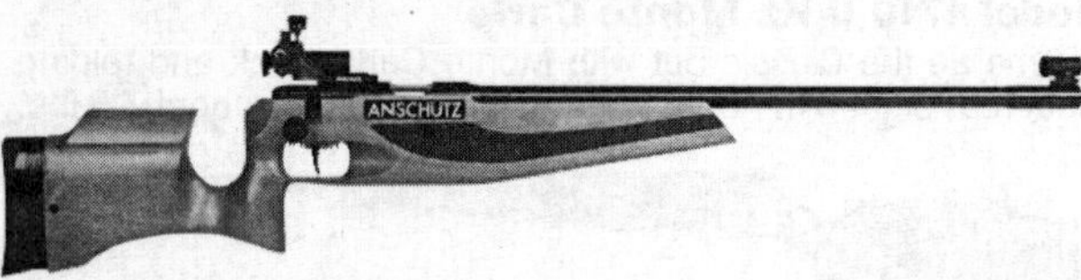

Model 1717 D Classic

This bolt-action model is chambered for the .17 HMR cartridge. Fitted with a 23.6" barrel with no sights. Checkered walnut stock. Weight is about 7.3 lbs.

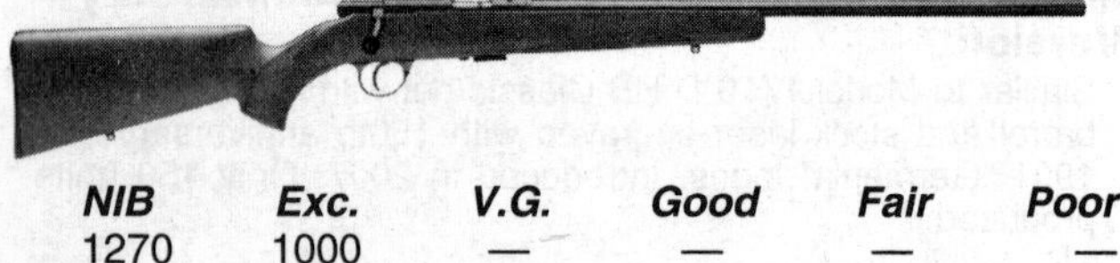

NIB	Exc.	V.G.	Good	Fair	Poor
1270	1000	—	—	—	—

Model 1717 D HB Classic

Same as above but with heavy barrel. Weight is about 8 lbs.

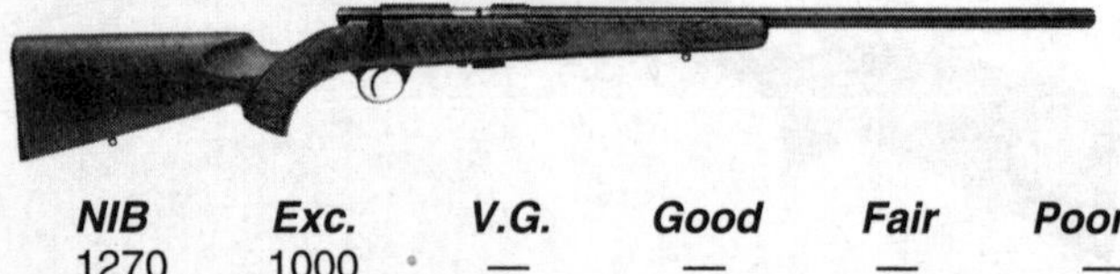

NIB	Exc.	V.G.	Good	Fair	Poor
1270	1000	—	—	—	—

Model 1730 D Classic

This bolt-action rifle is chambered for the .22 Hornet cartridge and fitted with a 23.6" barrel. Magazine capacity is 5 rounds. Checkered walnut stock. No sights. Weight is about 7.3 lbs.

NIB	Exc.	V.G.	Good	Fair	Poor
1425	1125	—	—	—	—

Model 1730 D HB Classic

Same as above but fitted with a heavy barrel. Weight is about 8 lbs.

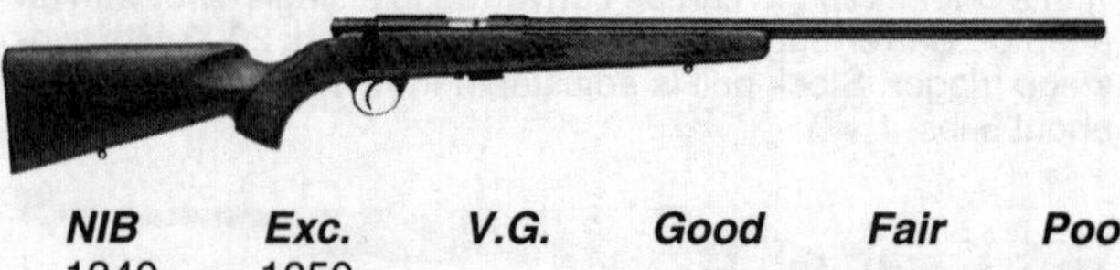

NIB	Exc.	V.G.	Good	Fair	Poor
1340	1050	—	—	—	—

Model 1730 D KL Monte Carlo

This model has a Monte Carlo stock and folding leaf rear sight with hooded front sight. Weight is about 7.5 lbs.

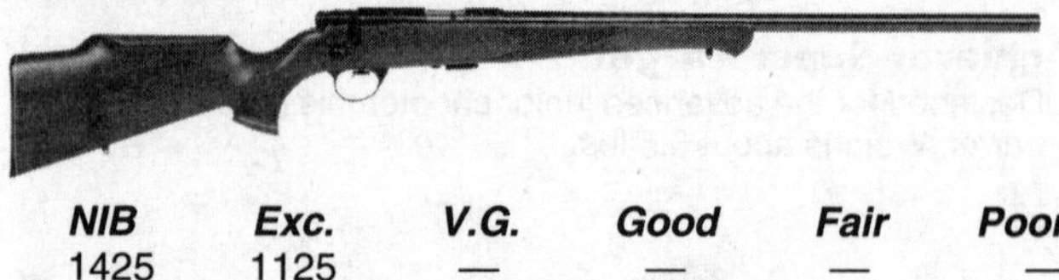

NIB	Exc.	V.G.	Good	Fair	Poor
1425	1125	—	—	—	—

Model 1733D KL Mannlicher

Introduced in 1993 this model features a Mannlicher stock built on a Match 54 action. The stock has a rosewood schnabel tip and checkering is done in a skip-line pattern. Chambered for .22 Hornet. Weighs about 6.25 lbs.

NIB	Exc.	V.G.	Good	Fair	Poor
1250	950	700	500	300	200

Model 1740 D Classic

This bolt-action model is chambered for the .222 Remington cartridge. Checkered walnut stock with no sights. Magazine capacity is 3 rounds. Weight is about 7.3 lbs.

NIB	Exc.	V.G.	Good	Fair	Poor
1425	1125	—	—	—	—

Model 1740 D HB Classic

Same as above but fitted with a heavy barrel. Weight is about 7.3 lbs.

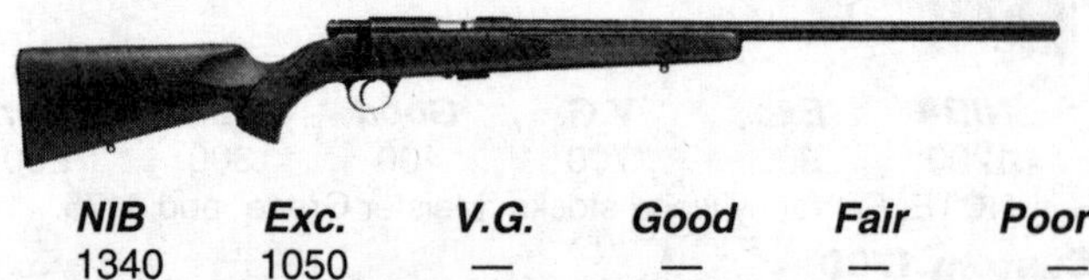

NIB	Exc.	V.G.	Good	Fair	Poor
1340	1050	—	—	—	—

Model 1740 D KL Monte Carlo

This model is fitted with a Monte Carlo stock and folding leaf rear sight and hooded front sight. Weight is about 7.3 lbs.

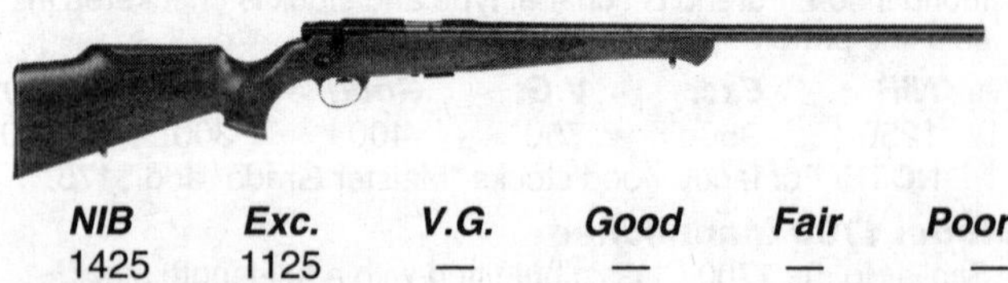

NIB	Exc.	V.G.	Good	Fair	Poor
1425	1125	—	—	—	—

Model 520/61

A blowback-operated, semi-automatic rifle that is chambered for the .22 LR cartridge. It has a 24" barrel and a 10-round, detachable magazine. The finish is blued with a checkered walnut stock. This rifle was discontinued in 1983.

NIB	Exc.	V.G.	Good	Fair	Poor
275	200	150	125	100	85

Model 525 Sporter

This semi-automatic rifle is chambered for the .22 LR cartridge. It has a 24" barrel with adjustable sights and a 10-round, detachable magazine. The finish is blued with a checkered Monte Carlo-type stock. It was introduced in 1984. A carbine version with a 20" barrel was originally offered but was discontinued in 1986.

NIB	Exc.	V.G.	Good	Fair	Poor
435	375	300	225	175	100

Exemplar

A bolt-action pistol that is built on the Model 64 Match Action. It is chambered for the .22 LR cartridge and has a 10" barrel with adjustable sights and a 5-shot, detachable magazine. It features an adjustable two-stage trigger with the receiver grooved for attaching a scope. The walnut stock and forend are stippled. It was introduced in 1987.

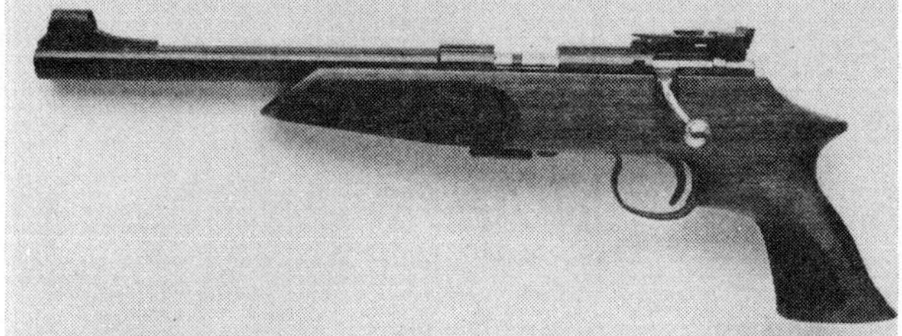

NIB	Exc.	V.G.	Good	Fair	Poor
500	425	350	225	175	100

Exemplar XIV

Similar to the standard Exemplar with a 14" barrel. It was introduced in 1988.

NIB	Exc.	V.G.	Good	Fair	Poor
550	475	375	250	200	100

Exemplar Hornet

Chambered for the .22 Hornet cartridge. It was introduced in 1988.

NIB	Exc.	V.G.	Good	Fair	Poor
750	600	400	300	200	100

ANTI GARROTTER

England

Percussion belt pistol, marked "Balls Pat. Steel." Oval is 7" long and the barrel protrudes 1-1/2"; approximately .45 caliber. A cord runs from the lock up and through the sleeve and is fired by pulling the cord. Beware of modern fakes.

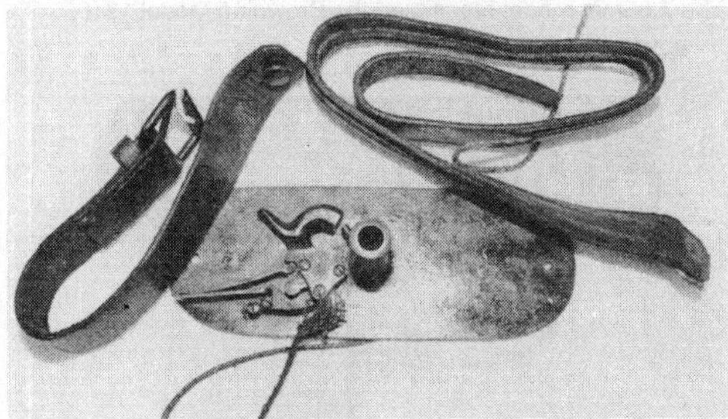

Exc.	V.G.	Good	Fair	Poor
—	6000	2500	800	400

APACHE

Eibar, Spain

SEE—Ojanguren Y Vidosa

APALOZO HERMANOS

Zumorraga, Spain

Spanish manufacturer from approximately 1920 to 1936. The trademark, a dove-like bird, is normally found impressed into the grips.

Apaloza

Copy of a Colt Police Positive Revolver.

Exc.	V.G.	Good	Fair	Poor
225	125	100	65	45

Paramount

Copy of the Model 1906 Browning chambered for 6.35mm. Paramount is stamped on the slide and at the top of each grip plate.

Courtesy James Rankin

Exc.	V.G.	Good	Fair	Poor
225	125	100	50	30

Triomphe

A copy of the Browning Model 1906 in caliber 6.35mm. The slide is inscribed "Pistolet Automatique Triomphe Acier Comprime." Cal. 6.35mm is stamped on each grip plate along with the dove logo.

Courtesy James Rankin

Exc.	V.G.	Good	Fair	Poor
225	125	100	50	30

AR-7 INDUSTRIES
Meriden, Connecticut

AR-7 Explorer
Semi-automatic .22 caliber takedown rifle fitted with a 16" barrel and 8-round magazine. Adjustable rear peep sight. Weight is 2.5 lbs.

NIB	Exc.	V.G.	Good	Fair	Poor
175	120	90	—	—	—

AR-7C Explorer
Same as above but with camo stock.

NIB	Exc.	V.G.	Good	Fair	Poor
175	130	100	—	—	—

AR-7 Sporter
Similar to the standard AR-7, but with a metal skeleton stock and aluminum ventilated shrouded barrel. Weight is about 3.8 lbs.

NIB	Exc.	V.G.	Good	Fair	Poor
250	150	120	—	—	—

AR-7 Target
This model features a tubular stock with cantilever 3x9x40mm scope. Fitted with 16" bull barrel. Weight is about 5.7 lbs.

NIB	Exc.	V.G.	Good	Fair	Poor
300	200	150	—	—	—

AR-7 Bolt-Action
This model is similar in all respects to the standard semi-automatic AR-7, but with a bolt action.

NIB	Exc.	V.G.	Good	Fair	Poor
225	120	90	—	—	—

ARCUS
Bulgaria

Arcus-94
Introduced in 1998 this is a semi-automatic pistol chambered for the 9mm cartridge. Fitted with an ambidextrous safety and 10-round magazine. Imported from Bulgaria.

NIB	Exc.	V.G.	Good	Fair	Poor
400	300	250	200	150	100

ARIZAGA, G.
Eibar, Spain

Spanish manufacturer prior to World War II.

Arizaga (Model 1915)
A 7.65mm semi-automatic pistol. Patterned after the Ruby-style military pistols. Magazine capacity is 9 or 12 rounds. Wood grips.

Exc.	V.G.	Good	Fair	Poor
250	150	100	75	45

Mondial
Similar design to the Astra pistol in the 100 series. Chambered for the 6.35mm cartridge. It has the Owl and Mondial on each grip plate.

Exc.	V.G.	Good	Fair	Poor
300	190	145	75	45

Pinkerton
Arizaga's standard model known to exist with a cartridge counter. Slide is marked "Pinkerton Automatic 6.35."

Exc.	V.G.	Good	Fair	Poor
250	150	100	75	45

Warwick
Same design as the Mondial but in caliber 7.65mm. Warwick appears on each grip plate.

Exc.	V.G.	Good	Fair	Poor
300	190	145	75	45

ARIZMENDI ZULAICA
Eibar, Spain

Cebra
A semi-automatic 7.65mm pistol patterned after the Ruby-style of Spanish automatics. The slide is marked "Pistolet Automatique Cebra Zulaica Eibar," together with the letters "AZ" in an oval. Generally found with checkered wood grips.

Courtesy James Rankin

Exc.	V.G.	Good	Fair	Poor
200	100	75	50	35

Cebra Revolver
Copy of a Colt Police Positive revolver marked "Made in Spain" with the word "Cebra" cast in the grips.

Exc.	V.G.	Good	Fair	Poor
225	125	125	75	50

ARIZMENDI, FRANCISCO
Eibar, Spain

Originally founded in the 1890s, the company was reformed in 1914 and manufactured semi-automatic pistols.

Singer
The Singer was manufactured in a number of different variations and in calibers 6.35mm and 7.65mm. It was earlier called the Victor. The 6.35mm models resembled the Browning 1906. The 7.65mm model resembled the Browning Model 1910.

6.35mm

Courtesy James Rankin

Exc.	V.G.	Good	Fair	Poor
150	100	75	50	35

7.65mm

Courtesy James Rankin

Exc.	V.G.	Good	Fair	Poor
150	100	75	50	35

Teuf Teuf

The Teuf Teuf was chambered in calibers 6.35mm and 7.65mm. The 7.65mm was only slightly larger than the 6.35mm model. The pistol copied its name from the Browning Model 1906 and from the Belgium Teuf Teuf. The pistol shown is a cartridge indicator model.

Courtesy James Rankin

6.35mm

Exc.	V.G.	Good	Fair	Poor
150	100	75	50	35

7.65mm

Exc.	V.G.	Good	Fair	Poor
150	100	75	50	35

Walman

The Walman was manufactured in a number of variations, and in calibers 6.35mm, 7.65mm, and .380. Earliest semi-automatic production was in 1908 through 1926. Certain variations were called the American Model. The model in .380 caliber had a squeeze grip safety.

6.35mm

Courtesy James Rankin

Exc.	V.G.	Good	Fair	Poor
150	100	75	50	35

7.65mm

Courtesy James Rankin

Exc.	V.G.	Good	Fair	Poor
175	125	90	60	35

.380

Courtesy James Rankin

Exc.	V.G.	Good	Fair	Poor
175	125	90	60	35

Arizmendi

Solid-frame, folding-trigger revolver chambered for 7.65mm or .32 caliber. Normal markings are the trademark "FA" and a circled five-pointed star.

Exc.	V.G.	Good	Fair	Poor
175	125	80	50	25

Boltun—1st Variation

The Bolton semi-automatic pistol was made in both calibers 6.35mm and 7.65mm. It was almost an exact copy of the Belgian Pieper. The 7.65mm model was only slightly larger than the 6.35mm model.

6.35mm

Exc.	V.G.	Good	Fair	Poor
175	125	90	60	35

7.65mm

Exc.	V.G.	Good	Fair	Poor
175	125	90	60	35

Boltun—2nd Variation

The Boltun 2nd variation is chambered for the 7.65mm cartridge and is almost an exact copy of the Browning Model 1910. It was made into the 1930s.

Exc.	V.G.	Good	Fair	Poor
175	125	90	60	35

Puppy

A variation of the "Velo-Dog" revolver with the barrel stamped "Puppy" and the frame bearing the "FA" trademark.

Exc.	V.G.	Good	Fair	Poor
175	125	80	50	25

Pistolet Automatique

Normal markings include the "FA" trademark.

Exc.	V.G.	Good	Fair	Poor
175	125	80	50	25

Kaba Spezial

A 6.35mm semi-automatic pistol patterned after the Browning Model 1906. The Kaba Spezial was originally made by August Menz of Suhl, Germany and sold by Karl Bauer of Berlin, Germany. The name "Kaba" was derived from the first two initials of Karl Bauer. These two pistols do not look alike.

Courtesy James Rankin

Exc.	V.G.	Good	Fair	Poor
200	100	75	50	35

Roland

Chambered for 6.35 and 7.65mm cartridges, this model was manufactured during the 1920s. The 7.65mm was only slightly larger than the 6.35mm model.

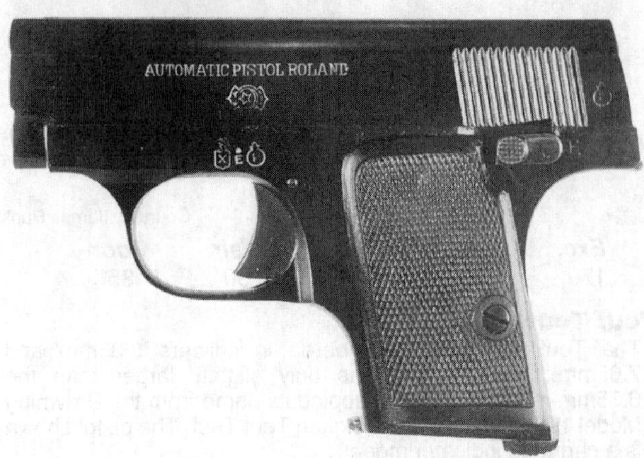

Courtesy James Rankin

6.35mm

Exc.	V.G.	Good	Fair	Poor
225	125	90	60	35

7.65mm

Exc.	V.G.	Good	Fair	Poor
225	125	90	60	35

Ydeal

The Ydeal was manufactured in four variations and in calibers 6.35mm, 7.65mm, and .380. All four variations resemble the Browning Model 1906, with the 7.65mm and .380 caliber being slightly larger.

Courtesy James Rankin

6.35mm

Exc.	V.G.	Good	Fair	Poor
175	125	90	60	35

7.65mm

Exc.	V.G.	Good	Fair	Poor
175	125	90	60	35

.380

Exc.	V.G.	Good	Fair	Poor
175	125	90	60	35

ARMALITE, INC.

Costa Mesa, California

Geneseo, Illinois (current production)

In 1995 Eagle Arms purchased the Armalite trademark and certain other assets. The new companies are organized under the Armalite name. The original company, formed in the mid 1950s, developed the AR-10, which in turn led to the development of the M-16 series of service rifles still in use today. All current models are produced at the Geneseo, Illinois, facility.

AR-24 Pistol

15-shot 9mm double-action semi-auto. Steel frame, fixed or adjustable sights. Compact version available. Introduced 2006. Pricing is for full-size pistol with adjustable sights. Deduct 15 percent for fixed sight versions.

NIB	Exc.	V.G.	Good	Fair	Poor
595	—	—	—	—	—

AR-17 Shotgun

A gas-operated semi-automatic 12 gauge shotgun, with a 24" barrel and interchangeable choke tubes. The receiver and the barrel are made of an aluminum alloy, with an anodized black or gold finish. The stock and forearm are of plastic. Approximately 2,000 were manufactured during 1964 and 1965.

NIB	Exc.	V.G.	Good	Fair	Poor
550	450	400	300	225	100

AR-7 Explorer Rifle

A .22 LR semi-auto carbine with a 16" barrel. The receiver and barrel are partially made of an alloy. The most noteworthy feature of this model is that it can be disassembled and the component parts stored in the plastic stock. Manufactured between 1959 and 1973. Reintroduced in 1999.

NIB	Exc.	V.G.	Good	Fair	Poor
170	125	100	75	50	—

AR-7 Custom

As above with a walnut cheekpiece stock, manufactured between 1964 and 1970.

NIB	Exc.	V.G.	Good	Fair	Poor
150	125	100	80	50	35

AR-180

A gas-operated semi-automatic rifle chambered for the .223 or 5.56mm cartridge. The AR-180 is the civilian version of the AR18, which is fully automatic. It is a simple and efficient rifle that was tested by various governments and found to have potential. This rifle was also manufactured by Howa Machinery Ltd. and Sterling Armament Co. of England. The most common version is manufactured by Sterling. Those built by Armalite and Howa bring a small premium.

Howa

NIB	Exc.	V.G.	Good	Fair	Poor
1500	1250	900	700	450	—

Sterling

NIB	Exc.	V.G.	Good	Fair	Poor
1250	900	700	500	350	—

AR-180B

Similar to the original AR-180. Chambered for the .223 cartridge and fitted with a 19.8" barrel with integral muzzlebrake. Lower receiver is polymer while the upper receiver is sheet steel. Trigger group is standard M15. Accepts standard M15 magazines. Weight is about 6 lbs.

NIB	Exc.	V.G.	Good	Fair	Poor
750	625	500	—	—	—

AR-10A4 Rifle

Introduced in 1995 this model features a 20" stainless steel heavy barrel chambered for the .308 Win. or .243 Win. cartridge. Has a flattop receiver, optional two-stage trigger, detachable carry handle, scope mount. Equipped with two 10-round magazines. Weight is about 9.6 lbs.

NIB	Exc.	V.G.	Good	Fair	Poor
1500	1250	900	700	500	—

NOTE: For stainless steel barrel add $100.

AR-10A4 Carbine

Similar to above model but chambered for .308 Win. cartridge and fitted with a 16" barrel. Flattop receiver. Sold with two 10-round magazines. Weight is approximately 9 lbs.

NIB	Exc.	V.G.	Good	Fair	Poor
1500	1250	900	700	500	—

NOTE: For stainless steel barrel add $100.

AR-10A2 Rifle

This model has a 20" heavy barrel chambered for the .308 cartridge but without the removable carry handle. Weight is about 9.8 lbs.

NIB	Exc.	V.G.	Good	Fair	Poor
1500	1250	900	700	500	—

NOTE: For stainless steel barrel add $100.

AR-10A2 Carbine

Similar to model above but fitted with a 16" barrel. Weight is approximately 9 lbs.

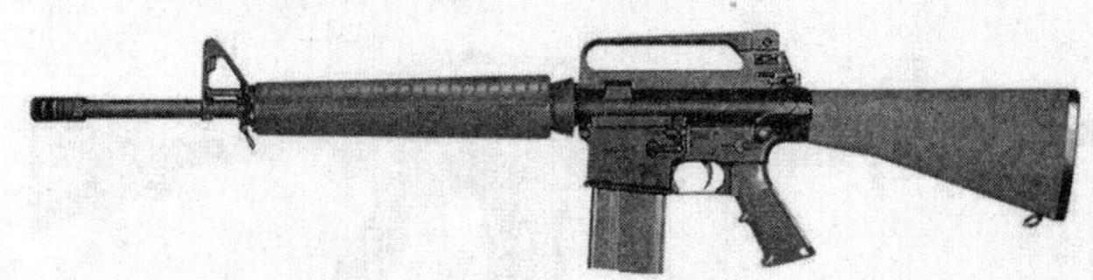

NIB	Exc.	V.G.	Good	Fair	Poor
1500	1250	900	700	500	—

NOTE: For stainless steel barrel add $100.

AR-10B

Chambered for the .308 cartridge and fitted with a 20" barrel. The trigger is a single-stage or optional 2-stage match type. This model has several of the early M16 features such as a tapered handguard, pistol grips, and short buttstock in original brown color. Fitted with early charging handle. Limited production. Weight is about 9.5 lbs. Introduced in 1999.

NIB	Exc.	V.G.	Good	Fair	Poor
1698	1250	900	—	—	—

AR-10(T) Rifle

This model features a 24" heavy barrel with a two-stage trigger. The front sight and carry handle are removable. The handguard is fiberglass. Weight is approximately 10.4 lbs.

NIB	Exc.	V.G.	Good	Fair	Poor
2125	1950	1500	1100	800	—

AR-10(T) Carbine

Similar to the AR-10T but fitted with a 16.25" target weight barrel. Weight is approximately 8.5 lbs.

NIB	Exc.	V.G.	Good	Fair	Poor
2400	1950	1500	1100	800	—

AR-10(T) Ultra

Chambered for the .300 Remington Short Action Ultra MAgnum cartridge. Barrel length is 24". Two stage National MAtch trigger. Offered in choice of green or black stock. Sold with a 5 round magazine.

NIB	Exc.	V.G.	Good	Fair	Poor
2340	1950	1500	1100	800	—

AR-10 SOF

Introduced in 2003 this model features an M4-style fixed stock. Flattop receiver. Chambered for the .308 cartridge. Offered in both A2 and A4 configurations.

NIB	Exc.	V.G.	Good	Fair	Poor
1500	1250	—	—	—	—

M15 SOF

This model is chambered for the .223 cartridge and is fitted with a flattop receiver and M4-style fixed stock. Introduced in 2003. Offered in both A2 and A4 configurations.

NIB	Exc.	V.G.	Good	Fair	Poor
1150	925	—	—	—	—

M15A2 HBAR

This model was introduced in 1995 and features a 20" heavy barrel chambered for .223 cartridge. A2-style forward assist, recoil check brake. Sold with a 10-round magazine. Weight is approximately 8.2 lbs.

NIB	Exc.	V.G.	Good	Fair	Poor
1000	850	600	500	—	—

M15A2 National Match

Chambered for the .223 cartridge this variation features a 20" stainless steel match barrel with two-stage trigger, A2 style forward assist and hard coated anodized receiver. Equipped with a 10-round magazine. Weight is about 9 lbs.

NIB	Exc.	V.G.	Good	Fair	Poor
1472	1200	850	600	—	—

M15A2-M4A1C Carbine

Similar to the M15A2 heavy barrel but with a 16" heavy barrel. Flattop receiver with detachable carry handle. Introduced in 1995.

NIB	Exc.	V.G.	Good	Fair	Poor
1100	900	700	500	—	—

NOTE: Add $100 for Match trigger.

M15A2-M4C Carbine

Similar to the M4A1C Carbine but with the flattop receiver and detachable carry handle.

NIB	Exc.	V.G.	Good	Fair	Poor
1000	850	600	500	—	—

M15A4(T) Eagle Eye

Chambered for the .223 cartridge and fitted with a 24" stainless steel heavy weight barrel this rifle has a National Match two-stage trigger, Picatinny rail, NM fiberglass handguard tube. Sold with a 7-round magazine and 4-section cleaning rod with brass tip, sling, owner's manual, and lifetime warranty.

NIB	Exc.	V.G.	Good	Fair	Poor
1500	1100	800	600	—	—

M15A4 Special Purpose Rifle (SPR)

This model is fitted with a 20" heavy barrel with detachable front sight, detachable carry handle with NM sights, Picatinny rail. Weight is about 7.8 lbs.

NIB	Exc.	V.G.	Good	Fair	Poor
1200	900	750	600	—	—

M15A4 Action Master

This variation features a 20" stainless steel heavy barrel with two-stage trigger, Picatinny rail, and fiberglass handguard tube. Weight is approximately 9 lbs.

NIB	Exc.	V.G.	Good	Fair	Poor
1450	1000	850	600	—	—

M15A4 Eagle Spirit

This version is similar to the Action Master above but fitted with a 16" stainless steel barrel. Weight is about 7.6 lbs.

NIB	Exc.	V.G.	Good	Fair	Poor
1450	1000	850	600	—	—

AR-30M

Chambered for the .338 Lapua, .300 Winchester Mag., or the .308 Winchester cartridges. Barrel length is 26" with muzzle-brake. Adjustable butt stock. Weight is about 12 lbs. This model is a reduced version of the AR-50.

NIB	Exc.	V.G.	Good	Fair	Poor
1460	1150	—	—	—	—

NOTE: Add $150 for .338 Lapua.

AR-50

Introduced in 2000 this rifle is chambered for the .50 BMG cartridge. Fitted with a 31" tapered barrel threaded for recoil check (muzzlebrake). Trigger is single-stage. Stock is a 3-section type with extruded forend. Pachmayr buttplate. Picatinny rail. Buttplate is adjustable. Finish is magnesium phosphated steel and hard anodized aluminum. Weight is about 33 lbs.

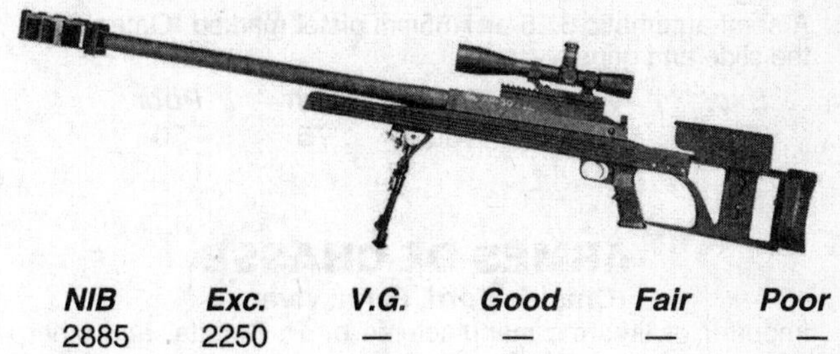

NIB	Exc.	V.G.	Good	Fair	Poor
2885	2250	—	—	—	—

PRE-BAN MODELS

Golden Eagle

Fitted with a 20" stainless extra-heavy barrel with NM two-stage trigger and NM sights. Sold with a 30-round magazine. Weight is about 9.4 lbs.

NIB	Exc.	V.G.	Good	Fair	Poor
1500	1200	950	800	—	—

HBAR

This pre-ban rifle has a 20" heavy barrel, a 30-round magazine, and sling. Weight is approximately 8 lbs.

NIB	Exc.	V.G.	Good	Fair	Poor
1300	1000	850	700	—	—

M4C Carbine

This pre-ban variation is fitted with a 16" heavy barrel, collapsible stock, and fixed flash suppressor. Weight is about 6.2 lbs.

NIB	Exc.	V.G.	Good	Fair	Poor
1300	1000	850	700	—	—

ARMAS DE FUEGO

Guernica, Spain

SEE—Alkartasuna Fabrica de Armas

ARMERO ESPECIALISTAS

Eibar, Spain

Alfa

"Alfa" was a trademark given a number of revolvers based upon both Colt and Smith & Wesson designs in calibers ranging from .22 to .44.

Exc.	V.G.	Good	Fair	Poor
200	150	100	75	50

Omega

A semi-automatic 6.35 or 7.65mm pistol marked "Omega" on the slide and grips.

Exc.	V.G.	Good	Fair	Poor
200	150	100	75	50

ARMES DE CHASSE
Chadds Ford, Pennsylvania

Importer of firearms manufactured by P. Beretta, and other arms manufactured in Germany.

Model EJ

An O/U Anson & Deeley action 12 gauge shotgun with double triggers as well as automatic ejectors. Blued barrels, silver finished receiver and checkered walnut stock. Manufactured in Germany and introduced in 1989.

NIB	Exc.	V.G.	Good	Fair	Poor
1000	950	800	650	500	250

Model EU

As above with a ventilated rib barrel and a nonselective single trigger. Introduced in 1989.

NIB	Exc.	V.G.	Good	Fair	Poor
1200	1000	850	650	500	250

Highlander

A side-by-side double-barrel 20 gauge shotgun with a boxlock action. Available in various barrel lengths and choke combinations, with double triggers and manual extractors. Blued with a checkered walnut stock. Manufactured in Italy and introduced in 1989.

NIB	Exc.	V.G.	Good	Fair	Poor
700	600	500	350	250	125

Chesapeake

As above but chambered for the 3.5" 12 gauge shell. The bores are chrome-lined and suitable for steel shot. Fitted with automatic ejectors and double triggers. Manufactured in Italy, it was introduced in 1989.

NIB	Exc.	V.G.	Good	Fair	Poor
800	700	600	475	400	200

Balmoral

English-style straight grip 12, 16, or 20 gauge boxlock shotgun, fitted with false side plates. Receiver and side plates case hardened, the barrels blued. Fitted with a single trigger and automatic ejectors. Manufactured in Italy and introduced in 1989.

NIB	Exc.	V.G.	Good	Fair	Poor
800	725	625	500	400	200

Model 70E

A 12, 16, or 20 gauge side-by-side shotgun fitted with 27" or 28" barrels. The action based upon the Anson & Deeley design with a Greener crossbolt. The receiver is case hardened, barrels are blued and the walnut stock checkered. Manufactured in Germany and introduced in 1989.

NIB	Exc.	V.G.	Good	Fair	Poor
800	725	625	500	400	200

Model 74E

As above with game scene engraving and more fully figured walnut stock. Introduced in 1989.

NIB	Exc.	V.G.	Good	Fair	Poor
1000	925	775	625	500	250

Model 76E

As above with engraved false side plates and fully figured walnut stock. Introduced in 1989.

NIB	Exc.	V.G.	Good	Fair	Poor
1500	1150	900	750	600	300

ARMINEX LTD.
Scottsdale, Arizona

Tri-Fire

A semi-automatic pistol chambered for 9mm, .38 Super or .45 ACP cartridges. Available with conversion units that add approximately $130 if in excellent condition. Fitted with 5", 6", or 7" stainless steel barrels. Presentation cases were available at an extra cost of $48. Approximately 250 were manufactured from 1981 to 1985.

Courtesy James Rankin

NIB	Exc.	V.G.	Good	Fair	Poor
800	650	500	300	175	100

Target Model

As above with a 6" or 7" barrel.

Courtesy James Rankin

NIB	Exc.	V.G.	Good	Fair	Poor
850	700	550	350	225	100

ARMINUS

SEE—Friedrich Pickert
SEE—Hermann Weirauch
SEE—F. I. E.

ARMITAGE INTERNATIONAL, LTD.
Seneca, South Carolina

Scarab Skorpion

A blowback-operated, semi-automatic pistol, patterned after the Czechoslovakian Scorpion submachine gun. Chambered for the 9mm cartridge with a 4.6" barrel having military-type sights. Fitted with a 32-round, detachable box magazine. The standard finish is matte black and the grips are plastic.

NIB	Exc.	V.G.	Good	Fair	Poor
650	550	400	300	175	100

ARMS CORPORATION OF THE PHILIPPINES

Armscor Precision
Marikina City, Philippines

Armscor Precision is an importer of a variety of firearms made in the Philippines.

KBI, Inc. also distributes some .22 caliber Armscor rifles.

MAP1 FS

Single/double-action 9mm semi-auto with 16+1 capacity. Fixed sights, 4.45" barrel, 40.5 oz. nickel alloy steel frame and slide. (Shorter, lighter MS model has 3.66" barrel.) Introduced 2006.

Exc.	V.G.	Good	Fair	Poor
350	—	—	—	—

MAPP1 FS

Single/double-action 9mm semi-auto with 16+1 capacity. Fixed sights, 4.45" barrel, 40.5 oz. polymer frame with integrated accessory rail, and nickel alloy steel slide. (Shorter, lighter MS model has 3.66" barrel.) Introduced 2006.

Exc.	V.G.	Good	Fair	Poor
350	—	—	—	—

SHOTGUNS

Model 30D

A slide-action 12 gauge shotgun fitted with either 28" or 30" barrels with various chokes. The magazine holds 6 cartridges. Weight is about 7.6 lbs.

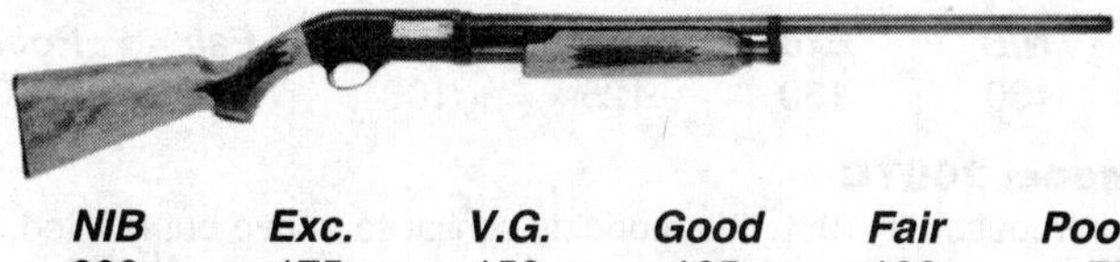

NIB	Exc.	V.G.	Good	Fair	Poor
200	175	150	125	100	75

Model 30DG

As above with a 20" barrel, fitted with rifle sights and a 7-shot magazine. Weight is about 7.2 lbs.

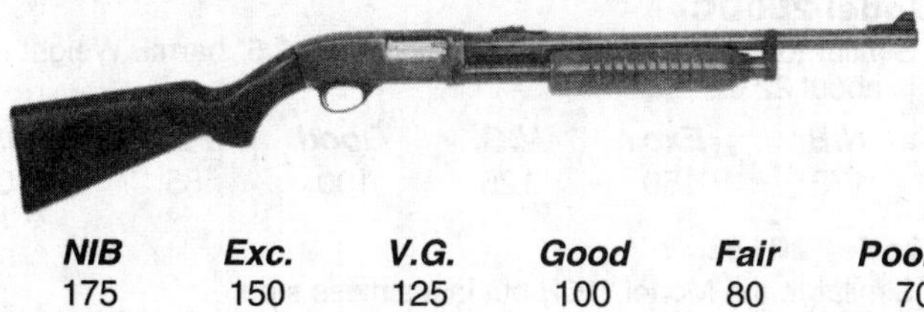

NIB	Exc.	V.G.	Good	Fair	Poor
175	150	125	100	80	70

Model 30R

As above with shotgun bead sights, 20" or 18.5" barrel. Weight is between 7 and 7.2 lbs. depending on barrel length.

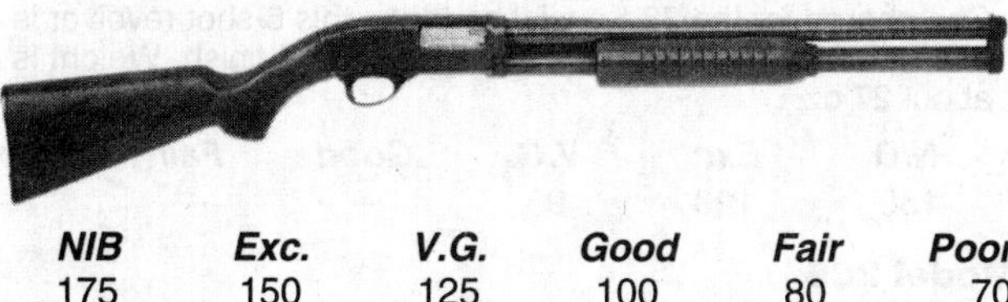

NIB	Exc.	V.G.	Good	Fair	Poor
175	150	125	100	80	70

Model 30RP

As above with an auxiliary black composition pistol grip and an 18.5" barrel.

NIB	Exc.	V.G.	Good	Fair	Poor
175	150	125	100	80	70

Model 30 SAS1

Slide-action 12 gauge with 20" barrel with heat shield. Chambered for the 3" shell. Open cylinder choke. Parkerized finish finish. Weight is about 8 lbs.

NIB	Exc.	V.G.	Good	Fair	Poor
200	150	—	—	—	—

RIFLES

Model M14P

A .22 caliber bolt-action rifle fitted with a 23" barrel, open sights, and a 5-shot detachable magazine. Mahogany stock.

NIB	Exc.	V.G.	Good	Fair	Poor
100	90	75	50	35	25

Model M14D

As above with an adjustable rear sight and checkered stock. Manufactured in 1987 only.

NIB	Exc.	V.G.	Good	Fair	Poor
125	100	85	60	40	25

Model 14Y

This bolt-action rifle is chambered for .22 LR cartridge. It is fitted with an 18" barrel and 10-round magazine. Weight is approximately 5.2 lbs.

NIB	Exc.	V.G.	Good	Fair	Poor
150	125	100	—	—	—

Model 12Y

This bolt-action rifle is a single-shot and chambered for the .22 LR. It is fitted with an 18" barrel. Weight is about 5 lbs.

NIB	Exc.	V.G.	Good	Fair	Poor
125	100	75	—	—	—

Model 1400

This is a bolt-action rifle chambered for the .22 LR cartridge. Fitted with a 22.5" barrel and a 10-round magazine. Weight is about 6.5 lbs.

NIB	Exc.	V.G.	Good	Fair	Poor
240	200	150	125	100	75

Model M1500

A .22 Magnum bolt-action rifle fitted with a 22.5" barrel, open sights, 5-shot magazine and checkered mahogany stock. Weight is approximately 6.5 lbs.

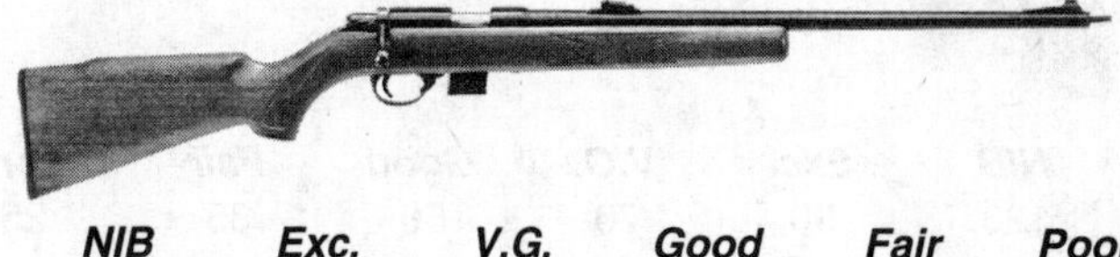

NIB	Exc.	V.G.	Good	Fair	Poor
250	200	150	125	100	75

Model M1600

A .22 caliber copy of the U.S. M16 rifle with an 18" barrel and detachable 15-round magazine. Weight is about 6.2 lbs.

NIB	Exc.	V.G.	Good	Fair	Poor
225	150	125	100	75	50

Model M1600R

As above with a stainless steel collapsible stock and shrouded barrel. No longer in production.

NIB	Exc.	V.G.	Good	Fair	Poor
250	200	150	125	100	75

Model M1600C

As above with a 20" barrel and fiberglass stock. No longer in production.

NIB	Exc.	V.G.	Good	Fair	Poor
135	110	90	70	50	35

Model M1600W

As above with a mahogany stock. No longer in production.

NIB	Exc.	V.G.	Good	Fair	Poor
150	125	100	75	50	35

Model M1800

A .22 Hornet bolt-action rifle fitted with a 22.5" barrel, 5-shot magazine and a mahogany Monte Carlo-style stock. Weight is approximately 6.6 lbs.

NIB	Exc.	V.G.	Good	Fair	Poor
150	125	100	75	50	35

Model 20C

Chambered for .22 LR with a 15-round magazine and fitted with an 18.25" barrel. Weight is about 6.2 lbs.

NIB	Exc.	V.G.	Good	Fair	Poor
150	120	90	70	50	40

Model M20P

A .22 caliber 15-shot semi-automatic rifle fitted with a 20.75" barrel, open sights and plain mahogany stock. Weight is about 6.3 lbs.

NIB	Exc.	V.G.	Good	Fair	Poor
100	80	65	50	35	25

Model M2000

As above with adjustable sights and a checkered stock. Weight is approximately 6.4 lbs.

NIB	Exc.	V.G.	Good	Fair	Poor
120	90	70	50	35	25

Model AK22S

A .22 caliber semi-automatic rifle resembling the Russian AKA47. Barrel length of 18.5", 15-round magazine and mahogany stock. Weight is about 7.5 lbs.

NIB	Exc.	V.G.	Good	Fair	Poor
215	165	140	100	75	50

Model AK22F

As above with a folding stock. No longer in production.

NIB	Exc.	V.G.	Good	Fair	Poor
225	175	150	100	75	50

HANDGUNS

Model M100

A double-action, swing-out cylinder revolver chambered for .22, .22 Magnum, and the .38 Special cartridges. Has a 4" ventilated rib barrel. Six-shot cylinder and adjustable sights. Blued with checkered mahogany grips. No longer in production.

NIB	Exc.	V.G.	Good	Fair	Poor
200	175	150	110	80	50

Model 200P

Introduced in 1990 this 6-shot revolver is chambered for the .38 Special cartridge. It is fitted with a 4" barrel, fixed sights and wood or rubber grips. Weighs about 26 ozs.

NIB	Exc.	V.G.	Good	Fair	Poor
180	150	125	100	85	60

Model 200TC

Introduced in 1990 this model is similar to above but is fitted with adjustable sights and checkered wood grips. Weight is about 28 oz.

NIB	Exc.	V.G.	Good	Fair	Poor
200	175	150	125	100	75

Model 200DC

Similar to the Model 200P but fitted with a 2.5" barrel. Weight is about 22 oz.

NIB	Exc.	V.G.	Good	Fair	Poor
175	150	125	100	85	60

Model 201S

Similar to the Model 200P but in stainless steel.

NIB	Exc.	V.G.	Good	Fair	Poor
200	175	150	125	100	75

Model 202

Chambered for the 38 Special cartridge this 6-shot revolver is fitted with a 4" barrel and fixed sights. Blued finish. Weight is about 27 oz.

NIB	Exc.	V.G.	Good	Fair	Poor
150	120	95	—	—	—

Model 206

Similar to the Model 202 but with a 2.88" barrel. Weight is about 25 oz.

NIB	Exc.	V.G.	Good	Fair	Poor
180	140	110	—	—	—

Model 210

Same as the Model 202 but with adjustable sights. Weight is about 27 oz.

NIB	Exc.	V.G.	Good	Fair	Poor
200	150	125	—	—	—

Model 1911-A1

A semi-automatic pistol similar in design to the Colt Model 1911 pistol. Chambered for the .45 ACP cartridge and fitted with a 5" barrel. Blued finish. Magazine capacity is 8 rounds. Weight is about 39 oz.

NIB	Exc.	V.G.	Good	Fair	Poor
500	400	—	—	—	—

Model 1911-A2

Same as above but fitted with a double column magazine with a 13-round capacity. Weight is approximately 43 oz.

NIB	Exc.	V.G.	Good	Fair	Poor
600	500	—	—	—	—

NOTE: For two-tone finish add $100. For chrome finish add $130.

ARMSCO FIREARMS CORP.

Ankara, Turkey
U.S.A.—Des Plaines, Illinois

Built by Huglu Hunting Firearms Corporation in Turkey, which was established in 1927. Armsco is the U.S. representive. First year of business in the U.S. was 2002.

SINGLE-SHOT

Model 301A

This single-shot model is offered in 12, 16, 20, 28 gauge as well as .410 bore. Barrel lengths from 22" to 32" depending on gauge. Checkered walnut stock. Weight varies from 5 lbs. to 5.5 lbs. depending on gauge.

NIB	Exc.	V.G.	Good	Fair	Poor
200	150	75	50	35	25

SIDE-BY-SIDE

Model 202B

Boxlock gun offered in 12, 16, 20, and 28 gauge as well as .410 bore with barrel lengths from 22" to 32" depending on gauge. Double triggers. Hand engraved about 50 percent coverage. Fixed chokes or choke tubes. Checkered walnut stock with cheekpiece. Weight is about 6.4 lbs. to 7.3 lbs. depending on gauge.

NIB	Exc.	V.G.	Good	Fair	Poor
520	400	300	200	125	50

Model 202A

Same as above but offered with standard buttstock.

NIB	Exc.	V.G.	Good	Fair	Poor
697	525	450	300	175	75

Model 201A

Offered in gauges from 12 to .410 with sideplates with 50 percent hand engraving. Choice of single or double triggers.

NIB	Exc.	V.G.	Good	Fair	Poor
695	525	450	300	175	75

Model 200A

Boxlock in gauges 12 to .410 with single trigger. Hand engraved 50 percent coverage.

NIB	Exc.	V.G.	Good	Fair	Poor
750	575	450	300	175	75

Model 205A

Offered in gauges 12 to .410 with barrel lengths 22" to 32" depending on gauge. Boxlock frame with 60 percent hand engraving coverage. Single trigger. Checkered walnut stock. Weights are 6.1 lbs. to 6.8 lbs. depending on gauge.

NIB	Exc.	V.G.	Good	Fair	Poor
990	750	600	425	200	100

Model 210AE

Offered in 12, 16, and 20 gauge with single trigger and automatic ejectors. Boxlock frame is 60 percent hand engraved. Optional fixed or choke tubes.

NIB	Exc.	V.G.	Good	Fair	Poor
1250	950	700	450	300	200

Model 210BE

Same as above but with double triggers.

NIB	Exc.	V.G.	Good	Fair	Poor
1150	850	675	450	300	200

OVER-AND-UNDER

Model 104A

Chambered for the 12 through .410 bores with double triggers and barrel lengths from 22" to 32" depending on gauge. Ventilated rib. Checkered walnut stock. Fixed or choke tubes. Weight is from 6.6 lbs. to 7.3 lbs. depending on gauge. Receiver is 15 percent hand engraved.

NIB	Exc.	V.G.	Good	Fair	Poor
425	300	250	200	125	75

Model 103D

Same as model above but with single trigger and schnabel forearm.

NIB	Exc.	V.G.	Good	Fair	Poor
595	475	375	325	175	75

Model 103DE

Same as above but with automatic ejectors.

NIB	Exc.	V.G.	Good	Fair	Poor
750	575	525	425	200	75

Model 103C

Similar to the Model 103D but with blued receiver with gold inlaid birds with 40 percent engraving coverage.

NIB	Exc.	V.G.	Good	Fair	Poor
720	550	525	425	200	75

Model 103CE

Same as above but with automatic ejectors.

NIB	Exc.	V.G.	Good	Fair	Poor
870	650	575	475	225	100

Model 103F

Similar to the Model 103D but with 80 to 100 percent hand engraved side plates.

NIB	Exc.	V.G.	Good	Fair	Poor
850	625	550	450	225	100

Model 103FE

Same as above but with automatic ejectors.

NIB	Exc.	V.G.	Good	Fair	Poor
970	750	600	475	250	125

Model 101SE

Offered in 12 gauge only with 28", 30", or 32" barrels with ventilated rib. Single trigger and automatic ejectors. Hand engraved receiver. Checkered walnut stock. Weight is from 6.6 lbs. to 7.3 lbs. depending on barrel length.

NIB	Exc.	V.G.	Good	Fair	Poor
1290	975	750	450	275	125

Model 101BE

Same as above but with adjustable comb.

NIB	Exc.	V.G.	Good	Fair	Poor
1290	975	750	450	275	125

SEMI-AUTO

Model 401A

This semi-automatic shotgun uses a short-recoil inertia-operated system. Chambered for the 12 gauge shell up to 3". Barrel lengths from 22" to 32". Ventilated rib. Plastic or walnut stock. Fixed or choke tubes. Fully engraved receiver. Weight is from 6.9 lbs. to 7.2 lbs. depending on barrel length. Magazine capacity is 6 rounds.

NIB	Exc.	V.G.	Good	Fair	Poor
400	350	275	225	125	75

Model 401B

Same as model above but with 4-round magazine capacity.

NIB	Exc.	V.G.	Good	Fair	Poor
400	350	275	225	125	75

Model 501GA

This is a gas-operated shotgun chambered for the 3" 12 gauge shell. Barrel lengths are from 22" to 32". Black receiver with 15 percent hand engraving coverage. Magazine capacity is 7 rounds. Walnut or plastic stock. Weight is from 6.8 lbs. to 7.3 lbs. depending on barrel length.

NIB	Exc.	V.G.	Good	Fair	Poor
400	350	275	225	125	75

Model 501GB

Same as above but with 4-round magazine.

NIB	Exc.	V.G.	Good	Fair	Poor
400	350	275	225	125	75

Model 601GB

Same as the Model 501GB but with a full engraving coverage silver receiver.

NIB	Exc.	V.G.	Good	Fair	Poor
400	350	275	225	125	75

Model 601GA

Same as Model 501GA with 7-round magazine capacity.

NIB	Exc.	V.G.	Good	Fair	Poor
400	350	275	225	125	75

Model 701GA

This model is chambered for the 20 gauge 3" shell and fitted with barrel lengths from 22" to 32". Ventilated rib. Walnut stock. Fixed or choke tubes. Magazine capacity is 7 rounds. Weight is 6 lbs. to 6.4 lbs. depending on barrel length.

NIB	Exc.	V.G.	Good	Fair	Poor
450	375	300	225	125	75

Model 701GB

Same as above but with 4-round magazine.

NIB	Exc.	V.G.	Good	Fair	Poor
450	375	300	225	125	75

PUMP ACTION

Model 801A

This is a slide-action 12 gauge shotgun with plastic stock. Barrel length is from 22" to 32". Fixed or choke tubes. Magazine capacity is 7 rounds. Weight is about 7 lbs.

NIB	Exc.	V.G.	Good	Fair	Poor
300	275	250	175	100	50

Model 801B

Same as above but with 4-round magazine.

NIB	Exc.	V.G.	Good	Fair	Poor
300	275	250	175	100	50

ARMSCORP OF AMERICA

Baltimore, Maryland

RIFLES

M14R

A civilian version of the U.S. M14 rifle manufactured from new and surplus parts. Introduced in 1986.

NIB	Exc.	V.G.	Good	Fair	Poor
600	500	400	300	200	100

M14 National Match

As above but built to A.M.T.U. MIL specifications. Introduced in 1987.

NIB	Exc.	V.G.	Good	Fair	Poor
1500	1150	800	500	400	200

FAL

A civilian version of the FN FAL rifle assembled from new and Argentine surplus parts. Introduced in 1987.

NIB	Exc.	V.G.	Good	Fair	Poor
800	650	500	400	300	150

M36 Israeli Sniper Rifle

A specialized weapon built upon the Armscorp M14 receiver in the Bullpup style. Barrel length 22" and of free floating design for accuracy, chambered for the .308 cartridge. There is an integral flash suppressor and a bipod. It is furnished with a 20-shot detachable magazine. This civilian version was first offered for sale in 1989.

NIB	Exc.	V.G.	Good	Fair	Poor
3000	2500	2000	1500	850	400

Expert Model

A .22 caliber semi-automatic rifle with a 21" barrel, open sights, and 10-shot magazine. Introduced in 1989.

NIB	Exc.	V.G.	Good	Fair	Poor
225	200	175	145	100	80

HANDGUNS

Hi-Power

An Argentine-made version of the Browning semi-automatic pistol chambered for 9mm with a 4.75" barrel. Matte finished with checkered synthetic grips. Introduced in 1989.

NIB	Exc.	V.G.	Good	Fair	Poor
375	350	300	250	200	100

Detective HP—Compact

As above with a 3.5" barrel.

NIB	Exc.	V.G.	Good	Fair	Poor
400	375	350	275	200	100

P22

A copy of the Colt Woodsman .22 caliber semi-automatic pistol available with either 4" or 6" barrels and a 10-shot magazine. Finish blued, grips of checkered hardwood. Introduced in 1989.

NIB	Exc.	V.G.	Good	Fair	Poor
200	150	125	100	75	50

SD9

An Israeli-made 9mm double-action semi-automatic pistol with a 3" barrel. Assembled extensively from sheet metal stampings. Loaded chamber indicator and 6-round magazine. This model is also known as the Sirkus SD9 manufactured by Sirkus Industries in Israel. Introduced in 1989.

Courtesy Jim Rankin

NIB	Exc.	V.G	Good	Fair	Poor
300	250	200	150	100	75

ARMY & NAVY CO-OPERATIVE SOCIETY

London, England

SEE—British Double Guns

ARNOLD ARMS

Arlington, Washington

This company offered a wide range of rifles and calibers including its own proprietary cartridges, from the 6mm Arnold to the .458 Arnold. Rifles were built on a choice of actions including the Apollo, Remington, Sako, and Winchester. These action choices affect the base price of the rifle. Went out of business in 2002. Values vary with geography.

NOTE: The prices listed are for a base rifle with Remington actions and matte blue finish unless otherwise noted.

Varminter I

This model features a heavy match grade barrel with straight taper. Lengths are from 24" to 26". Calibers are from .222 Rem. to .257 Arnold magnum. Choice of McMillian Varmint stock in various finishes and Pacific Research Varmint stock in flat black. Rifles weigh from 9 to 11 lbs. depending on caliber and configuration.

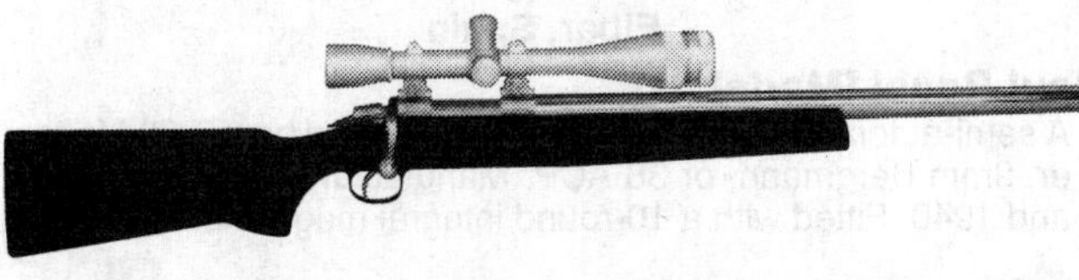

NIB	Exc.	V.G.	Good	Fair	Poor
2600	2000	—	—	—	—

NOTE: For Apollo action add approximately $1100.

Varminter II

This variation features a 24" to 26" medium weight match barrel with choice of McMillan or Pacific Research sporter stocks. Choice of triggers. Weight is 7.5 to 9 lbs. depending on configuration. Calibers from .223 Rem. to .257 Arnold Magnum.

NIB	Exc.	V.G.	Good	Fair	Poor
2600	2000	—	—	—	—

NOTE: For Apollo action add approximately $1100.

Alaskan Rifle

This is a bolt-action rifle chambered for calibers from .223 to .338 Win. Mag. Barrel lengths are from 22" to 26" depending on caliber. Stocks are synthetic in black woodland or arctic camo. Sights are optional. Rifle is drilled and tapped for scope mounts. Trigger is fully adjustable. Choice of chrome moly steel or stainless steel. Introduced in 1996.

NIB	Exc.	V.G.	Good	Fair	Poor
2600	2000	—	—	—	—

NOTE: Add $1100 for Apollo action.

Alaskan Trophy Rifle

Similar to the Alaskan Rifle except chambered for .300 Magnums to .458 Win. Mag. Barrel lengths are 24" to 26" depending on caliber. Choice of walnut, synthetic, or fibergrain stock. Fitted with iron sights. Choice of stainless or chrome moly steel. Introduced in 1996.

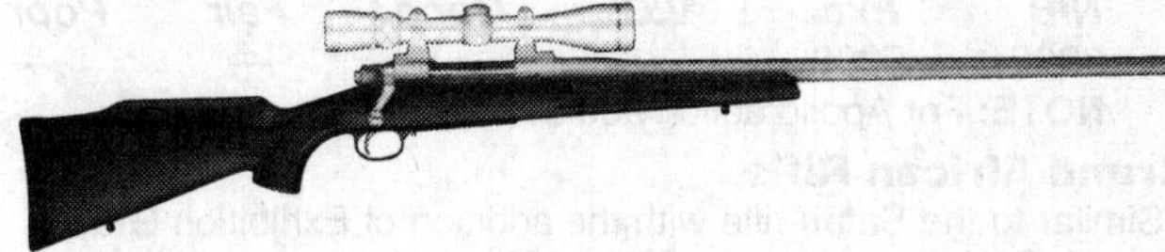

NIB	Exc.	V.G.	Good	Fair	Poor
3100	2500	—	—	—	—

NOTE: Add $1100 for Apollo action.

Alaskan Guide Rifle

This model is offered in choice of calibers from .257 to .338 Magnum. Barrel lengths are 22" to 26" depending on caliber. Buyer has a choice of "A" English walnut stock or deluxe synthetic stock. No open sights.

Synthetic Stock

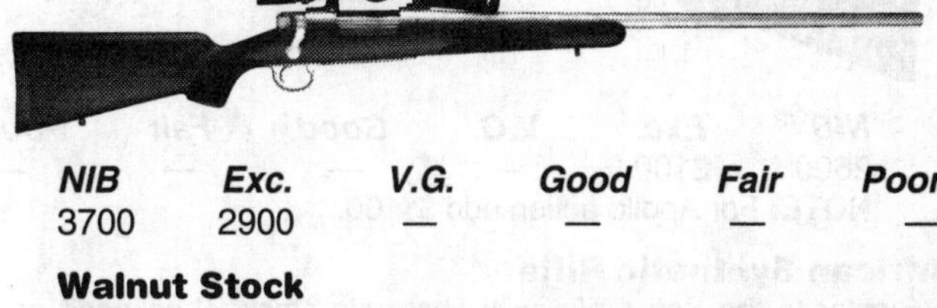

NIB	Exc.	V.G.	Good	Fair	Poor
3700	2900	—	—	—	—

Walnut Stock

NIB	Exc.	V.G.	Good	Fair	Poor
4300	3400	—	—	—	—

NOTE: For Apollo action add approximately $1100.

Grand Alaskan Rifle

This version is fitted with AAA fancy select or exhibition wood. Built in calibers from 300 Mag. to .458 Win. Mag.

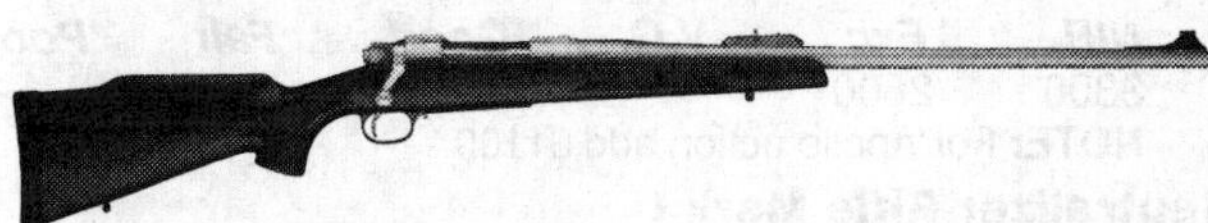

"AAA" English Walnut

NIB	Exc.	V.G.	Good	Fair	Poor
6300	5000	—	—	—	—

"Exhibition" Grade Walnut

NIB	Exc.	V.G.	Good	Fair	Poor
7400	6000	—	—	—	—

NOTE: For Apollo action add $1100.

Safari Rifle

Introduced in 1996 this model features calibers from .223 to .458 Win. Mag. Barrel lengths are from 22" to 26" depending on caliber. The Apollo is a controlled or push feed type with one-piece, cone-head bolt. Fully adjustable trigger with chrome moly or stainless steel construction. Sights are optional but the rifle is drilled and tapped for scope mounts. Choice of A fancy English or AA fancy English walnut.

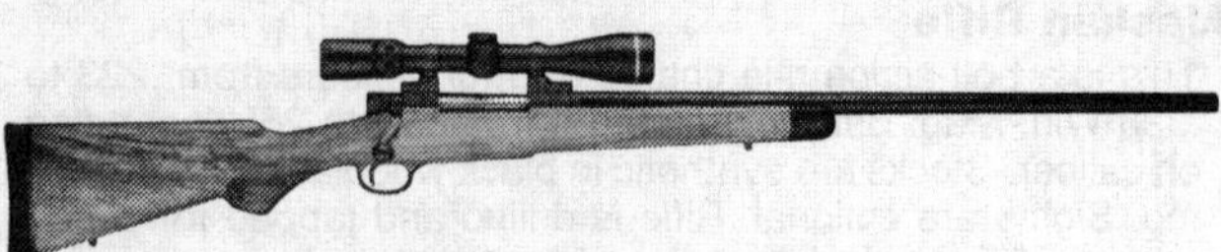

"A" Fancy English Walnut

NIB	Exc.	V.G.	Good	Fair	Poor
4300	3500	—	—	—	—

"AA" Fancy English Walnut

NIB	Exc.	V.G.	Good	Fair	Poor
4400	3500	—	—	—	—

NOTE: For Apollo action add $1100.

African Trophy Rifle

Similar to the Safari Rifle except stocked in AAA fancy walnut with wraparound checkering.

NIB	Exc.	V.G.	Good	Fair	Poor
6300	5000	—	—	—	—

NOTE: For Apollo action add $1100.

Grand African Rifle

Similar to the Safari rifle with the addition of Exhibition Grade wood. Calibers are from .338 to .458.

NIB	Exc.	V.G.	Good	Fair	Poor
7600	6100	—	—	—	—

NOTE: For Apollo action add $1100.

Serengeti Synthetic Rifle

Similar to the Safari rifle with a fibergrain stock in classic or Monte Carlo style. Checkering or stipple finish. Calibers are .243 to 300 Magnum. Introduced in 1996.

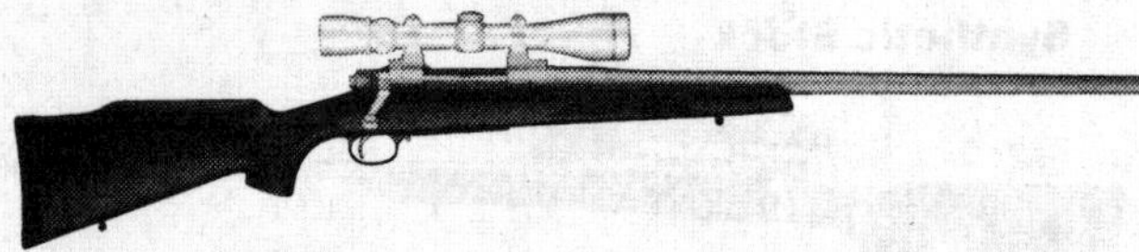

NIB	Exc.	V.G.	Good	Fair	Poor
2600	2100	—	—	—	—

NOTE: For Apollo action add $1100.

African Synthetic Rifle

Similar to the Safari rifle with fibergrain stock, checkering or stipple finish. Calibers are .338 Mag. to .458 Mag.

NIB	Exc.	V.G.	Good	Fair	Poor
3300	2600	—	—	—	—

NOTE: For Apollo action add $1100.

Neutralizer Rifle Mark I

Built on a Remington 700 or Winchester action this bolt-action rifle is chambered in a choice of calibers from .223 to .300 Win. Mag. Barrel lengths are from 24" to 26" depending on caliber with Magnum barrels up to 28". A fiberglass tactical stock with adjustable cheekpiece and buttplate is standard in various finishes. Winchester action is $400 less.

NIB	Exc.	V.G.	Good	Fair	Poor
2900	2300	—	—	—	—

Neutralizer Rifle Mark II

Same as above but with Apollo action.

NIB	Exc.	V.G.	Good	Fair	Poor
4000	3200	—	—	—	—

Benchrest Rifles

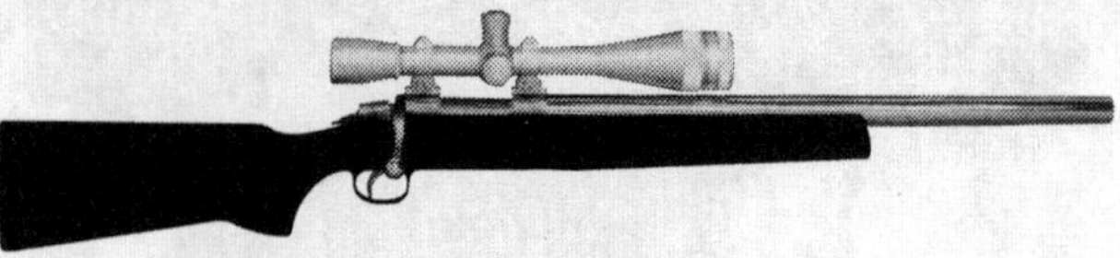

Custom built. Unable to price individual rifles.

Prone Rifles

Custom built. Unable to price individual rifles.

X-Course Rifles

Custom built. Unable to price individual rifles.

1,000 Yard Match Rifles

Custom built. Unable to price individual rifles.

Fully Accurized Production Rifles

These rifles are offered in standard blue or stainless steel with walnut or synthetic stock. Chambered from .223 to .338 Win. mag. and built on Remington, Ruger, or Winchester actions.

NIB	Exc.	V.G.	Good	Fair	Poor
1250	—	—	—	—	—

AROSTEGUI, EULOGIO
Eibar, Spain

Azul Royal (Model 31)

A semi-automatic or full automatic pistol in calibers 7.63 Mauser, 9mm Bergmann, or 38 ACP. Manufactured between 1935 and 1940. Fitted with a 10-round integral magazine.

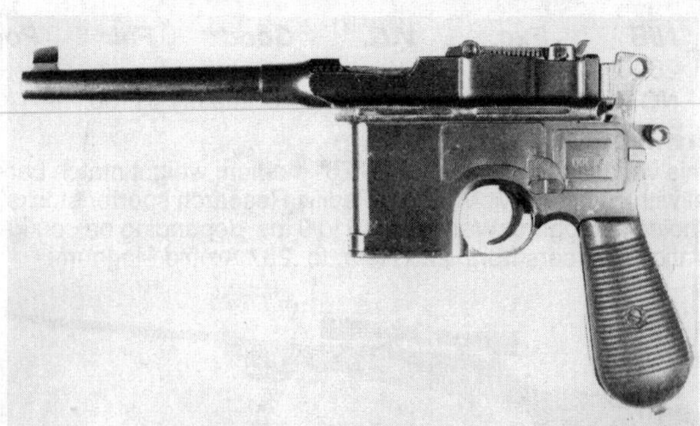

Courtesy James Rankin

Exc.	V.G.	Good	Fair	Poor
2200	1500	1000	500	300

NOTE: Add 200 percent for fully automatic machine pistol version.

Super Azul (M-34)

A semi-automatic or full automatic pistol in 7.63mm Mauser, 9mm Bergmann, and .38 ACP. Manufactured between 1935 and 1940. It has a removable box magazine with capacity of 10, 20, or 30 rounds. Also known as the War Model or the Standard Model.

Courtesy James Rankin

Exc.	V.G.	Good	Fair	Poor
2200	1500	1000	500	300

NOTE: Add 300 percent for fully automatic machine pistol version.

Azul 6.35mm

A 6.35mm semi-automatic pistol copied after the Model 1906 Browning. The frame is marked with the letters "EA" in a circle and a retriever is molded in the grips. Magazine capacity is 6 or 9 rounds.

Exc.	V.G.	Good	Fair	Poor
250	200	150	100	75

Azul 7.65mm

A 7.65mm semi-automatic pistol copied after the Model 1910 FN. Magazine capacity is 7 or 9 rounds.

Exc.	V.G.	Good	Fair	Poor
250	200	150	100	75

Velo-Dog

A folding trigger 5.5mm or 6.35mm revolver bearing the trademark "EA" on the grips.

Exc.	V.G.	Good	Fair	Poor
125	100	75	50	30

ARRIETA S.L.

Elgoibar, Spain

This company produces a wide variety of double-barrel shotguns in a price range from $450 to above $14,000. It is recommended that highly engraved examples, as well as small bore arms, be individually appraised.

490 Eder

A double-barrel boxlock shotgun with double triggers and extractors. Discontinued in 1986.

Exc.	V.G.	Good	Fair	Poor
475	425	325	250	100

500 Titan

A Holland & Holland-style sidelock double-barrel shotgun with French case hardened and engraved locks. Double triggers on extractors. No longer imported after 1986.

Exc.	V.G.	Good	Fair	Poor
575	500	400	300	150

501 Palomara

As above, but more finely finished. Discontinued in 1986.

Exc.	V.G.	Good	Fair	Poor
700	600	500	400	200

505 Alaska

As above, but more intricately engraved. Discontinued in 1986.

Exc.	V.G.	Good	Fair	Poor
800	700	600	500	250

510 Montana

A Holland & Holland-style sidelock double-barrel shotgun with the internal parts gold-plated.

NIB	Exc.	V.G.	Good	Fair	Poor
2200	1750	1250	850	500	250

550 Field

As above, without the internal parts gold-plated.

NIB	Exc.	V.G.	Good	Fair	Poor
2200	1750	1250	850	500	250

557 Standard

As above, but more finely finished.

NIB	Exc.	V.G.	Good	Fair	Poor
2750	2000	1750	1250	800	400

558 Patria

As above, but more finely finished.

NIB	Exc.	V.G.	Good	Fair	Poor
2650	2150	1750	1250	800	400

560 Cumbre

As above, but featuring intricate engraving.

NIB	Exc.	V.G.	Good	Fair	Poor
2800	2200	1800	1200	800	400

570 Lieja

NIB	Exc.	V.G.	Good	Fair	Poor
3400	2500	2000	1500	750	500

575 Sport

NIB	Exc.	V.G.	Good	Fair	Poor
3750	2750	2250	1700	1200	750

578 Victoria

This model is engraved in the English manner with floral bouquets.

NIB	Exc.	V.G.	Good	Fair	Poor
3500	2750	2000	1250	750	350

585 Liria

As above, but more finely finished.

NIB	Exc.	V.G.	Good	Fair	Poor
3800	3000	2250	1500	900	400

588 Cima

NIB	Exc.	V.G.	Good	Fair	Poor
3800	3000	2250	1500	900	400

590 Regina

NIB	Exc.	V.G.	Good	Fair	Poor
4250	3500	2700	1750	1000	500

595 Principe

As above, but engraved with relief-cut hunting scenes.

NIB	Exc.	V.G.	Good	Fair	Poor
6500	5000	4000	3000	2000	1000

600 Imperial

This double-barrel shotgun has a self-opening action.

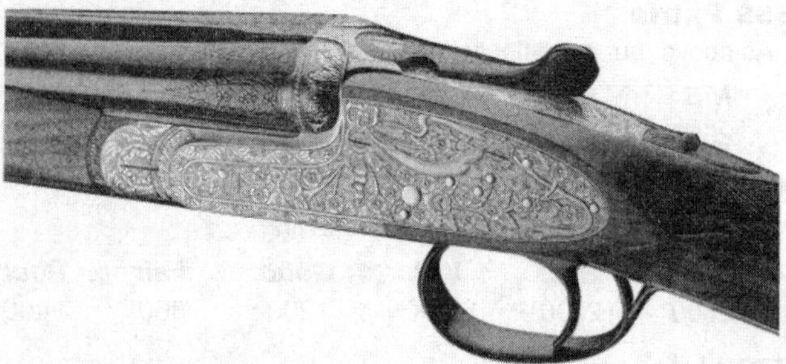

NIB	Exc.	V.G.	Good	Fair	Poor
5000	4250	3250	2000	1000	500

601 Imperial Tiro

As above, but nickel-plated. Fitted with a self-opening action.

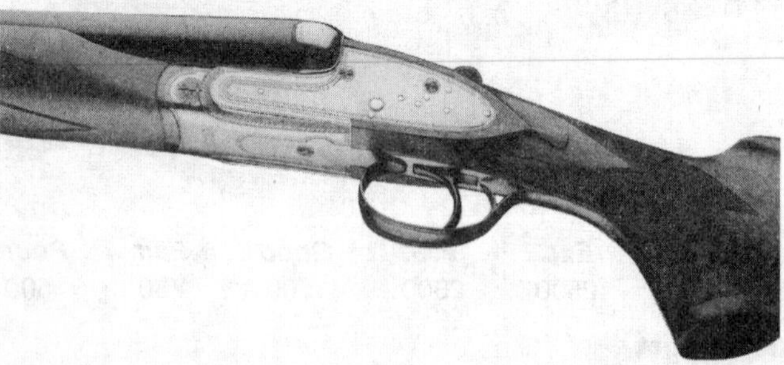

NIB	Exc.	V.G.	Good	Fair	Poor
5750	5000	4000	3000	2000	1000

801

A detachable sidelock, self-opening action, double-barrel shotgun engraved in the manner of Churchill.

NIB	Exc.	V.G.	Good	Fair	Poor
7950	7000	6500	4000	3000	1500

802

As above, with Holland & Holland-style engraving.

NIB	Exc.	V.G.	Good	Fair	Poor
7950	7000	6500	4000	3000	1500

803

As above, with Purdey-style engraving.

NIB	Exc.	V.G.	Good	Fair	Poor
5850	5000	4000	3000	2000	1000

871

This model features hand detachable sidelocks with Holland ejectors. Scroll engraving.

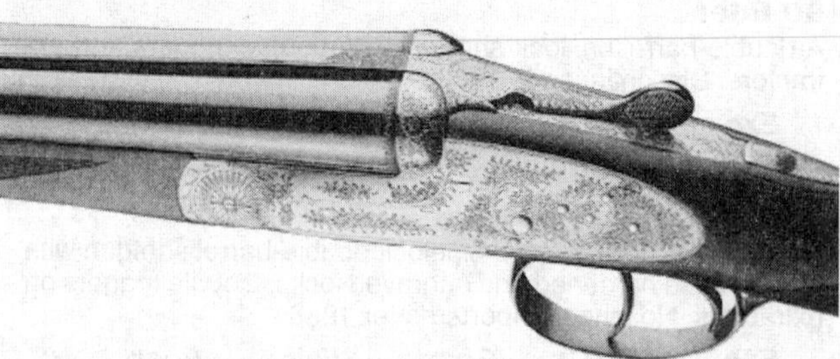

NIB	Exc.	V.G.	Good	Fair	Poor
4300	3600	2500	1500	1000	750

872

This model has same features as the Model 871 with the addition of more engraving coverage using a tighter scroll.

NIB	Exc.	V.G.	Good	Fair	Poor
9800	8250	7000	4000	3000	1000

873

This model features hand detachable sidelocks and game scene engraving.

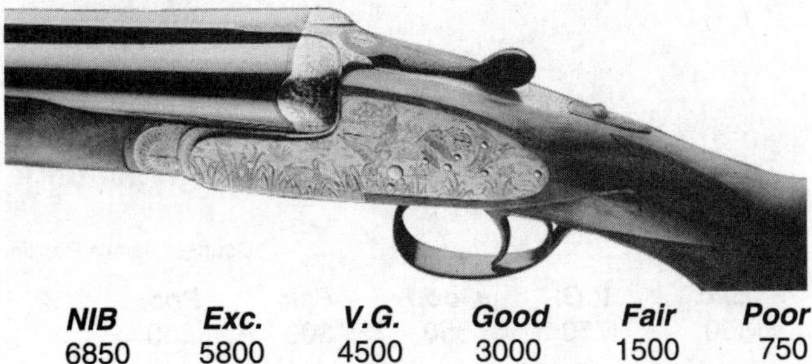

NIB	Exc.	V.G.	Good	Fair	Poor
6850	5800	4500	3000	1500	750

874

Same features as above model but with the addition of a blued frame with gold line outlines.

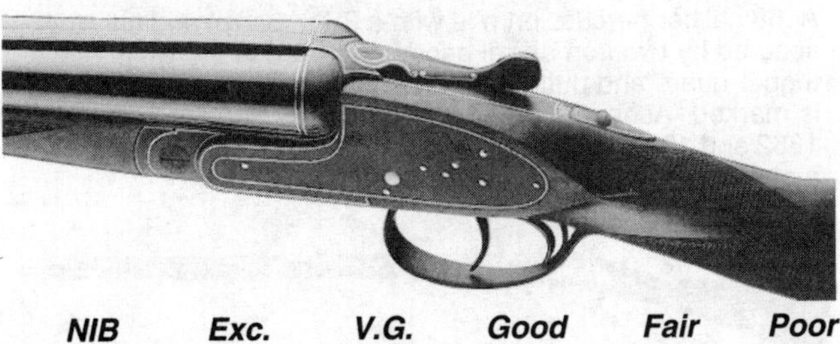

NIB	Exc.	V.G.	Good	Fair	Poor
8000	6750	5500	4500	3000	1000

875

A custom manufactured sidelock, double-barrel shotgun built solely to the customer's specifications.

NIB	Exc.	V.G.	Good	Fair	Poor
13000	10500	8500	6000	3000	1000

R-1 Double Rifle

NIB	Exc.	V.G.	Good	Fair	Poor
8950	7500	6000	4000	2000	1000

R-2 Double Rifle

NIB	Exc.	V.G.	Good	Fair	Poor
13000	10500	8500	6000	3000	1000

NOTE: Add 5 percent for gauges smaller than 16 gauge. Add 10 percent for matched pairs. There are a number of extra cost options that will affect the price of individual guns. Seek expert advice before a sale.

ARRIZABALAGA, HIJOS de C.

Eibar, Spain

Arrizabalaga

A 7.65mm semi-automatic pistol with a 9-shot magazine and a lanyard ring fitted to the butt. Checkered wood grips. ARRIZABALAGA on the slide.

Courtesy James Rankin

Exc.	V.G.	Good	Fair	Poor
275	175	125	75	50

Campeon

The Model 1919 6.35mm, 7.65mm, or 9mm Kurtz semi-automatic pistol with the slide marked "Campeon Patent 1919" and the plastic grips "Campeon." Supplied with 6- or 8-round magazines. CAMPEON appears on the slide.

Courtesy James Rankin

Exc.	V.G.	Good	Fair	Poor
275	175	125	75	50

NOTE: Add 25 percent for 9mm Kurtz.

Jo Lo Ar

The Model 1924 semi-automatic pistol with a tip-up barrel, cocking lever, and no trigger guard. The Jo Lo Ar was built in six calibers: 6.35mm, 7.65mm, 9mm Kurtz, 9mm Largo, and .45 ACP. Jo-Lo-Ar appears on the slide and the grips. Premium for larger calibers. Add 400 percent for .45.

Courtesy James Rankin

Exc.	V.G.	Good	Fair	Poor
1000	725	425	250	100

Sharpshooter

A 6.35mm, 7.65mm or 9mm Corto (short) semi-automatic pistol fitted with a cocking lever. The barrel tips up for cleaning or when using the pistol as a single-shot. SHARPSHOOTER appears on the slide.

Courtesy James Rankin

Exc.	V.G.	Good	Fair	Poor
400	300	225	150	100

ARSENAL, INC.

Las Vegas, Nevada

SA M-7

Semi-automatic rifles manufactured in U.S. similar to the AK-47 in appearance. Chambered for the 7.62x39 cartridge and fitted with a 16" barrel. Black polymer stock.

NIB	Exc.	V.G.	Good	Fair	Poor
750	600	—	—	—	—

SA M-7 Classic

As above but with blonde wood stock.

NIB	Exc.	V.G.	Good	Fair	Poor
875	700	—	—	—	—

SA M-7S

Similar to the SA M-7 but with scope rail added.

NIB	Exc.	V.G.	Good	Fair	Poor
825	650	—	—	—	—

SA RPK-7

Chambered for the 7.62x39 cartridge this rifle is similar to the RPK. Fitted with a 23" barrel with bipod. Solid blonde wood stock with trap in stock for cleaning kit.

NIB	Exc.	V.G.	Good	Fair	Poor
975	800	—	—	—	—

ASCASO

Cataluna, Spain

Spanish Rebublican Government

A copy of the Astra Model 400 chambered for the 9mm Largo cartridge. The barrel marked "F. Ascaso Tarrassa" in an oval. Built by the Spanish government during the Spanish Civil War. Very few were made during the Spanish Civil War.

Courtesy James Rankin

Exc.	V.G.	Good	Fair	Poor
850	750	550	300	200

ASHEVILLE ARMORY

Asheville, North Carolina

Enfield Type Rifle

A .58 caliber percussion rifle with a 32.5" barrel and full stock secured by two iron barrel bands. Finished in the white brass trigger guard and buttplate with a walnut stock. The lockplate is marked "Asheville, N.C." Approximately 300 were made in 1862 and 1863. Prospective purchasers are advised to secure a qualified appraisal prior to acquisition.

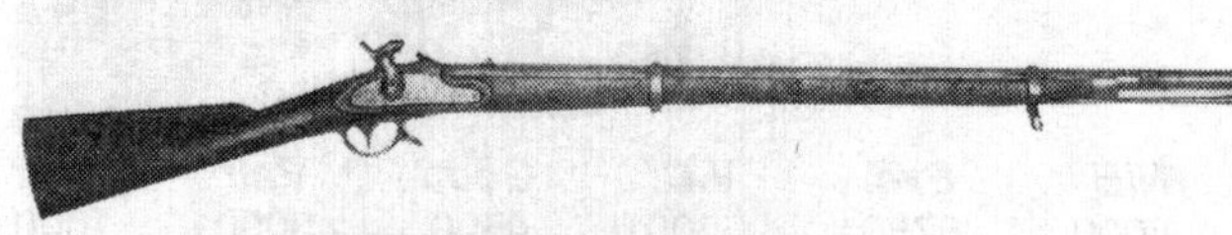

Courtesy Milwaukee Public Museum, Milwaukee, Wisconsin

Exc.	V.G.	Good	Fair	Poor
—	—	40000	17500	5000

ASHTON, PETER & WILLIAM

Middletown, Connecticut

Ashton Under Hammer Pistol

A .28 to .38 caliber single-shot percussion revolver with 4" or 5" half-octagonal barrels marked "P.H. Ashton" or "W. Ashton." Blued or browned with walnut grips. Active 1850s.

Exc.	V.G.	Good	Fair	Poor
—	—	1000	400	150

ASTON, H./H. ASTON & CO. PISTOLS

Middleton, Connecticut

Overall length 14"; barrel length 8-1/2"; caliber .54. Markings: on lockplate, forward of hammer "U S/H. ASTON" or "U S/H. ASTON & CO.," on tail "MIDDTN/CONN/(date)"; on barrel, standard government inspection marks. Henry Aston of Middleton, Connecticut received a contract from the U.S. War Department in February 1845 for 30,000 single-shot percussion pistols. These were delivered between 1846 and 1852, after which Ira N. Johnston continued production under a separate contract. Three thousand of these pistols were purchased for Navy usage and many of these were subsequently marked with a small anchor on the barrel near the breech. These Navy purchases will command a slight premium.

Courtesy Milwaukee Public Museum, Milwaukee, Wisconsin

Exc.	V.G.	Good	Fair	Poor
—	—	4500	1750	500

ASTRA-UNCETA SA
Guernica, Spain

Astra is a brand name placed on guns built by Esperanza y Unceta and then Unceta y Cia. This Spanish company has now incorporated its trade name into its corporate name and is now know as Astra-Unceta SA. The firm under the direction of Don Pedron Unceta and Don Juan Esperanza began business in Eibar on July 17, 1908 and moved to Guernica in 1913. The Astra trademark was adopted on November 25, 1914. Esperanza began production of the Spanish Army's Campo Giro pistol in 1913. The Model 1921 was marketed commercially as the Astra 400. After the Spanish Civil War Unceta was one of only four handgun companies permitted to resume manufacturing operations. An interesting and informative side note is that pistols with 1000 to 5000 model numbers were made after 1945.

Victoria

A 6.36mm semi-automatic pistol with a 2.5" barrel. Blued with black plastic grips. Manufactured prior to 1913.

Exc.	V.G.	Good	Fair	Poor
350	250	200	150	100

Astra 1911

A 6.35mm and 7.65mm semi-automatic pistol. External hammer and checkered hard rubber grips. The 7.65mm model was manufactured before the 6.35mm model.

Courtesy James Rankin

Exc.	V.G.	Good	Fair	Poor
350	250	175	100	75

Astra 1924

A 6.35mm semi-automatic pistol with a 2.5" barrel. The slide marked "Esperanza y Unceta Guernica Spain Astra Cal 6.35 .25." Blued with black plastic grips.

Exc.	V.G.	Good	Fair	Poor
300	200	125	100	75

Astra 100

A semi-automatic pistol in caliber 7.65mm. Checkered hard rubber grips. Magazine capacity is 12 rounds. Introduced after WWII.

Courtesy James Rankin

Exc.	V.G.	Good	Fair	Poor
550	400	300	200	100

REMINDER

An "N/A" or "—" instead of a price indicates that there is no known price available for that gun in that condition, or the sales for that particular model are so few that a reliable price cannot be given.

Astra 200

A 6.35mm semi-automatic pistol with a 2.5" barrel and 6-shot magazine fitted with a grip safety. Also known as the "Firecat" in the United States. Manufactured from 1920 to 1966.

Courtesy James Rankin

Exc.	V.G.	Good	Fair	Poor
300	200	125	100	75

Astra 400 or Model 1921

A 9x23 Bergman caliber semi-automatic pistol with a 6" barrel. Blued with black plastic grips. This model was adopted for use by the Spanish Army. Approximately 106,000 were made prior to 1946. Recent importation has depressed the price of these guns. Any with Nazi proofs marks are worth a 100 percent premium, but caution is advised.

Exc.	V.G.	Good	Fair	Poor
395	325	150	75	40

Astra 300

As above, in 7.65mm or 9mm short. Those used during World War II by German forces bear Waffenamt marks. Approximately 171,000 were manufactured prior to 1947.

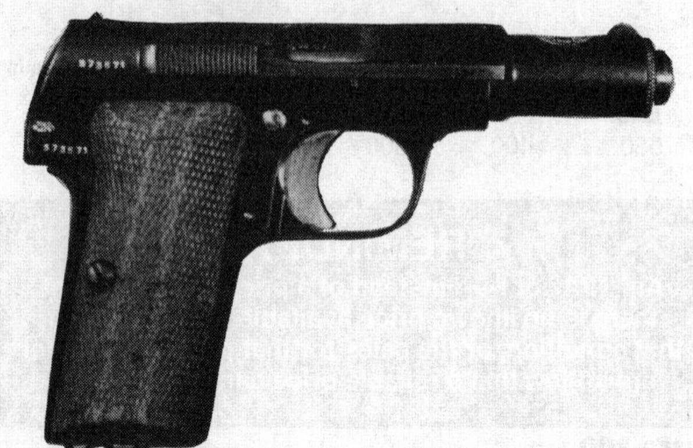

Courtesy Orvel Reichert

Exc.	V.G.	Good	Fair	Poor
400	350	250	150	100

NOTE: Nazi-proofed add 25 percent.

Astra 600

Similar to the Model 400, but in 9mm Parabellum. In 1943 and 1944 approximately 10,500 were manufactured. Some of these World War II guns will have Nazi proof stamp and bring a premium. A further 49,000 were made in 1946 and commercially sold.

Exc.	V.G.	Good	Fair	Poor
525	325	275	175	100

Astra 700

A single-action semi-automatic pistol in caliber 7.65mm. Magazine capacity is 9 rounds. Introduced in 1926.

Courtesy James Rankin

Exc.	V.G.	Good	Fair	Poor
400	300	200	150	100

Astra 800

Similar to the Model 600 with an external hammer and loaded chamber indicator. Blued with plastic grips having the tradename "Condor" cast in them. Approximately 11,400 were made from 1958 to 1969.

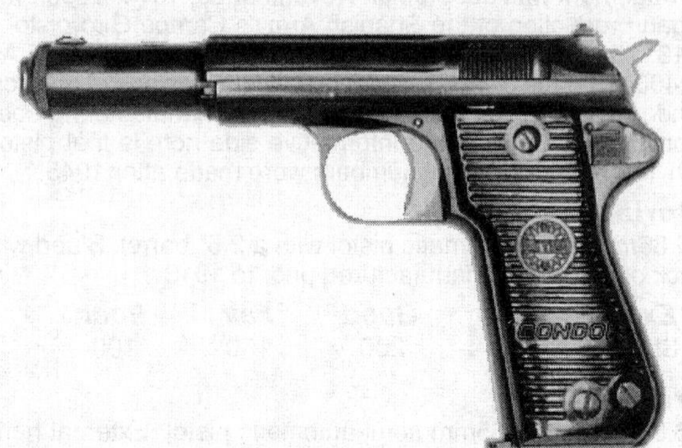

Exc.	V.G.	Good	Fair	Poor
1500	1200	850	500	300

Astra 900

A modified copy of the Mauser Model C96 semi-automatic pistol. Blued with walnut grips. Early examples with a small Bolo grip marked "Hope" on the chamber will bring a 20 percent premium. Serial numbers 32,788 through 33,774 were used by the German Army in WWII and bring a 50 percent premium. Add 50 percent for matching Astra-made stock.

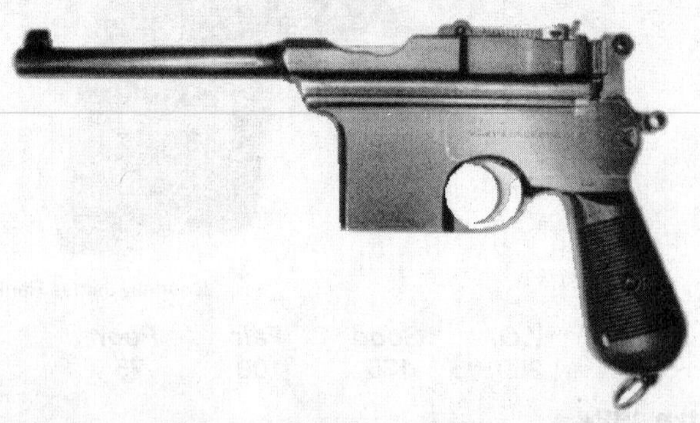

Exc.	V.G.	Good	Fair	Poor
2250	1750	1000	600	300

Astra 1000

A single-action semi-automatic pistol in caliber 7.65mm. Magazine capacity is 12 rounds. Introduced after WWII.

Courtesy James Rankin

Exc.	V.G.	Good	Fair	Poor
550	400	300	200	100

Astra 2000

As above, in .22 or 6.35mm caliber without a grip safety and with an external hammer. Blued with plastic grips.

Exc.	V.G.	Good	Fair	Poor
550	450	295	150	90

Astra 3000

The Model 300 in 7.65mm or 9mm short with a 6- or 7-shot magazine and loaded chamber indicator. Manufactured from 1948 to 1956.

Paul Goodwin photo

Exc.	V.G.	Good	Fair	Poor
575	475	325	200	100

Astra 4000

A semi-automatic pistol that was known later as the Falcon. Calibers were .22 LR, 7.65mm, and 9mmK with magazine capacity of 10, 8, and 7 rounds. Manufactured beginning 1955.

Courtesy James Rankin

Exc.	V.G.	Good	Fair	Poor
575	475	325	200	100

Astra 5000

A .22, 7.65mm or 9mm short semi-automatic pistol (resembling a Walther PP Pistol) with a 3.5" barrel. Blued, chrome-plated or stainless steel with plastic grips. Also available with a 6" barrel as a sport model. Introduced in 1965.

Exc.	V.G.	Good	Fair	Poor
575	475	325	200	100

Astra 7000

An enlarged version of the Model 2000 in .22 caliber.

Exc.	V.G.	Good	Fair	Poor
575	475	325	200	100

Astra A-80

A .38 Super, 9mm or .45 caliber double-action semi-automatic pistol with a 3.75" barrel and either a 9- or 15-shot magazine depending upon the caliber. Blued or chrome-plated with plastic grips. Introduced in 1982.

Courtesy James Rankin

NIB	Exc.	V.G.	Good	Fair	Poor
450	350	300	250	200	100

Astra A-90

As above, in 9mm or .45 caliber only. Introduced in 1986.

NIB	*Exc.*	*V.G.*	*Good*	*Fair*	*Poor*
400	350	300	250	200	100

Astra Cadix

A .22 or .38 Special double-action swing-out cylinder revolver with a 4" or 6" barrel and either 9- or 5-shot cylinder. Blued with plastic grips. Manufactured from 1960 to 1968.

Exc.	*V.G.*	*Good*	*Fair*	*Poor*
200	150	125	90	70

Constable A-60

A .380 caliber double-action semi-automatic pistol with a 3.5" barrel, adjustable sights and 13-shot magazine. Blued with plastic grips. Introduced in 1986.

NIB	*Exc.*	*V.G.*	*Good*	*Fair*	*Poor*
400	300	200	150	100	75

.357 Double-Action Revolver

As above, in .357 Magnum caliber with a 3", 4", 6", or 8.5" barrel, adjustable sights and 6-shot cylinder. Blued or stainless steel with walnut grips. Manufactured from 1972 to 1988.

NIB	*Exc.*	*V.G.*	*Good*	*Fair*	*Poor*
250	200	150	125	100	75

NOTE: Stainless steel add 10 percent.

.44/.45 Double-Action Revolver

As above, in .41 Magnum, .44 Magnum or.45 ACP caliber with 6" or 8.5" barrels and a 6-shot cylinder. Blued or stainless steel with walnut grips. Manufactured from 1980 to 1987.

Exc.	*V.G.*	*Good*	*Fair*	*Poor*
350	300	250	200	100

NOTE: Stainless steel add 25 percent.

Terminator

As above, in .44 Special or .44 Magnum with a 2.75" barrel, adjustable sights and 6-shot cylinder. Blued or stainless steel with rubber grips.

Exc.	*V.G.*	*Good*	*Fair*	*Poor*
350	300	250	200	100

NOTE: Stainless steel add 10 percent.

Convertible Revolver

Similar to the .357 D/A revolver but accompanied by a cylinder chambered for 9mm cartridges. Barrel length 3". Blued with walnut grips. Introduced in 1986.

Exc.	*V.G.*	*Good*	*Fair*	*Poor*
300	250	200	150	100

CURRENTLY IMPORTED PISTOLS

Hialeah, Florida

Model A-100

This semi-automatic service pistol is chambered for the 9mm Parabellum, .40 S&W, or .45 ACP cartridges. The trigger action is double-action for the first shot, single-action for follow-up shots. Equipped with a decocking lever. The barrel is 3.8" long and the overall length is 7.5". Magazine capacity for the 9mm is 17 rounds, .40 S&W is 13 rounds, while the .45 holds 9 rounds. A blue or nickel finish is standard. Weight is approximately 34 oz. Also available in a featherweight model 9mm only at 26.5 oz.

NIB	*Exc.*	*V.G.*	*Good*	*Fair*	*Poor*
400	350	300	250	200	100

NOTE: Add $35 for nickel finish.

Model A-100 Carry Comp

Similar to the Model A-100 but fitted with a 4.25" barrel and 1" compensator. Blue finish only. Weight is approximately 38 oz. Magazine capacity for 9mm is 17 rounds and for the .40 S&W and .45 ACP 10 rounds.

NIB	*Exc.*	*V.G.*	*Good*	*Fair*	*Poor*
475	375	—	—	—	—

This symbol denotes "Sleepers" with rapidly-rising values and/or significant collector potential.

Model A-70

This is a lightweight semi-automatic pistol chambered for the 9mm cartridge or .40 S&W cartridge. It is fitted with 3-dot combat sights. The barrel is 3.5" long and the magazine capacity is 8 rounds for 9mm and 7 rounds for the .40 S&W. Black plastic grips and blue finish are standard. Weight is 29 oz.

NIB	Exc.	V.G.	Good	Fair	Poor
350	275	225	175	150	100

NOTE: Add $35 for nickel finish.

Model A-75

Introduced in 1993 this model features all of the standard features of the Model 70 plus selective double or single trigger action and decocking lever. Chambered for 9mm, .40 S&W, or .45 ACP. Offered in blue or nickel finish and steel or alloy frame in 9mm only. Weight for steel frame in 9mm and .40 S&W is 31 oz., for .45 ACP weight is 34.4 oz. Featherweight 9mm weight is 23.5 oz.

NIB	Exc.	V.G.	Good	Fair	Poor
375	325	250	200	150	100

NOTE: Add $35 for nickel finish.

ATCSA

Armas de Tiro y Casa
Eibar, Spain

Colt Police Positive Copy

A .38 caliber 6-shot revolver resembling a Colt Police Positive.

Exc.	V.G.	Good	Fair	Poor
250	125	100	60	40

Target Pistol

A .22 caliber single-shot target pistol utilizing a revolver frame.

Exc.	V.G.	Good	Fair	Poor
300	175	125	100	55

ATKIN, HENRY

London, England
SEE—British Double Guns

AUBREY, A.J.

Meriden, Connecticut

Double-Barrel Shotguns

Good quality doubles made for Sears. Value depends on condition, grade, and model. Price range between $100 and $1,500. Seek an expert appraisal prior to sale.

AUER, B.

Louisville, Kentucky

Auer Pocket Pistol

A .60 caliber percussion pocket pistol with a 4" octagonal barrel and a long tang extending well back along the grip. Browned, silver furniture and a checkered walnut stock. The lock is marked "B. Auer." Produced during the 1850s.

Exc.	V.G.	Good	Fair	Poor
—	—	1500	600	250

AUGUSTA MACHINE WORKS

Augusta, Georgia

1851 Colt Navy Copy

A .36 caliber percussion revolver with an 8" barrel and 6-shot cylinder. Unmarked except for serial numbers with either 6 or 12 stop cylinder slots. Blued with walnut grips. This is a very rare revolver.

Exc.	V.G.	Good	Fair	Poor
—	—	40000	17500	5000

AUSTIN & HALLECK, INC.

Weston, Missouri; later Provo, Utah

Model 320 LR BLU

An in-line percussion, bolt-action rifle fitted with a 26" half octagon-half round barrel in .50 caliber. Receiver and barrel are blue. Adjustable trigger and receiver drilled and tapped for scope mount. Stock is black synthetic with checkering. Weight is about 7.87 lbs.

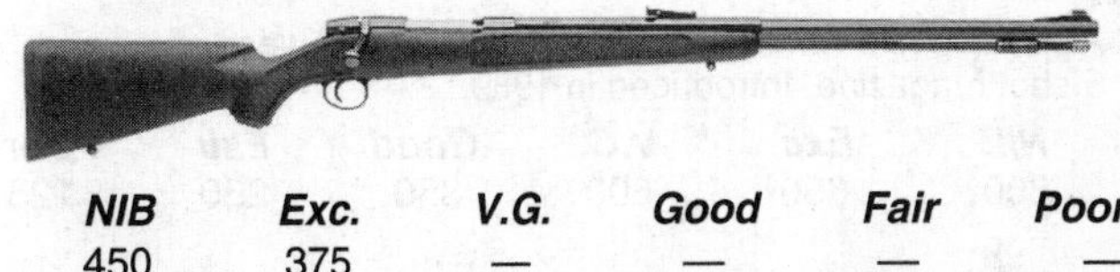

NIB	Exc.	V.G.	Good	Fair	Poor
450	375	—	—	—	—

Model 320 S/S

Similar to the above model but fitted with stainless steel barrel and action.

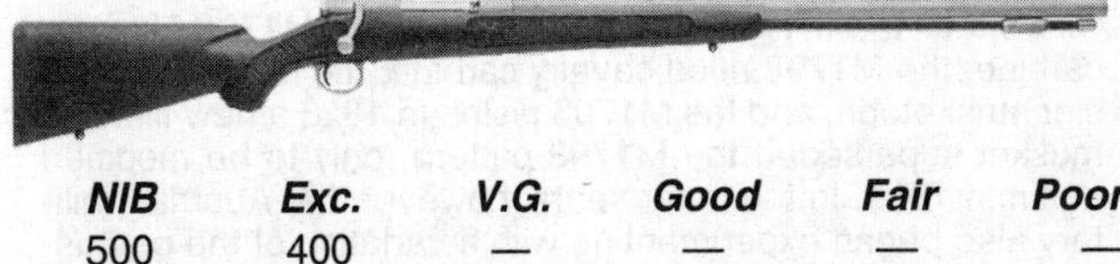

NIB	Exc.	V.G.	Good	Fair	Poor
500	400	—	—	—	—

Model 420 LR Classic

Similar to the Model 320 series but fitted with a standard lightly figured Maple stock in classic configuration. Available in blue or stainless steel. Premium for fancy wood.

NIB	Exc.	V.G.	Good	Fair	Poor
500	425	—	—	—	—

Model 420 LR Monte Carlo

Same as classic series but with Monte Carlo stock and cheekpiece. Premium for fancy wood.

Hand-select wood

NIB	Exc.	V.G.	Good	Fair	Poor
500	425	—	—	—	—

Mountain Rifle

This is a .50 caliber percussion or flintlock rifle with double-set triggers, 32" octagonal barrel, buckhorn sights, curly Maple stock and crescent steel buttplate. Weight is approximately 7.5 lbs. Premium for fancy wood.

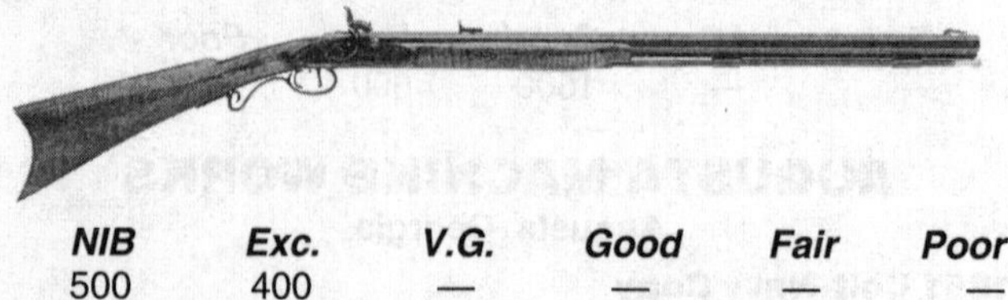

NIB	Exc.	V.G.	Good	Fair	Poor
500	400	—	—	—	—

AUSTRALIAN AUTOMATIC ARMS LTD.

Tasmania, Australia

SAR

A 5.56mm semi-automatic rifle with a 16.25" or 20" barrel, 5-shot or 20-shot magazine, black plastic stock and forend. Imported from 1986 to 1989.

NIB	Exc.	V.G.	Good	Fair	Poor
1000	800	500	350	250	125

SAP

A 10.5" barreled pistol version of the above. Imported from 1986 to 1989.

NIB	Exc.	V.G.	Good	Fair	Poor
1000	800	500	350	250	125

SP

A sporting rifle version of the SAR, fitted with a wood stock and 5-shot magazine. Introduced in 1989.

NIB	Exc.	V.G.	Good	Fair	Poor
800	650	500	350	250	125

AUSTRIAN MILITARY FIREARMS

The end of the Napoleonic Wars found the army of the Austria Hungarian Empire armed with a variety of flintlock firearms. The foot troops carried either the M1798 or the M1807 musket or the M1807 yager rifle. The mounted forces were armed with either the M1798 dragoon carbine, the M1798 Hussar-carbine, the M1798 rifled cavalry carbine, the M1781 Cuirassier musketoon, and the M1798 pistol. In 1828 a new flintlock musket superseded the M1798 pattern, only to be modified again in 1835. In the latter years, however, the Austrian military also began experimenting with a variation of the percussion system invented by Giuseppe Console, utilizing a small elongated copper cylinder filled with fulminate. In 1840, the flintlock muskets adopted in 1835 were adapted to a variation of this percussion system as modified by Baron von Augustin. This system was made army-wide in 1842 with the adoption of a new musket and yager rifle with locks specifically manufactured for the Augustin tubelocks. In 1849, a new rifle replaced the M1842 pattern; both of these rifles were based on the Devilgne chambered breech. In 1850, a cavalry carbine and a horse pistol were added to the tubelock series. All of these arms were either .69 or .71 caliber. The tubelock, however, was short-lived; in 1854, Austria abandoned the tubelock system in favor of standard percussion cap then widely used by the armies of Europe. At the same time it adopted a new smaller caliber (.54) which it applied to the new M1854 rifle-musket and the M1855 yager rifle. A horse pistol based on the same system (Lorenz's compressed, elongated ball) was adopted in 1859.

Large numbers of the Austrian longarms were imported to the United States in the first two years of the American Civil War. Beginning in 1863, the Confederate States also imported large numbers of the M1854 series rifle-muskets. Most of the tubelocks first being modified to standard percussion in Belgium before importation, arms of prime interest to American collectors, accordingly demand higher prices.

In 1867, the Austria-Hungarian Empire adopted two different breechloading mechanisms and the self-contained metallic cartridge. Those muzzleloading arms deemed acceptable for alteration (the M1854 series of rifle-muskets and rifles) were adapted to the Wanzel system. Newly made arms (the M1867 rifle) were made in conformity with Werndl's breechloading design.

During the period within the scope of this catalog, Austrian arms were generally made on contract with the major gun makers in and near Vienna ("Wien" in Austrian). These makers usually marked their products with their name upon the barrel of the arm, near the breech. The major makers included BENTZ, FERD. FRUWIRTH (who also simply marked his arms "F. F."), CARL HEISER, JOSEF JESCHER, ANNA OSTERLIEN, PIRKO, TH. ROTTME, G. SCHLAGER, TH. SEDERE, F. UMFAURER, WANZEL, and ZEILINGER (with the "Z" usually backwards). Lockplates were marked with the government ownership mark (a small double-headed eagle) and the date of manufacture (deleting the number "1" from the year, such as "847" for "1847.") Since the arms were not interchangeable, mating numbers are usually found on all the metal parts.

Austrian Musket, M1828

Overall length 57-3/4"; barrel length 42-1/2"; caliber .69. Basically following the pattern of the French M1822 musket, this arm still accepted the quadrangular M1799 bayonet, distinguished by having a solid socket with a hook ring at its rear, like the Prussian bayonet for the M1808 musket.

Exc.	V.G.	Good	Fair	Poor
—	—	2000	950	400

Austrian Musket, M1835

Overall length 57-3/4"; barrel length 42-1/2"; caliber .69. The M1835 musket follows the pattern of the Austrian M1807 musket, but is adapted for the Consule tubelock percussion system, which essentially replaced the frizzen and pan with a hinged tube retainer. This arm still uses the M1799 quadrangular bayonet.

Exc.	V.G.	Good	Fair	Poor
—	—	2500	1100	450

Austrian Musket, M1840

Overall length 57-3/4"; barrel length 42-1/2"; caliber .69. The M1840 musket was manufactured in flint. Its primary differences from the M1828 musket lie in its furniture (mainly the front band) and the bayonet attachment, which consists of a lug beneath the barrel and an elongated hook projecting from the forend of the stock to accept the new M1840 quadrangular bayonet. The bayonet is distinguished by having a straight slot in its socket, closed by a bridge.

Exc.	V.G.	Good	Fair	Poor
—	—	2500	1100	450

Austrian Musket, M1842

Overall length 57-3/4"; barrel length 42-1/2"; caliber .69 (.71). The M1842 musket was manufactured in Augustin tubelock. Its main distinction from the M1840 flintlock musket is the lock, which in addition to having the integral hinged tubelock mechanism in lieu of the frizzen, has a distinctly rounded rear tail. Although 25,000 of these muskets were imported into the United States for use by Fremont's forces in Missouri in 1861, many were subsequently altered to percussion. The Cincinnati contractors, Hall, Carroll & Co. or Greenwood & Co. accounted for 10,000 of these arms, all of which were altered to percussion by means of the cone-in-barrel system. These were also rifled and a portion of them sighted with a long range rear sight similar to the Enfield P1853 rifle-musket. Many of the balance were subsequently sent to the Frankfort Arsenal in Philadelphia, where they were subcontracted to Henry Leman of Lancaster for alteration to standard percussion. Those altered by Leman are distinguished by having a new breechpiece with integral bolster, the latter with a cleanout screw through its face. In addition to the 25,000 imported for Fremont, the firm of H. Boker & Co. of New York imported approximately 8,000 Austrian M1842 muskets which it had altered to percussion in Belgium. The French method of adding a reinforced bolster to the top right-hand side of the barrel was used. Many of those were also rifled and sighted in the manner of the French adaptations fashionable in Europe. George Heydecker of New York City imported another 4,000 in 1863 that were seized in transit to Canada, reputedly for delivery to Mexican republican forces.

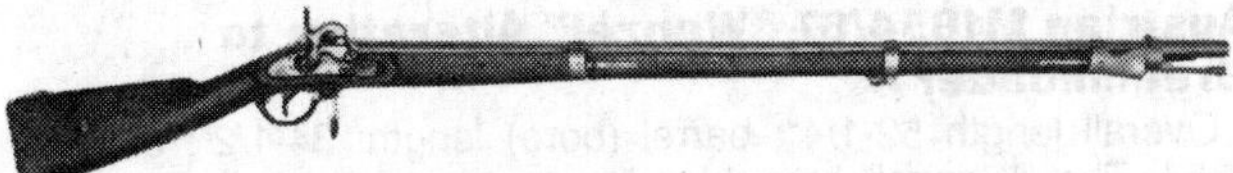

Courtesy Milwaukee Public Museum, Milwaukee, Wisconsin

In original tubelock

Exc.	V.G.	Good	Fair	Poor
—	—	3500	1500	600

Altered to percussion (Cincinnati contractors)

Exc.	V.G.	Good	Fair	Poor
—	—	1500	600	250

Altered to percussion (Leman)

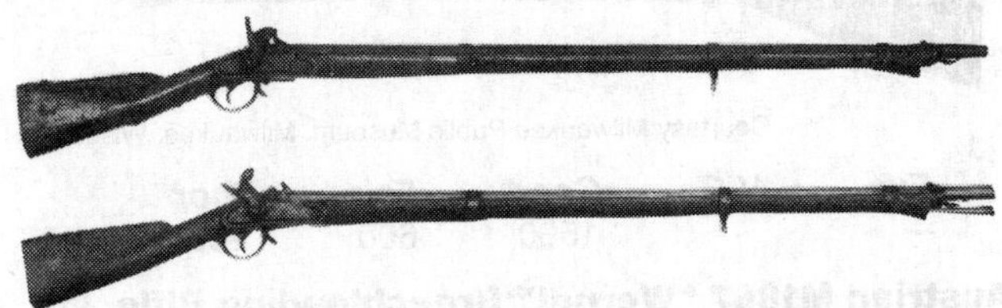

Courtesy Milwaukee Public Museum, Milwaukee, Wisconsin

Exc.	V.G.	Good	Fair	Poor
—	—	1500	600	250

Altered to percussion and rifled (Boker)

Exc.	V.G.	Good	Fair	Poor
—	—	1500	600	250

Austrian M1844 "Extra Corps" Musketoon

Overall length 48-3/8"; barrel length 33-1/2"; caliber .69 (.71). Is essentially a shortened version of the Austrian M1842 musket. In original Augustin tubelock, it is virtually unknown. Most of the production is thought to have been purchased by arms speculators at the beginning of the American Civil War and altered to standard percussion in Liege, Belgium. The Belgian alteration followed the second pattern adopted by that government to alter arms to percussion and consisted of brazing a "lump" of metal to the upper right-hand side of the barrel, into which a cone was threaded. The arms so altered were also rifled and sighted. The sights either copied the Austrian M1854 rifle-musket folding sight or the French "ladder" rear sight using the pattern utilized on the M1829 rifled cavalry musketoon. Over 10,000 of these arms were imported into the United States in 1861-1862 by Herman Boker & Co. of New York City.

Courtesy Milwaukee Public Museum, Milwaukee, Wisconsin

Courtesy Milwaukee Public Museum, Milwaukee, Wisconsin

Altered to percussion and rifled (Boker)

Exc.	V.G.	Good	Fair	Poor
—		2000	950	350

Austrian M1842 Yager Rifle

Overall length 48-1/4"; barrel length 33-1/4"; caliber .69/.71. The Austrian M1842 yager rifle ("Kammer Busche") was originally manufactured in tubelock for the rifle battalions of the Austrian Army. Its bore terminated in a Delvigne breech, i.e. a chamber of lesser diameter than the caliber whose lip served as a base for disfiguring the projectile to fill the rifling. Made obsolete by the Thouvenin and Minie systems, many M1842 yager rifles were altered in 1860 in Belgium to standard percussion and sold to the Italian revolutionaries led by Giuseppe Garibaldi, giving the gun that nickname. Two methods of alteration were applied. One, the "Belgian" system, brazed a "lump" of iron to the upper right surface of the breech, which was tapped for a standard percussion cone. The other, the "Prussian," involved fitting the breech with a new barrel section incorporating a new bolster. At least 500 of these altered arms were imported into the United States during the American Civil War, where they (and the M1849 yager rifles similarly altered) were called "Garibaldi Rifles."

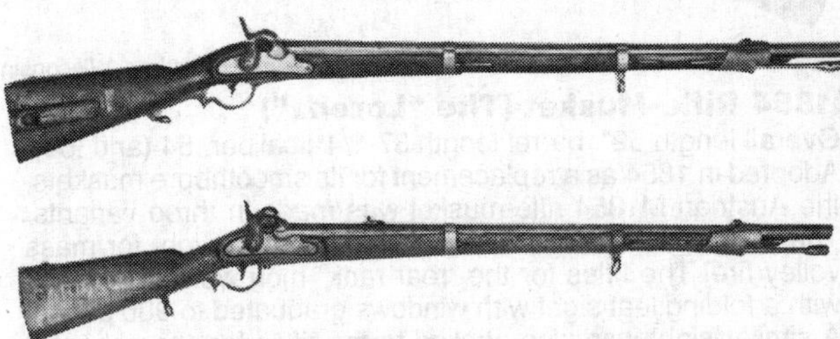

Courtesy Milwaukee Public Museum, Milwaukee, Wisconsin

Exc.	V.G.	Good	Fair	Poor
—	—	2500	1100	350

Austrian M1849 Yager Rifle

Overall length 48"; barrel length 33-1/4"; caliber .71. The successor to the M1842 Austrian "Kammer Busche," the M1849 model is distinguished by having its barrel wedge fastened rather than retained by bands. Both the M1842 and the M1849 yager rifles were adapted to socket bayonets having long straight knife blades; both socket types were slotted. That of the M1842 was secured to the barrel by the same method as the M1842 Austrian musket; that of the M1849, however, locked onto a lug on the right side of the barrel and was secured by a rotating ring on the back of the socket. Adapted to standard percussion in the same manner as the M1842 yager rifles, more than 25,000 were sold to the U.S. War Department in 1862 and 1863.

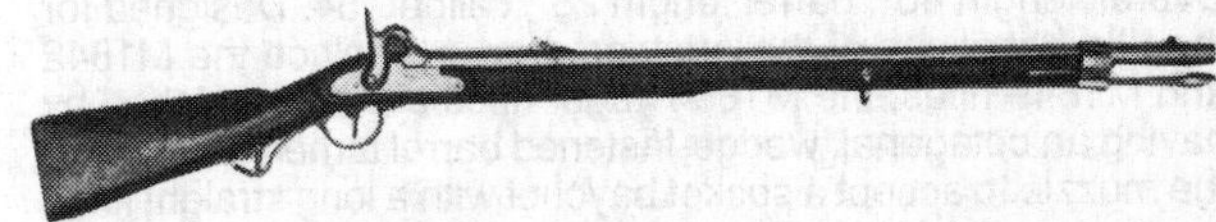

Courtesy Milwaukee Public Museum, Milwaukee, Wisconsin

Austrian M1850 Horse Pistol

Overall length 16"; barrel length 8-7/8"; caliber .69. A bulky brass mounted pistol with lanyard ring, this arm was made originally in tubelock. However, a small quantity appear to have been altered to standard percussion locks in Liege, Belgium. In the process the double-strapped front bands of the original were removed and the forestock cut away to adapt the stock to an iron ramrod. (In Austrian service the ramrod was hung from the crossbelt of the mounted trooper.) Quantities imported into the United States are uncertain but may have been included among the 346 foreign horse pistols purchased by the U.S. War Department from P.S. Justice in 1861.

Exc.	V.G.	Good	Fair	Poor
		1500	600	250

Austrian M1850 Carbine

Overall length 30"; barrel length 14-1/2"; caliber .71. Originally manufactured in tubelock for Austrian cavalry service, this large caliber, short-barreled rifled carbine (12-groove rifling) saw service in the United States when 10,000 were purchased by U.S. purchasing agent George Schuyler in 1861. Those purchased for U.S. service, however, had been altered in Liege, Belgium for standard percussion locks in the same manner that the Austrian M1842 and M1849 yager rifles had been altered.

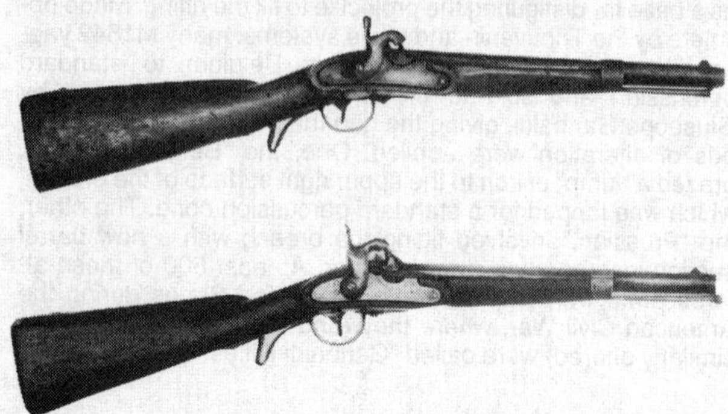

Courtesy Milwaukee Public Museum, Milwaukee, Wisconsin

Exc.	V.G.	Good	Fair	Poor
—	—	3000	1250	450

M1854 Rifle-Musket (The "Lorenz")

Overall length 52"; barrel length 37-1/4"; caliber .54 (and .58). Adopted in 1854 as a replacement for its smoothbore muskets, the Austrian M1854 rifle-musket was made in three variants. The standard infantry arm had a simple block sight for mass volley fire. The rifles for the "rear rank" men were similar but with a folding leaf sight with windows graduated to 900 paces. A similar sight was also applied to the rifles for sharpshooter battalions, which also had a cheekpiece built into the buttstock. The quadrangular socket bayonet locked onto the front sight, whose sides were angled to accept the diagonal slot in the bayonet's socket. The Austrian M1854 rifle-musket was the second most prolifically imported arm during the American Civil War, with some 89,000 being imported into the Confederacy and more than 175,000 into the Union. Thousands of the latter were bored up to .58 caliber before being imported.

Courtesy Milwaukee Public Museum, Milwaukee, Wisconsin

Exc.	V.G.	Good	Fair	Poor
—	—	2000	900	350

M1854 Yager Rifle

Overall length 43"; barrel length 28"; caliber .54. Designed for the rifle battalions of the Austrian army to replace the M1842 and M1849 rifles, the M1854 yager rifles are distinguished by having an octagonal, wedge-fastened barrel turned round near the muzzle to accept a socket bayonet with a long straight knife blade. An angled lug on the turned section engaged the diagonal slot in the bayonet's socket. The rear sight for these rifles is unusual, consisting of a curved slide that traverses two upright walls and can be locked with a turn key on its right side for various ranges up to 900 paces. These rifles were made for Austrian service without provision for a ramrod (that device being affixed to a crossbelt of the individual soldier). But the approximately 2,500 that were imported for U.S. service during the American Civil War were adapted for a ramrod by inletting a channel under the forestock.

Courtesy Milwaukee Public Museum, Milwaukee, Wisconsin

Austrian M1859 Horse Pistol

Overall length 16" (less stock); barrel length 10-3/8"; caliber .54. The M1850 tubelock pistol was replaced in the Austrian service in 1859 with a new standard percussion rifled horse pistol firing the Lorenz "compression" elongated ball. Like the U.S. M1855 horse pistol, this new pistol had a detachable shoulder stock so that it could be used as a carbine. Like its predecessors, no provision was made for a ramrod, which continued to be attached to a belt crossing the trooper's torso.

Exc.	V.G.	Good	Fair	Poor
—		1500	600	250

Austrian M1854/67 "Wanzel" Alteration to Breechloader

Overall length 52-1/4"; barrel (bore) length; 34-1/2"; caliber .54. The "Wanzel" breechloading mechanism applied to the Austrian M1854 rifle-muskets is much like the Allin "trapdoor" applied in the U.S. to long arms during the period 1865-1873. A breech block that hinges forward upon the barrel is released by a lever on the right side of the block, permitting insertion of a brass cartridge. In the process of altering these arms to breechloaders the sling swivels were moved from the middle band and trigger guard bow to the middle of the forestock and the buttstock.

Courtesy Milwaukee Public Museum, Milwaukee, Wisconsin

Exc.	V.G.	Good	Fair	Poor
—	—	1500	600	250

Austrian M1867 "Werndl" Breechloading Rifle

Overall length 48-1/4"; barrel (bore) length 31-1/4"; caliber 11mm. In 1867 the Austrian military adopted the breechloading system that had been invented by Joseph Werndl, director of the Austrian armory at Steyr. The breech of Werndl's design is rotated by means of a lever on its left side to expose the chamber for loading and extraction of cartridges. WERNDL appears on the top of the barrel in recognition of the designer's invention. In 1888 the Werndl rifles were superseded by the Mannlicher smokeless powder arms.

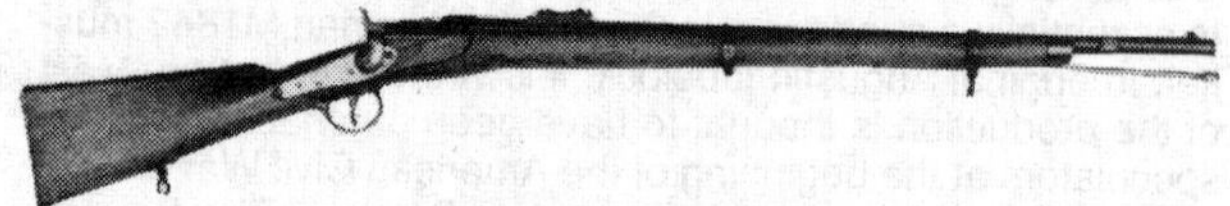

Courtesy Milwaukee Public Museum, Milwaukee, Wisconsin

Exc.	V.G.	Good	Fair	Poor
—	—	2500	1100	450

AUTAUGA ARMS INC.

Prattville, Alabama

Autauga MK II

This is a .32 ACP semi-automatic blowback pistol with a double-action trigger. Barrel length is 2.25". Fixed sights. Overall length 4.25". Weight is about 13.5 oz. Magazine capacity is 6 rounds. Introduced in 1999.

NIB	Exc.	V.G.	Good	Fair	Poor
400	325	—	—	—	—

AUTO MAG

Various Manufacturers

This popular stainless steel semi-automatic pistol was developed by the Sanford Arms Company of Pasadena, California, in the 1960s and was chambered for a special cartridge known as the .44 AMP which had a 240 grain .44 caliber bullet. Production of this arm has been carried out by a number of companies over the past 30 years. It is believed that less than 10,000 have been produced by the eight manufacturers involved.

AUTO MAG CORP.
Pasadena, California

Serial number range A0000 through A3300, made with a 6.5" vent rib barrel, chambered in .44 AMP only.

NIB	*Exc.*	*V.G.*	*Good*	*Fair*	*Poor*
2500	1700	1200	850	600	300

TDE CORP.
North Hollywood, California

Serial number range A3400 through A05015, made with a 6.5" vent rib barrel, chambered in .44 AMP and .357 AMP.

.44 AMP

NIB	*Exc.*	*V.G.*	*Good*	*Fair*	*Poor*
1950	1500	1100	850	600	300

.357 AMP

NIB	*Exc.*	*V.G.*	*Good*	*Fair*	*Poor*
2150	1650	1200	900	600	300

TDE CORP.
El Monte, California

Serial number range A05016 through A08300, 6.5" vent rib barrel standard. Also available in 8" and 10" barrel lengths chambered for .44 AMP and .357 AMP.

.44 AMP

NIB	*Exc.*	*V.G.*	*Good*	*Fair*	*Poor*
1800	1450	1000	800	600	300

.357 AMP

NIB	*Exc.*	*V.G.*	*Good*	*Fair*	*Poor*
1600	1200	900	700	500	300

HIGH STANDARD
Hamden, Connecticut

High Standard was the national distributor for Auto Mag in 1974 and 1975. These guns were chambered for the .44 AMP and .357 AMP. HS cat. no 9346 for .44 AMP, 9347 for .357 AMP.

High Standard sold 134 Auto Mags with the "H" prefix. Serial numbers are between H1 and H198, one at H1566 and three between H17219 and H17222. Of these 108 were .44AMP and 26 were .357 AMP.

High Standard also sold 911 Auto Mags between serial numbers A05278 and A07637. Of these 777 were .44 AMP and 108 were .357 AMP.

NIB	*Exc.*	*V.G.*	*Good*	*Fair*	*Poor*
2000	1750	1250	900	600	300

TDE-OMC

This is known as the solid-bolt or "B" series. The serial number range is B00001 through B00370. Either 6.5" vent rib or 10" tapered barrels are available.

NIB	*Exc.*	*V.G.*	*Good*	*Fair*	*Poor*
2400	2000	1500	1000	600	300

AMT "C" SERIES

There were 100 guns produced in this series. The first 50 were serial numbered with a "C" prefix. The second 50 were serial numbered "LAST 1" through "LAST 50." They were available with a 6.5" vent rib or 10" tapered barrel.

NIB	*Exc.*	*V.G.*	*Good*	*Fair*	*Poor*
2400	2000	1500	1250	700	350

L. E. JURRAS CUSTOM

This custom maker produced a limited number of Auto Mag pistols in 1977. These arms are worth approximately 35-50 percent more than standard production models.

KENT LOMONT

As pistols made by this maker are essentially prototypes, it is advised that potential purchasers secure a qualified appraisal.

AUTO MAG, INC.
Irwindale, California

In 1998 this company was formed to produce 1,000 Harry Sanford Commemorative pistols. Chambered for .44 AMP cartridge. Each pistol comes in a walnut display case with special serial number with Harry Sanford's signature and the name Auto Mag on the receiver.

The last retail price for the Auto Mag is $2,750.

AUTO ORDNANCE CORP.

West Hurley, New York

In 1999 Kahr Arms purchased Auto Ordnance Corp. Add 20 percent for Numrich/West Hurley models.

Model 1911TC

.45 ACP semi-auto with fixed sights and 7+1 capacity. Stainless frame and slide. 5" barrel, 39 oz. Laminate grips. MSRP: 775

Model 1911CAF

.45 ACP semi-auto with fixed sights and 7+1 capacity. Aluminum frame and stainless slide. 5" barrel, 31.5 oz. Laminate grips. MSRP: 775

Thompson 1911 A1—Standard

A 9mm, .38 Super or .45 caliber copy of the Colt Model 1911 A1. Pistol weighs 39 oz.

NIB	Exc.	V.G.	Good	Fair	Poor
375	300	250	200	150	100

NOTE: For 9mm and .38 Super add $20 to above prices. The 9mm and .38 Super models were discontinued in 1997.

Thompson 1911 A1—Parkerized

NIB	Exc.	V.G.	Good	Fair	Poor
375	295	250	225	200	150

Thompson 1911 A1—Deluxe

Same as above but Hi-profile 3 white dot sight system. Black textured, rubber wraparound grips.

NIB	Exc.	V.G.	Good	Fair	Poor
400	325	275	225	150	100

Thompson 1911 A1 Custom High Polish

Introduced in 1997 this model features a special high polish blued finish with numerous special options. Stocks are rosewood with medallion. Fitted with 5" barrel and chambered for .45 ACP. Weight is about 39 oz.

NIB	Exc.	V.G.	Good	Fair	Poor
575	475	—	—	—	—

Thompson 1911 A1—10mm

Same as above but chambered for the 10mm cartridge. Magazine capacity is 8 rounds. Discontinued in 1997.

NIB	Exc.	V.G.	Good	Fair	Poor
425	350	300	250	175	100

Thompson 1911 A1—Duo Tone

Chambered for the .45 ACP, the slide is blued and the frame is satin nickel. Discontinued in 1997.

NIB	Exc.	V.G.	Good	Fair	Poor
400	325	275	225	150	100

Thompson 1911 A—Satin Nickel

Chambered for .45 ACP or .38 Super the finish is a satin nickel on both frame and slide. Blade front sight and black checkered plastic grips. Discontinued in 1997.

NIB	Exc.	V.G.	Good	Fair	Poor
400	325	275	225	150	100

Thompson 1911 A1—Competition

Chambered for .45 ACP or .38 Super the pistol is fitted with a 5" barrel with compensator and other competition features such as custom Commander hammer, flat mainspring housing, beavertail grip safety, full length recoil guide rod, extended ejector, slide stop and thumb safety. Pistol weighs 42 oz. and is 10" overall. Discontinued in 1997.

NIB	Exc.	V.G.	Good	Fair	Poor
600	525	400	350	300	150

NOTE: For .38 Super add $10 to above prices.

Thompson 1911 A1—Pit Bull

Chambered for .45 ACP and fitted with a 3-1/2" barrel this model has high profile sights and black textured rubber wraparound grips. Magazine capacity is 7 rounds and weight is 36 oz.

NIB	Exc.	V.G.	Good	Fair	Poor
400	350	300	250	200	150

Thompson 1911 A1—General

This is a Commander-size pistol with 4-1/2" barrel, high profile sights. Chambered for .45 ACP or .38 Super. Weighs 37 oz. Discontinued in 1997.

NIB	Exc.	V.G.	Good	Fair	Poor
400	325	275	225	150	100

ZG-51 "Pit Bull"

Same as above, with a 3.5" barrel in .45 caliber. Introduced in 1988 and renamed "PIT BULL" in 1994. Discontinued.

NIB	Exc.	V.G.	Good	Fair	Poor
375	325	275	225	200	150

Thompson 1927 A1 Standard

A semi-automatic version of the Thompson submachine gun, chambered for the .45 ACP cartridge with a 16-1/2" barrel that is 18" with compensator. Blued with walnut stock. Weight is 13 lbs.

NIB	Exc.	V.G.	Good	Fair	Poor
950	750	500	400	300	150

1927 A1 Deluxe

As above, with a finned barrel, adjustable sights, pistol grip forearm, and a 50-round drum magazine costing an additional $140. The violin-shaped carrying case adds approximately $115 to the values listed.

NIB	Exc.	V.G.	Good	Fair	Poor
950	750	500	400	300	150

1927 A1C

As above, with an aluminum alloy receiver. Introduced in 1984.

NIB	Exc.	V.G.	Good	Fair	Poor
925	700	500	400	300	150

1927 A1 Commando

Introduced in 1998 this version features a 16.5" finned barrel with compensator. The finish is parkerized with black wood finish. Furnished with 30-round magazine and black nylon sling. Weight is about 13 lbs.

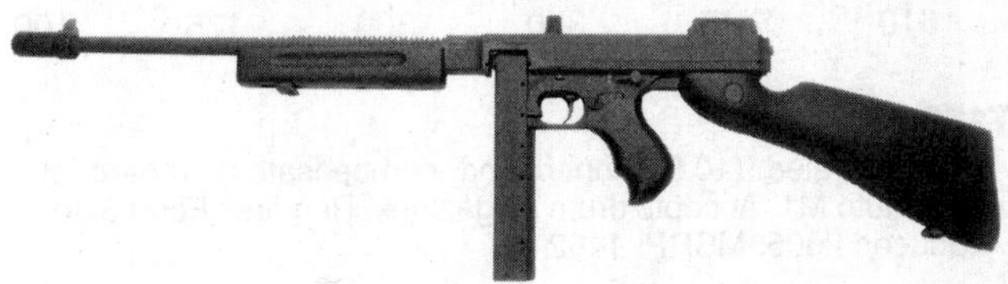

NIB	Exc.	V.G.	Good	Fair	Poor
950	750	500	400	300	100

1927 A5

A pistol version of the Model 1927 A1 with a 13" finned barrel, aluminum alloy receiver and no shoulder stock.

NIB	Exc.	V.G.	Good	Fair	Poor
1700	1300	1000	800	500	150

1927 A3

A .22 caliber variation of the Model 1927 A1 with a 16" barrel and aluminum alloy receiver. No longer in production.

NIB	Exc.	V.G.	Good	Fair	Poor
1250	1100	850	675	425	150

THE FUNNEST FUN GUN OF THEM ALL

DAN SHIDELER

No doubt about it, there's something about firing a Tommy gun that makes you feel 10 feet tall and a mile wide. A few years ago I spent an enjoyable afternoon with a WWII-vintage AutoOrdnance Thompson M1, and there was great consternation and gnashing of teeth among the bowling pin population of Noble County.

The ammunition bill, though, was nightmarish. But I—or you—can still own a semi-auto version of a Thompson submachinegun. Some are proving quite collectible, in fact.

The story of the semiauto Thompson began in 1927, with the original Model 1927 Thompson Semi-Automatic Carbine as manufactured by Auto-Ordnance Corp., a company established in 1916 by Tommy gun inventor Brig. Gen. John Taliaferro Thompson. Designed as a sem-auto clone of the famous Model 1921 (or "the Chicago Typewriter" or "the Chopper"), the Model 1927 wasn't exactly a big seller. Only 50 or so were produced.

Fast forward to 1967, when Auto-Ordnance Corp., then under the leadership of George Numrich, decided to offer an updated version of the Model 1927 semi-auto to the public. The U.S. Bureau of Alcohol, Tobacco and Firearms frowned on the original 1927's open-bolt design, deeming it too easily converted to full-auto operation, so Numrich redesigned its lockwork to prevent any unauthorized full-auto conversion. Numrich's first attempt failed to win BATF approval, but he gave it another go. And this time, the BATF signed off on the first semiauto Tommy gun made in nearly a half-century.

The first "new" Thompson semiauto—the Model 1927-A1—was offered in Deluxe and Standard versions beginning in 1975. Purists decried the new tommyguns, describing them in terms usually reserved for those born out of wedlock. Still, the Deluxe at least captured the spirit of the original, with its massive steel receiver milled out of forged bar stock, its finned and compensated barrel (now 16 inches long, to comply with the law) and its 50-round drum magazine. Other versions soon followed: a lightweight version with aluminum receiver (the 1927-A1C), a .22 Long Rifle version (the 1927-A3) and even a pistol version sans buttstock.

These Thompsons, bearing the legend "AUTO-ORDNANCE/WEST HURLEY, NY," were extremely well fit and finished. West Hurley 1927-A1s and 1927A1Cs regularly sell for $1,200 and more in excellent condition. (A scarce model chambered in 10 mm Auto is worth an additional 10 percent to 20 percent.) A West Hurley-marked C drum (50-round) or Japanese-made XL drum (39-round) magazine adds about another $225 to the price tag.

Of all the "new" Tommy gun semiautos, however, the one to have, at least in terms of collectibility, is the 1927-A5 pistol. With its 13-inch barrel, this odd little duck comes the closest of all the Numrich Thompsons in capturing the spirit of the original. At around 9 pounds, it was pretty unwieldy as a pistol, but when fired Dillinger-fashion from the hip, it sure looked the part. They rarely turn up on the market and when they do, they usually command $2,000 or more. Hoo boy!

Another little collector's gem is the 1927-A3 in .22 LR. These cheap-to-feed Tommy guns regularly sell for about $1,500 or more in excellent shape, and the 50-round accessory drum fetches almost as much all by itself. That's not bad for a gun that cost about $450 when new! It, too, is long out of production.

Today, Thompsons are manufactured by Kahr Arms. These models can be identified by the "K" prefix in their serial numbers. When Kahr absorbed Numrich in the late 1990s, inevitable production glitches occurred that resulted in the Kahr 1927s being slightly less desirable than the Numrich-made models. I have fired recent Kahr Tommy guns, however, and can honestly say their quality is comparable to that of their excellent pistols.

Will the Kahr tommyguns become collectible? That's a pretty safe bet. After all, no Thompson—full-auto or semiauto—has ever proven to be anything but.

Auto-Ordnance M1 Carbine

Introduced in 2004 this M1 carbine version is fitted with a birch stock, metal handguard and parkerized finish. Barrel length is 18". Weight is about 5.5 lbs.

NIB	Exc.	V.G.	Good	Fair	Poor
610	475	350	300	175	100

T1SB

Short-barreled (10.5" finned and compensated) variant of semi-auto M1. Accepts drum magazines. Requires Form 3. Introduced 2005. MSRP: 1482

M1SB

Short-barreled (10.5" finned and compensated) variant of semi-auto M1. Does not accept drum magazines. Requires Form 3. Introduced 2005. MSRP: 1482

M1 Carbine

Newly-manufactured replica of military M1 carbine chambered in .30 Carbine. Introduced 2005. Birch stock, parkerized finish. (Add 5 percent for walnut stock.) MSRP: 674

AUTO POINTER

Yamamoto Co.
Tokyo, Japan

Auto Pointer Shotgun

A 12 or 20 gauge semi-automatic shotgun with 26", 28" or 30" barrels and an aluminum alloy frame. Blued with a checkered walnut stock. Originally imported by Sloan's but no longer available. Clone of Browning A-5.

Exc.	V.G.	Good	Fair	Poor
375	300	250	175	100

AXTELL RIFLE CO.

(Riflesmith Inc.)
Sheridan, Montana

#1 Long Range Creedmore

This single-shot rifle is chambered for the .40-50BN, .40-70SS, .40-70BN, .40-90, .45-70, .45-90, .45-100. Weight is about 10 lbs. Numerous options will affect price.

NIB	Exc.	V.G.	Good	Fair	Poor
4700	3750	—	—	—	—

New Model Sharps 1877

Chambered for the .45-90, .45-100, and the .45-70 cartridges and fitted with a choice of 30" to 34" half round-half octagon barrel with double-set triggers.

NIB	Exc.	V.G.	Good	Fair	Poor
5200	4000	—	—	—	—

#2 Long Range

The Long Range #2 rifle is chambered for all the same calibers as the #1 Long Range Creedmore. Weight is about 10 lbs.

NIB	Exc.	V.G.	Good	Fair	Poor
3900	3000	—	—	—	—

Lower Sporting Rifle

Chambered for same calibers as above. Weight is between 9 and 12 lbs. depending on barrel options.

NIB	Exc.	V.G.	Good	Fair	Poor
2600	2000	—	—	—	—

Business Rifle

Same calibers as above. Weight is about 8.5 lbs.

NIB	Exc.	V.G.	Good	Fair	Poor
2400	1800	—	—	—	—

Overbaugh Schuetzen

Chambered for the .40-50BN and the .40-50 straight. Weight is 11 to 14 lbs. depending on barrel options.

NIB	Exc.	V.G.	Good	Fair	Poor
4400	3500	—	—	—	—

AZPIRI

Eibar, Spain

A Spanish manufacturer of pistols prior to World War II.

Avion

A 6.35mm semi-automatic pistol copied after the Model 1906 Browning. Marked "Pistolet Automatique Avion Brevete" on the slide as well as on each side of the grip plate along with an airplane logo. Manufactured from 1914 to 1918.

Courtesy James Rankin

Exc.	V.G.	Good	Fair	Poor
200	150	100	75	45

Colon

As above, in 6.35mm caliber and marked "Automatic Pistol Colon."

Exc.	V.G.	Good	Fair	Poor
200	125	100	75	50

B

B.R.F.
South Africa

B.R.F.
This is a .25 caliber semi-automatic pistol similar to the P.A.F. with a 2" barrel and 6-shot magazine. U-SA means Union of South Africa. Little is known about the manufacturer of this pistol, its origin, or dates of manufacture.

Exc.	V.G.	Good	Fair	Poor
250	175	125	100	70

REMINDER

An "N/A" or "—" instead of a price indicates that there is no known price available for that gun in that condition, or the sales for that particular model are so few that a reliable price cannot be given.

BABBIT, A. S.
Plattsburgh, New York
SEE—Adirondack Arms

BABCOCK, MOSES
Charlestown, Massachusetts

Babcock Under Hammer Cane Gun
A .52 caliber percussion cane gun with a 27" barrel and overall length of approximately 33". Folding trigger, under hammer with a wood handle. The hammer is marked "Moses Babcock/Charlestown." Active 1850s and 1860s.

Exc.	V.G.	Good	Fair	Poor
—	—	2250	950	350

BACON ARMS CO.
Norwich, Connecticut

Bacon Arms operated from 1862 until 1891. They have become known primarily for the production of cheaply made, solid-frame, rimfire revolvers known as "Suicide Specials." Bacon manufactured and sold under a number of different trademarks. They were: Bacon, Bonanza, Conqueror, Express, Gem, Governor, Guardian, and Little Giant. Collector interest is low, and values for all trademarks are quite similar.

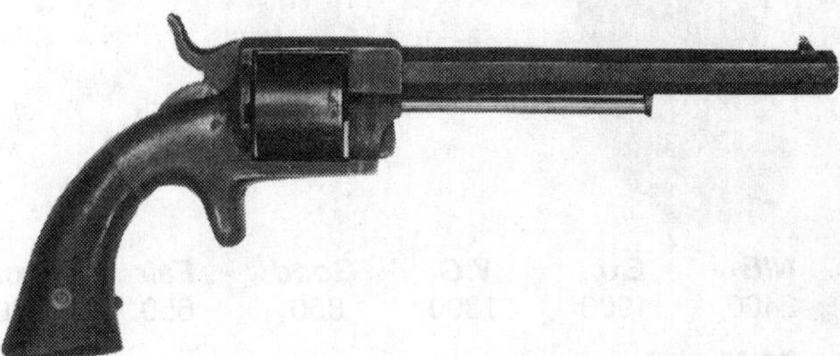

Courtesy Milwaukee Public Museum, Milwaukee, Wisconsin

Exc.	V.G.	Good	Fair	Poor
—	350	150	100	75

BAER CUSTOM, LES
Hillsdale, Illinois

This long-standing 1911 pistolsmith is now producing custom quality 1911 pistols on a semi-production basis. Each pistol features a large number of custom characteristics such as forged steel frame and full slide recoil rod, double-serrated slide, beveled magazine well, checkered front strap, beavertail safety, extended magazine release button, Bo-Mar sights, and many others depending on the specific model.

COMPETITION PISTOLS

Baer 1911 Ultimate Master Combat Pistol-Compensated
Chambered for the .45 ACP and fitted with a triple port, tapered cone compensator.

NIB	Exc.	V.G.	Good	Fair	Poor
2300	1750	1000	750	600	300

Baer 1911 Ultimate Master Steel Special
Designed for steel targets and Bianchi-style competition this model is similar to above but designed for light loads. Chambered for .38 Super. Hard chrome finish.

NIB	Exc.	V.G.	Good	Fair	Poor
2900	2250	1500	950	750	350

Baer 1911 Ultimate Master Combat Pistol
Similar to the other Baer Master series pistols this model is offered in .45 ACP, .400 Cor-Bon, and .38 Super. It is fitted with a large number of special features. Offered in a 5" or 6" version. The 5" version is also offered in 9x23 caliber.

6" Model

NIB	Exc.	V.G.	Good	Fair	Poor
2400	1900	1300	850	650	350

5" Model

NIB	Exc.	V.G.	Good	Fair	Poor
2500	1800	1200	800	600	350

Baer 1911 Ultimate Master Para

Designed for IPSC competition and offered either in Unlimited version with compensator and scope or Limited version with iron sights and no compensator.

Unlimited Model

.45 ACP, .38 Super, 9x23.

NIB	Exc.	V.G.	Good	Fair	Poor
3200	2500	1750	1200	850	400

Limited Model

.45 ACP, .38 Super, 9x23.

NIB	Exc.	V.G.	Good	Fair	Poor
2700	2000	1500	900	650	300

Baer 1911 IPSC Action Pistol

Chambered for .45 ACP with blued slide and frame.

NIB	Exc.	V.G.	Good	Fair	Poor
1500	1150	850	600	450	300

Baer 1911 National Match Hardball Pistol

Designed for DCM matches. Chambered for .45 ACP.

NIB	Exc.	V.G.	Good	Fair	Poor
1225	900	700	500	400	200

Baer 1911 Bullseye Wadcutter Pistol

Designed for use with wadcutter loads only. Chambered for .45 ACP.

NIB	Exc.	V.G.	Good	Fair	Poor
1500	1100	800	600	500	250

NOTE: This version is also offered with a Baer Optical mount. Add $125 for this option. For a 6" slide with LoMount BoMars sight add $200.

Baer 1911 Target Master

Designed for NRA centerfire matches. Chambered for .45 ACP.

NIB	Exc.	V.G.	Good	Fair	Poor
1250	1000	750	550	450	250

REMINDER

Prices paid for firearms is an ever-changing affair based on a large number of variables.

Baer 1911 P.P.C. Distinguished Match

Introduced in 1999 this pistol features a 5" barrel with an adjustable Aristrocrat rear sight. Many, many special features such as double serrated slide lowered and flared ejection port extended ambi safety, checkered front strap, etc. Offered in .45 ACP, and 9mm with supported chamber. Blued finish and one magazine.

NIB	Exc.	V.G.	Good	Fair	Poor
1600	1300	—	—	—	—

NOTE: Add approximately $300 for 9mm model.

Baer 1911 P.P.C. Open Class

Similar to the model above but fitted with a 6" barrel and slide. Chambered for .45 ACP, and 9mm with supported chamber. Blued finish. Introduced in 1999.

NIB	Exc.	V.G.	Good	Fair	Poor
1700	1350	—	—	—	—

NOTE: Add approximately $300 for 9mm model.

DUTY & DEFENSE PISTOLS

Baer 1911 Premier II

Designed as a duty or defense pistol this model is chambered for the .45 ACP, .400 Cor-Bon, and 9x23 cartridges. Fitted with a 5" slide.

NIB	Exc.	V.G.	Good	Fair	Poor
1425	1150	900	600	450	250

NOTE: For stainless steel version add $150 to above prices. Add $100 for .400 Cor-Bon and $250 for 9x23.

Baer 1911 Premier II—6" barrel

Same as above but fitted with a 6" match grade barrel.

NIB	Exc.	V.G.	Good	Fair	Poor
1700	1400	1100	900	700	350

NOTE: Add $100 for .400 Cor-Bon and $300 for .38 Super. 9x23 not offered with 6" slide.

Baer 1911 Premier II—Light Weight (LW1)

Has the same features as the standard Premier II but with reduced weight aluminum frame. Furnished with low mount LCB adjustable rear sight. Offered in .45 ACP only.

NIB	Exc.	V.G.	Good	Fair	Poor
1700	1400	1100	900	700	350

Baer 1911 Premier II—Light Weight (LW2)

Same as above but with fixed combat-style rear sight.

NIB	Exc.	V.G.	Good	Fair	Poor
1700	1400	1100	900	700	350

Baer 1911 Premier II Super-Tac

Similar to the standard Premier II models but with low mount adjustable rear night sight and front sight. Special BEAR COAT finish. Offered in .45 ACP, .40 S&W, .400 Cor-Bon.

NIB	Exc.	V.G.	Good	Fair	Poor
1900	1500	1200	900	700	350

NOTE: Dual caliber .45 ACP/.400 Cor-Bon combo add $200.

Baer 1911 Prowler III

Similar to the Premier II but with a tapered cone stub weight, a full-length guide rod, and a reverse plug. Special order only.

NIB	Exc.	V.G.	Good	Fair	Poor
1800	1500	1200	950	700	350

Baer 1911 Prowler IV

Chambered for .45 ACP or .38 Super this model is built on a Para-Ordnance oversize frame. Fitted with a 5" slide. Special order only.

NIB	Exc.	V.G.	Good	Fair	Poor
2300	1750	1250	900	650	300

NOTE: For optional 6" barrel and slide add $300.

Baer 1911 Custom Carry—Commanche Length

Chambered for .45 ACP this model has several options including 4-1/2" barrel, stainless steel slide and frame, lightweight aluminum frame with blued steel slide. As of 2000 this model is furnished with night sights.

NIB	Exc.	V.G.	Good	Fair	Poor
1640	1200	950	600	450	250

NOTE: For stainless steel add $40. For lightweight frame add $130.

Baer Custom Carry—5"

Same as above but offered with 5" slide. Not offered in aluminum frame.

NIB	Exc.	V.G.	Good	Fair	Poor
1600	1200	950	600	450	250

NOTE: Add $40 for stainless steel.

Baer 1911 Thunder Ranch Special

This model features a steel frame and slide with front and rear serrations. Deluxe fixed rear sight with tritium insert. Checkered front strap. Numerous special features. Slim line grips with Thunder Ranch logo. Seven-round magazine standard. Special serial numbers with "TR" prefix. Offered in .45 ACP.

NIB	Exc.	V.G.	Good	Fair	Poor
1600	1200	950	600	450	250

Baer 1911 Thunder Ranch Special Engraved Model

As above but with engraved frame and slide.

NIB	Exc.	V.G.	Good	Fair	Poor
6000	4750	—	—	—	—

Baer S.R.P. (Swift Response Pistol)

Chambered for .45 ACP and built on a Para-Ordnance frame this unit is similar to the one supplied to the FBI. Supplied with wooden presentation box.

NIB	Exc.	V.G.	Good	Fair	Poor
2800	2350	1750	1200	850	400

NOTE: For S.R.P. models built on a Baer frame or shorter 4-1/2" frame subtract $300 from NIB through Fair prices.

Baer 1911 Monolith

Introduced in 1999 this model features a 5" barrel and slide with extra long dust cover. Chambered in .45 ACP, .400 Cor-Bon, .40 S&W, 9x23, 9mm, or .38 Super all with supported chamber. Many special features such as BoMar sights, Commander-style hammer, speed trigger, etc. Blued finish with one magazine. Weight is approximately 37 oz.

NIB	Exc.	V.G.	Good	Fair	Poor
1650	1300	—	—	—	—

NOTE: For all other supported calibers add $250.

Baer 1911 Monolith Heavyweight

Introduced in 1999 this model is similar to the Monolith but with the addition of a heavier frame that adds 3.5 oz. Same calibers as available on the Monolith. Weight is approximately 40 oz.

NIB	Exc.	V.G.	Good	Fair	Poor
1650	1300	—	—	—	—

NOTE: For all other supported calibers add $200.

Baer 1911 Monolith Tactical Illuminator

This model, introduced in 1999, has the same features as the Monolith Heavyweight above but with the addition of light mounted under the dust cover. Offered in .45 ACP and .40 S&W with supported chamber. Weight with light is approximately 44 oz.

NIB	Exc.	V.G.	Good	Fair	Poor
1850	1500	—	—	—	—

NOTE: For all other supported calibers add $275.

Baer 1911 Monolith Commanche

Fitted with a 4.25" slide and a dust cover that covers the length of the slide. Has all the features of the standard Monolith. Comes with night sights and a deluxe fixed rear sight. Edges rounded for tactical carry. Chambered in .45 ACP only. Introduced in 2001.

NIB	Exc.	V.G.	Good	Fair	Poor
1600	1250	—	—	—	—

Baer 1911 Monolith Commanche Heavyweight

Exactly as above but with thicker dust cover to add an additional 2 oz. of weight. Introduced in 2001.

NIB	Exc.	V.G.	Good	Fair	Poor
1650	1275	—	—	—	—

Baer 1911 Stinger

This model features a shorter Officer's grip frame and Commanche slide and barrel. Many special features. Offered in .45 ACP. Choice of aluminum frame with blued slide, aluminum frame with stainless steel slide and stainless steel frame and slide. Weight in aluminum is about 28 oz., with stainless steel about 34 oz. Introduced in 1999.

NIB	Exc.	V.G.	Good	Fair	Poor
1500	1200	—	—	—	—

NOTE: For aluminum frame and blued slide with supported calibers add $300. For aluminum frame with stainless slide and supported chamber add $340. For stainless frame and slide with supported chamber add $140.

Baer 1911 Stinger Stainless

Same as above but with stainless steel frame and slide. Introduced in 2001.

NIB	Exc.	V.G.	Good	Fair	Poor
1500	1200	—	—	—	—

NEW CONCEPTS PISTOLS

This line of 1911 pistols offers custom features at a slightly lower cost. Each succeeding grade offers a few more features.

Baer 1911 Concept I

Chambered for .45 ACP and fitted with BoMar sights.

NIB	Exc.	V.G.	Good	Fair	Poor
1400	1150	900	750	550	300

Baer 1911 Concept II

Same as above but fitted with Baer adjustable sights.

NIB	Exc.	V.G.	Good	Fair	Poor
1400	1150	900	750	550	300

Baer 1911 Concept III

Same as above but with stainless steel frame with blued steel slide with BoMar sights.

NIB	Exc.	V.G.	Good	Fair	Poor
1520	1250	950	800	550	300

Baer 1911 Concept IV

Same as above but with Baer adjustable sights.

NIB	Exc.	V.G.	Good	Fair	Poor
1500	1250	950	800	550	300

Baer 1911 Concept V

This model has both stainless steel slide and frame with BoMar sights.

NIB	Exc.	V.G.	Good	Fair	Poor
1550	1350	1000	850	600	300

Baer 1911 Concept V 6"

This model is identical to the Concept V with the addition of a 6" barrel and slide. Introduced in 1999.

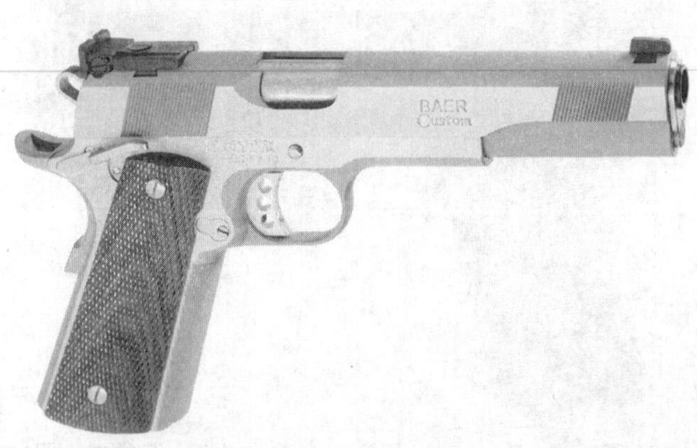

NIB	Exc.	V.G.	Good	Fair	Poor
1700	1350	—	—	—	—

Baer 1911 Concept VI
Same as above but fitted with Baer adjustable sights.

NIB	Exc.	V.G.	Good	Fair	Poor
1550	1350	975	850	600	300

Baer 1911 Concept VI L.W.
Same as above but built on aluminum frame with supported chamber and National Match barrel.

NIB	Exc.	V.G.	Good	Fair	Poor
1750	1400	1000	—	—	—

Baer 1911 Concept VII
Features all blued 4-1/2" steel frame and slide with Baer adjustable fixed night sights.

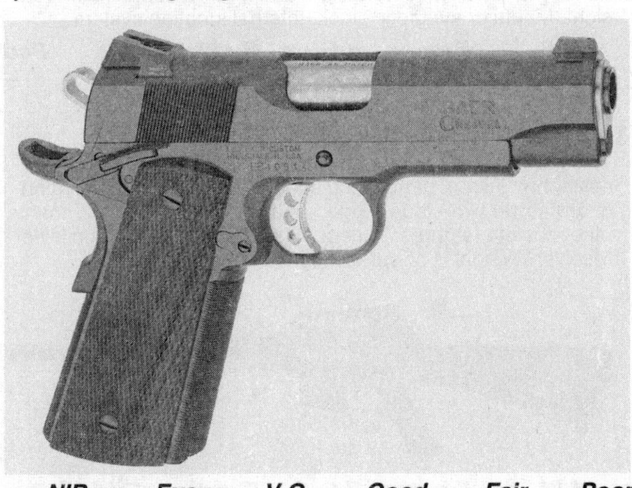

NIB	Exc.	V.G.	Good	Fair	Poor
1500	1250	950	800	550	300

Baer 1911 Concept VIII
Same as above but with stainless steel slide and frame. Fixed combat night sights standard.

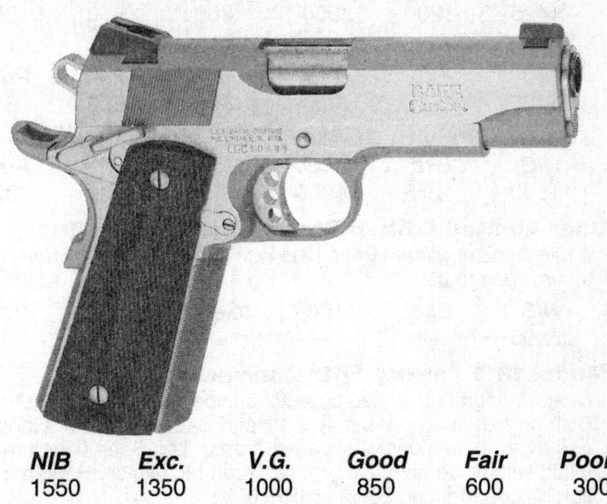

NIB	Exc.	V.G.	Good	Fair	Poor
1550	1350	1000	850	600	300

Baer 1911 Concept IX
This version has a lightweight aluminum frame with 4-1/2" steel slide.

NIB	Exc.	V.G.	Good	Fair	Poor
1600	1350	1000	850	600	300

Baer 1911 Concept X
This model features a 4-1/2" stainless steel slide with a lightweight aluminum frame.

NIB	Exc.	V.G.	Good	Fair	Poor
1600	1350	1000	850	600	300

Baer Lightweight .22 caliber 1911 Models

4-1/2" Model with fixed sights

NIB	Exc.	V.G.	Good	Fair	Poor
1425	1200	950	800	550	300

5" Model with fixed sights

NIB	Exc.	V.G.	Good	Fair	Poor
1425	1200	950	800	550	300

5" Model with Bo-Mar sights

NIB	Exc.	V.G.	Good	Fair	Poor
1500	1275	1000	850	600	300

Baer Limited Edition Presentation Grade 1911

A fully hand engraved Baer 1911 with special bluing in presentation wooden box.

NIB	Exc.	V.G.	Good	Fair	Poor
6000	—	—	—	—	—

Model 1911 Twenty-Fifth Anniversary

Custom-engraved limited collector edition .45 ACP semi-auto. Built on fully functional, fully equipped Baer Premier II. Hand engraved, both sides of slide and frame. Les Baer signature. Inlaid with white gold. Ivory grips. Deep blue finish. Presentation box. Introduced 2006. MSRP: 6595

Ultimate Recon

Semi-auto with integral Picatinny rail, 5" barrel, .45 ACP. Blue or chrome. Comes with SureFire X-200 light. Fixed sights. 4-pound trigger. Two 8-round magazines. Cocobolo grips. MSRP: 2988 (Blue), 3230 (Chrome)

RIFLES

AR .223 Ultimate Super Varmint

Fitted with a choice of 18", 20", or 24" heavy barrels with 1-in-12 twist. Flat top rail. Choice of single or two-stage trigger. Aluminum free-floating handguard. Bear Coat finish. Introduced in 2000.

NIB	Exc.	V.G.	Good	Fair	Poor
1975	1600	—	—	—	—

AR .223 Ultimate Super Match

Introduced in 2002 this model features a wide number of custom features with barrel lengths from 18" to 24". Special match carrier with integral rail system.

NIB	Exc.	V.G.	Good	Fair	Poor
2125	1700	—	—	—	—

AR .223 M4-A2 Flattop

This model features a flat-top rail and match bolt and carrier. The 16" barrel has a integral compensator. Single stage trigger. Knights Armament Systems rail adapter. Bear Coat finish. Introduced in 2000.

NIB	Exc.	V.G.	Good	Fair	Poor
2175	1700	—	—	—	—

AR .223 IPSC Action Model

Similar to the model above but with 18" Super Match heavy barrel with integral compensator. Introduced in 2000.

NIB	Exc.	V.G.	Good	Fair	Poor
2175	1700	—	—	—	—

AR .223 Ultimate NRA Match

This model features numerous custom features and is fitted with a 30" barrel, special front and rear sights.

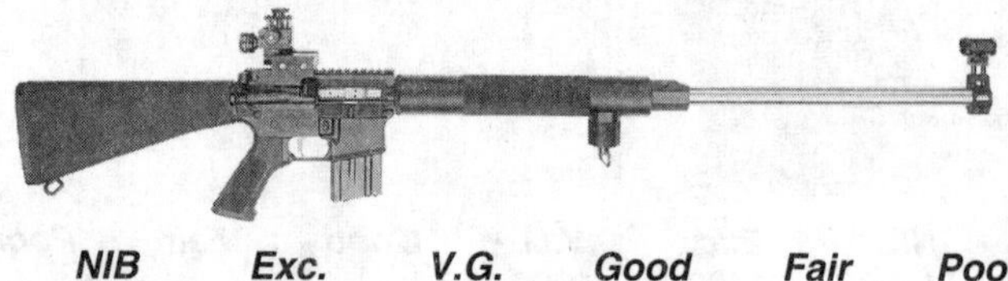

NIB	Exc.	V.G.	Good	Fair	Poor
2100	1700	—	—	—	—

NOTE: Add $750 for special sight pacakage.

Bullpup Muzzleloader

This .50 caliber muzzleloader is fitted with a 28" stainless steel barrel with a Williams front sight and M16 National Match rear sight. Maple or synthetic stock. Internal ignation system.

NIB	Exc.	V.G.	Good	Fair	Poor
320	250	—	—	—	—

NOTE: Add $30 for maple stock and stainless steel.

Thunder Ranch Rifle

This .223 model is fitted with a bench rest 16" barrel. Upper receiver has a carry handle and a toptop rail. Free floating handguard, jewel two-stage trigger, floading front sight, and many other custom features. Thunder Ranch logo stamped on lower receiver. Weight is about 7.5 lbs. Introduced in 2004.

NIB	Exc.	V.G.	Good	Fair	Poor
2490	1900	—	—	—	—

BAFORD, ARMS, INC.
Bristol, Tennessee

Thunder Derringer

A .410 bore or .44 Special single-shot pistol with 3" interchangeable barrels and a spur trigger. Additional interchangeable barrels are chambered in calibers from .22 to 9mm. Also available with a scope. Blued with a walnut grip. Introduced in 1988.

NIB	Exc.	V.G.	Good	Fair	Poor
150	100	85	70	55	35

NOTE: Add $50 for interchangeable barrel.

Fire Power Model 35

A 9mm semi-automatic pistol with a 4.75" barrel, Millett adjustable sights and 14-shot magazine. Fitted with a combat safety and hammer, and Pachmayr grips. Stainless steel. Introduced in 1988.

NIB	Exc.	V.G.	Good	Fair	Poor
525	425	350	300	250	125

BAIKAL
Russia

Baikal IJ-27E1C

A 12 or 20 gauge Magnum O/U shotgun with 26" Skeet-Skeet or 28" Modified-Full ventilated rib barrels, single-selective trigger and extractors. Blued with a walnut stock. **Mfg. List Price:** $449.95

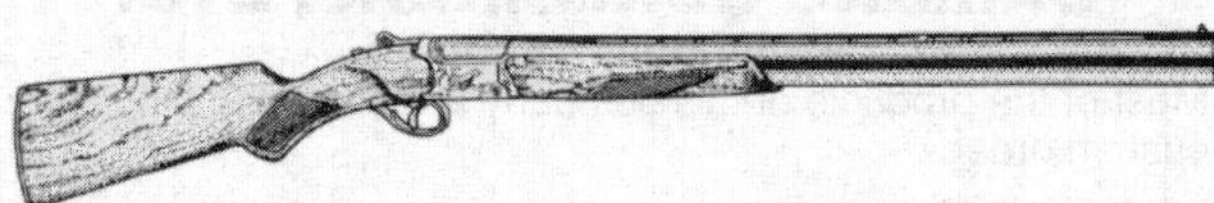

NIB	Exc.	V.G.	Good	Fair	Poor
375	275	200	150	100	75

Baikal TOZ - 34

A 12 or 28 gauge double-barrel shotgun with 26" or 28" barrels, double triggers, cocking indicators and extractors. Blued with a checkered walnut stock. This model was also available with a silver-plated receiver. **Mfg. List Price:** $465.95

NIB	Exc.	V.G.	Good	Fair	Poor
400	300	250	200	100	75

Model MC-8-0

A 12 gauge double-barrel shotgun with 26" Skeet-Skeet or 28 Full-Modified barrels, hand fitted action and engraved receiver. **Mfg. List Price:** $2,295.00

NIB	Exc.	V.G.	Good	Fair	Poor
2000	1250	950	700	500	250

Model MC-5-105

The Model TOZ-34 with an engraved receiver. **Mfg. List Price:** $1,325.00

NIB	Exc.	V.G.	Good	Fair	Poor
1200	850	700	500	300	150

Model MC-7

As above, with a relief engraved receiver. **Mfg. List Price:** $2,695.00

NIB	Exc.	V.G.	Good	Fair	Poor
2250	1750	1200	800	550	250

Model MC-109

A custom-made O/U shotgun with detachable sidelocks. Produced in limited quantities and most often to the purchaser's specifications. **Mfg. List Price:** $3,695.00

NIB	Exc.	V.G.	Good	Fair	Poor
2850	2000	1500	950	600	300

CURRENTLY IMPORTED BAIKAL SHOTGUNS
Importer—European American Armory

IZH18

This is a single-barrel shotgun chambered for 12, 20, or .410 bore. Choice of 26.5" or 29.5" barrels. Hardwood stock. Ejectors. Introduced in 1999.

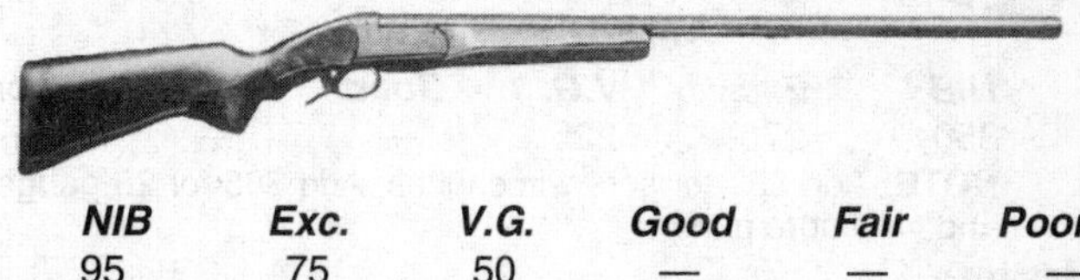

NIB	Exc.	V.G.	Good	Fair	Poor
95	75	50	—	—	—

IZK18MAX

Similar to the above model but with polished nickel receiver, vent rib, walnut stock, screw-in chokes, and ejectors. Offered in 12 and 20 gauge as well as .410 bore.

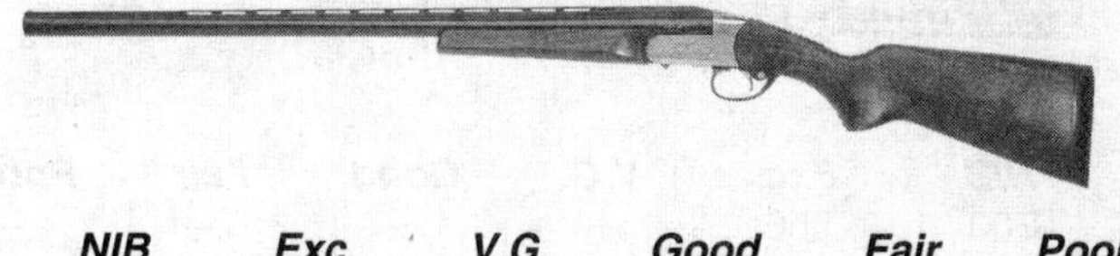

NIB	Exc.	V.G.	Good	Fair	Poor
170	125	100	—	—	—

IZH43

This side-by-side gun is available in 12, 16, 20, 28, and .410 bore. In barrel lengths for 20" to 28" depending on gauge. Internal hammers. Single-selective trigger, ejectors. Walnut stock.

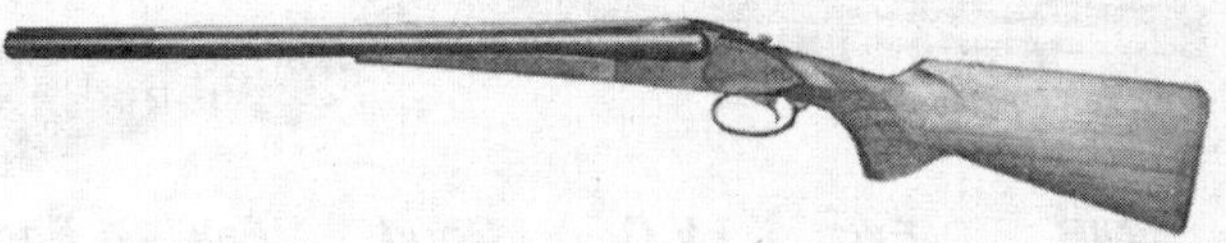

NIB	Exc.	V.G.	Good	Fair	Poor
350	275	200	—	—	—

NOTE: Add $80 for 28 gauge and .410 bore guns.

IZH43K

Introduced in 1999 this is a 12 gauge 3" side-by-side hammer gun with choice of barrel lengths of 18.5", 20", 24", 26", and 28". Single-selective trigger or double trigger. Engraved side plates. Walnut stock with pistol grip. Weight is about 7.3 lbs.

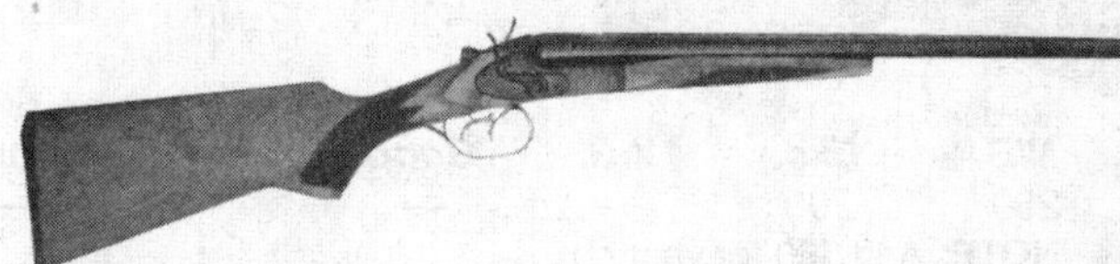

NIB	Exc.	V.G.	Good	Fair	Poor
375	300	250	—	—	—

NOTE: Deduct $40 for double triggers.

MP213 Coach Gun

Similar to the above model but with internal hammers. Single or double triggers. Weight is about 7 lbs.

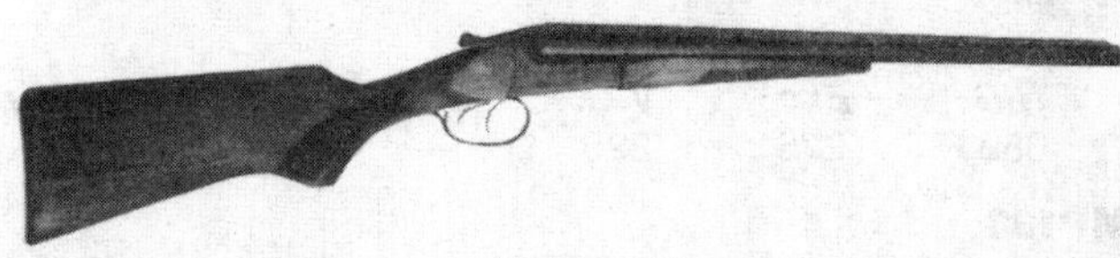

NIB	Exc.	V.G.	Good	Fair	Poor
275	255	175	—	—	—

NOTE: Deduct $40 for double triggers. Add $80 for 20 gauge.

IZH27

This is an over/under gun chambered for 12, 20, 28, and .410 bore. Choice of 26.5" or 28.5" barrels. Walnut stock. Single trigger with ejectors. Fixed chokes.

NIB	Exc.	V.G.	Good	Fair	Poor
350	275	225	—	—	—

NOTE: Add $35 for screw-in chokes. Add $85 for 28 gauge and .410 bore guns.

MP233

This over/under gun is chambered for the 12 gauge 3" shell with a choice of 26", 28", or 30" barrels. Walnut checkered stock. Single or double triggers. Screw-in chokes. Removable trigger assembly. Weight is about 7.3 lbs. Introduced in 1999.

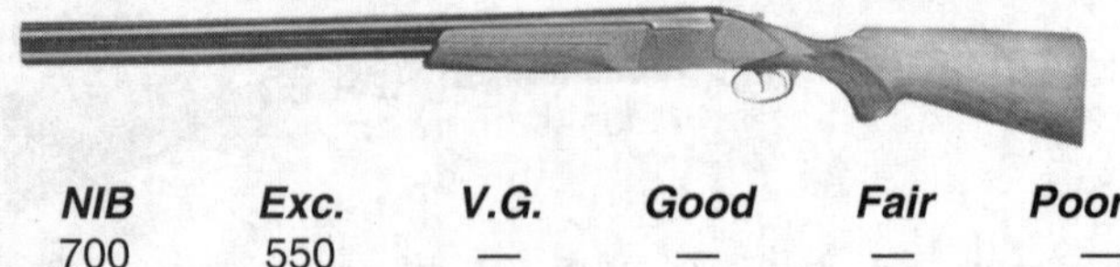

NIB	Exc.	V.G.	Good	Fair	Poor
700	550	—	—	—	—

IZH94

This is an over/under combination gun with a 12 gauge upper barrel and centerfire rifle barrel on the under barrel. Barrel length is 24" or 26". This model is offered as an over/under rifle in calibers from .222 to .30-06. Walnut stock single or double trigger. Weight is about 7.3 lbs. Open sights.

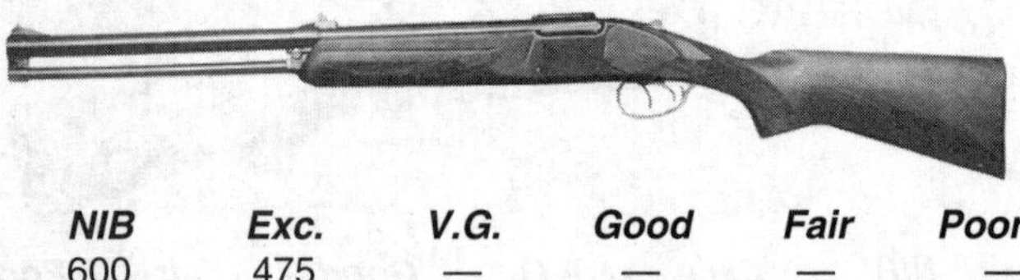

NIB	Exc.	V.G.	Good	Fair	Poor
600	475	—	—	—	—

IZH81

This is a pump-action shotgun chambered for 12 gauge 3" shells. Barrel lengths are a choice of 20", 26", or 28". Five-round detachable magazine. Walnut stock.

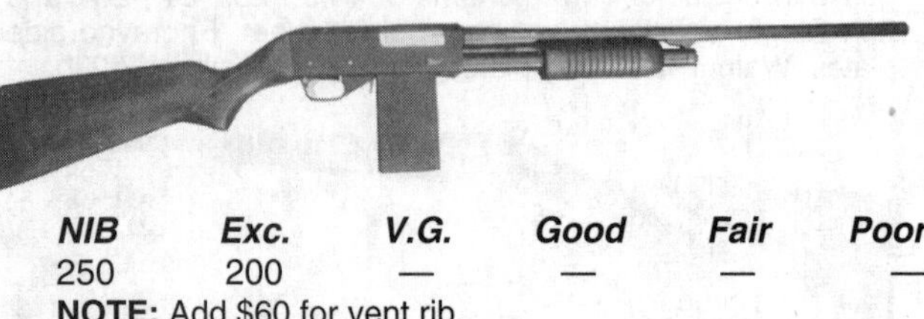

NIB	Exc.	V.G.	Good	Fair	Poor
250	200	—	—	—	—

NOTE: Add $60 for vent rib.

MP131K

This is a pump-action shotgun with a choice of two different feeding sources: a tubular magazine or a detachable 3-round or 5-round box magazine.

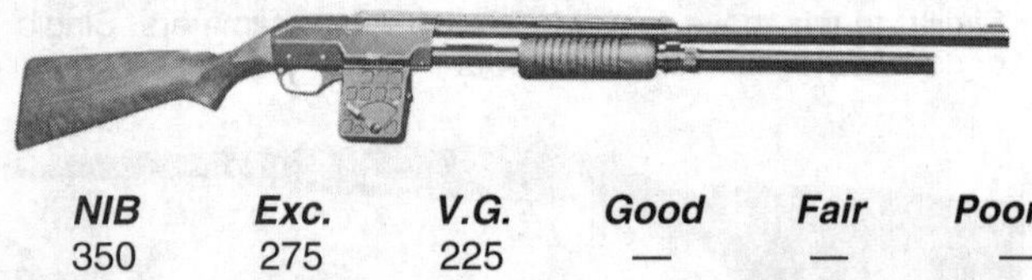

NIB	Exc.	V.G.	Good	Fair	Poor
350	275	225	—	—	—

MP133

This is a slide action shotgun chambered for the 12 gauge 3.5" shell. Available with barrel lengths of 20", 24", 26", or 28". Vent rib or all barrel lengths except 20". Walnut stock. Choke tubes for all barrel lengths except 20" (Cylinder choke). Introduced in 2001.

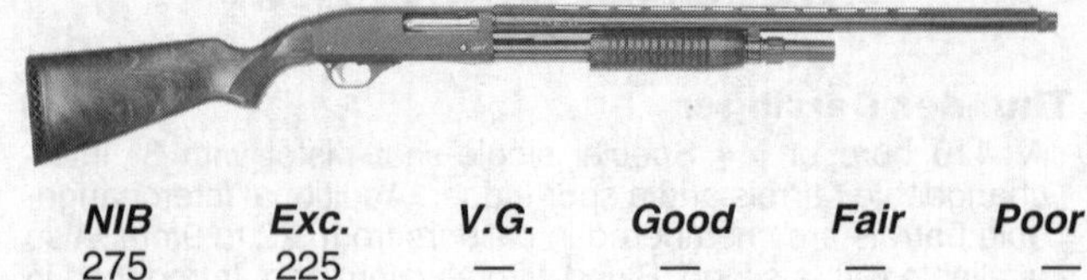

NIB	Exc.	V.G.	Good	Fair	Poor
275	225	—	—	—	—

MP153

This is a semi-automatic shotgun chambered for 12 gauge 3" shell. Choice of 26" or 28" barrels. Choice of walnut or black synthetic stock. Weight is about 7.8 lbs. Screw-in chokes. Introduced in 1999.

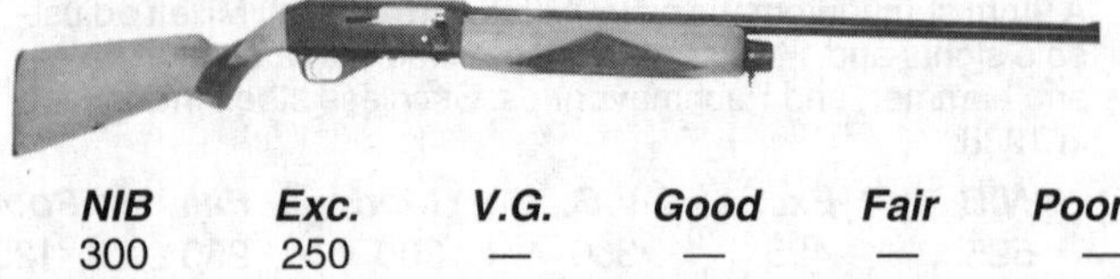

NIB	Exc.	V.G.	Good	Fair	Poor
300	250	—	—	—	—

IZH35

This is a semi-automatic pistol chambered for the .22 LR cartridge. Fully adjustable target grip, adjustable trigger assembly, cocking indicator, detachable scope. Fitted with a 6" barrel. Introduced in 2000.

NIB	Exc.	V.G.	Good	Fair	Poor
500	400	350	—	—	—

BAILONS GUNMAKERS, LTD.

Birmingham, England

Most of the products of this company are produced strictly on custom order.

Hunting Rifle

A bolt-action sporting rifle produced in a variety of calibers with a 24" barrel, open sights, double-set triggers and a 3- or 4-shot magazine. Blued with a well-figured walnut stock. The values listed are for a standard grade rifle.

NIB	Exc.	V.G.	Good	Fair	Poor
2250	1700	1250	900	600	300

BAKER GAS SEAL

London, England

A .577 caliber percussion revolver with a 6.5" octagonal barrel and 6-shot cylinder. When the hammer is cocked, the cylinder is forced forward tightly against the barrel breech, thus creating a gas seal. Blued, case hardened with walnut grips.

Exc.	V.G.	Good	Fair	Poor
1500	900	600	475	250

BAKER GUN & FORGING CO.

Batavia, New York

The Baker Gun & Forging Company was founded in early 1890, by Elias Baker, brother of William Baker. Made from drop forged parts, Baker single and double barrel shotguns quickly gained a reputation for strength and reliability among shooters of the period. Offered in a wide variety of grades, from plain utilitarian to heavily embellished models, Baker shotguns have in recent years become highly collectable. The company was sold on December 24, 1919, to H. & D. Folsom Arms Company of Norwich, Connecticut. The Folsom Company had for almost 20 years been the Baker Company's sole New York City agent and had marketed at least one Baker model that was only made for them. From 1919 to approximately 1923, Folsom continued to assemble and make Baker shotguns. Late model Bakers were made by the Crescent Firearms Company and have serial numbers with an "F" suffix.

The Baker Gun & Forging Company was the first American arms manufacturer to:

1. Make a single barrel trap shotgun.
2. Make a single barrel trap shotgun with a ventilated rib.

3. Make arms with an intercepting firing pin block safety.
4. Make a double barrel shotgun with hammers directly behind the firing pins.
5. Use a long swinging sear that once adjusted gave consistent trigger pull throughout the working life of an arm.

Those Baker shotguns manufactured between 1913 and 1923 that were engraved by Rudolph J. Kornbrath command substantial price premiums over the values listed.

Baker Trap Gun

A 12 gauge single barrel boxlock shotgun with either a 30" or 32" barrel. Blued, case hardened with a walnut stock.

Exc.	*V.G.*	*Good*	*Fair*	*Poor*
1600	1250	900	500	250

Elite Grade

Standard scrollwork and simple game scenes engraved on receiver.

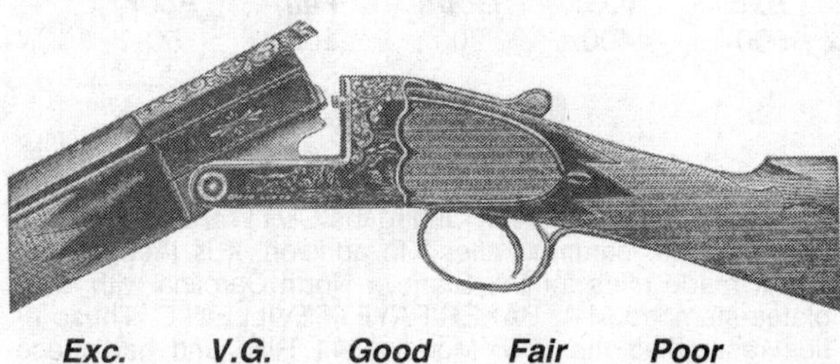

Exc.	*V.G.*	*Good*	*Fair*	*Poor*
2100	1500	1000	500	250

Superba

Heavily engraved on receiver and sides of barrel breech.

Exc.	*V.G.*	*Good*	*Fair*	*Poor*
4200	3000	1500	750	500

Expert Grade Double Shotgun

The highest grade shotgun manufactured by the Baker Gun & Forging Company. General specifications as above. The stock of imported English or French walnut. The engraving of full coverage type and partially chiselled. Automatic ejectors and single trigger if requested. Built on special order only.

Exc.	*V.G.*	*Good*	*Fair*	*Poor*
5300	4000	2000	1500	750

Deluxe Grade Double Shotgun

The designation given those Expert Grade shotguns produced by H. & D. Folsom from 1919 to 1923. Characteristics and values identical to those listed for the Baker Expert Grade Double Shotgun.

Black Beauty Double Shotgun

Made solely for H. & D. Folsom Arms Company. A 12 or 16 gauge double barrel shotgun with sidelocks and 26", 28", 30", or 32" barrels in 12 gauge and 26", 28", or 30" barrels in 16 gauge. The barrels are blued, the receiver is case hardened, the sideplates are finished with black oxide and the stock is walnut. Automatic ejectors and single trigger are extra cost options.

Exc.	*V.G.*	*Good*	*Fair*	*Poor*
900	750	650	500	250

Grade S Double Shotgun

As above, with simple engraving.

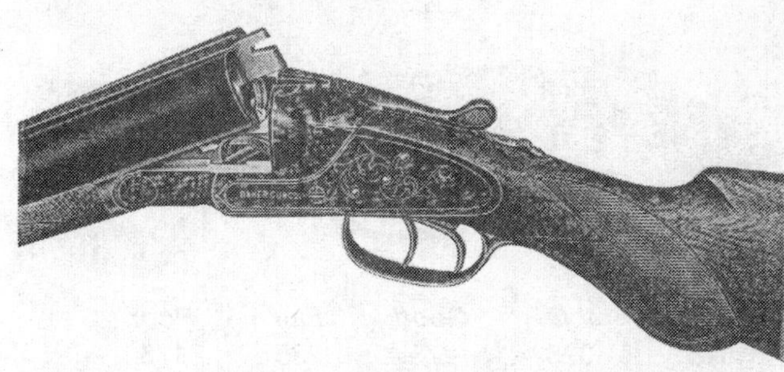

Exc.	*V.G.*	*Good*	*Fair*	*Poor*
1300	1000	750	400	250

Grade R Double Shotgun

As above, with case hardened sideplates and engraved with simple scrollwork and game scenes.

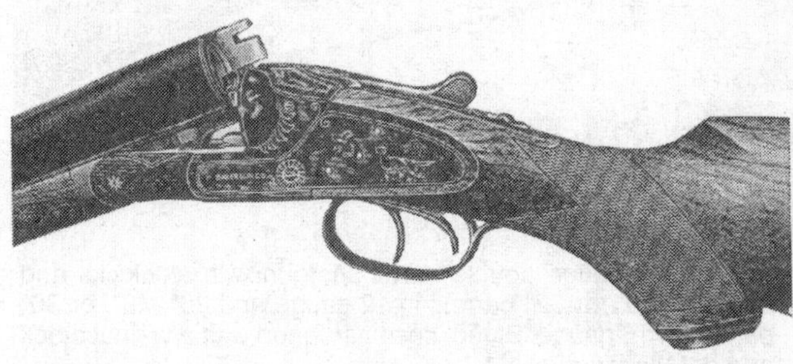

Exc.	*V.G.*	*Good*	*Fair*	*Poor*
1700	1250	900	500	300

Paragon Grade Shotgun

As above, with finely cut scrollwork and detailed game scenes engraved on the sideplates. The stock of finely figured walnut.

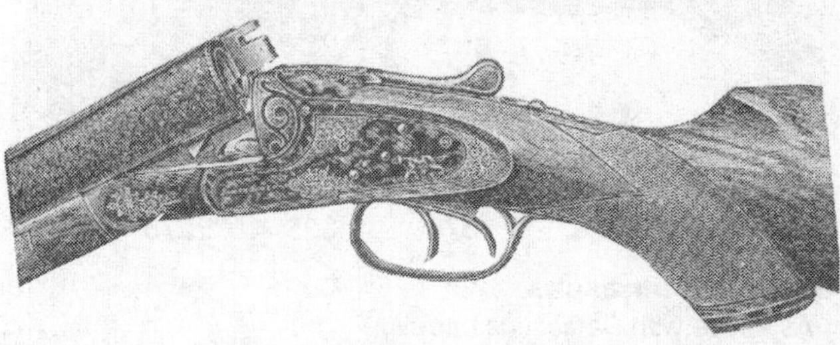

Exc.	*V.G.*	*Good*	*Fair*	*Poor*
2250	1750	1200	900	500

Paragon Grade—Model NN

As above, but more finely engraved. Built on special order only. Automatic ejectors.

Exc.	*V.G.*	*Good*	*Fair*	*Poor*
3300	2250	1400	900	500

Batavia Special

A 12 or 16 gauge double barrel shotgun with sidelocks and 28", 30", or 32" barrels in 12 gauge and 28" or 30" barrels in 16 gauge. Blued, case hardened with a walnut stock and double triggers.

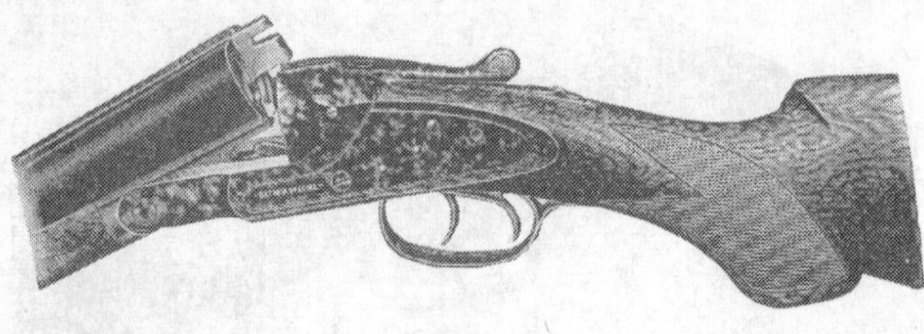

Exc.	V.G.	Good	Fair	Poor
625	325	275	225	175

Batavia Brush Gun

A 12 or 16 gauge double barrel shotgun with sidelocks and 26" barrels. Blued, case hardened with walnut stock. Sling rings and swivels optional.

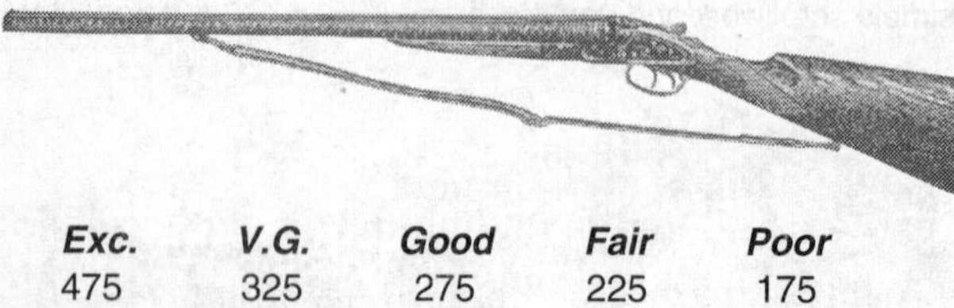

Exc.	V.G.	Good	Fair	Poor
475	325	275	225	175

Batavia Leader

A 12 or 16 gauge double barrel shotgun with sidelocks and 26", 28", 30", or 32" barrels in 12 gauge and 26", 28", or 30" barrels in 16 gauge. Blued, case hardened with a walnut stock and double triggers.

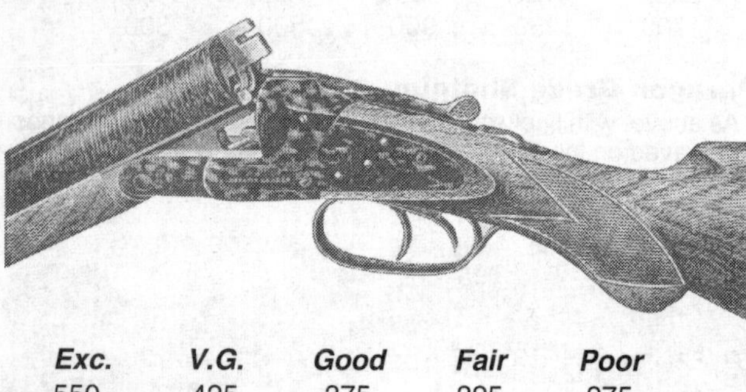

Exc.	V.G.	Good	Fair	Poor
550	425	375	325	275

Batavia Damascus

As above with Damascus barrels.

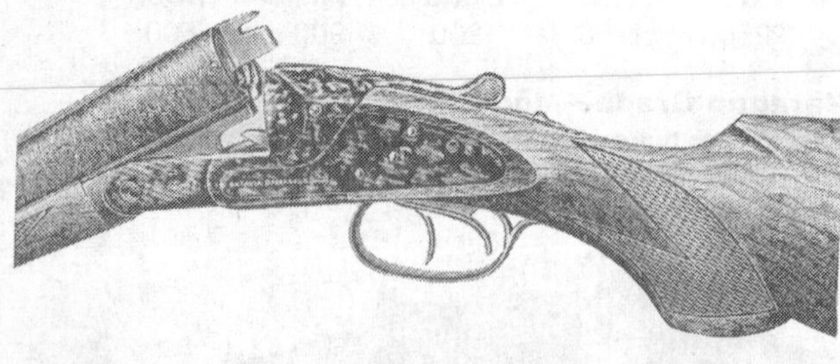

Exc.	V.G.	Good	Fair	Poor
400	325	275	225	175

Baker Hammer Gun

A 10, 12, or 16 gauge double barrel shotgun with sidehammers and 30" and 32" barrels in 10 gauge, 26" to 32" barrels in 12 gauge and 26" to 30" barrels in 16 gauge. Browned, case hardened with walnut stock and double triggers.

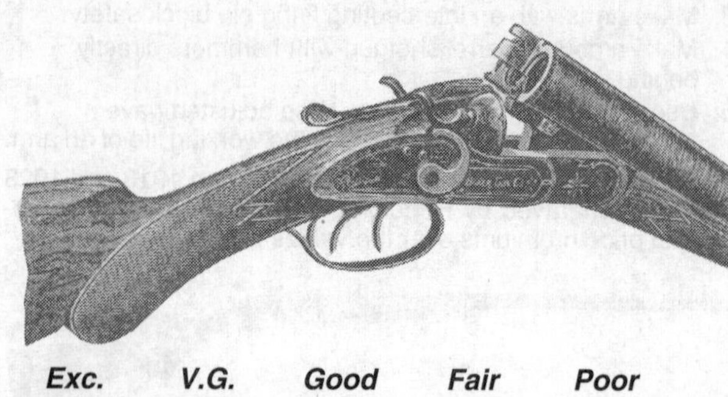

Exc.	V.G.	Good	Fair	Poor
350	250	175	125	100

Batavia Automatic Rifle

A .22 caliber semi-automatic rifle with a 24" round barrel and a detachable 7-shot magazine. Blued with a walnut stock.

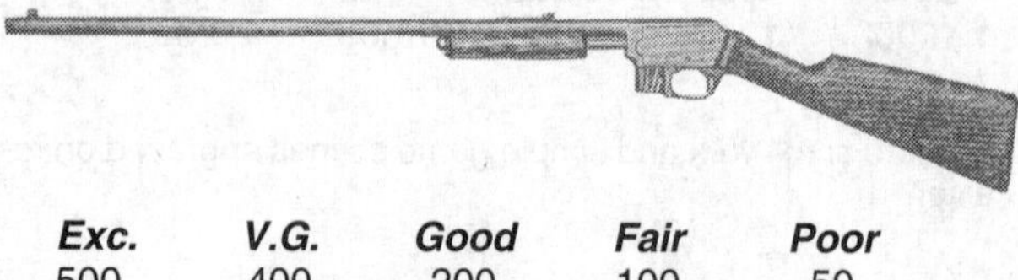

Exc.	V.G.	Good	Fair	Poor
500	400	200	100	50

BAKER, M.A.

Fayetteville, North Carolina

In business from 1857 through 1862, Baker produced sporting arms prior to the Civil War. During the Civil War Baker altered muskets and "common rifles." In addition, it is thought that Baker made rifles for the State of North Carolina with lockplates stamped M.A. BAKER/FAYETTEVILLE/N.C. These rifles resembled the U.S. Model 1841 Rifle and had these characteristics: Overall length 51-1/2"; Barrel length 35-1/8"; Caliber .50.

Exc.	V.G.	Good	Fair	Poor
—	—	25000	12500	2500

BAKER, THOMAS

Baker shotguns and rifles were extensively imported into the United States during the nineteenth and early twentieth centuries. His premises were as follows:

1 Stonecutter Street	1838-1844
Bury Street, St. James	1844-1850
34 St. James Street	1850
88 Fleet Street	1851-1881
88 Fleet Street & 21 Cockspur Street	1882-1898
88 Fleet Street & 29 Glasshouse Street	1899-1905
29 Glasshouse Street	1905-1915
64 Haymarket	1915

BAKER, WILLIAM

Marathon, Syracuse and Ithaca, New York

William Baker designed and built double barrel shotguns from approximately 1869 until his death in 1889. His hammerless designs were used by the Baker Gun & Forging Company of Batavia, New York, which was established by his brother Elias in early 1890.

BALL REPEATING CARBINE

Lamson & Co.
Windsor, Vermont

Ball Repeating Carbine

A .50 caliber lever action repeating carbine with a 20.5" round barrel and 7-shot magazine. The receiver is marked "E.G. Lamson & Co./Windsor, Vt./U.S./Ball's Patent/June 23, 1863/Mar. 15, 1864." Blued, case hardened with a walnut stock. Late production examples of this carbine have been noted with browned or bright barrels. In excess of 1,500 were made between 1864 and 1867.

Courtesy Milwaukee Public Museum, Milwaukee, Wisconsin

Exc.	V.G.	Good	Fair	Poor
—	5000	2500	900	400

BALLARD PATENT ARMS

(until 1873; after 1875, see MARLIN)

On Nov. 5, 1861, C.H. Ballard of Worcester, Massachusetts, received a patent for a breechloading mechanism that would remain in production for nearly thirty years. Ballard patented a breechblock that tilted down at its front to expose the breech by activating the lever/triggerguard. During the twelve years that followed, Ballard rifles, carbines, and shotguns were produced by five interrelated companies. Four of these were successive: Ball & Williams, R. Ball & Co. (both of Worcester, Massachusetts), Merrimack Arms & Manufacturing Co. and Brown Manufacturing Company (both of Newburyport, Massachusetts). These four companies produced Ballard arms in a successive serial range (1 through approximately 22,000), all marked upon the top of the frame and the top of the barrel where it joins the frame. In 1863, another company, Dwight, Chapin & Company of Bridgeport, Connecticut, also produced Ballard rifles and carbines in a larger frame size, but in a different serial range (1 through about 1,900), usually marked on the left side of the frame below the agents' mark. The large frame carbines and rifles were produced to fulfill a U.S. War Department contract initially for 10,000 of each, subsequently reduced to 1,000 of each, issued to Merwin & Bray, the sole agents for the Ballard patent arms between 1862 and 1866. Most of the production during this period concentrated on military contracts, either for the U.S. War Department or the state of Kentucky, although the state of New York also purchased 500 for its state militia.

Ballard (Ball & Williams) Sporting Rifles, First Type (Serial numbers 1-100)

Barrel length 24"; caliber .38 rimfire. Markings: BALL & WILLIAMS/Worcester, Mass., and BALLARD'S PATENT/Nov. 5, 1861 on octagonal barrel. The distinctive feature of the earliest production of the Ballard rifles is the presence of an internal extractor conforming to the patent specifications. After approximately 100 rifles, this feature was dropped in favor of a manual extractor located under the barrel.

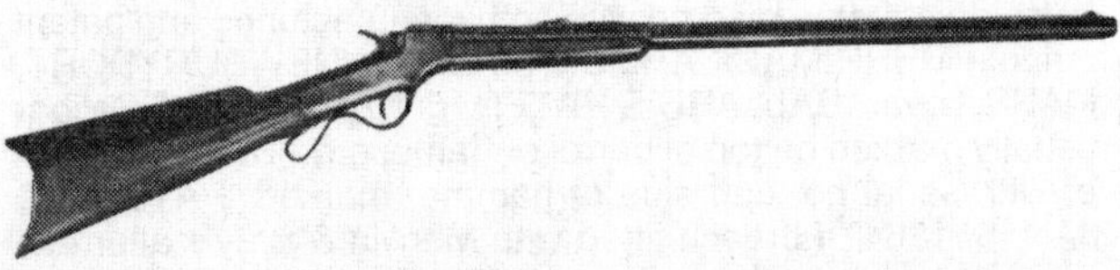

Courtesy Milwaukee Public Museum, Milwaukee, Wisconsin

Exc.	V.G.	Good	Fair	Poor
—	—	2750	1100	450

Ballard (Ball & Williams) Sporting Rifles, Second Type (Serial numbers 200-1600, and 1600-14,000, interspersed with martial production)

Barrel length 24", 28", or 30", usually octagonal, but part round/part octagonal as well; calibers .32, .38, and .44 rimfire. Markings: BALL & WILLIAMS/Worcester, Mass., BALLARD'S PATENT/Nov. 5, 1861, and MERWIN & BRAY, AGT'S/ NEW YORK, on facets of barrel until about serial no. 9000, thereafter the patent name and date on the right side of the frame and the manufacturer and agents on the left side of the frame. On early production (200 to 1500), the extractor knob is smaller and crescent shaped. Early production (prior to about serial no. 10,000) have solid breechblocks; after that number breechblocks are made in two halves. A few of these arms were made with bronze frames to facilitate engraving and plating. These should command a higher premium.

Exc.	V.G.	Good	Fair	Poor
—	—	1500	650	250

Ballard (Ball & Williams) Sporting Rifles, Third Type (Serial numbers 14,000-15,000)

These arms are essentially the same as the second type in characteristics but have Merwin & Bray's alternate percussion mechanism built into the breechblock. The hammer is accordingly marked on the left side "PATENTED JAN. 5, 1864."

Exc.	V.G.	Good	Fair	Poor
—	—	1000	500	200

Ballard (Ball & Williams) Military Carbines (Serial numbers 1500-7500, and 8500-10,500)

Overall length 37-1/4"; barrel (bore) length 22"; caliber .44 rimfire. Markings: same as Ballard/Ball & Williams sporting rifles, second type. Additional marks on U.S. War Department purchases include inspector's initials "MM" or "GH" on left side of frame, and "MM" on barrel, breechblock, buttplate, and on left side of buttstock in script within an oval cartouche. Three thousand of the earlier production (serial numbers 1700 through about 5000) of these carbines were sold to the state of Kentucky under an August 1862 contract, extended in April 1863. In November 1863, Kentucky contracted for an additional 1,000 carbines. In the interim, the state of New York purchased 500 for distribution to its militia. The U.S. War Department ordered 5,000 under a contract signed in January of 1864, but Ball & Williams delivered only 1,500 (serial numbers noted in range of 9800 through 10,600) while concentrating production on their more lucrative Kentucky contract. Another 600 of the federal contract were partially inspected (serial numbers about 6500 to 7100-MM in cartouche in stock only) but were rejected because the barrels had been rifled prior to proofing; these were sold to Kentucky in September 1864 on an open market purchase. The carbines marked with federal inspection marks usually bring a premium.

Courtesy Milwaukee Public Museum, Milwaukee, Wisconsin

Exc.	V.G.	Good	Fair	Poor
—	—	3750	1500	600

Ballard (Ball & Williams) "Kentucky" Half-Stock Rifles

Overall length 45-3/8"; barrel (bore) length 30"; caliber .44 rimfire. These half-stock rifles bear the standard Ball & Williams markings upon their barrels and in addition have the state ownership mark ("KENTUCKY") on the barrel forward of the rear sights. A total of 1,000 (serial numbers about 7100 through 8550) were contracted for by Kentucky in November 1863 and delivered between January and April 1864.

Courtesy Milwaukee Public Museum, Milwaukee, Wisconsin

Exc.	V.G.	Good	Fair	Poor
—	—	1750	700	300

Ballard (Ball & Williams) "Kentucky" Full-Stock Rifles

Overall length 45-1/4"; barrel (bore) length 30"; caliber .46 rimfire. Marked on the frame with standard Ball & Williams manufacturer (left), agent (left), and patent (right) markings, these rifles are additionally distinguished by the state ownership mark "KENTUCKY" stamped into the top of the frame near the breech. Kentucky contracted for 3,000 of these arms in November 1863, initially in .56 caliber. However, by mutual consent of the state and the contractors, in February 1864 the caliber of the arms was changed to .46. All deliveries were made in this caliber, beginning in July 1864 and continuing until March 1865 (serial numbers 10,400 to 14,500).

Courtesy Milwaukee Public Museum, Milwaukee, Wisconsin

Exc.	V.G.	Good	Fair	Poor
—	—	1600	550	250

Ballard (Dwight, Chapin & Co.) Carbines

Overall length 37-3/4"; barrel (bore) length 22"; caliber .56 rimfire. Markings: On left side of round-topped frame "BALLARD'S PATENT/NOV. 5 1861"; on right side of frame "DWIGHT, CHAPIN & CO./BRIDGEPORT CONN." (through serial no. about 125, deleted after that number) over "MERWIN & BRAY/AGT'S N.Y." over serial no. Inspection letters "D" frequently appear on carbines with the Dwight, Chapin, & Co. markings, indicative of preliminary inspection by E. M. Dustin, of the U.S. Ordnance Department.

Often mistaken as early Ballard production from a fictitious Fall River, Massachusetts factory, these carbines and their complementing rifles were in fact not placed into production until 1863, as evident by the split, two-piece breechblocks. Both carbines and rifles originated from a contract entered into between the U.S. War Department and Merwin & Bray in October 1862 for 10,000 of each arm, subsequently reduced to 1,000 of each by the Commission on Ordnance and Ordnance Stores. Because Ball & Williams facilities were tied up with Kentucky contracts, Merwin & Bray turned to the small parts maker of Dwight, Chapin & Co. in Bridgeport, Connecticut. Although they tooled for production, they fell short of scheduled delivery dates, and although about 100 carbines had been inspected, no deliveries were accepted (due to caliber problems) by the U.S. government, effectively bankrupting Dwight, Chapin & Co. The completed carbines and unfinished parts were sent to Worcester and assembled by Ball & Williams, and Merwin & Bray sold all 1,000 carbines in Kentucky in April 1864 on an open market purchase.

Courtesy Milwaukee Public Museum, Milwaukee, Wisconsin

Exc.	V.G.	Good	Fair	Poor
—	—	1800	750	300

Ballard (Dwight, Chapin & Co.) Full-Stock Rifles

Overall length 53"; barrel (bore) length 30"; caliber .56 rimfire. Markings: same as Dwight, Chapin & Co. carbines, but none found with "DWIGHT, CHAPIN & CO./BRIDGEPORT, CONN." stamping above agents marks. The history of these rifles is the same as the .56 caliber carbines, with serial numbers interspersed in the production of the carbines (1 through 1850). Evidently only about 650 of the rifles were completed of the 1,000 set up. Of these, 35 were sold to a U.S. agent in Florida in February 1864 and 600 to Kentucky in April 1864 with the 1,000 carbines.

Exc.	V.G.	Good	Fair	Poor
—	—	1800	750	300

Ballard (R. Ball) & Co. Sporting Rifles

Overall length varies according to barrel length; barrel (bore) length usually 24", 28", and 30"; calibers .32, .38, .44, and .46 rimfire. Markings: The frame markings of R. Ball & Co. rifles are similar to Ball & Williams production, only eliminating the Ball & Williams marking on the left side. Cartridge size, e.g. "No. 44," usually also stamped upon the top of the barrel or frame. Merwin & Bray's patented alternate ignition device usually present with left side of hammer usually marked "PATENTED JAN. 5, 1864." Serial numbers (which follow in sequence with Ball & Williams production. i.e. after no. about 15,800) appear on top of barrel and top of frame. After William Williams withdrew from the Ball & Williams partnership in mid-1865, the business continued under the name of R. Ball & Co., with Richard Ball's son-in-law, E.J. Halstead, in charge after the former's paralytic stroke in the fall of 1865.

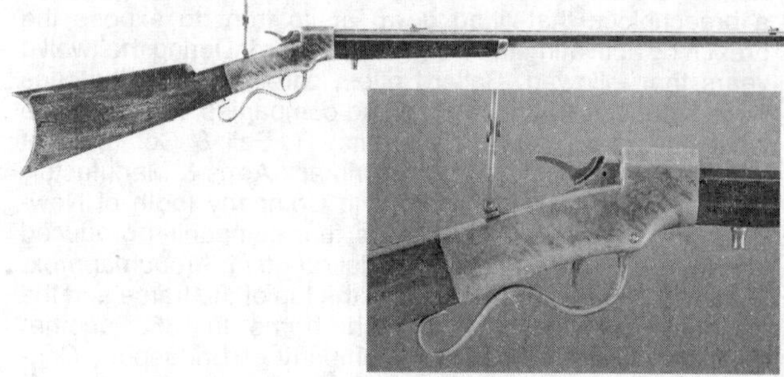

Courtesy Rock Island Auction Company

Exc.	V.G.	Good	Fair	Poor
—	—	2000	850	300

Ballard (R. Ball) & Co. Carbines

Overall length 37-1/4"; barrel (bore) length 22" caliber .44 rimfire. Markings: same as R. Ball & Co. sporting rifles; "No. 44" on top of frame near breech. Although firm evidence is elusive, approximately 1,000 of these carbines were manufactured in anticipation of a Canadian contract, which never came to fruition. Serial numbers are interspersed with sporting rifles, in the 16,400 through 17,700 range. All are equipped with the Merwin & Bray dual ignition block.

Exc.	V.G.	Good	Fair	Poor
—	—	1350	500	200

Ballard (Merrimack Arms & Manufacturing Co.) Sporting Rifles

Overall length varies with barrel length; usual barrel lengths 24", 28", 30"; calibers .22, .32, .44, .46, .50 rimfire. Markings: Left side of frame marked with both manufacturing and patent marks, "MERRIMACK ARMS & MFG. CO./NEWBURYPORT, MASS." over "BALLARD'S PATENT/ NOV. 5, 1861." Caliber usually marked on top of barrel or frame, e.g. "No. 38" together with serial no. Left side of hammer marked "PATENTED JAN. 5, 1864" if breech fitted with Merwin & Bray's alternate ignition device. In the spring of 1866, Edward Bray of Brooklyn, New York, and former partner of Joseph Merwin purchased the Ballard machinery from R. Ball & Co. and set up a new plant in Newburyport, Massachusetts primarily for the production of sporting rifles. The glut of surplus arms on the market following the American Civil War, however, forced him into bankruptcy in early 1869, after producing only about 2,000 Ballard rifles, carbines and a limited number of 20 gauge shotguns. Serial numbers continue in the sequence of the Ball & Williams/R. Ball & Co. production (serial numbers about 18,000 through 20,300). Prices of these rifles will vary considerably depending on the degree of finish or engraving.

Exc.	V.G.	Good	Fair	Poor
—	—	1750	700	300

Ballard (Merrimack Arms & Manufacturing Co.) Carbines

Overall length 37-1/4"; barrel (bore) length 22"; caliber .44 rimfire. Markings: same as Merrimack Arms & Mfg. Co. sporting rifles. In March 1866, the state of New York purchased 100 Ballard carbines (serial numbers about 18,500 to 18,600) for use by its prison guards. In January 1870, an additional 70 (serial numbers 19,400 to 19,500) were purchased from New York City arms merchants Merwin, Hulbert & Co. to arm guards at Sing Sing Prison. Between these two purchases Merrimack Arms & Mfg. Co. had shortened its new "tangless" frames by 1/8", the prime distinction between the two purchases. Despite the rarity of both types of carbines, they do not command high prices.

Exc.	V.G.	Good	Fair	Poor
—	—	1250	500	275

Ballard (Brown Manufacturing Co.) Sporting Rifles

Dimensions: same as Merrimack Arms & Mfg. Co. sporting rifles. Markings: left side of frame marked with manufacturer, "BROWN MFG. CO. NEWBURYPORT, MASS." over patent, "BALLARD'S PATENT/ NOV. 5, 1861." Serial no. on top of barrel and frame. Upon the failure of Merrimack Arms & Manufacturing Company in early 1869, the plant was purchased by John Hamilton Brown, who continued producing Ballard patent rifles until 1873 in a serial range consecutive with that of its three predecessors (Ball & Williams, R. Ball & Co., and Merrimack Arms & Mfg. Co.). Approximately 2,000 Ballard arms were produced during the period of Brown's manufacture of the Ballard (serial numbers about 20,325 through 22,100). Brown made Ballards tend to exhibit finer finishing than earlier produced rifles, accounting for their average higher value. Special features, such as breakdown facility and side extractors (on .22 cal. rifles) will also positively affect the prices.

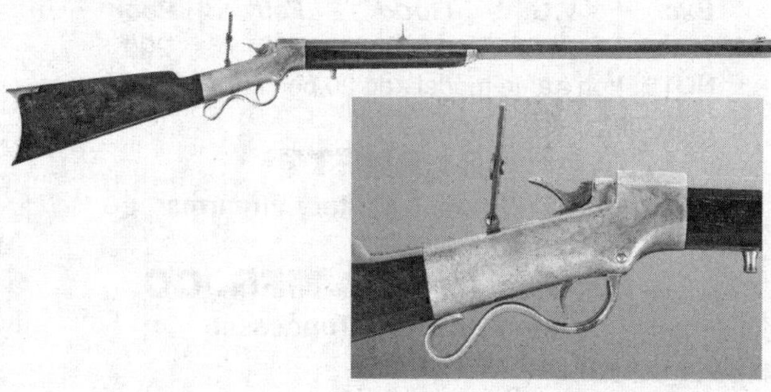

Courtesy Rock Island Auction Company

Exc.	V.G.	Good	Fair	Poor
—	—	1750	600	300

Ballard (Brown Mfg. Co.) Full-Stock Military Rifles

Overall length 52-1/2" barrel (bore) length 30"; caliber .46 rimfire. Markings: The same as Brown Mfg. Co. sporting rifles, with the addition of the caliber marking, "No. 46," on the top of the barrel forward of the rear sight. The cause for the production of the Ballard/Brown military rifle has yet to be determined, but it has been speculated that they were possibly manufactured in anticipation of a sale to France during the Franco-Prussian War. In any event, the sale was not culminated, and many, if not most, of the estimated 1,000 produced were "sporterized" by shortening the forestock and sold by commercial dealers in the United States. Serial numbers concentrate in the 20,500 through 21,600 range, with sporting rifles interspersed in the sequence. Rifles that have not been sporterized command a premium.

Exc.	V.G.	Good	Fair	Poor
—	—	1750	700	300

BALLARD RIFLE AND CARTRIDGE CO.

Cody, Wyoming

All models feature American black walnut stocks, case hardening, and rust blued barrels. There are a number of special order features that are available with these rifles. These extra-cost items should be appraised prior to a sale.

No. 1-3/4 Far West Rifle

Offered with 30" round barrel in standard or heavy weight. Single or double-set triggers, S lever, ring-style lever, blade front sight, and Rocky Mountain rear sight. Offered in calibers from .32-40 to .50-90. Weight with standard 30" barrel is approximately 10.5 lbs., with heavyweight barrel 11.75 lbs.

NIB	Exc.	V.G.	Good	Fair	Poor
2500	2000	1500	—	—	—

No. 4-1/2 Mid Range Model

This model features checkered fancy walnut stock, standard or heavy weight half octagon barrel 30" or 32" with single or double-set triggers, pistol grip, hard rubber or steel shotgun butt, horn forend cap, full-loop lever, and globe front sight. Offered in calibers from .32-40 to .40-70. Weight with standard barrel 10.75 lbs. and with heavy barrel 11.5 lbs.

NIB	Exc.	V.G.	Good	Fair	Poor
2800	2250	1700	—	—	—

No. 5 Pacific Model

This model features a 30" or 32" octagon barrel in either standard or heavy weight, stocks in rifle or shotgun configuration, double-set triggers, ring lever, blade front sight, and Rocky Mountain rear sight. Calibers from .38-55 to .50-90. Weight with standard 30" barrel is 10.75 lbs., with heavyweight barrel 12 lbs.

NIB	Exc.	V.G.	Good	Fair	Poor
2950	2200	1850	—	—	—

No. 7 Long Range Model

This model features a fancy walnut checkered stock with 32" or 34" standard or heavy weight half octagon barrel. Pistol-grip stock with rubber or steel shotgun butt, single or double-set triggers, full-loop lever, horn forend cap, and globe front sight. Calibers from .32-40 to .45-110. Weight with standard 32" barrel 11.75 lbs., with heavyweight barrel 12.25 lbs.

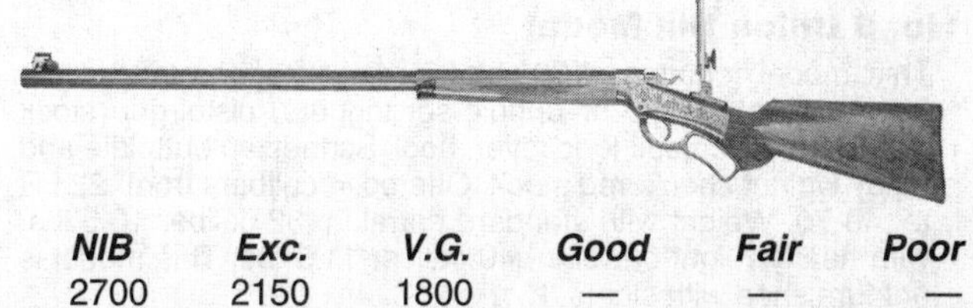

NIB	Exc.	V.G.	Good	Fair	Poor
2700	2150	1800	—	—	—

No. 1-1/2 Hunter's Rifle

This model features a 30" round barrel, single trigger, S lever, plain forend, and rifle buttstock. Blade front sight and Rocky Mountain rear sight are standard. Calibers from .32-40 to .50-70. Weight is about 10.5 lbs.

NIB	Exc.	V.G.	Good	Fair	Poor
2600	1950	1550	—	—	—

No. 2 Sporting Model

Stocked in plain walnut with crescent butt and offered in 24", 26", 28", or 30" octagon barrel with blade front and Rocky Mountain rear sights. A straight-grip action with S lever, in calibers .38-40, .44-40, and .45 Colt. Discontinued.

NIB	Exc.	V.G.	Good	Fair	Poor
1650	1250	900	—	—	—

No. 3 Gallery Rifle

Chambered for the .22 caliber rimfire cartridge this model features a choice of 24", 26", or 30" lightweight octagon barrel with rifle-style buttstock with steel crescent buttplate, S lever, blade and Rocky Mountain sights. Weight with standard 26" barrel is about 7.5 lbs.

NIB	Exc.	V.G.	Good	Fair	Poor
2600	2250	1900	—	—	—

No. 3F Fine Gallery Rifle

Same as above model but with fancy checkered walnut stock, pistol grip, single or double-set triggers, full-loop lever, light Schuetzen buttstock, Globe front sight and gallery tang sight. Weight with standard 26" barrel is approximately 7.75 lbs.

NIB	Exc.	V.G.	Good	Fair	Poor
3100	2600	2000	—	—	—

No. 4 Perfection Model

This model features a plain walnut stock with rifle or shotgun butt. Offered in 28", 30" or 32" octagon barrel with blade front sight and Rocky Mountain rear sight. Straight-grip action with single or double-set triggers with S lever or ring lever in calibers from .32-40 to .50-90.

NIB	Exc.	V.G.	Good	Fair	Poor
3000	2500	1900	—	—	—

No. 5-1/2 Montana Model

This model has a fancy walnut stock, double-set triggers, and ring lever. Shotgun steel butt. Barrels are either 28", 30" or 32", extra heavy octagon, in calibers .45-70, .45-110, and .50-90. Under barrel wiping rod. Weight is approximately 14.5 lbs.

NIB	Exc.	V.G.	Good	Fair	Poor
2900	2300	1700	—	—	—

No. 6 Off-Hand Rifle Model (Schuetzen)

This rifle features a fancy walnut checkered stock with hand rubbed finish, heavy Schuetzen buttplate, and horn insert on forend. Choice of 30", 32", or 34" half-octagon barrel with Globe front sight. Straight-grip action with double-set triggers, Schuetzen ball, spur lever and deluxe rust blueing. Offered in .22 LR, .32-40, .38-55, .40-65, and .40-70 calibers.

NIB	Exc.	V.G.	Good	Fair	Poor
2900	2300	1700	—	—	—

No. 8 Union Hill Model

This model features a 30" or 32" half-octagon standard or heavy barrel, single or double-set triggers, pistol-grip stock with cheekpiece, full-loop lever, hook Schuetzen buttplate and fancy walnut checkered stock. Offered in calibers from .22 LR to .40-70. Weight with standard barrel in .32 caliber 10.5 lbs, with heavyweight barrel in .40 caliber 11.5 lbs. This model is not furnished with sights.

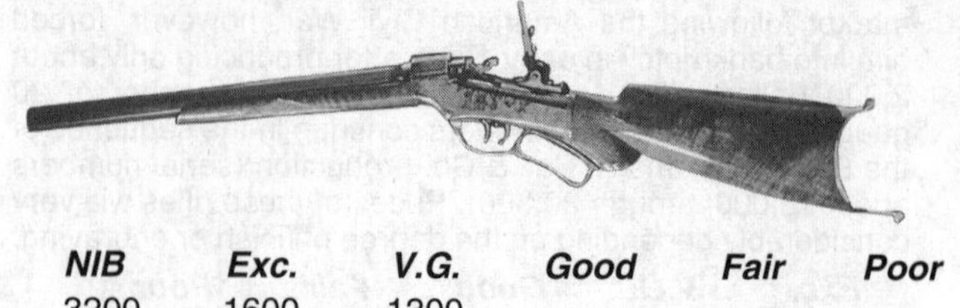

NIB	Exc.	V.G.	Good	Fair	Poor
3200	1600	1300	—	—	—

Model 1885 High Wall

This single-shot rifle is chambered for a wide variety of calibers from .18 Bee to .577 Express. Barrel lengths to 34". American walnut stock. Many options to choose from that will affect price. Introduced in 2000.

NIB	Exc.	V.G.	Good	Fair	Poor
2650	2100	1600	—	—	—

BALLESTER—MOLINA

SEE—Hafdasa

BALLARD, C. H.

Worcester, Massachusetts

Single-Shot Derringer

A .41 caliber rimfire spur trigger single-shot pistol with a 2.75" barrel marked "Ballard's." Blued with silver-plated frame and walnut grips. Manufactured during the 1870s.

Exc.	V.G.	Good	Fair	Poor
—	—	1250	500	200

NOTE: Iron frame model add 20 percent.

BARNETT

SEE—English Military Firearms

BARRETT F.A. MFG. CO.

Murfreesboro, Tennessee

Model 82 Rifle

A .50 caliber Browning semi-automatic rifle with a 37" barrel and 11-shot magazine. The barrel fitted with a muzzlebrake, and the receiver with a telescope. Approximate weight 35 lbs. Parkerized. Manufactured from 1985 to 1987.

NIB	Exc.	V.G.	Good	Fair	Poor
4200	3500	2750	2250	—	—

Model 82A1

As above, with a 29" barrel without sights, and a 10-round magazine. A 10X telescope and iron sights are optional. Comes with hard carrying case. Weight is 28.5 lbs.

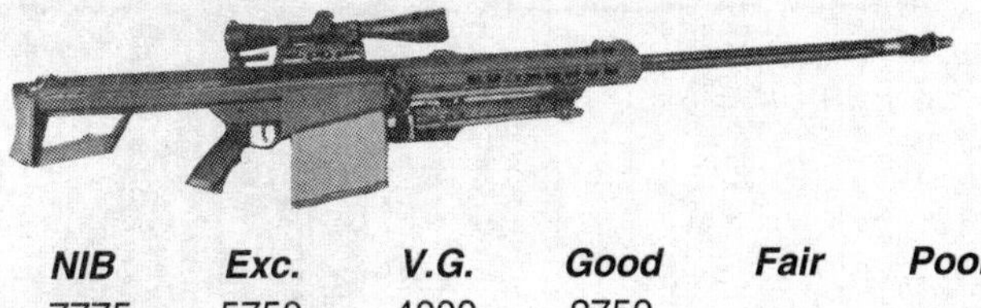

NIB	Exc.	V.G.	Good	Fair	Poor
7775	5750	4000	2750	—	—

Model 95M

Introduced in 1995 this .50 caliber BMG bolt-action model features a 29" barrel and 5-round magazine. Scope optional. Weight is 22 lbs.

NIB	Exc.	V.G.	Good	Fair	Poor
5540	4000	3000	2000	—	—

Model 99

This model is a single-shot bolt-action rifle chambered for the .50 BMG cartridge. Standard barrel length is 32". Optional barrel lengths of 29" or 25". Rifle weight is about 25 lbs. with 32" barrel.

NIB	Exc.	V.G.	Good	Fair	Poor
3675	2750	2000	—	—	—

NOTE: Add $200 for fluted barrel.

Model 99-1

Similar to the Model 99 but fitted with a 29" barrel. Weight is about 21 lbs.

NIB	Exc.	V.G.	Good	Fair	Poor
2800	2250	—	—	—	—

Model 107

Chambered for the .50 caliber cartridge this model is a semi-automatic rifle fitted with a 29" barrel with muzzlebrake. Bipod is detachable and adjustable. M1913 accessory rail. Supplied with two 10-round magazines. Weight is about 32 lbs.

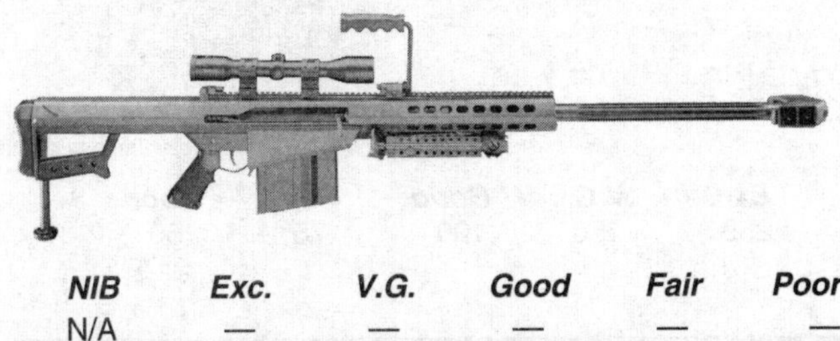

NIB	Exc.	V.G.	Good	Fair	Poor
N/A	—	—	—	—	—

Model 468

Built on a semi-automatic AR-15 style lower receiver, this rifle features a 16" barrel with muzzlebrake chambered for the 6.8 SPC cartridge. Folding front sight and integrated Rail system. Folding rear sight. Weight is about 7.3 lbs.

NIB	Exc.	V.G.	Good	Fair	Poor
2700	2000	—	—	—	—

BARRETT, J. B. and A.B. & CO.

Wytheville, Virginia

Barrett Muskets and Rifled Muskets

Overall length 57-3/4"; barrel length 41-1/2" to 42"; caliber .69. Markings: Although the Barretts placed no marks of their own on their alterations, most were effected on Virginia Manufactory muskets, whose lockplates are marked "VIRGINIA/Manufactory" forward of the hammer and "RICHMOND/(date)" on the tail.

For many years collectors considered the adaptations of Hall rifles and carbines from breechloaders to muzzleloaders to be the product of J.B. Barrett & Co. of Wytheville. Recent evidence, however, confirms that those adaptations were actually effected in Danville, Virginia, by another firm (see READ & WATSON). Nevertheless, the Barretts of Wytheville did adapt arms during the early years of the American Civil War. The adaptation, effected almost exclusively upon Virginia Manufactory flintlock muskets, consisted of percussioning by means of the cone-in-barrel and rifling of the barrels with seven narrow grooves. In 1861 and 1862, the Barretts percussioned a total of 1250 muskets, of which 744 were rifled.

Courtesy Milwaukee Public Museum, Milwaukee, Wisconsin

Exc.	V.G.	Good	Fair	Poor
—	—	15000	6000	2000

BAR-STO PRECISION MACHINE

Burbank, California

Bar-Sto 25

A .25 caliber semi-automatic pistol with a brushed stainless steel receiver and slide. Walnut grips. Produced in 1974.

Exc.	V.G.	Good	Fair	Poor
225	175	150	125	100

BASCARAN, MARTIN A.

Eibar, Spain

A Spanish manufacturer of pistols prior to World War II.

Martian 6.35mm

A 6.35mm semi-automatic pistol. The slide is marked "Automatic Pistol Martian." Blued with black plastic grips having the monogram "MAB" cast in them.

Exc.	V.G.	Good	Fair	Poor
250	175	135	100	75

Martian 7.65mm

A semi-automatic pistol patterned after the Ruby military pistols. "Martian" is stamped on the slide with wood grips and a lanyard loop.

Courtesy James Rankin

Exc.	V.G.	Good	Fair	Poor
250	175	135	100	75

Thunder

A semi-automatic pistol in caliber 6.35mm. Almost a duplicate of the Martian above except for the sight placement. "Thunder" is stamped on the slide and each grip plate.

Courtesy James Rankin

Exc.	V.G.	Good	Fair	Poor
250	175	100	75	45

BAUER F. A. CORP.

Fraser, Michigan

Bauer 25 Automatic

A .25 caliber semi-automatic pistol made of stainless steel with a 2.5" barrel and 6-shot magazine. Walnut or imitation pearl grips. Manufactured from 1972 to 1984. After 1984 this pistol was produced under the name of Fraser for a few years.

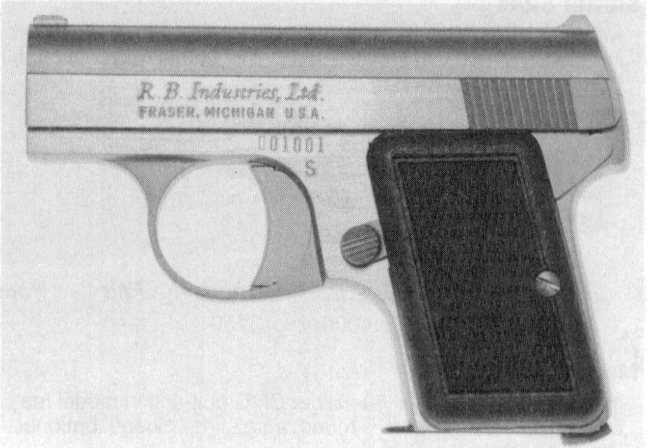

Courtesy James Rankin

Exc.	V.G.	Good	Fair	Poor
275	200	175	125	80

The Rabbit

A .22 caliber by .410 bore combination rifle/shotgun, with a tubular metal stock. Manufactured between 1982 and 1984. Similar to Gacria Bronco.

Exc.	V.G.	Good	Fair	Poor
325	300	225	125	75

BAYARD

SEE—Pieper, H. & N. and Bergmann

Herstal, Belgium

BAYONNE, MANUFACTURE D'ARMES

Bayonne, France
aka MAB

MAB Model A

Manufactured in 1921 and chambered for the 6.35mm cartridge. Patterned after the Browning Model 1906. Squeeze grip safety with a 6-round magazine.

Courtesy James Rankin

Exc.	V.G.	Good	Fair	Poor
250	150	90	75	50

REMINDER
An "N/A" or "—" instead of a price indicates that there is no known price available for that gun in that condition, or the sales for that particular model are so few that a reliable price cannot be given.

MAB Model B

Manufactured in 1932 and chambered for the 6.35mm cartridge. The pistol has an exposed hammer, no grip safety, and a 6-round magazine.

Courtesy James Rankin

Exc.	V.G.	Good	Fair	Poor
250	150	90	75	50

MAB Model C

Manufactured in 1933 and chambered for the 7.65mm and .380 cartridge. Patterned after the Browning Model 1910. Seven-round magazine.

Courtesy James Rankin

Exc.	V.G.	Good	Fair	Poor
325	225	200	125	90

MAB Model D

Manufactured in 1933 and chambered for the 7.65mm and .380 cartridge. Basically a Model C with a longer barrel and a 9-round magazine.

Courtesy James Rankin

Exc.	V.G.	Good	Fair	Poor
300	200	150	125	100

NOTE: Add 100 percent for Nazi-marked pistols.

MAB Model E

Manufactured in 1949 and chambered for the 6.35mm cartridge. Patterned after the Model D with streamlined grips and a 10-round magazine.

Exc.	V.G.	Good	Fair	Poor
325	225	200	150	125

MAB Model F

Manufactured in 1950 and chambered for the .22 LR cartridge. Interchangeable barrel lengths, target grips, and a 10-round magazine.

Courtesy James Rankin

Exc.	V.G.	Good	Fair	Poor
325	225	200	150	125

MAB Model G

Manufactured in 1951, chambered for the .22 LR cartridge and 7.65mm cartridge. Some with Dural frames. Magazine capacity is 10 rounds for .22 LR and 8 rounds for the 7.65mm.

Courtesy James Rankin

Exc.	V.G.	Good	Fair	Poor
350	250	225	150	125

MAB Model GZ

Manufactured in calibers .22 LR, 6.35mm, 7.65mm, and .380. Almost identical to the Model G. Dural frames and two-tone finishes on some variations.

Exc.	V.G.	Good	Fair	Poor
350	250	225	150	125

MAB Model P-8 & P-15

In 1966 MAB manufactured the Model P-8 and Model P-15 in 9mm Parabellum with 8- and 15-round magazine capacity. Basically it is the same gun with different magazine capacities. The Model P-15 went to the French military as well as some commercial sales.

Courtesy James Rankin

Exc.	V.G.	Good	Fair	Poor
450	350	300	250	175

Model P-15 M1 Target

The MAB Model P-15 was manufactured for target shooting using the 9mm Parabellum cartridge. Most M1 Target MABs were purchased by the French military for their target teams.

Courtesy James Rankin

Exc.	V.G.	Good	Fair	Poor
500	400	350	275	175

MAB Model R

Manufactured in caliber 7.65mm Long in 1951 the Model R was similar to the Model D. Model Rs were later produced in several calibers. The .22 LR was furnished with a 10-round magazine and two different barrel lengths. The 7.65mm had a 9-round magazine while the .380 and 9mm Parabellum were fitted with 8-round magazines.

.22 Long Rifle

Exc.	V.G.	Good	Fair	Poor
350	250	225	150	125

7.65mm & 7.65mm Long & .380

Exc.	V.G.	Good	Fair	Poor
350	250	225	150	125

9mm Parabellum

Exc.	V.G.	Good	Fair	Poor
400	300	250	150	125

MAB Model R PARA Experimential

In the late 1950s MAB began experimenting with the Model R in caliber 9mm Parabellum. There were many of these experimental-type pistols and the 8-round, rotating barrel Model R shown led directly to the Model P-15 series.

Courtesy James Rankin

Exc.	V.G.	Good	Fair	Poor
1500	1250	1000	500	250

Model "Le Chasseur"

Manufactured in 1953 the Le Chasseur was a target model in .22 LR and had a 9-round magazine. It had an external hammer, target sights, and target grips.

NOTE: MAB pistols that were sold in the U.S.A. were retailed by the Winfield Arms Company of Los Angeles, California, and are marked "Made in France for WAC." This does not affect value.

Exc.	V.G.	Good	Fair	Poor
300	200	150	125	90

BEATTIE, J.

London, England

Beattie produced a variety of revolvers during the percussion period, some of which were imported into the United States. During the period this firm was in business, it was located at these London addresses:

43 Upper Marylebone Street	1835-1838
52 Upper Marylebone Street	1838-1842
52 Upper Marylebone Street & 223 Regent Street	1842-1846
205 Regent Street	1851-1882
104 Queen Victoria Street	1882-1894

Beattie Gas Seal Revolver

A .42 caliber single-action percussion revolver with a 6.25" octagonal barrel. When the hammer is cocked, the cylinder is forced forward against the barrel breech, thus effecting a gas seal. Blued, case hardened with walnut grips.

Exc.	V.G.	Good	Fair	Poor
—	4500	3000	2000	1000

BEAUMONT

Maastrict, Netherlands

1873 Dutch Service Revolver, Old Model

A 9.4mm double-action 6-shot revolver weighing 2 lbs. 12 oz.

Exc.	V.G.	Good	Fair	Poor
—	600	350	150	100

1873 Dutch Service Revolver, New Model

As above, with a 6-shot cylinder.

Exc.	V.G.	Good	Fair	Poor
—	600	350	150	100

1873 KIM, Small Model

As above, with an octagonal barrel and 5-shot cylinder.

Exc.	V.G.	Good	Fair	Poor
—	700	400	175	100

BEAUMONT, ADAMS

SEE—Adams

BEAUMONT-VITALI

Holland

NOTE: For photos, historical data, and prices see *The Standard Catalog of Military Firearms, Netherlands, Rifles, Beaumont.*

BECKER AND HOLLANDER

Suhl, Germany

Beholla

A semi-automatic pistol in caliber 7.65mm. Introduced in 1908 in Germany. It was manufactured by Becker & Hollander until 1920. After that date three different companies produced the Beholla under the names Stenda, Menta, and Leonhardt.

Courtesy James Rankin

Exc.	V.G.	Good	Fair	Poor
500	350	225	175	100

BEEMAN PRECISION ARMS, INC.

Santa Rosa, California

Although primarily known as an importer and retailer of airguns, Beeman Precision Arms, Inc. has marketed several firearms.

MP-08

A .380 caliber semi-automatic pistol, with a 3.5" barrel and 6-shot magazine, resembling the German Luger. Blued. Introduced in 1968.

NIB	Exc.	V.G	Good	Fair	Poor
450	350	250	200	175	100

P-08

As above, in .22 caliber with an 8-shot magazine and walnut grips. Introduced in 1969.

NIB	Exc.	V.G.	Good	Fair	Poor
450	350	250	200	175	100

SP Standard

A .22 caliber single-shot target pistol with 8" to 15" barrels. Fitted with adjustable sights and walnut grips. Imported in 1985 and 1986.

NIB	Exc.	V.G.	Good	Fair	Poor
300	200	175	150	125	75

SP Deluxe

As above, with a walnut forend.

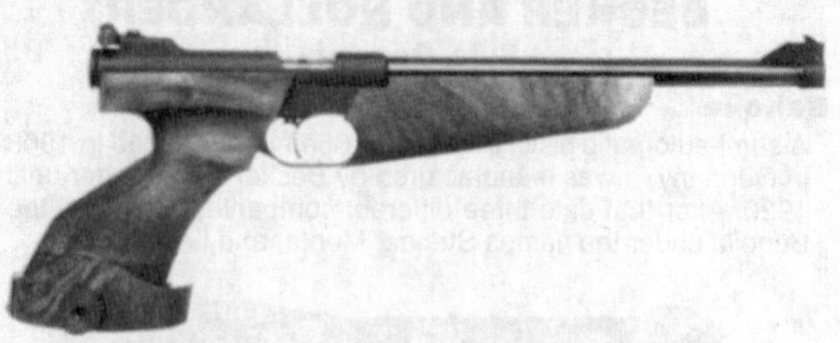

NIB	Exc.	V.G.	Good	Fair	Poor
325	225	200	175	125	75

BEERSTECHER, FREDERICK

Philadelphia, Pennsylvania (1846-1856)
Lewisburg, Pennsylvania (1857-1868)

Superposed Load Pocket Pistol

A .41 caliber superposed load percussion pistol with an average barrel length of 3", German silver mounts and walnut stock. The hammer is fitted with a moveable twin striker head so that the first charge in the barrel can be fired and then the second fired. The lock is normally marked "F. Beerstecher's/Patent 1855." Prospective purchasers are advised to secure a qualified appraisal prior to acquisition.

Exc.	V.G.	Good	Fair	Poor
—	5500	4000	3000	950

BEESLEY, FREDERICK

London, England
SEE—British Double Guns

BEHOLLA

SEE—Becker and Hollander

BEISTEGUI, HERMANOS

Eibar, Spain
SEE—Grand Precision

BENELLI

Italy

SHOTGUNS

Model SL-121 V

This is a semi-automatic 12 gauge with 3" chambers and various barrel lengths and chokes. It has a black anodized alloy receiver and was discontinued in 1985.

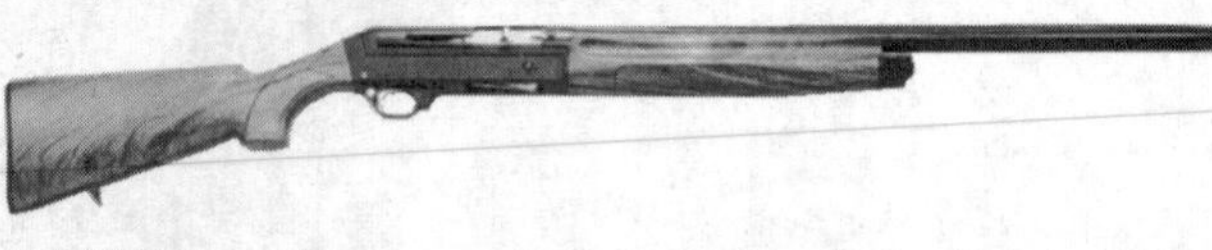

NIB	Exc.	V.G.	Good	Fair	Poor
500	450	400	350	300	150

Model SL 121 Slug

This model is similar to the SL-121 V with a 21" cylinder-bore barrel and rifle sights. It, too, was discontinued in 1985.

NIB	Exc.	V.G.	Good	Fair	Poor
500	450	400	350	300	150

Model SL-123 V

This model has the improved, fast, third-generation action. Otherwise it resembles the earlier SL-121.

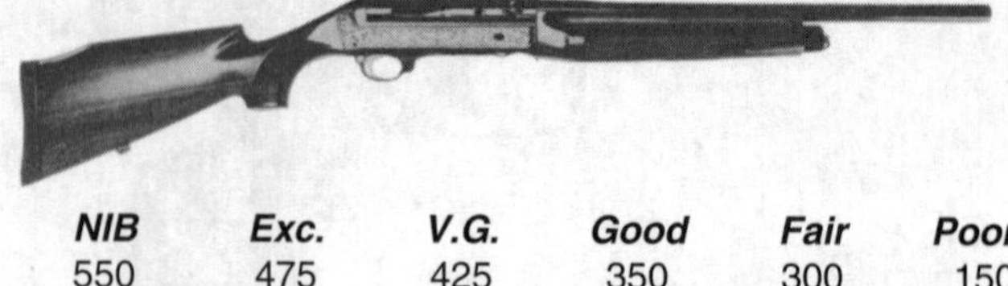

NIB	Exc.	V.G.	Good	Fair	Poor
550	475	425	350	300	150

Model SL 201

This is a 20 gauge with a 26", Improved Cylinder barrel. It is similar in appearance to the SL-123.

NIB	Exc.	V.G.	Good	Fair	Poor
500	475	425	350	300	150

M3 Super 90

This is an improved version of the Benelli pump action and semi-automatic inertia recoil system. The shotgun can be converted from pump to semi-automatic by turning a spring-loaded ring located at the end of the forearm. It has a rotating bolt system and is chambered for 12 gauge, with a 3" chamber. This model has a 19.75" barrel with cylinder bore and rifle sights with a 7-round tubular magazine. It has a matte black finish and a black fiberglass pistol-grip stock and forearm. This model was introduced in 1986.

NIB	Exc.	V.G.	Good	Fair	Poor
1185	900	700	600	450	300

NOTE: Add $50 for open rifle sights.

M3 Super 90 Folding Stock

Same as above but furnished with a folding tubular steel stock.

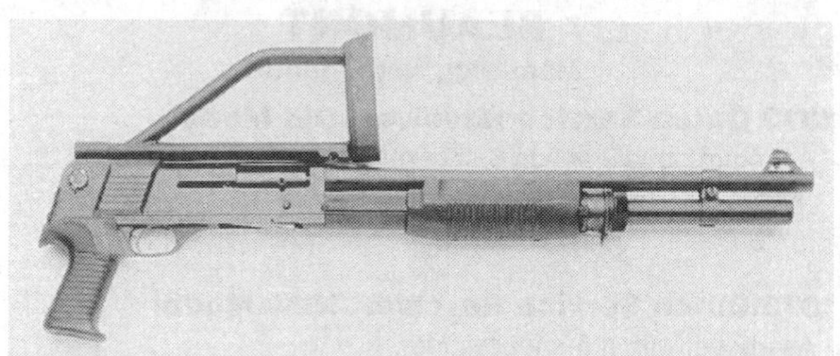

NIB	Exc.	V.G.	Good	Fair	Poor
2000	1500	1150	850	600	300

M4

Adopted by the U.S. Marine Corps this 12 gauge shotgun features a choice of three modular buttstock and two barrel configurations. Top-mounted Picatinny rail. Barrel length is 18.5". Magazine capacity is 6 rounds. Ghost ring sights. Weight is about 8.4 lbs. Matte black finish. Introduced in 2003. The civilian version does not have a collapsible buttstock.

M4 with non-collapsible stock with cheekpiece

M4 with standard stock

M4 with pistol-grip stock

NIB	Exc.	V.G.	Good	Fair	Poor
1530	1150	—	—	—	—

M1014 Limited Edition

Introduced in 2003 this version of the M4 is fitted with a skelton buttstock and a special U.S. flag engraving on the receiver. Fitted with an 18.5" barrel and Picatinny rail with ghost ring sights. Limited to 2,500 shotguns.

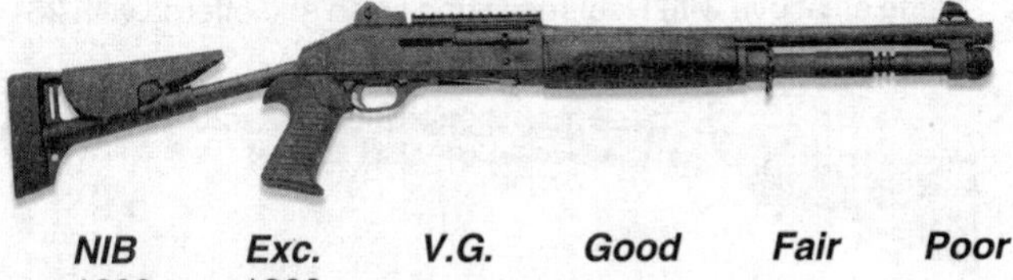

NIB	Exc.	V.G.	Good	Fair	Poor
1600	1200	—	—	—	—

M1 Practical

This model was designed for IPSC events and features an oversized safety, speed loader, larger bolt handle, muzzlebrake, and adjustable ghost ring sight and optics rail. Offered with 26" barrel with extended magazine tube. Weighs about 7.6 lbs.

NIB	Exc.	V.G.	Good	Fair	Poor
1150	900	750	500	—	—

M1 Super 90 Tactical

This is a semi-automatic 12 gauge shotgun with an inertia recoil system. It features an 18.5" plain barrel with three screw-in choke tubes. Available in either standard polymer stock or pistol-grip stock. Ghost ring sights are standard. Gun weighs 6.5 lbs. First introduced in 1993.

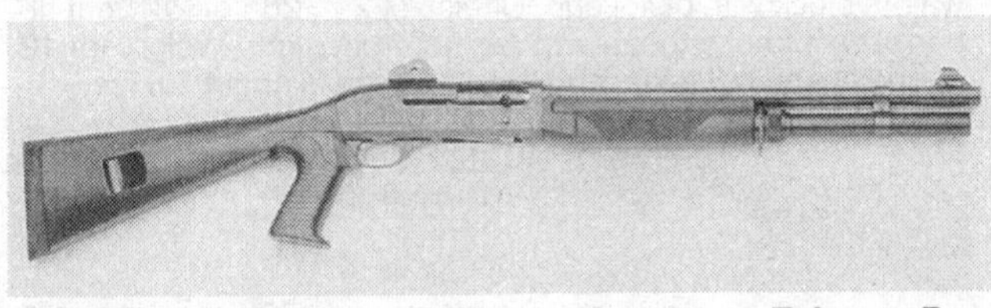

NIB	Exc.	V.G.	Good	Fair	Poor
900	700	600	500	450	250

M1 Super 90 Slug Gun

Equipped with a standard black polymer stock with 19.75" plain barrel. Fitted with a 7-shot magazine. Ghost ring sights are an option. Weighs 6.7 lbs. Camo model introduced in 2000.

NIB	Exc.	V.G.	Good	Fair	Poor
1000	750	550	450	350	250

NOTE: Add $100 for Camo model.

M1 Super 90 Entry Gun

This model is fitted with a black polymer pistol-grip stock with 14" plain barrel. Magazine holds 5 shells. Plain or ghost ring sights available. **CAUTION: NFA Weapon, Restricted sale, Class III Transfer required**. Manufacturer's retail price is $900.

M1 Super 90 Defense Gun

Comes standard with polymer pistol-grip stock, 19.75" barrel, plain sights, or ghost ring sights. Offered in 12 gauge only. Weighs 7.1 lbs.

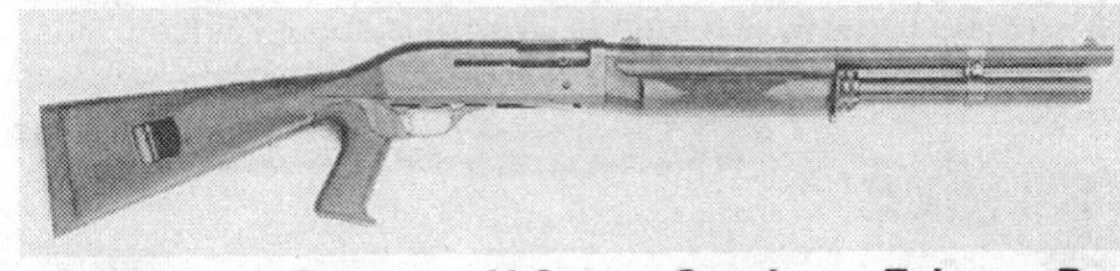

NIB	Exc.	V.G.	Good	Fair	Poor
900	700	600	500	450	250

M1 Super 90 Field

This model is similar to other Super 90 series guns with a 21", 24", 26", or 28" vent rib barrel with screw-in choke tubes. In 1998 this model was available with 24" rifled bore with matte rib. Add $80 for this barrel. Left-hand model added in 2000. In 2001 this model was offered in 20 gauge as well.

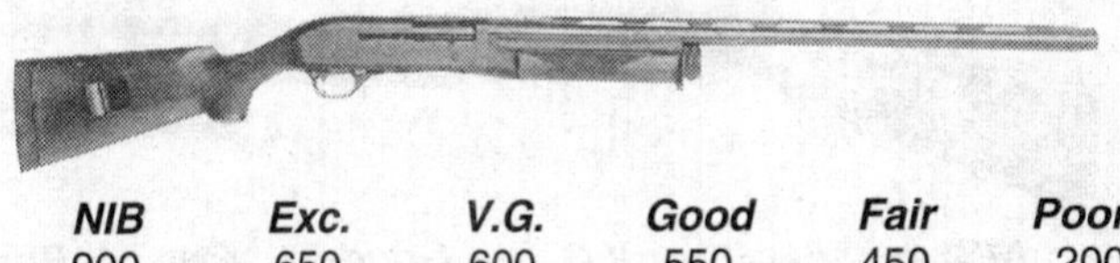

NIB	Exc.	V.G.	Good	Fair	Poor
900	650	600	550	450	200

M1 Super 90 Camo Field

Same as above but with camouflage receiver, barrel, buttstock and forearm. Offered in 24", 26", and 28" vent rib barrels. Introduced in 1997. In 1998 this model was also offered with a 21" vent rib barrel. Left-hand model added in 2000. In 2001 this model was offered in 20 gauge as well.

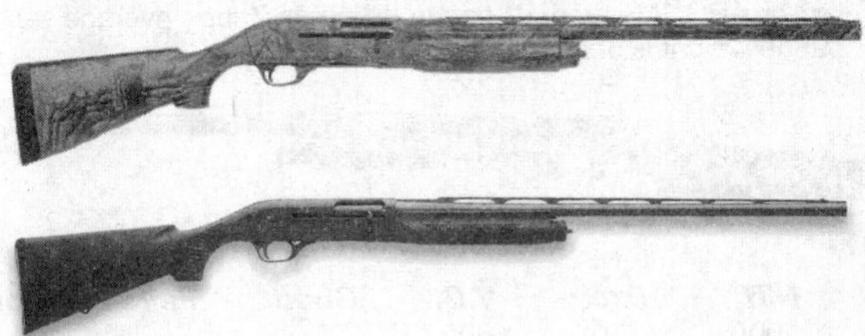

M1 20 gauge

NIB	Exc.	V.G.	Good	Fair	Poor
950	750	700	600	500	400

M1 Field Steady Grip

Introduced in 2003 this model features a vertical pistol grip, drilled and tapped receiver and extra Full choke tube. Barrel length is 24". Weight is about 7.3 lbs.

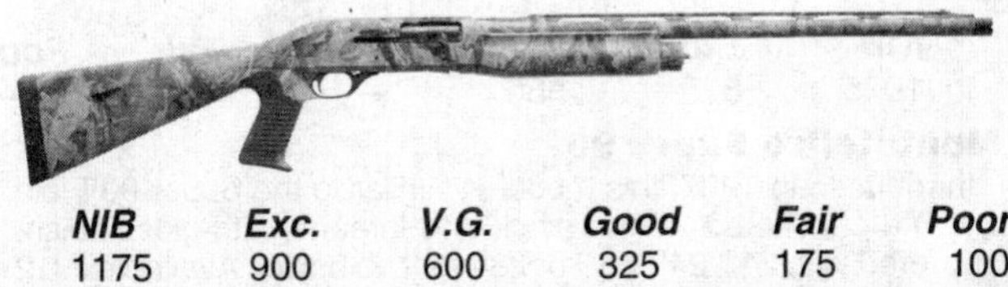

NIB	Exc.	V.G.	Good	Fair	Poor
1175	900	600	325	175	100

M1 Super 90 Sporting Special

Introduced in 1993 this 12 gauge shotgun is similar to the Super 90 with the addition of non-reflective surfaces, 18.5" plain barrel with 3 choke tubes (IC, Mod, Full). The gun is fitted with ghost ring sights.

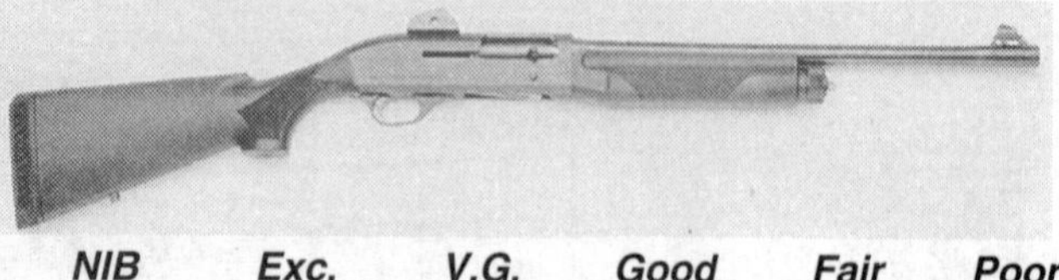

NIB	Exc.	V.G.	Good	Fair	Poor
725	600	500	400	350	200

M2 Practical with ComforTech

Introduced in 2005 this model is chambered for the 12 gauge 3" shell and fitted with a 25" plain barrel with compensator and ghost-ring rear sight. Receiver is fitted with a Picatinny rail. Magazine capacity is 8 rounds. Weight is about 7.6 lbs.

NIB	Exc.	V.G.	Good	Fair	Poor
1335	1000	750	—	—	—

M2 Tactical

This 12 gauge 3" gun is fitted with a 18.5" barrel with choke tubes and choice of rifle or ghost-ring sights. Pistol grip or extended pistol grip. Black synthetic stock. Magazine capacity is 5 rounds. Weight is about 7 lbs.

NIB	Exc.	V.G.	Good	Fair	Poor
1000	750	500	—	—	—

NOTE: Add $70 for ComforTech version and $65 for Ghost-ring sights.

M2 Field with ComforTech

In 12 gauge, this model is offered with a 21", 24", 26" or 28" barrel with a black matte synthetic finish or Max-4, Timber or APG camo. The 20 gauge has a 24" or 26" barrel in black, Timber or APG. Average 12 gauge weight is 7 lbs.; average 20 gauge weight is 5.8 lbs. Add $75 for camo.

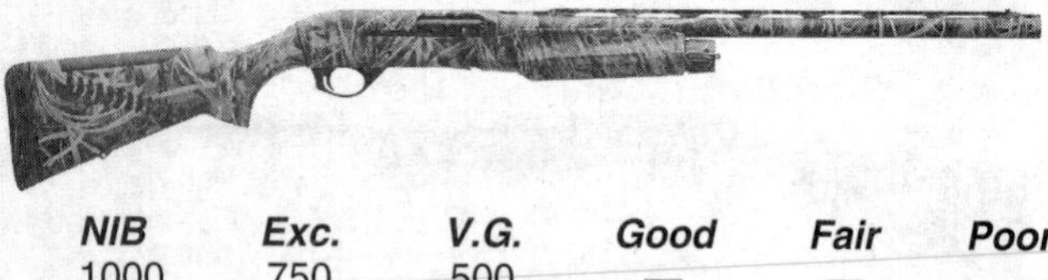

NIB	Exc.	V.G.	Good	Fair	Poor
1000	750	500	—	—	—

M2 Field without ComforTech

Same features as above without ComforTech features. Available only in satin walnut with 26" or 28" barrel.

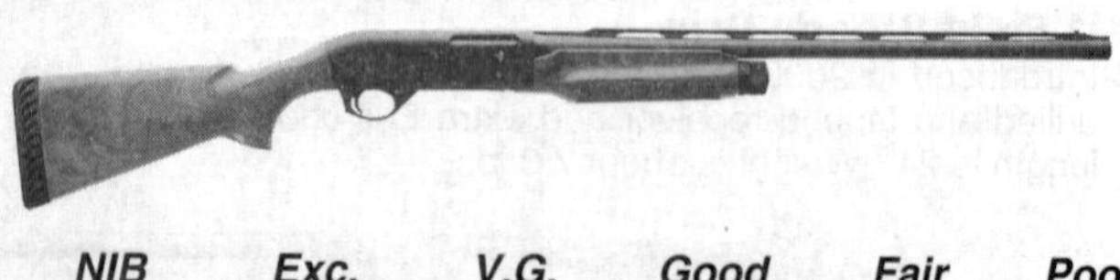

NIB	Exc.	V.G.	Good	Fair	Poor
1075	825	550	—	—	—

Montefeltro Super 90

Introduced in 1987, this model is similar to the Super 90 Field with a checkered walnut stock and forearm with gloss finish. Offered with 21", 24", 26", or 28" vent rib barrel. Available in 12 gauge only with 3" chambers. This shotgun offered in left-hand model also.

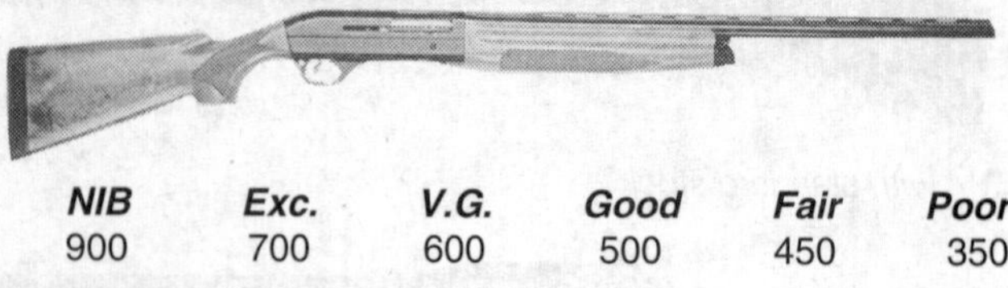

NIB	Exc.	V.G.	Good	Fair	Poor
900	700	600	500	450	350

Montefeltro 20 Gauge

Introduced in 1993, this model features a walnut checkered stock with 26" vent rib barrel. In 1995 a 24" vent rib barrel was offered as well. Gun weighs 5.75 lbs.

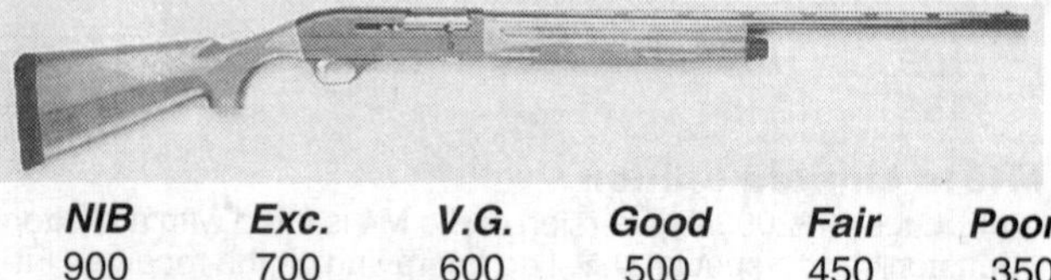

NIB	Exc.	V.G.	Good	Fair	Poor
900	700	600	500	450	350

NOTE: Add $75 for short stock model.

Montefeltro 20 Gauge Camo

Same as above with Realtree Camo finish and offered with 26" vent rib barrel. Introduced in 1998.

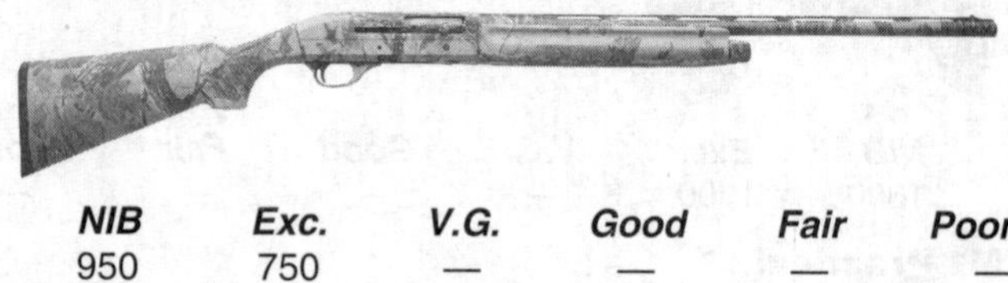

NIB	Exc.	V.G.	Good	Fair	Poor
950	750	—	—	—	—

Montefeltro 20 Gauge Limited

Introduced in 1995 this version features a finely etched nickel plate receiver with scroll and game scenes highlighted in gold. The stock is a select grade walnut and is fitted with a 26" vent rib barrel.

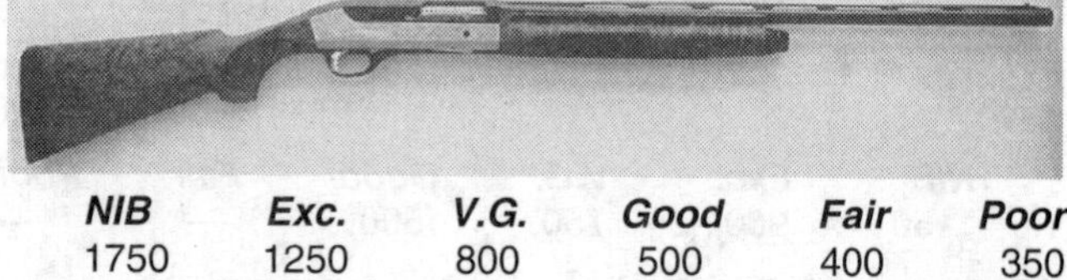

NIB	Exc.	V.G.	Good	Fair	Poor
1750	1250	800	500	400	350

Montefeltro (2005)

This is an updated version of the Montefeltro series of guns with a slight change in the receiver, a different trigger, upgraded wood, and the name "Montefeltro" in gold on the receiver. Offered in 12 or 20 gauge with 3" chambers. Checkered select walnut stock with pistol grip. Choice of 24", 26", or 28" vent rib barrel with choke tubes and red bar front sight. Weight for 12 gauge is about 6.9 lbs. and the 20 gauge is about 5.6 lbs.

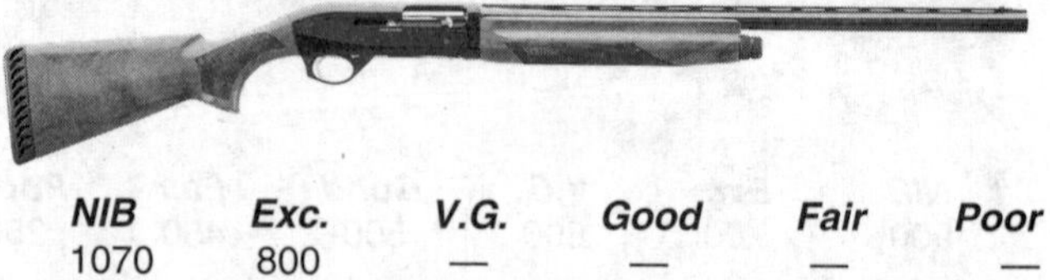

NIB	Exc.	V.G.	Good	Fair	Poor
1070	800	—	—	—	—

SUPER BLACK EAGLE II

This new series of guns was introduced in 2005. Major features are a new butt pad, grip, and cryogenically treated barrels for which specially designed longer choke tubes are required. Benelli offers this series with or without "ComforTech" features. This system reduces recoil up to 48 percent and muzzle climb by 15 percent.

Super Black Eagle II with ComforTech

Offered in 12 gauge with 3.5" chambers. Barrel lengths are 24", 26", or 28" with choke tubes and red bar front sight. Available in synthetic or various camo finishes. Magazine capacity is 3 rounds. Weight is about 7.2 lbs. with 26" barrel.

NIB	Exc.	V.G.	Good	Fair	Poor
1465	1100	700	—	—	—

Super Black Eagle II without ComforTech

This model, without ComforTech, has the same options as the one above with the addition of a walnut stock.

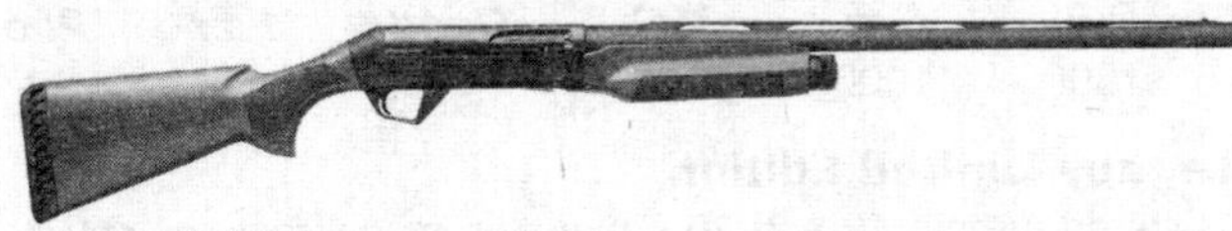

NIB	Exc.	V.G.	Good	Fair	Poor
1355	1000	650	—	—	—

NOTE: Add $60 for walnut stock. Add $110 for camo models.

Super Black Eagle II Rifled Slug with ComforTech

This is a 12 gauge 3" chamber gun with 24" rifled barrel with adjustable sights. Available with synthetic stock or Timber HD camo stock. Weight is about 7.4 lbs.

NIB	Exc.	V.G.	Good	Fair	Poor
1535	1150	650	—	—	—

NOTE: Add $120 for Camo version.

Super Black Eagle II Turkey Gun

This 12 gauge 3" chamber shotgun (3.5" chambers on non-ComforTech guns) is fitted with 24" smooth bore barrels with choke tubes. Red bar front sight. Weight is about 7.1 lbs. Available with Timber HD camo stock with or without ComforTech.

NIB	Exc.	V.G.	Good	Fair	Poor
1455	1050	600	—	—	—

NOTE: Add $130 for ComforTech version.

Super Black Eagle II Steady Grip

This 12 gauge 3.5" chamber gun is fitted with a 24" barrel with red bar front sight. Choke tubes. Stock is camo with steady grip pistol grip. Weight is about 7.3 lbs. This model comes without ComforTech.

NIB	Exc.	V.G.	Good	Fair	Poor
1200	950	750	600	—	—

Super Black Eagle

This model is similar to the Montefeltro Super 90 Hunter with a polymer or walnut stock and forearm. It is offered with a 24", 26", or 28" vent rib barrel with 5 screw-in choke tubes. Chambered for 12 gauge from 2-3/4" to 3-1/2". It was introduced in 1989. The 24" barrel was introduced in 1993.

NIB	Exc.	V.G.	Good	Fair	Poor
1200	800	750	600	500	400

Super Black Eagle Left-Hand

Introduced in 1999 this model is the same as the Black Eagle but in a left-hand version. A Camo version is available.

NIB	Exc.	V.G.	Good	Fair	Poor
1200	950	750	—	—	—

Super Black Eagle Custom Slug Gun

This 12 gauge model has a 24" rifled barrel with 3" chamber. It comes standard with matte metal finish. Gun weighs 7.6 lbs.

NIB	Exc.	V.G.	Good	Fair	Poor
1100	800	750	600	500	350

Super Black Eagle Camo Gun

Introduced in 1997 this model features 24", 26", or 28' vent rib barrels chambered for 12 gauge shells. Has a Realtree Xtra Brown Camo finish. Stock is camo polymer as is forearm.

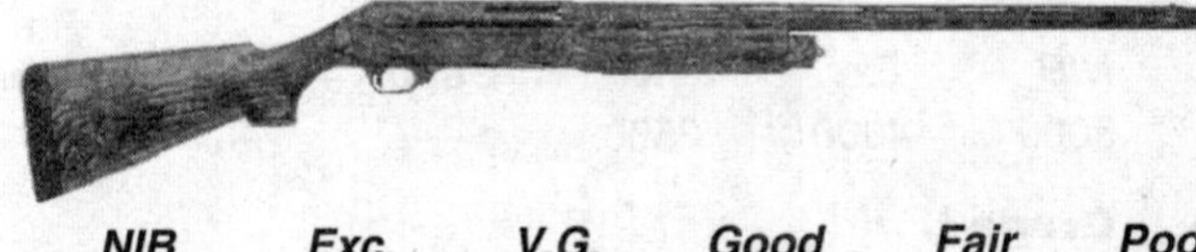

NIB	Exc.	V.G.	Good	Fair	Poor
1300	1000	750	600	500	400

Super Black Eagle Steady Grip

Similar to the model above but equipped with a vertical pistol grip. Drilled and tapped receiver. Extra Full choke tube. Barrel length is 24". Weight is about 7.3 lbs. Introduced in 2003.

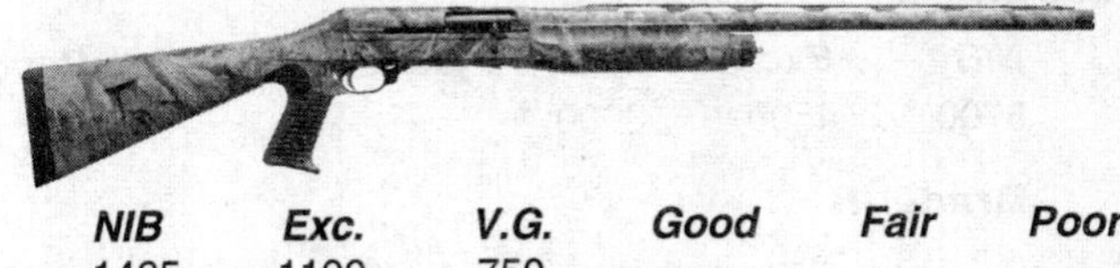

NIB	Exc.	V.G.	Good	Fair	Poor
1465	1100	750	—	—	—

Super Black Eagle Limited Edition

Introduced in 1997 this shotgun features a 26" vent rib barrel, matte metal finish, and satin select grade wood stock. The nickel plated receiver is finely etched with scroll and game scenes. Limited to 1,000 guns.

NIB	Exc.	V.G.	Good	Fair	Poor
2000	1500	1050	—	—	—

Black Eagle Competition Gun

Offered in 12 gauge only this model is fitted with an etched receiver, mid rib bead, competition stock, and 5 screw-in choke tubes. Available in either 26" or 28" vent rib barrel. The upper receiver is steel while the lower receiver is lightweight alloy. Weighs 7.3 lbs.

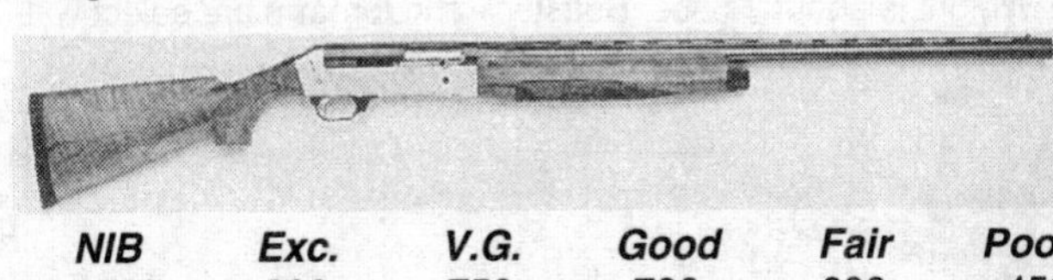

NIB	Exc.	V.G.	Good	Fair	Poor
1300	800	750	700	600	450

Black Eagle

Similar to the Black Eagle Competition Model but with standard grade wood and matte black finish on the receiver. Introduced in 1997.

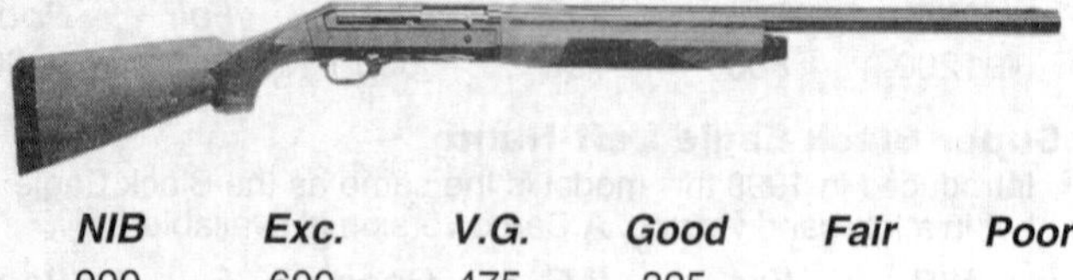

NIB	Exc.	V.G.	Good	Fair	Poor
900	600	475	325	—	—

Black Eagle Executive Series

Offered in 12 gauge only this is a special order only shotgun. It is offered with a choice of 21", 24", 26", 28" vent rib barrels. Each grade or level of gun is engraved with increasing levels of coverage. The stock is fancy walnut.

Grade I

NIB	Exc.	V.G.	Good	Fair	Poor
5000	4000	2500	—	—	—

Grade II

NIB	Exc.	V.G.	Good	Fair	Poor
5700	4500	3000	—	—	—

Grade III

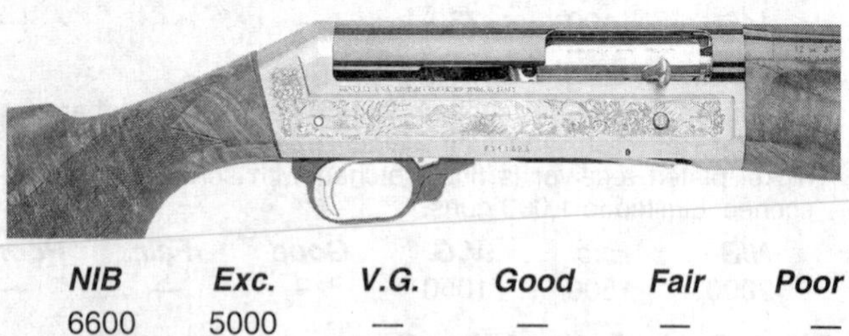

NIB	Exc.	V.G.	Good	Fair	Poor
6600	5000	—	—	—	—

Legacy

This model features a coin finished alloy receiver and is chambered for the 12 gauge 2-3/4" or 3" shell. It is fitted with a choice of 26" or 28" vent rib barrel with mid and front sights. Weight is about 7.5 lbs. Buttstock and forearm are select walnut.

NIB	Exc.	V.G.	Good	Fair	Poor
1300	1000	750	—	—	—

Legacy—20 Gauge

Offered for the first time in 1999 this model is chambered for 20 gauge shells and is fitted with either 24" or 26" vent rib barrels. Weight is about 6 lbs.

NIB	Exc.	V.G.	Good	Fair	Poor
1300	1000	—	—	—	—

Legacy Limited Edition

Offered in both 12 and 20 gauge this model features select walnut stock and etched game scenes with gold filled accents. The 12 gauge features waterfowl scenes while the 20 gauge has upland game scenes. The 12 gauge is fitted with a 28" barrel while the 20 gauge has a 26" barrel. This model was introduced in 2000 and is limited to 250 guns in each gauge.

Limited Edition, right side, 12 gauge

NIB	Exc.	V.G.	Good	Fair	Poor
1600	1200	900	—	—	—

Legacy (2005)

This is a updated version of the Legacy model with changes in the engraving pattern, upgraded wood, improved trigger, and a slightly different receiver style. Offered in 12 and 20 gauge with 3" chambers and choice of 26" or 28" vent rib barrel with choke tubes. Red bar front sight. Checkered select walnut stock with pistol grip. Magazine capacity is 4 rounds. Weight for 12 gauge is about 7.4 lbs. and the 20 gauge is about 5.8 lbs.

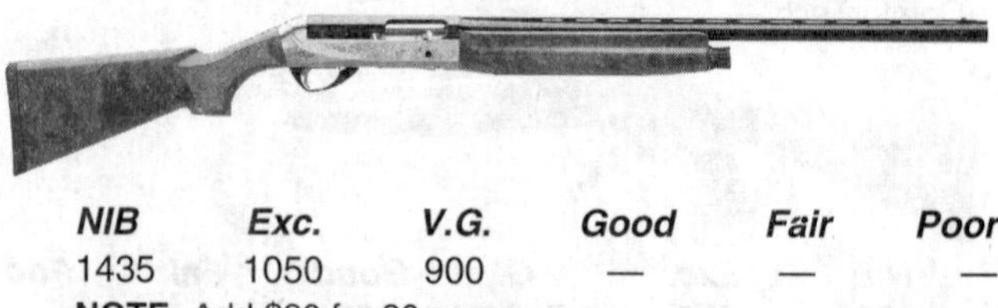

NIB	Exc.	V.G.	Good	Fair	Poor
1435	1050	900	—	—	—

NOTE: Add $30 for 20 gauge.

Cordoba

This model, introduced in 2005, is chambered for the 12 gauge 3" shell and fitted with cryogencially treated ported barrels in 28" or 30" lengths with extended choke tubes. Vent rib is 10mm width. Synthetic stock with adjustable length butt pads. Red bar front sight. Weight is about 7.25 lbs.

NIB	Exc.	V.G.	Good	Fair	Poor
1600	1250	1050	—	—	—

Nova

Introduced in 1999 this model features polymer molded frame with steel cage chambered for 3-1/2" shells. Choice of 24", 26", or 28" vent rib barrels. A 18.5" slug barrel is also offered. Two- or four-shot magazine extensions are offered as well. Weight with 28" barrel is 8 lbs. Choice of camo or black synthetic pistol-grip stock. In 2001 this model was offered in 20 gauge as well.

Nova Pump with vent rib barrel

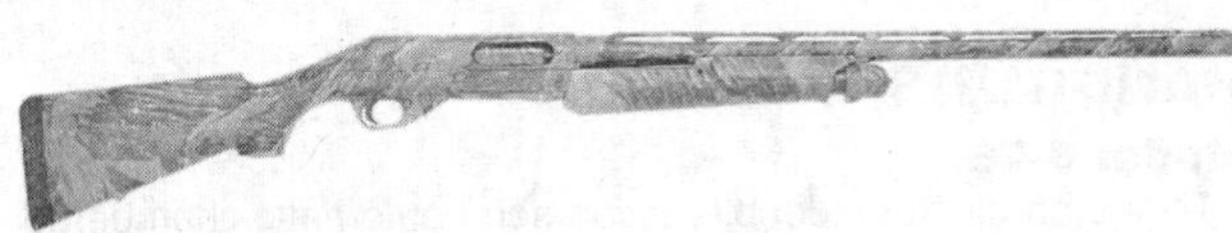

Nova Camo Model

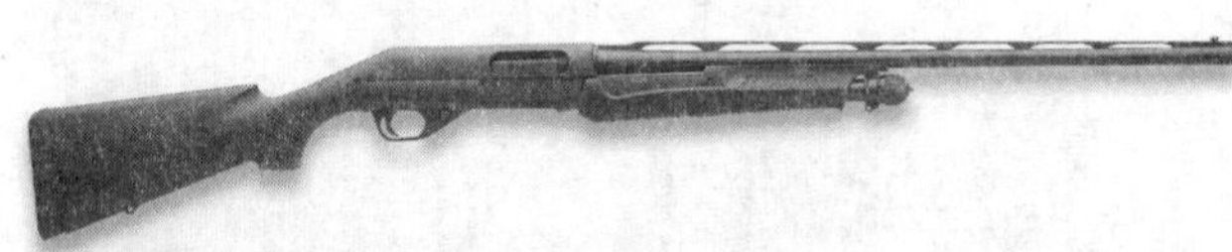

Nova 20 gauge

NIB	Exc.	V.G.	Good	Fair	Poor
350	275	225	175	150	—

Nova Slug

This 12 gauge shotgun has a 18.5" cylinder bored barrel with open rifle or ghost-ring sights. Black synthetic stock. Chambered for 2.75" or 3" shells. Magazine capacity is 4 rounds. Weight is about 7.2 lbs. Introduced in 2000.

NIB	Exc.	V.G.	Good	Fair	Poor
350	275	225	200	150	—

NOTE: Add $40 for ghost ring sights.

Nova Rifled Slug

Introduced in 2000 this 12 gauge model features a 24" rifled barrel with open rifle sights. Black synthetic stock or Timber HD camo stock. Chambered for 2.75" or 3" shells. Magazine capacity is 4 rounds. Weight is about 8 lbs.

NIB	Exc.	V.G.	Good	Fair	Poor
525	425	350	250	—	—

NOTE: Add $75 for Camo version.

Nova Field Slug Combo

This 12 gauge 3" gun is equipped with a 26" and 24" barrel. The 26" barrel is fitted with a vent rib and choke tube while the 24" barrel is rifled and fitted with a cantilever scope mount. Black synthetic stock.

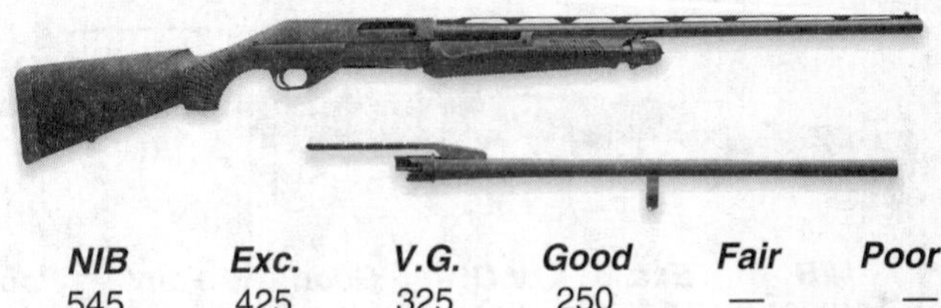

NIB	Exc.	V.G.	Good	Fair	Poor
545	425	325	250	—	—

Nova H_2O Pump

Introduced in 2003 this model features a largely polymer exterior with corrosion-resistant finish. Barrel, magazine tube, magazine cap, trigger group and other internal parts are nickel plated. Chambered for 12 gauge. Fitted with an 18.5" barrel. Black synthetic stock. Magazine capacity is 4 rounds. Open rifle sights. Weight is about 7.2 lbs.

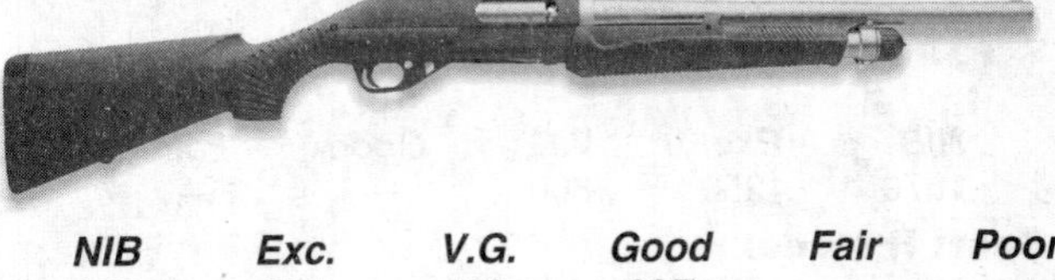

NIB	Exc.	V.G.	Good	Fair	Poor
465	375	295	225	—	—

Supernova

Introduced in 2006, the Supernova incorporates Benelli's ComforTech stock system into the Nova pump shotgun. Available in 24", 26" and 28" barrel lengths in matte black synthetic, 24" and 26" barrel lengths in Advantage Timber camo, and 26" and 28" barrel lengths in Max-4 camo. Weight is about 8 lbs. with 28" barrel. All versions are chambered for 3.5" shells. Three choke tubes. Add 15 percent for camo versions.

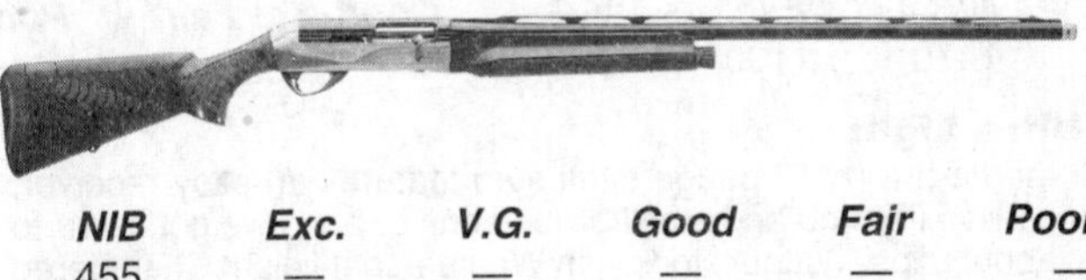

NIB	Exc.	V.G.	Good	Fair	Poor
455	—	—	—	—	—

Supernova SteadyGrip

As above but with extended pistol grip in 24" barrel only. Matte black synthetic or Advantage Timber stock. Add 15 percent for camo model.

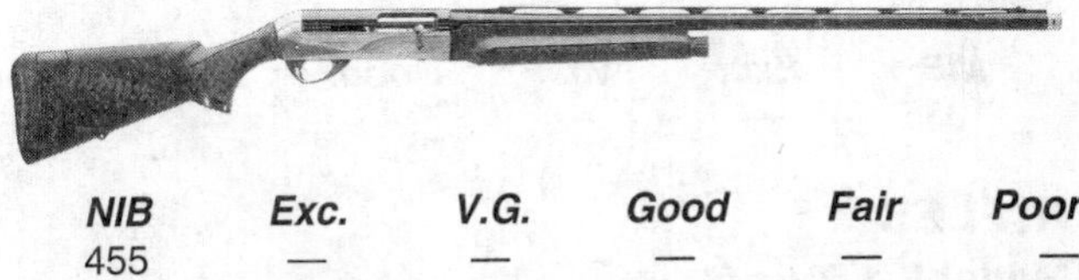

NIB	Exc.	V.G.	Good	Fair	Poor
455	—	—	—	—	—

Supernova Tactical

Matte black synthetic stock with 18" barrel. Available with ComforTech or pistol grip stock. Fixed cylinder bore. Open rifle sights. Ghost ring sights optional.

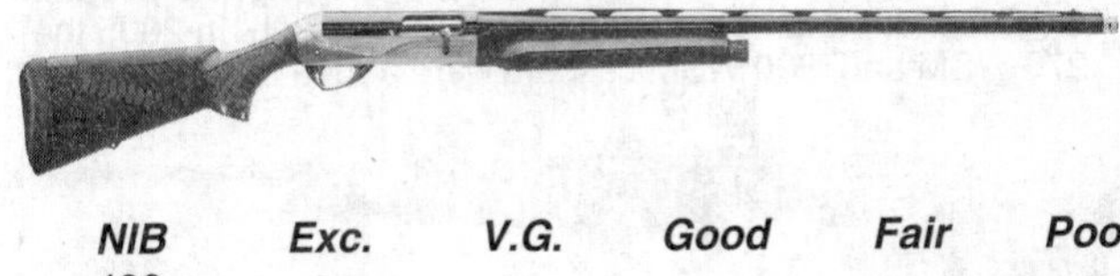

NIB	Exc.	V.G.	Good	Fair	Poor
400	—	—	—	—	—

Sport Model

This model was introduced in 1997 and is the first shotgun with removable, interchangeable carbon fiber vent ribs. This model is offered in 12 gauge only with choice of 26" or 28" barrels or 20-ga. with 28" barrel.. Buttpad is adjustable. Weight is 7 lbs. for 26" models and 7.3 lbs. for 28" models.

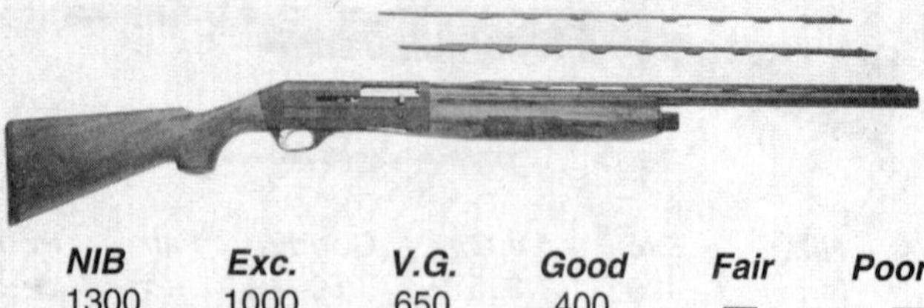

NIB	Exc.	V.G.	Good	Fair	Poor
1300	1000	650	400	—	—

SuperSport with ComforTech

Introduced in 2005 this model is offered in 12 gauge with 3" chamber or 20-ga. with 28" barrel. Choice of 28" or 30" carbon fiber barrel with choke tubes and red bar front sight. Weight is about 7.25 lbs.

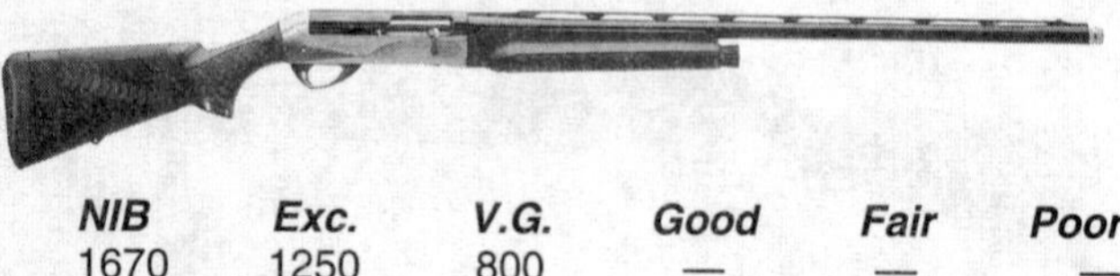

NIB	Exc.	V.G.	Good	Fair	Poor
1670	1250	800	—	—	—

Sport II Model

Introduced in 2003 this model features cryogenically treated barrels and extra-long choke tubes. Chambered for the 12 gauge shell in either 2.75" or 3" with 28" or 30" barrel or 20-ga. with 28" barrel. Vent rib and choke tubes. Magazine capacity is 4 rounds. Red bar front sight. Weight is approximately 7.9 lbs.

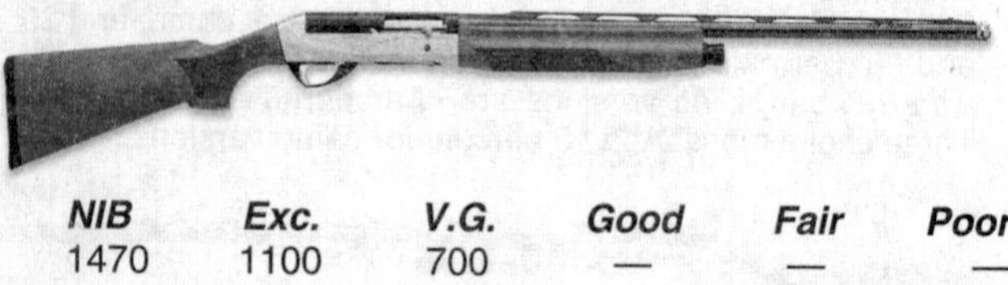

NIB	Exc.	V.G.	Good	Fair	Poor
1470	1100	700	—	—	—

Ultra Light

Inertia-driven 12 gauge semi-auto features an alloy receiver, carbon fiber rib and small proportions to bring weight down to about 6 lbs. Walnut stock with Weathercoat finish. Chambered for 3" shells. Offered in 24" or 26" barrel only with 5 Crio chokes. Introduced 2006.

NIB	Exc.	V.G.	Good	Fair	Poor
1335	—	—	—	—	—

RIFLES

Model R 1 Rifle

Introduced in 2003 this rifle is chambered for the .30-06 or .300 Win. Mag cartridge. Barrels are cryogenically treated. Action is gas operated. Interchangeable barrel offered in 20" and 22" in .30-06 and 20" and 24" in .300 Win. Mag. Walnut stock. Detachable magazine has a 4-round capacity. Weight is about 7 to 7.2 lbs. depending on caliber and barrel length. In 2005 the .270 WSM and .300 WSM calibers were added to the R 1 rifle.

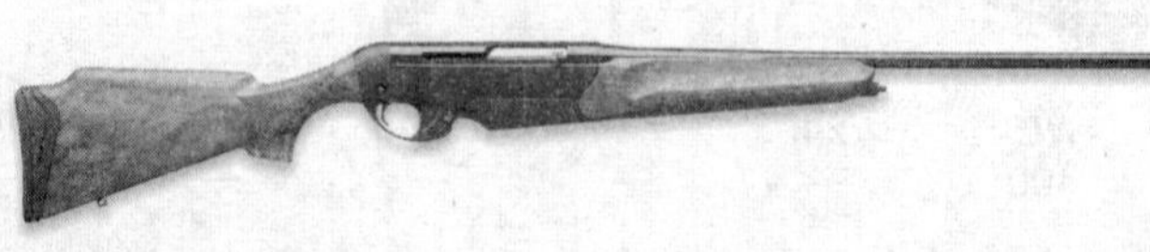

NIB	Exc.	V.G.	Good	Fair	Poor
1080	750	600	—	—	—

Model R 1 Carbine

As above but with 20" barrel chambered for the .30-06 or .300 Win. Mag calibers. Weight is about 7 lbs.

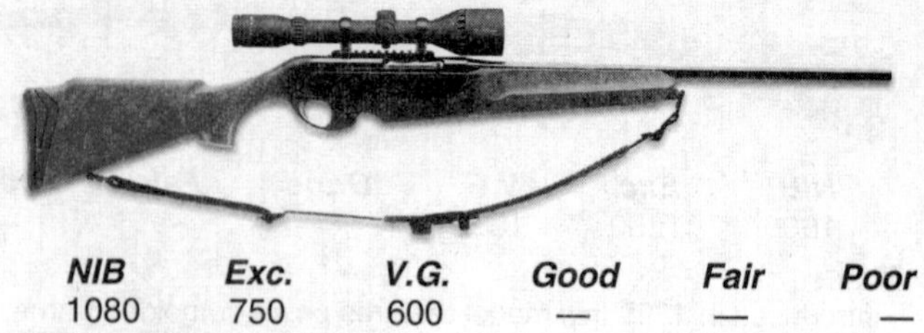

NIB	Exc.	V.G.	Good	Fair	Poor
1080	750	600	—	—	—

R1 ComforTech Rifle

Similar to Model R1 but with ComforTech recoil-absorbing stock. Additional chamberings .270 and .300 WSM. Introduced 2006. Add 10 percent for RealTree camo and adjustable comb.

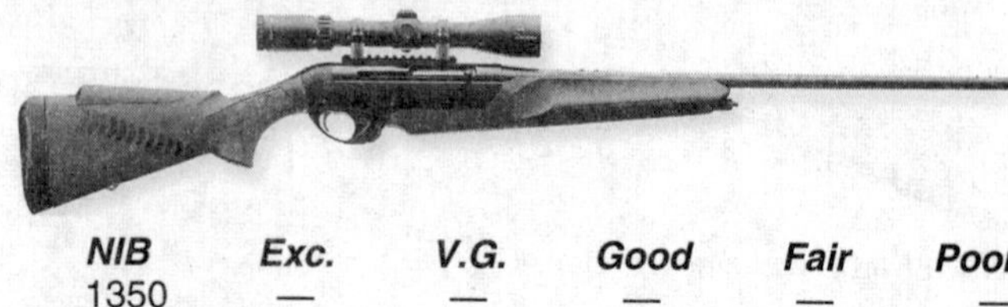

NIB	Exc.	V.G.	Good	Fair	Poor
1350	—	—	—	—	—

HANDGUNS

Model B-76

This is an all-steel, double-action semi-automatic chambered for the 9mm Parabellum. It has a 4.25" barrel, fixed sights, and an 8-round detachable magazine.

NIB	Exc.	V.G.	Good	Fair	Poor
500	400	350	300	200	100

Model B-76S

This is the target version of the B-76. It has a 5.5" barrel, adjustable sights, and target grips.

NIB	Exc.	V.G.	Good	Fair	Poor
600	500	400	300	200	100

Model B-77

This model is similar to the B-76 except that it is chambered for the .32 ACP.

NIB	Exc.	V.G.	Good	Fair	Poor
400	300	250	200	150	100

Model B-80

This is another model similar to the B-76 except that it is chambered for the .30 Luger cartridge.

NIB	Exc.	V.G.	Good	Fair	Poor
450	350	300	200	150	100

Model B-80S

This is the target version of the B-80 with a 5.5" barrel and adjustable sights. It also features target grips.

NIB	Exc.	V.G.	Good	Fair	Poor
550	450	400	300	200	100

Model MP90S Match (World Cup)

This is a semi-automatic single-action pistol chambered for the .22 Short, .22 LR, or .32 S&W wadcutter. It is fitted with a 4-3/8" barrel with walnut match style fully adjustable grips, blade front sight and fully adjustable rear sight. Barrel has adjustable weights below. Magazine capacity is 5 rounds. Weight is about 39 oz. Previously imported by European American Armory, now imported by Benelli USA. Add 10 percent for .32 S&W.

NIB	Exc.	V.G.	Good	Fair	Poor
1200	950	700	500	—	—

Model MP95E Match (Atlanta)

Similar to the above model but with anatomically shaped grips. Choice of blue or chrome finish. Previously imported by European American Armory, now imported by Benelli U.S.A.

NIB	Exc.	V.G.	Good	Fair	Poor
750	600	450	350	—	—

NOTE: Add $60 for chrome finish.

BENTLEY, DAVID

Birmingham, England

Bentley was a prolific maker of both percussion and cartridge arms between 1845 and 1883. Those arms in cases can be dated by the addresses listed.

New Church Street	1845-1849
55 Hockley Street	1849-1854
5 Lower Loveday Street	1855-1860
61 & 62 Lower Loveday Street	1860-1863
44 Shadwell Street	1863-1871
Tower Works, Aston	1871-1883

BENTLEY, JOSEPH

Birmingham and Liverpool, England

Best known for his transitional and later patented percussion revolvers, Bentley worked at these addresses:

Birmingham	11 Steelhouse Lane	1829-1837
	14 St. Mary's Row	1840-1864
Liverpool	143 Dale Street	1840-1842
	12 South Castle Street	1842-1851
	40 Lime Street & 65 Castle	1852-1857
	65 Castle & 37 Russell Street	1857-1862

Bentley Revolver

A .44 caliber double-action percussion revolver with a 7" barrel and 5-shot cylinder. Blued, case hardened with walnut grips.

Exc.	V.G.	Good	Fair	Poor
—	4000	2500	1500	500

BENTZ

SEE—Austrian Military Firearms

BERETTA, DR. FRANCO

Brescia, Italy

Black Diamond Field Grade

A boxlock O/U shotgun produced in a variety of gauges and barrel lengths with single triggers and automatic ejectors. Blued, French case hardened with a walnut stock.

NIB	Exc.	V.G.	Good	Fair	Poor
975	850	700	575	450	200

The above model is produced in four embellished grades.

Grade One

NIB	Exc.	V.G.	Good	Fair	Poor
1150	900	700	550	400	200

Grade Two

NIB	Exc.	V.G.	Good	Fair	Poor
1700	1250	900	700	500	300

Grade Three

NIB	Exc.	V.G.	Good	Fair	Poor
2500	1750	1200	850	600	300

Grade Four

NIB	Exc.	V.G.	Good	Fair	Poor
3250	2750	2200	1250	700	350

Gamma Standard

A 12, 16, or 20 gauge boxlock O/U shotgun with 26" or 28" barrels, single trigger and automatic ejectors. Blued, French case hardened with a walnut stock. Imported from 1984 to 1988.

NIB	Exc.	V.G.	Good	Fair	Poor
450	375	300	225	150	100

Gamma Deluxe

As above, but more finely finished.

NIB	Exc.	V.G.	Good	Fair	Poor
700	575	500	400	250	125

Gamma Target

As above, in a trap or skeet version. Imported from 1986 to 1988.

NIB	Exc.	V.G.	Good	Fair	Poor
600	500	450	375	300	150

America Standard

A .410 bore boxlock O/U shotgun with 26" or 28" barrels. Blued, French case hardened with a walnut stock. Imported from 1984 to 1988.

NIB	Exc.	V.G.	Good	Fair	Poor
400	275	225	175	150	100

America Deluxe

As above, but more finely finished.

NIB	Exc.	V.G.	Good	Fair	Poor
450	325	275	220	175	100

Europa

As above, with a 26" barrel and engraved action. Imported from 1984 to 1988.

NIB	Exc.	V.G.	Good	Fair	Poor
450	325	275	225	175	100

Europa Deluxe

As above, but more finely finished.

NIB	Exc.	V.G.	Good	Fair	Poor
475	375	300	250	200	125

Francia Standard

A .410 bore boxlock double-barrel shotgun with varying barrel lengths, double triggers and manual extractors. Blued with a walnut stock. Imported from 1986 to 1988.

NIB	Exc.	V.G.	Good	Fair	Poor
300	200	175	150	125	100

Alpha Three

A 12, 16, or 20 gauge boxlock double-barrel shotgun with 26" or 28" barrels, single triggers and automatic ejectors. Blued, French case hardened with a walnut stock. Imported from 1984 to 1988.

NIB	Exc.	V.G.	Good	Fair	Poor
450	350	300	225	150	100

Beta Three

A single-barrel, break-open, field-grade gun chambered for all gauges and offered with a ventilated rib barrel from 24" to 32" in length. The receiver chrome-plated, and the stock of walnut. Imported from 1985 to 1988.

NIB	Exc.	V.G.	Good	Fair	Poor
200	125	100	75	60	40

REMINDER

The prices listed in this book are given to assist the shooter and collector in pursuing their hobby with a better understanding of what is going on in the marketplace.

BERETTA, PIETRO

Brescia, Italy

PISTOLS

Model 1915

A 7.65mm and 9mm Glisenti caliber semi-automatic pistol with 3.5" barrel, fixed sights and 8-shot magazine. Blued with walnut grips. The 7.65mm pistol has a single-line inscription while the 9mm Glisenti has a double line. There are various styles of wood grips on this model. Manufactured between 1915 and 1922. Replaced by the Model 1915/19.

Model 1915 in 7.65mm — Courtesy James Rankin

Model 1915 in 9mm Glisenti — Courtesy James Rankin

Exc.	V.G.	Good	Fair	Poor
850	700	500	350	250

Model 1915/1919

This model is an improved version of the above pistol but chambered for the 7.65mm cartridge. It also incorporates a new barrel-mounting method and a longer cutout in the top of the slide.

Courtesy Orvel Reichert

Exc.	V.G.	Good	Fair	Poor
350	300	225	150	100

Model 1919

Similar to Model 1915, in 6.35mm caliber. Manufactured with minor variations and different names between 1919 and the 1940s.

Courtesy James Rankin

Exc.	V.G.	Good	Fair	Poor
500	400	300	250	100

Model 1923

A 9mm caliber semi-automatic pistol with 4" barrel and 8-shot magazine. Blued with steel grips. The slide is marked, "Brev 1915-1919 Mlo 1923." Manufactured from 1923 to 1935.

Exc.	V.G.	Good	Fair	Poor
525	425	350	225	150

Model 1931

A 7.65mm caliber semi-automatic pistol with 3.5" barrel and open-top slide. Blued with walnut grips and marked, "RM" separated by an anchor.

Exc.	V.G.	Good	Fair	Poor
450	375	275	200	150

Model 1934

As above, with 9mm short caliber. The slide is marked, "P. Beretta Cal. 9 Corto-Mo 1934 Brevet Gardone VT." This inscription is followed by the date of manufacture that was given numerically, followed by a Roman numeral that denoted the year of manufacture on the Fascist calendar which began in 1922. Examples are marked, "RM" (Navy), "RE" (Army), "RA" (Air Force), and "PS" (Police). Manufactured between 1934 and 1959.

Courtesy Orvel Reichert

Courtesy Orvel Reichert

Exc.	V.G.	Good	Fair	Poor
375	325	225	150	100

Air Force "RA" marked

Exc.	V.G.	Good	Fair	Poor
550	475	325	225	150

Navy "RM" marked

Exc.	V.G.	Good	Fair	Poor
625	550	375	250	175

Model 1934 Rumanian Contract

This model is identical to the Model 1934 except the slide is marked "9mm Scurt" instead of 9mm Corto.

Exc.	V.G.	Good	Fair	Poor
475	425	325	225	125

Model 1935

As above, in 7.65mm caliber. Post-war versions are known. Manufactured from 1935 to 1959.

Courtesy Orvel Reichert

Exc.	V.G.	Good	Fair	Poor
375	325	225	150	100

Model 318

An improved version of the old Model 1919 with the butt reshaped to afford a better grip. Chambered for the .25 ACP cartridge and has a 2.5" barrel. Variety of finishes with plastic grips. In the United States it is known as the "Panther." Manufactured between 1935 and 1946.

Exc.	V.G.	Good	Fair	Poor
300	250	200	150	100

Model 418

As above, with a rounded grip and a cocking indicator. It is known as the "Bantam" in the U.S. Introduced in 1947.

Exc.	V.G.	Good	Fair	Poor
250	200	150	125	90

Model 420

An engraved and chrome-plated Model 418.

Exc.	V.G.	Good	Fair	Poor
350	300	275	200	150

Model 421

An engraved, gold-plated Model 418 with tortoise-shell grips.

Exc.	V.G.	Good	Fair	Poor
475	425	325	250	150

Model 948

A .22 LR version of the Model 1934. It has either a 3.5" or 6" barrel.

Exc.	V.G.	Good	Fair	Poor
350	300	200	125	90

Model 949 Olympic Target

A .22 caliber semi-automatic pistol with 8.75" barrel, adjustable sights and muzzlebrake. Blued with checkered, walnut grips. Manufactured from 1959 to 1964.

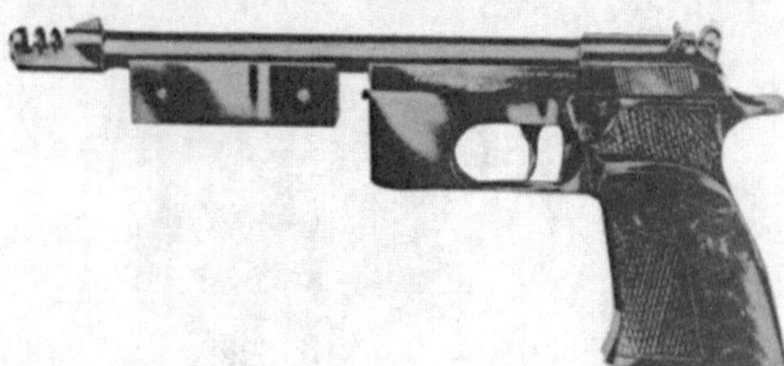

Exc.	V.G.	Good	Fair	Poor
750	600	500	400	200

U22 NEOS

U22 Neos 4.5/6.0

This semi-automatic .22 caliber pistol was first introduced in 2002. It is chambered for the .22 LR cartridge and fitted with a choice of 4.5" or 6" barrel with integral scope rail. Magazine capacity is 10 rounds. Weight is about 32 oz. to 36 oz. depending on barrel length.

NIB	Exc.	V.G.	Good	Fair	Poor
250	200	165	—	—	—

U22 Neos 4.5 Inox/6.0 Inox

Same as above but with special two-tone finish.

NIB	Exc.	V.G.	Good	Fair	Poor
300	250	195	—	—	—

U22 Neos 6.0/7.5 DLX

Introduced in 2003 this model features a 6" or 7.5" barrel with target sights and polymer grips with inlays. Adjustable trigger and interchangeable sights. Laser-engraved slide. Weight is about 36 oz.

NIB	Exc.	V.G.	Good	Fair	Poor
335	275	200	—	—	—

U22 Neos 6.0/7.5 Inox DLX

As above but with Inox finish.

This symbol denotes "Sleepers" with rapidly-rising values and/or significant collector potential.

NIB	Exc.	V.G.	Good	Fair	Poor
385	300	215	—	—	—

BERETTA 70 SERIES

These pistols began production in 1958 replacing Models 1934, 1935, 948, and 949. During the late 1960s several of these models briefly utilized a 100 series designation for the U.S. market. During the latter part of the 1970s a magazine safety was added to the 70 series and the pistols became known as the Model 70S. The 70S designation replaced model designations 70 through 75 making these older model numbers obsolete. Only the Model 76 designation continued.

The 70 Series design included a cross bolt safety, sear block safety, a slide hold-open device, and a push-button magazine release. Shorty after its introduction the cross bolt safety push-button was replaced with a lever-type sear block safety located in the same place.

NOTE: The above information was supplied by contributing editor John Stimson, Jr.

Model 70 (Model 100)

The Model 948 with cross bolt safety, hold-open device, and a push-button magazine release. Fixed sights. There are a number of subvariations available chambered for the .22 LR, .32 ACP, and the .380 ACP cartridges. Available with a 3.5" or 5.9" barrel and has a detachable magazine. Also known as the "Puma" when marketed in the U.S. by J.L. Galef & Sons. It was introduced in 1958 and discontinued in 1985.

NIB	Exc.	V.G.	Good	Fair	Poor
325	275	200	175	125	85

Model 70S

This is an improved Model 70. Chambered for the 7.65 (.32 ACP), 9mm Corto (.380 ACP), and the .22 LR cartridge. Magazine capacity is 7, 8, and 8 rounds respectively.

NIB	Exc.	V.G.	Good	Fair	Poor
325	275	200	175	125	85

Model 71/Jaguar (Model 101)

Similar to above model and chambered for .22 LR cartridge. Magazine capacity is 10 rounds. Frame is alloy and is fitted with a 5.9" barrel. Models imported into the U.S. prior to 1968 were fitted with 3.5" barrels.

NIB	Exc.	V.G.	Good	Fair	Poor
350	275	225	175	125	100

Model 72

This is essentially a Model 71 but sold with two sets of barrels; a 3.5" and 5.9". Fixed sights.

NIB	Exc.	V.G.	Good	Fair	Poor
350	300	275	225	150	125

Model 76 (102)

This is a .22 LR target pistol. The barrel is shrouded with an aluminum sleeve, with the rear part of the sleeve extended above the slide to hold an adjustable rear sight. Marketed in the U.S. as the Sable. Magazine capacity is 10 rounds. Briefly after 1968 imported into the U.S. as the Model 102, the New Sable.

Courtesy John J. Stimson, Jr.

NIB	Exc.	V.G.	Good	Fair	Poor
450	400	300	200	—	—

Model 950/Jetfire

A .22 caliber semi-automatic pistol with 2.25" barrel hinged at the front that could be pivoted forward for cleaning or loading, making this either a semi-auto or single-shot pistol. Blued with plastic grips. Introduced in 1955. A 4" barrel version also available. This model was known as the "Minx" in the U.S.

REMINDER

Join a firearms club or association. These groups have older, experienced collectors who are glad to help the beginner or veteran.

NIB	Exc.	V.G.	Good	Fair	Poor
200	150	135	110	85	50

Model 950B/Jetfire

As above, in .25 caliber, known as the "Jetfire" in the U.S.

NIB	Exc.	V.G.	Good	Fair	Poor
295	225	135	110	85	50

Model 950 Jetfire Inox

Same as the Model 950 Jetfire but with stainless steel finish. Introduced in 2000.

NIB	Exc.	V.G.	Good	Fair	Poor
310	250	175	135	—	—

Model 3032 Tomcat

This is a double-action semi-automatic pistol similar in appearance to the Model 950 but chambered for the .32 ACP cartridge. Barrel length is 2.45" and overall length is 5". Fixed blade front sight and drift adjustable rear sight. Plastic grips. Seven-round magazine. Blued or matte black finish. Weight is 14.5 oz.

NIB	Exc.	V.G.	Good	Fair	Poor
325	225	150	125	100	75

NOTE: For blued finish add $30.

Model 3032 Tomcat Inox

Same as above but with stainless steel finish. Introduced in 2000.

NIB	Exc.	V.G.	Good	Fair	Poor
400	325	250	195	125	75

Model 3032 Tomcat Titanium

Same as above but with titanium finish and plastic grips. Weight is about 16 oz. Introduced in 2001.

NIB	Exc.	V.G.	Good	Fair	Poor
575	450	350	290	210	150

Alley Cat

Introduced in 2001 as a special limited run promotion pistol. Chambered for the .32 ACP cartridge this model is a Tomcat with special features such as AO Big Dot night sights. Supplied with an Alcantara inside-the-pants holster.

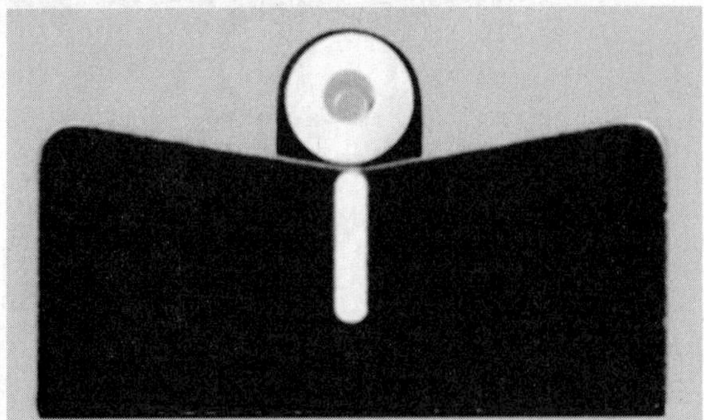

Alley Cat AO Big Dot night sights

NIB	Exc.	V.G.	Good	Fair	Poor
350	275	200	150	125	75

Model 951

A 9mm caliber semi-automatic pistol with 4.5" barrel and fixed sights. Blued with plastic grips. It was also known as the "Brigadier" at one time. Manufactured from 1952 to present day.

Exc.	V.G.	Good	Fair	Poor
350	300	200	150	100

Model 20

A .25 ACP double-action pistol with 2.5" barrel and 9-shot magazine. Blued with either walnut or plastic grips. Discontinued in 1985.

NIB	Exc.	V.G.	Good	Fair	Poor
200	175	150	125	90	75

Model 21/21 Bobcat

This small frame semi-automatic pistol, chambered for the .22 LR or .25 ACP cartridge, features a 2.4" tip-up barrel with fixed sights and a magazine capacity of 8 rounds (.25 ACP) or 7 rounds (.22 LR). Comes with either plastic or walnut grips and a deluxe version with gold line engraving. Pistol weighs about 11 to 11.8 oz. depending on caliber.

Standard Model

NIB	Exc.	V.G.	Good	Fair	Poor
200	175	150	125	100	75

Model 21EL

Gold engraved model.

NIB	Exc.	V.G.	Good	Fair	Poor
350	250	200	150	—	—

Model 21 Inox

Stainless steel.

NIB	Exc.	V.G.	Good	Fair	Poor
300	225	175	115	—	—

Model 90

A double-action, semi-automatic pocket pistol with a 3.5" barrel and 8-round magazine. Manufactured from 1969 to 1983.

Exc.	V.G.	Good	Fair	Poor
275	250	200	150	125

Model 92

A 9mm caliber double-action, semi-automatic pistol with a 5" barrel, fixed sights and a 16-round, double-stack magazine. Blued with plastic grips. Introduced in 1976 and is now discontinued.

NIB	Exc.	V.G.	Good	Fair	Poor
500	400	375	300	250	200

Model 92SB-P

As above, but with a polished finish. Manufactured from 1980 to 1985.

NIB	Exc.	V.G.	Good	Fair	Poor
550	425	375	325	250	200

Model 92SB Compact

As above, with a 4.3" barrel and a shortened grip frame that holds a 14-shot magazine. Either blued or nickel-plated with wood or plastic grips. The nickel version would be worth an additional 15 percent. The wood grips would add $20 to the value. Introduced in 1980 and discontinued in 1985.

NIB	Exc.	V.G.	Good	Fair	Poor
500	425	375	325	250	200

Model 92FS

The current production Model 92 chambered for the 9mm Parabellum cartridge. Barrel length is 4.9" and rear sight is a 3-dot combat drift adjustable. The magazine capacity is 15 rounds. This semi-automatic pistol features a double- or single-action operation. The safety is manual type. The frame is a light alloy sandblasted and anodized black. The barrel slide is steel. Grips are plastic checkered with black matte finish. Equipped with spare magazine cleaning rod, and hard carrying case. Pistol weighs 34.4 oz. empty.

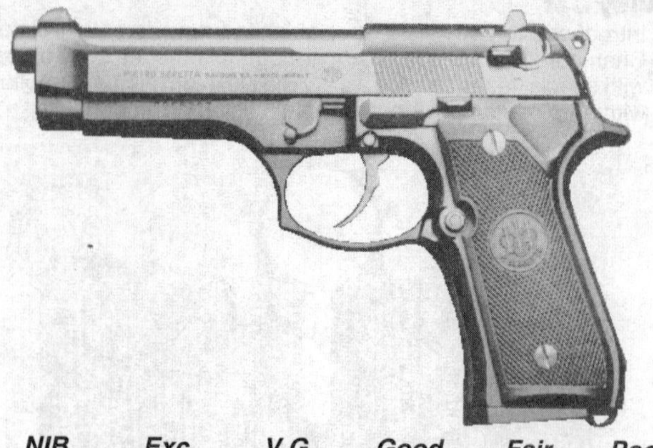

NIB	Exc.	V.G.	Good	Fair	Poor
550	450	350	300	200	150

Model 92FS Inox

Introduced in 2001 this pistol is chambered for the 9mm cartridge and fitted with a 4.9" barrel. The slide is black stainless steel with lightweight frame and combat-style trigger guard, reversible magazine release, and ambidextrous safety. Gray wrap-around grips. Weight is about 34 oz.

NIB	Exc.	V.G.	Good	Fair	Poor
725	575	425	350	—	—

Model 96

Identical to Model 92FS but fitted with a 10-round magazine and chambered for the .40 S&W. Introduced in 1992.

NIB	Exc.	V.G.	Good	Fair	Poor
550	450	350	300	200	150

Model 96 Combat

Introduced in 1997 this model is single-action-only with a competition tuned trigger. Developed for practical shooting competition. The barrel length is 5.9" and is supplied with a weight as standard. Rear sight is adjustable target type. Tool kit included as standard. Weight is 40 oz.

NIB	Exc.	V.G.	Good	Fair	Poor
1700	1300	950	—	—	—

Model 96 Stock

Similar to the Model 96 but in double-/single-action with a half-cock notch for cocked and locked carry. Fitted with a 4.9" barrel with fixed sights. Three interchangeable front sights are supplied as standard. Weight is 35 oz. Introduced in 1997. No longer in the U.S. product line.

NIB	Exc.	V.G.	Good	Fair	Poor
1350	950	775	—	—	—

Model 92/96FS Inox

Same as above except the barrel, slide, trigger, extractor, and other components are made of stainless steel. The frame is made of lightweight anodized aluminum alloy. The Model 96FS was discontinued in 1993.

NIB	Exc.	V.G.	Good	Fair	Poor
650	550	450	350	300	200

Model 92/96FS Centurion

Chambered for either the 9mm or .40 S&W this model features a 4.3" barrel, but retains a full grip to accommodate a 15-round magazine (9mm) or 10 rounds (.40 S&W). Pistol weighs approximately 33.2 oz. Introduced in 1993. Black sandblasted finish.

NIB	Exc.	V.G.	Good	Fair	Poor
550	450	400	300	200	150

Model 92FS/96 Brigadier

Same as the 92FS and 96 but with a heavier slide to reduce felt recoil. Removable front sight. Weight is about 35 oz.

NIB	Exc.	V.G.	Good	Fair	Poor
700	550	400	300	—	—

Model 92FS/96 Brigadier Inox

Same as above but with stainless steel finish. Introduced in 2000.

NIB	Exc.	V.G.	Good	Fair	Poor
750	600	475	325	—	—

Model 92G-SD/96G-SD

Introduced in 2003 this model features a decock mechanism built around a single-action/double-action trigger system. In addition, the pistol has an integral accessory rail on the frame. Fitted with a 9mm or .40 S&W 4.9" barrel with heavy slide and 3-dot tritium sights. Weight is about 35 oz.

NIB	Exc.	V.G.	Good	Fair	Poor
1000	750	500	—	—	—

Model 92F

A 9mm Parabellum caliber double-action semi-automatic pistol with a 4.9" barrel, fixed sights and a 15-shot double-stack magazine with an extended base. Matte blued finish with walnut or plastic grips. Introduced in 1984. No longer in production.

NIB	Exc.	V.G.	Good	Fair	Poor
500	400	350	300	200	150

Model 92F Compact

As above, with a 4.3" barrel and a 13-shot magazine. No longer in production.

NIB	Exc.	V.G.	Good	Fair	Poor
500	400	350	300	200	150

Model 92/96 Compact "Type M"

Essentially the same as the Model 92FS Compact but with the exception of a single column magazine that holds 8 rounds and reduces the grip thickness of the pistol. Pistol weighs 30.9 oz. Discontinued in 1993 and reintroduced in 1998. The Model 96 version (.40 S&W) was introduced in 2000.

NIB	Exc.	V.G.	Good	Fair	Poor
700	550	350	300	200	150

NOTE: Add $90 for Tritium night sights.

Model 92/96M Compact Inox

Same as above but with stainless steel slide and frame. Introduced in 2000.

NIB	Exc.	V.G.	Good	Fair	Poor
700	550	—	—	—	—

Model 92D Compact Type M

Same as above but with double-action-only trigger function.

NIB	Exc.	V.G.	Good	Fair	Poor
550	450	350	300	200	150

NOTE: Add $90 for Tritium night sights.

Model 92FS Deluxe

Identical dimensions to the full size Model 92FS with the addition of gold-plated engraved frame with gold-plated extra magazine in fitted leather presentation hard case. Grips are walnut briar with gold initial plate. Introduced in 1993.

NIB	Exc.	V.G.	Good	Fair	Poor
3750	3000	2000	1000	750	500

Model 92FS "470th Anniversary" Limited Edition

This model is limited to only 470 pistols worldwide. Features high polish finish with stainless steel, gold-filled engravings, walnut grips, Anniversary logo on top of slide and on the back of the chrome plated magazine. Supplied with walnut case.

NIB	Exc.	V.G.	Good	Fair	Poor
2075	1300	—	—	—	—

Model 92/96D

Same specifications as the standard Model 92 and Model 96 except that this variation has no visible hammer and is double-action-only. This model has no manual safety. Pistol weighs 33.8 oz.

NIB	Exc.	V.G.	Good	Fair	Poor
425	375	325	275	200	150

Model 92/96DS

Same as above but with the same manual safety as found on the 92FS pistol. Introduced in 1994.

NIB	Exc.	V.G.	Good	Fair	Poor
425	375	325	275	200	150

Model 92G/96G

Designed for the French Gendarmerie, this model has now been adopted for the French Air Force as well as other government agencies. This model features a hammer drop lever that does not function as a safety when the lever is released but lowers the hammer and returns to the ready to fire position automatically. Offered to law enforcement agencies only.

Model 92/96 Vertec

Introduced in 2002 this pistol is chambered for the 9mm or .40 S&W cartridges. Fitted with a 4.7" barrel. Double and single-action trigger. Features a new vertical grip design with a shorter trigger reach and thin grip panels. Removable front sight. and integral accessory rail on frame. Magazine capacity is 10 rounds. Weight is about 32 oz.

NIB	Exc.	V.G.	Good	Fair	Poor
700	575	—	—	—	—

Model 92 Competition Conversion Kit

The kit includes a 7.3" barrel with counterweight and elevated front sight, semi-automatic, walnut grips, and fully adjustable rear sight. Comes in special carrying case with the basic pistol.

Kit Price Only

NIB	Exc.	V.G.	Good	Fair	Poor
500	350	300	200	150	100

Model 92/96 Combo

This model features a specially designed Model 96 pistol with an extra 92FS slide and barrel assembly. Barrel lengths are 4.66". Sold with one 10-round magazine in both 9mm and .40 S&W.

NIB	Exc.	V.G.	Good	Fair	Poor
900	725	600	—	—	—

Model M9 Limited Edition

Introduced in 1995 to commemorate the 10th anniversary of the U.S. military's official sidearm this 9mm pistol is limited to 10,000 units. Special engraving on the slide with special serial numbers. Slide stamped "U.S. 9MM M9-BERETTA U.S.A.-65490."

Standard Model

NIB	Exc.	V.G.	Good	Fair	Poor
750	600	400	300	200	100

Deluxe Model

Walnut grips with gold plated hammer and grip screws.

NIB	Exc.	V.G.	Good	Fair	Poor
850	700	450	350	200	100

Model 92 Billennium

Introduced in 2001 this is a limited production pistol of 2,000 units world wide. Chambered for the 9mm cartridge. Steel frame with checkered front and backstrap. Nickel alloy finish with unique engraving. Carbon fiber grips. Interchangeable sights with adjustable rear sight. Carry case standard.

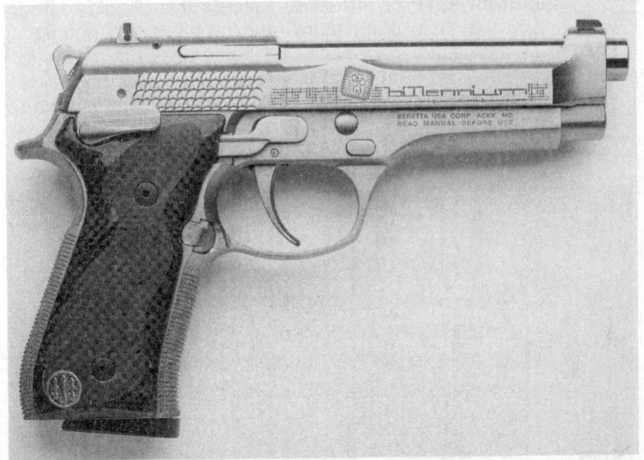

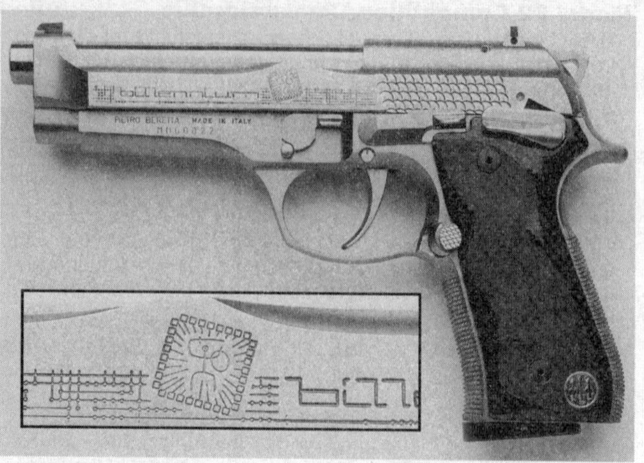

NIB	Exc.	V.G.	Good	Fair	Poor
1275	700	—	—	—	—

92 Steel-I

Steel-frame semi-auto in 9mm or .40 S&W. Single- or single/double-action. 15+1 capacity, 4.7" barrel, 42.3 oz. IDPA certified. Fixed, 3-dot sights. Introduced 2006. MSRP: 1029

M9A1

Semi-auto, single/double-action in 9mm developed for U.S. Marine Corps. Capacity 10+1 or 15+1. Fixed sights. Introduced 2006. MSRP: 850

ELITE TEAM SERIES

In 1999 Beretta introduced a new series of pistols based on the company's M92/96 pistol. Each of these pistols has specific features for specific shooting requirements.

Model 92G/96G Elite

Chambered for 9mm or .40 S&W calibers this pistol is fitted with a 4.7" stainless steel barrel and heavy-duty Brigadier-style slide. The action is decock only. Slide has both front and rear serrations. Hammer is skeletonized. Beveled magazine well. Special "ELITE" engraving on the slide. Weight is about 35 oz.

REMINDER

The prices given in this book are designed as a guide, not a quote. This is an important distinction because prices for firearms vary with the time of the year and geographical location.

NIB	Exc.	V.G.	Good	Fair	Poor
825	650	450	—	—	—

Model 92G Elite II

This version of the Elite was developed for the competition shooter. Fitted with a 4.7" barrel fitted with a heavy slide, it also has a skeletonized hammer. Beveled magazine well. Extended magazine release. Checkered front and backstrap grip. Weight is about 35 oz.

NIB	Exc.	V.G.	Good	Fair	Poor
925	725	550	—	—	—

Model 92/96 Border Marshall

This is the commercial version of the pistol built for the Immigration and Naturalization Service. It is fitted with a heavy-duty steel slide and short 4.7" I.N.S. style barrel. Rubber grips and night sights are standard. "BORDER MARSHALL" engraved on the slide. Offered in either 9mm or .40 S&W calibers.

NIB	Exc.	V.G.	Good	Fair	Poor
750	600	—	—	—	—

Model 92/96 Custom Carry

This model is fitted with a 4.3" barrel, shortened grip, and low profile control levers. Safety lever is left side only. Magazine capacity is 10 rounds. "CUSTOM CARRY" engraved on the slide. Chambered for either 9mm or .40 S&W calibers.

NIB	Exc.	V.G.	Good	Fair	Poor
625	500	400	—	—	—

Model 92FS INOX Tactical

This model has a satin matte finish on its stainless steel slide. The frame is anodized aluminum. Black rubber grips and night sights are standard. Offered in 9mm only.

NIB	Exc.	V.G.	Good	Fair	Poor
775	625	500	—	—	—

COUGAR SERIES

Model 8000/8040/8045 Cougar

This is a compact size pistol using a short recoil rotating barrel. It features a firing pin lock, chrome lined barrel, anodized aluminum alloy frame with Bruniton finish. Overall length is 7", barrel length is 3.6", overall height 5.5", and unloaded weight is 33.5 oz. Offered in double-/single-action as well as double-action-only. Magazine holds 10 rounds. Available in 9mm or .40 S&W. In 1998 Beretta added the .45 ACP caliber to this model.

NIB	Exc.	V.G.	Good	Fair	Poor
625	525	400	350	250	150

NOTE: Add $50 for .45 ACP models

Model 8000/8040/8045 Mini Cougar

This pistol was introduced in 1997 and is similar in design to the full size model. Offered in 9mm or .40 S&W or .45 ACP. The pistol is fitted with a 3.6" barrel (3.7" on .45 ACP). Empty weight is 27 oz. Offered in double-/single-action or double-action-only. Magazine capacity is 10 rounds for 9mm and 8 rounds for .40 S&W model. Weight is between 27 oz. and 30 oz. depending on caliber.

NIB	Exc.	V.G.	Good	Fair	Poor
700	550	450	—	—	—

NOTE: Add $50 for .45 ACP models

Model 8000F—Cougar L

Similar to the model above but fitted with a shortened grip frame. Chambered for the 9mm cartridge and fitted with a 3.6" barrel. Overall height as been reduced by .4". Weight is about 28 oz. Introduced in 2003.

NIB	Exc.	V.G.	Good	Fair	Poor
700	550	400	—	—	—

Model 9000F

Introduced in 2000 this pistol is chambered for the 9mm or .40 S&W cartridge. It is fitted with a 3.4" barrel and has a polymer frame. The "F" type has a single-action/double-action trigger. Fixed sights. Magazine capacity is 10 rounds. Weight is about 27 oz. Overall length is 6.6" and overall height is 4.8". External hammer and black finish.

NIB	Exc.	V.G.	Good	Fair	Poor
550	450	350	—	—	—

Model 9000D

Same as above but with double-action-only trigger.

NIB	Exc.	V.G.	Good	Fair	Poor
550	450	350	—	—	—

Model 9000S

This model is chambered for the 9mm or .40 S&W cartridges. Magazine capacity is 10 rounds. With optional spacer Model 92/96 magazines can also be used. Three-dot sight system. An accessory magazine bottom that extends when griped but retracts when holstered is standard. Steel alloy frame and slide. Weight is about 27 oz. Introduced in 2001.

NIB	Exc.	V.G.	Good	Fair	Poor
550	450	350	—	—	—

REMINDER

The prices listed in this book are given to assist the shooter and collector in pursuing their hobby with a better understanding of what is going on in the marketplace.

CHEETAH SERIES

Model 84/Cheetah

This is a small semi-automatic pistol chambered for the .380 cartridge. It has a double-column magazine that holds 13 rounds. Offered in blue or nickel finish. Grips are checkered black plastic or checkered wood.

NIB	Exc.	V.G.	Good	Fair	Poor
450	375	325	275	200	150

Model 84BB

Similar to the Model 84 but incorporates different features such as a firing pin blocking device and loaded chamber indicator. Single-column magazine holds 8 rounds of .380 shells. Discontinued in 1993.

NIB	Exc.	V.G.	Good	Fair	Poor
425	375	325	275	200	150

Model 85/Cheetah

Similar in appearance to the Model 84, but features a single-column magazine with a capacity of 8 rounds. Available in blue or nickel finish. Grips are checkered black plastic. Pistol weighs 22 oz.

NIB	Exc.	V.G.	Good	Fair	Poor
405	375	325	275	200	150

Model 86/Cheetah

This .380 ACP semi-automatic pistol has a 4.4" tip-up barrel. Magazine capacity is 8 rounds. Furnished with checkered wood grips. Pistol weighs 23 oz.

NIB	Exc.	V.G.	Good	Fair	Poor
425	350	300	250	200	150

Model 87/Cheetah

A .22 caliber double-action, semi-automatic target pistol with a 3.8" or 6" barrel, adjustable sights with a 7-shot magazine. Blued with checkered walnut grips. Introduced in 1986.

NIB	Exc.	V.G.	Good	Fair	Poor
550	425	300	250	200	150

Model 87 Target

This is a .22 caliber single-action target pistol. It features an adjustable rear sight, integral scope base, and external hammer. Anodized aluminum frame. Weight is about 41 oz. Introduced in 2000.

NIB	Exc.	V.G.	Good	Fair	Poor
650	500	350	—	—	—

Model 89/Gold Standard

A .22 caliber, semi-automatic target pistol with adjustable sights, and 10-shot, detachable magazine. Matte finish with hand-fitting walnut grips. Introduced in 1988.

NIB	Exc.	V.G.	Good	Fair	Poor
800	625	475	400	300	150

Px4 Storm Pistol, Type F

Introduced in 2005 this pistol features a single/double action trigger with decocker and is chambered for the 9mm or .40 S&W cartridges. Fitted with a 4" barrel. Interchangeable grip backstraps. Reversable magazine release button. Picatinny rail. Fixed sights. Magazine capacity is 14 rounds for the .40 S&W and 17 rounds for the 9mm. Weight is about 27.5 lbs.

NIB	Exc.	V.G.	Good	Fair	Poor
630	500	375	—	—	—

Stampede Blue

Introduced in 2003, this single-action revolver is chambered for the choice of .45 Colt, .44-40, or .357 Magnum cartridge. Choice of 4.75", 5.5", or 7.5" barrel. Blued with Beretta case color and black polymer grips. Weight is about 2.3 lbs. depending on barrel length.

NIB	Exc.	V.G.	Good	Fair	Poor
465	365	275	—	—	—

Stampede Nickel

As above but with brushed nickel finish and walnut grips.

NIB	Exc.	V.G.	Good	Fair	Poor
500	400	295	—	—	—

Stampede Deluxe

As above but with charcoal blue finish and Beretta case color with select walnut grips.

NIB	Exc.	V.G.	Good	Fair	Poor
620	500	375	—	—	—

Stampede Bisley

Single action 6-shot Bisley replica revolver in .45 Colt or .357 Magnum. Blued with 4-3/4", 5-1/2" or 7-1/2" barrel. Introduced 2006. MSRP: 625 (nickel-plated 698)

90-Two

Wrap-around polymer grip, standard or slim. Single/double-action semi-auto in 9mm (10+1, 15+1 or 17+1 capacity) or .40 S&W (10+1 or 12+1 capacity). Types D, F or G. Fixed sights. 4.9" barrel, 32.5 oz. Introduced 2006. Add 10 percent for luminous sights.

NIB	Exc.	V.G.	Good	Fair	Poor
575	450	350	290	210	150

Laramie

Break-open single-action revolver reminiscent of S&W #3 chambered for.45 LC or .38 Special. Six-shot cylinder. Adjustable rear sight. 5" or 6-1/2" barrels. Introduced 2006. Add 10 percent for nickel finish. Made by Beretta subsidiary Uberti.

NIB	Exc.	V.G.	Good	Fair	Poor
950	—	—	—	—	—

RIFLES

Cx4 Storm

Introduced in 2003, this semi-automatic carbine has a 16.6" barrel. Chambered for the 9mm, .40 S&W, or .45 ACP cartridge. Synthetic stock with rubber recoil pad has adjustable stock spacers. Ghost ring rear sight with adjustable post front sight. Forward accessory rail. Magazine capacity is 10 rounds for 9mm or .40 S&W and 8 rounds for the .45 ACP model. Weight is about 5.75 lbs.

NIB	Exc.	V.G.	Good	Fair	Poor
685	550	395	—	—	—

AR-70

A .223 caliber, semi-automatic rifle with a 17.7" barrel, adjustable diopter sights, and an 8- or 30-shot magazine. Black epoxy finish with a synthetic stock. Weight is approximately 8.3 lbs. No longer imported into the U.S.

NIB	Exc.	V.G.	Good	Fair	Poor
2100	1900	1500	1000	750	—

BM-59 Standard Grade

A gas operated semi-automatic rifle with detachable box magazine. Chambered for .308 cartridge. Walnut stock. Barrel length is 19.3" with muzzlebrake. Magazine capacity is 5,10, or 20 rounds. Weight is about 9.5 lbs.

NIB	Exc.	V.G.	Good	Fair	Poor
2000	1500	1100	700	400	—

Model 500 Custom

A bolt-action sporting rifle chambered for a variety of calibers with a 24" barrel, open sights, three action lengths and a 3- or 4-shot magazine. Blued with a checkered walnut stock.

Exc.	V.G.	Good	Fair	Poor
600	525	400	325	275

This model was offered in four other grades:

Model 500S

Exc.	V.G.	Good	Fair	Poor
625	550	425	350	300

Model 500DL

Exc.	V.G.	Good	Fair	Poor
1400	1250	1000	775	650

Model 500DEELL

Exc.	V.G.	Good	Fair	Poor
1600	1450	1200	975	800

Model 500DEELLS

Exc.	V.G.	Good	Fair	Poor
1625	1475	1225	1000	825

Model 501

A .243 or .308 caliber bolt-action rifle with a 23" barrel, furnished without sights and a 6-shot magazine. Blued with a checkered walnut stock. It was discontinued in 1986. It was offered in the same variations as the Model 500 series-501S, 501DL, 501DLS, 501EELL, and 501EELLS. The values for this series are the same as for the 500 series rifles.

Model 502

A .270, 7mm Remington Magnum, and .30-06 caliber bolt-action rifle with a 24" barrel (without sights) and a 5-shot magazine. Blued with a checkered walnut stock. Discontinued in 1986. It is also available in the same variations as the Model 500 and the Model 501 but is valued at approximately 10 percent higher in each variation.

Mato Deluxe

This bolt-action rifle was introduced into the Beretta product line in 1997. It is based on the Mauser 98 action and is fitted with a drop-out box magazine. The stock is XXX Claro walnut with a hand-rubbed oil finish and black forend tip. Chambered for .270 Win., .280, .30-06, 7mm Magnum, .300 Magnum, .338 Magnum, and .375 H&H. Weight is about 8 lbs.

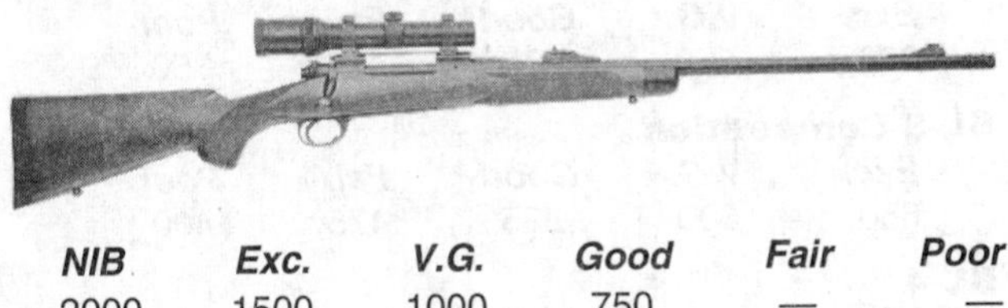

NIB	Exc.	V.G.	Good	Fair	Poor
2000	1500	1000	750	—	—

Mato Standard

Same as above but fitted with a matte gray Kevlar and graphite composite stock. Weight is approximately 7.9 lbs.

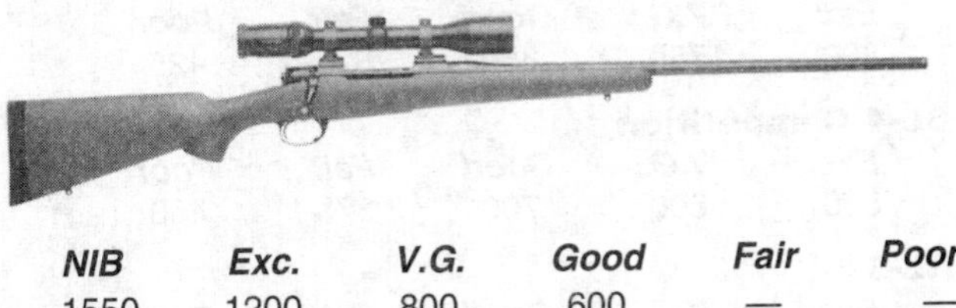

NIB	Exc.	V.G.	Good	Fair	Poor
1550	1200	800	600	—	—

PREMIUM RIFLES

Model S689 Sable

A 9.3x74R or the .30-06 caliber O/U rifle with a boxlock action, 23" ribbed barrels and express-type sights. Blued, case hardened or nickel-plated with checkered walnut stock. Double triggers and automatic ejectors. Offered in three grades.

Silver Sable

NIB	Exc.	V.G.	Good	Fair	Poor
3850	3000	2500	—	—	—

Gold Sable

NIB	Exc.	V.G.	Good	Fair	Poor
5750	4500	3500	—	—	—

Diamond Sable

NIB	Exc.	V.G.	Good	Fair	Poor
12750	10000	7500	—	—	—

NOTE: Extra 20 gauge barrel with forearm add $1,200. Scope with claw mounts add $2,000.

SSO Express

A .375 Holland & Holland and .458 Winchester Magnum caliber O/U, double barrel rifle with 23" barrels, folding express sights, double triggers, and automatic ejectors. Furnished with a fitted case. This firearm is available on a custom order basis and should be individually appraised.

NIB	Exc.	V.G.	Good	Fair	Poor
18000	13000	9500	—	—	—

SSO5 Express

A more finely finished version of the above.

NIB	Exc.	V.G.	Good	Fair	Poor
20000	15000	11000	—	—	—

SSO6

This is a premium grade sidelock over-and-under express rifle. Equipped with double triggers. It is offered in 9.3x74R, .375 H&H Magnum, and .458 Win. Magnum. It is fitted with a 24" barrel with express sights. Claw mounts for Zeiss scopes are available from the factory. The receiver is case-colored with light scroll engraving. Special select walnut is used in the stock and forearm with fine line checkering. Stock comes with cheekpiece and rubber recoil pad. Furnished with leather case. Rifle weighs about 11 lbs.

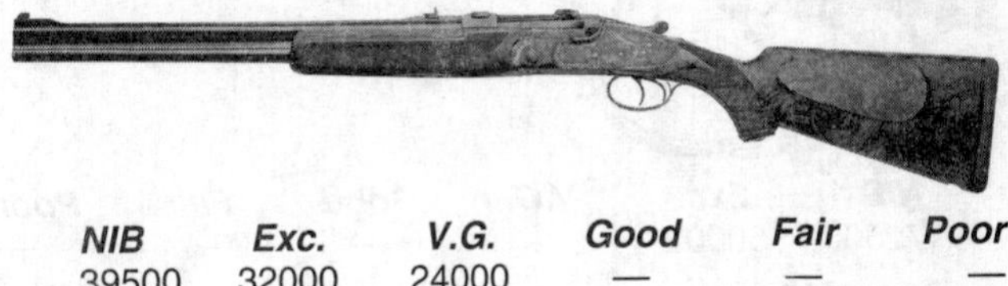

NIB	Exc.	V.G.	Good	Fair	Poor
39500	32000	24000	—	—	—

SSO6 EELL

Offered in the same calibers as above but furnished with hand engraved game scenes with gold inlays. Walnut stock is special select briar with fine diamond line checkering.

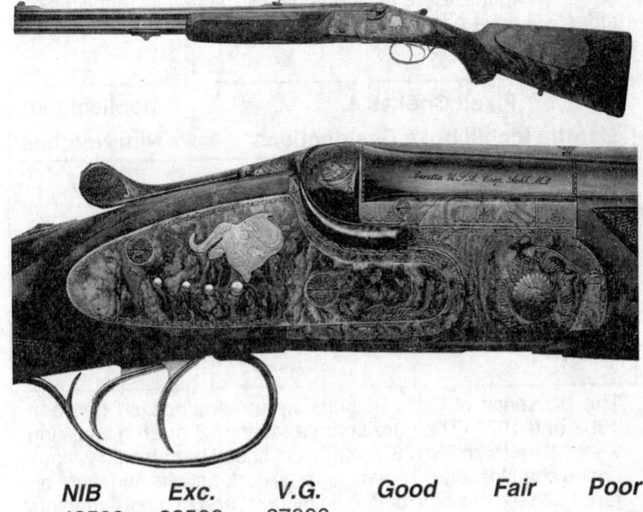

NIB	Exc.	V.G.	Good	Fair	Poor
42500	32500	27000	—	—	—

Model 455

This is a premium grade side-by-side express rifle with slide locks. Available in these calibers: .375 H&H Magnum, .458 Win. Magnum, .470 Nitro Express, .500 Nitro Express, and .416 Rigby. The receiver is case-colored without engraving and the walnut stock is highly figured with fine line checkering. Comes supplied with express sights. Claw mounts and Zeiss scope offered at customer's request only on .375, .458, and .416. Weighs about 11 lbs.

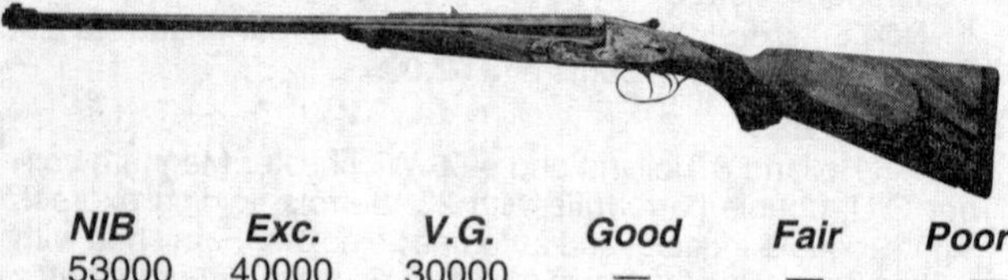

NIB	Exc.	V.G.	Good	Fair	Poor
53000	40000	30000	—	—	—

Model 455 EELL

Same as above model but furnished with case-colored game scene engraving with gold inlays. Walnut briar stock with fine diamond line checkering. Supplied with leather case and accessories.

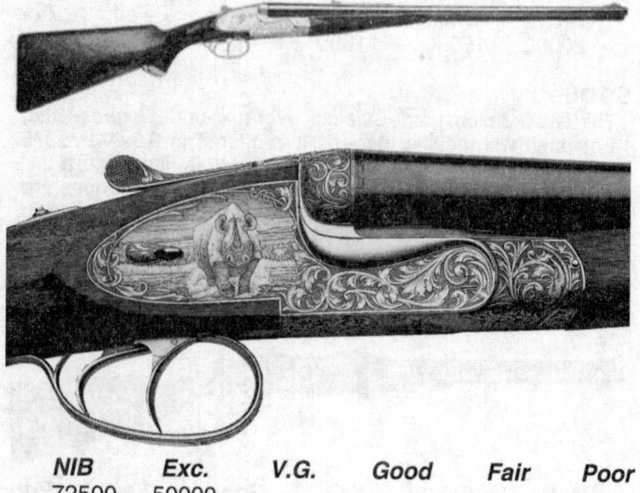

NIB	Exc.	V.G.	Good	Fair	Poor
72500	50000	—	—	—	—

SHOTGUNS

Beretta shotguns are marked with a symbol or 0 stamping to indicate the type of fixed choke in the barrel or barrels. Usually this stamping is on the side of the barrel in the rear near the receiver on semi-automatics and near the ejectors on double barrel shotguns. Beretta shotguns with screw-in Mobilchoke tubes will have notches cut in them to indicate the amount of choke placed in the tube.

Fixed Chokes & Beretta Mobilchoke Designations		Mobilechoke Rim Notches
0(*)	F (Full)	I
00(**)	IM (Improved Modified)	II
000(***)	M (Modified)	III
0000(****)	IC (Improved Cyl.)	IIII
C0000(C****)	CL (Cylinder)	IIIII
SK	SK (Skeet)	No Notches

The BL series of O/U shotguns were manufactured between 1968 and 1973. They are chambered for 12 or 20 gauge and were offered with 26", 28", or 30" vent ribbed barrels with various choke combinations. They feature boxlock actions and were offered with either single or double triggers, and manual extractors or automatic ejectors. The finishes are blued with checkered walnut stocks. The configurations differ basically in the quality of materials and workmanship and the degree of ornamentation.

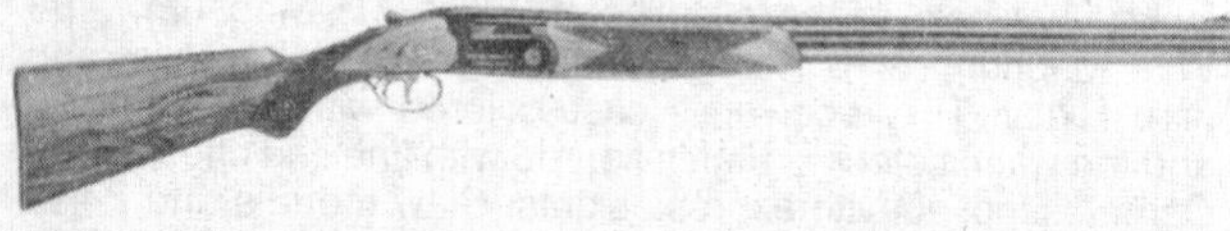

BL-1

Exc.	V.G.	Good	Fair	Poor
500	450	350	225	150

BL-2

Exc.	V.G.	Good	Fair	Poor
425	375	300	250	200

BL-2/S (Speed Trigger)

Exc.	V.G.	Good	Fair	Poor
450	400	325	275	225

BL-2 Stakeout

18" barrel.

Exc.	V.G.	Good	Fair	Poor
400	350	275	225	175

BL-3

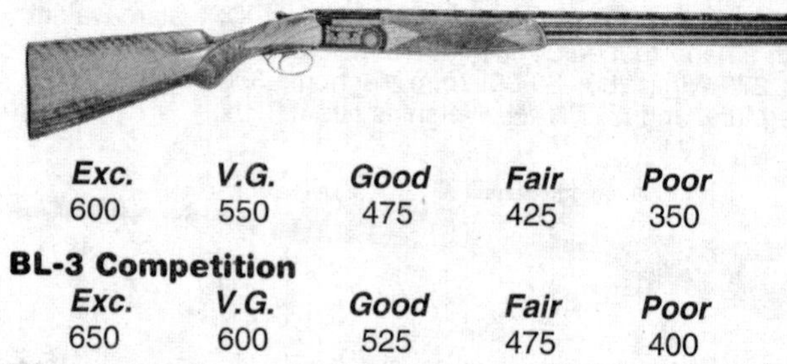

Exc.	V.G.	Good	Fair	Poor
600	550	475	425	350

BL-3 Competition

Exc.	V.G.	Good	Fair	Poor
650	600	525	475	400

BL-4

Exc.	V.G.	Good	Fair	Poor
800	750	650	525	425

BL-4 Competition

Exc.	V.G.	Good	Fair	Poor
850	800	700	575	450

BL-5

Exc.	V.G.	Good	Fair	Poor
900	850	725	575	450

BL-5 Competition

Exc.	V.G.	Good	Fair	Poor
950	900	775	600	475

BL-6

Sidelock.

Exc.	V.G.	Good	Fair	Poor
1250	1150	1000	850	675

BL-6 Competition

Exc.	V.G.	Good	Fair	Poor
1300	1200	1050	900	725

Model S55 B

A 12 or 20 gauge O/U shotgun with 26", 28", or 30" ventilated rib barrels, various choke combinations and boxlock action with a single-selective trigger and extractors. Blued with a checkered walnut stock.

Exc.	V.G.	Good	Fair	Poor
550	500	400	325	275

Model S56 E

As above, but more finely finished.

Exc.	V.G.	Good	Fair	Poor
600	550	450	375	325

Model S58 Competition

As above, with either 26" or 30" barrels, wide vent ribs and competition-type stocks.

Exc.	V.G.	Good	Fair	Poor
700	650	550	475	400

Silver Snipe

A 12 or 20 gauge O/U shotgun with 26", 28", or 30" barrels, boxlock action with a double trigger and extractors. Blued with a checkered walnut stock. Manufactured from 1955 through 1967. A single-selective trigger version with ventilated rib and automatic ejectors would be worth approximately 50 percent additional.

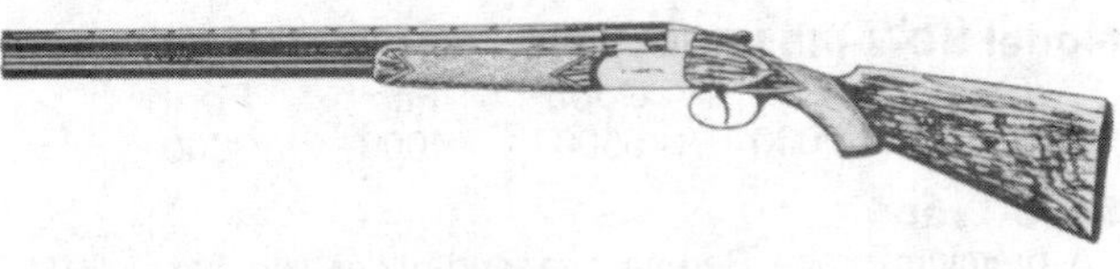

Exc.	V.G.	Good	Fair	Poor
475	375	325	275	200

Golden Snipe

As above with a ventilated rib and automatic ejectors. If it has a single-selective trigger, add 10 percent.

Exc.	V.G.	Good	Fair	Poor
675	600	500	350	200

Model 57 E

As above, but more finely finished. Manufactured between 1955 and 1967.

Exc.	V.G.	Good	Fair	Poor
825	775	600	475	250

ASEL Model

A 12 or 20 gauge O/U shotgun with 26", 28", or 30" ventilated rib barrel with various choke combinations. Single-selective trigger and automatic ejectors. Blued with a checkered pistol-grip stock. Manufactured between 1947 and 1964. Prices listed are for 20 gauge guns.

Exc.	V.G.	Good	Fair	Poor
4250	2500	1200	750	400

NOTE: For 12 gauge guns deduct $1000 from Exc. condition price. For EELL grade add 30 percent.

Model 409 PB

A 12, 16, 20, and 28 gauge boxlock, double-barrel shotgun with 27", 28", or 30" barrels with double triggers and extractors and various choke combinations. Blued with a checkered walnut stock. Manufactured between 1934 and 1964.

Exc.	V.G.	Good	Fair	Poor
775	700	625	500	250

Model 410 E

As above, but more finely finished.

Exc.	V.G.	Good	Fair	Poor
900	825	650	500	275

Model 410

As above, with a 32" Full-choke barrel. Blued with a checkered walnut stock. Introduced in 1934.

Exc.	V.G.	Good	Fair	Poor
1000	925	750	600	300

Model 411 E

The Model 410 with false sideplates and more heavily engraved. Manufactured between 1934 and 1964.

Exc.	V.G.	Good	Fair	Poor
1200	1125	950	800	425

Model 424

A 12 and 20 gauge boxlock shotgun with 26" or 28" barrels, double triggers, various choke combinations, and extractors. Blued with a checkered walnut stock. In 20 gauge it is designated the Model 426 and would be worth an additional $100.

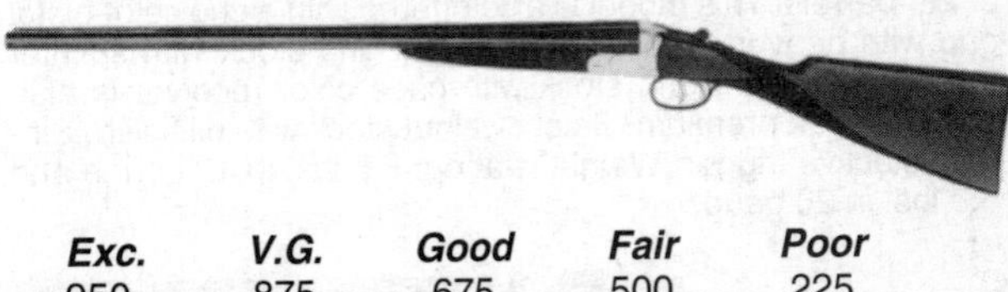

Exc.	V.G.	Good	Fair	Poor
950	875	675	500	225

Model 426 E

As above, with silver inlays and heavier engraving, single-selective trigger and automatic ejectors. Not imported after 1983.

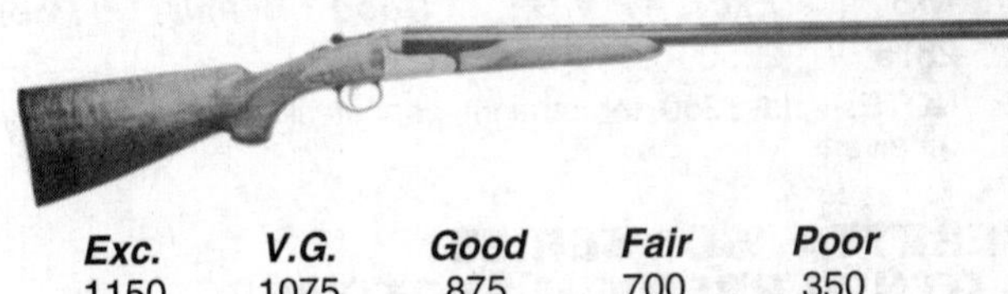

Exc.	V.G.	Good	Fair	Poor
1150	1075	875	700	350

Model 625

A 12 or 20 gauge boxlock, double-barrel shotgun with 26", 28", or 30" barrels, various choke combinations, double triggers and extractors. Moderately engraved and blued with a checkered walnut grip. Imported between 1984 and 1986.

Exc.	V.G.	Good	Fair	Poor
800	750	600	500	250

Silver Hawk

A 10 or 12 gauge boxlock, double-barrel shotgun with 30" barrels, double triggers and extractors. Blued with a silver-finished receiver and a checkered walnut stock. The 10 gauge version would be worth an additional 20 percent. Discontinued in 1967.

Exc.	V.G.	Good	Fair	Poor
500	450	375	250	150

Model 470 Silver Hawk

Introduced in 1997 to commemorate Beretta's 470 years in the gunmaking business, this shotgun is offered in either 12 or 20 gauge configurations.The receiver is silver chrome with engraving. The top lever is checkered with a gold inlaid hawk's head. The gun is fitted with a straight grip stock with splinter forearm of select walnut with oil finish. Choice of 26" or 28" barrels with auto ejection or manual extraction. Weight of 12 gauge about 6.5 lbs. The 20 gauge weighs approximately 6 lbs.

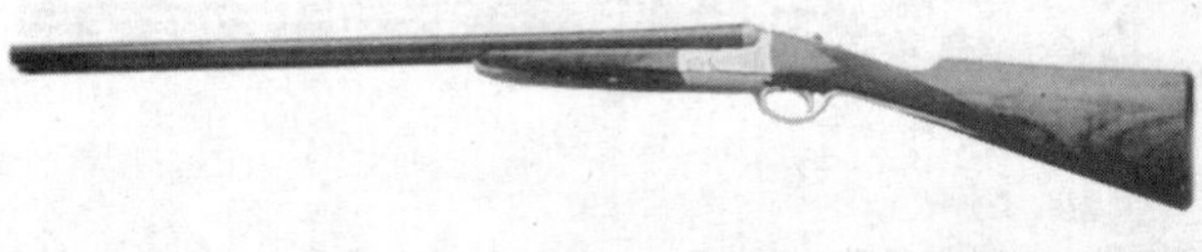

NIB	Exc.	V.G.	Good	Fair	Poor
3600	2800	1500	—	—	—

Model 470 Silver Hawk EL

Introduced in 2002 this model features color case hardened frame with side plates with gold filled game scene engraving. Offered in 12 or 20 gauge with choice of 26" or 28" barrels. Weight is 5.9 lbs. for 20 gauge and 6.5 lbs. for 12 gauge.

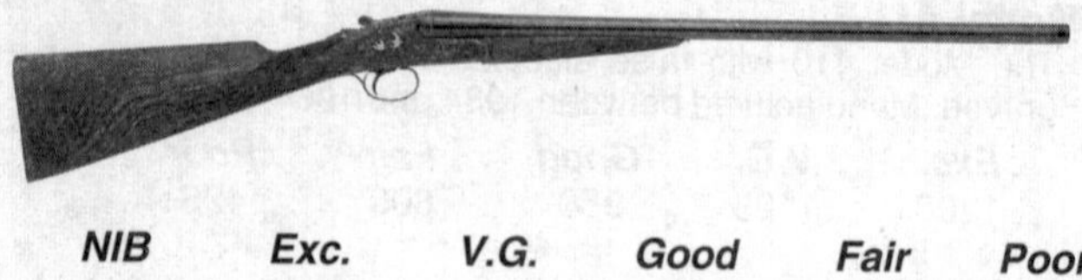

NIB	Exc.	V.G.	Good	Fair	Poor
5975	4700	—	—	—	—

471 Silver Hawk

Introduced in 2003, this side-by-side shotgun has a boxlock receiver and is offered in 12 and 20 gauge with a choice of 26" or 28" barrels. This model is also offered with a choice of pistol grip with beavertail forend or straight grip stock with splinter forend. A straight grip stock with case color receiver is also available at a premium. Select walnut stock with oil finish. Single-selective trigger. Weight is about 6.5 lbs. in 12 gauge and 5.9 lbs. in 20 gauge.

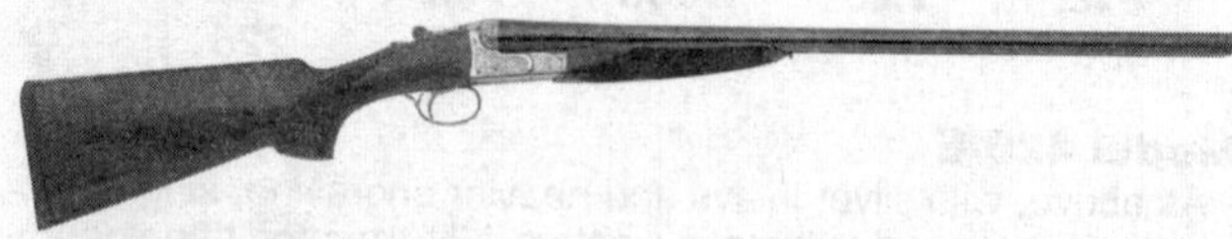

NIB	Exc.	V.G.	Good	Fair	Poor
2875	2250	—	—	—	—

NOTE: Add $350 for straight grip stock with case color receiver.

BERETTA "SO" SERIES & OTHER PREMIUM SHOTGUNS

These over-and-under shotguns were fitted with side locks, automatic ejectors, single or double triggers. Barrel ranges in length from 26" to 30" with a wide variety of choke combinations. These guns were introduced in 1948 in 12 gauge only and no longer imported as a production gun in 1986. Many of these SO guns were sold through the firm of Garcia, a sporting goods firm and distributor. The various grades are priced according to quality of wood, finish engraving coverage, and the like. Do not confuse these earlier Beretta shotguns with the present line of premium grade Berettas now being imported into the U.S.

Model SO-1

Exc.	V.G.	Good	Fair	Poor
2000	1600	1200	800	400

Model SO-2

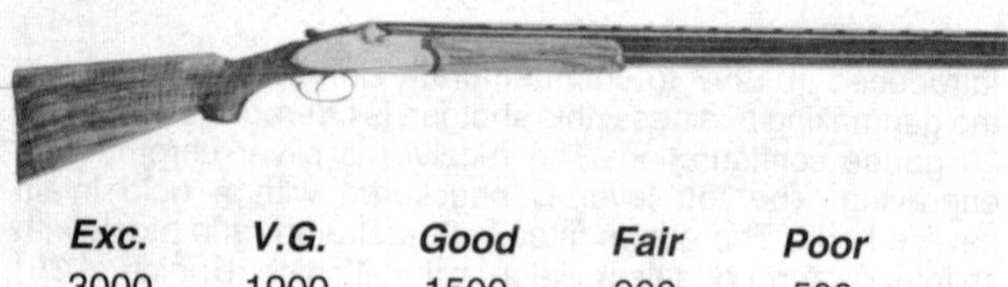

Exc.	V.G.	Good	Fair	Poor
3000	1900	1500	900	500

Model SO-3

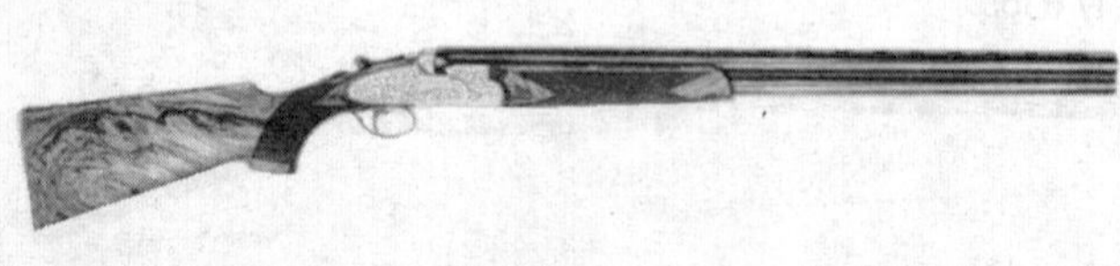

Exc.	V.G.	Good	Fair	Poor
4500	4000	2500	1500	1000

Model SO-4 (Garcia SO3EL)

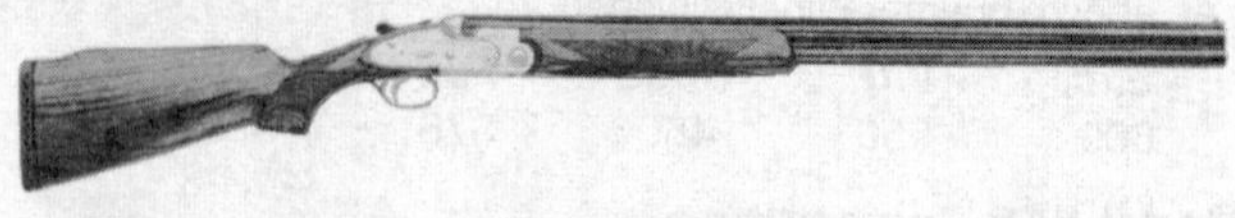

Exc.	V.G.	Good	Fair	Poor
7500	6500	3500	2000	1500

NOTE: For fully engraved Garcia Model SO3-EL add 80 percent.

Model SO-5 (Garcia SO-3 EELL)

Exc.	V.G.	Good	Fair	Poor
8000	7500	5000	3500	2500

Model SO-6 (450 or 451 EL) Side-by-Side

This model is fitted with Holland & Holland-style sidelocks and third fastener.

Exc.	V.G.	Good	Fair	Poor
7000	6000	5000	3500	2500

Model SO-7 (451 EELL) Side-by-Side

Exc.	V.G.	Good	Fair	Poor
8000	7000	5500	4000	3000

SO-5 Trap

A premium grade Beretta over-and-under shotgun built for competition trap shooting. Available in 12 gauge with 30" vent rib barrels standard. Barrels in 28" and 32" may be special ordered. Receiver is silver with light scroll engraving. The stock is select highly figured walnut with pistol grip and offered in International or Monte Carlo dimensions. Special trap rubber recoil pad is furnished. Weighs 8 lbs. 2 oz. Furnished with leather case and tools.

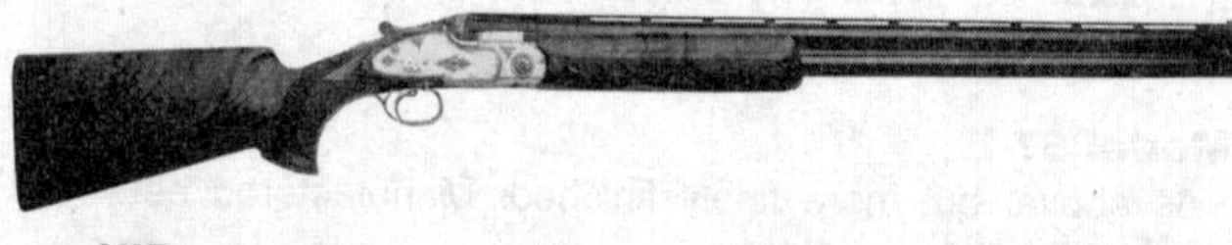

NIB	Exc.	V.G.	Good	Fair	Poor
19500	15000	—	—	—	—

SO-5 Trap 2 BBL Set

NIB	Exc.	V.G.	Good	Fair	Poor
22500	17500	—	—	—	—

SO-5 Sporting Clays

Offered in 12 gauge only with choice of 28", 30", or 32" barrels; 26" on special order. Sporting clay dimension walnut stock with pistol grip and rubber recoil pad. Weighs 7 lbs. 8 oz.

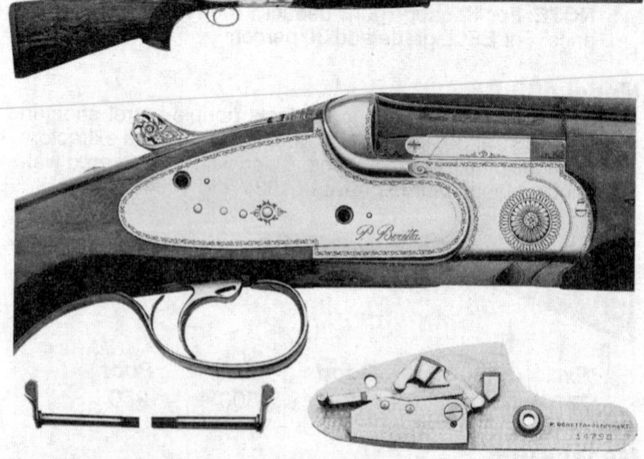

SO-5 sidelocks

NIB	Exc.	V.G.	Good	Fair	Poor
19500	9000	—	—	—	—

SO-5 Skeet

Same general specifications as SO-5 Trap but furnished to skeet dimensions. Offered in 12 gauge only with 26" or 28" vent rib barrels choked skeet. Weighs 7 lbs. 8 oz.

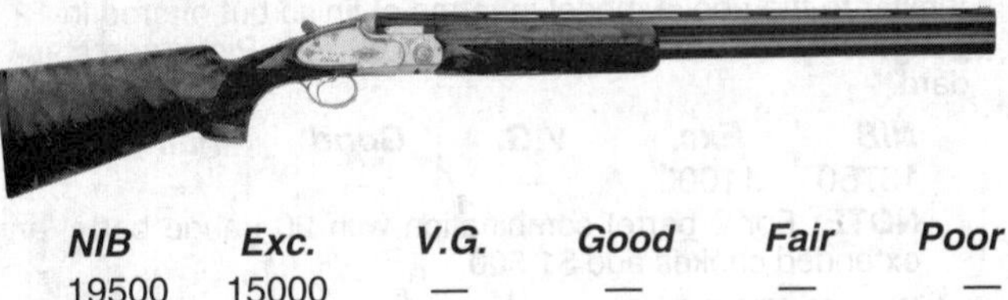

NIB	Exc.	V.G.	Good	Fair	Poor
19500	15000	—	—	—	—

SO-6 EL

This is a premium grade Beretta that is available in several different configurations similar to the SO-5. Available in 12 gauge only. It features a true side lock action, single-selective or non-selective trigger, fixed or screw-in choke tubes. The receiver is offered either in silver finish or case hardened without engraving. The walnut is highly select walnut with fine line checkering. A choice of pistol grip or straight grip is offered. Supplied with a leather fitted hard case. Weighs about 7 lbs. 4 oz. depending on barrel length.

SO-6 receiver

SO-6 Trap

NIB	Exc.	V.G.	Good	Fair	Poor
25500	12000	—	—	—	—

SO-6 Skeet

NIB	Exc.	V.G.	Good	Fair	Poor
25500	12000	—	—	—	—

SO-6 Sporting Clays

NIB	Exc.	V.G.	Good	Fair	Poor
25500	12000	—	—	—	—

SO-6 EELL

A higher grade in the SO-6 series that features a silver receiver with custom engraving with scroll or game scenes. Gold inlays are available on request. Choice of barrel lengths from 26" to 30". Choice of pistol grip or straight grip. All of the same features of the SO-6, but with higher fit and finish. Offered in 12 gauge only.

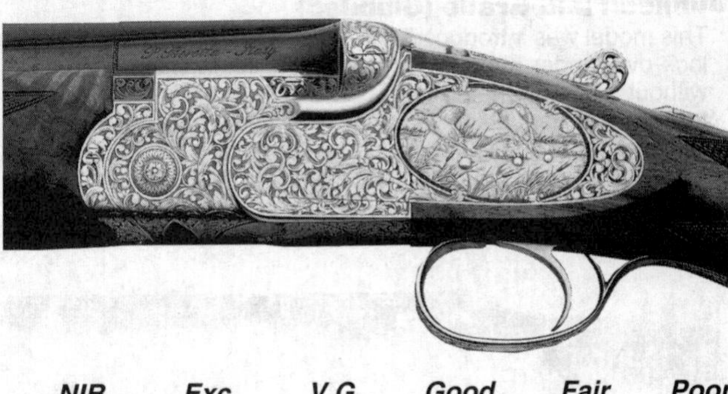

NIB	Exc.	V.G.	Good	Fair	Poor
42750	32500	—	—	—	—

SO-6 EESS

Same specifications as the SO-6 EELL grade but with ruby, sapphire, or emerald side plates with diamond brilliants.

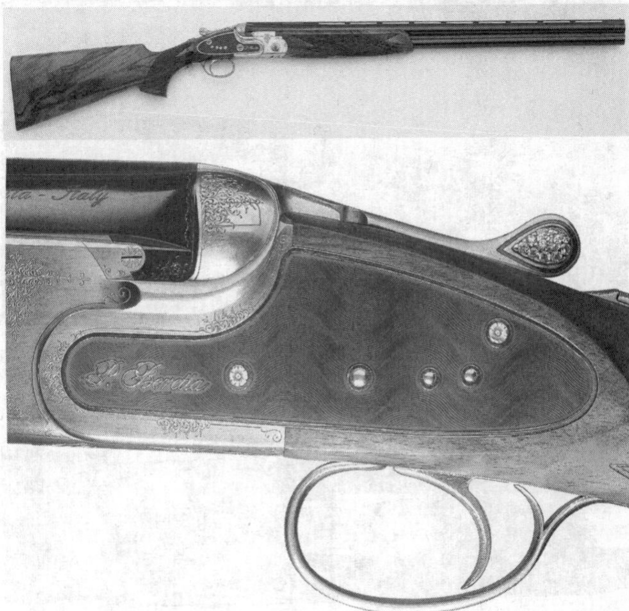

NIB	Exc.	V.G.	Good	Fair	Poor
86850	—	—	—	—	—

SO-7

One of Beretta's best-grade, sidelock, double-barrel shotgun. It is elaborately engraved and has the highest grade walnut in the stock. No longer in production.

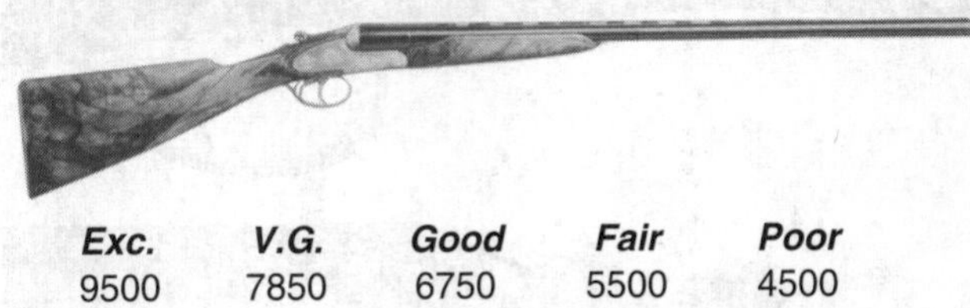

Exc.	V.G.	Good	Fair	Poor
9500	7850	6750	5500	4500

SO-9

This model O/U is Beretta's highest grade. Offered in 12, 20, and 28 gauge, and .410 bore. The true side lock (removable) receiver is highly engraved with scroll or game scenes by Italy's finest craftsmen. Barrel lengths are offered from 26" to 30" with solid hand filed rib. The walnut stock is the finest available with either pistol grip or straight grip. Stock dimensions to customers request. A custom fitted leather case with accessories is supplied with gun. A custom order gun. An independent appraisal is strongly suggested prior to a sale.

Suggester Retail Price: From $44,500 to $90,000.

Jubilee Field Grade (Giubileo)

This model was introduced in 1998 and is Beretta's finest boxlock over/under shotgun. The model is fitted with sideplates without screws. Offered in 12, 20, 28, and .410 bore with 26" to 30" barrel depending on gauge. Each gun is richly engraved with fine scroll and signed by master engravers. Highly figured walnut with pistol or straight grip. Weights range from about 7 lbs. in 12 gauge to 5.5 lbs. in .410 bore.

Single Gun

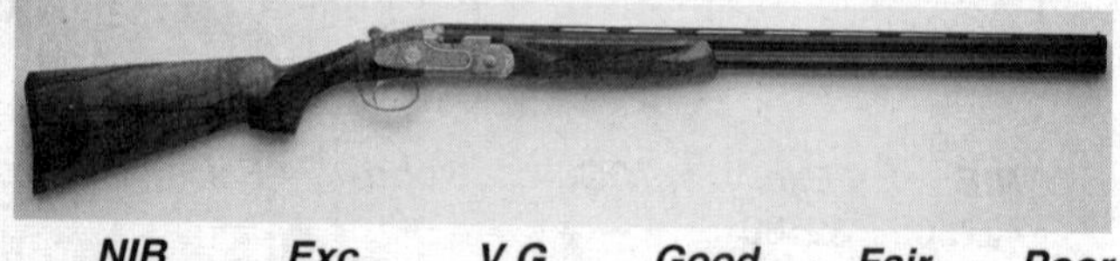

NIB	Exc.	V.G.	Good	Fair	Poor
13750	11000	—	—	—	—

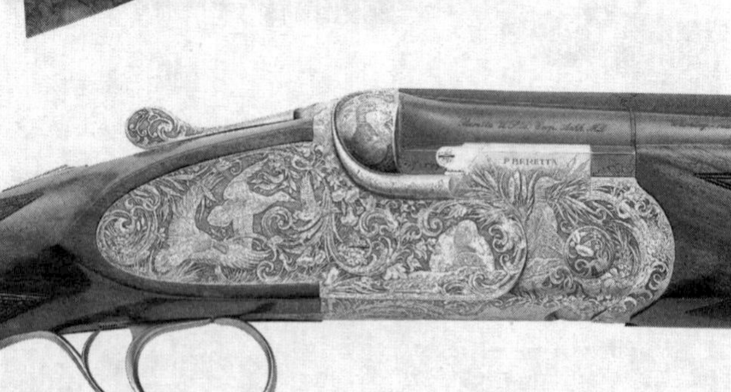

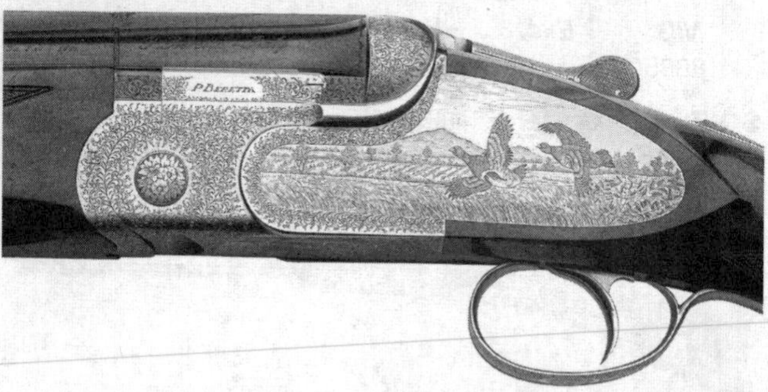

SO-9 with close-ups of engraving patterns

Matched Pair

NIB	Exc.	V.G.	Good	Fair	Poor
31650	—	—	—	—	—

Jubilee Sporting Grade

Similar to the above model in terms of finish but offered in 12 gauge only with choice of 30" or 32" barrels. Pistol grip standard.

NIB	Exc.	V.G.	Good	Fair	Poor
13750	11000	—	—	—	—

NOTE: For 2 barrel combination with 20 gauge barrel and extended chokes add $1,500.

Jubilee II (Giublio)

This is a side-by-side model offered in 12 or 20 gauge only with straight grip stocks. Choice of 26" or 28" barrels. Full coverage scroll engraving and highly figured walnut. Double triggers are by special order only. The 12 gauge weighs about 6.5 lbs. while the 20 gauge weighs about 6 lbs.

Single Gun

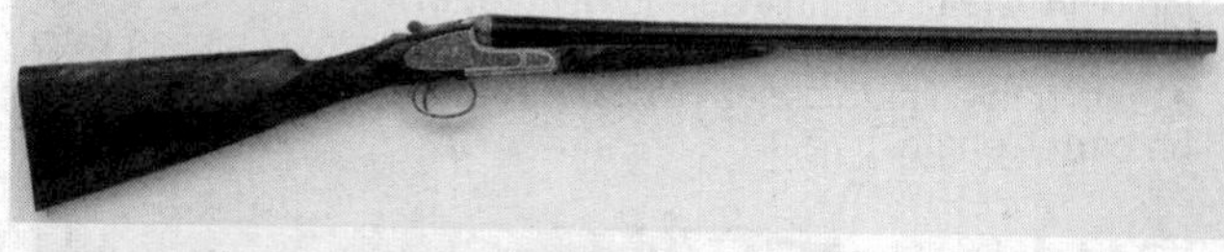

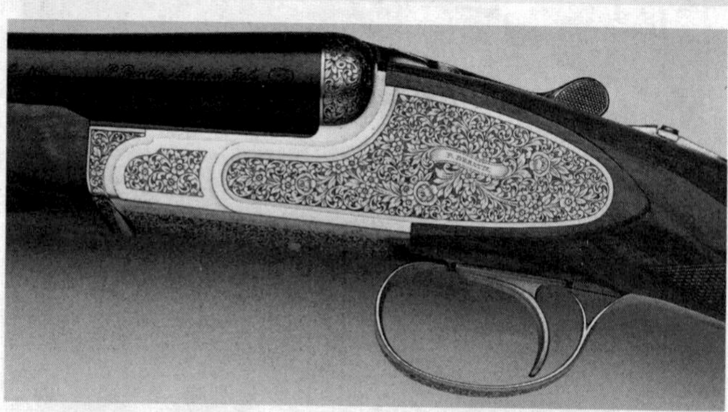

NIB	Exc.	V.G.	Good	Fair	Poor
13750	11000	—	—	—	—

Matched Pair

NIB	Exc.	V.G.	Good	Fair	Poor
31650	—	—	—	—	—

ASE Deluxe Sporting

This boxlock over/under gun is offered in 12 gauge only with choice of 28" or 30" barrels. Classic European scroll engraving. Offered in both field and competition configuration. Weights are about 7.5 lbs. for the 12 gauge.

NIB	Exc.	V.G.	Good	Fair	Poor
24000	17500	—	—	—	—

Model 687 EELL Gallery Special

A special version of this model. These are especially engraved guns with upgraded wood that are only made for the Beretta Galleries. Offered in 12, 20, 28, and .410 bore.

Single Gun

NIB	Exc.	V.G.	Good	Fair	Poor
7500	—	—	—	—	—

Special Combo—20/28 Gauge

NIB	Exc.	V.G.	Good	Fair	Poor
8500	—	—	—	—	—

Matched Pair

NIB	Exc.	V.G.	Good	Fair	Poor
16100	—	—	—	—	—

Imperiale Montecarlo

This is a side-by-side gun chambered for the 12, 20, or 28 gauge shell. True sidelock action. Choice of 26", 27", or 28" barrels with fixed chokes. Other lengths by special request. Weight is about 7.3 lbs. for 12 gauge, 6.5 lbs. for 20 gauge, and 6.2 lbs. for 28 gauge. Master engraved and signed.

NIB	Exc.	V.G.	Good	Fair	Poor
N/A	—	—	—	—	

Diana

This side-by-side gun is chambered for the 12 or 20 gauge with choice of barrel lengths. Action is true sidelock with exposed hammers. Weight for 12 gauge is about 7.2 lbs. and for the 20 gauge about 6.4 lbs. Master engraved and signed.

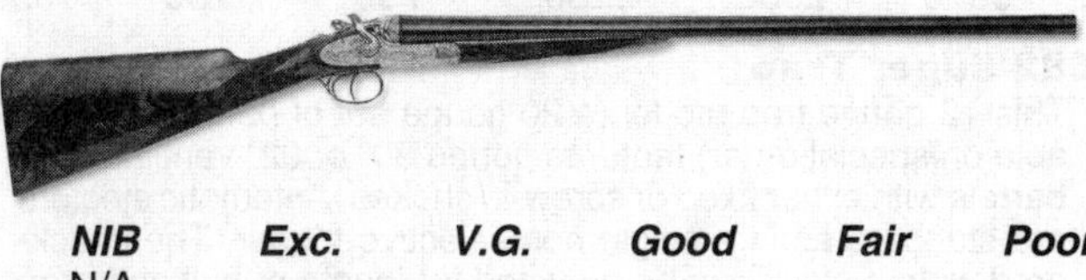

NIB	Exc.	V.G.	Good	Fair	Poor
N/A	—	—	—	—	

Model 451 Series

A custom order sidelock shotgun. The lowest priced version would be worth approximately $8,000 in excellent condition; and the top-of-the-line model, approximately $25,000. Prospective purchasers are advised to secure a qualified appraisal prior to acquisition.

Model 450 Series

This model is the same as the 451 series with the exception of being a Holland & Holland sidelock design. Prospective purchasers are advised to secure a qualified appraisal prior to acquisition.

Model 452

This is a premium grade side-by-side shotgun fitted with slide locks (removable). Offered in 12 gauge only with 26", 28", or 30" solid rib barrels. The receiver is a highly polished silver finish without engraving. Triggers may be double, single-selective, or single non-selective. The stock and forearm are special select walnut with fine line checkering with a choice of pistol or straight grip. Comes with leather hard case. Weighs about 6 lbs. 13 oz.

NIB	Exc.	V.G.	Good	Fair	Poor
22000	17000	12500	8500	4500	2500

Model 452 EELL

Same as above but furnished with fine scroll or game scene engraving. The highest grade of walnut is furnished for the stock and forearm. Leather case with accessories furnished.

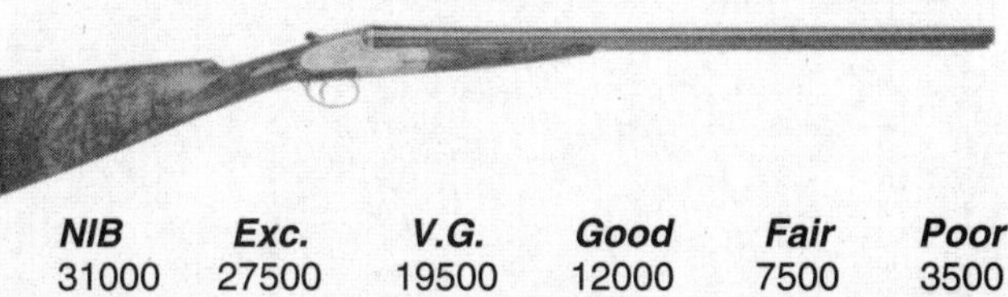

NIB	Exc.	V.G.	Good	Fair	Poor
31000	27500	19500	12000	7500	3500

BERETTA ONYX SERIES

This series designation was first used in 2003 to simplify the product line. Instead of using numeric model references the company now refers to these guns and others by series name.

Onyx

This over-and-under gun is offered in 12, 20, and for 2003, 28 gauge. With a choice of 26" or 28" barrels. It features a boxlock action with select checkered walnut stock, single-selective trigger, schnabel forend and auto safety. Black rubber recoil pad. Blued barrels and action. Weight is about 6.8 lbs. for 12 gauge.

NIB	Exc.	V.G.	Good	Fair	Poor
1580	1250	—	—	—	—

Onyx Waterfowler 3.5

As above but in 12 gauge with 3.5" chamber and matte black finish.

NIB	Exc.	V.G.	Good	Fair	Poor
1650	1300	—	—	—	—

White Onyx

Introduced in 2003 this model features a receiver machined in a jeweled pattern with satin nickel alloy. Offered in 12, 20, and 28 gauge with choice of 26" or 28" barrels. Select checkered walnut stock with schnabel forend. Weight is about 6.8 lbs. for 12 gauge.

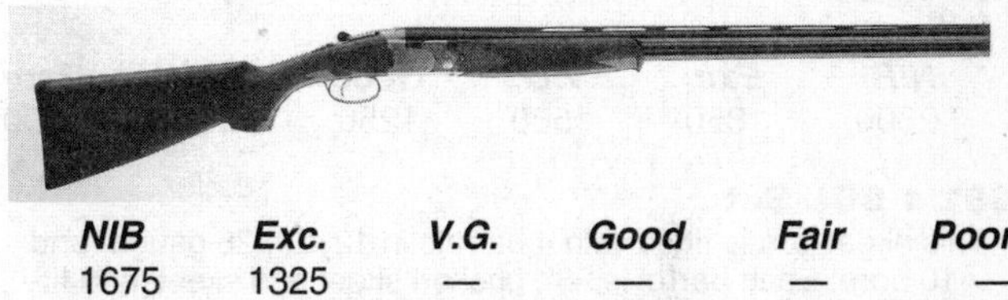

NIB	Exc.	V.G.	Good	Fair	Poor
1675	1325	—	—	—	—

BERETTA ONYX PRO SERIES

This series designation was first used in 2003 to simplify the product line. Instead of using numeric model references the company now refers to these guns and others by series name.

Onyx Pro

Introduced in 2003 this over-and-under shotgun is offered in 12, 20 and 28 gauge with a choice of 26" or 28" vent rib barrels with choke tubes. Single-selective trigger. Checkered X-Tra wood stock. Gel-Tek recoil pad. Supplied with plastic carry case. Weight is about 6.8 lbs.

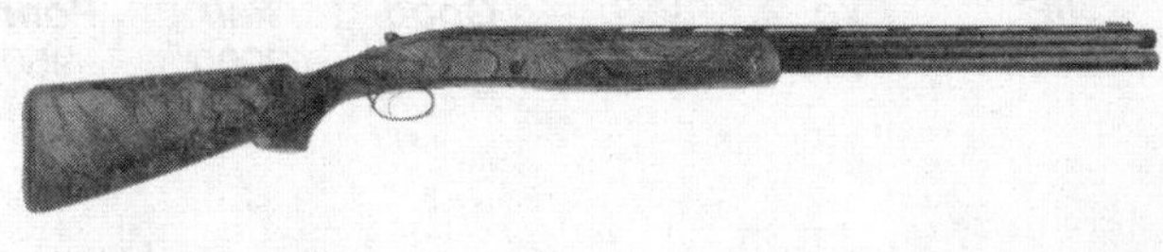

NIB	Exc.	V.G.	Good	Fair	Poor
1800	1375	—	—	—	—

Onyx Pro 3.5

As above in 12 gauge with 3.5" chamber. Weight is approximately 6.9 lbs. Introduced in 2003.

NIB	Exc.	V.G.	Good	Fair	Poor
1870	1450	—	—	—	—

BERETTA 682 SERIES

Model 682/682 Gold

This is a high-grade, quality-built O/U shotgun. Offered in 12 and 20 gauge, it is also available in some configurations in 28 gauge and .410 bore with barrel lengths from 26" to 34" depending on the type of shooting required. It is fitted with single-selective trigger and automatic ejectors. Barrels are fitted with ventilated rib and various fixed or screw-in choke combinations are available. The stock is a high-grade walnut with fine checkering in stock dimensions to fit the function of the gun. The frame is silver with light scroll borders on most models. This model covers a wide variety of applications and these are listed by grade and/or function:

NOTE: The Beretta Competition series shotguns have been renamed as of 1994. These shotguns are also referred to as the 682 Gold Competition Series guns, such as Model 682 Gold Trap or Model 682 Gold X Trap Combo and so forth.

682 Super Skeet

This model is offered in 12 gauge only with 28" vent rib barrels choked skeet and skeet. Single-selective trigger and auto ejectors are standard. This Super Skeet features ported barrels and adjustable length of pull and drop. A fitted hard case is standard. Gun weighs 7 lbs. 8 oz.

NIB	Exc.	V.G.	Good	Fair	Poor
2600	1850	1500	1250	950	750

682 Skeet

This is the standard 12 gauge skeet model that features a choice of 26" or 28" vent rib barrels choked skeet and skeet. Walnut stock is of International dimensions with special skeet rubber recoil pad. Gun is supplied with hard case. Weighs 7 lbs. 8 oz.

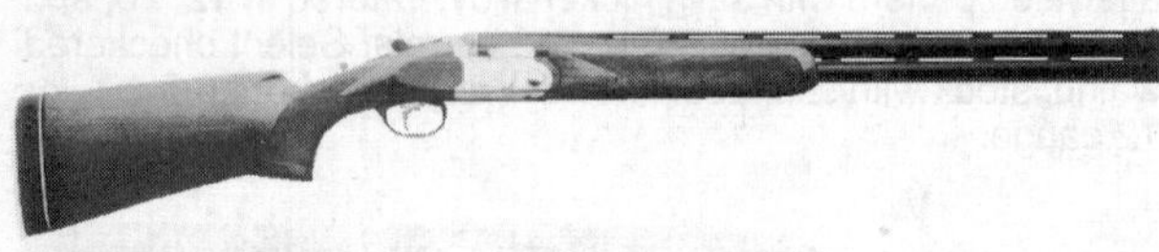

NIB	Exc.	V.G.	Good	Fair	Poor
2300	1850	1500	1250	950	700

682 4 BBL Set

This skeet gun is fitted with 4 barrels in 12, 20, 28 gauge, and .410 bore. Each barrel is 28", choked skeet and skeet, and fitted with a vent rib.

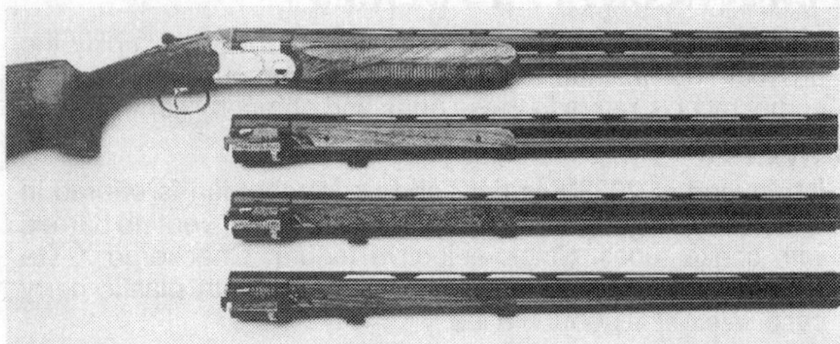

NIB	Exc.	V.G.	Good	Fair	Poor
5000	4000	3500	3000	2000	950

682 Super Sporting/682 Gold Sporting Ported

Built for sporting clays this 12 gauge or 20 gauge model features ported barrel and adjustable length of pull and drop. Fitted with 28" or 30" vent barrel with screw-in chokes; fixed chokes on special order. Checkered walnut stock with pistol grip and recoil pad. Supplied with case. Introduced in 1993. Weight of 12 gauge is 7 lbs. 8 oz. and 20 gauge weighs 6 lbs. 3 oz.

NIB	Exc.	V.G.	Good	Fair	Poor
2600	1000	750	—	—	—

682 Sporting/682 Gold Sporting

The standard version of the 12 gauge or 20 gauge Super Sporting model with a choice of 28" or 30" vent rib barrel with screw-in chokes. Checkered walnut stock with recoil pad. Introduced in 1993.

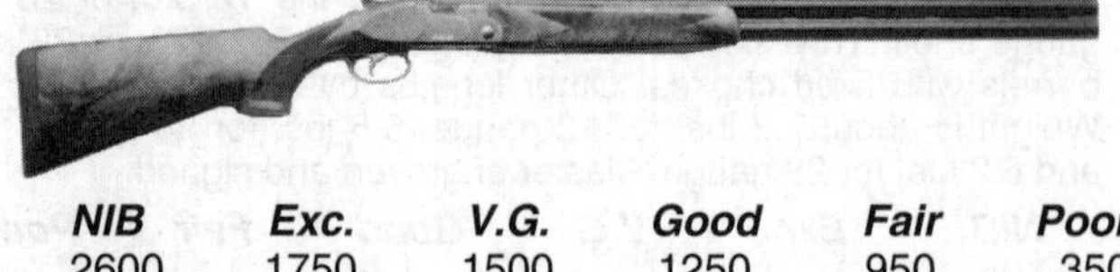

NIB	Exc.	V.G.	Good	Fair	Poor
2600	1750	1500	1250	950	350

682 Sporting Combo

Similar to the 682 Sporting with the addition of two 12 gauge 28" and 30" barrel fitted with screw-in chokes. Supplied with hard case.

NIB	Exc.	V.G.	Good	Fair	Poor
3200	2500	2250	1750	1250	650

682 Super Trap

This 12 gauge trap model (a 20 gauge set of barrels is available on special order) features ported 30" or 32" ventilated rib barrels with either fixed or screw-in chokes. Automatic ejectors are standard as is a single non-selective trigger. The checkered walnut stock can be adjusted for length of pull and drop of comb and is offered in either Monte Carlo or International dimensions. Weight is approximately 8 lbs. 6 oz.

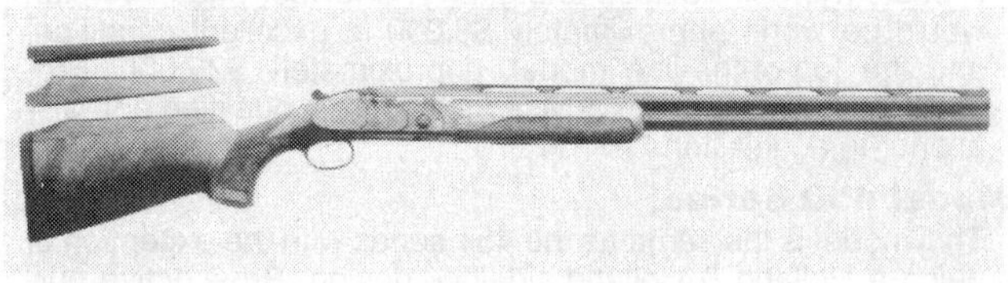

NIB	Exc.	V.G.	Good	Fair	Poor
2600	1850	1500	1250	950	500

Models 682 Skeet (top), 682 Super Trap (middle) and 682 Trap (bottom)

682 Top Single Super Trap

Same as the Super Trap but available in a single barrel configuration of either 32" or 34".

NIB	Exc.	V.G.	Good	Fair	Poor
2400	1950	1600	1350	950	500

682 Top Combo Super Trap

This configuration features a single barrel and an O/U barrel, both interchangeable. The combinations are: 30", 32", and 30", 34".

NIB	Exc.	V.G.	Good	Fair	Poor
3000	2750	2250	1750	1250	650

682 Trap

This model is the standard variation Beretta Trap gun. This 12 gauge comes standard with 30" vent rib barrels. However, 28" and 32" barrel can be special ordered. Fixed or screw-in chokes are available. The three-position sliding trigger allows for adjustable length of pull. A checkered walnut stock with recoil pad is standard. Stock is available in either Monte Carlo or International dimensions. Customer has choice of either silver or black receiver. Comes cased.

NIB	Exc.	V.G.	Good	Fair	Poor
2600	1750	1500	1250	900	450

682 Top Single Trap

This 12 gauge single barrel trap gun is available in 32" or 34" vent rib barrel.

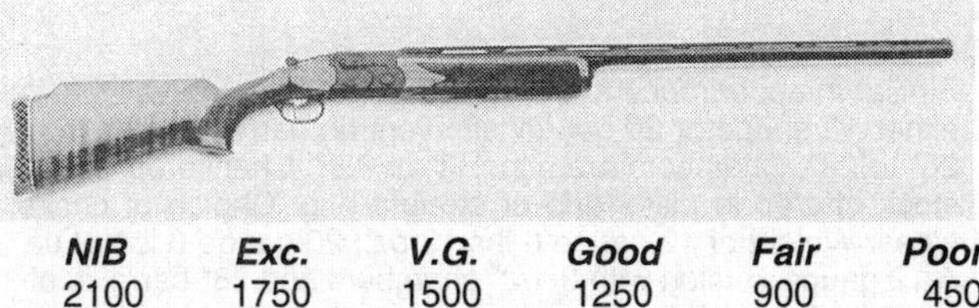

NIB	Exc.	V.G.	Good	Fair	Poor
2100	1750	1500	1250	900	450

682 Mono Combo Trap

A special configuration that features a single barrel with vent rib set to place single barrel in bottom position of what would normally be an O/U setup. A second barrel that is an O/U is also provided as part of the set. Single barrel is 34" and the O/U set is 32" in length.

NIB	Exc.	V.G.	Good	Fair	Poor
2700	2350	1850	1350	950	500

682 Top Combo

This trap combination features a standard placement single barrel with an interchangeable O/U barrel. Barrel available in 30", 32"; 30", 34"; and 32", 34". Barrels are fitted with ventilated rib.

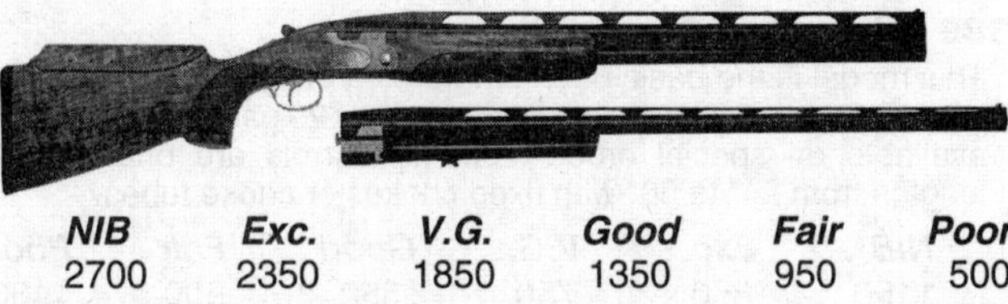

NIB	Exc.	V.G.	Good	Fair	Poor
2700	2350	1850	1350	950	500

682 Gold Trap with Adjustable Stock

Introduced in 1998 this over-and-under features a choice of 30" or 32" barrels with Monte Carlo stock and adjustable drop, cast, and comb. Trigger is adjustable for length of pull. Selected walnut stock with oil finish. Black rubber recoil pad standard. Weight is approximately 8.8 lbs.

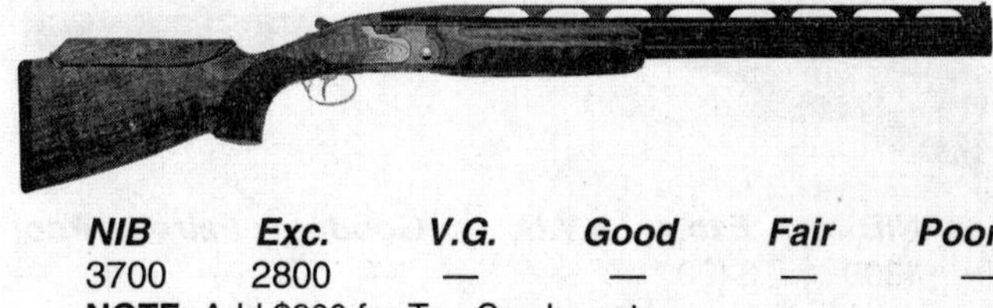

NIB	Exc.	V.G.	Good	Fair	Poor
3700	2800	—	—	—	—

NOTE: Add $800 for Top Combo set.

682 Gold Skeet with Adjustable Stock

Introduced in 1999 this 12 gauge model features skeet stock with adjustable comb. Stock drop and cast may also be adjusted. Greystone receiver. Comes with case. Offered in choice of 28" or 30" barrels. Single-selective trigger adjustable for length of pull. Black rubber recoil pad standard. Weight is about 7.5 lbs.

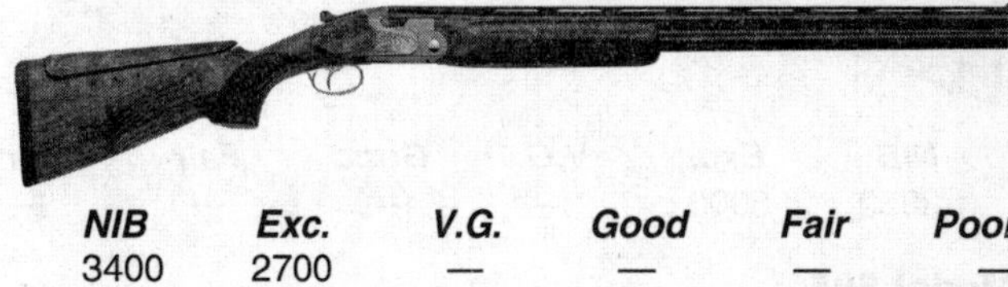

NIB	Exc.	V.G.	Good	Fair	Poor
3400	2700	—	—	—	—

682 Gold "Live Bird"

Introduced in 1995 this model has a gray receiver with select walnut stock. Single-selective is adjustable for length of pull. Offered in 12 gauge only with 30" barrels. Average weight is 8.8 lbs.

NIB	Exc.	V.G.	Good	Fair	Poor
2250	1750	1450	1150	850	400

S682 Gold E Trap

Chambered for 12 gauge 3" chambers with choice of 30" or 32" barrels with overbore and choke tubes. Highly select walnut stock with black rubber pad. Single-selective trigger with adjustable length of pull. Beavertail forend. Adjustable Monte Carlo stock. Front white bead with mid bead sight. Carry case standard. Weight is about 8.8 lbs. Introduced in 2001.

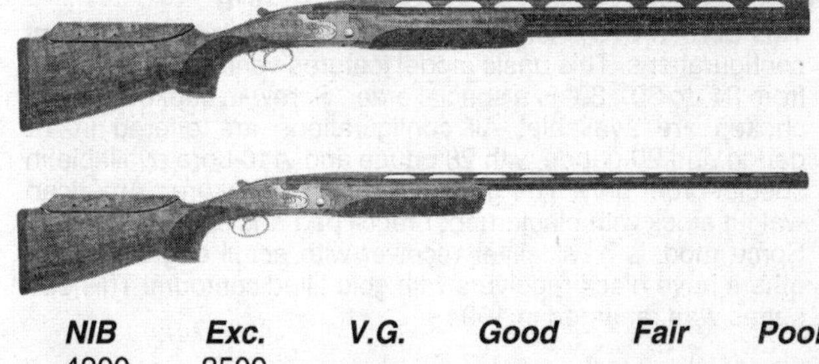

NIB	Exc.	V.G.	Good	Fair	Poor
4300	3500	—	—	—	—

S682 Gold E Trap Combo

Offers the same features as the Trap model but with interchangeable over-and-under barrels and top single barrel with under rib. Introduced in 2001.

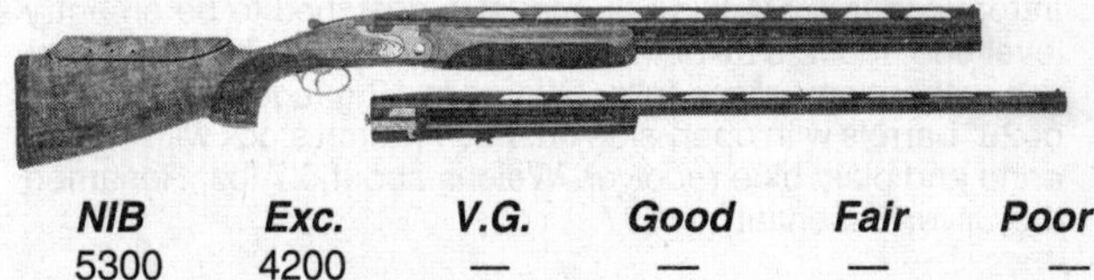

NIB	Exc.	V.G.	Good	Fair	Poor
5300	4200	—	—	—	—

S682 Gold E Skeet

This 12 gauge skeet gun features a special skeet-style stock with beavertail forend. Adjustable stock. Barrel lengths are 28" or 30". Single-selective trigger. Weight is about 7.5 lbs. Introduced in 2001.

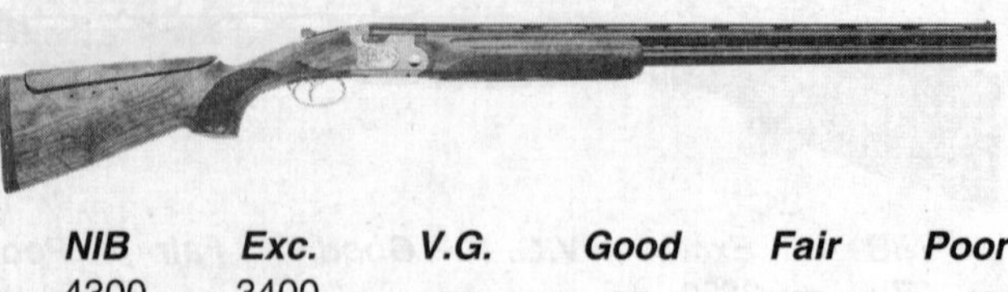

NIB	Exc.	V.G.	Good	Fair	Poor
4300	3400	—	—	—	—

S682 Gold E Sporting

This 12 gauge model has a choice of 28", 30", or 32" barrels with extended choke tubes and tapered top rib with white front sight and mid bead. Sporting clay-style stock of select walnut. Weight is about 7.6 lbs. Introduced in 2001.

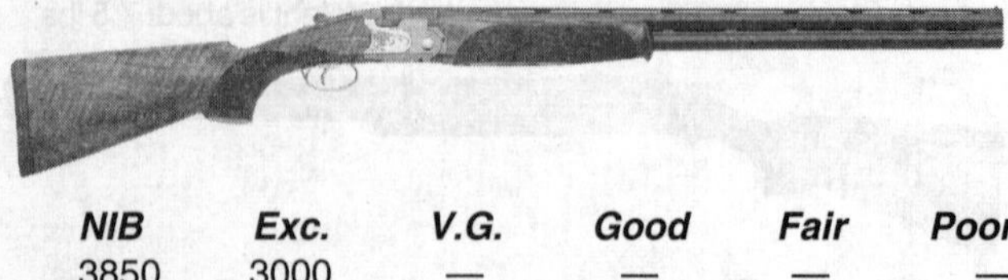

NIB	Exc.	V.G.	Good	Fair	Poor
3850	3000	—	—	—	—

Model 685

A lower priced O/U chambered for 12 or 20 gauge with 3" chambers, a satin-chromed boxlock action with a single trigger and extractors. Not imported after 1986.

Exc.	V.G.	Good	Fair	Poor
650	600	500	375	200

BERETTA 686 SERIES

Model 686/686 Silver Perdiz Sporting

This Beretta O/U shotgun is available in a number of different configurations. This basic model features ventilated rib barrels from 24" to 30"; 30" is a special order. Screw-in chokes or fixed chokes are available. All configurations are offered in 12 gauge and 20 gauge with 28 gauge and .410 bore available in special order only. The gun is fitted with checkered American walnut stock with black rubber recoil pad and special grip cap. Some models have silver receiver with scroll engraving and others have black receivers with gold-filled contours. This 686 series was renamed in 1994.

Model 686 Essential/Silver Essential

Introduced in 1994 this 686 model is designed to be an entry level 686. It offers all of the mechanical features of the 686 series without any of the frills. Offered in 12 gauge only with 26" or 28" barrels with open-side rib. Plain walnut stock with checkering and plain blue receiver. Weighs about 6.7 lbs. Renamed the Silver Essential in 1997.

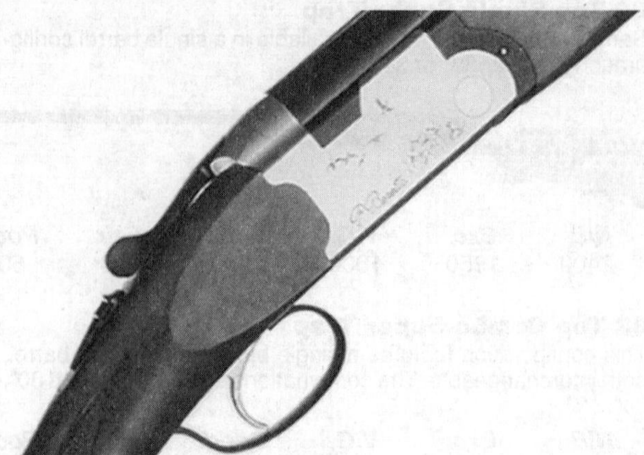

Beretta 686 Silver Essential close-up

NIB	Exc.	V.G.	Good	Fair	Poor
900	750	600	450	350	200

686 Ultra Light Onyx

This model features a black anodized light alloy receiver accented with an engraved gold-filled "P. Beretta" signature. Available in 12 gauge only with 26" or 28" vent rib barrels. Chokes are either fixed or screw-in type. Weighs 5 lbs. 1 oz.

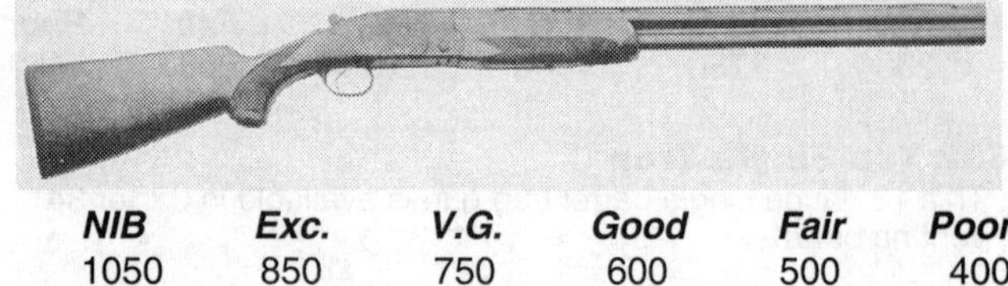

NIB	Exc.	V.G.	Good	Fair	Poor
1050	850	750	600	500	400

686 Onyx

Similar in appearance to the Ultra Light Onyx, but available in either 12 gauge or 20 gauge with vent rib barrel lengths from 26" to 28". Chambers are either 3" or 3.5". Checkered walnut stock offered in pistol grip or straight grip. Choice of choke types. Weight of 12 gauge 6 lbs.13 oz.; 20 gauge 6 lbs. 3 oz. A 12 gauge version with 3-1/2" chambers and 28" barrel is offered (new in 1999) with matte wood finish, matte black receiver, beavertail forend with fingerwells, and silver finish trigger.

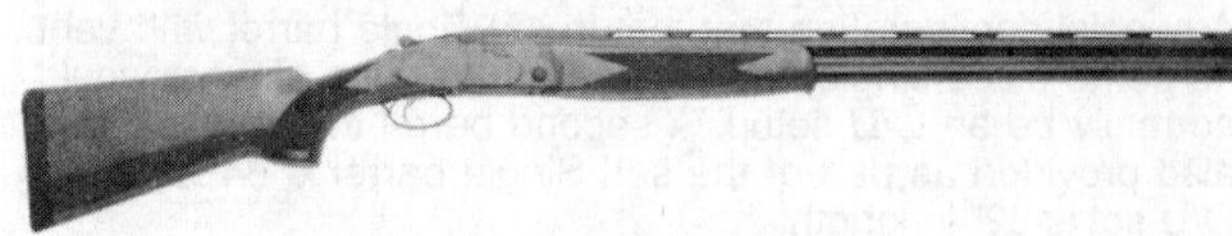

NIB	Exc.	V.G.	Good	Fair	Poor
1100	850	750	650	500	400

686 Onyx 2 BBL Set

Same as above but supplied with a 20 gauge 28" vent rib barrel and a 28 gauge 26" vent rib barrel.

NIB	Exc.	V.G.	Good	Fair	Poor
1600	1250	1000	800	650	500

686 Silver Receiver

This model is the basic 686. It features a plain semi-matte silver receiver and is available in either 12 or 20 gauge; 28 gauge available on special order. Vent rib barrels are offered in lengths from 24" to 30" with fixed chokes or choke tubes.

NIB	Exc.	V.G.	Good	Fair	Poor
1100	850	750	650	500	400

686 L/686 Silver Perdiz

Same as above but furnished with a scroll engraved silver receiver. Offered in 28 gauge with 26" or 28" vent rib barrels. Gun weighs 5 lbs. 5 oz.

NIB	Exc.	V.G.	Good	Fair	Poor
1100	850	750	650	500	400

686 Silver Pigeon

Introduced in 1996 this model replaces the Silver Perdiz. It has an electroless nickel finish on a scroll engraved receiver. Offered in 12, 20, and 28 gauge with 26" or 28" barrels. Average weight is 6.8 lbs. A new variation, introduced in 1999, features a 20 gauge gun with 28" barrels, straight grip stock, and matte nickel receiver.

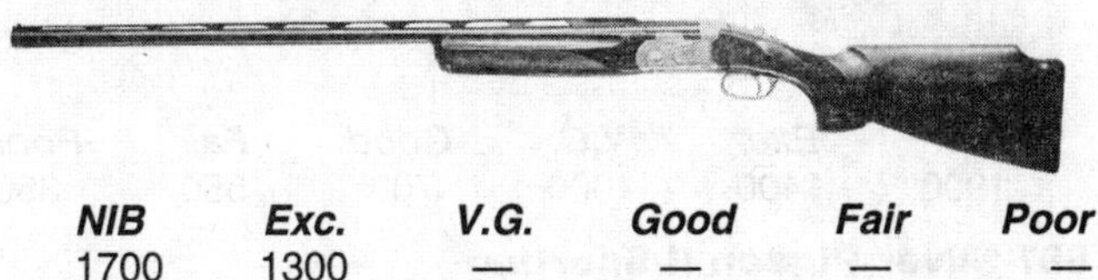

NIB	Exc.	V.G.	Good	Fair	Poor
1700	1350	950	600	—	—

686 Silver Pigeon Sporting

NIB	Exc.	V.G.	Good	Fair	Poor
1400	950	750	600	500	300

686 Silver Pigeon Trap (30")

NIB	Exc.	V.G.	Good	Fair	Poor
1700	1300	—	—	—	—

686 Silver Pigeon Trap Top Mono (32" or 34")

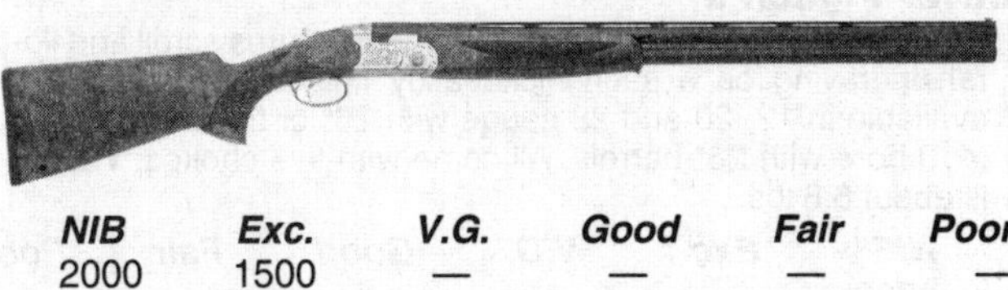

NIB	Exc.	V.G.	Good	Fair	Poor
1700	1300	—	—	—	—

686 Silver Pigeon S

Essentially the same as the Silver Pigeon models but packaged with a carrying case that includes five choke tubes, accessory recoil pad, and sling swivels. A .410-bore offering on a proportionally smaller receiver was added in 2006.

NIB	Exc.	V.G.	Good	Fair	Poor
1900	1500	—	—	—	—

NOTE: Add $700 for two barrel 20/28 gauge set.

686E Sporting

Offered in 12 or 20 gauge with choice of 28" or 30" barrels. Five Beretta screw-in chokes. Modern ellipsis receiver engraving. Special carrying case. Introduced with new styling in 2001.

NIB	Exc.	V.G.	Good	Fair	Poor
2000	1500	—	—	—	—

686 EL/Gold Perdiz

This model is available in 12 gauge or 20 gauge with 26" or 28" vent rib barrels. The receiver is silver with scroll engraving and fitted with side plates. A fitted hard case comes with the gun.

NIB	Exc.	V.G.	Good	Fair	Poor
1800	1250	1000	800	700	350

686 Hunter Sport

A sporting clay 12 gauge or 20 gauge shotgun that features a silver receiver with scroll engraving. Wide 12.5mm target rib. Radiused recoil pad. Offered in 26" or 28" vent rib barrels with screw-in chokes. Offered for the first time in 1993.

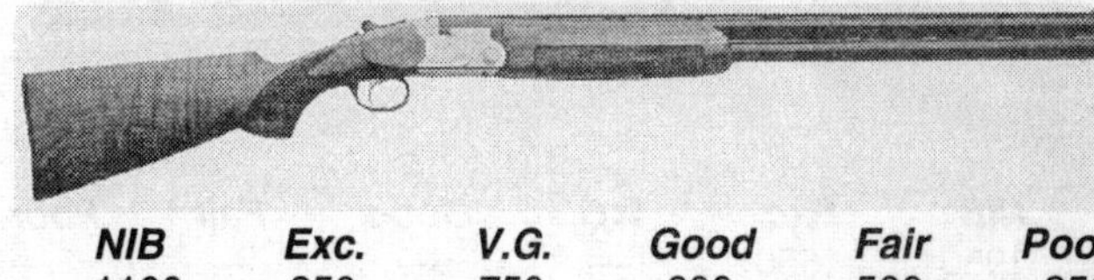

NIB	Exc.	V.G.	Good	Fair	Poor
1100	850	750	600	500	250

686 Onyx Hunter Sport

Same as above but offered in 12 gauge only with matte black finish on receiver and barrels. Weighs 6 lbs.13 oz. Introduced in 1993.

NIB	Exc.	V.G.	Good	Fair	Poor
1000	850	750	600	500	250

WING SERIES

This series designation was first used in 2003 to simplify the product line. Instead of using numeric model references the company now refers to these guns and others by series name.

686 Whitewing

Introduced in the fall of 1998, this over-and-under shotgun is chambered for the 12 gauge shell and fitted with 26" or 28" barrels with Beretta's choke system. The receiver is polished nickel with engraved game scenes, and gold-plated trigger. Walnut pistol-grip stock with gloss finish.

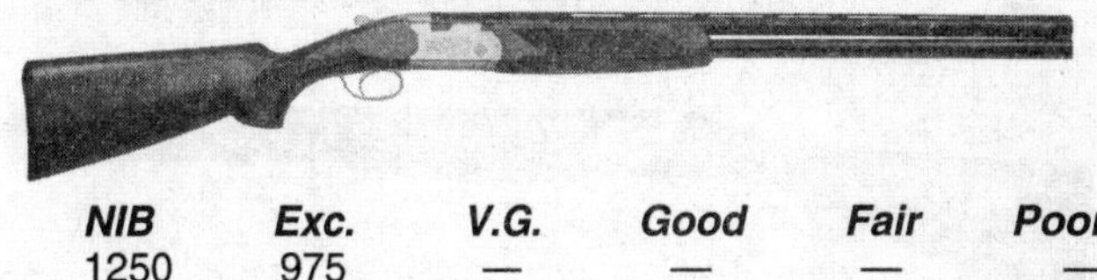

NIB	Exc.	V.G.	Good	Fair	Poor
1250	975	—	—	—	—

686 Blackwing

This model, introduced in 2002, is similar to the Whitewing model with the exception of a blued receiver and schnabel forend.

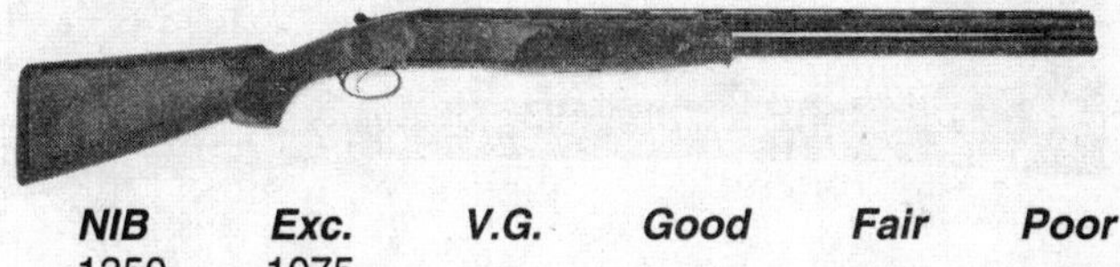

NIB	Exc.	V.G.	Good	Fair	Poor
1350	1075	—	—	—	—

686 Sporting Combo

Same specifications as the Hunter Sport with the addition of an interchangeable 30" 12 gauge barrel.

NIB	Exc.	V.G.	Good	Fair	Poor
1800	1500	1250	1000	800	550

686 Collection Trap

Introduced in 1996 this model features a special multi-colored stock and forend. Offered in 12 gauge only with 30" barrels. Factory recoil pad standard. Average weight is 7.7 lbs.

NIB	Exc.	V.G.	Good	Fair	Poor
1400	900	750	500	400	300

686 Collection Sport

Similar to above but offered with 28" barrels.

NIB	Exc.	V.G.	Good	Fair	Poor
1400	900	750	500	400	300

686 Quail Unlimited 2002 Covey Limited Edition

Offered in 20 or 28 gauge with 26" or 28" vent rib barrels. Choke tubes. Engraved receiver with gold quail inlays. Weight is about 6.8 lbs.

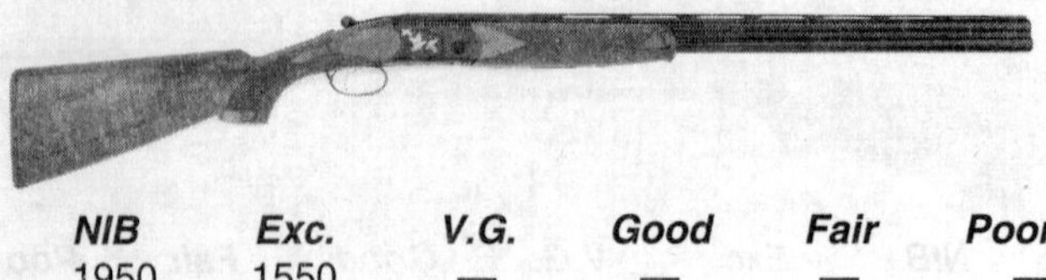

NIB	Exc.	V.G.	Good	Fair	Poor
1950	1550	—	—	—	—

686 Ringneck Pheasants Forever

Introduced in 2003 this model is chambered for 12 or 20 gauge and fitted with 26" or 28" vent rib barrels. Checkered walnut stock with pistol grip. Single-selective trigger. Gel-Tek recoil pad. Schnabel forend. Weight is about 6.8 lbs. on 12 gauge.

NIB	Exc.	V.G.	Good	Fair	Poor
2025	1550	—	—	—	—

ULTRALIGHT SERIES

This series designation was first used in 2003 to simplify the product line. Instead of using numeric model references the company now refers to these guns and others by series name.

Ultralight

This over-and-under model is chambered for 12 gauge 2-3/4" shells and fitted with a choice of 26" or 28" barrels. The receiver is light aluminum alloy with nickel finish with game scene engraving. Black rubber recoil pad is standard. Single-selective trigger, pistol grip, and schnabel forearm. Weight is approximately 5.75 lbs.

Ultralight Receiver

NIB	Exc.	V.G.	Good	Fair	Poor
1900	1500	900	600	—	—

Ultralight Deluxe

Similar to the above model but offered only with 28" barrels. Nickel receiver is gold game scene engraved. First offered in 1998.

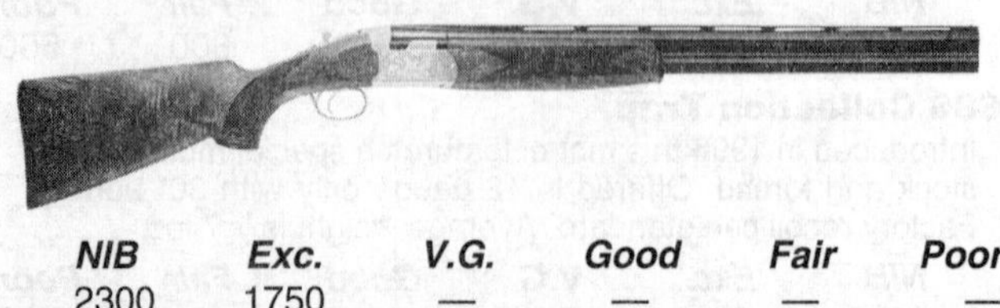

NIB	Exc.	V.G.	Good	Fair	Poor
2300	1750	—	—	—	—

BERETTA 687/PIGEON SERIES

This series designation was first used in 2003 to simplify the product line. Instead of using numeric model references the company now refers to these guns and others by series name.

Model 687/687 Silver Pigeon Sporting

This model is similar to the Model 686 but in a slightly more ornate version. This series was renamed in 1994.

687 L/Silver Pigeon

This model is offered in 12 gauge or 20 gauge with 26" or 28" vent rib barrels. The boxlock receiver is scroll engraved with game scenes. Auto ejectors and double or single triggers are offered.

NIB	Exc.	V.G.	Good	Fair	Poor
1800	1100	950	800	650	300

687 Silver Pigeon II

Introduced in 1999, this model features a deep relief game scene engraving on a silver receiver. Select walnut stock with oil finish. Available in 12 gauge only with choice of 26" or 28" vent rib barrels. Single-selective trigger. Weight is about 6.8 lbs.

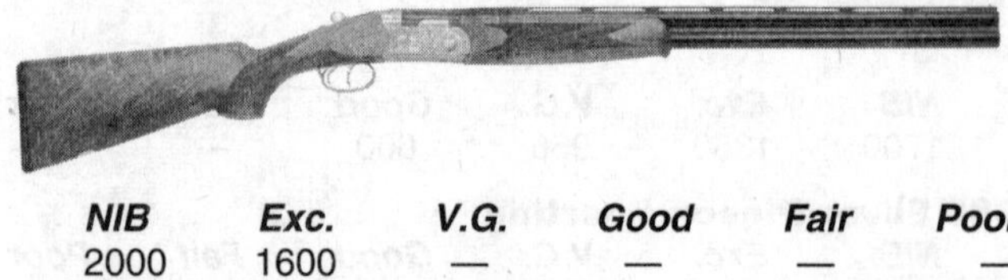

NIB	Exc.	V.G.	Good	Fair	Poor
2000	1600	—	—	—	—

687 Silver Pigeon Sporting

A sporting clays version available in 12 or 20 gauge with 28" or 30" barrels.

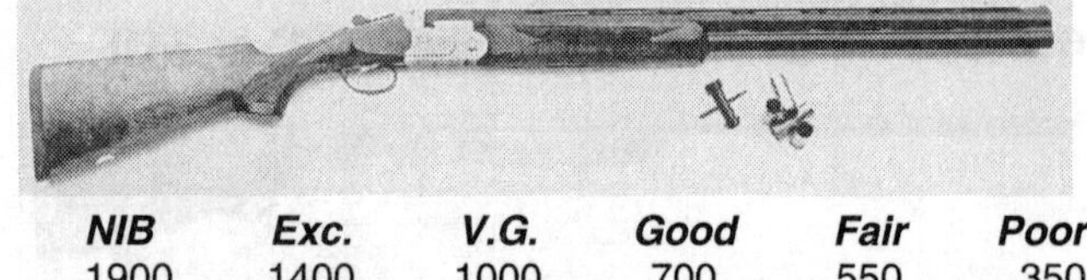

NIB	Exc.	V.G.	Good	Fair	Poor
1900	1400	1000	700	550	350

687 Silver Pigeon II Sporting

Introduced in 1999, this model features a deep relief engraving with oil finished select walnut stock with schnabel forend. Single-selective trigger. Offered in 12 gauge only with choice of 28" or 30" barrels. Black rubber recoil pad. Weight is about 7.7 lbs.

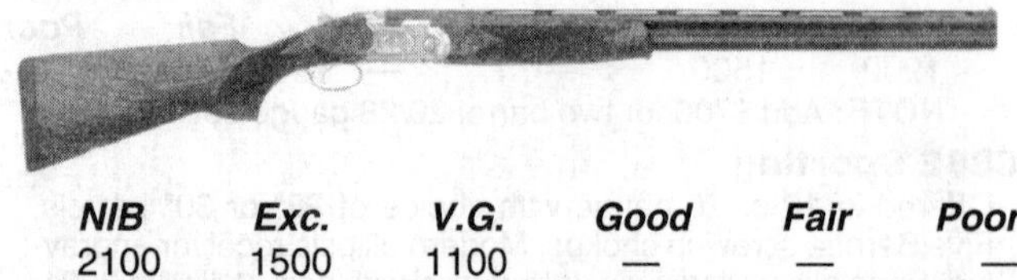

NIB	Exc.	V.G.	Good	Fair	Poor
2100	1500	1100	—	—	—

Silver Pigeon S

New in 2007, the Silver Pigeon S Series features scroll and floral engraving on a satin nickel-alloy finished receiver. It is available in 12, 20 and 28 gauge with 26" or 28" barrels, and .410 bore with 28" barrels. All come with five chokes. Weight is about 6.8 lbs.

NIB	Exc.	V.G.	Good	Fair	Poor
1700	—	—	—	—	—

Silver Pigeon S Combo

Combo model comes with 26" 20 gauge barrels and 28" 28 gauge barrels.

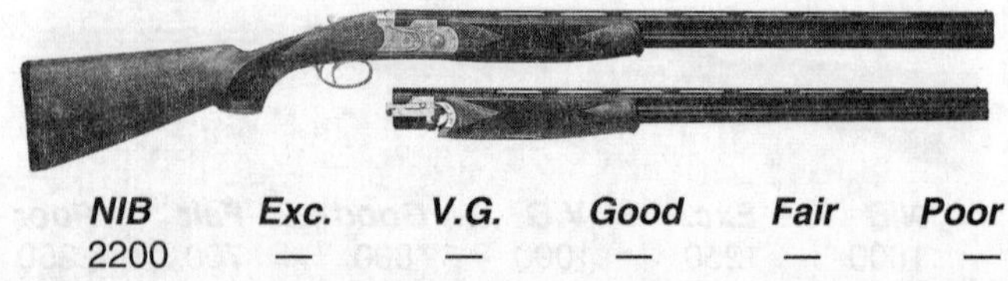

NIB	Exc.	V.G.	Good	Fair	Poor
2200	—	—	—	—	—

687 Sporting Combo

Offered in 12 gauge only with two sets of 12 gauge interchangeable vent rib barrels in 28" and 30".

NIB	Exc.	V.G.	Good	Fair	Poor
2400	2100	1850	1500	1150	600

687 Silver Pigeon IV

Introduced in 2003 for the U.S. market this shotgun features a black finish receiver with full scroll engraving with gold-filled game birds. Select oil-finished walnut stock with Gel-Tek recoil pad. Offered in 12, 20, or 28 gauge with 26" or 28" barrels. Single-selective trigger with fluted beavertail forend. Weight is about 6.8 lbs. in 12 gauge.

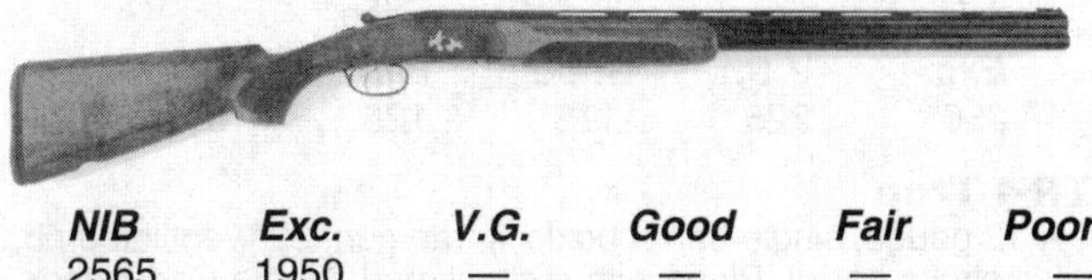

NIB	Exc.	V.G.	Good	Fair	Poor
2565	1950	—	—	—	—

687 Silver Pigeon V

This is the top-of-the-line model in the Silver Pigeon Series. Available in 12, 20 and 28 gauges with 26" and 28" barrels and .410-bore (added in 2006). Pistol-grip stock of richly figured walnut with oil finish. Color case-hardened receiver with gold-filled game bird inlays. English stocked versions of the 20 and 28 gauges and .410 bore were added in 2006.

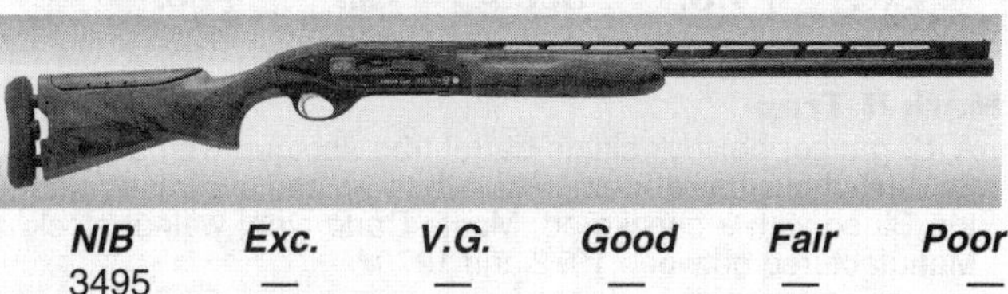

NIB	Exc.	V.G.	Good	Fair	Poor
3495	—	—	—	—	—

687 EL/687 Gold Pigeon

This model is offered with scroll engraved gold inlaid game animals. Fitted with side plates. The stock is highly figured walnut with fine line checkering. Available in 12, 20, 28 gauge or .410 bore in 26" or 28" vent rib barrels with screw-in chokes. Comes with fitted hard case. Weights for 12 gauge: 6 lbs. 13 oz.; 20 gauge: 6 lbs. 3 oz.; 28/.410: 5 lbs. 5 oz. Series was renamed in 1994.

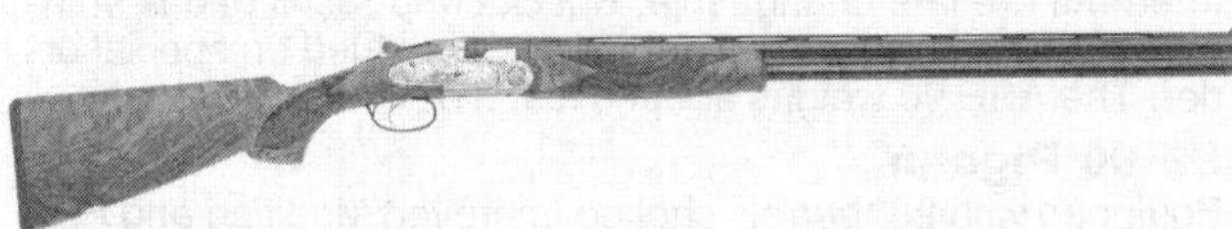

In 2001 Beretta enhanced the engraving on the Model 687EL Gold Pigeon

687 EL 12 and 20 gauge

NIB	Exc.	V.G.	Good	Fair	Poor
3200	2450	1800	1200	750	350

687 EL 28/.410

NIB	Exc.	V.G.	Good	Fair	Poor
3200	2500	1850	1250	800	400

687 EL Gold Pigeon Sporting

A sporting clays model chambered for 12 gauge and fitted with 28" or 30" vent rib barrels. Offered new in 1993. Comes with fitted hard case.

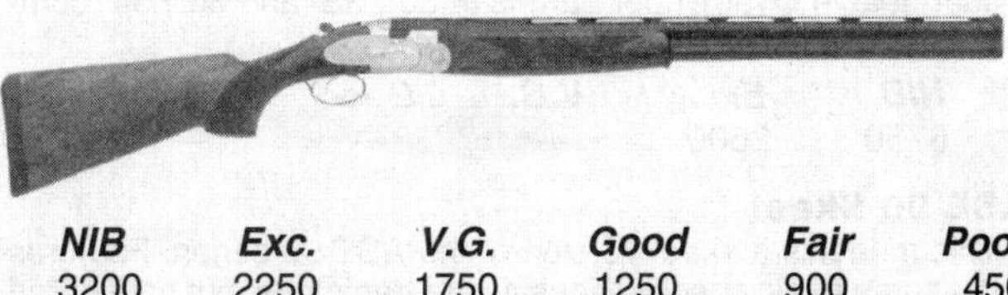

NIB	Exc.	V.G.	Good	Fair	Poor
3200	2250	1750	1250	900	450

687 EELL/Diamond Pigeon

Same as above, including gauge and barrel offerings, but furnished with more fully figured walnut and finer checkering. Fitted with side plates that are scroll engraved with fine cut game scenes. This grade is also available in a straight grip English stock version in 20 gauge as well as a combo set of 20 gauge and 28 gauge interchangeable 26" barrels. All 687 EELL Models are fitted with hard case. Series was renamed in 1994.

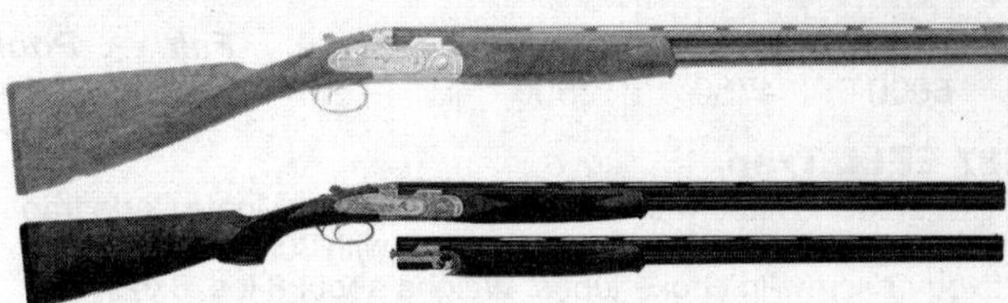

687 EELL 12 and 20 gauge

NIB	Exc.	V.G.	Good	Fair	Poor
5700	3250	2250	1500	1000	—

687 EELL 28 gauge and .410 bore

NIB	Exc.	V.G.	Good	Fair	Poor
5700	3500	2500	1750	1250	—

687 EELL Combo

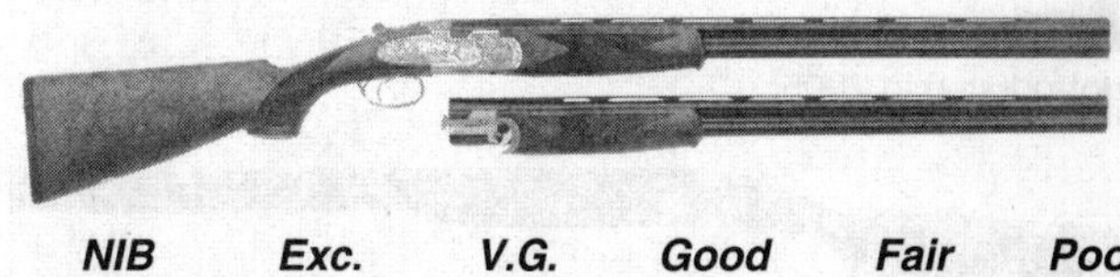

NIB	Exc.	V.G.	Good	Fair	Poor
6800	5250	4000	—	—	—

687 EELL Diamond Pigeon Skeet

Same as above with the addition of a skeet configuration. A 12 gauge version is offered with 28" vent rib barrels choked skeet and skeet. Weighs about 7 lbs. 8 oz. A 4 barrel set is also offered with interchangeable 12, 20, 28 gauge, and .410 bore barrels choked Skeet and Skeet.

687 EELL 12 gauge

NIB	Exc.	V.G.	Good	Fair	Poor
4700	3700	2500	—	—	—

687 EELL 4 BBL Set

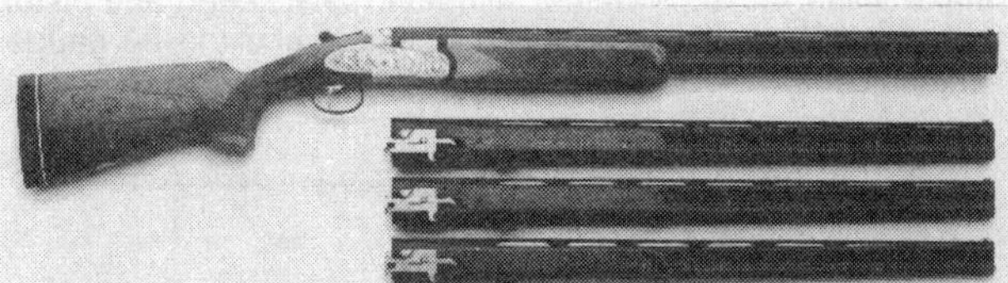

NIB	Exc.	V.G.	Good	Fair	Poor
6200	5000	4500	3750	2500	1500

687 EELL Diamond Pigeon Skeet with Adjustable Stock

Same as the Skeet version above but with adjustable comb, drop and cast. Introduced in 1999.

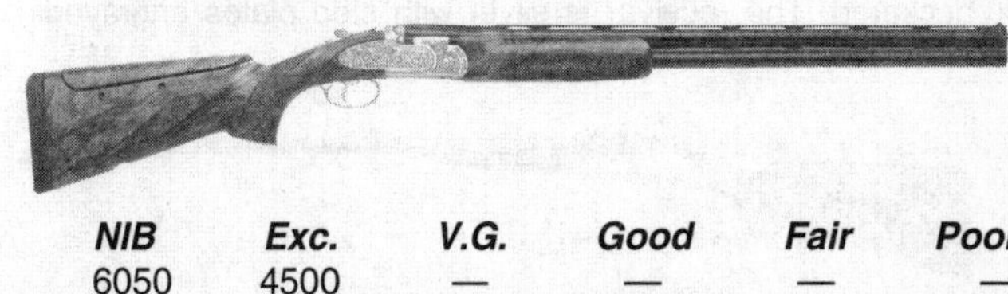

NIB	Exc.	V.G.	Good	Fair	Poor
6050	4500	—	—	—	—

687 EELL Diamond Pigeon Sporting

A sporting clays version of the 687 EELL in 12 gauge only with 28" vent rib barrels fitted with screw-in chokes.

NIB	Exc.	V.G.	Good	Fair	Poor
6000	4750	3500	—	—	—

687 EELL Trap

This model is fitted with either International or Monte Carlo trap stock dimensions. Offered in 12 gauge with 30" vent rib barrels fixed or screw-in choke tubes. Weighs about 8 lbs. 6 oz.

NIB	Exc.	V.G.	Good	Fair	Poor
3800	3000	2500	2000	1500	1000

687 EELL Top Combo

A single barrel trap gun with choice of one single barrel set and one Over/Under steel rod barrel in either 30" and 32" or 32" and 34".

NIB	Exc.	V.G.	Good	Fair	Poor
4500	3500	3000	2250	2000	1000

Model 687 EELL King Ranch

Introduced in 2005.

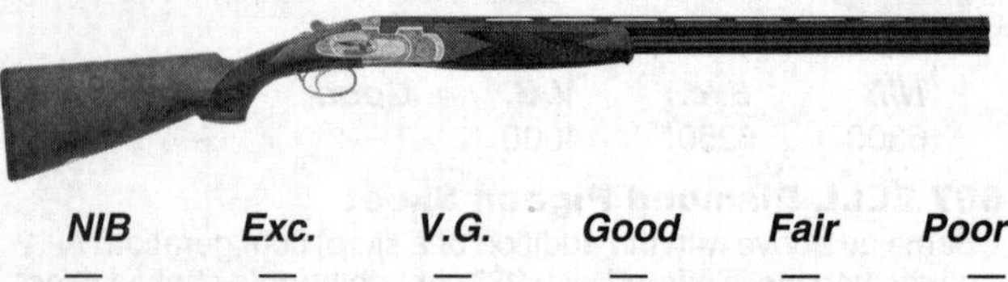

NIB	Exc.	V.G.	Good	Fair	Poor
—	—	—	—	—	—

Model 626 Field Grade

A 12 or 20 gauge boxlock double barrel shotgun with a 26" or 28" barrel, various choke combinations, single trigger and automatic ejectors. Engraved, blued with a checkered walnut stock. Imported between 1984 and 1988.

Exc.	V.G.	Good	Fair	Poor
900	825	700	575	475

626 Onyx

This model is a boxlock side-by-side shotgun offered in 12 gauge and 20 gauge. With choice of 26" or 28" solid rib barrels with screw-in chokes. Double triggers are standard but single trigger is available on request. Receiver is anti-glare black matte finish. Stock is walnut with hand checkering and pistol grip. The 12 gauge weighs 6 lbs. 13 oz. and the 20 gauge weighs 6 lbs. 13 oz.

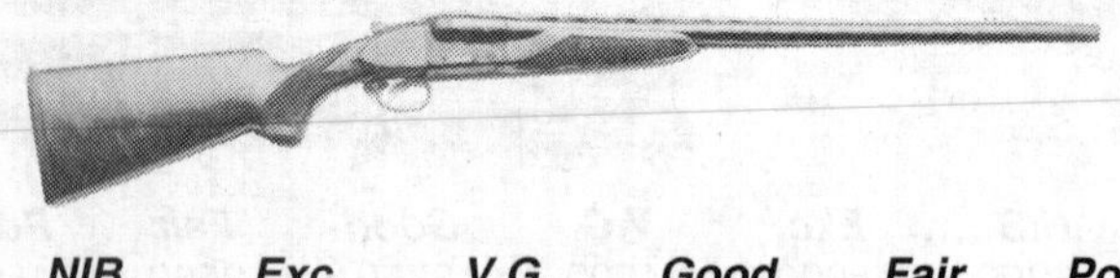

NIB	Exc.	V.G.	Good	Fair	Poor
1250	950	850	750	500	400

627 EL

This model is offered in 12 gauge only with choice of 26" or 28" solid rib barrels. The walnut is highly figured and fine cut checkered. The receiver is silver with side plates engraved with scroll. Comes with hard case.

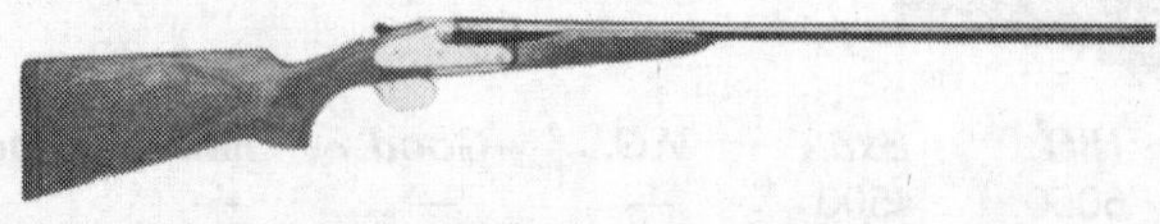

NIB	Exc.	V.G.	Good	Fair	Poor
2500	2000	1750	1500	1250	650

627 EELL

Same as above but fitted with scroll engraved side plates with game scenes. Walnut is highly figured with fine line checkering. A straight-grip stock is also offered in this model. Comes with hard case.

NIB	Exc.	V.G.	Good	Fair	Poor
3750	3500	3000	2500	1500	1000

Model FS-1

A single-barrel boxlock shotgun in all gauges and a 26" or 28", full choke barrel. Blued with a checkered walnut stock. This model was also known as the "Companion."

Exc.	V.G.	Good	Fair	Poor
250	225	175	125	90

TR-1 Trap

A 12 gauge, single-barrel boxlock trap gun, 32" ventilated rib, full choke barrel. Blued with a checkered, Monte Carlo stock. Manufactured between 1968 and 1971.

Exc.	V.G.	Good	Fair	Poor
275	250	200	150	100

TR-2 Trap

As above, with a high, competition-type vent rib. It was manufactured between 1969 and 1973.

Exc.	V.G.	Good	Fair	Poor
300	275	225	175	125

Mark II Trap

A 12 gauge, boxlock single-barrel trap shotgun with a 32" or 34", full-choke barrel, competition-type rib and automatic ejector. Blued with a checkered, Monte Carlo type, walnut stock. Manufactured between 1972 and 1976.

Exc.	V.G.	Good	Fair	Poor
700	625	525	450	275

Model ASE 90/Gold Series

This is a competition trap model Over/Under shotgun. It features a trigger lock assembly that is removable in the field so a spare can be used in the event of failure. The single non-selective trigger has a three way adjustment. The ventilated rib is wide and the side ribs are also ventilated. Walnut stock and forearms are interchangeable. Special trap recoil pad is standard. Receiver is silver with gold inlays or blued on special order. The ASE 90 weighs about 8 lbs. 6 oz.

ASE 90 Pigeon

Equipped with 28" barrels choked Improved Modified and Full.

NIB	Exc.	V.G.	Good	Fair	Poor
6500	5250	3750	2750	1500	1000

ASE 90 Trap

Comes standard with 30" vent rib barrels.

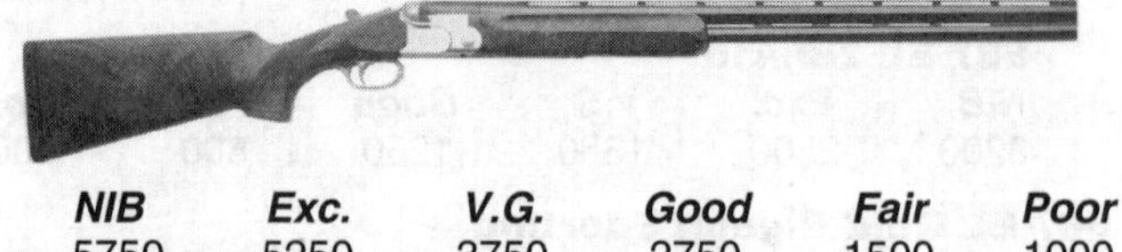

NIB	Exc.	V.G.	Good	Fair	Poor
5750	5250	3750	2750	1500	1000

ASE 90 Gold X Trap Combo

Introduced in 1993 this set features a single barrel and interchangeable Over/Under barrels in 30", 32" and 30", 34" combinations.

NIB	Exc.	V.G.	Good	Fair	Poor
6750	2500	—	—	—	1000

ASE 90 Skeet

This model is a skeet version of the ASE 90 series. Features the same basic specifications as the trap model but configured for competition skeet. Offered in 12 gauge only with 28" Skeet and Skeet chokes. Weighs about 7 lbs. 11 oz.

NIB	Exc.	V.G.	Good	Fair	Poor
5750	2500	—	—	—	1000

ASE 90 Sporting Clay

Configured for sporting clay competition. Offered in 12 gauge only with 28" or 30" vent rib barrels.

NIB	Exc.	V.G.	Good	Fair	Poor
6750	5000	4000	3000	1500	1000

Model SL-2

A 12 gauge slide action shotgun, 26", 28", or 30", ventilated rib barrels with various chokes. Blued with a checkered walnut stock. Manufactured between 1968 and 1971.

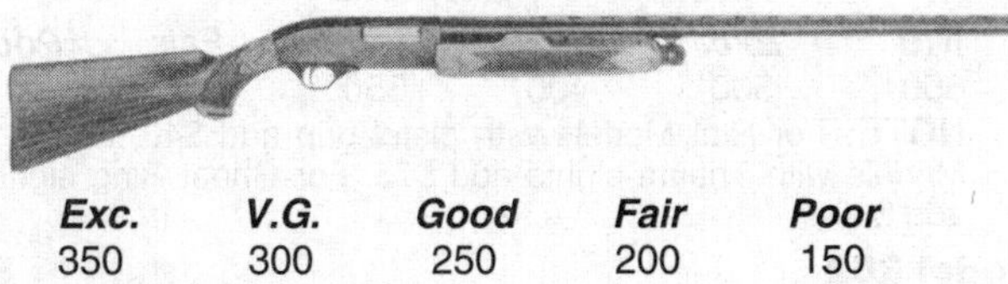

Exc.	V.G.	Good	Fair	Poor
350	300	250	200	150

Pigeon Series

As above, in three grades.

Silver Pigeon

Exc.	V.G.	Good	Fair	Poor
300	250	200	150	110

Gold Pigeon

Exc.	V.G.	Good	Fair	Poor
450	400	300	250	200

Ruby Pigeon

Exc.	V.G.	Good	Fair	Poor
600	550	450	375	275

DT 10 TRIDENT SERIES

These shotguns feature removable trigger mechanism, overbored barrels, and special choke tubes.

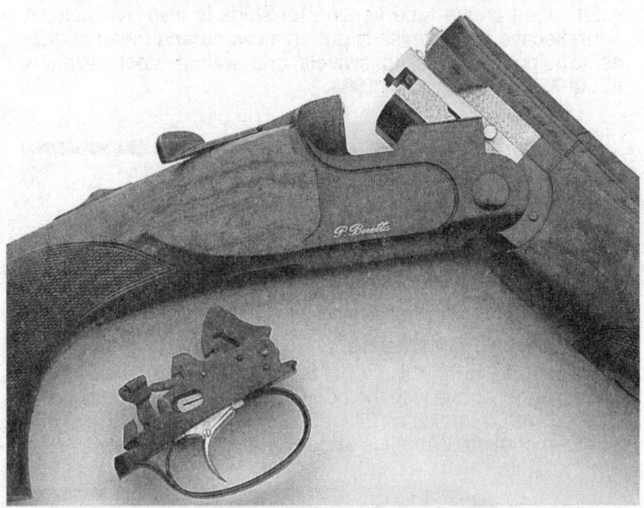

DT 10 Trident Trap

This is a 12 gauge over/under gun with a number of options. The barrel is 30" or 32" and the highly select walnut stock is fitted with a Monte Carlo comb. Stock is also adjustable. Rib type is 3/8" with progressive step. Full black rubber recoil pad. Weight is about 8.8 lbs. A top single model is also offered with 34" barrel. Introduced in 2000.

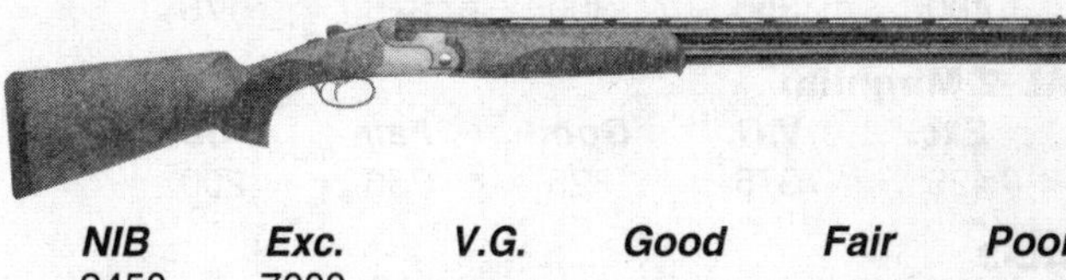

NIB	Exc.	V.G.	Good	Fair	Poor
9450	7000	—	—	—	—

DT 10 Trident Trap Combo Top

Same as above with both over/under barrels and single barrel combo.

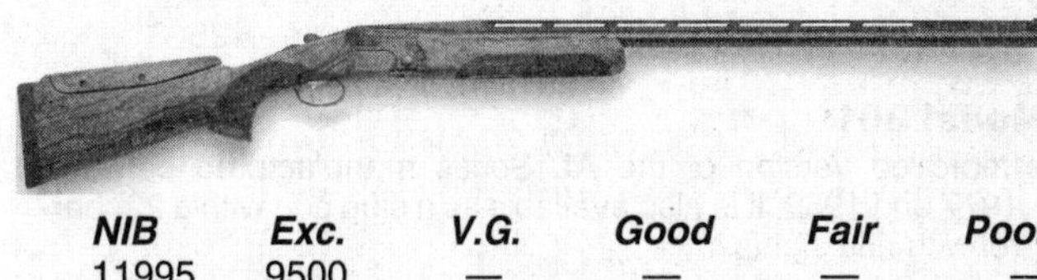

NIB	Exc.	V.G.	Good	Fair	Poor
11995	9500	—	—	—	—

DT 10 Trident Trap Bottom Single

Introduced in 2001 this model features a choice of 30"/34" barrel combo or 32"/34" barrel combo. Select walnut stock. Fitted with an adjustable point-of-impact rib. Weight is about 8.8 lbs.

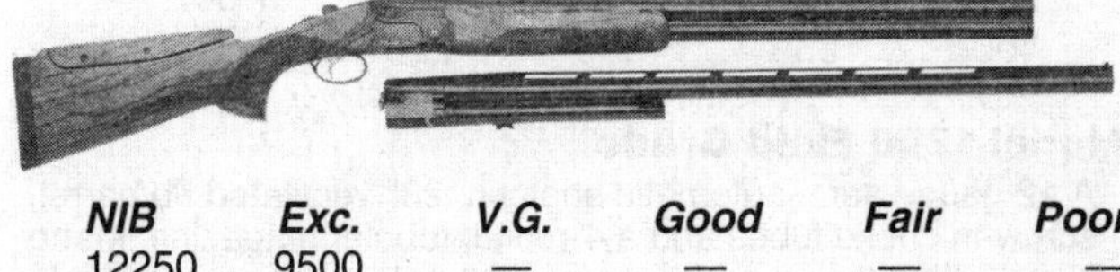

NIB	Exc.	V.G.	Good	Fair	Poor
12250	9500	—	—	—	—

DT 10 Trident Skeet

This 12 gauge skeet model is fitted with either 28" or 30" barrel. Walnut stock is adjustable. Weight is about 8 lbs. Introduced in 2000.

NIB	Exc.	V.G.	Good	Fair	Poor
9450	7000	—	—	—	—

DT 10 Trident Sporting

This 12 gauge over/under gun is fitted with a choice of 28", 30", or 32" barrels. Highly figured walnut stock with schnabel forend. Weight is about 8 lbs. Introduced in 2000.

NIB	Exc.	V.G.	Good	Fair	Poor
9200	7000	—	—	—	—

SEMI-AUTOMATIC SHOTGUNS

AL SERIES

A 12 or 20 gauge semi-automatic shotgun with 26", 28", or 30" barrels and various choke combinations. Blued with a checkered walnut stock. Manufactured between 1969 and 1976.

AL-1

Exc.	V.G.	Good	Fair	Poor
400	375	300	225	150

AL-2

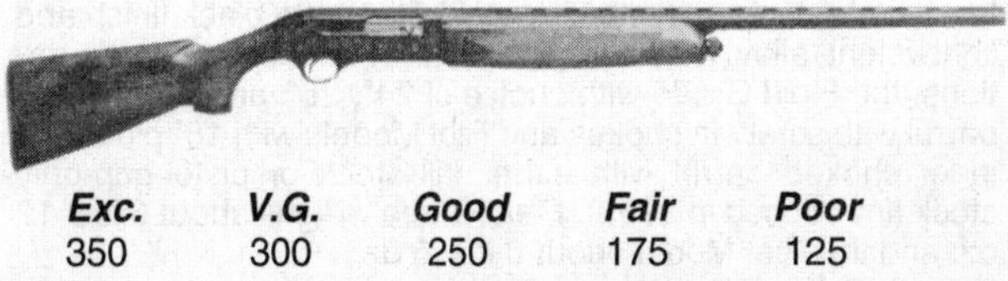

Exc.	V.G.	Good	Fair	Poor
350	300	250	175	125

AL-2 Competition

Exc.	V.G.	Good	Fair	Poor
400	350	300	225	175

AL-2 Magnum

Exc.	V.G.	Good	Fair	Poor
425	375	325	250	200

AL-3

Exc.	V.G.	Good	Fair	Poor
400	350	300	225	175

AL-3 Deluxe Trap

Exc.	V.G.	Good	Fair	Poor
775	700	600	500	425

Model 301

Improved version of the AL Series manufactured between 1977 and 1982. It is also available as a slug gun with a 22" barrel with rifle sights.

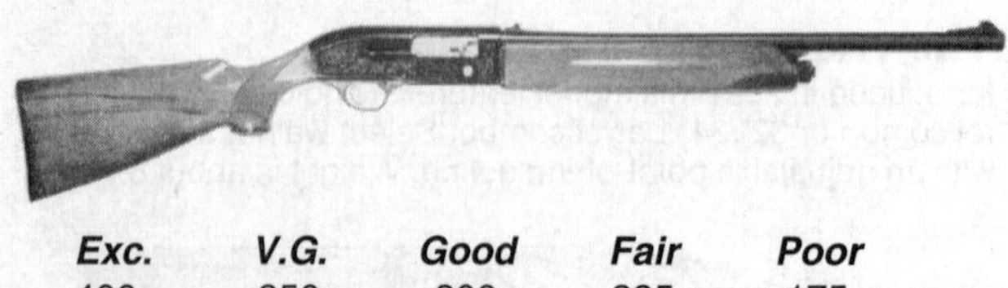

Exc.	V.G.	Good	Fair	Poor
400	350	300	225	175

Model 1200 Field Grade

A 12 gauge semi-automatic shotgun, 28" ventilated rib barrel, screw-in choke tubes and a 4-round, tubular magazine. Matte blued with either a checkered walnut or black synthetic stock. Introduced in 1984.

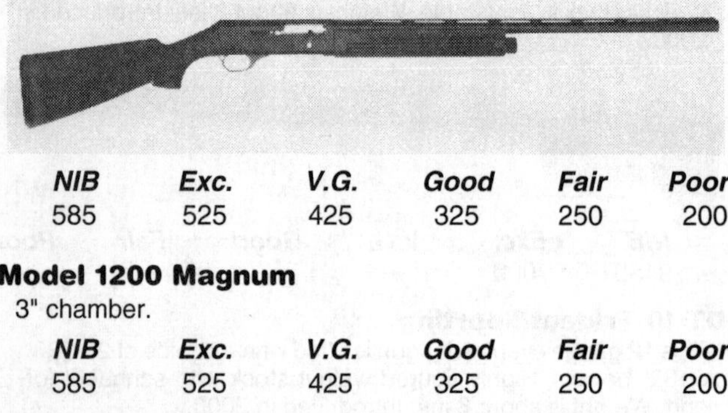

NIB	Exc.	V.G.	Good	Fair	Poor
585	525	425	325	250	200

Model 1200 Magnum

3" chamber.

NIB	Exc.	V.G.	Good	Fair	Poor
585	525	425	325	250	200

Model 1200 Riot

20" cyl. bore barrel.

NIB	Exc.	V.G.	Good	Fair	Poor
585	525	425	325	250	200

Model 1201

This 12 gauge semi-automatic shotgun has a short recoil system and features a synthetic stock with matte black finish and lightweight alloy receiver. Available in two basic configurations: the Field Grade with choice of 24", 26", and 28" vent rib barrel with screw-in chokes and Riot Models with 18" plain Cylinder choked barrel with either full stock or pistol-grip-only stock (introduced in 1993). Field Grade weighs about 6 lbs. 12 oz. and the Riot Model about 6 lbs. 5 oz.

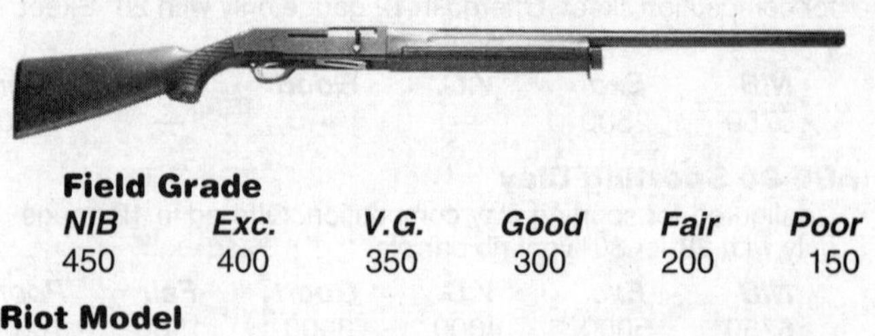

Field Grade

NIB	Exc.	V.G.	Good	Fair	Poor
450	400	350	300	200	150

Riot Model

NIB	Exc.	V.G.	Good	Fair	Poor
650	500	400	350	250	175

NOTE: For Riot Models with pistol grip add $40. For Riot Models with Tritium sights add $75. For Ghost Ring sights add $100.

Model 302

A 12 or 20 gauge semi-automatic shotgun using 2.75" or 3" shells interchangeably, various barrel lengths and screw-in choke tubes. Blued with a checkered walnut stock. Manufactured between 1982 and 1987.

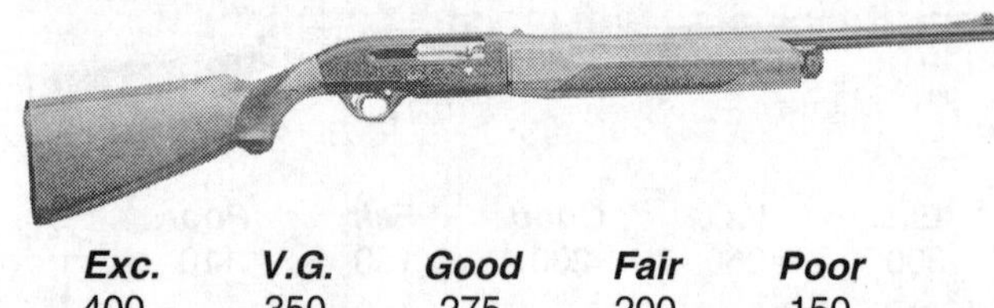

Exc.	V.G.	Good	Fair	Poor
400	350	275	200	150

Model 302 Super Lusso

As above, with a heavily engraved receiver and gold-plated, contrasting parts. Presentation grade walnut was used for the hand checkered stock. Discontinued in 1986.

Exc.	V.G.	Good	Fair	Poor
2150	2000	1600	1050	850

Model Vittoria/Pintail

This semi-automatic 12 gauge shotgun was introduced to the Beretta product line in 1993. It has a short recoil operation and is offered with a 24" or 26" vent rib barrel with screw-in chokes. A 24" rifled choke tube version for slugs is also available. A nonreflective matte finish is put on all wood and metal surfaces. Equipped with sling swivels and walnut stock. Weighs about 7 lbs. Renamed in 1994.

NIB	Exc.	V.G.	Good	Fair	Poor
600	550	500	400	350	250

ES100 Pintail Synthetic

Introduced in 1999, this model is essentially the same as the Pintail model above with the addition of a black synthetic stock. Offered with a choice of 24", 26", or 28" vent rib barrels with screw-in chokes. Weight is about 7 lbs.

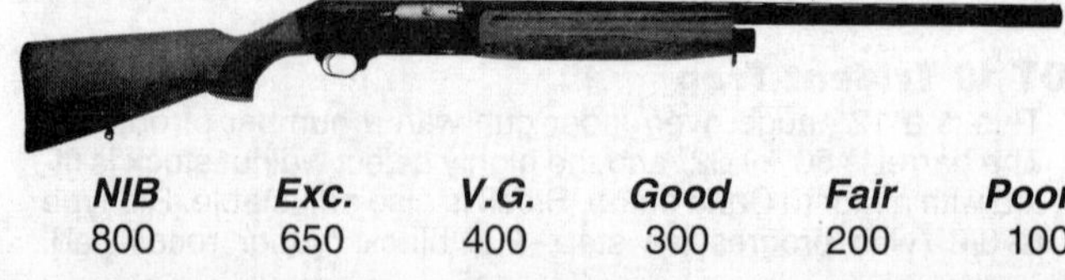

NIB	Exc.	V.G.	Good	Fair	Poor
800	650	400	300	200	100

ES100 Pintail Rifled Slug

Introduced in 1997 this model features a 24" fully rifled barrel with adjustable rear sight and removable blade front sight. The receiver is drilled and tapped for scope mount. Hardwood stock with matte finish. Anodized aluminum alloy receiver. Weight is approximately 7 lbs. Fitted with 3" chambers.

NIB	Exc.	V.G.	Good	Fair	Poor
1000	800	600	350	250	100

ES100 Rifled Slug

This variation is the same as the Pintail Rifled Slug model above with the addition of a black synthetic stock. Introduced in 1999.

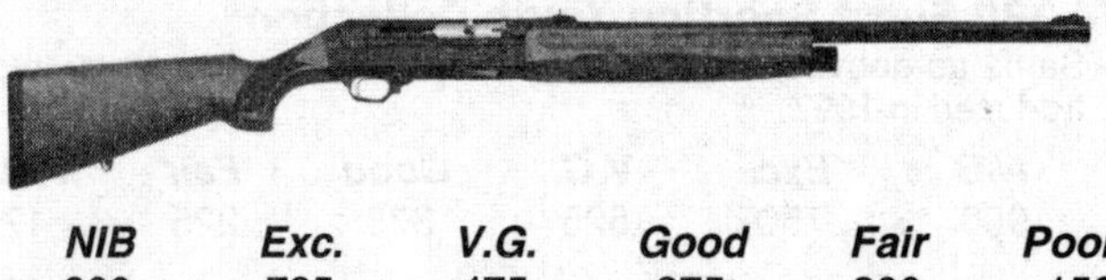

NIB	Exc.	V.G.	Good	Fair	Poor
900	725	475	375	200	150

ES100 Rifled Slug Combo

Same as above but with the addition of a 28" smooth bored barrel.

NIB	Exc.	V.G.	Good	Fair	Poor
1000	800	475	375	200	150

ES100 NWTF Special Camo

This 12 gauge model is fitted with a 24" barrel with 3" chambers. Stock is Mossy Oak camo. Metal is black matte finish. Weight is about 7.3 lbs. Introduced in 1999.

NIB	Exc.	V.G.	Good	Fair	Poor
925	750	550	375	210	150

A-303 SERIES

A 12 or 20 gauge semi-automatic shotgun, 26", 28", 30", or 32" ventilated rib barrels with screw-in choke tubes. Blued with a checkered walnut stock. Introduced in 1987. The various models offered differ slightly in configuration and/or quality of materials.

Model A-303

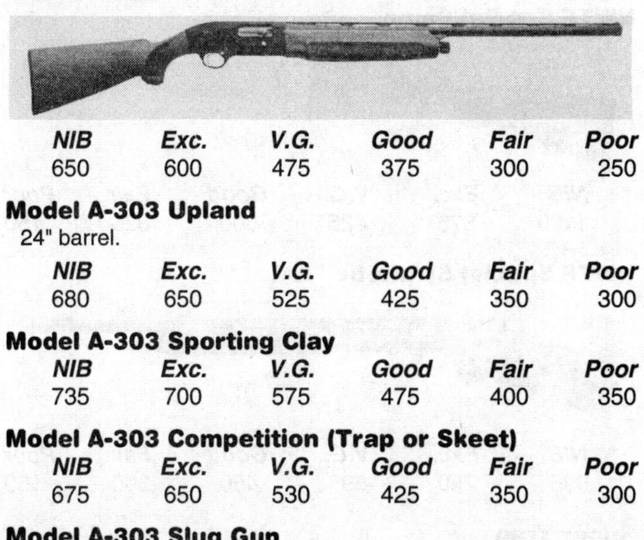

NIB	Exc.	V.G.	Good	Fair	Poor
650	600	475	375	300	250

Model A-303 Upland

24" barrel.

NIB	Exc.	V.G.	Good	Fair	Poor
680	650	525	425	350	300

Model A-303 Sporting Clay

NIB	Exc.	V.G.	Good	Fair	Poor
735	700	575	475	400	350

Model A-303 Competition (Trap or Skeet)

NIB	Exc.	V.G.	Good	Fair	Poor
675	650	530	425	350	300

Model A-303 Slug Gun

22" barrel with sights.

NIB	Exc.	V.G.	Good	Fair	Poor
680	650	525	425	350	300

Model 303 Youth Gun

This version of the Model 303 is available in 20 gauge with a shorter length of pull, 13.5", than standard. It is fitted with a rubber recoil pad, screw-in choke tubes, and checkered walnut stock.

NIB	Exc.	V.G.	Good	Fair	Poor
500	450	400	300	250	200

Model A-303 Ducks Unlimited

A commemorative version of the Model 303. It is chambered for 12 or 20 gauge. There were 5,500 manufactured in 12 gauge in 1986 and 1987. There were 3,500 manufactured in 20 gauge in 1987 and 1988. These are commemorative firearms and are collectible when NIB with all furnished materials.

12 Gauge

NIB	Exc.	V.G.	Good	Fair	Poor
575	500	425	325	275	225

20 Gauge

NIB	Exc.	V.G.	Good	Fair	Poor
675	600	525	425	375	325

MODEL AL390/MALLARD SERIES

This series of 12 gauge semi-automatic shotguns features a self-compensating, gas-operating recoil system. All loads from target to 3" Magnums can be used in the same gun. The Field Model features an anodized light alloy receiver with scroll engraving and matte black receiver top. Magazine capacity is 3 rounds. Checkered walnut stock with recoil pad. Available in vent rib barrel lengths from 24" to 30" with 32" on special request. A 22" or 24" slug plain barrel is also available. Chokes are fixed or screw-in at customer's option. Shotgun weighs about 7 lbs. Beginning in 1996 Beretta offered the Silver Mallard shotguns chambered for the 20 gauge shell and available with 24", 26, or 28" barrels. Average weight for these 20 gauge guns is 6.4 lbs.

Field Grade

NIB	Exc.	V.G.	Good	Fair	Poor
800	600	450	350	300	200

Slug Gun

NIB	Exc.	V.G.	Good	Fair	Poor
800	600	450	350	300	200

Synthetic Stock

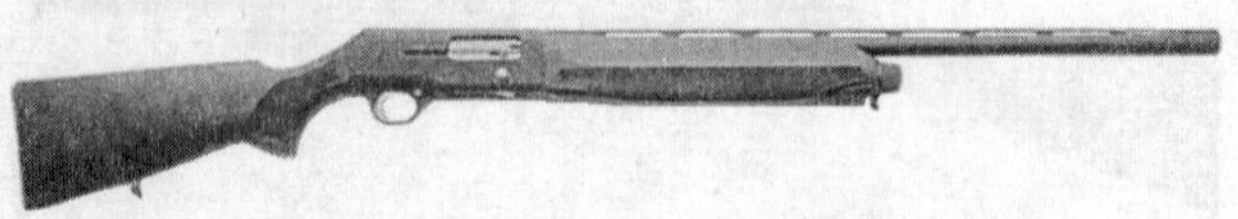

NIB	Exc.	V.G.	Good	Fair	Poor
800	600	450	350	300	200

Camouflage

NIB	Exc.	V.G.	Good	Fair	Poor
800	600	450	350	300	200

Deluxe Grade/Gold Mallard

Gold-filled game animals and select walnut stock.

NIB	Exc.	V.G.	Good	Fair	Poor
700	650	500	350	300	200

AL390 Trap

NIB	Exc.	V.G.	Good	Fair	Poor
675	600	500	400	300	200

AL390 Super Trap

Features ported barrels in 30" or 32", adjustable length of pull, adjustable comb.

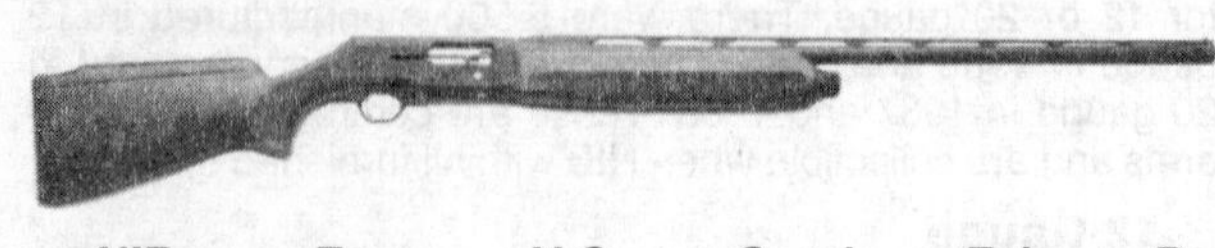

NIB	Exc.	V.G.	Good	Fair	Poor
1000	800	600	500	300	200

AL390 Skeet

NIB	Exc.	V.G.	Good	Fair	Poor
625	550	450	350	250	200

AL390 Super Skeet

Features ported barrel, adjustable cast and length of pull, and adjustable drop. 12 gauge only.

NIB	Exc.	V.G.	Good	Fair	Poor
1000	800	600	500	300	200

AL390 Sporting

NIB	Exc.	V.G.	Good	Fair	Poor
700	550	450	350	250	200

20 gauge

Same as above but in 20 gauge. Introduced in 1997. Weight about 6.8 lbs.

NIB	Exc.	V.G.	Good	Fair	Poor
800	600	450	350	250	200

Ported

NIB	Exc.	V.G.	Good	Fair	Poor
725	650	550	400	300	200

AL390 Sport Gold Sporting

Introduced in 1997 this model is similar to above models but with silver sided receiver with gold engraving. Select walnut stock. 12 gauge only with choice of 28" or 30" vent rib barrels. Weight about 7.6 lbs.

NIB	Exc.	V.G.	Good	Fair	Poor
1100	900	700	450	300	175

AL390 Sport Sporting Youth

This semi-automatic shotgun is offered in 20 gauge only with 26" vent rib barrel. Length of pull is 13.5" with adjustable drop and cast on the buttstock. Introduced in 1997. Weight is approximately 6.7 lbs.

NIB	Exc.	V.G.	Good	Fair	Poor
825	675	500	350	200	175

AL390 NWTF Special Youth

Introduced in 1999, this model features a shortened walnut stock with 24" 20 gauge vent rib barrel. Black matte finish. Weight is about 6.4 lbs.

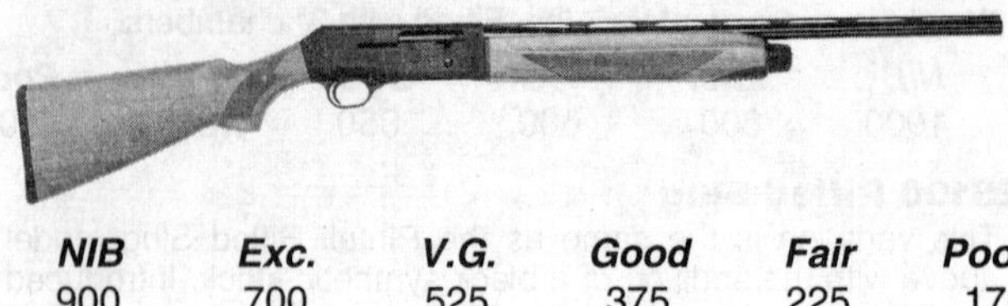

NIB	Exc.	V.G.	Good	Fair	Poor
900	700	525	375	225	175

AL390 Sport Sporting Youth Collection

Same as above but with multi-colored stock and forearm. Introduced in 1997.

NIB	Exc.	V.G.	Good	Fair	Poor
900	750	525	375	225	175

AL390 Sport Diamond Sporting

Introduced in 1998 this model features a silver sided receiver with gold engraving. Select walnut stock with oil finish and adjustable for drop and cast. Available in 12 gauge with 28" or 30" barrels. Sold with spare trigger group and orange front sight beads. Weight is approximately 7.6 lbs.

NIB	Exc.	V.G.	Good	Fair	Poor
3850	3000	1950	1300	600	300

AL390 Camo

This 12 gauge shotgun is offered with either a 24" or 28" vent rib barrel. Barrel, receiver, stock and forearm have woodland camo finish. Weight is about 7.5 lbs. Offered for first time in 1997.

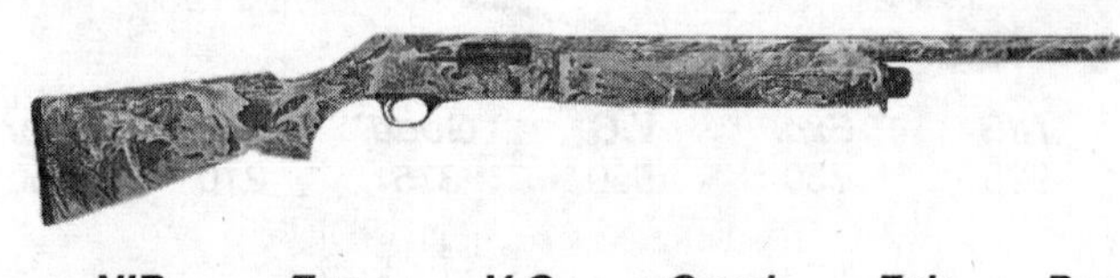

NIB	Exc.	V.G.	Good	Fair	Poor
995	775	595	450	300	150

Waterfowl/Turkey Model

Matte finish.

NIB	Exc.	V.G	Good	Fair	Poor
550	500	450	350	300	250

NWTF Special Camo

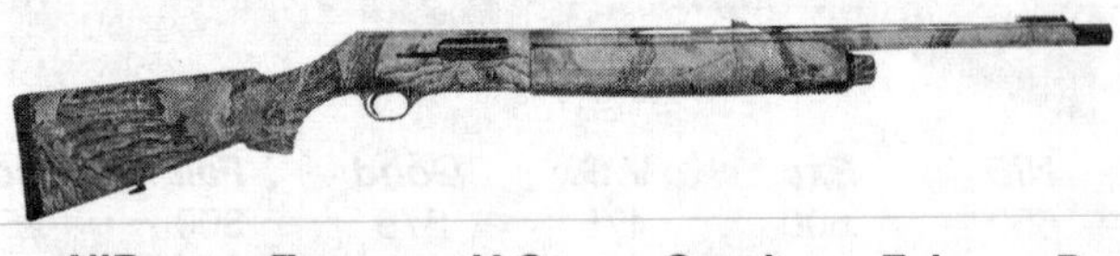

NIB	Exc.	V.G.	Good	Fair	Poor
1100	875	625	500	325	150

NWTF Special Synthetic

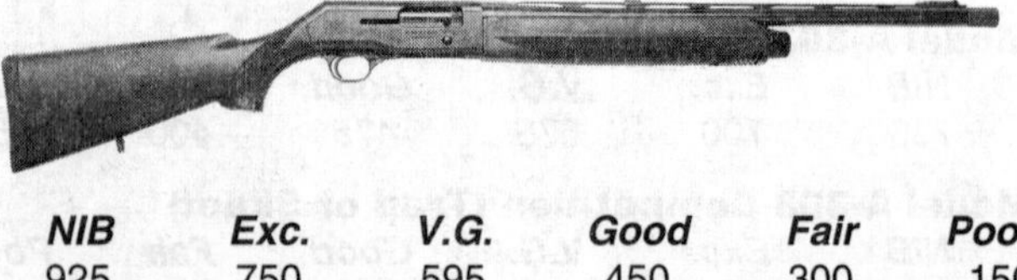

NIB	Exc.	V.G.	Good	Fair	Poor
925	750	595	450	300	150

Super Trap

Ported barrels, adjustable comb and length of pull.

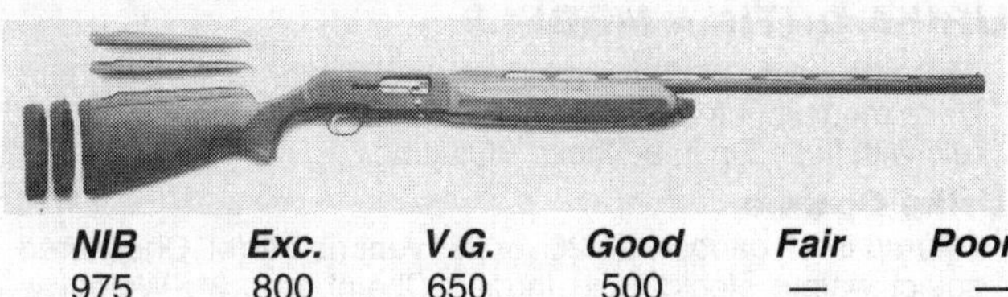

NIB	Exc.	V.G.	Good	Fair	Poor
975	800	650	500	—	—

Super Skeet

Ported barrels, adjustable comb and length of pull.

NIB	Exc.	V.G.	Good	Fair	Poor
950	800	650	500	—	—

3901 SERIES

This series was introduced in 2005 and is built around the A390 shotgun. The 3901 guns feature a gas operating system, choke tubes, and a removable trigger group.

Model 3901

Introduced in 2003, this semi-automatic shotgun is offered in 12 gauge with choice of 26" or 28" barrel. Charcoal gray synthetic stock. Black rubber recoil pad. Non-reflective black finish. Weight is about 7.5 lbs.

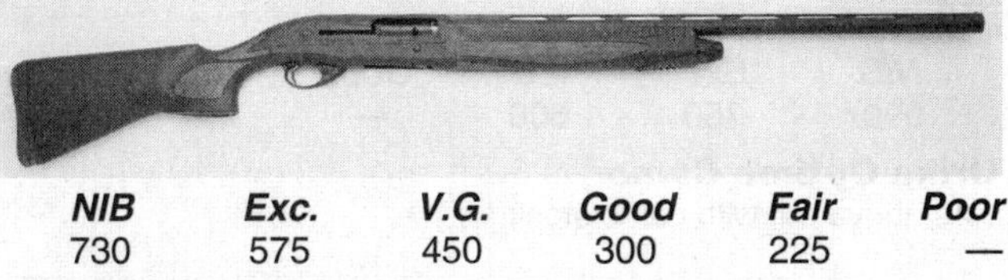

NIB	Exc.	V.G.	Good	Fair	Poor
730	575	450	300	225	—

Model 3901 RL

As above, but in 20 gauge with reduced-length buttstock. Introduced in 2003.

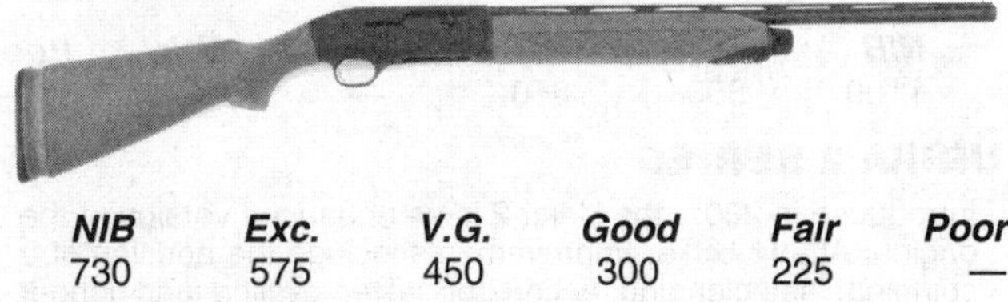

NIB	Exc.	V.G.	Good	Fair	Poor
730	575	450	300	225	—

Model 3901 Camo

This 12 gauge model is offered in Mossy Oak, Shadowgrass camo stock. Choice of 24" or 26" barrel. Introduced in 2003.

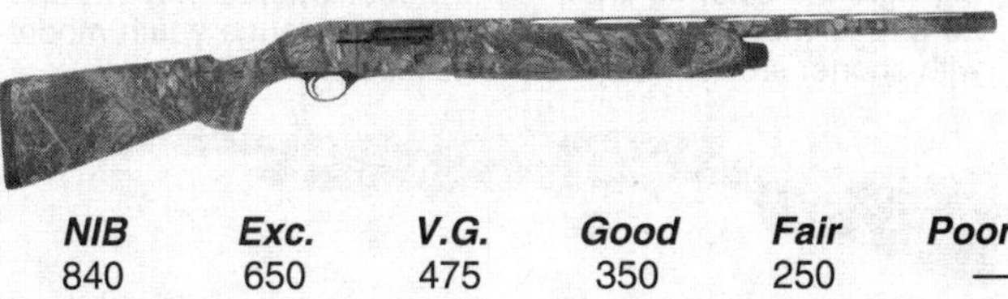

NIB	Exc.	V.G.	Good	Fair	Poor
840	650	475	350	250	—

3901 Citizen

Offered in 12 or 20 gauge with choice of 26" or 28" vent rib barrels with choke tubes. Black synthetic stock. Rubber recoil pad. Weight is about 7.6 lbs. for the 12 gauge and 7 lbs. for the 20 gauge.

NIB	Exc.	V.G.	Good	Fair	Poor
750	600	450	300	225	—

3901 Statesman

As above but with checkered walnut stock.

NIB	Exc.	V.G.	Good	Fair	Poor
850	675	475	325	250	—

3901 Ambassador

This model has all the features of the Statesman but is fitted with a select checkered X-tra wood stock with Gel-Tek recoil pad. Weight for 12 gauge is about 7.2 lbs. and 6.6 lbs. for the 20 gauge.

NIB	Exc.	V.G.	Good	Fair	Poor
950	750	525	450	350	—

3901 Target RL

Gas-operated semi-auto chambered in 3" 12-gauge. Specifically designed for smaller-stature shooters with adjustable length of pull from 12 to 13 inches. Stock is adjustable for cast on or cast off. Adjustable comb and Sporting style flat rib. Available in 12 gauge only with 26" or 28" barrel.

NIB	Exc.	V.G.	Good	Fair	Poor
895	—	—	—	—	—

AL 391 URIKA SERIES

Urika

Introduced in 2000 this semi-automatic shotgun is offered in both 12 and 20 gauge. Choice of barrels from 24" to 30" depending on gauge. Stock is walnut with checkered grip and forend. Rubber recoil pad. Gold trigger. Choke tubes. Weight for 12 gauge is about 7.3 lbs. while the 20 gauge is about 6 lbs.

NIB	Exc.	V.G.	Good	Fair	Poor
850	750	600	450	—	—

Urika Synthetic

Same as above but fitted with a black synthetic stock with gripping inserts. Offered in 12 gauge only. Introduced in 2000.

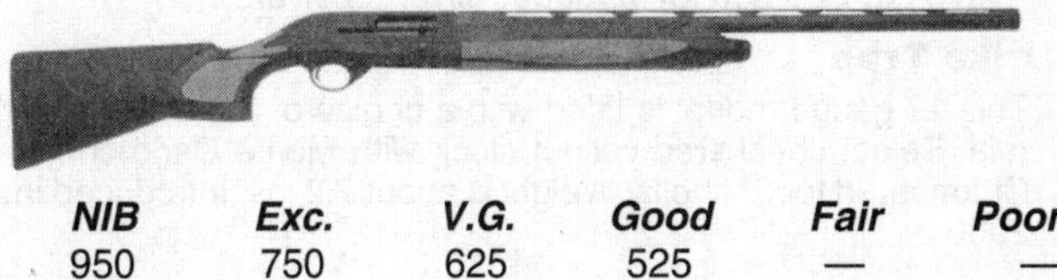

NIB	Exc.	V.G.	Good	Fair	Poor
950	750	625	525	—	—

Urika Camo

This 12 gauge model is offered with either Realtree Hardwoods camo or Advantage Wetlands camo. In 24" or 26" barrels. Weight is about 7.3 lbs. First introduced in 2000.

NIB	Exc.	V.G.	Good	Fair	Poor
1050	800	650	550	—	—

Urika Gold

This model features a 26" or 28" barrels with choke tubes. The black receiver model is offered in both 12 and 20 gauge with a weight of about 7.3 lbs. The silver receiver model (lightweight) is available in 12 gauge only and weighs about 6.6 lbs. Both configurations are fitted with highly figured walnut stock. Gold trigger. Introduced in 2000.

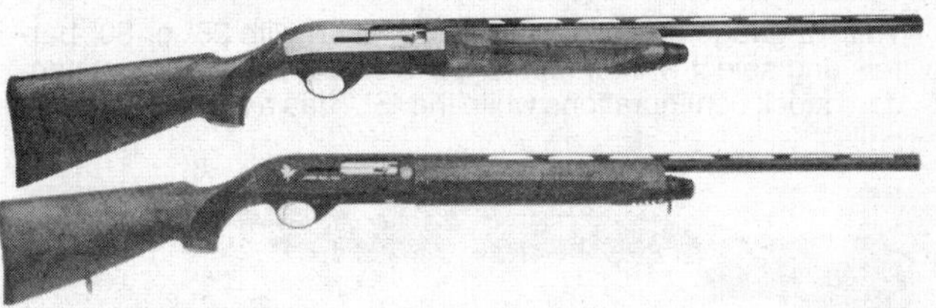

AL391 Gold receiver

NIB	Exc.	V.G.	Good	Fair	Poor
1150	900	750	675	—	—

Urika Youth

This 20 gauge model features a walnut stock with a shorter length of pull than standard and a 24" barrel. Weight is about 6 lbs. Introduced in 2000.

NIB	Exc.	V.G.	Good	Fair	Poor
950	750	600	450	—	—

Urika Sporting

This model is offered in both 12 and 20 gauge. Fitted 28" or 30" barrels. Select walnut checkered stock. Gold trigger. Chambered for 3" shells. Weight of 12 gauge is about 7.3 lbs. and the 20 gauge is about 6 lbs. Introduced in 2000.

NIB	Exc.	V.G.	Good	Fair	Poor
1000	750	600	500	350	175

Urika Gold Sporting

This model is offered in 12 gauge with a choice of black or silver receiver. The 20 gauge models are offered with black receiver only. Fitted with 28" or 30" barrels. Highly select checkered walnut stock. Chambered for 3" shells. Introduced in 2000.

NIB	Exc.	V.G.	Good	Fair	Poor
1195	950	700	600	450	175

NOTE: Add $30 for 12 gauge silver receiver.

Urika Trap

This 12 gauge model is fitted with a choice of 30" or 32" barrels. Select checkered walnut stock with Monte Carlo comb. Chambered for 3" shells. Weight is about 7.2 lbs. Introduced in 2000.

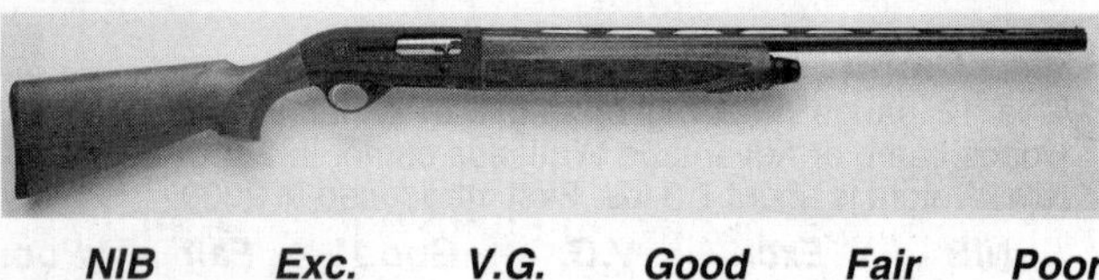

NIB	Exc.	V.G.	Good	Fair	Poor
1000	750	600	500	350	175

Urika Gold Trap

This model is similar to the standard Urika Trap but with highly selected checkered walnut stock and black receiver.

NIB	Exc.	V.G.	Good	Fair	Poor
1195	950	700	600	450	175

Urika Parallel Target RL/SL

This 12 gauge competition model is fitted with 28" or 30" barrels and select walnut Monte Carlo stock. The "RL" has standard stock configurations while the "SL" has a shorter length of pull.

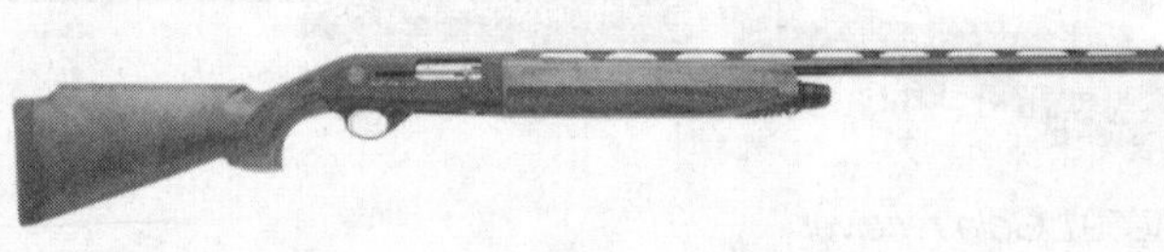

NIB	Exc.	V.G.	Good	Fair	Poor
1000	750	600	500	350	200

URIKA OPTIMA MODELS

First offered in 2003 this shotguns are similar to the standard Urika model but feature Beretta's Optima-Bore overbored barrels with flush Optima-Choke Plus tubes.

Urika Optima

Offered in 12 gauge with 26" or 28" vent rib barrel. Checkered select walnut stock. Gold trigger. Chamber is 3". Weight is about 7.3 lbs.

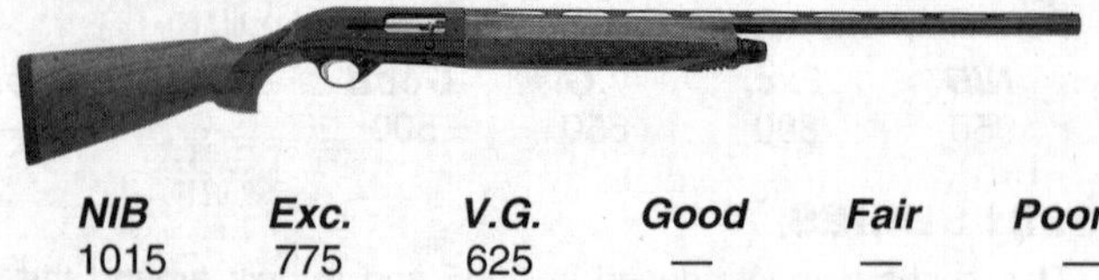

NIB	Exc.	V.G.	Good	Fair	Poor
1015	775	625	—	—	—

Urika Synthetic Optima

As above but with synthetic stock with rubber inserts. Weight is about 7.4 lbs.

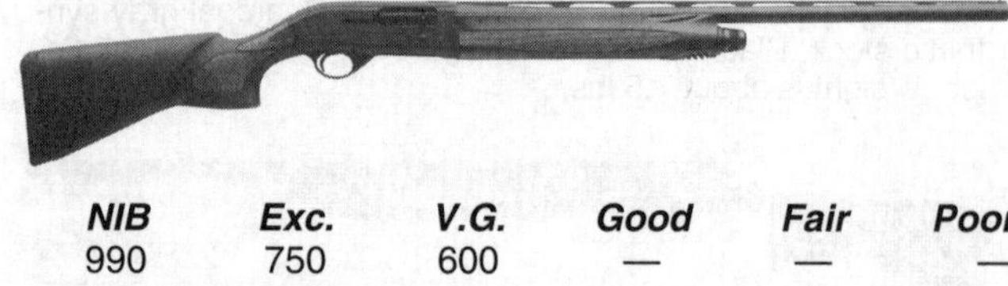

NIB	Exc.	V.G.	Good	Fair	Poor
990	750	600	—	—	—

Urika Optima Camo

As above but with camo stock.

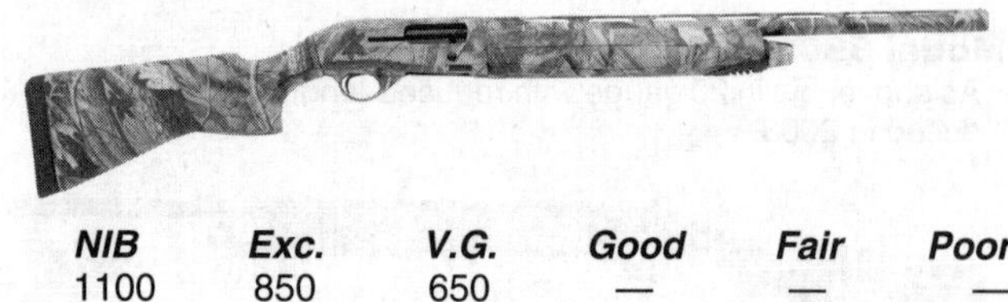

NIB	Exc.	V.G.	Good	Fair	Poor
1100	850	650	—	—	—

URIKA 2 SERIES

Introduced in 2007, the Urika 2 is an enhanced version of the original AL391 Urika. Improvements include the addition of a spinning, self-cleaning action for faster cycling and longer functioning periods between cleanings.

AL391 Urika2 X-Tra Grain

This series features Beretta's wood-enhancement treatment to highlight the color contrast of the wood. Offered in 3" 12 and 20 gauge with 26" and 28" barrels. A 20 gauge youth model with shorter stock and 24" barrel is also offered.

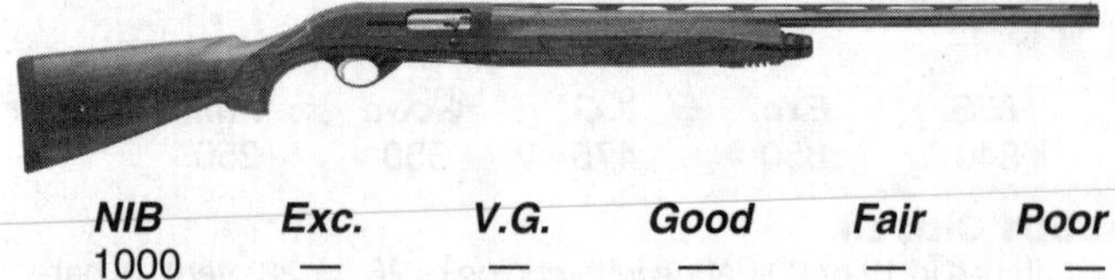

NIB	Exc.	V.G.	Good	Fair	Poor
1000	—	—	—	—	—

AL391 Urika 2 Gold

Select oil-finished wood stock and forend with gold-filled game bird inlays on the receiver. The 12 gauge has a 28" barrel and the 20 gauge has a 26" barrel.

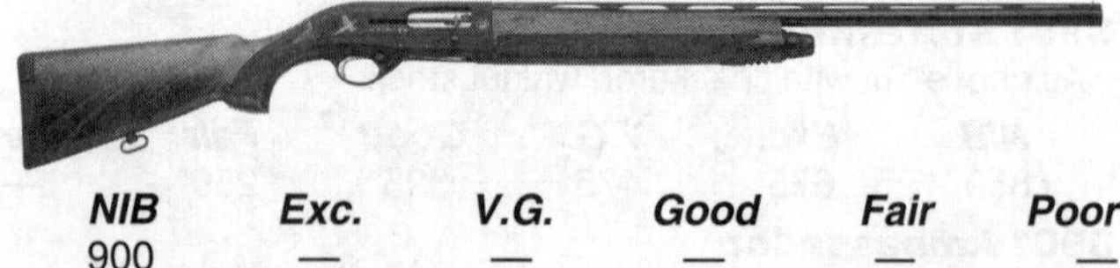

NIB	Exc.	V.G.	Good	Fair	Poor
900	—	—	—	—	—

AL391 Urika 2 Kick-Off

These waterfowl models feature Beretta's Kick-Off recoil reduction system. Matte black synthetic, Max-4 or Realtree AP

 *This symbol denotes "Sleepers" with rapidly-rising values and/or significant collector potential.*

finish with 26" or 28" barrel. MSRP: $1,250. Deduct 30 percent for models without Kick-Off. Add 10 percent for camo finish.

NIB	Exc.	V.G.	Good	Fair	Poor
1000	—	—	—	—	—

AL391 Urika 2 Sporting X-Tra Grain

Sporting clays models in 12 and 20 gauge with 28" or 30" barrel.

NIB	Exc.	V.G.	Good	Fair	Poor
1000	—	—	—	—	—

AL391 Urika 2 Gold Sporting

Enhanced wood with gold inlays and floral motif engraving on receiver in 12 gauge with 28" or 30" barrel.

NIB	Exc.	V.G.	Good	Fair	Poor
1100	—	—	—	—	—

AL391 Urika 2 Parallel Target X-Tra Grain

Target model in 12 gauge with 28", 30" or 32" barrel.

NIB	Exc.	V.G.	Good	Fair	Poor
1050	—	—	—	—	—

AL391 Urika 2 Gold Parallel Target

Enhanced wood with gold inlays and floral motif engraving on receiver in 12 gauge with 30" or 32" barrel.

NIB	Exc.	V.G.	Good	Fair	Poor
1200	—	—	—	—	—

AL391 Covey

Introduced in 2003 this model is offered in 20 gauge with a 26" or 28" vent rib barrel. Select walnut stock. Gold-filled game scenes. Weight is about 5.9 lbs. Limited to 1,000 guns.

NIB	Exc.	V.G.	Good	Fair	Poor
—	—	—	—	—	—

AL391 Ringneck

As above but with gold-filled pheasants. In 12 gauge only. Weight is about 7.3 lbs. Limited to 1,000 guns. Introduced in 2003.

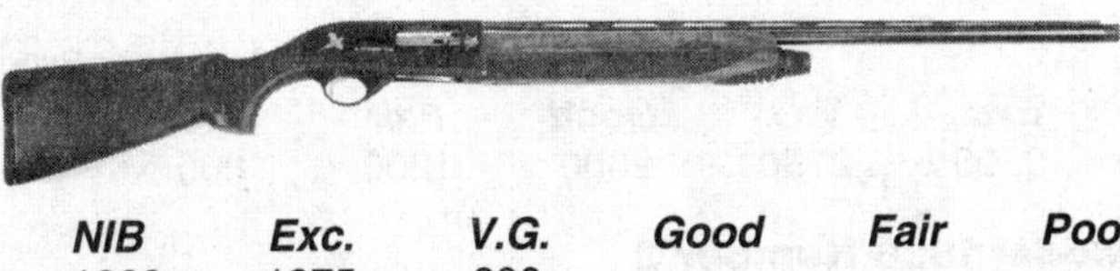

NIB	Exc.	V.G.	Good	Fair	Poor
1360	1075	800	—	—	—

AL391 Teknys

This model features a nickel receiver with polished sides and anti-glare top. Offered in 12 or 20 gauge with 26" or 28" vent rib barrel. X-wood stock with Gel-Tek recoil. Weight is about 7.2 lbs. for 12 gauge and 5.9 lbs. for the 20 gauge. Introduced in 2003.

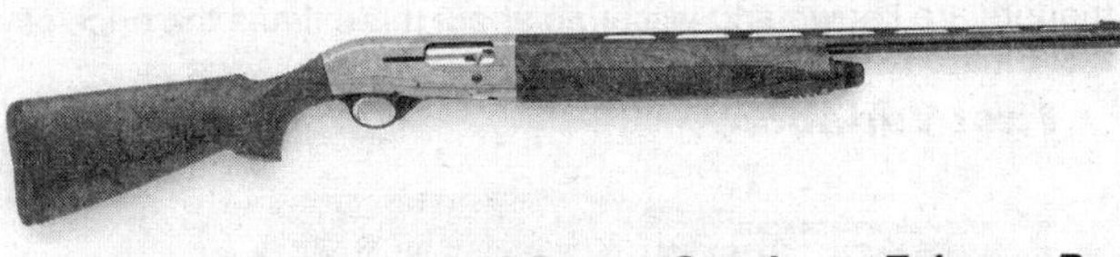

NIB	Exc.	V.G.	Good	Fair	Poor
1150	900	750	—	—	—

AL391 Teknys Gold

As above, but with engraved hunting scene on the receiver, gold plated trigger, jeweled breech bolt and carrier. Select walnut checkered stock with oil finish. Introduced in 2003.

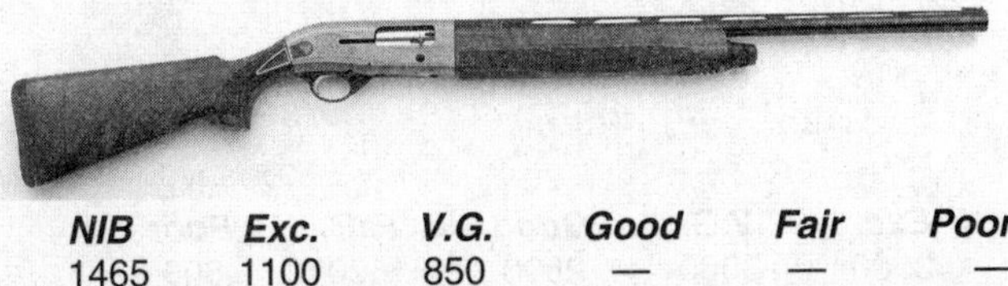

NIB	Exc.	V.G.	Good	Fair	Poor
1465	1100	850	—	—	—

A391 Teknys Gold Target

Similar to AL391 Teknys Gold but with adjustable comb, 8.5 oz. recoil reducer and additional stepped rib for trap shooting. 30" barrel. MSRP: 1995

AL391 Teknys King Ranch

Introduced in 2005.

NIB	Exc.	V.G.	Good	Fair	Poor
1650	1500	—	—	—	—

AL391 XTREMA SERIES

Xtrema 3.5

Introduced in 2002 this model features an overbuilt Urika to handle 12 gauge 3.5" super magnum loads. Offered with a choice of 24", 26", or 28" vent rib barrels with black synthetic stock or choice of various camo stocks. Weight is about 7.8 lbs.

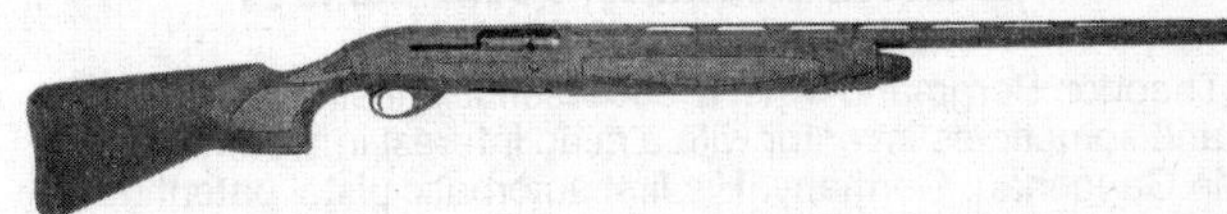

NIB	Exc.	V.G.	Good	Fair	Poor
1125	850	750	600	—	—

NOTE: Add $100 for camo finish.

A391 Xtrema2

An upgraded version of the Xtrema with additional recoil-reducing features was introduced in 2005. Available with 24", 26" or 28" barrels with black, Max-4 HD or Hardwoods HD synthetic stock. Optima-Bore five choke system. Optional Kick Off recoil reduction feature available. Add 10 percent for camo finish. Add 30 percent for Kick Off option.

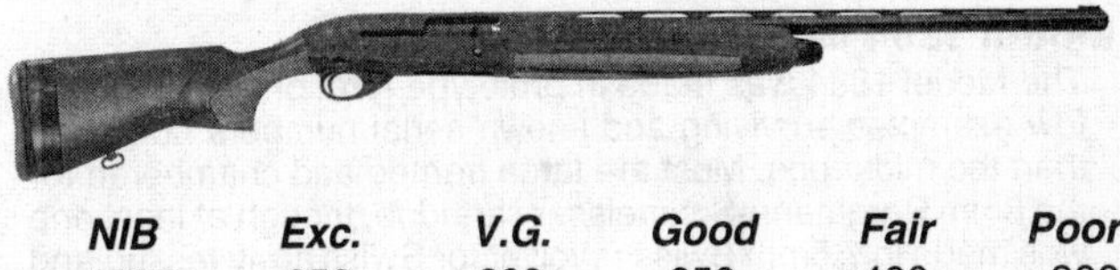

NIB	Exc.	V.G.	Good	Fair	Poor
1100	950	800	650	400	300

A391 Xtrema2 Slug Gun

24" rifled barrel version of Xtrema2. Introduced in 2006. Black synthetic only. Add 10 percent for Kick Off option. MSRP: 1450

NIB	Exc.	V.G.	Good	Fair	Poor
1000	900	800	650	400	300

UGB25 XCEL

Introduced in 2005 this is a semi-automatic break-open competition Trap gun chambered for the 12 gauge 2.75" shell. The gun is fed from the side with bottom ejection. Choice of 30" or 32" barrel with high trap-style interchangeable rib. Choke tubes. The checkered walnut has an adjustable comb and length of pull. Weight is about 7.7 to 9 lbs. depending on barrel length and rib.

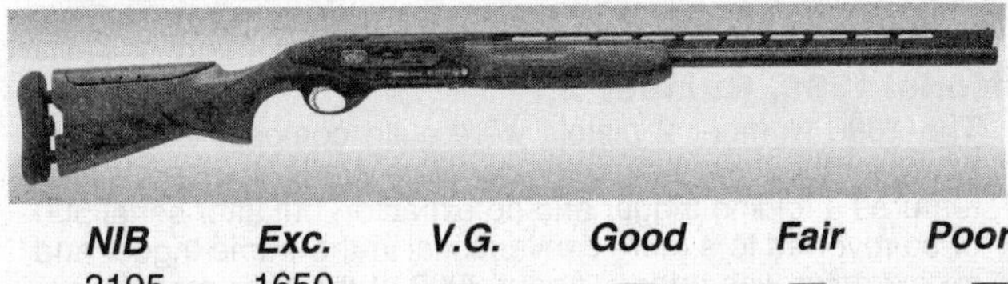

NIB	Exc.	V.G.	Good	Fair	Poor
3195	1650	—	—	—	—

BERGER, JEAN MARIUS

St. Etienne, France

Berger

The Berger was a magazine fed repeating pistol in 7.65mm. It was a self loader and self cocker. It had all the characteristics of a semi-automatic except for the recoil operating system.

Courtesy James Rankin

Exc.	V.G.	Good	Fair	Poor
5500	4500	3750	3000	2000

BERGMANN, THEODOR

Gaggenau, Germany

Theodor Bergmann was a successful industrialist, designer and sometimes inventor with a deep interest in firearms based in Gaggenau, Germany. His first automatic pistol patent dates from 1892, and by 1894 he had prototype pistols, refined with the help of Louis Schmeisser, being evaluated by various governments. When his designs went into commercial production in 1896, however, they were actually manufactured by the firm of V. Charles Schilling in Suhl, the heart of German arms manufacture. Later he licensed manufacture of his "Mars" pistol to Anciens Establishment Pieper ("Bayard"), and after WWI affiliated with the Lignose firm, producing a line of .25 caliber pocket pistols, first under the Bergmann name but later marketed as Lignose. Still later several pistol designs from the August Menz firm were marketed under the "Bergmann Erben" trademark, though it's doubtful if the Bergmann firm actually had much part in their production or sale.

Model 1894 Bergmann Schmeisser

The Model 1894 was made in prototype form only, with only a few examples surviving and known serial numbers no higher than the mid teens. Most are large framed and chambered for the 8mm Bergmann-Schmeisser cartridge, though at least one was made in 7.5mm Swiss revolver for Swiss army testing and a few very compact versions, with a unique folding trigger, for 5mm Bergmann. Early Bergmann pistols had no extractor, counting on gas pressure to blow the fired (rimless-grooveless) cartridge from the chamber. Too rare to price.

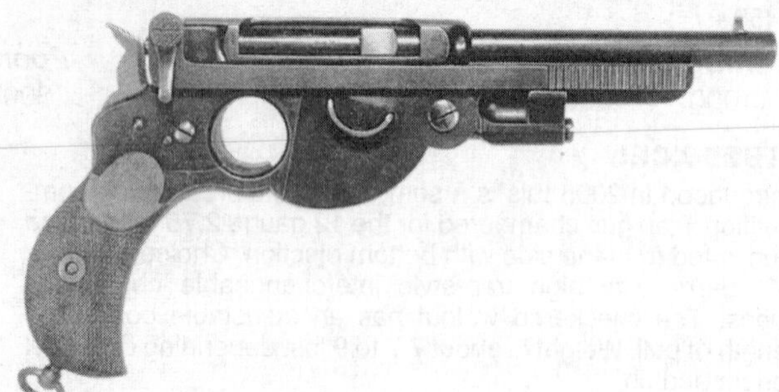

Bergmann Schmeisser

Model 1896, Number 2

The 1896 Number 2 pistols were quite compact and chambered for the 5mm Bergmann cartridge. Early Number 2s also featured a folding trigger and no extractor, but after serial 500 or so reverted to a more conventional in-the-frame trigger and an extractor was added. About 2000 of the later model were produced. Cased sets are known, and add about 50 percent to the value.

Folding Trigger Number 2

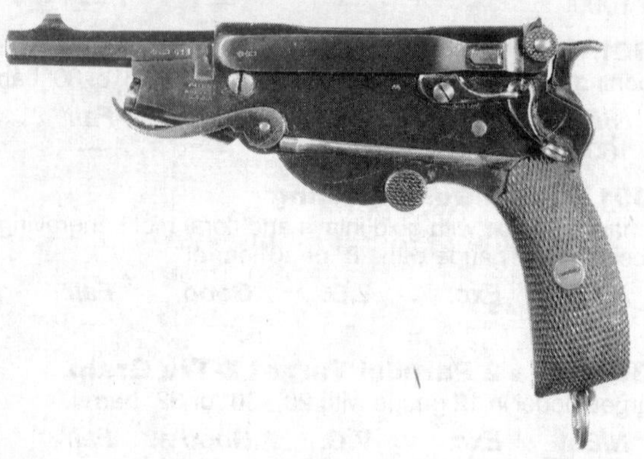

Courtesy James Rankin

Exc.	V.G.	Good	Fair	Poor
4200	3200	2500	1200	800

Conventional Number 2

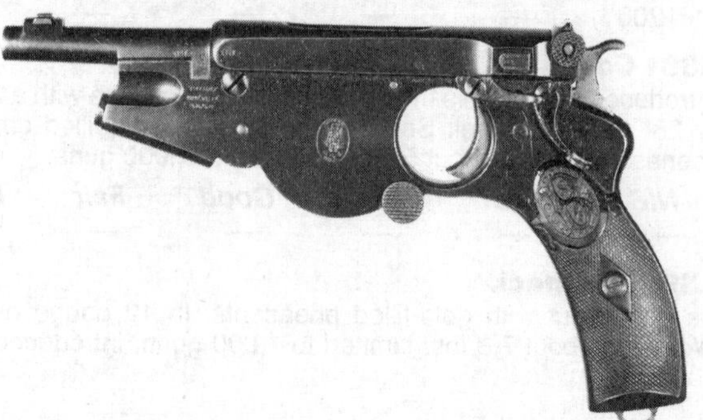

Courtesy James Rankin

Exc.	V.G.	Good	Fair	Poor
3200	2750	2000	1200	800

Model 1896 Number 3

The Number 3 was a larger version of the Number 2, chambered for the 6.5mm Bergmann cartridge. Early examples had a slim gripframe and, up to about serial 800, were made without extractor like the early Number 2s. These bring about a 20 percent premium over the later examples. Number 3 serials range to a little over 4000. Add about 20 percent for dealer markings (usually English), and 50 percent for cased sets. A few target models, with long barrel, adjustable sights and set triggers are known and will bring about three times the price of a standard Number 3.

First Variation

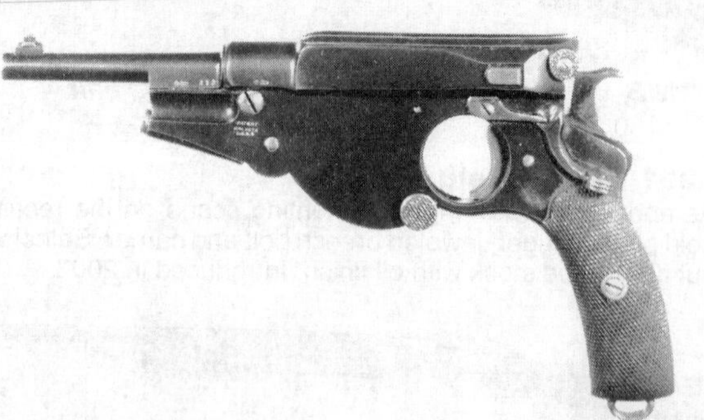

Courtesy James Rankin

Exc.	V.G.	Good	Fair	Poor
3500	3000	2500	1500	800

Second Variation

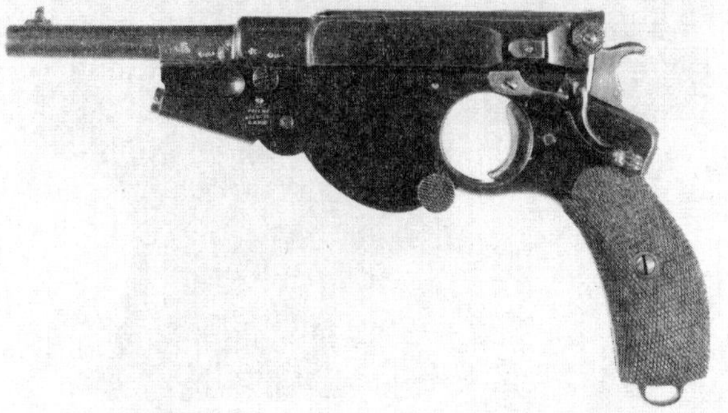

Courtesy James Rankin

Exc.	V.G.	Good	Fair	Poor
3000	2750	2200	1500	800

Third Variation

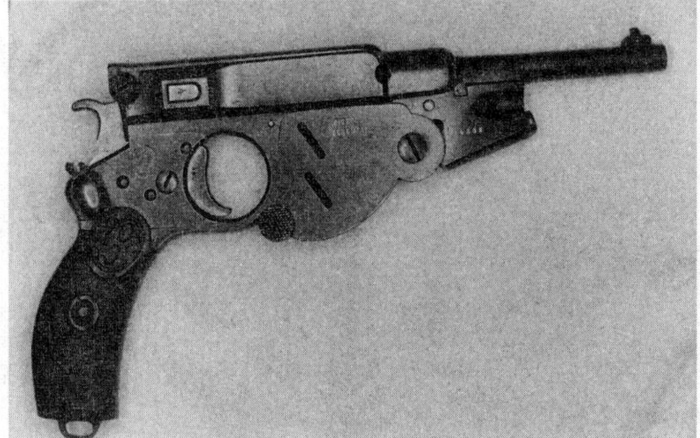

Courtesy James Rankin

Exc.	V.G.	Good	Fair	Poor
3200	2800	2200	1500	800

Holster and Stock Model

Model 1896 No. 3 with accessory holster stock

Courtesy James Rankin

Exc.	V.G.	Good	Fair	Poor
5500	5000	4500	3000	2500

Model 1896 Number 4

The Number 4 is identical to the Number 3 but chambered for a unique 8mm Bergmann cartridge and serialed in the same series with the Number 3. Both the Number 4 and its cartridge are rare; probably fewer than 200 were ever made.

Exc.	V.G.	Good	Fair	Poor
5500	4500	4000	3000	2500

Model 1897 Number 5

The was Bergmann's first attempt at a more powerful arm for the military market, with a unique side-moving locking system and a 10-shot removable box magazine. The 7.8mm cartridge resembled the 7.63mm Mauser, but with a longer neck. Add 60 percent for original metal framed leather holster-stock.

Exc.	V.G.	Good	Fair	Poor
7500	6000	4500	2750	1750

Model 1897 Number 5a Carbine

A limited number of the approximately 1000 Bergmann Model 5s were made with a 12-inch barrel and solid wood detachable buttstock and marked "Karabiner Bergmann" on the action cover. A very few were made with a full-length Mannlicher-type stock and sold as the Bergmann Model 1897/07 Sporting Carbine; these are worth about 50 percent more than the long barreled pistol with detachable stock.

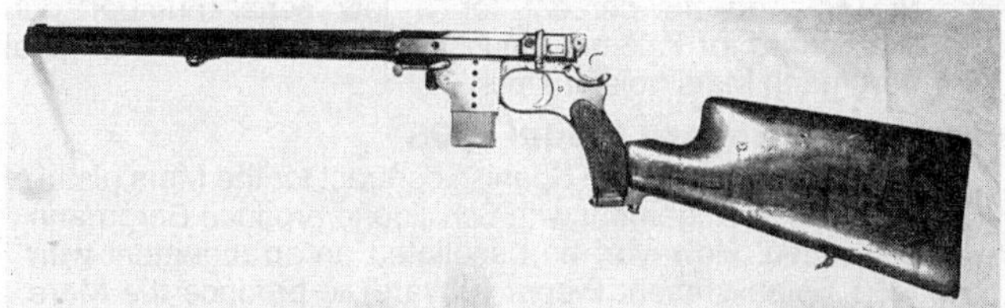

Courtesy Joe Schroeder

Exc.	V.G.	Good	Fair	Poor
12000	10000	6000	3000	2000

Bergmann Simplex

The Simplex combined some features of the 1896 pistols with improvements developed from the "Mars," resulting in a reasonable compact pocket pistol that came on the market in the early 1900s. It was chambered for the unique Bergmann-Simplex 8mm cartridge, however, and that and competition from better Browning and other designs doomed it to a short production life. Very early examples had checkered wood grips and bring a premium, as do very late examples (above serial 3000) that have the magazine release behind the magazine instead of on the front of the frame.

Exc.	V.G.	Good	Fair	Poor
3250	2800	2000	900	600

Bergmann "Mars"

The Mars was Bergmann's first really successful pistol aimed at the military market. Early examples, about 100 of the total 1000 or so Mars pistols made, were chambered for the 7.63mm Mauser cartridge but later Mars pistols, identified by a large "9mm" on the chamber, were chambered for the special

9mm cartridge that later became known as the 9mm Bergmann-Bayard. The Mars was adopted by the Spanish government in 1905 as their first military automatic pistol, but none were ever delivered by Bergmann. At least two Mars pistols were also made in .45 caliber for U.S. Army trials in 1906, but did not perform well and were dropped from the trials; these are too rare to price.

Exc.	*V.G.*	*Good*	*Fair*	*Poor*
5500	4500	3500	2200	1350

NOTE: Add 25 percent for a low serial number gun chambered for 7.63mm Mauser; add 50 percent for original Bergmann Mars holster stock.

Bergmann Bayard Model 1908

Shortly after receiving the Spanish contract for the Mars pistol, Bergmann's arrangement with Schilling to produce Bergmann pistols ended. However, he negotiated an arrangement with Anciens Establishment Pieper (Bayard) to produce the Mars and, after some minor modifications, AEP filled the Spanish contract. They also marketed the gun commercially, and later secured a production contract from the Danish army as the Model 1910. Spanish contract (proofed with a small circle divided into three segments) and very early commercial pistols have hard rubber grips that proved very fragile in service; these bring a premium as do original unmodified Danish contract guns (with a contract number and Danish letter D proof). A few Model 1908 Bergmann Bayards were equipped with leather and wood holster stocks; a complete rig is worth at least twice the price of an unslotted pistol.

Courtesy James Rankin

Exc.	*V.G.*	*Good*	*Fair*	*Poor*
1500	1200	850	700	500

Bergmann Post War Pistols

Shortly after WWI ended Bergmann came on the market with a line of .25 caliber pocket pistols; the 2 and 3 were conventional vest pocket designs with a short and long gripframe respectively; the 2a and 3a were identical except for an "Einhand" (one-hand) feature that enabled the user to cycle the slide by pulling the front of the trigger guard with his trigger finger. Soon into production (at about serial 8000) Bergmann affiliated with the Lignose firm and later Model 2 and 3 pistols were marketed under the Lignose name.

Courtesy Joe Schroeder

Model 2 and 3

Exc.	*V.G.*	*Good*	*Fair*	*Poor*
275	225	175	125	100

Model 2a and 3a

Exc.	*V.G.*	*Good*	*Fair*	*Poor*
350	275	225	175	125

Bergmann Erben Pistols

The Bergmann Erben pistols appear to be an attempt by the Bergmann family to keep the Bergmann name associated with firearms without actually investing any design or production effort. The Bergmann Erben pistols were all August Menz designs, and were undoubtedly made by Menz as well. Most noteworthy was the "Spezial" model, a very sophisticated double-action .32 pocket pistol that could be cocked for single-action fire by pulling and then releasing the trigger. Also noteworthy were several compact vest pocket .25s that also bore the Bergmann Erben name.

Bergmann Erben Spezial

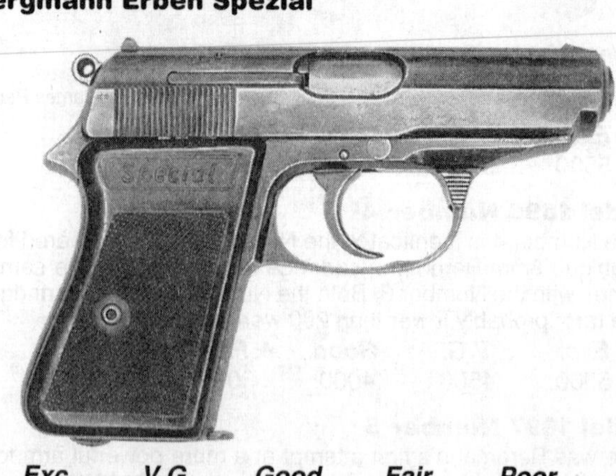

Exc.	*V.G.*	*Good*	*Fair*	*Poor*
1500	1200	750	500	300

Bergmann Erben Model II Pistol

Courtesy James Rankin

Exc.	V.G.	Good	Fair	Poor
450	400	300	200	100

Bergmann Einhand

SEE—Lignose.

BERN, WAFFENFABRIK

Bern, Switzerland

NOTE: For history, technical data, descriptions, photos, and prices see the *Standard Catalog of Military Firearms* under Switzerland.

BERNARDELLI, VINCENZO

Brescia, Italy

Established in the 1721, this company originally manufactured military arms and only entered the commercial sporting arms market in 1928.

HANDGUNS

Vest Pocket Model

Similar to the Walther Model 9, in a 6.35mm caliber semi-automatic pistol with a 2.25" barrel, and 5-shot magazine. An extended 8-shot version was also available. Blued with plastic grips. Manufactured between 1945 and 1948.

Exc.	V.G.	Good	Fair	Poor
300	225	155	100	75

Pocket Model

As above, in 7.65mm caliber. This model was also offered with extended barrels that protruded beyond the end of the slide. Introduced in 1947.

Exc.	V.G.	Good	Fair	Poor
275	200	150	100	75

Baby Model

As above, in .22 short or long rifle. Manufactured between 1949 and 1968.

Exc.	V.G.	Good	Fair	Poor
275	200	150	100	75

Sporter Model

A .22 caliber semi-automatic pistol with 6", 8", or 10" barrels and adjustable sights. Blued with walnut grips. Manufactured between 1949 and 1968.

Exc.	V.G.	Good	Fair	Poor
300	225	175	125	100

Revolvers

A .22 rimfire and .32 caliber double-action revolver with 1.5", 2", or 5" barrels. A .22 caliber, 7" barrel version with adjustable sights also available. Manufactured between 1950 and 1962.

Exc.	V.G.	Good	Fair	Poor
225	150	125	100	75

Model 60

A .22, .32 ACP or .380 ACP caliber semi-automatic pistol with 3.5" barrel and fixed sights. Blued with plastic grips. Manufactured since 1959.

Exc.	V.G.	Good	Fair	Poor
250	175	150	125	90

REMINDER
The prices given in this book are RETAIL prices.
They are a general guide as to what a willing buyer and willing seller might agree on.

Model 68

A .22 rimfire caliber or .25 ACP semi-automatic pistol with a 2" barrel and 5-shot magazine. Blued with plastic grips. No longer imported into the U.S.

Exc.	V.G.	Good	Fair	Poor
175	125	100	75	50

Model 80

A .22 or .380 ACP caliber semi-automatic pistol with a 3.5" barrel and adjustable sights. Blued with plastic grips. Imported between 1968 and 1988.

Exc.	V.G.	Good	Fair	Poor
225	175	125	100	80

Model AMR

As above, with a 6" barrel.

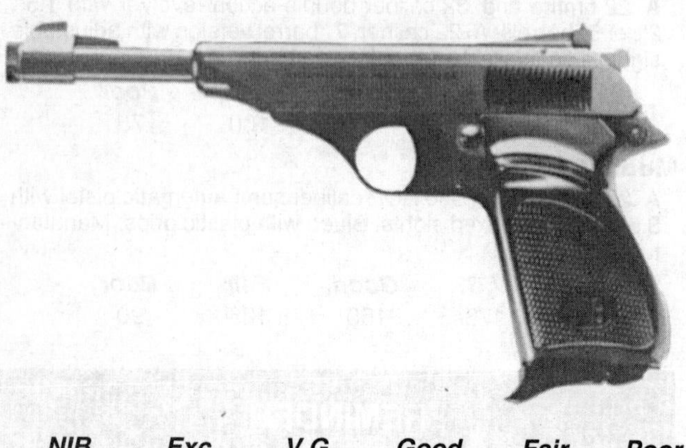

NIB	Exc.	V.G.	Good	Fair	Poor
450	350	200	150	100	90

Model 69

A .22 caliber semi-automatic target pistol with a 6" heavy barrel, and a 10-shot magazine. Blued with checkered walnut grips.

NIB	Exc.	V.G.	Good	Fair	Poor
450	375	300	225	150	100

Model PO10

A .22 caliber, single-action, semi-automatic target pistol with a 6" barrel, adjustable target sights, barrel weights, and an adjustable trigger. Matte-black finish with stippled walnut grips. Introduced in 1989. Weight 40 oz. sold with special hard case.

NIB	Exc.	V.G.	Good	Fair	Poor
800	700	500	300	200	100

Model PO18

A 7.65mm or 9mm Parabellum caliber, double-action, semi-automatic pistol with a 4.75" barrel and a 16-shot, double stack, detachable magazine. All-steel construction. Blued with plastic grips. Walnut grips are available for an additional $40. Introduced in 1985.

NIB	Exc.	V.G.	Good	Fair	Poor
650	550	400	275	200	100

Model PO18 Compact

As above, with a 4" barrel and a shorter grip frame with a 14-shot, double-column magazine. Introduced in 1989.

NIB	Exc.	V.G.	Good	Fair	Poor
650	550	400	275	200	100

Model P. One

A full-size semi-automatic pistol chambered for the 9mm or .40 S&W calibers. Fitted with a 4.8" barrel. Can be fired double-action or single-action. Ten-shot magazine. Weight is 2.14 lbs. Available in black or chrome finish. Add $50 for chrome finish.

NIB	Exc.	V.G.	Good	Fair	Poor
625	525	400	275	200	100

Model P. One-Compact

Same as above but with 4" barrel and offered in .380 caliber as well as 9mm and .40 S&W. Weight is 1.96 lbs.

NIB	Exc.	V.G.	Good	Fair	Poor
650	550	400	275	200	100

Practical VB Target

Designed for Practical shooting this 9mm pistol has a 6" barrel with choice of 2 or 4 port compensator. It is fitted with numerous extra features. Weights is 2.2 lbs.

NIB	Exc.	V.G.	Good	Fair	Poor
1500	1200	850	600	400	200

Practical VB Custom

As above but designed for IPSC rules.

NIB	Exc.	V.G.	Good	Fair	Poor
2250	1900	1400	900	600	300

Model USA

A .22, .32 ACP or .380 ACP caliber semi-automatic pistol with a 3.5" barrel, adjustable sights, steel frame and a loaded chamber indicator. Blued with plastic grips.

NIB	Exc.	V.G.	Good	Fair	Poor
450	350	200	150	100	90

SHOTGUNS

MODEL 115 SERIES

A 12 gauge Over/Under, boxlock, double-barrel shotgun with various barrel lengths and choke combinations, single triggers and automatic ejectors.

Model 115

NIB	Exc.	V.G.	Good	Fair	Poor
1525	1250	900	700	550	300

Model 115S

NIB	Exc.	V.G.	Good	Fair	Poor
2000	1750	1200	800	600	300

Model 115L

NIB	Exc.	V.G.	Good	Fair	Poor
2500	2000	1500	900	650	300

Model 115E

NIB	Exc.	V.G.	Good	Fair	Poor
5200	4800	4200	3500	2500	1850

Model 115 Trap

NIB	Exc.	V.G.	Good	Fair	Poor
2200	1950	1400	950	750	600

Model 115S Trap

NIB	Exc.	V.G.	Good	Fair	Poor
2700	2450	1900	1450	1150	900

Model 115E Trap

NIB	Exc.	V.G.	Good	Fair	Poor
5250	4800	4200	3500	2500	1850

MODEL 190 SERIES

A 12 gauge, Over/Under shotgun with various barrel lengths and choke combinations, a single-selective trigger and automatic ejectors. Engraved and silver-finished with a checkered walnut stock. Introduced in 1986. The various versions differ in the degree of ornamentation and quality of materials utilized in construction.

Model 190

NIB	Exc.	V.G.	Good	Fair	Poor
1050	950	750	600	475	400

Model 190MC

NIB	Exc.	V.G.	Good	Fair	Poor
1150	1050	850	700	575	500

Model 190 Special

NIB	Exc.	V.G.	Good	Fair	Poor
1350	1150	950	800	675	600

Model 190 Combo Gun

A .243, .308 or .30-06 caliber and 12, 16, or 20 gauge combination Over/Under rifle shotgun with a boxlock action, double triggers and automatic ejectors. Blued with a checkered walnut stock. Introduced in 1989.

NIB	Exc.	V.G.	Good	Fair	Poor
1625	1425	925	775	650	575

ORIONE SERIES

A 12 gauge boxlock Over/Under shotgun with various barrel lengths and choke combinations. Finishes and triggers were optional, as were extractors or automatic ejectors.

Orione

NIB	Exc.	V.G.	Good	Fair	Poor
1150	900	700	500	400	200

Orione S

NIB	Exc.	V.G.	Good	Fair	Poor
1150	900	700	500	400	200

Orione L

NIB	Exc.	V.G.	Good	Fair	Poor
1250	1000	800	600	500	250

Orione E

NIB	Exc.	V.G.	Good	Fair	Poor
1350	1150	850	600	500	250

S. Uberto I Gamecock

A 12, 16, 20, or 28 gauge boxlock side-by-side shotgun with either 25.75" or 27.5" barrels, various chokes, double triggers and extractors. Automatic ejectors were available and would be worth a 20 percent premium. Blued with a checkered stock.

Exc.	V.G.	Good	Fair	Poor
950	700	500	350	250

Brescia

A 12, 16, or 20 gauge sidelock double-barrel shotgun with exposed hammers, various barrel lengths, choke combinations, a sidelock action, double triggers, and manual extractors. Blued with an English-style, checkered walnut stock.

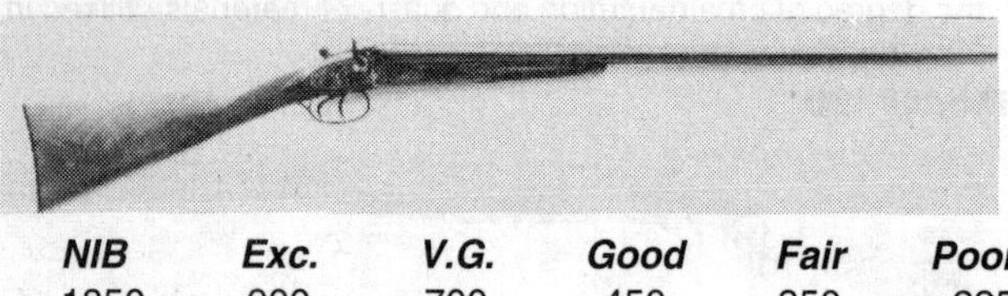

NIB	Exc.	V.G.	Good	Fair	Poor
1850	900	700	450	350	225

Italia

This is a higher grade version of the Brescia.

NIB	Exc.	V.G.	Good	Fair	Poor
2250	1250	750	600	400	250

Italia Extra

This is the highest grade hammer gun that Bernardelli produces.

NIB	Exc.	V.G.	Good	Fair	Poor
5900	2750	1500	1000	750	300

UBERTO SERIES

A 12, 16, 20 or 28 gauge Anson & Deeley boxlock double barrel shotgun with various barrel lengths and choke combinations. The increased value of the various models depends on the degree of engraving, options, and quality of materials and workmanship utilized in their construction.

S. Uberto I

NIB	Exc.	V.G.	Good	Fair	Poor
1000	800	650	475	350	250

S. Uberto 1E

NIB	Exc.	V.G.	Good	Fair	Poor
1100	900	700	500	350	250

S. Uberto 2

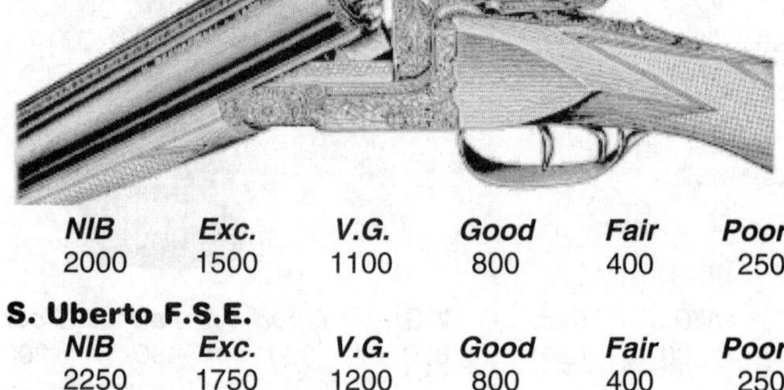

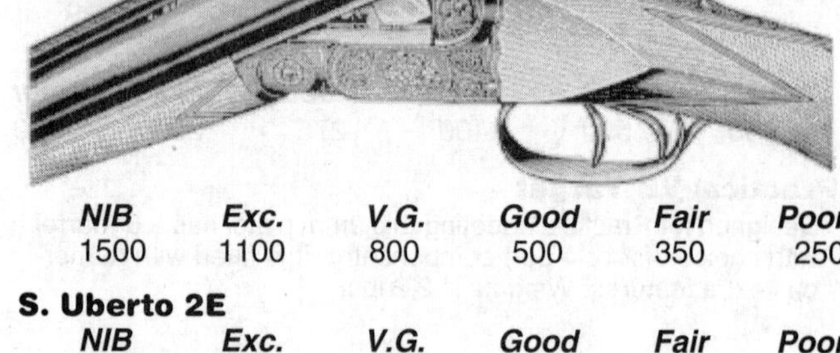

NIB	Exc.	V.G.	Good	Fair	Poor
1500	1100	800	500	350	250

S. Uberto 2E

NIB	Exc.	V.G.	Good	Fair	Poor
1750	1350	950	600	400	250

S. Uberto F.S.

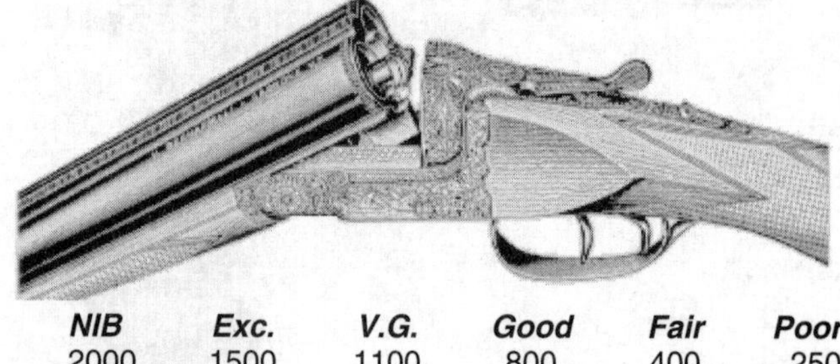

NIB	Exc.	V.G.	Good	Fair	Poor
2000	1500	1100	800	400	250

S. Uberto F.S.E.

NIB	Exc.	V.G.	Good	Fair	Poor
2250	1750	1200	800	400	250

ROMA SERIES

Similar to the S. Uberto Series with false sideplates. The values of the respective variations result from the degree of ornamentation and quality of materials and workmanship utilized in the construction.

Roma 3

NIB	Exc.	V.G.	Good	Fair	Poor
1550	1200	800	600	300	200

Roma 3E

NIB	Exc.	V.G.	Good	Fair	Poor
1750	1300	900	650	300	200

Roma 4

NIB	Exc.	V.G.	Good	Fair	Poor
1950	1400	1100	750	400	250

Roma 4E

NIB	Exc.	V.G.	Good	Fair	Poor
2000	1500	1200	750	400	250

Roma 6

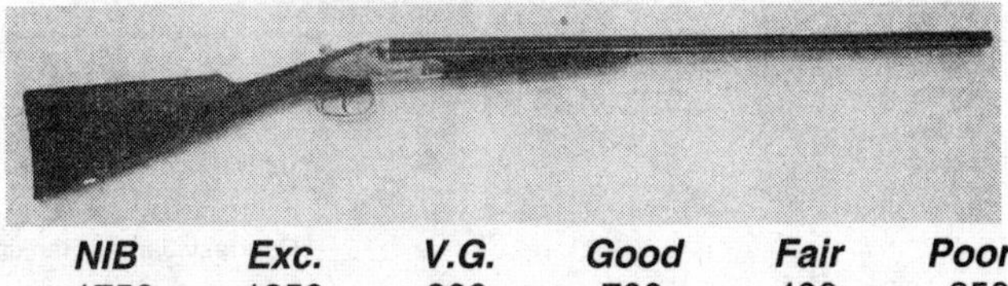

NIB	Exc.	V.G.	Good	Fair	Poor
2100	1750	1400	850	500	250

Roma 6E

NIB	Exc.	V.G.	Good	Fair	Poor
2200	1800	1400	850	500	250

Roma 7

NIB	Exc.	V.G.	Good	Fair	Poor
2900	2500	1800	1200	700	350

Roma 8

NIB	Exc.	V.G.	Good	Fair	Poor
3500	3000	2250	1550	850	400

Roma 9

NIB	Exc.	V.G.	Good	Fair	Poor
4000	3500	2750	1700	950	450

Elio

A 12 gauge boxlock double-barrel shotgun with various barrel lengths and choke combinations, lightweight frame, double triggers and extractors. Scroll-engraved, silver-finished receiver, blued barrels and a select, checkered walnut stock.

NIB	Exc.	V.G.	Good	Fair	Poor
1000	800	600	500	350	250

Elio E

As above, with automatic ejectors.

NIB	Exc.	V.G.	Good	Fair	Poor
1100	900	700	550	350	250

Hemingway

As above, with coin finished receiver, engraved with hunting scenes, 23.5" barrels, double triggers or single trigger and a select, checkered walnut stock. Available in 12, 20 and 28 gauge.

NIB	Exc.	V.G.	Good	Fair	Poor
1750	1350	900	700	400	250

Hemingway Deluxe

Same as above but fitted with full side plates.

NIB	Exc.	V.G.	Good	Fair	Poor
2250	1750	1200	800	400	250

Las Palomas Pigeon Model

A live Pigeon gun in 12 gauge with single trigger.

NIB	Exc.	V.G.	Good	Fair	Poor
3800	3250	2500	2000	1500	750

HOLLAND V.B. SERIES

A 12 or 20 gauge sidelock shotgun with various barrel lengths, detachable Holland & Holland-type locks, single triggers, and automatic ejectors. The models listed vary in the amount of engraving and the quality of their wood. Prospective purchasers are advised to secure a qualified appraisal prior to acquisition.

Holland V.B. Liscio

NIB	Exc.	V.G.	Good	Fair	Poor
8000	5500	4000	3000	2000	1000

Holland V.B. Inciso

NIB	Exc.	V.G.	Good	Fair	Poor
10250	7500	5250	4000	2500	1250

Holland V.B. Lusso

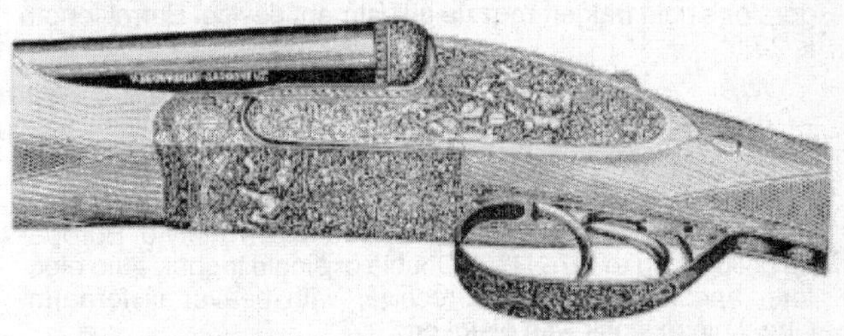

NIB	Exc.	V.G.	Good	Fair	Poor
11000	8000	6000	4500	2500	1250

Holland V.B. Extra

NIB	Exc.	V.G.	Good	Fair	Poor
13000	10000	7500	5500	3000	1500

Holland V.B. Gold

NIB	Exc.	V.G.	Good	Fair	Poor
45000	30000	22500	15000	7500	3000

Luck

An over-and-under shotgun with single-selective trigger or double triggers, automatic ejectors with choice of fixed chokes or choke tubes. Available in 12 gauge. Blued or coin finish receiver.

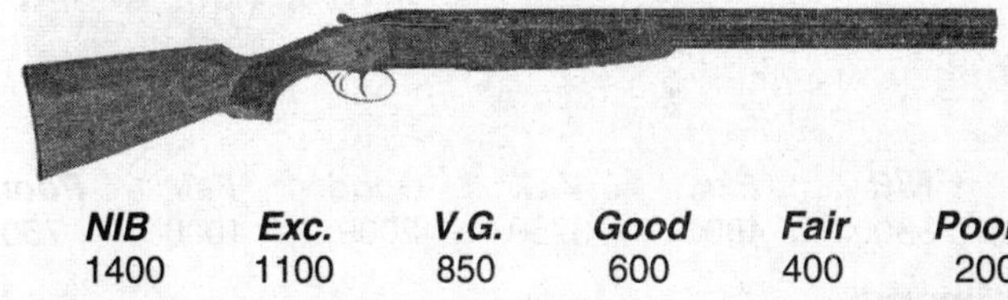

NIB	Exc.	V.G.	Good	Fair	Poor
1400	1100	850	600	400	200

Giardino

This is a semi-automatic shotgun chambered for the 9mm shot cartridge. Fitted with a 4-round magazine. Weight is 5 lbs.

NIB	Exc.	V.G.	Good	Fair	Poor
400	350	300	250	200	100

RIFLES

Carbina VB Target

A semi-automatic carbine chambered for the .22 LR cartridge. Barrel is 20.8" and magazine capacity is 10 rounds.

NIB	Exc.	V.G.	Good	Fair	Poor
650	550	400	300	200	100

Comb 2000

A rifle shotgun combination in 12 or 16 gauge with a variety of centerfire calibers to choose from. Barrels are 23.5" long. Set trigger, special rib for scope mount and cheekpiece stock with pistol grip. Weight is 6-3/4 lbs.

NIB	Exc.	V.G.	Good	Fair	Poor
2200	1700	1200	800	400	250

Express 2000

An over-and-under double rifle chambered for a variety of European calibers. Fitted with automatic ejectors, double-set triggers or single trigger, muzzle adjustment device. Barrel length is 23.5".

NIB	Exc.	V.G.	Good	Fair	Poor
2750	2350	1700	1200	600	300

Express VB

A side-by-side double rifle chambered for a variety of European calibers up to .375 H&H. Double or single trigger, auto ejectors, and finely engraved receiver with beavertail forearm. Cheekpiece stock with pistol grip.

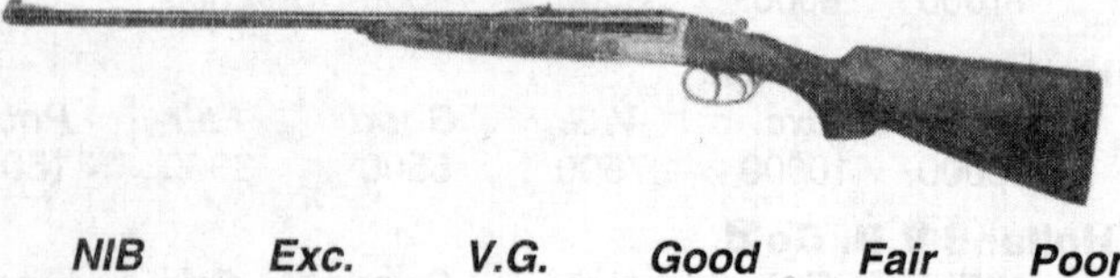

NIB	Exc.	V.G.	Good	Fair	Poor
5500	4700	3750	2000	1000	750

Express VB Deluxe

Same as above but with side plates and select walnut stock finely checkered.

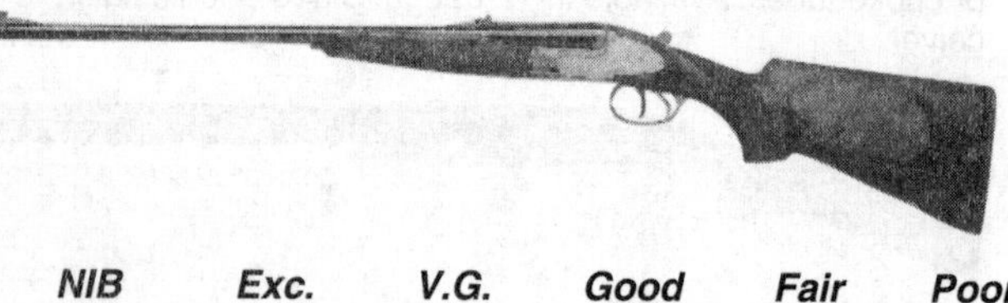

NIB	Exc.	V.G.	Good	Fair	Poor
5600	4800	3750	2000	1000	750

Minerva

A side-by-side double rifle with exposed hammers chambered for the 9.3x74R cartridge. Fitted with fancy walnut stock, double triggers, hand-cut rib, and other high-quality features.

NIB	Exc.	V.G.	Good	Fair	Poor
6000	5600	4250	2500	1200	750

BERNARDON MARTIN

St. Etienne, France

This small firm was active between 1906 and 1912. The gun designer was Martin and the money man was Bernadon.

1907/8 Model

A 7.65mm caliber semi-automatic pistol. The left side of the slide is marked "Cal. 7.65mm St. Etienne." The trademark "BM" is molded into the grips. Sometimes found with a 32-round horseshoe magazine.

Occasionally the Bernardon Martin pistol will be noted with the word "Hermetic" stamped on the slide in letters that do not match the other markings on the weapon. This was but another name for the Model 1907/8. Guns with this stamping were most likely assembled after the company ceased operations.

Courtesy James Rankin

Exc.	V.G.	Good	Fair	Poor
1000	800	650	400	250

NOTE: Add 50 percent for horseshoe magazine.

1908/9 Model

Introduced late in 1908 this model is similar to the Model 1907/8 with the addition of a grip safety.

Exc.	V.G.	Good	Fair	Poor
850	700	550	350	200

BERNEDO, VINCENZO

Eibar, Spain

B C

The B C is in caliber 6.35mm and most of the barrel is exposed. The recoil spring is housed in the rear of the receiver. The B C closely resembles the Tanque pistol.

Courtesy James Rankin

Exc.	V.G.	Good	Fair	Poor
300	200	175	150	125

Bernado

This model 7.65mm is in the Spanish style of the Ruby automatic pistols.

Courtesy James Rankin

Exc.	V.G.	Good	Fair	Poor
200	125	90	60	35

BERSA

Ramos Mejia, Argentina

Model 644

This model is a blowback pocket pistol chambered for the .22 LR. The trigger system is single-action. Barrel length is 3.5", overall length is 6.57", and empty weight is approximately 28 oz. This is the basic Bersa model from which its other models derive their design and function.

NIB	Exc.	V.G.	Good	Fair	Poor
275	175	150	125	100	75

Model 622

Similar to the Model 644 but with a slightly longer barrel.

NIB	Exc.	V.G.	Good	Fair	Poor
275	175	150	125	100	75

Model 97

This model is a slightly larger version of the Model 644 chambered for the 9mm Short.

NIB	Exc.	V.G.	Good	Fair	Poor
275	175	150	125	100	75

Model 23

A .22 rimfire caliber, double-action, semi-automatic pistol with a 3.5" barrel and 10-shot detachable magazine. Either blued or satin nickel-plated with checkered walnut grips.

NIB	Exc.	V.G.	Good	Fair	Poor
300	200	150	125	100	75

Model 223

As above, with a squared trigger guard and nylon grips. Imported after 1988.

Exc.	V.G.	Good	Fair	Poor
275	175	125	100	75

Model 224

As above, with a 4" barrel. Imported after 1988.

Exc.	V.G.	Good	Fair	Poor
275	175	125	100	75

Model 225

As above, with a 5" barrel. Discontinued in 1986.

Exc.	V.G.	Good	Fair	Poor
275	175	125	100	75

Model 226

As above, with a 6" barrel. Discontinued in 1988.

Courtesy John J. Stimson, Jr.

Exc.	V.G.	Good	Fair	Poor
275	175	125	100	75

Model 323

A .32 ACP caliber single-action semi-automatic pistol, with a 3.5" barrel, fixed sights and a 7-shot detachable magazine. Blued with molded plastic grips. Not imported after 1986.

Exc.	V.G.	Good	Fair	Poor
225	125	100	75	50

Model 383

As above, in .380 caliber. Discontinued in 1988.

Exc.	V.G.	Good	Fair	Poor
250	150	125	90	75

Model 383A

A .380 ACP caliber double-action semi-automatic pistol with a 3.5" barrel with fixed sights and 7-shot magazine. Blued with checkered walnut grips. Overall length is 6.6" and weight is about 24 oz. Available in blue or nickel finish.

NIB	Exc.	V.G.	Good	Fair	Poor
300	200	150	125	100	75

Model 83

Similar to the above model but with double-action operating system. Weighs about 26 oz. Introduced in 1988.

NIB	Exc.	V.G.	Good	Fair	Poor
300	200	150	125	100	75

Model 85

As above, with a double-column magazine. Introduced in 1988.

NIB	Exc.	V.G.	Good	Fair	Poor
350	250	200	150	100	75

Model 86

Similar to the Model 85 .380 caliber, but features a matte blue or satin nickel finish, wrap around rubber grips, and three-dot sight. Magazine capacity is 13 rounds.

NIB	Exc.	V.G.	Good	Fair	Poor
350	250	225	200	150	100

Thunder 9

Introduced in 1993 this model is a double-action 9mm pistol that features ambidextrous safety, reversible extended magazine release, ambidextrous slide release, adjustable trigger stop, combat-style hammer, three-dot sights, and matte blue finish. Magazine capacity is 15 rounds.

NIB	Exc.	V.G.	Good	Fair	Poor
350	275	250	200	150	100

Series 95/Thunder 380

This is a semi-automatic double-action pistol chambered for the .380 cartridge. Choice of matte blue or nickel finish. Barrel length is 3.5". Fixed sights. Magazine capacity is 7 rounds. Weight is about 23 oz. Add $50 for nickel.

NIB	Exc.	V.G.	Good	Fair	Poor
260	200	150	100	—	—

Thunder 380 Matte Plus

Semi-auto double-action blued pistol in .380 with 15-round magazine. Fixed sights and polymer grips. Introduced 2006.

NIB	Exc.	V.G.	Good	Fair	Poor
350	—	—	—	—	—

Thunder 9 Ultra Compact

Available blued or stainless with 10- or 13-round capacity. Double-action chambered for 9mm. 3.5" barrel, 25 oz., fixed sights and polymer grips. Introduced 2006. MSRP: 442 blued (500 stainless)

Thunder 9/40 High Capacity Series

Double-action semi-autos available chambered for 9mm or .40 S&W and in matte blued or satin nickel-plate. Fixed sights and polymer grips. LOA 7 1/2", 4 1/4" barrel, 26 oz. Introduced 2006. MSRP: 460 blued (485 satin nickel)

Thunder Deluxe

This semi-automatic double-action pistol is chambered for the .380 cartridge. Blued finish. Fixed sights. Barrel length is 3.5". Weight is about 23 oz. Magazine capacity is 9 rounds.

NIB	Exc.	V.G.	Good	Fair	Poor
325	225	175	100	—	—

BERTHIER

French State

NOTE: For photos, prices, and historical data See the *Standard Catalog of Military Firearms, France, Rifles, Berthier.*

BERTRAND, JULES

Liege, Belgium

Le Novo

A 6.35mm caliber double-action revolver. Manufactured in the 1890s. The only identifying markings are the "JB" trademark on the grips.

Exc.	V.G.	Good	Fair	Poor
300	225	175	100	50

Lincoln

As above, in 7.65mm caliber.

Exc.	V.G.	Good	Fair	Poor
300	225	175	100	50

Le Rapide

A 6.35mm caliber, semi-automatic pistol. The Jules Bertrand logo is on the slide, as well as LePapide. Both are on each side of the grip plates.

Courtesy James Rankin

Exc.	V.G.	Good	Fair	Poor
350	275	200	125	50

BERTUZZI

Brescia, Italy

SHOTGUNS OVER/UNDER

Zeus

A 12, 16, 20, or 28 gauge sidelock shotgun with automatic ejectors, single-selective trigger, and deluxe checkered walnut stock. Custom order in various barrel lengths and chokes. Engraved. Rarely seen on the used gun market.

NIB	Exc.	V.G.	Good	Fair	Poor
18000-35000	—	—	—	—	—

Zeus Extra Lusso

As above, but with best wood and engraving. Cased.

NIB	Exc.	V.G.	Good	Fair	Poor
35000-75000	—	—	—	—	—

Zeus Boss System

This gun is chamberd for the 12, 16, 20, or 28 gauge and is fitted with the Boss locking system with ejectors. One-of-a-kind gun with best quality wood and engraving.

NIB	Exc.	V.G.	Good	Fair	Poor
65000-125000	—	—	—	—	—

Gull Wing

This is Burtuzzi's best gun with a unique sidelock design mounted on a center plate with a release located on top of the safety to allow sidelock access. These shotguns usually take about three years to build. Consult the distributor about options and availability.

NIB	Exc.	V.G.	Good	Fair	Poor
125000+	—	—	—	—	—

Ariete Extra Lusso

This is a best quality hammer gun in all gauges from 12 to 28. Limited quantities.

NIB	Exc.	V.G.	Good	Fair	Poor
65000+	—	—	—	—	—

SHOTGUNS SIDE-BY-SIDE

Orione

A 12, 16, 20 or 28 gauge boxlock shotgun with Anson & Deeley through bolt, in various barrel lengths and chokes, single-selective trigger and automatic ejectors. Hand checkered, walnut stock with a semi-beavertail forearm. Engraving.

NIB	Exc.	V.G.	Good	Fair	Poor
25500-39950		—	—	—	—

Venere

This is a best quality sidelock gun with either a traditional or round frame. Special order to customer specifications. Engraved guns bring a premium.

NIB	Exc.	V.G.	Good	Fair	Poor
29000-69000		—	—	—	—

Ariete

Best quality hammer gun with or without self cocking hammers and ejectors. Offered in 12 bore through .410. Many options.

NIB	Exc.	V.G.	Good	Fair	Poor
25000-55000		—	—	—	—

Gull Wing

This is a one-of-a-kind custom built gun with quick release sidelocks. Delivery time about three years. Contact distributor for more information.

NIB	Exc.	V.G.	Good	Fair	Poor
85000+	—	—	—	—	—

BIGHORN ARMS CO.

Watertown, South Dakota

Target Pistol

A .22 caliber single-shot pistol resembling a semi-automatic. Ventilated rib barrel 6" in length. Stock of molded plastic.

Exc.	V.G.	Good	Fair	Poor
225	125	100	85	65

Shotgun

A single-shot 12 gauge shotgun with a 26" barrel. Blued with a plastic stock.

Exc.	V.G.	Good	Fair	Poor
175	85	65	50	30

BIGHORN RIFLE CO.

Orem, Utah

Bighorn Rifle

Custom order in any caliber, double-barrel, bolt-action rifle with optional barrel lengths and finishes. Double trigger and walnut stock.

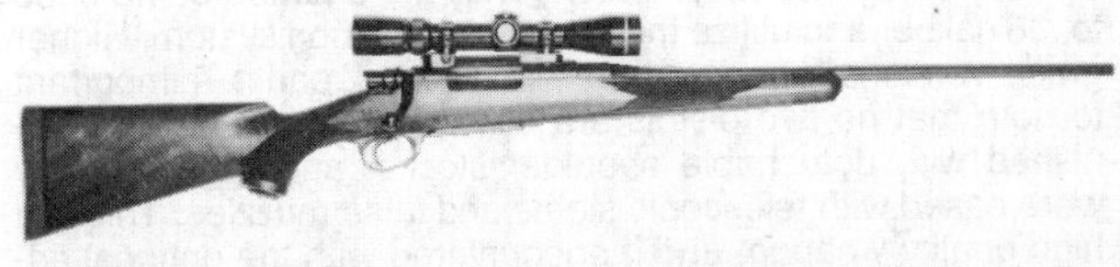

NIB	Exc.	V.G.	Good	Fair	Poor
2500	1750	1500	1000	750	400

BILHARZ, HALL & CO.

CONFEDERATE CARBINES

Bilharz, Hall & Co. Breechloading ("Rising Breech") Carbine

Overall length 40"; barrel length 21"; caliber 54. Markings: either "P" or "P/CS" on upper left side of barrel and top of rising breech. The peculiar feature of this carbine is the manner in which the breechblock exposes the chamber. A box-like chamber at the rear of the barrel rises vertically to expose the chamber for a paper cartridge by activating the lever/triggerguard mechanism. Only 100 of this type were delivered to the Confederacy in September 1862. Two types of front sight blades are known, but neither affects the value.

Courtesy Milwaukee Public Museum, Milwaukee, Wisconsin

Exc.	V.G.	Good	Fair	Poor
—	—	50000	22500	5000

Bilharz, Hall & Co. Muzzleloading Carbine

Overall length 37-1/2"; barrel length 22"; caliber .58. Markings: "P/CS" on upper left of barrel near breech; "CSA" on top near breech. Modeled after the Springfield U.S. M1855 rifle carbine, the Bilharz, Hall & Co. muzzleloading carbine has often been mistakenly identified as a product of D.C. Hodgkins & Sons of Macon, Georgia. Serial numbers (found internally) belie that identification. Instead these arms are part of deliveries made to Richmond from the middle of 1863 until March 1864. Serial numbers, noted in excess of 700, suggest that about 1,000 were produced. Two basic types, the earlier (through serial number 300) were made with brass nosecaps; the later type (about serial number 310 through at least 710) have pewter nosecaps on the short forestock; neither type affects value.

Exc.	V.G.	Good	Fair	Poor
—	—	25000	10000	3000

BILLINGHURST, WILLIAM

Rochester, New York

Billinghurst originally worked for James and John Miller of Rochester. After James Miller's death in 1837, Billinghurst established his own shop where he produced revolving rifles based upon Miller's 1829 patent. While these arms were originally made with percussion ignition systems (either pill or percussion cap), later examples using self-contained metallic cartridges are sometimes encountered. Billinghurst also established a well-deserved reputation for making extremely accurate percussion target pistols and rifles.

W. Billinghurst Under Hammer Pistol

This pistol is somewhat different than most of the under hammers encountered. The barrels are 12" to 18" in length and of a heavy octagonal construction. They are chambered from .30 to .38 caliber and utilize the percussion ignition system. Higher grade versions feature a part-round barrel, and it is important to note that no two pistols are alike. These pistols were furnished with detachable shoulder stocks, and a good many were cased with telescopic sights and false muzzles. This is a high quality weapon; and if encountered with the optional accessories, it would definitely warrant an individual appraisal. This firearm was manufactured in the 1850s and 1860s.

Exc.	V.G.	Good	Fair	Poor
—	—	4250	1750	800

NOTE: Shoulder stock add 50 percent.

Revolving Rifle

Calibers vary from .40 to .50 with barrels from 24" to 29"; walnut stocks. The barrels marked: "W. Billinghurst, Rochester, N.Y.," or "W. Billinghurst."

Exc.	V.G.	Good	Fair	Poor
—	—	7500	3000	950

BILLINGS

Location Unknown

Billings Pocket Pistol

A .32 rimfire caliber single-shot spur trigger pistol with a 2.5" round barrel and an unusually large grip. The barrel is stamped "Billings Vest Pocket Pistol Pat. April 24, 1866." Blued with walnut grips. Manufactured between 1865 and 1868.

Exc.	V.G.	Good	Fair	Poor
—	—	3500	1500	550

BINGHAM LTD.

Norcross, Georgia

PPS 50

A .22 rimfire caliber semi-automatic rifle patterned after the Soviet PPSH submachine gun with 16" barrel and a 50-round drum magazine. Blued, walnut or beech stock with a vented handguard. Manufactured between 1976 and 1985.

Exc.	V.G.	Good	Fair	Poor
450	300	175	125	100

AK-22

A .22 rimfire caliber semi-automatic rifle patterned after the Soviet AK-47 with either a 15- or 29-shot magazine. Walnut or beech stock. Manufactured between 1976 and 1985.

Exc.	V.G.	Good	Fair	Poor
325	200	150	100	75

Bantam

A .22 rimfire or .22 rimfire Magnum caliber bolt-action rifle with an 18.5" barrel. Manufactured between 1976 and 1985.

Exc.	V.G.	Good	Fair	Poor
200	85	70	50	35

BISMARCK

Location Unknown

Bismarck Pocket Revolver

A .22 caliber spur trigger revolver with a 3" round ribbed barrel and a 7-shot, unfluted cylinder. Brass frame and the remainder was plated with rosewood grips. The barrel is marked "Bismarck." Manufactured in the 1870s.

Exc.	V.G.	Good	Fair	Poor
—	—	500	200	90

BITTERLICH, FRANK J.

Nashville, Tennessee

A .41 caliber single-shot percussion pistol in a variety of octagonal barrel lengths, German silver mounts, walnut stock. The barrel and locks are marked "Fr.J. Bitterlich/Nashville, Tenn." Produced between 1861 and 1867.

Exc.	V.G.	Good	Fair	Poor
—	—	4500	1750	750

BITTNER, GUSTAV
Wieport, Bohemia

Bittner
A 7.7mm Bittner caliber repeating pistol with a 4.5" barrel. The bolt containing the firing pin rotates to lock the breech and is operated by the finger lever that encloses the trigger. Manufactured in mid 1890s. Fewer than 500 were made.

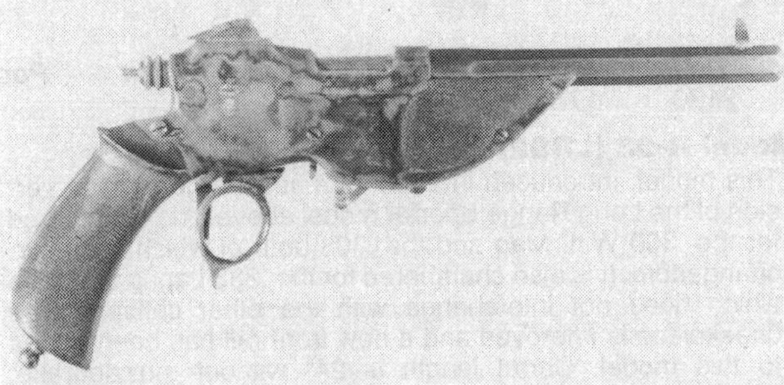

Exc.	V.G.	Good	Fair	Poor
6000	5000	3500	2000	1000

BLAKE, J. H.
New York, New York

Blake Bolt-Action Rifle
A .30-40 Krag caliber bolt-action rifle with a 30" barrel, and a 7-shot magazine. The stock is secured by three barrel bands. Blued with a walnut stock. Manufactured between 1892 and 1910.

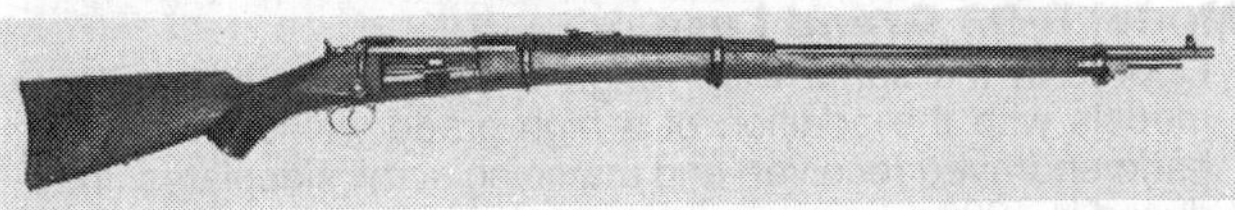

Courtesy Milwaukee Public Museum, Milwaukee, Wisconsin

Exc.	V.G.	Good	Fair	Poor
—	2750	950	400	200

BLANCH, JOHN
London, England

Blanch Percussion Pistol
A .69 caliber single-shot, percussion pistol with a 5" Damascus barrel. Engraved frame and hammer with a walnut grip. Manufactured in the 1830s.

Exc.	V.G.	Good	Fair	Poor
—	5750	2500	1300	800

Double Barrel Shotguns
SEE—British Double Guns

BLAND, THOMAS & SONS
London, England

Established in 1840, this firm has produced or marketed a wide variety of percussion and cartridge arms. Over the years, the firm has occupied a variety of premises in London, some of them concurrently.

41 Whittall Street	1840-1867
41, 42, 43 Whittall Street	1867-1886
106 Strand	1872-1900
430 Strand	1886-1900
2 William IV Street	1900-1919
4-5 William IV Street	1919-1973
New Row, St. Martin's Lane	1973-

T. Bland & Sons is perhaps best known for their double-barrel rifles and shotguns, which were made in a variety of grades.

Double Barrel Shotguns
SEE—British Double Guns

BLASER JAGDWAFFEN
Germany

SHOTGUNS

Blaser F3
This 12 gauge over/under shotgun with 3" chambers features Grade 4 walnut and is available with 28"-, 30"- or 32" barrels. Includes five choke tubes. Weight is about 8.2 lbs. Introduced 2006. NIB: 5200

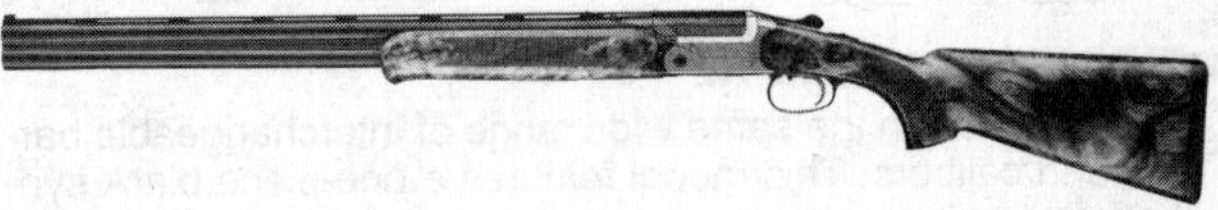

RIFLES

Model K77
A single-shot rifle chambered in a variety of calibers with a 24" barrel and silver-plated as well as engraved receiver. Walnut stock. Introduced in 1988.

NIB	Exc.	V.G.	Good	Fair	Poor
2500	1850	1500	1200	900	450

NOTE: Extra barrels add $750 per barrel.

Model R-84
A bolt-action sporting rifle chambered in a variety of calibers with either a 23" or 24" barrel. Interchangeable barrels are available for this model. Walnut stock. Imported beginning in 1988.

NIB	Exc.	V.G.	Good	Fair	Poor
2300	1850	1500	1200	900	450

Model R-93 LX
This is a straight-pull-back bolt-action rifle with interchangeable barrels in calibers from .22-250 to .416 Rem. Mag. Barrel length for standard calibers is 22" and for Magnum calibers 26". Magazine capacity is 3 rounds. Receiver is drilled and tapped for Blaser scope mounts. Weight is approximately 7 lbs. Two-piece walnut stock. Introduced by SIGARMS into the U.S. in 1998.

NIB	Exc.	V.G.	Good	Fair	Poor
1800	1400	—	—	—	—

NOTE: Add $200 for left-hand rifles, add $800 for .416 Remington Magnum.

Model R-93 Prestige

An updated and upgraded standard model with all the features of the R-93 LX. Light scroll engraving on receiver.

NIB	Exc.	V.G.	Good	Fair	Poor
2100	1650	—	—	—	—

Model R-93 Classic

Similar to the model above in choice of calibers and barrel lengths but with the addition of highly figured walnut stock and game scene engraved receiver.

NIB	Exc.	V.G.	Good	Fair	Poor
3500	2750	—	—	—	—

NOTE: Add $200 for left-hand rifles, add $800 for .416 Remington Magnum.

Model R-93 Luxus

This is an updated and upgraded model of the R-93 Classic. It features a high grade Turkish walnut stock with ebony forend. Side plates are engraved with game scenes.

NIB	Exc.	V.G.	Good	Fair	Poor
3000	2500	—	—	—	—

Model R-93 Synthetic

Also available in the same wide range of interchangeable barrels and calibers. This model features a one-piece black synthetic stock.

NIB	Exc.	V.G.	Good	Fair	Poor
1500	1200	—	—	—	—

NOTE: Add $200 for left-hand rifles, add $800 for .416 Remington Magnum.

Model R-93 Attache

This model features a custom made stock of highly figured walnut with cheekpiece, leather covered buttplate, silver pistolgrip cap, ebony forend tip, and custom checkering. Sold with a leather carrying case.

NIB	Exc.	V.G.	Good	Fair	Poor
5100	4000	—	—	—	—

NOTE: Add $200 for left-hand rifles.

Model R-93 Safari Synthetic

This model is chambered for the .416 Remington Magnum cartridge and fitted with a 24" heavy barrel with open sights. Weight is 9.5 lbs. Black synthetic stock. Other Blaser barrels will interchange on this model.

NIB	Exc.	V.G.	Good	Fair	Poor
2100	1700	—	—	—	—

Model R-93 Safari LX

Same as the R-93 Safari Synthetic with the exception of a two-piece walnut stock.

NIB	Exc.	V.G.	Good	Fair	Poor
2500	2000	—	—	—	—

Model R-93 Safari Classic

This model features an engraved receiver and fancy walnut stock.

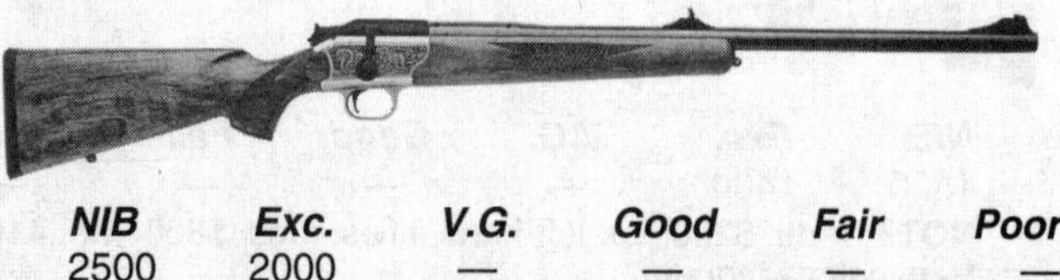

NIB	Exc.	V.G.	Good	Fair	Poor
2500	2000	—	—	—	—

Model R-93 Safari Attache

This is a top-of-the-line version of the R-93 series. It features engraved receiver, fancy walnut stock and other custom options found on the R-93 Attache model.

NIB	Exc.	V.G.	Good	Fair	Poor
5800	4500	—	—	—	—

Model R-93 Long Range Sporter

Introduced in 1998, this bolt-action rifle is chambered for the .308 Win. cartridge. The barrel length is 24" without muzzlebrake. Removable box magazine holds 10 rounds. The stock is aluminum and fully adjustable. Weight is approximately 10.4 lbs. No longer in production.

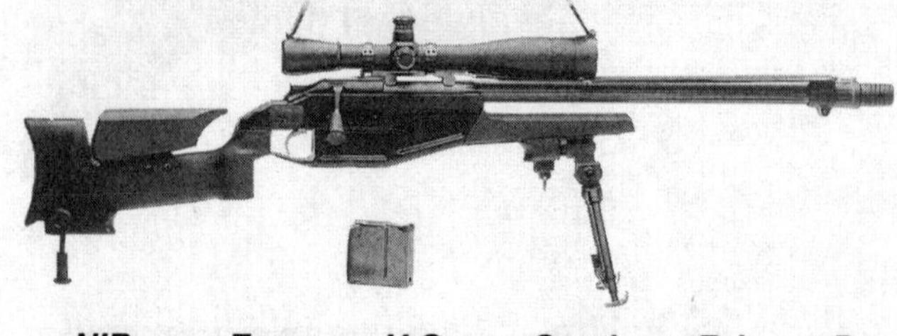

NIB	Exc.	V.G.	Good	Fair	Poor
2130	1700	—	—	—	—

Model R-93 (LRS2)

This model, introduced in 2000, is a second generation version of the Long Range Sporter model above. It is chambered for the .300 Win. Mag and the .308 both of which are interchangeable. It is also chambered for the .338 Lapua cartridge which does not interchange with the other calibers. The cheekpiece is improved and a new front rail has been added to this model. Barrel length is 24" without muzzlebrake. Weight is about 10.4 lbs.

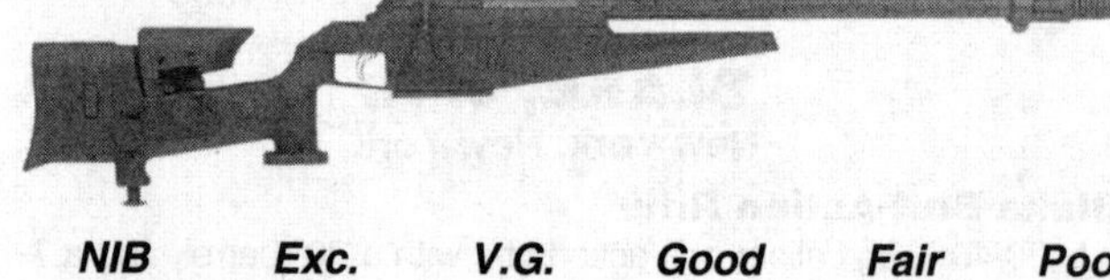

NIB	Exc.	V.G.	Good	Fair	Poor
3475	2700	—	—	—	—

NOTE: For .338 Lapua add $350.

Model R-93 Grand Luxe

Offered in the same wide range of calibers as other Blaser models with the addition of a high grade walnut stock, fully hand engraved receiver, and matching scroll sideplates. Introduced in 1999.

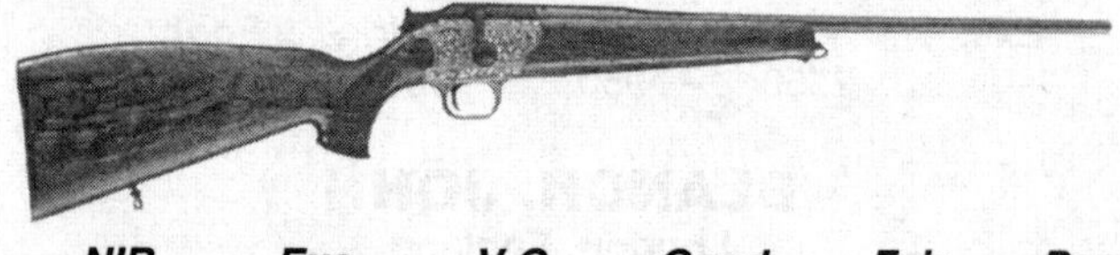

NIB	Exc.	V.G.	Good	Fair	Poor
4675	3700	—	—	—	—

NOTE: Add $200 for left-hand rifles.

Model K-95 Standard

This is a single-shot model with break-open action.The receiver is aluminum with engraving on the side plates. Barrel length is 23.6" for standard calibers and 25.6" for magnum calibers. Oil finish Turkish walnut stock. Interchangeable barrels in calibers from .243 to .300 Wby. Magnum. Weight is about 5.5 lbs. Introduced in 2001.

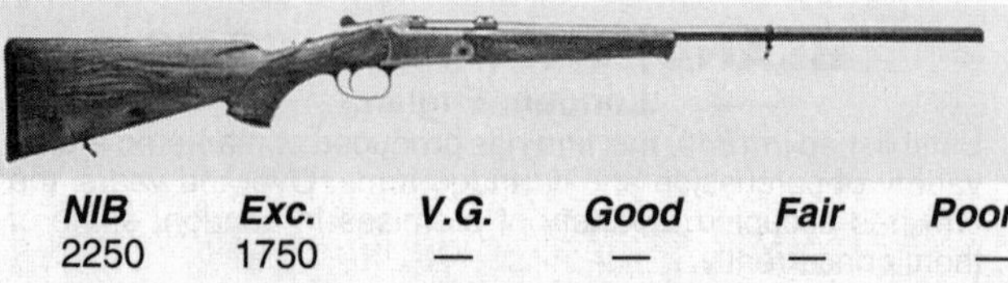

NIB	Exc.	V.G.	Good	Fair	Poor
2250	1750	—	—	—	—

Model K-95 Luxus

Same as above but with fancy Turkish walnut stock and hand engraving on receiver and side plates.

NIB	Exc.	V.G.	Good	Fair	Poor
2600	2000	—	—	—	—

Model K-95 Stutzen

Introduced in 2003 this break-action single-shot rifle is offered in 23 calibers. Fancy walnut Mannlicher-style, two-piece stock. Interchangeable barrels.

NIB	Exc.	V.G.	Good	Fair	Poor
3950	3200	—	—	—	—

Ultimate Bolt-Action

As above, with a silver-plated and engraved receiver as well as a set trigger.

NIB	Exc.	V.G.	Good	Fair	Poor
1500	1300	1050	825	700	375

Special Order Ultimate

The above model is available in a variety of finishes and degrees of decoration.

Ultimate Deluxe

NIB	Exc.	V.G.	Good	Fair	Poor
1600	1400	1150	925	800	400

Ultimate Super Deluxe

NIB	Exc.	V.G.	Good	Fair	Poor
4250	3750	3250	2500	2000	1000

Ultimate Exclusive

NIB	Exc.	V.G.	Good	Fair	Poor
5700	5000	4500	3500	2600	1300

Ultimate Super Exclusive

NIB	Exc.	V.G.	Good	Fair	Poor
8900	7900	6800	5000	4000	2000

Ultimate Royal

NIB	Exc.	V.G.	Good	Fair	Poor
11500	9500	7500	6000	4000	2000

NOTE: Extra interchangeable caliber barrels for the above rifles are available at $700 to $1,200 per barrel depending on the grade.

Blaser S2 Double Rifle

Chambered for the .375 H&H, .500/.416 NE, .470 NE, and the .500 NE cartridges. Offered in different grades from Standard, Luxus, Super Luxus, Exclusiv, Super Exclusiv, and the Royal. Prices range from $7,000 for the Standard to $26,500 for the Royal.

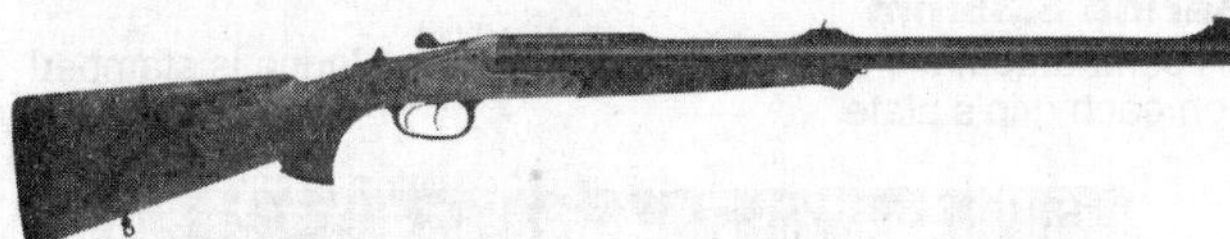

S2 rifle in Super Luxus grade

HANDGUNS

Blaser HHS

This single-shot pistol has an R93 receiver and is fitted with a 14" barrel and pistol-grip fancy Turkish walnut stock. All R93 calibers are offered. Offered in both right- and left-hand models. Introduced in 2003.

NIB	Exc.	V.G.	Good	Fair	Poor
2650	2100	—	—	—	—

NOTE: Add $100 for left-hand models.

BLISS, F. D.

New Haven, Connecticut

Bliss Pocket Revolver

A .25 caliber spur trigger revolver with a 3.25" octagon barrel, 6-shot magazine, and a square butt. Blued with either hard rubber or walnut grips. The barrel is stamped "F.D. Bliss New Haven, Ct." There was an all-brass framed version made early in the production, and this model would be worth approximately 50 percent more than the values listed here for the standard model. Approximately 3,000 manufactured circa 1860 to 1863.

Exc.	V.G.	Good	Fair	Poor
—	—	850	375	100

BLISS & GOODYEAR

New Haven, Connecticut

Pocket Model Revolver

A .28 caliber percussion revolver with a 3" octagonal barrel, 6-shot magazine, unfluted cylinder and a solid frame with a removable side plate. Blued with a brass frame and walnut grips. Approximately 3,000 manufactured in 1860.

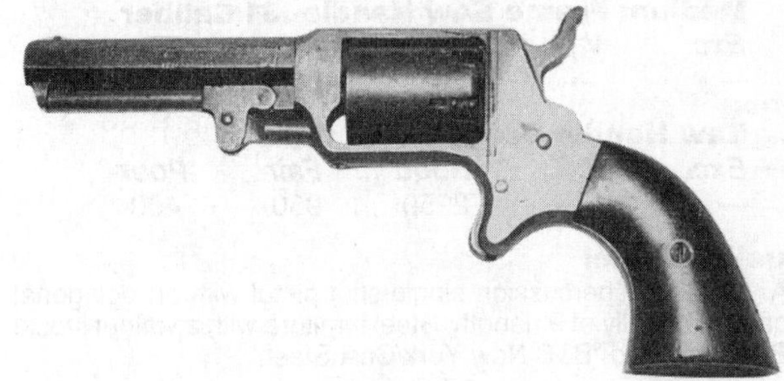

Exc.	V.G.	Good	Fair	Poor
—	—	1150	500	200

BLISSETT

SEE—English Military Firearms

BLUNT & SYMS

New York, New York

Under Hammer Pepperbox

Pepperboxes produced by Blunt & Syms are noteworthy for the fact that they incorporate a ring trigger cocking/revolving mechanism and a concealed under hammer. They were produced in a variety of calibers and the standard finish was blued. Normally these pistols are found marked simply "A-C" on the face of the barrel group. Some examples though are marked "Blunt & Syms New York."

This firm was in business from approximately 1837 to 1855.

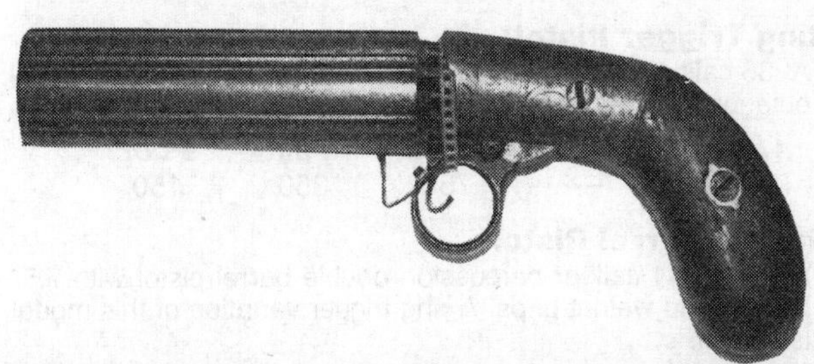

REMINDER

Perhaps the best advice is for the collector to take his time.

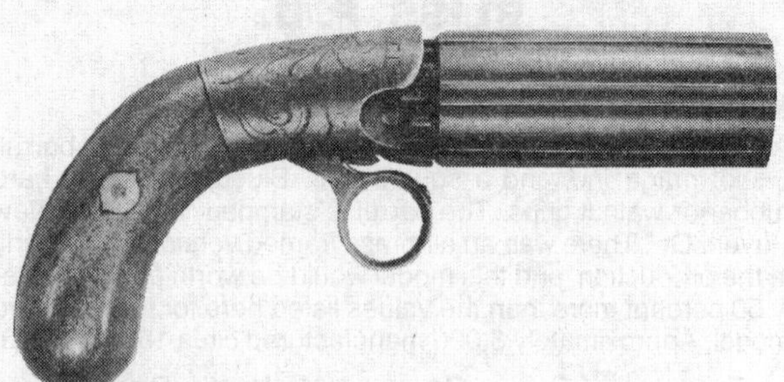

Small Frame Round Handle .25-.28 Caliber

Exc.	V.G.	Good	Fair	Poor
—	—	1250	600	200

Medium Frame Round Handle .31 Caliber

Exc.	V.G.	Good	Fair	Poor
—	—	1000	400	150

Round Handle Dragoon .36 Caliber

Exc.	V.G.	Good	Fair	Poor
—	—	2250	850	350

Medium Frame Saw Handle .31 Caliber

Exc.	V.G.	Good	Fair	Poor
—	—	1250	500	250

Saw Handle Dragoon .36 Caliber

Exc.	V.G.	Good	Fair	Poor
—	—	2250	950	400

Dueling Pistol

A .52 caliber percussion single-shot pistol with an octagonal barrel normally of 9" length. Steel furniture with a walnut stock. Barrel marked "B&S New York/Cast Steel."

Exc.	V.G.	Good	Fair	Poor
—	—	1500	650	300

Single-Shot Bar Hammer

A .36 caliber single-shot percussion pistol with a 6" half-octagonal barrel and a bar hammer. Blued or browned with walnut grips. Marked as above.

Exc.	V.G.	Good	Fair	Poor
—	—	900	400	200

Side Hammer Pocket Pistol

A .31 or .35 caliber single-shot percussion pistol with a 2.5" to 6" octagonal barrel. Blued with walnut grips.

Exc.	V.G.	Good	Fair	Poor
—	—	900	400	175

Side Hammer Belt Pistol

As above, in calibers ranging from .36 to .44 with barrel lengths of 4" or 6".

Exc.	V.G.	Good	Fair	Poor
—	—	1000	400	250

Ring Trigger Pistol

A .36 caliber percussion single-shot pistol with a 3" to 5" half-octagonal barrel and a ring trigger. Blued with walnut grips.

Exc.	V.G.	Good	Fair	Poor
—	—	750	350	150

Double Barrel Pistol

A .36 to .44 caliber percussion double barrel pistol with 7.5" barrels and walnut grips. A ring trigger variation of this model is known.

Exc.	V.G.	Good	Fair	Poor
—	—	950	400	150

Double Barrel Under Hammer Pistol

As above, with two under hammers and in .34 caliber with 4" barrels.

Exc.	V.G.	Good	Fair	Poor
—	—	1250	550	200

Derringer Style Pistol

A .50 caliber single-shot percussion pistol with a 3" barrel, German silver mounts and a walnut stock. The lock is marked "Blunt & Syms/New York."

Exc.	V.G.	Good	Fair	Poor
—	—	1250	500	250

BODEO

Italian Service Revolver

System Bodeo Modello 1889 (Enlisted Model)

Exc.	V.G.	Good	Fair	Poor
750	550	400	250	100

Modello 1889 (Officer's Model)

Exc.	V.G.	Good	Fair	Poor
750	550	400	250	100

BOLUMBURO, G.

Eibar, Spain

Bristol

A semi-automatic pistol in caliber 7.65mm made in the style of the Ruby military pistols. Bristol is stamped on the slide. Wood grips.

Courtesy James Rankin

Exc.	V.G.	Good	Fair	Poor
275	175	150	90	40

Marina 6.35mm

A semi-automatic pistol in caliber 6.35mm. Marina is stamped on each grip's plate.

Courtesy James Rankin

Exc.	V.G.	Good	Fair	Poor
250	175	150	90	40

Marina 7.65mm

As above but in 7.65mm with Marina stamped on the slide. Wood grips and a lanyard loop.

Courtesy James Rankin

Exc.	V.G.	Good	Fair	Poor
250	175	150	90	40

Rex

A semi-automatic pistol in caliber 7.65mm. "Rex" is stamped on the slide with wood grips and a lanyard loop.

Courtesy James Rankin

Exc.	V.G.	Good	Fair	Poor
250	175	150	90	40

BOND

SEE—English Military Firearms

BOND ARMS INC.

Grandbury, Texas

Texas Defender

This is a stainless steel over-and-under derringer chambered for a variety of calibers such as .45 Colt/.410, .357 Magnum, 9mm, .45 ACP, and .44 Magnum. Removable triggerguard. Barrels are interchangeable. Grips are laminated black ash or rosewood. Barrel length is 3" with blade front sight and fixed rear sight. Weight is approximately 21 oz. Introduced in 1997.

Exc.	V.G.	Good	Fair	Poor
330	275	—	—	—

Snake Slayer IV

Modern variation of the Remington over/under derringer. Interchangeable 4.5" barrel assemblies, rosewood grip panels, stainless finish, fixed sights. Chambered for .410-bore shotshell/.45 LC, 9mm, 10mm, .40 S&W, .45 ACP.

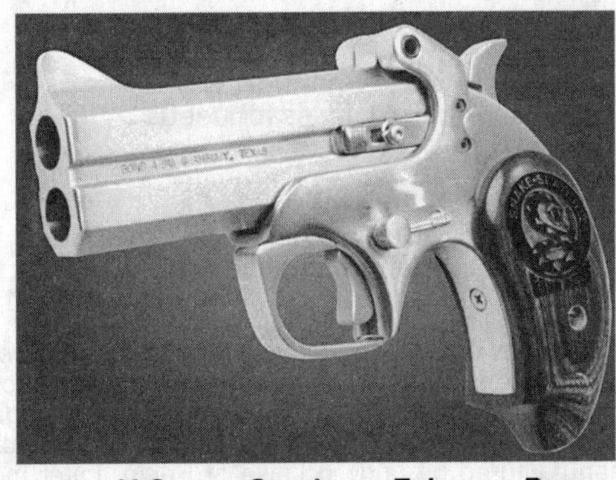

Exc.	V.G.	Good	Fair	Poor
400	325	—	—	—

Snake Slayer

3.5" barrels; weighs 22 oz. Interchangeable barrel assemblies, rosewood grip panels, stainless, fixed sights. Chambered for .410-bore shotshell/.45 LC, 9mm, 10mm, .40 S&W, .45 ACP).

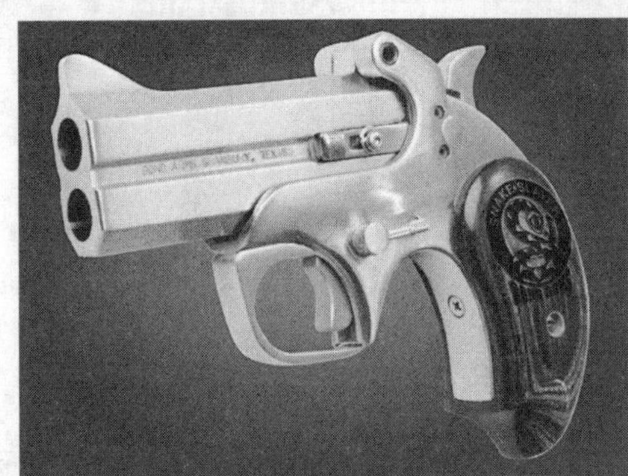

Exc.	V.G.	Good	Fair	Poor
375	315	—	—	—

Cowboy Defender

Derringer with 3" barrels. Weighs 19 oz. Interchangeable barrels, rosewood grip panels, stainless, fixed sights. Variety of chambering options such as .410-bore, .45 LC, .357 Mag, .38 Special, .45 ACP, .44 Special, .44-40 Win, .40 S&W, 10mm, etc. No trigger guard. Fixed triggerguard. Automatic extractor (except for 9mm, 10mm, .40 S&W, .45 ACP).

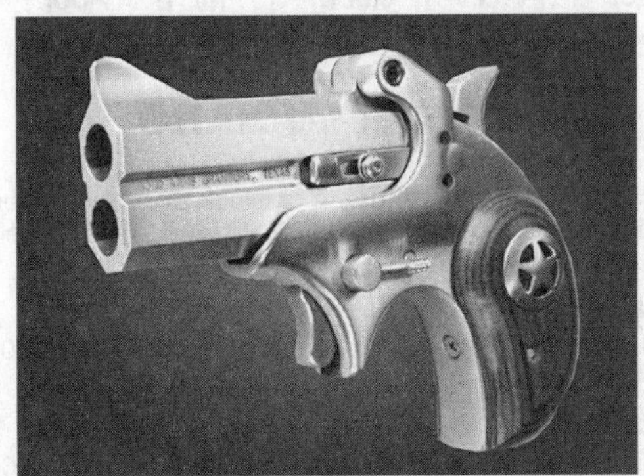

NIB	Exc.	V.G.	Good	Fair	Poor
389	350	300	225	150	75

Century 2000

Similar to Cowboy Defender but with 3.5" barrels to allow use of .410 Magnum, shotshells..357/.38 Special, .45 ACP, .44 Special, .44-40 Win, .40 S&W, 10mm, etc. Automatic extractor (except for 9mm, 10mm, .40 S&W, .45 ACP).

NIB	Exc.	V.G.	Good	Fair	Poor
389	350	300	225	150	75

BOOM

SEE—Shattuck, C.S.
Hatfield, Massachusetts

BORCHARDT

Berlin, Germany
Waffenfabrik Lowe

Borchardt

A forerunner of the German Luger. The Borchardt was a semi-automatic pistol chambered for the 7.65mm Borchardt cartridge. It was fitted with a 6.5" barrel and the magazine held 8 rounds. The pistol was designed by Hugo Borchardt and manufactured by Ludwig Lowe of Berlin. Later models were manufactured by DWM, Deutsch Waffen Und Munitionsfabriken, Berlin. Most Borchardts come with a case which holds shoulder stock, holster, extra magazines, and numerous other accessories.

Courtesy James Rankin

Pistol Only

Exc.	V.G.	Good	Fair	Poor
14000	10000	7500	5000	2500

Pistol with Case and Accessories

Exc.	V.G.	Good	Fair	Poor
19000	15000	10000	8000	4500

BORSIG

East Germany

The Borsig is the East German version of the Soviet Makarov pistol. It is a double-action, chambered for the Soviet 9x18mm cartridge. Its appearance is nearly identical to the Makarov.

Exc.	V.G.	Good	Fair	Poor
250	175	150	100	75

BOSIS, LUCIANO

Brescia, Italy

Bosis is a maker of high-grade sidelock over-and-under and side-by-side guns in gauges 12, 20, 28, and .410. These guns are made on a custom-order basis.

Over-and-Under

Values for used guns in excellent condition begin at $30,000. Secure an expert appraisal prior to sale.

Side-by-Side

Values for used guns in excellent condition begin at $20,000. Secure an expert appraisal prior to sale.

NOTE: Small gauge guns will bring a premium of 20 percent.

BOSS & CO.

London, England
SEE—British Double Guns

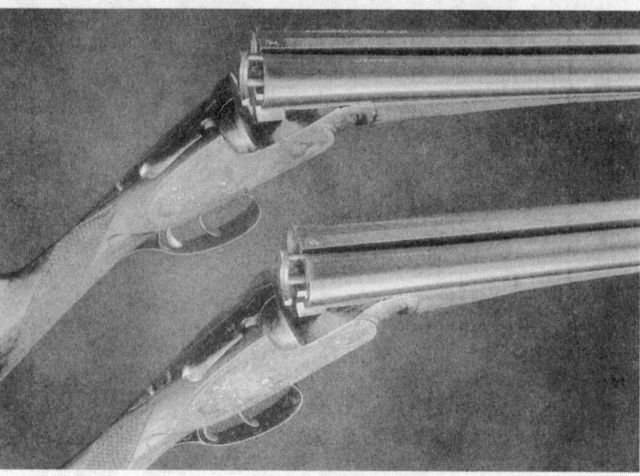

A cased pair of Boss & Co. sidelock shotguns

BOSWELL, CHARLES

London, England

One of England's more established makers of best-quality rifles and shotguns. In 1988 the company was purchased by an American consortium and the Cape Horn Outfitters of Charlotte, North Carolina, was appointed their sole agent.

Double Rifle, Boxlock

A .300 Holland & Holland, .375 Holland & Holland or .458 Winchester Magnum double-barrel boxlock rifle with double triggers and a walnut stock. Other features were made to the customer's specifications. A .600 Nitro Express version was also available.

Exc.	V.G.	Good	Fair	Poor
40000	32500	25000	17500	—

NOTE: .600 Nitro Express add 25 percent.

Double Rifle, Sidelock

As above, with Holland & Holland-style sidelocks.

Exc.	V.G.	Good	Fair	Poor
55000	40000	30000	20000	—

NOTE: .600 Nitro Express add 25 percent.

Double Barrel Shotguns

SEE—British Double Guns

BOSWORTH, B. M.

Warren, Pennsylvania

Bosworth Under Hammer Pistol

A .38 caliber single-shot percussion pistol with an under hammer and a 6" half-octagonal barrel. The frame is marked "BM Bosworth." Browned with brass grips forming part of the frame. Made circa 1850 to 1860.

Exc.	V.G.	Good	Fair	Poor
—	—	1500	550	200

BOWEN CLASSIC ARMS CORP.

Louisville, Tennessee

This firm was founded in 1980 by Hamilton Bowen and is a pioneer in the field of fine custom revolvers. The company offers an extensive number of modifications. Bowen Classic Arms only modifies customer's guns, it does not produce its own. Prices listed are for the modifications only on the customer-supplied revolver.

For Bowen Arms not listed, pricing is whatever the market will bear. Bowen Arms are (justifiably) highly valued by their owners.

Nimrod (RS09/RS09S & RS10/RS10S)

This package is performed on the Ruger single-action revolver. It has a 5.5" tapered barrel with integral muzzle band. Baughman ramp-style blade is pinned to the express front sight base. Chambered for .41 or .44 Magnum, .45 Colt, .454 Casull, or the .50 Action Express. Includes steel ejector housing. Also offered in .475 Linebaugh or the .500 Linebaugh. Offered in blue or stainless steel.

NIB	Exc.	V.G.	Good	Fair	Poor
1895	—	—	—	—	—

NOTE: Add $500 for stainless steel. Add $200 for blued .475 and .500 Linebaugh, and $500 for these calibers in stainless steel.

Alpine (RD02)

This package is done on the Ruger Redhawk revolver. The action is tuned with hammer nose refitted for maximum firing pin protrusion. Barrel cut to 4". Round butt frame and reshaped factory grips. The cylinder is beveled in the Colt blackpowder style. Fitted with Ashley Emerson sights for an additional $125.

NIB	Exc.	V.G.	Good	Fair	Poor
650	—	—	—	—	—

NOTE: Prices listed are for 6-shot Alpines. For 5-shot Alpines add $1,250.

Colt SAA Lightweight (CS02)

This conversion is done on the Colt SAA revolver. An action reliability package is performed. A 4" barrel with dovetail front sight (no 4.75" guns). Lightened/scalloped receiver. Rebluing and recoloring and a blackpowder cylinder chamfer.

NIB	Exc.	V.G.	Good	Fair	Poor
1395	—	—	—	—	—

BRAENDLIN ARMOURY

London, England

A .450 caliber 8-barrel pistol with hinged barrels, rotating firing pin and double-action lock. Manufactured during the 1880s.

Exc.	V.G.	Good	Fair	Poor
—	7500	4500	2750	1500

BRAND

Maker—E. Robinson
New York

Brand Breech Loading Carbine

A .50 rimfire caliber carbine with a 22" barrel secured by one barrel band. The frame is marked "Brand's Patent July 29,1862/E. Robinson Manfr/New York." This carbine was produced in limited numbers, primarily for trial purposes.

Exc.	V.G.	Good	Fair	Poor
—	—	5500	2500	900

BREDA, ERNESTO

Milan, Italy

Andromeda Special

A 12 gauge boxlock shotgun with various barrel lengths and chokes, single-selective triggers and automatic ejectors. Engraved, satin-finished with checkered walnut stock.

Exc.	V.G.	Good	Fair	Poor
950	650	550	425	300

Vega Special

A 12 gauge boxlock Over/Under shotgun with 26" or 28" barrels, various choke combinations, single-selective trigger and automatic ejectors. Engraved and blued with a checkered walnut stock.

Exc.	V.G	Good	Fair	Poor
750	600	500	375	275

Vega Special Trap

As above with a competition-styled stock and 30" or 32" barrels with full chokes.

Exc.	V.G.	Good	Fair	Poor
1250	900	750	500	350

Sirio Standard

Similar to the Vega with extensive engraving and a higher degree of finishing. There is a 28" barreled skeet version available in this model.

Exc.	V.G.	Good	Fair	Poor
2500	2000	1750	1250	650

Standard Semi-Automatic

A 12 gauge semi-automatic shotgun with 25" or 27" ventilated rib barrels, screw-in choke tubes, an engraved receiver, and checkered walnut stock.

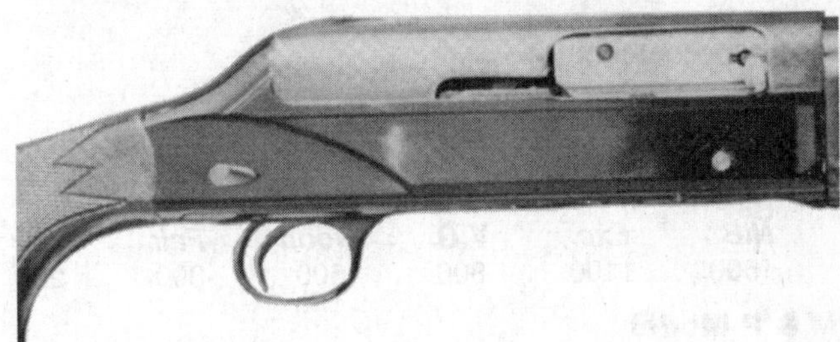

Exc.	V.G.	Good	Fair	Poor
350	275	225	175	125

Grade I

As above, with more engraving and finer wood.

Exc.	V.G.	Good	Fair	Poor
600	475	325	225	175

Grade II

A more elaborately engraved version of the Grade I.

Exc.	V.G.	Good	Fair	Poor
750	600	450	375	250

Grade III

The most deluxe version in this line with select walnut and extensive engraving.

Exc.	V.G.	Good	Fair	Poor
950	800	650	575	250

Magnum Model

Same as the standard but in 12 gauge Magnum.

Exc.	V.G.	Good	Fair	Poor
400	300	250	175	75

Gold Series Antares Standard

A 12 gauge semi-automatic shotgun with a 25" or 27" ventilated rib barrel and screw-in choke tubes. Blued with a checkered walnut stock.

Exc.	V.G.	Good	Fair	Poor
550	400	350	275	225

Gold Series Argus

As above, with alloy frame.

Exc.	V.G.	Good	Fair	Poor
600	425	375	300	250

Gold Series Aries

As above, except in 12 gauge Magnum.

Exc.	V.G.	Good	Fair	Poor
600	450	400	325	275

BREN 10

Dornaus & Dixon Inc.
Huntington Beach, California

Manufactured from 1983 until 1986.

Standard Bren 10

A 10mm caliber double-action semi-automatic pistol with a 5" barrel and 11-shot magazine. Stainless frame and satin-blued slide. Manufactured between 1983 and 1986.

NIB	Exc.	V.G.	Good	Fair	Poor
1500	1100	800	500	300	200

M & P Model

As above, with a matte black finish.

NIB	Exc.	V.G.	Good	Fair	Poor
1500	1100	800	500	300	200

Special Forces Model

Chambered for 10mm cartridge and is similar to the M&P model. Offered in two models: Model D has a dark finish while Model L has a light finish. Prices listed are for Model D, add 25 percent for Model L.

NIB	Exc.	V.G.	Good	Fair	Poor
1500	1200	900	700	500	250

Pocket Model

This model is fitted with a 4" barrel and 9-shot magazine.

NIB	Exc.	V.G.	Good	Fair	Poor
1150	1100	800	500	300	200

Dual-Master Presentation Model

As above, with a .45 caliber, extra barrel and slide and a fitted walnut case.

NIB	Exc.	V.G.	Good	Fair	Poor
3500	2500	1250	700	500	300

Marksman Model

Similar to the Standard Model but in .45 caliber. There were 250 manufactured for the "Marksman Shop" in Chicago, Illinois.

NIB	Exc.	V.G.	Good	Fair	Poor
1400	1000	750	500	300	200

Initial Commemorative

There were supposed to be 2,000 of these manufactured in 1986, but no one knows how many were actually produced. They are chambered for the 10mm and have a high-gloss blue finish with 22 kt. gold-plated details. The grips are laser engraved, and the whole affair is furnished in a walnut display case.

NIB	Exc.	V.G.	Good	Fair	Poor
3500	2500	—	—	—	—

BRETTON

Ste. Etienne, France

Baby Standard

A 12 or 20 gauge Over/Under shotgun with various barrel lengths and choke combinations and double triggers. Blued, checkered walnut stock.

NIB	Exc.	V.G.	Good	Fair	Poor
800	725	625	500	400	325

Deluxe Grade

A 12, 16, and 20 gauge Over/Under shotgun. Engraved, coin-finished receiver with walnut stock.

NIB	Exc.	V.G.	Good	Fair	Poor
1000	800	650	500	400	325

BRIGGS, H. A.

Norwich, Connecticut

Briggs Single-Shot Pistol

A .22 caliber single-shot spur trigger pistol with a 4" part-round/part-octagonal barrel with a downward rotating breech-block. Blued with walnut grips. Frame is marked "H.A. Briggs/Norwich, Ct." Manufactured in the 1850s and 1860s.

Exc.	V.G.	Good	Fair	Poor
—	—	2500	1100	400

BRILEY MANUFACTURING INC.

Houston, Texas

El Presidente Model—Unlimited

This 1911-style pistol can be built on a Caspian Arms, STI, or SVI frame. Includes scope mount, compensator, match barrel, cocking sight, lowered and flared ejection port, front and rear serrations, aluminum guide rod, and numerous other custom features. Offered in most calibers. Blued finish.

NIB	Exc.	V.G.	Good	Fair	Poor
2400	2000	—	—	—	—

Versatility Plus Model—Limited

Built on a 1911 frame with BoMar sight, checkered mainspring housing and checkered front strap. Many other custom features. Available in .45 ACP, .40 S&W, and 9mm.

This symbol denotes "Sleepers" with rapidly-rising values and/or significant collector potential.

NIB	Exc.	V.G.	Good	Fair	Poor
1750	1500	—	—	—	—

Versatility Model—Limited

Similar to the above model but without several features such as the checkered front strap. Available in .45 ACP, .40 S&W, 9mm.

NIB	Exc.	V.G.	Good	Fair	Poor
1250	1000	—	—	—	—

Lightning Model—Action Pistol

Built on a 1911 frame this pistol features many custom components including a titanium compensator. Weight no more than 40 oz. Available in 9mm and .38 Super only.

NIB	Exc.	V.G.	Good	Fair	Poor
2200	1800	—	—	—	—

Carry Comp Model—Defense

Built on a 1911 frame this model features a dual port cone compensator with many custom features. Barrel length is about 5". Offered in .45 ACP only.

NIB	Exc.	V.G.	Good	Fair	Poor
2150	1800	—	—	—	—

BRITISH DOUBLES

By Douglas Tate

ENGLISH GUNMAKERS IN NORTH AMERICA

Following is an alphabetic listing of British makers whose guns are most frequently encountered with dealers and at auctions.

Army & Navy Co-operative Society Limited, London

Started in 1871 as an organization by which military men could buy wine wholesale, the membership soon increased to include diplomats and foreign service bureaucrats, while the catalogue expanded to include every manner of household and sporting goods. Most guns were acquired in the Birmingham trade and many were Webley & Scott products.

Boxlock non-ejectors $1,000 to $3,000
Boxlock ejectors $1,500 to $5,000
Sidelock non-ejectors $2,000 to $7,000
Sidelock ejectors $3,000 to $15,000
Hammer Guns $1,000 to $3,000

Atkin, Henry

The first Henry Atkin was one of James Purdey' s original workman, his son started the family business in 1878. J. P. Morgan and Gough Thomas were both Atkin customers because they felt the Atkin's offered the same quality as Purdey's without as high a cost.

Boxlock non-ejectors $1,500 to $4,000
Boxlock ejectors $2,000 to $8,500
Sidelock non-ejectors $2,000 to $10,000
Sidelock ejectors $4,000 to $30,000
Hammer Guns $2,000 to $10,000

Beesley, Frederick

Frederick Beesley served his apprenticeship with Moore and Grey and worked for several London gun makers including James Purdey and Son before establishing his own business in 1879. His claim to fame is the self opening system he patented (No. 31 of 1880) and licensed to James Purdey for "five shillings for every gun made." To this day every side-by-side gun by Purdey is built on this system.

Boxlock non-ejectors $1,500 to $4,000
Boxlock ejectors $2,000 to $8,500
Sidelock non-ejectors $2,000 to $10,000
Sidelock ejectors $4,000 to $30,000
Hammer Guns $2,000 to $10,000
Over & Unders $5,000 to $30,000

Blanch, John

John Blanch apprenticed with Jackson Mortimer and married his master's daughter. Later he working with John Manton. Today the Blanch name is perhaps best remembered for *"A Cen-*

tury of Guns" first published in 1909 and written by H. J. Blanch grandson of the founder.

Boxlock non-ejectors $1,500 to $4,000
Boxlock ejectors $2,000 to $8,500
Sidelock non-ejectors $2,000 to $10,000
Sidelock ejectors $4,000 to $30,000
Hammer Guns $2,000 to $10,000

Bland, Thomas

Thomas Bland started in business in 1840 in Birmingham. Bland moved to London in 1875 and occupied a variety of premises close to Charing Cross Station until at least the 1960s. They well known for their wildfowling guns, particularly the "Brent" model which enjoyed a wide following. The Bland firm is still in business in Benton, Pennsylvania.

Boxlock non-ejectors $1,000 to $3,000
Boxlock ejectors $1,500 to $5,000
Sidelock non-ejectors $2,000 to $7,000
Sidelock ejectors $3,000 to $15,000
Hammer Guns $1,000 to $3,000

Boss & Co.

Thomas Boss worked for the great Joseph Manton before becoming a pieceworker to the London trade. In 1891 John Robertson, a Scotsman, was taken in as a partner. Under Robertson's control the firm established itself as London's best gun maker rivaled only by Purdey's. Beyond intrinsic quality Boss is famous for their single trigger and over-and-under designs which are both widely copied. A scarce 20 bore assisted opening over-and-under by Boss sold as Sotheby's, Glen-eagles sale in August 1998 for $76,500.

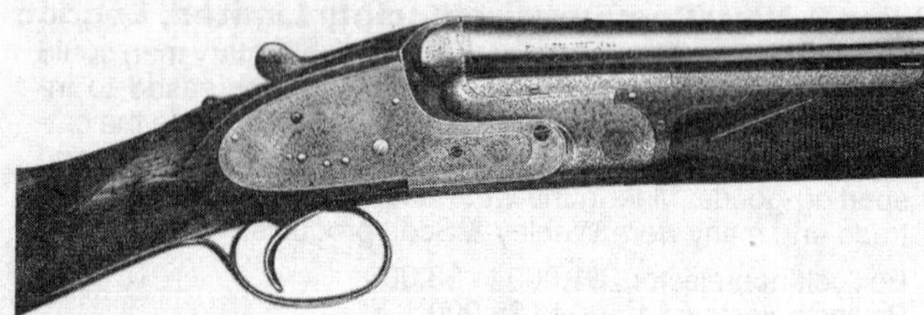

Boxlock non-ejectors $1,500 to $4,000
Boxlock ejectors $2,000 to $8,500
Sidelock non-ejectors $2,000 to $10,000
Sidelock ejectors $4,000 to $30,000
Hammer Guns $2,000 to $10,000
Over & Unders $20,000 to $100,000

Boswell, Charles

Charles Boswell worked for Thomas Gooch and the Enfield factory before establishing himself in 1872. He was a skillful pigeon shot and the firm's reputation rested for many years on their ability to build live bird guns. The records are currently in the hands of G. R. Beckstead in Florida.

Boxlock non-ejectors $1,000 to $3,000
Boxlock ejectors $1,500 to $5,000
Sidelock non-ejectors $2,000 to $7,000
Sidelock ejectors $3,000 to $15,000
Hammer Guns $1,000 to $3,000

Brazier, Joseph

Current Importer/Distributor FNGB, Colorado Springs, CO

Founded in 1831 and best known for high quality locks, receivers, and components supplied to the English gun trade. The majority of Best Guns have used Brazier components. Today, this firm makes close tolerance CNC parts, Best Guns of its own design. Made to order Best sidelock with interchangeable parts begin at $20,000.

Boxlock non-ejectors $2,000 to $3,000
Boxlock ejectors $2,000 to $4,500
Sidelock non-ejectors $20,000 to $25,000
Sidelock ejectors $20,000 to $250,000
Hammer Guns $4,000 to $15,000

Brown, A.A.

Albert Arthur Brown established his business in Whittal St., Birmingham in 1930. The firm has maintained a reputation as one of the finest makers to the trade having built guns for Churchill, H & H and Westley Richards. They still make guns today in Alverchurch, not far from Birmingham.

Boxlock non-ejectors $1,000 to $3,000
Boxlock ejectors $1,500 to $5,000
Sidelock non-ejectors $2,000 to $7,000
Sidelock ejectors $3,000 to $15,000

Brown, David McKay

David McKay Brown started his apprenticeship with Alex Martin in Glasgow and completed it with John Dickson in Edinburgh. His renown rest on his ability with traditional Scottish round action guns and his own patent over/under based on a trigger plate action. He works in Bothwell just outside Glasgow. A fine pair of 20 bore assisted opening round action guns by David McKay Brown sold at Sotheby's, Gleneagles sale in August 1998 for $52,200.

Round Action & O/U Guns $20,000 to $100,000

Churchill, E.J.

Edwin John Churchill served his time with William Jeffery & Son and was famous as a pigeon shot. Today the firm is best remembered for its 25" barreled guns introduced by Robert Churchill in the 1920s. The firm is still in business in West Wycombe, England.

Boxlock non-ejectors $1,500 to $4,000
Boxlock ejectors $2,000 to $8,500
Sidelock non-ejectors $2,000 to $10,000
Sidelock ejectors $4,000 to $30,000
Hammer Guns $2,000 to $10,000
Over & Unders $10,000 to $50,000

Cogswell & Harrison

Benjamin Cogswell claimed to be in business from 1770. The firm's reputation rests on its self-opening game guns. Today this tradition continues with ex-Purdey craftsman Allen Crewe. building fine Beesley action self-openers and Woodward-style O/U's. They are in Royal Berkshire just west of London.

Boxlock non-ejectors $1,000 to $3,000
Boxlock ejectors $1,500 to $5,000
Sidelock non-ejectors $2,000 to $7,000
Sidelock ejectors $3,000 to $30,000
Hammer Guns $1,000 to $3,000
Over & Unders $10,000 to $50,000

Dickson, John

John Dickson served his time with J. Wallace in Edinburgh. In 1882 he registered the first of a series of patents which would culminate in the famous Scottish round action gun. Dickson's continue to build these guns to this day at their Frederick Street premises.

Boxlock non-ejectors $1,000 to $3,000
Boxlock ejectors $1,500 to $5,000
Sidelock non-ejectors $2,000 to $7,000
Sidelock ejectors $3,000 to $15,000
Hammer Guns $2,000 to $10,000
Round Action Guns $5,000 to $50,000

Evans, William

William Evans worked for both Purdey and H & H before setting up on his own in 1883. Many of the Evans guns appear to have been made by Webley & Scott and other Birmingham gun makers. Today the firm builds its own guns and is located in St. James, central London.

Boxlock non-ejectors $1,000 to $3,000
Boxlock ejectors $1,500 to $5,000
Sidelock non-ejectors $2,000 to $7,000
Sidelock ejectors $3,000 to $50,000
Hammer Guns $1,000 to $3,000

Fraser, Daniel

Daniel Fraser apprenticed with Alexander Henry in Edinburgh before opening his own business on Leith St. He is perhaps best remembered for his rifles and distinctive, fancy back boxlocks. The firm he founded is once again in business in Scotland.

Boxlock non-ejectors $1,000 to $3,000
Boxlock ejectors $1,500 to $5,000
Sidelock non-ejectors $2,000 to $7,000
Sidelock ejectors $3,000 to $50,000
Hammer Guns $1,000 to $3,000

Grant, Stephen

Stephen Grant was apprenticed to Kavanagh of Dublin before working with Charles Lancaster and Thomas Boss in London. The firm is perhaps best remembered for its distinctive sidelever guns with fluted fences. The guns are made today in Essendon, Herts, England.

Boxlock non-ejectors $1,500 to $4,000
Boxlock ejectors $2,000 to $8,500
Sidelock non-ejectors $2,000 to $10,000
Sidelock ejectors $4,000 to $50,000
Hammer Guns $2,000 to $10,000

Gibbs, George

The Gibbs Company has been in Bristol, England since the 1830s. Though they have built many fine shotguns the name is also strongly associated with rifles. The firm is now owned by Ian Crudgington famous for his book *"The British Shotgun, Vol. I & II."*

Boxlock non-ejectors $1,000 to $3,000
Boxlock ejectors $1,500 to $5,000
Sidelock non-ejectors $2,000 to $7,000
Sidelock ejectors $3,000 to $15,000
Hammer Guns $1,000 to $3,000

Greener, W.W.

William Greener apprenticed with Burnand of Newcastle before working with John Manton in London. His son, W.W. Greener, took over in 1869 and built his reputation with "a medium-priced weapon of sound workmanship. The name will forever be associated with the "Greener crossbolt." In recent years the company, still based in Birmingham, has built a small quantity of high grade guns.

Boxlock non-ejectors $1,000 to $3,000
Boxlock ejectors $1,500 to $50,000
Sidelock non-ejectors $2,000 to $7,000
Sidelock ejectors $3,000 to $100,000
Hammer Guns $1,000 to $3,000

Hellis, Charles

Charles Hellis was established in 1884 in Westbourne Park, London. The most frequently encountered Hellis guns here in the U.S. are probably the 2" 12 bore and "featherweight" models. Charles Hellis is once again doing business from the west end of London.

Boxlock non-ejectors $1,000 to $3,000
Boxlock ejectors $1,500 to $5,000
Sidelock non-ejectors $2,000 to $7,000
Sidelock ejectors $3,000 to $15,000

Henry, Alexander

Alexander Henry has been Edinburg's rifle maker since 1853. Between 1860 and 1882 Henry registered over a dozen patents, mostly for falling block and double rifles. Henry built rifles for Queen Victoria, her husband Prince Albert and their son The Duke of Edinburg. The name and records were eventually acquired by Alex Martin of Glasgow and now reside with Dickson's in Edinburg.

Boxlock non-ejectors $1,500 to $3,000
Boxlock ejectors $2,000 to $6,000
Sidelock non-ejectors $2,000 to $9,000
Sidelock ejectors $4,000 to $15,000

Holland & Holland

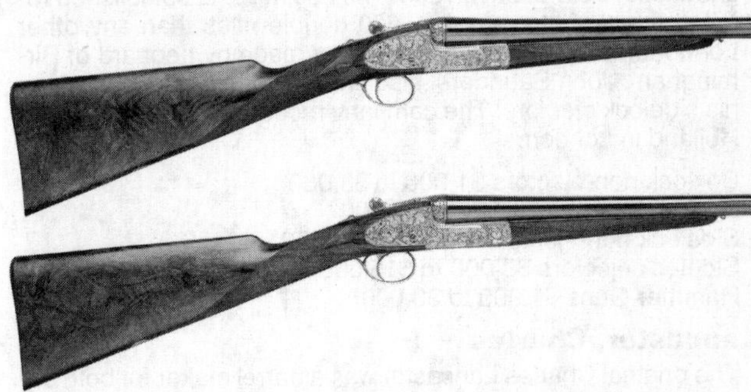

Pair of H&H Royal Deluxe Self-Opening Ejector Guns

Harris Holland started as a tobacconist but moved into guns around 1848. Famous for presentation quality guns built for figures as diverse as President Theodore Roosevelt and The Nizam of Hyderabad, they continue to trade under the auspices of Channel, the well-known French luxury goods company.

Boxlock non-ejectors $1,5000 to $4,000
Boxlock ejectors $2,000 to $9,000
Sidelock non-ejectors $2,000 to $10,000
Sidelock ejectors $4,000 to $100,000
Hammer Guns $2,000 to $10,000
Over & Unders $8,000 to $100,000

Horsley, Thomas

The firm was founded by Thomas Horsley in about 1832 in York, Yorkshire. Famous for their sliding thumb piece toplever hammer guns they are considered by many to be the best of the provincial gun makers. No longer in business.

Boxlock non-ejectors $1,000 to $3,000
Boxlock ejectors $1,500 to $5,000
Sidelock non-ejectors $2,000 to $7,000
Sidelock ejectors $3,000 to $15,000
Hammer Guns $1,000 to $3,000

Horton, William

William Horton was a Burmingham gunmaker who moved to Whitehaven in north-west England before settling in Glasgow in 1863. He died in 1896 but his son Oliver continued registering a series of patents that culminated in the firm's distinctive boxlock gun. Horton was acquired by another Glasgow gunmaker, Arthur Allen, in 1924.

Boxlock non-ejectors $1,500 to $3,000
Boxlock ejectors $2,000 to $6,000
Sidelock non-ejectors $2,000 to $9,000
Sidelock ejectors $4,000 to $15,000

Jeffrey, W.J.

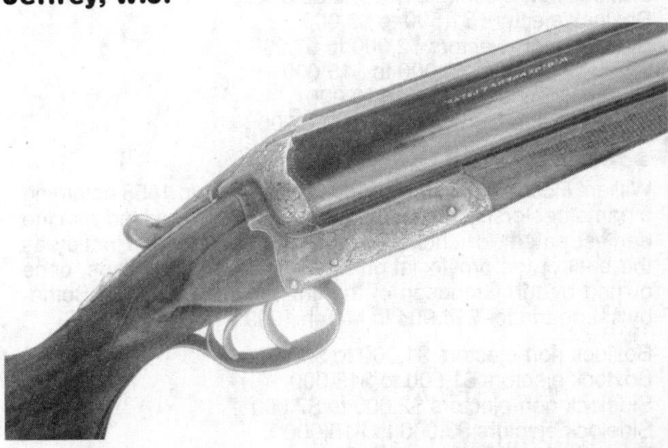

Courtesy Bonhams & Butterfields

William Jackman Jeffery managed Philip Webley's London showroom from 1887 to 1894. The business he established retailed more of the massive .600 double rifles than any other London maker. but these were likely made by Leonard of Birmingham. John Saunders, also of Birmingham, made many of his sidelock ejectors. The company records are with Holland & Holland in London.

Boxlock non-ejectors $1,000 to $3,000
Boxlock ejectors $1,500 to $5,000
Sidelock non-ejectors $2,000 to $7,000
Sidelock ejectors $3,000 to $15,000
Hammer Guns $1,000 to $3,000

Lancaster, Charles

The original Charles Lancaster was a barrel maker for both Joseph Manton and the first James Purdey. In 1878 the business was acquired by A.A. Thorn who established the firm's name with "The Art of Shooting," which ran to at least 14 editions and which he wrote under the pseudonym of "Charles Lancaster." The firm was famous for its four barrel pistols/rifles/shotguns and continues today from Bishopswood, Somerset.

Boxlock non-ejectors $1,000 to $3,000
Boxlock ejectors $1,500 to $5,000
Sidelock non-ejectors $2,000 to $7,000
Sidelock ejectors $3,000 to $15,000
Hammer Guns $1,000 to $3,000
Over & Unders $5,000 to $20,000

Lang, Joseph

Joseph Lang worked for Alexander Wilson before starting out on his own in 1821. The firm is best remembered for its "Vena Contracta" gun which had a 12 bore breech that tapered to 16 bore at the muzzle. The company was until recently owned by a Texan but has since returned to England.

Boxlock non-ejectors $1,000 to $3,000
Boxlock ejectors $1,500 to $5,000
Sidelock non-ejectors $2,000 to $7,000
Sidelock ejectors $3,000 to $35,000
Hammer Guns $1,000 to $3,000

Lewis, G.E.

George Edward Lewis was born in 1829 and apprenticed in "all branches" of the Birmingham gun trade. His fame rests on his magnum "gun of the period" which was popular with generations of wildfowlers. The firm continues today from Halesowen, West Midlands.

Boxlock non-ejectors $1,500 to $4,000
Boxlock ejectors $2,000 to $8,500
Sidelock non-ejectors $2,000 to $10,000
Sidelock ejectors $4,000 to $30,000
Hammer Guns $2,000 to $10,000

MacNaughton & Son

James MacNaughton started in business in 1864 in Edinburgh. His fame rests on his patent Edinburgh round action gun of 1879. The firm is back in business in Edinburgh.

Boxlock non-ejectors $1,000 to $3,000
Boxlock ejectors $1,500 to $5,000
Sidelock non-ejectors $2,000 to $7,000
Sidelock ejectors $3,000 to $15,000
Hammer Guns $2,000 to $10,000
Round Action Guns $3,000 to $20,000

Pape, W.R.

William Rochester Pape started his business in 1858 enlarging a game dealership owned by his family. He is credited with the earliest patent for choke boring (1866) and rivals Horsley as the best of the provincial gun makers. A 16 bore Pape, once owned by the Grandson of the firm's founder, sold at Sotheby's, London for $14,904 in March 1999.

Boxlock non-ejectors $1,000 to $3,000
Boxlock ejectors $1,500 to $15,000
Sidelock non-ejectors $2,000 to $7,000
Sidelock ejectors $3,000 to $15,000
Hammer Guns $1,000 to $3,000

Powell, William

William Powell started out in Birmingham in 1802. Their top "lift uplever" are considered highly desirable. They continue in Birmingham today.

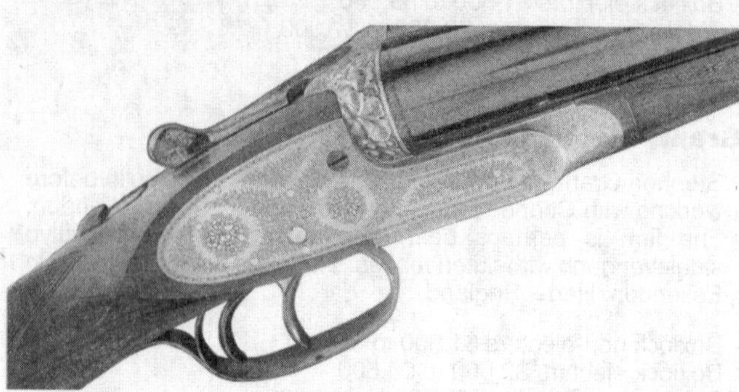

Courtesy Bonhams & Butterfields

Boxlock non-ejectors $1,000 to $3,000
Boxlock ejectors $1,500 to $5,000
Sidelock non-ejectors $2,000 to $7,000
Sidelock ejectors $3,000 to $35,000
Hammer Guns $1,000 to $3,000

Purdey & Son, James

James Purdey, one of Joseph Manton's earliest gun makers, starting in about 1803. The famous Purdey underbolt, developed in 1863 is perhaps the most widely disseminated of all shotgun patents. Today the company is still considered the world's greatest gun makers. A pair of Purdey 16 bore guns, once were owned by Edward VIII when he was Prince of Wales, sold at Sotheby's, Geneva, in 1991 for $196,428.

Boxlock non-ejectors $1,5000 to $4,000
Boxlock ejectors $2,000 to $9,000
Sidelock non-ejectors $2,000 to $10,000
Sidelock ejectors $4,000 to $100,000
Hammer Guns $2,000 to $10,000
Over & Unders $8,000 to $100,000

Richards, William Westley

William Westley Richards founded his own company in 1812 at 82 High St., Birmingham. In 1975 two of the firms workforce developed the famous Anson & Deeley boxlock action which was made hand detachable in 1897. The firm continues in Bournebrook to this day.

Boxlock non-ejectors $1,500 to $4,000
Boxlock ejectors $2,000 to $8,500
Sidelock non-ejectors $2,000 to $10,000
Sidelock ejectors $4,000 to $30,000
Hammer Guns $2,000 to $10,000
Over & Unders $10,000 to $100,000

Rigby, John

John Rigby started for himself in Dublin in 1775. The company enjoys a 200-year reputation as fine rifle makers and are famous for their .416 proprietary cartridge. They were recently sold and moved to California.

Boxlock non-ejectors $1,500 to $4,000
Boxlock ejectors $2,000 to $8,500
Sidelock non-ejectors $2,000 to $10,000
Sidelock ejectors $4,000 to $35,000
Hammer Guns $2,000 to $10,000

Rosson & Co., C. S.

C. S. Rosson was a provincial maker active from the turn of the century in Norwich. They produced a slide opener, self openers built on the Edwin V. Smith patent and a 2" chambered gun they called the "Twentieth Century." They failed in 1957.

Boxlock non-ejectors $1,000 to $3,000
Boxlock ejectors $1,500 to $5,000
Sidelock non-ejectors $2,000 to $7,000
Sidelock ejectors $3,000 to $15,000
Hammer Guns $1,000 to $3,000

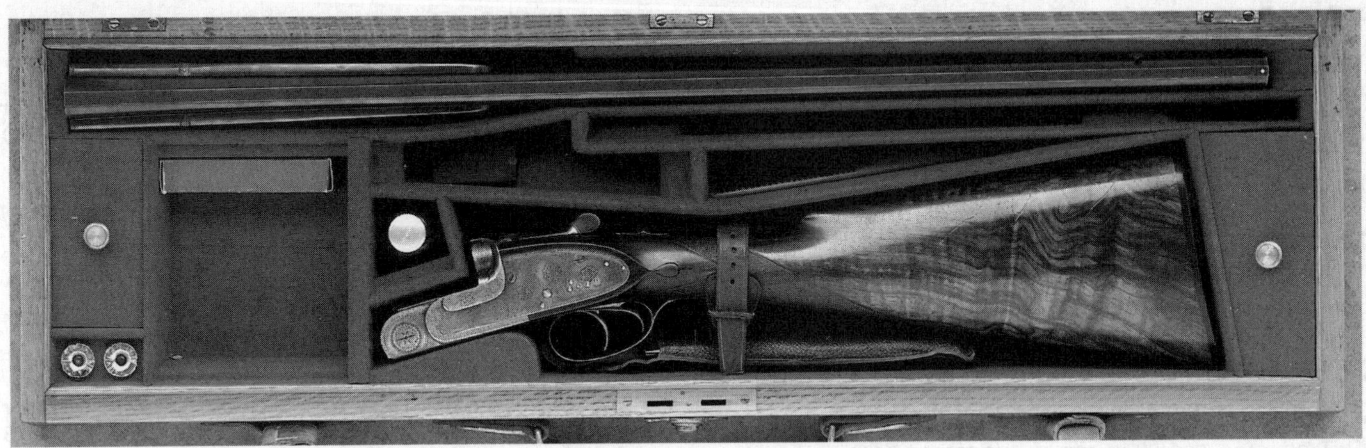

Scott, W & C

William Scott served an apprenticeship with a Bury St. Edmund's gun maker, possibly Ben or Charles Parker. In 1865 the firm contributed to the perfection of the English gun by developing the standard spindle, which connects the Purdey bolt to the top lever. They no longer trade.

Boxlock non-ejectors $1,000 to $3,000
Boxlock ejectors $1,500 to $5,000
Sidelock non-ejectors $2,000 to $7,000
Sidelock ejectors $3,000 to $15,000
Hammer Guns $1,000 to $3,000

Watson Brothers

Watson Brothers date from 1875 and are famous for their small bore guns. In recent years the company has been resuscitated by Mike Louca, who is establishing himself as a builder of round bodied over-and-unders.

Boxlock non-ejectors $1,000 to $3,000
Boxlock ejectors $1,500 to $5,000
Sidelock non-ejectors $2,000 to $7,000
Sidelock ejectors $3,000 to $15,000
Hammer Guns $1,000 to $3,000
Over & Unders $30,000 to $100,000

Webley & Scott

Philip Webley began his apprenticeship as a lockmaker in 1827, probably with Ryan & Watson. In 1897 he merged with W. & C. Scott and built semi machine-made shotguns using techniques previously employed on revolvers. The firm ceased operations in 1991.

Boxlock non-ejectors $1,000 to $3,000
Boxlock ejectors $1,500 to $5,000
Sidelock non-ejectors $2,000 to $7,000
Sidelock ejectors $3,000 to $15,000
Hammer Guns $1,000 to $3,000

Wilkes, John

The first John Wilkes was established in Birmingham in 1830. The firm's reputation rests on the intrinsic high quality of their work. They continue on 79 Beak St., London.

New guns built today have interchangeable parts and locks. Special Series over-and-under sidelock guns in 20 gauge only with custom features retail for $28500. Only 25 are to be built.

Boxlock non-ejectors $2,000 to $3,000
Boxlock ejectors $2,000 to $4,500
Sidelock non-ejectors $20,000 to $25,000
Sidelock ejectors $20,000 to $250,000
Hammer Guns $4,000 to $15,000

Woodward, James

James Woodward worked for Charles Moore, becoming a partner before establishing his own company. The firm's reputation rests in large part on its "Automatic" double rifles and to an even greater extent on its over-and-under shotguns, which are the only ones that have ever rivaled Boss's.

Boxlock non-ejectors $1,500 to $4,000
Boxlock ejectors $2,000 to $8,500
Sidelock non-ejectors $2,000 to $10,000
Sidelock ejectors $4,000 to $30,000
Hammer Guns $2,000 to $10,000
Over & Unders $20,000 to $200,000

BRIXIA
Brescia, Italy

Model 12

A commercial version of the Model 1910 Glisenti in 9mm Glisenti caliber. The Brixia was a simplified Glisenti and was made to replace the Glisenti for the military market. The Italian military did not accept them and only a few were made for the commercial market. The only markings are the monogram eagle holding a shield cast in the grips.

Courtesy James Rankin

Exc.	*V.G.*	*Good*	*Fair*	*Poor*
1000	800	600	400	300

BRNO ARMS
Uhersky Brod, Czech Republic

NOTE: Some but not all of the BRNO models listed in this section are currently imported into the U.S.

ZG-47

A bolt-action rifle based on the Mauser system. Chambered for .270, 7x57, 7x64, .30-06, 8x57, 8x60, 8x64S, 9.3x62, and on special order 10.75x68. Barrel length is 23.6". Adjustable trigger. Hinged floorplate. Weight is about 7.7 lbs.

Standard

Exc.	*V.G.*	*Good*	*Fair*	*Poor*
1000	900	800	650	400

Deluxe

Exc.	*V.G.*	*Good*	*Fair*	*Poor*
1100	950	850	600	450

ZH-SERIES

A double barrel Over/Under boxlock series of shotguns with interchangeable barrels in shotgun and rifle configurations, of various lengths, double triggers and automatic ejectors. The models listed represent the different gauges and/or calibers offered.

ZH-300

NIB	Exc.	V.G.	Good	Fair	Poor
800	675	575	400	325	250

ZH-301

12ga/12ga.

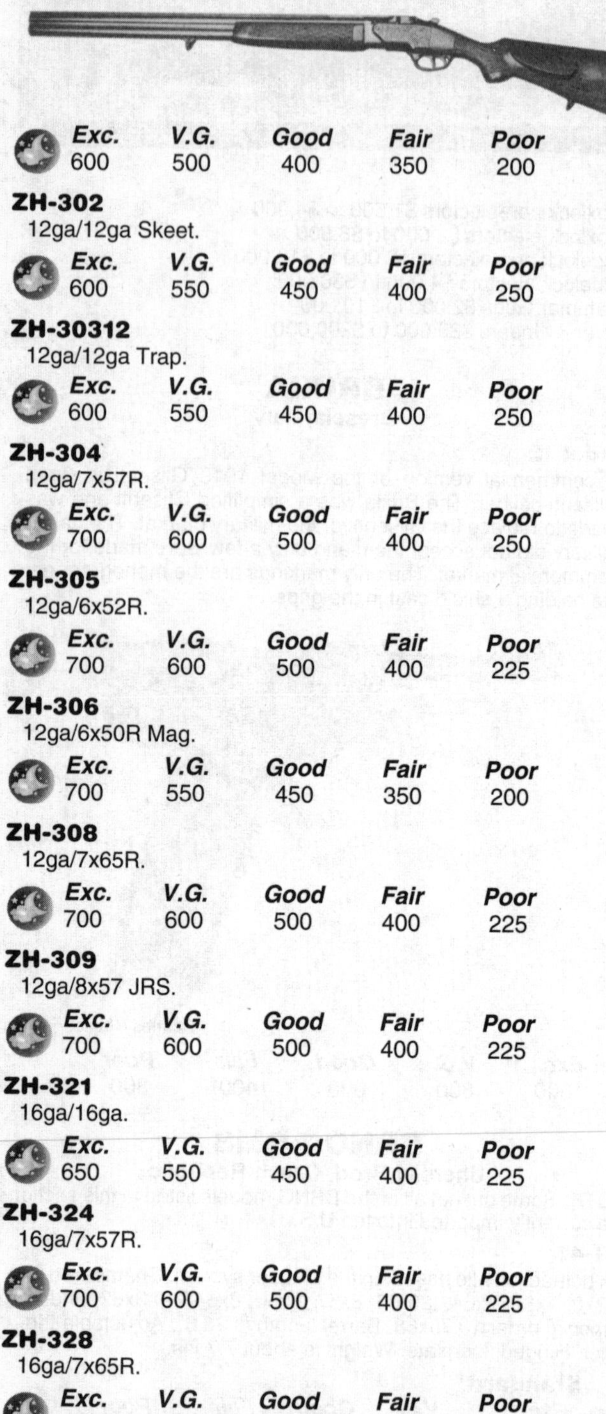

Exc.	V.G.	Good	Fair	Poor
600	500	400	350	200

ZH-302

12ga/12ga Skeet.

Exc.	V.G.	Good	Fair	Poor
600	550	450	400	250

ZH-30312

12ga/12ga Trap.

Exc.	V.G.	Good	Fair	Poor
600	550	450	400	250

ZH-304

12ga/7x57R.

Exc.	V.G.	Good	Fair	Poor
700	600	500	400	250

ZH-305

12ga/6x52R.

Exc.	V.G.	Good	Fair	Poor
700	600	500	400	225

ZH-306

12ga/6x50R Mag.

Exc.	V.G.	Good	Fair	Poor
700	550	450	350	200

ZH-308

12ga/7x65R.

Exc.	V.G.	Good	Fair	Poor
700	600	500	400	225

ZH-309

12ga/8x57 JRS.

Exc.	V.G.	Good	Fair	Poor
700	600	500	400	225

ZH-321

16ga/16ga.

Exc.	V.G.	Good	Fair	Poor
650	550	450	400	225

ZH-324

16ga/7x57R.

Exc.	V.G.	Good	Fair	Poor
700	600	500	400	225

ZH-328

16ga/7x65R.

Exc.	V.G.	Good	Fair	Poor
700	600	500	400	225

NOTE: For ZH models with set triggers and cheekpiece add $75. For interchangeable barrels add between $300 and $400 depending on gauge and caliber.

Model 300 Combo

The model ZH-300 with 8 interchangeable barrels in a fitted case. Introduced in 1986.

NIB	Exc.	V.G.	Good	Fair	Poor
6000	5000	4000	2750	2000	1500

Model 500

The model ZH-300 with acid-etched decoration, automatic ejectors and in 12 gauge.

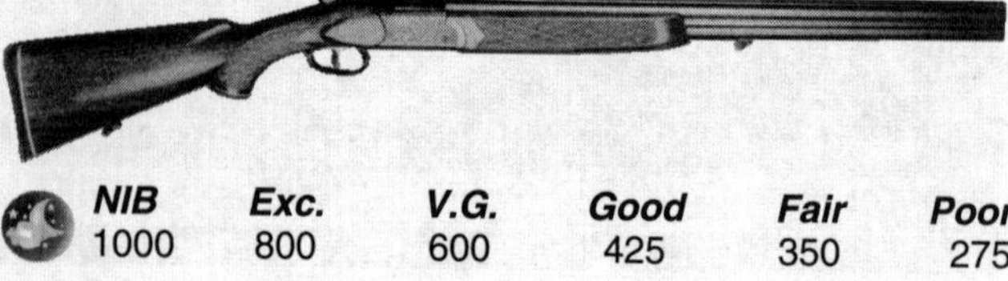

NIB	Exc.	V.G.	Good	Fair	Poor
1000	800	600	425	350	275

ZP-49

A 12 gauge sidelock double-barrel shotgun with double triggers and automatic ejectors. Blued with a walnut stock. Imported in 1986 only.

Exc.	V.G.	Good	Fair	Poor
950	800	650	450	325

ZP-149

As above, without engraving.

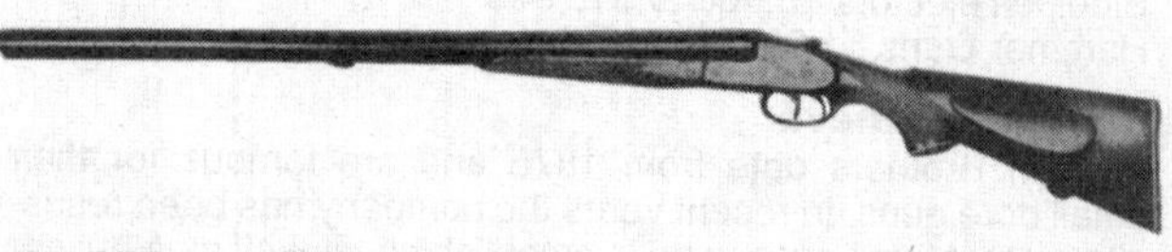

NIB	Exc.	V.G.	Good	Fair	Poor
700	600	500	400	300	200

ZP-349

As above, with the buttstock having a cheekpiece and a beavertail forearm.

Exc.	V.G.	Good	Fair	Poor
700	600	500	350	250

ZBK-100

A single barrel shotgun in 12 or 20 gauge with 27" barrel and walnut stock. Weight is approximately 5.5 lbs.

NIB	Exc.	V.G.	Good	Fair	Poor
250	200	150	—	—	—

RIFLES

ZKW-465 (Hornet Sporter)

A .22 Hornet caliber bolt-action rifle with a 23" barrel, express sights and double-set triggers. Blued with a walnut stock.

Exc.	V.G.	Good	Fair	Poor
1300	1100	950	800	550

Model 21H

A 6.5x57mm, 7x57mm or 8x57mm caliber bolt-action sporting rifle with a 23-5/8" barrel, express sights and double set triggers. Blued with a walnut stock.

Exc.	V.G.	Good	Fair	Poor
1150	1050	900	750	600

Model 22F
As above, with a Mannlicher-style stock. Barrel length is 20-1/2".

Exc.	V.G.	Good	Fair	Poor
1250	1100	900	650	500

Model I
A .22 caliber bolt-action rifle with a 22.75" barrel having folding leaf rear sights. Blued with a walnut stock.

Exc.	V.G.	Good	Fair	Poor
500	400	300	250	200

Model II
As above, with a more finely figured walnut stock.

Exc.	V.G.	Good	Fair	Poor
550	450	350	300	225

ZKM 611
This is a semi-automatic rifle chambered for the .22 WRM cartridge. It is fitted with a 20" barrel and has a magazine capacity of 6 rounds. Weight is approximately 6.2 lbs.

NIB	Exc.	V.G.	Good	Fair	Poor
500	425	325	225	175	125

ZKM 451
This is a semi-automatic rifle chambered for the .22 LR cartridge and fitted with a 22" barrel. Magazine capacity is 7 rounds. Weight is about 5.25 lbs.

NIB	Exc.	V.G.	Good	Fair	Poor
250	200	150	—	—	—

ZKM 451 LUX
Same as above but with select walnut stock.

NIB	Exc.	V.G.	Good	Fair	Poor
300	250	200	—	—	—

ZBK 680
A .22 Hornet or .222 caliber bolt-action rifle with a 23.5" barrel, double set triggers and 5-shot magazine. Blued with a walnut stock.

NIB	Exc.	V.G.	Good	Fair	Poor
800	700	550	400	325	225

Super Express Rifle
An Over/Under sidelock double-barrel rifle, with 23.5" barrels, double triggers and automatic ejectors. Engraved, blued with a walnut stock. Available in 6 grades:

Standard Model

NIB	Exc.	V.G.	Good	Fair	Poor
4500	3750	3000	2500	1750	1250

Grade I

NIB	Exc.	V.G.	Good	Fair	Poor
6500	5500	4750	4500	3600	3250

Grade II

NIB	Exc.	V.G.	Good	Fair	Poor
5500	4750	4000	3500	2750	2250

Grade III

NIB	Exc.	V.G.	Good	Fair	Poor
5250	4500	3950	3250	2750	2250

Grade IV

NIB	Exc.	V.G.	Good	Fair	Poor
5000	4000	3500	3000	2500	2250

Grade V

NIB	Exc.	V.G.	Good	Fair	Poor
4750	3850	3250	2750	2250	1750

Grade VI

NIB	Exc.	V.G.	Good	Fair	Poor
4600	3950	3100	2600	1950	1500

ZH-344/348/349
An over-and-under rifle chambered for 7x57R, 7x65R, or 8x57JRS.

NIB	Exc.	V.G.	Good	Fair	Poor
1100	850	600	—	—	—

Model 98 Standard
This bolt-action rifle is chambered for a variety of calibers from the 7x64 to the 9.3x62. It is fitted with a 23" barrel and figured walnut stock with buttplate and open sights. Weight is approximately 7.25 lbs.

NIB	Exc.	V.G.	Good	Fair	Poor
600	550	400	300	200	150

NOTE: For set trigger add $100.

Model 98 Full Stock
Same as above but with full one-piece stock and set trigger.

NIB	Exc.	V.G.	Good	Fair	Poor
700	600	500	400	350	200

ZK 99
This is a tip-up centerfire rifle chambered for a wide variety of calibers from 6.5x57R to .30-06. Barrel length is 23" and weight is about 5.75 lbs.

NIB	Exc.	V.G.	Good	Fair	Poor
900	700	550	—	—	—

ZBK 110
This is a single-shot tip-open rifle chambered for the .22 Hornet, .222 Rem., the 5.6x50R Mag., and the 5.6x52R. Barrel length is 23.5". Open sights. Walnut stock without checkering. Weight is about 6 lbs.

NIB	Exc.	V.G.	Good	Fair	Poor
250	200	150	—	—	—

ZBK 110 LUX
Same as above but with select walnut stock with checkering. Open sights.

NIB	Exc.	V.G.	Good	Fair	Poor
340	275	—	—	—	—

ZBK 110 Super Lux
Same as above but with fancy walnut stock with checkering. Open sights.

NIB	Exc.	V.G.	Good	Fair	Poor
450	350	—	—	—	—

HANDGUNS

ZKR 551
This is a double-action or single-action revolver with a 6-round cylinder. Adjustable rear sight. Walnut grips. Fitted with 6" barrel. Chambered for .38, .32 S&W Long, and .22 LR. Weight is about 35 oz.

NIB	Exc.	V.G.	Good	Fair	Poor
1500	1200	—	—	—	—

BROLIN ARMS
La Verne, California

LEGEND SERIES—1911 AUTO PISTOL

Model L45—Standard Auto Pistol
This is the standard model with 5" barrel chambered for the .45 ACP. Fitted with throated match barrel, polished feed ramp, lowered ejection port, beveled magazine well and fixed sights. Other custom features as well. Finish is matte blue with 7-round magazine. Weight is about 36 oz.

NIB	Exc.	V.G.	Good	Fair	Poor
450	350	—	—	—	—

Model L45C—Compact Auto Pistol

Similar to the above standard model but with a 4.5" barrel. Weight is about 32 oz.

NIB	Exc.	V.G.	Good	Fair	Poor
460	350	—	—	—	—

Model L45T

This version of the L45 series was introduced in 1997 and is fitted with a compact slide on a full-size frame. Weight is 36 oz.

NIB	Exc.	V.G.	Good	Fair	Poor
460	350	—	—	—	—

NOTE: For Novak sights add $50.

PATRIOT SERIES—DPC CARRY-COMP PISTOLS

Model P45 Comp—Standard Carry Comp

This model features a 4" barrel with integral compensator cut into the slide. Other features are a custom beavertail grip safety, adjustable aluminum trigger, flat top slide, and checkered wood grips. Weight is about 37 oz.

NIB	Exc.	V.G.	Good	Fair	Poor
550	500	—	—	—	—

Model P45C Comp—Compact Carry Comp

Similar to the above model but fitted with a 3.25" barrel. Weight is about 33 oz.

NIB	Exc.	V.G.	Good	Fair	Poor
580	500	—	—	—	—

NOTE: For two-tone finish add $20.

Model P45T

This addition to the Patriot Series was introduced in 1997 and has all of the features of the Patriot pistols but is fitted with a compact slide and full size frame. Weight is about 35 oz. Also available in two-tone finish for an additional $20.

NIB	Exc.	V.G.	Good	Fair	Poor
590	500	—	—	—	—

NOTE: For Novak sights add $50.

TAC SERIES—TACTICAL 1911 PISTOLS

Model TAC-11

This series and model were introduced in 1997 and have all of the features of the L45 series with the additions of a special 5" conical match barrel, Novak Low Profile sights, black rubber contour grips, "iron claw" extractor, and optional night sights. Chambered for the .45 ACP the pistol is supplied with an 8-round magazine. Weight is approximately 37 oz.

NIB	Exc.	V.G.	Good	Fair	Poor
550	500	—	—	—	—

NOTE: For Tritium night sights add $90.

TAC SERIES—DOUBLE-ACTION PISTOLS

MS45

This is a full-size double-action pistol chambered for the .45 ACP cartridge. It is fitted with an 8-round magazine and low-profile 3-dot sights. Standard finish is matte blue.

NIB	Exc.	V.G.	Good	Fair	Poor
400	300	—	—	—	—

NOTE: Add $20 for royal blue finish.

M45

Similar to the model above but with a longer barrel. Chambered for .45 ACP and 8-round magazine.

NIB	Exc.	V.G.	Good	Fair	Poor
400	300	—	—	—	—

NOTE: Add $20 for royal blue finish.

M40

Same as M45 but chambered for .40 S&W cartridge. Magazine capacity is 10 rounds.

NIB	Exc.	V.G.	Good	Fair	Poor
400	300	—	—	—	—

NOTE: Add $20 for royal blue finish.

M90

Same as M45 model but chambered for 9mm cartridge. Magazine capacity is 10 rounds.

NIB	Exc.	V.G.	Good	Fair	Poor
400	300	—	—	—	—

NOTE: Add $20 for royal blue finish.

MC40
This is compact version of the full-size double-action models. It is fitted with a full-size frame but shorter slide. Chambered for .40 S&W cartridge. Magazine capacity is 10 rounds.

NIB	Exc.	V.G.	Good	Fair	Poor
400	300	—	—	—	—

NOTE: Add $20 for royal blue finish.

MC90
Same as above but chambered for 9mm cartridge.

NIB	Exc.	V.G.	Good	Fair	Poor
400	300	—	—	—	—

MB40
This is super-compact double-action pistol. Features a concealed hammer. Chambered for .40 S&W cartridge. Magazine capacity is 6 rounds.

NIB	Exc.	V.G.	Good	Fair	Poor
430	350	—	—	—	—

NOTE: Add $20 for royal blue finish.

MB90
Same as above but chambered for 9mm cartridge.

NIB	Exc.	V.G.	Good	Fair	Poor
430	350	—	—	—	—

PRO SERIES—COMPETITION PISTOL

Model Pro-Stock—Competition Pistol
Chambered for the .45 ACP, this pistol is designed for the competition shooter. Many special features are standard such as full-length recoil guide, front strap high relief cut, serrated flat mainspring housing, ambidextrous thumb safety and fully adjustable rear sight. Barrel length is 5" and weight is about 37 oz.

NIB	Exc.	V.G.	Good	Fair	Poor
780	600	—	—	—	—

NOTE: For two-tone finish add $20.

Model Pro-Comp-Competition Pistol
Similar to the competition model above but fitted with an integral compensator and 4" barrel. Weight is about 37 oz.

NIB	Exc.	V.G.	Good	Fair	Poor
900	700	—	—	—	—

NOTE: For two-tone finish add $20.

SHOTGUNS

LAWMAN SERIES—PERSONAL SECURITY SHOTGUN

Model HL18SB
This is a pump-action 12 gauge shotgun with an 18.5" barrel, black synthetic stock and bead sights. Weight is about 7 lbs. Introduced in 1997.

NIB	Exc.	V.G.	Good	Fair	Poor
250	200	—	—	—	—

Model HL18SR
Same as above but fitted with rifle sights.

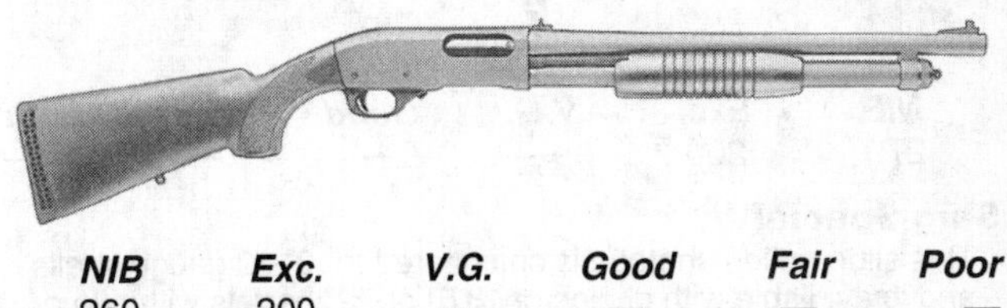

NIB	Exc.	V.G.	Good	Fair	Poor
260	200	—	—	—	—

Model HL18SBN
Same as above but with nickel finish and bead sights.

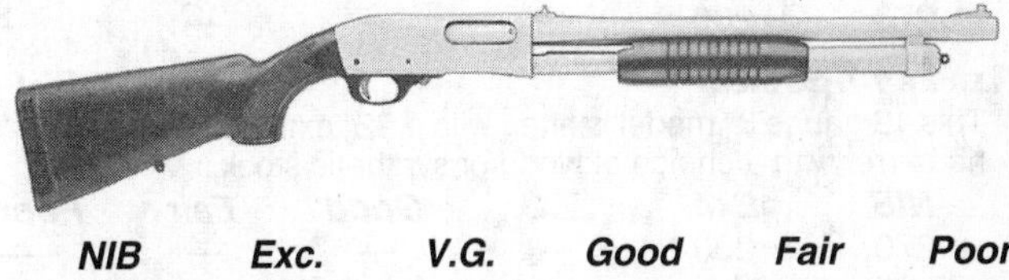

NIB	Exc.	V.G.	Good	Fair	Poor
270	200	—	—	—	—

Model HL18WB
This version has a wood stock and bead sights.

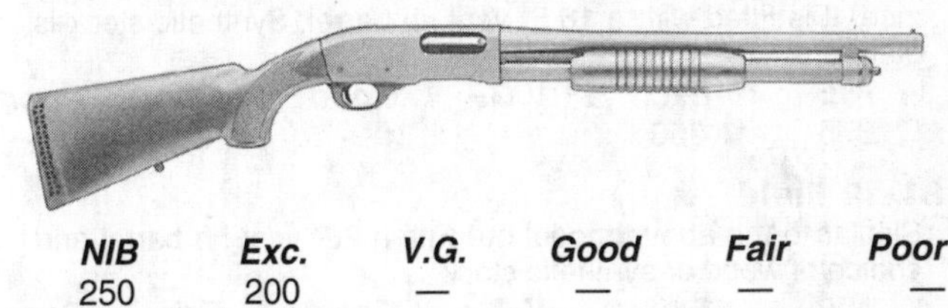

NIB	Exc.	V.G.	Good	Fair	Poor
250	200	—	—	—	—

Model HL18WR
Same as above but fitted with rifle sights.

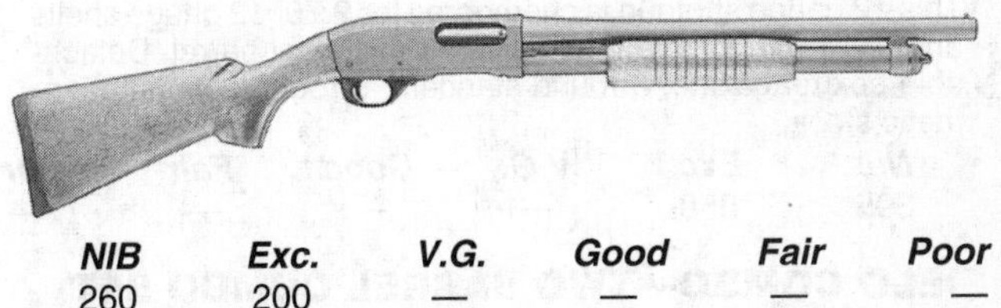

NIB	Exc.	V.G.	Good	Fair	Poor
260	200	—	—	—	—

FIELD SERIES—PUMP ACTION FIELD GUN

Model HF24SB
This is a 12 gauge pump action shotgun with a 24" barrel, matte finish, and black synthetic stock with bead sights. Weight is about 7.3 lbs. Introduced in 1997.

NIB	Exc.	V.G.	Good	Fair	Poor
270	200	—	—	—	—

Model HF28SB
Same as above but fitted with a 28" barrel. Weight is 7.4 lbs.

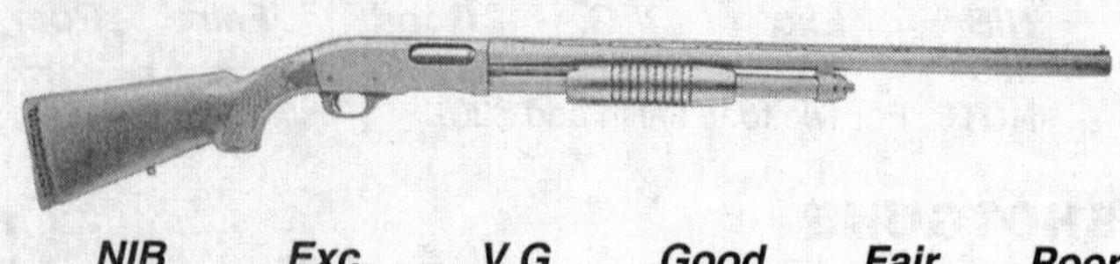

NIB	Exc.	V.G.	Good	Fair	Poor
270	200	—	—	—	—

Model HF24WB

This model features a 24" barrel with wood stock.

NIB	Exc.	V.G.	Good	Fair	Poor
270	200	—	—	—	—

Model HF28WB

Same as above but with 24" barrel.

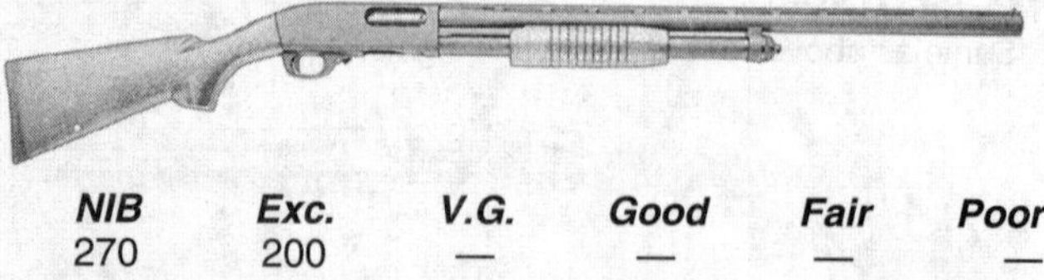

NIB	Exc.	V.G.	Good	Fair	Poor
270	200	—	—	—	—

Slug Special

This slide-action shotgun is chambered for 3" 12 gauge shells and is available with choice of 18.5" or 22" barrels with rifle or ghost ring sights. Available with fixed improved cylinder choke, 4" extended rifled choke, or fully rifled barrel. Choice of wood or synthetic stocks.

NIB	Exc.	V.G.	Good	Fair	Poor
270	200	—	—	—	—

Turkey Special

This 12 gauge 3" model is fitted with a 22" extra full choke vent rib barrel with a choice of wood or synthetic stock.

NIB	Exc.	V.G.	Good	Fair	Poor
270	200	—	—	—	—

SEMI-AUTOMATIC SHOTGUNS

BL-12 Security

This 12 gauge shotgun has a 3" chamber and 5 round magazine. It is fitted with a 18.5" vent rib barrel. Synthetic stock is standard.

NIB	Exc.	V.G.	Good	Fair	Poor
375	350	—	—	—	—

BL-12 Field

Similar to the above model but with a 28" vent rib barrel and choice of wood or synthetic stock.

NIB	Exc.	V.G.	Good	Fair	Poor
390	375	—	—	—	—

SAS-12 Security

This 12 gauge shotgun is chambered for 2.75" 12 gauge shells and fitted with 24" vent rib barrel or rifle sight barrel. Detachable box magazine; 3 round standard, 5 round optional. Synthetic stock.

NIB	Exc.	V.G.	Good	Fair	Poor
395	350	—	—	—	—

FIELD COMBO—TWO BARREL COMBO SET

Model HC28SB

This set consists of an 18.5" barrel and 28" barrel with synthetic stock pistol grip, and bead sights.

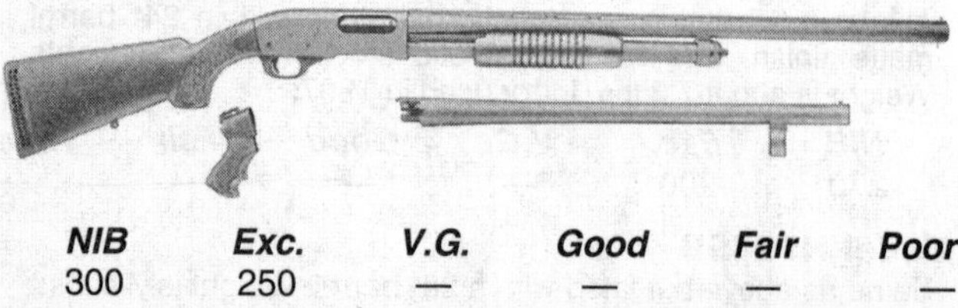

NIB	Exc.	V.G.	Good	Fair	Poor
300	250	—	—	—	—

Model HC28SR

Same as above but with rifle and bead sights.

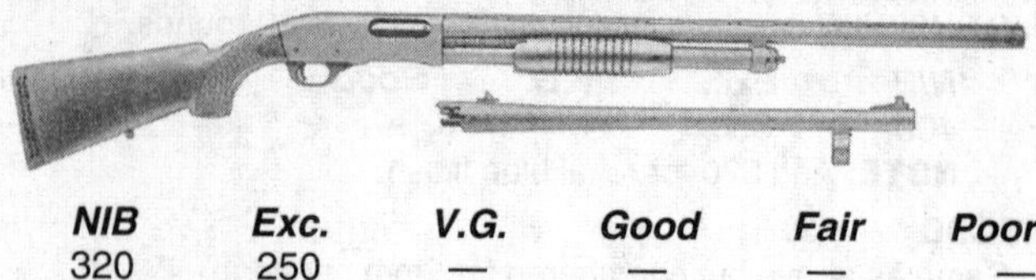

NIB	Exc.	V.G.	Good	Fair	Poor
320	250	—	—	—	—

Model HC28WB

This model features a wood stock, pistol grip, and bead sights.

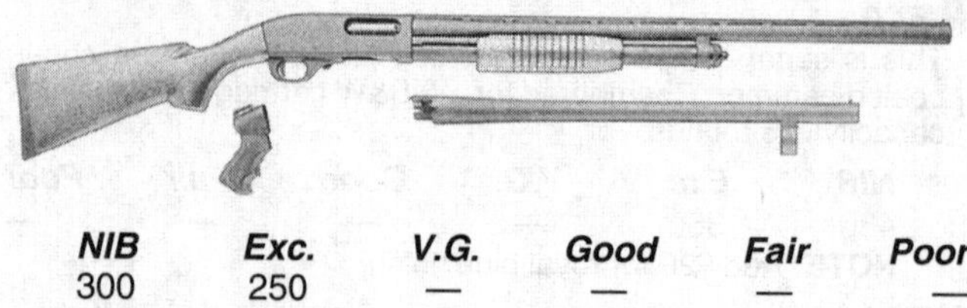

NIB	Exc.	V.G.	Good	Fair	Poor
300	250	—	—	—	—

Model HC28WR

Same as above but with wood stock with rifle and bead sights.

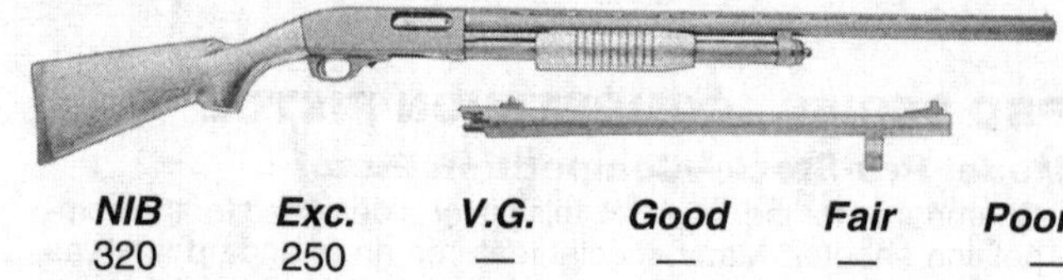

NIB	Exc.	V.G.	Good	Fair	Poor
320	250	—	—	—	—

RIFLES

Legacy

This is a .50 caliber muzzleloader with in-line ignition system. It has a walnut stain hardwood stock with recoil pad. Finish is blue or chrome.

NIB	Exc.	V.G.	Good	Fair	Poor
180	150	—	—	—	—

NOTE: Add $20 for chrome finish.

Mitchell PPS-50

This is a semi-automatic rifle chambered for the .22 LR cartridge. It has a detachable 10-round magazine. It is a copy of the Russian PPSh machine gun used in WWII.

NIB	Exc.	V.G.	Good	Fair	Poor
400	325	—	—	—	—

MAUSER RIFLES

All of these Mauser rifles were introduced in 1998 to the Brolin product line.

Lightning Model

This model features a sliding bolt that locks directly into the barrel. Chambered for 7.62x39mm cartridge as well as the .308 Win. Blue finish with choice of colored synthetic stocks. Open sights are standard.

NIB	Exc.	V.G.	Good	Fair	Poor
550	450	—	—	—	—

Lightning Hunter Model

This model features a detachable magazine, recoil pad, blued finish, checkered wood stock, and choice of open sights or no sights with scope mounts included. Calibers from .243 to .300 Win. Mag.

NIB	Exc.	V.G.	Good	Fair	Poor
750	600	—	—	—	—

NOTE: Add $50 for open sights, $50 for stainless steel.

Lightning Hunter All Weather Model

Same as above but with black synthetic stock.

NIB	Exc.	V.G.	Good	Fair	Poor
700	550	—	—	—	—

Lightning Varmint Model

The features of this model are the same as the Lightning Hunter Model with the addition of a heavy fluted barrel with special varmint wood or synthetic stock. Chambered for .22-250 and .243 cartridges.

NIB	Exc.	V.G.	Good	Fair	Poor
1000	800	—	—	—	—

Lightning Sniper

This model features a heavy fluted barrel with detachable magazine and a choice of special wood or synthetic stock with built-in bi-pod rail. Offered in .308 or 300 Win. Mag. calibers.

NIB	Exc.	V.G.	Good	Fair	Poor
1000	800	—	—	—	—

Lightning Professional

This model has a heavy fluted barrel, no sights, and recoil compensator. A tuned trigger system is standard. All weather adjustable stock with pistol grip. Available in .308 or .300 Win. Mag. calibers.

NIB	Exc.	V.G.	Good	Fair	Poor
1000	800	—	—	—	—

Model 2000 Classic

The 2000 Classic features an interchangeable caliber system for cartridges in the same action length. Detachable magazine. High-grade walnut stock with cut checkering and rosewood forend. Single set trigger is standard. Offered in .270, .308, .30-06, 7mm Rem. Mag., and .300 Win. Mag.

NIB	Exc.	V.G.	Good	Fair	Poor
1800	1400	—	—	—	—

Model 2000 Varmint

This model features a heavy fluted barrel with special varmint wood stock with accessory rail. Offered in .22-250, and .243 calibers. Standard without sights.

NIB	Exc.	V.G.	Good	Fair	Poor
2200	1700	—	—	—	—

Model 2000 Sniper

This model features an interchangeable caliber system, heavy fluted barrel, no sights, single set trigger, all-weather stock with built-in bi-pod rail. Offered in .308 and .300 Win. Mag. calibers.

NIB	Exc.	V.G.	Good	Fair	Poor
2200	1750	—	—	—	—

Model 2000 Professional

This model has all of the features of the Sniper rifle with the addition of a recoil compensator and special all-weather pistol-grip stock. Each rifle is custom built.

NIB	Exc.	V.G.	Good	Fair	Poor
3500	2750	—	—	—	—

Model 20/22

This is a high-quality .22 bolt-action rifle chambered for the .22 LR or .22 Magnum cartridge. Available in both a standard and deluxe configuration. Add $100 for deluxe version.

NIB	Exc.	V.G.	Good	Fair	Poor
700	550	—	—	—	—

Model 1898 Commemorative

This model celebrates the 100 year anniversary of the '98 Mauser. Chambered for the 8mm Mauser cartridge. This is a limited edition rifle.

NIB	Exc.	V.G.	Good	Fair	Poor
2300	—	—			

Model 98

This is the original Mauser action built to Safari calibers. Chambered for .375 H&H or .416 Rigby.

NIB	Exc.	V.G.	Good	Fair	Poor
10000	8000	—	—	—	—

CUSTOM SHOP

Formula One RZ

This is a high-performance competition race gun with many special features such as supported barrel chamber, 6-port compensator, tuned trigger, extended magazine release, and many other options as standard. Chambered for .38 Super, .40 S&W cartridges. Blue finish. Add $400 for double-action.

NIB	Exc.	V.G.	Good	Fair	Poor
2500	2000	—	—		

Formula One RS

Designed as a Limited Class competition gun with 5" barrel and chambered for .38 Super, .40 S&W, or .45 ACP calibers. Features adjustable rear sight, tuned trigger, checkered front strap and mainspring housing and other special features. Add $300 for double-action.

NIB	Exc.	V.G.	Good	Fair	Poor
2000	1600	—	—	—	—

Formula Z

This model is a custom-built combat pistol chambered for .40 S&W, .400 Cor-Bon, or .45 ACP calibers. Fitted with a 5" or 4" barrel. Features many extra-cost features as standard.

NIB	Exc.	V.G.	Good	Fair	Poor
1300	1000	—	—	—	—

MITCHELL SINGLE-ACTION REVOLVERS

Single-Action Army Model

Offered in 4.75", 5.5", or 7.5" barrel lengths and chambered for the .45 Long Colt, .357 Magnum, or .44-40 calibers. Offered in blue finish with case hardened frame or nickel finish. Also available with dual cylinders, i.e. .45 LC/.45 ACP. Add $50 for nickel finish, and $150 for dual cylinder models.

NIB	Exc.	V.G.	Good	Fair	Poor
395	350	—	—	—	—

BRONCO

SEE Echave & Arizmendi
Eibar, Spain
(SEE ALSO Firearms International & Garcia)

BROOKLYN F. A. CO.

Brooklyn, New York

Slocum Pocket Revolver

A .32 caliber spur-trigger revolver with a 3" round barrel. The frame is silver-plated brass and scroll engraved; the remainder is either blued or plated with walnut grips. The barrel is marked "B.A. Co. Patented April 14, 1863." Approximately 10,000 were manufactured in 1863 and 1864. The cylinder has five individual tubes that slide forward to open for loading and then for ejecting the spent cartridges.

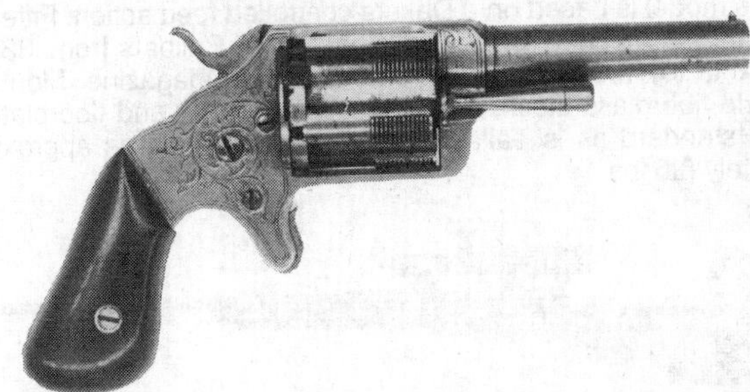

Exc.	V.G.	Good	Fair	Poor
—	—	800	300	100

Slocum Unfluted Cylinder Pocket Revolver

As above, but in .22 or .32 caliber with 5- or 7-shot cylinder. Approximately 250 were manufactured in .32 rimfire and 100 in .22 rimfire.

Exc.	V.G.	Good	Fair	Poor
—	—	1000	400	200

NOTE: .22 caliber add 25 percent.

BROWN CUSTOM, ED

Perry, Missouri

RIFLES

NOTE: There are a number of extra-cost options that are offered by this company on its rifles that may affect value. Consult the company or an expert prior to a sale.

Model 702, Savanna

Fitted with a long action and chambered for calibers from .257 Ackley to .338 Win. Mag. Barrel is a lightweight 24" for standard calibers and a 24" medium weight for magnum calibers. Talley scope mounts included. Fiberglass stock, recoil pad, steel trigger guard and floorplate are standard.

NIB	Exc.	V.G.	Good	Fair	Poor
2800	2250	—	—	—	—

Model 702, Ozark

This rifle is built on a short action with a blind magazine. A 21" lightweight barrel is fitted for standard calibers and a medium weight 21" barrel for magnum calibers. Chambered for calibers from .22-250 to .308. Talley scope mounts are included as is a fiberglass stock, recoil pad, steel trigger guard and floorplate.

NIB	Exc.	V.G.	Good	Fair	Poor
2800	2250	—	—	—	—

Model 702, Denali

This is a lighter-weight version of the Ozark with a 22" super lightweight barrel. Chambered for calibers .25-06 to .300 WSM. Weight is about 6.75 lbs.

NIB	Exc.	V.G.	Good	Fair	Poor
2800	2250	—	—	—	—

Model 76, Bushveld

This model is based on a Dakota controlled feed action. Fitted with a 24" medium- or heavyweight barrel. Calibers from .330 Dakota to .458 Win. Mag. Detachable box magazine. Monte Carlo fiberglass stock, recoil pad, steel trigger and floorplate are standard as is Talley scope mounts. Weight is approximately 8.5 lbs.

NIB	Exc.	V.G.	Good	Fair	Poor
3400	2750				

Model 702, Light Tactical

This is short-action rifle with light weight floorplate and trigger guard. Fitted with a 21" medium-weight barrel. Black fiberglass stock with aluminum bedding block. Available in calibers from .22-250 to .308.

NIB	Exc.	V.G.	Good	Fair	Poor
2800	2250	—	—	—	—

Model 702, Tactical

This is similar to the above model but built on a long action with heavy weight 26" blued barrel. McMillan A-3 black tactical stock. Available in .308 and .300 Win. Mag.

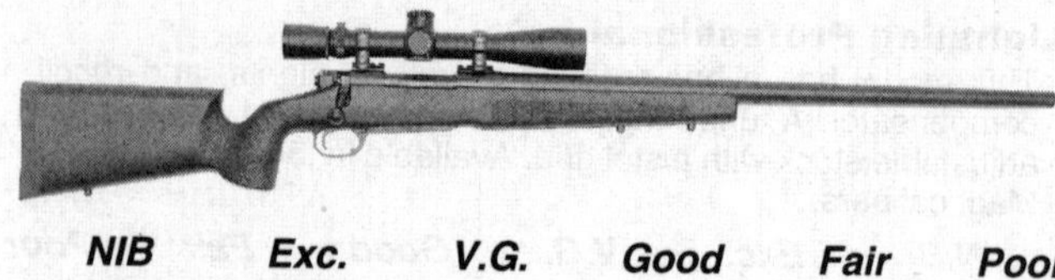

NIB	Exc.	V.G.	Good	Fair	Poor
2900	2350	—	—	—	—

Model 702, Marine Sniper

Similar to the Marine M40 with heavy 24" barrel and McMillan synthetic camo stock. Offered in .308 and .300 Win. Mag. calibers. Weight is about 9.25 lbs.

NIB	Exc.	V.G.	Good	Fair	Poor
2900	2350	—	—	—	—

Model 702, Varmint

This is a custom-made rifle with a short single-shot action. 26" medium weight barrel or 24" heavyweight barrel. H-S Precision stock. Available in calibers from .222 to 6.5/.284.

NIB	Exc.	V.G.	Good	Fair	Poor
2500	2000	—	—	—	—

Model 702, Peacekeeper

This is single-shot long-action rifle chambered for .30-378 Wby., .338-378 Wby., or the .338 Lapua caliber. Fitted with a heavy 26" barrel with muzzlebrake. Fiberglass tactical stock with recoil pad. Leupold Mark 4 scope mounts standard. Weight is approximately 13 lbs.

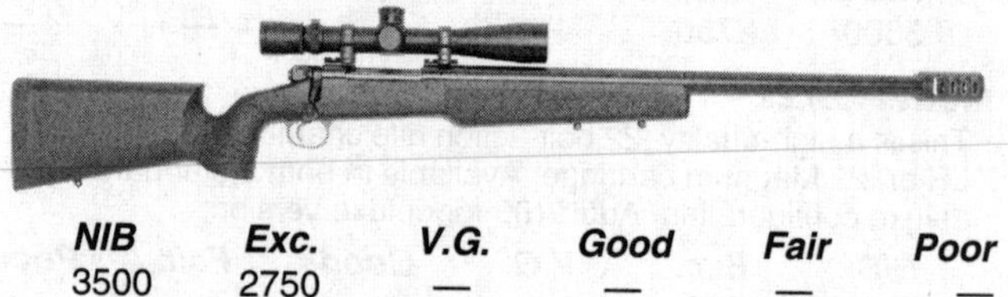

NIB	Exc.	V.G.	Good	Fair	Poor
3500	2750	—	—	—	—

BROWN PRODUCTS, INC., ED

Perry, Missouri

NOTE: There are a number of extra options offered on these pistols that may affect value.

Commander Bobtail

This model features a 4.25" barrel chambered for the .45 ACP, .400 Cor-Bon, .40 S&W, .38 Super, 9x23, or 9mm Luger cartridge. Modified Hogue grips from exotic wood are standard. This pistol is completely handmade and is built to the customer's specifications. Many available options. Retail prices begin at $2,400.

Classic Custom

Chambered for the .45 ACP cartridge. This is a custom built pistol with many extra features such as Videki trigger, Ed Brown wide thumb safety, stainless steel thumb safety, and extended safety, adjustable rear sight, etc. All hand-fitted parts.

NIB	Exc.	V.G.	Good	Fair	Poor
2750	2000	—	—	—	—

Class A Limited

This is a custom-built pistol offered in a number of different calibers from .45 ACP to 9mm Luger. Fitted with a 4.25" Commander length slide. Many special features. Price listed is for the basic pistol.

NIB	Exc.	V.G.	Good	Fair	Poor
2250	1750	—	—	—	—

Kobra Custom .45

Introduced in 2002 this pistol features a snakeskin treatment on forestrap, mainspring housing, and slide. Novak night sights and Hogue checkered wood grips standard. Many other custom features.

NIB	Exc.	V.G.	Good	Fair	Poor
1795	1400	—	—	—	—

Kobra Carry .45

Same as above but with shorter grip frame and barrel.

NIB	Exc.	V.G.	Good	Fair	Poor
1995	1500	—	—	—	—

Executive Target

1911 Executive Elite modified for target/range with adjustable BoMar rear sight, ambidextrous safety. 38 oz. 5" barrel chambered for .45 ACP. 7-round magazine.

NIB	Exc.	V.G.	Good	Fair	Poor
2350	2000	—	—	—	—

Executive Elite

Government model 5" barrel, 38 oz., chambered for .45 ACP. 7-round magazine. Fixed sights. Blue/blue, stainless/blue or all-stainless.

NIB	Exc.	V.G.	Good	Fair	Poor
2100	1800	—	—	—	—

Executive Carry

A 4.25" commander model .45 ACP with Ed Brown Bobtail. 38 oz. 7-round magazine, fixed sights. Blue/blue, stainless/blue or all-stainless.

NIB	Exc.	V.G.	Good	Fair	Poor
2200	1900	—	—	—	—

Special Forces

Blue/blue 1911 semi-auto with 5" barrel and fixed 3-dot night sights. Chambered for .45 ACP. 38 oz.; 7-round magazine. Cocobolo grips.

NIB	Exc.	V.G.	Good	Fair	Poor
1995	1600	—	—	—	—

RIFLES

Savanna

Bolt-action medium-weight centerfire rifle. Chambered in a variety of short- and long-action standard and magnum chamberings. Fluted bolt, McMillan stock, optional muzzlebrake, blackened stainless barrel.

NIB	Exc.	V.G.	Good	Fair	Poor
3200	—	—	—	—	—

Damara

Similar to Savannah but in a lightweight configuration with natural-finish stainless barrel.

NIB	Exc.	V.G.	Good	Fair	Poor
3200	—	—	—	—	—

Compact Varmint

Similar to Damara but with shorter barrel, beavertail forend.

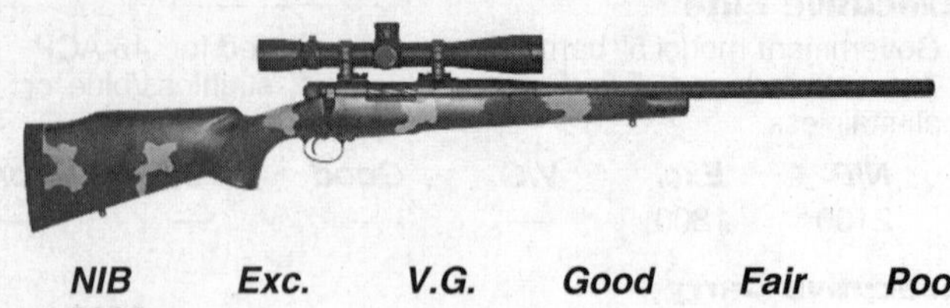

NIB	Exc.	V.G.	Good	Fair	Poor
3200	—	—	—	—	—

Bushveld

Generally similar to Damara but built to customer specs.

NIB	Exc.	V.G.	Good	Fair	Poor
3200	—	—	—	—	—

M-704 Express

Centerfire bolt-action rifle chambered for a wide variety of large Africa-class calibers. Dropped box magazine, fully controlled feed, fluted bolt, McMillan stock, iron sights.

NIB	Exc.	V.G.	Good	Fair	Poor
3600	—	—	—	—	—

Marine Sniper

Duplicate of Vietnam-era McMillan sniper rifle, controlled feed, fluted bolt, hinged floorplate, woodland camo stock, blackened stainless steel barrel and receiver.

NIB	Exc.	V.G.	Good	Fair	Poor
2900	—	—	—	—	—

A3 Tactical

Generally similar to Marine But with black fiberglass McMillan A-3 stock.

NIB	Exc.	V.G.	Good	Fair	Poor
2900	—	—	—	—	—

BROWN MANUFACTURING CO.

Newburyport, Massachusetts
Also SEE—Ballard Patent Arms

Southerner Derringer

A .41 caliber spur-trigger single-shot pocket pistol with a pivoted 2.5" or 4" octagonal barrel marked "Southerner." Silver-plated or blued with walnut grips. This pistol was manufactured by the Merrimack Arms Co. from 1867 to 1869 and by the Brown Manufacturing Co. from 1869 to 1873.

Courtesy W. P. Hallstein III and son Chip

Brass Framed

2.5" barrel.

Exc.	V.G.	Good	Fair	Poor
—	—	800	300	125

Iron Frame

2.5" barrel (Brown Mfg. only).

Exc.	V.G.	Good	Fair	Poor
—	—	950	400	200

Brass Frame 4" Barrel

Exc.	V.G.	Good	Fair	Poor
—	—	3250	1250	500

Brown Mfg. Co./Merrill Patent Breechloading Rifles

Overall length 54-3/4"; barrel (bore) length 35"; caliber .577. Markings: On breechblock-bolt mechanism, "BROWN MFG. CO. NEWBURYPORT, MASS./PATANTED OCT. 17, 1871." The patent issued to George Merrill in 1871, permitted the Brown Manufacturing Co. to alter probably up to 1,000 English P1853 rifle-muskets to a single-shot breechloading system. The large bolt handle projecting upward at the end of the breech readily distinguishes these arms.

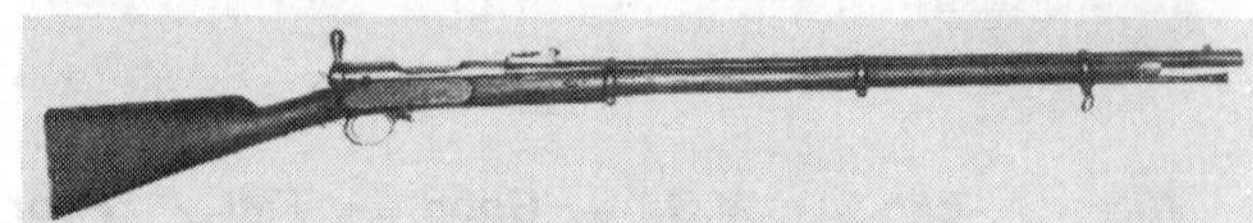

Courtesy Milwaukee Public Museum, Milwaukee, Wisconsin

Exc.	V.G.	Good	Fair	Poor
—	—	2000	800	300

BROWN PRECISION, INC.

Los Molinos, California

Although known as a manufacturer of stocks, this company also produces custom-order rifles.

High Country Standard

A .243 to .30-06 bolt-action rifle with a 22" barrel and Kevlar stock.

NIB	Exc.	V.G.	Good	Fair	Poor
985	775	600	500	400	200

Gray camo stock, stainless barrel and Leupold 2.5 x 10 scope add $650.

Open Country Varmint Rifle

Similar to the above, with a heavy barrel. Introduced in 1989.

NIB	Exc.	V.G.	Good	Fair	Poor
1100	800	650	550	400	200

Law Enforcement Model

A .308 caliber Remington Varmint action rifle with a 20" barrel, Zeiss telescope and Kevlar stock.

NIB	Exc.	V.G.	Good	Fair	Poor
1050	800	650	550	400	200

Pro-Hunter

A .375 Holland & Holland or .458 Winchester Magnum bolt-action rifle. Blued, electroless nickel-plated or Teflon coated.

NIB	Exc.	V.G.	Good	Fair	Poor
1800	1400	950	700	500	250

Brown Precision Rifle

A .270 or .30-06 bolt-action rifle with a 22" featherweight barrel and Kevlar stock.

NIB	Exc.	V.G.	Good	Fair	Poor
600	475	350	250	150	100

Blaser Rifle

Built on the Camex-Blaser action with a Brown Precision stock.

NIB	Exc.	V.G.	Good	Fair	Poor
1400	1100	750	550	400	200

BROWN, A.A.
Birmingham, England
SEE—British Double Guns

BROWN, DAVID MCKAY
Glasgow, Scotland
SEE—British Double Guns

BROWN, E.A. MANUFACTURING CO.
Alexandria, Minnesota

Brown Classic Single-Shot Pistol
This is a falling block single-shot pistol with 15" match grade barrel. Chambered for calibers from .17 Ackley to .45-70 Gov't. Walnut thumbrest grips. Handfitted. Introduced in 1998.

NIB	*Exc.*	*V.G.*	*Good*	*Fair*	*Poor*
900	750	—	—	—	—

Brown Model 97D Single-Shot Rifle
This is a single-shot falling block rifle chambered for calibers from .17 Ackley to .45-70 Gov't. Barrel lengths up to 26". Sporter-style stock with pistol grip, cheekpiece, and schnabel forend. Blue/black finish. Weight is about 6 lbs. No sights.

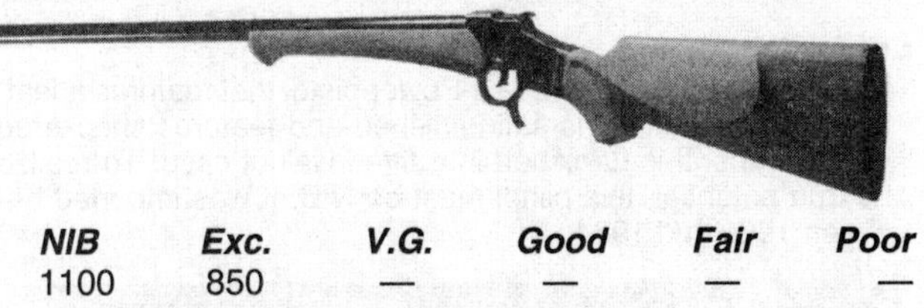

NIB	*Exc.*	*V.G.*	*Good*	*Fair*	*Poor*
1100	850	—	—	—	—

BROWNING ARMS CO.
Morgan, Utah

Contrary to popular belief, the firm of Browning Arms has really manufactured only one gun in its long and colorful history. This was the Model 1878 single-shot rifle, which was actually the first gun that the prolific inventor John M. Browning patented. This firm was founded in 1880 as J. M. Browning & Bro. in Ogden, Utah. John Browning is considered by many to be the greatest firearms genius of all time. He created 80 firearms designs and held 128 individual patents. He sold designs to Winchester, Stevens, Remington, and Colt, as well as to the Belgian firm of Fabrique Nationale (FN). He was directly responsible for designing many of the firearms with which we have come to be familiar, including the 1911 Colt Government Model, the 1885 Winchester Single-Shot (evolved from the Model 1878 that was actually Browning-manufactured), the Models 1886, 1892, 1894, and 1895 Lever Action Rifles, as well as the Model 1897 Shotgun. He was also directly responsible for producing the Model 1935 Hi-Power that achieved worldwide service pistol acceptance. In the 1890s Browning had difficulty dealing with the American arms corporations, so he went to Europe and established a lasting relationship with the firm of Fabrique Nationale in Herstal, Belgium. This agreement lasted until 1977 when FN purchased the Browning Company. In the early 1970s, the Browning corporation contracted with the firm of B. C. Miroku in Japan and has since marketed guns produced by them. In 1991 GIAT, a French state-owned firm, purchased FN and Browning. One should be cognizant of the fact that in the opinion of many experts Miroku-produced Browning firearms are as high in quality as any others produced; collector interest dictates greater values on the Belgian-manufactured versions.

> **CAUTION**
> Certain Browning long guns and pistols used wood that was salt-cured, causing a rusting problem to the underside of barrels and actions. This problem occurred from about 1966 to 1972. This should be carefully checked before purchase.

Early Semi-Automatic Pistols
In the period between 1900 and the development of the Model 1935 Hi-Power Pistol, Browning had a number of semi-automatic pistols manufactured by Fabrique Nationale of Herstal, Belgium. They were the Models 1900, 1903, 1905, 1910, 1922, the Baby, and the 1935 Model Hi-Power. These firearms will be listed in more detail with their respective values in the Fabrique Nationale section of this text.

Hi-Power Modern Production
This version of the FN Model 1935 is quite similar in appearance to the original described in the FN section. It is chambered for the 9mm Parabellum cartridge and has a 4.75" barrel. Models built before the passage of the crime bill have a double column, 13-round, detachable box magazine and is blued with checkered walnut grips. It has fixed sights and has been produced in its present configuration since 1954. Add a 10 percent premium for adjustable sights. A matte-nickel version, offered between 1980 and 1984, was also available and would be worth approximately 15 percent additional. This model is also avalable in .40 S&W.

Hi-Power with spur hammer and adjustable sights

Spur Hammer Version

NIB	*Exc.*	*V.G.*	*Good*	*Fair*	*Poor*
800'	600	450	300	200	150

Round Hammer Version

NIB	*Exc.*	*V.G.*	*Good*	*Fair*	*Poor*
750	500	400	250	200	150

NOTE: Add $60 for adjustable sights.

Hi-Power—.30 Luger

This version is similar to the standard Hi-Power except that it is chambered for the .30 Luger cartridge. There were approximately 1,500 imported between 1986 and 1989. The slide is marked "FN." The Browning-marked versions are quite rare and worth approximately 30 percent additional.

Exc.	V.G.	Good	Fair	Poor
800	650	450	300	200

Tangent Sight Model

This version is similar to the standard Hi-Power with the addition of an adjustable rear sight calibrated to 500 meters. There were approximately 7,000 imported between 1965 and 1978.

Exc.	V.G.	Good	Fair	Poor
950	800	650	450	200

NOTE: If the grip frame is slotted to accept a detachable shoulder stock, add approximately 20 percent to the value; but be wary of fakes. Add an additional 10 percent for "T" series serial numbers.

Renaissance Hi-Power

This is a heavily engraved version with a matte-silver finish. It features synthetic-pearl grips and a gold-plated trigger. Import on this model ended in 1979.

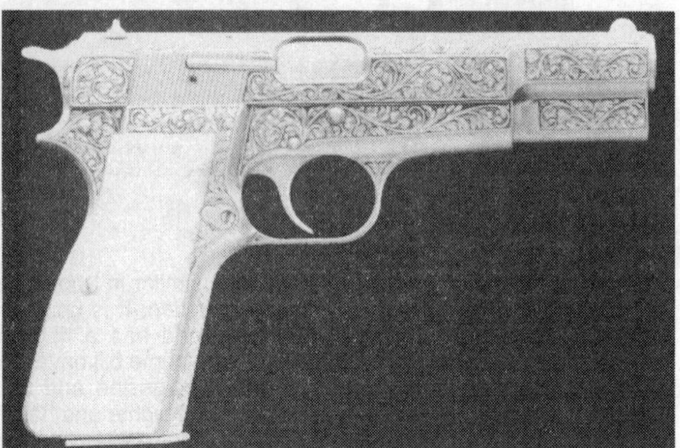

Spur Hammer Model

NIB	Exc.	V.G.	Good	Fair	Poor
1800	1500	1200	925	325	175

Ring Hammer Model

NIB	Exc.	V.G.	Good	Fair	Poor
1900	1600	1300	975	600	300

Adjustable Sight Spur Hammer Model

NIB	Exc.	V.G.	Good	Fair	Poor
1800	1350	975	700	575	300

Renaissance .25 Caliber

NIB	Exc.	V.G.	Good	Fair	Poor
950	825	700	500	400	250

Renaissance .380 Caliber

With pearl grips.

NIB	Exc.	V.G.	Good	Fair	Poor
1700	1300	1000	750	475	300

Renaissance .380 Caliber (Model 1971)

With wood grips and adjustable sights.

NIB	Exc.	V.G.	Good	Fair	Poor
1200	1000	750	525	375	200

Cased Renaissance Set

This features one example of a fully engraved and silver-finished .25 ACP "Baby," one .380 ACP pistol, and one Hi-Power. The set is furnished in a fitted walnut case or black leatherette and was imported between 1955 and 1969.

Courtesy Rock Island Auction Company

NIB	Exc.	V.G.	Good	Fair	Poor
4700	3700	2700	1800	1100	900

NOTE: For early coin finish sets add 30 percent.

Louis XVI Model

This is a heavily engraved Hi-Power pistol that features a leaf-and-scroll pattern. It is satin-finished and features checkered walnut grips. It is furnished in a fitted walnut case. To realize its true potential, this pistol must be NIB. It was imported between 1980 and 1984.

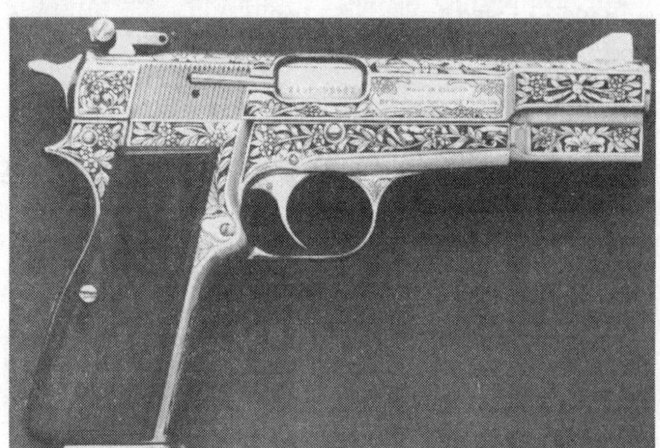

Diamond Grip Model

NIB	Exc.	V.G.	Good	Fair	Poor
1650	1050	800	675	400	300

Medallion Grip Model

NIB	Exc.	V.G.	Good	Fair	Poor
950	700	600	350	225	150

Hi-Power Centennial Model

This version is similar to the standard fixed-sight Hi-Power but is chrome-plated with the inscription, "Browning Centennial/1878-1978" engraved on the slide. It is furnished with a fitted case. There were 3,500 manufactured in 1978. As with all commemorative pistols, in order to realize its collector potential, this model should be NIB with all supplied material. Prices are for pistols built in Belgium

NIB	Exc.	V.G.	Good	Fair	Poor
1000	775	625	450	300	200

Hi-Power Capitan

This is a new version of the Hi-Power model fitted with tangent sights. Introduced in 1993. Furnished with walnut grips. Weighs about 32 oz. Assembled in Portugal.

This symbol denotes "Sleepers" with rapidly-rising values and/or significant collector potential.

NIB	Exc.	V.G.	Good	Fair	Poor
650	475	350	300	250	200

Hi-Power Practical

First introduced in 1993 this version is furnished with a blued slide and chrome frame. Has Pachmayr wraparound rubber grips, round-style serrated hammer, and removable front sight. Available with adjustable sights. Weighs 36 oz. Assembled in Portugal.

NIB	Exc.	V.G.	Good	Fair	Poor
845	625	500	300	200	175

Hi-Power Silver Chrome Model

Furnished in hard chrome and fitted with wraparound Pachmayr rubber grips. Weighs 36 oz. Assembled in Portugal. Add 10 percent for models with all Belgian markings. This pistol was introduced in 1981 and dropped from the Browning product line in 1984. It was reintroduced in 1991.

NIB	Exc.	V.G.	Good	Fair	Poor
650	425	325	275	225	200

Hi-Power .40 S&W

Introduced in 1994, this new version of the Hi-Power is furnished with adjustable sights, molded grips, 5" barrel and a 10-round magazine. Weighs about 35 oz.

NIB	Exc.	V.G.	Good	Fair	Poor
800	600	450	300	200	150

Hi-Power Mark III

The pistol, introduced in 1991, has a matte blued finish, low-profile fixed sights, and two-piece molded grips with thumb rest. Weighs 32 oz.

NIB	Exc.	V.G.	Good	Fair	Poor
780	600	500	300	200	175

PRO-9/Pro-40

This 9mm or .40 S&W double-action pistol is fitted with a 4" barrel. Stainless steel slide. Grips are composite with interchangeable backstrap inserts. Magazine capacity is 16 rounds for 9mm and 14 rounds for the .40 S&W. Weight is about 30 oz.

NIB	Exc.	V.G.	Good	Fair	Poor
625	500	375	—	—	—

BDA-380

This is a double-action, semi-automatic pistol chambered for the .380 ACP cartridge. It features a 3.75" barrel with a 14-round, double-stack, detachable magazine. The finish is either blued or nickel-plated with smooth walnut grips. This pistol was manufactured in Italy by Beretta and introduced in 1977.

NIB	Exc.	V.G.	Good	Fair	Poor
500	375	325	275	200	150

NOTE: Add 10 percent for nickel finish.

Model BDA

This is a double-action, semi-automatic pistol manufactured between 1977 and 1980 for Browning by SIG-Sauer of Germany. It is identical to the SIG-Sauer Model 220. It is chambered for

9mm Parabellum, .38 Super, and the .45 ACP cartridges. The .38 Super would be worth approximately 30 percent additional.

Exc.	V.G.	Good	Fair	Poor
525	425	375	300	235

BDM Pistol

This is a double-action, semi-automatic pistol chambered for the 9mm cartridge. The pistol is fitted with a selector switch that allows the shooter to choose between single-action model or double-action model. It features a 4.75" barrel with adjustable rear sight. The magazine capacity is 15 rounds. Weighs 31 oz. First introduced in 1991.

NIB	Exc.	V.G.	Good	Fair	Poor
560	450	350	250	200	150

Model BDM Silver Chrome

This variation of the BDM was introduced in 1997 and features a silver chrome finish on the slide and frame. The balance of the pistol is in a contrasting matte blue finish.

NIB	Exc.	V.G.	Good	Fair	Poor
560	450	350	250	200	150

Model BDM Practical

This model, also introduced in 1997, is the same as above but with the silver chrome on the frame only.

NIB	Exc.	V.G.	Good	Fair	Poor
560	450	350	250	200	150

Model BPM-D

Introduced in 1997 this new version of the BDM (Browning Pistol Model Decocker) features a double-action pistol with the first shot fired double-action and subsequent shots fired single-action. There is no manual safety. A decock lever also releases the slide.

NIB	Exc.	V.G.	Good	Fair	Poor
525	400	300	250	200	150

Model BRM-DAO

This 9mm pistol is a redesigned version of the Model BDM but the initials stand for "Browning Revolver Model Double-Action-Only." This pistol also has a finger support trigger guard for two-handed control. All other features are the same as the BPM-D pistol. Weight is approximately 31 oz.

NIB	Exc.	V.G.	Good	Fair	Poor
525	400	300	250	200	150

Nomad

This is a blowback-operated, semi-automatic pistol chambered for the .22 LR cartridge. It was offered with a 4.5" or 6.75" barrel. It has a 10-round, detachable magazine with adjustable sights and all-steel construction. The finish is blued with black plastic grips. It was manufactured between 1962 and 1974 by FN.

NIB	Exc.	V.G.	Good	Fair	Poor
350	250	200	150	75	50

Challenger

This is a more deluxe target pistol chambered for the .22 LR cartridge. It was offered with a 4.5" or 6.75" barrel and has a 10-round magazine. It is constructed entirely of steel and has adjustable sights. The finish is blued with a gold-plated trigger and checkered, wraparound, walnut grips. It was manufactured between 1962 and 1974 by FN.

Courtesy John J. Stimson, Jr.

NIB	Exc.	V.G.	Good	Fair	Poor
500	375	300	250	200	140

Renaissance Challenger

This version is fully engraved with a satin-nickel finish and furnished with a fleece-lined pouch.

This symbol denotes "Sleepers" with rapidly-rising values and/or significant collector potential.

NIB	Exc.	V.G.	Good	Fair	Poor
1600	1300	1000	750	500	350

Gold Line Challenger

This version is blued and has a gold-inlaid line around the outer edges of the pistol. It was cased in a fleece-lined pouch. Built in Belgium.

NIB	Exc.	V.G.	Good	Fair	Poor
1600	1300	1000	750	500	350

Challenger II

This is a blowback-operated, semi-automatic pistol chambered for the .22 LR cartridge. It has a 6.75" barrel with an alloy frame. The finish is blued with phenolic impregnated hardwood grips. This pistol was manufactured between 1976 and 1982 in Salt Lake City, Utah.

Exc.	V.G.	Good	Fair	Poor
350	225	175	140	100

Challenger III

This version features a 5.5" bull barrel with adjustable sights. It was manufactured between 1982 and 1984 in Salt Lake City, Utah. A 6.75", tapered-barrel version was also available and known as the Sporter.

Exc.	V.G.	Good	Fair	Poor
300	200	150	125	90

Browning Collector's Association Edition

Fully engraved, 100 manufactured. This model was fitted with a two-piece grip.

NIB	Exc.	V.G.	Good	Fair	Poor
2750	2250	—	—	—	—

Medalist

This is a high-grade, semi-automatic target pistol chambered for the .22 LR cartridge. It has a 6.75", vent rib barrel with adjustable target sights. It was supplied with three barrel weights and a dry-fire-practice mechanism. The finish is blued with target type, thumbrest, walnut grips. It was manufactured between 1962 and 1974 by FN. There were four additional high-grade versions of this pistol that differed in the degree of ornamentation.

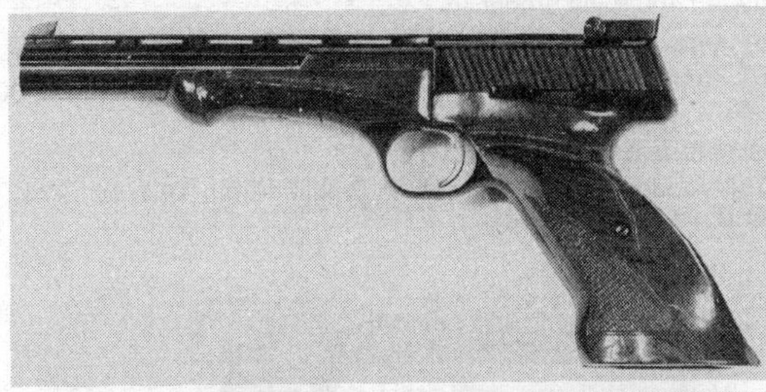

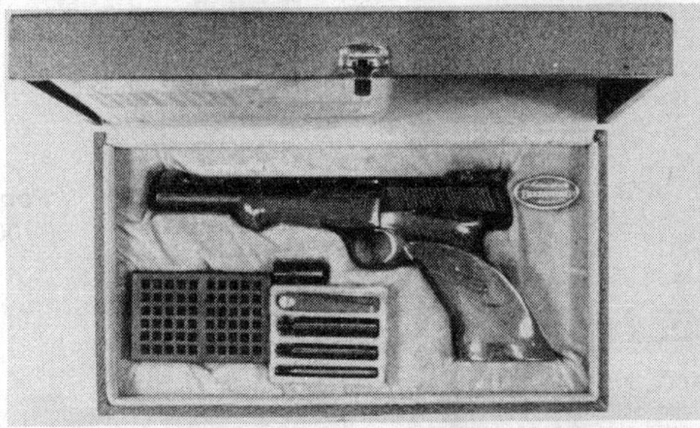

NIB	Exc.	V.G.	Good	Fair	Poor
900	750	575	475	375	250

International Medalist

About 700 were sold in the U.S. from 1977 to 1980. Barrels were 5-7/8" long. Built in Belgium.

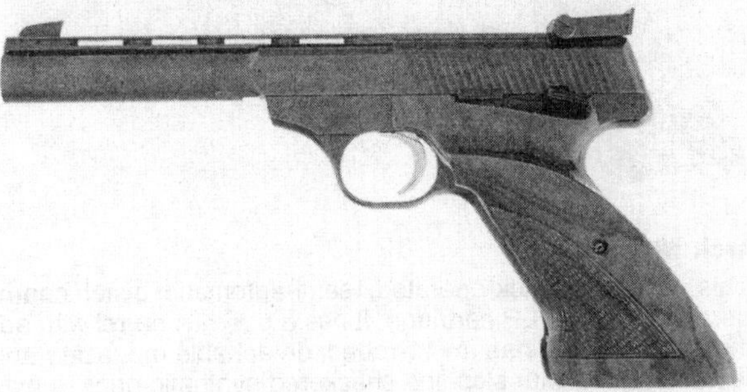

Courtesy John J. Stimson, Jr.

NIB	Exc.	V.G.	Good	Fair	Poor
950	800	600	450	300	150

Second Model International Medalist

Same as above but with flat-sided barrel, dull finish, and adjustable palm rest. Built in Belgium.

Courtesy John J. Stimson, Jr.

NIB	Exc.	V.G.	Good	Fair	Poor
875	725	450	300	200	150

Gold Line Medalist

Introduced in 1962 and discontinued in 1974 with only an estimated 400 guns produced.

NIB	Exc.	V.G.	Good	Fair	Poor
1750	1600	1250	1000	750	500

Renaissance Medalist

This model was built entirely in Belgium from 1970 to 1974. Built with a one-piece grip.

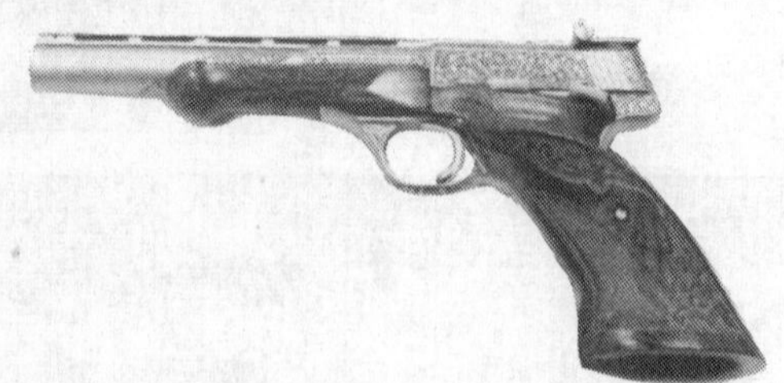

NIB	Exc.	V.G.	Good	Fair	Poor
2250	1900	1500	1200	900	700

BUCK MARK SERIES

Buck Mark

This is a blowback-operated, semi-automatic pistol chambered for the .22 LR cartridge. It has a 5.5" bull barrel with adjustable sights. It has an 11-round, detachable magazine and is matte blued with skip-line checkered synthetic grips. It was introduced in 1985. Produced in the U.S.

NIB	Exc.	V.G.	Good	Fair	Poor
320	250	175	135	110	85

NOTE: Add $25 for stainless steel version introduced in 2005.

Buck Mark Plus

This version is similar to the standard, with plain wood grips. It was introduced in 1987. Produced in the U.S.

NIB	Exc.	V.G.	Good	Fair	Poor
390	300	200	150	100	75

Buck Mark Plus Nickel

Introduced in 1991. Add $35 to above prices.

REMINDER
In most cases, condition determines price.

Buck Mark Varmint

This version has a 9.75" bull barrel with a full-length ramp to allow scope mounting. It has no sights. It was introduced in 1987 and produced in the U.S.

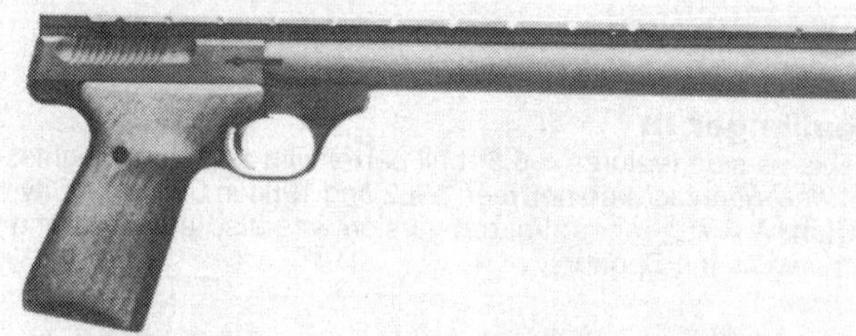

NIB	Exc.	V.G.	Good	Fair	Poor
375	285	250	200	175	125

Buck Mark Silhouette

This version features a 9.75" bull barrel with adjustable sights. Introduced in 1987.

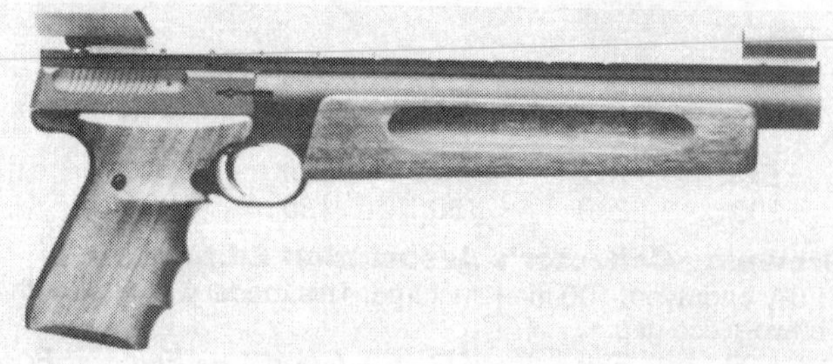

NIB	Exc.	V.G.	Good	Fair	Poor
425	325	285	220	185	140

Buck Mark 22 Micro

This version of the Buck Mark 22 is fitted with a 4" bull barrel. Available in blue, matte blue, or nickel finish. Also available in Micro Plus variation with walnut grips. Weighs 32 oz. Introduced in 1992.

NIB	Exc.	V.G.	Good	Fair	Poor
320	250	175	135	110	85

NOTE: Add $25 for stainless steel version introduced in 2005.

Micro Plus

NIB	Exc.	V.G.	Good	Fair	Poor
325	225	175	150	125	90

Micro Plus Nickel

Introduced in 1996. Add $75 to above price.

REMINDER
Prices paid for firearms is an ever-changing affair based on a large number of variables.

Buck Mark 5.5

This .22 caliber pistol has a 5.5" heavy bull barrel fitted with target sights. It is offered in three separate models:

5.5 Blued Target

This version has a blued finish, contoured walnut grips, target sights. Weighs 35.5 oz. Introduced in 1990.

NIB	Exc.	V.G.	Good	Fair	Poor
450	350	250	150	100	100

5.5 Blued Target (2005)

Introduced in 2005 this model features a new target-style Cocabolo grips, a full length scope mount, and hooded target sights. Weight is 35 oz.

NIB	Exc.	V.G.	Good	Fair	Poor
510	400	300	200	150	100

5.5 Gold Target

Same as above but has a gold anodized frame and top rib. Slide is blue. Walnut grips. Introduced in 1991.

NIB	Exc.	V.G.	Good	Fair	Poor
500	400	300	200	150	125

5.5 Field

Same action and barrel as the Target Model but with adjustable field sights. Sights are hoodless. Slide and barrel is blued while the rib and frame are anodized blue. Grips are walnut. Introduced in 1991.

NIB	Exc.	V.G.	Good	Fair	Poor
400	325	225	150	100	100

5.5 Field (2005)

This model features new target style grips and full-length scope rail. Introduced in 2005. Weight is about 35 oz.

NIB	Exc.	V.G.	Good	Fair	Poor
510	400	—	—	—	—

Buck Field Plus

This .22 caliber pistol has a 5.5" barrel with Truglo/Marbles' front sight. Grips are laminated rosewood. Barrel are polished blue. Weight is about 24 oz.

NIB	Exc.	V.G.	Good	Fair	Poor
390	300	225	—	—	—

Buck Mark Bullseye

Introduced in 1996 this pistol is designed for metallic silhouette competition. The fluted barrel is 7-1/4" long. Adjustable trigger pull, adjustable rear sight removable barrel are some of the features. Weight is about 36 oz. Choice of laminated wood grips or rubber grips.

NIB	Exc.	V.G.	Good	Fair	Poor
465	375	225	175	125	75

NOTE: For Rosewood target grips add $90.

Buck Mark Unlimited Match

This pistol is fitted with a 14" barrel with top rib. The front sight hood is slightly rearward of the muzzle for a maximum sight radius of 15". All other features are the same as the Silhouette model. Weighs 64 oz.

NIB	Exc.	V.G.	Good	Fair	Poor
425	325	275	225	175	125

Buck Mark Challenge

Introduced in 1999 this model features a lightweight 5.5" barrel with adjustable rear sight. Smaller grip diameter. Matte blue finish and 10-round magazine capacity. Weight is about 25 oz.

NIB	Exc.	V.G.	Good	Fair	Poor
350	250	200	175	—	—

Buck Mark Camper

This model is fitted with a heavy 5.5" barrel and has a matte blue finish. Ten-round magazine capacity. Weight is about 34 oz. Introduced in 1999.

NIB	Exc.	V.G.	Good	Fair	Poor
290	200	150	125	—	—

NOTE: Add $25 for stainless steel version introduced in 2005.

Buck Mark Hunter

This .22 pistol features a 7.25" heavy round barrel with Truglo/Marbles front sights, adjustable rear sight and integrated scope base. Grips are Cocabolo target-style. Weight is about 38 oz. Introduced in 2005.

NIB	Exc.	V.G.	Good	Fair	Poor
360	275	225	175	—	—

Buck Mark Limited Edition 25th Anniversary

This model is limited to 1,000 pistols and features a 6.75" barrel with matte blued finish and scrimshaw etched ivory grips. Pistol rug furnished as standard equipment.

NIB	Exc.	V.G.	Good	Fair	Poor
475	350	300	—	—	—

Buck Mark Bullseye Target Stainless

Blowback, single action .22 LR semi-auto. Matte blued, heavy 7.25" round and fluted stainless bull barrel. Laminated rosewood grip, adjustable sights. Introduced 2006. MSRP: 643

Buck Mark Bullseye Target URX

Blowback, single-action semi-auto in .22LR. Matte blued, heavy 7.25" round and fluted bull barrel. Grooved, rubberized grip, 39 oz., adjustable sights. Introduced 2006.

NIB	Exc.	V.G.	Good	Fair	Poor
450	—	—	—	—	—

Buck Mark Contour 5.5 URX

Blowback, single-action .222 semi-auto. Matte blued, contoured 5.5" barrel. Full-length scope base, 36 oz., adjustable sights. (Multiple barrel lengths and options.) Introduced 2006.

NIB	Exc.	V.G.	Good	Fair	Poor
400	—	—	—	—	—

Buck Mark Contour Lite 5.5 URX

.22 LR blowback, single-action semi-auto. Matte blued, contoured 5.5" barrel. Full-length scope base, 28 oz. Adjustable sights. (Multiple barrel lengths and options.) Introduced 2006.

NIB	Exc.	V.G.	Good	Fair	Poor
450	—	—	—	—	—

Buck Mark FLD Plus Rosewood UDX

22 LR blowback single-action semi-auto. "FLD" sculpted grip with rosewood panels. Blued, contoured 5.5" barrel, 34 oz., adjustable rear sight, fiber optic front sight. (Multiple barrel lengths and options.) Introduced 2006.

NIB	Exc.	V.G.	Good	Fair	Poor
450	—	—	—	—	—

Buck Mark Lite Splash 5.5 URX

Blowback single-action semi-auto. Matte blued finish, gold splash anodizing. Chambered for .22 LR, 5.5" barrel. Rubberized ambidextrous grip. Adjustable sights; fiber optic front sight. 28 oz. (Also available with 7.5" barrel.) Introduced 2006.

NIB	Exc.	V.G.	Good	Fair	Poor
430	—	—	—	—	—

Buck Mark Micro Standard Stainless URX

With a 4" stainless barrel, this .22 LR weighs 32 oz. Ambidextrous rubberized grip and adjustable sights. (Also available in alloy steel.) Introduced 2006.

NIB	Exc.	V.G.	Good	Fair	Poor
375	—	—	—	—	—

Buck Mark Micro Bull

4" stainless bull barrel; .22 LR; weight 33 oz. Plastic grip panels and adjustable sights. Introduced 2006.

NIB	Exc.	V.G.	Good	Fair	Poor
260	—	—	—	—	—

Buck Mark Plus Stainless Black Laminated UDX

Similar to Buck Mark Standard Stainless UDX but with ambidextrous grips. Introduced 2007.

NIB	Exc.	V.G.	Good	Fair	Poor
461	—	—	—	—	—

Buck Mark Plus UDX

Similar to Buck Mark FLD Plus but with ambidextrous walnut grips. Introduced 2007.

NIB	Exc.	V.G.	Good	Fair	Poor
425	—	—	—	—	—

Full Line Dealer Buck Mark Plus Rosewood UDX

Similar to Buck Mark Plus UDX but with ambidextrous rosewood grips. Available only to full-line and Medallion-level Browning dealers. Introduced 2007.

NIB	Exc.	V.G.	Good	Fair	Poor
425	—	—	—	—	—

Buck Mark Plus Stainless UDX

.22 LR semi-auto with finger-grooved wood grips. 5.5" barrel, 34 oz. Adjustable sights, fiber optic front sight. (Also available blued alloy steel.) Introduced 2006.

NIB	Exc.	V.G.	Good	Fair	Poor
440	—	—	—	—	—

Buck Mark Standard Stainless URX

.22 LR semi-auto. 5.5" stainless bull barrel; 34 oz. Ambidextrous rubberized grip and adjustable sights. (Also available in alloy steel.) Introduced 2006.

NIB	Exc.	V.G.	Good	Fair	Poor
380	—	—	—	—	—

CAUTION

Certain Browning long guns used wood that was salt-cured, causing a rusting problem to the underside of barrels and actions. This should be carefully checked before purchase. This problem is most prevalent during the years 1966 to 1972.

SHOTGUNS

SUPERPOSED SHOTGUNS

This series of Over/Under, double-barrel shotguns is chambered for 12, 20, and 28 gauges, as well as the .410 bore and is offered with vent rib barrels from 26.5" to 32" in length. It features various choke combinations. This shotgun is built on a boxlock action and features either double or single-selective triggers and automatic ejectors. There were a number of versions offered that differ in the amount of ornamentation and the quality of the materials and workmanship utilized in manufacture. Values for small-bore models are generally higher. This series was introduced in 1930 and is manufactured by Fabrique Nationale in Belgium. For factory restored guns or very fine non-factory restorations Superposed guns will bring close to factory original prices.

For extra factory installed barrels add $1000 to $2500 depending on the grade of the gun.

PRE-WAR SUPERPOSED, 1930-1940

Browning Superposed shotgun prices are divided into three different categories. The first category is for pre-war guns built from 1930 to 1940. *These pre-war Superposed guns were manufactured in 12 gauge only* from serial number 1 to around 17,000. These shotguns were offered in four different grades: Grade I, Pigeon, Diana, and Midas.

Grade I

Rock Island Auction Company, August, 2004

Exc.	V.G.	Good	Fair	Poor
2250	1750	1000	450	300

Pigeon

Exc.	V.G.	Good	Fair	Poor
3500	2500	1500	500	400

Diana

Exc.	V.G.	Good	Fair	Poor
6000	5200	3000	900	500

Midas

Exc.	V.G.	Good	Fair	Poor
9000	7500	3700	1200	750

NOTE: For twin-single triggers add 15 percent. For vent rib add 10 percent. For recoil pads or shorter than standard stocks deduct 25 percent.

SUPERPOSED FROM 1947-1959

The second category of Superposed was produced and sold from 1947 to 1959. These were built in 12 and 20 gauge as well as the 28 gauge and .410 bore which were introduced in 1959. These shotguns were graded using a Roman numeral system instead of names. They are: Grade I, Grade II, Grade III, Grade IV, Grade V, and Grade VI. The values listed are for 12 gauge. Add the premium or deductions as listed. The number of 28 gauge and .410 bore guns sold in late 1959 number less than 100.

NOTE: The number of Grade VIs sold in North America is unknown, but it was most likely very small. This is a very rare grade. Proceed with caution.

Grade I

Marked Lightning on frame.

NIB	Exc.	V.G.	Good	Fair	Poor
3000	2000	1100	900	300	250

Grade II

NIB	Exc.	V.G.	Good	Fair	Poor
4500	3300	2100	1200	600	375

Grade III

NIB	Exc.	V.G.	Good	Fair	Poor
5750	5000	3500	2200	750	450

Grade IV

NIB	Exc.	V.G.	Good	Fair	Poor
8500	7500	4000	2400	1200	550

Grade V

NIB	Exc.	V.G.	Good	Fair	Poor
7500	6000	3800	2400	1200	650

Grade VI

Built 1957 through 1959 only.

NIB	Exc.	V.G.	Good	Fair	Poor
13000	11000	7000	4000	2200	850

NOTE: 20 gauge add 45 percent. 28 gauge add 90 percent (1959 only). 410 add 45 percent (1959 only). Trap deduct 40 percent. Standard weight 12 gauge Grade I deduct 10 percent.

SUPERPOSED FROM 1960-1976

Browning Superposed shotguns built from 1960 to 1976 revert back to the older grade names. They are Grade I, Pigeon, Pointer, Diana, and Midas. These shotguns were available in 12, 20, and 28 gauge as well as .410 bore. This last production period is a little more complicated due to manufacturing changes that some collectors consider important such as round knobs, long tangs.

Prices listed reflect Superposed field guns produced from 1960 to 1965 in round pistol grip knob with long trigger guard tang in 12 gauge. For all other variations during this period one should consider:

For salt wood damage deduct a minimum of 60 percent. For round knob short tang (circa 1966-1969) deduct 50 percent. For flat knob short tang (circa 1969-1971) deduct 50 percent. For flat knob long tang (circa 1971-1976) deduct 25 percent. For New Style Skeet and Lightning Trap (recoil pad, flat knob, full beavertail forearm) with long trigger guard tang (1971-1976) deduct 35 percent; with short trigger guard tang deduct 40 percent; if Broadway rib deduct an additional 10 percent. For skeet chokes on field guns deduct 5 percent. For recoil pads on 2-3/4" chambered field guns deduct 20 percent. For Master engraver signed guns (Funken, Watrin, Vrancken) add 10 percent. For Standard weight Grade I guns deduct 10 percent. For shorter than standard stock length deduct 25 percent. For barrel lengths of 32" add 10 percent. For 20 gauge add 50 percent. For 28 gauge add 100 percent. For .410 bore add 35 percent.

Grade I

Lightning marked on frame.

NIB	Exc.	V.G.	Good	Fair	Poor
3000	2250	1200	700	500	250

Pigeon Grade

NIB	Exc.	V.G.	Good	Fair	Poor
5500	4500	3000	2000	1000	600

Pointer Grade—Rare

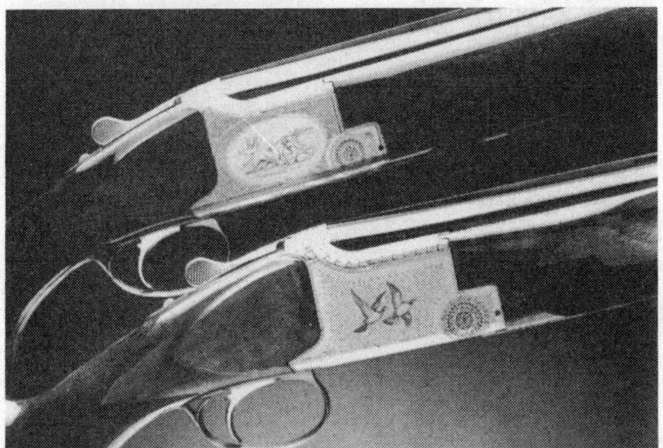

NIB	Exc.	V.G.	Good	Fair	Poor
8500	7250	5000	3000	2000	1000

Diana Grade

NIB	Exc.	V.G.	Good	Fair	Poor
8500	7250	5000	3000	2000	1000

Midas Grade

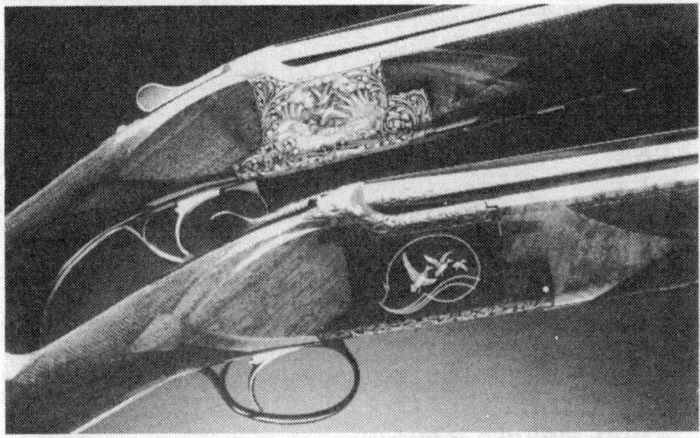

NIB	Exc.	V.G.	Good	Fair	Poor
11000	10000	8000	7000	5000	4000

Comment: FN also built Exhibition Grades that were sold in this country under the Browning name. Collectors consider a true Exhibition Grade as one not having a "C" prefix in the serial number. These particular guns are considered quite desirable and should be appraised on an individual basis. Superposed in this catageory can range in price from $10,000 to $20,000 depending on gauge, engraving coverage, and options.

The second type of Exhibition Grade is know as the "C" type that was first sold in the United States from about 1973 to 1977 and is so called because of the "C" prefix in the serial number. There were about 225 of these guns sold in the United States They came in quite a few grades and some were specially ordered. Although the lower grades are not considered by some to be true exhibitions (pre-C series) the highest "C" series grades are a match to the best of the older exhibitions. In 2000, an all option Superlight 2 barrel set with sideplates engraved by Vranken sold for $22,000. Generally, depending on the gun, prices will range between $6,000 and $25,000. These "C" grade guns should also be appraised individually.

SUPERPOSED SUPERLIGHT

This model was first introduced in 1967 in 12 gauge and in 1969 in 20 gauge. Special order 28 gauge as well as .410 bore are also seen. It was offered in 26.5" barrel lengths with 27.5" barrls in 12 gauge and 28" barrels in smaller bores available on special order. It features a rounded frame and straight grip stock with tapered solid or vent rib barrels. Regular production on the Superlight ended in 1976 for the grades listed. Production did continue for the Superlight in the P series begun in 1977.

Grade I

NIB	Exc.	V.G.	Good	Fair	Poor
3250	2750	1700	600	400	250

Pigeon Grade

NIB	Exc.	V.G.	Good	Fair	Poor
5000	3900	3000	1500	1000	800

Pointer Grade—Rare

NIB	Exc.	V.G.	Good	Fair	Poor
9000	7000	4700	2500	1500	1000

Diana Grade

NIB	Exc.	V.G.	Good	Fair	Poor
9000	7000	4700	2500	1500	850

Midas Grade

NIB	Exc.	V.G.	Good	Fair	Poor
11000	9000	6500	3700	2000	1000

NOTE: For 20 gauge guns add a 50 percent premium. For 28 gauge guns add a 100 percent premium. For .410 bore guns add 30 percent premium for high grades guns and 30 percent for Grade I.

SUPERPOSED PRESENTATION GRADE SERIES

The superposed shotguns listed were manufactured between 1977 and 1984 by FN in Belgium. The models listed differ in the amount of ornamentation and the quality of materials and workmanship utilized in construction. This series was also available in a superlight configuration.

NOTE: Due to the tremendous variation of P-Series guns, prices here reflect the Superlight configuration. An all option superlight with a checkered butt, oil finish, and three piece forend will bring 25-30 percent more. For all other variations one should consider:

For trap guns deduct 35 percent. For new style skeet deduct 30 percent. For skeet choked field guns deduct 5 percent. For recoil pads on field guns deduct 30 percent. For flat knob long tang hunting guns with no options deduct 35 percent. For flat knob long tang hunting guns with all options add 25 percent. For guns signed by J. Baerten add 5 percent. For P-4V guns with no gold deduct 20 percent. For hand filed vent rib add 5 percent.

For Presentation Grade guns with extra sets of barrels add approximately $1,500 to $2,500 depending on gauge and combination.

For P1, P2, and P3 grades add the premium listed:
For 20 gauge guns—55 percent.
For .28 gauge guns—100 percent.
For .410 bore—30 percent.

For the P4 grade add the premium listed:
For 20 gauge guns—55 percent.
For 28 gauge guns—100 percent.
For .410 bore—40 percent.

Presentation I (without gold inlays)

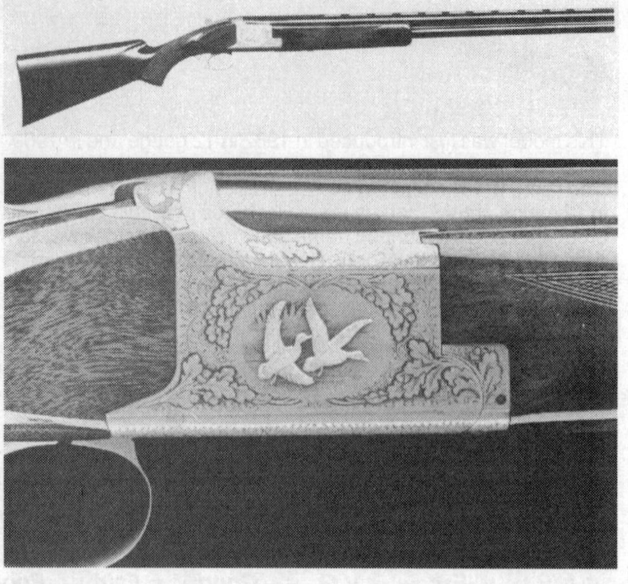

NIB	Exc.	V.G.	Good	Fair	Poor
3500	2700	1200	1000	600	500

Presentation 1 Gold-inlaid

NIB	Exc.	V.G.	Good	Fair	Poor
5250	4000	2700	1400	700	500

Presentation 2 (without gold inlays)

NIB	Exc.	V.G.	Good	Fair	Poor
5250	4250	3000	1800	1000	600

Presentation 2 Gold-inlaid

NIB	Exc.	V.G.	Good	Fair	Poor
7500	6500	4250	2500	1500	1000

NOTE: For early hand-engraved P3 models (approximately 25 produced) add 40 percent. These early guns are rare, proceed with caution.

Presentation 3 Gold-inlaid

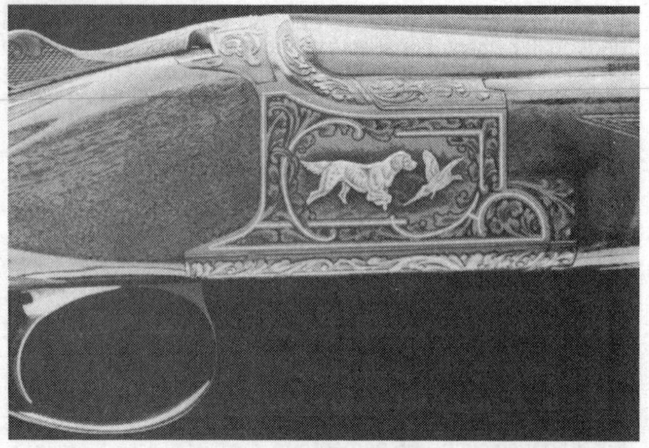

NIB	Exc.	V.G.	Good	Fair	Poor
9500	8000	5800	4000	2000	1300

Presentation 4 Gold-inlaid

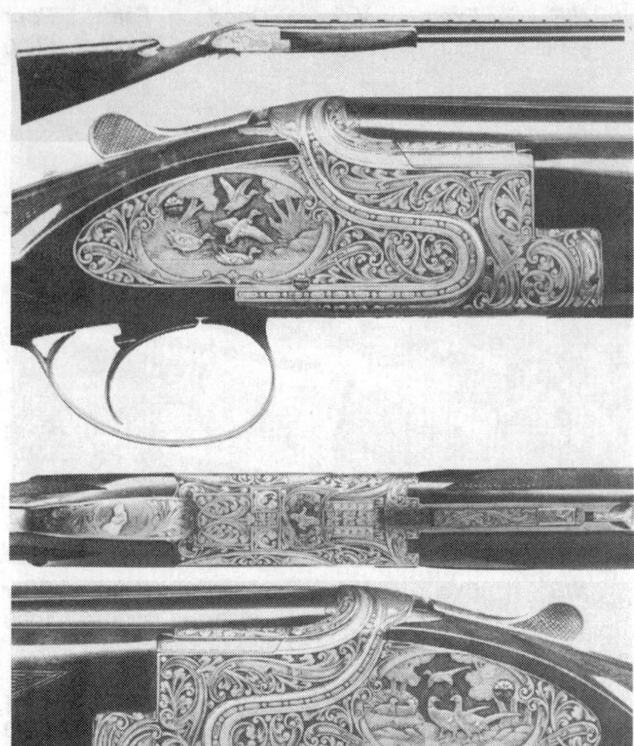

NIB	Exc.	V.G.	Good	Fair	Poor
13000	11500	9000	6750	5000	3500

NOTE: For P4 Grade guns with no gold deduct approximately 20 percent.

SUPERPOSED WATERFOWL LIMITED EDITION SERIES

This model was issued in three different versions; Mallard, Pintail, and Black Duck. Each edition was limited to 500 guns, all in 12 gauge.

1981 Mallard Issue

NIB	Exc.	V.G.	Good	Fair	Poor
7200	6000	4500	3300	1900	1100

1982 Pintail Issue

NIB	Exc.	V.G.	Good	Fair	Poor
7200	6000	4500	3300	1900	1100

1983 Black Duck Issue

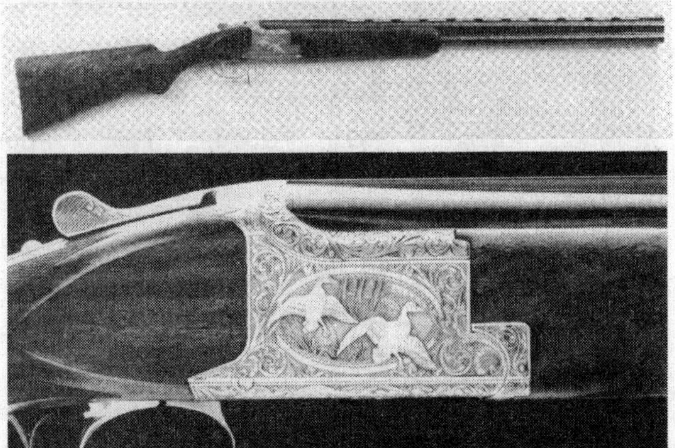

NIB	Exc.	V.G.	Good	Fair	Poor
7200	6000	4500	3300	1900	1100

Bicentennial Model

Produced in 1976 to commemorate the 200 year anniversary of America. A total of 53 guns were built in this special edition. All of these Superposed were 12 gauge with 28" barrels and each was numbered for one of the fifty states plus the District of Columbia. Two additional guns were built for the Smithsonian Institution and the Liege Firearms Museum. All were fitted with side plates with gold inlays. To reflect true value guns must be in unfired condition in their original case with all the papers.

NIB	Exc.	V.G.	Good	Fair	Poor
10000	8000	5500	2750	1500	1000

NOTE: Price often depends on the state.

FN/Browning Superposed

A number of FN Browning Superposed B-25 shotguns were imported into this country by Browning in various grades. These Superposed were intended originally for FN's European market. There are a large number of variations and grades. It is strongly suggested that an expert appraisal be sought prior to the sale. As a general rule these prices for NIB guns are: A grade-$1,200-1,600; B grade $1,600-2,500; C grade $2,500-3,500; D grade $3,500-5,000. These guns are marked with both the Browning and FN barrel address.

Classic

Produced in 1986 this model was offered in 20 gauge with 26" barrels. About 2,500 guns were produced. Silver gray receiver with engraving.

NIB	Exc.	V.G.	Good	Fair	Poor
2500	1750	—	—	—	—

Gold Classic

This shotgun was similar to the above model but more finely finished and engraved with gold inlays. About 350 of these guns were built in 1986.

NIB	Exc.	V.G.	Good	Fair	Poor
9500	6500	—	—	—	—

Custom Shop B25 & B125 Superposed

These special order Superposed are currently available with a delivery time of 6 to 8 months. A number of options are offered that affect price. B125 guns are assembled in Belgium with components made in other countries to hold down costs. The B25 is made entirely in Belgium and is the more expensive version of the Superposed. Prices listed are retail only.

NOTE: Retail prices for current production guns change often. Contact Browning for the present prices.

B-125

Trap — Retail Price—$8,125

12 Gauge Sporting

A Style — Retail Price—$4,475
B Style — Retail Price—$4,800
C Style — Retail Price—$5,275

12 & 20 Gauge Hunting and Superlight

A Style — Retail price—$4,475
B Style — Retail price—$4,800
C Style — Retail price—$5,275

B-25

Grade I — Retail price—$6,850
Pigeon Grade — Retail price—$8,625
Pointer Grade — Retail price—$9,950
Diana Grade — Retail price—$10,350
Midas Grade — Retail price—$14,500

Custom Shop BSL

This is a side-by-side shotgun is equiped with Browning sidelock barrel, Holland & Holland-type locks with double trigger and auto ejectors. The gun is assembled and finished by Labeau-Courally. It is offered in both 12 and 20 gauge. Engraved grayed receiver or case colored receiver. Introduced into the Browning product line in 2001.

Case Colored Receiver (BSL Grade LC1)

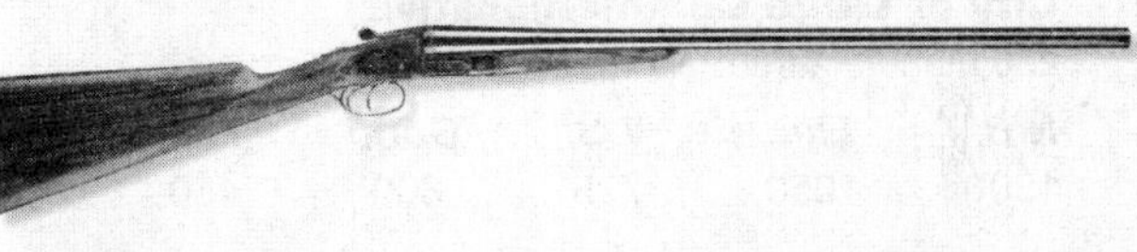

NIB	Exc.	V.G.	Good	Fair	Poor
10200	—	—	—	—	—

Engraved Gray Receiver (BSL Grade LC2)

NIB	Exc.	V.G.	Good	Fair	Poor
12275	—	—	—	—	—

Liege

This is an Over/Under shotgun chambered for 12 gauge. It was offered with 26.5", 28", or 30" vent rib barrels with various choke combinations. It features a boxlock action with a nonselective single trigger and automatic ejectors. The finish is blued with a checkered walnut stock. There were approximately 10,000 manufactured between 1973 and 1975. U.S. versions were marked Browning Arms Company on the barrel.

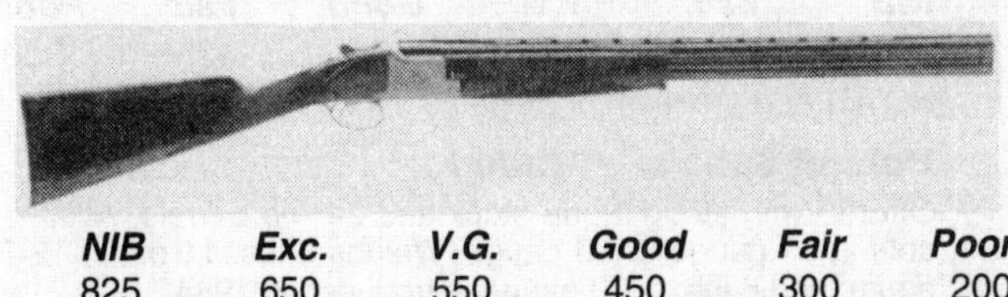

NIB	Exc.	V.G.	Good	Fair	Poor
825	650	550	450	300	200

B27

This improved version of the Liege was imported into the U.S., some without the Browning Arms Company markings and only the FN barrel address. Others may have both barrel addresses. It was offered in a number of variations that differed in the amount of ornamentation and quality of materials and workmanship utilized. It features the same action as the Liege Over/Under gun.

Standard

NIB	Exc.	V.G.	Good	Fair	Poor
750	550	450	350	250	200

Deluxe

NIB	Exc.	V.G.	Good	Fair	Poor
1100	900	650	500	350	250

Deluxe Trap

NIB	Exc.	V.G.	Good	Fair	Poor
1000	825	550	450	300	250

Deluxe Skeet

NIB	Exc.	V.G.	Good	Fair	Poor
1000	825	550	450	300	250

Grand Deluxe

NIB	Exc.	V.G.	Good	Fair	Poor
1500	1100	775	650	500	400

City of Liege Commemorative

250 manufactured.

NIB	Exc.	V.G.	Good	Fair	Poor
1500	1050	725	600	450	300

ST-100

This is an Over/Under trap gun that features separated barrels with an adjustable point of impact. It is chambered for 12 gauge and has a 30" or 32" barrel with full choke and a floating ventilated rib. It features a single trigger and automatic ejectors. The finish is blued with a checkered walnut stock. It was manufactured by FN between 1979 and 1981.

NIB	Exc.	V.G.	Good	Fair	Poor
2750	1700	1400	1000	700	400

CITORI SERIES

This is an Over/Under, double-barrel shotgun chambered for all gauges and offered with vent rib barrels of 26" through 30" in length. It has a boxlock action with a single-selective trigger and automatic ejectors. The various grades differ in the amount of ornamentation and the quality of materials and workmanship utilized in construction. This series is manufactured in Japan by B.C. Miroku and was introduced in 1973.

NOTE: For all Citori models, add a 15-20 percent premium for 28 gauge and .410.

Grade I

NIB	Exc.	V.G.	Good	Fair	Poor
900	800	725	550	425	300

NOTE: Add premium of 30 percent for 16 gauge guns.

Upland Special—Grade I

Offered with straight-grip stock and 24" rib barrels. Available in 12 gauge or 20 gauge. Weighs 6 lbs. 11 oz. in 12 gauge and 6 lbs. in 20 gauge. Introduced in 1984.

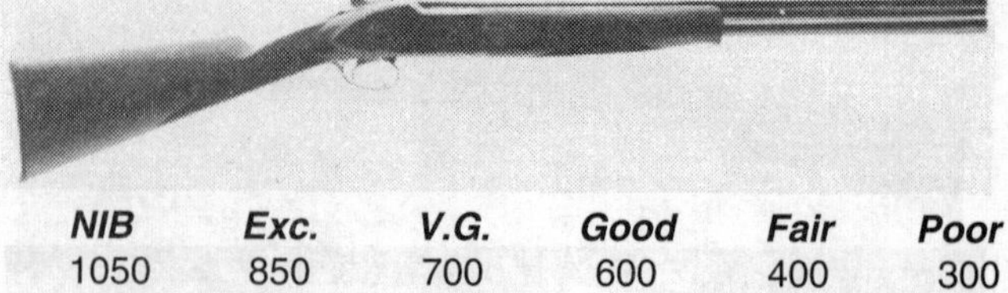

NIB	Exc.	V.G.	Good	Fair	Poor
1050	850	700	600	400	300

Grade II—1978 to 1983

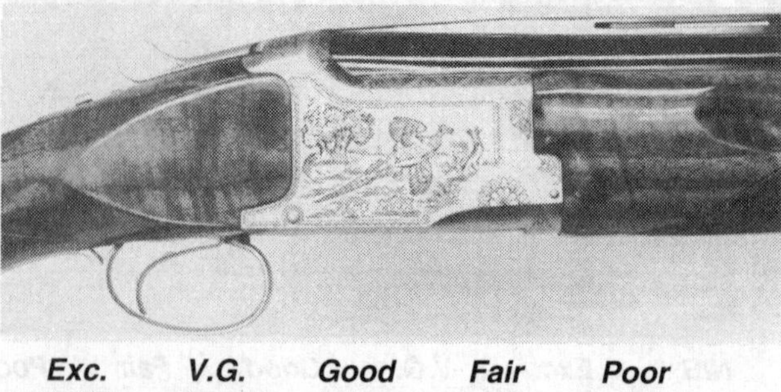

Exc.	V.G.	Good	Fair	Poor
1500	1200	1000	650	400

Grade II—Choke Tubes

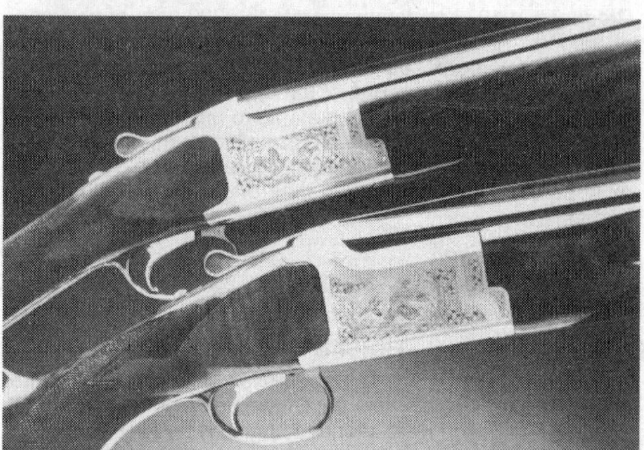

NIB	Exc.	V.G.	Good	Fair	Poor
1600	1400	1000	775	650	400

Grade V—1978 to 1984

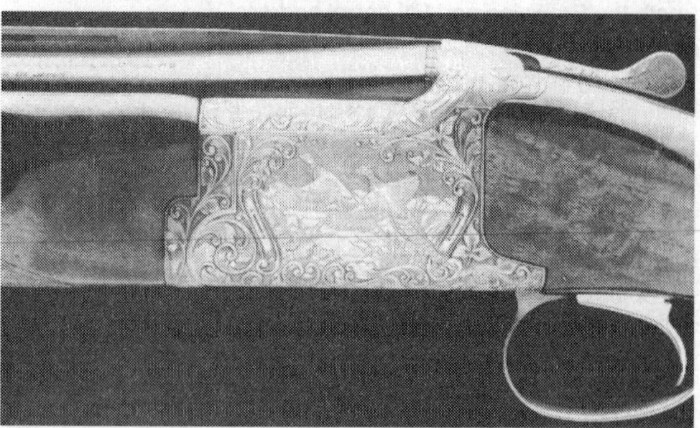

NIB	Exc.	V.G.	Good	Fair	Poor
2600	2100	1600	950	750	400

Grade V with sideplates—1981 to 1984

NIB	Exc.	V.G.	Good	Fair	Poor
2900	2500	2100	1500	800	400

NOTE: Add 10 percent for small gauges.

Grade VI—Choke Tubes

Introduced 1983.

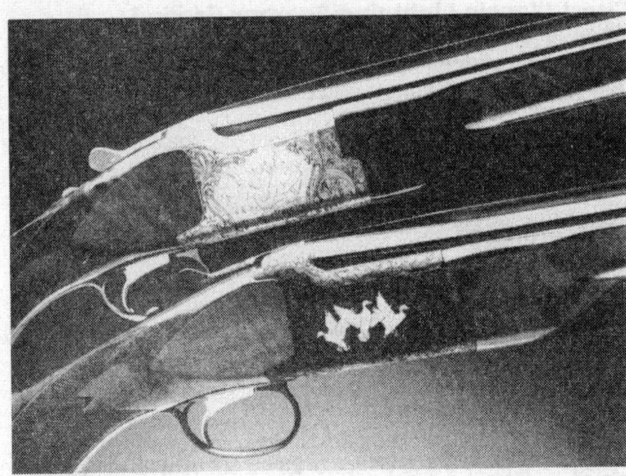

NIB	Exc.	V.G.	Good	Fair	Poor
1750	1500	1200	1000	750	500

Citori Hunter

This model features a full pistol-grip stock with beavertail forearm with high-gloss walnut. Chambered for 12 with 2.75", 3", or 3.5" chambers and choice of 26", 28" or 30" barrels in 12 gauge. The 20 gauge models have a choice of 26" or 28" barrels. Twelve gauge guns weigh from 7 lbs. 13 ozs. to 8 lbs. 9 ozs. depending on barrel length. Twenty gauge guns weigh about 6.75 lbs.

NIB	Exc.	V.G.	Good	Fair	Poor
1300	1000	850	650	550	450

NOTE: Add $75 for 3.5" models.

Citori Sporting Hunter

This model has the same features as the Hunting model with the exception of the stock configuration. The Sporting Hunter has a Sporting model buttstock and a Superposed style forearm. Fitted with a contoured sporting recoil pad. Introduced in 1998.

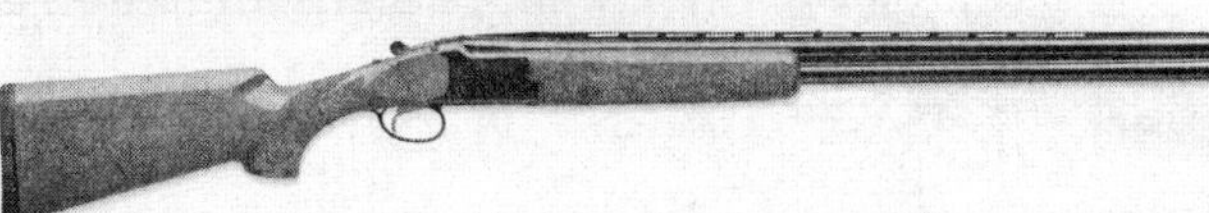

NIB	Exc.	V.G.	Good	Fair	Poor
1400	1300	1050	750	550	450

NOTE: Add $75 for 3.5" models.

Citori Satin Hunter

This model is chambered for 12 gauge shells, has a hunting-style stock, choice of 26" or 28" barrels, and a special satin wood finish with matte black receiver and barrels. Offered in Grade I only. Weight is about 8 lbs. Introduced in 1999.

NIB	Exc.	V.G.	Good	Fair	Poor
1250	1000	825	700	—	—

NOTE: Add $100 for 3.5" chamber.

Citori Lightning

This is a lightweight version that features a slimmer profile and has a checkered, round-knob, pistol-grip stock. It is offered in all gauges and in the same barrel lengths as the standard Citori. It features screw-in choke tubes known as Invectors. It was introduced in 1988. Offered in 12, 20 and 28 gauge and .410 bore. Weights are 6.5 lbs. to 8 lbs. depending on gauge and barrel length. The models differ in the amount of ornamentation and quality of materials and workmanship utilized.

Grade I

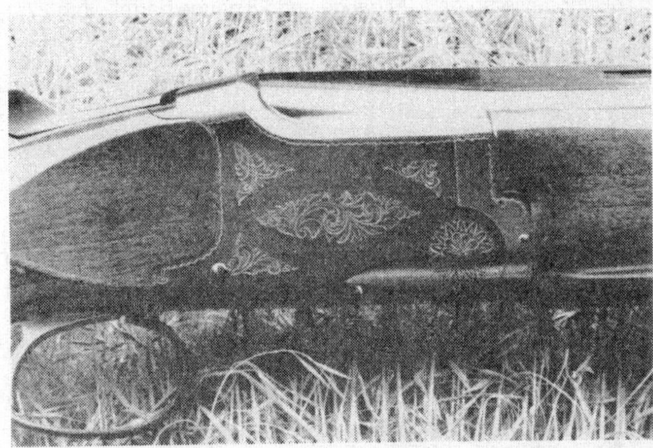

NIB	Exc.	V.G.	Good	Fair	Poor
1645	1200	900	600	450	375

Grade III

NIB	Exc.	V.G.	Good	Fair	Poor
2450	1900	1400	975	—	—

Grade IV

Introduced in 2005.

NIB	Exc.	V.G.	Good	Fair	Poor
2610	1950	—	—	—	—

Grade VI

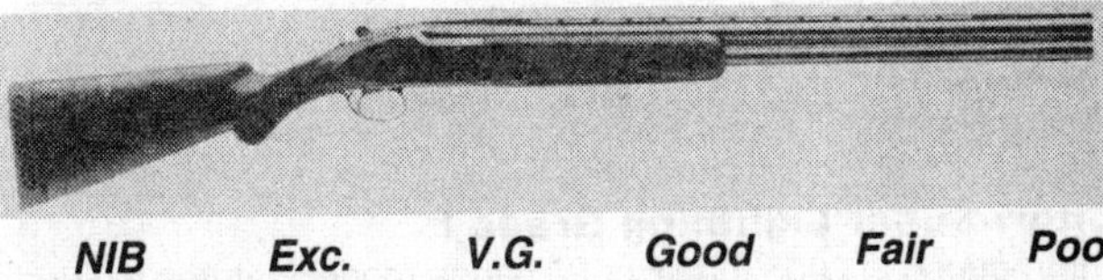

NIB	Exc.	V.G.	Good	Fair	Poor
3800	3000	2250	1500	—	—

Grade VII

Introduced in 2005.

NIB	Exc.	V.G.	Good	Fair	Poor
4145	3100	—	—	—	—

NOTE: Add $300 for 28 and .410 models.

Citori Lightning Feather

Introduced in 1999 this model features a lightweight alloy receiver. Offered in 12 gauge Grade I only with choice of 26" or 28" barrels. Weight with 28" barrels is about 7 lbs. 11 ozs. In 2000 this model was offered in 20 gauge as well with 26" or 28" barrels with 3" chambers. Weight of 20 gauge is about 6.5 lbs.

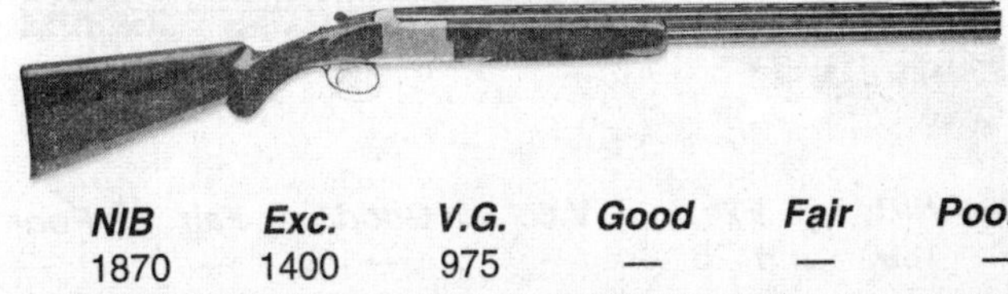

NIB	Exc.	V.G.	Good	Fair	Poor
1870	1400	975	—	—	—

Citori Lightning Feather Combo

This model features a 20 gauge and 28 gauge barrel, both 27" long. The 20 gauge with 3" chambers the 28 gauge with 2.75" chambers. Pistol grip stock. Weight is about 6.25 lbs. Supplied with Browning luggage case. Introduced in 2000.

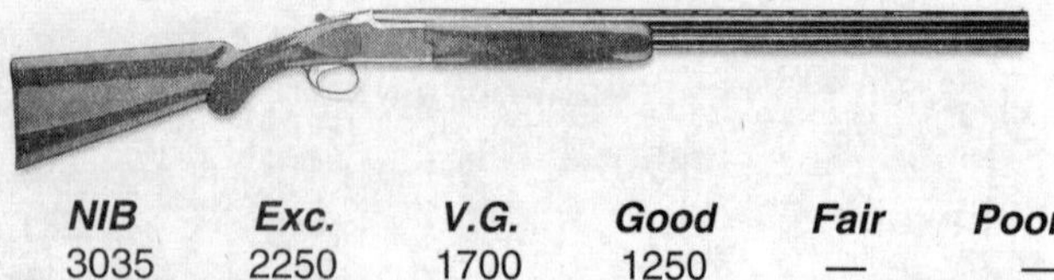

NIB	Exc.	V.G.	Good	Fair	Poor
3035	2250	1700	1250	—	—

Citori Feather XS

This model is offered in 12, 20, 28, and .410 bore. It has a lightweight alloy receiver. Fitted with a walnut stock with pistol grip, black recoil pad and schnabel forearm. Triple trigger system and Hi-Viz Comp sight system standard. Weight is about 7 lbs. for 12 gauge; 6.5 lbs. for 20 gauge; 6 lbs. for 28 gauge; and 6 lbs. for .410 bore. Introduced in 2000.

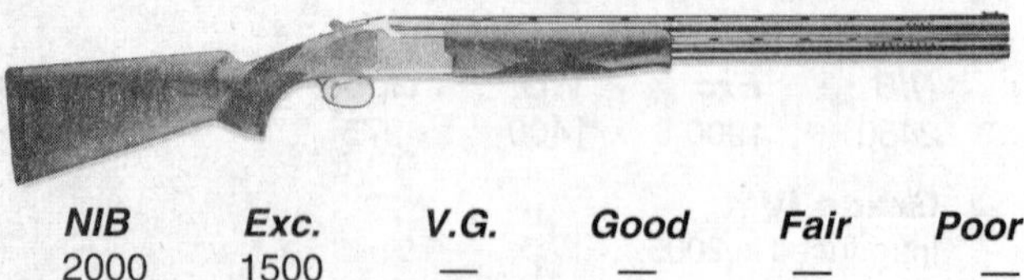

NIB	Exc.	V.G.	Good	Fair	Poor
2000	1500	—	—	—	—

Citori Superlight Feather

Chambered for the 12 or 20 gauge with straight grip stock and schnabel forearm. This model has an alloy receiver. Checkered walnut stock. Offered with 26" barrels. Weight is about 6 lbs. Introduced in 2002.

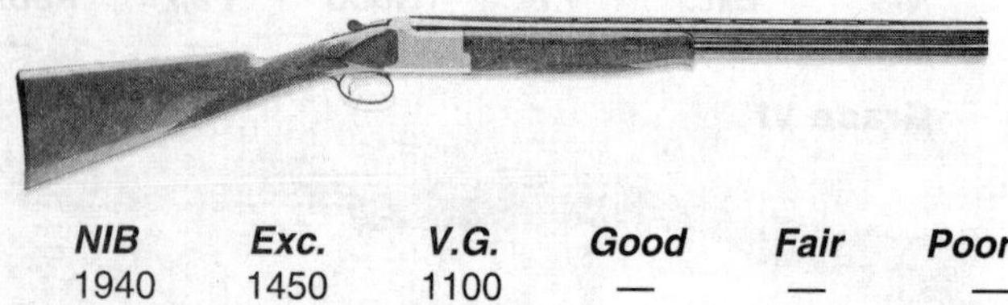

NIB	Exc.	V.G.	Good	Fair	Poor
1940	1450	1100	—	—	—

Citori Super Lightning Grade I

Introduced in 2005 this12 or 20 gauge model features a blued receiver with gold line border. Checkered satin finished select walnut stock with pistol grip and Schnabel forearm. Barrels are 26" or 28" with choke tubes. Recoil pad on 12 gauge. Weight is about 8 lbs. for the 12 gauge and 6.75 lbs. for the 20 gauge.

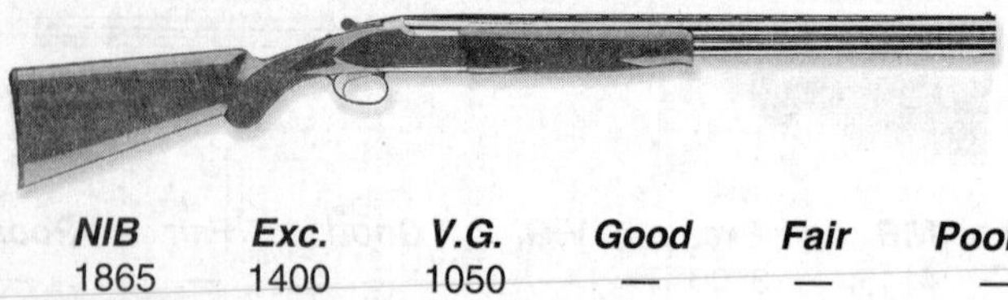

NIB	Exc.	V.G.	Good	Fair	Poor
1865	1400	1050	—	—	—

Citori Classic Lightning Grade I

Offered in 12 or 20 gauge with choice of 26" or 28" vent rib barrels with choke tubes. Receiver is scroll engraved on a silver nitride finish. Checkered select walnut stock with oil finish. Forearm is Lightning style. Recoil pad on 12 gauge. Weight is about 8 lbs. for 12 gauge and about 6.75 lbs. for the 20 gauge. Introduced in 2005.

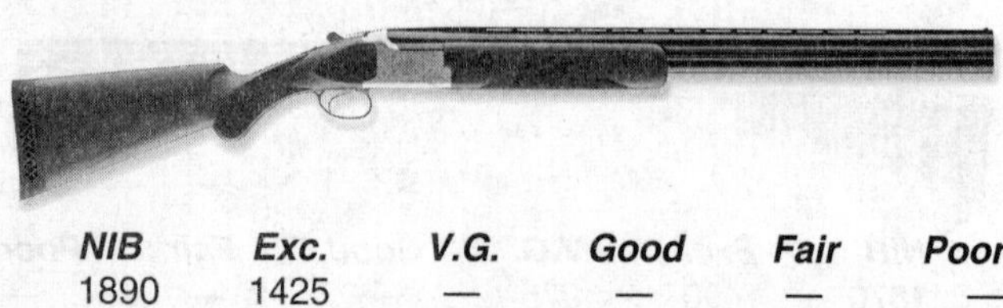

NIB	Exc.	V.G.	Good	Fair	Poor
1890	1425	—	—	—	—

Citori Classic Lightning Feather Grade I

This model, introduced in 2005, features a high relief engraved alloy receiver. Chambered for the 12 or 20 gauge and fitted with 26" or 28" vent rib barrels with choke tubes. Checkered select stock with Schnable forearm. Recoil pad on 12 gauge. Weight is about 7 lbs. for 12 gauge and about 6.25 lbs. for 20 gauge.

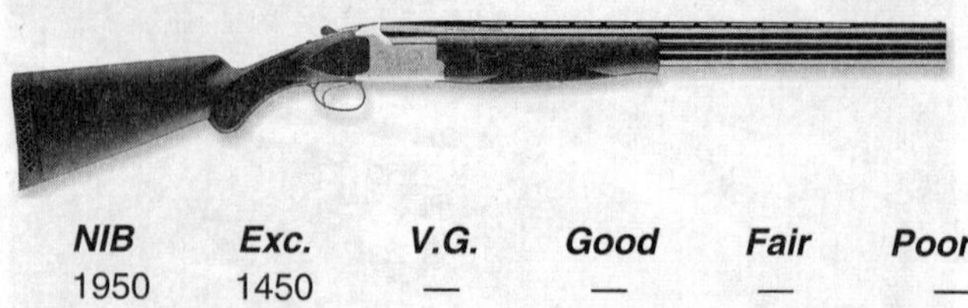

NIB	Exc.	V.G.	Good	Fair	Poor
1950	1450	—	—	—	—

Citori 525 Sporting

Introduced in 2002 this model is chambered for the 12 or 20 gauge and fitted with a choice of 28" or 30" vent rib ported barrels. The stock is redesigned with a Euro checkering pattern and more pronounced palm swell. Weight is about 8 lbs. for the 12 gauge and 7 lbs. for the 20. In 2003 this model was offered in both 28 gauge and .410 bore.

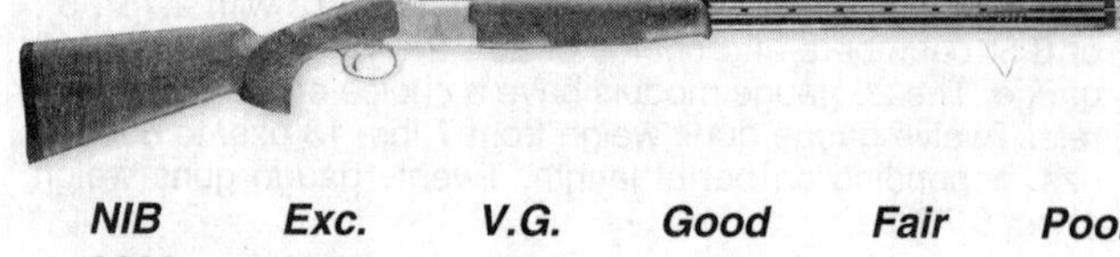

NIB	Exc.	V.G.	Good	Fair	Poor
2320	1750	1250	—	—	—

NOTE: Add $275 for adjustable comb.

Citori 525 Field

As above but with a choice of 26" or 28" barrels. Barrels are unported. Ventilated recoil pad. Introduced in 2002. In 2003 this model was offered in both 28 gauge and .410 bore.

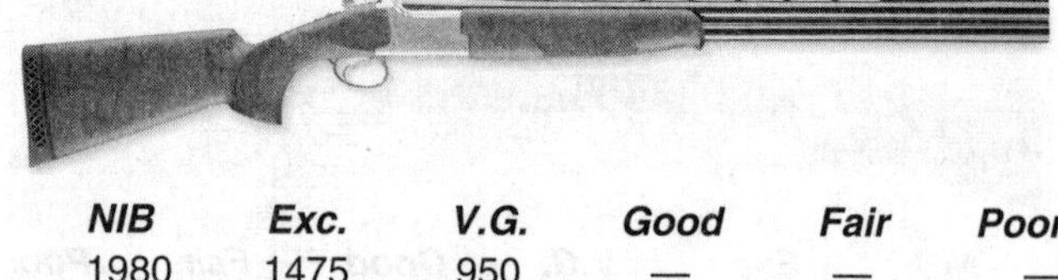

NIB	Exc.	V.G.	Good	Fair	Poor
1980	1475	950	—	—	—

Citori 525 Golden Clays Sporting

This model has the same features as the 525 Sporting but with an oil-finished high stock and engraved receiver with gold inlays. In 2003 this model was offered in both 28 gauge and .410 bore.

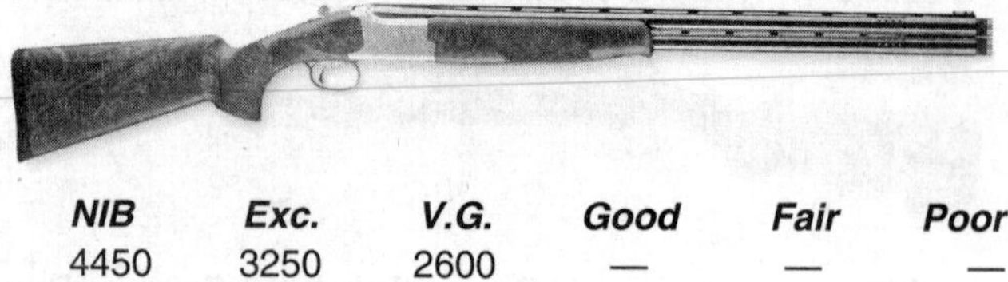

NIB	Exc.	V.G.	Good	Fair	Poor
4450	3250	2600	—	—	—

Citori Esprit

Introduced in 2002 this model features removable decorative sideplates, schnabel forearm, and high-grade walnut stock. Offered in 12 gauge only with 28" vent rib barrels. Weight is about 8.25 lbs.

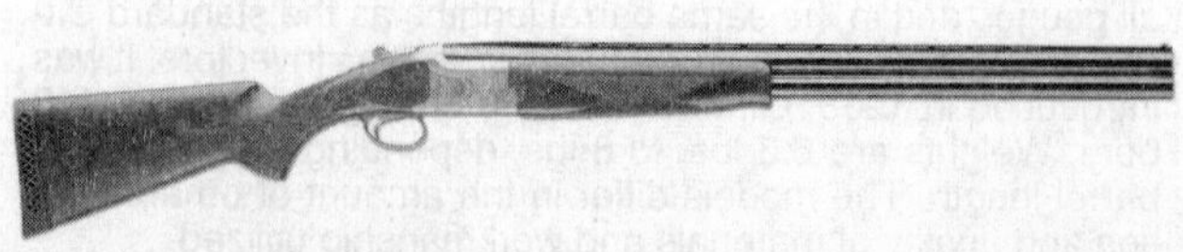

This symbol denotes "Sleepers" with rapidly-rising values and/or significant collector potential.

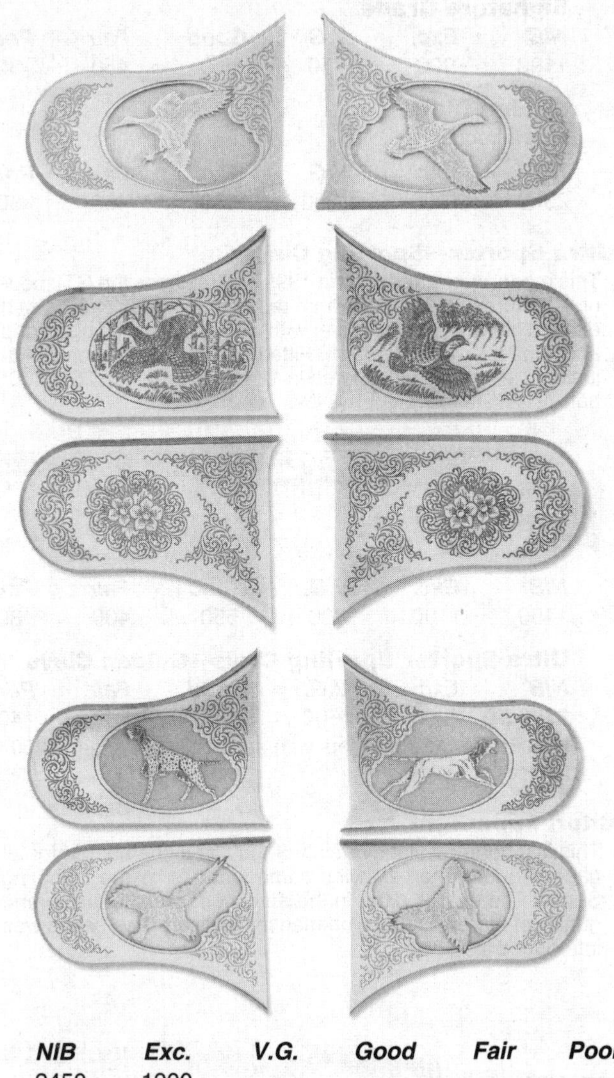

NIB	Exc.	V.G.	Good	Fair	Poor
2450	1900	—	—	—	—

Citori Sporting Clays

Specifically designed for sporting clays shooting. Offered in 12 gauge only, each model is back-bored, ported and fitted with Invector-Plus choke tubes. Barrels are chrome-plated. Receiver is blued with gold inscription. Pigeon Grade has gold detailing and high grade gloss walnut stock. Signature Grade features a red and black print on the stock with gold decals. Trigger is adjustable to three length of pull positions. Comes with three interchangeable trigger shoes. Each model is fitted with rubber recoil pad.

Lightning Sporting Model

This model features a rounded pistol grip and Lightning forearm with choice of high or low vent rib. Chambered for 3" shells. Offered in 28" or 30" barrels. Weighs about 8.5 lbs. Introduced in 1989.

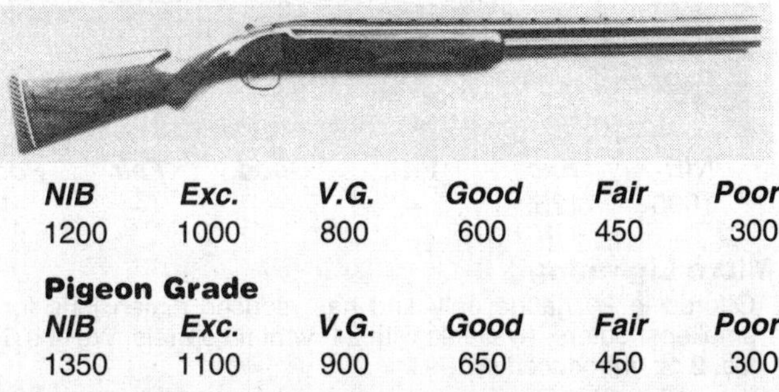

NIB	Exc.	V.G.	Good	Fair	Poor
1200	1000	800	600	450	300

Pigeon Grade

NIB	Exc.	V.G.	Good	Fair	Poor
1350	1100	900	650	450	300

Golden Clays

First introduced in 1994.

NIB	Exc.	V.G.	Good	Fair	Poor
2600	2250	1650	900	450	300

Citori Privilege

This high-grade model features game scene engraved sideplates, unique checkering pattern, oil finish high-grade walnut stock with pistol grip. Offered in 12 gauge only with choice of 26" or 28" barrels. Weight is about 8 lbs. Introduced in 2000. In 2001 a 20 gauge version with 26" or 28" barrels was introduced.

Citori Privilege left side

NIB	Exc.	V.G.	Good	Fair	Poor
5375	4250	3500	—	—	—

Citori XS Sporting Clays

Introduced in 1999, this model features silver nitride receiver with gold accents and European-style stock with schnabel forend. Available in 12 or 20. Choice of 28", 30" or 32" barrels. Weight varies from 8 lbs. in 12 gauge to 7 lbs. for the 20 gauge.

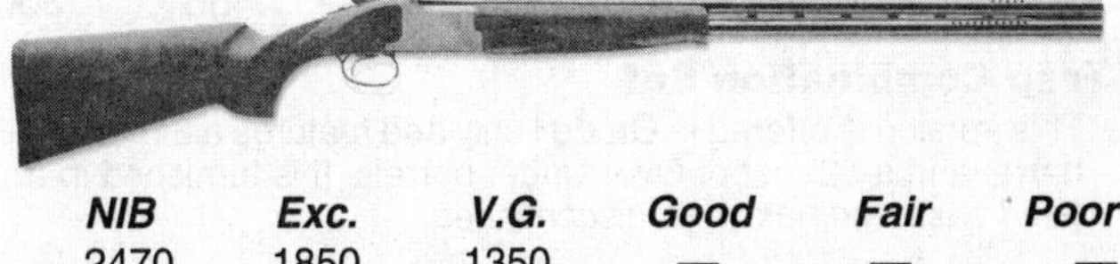

NIB	Exc.	V.G.	Good	Fair	Poor
2470	1850	1350	—	—	—

Citori Ultra XS Skeet

This model is offered in 12 gauge only with choice of 28" or 30" ported barrels chambered for 2.75" shells. Semi-beavertail forearm. Triple trigger system standard. Adjustable comb optional. Walnut stock with pistol grip and black recoil pad. Weight is about 7.75 lbs. Introduced in 2000. In 2001 a 20 gauge version was introduced with a choice of 28" or 30" barrels.

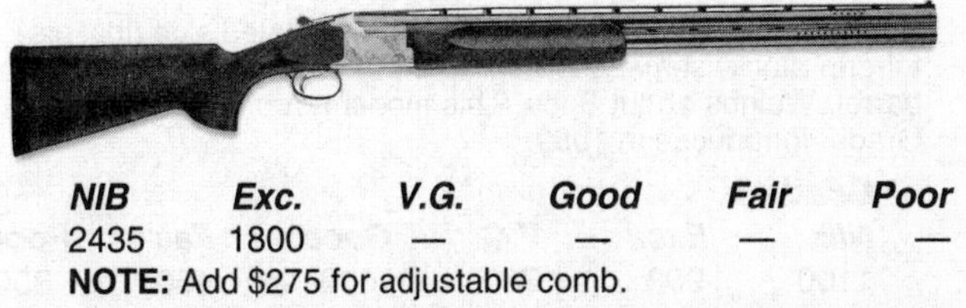

NIB	Exc.	V.G.	Good	Fair	Poor
2435	1800	—	—	—	—

NOTE: Add $275 for adjustable comb.

Citori XS Special

This is a 12 gauge 2.75" chamber gun with choice of 30" or 32" vent rib barrels with porting and extended choke tubes. Checkered walnut stock with adjustable comb and pistol grip. Semi-beavertail forearm. Silver engraved receiver. Weight is about 8.7 lbs.

NIB	Exc.	V.G.	Good	Fair	Poor
2725	2050	—	—	—	—

Citori Plus

This model features an adjustable point of impact from 3" to 12" above point of aim. Receiver on Grade I is blued with scroll engraving. Walnut stock is adjustable and forearm is a modified beavertail style. Available in 30" or 32" barrels that are backbored and ported. Non-ported barrels are optional. Weighs about 9 lbs. 6 oz. Introduced in 1989.

Grade I

NIB	Exc.	V.G.	Good	Fair	Poor
1200	1000	750	500	400	300

Pigeon Grade

NIB	Exc.	V.G.	Good	Fair	Poor
1750	1500	950	700	500	300

Signature Grade

NIB	Exc.	V.G.	Good	Fair	Poor
1650	1450	950	700	500	300

Golden Clays

First introduced in 1994.

NIB	Exc.	V.G.	Good	Fair	Poor
2750	2250	1500	900	450	300

Trap Combination Set

This version is offered in Grade I only and features a 34" single barrel and a 32" set of Over/Under barrels. It is furnished in a fitted case and has been discontinued.

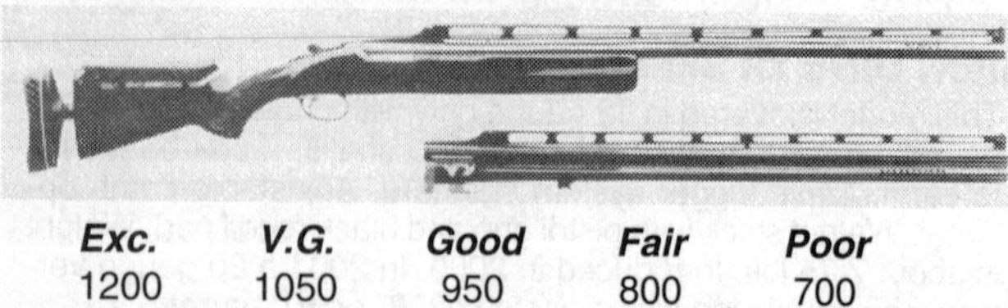

Exc.	V.G.	Good	Fair	Poor
1200	1050	950	800	700

GTI Model

This model features a 13mm wide rib, ventilated side ribs, pistol-grip stock, semi-beavertail forearm. Offered in 28" or 30" barrel. Weighs about 8 lbs. This model not offered in Pigeon Grade. Introduced in 1989.

Grade I

NIB	Exc.	V.G.	Good	Fair	Poor
1100	900	750	600	450	300

Signature Grade

NIB	Exc.	V.G.	Good	Fair	Poor
1100	900	750	600	450	300

Golden Clays

First introduced in 1994.

NIB	Exc.	V.G.	Good	Fair	Poor
2350	1900	1250	900	450	300

Ultra Sporter—Sporting Clays

This model was introduced in 1995 and replaces the GTI model. It features a 10mm to 13mm tapered rib and is offered with either a blued or gray receiver with walnut stock with pistol grip and semi-beavertail forearm. Fitted with adjustable comb. Adjustable length of pull. Offered in 12 gauge only with 28" or 30" barrels. Average weight is 8 lbs.

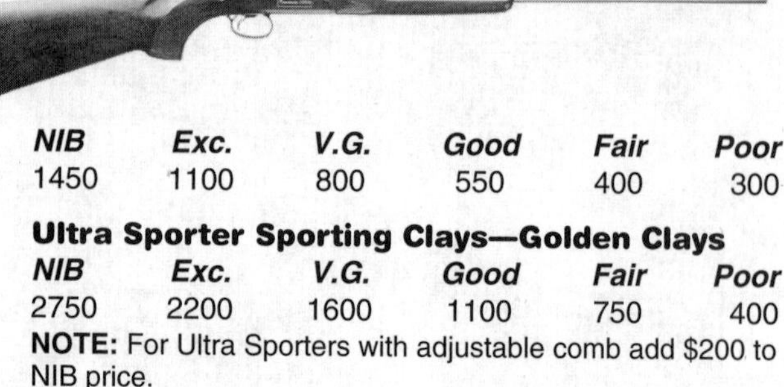

NIB	Exc.	V.G.	Good	Fair	Poor
1450	1100	800	550	400	300

Ultra Sporter Sporting Clays—Golden Clays

NIB	Exc.	V.G.	Good	Fair	Poor
2750	2200	1600	1100	750	400

NOTE: For Ultra Sporters with adjustable comb add $200 to NIB price.

Citori Superlight

This is a lighter-weight version of the Citori chambered for all gauges and offered with the same features as the Lightning Series. The grades differ in the amount of ornamentation and quality of materials and workmanship utilized. This series was introduced in 1983.

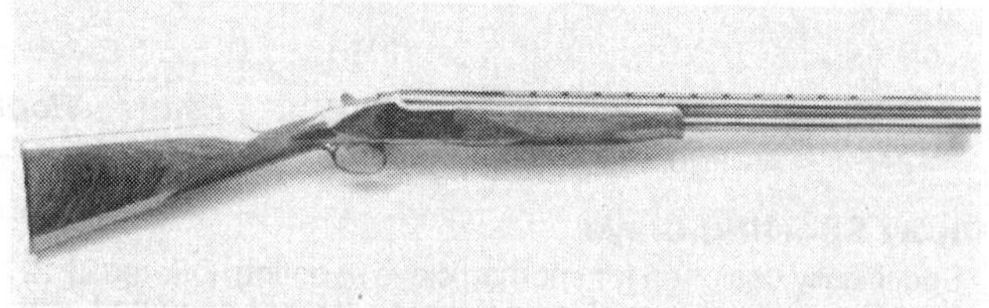

Citori Superlight Feather

Introduced in 1999 this model features a straight grip stock with schnabel forend. Lightweight alloy receiver. Offered in 12 gauge Grade I only with choice of 26" or 28" barrels. Weight with 28" barrels is about 6 lbs. 6 ozs.

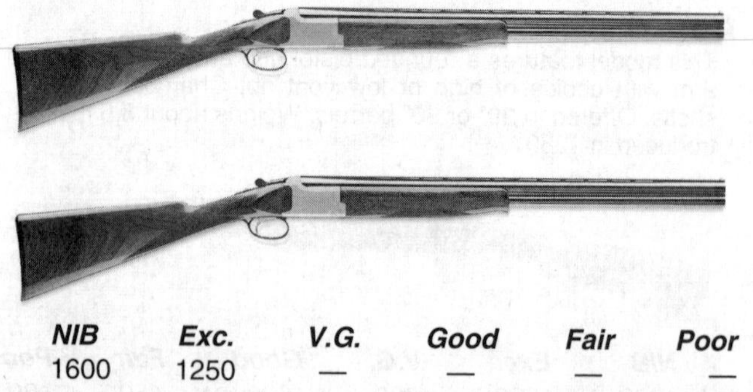

NIB	Exc.	V.G.	Good	Fair	Poor
1600	1250	—	—	—	—

Micro Lightning

Offered in 20 gauge only and has reduced dimensions for smaller shooters. Available with 24" vent rib barrels. Weighs 6 lbs. 3 oz. Introduced in 1991.

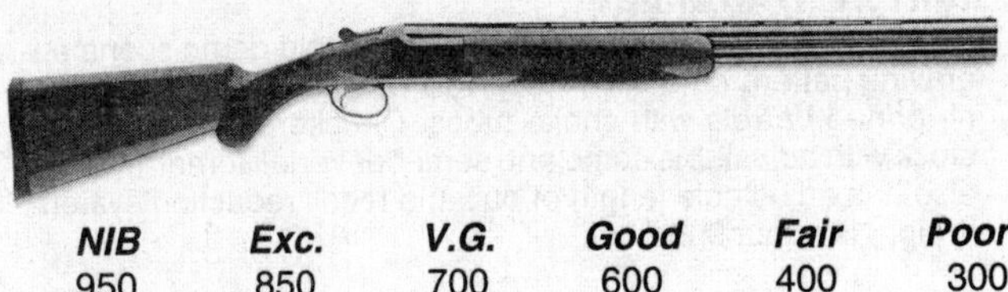

NIB	Exc.	V.G.	Good	Fair	Poor
950	850	700	600	400	300

Gran Lightning

This is essentially a Grade I Lightning with a high grade select walnut stock with satin finish. Receiver and barrels are blued. Offered in 12 gauge and 20 gauge with choice of 26" or 28" vent rib barrels. Choke tubes standard. Weighs about 8 lbs. in 12 gauge and 6 lbs. 11 oz. in 20 gauge. Introduced in 1990. In 2004 the 28 gauge and .410 bore were added.

NIB	Exc.	V.G.	Good	Fair	Poor
2430	1800	1300	975	650	350

Grade I

NIB	Exc.	V.G.	Good	Fair	Poor
1100	950	750	500	425	350

Grade III

NIB	Exc.	V.G.	Good	Fair	Poor
1500	1350	1050	750	550	450

Grade V

Discontinued 1984.

Exc.	V.G.	Good	Fair	Poor
1600	1250	950	750	500

Grade VI

NIB	Exc.	V.G.	Good	Fair	Poor
1800	1600	1300	1000	800	500

Citori White Lightning

Introduced in 1998 this model features a silver nitride scroll engraved receiver. Offered in 3" 12 and 3" 20 gauge with choice of 26" or 28" barrels. In 2004 this model is also available in 28 gauge as well as .410 bore. Weight is approximately 8 lbs. for 12 gauge models and 6.8 lbs. for 20 gauge models. Invector-Plus chokes standard. Lightning-style stock.

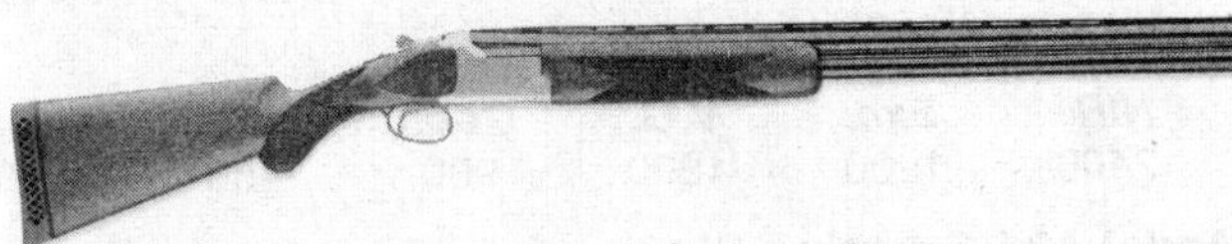

NIB	Exc.	V.G.	Good	Fair	Poor
1715	1300	950	700	—	—

NOTE: Add $75 for 28 and .410 models.

Citori White Upland Special

Introduced in 2000 this model features a shortened straight-grip stock, schnabel forearm, and 24" barrel. Fitted with 2.75" chambered for 12 gauge and 20 gauge only. Weight is about 6.75 lbs.

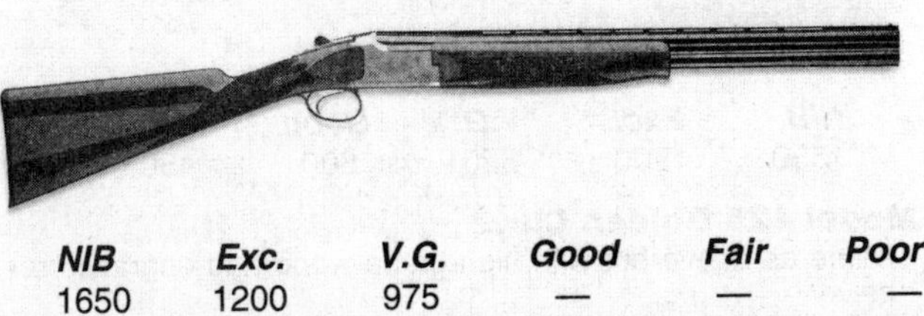

NIB	Exc.	V.G.	Good	Fair	Poor
1650	1200	975	—	—	—

Citori Skeet

This series of guns was chambered for all gauges and was designed for competition skeet shooting. It is similar to the standard Citori with a high-post target rib and 26" or 28" barrels. The versions differ in the amount of engraving and the quality of materials and workmanship utilized.

Grade I

NIB	Exc.	V.G.	Good	Fair	Poor
1000	925	750	550	425	350

Grade II

Discontinued 1983.

Exc.	V.G.	Good	Fair	Poor
1000	900	750	450	300

Grade III

NIB	Exc.	V.G.	Good	Fair	Poor
1500	1200	900	750	450	300

Grade V

Discontinued 1984.

NIB	Exc.	V.G.	Good	Fair	Poor
1600	1200	900	750	450	300

Grade VI

NIB	Exc.	V.G.	Good	Fair	Poor
2000	1750	1200	900	450	300

Golden Clays

First introduced in 1994.

NIB	Exc.	V.G.	Good	Fair	Poor
2400	2000	1500	900	450	300

3 Gauge Set

Consists of 20 gauge, 28 gauge, and .410 bore interchangeable 28" vent rib barrels. Introduced in 1987.

Grade I

NIB	Exc.	V.G.	Good	Fair	Poor
2100	1950	1700	1250	900	700

Grade III

NIB	Exc.	V.G.	Good	Fair	Poor
2500	2250	1900	1400	1100	800

Grade VI

NIB	Exc.	V.G.	Good	Fair	Poor
2950	2500	2000	1500	1200	900

4 Gauge Set

This set has a 12 gauge, 20 gauge, 28 gauge, and .410 bore interchangeable vent rib barrels in either 26" or 28" lengths. Introduced in 1981.

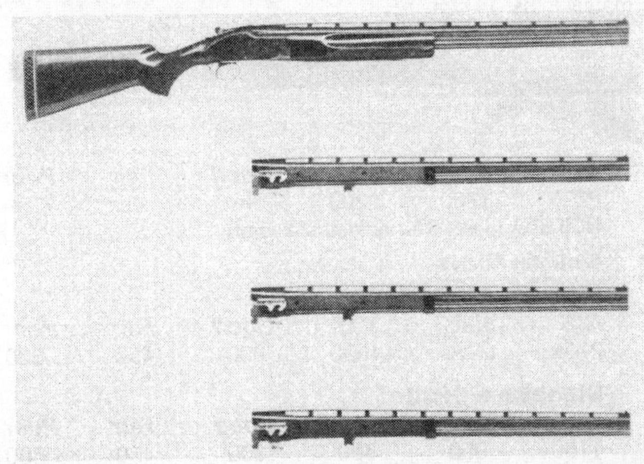

Grade I

NIB	Exc.	V.G.	Good	Fair	Poor
3300	2750	2250	1700	1250	900

Grade III

NIB	Exc.	V.G.	Good	Fair	Poor
3400	2900	2500	1900	1350	900

Grade VI

NIB	Exc.	V.G.	Good	Fair	Poor
3800	3300	2900	2250	1400	950

Citori Trap

This version is similar to the standard Citori, offered in 12 gauge only with 30" or 32" barrels. It features a high rib and a Monte Carlo-type stock with recoil pad. The versions differ as to the amount of ornamentation and the quality of materials and workmanship utilized.

Grade I

NIB	Exc.	V.G.	Good	Fair	Poor
1000	900	750	550	425	350

Plus Trap

Adjustable rib and stock. Introduced in 1989.

NIB	Exc.	V.G.	Good	Fair	Poor
1500	1350	1000	750	600	500

Grade II

Discontinued 1983.

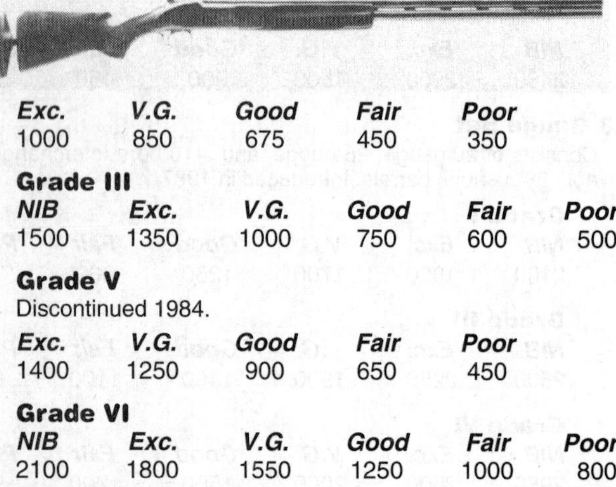

Exc.	V.G.	Good	Fair	Poor
1000	850	675	450	350

Grade III

NIB	Exc.	V.G.	Good	Fair	Poor
1500	1350	1000	750	600	500

Grade V

Discontinued 1984.

Exc.	V.G.	Good	Fair	Poor
1400	1250	900	650	450

Grade VI

NIB	Exc.	V.G.	Good	Fair	Poor
2100	1800	1550	1250	1000	800

Citori XT Trap

Introduced in 1999, this Trap model is fitted with contoured beavertail with Monte Carlo stock with or without adjustable comb. The grayed receiver is highlighted in gold with light scroll work. Choice of 32" or 30" barrels. Weight is approximately 8 lbs. 11 ozs.

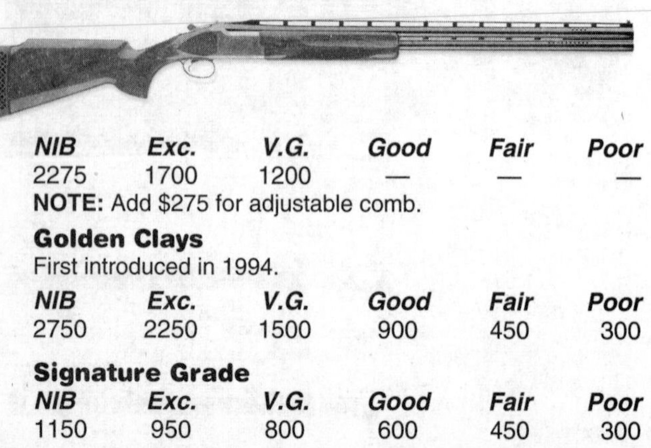

NIB	Exc.	V.G.	Good	Fair	Poor
2275	1700	1200	—	—	—

NOTE: Add $275 for adjustable comb.

Golden Clays

First introduced in 1994.

NIB	Exc.	V.G.	Good	Fair	Poor
2750	2250	1500	900	450	300

Signature Grade

NIB	Exc.	V.G.	Good	Fair	Poor
1150	950	800	600	450	300

Citori XT Trap Gold

Introduced in 2005 this model features a gold game scene engraving pattern on a silver receiver. Choice of 30" or 32" vent rib ported barrels with choke tubes. Checkered select walnut stock with adjustable comb and semi-beavertail forearm. Stock also has adjustable length of pull and recoil reduction system. Weight is about 9 lbs.

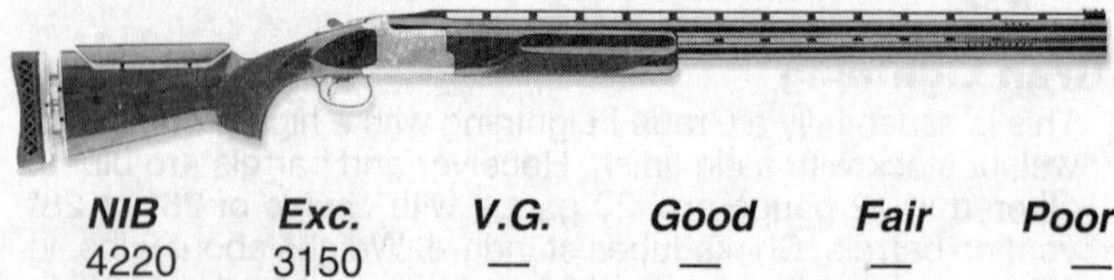

NIB	Exc.	V.G.	Good	Fair	Poor
4220	3150	—	—	—	—

Model 325 Sporting Clays

Introduced in 1993 this model has a European design that features a scroll-engraved, grayed receiver schnabel forearm, 10mm wide vent rib, three interchangeable and adjustable trigger shoes, and back-bore barrels that are ported and fitted with choke tubes. Available in 12 gauge and 20 gauge. The 12 gauge is offered with 28", 30", or 32" barrels while the 20 gauge is offered with 28" or 30" barrel fitted with conventional chokes. The 12 gauge weighs about 7 lbs. 14 oz., while the 20 gauge weighs about 6 lbs. 12 oz.

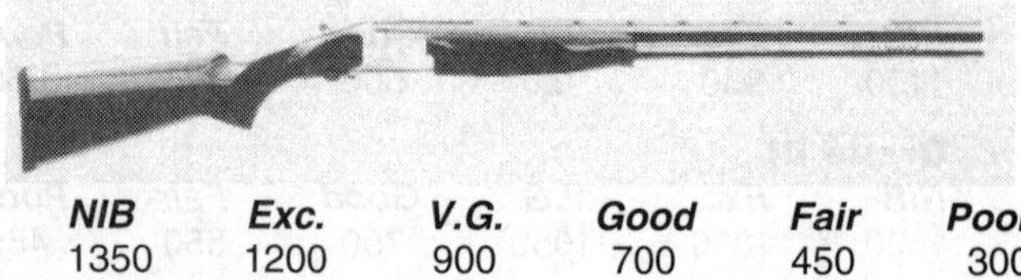

NIB	Exc.	V.G.	Good	Fair	Poor
1350	1200	900	700	450	300

Special Sporting

Similar to the Sporting model but fitted with a 2-3/4" chamber and choice of 28", 30", or 32" barrels. Barrels are ported. Barrels are also fitted with a high post rib. Stock has a full pistol grip and optional adjustable comb. Depending on barrel length weighs about 8.3 lbs.

Grade I

NIB	Exc.	V.G.	Good	Fair	Poor
1150	900	750	600	450	300

Signature Grade

NIB	Exc.	V.G.	Good	Fair	Poor
1150	900	750	600	450	300

Pigeon Grade

NIB	Exc.	V.G.	Good	Fair	Poor
1300	1100	850	600	450	300

Golden Clays

NIB	Exc.	V.G.	Good	Fair	Poor
2400	1900	1250	900	450	300

Model 425 Sporting Clays

This Citori over-and-under gun is offered in both 12 and 20 gauge with a choice of 28" and 30" barrel with 32" barrels available on the 12 gauge as well. The 425 is adjustable for length of pull and has an adjustable comb. Barrels are fitted with a 10mm wide rib. Invector chokes are standard. Average weight is 7 lbs. 14 oz. Introduced in 1995.

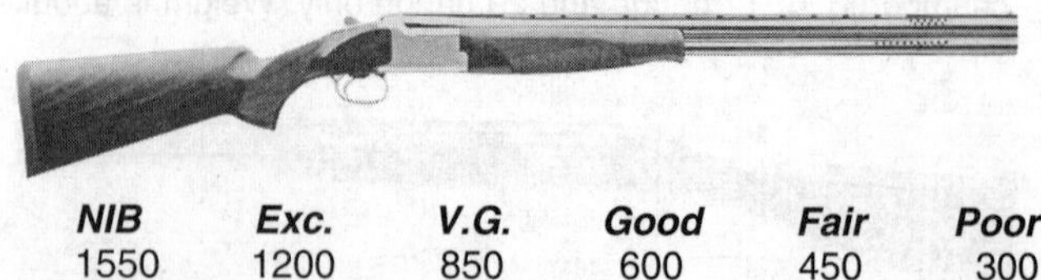

NIB	Exc.	V.G.	Good	Fair	Poor
1550	1200	850	600	450	300

Model 425 Golden Clays

Same as above but with high-grade wood and engraved receiver.

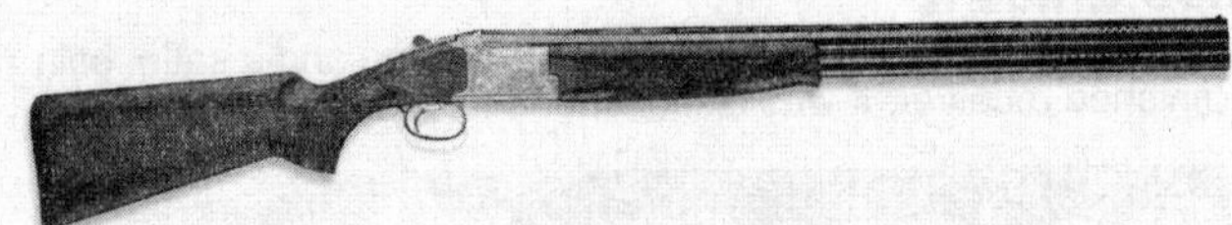

NIB	Exc.	V.G.	Good	Fair	Poor
2950	2350	1650	1100	600	300

NOTE: For Model 425 with adjustable comb add $200 to NIB price.

Light Sporting 802ES (Extended Swing)

Introduced in 1996 this model features a 28" vent rib barrel with 2" stainless steel extension tubes for an extended swing of 30". An additional 4" extension is also included. Thus the barrel can be 28", 30" or 32" according to needs. Chambered for 12 gauge with adjustable length of pull. Walnut stock with pistol grip and schnabel forearm. Weight is about 7.5 lbs.

NIB	Exc.	V.G.	Good	Fair	Poor
1700	1400	900	700	500	250

BT-99

This is a break-open, single-barrel trap gun chambered for 12 gauge only. It is offered with a 32" or 34", vent rib barrel with screw-in choke tubes. It features a boxlock action with automatic ejectors. The finish is blued with a checkered walnut stock and beavertail forearm. It was introduced in 1968 by B.C. Miroku.

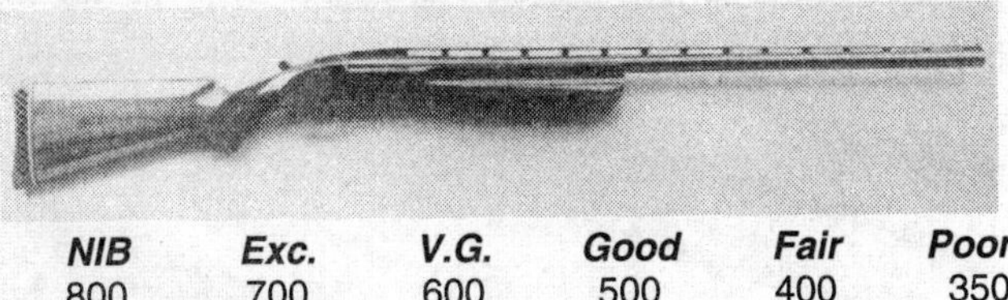

NIB	Exc.	V.G.	Good	Fair	Poor
800	700	600	500	400	350

Citori Plus Combo

This model features a single-barrel trap and an interchangeable Over/Under set of barrels. Other features are similar to Citori Plus Grade 1. Barrel combinations are 32" Over/Under with 34" single barrel or 30" Over/Under barrel with 32" or 34" single barrel. Introduced in 1989.

NIB	Exc.	V.G.	Good	Fair	Poor
2500	2100	1750	1100	700	450

BT-99 SERIES

BT-99 Stainless

First introduced in 1993.

NIB	Exc.	V.G.	Good	Fair	Poor
1275	1150	900	700	550	350

BT-99 Signature Grade I

First introduced in 1993.

NIB	Exc.	V.G.	Good	Fair	Poor
975	850	700	600	500	300

BT-99 Pigeon Grade

First introduced in 1993.

NIB	Exc.	V.G.	Good	Fair	Poor
1200	950	800	650	500	300

BT-99 Golden Clays

First introduced in 1994. In 2003 this model was offered with an adjustable comb. Weight is about 9 lbs. Available with either a 32" or 34" barrel.

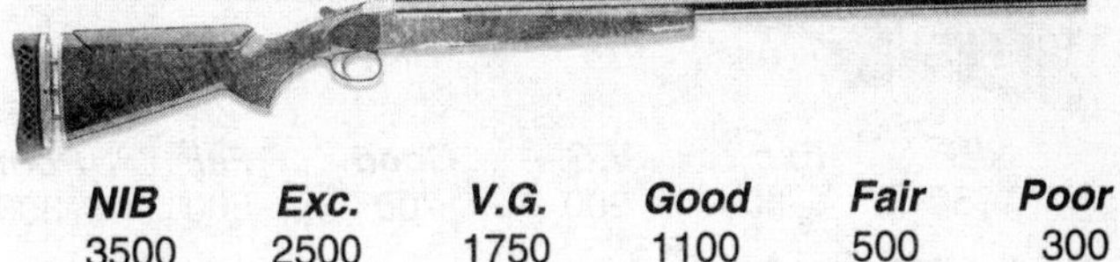

NIB	Exc.	V.G.	Good	Fair	Poor
3500	2500	1750	1100	500	300

BT-99 Plus

This version features an adjustable vent rib and a recoil reduction system. It has an adjustable stock and recoil pad, as well as a back-bored barrel. It was introduced in 1989.

NIB	Exc.	V.G.	Good	Fair	Poor
1350	1200	900	700	500	300

BT-99 Plus—Pigeon Grade

NIB	Exc.	V.G.	Good	Fair	Poor
1500	1200	900	800	550	350

BT-99 Plus—Signature Grade

NIB	Exc.	V.G.	Good	Fair	Poor
1400	1100	850	700	500	300

BT-99 Plus Stainless—Grade I

Same as standard version but offered in stainless steel. First introduced in 1993. Available in 32" and 34" barrels. Weighs about 8 lbs. 11 oz.

NIB	Exc.	V.G.	Good	Fair	Poor
1600	1350	900	700	500	350

BT-99 Plus—Golden Clays

First introduced in 1994.

NIB	Exc.	V.G.	Good	Fair	Poor
2600	2250	1750	900	450	300

BT-99 Plus Micro

Slightly reduced dimensions and offered in barrel lengths from 28" to 34". Weighs about 8 lbs. 6 oz. Introduced in 1991.

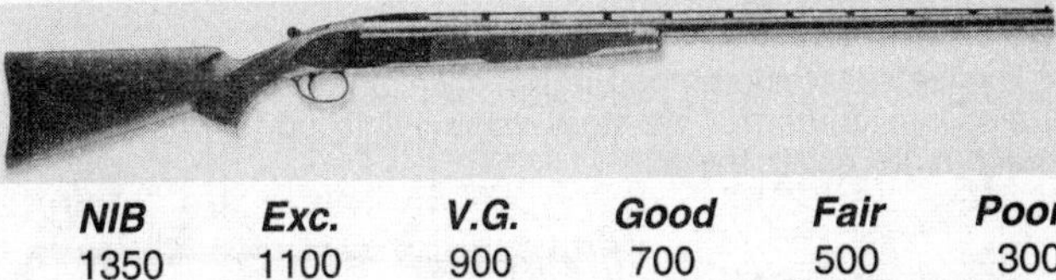

NIB	Exc.	V.G.	Good	Fair	Poor
1350	1100	900	700	500	300

Model BT-100

First introduced in 1995 this single-barrel trap features an adjustable trigger pull and length of pull. The stock is either a Monte Carlo version or an adjustable comb version. Barrel is either 32" or 34". Choice of blue or stainless finish. Weight is about 8.9 lbs.

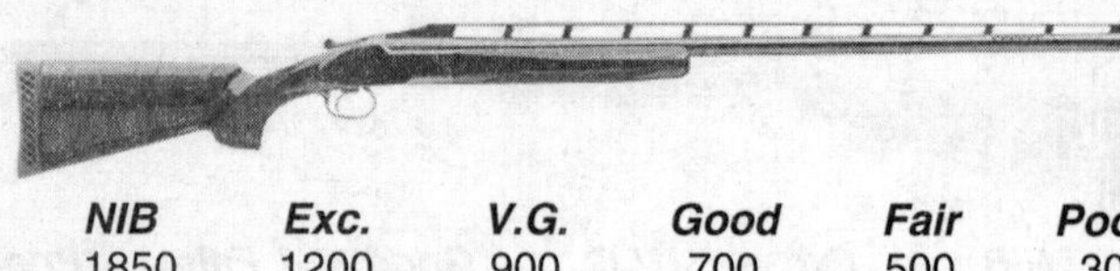

NIB	Exc.	V.G.	Good	Fair	Poor
1850	1200	900	700	500	300

Model BT-100 Satin

Introduced in 1999, this model features a matte black receiver and barrels without ejector selector. Available in 32" or 34" barrels. Available in Grade I only.

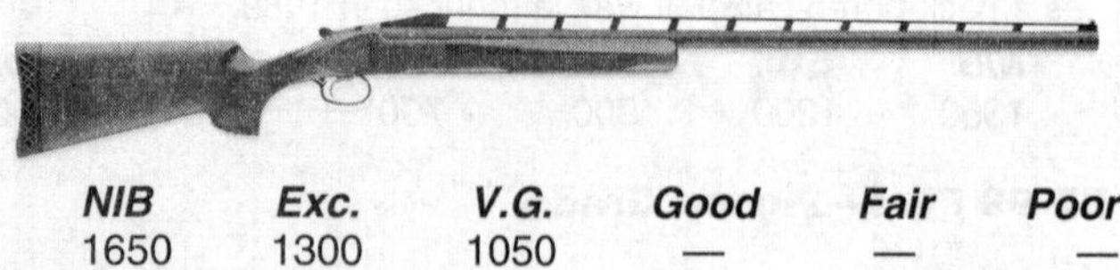

NIB	Exc.	V.G.	Good	Fair	Poor
1650	1300	1050	—	—	—

Model BT-100 Thumbhole

This model is the same as the standard BT-100, but with the additional feature of a thumbhole stock. Offered in both blue and stainless.

NIB	Exc.	V.G.	Good	Fair	Poor
2375	1900	1350	—	—	—

Recoilless Trap

First introduced in 1993 this model features an advanced design that eliminates recoil up to 72 percent. The receiver is a special bolt-action single-shot. Receiver is black anodized. It is fitted with an adjustable ventilated rib so the point of impact can be moved. Adjustable length of pull. The Standard Model is a 12 gauge with 30" barrel while the Micro Model is fitted with 27" barrels. Choke tubes are supplied. Standard Model weighs 9 lbs. 1 oz., while the Micro Model weighs 8 lbs. 10 oz.

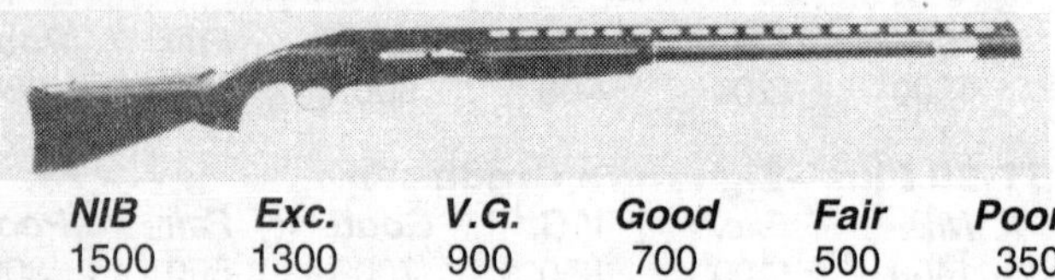

NIB	Exc.	V.G.	Good	Fair	Poor
1500	1300	900	700	500	350

BSS

This is a side-by-side, double-barrel shotgun chambered for 12 or 20 gauge. It was offered with a 26", 28", or 30" barrel with various choke combinations. It features a boxlock action and automatic ejectors. Early guns had a nonselective single trigger; late production, a selective trigger. The finish is blued with a checkered walnut stock and beavertail forearm. It was manufactured between 1978 and 1987 by B.C. Miroku.

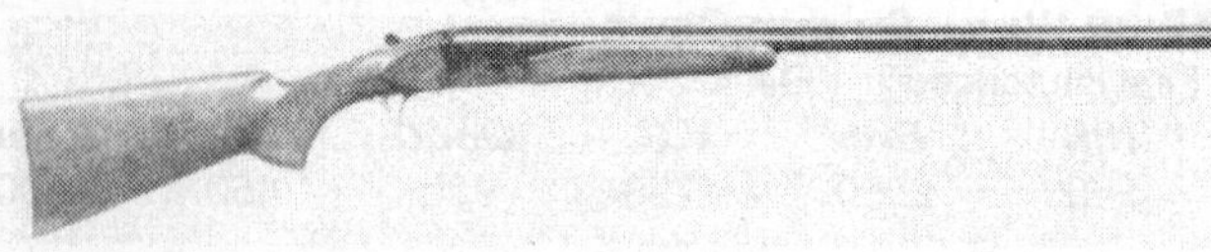

Exc.	V.G.	Good	Fair	Poor
1400	1050	775	650	400

NOTE: Single-selective trigger add 20 percent. 20 gauge add 20 percent.

BSS Sporter

This version features an English-style, straight-grip stock and a splinter forearm. The stock was oil-finished. It was offered with a 26" or 28" barrel.

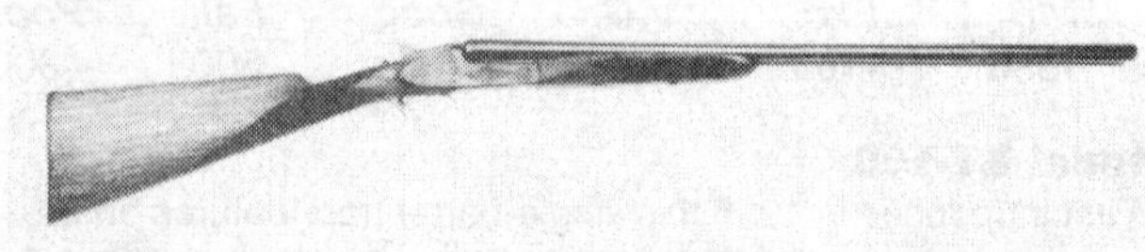

Exc.	V.G.	Good	Fair	Poor
1200	950	775	650	400

NOTE: For 20 gauge add 20 percent.

BSS Grade II

This version features game scene engraving and a satin, coin finished receiver. It was discontinued in 1984.

Exc.	V.G.	Good	Fair	Poor
1750	1350	1100	850	500

BSS Sidelock

This version features an engraved sidelock action and was offered in 12 or 20 gauge. It was offered with a 26" or 28" barrel and has a straight-grip stock and splintered forearm. It was manufactured in Korea between 1983 and 1987.

NOTE: The last few dozen 12 gauge sidelocks produced were an uncatalogued version of earlier guns. These guns had very finely engraved game scenes with English scroll. Add a 30 percent premium for this variation.

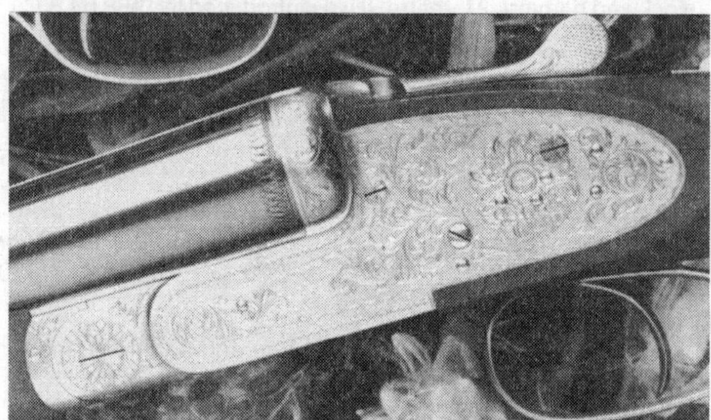

NIB	Exc.	V.G.	Good	Fair	Poor
2750	2100	1600	1250	800	500

NOTE: Add 30 percent to above prices for 20 gauge guns.

CYNERGY SERIES

This series was introduced in 2004. Browning calls it the third generation over-and-under gun. The Cynergy has a number of new design features such as a monolock hinge system for a lower profile, an inflex recoil pad, a new mechanical trigger system, an adjustable comb, back-bored barrels, and impact ejectors.

Cynergy Field

This 12 gauge 3" model features a checkered walnut stock and forearm. Silver nitrate receiver with engraving. Choice of 26" or 28" vent rib barrels with choke tubes. Weight is about 7.75 lbs. A synthetic stock with adjustable comb is also offered.

NIB	Exc.	V.G.	Good	Fair	Poor
2050	1500	—	—	—	—

NOTE: Deduct $40 for synthetic stock.

Cynergy Classic Field

This more traditionally styled 12 gauge was added to the Cynergy line in 2006. It features a steel receiver with silver nitride finish and game bird scenes on each side. Satin finish walnut stock and Schnabel style forend. Three choke tubes. Available in barrel lengths of 26" and 28" with an average weight of 7.75 lbs.

 *This symbol denotes "Sleepers" with rapidly-rising values and/or significant collector potential.*

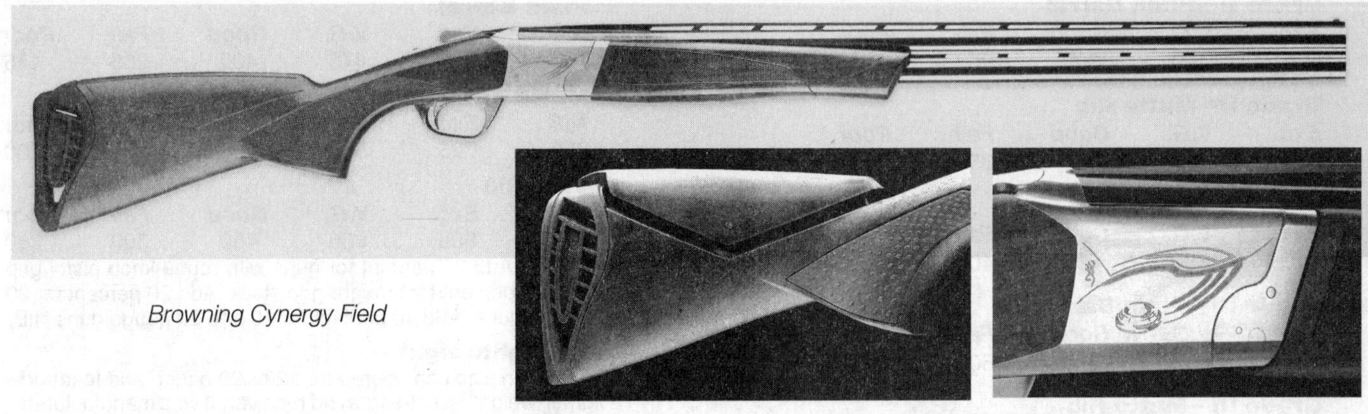

Browning Cynergy Field

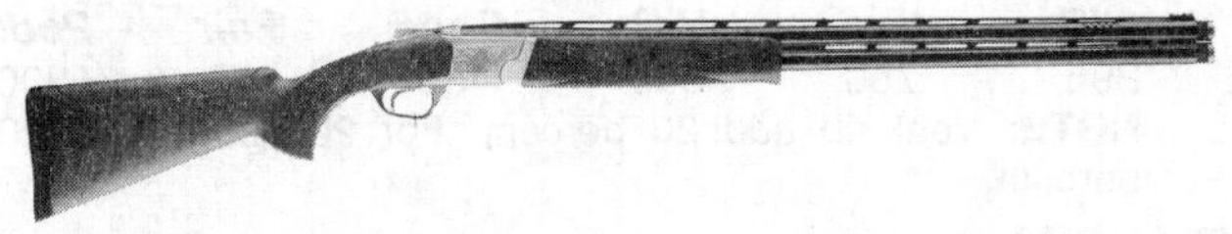

NIB	Exc.	V.G.	Good	Fair	Poor
2150	—	—	—	—	—

Cynergy Field Small Gauge

Introduced in 2005 this model is chambered for the 20 or 28 gauge. Choice of 26" or 28" vent rib barrels. Weight is about 6.25 lbs.

NIB	Exc.	V.G.	Good	Fair	Poor
2060	1600	—	—	—	—

Cynergy Sporting

As above but with higher grade walnut stock and choice of 28", 30", or 32" vent rib barrels with choke tubes. Ported barrels. Hi-Viz front sight. Weight is about 8 lbs. A synthetic stock with adjustable comb is also offered.

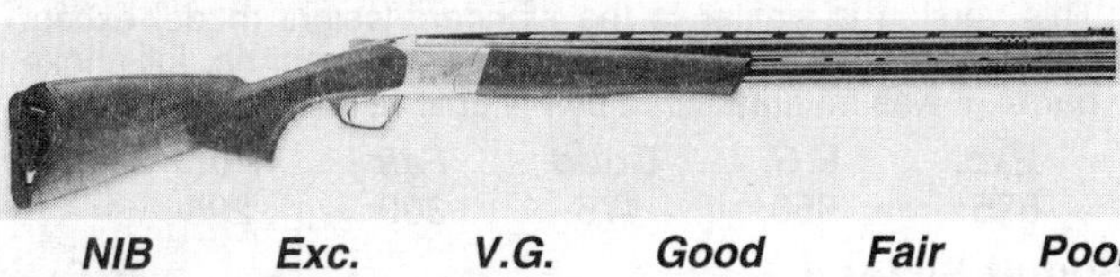

NIB	Exc.	V.G.	Good	Fair	Poor
2690	2100	—	—	—	—

NOTE: For synthetic stock deduct $40.

Cynergy Classic Sporting

New for 2006, this traditionally styled version of the Cynergy Sporting is available in 12 gauge with 28", 30" or 32" ported barrels. Oil finish walnut stock with Schnabel forend and Browning logo on steel receiver with silver nitride finish. Three Invector-Plus Midas Grade choke tubes. Average weight 7.75 lbs.

NIB	Exc.	V.G.	Good	Fair	Poor
2500	—	—	—	—	—

Cynergy Sporting, Adjustable Comb

Similar to Cynergy Sporting but with a comb adjustable for cast and drop. Average weight 8.2 lbs. Introduced 2006.

NIB	Exc.	V.G.	Good	Fair	Poor
2800	—	—	—	—	—

Cynergy Sporting Small Gauge

As above but in 20" or 28" gauge. Choice of 28", 30", or 32" ported barrels in 20 gauge and 28" or 30" ported barrels in 28 gauge. Weight is about 6.25 to 6.5 lbs. depending on barrel length. Introduced in 2005.

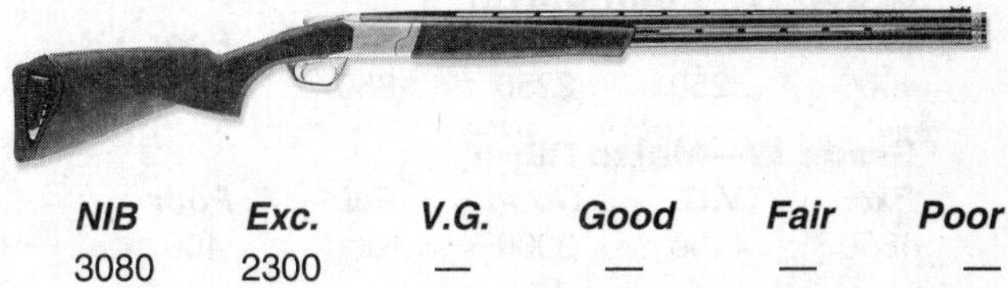

NIB	Exc.	V.G.	Good	Fair	Poor
3080	2300	—	—	—	—

AUTO-5 SHOTGUN

Early Production Auto-5

This series of recoil-operated, semi-automatic shotguns was designed by John M. Browning and was offered in 12 or 16 gauge. The barrel lengths were 26", 28", 30", or 32" with various chokes and ribs. It has a unique, square-back action that has become instantly recognizable. The finish is blued with a checkered, walnut, round-knob stock. The various versions differ in the amount of ornamentation, type of rib, and quality of materials and workmanship utilized in construction. This series was manufactured in Belgium by FN between 1903 and 1939. The first example appeared in the United States in 1923. Pre-WWI 16 gauge guns, introduced in 1936, had 2-9/16" chambers; early models should be inspected by a qualified gunsmith before firing.

NOTE: For 16 gauge not converted to 2-3/4" chamber deduct 30 percent. Grade III or Grade IV prices are not nearly as affected by chamber length because of their rarity. Original prewar barrels were serial numbered to the gun. For extra barrels serial numbered to the gun add $100 for plain barrels, $200 for matte rib barrels, $275 for vent rib barrels. For extra barrels on Grade IV guns add an additional 30 percent to these barrel prices. Prices given are for guns with original barrels serial numbered to the gun. Remember the safety is located in front of the trigger guard.

Grade I—Plain Barrel

Exc.	V.G.	Good	Fair	Poor
500	400	300	250	150

Grade I—Matte Rib

Exc.	V.G.	Good	Fair	Poor
650	550	375	300	175

Grade I—Vent Rib

Exc.	V.G.	Good	Fair	Poor
825	650	475	375	200

Grade II—Plain Barrel

Exc.	V.G.	Good	Fair	Poor
550	450	300	250	150

Grade II—Matte Rib

Exc.	V.G.	Good	Fair	Poor
825	650	450	350	175

Grade II—Vent Rib

Exc.	V.G.	Good	Fair	Poor
1400	850	600	400	200

Grade III—Plain Barrel

Exc.	V.G.	Good	Fair	Poor
1900	1500	850	500	250

Grade III—Matte Rib

Exc.	V.G.	Good	Fair	Poor
3000	2500	1350	600	250

Grade III—Vent Rib

Exc.	V.G.	Good	Fair	Poor
3000	2500	1350	600	300

Grade IV—Plain Barrel

Exc.	V.G.	Good	Fair	Poor
4000	3250	2250	850	350

Grade IV—Matte Rib

Exc.	V.G.	Good	Fair	Poor
4850	4150	3000	1000	400

Grade IV—Vent Rib

Exc.	V.G.	Good	Fair	Poor
5500	4750	3500	1500	500

Browning Grade IV Courtesy Amoskeag Auction Company

American Browning Auto-5

This recoil-operated, semi-automatic shotgun was another variation of the early-production Auto-5. It was chambered for 12, 16, or 20 gauge and was manufactured by the Remington Company for Browning. It is quite similar to Remington's Model 11 shotgun but features the Browning logo and a different type of engraving. There were approximately 45,000 manufactured between 1940 and 1942.

Exc.	V.G.	Good	Fair	Poor
675	575	450	375	200

NOTE: Vent rib add 20 percent. 20 gauge add 10 percent.

MID-PRODUCTION AUTO-5—FN MANUFACTURE STANDARD WEIGHT

This version of the recoil-operated, semi-automatic Auto-5 shotgun was manufactured by FN in Belgium between 1952 and 1976. It was offered in 12 or 16 gauge with 26" through 32" barrels with various chokes. The finish is blued with a checkered walnut stock and a black buttplate that was marked "Browning Automatic" with "FN" in center oval. Guns made prior to 1967 will be found with round knob pistol grips. The flat-bottom variation was introduced in 1967.

Plain Barrel

NIB	Exc.	V.G.	Good	Fair	Poor
750	600	475	400	250	175

Matte Rib

NIB	Exc.	V.G.	Good	Fair	Poor
825	725	500	400	275	200

Vent Rib

NIB	Exc.	V.G.	Good	Fair	Poor
950	800	600	450	300	250

NOTE: Add 25 percent for guns with round-knob pistol grip and 35 percent for straight-grip stock. Add 20 percent for 20 gauge guns. Add 40 percent for 16 and 20 gauge guns NIB.

Auto-5 Lightweight

This version was chambered for 12 or 20 gauge and featured a lighter-weight, scroll-engraved receiver. It was manufactured between 1952 and 1976 by FN. The 20 gauge was not introduced until 1958.

NIB	Exc.	V.G.	Good	Fair	Poor
895	750	600	450	275	200

NOTE: Vent rib add 20 percent. For 20 gauge add 20 percent.

Auto-5 Magnum

This version featured 3" chambers and was offered with 26" through 32", full-choke barrels. It was manufactured between 1958 and 1976 by FN. The 12 gauge was introduced in 1958 and the 20 gauge brought out in 1967.

Exc.	V.G.	Good	Fair	Poor
750	650	500	375	200

NOTE: Vent rib add 20 percent.

Auto-5 Skeet

This version is similar to the Lightweight Model, chambered for 12 or 20 gauge with a 26" or 28", vent rib, skeet-choked barrel.

Exc.	V.G.	Good	Fair	Poor
795	575	525	425	250

Auto-5 Trap Model

This version is similar to the standard-weight model except chambered for 12 gauge only, with a 30", vent rib, full-choke barrel. It was manufactured by FN until 1971.

Exc.	V.G.	Good	Fair	Poor
675	550	475	300	225

Sweet Sixteen

This version is similar to the standard-weight and is chambered for 16 gauge only. It has a gold-plated trigger and was manufactured by FN between 1936 and 1976.

NOTE: Not all A-5 16-gauges are Sweet Sixteens. Look for the gold-plated trigger and the lack of a suicide safety.

NIB	Exc.	V.G.	Good	Fair	Poor
1250	850	700	400	300	200

NOTE: Matte rib add 25 percent. Vent rib add 50 percent.

Buck Special

This version features a 24", cylinder-bore barrel with adjustable rifle sights. It was produced in 12 and 20 gauge 2-3/4" and 3" Magnum, and in 16 gauge with 2-3/4" chambers. It was manufactured by FN between 1963 and 1976. Prices are for 12 gauge guns.

Exc.	V.G.	Good	Fair	Poor
750	650	525	400	275

Two Millionth Commemorative

This version commemorated the two millionth Auto-5 shotgun produced by FN. It was engraved with a special high-polish blue finish and high-grade, checkered walnut in the stock. It was furnished in a black fitted case along with a book on the Browning Company. There were 2,500 manufactured between 1971 and 1974. As with all commemoratives, it must be NIB to realize its top potential.

NIB	Exc.	V.G.	Good	Fair	Poor
2750	1700	950	625	—	—

LATE PRODUCTION AUTO-5—B.C. MIROKU MANUFACTURE

In 1976 production of the Auto-5 shotgun was begun by B.C. Miroku in Japan. This move was accomplished after approximately 2,750,000 Auto-5 shotguns were manufactured by FN in Belgium between 1903 and 1976. The Japanese-manufactured guns, in the opinion of many knowledgeable people, show no less quality or functionality but are simply not as desirable from a collector's standpoint. In 1999 Browning discontinued production of the Auto-5 shotgun.

Auto-5 Light 12

This version is chambered for 12 gauge 2-3/4" chamber only and is offered with a lightweight receiver. The barrel has a vent rib and choke tubes. It was introduced in 1975.

NIB	Exc.	V.G.	Good	Fair	Poor
750	650	500	400	350	250

Auto-5 Light 20

This version is similar to the Light 12 except chambered for 20 gauge only.

NIB	Exc.	V.G.	Good	Fair	Poor
800	650	550	425	350	250

Auto-5 Magnum

This version features 3" chambers and is offered with 26", 28", 30", or 32" barrels. It was introduced in 1976 by Miroku and discontinued in 1996.

NIB	Exc.	V.G.	Good	Fair	Poor
775	625	575	450	325	250

Auto-5 Buck Special

This version has a 24" barrel cylinder-bored with adjustable sights. It was introduced by Miroku in 1976.

NIB	Exc.	V.G.	Good	Fair	Poor
725	625	500	425	300	200

Auto-5 Skeet

This is a competition model that features 26" or 28", skeet-bored barrels with a vent rib. It was manufactured between 1976 and 1983 by Miroku.

NIB	Exc.	V.G.	Good	Fair	Poor
825	550	450	350	275	200

Sweet Sixteen

This version is similar to the Belgian-produced Sweet Sixteen, but is offered standard with a vent rib and screw-in Invector choke tubes. It was introduced in 1988 by Miroku and discontinued in 1992.

NIB	Exc.	V.G.	Good	Fair	Poor
1250	1000	750	550	375	225

A-5 DU 50th Anniversary

This was a high-grade version of the Auto-5 produced to commemorate the 50th anniversary of Ducks Unlimited. It is highly engraved and features high-gloss bluing and a fancy checkered walnut stock. There were approximately 5,500 manufactured by Miroku in 1987. They were auctioned by the Ducks Unlimited chapters to raise money for the organization, and because of this fact, it is difficult to furnish an accurate value. This is a commemorative firearm and, as such, must be NIB with all furnished materials to command premium collector value. We furnish what we feel is a general value.

NIB	Exc.	V.G.	Good	Fair	Poor
1550	1000	800	600	450	300

A-5 DU Sweet Sixteen

This was a special version of the Miroku-manufactured Sweet Sixteen that was auctioned by the Ducks Unlimited chapters in 1988. There were 5,500 produced. All specifications and cautions that were furnished for the 50th Anniversary gun also apply here.

NIB	Exc.	V.G.	Good	Fair	Poor
1350	105	0850	600	400	300

Auto-5 Classic

This is a special limited edition series of A-5 shotguns built in 12 gauge only. The Classic is photo-etched with game scenes on a silver gray receiver. 5,000 of these guns were manufactured in 1984. The Gold Classic is similar in appearance but features gold inlays and is limited to 500 guns.

Classic

NIB	Exc.	V.G.	Good	Fair	Poor
1750	1400	1050	775	600	400

Gold Classic

Produced by FN.

NIB	Exc.	V.G.	Good	Fair	Poor
4500	3250	2500	2000	1000	500

Auto-5 Light Buck Special

This model is a lightweight version of the Buck Special. Chambered for the 2-3/4" shell and fitted with a 24" vent rib barrel. Conventional choked for slug or buckshot. Barrel has adjustable rear sight and ramp front sight. Weighs 8 lbs.

NIB	Exc.	V.G.	Good	Fair	Poor
750	650	550	450	375	225

Auto-5 Stalker

New for 1992 this model is available in either a lightweight version or a Magnum version. The Light Stalker is available in 12 gauge with either 26" or 28" barrel with choke tubes. The Magnum Stalker is offered in 12 gauge (3" chamber) with 28" or 30" barrel and choke tubes. The Light Stalker weighs 8 lbs. 4 oz. and the Magnum Stalker weighs 8 lbs. 11 oz.

Light Stalker

NIB	Exc.	V.G.	Good	Fair	Poor
675	600	550	400	300	225

Magnum Stalker

NIB	Exc.	V.G.	Good	Fair	Poor
725	650	600	375	275	250

Auto-5 Final Tribute Limited Edition

Introduced in 1999, this commemorative A-5 is limited to 1,000 shotguns. It represents the final production of this model. Chambered for the 12 gauge shell and fitted with a 28" vent rib barrel this shotgun has a special engraved receiver.

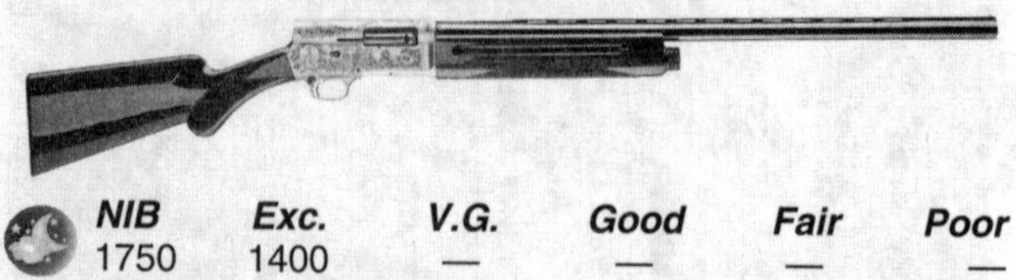

NIB	Exc.	V.G.	Good	Fair	Poor
1750	1400	—	—	—	—

Double Automatic Shotgun

This is a short recoil-operated, semi-automatic shotgun chambered for 12 gauge only. It was offered with a 26", 28", or 30" barrel that was either plain or vent ribbed. It has various chokes. The receiver is steel, and the finish is blued or silver with a checkered walnut stock. The tubular magazine holds only two shots—hence its name. It was manufactured between 1954 and 1972.

Exc.	V.G.	Good	Fair	Poor
525	425	350	275	225

NOTE: Vent rib add 25 percent.

Twelvette Double Auto

This version is similar to the Double Automatic except that it has an aircraft aluminum alloy frame color-anodized in either blue, silver, green, brown, or black. Red-, gold-, or royal blue-colored receivers were the rarest colors and would command approximately a 50 percent premium. It was offered with either a plain or vent rib barrel. There were approximately 65,000 produced between 1954 and 1972.

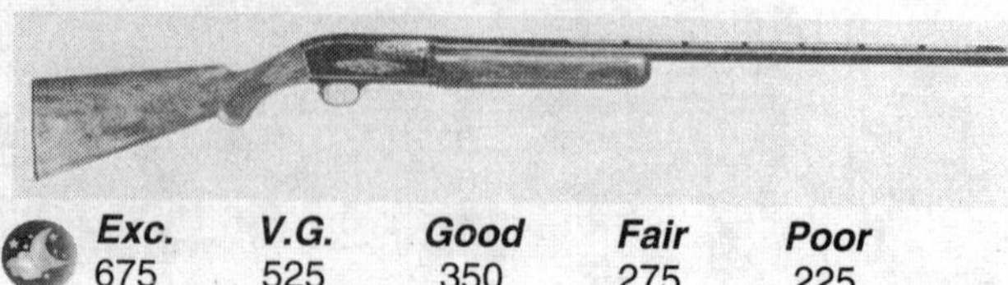

Exc.	V.G.	Good	Fair	Poor
675	525	350	275	225

NOTE: Vent rib add 25 percent.

Twentyweight Double Auto

This version is similar in all respects to the Twelvette except that it is three-quarters of a pound lighter and was offered with a 26.5" barrel. It was manufactured between 1952 and 1971.

Exc.	V.G.	Good	Fair	Poor
750	575	375	300	250

NOTE: Vent rib add 25 percent.

2000 SERIES

B-2000

This is a gas-operated, semi-automatic shotgun chambered for 12 or 20 gauge and offered with a 26", 28", or 30", vent rib barrel with various chokes. The finish is blued with a checkered walnut stock. This shotgun was assembled in Portugal from parts that were manufactured by FN in Belgium. There were approximately 115,000 imported between 1974 and 1981.

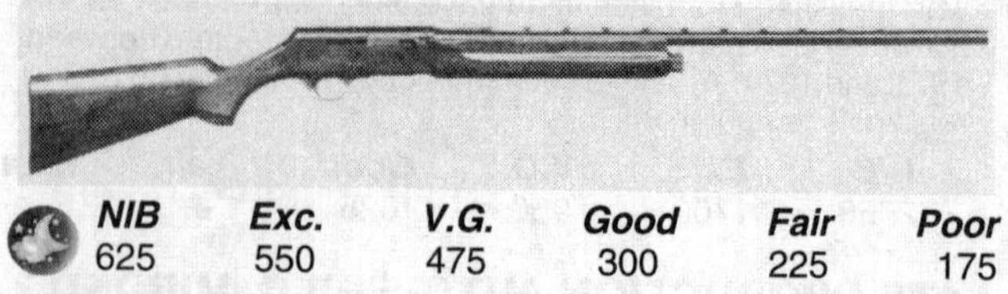

NIB	Exc.	V.G.	Good	Fair	Poor
625	550	475	300	225	175

B-2000 Magnum

This version features a barrel with 3" chambers and was offered standard with a recoil pad.

NIB	Exc.	V.G.	Good	Fair	Poor
675	575	500	300	225	175

B-2000 Buck Special

This version has a 24", cylinder-bored barrel with rifle sights.

NIB	Exc.	V.G.	Good	Fair	Poor
575	475	425	275	225	175

B-2000 Trap

This version has a 30", full-choke barrel with a floating rib and a Monte Carlo-type trap stock.

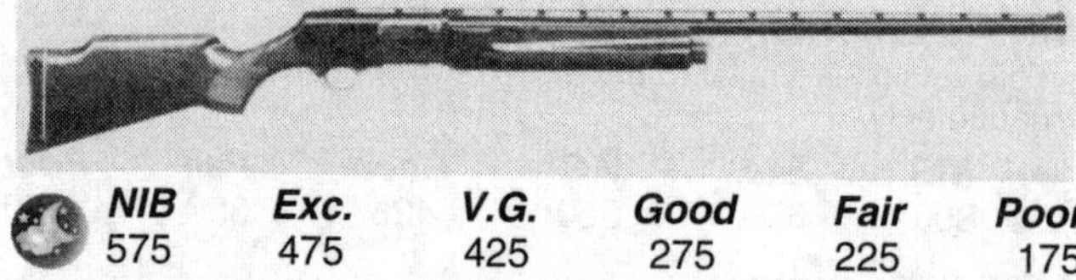

NIB	Exc.	V.G.	Good	Fair	Poor
575	475	425	275	225	175

B-2000 Skeet

This version features a 26", skeet-bored barrel with a floating vent rib and a skeet-type stock.

Exc.	V.G.	Good	Fair	Poor
500	450	375	275	200

NOTE: Add 20 percent for 20 gauge guns.

Model B-80

This is a gas-operated, semi-automatic shotgun chambered for 12 or 20 gauge. It features 3" magnum potential by simply exchanging the barrel. It features various-length barrels and was offered with screw-in Invector chokes as of 1985. The receiver is either steel or lightweight aluminum alloy. The finish is blued with a checkered walnut stock. This gun was assembled in Portugal from parts manufactured by Beretta in Italy. It was manufactured between 1981 and 1988.

Exc.	V.G.	Good	Fair	Poor
500	450	375	325	225

NOTE: Add 20 percent for 20 gauge guns.

Model B-80 Buck Special

This version features a 24", cylinder-bored barrel with rifle sights. It was discontinued in 1984.

Exc.	V.G.	Good	Fair	Poor
450	400	350	300	200

Model B-80 DU Commemorative

This version was produced to be auctioned by American Ducks Unlimited chapters. In order to realize the collector potential, it must be NIB with all supplied materials. Values supplied are general.

NIB	Exc.	V.G.	Good	Fair	Poor
950	750	550	425	325	275

GOLD SERIES

Model Gold 10

Introduced for the first time in 1993 this is a gas-operated 5-shot semi-automatic shotgun chambered for the 10 gauge shell. Offered with 26", 28", or 30" vent rib barrel. The standard model has a walnut stock, blued receiver and barrel while the Stalker Model is fitted with a graphite composite stock with nonglare finish on receiver and barrel. Both models are fitted with choke tubes. Weighs about 10 lbs. 10 oz.

NIB	Exc.	V.G.	Good	Fair	Poor
950	700	550	450	300	150

Gold Evolve

Introduced in 2004 this model is an updated version of the original Gold gun. It features newly designed receiver, magazine cap, ventilated rib design, checkering pattern and Hi-Viz sights. Offered in 12 gauge 3" with choice of 26", 28", or 30" barrel with choke tubes. Weight is about 7 lbs. for the 28" model.

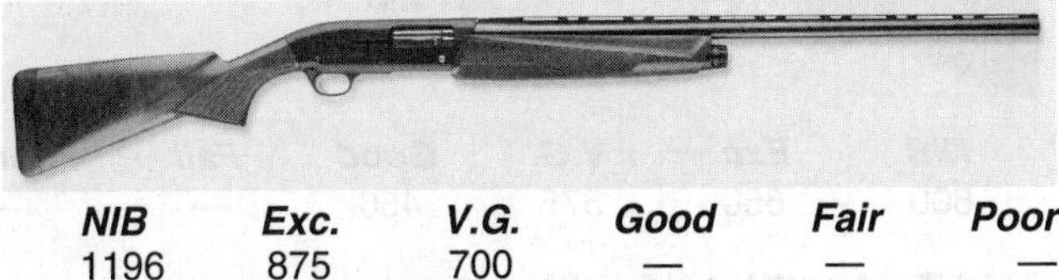

NIB	Exc.	V.G.	Good	Fair	Poor
1196	875	700	—	—	—

Gold Light 10 Gauge Camo

This 10 gauge model is offered with 26" or 28" barrels with Mossy Oak or Shadow Grass camo. Lightweight alloy receiver reduces weight to 9 lb. 10 oz. Introduced in 2001.

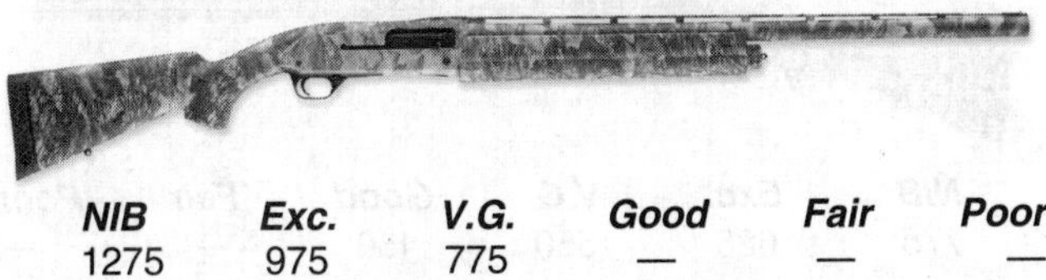

NIB	Exc.	V.G.	Good	Fair	Poor
1275	975	775	—	—	—

Gold 10 Gauge Combo

This 10 gauge model has a choice of two vent rib barrels in lengths of 24" and 26", or 24" and 28". Walnut stock with black ventilated recoil pad. Weight with 28" barrels is about 10 lbs. 10 ozs.

NIB	Exc.	V.G.	Good	Fair	Poor
1050	800	675	—	—	—

Gold Stalker

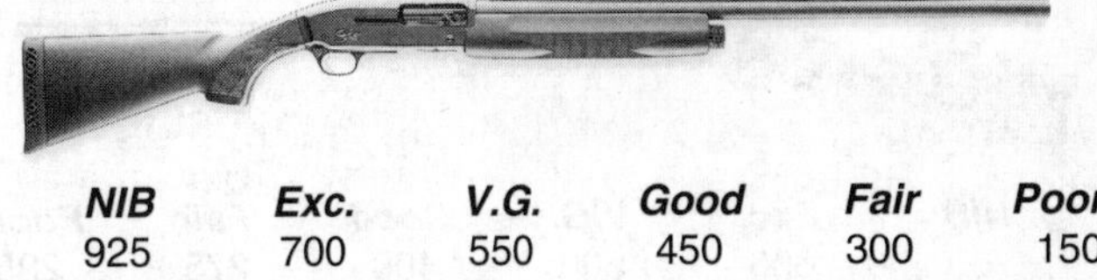

NIB	Exc.	V.G.	Good	Fair	Poor
925	700	550	450	300	150

Gold Classic Stalker

Introduced in 1999 this model features a classic Browning squared receiver and fully adjustable stock. This model is chambered for 12 gauge shells with choice 26" or 28" vent rib barrels. Gun has 3" chambers. Black synthetic stock. Weight is about 7 lbs. 3 ozs.

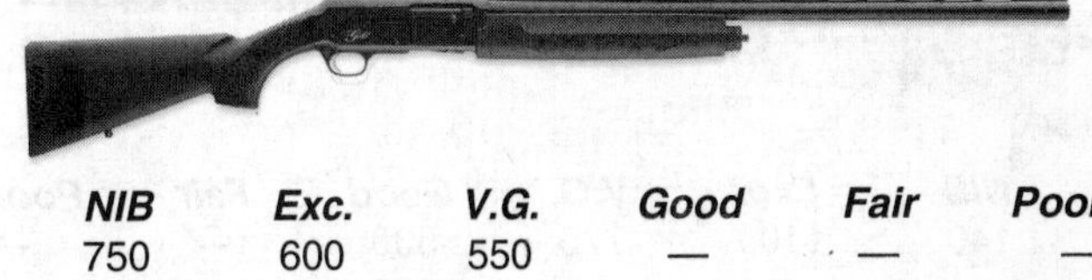

NIB	Exc.	V.G.	Good	Fair	Poor
750	600	550	—	—	—

Gold 3-1/2" 12 Gauge

Introduced in 1997 this model features a 3-1/2" chamber. It can operate 2-3/4", or 3" shells as well. Choice of barrel lengths from 26" to 30". Invector-Plus chokes. Magazine capacity is four 2.75" shells or three 3" shells or three 3.5" shells. The weight is approximately 7 lbs. 10 oz.

NIB	Exc.	V.G.	Good	Fair	Poor
900	700	550	450	—	—

Gold 12 Gauge Hunter

Introduced in 1994 this semi-automatic shotgun is built on the same gas operating system as the Gold 10. Offered with 26", 28", or 30" barrel it has a magazine capacity of four 3" shells. Walnut stock has full checkered pistol grip with black rubber recoil pad. Invector-Plus choke tubes supplied. Weighs about 7.5 lbs. Also available (1998) in Stalker version with non-glare matte metal parts and stocks.

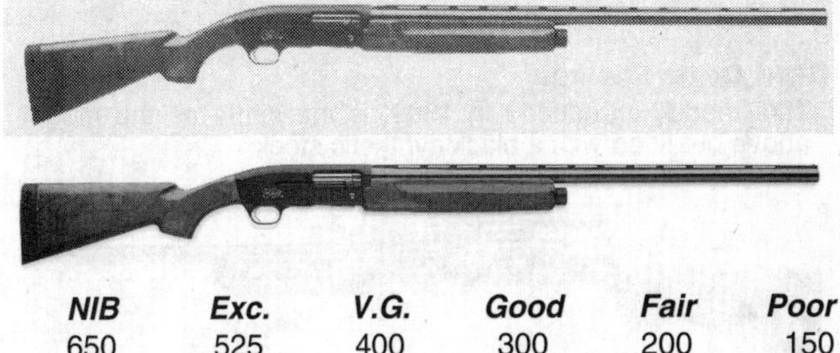

NIB	Exc.	V.G.	Good	Fair	Poor
650	525	400	300	200	150

Gold Classic Hunter

Introduced in 1999, this model features a squared receiver, fully adjustable stock, selected walnut stock, and deep blued barrels. Choice of 26", 28", or 30" vent rib barrel. Offered with 3" chamber 12 gauge only.

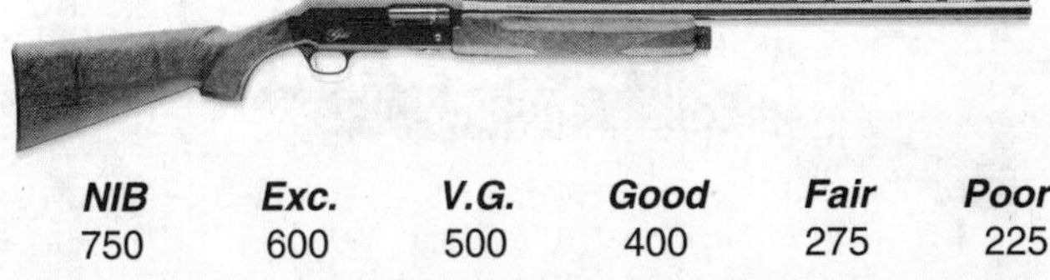

NIB	Exc.	V.G.	Good	Fair	Poor
750	600	500	400	275	225

Gold Classic 20 Gauge

Offered with choice of 26" or 28" vent rib barrels with select walnut stock. Adjustable comb. Squared receiver. Weight is about 6 lbs. 12 ozs. Introduced in 1999.

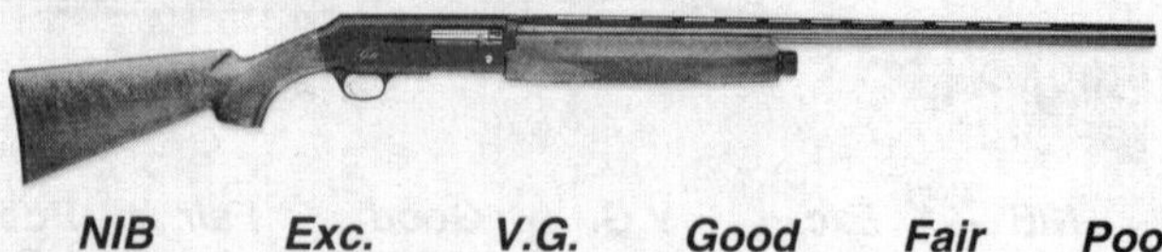

NIB	Exc.	V.G.	Good	Fair	Poor
750	600	500	400	275	225

Gold Classic High Grade

Introduced in 1999, this model features a traditional square receiver with engraved silver gray finish. Offered in 12 gauge only with 3" chambers and 28" vent rib barrel. Select walnut stock. Weight is about 7 lbs. 6 ozs.

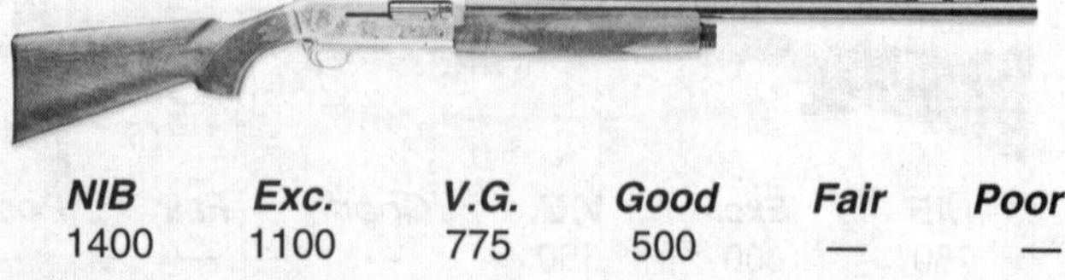

NIB	Exc.	V.G.	Good	Fair	Poor
1400	1100	775	500	—	—

Gold Deer Hunter

Introduced in 1997, this model features a choice of a fully rifled barrel or a smooth bore barrel with Invector choke system. Both versions come with a cantilever scope mount. Stock and forearm are of select walnut. Receiver has non-glare black finish. Barrel is satin finish. Barrel length is 22" on both barrels. Weight is about 7 lbs. 12 oz. Price listed are for smoothbore barrel.

NIB	Exc.	V.G.	Good	Fair	Poor
775	600	500	400	200	150

NOTE: For fully rifled version add $40.

Gold Deer Hunter—20 gauge

Same as above but chambered for 20 gauge 3" shell. Furnished with fully rifled 22" barrel. Cantilever scope mount. Introduced in 2001.

NIB	Exc.	V.G.	Good	Fair	Poor
975	800	625	—	—	—

Gold Deer Stalker

This model, introduced in 1999, is the same as the model above but fitted with a black synthetic stock.

NIB	Exc.	V.G.	Good	Fair	Poor
980	750	600	500	300	—

Gold Deer—Mossy Oak

Introduced in 1999 with camo finish.

NIB	Exc.	V.G.	Good	Fair	Poor
825	675	575	450	—	—

Gold Waterfowl—Mossy Oak Shadow Grass

Introduced in 1999 with camo finish.

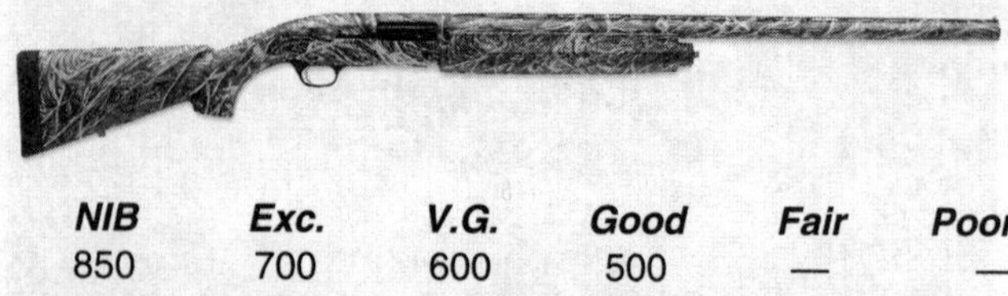

NIB	Exc.	V.G.	Good	Fair	Poor
850	700	600	500	—	—

Gold Waterfowl—Mossy Oak Breakup

Introduced in 2000 with camo finish.

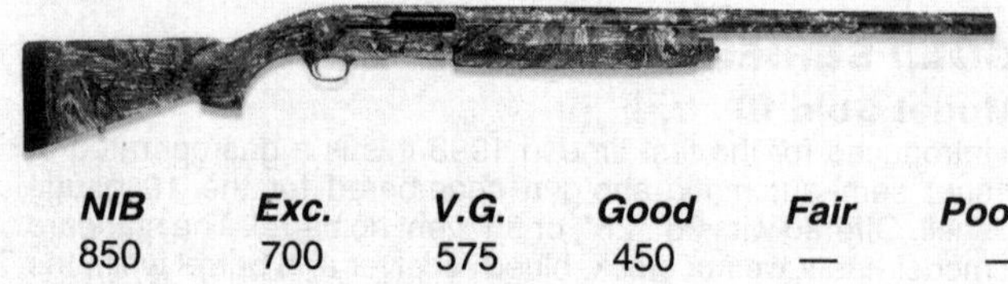

NIB	Exc.	V.G.	Good	Fair	Poor
850	700	575	450	—	—

Gold Turkey/Waterfowl—Mossy Oak

Introduced in 1999 with camo finish.

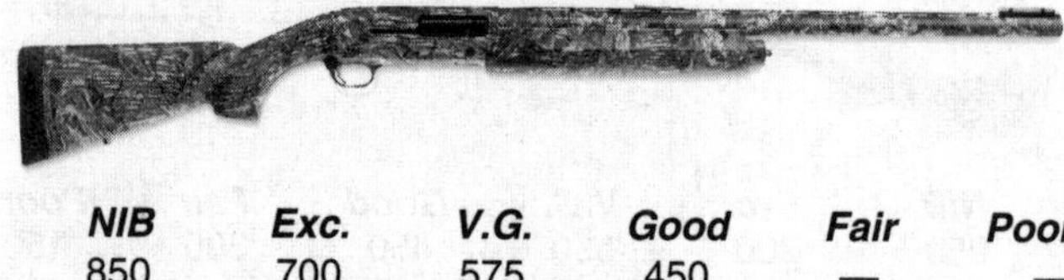

NIB	Exc.	V.G.	Good	Fair	Poor
850	700	575	450	—	—

Gold Turkey/Waterfowl Stalker

Introduced in 1999, this model features a black synthetic stock, 24" barrel, Hi-Viz sight, and 3" or 3.5" chambers. Weight is approximately 7 lbs. 4 ozs.

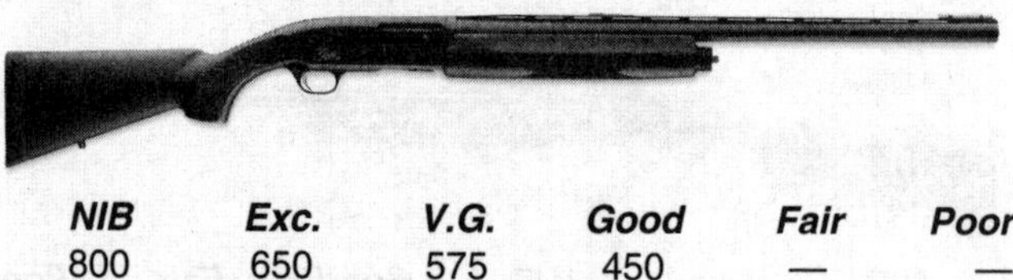

NIB	Exc.	V.G.	Good	Fair	Poor
800	650	575	450	—	—

Gold Turkey/Waterfowl Hunter

This 12 gauge 3" or 3.5" chambered gun is offered with 24" vent rib barrel. Select walnut stock with black ventilated recoil pad. Weight is about 7 lbs. Introduced in 1999.

NIB	Exc.	V.G.	Good	Fair	Poor
775	625	550	450	—	—

Gold NWTF Series

This model is finished in a Mossy Oak Breakup pattern and bears the NWTF logo on the buttstock. Fitted with a 24" barrel, Hi-Viz front sight, X-full extended Turkey choke. Offered in the configurations listed.

Gold Light 10 Gauge

NIB	Exc.	V.G.	Good	Fair	Poor
1250	950	775	—	—	—

Gold 12 Gauge

3.5" Chamber, Shadow Grass

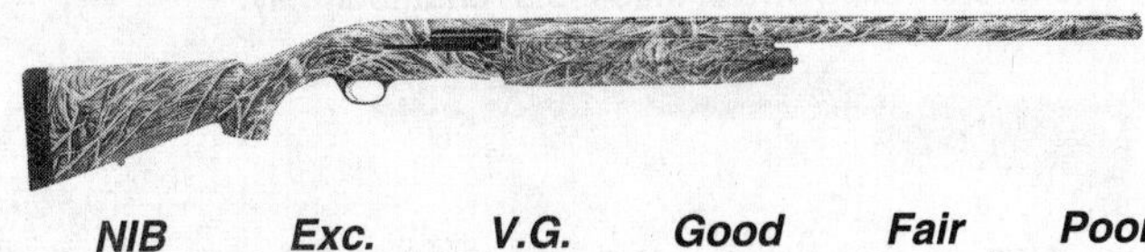

NIB	Exc.	V.G.	Good	Fair	Poor
1175	900	800	700	—	—

3" Chamber

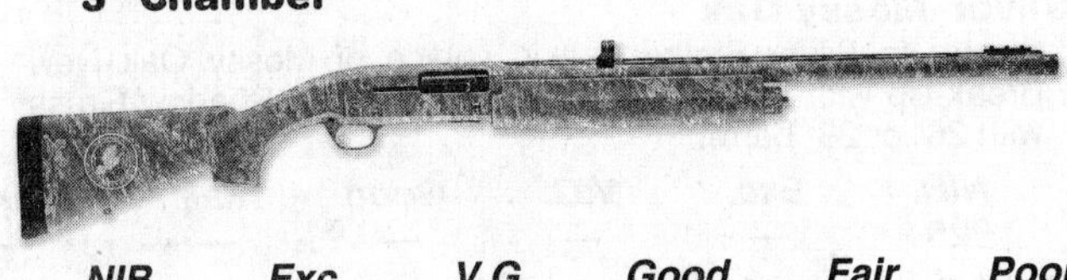

NIB	Exc.	V.G.	Good	Fair	Poor
1000	775	650	575	—	—

3.5" Chamber Ultimate Turkey Gun

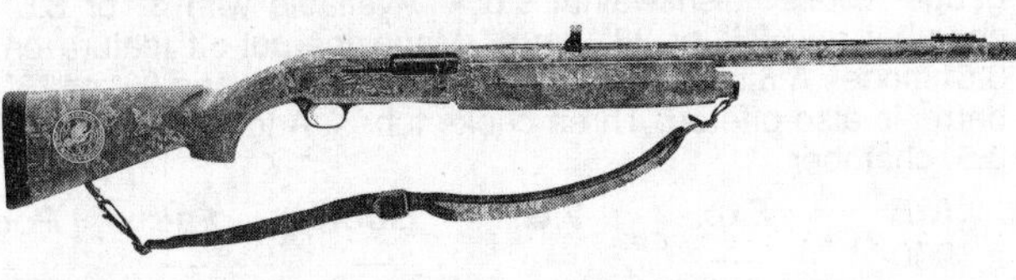

NIB	Exc.	V.G.	Good	Fair	Poor
1280	1000	900	725	—	—

Gold 20 Gauge Hunter

Same as above but chambered for 20 gauge and offered in 26" or 28" barrel lengths. Weighs about 6.8 lbs.

NIB	Exc.	V.G.	Good	Fair	Poor
650	525	400	300	200	150

Gold Sporting Clays

Introduced in 1996, this model features a ported barrel in 28" or 30" lengths. Recoil pad is standard. Weight is about 7.5 lbs.

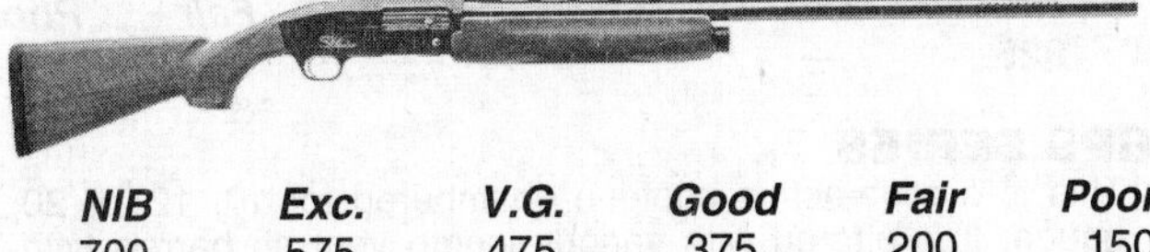

NIB	Exc.	V.G.	Good	Fair	Poor
700	575	475	375	200	150

Gold Ladies/Youth Sporting Clays

Offered in 12 gauge only with 2.75" chambers this model features a 28" vent rib barrel. Overall dimensions have been adjusted to fit women. Black solid recoil pad. Weight is about 7 lbs. 6 ozs. Introduced in 1999.

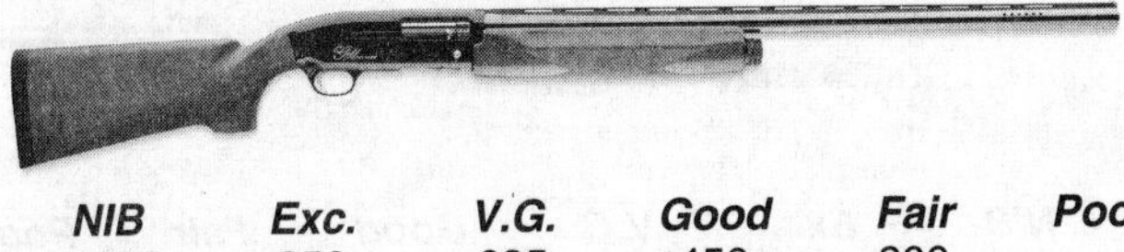

NIB	Exc.	V.G.	Good	Fair	Poor
1100	850	625	450	300	—

Gold "Golden Clays" Ladies Sporting Clays

Introduced in 2005 this 12 gauge 2.75" chambered gun is fitted with a 28" vent rib ported barrel with 4 choke tubes. Silver receiver is engraved with gold enhancements. Weight is about 7.75 lbs.

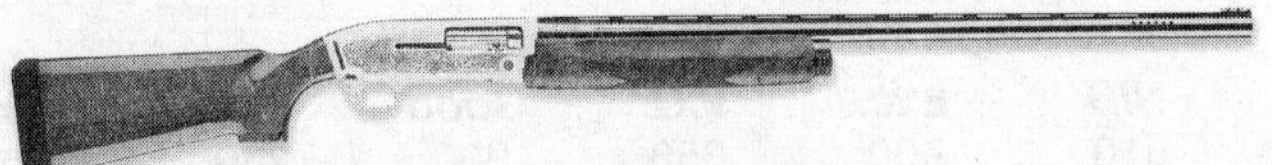

NIB	Exc.	V.G.	Good	Fair	Poor
1810	1300	1050	800	—	—

Gold "Golden Clays" Sporting Clays

As above but with standard stock dimensions and choice of 28" or 30" barrels. Introduced in 2005.

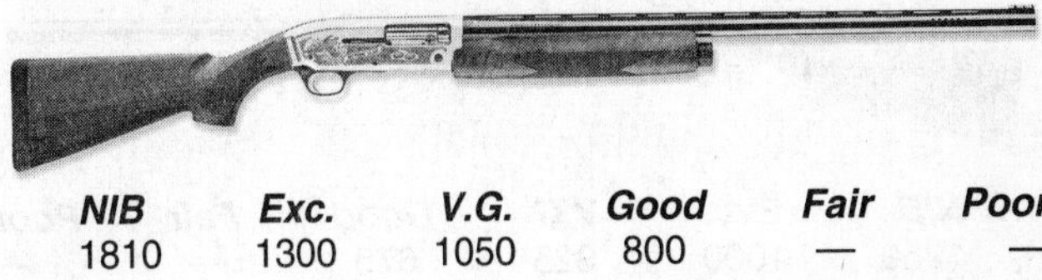

NIB	Exc.	V.G.	Good	Fair	Poor
1810	1300	1050	800	—	—

Gold Micro

Introduced in 2001 this model features a 20 gauge gun with 26" barrel, smaller pistol grip, shorter length of pull, and back-bored barrel with choke tubes. Weight is about 6 lb. 10 oz.

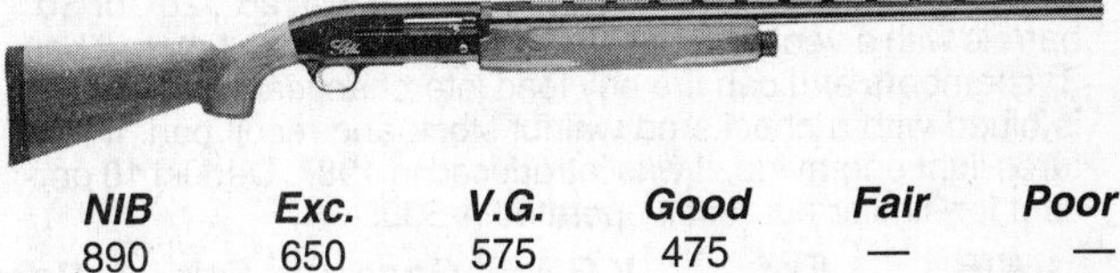

NIB	Exc.	V.G.	Good	Fair	Poor
890	650	575	475	—	—

Gold Upland

Offered in 12 or 20 gauge. The 12 gauge offered with 24" barrel and the 20 gauge with 26" barrel. Straight grip stock with 3" chamber. Weight is 7 lbs. for 12 gauge and 6.75 lbs. for 20 gauge. Introduced in 2001.

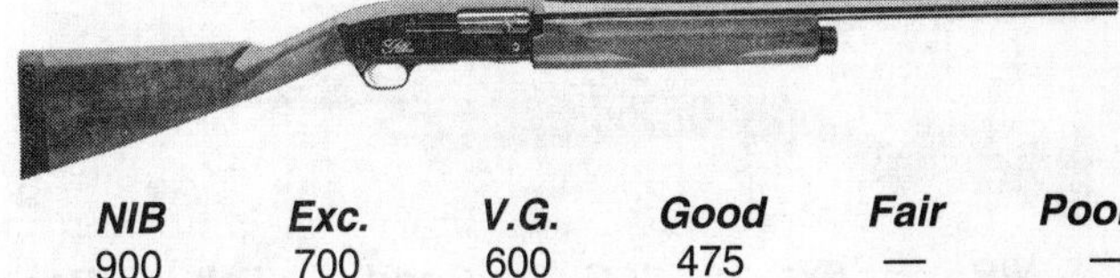

NIB	Exc.	V.G.	Good	Fair	Poor
900	700	600	475	—	—

Gold Fusion

This model features a new style vent rib, adjustable comb pro-comp sight, and five choke tubes. Offered in 12 gauge with 3" chambers with 26" or 28" barrels. Introduced in 2001. In 2002 this model was offered in 20 gauge as well as 12 with choice of 26" or 28" vent rib barrel. Weight for 12 gauge is about 7 lbs. anbd for 20 gauge about 6.5 lbs.

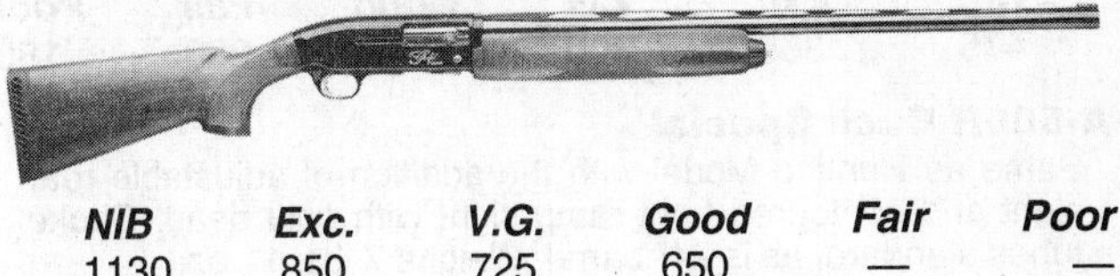

NIB	Exc.	V.G.	Good	Fair	Poor
1130	850	725	650	—	—

Gold Fusion High Grade

Similar to the Gold Fusion with the addition of a high grade Turkish walnut stock, silver nitride receiver with game scene in gold. Five choke tubes and a hard case are standard. Introduced in 2005.

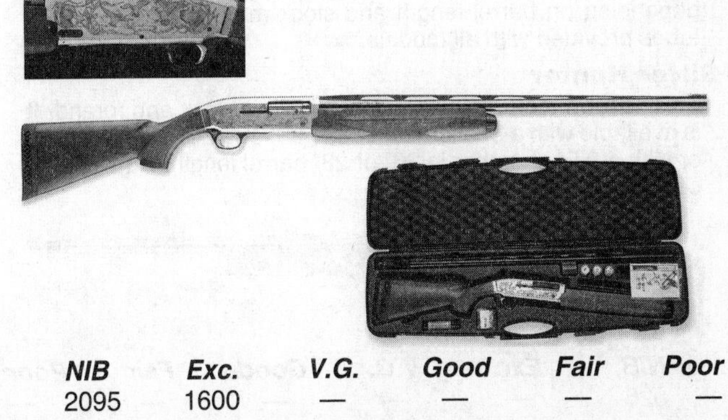

NIB	Exc.	V.G.	Good	Fair	Poor
2095	1600	—	—	—	—

Golden Clays

Introduced in 1999, this model features chambered for the 12 gauge shell with 2.74" chambers. Choice of 28" or 30" vent rib ported barrels. Engraved silver gray receiver. Select walnut stock. Weight is about 7 lbs. 3 ozs.

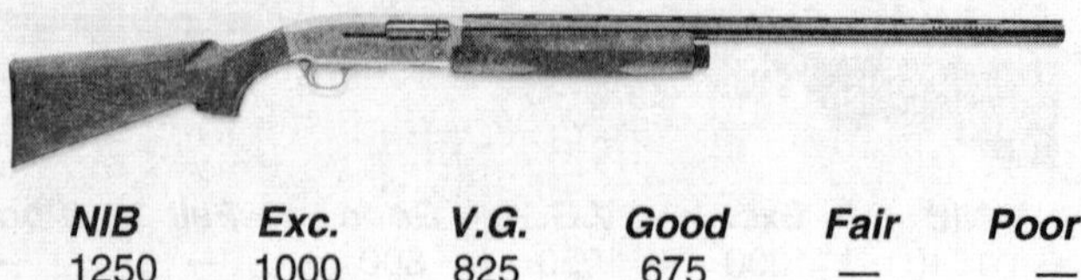

NIB	Exc.	V.G.	Good	Fair	Poor
1250	1000	825	675	—	—

500 SERIES

A-500G/A-500R

This is a self-adjusting, gas-operated, semi-automatic shotgun chambered for 12 gauge only. It is offered with 26", 28", or 30" barrels with a vent rib and screw-in Invector choke tubes. It has 3" chambers and can fire any load interchangeably. The finish is blued with a checkered walnut stock and recoil pad. It features light engraving. It was introduced in 1987. Deduct 10 percent for similar but recoil-operated A-500R.

NIB	Exc.	V.G.	Good	Fair	Poor
560	490	425	350	275	225

A-500G Sporting Clays

This gas-operated version is designed for sporting clays and features a choice of 28" or 30" vent rib barrel with semi-gloss finish with gold lettering "Sporting Clays." Ventilated recoil pad standard. Weighs about 8 lbs.

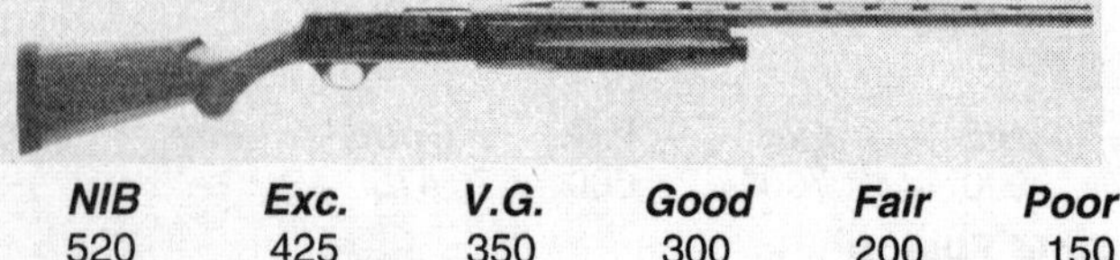

NIB	Exc.	V.G.	Good	Fair	Poor
520	425	350	300	200	150

A-500R Hunting Model

Similar in appearance to the A-500G with the exception that this model operates on a short recoil design. The buttstock features a full pistol grip. Available with 26", 28", or 30" vent rib barrels. Choke tubes standard. Weighs about 7 lbs. 13 oz.

NIB	Exc.	V.G.	Good	Fair	Poor
475	385	300	250	200	150

A-500R Buck Special

Same as Hunting Model with the addition of adjustable rear sight and contoured front ramp sight with gold bead. Choke tubes standard, as is 24" barrel. Weighs 7 lbs. 11 oz.

NIB	Exc.	V.G.	Good	Fair	Poor
500	425	350	300	225	150

SILVER SERIES

This value-priced series of gas-operated autoloaders was introduced in 2006. All models feature a semi-humpback design and aluminum alloy receiver. Weights vary from 7.25 to 7.5 lbs. depending on barrel length and stock material. Three choke tubes provided with all models.

Silver Hunter

This version features a satin finish walnut stock and forend. It is available with a 3" chamber in 26", 28" and 30" barrel lengths or with a 3.5" chamber in 26" or 28" barrel length. Add 15 percent for 3.5" chamber.

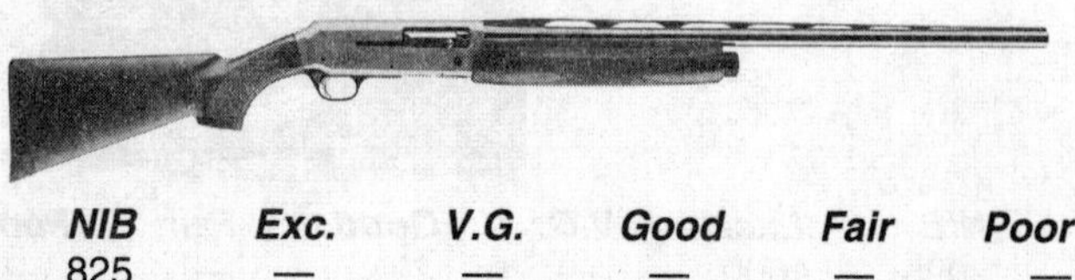

NIB	Exc.	V.G.	Good	Fair	Poor
825	—	—	—	—	—

Silver Stalker

Similar to Silver Hunter but with matte black composite stock and forend. Sling swivel studs. 3.5" chamber only.

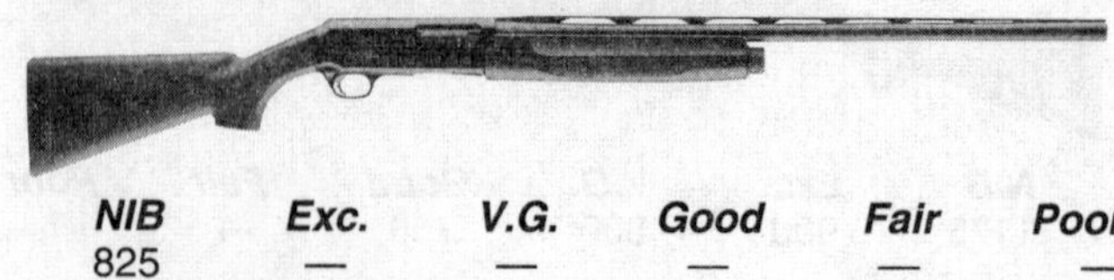

NIB	Exc.	V.G.	Good	Fair	Poor
825	—	—	—	—	—

Silver-Mossy Oak

Similar to Silver Stalker but in choice of Mossy Oak New Break-Up with 26" barrel or Mossy Oak New Shadow Grass with 26" or 28" barrel.

NIB	Exc.	V.G.	Good	Fair	Poor
925	—	—	—	—	—

Gold Superlite Hunter

Introduced in 2006, this gun uses an aluminum alloy receiver and alloy magazine tube to reduce weight to about 7 lbs. in 12 gauge. Gloss finish walnut stock. Available with 3" or 3.5" chamber and 26" or 28" barrel. Magazine cut-off feature on 3.5" model. A 6.5 lb. 20 gauge with 3" chamber and 26" or 28" barrel is also offered. Three choke tubes. Add 15 percent for 3.5" chamber.

NIB	Exc.	V.G.	Good	Fair	Poor
900	—	—	—	—	—

Gold Superlite FLD Hunter

Similar to Gold Superlite Hunter but with semi-humpback style receiver and satin finish walnut stock and 3" chamber only. Magazine cut-off on 12 gauge models. Adjustable shim system and three choke tubes.

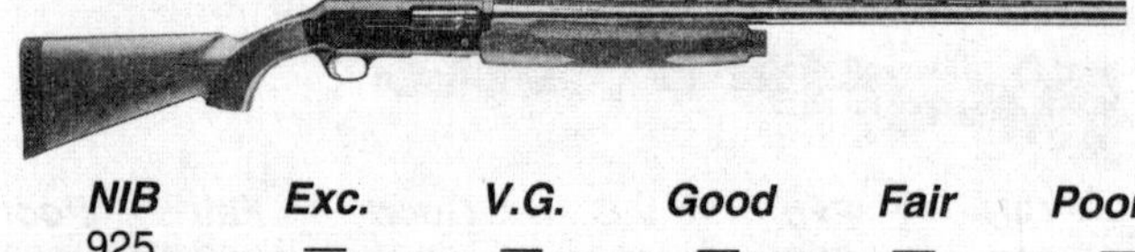

NIB	Exc.	V.G.	Good	Fair	Poor
925	—	—	—	—	—

Gold Superlite Micro

Similar to Gold Superlite Hunter but with compact dimensions for smaller shooters. Only in 20 gauge with 26" barrel. Weighs about 6.25 pounds. Three choke tubes.

NIB	Exc.	V.G.	Good	Fair	Poor
925	—	—	—	—	—

BPS SERIES

This is a slide-action shotgun chambered for 10, 12, or 20 gauge. It is offered with various length vent rib barrels with screw-in Invector chokes. It features 3" magnum chambers and a bottom-ejection system that effectively makes it ambidextrous. It has double slide bars and a 5-shot tubular magazine. It is constructed of all steel. It was introduced by B.C. Miroku in 1977.

BPS Field Grade

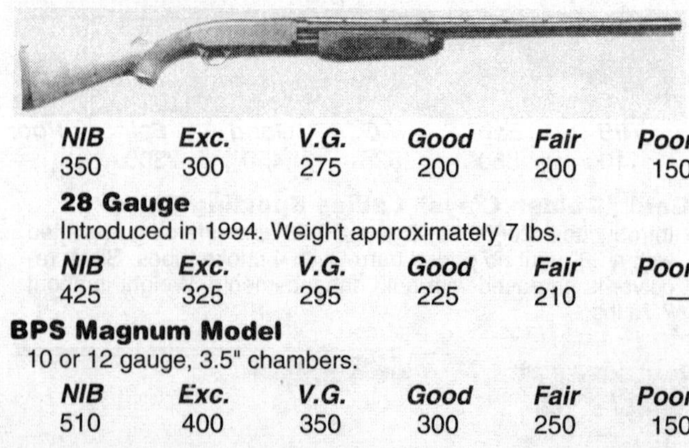

NIB	Exc.	V.G.	Good	Fair	Poor
350	300	275	200	200	150

28 Gauge

Introduced in 1994. Weight approximately 7 lbs.

NIB	Exc.	V.G.	Good	Fair	Poor
425	325	295	225	210	—

BPS Magnum Model

10 or 12 gauge, 3.5" chambers.

NIB	Exc.	V.G.	Good	Fair	Poor
510	400	350	300	250	150

BPS 12 Gauge Waterfowl Camo (1999)

NIB	Exc.	V.G.	Good	Fair	Poor
525	425	350	300	—	—

Waterfowl Mossy Oak Break-Up

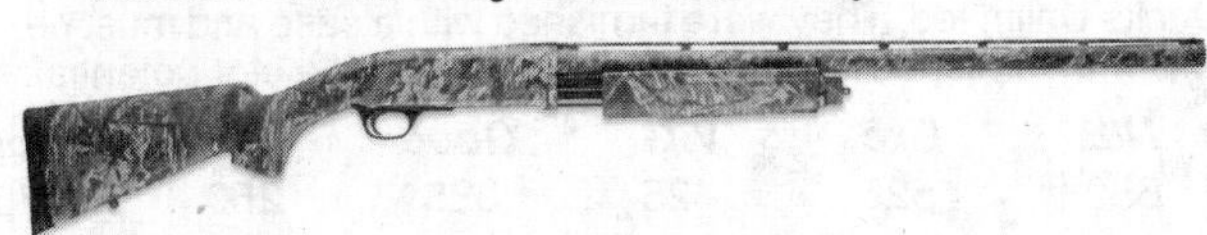

NIB	Exc.	V.G.	Good	Fair	Poor
575	475	375	325	—	—

BPS 10 Gauge Mossy Oak Shadow Grass Camo (1999)

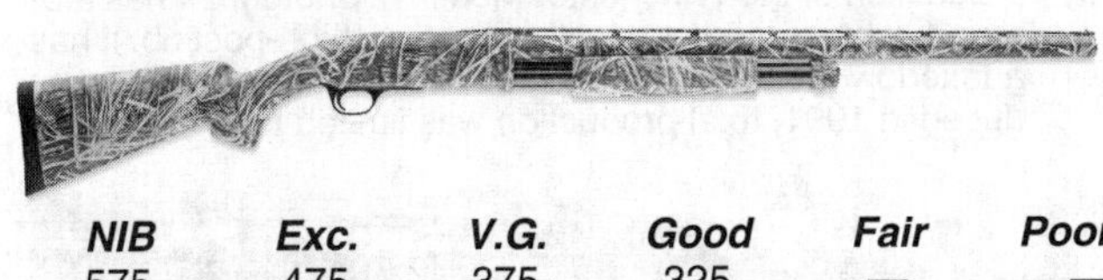

NIB	Exc.	V.G.	Good	Fair	Poor
575	475	375	325	—	—

BPS NWTF Series

This model is finished in a Mossy Oak Breakup pattern and bears the NWTF logo on the buttstock. Fitted with a 24" barrel, Hi-Viz front sight, Extra Full extended turkey choke. Introduced in 2001. Offered in the configurations listed.

BPS 10 Gauge

NIB	Exc.	V.G.	Good	Fair	Poor
625	475	400	325	—	—

BPS 12 Gauge

3.5" Chamber

NIB	Exc.	V.G.	Good	Fair	Poor
625	475	400	325	—	—

3" Chamber

NIB	Exc.	V.G.	Good	Fair	Poor
550	450	375	325	—	—

BPS Upland Special 22" Barrel, Straight Stock

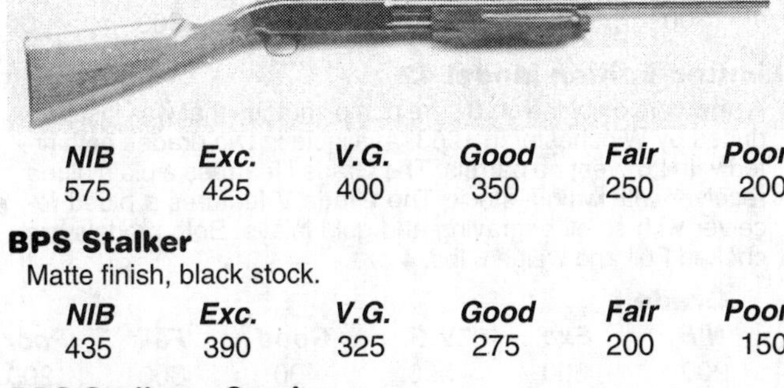

NIB	Exc.	V.G.	Good	Fair	Poor
575	425	400	350	250	200

BPS Stalker

Matte finish, black stock.

NIB	Exc.	V.G.	Good	Fair	Poor
435	390	325	275	200	150

BPS Stalker—Combo

A combination of a 28" vent rib barrel and a choice of 22" fully rifles barrel or 20.5" Invector barrel with Extra Full turkey choke. Introduced in 2000.

NIB	Exc.	V.G.	Good	Fair	Poor
650	525	475	—	—	—

BPS 10 Gauge Turkey

Fitted with a 24" vent rib barrel and black synthetic stock with black solid recoil pad, this model was introduced in 1999. Weight is about 9 lbs. 2 ozs.

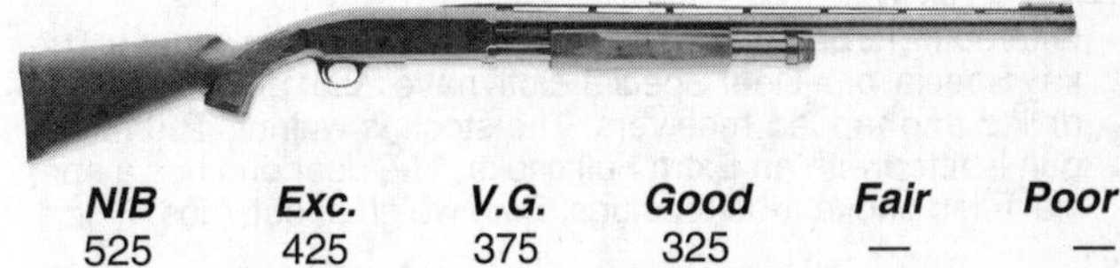

NIB	Exc.	V.G.	Good	Fair	Poor
525	425	375	325	—	—

BPS Game Gun

These models are designed for turkey and deer with 20.5" barrels with Invector chokes or rifled barrels. Deer model has 5" rifled choke tube while the turkey model has Extra Full choke tube. The Cantilever model has a fully rifled barrel. Weight is approximately 7.7 lbs. Introduced in 1998. Add $30 for deer model and $60 for Cantilever model.

NIB	Exc.	V.G.	Good	Fair	Poor
450	350	300	250	—	—

BPS Micro 20 Gauge

This model features a 22" vent rib barrel with shorter pistol grip stock and lighter weight. Weight is about 6.75 lbs. Introduced in 2001.

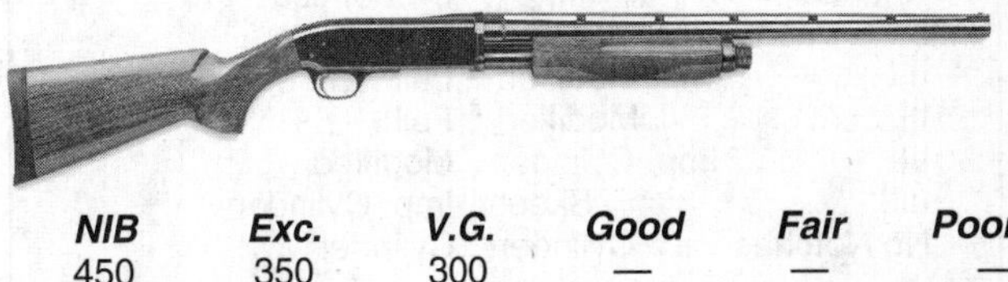

NIB	Exc.	V.G.	Good	Fair	Poor
450	350	300	—	—	—

BPS Upland Special

This model is chambered for the 20 gauge shell and fitted with a 22" vent rib barrel. The walnut stock is a straight grip. Weight is about 6.5 lbs.

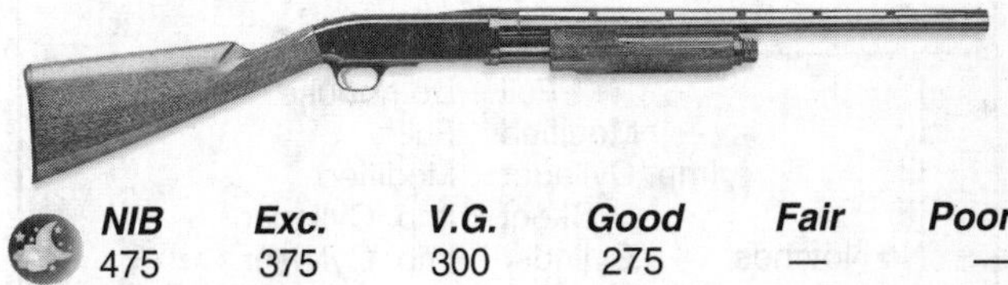

NIB	Exc.	V.G.	Good	Fair	Poor
475	375	300	275	—	—

BPS Small Gauge

Introduced in 2000 this model is chambered for the 28 gauge and the .410 bore. The 28 gauge is offered with a choice of 26" or 28" vent rib barrel with Invector chokes. The .410 is available with 26" vent rib barrel with Invector chokes. Both the 28 gauge and .410 bore weigh about 6.75 lbs.

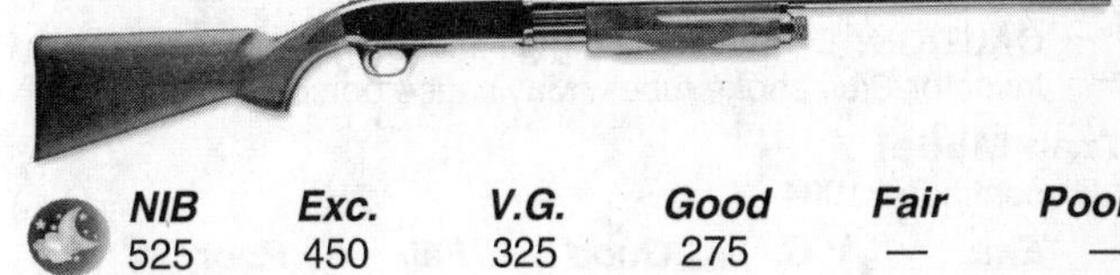

NIB	Exc.	V.G.	Good	Fair	Poor
525	450	325	275	—	—

BPS Pigeon Grade

Furnished in 12 gauge only with high grade walnut stock and gold trimmed receiver.

NIB	Exc.	V.G.	Good	Fair	Poor
500	400	300	225	175	125

Game Gun

Offered in 12 gauge only this model is available in either a Turkey Special or a Deer Special. Both have 20.5" plain barrel and drilled and tapped receivers. The stock is walnut. The turkey gun is fitted with an Extra Full choke. The deer gun has a special rifled choke tube for slugs. Both weigh about 7 lbs. 7 oz.

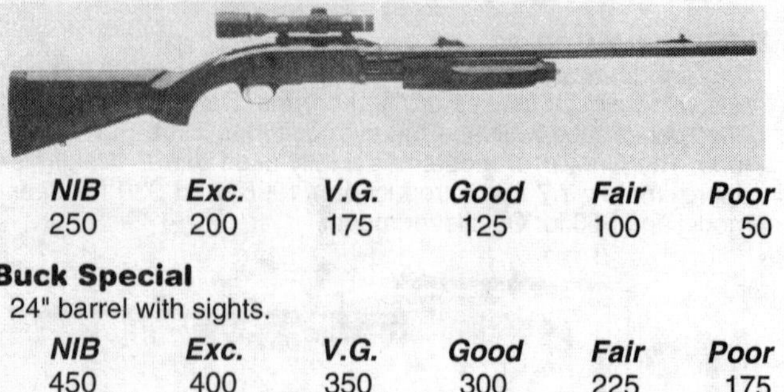

NIB	Exc.	V.G.	Good	Fair	Poor
250	200	175	125	100	50

Buck Special

24" barrel with sights.

NIB	Exc.	V.G.	Good	Fair	Poor
450	400	350	300	225	175

BROWNING CHOKE TUBE SELECTION

Rim Notches	Pattern w/Lead Shot	Pattern w/Steel Shot
12 Gauge Invector-Plus for Back-Bored Guns		
Knurled	X-Full Turkey	Do not use
I	Full	Do not use
II	Imp. Modified	Full
III	Modified	Full
IIII	Imp. Cylinder	Modified
IIIII	Skeet	Imp. Cylinder
No Notches	Cylinder	Cylinder
10 Gauge Invector		
Knurled	X-Full Turkey	Do not use
I	Full	Do not use
II	Modified	Full
III	Imp. Modified	Modified
16 Gauge Invector		
I	Full	Do not use
II	Modified	Full
III	Imp. Cylinder	Modified
IIII	Skeet	Imp. Cylinder
No Notches	Cylinder	Imp. Cylinder
20 Gauge Invector		
I	Full	Full
II	Modified	Imp. Modified
III	Imp. Cylinder	Modified
IIII	Skeet	Modified
No Notches	Cylinder	Imp. Cylinder

CAUTION: Do not interchange Invector choke tubes with Invector-Plus choke tubes. May cause personal injury.

Trap Model

Discontinued 1984.

Exc.	V.G.	Good	Fair	Poor
375	325	275	200	150

Youth Model

Short stock, 22" barrel.

NIB	Exc.	V.G.	Good	Fair	Poor
435	390	325	275	200	150

Waterfowl Deluxe

This version is chambered for 12 gauge with a 3" chamber and features an etched receiver with a gold-plated trigger. Otherwise, it is similar to the standard BPS.

Exc.	V.G.	Good	Fair	Poor
600	525	425	325	250

Ducks Unlimited Versions

These were limited-edition guns produced to be auctioned by Ducks Unlimited. They were furnished with a case and must be NIB with furnished materials to realize their colle ctor potential.

NIB	Exc.	V.G.	Good	Fair	Poor
650	525	425	325	250	175

Model 12

Grade I

This is a slide-action shotgun chambered for 20 and 28 gauge with a 26", modified choke, vent rib barrel. It is a reproduction of the Winchester Model 12 shotgun. It has a 5-round, tubular magazine with a floating, high-post rib. It has a takedown feature and is blued with a walnut stock. Introduced in 1991, total production was limited to 7,000 guns.

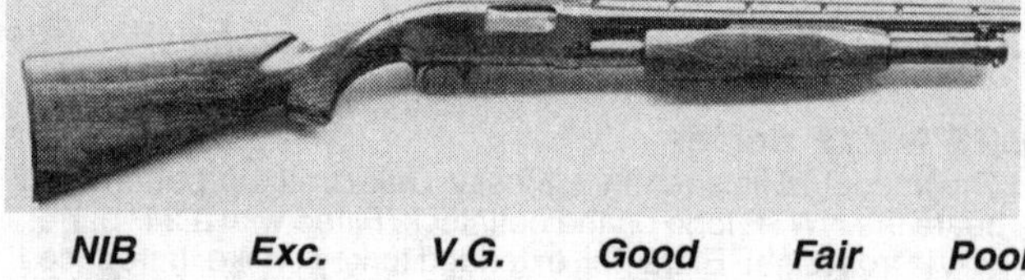

NIB	Exc.	V.G.	Good	Fair	Poor
825	625	425	300	250	200

Grade IV

This is an extensively engraved version of the Grade I Model 12. It features a select walnut stock with deluxe checkering and a high-gloss finish. There are gold inlays. It was introduced in 1991, and production was limited to 5,000 guns. Discontinued 1992.

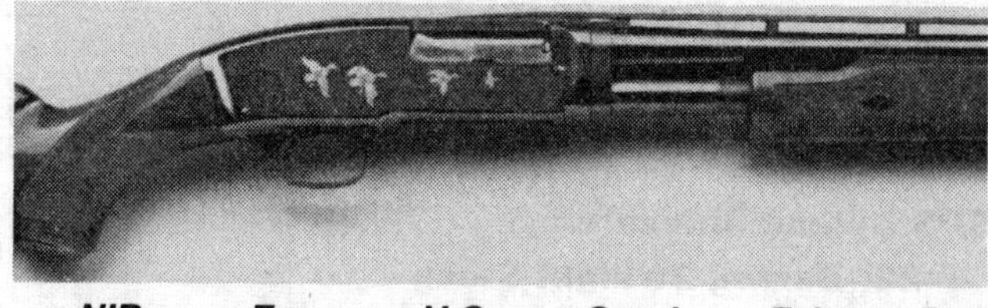

NIB	Exc.	V.G.	Good	Fair	Poor
1200	950	700	450	300	200

Limited Edition Model 42

A new version of the .410 bore pump shotgun that was last produced by Winchester in 1963. Available in two grades both fitted with 26" vent rib barrels. The Grade I features a plain blued receiver with walnut stock. The Grade V features a blued receiver with scroll engraving and gold inlays. Both models are choked Full and weigh 6 lbs. 4 oz.

Grade I

NIB	Exc.	V.G.	Good	Fair	Poor
900	600	500	400	300	200

Grade V

NIB	Exc.	V.G.	Good	Fair	Poor
1150	900	700	500	350	200

A-Bolt Shotgun

Introduced in 1995 this bolt-action shotgun was offered in 12 gauge with 3" chamber. Rifled barrel version is 22" long while the Invector barrel version is 23" long with a 5" rifle tube installed. Has a 2-shot detachable magazine. Average weight is about 7 lbs.

Hunter Version

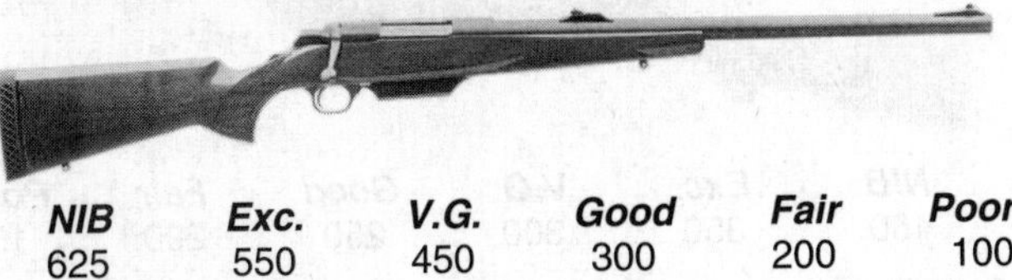

NIB	Exc.	V.G.	Good	Fair	Poor
625	550	450	300	200	100

Stalker Version

NIB	Exc.	V.G.	Good	Fair	Poor
500	400	300	250	200	100

NOTE: For Invector rifled choke tube model deduct $50.

RIFLES

High-Power Bolt-Action Rifle

This was a high-grade, bolt-action sporting rifle manufactured by FN in Belgium (from 1959 to 1975) or Sako of Finland (from 1961 to 1975). It was built on either a Mauser or a Sako action and chambered for a number of popular calibers from the .222 Remington up to the .458 Winchester Magnum. There were three basic grades that differed in the amount of ornamentation and the quality of materials and workmanship utilized. Certain calibers are considered to be rare and will bring a premium from collectors of this firearm. We recommend securing a qualified appraisal on these rifles if a transaction is contemplated. We furnish general values only.

NOTE: From 1959 through 1966 FN Mauser actions with long extractors were featured. These Mauser actions will bring a premium depending on caliber. From 1967 on, FN Supreme actions with short extractors were used. *Only* .30-06 and .270 calibers continued with long extractor Mauser actions.

CAUTION: For buyer and seller alike some rare calibers may be worth as much as 100 percent or more over prices listed for rare calibers such as .284 Win., .257 Roberts, 300 H&H, and .308 Norma Magnum. The High-Power bolt-action rifles seemed to be particularly hard hit by salt wood. That is why short extractors rifles bring less than long extravtor guns. No factory replacement stocks are known to still be available. Deduct 20-25 percent for short extractor rifles. Proceed with caution.

Safari Grade

Standard model, standard calibers.

Exc.	V.G.	Good	Fair	Poor
900	700	550	400	400

Medallion Grade

Scroll engraved, standard calibers.

Exc.	V.G.	Good	Fair	Poor
2000	1500	1100	750	400

Olympian Grade

Extensive game scene engraving, standard calibers.

Exc.	V.G.	Good	Fair	Poor
5000	4250	3250	2500	1500

Model BBR

This is a bolt-action sporting rifle chambered for various popular calibers. It has a 24" barrel with an adjustable trigger and fluted bolt. It features a detachable magazine under the floorplate and was furnished without sights. The finish is blued with a checkered, walnut, Monte Carlo stock. It was manufactured between 1978 and 1984 by Miroku.

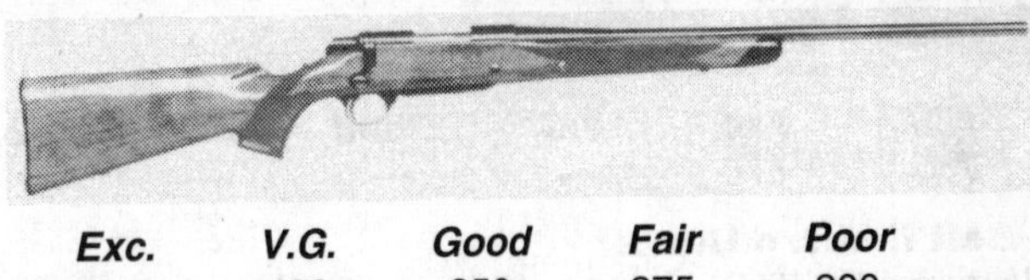

Exc.	V.G.	Good	Fair	Poor
525	400	350	275	200

BOSS™ SYSTEM

Introduced by Browning in 1994 this new accuracy system allows the shooter to fine-tune his Browning rifle to the particular load he is using. Consists of a tube on the end of the rifle muzzle that allows the shooter to select the best setting for the ammunition type. The system also reduces recoil. BOSS stands for Ballistic Optimizing Shooting System. This option will add approximately $80 to the value of the particular Browning rifle on which it is fitted.

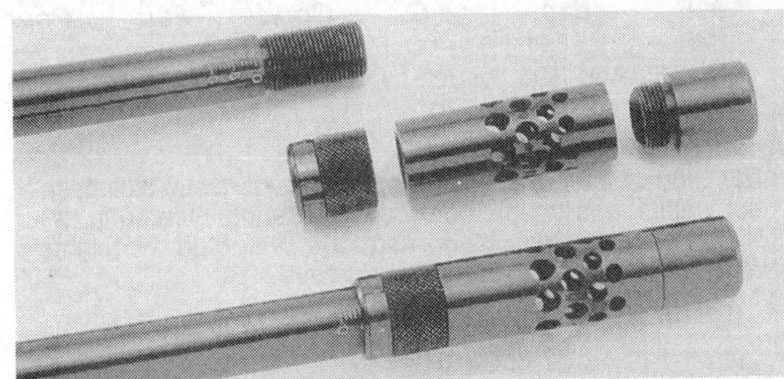

A-BOLT SERIES

NOTE: In 2004 new calibers were offered for the A-Bolt series depending on model. They are the .25 WSSM and the .223 Rem. SSA.

All A-Bolt II Descriptions: "II" designation dropped from A-Bolt name in 2006.

A-Bolt Hunter

This is the current bolt-action rifle manufactured by B.C. Miroku. It is chambered for various popular calibers and offered with a 22", 24", or 26" barrel. It has either a short or long action, an adjustable trigger, and a detachable box magazine that is mounted under the floorplate. It is furnished without sights and is blued with a checkered walnut stock. It was introduced in 1985.

NIB	Exc.	V.G.	Good	Fair	Poor
525	400	350	300	250	200

A-Bolt II Hunter

Introduced in 1994 this new model features a newly designed anti-bind bolt and improved trigger system. In 2001 the .300 Winchester Short Magnum cartridge was offered for this model. In 2003 a left-hand model was introduced.

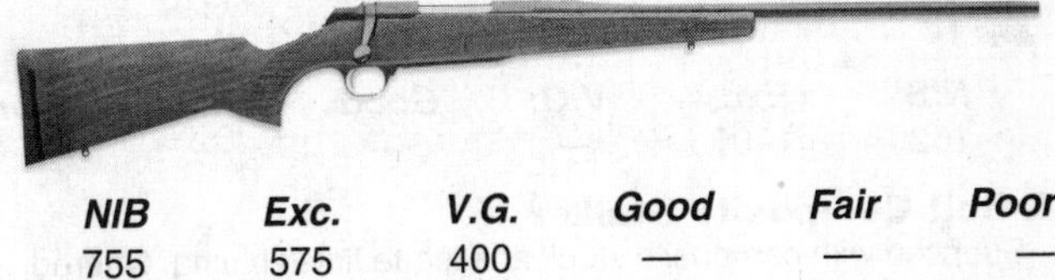

NIB	Exc.	V.G.	Good	Fair	Poor
755	575	400	—	—	—

A-Bolt II Hunter WSSM

Similar to the A-Bolt Hunter but chambered for the .223 WSM and .243 WSM cartridges. The stock design is also different from the A-Bolt Hunter with the addition of a longer pistol grip and thicker forearm. Weight is about 6.25 lbs. Introduced in 2003.

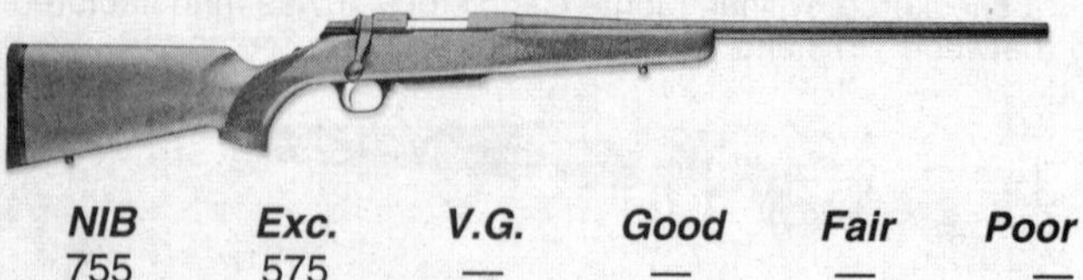

NIB	Exc.	V.G.	Good	Fair	Poor
755	575	—	—	—	—

A-Bolt II Micro Hunter

Introduced in 1999, this model features a shorter length of pull and a shorter barrel length than the Hunter model. Offered in .22 Hornet, .22-250, 7mm-08, .308, .243, and .260 calibers. Weight is about 6 lbs. In 2003 the .270 WSM, 7mm WSM, and .300 WSM calibers were added for this model as well as a left-hand version.

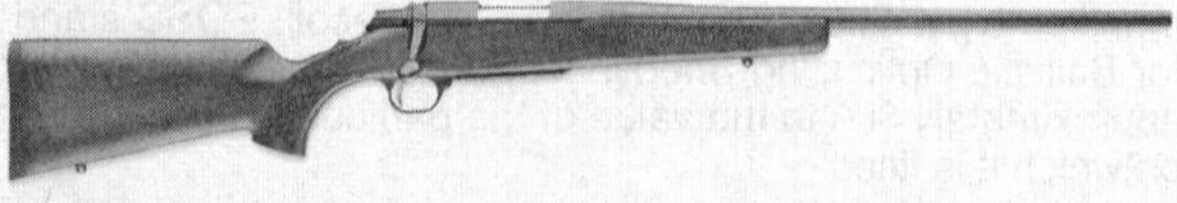

NIB	Exc.	V.G.	Good	Fair	Poor
625	525	400	—	—	—

NOTE: Add $30 for left-hand model and $30 for WSM calibers.

A-Bolt II Classic Hunter

This model features a Monte Carlo stock, low luster bluing, select walnut, and double bordered checkering. Offered in .30-06, .270, 7mm Rem. Mag., and .300 Win. Mag. No sights. Weight is about 7 lbs. Introduced in 1999.

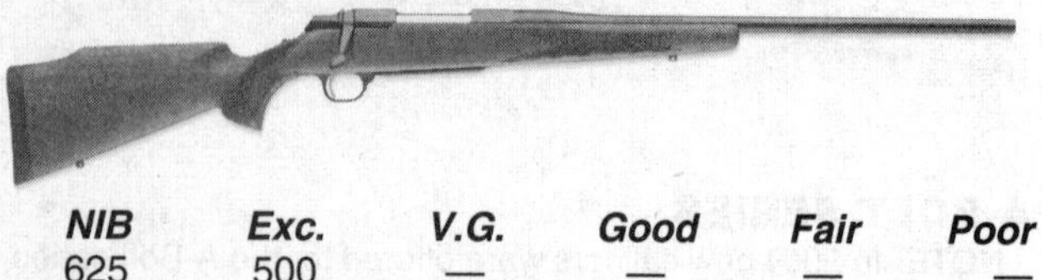

NIB	Exc.	V.G.	Good	Fair	Poor
625	500	—	—	—	—

A-Bolt Classic Hunter WSSM

As above but chambered for the .223 WSSM and .243 WSSM cartridges. Weight is about 6.25 lbs. Introduced in 2003.

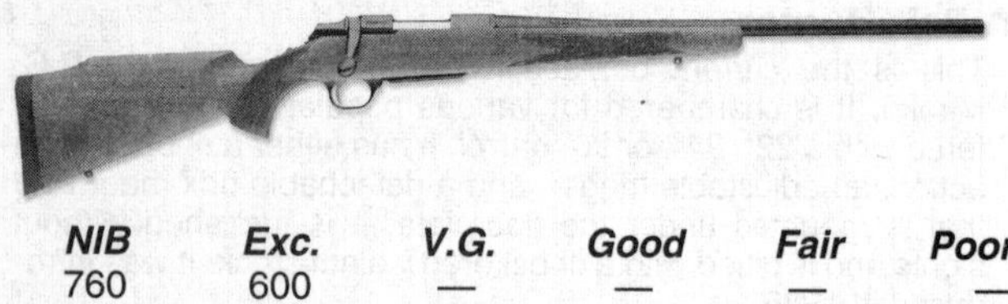

NIB	Exc.	V.G.	Good	Fair	Poor
760	600	—	—	—	—

A-Bolt Mountain, Ti

This model features a lightweight stainless steel 23" barrel, titanium receiver, and lightweight fiberglass stock. Chambered for the .270 WSM, 7mm WSM, and the .300 WSM cartridges. Weight is about 5.5 lbs. Calibers: .243, 7mm-08, .308, .325 WSM. Introduced in 2004.

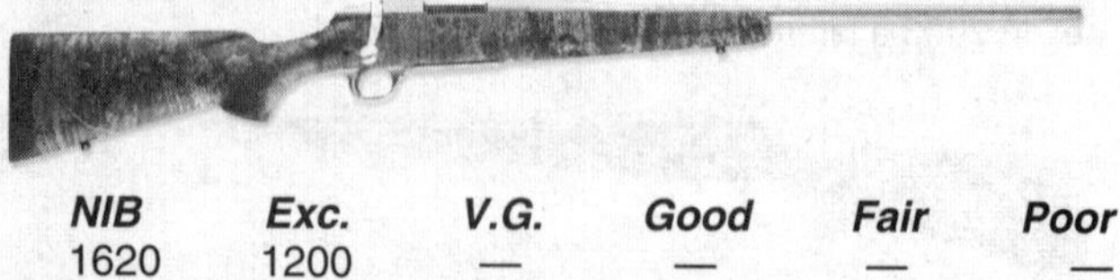

NIB	Exc.	V.G.	Good	Fair	Poor
1620	1200	—	—	—	—

A-Bolt Composite Stalker

Supplied with composite stock and matte finish bluing. Offered in .338 Win. Mag., .300 Win. Mag., 7mm Rem. Mag., .25-06, .270, .280, .30-06. Introduced in 1988. In 2001 the .300 Winchester Short Magnum cartridge was offered for this model. Calibers: .223 WSSM, .243 WSSM, .25 WSSM, .223, .243, .7mm-08, .270 WSM, 7mm WSM, .300 WSM, .325 WSM, .25-06, .270, .280, .30-06, 7mm RM, .300 WM, .338 WM. Add 10 percent for BOSS or left-hand version.

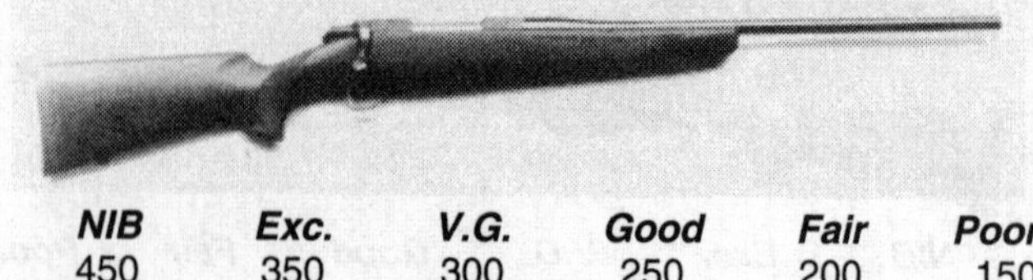

NIB	Exc.	V.G.	Good	Fair	Poor
450	350	300	250	200	150

A-Bolt II Composite Stalker

Same as above but with 1994 improvements.

NIB	Exc.	V.G.	Good	Fair	Poor
670	525	400	300	250	200

NOTE: Add $80 for BOSS system.

A-Bolt Composite Stalker WSSM

As above but chambered for the .223 WSSM or the .243 WSSM cartridge. Weight is about 6 lbs. Introduced in 2003.

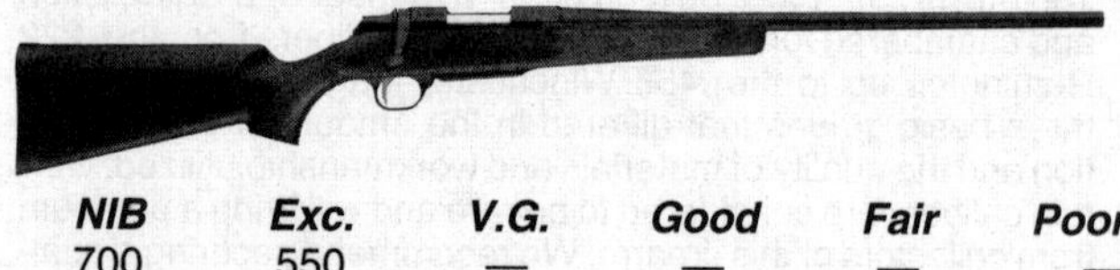

NIB	Exc.	V.G.	Good	Fair	Poor
700	550	—	—	—	—

A-Bolt Stainless Stalker

Bolt-action rifle. Calibers: .223 WSSM, .243 WSSM, .25 WSSM, .223, .243, .7mm-08, .270 WSM, 7mm WSM, .300 WSM, .325 WSM, .25-06, .270, .280, .30-06, 7mm RM, .300 WM, .338 WM, .375 H&H. Barrel: 22-inch, 23-inch, 24-inch, 26-inch stainless steel, sightless (except for .375 H&H). Magazine: Detachable box. Stock: Black composite. Add 10 percent for BOSS system and left-hand version.

NIB	Exc.	V.G.	Good	Fair	Poor
600	450	400	350	300	250

NOTE: For .300 and .338 calibers add $30.

A-Bolt II Composite Stainless Stalker

Same as above but with 1994 improvements.

NIB	Exc.	V.G.	Good	Fair	Poor
850	650	550	400	300	250

NOTE: For Magnum calibers add $30. For BOSS system add $110.

A-Bolt Stainless Stalker, WSSM

As above but chambered for the .223 WSSM and .243 WSSM calibers. Stock design is slightly different from standard A-Bolt Stalker. Weight is about 6 lbs. Introduced in 2003.

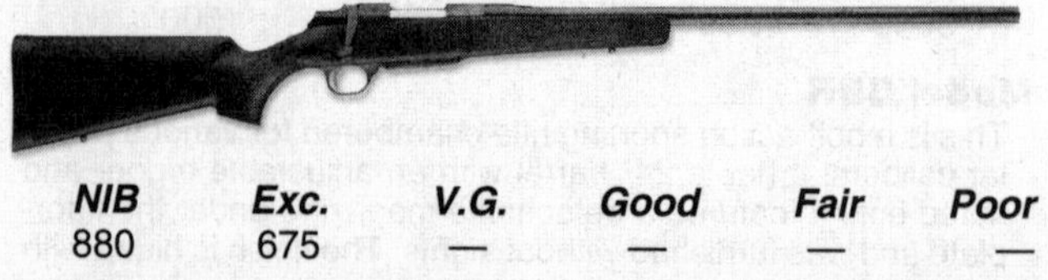

NIB	Exc.	V.G.	Good	Fair	Poor
880	675	—	—	—	—

A-Bolt Carbon Fiber Stainless Stalker

This model features a Christensen Arms patent carbon barrel. Chambered for .22-250 or .300 Win. Mag. Weight is about 6.25 lbs. for short action and 7 lbs. for long action. Introduced in 2000. In 2001 the .300 Winchester Short Magnum cartridge was offered for this model.

NIB	Exc.	V.G.	Good	Fair	Poor
1400	1200	1000	900	700	—

A-Bolt II Heavy Barrel Varmint

Introduced in 1994 this model features all of the A-Bolt II improvements in a heavy barrel varmint rifle. Offered in .22-250 and .223 Rem. calibers with 22" barrel. Equipped with black laminated wood stock.

NIB	Exc.	V.G.	Good	Fair	Poor
685	600	525	425	325	250

A-Bolt Varmint Stalker

Introduced in 2002 this model features a new armor coated synthetic stock. Matte blue metal finish. Chambered for the .223 Rem. and .22-250 Rem. cartridges. Fitted with a 24" barrel on the .223 and a 26" barrel on the .22-250. Weight is about 8 lbs.

NIB	Exc.	V.G.	Good	Fair	Poor
790	650	—	—	—	—

A-Bolt Varmint Stalker WSSM

As above but chambered for the .223 WSSM and .243 WSSM cartridges. Weight is about 7.75 lbs. Introduced in 2003.

NIB	Exc.	V.G.	Good	Fair	Poor
815	650	—	—	—	—

A-Bolt Eclipse M-1000

Thumbhole stock. Calibers: .270, .30-06, 7mm RM, .22-250, .308, .270 WSM, .7mm WSM, .300 WSM. Add 10 percent for BOSS. The rifle is fitted with a 26" barrel with BOSS system. The stock is a laminated hardwood with gray/black finish. The forearm is a benchrest style. Weight is approximately 9 lbs. 13 oz.

NIB	Exc.	V.G.	Good	Fair	Poor
1135	700	625	450	350	250

A-Bolt Eclipse M-1000 WSM & Stainless

Introduced in 2004 this model is offered in all of the WSM calibers. The M-1000 is blued with a heavy barrel, while the stainless is fitted with a heavy bull barrel. Barrel length is 26". Weight is 9.85 lbs. No sights.

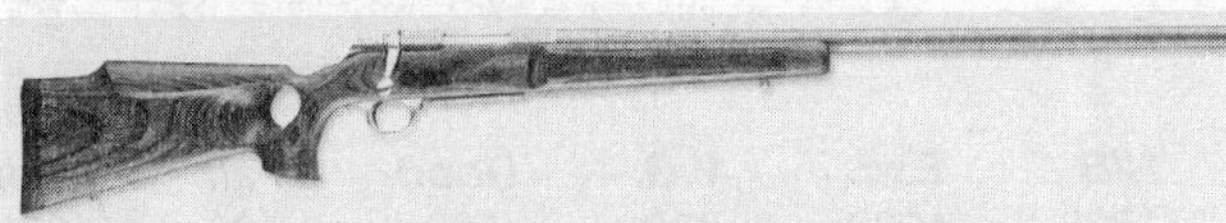

A-Bolt Eclipse M-1000 Stainless

NIB	Exc.	V.G.	Good	Fair	Poor
1050	825	675	500	—	—

NOTE: Add $200 for the stainless model.

A-Bolt Eclipse Varmint

Introduced in 1996 this model features a thumbhole stock made from gray/black laminated hardwood. Offered in two version: a short-action, heavy-barrel version, and a long and short action with standard-weight barrel. Eclipse Varmint weighs about 9 lbs. and the standard-barrel version weighs about 7.5 lbs. depending on caliber.

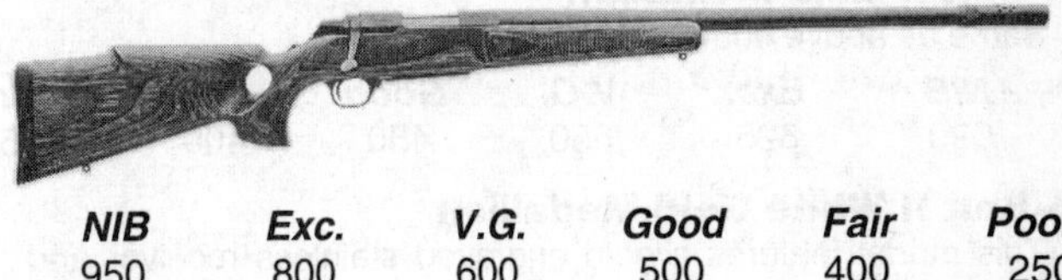

NIB	Exc.	V.G.	Good	Fair	Poor
950	800	600	500	400	250

Euro-Bolt

First introduced in 1993 this A-Bolt variation features a rounded bolt shroud, Mannlicher-style bolt handle, continental-style stock with cheekpiece, schnabel-style forearm. The finish is a low-luster blue. Offered in .270, .30-06, and 7mm Rem. Mag. calibers. Weighs about 7 lbs.

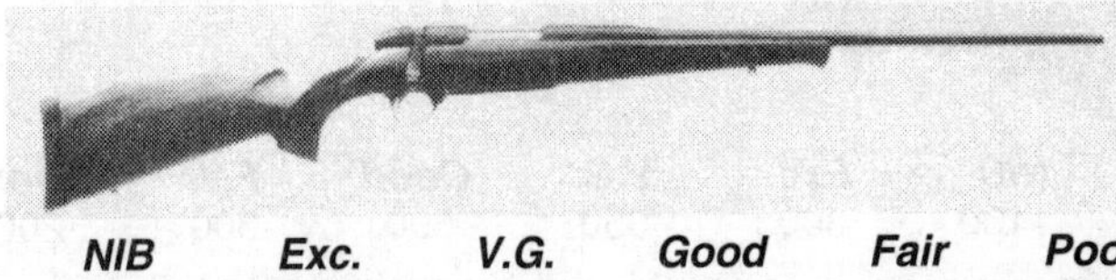

NIB	Exc.	V.G.	Good	Fair	Poor
550	500	450	350	250	150

A-Bolt II Euro Bolt

Same as above but with 1994 improvements.

NIB	Exc.	V.G.	Good	Fair	Poor
550	500	450	350	250	150

A-Bolt Medallion Model

Calibers: .223 WSSM, .243 WSSM, .25 WSSM, .223, .243, .7mm-08, .270 WSM, 7mm WSM, .300 WSM, .325 WSM, .25-06, .270, .280, .30-06, 7mm RM, .300 WM, .338 WM. Add 10 percent for BOSS or left-hand version.

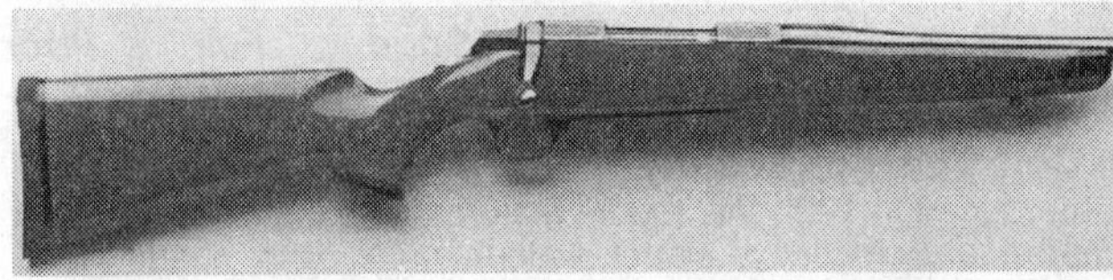

NIB	Exc.	V.G.	Good	Fair	Poor
800	600	500	400	300	250

NOTE: Add $35 for .300 and .338 calibers.

A-Bolt II Medallion

Same as above but with 1994 improvements. In 2003 this model was offered in a left-hand version.

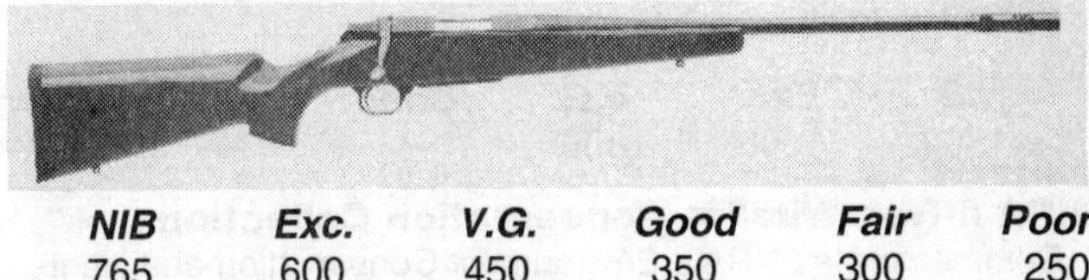

NIB	Exc.	V.G.	Good	Fair	Poor
765	600	450	350	300	250

A-Bolt II Medallion WSSM

As above but chambered for the .223 WSSM or the .243 WSSM cartridge. Weight is about 6.25 lbs. Introduced in 2003.

NIB	Exc.	V.G.	Good	Fair	Poor
795	650	525	—	—	—

Gold Medallion

This version has a fancy grade walnut stock with a cheekpiece. It is lightly engraved and has gold-inlaid letters. It was introduced in 1988.

NIB	Exc.	V.G.	Good	Fair	Poor
690	625	550	450	400	325

A-Bolt II Gold Medallion

Same as above but with 1994 improvements.

NIB	Exc.	V.G.	Good	Fair	Poor
690	625	550	450	400	325

A-Bolt II White Gold Medallion

This model features a gold engraved stainless receiver and barrel, select walnut stock with brass spacers and rosewood caps. European-style cheekpiece. No sights. Introduced in 1999. Offered in .30-06, .270, 7mm Rem. Mag., and .300 Win. Mag. Weight is about 7 lbs. 8 ozs.

NIB	Exc.	V.G.	Good	Fair	Poor
1100	800	650	500	300	200

A-Bolt White Gold Medallion, RMEF

Introduced in 2003 this model is a special edition for the Rocky Mountain Elk Foundation. Chambered for the 7mm Rem. Mag. and fitted with a 26" barrel. Both action and barrel are stainless steel. Special RMEF logo on the grip cap. Weight is about 7.75 lbs. Add 5 percent for WSM calibers.

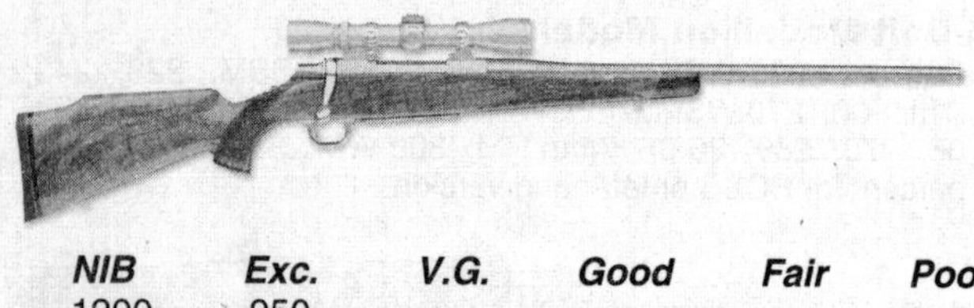

NIB	Exc.	V.G.	Good	Fair	Poor
1200	950	—	—	—	—

A-Bolt Custom Trophy

Introduced in 1998 this model features gold highlights on the barrel and receiver, select walnut stock, with shadowline cheekpiece and skeleton pistol grip. The barrel is octagonal. Chambered for .270 and .30-06 with 24" barrel and 7mm Rem. Mag. and .300 Win. Mag. with 26" barrel. Weight varies from 7 lbs. 11 oz. to 7 lbs. 3 oz. depending on caliber.

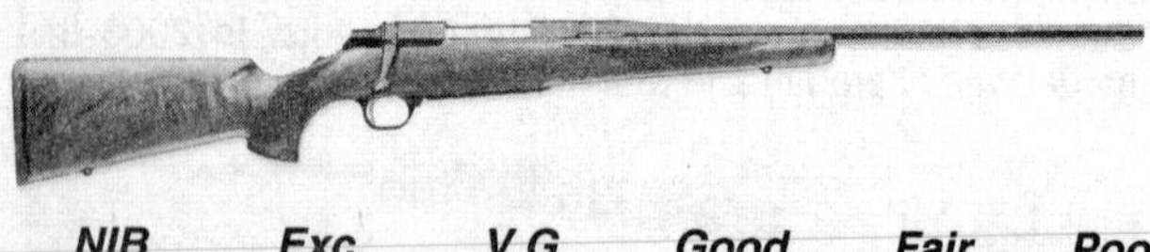

NIB	Exc.	V.G.	Good	Fair	Poor
1300	1000	800	—	—	—

NRA A-Bolt Wildlife Conservation Collection

Commemorates NRA's Environment Conservation and Hunting Outreach Program. Caliber: .243 Win. Barrel: 22-inch blued sightless. Stock: Satin-finish walnut with NRA Heritage logo lasered on buttstock. MSRP: 797

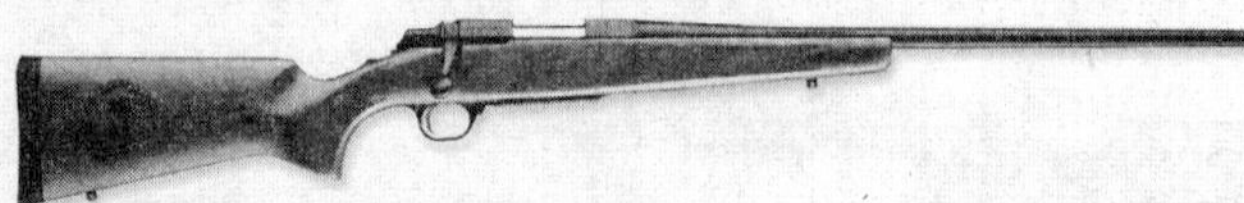

A-Bolt Big Horn Sheep Issue

This is a high-grade version of the A-Bolt chambered for the .270 cartridge. It features a deluxe skipline checkered walnut stock with a heavily engraved receiver and floorplate. It has two gold sheep inlays. There were 600 manufactured in 1986 and 1987.

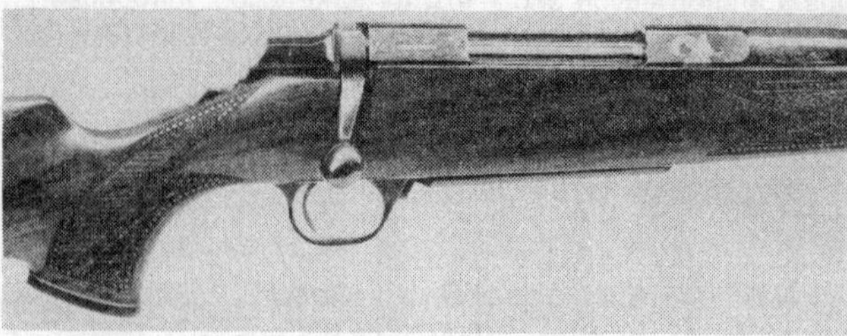

NIB	Exc.	V.G.	Good	Fair	Poor
1050	800	600	450	400	325

Micro-Medallion Model

This is a smaller version of the A-Bolt Hunter chambered for popular cartridges that fit a short action. It has a 20" barrel without sights and a 3-round magazine. It was introduced in 1988.

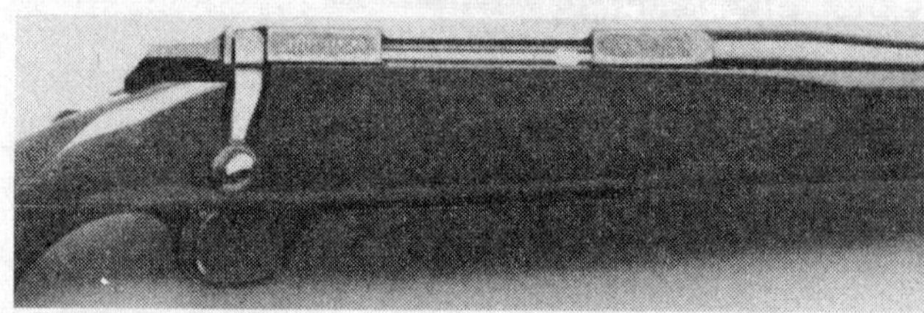

NIB	Exc.	V.G.	Good	Fair	Poor
525	475	400	350	300	250

A-Bolt II Micro-Medallion

Same as above but with 1994 improvements.

NIB	Exc.	V.G.	Good	Fair	Poor
525	475	400	350	300	250

A-Bolt Pronghorn Issue

This is a deluxe version of the A-Bolt chambered for the .243 cartridge. It is heavily engraved and gold inlaid and features a presentation-grade walnut stock with skipline checkering and pearl-inlaid borders. There were 500 manufactured in 1987.

NIB	Exc.	V.G.	Good	Fair	Poor
1300	1000	750	500	400	325

A-Bolt Special Hunter RMEF

Similar to A-Bolt Hunter but honors Rocky Mountain Elk Foundation. Chambered in .325 WSM. Satin finish. Introduced 2007.

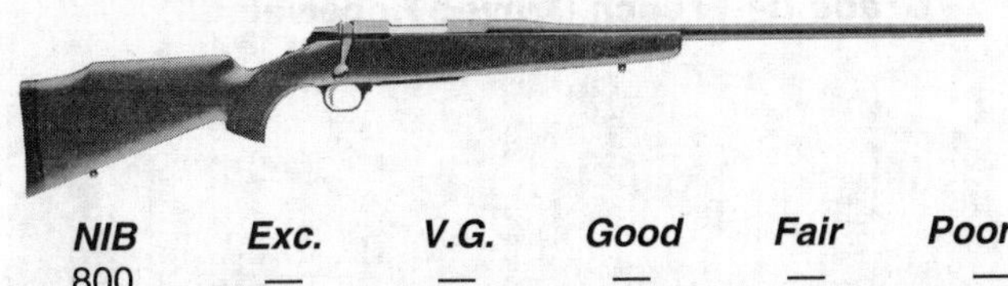

NIB	Exc.	V.G.	Good	Fair	Poor
800	—	—	—	—	—

A-Bolt White Gold RMEF

Similar to A-Bolt Special Hunter RMEF but with stainless barrel and receiver and glossy finish. Introduced 2007.

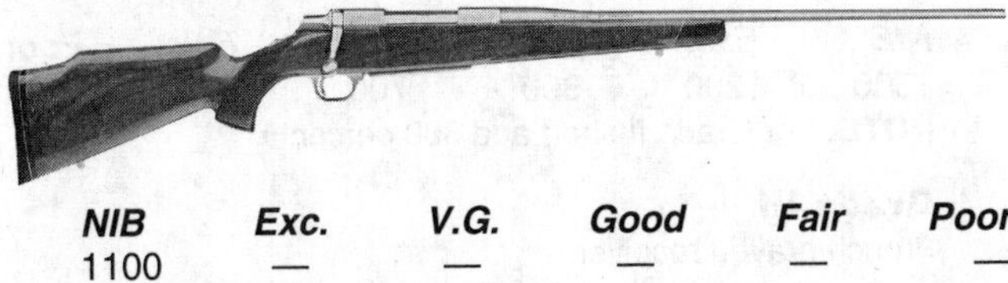

NIB	Exc.	V.G.	Good	Fair	Poor
1100	—	—	—	—	—

Acera Straight Pull Rifle

Introduced in 1999, this model features a straight action bolt system. It is chambered for the .30-06 with a 22" barrel and the .300 Win. Mag. with 24" barrel. Open sights are optional as is the BOSS system. Detachable box magazine. Checkered walnut stock. Prices listed are for .30-06 with no sights and no BOSS.

NIB	Exc.	V.G.	Good	Fair	Poor
1000	775	600	475	—	—

NOTE: Add $100 for .300 Win. Mag with no sights and no BOSS.

Grade I A—Bolt .22

This is a bolt-action sporting rifle chambered for the .22 LR or .22 Magnum cartridges. It features a 60-degree bolt and a 22" barrel available either with or without open sights. It has a 5-round, detachable magazine and an adjustable trigger. The finish is blued with a checkered walnut stock. It was introduced in 1986.

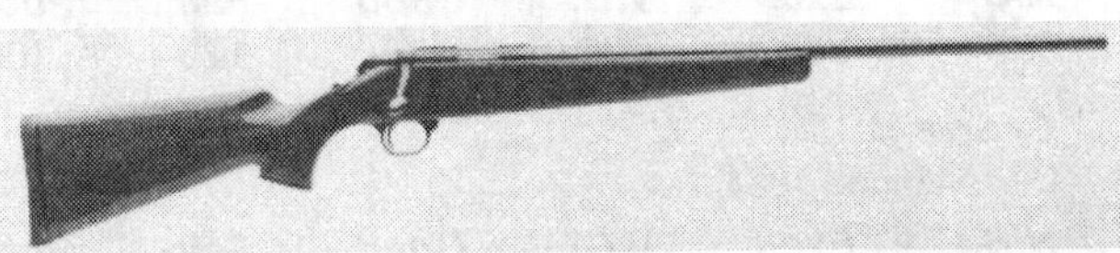

NIB	Exc.	V.G.	Good	Fair	Poor
340	275	210	150	125	100

NOTE: .22 Magnum add 15 percent.

Gold Medallion A-Bolt .22

This deluxe, high-grade version features a select stock with rosewood pistol-grip cap and forend tip. It is lightly engraved and has gold-filled letters. It was introduced in 1988.

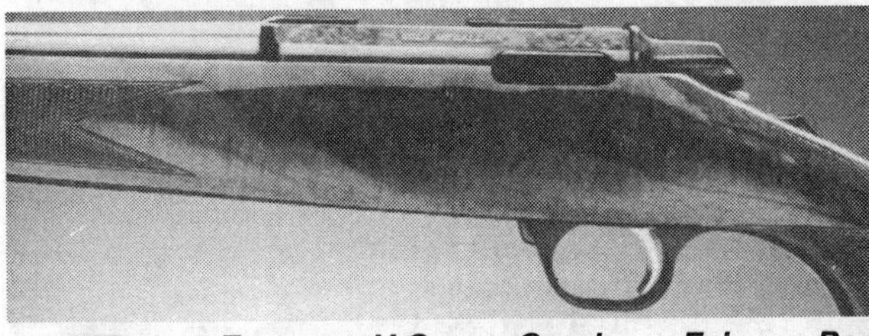

NIB	Exc.	V.G.	Good	Fair	Poor
450	400	350	300	225	175

T-Bolt Model T-1

This is a unique, straight-pull, bolt-action sporting rifle chambered for .22 caliber cartridges. It has a 22" barrel with open sights and a 5-round magazine. The finish is blued with a plain walnut stock. It was manufactured between 1965 and 1974 by FN. Many T-Bolt rifles were affected by salt wood. Proceed with caution. Reintroduced 2006 with rotary magazine.

Exc.	V.G.	Good	Fair	Poor
550	395	350	150	100

T-Bolt Model T-2

This version is similar to the T-1 with a select, checkered walnut stock and a 24" barrel.

Exc.	V.G.	Good	Fair	Poor
600	450	375	250	200

T-Bolt (2006)

Reintroduction of classic and collectible T-bolt straight-pull .22 rifle. Introduced 2006.

NIB	Exc.	V.G.	Good	Fair	Poor
600	—	—	—	—	—

T-Bolt Target/Varmint

Similar to reintroduced T-Bolt but with floating heavy target barrel and other accurizing refinements. Introduced 2007.

NIB	Exc.	V.G.	Good	Fair	Poor
650	—	—	—	—	—

Model 52 Limited Edition

This model is based on the design of the original Winchester Model 52 .22 caliber bolt-action rifle. Fitted with a 24" barrel and walnut stock with oil finish. Metal pistol-grip cap and rosewood forend tip. Drilled and tapped for scope. Five-round detachable magazine. Blued finish. Weight is about 7 lbs. From 1991 to 1992 5,000 Model 52s were built.

NIB	Exc.	V.G.	Good	Fair	Poor
700	435	325	225	—	—

Trombone Model

This is a slide-action rifle chambered for the .22 LR cartridge. It has a 24" barrel with open sights and a takedown design. It has a tubular magazine and a hammerless action. There were approximately 150,000 manufactured by FN between 1922 and 1974. Approximately 3,200 were imported by Browning in the 1960s. They are marked with either the FN barrel address or the Browning Arms address. The Browning-marked guns are worth approximately 20 percent additional. The values given are for FN-marked guns.

NIB	Exc.	V.G.	Good	Fair	Poor
900	750	600	450	375	275

BPR-22

This is a short-stroke, slide action rifle chambered for the .22 LR and Magnum cartridges. It has a 20.25" barrel with open sights and an 11-round, tubular magazine. The finish is blued with a checkered walnut stock. It was manufactured between 1977 and 1982.

Exc.	V.G.	Good	Fair	Poor
400	300	215	125	95

NOTE: Add $100 for models chambered for .22 Magnum.

BPR-22 Grade II

This version is engraved and has a select walnut stock.

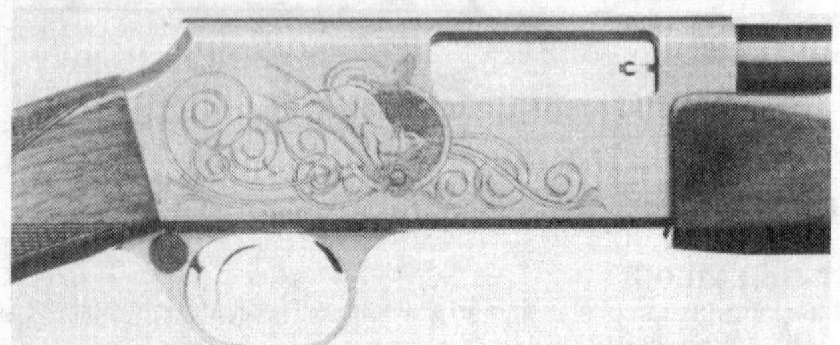

Exc.	V.G.	Good	Fair	Poor
500	375	275	225	150

NOTE: Add 20 percent for models chambered for .22 Magnum.

.22 Caliber Semi-Auto

This is a blowback-operated, semi-automatic rifle chambered for the .22 Long Rifle or Short cartridge. It features a take-down barrel design with a 19.25" barrel and an 11-round, tubular magazine inside the buttstock. It is loaded through a hole in the middle of the buttstock. The finish is blued with a checkered walnut stock and beavertail forearm. This lightweight, compact firearm was manufactured by FN between 1956 and 1974 for U.S. marked guns. There are a number of versions that differ in the amount of ornamentation and the quality of materials and workmanship.

Grade I

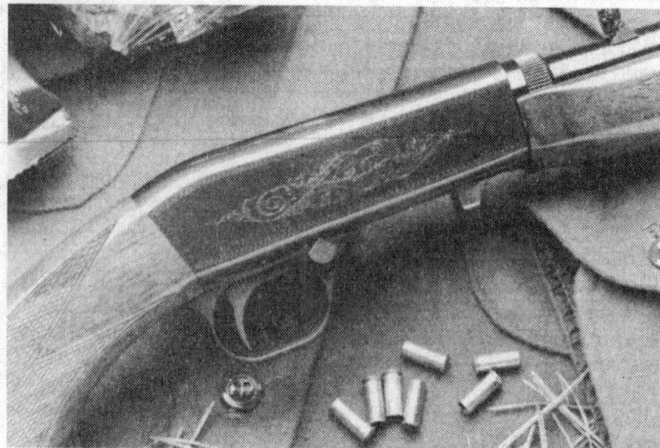

NIB	Exc.	V.G.	Good	Fair	Poor
650	475	400	325	220	125

NOTE: For Grade I short add 20 percent. Early Wheel Sight manufactured 1956-1960 add 10 percent.

Grade II—French Grayed Receiver

NIB	Exc.	V.G.	Good	Fair	Poor
1500	1200	900	700	300	200

NOTE: For Grade II short add 300 percent.

Grade III

French grayed receiver.

NIB	Exc.	V.G.	Good	Fair	Poor
3000	2400	1900	1200	700	400

NOTE: For premium engravers add 40 percent to Grade III. For Grade III short add 800 percent. For unsigned Grade III, 1956-1960 deduct 20 percent.

.22 Semi-Auto/Model SA-22 (Miroku Mfg.)

This model is similar to the Belgian FN except that it was produced as of 1976 by B.C. Miroku in Japan. Collector interest is not as high as in the FN version.

Grade I

NIB	Exc.	V.G.	Good	Fair	Poor
325	275	200	175	125	100

Grade II

Discontinued 1984.

NIB	Exc.	V.G.	Good	Fair	Poor
475	400	325	275	225	150

Grade III

Discontinued 1983.

NIB	Exc.	V.G.	Good	Fair	Poor
750	675	500	400	300	200

Grade VI

Gold plated animals.

NIB	Exc.	V.G.	Good	Fair	Poor
725	650	500	425	325	275

BAR-22

This is a blowback-operated, semi-automatic rifle chambered for the .22 LR cartridge. It has a 20.25" barrel with open sights and a 15-round, tubular magazine. It features a polished, lightweight alloy receiver. It was finished in blue with a checkered walnut stock. It is manufactured between 1977 and 1985 by Miroku.

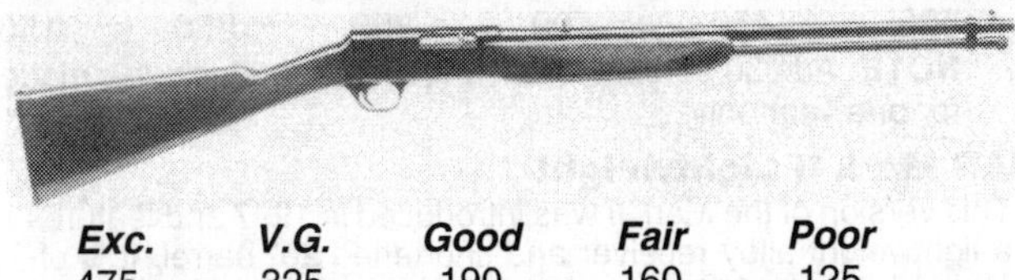

Exc.	V.G.	Good	Fair	Poor
475	325	190	160	125

BAR-22 Grade II

This is a deluxe version with an engraved, silver-finished receiver. It has a select walnut stock. It was discontinued in 1985.

Exc.	V.G.	Good	Fair	Poor
495	375	200	150	120

Buck Mark Rifle

This model uses the same design as the Buck Mark pistol. It is fitted with an 18" barrel (heavy on the target model) and thumbhole pistol grip. Magazine capacity is 10 rounds. Integral rail scope mount. Introduced in 2001. Weight is about 4.25 lbs. for Sporter and 5.5 lbs. for the Target model.

Sporter Model

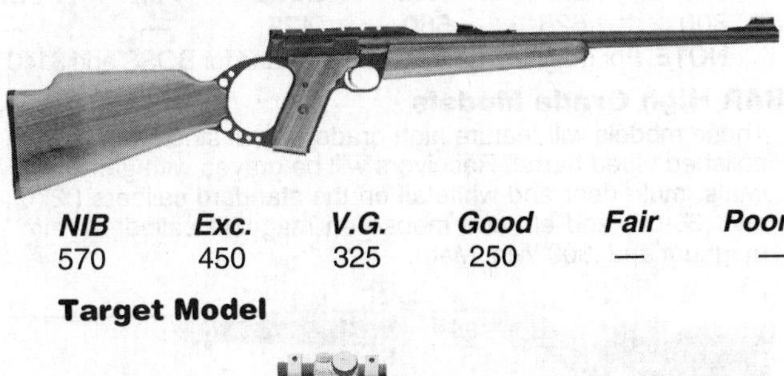

NIB	Exc.	V.G.	Good	Fair	Poor
570	450	325	250	—	—

Target Model

NIB	Exc.	V.G.	Good	Fair	Poor
570	450	325	250	—	—

Buck Mark Field Target Gray Laminate Rifle

Introduced in 2003 this model features a lightweight carbon composite barrel, gray laminate stock and integral scope rail. Chambered for the .22 cartridge and fitted with an 18" barrel. Weight: 5.5 lbs. for standard; 3.75 lbs. for Lite model..

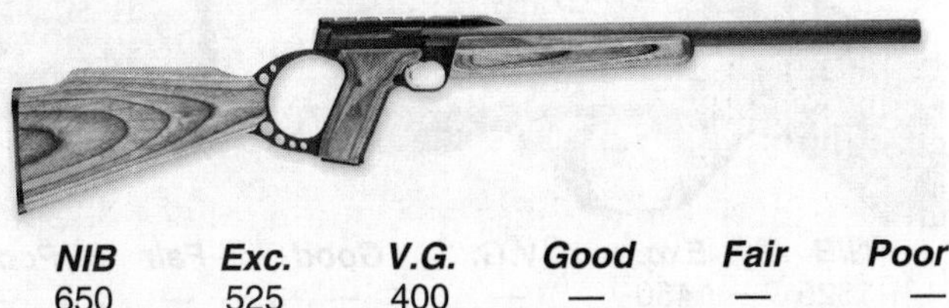

NIB	Exc.	V.G.	Good	Fair	Poor
650	525	400	—	—	—

Patent 1900 High Power

This is a semi-automatic sporting rifle chambered for the .35 Remington cartridge. It is similar in configuration to the Remington Model 8 rifle. It has a 22" barrel with open sights and a 5-round, integral magazine. The finish is blued with a plain walnut stock. There were approximately 5,000 manufactured between 1910 and 1931. A deluxe model with a ribbed barrel and checkered walnut stock was also available and would be worth approximately 15 percent additional.

Exc.	V.G.	Good	Fair	Poor
675	600	500	375	300

BAR HIGH POWER RIFLE

This is a gas-operated, semi-automatic sporting rifle chambered for various popular calibers from the .243 up to the .338 Magnum cartridges. It was offered with either a 22" or 24" barrel with folding leaf sight until 1980. The finish is blued with a checkered walnut stock. The various grades offered differed in the amount of ornamentation and the quality of materials and workmanship utilized. Earlier models were manufactured in Belgium by FN; these guns would be worth approximately 15 percent additional over guns assembled in Portugal from parts manufactured by FN. The early .338 Magnum model is rarely encountered and would be worth approximately 25 percent additional. The Grade I values furnished are for Portuguese-assembled guns from 1977 until the introduction of the BAR Mark II in 1993. This model was introduced in 1967 and discontinued in 1977.

Grade I

NIB	Exc.	V.G.	Good	Fair	Poor
600	425	350	275	225	100

Grade I Magnum

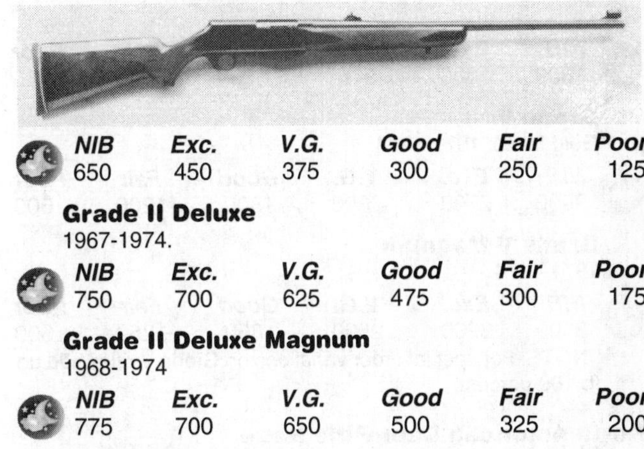

NIB	Exc.	V.G.	Good	Fair	Poor
650	450	375	300	250	125

Grade II Deluxe

1967-1974.

NIB	Exc.	V.G.	Good	Fair	Poor
750	700	625	475	300	175

Grade II Deluxe Magnum

1968-1974

NIB	Exc.	V.G.	Good	Fair	Poor
775	700	650	500	325	200

Grade III

Discontinued 1984.

NOTE: The Grade III was offered in two variations. The first was hand-engraved and produced in Belgium. The second was photo-etched and built in Belgium and assembled in Portugal. This second variation will not be as valuable as the first.

NIB	Exc.	V.G.	Good	Fair	Poor
1250	1000	700	550	375	250

Grade III Magnum

Discontinued 1984.

NIB	Exc.	V.G.	Good	Fair	Poor
1400	1200	850	600	400	275

NOTE: Prices indicated above are for 1970 through 1974 production. For guns assembled in Portugal deduct 30 percent. .338 Win. Mag caliber is rare in Grade III; add 75 percent premium.

Grade IV

Gamescene engraved. This grade was hand-engraved from 1970 through 1976 then was etched thereafter. Grade IV rifles were discontinued in 1984.

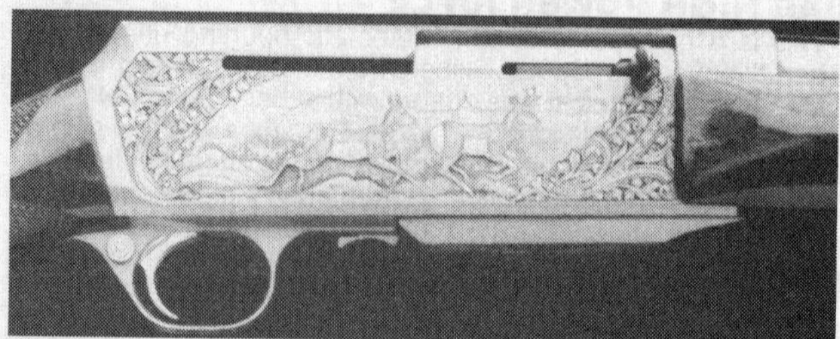

NIB	Exc.	V.G.	Good	Fair	Poor
1700	1300	950	800	650	400

NOTE: Pre-1977 rifles add 40 percent. Premium engraving add 10 percent.

Grade IV Magnum

NIB	Exc.	V.G.	Good	Fair	Poor
1800	1300	975	850	650	425

Grade V

Gold Inlaid. 1971-1974.

NIB	Exc.	V.G.	Good	Fair	Poor
3000	2700	2300	1800	1200	600

Grade V Magnum

1971-1974.

NIB	Exc.	V.G.	Good	Fair	Poor
3500	3200	2500	1850	1250	600

NOTE: For special order variations on Grade V rifles add up to 100 percent.

North American Deer Rifle Issue

This is a deluxe version of the BAR chambered for .30-06 only. It features a photo etched, silver-finished receiver and a deluxe, checkered walnut stock. There were 600 produced and furnished with a walnut case and accessories. This model was discontinued in 1983. As with all commemoratives, it must be NIB to command premium values.

NIB	Exc.	V.G.	Good	Fair	Poor
2700	1800	1400	1000	450	250

BAR Mark II Safari Rifle

This is an improved version of the BAR first introduced by Browning in 1967. Announced in 1993 this Mark II design uses a new gas system with a newly designed buffering system to improve reliability. This model also has a new bolt release lever, a new easily removable trigger assembly. Available with or without sights. Walnut stock with full pistol grip and recoil pad on magnum gun are standard. The receiver is blued with scroll engraving. Rifles with magnum calibers have a 24" barrel while standard calibers are fitted with a 22" barrel. Available in .243, .308, .270, .30-06, 7mm Rem. Mag., .300 Win. Mag., .338 Win. Mag. Standard calibers weigh about 7 lbs. 9 oz. and magnum calibers weigh about 8 lbs. 6 oz.

NIB	Exc.	V.G.	Good	Fair	Poor
525	450	400	350	250	150

NOTE: Add 30 percent for .270 Wby. Mag., which was made for one year only.

BAR Mark II Lightweight

This version of the Mark II was introduced in 1997 and features a lightweight alloy receiver and shortened 20" barrel. It is offered in .30-06, .270 Win., .308 Win., and .243 Win. calibers. It is not offered with the BOSS system. Weight is approximately 7 lbs. 2 oz.

NIB	Exc.	V.G.	Good	Fair	Poor
700	550	400	300	—	—

BAR Composite Stalker

Introduced in 2001 this model features a composite buttstock and forend with removable magazine. It is offered in short action (.243 and .308) with sights, and in standard action (.270 and .30-06) with no sights. In magnum calibers (7mm, .330 Win., and .338) it is offered with no sights and with the BOSS system as well.

NIB	Exc.	V.G.	Good	Fair	Poor
800	625	550	425	—	—

NOTE: For magnum calibers add $75, and for BOSS add $140.

BAR High Grade Models

These models will feature high grade walnut stock with highly polished blued barrel. Receivers will be grayed with game animals: mule deer and whitetail on the standard calibers (.270 and .30-06) and elk and moose on magnum calibers (7mm magnum and .300 Win. Mag).

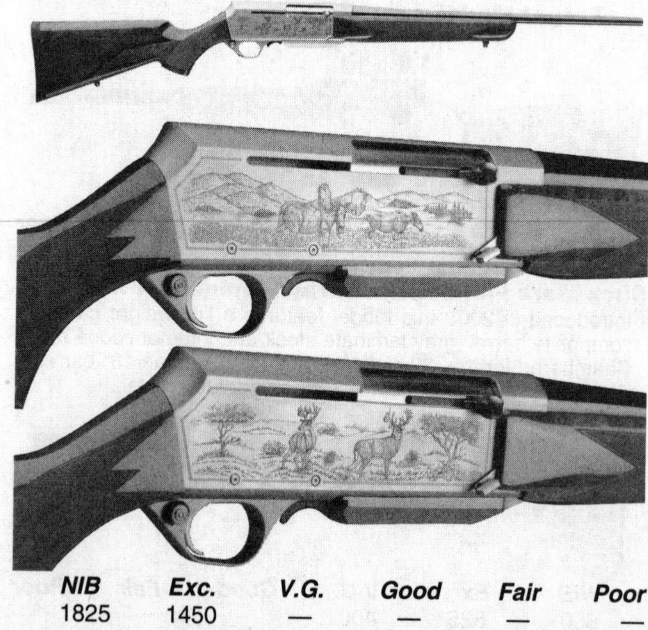

NIB	Exc.	V.G.	Good	Fair	Poor
1825	1450	—	—	—	—

This symbol denotes "Sleepers" with rapidly-rising values and/or significant collector potential.

BAR Short Trac

Introduced in 2004 this model features the ability to chamber magnum cartridges. Offered in .270 WSM, 7mm WSM, and .300 WSM as well as .243 and .308. Fitted with a 23" barrel in magnum calibers and 22" barrel in non-magnum. Receiver is alloy steel. Redesigned stock adjustable length of pull. Weight is about 7.25 lbs. for magnum calibers and 6 75 lbs. for others. Add 10 percent for camo finish.

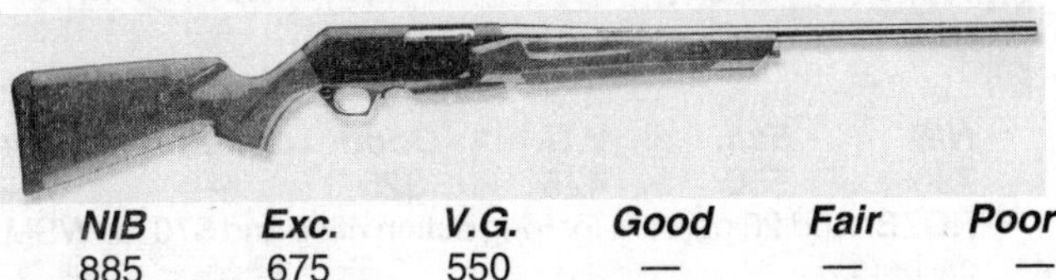

NIB	Exc.	V.G.	Good	Fair	Poor
885	675	550	—	—	—

BAR Long Trac

Similar to the above model but made for long action calibers such as .270, .30-06, 7mm Rem. Mag, and .300 Win. Mag. Barrel length is 22" for the .270 and .30-06 and 24" for the other two calibers. Weight is about 7 lbs. for .270 and .30-06 and 7.5 lbs. for 7mm and .300. Introduced in 2004. Add 10 percent for camo finish.

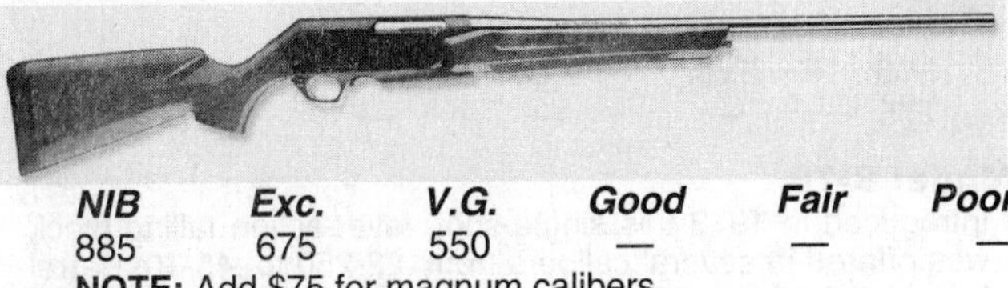

NIB	Exc.	V.G.	Good	Fair	Poor
885	675	550	—	—	—

NOTE: Add $75 for magnum calibers.

BAR ShortTrac Stalker

Similar to BAR ShortTrac but with matte blue barrel and composite stock. Introduced 2006.

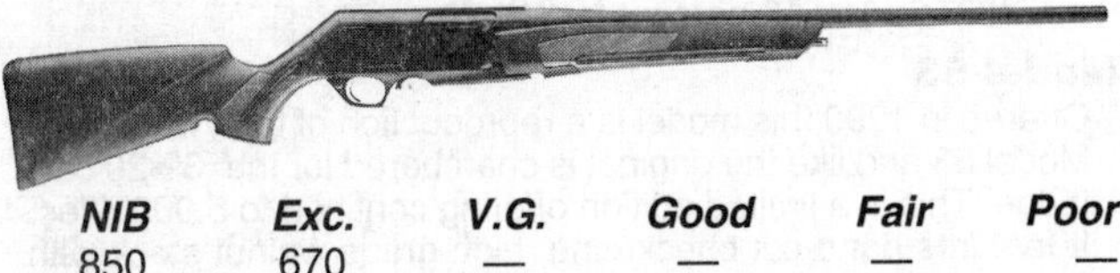

NIB	Exc.	V.G.	Good	Fair	Poor
850	670	—	—	—	—

BAR LongTrac Stalker

Long-action version of the BAR ShortTrac Stalker.

NIB	Exc.	V.G.	Good	Fair	Poor
850	670	—	—	—	—

BAR ShortTrac Left-Hand

Similar to BAR ShortTrac but in left hand. Introduced 2007.

NIB	Exc.	V.G.	Good	Fair	Poor
950	—	—	—	—	—

BAR LongTrac Left-Hand

Similar to BAR Long-Trac but in left hand. Introduced 2007.

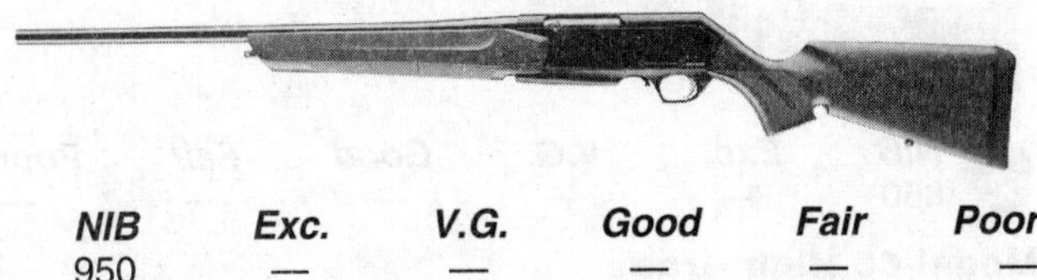

NIB	Exc.	V.G.	Good	Fair	Poor
950	—	—	—	—	—

Model BPR

The initials "BPR" stand for Browning Pump Rifle. It was introduced in 1997 and is similar in appearance to the BAR. Offered in both long action and short action calibers with barrel lengths from 22" to 24". Short action calibers are: .243 Win., and .308 Win. Long Action calibers are: .270 Win., .30-06, 7mm Rem. Mag., and .300 Win. Mag. Weight is about 7 lbs. 3 oz. Discontinued 2003.

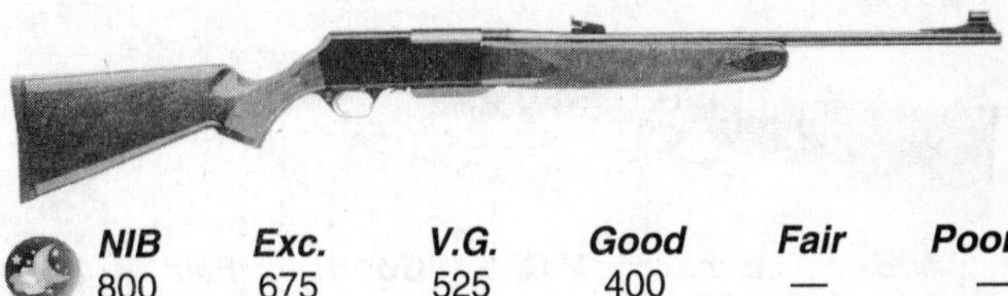

NIB	Exc.	V.G.	Good	Fair	Poor
800	675	525	400	—	—

BL-22 Grade I

This is a lever-action rifle chambered for the .22 rimfire cartridge. It has an 18" barrel with a tubular magazine and a folding leaf rear sight. It is a Western-style firearm that features an exposed hammer. The finish is blued with a walnut stock. It was introduced in 1970 by Miroku.

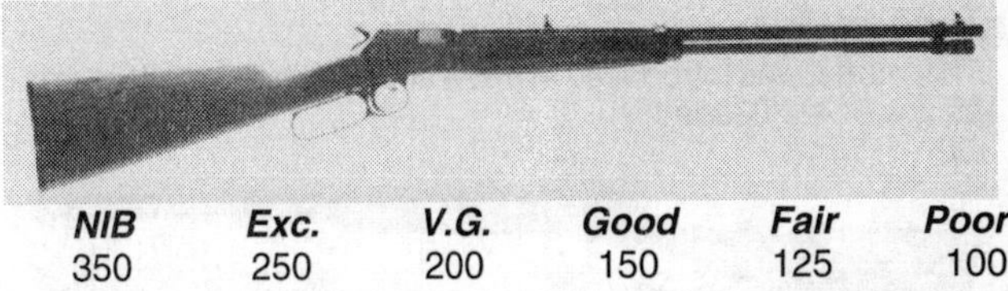

NIB	Exc.	V.G.	Good	Fair	Poor
350	250	200	150	125	100

BL-22 Grade II

This version is similar with a scroll-engraved receiver and a checkered, select walnut stock.

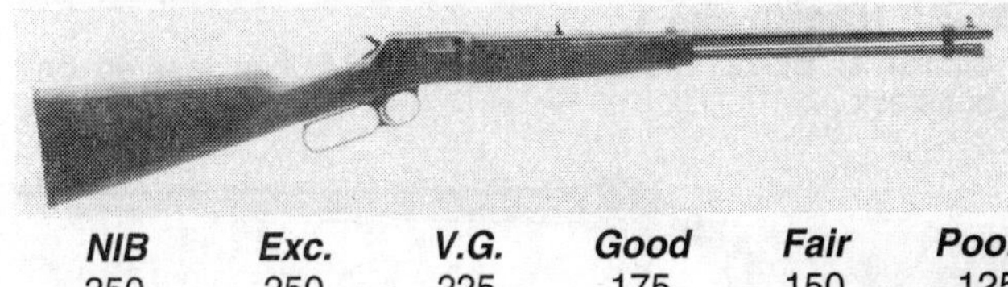

NIB	Exc.	V.G.	Good	Fair	Poor
350	250	225	175	150	125

BL-22 Field Series Grade I

Introduced in 2005 this rifle features a satin nickel receiver. Walnut stock with no checkering. Blued trigger. Magazine capacity is 16 rounds. Weight is about 5 lbs.

NIB	Exc.	V.G.	Good	Fair	Poor
495	375	—	—	—	—

BL-17 Field Series Grade I

As above but chambered for the .17 Mach 2 cartridge. Weight is about 5.2 lbs.

NIB	Exc.	V.G.	Good	Fair	Poor
515	400	—	—	—	—

BL-22 Field Series Grade II

As above but with checkered stock, gold trigger, and scroll engraving on the receiver.

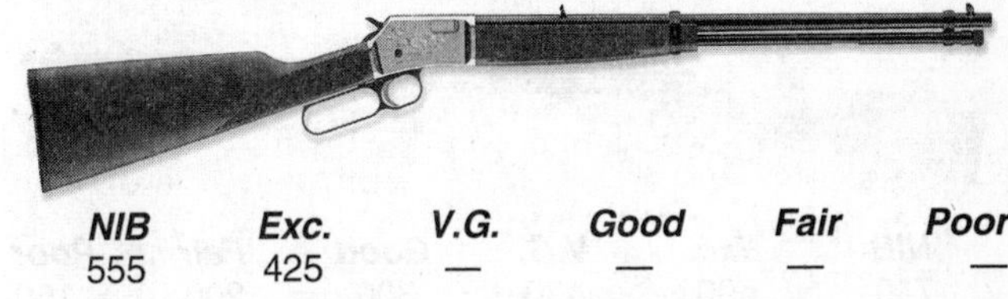

NIB	Exc.	V.G.	Good	Fair	Poor
555	425	—	—	—	—

BL-17 Field Series Grade II

As above but chambered for the .17 Mach 2 cartridge.

NIB	Exc.	V.G.	Good	Fair	Poor
545	425	—	—	—	—

BL-22 Grade II Octagon

Introduced in 2005 this model has a 24" octagon barrel chambered for the .22 Long and Long Rifle cartridges. Receiver is silver nitride with scroll engraving and gold trigger. Magazine capacity is 16 rounds. Gold bead front sight. Weight is about 5.25 lbs.

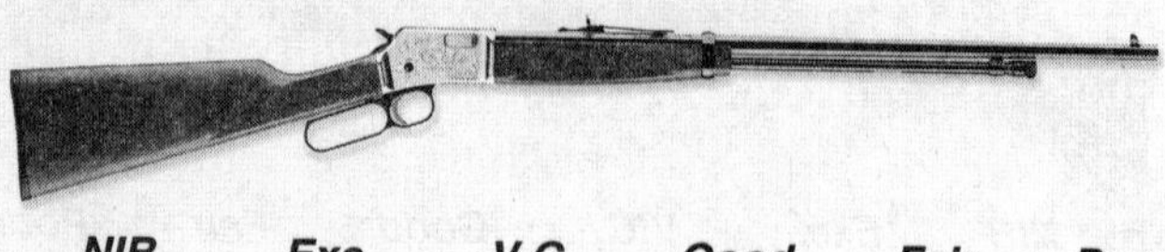

NIB	Exc.	V.G.	Good	Fair	Poor
725	550	—	—	—	—

BL-17 Grade II Octagon

As above but chambered for the .17 Mach 2 cartridge. Magazine capacity is 16 rounds. Weight is about 5.35 lbs. Introduced in 2005.

NIB	Exc.	V.G.	Good	Fair	Poor
750	575	—	—	—	—

BL-22 Classic

This model was introduced in 1999 and has the same features as the BL-22 Grade I.

NIB	Exc.	V.G.	Good	Fair	Poor
425	375	275	200	175	—

BL-22 NRA Grade 1

Similar to BL-22 Grade 1 but with NRA logo lasered on buttstock.

BL-22 Gray Laminate Stainless

Similar to BL-22 but with gray laminated stock, nickeled receiver and stainless steel barrel. Introduced 2006. MSRP: 690

Model BLR Lightning (Lightweight)

Introduced in 1996 this model features a lightweight aluminum receiver with walnut stock and checkered pistol grip. Offered in both long and short action calibers from .223 Rem. to 7mm Rem. Mag. Barrel length is 20" for short action calibers and 22" to 24" for long action calibers. Open sights are standard. Weight is about 7 lbs. depending on caliber. In 2003 a straight-grip stock was introduced.

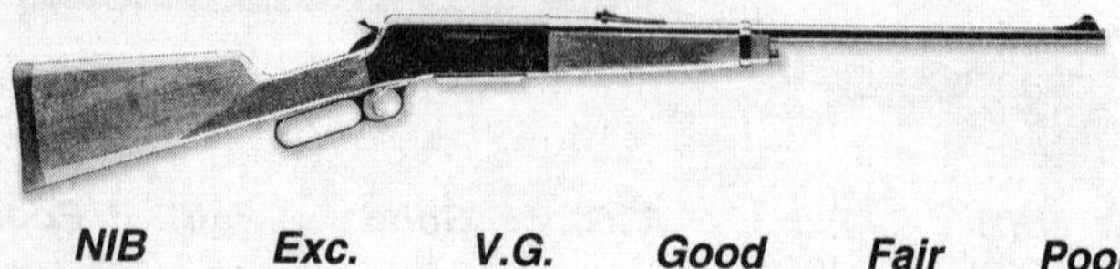

NIB	Exc.	V.G.	Good	Fair	Poor
740	600	450	300	200	150

Model BLR Lightweight '81

This model features a straight grip checkered walnut stock. Fitted with a 20" or 22" barrel depending on caliber. Magazine capacity is 4 or 5 rounds depending on caliber. Chambered for calibers .22-25-, .243, 7mm-08, .308, .358, .450 Marlin, .270 WSM, .300 WSM, and .325 WSM. Also offered in a long action version chambered for the .270, .30-06, 7mm Rem. mag, and the .300 Win. mag. Weight is from 6.5 lbs. to 7.75 lbs. depending on caliber.

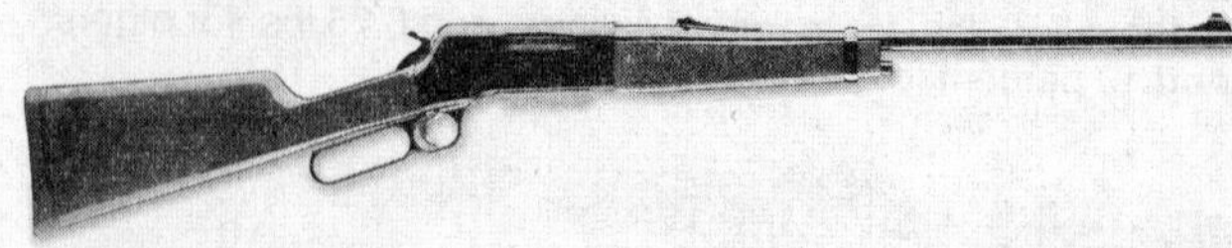

NIB	Exc.	V.G.	Good	Fair	Poor
730	550	425	325	—	—

NOTE: Add 20 percent for long action rifles and $70 for WSM calibers.

BLR Lightweight Takedown

Similar to BLR Lightweight but with takedown feature. Introduced 2007.

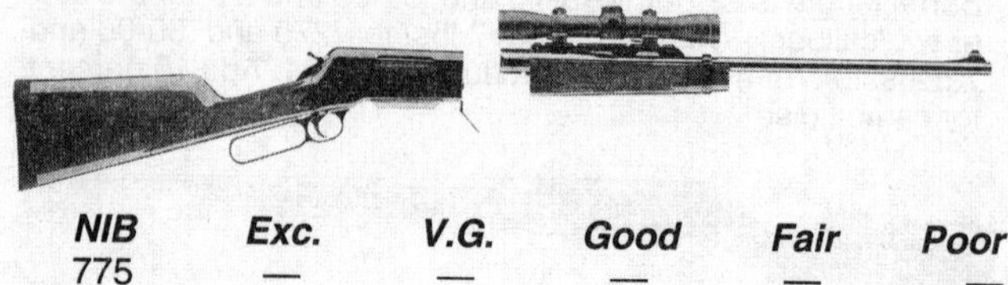

NIB	Exc.	V.G.	Good	Fair	Poor
775	—	—	—	—	—

Model B-78

Introduced in 1973 this single-shot, lever-action falling block was offered in several calibers from .22-250 to .45-70. Barrel lengths from 24" to 26" in either round or octagonal shape with no sights except .45-70. Checkered walnut stock. First built in 1973 and discontinued in 1983.

NIB	Exc.	V.G.	Good	Fair	Poor
800	650	550	300	200	100

NOTE: Add 15 percent for .45-70 caliber.

Model 53

Offered in 1990 this model is a reproduction of the Winchester Model 53 and like the original is chambered for the .32-20 cartridge. This is a limited edition offering confined to 5,000 rifles. It features hand-cut checkering, high-grade walnut stock with full pistol grip and semi-beavertail forend. Pistol grip is fitted with a metal grip cap. Barrel length is 22" and the finish is blue.

NIB	Exc.	V.G.	Good	Fair	Poor
725	625	550	450	325	200

Model 65 Grade I

This was a limited-edition, lever-action rifle chambered for the .218 Bee cartridge. It has a tapered, round, 24" barrel with open sights. It was patterned after the Winchester Model 65 rifle. It has a 7-round, tubular magazine. The finish is blued with a plain walnut stock and metal buttplate. There were 3,500 manufactured in 1989.

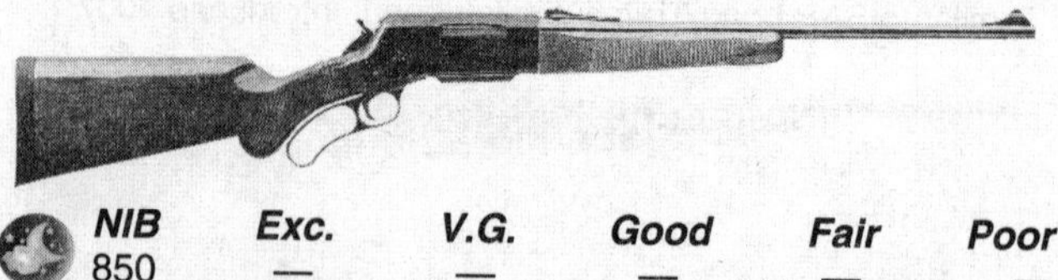

NIB	Exc.	V.G.	Good	Fair	Poor
850	—	—	—	—	—

Model 65 High Grade

This is a deluxe version that features a silver-finished, scroll engraved receiver with gold animal inlays and a gold-plated trigger. It features a select, checkered walnut stock. There were 1,500 manufactured in 1989.

This symbol denotes "Sleepers" with rapidly-rising values and/or significant collector potential.

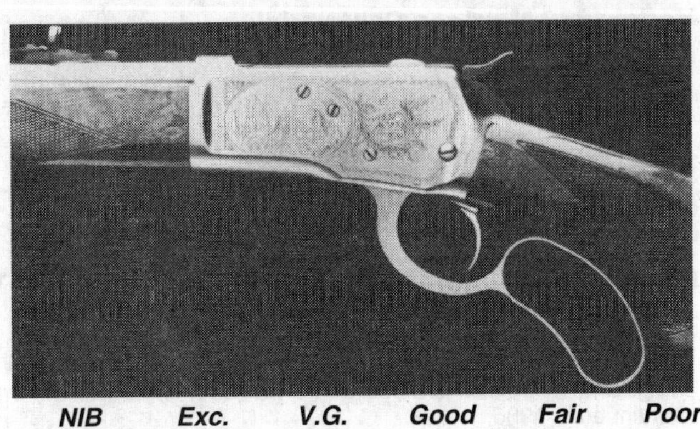

NIB	Exc.	V.G.	Good	Fair	Poor
1150	—	—	—	—	—

Model 71 Grade I

This was a reproduction of the Winchester Model 71, chambered for the .348 cartridge. It has either a 20" or 24" barrel with open sights and a 4-round, tubular magazine. The finish is blued with a plain walnut stock. There were 4,000 20" carbines and 3,000 24" rifles manufactured in 1986 and 1987.

Exc.	V.G.	Good	Fair	Poor
950	750	—	—	—

Model 71 High Grade

This version was similar to the Grade I except that it had a scroll engraved, grayed receiver with a gold-plated trigger and gold inlays. There were 3,000 rifles and 3,000 carbines manufactured in 1986 and 1987.

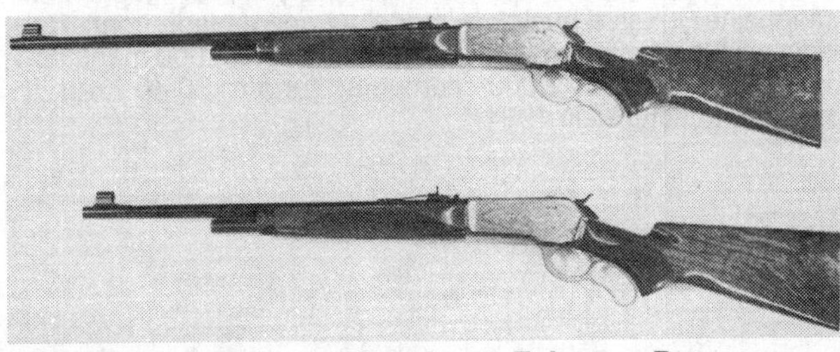

Exc.	V.G.	Good	Fair	Poor
1400	950	—	—	—

Model 81 BLR

This is a contemporarily designed, lever-action sporting rifle chambered for various popular calibers from .22-250 up to .358 Winchester. It has a 20" barrel with adjustable sights. It features a 4-round, detachable magazine and a rotary locking bolt. The finish is blued with a checkered walnut stock and recoil pad. It was introduced in 1971 and manufactured that year in Belgium. In 1972 manufacture moved to Miroku in Japan. In 2003 a straight-grip stock was introduced and WSM calibers were added from .270 to .300. Weight is about 6.5 lbs.

NIB	Exc.	V.G.	Good	Fair	Poor
695	550	400	300	200	150

NOTE: Belgian-manufactured version add 20 percent.

Jonathan Browning Centennial Mountain Rifle

This is a limited edition blackpowder rifle chambered for the .50 ball. It is fitted with a 30" octagon barrel with single set trigger. Figured walnut stock and engraved lock plate. Cased with powder horn. Limited to 1,000 rifles in 1978.

NIB	Exc.	V.G.	Good	Fair	Poor
1250	750	—	—	—	—

Jonathan Browning Mountain Rifle

Same as above but without fancy wood, case, or engraving. Also chambered for .45 or .54 caliber.

NIB	Exc.	V.G.	Good	Fair	Poor
800	500	400	300	—	—

Model 1878

Based on John M. Browning's first patent this single-shot rifle was the only firearm manufactured by the Browning brothers. Offered in several calibers only a few hundred probably exist with the Ogden, Utah, barrel address. This design was later sold to Winchester and sold under that company's name as the Model 1885 High Wall.

Exc.	V.G.	Good	Fair	Poor
7500	5500	3500	2000	1000

Model 1885 High Wall

This is a single-shot rifle with falling block action and octagonal free-floating barrel similar to the Model 78. Introduced in 1985. The stock is a high grade walnut with straight grip and recoil pad. Furnished with 28" barrel it is offered in these calibers: .223, .22-250, .270, .30-06, 7mm Rem. Mag., .45-70 Gov't. Weighs about 8 lbs. 12 oz.

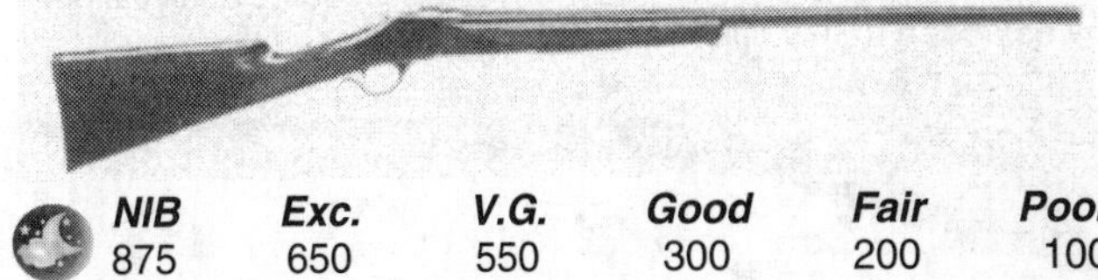

NIB	Exc.	V.G.	Good	Fair	Poor
875	650	550	300	200	100

Model 1885 Low Wall

Introduced in 1995 this rifle is similar to the above but in a more accurate version of the original Low Wall. The thin octagon barrel is 24" in length. Trigger pull is adjustable. The walnut stock is fitted with a pistol grip and schnabel forearm. Offered in .22 Hornet, .223 Rem. and the .243 Win. calibers. Weight is about 6.4 lbs.

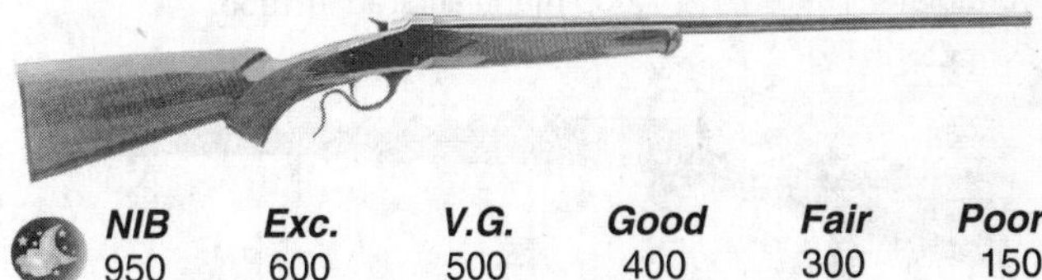

NIB	Exc.	V.G.	Good	Fair	Poor
950	600	500	400	300	150

Model 1885 Low Wall Traditional Hunter

Introduced in 1998 this model is similar to the Low Wall but with a half-octagon half-round 24" barrel chambered for the .357 Magnum, .44 Magnum, and .45 Colt cartridges. Case colored receiver and crescent butt with tang sight are also features. Weight is approximately 6.5 lbs.

NIB	Exc.	V.G.	Good	Fair	Poor
900	750	650	525	—	—

Model 1885 BPCR (Black Powder Cartridge Rifle)

This model was introduced in 1996 for BPCR metallic silhouette shoots. Chambered for the .45-70 or .40-60 caliber the receiver is case colored and the 28" round barrel is fitted with vernier sight with level. The walnut stock has a checkered pistol grip and is fitted with a tang sight. Weight is approximately 11 lbs.

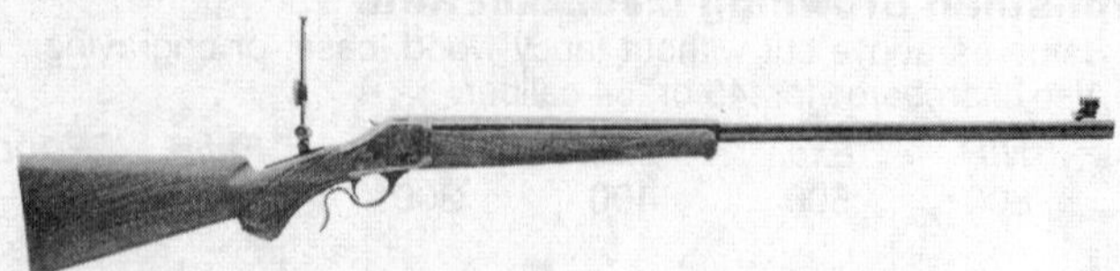

NIB	Exc.	V.G.	Good	Fair	Poor
1500	1300	800	400	300	150

Model 1885 BPCR Creedmore Type

Introduced in 1998 this model is chambered for the 45/90 cartridge and features a 34" heavy half-round barrel with long range tang sight and wind gauge front sight. Weight is approximately 11 lbs. 13 oz.

NIB	Exc.	V.G.	Good	Fair	Poor
1250	1000	875	750	—	—

Model 1885 High Wall Traditional Hunter

This variation of the Model 1885 series was introduced in 1997. It is fitted with an oil finish walnut stock with crescent buttplate. The barrel is octagonal and 28" in length. The rear sight is buckhorn and the rifle is fitted with a tang-mounted peep sight. The front sight is gold bead classic style. The rifle is chambered for the .30-30, .38-55, and .45-70 cartridges. Weight is approximately 9 lbs. In 1998 the .454 Casull caliber was added to this rifle.

NIB	Exc.	V.G.	Good	Fair	Poor
1100	900	700	575	—	—

Model 1886 Grade I

This was a lever action sporting rifle patterned after the Model 1886 Winchester rifle. It was chambered for the .45-70 cartridge and has a 26", octagonal barrel with a full-length, tubular magazine. The finish is blued with a walnut stock and crescent buttplate. There were 7,000 manufactured in 1986.

NIB	Exc.	V.G.	Good	Fair	Poor
1350	950	725	600	450	300

Model 1886 Grade I Carbine

NIB	Exc.	V.G.	Good	Fair	Poor
950	650	550	400	325	250

Model 1886 High Grade

This deluxe version of the Model 1886 features game scene engraving with gold accents and a checkered, select walnut stock. "1 of 3,000" is engraved on the top of the barrel. There were 3,000 manufactured in 1986.

NIB	Exc.	V.G.	Good	Fair	Poor
1600	1150	900	700	550	425

Model 1886 High Grade Carbine

NIB	Exc.	V.G.	Good	Fair	Poor
1200	950	750	600	450	300

Model 1886 Montana Centennial

This version is similar to the High Grade with a different engraving pattern designed to commemorate the centennial of the State of Montana. There were 2,000 manufactured in 1986. As with all commemoratives, it must be NIB with all supplied materials to command collector interest.

NIB	Exc.	V.G.	Good	Fair	Poor
1300	950	750	600	450	375

B-92 Carbine

This is a lever action sporting rifle patterned after the Winchester Model 92. It was chambered for the .357 Mag. and the .44 Mag. cartridges. It has a 20" barrel with an 11-round, tubular magazine. The finish is blued with a walnut stock. It was discontinued in 1986.

Exc.	V.G.	Good	Fair	Poor
650	425	295	150	120

NOTE: Add 10 percent for Centennial Model. For .357 Magnum add 30 percent.

Model 1895 Grade I

This is a lever action sporting rifle chambered in .30-40 Krag and the .30-06 cartridge. It was patterned after the Model 1895 Winchester rifle. It has a 24" barrel and a 4-round, integral box magazine. It has a buckhorn rear sight and a blade front. The finish is blued with a walnut stock. There were 6,000 manufactured in .30-06 and 2,000 chambered for the .30-40 Krag. It was manufactured in 1984.

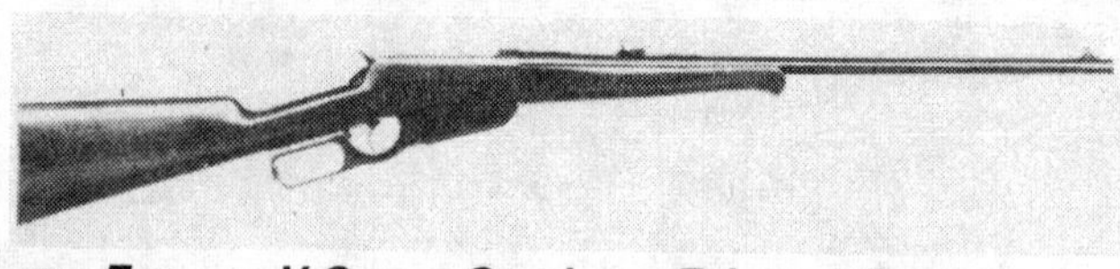

Exc.	V.G.	Good	Fair	Poor
950	675	475	375	275

Model 1895 High Grade

This is the deluxe engraved version of the Model 1895. It has gold-inlaid game scenes and a gold-plated trigger and features a checkered select walnut stock. There were 2,000 produced in 1984—1,000 in each caliber.

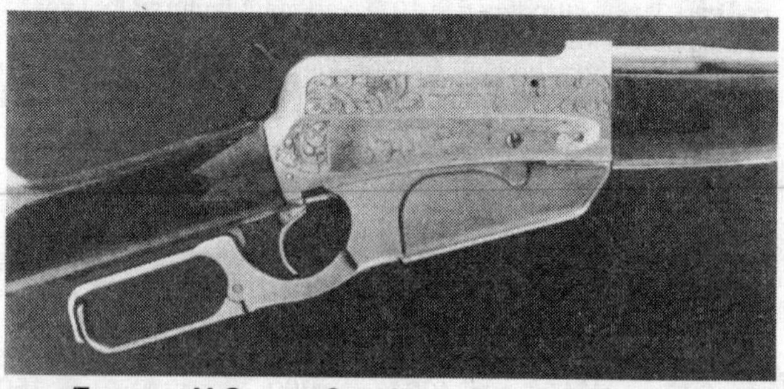

Exc.	V.G.	Good	Fair	Poor
1500	1250	900	700	400

Express Rifle

This is an Over/Under, superposed rifle chambered for the .270 Winchester or the .30-06 cartridges. It has 24" barrels with folding express sights and automatic ejectors. It features a single trigger. The receiver is engraved and is finished in blue with a deluxe checkered walnut stock. Introduced in 1980 and discontinued in 1986.

This symbol denotes "Sleepers" with rapidly-rising values and/or significant collector potential.

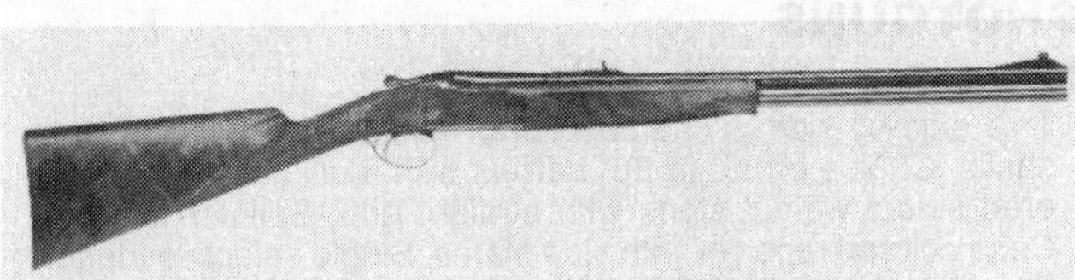

Exc.	V.G.	Good	Fair	Poor
3200	2000	1500	1100	800

Custom Shop Express Rifles

Produced in two different models; the Herstall and the CCS 375. Both are custom-built with choice of engraving patterns.

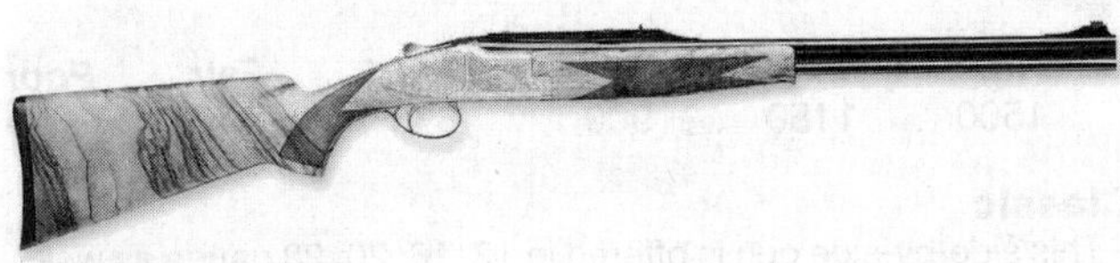

Herstal Express Rifle

NIB	Exc.	V.G.	Good	Fair	Poor
N/A	23000	17500	—	—	—

Continental Set

This consists of an Express Rifle chambered for the .30-06 cartridge and furnished with an extra set of 20 gauge, Over/Under barrels. The shotgun barrels are 26.5" in length. There is a single trigger, automatic ejectors, and a heavily engraved receiver. The select walnut stock is hand checkered and oil-finished. It was furnished with a fitted case. There were 500 manufactured between 1978 and 1986.

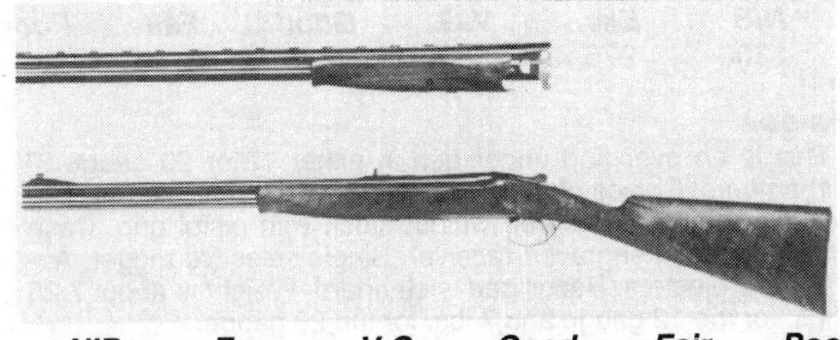

NIB	Exc.	V.G.	Good	Fair	Poor
7000	5500	3500	2250	1300	1000

BRUCE & DAVIS

Webster, Massachusetts

Double-Barreled Pistol

A .36 caliber double-barrel percussion pistol with 3" to 6" round barrels. The barrel rib marked "Bruce & Davis." Blued with walnut grips. Manufactured during the 1840s.

Exc.	V.G.	Good	Fair	Poor
—	—	800	350	150

BRUCHET

Ste. Etienne, France

Model A Shotgun

A 12 or .410 bore side-by-side shotgun with double triggers, and automatic ejectors. The barrel lengths and chokes are to customer specifications. Produced on a limited basis (50 per year) since 1982. Base price is listed.

NIB	Exc.	V.G.	Good	Fair	Poor
2500	1750	1500	1250	1000	500

Model B

As above, with a finer finish and a spring-assisted action opener. Imported since 1982.

NIB	Exc.	V.G.	Good	Fair	Poor
6750	5250	4000	3000	2250	1250

BRUFF, R.P.

New York, New York

Bruff Pocket Pistol

A .41 caliber single-shot percussion pistol with 2.5" to 3" barrels The pistol is marked "R.P. Bruff NY" in an arch and "Cast Steel." German silver with a checkered walnut stock. Manufactured between 1861 and 1870.

Exc.	V.G.	Good	Fair	Poor
—	—	1750	750	200

BRYCO ARMS

Carson City, Nevada

SEE—Jennings

BSA GUNS LTD.

Birmingham, England

Established in 1861, this firm has produced a wide variety of firearms over the years. The more common of these arms that are currently available in the United States are listed.

SINGLE-SHOT

No. 12 Cadet Martini

A .310 caliber single-shot Martini action rifle with a 29" barrel, adjustable sights and straight-gripped walnut stock. Approximately 80,000 were manufactured from 1911 to 1913. Many of those imported into the United States were altered to .22 caliber.

Exc.	V.G.	Good	Fair	Poor
450	300	200	150	100

Centurian Match Rifle

As above, in .22 caliber with a 24" barrel, adjustable sights and a pistol-grip walnut stock.

Exc.	V.G.	Good	Fair	Poor
500	350	300	200	100

Model 13 Sporter

As above, in .22 Hornet with hunting sights.

Exc.	V.G.	Good	Fair	Poor
450	325	300	225	100

Martini International Match

As above, with a heavy match barrel, ISU-style sights and a match stock. Manufactured from 1950 to 1953.

Exc.	V.G.	Good	Fair	Poor
500	375	325	250	125

Martini International Light

As above, with a 26" barrel of lighter weight.

Exc.	V.G.	Good	Fair	Poor
500	375	325	250	125

Martini International ISU

As above, meeting ISU specifications with a 28" barrel. Manufactured from 1968 to 1976.

Exc.	V.G.	Good	Fair	Poor
600	450	400	325	200

BOLT-ACTIONS

Royal

A bolt-action sporting rifle manufactured in a variety of calibers and a 24" barrel, with a checkered French walnut stock.

Exc.	V.G.	Good	Fair	Poor
450	300	250	200	100

Majestic Deluxe

A .22 Hornet, .222, .243, 7x57mm, .308 or .30-06 bolt-action sporting rifle with a 22" barrel, having a folding rear sight and a checkered walnut stock with a schnabel forend tip. Imported from 1959 to 1965.

Exc.	V.G.	Good	Fair	Poor
450	300	250	200	100

Majestic Deluxe Featherweight

As above, in .270 or .458 Magnum with a thinner barrel.

Exc.	V.G.	Good	Fair	Poor
450	300	250	200	100

Monarch Deluxe

As above, drilled and tapped for telescopic sight and also available in a heavy barreled varmint version in .222 or .243 caliber. Imported from 1966 to 1974.

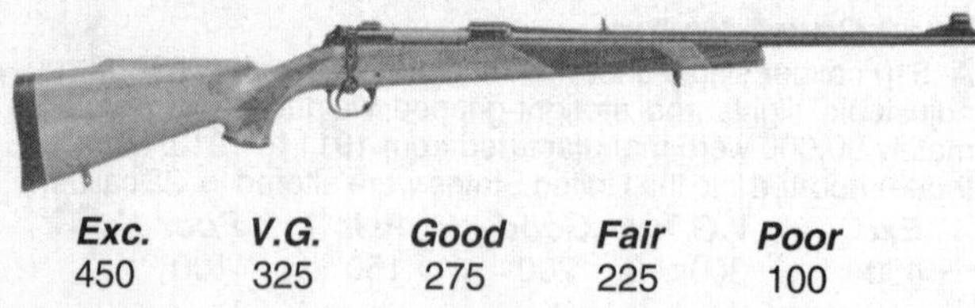

Exc.	V.G.	Good	Fair	Poor
450	325	275	225	100

Herters U9

The firm of Herters, Inc. of Waseca, Minnesota, imported BSA rifle actions beginning in 1965 that were used for custom-made rifles. Commencing in 1986, BSA began production of a new line of bolt-action sporting rifles on the Model CF-2 action. The standard production models are listed.

Sporter/Classic

A hunting rifle available in a variety of calibers with a checkered walnut stock. Introduced in 1986.

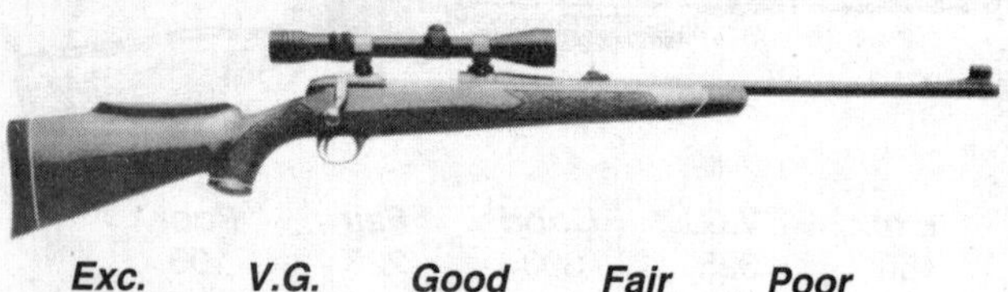

Exc.	V.G.	Good	Fair	Poor
450	325	275	200	100

Varminter

As above, with a matte-finished heavy barrel in .222, .22-250 or .243 caliber. Introduced in 1986.

Exc.	V.G.	Good	Fair	Poor
350	275	225	175	100

Stutzen Rifle

As above, with a 20.5" barrel and a Mannlicher-style stock.

Exc.	V.G.	Good	Fair	Poor
475	350	275	225	100

Regal Custom

As above, with an engraved receiver, checkered walnut stock and an ebony forend. Imported only in 1986.

Exc.	V.G.	Good	Fair	Poor
925	750	600	500	250

CFT Target Rifle

A .308 caliber single-shot version of the above with a 26.5" barrel and adjustable sights. Imported only in 1987.

Exc.	V.G.	Good	Fair	Poor
750	600	550	400	200

SHOTGUNS

Royal

This side-by-side is chambered for either 12 or 20 gauge 3" shells. Choice of 26" or 28" barrels with multi chokes. Checkered select walnut stock with straight grip. Splinter forearm. Case colored receiver with side plates. Single selective trigger. Recoil pad standard. Weight is about 7.25 lbs. for 12 gauge and about 6.75 lbs. for the 20 gauge.

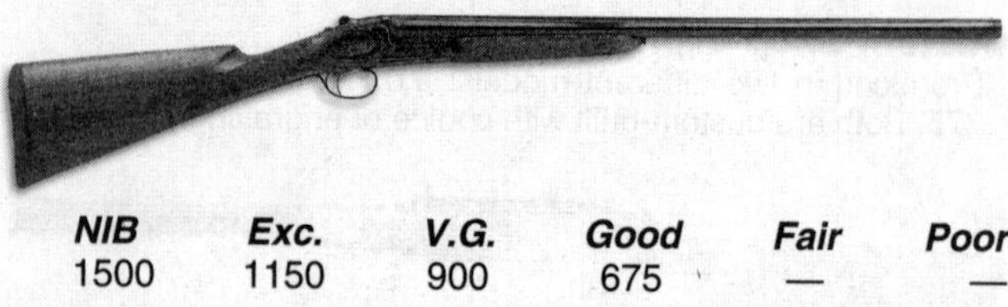

NIB	Exc.	V.G.	Good	Fair	Poor
1500	1150	900	675	—	—

Classic

This side-by-side gun is offered in 12, 16, 20, 28 gauge as well as .410 bore. Choice of 26" or 28" barrels except for 28 and .410 where 26" barrels are the only length offered. Checkered walnut stock with pistol grip. Case colored box lock receiver with scroll engraving. Semi-beavertail forearm. Recoil pad standard. Choke tubes standard. Weight is about 7.25 lbs. for 12 gauge, 6.75 lbs. for 16 gauge, 6.6 lbs. for 20 gauge, 6.25 lbs. for 28 gauge. .410 bore weighs about 6.5 lbs.

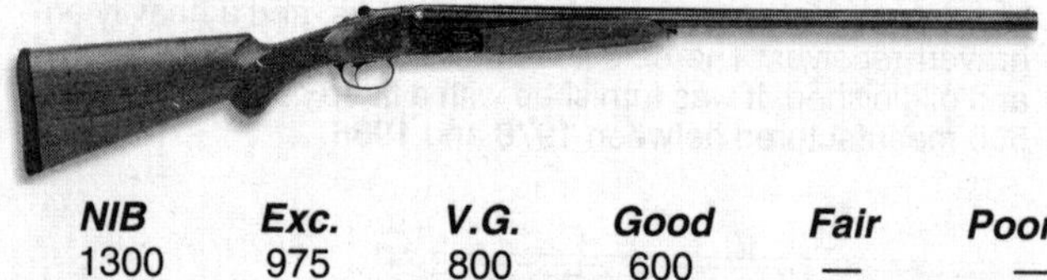

NIB	Exc.	V.G.	Good	Fair	Poor
1300	975	800	600	—	—

Falcon

This is an over and under gun in either 12 or 20 gauge 3" chambers. Choice of 26" or 28" barrels with ventilated rib and choke tubes. Checkered walnut stock with pistol grip. Case colored scroll engraved receiver. Single selective trigger. Automatic ejectors. Recoil pad is standard. Weight is about 7.25 lbs. for the 12 gauge and 7 lbs. for the 20 gauge.

NIB	Exc.	V.G.	Good	Fair	Poor
1200	900	875	500	—	—

Falcon Sporting

Similar to the Falcon but offered only in 12 gauge with 2 3/4" chambers. Choice of 28" or 30" ventilated rib barrels with 5 chokes tubes. Barrels are ported. Checkered walnut stock with Schnabel forearm. Weight is about 7.7 lbs.

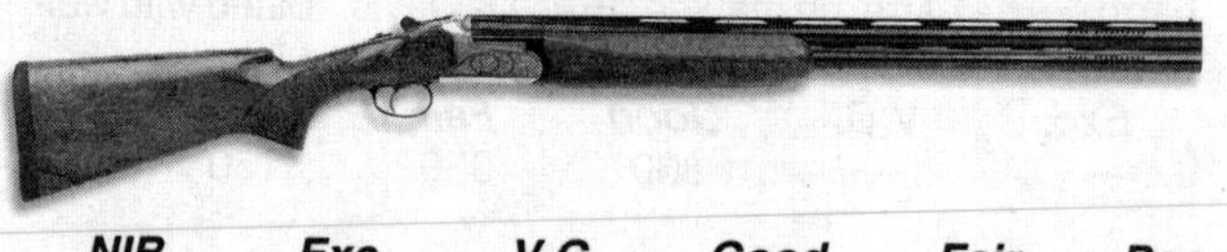

NIB	Exc.	V.G.	Good	Fair	Poor
1250	950	775	475	—	—

Silver Eagle

This over and under gun is chambered for either the 12 or 20 gauge 3" shell. Fitted with 26" or 28" vent rib barrels with choke tubes. Checkered walnut stock with pistol grip. Single selective trigger. Blued box lock receiver. Recoil is standard. Weight for 12 gauge is about 7.2 lbs. and 6.75 lbs. for the 20 gauge.

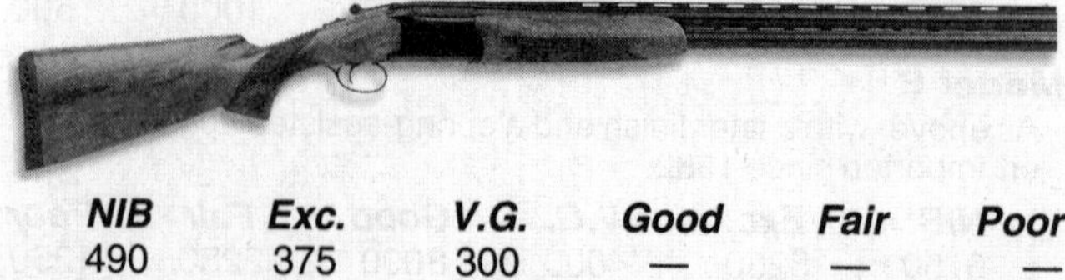

NIB	Exc.	V.G.	Good	Fair	Poor
490	375	300	—	—	—

Silver Eagle II

Similar to the Silver Eagle above with the addition of automatic ejectors.

NIB	Exc.	V.G.	Good	Fair	Poor
590	425	275			—

200 Series

This is a series of semi-automatic shotgun chambered for 12, 16, 20, 28 gauge as well as the .410 bore. The 12, 16, and 20 gauge guns are offered with choice of 26" or 28" vent rib barrels with choke tubes. The 28 and .410 are available in 26" barrels only. All gauges are offered with a choice of walnut or synthetic stocks. The 20 gauge gun is offered in a youth model with shortened stock. All gauges have 3" chambers except for the 28 gauge with 2.75" chambers. Weights range from 7.4 lbs. to 6.5 lbs.

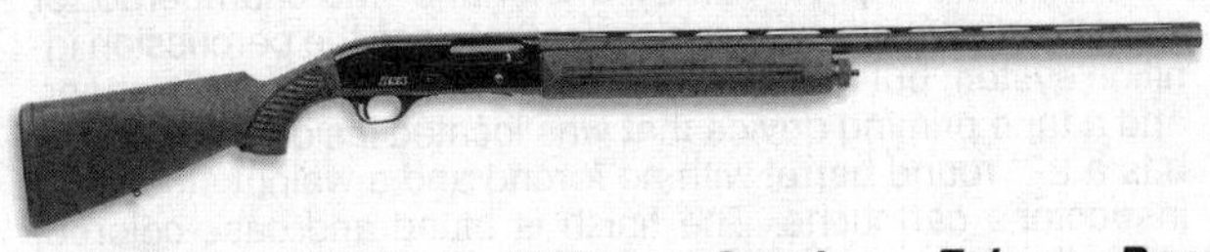

NIB	Exc.	V.G.	Good	Fair	Poor
390	290	225	200	—	—

NOTE: Add $70 for walnut stock.

300 SM Series

This semi-automatic series is offered in 12 gauge only with 3.5" chambers. Choice of 24", 26", or 28" vent rib barrels with choke tubes. Synthetic stock. Weights are about 7.3 lbs.

NIB	Exc.	V.G.	Good	Fair	Poor
420	315	250	225	—	—

BUCO
Germany

Buco Gas Pistol

This odd firearm looks more like a telescope than a pistol. It is chambered for a 10.55mm gas cartridge and is a single-shot. Overall it is approximately 5.5" long in its open or cocked position. The barrel is smooth bore and 3.75" in length. This pistol has no sights and no safety—one simply pulls the inner tube back much like extending a telescope, unscrews the end cap, inserts the round, and screws the cap back into place. When it is needed, a thumbnail is used to depress the sear and fire the pistol. They are marked on the end cap "Buco DRGM." No more information is available as to quantity or year of manufacture.

Exc.	V.G.	Good	Fair	Poor
—	650	500	350	150

BUDISCHOWSKY
Norton Armament Corp.
Mt. Clemens, Michigan

TP-70

A .22 or .25 ACP caliber semi-automatic pistol with a 2.5" barrel, fixed sights and 6-shot magazine. Stainless steel with plastic grips. Manufactured between 1973 and 1977.

NOTE: The German-designed Budischowsky was originally made in Michigan by Norton Armament Corp. Michigan-made Budischowsky's are considered better quality than later examples made in Florida and Utah.

.22 Rimfire Caliber

NIB	Exc.	V.G.	Good	Fair	Poor
475	425	350	300	225	150

.25 ACP Caliber

NIB	Exc.	V.G.	Good	Fair	Poor
400	325	250	200	175	125

BUL TRANSMARK LTD.
Tel-Aviv, Israel

Model M5

Introduced for the first time in the U.S. in 1996 this semi-automatic pistol bears a resemblance to the Model 1911. The frame is polymer and the slide is stainless steel. Available in 9mm, 38 Super, .40 S&W, and .45 ACP. Magazine limited to 10 rounds.

NIB	Exc.	V.G.	Good	Fair	Poor
750	600	450	350	—	—

BULLARD REPEATING ARMS CO.
Springfield, Massachusetts

Designed by James H. Bullard, the rifles listed were manufactured in competition with those produced by the Whitney Arms Company and the Winchester Repeating Arms Company. Approximately 12,000 were made between 1886 and 1890.

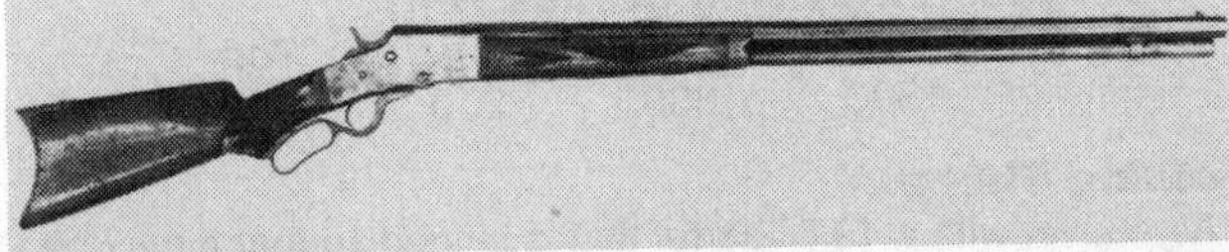

Courtesy Milwaukee Public Museum, Milwaukee, Wisconsin

Small Frame

A .32-40 and .38-45 caliber lever action rifle with a 26" octagonal barrel and either a half or full length magazine tube. Blued or case hardened with a walnut stock. The receiver is stamped "Bullard Repeating Arms Company/Springfield, Mass., U.S.A. Pat. Aug. 16, 1881." The caliber is marked on top of the frame.

Exc.	V.G.	Good	Fair	Poor
—	3500	1500	600	300

Large Frame

A .40-75 through .45-85 caliber lever action rifle with 28" octagonal barrel. Other features and markings as above. Can be custom ordered in .50-95 and .50-115.

Exc.	V.G.	Good	Fair	Poor
—	4500	2000	800	400

Carbine

A .45-70 caliber lever action rifle with a 22" round barrel and a sliding dust cover on the receiver. Marking and finish as above.

Exc.	V.G.	Good	Fair	Poor
—	7000	3250	1250	500

Musket

A .45-70 caliber lever action rifle with a 30" round barrel with a full-length stock secured by two barrel bands. There is a rod under the barrel, military sights, and the same sliding cover on the receiver as found on the Carbine. There have been examples noted without the manufacturer's markings.

Exc.	V.G.	Good	Fair	Poor
—	6250	3000	1250	500

BULLDOG SINGLE-SHOT PISTOL

Connecticut Arms & Manufacturing Co.
Naubuc, Connecticut

Bulldog

A .44 or .50 caliber single-shot spur trigger pistol with 4" or 6" barrels, and a pivoting breechblock that moves to the left for loading. Blued, case hardened and stamped "Connecticut Arms & Manf. Co. Naubuc Conn. Patented Oct. 25, 1864." There were only a few hundred manufactured, and the .50 caliber, 6" barreled versions would be worth an additional 40 percent. Produced between 1866 and 1868.

Exc.	V.G.	Good	Fair	Poor
—	1500	600	250	150

BURGESS GUN CO.

Buffalo, New York
Also SEE—Colt and Whitney

One of the most prolific 19th century designers was Andrew Burgess who established his own company in 1892. The Burgess Gun Company manufactured slide action shotguns and rifles operated by a unique pistol grip prior to their being purchased by the Winchester Repeating Arms Company in 1899. Arms based on Burgess' patents were manufactured by a variety of American gun makers. Serial numbers for all Burgess shotguns begin at 1000.

12 Gauge Slide Action Shotgun

A 12 gauge slide-action shotgun with a 28" or 30" barrel. Blued with a walnut stock. This model was available with 6 grades of engraving. The values listed are for the standard, plain model.

Burgess engraving grades (1-4)

Exc.	V.G.	Good	Fair	Poor
—	1500	600	250	125

Folding Shotgun

As above, with a 19.5" barrel that is hinged so that it may be folded back against the buttstock.

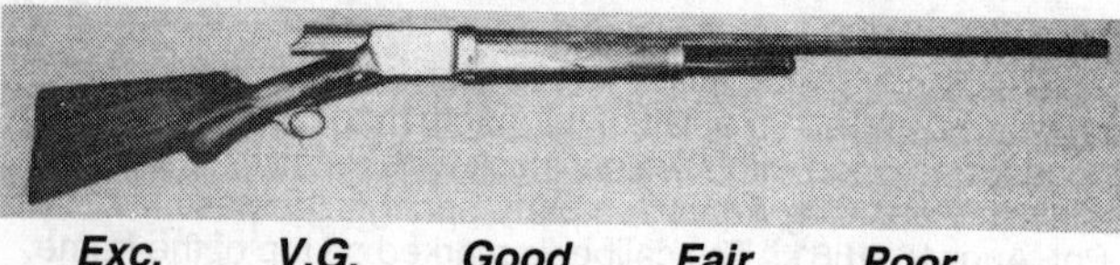

Exc.	V.G.	Good	Fair	Poor
—	4250	1750	650	300

Slide Action Rifle

An extremely rare rifle based upon the shotgun design described above. Manufactured in at least three calibers with varying barrel lengths. Blued with a walnut stock.

Exc.	V.G.	Good	Fair	Poor
—	3750	1500	500	250

BURGSMULLER, K.

Krelensen, Germany

Burgo

The Rohm RG10 under another name. It is a poor quality, inexpensive .38 caliber revolver. The examples marketed by Burgsmuller are so marked.

Exc.	V.G.	Good	Fair	Poor
175	125	90	50	25

Regent

The Regent is a .22 caliber revolver that resembles the Colt Police Positive in appearance. It is of a higher quality than the Burgo. The manufacturer is not known.

Exc.	V.G.	Good	Fair	Poor
250	175	125	75	50

BURNSIDE RIFLE CO.

Bristol Firearms Co.
Providence, Rhode Island

Bristol, Rhode Island

This is a historically desirable firearm for Civil War collectors as the designer, Ambrose E. Burnside, was to become a well-known Union general. The rifle, of which there were four distinct models, was used quite extensively in the Civil War.

This carbine was manufactured first by the Bristol Firearms Co., which made the entire production of the first model and also some of the second model. In 1862 the Burnside Firearms Co. was formed, and they produced the remainder of the second models and all of the third and fourth models. Production ceased entirely in 1865.

Burnside Carbine 1st Model

This model was produced by Bristol and was chambered for the .54 caliber. It is a breechloader that uses the percussion ignition system but features a cartridge of sorts made of copper, and a tape priming device that was located inside the frame. It has a 22" round barrel with no forend and a walnut stock with inspector's cartouche. The finish is blued and case-colored, and the frame is stamped "Burnside's /Patent/March 25th/1856." There were approximately 250 1st Models manufactured.

Exc.	V.G.	Good	Fair	Poor
—	—	15000	6000	1500

2nd Model

The 2nd Model features an improved breechblock opening mechanism located inside the trigger guard. The barrel is 21" long, and the other features are similar to the 1st Model. They are marked either "Bristol Firearm Co." or "Burnside Rifle Co./Providence-R.I." The barrel is marked "Cast Steel 1861," and some of the breechblock devices are marked "G.P. Foster Pat./April 10th 1860." There were approximately 1,500 2nd Models manufactured in 1861 and 1862.

Courtesy Milwaukee Public Museum, Milwaukee, Wisconsin

Exc.	V.G.	Good	Fair	Poor
—	—	5500	2500	750

3rd Model

This model differs from the 2nd Model in that it has a forend with a barrel band and a slightly modified hammer. The markings are the same as the Burnside-manufactured 2nd Models. There were approximately 2,000 produced in 1862.

Exc.	V.G.	Good	Fair	Poor
—	—	3500	1250	500

4th Model

This model differs from the others in that it features a hinged breech that permits simpler loading of the odd-shaped Burnside percussion cartridge. The frame is marked "Burnside's Patent/Model of 1864." The other features are similar to the 3rd Model. There were approximately 50,000 manufactured between 1862 and 1865.

Courtesy Milwaukee Public Museum, Milwaukee, Wisconsin

Exc.	V.G.	Good	Fair	Poor
—	4000	2000	800	400

BUSHMASTER FIREARMS INC.

Windham, Maine

Bushmaster XM15-E2S Target Model

Furnished with a 20" heavy barrel and A-2 stock. Weight is 8.35 lbs.

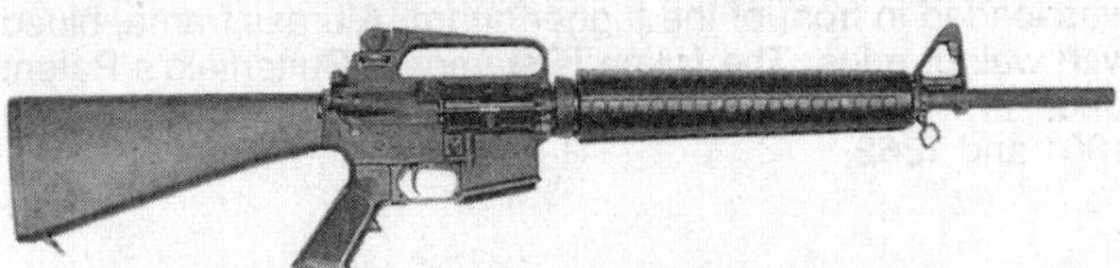

NIB	Exc.	V.G.	Good	Fair	Poor
800	675	550	400	300	200

NOTE: Add $10 for 24" barrel and $20 for 26" barrel. Add $75 for A3 carry handle.

Bushmaster XM15-E2S V-Match Competition Rifle

This model is a specially designed competition rifle with 20", 24", or 26" barrel lengths. Fitted with a black anodized aluminum handguard. Weight is about 8.1 lbs.

NIB	Exc.	V.G.	Good	Fair	Poor
850	700	575	450	350	250

NOTE: Add $75 for A3 carry handle.

Bushmaster XM15-E2S V-Match Carbine

As above but with 16" barrel. Weight is about 6.9 lbs.

NIB	Exc.	V.G.	Good	Fair	Poor
900	700	575	450	350	250

NOTE: Add $75 for A3 carry handle.

Bushmaster XM15-E2S Shorty Carbine

This "post-ban" model of the M16 is a gas-operated semi-automatic rifle chambered for the .223 Remington cartridge. It is fitted with a heavy 16" barrel and a 30-round magazine (while supplies last). Overall length is 35" and empty weight is 6.72 lbs.

NIB	Exc.	V.G.	Good	Fair	Poor
800	675	550	450	300	200

NOTE: Add $50 for fluted barrel. Add $75 for A3-type carry handle.

Bushmaster XM15-E2S Dissipator

Similar to the above model with a 16" barrel but fitted with a longer plastic handguard to give a longer sight radius. Weight is 7.2 lbs.

NIB	Exc.	V.G.	Good	Fair	Poor
800	675	550	450	300	200

NOTE: Add $75 for A3 carry handle.

Bushmaster M4 Post-Ban Carbine

Introduced in 2001 this rifle features a 14.5" barrel with permanently attached Mini Y Comp muzzlebrake (total length 16") and pinned, fixed-length Tele-style stock. Chambered for .223 caliber. M16A2 rear sight. Supplied with 10-round magazine. Weight is about 6.6 lbs.

NIB	Exc.	V.G.	Good	Fair	Poor
900	700	550	450	300	200

Bushmaster M4A3 Post-Ban Carbine

Same as above but with removable carry handle. Introduced in 2001.

NIB	Exc.	V.G.	Good	Fair	Poor
975	775	600	500	400	300

Bushmaster DCM Competition Rifle

This model features a 20" extra heavy barrel with free floating forend. Competition sights and trigger. Supplied with buttstock weight and hard carrying case. 10-round magazine.

NIB	Exc.	V.G.	Good	Fair	Poor
1350	1075	800	600	—	—

Bushmaster M17S Bullpup

This model is a gas-operated semi-automatic rifle in the bullpup design. Chambered for the .223 cartridge and fitted with a 21.5" barrel. Weight is 8.2 lbs.

NIB	Exc.	V.G.	Good	Fair	Poor
1000	875	675	400	300	200

Carbon 15 9mm Carbine

Semi-auto carbine chambered in 9mm Parabellum. Carbon fiber frame, 16-inch steel barrel, six-position telescoping stock, 30-rd. detachable magazine. Introduced 2006.

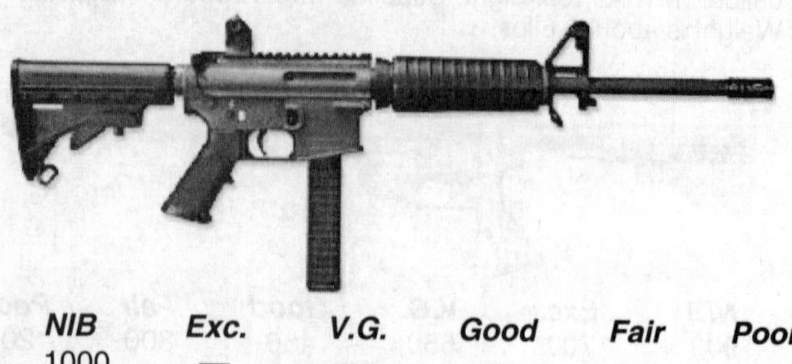

NIB	Exc.	V.G.	Good	Fair	Poor
1000	—	—	—	—	—

Carbon 15 Top Loading Rifle

Semi-auto rifle chambered in .223. Carbon fiber frame, 16-inch steel barrel, retractable stock, Picatinny rail, 10-rd. fixed magazine. Based on AR-15. Introduced 2006.

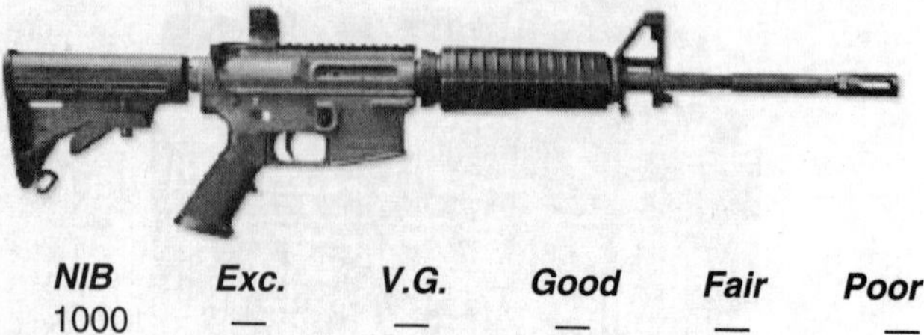

NIB	Exc.	V.G.	Good	Fair	Poor
1000	—	—	—	—	—

Predator

Semi-auto rifle chambered in .223. 20-inch DCM-type barrel, fixed composite buttstock, 2-stage competition trigger, Picatinny rail, 1/2" scope risers. Based on AR-15. Introduced 2006.

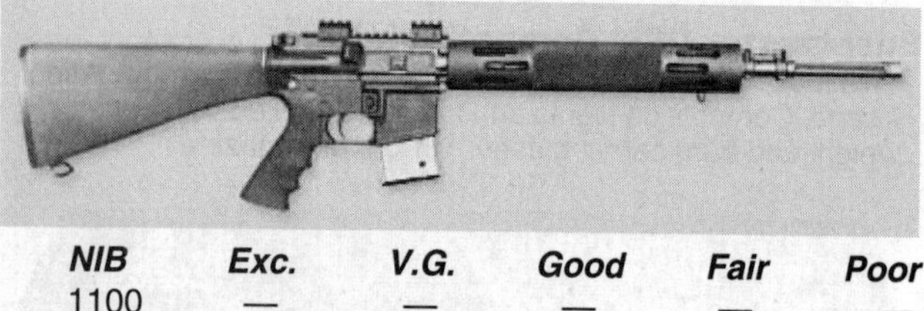

NIB	Exc.	V.G.	Good	Fair	Poor
1100	—	—	—	—	—

Carbon 15 .22 Rimfire Rifle

Similar to Shorty carbine but chambered in .22 LR. Blowback; 10-rd. magazine. MSRP: 790

BUTLER, WM. S.

Rocky Hill, Connecticut

Butler Single-Shot Pistol

A .36 caliber single-shot percussion pocket pistol with a 2.5" barrel and the frame and grip made in one piece. The frame marked "Wm. S. Butler's Patent/Patented Feb.3, 1857."

Exc.	V.G.	Good	Fair	Poor
—	—	900	350	150

BUTTERFIELD, JESSE

Philadelphia, Pennsylvania

Butterfield Army Revolver

A .41 caliber revolver with a 7" octagonal barrel, an unfluted 5-shot cylinder and features a special priming device, a disk that was loaded in front of the trigger guard. A brass frame, blued with walnut grips. The frame is stamped "Butterfield's Patent Dec. 11, 1855/Phila." Approximately 650 manufactured in 1861 and 1862.

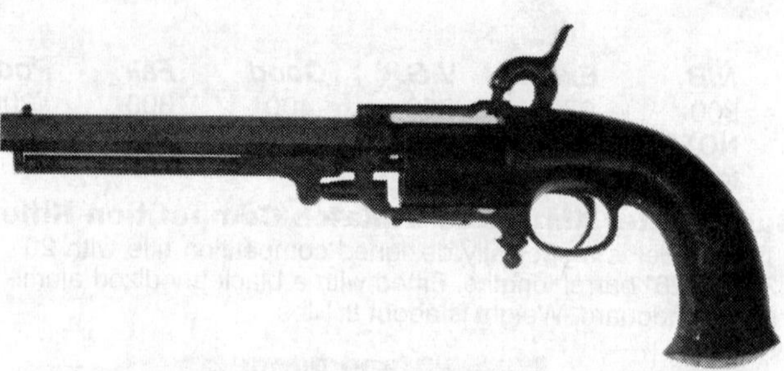

Courtesy Milwaukee Public Museum, Milwaukee, Wisconsin

Exc.	V.G.	Good	Fair	Poor
—	—	5500	2000	800

Butterfield Pocket Pistol

A .41 caliber single-shot percussion pistol with a 2" to 3.5" barrel. German silver with walnut stocks. The lock is marked "Butterfield's/Patent Dec 11, 1855." Extremely rare. Manufactured in the 1850s.

Exc.	V.G.	Good	Fair	Poor
—	—	8500	3750	1500

CABANAS, INDUSTRIAS S.A.

Aguilas, Mexico

This company manufactures a variety of bolt-action single-shot rifles that utilize .22 caliber blanks to propel a .177 caliber pellet.

Mini-82 Youth

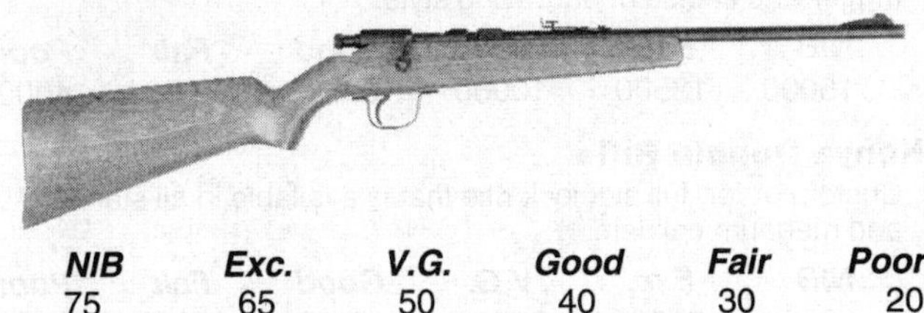

NIB	Exc.	V.G.	Good	Fair	Poor
75	65	50	40	30	20

R-83 Larger Youth

NIB	Exc.	V.G.	Good	Fair	Poor
85	75	60	50	40	30

Safari A

NIB	Exc.	V.G.	Good	Fair	Poor
100	90	75	50	40	30

Varmint

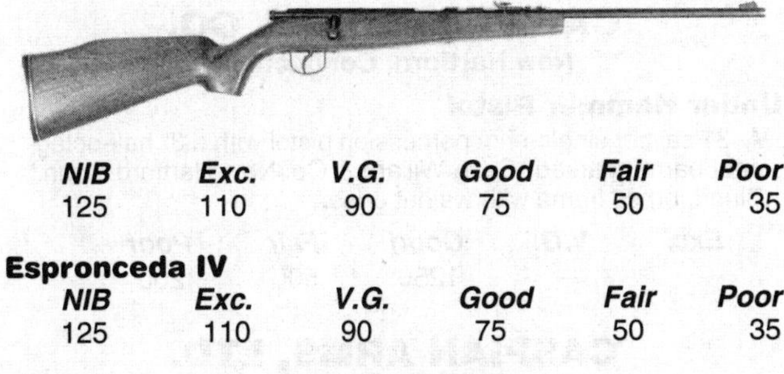

NIB	Exc.	V.G.	Good	Fair	Poor
125	110	90	75	50	35

Espronceda IV

NIB	Exc.	V.G.	Good	Fair	Poor
125	110	90	75	50	35

Leyre

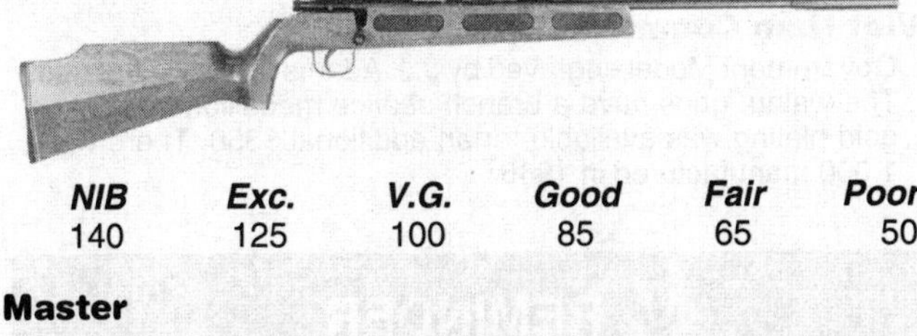

NIB	Exc.	V.G.	Good	Fair	Poor
140	125	100	85	65	50

Master

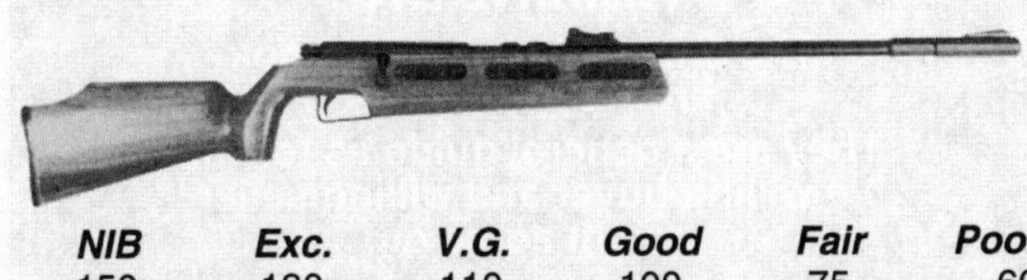

NIB	Exc.	V.G.	Good	Fair	Poor
150	130	110	100	75	60

CABELAS, INC.

Sidney, Nebraska

AYA Grade II Custom

A 12, 16, and 20 gauge boxlock shotgun in various barrel lengths and chokes, a single-selective trigger, and automatic ejectors. Engraved with a hand checkered walnut stock. This model is no longer available.

Exc.	V.G.	Good	Fair	Poor
1250	1175	950	700	575

Hemingway Model

A 12 or 20 gauge boxlock shotgun with 28" barrels, various chokes, a single-selective trigger and automatic ejectors. Engraved with a hand checkered walnut stock.

NIB	Exc.	V.G.	Good	Fair	Poor
975	900	750	600	525	450

CALICO

SEE—American Industries, Inc.
Cleveland, Ohio

CAMEX-BLASER USA, INC.

SEE—Blaser Jagdwaffen
Ft. Worth, Texas

CAMPO GIRO

Eibar, Spain

Esperanza y Unceta Model 1904

Designed by Lt. Col. Venancio Aguirre. This pistol was produced in limited numbers.

Exc.	V.G.	Good	Fair	Poor
3000	2000	1500	1000	800

Model 1910

Similar to the above, in 9mm Largo. Tested, but not adopted, by the Spanish army.

Exc.	V.G.	Good	Fair	Poor
2000	1500	1000	800	600

Model 1913

An improved version of the above, about 1,300 made.

Courtesy James Rankin

Exc.	V.G.	Good	Fair	Poor
1500	1250	850	600	500

Model 1913/16

An improved version of the above, about 13,000 built.

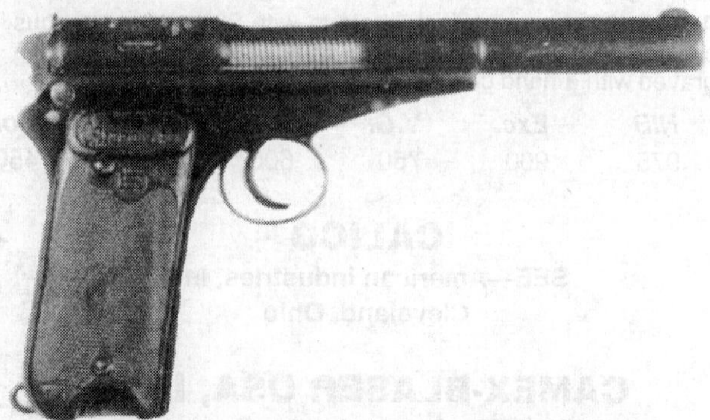

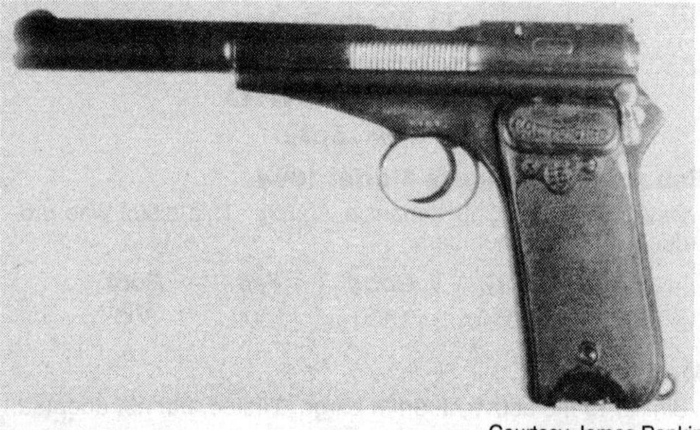

Courtesy James Rankin

Exc.	V.G.	Good	Fair	Poor
800	750	500	400	250

CARCANO
Turin, Italy

NOTE: For prices, historical data, and photos *see The Standard Catalog of Military Firearms, Italy, Rifles, Carcano.*

CARD, S. W.
Location Unknown

Under Hammer Pistol

A .34 caliber single-shot percussion pocket pistol with a 7.75" half octagonal barrel marked "S.W. Card" and "Cast Steel". Blued with walnut grips.

Exc.	V.G.	Good	Fair	Poor
—	—	1200	450	150

CARLTON, M.
Haverhill, New Hampshire

Under Hammer Pistol

A .34 caliber percussion under hammer single-shot pistol with a 3.5" to 7.75" half-octagonal barrel marked "M. Carleton & Co." Browned with walnut grips. Active 1830s and 1840s.

Exc.	V.G.	Good	Fair	Poor
—	—	1500	600	200

CASARTELLI, CARLO
Brescia, Italy

Sidelock Shotgun

Custom order sidelock shotgun that is available in any gauge, barrel length, choke, automatic ejectors and single-selective trigger and choice of engraving style.

NIB	Exc.	V.G.	Good	Fair	Poor
15000	13500	10000	8250	6000	4000

Kenya Double Rifle

Custom order, full sidelock rifle that is available in all standard and magnum calibers.

NIB	Exc.	V.G.	Good	Fair	Poor
30000	27000	22500	18000	13000	9000

Africa Model

A bolt-action rifle built on a square-bridge magnum Mauser action. It is chambered for the heavy magnum calibers and can be taken down for transport. The other features are on a custom order basis.

NIB	Exc.	V.G.	Good	Fair	Poor
8750	8000	7000	5750	4750	3750

Safari Model

Built on a standard Mauser bolt-action and is chambered for the non-magnum calibers.

NIB	Exc.	V.G.	Good	Fair	Poor
7000	6500	5500	4500	3250	2500

CASE WILLARD & CO.
New Hartford, Connecticut

Under Hammer Pistol

A .31 caliber single-shot percussion pistol with a 3" half-octagonal barrel marked "Case Willard & Co./New Hartford Conn." Blued, brass frame with walnut grips.

Exc.	V.G.	Good	Fair	Poor
—	—	1250	500	200

CASPIAN ARMS, LTD.
Hardwick, Vermont

This company is primarily a 1911 component manufacturer.

Viet Nam Commemorative

Government Model engraved by J.J. Adams and nickel-plated. The walnut grips have a branch service medallion inlaid, and gold plating was available for an additional $350. There were 1,000 manufactured in 1986.

REMINDER

The prices given in this book are RETAIL prices. They are a general guide as to what a willing buyer and willing seller might agree on.

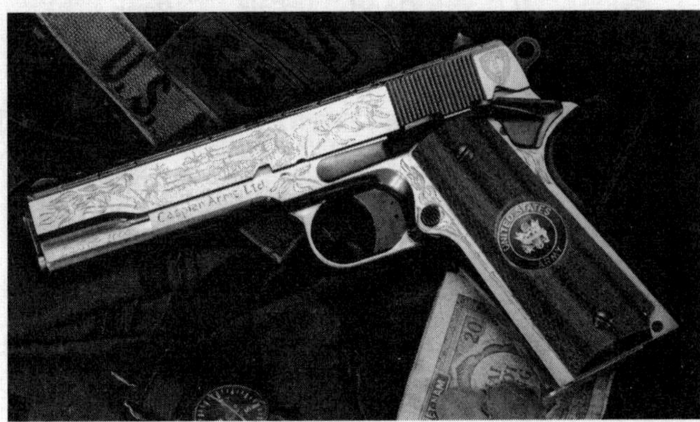

Courtesy James Rankin

NIB	Exc.	V.G.	Good	Fair	Poor
1200	1000	800	600	475	300

CASULL ARMS, INC.

Afton, Wyoming

CA 2000

Chambered for the .22 caliber LR cartridge this stainless steel revolver has a 5-round cylinder with fold-up trigger. Double-action-only. Palm sized.

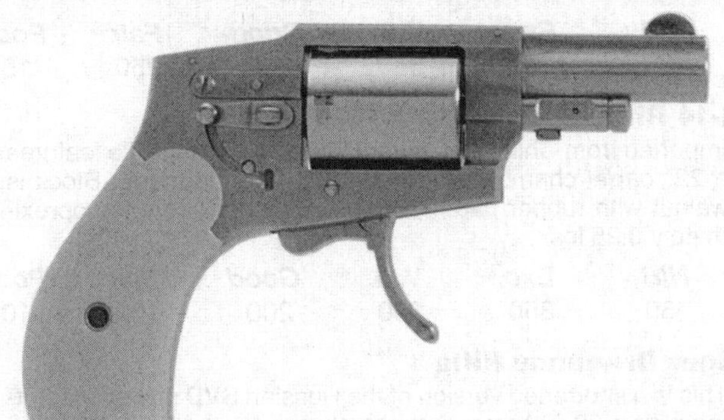

NIB	Exc.	V.G.	Good	Fair	Poor
500	425	350	250	—	—

CA 3800

Chambered for the .38 Casull cartridge (124 gr. 1800+fps) this pistol is fitted with a 6" match barrel and has a magazine capacity of 8 rounds. Full-length two-piece guide rod. Checkering on front strap and mainspring housing is 20 lpi. Match trigger and numerous other special features. Weight is about 40 oz. Introduced in 2000.

NIB	Exc.	V.G.	Good	Fair	Poor
2600	2050	1700	—	—	—

NOTE: Add $300 for extra .45 ACP barrel.

CENTURY GUN COMPANY/NEW CENTURY MANFACTURING

Evansville, Knightstown & Greenfield, Indiana

This revolver design was originally manufactured in 1972 by Russell Wilson, who sandcasted the bronze frame (cloned from the Colt SAA configuration) in Evansville, IN. Gene Phelps purchased the manufacturing rights for this gun and formed a partnership with Earl Keller to produce a redesigned frame, also using sandcast bronze.

The original Century revolver was made in Evansville, IN beginning in 1973 (1973 was the 100th anniversary of the .45-70 Govt. cartridge — hence the term Century) and production was halted in 1976 at ser. no. 524. In late 1976, Phelps and Keller (the two original partners on the venture) dissolved their partnership and each began manufacturing their own version of the .45-70 revolver. Gene Phelps completely redesigned the gun's interior and began manufacturing the Heritage I, with an investment-cast steel frame, and without the Century's novel cross-bolt safety. Keller's Century Manufacturing, Inc. continued to produce the original Century, with some design refinements, and in 1985 the company was purchased by Dr. Paul Majors, who died in Dec. of 2001.

The most recent Century revolver featured a manganese bronze frame and other components in addition to having a cross-bolt safety. They were produced in .45-70 and various other cals., in Greenfield, IN. Earl Keller died in 1986. The second series was made in Greenfield, IN with limited production resuming in 1986. Earlier handmade "Evansville" Model 100s (disc.) are currently selling for between $2,500-$3,500, depending on the region and condition. Post-Evansville guns retail from a high around $1700 (Excellent) to $9000 (Good) in .45-70; other chamberings such as .444 Marlin and .50-70 Government generally bring 10 percent to 20 percent more.

In Feb., 2002, Century Mfg. was purchased by Dave Lukens & Jeff Yelton and moved to Knightstown, IN. Dave and Jeff produced approximately 500 guns.

In June, 2004, Century Mfg. was purchased by Bill, Stephen, Robert, and Thomas Jordan and renamed the company to New Century Manufacturing, LLC. Production was expected to begin in late 2004.

(Courtesy New Century Manufacturing)

CENTURY INTERNATIONAL ARMS CO.

St. Albans, Vermont

Century International Arms is a leading importer of military firearms primarily of foreign manufacture. These low-cost firearms are excellent shooters and many have been restocked to make satisfactory hunting rifles. The listing offers a representative sample of imports from Century. The company is always providing new surplus firearms that may not appear in this edition.

Centurion Shotgun

This is a new over/under shotgun in 12, 20, and 28 gauge as well as .410 bore with 2-3/4" chambers. The walnut stock is checkered. The receiver is blue. Offered in 28" vent-rib barrels in full and modified chokes. Weight is about 7.35 lbs. for the 12 gauge and 5.3 lbs. for the .410 bore.

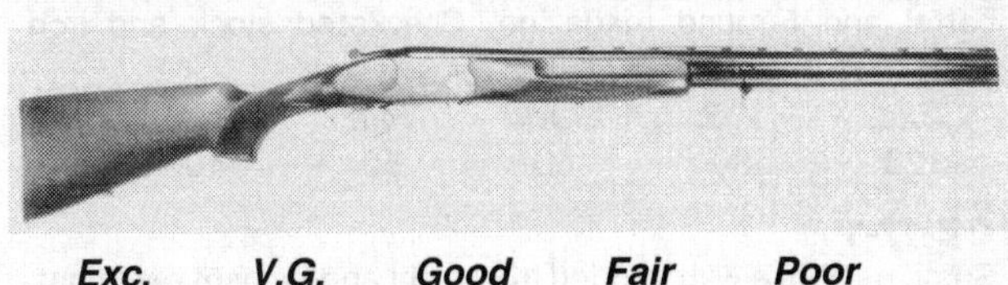

Exc.	V.G.	Good	Fair	Poor
325	275	225	175	125

Centurion 98 Sporter

This is a refinished and rebuilt on a surplus German Mauser 98 action with new commercial 22" barrel. No sights. A synthetic stock with recoil pad is standard. Chambered for .270 or .30-06. Weighs about 7 lbs. 13 oz.

Exc.	V.G.	Good	Fair	Poor
230	200	175	150	100

Century Centurion 14

This bolt-action rifle uses an Enfield Pattern 14 action drilled and tapped for scope mount. Barrel is 24" and chambered for 7mm Rem. Mag. Walnut stock is checkered with pistol grip and Monte Carlo comb. No sights.

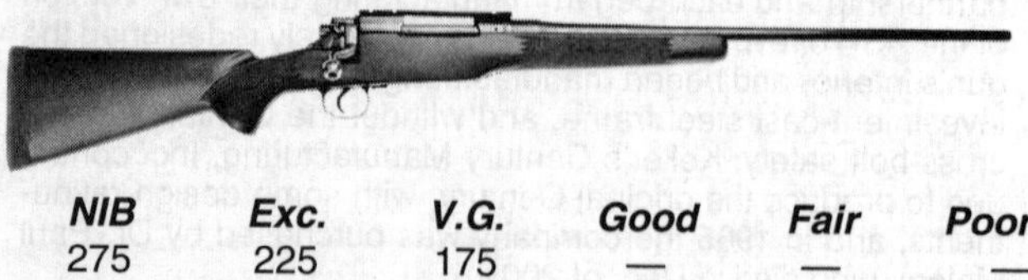

NIB	Exc.	V.G.	Good	Fair	Poor
275	225	175	—	—	—

Enfield Sporter No. I Mark III

This refinished rifle has a cut down Sporter-style stock. Action and sights are original. Caliber is .303.

Exc.	V.G.	Good	Fair	Poor
120	80	60	50	40

Enfield Sporter No. 4 Mark I

Similar to above with cut down stock. Caliber .303.

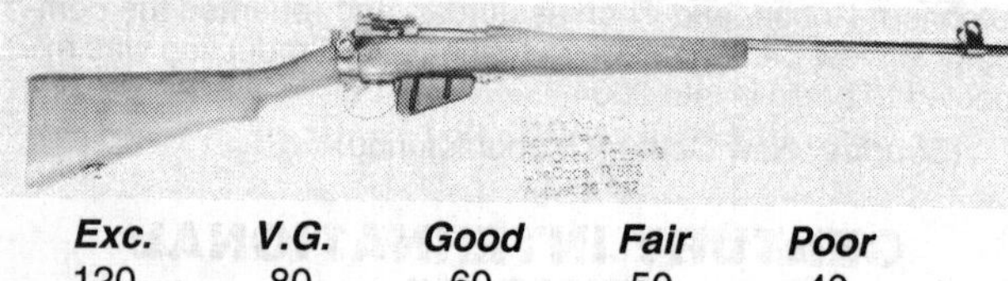

Exc.	V.G.	Good	Fair	Poor
120	80	60	50	40

With new walnut stock.

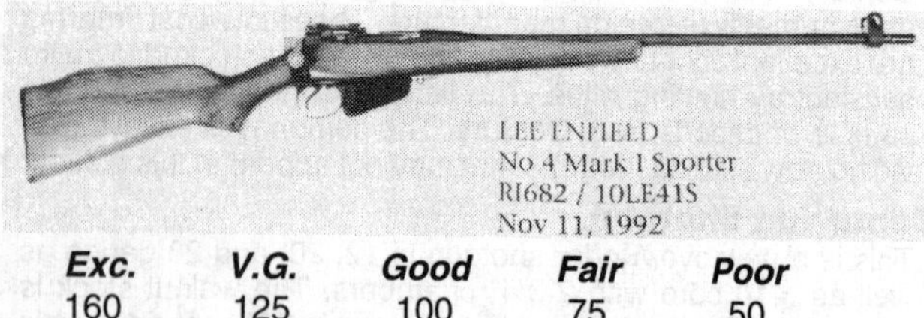

Exc.	V.G.	Good	Fair	Poor
160	125	100	75	50

TOZ-17

An original Russian rifle chambered for the .22 LR. Has a 21" barrel and 5-round magazine. Checkered stock and iron sights. Weighs about 5.4 lbs.

Exc.	V.G.	Good	Fair	Poor
120	80	60	50	40

TOZ-17-1

Same as above with hooded front sight and tangent rear sight. Receiver is grooved for scope mount.

Exc.	V.G.	Good	Fair	Poor
80	65	50	40	35

Mexican Mauser Model 1910 Sporter

This rifle has been converted from a military rifle to a sporter by cutting down the stock. The metal is refinished and the barrel has been rebored and rechambered for the .30-06 cartridge. The box magazine holds 5 rounds. Barrel is 23" and rifle weighs about 8 lbs.

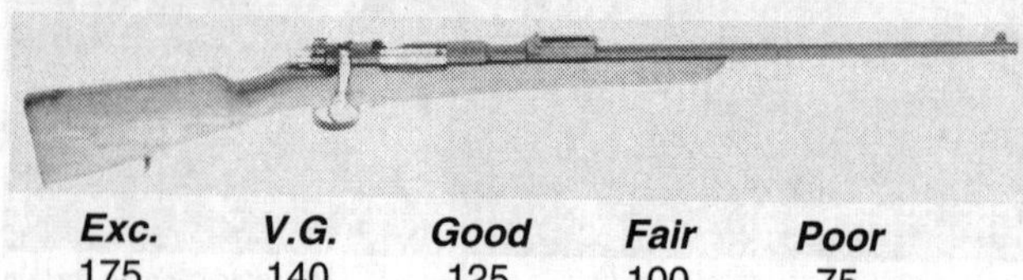

Exc.	V.G.	Good	Fair	Poor
175	140	125	100	75

FAL Sporter

This is a refinished FAL receiver and barrel installed in a synthetic thumbhole stock. The flash suppressor and bayonet lug have been removed. Barrel is 20.75" and weight is approximately 10 lbs.

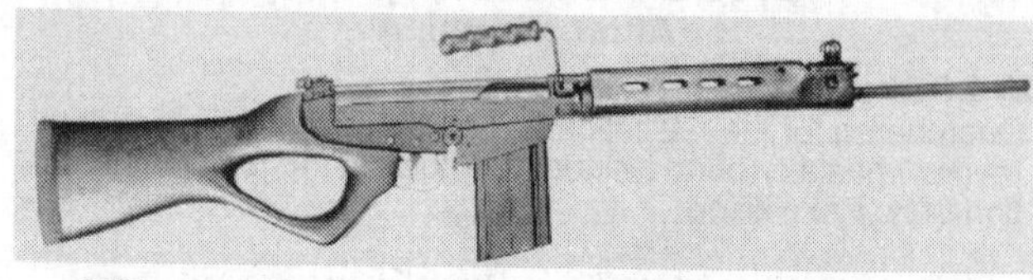

NIB	Exc.	V.G.	Good	Fair	Poor
625	500	350	300	250	150

M-14 Rifle

Imported from China by Century International this rifle features a 22" barrel chambered for the .308 Win. cartridge. Stock is walnut with rubber pad. Parkerized finish. Weight is approximately 8.25 lbs.

NIB	Exc.	V.G.	Good	Fair	Poor
450	350	250	200	150	100

Tiger Dragunov Rifle

This is a shortened version of the Russian SVD sniper rifle. Fitted with a 20.8" barrel and chambered for the 7.62x54R cartridge the rifle is sold with a 5-round magazine and a 4x range finding scope. Imported from Russia. Weight is about 8.5 lbs.

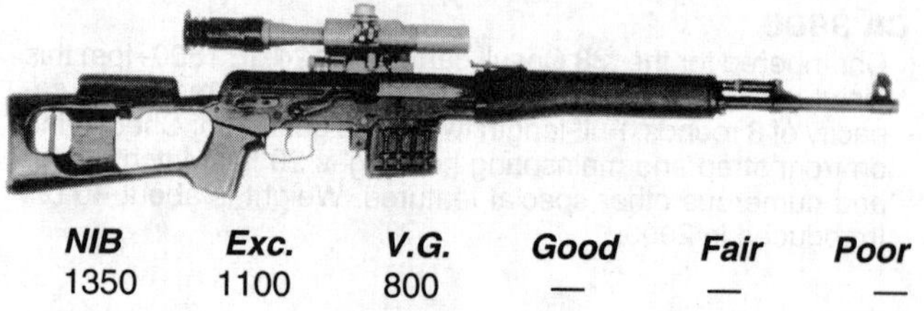

NIB	Exc.	V.G.	Good	Fair	Poor
1350	1100	800	—	—	—

CETME

Madrid, Spain

Cetme Autoloading Rifle

A .308 caliber semi-automatic rifle with a fluted chamber, a 17.74" barrel, an aperture rear sight and a 20-round detachable magazine. Black with a military-style wood stock. It is identical in appearance to the H&K 91 assault rifle.

NIB	Exc.	V.G.	Good	Fair	Poor
2500	2000	1500	900	—	—

CHAMELOT-DELVIGNE

Liege, Belgium

NOTE: For full details, prices, and photos by country of issue see the *Standard Catalog of Military Firearms.*

CHAMPLIN FIREARMS

Enid, Oklahoma

Champlin Firearms Company manufactures custom order rifles built to the customer's specifications. Prospective purchasers are advised to secure a qualified appraisal prior to acquisition.

Bolt-Action Rifle

These arms featured round or octagonal barrels, set triggers, a variety of sights and well figured walnut stocks.

NIB	Exc.	V.G.	Good	Fair	Poor
5500	4500	3500	2900	2200	1500

CHAPMAN C.

Location Unknown

Chapman Rifle

This rare Confederate weapon was patterned after the U.S. Model 1841. It is chambered for .58 caliber and utilizes the percussion ignition system. The round barrel is 33" long, with a full-length stock and two barrel bands. The mountings are brass, and the stock is walnut. "C.Chapman" was stamped on the lock. This weapon was manufactured somewhere in the Confederate States of America during the Civil War, but little else is known.

CHAPMAN CHARLES

Chattanooga, Tennessee

Chapman produced a limited number of percussion carbines and rifles during the Civil War. Carbines had an overall length of 39-1/2" and .54 caliber barrels 24" in length. Their furniture was of brass. Chapman rifles resembled the U.S. Model 1841 Rifle, but did not have patchboxes. Overall length 48-1/2", barrel length 33", caliber .58. Chapman rifles and carbines are marked "C. CHAPMAN" on the lockplates.

Prospective purchasers are strongly advised to secure an expert appraisal prior to acquisition.

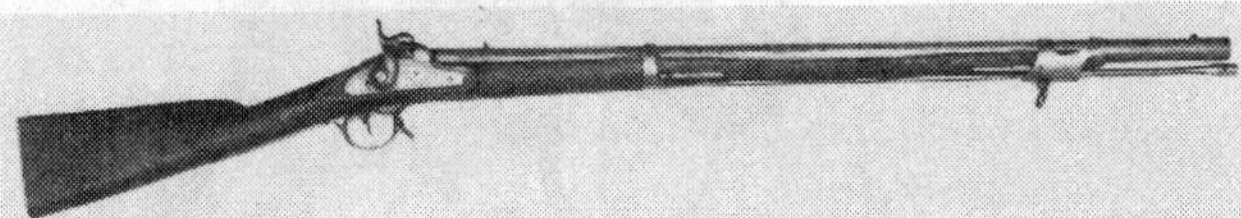

Courtesy Milwaukee Public Museum, Milwaukee, Wisconsin

Exc.	V.G.	Good	Fair	Poor
—	—	35000	15000	3000

CHAPMAN, G. & J.

Philadelphia, Pennsylvania

Chapman Pocket Revolver

A .32 caliber revolver with a 4" round barrel and 7-shot cylinder. The frame is made of brass while the barrel and cylinder are of steel. The barrel is marked "G.& J. Chapman/Phila-da/Patent Applied For/1861." Manufactured during the1860s.

Exc.	V.G.	Good	Fair	Poor
—	—	2250	950	250

CHAPUIS ARMES

France

RG Progress

A 12, 16, or 20 gauge boxlock shotgun. Most options are available on order.

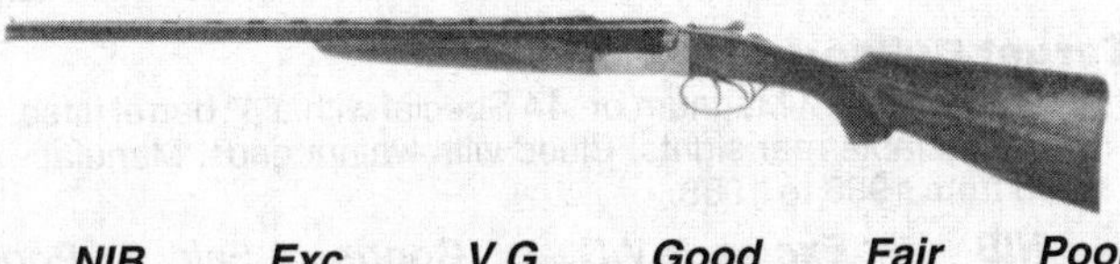

NIB	Exc.	V.G.	Good	Fair	Poor
2500	2250	2000	1800	1250	900

RG Express Model 89

A 7 x 65R, 8 x 57 JRS, 9.3 x 74R, and .375 Holland & Holland caliber sidelock, double-barreled rifle. The other features are at the customer's order.

NIB	Exc.	V.G.	Good	Fair	Poor
6500	5750	4800	4000	3000	1500

Utility Grade Express Model

A side-by-side boxlock-action double rifle with case colored or coin finish receiver. Offered in a variety of calibers: 9.3x74R, 8x57JRS, 7x65R, 8x75RS, and .30-06. Checkered walnut stock with pistol grip.

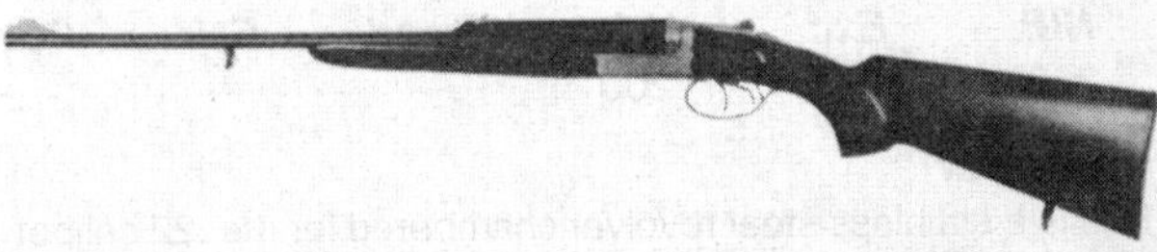

NIB	Exc.	V.G.	Good	Fair	Poor
6000	4800	4000	3000	1500	750

St. Bonnet Model

This model is a side-by-side shotgun with sideplates on a box-lock-action. Scroll engraved case colored receiver. Straight grip stock and double triggers. Offered in 12, 16, or 20 gauge.

NIB	Exc.	V.G.	Good	Fair	Poor
4000	3250	2000	1250	800	500

African PH Model Grade I

A boxlock-action double rifle offered in a wide variety of calibers. Caliber determines retail price. Hand engraved case colored receiver. Pistol grip stock with European-style cheekpiece.

.470 Nitro & .416 Rigby

NIB	Exc.	V.G.	Good	Fair	Poor
12500	9500	8500	—	—	—

375 H&H

NIB	Exc.	V.G.	Good	Fair	Poor
9500	7500	6250	—	—	—

.300 Win. Mag.

NIB	Exc.	V.G.	Good	Fair	Poor
8500	6500	5250	—	—	—

.30-06, 9.3x74 R

NIB	Exc.	V.G.	Good	Fair	Poor
8000	6000	5000	—	—	—

African PH Model Grade II

Same as above but with master engraving with game scenes. Add 20 percent to 25 percent to above NIB prices.

CHARLEVILLE

("Manufre Royle de Charleville"
SEE—French Military Firearms)

CHARTER 2000, INC.

Shelton, Connecticut

Bulldog

Chambered for the .44 Special cartridge and fitted with a 2.5" barrel. Stainless steel or blued frame with 5-round cylinder. Round butt and fixed sights. Weight is 21 oz.

NIB	Exc.	V.G.	Good	Fair	Poor
320	250	175	125	—	—

NOTE: For stainless steel add $20.

Police Bulldog

This model is chambered for the .38 Special cartridge and fitted with a 4" bull or tapered barrel. Full rubber grips. Blued finish. Weight is about 24 oz. Introduced in 2002.

NIB	Exc.	V.G.	Good	Fair	Poor
320	250	175	125	—	—

Undercover

Chambered for the .38 Special cartridge and fitted with a 2" barrel. Stainless steel or blued frame with 5-round cylinder. Round butt. Weight is about 20 oz.

NIB	Exc.	V.G.	Good	Fair	Poor
280	225	175	150	100	75

NOTE: For stainless steel add $20.

Off Duty

This .38 Special revolver has an aluminum frame and 2" barrel. Combat grips. Double-action-only. Weight is about 12 oz. Introduced in 2002.

NIB	Exc.	V.G.	Good	Fair	Poor
350	250	200	—	—	—

Pathfinder

This is a stainless steel revolver chambered for the .22 caliber cartridge. Fitted with a 2" barrel and wood grips. Weight is about 17 oz. Introduced in 2002.

NIB	Exc.	V.G.	Good	Fair	Poor
265	200	165	125	—	—

Mag Pug

Chambered for the .357 Magnum cartridge and fitted with a 2.2" ported barrel. Stainless steel or blued frame. Weight is about 24 oz.

NIB	Exc.	V.G.	Good	Fair	Poor
320	250	175	125	—	—

Dixie Derringer

Stainless steel with 1.125" barrels. Chambered for the .22 LR or .22 Mag cartridges. Weight is about 8 oz. Introduced in 2002.

NIB	Exc.	V.G.	Good	Fair	Poor
190	150	125	100	—	—

NOTE: For .22 Mag. model add $10.

Field King Rifle

Available with blue or stainless steel finish and chambered for .25-06, .270, .30-06, or .308 with 22" barrel. Magazine capacity is 4 rounds. Checkered fiberglass stock with cheekpiece. Weight is about 8 lbs.

NIB	Exc.	V.G.	Good	Fair	Poor
300	225	175	125	—	—

Field King Carbine

Same as above but with 18" barrel with compensator (20" total) and chambered for .308.

NIB	Exc.	V.G.	Good	Fair	Poor
350	250	200	150	—	—

REMINDER
Go to gun shows, not just to buy or sell, but to observe and learn.

CHARTER ARMS CORP.

Ansonia, Connecticut

Police Undercover

This model is chambered for the .38 Special or the .32 Magnum. It is fitted with a 2" barrel in blue or stainless steel finish. Offered with walnut or rubber grips. The overall length is 6.25" and weight is between 16 oz. and 19 oz. depending on grips and finish.

NIB	Exc.	V.G.	Good	Fair	Poor
250	200	175	150	100	75

Undercover Stainless Steel

As above, in stainless steel.

NIB	Exc.	V.G.	Good	Fair	Poor
300	250	225	175	125	100

Undercoverette

As above, with a thinner grip and in .32 S&W.

Exc.	V.G.	Good	Fair	Poor
200	150	125	100	75

Pathfinder

Similar to the above, but in .22 or .22 Magnum caliber with a 2", 3", or 6" barrel with adjustable sights.

NIB	Exc.	V.G.	Good	Fair	Poor
250	200	175	150	100	75

Pathfinder Stainless Steel

As above, in stainless steel.

NIB	Exc.	V.G.	Good	Fair	Poor
300	250	200	175	125	100

Bulldog

Similar to the Undercover model, but in .44 Special caliber with a 2.5" or 3" barrel and 5-shot cylinder.

NIB	Exc.	V.G.	Good	Fair	Poor
325	275	225	175	125	100

Stainless Steel Bulldog

As above, in stainless steel.

NIB	Exc.	V.G.	Good	Fair	Poor
350	300	250	200	150	125

Target Bulldog

As above, in .357 Magnum or .44 Special with a 4" barrel fitted with adjustable rear sights. Blued with walnut grips. Manufactured from 1986 to 1988.

NIB	Exc.	V.G.	Good	Fair	Poor
350	300	250	200	150	125

Bulldog Pug

Chambered for the .44 Special cartridge it is fitted with a 2.5" barrel. Available with walnut or neoprene grips in blue or stainless steel finish with choice of spur or pocket hammer. The cylinder holds 5 rounds. Overall length is 7" and weight is between 20 oz. and 25 oz. depending on grip and finish.

NIB	Exc.	V.G.	Good	Fair	Poor
325	275	225	175	125	100

Stainless Steel Bulldog

As above, in stainless steel.

NIB	Exc.	V.G.	Good	Fair	Poor
350	300	250	200	150	125

Bulldog Tracker

As above, with a 2.5", 4", or 6" barrel in .357 Magnum only.

NIB	Exc.	V.G.	Good	Fair	Poor
275	225	200	165	140	110

Police Bulldog

As above, in .32 H&R Magnum, .38 Special or .44 Special with 3.5" or 4" barrel.

NIB	Exc.	V.G.	Good	Fair	Poor
250	200	175	150	125	100

REMINDER

An "N/A" or "—" instead of a price indicates that there is no known price available for that gun in that condition, or the sales for that particular model are so few that a reliable price cannot be given.

Stainless Steel Police Bulldog

As above, in stainless steel and available also in .357 Magnum.

NIB	Exc.	V.G.	Good	Fair	Poor
300	250	210	175	145	110

Off Duty

Chambered for the .38 Special or .22 LR this revolver is fitted with a 2" barrel. Offered with either walnut or rubber grips in blue or stainless steel finish with choice of spur or pocket hammer. Weight of the .38 special version is between 17 oz. and 23 oz., depending on grip and finish. The .22 LR version weighs between 19 oz. and 22 oz. The overall length is 4.75". A nickel finish with rubber grips is also offered.

NIB	Exc.	V.G.	Good	Fair	Poor
200	150	125	100	75	60

Pit Bull

A 9mm Federal, .38 Special or .357 Magnum caliber double-action revolver with a 2.5", 3.5", or 4" barrel. Blued with rubber grips.

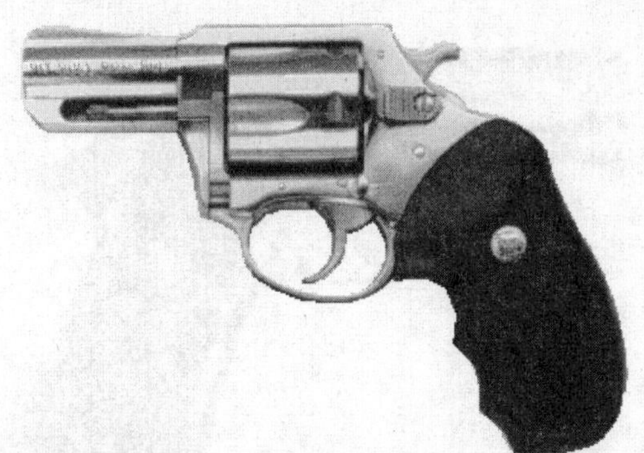

NIB	Exc.	V.G.	Good	Fair	Poor
300	250	200	175	125	90

The Mag Pug

A 5-shot revolver chambered for .357 Magnum. Stainless or blue. Ported 2.2" barrel. 23 oz. Fixed sights, rubber grips. Stainless or black.

NIB	Exc.	V.G.	Good	Fair	Poor
290	235	175	—	—	—

Dixie Derringer

Stainless mini-revolver chambered for .22 LR (5 oz.) or .22 Mag (6 oz.). 5-shot, 1.175" barrel.

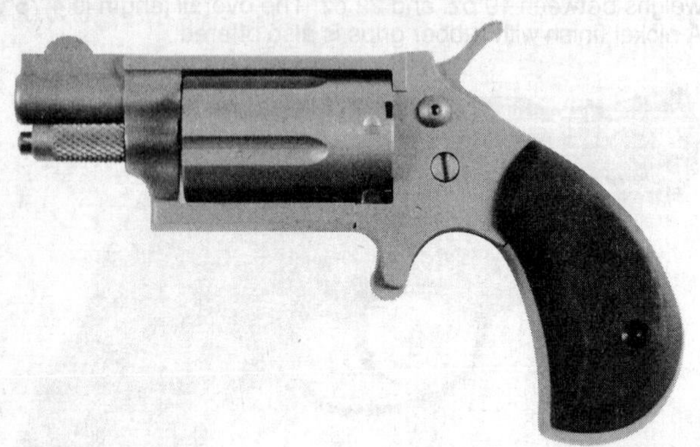

NIB	Exc.	V.G.	Good	Fair	Poor
175	140	—	—	—	—

Explorer II Pistol

A .22 caliber semi-automatic pistol with 6", 8", or 10" barrels. Available with a camo, black, silver, or gold finish and plastic grips. Discontinued in 1986.

NIB	Exc.	V.G.	Good	Fair	Poor
175	150	100	65	45	25

Model 40

A .22 caliber double-action semi-automatic pistol with a 3.5" barrel and 8-shot magazine. Stainless steel with plastic grips. Manufactured from 1984 to 1986.

Exc.	V.G.	Good	Fair	Poor
275	225	200	150	100

Model 79K

A .32 or .380 caliber double-action semi-automatic pistol with a 3.5" barrel and 7-shot magazine. Stainless steel with plastic grips. Manufactured from 1986 to 1988.

Exc.	V.G.	Good	Fair	Poor
350	300	250	180	125

Model 42T

A .22 caliber semi-automatic pistol with a 6" barrel and adjustable sights. Blued with walnut grips. Manufactured in 1984 and 1985.

NIB	Exc.	V.G.	Good	Fair	Poor
500	450	400	325	—	200

AR-7 Explorer Rifle

A .22 caliber semi-automatic rifle with a 16" barrel, 8-shot magazine and hollow plastic stock which can house the barrel when detached.

NIB	Exc.	V.G.	Good	Fair	Poor
125	1100	80	60	40	25

CHASSEPOT
French Military

MLE 1866

An 11mm caliber bolt-action rifle with a 32" barrel, a full-length walnut stock held on by two barrel bands, a cleaning rod mounted under the barrel and a bayonet lug that allows the attaching of a brass-handled, saber-type bayonet. White with a walnut stock.

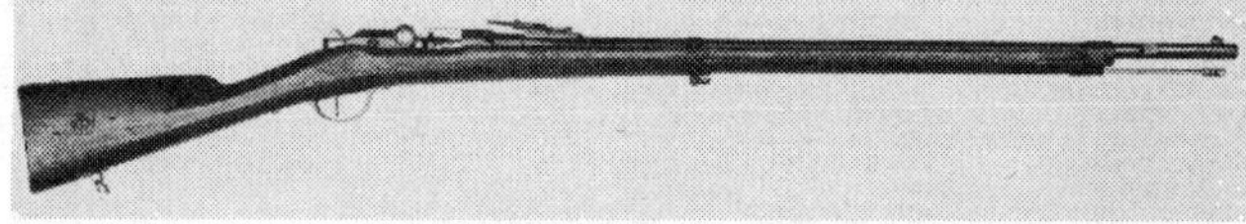

Courtesy Milwaukee Public Museum, Milwaukee, Wisconsin

Exc.	V.G.	Good	Fair	Poor
1500	850	500	150	100

CHEYTAC
Arco, Idaho

M-200

This bolt action rifle is chambered for the .408 CheyTac cartridge. Detachable barrel length is 30" with muzzlebrake. Magazine capacity is 7 rounds. Integral bipod. No sights, but receiver has attachable Picatinny rail. Weight is about 27 lbs.

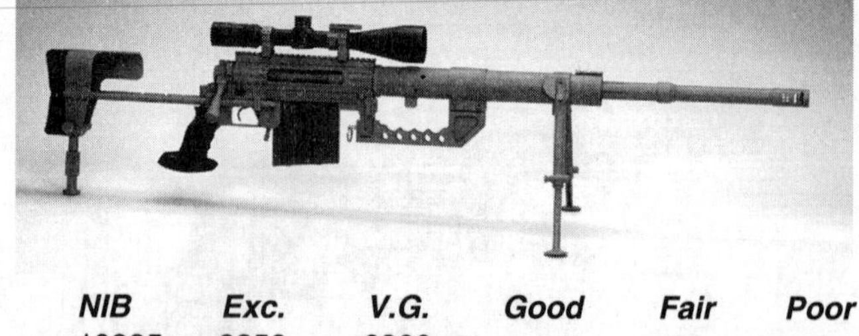

NIB	Exc.	V.G.	Good	Fair	Poor
10995	8250	6900	—	—	—

M-310

This is a single shot bolt action rifle chambered for the .408 CheyTac cartridge. Fitted with a 25" barrel with muzzlebrake. McMillian A-5 stock with adjustable cheekpiece. Match grade trigger. Picatinny rail. Weight is about 16.5 lbs.

NIB	Exc.	V.G.	Good	Fair	Poor
4395	3250	2750	—	—	—

CHICAGO F. A. CO.

Chicago, Illinois

Protector Palm Pistol

A .32 caliber radial cylinder revolver designed to fit in the palm of the hand and to be operated by a hinged lever mounted to the rear of the circular frame. The sideplates are marked "Chicago Firearms Co., Chicago, Ill." and "The Protector". Blued with hard rubber grip panels or nickel-plated with pearl grip panels. Manufactured by the Ames Manufacturing Company.

Standard Model Nickel-Plated/Black Grips

Exc.	V.G.	Good	Fair	Poor
—	2500	1000	500	250

NOTE: Blued finish add 50 percent. Pearl grips add 20 percent.

CHIPMUNK RIFLES/ROGUE RIFLE CO.

Lewiston, Idaho

Chipmunk Single-Shot Standard Rifle

A .22 or the .22 rimfire Magnum caliber bolt-action rifle with 16.25" barrel, and open sights. Weight is approximately 3.5 lbs.

NIB	Exc.	V.G.	Good	Fair	Poor
185	150	125	100	80	60

Deluxe Chipmunk

As above, with a hand-checkered walnut stock.

NIB	Exc.	V.G.	Good	Fair	Poor
230	180	135	100	80	60

Chipmunk .17 HMR

Similar to the Standard Model but chambered for the .17 HMR cartridge. Introduced in 2002.

NIB	Exc.	V.G.	Good	Fair	Poor
200	160	—	—	—	—

Chipmunk TM

Introduced in 2002 this model features a micrometer rear sight. Stock has accessory rail installed and is adjustable for length of pull. Barrel is an 18" heavy type. Weight is about 5 lbs.

NIB	Exc.	V.G.	Good	Fair	Poor
325	250	—	—	—	—

Silhouette Pistol

A .22 caliber bolt-action pistol with a 14.5" barrel, open sights and rear pistol-grip walnut stock.

NIB	Exc.	V.G.	Good	Fair	Poor
150	125	100	80	60	40

CHRISTENSEN ARMS

Fayette, Utah

NOTE: There are a number of custom options offered by this company for its rifles. Many of these options may affect price. Prices listed are for standard models with standard features.

Carbon One

This is a bolt-action rifle with Remington 700 action chambered for .17 through .243 caliber. It is fitted with a custom trigger, Match grade stainless steel barrel and black synthetic stock. Weight is about 6 lbs.

NIB	Exc.	V.G.	Good	Fair	Poor
2750	2250	—	—	—	—

Carbon Lite

This model is similar to above but weighs about 5 lbs.

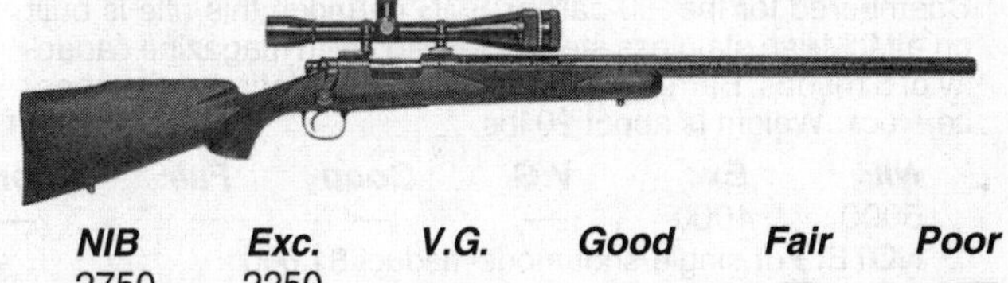

NIB	Exc.	V.G.	Good	Fair	Poor
2750	2250	—	—	—	—

Carbon King

This model utilizes a Remington 700 BDL long action and is chambered for .25 caliber through .30-06. Stainless steel barrel, custom trigger, and black synthetic stock are standard. Weight is approximately 6.5 lbs.

NIB	Exc.	V.G.	Good	Fair	Poor
2750	2250	—	—	—	—

Carbon Cannon

Similar to above model and chambered for belted magnum calibers. Weight is about 7 lbs.

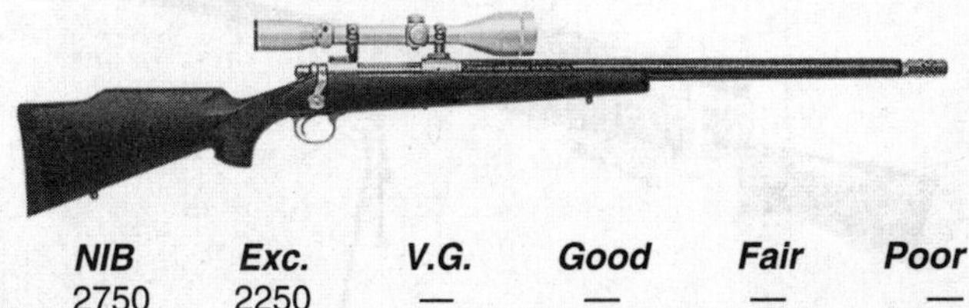

NIB	Exc.	V.G.	Good	Fair	Poor
2750	2250	—	—	—	—

Carbon Challenge I

This rifle is built on a Ruger 10/22 action. It is fitted with a Volquartsen trigger, stainless steel bull barrel and black synthetic stock. Weight is approximately 3.5 lbs.

NIB	Exc.	V.G.	Good	Fair	Poor
995	800	—	—	—	—

Carbon Challenge II

Similar to above model but fitted with an AMT action and trigger. Weight is about 4.5 lbs.

NIB	Exc.	V.G.	Good	Fair	Poor
1095	900	—	—	—	—

Carbon Tactical

This bolt-action model uses a Remington 700 BDL action and is available in most any caliber. It is fitted with a custom trigger, Match grade stainless steel barrel and black synthetic stock. Weight is about 7 lbs.

NIB	Exc.	V.G.	Good	Fair	Poor
2750	2250	—	—	—	—

Carbon Conquest

Chambered for the .50 caliber BMG cartridge this rifle is built on a McMillan stainless steel bolt-action with magazine capacity of 5 rounds. Barrel length is 32" with muzzlebrake. Composite stock. Weight is about 20 lbs.

NIB	Exc.	V.G.	Good	Fair	Poor
5000	4000	—	—	—	—

NOTE: For single-shot model deduct $1,000.

Carbon One Hunter

Semi-custom bolt action rifle built around choice of receivers; steel barrel encased in carbon alloy shroud; synthetic stock. All popular calibers. Weight: 6.5-7 lbs.

NIB	Exc.	V.G.	Good	Fair	Poor
1500	1300	—	—	—	—

Carbon Ranger Repeater

Semi-custom bolt-action rifle chambered in .50 BMG. Five-shot magazine; steel Pac-Nor barrel encased in carbon alloy. Muzzle brake. Weight: 20 lbs.

NIB	Exc.	V.G.	Good	Fair	Poor
5250	4600	—	—	—	—

Carbon Ranger Single Shot

Similar to repeater but single shot.

NIB	Exc.	V.G.	Good	Fair	Poor
4700	4000	—	—	—	—

CHURCHILL

Various European Manufacturers and Importers

Windsor I

A 10, 12, 16, 20, 28, and .410 bore Anson & Deeley double-barrel boxlock shotgun with barrel lengths from 23" through 32", various choke combinations, double triggers and extractors. Scroll-engraved, silver-finished, with checkered walnut pistol grip and forend.

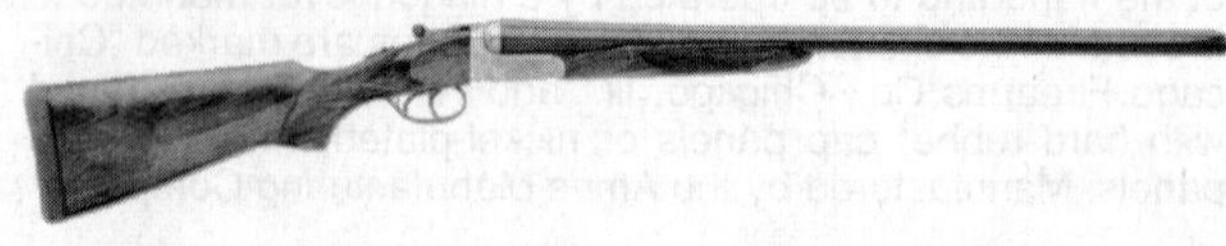

NIB	Exc.	V.G.	Good	Fair	Poor
800	600	500	400	300	200

Windsor II

As above, in 10, 12, and 20 gauge only with automatic ejectors. Not imported after 1987.

NIB	Exc.	V.G.	Good	Fair	Poor
800	600	550	450	350	250

Windsor VI

As above with sidelocks. Chambered for 12 and 20 gauge only with automatic ejectors. Not imported after 1987.

NIB	Exc.	V.G.	Good	Fair	Poor
1100	800	750	650	500	350

Royal

A 12, 20, 28 and .410 bore boxlock double-barrel shotgun with various barrel lengths and chokes, double triggers and extractors. Case hardened with checkered walnut stock. Introduced in 1988.

NIB	Exc.	V.G.	Good	Fair	Poor
650	500	425	350	275	125

OVER/UNDERS

Monarch

A 12, 20, 28, or .410 bore Over/Under shotgun with a boxlock-action, 25", 26", or 28" ventilated-rib barrels, either double- or a single-selective trigger, extractors, and a checkered walnut stock.

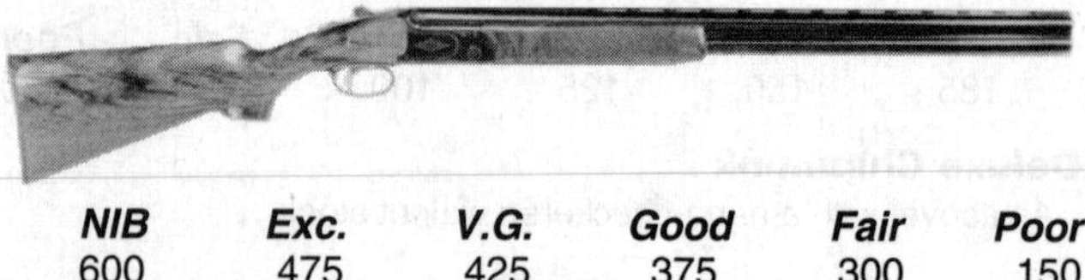

NIB	Exc.	V.G.	Good	Fair	Poor
600	475	425	375	300	150

Windsor III

A 12 and 20 and .410 bore boxlock double-barrel shotgun with 27" or 30" ventilated-rib barrels, extractors, a single-selective trigger, scroll-engraved, silver finished and a checkered walnut stock.

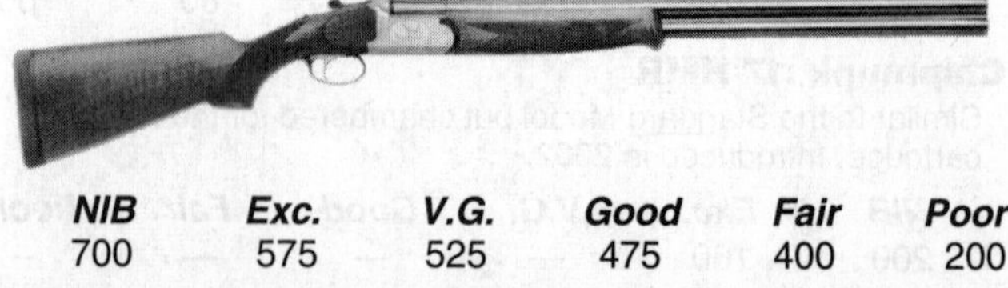

NIB	Exc.	V.G.	Good	Fair	Poor
700	575	525	475	400	200

Windsor IV

As above, with screw-in choke tubes standard. Introduced in 1989.

NIB	Exc.	V.G.	Good	Fair	Poor
975	775	650	500	425	200

Regent

As above, in 12 and 20 gauge with 27" ventilated-rib barrels, screw-in choke tubes, scroll-engraved false sideplates, automatic ejectors, a single-selective trigger, and a checkered walnut stock. Not imported after 1986.

NIB	Exc.	V.G.	Good	Fair	Poor
950	750	650	550	450	250

Regent II

As above with finer overall finishing.

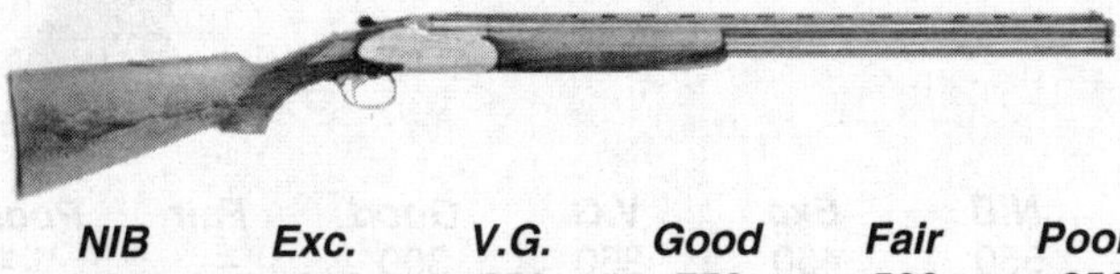

NIB	Exc.	V.G.	Good	Fair	Poor
1250	1000	850	750	500	250

Regent Shotgun/Rifle Combination

A .222, .223, .243, .270, .308, or .30-06 caliber/12 gauge Over/Under rifle/shotgun with a 25" ventilated rib, automatic ejectors and single-selective trigger. Silver finished, scroll engraved with a checkered walnut stock.

NIB	Exc.	V.G.	Good	Fair	Poor
1050	825	725	600	450	250

Windsor Grade Semi-Automatic

A 12 gauge semi-automatic shotgun with 26", 28", or 30" ventilated-rib barrels and screw-in choke tubes. An etched and anodized alloy receiver with a checkered walnut stock.

NIB	Exc.	V.G.	Good	Fair	Poor
500	375	325	275	225	175

Regent Grade Semi-Automatic

Chambered for 12 gauge with choice of 26", 28", or 30" barrels. Standard chokes or choke tubes. Walnut stock with pistol grip. Introduced in 1984 and discontinued in 1986. Weight is about 7-1/2 lbs.

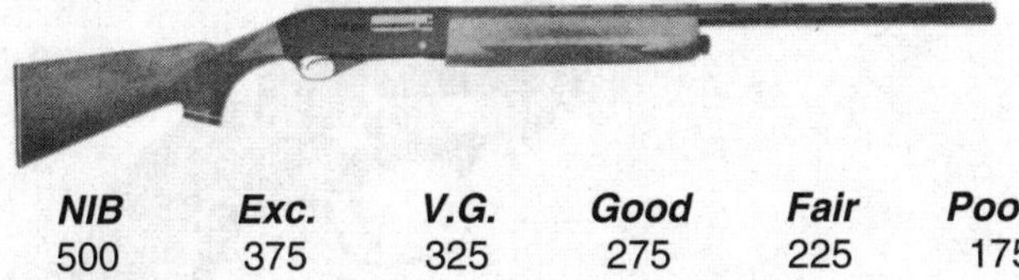

NIB	Exc.	V.G.	Good	Fair	Poor
500	375	325	275	225	175

Windsor Grade Slide-Action

A 12 gauge slide-action shotgun with a 26" through 30" ventilated-rib barrel, various chokes, double slide rails, and an anodized alloy receiver. Checkered walnut stock. Discontinued in 1986.

Exc.	V.G.	Good	Fair	Poor
500	375	300	250	175

RIFLES

Highlander

A .25-06 through .300 Winchester Magnum caliber bolt-action rifle with a 22" barrel, with or without sights, a 3-shot magazine, and a checkered walnut stock.

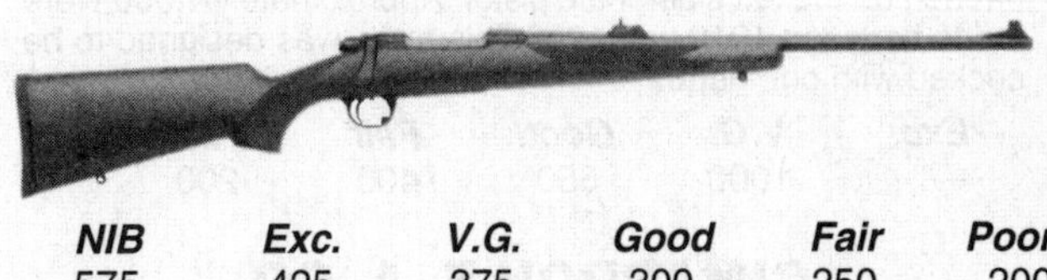

NIB	Exc.	V.G.	Good	Fair	Poor
575	425	375	300	250	200

Regent

As above, with a Monte Carlo-style comb and cheekpiece. Discontinued in 1988.

Exc.	V.G.	Good	Fair	Poor
650	500	425	350	275

CHURCHILL, E. J. LTD.

London, England

One of One Thousand Rifle

A .270 to .458 Magnum caliber bolt-action rifle with 24" barrel and a select French walnut stock with a trap pistol-grip cap and recoil pad. Only 100 produced for the 20th anniversary of Interarms in 1973.

Exc.	V.G.	Good	Fair	Poor
1500	1250	1000	700	550

Premier Over-and-Under

This is a sidelock ejector gun available in 12, 20 or 28 gauge. Single- or double-trigger with choice of finish. Barrel lengths built to order. Deluxe Turkish walnut with choice of grip. Fine scroll engraving. Weight for 12 gauge gun about 7 lbs., for 20 gauge guns about 6.75 lbs. Many extra cost options available. Seek expert advice prior to a sale.

NIB	Exc.	V.G.	Good	Fair	Poor
45000	—	—	—	—	—

NOTE: Add $3,000 for 28 gauge guns.

Premier Side-by-Side

Similar to the over-and-under gun but with side-by-side barrels. Also offered in 16 gauge as well as 12, 20, and 28 gauge. Weights are about 6.5 lbs. for 12 gauge; 6 lbs. for 16 gauge; and 5.8 lbs. for 20 gauge. Many extra options are available. Seek expert advice prior to a sale.

NIB	Exc.	V.G.	Good	Fair	Poor
36500	—	—	—	—	—

NOTE: Add $3,000 for 28 gauge guns.

Premier Double Rifle

Similar in construction to the side-by-side shot this rifle is chambered for the .300 H&H, .375 H&H, or .500 Nitro Express. Weight is 9.5 lbs. for the .300, 9.75 lbs. for the 375, and 12.5 lbs. for the .500. Many extra-cost options. Seek an expert opinion prior to a sale.

NIB	Exc.	V.G.	Good	Fair	Poor
52000	—	—	—	—	—

NOTE: Add $3,000 for .500 N.E. guns.

Baronet Magazine Rifle

This rifle uses the standard Mauser 98 action with fully adjustable trigger, 3 position safety, and box release floor plate. Barrel length is custom to order. Border engraving. Chambered for the .30-06 or .375 H&H. Weight for .30-06 is about 8.5 lbs., for the .375 about 9 lbs. Many extra-cost options offered. Seek an expert opinion prior to a sale.

NIB	Exc.	V.G.	Good	Fair	Poor
11500	—	—	—	—	—

Double Barrel Shotguns

SEE—British Double Guns for older guns

CHYLEWSKI, WITOLD

Switzerland

A 6.35mm caliber semi-automatic pistol with a 6-round magazine, marked "Brevete Chylewski" and bears the name Neuhausen on the left side of the pistol. Approximately 1,000 were made between 1910 and 1918. This pistol was designed to be cocked with one hand.

Exc.	V.G.	Good	Fair	Poor
—	1000	650	400	200

CIMARRON F. A. CO.

Fredericksburg, Texas

In business since 1984 this company imports quality single-action revolvers and rifles from Uberti, Armi San Marco, and Pedersoli.

NOTE: Cimarron also sells Uberti-manufactured blackpowder Colt reproductions, from the Patterson to the Model 1862 Pocket. For prices and specifications on these models see the Uberti section.

Model No. 3 Schofield

This version of the Schofield is manufactured for Cimarron by Armi San Marco in Italy. Its parts are interchangeable with the original. It is offered in several variations and calibers. Discontinued. Beware of latch locking problems.

Schofield Civilian Model

Fitted with 7" barrel and offered in .44 Russian & .44 Special, .44 WCF, .45 Schofield, .45 Long Colt.

NIB	Exc.	V.G.	Good	Fair	Poor
849	600	525	425	—	—

Schofield Military Model

Essentially the same as the Civilian Model except for its markings.

NIB	Exc.	V.G.	Good	Fair	Poor
849	600	525	425	—	—

Schofield Wells Fargo

Similar to the Military and Civilian Model but fitted with a 5" barrel. Calibers are the same.

NIB	Exc.	V.G.	Good	Fair	Poor
849	600	525	425	—	—

NOTE: For standard nickel finish add $100 and for custom nickel finish add $150.

Model 1872 Open Top

This revolver is offered in a number of different calibers and configurations. It is chambered for the .44 SP, .44 Colt, .44 Russian, .45 Schofield, .38 Colt, .38 Special. It can be fitted with Army or Navy grips. Barrel lengths are 4.75", 5.5", or 7.5". Offered in regular blued finish, charcoal blue finish, or original finish.

NIB	Exc.	V.G.	Good	Fair	Poor
530	425	350	—	—	—

NOTE: Add $40 for charcoal finish and $50 for original finish. Add $25 for silver-plated back strap and trigger guard.

COLT SINGLE-ACTION ARMY CONFIGURATIONS

Cimarron Arms reproduction of the 1873 Colt Single-Action Army revolver comes in two basic configurations. First is the "Old Model" with the black powder frame screw-in cylinder pin retainer and circular bull's eye ejector head. Second is the "pre-war Model" style frame with spring loaded cross-pin cylinder retainer and half moon ejector head. Old Model revolvers are available in authentic old style charcoal blue finish at an extra charge. Unless otherwise stated all of these Colt reproductions are produced by Uberti of Italy. Plain walnut grips are standard unless noted.

General Custer 7th Cavalry Model

Has US military markings and is fitted with 7-1/2" barrel on an Old Model frame. Offered in .45 Long Colt only.

NIB	Exc.	V.G.	Good	Fair	Poor
550	450	350	300	—	—

Rough Rider U.S. Artillery Model

This version of the Old Model is fitted with a 5-1/2" barrel and chambered for .45 Long Colt.

NIB	Exc.	V.G.	Good	Fair	Poor
550	450	350	300	—	—

Frontier Six Shooter

This revolver is offered with a choice of 4-3/4", 5-1/2", or 7-1/2" barrel. It is chambered for .38 WCF, .357 Magnum, .44 WCF, .45 Long Colt, or .45 LC with extra .45 ACP cylinder.

NIB	Exc.	V.G.	Good	Fair	Poor
475	350	300	275	—	—

NOTE: For charcoal blue finish add $40 to NIB price. For extra .45 ACP cylinder add $30. For stainless steel add $50.

Sheriff's Model w/no ejector

Fitted with a 3" barrel and chambered in .44 WCF or .45 Long Colt. Built on an Old Model frame.

NIB	Exc.	V.G.	Good	Fair	Poor
469	350	300	275	—	—

New Sheriff's Model w/ejector

This variation is fitted with a 3-1/2" barrel with ejector and is available in .357 Magnum, .44 WCF, .44 Special, and .45 Long Colt. For checkered walnut grips add $35.

NIB	Exc.	V.G.	Good	Fair	Poor
500	400	325	275	—	—

Wyatt Earp Buntline

This is a limited edition model fitted with a 10" barrel chambered for the .45 Long Colt cartridge. Model P frame. Silver shield inlaid in grip.

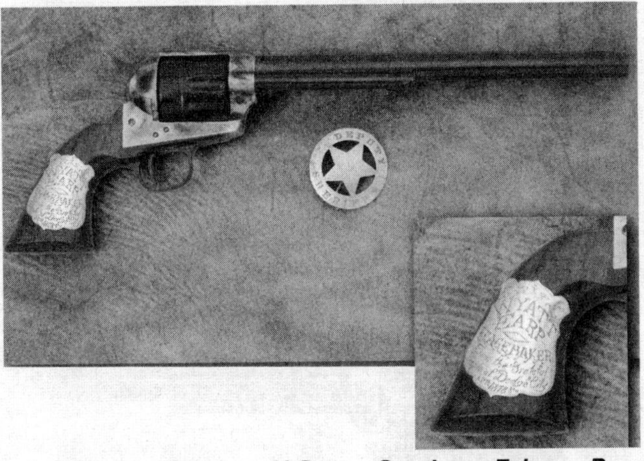

NIB	Exc.	V.G.	Good	Fair	Poor
760	600	500	425	—	—

New Thunderer

The frame is based on the Old Model fitted with a bird's-head grip with a choice of plain or checkered walnut grips. Originally offered in 3-1/2" or 4-3/4" barrel lengths; in 1997 5-1/2" barrels were offered. Chambered for .357 Magnum, .44 WCF, .44 Special, or .45 Long Colt/.45 ACP. Add $35 for checkered grips.

NIB	Exc.	V.G.	Good	Fair	Poor
520	400	325	275	—	—

Thunderer Long Tom

Same as the New Thunderer except for a barrel length of 7.5".

NIB	Exc.	V.G.	Good	Fair	Poor
520	425	350	275	—	—

Lightning

Similar to the Thunderer but with a smaller grip frame. Chambered for the .38 Special cartridge or .22 LR and fitted with 3.5", 4.75", or 5.5" barrel. Finish is blue with case hardened frame.

NIB	Exc.	V.G.	Good	Fair	Poor
450	375	315	—	—	—

Lightning .32s

This model features two cylinders chambered for the .32-20 and the .32 H&R cartridges. Choice of 3.5", 4.75", or 5.5" barrel. Introduced in 2004.

NIB	Exc.	V.G.	Good	Fair	Poor
500	400	350	—	—	—

New Model P

Offered in either Old Model or pre-war styles in a choice of 4-3/4", 5-1/2", or 7-1/2" barrel. Chambered for .32 WCF, .38 WCF, .44 WCF, .44 Special, or .45 Long Colt.

NIB	Exc.	V.G.	Good	Fair	Poor
445	400	325	275	—	—

Stainless Frontier Model P

This model is a Model P in stainless steel. Chambered for the .357 Mag or .45 Colt cartridge. Barrels are 4.75", 5.5", or 7.5". Introduced in 2004.

NIB	Exc.	V.G.	Good	Fair	Poor
600	450	400	—	—	—

A.P. Casey Model P U.S. Cavalry

Fitted with a 7-1/2" barrel and chambered for .45 Long Colt this revolver has US markings (APC) on an Old Model frame.

NIB	Exc.	V.G.	Good	Fair	Poor
500	375	325	—	—	—

Rinaldo A. Carr Model P U.S. Artillery

This is a Model P built on an Old Model frame and chambered for .45 Long Colt and fitted with a 5-1/2" barrel. US markings (RAC).

NIB	Exc.	V.G.	Good	Fair	Poor
550	425	375	—	—	—

Evil Roy Model

This model features a Model P frame with wide square-notch rear sight and wide-width front sight. Slim grips checkered or smooth. Tuned action with lightened trigger. Chambered for the .357 Mag, .45 Colt, or .44-40 cartridge. Barrel lengths are 4.75" or 5.5". Introduced in 2004.

NIB	Exc.	V.G.	Good	Fair	Poor
720	575	500	—	—	—

Model P Jr.

Similar to the Model P but sized 20 percent smaller. Chambered for the .38 Special cartridge and fitted with 3.5" or 4.75" barrels. Blue with case hardened frame.

NIB	Exc.	V.G.	Good	Fair	Poor
490	400	325	250	—	—

Model P Jr. .32s

This model, introduced in 2004, features two cylinders chambered for the .32-20 and the .32 H&R cartridges. Choice of 3.5", 4.75", or 5.5" barrel.

NIB	Exc.	V.G.	Good	Fair	Poor
550	400	350	—	—	—

Cimarron 1880 Frontier Flat Top

Introduced in 1998 this model is a target version of the Colt single-action army. Rear sight is adjustable for windage and front adjustable for elevation. Offered with choice of 4.75", 5.5", or 7.5" barrels and chambered for .45 Colt, .45 Schofield, .44 WCF, and .357 Magnum. Choice of model P frame or pre-war frame.

NIB	Exc.	V.G.	Good	Fair	Poor
480	350	325	—	—	—

Cimarron Bisley

Exact copy of the Colt Bisley with case hardened frame. Choice of 4.75", 5.5", or 7.5" barrels and calibers from .45 Colt, .45 Schofield, .44 WCF, to .357 Magnum. Introduced in 1998.

NIB	Exc.	V.G.	Good	Fair	Poor
525	400	325	275	—	—

Cimarron Bisley Flat Top

Offered in the same barrel lengths and caliber as the standard Bisley with the addition of a windage adjustable rear sight and elevation adjustable front sight. Introduced in 1998.

NIB	Exc.	V.G.	Good	Fair	Poor
525	400	325	275	—	—

El Pistolero

This budget-priced revolver was introduced in 1997 and features a brass backstrap and trigger guard with plain walnut grips. Offered in 4-3/4", 5-1/2", and 7-1/2" barrel lengths. Chambered for .45 Long Colt or .357 Magnum.

NIB	Exc.	V.G.	Good	Fair	Poor
340	250	200	—	—	—

RICHARDS CONVERSIONS

Model 1851

Chambered for .38 Special, .38 Colt, and .44 Colt. Fitted with 5" or 7" barrels.

NIB	Exc.	V.G.	Good	Fair	Poor
530	425	350	—	—	—

Model 1861

Chambered for .38 Special, .38 Colt, and .44 Colt. Fitted with 5" or 7" barrels.

NIB	Exc.	V.G.	Good	Fair	Poor
530	425	350			

Model 1860

Chambered for .38 Special, .38 Colt, and .44 Colt. Fitted with 5" or 7.5" barrels.

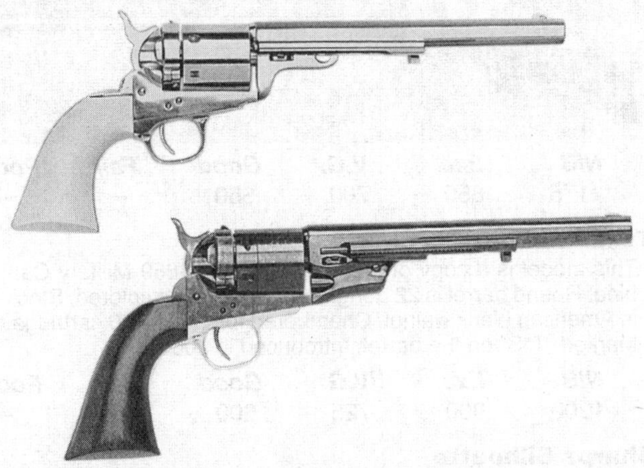

NIB	Exc.	V.G.	Good	Fair	Poor
530	425	350	—	—	—

Relic Finish

Offered by Cimarron as an extra cost item on its revolvers. This finish duplicates the old worn antique finish seen on many used historical Colts. Add $40 to the NIB price for any Cimarron revolver with this finish.

Relic finish

RIFLES

Model 1855 Spencer

Chambered for the .56-50 centerfire cartridge.

NIB	Exc.	V.G.	Good	Fair	Poor
1150	875	775	—	—	—

Henry Civil War Model

Offered in .44 WCF or .45 Long Colt with 24-1/4" barrel.

NIB	Exc.	V.G.	Good	Fair	Poor
1200	925	750	625	—	—

NOTE: For charcoal blue or white finish add $80.

Henry Civilian Model

Same as above but without military markings.

NIB	Exc.	V.G.	Good	Fair	Poor
1200	925	750	625	—	—

Model 1866 Yellowboy Carbine

Reproduction of the Winchester model 1866. Fitted with a 19" barrel and chambered for .38 Special, .44 WCF, or .45 Long Colt.

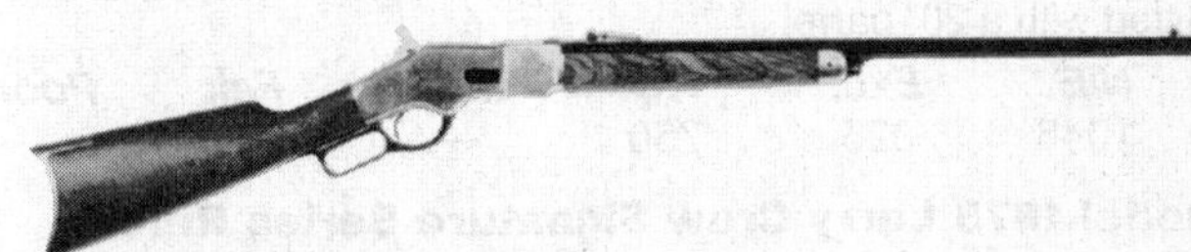

NIB	Exc.	V.G.	Good	Fair	Poor
965	750	600	525	—	—

NOTE: For charcoal blue add $40.

Model 1866 Yellowboy Rifle

Same as above but fitted with a 24-1/4" barrel.

NIB	Exc.	V.G.	Good	Fair	Poor
965	750	600	525	—	—

NOTE: For charcoal blue add $40.

Model 1866 Yellowboy Trapper

As above but with a 16" barrel.

NIB	Exc.	V.G.	Good	Fair	Poor
925	725	600	525	—	—

Model 1873 Winchester Rifle

This lever-action rifle is offered in .357 Magnum, .44 WCF, or .45 Long Colt. Fitted with a 24-1/4" barrel.

NIB	Exc.	V.G.	Good	Fair	Poor
1150	925	750	675		—

NOTE: For charcoal blue add $40. For pistol grip option add $140.

Model 1873 Long Range Rifle

Similar to the Model 1873 but fitted with a 30" barrel. For pistol grip option add $140.

NIB	Exc.	V.G.	Good	Fair	Poor
1120	850	725	675		—

NOTE: For 1 of 1000 engraving option add $1,250.

Model 1873 Carbine

Same as the standard Model 1873 but fitted with a 19" barrel.

NIB	Exc.	V.G.	Good	Fair	Poor
1045	825	700	650	—	—

NOTE: For charcoal blue add $40.

Model 1873 Short Rifle

This model is fitted with a 20" barrel. Production ceased in 1998.

NIB	Exc.	V.G.	Good	Fair	Poor
1150	925	750	675	—	—

NOTE: For charcoal blue add $40.

Model 1873 Trapper
As above but with 16" barrel.

NIB	Exc.	V.G.	Good	Fair	Poor
1045	825	750	—	—	—

Model 1873 Deluxe Sporting Rifle
This model is fitted with a 24" barrel, checkered walnut stock with pistol grip.

NIB	Exc.	V.G.	Good	Fair	Poor
1220	925	850	—	—	—

Model 1873 Evil Roy Rifle
This model is chambered for the .357 or .45 Colt cartridge and fitted with a 20" barrel.

NIB	Exc.	V.G.	Good	Fair	Poor
1045	825	750	—	—	—

Model 1873 Larry Crow Signature Series Rifle
Chambered for the .357 or .45 Colt cartridge and fitted with a 20" barrel.

NIB	Exc.	V.G.	Good	Fair	Poor
1045	825	750	—	—	—

Model 1892 Solid Frame Rifle
Offered with either 20" or 24" octagon barrels and chambered for the .357, .44WCF, or .45 Colt cartridges.

NIB	Exc.	V.G.	Good	Fair	Poor
850	675	575	—	—	—

Model 1892 Takedown Rifle
As above but with takedown feature.

NIB	Exc.	V.G.	Good	Fair	Poor
975	775	675	—	—	—

Billy Dixon Model 1874 Sharps (Pedersoli)
A reproduction of the Model 1874 Sharps rifle chambered for the .45-70 cartridge. Fitted with a 32" tapered octagon barrel. Stock is hand checkered with oil finish walnut. Double set triggers standard. First introduced to the Cimarron product line in 1997.

NIB	Exc.	V.G.	Good	Fair	Poor
1650	1225	1100	—	—	—

Remington Rolling Block
This Remington reproduction was introduced to Cimarron in 1997 and represents the Rolling Block Sporting rifle with 30" tapered octagon barrel and chambered for .45-70 cartridge. Hand-checkered, satin-finished walnut stock.

NIB	Exc.	V.G.	Good	Fair	Poor
1300	1000	900	—	—	—

Adobe Walls Rolling Block
This model is chambered for the .45-70 cartridge and is fitted with a 30" octagon barrel. Hand-checkered walnut stock with hand finishing. Case colored receiver and German silver nose cap. Weight is about 10.13 lbs. Introduced in 2004.

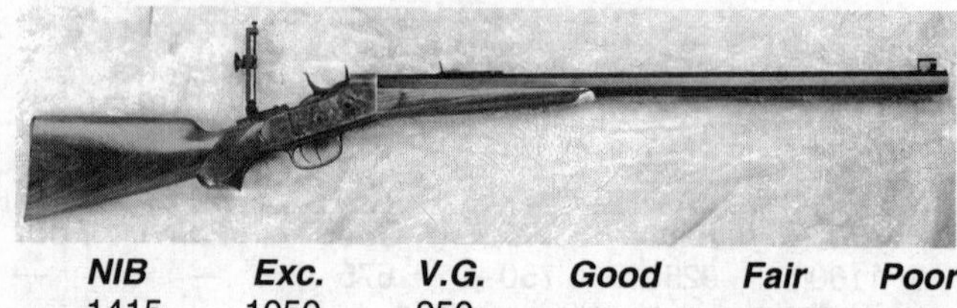

NIB	Exc.	V.G.	Good	Fair	Poor
1415	1050	950	—	—	—

Model 1885 High Wall
Reproduction of the Winchester Model 1885 chambered for .45-70, .45-90, .45-120, .40-65, .348 Win., .30-40 Krag, or .38-55 cartridges. Fitted with a 30" barrel. Walnut stock and case colored receiver.

NIB	Exc.	V.G.	Good	Fair	Poor
995	800	650	500	—	—

Model 1885 Deluxe High Wall
As above but with checkered walnut stock with pistol grip.

NIB	Exc.	V.G.	Good	Fair	Poor
1175	875	700	550	—	—

Model 1885 Low Wall
Introduced in 2004 this model is chambered for the .22 Long Rifle, .22 Hornet, .30-30, .32-20, .38-40, .357 Mag, .44-40, and .44 Mag cartridges. Hand checkered walnut stock with pistol grip. Octagon barrel is 30" long. Single or double-set trigger.

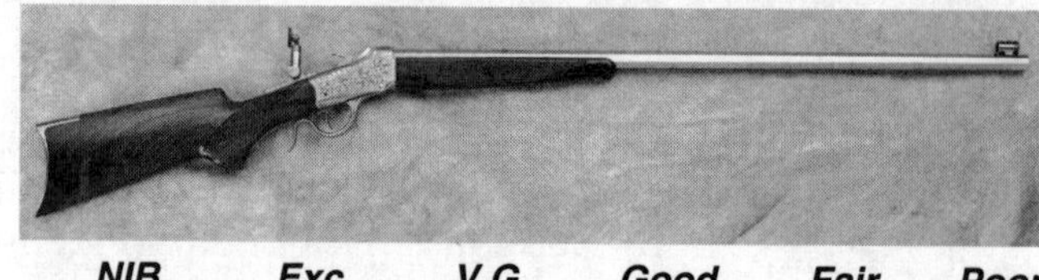

NIB	Exc.	V.G.	Good	Fair	Poor
1175	850	700	550	—	—

Texas Ranger Carbine
This model is a copy of the Sharps Model 1859 Military Carbine. Round barrel is 22" long. Receiver is case colored. Stock is American black walnut. Chambered for the .45-70 cartridge. Marked "T*S" on the barrel. Introduced in 2004.

NIB	Exc.	V.G.	Good	Fair	Poor
1200	900	725	600	—	—

Sharps Silhoutte
Offered in .45-70 or .40-65 calibers with 32" octagon barrel. Introduced in 1998.

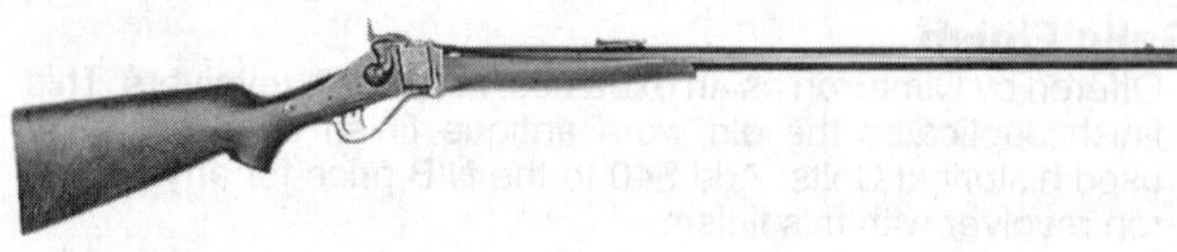

NIB	Exc.	V.G.	Good	Fair	Poor
1095	850	700	600	—	—

Quigley Sharps Sporting Rifle
This rifle is chambered for the .45-70 or .45-120 caliber and fitted with a heavy 34" octagon barrel. Introduced in 1998.

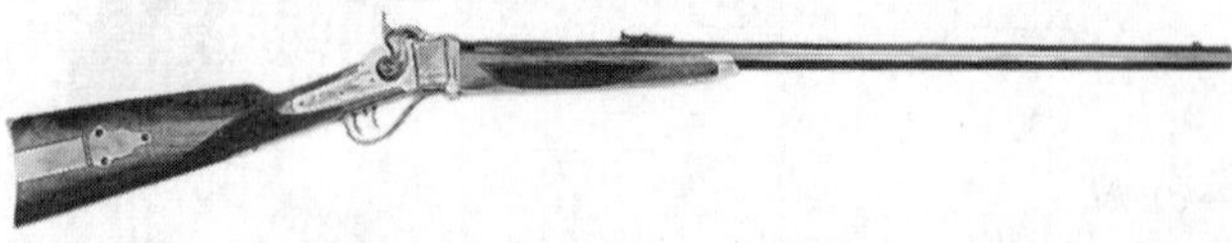

NIB	Exc.	V.G.	Good	Fair	Poor
1725	1350	1175	—	—	—

Billy Dixon 1874 Sharps (Armi-Sport)
Fitted with a 32" barrel and chambered for the .45-70, .45-90, or the .50-70. Introduced in 1995.

NIB	Exc.	V.G.	Good	Fair	Poor
1350	1025	875	—	—	—

This symbol denotes "Sleepers" with rapidly-rising values and/or significant collector potential.

Sharp's No. 1 Sporting Rifle

Plain walnut stock with pistol grip. Fitted with a 32" barrel. Chambered for the .45-70 cartridge.

NIB	Exc.	V.G.	Good	Fair	Poor
1350	1050	900	—	—	—

Pride of the Plains Model

Based on the Sharps Model 1874 Sporting Rifle, this model, chambered for the .45-70 cartridge, features a 32" octagon barrel, hand-checkered walnut stock with pistol grip, coin nickel receiver, Creedmore tang sight, and target front sight with inserts. Introduced in 2004.

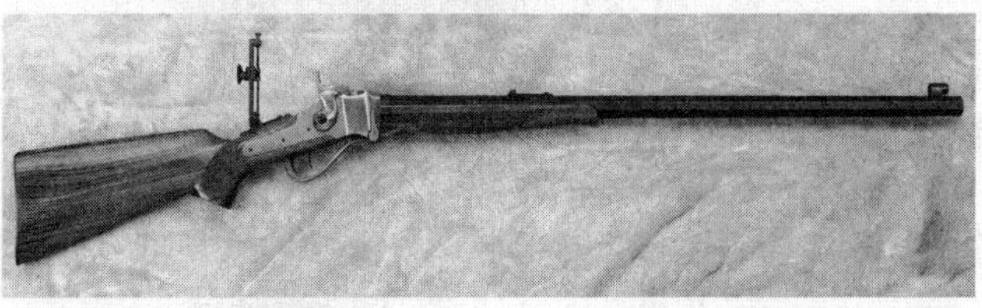

NIB	Exc.	V.G.	Good	Fair	Poor
1620	1200	1050	—	—	—

Professional Hunter Model

This model is the basic Sharps Model 1874 chambered for the .45-70 cartridge. Fitted with a 32" barrel, case colored receiver, walnut stock with shotgun butt and double-set triggers. Introduced in 2004.

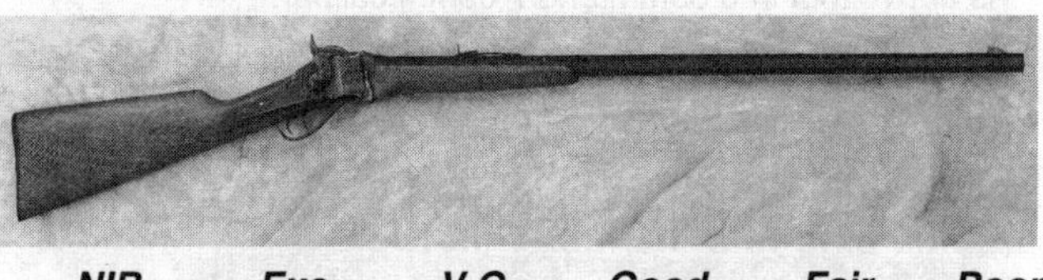

NIB	Exc.	V.G.	Good	Fair	Poor
1160	850	725	—	—	—

Big Fifty Model

Chambered for the .50-90 cartridge and fitted with a 34" half-octagon barrel. Fancy walnut stock with hand checkering and pistol grip. Case colored receiver, German silver nose cap, and Hartford-style Soule Creedmore sights with spirit level and globe front sight. Weight is about 11 lbs. Introduced in 2004.

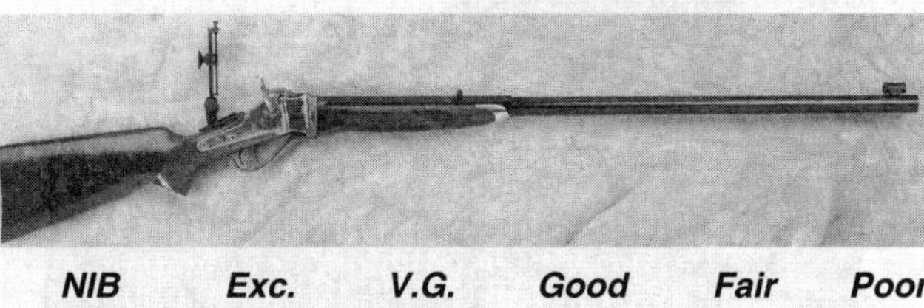

NIB	Exc.	V.G.	Good	Fair	Poor
1890	1400	1150	—	—	—

Springfield Trapdoor Carbine

Based on the famous Springfield design. Chambered for the .45-70.

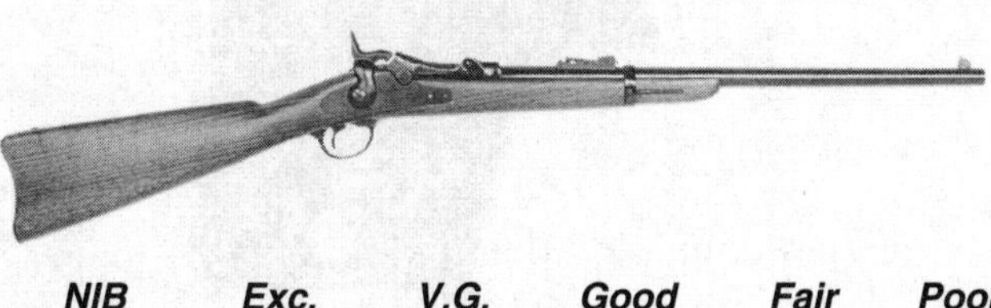

NIB	Exc.	V.G.	Good	Fair	Poor
995	800	625	—	—	—

Springfield Trapdoor Officer's Model

This is the Officer's version of the Springfield Trapdoor model. Chambered for .45-70.

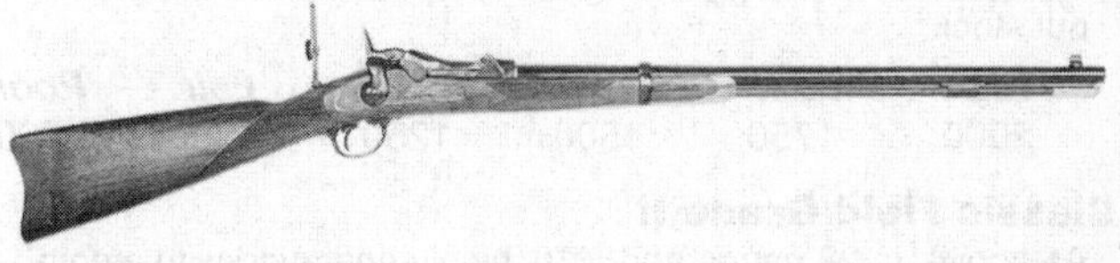

NIB	Exc.	V.G.	Good	Fair	Poor
1150	900	775	—	—	—

CLAPP, HOFFMAN & CO. CLAPP, GATES & CO. RIFLES

Alamance, North Carolina

Overall length: Types I, II, & III 51-1/4" to 52", Type IV varies between 46-1/2" and 51"; barrel length: Types I, II, & III 35-1/4" to 36", Type IV varies between 31-1/4" and 35-7/8"; caliber: Types I, II, & III .50, Type IV .577; markings: none. Despite the absence of makers marks, the Clapp, Gates & Co. products are readily distinguished by their part-round, part-octagonal (octagonal section on Types I to III, about 4" long, 4-3/4" to 5-1/2" on Type IV rifles) barrels having only a slightly raised bolster projecting from the upper right quarter. This small bolster accommodates the boxlock that distinguished the first 100 rifles produced. This gave way to a standard percussion lock on subsequent production, which required that the hammer bend sharply to the left to strike the cone. Type I and Type II rifles were adapted to a "footprint" saber bayonet lug on the right side of the barrel; Types III and IV also had a saber bayonet lug on the right side of the barrel but of the standard pattern. Types III and IV are distinguished by their caliber, the former being .50, the latter .577. Prices reflect Type II through IV production; Type I (while extant) has never been offered for sale and would presumably bring a significantly higher premium.

Exc.	V.G.	Good	Fair	Poor
—	—	32500	15000	3000

CLARK, F. H.

Memphis, Tennessee

Pocket Pistol

A .41 caliber single-shot percussion pistol with a 3.5" to 5" barrel, German silver mounts and end cap, and the barrel is stamped "F.H. Clark & Co./Memphis." Manufactured in the 1850s and 1860s.

Exc.	V.G.	Good	Fair	Poor
—	—	4250	1750	500

CLASSIC DOUBLES

Tochigi City, Japan

Importer of the Japanese shotgun formerly imported by Winchester as the Model 101 and Model 23. These models were discontinued by Winchester in 1987.

Model 201 Classic

A 12 or 20 gauge boxlock double-barrel shotgun with 26" ventilated-rib barrels, screw-in choke tubes single-selective trigger and automatic ejectors. Blued with checkered walnut stock and beavertail forearm.

NIB	Exc.	V.G.	Good	Fair	Poor
2400	1950	1700	1500	1250	900

Model 201 Small Bore Set

As above, with a smaller receiver and two sets of barrels chambered for 28 gauge and .410. The barrels are 28" in length.

NIB	Exc.	V.G.	Good	Fair	Poor
3850	3200	2750	2250	1750	1250

Model 101 Classic Field Grade I

A 12 or 20 gauge Over/Under shotgun with 25.5" or 28" ventilated-rib barrels, screw-in choke tubes, automatic ejectors and a single-selective trigger. Engraved, blued with checkered walnut stock.

NIB	Exc.	V.G.	Good	Fair	Poor
2000	1750	1500	1250	1000	700

Classic Field Grade II

As above, in 28 gauge and .410, highly engraved with a coin-finished receiver and a deluxe walnut stock with a round knob pistol grip and fleur-de-lis checkering.

NIB	Exc.	V.G.	Good	Fair	Poor
2500	2000	1750	1500	1250	900

Classic Sporter

As above, in 12 gauge only with 28" or 30" barrels, ventilated rib and screw-in choke tubes. The frame is coin-finished with light engraving and a matted upper surface to reduce glare. The stock is select walnut. This model was designed for sporting clays.

NIB	Exc.	V.G.	Good	Fair	Poor
2250	1800	1500	1250	1000	700

Waterfowl Model

As above with 30" barrels, 3" chambers, vent-rib, and screw-in choke tubes. The overall finish is a subdued matte with light engraving.

NIB	Exc.	V.G.	Good	Fair	Poor
1650	1350	1000	850	650	500

Classic Trap Over-and-Under

Designed for competition trap shooting with 30" or 32" barrels, a ventilated center and top rib, automatic ejectors, screw-in choke tubes, and a single trigger. Blued with light engraving and a walnut stock in straight or Monte Carlo style.

NIB	Exc.	V.G.	Good	Fair	Poor
2250	1750	1500	1250	1000	700

Classic Trap Single

As above, with a single 32" or 34" barrel.

NIB	Exc.	V.G.	Good	Fair	Poor
2250	1800	1500	1250	1000	700

Classic Trap Combo

As above, with a single barrel and a set of over-and-under barrels.

NIB	Exc.	V.G.	Good	Fair	Poor
3000	2500	2000	1750	1250	1000

Classic Skeet

As above, with 27.5" barrels.

NIB	Exc.	V.G.	Good	Fair	Poor
2250	1750	1500	1250	1000	700

Classic Skeet 4 Gauge Set

As above, furnished with four sets of barrels chambered for 12, 20, 28 gauge, and .410.

NIB	Exc.	V.G.	Good	Fair	Poor
3700	3000	2500	2250	1850	1500

REMINDER

An "N/A" or "—" instead of a price indicates that there is no known price available for that gun in that condition, or the sales for that particular model are so few that a reliable price cannot be given.

CLEMENT, CHAS.

Liege, Belgium

Model 1903

A 5.5mm Glisenti caliber semi-automatic pistol. Barrel raises at the muzzle to begin the loading procedure.

Courtesy James Rankin

Exc.	V.G.	Good	Fair	Poor
500	400	275	200	100

Model 1907

As above, but in 6.35mm and 7.65mm caliber.

Courtesy Orvel Reichert

Exc.	V.G.	Good	Fair	Poor
450	375	300	200	100

Model 1908

Similar to the Model 1907 but with the magazine release at the bottom of the frame. Fitted with a larger grip.

Courtesy J.B. Wood

Exc.	V.G.	Good	Fair	Poor
500	400	250	175	100

Model 1909

A semi-automatic pistol in 6.35mm and 7.65mm calibers. Similar to the Model 1908 but with barrel and chamber housing in one piece.

Courtesy James Rankin

Exc.	V.G.	Good	Fair	Poor
500	400	250	175	100

Model 1910

Redesigned version of the above with the barrel and housing all one piece. This unit is held in position by the trigger guard.

Courtesy Orvel Reichert

Courtesy Orvel Reichert

Exc.	V.G.	Good	Fair	Poor
500	400	350	300	250

Model 1912

A 6.35mm caliber semi-automatic pistol marked "Clement's Patent"; others, "Model 1912 Brevet 243839." This model is quite different from earlier Clement models.

Courtesy James Rankin

Exc.	V.G.	Good	Fair	Poor
350	250	200	150	100

American Model

Revolver copy of the Colt Police Positive. It was chambered for .38 caliber.

Exc.	V.G.	Good	Fair	Poor
350	250	200	125	90

CLERKE PRODUCTS

Santa Monica, California

Hi-Wall

A copy of the Winchester Model 1885 High Wall rifle with the action activated by a lever, and the receiver is case colored. This rifle is chambered for almost all of the modern calibers and features a 26" barrel and a walnut stock with a pistol grip and a schnabel forend. It was manufactured between 1972 and 1974.

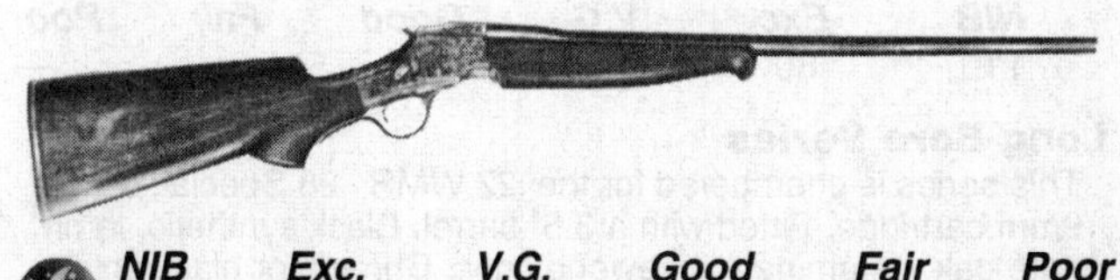

NIB	Exc.	V.G.	Good	Fair	Poor
900	800	625	425	300	200

Deluxe Hi-Wall

As above, with a half-round/half-octagonal barrel, select walnut stock, and a recoil pad. It was manufactured between 1972 and 1974.

NIB	Exc.	V.G.	Good	Fair	Poor
1000	900	725	525	400	250

COBRA ENTERPRISES, INC.

Salt Lake City, Utah

DERRINGERS

Standard Series

Offered chambered in .22 LR, .22 WMR, .25 ACP, and .32 ACP. Over-and-under barrels are 2.4". Pearl or laminate wood grips. Weight is about 9.5 oz. grips. Introduced in 2002.

NIB	Exc.	V.G.	Good	Fair	Poor
90	70	50	—	—	—

Big Bore Series

Chambered for the .22 WMR, .32 H&R Mag., and the .38 Special. Barrel length is 2.75". Choice of black synthetic, laminate oak, or laminate rosewood grips. Chrome or black finish. Weight is about 14 oz.

NIB	Exc.	V.G.	Good	Fair	Poor
110	80	50	—	—	—

Long Bore Series

This series is chambered for the .22 WMR, .38 Special, or the 9mm cartridge. Fitted with a 3.5" barrel. Black synthetic, laminate oak, or laminate rosewood grips. Chrome or black finish. Weight is about 16 oz.

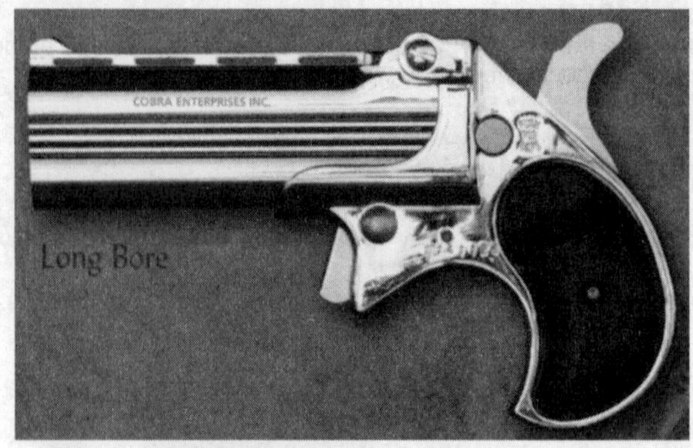

NIB	Exc.	V.G.	Good	Fair	Poor
110	80	50	—	—	—

SEMI-AUTO PISTOLS

C-32/C-380

Chambered for the .32 ACP or .380 cartridges. Fitted with a 2.8" barrel. Chrome or black finish. Magazine capacity is 5 rounds for the .380 and 6 rounds for the .32 ACP. Weight is about 22 oz.

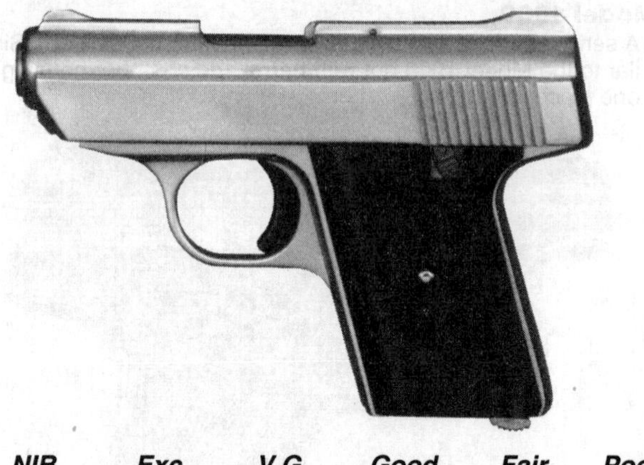

NIB	Exc.	V.G.	Good	Fair	Poor
100	80	—	—	—	—

C-9mm

This is a double-action-only pistol chambered for the 9mm cartridge. Fitted with a 3.3" barrel. Magazine capacity is 10 rounds. Load indicator. Polymer grips. Weight is about 21 oz.

NIB	Exc.	V.G.	Good	Fair	Poor
130	100	—	—	—	—

Patriot .45

This is double-action-only pistol chambered for the .45 ACP cartridge. Barrel length is 3". Frame is black polymer. Slide is stainless steel. Magazine capacity is 6 rounds. Weight is about 20 oz.

NIB	Exc.	V.G.	Good	Fair	Poor
250	200	—	—	—	—

COBRAY INDUSTRIES

S.W.D., Inc.
Atlanta, Georgia

M-11 Pistol

A 9mm caliber semi-automatic pistol. It fires from the closed bolt and is made of steel stampings with a parkerized finish. It is patterned after, though a good deal smaller than, the Ingram Mac 10. It is currently out of production and difficult to accurately price. If purchase or sale is contemplated, please check local values.

Exc.	V.G.	Good	Fair	Poor
300	200	150	100	75

NOTE: Add $70 for stainless steel. Add $150 for pre-ban models.

M-12

Same as above but chambered for the .380 ACP cartridge.

Exc.	V.G.	Good	Fair	Poor
300	200	150	100	75

NOTE: Add $150 for pre-ban models.

TM-11 Carbine

As above in 9mm caliber, with a 16.25" shrouded barrel and a telescoping metal shoulder stock.

Exc.	V.G.	Good	Fair	Poor
350	250	200	150	100

TM-12 Carbine

As above but chambered for the .380 ACP cartridge.

Exc.	V.G.	Good	Fair	Poor
350	250	200	150	100

Terminator Shotgun

A single-shot 12 or 20 gauge shotgun that fires from an open bolt position. The cocked bolt is released to slam home on the shell when the trigger is pulled. The 18" barrel is cylinder bored. There is a telescoping wire stock and the finish is Parkerized.

Exc.	V.G.	Good	Fair	Poor
175	125	80	60	40

COCHRAN TURRET

C. B. Allen
Springfield, Massachusetts

Under Hammer Turret Rifle

A .36 or .40 caliber percussion radial cylinder rifle with 31" or 32" octagonal barrels and walnut stocks. The barrel marked "Cochrans/Many/Chambered/&/Non Recoil/Rifle" and the top strap "C.B. Allen / Springfield." These rifles were produced in the variations listed. Manufactured during the late 1830s and 1840s.

1st Type

Fitted with a circular top strap secured by two screws. Serial numbered from 1 to approximately 30.

Exc.	V.G.	Good	Fair	Poor
—	—	12000	5000	1500

2nd Type

Fitted with a rectangular hinged top strap, the locking catch of which serves as the rear sight. Serial numbered from approximately 31 to 155.

Exc.	V.G.	Good	Fair	Poor
—	—	10500	4000	1500

3rd Type

As above, with a smaller hammer and a plain trigger guard.

Exc.	V.G.	Good	Fair	Poor
—	—	10500	4000	1500

Pistol

Action similar to above with 4" to 7" barrels.

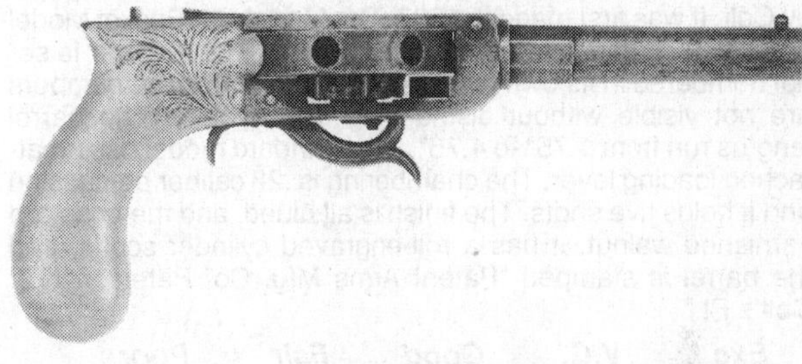

Exc.	V.G.	Good	Fair	Poor
—	—	16000	7000	2000

CODY, MICHAEL & SONS

Nashville, Tennessee

Received a contract with the State of Tennessee for "Mississippi" rifles with brass patchboxes in late 1861. Barrel length 36"; caliber .54. Cody often used reworked Model 1817 Rifle barrels and sporting pattern single screw lockplates. Rifles are unmarked except for large engraved serial number on top of breech plug tang.

Exc.	V.G.	Good	Fair	Poor
—	—	25000	10000	1500

COFER, T. W.

Portsmouth, Virginia

Cofer Navy Revolver

A .36 caliber spur trigger percussion revolver with a 7.5" octagonal barrel and 6-shot cylinder. The top strap is marked "T.W. Cofer's/Patent." and the barrel "Portsmouth, Va." This revolver was manufactured in limited quantities during the Civil War.

Exc.	V.G.	Good	Fair	Poor
—	—	100000	35000	5000

COGSWELL

London, England

Cogswell Pepperbox Pistol

A .47 caliber 6-shot percussion pepperbox with case hardened barrels, German silver frame and walnut grips. Normally marked "B. Cogswell, 224 Strand, London" and "Improved Revolving Pistol."

Exc.	V.G.	Good	Fair	Poor
—	—	3500	1250	750

COGSWELL & HARRISON, LTD.

London, England

SEE—British Double Guns

COLT'S PATENT FIRE ARMS MANUFACTURING COMPANY

Hartford, Connecticut

COLT PATERSON MODELS

Pocket or Baby Paterson Model No. 1

The Paterson was the first production revolver manufactured by Colt. It was first made in 1837. The Model 1 or Pocket Model is the most diminutive of the Paterson line. The revolver is serial numbered in its own range, #1 through #500. The numbers are not visible without dismantling the revolver. The barrel lengths run from 1.75" to 4.75". The standard model has no attached loading lever. The chambering is .28 caliber percussion and it holds five shots. The finish is all blued, and the grips are varnished walnut. It has a roll-engraved cylinder scene, and the barrel is stamped "Patent Arms Mfg. Co. Paterson N.J. Colt's Pt."

Exc.	V.G.	Good	Fair	Poor
—	—	30000	12500	—

Belt Model Paterson No. 2

The Belt Model Paterson is a larger revolver with a straight-grip and an octagonal barrel that is 2.5" to 5.5" in length. It is chambered for .31 caliber percussion and holds five shots. The finish is all blued, with varnished walnut grips and no attached loading lever. It has a roll-engraved cylinder scene, and the barrel is stamped "Patent Arms Mfg. Co. Paterson N.J. Colt's Pt." The serial number range is #1-#850 and is shared with the #3 Belt Model. It was made from 1837-1840.

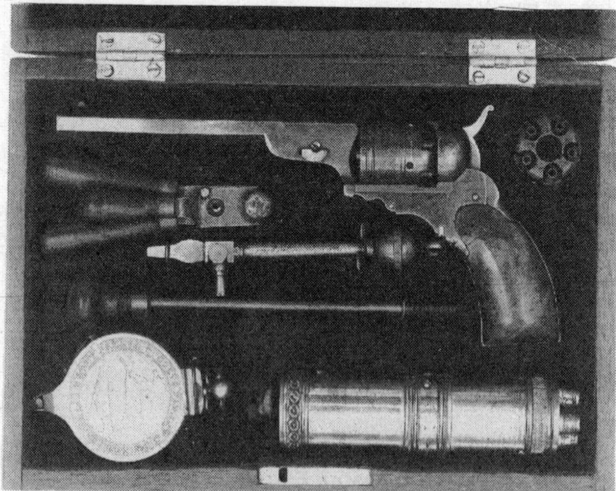

Courtesy Buffalo Bill Historical Center, Cody, Wyoming

Exc.	V.G.	Good	Fair	Poor
—	—	50000	20000	—

Belt Model Paterson No. 3

This revolver is quite similar to the Model #2 except that the grips are curved outward at the bottom to form a more handfilling configuration. They are serial numbered in the same #1-#850 range. Some attached loading levers have been noted on this model, but they are extremely rare and would add approximately 35 percent to the value.

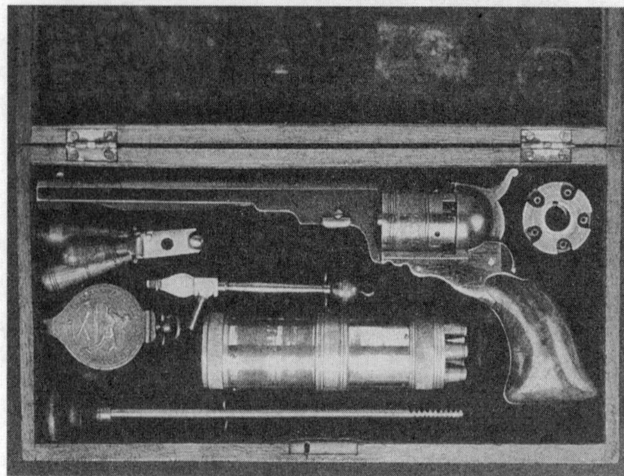

Exc.	V.G.	Good	Fair	Poor
—	—	75000	30000	—

Ehlers Model Pocket Paterson

John Ehlers was a major stockholder and treasurer of the Patent Arms Mfg. Co. when it went bankrupt. He seized the assets and inventory. These revolvers were Pocket Model Patersons that were not finished at the time. Ehlers had them finished and marketed them. They had an attached loading lever, and the abbreviation "Mfg Co." was deleted from the barrel stamping. There were 500 revolvers involved in the Ehlers variation totally, and they were produced from 1840-1843.

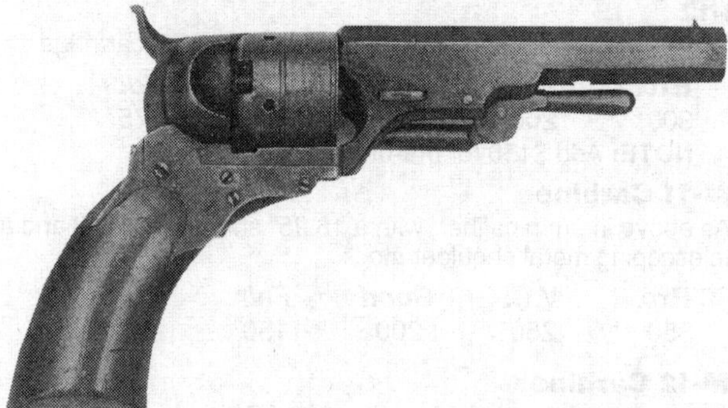

Exc.	V.G.	Good	Fair	Poor
—	—	50000	20000	—

Ehlers Belt Model Paterson

The same specifications apply to this larger revolver as they do to the Ehlers Pocket Model. It falls within the same 500 revolver involvement and is rare.

Exc.	V.G.	Good	Fair	Poor
—	—	50000	20000	—

Texas Paterson Model No. 5

This is the largest and most sought after of the Paterson models. It is also known as the Holster Model. It has been verified as actually seeing use by both the military and civilians on the American frontier. It is chambered for .36 caliber percussion, holds five shots, and has an octagonal barrel that ranges from 4" to 12" in length. It has been observed with and without the attached loading lever, but those with it are rare. The finish is blued, with a case-colored hammer. The grips are varnished walnut. The cylinder is roll-engraved; and the barrel is stamped "Patent Arms Mfg. Co. Paterson, N.J. Colts Pt." Most Texas Patersons are well used and have a worn appearance. One in excellent or V.G. condition would be highly prized. A verified

This symbol denotes "Sleepers" with rapidly-rising values and/or significant collector potential.

military model would be worth a great deal more than standard, so qualified appraisal would be essential. The serial number range is #1-#1000, and they were manufactured from 1838-1840. The attached loading lever brings approximately a 25 percent premium.

Exc.	V.G.	Good	Fair	Poor
—	—	125000	50000	—

COLT REVOLVING LONG GUNS 1837-1847

First Model Ring Lever Rifle

This was actually the first firearm manufactured by Colt; the first revolver appeared a short time later. There were 200 of the First Models made in 1837 and 1838. The octagonal barrel of the First Model is 32" long and browned, while the rest of the finish is blued. The stock is varnished walnut with a cheekpiece inlaid with Colt's trademark. The ring lever located in front of the frame is pulled to rotate the 8-shot cylinder and cock the hammer. The rifle is chambered for .34, .36, .38, .40, and .44 caliber percussion. The cylinder is roll-engraved, and the barrel is stamped "Colt's Patent/Patent Arms Mfg. Co., Paterson, N. Jersey." This model has a top strap over the cylinder. They were made both with and without an attached loading lever. The latter is worth approximately 10 percent more.

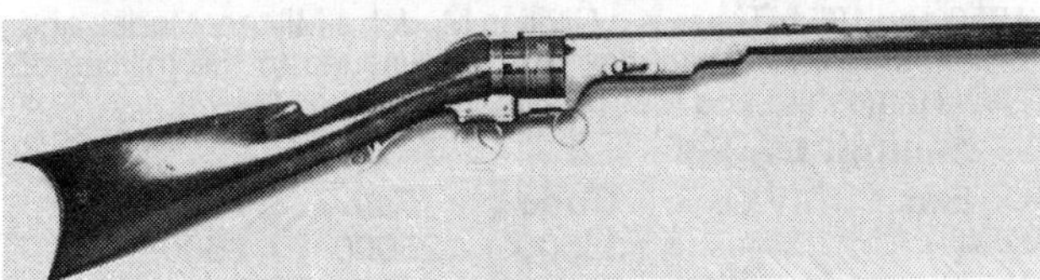

Courtesy Bonhams & Butterfields, San Francisco, California

Exc.	V.G.	Good	Fair	Poor
—	—	60000	20000	—

Second Model Ring Lever Rifle

This model is quite similar in appearance to the First Model. Its function is identical. The major difference is the absence of the top strap over the cylinder. It had no trademark stamped on the cheekpiece. The Second Model is offered with a 28" and a 32" octagonal barrel and is chambered for .44 caliber percussion, holding 8 shots. There were approximately 500 produced from 1838-1841. The presence of an attached cheekpiece would add approximately 10 percent to the value.

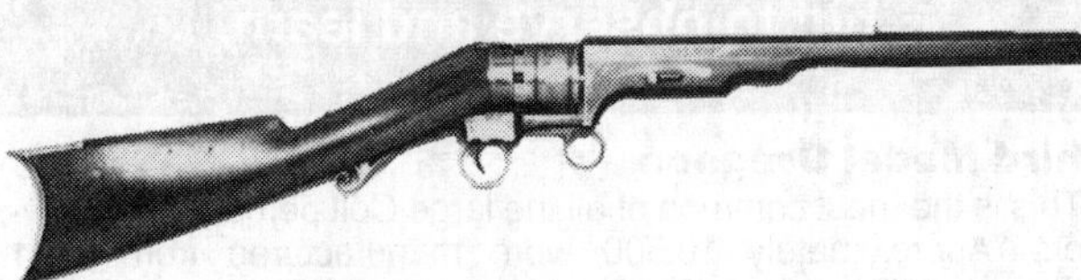

Courtesy Bonhams & Butterfields, San Francisco, California

Exc.	V.G.	Good	Fair	Poor
—	—	40000	12500	—

Model 1839 Shotgun

This model is quite similar in appearance to the 1839 Carbine. It is chambered for 16 gauge and holds six shots. It has a Damascus pattern barrel, and the most notable difference is a 3.5" (instead of a 2.5") long cylinder. There were only 225 of these made from 1839-1841. The markings are the same as on the Carbine.

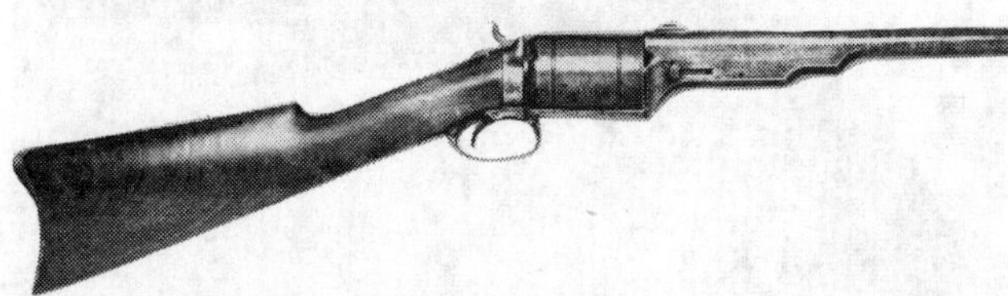

Courtesy Bonhams & Butterfields, San Francisco, California

Exc.	V.G.	Good	Fair	Poor
—	—	25000	10000	—

Model 1839 Carbine

This model has no ring but features an exposed hammer for cocking and rotating the 6-shot cylinder. It is chambered for .525 smoothbore and comes standard with a 24" round barrel. Other barrel lengths have been noted. The finish is blued, with a browned barrel and a varnished walnut stock. The cylinder is roll-engraved, and the barrel is stamped "Patent Arms Mfg. Co. Paterson, N.J.-Colt's Pt." There were 950 manufactured from 1838-1841. Later variations of this model are found with the attached loading lever standard, and earlier models without one would bring approximately 25 percent additional. There were 360 purchased by the military and stamped "WAT" on the stock. These would be worth twice what a standard model would bring.

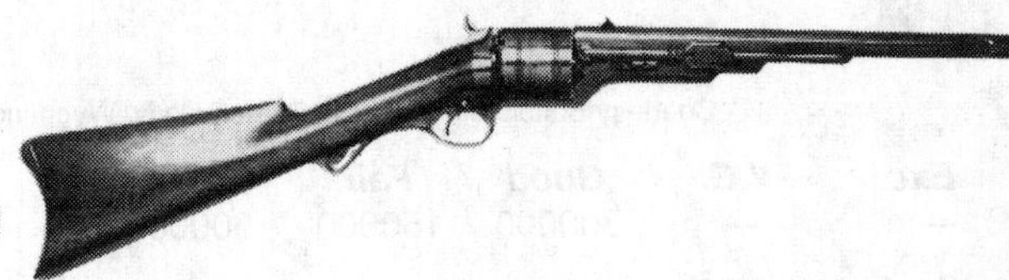

Courtesy Bonhams & Butterfields, San Francisco, California

Exc.	V.G.	Good	Fair	Poor
—	—	25000	9500	—

Model 1839/1850 Carbine

In 1848 Colt acquired a number of Model 1839 Carbines (approximately 40) from the state of Rhode Island. In an effort to make them marketable they were refinished and the majority fitted with plain cylinders (brightly polished) having integral ratchets around the arbor hole.

Barrel length 24"; caliber .525; barrel browned; cylinder polished; frame blued; furniture case hardened; walnut stock varnished.

Exc.	V.G.	Good	Fair	Poor
—	—	35000	12500	—

Model 1854 Russian Contract Musket

In 1854 Colt purchased a large number of U.S. Model 1822 flintlock muskets that the company altered to percussion cap ignition and rifled. The reworked muskets are dated 1854 on the barrel tang and at the rear of the lockplate. In most instances the original manufactory marks, such as Springfield or Harpers Ferry at the rear of the lockplate, have been removed, while the U.S. and eagle between the hammer and bolster remain. The percussion nipple bolster is marked COLT'S PATENT. Some examples have been noted with the date 1858.

Barrel length 42"; caliber .69; lock and furniture burnished bright; walnut stock oil finished.

Exc.	V.G.	Good	Fair	Poor
—	—	4000	1500	750

Breech-loading examples made in two styles are also known. Production of this variation is believed to have only taken place on an experimental basis.

Exc.	V.G.	Good	Fair	Poor
—	—	6500	2500	1000

COLT WALKER-DRAGOON MODELS

Hartford, Connecticut

Walker Model Revolver

The Walker is a massive revolver. It weighs 4 lbs., 9 oz. and has a 9" part-round/part-octagonal barrel. The cylinder holds six shots and is chambered for .44 caliber percussion. There were 1,000 Walker Colts manufactured in 1847, and nearly all of them saw extremely hard use. Originally this model had a roll-engraved cylinder, military inspection marks, and barrel stamping that read "Address Saml. Colt-New York City." Practically all examples noted have had these markings worn or rusted beyond recognition. Because the Walker is perhaps the most desirable and sought-after Colt from a collector's standpoint and because of the extremely high value of a Walker in any condition, qualified appraisal is definitely recommended. These revolvers were serial numbered A, B, C, and D Company 1-220, and E Company 1-120.

Courtesy Buffalo Bill Historical Center, Cody, Wyoming

Exc.	V.G.	Good	Fair	Poor
—	—	300000	150000	50000

Civilian Walker Revolver

This model is identical to the military model but has no martial markings. They are found serial numbered 1001 through 1100.

Exc.	V.G.	Good	Fair	Poor
—	—	300000	150000	50000

Whitneyville Hartford Dragoon

This is a large, 6-shot, .44 caliber percussion revolver. It has a 7.5" part-round/part-octagonal barrel. The frame, hammer, and loading lever are case colored. The remainder is blued, with a brass trigger guard and varnished walnut grips. There were only 240 made in late 1847. The serial numbers run from 1100-1340. This model is often referred to as a Transitional Walker. Some of the parts used in its manufacture were left over from the Walker production run. This model has a roll-engraved cylinder scene, and the barrel is stamped "Address Saml. Colt New York-City." This is an extremely rare model.

Exc.	V.G.	Good	Fair	Poor
—	—	60000	35000	18500

Walker Replacement Dragoon

This extremely rare Colt (300 produced) is sometimes referred to as the "Fluck" in memory of the gentleman who first identified it as a distinct and separate model. They were produced by Colt as replacements to the military for Walkers that were no longer fit for service due to mechanical failures. They were large, 6-shot, .44 caliber percussion revolvers with 7.5" part-round/part-octagonal barrels. Serial numbers ran from 2216 to 2515. The frame, hammer, and loading lever are case-colored; the remainder, blued, The grips, which are longer than other Dragoons and similar to the Walkers, are of varnished walnut and bear the inspectors mark "WAT" inside an oval cartouche on one side and the letters "JH" on the other. The frame is stamped "Colt's/ Patent/U.S." The letter "P" appears on various parts of the gun.

Exc.	V.G.	Good	Fair	Poor
—	—	45000	25000	6000

First Model Dragoon

Another large, 6-shot, .44 caliber percussion revolver. It has a 7.5" part-round/part-octagonal barrel. The frame, hammer, and loading lever are case colored; the remainder, blued with a brass grip frame and square backed trigger guard. The trigger guard is silver-plated on the Civilian Model only. Another distinguishing feature on the First Model is the oval cylinder stop notches. The serial number range is 1341-8000. There were approximately 5,000 made. The cylinder is roll-engraved; and the barrel stampings read "Address Saml. Colt, New York City." "Colt's Patent" appears on the frame. On Military Models the letters "U.S." also appear on the frame.

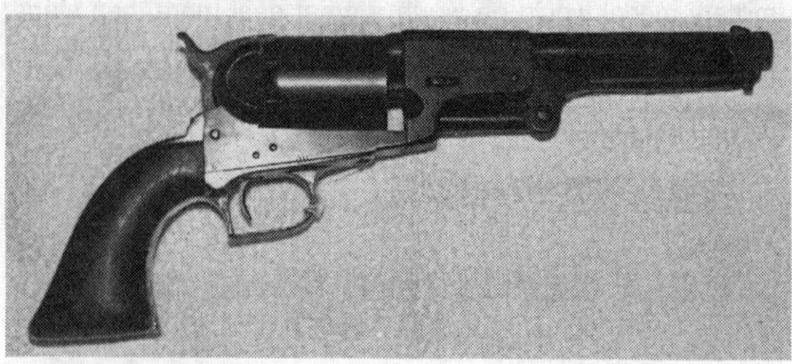

Military Model

Exc.	V.G.	Good	Fair	Poor
—	—	40000	20000	3500

Civilian Model

Exc.	V.G.	Good	Fair	Poor
—	—	35000	18000	3000

Second Model Dragoon

Most of the improvements that distinguish this model from the First Model are internal and not readily apparent. The most obvious external change is the rectangular cylinder-stop notches. This model is serial numbered from 8000-10700, for a total production of approximately 2,700 revolvers manufactured in 1850 and 1851. There is a Civilian Model, a Military Model, and an extremely rare variation that was issued to the militias of New Hampshire and Massachusetts (marked "MS.").

Civilian Model

Exc.	V.G.	Good	Fair	Poor
—	—	35000	25000	3500

Military Model

Exc.	V.G.	Good	Fair	Poor
—	—	40000	30000	3000

Militia Model

Exc.	V.G.	Good	Fair	Poor
—	—	45000	30000	3000

REMINDER
Go to gun shows, not just to buy or sell, but to observe and learn.

Third Model Dragoon

This is the most common of all the large Colt percussion revolvers. Approximately 10,500 were manufactured from 1851 through 1861. It is quite similar in appearance to the Second Model, and the most obvious external difference is the round trigger guard. The Third Model Dragoon was the first Colt revolver available with a detachable shoulder stock. There are three basic types of stocks, and all are quite rare as only 1,250 were produced. There are two other major variations we will note—the "C.L." Dragoon, which was a militia-issued model and is rare, and the late-issue model with an 8" barrel. These are found over serial number 18000, and only 50 were produced.

Courtesy Buffalo Bill Historical Center, Cody, Wyoming

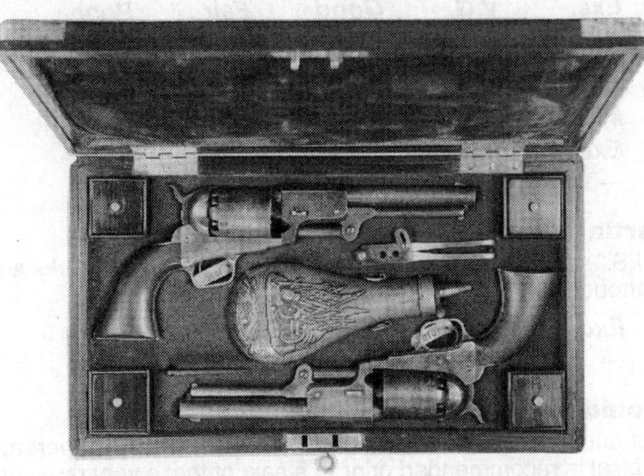

Courtesy Buffalo Bill Historical Center, Cody, Wyoming

Civilian Model

Exc.	V.G.	Good	Fair	Poor
—	—	27500	15000	2500

Military Model

Exc.	V.G.	Good	Fair	Poor
—	—	30000	17500	3000

Shoulder Stock Cut Revolvers

Exc.	V.G.	Good	Fair	Poor
—	—	35000	20000	3000

Shoulder Stocks

Exc.	V.G.	Good	Fair	Poor
—	15000	8000	4000	2000

C.L. Dragoon

Hand engraved, not stamped.

Exc.	V.G.	Good	Fair	Poor
—	—	57500	17500	3000

8" Barrel Late Issue

Exc.	V.G.	Good	Fair	Poor
—	—	42500	25000	3000

Hartford English Dragoon

This is a variation of the Third Model Dragoon. The only notable differences are the British proofmarks and the distinct #1-#700 serial number range. Other than these two features, the description given for the Third Model would apply. These revolvers were manufactured in Hartford but were finished at Colt's London factory from 1853-1857. Some bear the hand-engraved barrel marking "Col. Colt London." Many of the English Dragoons were elaborately engraved, and individual appraisal would be a must. Two hundred revolvers came back to America in 1861 to be used in the Civil War.

Exc.	V.G.	Good	Fair	Poor
—	—	25000	12000	3000

Model 1848 Baby Dragoon

This is a small, 5-shot, .31 caliber percussion revolver. It has an octagonal barrel in lengths of 3", 4", 5", and 6". Most were made without an attached loading lever, although some with loading levers have been noted. The frame, hammer, and loading lever (when present) are case colored; the barrel and cylinder, blued. The grip frame and trigger guard are silver-plated brass. There were approximately 15,500 manufactured between 1847 and 1850. The serial range is between 1-5500. The barrels are stamped "Address Saml. Colt/New York City." Some have been noted with the barrel address inside brackets. The frame is marked "Colt's/Patent." The first 10,000 revolvers have the Texas Ranger/Indian roll-engraved cylinder scene; the later guns the stagecoach holdup scene. This is a popular model, and many fakes have been noted.

Texas Ranger/Indian Scene

Exc.	V.G.	Good	Fair	Poor
—	—	12000	6500	2000

NOTE: Attached loading lever add 15 percent.

Courtesy Bonhams & Butterfields, San Francisco, California

Courtesy Bonhams & Butterfields, San Francisco, California

Stagecoach Holdup Scene

Exc.	V.G.	Good	Fair	Poor
—	—	13000	7000	2000

Model 1849 Pocket Revolver

This is a small, either 5- or 6-shot, .31 caliber percussion revolver. It has an octagonal barrel 3", 4", 5", or 6" in length. Most had loading gates, but some did not. The frame, hammer, and loading lever are case colored; the cylinder and barrel are blued. The grip frame and round trigger guard are made of brass and are silver plated. There are both large and small trigger guard variations noted. This is the most plentiful of all the Colt percussion revolvers, with approximately 325,000 manufactured over a 23-year period, 1850-1873. There are over 200 variations of this model, and one should consult an expert for individual appraisals. There are many fine publications specializing in the field of Colt percussion revolvers that would be helpful in the identification of the variations. The values represented here are for the standard model.

Courtesy Rock Island Auction Company

Exc.	V.G.	Good	Fair	Poor
—	—	1800	1200	300

London Model 1849 Pocket Revolver

Identical in configuration to the standard 1849 Pocket Revolver, the London-made models have a higher quality finish and their own serial number range, 1-11000. They were manufactured from 1853 through 1857. They feature a roll-engraved cylinder scene, and the barrels are stamped "Address Col. Colt/London." The first 265 revolvers, known as early models, have brass grip frames and small round trigger guards. They are quite rare and worth approximately 50 percent more than the standard model that has a steel grip frame and large oval trigger guard.

Exc.	*V.G.*	*Good*	*Fair*	*Poor*
—	—	1800	1200	300

Model 1851 Navy Revolver

This is undoubtedly the most popular revolver Colt produced in the medium size and power range. It is a 6-shot, .36-caliber percussion revolver with a 7.5" octagonal barrel. It has an attached loading lever. The basic model has a case colored frame hammer, and loading lever, with silver-plated brass grip frame and trigger guard. The grips are varnished walnut. Colt manufactured approximately 215,000 of these fine revolvers between 1850 and 1873. The basic Navy features a roll-engraved cylinder scene of a battle between the navies of Texas and Mexico. There are three distinct barrel stampings—serial number 1-74000, "Address Saml. Colt New York City"; serial number 74001-101000 "Address Saml. Colt. Hartford, Ct."; and serial number 101001-215000 "Address Saml. Colt New York U.S. America." The left side of the frame is stamped "Colt's/Patent" on all variations. This model is also available with a detached shoulder stock, and values for the stocks today are nearly as high as for the revolver itself. Careful appraisal should be secured before purchase. The number of variations within the 1851 Navy model designation makes it necessary to read specialized text available on the subject.

Square Back Trigger Guard, 1st Model, Serial #1-1000

Courtesy Rock Island Auction Company

Exc.	*V.G.*	*Good*	*Fair*	*Poor*
—	—	35000	25000	5500

Square Back Trigger Guard, 2nd Model, Serial #1001-4200

Exc.	*V.G.*	*Good*	*Fair*	*Poor*
—	—	25000	10000	2500

Small Round Trigger Guard, Serial #4201-85000

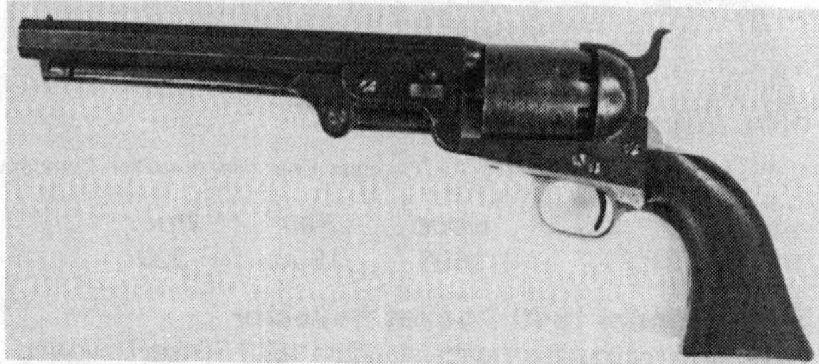

Courtesy Milwaukee Public Museum, Milwaukee, Wisconsin

Exc.	*V.G.*	*Good*	*Fair*	*Poor*
—	—	5000	2500	500

Large Round Trigger Guard, Serial #85001-215000

Exc.	*V.G.*	*Good*	*Fair*	*Poor*
—	—	4500	2200	500

Martial Model

"U.S." stamped on the left side of frame; inspector's marks and cartouche on the grips.

Exc.	*V.G.*	*Good*	*Fair*	*Poor*
—	—	12000	4000	1000

Shoulder Stock Variations

1st and 2nd Model Revolver cut for stock only. An expert appraisal is recommended prior to a sale of these very rare variations.

Stock Only

Exc.	*V.G.*	*Good*	*Fair*	*Poor*
—	—	8000	4000	1250

3rd Model Cut For Stock

Revolver only.

Exc.	*V.G.*	*Good*	*Fair*	*Poor*
—	—	9500	4000	1250

Stock

Exc.	*V.G.*	*Good*	*Fair*	*Poor*
—	—	7000	3750	1000

London Model 1851 Navy Revolver

These revolvers are physically similar to the U.S.-made model with the exception of the barrel address, which reads "Address Col. Colt. London." There are also British proofmarks stamped on the barrel and cylinder. There were 42,000 made between 1853 and 1857. They have their own serial number range, #1-#42,000. There are two major variations of the London Navy, and again a serious purchaser would be well advised to seek qualified appraisal as fakes have been noted.

1st Model

Serial #1-#2,000 with a small round brass trigger guard and grip frame. Squareback guard worth a 40 percent premium.

Exc.	*V.G.*	*Good*	*Fair*	*Poor*
—	—	4250	1750	700

2nd Model

Serial #2,001-#42,000, steel grip frame, and large round trigger guard.

Exc.	*V.G.*	*Good*	*Fair*	*Poor*
—	—	4000	1500	600

Hartford Manufactured Variation

Serial numbers in the 42,000 range.

Exc.	*V.G.*	*Good*	*Fair*	*Poor*
—	—	4500	3000	600

COLT SIDE HAMMER MODELS

Model 1855 Side Hammer "Root" Pocket Revolver

The "Root," as it is popularly known, was the only solid-frame revolver Colt ever made. It has a spur trigger and walnut grips, and the hammer is mounted on the right side of the frame. The standard finish is a case colored frame, hammer, and loading lever, with the barrel and cylinder blued. It is chambered for both .28 caliber and .31 caliber percussion. Each caliber has its own serial number range—1-30000 for the .28 caliber and 1-14000 for the .31 caliber. The model consists of seven basic variations, and the serious student should avail himself of the fine publications dealing with this model in depth. Colt produced the Side Hammer Root from 1855-1870.

Models 1 and 1A Serial #1-384
3.5" octagonal barrel, .28 caliber, roll-engraved cylinder, Hartford barrel address without pointing hand.

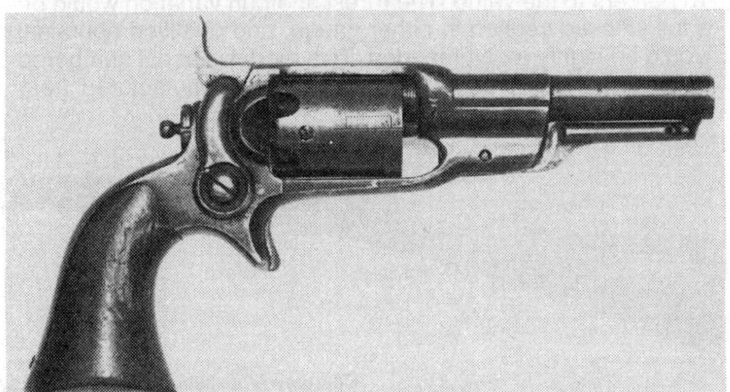
Courtesy Milwaukee Public Museum, Milwaukee, Wisconsin

Exc.	V.G.	Good	Fair	Poor
—	—	6000	3500	1200

Model 2 Serial #476-25000
Same as Model 1 with pointing hand barrel address.

Exc.	V.G.	Good	Fair	Poor
—	—	1800	1200	500

Model 3 Serial #25001-30000
Same as the Model 2 with a full fluted cylinder.

Exc.	V.G.	Good	Fair	Poor
—	—	1800	1200	500

Model 3A and 4 Serial #1-2400
.31 caliber, 3.5" barrel, Hartford address, full fluted cylinder.

Exc.	V.G.	Good	Fair	Poor
—	—	2500	1500	600

Model 5 Serial #2401-8000
.31 caliber, 3.5" round barrel, address "Col. Colt New York."

Exc.	V.G.	Good	Fair	Poor
—	—	1800	1200	500

Model 5A Serial #2401-8000
Same as Model 5 with a 4.5" barrel.

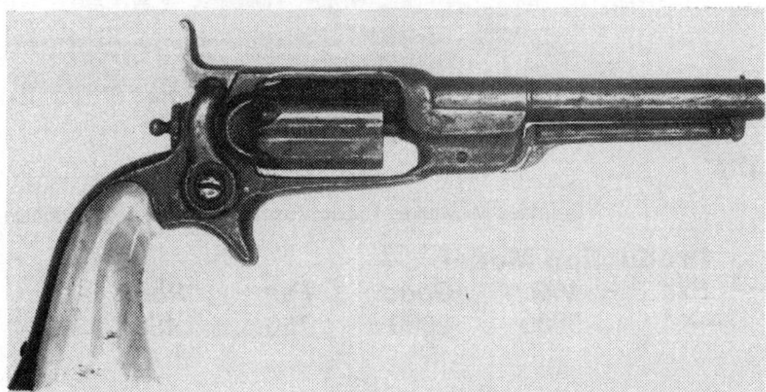
Courtesy Milwaukee Public Museum, Milwaukee, Wisconsin

Exc.	V.G.	Good	Fair	Poor
—	—	3200	1600	600

Models 6 and 6A Serial #8001-11074
Same as Model 5 and 5A with roll-engraved cylinder scene.

Exc.	V.G.	Good	Fair	Poor
—	—	1800	1200	500

Models 7 and 7A Serial #11075-14000
Same as Models 6 and 6A with a screw holding in the cylinder pin.

Exc.	V.G.	Good	Fair	Poor
—	—	3500	2200	800

COLT SIDE HAMMER LONG GUNS

1855 Sporting Rifle, 1st Model
This is a 6-shot revolving rifle chambered for .36 caliber percussion. It comes with a 21", 24", 27", or 30" round barrel that is part octagonal where it joins the frame. The stock is walnut with either an oil or a varnish finish. The frame, hammer, and loading lever are case colored; the rest of the metal, blued. The hammer is on the right side of the frame. The 1st Model has no forend, and an oiling device is attached to the barrel underlug. The trigger guard has two spur-like projections in front and in back of the bow. The roll-engraved cylinder scene depicts a hunter shooting at five deer and is found only on this model. The standard stampings are " Colt's Pt./1856" and "Address S. Colt Hartford, Ct. U.S.A."

Early Model
Low serial numbers with a hand-engraved barrel marking "Address S. Colt Hartford, U.S.A."

Exc.	V.G.	Good	Fair	Poor
—	—	15000	5500	1500

Production Model

Exc.	V.G.	Good	Fair	Poor
—	—	12000	3000	1000

1855 1st Model Carbine
Identical to the 1st Model Rifle but offered with a 15" and 18" barrel.

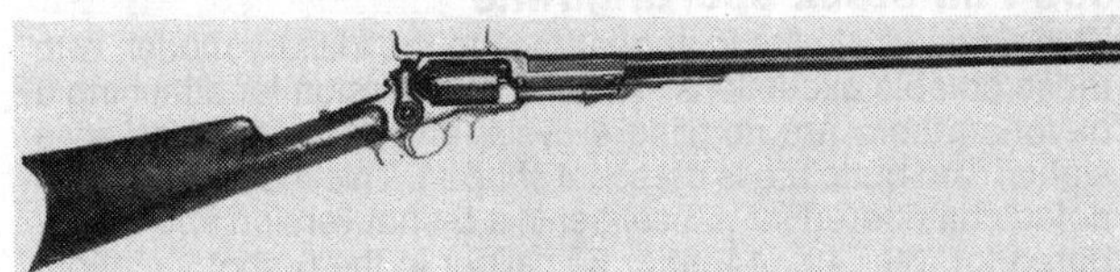
Courtesy Milwaukee Public Museum, Milwaukee, Wisconsin

Exc.	V.G.	Good	Fair	Poor
—	—	9500	3000	1000

1855 Half Stock Sporting Rifle
Although this rifle is quite similar in appearance and finish to the 1st Model, there are some notable differences. It features a walnut forend that protrudes halfway down the barrel. There are two types of trigger guards—a short projectionless one or a long model with a graceful scroll. There is a 6-shot model chambered for .36 or .44 caliber or a 5-shot model chambered for .56 caliber. The cylinder is fully fluted. The markings are "Colt's Pt/1856" and "Address Col. Colt/Hartford Ct. U.S.A." There were approximately 1,500 manufactured between 1857 and 1864.

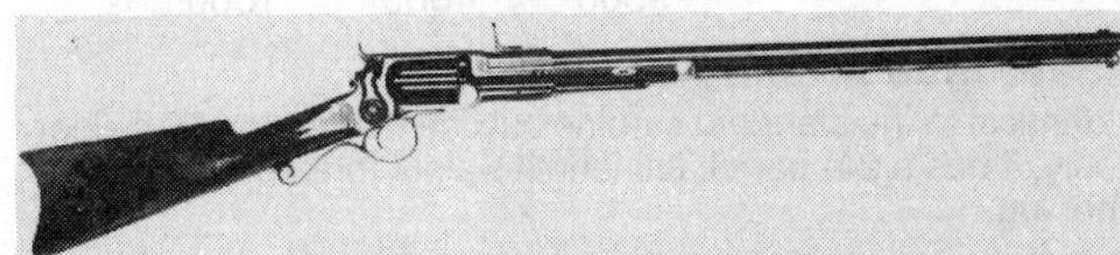
Courtesy Milwaukee Public Museum, Milwaukee, Wisconsin

Exc.	V.G.	Good	Fair	Poor
—	—	9500	3500	1000

1855 Full Stock Military Rifle
This model holds 6 shots in its .44 caliber chambering and 5 shots when chambered for .56 caliber. It is another side hammer revolving rifle that resembles the Half Stock model. The barrels are round and part-octagonal where they join the frame. They come in lengths of 21", 24", 27", 31", and 37". The hammer and loading lever are case colored; the rest of the metal parts, blued. The walnut buttstock and full length forend are oil finished, and this model has sling swivels. The cylinder is fully fluted. Military models have provisions for affixing a bayonet and military-style sights and bear the "U.S." martial mark on examples that were actually issued to the military. The standard stampings found on this model are "Colt's Pt/1856" and

"Address Col. Colt Hartford, Ct. U.S.A." There were an estimated 9,300 manufactured between 1856 and 1864.

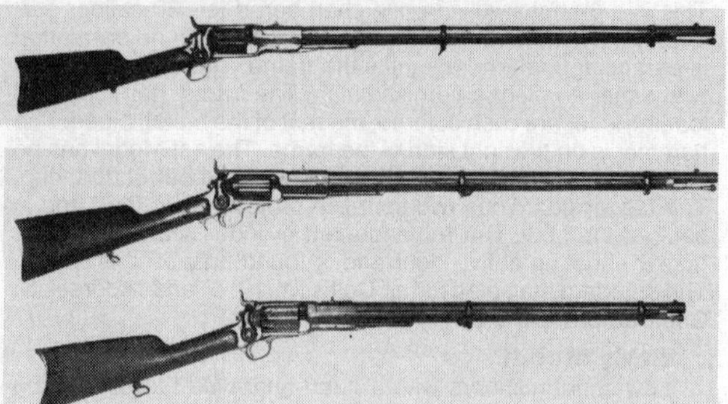

Courtesy Milwaukee Public Museum, Milwaukee, Wisconsin

Martially Marked Models

Exc.	V.G.	Good	Fair	Poor
—	—	25000	9500	2000

Without Martial Markings

Exc.	V.G.	Good	Fair	Poor
—	—	8000	3500	1000

1855 Full Stock Sporting Rifle

This model is similar in appearance to the Military model, with these notable exceptions. There is no provision for attaching a bayonet, there are no sling swivels, and it has sporting-style sights. The buttplate is crescent shaped. This model has been noted chambered for .56 caliber in a 5-shot version and chambered for .36, .40, .44, and .50 caliber in the 6-shot variation. They are quite scarce in .40 and .50 caliber and will bring a 10 percent premium. The standard markings are "Colt's Pt/1856" and "Address Col. Colt/Hartford Ct. U.S.A." Production on this model was quite limited (several hundred at most) between the years 1856 and 1864.

Exc.	V.G.	Good	Fair	Poor
—	—	10500	4000	1000

Model 1855 Revolving Carbine

This model is similar in appearance to the 1855 Military Rifle. The barrel lengths of 15", 18", and 21" plus the absence of a forend make the standard Carbine Model readily identifiable. The markings are the same. Approximately 4,400 were manufactured between 1856 and 1864.

Exc.	V.G.	Good	Fair	Poor
—	—	9500	4000	1000

Model 1855 Artillery Carbine

Identical to the standard carbine but chambered for .56 caliber only, it has a 24" barrel, full-length walnut forend, and a bayonet lug.

Exc.	V.G.	Good	Fair	Poor
—	—	17000	5500	1500

Model 1855 British Carbine

This is a British-proofed version with barrel lengths of up to 30". It has a brass trigger guard and buttplate and is chambered for .56 caliber only. This variation is usually found in the 10000-12000 serial number range.

Exc.	V.G.	Good	Fair	Poor
—	—	9000	3750	1000

Model 1855 Revolving Shotgun

This model very much resembles the Half Stock Sporting Rifle but was made with a 27", 30", 33", and 36" smoothbore barrel. It has a 5-shot cylinder chambered for .60 or .75 caliber (20 or 10 gauge). This model has a case-colored hammer and loading lever; the rest of the metal is blued, with an occasional browned barrel noted. The buttstock and forend are of walnut, either oil or varnish-finished. This model has no rear sight and a small trigger guard with the caliber stamped on it. Some have been noted with the large scroll trigger guard; these would add 10 percent to the value. The rarest shotgun variation would be a full stocked version in either gauge, and qualified appraisal would be highly recommended. This model is serial numbered in its own range, #1-#1100. They were manufactured from 1860-1863.

Courtesy Amoskeag Auction Company

.60 Caliber (20 gauge)

Exc.	V.G.	Good	Fair	Poor
—	—	8000	3500	1000

.75 Caliber (10 gauge)

Exc.	V.G.	Good	Fair	Poor
—	—	8000	3500	1000

Model 1861 Single-Shot Rifled Musket

With the advent of the Civil War, the army of the Union seriously needed military arms. Colt was given a contract to supply 112,500 1861-pattern percussion single-shot muskets. Between 1861 and 1865, 75,000 were delivered. They have 40" rifled barrels chambered for .58 caliber. The musket is equipped with military sights, sling swivels, and a bayonet lug. The metal finish is bright steel, and the stock is oil-finished walnut. Military inspector's marks are found on all major parts. "VP" over an eagle is stamped on the breech along with a date. The Colt address and a date are stamped on the lockplate. A large number of these rifles were altered to the Snyder breech loading system for the Bey of Egypt.

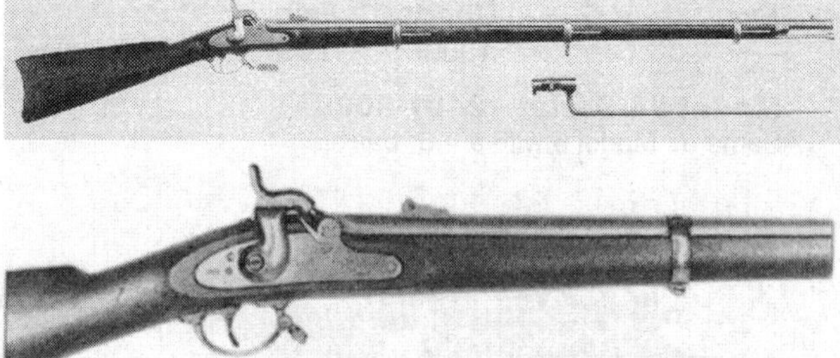

Courtesy Milwaukee Public Museum, Milwaukee, Wisconsin

Production Model

Exc.	V.G.	Good	Fair	Poor
—	5500	2000	750	450

COLT PERCUSSION REVOLVERS

Model 1860 Army Revolver

This model was the third most produced of the Colt percussion handguns. It was the primary revolver used by the Union Army during the Civil War. Colt delivered 127,156 of these revolvers to be used during those hostilities. This is a 6-shot .44 caliber percussion revolver. It has either a 7.5" or 8" round barrel with an attached loading lever. The frame, hammer, and loading lever are case colored; the barrel and cylinder are blued. The trigger guard and front strap are brass, and the backstrap is blued steel. The grips are one-piece walnut. The early models have the barrels stamped "Address Saml. Colt Hartford Ct." Later models are stamped "Address Col. Saml. Colt New-York U.S. America." "Colt's/Patent" is stamped on the left side of the frame; ".44 Cal.," on the trigger guard. The cylinder is roll engraved with the naval battle scene. There were a total of 200,500 1860 Army Revolvers manufactured between 1860 and 1873.

Martial Marked Model

Exc.	V.G.	Good	Fair	Poor
—	—	7500	3500	900

Civilian Model

This model is found in either 3- or-4 screw variations and it may or may not be cut for a shoulder stock. Civilian models are usually better finished.

Courtesy Milwaukee Public Museum, Milwaukee, Wisconsin

Exc.	V.G.	Good	Fair	Poor
—	—	6000	3000	800

Full Fluted Cylinder Model

Approximately 4,000 Army's were made with full fluted cylinders. They appear in the first 8,000 serial numbers.

Courtesy Milwaukee Public Museum, Milwaukee, Wisconsin

Exc.	V.G.	Good	Fair	Poor
—	—	15000	7000	2000

Shoulder Stock 2nd Type (Fluted Cylinder Model)

Courtesy Milwaukee Public Museum, Milwaukee, Wisconsin

Courtesy Milwaukee Public Museum, Milwaukee, Wisconsin

Model 1861 Navy Revolver

This model is a 6-shot, 7.5" round-barreled, .36 caliber percussion revolver. The frame, hammer, and attached loading lever are case colored. The barrel and cylinder are blued. The grip frame and trigger guard are silver-plated brass. The grips are of one-piece walnut. The cylinder has the roll-engraved naval battle scene, and the barrel stamping is "Address Col. Saml. Colt New-York U.S. America." The frame is stamped "Colts/Patent" with "36 Cal." on the trigger guard. There are not many variations within the 1861 Navy model designation, as less than 39,000 were made between 1861 and 1873.

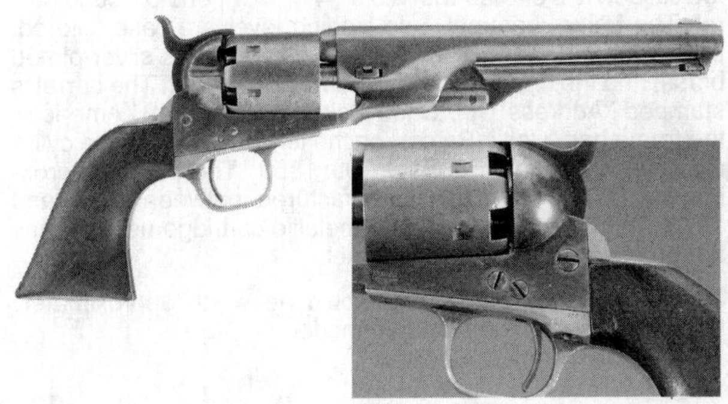

Courtesy Rock Island Auction Company

Civilian Model

Exc.	V.G.	Good	Fair	Poor
—	—	7500	3500	900

Military Model

Marked "U.S." on frame, inspector's cartouche on grip. 650 were marked "U.S.N." on the butt.

Exc.	V.G.	Good	Fair	Poor
—	—	18000	5500	1800

Shoulder Stock Model

Only 100 3rd-type stocks were made. They appear between serial #11000-#14000. These are very rare revolvers.

Revolver

Exc.	V.G.	Good	Fair	Poor
—	—	17500	5000	1500

Stock

Exc.	V.G.	Good	Fair	Poor
—	—	9500	4250	1000

Fluted Cylinder Model

Approximately the first 100 were made with full fluted cylinders.

Exc.	V.G.	Good	Fair	Poor
—	—	45000	7500	2000

Model 1862 Pocket Navy Revolver

This is a smaller, 5-shot, .36 caliber percussion revolver that resembles the configuration of the 1851 Navy. It has a 4.5", 5.5", or 6.5" octagonal barrel with an attached loading lever. The frame, hammer, and loading lever are case colored; the barrel and cylinder, blued. The grip frame and trigger guard are silver-plated brass; and the one-piece grips, of varnished walnut. The stagecoach holdup scene is roll-engraved on the cylinder. The frame is stamped "Colt's/Patent"; and the barrel, "Address Col. Saml. Colt New-York U.S. America." There were approximately 19,000 manufactured between 1861 and 1873. They are serial numbered in the same range as the Model 1862 Police. Because a great many were used for metallic cartridge conversions, they are quite scarce today.

The London Address Model with blued steel grip frame would be worth more than the standard model.

Standard Production Model

Exc.	V.G.	Good	Fair	Poor
—	—	3000	1200	500

NOTE: Longer barrels will bring a premium over the 4.5" length.

Model 1862 Police Revolver

This is a slim, attractively designed revolver that some consider to be the most aesthetically pleasing of all the Colt percussion designs. It has a 5-shot, half-fluted cylinder chambered for .36 caliber. It is offered with a 3.5", 4.5", 5.5", or 6.5" round barrel. The frame, hammer, and loading lever are case colored; the barrel and cylinder, blued. The grip frame is silver-plated brass; and the one-piece grips, varnished walnut. The barrel is stamped "Address Col. Saml Colt New-York U.S. America"; the frame has "Colt's/Patent" on the left side. One of the cylinder flutes is marked "Pat Sept. 10th 1850." There were approximately 28,000 of these manufactured between 1861 and 1873. Many were converted to metallic cartridge use, so they are quite scarce on today's market.

The London Address Model would be worth approximately twice the value of the standard model.

Courtesy Milwaukee Public Museum, Milwaukee, Wisconsin

Standard Production Model

Exc.	V.G.	Good	Fair	Poor
—	—	2250	1000	400

NOTE: Longer barrels will bring a premium over the 3.5" or 4.5" length.

COLT METALLIC CARTRIDGE CONVERSIONS

Thuer Conversion Revolver

Although quite simplistic and not commercially successful, the Thuer Conversion was the first attempt by Colt to convert the percussion revolvers to the new metallic cartridge system. This conversion was designed around the tapered Thuer cartridge and consists of a ring that replaced the back part of the cylinder, which had been milled off. This ring is stamped "Pat. Sep. / 15. 1868." The ejection position is marked with the letter "E." These conversions have rebounding firing pins and are milled to allow loading from the front of the revolver. This conversion was undertaken on the six different models listed; and all other specifications, finishes, markings, etc., not directly affected by the conversion would be the same as previously described. From a collectible and investment standpoint, the Thuer Conversion is very desirable. Competent appraisal should be secured if acquisition is contemplated.

Model 1849 Pocket Conversion

Exc.	V.G.	Good	Fair	Poor
—	—	12500	4000	2000

Model 1851 Navy Conversion

Exc.	V.G.	Good	Fair	Poor
—	—	15000	5000	2000

Courtesy Milwaukee Public Museum, Milwaukee, Wisconsin

Model 1860 Army Conversion

Exc.	V.G.	Good	Fair	Poor
—	—	17500	6000	2000

Model 1861 Navy Conversion

Exc.	V.G.	Good	Fair	Poor
—	—	17500	6000	2000

Models 1862 Police Conversion

Exc.	V.G.	Good	Fair	Poor
—	—	11500	3500	1500

Model 1862 Pocket Navy Conversion

Exc.	V.G.	Good	Fair	Poor
—	—	11500	3500	1500

NOTE: Blued models will bring higher prices than nickel models in the same condition.

Richards Conversion, 1860 Army Revolver

This was Colt's second attempt at metallic cartridge conversion, and it met with quite a bit more success than the first. The Richards Conversion was designed for the .44 Colt cartridge and has a 6-shot cylinder and an integral ejector rod to replace the loading lever that had been removed. The other specifications pertaining to the 1860 Army Revolver remain as previously described if they are not directly altered by the conversion. The Richards Conversion adds a breechplate with a firing pin and its own rear sight. There were approximately 9,000 of these Conversions manufactured between 1873 and 1878.

Civilian Model

Exc.	V.G.	Good	Fair	Poor
—	—	5250	2000	600

Martially Marked Variation

This variation is found with mixed serial numbers and a second set of conversion serial numbers. The "U.S." is stamped on the left side of the barrel lug, and inspector's cartouche appears on the grip. This is a very rare Colt revolver.

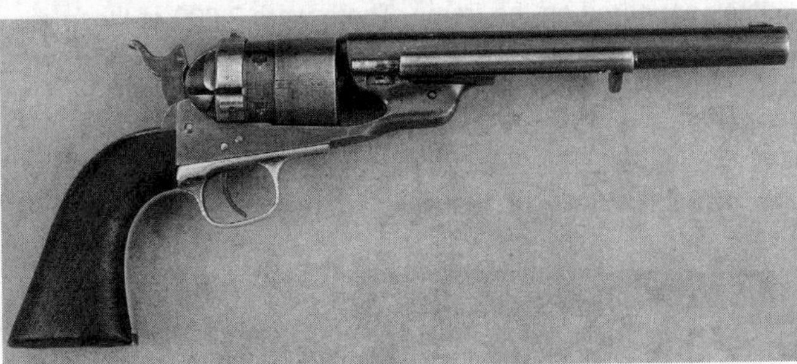

Courtesy Little John's Auction Service, Inc., Paul Goodwin photo

Exc.	V.G.	Good	Fair	Poor
—	—	15000	7000	2000

NOTE: Blued models will bring higher prices than nickel models in the same condition.

Transition Richards Model

This variation is marked by the presence of a firing pin hammer.

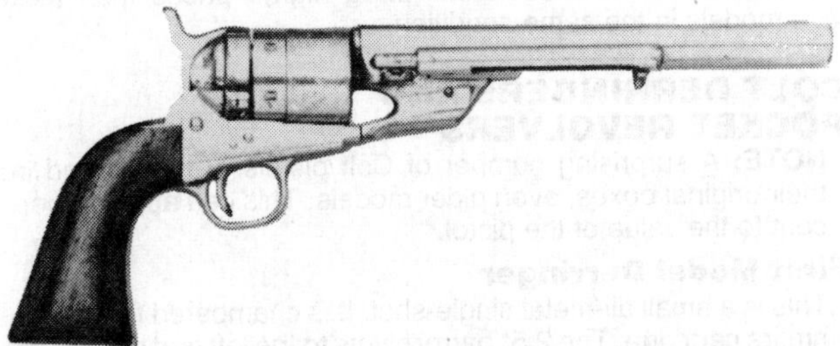

Courtesy Bonhams & Butterfields, San Francisco, California

Exc.	V.G.	Good	Fair	Poor
—	—	6000	3000	1200

NOTE: Blued models will bring higher prices than nickel models in the same condition.

Richards-Mason Conversion, 1860 Army Revolver

This conversion is different from the Richards Conversion in a number of readily apparent aspects. The barrel was manufactured with a small lug much different in appearance than seen on the standard 1860 Army. The breechplate does not have its own rear sight, and there is a milled area to allow the hammer to contact the base of the cartridge. These Conversions were also chambered for the .44 Colt cartridge, and the cylinder holds 6 shots. There is an integral ejector rod in place of the loading lever. The barrels on some are stamped either "Address Col. Saml. Colt New-York U.S. America" or "Colt's Pt. F.A. Mfg. Co. Hartford, Ct." The patent dates 1871 and 1872 are stamped on the left side of the frame. The finish of these revolvers, as well as the grips, were for the most part the same as on the unconverted Armies; but for the first time, nickel-plated guns are found. There were approximately 2,100 of these Conversions produced in 1877 and 1878.

Exc.	V.G.	Good	Fair	Poor
—	—	6000	2500	800

NOTE: Blued models will bring higher prices than nickel models in the same condition.

Richards-Mason Conversions 1851 Navy Revolver

These revolvers were converted in the same way as the 1860 Army previously described, the major difference being the caliber .38, either rimfire or centerfire. Finishes are mostly the same as on unconverted revolvers, but nickel-plated guns are not rare.

Production Model Serial #1-3800

Exc.	V.G.	Good	Fair	Poor
—	—	4500	2000	800

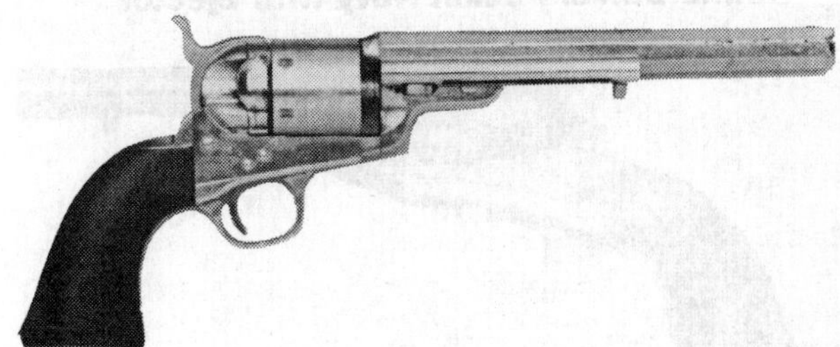

Courtesy Bonhams & Butterfields, San Francisco, California

U.S. Navy Model Serial #41000-91000

"USN" stamped on butt; steel grip frame.

Exc.	V.G.	Good	Fair	Poor
—	—	7000	3000	1000

NOTE: Blued models will bring higher prices than nickel models in the same condition.

Richards-Mason Conversion 1861 Navy Revolver

The specifications for this model are the same as for the 1851 Navy Conversion described above, with the base revolver being different. There were 2,200 manufactured in the 1870s.

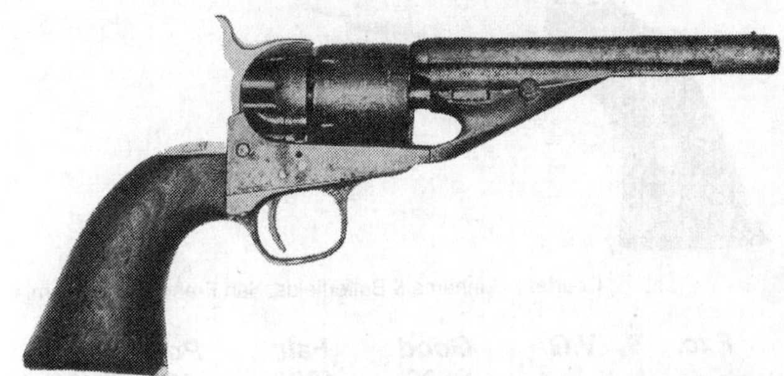

Courtesy Wallis & Wallis, Lewes, Sussex, England

Standard Production Model Serial #100-3300

Exc.	V.G.	Good	Fair	Poor
—	—	4250	1500	500

U.S. Navy Model Serial #1000-9999

Exc.	V.G.	Good	Fair	Poor
—	—	6500	3500	1000

NOTE: Blued models will bring higher prices than nickel models in the same condition.

Model 1862 Police and Pocket Navy Conversions

The conversion of these two revolver models is the most difficult to catalogue of all the Colt variations. There were approximately 24,000 of these produced between 1873 and 1880. There are five basic variations with a number of sub-variations. The confusion is usually caused by the different ways in which these were marked. Depending upon what parts were utilized, caliber markings could be particularly confusing. One must also consider the fact that many of these conversion revolvers found their way into secondary markets, such as Mexico and Central and South America, where they were either destroyed or received sufficient abuse to obliterate most identifying markings. The five basic variations are all chambered for either the .38 rimfire or the .38 centerfire cartridge. All held 5 shots, and most were found with the round roll-engraved stagecoach holdup scene. The half-fluted cylinder from the 1862 Police is quite rare on the conversion revolver and not found at all on some of the variations. The finishes on these guns were pretty much the same as they were before conversion, but it is not unusual to find nickel-plated specimens. Blued models will bring a premium over nickel in the same condition. The basic variations are listed.

Round Barrel Pocket Navy with Ejector

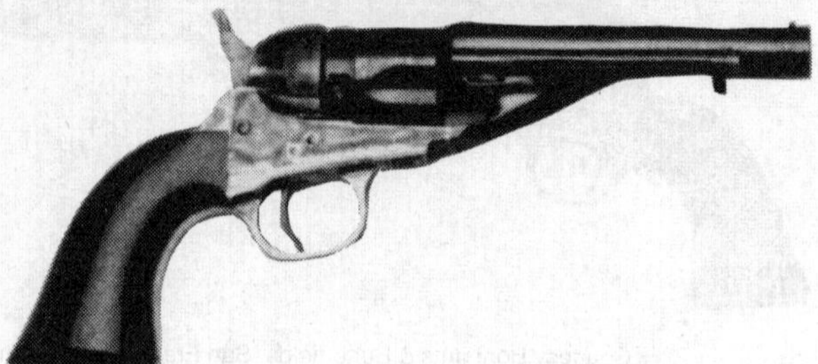

Courtesy Bonhams & Butterfields, San Francisco, California

Exc.	V.G.	Good	Fair	Poor
—	—	3500	1600	800

3.5" Round Barrel Without Ejector

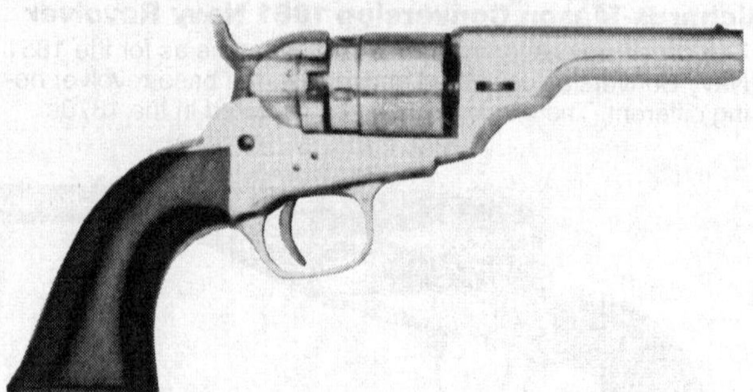

Courtesy Bonhams & Butterfields, San Francisco, California

Exc.	V.G.	Good	Fair	Poor
—	—	2500	1000	300

4.5" Octagonal Barrel Without Ejector

Exc.	V.G.	Good	Fair	Poor
—	—	3000	1200	400

NOTE: Blued models will bring higher prices than nickel models in the same condition.

Model 1862 Pocket Navy Octagon Barrel with Ejector

Exc.	V.G.	Good	Fair	Poor
—	—	3250	1500	600

NOTE: Half-fluted cylinder add 20 percent.

Model 1862 Police Round Barrel with Ejector

Exc.	V.G.	Good	Fair	Poor
—	—	3250	1500	600

NOTE: Blued models will bring higher prices than nickel models in the same condition.

Model 1871-1872 Open Top Revolver

This model was the first revolver Colt manufactured especially for a metallic cartridge. It was not a conversion. The frame, 7.5" or 8" round barrel, and the 6-shot cylinder were produced for the .44 rimfire metallic cartridge. The grip frame and some internal parts were taken from the 1860 Army and the 1851 Navy. Although this model was not commercially successful and was not accepted by the U.S. Ordnance Department, it did pave the way for the Single-Action Army that came out shortly thereafter and was an immediate success. This model is all blued, with a case colored hammer. There are some with silver-plated brass grip frames, but most are blued steel. The one-piece grips are of varnished walnut. The cylinder is roll-engraved with the naval battle scene. The barrel is stamped "Address Col. Saml. Colt New-York U.S. America." The later production revolvers are barrel stamped "Colt's Pt. F.A. Mfg. Co. Hartford, Ct. U.S.A." The first 1,000 revolvers were stamped "Colt's/Patent." After that, 1871 and 1872 patent dates appeared on the frame. There were 7,000 of these revolvers manufactured in 1872 and 1873.

1860 Army Grip Frame

Exc.	V.G.	Good	Fair	Poor
—	—	10000	3000	800

1851 Navy Grip Frame

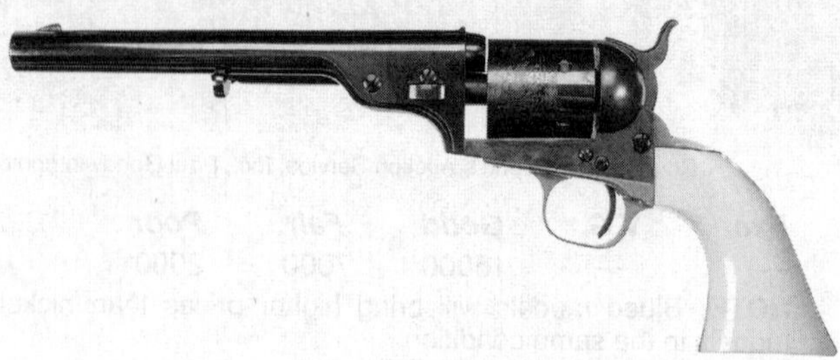

Courtesy Rock Island Auction Company

Exc.	V.G.	Good	Fair	Poor
—	—	11500	4000	1200

NOTE: Blued models will bring higher prices than nickel models in the same condition.

COLT DERRINGERS AND POCKET REVOLVERS

NOTE: A surprising number of Colt pistols are still found in their original boxes, even older models. This can add 100 percent to the value of the pistol.

First Model Derringer

This is a small all-metal single-shot. It is chambered for the .41 rimfire cartridge. The 2.5" barrel pivots to the left and downward for loading. This model is engraved with a scroll pattern and has been noted blued, silver, or nickel-plated. The barrel is stamped "Colt's Pt. F.A. Mfg. Co./Hartford Ct. U.S.A/ No.1." ".41 Cal." is stamped on the frame under the release catch. There were approximately 6,500 of this model manufactured from 1870-1890. It was the first single-shot pistol Colt produced.

A Colt Model 1871-72 Open-Top Revolver sold at auction for $42,187.50. Chambered for the .44 rimfire and fitted with a 7 1.2-inch barrel. Condition is 80 percent original blued finish. The cylinder scene is 100 percent. Walnut grips are mint.
Greg Martin Auctions

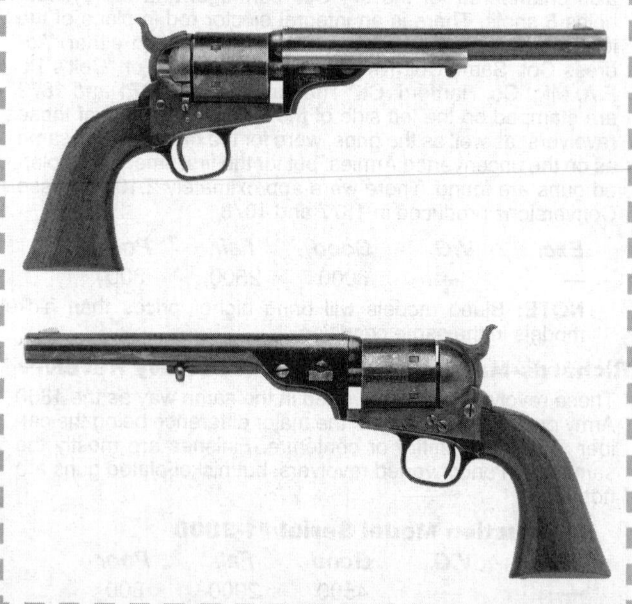

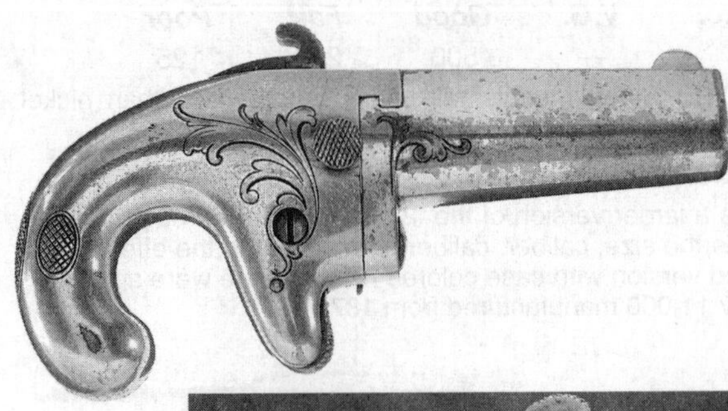

Courtesy Rock Island Auction Company

Exc.	V.G.	Good	Fair	Poor
—		2500	1200	400

Second Model Derringer

Although this model has the same odd shape as the First Model, it is readily identifiable by the checkered varnished walnut grips and the "No 2" on the barrel after the address. It is also .41 rimfire and has a 2.5" barrel that pivots in the same manner as the First Model. There were approximately 9,000 of these manufactured between 1870 and 1890.

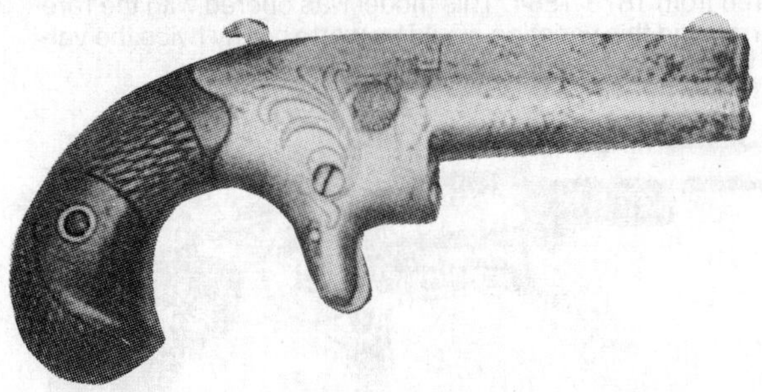

Courtesy Wallis & Wallis, Lewes, Sussex, England

Exc.	V.G.	Good	Fair	Poor
—	—	2000	900	400

Third Model Derringer

This model was designed by Alexander Thuer who was also responsible for Colt's first metallic cartridge conversion. It is often referred to as the "Thuer Model" for this reason. It is also chambered for the .41 rimfire cartridge and has a 2.5" barrel that pivots to the right (but not down) for loading. The Third Model has a more balanced appearance than its predecessors, and its commercial success (45,000 produced between 1875 and 1910) reflects this. The barrel on this model is stamped "Colt" in small block letters on the first 2,000 guns. The remainder of the production features the "COLT" in large italicized print. The ".41 Cal." is stamped on the left side of the frame. This model will be found with the barrel blued or plated in either silver or nickel and the bronze frame plated. The grips are varnished walnut.

First Variation, Early Production

This has a raised area on the underside of the frame through which the barrel screw passes, and the spur is not angled. Small block "Colt" lettering on barrel.

Exc.	V.G.	Good	Fair	Poor
—	—	6500	2200	1000

First Variation, Late Production

This is similar to early production but has large italicized "COLT" on barrel.

Exc.	V.G.	Good	Fair	Poor
—	—	3250	1500	600

Production Model

Exc.	V.G.	Good	Fair	Poor
—	—	800	400	200

NOTE: Blued models will bring a premium over nickel in the same condition.

House Model Revolver

There are two basic versions of this model. They are both chambered for the .41 rimfire cartridge. The 4-shot version is known as the "Cloverleaf" due to the shape of the cylinder when viewed from the front. Approximately 7,500 of the nearly 10,000 House revolvers were of this 4-shot configuration. They are offered with a 1.5" or 3" barrel. The 1.5" length is quite rare, and some octagonal barrels in this length have been noted. The 5-shot round-cylinder version accounts for the rest of the production. It is found with serial numbers over 6100 and is offered with a 2-7/8" length barrel only. This model is stamped on the top strap "Pat. Sept. 19, 1871." This model has brass frames that were sometimes nickel-plated. The barrels are found either blued or plated. The grips are varnished walnut or rosewood. There were slightly fewer than 10,000 of both variations manufactured from 1871-1876.

Cloverleaf with 1.5" Round Barrel

Exc.	V.G.	Good	Fair	Poor
—		3000	1250	400

NOTE: Blued models will bring a premium over nickel in the same condition.

Cloverleaf with 3" Barrel

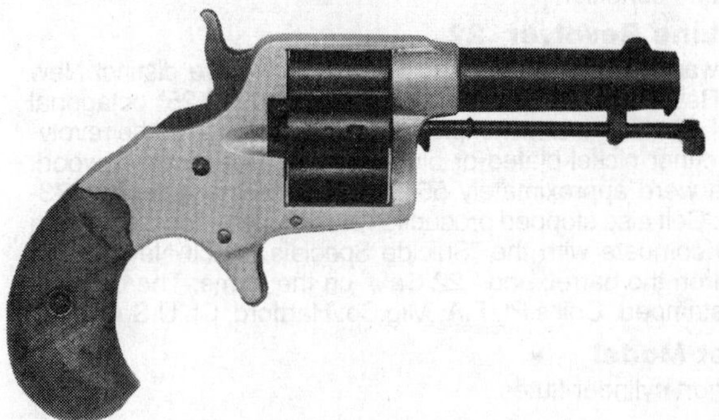

Courtesy Buffalo Bill Historical Center, Cody, Wyoming

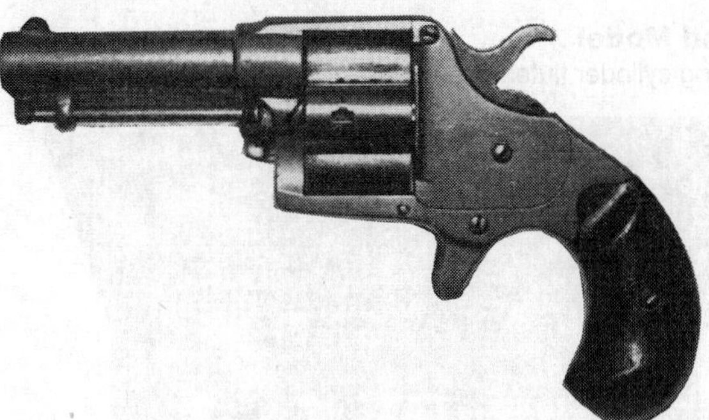

Exc.	V.G.	Good	Fair	Poor
—	—	1500	500	200

House Pistol with 5-Shot Round Cylinder

Exc.	V.G.	Good	Fair	Poor
—	—	1300	500	200

Open Top Pocket Revolver

This is a .22-caliber rimfire, 7-shot revolver that was offered with either a 2-3/8" or a 2-7/8" barrel. The model was a commercial success, with over 114,000 manufactured between 1871 and 1877. There would undoubtedly have been a great deal more sold had not the cheap copies begun to flood the market at that time, forcing Colt to drop this model from the line. This revolver has a silver or nickel-plated brass frame and a nickel-plated or blued barrel and cylinder. The grips are varnished walnut. The cylinder bolt slots are found toward the front on this model. "Colt's Pt. F.A. Mfg. Co./Hartford, Ct. U.S.A." is stamped on the barrel and ".22 Cal." on the left side of the frame.

Early Model with Ejector Rod

Courtesy Bonhams & Butterfields

Exc.	V.G.	Good	Fair	Poor
—	—	1750	800	400

Production Model without Ejector Rod

Exc.	V.G.	Good	Fair	Poor
—	—	600	300	150

NOTE: Blued models will bring a premium over nickel in the same condition.

New Line Revolver .22

This was the smallest framed version of the five distinct New Line Revolvers. It has a 7-shot cylinder and a 2.25" octagonal barrel. The frame is nickel-plated, and the balance of the revolver is either nickel-plated or blued. The grips are of rosewood. There were approximately 55,000 of these made from 1873-1877. Colt also stopped production of the New Lines rather than try to compete with the "Suicide Specials." "Colt New .22" is found on the barrel; and ".22 Cal.," on the frame. The barrel is also stamped "Colt's Pt. F.A. Mfg.Co./Hartford, Ct. U.S.A."

1st Model

Short cylinder flutes.

Exc.	V.G.	Good	Fair	Poor
—	—	600	300	150

2nd Model

Long cylinder flutes.

Courtesy Bonhams & Butterfields, San Francisco, California

Exc.	V.G.	Good	Fair	Poor
—	—	500	250	125

NOTE: Blued models will bring higher prices than nickel models in the same condition.

New Line Revolver .30

This is a larger version of the .22 New Line. The basic difference is the size, caliber, caliber markings, and the offering of a blued version with case colored frame. There were approximately 11,000 manufactured from 1874-1876.

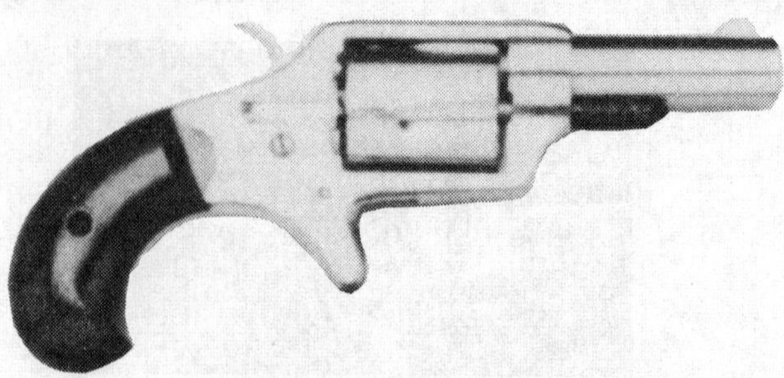

Courtesy Wallis & Wallis, Lewes, Sussex, England

Exc.	V.G.	Good	Fair	Poor
—	—	600	300	150

NOTE: Prices above are for nickel finish. Blued models will bring a premium of 100 percent.

New Line Revolver .32

This is the same basic revolver as the .30 caliber except that it is chambered for the .32-caliber rimfire and .32-caliber centerfire and is so marked. There were 22,000 of this model manufactured from 1873-1884. This model was offered with the rare 4" barrel, and this variation would be worth nearly twice the value of a standard model.

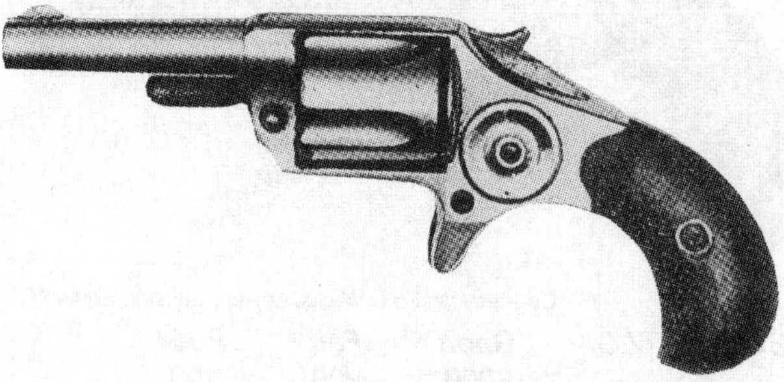

Courtesy Bonhams & Butterfields, San Francisco, California

Exc.	V.G.	Good	Fair	Poor
—	—	600	300	150

NOTE: Prices above are for nickel finish. Blued models will bring a premium of 100 percent.

REMINDER
Go to gun shows, not just to buy or sell, but to observe and learn.

New Line Revolver .38

There were approximately 5,500 of this model manufactured between 1874 and 1880. It is chambered for either the .38 rimfire or .38 centerfire caliber and is so marked. This model in a 4" barrel would also bring twice the value.

Courtesy Rock Island Auction Company

Exc.	V.G.	Good	Fair	Poor
—	—	800	400	200

NOTE: Blued models will bring a premium over nickel in the same condition.

New Line Revolver .41

This is the "Big Colt," as it was sometimes known in advertising of its era. It is chambered for the .41 rimfire and the .41 centerfire and is so marked. The large caliber of this variation makes this the most desirable of the New Lines to collectors. There were approximately 7,000 of this model manufactured from 1874-1879. A 4"-barreled version would again be worth a 100 percent premium.

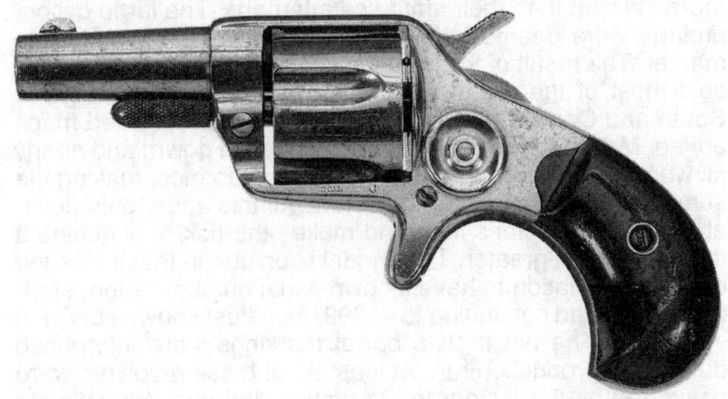

Exc.	V.G.	Good	Fair	Poor
—	—	1000	550	300

NOTE: Prices above are for nickel finish. Blued models will bring a premium of 100 percent.

New House Model Revolver

This revolver is similar to the other New Lines except that it features a square-butt instead of the bird's-head configuration, a 2.25" round barrel without ejector rod, and a thin loading gate. It is chambered for the .32 (rare), .38, and the .41 centerfire cartridges. The finish was either full nickel-plated or blued, with a case colored frame. The grips are walnut, rosewood or (for the first time on a Colt revolver) checkered hard rubber, with an oval around the word "Colt." The barrel address is the same as on the other New Lines. The frame is marked "New House," with the caliber. There were approximately 4,000 manufactured between 1880-1886. .32 caliber model would bring a 10 percent premium.

REMINDER
Prices paid for firearms is an ever-changing affair based on a large number of variables.

Courtesy Milwaukee Public Museum, Milwaukee, Wisconsin

Exc.	V.G.	Good	Fair	Poor
—	—	1000	450	250

NOTE: Prices above are for nickel finish. Blued models will bring a premium of 100 percent.

New Police Revolver

This was the final revolver in the New Line series. It is chambered for .32, .38, and .41 centerfire caliber. The .32 and .41 are quite rare. It is offered in barrel lengths of 2.25", 4.5", 5.5", and 6.5". An ejector rod is found on all but the 2.5" barrel. The finish is either nickel or blued and case colored. The grips are hard rubber with a scene of a policeman arresting a criminal embossed on them; thusly the model became known to collectors as the "Cop and Thug" model. The barrel stamping is as the other New Lines, and the frame is stamped "New Police .38." There were approximately 4,000 of these manufactured between 1882-1886.

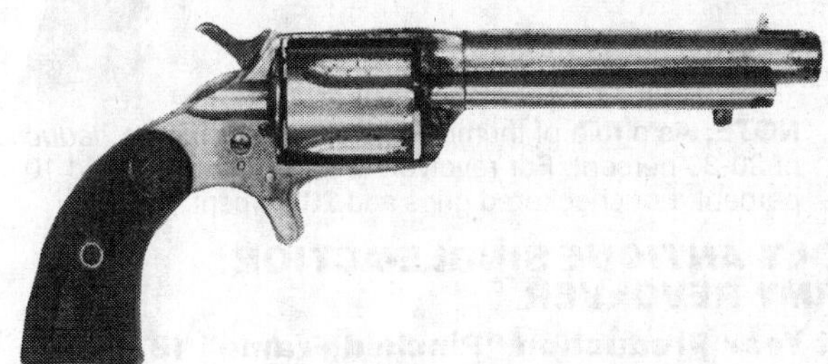
Courtesy Milwaukee Public Museum, Milwaukee, Wisconsin

Long Barrel Model with Ejector

Exc.	V.G.	Good	Fair	Poor
—	—	3250	1400	700

NOTE: The .32 and .41 caliber versions of this model will bring a 40-50 percent premium. Blued models and models with 5.5" or 6.5" barrels will bring a premium. Short barrel model will bring about 50 percent of the listed prices.

COLT'S SINGLE-ACTION ARMY REVOLVER

The Colt Single-Action Army, or Peacemaker as it is sometimes referred to, is one of the most widely collected and recognized firearms in the world. With few interruptions or changes in design, it has been manufactured from 1873 until the present. It is still available on a limited production basis from the Colt Custom Shop. The variations in this model are myriad. It has been produced in 30 different calibers and barrel lengths from 2.5" to 16", with 4.75", 5.5", and 7.5" standard. The standard finish is blued, with a case colored frame. Many are nickel-plated. Examples have been found silver- and gold-plated, with combinations thereof. The finest engravers in the world have used the SAA as a canvas to display their artistry. The standard grips from 1873-1883 were walnut, either oil-stained or varnished. From 1883 to approximately 1897, the standard grips were hard rubber with eagle and shield. After this date, at serial number 165000, the hard rubber grips featured the Rampant Colt. Many special-order grips were available, notably pearl and ivory, which were often checkered or carved in ornate fashion. The variables involved in establishing values on this model are extreme. Added to this, one must also consider historical significance, since the SAA played a big part in the formative years of the American West. Fortunately for those among us interested in the SAA, there are a number of fine publications available dealing exclusively with this model. It is my strongest recommendation that they be acquired and studied thoroughly to prevent extremely expensive mistakes. The Colt factory records are nearly complete for this model, and research should be done before acquisition of rare or valuable specimens.

For our purposes we will break down the Single-Action Army production as follows:

Antique or Black Powder, **1873-1898, serial number 1-175000**

The cylinder axis pin is retained by a screw in the front of the frame.

Pre-war, **1899-1940, serial number 175001-357859**

The cylinder axis pin is retained by a spring-loaded button through the side of the frame. This method is utilized on the following models, as well.

Post-war 2nd Generation, **1956-1978, serial number 0001SA-99999SA**

3rd Generation, **1978-Present, serial #SA1001.** A breakdown of production by caliber will follow the chapter. It is important to note that the rarer calibers and the larger calibers bring higher values in this variation.

NOTE: As a rule of thumb nickel guns will bring a *deduction* of 20-30 percent. For revolvers with 4.75" barrels add 10-15 percent. For checkered grips add 20 percent.

COLT *ANTIQUE* SINGLE-ACTION ARMY REVOLVER

1st Year Production "Pinched Frame" 1873 Only

It is necessary to categorize this variation on its own. This is one of the rarest and most interesting of all the SAAs—not to mention that it is the first. On this model the top strap is pinched or constricted approximately one-half inch up from the hammer to form the rear sight. The highest surviving serial number having this feature is #156, the lowest #1. From these numbers, it is safe to assume that the first run of SAAs were all pinched-frame models; but there is no way to tell how many there were, since Colt did not serial number the frames in the order that they were manufactured. An educated guess would be that there were between 50 and 150 pinched frame guns in all and that they were all made before mid-July 1873. The reason for the change came about on the recommendation of Capt. J.R. Edie, a government inspector who thought that the full fluted top strap would be a big improvement in the sighting capabilities of the weapon. The barrel length of the first model is 7.5"; the standard caliber, .45 Colt; and the proper grips were of walnut. The front sight blade is German silver. Needless to say, this model will rarely be encountered; and if it is, it should never be purchased without competent appraisal.

Exc.	V.G.	Good	Fair	Poor
—	60000	45000	30000	10000

Early Military Model 1873-1877

The serial number range on this first run of military contract revolvers extends to #24000. The barrel address is in the early script style with the # symbol preceding and following. The frame bears the martial marking "US," and the walnut grips have the inspector's cartouche stamped on them. The front sight is steel as on all military models; the barrel length, 7.5". The caliber is .45 Colt, and the ejector rod head is the bull's-eye or donut style with a hole in the center of it. The finish features the military polish and case colored frame, with the remainder blued. Authenticate any potential purchase; many spurious examples have been noted.

Exc.	V.G.	Good	Fair	Poor
35000	25000	12000	8000	5000

NOTE: Certain 3-digit and 4-digit serial numbers will command a substantial premium. Seek an expert appraisal prior to sale.

Early Civilian Model 1873-1877

This model is identical to the Early Military Model but has no military acceptance markings or cartouches. Some could have the German silver front sight blade. The early bull's-eye ejector rod head is used on this model. The Civilian Model has a higher degree of polish than is found on the military models, and the finish on these early models could be plated or blued with a case colored frame. This model also has a script barrel address. The grips are standard one-piece walnut. Ivory-grip models are worth a premium.

Exc.	V.G.	Good	Fair	Poor
30000	24000	12000	9000	6000

NOTE: Certain 3-digit and 4-digit serial numbers will command a substantial premium. Seek an expert appraisal prior to sale.

.44 Rimfire Model 1875-1880

This model was made to fire the .44 Henry Rimfire cartridge. It was to be used as a compatible companion sidearm to the Henry and Winchester 1866 rifles that were used extensively during this era. However, this was not the case; and the .44 Rimfire was doomed to economic failure as soon as it appeared on the market. By that time, it had already been established that large-caliber centerfire cartridges were a good deal more efficient than their rimfire counterparts. The large-caliber rimfires were deemed obsolete before this Colt ever hit the market. The result of this was that Colt's sales representatives sold most of the production to obscure banana republics in South and Central America, where this model received much abuse. Most had the original 7.5" barrels cut down; and nearly all were denied even the most basic maintenance, making the survival rate of this model quite low. All this adds to its desirability as a collector's item and makes the risk of acquiring a fake that much greater. This model is unique in that it was the only SAA variation to have its own serial number range, starting with #1 and continuing to #1892, the latest known surviving specimen. The block style barrel markings were introduced during this production run. At least 90 of these revolvers were converted by the factory to .22 rimfire, and one was shipped chambered for .32 rimfire.

Exc.	V.G.	Good	Fair	Poor
40000	33000	17000	7500	4000

Late Military Model 1878-1891

The later Military Models are serial numbered to approximately #136000. They bear the block-style barrel address without the # prefix and suffix. The frames are marked "US," and the grips have the inspector's cartouche. The finish is the military-style polish, case colored frame; and the remainder, blued. Grips are oil-stained walnut. On the military marked Colts, it is imperative that potential purchases be authenticated as many fakes have been noted.

Exc.	V.G.	Good	Fair	Poor
35000	24000	14000	10000	6000

NOTE: Revolvers produced from 1878 to 1885 will command a premium. Seek an expert appraisal prior to sale.

Artillery Model 1895-1903

A number of "US" marked SAAs were returned either to the Colt factory or to the Springfield Armory, where they were altered and refinished. These revolvers have 5.5" barrels and any combination of mixed serial numbers. They were remarked by the inspectors of the era and have a case colored frame and a blued cylinder and barrel. Some have been noted all blued within this variation. This model, as with the other military marked Colts, should definitely be authenticated before purchase. Some of these revolvers fall outside the 1898 antique cutoff date that has been established by the government and, in our experience, are not quite as desirable to investors. They are generally worth approximately 20 percent less.

Exc.	V.G.	Good	Fair	Poor
18000	12500	8000	4000	3000

London Model

These SAAs were manufactured to be sold through Colt's London Agency. The barrel is stamped "Colt's Pt. F.A. Mfg. Co. Hartford, Ct. U.S.A. Depot 14 Pall Mall London." This model is available in various barrel lengths. They are generally chambered for .45 Colt, .450 Boxer, .450 Eley, .455 Eley, and rarely .476 Eley, the largest of the SAA chamberings. A good many of these London Models were cased and embellished, and they should be individually appraised. This model should be authenticated as many spurious examples have been noted.

Exc.	V.G.	Good	Fair	Poor
22000	15000	10000	4500	2000

Frontier Six-Shooter 1878-1882

Several thousand SAAs were made with the legend "Colt's Frontier Six Shooter" acid-etched into the left side of the barrel instead of being stamped. This etching is not deep, and today collectors will become ecstatic if they discover a specimen with mere vestiges of the etched panel remaining. These acid-etched SAAs are serial numbered #45000-#65000. They have various barrel lengths and finishes, but all are chambered for the .44-40 caliber.

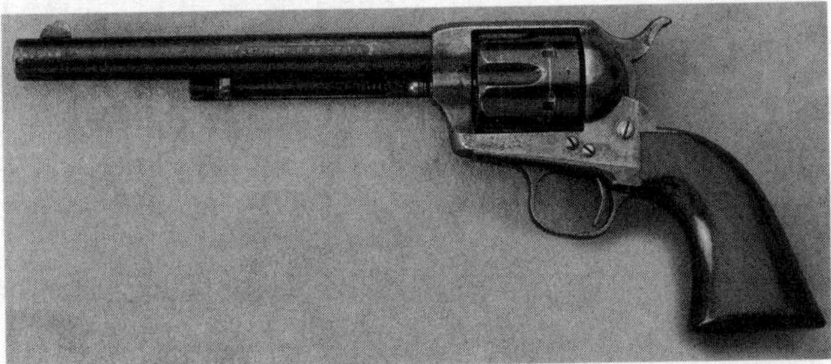

Courtesy Little John's Auction Service, Inc., Paul Goodwin photo

Exc.	V.G.	Good	Fair	Poor
40000	20000	14000	7000	5000

Sheriff's or Storekeeper's Model 1882-1898

This model was manufactured with a short barrel (2.5"-4.75"). Most have 4" barrels. It features no ejector rod or housing, and the frame is made without the hole in the right forward section to accommodate the ejector assembly. The Sheriff's or Storekeeper's Model is numbered above serial #73000. It was manufactured with various finishes and chambered for numerous calibers. This model continued after 1898 into the smokeless or modern era. Examples manufactured in the pre-war years are worth approximately 20 percent less. Although faking this model is quite difficult, it has been successfully attempted.

Courtesy Little John's Auction Service, Inc., Paul Goodwin photo

Exc.	V.G.	Good	Fair	Poor
35000	22000	14000	9000	5000

Flattop Target Model 1888-1896

This model is highly regarded and sought after by collectors. It is not only rare (only 925 manufactured) but is an extremely attractive and well-finished variation. It is chambered for 22 different calibers from .22 rimfire to .476 Eley. The .22 rimfire, .38 Colt, .41, and .45 Colt are the most predominant chamberings. The 7.5" barrel length is the most commonly encountered.

The serial number range is between #127000-#162000. Some have been noted in higher ranges. The finish is all blued, with a case colored hammer. The checkered grips are either hard rubber or walnut. The most readily identifying feature of the flattop is the lack of a groove in the top strap and the sight blade dovetailed into the flattop. The front sight has a removable blade insert. The values given are for a standard production model chambered for the calibers previously mentioned as being the most common. It is important to have other calibers individually appraised as variance in values can be quite extreme.

Exc.	V.G.	Good	Fair	Poor
35000	25000	15000	8000	4000

NOTE: Nickel models will command a premium.

Bisley Model 1894-1915

This model was named for the target range in Great Britain, where their National Target Matches were held since the nineteenth century. The model was designed as a target revolver with an odd humped-back grip that was supposed to better fill the hand while target shooting. It is also easily identified by the wide low profile hammer spur, wide trigger, and the name "Bisley" stamped on the barrel. The Bisley production fell within the serial number range #165000-#331916. There were 44,350 made.

It was offered in 16 different chamberings from .32 Colt to .455 Eley. The most common calibers were .32-20, .38-40, .41, .44-40, and .45 Colt. The barrel lengths are 4.75", 5.5", and 7.5". The frame and hammer are case-colored; the remainder, blued. Smokeless powder models produced after 1899 utilized the push-button cylinder pin retainer. The grips are checkered hard rubber. This model was actually designed with English sales in mind; and though it did sell well over there, American sales accounted for most of the Bisley production. The values we provide here cover the standard calibers and barrel lengths. Rare calibers and/or other notable variations can bring greatly fluctuating values.

Exc.	V.G.	Good	Fair	Poor
9000	6500	4500	2500	1200

Bisley Model Flattop Target 1894-1913

This model is quite similar to the Standard Bisley Model, with the flattop frame and dovetailed rear sight feature. It also has the removable front sight insert. It has an all-blued finish with case-colored hammer only and is available with a 7.5" barrel. Smokeless powder models produced after 1899 utilized the push-button cylinder pin retainer. The calibers are the same as the standard Bisley. Colt manufactured 976 of these revolvers. The advice regarding appraisal would also apply.

Exc.	V.G.	Good	Fair	Poor
25000	16000	9500	3500	1800

NOTE: Nickel models will command a premium.

Standard Civilian Production Models 1876-1898

This final designated category for the black powder or antique SAAs includes all the revolvers not previously categorized. They have barrel lengths from 4.75", 5.5", and 7.5" and are chambered for any one of 30 different calibers. The finishes could be blued, blued and case colored, or plated in nickel, silver, gold, or combinations thereof. Grips could be walnut, hard rubber, ivory, pearl, stag, or bone. The possibilities are endless. The values given here are for the basic model, and we again strongly advise securing qualified appraisal when not completely sure of any model variation.

NOTE: For Standard Civilian Production Models with screw-in frame, serial number to 163,000 add a 25-100 percent premium depending on year built. Seek an expert appraisal prior to sale.

Exc.	*V.G.*	*Good*	*Fair*	*Poor*
25000	16000	12000	8000	3000

At this time it is important to note that the Colt's Single-Action Army Revolvers we have discussed to this point are in the antique category as established by our federal government. The arbitrary cutoff date of 1898 has been established, and any weapon made prior to this date is considered an antique and, as such, not subject to the restraints placed on collectors and dealers by the Gun Control Act of 1968. This is important because firearms falling into this category will usually bring higher values due to the demand by pure investors who do not relish paperwork on collectible investments. There will be those who disagree with me on this line of reasoning, but my experience tells me that it is correct.

COLT PRE-WAR SINGLE-ACTION ARMY REVOLVER 1899-1940

NOTE: A surprising number of Colt pistols are still found in their original boxes, even older models. This can add 100 percent to the value of the pistol.

Standard Production Pre-war Models

The 1899 cutoff has been thoroughly discussed, but it is interesting to note that the actual beginning production date for smokeless models was 1900. The pre-war Colts are, all in all, quite similar to the antiques—the finishes, barrel lengths, grips, etc. Calibers are also similar, with the exception of the obsolete ones being dropped and new discoveries added. The most apparent physical difference between the smokeless powder and black powder models is the previously discussed method of retaining the cylinder axis pin. The pre-war Colts utilized the spring-loaded button through the side of the frame. The black powder models utilized a screw in the front of the frame. The values we furnish for this model designation are for these standard models only. The serial number range on the pre-war SAAs is 175001-357859. Note that any variation can have marked effects on value fluctuations, and qualified appraisal should be secured. Note: Scarce chamberings command 30 percent to 100 percent premium.

Exc.	*V.G.*	*Good*	*Fair*	*Poor*
10000	7000	3500	2500	1500

Colt Single-Action Army Production Breakdown by Caliber Antique and Pre-war

NOTE: Rare calibers can increase values 300-500 percent in extreme cases.

CALIBER	SAA	FLATTOP SAA	BISLEY	FLATTOP BISLEY
.22 R.F.	107	93	0	0
.32 R.F.	1	0	0	0
.32 Colt	192	24	160	44
.32 S&W	32	30	18	17
.32-44	2	9	14	17
.32-20	29,812	30	13,291	131
.38 Colt (1914)	1,011	122	412	96
.38 Colt (1922)	1,365	0	0	0
.38 S&W	9	39	10	5
.38 Colt Sp.	82	7	0	0
.38 S&W Sp.	25	0	2	0
.38-44	2	11	6	47
.357 Mag.	525	0	0	0
.380 Eley	1	3	0	0
.38-40	38,240	19	12,163	98
.41	16,402	91	3,159	24
.44 SmBr.	15	0	1	0
.44 R. F.	1,863	0	0	0
.44 Germ.	59	0	0	0
.44 Russ.	154	51	90	62
.44 S&W	24	51	29	64
.44 S&W Sp.	506	1	0	0
.44-40	64,489	21	6,803	78
.45 Colt	150,683	100	8,005	97
.45 SmBr.	4	0	2	0
.45 ACP	44	0	0	0
.450 Boxer	729	89	0	0
.450 Eley	2,697	84	5	0
.455 Eley	1,150	37	180	196
.476 Eley	161	2	0	0
Total	**310,386**	**914**	**44,350**	**976**

The above chart covers the production by caliber of the Single-Action Army Revolvers manufactured between 1873 and 1940. These are the antique and the pre-war firearms. This chart readily informs us as to which are the rare calibers.

Long Fluted Cylinder Model 1913-1915

Strange as it may seem, the Colt Company has an apparent credo they followed to never throw anything away. That credo was never more evident than with this model. These Long Flute Cylinders were actually left over from the model 1878 Double-Action Army Revolvers. Someone in the hierarchy at Colt had an inspiration that drove the gunsmiths on the payroll slightly mad: to make these cylinders fit the SAA frames. There were 1,478 of these Long Flutes manufactured. They are chambered for the .45 Colt, .38-40, .32-20, .41 Colt, and the .44 Smith & Wesson Special. They were offered in the three standard barrel lengths and were especially well-polished, having what has been described as Colt's "Fire Blue" on the barrel and cylinder. The frame and hammer are case colored. They are fitted with checkered hard rubber grips and are particularly fine examples of Colt's craft. Rare.

Exc.	V.G.	Good	Fair	Poor
15000	8500	6000	3250	2000

COLT POST-WAR SINGLE-ACTION ARMY REVOLVER

NOTE: A surprising number of Colt pistols are still found in their original boxes, even older models. This can add 100 percent to the value of the pistol.

Standard Post-war Model 1956-1975

In 1956 the shooting and gun-collecting fraternity succeeded in convincing Colt that there was a market for a re-introduced SAA. The revolver was brought back in the same external configuration. The only changes were internal. The basic specifications as to barrel length and finish availability were the same. The calibers available were .38 Special, .357 Magnum, .44 Special, and .45 Colt. The serial number range of the re-introduced 2nd Generation, as it is sometimes known, Colt is #000ISA-73000SA. Values for the standard post-war Colts are established by four basic factors: caliber (popularity and scarcity), barrel length, finish, and condition. Shorter barrel lengths are generally more desirable than the 7.5". The .38 Special is the rarest caliber, but the .45 Colt and .44 Special are more sought after than the .357 Magnum. Special feature revolvers, such as the 350 factory-engraved guns produced during this period, must be individually appraised. The ivory situation in the world today has become quite a factor, as ivory grips are found on many SAAs. We will attempt to take these factors into consideration and evaluate this variation as accurately and clearly as possible. Remember as always, when in doubt secure a qualified appraisal.

NOTE: 4.75" barrel add 25 percent. 5.5" barrel add 15 percent. Nickel finish add 20 percent. Ivory grips add $250.

7.5" Barrel Model

.38 Special

NIB	Exc.	V.G.	Good	Fair	Poor
2450	1850	1200	900	700	600

.357 Magnum

NIB	Exc.	V.G.	Good	Fair	Poor
1850	1350	900	750	700	650

.44 Special

NIB	Exc.	V.G.	Good	Fair	Poor
2950	2250	1750	1100	1000	750

.45 Colt

NIB	Exc.	V.G.	Good	Fair	Poor
2000	1650	1400	1000	900	750

Sheriff's Model 1960-1975

Between 1960 and 1975, there were approximately 500 Sheriff's Models manufactured. They have 3" barrels and no ejector rod assemblies. The frames were made without the hole for the ejector rod to pass through. They were blued, with case colored frames; 25 revolvers were nickel-plated and would bring a sizable premium if authenticated. The barrels are marked "Colt Sheriff's Model." The serial number has an "SM" suffix. They are chambered for the .45 Colt cartridge.

NIB	Exc.	V.G.	Good	Fair	Poor
3000	2200	1800	1200	850	600

NOTE: Nickel finish add 20 percent.

Buntline Special 1957-1975

The "Buntline Special" was named after a dime novelist named Ned Buntline, who supposedly gave this special long barrel revolver to Wyatt Earp. The story is suspected to be purely legend as no Colt records exist to lend it credence. Be that as it may, the Colt factory decided to take advantage of the market and produced the 12" barreled SAA from 1957-1974. There were approximately 3,900 manufactured. They are chambered for the .45 Colt cartridge and are offered in the blued and case colored finish. Only 65 Buntlines are nickel-plated, making this an extremely rare variation that definitely should be authenticated before purchase. Walnut grips are the most commonly noted, but they are also offered with the checkered hard rubber grips. The barrels are marked on the left side "Colt Buntline Special .45."

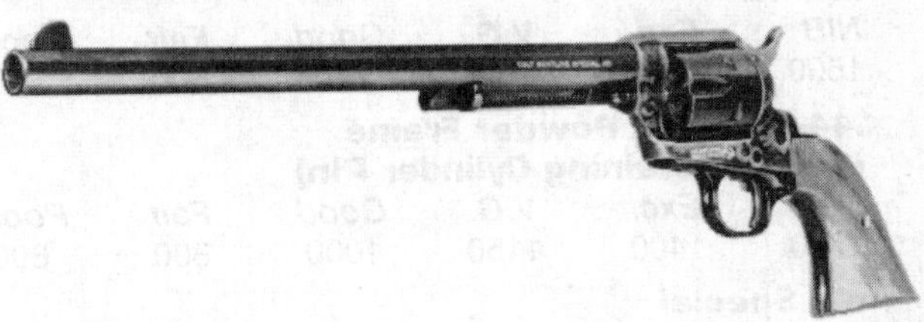

NIB	Exc.	V.G.	Good	Fair	Poor
2000	1650	1250	850	600	500

NOTE: Nickel finish add 60 percent.

New Frontier 1961-1975

The New Frontier is readily identified by its flattop frame and adjustable sight. It also has a high front sight. Colt manufactured approximately 4,200 of them. They are chambered for the .357 Magnum, .45 Colt, .44 Special (255 produced), and rarely (only 49 produced) in .38 Special. A few were chambered for the .44-40 cartridge. The 7.5" barrel length is by far the most common, but the 4.75" and 5.5" barrels are also offered. The standard finish is case colored and blued. Nickel-plating and full blue are offered but are rarely encountered. Standard grips are walnut. The barrel is stamped on the left side "Colt New Frontier S.A.A." The serial has the "NF" suffix.

NIB	Exc.	V.G.	Good	Fair	Poor
1750	1400	1000	800	600	500

NOTE: 4.75" barrel add 25 percent. 5.5" barrel add 20 percent. Full Blue add 50 percent. .38 Special add 50 percent. .44 Special add 30 percent. 44-40 add 30 percent

New Frontier Buntline Special 1962-1967

This model is rare, as Colt only manufactured 70 during this five-year period. They are similar to the standard Buntline, with a 12" barrel. They are chambered for .45 Colt only.

NIB	Exc.	V.G.	Good	Fair	Poor
4000	3000	2000	1500	1000	700

COLT THIRD GENERATION SINGLE-ACTION ARMY 1976-1981

In 1976 Colt made some internal changes in the SAA. The external configuration was not altered. The serial number range began in 1976 with #80000SA, and in 1978 #99999SA was reached. At this time the suffix became a prefix, and the new serial range began with #SA01001. This model's value is determined in much the same manner as was described in the section on the 2nd Generation SAAs. Caliber, barrel length, finish, and condition are once again the four main determining factors. The prevalence of special-order guns was greater during this period, and many more factory-engraved SAAs were produced. Colt's Custom Shop was quite active during this period. We feel that it is not advisable to undertake evaluation of specially embellished guns and strongly advise that competent appraisal be secured on any firearms that deviate from the standard. There are, quite frankly, too many fraudulent Colt SAAs out there; and the financial risks are great.

7.5" Barrel

.357 Magnum

NIB	Exc.	V.G.	Good	Fair	Poor
1200	1100	895	750	600	500

.44-40

NIB	Exc.	V.G.	Good	Fair	Poor
1500	1250	900	750	600	500

.44-40 Black Powder Frame (Screw Retaining Cylinder Pin)

NIB	Exc.	V.G.	Good	Fair	Poor
1700	1400	1150	1000	800	600

.44 Special

NIB	Exc.	V.G.	Good	Fair	Poor
1400	1200	900	700	550	500

.45 Colt

NIB	Exc.	V.G.	Good	Fair	Poor
1500	1300	900	750	600	500

NOTE: 4.75" barrel add 25 percent. 5.5" barrel add 10 percent. Nickel plated add 10 percent. Ivory grips add $250.

Sheriff's Model 3rd Generation

This model is similar to the 2nd Generation Sheriff's Model. The serial number and the fact that this model is also chambered for the .44-40 are the only external differences. Colt offered this model with interchangeable cylinders—.45 Colt/.45 ACP or .44-40/.44 Special—available in 3" barrel, blued and case colored finish standard.

NIB	Exc.	V.G.	Good	Fair	Poor
1050	875	750	600	450	400

NOTE: Interchangeable cylinders add 30 percent. Nickel finish add 10 percent. Ivory grips add $250.

Buntline Special 3rd Generation

This is the same basic configuration as the 2nd Generation with the 12" barrel. Standard finish blued and case-colored, it is chambered for .45 Colt and has checkered hard rubber grips.

NIB	Exc.	V.G.	Good	Fair	Poor
1050	875	750	600	450	400

NOTE: Nickel finish add 20 percent.

New Frontier 3rd Generation

This model is similar in appearance to the 2nd Generation guns. The 3rd Generation New Frontiers have five-digit serial numbers; the 2nd Generation guns, four-digit numbers. That and the calibers offered are basically the only differences. The 3rd Generations are chambered for the .44 Special and .45 Colt and are rarely found in .44-40. Barrel lengths are 7.5" standard, with the 4.75" and 5.5" rarely encountered.

NIB	Exc.	V.G.	Good	Fair	Poor
950	725	650	550	500	400

NOTE: .44-40 add 20 percent. 4.75" barrel add 35 percent. 5.5" barrel add 25 percent.

COLT CURRENT PRODUCTION SINGLE-ACTION ARMY 1982-PRESENT

NOTE: A surprising number of Colt pistols are still found in their original boxes, even older models. This can add 100 percent to the value of the pistol.

Standard Single-Action Army

The SAA, it is sad to note, has all but faded from the firearms picture. They are currently available as a special-order custom shop proposition. The cost is great; and the availability, low. The heyday of one of the most venerable firearms of them all is pretty much at an end. The SAAs have been available in .357 Magnum, .38-40, .44-40, .44 Special, and .45 Colt. Barrels were available in 3" through 10" lengths. The finishes are nickel-plated and blued, with case-colored frames. A number of optional finishes are available on request. Grips are available on a custom order basis. This model is available on special-order only.

NOTE: As of 2000 the Custom Shop is offering this revolver in the configurations listed:

P1840—Blued .45 Colt with 4.75" barrel.
P1841—Nickel .45 Colt with 4.75" barrel.
P1850—Blued .45 Colt with 5.5" barrel.
P1856—Nickel .45 Colt with 5.5" barrel.
P1940—Blued .44-40 with 4.75" barrel.
P1941—Nickel .44-40 with 4.75" barrel.
P1950—Blued .44-40 with 5.5" barrel.
P1956—Nickel .44-40 with 5.5" barrel.
P1640—Blued .357 Magnum with 4.75" barrel.
P1650—Blued .357 Magnum with 5.5" barrel.

Optional Features:

Nickel finish add $125. Royal blue finish add $200. Mirror brite finish add $225. Gold plate add $365. Silver plate add $365. Class A engraving add $875. Class B engraving add $1,200. Class C engraving add $1,500. Class D engraving add $1,750. Buntline engraving add 15 percent.

NIB	Exc.	V.G.	Good	Fair	Poor
1200	1100	850	—	—	—

Colt Cowboy (CB1850)

Introduced in 1998 this model is a replica of the Single-Action Army that features a modern transfer bar safety system. Offered with 5.5" barrel and chambered for .45 Colt. Sights are fixed with walnut grips. Blued barrel with case colored frame. Weight is about 42 oz.

NIB	Exc.	V.G.	Good	Fair	Poor
650	500	—	—	—	—

Colt Single-Action Army "The Legend"

A limited-edition revolver built to commemorate Colt's official PRCA sponsorship. Limited to 1,000. Chambered for .45 Long Colt fitted with a 5-1/2" barrel. Nickel finish Buffalo horn grips with gold medallions. Machine engraved and washed in gold.

This symbol denotes "Sleepers" with rapidly-rising values and/or significant collector potential.

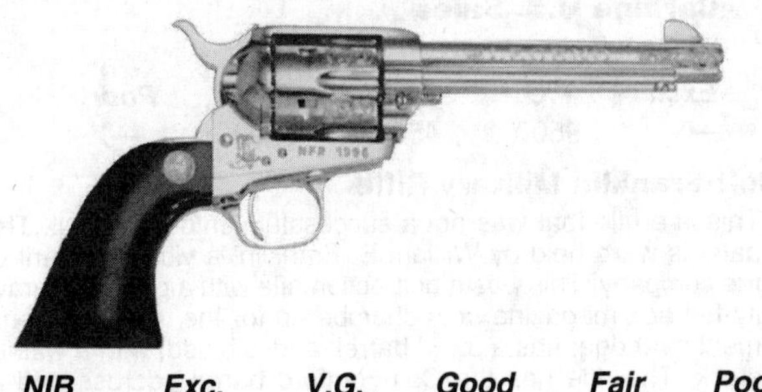

NIB	Exc.	V.G.	Good	Fair	Poor
2750	2250	—	—	—	—

COLT SCOUT MODEL SINGLE-ACTION ARMY

NOTE: A surprising number of Colt pistols are still found in their original boxes, even older models. This can add 100 percent to the value of the pistol.

Anyone wishing to procure a factory letter authenticating a Single-Action Army should do so by writing to: COLT HISTORIAN, P.O. BOX 1868, HARTFORD, CT 06101. There is a charge of $50 per serial number for this service. If Colt cannot provide the desired information, $10 will be refunded. Enclose the Colt model name, serial number, and your name and address, along with the check.

Frontier Scout 1957-1971

This is a scaled-down version of the SAA that is chambered for the .22 LR with an interchangeable .22 Magnum cylinder. It is offered with a 4.25", 4.75", or a 9.5" barrel. The frame is alloy. First year production frame were duotone with frame left in the white and the balance of the revolver blued. All blue models and wood grips became available in 1958. In 1961 the duotone model was dropped from production. A .22 Magnum model was first offered in 1959. In 1964 dual cylinders were introduced. These revolvers have "Q" or "F" serial number suffixes. In 1960 the "K" series Scout was introduced and featured a heavier frame, nickel plating, and wood grips. The majority of commemorative revolvers are of this type. This series was discontinued in 1970. Prices are about 15 percent higher than for the "Q" and "F" series guns.

NIB	Exc.	V.G.	Good	Fair	Poor
450	325	200	175	125	90

NOTE: 9.5" Buntline add 50 percent. Extra cylinder add 10 percent.

THE BRIEF LIFE OF COLT'S COWBOY

DAN SHIDELER

What? You don't remember the Colt Cowboy? You're not alone. Many people have a hazy, faint recollection of the Colt Cowboy, much as you might remember an all-night poker game after a fifth of Jim Beam and some bad sausages. Like Colt's All-American 2000 semi-auto pistol, the Cowboy was another of Colt's failed yet well-intentioned efforts at throwing something—anything—up against a wall to see if it would stick.

The All-American 2000 didn't stick. Neither did the Cowboy.

The Colt Cowboy was rolled out at the 1998 SHOT Show. Well-known gunwriter John Taffin wasn't impressed with the prototype.

"When I saw it," he writes in *Single Action Sixguns* (Krause Publications, 2005), "I must admit I was totally underwhelmed…I went directly to the Colt rep to ask if it was made in Germany. They assured me it was not. But it did not look, feel or smell like a Colt. It did say COLT on the barrel, however."

That was the prototype. Taffin was not quite so critical of the production model, saying the final version of the Cowboy was tight, reasonably accurate and compared well to other Single Action Army knockoffs. But there were four characteristics that distinguished the Cowboy from other 1873 replicas: the letters "C," "O," "L" and "T."

The Cowboy vanished from the market after only five years. Why?

Part of the reason was the Cowboy's street price, which ran from $500 to $600. That's about half of what a Single Action Army ran at the time, but it was about 25 percent more expensive than the comparable Ruger Vaquero. And that wasn't all: When you cocked the Cowboy, it made only three clicks, not four, another result of the transfer bar. "Real" Colts made four.

The Cowboy was advertised as being made in America, and therein lies a tale. In 2002, American Western Arms, importer of several high-quality SAA clones, was sued by New Colt Holding Corp. and Colt Manufacturing Corp. for "infringement of trade dress." In this lawsuit, Colt claimed that, in putting a running-horse emblem on the grips of its Longhorn single-action revolver, AWA was attempting to pass off the Longhorn as a genuine Colt.

Even by the standards of the legal profession, the Colt/AWA lawsuit was a nasty affair. In fact, in his ruling, District Court Judge Peter C. Dorsey noted, "It bears mentioning at the outset that the hostility evident in both parties' briefs is entirely inappropriate and unprofessional. Referring to another party's argument as preposterous, ludicrous, absurd, or anything similar does nothing to advance rational discussion of an issue or aid in its resolution."

Was the Cowboy really made in America? Yes, at least in a strictly legal sense. According to the recollection of a friend who was deposed for the lawsuit, the Cowboy was assembled and packaged in the Colt plant in Hartford, Conn. Judge Dorsey acknowledged in his ruling that Colt was legally entitled to claim the Cowboy was made in America, even though its "frame, trigger guard, hammer, frontstrap, backstrap, ejector rod, and ejector rod housing are all cast in Canada…."

In a nutshell, then, the Cowboy was assembled in the United States from Canadian investment-cast components. So, was it really "made in America" as most shooters understand it? Take your choice.

But it's a fine-looking revolver regardless. After all, it's got those four magic letters right there on its barrel.

Peacemaker Scout & New Frontier

This model is similar to the Frontier Scout, with a steel case-colored or blued frame. Fitted with old style black plastic eagle grips.The barrel lengths offered are 4.75", 6", or 7.5" (Buntline model). It also has an interchangeable .22 Magnum cylinder. Most of these revolvers had a "G" suffix although some built in 1974 had a "L" suffix. In 1982 through 1986 a New Frontier model with cross-bolt safety was offered. This model is often referred to as the "GS" series. This revolver was offered with adjustable sights only. No Peacemakers were offered in this series.

NIB	Exc.	V.G.	Good	Fair	Poor
550	475	300	200	150	100

Scout Model SAA 1962-1971

This is basically a scaled-down version of the SAA chambered for the .22 LR cartridge. This model is offered with a 4.75", 6", or 7" barrel. The earlier production has case-colored frames with the remainder blued; later production is all blued. Grips are checkered hard rubber. This model was discontinued in 1986.

NIB	Exc.	V.G.	Good	Fair	Poor
400	275	200	150	100	75

COLT ANTIQUE LONG ARMS

Berdan Single-Shot Rifle

This is a scarce rifle on today's market. There were approximately 30,200 manufactured, but nearly 30,000 of them were sent to Russia. This rifle was produced from 1866-1870. It is a trapdoor-type action chambered for .42 centerfire. The standard model has a 32.5" barrel; the carbine, 18.25". The finish is blued, with a walnut stock. This rifle was designed and the patent held by Hiram Berdan, Commander of the Civil War "Sharpshooters" Regiment. This was actually Colt's first cartridge arm. The 30,000 rifles and 25 half-stocked carbines that were sent to Russia were in Russian Cyrillic letters. The few examples made for American sales have Colt's name and Hartford address on the barrel.

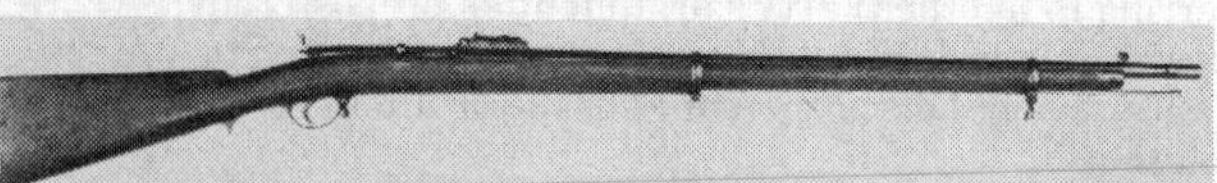

Courtesy Milwaukee Public Museum, Milwaukee, Wisconsin

Rifle Russian Order

30,000 manufactured.

Exc.	V.G.	Good	Fair	Poor
—	2000	750	450	—

Carbine Russian Order

25 manufactured.

Exc.	V.G.	Good	Fair	Poor
—	5500	3000	1250	—

Rifle U.S. Sales

100 manufactured.

Exc.	V.G.	Good	Fair	Poor
—	5000	2250	1250	—

Carbine U.S. Sales

25 manufactured.

Exc.	V.G.	Good	Fair	Poor
—	9500	4500	2000	—

Colt-Franklin Military Rifle

This is a rifle that was not a successful venture for Colt. The patents were held by William B. Franklin, a vice-president of the company. This was a bolt-action rifle with a primitive, gravity-fed box magazine. It is chambered for the .45-70 government cartridge, has a 32.5" barrel, and is blued, with a walnut stock. The rifle has the Colt Hartford barrel address and is stamped with an eagle's head and U.S. inspectors marks. There were only 50 of these rifles produced, and it is believed that they were prototypes intended for government sales. This was not to be, and production ceased after approximately 50 were manufactured in 1887 and 1888.

Exc.	V.G.	Good	Fair	Poor
—	8000	4500	2000	—

Colt-Burgess Lever-Action Rifle

This represented Colt's only attempt to compete with Winchester for the lever-action rifle market. It is said that when Winchester started to produce revolving handguns for prospective marketing, Colt dropped the Burgess from its line. This rifle is chambered for .44-40. It has a 25.5" barrel and a 15-shot tubular magazine. The Carbine version has a 20.5" barrel and 12-shot magazine. The finish is blued, with a case-colored hammer and lever. The stock is walnut with an oil finish. The Colt Hartford address is on the barrel, and "Burgess Patents" is stamped on the bottom of the lever. There were 3,775 rifles manufactured—1,219 with round barrels and 2,556 with octagonal barrels. There were also 2,593 Carbines. The Burgess was produced from 1883-1885.

Courtesy Buffalo Bill Historical Center, Cody, Wyoming

Rifle

Octagonal barrel.

Exc.	V.G.	Good	Fair	Poor
—	—	3500	1500	550

Rifle

Round barrel.

Exc.	V.G.	Good	Fair	Poor
—	—	3500	1500	550

Carbine

Exc.	V.G.	Good	Fair	Poor
—	—	5000	2000	950

Baby Carbine

Lighter frame and barrel (RARE).

Exc.	V.G.	Good	Fair	Poor
—	—	6000	2500	1150

Lightning Slide-Action, Medium-Frame

This was the first slide-action rifle Colt produced. It is chambered for .32-20, .38-40, and .44-40 and was intended to be a companion piece to the SAAs in the same calibers. The rifle has a 26" barrel with 15-shot tube magazine; the carbine, a 20" barrel with 12-shot magazine. The finish is blued, with case-colored hammer; the walnut stock is oil-finished; and the forend, usually checkered. The Colt name and Hartford address are stamped on the barrel along with the patent dates. There were approximately 89,777 manufactured between 1884 and 1902.

This symbol denotes "Sleepers" with rapidly-rising values and/or significant collector potential.

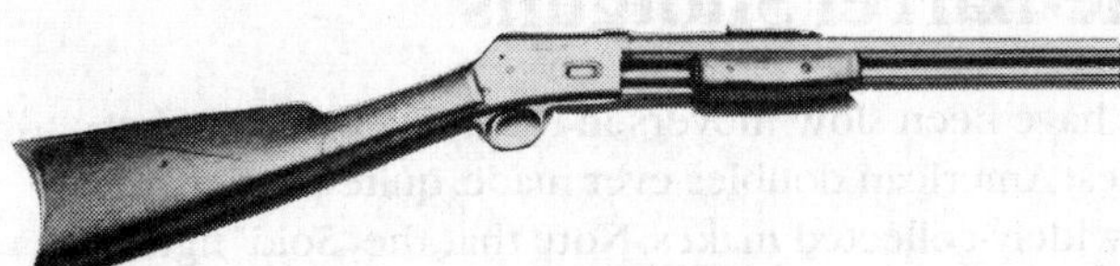

Courtesy Bonhams & Butterfields, San Francisco, California

Rifle

Exc.	V.G.	Good	Fair	Poor
—	2000	1250	750	400

Carbine

Exc.	V.G.	Good	Fair	Poor
—	3000	1750	800	500

Military Rifle or Carbine

.44-40 caliber, short magazine tube, bayonet lug, and sling swivels.

Exc.	V.G.	Good	Fair	Poor
—	4000	2000	1000	600

Baby Carbine

1 lb., lighter version of standard carbine.

Courtesy Richard M. Kumor Sr.

Exc.	V.G.	Good	Fair	Poor
—	4500	2500	1250	750

San Francisco Police Rifle

.44-40 caliber, #SFP 1-SFP401 on bottom tang.

Exc.	V.G.	Good	Fair	Poor
—	3250	1250	800	500

Lightning Slide-Action Small-Frame

This is a well-made rifle and the first of its type that Colt manufactured. It is chambered for the .22 Short and Long. The standard barrel length is 24"; the finish, blued with a case-colored hammer. The stock is walnut; some were checkered; some, not. The barrel is stamped with the Colt name and Hartford address and the patent dates. There were 89,912 manufactured between 1887 and 1904.

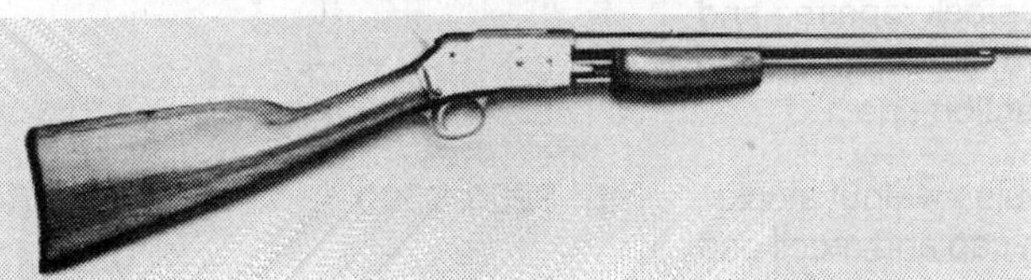

Courtesy Bonhams & Butterfields, San Francisco, California

Exc.	V.G.	Good	Fair	Poor
2500	1100	700	500	300

Lightning Slide-Action, Large-Frame

This rifle is similar in appearance to the medium-frame Lightning, though larger in size. It is chambered in larger rifle calibers of the era, from .38-56 up to .50-95 Express. The larger calibers are more desirable from a collector's standpoint. The rifle has a 28" barrel; the carbine, a 22" barrel. The finish is blued, with a case-colored hammer. The stock is oiled walnut; the forend, checkered. The Colt name and Hartford address are stamped on the barrel along with the patent dates. This rifle is quite large and has come to be known as the "Express model." Colt manufactured 6,496 between 1887 and 1894.

Rifle

28" octagonal barrel.

Exc.	V.G.	Good	Fair	Poor
—	4500	2000	750	500

Rifle

28" round barrel.

Exc.	V.G.	Good	Fair	Poor
—	4000	1750	750	500

Carbine

22" barrel.

Exc.	V.G.	Good	Fair	Poor
—	7500	3500	1500	750

Baby Carbine

22" barrel 1 lb. lighter.

Exc.	V.G.	Good	Fair	Poor
—	10000	5000	2250	950

Model 1878 Double-Barrel Shotgun

This model is chambered in 10 or 12 gauge and has 28", 30", or 32" barrels. It is a sidelock double-trigger hammer gun with case-colored locks and breech. The barrels are browned Damacus-patterned. The checkered walnut stock is varnished or oil-finished. The Colt's Hartford address is stamped on the barrel rib; and Colt's name, on the lock. This has been regarded as one of the finest shotguns made in America, although Colt had difficulty competing with the less expensive European imports of the day. They ceased production after only 22,690 were manufactured between 1878 and 1889.

Exc.	V.G.	Good	Fair	Poor
—	1500	900	500	300

NOTE: Fully engraved model add 300 percent.

Model 1883 Double-Barrel Shotgun

This model is a hammerless boxlock, chambered for 10 or 12 gauge. The barrels are 28", 30", or 32"; and it features double triggers. The frame and furniture are case-colored; the barrels, browned with Damascus pattern. The checkered walnut stock is varnished or oil-finished. Colt's Hartford address is stamped on the barrel rib. "Colt" is stamped on each side of the frame. Again, as in the Model 1878, this is rated as one of the finest of all American-made shotguns. There were many special orders, and they require individual appraisal. Colt manufactured 7,366 of these guns between 1883 and 1895.

Exc.	V.G.	Good	Fair	Poor
—	2000	1400	775	400

NOTE: Fully engraved model add 300 percent.

Double-Barrel Rifle

This is one of the rarest of all Colt firearms and is a prize for the Colt collector. There were only 35 of these guns manufactured. They were said to be the special interest of Caldwell Hart Colt, Samuel Colt's son, who was an avid arms collector. It is said that most of the 35 guns produced wound up in his collection or those of his friends. This gun is chambered for .45-70 or one of the larger variations thereof. It is an exposed hammer sidelock with double triggers. The locks, breech, and furniture are case-colored; the barrels, browned or blued. The barrels are 28" in length, and the checkered stock was oil-finished or varnished walnut. The barrel rib is stamped with the Colt name and Hartford address. The locks are also stamped "Colt." One must exercise extreme caution in dealing with this model as there have been model 1878 Shotguns converted into double rifles. Colt manufactured the 35 guns over the period 1879-1885.

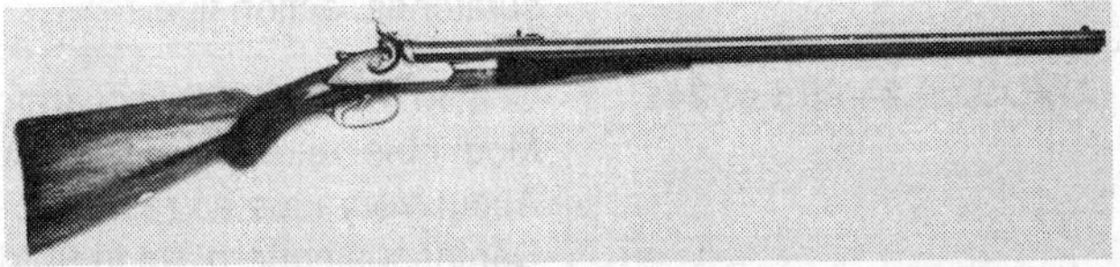

Courtesy Bonhams & Butterfields, San Francisco, California

Exc.	V.G.	Good	Fair	Poor
—	30000	17500	7000	1750

Value Tracker: Colt Double-Barrel Shotguns

Until relatively recently, Colt double shotguns from the late 1800s have been slow movers in the collectibles market. Today, Colt doubles are increasingly recognized as some of the finest American doubles ever made, quite properly keeping company with Parkers, Bakers, LeFevers and other more widely-collected makes. Note that the "Sold" figures below may include a buyer's premium.

*Legend: **RIA** = Rock Island Auctions; **B&B** = Butterfield & Butterfield; **AMOS** = Amoskeag; **JCD** = J. C. Devine; **JDJ** + James D. Julia; **GMA** = Greg Martin. Contact information for these fine auction houses can be found in the front pages of this book.*

Auction House/Date/Lot No.	Item Description	Estimated Value	Actually Sold For
RIA 08/27-29/05 Lot 24	Colt M1878 #3140, 10 ga., 30" solid-rib bbls., extra fancy feather-grain walnut round knob pistol grip stock and forearm w/inlaid ebony tip. "Very Good," 60 percent brown on strong Damascus pattern bbls., mostly gray patina overall, wood good w/several repaired areas, wrist cracks, chips and repairs.	E: $1,800-$2,250	$1,265
RIA 08/27-29/05 Lot 26	Colt M1878 #11820, 12 ga., 28" solid-rib bbls. shortened from orig. length, walnut stock. "Fair," gray-brown patina w/scattered spots of surface rust, wood w/normal scratches and dents, action good.	E: $600-$900	$862.50
RIA 08/27-29/05 Lot 27	Colt M1878 #7917, 10 ga., 32" solid-rib bbls., replacement wood, "an extra barrel *[sic]* #1897 accompanies it." About Good as configured, metal worn to gray-brown patina, wood worn smooth in spots w/repairs and a splinter, action tight.	E: $300-$600	$805
RIA 08/27-29/05 Lot 28	Colt M1883 #1264, 10 ga., 32" solid-rib bbls., walnut stock with recoil pad added, grip cap and forearm replaced. "Good as refurbished," retains most of new brown on bbls. and reblue elsewhere, stock repaired w/steel pins, refinished with later scratches, scrapes, mechanically fine.	E: $400-$600	$575
RIA 08/27-29/05 Lot 285	Colt M1878 #3429 (mfg 1880), 12 ga., 30" solid-rib bbls., walnut stock. "Excellent," 80 percent brown finish on Damascus bbls., up to 90 percent case color, wood excellent except for minor dents, forearm gouge and second coat of varnish at rear of stock, action tight.	E: $3,000-$5,000	$2,070
RIA 08/27-29/05 Lot 619	Colt 1883 #4490, 10 ga., 32" solid-rib bbls., walnut stock. "Fine," strong Damascus pattern on bbls., stock repaired and refinished at wrist near rear of trigger guard, some good case color, one trigger guard screw replaced, action fine.	E: $800-$1,500	$575
RIA 08/27-29/05 Lot 644	Colt M1883 #4455, 12 ga., 30" solid-rib bbls., walnut stock. "About Good," buttstock replaced with grip cap and recoil pad probably added at the same time, strong Damascus pattern but little brown on bbls., faded case color, wood sound, action good.	E: $250-$500	$373.75
RIA 08/27-29/05 Lot 645	Colt M1883 #2329, 12 ga., 30" solid-rib bbls., walnut stock. About Fair to Good without finish, all metal cleaned to gray w/some dents, stains remaining, wood sound w/dents and scratches, action fine.	E: $300-$600	$517.50
AMOS 09/24/05 Lot 241	Colt M1878 #G305 *[sic]*, (mfg 1880), 12 ga., 30" solid-rib Mod. bbls., straight grip walnut stock and splinter forend. About Very Fine as restored, bbls. w/brown and gray Damascus pattern, up to 99 percent restored case color, wood excellent as professionally restored and recheckered, mechanically excellent.	E: $1,500-$2,000	$1,035

Auction House/Date/Lot No.	Item Description	Estimated Value	Actually Sold For
AMOS 08/06/05 Lot 174	Colt M1883 #2740, 10 ga., 32" bbls., checkered walnut pistol grip stock w/cap and splinter forend w/ebony tip. About Fine to Very Fine but for crack through wrist, 75-95 percent case color, bbls. w/Damascus pattern full length, "locks up nice and tight."	E: $800-$1,200	UNSOLD
B&B 06/29/05 Lot 2066	Colt M1883 #1094, 10 ga., 30" bbls., casehardened boxlock action engraved w/game scenes, deluxe burl walnut checkered forend w/pistol grip stock. "Poor," much Damascus finish on bbls., trigger guard bow broken, stock broken and repaired at wrist.	E: $500-$800	$460
RIA 4/29-5/1/06 Lot 1191	Colt M1878 #9201, 10 ga., 32" solid concave-rib bbls., extra fancy walnut checkered round-knob pistol grip stock and forearm w/ inlaid ebony forearm tip, blank initial escutcheon. "Very Good," 75 percent finish intact, fine Damascus pattern on bbls., 50 percent case color, stock fine, action excellent.	E: $1,500-$2,250	$2,070
RIA 4/29-5/1/06 Lot 1192	Colt M1878 #3429 (mfg 1880), 12 ga., 30" solid-rib bbls., walnut checkered round-knob pistol grip stock and forearm. "Excellent," 90 percent brown finish on Damascus pattern bbls., up to 90 percent case color, ding on left forearm, action tight.	E: $3,000-$5,000	$2,875
RIA 4/29-5/1/06 Lot 1195	Colt M1883 #6884 (mfg 1893), 12 ga., 28" solid concave-rib bbls., extra fancy walnut checkered stock and forearm w/ebony forearm tip and horn Colt buttplate. "Fine," 85 percent finish, slight scuffs and dings overall, wood excellent w/no finish loss.	E: $1,500-$2,500	$1,150
RIA 12/3-5/05 Lot 3560	Colt M1883 #8096 (mfg 1895), 12 ga., 28" solid-rib bbls., fine walnut stock and forearm. "Very Good +," Damascus pattern retains 50 percent brown, good case color, wood w/many dents and scratches, butt plate missing bottom tip.	E: $1,000-$1,500	$488.75
RIA 12/3-5/05 Lot 3595	Colt M1878 #859, 12 ga., 30" solid-rib bbls. About Good, traces of finish in protected areas, faded Damascus pattern on bbls., wood lightly cleaned w/some thinning of checkering, chips missing from forearm.	E: $550-$1,100	$862.50
RIA 12/3-5/05 Lot 3596	Colt M1878 #8245, 10 ga., 30" solid-rib bbls. About Fair to Good, traces of finish in protected areas, mostly gray patina overall, bbl. dents, forearm repaired and refinished, mechanically good.	E: $650-$1,100	$862.50
RIA 09/16-18/06 Lot 597	Colt M1883 #5000 (mfg 1878-89), 12 ga., 28" solid concave-rib bbls., fancy checkered pistol grip stock w/blank silver initial oval and checkered horn buttplate. "Very Good," excellent Damascus pattern on bbls., frame is a smooth silver, stock very good, action crisp.	E: $1,200-$1,500	$1,092.50
JCD 04/23/06 Lot 284	Colt M1878 #1849 (mfg 1878-89), 12 ga., 30" bbls. w/very good bores, splinter forend, good checkering on round knob pistol grip buttstock. "Antique - Fine," excellent Damascus pattern, 30 percent case color in places but mottled receiver.	E: $600-$800	$920
JCD 04/23/06 Lot 285	Colt M1883 #6431 (mfg 1883-95), 12 ga., 30" bbls. w/fair bores, left barrel with rifle cartridge tube insert. "Antique - Good," good Damascus pattern, good figure to checkered pistol grip buttstock and splinter forend.	E: $400-$600	$575

Auction House/Date/Lot No.	Item Description	Estimated Value	Actually Sold For
JCD 04/23/06 Lot 622	Colt M1878 #18921 (mfg 1878-89), 10 ga., 30" Full and Modified bbls. w/rusted, pitted bores, round knob pistol grip buttstock and splinter forend. "Fair," stress cracks from the back of each lockplate over the wrist.	E: $200-$400	$460
JCD 04/23/06 Lot 62	Colt M1878 #11727 (mfg 1878-89), 12 ga., 28.5" w\ Full and Modified bbls. w/fair bores, round knob pistol grip buttstock and splinter forend. About Good to Very Good, w/good Damascus pattern, gray receivers, lockplates and hammers, forearm w/splinter, buttstock w/repaired crack.	E: $200-$400	$402.50
JCD 11/21/04 Lot 269	Colt M1878 #15995 (mfg 1883), 12 ga., 30" Imp. Cyl. bbls., bores w/light pitting and dents, "plainest grade." About Good to Very Good, gun broken through at wrist, bbls. gray brown, frame and locks apparently re-colored.	E:200-$300	$287.50
B&B 08/16/04 Lot 1019 –	Colt M1883 #6498, 12 ga., 28" bbls., figured walnut pistol grip stock and forend w/checkered panels. Very Good to Fine, 90 percent Damascus pattern, action 20-30 percent faded case colors, wood w/95 percent + varnish, bore w/some light pitting.	E:$1,000-$1,800	$862.50
AMOS 09/25/04 Lot 324	Colt M1878 #20004, 12 ga. 28" Imp. Cyl. and Mod. bbls. w/very good bores but one with odd pitting, sound checkered round-knob pistol grip stock and splinter forend rate very good. About Good to Very Good.	E: $400-$600	$460
AMOS 09/25/04 Lot 325 –	Colt M1878 #2888, 12 ga. 30" bbls. "choked about a light Modified with fair bores" w/pitting, fading Damascus pattern. About Very Good w/checkered stock and forend rating very good +, no cracking or refinishing.	E: $350-$550	$488.75
AMOS 09/25/04 Lot 326	Colt M1883 #7770, 12 ga. 28" Imp. Cyl. and Mod. bbls. w/ good to fair bores. About Very Good to Fine, full Damascus pattern, receiver mostly gray, wood very good with much original finish.	E: $450-$650	$488.75
JDJ 10/04-07/04 Lot 732	Grade 2 Colt M1883 #4425 (mfg 1889), 12 ga., 30" straight, matted rib bbls., engraved receiver w/game scenes, checkered, figured walnut Prince of Wales stock and black-tipped splinter forearming w/game scenes on receiver. "Very Fine," 90 percent Damascus pattern w/scrape at forearm, 75-80 percent case color, wood w/95 percent orig. varnish, mechanics fine.	E: $3,000-$5,000	$4,680
JDJ 10/04-07/04 Lot 733	M1878 #8596, 12 ga., 30" bbls. w/tapered, concave rib nicely figured walnut semi-pistol grip stock and black-tip splinter forearm, steel buttplate. "Extremely Fine," 90-92 percent Damascus pattern, 50-60 percent case color, wood sound w/most of what may be a restored varnish finish.	E: $3,000-$5,000	$4,600
JDJ 10/04-07/04 Lot 734	M1878 #1008, 12 ga., 30" Modified bbls., coarse-checkered straight-grain walnut semi-pistol grip stock and Schnabel forearm. "Very Good," 75-80 percent Damascus pattern w/dent near right muzzle, 25-60 percent case color, wood sound w/moderate to heavy wear.	E: $800-$1,200	$1,170

COLT DOUBLE-ACTION REVOLVERS

Model 1877 "Lightning" and "Thunderer"

The Model 1877 was Colt's first attempt at manufacturing a double-action revolver. It shows a striking resemblance to the Single-Action Army. Sales on this model were brisk, with over 166,000 produced between 1877 and 1909. Chambered for two different cartridges, the .38 Colt, known as the "Lightning," and .41 Colt, as the "Thunderer." The standard finishes are blued, with case-colored frame and nickel plate. The bird's-head grips are of checkered rosewood on the early guns and hard rubber on the majority of the production run. The barrel lengths most often encountered are 2.5" and 3.5" without an ejector rod, and 4.5" and 6" with the rod. Other barrel lengths from 1.5" through 10" were offered. The Model 1877 holds 6 shots in either caliber. There were quite a few different variations found within this model designation. Values furnished are for the standard variations. Antiques made before 1898 would be more desirable from an investment standpoint.

Without Ejector, 2.5" and 3.5" Barrel

Exc.	*V.G.*	*Good*	*Fair*	*Poor*
3000	2000	1000	500	350

With Ejector, 4.5" and 6" Barrel

Exc.	*V.G.*	*Good*	*Fair*	*Poor*
3000	1800	1000	750	450

NOTE: Premium for blued guns add 25 percent. Premium for shorter than 2-1/2" add 50 percent. .41 Caliber "Thunderer" add 10 percent. Over 6" barrel add 50 percent. London barrel address add 20 percent. .32 caliber add 50 percent. Rosewood grips add 10 percent.

Model 1878 "Frontier"

This model is a large and somewhat ungainly looking revolver. It has a solid frame with a removable trigger guard. The cylinder does not swing out, and there is a thin loading gate. It has bird's-head grips made of checkered hard rubber; walnut would be found on the early models. The finish is either blued and case-colored or nickel-plated. The Model 1878 holds 6 shots, and the standard barrel lengths are 4.75", 5.5", and 7.5" with an ejector assembly and 3", 3.5", and 4" without. The standard chamberings for the Model 1878 are .32-20, .38-40, .41 Colt, .44-40, and .45 Colt. This model was fairly well received because it is chambered for the large calibers that were popular in that era. Colt manufactured 51,210 between 1878 and 1905. Antique models made before 1898 would be more desirable from an investment standpoint.

Model 1878 "Frontier" Standard

Courtesy Bonhams & Butterfields, San Francisco, California

Exc.	*V.G.*	*Good*	*Fair*	*Poor*
4200	3000	1200	800	400

NOTE: Add a 15 percent premium for blued revolvers. Add 10-50 percent premium for calibers other than .44-40 or .45.

Model 1878 "Frontier" Omnipotent

This is a special order version of the model above with the name "Omnipotent" stamped on the barrel.

Exc.	*V.G.*	*Good*	*Fair*	*Poor*
16000	10000	6000	3000	1000

Sheriff's Model

Chambered for .44-40 or .45 Colt with barrels lengths of 3.5" or 4".

Exc.	*V.G.*	*Good*	*Fair*	*Poor*
6000	4000	2000	1000	800

Model 1902 (Philippine or Alaskan Model)

This is a U.S. Ordnance contract Model 1878. It has a 6" barrel and is chambered for .45 Colt. The finish is blued, and there is a lanyard swivel on the butt. This model bears the U.S. inspector's marks. It is sometimes referred to as the Philippine or the Alaskan model. The trigger guard is quite a bit larger than standard.

Courtesy Bonhams & Butterfields

Exc.	*V.G.*	*Good*	*Fair*	*Poor*
5500	3500	1800	1000	600

Model 1889 Navy—Civilian Model

The 1889 Navy is an important model from a historical standpoint as it was the first double-action revolver Colt manufactured with a swing-out cylinder. They produced 31,000 of them between 1889 and 1894. The Model 1889 is chambered for the .38 Colt and the .41 Colt cartridges. The cylinder holds 6 shots.

It is offered with a 3", 4.5", or 6" barrel; and the finish was either blued or nickel-plated. The grips are checkered hard rubber with the "Rampant Colt" in an oval molded into them. The patent dates 1884 and 1888 appear in the barrel marking, and the serial numbers are stamped on the butt.

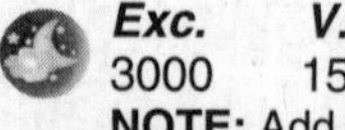

Exc.	V.G.	Good	Fair	Poor
3000	1500	1000	600	300

NOTE: Add premium for blued models. For 3" barrel add 20 percent.

REMINDER
Prices paid for firearms is an ever-changing affair based on a large number of variables.

Model 1889 U.S. Navy—Martial Model

This variation has a 6" barrel, is chambered for .38 Colt, and is offered in blued finish only. "U.S.N." is stamped on the butt. Most of the Navy models were altered at the Colt factory to add the Model 1895 improvements. An original unaltered specimen would be worth as much as 50 percent premium over the altered values listed.

Courtesy Bonhams & Butterfields, San Francisco, California

Exc.	V.G.	Good	Fair	Poor
9000	5000	2500	1000	500

Model 1892 "New Army and Navy"—Civilian Model

This model is similar in appearance to the 1889 Navy. The main differences are improvements to the lockwork function. It has double bolt stop notches, a double cylinder locking bolt, and shorter flutes on the cylinder. The .38 Smith & Wesson and the .32-20 were added to the .38 Colt and .41 Colt chamberings. The checkered hard rubber grips are standard, with plain walnut grips found on some contract series guns. Barrel lengths and finishes are the same as described for the Model 1889. The patent dates 1895 and 1901 appear stamped on later models. Colt manufactured 291,000 of these revolvers between 1892 and 1907. Antiques before 1898 are more desirable from an investment standpoint.

Exc.	V.G.	Good	Fair	Poor
2000	800	500	200	100

NOTE: For 3" barrel add 20 percent.

Model 1892 U.S. Navy—Martial Model

Exc.	V.G.	Good	Fair	Poor
3500	2000	800	600	400

Courtesy Bonhams & Butterfields, San Francisco, California

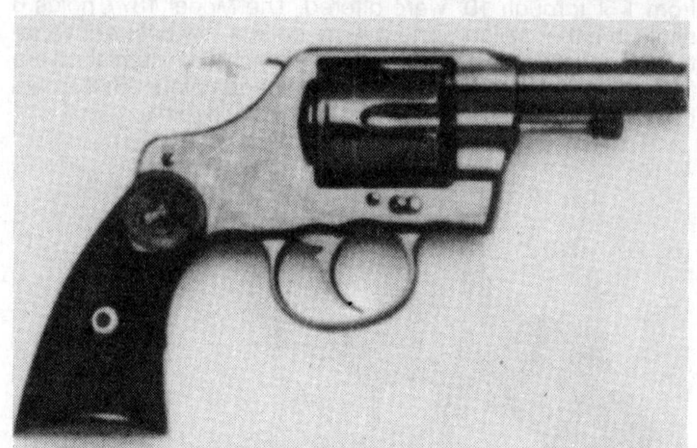

Courtesy Bonhams & Butterfields, San Francisco, California

Model 1892 U.S. Army—Martial Model

Exc.	V.G.	Good	Fair	Poor
3500	2000	800	600	400

Model 1896/1896 Army

Exc.	V.G.	Good	Fair	Poor
3500	2000	800	600	400

Model 1905 Marine Corps

This model is a variation of the New Army and Navy Model. It was derived from the late production with its own serial range #10001-10926. With only 926 produced between 1905 and 1909, it is quite rare on today's market and is eagerly sought after by Colt Double-Action collectors. This model is chambered for the .38 Colt and the .38 Smith & Wesson Special cartridges. It holds 6 shots, has a 6" barrel, and is offered in a blued finish only. The grips are checkered walnut and are quite different than those found on previous models. "U.S.M.C." is stamped on the butt; patent dates of 1884, 1888, and 1895 are stamped on the barrel. One hundred twenty-five of these revolvers were earmarked for civilian sales and do not have the Marine Corps markings; these will generally be found in better condition. Values are similar.

Courtesy Faintich Auction Services, Inc., Paul Goodwin photo

Exc.	V.G.	Good	Fair	Poor
4500	3500	2000	1500	750

This symbol denotes "Sleepers" with rapidly-rising values and/or significant collector potential.

New Service Model

This model was in continual production from 1898 through 1944. It is chambered for 11 different calibers: .38 Special, .357 Magnum, .38-40, .44 Russian, .44 Special, .44-40, .45 ACP, .45 Colt, .450 Eley, .455 Eley, and .476 Eley. It is offered in barrel lengths from 2" to 7.5", either blued or nickel-plated. Checkered hard rubber grips were standard until 1928, and then checkered walnut grips were used with an inletted Colt medallion. This was the largest swing-out cylinder double-action revolver that Colt ever produced, and approximately 356,000 were manufactured over the 46 years they were made. There are many different variations of this revolver, and one should consult a book dealing strictly with Colt for a thorough breakdown and description.

Courtesy Cherry's Collector Firearms Auction, Paul Goodwin photo

Early Model, #1-21000

Exc.	V.G.	Good	Fair	Poor
1000	650	350	200	125

Early Model Target, #6000-15000

Checkered walnut grips, flattop frame, 7.5" barrel.

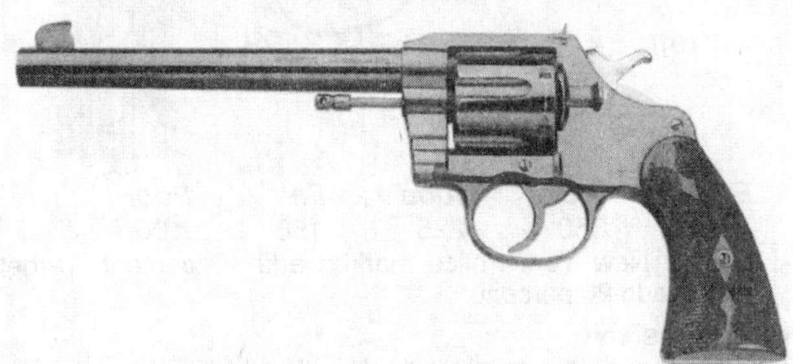

Courtesy Faintich Auction Services, Inc., Paul Goodwin photo

Exc.	V.G.	Good	Fair	Poor
3000	1500	550	300	200

Improved Model, #21000-325000

Has internal locking improvements.

Courtesy Faintich Auction Services, Inc., Paul Goodwin photo

Exc.	V.G.	Good	Fair	Poor
850	550	300	175	150

Improved Target Model, #21000-325000

Courtesy Faintich Auction Services, Inc., Paul Goodwin photo

Exc.	V.G.	Good	Fair	Poor
2250	1500	550	300	200

U.S. Army Model 1909, #30000-50000

5.5" barrel, .45 Colt, walnut grips, "U.S. Army Model 1909" on butt.

Exc.	V.G.	Good	Fair	Poor
1500	900	550	300	200

U.S. Navy Model 1909, #50000-52000

Same as above with "U.S.N." on butt.

Exc.	V.G.	Good	Fair	Poor
2600	1800	1000	350	250

U.S. Marine Corps Model 1909, #21000-23000

Checkered walnut grips, "U.S.M.C." on butt.

Exc.	V.G.	Good	Fair	Poor
3000	2000	1200	650	450

U.S. Army Model 1917, #150000-301000

Smooth walnut grips, 5.5" barrel, .45 ACP. Model designation stamped on butt.

Courtesy Faintich Auction Services, Inc., Paul Goodwin photo

Exc.	V.G.	Good	Fair	Poor
850	600	400	300	225

Model 1917 Civilian, #335000-336000

Approximately 1,000 made in .45 ACP only from Army parts overrun. No military markings.

Exc.	V.G.	Good	Fair	Poor
750	550	400	250	200

Late Model New Service, #325000-356000

Checkered walnut grips and internal improvements.

Exc.	V.G.	Good	Fair	Poor
850	650	400	200	125

Shooting Master, #333000-350000

Round-butt, checkered walnut grips with Colt medallion, 6" barrel, "Colt Shooting Master" on barrel, flattop frame with target sights. Chambered for the .38 Special cartridge.

Courtesy Faintich Auction Services, Inc., Paul Goodwin photo

Exc.	V.G.	Good	Fair	Poor
1750	1200	850	400	300

NOTE: Add 100 percent premium for .357 Magnum, .44 Special, .45 ACP, and .45 Colt.

Magnum Model New Service, Over #340000

Chambered for .357 Magnum, .38 Special.

Exc.	V.G.	Good	Fair	Poor
950	600	350	250	200

NOTE: Deduct $100 for .38 Special.

New Pocket Model

This was the first swing-out cylinder, double-action pocket revolver made by Colt. It is chambered for .32 Colt and .32 Smith & Wesson. It holds 6 shots and is offered with barrel lengths of 2.5", 3.5", 5", and 6". The finish is blued or nickel-plated, and the grips are checkered hard rubber with the oval Colt molded into them. "Colt's New Pocket" is stamped on the frame. 1884 and 1888 patent dates are stamped on the barrel of later-production guns. There were approximately 30,000 of these manufactured between 1893 and 1905. Antiques made before 1898 are more desirable.

Exc.	V.G.	Good	Fair	Poor
600	450	300	250	150

NOTE: Early production without patent dates add 25 percent. 5" barrel add 10 percent.

Pocket Positive

Externally this is the same revolver as the New Pocket, but it has the positive lock feature. It was manufactured between 1905 and 1940.

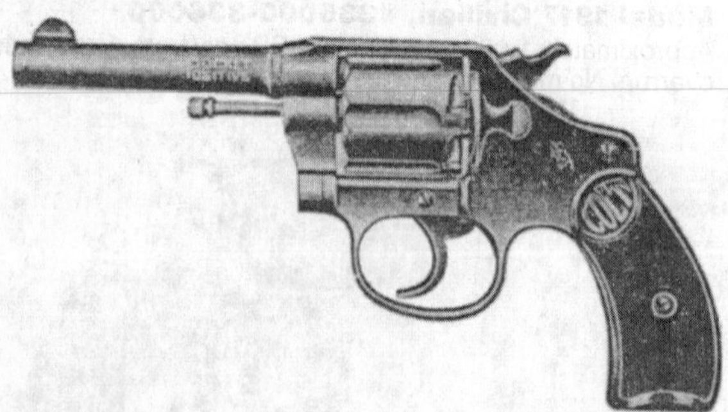

Exc.	V.G.	Good	Fair	Poor
600	375	275	225	125

Army Special Model

This is a heavier-framed improved version of the New Army and Navy revolver. It is chambered for the .32-20, .38 Colt, .38 Smith & Wesson, and .41 Colt. It is offered with a 4", 4.5", 5", and 6" barrel. The finish is blued or nickel-plated, and the grips are checkered hard rubber. The serial number range is #291000-#540000, and they were manufactured between 1908-1927.

Exc.	V.G.	Good	Fair	Poor
550	400	250	200	150

New Police Model

This model appears similar to the New Pocket Model. The frame is stamped "New Police." It is chambered for the .32 Colt, .32 Colt New Police, and .32 Smith & Wesson cartridges. The barrel lengths are 2.5", 4", and 6". The finishes are blued or nickel-plated. Colt manufactured 49,500 of this model from 1896-1907. The New York City Police Department purchased 4,500 of these revolvers, and the backstraps are so marked. There was also a target model of this revolver, which features a 6" barrel with a flattop frame and target sights, of which 5,000 were produced.

Exc.	V.G.	Good	Fair	Poor
500	350	225	150	100

NOTE: New York Police marked add 10 percent. Target model add 20 percent.

Police Positive

This is externally the same as the New Police with the addition of the positive lock feature and two new chamberings—the .38 New Police and the .38 Smith & Wesson. They were manufactured from 1905-1947.

Exc.	V.G.	Good	Fair	Poor
450	300	250	200	150

Police Positive Target

This is basically the same as the New Police Target with the positive lock feature. It is chambered in .22 LR, the .22 WRF, as well as the other cartridges offered in the earlier model.

 *This symbol denotes "Sleepers" with rapidly-rising values and/or significant collector potential.*

NOTE: A .22 caliber Police Positive chambered for the .22 Short and Long cartridge may be seen with British proofs. Several such revolvers were sold to London Armory in this configuration during the late 1920s. A NIB example recently sold for $1,200.

Exc.	V.G.	Good	Fair	Poor
650	450	300	175	100

Police Positive Special

This model is similar to the Police Positive but has a slightly larger frame to accept the longer cylinder needed to chamber more powerful cartridges such as the .38 Special, in addition to the original chamberings. They were manufactured from 1907-1973.

Exc.	V.G.	Good	Fair	Poor
400	300	250	150	100

Police Positive Special Mark V

Introduced in 1994 this is an updated version of the Police Positive Special. This model features an underlug 4" barrel with rubber grips and fixed sights. The butt is rounded. The revolver is rated to fire .38 caliber +P rounds. Overall length is 9" and weighs approximately 30 oz.

NIB	Exc.	V.G.	Good	Fair	Poor
350	250	200	150	100	85

Officer's Model Target 1st Issue

This revolver is chambered for the .38 Special cartridge. It has a 6" barrel and is blued. It has a flattop frame with adjustable target sights. Colt manufactured this model from 1904-1908.

Exc.	V.G.	Good	Fair	Poor
1000	750	350	300	200

Officer's Model Target 2nd Issue

This model is similar to the 1st Issue but is offered in .22 LR and .32 Police Positive caliber, as well as in .38 Special. It also is furnished with a 4", 4.5", 5", 6", and 7.5" barrel in .38 Special only. It has checkered walnut grips. Colt manufactured this model between 1908 and 1940.

Courtesy Faintich Auction Services, Inc., Paul Goodwin photo

Exc.	V.G.	Good	Fair	Poor
700	550	300	250	150

Camp Perry Single-Shot

This model was created by modifying an Officer's Model frame to accept a special flat single-shot "cylinder." This flat chamber pivots to the left side and downward for loading. The pistol is chambered for .22 LR and is offered with an 8" (early production) or 10" (late production) barrel. The finish is blued, with checkered walnut grips. The name "Camp Perry Model" is stamped on the left side of the chamber; the caliber is on the barrel. Colt named this model after the site of the U.S. Target Competition held annually at Camp Perry, Ohio. They manufactured 2,525 of these between 1920 and 1941.

Exc.	V.G.	Good	Fair	Poor
2500	1750	950	600	400

NOTE: Add 100 percent premium for 10" barrel. Add 50 percent premium for original box.

Officer's Model Match

Introduced in 1953 this model is similar to the Officer's Model Target and chambered for either the .22 caliber cartridge or the .38 Special with 6" barrel. The revolver is fitted with a heavy tapered barrel and wide hammer spur with adjustable rear sight and ramp front sight. It was sold with checkered walnut target grips. Blued finish is standard. Discontinued in 1970. The standard of long action could be fired both double- or single-action. The .22 caliber version prices are listed. Officer's Model Match in .38 caliber will bring approximately 20 percent less.

Exc.	V.G.	Good	Fair	Poor
750	600	450	350	250

.22 Caliber in Short Action—Single-Action-Only

Exc.	V.G.	Good	Fair	Poor
1000	750	600	500	350

Official Police

This was a popular revolver in the Colt line for many years. It was manufactured from 1927 to 1969. It is chambered for .32-20 and .41 Colt. These calibers were discontinued in 1942 and 1930, respectively. The .38 Special was chambered throughout the entire production run, and .22 LR was added in 1930. This model holds 6 shots, has a square-butt, and is offered with 2", 4", 5", and 6" barrel lengths. The grips are checkered walnut. The finish is either blued or nickel-plated.

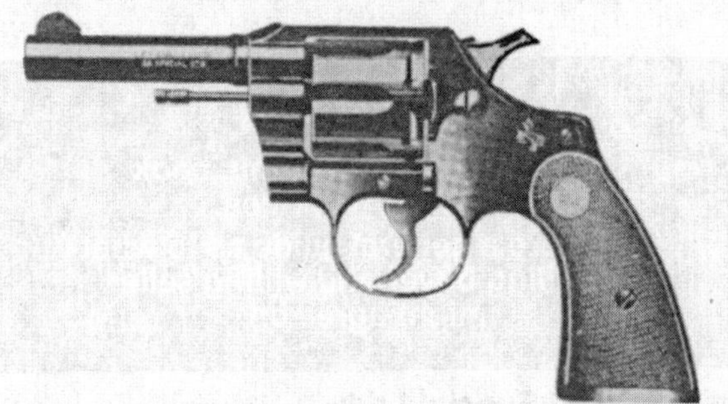

Exc.	V.G.	Good	Fair	Poor
450	325	250	200	150

NOTE: Nickel-plated add 10 percent. .22 LR add 20 percent.

Commando Model

This model, for all intents and purposes, is an Official Police chambered for .38 Special, with a 2", 4", or 6" barrel. This model is Parkerized and stamped "Colt Commando" on the barrel. There were approximately 50,000 manufactured between 1942-1945 for use in World War II.

Courtesy Richard M. Kumor, Sr.

Exc.	V.G.	Good	Fair	Poor
550	450	275	150	100

NOTE: Add 30 percent for 2" barrel.

Marshall Model

This is an Official Police that is marked "Colt Marshall" on the barrel and has an "M" suffix in the serial number. It has a 2" or 4" barrel and a round butt. The finish is blued. There were approximately 2,500 manufactured between 1954 and 1956.

Exc.	V.G.	Good	Fair	Poor
500	400	300	250	150

Colt .38 SF-VI

Introduced in 1995 this model is essentially a Detective Special in stainless steel with a new internal mechanism. Has a transfer bar safety mechanism. Fitted with a 2" barrel and cylinder holds 6 rounds of .38 Special. A 4" barrel in bright stainless steel is also available. Weight is 21 oz. and overall length is 7".

NIB	Exc.	V.G	Good	Fair	Poor
400	325	275	225	150	100

REMINDER

The prices given in this book are RETAIL prices. They are a general guide as to what a willing buyer and willing seller might agree on.

Colt .38 SF-VI Special Lady

Introduced in 1996 this 2" barrel version is similar to the above model with the addition of a bright finish and bobbed hammer. Weight is 21 oz.

NIB	Exc.	V.G.	Good	Fair	Poor
475	350	275	225	150	100

Detective Special 1st Issue

This model is actually a duplication, as it is nothing more than a Police Positive Special with a 2" barrel standard. It was originally chambered for .32 New Police, .38 New Police, (which were discontinued) and .38 Special, which continued until the end of the production run. The finish is blued, and it is offered with wood or plastic grips. There were over 400,000 manufactured between 1926 and 1972.

Exc.	V.G.	Good	Fair	Poor
750	550	285	175	100

Detective Special 2nd Issue

This is basically a modernized, streamlined version of the 1st issue. It is similar except that it has a 2" or 3" barrel with a shrouded ejector rod and wraparound checkered walnut grips and is chambered for .38 Special. It was finished in blue or nickel plate. Reintroduced in 1993.

This symbol denotes "Sleepers" with rapidly-rising values and/or significant collector potential.

NIB	Exc.	V.G.	Good	Fair	Poor
425	325	250	175	125	75

NOTE: Add $25 for nickel finish.

Detective Special II (DS-II)

Introduced in 1997 this version of the Detective special features new internal lock work and a transfer bar safety mechanism. It is fitted with a 2" barrel, has a capacity of six rounds, and is chambered for the .38 Special. In 1998 this model was offered chambered for .357 Magnum cartridge as well. Rubber combat style grips are standard. Weight is approximately 21 oz. Stainless steel finish.

NIB	Exc.	V.G.	Good	Fair	Poor
550	425	300	225	—	—

Colt Magnum Carry

Introduced in 1998 this model is essentially a renamed Detective Special II. Stainless steel finish. Weight is 21 oz.

NIB	Exc.	V.G.	Good	Fair	Poor
550	425	300	250	—	—

Banker's Special

The Bankers Special is a 2" barreled, easily concealed revolver. It was designed with bank employees in mind. It is chambered for .38 Special and was offered in blued finish. The revolver was also offered in .22 caliber. The grips are rounded but full-sized, and Colt utilized this feature in advertising this model. The U.S. Postal Service equipped its railway mail clerks with this model. There were approximately 35,000 manufactured between 1926 and 1943.

Exc.	V.G.	Good	Fair	Poor
1200	800	400	250	150

NOTE: Nickel models will command a premium. A Banker's Special in .22 caliber will command a premium.

Cobra 1st Issue

The Cobra is simply an alloy-framed lightweight version of the Detective Special. It weighs only 15 oz. The Cobra is chambered for .32, .38 Special, and .22 LR. This model is available in either a round-butt or square-butt version with a 4" barrel only. They were manufactured between 1950 and 1973.

Exc.	V.G.	Good	Fair	Poor
550	350	225	150	100

Cobra 2nd Issue

The same as the 1st Issue in .38 Special only, this is streamlined with wraparound walnut grips and shrouded ejector rod.

Exc.	V.G.	Good	Fair	Poor
425	325	250	150	100

NOTE: For nickel add 30 percent.

Agent 1st Issue

This revolver is basically the same as the 1st Issue Cobra with a shortened grip frame. This was done to make the Agent more concealable. Colt manufactured the Agent 1st Issue from 1955-1973.

Exc.	V.G.	Good	Fair	Poor
550	350	225	150	100

Border Patrol

This model is quite rare, as Colt manufactured only 400 of them in 1952. It is basically a Police Special with a heavy 4" barrel. It is chambered for the .38 Special and was built to be strong. The finish is blued and serial numbered in the 610000 range.

Exc.	V.G.	Good	Fair	Poor
5000	3000	2000	1000	500

Agent L.W. 2nd Issue

This is a streamlined version with the shrouded ejector rod. In the last four years of its production, it was matte finished. Colt manufactured this model between 1973 and 1986.

Exc.	V.G.	Good	Fair	Poor
375	275	225	175	150

Aircrewman Special

This model was especially fabricated for the Air Force to be carried by their pilots for protection. It is extremely lightweight at 11 oz. The frame and the cylinder are made of aluminum alloy. It has a 2" barrel and is chambered for the .38 Special. The finish was blued, with checkered walnut grips. There were approximately 1,200 manufactured in 1951, and they are marked "U.S." or "A.F."

Exc.	V.G.	Good	Fair	Poor
4500	2500	1500	800	250

Courier

This is another version of the Cobra. It features a shorter grip frame and a 3" barrel. This model is chambered for .32 and .22 rimfire. There were approximately 3,000 manufactured in 1955 and 1956.

NIB	Exc.	V.G.	Good	Fair	Poor
1000	750	600	500	350	150

NOTE: .22 Rimfire add 20 percent.

Trooper

This model was designed specifically by Colt to fill the need for a large, heavy-duty, powerful revolver that was accurate. The Trooper filled that need. It was offered with a 4" or 6" barrel and blued or nickel finishes with checkered walnut grips. The Trooper is chambered for the .38 Special/.357 Magnum, and there is a .22 rimfire version for the target shooters. This model was manufactured between 1953 and 1969.

Exc.	V.G.	Good	Fair	Poor
500	325	250	150	100

Colt .357 Magnum

This is a deluxe version of the Trooper. It is offered with a special target wide hammer and large target-type grips. The sights are the same as Accro target model. It features a 4" or 6" barrel and a blued finish and was manufactured between 1953 and 1961. There were fewer than 15,000 produced.

Exc.	V.G.	Good	Fair	Poor
550	375	300	200	150

Diamondback

This model is a medium-frame, duty-type weapon suitable for target work. It has the short frame of the Detective Special with the ventilated rib 2.5", 4", or 6" barrel. It is chambered for .38 Special and .22 rimfire for the target shooters. The finish is blued or nickel-plated, with checkered walnut grips. The Diamondback features adjustable target sights, wide target hammer, and a steel frame. It was manufactured between 1966 and 1986.

NIB	Exc.	V.G.	Good	Fair	Poor
750	525	375	300	250	150

NOTE: For .22 caliber 2.5" barrel add 30 percent. If finish is nickel add 60 percent.

Viper

This is an alloy-framed revolver chambered for the .38 Special. It has a 4" barrel and was manufactured between 1977 and 1984. The Viper is essentially a lightweight version of the Police Positive.

NIB	Exc.	V.G.	Good	Fair	Poor
550	425	325	200	125	100

Python

The Python is the Cadillac of the Colt double-action line. It has been manufactured since 1955 and is still the flagship of the Colt line. It is chambered for the .357 Magnum cartridge, holds 6 shots, and has been offered in barrel lengths of 2.5", 3", 4", 6", and 8". This revolver is offered finished in high polished Colt Royal Blue, nickel-plate, matte-finish stainless steel, or what is known as "The Ultimate"—a high polished stainless steel. The 3" barrel, as well as the nickel plating, has been discontinued. The grips are checkered walnut. It is possible that the nickel-plated specimens may bring a 10 percent premium. In my experience this is not always the case as many potential purchasers have a definite preference for the blued finish. Reintroduced into the Colt product line in 2001 as the Python Elite. Early (pre-1966) models command 10 percent to 25 percent premium in Exc. or better condition. Discontinued 2005.

NIB	Exc.	V.G.	Good	Fair	Poor
1050	800	700	500	400	225

Matte Stainless Steel

NIB	Exc.	V.G.	Good	Fair	Poor
1200	900	775	600	500	275

"The Ultimate" Bright Stainless

NIB	Exc.	V.G.	Good	Fair	Poor
1250	925	800	600	500	300

Python Elite

Reintroduced in 2001 this model features a stainless steel satin finish or blued finish. Adjustable red ramp front sight. Custom wood grips and choice of 4" or 6" barrel. Weight is about 43 oz.

NIB	Exc.	V.G.	Good	Fair	Poor
1250	925	700	500	—	—

Python .38 Special

This is an 8" barreled Python chambered for the .38 Special only. It was a limited-production venture that was not a success. It was offered in blue only.

Exc.	V.G.	Good	Fair	Poor
750	600	475	300	225

Python Hunter

The Hunter was a special 8" .357 Magnum Python with an extended eye relief Leupold 2X scope. The grips are neoprene with gold Colt medallions. The revolver, with mounted scope and accessories, was fitted into a Haliburton extruded aluminum case. The Hunter was manufactured in 1981 only.

NIB	Exc.	V.G.	Good	Fair	Poor
1300	950	750	500	400	300

Metropolitan MK III

This revolver is basically a heavier-duty version of the Official Police. It is chambered for .38 Special and fitted with a 4" heavy barrel. It is finished in blue only and was manufactured from 1969-1972.

NIB	Exc.	V.G.	Good	Fair	Poor
425	325	225	150	100	75

Lawman MK III

This model is offered chambered for the .357 Magnum with a 2" or 4" barrel. It has checkered walnut grips and is either blued or nickel-plated. Colt manufactured the Lawman between 1969 and 1983.

Exc.	V.G.	Good	Fair	Poor
450	400	300	200	100

Lawman MK V

This is an improved version of the MK III. It entailed a redesigned grip, a shorter lock time, and an improved double-action. It was manufactured 1982-1985.

NIB	Exc.	V.G.	Good	Fair	Poor
425	375	300	200	150	100

Trooper MK III

This revolver was intended to be the target-grade version of the MK III series. It is offered with a 4", 6", or 8" vent-rib barrel with a shrouded ejector rod similar in appearance to the Python. It is chambered for the .22 LR and the .22 Magnum, as well as .357 Magnum. It features adjustable target sights, checkered walnut target grips, and is either blued or nickel-plated. This model was manufactured between 1969 and 1983.

NIB	Exc.	V.G.	Good	Fair	Poor
450	375	325	200	150	100

Trooper MK V

This improved version of the MK III was manufactured between 1982 and 1985.

NIB	Exc.	V.G.	Good	Fair	Poor
425	350	275	200	150	100

Boa

This is basically a deluxe version of the Trooper MK V. It has all the same features plus the high polished blue found on the Python. Colt manufactured 1,200 of these revolvers in 1985, and the entire production was purchased and marketed by Lew Horton Distributing Company in Southboro, Massachusetts.

NIB	Exc.	V.G.	Good	Fair	Poor
700	550	400	325	250	150

Peacekeeper

This model was designed as a duty-type weapon with target capabilities. It is offered with a 4" or 6" barrel chambered for .357 Magnum. It features adjustable sights and neoprene combat-style grips and has a matte blued finish. This model was manufactured between 1985 and 1987.

NIB	Exc.	V.G.	Good	Fair	Poor
425	350	275	200	150	100

King Cobra

This model has become the workhorse of the Colt revolver line. The King Cobra has a forged steel frame and barrel and a full length ejector rod housing. The barrel is fitted with a solid rib. This model is equipped with an adjustable, white outline rear sight and a red insert front sight. Colt black neoprene combat style grips are standard. The blued model is no longer offered. Discontinued.

NOTE: In 1998 all King Cobras were drilled and tapped for scope mounts.

Blued

NIB	Exc.	V.G.	Good	Fair	Poor
750	500	375	250	200	100

Stainless Steel

Offered in 4" or 6" barrel lengths. In 1997 this model was introduced with optional barrel porting. No longer in production.

NIB	Exc.	V.G.	Good	Fair	Poor
775	525	375	275	200	125

High Polish Stainless Steel

NIB	Exc.	V.G.	Good	Fair	Poor
775	525	375	275	200	125

Anaconda

This double-action .44 Magnum revolver was introduced in 1990. It is offered with 4", 6", or 8" barrel lengths. The 4" model weighs 47 oz., the 6" model weighs 63 oz., and the 8" model weighs 59 oz. The Anaconda holds 6 rounds and is available with a matte stainless steel finish. For 1993 a new chambering in .45 Colt was offered for the Anaconda. This model was offered with a 6" or 8" barrel in a matte stainless steel finish revolver chambered for the .44 Remington Magnum cartridge. It is currently offered with a 6" or 8" barrel and adjustable red-insert front and white-outline rear sights. It is constructed of matte-finished stainless steel and has black neoprene finger-groove grips with gold Colt medallions. In 1996 the Realtree model was offered with 8" barrel. Chambered for the .44 Magnum cartridge. Furnished with either adjustable rear sight and ramp front sights or special scope mount. No longer in production. Reintroduced in 2001 In .44 Magnum with 4", 6", or 8" barrel. Once again, discontinued.

NOTE: In 1998 the Anaconda was drilled and tapped for scope mounts and buyers had the option of barrel porting.

Colt Anaconda with optional ported barrel

Colt Anaconda with optional Colt optics

.44 Magnum

NIB	Exc.	V.G.	Good	Fair	Poor
1000	750	600	450	300	200

.45 Colt

NIB	Exc.	V.G.	Good	Fair	Poor
1100	800	600	450	300	200

Realtree Camo Model—Adjustable Sights

NIB	Exc.	V.G.	Good	Fair	Poor
1100	800	600	450	300	200

Realtree Camo Model—Scope Mounts

NIB	Exc.	V.G.	Good	Fair	Poor
1150	850	650	500	400	250

COLT SEMI-AUTOMATIC PISTOLS

The Colt Firearms Co. was the first of the American gun manufacturers to take the advent of the semi-automatic pistol seriously. This pistol design was becoming popular among European gun makers in the late 1880s and early 1900s. In the United States, however, the revolver was firmly ensconced as the accepted design. Colt realized that if the semi-auto could be made to function reliably, it would soon catch on. The powers that be at Colt were able to negotiate with some of the noted inventors of the day, including Browning, and to secure or lease the rights to manufacture their designs. Colt also encouraged the creativity of their employees with bonuses and incentives and, through this innovative thinking, soon became the leader in semi-auto pistol sales—a position that they have never really relinquished to any other American gun maker. The Colt semi-automatic pistols represent an interesting field for the collector of Colt handguns. There were many variations with high enough production to make it worthwhile to seek them out. There are a number of fine books on the Colt semi-automatics, and anyone wishing to do so will be able to learn a great deal about them. Collector interest is high in this field, and values are definitely on the rise.

Model 1900

This was the first of the Colt automatic pistols. It was actually a developmental model with only 3,500 being produced. The Model 1900 was not really a successful design. It was quite clumsy and out of balance in the hand; however it was reliable in function during Army trials. This model is chambered for the .38 Rimless smokeless cartridge. It has a detachable magazine that holds seven cartridges. The barrel is 6" in length. The finish is blued, with a case-colored hammer and safety/sight combination. The grips are either plain walnut, checkered walnut, or hard rubber. This pistol is a Browning design, and the left side of the slide is stamped "Browning's Patent" with the 1897 patent date. Colt sold 200 pistols to the Navy and 200 to the Army for field trials and evaluation. The remaining 3,300 were sold on the civilian market. This model was manufactured from 1900-1903.

NOTE: Many of the original 1900 pistols had the original sight/safety converted to Model 1902 configuration. These are worth about 50 percent less than unconverted pistols.

Standard Civilian Production

Exc.	V.G.	Good	Fair	Poor
7500	4000	2250	1250	750

U.S. Navy Military Model

Exc.	V.G.	Good	Fair	Poor
7500	6000	5000	2500	1000

U.S. Army Military Model—1st Contract

Exc.	V.G.	Good	Fair	Poor
20000	15000	10000	4000	2000

U.S. Army Military Model—2nd Contract

Exc.	V.G.	Good	Fair	Poor
10000	7500	5500	2000	1500

Model 1902 Sporting Pistol

This model is chambered for the .38 Rimless smokeless cartridge. It has a 7-round detachable magazine and a 6" barrel and is blued, with checkered hard rubber grips featuring the "Rampant Colt" molded into them. The most notable features of the 1902 Sporting Model are the rounded butt, rounded hammer spur, dovetailed rear sight, and the 1897-1902 patent dates. Colt manufactured approximately 7,500 of these pistols between 1903 and 1908.

Paul Goodwin photo

Exc.	V.G.	Good	Fair	Poor
3500	2000	1250	750	450

Model 1902 Military Pistol

Early Model with Front of Slide Serrated

Exc.	V.G.	Good	Fair	Poor
3500	2000	1250	750	450

Standard Model with Rear of Slide Serrated

Exc.	V.G.	Good	Fair	Poor
2500	1750	1000	500	400

U.S. Army Marked, #15001-15200 with Front Serrations

Exc.	V.G.	Good	Fair	Poor
6000	5000	2500	1250	600

Model 1903 Pocket Pistol

This was the first automatic pocket pistol Colt produced. It is essentially identical to the 1902 Sporting Model with a shorter slide. The barrel length is 4.5", and it is chambered for the .38 Rimless smokeless cartridge. It is blued, with a case-colored hammer, with checkered hard rubber grips that have the "Rampant Colt" molded into them. The detachable magazine holds 7 rounds. There were approximately 26,000 manufactured between 1903 and 1929.

Paul Goodwin photo

Exc.	V.G.	Good	Fair	Poor
1100	850	650	350	200

Model 1903 Hammerless, .32 Pocket Pistol

Model 1903 Hammerless with 4" barrel

Courtesy Richard M. Kumor, Sr.

This was the second pocket automatic Colt manufactured. It was another of John Browning's designs, and it developed into one of Colt's most successful pistols. This pistol is chambered for the .32 ACP cartridge. Initially the barrel length was 4"; this was shortened to 3.75". The detachable magazine holds 8 rounds. The standard finish is blue, with quite a few nickel plated. The early model grips are checkered hard rubber with the "Rampant Colt" molded into them. Many of the nickel plated pistols had pearl grips. In 1924 the grips were changed to checkered walnut with the Colt medallions. The name of this model can be misleading as it is not a true hammerless but a concealed hammer design. It features a slide stop and a grip safety. Colt manufactured 572,215 civilian versions of this pistol and approximately 200,000 more for military contracts. This model was manufactured between 1903 and 1945.

Courtesy Orvel Reichert

Exc.	*V.G.*	*Good*	*Fair*	*Poor*
550	500	450	300	200

NOTE: Early Model 1897 patent date add 40 percent. Nickel-plated with pearl grips add $100. 4" barrel to #72,000 add 20 percent.

U.S. Military Model

Serial prefix M, marked "U.S. Property" on frame, Parkerized finish.

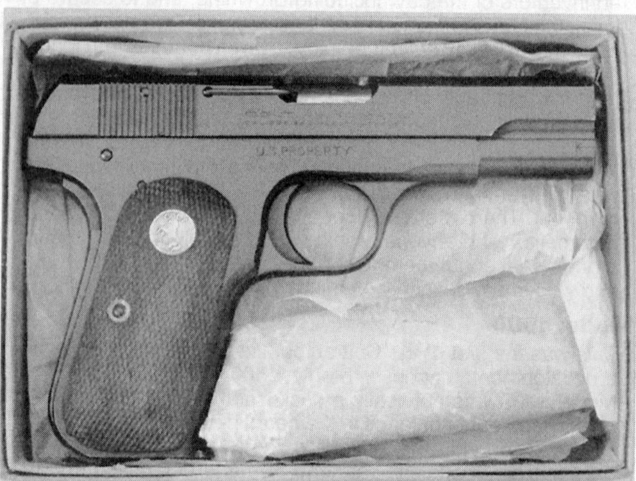

Exc.	*V.G.*	*Good*	*Fair*	*Poor*
1200	850	400	300	250

NOTE: Pistols issued to General Officers will command a premium.

Model 1908 Hammerless .380 Pocket Pistol

This model is essentially the same as the .32 Pocket Pistol, chambered for the more potent .380 ACP, also known as the 9mm Browning short. Other specifications are the same. Colt manufactured approximately 138,000 in this caliber for civilian sales. An unknown number were sold to the military.

Standard Civilian Model

Exc.	*V.G.*	*Good*	*Fair*	*Poor*
800	650	475	350	250

NOTE: Nickel with pearl grips add $100.

Military Model

Serial prefix M, marked "U.S. Property" on frame, parkerized finish.

Exc.	*V.G.*	*Good*	*Fair*	*Poor*
1500	1000	750	500	300

Model 1908 Hammerless .25 Pocket Pistol

This was the smallest automatic Colt made. It is chambered for the .25 ACP cartridge, has a 2" barrel, and is 4.5" long overall. It weighs a mere 13 oz. This is a true pocket pistol. The detachable magazine holds 6 shots. This model was offered in blue or nickel-plate, with grips of checkered hard rubber and checkered walnut on later versions. This model has a grip safety, slide lock, and a magazine disconnector safety. This was another Browning design, and Fabrique Nationale manufactured this pistol in Belgium before Colt picked up the rights to make it in the U.S. This was a commercial success by Colt's standards, with approximately 409,000 manufactured between 1908 and 1941.

REMINDER

An "N/A" or "—" instead of a price indicates that there is no known price available for that gun in that condition, or the sales for that particular model are so few that a reliable price cannot be given.

 *This symbol denotes "Sleepers" with rapidly-rising values and/or significant collector potential.*

Courtesy Orvel Reichert

Civilian Model

Exc.	*V.G.*	*Good*	*Fair*	*Poor*
500	350	300	200	100

Military Model

"U.S. Property" marked on right frame. Very rare.

Exc.	*V.G.*	*Good*	*Fair*	*Poor*
2500	1500	600	450	300

Model 1905 .45 Automatic Pistol

The Spanish American War and the experiences with the Moros in the Philippine campaign taught a lesson about stopping power or the lack of it. The United States Army was convinced that they needed a more powerful handgun cartridge. This led Colt to the development of a .45 caliber cartridge suitable for the semi-automatic pistol. The Model 1905 and the .45 Rimless round were the result. In actuality, this cartridge was not nearly powerful enough to satisfy the need, but it led to the development of the .45 ACP. Colt believed that this pistol/cartridge combination would be a success and was geared up for mass production. The Army actually bought only 200 of them, and the total production was approximately 6,300 from 1905 to 1911. The pistol has a 5" barrel and detachable 7-shot magazine and is blued, with a case-colored hammer. The grips are checkered walnut. The hammer was rounded on the first 3,600 pistols and was changed to a spur hammer on the later models. The right side of the slide is stamped "Automatic Colt / Calibre 45 Rimless Smokeless." This model was not a commercial success for Colt—possibly because it has no safety whatsoever except for the floating inertia firing pin. The 200 military models have grip safeties only. A small number (believed to be less than 500) of these pistols were grooved to accept a shoulder stock. The stocks were made of leather and steel and made to double as a holster. These pistols have been classified "Curios and Relics" under the provisions of the Gun Control Act of 1968.

Civilian Model

Exc.	*V.G.*	*Good*	*Fair*	*Poor*
4000	3500	1750	950	400

Military Model, Serial #1-201

Exc.	*V.G.*	*Good*	*Fair*	*Poor*
8500	6500	4500	1500	500

COLT 1911/1911A1

Verified proof Courtesy Karl Karash

Early Colt "1911 Commercial Government Model"

Serial numbers through about C4500, high polish on all parts and fire-blue finish on the trigger, slide stop, thumb safety, hammer pins, ejector, and stock screws. Pistols in the latter part of the serial range did not have fire blued stock screws. Pistols through about serial C350 had the dimpled magazine catch. The main spring housing pin was rounded on both ends in the pistols through about serial C2000. Keyhole (punch and sawcut) magazines were shipped on pistols through serial C3500.

Courtesy Karl Karash

Exc.	*V.G.*	*Good*	*Fair*	*Poor*
6000	3600	2200	1400	900

NOTE: Three-digit serial number add 20 percent. Two-digit serial number add 40 percent. For finish 99-100 percent add 30-50 percent.

Standard Colt "1911 Commercial Model" with Un-numbered Slide

Above about serial # C4500 with un-numberd slide to about serial #C127300. No fire blue. Polished finished but not mirror finish. Loop magazine until about C90000. A number of variations exist within this wide serial range such as slide nomenclature and position of the "Rampant Colt," but none currently receives any particular premium.

Exc.	V.G.	Good	Fair	Poor
3500	2100	1500	900	700

NOTE: Finish 99-100 percent add 20-50 percent.

Standard Colt "1911 Commercial Government Model" with Numbered Slide

Colt started to number the slide with the receiver's serial number at about serial #C127300. This practice continued for commercial production through WWII, and all 1911 commercial pistols after about serial C127300 to about serial C136000 (when 1911A1 production had taken over). The first numberd slide pistols (in the C127xxx range) had the slide numbered on the bottom of the slide rail. This only lasted a short time and the numbering was moved to behind the firing pin stop plate by serial C128000. Subtract 20 percent for a mismatched slide number. The changes between the 1911 Commercial Government Model and the 1911A1 Commercial Government were phased in during this period.

Exc.	V.G.	Good	Fair	Poor
3500	2100	1400	900	650

NOTE: Finish 99-100 percent add 20-50 percent.

FOREIGN CONTRACTS

Colt "1911 Commercial Government Model" Argentine Contracts

Multiple contracts were awarded by Argentina between 1914 and 1948 to supply .45 caliber pistols to their armed forces, police, and government agencies. these contracts totaled 21,616 pistols of which 2,151 were the 1911 model. Pistols differ from the Standard Government Model in that they are usually marked with an Argentine crest as well as the normal Colt commercial markings including the C prefix serial number. Colt also supplied Argentina the 1911A1 model "MODELO 1927" that had its own serial number range of #1 to #10000 with no C prefix. Most of these pistols are well used, reblued, had mixed parts, and have import markings. Prices listed are for completely original pistols. Reblue=Fair/Poor.

An example of one style of Argentine crest Courtesy Karl Karash

Exc.	V.G.	Good	Fair	Poor
1500	1100	750	500	400

NOTE: Finish 99-100 percent add 20-100 percent.

Colt "1911 Commercial Government Model" Russian Order

This variation is chambered for .45 ACP and has the Russian version of "Anglo Zakazivat" stamped on the frame. There were about 51,000 of these blued pistols manufactured in 1915-1916. They are found between serial numbers C21000 and C89000.

This variation is rarely encountered today, but a few have recently been imported and advertised. One should be extremely cautious and verify the authenticity if contemplating a purchase, as fakes have been noted. Despite market uncertainties demand for original pistols is high. (Reblue=Fair/Poor)

Russian frame stamping Courtesy Karl Karash

Exc.	V.G.	Good	Fair	Poor
5500	3900	2350	1600	1000

NOTE: Finish 99-100 percent add 30-100 percent.

Colt "1911 Commercial Government Model" Canadian Contract

This group of 5099 pistols serial numbered between about C3077 and C13500 were purchased by the Canadian Government in 1914. Most observed pistols appear to be unmarked and can be identified only by a Colt factory letter. Others have been observed with the Canadian Broad Arrow property mark as well as unit markings. Often these unit markings are applied in a very rudimentary manner that detracts considerably from the appearance. (Any applied markings done crudely, deduct 10-50 percent.) Due to the nature of these markings, a Colt factory letter is probably a requirement to authenticate these pistols. Refinish=Fair/Poor.

Exc.	V.G.	Good	Fair	Poor
3100	2200	1450	950	650

NOTE: Finish. 99-100 percent add 20-50 percent.

Colt "1911 Commercial Government Model" British Contract

This series is chambered for the British .455 cartridge and is so marked on the right side of the slide. The British "Broad Arrow" proofmark will often be found. These pistols were made in 1915-1919 and follow the same numeric serial number sequence as the normal Government models, except that the "C" prefix was replaced with a "W." They are commercial series pistols. The magazine well of these .455 pistols is slightly larger than a standard Cal. .45 Auto pistol and will accept a Cal.45 magazine, but a standard Cal. 45 will not accept a Cal. .455 magazine. All pistols in the W19001 to W19200 range as well as some in the W29000 range are believed to be JJ marked above the left trigger guard bow. Add 25 percent for JJ marked. Some pistols in the C101000 to about C109000 range have RAF marks as well as a welded ring in the lanyard loop. Most RAF pistols have been refinished and many have been converted to .45 cal. by changing the barrels. Refinish=Fair/Poor.

Broad Arrow Courtesy Karl Karash

Exc.	V.G.	Good	Fair	Poor
3200	2000	1250	850	650

NOTE: Finish. 99-100 percent add 20-50 percent. Add 25 percent for RAF. Wrong barrel less 35 percent.

Norwegian Kongsberg Vapenfabrikk Pistol Model 1912 (Extremely Rare)

Serial number 1-96.

Exc.	V.G.	Good	Fair	Poor
5000	3200	2200	1600	1200

NOTE: These pistols are so rare that almost any price would not be out of order for an original pistol. Finish 99-100 percent add 20-30 percent.

Norwegian Kongsberg Vapenfabrikk Pistol Model 1914

Serial number 97-32854.

Exc.	V.G.	Good	Fair	Poor
1350	1050	900	770	600

NOTE: Finish 99-100 percent add 20-50 percent.

Kongsberg Vapenfabrikk Model 1914 (Norwegian) Copy

Serial number 29615 to 30535. Waffenamt marked on slide and barrel. **CAUTION:** Fakes have been reported. Any Waffenamt-marked pistol outside this serial range is probably counterfeit.

Exc.	V.G.	Good	Fair	Poor
4500	2700	2000	1200	900

NOTE: Finish 99-100 percent add 20-30 percent.

MODEL 1911 AUTOMATIC PISTOL, MILITARY SERIES

NOTE: For a complete listing of Colt 1911 military pistols with photos, technical data, and prices see the *Standard Catalog of Military Firearms*.

COLT 1911A1 COMMERCIAL GOVERNMENT MODEL

The commercial "Government Models" made by Colt between the wars may be the best pistols that Colt ever produced. The civilian configurations of the 1911 and 1911A1 were known as "Government Models." They were identical to the military models, with the exception of the fit, finish, and markings. However, commercial production of the 1911A1 pistols was stopped when WWII started. Therefore, production changes of the 1911A1 pistols were not carried over to the contemporary commercial pistols because there was no contemporary commercial production. The "C" serial number prefix designated the commercial series until 1950, when it was changed to a "C" suffix. The "Government Model" pistols were polished and blued until about serial number C230,000, when the top, bottom, and rear were matte finished. The words "Government Model" as well as the usual "Verified Proof" mark were stamped on all but about the first 500 pistols when post-war production commenced at C220,000. Some of these first 500 also lacked the verified proof mark. These first post-war pistols used some leftover military parts such as triggers and stocks. Pre-war pistols all had checkered walnut grips. Post-war pistols generally had plastic grips until the "midrange" serial when the wood grips returned. There were a number of different commercial models manufactured. They are individually listed.

PRE-WWII COLT "1911A1 COMMERCIAL GOVERNMENT MODEL"

Manufactured by Colt from 1925-1942 from about serial number C136000 to about serial number C215000. Only a few pistols from serial #C202000 to C215000 were shipped domestically, as most were shipped to Brazil or renumbered into military models. *See Model 1911A1 commercial to military conversions.*

Standard Colt "1911A1 Commercial Government Model" Domestic Sales

These pistols have numbered slides, no foreign markings, no Swartz safeties and no additions whatsoever.

Exc.	V.G.	Good	Fair	Poor
2500	1600	1150	750	500

NOTE: Finish 99-100 percent add 30-60 percent.

Standard Colt "1911A1 Commercial Government Model" Export Sales

Usually with foreign crest or foreign inscription of a county such as Argentina or Brazil. This pistol has a numbered slide. Some variations with the foreign markings are more rare than the standard domestic pistols and have a developed local followings who have raised their prices considerably. The Argentine pistols do not have the collector interest that the others or the "Standard" domestic pistols have. Four factors have reduced collector interest in the Argentine Colt pistols compared to the rest:

1. Most of the Argentine-marked pistols have been recently imported and have the legally required important markings.
2. Many of the Argentine-marked pistols have been advertised and sold in the wholesale trade publications at utility prices.
3. Most of the recent import pistols from Argentina have been refinished or are in "well used" condition.
4. Most of the recent import pistols from Argentina have had some parts changed or swapped with other pistols and are not in original condition.

The few Argentine pistols that remain in original and excellent or better condition usually sell for less than their "plain Jane" counterparts, and they sell for much less than the rarer Brazilian and Mexican pistols.

Argentine Colt-made 1911A1 model pistols without Swartz safeties

Exc.	V.G.	Good	Fair	Poor
1100	800	650	550	450

NOTE: Finish 99-100 percent add 20-30 percent.

Brazilian, Mexican, and other South American (except Argentina)

Colt-made "1911A1 Commercial Government Model" pistols.

Exc.	V.G.	Good	Fair	Poor
6500	4500	2800	1700	1000

NOTE: Finish 99-100 percent add 20-100 percent.

Colt National Match Caliber .45, Pre-WWII, .45 (without Swartz safeties)

The National Match Commercial pistol was introduced by Colt at the 1930 National Matches at Camp Perry. Production began in 1932. The right side of the slide was marked "NATIONAL MATCH" and the mainspring housing had no lanyard loop. The National Match modifications to the standard pistol, as described in Colt literature included: "A tighter barrel, better sights, and a hand polished action." The "tighter barrel" probably amounted to a tighter fit between the barrel bushing and barrel. The hand polishing of the action probably produced a greatly improved trigger pull, but overall, the barrel slide lockup was probably only superficially improved. Colt also advertised a "Selected Match Grade" barrel. Colt advertising indicated that scores using the National Match pistols improved greatly and they probably did to a degree, but most of the improvement was probably due to the improved (wider) sights and improved trigger pull. The very first pistols had fixed sights, but by about SN C177,000 the "Stevens Adjustable Rear Target Sight" was available. Both fixed and adjustable sights were available thereafter throughout production. The total number of National Match pistols with each type of sight is not known, but one author (Kevin Williams, *Collecting Colt's National Match Pistols*) estimates that the percentage of adjustable sight equipped National Match pistols may have been only 20 percent. Note that the Colt National Match pistol is not referred to here as a "1911A1" because this pistol lacks the military lanyard loop that is present in all Standard Government Models. This is simply a matter of personal preference. Also note that "Colt National Match" Pre-war pistols are also "Government models" as the receiver was marked as such throughout production.

With Adjustable Sights

Exc.	V.G.	Good	Fair	Poor
4800	2900	1700	1050	900

NOTE: Finish 99-100 percent add 30-60 percent.

Stevens adjustable sight
Courtesy Karl Karash

Fixed Sights

Exc.	*V.G.*	*Good*	*Fair*	*Poor*
3700	2500	1400	900	750

SWARTZ SAFETIES, PRE-WWII, FIRING PIN AND HAMMER/SEAR

The "Swartz Safeties" are a pair of devices that Colt installed in 1911A1 Commercial Government Models" and 1911A1 Commercial National Match pistols in the late 1930s and early 1940s. The first device, a firing pin block that was actuated by the grip safety, prevented the firing pin from moving forward unless the grip safety was squeezed. The second Swartz safety device, the Hammer/Sear safety prevented a possible unsafe half cock position. The Swartz firing pin block safety can be observed by pulling the slide back all the way and looking at the top of the frame. A Swartz-safety-equipped 1911A1 pistol will have a second pin protruding up, next to the conventional disconnector pin. This second pin pushes a spring loaded piston in the rear part of the slide that is visible when the slide is pulled back and the slide is viewed from underneath. This piston, in turn, blocks the firing pin when relaxed. A second Swartz safety (the Swartz Sear Safety), is usually built into pistols equipped with the Swartz firing pin block safety. The sear safety can sometimes be detected by the drag marks of the notched sear on the round portion of the hammer that the sear rides on. Pulling the hammer all the way back will expose these drag marks if they are visible. Presence of the drag marks, however, does not ensure that the Swartz-modified sear safety parts are all present. Disassembly may be required to verify the correct parts are all present. The Swartz Safeties are referred to in Colt Factory letters as the "NSD" (New Safety Device).

(From SN C162,000 to C215,000 about 3,000 total National Match pistols were made with and without Swartz safeties.) The number of National Match pistols having the Swartz safeties is unknown. However only a few pistols below serial C190000 had the safeties installed and of the pistols made after C190000, most were Standard Models shipped to Brazil and Argentina. The Brazilian pistols were without the safeties or the cutouts. The Argentine pistols were shipped in two batches of 250 pistols each. Both of these Argentine batches appear to have had the safeties installed as a number of them have recently been imported into the U.S.A. Probably much less than half of the total Colt made National Match pistols had the Swartz safeties. The total number of pistols (both Standard Government Model and National Match) shipped with Swartz safeties is probably much less than 3,000. And probably much less than half of the total Colt made National Match pistols had the Swartz safeties. Swartz safeties were also installed in late Super .38 and Super Match .38 pistols.

The Swartz pin is the smaller of the two pins, as seen from the top of the ejection port. The Swartz piston is located to the side of the disconnector notch in the slide.
Courtesy Karl Karash

Colt 1911/1911A1 Pistols

Photos courtesy of Karl Karash

Arched mainspring

Flat mainspring

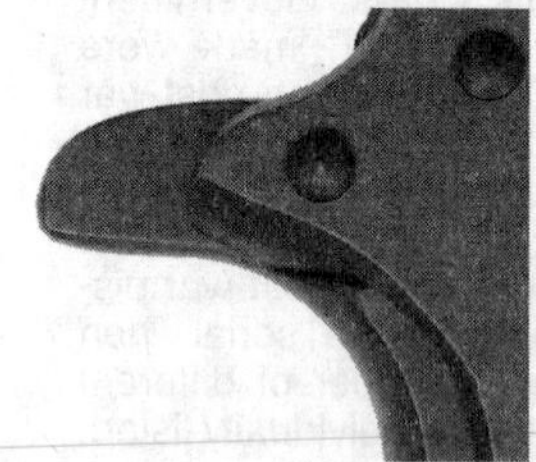

Long grip safety

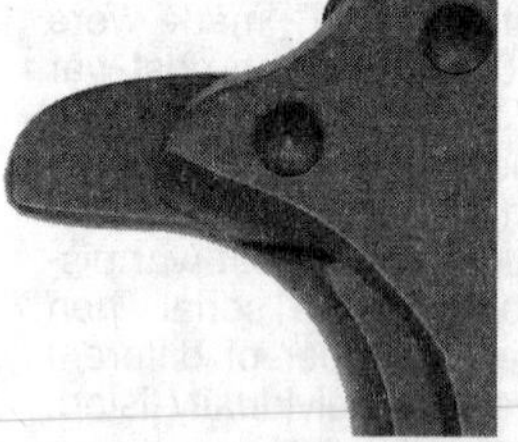

Short grip safety

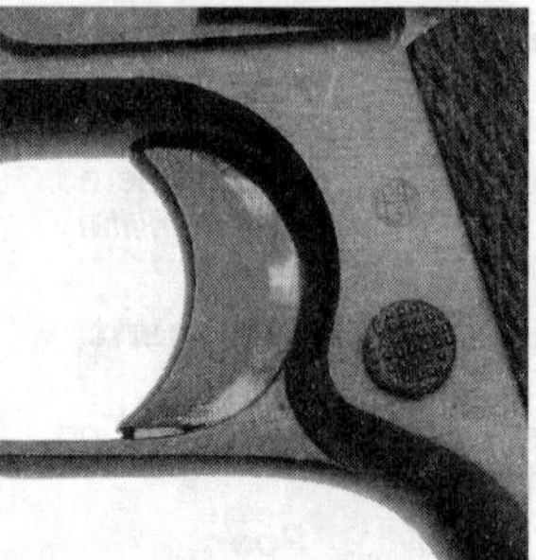

No finger groove

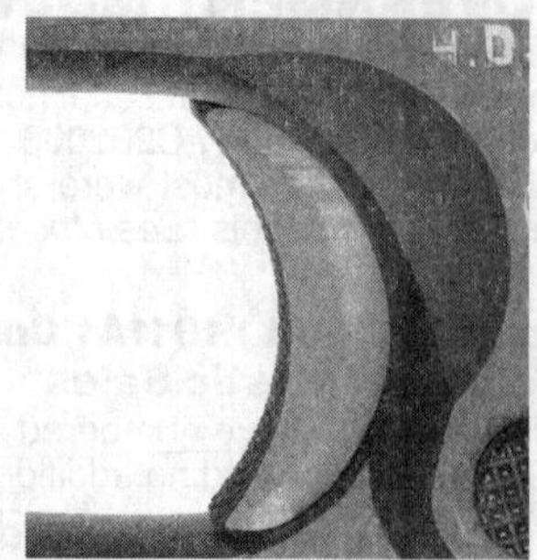

Finger groove

This symbol denotes "Sleepers" with rapidly-rising values and/or significant collector potential.

tandard Colt 1911A1 Commercial "GOVERNMENT IODEL" Marked Pistol with Numbered Slide

"Swartz safeties," no foreign markings. Fixed sights only, no additions whatsoever. Rare, seldom seen.

Exc.	V.G.	Good	Fair	Poor
3750	2500	1900	1150	850

NOTE: Finish 99-100 percent add 20-50 percent.

lt National Match Caliber Pre-WWII, .45. re-WWII (with "Swartz Safeties")

Serial number C186,000-C215,000 probably less than 1,500 pistols. Colt would rework fixed sights equipped pistols on a repair order with Stevens adjustable sight. Therefore, a Colt letter showing that the pistol was originally shipped with adjustable sights is in order for any adjustable sight-equipped pistol.

Stevens Adjustable Sights

Exc.	V.G.	Good	Fair	Poor
6200	3550	2400	1350	1000

Fixed Sights

Exc.	V.G.	Good	Fair	Poor
4700	2750	1700	1050	800

NOTE: Finish 99-100 percent add 30-60 percent.

tandard 1911A1 Pre-WWII, "GOVERNMENT IODEL" Export Sales

With "Swartz Safeties" and usually a foreign crest or foreign inscription mainly from Argentina. The vast majority of Swartz equipped foreign contract pistols were shipped to Argentina, but Argentine pistols do not have the collector interest that the others or the plain domestic pistols have. Four factors reduce collector interest in the Colt made Argentine pistols compared to the rest:

1. Most of the Argentine-marked pistols have been recently imported and have the legally required Import Markings.
2. Many of the Argentine-marked pistols have been advertised and sold in the wholesale trade publications at utility prices.
3. Most of the recent import Argentine pistols have been refinished or are in "well used" condition.
4. Most of the recent import pistols from Argentina have had some parts changed or swapped with other pistols and are not in original condition.

The few of these Argentine Swartz equipped pistols that remain in original and excellent or better condition usually sell for less than their "plain Jane" domestic counterparts, and they sell for much less than the much rarer Brazilian and Mexican pistols. Perhaps these depressed prices represent a bargin for collectors with an eye to the future when the supply of these extremely rare pistols dries up. 100 percent reblue = Fair/Poor.

Exc.	V.G.	Good	Fair	Poor
1400	1050	900	650	550

NOTE: Finish 99-100 percent add 20-30 percent.

Iormal Brazilian and Mexican Pistols w/Swartz Safeties)

These pistols do not normally have Swartz safeties, but if any were found, they would be expected to sell for at least the amount listed.

Exc.	V.G.	Good	Fair	Poor
9500	7000	4000	2500	1200

NOTE: Finish 99-100 percent add 20-30 percent.

rgentine Contract Pistols "Modelo Argentino 927, Calibre .45"

These pistols were delivered to Argentina in 1927. The right side of the slide is marked with the two-line inscription "Ejercito Argentino Colt Cal .45 Mod. 1927." There is also the Argentine National Seal and the "Rampant Colt." SN 1-10,000. Verified proof, Assembler's mark, and Final inspectors mark under left stock by upper bushing. None had Swartz Safeties. Most of these pistols were reblued. Reblued = Fair/Poor.

Exc.	V.G.	Good	Fair	Poor
1400	1050	850	600	400

NOTE: The abundance of these and other refinished Argentine pistols has depressed the prices of all original finish Argentine pistols. Finish 99-100 percent add 20-50 percent.

"Military to Commercial Conversions"

Some 1911 Military pistols that were brought home by GIs were subsequently returned to the Colt factory by their owners, for repair or refinishing. If the repair included a new barrel, the pistol would have been proof fired and a normal Verified proof mark affixed to the trigger guard bow in the normal commercial practice. If the pistol was refinished between about 1920 and 1942, the slide would probably be numbered to the frame again in the normal commercial practice. These pistols are really remanufactured Colt pistols of limited production and should be valued at least that of a contemporary 1911A1 commercial pistol. Only pistols marked with identifiable Colt markings should be included in this category. Very seldom seen.

"C" prefix until 1950, when it was changed to a suffix

Exc.	V.G.	Good	Fair	Poor
1900	1300	975	550	425

NOTE: Finish 99-100 percent add 30 percent.

Reworks of Colt 1911 and 1911A1 Commercial "GOVERNMENT MODEL" Pistols

Since Colt rework records are lost, reworked and refinished pistols without identifiable Colt applied markings are probably not verifiable as Colt reworks, and should be considered refinished pistols of unknown pedigree. The standard rule of thumb is that the value of a reworked/refinished pistol is equivalent to a similar original pistol in "Poor" condition. Many beginning collectors start by buying a pistol with either no original finish or it has been refinished. The first thing they ask is where can I get it refinished, and second is how much will it cost? A quality restoration will often cost $1,000, and that added to an initial cost of $600 will produce a pistol that might sell for $1,000 to $1,200. The lesson is that the cost to rework and refinish will seldom be recovered when the pistol is sold. Since these pistols are not original pistols, their prices are much closer to a utility shooter and depend a lot on the overall appearance of the pistol. A professionally restored example might sell for as high as $1,100 but a poorly refinished example would probably rank with the import-marked refinished pistols ($300).

POST WWII COMMERCIAL PRODUCED, DOMESTIC SALES, 1946-1969

SN C220,000 to about C220,500

No "GOVERNMENT MODEL" marking, a few have no verified proof. Many parts are leftover military.

Exc.	V.G.	Good	Fair	Poor
2300	1650	1150	950	750

NOTE: Finish 99-100 percent add 20-50 percent.

SN C220,500 to about C249,000 verified proof and "GOVERNMENT MODEL" marking

Many parts are leftover military in the first few thousand pistols. No foreign markings.

Exc.	*V.G.*	*Good*	*Fair*	*Poor*
1450	950	650	535	450

NOTE: Finish 99-100 percent add 20-30 percent. Less 30 percent for foreign markings.

SN 255,000-C to about 258,000-C Slide Factory Roll Marked "PROPERTY OF THE STATE OF NEW YORK," verified proof, and "GOVERNMENT MODEL" marking (250 pistols total)

A few leftover military parts are still used. A few pairs of pistols remain as consecutive pairs.

Courtesy Karl Karash

Exc.	*V.G.*	*Good*	*Fair*	*Poor*
1600	900	600	550	450

NOTE: Finish 99-100 percent add 20-50 percent. Add 10 percent for consecutive pairs.

SN 249,500-C to about 335,000-C, verified proof and "GOVERNMENT MODEL" marking

No foreign markings.

Exc.	*V.G.*	*Good*	*Fair*	*Poor*
1100	900	625	500	400

NOTE: Finish 99-100 percent add 20-30 percent. Less 30 percent for foreign markings.

SN 334,500-C to about 336,169-C, BB (Barrel Bushing) marked

About 1000 pistols. Verified proof and "GOVERNMENT MODEL" marking.

Exc.	*V.G.*	*Good*	*Fair*	*Poor*
1375	900	700	575	450

NOTE: Finish 99-100 percent add 20-50 percent.

Super .38 1929 Model, Pre-WWII

This pistol is identical in outward physical configuration to the .45 ACP Colt Commercial. It is chambered for the .38 Super cartridge and has a magazine that holds 9 rounds. The right side of the slide is marked "Colt Super .38 Automatic" in two lines, followed by the "Rampant Colt." The last few thousand pre-war Super .38 pistols made had the Swartz Safety parts installed, but some pistols were assembled post-war with leftover parts. These post-war-assembled pistols did not have the Swartz safeties installed but most (possibly all) had the cutouts. In 1945, 400 pistols were purchased by the U.S. Government. These 400 pistols bear the G.H.D. acceptance mark as well as the Ordnance crossed cannons. (G.H.D. and Ordnance marked add 30-50 percent. A factory letter is probably necessary here.) Some collectors feel that post-war assembly and post-war chemical tank blueing adds a premium, others feel that it requires a deduction. Post-war assembly may add 15 percent or it may deduct 15 percent.)

A Colt Super Match .38 pistol sold at auction for $12,650. This is a rare pre-war/post-war variation. Shipped in 1946. Condition is 99 percent.
Amoskeag Auction Company, April 2005

Exc.	*V.G.*	*Good*	*Fair*	*Poor*
3600	2400	1400	1100	800

NOTE: Finish 99-100 percent add 33 percent. Swartz Safeties add 20 percent.

Super Match .38 1935 Model, Pre-WWII

Only 5,000 of these specially fit and finished target-grade pistols were manufactured. They have fixed sights or the Stevens adjustable sights, and the top surfaces are matte-finished to reduce glare. Twelve hundred of these pistols were purchased and sent to Britain in 1939, at the then-costly rate of $50 per unit. The last few thousand pre-war Super .38 pistols made had the Swartz safety parts installed, but some pistols were assembled post-war with leftover parts. These post-war-assembled pistols did not have the Swartz safeties installed but most (possibly all) had the cutouts. In 1945, 400 pistols were purchased by the U.S. Government. These 400 pistols bear the G.H.D. acceptance mark as well as the Ordnance crossed cannons. G.H.D. and Ordnance marked add 30-50 percent. A factory letter is probably necessary here. Swartz Safeties add 20 percent. Some collectors feel that post-war assembly and post-war chemical tank bluing adds a premium, others feel that it requires a deduction. Post-war assembly may add 15 percent or it may deduct 15 percent.

Adjustable Sights

Exc.	*V.G.*	*Good*	*Fair*	*Poor*
7500	4200	3000	1800	1200

Fixed Sights

Exc.	*V.G.*	*Good*	*Fair*	*Poor*
6000	3850	2850	1600	1150

NOTE: Finish 99-100 percent add 20-75 percent for both models.

ACE and SERVICE MODEL ACE

Ace Model .22 Pistol

Starting on June 21, 1913, the U.S. Military along with "Springfield Armory" and "Colt Patented Firearms Manufacturing Co." attempted to develop a .22 cal rimfire pistol that could be used for training purposes. By 1927, the military became convinced that a pistol identical to the standard "Service Pistol" but in .22 cal rimfire was impractical and dropped the idea. In 1930 Colt purchased advertising that, in effect, requested the shooting public to let the company know if they would be interested in a .22 rimfire pistol built similar to the Government Model. The response must have been positive because in 1931 the Colt Ace appeared on the market. The Ace uses the same frame as the Government Model with a highly modified slide and a heavy barrel. It is chambered for .22 LR cartridge only. The size is the same as the larger-caliber version, and the weight is 36 oz. The operation is straight blowback. The Ace has a 10-round detachable magazine and features the "Improved Ace Adjustable Target Sight." The markings on the left side of the slide are the same as on the Government Model; the right side reads "Colt Ace 22 Long Rifle." At first the Army purchased a few pistols (totaling 206) through 1936. The Army concluded that the function of the Ace was less than perfect, as they concluded the .22 rimfire lacked the power to consistently and reliably operate the slide. Approximately 11,000 Ace pistols were manufactured, and in 1941 they were discontinued. Many owners today find that although the ACE is somewhat selective to ammunition, with full power loads, it is a highly reliable pistol when properly cleaned and maintained.

Exc.	*V.G.*	*Good*	*Fair*	*Poor*
2500	1750	1100	1000	900

NOTE: Finish 99-100 percent add 33 percent.

Pre-1945 Service Model Ace .22 R. F. Pistol

In 1937 Colt introduced this improved version of the Ace Pistol. It utilizes a floating chamber invented by David "Carbine" Williams, the firearm's designer who invented the "Short Stroke Gas Piston" that is the basis of the MI carbine while serving time on a Southern chain gang. Colt's advertised that this pistol with its floating chamber would give the Service Model Ace the reliability and "feel" of a .45 Auto. Today, owners of the Service Model ACE pistols find that they require regular maintenance and cleaning in order to keep the close-fitting floating chamber from binding. Furthermore, fouling appears to be much worse with some brands and types of ammunition. Most owners feel that although the perceived recoil of the Service Model ACE is noticeably greater than that of the ACE, it falls far short of a .45 Auto's recoil. The serial number is prefixed by the letters "SM." The external configuration is the same as the Ace, and the slide is marked "Colt Service Model Ace .22 Long Rifle." Most were sold to the Army and some on a commercial basis. There were a total of 13,803 manufactured before production ceased in 1945.

Blued pistols (before about SN SM 3840)

Exc.	*V.G.*	*Good*	*Fair*	*Poor*
3900	2300	1700	1150	1000

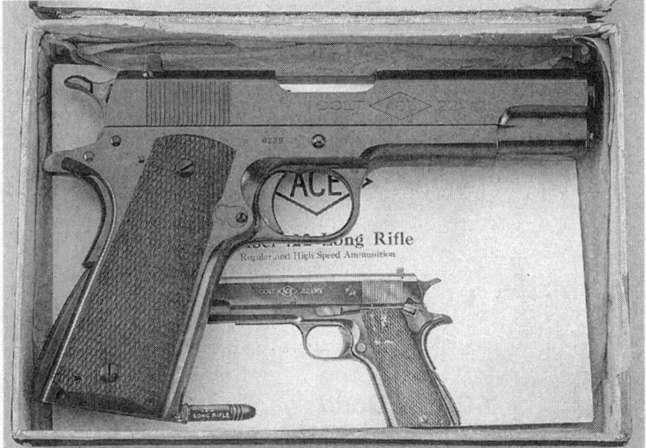

Paul Goodwin photo

Parkerized pistols (after about SN SM 3840)

Exc.	*V.G.*	*Good*	*Fair*	*Poor*
2800	1850	1300	950	700

NOTE: Finish 99-100 percent add 20-30 percent for both models. Add 20 percent for "US Property" marking.

Service Model Ace-Post-War

Introduced in 1978 this model is similar to the pre-war model. Production ceased in 1982.

Exc.	*V.G.*	*Good*	*Fair*	*Poor*
1100	950	875	800	600

NOTE: Finish 99-100 percent add 20-30 percent.

Conversion Units .22-.45, .45-.22

In 1938 Colt released a .22-caliber conversion unit. With this kit, one who already owned a Government Model could simply switch the top half and fire inexpensive .22 rimfire ammunition. The unit consists of a slide marked "Service Model Ace," barrel with floating chamber, ejector, slide lock, bushing, recoil spring, 10-shot magazine, and box. The Conversion Units feature the Stevens adjustable rear sight. Later that same year, a kit to convert the Service Model Ace to .45 ACP was offered. In 1942 production of these units ceased. The .22 kit was reintroduced in 1947; the .45 kit was not brought back. (Finish 99-100 percent add 20-30 percent.) Subtract 20 percent if box is missing. Be alert, as sometimes a conversion unit is found on a Service Model ACE receiver and a Service model Ace upper is sold as a "Conversion Unit." Conversion Units are ALWAYS marked "Conversion Unit." Service Model ACE" pistols lack the "Conversion Unit" marking.

Pre-war and Post-war "U" numbered Service Model Ace Conversion Unit, .22-.45 (to convert .45 cal. to .22 cal.)

The pre-war conversion units were serial numbered U1-U2000.

Exc.	*V.G.*	*Good*	*Fair*	*Poor*
900	650	550	500	450

NOTE: Finish 99-100 percent add 20-30 percent.

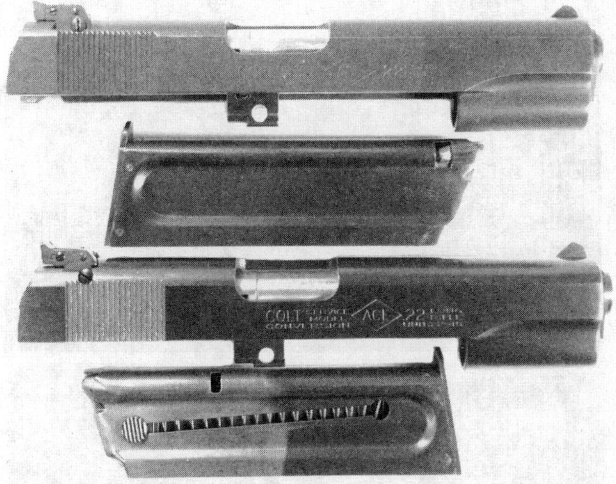

Courtesy Karl Karash

Post-war Conversion Units

These were serial numberd U2001-U2670.

Exc.	*V.G.*	*Good*	*Fair*	*Poor*
650	550	500	450	425

NOTE: Finish 99-100 percent add 20-30 percent.

Pre-war Service Model Ace (Re-)Conversion Unit, .45-22

To convert Convert SMA .22 Cal. to .45 Cal. SN 1-SN 112. <u>Watch out for fakes</u>.

Exc.	*V.G.*	*Good*	*Fair*	*Poor*
3500	2500	1500	750	550

NOTE: Finish 99-100 percent add 20-30 percent.

Post-war .22 Conversion Unit Unnumbered

30 percent premium for Stevens adjustable sights, 1946 only.

Exc.	V.G.	Good	Fair	Poor
400	350	250	225	175

NOTE: Finish 99-100 percent add 20-30 percent.

Military National Match .45 pistols

Rebuilt from service pistols at Springfield Armory between 1955 and about 1967 and at Rock Island in 1968. These pistols were built and rebuilt each year with a portion being sold to competitors by the NRA. Each year improvements were added to the rebuild program. Four articles in the "National Rifleman" document these pistols well: August 1959, April 1963, June 1966, and July 1966. Many parts for these pistols have been available and many "Look Alike" pistols have been built by basement armorers. Pistols generally came with a numbered box and shipping papers. Prices listed are for pistols with numbered box or papers. Less box and papers deduct 30 percent. When well-worn, these pistols will offer little over a standard pistol. Early pistols are much less commonly seen, but seem to be less sought after since they look largely like normal issue pistols.

Paul Goodwin photo

Exc.	V.G.	Good	Fair	Poor
1500	1075	775	600	475

NOTE: Finish 99-100 percent add 20-30 percent.

Military National Match Pistols (Drake Slide)

In 1964, Springfield Armory used some of these specially machined and hardened slides to build the Military National Match pistols that year. This year's pistol is perhaps the most identifiable NM pistol due to the unique slide marking. However, Drake was only the supplier of the slides that year. Colt supplied the slides in the following year (1965).

Courtesy Karl Karash

Exc.	V.G.	Good	Fair	Poor
1550	1100	790	610	485

NOTE: Finish 99-100 percent add 20-30 percent.

Gold Cup National Match (pre-series 70)

This model is chambered for the .45 ACP, features the flat mainspring housing of the 1911, and has a match-grade barrel and bushing. The parts were hand fitted, and the slide has an enlarged ejection port. The trigger is the long version with an adjustable trigger stop, and the sights are adjustable target type. The finish is blued, with checkered walnut grips and gold medallions. The slide is marked "Gold Cup National Match," and the serial number is prefixed by the letters "NM." This pistol was manufactured from 1957 to 1970.

Exc.	V.G.	Good	Fair	Poor
1100	850	625	500	400

NOTE: Finish 99-100 percent add 20-30 percent.

Gold Cup MKIII National Match

This pistol is identical to the Gold Cup .45 except that it is chambered for the .38 Mid-Range Wad Cutter round. It was manufactured from 1961 until 1974.

Courtesy John J. Stimpson

Exc.	V.G.	Good	Fair	Poor
1050	875	600	450	350

NOTE: Finish 99-100 percent add 20-30 percent.

Colt 1911A1 AMU (Army Marksmanship Unit)

Exc.	V.G.	Good	Fair	Poor
2700	2250	1450	900	400

NOTE: For Army modified pistols deduct 70 percent.

COLT LICENSED AND UNLICENSED FOREIGN-MADE 1911A1 AND VARIATIONS

Argentine D.G.F.M.

Direccion General de Fabricaciones Militares made at the F.M.A.P. (Fabrica Militar de Arms Portatiles [Military Factory of Small Arms]). Licensed copies SN 24,000 to 112,494. Parts are generally interchangeable with Colt-made 1911A1 type pistols. Most pistols were marked "D.G.F.M. - (F.M.A.P.)." Late pistols were marked FM within a cartouche on the right side of the slide. These pistols are found both with and without import markings, often in excellent condition, currently more often in refinished condition, and with a seemingly endless variety of slide markings. None of these variations have yet achieved any particular collector status or distinction, unless new in box. A new in the box DGFM recently sold at auction for $1,200. In fact many of these fine pistols have and continue to be used as the platforms for the highly customized competition and target pistols that are currently popular. Refinished=Fair/Poor.

Courtesy Karl Karash

Courtesy Karl Karash

Exc.	V.G.	Good	Fair	Poor
575	475	400	350	300

NOTE: Finish 99-100 percent-NIB add 10-30 percent)

Argentine-Made Ballester Molina

Un-licensed, Argentine redesigned versions. (Parts are NOT interchangeable with Colt except for the barrel and magazine.) These pistols are found both with and without import markings. Pistols without import markings usually have a B prefix number stamped on the left rear part of the mainspring housing and are often in excellent to new original condition. The vast majority of currently available pistols are found in excellent but refinished condition. Only the pistols with no import markings that are in excellent-to-new original condition have achieved any particular collector status. Most of these pistols that are being sold today are being carried and shot rather than being collected. Refinished = Fair/Poor.

Courtesy Karl Karash

Exc.	V.G.	Good	Fair	Poor
600	375	300	215	190

NOTE: Finish 99-100 percent-NIB add 10-30 percent)

Brazilian Models 1911A1

Made by "Fabrica de Itajuba" in Itajuba, Brazil, and the Imbel Model 973, made by "Industriade Material Belico do Brazil" in Sao Paulo, Brazil. The Itajuba is a true copy of the Colt 1911A1, and the Imbel is also believed to be a true copy. However, an Imbel has yet to be examined by the author. Too rarely seen in the U.S.A. to establish a meaningful price.

MODEL 1911A1 AUTOMATIC PISTOL MILITARY MODEL

NOTE: For Colt military Model 1911A1 pistols see a complete listing with photos, prices, technical data, and history in the *Standard Catalog of Military Firearms, 2nd Edition.*

MODEL 1911A1 SEMI-AUTOMATIC PISTOL

The Model 1911A1 was manufactured by Colt until 1971 when the Series 70 Government Model superceded it. The modifications in the new model were a slightly heavier slide and a slotted collet barrel bushing. In 1983 Colt introduced the Series 80 models which had an additional passive firing pin safety lock. The half-cock notch was also redesigned. At the beginning of 1992 another change was made to the Model 1911A1 model in the form of an enhanced pistol. Included were the Government models, the Commander, the Officer's model, the Gold Cup, and the Combat Elite. These modifications are the result of Colt's desire to meet the shooters demand for a more "customized" pistol. Colt chose some of the most popular modifications to perform on their new enhanced models. They include beavertail safety grip, a slotted Commander-style hammer, a relief cut under the trigger guard, a beveled magazine well, a slightly longer trigger, a flat top rib, and angled slide serrations. The Model 1911A1 may be the most modified handgun in the world.

MKIV Series 70 Government Model

This model is essentially a newer version of the 1911A1. It has the prefix "70G" from 1970-1976, "G70" from 1976-1980, and "70B" from 1980-1983, when production ceased. This model is offered in blue or nickel plate and has checkered walnut grips with the Colt medallion. It is chambered for .45 ACP, .38 Super, 9mm, and 9mm Steyr (foreign export only).

NIB	*Exc.*	*V.G.*	*Good*	*Fair*	*Poor*
600	500	400	300	250	200

MKIV Series 70 Gold Cup National Match

This is the newer version of the 1957 National Match. It features a slightly heavier slide and Colt Elliason sights. The chambering is .45 ACP only. The Accurizer barrel and bushing was introduced on this model. It was manufactured from 1970-1983.

NIB	*Exc.*	*V.G.*	*Good*	*Fair*	*Poor*
800	700	600	550	500	400

Series 70 1911 Service Model WWI

Introduced in 2004 this model is a reproduction of the famous WWI 1911 model with the original roll marks and inspector marks. Straight mainspring housing with lanyard loop. Double diamond walnut grips. Other WWI features. Two 7-round magazines included.

NIB	*Exc.*	*V.G.*	*Good*	*Fair*	*Poor*
990	775	—	—	—	—

Series 70 Gunsite Pistol

This model features a 5" barrel, thin rosewood grips, Gold Cup serrations, Heinie front sight and Novak rear sight, and several other special features. Available in blue of stainless steel. Introduced in 2004.

NIB	*Exc.*	*V.G.*	*Good*	*Fair*	*Poor*
1400	1100	—	—	—	—

Series 70 Gunsite Pistol Commander

As above but with 4.25" barrel.

NIB	*Exc.*	*V.G.*	*Good*	*Fair*	*Poor*
1400	1100	—	—	—	—

COLT ENHANCED GOVERNMENT MODELS

In 1992 Colt introduced a new set of features for its Model 1911A1 series pistols. These new features include: a flattop slide, angled rear slide serrations, scalloped ejection port, combat style hammer, beavertail grip safety, relief cut-under trigger guard, and long trigger. The models that are affected by this new upgrade are the: Delta Elite, Combat Elite, Government Model, Combat Commander, Lightweight Commander, Officer's ACP, Officer's ACP Lightweight.

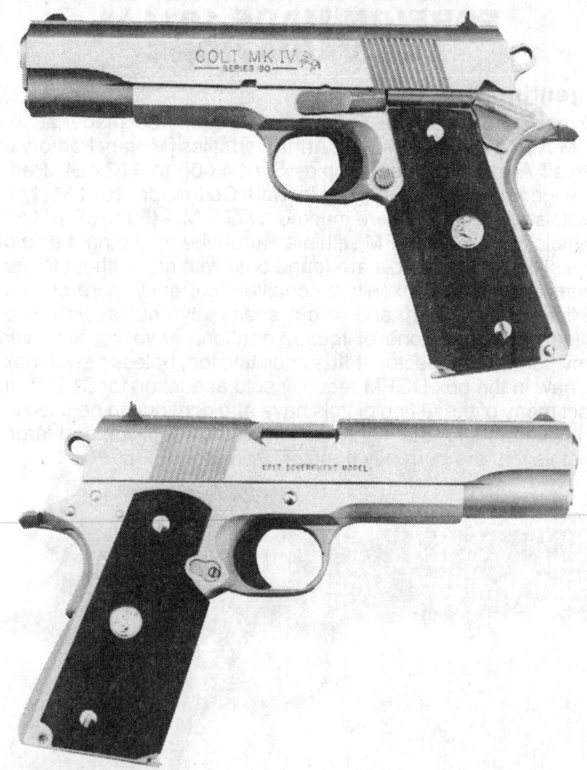

Commander

This is a shortened version of the Government model. It has a 4.25" barrel, a lightweight alloy frame, and a rounded spur hammer. The total weight of the Commander is 27.5 oz. The serial number has the suffix "LW." The Commander is chambered for the .45 ACP, 9mm, and .38 Super. The latter two have been discontinued. Some were chambered for 7.65 Parabellum for export only. The Commander was introduced in 1949. No longer in production.

NIB	Exc.	V.G.	Good	Fair	Poor
700	550	450	350	300	200

Combat Commander

The Combat Commander was produced in response to complaints from some quarters about the excessive recoil and rapid wear of the alloy-framed Commander. This model is simply a Commander with a steel frame. The Combat Commander weighs 32 oz. and is offered in blue or satin nickel with walnut grips. No longer in production.

NIB	Exc.	V.G.	Good	Fair	Poor
700	550	475	375	300	200

MK IV Series 80 Government Model

This model was introduced in 1983. It is, for all purposes, the same externally as the Series 70. The basic difference is the addition of the new firing pin safety on this model. No longer in production.

NOTE: In 1997 Colt offered this model with fixed white dot sights.

Blued

NIB	Exc.	V.G.	Good	Fair	Poor
650	500	400	350	300	250

Nickel Plated

NIB	Exc.	V.G.	Good	Fair	Poor
750	600	500	375	300	250

Stainless Steel

NIB	Exc.	V.G.	Good	Fair	Poor
675	625	500	400	325	275

Polished Stainless Steel

NIB	Exc.	V.G.	Good	Fair	Poor
750	650	550	450	350	300

REMINDER
In most cases, condition determines price.

Colt 1991A1

Introduced in 1992 this Colt Government Model is designed to resemble the original GI service issue Government Model. Offered in .45 ACP, a 5" barrel, 7-round magazine, black composition grips, and a special parkerized finish. In 1996 this model was also chambered for the 9x23 cartridge. No longer in production.

NIB	Exc.	V.G.	Good	Fair	Poor
550	450	350	300	150	125

NOTE: This pistol was offered in stainless steel in 1996. Add $50 to the above prices.

M1991A1 Commander

Chambered for the .45 ACP this model has all of the same features as the standard M1991A1 with a slightly shorter 4.25" barrel. Reintroduced in 2004.

NIB	Exc.	V.G.	Good	Fair	Poor
700	550	400	300	225	125

NOTE: In 1997 Colt offered this model in stainless steel with fixed white dot sights. Add $100 to NIB price.

M1991A1 Compact

Chambered for the .45 ACP this model has a 3.25" barrel. It is 1.5" shorter than the standard M1991A1 model and .375" shorter in height. Its magazine holds 6 rounds. No longer in production.

REMINDER

Perhaps the best advice is for the collector to take his time. Do not be in a hurry, and do not allow yourself to be rushed into making a decision. Learn as much as possible about the firearm you are interested in collecting or shooting. Try to keep current with pricing.

NIB	Exc.	V.G.	Good	Fair	Poor
550	400	250	200	150	125

NOTE: In 1997 Colt offered this model in stainless steel with fixed white dot sights. Add $50 to NIB price.

MK IV Series 80 Gold Cup National Match

Externally the same as the Series 70 Gold Cup with the new firing pin safety. No longer in production.

Blued

NIB	Exc.	V.G.	Good	Fair	Poor
850	725	600	500	350	250

Stainless Steel

NIB	Exc.	V.G.	Good	Fair	Poor
925	775	650	500	400	300

Polished Stainless Steel

NIB	Exc.	V.G.	Good	Fair	Poor
975	850	725	600	450	350

Officer's ACP

This is a shortened version of the Government Model. It has a 3.5" barrel and weighs 37 oz. It is chambered for the .45 ACP only and has checkered walnut grips. The Officer's ACP was introduced in 1985. No longer in production.

Blued

NIB	Exc.	V.G.	Good	Fair	Poor
625	500	400	325	250	200

Matte Blued

NIB	Exc.	V.G.	Good	Fair	Poor
600	475	375	300	225	200

Satin Nickel

Discontinued 1985.

Exc.	V.G.	Good	Fair	Poor
450	350	275	200	150

Stainless Steel

NIB	Exc.	V.G.	Good	Fair	Poor
750	625	450	350	300	250

Lightweight Officer's ACP

This is an alloy-framed version that weighs 24 oz. It was introduced in 1986. No longer in production.

NIB	Exc.	V.G.	Good	Fair	Poor
675	550	450	375	300	200

Concealed Carry Officer's Model

This model features a lightweight aluminum frame with stainless steel Commander slide. Barrel length is 4.25" and it is chambered for .45 ACP cartridge. Fitted with lightweight trigger, combat style hammer, and Hogue grips. Weight is approximately 34 oz. Introduced in 1998. No longer in production.

NIB	Exc.	V.G.	Good	Fair	Poor
800	650	—	—	—	—

Delta Gold Cup

Introduced in 1992 the Delta Gold Cup is chambered for the 10mm, features a 5" barrel, stainless steel finish, adjustable Accro sights, special trigger, and black rubber wraparound grips. Features all of the new "Enhanced" model features. No longer in production.

NIB	Exc.	V.G.	Good	Fair	Poor
1000	825	700	600	400	200

Delta Elite

This model is chambered for the 10mm Norma cartridge. It is offered in blue or stainless steel. The grips are black neoprene with the Delta medallion. It features a high-profile three-dot combat sight system. The Delta Elite was introduced in 1987. No longer in production.

Blued

NIB	Exc.	V.G.	Good	Fair	Poor
700	525	425	350	300	250

Stainless Steel

NIB	Exc.	V.G.	Good	Fair	Poor
750	575	450	375	300	250

Polished Stainless Steel

NIB	Exc.	V.G.	Good	Fair	Poor
850	675	550	425	350	250

Combat Elite

This is a specialized Government model that has a 5" barrel and adjustable Accro sights. It is chambered either in .45 ACP or .38 Super. It weighs 38 oz. and has an 8-round magazine for the .45 ACP and a 9-round magazine for the .38 Super. Finish can be either blue or matte stainless steel. No longer in production.

NIB	Exc.	V.G.	Good	Fair	Poor
775	625	500	400	300	200

Combat Target Model

Introduced in 1996 this 5" barrel 1911 model features a fitted barrel, Gold Cup-style trigger, tuned action, flat top slide, relieved ejection port, skeletonized hammer, wide grip safety, high cut trigger guard, beveled magazine well, and adjustable sights. Weight is 39 oz. Offered in both blue and stainless steel. In 1996 this model was also chambered for the new 9x23 cartridge as well as the .45 ACP and the .38 Super. No longer in production.

NOTE: In 1997 Colt expanded this Target Model to include a number of different variations. They are listed.

NIB	Exc.	V.G.	Good	Fair	Poor
800	650	550	500	400	200

NOTE: Add $50 for stainless steel version.

Combat Target Combat Commander

Barrel length is 4-1/4". Chambered for .45 ACP. Stainless steel finish. Weight is 36 oz. Has all other Combat Target features. No longer in production.

NIB	Exc.	V.G.	Good	Fair	Poor
800	675	575	500	400	200

Combat Target Officer's ACP

Fitted with a 3-1/2" barrel and chambered for .45 ACP. Stainless steel finish. Weight is about 34 oz. Has all other Combat Target features. No longer in production.

NIB	Exc.	V.G.	Good	Fair	Poor
800	675	575	500	400	200

Special Combat Government

This pistol features a 5" barrel, double diamond rosewood grips, extended ambidextrous thumb safety, and steel checkered mainspring housing with extended magazine well. Chambered for the .45 ACP or .38 Super cartridges. Adjustable Bomar rear sight. Magazine capacity is 8 rounds. Choice of hard chrome or blue/satin nickel finish.

NIB	Exc.	V.G.	Good	Fair	Poor
2000	1500	—	—	—	—

XSE SERIES MODEL O PISTOLS

Introduced in 1999, these models are an enhanced version of the Colt 1911 and features front slide serrations, checkered, double diamond rosewood grips, adjustable McCormick trigger, three-dot dovetail rear sights, ambidextrous safety, enhanced tolerances, aluminum frame, and stainless steel slide. Chambered for .45 ACP cartridge.

Colt O-Model Government (01070XS)

Fitted with a 5" barrel and 8-round magazine.

NIB	Exc.	V.G.	Good	Fair	Poor
1100	825	—	—	—	—

This symbol denotes "Sleepers" with rapidly-rising values and/or significant collector potential.

Colt O-Model Concealed Carry Officer's (09850XS)

Fitted with a 4.25" barrel and 7-round magazine.

NIB	Exc.	V.G.	Good	Fair	Poor
1100	825	—	—	—	—

Colt O-Model Commander (04012XS)

Fitted with a 4.25" barrel and 8-round magazine.

NIB	Exc.	V.G.	Good	Fair	Poor
1100	825	—	—	—	—

Colt O-Model Lightweight Commander (04860XS)

Fitted with a 4.25" barrel and 8-round magazine. Weight is about 26 oz.

NIB	Exc.	V.G.	Good	Fair	Poor
1100	825	—	—	—	—

1991 SERIES MODEL O PISTOLS

This series of pistol was introduced in 1991 and is to replace the standard Colt 1911 series pistols. These pistols feature checkered rubber composite grips, smooth trigger, fixed sights, beveled magazine well and standard thumb safety and service style grip safety. Chambered for .45 ACP cartridge and 7-round magazines.

Colt O-Model Government Matte (01991)

Fitted with a 5" barrel, black matte finish, carbon steel frame and slide.

NIB	Exc.	V.G.	Good	Fair	Poor
870	650	—	—	—	—

Colt O-Model Government Stainless (01091)

Fitted with a 5" barrel, mattel stainless finish on stainless steel frame and slide.

NIB	Exc.	V.G.	Good	Fair	Poor
920	700	—	—	—	—

Colt O-Model Commander Stainless (04091U)

Fitted with a 4.25" barrel and matte stainless finish with stainless steel frame and slide.

NIB	Exc.	V.G.	Good	Fair	Poor
920	700	—	—	—	—

Colt O-Model Commander (04691)

Fitted with a 4.25" barrel and black matte finish with carbon steel frame and slide.

NIB	Exc.	V.G.	Good	Fair	Poor
870	650	—	—	—	—

Colt O-Model Gold Cup

This model has the same features as the O-Model Commander with the addition of a 5" barrel with a stainless steel frame and slide. Slide top is rounded. Magazine capacity is 8 rounds. Weight is about 39 oz. Introduced in 1999.

NIB	Exc.	V.G.	Good	Fair	Poor
1400	1050	—	—	—	—

Colt Defender

This single-action pistol was introduced in 1998. This model features a lightweight aluminum alloy frame and stainless steel slide. It is chambered for the .45 ACP or .40 S&W cartridge and is fitted with a 3" barrel. Magazine capacity is 7 rounds. Rubber wraparound grips. Weight is approximately 23 oz. and overall length is 6.75". No longer in production.

NIB	Exc.	V.G.	Good	Fair	Poor
840	650	475	—	—	—

Colt Defender Model O (07000D)

This model takes the place of Defender and was introduced in 2000. It has a brushed stainless finish with a 3" barrel. Skeletonized composite trigger, beveled magazine well, extended thumb safety and upswept beavertail with palm swell. Chambered for .45 ACP only.

NIB	Exc.	V.G.	Good	Fair	Poor
950	700	—	—	—	—

1911 - WWI Replica

Single-action semi-auto chambered in .45 ACP. Faithful external reproduction of the WWI-era service pistol with original-style rollmarks, grips, sights, etc. Series 70 lockwork.

NIB	Exc.	V.G.	Good	Fair	Poor
900	750	625	—	—	—

Colt Concealed Carry

Chopped, lightweight 1911-style semi-auto chambered in .45 ACP. Weighs 25 oz. unloaded; overall length 6.75"; 7+1 capacity; Series 80 lockwork; black anodized aluminum frame with double-diamond wood grips. Introduced 2007.

NIB	Exc.	V.G.	Good	Fair	Poor
885	—	—	—	—	—

.38 Super (2006)

1911-style single-action semi-auto chambered in .38 Super. Nine-shot magazine, double-diamond walnut or checkered hard rubber stocks, fixed 3-dot sights, 5" barrel. Stainless, bright stainless or blued finish.

NIB	Exc.	V.G.	Good	Fair	Poor
837	695	525	—	—	—

Double Eagle

This is a double-action semi-automatic pistol chambered for the 10mm Auto and the .45 ACP cartridges. It has a 5" barrel and an 8-round detachable box magazine. It is constructed of stainless steel and has checkered black synthetic grips. The sights are fixed and utilize the three-dot system. No longer in production.

NIB	Exc.	V.G.	Good	Fair	Poor
500	425	350	300	250	200

Double Eagle Officer's Model

This is a compact version of the double-action Double Eagle pistol chambered for .45 ACP only. No longer in production.

NIB	Exc.	V.G.	Good	Fair	Poor
480	425	375	300	250	200

Double Eagle Combat Commander

Based on the standard Double Eagle design but with a slightly shorter 4.25" barrel, the Double Eagle Combat Commander fits between the standard model and the smaller Officer's Model. Available in .45 ACP and .40 S&W (1993) this model weighs about 36 oz., holds 8 rounds, has white dot sights, and checkered Xenoy grips. The finish is matte stainless steel. No longer in production.

NIB	Exc.	V.G.	Good	Fair	Poor
625	550	500	400	300	200

Double Eagle First Edition

This version of the double-action Double Eagle pistol is chambered for the 10mm Auto and is furnished with a Cordura holster, double-magazine pouch, and three magazines, as well as a zippered black Cordura case.

NIB	Exc.	V.G.	Good	Fair	Poor
700	650	550	475	375	300

Pocket Nine

This double-action semi-automatic pistol is chambered for the 9mm cartridge. The frame is aluminum alloy and the slide is stainless steel. Barrel length is 2.75". Magazine capacity is 6 rounds. Wraparound rubber grips standard. Overall length is 5.5". Weight is approximately 17 oz. No longer in production.

NIB	Exc.	V.G.	Good	Fair	Poor
550	450	325	—	—	—

Tac Nine

Introduced in 1999, this double-action-only semi-automatic pistol is chambered for the 9mm cartridge. It has a 2.75" barrel

 *This symbol denotes "Sleepers" with rapidly-rising values and/or significant collector potential.*

with an aluminum alloy frame and stainless steel slide. Tritium night sights. Wraparound rubber grips are standard. The finish is black oxide. Enhanced tolerances. Weight is about 17 oz. No longer in production.

NIB	Exc.	V.G.	Good	Fair	Poor
725	—	—	—	—	—

Mustang

This is a more compact version of the .380 Government Model. It has a 2.75" barrel and a 5-round detachable magazine. No longer in production.

NIB	Exc.	V.G.	Good	Fair	Poor
350	300	250	200	175	125

NOTE: Nickel finish add 10 percent. Stainless steel add 10 percent.

Mustang PocketLite

A lightweight version of the Mustang that features an aluminum alloy receiver. The finish is blued only, and it has synthetic grips. It was introduced in 1987. No longer in production.

NIB	Exc.	V.G.	Good	Fair	Poor
450	300	250	200	175	125

Government Pocketlite LW

Similar to the Mustang but fitted with a 3.25" barrel and a 7-round magazine. This model has an aluminum frame and stainless steel slide. Fixed sights. Black composition grips. Weight is approximately 15 oz. No longer in production.

NIB	Exc.	V.G.	Good	Fair	Poor
450	300	250	200	175	125

Mustang Plus II

This version of the Mustang pistol features the 2.75" barrel with the longer grip frame that accommodates a 7-round magazine. It was introduced in 1988 and is offered in blue, as well as stainless steel. No longer in production.

NIB	Exc.	V.G.	Good	Fair	Poor
385	300	250	200	175	125

NOTE: Stainless steel add 10 percent.

Colt Pony

Introduced in 1997 this semi-automatic pistol is chambered for the .380 ACP. It is fitted with a 2-3/4" barrel and a bobbed hammer. It is double-action-only. The grips are black composition. Sights are a ramp front with fixed rear. Finish is Teflon and stainless steel. Magazine capacity is 6 rounds. Overall length is 5-1/2". Weight is 19 oz. No longer in production.

NIB	Exc.	V.G.	Good	Fair	Poor
475	400	300	—	—	—

Colt Pony PocketLite

Same as above but with aluminum and stainless steel frame. Weight is approximately 13 oz. No longer in production.

NIB	Exc.	V.G.	Good	Fair	Poor
550	475	350	275	—	—

This symbol denotes "Sleepers" with rapidly-rising values and/or significant collector potential. 

.380 Series 80 Government Model

This is a single-action, blowback-operated semi-automatic pistol chambered for the .380 ACP cartridge. It has a 3.25" barrel and a 7-round magazine. The sights are fixed. It is available either blued, nickel plated, or stainless steel. It has synthetic grips and was introduced in 1985. No longer in production.

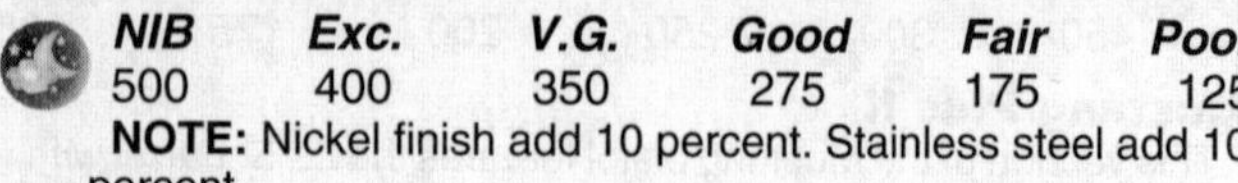

NIB	Exc.	V.G.	Good	Fair	Poor
500	400	350	275	175	125

NOTE: Nickel finish add 10 percent. Stainless steel add 10 percent.

Colt CZ40

Introduced in 1998 this double-action .40 S&W pistol was built for Colt by CZ in the Czech Republic. It is fitted with a 4" barrel and has black polymer grips. The frame is alloy with a carbon steel slide with blue finish. Magazine capacity is 10 rounds. Weight is approximately 34 oz. No longer in production.

NIB	Exc.	V.G.	Good	Fair	Poor
750	600	—	—	—	—

Colt Model 2000

Introduced in 1992, the Model 2000 is a new departure for Colt from its traditional service style semi-automatic pistols. Chambered for the 9mm, the Model 2000 is a double-action-only pistol with a 4.5" barrel and a choice between a polymer frame or an aluminum alloy frame. The polymer frame model weighs 29 oz. while the aluminum alloy frame weighs 33 oz. Grips are black composition and sights are white dot. Pistol was dropped from the Colt line in 1994.

NIB	Exc.	V.G.	Good	Fair	Poor
525	475	400	300	250	200

COLT .22 RIMFIRE SEMI-AUTOMATIC PISTOLS

For the Colt Ace see the Model 1911 section.

COLT WOODSMAN

Text and photos by Bob Rayburn

The original Colt .22 Target Model was designed by John Moses Browning and improved by engineers at Colt Firearms prior to the start of production in 1915, and major design updates were made in 1947 and again in 1955. Those three designs constitute what collectors call the three series of Woodsman pistols. First Series refers to all those built on the frame used prior to and during World War II. Second Series includes all versions built on the second frame design from 1947 until 1955, and Third Series means the third frame design as used from 1955 to the end of production in 1977.

Each series had a Target Model, a Sport Model, and a Match Target Model. All models are very similar: the Sport Model, for example, is merely the Target Model with a short barrel, and in some cases different sights or grips. The Match Target is nearly the same as the Sport or Target Model, but with a heavier, slab-sided barrel, a squared-off frame at the front of the receiver to mate with the heavy barrel, and improved sights. In the post-war years only there were also three very similar economy models: First the Challenger, then the Huntsman, and finally the Targetsman. The actions of the economy models are identical to the higher-end models of the same period internally; they lack only some of the refinements.

These guns were not assembled in strict numerical sequence. Furthermore, even when changes were made, old parts were used up at the same time new parts were being introduced. As a result, there is no hard and fast serial number dividing line for any particular feature, and serial number overlaps of several thousand are common.

All models of the Woodsman line, in all three series, are discussed here, but there are numerous variations in details that are primarily of interest to specialized collectors. For more details see Bob Rayburn's ***Colt Woodsman Pocket Guide***, a 96-page pocket-sized guide to the Colt Woodsman line, available for $10 (including shipping) from:

Bob Rayburn
PO Box 97104
Lakewood, WA 98497

Or online at http://www.colt22.com or http://www.coltwoodsman.com

Values listed here are for the pistol only, without extras, for guns in the middle of each condition range. These are guidelines to the prevailing retail values for the collector or shooter who is buying it as the end user, ***not*** what one might expect to receive from a gun dealer who is buying it to resell. Furthermore, within the Excellent and Very Good condition categories, there is a considerable spread in value, especially for the older and more collectible versions. Excellent, for example, means 98 percent ***or more*** original blue, but a very nice pre-Woodsman with 100 percent of the original blue would likely be worth twice as much to a serious collector as one with only 98 percent. At the other end of the condition scale, in the Fair and Poor categories, the individual values of component parts become significant, and effectively set a floor value. A poor condition, rusty, pitted pre-Woodsman or First Series Match Target would still have good value if it included the original magazine and grips in nice condition, for example. In addition, there are sometimes rare variations within the broad categories that can significantly enhance the value. Include the original crisp condition box, instructions, and tools, and the value goes up more, especially for high condition early guns. On the other hand, rust, pitting (even very minor), rebluing, or other non-factory modifications will significantly reduce the values from those listed in the Very Good category or better.

FIRST SERIES

In 1915 the intended market was the target shooter, and there was only one model: the Colt .22 LR Automatic Target Pistol. That model, however, proved to be very popular not only with target shooters, but also with hunters, trappers, campers, and other outdoorsmen. Management at Colt noticed this, of course, and decided to give the pistol a new name that more closely reflected its widespread use. THE WOODSMAN was the name chosen, and that roll mark was added to the side of the receiver in 1927, at approximately serial number 54000.

To further satisfy the broader market, Colt introduced the Sport Model in 1933, and the Match Target Model in 1938. The compact and beautifully balanced Sport Model was a near perfect "kit gun" for the outdoorsman, and the Match Target was designed for the special needs of the serious target shooters.

Approximately 54,000 pre-Woodsmans (all with 6-5/8 inch barrels) and a combined total of approximately 110,000 Woodsman marked Sport and Target Models were produced in the first series. The Sport Model and Target Model were serial numbered together after the Sport Model was added to the line in 1933, so it is not possible to easily determine how many of each were manufactured. It is safe to say that the Target Model far outnumbered the Sport Model.

During the war years of 1942-45 the Match Target was the only Woodsman model built, and virtually the entire production was for the US military.

Pre-Woodsman

This model was made from 1915-1927. It has a 10-round magazine capacity, blue finish, checkered walnut grips, and 6-5/8" barrel. It was designed for .22 LR standard velocity ammunition. The rear sight is adjustable for windage, the front sight for elevation. Up until approximately serial number 31000 the barrel was a very thin, so-called "pencil barrel." The barrel weight and diameter were increased slightly in 1922 to what collectors now call the "medium weight barrel." There were also numerous small changes in the grips, magazines, and markings over the years. Approximately 54,000 were made in all variations.

An early pre-Woodsman

Exc.	V.G.	Good	Fair	Poor
1400	900	400	250	200

*A checkered pattern in an oval on the mainspring housing (left) indicates a pre-Woodsman or First Series Woodsman Target model that was designed for standard velocity .22 Long Rifle ammunition only. A series of horizontal parallel lines in a rectangular pattern (right) indicates one that was designed for high-velocity .22 Long Rifle ammunition. All guns in the series made after 1932 were designed for high-velocity ammunition, and that includes **all** Sport, Match Target, Challenger, Huntsman, and Targetsman models. The post-WWII guns have no pattern on the mainspring housing but they were all made for high-velocity ammunition.*

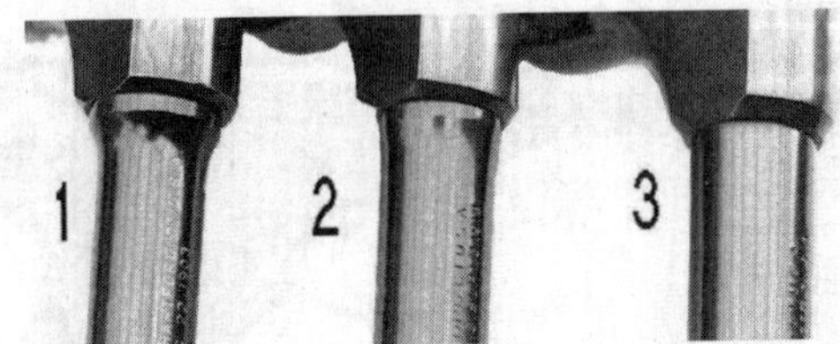

The three barrel profiles used with the Colt pre-Woodsman and First Series Target Model: from left to right, in order used, the pencil barrel, medium weight barrel, and straight taper barrel.

Woodsman Target

Initially this was exactly the same as the late pre-Woodsman, with the exception of THE WOODSMAN marking on the side of the receiver. Later there were small changes in the sights, trigger, and markings. In 1934 the barrel profile was again modified to a larger diameter, heavier barrel. This third and final pre-WWII barrel profile lacked the fillet, or step-down, as was present on the earlier pencil barrel and medium barrel, and is therefore commonly called the "straight taper" barrel.

A significant modification occurred in 1932 when a new heat-treated mainspring housing and stiffer recoil spring were phased in to allow the use of the increasingly popular *high velocity* .22 LR ammunition. While this change has been widely reported to have taken place at serial number 83790, it was actually phased in over a period of time and a range of serial numbers, spanning at least 81000-86000, within which range both standard and high speed versions can be found. Fortunately Colt changed the marking on the back of the mainspring housing (see photo) to allow visual differentiation. Colt also sold a conversion kit to modify the older guns for use with high velocity ammunition. The kit consisted of a new style mainspring housing, a stiffer recoil spring, and a coil type magazine spring for use in the very early guns that had a Z type magazine spring.

First Series Target Model

Exc.	V.G.	Good	Fair	Poor
1100	750	400	250	200

Woodsman Sport

With the Woodsman proving to be increasingly popular with outdoorsmen of all types, Colt decided to market a Woodsman better suited for a "take along" gun for hiking, camping, etc. This was accomplished in 1933 by merely shortening the barrel from 6-5/8 inches to 4-1/2 inches, and announcing the new Sport Model. Other than barrel length, the only difference between the Target Model and the Sport Model was an adjustable front sight on the Target Model and a fixed front sight on the Sport Model. Later a front sight adjustable for elevation would be an available option for the Sport Model. Colt called this arrangement "Target Sights," and indeed it was the same front sight used on the Target Model. A First Series Sport Model with an adjustable front sight will command a premium of approximately 25 percent over the values listed.

First Series Sport Model

Exc.	V.G.	Good	Fair	Poor
1400	1000	500	250	200

Woodsman Match Target

Colt introduced the Match Target Woodsman in 1938, with its own serial number series beginning at MT1, and continuing until 1944 with serial number MT16611. The new features included larger grips, a heavier barrel (6-5/8"), and a rear sight fully adjustable for both windage and elevation. To signify its intended market a Bullseye Target pattern was placed on the side of the barrel. That led to its nickname of "Bullseye Match Target." The elongated, one-piece wraparound walnut grips also picked up a nickname, due to their unusual shape. Unfortunately, the so-called "Elephant Ear" grips are somewhat fragile and are often broken. In addition, many of the serious target shooters of the day replaced them with custom grips with thumb rest and palm swell, and the original grips were set aside and eventually lost or discarded. For those reasons the original grips are often missing, and that severely affects the value. Values listed assume original one-piece walnut wraparound Elephant Ear grips with no cracks, repairs, or modifications, and a correct Match Target marked magazine. The values listed for Fair and Poor condition are primarily salvage value, and reflect the high value of original "Elephant Ear" grips and Match Target marked magazines for spare parts. Approximately 11,000 were produced for the civilian market from 1938-1942.

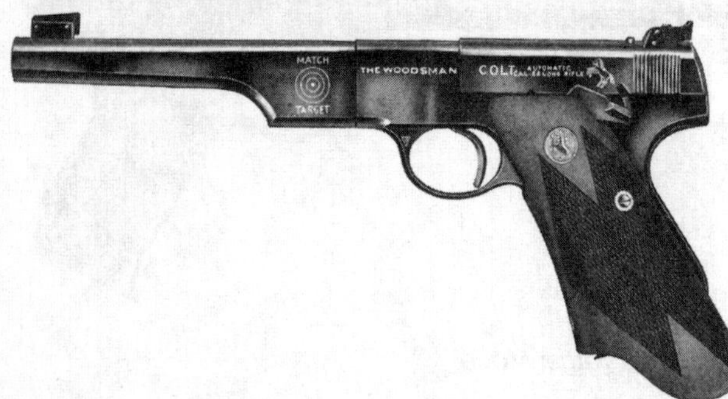

First Series Match Target

Exc.	V.G.	Good	Fair	Poor
3000	1600	750	650	550

Military Woodsman Match Target

After the United States entered World War II at the end of 1941, civilian production at Colt was stopped and the total effort was devoted to the U.S. military. Slightly more than 4000 First Series Match Target Woodsmans were delivered on U.S. Government contract from 1942-1944. Most of them, but not all, had serial numbers above MT12000. With possible rare exceptions they all had U.S. Property or U.S. military markings, standard blue finish, 6-5/8" barrel, and extended length plastic stocks. The plastic stocks are sometimes erroneously called elephant ear stocks. The military plastic stocks are still relatively easy to find and inexpensive and, since they will fit any First Series Colt Woodsman, they are often used as replacement grips on non-military guns. Since the military guns had plastic grips, rather than the costly and desirable "Elephant Ear" grips, the salvage value in the Fair and Poor condition range is less than that for the civilian model.

A Colt Woodsman First Model Match Target pistol sold at auction for $4,025. Condition is NIB with papers.
Amoskeag Auction Company, January 2005

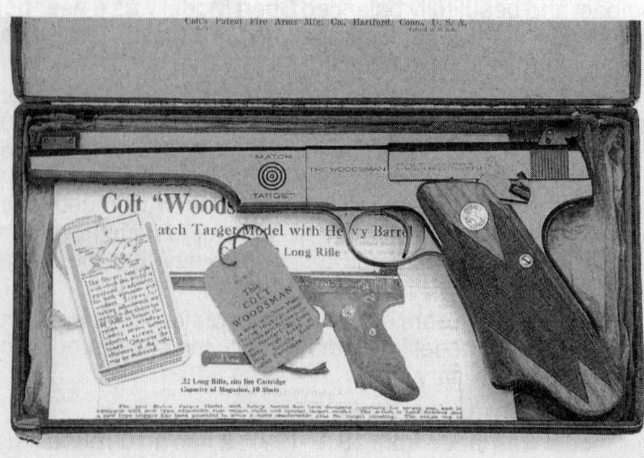

Exc.	V.G.	Good	Fair	Poor
3200	1800	850	550	350

SECOND SERIES

After World War II Colt entered a lengthy period of clearing up government contracts and retooling for the civilian market. The Woodsman line was extensively revised and modernized. The second series guns began appearing near the end of 1947, although no appreciable numbers were shipped until 1948. The Second Series Woodsman had essentially the same action and many of the same internals as the first series guns, but were larger and heavier, with a longer grip frame. New features included a magazine safety, automatic slide stop when the magazine was emptied, fully adjustable rear sight, heavier barrels, and a 6-inch barrel length on the Target and Match Target Models, rather than 6-5/8 inches, as on the first series. Other new features included a push button magazine release just aft of the trigger guard, like that on the large frame Govern-

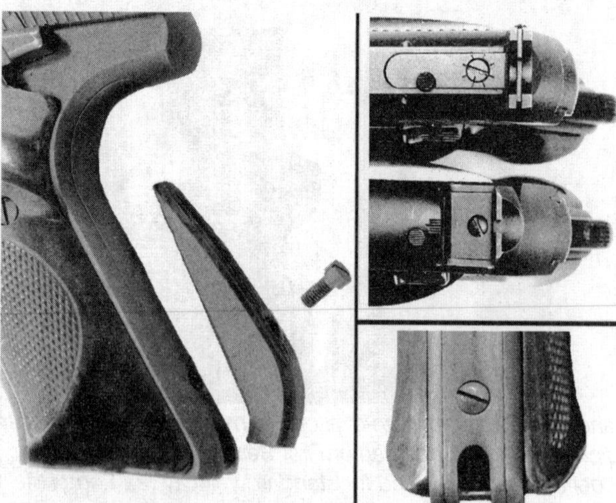

(Above left) The Second Series Woodsman came with two grip adapters, to provide for different sized hands.

(Above, bottom right) This shows the screw for mounting the grip adapter, and below that the concealed lanyard ring.

(Above, top right) In 1953 the Woodsman rear sight was changed from the Coltmaster (bottom) to the Accro (top).

ment Model semi-automatics, a lanyard ring concealed in the butt, and a provision for attaching a plastic grip adapter to the backstrap, thereby accommodating different sized hands. Elevation adjustment was incorporated into the rear sight of all Woodsman models, and the adjustable front sight was replaced with a fixed blade. Serial numbers were restarted at 1-S, and are intermixed for all three models. Approximately 146,000 of the three models were produced.

In 1950 Colt added the Challenger to the line of second series pistols, the first of the economy models. Internally the Challenger is nearly identical to the Woodsman pistols of the same era, but externally it lacks most of the refinements introduced with the Second Series Woodsman. It has no magazine safety, automatic slide stop, adjustable sights, push button magazine release, lanyard ring, or grip adapters. It was available with either a 6-inch or 4-1/2 inch barrel, and had its own serial number series beginning with 1-C. Approximately 77,000 were produced.

Woodsman Target

6 inch barrel

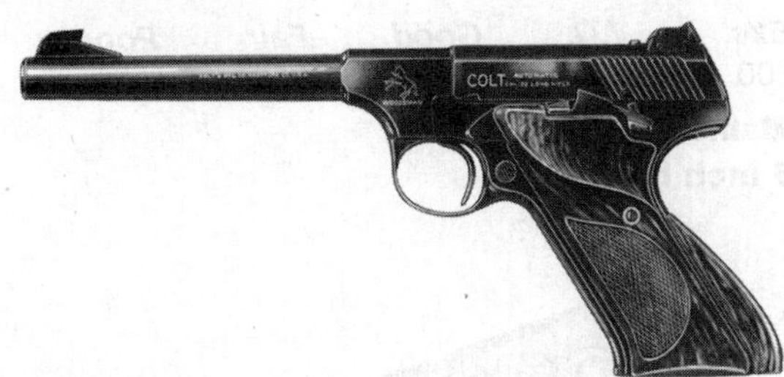

Second Series Target Model

Exc.	V.G.	Good	Fair	Poor
750	550	300	250	150

Woodsman Sport

4-1/2 inch barrel

Second Series Sport Model

Exc.	V.G.	Good	Fair	Poor
850	600	350	250	150

Woodsman Match Target

6 inch barrel

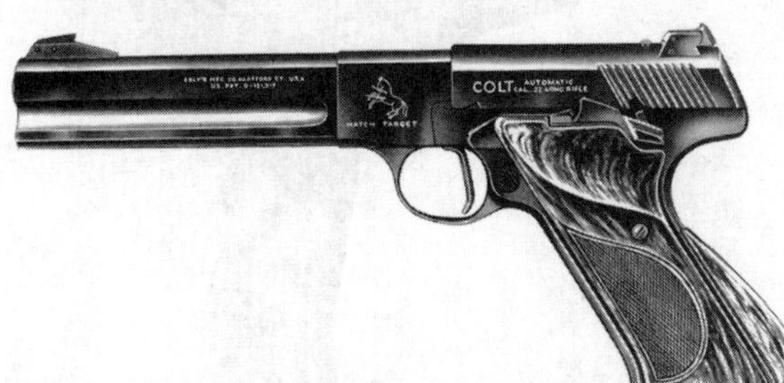

Second Series Match Target Model with 6 inch barrel.

Exc.	V.G.	Good	Fair	Poor
1000	650	450	350	150

Woodsman Match Target

4-1/2 inch barrel

Introduced in 1950.

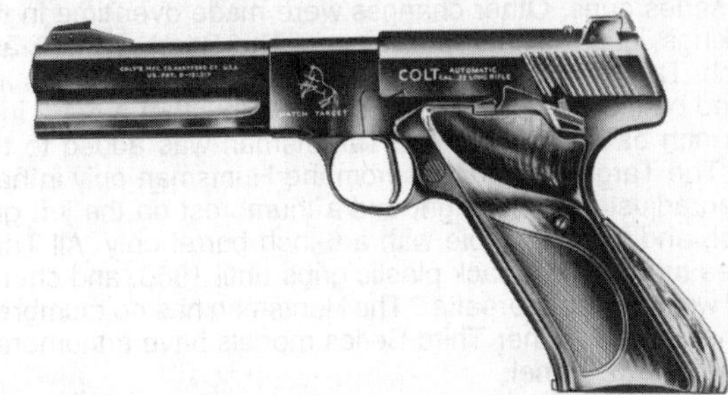

Second Series Match Target Model with 4-1/2 inch barrel.

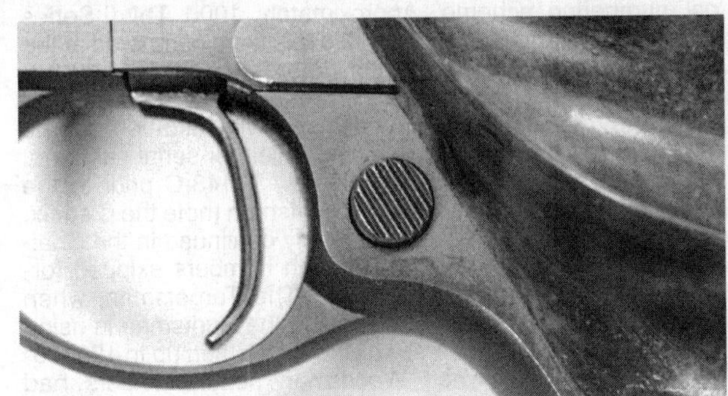

Second Series Woodsman magazine catch

Exc.	V.G.	Good	Fair	Poor
1200	750	500	350	150

Challenger

4-1/2 inch barrel

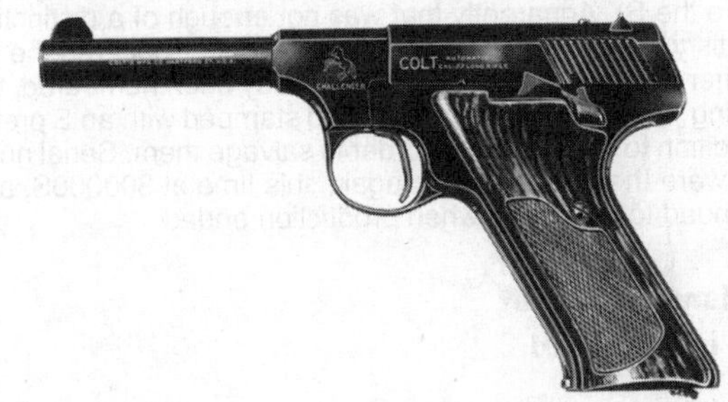

Colt Challenger (Second Series only) with 4-1/2 inch barrel.

Exc.	V.G.	Good	Fair	Poor
550	350	250	200	150

Challenger

6 inch barrel

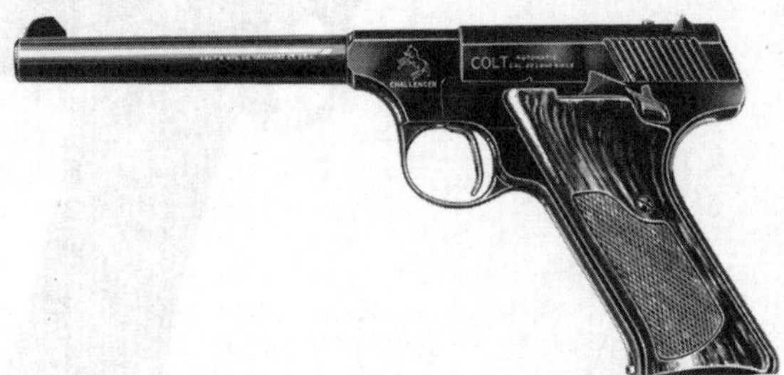

Colt Challenger (Second Series only) with 6 inch barrel.

Exc.	V.G.	Good	Fair	Poor
550	350	250	200	150

THIRD SERIES

In 1955 Colt again redesigned the Woodsman line. The most obvious change was in the location of the magazine release, which was again placed at the heel of the butt, just as on the first series guns. Other changes were made over time in the markings, grips, sights, and trigger. The Sport, Target, and Match Target models continued. The Challenger was replaced by the very similar Huntsman, with either a 4-1/2 inch or 6 inch barrel. In 1959 the Targetsman was added to the line. The Targetsman differs from the Huntsman only in having an adjustable rear sight and a thumbrest on the left grip panel, and was available with a 6-inch barrel only. All Third Series models had black plastic grips until 1960, and checkered walnut grips thereafter. The Huntsman has no thumbrest on the grips. All other Third Series models have a thumbrest on the left grip panel.

It is difficult to impossible to determine how many of each model were produced in the third series, due to a very complex serial numbering scheme. Approximately 1000 Third Series Sport, Target, and Match Target Models were numbered at the end of the second series serial number range, from 146138-S to 147138-S. Numbers were then restarted at 160001-S, so there are no post-WWII Woodsmans with numbers in the 148xxx-S to 159xxx-S range. The Challenger serial numbers, meantime, had reached approximately 77143-C prior to the Challenger being replaced by the Huntsman (note the C suffix, for Challenger). The Huntsman initially continued in the Challenger serial number series, although numbers skipped forward to 90000-C before restarting. The Targetsman, when added to the line early in 1959, joined the Huntsman in using the -C suffix serial numbers, which were by then up to 129300-C. Then in 1969, when Woodsman serial numbers had reached 241811-S and the -C numbers had reached 194040-C, Colt decided to integrate the serial numbers for all versions of the Woodsman, Huntsman, and Targetsman and restart numbering again. This time they started with 001001S. That worked fine until numbers reached 099999S, and rolled over to 100000S. Numbers used in 1951-52 were then being inadvertently duplicated, with one small exception: the earlier guns had a -S suffix while the later ones had only an S (no hyphen before the S). Apparently that was not enough of a distinction to satisfy federal regulations, so when Colt discovered the error after approximately 1,330 had already been numbered, the existing "double headers" were hand stamped with an S prefix, in addition to the S suffix, in order to salvage them. Serial numbers were then restarted yet again, this time at 300000S, and continued to 317736S, when production ended.

Woodsman Target

6 inch barrel

Exc.	V.G.	Good	Fair	Poor
700	450	300	250	150

Woodsman Sport

4-1/2 inch barrel

Exc.	V.G.	Good	Fair	Poor
800	500	300	250	150

Woodsman Match Target

6 inch barrel

Exc.	V.G.	Good	Fair	Poor
900	650	450	350	150

4-1/2 inch barrel

Added to the line in 1950.

Exc.	V.G.	Good	Fair	Poor
1000	750	500	350	150

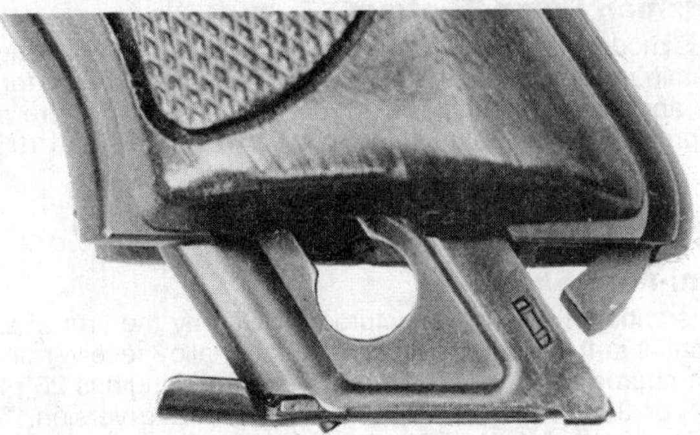

With the introduction of the Third Series guns, Colt moved the magazine catch back to the heel of the butt, where it had been on the first series.

Huntsman

4-1/2 or 6 inch barrel

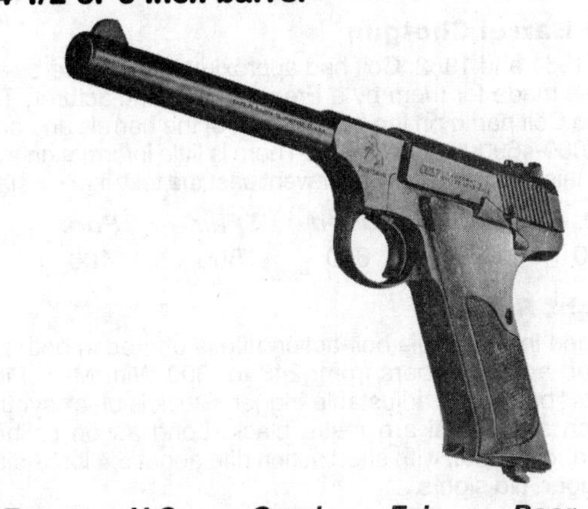

Exc.	V.G.	Good	Fair	Poor
500	350	250	200	150

Targetsman

6 inch barrel, 4-1/2 inch (rare)

Exc.	V.G.	Good	Fair	Poor
550	400	250	200	150

Colt Junior Pocket Model

This diminutive unit is only 4.5" long overall and weighs 12 oz. Colt did not manufacture this pistol, but rather had it made for them by Astra in Spain. The pistol was introduced in 1958 chambered for .25 ACP. One year later a .22 Short version appeared. Both had external hammers and detachable 6-round magazines. The passage of the 1968 Gun Control Act made import of a weapon of this size illegal, so Colt discontinued its relationship with Astra. The pistol was re-introduced in 1970 as an American-made product and was produced for two more years. Production ceased in 1972. Astra also made this pistol and called it the Cub.

NIB	Exc.	V.G.	Good	Fair	Poor
300	250	200	175	125	75

NOTE: .22 Short add 25 percent.

Cadet / Colt .22

Introduced in 1994 this .22 caliber semi-automatic pistol is offered with a 4-1/2" barrel and stainless steel finish. The model was renamed Colt .22 in 1995. The sights are fixed and magazine capacity is 11 rounds. Overall length is 8-5/8" and weight is approximately 33 oz.

NIB	Exc.	V.G.	Good	Fair	Poor
250	200	165	125	75	50

Colt .22 Target

Introduced in 1995 this model features a 6" bull barrel with removable front sight and adjustable rear sight. Black composite monogrip stock. Stainless steel finish. Weight is 40.5 oz.

NIB	Exc.	V.G.	Good	Fair	Poor
325	275	225	150	100	75

COLT MODERN LONG ARMS

Colteer I-22

This is a single-shot bolt-action rifle chambered for .22 LR or .22 Magnum. It has a plain uncheckered walnut stock, 20" barrel, and adjustable sights. There were approximately 50,000 manufactured between 1957 and 1966.

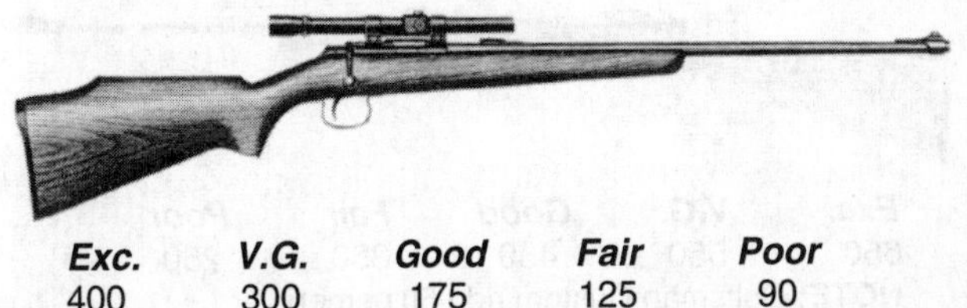

Exc.	V.G.	Good	Fair	Poor
400	300	175	125	90

This symbol denotes "Sleepers" with rapidly-rising values and/or significant collector potential.

Stagecoach

This is a semi-automatic, saddle ring carbine. It is chambered for .22 LR and has a 16.5" barrel and a 13-shot tubular magazine. The stock is fancy walnut, and the receiver has the stagecoach holdup scene roll-engraved on it. There were approximately 25,000 manufactured between 1965 and 1975.

Exc.	V.G.	Good	Fair	Poor
450	350	200	150	100

Courier

This model is similar to the Stagecoach, with a pistol-grip stock and beavertail forearm. It was manufactured between 1970 and 1975.

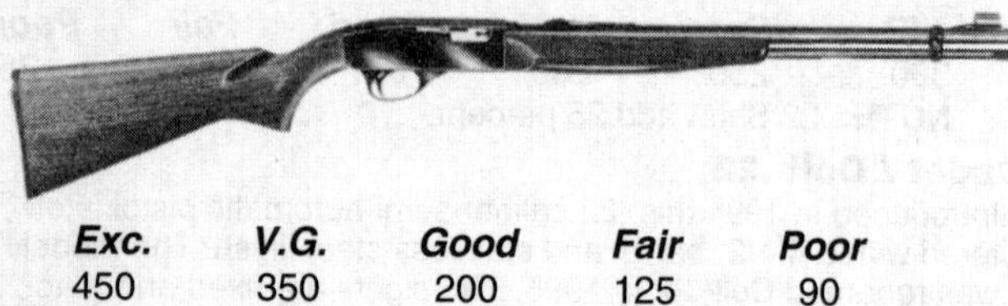

Exc.	V.G.	Good	Fair	Poor
450	350	200	125	90

Colteer

This is a less-expensive version of the Stagecoach. It features a 19.5" barrel, has a 15-shot tubular magazine, and is stocked in a plainer grade walnut. There is no roll engraving. Approximately 25,000 were manufactured between 1965 and 1975.

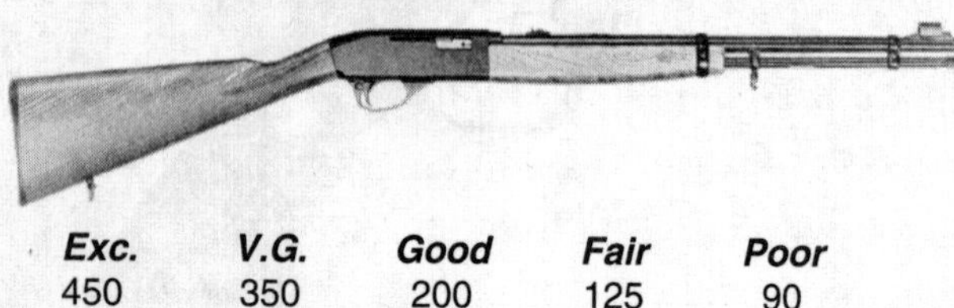

Exc.	V.G.	Good	Fair	Poor
450	350	200	125	90

Colt "57" Bolt-Action Rifle

This rifle was manufactured for Colt by the Jefferson Mfg. Co of New Haven, Connecticut. It utilizes a Fabrique Nationale Mauser action and has a checkered American walnut stock with a Monte Carlo comb. The rifle is offered with adjustable sights. It is chambered for .243 or .30-06. There is also a deluxe version that features higher-grade wood. There were approximately 5,000 manufactured in 1957.

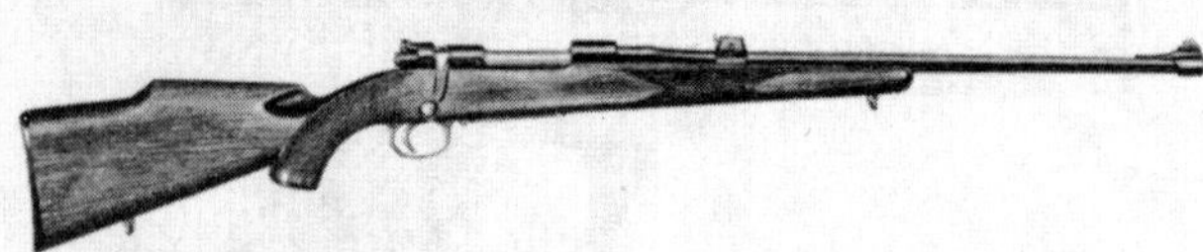

Exc.	V.G.	Good	Fair	Poor
550	450	350	300	225

NOTE: Deluxe version add 20 percent.

Coltsman Bolt-Action Rifle

The Coltsman was manufactured for Colt by Kodiak Arms. It utilizes either a Mauser or Sako action. The rifle is offered in .243, .308, .30-06, and .300 Winchester Magnum. It has a barrel length of 22", 24" in the Magnum chambering. The stock is checkered American walnut. There were approximately 10,000 manufactured between 1958 and 1966. There is a deluxe version that features a higher-grade, skipline-checkered walnut stock and rosewood forend tip; this is called "The Coltsman Custom."

Exc.	V.G.	Good	Fair	Poor
650	550	450	350	250

NOTE: Coltsman Custom add 50 percent.

Coltsman Pump Shotgun

This model was manufactured by Jefferson Arms, utilizing an aluminum alloy frame made by Franchi. It is chambered for 12, 16, and 20 gauge and has a 26" or 28" plain barrel. There were approximately 2,000 manufactured between 1961 and 1965.

Exc.	V.G.	Good	Fair	Poor
350	300	275	200	150

Semi-Auto Shotgun

This shotgun was manufactured for Colt by the firm of Luigi Franchi in Italy. It features an aluminum alloy receiver and is chambered for 12 or 20 gauge. The barrel length is 26", 28", 30", or 32"—either vent-rib or plain. A deluxe version, "The Custom Auto," features a fancy walnut stock and a hand engraved receiver. There were approximately 5,300 manufactured between 1962 and 1966.

Exc.	V.G.	Good	Fair	Poor
375	325	300	225	175

NOTE: Custom Auto add 25 percent.

Double-Barrel Shotgun

During 1961 and 1962, Colt had approximately 50 side-by-side shotguns made for them by a French gun manufacturer. They have the Colt name on the breech area of the barrels and are in the 467000-469000 serial range. There is little information available on this gun, and Colt never went past the test-market stage.

Exc.	V.G.	Good	Fair	Poor
1000	750	650	500	400

Colt Light Rifle

Introduced in 1999, this bolt-action rifle is offered in both long and short action calibers from .243 to .300 Win. Mag. Fitted with a 24" barrel and adjustable trigger. Stock is black synthetic. Action and barrel are matte black. Long action calibers. Weight about 6 lbs., with short action rifle about 5.4 lbs. Adjustable trigger. No sights.

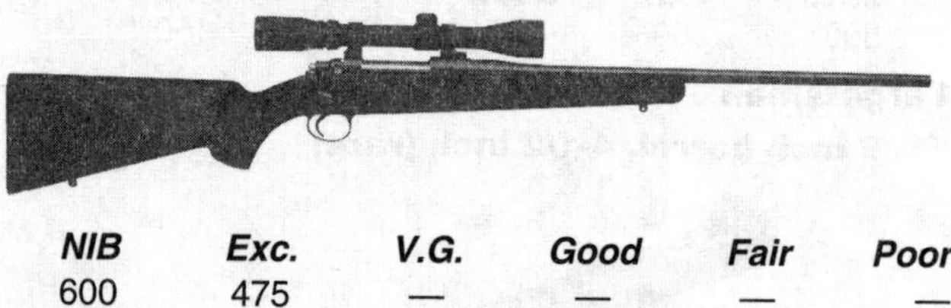

NIB	Exc.	V.G.	Good	Fair	Poor
600	475	—	—	—	—

Colt Sauer Bolt-Action Rifle

This is a high quality and unique rifle manufactured for Colt by the firm of J.P. Sauer & Son of Germany. The rifle features a non-rotating bolt that makes the Colt Sauer action smoother functioning than most. It has a 24" barrel, skipline-checkered walnut stock with rosewood forend tip, pistol grip cap, and recoil pad. There are five basic configurations: the Standard Action, chambered for .25-06, .270 Winchester, and .30-06; the Short Action, chambered for .22-250, .243 Winchester, and .308 Winchester; the Magnum Action, chambered for .7mm Remington Magnum, .300 Winchester Magnum, and .300 Weatherby Magnum; also the "Grand Alaskan" and the "Grand African," heavier versions chambered for .375 Holland & Holland Magnum and .458 Winchester Magnum, respectively. These rifles were all discontinued by Colt in 1985.

Colt Sauer Short Action

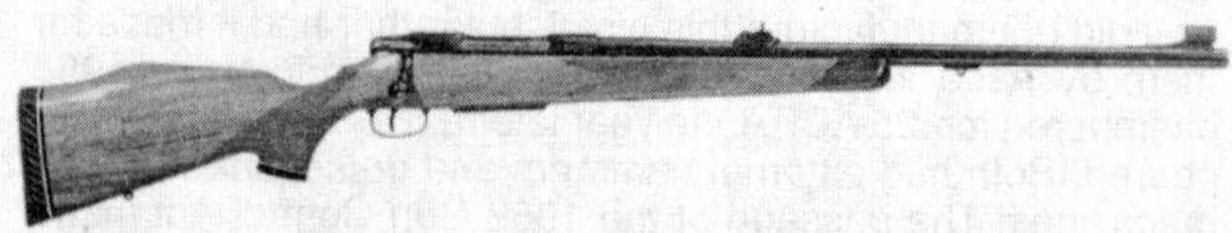

Exc.	V.G.	Good	Fair	Poor
995	850	700	600	500

NOTE: Standard Action add $50. Magnum Action add $200. "Grand Alaskan" add $400. "Grand African" add $450.

Colt Sauer Drilling

This is a rather unique firearm and one with which many American enthusiasts are not familiar—a 3-barreled gun. It features a side-by-side shotgun in 12 gauge over a .30-06 or .243 rifle barrel. The name was based on the German word for three, as this is where the concept was developed. They are quite popular in Europe where the game preserve style of hunting is prevalent but have little use in America where our hunting seasons don't often overlap. This drilling has 25" barrels and pop-up sights for the rifle barrel and is nicely engraved. It was discontinued by Colt in 1985.

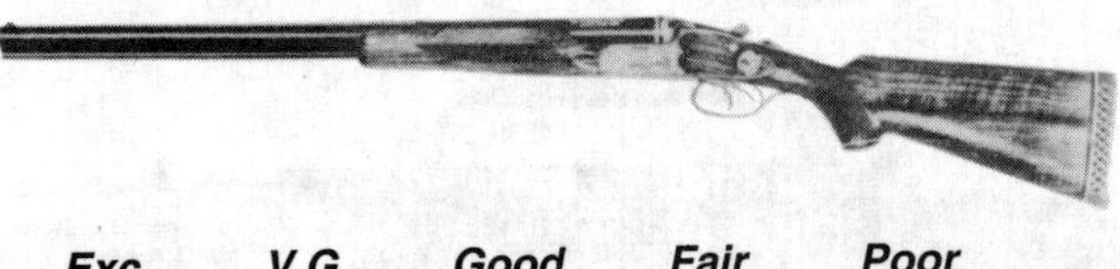

Exc.	V.G.	Good	Fair	Poor
3500	2750	2000	1500	1100

Colt-Sharps Rifle

Introduced in 1970 as the last word in sporting rifles, the Colt-Sharps is a falling-block action that was advertised as a modern Sharps-Borchardt. This undertaking was first-class all the way. The finish is high polish blue with a deluxe-grade hand-checkered walnut stock and forend. This rifle is chambered for .17 Remington, .22-250, .243, .25-06, 7mm Remington Magnum, .30-06, and .375 Holland & Holland Magnum; and it was offered cased with accessories. This model was manufactured between 1970 and 1977.

NIB	Exc.	V.G.	Good	Fair	Poor
2500	2000	1200	850	500	300

AR-15 & SPORTER RIFLES

PRICING NOTICE: It is estimated that the value of pre-ban AR-15s have declined 10-15 percent since the Assault Weapons ban has lapsed. The pricing status of the AR-15 Sporter is still volatile.

AR-15 Sporter (Model #6000)

A semi-automatic rifle firing from a closed bolt was introduced into the Colt product line in 1964. Similar in appearance and function to the military version, the M-16. Chambered for the .223 cartridge. It is fitted with a standard 20" barrel with no forward assist, no case deflector, but with a bayonet lug. Weighs about 7.5 lbs. Dropped from production in 1985.

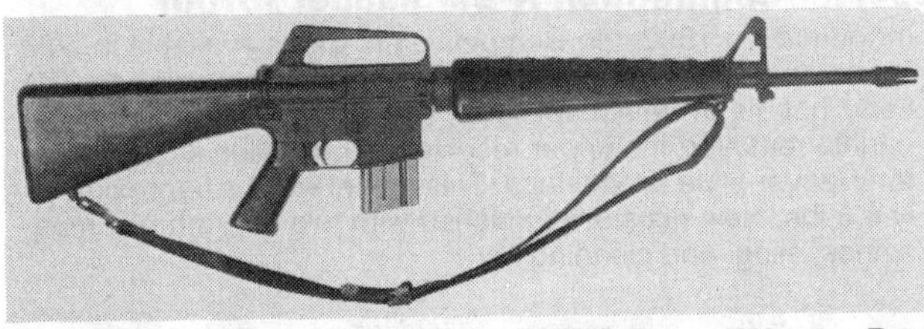

NIB	Exc.	V.G.	Good	Fair	Poor
2150	1600	1200	700	600	400

AR-15 Sporter w/Collapsible Stock (Model #6001)

Same as above but fitted with a 16" barrel and folding stock. Weighs approximately 5.8 lbs. Introduced in 1978 and discontinued in 1985.

NIB	Exc.	V.G.	Good	Fair	Poor
1800	1450	1000	750	600	400

AR-15 Carbine (Model #6420)

Introduced in 1985 this model has a 16" standard weight barrel. All other features are the same as the previous discontinued AR-15 models. This version was dropped from the Colt product line in 1987.

NIB	Exc.	V.G.	Good	Fair	Poor
1450	1200	900	750	600	400

Colt AR-15 and Colt Sporter Terminology

There are three different and distinct manufacturing cycles that not only affect the value of these rifles but also the legal consequences of their modifications.

Pre-Ban Colt AR-15 rifles (Pre-1989): Fitted with bayonet lug, flash hider, and stamped AR-15 on lower receiver. Rifles that are NIB have a green label. It is legal to modify this rifle with any AR-15 upper receiver. These are the most desirable models because of their pre-ban features.

Colt Sporters (Post-1989-pre-September 1994): This transition model has no bayonet lug, but it does have a flash hider. There is no AR-15 designation stamped on the lower receiver. Rifles that are NIB have a blue label. It is legal to modify this rifle with upper receivers made after 1989, i.e. no bayonet lug. These rifles are less desirable than pre-ban AR-15s.

Colt Sporters (Post-September 1994): This rifle has no bayonet lug, no flash hider, and does not have the AR-15 designation stamped on the lower receiver. Rifles that are NIB have a blue label. It is legal to modify this rifle only with upper receivers manufactured after September 1994. These rifles are the least desirable of the three manufacturing periods because of their lack of pre-ban military features and current manufacture status.

AR-15 9mm Carbine (Model #6450)

Same as above, chambered for 9mm cartridge. Weighs 6.3 lbs.

NIB	Exc.	V.G.	Good	Fair	Poor
1300	1150	1000	800	700	400

AR-15A2 Sporter II (Model #6500)

Introduced in 1984 this was an updated version with a heavier barrel and forward assist. The AR sight was still utilized. Weighs approximately 7.8 lbs.

NIB	Exc.	V.G.	Good	Fair	Poor
1450	1100	950	750	550	400

AR-15A2 Government Model Carbine (Model #6520)

Added to the Colt line in 1988 this 16" standard barrel carbine featured for the first time a case deflector and the improved A2 rear sight. This model is fitted with a 4-position telescoping buttstock. Weighs about 5.8 lbs.

NIB	Exc.	V.G.	Good	Fair	Poor
1450	1300	1000	800	700	500

AR-15A2 Government Model (Model #6550)

This model was introduced in 1988 is the rifle equivalent to the Carbine. It features a 20" A2 barrel, forward assist, case deflector, but still retains the bayonet lug. Weighs about 7.5 lbs. Discontinued in 1990. USMC model.

NIB	Exc.	V.G.	Good	Fair	Poor
2300	2000	1250	950	700	500

AR-15A2 H-Bar (Model #6600)

Introduced in 1986 this version features a special 20" heavy barrel. All other features are the same as the A2 series of AR15s. Discontinued in 1991. Weighs about 8 lbs.

NIB	Exc.	V.G.	Good	Fair	Poor
1650	1450	1250	850	700	500

AR-15A2 Delta H-Bar (Model #6600DH)

Same as above but fitted with a 3x9 scope and detachable cheekpiece. Dropped from the Colt line in 1990. Weighs about 10 lbs.

NIB	Exc.	V.G.	Good	Fair	Poor
1900	1750	1300	1000	850	600

Sporter Lightweight Rifle

This lightweight model has a 16" barrel and is finished in a matte black. It is available in either a .223 Rem. caliber (Model #6530) that weighs 6.7 lbs., a (Model #6430) 9mm caliber weighing 7.1 lbs., or a (Model #6830) 7.65x39mm that weighs 7.3 lbs. The .223 is furnished with two five-round box magazines as is the 9mm and 7.65x39mm. A cleaning kit and sling are also supplied with each new rifle. The buttstock and pistol grip are made of durable nylon and the handguard is reinforced fiberglass and aluminum lined. The rear sight is adjustable for windage and elevation. These newer models are referred to simply as Sporters and are not fitted with a bayonet lug and receiver block has different size pins.

NIB	Exc.	V.G.	Good	Fair	Poor
950	850	750	600	400	300

NOTE: The Model 6830 will bring about $25 less than the above prices. For post-9/94 guns deduct 30 percent.

Sporter Target Model Rifle (Model #6551)

This 1991 model is a full size version of the Lightweight Rifle. The Target Rifle weighs 7.5 lbs. and has a 20" barrel. Offered in .223 Rem. caliber only with target sights adjustable to 800 meters. New rifles are furnished with two 5-round box magazines, sling, and cleaning kit.

NIB	Exc.	V.G.	Good	Fair	Poor
1200	1100	850	650	400	300

NOTE: For post-9/94 guns deduct 30 percent.

Sporter Match H-Bar (Model #6601)

This 1991 variation of the AR-15 is similar to the Target Model but has a 20" heavy barrel chambered for the .223 caliber. This model weighs 8 lbs. and has target type sights adjustable out to 800 meters. Supplied with two 5-round box magazines, sling, and cleaning kit.

NIB	Exc.	V.G.	Good	Fair	Poor
1300	1150	1000	650	400	300

NOTE: For post-9/94 guns deduct 35 percent.

Colt AR-15 (XM16E1)

This rifle was made upon request for foreign contracts. Very rare. Proceed with caution. This variation will command a premium price over the standard AR-15 rifle. Secure an appraisal before a sale.

Courtesy Richard M. Kumor, Sr.

Sporter Match Delta H-Bar (Model #6601 DH)

Same as above but supplied with a 3x9 scope. Weighs about 10 lbs. Discontinued in 1992.

NIB	Exc.	V.G.	Good	Fair	Poor
1400	1200	1100	850	600	400

Match Target H-BAR Compensated (Model #6601C)

Same as the regular Sporter H-BAR with the addition of a compensator.

NIB	Exc.	V.G.	Good	Fair	Poor
1250	900	750	—	—	—

Sporter Competition H-Bar (Model #6700)

Introduced in 1992, the Competition H-Bar is available in .223 caliber with a 20" heavy barrel counterbored for accuracy. The carry handle is detachable with target sights. With the carry handle removed the upper receiver is dovetailed and grooved for Weaver-style scope rings. This model weighs approximately 8.5 lbs. New rifles are furnished with two 5-round box magazines, sling, and cleaning kit.

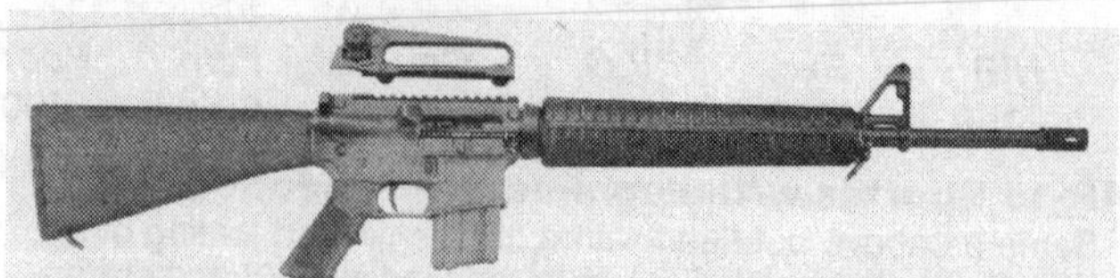

NIB	Exc.	V.G.	Good	Fair	Poor
1100	1000	900	700	500	350

NOTE: For post-9/94 guns deduct 35 percent.

Sporter Competition H-Bar Select w/scope (Model #6700CH)

This variation, also new for 1992, is identical to the Sporter Competition with the addition of a factory mounted scope. The rifle has also been selected for accuracy and comes complete with a 3-9X rubber armored variable scope, scope mount, carry handle with iron sights, and nylon carrying case.

NIB	Exc.	V.G.	Good	Fair	Poor
1200	1100	950	800	600	400

Match Target Competition H-BAR Compensated (Model #6700C)

Same as the Match Target with a compensator.

NIB	Exc.	V.G.	Good	Fair	Poor
1250	900	—	—	—	—

AR-15 Carbine Flat-top Heavyweight/Match Target Competition (Model #6731)

This variation in the Sporter series features a heavyweight 16" barrel with flat-top receiver chambered for the .223 cartridge. It is equipped with a fixed buttstock. Weight is about 7.1 lbs.

NIB	Exc.	V.G.	Good	Fair	Poor
1200	1000	800	600	400	300

NOTE: For post-9/94 guns deduct 30 percent.

AR-15 Tactical Carbine (Model #6721)

This version is similar to the above model with the exception of the buttstock which is telescoping and adjusts to 4 positions. Chambered for the .223 cartridge with a weight of about 7 lbs. A majority of these guns were for law enforcement only. Only 134 rifles are pre-ban.

NIB	Exc.	V.G.	Good	Fair	Poor
1400	1200	1000	800	600	400

Sporter H-Bar Elite/Accurized Rifle (Model #6724)

This variation was introduced in 1996 and features a free floating 24" stainless steel match barrel with an 11 degree target crown and special Teflon coated trigger group. The handguard is all-aluminum with twin swivel studs. Weight is approximately 9.26 lbs.

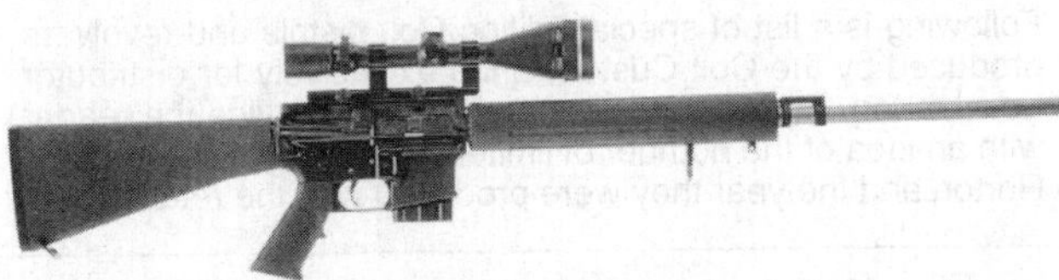

NIB	Exc.	V.G.	Good	Fair	Poor
1000	850	700	550	400	300

COLT CUSTOM SHOP

The Colt Custom Shop has developed several models over the years that are available to the public. The basis of these offerings are standard Colt Models upgraded to perform special functions.

Special Combat Government Model (Competition)

This is a competition ready model. Chambered for the .45 ACP it comes fitted with a skeletonized trigger, upswept grip safety, custom tuned action, polished feed ramp, throated barrel, flared ejection port, cutout commander hammer, two 8-round magazines, hard chromed slide and receiver, extended thumb safety, Bomar rear sight, Clark dovetail front sight, and flared magazine funnel. The pistol has been accurized and is shipped with a certified target.

NIB	Exc.	V.G.	Good	Fair	Poor
1450	1100	800	500	300	200

Special Combat Government Model (Carry)

This model has all of the same features as the competition model except that it has a royal blue finish, special bar-dot night sights, ambidextrous safety. It has also been accurized and shipped with a certified target.

NIB	Exc.	V.G.	Good	Fair	Poor
1250	900	700	400	300	200

Gold Cup Commander

Chambered for the .45 ACP and has these features: heavy-duty adjustable target sights, beveled magazine well, serrated front strap, checkered mainspring housing, wide grip safety, Palo Alto wood grips, and stainless steel or royal blue finish.

NIB	Exc.	V.G.	Good	Fair	Poor
875	775	650	600	500	375

U.S. Shooting Team Gold Cup

This is a limited edition Gold Cup .45 ACP with special blue, sights, grips. The U.S. Shooting Team logo is rolled on the slide. Limited to 500 pistols and built for Lew Horton.

Suggested Retail Price: $1,025

Gold Cup Trophy

Introduced in 1997 this model features .45 ACP 5" barrel 1911 with a choice of stainless steel or blue finish. Several custom features such as skeletonized hammer and trigger. Adjustable rear sight and wraparound rubber grips are standard. The pistol has been accurized and is shipped with a target. Magazine capacity is 7 or 8 rounds. Weight is approximately 39 oz. Add $60.00 for stainless steel finish.

NIB	Exc.	V.G.	Good	Fair	Poor
1000	800	—	—	—	—

McCormick Commander

This is a limited edition pistol made for Lew Horton in 1995 and limited to 100 pistols. It has many special features. The slide is engraved and there is a gold rampant colt on the slide.

Suggested Retail Price: $1,125

McCormick Officer

This Lew Horton exclusive pistol has factory installed McCormick parts and a hard chrome finish. A total of 500 guns were built in 1995.

Suggested Retail Price: $950

McCormick Factory Racer

This is a limited edition pistol from Lew Horton. It is a full size government model with hard chrome finish, special barrel, trigger safety, and other custom features. Each gun is rollmarked "McCormick Factory Racer" on the slide. Special serial numbers from MFR001 to MFR500.

Suggested Retail Price: $1,100

Colt Classic .45 Special Edition

This Lew Horton model is limited to 400 pistols and features a royal blue polish with special "Classic .45" gold etched on the slide. Pearlite grips.

Suggested Retail Price: $960

125th Anniversary Edition Peacemaker

Introduced in 1998 this model features a V-shaped rear sight with two-line patent date. Barrel is 4.75" and is chambered for .45 Colt cartridge. The cylinder is the second generation type and the hammer is knurled. Frame and hammer are case colored with blue barrel. Grips are two piece walnut with oil finish. Special serial number range SA74000 to SA75999.

Suggested Retail Price: $1,615

Custom Anaconda

Custom-tuned action, Magnaported barrel, with Elliason rear sight. The contoured trigger is polished smooth. Comes with Pachmayr grips and brushed stainless steel finish.

NIB	Exc.	V.G.	Good	Fair	Poor
650	575	500	400	300	200

Ultimate Python

Custom tuned action with both Elliason and Accro sighting systems. Both rubber and walnut grips are included. Bright stainless steel or royal blue finish. Available only with 6" barrel.

NIB	Exc.	V.G.	Good	Fair	Poor
1150	950	800	650	450	275

Python Elite

This model has a hand-tuned .357 Magnum action with a choice of 4" or 6" barrel with adjustable rear sight and red ramp front sight. On the 4" barrel models grips are rubber service, while on the 6" models they are rubber target style. Finish is stainless steel or royal blue. Weight is about 38 oz. with 4" barrel and 43 oz. with 6" barrel.

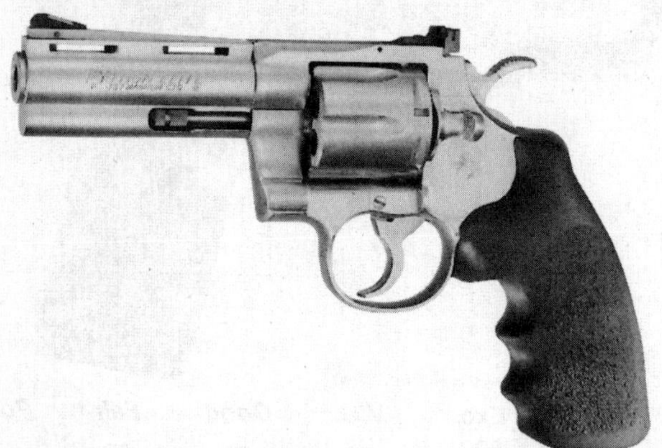

NIB	Exc.	V.G.	Good	Fair	Poor
1150	900	—	—	—	—

Anaconda Hunter

Comes with a Leupold 2X scope, heavy-duty mounts, cleaning accessories, both walnut and rubber grips, in a hard case. Furnished only with an 8" barrel.

NIB	Exc.	V.G.	Good	Fair	Poor
975	900	800	600	400	250

Bobbed Detective Special

First offered in 1994 this model features a bobbed hammer, a front sight with night sight, and honed action. Available in either chrome or blue finish.

NIB	Exc.	V.G.	Good	Fair	Poor
475	400	300	200	150	100

Limited Class .45 ACP

Designed for tactical competition. Supplied with a parkerized matte finish, lightweight composite trigger, extended ambidextrous safety, upswept grip safety, beveled magazine well, accurized, and shipped with a signed target. Introduced in 1993.

NIB	Exc.	V.G.	Good	Fair	Poor
750	675	600	450	300	200

Compensated Model .45 ACP

This competition pistol has a hard chrome receiver, bumper on magazine, extended ambidextrous safety, blue slide with full profile BAT compensator, Bomar rear sight, and flared funnel magazine well. Introduced in 1993.

NIB	Exc.	V.G.	Good	Fair	Poor
1850	1350	900	650	400	250

Compensated .45 ACP Commander

Introduced in 1998 and limited to 500 pistols. This model is fitted with a full-length guide rod, extended beavertail safety, skeletonized hammer, Novak-style sights, and checkered walnut double-diamond grips.

Suggested Retail Price: $890

Nite Lite .380

Supplied with a bar-dot night sight, special foil mark on barrel slide, Teflon-coated alloy receiver, stainless slide, high-capacity grip-extension magazine, and a standard magazine. Shipped with a soft carrying case. Introduced in 1993.

NIB	Exc.	V.G.	Good	Fair	Poor
450	400	325	275	225	150

Standard Tactical Model

Built for 20th Anniversary of IPSC competition shooting in 1996. Built on the Colt Government model with round top slide and chamber for .45 ACP. Many special features special serial numbers. Limited to 1,500 pistols.

Suggested Retail Price: $1,400

Superior Tactical Model

Same as above but built on an enhanced frame with many custom features.

Special serial numbers limited to 500 pistols.
Suggested Retail Price: $1,800

Deluxe Tactical Model

Same as above but with added features. Limited to 250 pistols.
Suggested Retail Price: $2,660

Following is a list of special edition Colt pistols and revolvers produced by the Colt Custom Shop exclusively for distributor Lew Horton. These handguns are listed to provide the reader with an idea of the number of limited edition Colts sold by Lew Horton and the year they were produced with the retail price.

Model	Qty. Built	Year Made	Retail Price
Horse Pistol, SAA	100	1983	$1100.00
Ultimate Officer's .45 ACP	500	1989	777.00
Lt. Commander .45 ACP	800	1985	590.00
Combat Cobra 2-1/2"	1000	1987	500.00
Lady Colt (MKIV .380 ACP)	1000	1989	547.00
Night Commander .45 ACP	250	1989	725.00
El Presidente .38 Super	350	1990	995.00
El Comandante .38 Super	500	1991	995.00
El General .38 Super	500	1991	995.00
El Capitan	500	1991	995.00
Colt Boa-4" & 6"	600	1985	525.00
El Dorado	750	1992	1195.00
El Coronel	750	1993	995.00
El Teniente	400	1992	1195.00
Classic Gold Cup	300	1993	1849.95
Night Officer	350	1993	679.95
El Presidente Premier Edition	10	1993	3000.00

COLT COMMEMORATIVES

The field of commemoratives can be fascinating and frustrating, depending on one's point of view. For someone who collects things from purely an aesthetic sense, commemoratives are quite desirable. Most are embellished and have had great care put into their fit and finish. They are attractively cased, and the proliferation of them makes acquisition relatively simple except from a financial standpoint. On the other hand, the collector who has an eye for the investment potential of his collections has found that the commemorative market has been soft and as investments they historically have not done well. The reason for this is twofold. The limited production appeal is not always what it seems. Many times the amounts produced are greater than one would consider limited. It is also a fact that if one fires a commemorative, its collectibility is gone. Even excessive handling can cause this problem. This means that since the majority of these firearms are kept new in the original boxes, the supply will usually outstrip the demand. Because of the limited numbers built, it is difficult to furnish accurate prices for the secondary market. Today's collectors are attracted to those Commemoratives with low production numbers and are willing to pay modest premiums for those where production was 2,500 or less.

Few commemoratives are ever lost or worn out. Collectors who seek firearms for their historic significance are usually not interested in the commemoratives, as even though they may have been issued to commemorate a specific historic person or event, they are not a part of the era and are regarded as "instant" collectibles. In some areas one will find that the Colt Commemoratives are not as desirable, saleable, or expensive as the plain out-of-the-box versions. This is especially true in the Single-Action Army Models. We list the commemoratives made by Colt in chronological order. Remember that the prices reflect new-in-the-box as it came from the factory—all papers, books, etc., intact and included. We also include the issue price for comparison. If the model with which you are concerned has been fired or is not in its original casing or box, deduct as much as 50 percent from these prices. It is interesting to note that in some areas shooters are taking advantage of the soft commemorative market and are buying SAAs at lower prices than the plain 3rd Generation guns—then shooting them. This can perhaps have a positive effect on appreciation.

One final note. There are a number of Colt Commemoratives that were produced by Colt but offered for sale by private companies to commemorate an event of their choosing. This publication does not cover most of these private commemoratives because it is difficult, if not impossible, to determine a secondary market value. It is also difficult to construct any meaningful comprehensive list of these private offerings. While the market for Colt factory remains soft the market for private commemoratives is usually very soft. the few that come on the market sometimes sell for less than half of their initial offering price. For those who enjoy collecting these firearms without investment goals these private commemoratives offer an additional outlet.

1961	Issue Price	NIB	Amount Mfg.
Geneseo, IL. 125th Anniv. Derringer	$ 28	$ 650	104
Sheriff's Model (Blue & Case)	130	2250	478
Sheriff's Model (Nickel)	140	6000	25
Kansas Statehood Scout	75	450	6,197
125th Anniv. Model SAA .45	150	1495	7,390
Pony Express Cent. Scout	80	475	1,007
Civil War Cent. Pistol	75	175	24,114
1962			
Rock Island Arsenal Cent. Scout	$ 39	$ 250	550
Columbus, OH. Sesquicent. Scout	100	550	200
Ft. Findlay, OH. Sesquicent. Scout	90	650	110
Ft. Findlay Cased Pair	185	2500	20
New Mex. Golden Anniv. Scout	80	450	1,000
Ft. McPherson, Nebraska Cent. Derringer	29	395	300
West Virginia Statehood Cent. Scout	75	450	3,452
1963			
West Virginia Statehood Cent. SAA .45	$ 150	$1495	600
Ariz. Terr. Cent. Scout	75	450	5,355
Ariz. Terr. Cent. SAA .45	150	1495	1,280
Carolina Charter Tercent Scout	75	450	300
Carolina Charter Tercent .22/.45 Comb.	240	1895	251
H. Cook 1 To 100 .22/.45 Comb.	275	1995	100
Ft. Stephenson, Oh. Sesquicent. Scout	75	550	200
Battle of Gettysburg Cent. Scout	90	450	1,019
Idaho Terr. Cent. Scout	75	450	902
Gen. J.H. Morgan Indiana Raid Scout	75	650	100
1964			
Cherry's 35th Anniv. .22/.45 Comb.	$ 275	$1995	100
Nevada Statehood Cent. Scout	75	450	3,984
Nevada Statehood Cent. SAA .45	150	1495	1,688
Nevada Statehood Cent. .22/.45 Comb.	240	1895	189
Nevada Statehood Cent. .22/.45 W/extra Cyls.	350	1995	577
Nevada Battle Born Scout	85	450	981
Nevada Battle Born SAA .45	175	1495	80
Nevada Battle Born .22/.45 Comb.	265	2595	20
Montana Terr. Cent. Scout	75	450	2,300

1964 *(cont.)*	Issue Price	NIB	Amount Mfg.
Montana Terr. Cent. SAA .45	150	1495	851
Wyoming Diamond Jubilee Scout	75	450	2,357
General Hood Cent. Scout	75	450	1,503
New Jersey Tercent Scout	$ 75	450	1,001
New Jersey Tercent SAA .45	150	1495	250
St. Louis Bicent. Scout	75	450	802
St. Louis Bicent. SAA .45	150	1495	200
St. Louis Bicent .22/.45 Comb.	240	1895	250
California Gold Rush Scout	80	475	500
Pony Express Pres. SAA .45	250	1495	1,004
Chamizal Treaty Scout	85	450	450
Chamizal Treaty SAA .45	170	1495	50
Chamizal Treaty .22/.45 Comb	280	1995	50
Col. Sam Colt Sesquicent. SAA .45	225	1495	4,750
Col. Sam Colt Deluxe SAA .45	500	2500	200
Col. Sam Colt Special Deluxe SAA .45	1000	4000	50
Wyatt Earp Buntline SAA .45	250	2750	150
1965			
Oregon Trail Scout	$ 75	$ 450	1,995
Joaquin Murietta .22/.45 Comb.	350	1995	100
Forty-Niner Miner Scout	85	450	500
Old Ft. Des Moines Reconst. Scout	90	475	700
Old Ft. Des Moines Reconst. SAA .45	170	1495	100
Old Ft. Des Moines Reconst. .22/.45 Comb.	290	1995	100
Appomattox Cent. Scout	75	450	1,001
Appomattox Cent. SAA .45	150	1495	250
Appomattox Cent. .22/.45 Comb.	240	1895	250
General Meade Campaign Scout	75	450	1,197
St. Augustine Quadracent. Scout	85	475	500
Kansas Cowtown Series Wichita Scout	85	450	500
1966			
Kansas Cowtown Series Dodge City Scout	$ 85	$ 450	500
Colorado Gold Rush Scout	85	475	1,350
Oklahoma Territory Scout	85	450	1,343
Dakota Territory Scout	85	450	1,000
General Meade SAA .45	165	1495	200
Abercrombie & Fitch Trailblazer N.Y.	275	1295	200
Abercrombie & Fitch Trailblazer Chic.	275	1295	100
Abercrombie & Fitch Trailblazer S.F.	275	1295	100
Kansas Cowtown Series Abilene Scout	95	450	500
Indiana Sesquicent. Scout	$ 85	$ 450	1,500
Pony Express 4-Square Set .45 4 Guns	1,400	5995	N/A
California Gold Rush SAA .45	175	1495	130
1967			
Lawman Series Bat Masterson Scout	$ 90	$ 475	3,000
Lawman Series Bat Masterson SAA .45	180	1500	500
Alamo Scout	85	450	4,250
Alamo SAA .45	165	1495	750
Alamo .22/.45 Comb.	265	1895	250
Kansas Cowtown Series Coffeyville Scout	95	450	500
Kansas Trail Series Chisolm Trail Scout	100	450	500
WWI Series Chateau Thierry .45 Auto	200	795	7,400
WWI Series Chateau Thierry Deluxe	500	1350	75
WWI Series Chateau Thierry Sp. Deluxe	1000	2750	25
1968			
Nebraska Cent. Scout	$ 100	$ 450	7,001
Kansas Trail Series Chisolm Trail Scout	100	450	500
WWI Series Belleau Wood .45 Auto	200	795	7,400
WWI Series Belleau Wood Deluxe	500	1350	75
WWI Series Belleau Wood Sp. Deluxe	1000	2750	25
Lawman Series Pat Garrett Scout	110	475	3,000
Lawman Series Pat Garrett SAA .45	220	1495	500

1969	Issue Price	NIB	Amount Mfg.
Nathan B. Forrest Scout	$ 110	$ 450	3,000
Kansas Trail Series Santa Fe Trail Sct.	120	450	501
WWI Ser. 2nd Battle of Marne .45 Auto	220	795	7,400
WWI Ser. 2nd Battle of Marne Deluxe	500	1350	75
WWI Ser. 2nd Battle of Marne Sp. Del.	1000	2750	25
Alabama Sesquicent. Scout	110	450	3,001
Alabama Sesquicent. SAA .45	N/A	15000	1
Golden Spike Scout	135	475	11,000
Kansas Trail Ser. Shawnee Tr. Scout	120	450	501
WWI Ser. Meuse-Argonne .45 Auto	220	795	7,400
WWI Ser. Meuse-Argonne Deluxe	500	1350	75
WWI Ser. Meuse-Argonne Sp. Deluxe	1000	2750	25
Arkansas Terr. Sesquicent. Scout	110	450	3,500
Lawman Ser. Wild Bill Hickok Scout	117	475	3,000
Lawman Ser. Wild Bill Hickok SAA .45	220	1495	500
California Bicent. Scout	135	450	5,000
1970			
Kansas Ft. Ser. Ft. Larned Scout	$ 120	$ 450	500
WWII Ser. European Theatre	250	795	11,500
WWII Ser. Pacific Theatre	250	795	11,500
Texas Ranger SAA .45	650	2250	1,000
Kansas Ft. Ser. Ft. Hays Scout	130	425	500
Marine Sesquicent. Scout	120	450	3,000
Missouri Sesquicent. Scout	125	450	3,000
Missouri Sesquicent. SAA .45	220	1495	900
Kansas Ft. Ser. Ft. Riley Scout	130	450	500
Lawman Ser. Wyatt Earp Scout	125	495	3,000
Lawman Ser. Wyatt Earp SAA .45	395	2750	500
1971			
NRA Centennial SAA .45	$ 250	$ 1495	5,000
NRA Centennial SAA .357 Mag.	250	1295	5,000
NRA Centennial Gold Cup .45 Auto	250	1295	2,500
U.S. Grant 1851 Navy	250	595	4,750
Robt. E. Lee 1851 Navy	250	595	4,750
Lee - Grant Set 1851 Navies	500	1350	250
Kansas Ft. Ser. Ft. Scott Scout	130	450	500
1972			
Centennial Cased Set Florida Terr. Sesquicent. Scout	$ 125	$ 450	2,001
Arizona Ranger Scout	135	450	3,001
1975			
Peacemaker Centennial SAA .45	$ 300	$ 1495	1,500
Peacemaker Centennial SAA .44-40	300	1495	1,500
Peacemaker	625	3250	500
1976			
U.S. Bicentennial Set	$ 1695	$ 2995	1,776
1977			
2nd Amendment .22	$ 195	$ 450	3,020
U.S. Cavalry 200th Anniversary Set	995	1250	3,000
1978			
Statehood 3rd Model Dragoon	$ 12500	$ 7500	52
1979			
Ned Buntline SAA N.F. .45	$ 895	$ 1295	3,000
Ohio President's Spec. Edit. .45 Auto	N/A	995	250
Tombstone Cent. .45 SAA	550	1395	300

	Issue Price	NIB	Amount Mfg.
1980			
Drug Enforcement Agency .45 Auto	$ 550	$ 1100	910
Olympics Ace Spec. Edition .22	1000	1295	200
Heritage Walker .44 Percussion	1495	950	1,847
1981			
John M. Browning .45 Auto	$ 1100	$ 995	3,000
Ace Signature Series .22	1000	1050	1,000
1982			
John Wayne SAA	$ 2995	$ 2250	3,100
John Wayne SAA Deluxe	10000	7500	500
John Wayne SAA Presentation	20000	12000	100
1983			
Buffalo Bill Wild West Show Cent. SAA	$ 1350	$ 1595	500
1984			
1st Edition Govt. Model .380 ACP	$ 425	$ 475	1,000
Duke Frontier .22	475	495	1,000
Winchester/Colt SAA .44-40	N/A	2250	4,000
USA Edition SAA .44-40	4995	3500	100
Kit Carson New Frontier .22	550	450	1,000
2nd Edition Govt. Model .380 ACP	525	475	1,000
Officer's ACP Commencement Issue	700	795	1,000
Theodore Roosevelt SAA .44-40	1695	1995	500
No Amer. Oilmen Buntline SAA .45	3900	3500	200
1985			
Mustang 1st Edition .380 ACP	$ 475	$ 450	1,000
Officer's ACP Heirloom Edition	1575	1550	N/A
Klay-Colt 1851 Navy	1850	1850	150
Klay-Colt 1851 Navy Engraved Edit.	3150	3150	50
Double Diamond Set .357 & .45 Auto	1575	1795	1,000
1986			
150th Anniversary SAA .45	$ 1595	$ 1995	1,000
150th Anniv. Engraving Sampler	1613	2750	N/A
150th Anniv. Engraving Sampler .45 Auto	1155	1295	N/A
Texas 150th Sesquicent. Sheriff's .45	836	1695	N/A
1987			
Combat Elite Custom Edition .45 Auto	$ 900	$ 995	500
12th Man Spirit of Aggieland .45 Auto	950	995	999
1989			
Snake Eyes Ltd. Edit. 2-2.5" Pythons	$ 2950	$ 1995	500

REPRODUCTION COLT PERCUSSION REVOLVERS

NOTE: The revolvers listed were manufactured in a variety of styles (cylinder form, stainless steel, etc.) that affect prices. Factory engraved examples command a considerable premium over the prices listed. Imported from Italy.

Walker

Made from 1979 to 1981; serial numbers 1200-4120 and 32256 to 32500.

NIB	*Exc.*	*V.G.*
895	750	500

Walker Heritage Model

NIB
950

First Model Dragoon

Made from 1980 to 1982; serial numbers 24100-34500.

NIB	*Exc.*	*V.G.*
395	300	100

Second Model Dragoon

Made from 1980 to 1982; serial numbers as above.

NIB	*Exc.*	*V.G.*
395	300	100

Third Model Dragoon

Made from 1980 to 1982; serial numbers as above.

NIB	*Exc.*	*V.G.*
395	300	100

This symbol denotes "Sleepers" with rapidly-rising values and/or significant collector potential.

Model 1848 Pocket Pistol

Made in 1981; serial numbers 16000-17851.

NIB	Exc.	V.G.
425	300	100

Model 1851 Navy Revolver

Made from 1971 to 1978; serial numbers 4201-25100 and 24900-29150.

NIB	Exc.	V.G.
395	400	325

Model 1860 Army Revolver

Made from 1978 to 1982; serial numbers 201000-212835.

NIB	Exc.	V.G.
550	500	475

Model 1861 Navy Revolver

Made during 1980 and 1981; serial numbers 40000-43165.

NIB	Exc.	V.G.
500	450	400

Model 1862 Pocket Pistol

Made from 1979 to 1984; serial numbers 8000-58850.

NIB	Exc.	V.G.
425	350	300

Model 1862 Police Revolver

Made from 1979 to 1984; serial numbers in above range.

NIB	Exc.	V.G.
425	400	300

COLT BLACKPOWDER ARMS

Brooklyn, New York

These blackpowder revolvers and rifles were made under license from Colt. Imported from Italy. No longer in business.

1842 Paterson Colt No. 5 Holster Model

This model is a copy of the No. 5 Holster model and is chambered for the .36 caliber ball. Fitted with a 7.5" octagon barrel. Hand engraved. This is a special order revolver.

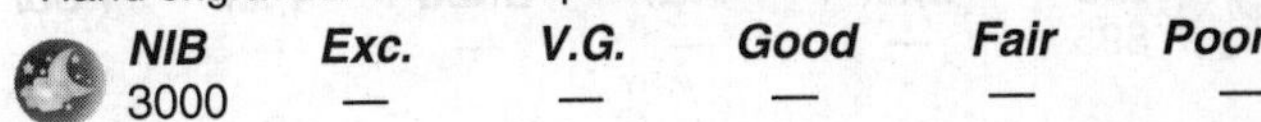

NIB	Exc.	V.G.	Good	Fair	Poor
3000	—	—	—	—	—

Walker

This .44 caliber large-frame revolver is fitted with a 9" barrel.

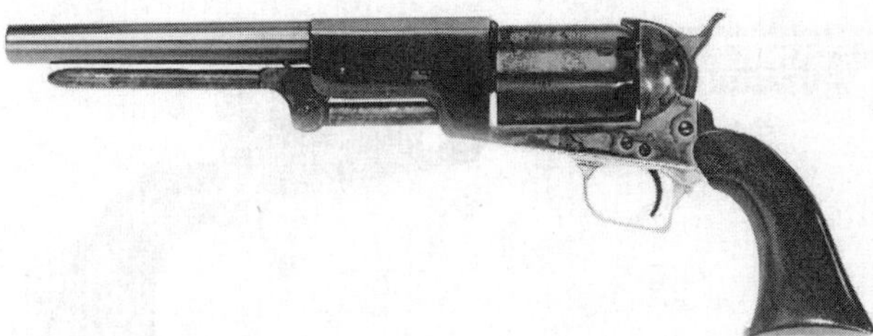

NIB	Exc.	V.G.	Good	Fair	Poor
475	400	350	300	200	150

Walker 150th Anniversary Model

Marked "A Company No. 1" in gold. Introduced 1997.

NIB	Exc.	V.G.	Good	Fair	Poor
600	500	—	—	—	—

Whitneyville Hartford Dragoon

Similar in appearance to the Walker colt this revolver is fitted with a 7-1/2" barrel and a silver plated iron backstrap and trigger guard. This is a limited edition with a total of 2,400 guns built with serial numbers between 1100 through 1340.

NIB	Exc.	V.G.	Good	Fair	Poor
475	400	350	300	200	150

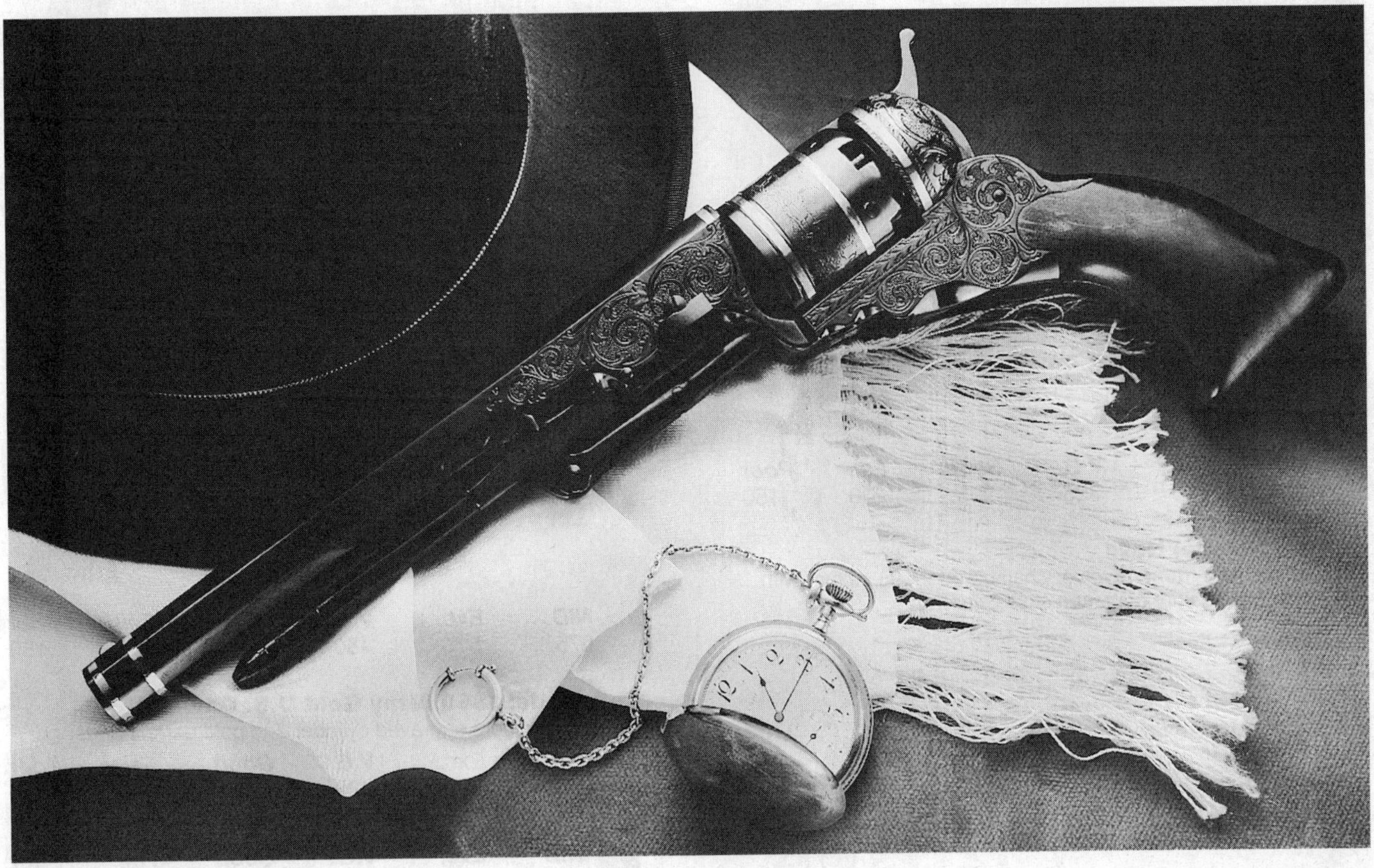

Special order Paterson Colt No. 5 Holster Model

Marine Dragoon

Special limited edition presentation grade in honor of U.S. Marine Corps.

NIB	Exc.	V.G.	Good	Fair	Poor
895	—	—	—	—	—

3rd Model Dragoon

Another large-frame revolver with 7-1/2" barrel with a brass backstrap, 3-screw frame, and unfluted cylinder.

NIB	Exc.	V.G.	Good	Fair	Poor
475	400	350	300	200	150

Steel Backstrap

NIB	Exc.	V.G.	Good	Fair	Poor
500	425	375	325	200	150

Fluted Cylinder

NIB	Exc.	V.G.	Good	Fair	Poor
510	435	375	325	200	150

Cochise Dragoon

This is a commemorative issue Third Model with gold inlay frame and barrel with special grips.

NIB	Exc.	V.G.	Good	Fair	Poor
895	—	—	—	—	—

Colt 1849 Model Pocket

A small-frame revolver chambered in .31 caliber with a 4" barrel. Fitted with one-piece walnut grips.

NIB	Exc.	V.G.	Good	Fair	Poor
435	375	325	275	200	150

Colt 1851 Model Navy

This is medium-frame revolver chambered in .36 caliber with 7-1/2" barrel. Walnut grips and case color frame.

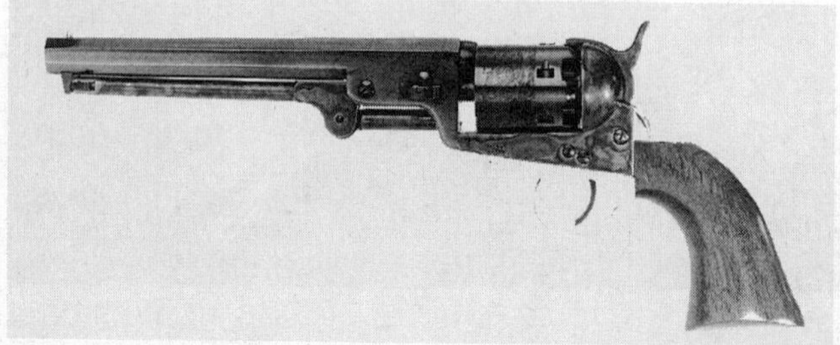

NIB	Exc.	V.G.	Good	Fair	Poor
435	375	325	275	200	150

Dual Cylinder

NIB	Exc.	V.G.	Good	Fair	Poor
475	400	350	300	200	150

Colt Model 1860 Army

This model is chamber in .44 caliber with roll engraved cylinder and one piece walnut grips. Barrel length is 8".

NIB	Exc.	V.G.	Good	Fair	Poor
435	375	325	275	200	150

Dual Cylinder

NIB	Exc.	V.G.	Good	Fair	Poor
475	400	350	300	200	150

Fluted Cylinder

NIB	Exc.	V.G.	Good	Fair	Poor
450	400	350	300	200	150

Colt 1860 Officer's Model

This is a deluxe version of the standard 1860 with a special blued finish and gold crossed sabres. This is a 4-screw frame with 8" barrel and 6-shot rebated cylinder.

NIB	Exc.	V.G.	Good	Fair	Poor
675	575	450	375	250	150

Colt Model 1860 Army Gold U.S. Cavalry

Features a gold engraved cylinder and gold barrel bands.

NIB	Exc.	V.G.	Good	Fair	Poor
650	575	450	375	250	150

Stainless Steel

NIB	Exc.	V.G.	Good	Fair	Poor
475	400	350	300	200	150

This symbol denotes "Sleepers" with rapidly-rising values and/or significant collector potential.

Colt 1860 Heirloom Edition

This is an elaborately engraved revolver done in the Tiffany-style and fitted with Tiffany-style grips.

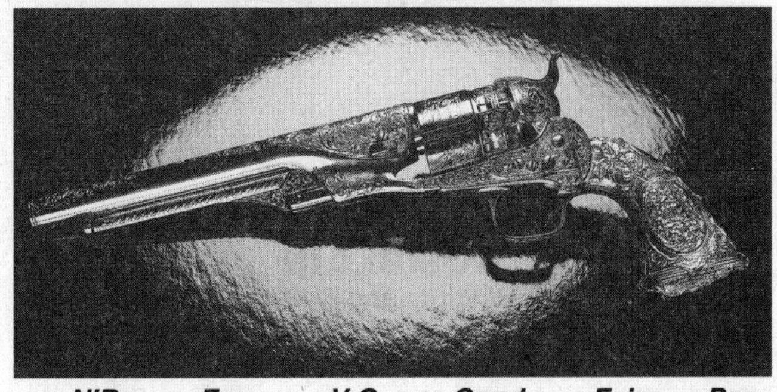

NIB	Exc.	V.G.	Good	Fair	Poor
5000	—	—	—	—	—

Colt Model 1861 Navy

This .36 caliber revolver features a 7-1/2" barrel with engraved cylinder, case colored frame and one piece walnut grips.

NIB	Exc.	V.G.	Good	Fair	Poor
500	400	350	300	200	150

Colt Model 1861 Navy General Custer

Same as above but with engraved frame and cylinder.

NIB	Exc.	V.G.	Good	Fair	Poor
975	850	700	500	300	200

Colt Model 1862 Pocket Navy

This small-frame revolver is fitted with a round engraved cylinder with a 5" octagon barrel with hinged loading lever. Chambered for .36 caliber.

NIB	Exc.	V.G.	Good	Fair	Poor
450	375	325	275	200	150

Colt Model 1862 Trapper-Pocket Police

This small-frame revolver is fitted with a 3-1/2" barrel, silver backstrap, and trigger guard. The cylinder is semi-fluted and chambered in .36 caliber.

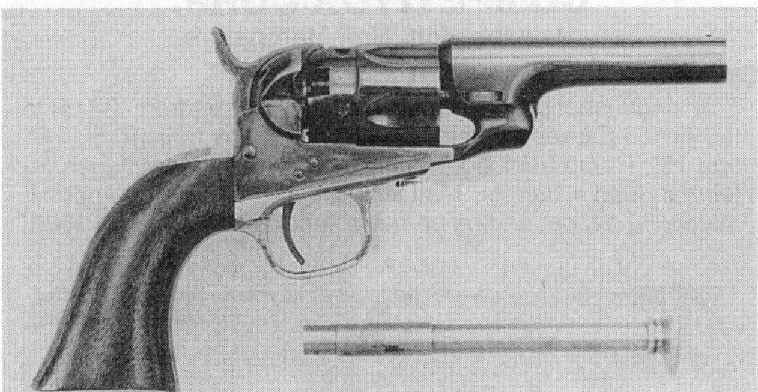

NIB	Exc.	V.G.	Good	Fair	Poor
435	375	325	275	200	150

Colt 1861 Musket

This Civil War musket is chambered in the .58 caliber. Lockplate, hammer, buttplate, and three barrel bands, and 40" barrel are finished bright. The stock is a one-piece oil-finish affair. Bayonet and accessories are extra.

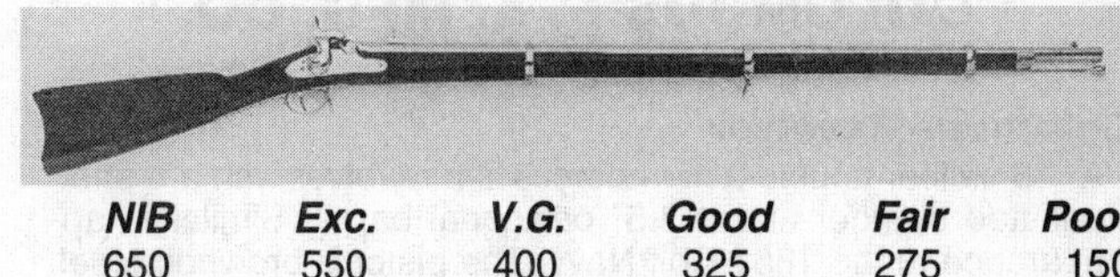

NIB	Exc.	V.G.	Good	Fair	Poor
650	550	400	325	275	150

Colt 1861 Musket—Artillery Model

Same as above but fitted with a 31-1/2" barrel.

NIB	Exc.	V.G.	Good	Fair	Poor
650	550	400	325	275	150

Colt 1861 Musket Presentation 1 of 1000

Limited to 1,000 guns these are special finished with a high polish and Colt's signature in gold on the trigger guard. Sold with special custom wooden case.

NIB	Exc.	V.G.	Good	Fair	Poor
2100	1500	750	600	450	300

Colt 1861 Musket Presentation 1 of 1000—Artillery Model

Same as above but 31-1/2" barrel.

NIB	Exc.	V.G.	Good	Fair	Poor
2100	1500	750	600	450	300

Colt Gamemaster .50

Introduced in 1997 this rifle is chambered for the .50 caliber. It is fitted with a 31.5" barrel and weighs about 13 lbs.

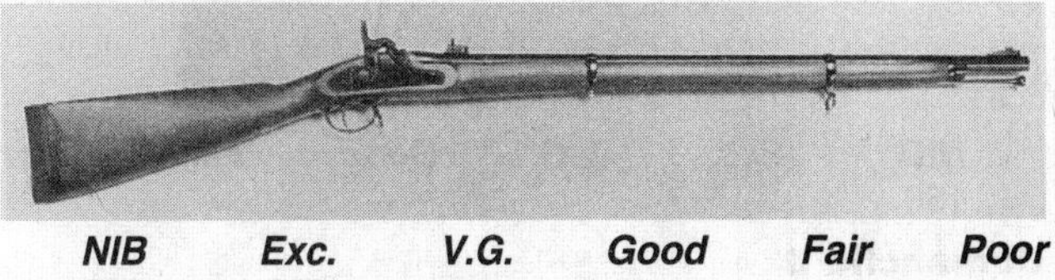

NIB	Exc.	V.G.	Good	Fair	Poor
800	650	—	—	—	—

COLTON MANUFACTURING CO.

Toledo, Ohio

The Colton Manufacturing Co. provided Sears with its first American-made hammerless house brand double. Sears advertised their sidelock hammerless gun as "the equal of any gun made, regardless of price" in their 1900 Fall catalog No. 110. There were four models: three sideplated boxlock-types and a unique unitized coil spring driven striker assembly version. All these, especially the latter, were designed to be mass produced. Many of the distinctive sidelock-within-a-sideplated model were produced but they are seldom seen today either because they were used-up or did not hold up well and were scrapped. Sears replaced Colton with the more traditional design Fryberg gun in 1902. Values depend on grade. There appear to be a least two levels of quality and condition ranging from $300 to $1,500. Colton-marked guns are scarce.

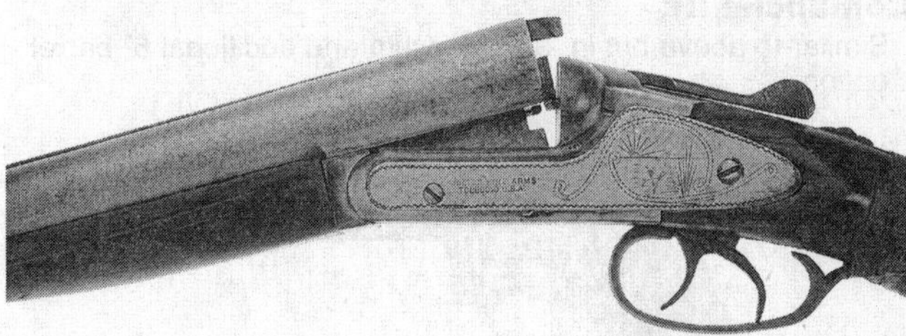

Courtesy Nick Niles, Paul Goodwin photo

COLUMBIA ARMORY

Columbia, Tennessee

A trade name applied to a variety of solid frame cartridge revolvers made by John T. Smith Company of Rock Falls, Connecticut. They were marked "SAFETY HAMMERLESS REVOLVER." This model was made under several trade names.

Exc.	V.G.	Good	Fair	Poor
—	200	100	75	50

COLUMBUS F. A. MFG. CO.
Columbus, Georgia

Columbus Revolver
A .36-caliber double-action percussion revolver with a 6-shot, unfluted cylinder and a 7.5" octagonal barrel. Similar in appearance to the 1851 Colt Navy. The pistol is browned steel, with brass gripstraps and walnut grips. The barrel is marked "Columbus Fire Arms Manuf. Co/Columbus Ga." 100 revolvers were manufactured in 1863 and 1864.

Exc.	V.G.	Good	Fair	Poor
—	—	100000	50000	—

COMANCHE (also see FIRESTORM)
Buenos Aires, Argentina

Comanche I
Single-/double-action revolver chambered in .22 LR. Nine-shot cylinder, 6" barrel, adjustable sights, blued or stainless steel construction with rubber grips.

NIB	Exc.	V.G.	Good	Fair	Poor
150	—	—	—	—	—

Comanche II
Similar to above but in .38 Special with 2", 3" or 4" barrel.

NIB	Exc.	V.G.	Good	Fair	Poor
175	—	—	—	—	—

Comanche III
Similar to above but in .357 Magnum and additional 6" barrel option.

NIB	Exc.	V.G.	Good	Fair	Poor
190	—	—	—	—	—

Super Comanche
Single-shot break-action pistol chambered in.410/.45 Colt. Matte black finish, rubber grips.

NIB	Exc.	V.G.	Good	Fair	Poor
150	—	—	—	—	—

COMBLAIN
Belgium and Brazil

Single-Shot Rifle
A 11x53Rmm caliber rifle with a falling block-action. Manufactured both in a hammerless and hammer version. Full stock secured by two barrel bands.

Courtesy Milwaukee Public Museum, Milwaukee, Wisconsin

Exc.	V.G.	Good	Fair	Poor
750	650	500	350	250

COMMANDO ARMS
Knoxville, Tennessee

Formerly known as Volunteer Enterprises. The name change took place in 1978.

Mark III Carbine
A .45 ACP caliber semi-automatic rifle with a 16.5" barrel, a peep rear sight and a vertical foregrip. Manufactured between 1969 and 1976.

NIB	Exc.	V.G.	Good	Fair	Poor
575	475	375	300	225	150

Mark 9 Carbine
As above, in 9mm caliber.

NIB	Exc.	V.G.	Good	Fair	Poor
575	475	375	300	225	150

Mark .45
The new designation for the Mark III after the company changed its name.

NIB	Exc.	V.G.	Good	Fair	Poor
575	475	375	300	225	150

COMPETITOR CORP.
New Ipswich, New Hampshire

Competitor Single-Shot
This single-shot pistol is chambered for calibers from .22 LR to .50 Action Express. Choice of barrels lengths from 10.5", 14", and 16". Ramp front sight. Adjustable single stage trigger. Interchangeable barrels. Matte blue finish. Weight is approximately 59 oz. depending on barrel length. Introduced in 1988.

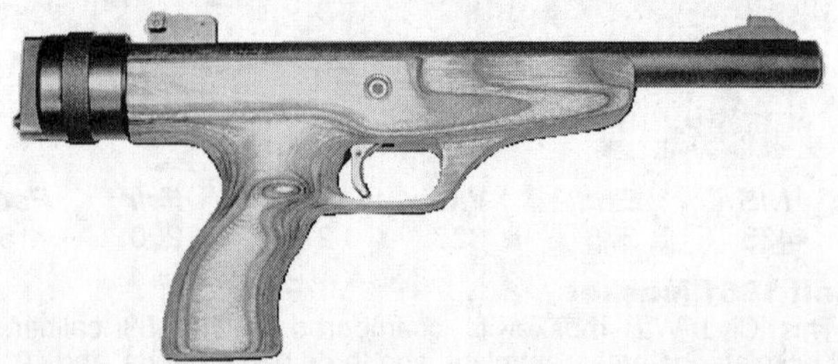

NIB	Exc.	V.G.	Good	Fair	Poor
450	325	275	225	175	125

CONNECTICUT ARMS CO.

Norfolk, Connecticut

Pocket Revolver

A .28 caliber spur trigger revolver with 3" octagonal barrel, 6-shot unfluted cylinder, using a cup-primed cartridge and loads from the front of the cylinder. There is a hinged hook on the side of the frame under the cylinder that acts as the extractor. Silver-plated brass, blued with walnut grips. The barrel is marked "Conn. Arms Co. Norfolk, Conn." Approximately 2,700 manufactured in the 1860s.

Exc.	V.G.	Good	Fair	Poor
—	—	750	300	100

CONNECTICUT VALLEY ARMS CO.

Norcross, Georgia

RIFLES

Express Rifle

A .50 caliber double-barrel percussion rifle with 28" barrels. Blued with a walnut stock.

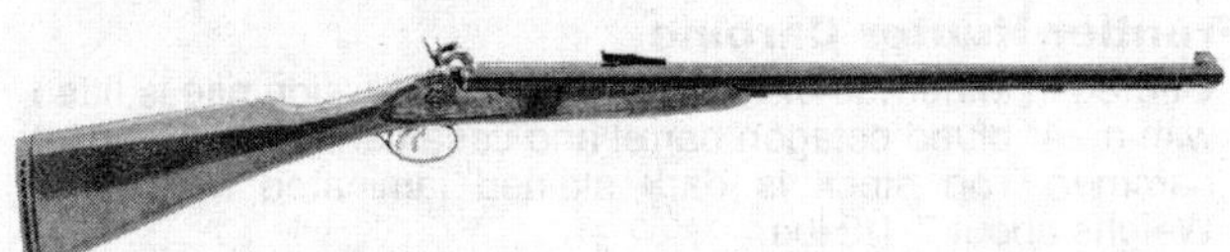

NIB	Exc.	V.G.	Good	Fair	Poor
625	475	425	375	325	200

NOTE: Deluxe version add 25 percent.

Over-and-Under Rifle

A .50 caliber double-barrel over-and-under rifle with 26" barrels. Blued with a walnut stock.

NIB	Exc.	V.G.	Good	Fair	Poor
600	475	425	375	325	200

Hawken Rifle

A .50 caliber with a 28" octagonal barrel, double set triggers and a walnut stock.

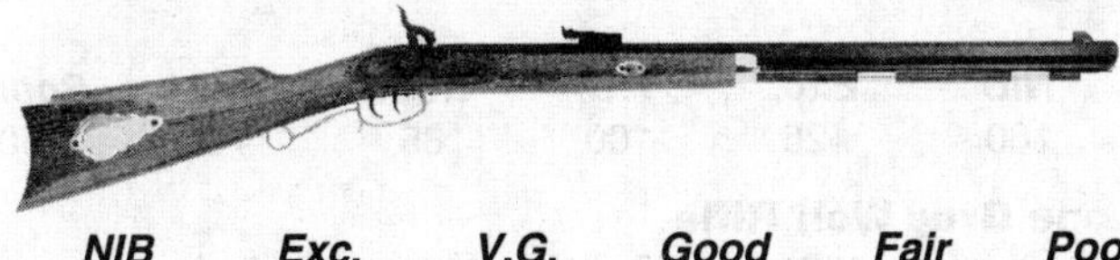

NIB	Exc.	V.G.	Good	Fair	Poor
450	325	275	225	150	100

Presentation Grade Hawken

As above, with an engraved lock, patchbox, and finely figured stock.

NIB	Exc.	V.G.	Good	Fair	Poor
550	425	375	325	275	200

Pennsylvania Long Rifle

A .50 caliber flintlock rifle with a 40" octagonal barrel, double set triggers and a walnut stock.

NIB	Exc.	V.G.	Good	Fair	Poor
475	400	350	300	250	175

Kentucky Rifle

A .45 caliber percussion rifle with a 33.5" octagonal barrel and walnut stock.

NIB	Exc.	V.G.	Good	Fair	Poor
275	225	175	150	100	75

Mountain Rifle

A .50 or .54 caliber percussion half-stock rifle.

NIB	Exc.	V.G.	Good	Fair	Poor
300	225	175	125	100	75

Blazer Rifle

A .50 caliber percussion rifle with a 28" octagonal barrel and walnut stock.

NIB	Exc.	V.G.	Good	Fair	Poor
150	125	100	85	65	45

Apollo Shadow SS

Introduced in 1993 this rifle features an in-line stainless steel bolt spring-action, a 24" blued round barrel with octagonal one piece receiver, drilled and tapped. Stock is black hardwood-textured with Dura Grip with pistol grip and recoil pad. Offered in either .50 or .54 caliber. Weighs about 9 lbs.

NIB	Exc.	V.G.	Good	Fair	Poor
175	150	125	100	75	50

Apollo Classic

Similar to the above Apollo Model but with dark brown stained laminated hardwood stock with pistol grip, raised comb, and recoil pad. Weighs about 8-1/2 lbs.

NIB	Exc.	V.G.	Good	Fair	Poor
215	175	150	125	100	75

Apollo Carbelite

Offered in .50 caliber with percussion bolt and 27" blued round taper barrel with octagonal receiver, drilled and tapped. Fitted with Carbelite composite stock with Monte Carlo and cheekpiece with pistol grip. Weighs approximately 7-1/2 lbs.

NIB	Exc.	V.G.	Good	Fair	Poor
280	225	175	150	100	75

Apollo Starfire

Chambered for the .50 caliber bullet this rifle is an in-line type with 24" stainless steel barrel with synthetic stock with checkered pistol grip, raised comb, and cheekpiece. Weight is about 6.5 lbs.

NIB	Exc.	V.G.	Good	Fair	Poor
225	175	150	125	100	75

Apollo Eclipse Rifle

Offered in either .50 or .54 caliber with 24" round barrel with blued steel receiver. Synthetic stock with checkered pistol, raised comb, and cheekpiece. Approximate weight is 6.5 lbs.

NIB	Exc.	V.G.	Good	Fair	Poor
175	150	125	100	85	65

Apollo Dominator

Fitted with a synthetic thumbhole stock and a 24" round barrel this rifle is chambered for the .50 caliber bullet. Introduced in 1996. Weight is approximately 8.5 lbs.

NIB	Exc.	V.G.	Good	Fair	Poor
300	225	175	150	100	75

Apollo Brown Bear

This .50 caliber rifle is fitted with a hardwood stock with pistol grip with raised comb and cheekpiece. The barrel is round and 24". Introduced in 1996. Weight is about 6.5 lbs.

NIB	Exc.	V.G.	Good	Fair	Poor
200	175	150	125	100	75

Frontier Carbine

Fitted with a 24" blued barrel this rifle is offered in .50 caliber percussion or flintlock. Case hardened lock with hardwood stock. Weighs about 6-3/4 lbs.

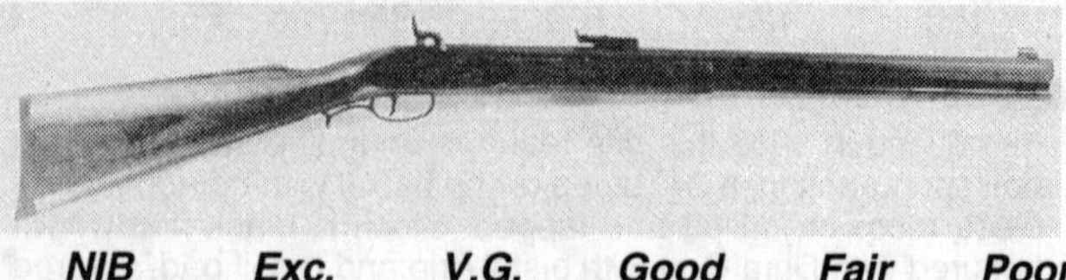

NIB	Exc.	V.G.	Good	Fair	Poor
150	125	100	85	75	50

Plainsman Rifle

This .50 caliber percussion rifle has a 26" octagonal barrel with case hardened lock and hardwood stock. Weight is about 6-1/2 lbs.

NIB	Exc.	V.G.	Good	Fair	Poor
130	115	100	85	75	50

Panther Carbine

This percussion rifle is available in either .50 or .54 caliber. It is fitted with a 24" blued octagonal barrel with Hawken-style case hardened lock. Stock is textured black Dura Grip over hardwood with Monte Carlo comb, cheekpiece, and pistol grip. Weight approximately 7-1/2 lbs.

NIB	Exc.	V.G.	Good	Fair	Poor
150	125	100	85	75	50

Bushwacker Rifle

This .50 caliber percussion rifle is fitted with a 26" octagonal barrel with case hardened engraved lock and brown stained hardwood stock with rounded nose. Weight is about 7-1/2 lbs.

NIB	Exc.	V.G.	Good	Fair	Poor
135	115	100	85	75	50

Trophy Carbine

This carbine is fitted with a 24" half-round half-octagon barrel with Hawken-style lock. The stock is walnut with Monte Carlo comb, cheekpiece, and pistol grip. Offered in .50 or .54 caliber percussion and weighs about 6-3/4 lbs.

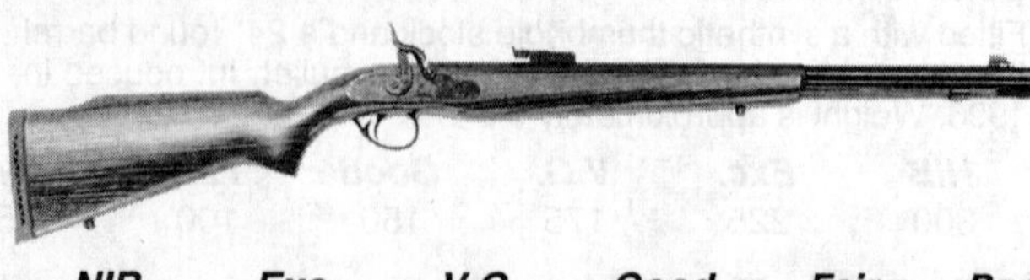

NIB	Exc.	V.G.	Good	Fair	Poor
215	175	150	125	100	75

Varmint Rifle

This is a lightweight percussion rifle in .32 caliber with 24" octagon barrel and case-colored lock. The stock is hardwood. Weighs about 6-3/4 lbs.

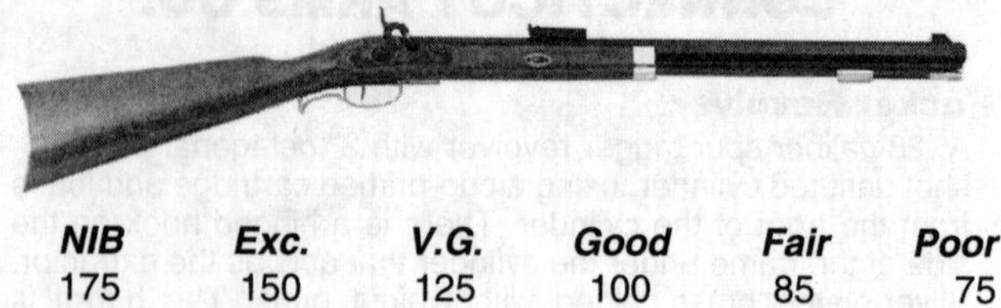

NIB	Exc.	V.G.	Good	Fair	Poor
175	150	125	100	85	75

Woodsman Rifle LS

Introduced in 1994 this rifle features a 26" blued octagon barrel with dark brown stained laminated hardwood stock. Offered in .50 or .54 caliber percussion. Weighs about 6-1/2 lbs.

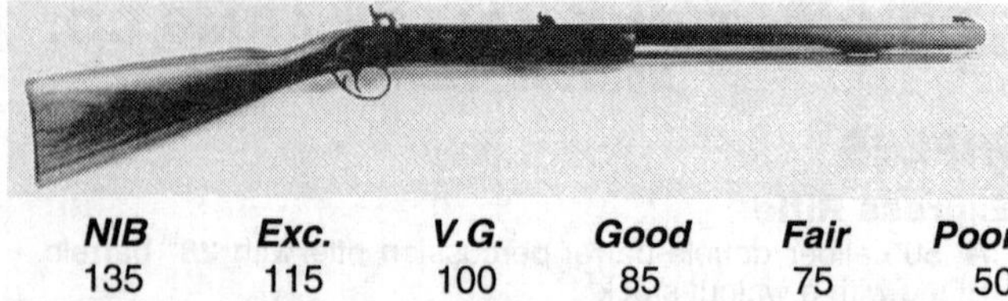

NIB	Exc.	V.G.	Good	Fair	Poor
135	115	100	85	75	50

Frontier Hunter Carbine

Offered in either .50 or .54 caliber this percussion rifle is fitted with a 24" blued octagon barrel and case hardened 45˚ offset hammer. The stock is dark stained laminated hardwood. Weighs about 7-1/2 lbs.

NIB	Exc.	V.G.	Good	Fair	Poor
170	150	125	100	75	50

Grey Wolf Rifle

Offered in either .50 or .54 caliber percussion this rifle is fitted with a 26" matte blue octagon barrel with a case hardened engraved lock. The stock is matte gray composite with raised comb, checkered pistol grip, and buttplate. Weighs about 6-1/2 lbs.

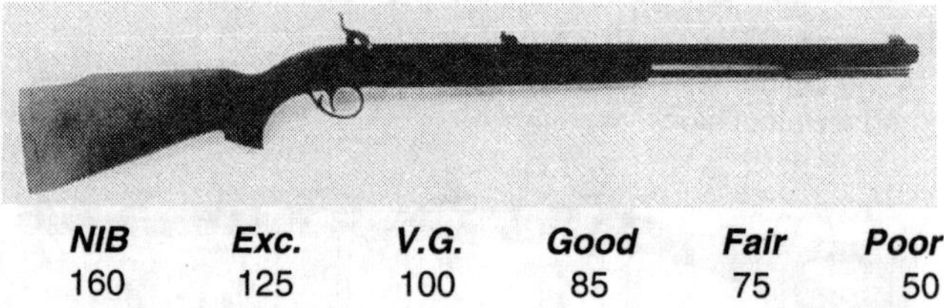

NIB	Exc.	V.G.	Good	Fair	Poor
160	125	100	85	75	50

Lone Grey Wolf Rifle

Introduced in 1994 this .50 caliber percussion rifle features a 26" matte blued octagon barrel. The trigger guard is oversized. The composite stock is black and has a raised comb, checkered pistol grip, and recoil pad. Weighs about 6-1/2 lbs.

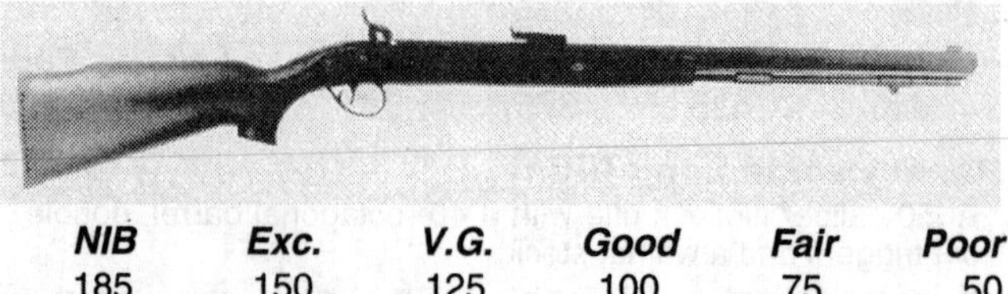

NIB	Exc.	V.G.	Good	Fair	Poor
185	150	125	100	75	50

Timber Wolf Rifle

Introduced in 1994 this model is similar to the above model but is furnished with Realtree composite stock with raised comb, checkered pistol grip, and buttplate. Weighs about 6-1/2 lbs.

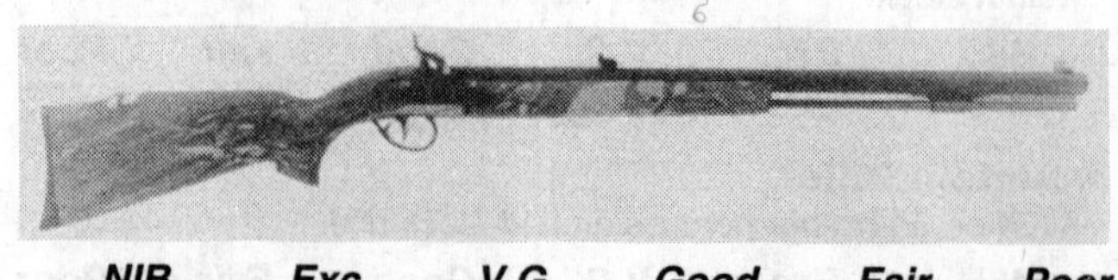

NIB	Exc.	V.G.	Good	Fair	Poor
185	165	140	100	75	50

Tracker Carbine LS

Introduced in 1994 this carbine is fitted with a 21" blued, half-round, half-octagon barrel with a Hawken-style lock. The stock is laminated dark brown with matte finish, and straight grip. Chambered for .50 caliber percussion. Weighs about 6-1/2 lbs.

NIB	Exc.	V.G.	Good	Fair	Poor
185	165	140	100	75	50

Stag Horn

Introduced in 1996 this in-line rifle is chambered for the .50 or .54 caliber bullet. The round barrel is 24" with blued finish. The stock is synthetic with checkered pistol grip, raised comb, and cheekpiece. Weight is about 6.5 lbs.

NIB	Exc.	V.G.	Good	Fair	Poor
175	150	125	100	85	65

Electra

A .50-caliber inline muzzleloader that uses electronic-arc ignition rather than caps or primers. Powered by common 9v battery. Finishes include stainless/camo, stainless/black composite, and blued/black composite. Introduced in 2007. Price given is for stainless/camo version.

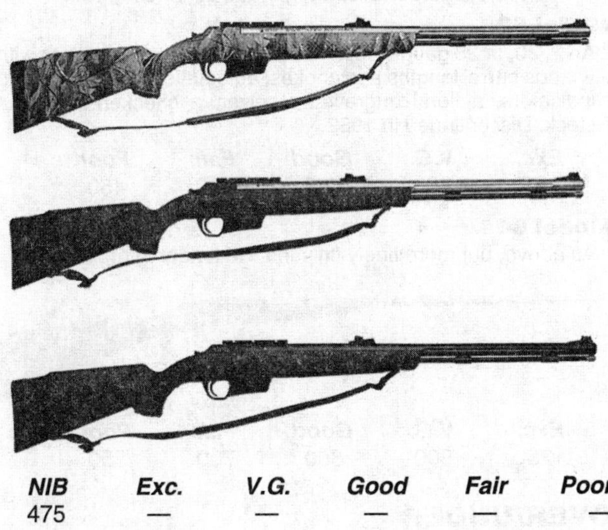

NIB	Exc.	V.G.	Good	Fair	Poor
475	—	—	—	—	—

SHOTGUNS

Brittany 11 Shotgun

A .410 bore double-barrel percussion shotgun with 24" barrels, double triggers and a walnut stock.

NIB	Exc.	V.G.	Good	Fair	Poor
300	250	200	150	125	75

Trapper Shotgun

A 12 gauge percussion single barrel shotgun with a 28" barrel threaded for choke tubes, and a walnut stock.

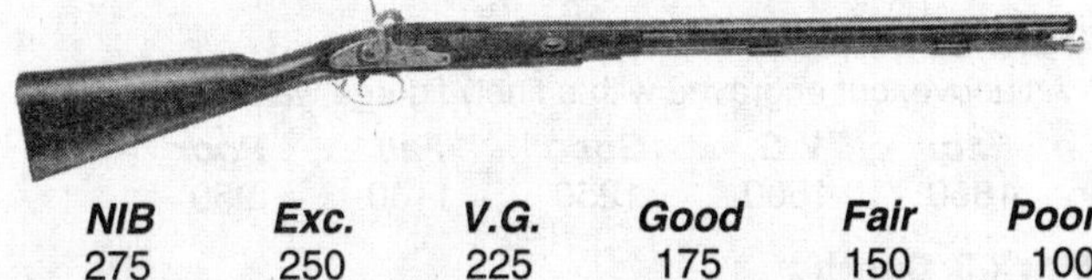

NIB	Exc.	V.G.	Good	Fair	Poor
275	250	225	175	150	100

Classic Turkey Double-Barrel Shotgun

This is a 12 gauge percussion breech-loading shotgun with 28" barrel. The checkered stock is European walnut with straight grip. Weighs about 9 lbs.

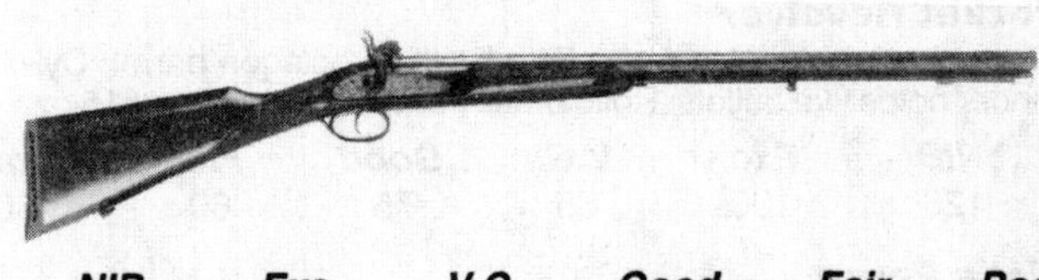

NIB	Exc.	V.G.	Good	Fair	Poor
375	325	275	200	175	100

Trapper Shotgun

This is a single barrel 12 gauge shotgun with a 28" barrel. The stock is a straight grip hardwood with checkering. Supplied with three interchangeable chokes. Weighs about 6 lbs.

NIB	Exc.	V.G.	Good	Fair	Poor
275	250	200	150	100	75

PISTOLS

Siber

A .45 caliber percussion pistol patterned after the Swiss Siber.

NIB	Exc.	V.G.	Good	Fair	Poor
400	325	275	225	150	100

Kentucky

A .45 caliber single-shot percussion pistol with a 10" barrel and walnut stock.

NIB	Exc.	V.G.	Good	Fair	Poor
140	125	100	80	60	40

Philadelphia Derringer

A .45 caliber single-shot percussion pistol with a 3.25" barrel and walnut stock.

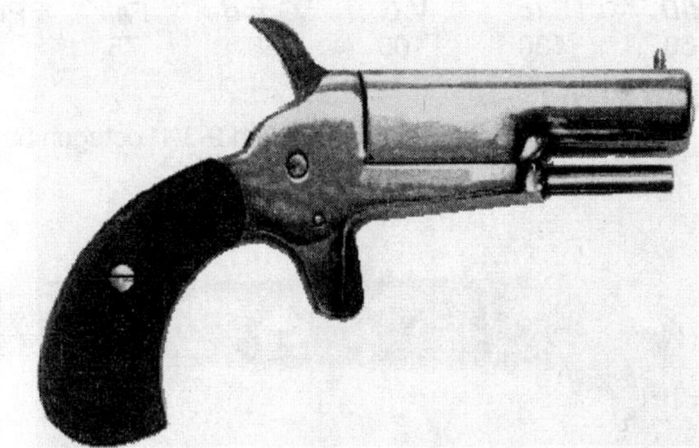

NIB	Exc.	V.G.	Good	Fair	Poor
75	65	50	40	30	20

Sheriff's Model

A .36 caliber percussion revolver, nickel-plated with walnut grips.

NIB	Exc.	V.G.	Good	Fair	Poor
225	200	175	150	125	100

3rd Model Dragoon

NIB	Exc.	V.G.	Good	Fair	Poor
225	200	175	150	125	100

Colt Walker Replica

NIB	Exc.	V.G.	Good	Fair	Poor
275	250	225	200	175	150

Remington Bison

NIB	Exc.	V.G.	Good	Fair	Poor
250	225	200	175	150	125

Pocket Police

NIB	Exc.	V.G.	Good	Fair	Poor
135	110	100	85	65	45

Pocket Revolver

Chambered for .31 caliber. Fitted with 4" octagon barrel. Cylinder holds five bullets. Solid brass frame. Weighs about 15 oz.

NIB	Exc.	V.G.	Good	Fair	Poor
125	100	85	75	60	50

Wells Fargo

NIB	Exc.	V.G.	Good	Fair	Poor
165	145	125	100	75	50

1851 Navy

NIB	Exc.	V.G.	Good	Fair	Poor
135	110	100	85	65	45

1861 Navy

NIB	Exc.	V.G.	Good	Fair	Poor
150	135	110	90	75	50

1860 Army

NIB	Exc.	V.G.	Good	Fair	Poor
220	200	175	150	125	100

1858 Remington

NIB	Exc.	V.G.	Good	Fair	Poor
175	150	125	100	75	50

1858 Remington Target

As above, but fitted with adjustable sights.

NIB	Exc.	V.G.	Good	Fair	Poor
235	200	175	125	100	75

Bison

A 6-shot .44 caliber revolver with 10-1/4" octagonal barrel. Solid brass frame. Weighs about 48 oz.

NIB	Exc.	V.G.	Good	Fair	Poor
160	130	100	85	75	50

Hawken Pistol

This is a .50 caliber percussion pistol with 9-3/4" octagon barrel. The stock is hardwood. Weighs about 50 oz.

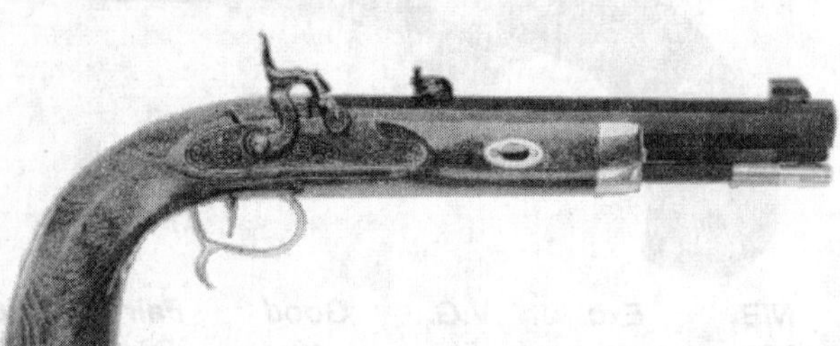

NIB	Exc.	V.G.	Good	Fair	Poor
135	110	85	75	65	50

CONSTABLE, R.

Philadelphia, Pennsylvania

Pocket Pistol

A single-shot percussion pistol with a 3" round or octagonal barrel. German-silver mounts and walnut stock. These pistols are marked "R. Constable Philadelphia" and were manufactured during the late 1840s and 1850s.

Exc.	V.G.	Good	Fair	Poor
—	1900	900	500	200

CONTENTO/VENTUR

SIDE-BY-SIDE

Model 51

A 12, 16, 20, 28, and .410 bore boxlock double-barrel shotgun with 26", 28", 30", and 32" barrels, various chokes, extractors and double triggers. Checkered walnut stock. Introduced in 1980 and discontinued in 1985.

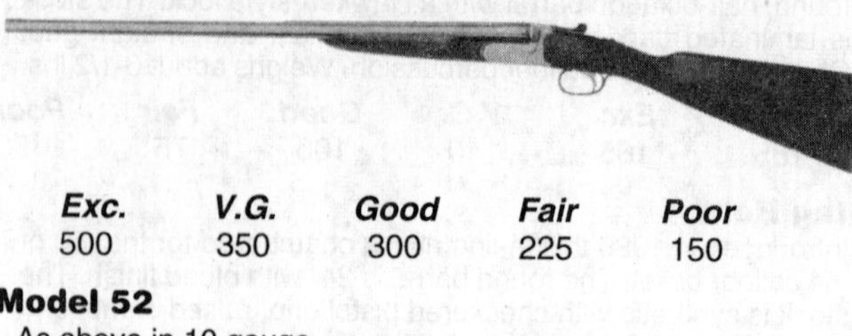

Exc.	V.G.	Good	Fair	Poor
500	350	300	225	150

Model 52

As above in 10 gauge.

Exc.	V.G.	Good	Fair	Poor
500	350	300	225	150

Model 53

As above, with scalloped receiver, automatic ejectors and available with a single-selective trigger. Discontinued in 1985.

Exc.	V.G.	Good	Fair	Poor
550	400	350	250	200

NOTE: Single-selective trigger add 25 percent.

Model 62

A 12, 20, or 28 gauge Holland & Holland sidelock shotgun with various barrel lengths and chokes, automatic ejectors, cocking indicators, a floral engraved receiver, a checkered, walnut stock. Discontinued in 1982.

Exc.	V.G.	Good	Fair	Poor
1150	800	750	600	450

Model 64

As above, but more finely finished. No longer in production.

Exc.	V.G.	Good	Fair	Poor
1250	900	850	700	550

OVER/UNDER

A 12 gauge Over/Under shotgun with 32" barrels, screw-in choke tubes, a high ventilated rib, automatic ejectors, and a standard single-selective trigger. Checkered, with Monte Carlo walnut stock.

Exc.	V.G.	Good	Fair	Poor
1250	900	750	600	500

Mark 2

As above, with an extra single barrel and fitted in a leather case.

Exc.	V.G.	Good	Fair	Poor
1500	1200	1050	900	800

Mark 3

As above, but engraved with a finely figured walnut stock.

Exc.	V.G.	Good	Fair	Poor
1850	1500	1250	1100	950

Mark 3 Combo

As above, with an extra single barrel and fitted in a leather case.

Exc.	V.G.	Good	Fair	Poor
3200	2600	2250	1750	1300

CONTINENTAL
RWM
Cologne, Germany

Continental Pocket Pistol (6.35mm)

A 6.35mm caliber semi-automatic pistol with a 2" barrel, internal hammer, and a 7-shot detachable magazine. Blued with plastic grips, and the slide is marked "Continental Kal. 6.35." Produced during the 1920s.

NOTE: This pistol may have been manufactured in Spain and carried German proof marks, because it was sold by RWM in Germany.

Exc.	V.G.	Good	Fair	Poor
300	150	125	100	75

Continental Pocket Pistol (7.65mm)

This is a German-made pistol chambered for the 7.65mm cartridhe. It is fitted with a 3.9" barrel. Rear sight is a U-notch in the slide. Magazine capacity is 8 rounds. Weight is about 20 oz. Made prior to 1914.

Exc.	V.G.	Good	Fair	Poor
500	300	225	150	100

CONTINENTAL ARMS CO.
Liege, Belgium

Double Rifle

A .270, .303, .30-40, .30-06, .348, 375 H&H, .400 Jeffreys, .465, .475, .500, and .600 Nitro Express caliber Anson & Deeley boxlock double-barreled rifle with 24" or 26" barrels, and double triggers. Checkered walnut stock.

Exc.	V.G.	Good	Fair	Poor
6500	4500	3750	3000	2250

CONTINENTAL ARMS CO.
Norwich, Connecticut

Pepperbox

A .22 caliber 5-barrel pepperbox with a spur trigger and 2.5" barrels marked "Continental Arms Co. Norwich Ct. Patented Aug. 28, 1866." Some examples of this pistol are to be found marked "Ladies Companion."

Courtesy Milwaukee Public Museum, Milwaukee, Wisconsin

Exc.	V.G.	Good	Fair	Poor
—	1850	850	350	250

COOK & BROTHER RIFLES AND CARBINES
New Orleans

In early 1861, Ferdinand W.C. Cook and his brother, Francis L. Cook, both English emigres, joined to form Cook & Brother in New Orleans to manufacture rifles and carbines following the English P1853 series for the newly seceded state of Louisiana and its neighbors. Between June 1861 and the federal occupation of New Orleans in April 1862, this firm produced about 200 cavalry and artillery carbines and about 1000 rifles. Having successfully moved the armory's machinery before federal occupation, the firm continued manufacture of rifles in Selma, Alabama, during 1862, probably completing another 1,000 rifles with the New Orleans lock markings from the parts brought with them. Re-established in Athens, Georgia, in early 1863, the firm continued to build both carbines and rifles, manufacturing more than 5,500 above the New Orleans production through 1864. The firm's products were clearly among the best small arms made within the Confederacy.

Cook & Brother Rifles (New Orleans & Selma production)

Overall length 48-3/4"; barrel length 33"; caliber .58. Markings: representation of a Confederate flag ("Stars & Bars") and "COOK & BROTHER/N.O./1861 (or) 1862" on lock; same usually on barrel, together with serial number and "PROVED" near breech. Rifles in the early production have long range rear sights and unusual two piece block and blade front sights as well as an integral bayonet lug with guide on right side of barrel. Later production utilizes a brass clamping ring for the bayonet, a block open rear sight and a simple block and blade front sight. Earlier production will claim a premium if in good condition.

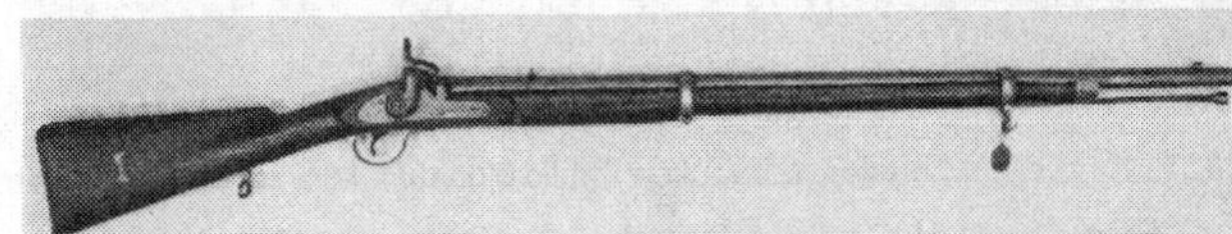

Courtesy Milwaukee Public Museum, Milwaukee, Wisconsin

Exc.	V.G.	Good	Fair	Poor
—	—	30000	12500	3000

Cook & Brother Carbines (New Orleans production)

Overall length 40" (artillery), 37" (cavalry); barrel length 24" (artillery), 21" to 21-1/2" (cavalry); caliber .58. Markings: As on Cook & Brother rifles (New Orleans production) artillery and cavalry carbines were produced in New Orleans in a separate serial range from the rifles. Total production is thought not to have exceeded 225, divided evenly between 1861 and 1862 dates. In addition to the overall and barrel lengths, the main difference between the artillery and cavalry carbines is the manner in which they were carried. The former bears standard sling rings on the upper band and the trigger guard strap, the latter has a bar with a ring on the left side of the stock. Both are exceedingly rare.

Exc.	V.G.	Good	Fair	Poor
—	—	17500	6500	5000

Cook & Brother Rifles (Athens production)

Overall length 49"; barrel length 33"; caliber .58. Markings: representation of a Confederate flag ("Stars & Bars") and "COOK & BROTHER/ATHENS GA./date (1863 or 1864), and serial number on lock; "PROVED" on barrel near breech; serial number on various metal parts. After re-establishing their plant at Athens, Georgia, in the spring of 1863, Cook & Brother continued to manufacture rifles in a consecutive serial range after their New Orleans/Selma production (beginning about serial number 2000) and continued to make arms well into 1864 (through at least serial number 7650) until Sherman's army threatened the plant and necessitated the employment of its workforce in a military capacity as the 23rd Battalion Georgia State Guard.

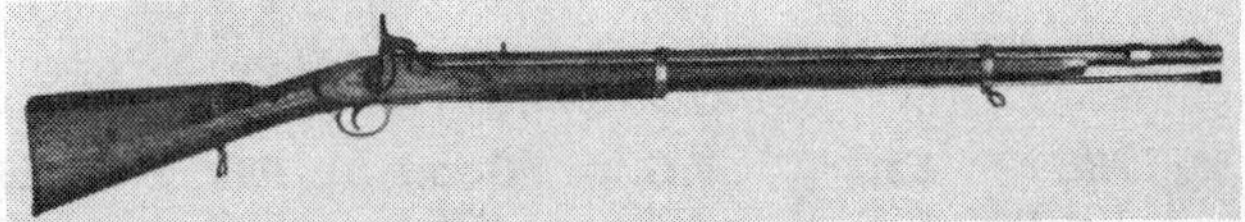

Courtesy Milwaukee Public Museum, Milwaukee, Wisconsin

Exc.	V.G.	Good	Fair	Poor
—	—	17500	7500	3000

Cook & Brother Carbines (Athens production)

Overall length 40" (artillery) or 37" (cavalry); barrel lengths 24" (artillery) or 21" to 21-1/2" (cavalry); caliber .58. Markings: same as on Athens production rifles. Artillery and cavalry carbines were manufactured in the same serial range as the Athens production rifles (about 2000 through 7650). As in New Orleans production, the artillery and cavalry carbines are distinguished from one another by their respective lengths. Unlike New Orleans/Selma production, however, some of the cavalry carbines are mounted with sling swivels of the artillery style, while others bear the sling ring on the left side and additionally have a swivel ring to secure the ramrod.

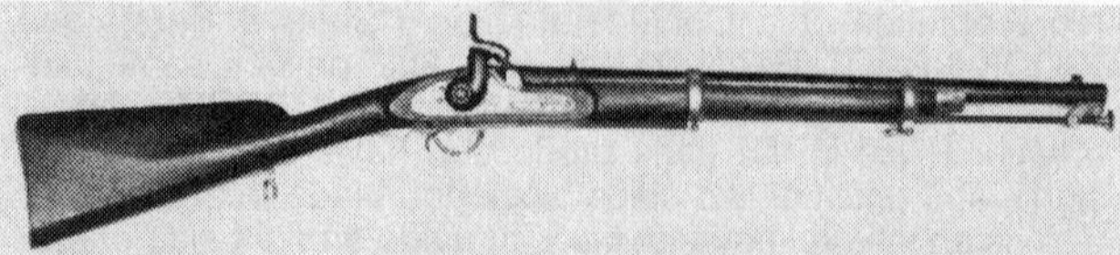

Courtesy Milwaukee Public Museum, Milwaukee, Wisconsin

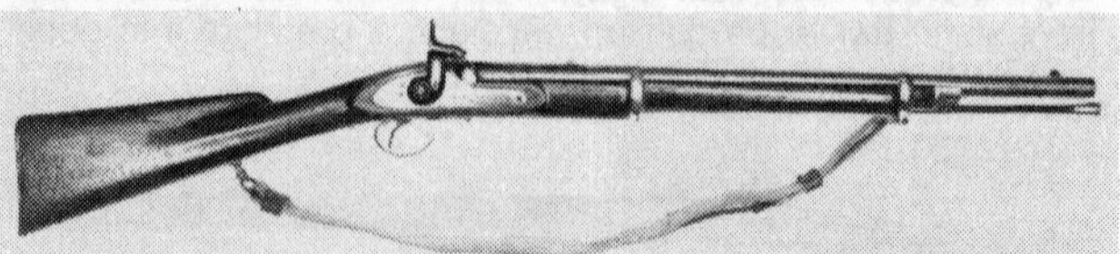

Courtesy Milwaukee Public Museum, Milwaukee, Wisconsin

Exc.	V.G.	Good	Fair	Poor
—	—	22500	8000	3500

COONAN ARMS CO.

Maplewood, Minnesota

Model A

A .357 Magnum semi-automatic pistol with a 5" barrel, a 7-shot, detachable magazine, and fixed sights. Stainless steel with walnut grips. Introduced in 1981 and discontinued in 1984.

NIB	Exc.	V.G.	Good	Fair	Poor
900	775	675	500	350	275

Model B

An improved version of the above with a linkless barrel system, extended grip safety, enclosed trigger bar, and a more contoured grip. A 6" barrel is available, as are adjustable sights, as extra cost options. A .38 Special conversion is also available. Introduced in 1985. A number of other options are also available that will affect value.

NIB	Exc.	V.G.	Good	Fair	Poor
1050	900	775	675	500	300

NOTE: For 6" barrel add $40, Bomar adjustable sights add $130, .38 Special Conversion add $40, checkered walnut grips add $40, with Teflon slide add $100, with Teflon frame add $100.

Comp I

As above, with 6" barrel and attached compensator and a stippled front grip strap. Introduced in 1989.

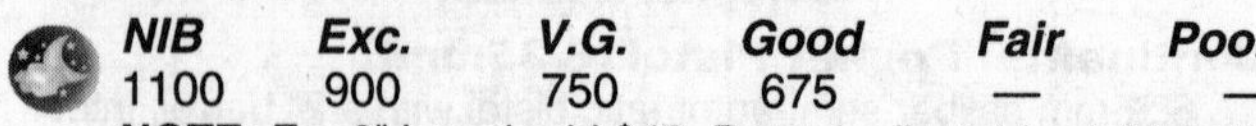

NIB	Exc.	V.G.	Good	Fair	Poor
1100	900	750	675	—	—

NOTE: For 6" barrel add $40; Bomar adjustable sights add $130; .38 Special conversion add $40; checkered walnut grips add $40; with Teflon slide add $100; with Teflon frame add $100.

Comp I Deluxe

As above, with a blued stainless steel slide, checkered grip straps, and a finer finishing.

NIB	Exc.	V.G.	Good	Fair	Poor
1750	1450	1250	975	800	600

Classic

This model features an integrated compensator with 5" barrel. Pistol is supplied with checkered walnut grips, Millett adjustable rear sight, and two-tone Teflon finish. Magazine capacity is 7 rounds, weight is 42 oz., and overall length is 8.3".

NIB	Exc.	V.G.	Good	Fair	Poor
1400	1100	850	600	500	—

Cadet

Chambered for the .357 magnum cartridge this model has a 3.9" barrel with smooth walnut grips, and fixed rear sight. Magazine capacity is 6 rounds; weight is about 39 oz., and overall length is 7.8". Height of the pistol is 5.3". Coonan Arms refers to this model as the "Short Grip."

NIB	Exc.	V.G.	Good	Fair	Poor
855	675	575	500	—	—

NOTE: For 6" barrel add $40, Bomar adjustable sights add $130, .38 Special Conversion add $40, checkered walnut grips add $40, with Teflon slide add $100, with Teflon frame add $100.

Cadet II

Same as above but with a standard grip. Magazine capacity of this model is 7 rounds.

NIB	Exc.	V.G.	Good	Fair	Poor
855	675	575	500	—	—

NOTE: For 6" barrel add $40; Bomar adjustable sights add $130; .38 Special conversion add $40; checkered walnut grips add $40; with Teflon slide add $100; with Teflon frame add $100.

.41 Magnum Model

Introduced in 1997 this model is chambered for the .41 Magnum cartridge and fitted with a 5" barrel with smooth walnut grips and fixed sights.

NIB	Exc.	V.G.	Good	Fair	Poor
1000	875	800	725	—	—

NOTE: For 6" barrel add $40; Bomar adjustable sights add $130; .38 Special conversion add $40; checkered walnut grips add $40; with Teflon slide add $100; with Teflon frame add $100.

COOPER ARMS
Stevensville, Montana

Model 36 Marksman

This is a premium bolt-action rifle chambered for the .22 LR cartridge and in centerfire calibers of .17 CCM and .22 Hornet. The 23" Shilen barrel is mated to a solid bar stock receiver. High grade walnut is used in stocks that are fine-lined checkered.

Standard

NIB	Exc.	V.G.	Good	Fair	Poor
1400	800	700	500	300	—

Classic

NIB	Exc.	V.G.	Good	Fair	Poor
1600	1100	800	600	400	—

Custom Classic

NIB	Exc.	V.G.	Good	Fair	Poor
1900	1550	1150	850	600	—

Western Classic

Octagon barrel and case color metal.

NIB	Exc.	V.G.	Good	Fair	Poor
2200	1800	—	—	—	—

BR-50 w/Jewell Trigger

NIB	Exc.	V.G.	Good	Fair	Poor
1800	1450	1100	800	600	—

IR-50-50 w/Jewell Trigger

NIB	Exc.	V.G.	Good	Fair	Poor
1800	1450	1100	800	600	—

Featherweight w/Jewell Trigger

NIB	Exc.	V.G.	Good	Fair	Poor
1800	1450	1100	800	600	—

Model 38/40

This bolt-action rifle is chambered for the .17 AK Hornet, .22 K Hornet, or the .22 Hornet.

Classic

NIB	Exc.	V.G.	Good	Fair	Poor
1800	1500	1100	800	600	—

Custom Classic

NIB	Exc.	V.G.	Good	Fair	Poor
2000	1750	1250	850	600	—

Western Classic

Octagon barrel and case color metal.

NIB	Exc.	V.G.	Good	Fair	Poor
2200	1800	—	—	—	—

Model 21

This bolt-action rifle is chambered for these cartridges: .221 Fireball, .222, .223, 6x45, 6x47, .17 Mach IV, and the .17 Rem. A 24" stainless steel Shilen match grade barrel is fitted. AAA claro walnut is used. Oval forearm, ambidextrous palm swell, 22 lpi checkering, oil finish, and Pachmayr buttpad are all standard features. Weighs approximately 8 lbs.

Varmint Extreme

NIB	Exc.	V.G.	Good	Fair	Poor
1600	1250	900	700	500	—

Classic

NIB	Exc.	V.G.	Good	Fair	Poor
1600	1250	900	700	500	—

Custom Classic

NIB	Exc.	V.G.	Good	Fair	Poor
1900	1700	1300	850	600	—

Western Classic

Octagon barrel and case color metal.

NIB	Exc.	V.G.	Good	Fair	Poor
2200	1800	—	—	—	—

Benchrest w/Jewell Trigger

NIB	Exc.	V.G.	Good	Fair	Poor
2100	1800	1300	900	650	—

Model 22

This is a bolt-action single rifle chambered for a variety of calibers: 6mm PPC, .22-250, .220 Swift, .243, .25-06, .308, .22 BR, 7.62x39, 6.5x55. A Pachmayr decelerator pad is standard. Weight is approximately 8.5 lbs.

Pro Varmint Extreme

NIB	Exc.	V.G.	Good	Fair	Poor
1750	1500	1200	800	600	—

Benchrest w/Jewell Trigger

NIB	Exc.	V.G.	Good	Fair	Poor
2100	1800	1300	900	650	—

Model 22 Repeater

Same as above but with magazine and chambered for .22-25, .308, 7mm-08, and .243.

Classic

NIB	Exc.	V.G.	Good	Fair	Poor
2400	2000	1750	1250	800	—

Custom Classic

NIB	Exc.	V.G.	Good	Fair	Poor
2650	2200	1850	1400	900	—

Western Classic

Octagon barrel and case color metal.

NIB	Exc.	V.G.	Good	Fair	Poor
2200	1800	—	—	—	—

Model 72/Montana Plainsman

Introduced in 1997 this High Wall single-shot rifle is available in a wide variety of calibers. It is offered with single or double set triggers.

NIB	Exc.	V.G.	Good	Fair	Poor
2200	1800	—	—	—	—

NOTE: There are a number of extra cost options that can affect the price of each of these models. Options such as Skelton buttplate, quarter ribs, ribbon checkering, etc. can add hundreds of dollars to the price of the gun. Check these options carefully before a sale.

COOPER, J. M. & CO.

Philadelphia, Pennsylvania

Pocket Revolver

A .31 caliber percussion double-action revolver with 4", 5", or 6" octagonal barrel, and a 6-shot unfluted cylinder. Blued with walnut grips. During the first two years of production they were made in Pittsburgh, Pennsylvania, and were so marked. Approximately 15,000 were manufactured between 1864 and 1869.

Courtesy Milwaukee Public Museum, Milwaukee, Wisconsin

Exc.	V.G.	Good	Fair	Poor
—	—	1500	600	150

NOTE: Pittsburgh-marked models add 20 percent.

COOPERATIVA OBRERA

Eibar, Spain

Longines

A 7.65mm caliber semi-automatic pistol. The slide is marked "Cal. 7.65 Automatic Pistol Longines."

Exc.	V.G.	Good	Fair	Poor
250	175	150	110	85

COPELAND, FRANK

Worcester, Massachusetts

Copeland Pocket Revolver .22

A .22 cartridge spur trigger revolver with a 2.5" barrel, 7-shot magazine, an unfluted cylinder and lock notches on the front. Frame is brass, blued walnut, or rosewood grips. The barrel marked "F. Copeland, Worcester, Mass." Manufactured in the 1860s.

Exc.	V.G.	Good	Fair	Poor
—	650	300	125	100

Copeland .32 Revolver

A .32 caliber spur trigger revolver with a 5-shot fluted cylinder and an iron frame. Nickel-plated. The barrel marked "F. Copeland, Sterling, Mass." Manufactured in the 1860s.

Exc.	V.G.	Good	Fair	Poor
—	650	300	150	75

COSMI, A. & F.

Torrette, Italy

Semi-Automatic

A 12 and 20 gauge top-break semi-automatic shotgun with various barrel lengths and chokes, an 8-shot magazine, and a ventilated rib. This is basically a custom-built, made-to-order gun. There is a standard and a deluxe model, with differences in the degree of embellishment.

Standard Model

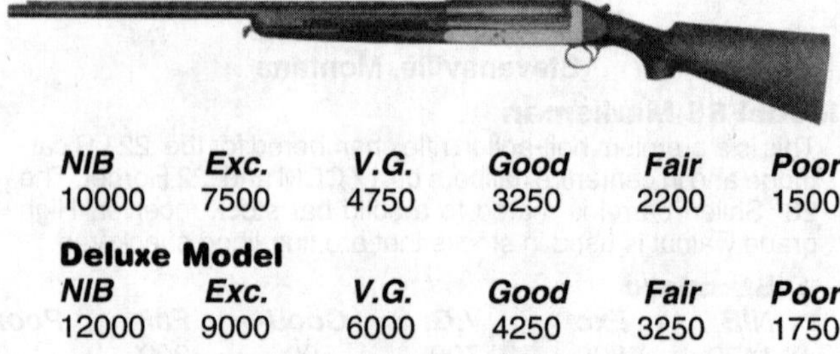

NIB	Exc.	V.G.	Good	Fair	Poor
10000	7500	4750	3250	2200	1500

Deluxe Model

NIB	Exc.	V.G.	Good	Fair	Poor
12000	9000	6000	4250	3250	1750

COSMOPOLITAN ARMS CO.

Hamilton, Ohio

Breech Loading Rifle

A .52 single-shot percussion rifle with a 31" round barrel. The frame marked "Cosmopolitan Arms Co. Hamilton 0. U.S./Gross Patent." Blued with a walnut buttstock. Approximately 100 were made between 1859 and 1862.

Exc.	V.G.	Good	Fair	Poor
—	—	6250	2500	700

COWLES & SON

Chicopee, Massachusetts

Single-Shot

A .22 or .30 caliber single-shot spur trigger pistol with a 3.25" round barrel. Silver-plated brass frame, blued with walnut grip. Approximately 200 manufactured in 1865.

Courtesy Richard M. Kumor Sr.

Exc.	V.G.	Good	Fair	Poor
—	1250	600	250	100

CPA RIFLES

Dingman's Ferry, Pennsylvania

This company builds rifles based on the Stevens Model 44-1/2. Several different configurations are offered, which are listed. Note there there are a number of special order options and custom features available at extra charge that will affect value.

Schuetzen Rifle

This model is usually built to order as to stock style, caliber, and barrel size, shape and length. Many calibers are available from .22 Short to .40-65 Winchester. Sights are extra.

NIB	Exc.	V.G.	Good	Fair	Poor
2450	—	—	—	—	—

Silhouette Rifle

This model as produced is approved for BPCR competition by the NRA. This model has either a sporting-style stock with low comb or the Model 52 style with more drop. Calibers are from .38-55 to .45-110 with other calibers available. Standard barrel is #4 part octagon 30" in length. Sights are extra.

NIB	Exc.	V.G.	Good	Fair	Poor
2100	—	—	—	—	—

Sporting Rifle

This model uses a sporting-style stock with standard forearm with Schnabel tip. Rifles are offered in rimmed calibers including .222, .225, .22 Hornet and others. Standard barrels are round or part octagon with weights from #1 to #5 and up to 28" in length. Sights are extra.

NIB	Exc.	V.G.	Good	Fair	Poor
2025	—	—	—	—	—

Varmint Rifle

As above but with a semi-beavertail forearm.

NIB	Exc.	V.G.	Good	Fair	Poor
2025	—	—	—	—	—

CRAUSE, CARL PHILLIP MUSKETS AND RIFLES

Herzberg, Germany

Carl Phillip Crause (who signed his products only with his last name) operated a gun manufactory in Herzberg on the Harz in the northwestern German kingdom of Hannover from the close of the Napoleonic Wars until 1857. The main production of his factory was devoted to military arms for Hannover and the surrounding principalities. Weapons of his manufacture included the Brunswick M1835 and M1848 rifles, the Hannovarian M1850 and M1854 rifle-muskets and yager rifles, and the M1840 and M1849 rifle-muskets of the Hanseatic League (a coalition of the north German states of Oldenberg, Hamburg, Bremen, and Lubeck). The latter two arms were subsequently altered to accept the elongated projectiles popular during the 1850s, and a few thousand evidently were imported into the United States and saw service during the American Civil War.

Hanseatic League M1840 Rifled Musket

Overall length 55-1/2"; barrel length 40-1/4"; caliber .70. Markings: on lockplate forward of hammer, "Crause in Herzberg" in script, the "s" in the archaic form, appearing as an "f." Of the 6,000 muskets of this type made, approximately half were sent to the United States in 1861 during the arms crisis that accompanied the outbreak of the American Civil War. A total of 2,680 of these were issued to Ohio and at least one regiment (the 56th Ohio) was armed with these rifled muskets. These arms were mistakenly identified during the period as being Saxon due to the similarity of the large squared off foresection of the lockplate.

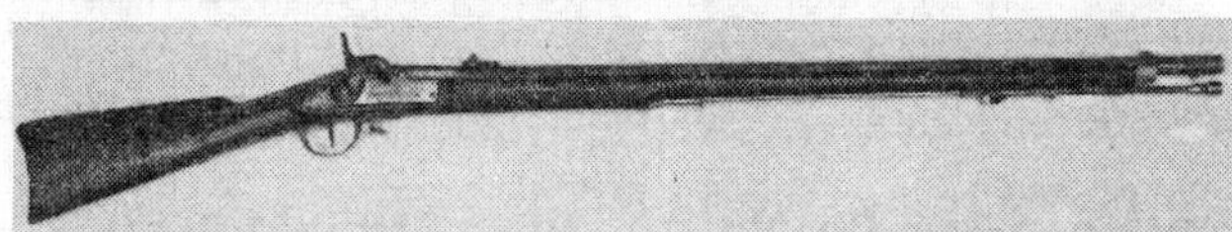

Courtesy Milwaukee Public Museum, Milwaukee, Wisconsin

Exc.	V.G.	Good	Fair	Poor
—	1700	800	375	200

Oldenberg M1849 Rifled Musket

Overall lengths 55-1/2" to 56-5/8" (long version), 49-1/2" (short version); barrel lengths 39" to 39-1/8" (long version), 33" (short version); caliber .69-.72 (rifled). Markings: "Crause in Herzberg" inscribed in script on the backstrap of the hammer housing, the "s" in archaic form, appearing as an "f." Nicknamed the "Cyclops" because its large, center-hung hammer is pierced with a large window that served as its rear sight, a few hundred of these clumsy rifled muskets may have been intermixed with the shipments of "Saxon" muskets imported in 1861 or 1862 into the United States during the American Civil War.

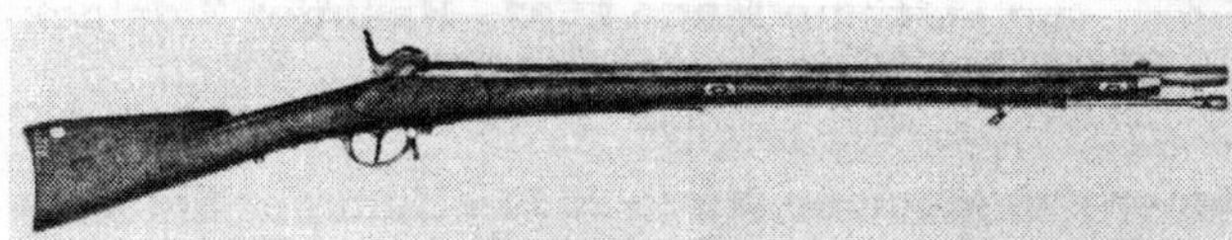

Courtesy Milwaukee Public Museum, Milwaukee, Wisconsin

Exc.	V.G.	Good	Fair	Poor
—	1800	850	400	250

CRESCENT F. A. CO.

Norwich, Connecticut

Text and prices by Nick Niles

The company made good quality inexpensive single and double-barrel shotguns at its Norwich works, beginning about 1892. It was bought by H&D Folsom of New York City, large importers and distributors of firearms and sporting goods, so they could add an American-made sidelock hammer, side-by-side to their extensive range of imported guns. The Crescent guns were offered in 12, 16, 20, and 28 gauges and later, 44XL shot caliber with Damascus twist laminated or Armory steel barrels depending on the shooter's wants. In 1898 VL&D said these were the best American hammer guns in the market for the money.

Huge quantities of these "Hardware Guns" were produced in a profusion of private brands as well as in Folsom's house brand "American Gun Co. of NY." In 1922 the Crescent brand replaced the "American Gun Co. of NY" and can be found on many thousands of doubles. In 1905 Crescent's first hammerless sidelock was introduced as the American Gun Co. "Knickerbocker" Model No. 6. This very popular model became the Crescent "Peerless" No. 6 in 1922. In 1928 it became the Crescent "Empire" No. 60 and in 1931 the Crescent-Davis "New Empire" No. 88, "New Empire" No. 9, and "Empire" No. 9.

Crescent was bought by J. Stevens Arms Co., Division of Savage Arms Corp. about 1930. It was merged with Davis-Warner Arms Corp. successors to N.R. Davis & Sons Co. and became Crescent-Davis Arms Corp. In 1932 the operation was moved to the Stevens plant at Springfield, Mass. where some sidelock doubles were assembled, Crescent-Davis brand guns remained in Steven's full line catalog until 1941 but from 1937 to 1941 the doubles sold in the C-D brand were on either Stevens or Davis boxlock frames.

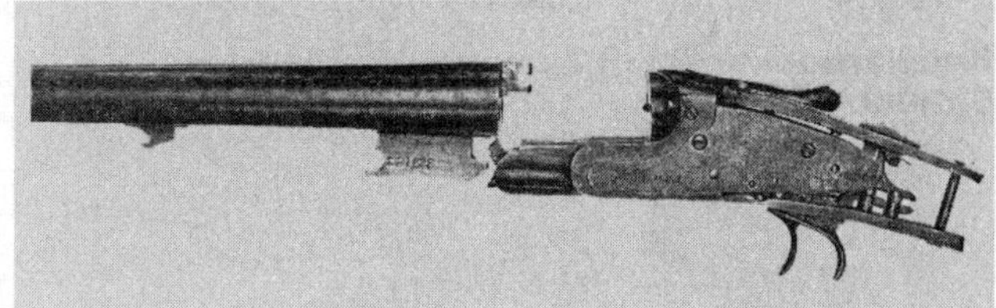

DOUBLES

Triumph—Hammerless Boxlock

Exc.	V.G.	Good	Fair	Poor
800	650	425	300	200

Model 2655—Laminated Barrels Hammer Sidelock

Exc.	V.G.	Good	Fair	Poor
575	450	325	200	150

Model 2665—Damascus Barrels Hammer Sidelock

Exc.	V.G.	Good	Fair	Poor
575	450	325	200	150

Crescent American Hammer Gun No. 0—Hammer Sidelock

Exc.	V.G.	Good	Fair	Poor
400	325	250	200	100

American Machine Made 2641—Hammer Sidelock

Exc.	V.G.	Good	Fair	Poor
450	350	300	250	200

American Machine Made 2650—Hammer Sidelock

Exc.	V.G.	Good	Fair	Poor
575	450	325	200	150

American Machine Made 2660—Damascus Barrels Hammer Sidelock

Exc.	V.G.	Good	Fair	Poor
700	550	400	275	175

American Gun Co. NY No. 1 Armory—Hammerless Sidelock

Exc.	V.G.	Good	Fair	Poor
450	325	250	200	100

American Gun Co. NY No. 2—Hammerless Sidelock

Exc.	V.G.	Good	Fair	Poor
575	450	300	250	200

American Gun Co. No. 3—Damascus Barrels Hammer Sidelock

Exc.	V.G.	Good	Fair	Poor
700	550	425	300	250

American Gun Co. No. 4—Hammer Sidelock

Exc.	V.G.	Good	Fair	Poor
800	650	525	400	300

American Gun Co. No. 5—Damascus Barrels Hammer Sidelock

Exc.	V.G.	Good	Fair	Poor
925	800	650	450	350

Folsom Arms Co. No. 0 Armory—Hammer Sidelock

Exc.	V.G.	Good	Fair	Poor
450	325	250	200	100

Folsom Arms Co. No. 2—Hammer Sidelock

Exc.	V.G.	Good	Fair	Poor
575	450	300	200	150

Folsom Arms Co. No. 3—Damascus Barrel

Exc.	V.G.	Good	Fair	Poor
700	550	425	300	200

Knickerbocker No. 6 Armory—Hammerless Sidelock

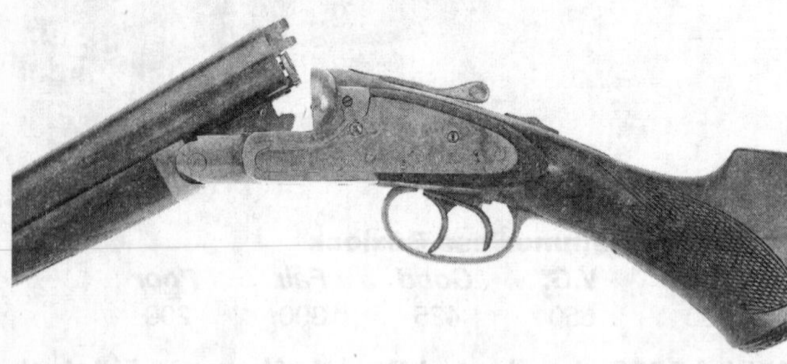

Courtesy Nick Niles, Paul Goodwin photo

Exc.	V.G.	Good	Fair	Poor
450	325	250	200	100

Knickerbocker No. 7—Hammerless Sidelock

Exc.	V.G.	Good	Fair	Poor
450	325	250	200	100

Knickerbocker No. 8—Damascus Barrels Hammerless Sidelock

Exc.	V.G.	Good	Fair	Poor
575	450	300	250	200

New Knickerbocker Armory—Hammerless Sidelock

Exc.	V.G.	Good	Fair	Poor
450	325	250	200	100

New Knickerbocker WT—Hammerless Sidelock

Courtesy Nick Niles, Paul Goodwin photo

Exc.	V.G.	Good	Fair	Poor
500	375	250	200	150

New Knickerbocker Damascus Barrels—Hammerless Sidelock

Exc.	V.G.	Good	Fair	Poor
575	450	300	250	200

American Gun Co. Small Bore No. 28—Straight Stock Hammer Sidelock

Exc.	V.G.	Good	Fair	Poor
925	775	650	400	300

American Gun Co. Small Bore No. 44—Straight Stock Hammer Sidelock

Exc.	V.G.	Good	Fair	Poor
1025	825	700	475	350

American Gun Co. No. 0—Armory Straight Stock—Hammer Sidelock

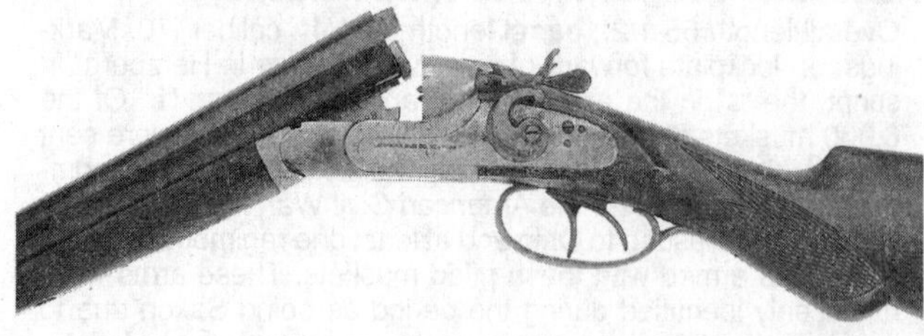

Courtesy Nick Niles, Paul Goodwin photo

Exc.	V.G.	Good	Fair	Poor
400	300	250	200	100

American Gun Co. No. 28—Nitro Straight Stock—Hammer Sidelock

Exc.	V.G.	Good	Fair	Poor
925	775	650	400	300

American Gun Co. No. 44—Nitro Straight Stock—Hammer Sidelock

Exc.	V.G.	Good	Fair	Poor
1025	825	700	475	350

American Gun Co. Midget Field No. 28—Hammer Sidelock

Exc.	V.G.	Good	Fair	Poor
925	775	650	400	300

American Gun Co. Midget Field No. 44—Hammer Sidelock

Courtesy Nick Niles, Paul Goodwin photo

Exc.	V.G.	Good	Fair	Poor
1025	825	700	500	350

Crescent 1922 Model No. 66—Quail—Hammerless Sidelock

Exc.	V.G.	Good	Fair	Poor
700	550	400	275	175

Crescent Firearms Co. No. 0—Hammer Sidelock

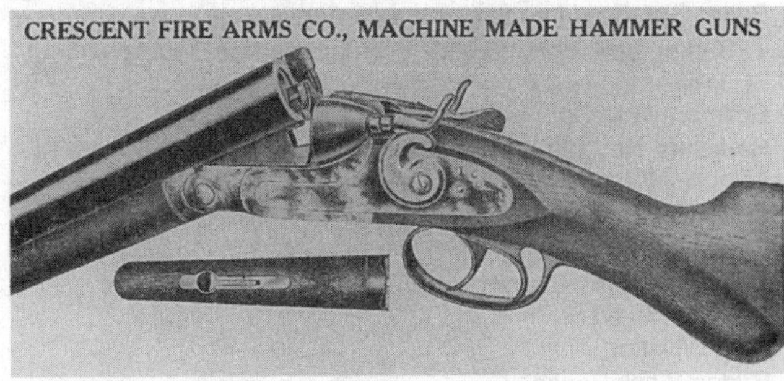

Exc.	V.G.	Good	Fair	Poor
450	350	250	200	150

Crescent Firearms Co. No. 0—Nickel—Hammer Sidelock

Exc.	V.G.	Good	Fair	Poor
600	450	350	250	200

Crescent Firearms Co. No. 6—Peerless—Hammerless Sidelock

Exc.	V.G.	Good	Fair	Poor
450	350	250	200	150

Crescent Firearms Co. No. 6E—Peerless Engraved—Hammerless Sidelock

Exc.	V.G.	Good	Fair	Poor
700	550	400	275	175

Crescent Firearms Co. No. 66—Quail—Hammerless Sidelock

Exc.	V.G.	Good	Fair	Poor
750	550	425	300	200

Crescent Firearms Co. No. 60—Empire—Hammerless Sidelock

Courtesy Nick Niles, Paul Goodwin photo

Exc.	V.G.	Good	Fair	Poor
500	400	350	300	200

Crescent Firearms Co. No. 6—Peerless—Hammerless Sidelock

Courtesy Nick Niles, Paul Goodwin photo

Exc.	V.G.	Good	Fair	Poor
450	350	300	200	150

Crescent Firearms Co. No. 44—Improved—Hammer Sidelock

Exc.	V.G.	Good	Fair	Poor
800	600	500	400	300

Crescent Empire No. 60—Hammerless Sidelock

Exc.	V.G.	Good	Fair	Poor
400	300	250	200	100

New Crescent Empire Red Butt—Hammerless Sidelock

Exc.	V.G.	Good	Fair	Poor
450	350	250	200	150

Crescent New Empire No. 88—Hammerless Sidelock

Exc.	V.G.	Good	Fair	Poor
450	350	250	200	150

Crescent New Empire No. 9—Hammerless Sidelock

Courtesy Nick Niles, Paul Goodwin photo

Exc.	V.G.	Good	Fair	Poor
400	300	250	200	100

Crescent Certified Empire No. 60—Hammerless Sidelock

Exc.	V.G.	Good	Fair	Poor
450	300	250	200	150

Crescent Certified Empire No. 9—Hammerless Sidelock

Exc.	V.G.	Good	Fair	Poor
500	375	300	250	200

Crescent Certified Empire No. 88—Hammerless Sidelock

Courtesy Nick Niles, Paul Goodwin photo

Exc.	*V.G.*	*Good*	*Fair*	*Poor*
575	450	400	350	300

Crescent Davis No. 600—Hammerless Boxlock

Courtesy Nick Niles, Paul Goodwin photo

Exc.	*V.G.*	*Good*	*Fair*	*Poor*
450	350	300	250	200

Crescent Davis No. 900—Hammerless Boxlock

Exc.	*V.G.*	*Good*	*Fair*	*Poor*
575	450	400	350	300

Single-Shot

Made in 12, 16, 20, and 28 gauge and .410. Barrel lengths were 26", 28", 30", and 32", with various chokes. It had an exposed hammer, fluid steel barrel, and walnut pistol grip stock.

Exc.	*V.G.*	*Good*	*Fair*	*Poor*
200	125	100	75	50

Revolver

A typical S&W copy made by Crescent in Norwich, Connecticut. It was a top-break, double-action, that was found either blued or nickel-plated with checkered, black hard rubber grips. The cylinder held 5 shots and was chambered for the .32 S&W cartridge.

Exc.	*V.G.*	*Good*	*Fair*	*Poor*
250	150	125	85	40

Crescent Certified Shotgun NFA, CURIO OR RELIC

The Crescent Certified Shotgun is a .410 smooth bore pistol with a 12.25" barrel manufactured from approximately 1930 to 1932 by the Crescent-Davis Arms Corp., Norwich, Connecticut, and possibly thereafter until 1934 by the J. Stevens Arms Co., which purchased the company. In various distributor catalogs it is termed the "Ever-Ready" Model 200, and advertised with a blued frame. Specimens have been observed with "tiger-stripe" (like an H&R Handy-Gun) or Colt SAA or Winchester-type case hardening. Total production is unknown but serial numbers ranging from 1305 to 3262 have been observed, suggesting it may have been fewer than 4,000. The Treasury Department ruled the .410 Crescent to be a "firearm" in the "any other weapon" category under the NFA in 1934, when its retail price was about $11.

Exc.	*V.G.*	*Good*	*Fair*	*Poor*
975	725	550	350	250

NOTE: Add $100 to $300 for original cardboard box.

The barrel is marked ***PROOF TESTED 410 GAUGE*** on top and **2-1/2 IN SHELLS** on the middle left side. The receiver's left side is stamped **CRESCENT CERTIFIED SHOTGUN/CRESCENT-DAVIS ARMS CORPORATION/NORWICH, CONN., U.S.A.** The earliest guns also have **.410** stamped at the top of the left side of the receiver near the breech, but this marking does not appear on later guns. It is a rather heavy (57 oz. unloaded) handgun.

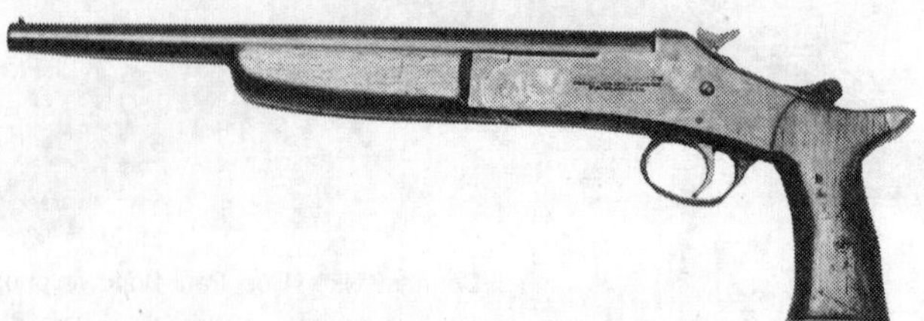

BRAND NAMES USED BY CRESCENT ARMS

American Bar Lock Wonder made for Sears, Roebuck & Co.
American Boy made for Townley Metal & Hardware Co.
American Gun Co. (H & D Folsom house brand)
American Gun Company of New York
American Nitro
Armory Gun Co.
Baker Gun Co. (if no foreign proof marks)
T. Barker New York-if a sidelock hammerless double without proofs.
Bellmore Gun Co.
Berkshire No. 3000 made for Shapleigh Hardware Co. of St. Louis, MO
Black Beauty-hammerless doubles
Bluefield Clipper
Bluegrass Arms Co. made for Belknap Hardware Co. of Louisville, KY
Blue Whistler
Bridge Black Prince
Bridge Gun Co.
Bridge Gun Works
Bridgeport Arms Co. (if no foreign proof marks)
Bright Arms Co.
Canadian Belle
Carolina Arms Co. made for Smith Wadsworth Hardware Co. of Charlotte, NC
Caroline Arms
Central Arm Co. made for Shapleigh Hardware Co. of St. Louis, MO
Chatham Arms Co.
Cherokee Arms Co. made for C. M. McClung Co. of Knoxville, TN
Chesapeake Gun Co.
Chicago Long Range Wonder 1908-1918 made for Sears, Roebuck & Co. of Chicago, IL
Colonial
Columbian New York Arms Co.
Compeer made for Van Camp Hardware & Iron Co. of Indianapolis, IN
Connecticut Arms Co.
Cumberland Arms Co.
Crescent Fire Arms Co.
Creve Cour (if no foreign proof marks) made for Isaac Walker Hardware Co. of Peoria, IL
Cruso
Daniel Boone Gun Co. made for Belknap Hardware Co. of Louisville, KY
Delphian Arms Co. (some models without foreign proof marks) made for Supplee-Biddle Hardware Co. of Philadelphia, PA
Delphian Manufacturing Co. (some models)
Diamond Arms Co. (some models) made for Shapleigh Hardware Co. of St. Louis, MO
Dunlap Special made for Dunlap Hardware Co. of Macon, GA
E.C. Mac made for E.C. Meacham Arms Co. of St. Louis, MO

Elgin Arms Co. made for Strauss & Schram and Fred Biffar & Co. both of Chicago, IL
Elmira Arms Co.
Empire Arms Co. made for Sears, Roebuck & Co. of Chicago, IL
Empire State Arms Co.
Enders Oakleaf made for Shapleigh Hardware Co. of St. Louis, MO
Enders Special Service made for Shapleigh Hardware Co.
Enders Royal Service made for Shapleigh Hardware Co.
Essex made for Belknap Hardware Co. of Louisville, KY
Excel made for Montgomery Ward & Co. of Chicago, IL
Farwell Arms Co. made for Farwell, Ozmun & Kirk of St. Paul, MN
Faultless made for John M. Smythe Co. of Chicago, IL
Faultless Goose Gun made for John M. Smyth Co. of Chicago, IL

The Field after 1894
Folsom Arms Co. (also used by H & D Folsom on Belgian imports)
F.F. Forbes (H & D Folsom house brand)
Fort Pitt Arms Co.
Fremont Arms Co. (also used on Belgian imports)
Gold Medal Wonder
Greenfield (some models) made for Hibbard, Spencer, Bartlett & Co. of Chicago, IL
H.B.C. (some models) made for Hudson's Bay Co. of Canada.
H.S.B. & Co. (some models) made for Hibbard, Spencer, Bartlett & Co. of Chicago, IL
Hanover Arms Co. (if no foreign proof marks)
S.H. Harrington (if no foreign proof marks)
Hartford Arms Co. made for both Simmons Hardware and Shapleigh Hardware Co. of St. Louis, MO
Harvard (H & D Folsom house brand)
Hermitage (some models) made for Grey-Dusley Hardware Co. of Nashville, TN
Hip Spe Bar (some models) made for Hibbard, Spencer, Bartlett & Co. of Chicago, IL
Hibbard (some models) made for Hibbard, Spencer, Bartlett & Co. of Chicago, IL
Howard Arms Co. made for Fred Biffar & Co. of Chicago, IL
Hudson (some models) made for Hibbard, Spencer, Bartlett & Co. of Chicago, IL
Hunter made for Belknap Hardware Co. Louisville, KY
Interstate Arms Co. made for Townley Metal & Hardware Co. of Kansas City, MO
Jackson Arms Co. made for C.M. McClung & Co. of Knoxville, TN
Joseph Arms Co. Norwich, Conn.
K K and Keen Kufter (some models) made for Shapleigh Hardware Co. of St. Louis, MO
Kingsland Special and Kingsland 10 Star made for Geller, Ward & Hasner of St. Louis, MO
Kirk Gun Co. made for Farwell, Ozmun & Kirk of St. Paul, MN
Knickerbocker (up to 1915, H & D Folsom house brand)
Knockabout (before 1925) made for Montgomery Ward & Co. of Chicago, IL
Knoxall (only hammerless doubles)
Laclede Gun Co.
Lakeside made for Montgomery Ward & Co. of Chicago, IL
Leader Gun Co. made for Charles Williams Stores of New York, NY
Lee's Special and Lee's Munner Special made for Lee Hardware Co. of Salina, KS
Long Range Marvel, Long Range Winner, and Long Range Wonder made between 1893 to 1909 for Sears, Roebuck & Co. of Chicago, IL F.A. Loomis
Marshwood
Massachusetts Arms Co. made before 1920 for Blish, Mizet and Silliman Hardware Co. of Atchison, KS
Mears (if no foreign proof marks)
Metropolitan made for Siegal-Cooper Co. of New York, NY
Minnesota Arms Co. made for Farwell, Ozmun, Kirk & Co. of St. Paul, MN
Mississippi Arms Co. St. Louis (some models) made for Shepleigh Hardware Co. of St. Louis, MO
Mississippi Valley Arms Co. (some models) made for Shapleigh Hardware Co. of St. Louis, MO
Mohawk made for Glish, Mizet and Lilliman Hardware Co. of Atchinson, KS
Monitor
R. Murdock, National Firearms Co. (some models)
National Arms Co. hammer doubles (without foreign proof marks) and hammerless doubles made for May Hardware Co. of Washington, D.C. and Moskowitz and Herbach Co. of Philadelphia, PA
New Britain Arms Co.'s Monarch
New Elgin Arms Co.
New Empire
New England (some models after 1914) made for Sears, Roebuck & Co.
New England Arms Co. (some models)
Newport Model CN made for Hibbard, Spencer, Bartlett and Co. of Chicago
Newport Model WN (some models) made for Hibbard, Spencer, Bartlett and Co. of Chicago
New Rival made for Van Camp Hardware and Iron Co. of Indianapolis, IN
New York Arms Co. made for Garnet Carter Co. of Chattanooga, TN
New York Machine Made (some models)
New York Match Gun (some models)
New York Nitro Hammerless
Nitro Bird made for Conover Hardware Co. of Kansas City, MO
Nitro Hunter made for Belknap Hardware Co. of Louisville, KY
Nitro King 1908 to 1917 made for Sears, Roebuck & Co. of Chicago, IL
Norwich Arms Co.
Not-Noc Manufacturing Co. made for Belknap Hardware Co. of Louisville, KY and Canton Hardware Co. of Canton, OH
Osprey made for Lou J. Eppinger, Detroit, MI
Oxford made for Belknap Hardware Co. of Louisville, KY
Peerless (H & D Folsom house brand)
Perfection made for H. G. Lipscomb & Co. of Nashville, TN Piedmont made for Piedmont Hardware Co. of Danville, PA
Piedmont Arms Co.
Pioneer Arms (if no foreign proof marks) made for Kruse and Baklmann Hardware Co. of Cincinnati, OH

Quail (H & D Folsom house brand)
Queen City made for Elmira Arms Co. of Elmira, NY

Red Chieftan (model 60) made for Supplee Biddle Hardware Co. of Philadelphia, PA

Rev-O-Noc (some models) made for Hibbard, Spencer, Bartlett & Co. of Chicago, IL

Rich-Con made for Richardson & Conover Hardware Co.

Charles Richter (some models) made for New York Sporting Goods Co. of New York, NY

Rickard Arms Co. made for J. A. Rickard Co. of Schenectady, NY

Rival (some models) made for Van Camp Hardware and Iron Co. of Indianapolis, IN

Rocket Special

Royal Service made for Shapleigh Hardware Co. of St. Louis, MO

Rummel Arms Co. made for A. J. Rummel Arms Co. of Toledo, OH

Ruso (if no foreign proof marks)

St. Louis Arms Co. (sidelock hammerless doubles) made for Shapleigh Hardware Co. of St. Louis, MO

Seminole (hammerless) unknown

Shue's Special made for Ira M. Shue of Hanover, PA

Smithsonian (some models)

John M. Smythe & Co. made for John M. Smythe Hardware Co. of Chicago, IL

Southern Arms Co. (some models)

Special Service made for Shapleigh Hardware Co. of St. Louis, MO

Spencer Gun Co. made for Hibbard, Spencer, Bartlett & Co. of Chicago, IL

Sportsman (some models) made for W. Bingham & Co. of Cleveland, OH

Springfield Arms Co. used until 1930. (H & D Folsom house brand). This brand was also used by Stevens and James Warner guns.

Square Deal made for Stratton, Warren Hardware Co. of Memphis, TN

Star Leader (some models)

State Arms Co. made for J.H. Lau & Co. of New York, NY

Sterling Arms Co.

Sullivan Arms Co. made for Sullivan Hardware Co. of Anderson, SC

Superior (some models) made for Paxton & Gallagher Co. of Omaha, NE

Syco (some models) made for Wyeth Hardware Co. of St. Joseph, MO

Ten Star & Ten Star Heavy Duty (if no foreign proof marks) made for Geller, Ward & Hasner Co. of St. Louis, MO

Tiger (if no foreign proof marks) made for J.H. Hall & Co. of Nashville, TN

Townley's Pal and Townley's American Boy made for Townley Metal & Hardware Co. of Kansas City, MO

Trap's Best made for Watkins, Cottrell Co. of Richmond, VA

Triumph (some models) made for Sears, Roebuck & Co. of Chicago, IL

Tryon Special (some models) made for Edward K. Tryon Co. of Philadelphia, PA

U.S. Arms Co. (if no foreign proof marks) made for Supplee-Biddle Hardware Co. of Philadelphia, PA

U.S. Field

Utica Firearms Co. (some models) made for Simmons Hardware Co. of St. Louis, MO

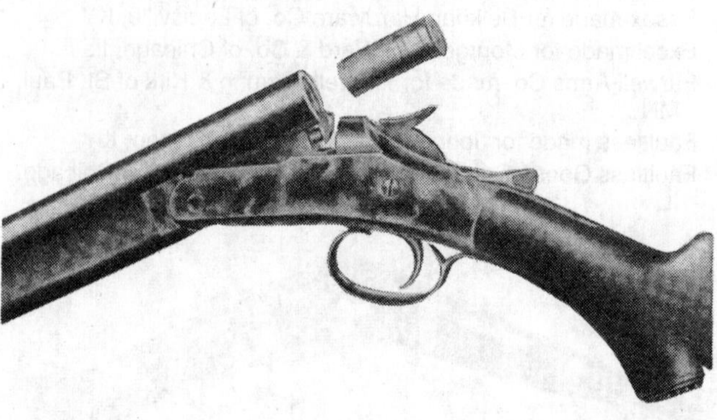

Victor & Victor Special made for Hibbard, Spencer, Bartlett & Co. of Chicago, IL

Virginia Arms Co. made for Virginia-Carolina Co. of Richmond, VA

Volunteer (some models) made for Belknap Hardware Co. of Louisville, KY

Vulcan Arms Co. made for Edward K. Tryon Co. of Philadelphia, PA

Warren Arms Co. (if no foreign proof marks)

Washington Arms Co. (some models)

Wauregan (some models)

Wautauga (some models) made for Wallace Hardware Co. Morristown, TN

Wildwood made for Sears, Roebuck & Co. of Chicago, IL

Wilkinson Arms Co. (if no foreign proof marks) made for Richmond Hardware Co. of Richmond, VA

Wilshire Arms Co. made for Stauffer, Eshleman & Co. of New Orleans, LA

Winfield Arms Co. (H & D Folsom house brand)

Winoca Arms Co. made for Jacobi Hardware Co. of Philadelphia, PA

Witte Hardware Co. (some models) made for Witte Hardware Co. of St. Louis, MO

Wolverine Arms Co. made for Fletcher Hardware Co. of Wilmington, NC

Worthington Arms Co. made for George Worthington Co. of Cleveland, OH

CRISPIN, SILAS

New York, New York

Crispin Revolver

A .32 Crispin caliber 5- or 6-shot revolver produced in limited quantities. Some are marked "Smith Arms Co., New York City. Crispin's Pat. Oct. 3, 1865." The most noteworthy feature of these revolvers is that the cylinder is constructed in two pieces so that the belted Crispin cartridge can be used. It is believed that these revolvers were only made on an experimental basis, between 1865 and 1867.

Exc.	*V.G.*	*Good*	*Fair*	*Poor*
—	—	18000	7000	2500

 *This symbol denotes "Sleepers" with rapidly-rising values and/or significant collector potential.*

CROSSFIRE

LaGrange, Georgia

This combination rifle/shotgun is manufactured by Saco Defense, Inc. for Crossfire. It is the first production firearm to combine the shotgun and rifle into a pump action, multi-shot weapon.

MK-1

This model is designed to fire both a .223 Rem. cartridge and a 12 gauge 3" shotgun shell from two different barrels. It is a dual action long gun operated with a pump action. Overall length of the gun is 38". The shotgun has a 4-round detachable magazine while the rifle has an AR-15 type 5-round magazine. Shotgun barrel is furnished with choke tubes. Offered in black oxide finish or camo finish. Weight is approximately 8.6 lbs. Introduced in 1999.

NIB	Exc.	V.G.	Good	Fair	Poor
1895	1450	—	—	—	—

NOTE: Add $100 for camo finish.

CRUCELEGUI, HERMANOS

Eibar, Spain

A 5mm, 6.35mm, 7.65mm, and 8mm caliber double-action revolver. The trade names used were; Puppy, Velo-Mith, Le-Brong, Bron-Sport, C.H., and Brong-Petit.

Exc.	V.G.	Good	Fair	Poor
200	100	80	60	35

CUMMINGS, O. S.

Lowell, Massachusetts

Cummings Pocket Revolver

A .22 caliber spur trigger revolver with a 3.5" ribbed round barrel, and a 7-shot fluted cylinder. Nickel-plated with rosewood grip. The barrel is stamped "O.S. Cummings Lowell, Mass." Approximately 1,000 manufactured in the 1870s.

Exc.	V.G.	Good	Fair	Poor
—	650	300	150	100

CUMMINGS & WHEELER

Lowell, Massachusetts

Pocket Revolver

Similar to the Cummings Pocket Revolver with subtle differences such as the length of the flutes on the cylinder and the size and shape of the grip. The barrel is slightly longer and is marked "Cummings & Wheeler, Lowell, Mass."

Exc.	V.G.	Good	Fair	Poor
—	700	350	150	100

CUSTOM GUN GUILD

Doraville, Georgia

Wood Model IV

A falling block single-shot rifle produced in a number of popular calibers with barrel lengths from 22" to 28". The stock of select checkered walnut. This is a lightweight rifle, at approximately 5.5 lbs. It was manufactured for one year only, 1984, and is not often encountered on today's market.

Exc.	V.G.	Good	Fair	Poor
3750	2750	2500	1750	1000

CZ

(Ceska Zbrojovka)
Uhersky Brod, Czech Republic

Established by Karel Bubla and Alois Tomiska in 1919. This company later merged with Hubertus Engineering Company. In 1949 the company was nationalized. CZ regularly exports 90 percent of its production to over 80 countries.

NOTE: As of 1998, CZ firearms have been imported exclusively by CZ-USA, a wholly-owned distribution subsidiary of Ceska Zbrojovka a.s. Uhersky Brod, (CZUB) of the Czech Republic.

Fox

A 6.35mm caliber semi-automatic pistol with a 2-1/8" barrel, tubular slide, a folding trigger and no trigger guard. Fox and CZ are inscribed on the slide. The CZ logo is on each grip plate. Blued with plastic grips. Manufactured between 1919 and 1936.

Courtesy James Rankin

Exc.	V.G.	Good	Fair	Poor
900	750	600	400	200

Army Pistol 1922 (Nickl-Pistole)

Designed by Josef Nickl of Mauser. First approved by the Army in 1921, this pistol was chambered for the .380 ACP (9mmKurtz/9x17mm) cartridge. Plagued by design problems, it was produced only in 1922 and 1923. Fewer than 22,000 were built.

Exc.	V.G.	Good	Fair	Poor
650	500	350	200	150

CZ 1921 Praga

A semi-automatic pistol in 7.65mm caliber. The first service pistol manufactured in Czechoslovakia. Production began in 1920. Praga is stamped on the slide and on each grip plate for commercial models. The service models were fitted with wood grips.

Courtesy James Rankin

Exc.	V.G.	Good	Fair	Poor
650	550	475	350	200

CZ 1922

A semi-automatic pistol in caliber 6.35mm. Very similar to the Fox above. It has no sights but is fitted with a conventional trigger guard. CZ is stamped on the slide and the CZ logo on each grip plate. Grips are plastic or wood. Manufactured between 1922 and 1936.

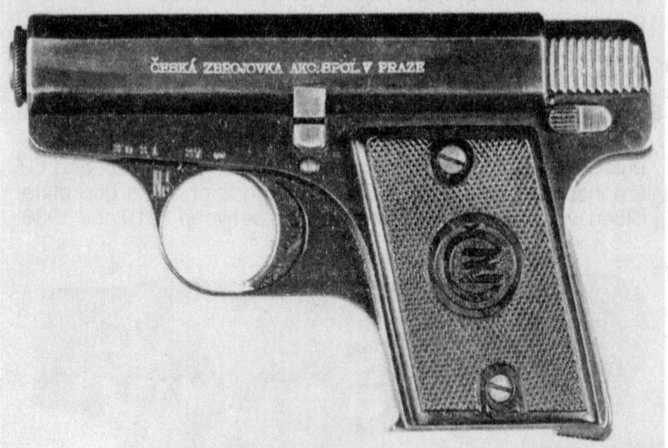

Courtesy James Rankin

Exc.	V.G.	Good	Fair	Poor
550	450	350	300	200

CZ 1924

The first large-production military pistol produced by CZ. Chambered for the 9mmK cartridge. It is the first of the CZ models with wraparound grips of both wood and plastic. CZ logo is seen on plastic grips. A lanyard loop is attached to the base of the butt. Manufactured from 1925 to 1932.

Courtesy James Rankin

Exc.	V.G.	Good	Fair	Poor
650	500	400	300	200

CZ 1927

A semi-automatic pistol chambered for the 7.65mm cartridge, marked the same as the CZ 1924, but the cocking grooves on the slide are cut vertically instead of sloped as on the earlier model. This model was blued with checkered, wrap-around, plastic grips. These early guns were beautifully made and marked, "Ceska Zbrojovka AS v Praze." After the war, these pistols continued in production until 1951. There were more than 500,000 manufactured.

NOTE: Some of these pistols were made with an extended barrel for the use of a silencer. This variation brings a large premium. Fewer than 10 CZ27s were made in .22 caliber. An expert opinion is suggested if a sale is contemplated.

Commercial markings Courtesy Orvel Reichert

Exc.	V.G.	Good	Fair	Poor
450	375	300	200	165

NOTE: Nazi-proofed add 50 percent.

CZ 1936

A 6.35mm caliber semi-automatic pistol with 2.5" barrel, and double-action-only lockwork. It has plastic wraparound grips with the CZ logo on each side. It replaced the Model 1922 in 1936. Discontinued in 1940 because of wartime production.

Courtesy James Rankin

Exc.	V.G.	Good	Fair	Poor
450	350	300	200	100

CZ 1938

A semi-automatic double-action pistol in caliber 9mmK. Manufactured for the Czechoslovakian military from 1938 to 1940. Barrel length is 4.7". Weight is about 32 oz. Magazine capacity is 8 rounds. Wraparound plastic grips with the CZ logo on each side.

Courtesy James Rankin

Exc.	V.G.	Good	Fair	Poor
550	500	400	300	200

CZ 1945

This model is a small .25 caliber (6.35mm) pocket pistol that is double-action-only. It was produced and sold after World War II. It is a modified version of the CZ 1936. Approximately 60,000 were built between 1945 and 1949.

Courtesy James Rankin

Exc.	V.G.	Good	Fair	Poor
350	300	250	175	125

CZ 1950

This is a blowback-operated, semi-automatic, double-action pistol chambered for the 7.65mm cartridge. It is patterned after the Walther Model PP with a few differences. The safety catch is located on the frame instead of the slide; and the trigger guard is not hinged, as on the Walther. It is dismantled by means of a catch on the side of the frame. Although intended to be a military pistol designed by the Kratochvil brothers, it proved to be underpowered and was adopted by the police. There were few released on the commercial market.

Courtesy James Rankin

Exc.	V.G.	Good	Fair	Poor
150	100	75	50	50

CZ 1952

This Czech army sidearm is a semi-automatic pistol chambered for the 7.62mm cartridge and fitted with a 4.7" barrel. It has a very complex locking system using two rollers inside the frame. Magazine capacity is 8 rounds. Weight is about 34 oz. Production ended in 1956.

Exc.	V.G.	Good	Fair	Poor
300	275	225	125	75

Model 1970

This model was an attempt to correct dependability problems with the Model 50. There is little difference to see externally between the two except for markings and the grip pattern. Production began during the 1960s and ended in 1983.

Courtesy Rock Island Auction Company

Exc.	V.G.	Good	Fair	Poor
250	200	150	100	75

RIFLES

Model 52 (7.62 x 45)

Exc.	V.G.	Good	Fair	Poor
350	300	250	200	125

Model 52/57 (7.62 x 39)

Exc.	V.G.	Good	Fair	Poor
375	325	275	225	150

CURRENTLY IMPORTED CZ RIFLES

CZ-USA

Kansas City, Kansas

CZ first entered the U.S. market in 1990 through various distributors. In January 1998 CZ-USA opened its office in Kansas City, Kansas. This office includes full sales and warranty service as well as an on-site gunsmith.

LONG GUNS

CZ Model 3

This bolt-action rifle, introduced in 2004, is produced in the U.S.A. Offered in both right- and left-hand configurations. Chambered for the Winchester Short Magnums: .270, 7mm, and .300. Walnut stock with choice of stainless steel or blue finish. Fitted with a 24" barrel. No sights. Magazine is 3 rounds. Weight is about 7.5 lbs.

NIB	Exc.	V.G.	Good	Fair	Poor
870	675	575	—	—	—

NOTE: Add $30 for stainless steel.

CZ 452-2E LUX

This bolt-action rifle is chambered for the .22 LR or .22 Win. Mag. cartridge. It is fitted with a 24.8" barrel with hooded front and adjustable rear sight. Trigger is adjustable for pull. The pistol grip stock is a European-style Turkish walnut. Supplied with a 5-round magazine. Blued finish. Weight is approximately 6.6 lbs.

NIB	Exc.	V.G.	Good	Fair	Poor
390	300	225	150	125	—

NOTE: Add $40 for .22 WMR.

CZ ZKM-452D

As above, with a walnut, Monte Carlo-style stock.

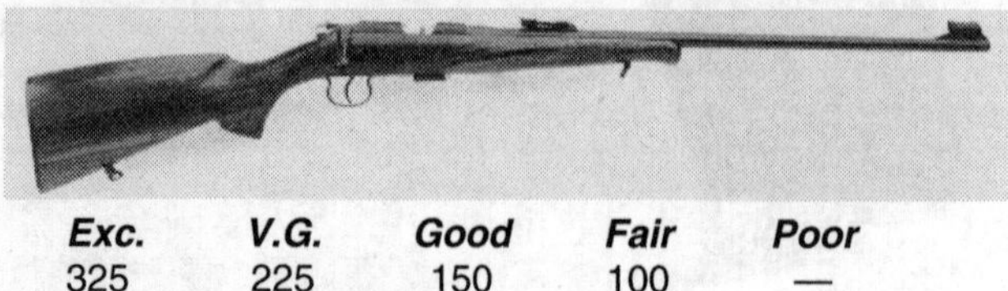

Exc.	V.G.	Good	Fair	Poor
325	225	150	100	—

CZ 452-2E ZKM Style

Similar to the above model but chambered for .22 LR only and fitted with a black synthetic stock and matte nickel finish. Fitted with a 22.5" barrel. Weight is about 6 lbs.

NIB	Exc.	V.G.	Good	Fair	Poor
375	275	225	175	125	—

CZ452 Training Rifle

Chambered for the .22 LR cartridge and fitted with a 24.8" barrel. Detachable magazine has a 5-round capacity. Beechwood stock. Adjustable sights. Weight is about 5.4 lbs.

NIB	Exc.	V.G.	Good	Fair	Poor
280	225	175	150	—	—

CZ 452 American Classic

This model is chambered for the .22 LR and .22 Win. Mag. cartridge and features an American-style Circassian walnut stock with 18 lpi checkering. Fitted with a 21" barrel with recessed target crown. Supplied with a 5-round magazine. Blued finish. Weight is about 6.5 lbs. Introduced in 1999. In 2005 the .17 Mach 2 caliber was offered.

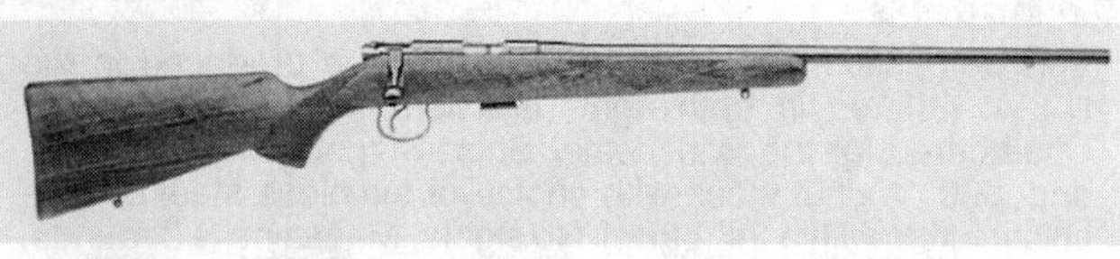

NIB	Exc.	V.G.	Good	Fair	Poor
390	300	250	—	—	—

NOTE: Add $40 for .22 WMR. or .17 HMR.

CZ 452 Varmint

This bolt-action rifle is chambered for the .22 LR cartridge and is fitted with a 20" barrel. American-style Turkish walnut stock. Blued finish. Weight is about 7.5 lbs. In 2005 the .17 Mach 2 was offered.

NIB	Exc.	V.G.	Good	Fair	Poor
420	300	250	200	150	—

NOTE: Add $20 for .17 Mach 2 caliber.

CZ 452 Scout

This model is designed for the younger shooter and features a shortened buttstock, 16.2" barrel, and reduced weight receiver. Chambered for the .22 LR cartridge. Open adjustable sights. Weight is 3.9 lbs. Introduced in 2000.

NIB	Exc.	V.G.	Good	Fair	Poor
250	200	150	—	—	—

CZ 452 Style

Chambered for the .22 LR cartridge and fitted with a 22.5" barrel, this model features a synthetic stock with matte nickel finish. Magazine capacity is 5 or 10 rounds. Weight is about 5.3 lbs.

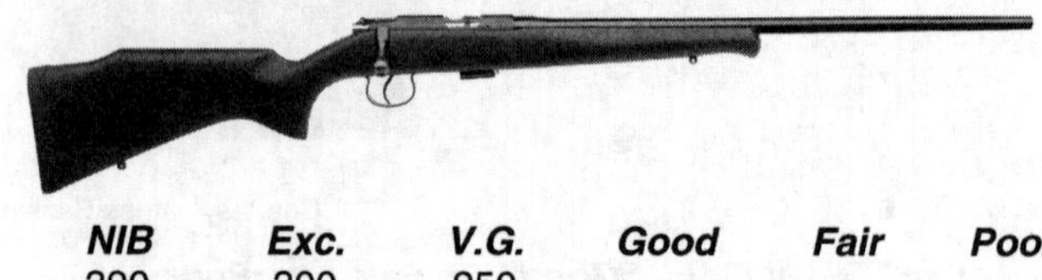

NIB	Exc.	V.G.	Good	Fair	Poor
390	300	250	—	—	—

CZ 452 Silhouette

Designed for small silhouette competition shooting, this .22 caliber rifle has a synthetic stock and blued finish. Barrel length is 22.5". Weight is about 5.3 lbs.

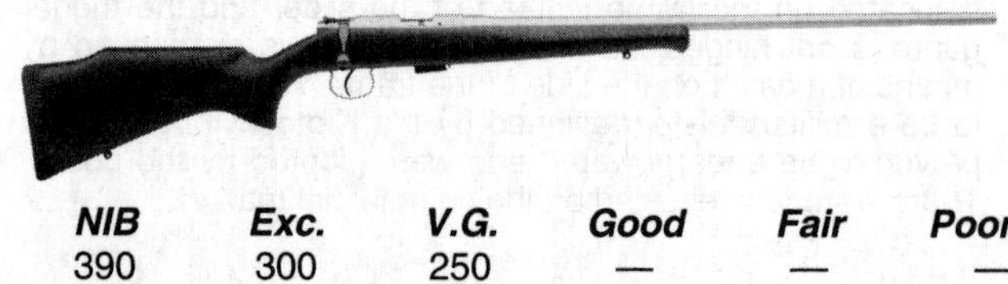

NIB	Exc.	V.G.	Good	Fair	Poor
390	300	250	—	—	—

CZ 452 FS

This model, introduced in 2004, is chambered for the .22 Long Rifle or .22 WMR cartridge and fitted with a full-length Turkish walnut stock. Barrel length is 20.5". Adjustable sights. Weight is about 6.5 lbs.

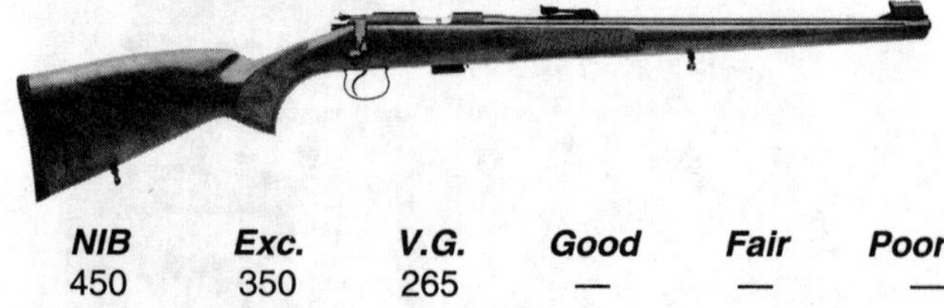

NIB	Exc.	V.G.	Good	Fair	Poor
450	350	265	—	—	—

CZ 513 Basic

This model is a simplified version of the CZ 452. It features a plain beechwood stock with no checkering. Iron sights. Chambered for the .22 Long Rifle cartridge. Barrel length is 21". Weight is about 5.4 lbs. Introduced in 2004.

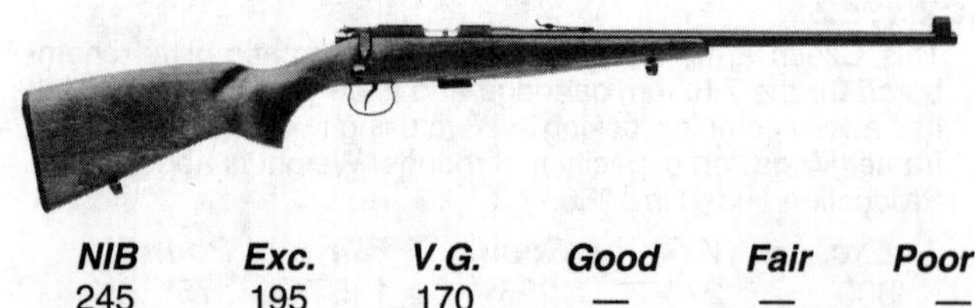

NIB	Exc.	V.G.	Good	Fair	Poor
245	195	170	—	—	—

CZ 511

This is a semi-automatic rifle chambered for the .22 LR cartridge. Fitted with a 22" barrel. Two-position rear sight. Supplied with an 8-round magazine. Cross bolt safety. Turkish walnut stock. Blued finish. Weight is approximately 5.4 lbs.

NIB	Exc.	V.G.	Good	Fair	Poor
390	300	250	175	125	—

CZ Model 527

This bolt-action model is chambered for the .22 Hornet, .222 Rem., and the .223 Rem. The rear sight is adjustable and the checkered stock is walnut. Barrel length is 23.6" and magazine capacity is 5 rounds. Weight is approximately 6.2 lbs.

NIB	Exc.	V.G.	Good	Fair	Poor
600	500	400	300	225	—

CZ 527 American Classic

Introduced in 1999, this model features a 20.5" barrel with American-style Turkish walnut stock. Weight is approximately 7.6 lbs. Blued finish. In 2005 this model was chambered for the .204 Ruger cartridge with 22" barrel.

NIB	Exc.	V.G.	Good	Fair	Poor
600	500	400	—	—	

NOTE: Add $170 for English walnut stock, $200 for fancy American walnut, $30 for maple, and $30 for laminate stock.

CZ 527 Lux

This is a bolt-action center fire rifle chambered for the .22 Hornet, .222 Rem., or the .223 Rem. cartridge. Fitted with a 23.6" barrel with a hooded front sight and fixed rear sight. The trigger is an adjustable single-set type. The Turkish walnut stock is in the Bavarian style. Blued finish. Supplied with a 5-round magazine. Weight is approximately 6.6 lbs.

NIB	Exc.	V.G.	Good	Fair	Poor
600	475	350	250	—	—

CZ 527 Premium (Lux)

Introduced in 2000 this model features hand fitted actions, fancy walnut stock, 18 lpi checkering, and satin finish. Offered in .22 Hornet and .223 Rem. Barrel length is 22". Magazine capacity is 5 rounds. Weight is about 6.2 lbs.

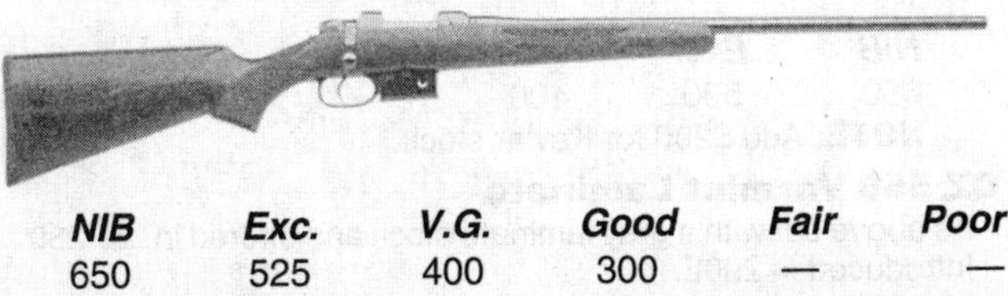

NIB	Exc.	V.G.	Good	Fair	Poor
650	525	400	300	—	—

CZ 527 FS

Similar to the above model but fitted with a 20.5" barrel with Mannlicher-style stock. Blued finish. Weight is about 6 lbs.

NIB	Exc.	V.G.	Good	Fair	Poor
690	525	400	300	—	—

CZ 527 Varmint

Chambered for the .17 Remington or .204 Ruger cartridge and fitted with a 24" heavy barrel. Checkered Turkish walnut stock. No sights. Detachable magazine. Weight is about 7.2 lbs.

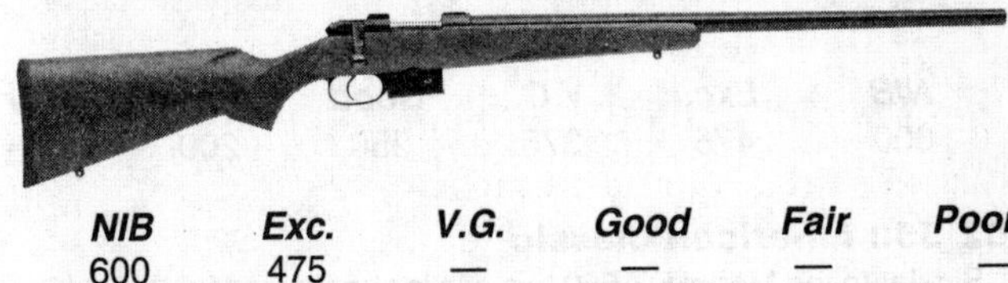

NIB	Exc.	V.G.	Good	Fair	Poor
600	475	—	—	—	—

CZ 527 Varmint Laminate

Chambered for the .223 Rem. cartridge and fitted with a 24" heavy barrel. Gray laminate stock. Magazine capacity is 5 rounds. Weight is about 8 lbs. Introduced in 2002.

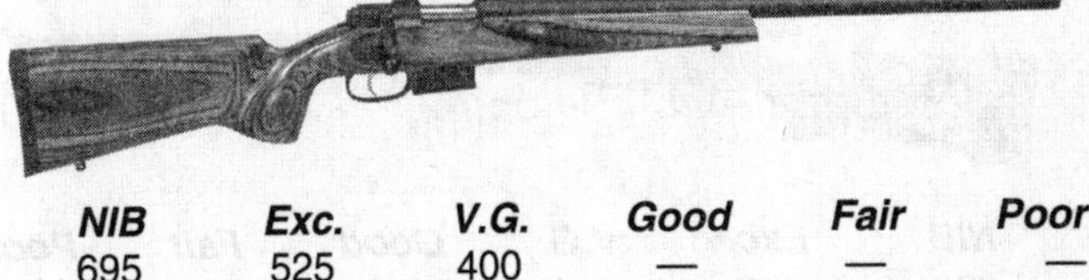

NIB	Exc.	V.G.	Good	Fair	Poor
695	525	400	—	—	—

CZ 527 Varmint

As above but with an H-S Kevlar stock. Weight is about 7.5 lbs. Introduced in 2002. In 2004 this model was also offered with a Turkish walnut stock.

NIB	Exc.	V.G.	Good	Fair	Poor
800	625	—	—	—	—

CZ 527 Carbine

This model, introduced in 2000, is chambered for the 7.62x39 cartridge and fitted with a 18.5" barrel. Detachable magazine capacity is 5 rounds. Open sights. Weight is about 6 lbs.

NIB	Exc.	V.G.	Good	Fair	Poor
600	475	350	—	—	—

CZ 527 Prestige

An upgraded CZ 527 American with jeweled bolt and semi-fancy Turkish walnut with hand rubbed finish. Chambered for the .22 Hornet or .223 Remington cartridges. Barrel length is 21.9". Weight is about 6.2 lbs. Introduced in 2001.

NIB	Exc.	V.G.	Good	Fair	Poor
880	675	600	475	—	—

CZ Model 537

This bolt-action rifle is chambered for the .270, .308, and .30-06 cartridges. The rear sight is adjustable and the stock is checkered walnut. Barrel length is 23.6". Magazine capacity is 5 rounds. Weight is approximately 7.9 lbs. Discontinued

NIB	Exc.	V.G.	Good	Fair	Poor
600	475	375	250	200	—

CZ 550 American Classic

Similar to the Model CZ 550 this rifle is chambered for the .243, .308, .270,and .30-06 cartridges. It is fitted with a 20.5" barrel and American-style Turkish walnut stock. No sights. Supplied with 5-round internal magazine. Blued finish. Weight is about 7.6 lbs. Introduced in 1999.

NIB	Exc.	V.G.	Good	Fair	Poor
620	500	400	300	—	—

CZ Model 550

Chambered for the .243, .270, .308, and .30-06 cartridges, this bolt-action rifle features a 24" barrel and high comb walnut stock. No open sights. Weight is about 7.25 lbs.

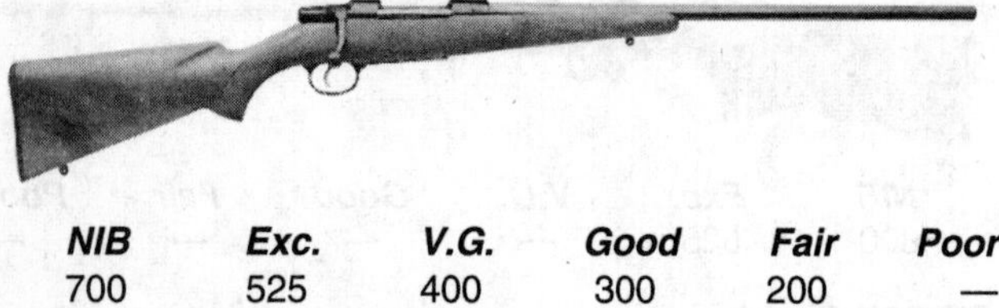

NIB	Exc.	V.G.	Good	Fair	Poor
700	525	400	300	200	—

CZ Model 550 Battue Lux

Chambered for the .30-06 cartridge. Ramp rear sight. Barrel length is 20.25". Weight is approximately 7.25 lbs. Checkered walnut stock.

NIB	Exc.	V.G.	Good	Fair	Poor
700	525	400	300	—	—

CZ Model 550 FS Battue

Same as above but with full-length stock.

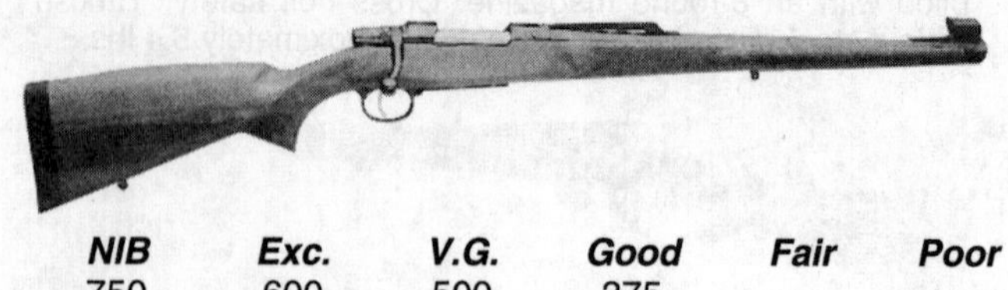

NIB	Exc.	V.G.	Good	Fair	Poor
750	600	500	375	—	—

CZ Model 550 Minnesota

This model is chambered for the .270 Win. and .30-06 calibers. Barrel length is 23.5". Weight is approximately 7.25 lbs. No sights. Supplied with recoil pad.

NIB	Exc.	V.G.	Good	Fair	Poor
650	550	450	325	—	—

CZ Model 550 Minnesota DM

Same as above but with detachable magazine. Calibers are .270 Win. and .308.

NIB	Exc.	V.G.	Good	Fair	Poor
725	575	475	350	—	—

CZ 550 Prestige

This model is similar to the CZ 550 American with the added features of jeweled bolt, semi-fancy walnut and hand rubbed finish. Chambered for the .270 or .30-06 cartridges with 23.6" barrel. Weight is approximately 7.3 lbs. Introduced in 2001.

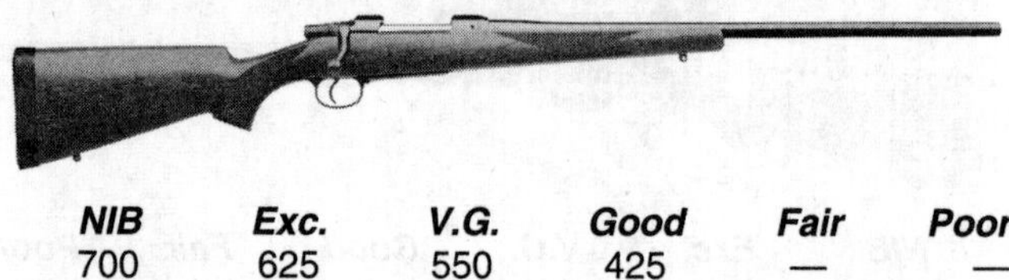

NIB	Exc.	V.G.	Good	Fair	Poor
700	625	550	425	—	—

CZ 550 Lux

This rifle is chambered for the 7x57, 6.5x55 SE, and the 9.3x62 cartridges. Barrel length is 23.6". Fixed magazine capacity is 5 rounds. Bavarian-style stock with Turkish walnut. Open sights. Weight is about 7.3 lbs.

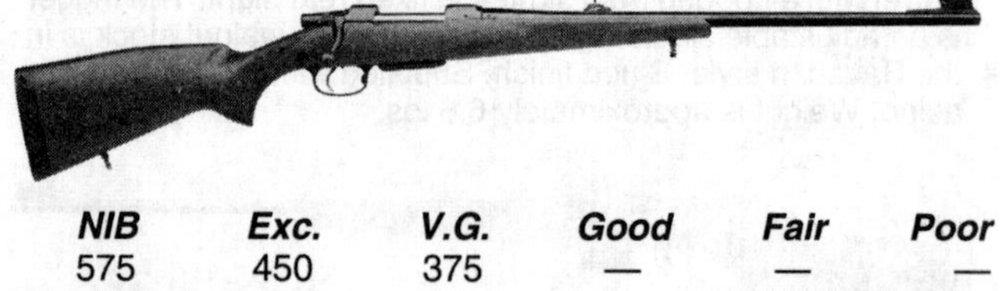

NIB	Exc.	V.G.	Good	Fair	Poor
575	450	375	—	—	—

CZ 550 Varmint

This model is chambered for the .308 Win. cartridge and is fitted with a 25.6" heavy barrel. No sights. Checkered walnut varmint-style stock. Ventilated recoil pad. Single set trigger. Detachable magazine holds 4 rounds. Weight is about 9.3 lbs. In 2004 an HS Precision Kevlar stock was also offered on this model.

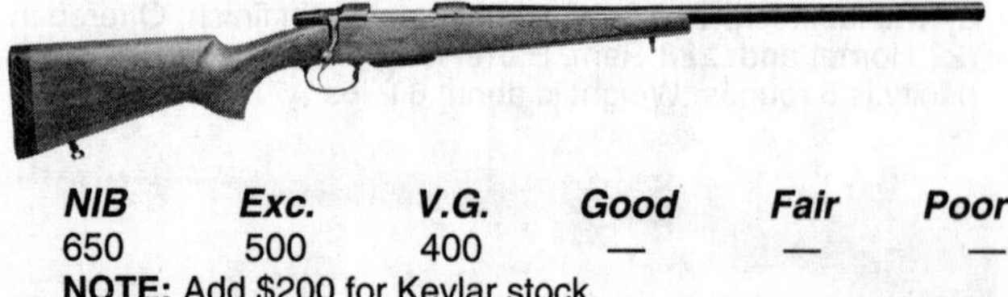

NIB	Exc.	V.G.	Good	Fair	Poor
650	500	400	—	—	—

NOTE: Add $200 for Kevlar stock.

CZ 550 Varmint Laminate

As above but with a gray laminate stock and offered in .22-250. Introduced in 2002.

NIB	Exc.	V.G.	Good	Fair	Poor
750	600	450	—	—	—

CZ 550 Safari Magnum

Chambered for the .300 Win. Mag., .375 H&H, .458 Win. Mag., and the .416 Rigby cartridges, this bolt-action rifle is fitted with a 25" barrel and 5-round internal magazine. Sights are one standing and two folding express rear with a hooded front sight. Blued finish. Bavarian-style Turkish walnut stock. Weight is about 9.2 lbs.

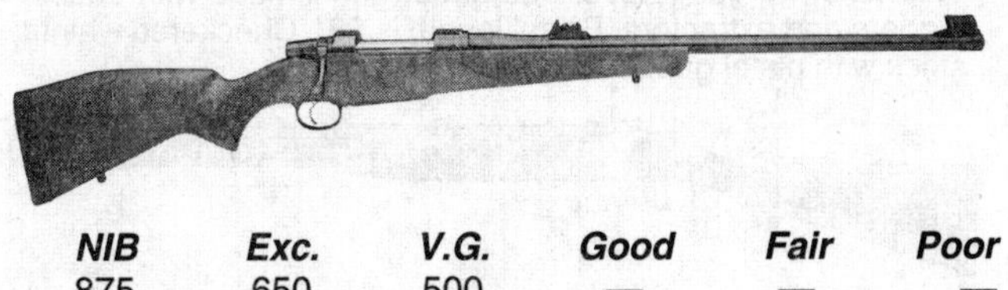

NIB	Exc.	V.G.	Good	Fair	Poor
875	650	500	—	—	—

CZ 550 American Safari Magnum

Introduced in 2004 this model is similar to the Safari Magnum above but with an American pattern stock. Offered with American walnut, brown laminate, or camo laminate stock. This model is also offered with fancy American walnut stock.

NIB	Exc.	V.G.	Good	Fair	Poor
875	675	550	—	—	—

NOTE: For laminate stock add $200, for fancy wood stock add $600.

CZ 550 Ultimate Hunting Rifle

Similar to CZ550 Safari Magnum but chambered for .300 WM only and with custom select wood. 23.6-inch barrel. Accuracy guaranteed at one MOA to 1000 yards. Introduced 2006. MSRP: 2500+

CZ 550 Premium

Introduced in 2000 this model features a hand fitted action with fancy walnut stock and 18 lpi checkering. Chambered for .30-06 and .270 Win. cartridges. Barrel length is 23.6". Weight is about 7.3 lbs.

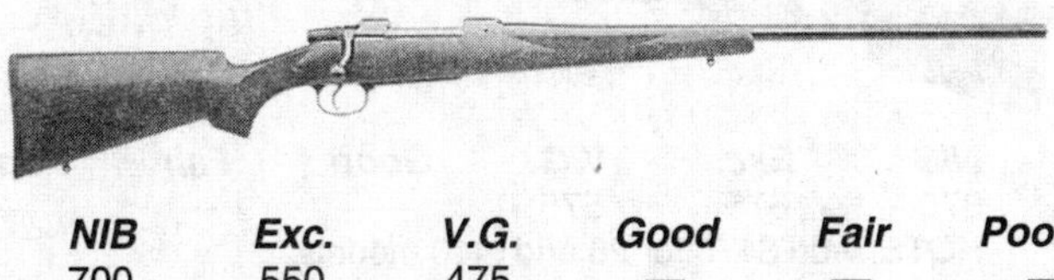

NIB	Exc.	V.G.	Good	Fair	Poor
700	550	475	—	—	—

CZ 550 Medium Magnum

This model is designed around a mid-sized magnum action. Fitted with a 23.6" barrel and has a fixed magazine capacity of 5 rounds. Chambered for the .300 Win. Mag or the 7mm Rem. Mag. Single set trigger and adjustable rear sight. Weight is about 7.3 lbs. Introduced in 2001.

NIB	Exc.	V.G.	Good	Fair	Poor
690	550	425	—	—	—

CZ 550 Safari Classic Custom

Chambered for the .404 Jeffery, .450 Rigby, or the .505 Gibbs. Fancy grade checkered walnut stock. Single set trigger. Express sights.

NIB	Exc.	V.G.	Good	Fair	Poor
1750	1300	1050	—	—	—

NOTE: Add $100 for .505 Gibbs.

CZ-581

A 12 gauge O/U double-barrel boxlock shotgun with 28" ventilated rib barrels, single trigger, and automatic ejectors. Blued with a walnut stock.

NIB	Exc.	V.G.	Good	Fair	Poor
870	700	600	450	400	—

CZ-584

A combination 12 gauge/7x57Rmm, .222 or .308 caliber Over/Under combination rifle/shotgun with 24.5" ventilated rib barrels, single triggers and automatic ejectors. Blued with a walnut stock.

NIB	Exc.	V.G.	Good	Fair	Poor
900	700	600	500	—	—

CZ ZKK 600

Offered in 7x57mm, 7x64mm, .270, or .30-06. Features a Mauser-type bolt-action with controlled feed, non-rotating extractor, and dovetailed receiver in three action lengths.

NIB	Exc.	V.G.	Good	Fair	Poor
700	600	500	425	325	—

NOTE: Add $100 to prices for pop-up receiver sight that was discontinued in 1977.

CZ ZKK 601

As above, in .243 or .308 caliber.

NIB	Exc.	V.G.	Good	Fair	Poor
700	600	500	425	325	—

CZ ZKK 602

As above, in .300 Holland & Holland, .375 Holland & Holland or .458 Winchester Magnum.

NIB	Exc.	V.G.	Good	Fair	Poor
800	700	600	500	400	—

CZ 700 Sniper M1

Introduced in 2001 this rifle is chambered for the .308 Winchester cartridge and fitted with a 25.6" heavy barrel. Receiver has permanently attached Weaver rail. Laminated stock has adjustable cheekpiece and buttplate with adjustable trigger. Magazine capacity is 10 rounds. Weigh is approximately 12 lbs.

NIB	Exc.	V.G.	Good	Fair	Poor
2100	1700	—	—	—	—

CZ 750 Sniper

Bolt-action rifle; .308 Win. 10-shot detachable magazine, 26-inch blued barrel, two scope mount systems, polymer stock, weighs 12 lbs. Introduced 2006. MSRP: 2000

SHOTGUNS

CZ 712

This is a gas-operated semi-automatic 12 gauge 3" chamber shotgun built on a lightweight alloy receiver. Offered with a choice of 26" or 28" vent rib barrels. Magazine is 4 rounds. Checkered walnut stock with blued finish. Weight is about 7 lbs. Introduced in 2004.

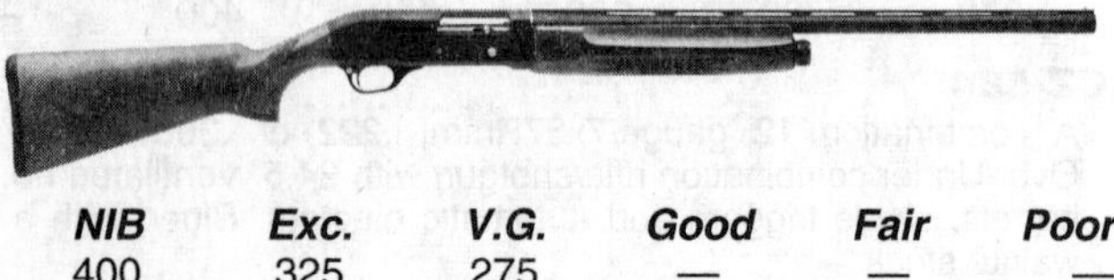

NIB	Exc.	V.G.	Good	Fair	Poor
400	325	275	—	—	—

CZ 720

This model is similar to the above but chambered for the 20 gauge 3" shell. Offered with a choice of 26" or 28" vent rib barrels. Walnut stock. Weight is about 6 lbs. Introduced in 2004.

NIB	Exc.	V.G.	Good	Fair	Poor
425	325	275	—	—	—

Redhead

This over and under is available in 12, 20, or 28 gauge with choke tubes, and .410 bore with fixed chokes. Barrel lengths are 26" or 28". Single-selective trigger with extractors on 28 and .410 models. Checkered walnut stock with pistol grip. Receiver finish is silver. Weight from 8 lbs. to 6 lbs. depending on gauge.

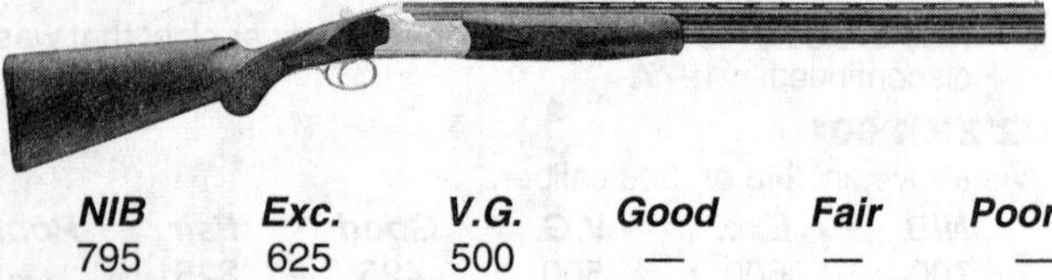

NIB	Exc.	V.G.	Good	Fair	Poor
795	625	500	—	—	—

Canvasback

This over and under gun is offered in 12 or 20 gauge fitted with 26" or 28" barrels with choke tubes. Single-selective trigger with extractors. Black receiver finish. Weight is about 7.5 lbs.

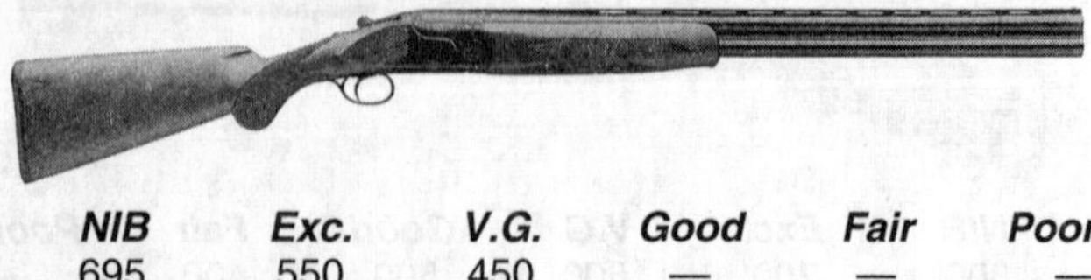

NIB	Exc.	V.G.	Good	Fair	Poor
695	550	450	—	—	—

Woodcock

Available in 12, 20, 28 and .410 bore with 26" or 28" barrel with chokes tubes except for fixed chokes on the .410. Single-selective trigger with ejectors except for the 12 and 20 gauge. Receiver is case colored with sideplate. Checkered walnut stock with pistol grip.

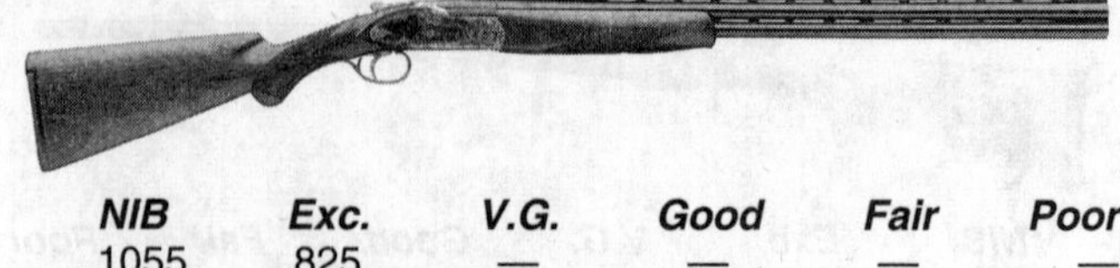

NIB	Exc.	V.G.	Good	Fair	Poor
1055	825	—	—	—	—

NOTE: Add $75 for 28 and .410 models.

Woodcock Custom Grade

Similar to the Woodcock model, but stocked with Grade IV walnut and offered only in 20 gauge with 28" barrels.

NIB	Exc.	V.G.	Good	Fair	Poor
1500	—	—	—	—	—

Mallard

This 12 or 20 gauge over and under gun is fitted with double triggers and extractors. Barrel length is 28". Checkered walnut stock with pistol grip. Coin finish receiver.

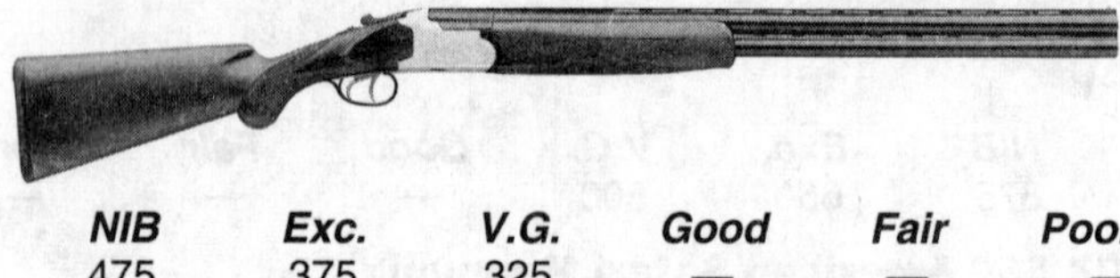

NIB	Exc.	V.G.	Good	Fair	Poor
475	375	325	—	—	—

Durango

This side-by-side gun is offered in 12 or 20 gauge with 20" barrels with choke tubes. Extractors. Case colored receiver. Single trigger. Checkered walnut with pistol grip.

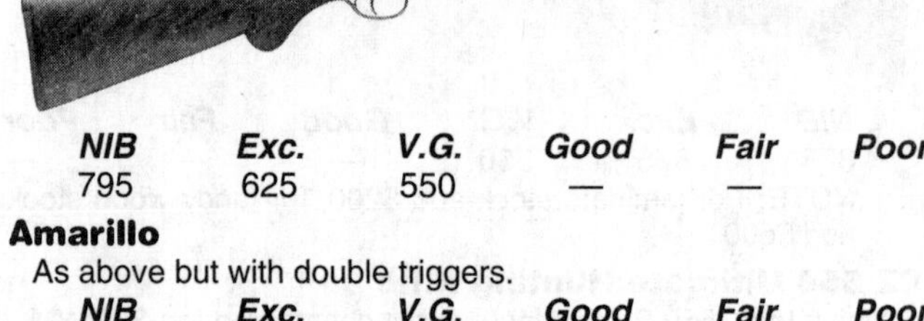

NIB	Exc.	V.G.	Good	Fair	Poor
795	625	550	—	—	—

Amarillo

As above but with double triggers.

NIB	Exc.	V.G.	Good	Fair	Poor
700	550	425	—	—	—

Ringneck

This side-by-side gun is chambered for the 12, 16, 20, 28, or .410 bore with 26" or 28" barrels with choke tubes. Case colored receiver with side plates. Single-selective trigger with extractors. Checkered walnut stock with pistol grip. Add $100 for 16 gauge.

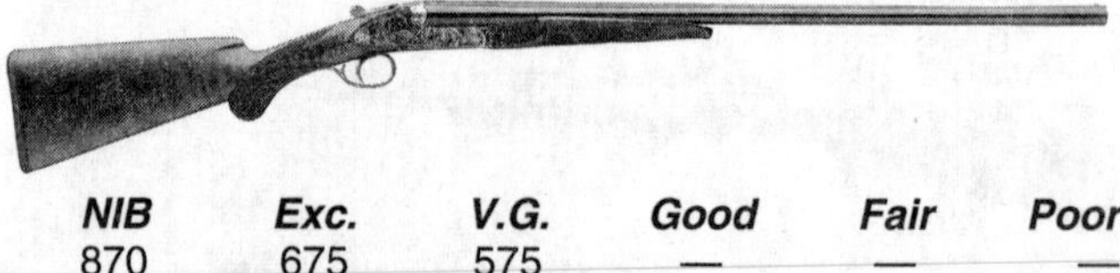

NIB	Exc.	V.G.	Good	Fair	Poor
870	675	575	—	—	—

NOTE: Add $175 for 28 and .410 models.

Ringneck Custom Grade

Select Grade IV walnut is used in the manufacture of this 20 gauge with 28" barrels.

NIB	Exc.	V.G.	Good	Fair	Poor
1200	—	—	—	—	—

Bobwhite

As above but with straight grip stock and double triggers.

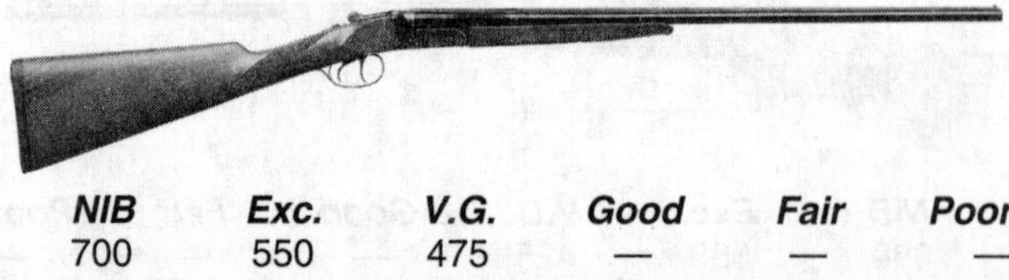

NIB	Exc.	V.G.	Good	Fair	Poor
700	550	475	—	—	—

Hammer Coach

12-gauge cowboy gun with double triggers, color case hardened receiver, external hammers and Turkish walnut pistol grip stock and forend. Fixed IC and modified chokes. Introduced 2006. MSRP: 795

PISTOLS

All currently imported CZ pistols can be ordered with tritium night sights with the exception of models CZ 97B and CZ 100. Add $80 for this option.

CZ 75

Designed by the Koucky brothers in 1975, this model bears little resemblance to previous CZ pistols. Considered by many to be the best pistol ever to come from the Czech Republic. Chambered for the 9mm Parabellum cartridge it is copied in many countries. This pistol has a breechlock system utilizing a Browning-style cam. The slide rides on the inside of the slide rails. Magazine capacity is 15 rounds, barrel length is 4.72", overall length is 8", and the empty pistol weighs 34.5 oz. Offered in black paint, matte or polished blue finish.

NIB	Exc.	V.G.	Good	Fair	Poor
600	500	425	400	325	250

CZ 74 30th Anniversary

Introduced in 2005 this model features special 30th anniversary engraving, gold inlays, gold plated controls, high gloss blue finish, engraved blonde finished birch grips. Magazine capacity is 15 rounds. Limited to 1,000 pistols.

NIB	Exc.	V.G.	Good	Fair	Poor
760	600	—	—	—	—

CZ 75 B

Introduced in 1994 this CZ model is an updated version of the original CZ 75. It features a pinned front sight, a commander hammer, non-glare ribbed barrel, and a squared trigger guard. Also offered in .40 S&W chamber.

NIB	Exc.	V.G.	Good	Fair	Poor
510	400	300	250	175	125

NOTE: For .40 S&W add $30. For glossy blue add $20, for dual tone finish $25, and for nickel add $25. For tritium night sights add $80.

CZ 75 Compact

Introduced in 1992, this is a compact version of the CZ 75. The barrel length is 3.9", the overall length is 7.3", and the weight is about 32 oz. Offered in black paint, matte or polished blue finish. Traditional single-action double-action.

NIB	Exc.	V.G.	Good	Fair	Poor
540	425	300	250	175	125

NOTE: For .40 S&W add $30. For glossy blue add $20, for dual tone finish $25, and for nickel add $25. For tritium night sights add $80.

In 2005 this model was offered with accessory rail and ambidextrous manual safety. Add $50 to above prices.

CZ 75 Compact D

Essentially the same as the CZ 75 Compact but with a decocking double-action system and lightweight alloy frame. Weight approximately 25 oz.

NIB	Exc.	V.G.	Good	Fair	Poor
555	450	—	—	—	—

NOTE: Only 20 of these pistols were imported into the U.S. No longer in production. Expert appraisal suggested prior to sale. Only the NIB retail price is listed above.

CZ 75 B Tactical

Chambered for the 9mm Luger cartridge and fitted with a 4.7" barrel. This pistol has a single-action/double-action trigger. Fixed sights. Rubber grips. Slide is black polycoat and the frame is a military green finish. Weight is about 35 oz.

NIB	Exc.	V.G.	Good	Fair	Poor
500	400	325	—	—	—

CZ 75 BD

Has all the same features as the Model 75 B but with the addition of a decocking double-action. Black polycoat finish.

NIB	Exc.	V.G.	Good	Fair	Poor
520	400	300	—	—	—

CZ BD Compact

Introduced in 2001 this model features a 3.9" barrel with decocking lever. Chambered for the .40 S&W cartridge. Blued finish. Magazine capacity is 10 rounds. Weight is about 32 oz. All other features same as CZ 75 B Compact.

NIB	Exc.	V.G.	Good	Fair	Poor
450	350	300	—	—	—

CZ BD Compact Carry

Same as the model above but with rounded edges including trigger guard.

NIB	Exc.	V.G.	Good	Fair	Poor
450	350	300	—	—	—

CZ 75 B SA

This model was introduced in 2000 and features a single-action trigger designed for competitive shooting that can be carried in condition one. Fitted with a straight trigger, manual safety, and chambered for the 9mm cartridge. Weight is about 35 oz.

NIB	Exc.	V.G.	Good	Fair	Poor
520	400	325	—	—	—

CZ 75 Semi-Compact

This model was introduced in 1994 and has the same barrel length as the Compact (3.9") but has the same full-size grip as the CZ 75. Magazine capacity is 15 rounds of 9mm. Overall length is 7.3".

NIB	Exc.	V.G.	Good	Fair	Poor
450	350	300	250	175	—

CZ 75 D PCR Compact

Introduced in 2000 this pistol is chambered for the 9mm cartridge and features a light alloy frame and 3.9" barrel. Trigger is both single and double-action with decocking lever. Low profile sights. Serrated front and rear backstrap. Designed for the Czech national police force. Magazine capacity is 10 rounds. Weight is about 27 oz.

NIB	Exc.	V.G.	Good	Fair	Poor
525	425	350	—	—	

CZ 75 Champion

This model is chambered for the .40 S&W, 9mm, and 9x21 cartridges. Single-action-only trigger with straight trigger. Fitted with a 4.5" barrel with low profile adjustable sights and three port compensator. Furnished with blue slide and nickel frame. Hand fitted. Weight is about 36 oz.

NIB	Exc.	V.G.	Good	Fair	Poor
1475	1150	975	—	—	—

CZ 75 DAO

This model is similar to the CZ 75 but with a double-action-only trigger, no safety lever and a spurless hammer. Offered in 9mm and .40 S&W. Barrel length is 4.7". Weight is about 35 oz. Introduced in 2000.

NIB	Exc.	V.G.	Good	Fair	Poor
450	350	300	—	—	—

CZ P-01

Introduced in 2002 this pistol replaced the CZ 75 with the Czech National Police. It features a forged aluminum alloy frame and 3.8" barrel. Decocker single-action/double-action. Fixed sights. Fitted with M3 accessory rail. Rubber grips. Ten-round magazine. Black polycoat finish. Weight is about 29 oz.

NIB	Exc.	V.G.	Good	Fair	Poor
585	450	375	—	—	—

CZ 75 Standard IPSC (ST)

Designed and built for IPSC competition. Chambered for .40 S&W and fitted with a 5.4" barrel. Single-action-only trigger. Special high-profile sights. Weight is about 45 oz.

NIB	Exc.	V.G.	Good	Fair	Poor
1150	850	775	—	—	—

CZ 75 M IPSC

Similar to the CZ 75 Standard IPSC with the addition of a two-port compensator with blast shield to protect frame-mounted optics. Slide racker standard. Red Dot optics. Barrel length is 3.9". Weight is about 45 oz. Introduced in 2001.

NIB	Exc.	V.G.	Good	Fair	Poor
1500	1200	1050	—	—	—

CZ 75 Silver Anniversary Model

This model commemorates the 25th anniversary of the CZ Model 75 pistol. It features a high polish nickel finish with walnut grips. The number "25" is inlaid in the grips. A total of 1000 pistols will be produced with about 500 allocated for the U.S. market.

NIB	Exc.	V.G.	Good	Fair	Poor
700	600	—	—	—	—

CZ 75 Stainless

All steel construction, double-stack magazines, 3-dot fixed sights and chambered for 9mm. 16+1 or 10+1 capacity with 4.72" barrel. The first stainless from CZ. Introduced 2006. MSRP: 565

CZ 75 SP-01 Shadow

Chambered 9mm for IPSC "Production" Division competition. 19+1 capacity, 4.72" barrel. 41 oz., wood grip. Introduced 2006. MSRP: 795

CZ 75 Tactical Sport

Single-action for IPSC competition. Chambered in 9mm and .40 S&W. Dual tone (nickel/blued). Capacity 20+1 (9mm) or 16+1 (.40 S&W). 5.4" barrel; 45 oz. Introduced 2006. MSRP: 1152

CZ 85 B

This model is similar in appearance to the CZ 75 but offers some new features such as ambidextrous safety and slide stop levers, squared trigger guard, adjustable sight, and ribbed slide. Caliber, magazine capacity, and weight are same as CZ 75.

NIB	Exc.	V.G.	Good	Fair	Poor
535	425	300	250	175	125

NOTE: For .40 S&W add $30. For glossy blue add $20, for dual tone finish $25, and for nickel add $25.

CZ 85 Combat

Similar to the CZ 85 but with the addition of adjustable sights, walnut grips, round hammer, and free dropping magazine.

NIB	Exc.	V.G.	Good	Fair	Poor
600	450	325	250	175	125

NOTE: For .40 S&W add $30. For glossy blue add $20, for dual tone finish $25, and for nickel add $25.

CZ 40B

Introduced in 2002 this model is similar to the CZ 75 but features an alloy frame similar in shape to the Colt Model 1911. It is a single-action/double-action design. Barrel length is 4.7". Magazine capacity is 10 rounds. Chambered for the .40 S&W cartridge. Weight is about 35 oz.

NIB	Exc.	V.G.	Good	Fair	Poor
500	400	325	—	—	—

CZ Kadet

Chambered for the .22 LR cartridge and fitted with a 4.7" barrel. This model is a fixed barrel blowback semi-automatic pistol. Adjustable sights and blue finish. Weight is about 36 oz.

NIB	Exc.	V.G.	Good	Fair	Poor
510	400	300	225	—	—

CZ 75 Kadet Conversion

This is a separate conversion kit for the CZ 75/85 series. It converts these pistols to .22 LR. Adjustable rear sight. Supplied with 10-round magazine.

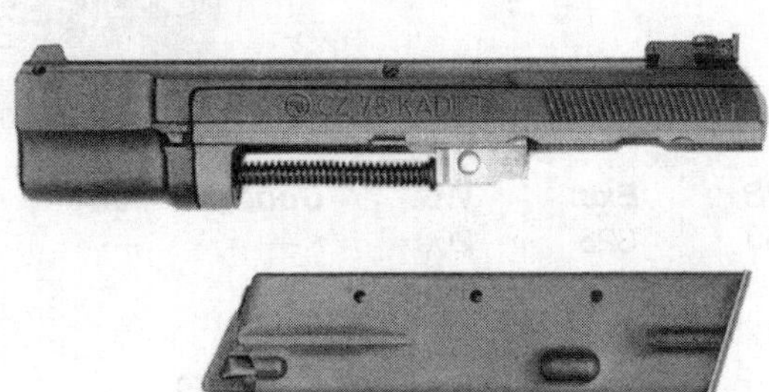

NIB	Exc.	V.G.	Good	Fair	Poor
300	225	200	—	—	—

CZ 2075 RAMI

Introduced in 2004 this 9mm or .40 S&W pistol is fitted with a 3" barrel. It has a single-action/double-action trigger. The design is based on the CZ Model 75. Magazine capacity is 10 rounds for the 9mm and 8 rounds for the .40 S&W. Weight is about 25 oz.

NIB	Exc.	V.G.	Good	Fair	Poor
575	425	—	—	—	—

CZ 83

This is a fixed-barrel .380 caliber pistol. It features an ambidextrous safety and magazine catch behind the trigger guard. The pistol is stripped by means of a hinged trigger guard. Barrel length is 3.8", overall length is 6.8", and weight is about 23 oz.

NIB	Exc.	V.G.	Good	Fair	Poor
420	325	200	175	150	125

NOTE: For nickel finish add $5. In 1993 Special Editions of the above pistols were introduced. These Special Editions consist of special finishes for the then-currently imported CZ pistols. They are high polish blue, nickel, chrome, gold, and a combination of the above finishes. These Special Edition finishes may affect price; they add between $100 and $250 to the cost of the pistol when new.

CZ Engraved Model 75 and Model 83 Pistols

CZ USA imports into this country factory engraved CZ 75 and CZ 83 pistols. These engraved pistols are special order and prices are quoted at the time of the order. It is strongly advised that a qualified appraisal be given before a sale.

Model CZ 75 Grade I

Model CZ 75 Grade II

Model CZ 75 Grade III

Model CZ 83 Grade I

Model CZ 83 Grade II

CZ 97 B

This pistol was planned for production in the summer of 1997. It is chambered for the .45 ACP cartridge. It is fitted with a 4.8" barrel and has a single-action/double-action mode. Magazine capacity is 10 rounds. Wood grips with blue finish. Weight is approximately 40 oz.

NIB	Exc.	V.G.	Good	Fair	Poor
665	525	400	300	—	—

CZ 100

This is a semi-automatic pistol, introduced in 1996, chambered for the 9mm or .40 S&W cartridge. It has a plastic frame and steel slide. Barrel length is 3.75". Weight is approximately 24 oz. U.S. magazine capacity is 10 rounds.

NIB	Exc.	V.G.	Good	Fair	Poor
450	325	200	—	—	—

CZ

Strakonice, Czech Republic

This firm is a separate company from the one located in Uhershy Brod. Prior to the collapse of the Soviet Union both companies were owned and operated by the state.

Model TT 40/45/9

This is semi-automatic pistol chambered for the .40 S&W, .45 ACP, or 9mm cartridges. Fitted with a 3.8" barrel. Trigger is single-action/double-action or double-action-only. Magazine capacity is 10 rounds. Weight is about 26 oz.

NIB	Exc.	V.G.	Good	Fair	Poor
560	425	—	—	—	—

D (anchor) C

(probably either "Dejardine & Cie," "L. Demousse & Cie," or "DeFooze & Cie," all of Liege, Belgium)
SEE—English Military Firearms

D. W. M.

Berlin, Germany
ALSO SEE—Luger & Borchardt

Model 22

A 7.65mm caliber semi-automatic pistol with 3.5" barrel. Blued with walnut grips; later changed to plastic grips. Approximately 40,000 manufactured between 1921 and 1931.

Exc.	V.G.	Good	Fair	Poor
750	675	500	400	250

DAEWOO

Pusan, Korea

DH-40

This semi-automatic pistol is chambered for the .40 S&W cartridge. It has a 4.13" barrel and a magazine capacity of 11 rounds. Weight is approximately 32 oz.

NIB	Exc.	V.G.	Good	Fair	Poor
450	350	300	250	175	100

DP-51B

This semi-automatic pistol is chambered for the 9mm cartridge and is fitted with a 4.13" barrel. Magazine capacity is 13 rounds. Overall length is 7.5" and weight is approximately 28 oz.

NIB	Exc.	V.G.	Good	Fair	Poor
375	325	275	225	175	100

DP-51SB

This is a more compact design with 3.6" barrel and 10-round magazine. Weight is 27 oz. Stainless steel finish.

NIB	Exc.	V.G.	Good	Fair	Poor
400	350	275	225	175	100

DP-51CB

Same as above but fitted with a 3.6" barrel. Magazine capacity is 10 rounds. Weight is about 26 oz.

NIB	Exc.	V.G.	Good	Fair	Poor
425	375	300	250	175	100

DP-52

This semi-automatic pistol is chambered for the .22 LR cartridge. It has a 3.82" barrel length and a magazine capacity of 10 rounds. It operates in double-action and single-action modes. Overall length is 6.7" and weight is approximately 23 oz.

NIB	Exc.	V.G.	Good	Fair	Poor
350	300	250	200	150	100

DH380

Introduced in 1996 this semi-automatic pistol is chambered for the .380 ACP cartridge. It is fitted with a 3.8" barrel and has a magazine capacity of 8 rounds. The firing model is double- or single-action. Weight is approximately 24 oz.

NIB	*Exc.*	*V.G.*	*Good*	*Fair*	*Poor*
375	325	275	225	150	100

DR200

Introduced in 1996 this post-ban semi-automatic rifle is chambered for the .223 Rem. cartridge. It features a black matte finish with a synthetic thumbhole stock. Barrel length is 18.3". Uses AR-15 magazines, not included with the rifle. Weight is about 9 lbs.

NIB	*Exc.*	*V.G.*	*Good*	*Fair*	*Poor*
675	625	500	400	300	150

K-2/AR-100 (Max I)

A 5.56mm caliber pre-ban semi-automatic rifle with an 18" barrel, gas-operated rotary bolt-action, magazines interchangeable with those from the M-16. Black. Introduced in 1985, but is no longer imported.

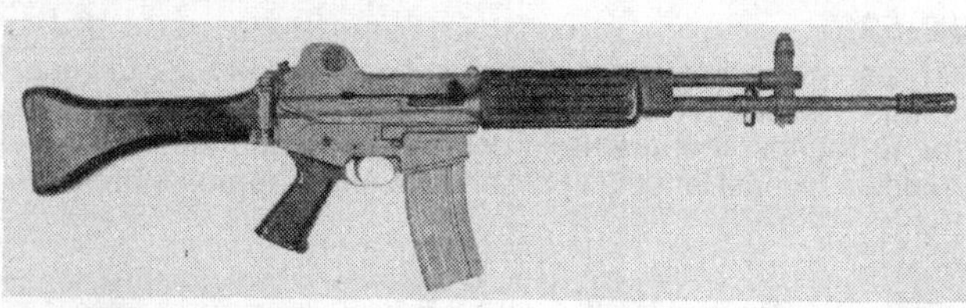

NIB	*Exc.*	*V.G.*	*Good*	*Fair*	*Poor*
1450	1200	950	700	500	400

K1A1 (Max II)

This rifle is quite similar to the K-2/AR-100 but with a folding composite stock.

NIB	*Exc.*	*V.G.*	*Good*	*Fair*	*Poor*
1450	1200	950	700	500	400

DAISY

Rogers, Arkansas

VL Rifle

A .22 combustible cartridge single-shot rifle with an 18" barrel and plastic stock. Cartridge is ignited by compressed air. Manufactured during 1968 and 1969. It is believed that fewer than 20,000 were made.

NIB	*Exc.*	*V.G.*	*Good*	*Fair*	*Poor*
150	100	85	75	50	25

VL Presentation Model

As above, with a walnut stock. Approximately 4,000 were made in 1968 and 1969.

NIB	*Exc.*	*V.G.*	*Good*	*Fair*	*Poor*
225	150	125	100	75	50

VL Cased Presentation Model

As above, with a gold plaque inlaid in the stock and with a fitted case containing 300 VL cartridges.

NIB	*Exc.*	*V.G.*	*Good*	*Fair*	*Poor*
275	200	175	125	100	75

Model 2201/2211

A bolt-action single-shot rifle chambered for .22 LR cartridge. Fitted with a 19" barrel with octagon shroud. Ramp blade front sight with adjustable notch rear sight. Synthetic stock on Model 2211 and walnut stock on Model 2201. Trigger is adjustable. Weight is about 6.5 lbs.

NIB	*Exc.*	*V.G.*	*Good*	*Fair*	*Poor*
150	100	75	60	50	25

Model 2202/2212

Similar to the above model in appearance but fitted with a 10-round rotary magazine. The synthetic stock is Model 2212 and the walnut stock is Model 2202. Weight is about 6.5 lbs.

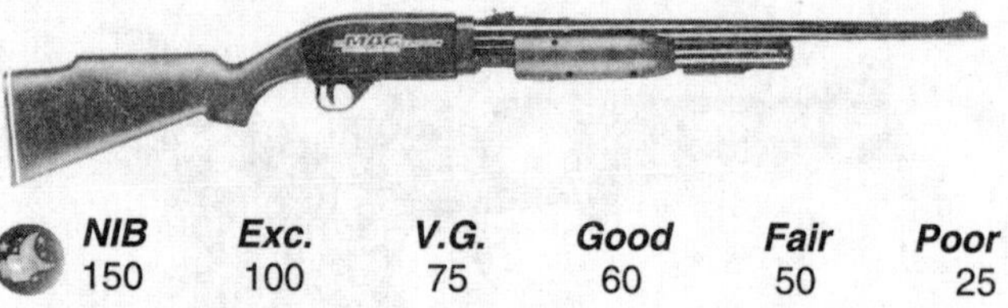

NIB	*Exc.*	*V.G.*	*Good*	*Fair*	*Poor*
150	100	75	60	50	25

Model 2203/2213

This is a semi-automatic rifle chambered for .22 long rifle cartridge. Has a 7-round magazine and a 19" barrel. The synthetic stock is Model 2213 and the walnut stock is Model 2203. Weight is approximately 6.5 lbs.

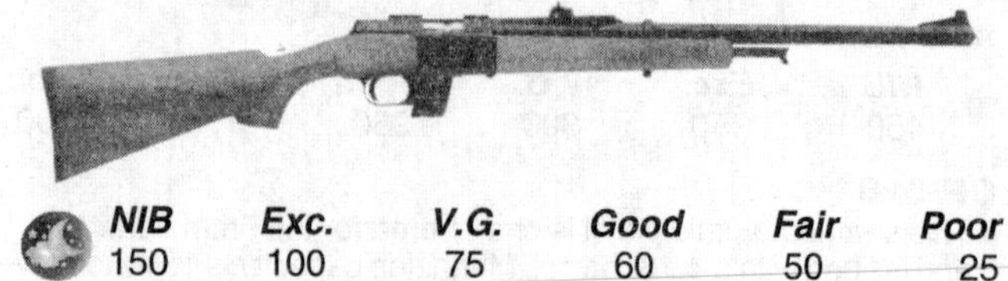

NIB	*Exc.*	*V.G.*	*Good*	*Fair*	*Poor*
150	100	75	60	50	25

DAKIN GUN CO.

San Francisco, California

Model 100

A 12 and 20 gauge boxlock double-barrel shotgun with 26" or 28" barrels, various chokes, extractors and double triggers. Engraved, blued, with a checkered walnut stock. Manufactured in the 1960s.

Exc.	*V.G.*	*Good*	*Fair*	*Poor*
400	325	275	200	100

Model 147

As above, with ventilated rib barrels.

Exc.	*V.G.*	*Good*	*Fair*	*Poor*
450	375	250	200	100

This symbol denotes "Sleepers" with rapidly-rising values and/or significant collector potential.

Model 160

As above with a single-selective trigger.

Exc.	V.G.	Good	Fair	Poor
475	400	350	250	150

Model 215

As above, but more finely finished.

Exc.	V.G.	Good	Fair	Poor
950	850	700	500	250

Model 170

A 12, 16, and 20 gauge Over/Under shotgun with 26" or 28" ventilated rib barrels, various chokes, and double triggers. Blued and lightly engraved. Discontinued in the 1960s.

Exc.	V.G.	Good	Fair	Poor
500	425	350	275	150

DAKOTA ARMS, INC.

Sturgis, South Dakota

This company was formed by Don Allen. He was a fine craftsmen in the field of custom rifles. The company offers four basic models with a number of options to fit the customers' needs or wants. The workmanship and materials are of the highest quality. They have been in business since 1987.

NOTE: All prices are base prices. Dakota offers a number of extra cost options that can greatly affect the value of its rifles and shotguns.

Dakota 76 Classic

A .257 Roberts, .270 Winchester, .280 Remington, .3006, 7mm Remington Magnum, .338, .300 Winchester Magnum, and the .458 Winchester Magnum bolt-action rifle with a 23" barrel, and Mauser-type extractor. Checkered walnut stock. Manufactured in 1987.

NIB	Exc.	V.G.	Good	Fair	Poor
3495	2750	1500	950	800	400

Dakota 76 Varmint

Introduced in 1996 this rifle is chambered for a variety of cartridges from the .22 Hornet to the 6mm PPC. This is a single-shot bolt-action design available in right- or left-hand versions. Barrel length is 24". The Varmint-style stock is semi-fancy walnut with oil finish and no checkering. Many extra cost options are offered for this model. This model is no longer in production as of 1998.

NIB	Exc.	V.G.	Good	Fair	Poor
2500	2200	1650	1100	850	400

Varmint Grade

Offered in a wide variety of calibers from the .222 Rem. to the .22-250 Rem. Furnished with X grade English walnut. This model was discontinued in 1998.

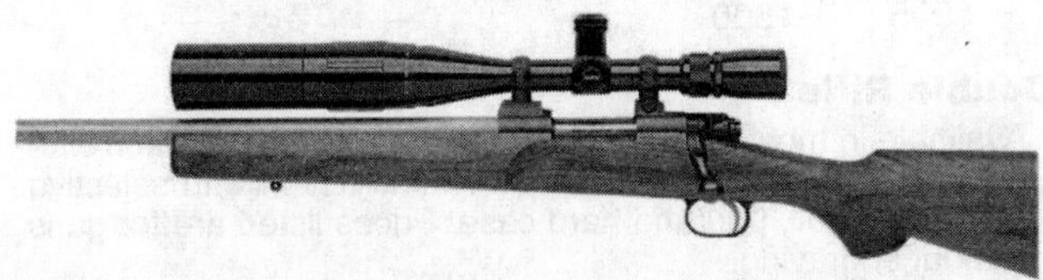

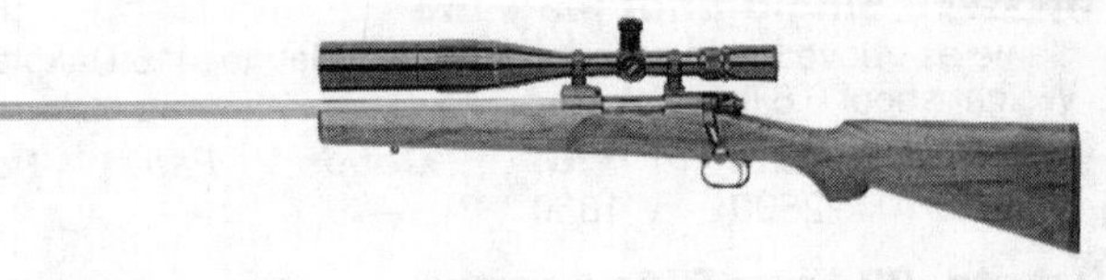

NIB	Exc.	V.G.	Good	Fair	Poor
2000	1850	1500	1200	900	400

Varmint Hunter

This model is built on a Model 97 action. Standard features are fiberglass stock, round-action single-shot, adjustable trigger, and black recoil pad. Barrel length is 24". Offered in calibers from .220 Swift to .308 Winchester. Weight is about 8 lbs. Introduced in 1999.

NIB	Exc.	V.G.	Good	Fair	Poor
1795	1400	1000	—	—	—

Safari Grade

As above, in .375 Holland & Holland, .458 Winchester Magnum, and other short Magnum calibers. Features an ebony forend tip, one-piece magazine assembly and open sights. Weighs approximately 8-1/2 lbs.

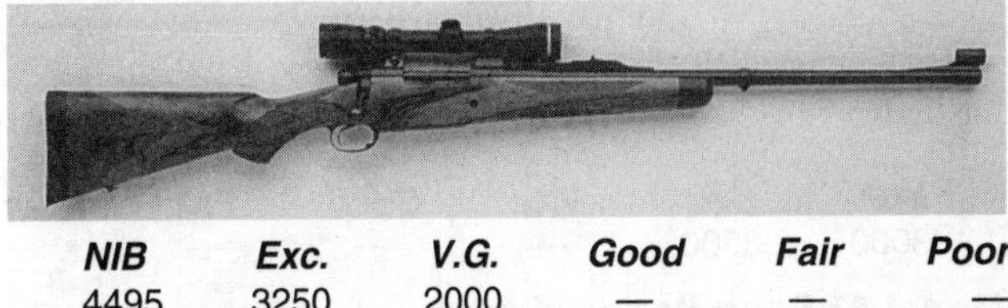

NIB	Exc.	V.G.	Good	Fair	Poor
4495	3250	2000	—	—	—

Alpine Grade

As above, but lighter in weight and chambered for .22-250, .243, 6mm, 250-3000, 7mm/08, .308, and .358. Introduced in 1989. This model is no longer in production.

NIB	Exc.	V.G.	Good	Fair	Poor
1850	1750	1400	1250	800	400

African Grade

As above in .416 Rigby, .416 Dakota, .404 Jeffery, and .450 Dakota with walnut especially selected for strength, with cross-bolts through the stock. Weighs between 9 and 10 lbs.

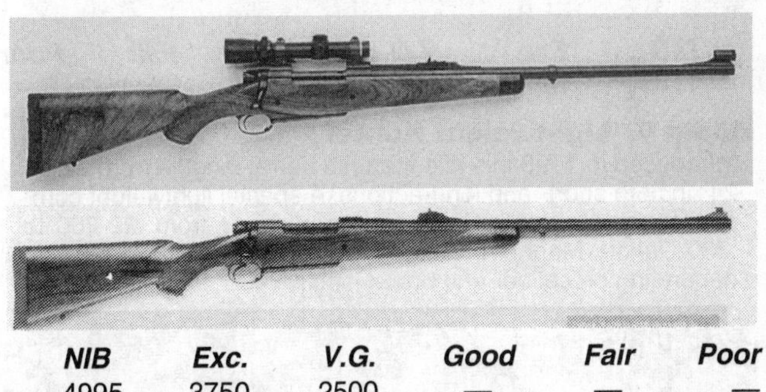

NIB	Exc.	V.G.	Good	Fair	Poor
4995	3750	2500	—	—	—

Model 10 Single-Shot

Built on a single-shot falling action this rifle features a 23" barrel and choice of XX grade wood with oil finish. Fine line checkering, steel gripcap, and 1/2" recoil pad are also standard. Weighs about 5.5 lbs.

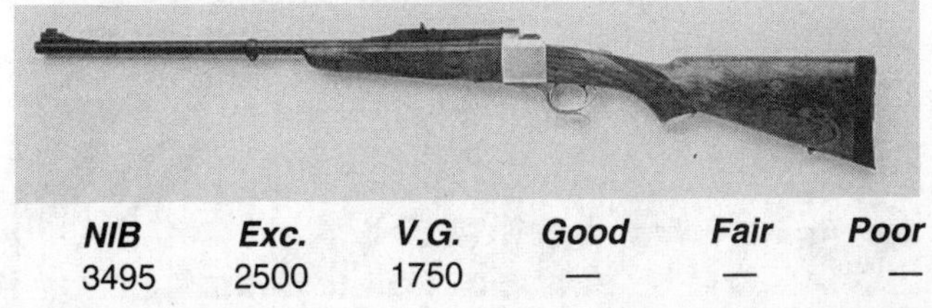

NIB	Exc.	V.G.	Good	Fair	Poor
3495	2500	1750	—	—	—

Model 10 Single-Shot Magnum

Same as above but in calibers .338 Win. Mag to .416 Dakota. Weight about 6.5 lbs.

NIB	Exc.	V.G.	Good	Fair	Poor
3595	2600	1850	—	—	—

Dakota .22 Long Rifle Sporter

Fitted with a 22" barrel and X grade oil finish walnut with fine line checkering and steel gripcap. A 1/2" black recoil pad is standard. Weighs about 6-1/2 lbs. This model ceased production in 1998.

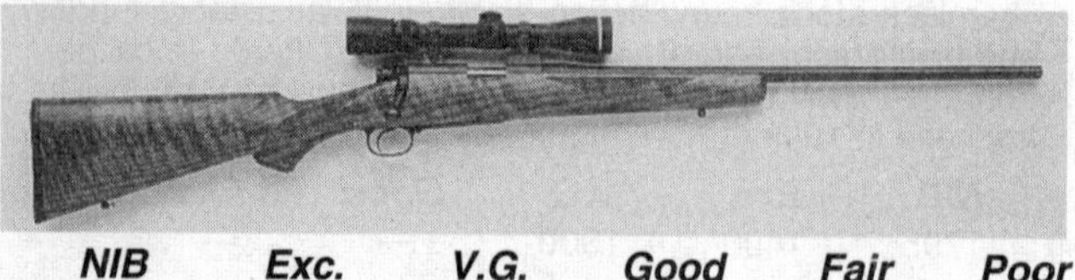

NIB	Exc.	V.G.	Good	Fair	Poor
1250	1000	800	650	500	300

Dakota .22 Long Rifle Sporter (New Model)

This is a reintroduction (2003) of the Dakota .22 rifle.

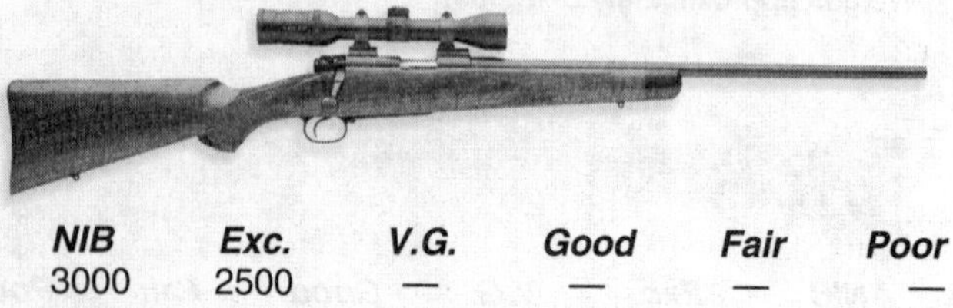

NIB	Exc.	V.G.	Good	Fair	Poor
3000	2500	—	—	—	—

Model 97 Long Range Hunter

Introduced in 1997 this bolt-action rifle is offered in 13 calibers: .250-6, .257 Roberts, .270 Win., .280 Rem., 7mm Rem. Mag., 7mm Dakota Mag., .30-06, .300 Win. Mag., .300 Dakota Mag., .338 Win. Mag., .330 Dakota Mag., .375 H&H, .375 Dakota Mag. Barrel lengths depend on caliber but are either 24" or 26". The trigger is fully adjustable. Many other special features. Stock is black synthetic with one-piece bedding. Black recoil pad is standard. Weight is approximately 7.7 lbs.

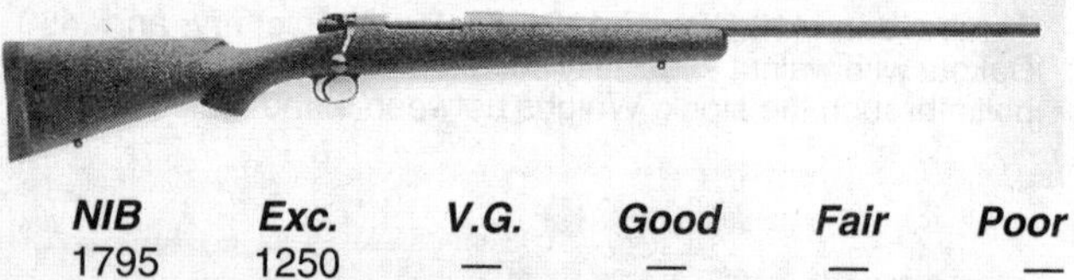

NIB	Exc.	V.G.	Good	Fair	Poor
1795	1250	—	—	—	—

Model 97 Lightweight Hunter

Introduced in 1998 this rifle features barrel lengths from 22" to 24" in both short- and long-actions. A special lightweight composite stock is used. Calibers offered range from .22-250 to .330 Dakota Magnum. Weights are between 6.15 to 6.5 lbs. depending on caliber and barrel length.

NIB	Exc.	V.G.	Good	Fair	Poor
1795	1250	—	—	—	—

Model T-76 Longbow Tactical Rifle

This long range tactical bolt-action rifle is available in 3 calibers: .338 Lapua, .300 Dakota Mag., and .330 Dakota Mag. The fiberglass stock is an A-2 McMillan in black or olive green. Adjustable length of pull with bipod spike in forearm. The 28" stainless steel is .950 diameter at the muzzle with muzzle-brake. The rifle is sold with a number of accessories such as a case with bipod, tool kit and tool box. Weight is about 13.7 lbs.

NIB	Exc.	V.G.	Good	Fair	Poor
4250	3000	—	—	—	—

Model 76 Traveler

This model was introduced in 1999 and is built on a modified Model 76 design and stocked in wood. Disassembly is threadless. It is offered in standard length action, short magnum-action, and long-actions in both left and right hand. Offered in three grades.

Traveler Classic

NIB	Exc.	V.G.	Good	Fair	Poor
4495	3200	—	—	—	—

Traveler Safari

NIB	Exc.	V.G.	Good	Fair	Poor
5495	3900	—	—	—	—

Traveler African

NIB	Exc.	V.G.	Good	Fair	Poor
5995	4500	—	—	—	—

Classic Predator

This bolt action rifle is chambered for the .17 VarTarg, .17 Rem., .17 Tactical, .20 VarTarg, .20 Tactical, .20 PPC, .204 Ruger, .221 Rem. Fireball, .222 Rem., .222 Rem. Mag., .223 Rem., .22 BR, 6 PPC, and the 6 BR. Fitted with a 22" stainless steel barrel, Checkered special select Claro walnut stock with cheekpiece.

NIB	Exc.	V.G.	Good	Fair	Poor
2675	2050	—	—	—	—

Serious Predator

As above but with AAA Claro walnut stock.

NIB	Exc.	V.G.	Good	Fair	Poor
2495	1850	—	—	—	—

All-Weather Predator

As above but with varmint style composite stock.

NIB	Exc.	V.G.	Good	Fair	Poor
1995	1500	—	—	—	—

Double Rifle

Available in most common calibers. Fitted with exhibition walnut with pistol grip. Barrel is 25". Round-action with selective ejectors, recoil, pad and hard case. Prices listed are for guns without engraving.

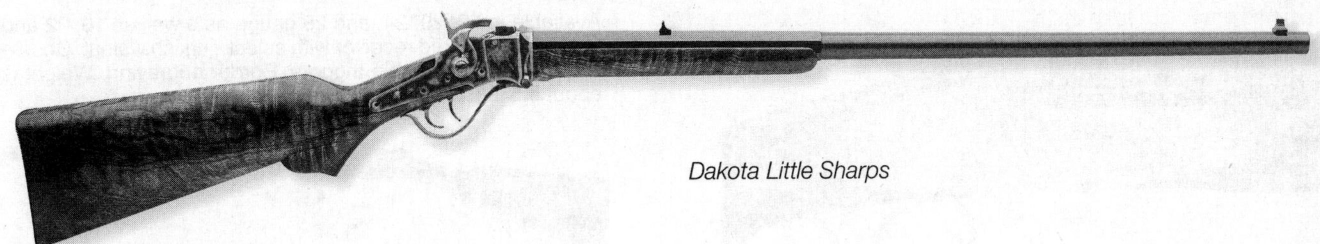

Dakota Little Sharps

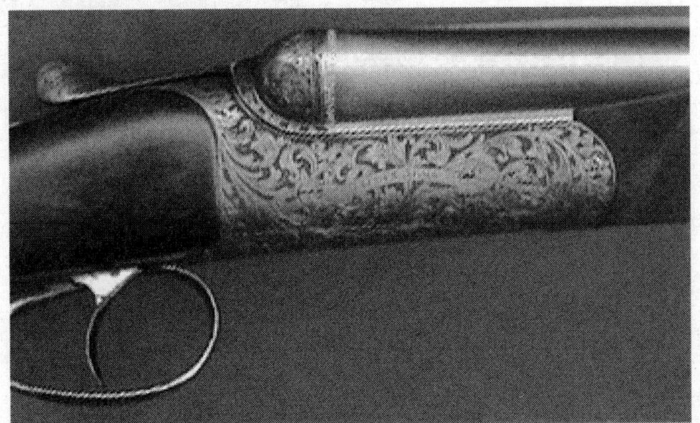

NIB	Exc.	V.G.	Good	Fair	Poor
25000	—	—	—	—	—

Little Sharps Rifle

Introduced in 2003 this is a smaller version (20 percent) of the full size Sharps rifle. Standard rifle has a 26" octagon barrel, straight grips stock with XX walnut, steel buttplate and blade front sight. Offered in calibers from .17 HMR to .30-40 Krag. Weight is around 8 lbs.

NIB	Exc.	V.G.	Good	Fair	Poor
3500	2750	—	—	—	—

Limited Edition .30-06 Model 76

Ultra-decked-out version of Model 76; commemorates 100th anniversary of .30-06 cartridge; production limited to 101 units. Introduced 2006. MSRP: 8945

Limited Edition .30-06 Model 10

Ultra-decked-out version of Model 76; commemorates 100th anniversary of .30-06 cartridge; production limited to 101 units. Introduced 2006. MSRP: 8195

SHOTGUNS

Classic Grade

This grade features a case colored round-action with straight grip and fancy walnut oil finish stock. Forearm is splinter type. Double trigger standard with choice of chokes. This model is no longer in production.

NIB	Exc.	V.G.	Good	Fair	Poor
7950	5200	—	—	—	—

Premier Grade

This grade features a case colored round-action with 50 percent engraving coverage. Exhibition grade English walnut stock with straight grip and splinter forearm. Oil rubbed finish. Double triggers are standard with choice of chokes.

NIB	Exc.	V.G.	Good	Fair	Poor
13950	9500	—	—	—	—

NOTE: Add 10 percent for 28 gauge and .410 bore.

Dakota American Legend

Introduced in 1996, this side-by-side shotgun is offered in 12, 20 and 28 gauge, and .410 bore with 27" barrels, concave rib, splinter forearm, double triggers, straight grips stock, and full scroll engraving on the frame. Many additional extra cost options are offered that can greatly affect the price. The base price is listed.

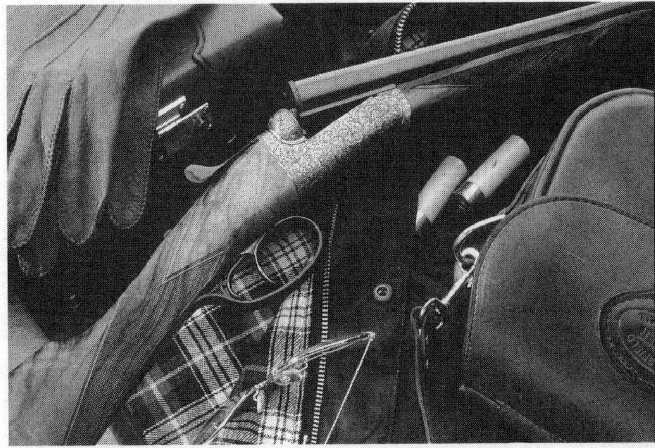

The American Legend

NIB	Exc.	V.G.	Good	Fair	Poor
18000	14000	—	—	—	—

Dakota Shotgun

Similar to the American Legend but offered in two grades of finish. These new grades were first offered in 1997.

DAKOTA ARMS INC.—FERLIB SHOTGUNS

In 2000 Dakota Arms Inc. became the exclusive importer of Ferlib shotgun in the U.S. The models listed are imported and sold by Dakota Arms Inc.

Model 7

NIB	Exc.	V.G.	Good	Fair	Poor
10950	8000	—	—	—	—

Prince Model

NIB	Exc.	V.G.	Good	Fair	Poor
11950	9000	—	—	—	—

Prince Model Side Lever

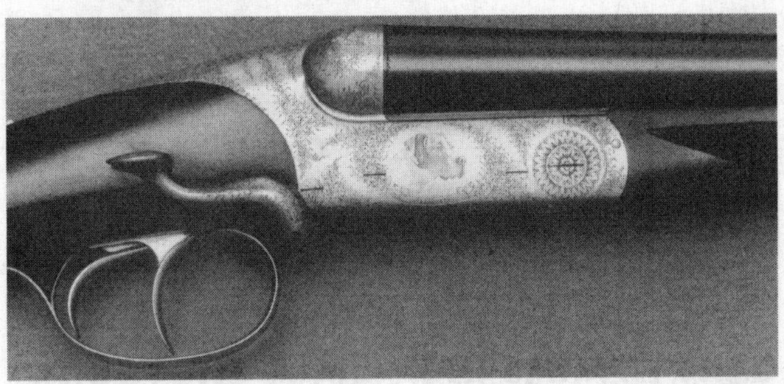

NIB	Exc.	V.G.	Good	Fair	Poor
14500	10500	—	—	—	—

Rex

NIB	Exc.	V.G.	Good	Fair	Poor
14950	11000	—	—	—	—

Premier

NIB	Exc.	V.G.	Good	Fair	Poor
16950	12500	—	—	—	—

Sideplate Model

NIB	Exc.	V.G.	Good	Fair	Poor
14400	10500	—	—	—	—

Sideplate Model with Gold

NIB	Exc.	V.G.	Good	Fair	Poor
15100	11250	—	—	—	—

Sideplate with Scroll

NIB	Exc.	V.G.	Good	Fair	Poor
14000	10500	—	—	—	—

Hammer Gun

NIB	Exc.	V.G.	Good	Fair	Poor
19000	14000	—	—	—	—

H.H. Model—no engraving

NIB	Exc.	V.G.	Good	Fair	Poor
20000	15000	—	—	—	—

Esposizione

NIB	Exc.	V.G.	Good	Fair	Poor
25500	18000	—	—	—	—

L'Inglesina

NIB	Exc.	V.G.	Good	Fair	Poor
25500	18000	—	—	—	—

Model E "Fantasy"

NIB	Exc.	V.G.	Good	Fair	Poor
39500	27500	—	—	—	—

Boss—no engraving

NIB	Exc.	V.G.	Good	Fair	Poor
29500	20000	—	—	—	—

DAKOTA ARMS INC.—SIACE SHOTGUNS

Imported from Italy in 2004 and called the Dakota SuperLight. These shotguns are side-by-sides with boxlock actions.

Field

Available in 12, 20, 24, and 28 gauge as a well as 16, 32 and .410. Case colored receiver with select Turkish walnut. Checkereing is 24 lpi. Double triggers. Border engraving. Weight is about 5.5 lbs. for the 20 gauge.

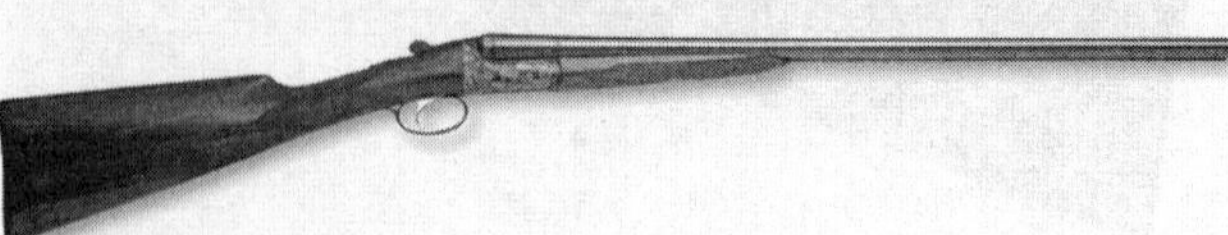

NIB	Exc.	V.G.	Good	Fair	Poor
4500	3500	—	—	—	—

Note: Add $600 for 16, 32, and .410 bores.

Grade II

As above but with 65 percent coverage of English scroll.

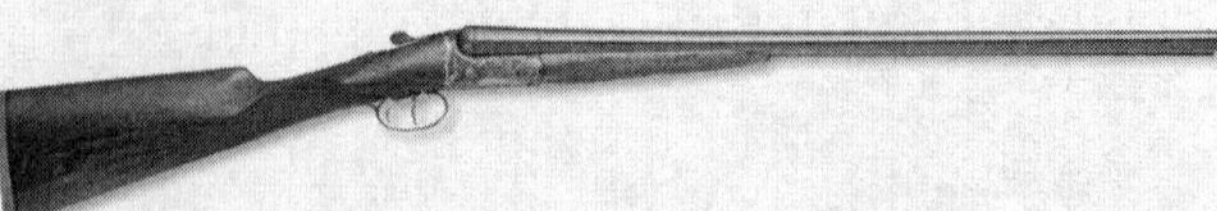

NIB	Exc.	V.G.	Good	Fair	Poor
5500	4250	—	—	—	—

Note: Add $700 for 16, 32, and .410 bores.

Grade III

As above but with deeply cut vine and leaf scroll with deluxe Turkish walnut and 65 percent coverage of English scroll.

NIB	Exc.	V.G.	Good	Fair	Poor
6500	5000	—	—	—	—

Note: Add $800 for 16, 32, and .410 bores.

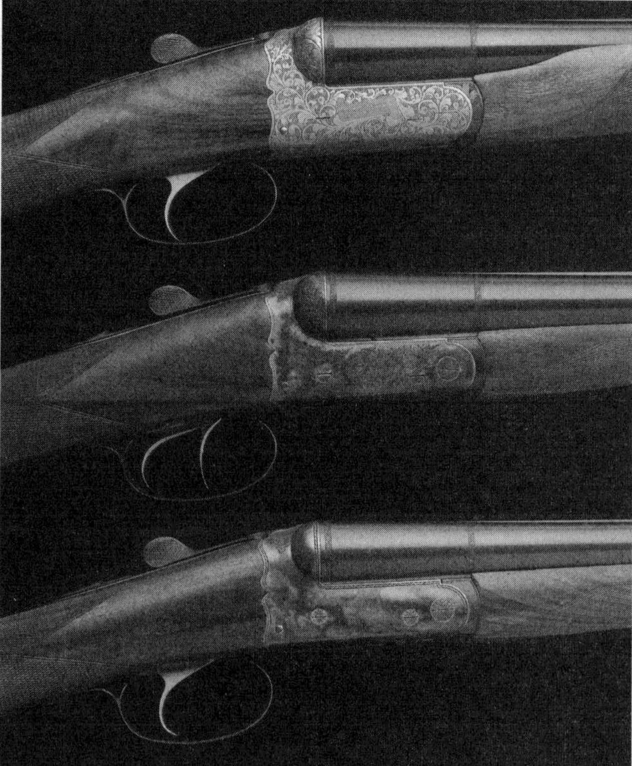

Dakota Grades II, II, and Field from top to bottom

DALY, CHARLES

An importer of German, Japanese, and Italian shotguns and combination guns.

CHARLES DALY, EARLY PRUSSIAN GUNS

Commanidor Over-and-Under Model 100

A boxlock over-and-under Anson & Deeley action shotgun chambered all gauges, choice of barrel length and chokes, double triggers (standard) or single-selective trigger. Blued with a checkered walnut stock. Manufactured in Belgium in the late 1930s.

Exc.	*V.G.*	*Good*	*Fair*	*Poor*
800	600	475	275	200

Commanidor Over-and-Under Model 200

As above, with a better-grade walnut stock.

Exc.	*V.G.*	*Good*	*Fair*	*Poor*
900	700	500	300	200

Superior Side-by-Side

As above, with an Anson & Deeley boxlock action and double triggers. Blued with a walnut stock. Not manufactured after 1933.

Exc.	*V.G.*	*Good*	*Fair*	*Poor*
1200	850	650	450	250

Empire Side-by-Side

As above, but engraved with a better grade of walnut.

Exc.	*V.G.*	*Good*	*Fair*	*Poor*
2500	2000	1750	1250	600

Diamond Grade Side-by-Side

A deluxe version of the above.

Exc.	*V.G.*	*Good*	*Fair*	*Poor*
5000	4500	3750	3000	1200

Regent Diamond Grade Side-by-Side

A custom order version of the above.

Exc.	*V.G.*	*Good*	*Fair*	*Poor*
10000	8500	7000	5500	2500

Empire Over-and-Under

A 12, 16, and 20 gauge Anson & Deeley boxlock shotgun with choice of barrel length and choke, double triggers and automatic ejectors. Engraved with fine quality scrollwork and walnut stock. Discontinued in 1933.

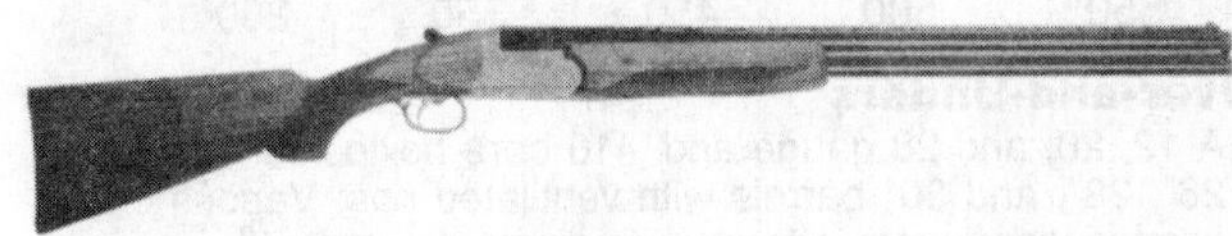

Exc.	*V.G.*	*Good*	*Fair*	*Poor*
2250	2000	1500	1150	500

Diamond Grade Over-and-Under

As above, but more finely finished.

Exc.	*V.G.*	*Good*	*Fair*	*Poor*
5000	4500	3750	3000	1250

SEXTUPLE SINGLE-BARREL TRAP

Empire Grade

A 12 gauge boxlock single-barrel shotgun with 30"-34" Full choke barrels, ventilated rib and automatic ejectors. The strong action features six locking lugs. Engraved with a walnut stock. Manufactured after 1933.

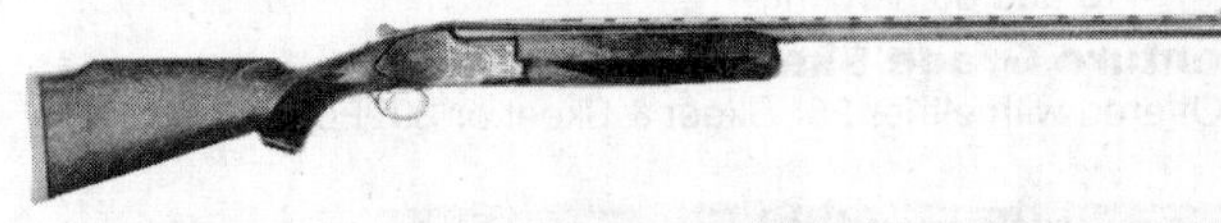

Exc.	*V.G.*	*Good*	*Fair*	*Poor*
2500	2250	1850	1500	750

Regent Diamond Grade

As above, with more engraving and a better grade walnut stock.

Exc.	*V.G.*	*Good*	*Fair*	*Poor*
7000	6300	5500	4500	2000

DRILLINGS

Superior Grade Drilling

A 12, 16, and 20 gauge Over/Under rifle/shotgun with a rifle barrel in .25-20, .25-35, or .30-30. Engraved with a walnut stock. Not manufactured after 1933.

Exc.	*V.G.*	*Good*	*Fair*	*Poor*
2500	2250	1800	1450	800

Diamond Grade Drilling

As above, with more engraving and a better grade of walnut in the stock.

Exc.	*V.G.*	*Good*	*Fair*	*Poor*
4500	4000	3750	3000	1500

Regent Diamond Grade Drilling

As above, with elaborate engraving and the highest quality walnut stock.

Exc.	*V.G.*	*Good*	*Fair*	*Poor*
10000	8500	7200	5800	3000

CHARLES DALY, B.C. MIROKU GUNS

Empire Grade Side-by-Side

A 12, 16, and 20 gauge Anson and Deeley boxlock shotgun with 26", 28", and 30" barrels, various chokes, extractors, and a single trigger. Blued with a checkered walnut stock. Manufactured between 1968 and 1971.

Exc.	*V.G.*	*Good*	*Fair*	*Poor*
600	450	300	200	100

NOTE: Add 10 percent for ventilated rib barrels and/or 20 gauge.

Superior Grade Single Barrel Trap

A 12 gauge boxlock shotgun with 32" or 34" ventilated rib barrels, Full choke, and automatic ejector. Blued with Monte Carlo walnut stock. Manufactured between 1968 and 1976.

Exc.	V.G.	Good	Fair	Poor
550	500	450	350	200

Over-and-Unders

A 12, 20, and 28 gauge and .410 bore boxlock shotgun with 26", 28", and 30" barrels with ventilated ribs. Various choke combinations were offered with single-selective triggers and automatic ejectors. Blued with checkered walnut stocks. The differences between the grades are the degree and quality of the engraving and the grade of walnut used for the stock. The smaller-bore guns bring a premium as listed. Manufactured between 1963 and 1976 by B.C. Miroku.

Venture Grade

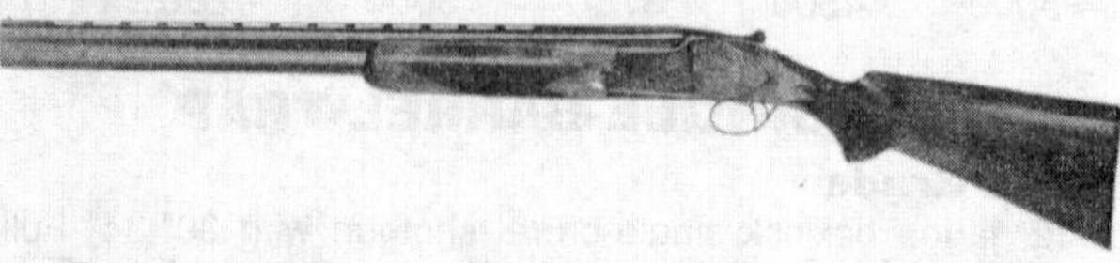

Exc.	V.G.	Good	Fair	Poor
550	500	450	375	200

NOTE: 20 gauge add 10 percent. 28 gauge add 20 percent. .410 add 30 percent.

Venture Grade Skeet or Trap

Offered with either 26" Skeet & Skeet or 30" Full choke.

Exc.	V.G.	Good	Fair	Poor
575	525	475	375	200

NOTE: 20 gauge add 10 percent. 28 gauge add 20 percent. .410 add 30 percent.

Field Grade

Chambered for 12 and 20 gauge only.

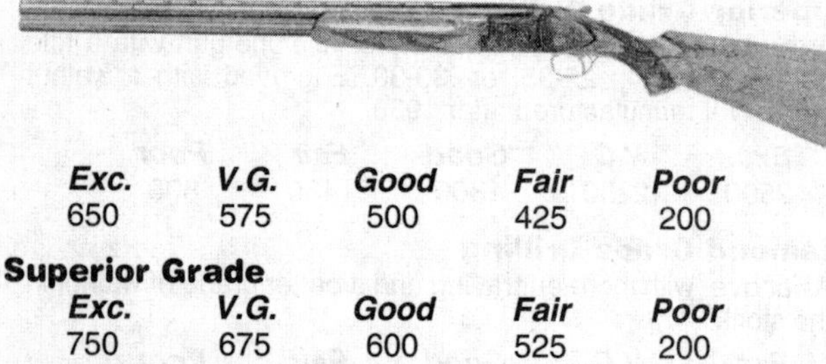

Exc.	V.G.	Good	Fair	Poor
650	575	500	425	200

Superior Grade

Exc.	V.G.	Good	Fair	Poor
750	675	600	525	200

Superior Grade Trap

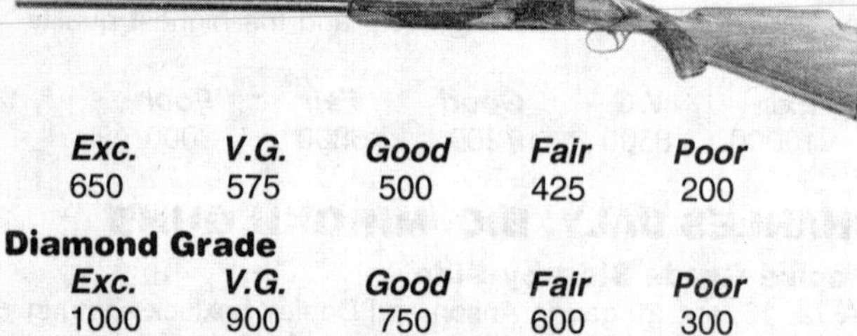

Exc.	V.G.	Good	Fair	Poor
650	575	500	425	200

Diamond Grade

Exc.	V.G.	Good	Fair	Poor
1000	900	750	600	300

Diamond Grade Trap or Skeet

With either 26" Skeet & Skeet or 30" Full choke barrels and Monte Carlo stocks.

Exc.	V.G.	Good	Fair	Poor
1050	950	800	650	350

NOTE: Wide rib add 5 percent.

CHARLES DALY, ITALIAN MANUFACTURE

Manufactured by the firm of Breda in Milan, Italy. The semi-automatic "Novamatic" was produced in 1968. All other models began Italian production in 1976. Imported by KBI, Inc.

SEMI-AUTOMATIC SHOTGUNS

Novamatic Lightweight

A 12 gauge semi-automatic shotgun with a 26" or 28" ventilated-rib barrel and screw-in choke tubes. The receiver is alloy, with checkered walnut stock. Imported under the Daly name in 1968 only.

Exc.	V.G.	Good	Fair	Poor
300	275	225	175	125

Novamatic Trap

As above, with a Monte Carlo stock and a 30" full choke barrel.

Exc.	V.G.	Good	Fair	Poor
350	300	250	200	150

Charles Daly Automatic

A 12 gauge Magnum semi-automatic shotgun with 26" or 28" ventilated rib barrels, screw-in choke tubes and a 5-shot magazine. There is a slug gun available with rifle sights. Checkered walnut grip in two versions—a pistol grip and an English-style straight grip.

Exc.	V.G.	Good	Fair	Poor
375	325	275	225	150

NOTE: The choke-tube model would be worth a 10 percent premium.

Field Grade

Introduced in 1999, this model has several variations all in 12 gauge. The standard gun has a choice of 24", 26", 28", or 30" barrels with screw-in chokes and synthetic stocks. A slug gun is offered with 22" barrel in blue or nickel finish. A full coverage camo model is offered in the same configurations as the field grade.

NIB	Exc.	V.G.	Good	Fair	Poor
390	300	225	—	—	—

NOTE: Add $30 for nickel slug gun, add $100 for camo gun.

Superior Grade Hunter

Offered in 12 gauge with choice of 26", 28", or 30" vent-rib barrels. Walnut stock with hand checkering. Gold trigger and gold highlights. Introduced in 1999.

NIB	Exc.	V.G.	Good	Fair	Poor
540	400	—	—	—	—

Superior Grade Sporting

Same as above but with a 28" or 30" ported barrel and select walnut stock.

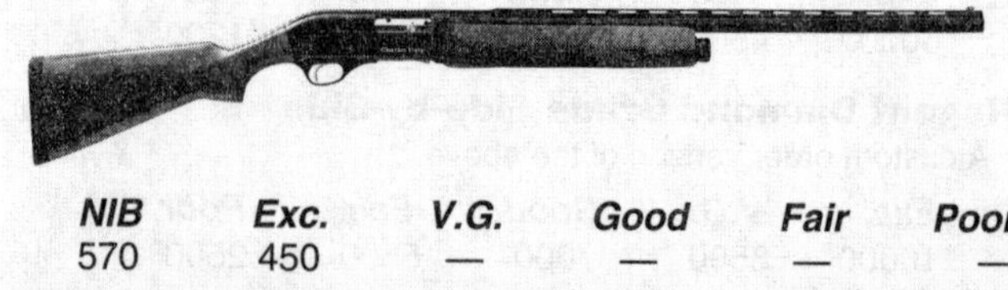

NIB	Exc.	V.G.	Good	Fair	Poor
570	450	—	—	—	—

Superior Grade Trap

This 12 gauge model is offered with a choice of 30" or 32" vent-rib barrel. Walnut stock with hand checkering. Introduced in 1999.

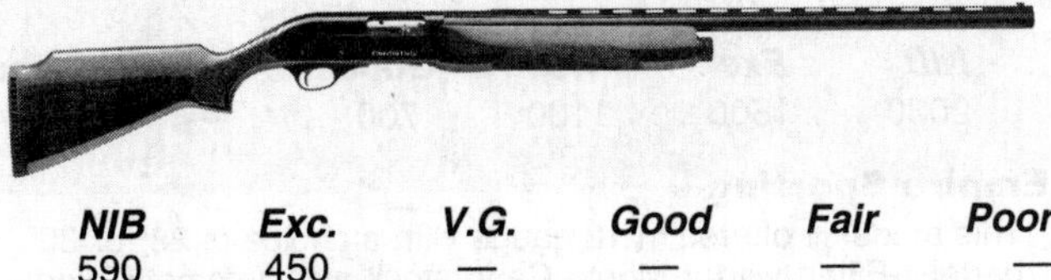

NIB	Exc.	V.G.	Good	Fair	Poor
590	450	—	—	—	—

Field Hunter VR-MC

This series of 3" semi-automatic 12 gauges is finished in one of four Realtree/Advantage camo patterns or matte black. Barrels are 24", 26" or 28". Advantage Timber model is available in 20 gauge and black matte is available in 20 and 28 gauge. Add 15 percent for camo.

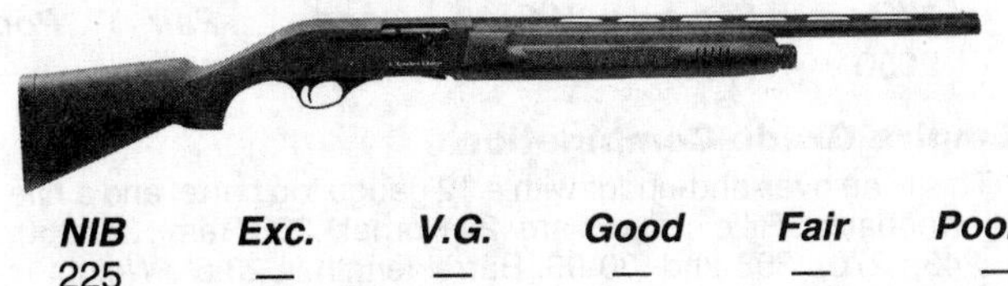

NIB	Exc.	V.G.	Good	Fair	Poor
225	—	—	—	—	—

Field Hunter VR-MC Youth

As above but with a 1.6-inch shorter stock and 22" barrel. In 20 gauge only.

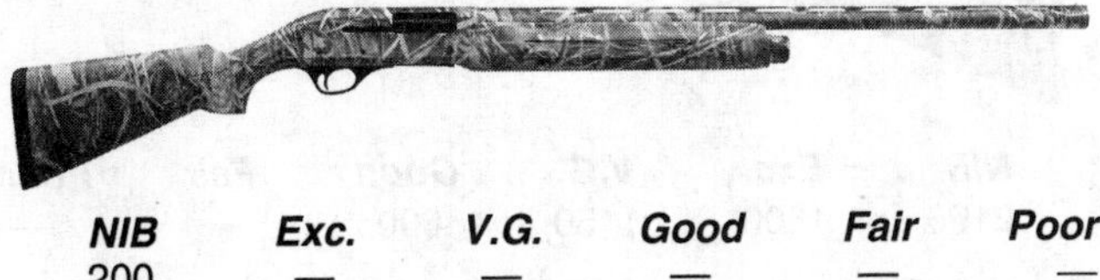

NIB	Exc.	V.G.	Good	Fair	Poor
200	—	—	—	—	—

Superior II

New in 2007, the Superior II line of semi-autos features oil-finished Turkish walnut stocks and three chokes.

NIB	Exc.	V.G.	Good	Fair	Poor
325	—	—	—	—	—

Superior II Hunter

Available in 12 and 20 gauge with 26" or 28" barrel and 28 gauge with 26" barrel.

NIB	Exc.	V.G.	Good	Fair	Poor
300	—	—	—	—	—

Superior II Sport

In 12 gauge only with 28" or 30" ported barrel and wide rib.

NIB	Exc.	V.G.	Good	Fair	Poor
300	—	—	—	—	—

Superior II Trap

In 12 gauge, 30" ported barrel only with Monte Carlo comb and wide rib.

NIB	Exc.	V.G.	Good	Fair	Poor
350	—	—	—	—	—

Field Hunter Maxi-Mag VR-MC Semi-Auto

This 3.5" 12 gauge comes in one of three Realtree/Advantage camos and matte black with 24", 26" or 28" ported barrel. MSRP: Add 15 percent for camo.

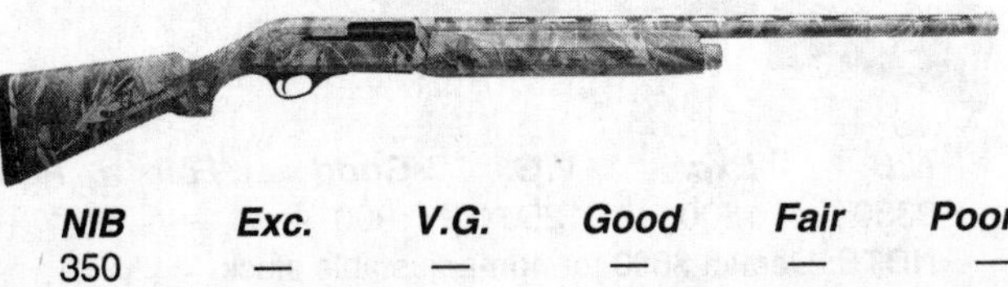

NIB	Exc.	V.G.	Good	Fair	Poor
350	—	—	—	—	—

TURKISH SHOTGUNS

Model 105

This 3" 12 gauge over-and-under features an engraved nickel-plated steel receiver, double triggers and extractors. Chokes are fixed Modified and Full with 28" barrels or Modified and Improved Cylinder with 26" barrels.

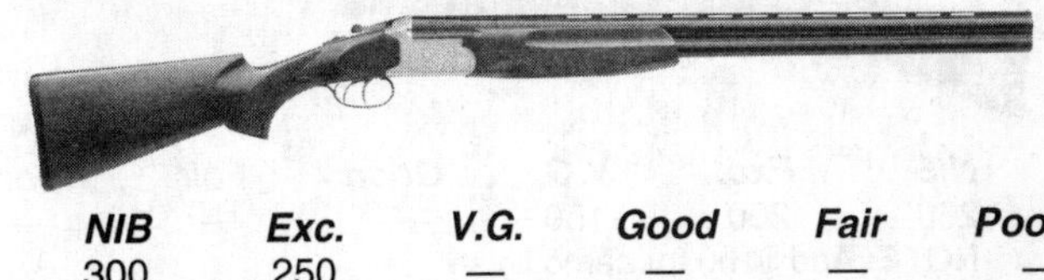

NIB	Exc.	V.G.	Good	Fair	Poor
300	250	—	—	—	—

Model 106

Similar to Model 105 but in 12, 20 and 28 gauge and .410 bore. The Model 106 has a blued receiver with raised gold ducks and a rounded pistol grip. All but the .410 include three screw-in chokes. Barrels are 26" or 28" in 12 and 20 gauge and 26" in 28 gauge and .410. Frames are scaled to gauge. Add $50 for 28 and .410.

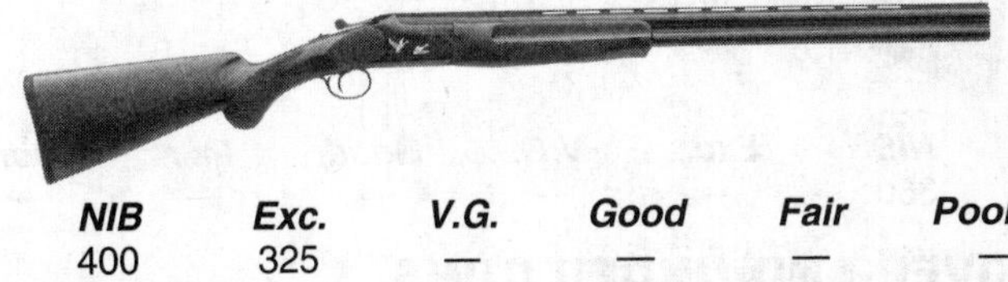

NIB	Exc.	V.G.	Good	Fair	Poor
400	325	—	—	—	—

Model 306

This 3" side-by-side is offered in 12 and 20 gauge with 26" or 28" barrels. Turkish walnut stock, gold-plated single selective trigger and extractors. Three choke tubes.

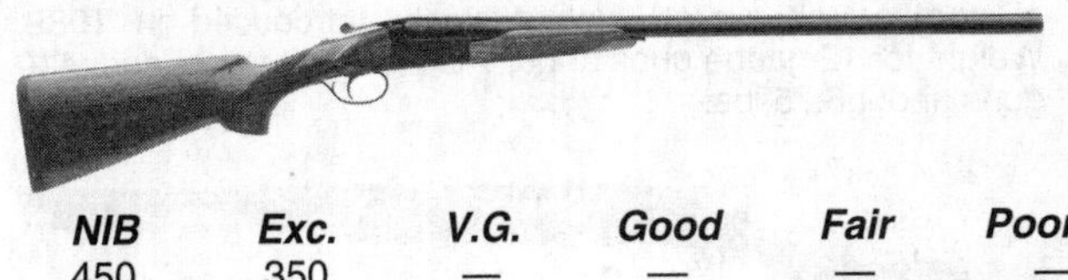

NIB	Exc.	V.G.	Good	Fair	Poor
450	350	—	—	—	—

PUMP SHOTGUNS

Field Grade

This 12 gauge pump gun is offered with 24", 26", 28", or 30" barrels. With fixed chokes. A slug gun is offered with 18.5" barrels with blue or nickel finish. A camo version is also offered. First introduced in 1999. This model is also offered in 20 gauge in both full size and youth.

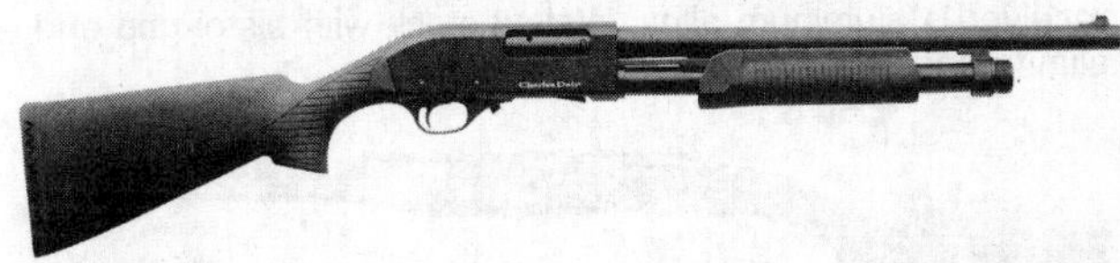

NIB	Exc.	V.G.	Good	Fair	Poor
240	190	—	—	—	—

NOTE: Add $10 for nickel gun, add $80 for full camo gun.

Field Tactical

This pump gun is chambered for the 12 gauge shell and fitted with an 18.5" barrel with fixed blade front sight. An 18.5" slug barrel with adjustable sights is also offered. Black synthetic stock. Blued or nickel finish.

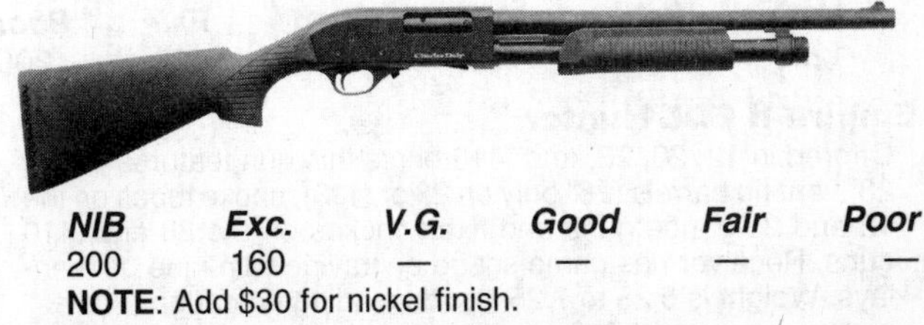

NIB	Exc.	V.G.	Good	Fair	Poor
200	160	—	—	—	—

NOTE: Add $30 for nickel finish.

Field Hunter MM (Maxi-Mag)

This is a 12 gauge pump gun chambered for the 3.5" Magnum shell. Offered with choice of 24", 26", or 28" vent-rib ported barrels. Black synthetic stock with camo stock also available. Weight is about 6.75 lbs.

NIB	Exc.	V.G.	Good	Fair	Poor
260	200	150	—	—	—

NOTE: Add $100 for camo finish.

Field Hunter Maxi-Mag VR-MC Pump

Newer versions of the Maxi-Mag are recognized by an updated forend and availability in Timber or Hardwoods camo or matte black. All are 3.5" 12 gauges with a 24", 26" or 28" ported barrel. Add 15 percent for camo.

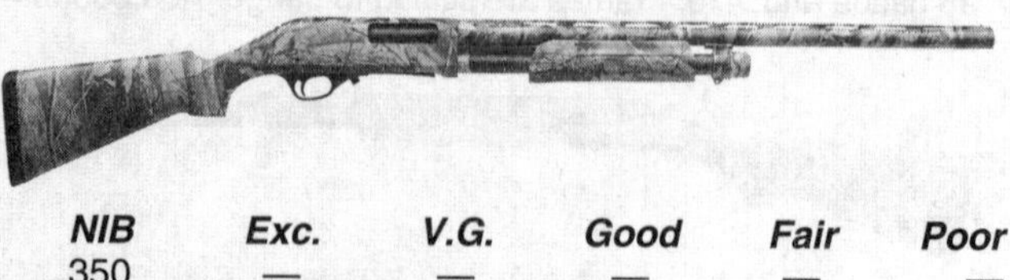

NIB	Exc.	V.G.	Good	Fair	Poor
350	—	—	—	—	—

OVER-AND-UNDER GUNS

Charles Daly Field Grade Over-and-Under

A 12, 20, 28, and .410 gauge over-and-under shotgun with 26" or 28" chrome-lined ventilated rib barrels with a crossbolt boxlock-action, single-selective trigger, and extractors. Blued with a stamped checkered walnut stock. Introduced in 1989. Weight for 12 gauge guns about 7 lbs. Weight for 28 and .410 guns about 6.75 lbs.

NIB	Exc.	V.G.	Good	Fair	Poor
1030	775	575	400	250	200

NOTE: Add $150 for ejectors.

Charles Daly Field Ultra Light

Introduced in 1999, this model is offered in either 12 or 20 gauge with 26" barrel choked Improved Cylinder/Modified. The receiver is aluminum alloy. Walnut stock with pistol grip and slim forend. Weight is approximately 5.5 lbs.

NIB	Exc.	V.G.	Good	Fair	Poor
1200	900	650	450	—	—

Charles Daly Empire Over-and-Under

As above with automatic ejectors, screw-in choke tubes, and a silver-finished receiver. The walnut stock is hand-checkered. Introduced in 1989.

NIB	Exc.	V.G.	Good	Fair	Poor
1250	1000	750	500	400	200

Empire II EDL Hunter

Offered in 12, 20, 28, and .410 bores this gun features 26" or 28" vent rib barrels (26" only on 28 or .410), choke tubes on the 12 and 20 gauge guns and fixed chokes on the 28 and .410 guns. Receiver has game scene engraving with nine gold enlays. Weight is 6.25 to 7.25 lbs. depending on gauge.

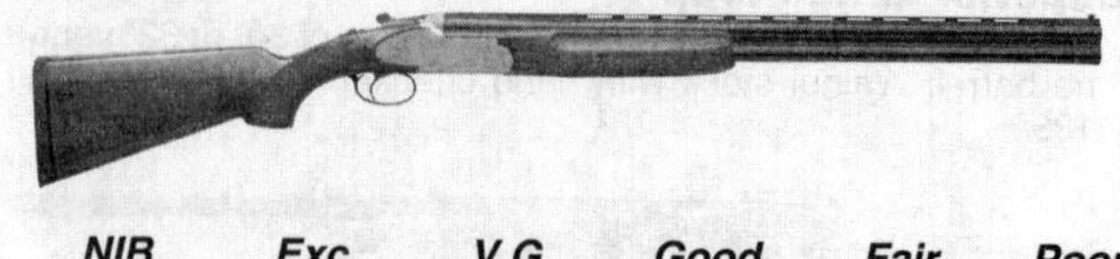

NIB	Exc.	V.G.	Good	Fair	Poor
2030	1500	1100	700	—	—

Empire Sporting

This model is offered in 12 gauge with a choice of 28" or 30" barrels. Fitted with a Monte Carlo stock and automatic ejectors.

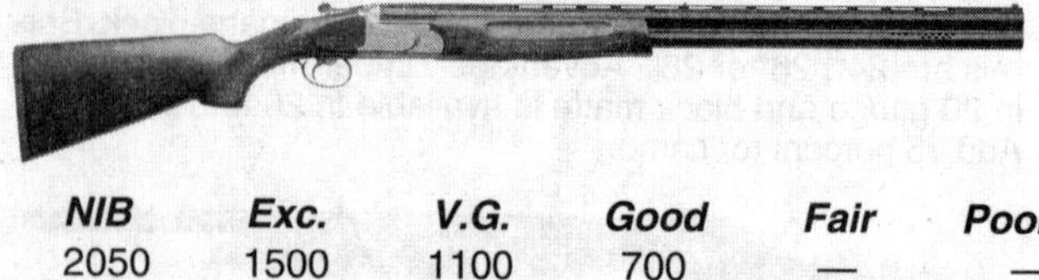

NIB	Exc.	V.G.	Good	Fair	Poor
2050	1500	1100	700	—	—

Empire Grade Combination

This is an over-and-under with a 12 gauge top barrel and a rifle lower barrel. Rifle calibers are .22 Hornet, .223 Rem., .22-250, .243, .270, .308 and .30-06. Barrel length is 23.5". Weight is about 7.25 lbs.

NIB	Exc.	V.G.	Good	Fair	Poor
2190	1600	1150	800	—	—

Empire Express

Chambered for the .30-06, .375H&H, or .416 Rigby cartridge with open sights and dovetail receiver for scope mounting. Barrel length is 23.5". Checkered walnut stock with Bavarian-style cheekpiece. Silver game scene engraved receiver. Weight is about 8 lbs.

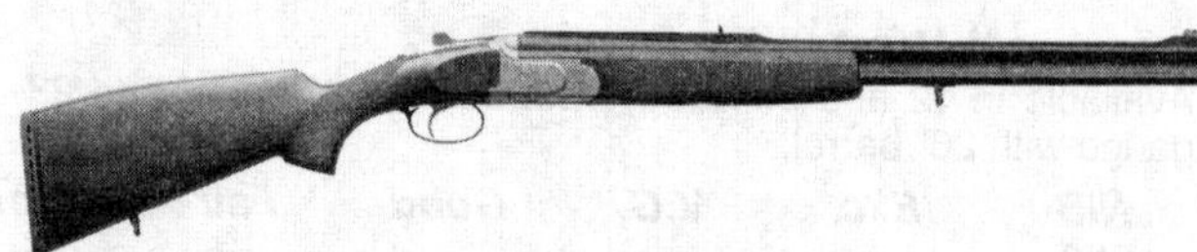

NIB	Exc.	V.G.	Good	Fair	Poor
2950	2200	—	—	—	—

NOTE: Add $700 for .375H&H and .416 Rigby models.

Empire Trap

This 12 gauge model features a Monte Carlo stock with 30" barrels.

NIB	Exc.	V.G.	Good	Fair	Poor
2100	1550	1150	750	—	—

Empire Trap Mono

This is a single barrel trap gun with choice of 30" or 32" barrels. Automatic ejectors and Monte Carlo fully adjustable stock.

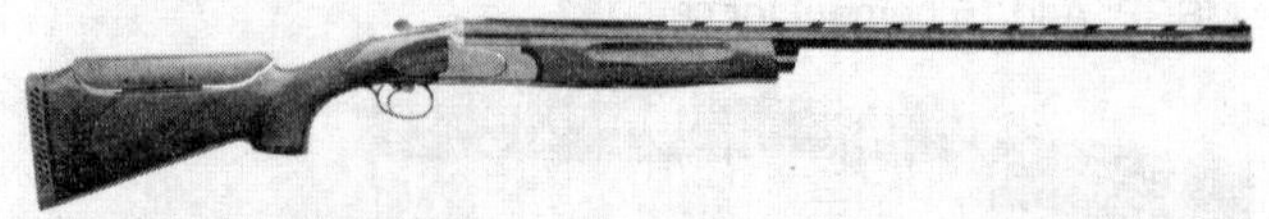

NIB	Exc.	V.G.	Good	Fair	Poor
2350	1800	1250	900	—	—

NOTE: Deduct $600 for non-adjustable stock.

Empire Grade Trap Combo

This model features a 30" over/under barrel with an additional 32" single barrel. Buttstock has fully adjustable comb. Introduced in 1999.

NIB	Exc.	V.G.	Good	Fair	Poor
3920	2900	2000	—	—	—

NOTE: Deduct $600 for non-adjustable stock.

Diamond Grade Over-and-Under

As above in 12 and 20 gauge Magnum with various barrel lengths and screw-in choke tubes, single trigger, automatic ejectors, and select walnut stock. Extra fancy walnut stock and hand engraved frame.

NIB	Exc.	V.G.	Good	Fair	Poor
5400	4250	2500	1250	900	450

Diamond Grade Sporting

This 12 gauge model features a choice of 28" or 30" barrels with automatic ejectors and Monte Carlo stock.

NIB	Exc.	V.G.	Good	Fair	Poor
5600	4500	2750	1250	—	—

Diamond Grade Trap or Skeet

As above, with 26" or 30" barrels. Available in 1989.

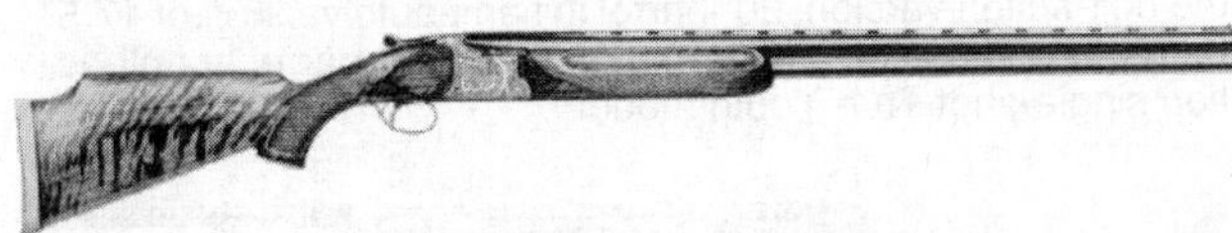

NIB	Exc.	V.G.	Good	Fair	Poor
5200	4000	1750	950	500	250

Diamond Grade Mono

This model has a fully adjustable stock. Barrel choice is 30". Automatic ejectors are standard.

NIB	Exc.	V.G.	Good	Fair	Poor
6300	5000	3500	2000	—	—

Diamond Grade Trap Combo

This model has a fully adjustable stock. Choice of 30" over/under barrels and 32" single barrel.

NIB	Exc.	V.G.	Good	Fair	Poor
7100	5500	4000	2500	—	—

Presentation Grade Over-and-Under

As above, with a Purdy-type boxlock action and engraved false sideplates. The stock is of deluxe French walnut. Discontinued in 1986.

Exc.	V.G.	Good	Fair	Poor
5000	3500	1500	900	450

Superior Over-and-Under

A 12, 20, 28, and .410 gauge over-and-under shotgun with 26" or 28" ventilated rib barrels, various chokes, single trigger, and automatic ejectors. Engraved, blued with a walnut stock. Weight for 12 and 20 gauge guns about 7 lbs. For 28 and .410 guns weight is about 6.75 lbs.

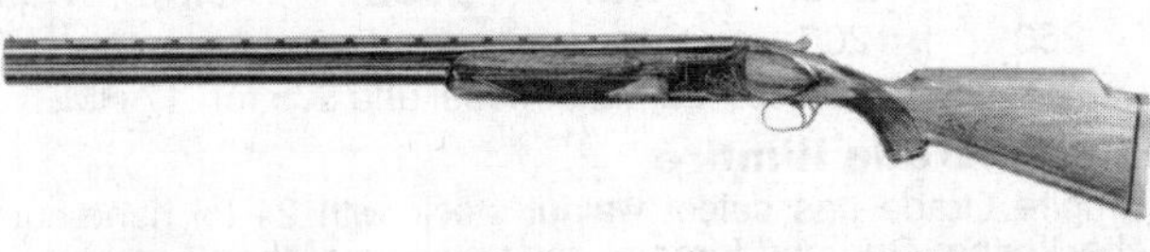

NIB	Exc.	V.G.	Good	Fair	Poor
1520	1100	800	550	350	200

Superior Grade Sporting

This 12 gauge model is fitted with a choice of 28" or 30" barrels. Monte Carlo stock and automatic ejectors.

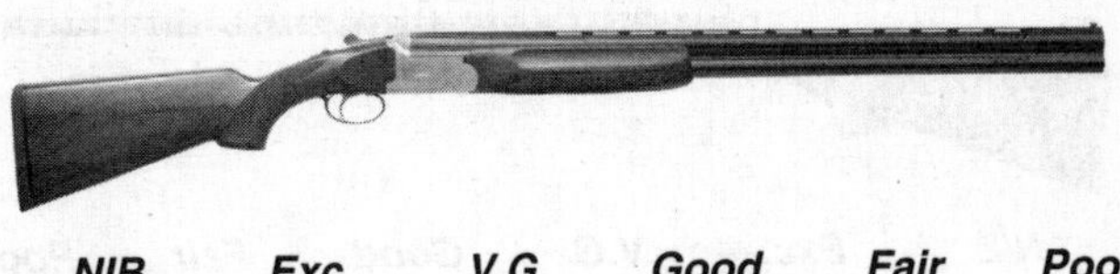

NIB	Exc.	V.G.	Good	Fair	Poor
1660	1200	875	600	400	—

Superior Grade Trap

This 12 gauge gun is fitted with 30" barrels, Monte Carlo stock and automatic ejectors.

NIB	Exc.	V.G.	Good	Fair	Poor
1700	1250	900	625	425	—

Superior Grade Combination

This is an over-and-under with a 12 gauge top barrel and a rifle lower barrel. Rifle calibers are .22 Hornet, .223 Rem., and .30-06. Barrel length is 23.5". Weight is about 7.25 lbs.

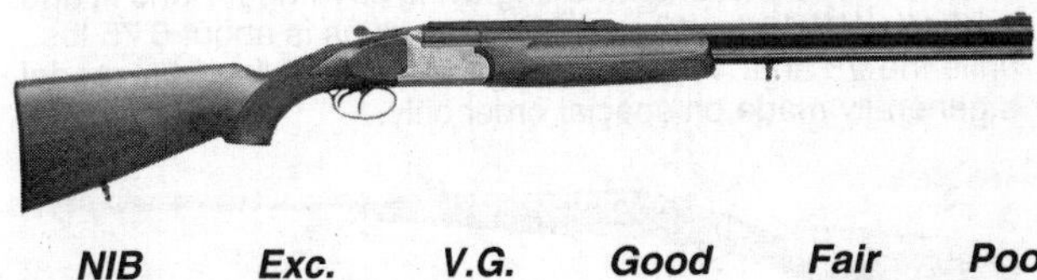

NIB	Exc.	V.G.	Good	Fair	Poor
1480	1100	800	550	350	—

Superior Grade Express

Chambered for the .30-06 cartridge and fitted with 23.5" barrel. Open sights with dovetail receiver for scope mounting. Silver receiver with game scene engraving. Checkered walnut stock with sling swivels. Weight is about 7.75 lbs.

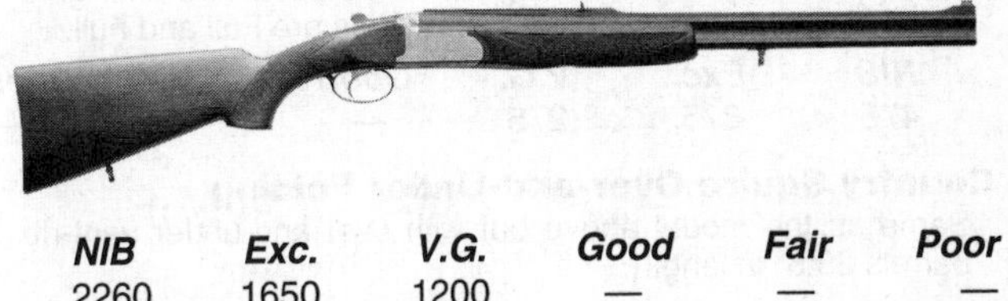

NIB	Exc.	V.G.	Good	Fair	Poor
2260	1650	1200	—	—	—

SIDE-BY-SIDE GUNS

Field Hunter

A side-by-side boxlock gun chambered for 10, 12, 20, 28 and .410. Barrel length from 26" to 32" depending on gauge. Extractors are standard. Add $100 for ejectors. Weight from 8.75 lbs. to 6.75 lbs. depending on gauge. Nickel receiver with game scene engraving.

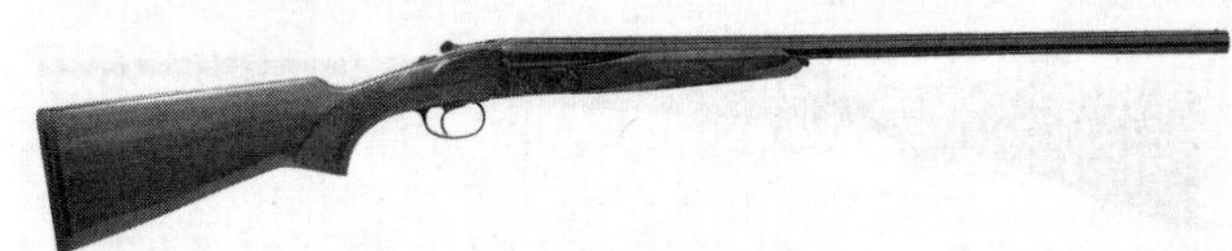

NIB	Exc.	V.G.	Good	Fair	Poor
1190	850	600	400	250	—

NOTE: Add $40 for 28 and .410 guns, add $100 for automatic ejectors.

Superior Hunter

A 12, 20, and 28 gauge as well as .410 bore boxlock double-barrel shotgun with 26" or 28" barrels, various chokes, a boxlock action and single trigger. Blued with a walnut stock. In 2002 this model was offered in 10 gauge with 28" barrels.

NIB	Exc.	V.G.	Good	Fair	Poor
1660	1200	850	600	—	—

NOTE: Add $50 for 28 and .410 gauge guns.

Empire Side-by-Side

Offered in 12 and 20 gauge with 26" or 28" barrels. Chokes are fixed. Weight is about 7 lbs. Silver receiver with game scene engraving, straight stock, splinter forearm, automatic ejectors.

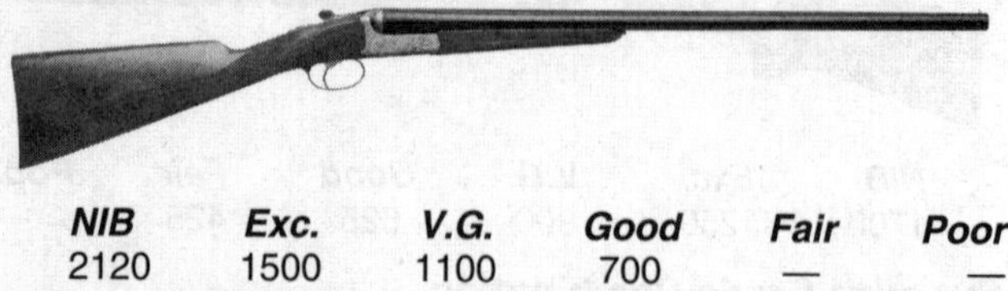

NIB	Exc.	V.G.	Good	Fair	Poor
2120	1500	1100	700	—	—

Diamond Side-by-Side

Offered in 12, 20, 28, and .410 with 26" or 28" barrels and fixed chokes. Fancy walnut straight grip stock, hand detachable sidelocks, 100 percent hand engraving coverage. Hand fit and finished. Weight for 12 and 20 gauge guns is about 6.75 lbs., while the 28 and .410 guns weigh about 5.75 lbs. This model is generally made on special order only.

NIB	Exc.	V.G.	Good	Fair	Poor
6700	5000	3500	1500	—	—

NOTE: Add $450 for 28 and .410 bores.

Country Squire Side-by-Side Folding

This model features a folding stock with 25.5" barrels, gold double triggers and walnut stock. Chokes are Full and Full.

NIB	Exc.	V.G.	Good	Fair	Poor
475	375	275	—	—	—

Country Squire Over-and-Under Folding

Same as the model above but with over-and-under vent-rib barrels 25.5" in length.

NIB	Exc.	V.G.	Good	Fair	Poor
550	450	325	—	—	—

RIFLES

Field Grade Mauser 98

This bolt-action rifle is offered in a wide variety of calibers from .243 Win. to .458 Win. Mag. Barrel length is 23" for all calibers. Stock is black synthetic. Open sights. Add $175 for .375 H&H and .458 Win. Mag.

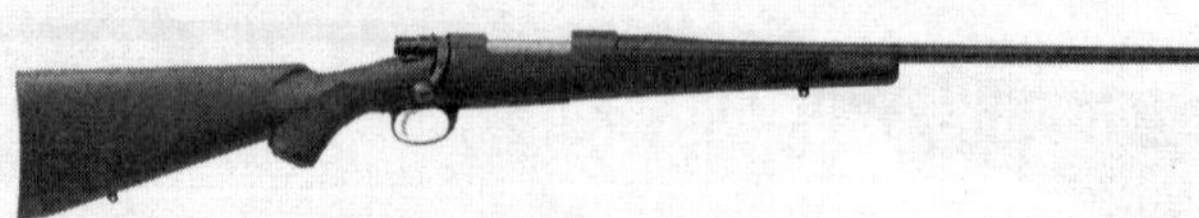

NIB	Exc.	V.G.	Good	Fair	Poor
460	350	300	—	—	—

NOTE: Add $50 for stainless steel.

Field Grade Mini-Mauser 98

This version is chambered for short cartridges such as the .22 Hornet, .223, .22-250, and 7.62x39mm. Barrel length is 19.25". Magazine capacity is 5 rounds.

NIB	Exc.	V.G.	Good	Fair	Poor
600	475	350	—	—	—

Superior Grade Mauser 98

This model is similar to the Field Grade Mauser with the addition of a hand-checkered walnut stock.

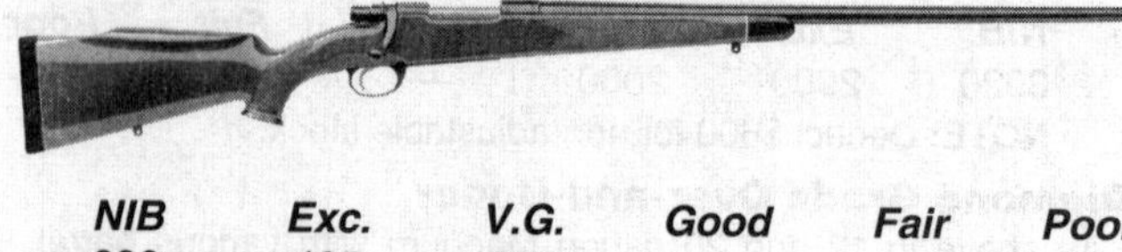

NIB	Exc.	V.G.	Good	Fair	Poor
600	425	325	—	—	—

Superior Grade Mini-Mauser 98

Same as the Field Grade Mini-Mauser with the addition of a hand-checkered walnut stock.

NIB	Exc.	V.G.	Good	Fair	Poor
600	450	325	—	—	—

Field Grade Rimfires

Chambered for .22 LR cartridge and fitted with a 22" barrel in the bolt-action version, 20" barrel in semi-auto version or 17.5" barrel in bolt-action. Youth model, or 16.25" barrel in bolt-action single-shot True Youth model.

NIB	Exc.	V.G.	Good	Fair	Poor
120	100	—	—	—	—

NOTE: Add $25 for True Youth model.

Superior Grade Rimfire

Chambered for .22 LR or .22 Mag, or .22 Hornet in bolt-action or .22 LR semi-auto. Walnut stock with checkering. Open sights.

NIB	Exc.	V.G.	Good	Fair	Poor
175	125	—	—	—	—

NOTE: Add $20 for .22 Mag. model and $170 for .22 Hornet model.

Superior II Grade Rimfire

This version was introduced in 2005 and is chambered for the .22 Long Rifle, .22 WMR, or the .17 HMR cartidges. Fitted with a 22" barrel with open sights on the .22 LR and drilled and tapped for scope mounts on the .22 WMR and .17 HMR models. Oiled walnut stocks with checkering.

NIB	Exc.	V.G.	Good	Fair	Poor
260	200	—	—	—	—

NOTE: Add $40 for .22 Mag. model and $75 for .17 HMR.

Empire Grade Rimfire

Empire Grade has select walnut stock with 24 lpi hand-cut checkering. Grip and forearm caps highly polished and blued metal finish. Same configurations as Superior Grade rifles.

NIB	Exc.	V.G.	Good	Fair	Poor
335	275	—	—	—	—

NOTE: Add $20 For .22 Mag. model and $100 for .22 Hornet model.

PISTOLS

Daly ZDA

Introduced in 2005 this pistol is chambered for the 9mm or .40 S&W cartridge. Fitted with a 4.5" ramped barrel. Ambidextrous slide release/dececker/lock as well as magazine release. Loaded chamber indicator. Magazine capacity is 15 rounds for 9mm and 12 rounds for the .40 S&W.

NIB	Exc.	V.G.	Good	Fair	Poor
590	450	—	—	—	—

Field 1911-A1 FS/MS/CS

Chambered for .45 ACP with a choice of 5" (FS), 4" (MS), or 3.5" (CS) barrel and various special features such as front and rear slide serrations, extended beavertail safety, and lightweight trigger. Magazine capacity is 8 rounds. Overall length is 8.75".

NIB	Exc.	V.G.	Good	Fair	Poor
530	400	300	—	—	—

Superior 1911-A1 EFS/EMS/ECS

Same as the Field Grade described above but with a blued frame and stainless steel slide. Introduced in 1999.

NIB	Exc.	V.G.	Good	Fair	Poor
550	450	350	—	—	—

Empire 1911-A1 EFS

Same as the Field Grade but in full stainless with both stainless steel slide and frame. Introduced in 1999.

NIB	Exc.	V.G.	Good	Fair	Poor
630	475	350	—	—	—

Field 1911-A2P

Same as above but with 10-round magazine.

NIB	Exc.	V.G.	Good	Fair	Poor
570	450	—	—	—	—

.22 Caliber Conversion Kit

Offered with adjustable sights for models with 5" barrel only. First offered in 1999.

NIB	Exc.	V.G.	Good	Fair	Poor
200	150	—	—	—	—

Field 1911-A1 PC

This model is fitted with a 4" barrel and slide. It also has a polymer frame. Produced under license from STI. Introduced in 1999.

NIB	Exc.	V.G.	Good	Fair	Poor
500	400	—	—	—	—

Superior 1911-A1 PC

Same as the model above but with stainless steel slide and black polymer frame. Introduced in 1999.

NIB	Exc.	V.G.	Good	Fair	Poor
525	425	—	—	—	—

Field 1911 Target EFST

Fitted with a 5" barrel and chambered for the .45 ACP cartridge. Eight-round magazine. Blued finish. Fully adjustable rear sight with dovetail front sight. Weight is about 40 oz.

NIB	Exc.	V.G.	Good	Fair	Poor
620	475	—	—	—	—

Empire 1911 Target EFST

As above but with stainless steel finish.

NIB	Exc.	V.G.	Good	Fair	Poor
790	600	—	—	—	—

Empire Custom Match Target

Same as Empire target but with hand polished stainless steel finish with 20 lpi checkered front strap.

NIB	Exc.	V.G.	Good	Fair	Poor
800	600	—	—	—	—

Daly HP

Introduced in 2003 this U.S.-made 9mm pistol is similar to the famous Browning Hi-Power. Fitted with a 5" barrel. XS sighting system. Weight is about 35 oz.

NIB	Exc.	V.G.	Good	Fair	Poor
550	400	—	—	—	—

Daly M-5 Government

This is a polymer frame pistol chambered for the 9mm, .40 S&W, or the .45 ACP cartridge. Fitted with a 5" barrel, high rise beavertail and ambidextrous safety. Low profile sights. Weight is around 34 oz. Made in Israel by BUL. Introduced in 2003.

NIB	Exc.	V.G.	Good	Fair	Poor
720	575	—	—	—	—

Daly M-5 Commander

Same as above but fitted with a 4.375" barrel. Weight is about 30 oz.

NIB	Exc.	V.G.	Good	Fair	Poor
720	575	—	—	—	—

Daly M-5 Ultra-X

This is an ultra compact model.

NIB	Exc.	V.G.	Good	Fair	Poor
720	575	—	—	—	—

Daly M-5 IPCS

This model has a 5" barrel and is fitted with a stainless steel slide with adjustable sights. Flared and lowered ejection port and extended mag release. Weight is about 34 oz.

NIB	Exc.	V.G.	Good	Fair	Poor
1500	1150	—	—	—	—

Daly Classic 1873 Single Action

Chambered for the .45 Colt or the .357 Mag., this revolver is offered with 4.75", 5.5", or 7.5" barrel. Choice of walnut or simulated Ivory grips. Stainless steel, blue or case colored finish. Introduced in 2005.

NIB	Exc.	V.G.	Good	Fair	Poor
450	350	—	—	—	—

NOTE: Add $30 for steel backstrap and trigger guard. Add $200 for stainless steel.

DAN ARMS OF AMERICA

Allentown, Pennsylvania

These are Italian-made shotguns manufactured by Silmer and imported by Dan Arms of America. Production ceased in 1988.

SIDE-BY-SIDES

Field Grade

A boxlock shotgun chambered for all gauges with 26" or 28" barrels, various choke combinations, double triggers and extractors. Blued with a walnut stock.

Exc.	V.G.	Good	Fair	Poor
300	265	225	150	125

Deluxe Field Grade

As above, with a single trigger and automatic ejectors.

Exc.	V.G.	Good	Fair	Poor
450	400	325	250	200

OVER/UNDERS

Lux Grade I

A 12 and 20 gauge Over/Under shotgun with a 26", 28" or 30" ventilated rib barrels, double triggers and extractors. Blued finish with a walnut stock.

Exc.	V.G.	Good	Fair	Poor
275	250	200	150	100

Lux Grade II

As above, in 12 gauge only with a single trigger.

Exc.	V.G.	Good	Fair	Poor
325	300	250	200	150

Lux Grade III

As above, in 20 gauge only with automatic ejectors.

Exc.	V.G.	Good	Fair	Poor
400	325	275	225	175

Lux Grade IV

As above in 12 gauge only with screw-in choke tubes.

Exc.	V.G.	Good	Fair	Poor
450	375	325	275	200

Silver Snipe

A 12 or 20 gauge shotgun manufactured to custom order with engraved false sideplates and a select walnut stock.

Exc.	V.G.	Good	Fair	Poor
1250	1000	800	600	350

DANCE & BROTHERS CONFEDERATE REVOLVERS

Columbia, Texas

J.H., G.P., and D.E. Dance began production of percussion revolvers for the Confederate States of America in Columbia, Texas, in mid-1862, moving to Anderson, Texas, in early 1864. Based on surviving serial numbers, the combined output at both places did not exceed 350 pistols. Most of these were in the "Army" (.44 caliber) size but a limited number of "Navy" (.36 caliber) were also manufactured. Nearly all are distinguished by the absence of a "recoil shield" on the frame behind the cylinders. As Colt M1851 "Navy" revolvers closely resemble the Dance Navy revolvers, great care must be exercised in examining revolvers purported to be Dance Navies.

.44 Caliber

Exc.	V.G.	Good	Fair	Poor
—	—	62500	18500	5000

.36 Caliber

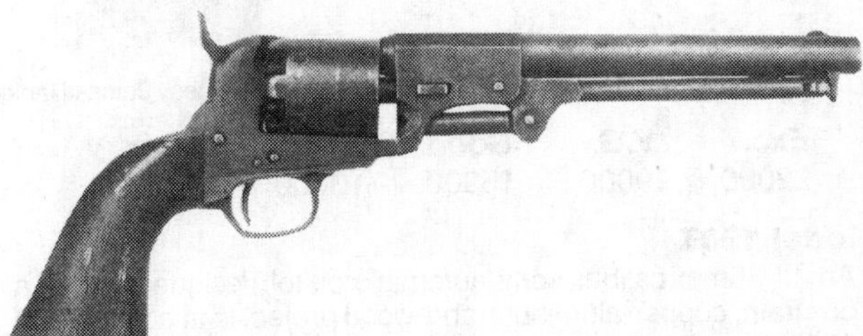

Courtesy Milwaukee Public Museum, Milwaukee, Wisconsin

Exc.	V.G.	Good	Fair	Poor
—	—	67500	20000	7000

DANDOY, C/A LIEGE

SEE—French Military Firearms

DANSK REKYLRIFFEL SYNDIKAT

Copenhagen, Denmark

This firm was founded in 1896. In 1936 it became known as Madsen, makers of the famous Madsen light machine gun.

The Schouboe pistols were designed by Jens Schouboe, the chief engineer for Dansk. They were developed in 1900-1902. The first year of manufacture was in 1902.

Schouboe 1902

A 7.65mm caliber semi-automatic pistol with a conventional blowback design. Production began in 1903 and ended in 1908, with fewer than 1,000 manufactured.

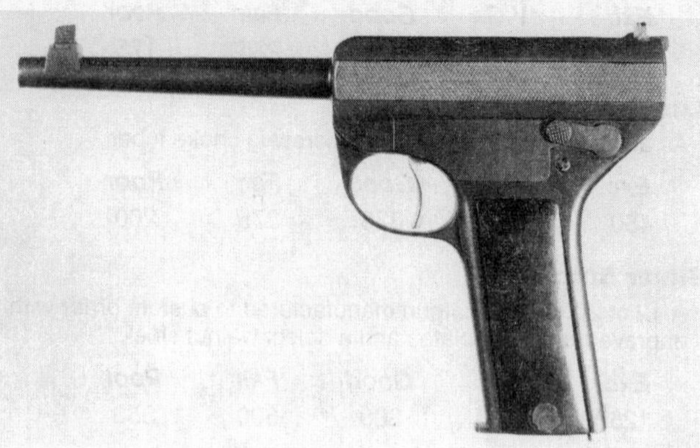

Courtesy James Rankin

Exc.	V.G.	Good	Fair	Poor
12000	10000	7500	5000	3000

Schouboe 1904

A semi-automatic pistol in caliber 11.35mm. The Model 1904 was an enlarged Model 1902. The name Dansk Rekylriffel is stamped on the slide.

Courtesy James Rankin

Exc.	V.G.	Good	Fair	Poor
22000	19000	15000	10000	5000

Model 1907

An 11.35mm caliber semi-automatic pistol designed to fire a 55-grain, copper-aluminum-and-wood projectile at a velocity of 1625 fps. The pistol has the name Dansk Rekylriffel and Schouboe stamped on the slide. Some of these pistols had grip frames slotted for stocks. Five hundred were manufactured before production stopped in 1917.

Courtesy James Rankin

Exc.	V.G.	Good	Fair	Poor
22000	19000	15000	10000	5000

NOTE: Combination holster/shoulder stocks were made for this model, but are extremely rare. If present with a pistol, they would add approximately $5,000 to the value.

Schouboe Model 1907 9mm

As above but chambered for the 9mm cartridge. Very few of these pistols were built.

Courtesy James Rankin

Exc.	V.G.	Good	Fair	Poor
12000	10000	7500	5000	3000

Schouboe Model 1910/12

This model is chambered for the 11.35mm cartridge, and was involved in U.S. military tests in 1912.

Courtesy James Rankin

Exc.	V.G.	Good	Fair	Poor
22000	19000	15000	10000	5000

Schouboe Model 1916

This model is also chambered for the 11.35mm cartridge. It is fitted with a very large slide release and safety lever on the left side of the pistol. The name of the manufacturer is stamped on the slide.

Courtesy James Rankin

Exc.	V.G.	Good	Fair	Poor
22000	19000	15000	10000	5000

DARDICK CORP.

Hamden, Connecticut

Perhaps one of the most unusual firearms to have been designed and marketed in the United States during the 20th century. It utilizes a "tround," which is a triangular plastic case enclosing a cartridge. The action of these arms consists of a revolving carrier that brings the trounds from the magazine into line with the barrel. Discontinued in 1962.

Series 1100

3" barrel. Chambered in .38 Dardick only.

Exc.	V.G.	Good	Fair	Poor
800	650	550	400	200

Series 1500

6" barrel. Chambered for the .22, .30, and the .38 Dardick.

Exc.	V.G.	Good	Fair	Poor
950	850	750	600	300

A carbine conversion kit consisting of a long barrel and shoulder stock was available and would bring a premium of $250 to $400 depending on the condition.

DARLING, B. & B. M.

Belingham, Massachusetts

Darling Pepperbox Pistol

A .30 caliber percussion 6-shot pepperbox with 3.25" length barrels. Blued with walnut grips. This is one of the rarest American pepperboxes and copies are known to have been made. Consequently, prospective purchasers are advised to secure a qualified appraisal prior to acquisition. Manufactured during the late 1830s.

Exc.	V.G.	Good	Fair	Poor
—	—	4250	1500	550

DARNE, S. A.

St. Etienne, France

Darne Side-by-Side Shotguns

A 12, 16, 20, or 28 gauge sliding breech double-barrel shotgun manufactured in a variety of barrel lengths and with numerous optional features. Manufactured from 1881 to 1979.

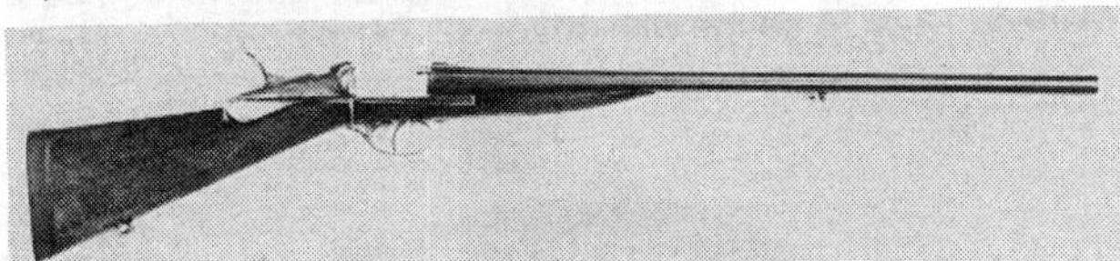

Model R11

Exc.	V.G.	Good	Fair	Poor
1000	900	750	600	350

Model R15

Exc.	V.G.	Good	Fair	Poor
2500	2000	1750	1500	750

Model V19

Exc.	V.G.	Good	Fair	Poor
3250	3000	2750	2250	1250

Model V22

Exc.	V.G.	Good	Fair	Poor
3750	3500	3000	2500	1200

Model V Hors Series No. I

Exc.	V.G.	Good	Fair	Poor
4500	4000	3750	3250	1500

DAUDETEAU

St. Denis, France

Model 1896

A 6.5mm caliber bolt-action rifle with a 26" barrel, full length stock secured by two barrel bands and a fixed magazine. Blued with a walnut stock.

Exc.	V.G.	Good	Fair	Poor
—	300	175	100	75

DAVENPORT FIREARMS CO.

Providence, Rhode Island
Norwich, Connecticut

DOUBLE-BARREL SHOTGUNS

Text and prices by Nick Niles

William Hastings Davenport's company also made and marked double-barrel, visible hammer guns in Providence, R.I. on Orange St., 1880-1882 and in Norwich, Conn. ca. 1890-1909. All are monbloc designs of which there were four models. The 1st model made at Providence, ca. 1881, had hammers rising out of the boxlock frame. The 2nd model, made in Norwich, Conn. about 1898, is a typical boxlock. The 3rd model made in Norwich, Conn., ca. 1909, has small sidelocks set in larger boxlock frames. Its barrels have unnotched extensions and notched underlugs. The 4th model, also from Norwich, possibly made after the 1901 takeover by Hopkins & Allen, also has sidelocks set in boxlock frames but the barrels have half moon lugs and notched barrel extensions. Few Davenport doubles are seen although single barrel guns are often found.

1st Model

Exc.	V.G.	Good	Fair	Poor
1200	875	500	400	300

2nd Model

Courtesy Nick Niles

Exc.	V.G.	Good	Fair	Poor
700	450	300	200	150

3rd Model

Exc.	V.G.	Good	Fair	Poor
1200	875	500	400	300

4th Model

Exc.	V.G.	Good	Fair	Poor
900	450	300	250	200

Single Barrel Shotgun

A 10, 12, 16, or 20 gauge side-hammer single-barrel shotgun with 26" to 36" barrels and extractors. Blued, case hardened with a walnut stock. Manufactured from approximately 1880 to 1915.

Exc.	V.G.	Good	Fair	Poor
—	450	300	150	75

8 Gauge Goose Gun

As above, in 8 gauge.

Exc.	V.G.	Good	Fair	Poor
—	550	250	175	100

Falling Block Single-Shot Rifle

A .22, .25, or .32 rimfire single-shot rifle with a 24" round barrel and exposed hammer. Blued with a walnut stock. The barrel marked "The W.H. Davenport Fire Arms Co. Norwich, Conn. U.S.A. Patented Dec. 15, 1891." Manufactured between 1891 and 1910.

Exc.	V.G.	Good	Fair	Poor
—	675	425	325	200

DAVIDSON F. A.

Eibar, Spain

Arms bearing this name were manufactured in Spain by Fabrica De Armas.

Model 63B

A 12, 16, 20, 28, or .410 bore double-barrel boxlock shotgun with 25" to 30" barrels. Engraved, nickel-plated with a walnut stock. Made from 1963 to 1976.

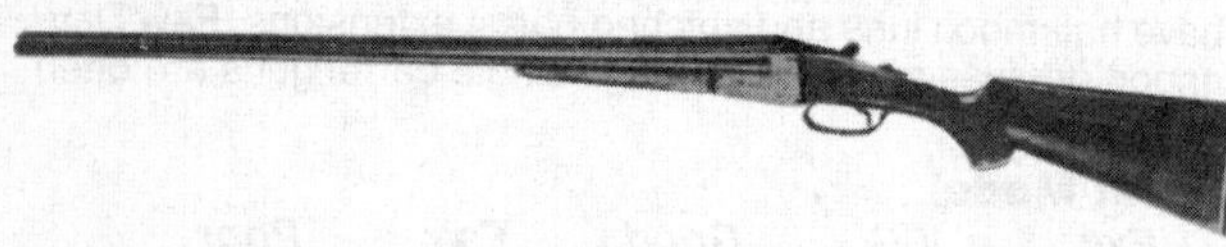

Exc.	V.G.	Good	Fair	Poor
325	225	200	150	100

Model 69 SL

A 12 or 20 gauge sidelock double-barrel shotgun with 26" or 28" barrels and finished as above.

Exc.	V.G.	Good	Fair	Poor
400	350	300	225	125

Stagecoach Model 73

A 12 or 20 gauge Magnum sidelock double-barrel shotgun with 20" barrels and exposed hammers.

Exc.	V.G.	Good	Fair	Poor
275	225	175	150	100

DAVIS, A. JR.

Stafford, Connecticut

Under Hammer Pistol

A .31 caliber single-shot under hammer percussion pistol with a 7.5" half octagonal barrel and brass frame. The grips are of maple and formed with a bottom tip. The top strap marked "A. Davis Jr./Stafford Conn."

Exc.	V.G.	Good	Fair	Poor
—	950	600	300	100

DAVIS, N.R. & CO.
DAVIS, N.R. & SONS

Manufacturer of percussion, and later, cartridge shotguns from 1853 to 1919. The cartridge shotguns embodied Nathan R. Davis' patented improvements of 1879, 1884, and 1886. Though only made in plain, serviceable grades, Davis shotguns were extremely well made and lived up to the company's motto "As Good as the Best."

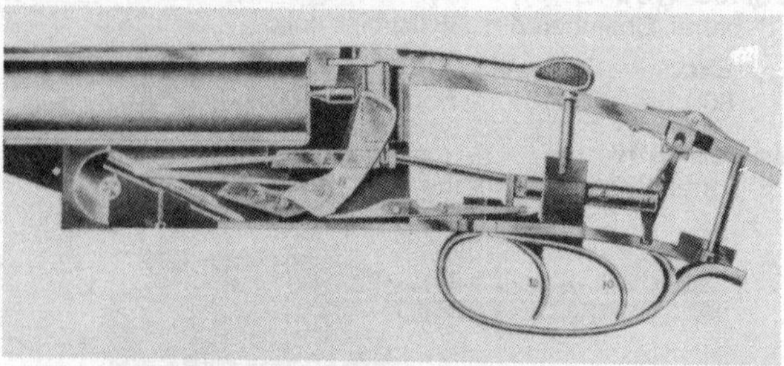

Grade A and B Hammerless Shotguns

Made in 12 or 16 gauge with 28", 30", or 32" barrels.

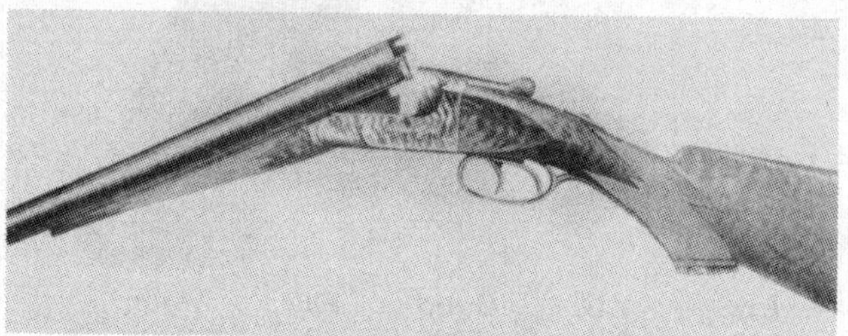

Exc.	V.G.	Good	Fair	Poor
850	650	400	200	100

Grade C Hammerless Shotgun

Made in 10 gauge with 30" or 32" barrels.

Exc.	V.G.	Good	Fair	Poor
850	650	400	200	100

Grade D and DS Hammer Shotguns

Made in 12 or 16 gauge with 28", 30", or 32" barrels.

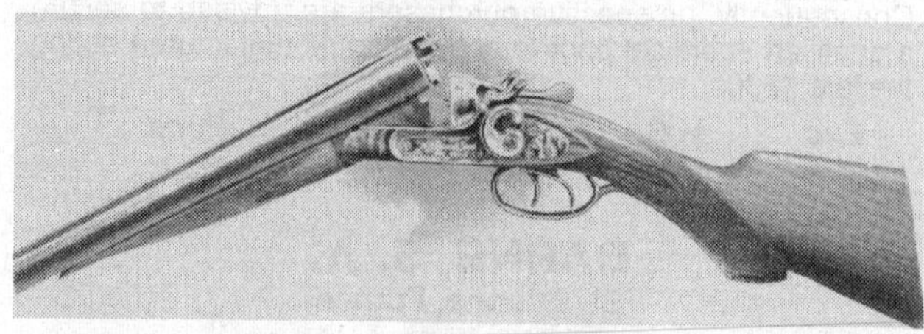

Exc.	V.G.	Good	Fair	Poor
850	650	400	200	100

Grade E and F Single-Barrel Shotguns

Made in 12 or 16 gauge with 30" or 32" barrels.

Exc.	V.G.	Good	Fair	Poor
300	225	100	75	50

N.R. DAVIS BRANDS

1st Button Opener—Hammer Boxlock

Exc.	V.G.	Good	Fair	Poor
475	325	250	150	100

1st Sidelever—Hammer Boxlock

Exc.	V.G.	Good	Fair	Poor
475	325	250	150	100

2nd Sidelever—Hammer Boxlock

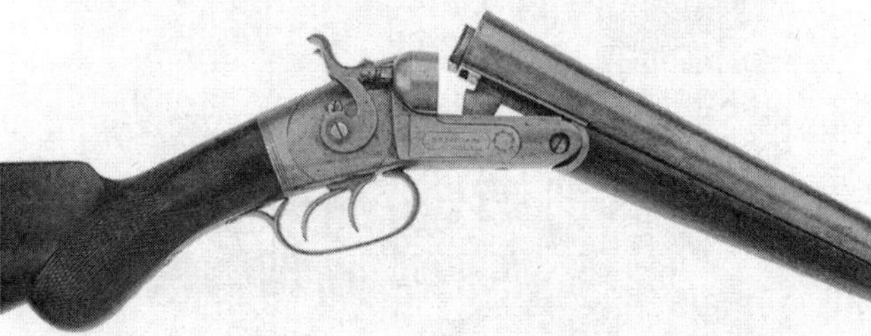

Courtesy Nick Niles, Paul Goodwin photo

Exc.	V.G.	Good	Fair	Poor
475	325	250	150	100

1st Toplever—Hammer Boxlock

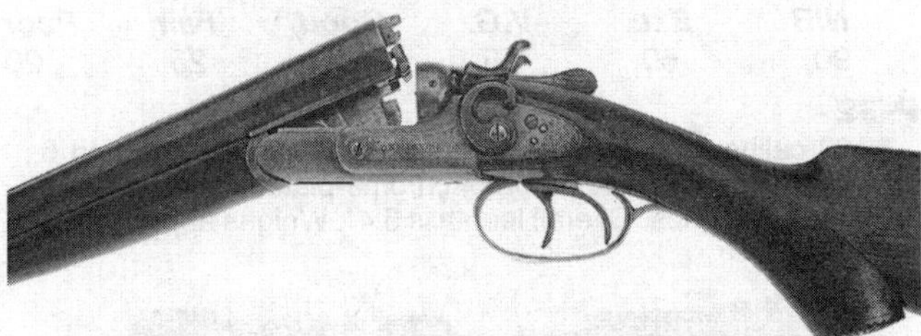

Courtesy Nick Niles, Paul Goodwin photo

Exc.	V.G.	Good	Fair	Poor
475	325	250	150	100

2nd Toplever—Hammer Boxlock

Exc.	V.G.	Good	Fair	Poor
475	325	250	150	100

3rd Toplever—Hammer Boxlock

Exc.	V.G.	Good	Fair	Poor
475	325	250	150	100

1879 1st Model—Hammer Boxlock

Exc.	V.G.	Good	Fair	Poor
475	325	250	150	100

1879 2nd Model—Damascus Barrels—Hammer Boxlock

Exc.	V.G.	Good	Fair	Poor
475	325	250	150	100

1885 "Hammerless"—Hammerless Boxlock

Exc.	V.G.	Good	Fair	Poor
475	325	250	150	100

1886 Rival—Hammerless Boxlock

Exc.	V.G.	Good	Fair	Poor
350	275	200	150	100

1886 Rival Improved—Hammerless Boxlock

Exc.	V.G.	Good	Fair	Poor
350	275	200	150	100

1897 "G"—Hammer Sidelock

Exc.	V.G.	Good	Fair	Poor
350	275	200	150	100

N.R. DAVIS & SONS BRAND

Hammerless 1900—Hammerless Boxlock

Exc.	V.G.	Good	Fair	Poor
350	275	200	150	100

Hammerless A—Damascus Barrels—Hammerless Boxlock

Exc.	V.G.	Good	Fair	Poor
350	275	200	150	100

Hammerless B—Hammerless Boxlock

Exc.	V.G.	Good	Fair	Poor
350	275	200	150	100

Hammerless C—Engraved Damascus Barrel—Hammerless Boxlock

Exc.	V.G.	Good	Fair	Poor
400	325	250	150	100

Hammerless D—Engraved—Hammerless Boxlock

Exc.	V.G.	Good	Fair	Poor
475	375	300	250	200

New Model—Hammerless Boxlock

Exc.	V.G.	Good	Fair	Poor
350	275	200	150	100

"D.S." Straight Stock—Engraved—Hammerless Boxlock

Exc.	V.G.	Good	Fair	Poor
350	275	200	150	100

Davis Special—Hammerless Boxlock

Exc.	V.G.	Good	Fair	Poor
925	650	500	400	250

Davis "B" Manga Steel—Hammerless Boxlock

Exc.	V.G.	Good	Fair	Poor
925	650	500	400	250

DAVIS-WARNER BRANDS

SEE—Davis-Warner

CRESCENT-DAVIS BRANDS

Model No. 600—Hammerless Boxlock

Exc.	V.G.	Good	Fair	Poor
700	550	300	200	100

Model No. 900—Hammerless Boxlock

Exc.	V.G.	Good	Fair	Poor
700	550	300	200	100

DAVIS & BOZEMAN

Central, Alabama

Pattern 1841 Rifle

A .58 caliber single-shot percussion rifle with a 33" round barrel, full walnut stock, two barrel bands, brass furniture and an iron ramrod. The lock marked "D. & B. Ala." as well as the serial number and date of manufacture.

Exc.	V.G.	Good	Fair	Poor
—	—	35000	15000	3500

DAVIS INDUSTRIES

Mira Loma, California

This company was founded in 1987 by Jim Davis in Chino, California. The company ceased operations in 2001. Remaining stocks and production machinery purchased by Cobra Enterprises, 1960 S. Milestone Drive, Suite F, Salt Lake City, UT 84104.

D-Series Deringer

A .22 LR, .22 WMR, .25 ACP and .32 ACP caliber double-barrel Over/Under derringer with 2.4" barrels. Black Teflon or chrome-plated finish with laminated wood grips. Weighs approximately 9.5 oz.

NIB	Exc.	V.G.	Good	Fair	Poor
75	50	40	30	25	20

Big Bore D-Series

Similar to the above model but chambered for the .38 Special and .32 H&R Magnum. Barrel length is 2.75". Weighs about 11.5 oz.

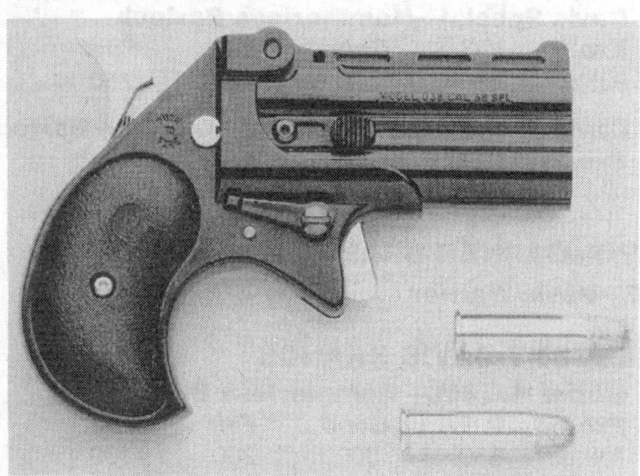

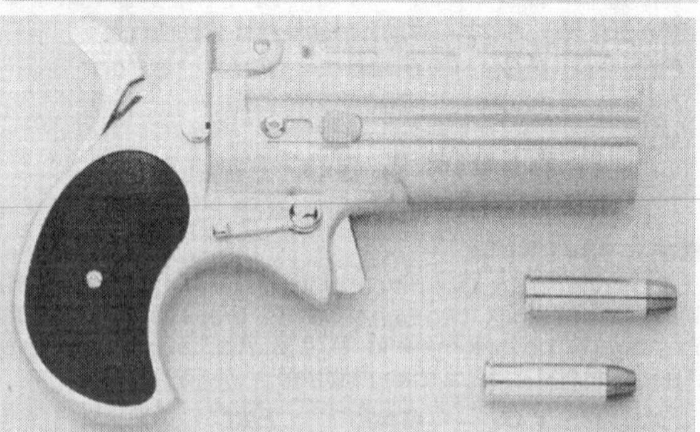

NIB	Exc.	V.G.	Good	Fair	Poor

Long Bore D-Series

Introduced in 1994 this two-shot pistol is chambered for the .22 LR , .22 WMR, .32 ACP, .32 H&R Mag., .380 ACP, 9mm, and .38 Special cartridges. Barrel length is 3.75", overall length is 5.65" and weight is approximately 13 oz.

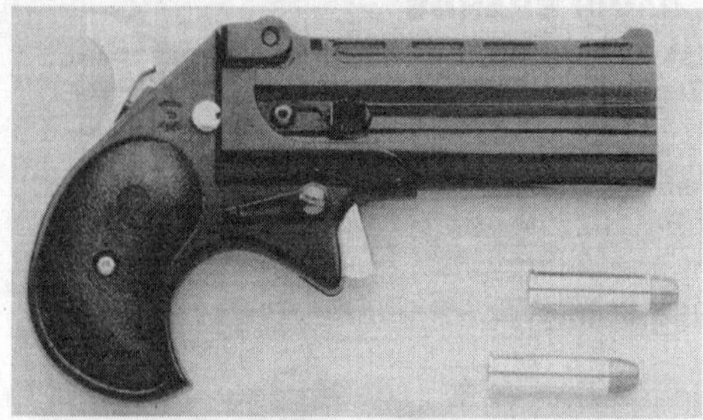

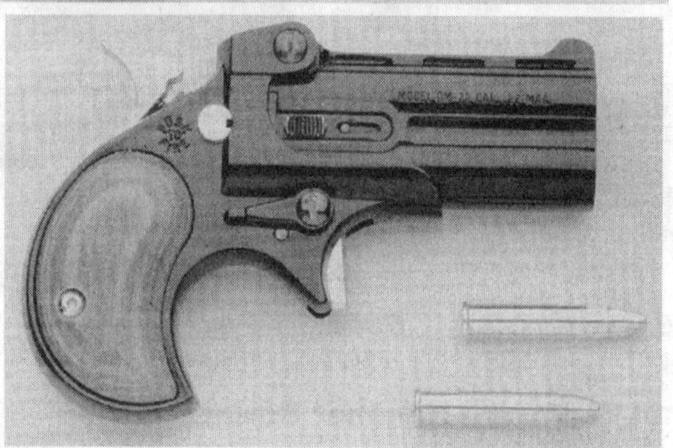

NIB	Exc.	V.G.	Good	Fair	Poor
90	60	45	30	25	20

P-32

A .32 caliber semi-automatic pistol with a 2.8" barrel and 6-shot magazine. Black Teflon or chrome-plated finish with laminated wood grips. Overall length is 5.4". Weighs approximately 22 oz.

NIB	Exc.	V.G.	Good	Fair	Poor
95	75	60	45	35	25

P-380

As above, in .380 caliber.

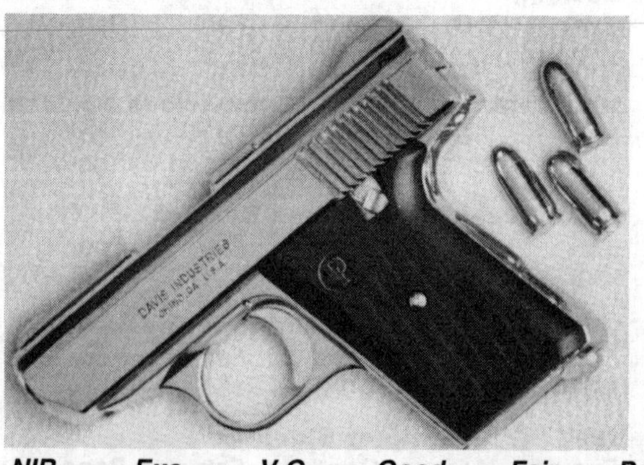

NIB	Exc.	V.G.	Good	Fair	Poor
125	80	65	50	40	30

DAVIS-WARNER ARMS CORPORATION

Norwich, Connecticut

Established in 1917, when N.R. Davis & Sons purchased the Warner Arms Company. Manufactured shotguns, as well as revolvers and semi-automatic pistols. Ceased operations in 1930. The Crescent Arms Company purchased the proprietary rights to the name and briefly assembled shotguns under the name (probably from parts acquired in the purchase) until Crescent was in turn purchased by J.C. Stevens.

Initially, the Davis-Warner shotguns were identical to those made by Davis, (page 360), but they subsequently made a Davis Grade B.S. Hammerless, Davis-Warner Expert and Davis Grade D.S. The pistols made by the company included .32 caliber revolvers and two Browning Patent semi-automatics made in Belgium for the company.

Davis Grade B.S. Hammerless Shotgun

Made in 12, 16, or 20 gauge with 28", 30", or 32" barrels.

Courtesy William Hammond

Exc.	V.G.	Good	Fair	Poor
875	650	400	200	100

Davis-Warner Expert Hammerless

Made in 12, 16, or 20 gauge with 26", 28", 30", or 32" barrels.

Courtesy Nick Niles, Paul Goodwin photo

Exc.	V.G.	Good	Fair	Poor
875	650	400	200	100

"BS"—Hammerless Boxlock

Exc.	V.G.	Good	Fair	Poor
350	275	200	150	100

"Maximin"—Hammerless Boxlock

Courtesy Nick Niles, Paul Goodwin photo

Exc.	V.G.	Good	Fair	Poor
475	325	250	200	150

"DS"—Hammerless Boxlock

Exc.	V.G.	Good	Fair	Poor
350	275	200	150	100

Deluxe—Hammerless Boxlock

Exc.	V.G.	Good	Fair	Poor
350	275	200	150	100

Premier—Hammerless Boxlock

Exc.	V.G.	Good	Fair	Poor
350	275	200	150	100

Peerless Ejector—Hammerless Boxlock

Courtesy Nick Niles, Paul Goodwin photo

Exc.	V.G.	Good	Fair	Poor
475	325	250	200	150

Hypower—Hammerless Boxlock

Exc.	V.G.	Good	Fair	Poor
475	325	250	200	150

Ajax—Hammerless Boxlock

Courtesy Nick Niles, Paul Goodwin photo

Exc.	V.G.	Good	Fair	Poor
350	275	200	150	100

Certified (Savage)

Courtesy Nick Niles, Paul Goodwin photo

Exc.	V.G.	Good	Fair	Poor
475	325	250	150	100

Deluxe Special (Model 805)

Automatic ejectors.

Exc.	V.G.	Good	Fair	Poor
575	450	300	200	150

Premier Special (Model 802)

Exc.	V.G.	Good	Fair	Poor
575	450	300	200	150

Premier (Model 801)

Exc.	V.G.	Good	Fair	Poor
475	325	250	150	100

Ajax (Model 800)

Courtesy Nick Niles, Paul Goodwin photo

Exc.	V.G.	Good	Fair	Poor
475	325	250	150	100

Davis-Warner Swing Out Revolver

Double-action .32 caliber revolver with a 5" or 6" barrel.

Exc.	V.G.	Good	Fair	Poor
175	125	100	75	50

Davis-Warner Semi-Automatic Pistols

Browning Patent .25 ACP, .32 ACP or .380 caliber pistols.

Exc.	V.G.	Good	Fair	Poor
350	275	175	125	75

Warner Infallible Semi-Automatic Pistol

Fyrberg Patent .32 ACP.

Courtesy J.B. Wood

Exc.	V.G.	Good	Fair	Poor
350	275	175	125	75

DAW, G. H.
London, England

Daw Revolver

A .38 caliber double-action percussion revolver with a 5.5" barrel marked "George H. Daw, 57 Threadneedle St. London, Patent No. 112." Blued, with walnut grips. Manufactured in the 1860s.

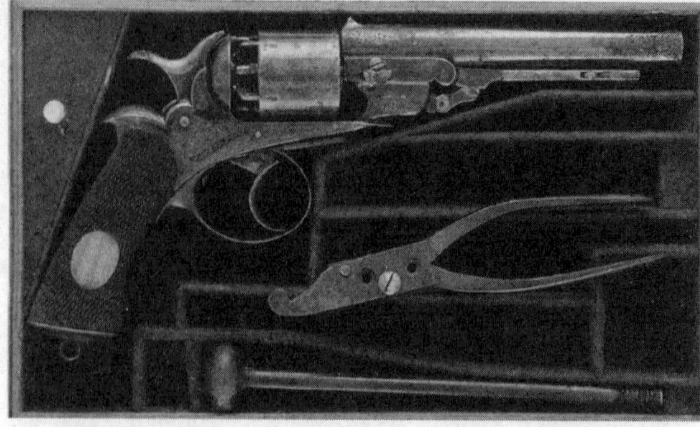

Exc.	V.G.	Good	Fair	Poor
—	5000	3000	1750	1000

DEANE, ADAMS & DEANE
London, England
SEE—Adams

DEANE-HARDING
London, England

Deane-Harding Revolver

A .44 caliber percussion revolver with a 5.25" barrel and 5-shot cylinder. Blued, case hardened with walnut grips. Manufactured during the late 1850s.

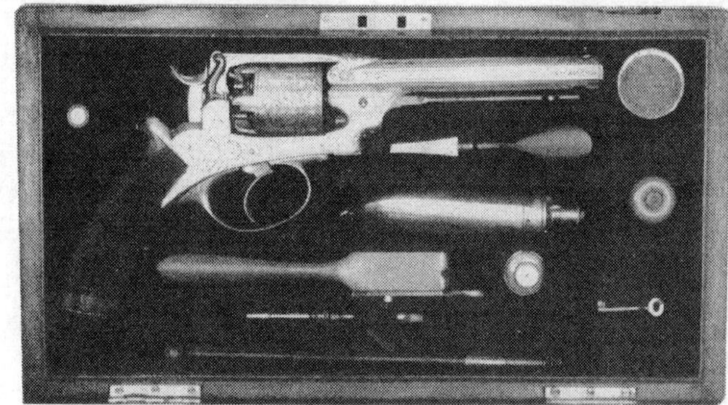

Courtesy Bonhams & Butterfields, San Francisco, California

Exc.	V.G.	Good	Fair	Poor
—	7500	1750	1250	800

DECKER, WILHELM
Zella St. Blasii, Germany

A 6.35mm double-action revolver with a 6-shot cylinder and concealed hammer. Unusual bar-type trigger design. Blued with plastic grips. Manufactured prior to 1914. Very few of these revolvers were produced.

Exc.	V.G.	Good	Fair	Poor
1500	750	450	300	100

DEFIANCE ANTI-BANDIT GUN
Distributed by California Arms Co.
San Francisco, California

Defiance Anti-Bandit Gun CURIO OR RELIC, NFA

The Defiance Anti-Bandit Gun is a double-barreled smooth bore pistol designed for 2.5" 20 gauge shotgun or tear gas shells. It was manufactured in 1926-27 by The American Machine Company for the California Arms Co., San Francisco, California, a law enforcement supply manufacturer and distributor, and distributed by them from about 1926-30. Because few specimens exist establishing reliable values may be difficult, but could logically be expected to approximate those for a nonstandard or special-order Ithaca Auto & Burglar Gun (*q.v.*).

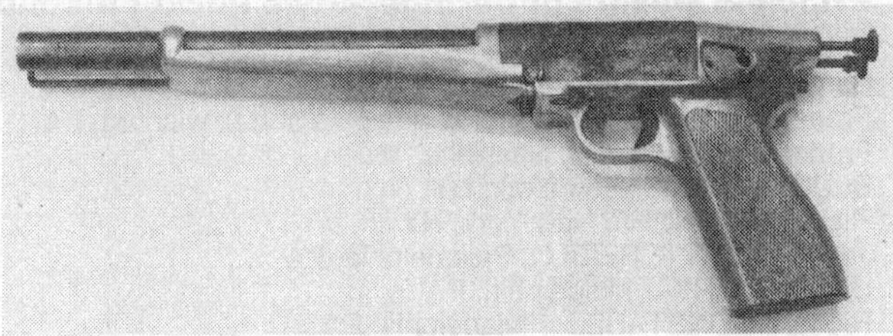

DEMIRETT, J.

Montpelier, Vermont

Under Hammer Pistol

A .27 caliber single-shot percussion pistol with 3" to 8" barrels and an under hammer. The barrel marked "J. Demerrit / Montpelier / Vermont." Blued with maple, walnut or stag horn grips. Active from 1866 to the mid-1880s.

Exc.	V.G.	Good	Fair	Poor
—	—	1950	750	300

DEMRO

Manchester, Connecticut

XF-7 Wasp Carbine

A 9mm or .45 caliber semi-automatic carbine with a 16.5" barrel and folding stock.

Exc.	V.G.	Good	Fair	Poor
500	350	250	200	150

T.A.C. Model 1

As above, with a fixed stock.

Exc.	V.G.	Good	Fair	Poor
500	350	250	200	150

DERINGER REVOLVER AND PISTOL CO.

Philadelphia, Pennsylvania

After Henry Deringer's death, his name was used by I.J. Clark who manufactured rimfire revolvers on Charles Foehl's patents between 1870 and 1879.

Deringer Model I

A .22 caliber spur trigger revolver with a hinged octagonal barrel and 7-shot cylinder. Manufactured circa 1873.

Exc.	V.G.	Good	Fair	Poor
—	—	650	275	150

Deringer Model II

As above, with a round barrel and also available in .32 caliber.

Exc.	V.G.	Good	Fair	Poor
—	—	425	200	100

Centennial 1876

A .22, .32, or .38 caliber solid frame revolver.

Exc.	V.G.	Good	Fair	Poor
—	—	900	450	200

DERINGER, HENRY RIFLES AND PISTOLS

Philadelphia, Pennsylvania

Henry Deringer Sr. and his son, Henry Jr., were well established in Philadelphia by the close of the War of 1812, having made both sporting and military rifles at that place since the turn of the century. Henry Jr. continued in the gun trade until the outbreak of the American Civil War, primarily producing flintlock and percussion military rifles, at least 2,500 "Northwest guns" and 1,200 rifles for the Indian trade, a few percussion martial pistols, but most importantly the percussion pocket pistols that became so popular that they took on his misspelled name as a generic term, the "derringers."

Deringer U.S. M1814 Military Rifle

Overall length 48-1/2"; barrel length 32-3/4"; caliber .54. Markings: on lockplate, "US/H. DERINGER/PHILADA," on top flat of barrel, "H. DERINGER/PHILADA" and standard U.S. proofmarks. The U.S. M1814 rifle is distinguished by its part octagonal barrel, whose bands were secured by wedge-shaped spring bands, and the distinctive finger ridges on the triggerguard strap. Henry Deringer Sr. received a contract for 2,000 of these rifles in 1814, but delivered only 50 that year, devoting his resources instead to a more lucrative Pennsylvania state contract for rifles.

Exc.	V.G.	Good	Fair	Poor
—	7700	2500	1200	850

Deringer U.S. M1817 Military Rifle (Types I & II)

Overall length 51-1/4"; barrel length 36"; caliber .54. Markings: on lockplate, "US/H. DERINGER/PHILADA" forward of cock, date on tail; standard U.S. proofmarks on barrel. The U.S. M1817 "common" rifle followed much of the same design elements as its predecessor, the U.S. M1814 rifle; however, the barrel is fully round with its bands secured by full band springs, and on the earlier production, the finger ridges on the triggerguard strap were eliminated in favor of a plain strap formed into a handgrip. On the 6,000 rifles manufactured under his 1840 contract, Deringer eliminated the "pistol grip" in favor of a plain strap, distinguishing Type 11 production from Type 1. As one of the four major contractors for the U.S. M1817 rifle, Deringer produced a total of 111,000 rifles for the U.S. War Department. Many of the rifles from first two contracts (2,000 in 1821, 3,000 in 1823) were distributed to Southern states under the 1808 Militia Act. Accordingly, Deringer M1817 rifles altered to percussion by traditional Southern methods may generate a premium.

(in flintlock)

Exc.	V.G.	Good	Fair	Poor
—	6700	2800	1200	800

(altered to percussion)

Exc.	V.G.	Good	Fair	Poor
—	3200	950	550	400

Deringer Original Percussion Martial Rifles (Types I & II)

Overall length 51-1/4"; barrel length 36"; caliber .54. Markings: Type I-on lockplate forward of hammer "DERINGER/PHILA"; also known to exist with standard U.S. M1817 lock markings and barrel marks; Type II-on lockplate forward of hammer "US/DERINGER/PHILADELA" or "DERINGER/PHILADELA" and same on top of barrel.

Although the Type I rifle of this series appears at first glance to be a late contract rifle altered to percussion by means of the cone-in barrel method, in fact it is an original percussion rifle made by Deringer from modified spare parts that remained after the completion of his 1840 contract. The Type 11 rifle also evidences having been made from modified parts; however, its cone is set in an elongated bolster brazed to the right side of the barrel. Speculation concerning these rifles is rampant; however, the available evidence indicates that Deringer produced about 600 of these most likely produced at the beginning of the American Civil War.

Courtesy Milwaukee Public Museum, Milwaukee, Wisconsin

Exc.	V.G.	Good	Fair	Poor
—	3700	1100	650	450

Deringer Original Percussion Rifle-Muskets

Overall length 57-3/4"; barrel length 42"; caliber .69. Markings: on lock forward of hammer, "US/DERINGER/PHILADELA."

Just as the original percussion rifle appears to be an altered arm, the rare Deringer rifle muskets at first appear to have been flintlocks. However, these arms are original percussion, having been made from spare or rejected parts from the U.S. M1816 muskets. The brazed bolsters are identical in style to that of the Type 11 original percussion rifles made by Deringer. Barrels are rifled with seven grooves, and the barrels accordingly bear a rear sight. Deringer probably assembled a hundred of these rifles in 1861 to arm some company of Pennsylvania's early war regiments.

Courtesy Milwaukee Public Museum, Milwaukee, Wisconsin

Exc.	*V.G.*	*Good*	*Fair*	*Poor*
—	3200	900	650	450

Deringer U.S. Navy Contract "Boxlock" Pistols

Overall length 11-5/8"; barrel length 6"; caliber .54. Markings: on lockplate, "US/DERINGER/ PHILADELIA" or merely "DERINGER/PHILADEL'A" in center, the tail either plain or marked "U.S.N./(date)"; barrels sometimes marked with U.S. Navy inspection marks.

Deringer was granted a contract with the U.S. Navy in 1845 for 1,200 of the new "boxlock" percussion pistols also made by Ames. All of these appear to have been delivered. From the extra parts, Deringer is thought to have assembled several hundred extra pistols, some of which he rifled. The latter bring a premium, even though quantities remain enigmatic.

Exc.	*V.G.*	*Good*	*Fair*	*Poor*
—	3700	1400	1100	750

Deringer Percussion Pocket Pistols

Overall length varies with barrel length; barrel length 1-1/2" to 6" in regular 1/8" gradiants; caliber .41 (usually, other calibers known). Markings: "DERINGER/PHILADELA" on back action lock and rear section of top barrel flat; "P" impressed in circle with serrated edges on left side of breech; agent marks occasionally on top of barrel.

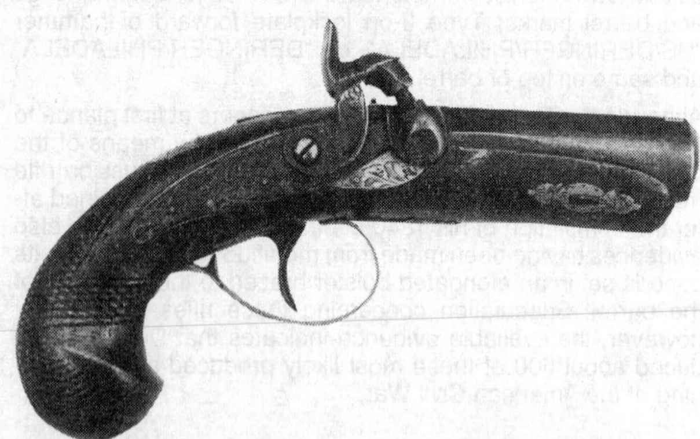

Courtesy Milwaukee Public Museum, Milwaukee, Wisconsin

The most famous of Henry Deringer's products, an estimated 15,000 were produced between the Mexican War through the Civil War, usually in pairs. The popularity of the pistol is attested in the large number of imitations and the nickname "Derringer" applied to them, even when clearly not Deringer's products. Prices can fluctuate widely based on agent marks occasionally found on barrel. Care is advised in purchasing purported "true" derringers.

Exc.	*V.G.*	*Good*	*Fair*	*Poor*
—	4700	1600	1200	800

Principal Makers of Deringer-Style Pocket Pistols

William AFFLERBACH, Philadelphia, PA
Balthaser AUER, Louisville, KY
Frederick BEERSTECHER, Philadelphia and Lewisburg, PA
Franz J. BITTERLICH, Nashville, TN
BLUNT & SYMS, New York, NY
Richard P. BRUFF, New York, NY
Jesse S. BUTTERFIELD, Philadelphia, PA
Daniel CLARK, Philadelphia, PA
Richard CONSTABLE, Philadelphia, PA
DELONG & SON, Chattanooga, TN
MOSES DICKSON, Louisville, KY
Horace E. DIMICK, St. Louis, MO
Gustau ERICHSON, Houston, TX
B.J. EUSTACE & Company, St. Louis, MO
James E. EVANS, Philadelphia, PA
W.S. EVANS, Philadelphia, PA
FIELD, LANGSTROTH & Company, Philadelphia, PA
Daniel FISH, New York, NY
FOLSOM BROTHERS & Company, New Orleans, LA
August G. GENEZ, New York, NY
George D. H. GILLESPIE, New York, NY
Frederick G. GLASSICK, Memphis, TN
James GOLCHER, Philadelphia, PA
Joseph GRUBB & Company, Philadelphia, PA
John H. HAPPOLDT, Charlestown, SC
John M. HAPPOLDT, Columbus, George, and Charlestown, SC
HAWS & WAGGONER, Columbia, SC
HODGKINS & SONS, Macon, GA
Louis HOFFMAN, Vicksburg, MS
HYDE & GOODRICH, New Orleans, LA
Joseph JACOB, Philadelphia, PA
William W. KAYE, Philadelphia, PA
Benjamin KITTERIDGE, Cincinnati, OH
Peter W. KRAFT, Columbia, SC
John KRIDER, Philadelphia, PA
Jacob KUNTZ, Philadelphia, PA
Martille La FITTE, Natchitoches, LA
A. Frederichk LINS, Philadelphia, PA
C. LOHNER, Philadelphia, PA
John P. LOWER, Denver, CO
A.R. MENDENHALL, Des Arc, AK
John MEUNIER, Milwaukee, WI
William D. MILLER, New York, NY
MURPHY & O'CONNELL, New York, NY
—— NEWCOMB, Natchez, MS
Charles A. OBERTEUFFER, Philadelphia, PA
Stephen O'DELL, Natchez, MS
Henry C. PALMER, St. Louis, MO
R. PATRICK, New York, NY
REID & TRACY, New York, NY
William ROBERTSON, Philadelphia, PA
ROBINSON & KRIDER, Philadelphia, PA
Ernst SCHMIDT & Company, Houston, TX
SCHNEIDER & GLASSICK, Memphis, TN
W.A. SEAVER, New York, NY
Paul J. SIMPSON, New York, NY
SLOTTER & Company, Philadelphia, PA
Patrick SMITH, Buffalo, NY
SPRANG & WALLACE, Philadelphia, PA
Adam W. SPIES, New York, NY
Casper SUTER, Selma, AL
Jacob F. TRUMPLER, Little Rock, AK
Edward TRYON, Jr., Philadelphia, PA
George K. TRYON, Philadelphia, PA
TUFTS & COLLEY, New York, NY
WOLF, DASH & FISHER, New York, NY
Alfred WOODHAM, New York, NY
Andrew WURFFLEIN, Philadelphia, PA
John WURFFLEIN, Philadelphia, PA

Agent Names Found On Deringer Pocket Pistols

W.C. ALLEN, San Francisco, CA
W.H. CALHOUN, Nashville, TN

CANFIELD & BROTHERS, Baltimore, MD
F. H. CLARK & CO., Memphis, TN
COLEMAN & DUKE, Cahaba, AL
M.W. GALT & BROTHER, Washington, DC
J.B. GILMORE, Shreveport, LA
A.B. GRISWOLD & CO., New Orleans, LA
HYDE & GOODRICH, New Orleans, LA
LULLMAN & VIENNA, Memphis, TN
A.J. MILLSPAUGH, Shreveport, LA
H.G. NEWCOMB, Natchez, MS
A.J. PLATE, San Francisco, CA
J.A. SCHAFER, Vicksburg, MS
S.L. SWETT, Vicksburg, MS
A.J. TAYLOR, San Francisco, CA
WOLF & DURRINGER, Louisville, KY

DESENZANI, LABORATORIES ARMI

Brescia, Italy

OVER-AND-UNDER

These custom made guns are all unique. Used guns in excellent condition will bring $30,000. Values increase depending on the small gauges and amount and coverage of engraving.

SIDE-BY-SIDE

These custom made guns are all unique. Used guns in excellent condition will bring $20,000. Values increase depending on the small gauges and amount and coverage of engraving.

DESERT EAGLE/ISRAELI MILITARY INDUSTRIES

The Desert Eagle is a semi-automatic gas-operated pistol chambered for the .357 Magnum, .41 Magnum, .44 Magnum, and .50 Action Express. It is produced by Israel Military Industries. The pistols are furnished with a standard 6" barrel but 10" and 14" interchangeable barrels are offered as options. Also available are these interchangeable barrels that are Mag-Na-Ported. The standard material used for frame is steel, but stainless and aluminum are also available. The standard finish for these pistols is black oxide but custom finishes are available on special order. These special finishes are: gold, stainless steel, satin nickel, bright nickel, polished blue, camo, matte chrome, polished chrome, brushed chrome, and matte chrome with gold. All of these special order finishes as well as the optional barrels will affect the prices of the pistols. Prices listed here will reflect standard pistols only.

Desert Eagle .357 Magnum

Standard with 6" barrel and black oxide finish. Magazine capacity is 9 rounds. Standard weight is 58 oz.

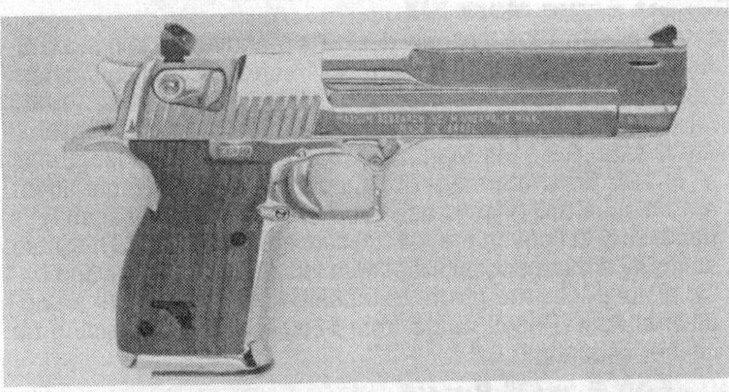

NIB	Exc.	V.G.	Good	Fair	Poor
1250	900	700	500	400	250

Desert Eagle .41 Magnum/.44 Magnum

Standard barrel length is 6" with black oxide finish. Magazine capacity is 8 rounds. Weight for standard pistol is 63 oz.

NIB	Exc.	V.G.	Good	Fair	Poor
1350	900	700	500	400	250

Desert Eagle .50 Action Express

Standard barrel length is 10" with black oxide finish. Magazine capacity is 7 rounds. Standard weight is 72 oz.

NIB	Exc.	V.G.	Good	Fair	Poor
1450	900	700	500	400	250

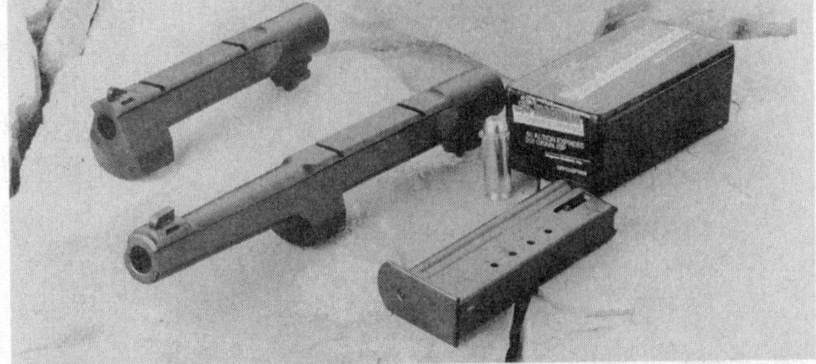

Interchangeable barrels make the Desert Eagle a truly versatile handgun. The .50 AE shown here will handle the biggest game in North America.

Desert Eagle Mark XIX

Introduced in 1996 this new design is manufactured in the U.S. and allows the interchangeability of barrels to switch calibers between the same receiver. A single receiver can be turned into six different pistols in three Magnum calibers. Available are the .50 A.E., .44 Mag., and .357 Mag. in barrel lengths of 6" or 10". Separate magazines are also required. Eight different finishes are offered as well. A separate bolt assembly is necessary to convert the .44/.50 calibers to the .357. There are so many different possibilities with this design that only the basic pistol prices are given. Extra barrel assemblies are an additional cost. Prices range from $280 to $160 depending on caliber and length.

.50A.E. w/6" Barrel

NIB	Exc.	V.G.	Good	Fair	Poor
1450	900	700	500	—	—

.50A.E. w/10" Barrel

NIB	Exc.	V.G.	Good	Fair	Poor
1350	1000	750	500	—	—

.44 Mag. w/6" Barrel

NIB	Exc.	V.G.	Good	Fair	Poor
1250	900	700	450	—	—

.44 Mag. w/10" Barrel

NIB	Exc.	V.G.	Good	Fair	Poor
1350	1000	750	500	—	—

.357 Mag. w/6" Barrel

NIB	Exc.	V.G.	Good	Fair	Poor
1250	900	700	450	—	—

.357 Mag. w/10" Barrel

NIB	Exc.	V.G.	Good	Fair	Poor
1350	1000	750	500	—	—

.440 Cor-Bon w/6" Barrel (1999)

NIB	Exc.	V.G.	Good	Fair	Poor
1200	950	—	—	—	—

.440 Cor-Bon w/10" Barrel (1999)

NIB	Exc.	V.G.	Good	Fair	Poor
1300	1000	—	—	—	—

Bolt Assembly—.44/.50 or .357

NIB	Exc.	V.G.	Good	Fair	Poor
220	175	—	—	—	—

Mark XIX Component System

Introduced in 2000 this system features a Mark XIX frame with a .44 magnum 6" and 10" barrels; .50AE with 6" and 10" barrel; and .357 magnum with 6" and 10" barrel. Supplied with ICC aluminum case. Also offered with 6" only barrel components or 10" only barrel components.

6" & 10" Component System

NIB	Exc.	V.G.	Good	Fair	Poor
3990	2990	—	—	—	—

6" Component System

NIB	Exc.	V.G.	Good	Fair	Poor
2575	1900	—	—	—	—

10" Component System

NIB	Exc.	V.G.	Good	Fair	Poor
2815	2100	—	—	—	—

Baby Eagle

The Baby Eagle is a smaller version of the Desert Eagle. It is an all-steel construction, extra long slide rail, nylon grips, combat style trigger guard, ambidextrous thumb safety, decocking safety. It is a double-action design and available in 9mm, .40 S&W, .41 Action Express. Standard finish is black oxide but matte chrome and brushed are offered as optional finishes. Fixed sights are standard. Fixed night sights and adjustable night sights are options.

Baby Eagle .40 S&W (Standard)

Supplied with 4.5" barrel and black oxide finish, it has a magazine capacity of 10 rounds. Empty weight is 38 oz.

NIB	Exc.	V.G.	Good	Fair	Poor
500	400	350	300	250	200

Baby Eagle 9mm (Standard)

Fitted with a 4.5" barrel and black oxide finish, this model has a magazine capacity of 16 rounds. Empty weight is 38 oz.

NIB	Exc.	V.G.	Good	Fair	Poor
500	400	350	300	250	200

Baby Eagle .41 Action Express

This model also has a 4.7" barrel and black oxide finish. Magazine capacity is 11 rounds. Empty weight is 38 oz.

NIB	Exc.	V.G.	Good	Fair	Poor
500	400	350	300	250	200

Baby Eagle Short Barrel (Semi-Compact)

This 9mm, 40 S&W, or .45 ACP model features a 3.6" barrel with frame-mounted safety. Weight is about 36 oz. Magazine holds 10 rounds.

NIB	Exc.	V.G.	Good	Fair	Poor
500	400	350	300	250	200

Baby Eagle Short Barrel/Short Grip (Compact)

This 9mm or .40 S&W version has a 3.6" barrel and shorter grip (3.25") than standard. Magazine capacity is still 10 rounds. Weight is about 38 oz. Frame-mounted safety.

NIB	Exc.	V.G.	Good	Fair	Poor
500	400	350	300	250	200

Baby Eagle Semi-Compact Polymer

This pistol has a polymer frame and a 3.9" barrel chambered for the 9mm or .40 S&W cartridge. Weight is about 29 oz.

NIB	Exc.	V.G.	Good	Fair	Poor
500	400	325	—	—	—

Baby Eagle Compact Polymer

As above but with 3.6" barrel and short grip. Weight is about 27 oz.

NIB	Exc.	V.G.	Good	Fair	Poor
500	400	325	—	—	—

NOTE: These custom shop finishes for Desert Eagle pistols are available: Satin nickel, bright nickel, polished and deep blued, matte hard chrome, polished hard chrome, brushed hard chrome, 24K gold. All finishes *except* gold add $195 to price of pistol. For gold finish add $500. For gold appointments add $195.

Mountain Eagle

This semi-automatic pistol is chambered for the .22 LR cartridge. It features a 6.5" barrel with adjustable rear sight. The grip is a one-piece molded plastic, checkered with raised side panels. The magazine capacity is 15 rounds with 20-round magazine available as an option. A black oxide finish is standard. The pistol weighs 21 oz.

NIB	Exc.	V.G.	Good	Fair	Poor
200	175	150	125	100	75

Mountain Eagle Target Edition

Similar to the standard Mountain Eagle but fitted with an 8" accurized barrel, two-stage target trigger, jeweled bolt, adjustable sights with three interchangeable blades, and range case.

NIB	Exc.	V.G.	Good	Fair	Poor
250	200	175	150	125	85

Mountain Eagle Compact Edition

Similar to above but fitted with a 4.5" barrel and short grip.

NIB	Exc.	V.G.	Good	Fair	Poor
200	150	125	100	85	70

Lone Eagle

This is a single-shot rotating breech pistol designed to fire centerfire cartridges. The standard finish is a black oxide blue luster. The barrel is drilled and tapped for scope mounts. Standard barrel length is 14". Fixed, adjustable, or silhouette sights are offered as options. Stock assembly is made from Lexan. The handgun is offered in these calibers: .22-250, .223, .22 Hornet, .243, .30-30, .30-06, .308, .357 Mag., .358 Win., .35 Rem., .44 Mag., .444 Marlin, 7mm-08, 7mm Bench Rest. Weighs between 4 lbs. 3 oz. to 4 lbs. 7 oz. depending on caliber.

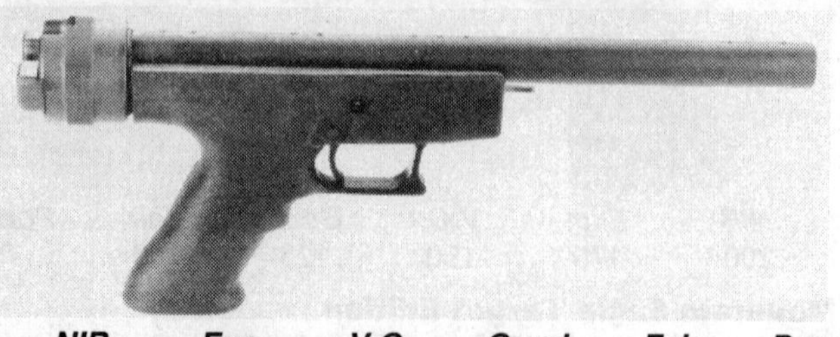

NIB	Exc.	V.G.	Good	Fair	Poor
375	300	275	250	200	125

Lone Eagle (New Model)

Introduced in 1996 this new Lone Eagle model features 15 interchangeable barreled actions from .22 Hornet to .444 Marlin. Available in both black and chrome actions with or without muzzlebrake. The 7.62x39 action was introduced in 1996 also. Sights can be fixed, adjustable or silhouette type. Weight is from 4 lbs. 3 oz. to 4 lbs. 7 oz. depending on caliber. Prices listed reflect black action and fixed sights.

NIB	Exc.	Good	Good	Fair	Poor
410	325	175	150	125	100

NOTE: Add $100 for muzzlebrake; $30 for chrome action; $35 for adjustable sights; $130 for silhouette sights.

Mountain Eagle Rifle

A limited edition rifle (1,000) with a Sako action and composite stock. Chambered for the .270, .280, .30-06, .300 Win., .338 Win, 7mm Mag. Introduced in 1994. Additional calibers are .300 Weatherby, .375 H&H, .416 Rem., and 7mm STW. Barrel length is 24". Average weight is about 7.74 lbs.

NIB	Exc.	V.G.	Good	Fair	Poor
2295	1700	1150	800	400	—

NOTE: For muzzlebrake add $150. For .375 H&H and .416 Rem. add $300. For left-hand actions add $100.

Mountain Eagle Varmint Edition

Chambered for the .222 Rem. and the .223 Rem. cartridges and fitted with a 26" stainless Krieger barrel. Kevlar-graphite stock. Weight is approximately 9 lbs. 13 oz.

NIB	Exc.	V.G.	Good	Fair	Poor
2295	1750	1150	800	400	—

Magnum Lite Rimfire Rifles

These rifles are built with Ruger 10/22 actions and graphite barrels. There are several variations depending on stock configuration.

Hogue and Fajen Scope-Hi Stock

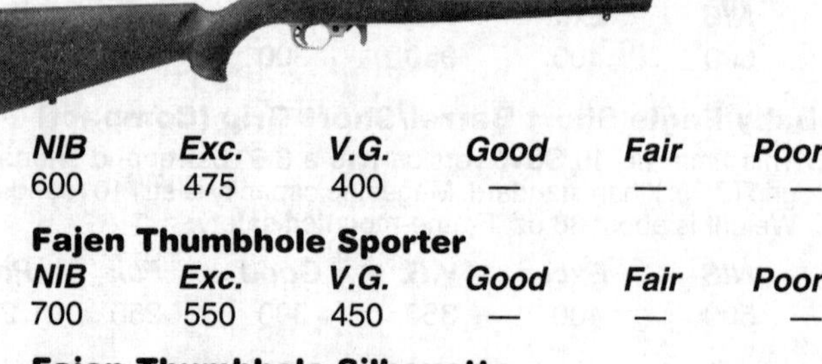

NIB	Exc.	V.G.	Good	Fair	Poor
600	475	400	—	—	—

Fajen Thumbhole Sporter

NIB	Exc.	V.G.	Good	Fair	Poor
700	550	450	—	—	—

Fajen Thumbhole Silhouette

NIB	Exc.	V.G.	Good	Fair	Poor
800	650	500	—	—	—

Turner Barracuda

NIB	Exc.	V.G.	Good	Fair	Poor
800	650	500	—	—	—

NOTE: For Clark Custom Upgrades add $130 to price of each Magnum Lite rifle.

Magnum Lite Centerfire Rifles

These rifles are built on Sako actions and are fitted with graphite barrels. Introduced in 1999. Offered in two configurations, both with synthetic stock.

Heavy Barrel

Fitted with a 26", 1.2" diameter barrel with a 1-in-14 twist. Chambered for .223 cartridge. Weight is approximately 7.8 lbs.

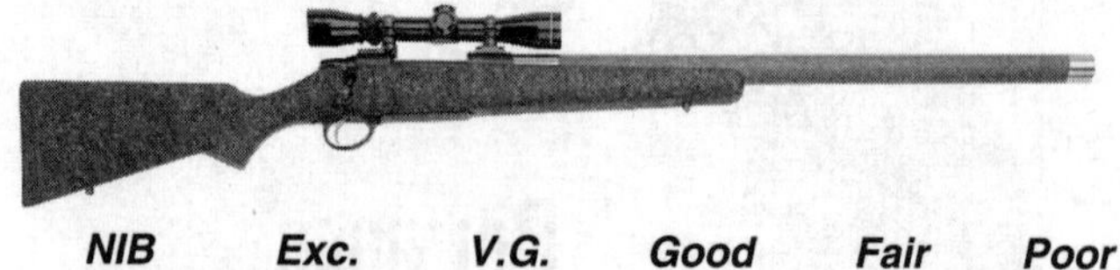

NIB	Exc.	V.G.	Good	Fair	Poor
2295	1700	1150	800	400	—

Sport Taper Barrel

Fitted with a 24" tapered barrel and chambered for the .280 Rem., 7mm Mag, .30-06, .300 Win. Mag. Weight is about 6.4 lbs.

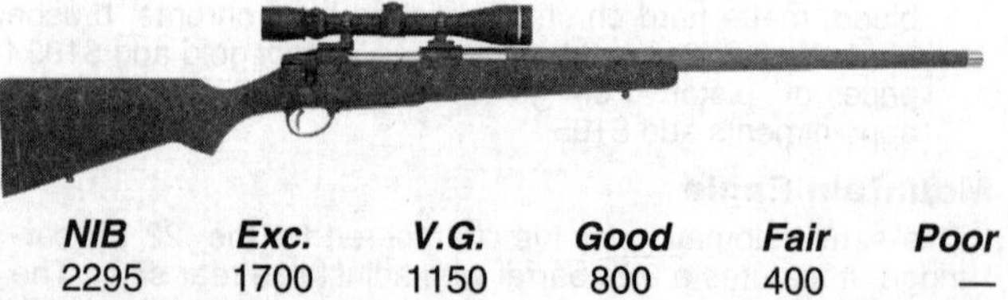

NIB	Exc.	V.G.	Good	Fair	Poor
2295	1700	1150	800	400	—

Tactical Rifle

Introduced in 2000 this rifle features a 26" match grade barrel chambered for the .223, .22-250, .308, or .300 Win. Mag. cartridges. The barrel is made from carbon fiber. The action is a Remington Model 700. H-S Precesion tactical stock with adjustable comb. Adjustable trigger. Weight is approximately 8.3 lbs.

NIB	Exc.	V.G.	Good	Fair	Poor
2400	1800	1250	850	—	—

DESERT INDUSTRIES

Las Vegas, Nevada

SEE—Steel City Arms

DESTROYER CARBINE

Spain

Destroyer Carbine

A 9mm Bayard/Largd caliber bolt-action rifle with a 20" barrel and 7-shot magazine. Full length stock with two barrel bands.

Exc.	V.G.	Good	Fair	Poor
425	350	200	100	35

DETONICS MANUFACTURING CORP.

Bellevue, Washington

This company manufactured semi-automatic pistols based upon the Colt Model 1911. It is no longer in business.

Mark I

A .45 caliber semi-automatic pistol with a 3.25" barrel and 6-shot magazine. Matte blued with walnut grips. Discontinued in 1981.

Exc.	V.G.	Good	Fair	Poor
550	450	400	300	200

Mark II

As above, with satin nickel-plated finish. Discontinued in 1979.

Exc.	V.G.	Good	Fair	Poor
550	450	400	300	200

Mark III

As above, with hard chrome plating. Discontinued in 1979.

Exc.	V.G.	Good	Fair	Poor
600	500	450	350	250

Mark IV

As above, with polished blue finish. Discontinued in 1981.

Exc.	V.G.	Good	Fair	Poor
550	450	400	300	200

Combat Master

The Mark I in 9mm, .38 Super, or .45 caliber.

NIB	Exc.	V.G.	Good	Fair	Poor
975	800	600	500	400	250

Combat Master Mark V

As above, in stainless steel with a matte finish. Discontinued in 1985.

NIB	Exc.	V.G.	Good	Fair	Poor
975	800	600	500	400	250

Combat Master Mark VI

As above, with adjustable sights and the sides of the slide polished. 1,000 were made in .451 Detonics Magnum caliber.

NIB	Exc.	V.G.	Good	Fair	Poor
900	750	600	500	400	250

NOTE: .451 Detonics Magnum add 40 percent.

Combat Master Mark VII

As above, without sights.

NIB	Exc.	V.G.	Good	Fair	Poor
900	750	600	500	400	250

NOTE: .451 Detonics Magnum add 40 percent.

Military Combat MC2

As above, in 9mm, .38 Super or .45 caliber with fixed sights, dull finish and Pachmayr grips. Discontinued in 1984.

NIB	Exc.	V.G.	Good	Fair	Poor
675	600	500	425	300	200

Scoremaster

As above, in .45 or .451 Detonics Magnum with a 5" or 6" barrel, Millet sights and a grip safety.

NIB	Exc.	V.G.	Good	Fair	Poor
1250	1000	800	600	400	250

Janus Competition Scoremaster

As above, in .45 caliber with a compensated barrel. Introduced in 1988.

NIB	Exc.	V.G.	Good	Fair	Poor
1750	1450	1250	850	650	300

Servicemaster

As above, with a 4.25" barrel, interchangeable sights and matte finish. Discontinued in 1986.

Exc.	V.G.	Good	Fair	Poor
1000	800	600	400	200

Pocket 9

A 9mm double-action semi-automatic pistol with a 3" barrel and 6-shot magazine. Matte finish stainless steel. Discontinued in 1986.

Exc.	V.G.	Good	Fair	Poor
400	350	275	225	175

DETONICS USA, LLC

Pendergrass, Georgia

This is a new company using improved materials and manufacturing techiques to built a new Detonics line of pistols.

Some of the features of the new Detonics line are: cone-shaped barrel, recoil system with counter-recoiling springs, recoil spring with guide rod with buffer, lowered ejection port, loaded magazine indicator, heavier firing pin than conventional 1911-style pistols, polished feed ramp, and other refinements.

Combat Master

Fitted with a 3.5" barrel chambered for the .45 ACP, .40 S&W, .357 SIG, .38 Super, or the 9mm Para cartridges. Checkered rosewood grips. Low profile fixed sights. Magazine capacity is 6 rounds. Height of pistol is 4.75". Overall length is 7". Weight is about 34 oz. All stainless steel including springs. Introduced in 2005.

NIB	Exc.	V.G.	Good	Fair	Poor
1200	—	—	—	—	—

Street Master

Chambered for the .45 ACP cartridge and fitted with a 5" barrel. Checkered rosewood grips. All stainless steel including springs. Height is 4.75". Overall length is 8.5". Weight is about 39 oz. Magazine capacity is 6 rounds.Fixed sights. Introduced in 2005.

NIB	Exc.	V.G.	Good	Fair	Poor
1200	—	—	—	—	—

Model 9-11-01

This model, introduced in 2005, is chambered for the .45 ACP cartridge and fitted with a 5" barrel. All stainlees steel construction. Checkered rosewood grips. Height is about 5.5". Overall length is 8.625". Weight is about 43 oz. Magazine capacity is 7 rounds. Fixed sights.

NIB	Exc.	V.G.	Good	Fair	Poor
1200	—	—	—	—	—

DEUTSCHE WERKE

Erfurt, Germany

Ortgies

A semi-automatic pistol in 6.35mm and 7.65mm. The 6.35mm pistol was manufactured in 1921 and the 7.65mm model in 1922 by the Ortgies Company. The pistols had the "HO" logo for Heinrich Ortgies on each grip. Later the Ortgies Company was bought by Deutsche Werke. The grip logo was "D." Over the period the Ortgies were manufactured with four different slide legends.

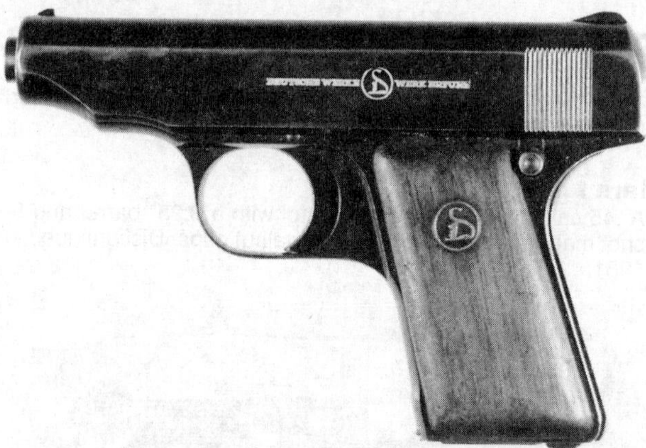

Courtesy James Rankin

Exc.	V.G.	Good	Fair	Poor
400	300	250	200	100

Ortgies 9mmk

As above but with the addition of a hold-open button on the left side of the slide. Caliber is 9mm.

Courtesy James Rankin

Exc.	V.G.	Good	Fair	Poor
450	375	250	175	100

 *This symbol denotes "Sleepers" with rapidly-rising values and/or significant collector potential.*

DEVISME, F. P.
Paris, France

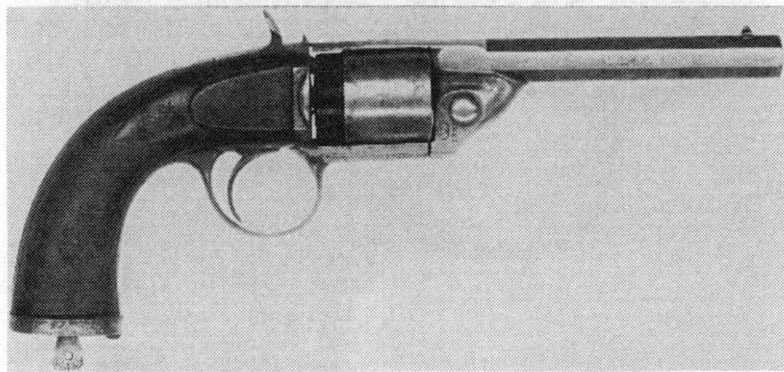

One of the more popular French gunsmiths of the mid-19th century, F.P. Devisme manufactured a wide variety of firearms including single-shot percussion pistols, double-barrel percussion rifles and shotguns, percussion revolvers and cane guns. After 1858 this maker manufactured cartridge weapons of the same style as his percussion arms. The quality of all of his products is uniformly high and it is impossible to provide generalized price guide.

DIAMOND
Turkey

Gold Series Auto
Chambered for the 12 gauge shell with 3" chamber. Barrel length is 28". Turkish walnut stock or synthetic stock. Black receiver with gold-filled engraving. Also available with 24" slug barrel with sights

NIB	Exc.	V.G.	Good	Fair	Poor
350	300	—	—	—	—

Note: Add $50 for walnut stock.

Gold Series Pump
Offered with the same features as the semi-auto Gold gun but with a slide-action.

NIB	Exc.	V.G.	Good	Fair	Poor
350	275	—	—	—	—

Note: Add $25 for walnut stock.

Silver Series Mariner Semi-Auto
This is a 12 gauge stainless steel and anodized alloy semi-auto gun with 3" chambers and fitted with 22" vent-rib barrel and synthetic stock.

NIB	Exc.	V.G.	Good	Fair	Poor
425	350	—	—	—	—

Silver Series Mariner Pump
A 12 gauge pump gun with 20" slug barrel and symthetic stock. Stainless steel and alloy.

NIB	Exc.	V.G.	Good	Fair	Poor
300	250	—	—	—	—

Diamond Elite Semi-Auto
This 12 gauge 3" chamber shotgun is offered with 22" to 28" barrels with 3 choke tubes. Engraved receiver.

NIB	Exc.	V.G.	Good	Fair	Poor
325	275	—	—	—	—

Diamond Elite Pump
As above but in a slide-action configuration.

NIB	Exc.	V.G.	Good	Fair	Poor
250	200	—	—	—	—

Diamond Panther Semi-Auto
A 12 gauge gun with 3" chambers with 20" or 28" vent-rib barrel. Furnished with three choke tubes. Synthetic stock.

NIB	Exc.	V.G.	Good	Fair	Poor
325	275	—	—	—	—

Diamond Elite Pump
As above but with slide-action. Also offered with 18.5" slug barrel.

NIB	Exc.	V.G.	Good	Fair	Poor
225	175	—	—	—	—

DICKINSON
SEE—Dickinson, E.L. & J.

DICKINSON, E. L. & J.
Springfield, Massachusetts

Ranger
A .32 caliber spur trigger revolver with a 6-shot cylinder.

Exc.	V.G.	Good	Fair	Poor
—	—	450	200	100

Single-Shot
A .32 caliber single-shot pistol with a 3.75" hinged barrel, silver plated brass frame, blued barrel and walnut grips.

Exc.	V.G.	Good	Fair	Poor
—	—	650	250	100

DICKSON, JOHN
Edinburg, Scotland
SEE—British Double Guns

DICKSON, NELSON & CO.
Dawson, Georgia

Dickson, Nelson Rifle
A .58 caliber single-shot percussion rifle with a 34" barrel, full stock secured by two barrel bands, brass furniture and iron loading rod. The lock marked "Dickson/Nelson & Co./C.S." as well as "Ala." and the date of manufacture. Prospective purchasers are advised to secure a qualified appraisal prior to acquisition. A carbine version of this arm is known and has a 24" barrel.

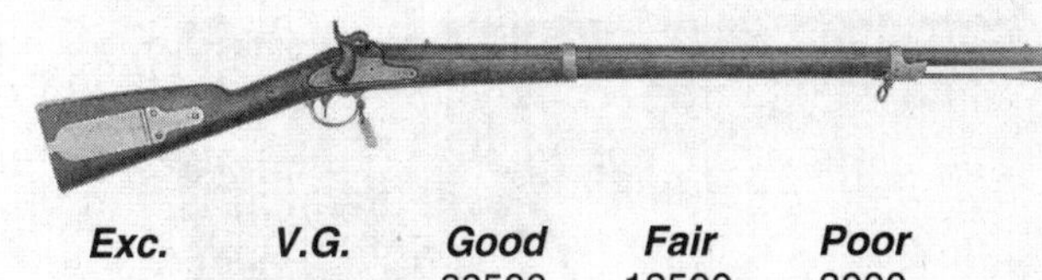

Exc.	V.G.	Good	Fair	Poor
—	—	32500	12500	3000

DIMICK, H.E.
St. Louis, Missouri

While this maker is primarily known for half stock Plains Rifles, he also manufactured a limited number of percussion pistols. These vary in length, caliber, stock form and type of furniture. The values listed should only be used as a rough guide. Prospective purchasers should secure a qualified appraisal prior to acquisition. Active 1849 to 1873.

Exc.	V.G.	Good	Fair	Poor
—	—	5000	2000	900

DOMINGO ACHA
SEE—Acha

DOMINO
Brescia, Italy

Model OP 601 Match Pistol
A .22 caliber short semi-automatic pistol with a 5.6" vented barrel, target sights, adjustable and removable trigger. Blued with adjustable walnut grips.

NIB	Exc.	V.G.	Good	Fair	Poor
1300	1000	800	550	—	—

Model SP 602 Match Pistol

As above, in .22 LR caliber.

Courtesy John J. Stimsom, Jr.

NIB	Exc.	V.G.	Good	Fair	Poor
1300	1000	800	550	—	—

DORMUS
Austria

8MM Special

Made in Austria in 1894 by M. Dormus from a design by Carlos Salvador. Fired a special 8mm cartridge. Fewer than 30 of these pistols were produced.

Courtesy James Rankin

Exc.	V.G.	Good	Fair	Poor
18000	15000	10000	7500	4000

DORNHAUS & DIXON
Huntington Beach, California

SEE—Bren 10

DORNHEIM, G.C.
Suhl, Germany

Gecado Model 11

A 6.35mm semi-automatic pistol bearing the name "Gecado" on the slide. Fitted with a 2.2" barrel. Magazine capacity is 6 rounds. Weight is about 15 oz. Marketed by G.C. Dornheim. Copy of the FN Browning Model 1906.

Courtesy James Rankin

Exc.	V.G.	Good	Fair	Poor
200	150	100	75	50

Gecado 7.65mm

A 7.65mm semi-automatic pistol bearing the name "Gecado" on the slide. Fitted with a 2.6" barrel. Magazine capacity is 7 rounds. Weight is about 21 oz. Marketed by G.C. Dornheim.

Exc.	V.G.	Good	Fair	Poor
275	150	125	75	50

DOUBLESTAR, CORP.
Winchester, Kentucky

Star EM-4

Chambered for the .223 cartridge and fitted with a 16" barrel. Rifle is supplied with A-2 or flat top upper and Colt M-4 handguard.

NIB	Exc.	V.G.	Good	Fair	Poor
915	750	—	—	—	—

Star-15

This model has a 20" barrel, A-2 buttstock, and A-2 handguard. Supplied with A-2 or flat top upper.

NIB	Exc.	V.G.	Good	Fair	Poor
775	625	—	—	—	—

Star Lightweight Tactical Rifle

Fitted with a 15" fluted barrel with permanently attached muzzlebrake. Fitted with a shot tactical buttstock. Supplied with an A-2 or flat top upper.

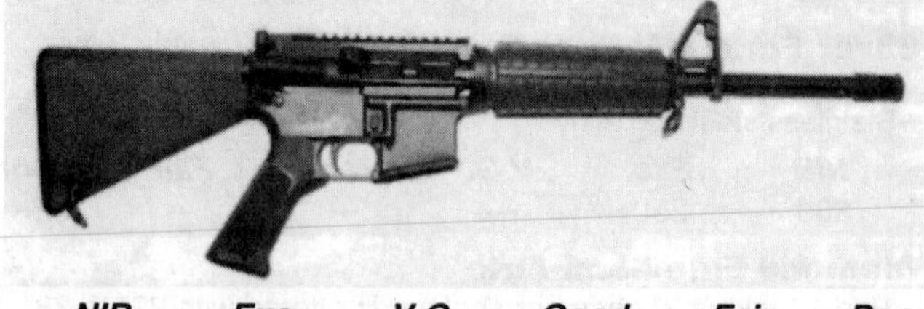

NIB	Exc.	V.G.	Good	Fair	Poor
880	700	—	—	—	—

Star Carbine

This model has a 16" match grade barrel. Supplied with either an A-2 buttstock or non-collapsing CAR buttstock. Upper receiver is A-2 style or flat top.

NIB	Exc.	V.G.	Good	Fair	Poor
775	625	—	—	—	—

Star DS-4 Carbine

This model features a 16" M-4 barrel with 6 position buttstock, oval handguard, and A2 flash hider. Weight is about 6.75 lbs. Choice of A2 or flattop upper receiver.

NIB	Exc.	V.G.	Good	Fair	Poor
875	700	—	—	—	—

Star Super Match Rifle

Choice of match grade barrel lengths of 16", 20", 22", or 24". Rifle supplied with flat top upper or tactical Hi-Rise upper.

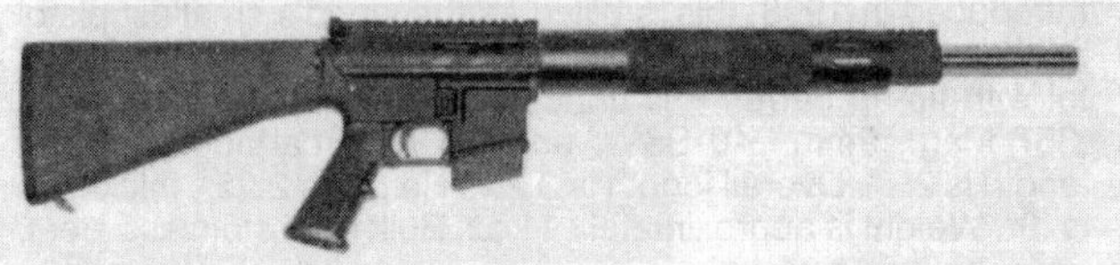

NIB	Exc.	V.G.	Good	Fair	Poor
875	700	—	—	—	—

Star Critterslayer

This model is fitted with a 24" fluted super match barrel with a flat top upper and free floating handguard. Match 2 stage trigger. Fitted with a Harris LMS swivel bipod and Ergo grip with palm swell.

NIB	Exc.	V.G.	Good	Fair	Poor
1300	1000	—	—	—	—

DSC Expedition Rifle

Offered with a 16" or 20" lightweight barrel with integral muzzle-brake. Stock, sights, and receiver are A2 configuration.

NIB	Exc.	V.G.	Good	Fair	Poor
825	650	—	—	—	—

DSC Star-15 CMP Service Rifle

Fitted with a 20" chrome lined heavy match barrel. National Match front and rear sights. CMP free float handguard. National Match trigger. A2 upper receiver.

NIB	Exc.	V.G.	Good	Fair	Poor
999	750	—	—	—	—

DSC Star CMP Improved Service Rifle

Similar to the above model but with 20" Wilson Arms premium grade heavy match barrel. McCormick single- or two-stage Match trigger and Tippie Competition rear sight.

NIB	Exc.	V.G.	Good	Fair	Poor
1299	975	—	—	—	—

DSC Star 15 Lightweight Tactical

This model is fitted with a 16" fluted heavy barrel with tactical "shorty" A-2 buttstock.

NIB	Exc.	V.G.	Good	Fair	Poor
880	700	—	—	—	—

DSC Star Dissipator

This model features a 16" barrel with full length handguard. Available with A2 or flattop upper receiver.

NIB	Exc.	V.G.	Good	Fair	Poor
875	700	—	—	—	—

DSC Star 15 9mm Rifle

Chambered for the 9mm cartridge and fitted with a 16" heavy barrel. A2 or flattop upper receiver. Available with A2 or CAR buttstock.

NIB	Exc.	V.G.	Good	Fair	Poor
995	750	—	—	—	—

DOUG TURNBULL RESTORATION, INC.

Bloomfield, New York

This company began operation in 1983 as a one-man shop. Today the company numbers 14 people and does finish work for most major firearms manufacturers. The company also installs Miller single triggers. The models listed are a series of special run firearms produced by Turnbull.

DT Colt

This model is a current Colt SAA reworked to look like the pre-1920 SAA. Assigned serial numbers beginning with 001DT these revolvers are offered in .45 Colt, .44-40, and .38-40 calibers. Barrel lengths are 4.75", 5.5", and 7.5". The standard DT has color case hardened frame and the rest of the gun charcoal blue. Cylinder flutes are enlarged and the front of the cylinder is beveled. Many special options offered which will affect cost. Prices listed are for standard revolvers.

Year Offered—1998

NIB	Exc.	V.G.	Good	Fair	Poor
1495	—	—	—	—	—

Year Offered—1999

NIB	Exc.	V.G.	Good	Fair	Poor
1995	—	—	—	—	—

Year Offered—2000

NIB	Exc.	V.G.	Good	Fair	Poor
2200					

EHBM Colt

This is a Colt SAA current production revolver limited to 50 guns chambered of the .45 Colt and fitted with a 5.5" barrel. Special features. Serial numbers EHBM01 to EHBM50. First offered in 2000.

NIB	Exc.	V.G.	Good	Fair	Poor
2150	—	—	—	—	—

Smith & Wesson No. 3 Schofield

Introduced in 2002 this is a special new production S&W Schofield with special serial numbers with a "DTR" prefix starting with serial number 0001. The frame, barrel, and cylinder are charcoal blued while the trigger, trigger guard, and barrel latch are bone color case hardened. Factory wood grips are standard. Engraving is optional.

NIB	Exc.	V.G.	Good	Fair	Poor
1995	—	—	—	—	—

Colt/Winchester Cased Set

A cased set with a Colt Model 1873 engraved revolver and a Winchester Model 1894. Colt is chambered for the .45 Colt cartridge and fitted with a 7.5" barrel. Engraving is "B" coverage. Model 1894 is chambered for the .45 Colt cartridge and is in the saddle ring configuration. Engraving pattern is #9 with deer. Checkered walnut stock. Limited to five sets total. Serial numbers 160DT to 164DT.

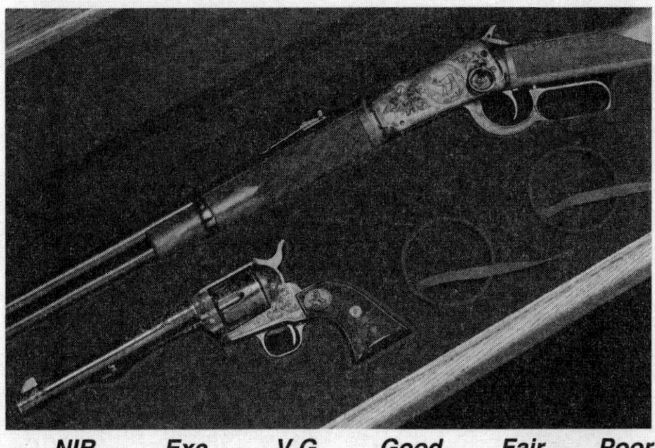

NIB	Exc.	V.G.	Good	Fair	Poor
5500	—	—	—	—	—

General Patton Colt

This limited run of engraved Colt Model 1873 single-action army revolvers is fitted with ivory grips and full-coverage engraving. Chambered for the .45 Colt cartridge and fitted with a 4.75" barrel. Helfricht-style engraving. Silver-plated finish. Limited to 10 revolvers total. Serial numbers GP01 to GP10.

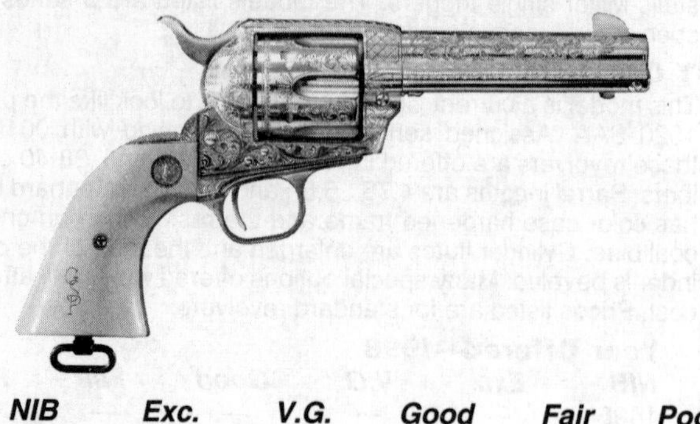

NIB	Exc.	V.G.	Good	Fair	Poor
5000	—	—	—	—	—

Theodore Roosevelt Colt

This Colt single-action army revolver features carved ivory grips, full coverage engraving with gold cylinder, hammer and ejector rod. Chambered for the .44-40 cartridge and fitted with a 7.5" barrel. Nimschke-style engraving. Balance of gun is silver plated. Supplied with fitted case. Limited to 25 revolvers total. Serial numbers TR01 to TR25.

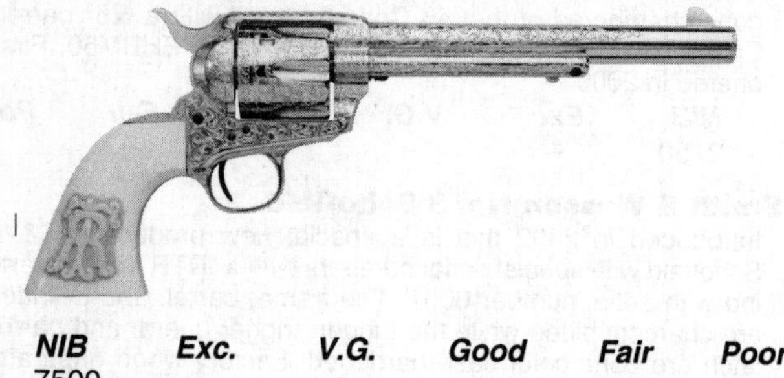

NIB	Exc.	V.G.	Good	Fair	Poor
7500	—	—	—	—	—

Theodore Roosevelt Winchester Model 1876

This custom rifle is limited to 25 pieces and will be serial numbered from TR01 to TR-25. Each rifle is engraved and checkered in the style of the original and chambered for the .45-70 cartridge. It is fitted with a 28" half round barrel. Gold inlaid stock oval. A portion of the proceeds of each rifle goes to benefit the Doug Turnbull Conservation Laboratory at the National Firearms Museum.

NIB	Exc.	V.G.	Good	Fair	Poor
28000	—	—	—	—	—

Classic Cowboy

Custom-tuned and authentically-finished USFA 1873-style single action revolver. Chambered in virtually all historically-correct centerfire cartridges. Barrel: 4.75, 5.5 and 7.5 inches. Black hard rubber grips standard. Bone charcoal case-hardened and charcoal blue finish. Introduced 2006. MSRP: 1150.

DOWNSIZER CORPORATION

Santee, California

Model WSP

Introduced in 1998, this is billed as the world's smallest pistol by the manufacturer. It is a single-shot, double-action-only pistol with tip-up barrel. It is chambered for .22 Mag., .32 Mag, .357 Mag., 9mm, .40 S&W, and .45 ACP cartridges. Barrel length is 2.1". Overall length is 3.25". Height is 2.25", thickness is .9". Weight is approximately 11 oz. Built from stainless steel.

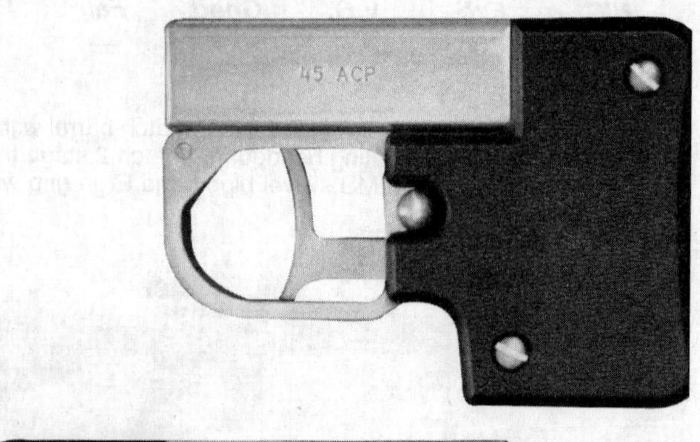

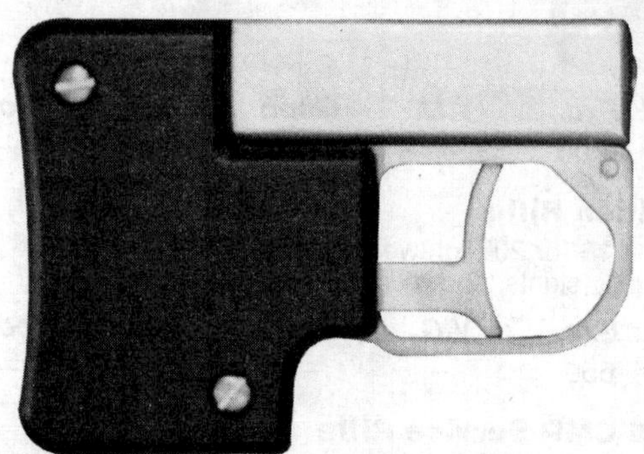

NIB	Exc.	V.G.	Good	Fair	Poor
330	250	—	—	—	—

DPMS

St. Cloud, Minnesota

Panther Bull A-15

This A-15 type rifle is chambered for the .223 cartridge and fitted with a 20" stainless steel bull barrel. A2-style buttstock. No sights. Barrel has 1:9 twist. Flat top receiver. Handguard is aluminum free float tube. Upper and lower receivers are hard coated black. Weight is about 9.5 lbs. Each rifle comes standard with two 7-round magazines, sling, and cleaning kit.

NIB	Exc.	V.G.	Good	Fair	Poor
900	700	550	—	—	—

Panther Bull 24

Similar to the model above but fitted with a 24" bull barrel. Flat top receiver. Weight is about 10 lbs.

 *This symbol denotes "Sleepers" with rapidly-rising values and/or significant collector potential.*

NIB	Exc.	V.G.	Good	Fair	Poor
950	750	600	—	—	—

Panther Deluxe Bull 24 Special

This model is fitted with a 24" stainless steel fluted bull barrel. Adjustable A2 style buttstock. Flat top receiver. Adjustable sniper pistol grip. Weight is about 10 lbs.

NIB	Exc.	V.G.	Good	Fair	Poor
1150	900	750	—	—	—

Panther Extreme Super Bull 24

This model is fitted with a 24" stainless steel extra heavy bull barrel (1.150" dia.). Skeletonized stock. Flat top receiver. Weight is about 11.75 lbs.

NIB	Exc.	V.G.	Good	Fair	Poor
1200	800	650	—	—	—

Panther Bulldog

Fitted with a 20" stainless steel fluted bull barrel with black synthetic A2-style buttstock. Flat top receiver. Adjustable trigger. Weight is about 10 lbs.

NIB	Exc.	V.G.	Good	Fair	Poor
1200	975	800	—	—	—

Panther Bull Sweet 16

This model is fitted with a 16" stainless steel bull barrel with flat top receiver. Weight is about 7.75 lbs.

NIB	Exc.	V.G.	Good	Fair	Poor
875	700	550	—	—	—

Panther Bull SST 16

Similar to the model above but with stainless steel lower receiver. Weight is about 9 lbs.

NIB	Exc.	V.G.	Good	Fair	Poor
875	700	550	—	—	—

Panther Bull Classic

This model is fitted with a 20" 4150 steel bull barrel. Square front post sight, adjustable A2 rear sight. Weight is about 9.75 lbs.

REMINDER

An "N/A" or "—" instead of a price indicates that there is no known price available for that gun in that condition, or the sales for that particular model are so few that a reliable price cannot be given.

NIB	Exc.	V.G.	Good	Fair	Poor
900	650	500	—	—	—

Panther Arctic

This model is similar to the model above but with 20" fluted bull barrel and flat top receiver. Black A2-style buttstock with white coat finish on receiver and handguard. Black Teflon finish on barrel. Weight is about 8.25 lbs.

NIB	Exc.	V.G.	Good	Fair	Poor
1075	850	700	—	—	—

Panther Classic

Fitted with a 20" 4150 steel heavy barrel with square front post sight and A2 rear sight. A2 round handguard. Weight is about 9.5 lbs.

NIB	Exc.	V.G.	Good	Fair	Poor
775	600	500	—	—	—

Panther DCM

This model is similar to the model above but with 20" stainless steel heavy barrel and NM rear sight. DCM free-float handguard. Adjustable trigger. Weight is about 9.5 lbs.

NIB	Exc.	V.G.	Good	Fair	Poor
1075	750	600	—	—	—

Panther Classic 16 Post Ban

This model is fitted with a 1" 4150 steel heavy barrel. A2-style sights. Round handguard. Weight is about 7.25 lbs.

NIB	Exc.	V.G.	Good	Fair	Poor
775	600	500	—	—	—

Panther Free Float 16 Post Ban

Similar to the model above with 16" barrel but fitted with a vented free-floated barrel and vented free-float tube handguard. Weight is approximately 7.25 lbs.

NIB	Exc.	V.G.	Good	Fair	Poor
825	650	550	—	—	—

Panther Southpaw Post Ban

This model is fitted with a 20" 4150 steel heavy barrel with A2-style sights. Upper receiver has been modified for left-hand ejection. Weight is about 9.5 lbs.

NIB	Exc.	V.G.	Good	Fair	Poor
875	700	600	—	—	—

Panther Race Gun

Similar to Panther Bull but with 24-inch fluted bull barrel. Sights: JP Micro adjustable rear, JP front sight adjustable for height. Includes Lyman globe and Shaver inserts. MSRP: 1719

Panther Tuber

Similar to Panther Bull 24 but with 16-inch barrel with cylindrical aluminum shroud.

NIB	Exc.	V.G.	Good	Fair	Poor
700	—	—	—	—	—

Single Shot Rifle

AR-15-style single-shot rifle with manually-operated bolt, no magazine.

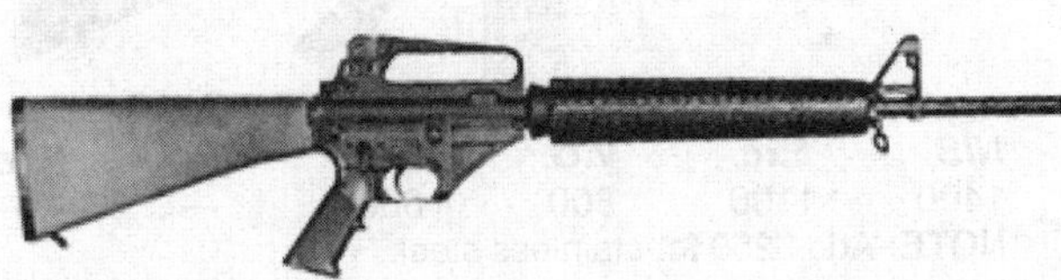

NIB	Exc.	V.G.	Good	Fair	Poor
775	—	—	—	—	—

Panthera Pardus

Similar to Panther Post-ban but with 16-inch bull barrel, telescoping buttstock and tan Teflon finish. Introduced 2006.

NIB	Exc.	V.G.	Good	Fair	Poor
1200	—	—	—	—	—

Panther 20th Anniversary Rifle

Similar to Panther Post-ban but with 20-inch bull barrel and engraved, chrome-plated lower receiver. Introduced 2006.

NIB	Exc.	V.G.	Good	Fair	Poor
2500	—	—	—	—	—

Panther 6.8 Rifle

Similar to Panther DCM but with 20-inch chrome-moly barrel and chambered for 6.8x43 Remington SPC. Introduced 2006.

NIB	Exc.	V.G.	Good	Fair	Poor
950	—	—	—	—	—

Panther Mark 12

Similar to Panther but with flash hider and other refinements. Introduced 2007.

NIB	Exc.	V.G.	Good	Fair	Poor
1300	—	—	—	—	—

Panther SDM-R

Similar to Panther but with stainless steel barrel and Harris bipod. Introduced 2007.

NIB	Exc.	V.G.	Good	Fair	Poor
1200	—	—	—	—	—

LRT-SASS

Semi-automatic rifle based on AR-15 design. Chambered in .308 Win. With 18-inch stainless steel barrel with flash hider, collapsible Vitor Clubfoot carbine stock and 19-rd. detachable magazine.Introduced 2006.

NIB	Exc.	V.G.	Good	Fair	Poor
1900	—	—	—	—	—

LR-260

Similar to LRT-SASS but with 24-inch stainless steel barrel and chambered in .260 Remington. Also available with 20-inch chrome-moly barrel as LR-260H. Introduced 2006.

NIB	Exc.	V.G.	Good	Fair	Poor
1100	—	—	—	—	—

LR-243

Similar to LR-260 but with 20-inch chrome-moly barrel and chambered in .243 Win. Introduced 2006.

NIB	Exc.	V.G.	Good	Fair	Poor
1100	—	—	—	—	—

LR-204

Similar to LRT-260 but chambered in .204 Ruger. Introduced 2006.

NIB	Exc.	V.G.	Good	Fair	Poor
1100	—	—	—	—	—

Panther A-15 Pump Rifle

This model has a 20" 4150 steel heavy barrel with A2-style sights. Fitted with an A2 compensator and modified to slide-action. Weight is about 8.5 lbs.

NIB	Exc.	V.G.	Good	Fair	Poor
1400	1050	700	—	—	—

Panther A-15 Pump Pistol

Same as above but fitted with a 10.5" barrel. Weight is about 5 lbs.

NIB	Exc.	V.G.	Good	Fair	Poor
1450	1100	750	—	—	—

DREYSE

SEE—Rheinmetall

DRISCOLL, J.B.

Springfield, Massachusetts

Single-Shot Pocket Pistol

A small pistol chambered for .22 rimfire. It has a 3.5" octagonal barrel that pivots downward for loading after a trigger-like hook under the breech is pulled. It has a spur trigger, silver-plated brass frame, and a blued barrel. The square butt is flared at the bottom, and the grips are walnut. There were approximately 200 manufactured in the late 1860s.

Exc.	V.G.	Good	Fair	Poor
—	—	900	350	100

DSA, INC.

Barrington, Illinois

DSA, Inc. began selling its rifles to the public in 1996. Based on actual blueprints of the famous FN/FAL rifle, DSA rifles are made in the US. All SA58 rifles are fitted with fully adjustable gas system, Type I, II, or III forged receiver, hand-lapped barrel, muzzlebrake, elevation adjustable post front sight, windage adjustable rear peep sight with 5 settings from 200 to 600 meters, detachable metric magazine, adjustable sling and hard case.

SA58 24" Bull

Fitted with a 24" stainless steel barrel with .308 match chamber. Overall length is 44.5". Weight is approximately 11.5 lbs.

NIB	Exc.	V.G.	Good	Fair	Poor
1795	1400	1050	800	—	—

SA58 21" Bull

Same as the above but fitted with a 21" stainless steel barrel. Weight is about 11.1 lbs.

NIB	Exc.	V.G.	Good	Fair	Poor
1795	1400	1050	800	—	—

SA58 Medium Contour

This model is offered with a 21" barrel in either stainless steel or blued steel. Weight is about 10.5 lbs.

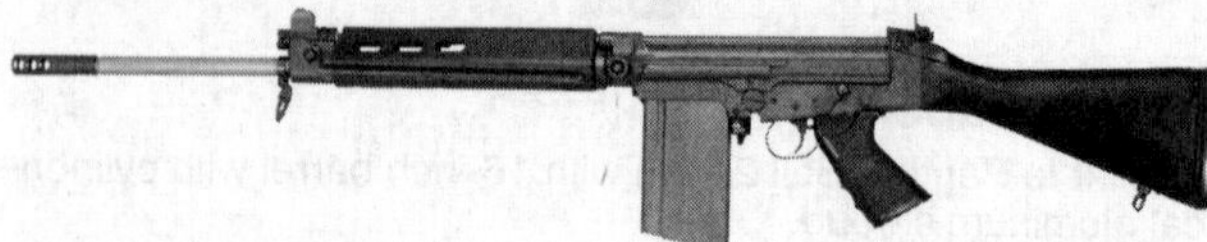

Medium contour stainless steel

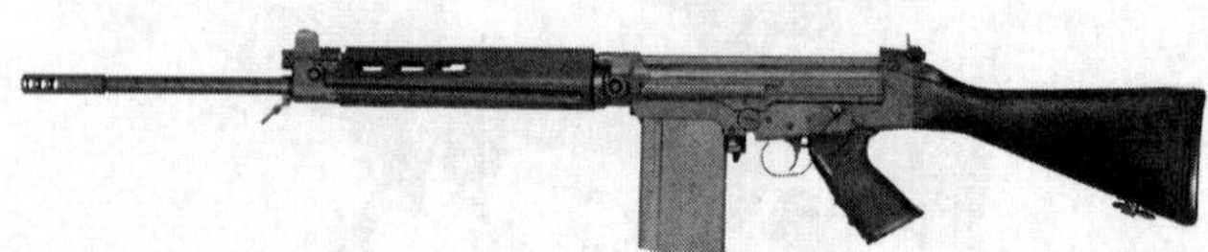

Medium contour blued

NIB	Exc.	V.G.	Good	Fair	Poor
1475	1200	950	700	—	—

NOTE: Add $250 for stainless steel.

SA58 Carbine

This model is fitted with a 16.25" barrel. Barrel is cut for factory light bipod. Blued finish. A stainless steel version is also available. Overall length is 37.5". Weight is about 8.35 lbs.

NIB	Exc.	V.G.	Good	Fair	Poor
1400	1100	800	600	—	—

NOTE: Add $250 for stainless steel.

SA58 Standard

This model has a 21" barrel cut for factory light bipod. Weight is about8.75 lbs. Blued finish.

NIB	Exc.	V.G.	Good	Fair	Poor
1500	1200	900	700	—	—

SA58 Tactical

Fitted with a 16.25" fluted barrel, black synthetic stock, Type I receiver, adjustable sights, and detachable magazine. Blued finish. Weight is about 8.25 lbs.

NIB	Exc.	V.G.	Good	Fair	Poor
1475	1100	—	—	—	—

SA58 Congo

This .308 model features a 18" bipod-cut barrel with short Belgian-style flase hider. Type I receiver with carry handle. Synthetic buttstock and pistol grip. Aluminum lower. Detachable magazine. Adjustable sights. Weight is about 8.6 lbs.

NIB	Exc.	V.G.	Good	Fair	Poor
1695	1350	950	—	—	—

SA58 Para Congo

This model is fitted with a Type II receiver with carry handle and a 18" bipod-cut barrel with short Belgian-style flash hider. Steel lower. Folding steel Para stock. Adjustable sights. Weight is about 9.85 lbs.

NIB	Exc.	V.G.	Good	Fair	Poor
1995	1550	1200	—	—	—

SA58 Predator

Offered in .308, .260 Rem., or .243. This rifle has a Type I receiver, a 16" medium carbine barrel with target crown or 19" medium barrel with target crown. Green furniture. Aluminum lower. Picatinny rail. Weight is about 9 lbs. with 16" barrel.

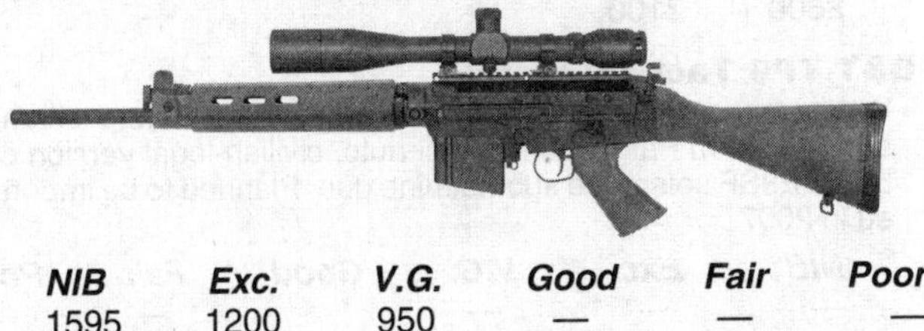

NIB	Exc.	V.G.	Good	Fair	Poor
1595	1200	950	—	—	—

SA58 Graywolf

This .308 model is fitted with a 21" match grade barrel with target crown. Type I receiver. Aluminum lower. Extended safety. Picatinny rail. Target pistol grip with standard or X-series buttstock. Versa-pod bipod. Weight is about 13 lbs.

NIB	Exc.	V.G.	Good	Fair	Poor
2100	1600	—	—	—	—

SA58 T48 Replica

Chambered for the .308 cartridge and fitted with a 21" barrel with replica Browning flash hider. Supplied with 10- or 20-round fixed magazine with stripper clip top cover. Wooden stock. Weight is about 9.7 lbs.

NIB	Exc.	V.G.	Good	Fair	Poor
1795	1400	—	—	—	—

SA58 Stainless Steel Carbine

Similar to SA58 carbine but in stainless steel. Introduced 2006.
MSRP: 1350

SR58 Medium Contour Stainless Steel

Similar to SA50 Standard but with flash hider and stainless steel lower, top cover and loading handle. Introduced 2006.
MSRP: 1350

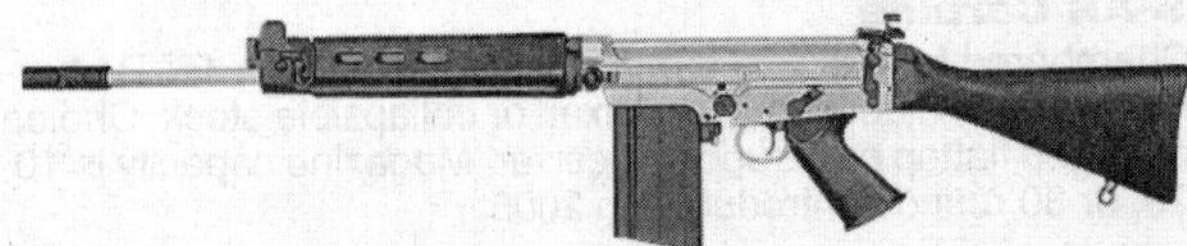

DS-MP1 .308 Custom Bolt Action

Based on Remington 700 short action. 22-inch stainless steel recessed Badger match barrel, black Duracote finish, black McMillan synthetic stock and Picatinny rail. Introduced in 2006.
MSRP: 2200

DS-AR

S1 Rifle

Introduced in 2004 this 5.56 caliber rifle features a 20" or 24" bull barrel with Picatinny gas black sight base. Flattop receiver. Free floating aluminum handguard. A2 stock. Ten-round magazine. Discontinued.

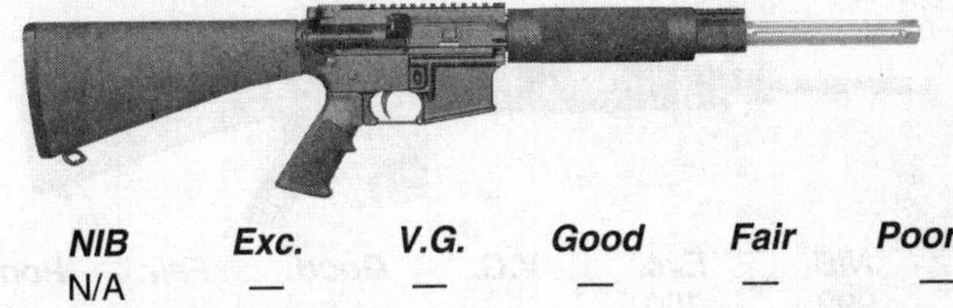

NIB	Exc.	V.G.	Good	Fair	Poor
N/A	—	—	—	—	—

CVI Carbine

Similar to the model above but with a 16" barrel with forged front sight base and integral muzzlebrake. D-4 handguard. Fixed CAR buttstock. Ten-round magazine. Discontinued

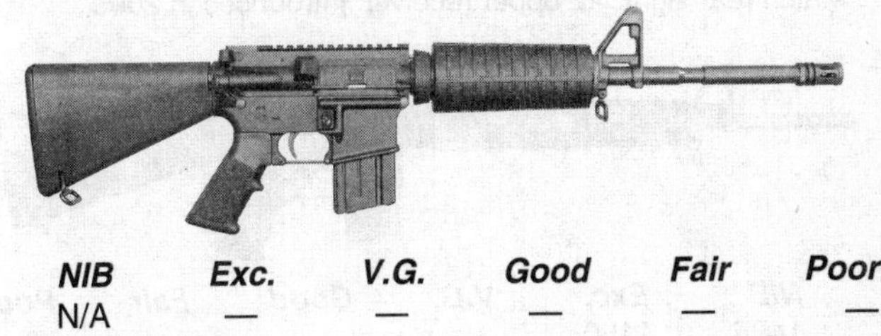

NIB	Exc.	V.G.	Good	Fair	Poor
N/A	—	—	—	—	—

LE4 Carbine

As above but with pre-ban features. For law enforcement only. Discontinued.

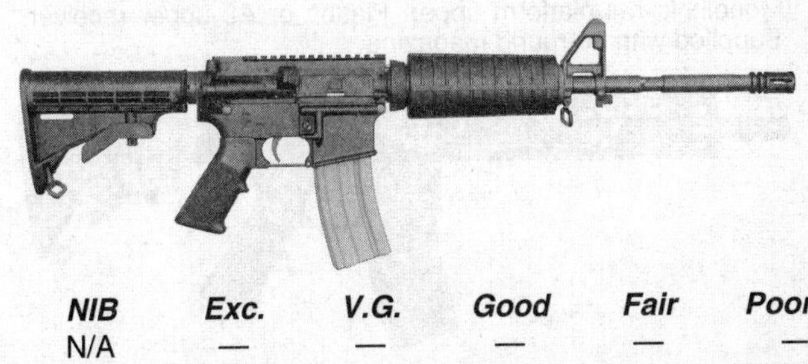

NIB	Exc.	V.G.	Good	Fair	Poor
N/A	—	—	—	—	—

DS-AR S Series Rifle

Introduced in 2005 this rifle is chambered for the .223 cartridge and fitted with a choice of 16", 20", or 24" stainless steel match grade bull barrel. A2 stock with free floating handguard. Flattop receiver, National Match 2 stage trigger. Magazine capacity is 10, 20, or 30 rounds.

NIB	Exc.	V.G.	Good	Fair	Poor
1130	850	—	—	—	—

DS-AR Carbine

Chambered for the .223 cartridge and fitted with a 16" D4 barrel with flash hider. Choice of fixed or collapsible stock. Choice of forged flattop or A2 upper receiver. Magazine capacity is 10, 20, or 30 rounds. Introduced in 2005.

NIB	Exc.	V.G.	Good	Fair	Poor
999	750	—	—	—	—

DS-AR Rifle

As above but with 20" heavy barrel with flash hider and fixed stock. Introduced in 2005.

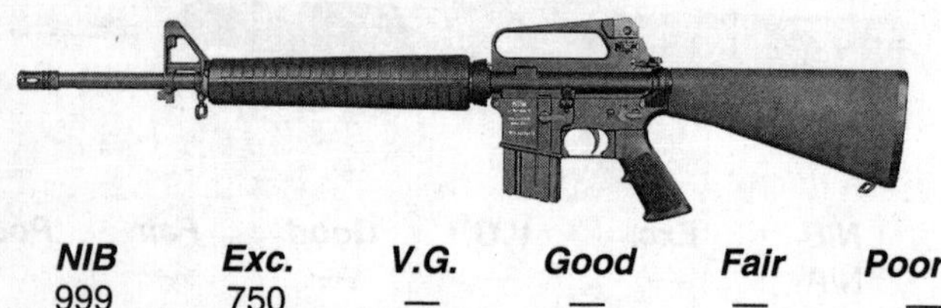

NIB	Exc.	V.G.	Good	Fair	Poor
999	750	—	—	—	—

DS-AR DCM Rifle

Chambered for the .223 cartridge with Wylde chamber. Fitted with a 20" match grade Badger barrel. DCM free float handguard system. National Match two-stage trigger. National Match rear sight. A2 upper receiver. Introduced in 2005.

NIB	Exc.	V.G.	Good	Fair	Poor
1495	1150	—	—	—	—

DS-AR CQB MRP

Introduced in 2005 this model features a 16" chrome lined barrel with A2 flash hider. Collapsible stock with MRP quad rail. Monolithic rail platform upper. Flattop or A2 upper receiver. Supplied with 30-round magazine.

NIB	Exc.	V.G.	Good	Fair	Poor
2395	1750	—	—	—	—

DSA Z4 Gas Trap Carbine (GTC)

This model, introduced in 2005, is fitted with a 16" chrome lined barrel with M4 profile fluted with Vortec flash hider. Collapsible 6-position stock with free float tactical rail. Gas trap system. Flattop upper receiver. Magazine capacity is 10, 20, or 30 rounds.

NIB	Exc.	V.G.	Good	Fair	Poor
1675	1250	—	—	—	—

BOLT ACTION RIFLES

DS-MP1

This is a bolt action rifle chambered for the .308 cartridge. It is built on a custom Remington 700 action and fitted with a 21" Badger barrel with target crown. Black McMillian A5 stock. Matte black finish. Introduced in 2004.

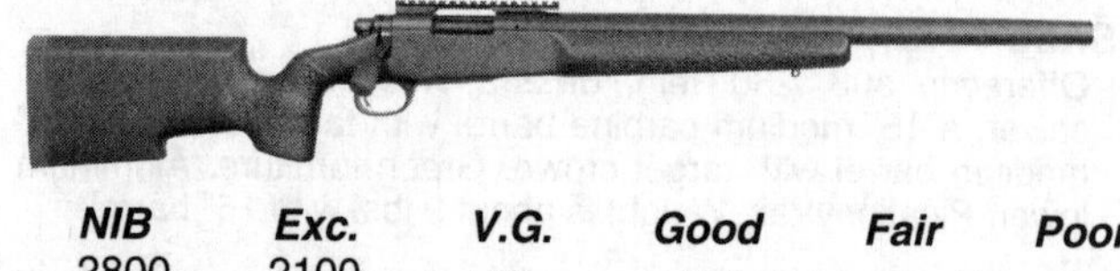

NIB	Exc.	V.G.	Good	Fair	Poor
2800	2100	—	—	—	—

B&T TP9 Tactical Pistol

Swiss made recoil-operated, rotating-bolt semi-auto chambered in 9mm Parabellum. Semi-auto, civilian-legal version of B&T TP9SF select-fire submachine gun. Planned to be imported in 2007.

NIB	Exc.	V.G.	Good	Fair	Poor
—	—	—	—	—	—

DUBIEL ARMS CO.

Sherman, Texas

Established in 1975 by Joseph Dubiel and Dr. John Tyson. They are engaged in the manufacture of high-quality, custom built, bolt-action rifles. The rifles are constructed from patented Dubiel actions that feature a 5-lug bolt locking mechanism and a 36-degree bolt rotation. They are chambered for all calibers from .22-250 through .458 Winchester Magnum. Barrel lengths, weights, and stock styles are made to the customer's order. Douglas Premium barrels and Canjar triggers are used, and there are six basic stock designs available. The rifles are guaranteed to group in 1.5" at 100 yards with factory ammunition. The values listed are basic retail prices.

NIB	Exc.	V.G.	Good	Fair	Poor
2750	2000	1500	950	700	—

DUMOULIN

Herstal, Belgium

The guns produced by Ernest Dumoulin are essentially handmade to the customer's order. They are of the highest quality, both in materials and workmanship. There are many options available that have a tremendous impact on value fluctuations. The models and values listed here are base prices.

SHOTGUNS

Europa Model

A side-by-side double-barrel chambered for 12, 20, and 28 gauge and .410 bore. It is available in any length barrel and choke combination, with an Anson & Deeley boxlock action and automatic ejectors. One has the option of double- or single-selective triggers and a choice of six different moderate engraving patterns. The select walnut stock is oil-finished. This model was introduced in 1989. Basic values are listed.

NIB	Exc.	V.G.	Good	Fair	Poor
3500	2750	1950	1250	800	—

Leige Model

A side-by-side double chambered for 12, 16, 20, and 28 gauge. It is similar to the Europa, with a greater degree of finish and more engraving. The walnut is of a higher grade. This model was introduced in 1986.

NIB	Exc.	V.G.	Good	Fair	Poor
5750	4200	2750	1500	950	—

Continental Model

A side-by-side chambered for 12, 20, and 28 gauge and .410. Barrel lengths and chokes are on a custom-order basis. This is a true sidelock action with automatic ejectors and choice of triggers. There are six different engraving patterns, and the stock is made of high grade, hand-checkered, oil-finished walnut. This model was introduced in 1989.

NIB	Exc.	V.G.	Good	Fair	Poor
7500	6000	4500	3000	1500	—

Etendart Model

A side-by-side chambered for 12, 20, and 28 gauge. This best grade side-by-side is built on a purely made-to-order basis. It is profusely engraved and uses exhibition grade walnut in its stock. There are 12 different engraving patterns from which to choose, and the cost is according to embellishments chosen. Values given here are for the basic model.

NIB	Exc.	V.G.	Good	Fair	Poor
14500	11000	8500	4000	3000	—

Superposed Express International

An Over/Under chambered for 20 gauge and is furnished with a set of rifle barrels in the customer's choice of seven calibers. The walnut is of a deluxe grade, and engraving is available at extra cost. This is a made-to-order gun, and the value here is for the most basic model. This gun was discontinued in 1985.

Exc.	V.G.	Good	Fair	Poor
2500	2000	1250	750	—

Boss Royal Model

The best grade Over/Under, chambered for 12, 20, and 28 gauge. It is a full sidelock gun that is made to the customer's specification using the finest materials and workmanship available. This model was introduced in 1987.

NIB	Exc.	V.G.	Good	Fair	Poor
18500	15000	12000	8000	4500	—

Eagle Model Combination Gun

This model has a rifle barrel or the shotgun barrel that is chambered for 12 or 20 gauge. The rifle calibers available are .22 Hornet, .222 Remington, .222 Remington Magnum, 6mm, .243, .25-06, .30-06, 6.5 x 57R, 7 x 57R, 8 x 57JRS, and 9.3 x 74R. The action is a boxlock with automatic ejectors, and the other specifications are on a custom-order basis. This model was introduced in 1989.

NIB	Exc.	V.G.	Good	Fair	Poor
2750	2250	1500	950	750	—

DOUBLE RIFLES

Europa I

A made-to-order, Over/Under, double-barreled rifle available in the same calibers as the Eagle Combination gun. It has an Anson & Deeley boxlock and all other options to the customer's specifications.

NIB	Exc.	V.G.	Good	Fair	Poor
5000	4000	3000	2000	1000	—

Continental I Model

A more deluxe Over/Under rifle with a true sidelock-action. The calibers are the same as the Europa. The specifications are to the customer's order with 12 engraving patterns to choose from at extra cost. This model was introduced in 1989.

NIB	Exc.	V.G.	Good	Fair	Poor
8500	6750	5500	4000	2000	—

Pionier Express Rifle

A side-by-side double rifle chambered for the .22 Hornet through the .600 Nitro Express. It has the Anson & Deeley boxlock-action and is quite deluxe throughout. The specifications are to the customer's order, and there are basically 12 models available (P-1 through P-XII). The differences among these models are in the degree of ornamentation and quality of the walnut used for the stock. The prices of these models would have to be ascertained through appraisal, as a book of this nature could not possibly consider the variables that one could encounter with a gun of this type. Values range from approximately $8,000 to $12,000 for the basic models.

Aristocrat Model

A low-profile single-shot chambered for all calibers up to .375 Holland & Holland. This is a deluxe, made-to-order rifle with exhibition-grade walnut and 12 engraving patterns available.

Exc.	V.G.	Good	Fair	Poor
9000	7000	5500	3000	—

BOLT-ACTION RIFLES

Centurion Model

A custom-order rifle built on a Mauser or Sako action and chambered for all calibers from .270 to .458 Winchester Magnum. The barrel lengths available were 21.5", 24", and 25.5"; and there were many engraving options from which to choose. The stock is of deluxe French walnut, with rosewood forend tip and pistol gripcap. This rifle was discontinued in 1986.

NIB	Exc.	V.G.	Good	Fair	Poor
800	650	500	400	300	200

Centurion Classic

Similar to the Mauser-actioned Centurion chambered for the non-Magnum calibers only. The walnut used for the stock is a better grade.

NIB	Exc.	V.G.	Good	Fair	Poor
950	750	600	500	400	200

Diane

A more deluxe version of the Centurion Classic.

NIB	Exc.	V.G.	Good	Fair	Poor
1550	1250	900	650	500	300

Amazone

A 20" barreled, full-length stocked, upgraded version of the Diane.

NIB	Exc.	V.G.	Good	Fair	Poor
1750	1400	950	700	500	300

Bavaria Deluxe

Similar to the Centurion, with the same barrel lengths and calibers available. The engraving styles available are more deluxe. This model was discontinued in 1985.

NIB	Exc.	V.G.	Good	Fair	Poor
1900	1500	1000	800	500	300

Safari Model

Similar to the Bavaria Deluxe, but it is chambered for the heavy Magnum calibers only.

NIB	Exc.	V.G.	Good	Fair	Poor
2400	1900	1450	900	500	300

Safari Sportsman

Built on a Magnum Mauser action and is chambered for the .375 Holland & Holland, .404 Jeffreys, .416 Rigby, and the .505 Gibbs. This is a true big game rifle that was made available in 1986.

NIB	Exc.	V.G.	Good	Fair	Poor
4000	3250	2000	1250	900	—

African Pro

A more deluxe version of the Safari Sportsman, with a folding leaf rear sight, hooded front sight, and an ebony or buffalo horn forend tip.

NIB	Exc.	V.G.	Good	Fair	Poor
4800	3750	2500	1500	1000	—

NOTE: Again it is important to note that all values furnished in this section are estimates based on the most basic model in each designation. There are many options that will radically affect values.

DURLOV

Czech Republic

This company was part of the national co-operative under communist rule when the Czech Republic was part of Czechoslovakia. The company was formed in 1948. The company specialized in low-cost but well made rimfire target pistols.

Durlov Model 70 Standard

This model is a bolt-action single-shot pistol chambered for the .22 Long Rifle. A knob at the rear of the frame opened the bolt. When the bolt is closed the firing pin is cocked. The barrel is 9.75" long with an adjustable front sight for windage. The rear sight is adjustable for elevation. Wooden wraparound grips with thumb rest are standard. Weighs about 44 oz.

Exc.	V.G.	Good	Fair	Poor
300	200	175	100	75

Durlov Model 70 Special

Same as above but with the addition of a set trigger.

Exc.	V.G.	Good	Fair	Poor
350	250	200	150	100

Durlov Model 75

This model features a set trigger, better sights, and grip. The rear sight is fully adjustable.

Exc.	V.G.	Good	Fair	Poor
400	300	250	200	150

Pav

This target pistol was introduced between World War I and World War II. It is an inexpensive pistol with a fixed front sight and a notch for the rear sight. Like the other models above it is also a single-shot chambered for the .22 Long Rifle cartridge. The barrel is 10.25" and weighs about 35 oz.

Courtesy Orvel Reichert

Exc.	V.G.	Good	Fair	Poor
175	150	100	75	50

DUSEK, F.

Opocno, Czech Republic

Dusek commenced business in the mid-1920s and continued to make firearms through WWII. They manufactured pistols for Nazi Germany under the contract code "aek." After the war the communists took over, and Dusek's designs were relegated to the CZ factory.

Perla

This 6.35mm pistol has a fixed barrel and open-topped slide. It resembles a Walther design and is striker-fired. The slide is marked "Automat Pistole Perla 6.35mm"; the grips, "Perla 6.35." Dusek made this model from the early 1930s until WWII.

Exc.	V.G.	Good	Fair	Poor
300	200	150	100	80

Duo

Introduced in 1926, this 6.35mm pistol is based on the 1906 Browning design. It has a 2.25" barrel and 6-shot detachable magazine. The Duo was successful from a commercial standpoint and was exported throughout the world. During WWII the slide markings were in German; and the name "Eblen," Dusek's German sales agent, may sometimes be found on the slide. The Duo may also be found marked Ideal, Jaga, and Singer.

Courtesy J.B. Wood

Exc.	V.G.	Good	Fair	Poor
300	200	150	100	80

NOTE: Nazi-marked examples will bring a 25 percent premium.

E

E.M.F. CO., INC.

Santa Ana, California
SEE—Uberti, Aldo

An importer and a distributor of quality Italian-made reproduction firearms. Its offerings are listed in the section dealing with Aldo Uberti firearms. Included are new products for this company as of 1997.

Hartford Bisley

This single-action revolver is fitted with a Colt Bisley grip. Chambered for .45 Long Colt as well as .32-20, .357 Magnum, .38-40, and .44-40 calibers. Barrel lengths are 4-3/4", 5-1/2", and 7-1/2". Plain walnut grips.

NIB	Exc.	V.G.	Good	Fair	Poor
450	350	—	—	—	—

Hartford Express

A single Colt SAA frame and barrel with a Colt Lightning-style grip. Chambered for .45 Long Colt in 4-3/4", 5-1/2", or 7-1/2" barrel lengths.

NIB	Exc.	V.G.	Good	Fair	Poor
450	350	—	—	—	—

Hartford Pinkerton

This model features a 4" barrel with ejector and a bird's-head grip. Chambered for 45 Long Colt, .32-20, .357 Magnum, .38-40, .44-40, and .44 Special.

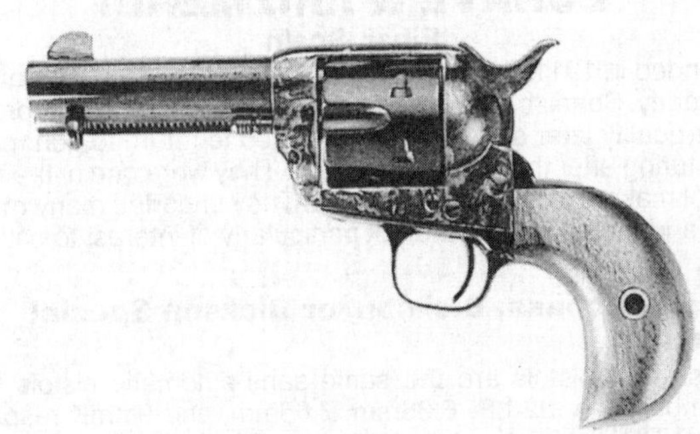

NIB	Exc.	V.G.	Good	Fair	Poor
450	350	—	—	—	—

EAGLE ARMS CO.

New Haven, Connecticut
SEE—Plant's Manufacturing Co.

EAGLE ARMS

Division of Armalite
Geneseo, Illinois

PRE-BAN MODELS

Golden Eagle

This model is identical in design to the AR-15. Fitted with a 20" stainless steel extra-heavy barrel with National Match sights and two-stage trigger. Weight is about 9.4 lbs.

NIB	Exc.	V.G.	Good	Fair	Poor
1500	1200	850	—	—	—

HBAR

Similar to the above model but with a heavy 20" barrel. Weight is approximately 8 lbs.

NIB	Exc.	V.G.	Good	Fair	Poor
1100	800	600	—	—	—

SPR

This is similar to the above model with the exception of a detachable carry handle. Weight is about 7.6 lbs.

NIB	Exc.	V.G.	Good	Fair	Poor
1150	850	650	—	—	—

M4C Carbine

This model features a 16" barrel with a 4.33" flash suppressor. Retractable stock. Weight is approximately 6.2 lbs.

NIB	Exc.	V.G.	Good	Fair	Poor
1100	800	600	—	—	—

M4A1C Carbine

Similar to the above model but with detachable carry handle. Weight is about 6 lbs.

NIB	Exc.	V.G.	Good	Fair	Poor
1150	800	600	—	—	—

POST-BAN MODEL

Golden Eagle

This model features a 20" stainless steel extra-heavy barrel with two-stage trigger. Weight is about 9.2 lbs.

NIB	Exc.	V.G.	Good	Fair	Poor
1200	900	700	—	—	—

ECHAVE & ARIZMENDI

Eibar, Spain

Founded in 1911, this company produced the usual poor quality, early Spanish semi-automatic pistols. They did improve their quality later on and were permitted to return to gun manufacturing after the Spanish civil war. They were one of the few pistol makers to survive this period. They imported many models, and their products are not particularly of interest to collectors.

Basque, Echasa, Dickson, or Dickson Special Agent

These four pistols are the same semi-automatic pistols but chambered in .22 LR, 6.35mm, 7.65mm, and 9mmK respectively. Their magazine capacities are 10, 9, 7, and 6 rounds. They are manufactured with alloy frames and various finish combinations. The specific model names are stamped on the slides and grip plates.

Courtesy James Rankin

Exc.	V.G.	Good	Fair	Poor
250	150	125	90	50

Bronco Model 1913

A semi-automatic pistol in caliber 6.35mm. Patterned after the Browning Model 1906 with a squeeze grip safety. Bronco is stamped on the slide and on each side of the grip plate.

Courtesy James Rankin

Exc.	V.G.	Good	Fair	Poor
200	150	100	70	40

Bronco Model 1918

A semi-automatic pistol chambered for both 6.35mm or 7.65mm. Both are patterned after the Browning Model 1906 with a squeeze grip safety. The 7.65mm pistol is approximately 1/2" longer and higher than the 6.35mm. It has a magazine capacity of 7 rounds. The 6.35mm pistol has a magazine capacity of 6 rounds.

Courtesy James Rankin

Exc.	V.G.	Good	Fair	Poor
200	150	100	70	40

Echasa

Similar to the 6.35mm Bronco, without a grip safety. It is marked "Model 1916."

Exc.	V.G.	Good	Fair	Poor
175	125	100	75	50

Lightning

A renamed version of the Bronco in 6.35mm.

Exc.	V.G.	Good	Fair	Poor
175	125	100	75	50

Lur Panzer

A copy of the Luger toggle-lock-action, chambered for .22 rimfire. This is an almost exact copy except for a different trigger assembly and a less robust mainspring. It is marked "Lur Cal.22 LR Made in Spain." The plastic grips have "Panzer" molded into them.

Exc.	V.G.	Good	Fair	Poor
250	200	150	125	100

Pathfinder

A semi-automatic pistol similar to the Bronco above but in caliber 6.35mm and 7.65mm. Sold in the U.S. by Stoeger. The 7.65mm Pathfinder holds 12 rounds. The values listed are for both pistol models.

Exc.	V.G.	Good	Fair	Poor
225	175	125	90	50

Protector Model 1915 and 1918

A semi-automatic pistol in caliber 6.35mm. Similar to the Echasa model. "Protector" is stamped on the slide while the grip plates have various logos of the firms that marketed the pistol.

Courtesy James Rankin

Exc.	V.G.	Good	Fair	Poor
200	150	100	70	40

Selecta Model 1918

A semi-automatic pistol chambered for 7.65mm cartridge. Patterned after the Protector but chambered for the 7.65mm. "Selecta" is stamped on the slide and Echave Arizmendi logo is on each of the grip plates.

Courtesy James Rankin

Exc.	V.G.	Good	Fair	Poor
200	150	100	70	40

ECHEVERRIA, STAR-BONIFACIO SA

Eibar, Spain

An old-line Spanish company that survived the Spanish civil war. It was founded in 1908 by Jean Echeverria, but the early records of the company were lost during the civil war. The early pistols the company produced were patterned after the Mannlicher designs, and the trade name Star was the closest thing to Steyr that could be used. After the close of WWI, the company began production of the open-topped slide Star for which they have become known. They also produced a large 1911-type pistol that was successful. During the civil war, the plant was damaged and the company records destroyed; but after the cessation of hostilities, they were one of only three gun companies that were allowed to remain in business. They survive to this day and are known for the manufacture of quality firearms.

Star Model 1908

The first pistol produced under the Star banner. It is a Mannlicher copy that is chambered for 6.35mm. It has a 3" fixed barrel and an open-topped slide. The detachable magazine holds 8 shots. The finish is blued, and the grips are checkered plastic. The slide is marked "Automatic Pistol Star Patent."

Courtesy James Rankin

Exc.	V.G.	Good	Fair	Poor
300	250	200	150	100

Star Model 1914

Similar to the Model 1908, with a 5" barrel and larger grips that have the Star name molded into them. This model was the first to have the six-pointed star surrounded by rays of light (that became the Star trademark) stamped on its slide.

Courtesy James Rankin

Exc.	V.G.	Good	Fair	Poor
300	250	200	150	100

Star Model 1919

Also a copy of a Mannlicher design and differs from its predecessors chiefly in the way the pistol is disassembled. This model has a spring catch at the top of the trigger guard. This model also has a small spur on the hammer, and the magazine release was relocated to a button behind the trigger guard instead of a catch at the bottom of the butt. This model was chambered for 6.35mm, 7.65mm and 9mm short, with various barrel lengths offered. The maker's name, as well as the Star trademark, is stamped into the slide. This model was produced until 1929.

Courtesy James Rankin

Exc.	V.G.	Good	Fair	Poor
300	250	200	150	100

Star Model 1919 New Variation

Same as above but with full spur hammer.

Courtesy James Rankin

Exc.	V.G.	Good	Fair	Poor
300	250	200	150	100

Modelo Militar

Represents the first pistol Star produced that was not a Mannlicher design copy. This model was copied from the Colt 1911. It was chambered initially for the 9mm Largo in hopes of securing a military contract. When this contract was awarded to Astra, Star chambered the Model 1919 for the .38 Super and the .45 ACP and put it on the commercial market. This model is like the Colt 1911—it has a Browning-type swinging link and the same type of lock up. However there is no grip safety, and the thumb safety functions differently. This model was produced until 1924.

Exc.	V.G.	Good	Fair	Poor
300	250	200	175	125

Star Model A

A modification of the Model 1919, chambered for the 7.65mm, 7.63mm Mauser, 9mm Largo, and the .45 ACP cartridge. The slide is similar in appearance to the 1911 Colt, and the spur hammer has a small hole in it. Early models had no grip safety, but later production added this feature. Some models are slotted for addition of a shoulder stock.

Courtesy James Rankin

Exc.	V.G.	Good	Fair	Poor
375	275	175	150	100

Star Model B

Similar to the Model A except that it is almost an exact copy of the Colt 1911. It is chambered for 9mm Parabellum and has a spur hammer with no hole. This model was introduced in 1928.

Courtesy Orvel Reichert

Exc.	V.G.	Good	Fair	Poor
350	250	200	175	125

Star Model C

The Model B chambered for the 9mm Browning long cartridge. It was manufactured in the 1920s.

Exc.	V.G.	Good	Fair	Poor
250	175	150	125	90

Star Model CO

A pocket pistol similar to the early open-topped Star pistols. It is chambered for the 6.35mm cartridge, and the finish is blued with checkered plastic grips that bear the Star name and logo. This model was manufactured between 1930 and 1957.

Courtesy James Rankin

Exc.	V.G.	Good	Fair	Poor
250	150	125	100	75

Star Model D

A medium-sized pistol that is similar in appearance to a smaller Model A. It is chambered for the 9mm short cartridge and was called the "Police and Pocket Model" after it was adopted by the Spanish police. It was manufactured between 1930 and 1941.

Exc.	V.G.	Good	Fair	Poor
275	175	150	110	80

Star Model E

A pocket pistol chambered for the 6.35mm cartridge. It has a 2.5" barrel and an external hammer. The detachable magazine holds 5 rounds, and the finish is blued with checkered plastic grips. This model was manufactured between 1932 and 1941.

Exc.	V.G.	Good	Fair	Poor
225	175	150	110	80

Star Model F

The first of the .22 caliber Star pistols. It has a 4" barrel, a 10-shot magazine, and fixed sights. The finish is blued, and the plastic grips are checkered. This model was manufactured between 1942 and 1967.

Exc.	V.G.	Good	Fair	Poor
225	175	125	100	75

Star Model F Target

Similar to the Model F, with a 6" barrel.

Exc.	V.G.	Good	Fair	Poor
250	200	150	125	100

Star Model F Sport

Has a 5" barrel and was also manufactured between 1962 and 1967.

Exc.	V.G.	Good	Fair	Poor
225	175	150	125	100

Star Model F Olympic

Has a 6" barrel and adjustable sights. It is furnished with a muzzlebrake and barrel weights. It was manufactured between 1942 and 1967.

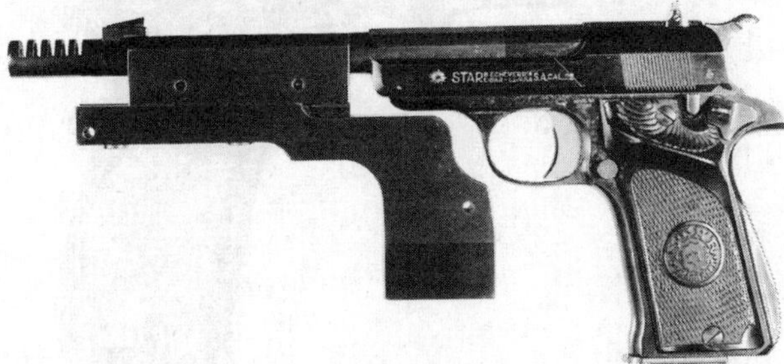

Courtesy James Rankin

Exc.	V.G.	Good	Fair	Poor
325	225	175	150	125

Star Model F Olympic Rapid Fire

Similar to the Olympic but is chambered for .22 Short only.

Exc.	V.G.	Good	Fair	Poor
325	225	175	150	125

Star Model FR

Has an adjustable sight and a slide stop. The 4" barrel is heavier, with flattened sides. It was manufactured between 1967 and 1972.

Exc.	V.G.	Good	Fair	Poor
225	175	145	125	100

Star Model FRS

Similar to the Model FR, with a 6" barrel. It is also available chrome-plated with white checkered plastic grips. It was introduced in 1967 and is still in production.

Exc.	V.G.	Good	Fair	Poor
225	175	145	125	100

Star Model FM

A heavier-framed version of the Model FRS. It has a 4.5" barrel and is available in blue or chrome-plated. It was introduced in 1972 and is still made.

Exc.	V.G.	Good	Fair	Poor
225	175	145	125	100

Star Model H

Similar to the old Model CO—only larger in size. It is chambered for the 7.65mm cartridge and was manufactured between 1932 and 1941.

Exc.	V.G.	Good	Fair	Poor
225	175	150	125	100

Star Model HK

A pocket-sized version of the Model F chambered for .22 Short. It has a 2.5" barrel and is quite scarce on today's market.

Exc.	V.G.	Good	Fair	Poor
250	200	150	125	100

Star Model HN

Simply the Model H chambered for the 9mm Short cartridge. It was manufactured and discontinued at the same time as the Model H was.

Exc.	V.G.	Good	Fair	Poor
250	200	150	125	100

Star Model I

An improved version of the Model H with a 4" barrel and a recontoured grip. It was chambered for 7.65mm and was produced until 1941. After the war it was resumed and survived until the mid-1950s, when it was replaced by the modernized Model IR that would be valued approximately the same.

Exc.	V.G.	Good	Fair	Poor
200	150	125	100	75

Star Model M

Similar to the Model B, chambered for the .38 Auto cartridge.

Exc.	V.G.	Good	Fair	Poor
275	225	175	125	100

Star Model P

The post-war version of the Model B, fitted with a 5" barrel and chambered for the .45 ACP cartridge. Checkered walnut grips and blued finish.

Exc.	V.G.	Good	Fair	Poor
350	300	225	175	125

Star Model CU "Starlet"

Similar to the Model CO, with an alloy frame that was anodized in black, blue, gray, green, or gold. It has a steel slide that is blued or chrome-plated. It has checkered, white plastic grips and is chambered for the .25 ACP cartridge. It has a 2.5" barrel, fixed sights, and a 5-shot magazine. This model was introduced in 1975 and was not imported after 1986.

Exc.	V.G.	Good	Fair	Poor
200	150	125	100	75

Star Model 1941 S

Add 100 percent to prices listed for pistols issued to Spanish Air Force with box, cleaning rod, instruction sheet, and two numbered magazines.

Courtesy Richard M. Kumor Sr.

Exc.	V.G.	Good	Fair	Poor
200	175	150	100	75

Star Model BKS "Starlight"

The smallest locked-breech automatic chambered for the 9mm cartridge at the time. It has an alloy frame and a 4.25" barrel. It is similar in appearance to a scaled-down Colt 1911 without a grip safety. It has an 8-shot magazine and is either blued or chrome-plated, with checkered plastic grips. This model was manufactured between 1970 and 1981.

Exc.	V.G.	Good	Fair	Poor
275	225	200	150	125

Star Model PD

Chambered for the .45 ACP cartridge and has a 4" barrel. It has an alloy frame and a 6-shot magazine and adjustable sights and is blued with checkered walnut grips. It was introduced in 1975.

NIB	Exc.	V.G.	Good	Fair	Poor
400	325	275	225	175	125

Star Model BM

A steel-framed 9mm that is styled after the Colt 1911. It has an 8-shot magazine and a 4" barrel. It is available either blued or chrome-plated.

NIB	Exc.	V.G.	Good	Fair	Poor
350	300	250	200	150	125

Star Model BKM

Similar to the BM, with an alloy frame.

NIB	Exc.	V.G.	Good	Fair	Poor
375	325	275	225	175	125

Star Model 28

The first of Star's Super 9s. It is a double-action semi-automatic chambered for the 9mm Parabellum cartridge. It has a 4.25" barrel and a steel frame. The magazine holds 15 shots. The construction of this pistol was totally modular, and it has no screws in its design. It is blued with checkered synthetic grips and was manufactured in 1983 and 1984.

NIB	Exc.	V.G.	Good	Fair	Poor
400	300	250	200	150	100

Star Model 30M

An improved version of the Model 28, that is quite similar in appearance. It was introduced in 1985.

NIB	Exc.	V.G.	Good	Fair	Poor
450	350	300	250	200	125

Star Model 30/PK

Similar to the Models 28 and 30M, with a lightweight alloy frame.

NIB	Exc.	V.G.	Good	Fair	Poor
450	350	300	250	200	125

ECHEVERRIA
(Star)

Megastar

This is a double-action semi-automatic pistol chambered for the 10mm or .45 ACP cartridge. It features a three-position ambidextrous selective decocking lever, rubber grips, combat-style trigger guard, slotted hammer, and checkered mainspring housing. Barrel length is 4.6" and the magazine capacity is 12 rounds. Available in either blue or starvel (brushed chrome). The pistol weighs 47.6 oz.

NIB	Exc.	V.G.	Good	Fair	Poor
500	450	350	250	200	100

Firestar-M/43, M/40, and M45

This is a compact large caliber semi-automatic pistol offered in 9mm, the M43, .40 S&W, the M40, and the .45 ACP, the M45. It features an ambidextrous safety, steel frame and slide, checkered rubber grips. The barrel is 3.4" on the M43 and M40 and 3.6" on the M45. Choice of finish is blue or starvel (brushed chrome). A finger rest magazine is optional. Weight for the M43 and M40 is 30 oz. while the M56 weighs 35 oz. Introduced in 1990.

NIB	Exc.	V.G.	Good	Fair	Poor
400	300	250	200	150	100

Firestar Plus

This is a lightweight version of the Firestar Series with the addition of a double column magazine. Offered in the 9mm caliber in either blue or starvel finish this pistol has a magazine capacity of 10 rounds and weighs 24 oz. Introduced in 1992.

NIB	Exc.	Good	Good	Fair	Poor
450	350	300	250	175	125

Starfire Model 31P

This model evolved from the Models 28 and 30. It is chambered for either the 9mm Parabellum or .40 S&W. The trigger action is double-action/single-action. Barrel length is 3.9". It is fitted with a two position safety/decocking lever. The magazine capacity for the 9mm is 15 rounds while the .40 S&W holds 11 rounds. The pistol weighs 39 oz.

NIB	Exc.	V.G.	Good	Fair	Poor
425	350	300	250	200	100

Starfire Model 31PK

Similar to the Model 31P but built on an alloy frame. Chambered for 9mm only with a 15-round magazine capacity. Weight is 30 oz.

NIB	Exc.	V.G.	Good	Fair	Poor
400	325	275	225	200	100

Ultrastar

Introduced in 1994 this compact 9mm or .40 S&W semi-automatic pistol with a polymer frame features a 3.57" barrel, a 9-round magazine, a blued finish and an overall length of 7". It weighs about 26 oz. It has a double-action operating system, a windage adjustable rear sight, and an ambidextrous two-position safety.

NIB	Exc.	V.G.	Good	Fair	Poor
475	375	325	275	200	100

ECLIPSE

Enterprise Gun Works
Pittsburgh, Pennsylvania

Single-Shot Derringer

This pocket pistol was made by the firm of James Bown & Son, doing business as the Enterprise Gun Works. It is chambered for .22 or .32-caliber rimfire cartridges. A few in .25 rimfire have been noted and would add approximately 25 percent to the values listed. The barrel is 2.5" in length and is part-round/part-octagonal. It pivots sideways for loading. It has a spur trigger and a bird's-head grip. The barrel is stamped "Eclipse." It is made of nickel-plated iron, with walnut grips. There were approximately 10,000 manufactured between 1870 and 1890.

Exc.	V.G.	Good	Fair	Poor
—	600	250	100	75

84 GUN CO.

Eighty Four, Pennsylvania

In business for a brief time in the early 1970s, this company produced three basic bolt-action rifles—each in four grades that differ in amounts of embellishment and grades of wood. There is little known about this company and its products. An accurate appraisal with hands-on would be the only proper way to place a value on these rifles as there are not enough traded to establish correct values. The basic models are listed.

Classic Rifle

Grade 1-Grade 4 available
$450—$1600

Lobo Rifle

Grade 1-Grade 4 available
$425—$2500

Pennsylvania Rifle

Grade 1-Grade 4 available
$425—$2500

EL DORADO ARMS

SEE—United Sporting Arms, Inc.

ELGIN CUTLASS

Springfield, Massachusetts

Manufactured by two companies—C.B. Allen of Springfield, Massachusetts, and Morill, Mosman and Blair of Amherst, Massachusetts. It is a unique pistol that has an integral knife attachment affixed to the gun barrel. It was designed and patented by George Elgin and simultaneously produced by the two companies. The inspiration for this weapon was supposedly Jim Bowie, who at that time had made a name as a knife fighter with his large "Bowie" knife. The blades for these pistols were supplied by N.P. Ames of the famed Ames Sword Co. These pistols are much sought after, and one must exercise caution as fraudulent examples have been noted.

C. B. ALLEN-MADE PISTOLS

U.S. Navy Elgin Cutlass Pistol

Chambered for .54 caliber percussion and has a 5" octagonal smooth-bore barrel. The Bowie-style blade is 11" long by 2" wide and is forged together with the trigger guard and the knuckle guard that protects the grip. The handle is walnut. This pistol was issued to the U.S. Navy's Wilkes-South Sea Exploration Expedition, and the markings are "C.B. Allen / Springfield / Mass." "Elgin's Patent" and the letters "CB", "CBA" along with the date 1837. If the sheath that was issued with this knife pistol is included and in sound condition, it would add approximately $700 to the value. There were 150 manufactured for the U.S. Navy in 1838.

Exc.	V.G.	Good	Fair	Poor
—	10000	8000	6500	4750

Civilian Model

Chambered for .35 or .41 caliber percussion and has a 4" octagonal barrel with a 7.5"-10" knife blade. It has a round trigger guard but does not have the knuckle bow across the grip, as found on the military model. They are marked "C.B. Allen Springfield, Mass." Blades marked "N.P. Ames" have been noted. There were approximately 100 manufactured in 1837.

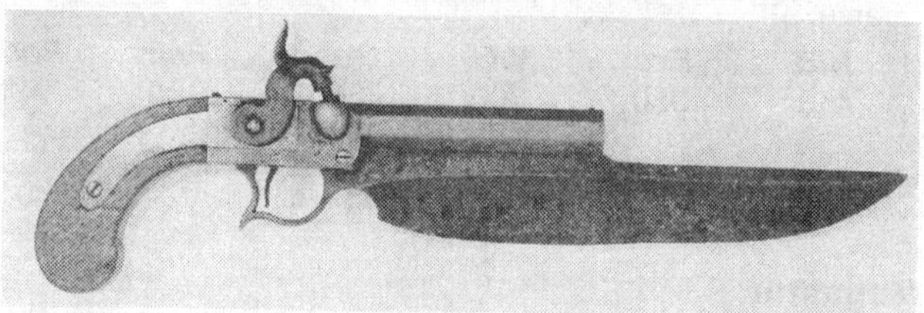

Exc.	V.G.	Good	Fair	Poor
—	9000	6000	3250	2750

MORILL, MOSMAN AND BLAIR-MADE PISTOLS

Small Model

The main difference in the pistols of the two makers is that this model has a round barrel and a square-back trigger guard that comes to a point at the rear. This version is chambered for .32 caliber percussion and has a 2.75" barrel. The knife blade is 7.5" in length and is screwed to the frame. This model is unmarked except for a serial number. The number produced is unknown, and they were manufactured in 1837.

Exc.	V.G.	Good	Fair	Poor
—	9000	6000	3250	2750

Large Model

Chambered for .36 caliber percussion and has a 4" round barrel and a 9" knife blade. The pistol is usually marked "Cast Steel" and serial numbered. The blade is etched with an American eagle, stars, and an urn with flowers. "Elgin Patent" is etched in the center. This model was also manufactured in 1837.

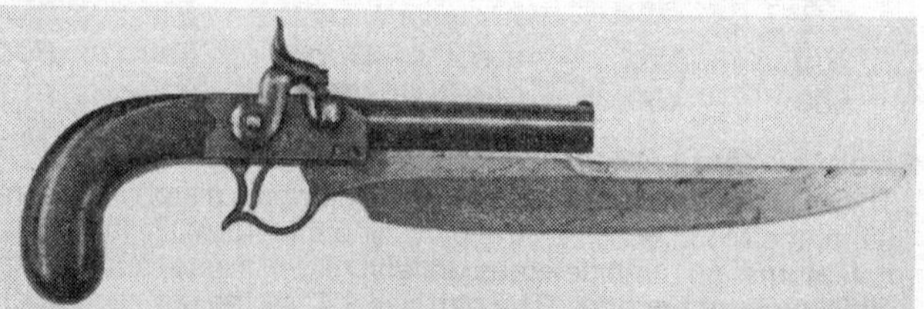

Courtesy Milwaukee Public Museum, Milwaukee, Wisconsin

Exc.	V.G.	Good	Fair	Poor
—	10000	7000	3500	3000

ELLS, JOSIAH
Pittsburgh, Pennsylvania

Pocket Revolver
Three distinct variations of this percussion revolver. They are chambered for .28 and .31 caliber and have 6-shot unfluted cylinders. They have been noted with 2.5", 3", and 3.75" octagonal barrels.

Model 1
The first model has an open-topped frame and is chambered for .28 caliber. The cylinder holds 5 or 6 shots, and the hammer is of the bar type. It was offered with a 2.5" or 3" barrel. The markings are "J. Ells; Patent; 1854." There were approximately 625 manufactured between 1857 and 1859.

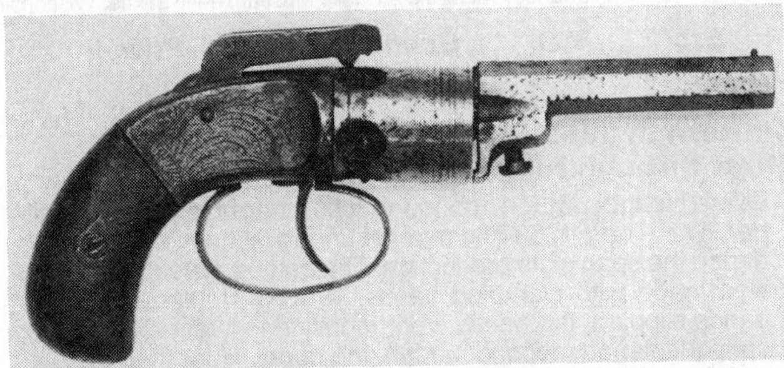

Courtesy Milwaukee Public Museum, Milwaukee, Wisconsin

Exc.	V.G.	Good	Fair	Poor
—	1500	650	300	200

Model 2
The second model is similar to the first, with a solid-topped frame. They have 5-shot cylinders and 3.75" long barrels. There were approximately 550 manufactured.

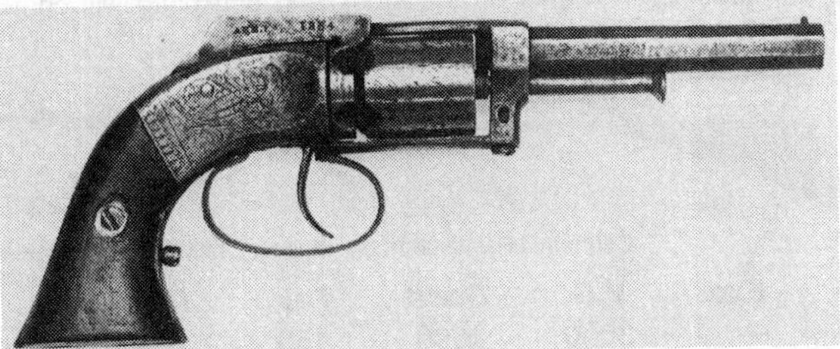

Courtesy Milwaukee Public Museum, Milwaukee, Wisconsin

Exc.	V.G.	Good	Fair	Poor
—	1500	650	300	200

Model 3
The third model is radically different from its forerunners. It has a closed-top frame and a conventional spur-type hammer that strikes from the right side. It functions either as a double- or single-action. It is chambered for .28 caliber and has a 5-shot cylinder and a 3.75" barrel. There were only about 200 manufactured between 1857 and 1859.

Exc.	V.G.	Good	Fair	Poor
—	1750	950	400	200

ENDERS, CARL
Suhl, Germany

Side-by-Side Shotgun
Percussion damascus double-barrel side-by-side in 12 gauge. Ornate checkering with cheekpiece and engraved metal work. This firm made high-quality firearms, mostly side-by-side guns. The gun pictured was made circa 1850-1860. The firm was in business from about 1835 to approximately 1890.

Courtesy Jim Cate

Exc.	V.G.	Good	Fair	Poor
—	1150	500	—	—

ENFIELD ROYAL SMALL ARMS FACTORY
Middlesex, England

NOTE: For technical details, descriptions, photos, and prices see the *Standard Catalog of Military Firearms, 2nd Edition* under Great Britain, Handguns and Rifles.

ENFIELD AMERICAN, INC.
Atlanta, Georgia

MP-45
A blowback-operated, semi-automatic assault pistol chambered for the .45 ACP cartridge. It was offered with a barrel length of 4.5" through 18.5". The long barrel features a shroud. The finish is Parkerized, and there were four different magazines available in 10, 20, 30, and 50-round capacities. This firearm was manufactured in 1985 only.

Exc.	V.G.	Good	Fair	Poor
300	275	225	175	125

ENGLISH MILITARY FIREARMS
Enfield, England

Until the establishment of the Royal Armory at Enfield in 1816, the government of England relied solely upon the contract system to obtain small arms for its naval and military forces. Even after the Enfield Armory began is first major production in 1823, the contractors continued to dominate the production of arms for the military. These contractors were concentrated in two major cities, Birmingham and London. Although a number of makers from Birmingham were capable of manufacturing arms, "lock, stock, and barrel," and of assembling them, most of the makers of that city specialized in the making of specific parts, which could be assembled into complete arms on the "factory system" then prevalent in Liege. When the English War Department was the purchaser, the parts were usually delivered to the Tower of London for assembly. Most military arms made in Birmingham accordingly are seldom marked with a single maker's name. Rather they bear the English crown and the name "TOWER" on the lock. Those barrels that passed proof at Birmingham after 1813 were marked with the view and proofmarks derived from Ketland's only proofmarks; these consisted of a pair of crowned, crossed scepters, one pair of which had the letter "V" in the lower quarter and the other of which had the letters "B," "C," and "P" respectively in the left, right, and lower quarters. In contrast, the arms manufactured at London were almost always completed by their manufacturers, and bear their names usually upon the lockplates and barrels. The London gunmakers also marked their barrels with a pair of proofmarks, consisting of a crown over a "V" and a crown over an intertwined "G" and "P." Prominent martial arms makers in the London trade through the 1860s included, "BOND," "BARNETT," "BLISSETT," "GREENER," "HOLLIS & SONS," "LONDON ARMORY CO," "KERR," "PARKER, FIELD & SONS," "PRITCHETT," "POTTS & HUNT," "ROBERT WHEELER," "WILSON & CO.," and "YEOMANS." (It should be noted that most of these London makers also manufactured sporting and other trade arms, which will bear similar marks.) During the period of transition from the contract system to the reliance upon the works at Enfield (roughly 1816 through 1867), the arms themselves underwent major transitions, first from flintlock to percussion ignition systems and then from smoothbore to rifled bore, first in large and then in small bore sizes. The major infantry types include:

New Land Pattern Musket

Overall length 58-1/2"; barrel length 42"; caliber .75. The mainstay of the British Army during the Napoleonic Wars, this flintlock arm continued, primarily, in service until 1838, with major quantities (5,000 from each) being ordered from Enfield and from the contractors as late as 1823.

Exc.	*V.G.*	*Good*	*Fair*	*Poor*
—	3500	1500	850	600

Pattern of 1839 (P1839) Musket

Overall length 55"; barrel length 39"; caliber .76. In 1838 the British War Department contracted for the parts for 30,000 new flintlock arms. However, before these arms could be assembled, the War Department adopted the percussion system of ignition and ordered that these arms be made as percussion. Obsolete by 1861, large numbers were purchased by the Southern Confederacy and imported for use in the American Civil War. Arms with firm evidence of Confederate military usage increases the value of the arm considerably.

Exc.	*V.G.*	*Good*	*Fair*	*Poor*
—	2000	500	450	350

Pattern of 1842 (P1842) Musket (and Rifled Musket)

Overall length 55"; barrel length 39-1/4"; caliber .75. The first English-made as percussion musket to be issued to the Line Regiments of the British Army, continued in production through the Crimean War. The final production (1851-1855) of 26,400 were made with rifled barrel and a long range rear sight soldered to the barrel, similar in configuration to that of the P1851 rifle-musket. These rifled versions of the P1842 musket will command a premium.

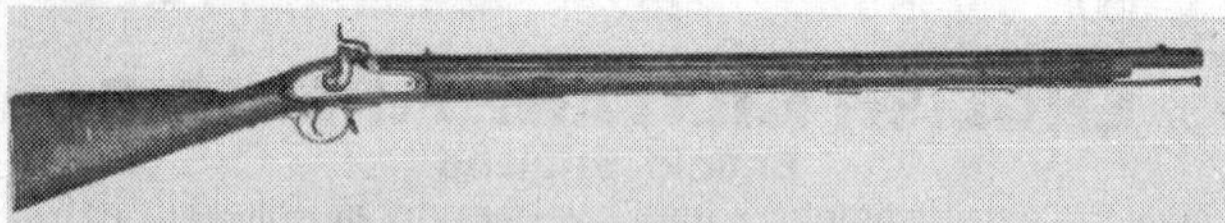

Courtesy Milwaukee Public Museum, Milwaukee, Wisconsin

Exc.	*V.G.*	*Good*	*Fair*	*Poor*
—	2000	500	450	350

"Brunswick" Rifles (first model or P1837) and (second model or P1845)

Overall length 46-1/2" (P1837), 45-3/4" (P1845); barrel length 33" (P1837), 30" (P1845); caliber .704. The "Brunswick" rifle differed from its predecessors (the "Baker rifle") adopted for the English "Rifle Brigade" in having a large bore cut with only two spiraling grooves. These grooves engaged a specially cast ball having a raised belt circumventing it. The first model of the "Brunswick rifle" adopted in 1837 is primarily distinguished by having a "backaction" percussion lock, which continued in production until 1844 despite having been officially changed to the standard "barlock" in 1841. Those made after 1844 bear the standard percussion lock. The value of these rifles is enhanced by virtue of the importation of at least 2,000 (probably first model variants) into the Southern Confederacy during the American Civil War. (It should be noted that Russia also adopted a variant of the "Brunswick" style rifle, having them made in Liege, Belgium and so marked with Liege proofmarks. These rifles are distinguished by having a distinctive rear sight with an adjustable arcing ladder.)

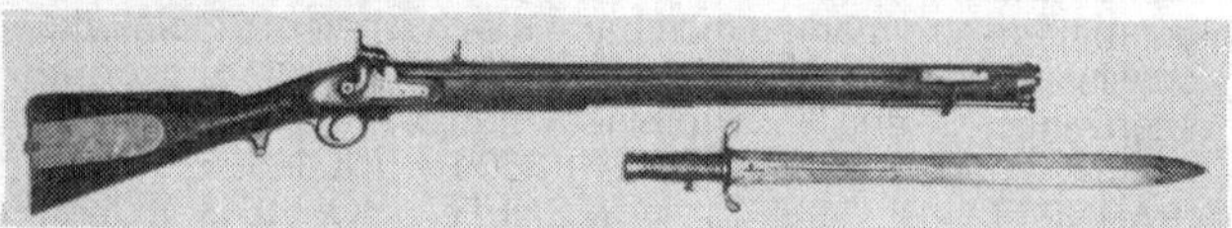

Courtesy Milwaukee Public Museum, Milwaukee, Wisconsin

Exc.	*V.G.*	*Good*	*Fair*	*Poor*
—	3000	1250	700	450

Pattern of 1851 (P1851) Rifle Musket

Overall length 55"; barrel length 39"; caliber .702. With the success of the "Minie ball" projectile in France, England in 1851 adopted its first production rifle musket. Externally resembling the P1842 musket, the P1851 is distinguished by the long range rear sight soldered to the barrel and its smaller caliber (.70) rifled bore. Approximately 35,000 were manufactured until 1855, with a substantial number being imported to the United States during the early years of the American Civil War.

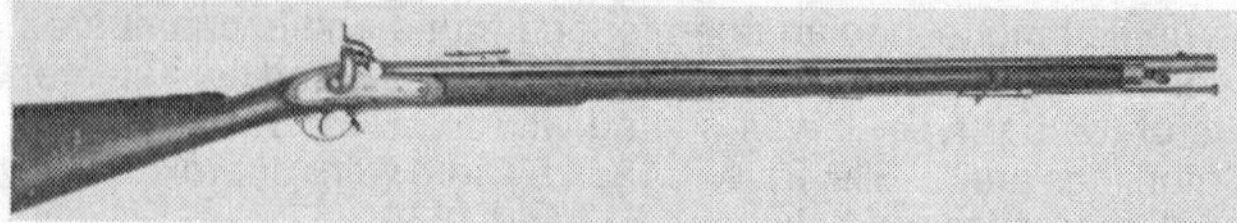

Courtesy Milwaukee Public Museum, Milwaukee, Wisconsin

Exc.	*V.G.*	*Good*	*Fair*	*Poor*
—	3500	1500	700	450

Pattern of 1853 (P1853) Rifle Musket (first through fourth types)

Overall length 55" (54" on fourth type); barrel length 39"; caliber .577. The P1853 rifle musket underwent several changes during the span of its production. The earliest type (first model) was made with clamping bands. Due to problems with the bands slipping, the bands were modified in late 1855 to solid, spring fastened (second model), the upper wider than the other two. However, in 1858 the government reverted to clamping bands continuing production in this style through 1863. Those made at Enfield after 1859 were one inch shorter in the butt stock, but the contractors continued to deliver them in 55-inch length well into the 1860s. The fourth model is distinguished by the "Baddeley patent" clamping barrel bands, wherein the screwheads are recessed into the bands. The third model saw the greatest production, with more than 600,000 being imported into the north and about 300,000 into the south during the American Civil War. P1853 rifle muskets with early Confederate importation marks on the stock and butt plate will command a premium if authentic.

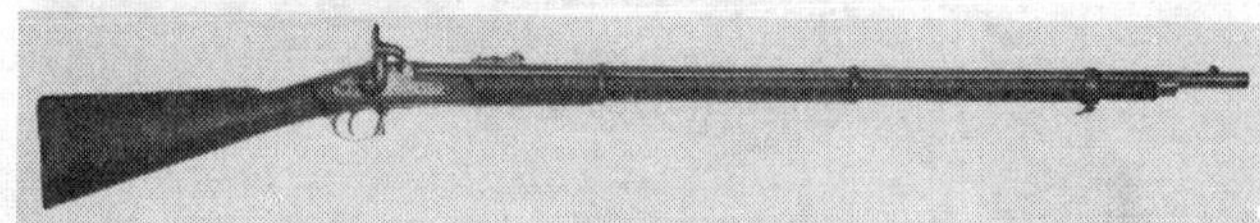

Courtesy Milwaukee Public Museum, Milwaukee, Wisconsin

Exc.	*V.G.*	*Good*	*Fair*	*Poor*
—	3000	1000	450	350

American-Made Copies of the English P1853 Rifle Musket

Three firms during the period from 1855 through 1862 produced copies of the P1853 rifle musket, Robbins & Lawrence of Windsor, Vermont; Orison Blunt of New York City; and John Moore of New York City. All three types command a premium over the standard imported muskets and may be distinguished as follows:

Robbins & Lawrence P1853 Rifle Muskets

During the Crimean War, Robbins & Lawrence received a contract for 25,000 P1853 rifle muskets of the second model. Due to production delays, the company had delivered only 10,400 when the war ended. Due to the penalties for non-deliveries, Robbins & Lawrence declared bankruptcy. An additional 5,600 arms were made on the firms machinery while in receivership by the "Vermont Arms Co." before the machinery was sold to Sharps and Eli Whitney, Jr. The Robbins & Lawrence-made P1853 rifle muskets are distinguished by the lock marking "WINDSOR" beneath the date (such as "1856") on the forward part of the lock and by non-English proofmarks on the barrel. Many of these arms saw service in the American Civil War, with Alabama obtaining several hundred in 1861. Arms with confirmed southern usage will bring substantial premiums.

Exc.	*V.G.*	*Good*	*Fair*	*Poor*
—	—	3750	1250	600

Orison Blunt P1853 Rifle Muskets

At the beginning of the Civil War, Orison Blunt of New York City attempted to produce a copy of the P1853 rifle musket but with a 40-inch barrel and in .58 caliber. After making several hundred, his proposed contract with the U.S. War Department was declined. Nevertheless, in mid-1862, it is thought that about 1,000 of his rifle muskets were purchased by the U.S. government and sent to Illinois to arm volunteers. Blunt "Enfields" are distinguished by two distinct markings. While most lockplates are totally unmarked, a few are known with the mark "UNION" on the forward part of the lockplate and an eagle impressed into the rounded tail. More importantly, Blunt barrels bear an oval with the letters "DP/B" near the breech. (Note: Not all P1853 rifle muskets with 40-inch barrels were made by Blunt; Birmingham and Liege contractors supplied the Spanish government with a 40-inch barrel copy of the P1853 English rifle musket as well, and some of these were diverted to the American market during the Civil War. These are usually distinguished by the letter "C" in a diamond near the breech of the barrel surrounded by proofmarks.)

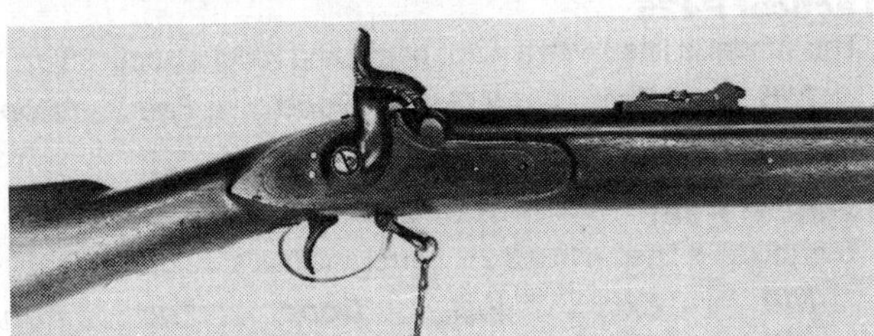

Courtesy Milwaukee Public Museum, Milwaukee, Wisconsin

Exc.	V.G.	Good	Fair	Poor
—	—	3750	1250	600

John P. Moore P1853 Rifle Muskets

During the American Civil War arms merchant John P. Moore of New York City received a contract for the delivery of 20,000 P1853 rifle muskets, supposedly to be made in the United States. In fact, most of his contract was made in Birmingham, England, with only 1,080 completely made in the United States. These are distinguished by having an unusual script proofmark on the barrel near the breech instead of the standard Birmingham crossed scepters. These script letters have been interpreted as either "V LB" or "EP I" depending on how they are read. All of Moore's P1853 deliveries bear a distinctive lock marking, consisting of the date forward of the hammer ("1861", "1862", or "1863") and an eagle perched on a shield on the tail. The shield bears the letter "M" in its chief. Moore also delivered 999 short rifles (33" barrels) with the same lock markings. Likewise, all of the barrels on the Moore P1853 rifle musket contract are serially numbered, either on the forward side near the muzzle or on the side of the bayonet lug/front sight. Because the Moore rifles have been misidentified as a product of a North Carolina arms merchant, they tend to command higher prices than are warranted by their numbers.

Exc.	V.G.	Good	Fair	Poor
—	—	2250	900	450

"Brazilian Naval Rifle"

Overall length 48"; barrel length 32"; caliber .58. Markings: on lockplate forward of hammer "D (anchor) C"; the same mark stamped in the wood and metal in various places on the rifle; on barrel, same mark and Liege proofmarks (an oval encompassing the letters E/LG/(star). Although neither made for the English government nor in England, this rifle copies so many features of the English P1856 series rifles as to be easily mistaken for it. The major differences consist of a longer (3-3/8") sight base than the English rifles and a front band/nosecap that also serves as the ramrod funnel. These Liege-made rifles were supposedly made for the Brazilian government, but at the beginning of the American Civil War they were diverted to the United States, about 10,000 being imported. To show their new ownership, a brass shield bearing the U.S. coat of arms was screwed into the wrist of the stock.

Courtesy Milwaukee Public Museum, Milwaukee, Wisconsin

Exc.	V.G.	Good	Fair	Poor
—	—	1750	650	275

Patterns of 1856, 1858, 1860, and 1861 (P1856, P1858, P1860, P1861) Sergeant's Rifles

Overall length 49"; barrel length 33"; caliber .577. The four variations of the short rifle adopted for sergeants in the British Army in 1856 are relatively minor. The P1856 is mainly distinguished by having a short (1/2") key forward of the saber bayonet lug on the right side of the barrel. The P1858 rifle moved this lug to the forward band, permitting the extension of the length of the forestock. (A brass furnished rifle also without the key but with the lug on the barrel was also adopted in 1858 for the Navy; it is distinguished by having its rear sling swivel attached to the trigger guard bow instead of the tail of the trigger guard strap.) The P1860 rifle differed from its predecessors by having five groove rifling instead of three groove. The introduction of a new gunpowder in 1861 permitted the resighting of the ladder on the P1861 rifle to 1,250 yards instead of the 1,100 yards that had been previously used. Significant quantities of these rifles were purchased by both billigerents during the American Civil War; those with proven Southern history will command a premium.

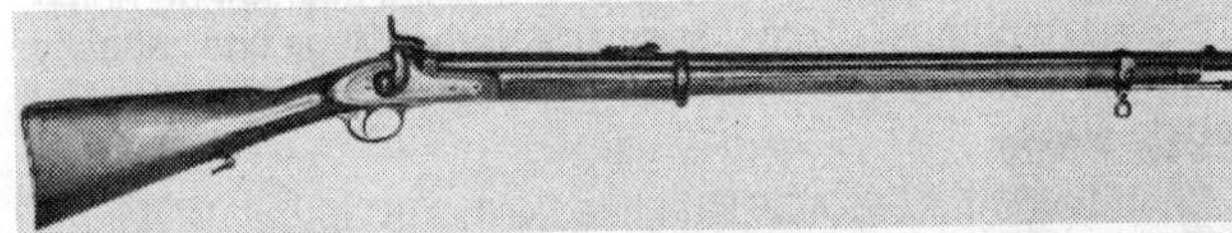

Courtesy Milwaukee Public Museum, Milwaukee, Wisconsin

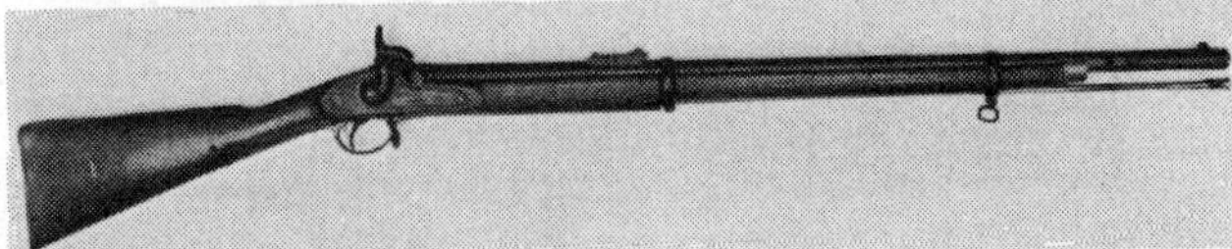

Courtesy Milwaukee Public Museum, Milwaukee, Wisconsin

Exc.	V.G.	Good	Fair	Poor
—	—	1650	650	450

Pattern of 1853 (P1853) Artillery Carbine (First, Second, and Third Models)

Overall length 40"; barrel length 24"; caliber .577. Designed for the gunners of the Royal Artillery, this carbine was meant to be slung over the shoulder and accordingly has a sling swivel on the upper band and upon a lug inset into the buttstock. The first model (adopted in 1853), like the sergeant's rifle has a 112" key forward of the saber bayonet lug on the right side of the barrel; in addition to other minor improvements, this key was eliminated in the second model, adopted in 1858. In 1861, a third model was adopted, having five groove rifling and improved rear sight. Approximately 1,000 of the latter type saw service in the American Civil War. Carbines with Confederate stock and buttplate markings will command a premium.

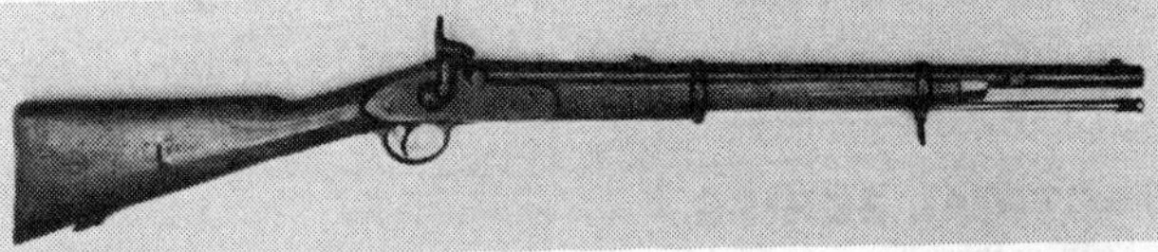

Courtesy Milwaukee Public Museum, Milwaukee, Wisconsin

Exc.	V.G.	Good	Fair	Poor
—	—	1650	650	450

Patterns of 1856 (P1856) and Pattern of 1861 (P1861) Cavalry Carbines

Overall length 37" (P1856), 36-1/2" (P1861) barrel length 21"; caliber .577. Due to inadequacies in the various breechloading carbines tried by the British mounted service, in 1856 the War Department adopted a muzzle-loading carbine incorporating the features of the P1853 series small arms. The earlier version had three groove rifling and a small rear sight with two leaves. In 1861 this was replaced by a larger ladder sight and five groove rifling adopted. More than 6,000 P1856 carbines were imported by the Southern Confederacy during the Civil War to make up for the inadequate supply of carbines. Carbines with verifiable Southern history will command a premium.

Courtesy Milwaukee Public Museum, Milwaukee, Wisconsin

Exc.	V.G.	Good	Fair	Poor
—	—	1650	650	450

ENTREPRISE ARMS, INC.

Irwindale, California

ELITE SERIES

This is the basic model with stainless steel barrels, fixed sights, squared trigger guard, adjustable match trigger, checkered slide release, high ride grip safety, flat mainspring housing, and a number of other special features. Magazine capacity is 10 rounds.

Elite P500

Chambered for .45 ACP and fitted with a 5" barrel. Weight is about 40 oz.

NIB	Exc.	V.G.	Good	Fair	Poor
740	600	—	—	—	—

Elite P425

This model has a 4.25" barrel. Weight is approximately 38 oz.

NIB	Exc.	V.G.	Good	Fair	Poor
740	600	—	—	—	—

Elite 325

This model has a 3.25" barrel with a weight of 36 oz.

NIB	Exc.	V.G.	Good	Fair	Poor
740	600	—	—	—	—

TACTICAL SERIES

This model has an ambidextrous thumb lock with lightweight match hammer with matching sear. National match barrel with match extractor, full length one-piece guide rod, Novak sights, dovetail front sight, matte black finish, and a host of other features. Magazine capacity is 10 rounds.

Tactical P500

This model is chambered for the .45 ACP cartridge and has a 5" barrel and a weight of approximately 40 oz.

NIB	Exc.	V.G.	Good	Fair	Poor
980	780	—	—	—	—

Tactical P425

This model is fitted with a 4.25" barrel and weighs about 38 oz.

NIB	Exc.	V.G.	Good	Fair	Poor
980	780	—	—	—	—

Tactical P325

This model is fitted with a 3.25" barrel and has a weight of 36 oz.

NIB	Exc.	V.G.	Good	Fair	Poor
980	780	—	—	—	—

Tactical P325 Plus

This model features a 3.25" barrel and is fitted to a full size Government model frame. Weight is about 37 oz.

NIB	Exc.	V.G.	Good	Fair	Poor
1050	800	—	—	—	—

TITLEIST NATIONAL MATCH SERIES

This model is chambered for either the .45 ACP or .40 S&W cartridge. It has all the features of the Elite Series with an adjustable rear sight and dovetail Patridge front sight. Many other special features.

Titleist P500

This model is fitted with a 5" barrel. Weight is about 40 oz.

NIB	Exc.	V.G.	Good	Fair	Poor
980	780	—	—	—	—

NOTE: Add $20 for .40 S&W chambering.

Boxer Model

Chambered for the .45 ACP cartridge and fitted with a 5" barrel this model features a ramped bull barrel, wide ambi safety and high-mass chiseled slide. Weight is approximately 44 oz.

 *This symbol denotes "Sleepers" with rapidly-rising values and/or significant collector potential.*

NIB	Exc.	V.G.	Good	Fair	Poor
1100	875	—	—	—	—

TOURNAMENT SERIES

These are the top-of-the-line models that feature all of the Elite Series features plus oversized magazine release button, checkered front strap, and flared extended magazine well.

TSM I

This is a limited class competition pistol. All these model are hand crafted. Fitted with a 5" barrel and choice of calibers. Weight is about 40 oz.

NIB	Exc.	V.G.	Good	Fair	Poor
2300	1750	—	—	—	—

TSM II

This is a long slide model with cocking serrations on front and rear of slide. Barrel is 6". Weight is about 44 oz.

NIB	Exc.	V.G.	Good	Fair	Poor
2000	1500	—	—	—	—

TSM III

This is an open class pistol designed for scope mount. Barrel is 5.5" long. Fitted with 7 port compensator. Many other custom features.Weight is about 44 oz.

NIB	Exc.	V.G.	Good	Fair	Poor
2700	2000	—	—	—	—

ERA
Brazil

Era Double Barrel Shotgun

An inexpensive shotgun chambered for 12 and 20 gauge, as well as .410. It was offered with 26", 28", or 30" barrels with various choke combinations. It has double triggers and extractors, with a checkered hardwood pistol-grip stock. This gun is also available as a Quail model with a 20" barrel and as a Riot model with an 18" barrel. These two models are not offered in .410 bore.

Exc.	V.G.	Good	Fair	Poor
200	150	125	100	75

Era Over-and-Under Shotgun

Chambered for 12 or 20 gauge, with 28" ventilated rib barrels that were choked full and modified. It is a boxlock with double triggers, extractors, and a hardwood stock. It was also offered in a trap model and a skeet model chambered for 12 gauge only and appropriately choked. These latter two models would be worth a 10 percent premium over the values listed.

Exc.	V.G.	Good	Fair	Poor
325	275	250	200	150

ERICHSON, G.
Houston, Texas

Erichson Pocket Pistol

A close copy of the Philadelphia-style Henry Deringer. It is chambered for .45-caliber percussion and has a 3.25" barrel. The mountings are German silver and not engraved; the stock is walnut. The hammer is deeply fluted; and the forend, carved. The barrel is marked "G. Erichson / Houston, Texas." The number produced is unknown, but examples are scarce. They were manufactured in the 1850s and 1860s.

Exc.	V.G.	Good	Fair	Poor
—	—	6000	3000	1000

ERMA WERKE WAFFENFABRIK
Erfurt, Germany
Post-war
Dachau, Germany

Known primarily as a manufacturer of submachine guns, but they are also in the handgun and rifle business. In 1933 they answered the German army's need for an inexpensive practice weapon by producing a .22 rimfire conversion unit for the Luger pistol. This was marketed commercially and was available for many years. The success of this unit led the company to produce other inexpensive target and plinking pistols. After the war they were reorganized in the western sector and resumed submachine gun production. In 1964 they returned to the sporting firearms business with the introduction of their .22 rimfire Luger-lookalike pistol. Since then, they have produced many like-quality firearms. They were imported by Excam of Hialeah, Florida. This association is now terminated, and they are currently imported by Beeman Precision in Santa Rosa, California, and Mandell Shooting Supplies in Scottsdale, Arizona.

Erma .22 Luger Conversion Unit

Produced for the German army in 1933 and then became a successful commercial item. It would turn a standard 9mm or 7.65mm Luger into an inexpensive-to-shoot .22 rimfire. The unit consists of a barrel insert, a breech block, and toggle unit with its own lightened recoil spring, and a .22 magazine. This unit was furnished with a wooden box. There were many different sized units to fit various caliber and barrel-length Lugers, but all used the same parts and concept. These units have become desirable to Luger collectors.

Exc.	V.G.	Good	Fair	Poor
500	425	350	275	200

.22 Target Pistol (Old Model)

A semi-automatic target pistol in caliber .22 LR. This model was offered with 4", 6", or 8" barrels. The frame is made from a cast zinc alloy, and there is an external hammer. There are adjustable sights, and balance weights were available. Magazine capacity is 10 rounds. Weight is about 35 oz. This pistol was manufactured in 1936 and 1937.

Courtesy James Rankin

Exc.	V.G.	Good	Fair	Poor
600	500	400	300	100

.22 Target Pistol (New Model) Master Model

An improved version of the old model that features a new grip angle and a magazine and takedown device like that of the Luger. There were interchangeable barrels and three basic models — the "Sport," "Hunter," and the "Master." The difference was the length of the barrels — 4", 8", and 12", respectively. Magazine capacity is 10 rounds. Weight is about 39 oz. These pistols were manufactured between 1937 and 1940, when they were discontinued due to Erma's involvement in the war effort.

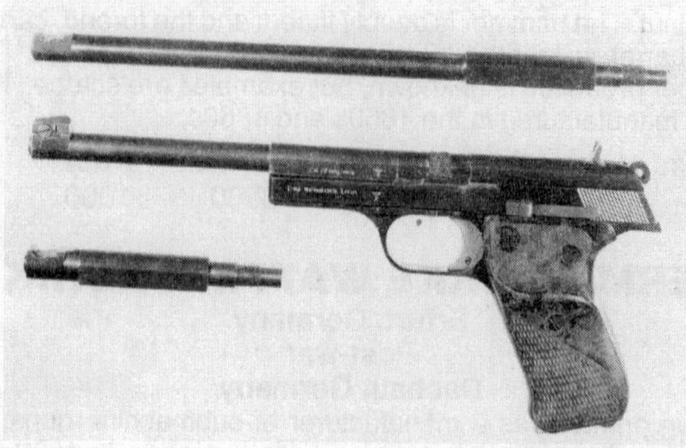

Courtesy James Rankin

Exc.	V.G.	Good	Fair	Poor
650	500	400	300	100

KGP-Series

Made to resemble the Luger quite closely. They utilized the mechanical features of the .22 conversion unit and developed a pistol around it. There are many different versions of this pistol chambered for .22 rimfire, .32 ACP, and .380 ACP. The original designation was the KGP-68; but the Gun Control Act of 1968 required that a magazine safety be added, and the model was redesignated the KGP-68A. The last designations for the three calibers are KGP-22, KGP-32, and KGP-38. These pistols were manufactured between 1964 and 1986, and their values are listed.

KGP-68

A 4" barrel and is chambered for the .32 ACP and the .380 ACP cartridges. It has a 6-shot magazine and an anodized alloy receiver. Weight is about 23 oz. This model is also known as the Beeman MP-08.

Courtesy James Rankin

Exc.	V.G.	Good	Fair	Poor
500	400	300	200	100

KGP-69

A .22 rimfire version of this series, with an 8-shot magazine capacity. Weight is about 30 oz. It is also known as the Beeman P-08.

Exc.	V.G.	Good	Fair	Poor
300	200	150	100	75

ET-22 Luger Carbine

A rare firearm. According to some estimates only 375 were produced. It features a 11.75" barrel and is chambered for the .22 rimfire cartridge. It has an artillery Luger-type rear sight and checkered walnut grips, with a smooth walnut forend. The pistol was furnished with a red-felt-lined, black leatherette case.

Exc.	V.G.	Good	Fair	Poor
400	350	300	200	150

KGP-22

The later version of the KGP-69 chambered for .22 rimfire.

Exc.	V.G.	Good	Fair	Poor
350	300	250	200	125

KGP-32 & KGP-38

These two designations are the later versions of the KGP-68 and 68A.

Exc.	V.G.	Good	Fair	Poor
350	300	250	200	125

ESP 85A

A high quality target pistol imported by Mandall Shooting Supply. It features an interchangeable barrel system that converts the chambering from .22 rimfire to .32 S&W long wad cutter. The barrels are both 6" in length, and there are adjustable and interchangeable sights and a 5- or 8-shot detachable magazine. Weight is about 41 oz. The finish is blued, and the grips are stippled target types. The gun is furnished in a padded hard case with two extra magazines and takedown tools. This unit was introduced in 1989.

NIB	Exc.	V.G.	Good	Fair	Poor
1100	1000	850	700	550	450

EP-25

A semi-automatic pistol in caliber 6.35mm. Fitted with 2.75" barrel. Weight is about 18 oz. Mostly marketed outside of Germany. It has a polished blue finish and wood grips. Erma is stamped on the slide and on each of the grip's plates.

Courtesy James Rankin

Exc.	V.G.	Good	Fair	Poor
200	175	150	100	75

RX-22 and PX-22

A semi-automatic .22 rimfire copy of the Walther PPK. It has a 7-round magazine. Assembled in the U.S. with parts from Germany by various companies that marketed the pistol in the U.S. It has a black plastic wraparound grips with the Erma logo on each side.

Courtesy James Rankin

Exc.	V.G.	Good	Fair	Poor
200	175	150	100	75

REVOLVERS

ER-772 Match

A target revolver chambered for the .22 rimfire and has a 6" shrouded barrel with a solid rib. The swing-out cylinder holds 6 shots, and the sights are adjustable. The finish is blued, with stippled target grips. This model was introduced in 1989.

NIB	Exc.	V.G.	Good	Fair	Poor
500	450	400	350	250	200

ER-773 Match

Similar to the ER-772 except that it is chambered for the .32 S&W long cartridge.

NIB	Exc.	V.G.	Good	Fair	Poor
500	450	400	350	250	200

ER-777

Basically a similar revolver to the ER-773 except that it has a 4.5" or 5" barrel and is chambered for the .357 Magnum cartridge. The revolver is larger and has standard sport grips. This model was introduced in 1989.

NIB	Exc.	V.G.	Good	Fair	Poor
500	450	400	350	250	200

RIFLES

EM1.22

A semi-automatic .22 rimfire version of the M1 Carbine. It has an 18" barrel and a 15-round magazine. It was manufactured between 1966 and 1976.

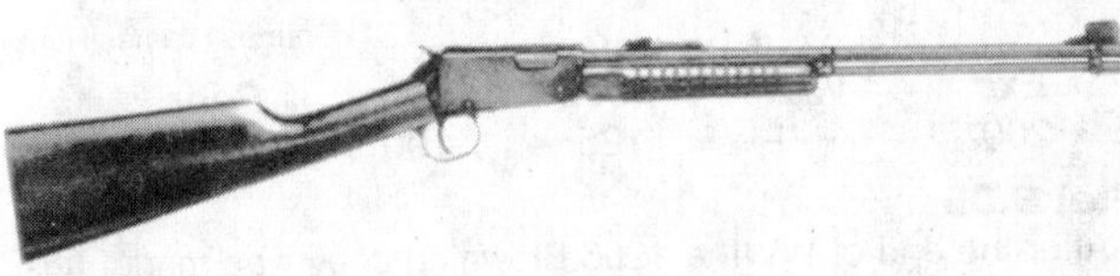

Exc.	V.G.	Good	Fair	Poor
200	175	150	125	100

EG-72, EG-722

A 15-shot slide-action carbine chambered for .22 rimfire, with a 18.5" barrel and open sights. The finish is blued, and it was manufactured between 1970 and 1985.

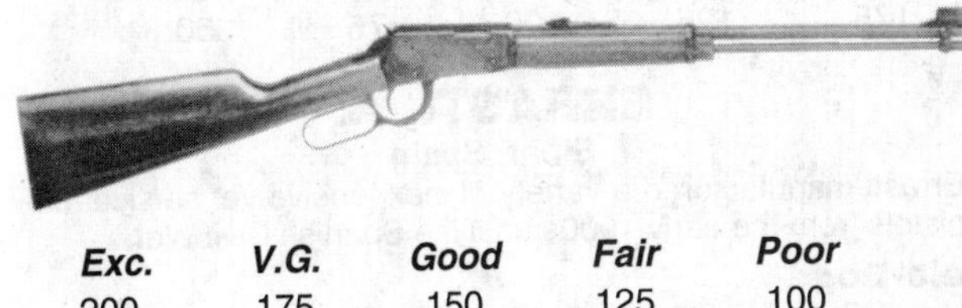

Exc.	V.G.	Good	Fair	Poor
150	110	100	75	50

EG-712, EG-73

A lever copy of the Winchester 94 Carbine chambered for the .22 rimfire or the .22 rimfire Magnum (EG-73). It has an 18.5" barrel and holds 15 shots in a tubular magazine. It was manufactured between 1973 and 1985.

Exc.	V.G.	Good	Fair	Poor
200	175	150	125	100

SR-100

This is long-range precision bolt-action rifle chambered for .308 Win., .300 Win. Mag., or .338 Lapua calibers. Barrel length on the .308 Win. caliber is 25.25", other calibers are 29.25". All barrels are fitted with a muzzlebrake. Trigger is adjustable. Stock is laminated with thumbhole and adjustable recoil pad and cheekpiece. Weight is approximately 15 lbs.

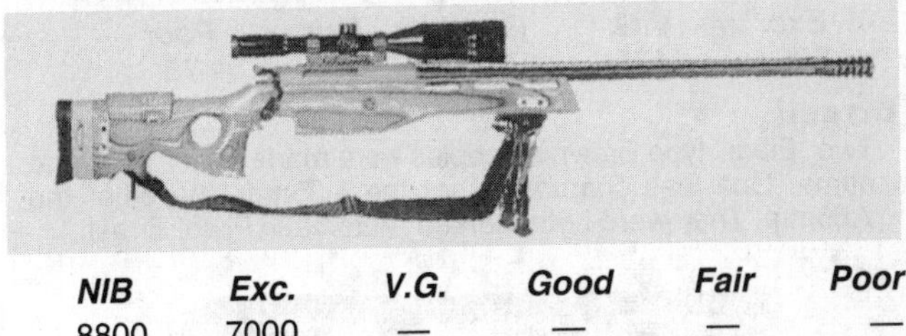

NIB	Exc.	V.G.	Good	Fair	Poor
8800	7000	—	—	—	—

ERQUIAGA

Eibar, Spain

Another Spanish company that commenced business during WWI as a subcontractor on the French "Ruby" contract. They manufactured the usual poor quality, 7.65mm Eibar-type pistol.

Fiel

The trade name found on the Ruby subcontract pistol described above. It is marked "Erquiaga y Cia Eibar Cal. 7.65 Fiel."

Courtesy James Rankin

Exc.	V.G.	Good	Fair	Poor
200	150	125	100	75

Fiel 6.35

After the end of WWI, a 1906 Browning copy was made. It is chambered for the 6.35mm cartridge. The markings are "Automatic Pistol 6.35 Fiel No. 1." Later models had "EMC" molded into the grip.

Exc.	V.G.	Good	Fair	Poor
175	125	100	75	50

Marte

Another poor-quality "Eibar"-type pistol that is chambered for the 6.35mm and that was made in the early 1920s.

Exc.	V.G.	Good	Fair	Poor
175	125	100	75	50

ERRASTI, A.

Eibar, Spain

Errasti manufactured a variety of inexpensive yet serviceable pistols from the early 1900s until the Spanish Civil War.

Velo-Dog

Usual cheap solid-frame folding-trigger revolvers one associates with the model designation. They were chambered in 5.5mm and 6.35mm and were made in the early 1900s.

Exc.	V.G.	Good	Fair	Poor
175	125	100	75	50

M1889

In 1915-1916 Errasti produced the 10.4mm Italian army service revolver. The quality was reasonably good. They were marked "Errasti Eiber" on the right side of the frame.

Exc.	V.G.	Good	Fair	Poor
225	175	150	100	75

Errasti

Two "Eibar" type Browning copies were made under this trade name. One was chambered for the 6.35mm, the other the 7.65mm. They were both marked "Automatic Pistol Errasti."

Courtesy James Rankin

Exc.	V.G.	Good	Fair	Poor
175	125	100	75	50

Errasti Oscillante

Manufactured in the 1920s, these revolvers were copied from the Smith & Wesson Military & Police design. They were chambered for the .32, .38, and .44 calibers with the .38 being the most frequently encountered.

Exc.	V.G.	Good	Fair	Poor
175	125	100	75	50

Dreadnaught, Goliath and Smith Americano

These three trade names were found on a group of poor quality nickel-plated revolvers. They were made from 1905 through 1920 and were obvious copies of the Iver Johnson design. They had break-open actions, ribbed barrel, and were chambered for .32, .38, and .44 calibers. They are scarce today, as most have long since fallen apart.

Exc.	V.G.	Good	Fair	Poor
175	125	100	75	50

ESCODIN, M.

Eibar, Spain

This company made a Smith & Wesson revolver copy from 1924 through 1931. It is chambered for the .32 and the .38 Special. The only marking is a coat of arms stamped on the left side of the frame.

Exc.	V.G.	Good	Fair	Poor
175	125	100	75	50

ESPIRIN, HERMANOS

Eibar, Spain

Euskaro

This poor-quality, often unsafe revolver was manufactured from 1906 until WWI. They are copies of the Iver Johnson design break-open actions, chambered for .32. .38, and .44. This product epitomizes the worst Eibar had to offer during the pre-Civil War era.

Exc.	V.G.	Good	Fair	Poor
—	125	75	50	25

ESCORT

Turkey

SEMI-AUTOMATIC SHOTGUNS

Model AS

This 12 gauge 3" model is fitted with a 28" vent rib barrel with choke tubes. Walnut stock. Black finish. Magazine capacity is 4 rounds. Weight is about 7 lbs.

NIB	Exc.	V.G.	Good	Fair	Poor
385	300	—	—	—	—

Model PS

This 12 gauge 3" model is similar to the above but with a black polymer stock and black finish. Also offered in Shadow Grass camo or Mossy Oak Break-Up camo. Choice of Spark or TriViz front sights. Barrel length is 28" except for TriViz variation with 24" barrel. Weight is about 7 lbs.

NIB	Exc.	V.G.	Good	Fair	Poor
400	300	—	—	—	—

NOTE: Add $45 for TriViz model.

Model PS AimGuard

This 12 gauge 3" model is fitted with a 20" fixed choke barrel in Cylinder bore. Black polymer stock with black finish. Magazine capacity is 5 rounds. Weight is about 6.4 lbs.

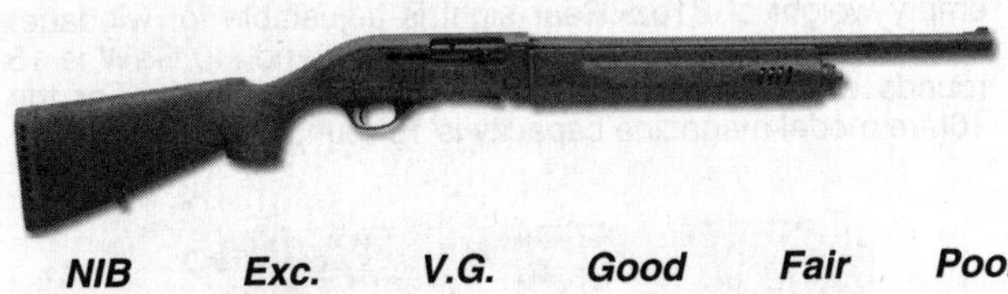

NIB	Exc.	V.G.	Good	Fair	Poor
360	275	—	—	—	—

Combo Model

This 12 gauge 3" model is offered with two sets of barrels: one 28" with Full choke tube and the other 24" with Turkey choke tube. Polymer stock with Mossy Oak Break-Up. Receiver is fitted with a dovetail mount. Weight is about 7 lbs.

NIB	Exc.	V.G.	Good	Fair	Poor
520	400	—	—	—	—

PUMP ACTION SHOTGUNS

Field Hunter

This 12 gauge 3" model is fitted with a 28" vent rib barrel with choke tubes. Offered with a black polymer stock of Mossy Oak Break-Up or Shadow Grass camo pattern. A 24" barrel with TriViz is also offered. Magazine capacity is 4 rounds. Weight is about 7 lbs.

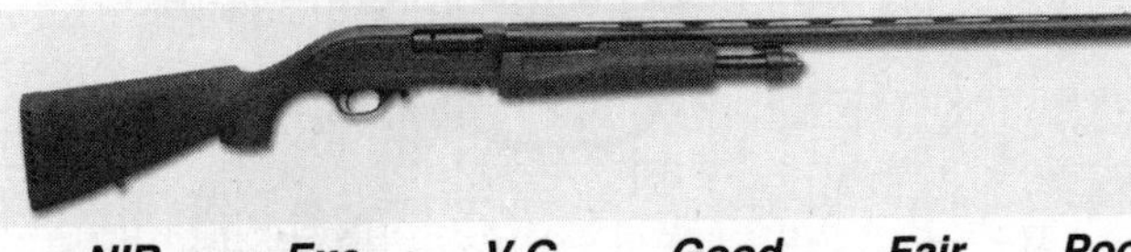

NIB	Exc.	V.G.	Good	Fair	Poor
225	175	—	—	—	—

NOTE: For camo finish add $50. For TriViz sights add $100.

AimGuard

This 12 gauge 3" model is fitted with a 20" barrel with fixed Cylinder bore choke. Black polymer stock. Magazine capacity is 5 rounds. Weight is about 6.4 lbs.

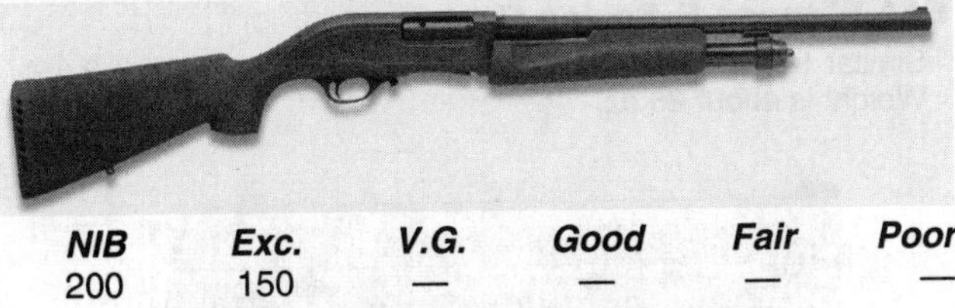

NIB	Exc.	V.G.	Good	Fair	Poor
200	150	—	—	—	—

EUROARMS OF AMERICA

Winchester, Virginia

An importer of blackpowder muzzle-loading firearms, primarily replicas of early American weapons.

REVOLVERS

1851 Navy

A replica of the Colt revolver chambered for .36 or .44 caliber percussion. It has a squareback, silver-plated trigger guard and a 7.5" barrel.

NIB	Exc.	V.G.	Good	Fair	Poor
175	125	110	80	65	45

1851 Navy Police Model

Chambered for .36 caliber with a 5-shot, fluted cylinder and a 5.5" barrel.

NIB	Exc.	V.G.	Good	Fair	Poor
175	125	110	80	65	45

1851 Navy Sheriff's Model

A 5" barrelled version of the Navy Model.

NIB	Exc.	V.G.	Good	Fair	Poor
150	100	80	60	50	35

1851 "Schneider & Glassick" Navy

A replica of the Confederate revolver chambered for .36 or .44 caliber percussion.

NIB	Exc.	V.G.	Good	Fair	Poor
150	100	80	60	50	35

1851 "Griswold & Gunnison" Navy

A replica of this Confederate revolver chambered for .36 or .44 caliber percussion.

NIB	Exc.	V.G.	Good	Fair	Poor
150	90	75	60	40	25

1862 Police

A replica of the Colt Model 1862 chambered for .36 caliber percussion, with a 7.5" barrel and a steel frame.

NIB	Exc.	V.G.	Good	Fair	Poor
175	125	110	90	65	45

1860 Army

A replica of the Colt revolver chambered for .44 caliber percussion. It was offered with a 5" or 8" barrel.

NIB	Exc.	V.G.	Good	Fair	Poor
175	125	100	75	50	30

1861 Navy

A replica of the Colt revolver chambered for .36 caliber percussion.

NIB	Exc.	V.G.	Good	Fair	Poor
175	135	110	80	60	40

1858 Remington Army or Navy

Replicas of the Remington percussion revolvers chambered for .26 or .44 caliber.

NIB	Exc.	V.G.	Good	Fair	Poor
200	150	125	100	75	50

RIFLES

The rifles listed are modern replicas of early American and British firearms. They are of good quality and are quite serviceable. There is little collector interest, and they are listed along with their values.

Cook & Brother Carbine

NIB	Exc.	V.G.	Good	Fair	Poor
375	325	250	200	150	100

1863 J.P. Murray

NIB	Exc.	V.G.	Good	Fair	Poor
350	300	225	175	125	100

1853 Enfield Rifled Musket

NIB	Exc.	V.G.	Good	Fair	Poor
400	350	300	250	175	125

1858 Enfield Rifled Musket

NIB	Exc.	V.G.	Good	Fair	Poor
375	325	250	200	150	100

1861 Enfield Musketoon

NIB	Exc.	V.G.	Good	Fair	Poor
350	300	225	175	125	90

1803 Harper's Ferry

NIB	Exc.	V.G.	Good	Fair	Poor
500	425	350	300	225	150

1841 Mississippi Rifle

NIB	Exc.	V.G.	Good	Fair	Poor
475	400	325	275	200	125

Pennsylvania Rifle

NIB	Exc.	V.G.	Good	Fair	Poor
300	250	225	200	150	100

Hawken Rifle

NIB	Exc.	V.G.	Good	Fair	Poor
300	250	200	150	100	80

Cape Gun

NIB	Exc.	V.G.	Good	Fair	Poor
400	350	275	225	175	125

Buffalo Carbine

NIB	Exc.	V.G.	Good	Fair	Poor
400	350	300	250	175	100

1862 Remington Rifle

NIB	Exc.	V.G.	Good	Fair	Poor
300	250	225	200	125	60

Zouave Rifle

NIB	Exc.	V.G.	Good	Fair	Poor
325	275	225	175	125	90

Duck Gun

A single-barreled percussion fowling piece chambered for 8, 10, or 12 gauge. It has a 33" smooth-bore barrel and a case-colored hammer and lock. The stock is walnut with brass mountings. This model was introduced in 1989.

NIB	Exc.	V.G.	Good	Fair	Poor
400	350	300	250	175	100

Standard Side-by-Side

A side-by-side, chambered for 12 gauge percussion. It has 28" barrels with engraved locks and a walnut stock.

NIB	Exc.	V.G.	Good	Fair	Poor
425	375	325	275	200	125

EUROPEAN AMERICAN ARMORY CORP.

EAA CORP.

Witness Pistols

These quality pistols are produced by Tanfoglio, an Italian firm, and imported into the U.S. by European American Armory. These handguns are based on the CZ design and offer many features that are sought after by the shooter such as: competition sights, double-action/single-action trigger system, and internal firing pin lock. The firm was founded by Giuseppe Tanfoglio after WWII. He formed a partnership with Antonio Sabbati and began to manufacture small caliber pistols. During the 1960s the firm also produced derringers and Colt SAA copies. In 1980 the Tanfoglio company decided to enter the service pistol market and copied the respected Czech CZ design. The Tanfoglio company currently produces the P9 series for Springfield Armory and the Desert Eagle line for IMI. In 1993 EAA converted from two frame sizes to one and redesigned the trigger guard and beavertail. This redesigned frame enables all of the different caliber slide assemblies to be interchangeable with one frame. This new configuration began to appear in mid-1993. The buyer should be aware that the EAA Custom Shop offers a wide variety of accessories for its pistols, such as compensators, hammers, ported barrels, grips, etc., that will affect price.

NOTE: Any of the EAA Witness pistols can be supplied with double-action-only triggers at no additional charge.

EAA Witness P-Series Full Size

Introduced in 1998 this is a full size polymer frame pistol chambered for 9mm, .40 S&W, .45 ACP, .38 Super, and 10mm cartridges. Barrel length is 4.55". Overall length is 8.5" with an empty weight of 31oz. Rear sight is adjustable for windage. Magazine capacity for 9mm is 28 rounds and .40 S&W is 15 rounds while the .45 ACP model holds 10 rounds. For the 10mm model magazine capacity is 15 rounds.

NIB	Exc.	V.G.	Good	Fair	Poor
425	325	225	180	140	100

NOTE: Add $30 for ported barrel.

EAA Witness P-Series Carry-Comp

This model is fitted with a 4.25" ported barrel. Chambered for .45 ACP.

NIB	Exc.	V.G.	Good	Fair	Poor
470	375	275	200	150	100

EAA Witness P-Series Compact

Similar to the above model but with a barrel length of 3.55". Weight is about 26 oz.

NIB	Exc.	V.G.	Good	Fair	Poor
450	350	250	200	150	100

NOTE: Add $30 for ported barrel.

EAA Witness P-S Series

Built on a different frame size from the P-Series pistols. This model is chambered for the .22 LR, 9mm, or .40 S&W cartridges. Barrel length is 4.55". Weight is about 31 oz.

NIB	Exc.	V.G.	Good	Fair	Poor
400	325	275	—	—	—

EAA Witness Carry Comp

This model is offered in 9mm, .41 AE, .40 S&W, and .45 ACP. It features a 1" steel compensator. The barrel is 4.1" long. Overall length is the same as the standard model as is magazine capacity. Offered in blue or blue chrome finish. Weighs 34 oz.

Old Configuration

NIB	Exc.	V.G.	Good	Fair	Poor
500	450	375	325	250	175

New Configuration

NIB	Exc.	V.G.	Good	Fair	Poor
425	350	300	250	200	175

NOTE: For .45 ACP add 15 percent to above prices.

EAA Witness Standard

Available in 9mm, .41 AE, .40 S&W, and .45 ACP with 4.5" barrel. Magazine capacity: 9mm-16 rounds, .41 AE-11 rounds, .40 S&W-12 rounds, .45 ACP-10 rounds. Offered in blue, chrome, two-tone, and stainless steel. Weighs approximately 33 oz.

Old Configuration

NIB	Exc.	V.G.	Good	Fair	Poor
385	325	275	225	175	125

New Configuration

NIB	Exc.	V.G.	Good	Fair	Poor
460	350	275	225	175	125

NOTE: For chrome, two-tone, and stainless steel add 5 percent to above prices.

EAA Witness Subcompact

Offered in the same calibers as the standard model but fitted with a 3.66" barrel and shorter grip. Magazine capacity: 9mm-13 rounds, .41 AE-9 rounds, .40 S&W 9 rounds, .45 ACP-8 rounds. Weighs about 30 oz. Offered in blue, chrome, two-tone, and stainless steel.

Old Configuration

NIB	Exc.	V.G.	Good	Fair	Poor
385	325	275	225	175	125

New Configuration

NIB	Exc.	V.G.	Good	Fair	Poor
460	350	275	225	175	125

NOTE: For chrome, two-tone, and stainless steel add 5 percent to above prices.

EAA Witness Sport L/S

This model features a longer slide for its 4.75" barrel. Offered in 9mm, .41 AE, .40 S&W, and .45 ACP. Magazine capacity: 9mm-19 rounds, .41 AE-13 rounds, .40 S&W 14 rounds, and .45 ACP-11 rounds. This model is also fitted with adjustable rear sight and extended safety. Available in two-tone finish. Weighs about 34.5 oz. A ported barrel is offered as an option.

Old Configuration

NIB	Exc.	V.G.	Good	Fair	Poor
625	550	500	400	300	200

New Configuration

NIB	Exc.	V.G.	Good	Fair	Poor
625	550	500	400	300	200

NOTE: For .45 ACP add 10 percent to prices.

EAA Witness Combo 9/40

This model offers a 9mm conversion kit, and a .40 S&W conversion kit. These kits consist of a slide, barrel, recoil spring and guide, and magazine. Available in standard or subcompact size in blue, chrome, or two-tone finish.

NIB	Exc.	V.G.	Good	Fair	Poor
550	475	400	350	275	175

NOTE: For chrome or two-tone finish add 5 percent to above prices.

EAA Witness Silver Team Match

This is designed as a competition pistol. It is fitted with a 5.25" barrel. It has these features: dual chamber compensator, single-action trigger, extended safety, competition hammer, paddle magazine release, checkered walnut grips, and adjustable rear sight or drilled and tapped for scope mount. Offered in 9mm-19 rounds, .40 S&W 14 rounds, .41 AE-13 rounds, .45 ACP-11 rounds, and 9 x 21. Finish is blue and weight is approximately 34 oz.

NIB	Exc.	V.G.	Good	Fair	Poor
900	800	700	600	450	300

EAA Witness Sport

This model is built on the standard Witness frame with the addition of an adjustable rear sight and extended safety. Offered in 9mm, .41 AE, .40 S&W, .45 ACP in standard model magazine capacity. Weighs 33 oz. Available in two-tone finish.

Old Configuration

NIB	Exc.	V.G.	Good	Fair	Poor
550	475	400	300	200	150

New Configuration

NIB	Exc.	V.G.	Good	Fair	Poor
550	475	400	300	200	150

NOTE: For .45 ACP add 10 percent to above prices.

EAA Witness Hunter

This model features a camo finish with a 6" barrel. Chambered for the .45 ACP or 10mm cartridge. Drilled and tapped for scope mount and adjustable sights. Magazine capacity is 10 rounds. Weight is about 41 oz. Also available with blued finish.

NIB	Exc.	V.G.	Good	Fair	Poor
940	750	—	—	—	—

EAA Witness Gold Team Match

This is a full race competition pistol with triple chamber compensator, beaver tail grip safety, beveled magazine well, adjustable rear sight or drilled and tapped for scope mount, extended safety and magazine release, competition hammer, square trigger guard, checkered front and backstrap, competition grips, and hard chrome finish. Same barrel length, magazine capacity, and calibers as the Silver Team Match. Weighs 38 oz.

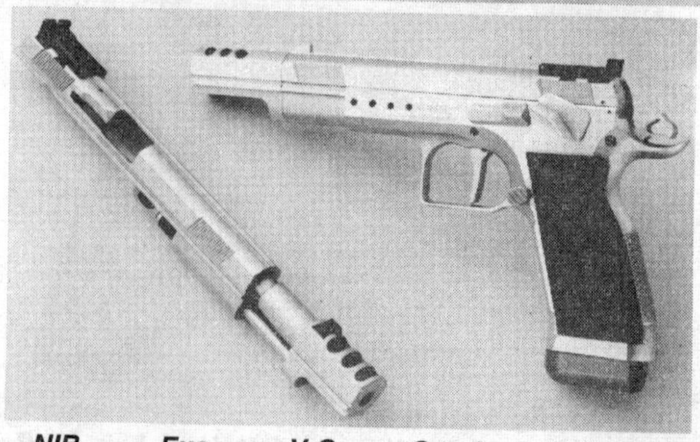

NIB	Exc.	V.G.	Good	Fair	Poor
1700	1250	900	750	600	400

EAA Witness Limited Class Pistol

This model is built on the Witness Match frame with competition grips, high capacity magazine, extended safety and magazine release, single-action trigger, long slide with adjustable rear sight, and match grade barrel. Offered in 9mm, .40 S&W, .38 Super, and .45 ACP with blue finish.

NIB	Exc.	V.G.	Good	Fair	Poor
1000	775	650	550	400	300

EAA Stock

Introduced in 2005 this pistol features a 4.5" tapered cone barrel chambered for the 9mm, .40S&W, .45ACP, or .10mm cartridge. Hard chrome finish, extended safety, wood checkred grips, and fully adjustable sights.Weight is about 33 oz.

NIB	Exc.	V.G.	Good	Fair	Poor
780	650	—	—	—	—

EAA Witness Multi Class Pistol Package

This package consists of one Witness Limited Class pistol with a complete unlimited class top half. The top half is made up of a standard length slide with super sight, recoil guide and spring, match grade competition barrel (threaded for compensator), and a dual chamber compensator. Available in 9mm, .40 S&W, 9 x 21, .45 ACP, 9 x 23, and .38 Super. Finish is blue.

NIB	Exc.	V.G.	Good	Fair	Poor
1500	1200	850	600	300	200

Witness Elite Match

Single action semi-auto featuring 4.5" polygonal rifled steel barrel, adjustable rear sights, rubber grips. Two-tone finish. Chambered for 9 mm (18+1), 10 mm (15+1), 38 Super (15+1), .40 S&W (15+1) and .45 ACP (10+1). 33 oz. Introduced 2006. MSRP: 579

Witness FCP

Novel semi-auto pistol that uses reusable tubular chambers that encase each cartridge. Chambered in .45 ACP, .38 Special, .380 ACP, 9mm Parabellum, .40 S&W, and .38 Super. Six-shot capacity. Built on EAA Witness polymer frame. Introduced 2007.

NIB	Exc.	V.G.	Good	Fair	Poor
415	—	—	—	—	—

Zastava EZ Pistol

CZ75 clone. Single-/double-action pistol with four-inch (Full Size) or 3.5-inch (Compact) barrel, polymer frame. Chambered in 9mm, .40 S&W or .45 ACP. Magazine capacity varies from 7 rounds (.45 ACP) to 15 (9mm).

NIB	Exc.	V.G.	Good	Fair	Poor
325	—	—	—	—	—

Thor

This is a single shot pistol chambered for the .223 Rem., .270 Win., .30-06, .300 Win., .308, .375 Win., .44 Mag., .45-70, .50 S&W, .7mm-08, or the .7mm Rem. Mag. Fitted with a 14" barrel, the receiver has an integral top rail for scope mount. Weight is about 5 lbs.

NIB	Exc.	V.G.	Good	Fair	Poor
1100	850	—	—	—	—

OTHER EAA IMPORTED FIREARMS

BUL 1911 SERIES

BUL Government

Chambered for the .45 ACP cartridge and fitted with 4.8" barrel. Polymer frame. Tactical rear sight with dovetail front sight. Fully checkered grip. Black or stainless steel slide. Weight is about 24 oz. Magazine capacity is 10 rounds. Introduced in 2002.

NIB	Exc.	V.G.	Good	Fair	Poor
550	450	—	—	—	—

NOTE: Add $50 for stainless steel slide.

BUL Commander

Same as above but fitted with 3.8" barrel.

NIB	Exc.	V.G.	Good	Fair	Poor
550	450	—	—	—	—

NOTE: Add $50 for stainless steel slide.

BUL Stinger

This model has a 3" barrel.

NIB	Exc.	V.G.	Good	Fair	Poor
550	450	—	—	—	—

NOTE: Add $50 for stainless steel slide.

EAA Big Bore Bounty Hunter

This model is a single-action revolver made in Germany. It features three-position hammer, forged barrel, and walnut grips. Offered in .357 Mag., .45 Long Colt, and .44 Mag. in 4.5", 5.5", or 7.5" barrel lengths. Choice of finish includes blue or case-colored frame, chrome, gold, or blue and gold.

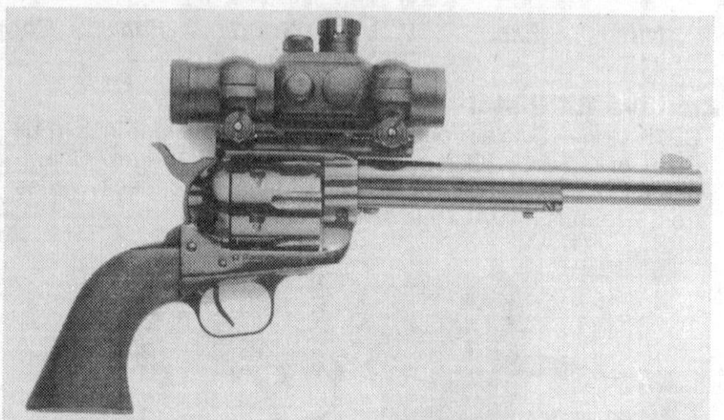

NIB	Exc.	V.G.	Good	Fair	Poor
300	225	175	150	125	100

NOTE: For chrome, gold, or blue and gold finish add 20 percent.

EAA Small Bore Bounty Hunter

This is a single-action .22 caliber revolver. It has wood grips and is available in blue or blue and brass finish. Barrel lengths are 4.75", 6", and 9". It is chambered for .22 LR or .22 Winchester Rimfire Magnum.

NIB	Exc.	V.G.	Good	Fair	Poor
225	175	125	100	75	60

EAA Bounty Hunter Shotgun—External Hammers

This is a side-by-side shotgun with external hammers chambered for 10, 12, 16, 20, 28, and .410 bores. It is offered in barrel lengths of 20", 24", and 26".

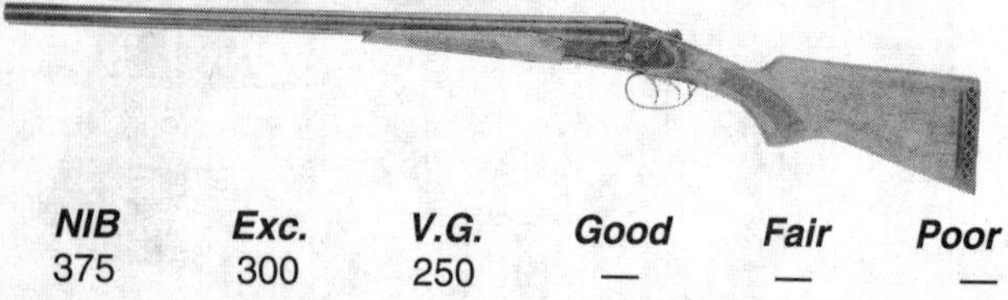

NIB	Exc.	V.G.	Good	Fair	Poor
375	300	250	—	—	—

EAA Bounty Hunter Shotgun—Traditional

Same as above but with internal hammers. Offered in 12 or 20 gauge.

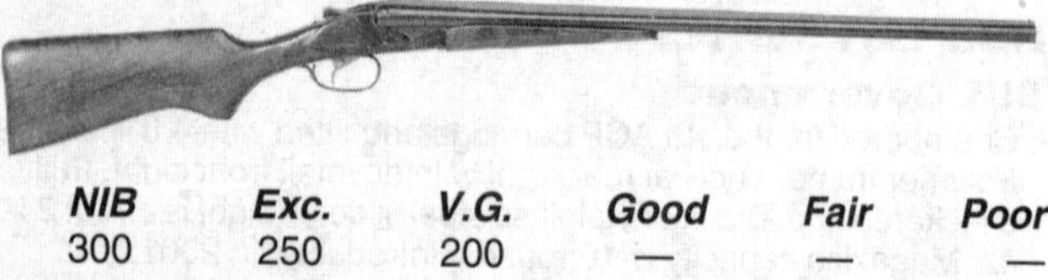

NIB	Exc.	V.G.	Good	Fair	Poor
300	250	200	—	—	—

EAA F.A.B. 92 Pistol

This model is a semi-automatic pistol similar to the Witness, but fitted with a hammer drop safety and slide mounted safety, that is both a double-action or single-action. It is available in either a full size (33 oz.) or compact size (30 oz.). The full size version has a 4.5" barrel while the compact is fitted with a 3.66" barrel. Offered in 9mm or .40 S&W in blue, two-tone, or chrome finish.

NIB	Exc.	V.G.	Good	Fair	Poor
350	275	225	175	125	100

EAA European Standard Pistol

This is a single-action semi-automatic pistol with external hammer, slide grip serrations, wood grips, and single column magazine. The barrels length is 3.2" and overall length is 6.5". Chambered for .22 LR, 380 ACP, and .32 ACP. The magazine capacity is 10 rounds for the .22 LR, 7 rounds for .380, and 7 rounds for .32. Offered in blue, blue/chrome, chrome, blue/gold. Weighs 26 oz.

NIB	Exc.	V.G.	Good	Fair	Poor
165	135	110	95	75	50

EAA European Target Pistol

This model features adjustable rear sight, external hammer, single-action trigger, walnut target grips, and adjustable weight system. Chambered for .22 LR. Offered in blue finish and weighs 40 oz.

NIB	Exc.	V.G.	Good	Fair	Poor
325	275	225	175	150	100

EAA Windicator Standard Grade

This German-built model is a double-action revolver chambered for the .22 LR, .22 Winchester Rimfire Magnum, .32 H&R, and .38 Special. It is offered in 2", 4", and 6" barrel lengths. The cylinder capacity for the .22 LR/.22 WRM is 8 rounds, .32 H&R is 7 rounds, and the .38 Special is 6 rounds. The cylinder is unfluted. Finish is blue.

NIB	Exc.	V.G.	Good	Fair	Poor
185	140	120	95	75	60

EAA Windicator Basic Grade

This model is chambered for the .38 Special or the .357 Magnum with 2" barrel. The fluted cylinder holds 6 rounds. Finish is blue.

NIB	Exc.	V.G.	Good	Fair	Poor
175	130	110	85	65	50

EAA Windicator Tactical Grade

This model is similar in appearance to the standard grade but is chambered for the .38 Special with 2" or 4" barrel. The 4" barrel has an integral compensator. Finish is blue.

2" Barrel

NIB	Exc.	V.G.	Good	Fair	Poor
190	150	125	100	80	60

4" Barrel

NIB	Exc.	V.G.	Good	Fair	Poor
250	200	150	125	100	75

EAA Windicator Target Grade

This model has these special features: adjustable trigger pull, walnut grips, adjustable rear sight, drilled and tapped for scope mount, target hammer, adjustable trigger stop. Fitted with 6" target barrel. Chambered for .22 LR, .38 Special, .357 Mag. Blue finish.

NIB	Exc.	V.G.	Good	Fair	Poor
350	275	225	200	150	100

EAA PM2 Shotgun

This is a pump-action 12 gauge shotgun with 6-round box magazine. Barrel length is 20" and finish is either blue or chrome. Stock is black composite. Weight is 6.8 lbs. This model was discontinued in 1993.

NIB	Exc.	V.G.	Good	Fair	Poor
450	350	300	250	200	150

NOTE: Add $100 for optional night sights.

EAA HW 60 Rifle

This German-made target rifle is chambered for the .22 LR. It features an adjustable trigger and other target and match grade components. The barrel length is 26.8", the stock is stippled walnut, and the finish is blue. Weighs approximately 10.8 lbs.

Target Grade

NIB	Exc.	V.G.	Good	Fair	Poor
670	575	500	400	300	200

Match Grade

NIB	Exc.	V.G.	Good	Fair	Poor
760	650	550	450	350	250

EAA Sabatti

These firearms are made by the Sabatti firm in Gardone, Italy. It is a old line company, having been in the firearms business since 1674. The company also produces and supplies component parts to many of Italy's premier gun makers. These shotguns and rifles are manufactured for the cost-conscious buyer.

EAA Sabatti Falcon

This is a field grade Over/Under shotgun with checkered walnut stock with pistol grip, boxlock action, double triggers, and extractors. Offered in 12 or 20 gauge with 3" chambers. Also available in 28 gauge and .410 bore with 26" or 28" barrels. Barrel lengths are available in 26", 28", or 30". Chokes are fixed.

NIB	Exc.	V.G.	Good	Fair	Poor
575	425	400	350	300	250

28/.410

NIB	Exc.	V.G.	Good	Fair	Poor
625	480	425	375	325	275

EAA Sporting Clay Basic

This model features a single-selective trigger, extractors, checkered walnut stock with pistol grip, extra wide rib, and blued receiver with scroll engraving. Offered in 12 gauge only with 28" fixed choke barrel.

NIB	Exc.	V.G.	Good	Fair	Poor
350	275	250	200	150	100

EAA Sporting Clay Pro

This model is similar to the basic sporting clay model with the addition of a select walnut stock, screw-in choke tubes, automatic ejectors, recoil pad. Comes with hard shell case.

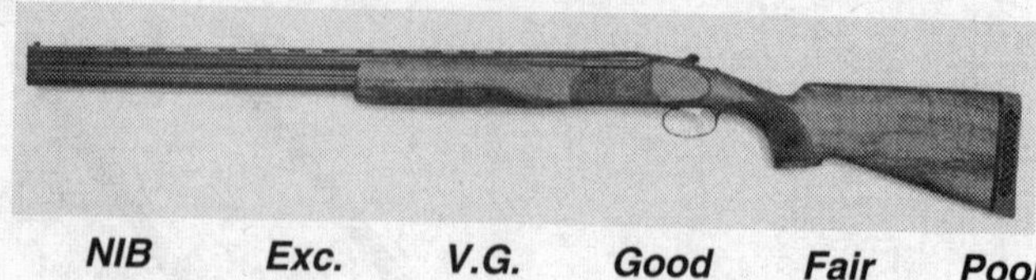

NIB	Exc.	V.G.	Good	Fair	Poor
950	720	650	550	450	300

EAA Sporting Clay Pro Gold

Same as above but with gold inlay receiver.

NIB	Exc.	V.G.	Good	Fair	Poor
1000	750	650	550	450	300

EAA Saba

This model is a side-by-side shotgun that features an engraved silver boxlock receiver, double or single triggers, selective ejectors, solid raised matted rib, and select European walnut checkered stock. Offered in 12, 20, and 28 gauge as well as .410 bore. Barrel length are 26" or 28" with fixed chokes.

NIB	Exc.	V.G.	Good	Fair	Poor
775	600	500	400	300	250

EAA/BAIKAL SHOTGUNS

SEE—Baikal

EAA/Saiga Shotgun

A semi-automatic shotgun based on the AK-47 design. Chambered for the 12, 20 and .410 bore. Barrel length are 20", 24", 26", or 28". Blued finish with optional camo finish. Detachable 5-round box magazine. Introduced in 1999.

NIB	Exc.	V.G.	Good	Fair	Poor
450	350	—	—	—	—

NOTE: Deduct $175 for .410 variation.

EAA/Saiga Rifle

Same as above but chambered for 7.62x39 or .308 cartridge. Fitted with a 20" barrel. Choice of wood or stnthetic stock. Introduced in 1999.

NIB	Exc.	V.G.	Good	Fair	Poor
275	225	—	—	—	—

NOTE: Add $100 for .308 caliber.

EAA Rover 870

This is a high-quality bolt-action rifle. The walnut stock is checkered with rubber recoil pad. Adjustable rear sight and receiver is drilled and tapped for scope mount. Barrel length is 22". Chambered for these cartridges: .22-250, .243, .25-06, .270, .308, .30-06, 7mm Rem. Mag., .300 and .338 Win. Mag.

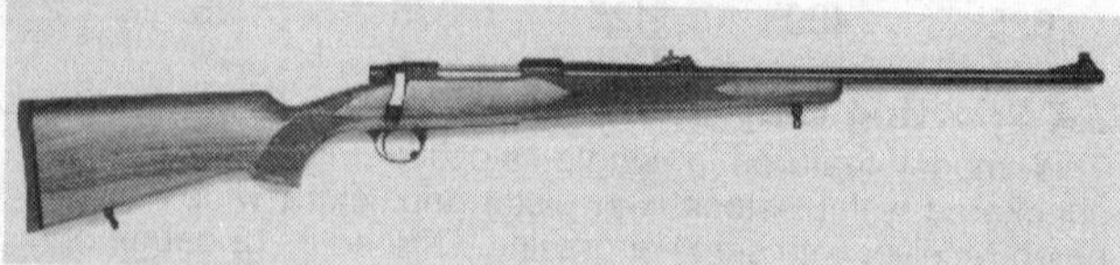

NIB	Exc.	V.G.	Good	Fair	Poor
560	425	375	300	200	125

EAA SP 1822

This Sabatti rifle is chambered for the .22 LR. It is a semi-automatic carbine with a two-piece adjustable stock.

NIB	Exc.	V.G.	Good	Fair	Poor
200	150	125	100	85	60

EAA SP 1822H

This a heavy barrel version of the above model without sights. The receiver is fitted with scope mount base.

NIB	Exc.	V.G.	Good	Fair	Poor
200	150	125	100	85	60

EAA SP 1822TH

This variation also has a heavy barrel without sights but with base mounts. A one-piece Bell and Carlson thumb hole stock is the feature of this model.

NIB	Exc.	V.G.	Good	Fair	Poor
350	260	225	175	125	90

EAA Benelli Silhouette Pistol

This is a specialized competition pistol with a semi-automatic action. The stocks are match type walnut with stippling. The palm shelf is adjustable. The barrel is 4.3" long. Fully adjustable sights. It is chambered for the .22 LR, .22 Short, and the .32 WC. Supplied with loading tool and cleaning rod. The .22 Caliber version weighs 38.5 oz. Overall length is 11.7".

NIB	Exc.	V.G.	Good	Fair	Poor
1850	1250	950	750	600	400

EAA Astra Pistol

SEE—Astra

EVANS REPEATING RIFLE CO.

Mechanic Falls, Maine

Incorporated in 1873, this firm produced repeating rifles based upon patents issued to Warren R. Evans (1868-1871) and later George F. Evans (1877, 1878 and 1879). The most distinctive feature of these arms is that they used a butt magazine operating on the principle of an Archimedean screw. Distributed by Merwin, Hulbert & Company, as well as Schuyler, Hartley & Graham, Evans rifles met with some success. One of their earliest advocates was William F. Cody (Buffalo Bill). The company ceased operations in 1879, after approximately 15,000 arms had been made.

Lever-Action Rifle

This rifle is totally unique for a number of reasons. It holds the most rounds of any repeating rifle that did not have a detachable magazine, with capacities up to 38 rounds on some models. This rifle was chambered for its own cartridge—the .44 Evans of which there were two versions: a 1" cartridge in the "Old Model" and the "Transition Model" and a 1.5" cartridge in the "New Model." The finish on these rifles is blued, with nickel-plated levers and buttplates noted on some examples. The stocks are walnut. There were approximately 12,250 of all models manufactured between 1873 and 1879.

Old Model

This variation is chambered for the 1" .44 Evans cartridge and has a butt stock that covers only the top half of the revolving 34-shot magazine located in the butt of the rifle. The buttplate appears as if it is reversed, and the markings on the "Old Model" are "Evans Repeating Rifle/Pat. Dec. 8, 1868 & Sept. 16, 1871." There are three versions of the Old Model listed. They were manufactured between 1874 and 1876 and serial numbered 1-500.

Military Musket

This version has a 30" barrel, with two barrel bands and provisions for a bayonet. There were only 50 estimated manufactured.

Exc.	V.G.	Good	Fair	Poor
—	—	3500	1500	500

Sporting Rifle

Approximately 300 of this model produced with a 26", 28", or 30" octagonal barrel.

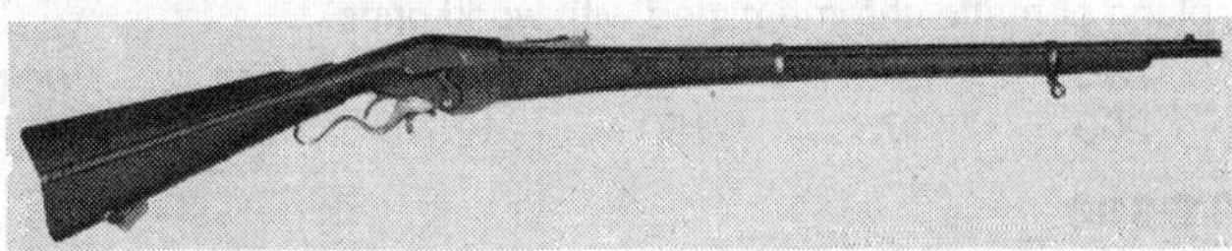

Courtesy Milwaukee Public Museum, Milwaukee, Wisconsin

Exc.	V.G.	Good	Fair	Poor
—	—	1850	800	400

Carbine

This variation has a 22" barrel, with one barrel band and a sling swivel. There were 150 produced.

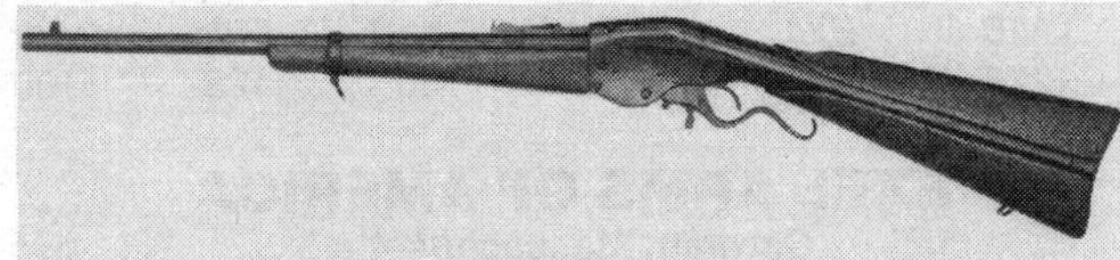

Courtesy Milwaukee Public Museum, Milwaukee, Wisconsin

Exc.	V.G.	Good	Fair	Poor
—	—	3000	1150	500

Transitional Model

Has a buttstock that covers both the top and bottom of the rotary magazine, with an exposed portion in the middle of the butt. The buttplate does not have the backward appearance, and the barrel is marked "Evans Repeating Rifle Mechanic Falls Me./Pat Dec. 8, 1868 & Sept. 16, 1871." This version was manufactured in 1876 and 1877 and was serial numbered between 500-2185, for a total of approximately 1,650 manufactured.

Military Musket

Has a 30" barrel and two barrel bands. 150 were produced.

Exc.	V.G.	Good	Fair	Poor
—	—	2750	1200	450

Carbine

Four hundred-fifty of these were produced, with a 22" barrel and one barrel band.

Exc.	V.G.	Good	Fair	Poor
—	—	2250	700	375

Sporting Rifle

Has a 26", 28", or 30" barrel. There were 1,050 produced.

Exc.	V.G.	Good	Fair	Poor
—	—	1750	800	300

"Montreal Carbine"

A special issue marked "Montreal," sold by R.H. Kilby, Evans' Canadian sales agent. There were between 50 and 100 produced.

Exc.	V.G.	Good	Fair	Poor
—	—	2750	1150	450

New Model

Approximately 10,000 of the New Model were produced, chambered for the 1.5" .44 Evans cartridge with a magazine capacity reduced to 28. The frame was redesigned and rounded at the top, and the forend fit flush to the receiver. The lever and hammer are streamlined, and there is a dust cover over the loading gate. The markings are the same as on the Transitional Model with "U.S.A." added to the last line. This version was not serial numbered, and any numbers found are assembly numbers only.

Military Musket

3,000 produced, with a 30" barrel and two barrel bands.

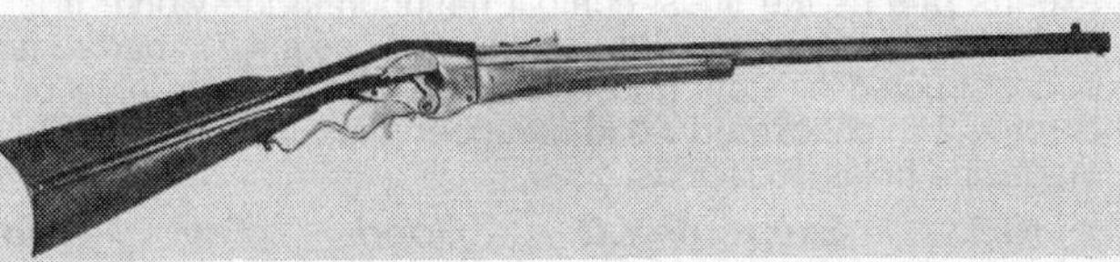

Courtesy Bonhams & Butterfields, San Francisco, California

Exc.	V.G.	Good	Fair	Poor
—	—	3250	1250	450

Carbine

4,000 produced with a 22" barrel, one barrel band, and a sling swivel.

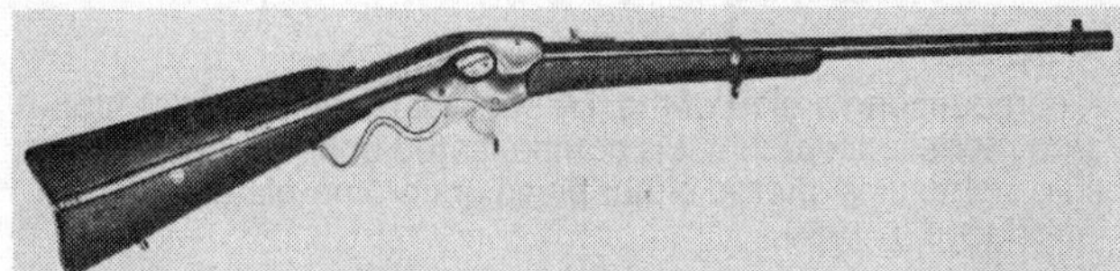

Courtesy Buffalo Bill Historical Center, Cody, Wyoming

Exc.	V.G.	Good	Fair	Poor
—	—	1750	750	400

Sporting Rifle

3,000 produced with 26", 28", or 30" octagonal barrels.

Exc.	V.G.	Good	Fair	Poor
—	—	2000	800	400

EVANS, J. E.

Philadelphia, Pennsylvania

Evans Pocket Pistol

A copy of the Philadelphia-made Henry Deringer pistol and is chambered for .41 caliber. It utilizes the percussion ignition system and has barrels from 2.5" to 3" in length. The stock is of walnut with a checkered grip, and the mountings are scroll engraved German silver. The barrel is marked "J.E. Evans Philada." These pistols were manufactured in the 1850s.

Exc.	V.G.	Good	Fair	Poor
—	—	1750	700	350

EVANS, WILLIAM

London, England

SEE—British Double Guns

EXCAM

Hialeah, Florida

An importer of firearms; not a manufacturer. The Erma and Uberti products imported by this company are under their own heading in this book. The other products that they imported are listed here. They are no longer in business.

TA 76

Patterned after the Colt Single Action Army and is chambered for the .22 rimfire cartridge. It has a 4.75", 6", or 9" barrel and blue finish with wood grips. It is offered with brass trigger guard and backstrap and also offered chrome-plated. A combo model with an extra .22 Magnum cylinder is available and would add 10 percent to the listed values.

Exc.	V.G.	Good	Fair	Poor
100	75	65	40	25

TA 38 Over-and-Under Derringer

A two-shot derringer patterned after the Remington derringer. It is chambered for the .38 Special cartridge, has 3" barrels that pivot upward for loading, and is blued with checkered nylon grips. This model was discontinued in 1985.

Exc.	V.G.	Good	Fair	Poor
100	75	65	40	25

TA 90

A double-action, semi-automatic copy of the CZ-75 that some experts rate as the finest combat handgun in the world. It is chambered for the 9mm Parabellum and has a 4.75" barrel. It is constructed of steel and is finished with a matte blue or chrome with checkered wood or rubber grips. The detachable magazine holds 15 rounds.

NIB	Exc.	V.G.	Good	Fair	Poor
425	375	325	275	200	150

BTA-90B

A compact version of the TA 90, that has a 3.5" barrel and a 12-round detachable magazine. It is similar in all other respects to the standard model, with rubber grips only.

NIB	Exc.	V.G.	Good	Fair	Poor
425	375	325	275	200	150

TA 90 SS

A competition version of the TA 90, that is similar to the standard model except that it is compensated and features adjustable sights. It is offered either blued or chrome-plated and was introduced in 1989.

NIB	Exc.	V.G.	Good	Fair	Poor
650	575	500	400	325	225

TA 41, 41C, and 41 SS

This series of pistols is identical to the TA 90 series except that they are chambered for the .41 Action Express cartridge. Their values are about 10 percent higher than the 9mm versions. They were introduced in 1989.

Warrior Model W 722

A double-action revolver chambered for the .22 rimfire and the .22 rimfire Magnum with an interchangeable cylinder. It has a 6" barrel, adjustable sights, and an 8-shot cylinder capacity. It is blued, with checkered plastic grips. This model was not imported after 1986.

Exc.	V.G.	Good	Fair	Poor
100	75	50	35	20

Model W384

A double-action revolver chambered for the .38 Special cartridge, with a 4" or 6" vent rib barrel, blued finish, and plastic grips. It was discontinued in 1986.

Exc.	V.G.	Good	Fair	Poor
175	125	100	75	50

Model W357

Similar to the W384 except that it is chambered for the .357 Magnum cartridge. It was discontinued in 1986.

Exc.	V.G.	Good	Fair	Poor
200	150	125	100	75

Targa GT 26

A blowback-operated, semi-automatic pistol chambered for the .25 ACP cartridge. It has a 2.5" barrel and a 6-shot detachable magazine. It is finished in blue or matte chrome, with a choice of alloy or steel frame. The grips are wood.

Steel Frame Version

NIB	Exc.	V.G.	Good	Fair	Poor
125	90	75	50	40	30

Alloy Frame Version

NIB	Exc.	V.G.	Good	Fair	Poor
100	75	50	35	30	25

GT 22

A semi-automatic pistol chambered for the .22 LR cartridge. It has a 4" barrel, fixed sights, and a 10-round magazine. Available either blued or matte chrome-plated and has wooden grips.

NIB	Exc.	V.G.	Good	Fair	Poor
200	175	150	125	90	70

GT 22T

Similar to the GT 22, with a 6" barrel and adjustable target-type sights.

NIB	Exc.	V.G.	Good	Fair	Poor
225	200	175	150	100	75

GT 32

A blowback-operated semi-automatic pistol chambered for the .32 ACP cartridge. It has a 7-round magazine and is either blued or matte chrome-plated with wood grips.

NIB	Exc.	V.G.	Good	Fair	Poor
200	175	150	125	90	75

GT 380

Similar to the GT 32 except that it is chambered for the .380 ACP cartridge.

NIB	Exc.	V.G.	Good	Fair	Poor
225	175	150	125	100	75

GT 380XE

Similar to the GT 380, with an 11-shot, high-capacity, detachable magazine.

NIB	Exc.	V.G.	Good	Fair	Poor
225	200	175	150	125	100

EXEL ARMS OF AMERICA

Gardner, Massachusetts

SEE—Lanber

Laurona & Ugartechia

This firm was engaged in the import of Spanish shotguns. They ceased importing them in 1967, and the specific models will be found listed under the manufacturers' names.

EXCEL INDUSTRIES

Chino, California

Accelerator Pistol

This is a semi-automatic pistol available in .22 WMR or .17 HMR. Barrel length is 8.5" with a .875" diameter. Stainless steel with polymer grip. The barrel is fitted with an aluminum rib with target sights and a Weaver base. Magazine capacity is 9 rounds. Weight is about 54 oz. Introduced in 2004.

NIB	Exc.	V.G.	Good	Fair	Poor
385	300	—	—	—	—

Accelerator Rifle

As above but with an 18" fluted stainless steel barrel and black polymer pistol-grip stock. Fully adjustable removable sights on a Weaver rail. Weight is about 8 lbs. Introduced in 2004.

NIB	Exc.	V.G.	Good	Fair	Poor
465	350	—	—	—	—

F&T
(Falise & Trappman of Liege, Belgium)
SEE—French Military Firearms

F.A.S.
Italy

Model 601
A high-grade, competition target pistol chambered for the .22 Short cartridge. It is a semi-automatic, with a 5.5" barrel and adjustable target sights. The detachable magazine holds 5 rounds, and the finish is blued with wraparound target grips. This model was discontinued in 1988.

Exc.	V.G.	Good	Fair	Poor
1250	1000	750	550	300

Model 602
Similar to the Model 601 except that it is chambered for the .22 LR. It was discontinued in 1987.

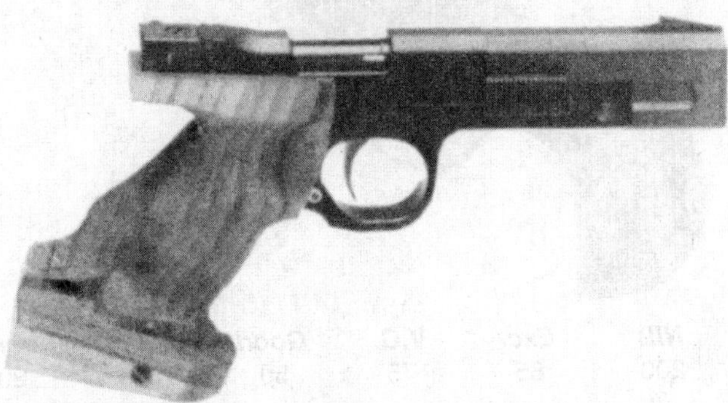

Exc.	V.G.	Good	Fair	Poor
1100	900	700	500	250

Model 603
Chambered for the .32 S&W wadcutter cartridge and features adjustable grips. It was discontinued in 1987.

Exc.	V.G.	Good	Fair	Poor
1100	900	700	500	250

F.I.E.
Hialeah, Florida

Firearms Import and Export was engaged in the business of importing the Franchi shotgun (which is listed under its own heading) and the Arminius revolver (which is made in Germany). They were also distributors for the Titan semi-automatic pistols, which are manufactured in the U.S.A. They were also importing a series of 9mm pistols from Italy that are produced by Tanfoglio and known as the TZ series. F.I.E. was no longer in business as of 1990.

TZ 75
A copy of the CZ 75 Czechoslovakian combat pistol produced by Tanfoglio in Italy. It is a 9mm, double-action semi-automatic with a 4.75" barrel, all-steel construction, fixed sights, and a 15-shot magazine. It is offered either blued or matte chrome plated, with wood or rubber grips.

NIB	Exc.	V.G.	Good	Fair	Poor
450	350	300	250	200	150

TZ 75 Series 88
An improved version that is also chambered for the .41 Action Express cartridge. It has a firing pin safety and can be carried cocked and locked. There are a few other minor changes. It was introduced in 1988.

NIB	Exc.	V.G.	Good	Fair	Poor
500	375	325	250	200	150

KG-99
A blowback-operated, semi-automatic assault pistol chambered for the 9mm Parabellum cartridge. It has a 36-round magazine. It was discontinued in 1984.

NIB	Exc.	V.G.	Good	Fair	Poor
550	450	350	250	200	150

Spectre Assault Pistol
An assault-type semi-automatic pistol chambered for the 9mm Parabellum. It has a 30- or 50-round magazine available. It was introduced in 1989.

NIB	Exc.	V.G.	Good	Fair	Poor
700	575	475	400	300	200

Titan II .22
A semi-automatic pistol chambered for the .22 LR. It has a 10-shot magazine and a blued finish with walnut grips. It is made in the U.S.A.

NIB	Exc.	V.G.	Good	Fair	Poor
275	150	100	75	50	25

Titan E32
A single-action, blowback-operated, semi-automatic pistol that was chambered for the .32 ACP and is now chambered for the .380 ACP cartridge. The finish is blue or chrome-plated, and the grips are walnut.

NIB	Exc.	V.G.	Good	Fair	Poor
300	175	150	125	100	75

Super Titan 11
Similar to the Titan except that it has a 12-round, high-capacity magazine.

NIB	Exc.	V.G.	Good	Fair	Poor
325	200	175	150	100	75

Titan 25

A smaller version of the Titan Series chambered for the .25 ACP cartridge. It is blued or chrome-plated.

NIB	Exc.	V.G.	Good	Fair	Poor
200	75	50	40	30	20

Titan Tigress

Similar to the Titan 25 except that it is gold-plated and cased.

NIB	Exc.	V.G.	Good	Fair	Poor
225	115	90	75	50	30

D38 Derringer

A two-shot, Over/Under, Remington-style derringer chambered for the .38 Special cartridge. It is chrome-plated and was dropped from the line in 1985.

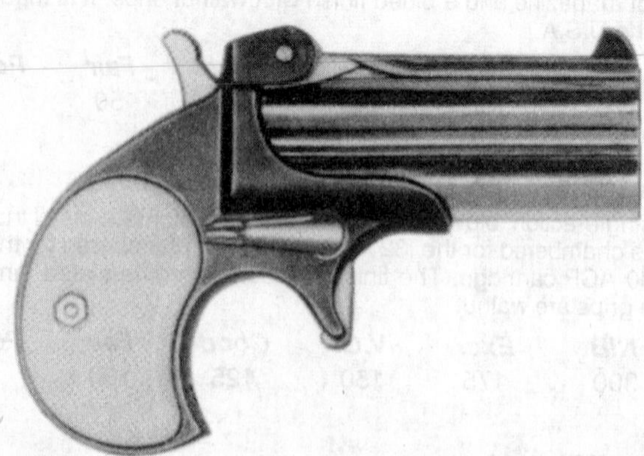

NIB	Exc.	V.G.	Good	Fair	Poor
150	60	45	35	25	20

D86 Derringer

A single-shot derringer with a 3" barrel. It is chambered for the .38 Special cartridge and is chrome-plated. There is an ammntion storage compartment in the butt and a transfer bar safety that makes it safer to carry. This model was introduced in 1986.

NIB	Exc.	V.G.	Good	Fair	Poor
150	80	65	50	35	20

SINGLE-ACTION ARMY REPLICA REVOLVERS

There is a series of single-action, .22 caliber revolvers that were patterned after the Colt Single-Action Army. They were manufactured in the U.S.A. or Brescia, Italy. They are inexpensive and of fair quality. The differences between these models are basically barrel lengths, type of sights, and finish. They all are chambered for the .22 LR and have interchangeable .22 Magnum cylinders. We list them for reference purposes.

Cowboy

NIB	Exc.	V.G.	Good	Fair	Poor
200	75	50	40	35	20

Gold Rush

NIB	Exc.	V.G.	Good	Fair	Poor
250	125	100	80	75	50

Texas Ranger

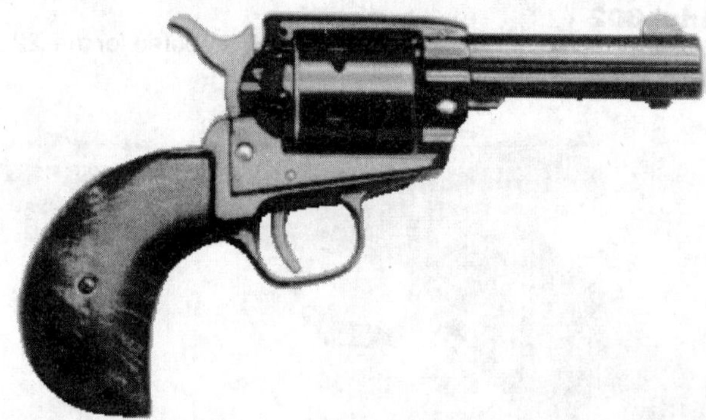

NIB	Exc.	V.G.	Good	Fair	Poor
200	85	75	50	35	20

Buffalo Scout

NIB	Exc.	V.G.	Good	Fair	Poor
175	80	70	50	35	20

Legend S.A.A.

NIB	Exc.	V.G.	Good	Fair	Poor
225	110	85	65	50	30

Hombre

A single-action made in Germany by Arminius. It is patterned after the Colt Single-Action Army revolver. The Hombre is chambered for the .357 Magnum, .44 Magnum, and .45 Colt cartridges. It is offered with a 5.5", 6", or 7.5" barrel, case-colored frame, and blued barrel and cylinder, with smooth walnut grips. The backstrap and trigger guard are offered in brass and will bring a 10 percent premium.

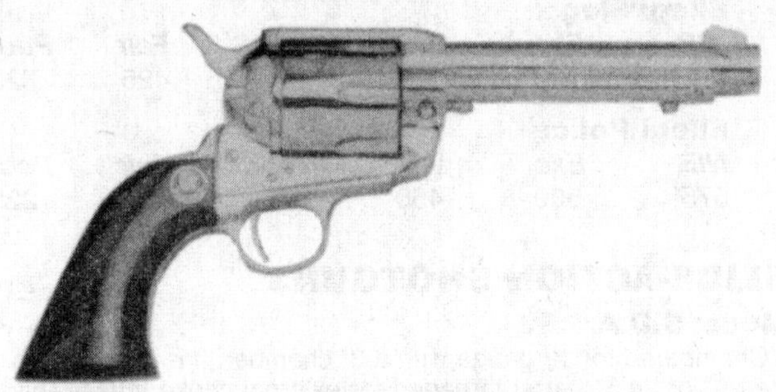

NIB	Exc.	V.G.	Good	Fair	Poor
320	200	175	125	100	75

ARMINIUS REVOLVERS

Model 522TB

A swing-out cylinder, double-action revolver chambered for the .22 rimfire cartridge. It has a 4" barrel and is blued with wood grips.

NIB	Exc.	V.G.	Good	Fair	Poor
250	125	100	75	50	30

722

Similar to the 522, with an 8-shot cylinder and a 6" barrel. It is available with a chrome finish.

NIB	Exc.	V.G.	Good	Fair	Poor
250	125	100	75	50	30

532TB

A 7-shot, double-action revolver chambered for the .32 S&W cartridge. It has a 4" barrel and adjustable sights and is finished in either blue or chrome.

NIB	Exc.	V.G.	Good	Fair	Poor
250	130	110	80	60	40

732B

Similar to the 532TB, with a 6" barrel and fixed sights. It was discontinued in 1988.

NIB	Exc.	V.G.	Good	Fair	Poor
225	100	80	65	50	35

Standard Revolver

A double-action, swing-out cylinder revolver chambered for .32 Magnum or .38 Special. It has a 4" or 6" barrel and fixed sights and is blued with wood grips. This model is made in the U.S.A. and was introduced in 1989.

NIB	Exc.	V.G.	Good	Fair	Poor
225	100	75	50	35	20

Models 384TB and 386TB

These two models are double-action chambered for the .38 Special cartridge. The 384 has a 4" barrel; and the 386, a 6" barrel. They are available in blue or chrome plate and were discontinued in 1985.

NIB	Exc.	V.G.	Good	Fair	Poor
250	125	100	85	65	50

Model 357TB

Similar to the 384TB except that it is chambered for the .357 Magnum cartridge and is offered with a 3", 4", or 6" barrel.

NIB	Exc.	V.G.	Good	Fair	Poor
250	125	100	85	65	50

222, 232, and 382TB

These models are double-action swing-out cylinder revolvers chambered for .22 rimfire, .32 S&W, and .38 Special. They are 2"-barreled snub-nosed revolvers, with either blued or chrome-plated finishes. They were discontinued in 1985.

NIB	Exc.	V.G.	Good	Fair	Poor
200	100	75	50	40	25

Model 3572

A similar revolver to the 382TB except that it is chambered for the .357 Magnum cartridge. It was discontinued in 1984.

NIB	Exc.	V.G.	Good	Fair	Poor
250	125	100	85	65	50

SHOTGUNS AND RIFLES

Model 122

A bolt-action rifle chambered for .22 rimfire, with a 21" barrel and adjustable sights. It has a 10-shot magazine and a walnut Monte Carlo stock. It was introduced in 1986.

NIB	Exc.	V.G.	Good	Fair	Poor
200	100	75	50	35	25

Single-Shot

Brazilian made and chambered for 12 or 20 gauge and .410. It is a single-barreled break open, with 25" through 30" barrel and various chokes. It is blued with a wood stock and was introduced in 1985.

NIB	Exc.	V.G.	Good	Fair	Poor
150	100	60	45	35	25

S.O.B.

Similar to the single-shot, with an 18.5" barrel and a pistol grip instead of a standard stock. This model was discontinued in 1984.

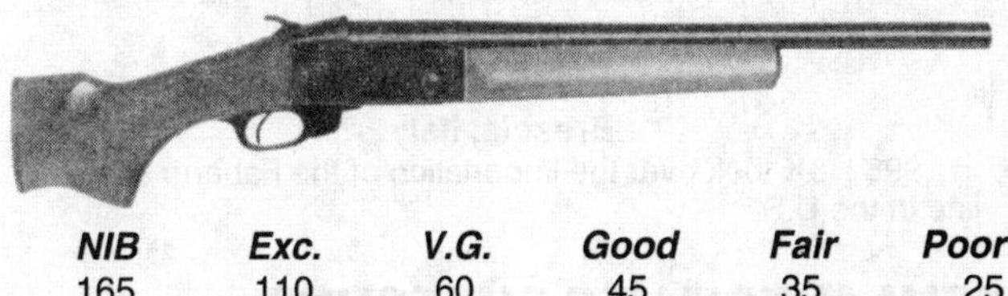

NIB	Exc.	V.G.	Good	Fair	Poor
165	110	60	45	35	25

Sturdy Over-and-Under

Chambered for 12 and 20 gauge and has 3" chambers and 28" vent-rib barrels with various chokes. This is an over-and-under with double triggers and extractors. The frame is engraved and silver finished. It was manufactured in Italy by Maroccini and imported between 1985 and 1988.

NIB	Exc.	V.G.	Good	Fair	Poor
400	300	225	175	150	100

Brute

A side-by-side chambered for 12 and 20 gauge and .410. It has 19" barrels, double triggers, and extractors. It has a wood stock and was dropped from the line in 1984.

NIB	Exc.	V.G.	Good	Fair	Poor
300	200	125	100	75	50

SPAS-12

A unique shotgun in that it can function as a pump or an automatic with the touch of a button. It is a paramilitary-type shotgun chambered for 12 gauge, with a 21.5" barrel and a 9-shot tube magazine. It has an alloy receiver and a folding stock. The finish is all black. This model is manufactured by Franchi in Italy.

NIB	Exc.	V.G.	Good	Fair	Poor
1500	1100	900	700	400	300

Law-12

A paramilitary-type, 12-gauge, semi-automatic shotgun that is gas-operated and has a 9-shot tube magazine. The barrel is 21.5" in length and choked cylinder bore. It has a military special black finish and a black synthetic stock.

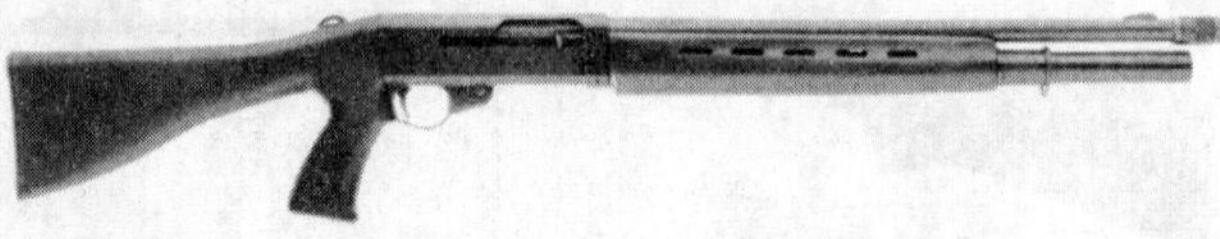

NIB	Exc.	V.G.	Good	Fair	Poor
750	550	400	300	200	100

SAS-12

A paramilitary-type, slide-action shotgun chambered for 12 gauge. It has a 21.5" barrel, choked cylinder bore. The finish is similar to the LAW-12, and it is manufactured by Franchi in Italy.

NIB	Exc.	V.G.	Good	Fair	Poor
850	650	500	400	300	200

F.L. SELBSTLADER

SEE—Langenhan

This is not a manufacturer but the German designation for the self-loader used on pistols made by Friedrich Langenhan.

FABARM

Brescia, Italy

In 1998 H&K took over the importation of the Fabarm shotgun line in the U.S.

SEMI-AUTOMATIC SHOTGUNS

Ellegi Standard

A gas-operated, semi-automatic shotgun chambered for 12 gauge. It has a 28" vent-rib barrel with choice of choke. The receiver is blue anodized alloy with a photo-etched game scene, and the stock and forearm are checkered walnut. This model was introduced in 1989.

NIB	Exc.	V.G.	Good	Fair	Poor
700	625	525	450	350	250

The Ellegi Model is available in six other configurations. The differences are in the barrel length and choke, type of choke tubes, and finish. Basically the guns are quite similar to the standard model. These variations are listed.

Ellegi Multichoke

NIB	Exc.	V.G.	Good	Fair	Poor
700	625	525	450	350	250

Ellegi Innerchoke

NIB	Exc.	V.G.	Good	Fair	Poor
725	650	550	475	375	275

Ellegi Magnum

NIB	Exc.	V.G.	Good	Fair	Poor
725	650	550	475	375	275

Ellegi Super Goose

NIB	Exc.	V.G.	Good	Fair	Poor
800	725	625	550	450	350

Ellegi Slug

NIB	Exc.	V.G.	Good	Fair	Poor
775	700	600	525	425	325

Ellegi Police

NIB	Exc.	V.G.	Good	Fair	Poor
575	500	450	400	300	225

SLIDE-ACTION SHOTGUNS

Model S.D.A.S.S.

Chambered for 12 gauge with a 3" chamber. It is offered with a 20" or 24.5" barrel threaded for external choke tubes. This model has an 8-shot tube magazine, twin action bars, an alloy receiver, and a matte black finish. It is a defensive-type shotgun and has been imported since 1989.

NIB	Exc.	V.G.	Good	Fair	Poor
500	450	400	350	250	175

The Special Police and the Martial Model are variations of the basic slide-action and differ in barrel length and choke. The Police Model has a shrouded barrel.

Special Police

NIB	Exc.	V.G.	Good	Fair	Poor
525	475	425	350	275	200

Martial Model

NIB	Exc.	V.G.	Good	Fair	Poor
475	425	375	300	225	175

SINGLE-SHOT SHOTGUNS

Omega Standard

Has an alloy receiver and is chambered for 12 and 20 gauge, as well as .410. It has 26" or 28" barrels with various chokes. The finish is black with a beech stock. It was introduced in 1989.

NIB	Exc.	V.G.	Good	Fair	Poor
150	125	100	75	50	40

Omega Goose Gun

Chambered for 12 gauge only, with a 35.5" full-choke barrel.

NIB	Exc.	V.G.	Good	Fair	Poor
160	140	125	100	75	50

SIDE-BY-SIDE SHOTGUNS

Beta Model

This double-barrel is chambered for 12 gauge only, with choice of barrel length and choke. It has a boxlock action with false side plates. It has a single trigger and automatic ejectors, and the finish is blued with a checkered, select walnut stock. This model was introduced in 1989.

NIB	Exc.	V.G.	Good	Fair	Poor
925	850	750	600	450	300

Beta Europe

A deluxe version that features single-selective triggers and a game scene engraved, coin-finished receiver. The stock is the straight English style with a splinter forend. This model was introduced in 1989.

NIB	Exc.	V.G.	Good	Fair	Poor
1750	1500	1250	1000	750	500

OVER/UNDER SHOTGUNS

Field Model

Chambered for 12 gauge and has 29" vent-rib barrels with various chokes. The receiver is coin-finished, and the stock is checkered walnut. This Model was discontinued in 1985.

NIB	Exc.	V.G.	Good	Fair	Poor
900	700	600	500	400	300

Gamma Field

Chambered for 12 or 20 gauge and is offered with 26", 28", or 29" vent-rib barrels and various choke combinations. Screw-in choke tubes are available and would be worth a 10 percent premium. This model has a boxlock, coin-finished receiver that is moderately engraved and a checkered walnut stock.

NIB	Exc.	V.G.	Good	Fair	Poor
925	850	775	650	500	350

Gamma Paradox Gun

Chambered for 12 gauge only, and the top barrel is rifled for accurate placement of slugs. The barrels are 25" long with vent-rib, and the bottom barrel has three screw-in choke tubes. This model has a single-selective trigger and automatic ejectors. The finish is similar to the Field Model. It was introduced in 1989.

NIB	Exc.	V.G.	Good	Fair	Poor
1000	900	825	750	600	450

Gamma Trap or Skeet

Competition-grade guns with either a 27.5" barrel with five screw-in choke tubes on the skeet model or a 29" barrel with screw-in trap chokes. Both models feature single-selective triggers and automatic ejectors; and the trap model has a Monte Carlo stock. They have moderately engraved, coin-finished boxlock actions and were introduced in 1989.

NIB	Exc.	V.G.	Good	Fair	Poor
1000	900	825	750	600	450

Gamma Sporting Competition Model

Designed for Sporting Clays and is chambered for 12 gauge only. The 29" barrel has a wide rib and is furnished with five screw-in choke tubes. It has a single-selective trigger, automatic ejectors, and a checkered walnut stock with a competition recoil pad. It is finished like the skeet and trap models and was introduced in 1989.

NIB	Exc.	V.G.	Good	Fair	Poor
1000	900	825	750	600	450

CURRENTLY IMPORTED SHOTGUNS (H&K-POST 1997)

SEMI-AUTOMATIC & PUMP SHOTGUNS

Camo Lion

Introduced in 1999, this 12 gauge model features a ported barrel system in 24", 26", or 28" lengths. Wetlands camo finish. Five chokes tubes and hard plastic case included. Weight is about 7 lbs.

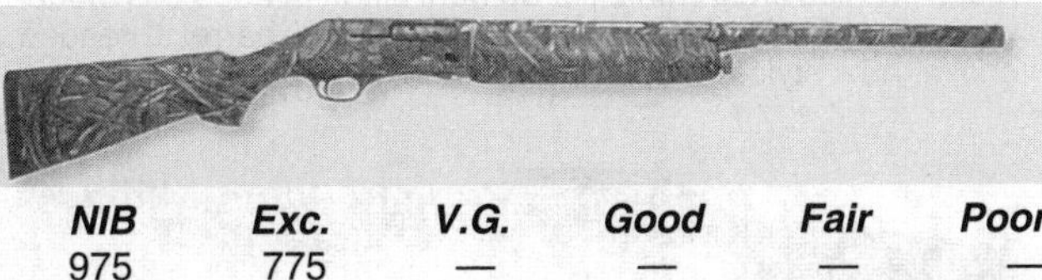

NIB	Exc.	V.G.	Good	Fair	Poor
975	775	—	—	—	—

Red Lion

This is a 12 gauge semi-auto with 3" chambers, three-shot magazine, matte finish, walnut stock, rubber vented recoil pad with leather cover, and set of five choke tubes. Available with 24", 26", or 28" vent-rib barrel. Weight is about 7 lbs.

NIB	Exc.	V.G.	Good	Fair	Poor
500	450	300	—	—	—

Red Lion Ducks Unlimited 2001

This model is offered only through the Ducks Unlimited banquet program only. This is a 12 gauge 28" barrel with select walnut stock. Oil finish. Unique serial numbers from 0001DU2001 to 3600DU2001. Receiver is engraved with waterfowl scene and DU logo. Comes with lockable case. Limited to 3,600 shotguns.

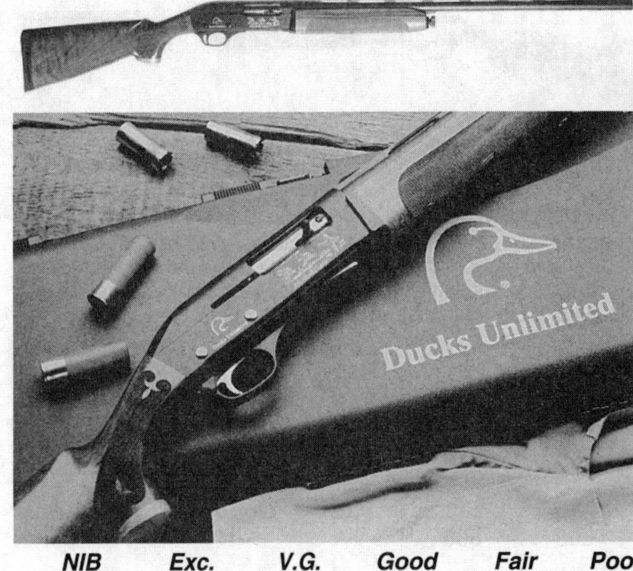

NIB	Exc.	V.G.	Good	Fair	Poor
700	575	—	—	—	—

Gold Lion

Has many of the features of the Red Lion model with the addition of a high-grade oil-finished walnut stock with Olive wood pistol grip cap. Trigger is gold plated.

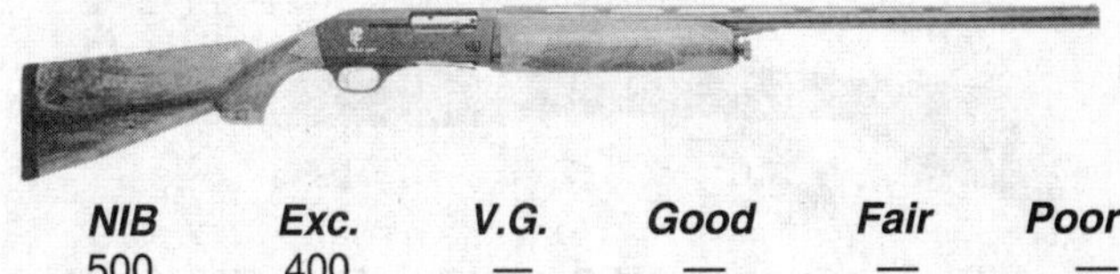

NIB	Exc.	V.G.	Good	Fair	Poor
500	400	—	—	—	—

Gold Lion Mark III

This semi-automatic model is an improved version of the Gold Lion with the addition of an enhanced walnut stock, lightweight receiver with scroll and engraving and gold enlays. Fitted with a 28" TriBore barrel and chambered for the 3" 12 gauge shell. Supplied with five choke tubes. Weight is about 7.2 lbs.

NIB	Exc.	V.G.	Good	Fair	Poor
450	375	—	—	—	—

Sporting Clays Lion

This model, introduced in 1999, features a ported barrel and special "TriBore" system. Offered in 12 gauge with 28" barrel. Walnut stock with rubber recoil pad, gold-plated trigger, matte blue finish, red front sight bar, 10mm channeled rib, two extra front sights (green and white), and a set of five choke tubes. Weight is about 7.2 lbs.

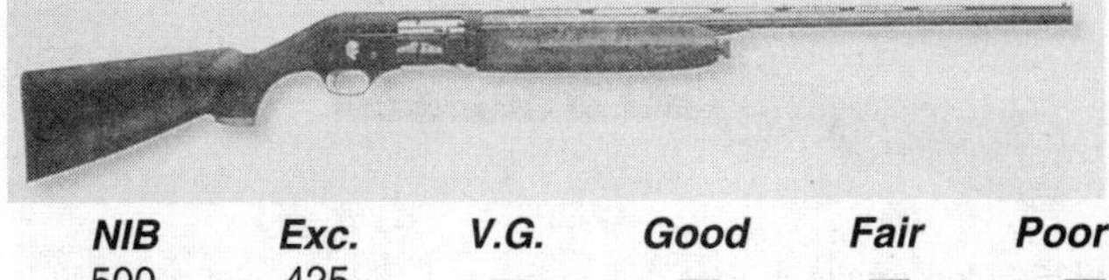

NIB	Exc.	V.G.	Good	Fair	Poor
500	425	—	—	—	—

Rex Lion

Introduced in 2002 this model features a 12 gauge gun with 3" chambers with 26" or 28" vent-rib barrel. Choke tubes. High-grade walnut stock with Olive wood grip cap. Silver and black frame with scroll engraving with gold inlay. Weight is about 7 lbs. A limited edition.

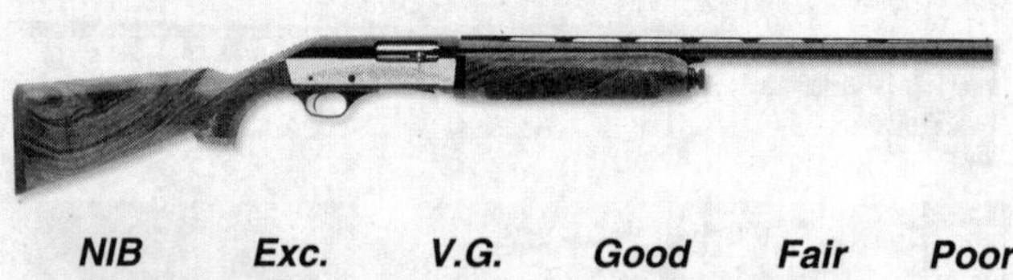

NIB	Exc.	V.G.	Good	Fair	Poor
1050	800	—	—	—	—

Sporting Clays Extra

Introduced in 2000 this model features a 28" or 30" vent-rib barrel with carbon fiber finish on both barrel and receiver. This model also supplied with eight competition choke tubes. Stock is adjustable. Supplied with fitted luggage case. Weight is about 7.3 lbs.

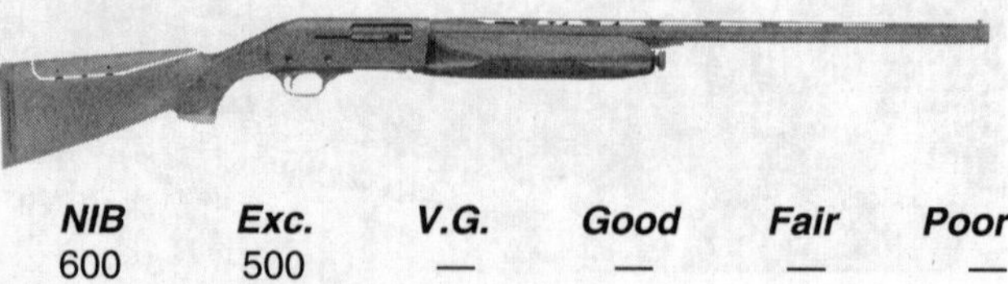

NIB	Exc.	V.G.	Good	Fair	Poor
600	500	—	—	—	—

Tactical Semi-Auto

This is a 12 gauge semi-automatic shotgun fitted with a 20" barrel threaded for chokes. Receiver-mounted Picatinny rail. Flip-up front sight. Optional magazine extension has 7-round capacity. Also optional pistol grip. Weight is about 6.6 lbs. Introduced in 2001.

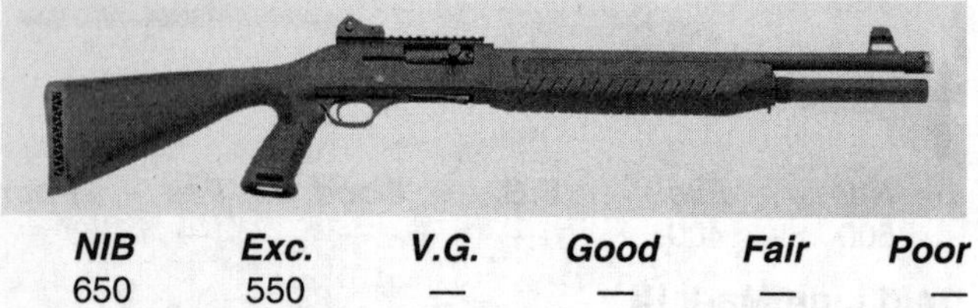

NIB	Exc.	V.G.	Good	Fair	Poor
650	550	—	—	—	—

Home Security HD

This semi-automatic shotgun is chambered for the 12 gauge 3" shell. Fitted with a 20" plain barrel with cylinder screw-in choke. Matte black finish. Black polymer stock. Magazine capacity is 5 rounds. Weight is about 7.5 lbs.

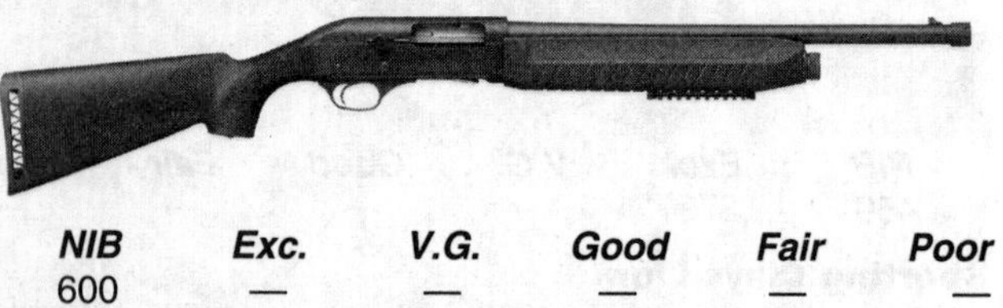

NIB	Exc.	V.G.	Good	Fair	Poor
600	—	—	—	—	—

H368

This 12 gauge 3" model features a 28" tri-bore vent rib barrel, matte black synthetic stock or Realtree camo stock. Lightweight alloy matte black receiver. Magazine capacity is 2 rounds. Weight is about 7.2 lbs. Introduced in 2003. Also available in a left-hand model.

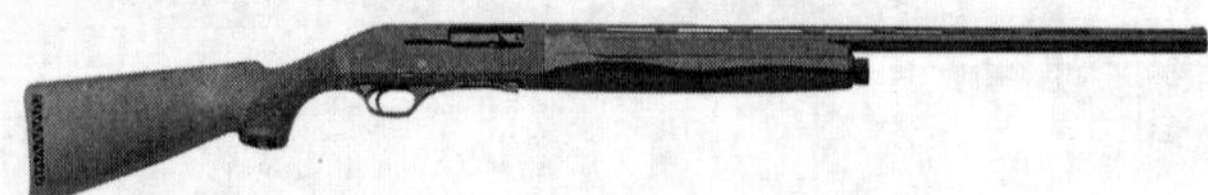

H368 Composite model

H368 Camo model

NIB	Exc.	V.G.	Good	Fair	Poor
500	425	—	—	—	—

NOTE: Add $60 for camo stock and $90 for left-hand model.

SLIDE ACTION

FP6 Field Pump

Introduced in 2001 this model features a black alloy receiver with screw-in chokes. Chambered for 12 gauge with 28" barrel. Black synthetic stock. Optional 24" rifles barrel. Weight is about 7 lbs.

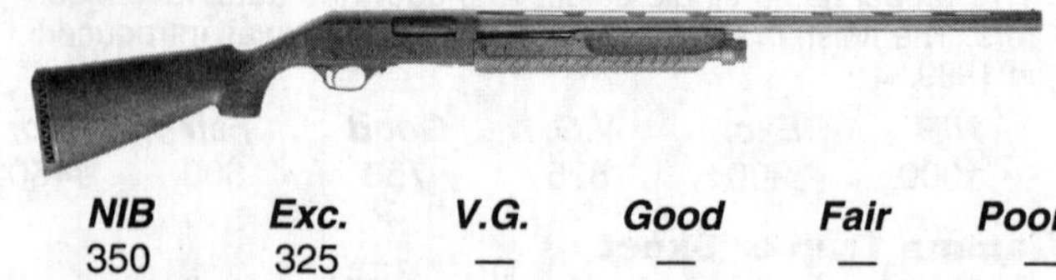

NIB	Exc.	V.G.	Good	Fair	Poor
350	325	—	—	—	—

FP6 Field Pump Camo

Same as above but with Mossy Oak Break-up camo pattern.

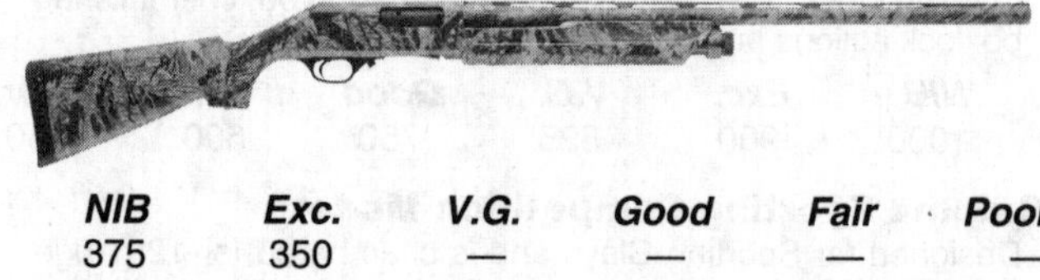

NIB	Exc.	V.G.	Good	Fair	Poor
375	350	—	—	—	—

FP6

This model is a 12 gauge slide-action shotgun with 3" chamber, 20" barrel with heat shield, black polymer stock, threaded barrel for exterior chokes. Weight is about 6.6 lbs. This model is also available with a carbon fiber finish.

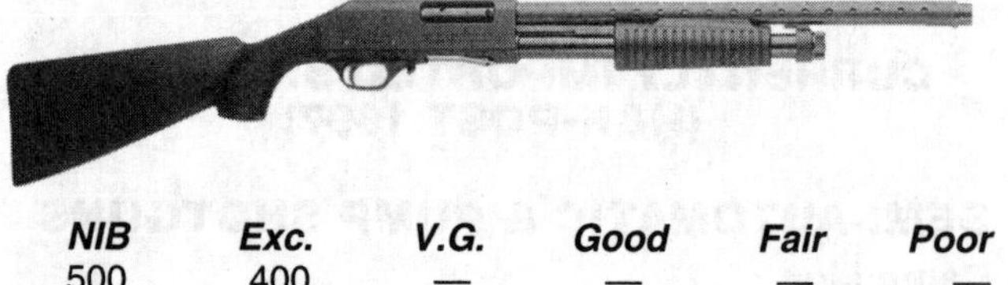

NIB	Exc.	V.G.	Good	Fair	Poor
500	400	—	—	—	—

FP6 with Rail

Introduced in 1999, this model is similar to the standard FP6 with the addition of a Picatinny rail mounted on the top of the receiver. Also fitted with a flip-up front sight. In 2003 this model was offered with a 20" tri-bore barrel with barrel threaded choke, new style front sight, and ghost ring rear sight.

NIB	Exc.	V.G.	Good	Fair	Poor
510	410	300	—	—	—

NOTE: This model is also available with 14" barrel. This requires a BATF tax and all NFA rules apply to purchase and sale of this restricted shotgun. An accessory wire stock and pistol grip are available for an additional $150.

OVER/UNDER GUNS

Max Lion

This over/under gun is chambered for the 12 or 20 gauge, 3" shell and fitted with single-selective trigger, auto ejectors, high grade walnut stock, leather covered recoil pad, set of five choke tubes and a fitted luggage-style case. Choice of 26", 28", or 30" barrels on 12 gauge guns and 26" or 28" on 20 gauge guns. Weight is about 7.5 lbs. for 12 gauge and 7 lbs. for 20 gauge.

Max Lion 12 gauge

NIB	Exc.	V.G.	Good	Fair	Poor
1200	900	700	—	—	—

NOTE: In 1999 the Max Lion was offered with the TriBore barrel system. For models with this system add $70 to above NIB prices.

Max Lion Light

Introduced in 2000 this model features 24" barrels in both 12 and 20 gauge. Receiver has gold game bird inlay. Single trigger, automatic ejectors and select walnut stock. Weight is about 7 lbs.

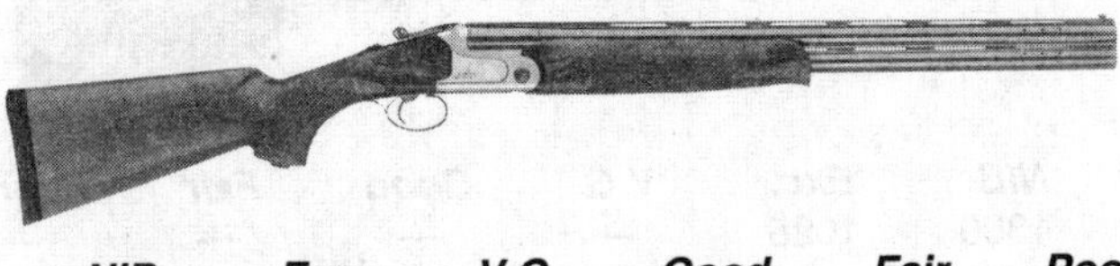

NIB	Exc.	V.G.	Good	Fair	Poor
1200	900	—	—	—	—

Max Lion Paradox

Introduced in 2002 this model features a 12 gauge 3" gun with 24" barrels. The bottom barrel is rifled. Case hardened receiver with checkered walnut stock. Weight is about 7.6 lbs.

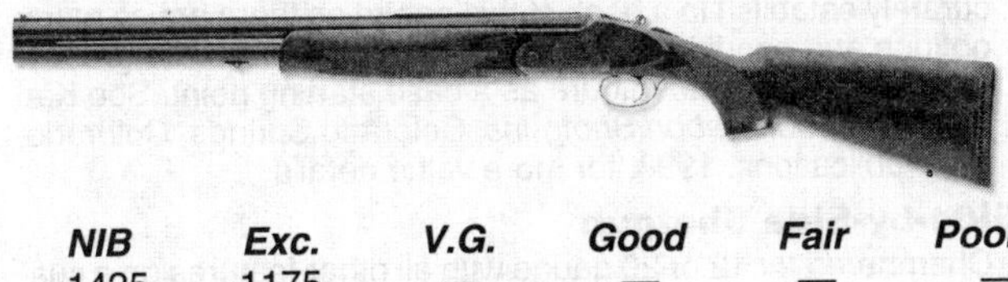

NIB	Exc.	V.G.	Good	Fair	Poor
1425	1175	—	—	—	—

Sporting Clays Competition Lion

This model is available in 12 or 20 gauge with 28" 10mm channeled rib barrels. Single-selective trigger and automatic ejectors. Recoil reducer installed in buttstock. Ported barrels. Set of 5 choke tubes standard. Leather covered recoil pad. High grade walnut stock. Introduced in 1999.

NIB	Exc.	V.G.	Good	Fair	Poor
675	550	—	—	—	—

Sporting Clays Max Lion

Chambered for the 12 gauge 3" shell and fitted with a 32" tribore vent rib barrel. Select walnut stock with hand checkering, adjustable trigger, and leather covered recoil pad. Engraved gold inlay receiver is case colored. Supplied with eight choke tubes. Weight is approximately 7.9 lbs. Introduced in 2003.

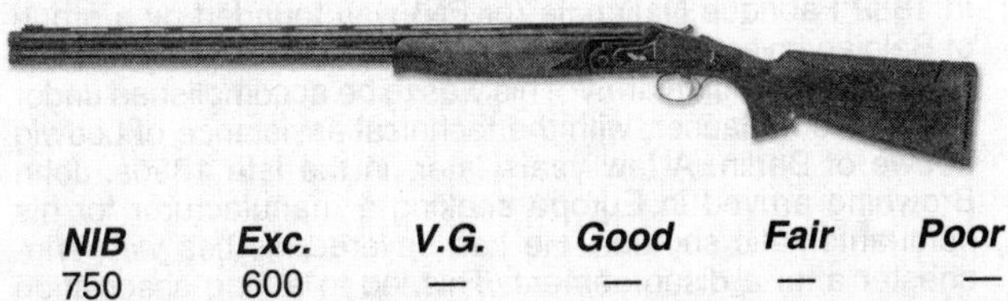

NIB	Exc.	V.G.	Good	Fair	Poor
750	600	—	—	—	—

Sporting Clays Competition Extra

This 12 gauge model features a a choice of 28" or 30" barrels. Walnut stock is adjustable. Finish is carbon fiber. Gun is supplied with set of eight choke tubes. Introduced in 2000. Weight is about 7.8 lbs.

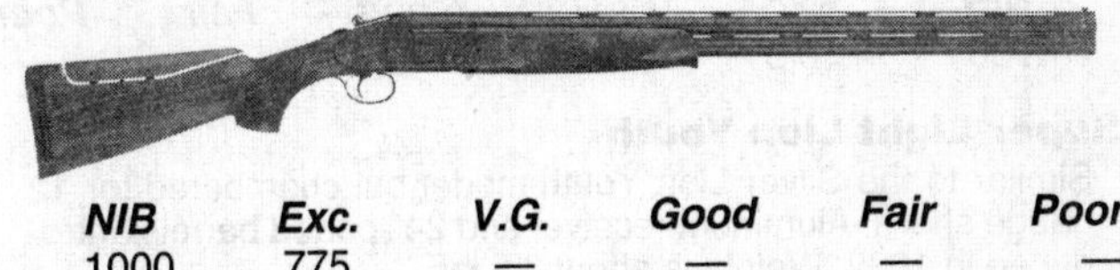

NIB	Exc.	V.G.	Good	Fair	Poor
1000	775	—	—	—	—

Black Lion Competition

Similar to the Max Lion in choice of gauges and barrel lengths and features but with less figured walnut stock and black receiver finish.

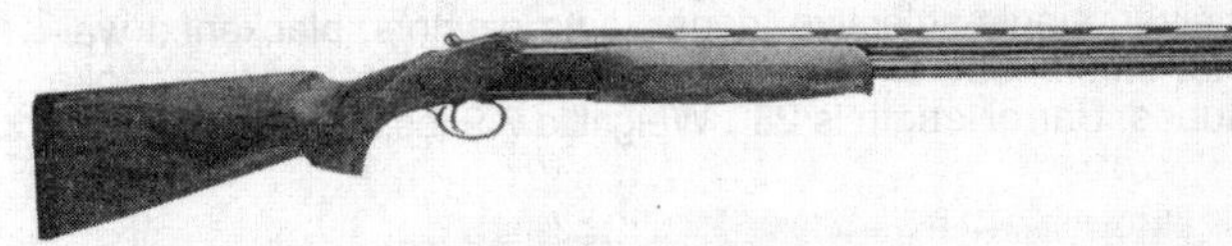

Black Lion 12 gauge

NIB	Exc.	V.G.	Good	Fair	Poor
1050	750	—	—	—	—

Monotrap

This is a single barrel trap gun with 30" vent-rib barrel. Forearm has built-in recoil reduction system. Single-selective trigger and automatic ejectors. Adjustable comb. This shotgun is a 12 gauge built on a 20 gauge receiver. Weight is about 6 lbs. Introduced in 2000.

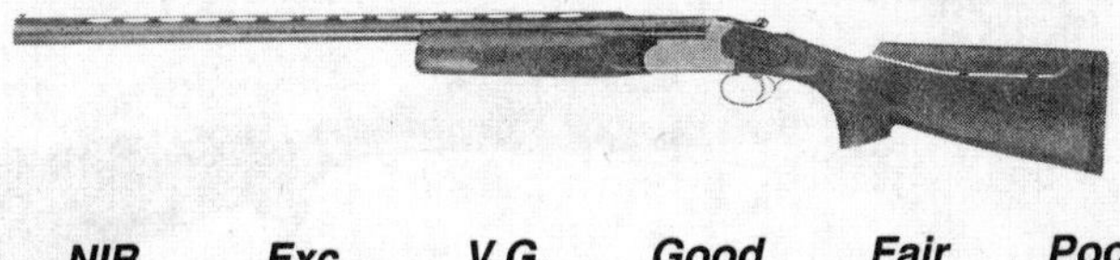

NIB	Exc.	V.G.	Good	Fair	Poor
1500	1150	—	—	—	—

Silver Lion

This model is available in both 12 and 20 gauge and with 26", 28" barrel and 30" barrels in 12 gauge. The silver finish receiver is etched and stock is high quality walnut with leather covered pad. Scalable forearm is standard and is single-selective trigger and auto ejectors. Five chokes tubes are included. Weight is about 7.5 lbs. for 12 gauge guns and 7 lbs. for 20 gauge.

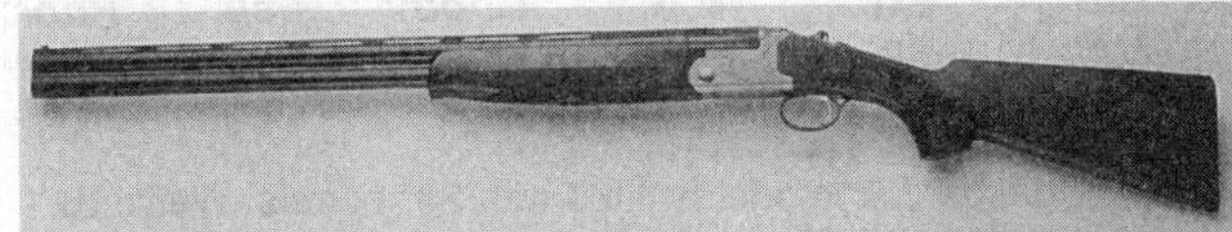

Silver Lion 12 gauge

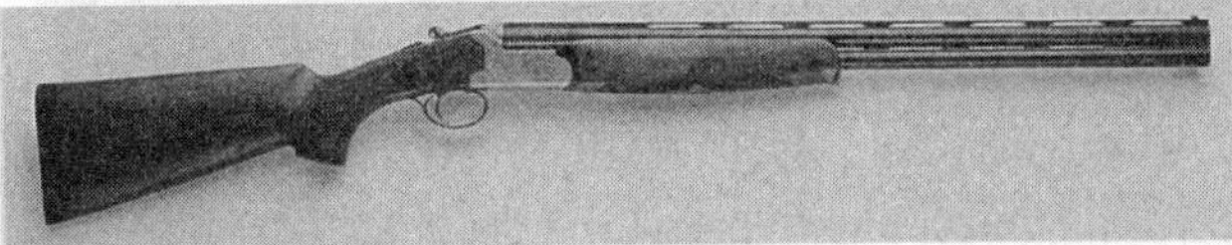

Silver Lion 20 gauge

NIB	Exc.	V.G.	Good	Fair	Poor
750	600	—	—	—	—

Silver Lion Youth

This 20 gauge over-and-under features a shortened buttstock and 24" ported barrels. Single-selective trigger and automatic ejectors standard. Walnut stock. Rubber recoil pad. Silver steel receiver. Weight is approximately 6 lbs. Introduced in 1999.

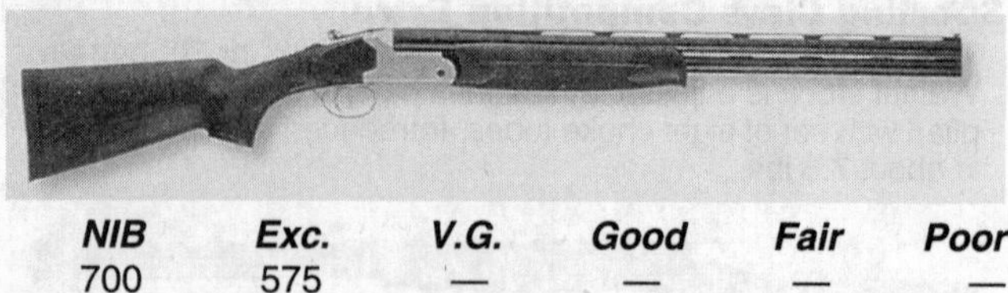

NIB	Exc.	V.G.	Good	Fair	Poor
700	575	—	—	—	—

Super Light Lion Youth

Similar to the Silver Lion Youth model but chambered for 12 gauge shells. Aluminum receiver and 24" ported barrels. Introduced in 1999. Weight is about 6.5 lbs.

NIB	Exc.	V.G.	Good	Fair	Poor
675	550	—	—	—	—

Ultra Mag Lion

This model is a 12 gauge gun with 3.5" chambers, black receiver, single-selective trigger, auto ejectors, blackened walnut stock, leather covered recoil pad, and set of five choke tubes. Barrel length is 28". Weight is 7.9 lbs.

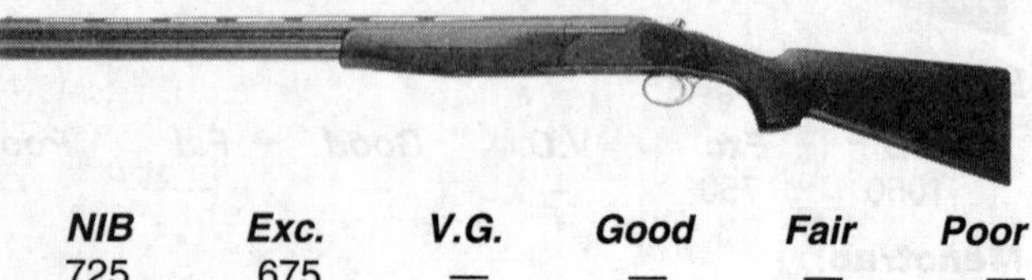

NIB	Exc.	V.G.	Good	Fair	Poor
725	675	—	—	—	—

Super Light Lion

This model features a lightweight alloy receiver with 12 gauge 24" barrels, single-selective trigger, non-auto ejectors, walnut stock, five choke tubes, and leather covered recoil pad. Weight is about 6.5 lbs.

NIB	Exc.	V.G.	Good	Fair	Poor
700	600	—	—	—	—

NOTE: For TriBore system add $125.

Camo Turkey Mag.

Introduced in 1999, this model features an unported TriBore 20" barrel. Receiver has Picatinny rail on top. Full extra brown camo finish. Chambered for 12 gauge with 3.5" chambers. Weight is about 7.5 lbs.

NIB	Exc.	V.G.	Good	Fair	Poor
600	525	—	—	—	—

Ultra Camo Mag. Lion

This 12 gauge 3.5" model is fitted with 28" barrels. Wetlands camo pattern finish. Non-automatic ejectors. Weight is about 8 lbs. Introduced in 1999. Standard with steel screw-in chokes and regular screw-in chokes.

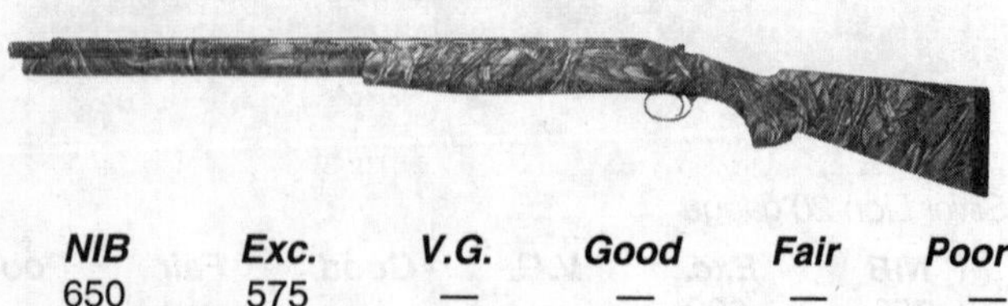

NIB	Exc.	V.G.	Good	Fair	Poor
650	575	—	—	—	—

SIDE-BY-SIDE GUNS

Classic Lion Grade I

Offered in 12 gauge with 3" chambers, single-selective trigger, auto-ejectors, walnut stock, buttplate, and fitted with 26" barrels. Weight is about 7 lbs.

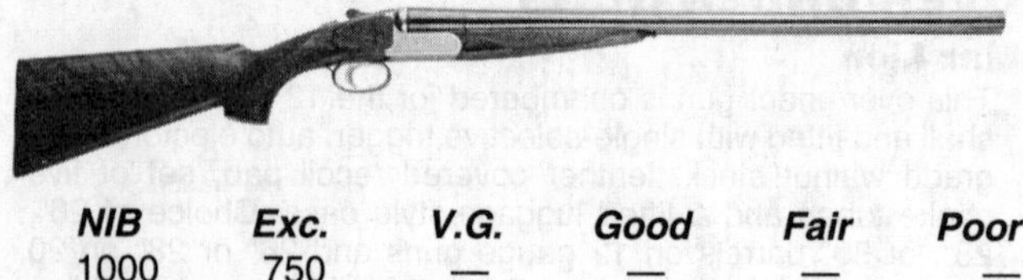

NIB	Exc.	V.G.	Good	Fair	Poor
1000	750	—	—	—	—

Classic Lion Grade II

Similar to the Grade I but with the addition of oil finished stock and removable sideplates with game scene engraving. Weight is 7.2 lbs.

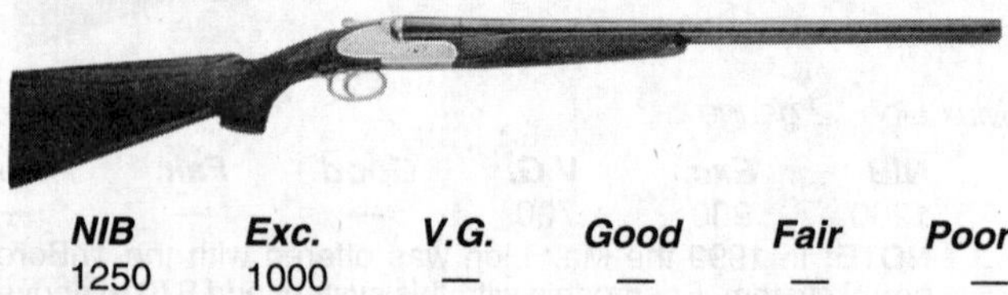

NIB	Exc.	V.G.	Good	Fair	Poor
1250	1000	—	—	—	—

Classic Lion Elite

Introduced in 2002, this 12 gauge model features 26" or 28" barrels with case colored receiver and straight grip stock. Fixed chokes. Weight is about 7 lbs.

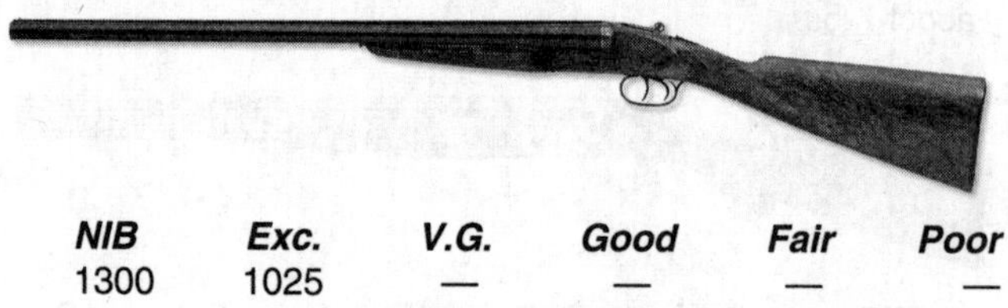

NIB	Exc.	V.G.	Good	Fair	Poor
1300	1025	—	—	—	—

FABBRI, ARMI

Gardone V.T., Italy

Fabbri Armi currently manufactures one of the best shotguns in the world. They are available as a custom made-to-order item, and they are not often seen in the used gun market. The values for guns of this nature and quality are impossible to accurately establish in a book of this nature as there are so many options and conditions that make the prices fluctuate greatly. We give an estimated figure as a base starting point. See Karl Lippard's book *Fabbri Shotguns*, Colorado Springs, Colorado, VM Publications, 1998, for more value details

Side-by-Side Shotgun

Chambered for 12 or 20 gauge with all other features on a custom-order basis. This model is no longer in production.

NIB	Exc.	V.G.	Good	Fair	Poor
38500	25000	17500	15000	10000	8000

NOTE: Deduct $10,000 for type One Model.

Over-and-Under Shotgun

Chambered for 12 or 20 gauge with all other features on a custom-order basis. Prices listed are for Boehler barrels.

NIB	Exc.	V.G.	Good	Fair	Poor
39500	25000	17500	15000	10000	8000

NOTE: Add 50 percent for vacuum arc remelted steel barrels. Deduct 50 percent for Phoenix barrels.

FABRIQUE NATIONALE

Herstal, Belgium

In 1889 Fabrique Nationale (or FN) was founded by a group of Belgian investors for the purpose of manufacturing Mauser rifles for the Belgian army. This was to be accomplished under license from Mauser, with the technical assistance of Ludwig Loewe of Berlin. A few years later, in the late 1890s, John Browning arrived in Europe seeking a manufacturer for his semi-automatic shotgun. He had severed his ties with Winchester after a disagreement. This led to a long association that worked out extremely well for both parties. Later Browning became associated with Colt, and the world market was divided—with the Eastern Hemisphere going to FN and the Western Hemisphere to Colt.

In this section, we list arms that bear the FN banner. The FN-manufactured firearms produced under the Browning banner are listed in the Browning section of this book.

Model 1900

A blowback-operated semi-automatic pistol chambered for the 7.65mm cartridge. It has a 4" barrel and fixed sights and is blued with molded plastic grips. This model is notorious as the pistol that was used to assassinate Archduke Ferdinand, an event that touched off WWI. It was manufactured between 1899 and 1910. This model is referred to as the "Old Model."

Exc.	V.G.	Good	Fair	Poor
500	375	310	200	150

Model 1903

A considerable improvement over the Model 1900. It is also a blowback-operated semi-automatic; but the recoil spring is located under the barrel, and the firing pin travels through the slide after being struck by a hidden hammer. The barrel is held in place by five locking lugs that fit into five grooves in the frame. This pistol is chambered for the 9mm Browning long cartridge and has a 5" barrel. The finish is blued with molded plastic grips, and the detachable magazine holds 7 rounds. There is a detachable shoulder stock/holster along with a 10-round magazine that was available for this model. These accessories are extremely rare and if present would make the package worth approximately five times that of the pistol alone. There were approximately 58,000 manufactured between 1903 and 1939.

Exc.	V.G.	Good	Fair	Poor
550	425	375	275	175

Model 1906

A smaller version of the Model 1903, designed to be a pocket pistol and chambered for the 6.35mm cartridge. It became known as the "Vest Pocket" model and was also the basis for many Eibar copies. It has a 2.5" barrel and was produced in two distinct variations. The first variation had no safety lever or slide lock and relied on the grip safety. The second variation, that occurred at approximately serial number 100000, added this safety lever and slide lock, which helped simplify dismantling of the pistol. This model was available either blued or nickel-plated. The plated models would bring a 10 percent premium. There were approximately 1,086,100 manufactured between 1906 and 1959.

1st Variation, Under Serial Number 100000

Exc.	V.G.	Good	Fair	Poor
425	300	250	200	125

2nd Variation, Over Serial Number 100000

Exc.	V.G.	Good	Fair	Poor
400	275	200	175	100

Model 1910 "New Model"

Chambered for 7.65mm and 9mm short. It has a 3.5" barrel, is blued, and has molded plastic grips. The principal difference between this model and its predecessors is that the recoil spring on the Model 1910 is wrapped around the barrel. This gives the slide a more graceful tubular appearance instead of the old slab-sided look. This model has the triple safety features of the 1906 Model 2nd variation and is blued with molded plastic grips. This model was adopted by police forces around the world. It was manufactured between 1912 and 1954.

Courtesy Orvel Reichert

Exc.	V.G.	Good	Fair	Poor
425	300	250	175	125

Model 1922

Exc.	V.G.	Good	Fair	Poor
350	225	175	125	100

"Baby" Model

A smaller and lighter version of the Model 1906. It is chambered for the 6.35mm cartridge and has a 2" barrel. There is no grip safety or slide lock on this model, and it appears to be more square in shape than the Model 1906. This model was offered in blue, with molded plastic grips. Early models have the word "Baby" molded into the grips; post-1945 versions do not. There is also a nickel-plated version with pearl grips. There were over 500,000 of these manufactured between 1931 and 1983.

Courtesy Orvel Reichert

Courtesy Orville Reichert

Exc.	V.G.	Good	Fair	Poor
525	375	300	225	150

Model 1935

The last design from John Browning and was developed between 1925 and 1935. This pistol is known as the Model 1935, the P-35, High-Power or HP, and also as the GP (which stood for "Grand Puissance") and was referred to by all those names at one time or another. The HP is essentially an improved version of the Colt 1911 design. The swinging link was replaced with a fixed cam, which was less prone to wear. It is chambered for the 9mm Parabellum and has a 13-round detachable magazine. The only drawback to the design is that the trigger pull is not as fine as that of the 1911, as there is a transfer bar instead of a stirrup arrangement. This is necessary due to the increased magazine capacity resulting in a thicker grip. The barrel is 4.75" in length. It has an external hammer with a manual and a magazine safety and was available with various finishes and sight options and was furnished with a shoulder stock. The Model 1935 was used by many countries as their service pistol as such there are many variations. We list these versions and their approximate values.

Pre-war Commercial Model

Found with either a fixed sight or a sliding tangent rear sight and is slotted for a detachable shoulder stock. It was manufactured from 1935 until 1940.

Fixed Sight Version

Exc.	V.G.	Good	Fair	Poor
725	600	475	375	275

Tangent Sight Version

Exc.	V.G.	Good	Fair	Poor
1200	850	675	550	400

NOTE: Wood holster stock add 50 percent.

Pre-war Military Contract

The Model 1935 was adopted by many countries as a service pistol, and they are listed.

Belgium

Exc.	V.G.	Good	Fair	Poor
1200	1050	900	600	375

Canada and China (*See John Inglis & Company*)

Denmark

Exc.	V.G.	Good	Fair	Poor
1250	1100	950	650	400

Great Britain

Exc.	V.G.	Good	Fair	Poor
1150	1000	850	550	325

Estonia

Exc.	V.G.	Good	Fair	Poor
1200	1050	900	600	375

Holland

Exc.	V.G.	Good	Fair	Poor
1250	1100	950	650	400

Latvia

Exc.	V.G.	Good	Fair	Poor
1500	1350	1050	775	500

Lithuania

Exc.	V.G.	Good	Fair	Poor
1250	1100	950	650	400

Romania

Exc.	V.G.	Good	Fair	Poor
1500	1350	1050	775	500

German Military Pistole Modell 640(b)

In 1940 Germany occupied Belgium and took over the FN plant. The production of the Model 1935 continued, with Germany taking the output. The FN plant was assigned the production code "ch," and many thousands were produced. The finish on these Nazi guns runs from as fine as the Pre-war Commercial series to downright crude, and it is possible to see how the war was progressing for Germany by the finish on their weapons. One must be cautious with some of these guns as there have been fakes noted with their backstraps cut for shoulder stocks, producing what would appear to be a more expensive variation. Individual appraisal should be secured if any doubt exists.

Fixed Sight Model

Exc.	V.G.	Good	Fair	Poor
600	450	400	300	250

Tangent Sight Model

50,000 manufactured.

Courtesy Orvel Reichert

Exc.	V.G.	Good	Fair	Poor
900	750	700	550	400

Captured Pre-war Commercial Model

These pistols were taken over when the plant was occupied. They are slotted for stocks and have tangent sights. There were few produced between serial number 48,000 and 52,000. All noted have the WA613 Nazi proof mark. Beware of fakes!

Exc.	V.G.	Good	Fair	Poor
1700	1400	1150	750	500

Post-war Military Contract

Manufactured from 1946, and they embody some design changes—such as improved heat treating and barrel locking. Pistols produced after 1950 do not have barrels that can interchange with the earlier model pistols. The earliest models have an "A" prefix on the serial number and do not have the magazine safety. These pistols were produced for many countries, and there were many thousands manufactured.

Fixed Sight

Exc.	V.G.	Good	Fair	Poor
525	425	375	300	250

Tangent Sight

Exc.	V.G.	Good	Fair	Poor
800	675	575	400	300

Slotted and Tangent Sight

Exc.	V.G.	Good	Fair	Poor
1300	1050	750	500	400

Post-war Commercial Model

Introduced in 1950 and in 1954. Those imported into the U.S.A. are marked Browning Arms Co. These pistols have the commercial polished finish.

Fixed Sight

Exc.	V.G.	Good	Fair	Poor
550	425	350	300	250

Tangent Sight

Exc.	V.G.	Good	Fair	Poor
850	650	500	400	350

Slotted and Tangent Sight

Exc.	V.G.	Good	Fair	Poor
1350	1100	800	550	450

WARNING

A large number of counterfeit FN Hi-Powers have been shipped to the United States, possibly from the Balkans. The slides are marked just like the FN originals but the fit and finish is of poor quality. These pistols are missing numerous small proof stamps and markings normally found on FN pistols. These counterfeits have a serial number on the front of the grip strap with a single letter prefix. All are fitted with the late style extractor. Metal finish is either a military matte blue or a commercial high gloss blue.

RIFLES

Model 1889

Exc.	V.G.	Good	Fair	Poor
350	250	200	125	100

Model 1949 or SAFN 49

Exc.	V.G.	Good	Fair	Poor
600	500	300	225	150

Model 30-11 Sniper Rifle

Exc.	V.G.	Good	Fair	Poor
5000	4500	3500	2750	2000

FN-FAL

50.00—21" Rifle Model

NIB	Exc.	V.G.	Good	Fair	Poor
3000	2750	2250	2000	1850	1000

50.63—18" Paratrooper Model

NIB	Exc.	V.G.	Good	Fair	Poor
3800	3350	2950	2750	2450	1100

50.64—21" Paratrooper Model

NIB	Exc.	V.G.	Good	Fair	Poor
3300	3000	2700	2200	1900	1000

50.41—Synthetic Butt H-Bar

NIB	Exc.	V.G.	Good	Fair	Poor
2800	2400	2000	1800	1200	1000

50.42—Wood Butt H-Bar

NIB	Exc.	V.G.	Good	Fair	Poor
2800	2400	2000	1800	1200	1000

FN FAL "G" Series (Type I Receiver)

Standard

NIB	Exc.	V.G.	Good	Fair	Poor
6500	5000	4000	3000	2000	1000

Lightweight

NIB	Exc.	V.G.	Good	Fair	Poor
6500	5000	4000	3000	2000	1000

FN CAL

NIB	Exc.	V.G.	Good	Fair	Poor
7000	6500	5000	3000	1500	1000

FNC

Standard

Fixed stock, 16" or 18" barrel.

NIB	Exc.	V.G.	Good	Fair	Poor
3000	2800	2500	2000	1500	1000

Paratrooper Model

Folding stock, 16" or 18" barrel.

NIB	Exc.	V.G.	Good	Fair	Poor
3000	2800	2500	2000	1500	1000

NOTE: The above prices are for Belgian-made guns only.

Musketeer Sporting Rifles

A bolt-action rifle built on the Mauser-action chambered for various popular cartridges. It has a 24" barrel and is blued, with a checkered walnut stock. It was manufactured between 1947 and 1963.

Exc.	V.G.	Good	Fair	Poor
450	350	300	250	200

Deluxe Sporter

A higher-grade version of the Musketeer with the same general specifications. It was also manufactured between 1947 and 1963.

Exc.	V.G.	Good	Fair	Poor
550	450	400	275	200

FN Supreme

Chambered for the popular standard calibers and has a 24" barrel with an aperture sight and a checkered walnut stock. It was manufactured between 1957 and 1975.

Exc.	V.G.	Good	Fair	Poor
800	650	500	400	400

Supreme Magnum Model

Similar to the standard Supreme except that it is chambered for .264 Win. Mag., 7mm Rem. Mag., and .300 Win. Mag. It is furnished with a recoil pad and was manufactured between the same years as the standard model.

Exc.	V.G.	Good	Fair	Poor
800	650	500	400	400

FAIRBANKS, A. B.

Boston, Massachusetts

Fairbanks All Metal Pistol

This odd pistol was produced of all metal, with a one-piece cast brass frame and handle and an iron barrel and lock system. It is chambered for .33 caliber and utilizes the percussion ignition system. The barrel lengths noted are of 3" to 10". The barrels are marked "Fairbanks Boston. Cast Steel." They were manufactured between 1838 and 1841.

Exc.	V.G.	Good	Fair	Poor
—	—	850	350	150

FALCON FIREARMS

Northridge, California

Portsider

A copy of the Colt 1911 built for a left-handed individual. It is constructed of stainless steel and is similar in all other respects to the Colt. It was introduced in 1986.

NIB	Exc.	V.G.	Good	Fair	Poor
625	500	425	375	300	225

Portsider Set

A matching serial numbered pair consisting of a left-handed and a right-handed version of this model. It was cased, and there were only 100 manufactured in 1986 and 1987.

NIB	Exc.	V.G.	Good	Fair	Poor
1400	1250	1000	750	600	475

Gold Falcon

The frame was machined from solid 17-karat gold. The slide is stainless steel, and the sights have diamond inlays. It was engraved to the customer's order, and there were only 50 manufactured.

NIB	Exc.	V.G.	Good	Fair	Poor
30000	25000	20000	15000	—	—

FAMARS, A. & S.

Brescia, Italy

The Famars shotgun is one of the world's finest and is available on a custom-order basis. This makes it quite difficult to accurately establish values in a book of this nature. We list them and give an estimated value in their basic form only.

Engraving Pattern Descriptions (Older Discontinued Patterns)

S2—Traditional fully engraved fine English scroll with coverage highlighting selected areas of the receiver and forend metal. Wood grade is AA.

S3—Traditional hand-engraved scroll with some open areas around the scroll coverage on the receiver and forend metal. Wood grade is AAA.

S4—Traditional full coverage, intricate and high in detail. Patterns may be English, German, or game scene. Wood grade is AAAA.

S5—Grade S4 patterns with animals inlaid in 24k gold. Wood grade is AAAA.

S4E—Extremely high detail scenes and elaborate ornamental work where the subject matter is selected by the customer. Wood grade is AAAAA.

S5E—Similar to the S4E level but with raised or flush gold inlay work. Wood grade is AAAAA.

SXO—The best work by the world's best engravers. Museum quality. Wood grade is AAAAAA.

Zeus

An engraved side-by-side boxlock in 12, 20, 28, and .410 bore.

In the white

NIB	Exc.	V.G.	Good	Fair	Poor
19000	12000	—	—	—	—

D2 pattern

NIB	Exc.	V.G.	Good	Fair	Poor
20000	12000	—	—	—	—

S3 pattern

NIB	Exc.	V.G.	Good	Fair	Poor
22000	20000	—	—	—	—

NOTE: Add 10 percent for smaller gauges.

Tribute

An engraved side-by-side droplock offered in 12 or 20 gauge.

In the white

NIB	Exc.	V.G.	Good	Fair	Poor
21400	20800	—	—	—	—

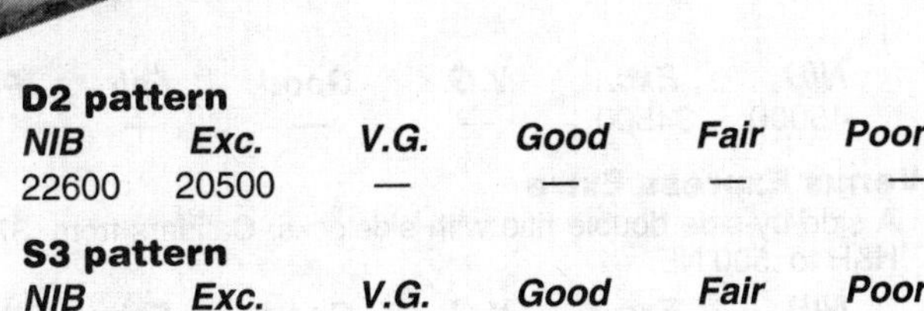

D2 pattern

NIB	Exc.	V.G.	Good	Fair	Poor
22600	20500	—	—	—	—

S3 pattern

NIB	Exc.	V.G.	Good	Fair	Poor
24300	22000	—	—	—	—

Venus

A side-by-side sidelock shotgun with choice of engraving patterns and coverage. Offered in 12,20, 28, or .410 bore.

In the white

NIB	Exc.	V.G.	Good	Fair	Poor
32700	30500	—	—	—	—

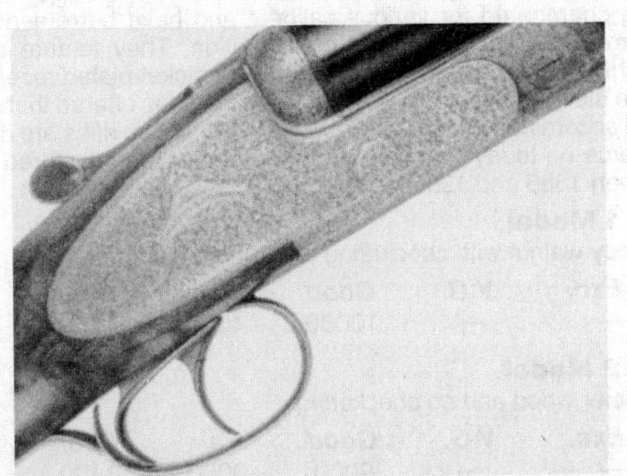

D2 pattern

NIB	Exc.	V.G.	Good	Fair	Poor
33900	31500	—	—	—	—

D3 pattern

NIB	Exc.	V.G.	Good	Fair	Poor
37000	10500	—	—	—	—

D4 pattern

NIB	Exc.	V.G.	Good	Fair	Poor
42800	39000	—	—	—	—

D5 pattern

NIB	Exc.	V.G.	Good	Fair	Poor
48200	42000	—	—	—	—

D4E pattern

NIB	Exc.	V.G.	Good	Fair	Poor
53500	47500	—	—	—	—

D5E pattern

NIB	Exc.	V.G.	Good	Fair	Poor
58500	51500	—	—	—	—

DXO pattern

NIB	Exc.	V.G.	Good	Fair	Poor
85000	55000	—	—	—	—

Veneri

A side-by-side sidelock shotgun.

NIB	Exc.	V.G.	Good	Fair	Poor
32000	30000	—	—	—	—

D2 pattern

NIB	Exc.	V.G.	Good	Fair	Poor
32700	30500	—	—	—	—

Jorema Royal

An over-and-under shotgun with sidelocks. Offered in 12, 20, 28, and .410 bore

In the white

NIB	Exc.	V.G.	Good	Fair	Poor
32700	26000	—	—	—	—

S2 pattern

NIB	Exc.	V.G.	Good	Fair	Poor
33900	20000	—	—	—	—

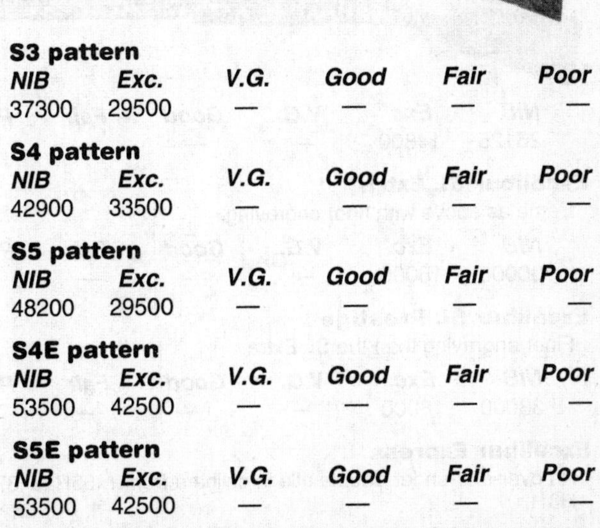

S3 pattern

NIB	Exc.	V.G.	Good	Fair	Poor
37300	29500	—	—	—	—

S4 pattern

NIB	Exc.	V.G.	Good	Fair	Poor
42900	33500	—	—	—	—

S5 pattern

NIB	Exc.	V.G.	Good	Fair	Poor
48200	29500	—	—	—	—

S4E pattern

NIB	Exc.	V.G.	Good	Fair	Poor
53500	42500	—	—	—	—

S5E pattern

NIB	Exc.	V.G.	Good	Fair	Poor
53500	42500	—	—	—	—

SXO pattern

NIB	Exc.	V.G.	Good	Fair	Poor
85000	66500	—	—	—	—

NOTE: Add 15 percent for smaller gauges.

Excaliber BL

An over-and-under shotgun with removable trigger group. Offered in 12, 20, 28, and .410 bore with single trigger.

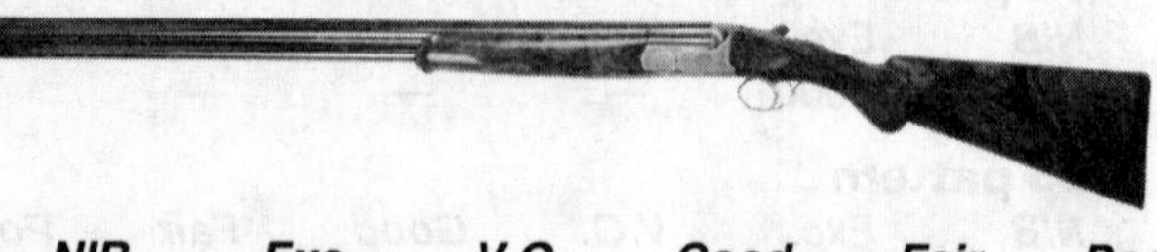

NIB	Exc.	V.G.	Good	Fair	Poor
11800	6500	—	—	—	—

Excalibur BL Extra

Finer engraving than standard.

NIB	Exc.	V.G.	Good	Fair	Poor
15455	8900	—	—	—	—

Excalibur BL Prestige

Finer engraving than BL Extra.

NIB	Exc.	V.G.	Good	Fair	Poor
17820	10750	—	—	—	—

Excalibur BLX

Over-and-under shotgun with sideplates.

NIB	Exc.	V.G.	Good	Fair	Poor
11150	9000	—	—	—	—

Excalibur BLX Extra

Same as above but with finer engraving.

NIB	Exc.	V.G.	Good	Fair	Poor
16759	14000	—	—	—	—

Excalibur BLX Prestige

Finer engraving than the BLX Extra.

NIB	Exc.	V.G.	Good	Fair	Poor
16900	13750	—	—	—	—

Excalibur SL

Over-and-under shotgun with sidelocks.

NIB	Exc.	V.G.	Good	Fair	Poor
26125	14800	—	—	—	—

Excalibur SL Extra

Same as above with finer engraving.

NIB	Exc.	V.G.	Good	Fair	Poor
30000	16000	—	—	—	—

Excalibur SL Prestige

Finer engraving than the SL Extra.

NIB	Exc.	V.G.	Good	Fair	Poor
33000	18000	—	—	—	—

Excalibur Express

An over-and-under double rifle in calibers from 7x65R to .375 H&H.

NIB	Exc.	V.G.	Good	Fair	Poor
20196	11500	—	—	—	—

Excalibur Express Extra

Same as above but with finer engraving.

NIB	Exc.	V.G.	Good	Fair	Poor
27060	12000	—	—	—	—

Excalibur Express Prestige

Finer engraving than the Express Extra.

NIB	Exc.	V.G.	Good	Fair	Poor
32065	15250	—	—	—	—

African Express

A side-by-side boxlock double rifle. Calibers from .22 Long Rifle to .600 NE.

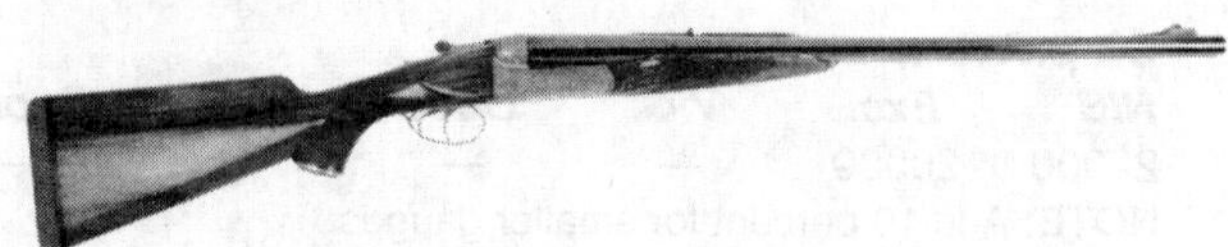

NIB	Exc.	V.G.	Good	Fair	Poor
34000	17500	—	—	—	—

Venus Express Professional

A side-by-side double rifle with sidelocks.

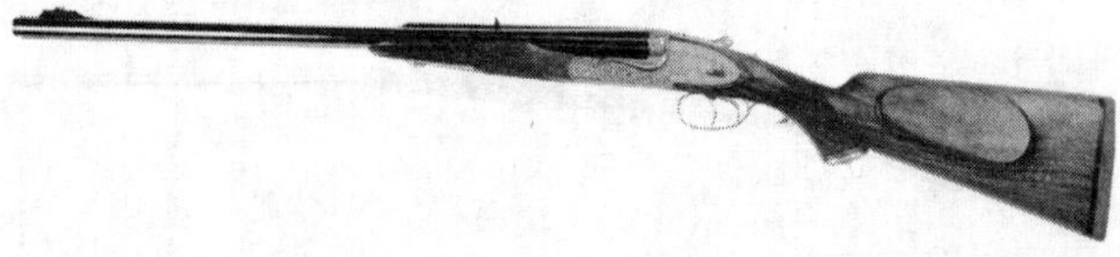

NIB	Exc.	V.G.	Good	Fair	Poor
45000	34500	—	—	—	—

Venus Express Extra

A side-by-side double rifle with sidelocks. Calibers from .375 H&H to .500 NE.

NIB	Exc.	V.G.	Good	Fair	Poor
95750	50000	—	—	—	—

FARROW ARMS CO.

Holyoke, Massachusetts
Mason, Tennessee

Farrow Falling Block Rifle

Designed by W.M. Farrow, a target shooter who had worked on the Ballard rifles for the Marlin company. The Farrow rifles are chambered for various calibers and have barrel lengths from 28"-36" of octagonal configuration. They feature tang sights and are either all blued or have a nickel-plated receiver. The stocks are walnut. There were two grades offered that varied according to the grade of wood used. These rifles are quite scarce on today's market, and the number manufactured between 1885 and 1900 is unknown.

No. 1 Model

Fancy walnut with checkering and a Schutzen buttplate.

Exc.	V.G.	Good	Fair	Poor
—	—	10000	4000	1750

No. 2 Model

Plainer wood and no checkering.

Exc.	V.G.	Good	Fair	Poor
—	—	9000	3000	1400

This symbol denotes "Sleepers" with rapidly-rising values and/or significant collector potential.

FAYETTEVILLE ARMORY PISTOLS AND RIFLES

Fayetteville, North Carolina

In 1861, the U.S. Arsenal at Fayetteville, North Carolina, was seized by the officials of that state and later turned over to the government of the Confederate States of America. While still controlled by the state of North Carolina, a number of inferior flintlock arms were altered at the arsenal from flint to percussion, including a number of U.S. M1836 pistols and U.S. M1819 Hall rifles (the latter also shortened and remodeled into cavalry carbines). In accordance with an agreement between the governors of Virginia and North Carolina, the rifle machinery seized at the former U.S. Armory at Harpers Ferry, Virginia, was also sent to Fayetteville, where in 1862 the Confederacy began the construction of rifles modeled after the U.S. M1855 rifle. Production continued until 1865 when the advance of Sherman's armies necessitated the evacuation of the armory.

Fayetteville Armory Percussion Pistols (U.S. M1836 Pistols, Altered)

Overall length 13-1/4"; barrel length 8-1/2"; caliber .54. Markings: same as U.S. M1836 contact pistols, i.e. the locks either marked with eagle head over "A. WATERS/MILBURY MS./(date)" or "US/R. JOHNSON/MIDDN CONN./(date)" and various barrel proofmarks; also occasionally marked "N. CAROLINA."

The Fayetteville Armory altered approximately 900 U.S. M1836 pistols from flintlock to percussion. These arms were altered by enlarging the flint touchhole and screwing in a cylindrical drum in place of the pan and frizzen. The distinguishing feature of the Fayetteville alteration is the clean-out screw at the face of the cylinder and the "S" shaped hammer, not unlike that used on post-1862 dated rifles.

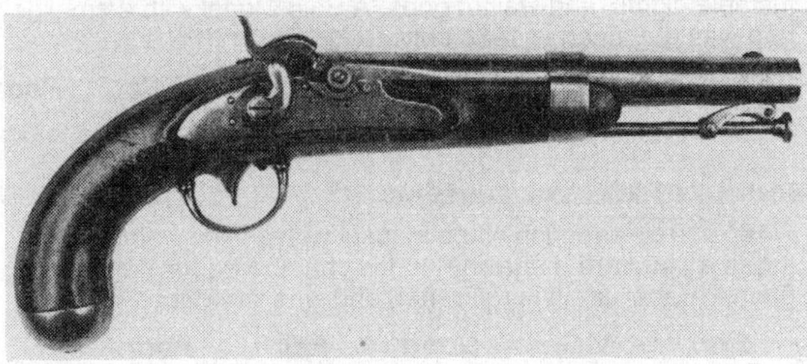

Courtesy Milwaukee Public Museum, Milwaukee, Wisconsin

Exc.	V.G.	Good	Fair	Poor
—	—	2500	1200	900

Fayetteville Armory Rifles (Types I through IV)

Overall length 49-1/8"; barrel length 33"; caliber .58. Markings: on barrel, an eagle over "C.S.A./FAYETTEVILLE" forward of the hammer and the date on the rounded tail. "CSA" also found on buttplates; date on top of barrel; proofmarks (eagle head, "V" and "P") on left quarter of barrel near breech.

From 1862 to early 1865, the Fayetteville Armory produced four variants of the old U.S. M1855 rifle on the machinery that had been lent to North Carolina by Virginia after its capture in April 1861. The earliest 1862 production (Type I) utilized unmilled lockplates captured at Harpers Ferry and are distinguished by having a "hump" (where the Maynard primer would have been milled) that extends to the arc of the hammer. Type II production utilized the newly made locks received from Richmond during the balance of 1862; they had a relatively low "hump" whose upper surface matched the contour of the stock. By the end of 1862, Fayetteville was producing its own lock, the plate of which resembled the U.S. M1861 rifle musket, but with a distinctive "S" shaped hammer. This lock distinguishes both type III and type IV production. All rifles made through 1863 continued to bear a saber bayonet lug on the right side of the barrel. In 1864, however, this was eliminated in favor of a triangular socket bayonet. The absence of the saber bayonet lug and remodeled front sight distinguishes type IV production. Because the barrel machinery went to Richmond, production at Fayetteville was continually hindered, seldom reaching more than 300 per month in the three years that the Fayetteville rifle was manufactured. (Note: The rarity of Type I production will usually generate a premium for that variant.)

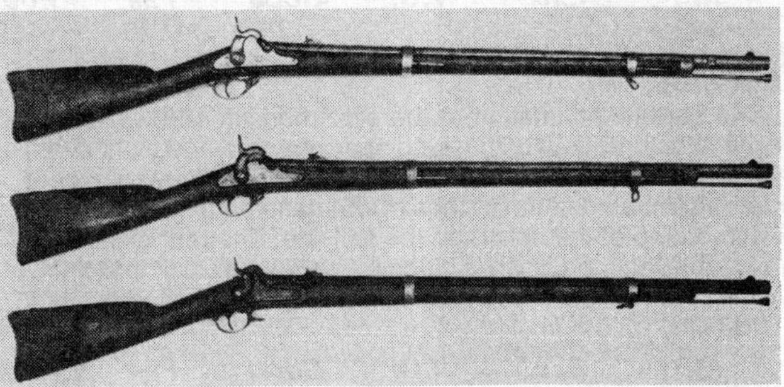

Courtesy Milwaukee Public Museum, Milwaukee, Wisconsin

Exc.	V.G.	Good	Fair	Poor
—	—	22500	9500	4000

FEATHER INDUSTRIES, INC.

Trinidad, Colorado

AT-22

A blowback-operated semi-automatic chambered for the .22 LR cartridge. It has a removable, shrouded 17" barrel and a folding metal stock. There are adjustable sights, and the finish is black. There is a detachable 20-round magazine. This model was introduced in 1986.

NIB	Exc.	V.G.	Good	Fair	Poor
325	200	175	150	110	75

AT-9

Similar to the AT-22 except that it is chambered for the 9mm Parabellum cartridge and has a 16" barrel and 32-round magazine. It was introduced in 1988.

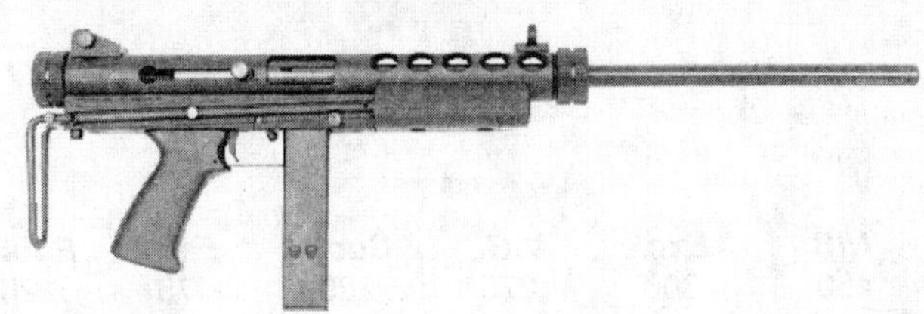

NIB	Exc.	V.G.	Good	Fair	Poor
800	675	300	250	175	125

KG-9

A 9mm, semi-automatic assault rifle that was introduced in 1989.

NIB	Exc.	V.G.	Good	Fair	Poor
725	500	425	375	300	250

KG-22

Similar in appearance to the KG-9 except that it is chambered for .22 LR and has a 20-round detachable magazine. It was introduced in 1989.

NIB	Exc.	V.G.	Good	Fair	Poor
400	275	225	175	125	100

SAR-180

The current incarnation of the old American 180, which was manufactured in Austria a number of years ago. It is chambered for .22 LR and has a 17.5" barrel. It is a blowback-operated semi-automatic that has a 165-round drum magazine that sits on top of the action on the flat side. The rear sight is adjustable, and the finish is blued with a walnut stock, pistol grip, and forend. This model was revived by Feather Industries in 1989.

NIB	Exc.	V.G.	Good	Fair	Poor
750	675	600	475	300	200

Mini-AT

A blowback-operated semi-automatic pistol chambered for the .22 LR cartridge. It is a 5.5"-barreled version of the AT-22 rifle-and has a 20-round magazine. This model was manufactured between 1986 and 1989.

NIB	Exc.	V.G.	Good	Fair	Poor
350	200	175	150	125	100

Guardian Angel

A two-shot, Over/Under, derringer-style pistol. It is chambered for the 9mm Parabellum and can be converted to fire the .38 Super cartridge. It is constructed of stainless steel and has an internal hammer and fully enclosed trigger. It was introduced in 1988.

NIB	Exc.	V.G.	Good	Fair	Poor
225	125	100	75	50	40

FEDERAL ENGINEERING CORP.

Chicago, Illinois

XC-220

A blowback-operated, semi-automatic rifle chambered for the .22 LR cartridge. It has a 16.5" barrel and a steel receiver that is blued. The stock is black synthetic. This model was introduced in 1984.

NIB	Exc.	V.G.	Good	Fair	Poor
450	300	275	225	175	125

XC-450

Similar in appearance to the XC-220 except that it is chambered for the .45 ACP cartridge. It has a 30-round detachable magazine.

NIB	Exc.	V.G.	Good	Fair	Poor
650	525	450	400	300	250

XC-900

A 9mm Parabellum version of the same basic firearm. It has a 32-round magazine and was introduced in 1984.

NIB	Exc.	V.G.	Good	Fair	Poor
600	500	425	350	275	200

FEDERAL ORDNANCE, INC.

South El Monte, California

An importer as well as a manufacturer that basically fabricates new and custom firearms out of existing older military parts. The firearms they import are military surplus weapons. The firearms covered here are of Federal Ordnance manufacture.

M-14 Semi-Automatic

A semi-automatic version of the M-14 service rifle. It is constructed of a newly manufactured receiver that has no selector and select surplus G.I. parts. The rifle is refinished to original specifications and furnished with a 20-round magazine and either a wood or fiberglass stock. This model was introduced in 1986. Although this model is a battle rifle and falls into the category affected by the wild price fluctuations we have been experiencing, prices for this gun have stayed fairly stable due to a fairly constant supply. This model has been manufactured since 1986.

Exc.	V.G.	Good	Fair	Poor
700	600	550	450	375

Model 714 Broomhandle Mauser

A remanufactured C96-type pistol chambered for 7.63mm or 9mm Parabellum. It utilizes a new manufactured frame and surplus parts. It features a 10-round detachable magazine, adjustable sights, and walnut grips. A Bolo Model with a smaller grip was produced in 1988 only.

NIB	Exc.	V.G.	Good	Fair	Poor
650	500	400	300	250	100

Model 713 Mauser Carbine

A 16"-barreled version of the Mauser with a fixed walnut stock. It has a standard magazine and is chambered for 7.63mm or 9mm Parabellum. It is refinished and was introduced in 1987.

Exc.	V.G.	Good	Fair	Poor
1250	1000	900	700	575

Model 713 Deluxe

Chambered for 7.63mm and has a 16" barrel with a detachable shoulder stock made of deluxe walnut. It has been modified to accept detachable magazines and is furnished with two 20-shot units. It has a 1000-meter adjustable sight and is furnished in a fitted leather case. There were only 1,500 manufactured in 1986.

NIB	Exc.	V.G.	Good	Fair	Poor
2000	1750	1500	1250	1000	800

Standard Broomhandle

A refurbished surplus C-96 Mauser pistol with a new 7.63mm or 9mm barrel. All springs are replaced, and the entire gun is refinished. It is furnished with a shoulder stock/holster of Chinese manufacture.

NIB	Exc.	V.G.	Good	Fair	Poor
800	650	525	450	350	275

Ranger 1911A1

Federal Ordnance's version of the 1911A1 Colt service pistol. It is made of all steel, is chambered for .45 ACP, and has checkered walnut grips. It was introduced in 1988.

NIB	Exc.	V.G.	Good	Fair	Poor
500	375	325	275	225	150

FEG (FEGYVER ES GAZKESZULEKGYAR)

Budapest, Hungary

Rudolf Frommer was a first-class engineer who became associated with Fegyvergyar in 1896. In 1900 he became the manager and held that position until his retirement in 1935. He died one year later in 1936. His designs were successful and prolific. They were used militarily and sold on the commercial market as well.

Model 1901

An odd pistol that was not successful at all. It was chambered for an 8mm cartridge that was the forerunner of the 8mm Roth Steyr. It has a long, slender barrel, which was actually a collar with the barrel within. It has a rotary bolt and external hammer and is recoil-operated. There is a 10-round integral magazine, and it is loaded from the top via a stripper clip. This pistol was manufactured from 1903 to 1905.

Courtesy James Rankin

Exc.	V.G.	Good	Fair	Poor
2000	1600	950	700	350

Model 1906

An improved version of the 1901, chambered for the 7.65mm Roth-Sauer cartridge. It is, for all intents and purposes, the same action; but on later models a detachable 10-round magazine was adopted. It was manufactured between 1906 and 1910 in small quantity.

Exc.	V.G.	Good	Fair	Poor
2000	1600	950	700	350

Model 1910

The final version in this series of pistols and is similar with the addition of a grip safety. Chambered for 7.65mm Browning.

Exc.	V.G.	Good	Fair	Poor
1250	1000	750	550	300

Frommer Stop Model 1912

A semi-automatic pistol in caliber 7.65mm or 9mmK. It is unusual in that it operates on a long recoil system. Frommer is stamped on the slide as well as the Frommer Stop logo on each side of the wood or plastic grip plates.

Courtesy James Rankin

Exc.	V.G.	Good	Fair	Poor
400	275	200	150	50

Frommer Baby Model

A smaller version of the Stop that was designed as a pocket pistol with a 2" barrel and chambered for the same calibers. It was manufactured at the same time as the Stop Model.

Courtesy James Rankin

Exc.	V.G.	Good	Fair	Poor
350	225	175	125	75

Frommer Lilliput

This pocket pistol is chambered for 6.35mm and outwardly resembles the Baby. It is actually a simple, blowback-operated, semi-automatic pistol and was a good deal less complex to produce. This model was introduced in 1921.

Courtesy James Rankin

Exc.	V.G.	Good	Fair	Poor
300	200	150	125	75

Model 1929

A semi-automatic pistol in 9mmK. It is based on the Browning designed block-back-action. This pistol replaced the earlier models. A few of these pistols were made in .22 Long Rifle.

Courtesy James Rankin

Exc.	V.G.	Good	Fair	Poor
400	300	200	175	100

.22 Caliber

Exc.	V.G.	Good	Fair	Poor
900	750	650	400	250

Model 1937

A semi-automatic pistol in caliber 7.65mm or 9mmK. This pistol was designed by Frommer and manufactured by Femaru. It is also known as the Model 1937.

Courtesy James Rankin

Nazi Proofed 7.65mm Version

Exc.	V.G.	Good	Fair	Poor
400	300	200	175	100

9mm Short Hungarian Military Version

Exc.	V.G.	Good	Fair	Poor
400	275	200	175	100

Model R-9

A copy of the Browning Hi-Power semi-automatic pistol. It is chambered for 9mm Parabellum and has a 4.75" barrel. The frame is steel, and the finish is blued with checkered wood grips. The detachable magazine holds 13 shots, and the sights are fixed. This model was imported in 1986 and 1987 only.

Exc.	V.G.	Good	Fair	Poor
350	225	200	150	100

Model PPH

A copy of the Walther PP, chambered for the .380 ACP cartridge. It is a double-action semi-automatic with a 3" barrel, alloy frame, and a blued finish, with thumb rest checkered plastic grips. It was imported in 1986 and 1987 only.

Exc.	V.G.	Good	Fair	Poor
300	175	150	100	75

Model B9R

This semi-automatic pistol is chambered for the .380 ACP cartridge and fitted with a 4" barrel, it features double or single-action trigger operation. The frame is alloy and weighs about 25 oz. Magazine capacity is 15 rounds.

NIB	Exc.	V.G.	Good	Fair	Poor
325	200	175	150	125	75

Model AP-9

This pistol has been manufactured in Hungary under a number of different names. It is known as the AP-9, Walam 48, AP-66, and the Attila. It is a semi-automatic pistol in calibers 7.65mm and 9mmK. It is similar to the Walther Model PP. It has a 7-round magazine and alloy frame. There are various styles of grip plates.

Courtesy James Rankin

Exc.	V.G.	Good	Fair	Poor
300	175	150	100	50

Model PA-63

Same as above but chambered for the 9mm Makarov (9x18mm) cartridge.

Exc.	V.G.	Good	Fair	Poor
200	90	75	60	50

Model FP-9

This model is a copy of the Browning Hi-Power pistol. Chambered for the 9mm Luger cartridge. It features a walnut checkered grip with blue finish. Barrel is 5" and overall length is 8". The top of the slide features a full-length ventilated rib with fixed sights. Weighs 35 oz. Magazine capacity is 14 rounds.

NIB	Exc.	V.G.	Good	Fair	Poor
300	175	150	125	90	70

Model P9R

This is similar to the model above and follows the Browning Hi-Power lines with the exception of the ventilated rib. Barrel length is 4.66" and the pistol is offered in blue or chrome finish. Magazine capacity is 15 rounds.

Blue

NIB	Exc.	V.G.	Good	Fair	Poor
325	200	150	125	90	70

Chrome

NIB	Exc.	V.G.	Good	Fair	Poor
350	225	175	150	120	80

Model P9RK

Similar to model above but fitted with 4.12" barrel and 7.5" overall length. Finger grooves on front strap and backstrap is serrated. Weighs about 34 oz.

NIB	Exc.	V.G.	Good	Fair	Poor
300	200	150	125	90	70

RIFLES

SA-2000-M

Introduced in 1999, this model is a semi-automatic rifle chambered for the 7.62x39mm cartridge or the .223 cartridge. Fitted with a detachable 10-round magazine, synthetic stock and muzzlebrake.

NIB	Exc.	V.G.	Good	Fair	Poor
475	350	—	—	—	—

FEINWERKBAU

Oberndorf, Germany

Known predominately for the production of high quality, extremely accurate air rifles and pistols. They also produce some of the most accurate target .22 caliber firearms in the world today. These firearms are listed:

Model 2000 Universal

A single-shot, bolt-action target rifle chambered for the .22 rimfire cartridge. It has a 26.5" barrel with adjustable aperture sights and a fully adjustable trigger. There were four different stock configurations offered with stippled pistol grips and forearms. An electronic trigger was available as a $450 option. This model was discontinued in 1988.

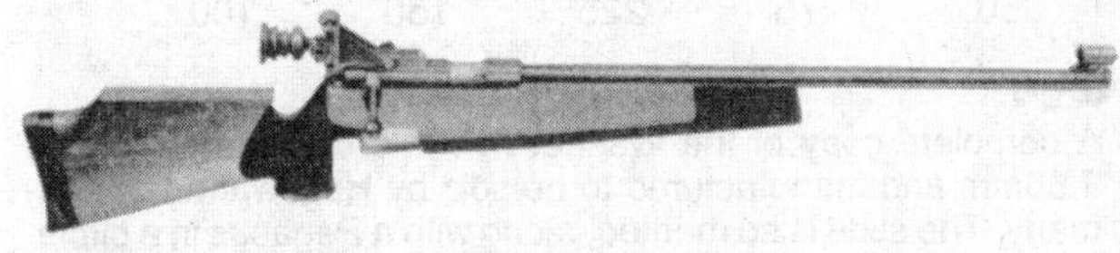

Exc.	V.G.	Good	Fair	Poor
1500	1050	850	650	550

Mini 2000

Has a 22" barrel, and the electronic trigger was available at the additional cost.

Exc.	V.G.	Good	Fair	Poor
1250	850	750	550	450

Running Boar Rifle

Has a thumbhole stock with an adjustable cheekpiece and is furnished without sights. It was specially designed for the offhand Running Boar Competitions.

Exc.	V.G.	Good	Fair	Poor
1500	1050	850	650	550

Match Rifle

Has a 26.75" barrel and an adjustable cheekpiece stock.

Exc.	V.G.	Good	Fair	Poor
1400	950	750	550	450

Model 2600 Ultra Match Free Rifle

Similar to the Model 2000, with a laminated thumbhole stock and a heavy 26" barrel, fully adjustable sights, and trigger. It is offered with an electronic trigger for an additional $400. This model was introduced in 1986.

NIB	Exc.	V.G.	Good	Fair	Poor
1750	1200	1000	850	650	550

FEMARU

Budapest, Hungary

Hungary became a communist satellite in the mid-1950s. At this time the Femaru company was designated to replace the firm of Fegyvergyar as the official Hungarian arms manufacturer. The products are of good quality.

Model 37

This semi-automatic pistol was built in both 7.65mm and 9mm Short calibers. It is well designed pistol of quality construction. It is fitted with a grip safety and exposed hammer. The Hungarian military adopted the pistol in 1937. It was produced until the late 1940s. Early guns were marked "Femaru Fegyver es Gepgyar RT Budapest" but during the war the Nazi code for these guns was "jhv." The 9mm models have a 7-round magazine while the 7.65 models have an 8-round magazine. During World War II the Germans designed this pistol the "Pistol Mod 37 Kal 7.65 (Ung)." Add 75 percent for Nazi proofed examples.

Courtesy Richard M. Kumor, Sr.

Exc.	V.G.	Good	Fair	Poor
350	275	225	150	100

Hege

A complete copy of the Walther PP. It is chambered for the 7.65mm and manufactured to be sold by Hegewaffen of Germany. The slide is so marked, along with a Pegasus in a circle. The designation "AP 66 Cal.7.65" also appears. The pistol was intended for export sales in the U.S. and other western countries.

Exc.	V.G.	Good	Fair	Poor
350	225	175	125	100

Tokagypt

15,000 of these pistols were built in 1958, under contract for the Egyptian army. It is a modified version of the Soviet TT-33 Tokarev chambered for the 9mm Parabellum with a safety added. The balance were sold commercially, some under the trademark "Firebird."

Exc.	V.G.	Good	Fair	Poor
475	350	275	200	125

Walam

Another Walther PP copy of excellent quality chambered for the 9mm short or .380 ACP. The pistols were sold on the commercial market—some designated Model 48.

Exc.	V.G.	Good	Fair	Poor
350	225	175	125	100

FERLACH

Ferlach, Austria

Text by Joseph M. Cornell Ph.D., A.M.A.

The history of gun making in Ferlach began in the early 1500s and continues to the present. Today, there are 13 companies making guns in this beautiful city of about 5,000 inhabitants, which is located in a remote corner of southern Austria. These companies make guns that are among the world's most beautiful and finest. Their price range, at the low end, for a bolt-action rifle is from $5,000 to the high end, for one of their high art guns, at $500,000, or perhaps even more.

These companies are family groupings. Many of these families have been making guns for centuries. For them, gun making is an all-consuming tradition. Some of the best known of these families, and most often encountered in the United States, have names such as Just, Hauptmann, Winkler, Michelitsch, Hambrusch, Scheiring, and Borovnik, etc. Other less well-known makers include Juch, Fanzoj, Glanzig, Koschat, Hofer and Zauner. Some of the companies from the past, such as Franz Sodia are no longer in business and guns from these now extinct companies will be occasionally encountered. But whether or not the families are still in business, Ferlach guns are some of the most beautiful and remarkable examples of the gunmaker's art that are to be found anywhere in the world. A Ferlach gun can be recognized, although not always easily, by the following:

1. Many times the city name "Ferlach" will be found on the gun.
2. Many times a recognizable Ferlach maker's name will be found on the guns, such as ones listed above, but not all Ferlach-made guns will have a maker's name on the gun.
3. Ferlach guns are usually made in the typical "German" style.
4. Ferlach guns usually have a unique type of serial number, which contains a two-digit number followed by a period, ".", e.g. XX.XXX. This serial number can sometimes by used to identify the maker.

Along with the companies in Ferlach, which make guns, there is also a Gunmaker's Consortium, which is owned by 12 of these companies. This Consortium provides a variety of services and products for gun makers both in Ferlach and in other locations as well. The Consortium acts as an engineering and mechanical "Center" that is an essential resource for many of the Ferlach gun makers. The Consortium uses three basic types of the steel to make the barrels: Boehler Antinit, Blitz and Super Blitz. The latter allows the thickness of the barrels to be reduced to a minimum, thus reducing the gun's final weight. Antinit is the most often encountered steel and the least expensive of the steel used in Ferlach guns.

While it is not generally known, many of the makers outside Ferlach, who make some of the world's most expensive guns, do not make their own barreled actions. They buy the actions and put their names on them. This is not true of the Ferlach maker. The actions used in their guns, with the exception of bolt-action rifles, are made right there in Ferlach by the Consortium and then finished by the individual maker. This allows for maximum efficiency and the technical control of the guns being made.

Ferlach gun makers produce almost all types of hunting weapons; these include bolt-action rifles, double rifles, three barreled rifles, drillings, shotguns, guns combining both rifles and shotguns called "combination guns," four barreled guns and even five barreled guns. Ferlach makers are very talented gunsmiths and as a result not only can they make the finest possible guns but they are also able to make guns that would be difficult or impossible for other makers to construct. Furthermore, Ferlach is one of the few centers of gun making in the world where it is still possible to order guns in almost any configuration and in almost any caliber from the small .22 LR to the .600 nitro express or even larger.

In addition to the companies that manufacture guns, Ferlach is the home of many of the world's best engravers. Many of the Ferlach makers have in-house engravers but many do not and almost all the companies send out work for special situations. A list of some of the engravers whose work will be found on Ferlach guns would include names such as Krondofer, Mack, Orou, Schaschl, Singer, Maurer, Widmann, Stogner, de Florian, Plucher and Obiltschnig.

Almost all Ferlach guns are "custom" made guns. This makes each gun somewhat unique, which makes their valuation difficult. There is, however, as with other gunmakers, almost always a relationship between quality, complexity of construction, functionality, beauty, rarity and value/pricing.

FERLIB

Gardone V.T., Italy

Model F.VI

A high-grade, side-by-side shotgun chambered for all gauges and is essentially custom-ordered. It is available in various barrel lengths and chokes and has an Anson and Deeley boxlock-action, double triggers, and automatic ejectors. The action is case-colored, and the stock is hand-checkered select walnut. Single-selective triggers are available for an additional $375.

NIB	Exc.	V.G.	Good	Fair	Poor
4500	3500	—	—	—	—

NOTE: 28 gauge and .410 add 10 percent.

Model F.VII

Has a scroll-engraved, coin-finished frame but otherwise is similar to the Model F.VI. Single trigger option and small gauge premium are the same.

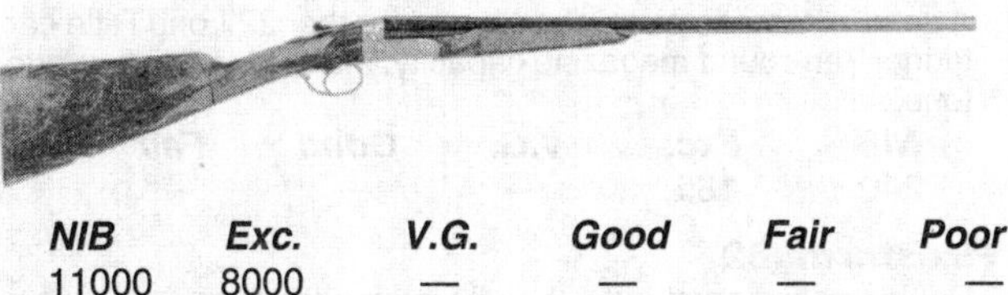

NIB	Exc.	V.G.	Good	Fair	Poor
11000	8000	—	—	—	—

Model F.VII/SC

A more deluxe version with gold inlays and a game scene-engraved receiver. Options and premium are the same.

NIB	Exc.	V.G.	Good	Fair	Poor
12000	9000	—	—	—	—

Model F.VII Sideplate

Features false sideplates that are completely covered with game scene engraving. This model is standard with a single-selective trigger, but the small gauge premium is applicable.

NIB	Exc.	V.G.	Good	Fair	Poor
14000	10000	—	—	—	—

Model F.VII/SC Sideplate

The false sideplate model with gold inlays accenting the full coverage engraving.

NIB	Exc.	V.G.	Good	Fair	Poor
15000	11000	—	—	—	—

NOTE: 28 gauge and .410 add 10 percent.

Hammer Gun

Features a boxlock action with external hammers. Its other features are custom ordered to the purchaser's specifications.

NIB	Exc.	V.G.	Good	Fair	Poor
19000	14000	—	—	—	—

FERRY, ANDREWS & CO.

Stafford, Connecticut

Under Hammer Pistol

This boot pistol is chambered for .36 caliber percussion and has a 3" part-round, part-octagonal barrel. They are similar to the other under hammer pistols that were produced in Connecticut and Massachusetts. The top strap was marked "Andrews Ferry & Co." The number manufactured is unknown. They were produced in the 1850s.

Exc.	V.G.	Good	Fair	Poor
—	1250	600	350	125

FIALA ARMS COMPANY

New Haven, Connecticut

Fiala Repeating Target Pistol

A different type of pistol than what is commonly encountered. Outwardly it resembles a semi-automatic Colt Woodsman; in actuality it is a manually operated firearm that must be cycled by hand after every shot. It was chambered for the .22 rimfire and was offered with interchangeable barrels in lengths of 3", 7.5", and 20". Also offered was a detachable buttstock. The finish is blued, and the grips are found in both smooth and ribbed walnut. The rear sight is a square-notched blade that tips up into an elevation-adjustable peep sight. They are marked "Fiala Arms and Equipment Co. Inc. / New Haven Conn. / Patents Pending" on the right side of the frame behind the grip and Model 1920/Made in U.S.A. on the right side of the frame above the trigger guard. The left side of the frame was marked "FIALA ARMS" above the image of the polar bear with the "TRADE MARK" below the polar bear in the area above the trigger guard. This pistol was also furnished in one of three variations of cases that were optionally available: a canvas case, a black leatherette case, velvet-lined and fitted with a lock and key, and a tan leather version of the leatherette case. A fixed 7.5" barrel variation was also produced. A 7.5" smoothbore barrel was catalogued as a silencer. Some 20" smoothbore barrels were produced. Some pistols bear the names "Columbia Arms Company," and "Botwinik Brothers." The government has classified this pistol with its stock as a "Curio or Relic" and in its complete state is a very desirable collectible.

NOTE: *See also Schall & Co.*

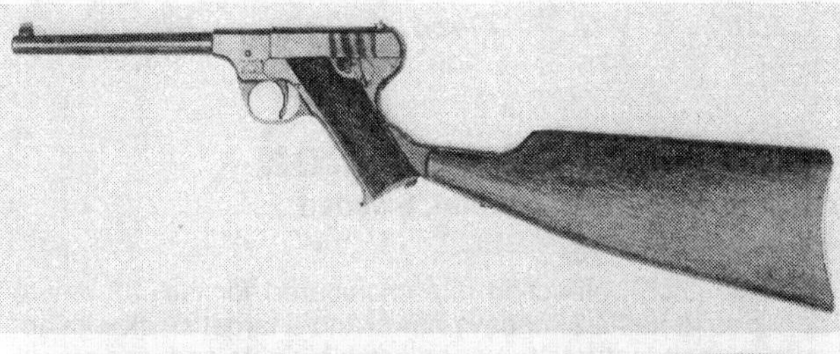

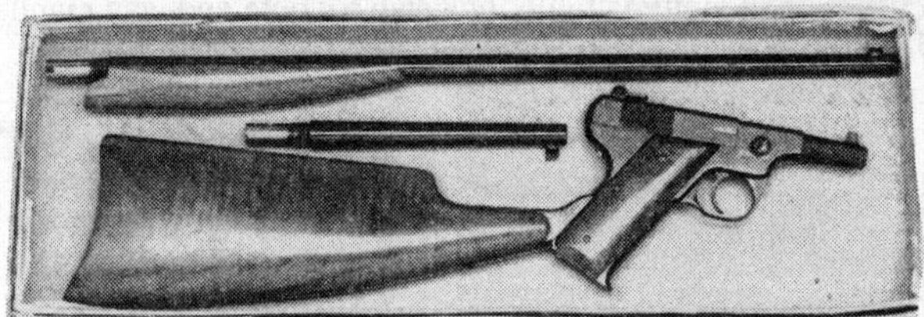

Courtesy Butterfield & Butterfield, San Francisco, California

Complete, Three Barrels, Stock, Tools, and Case

Exc.	V.G.	Good	Fair	Poor
2500	2100	1250	675	550

Gun Only

Courtesy Dr. Jon Miller

Exc.	V.G.	Good	Fair	Poor
550	375	300	240	175

FINNISH LION

Valmet, Sweden

ISU Target Rifle

A single-shot, bolt-action rifle chambered for the .22 rimfire cartridge. It has a 27" heavy barrel and a target stock with accessories. It features target adjustable sights and was manufactured between 1966 and 1977.

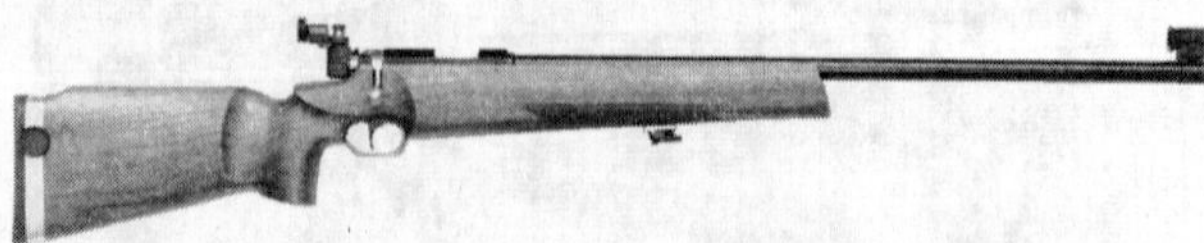

Exc.	V.G.	Good	Fair	Poor
425	300	250	200	125

Champion Free Rifle

Has a 29" heavy barrel and double-set triggers. Otherwise it is similar to the ISU model. It was manufactured between 1965 and 1972.

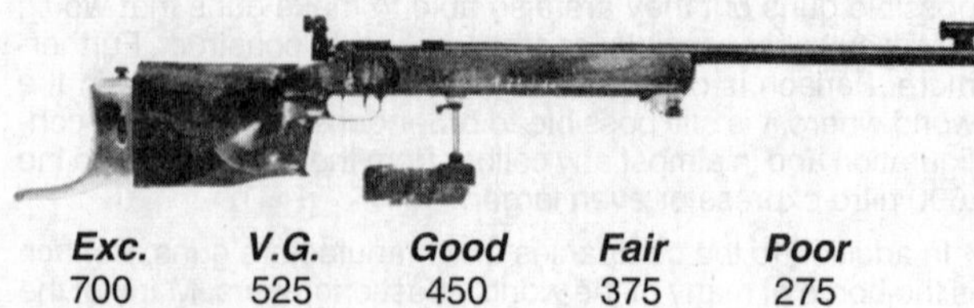

Exc.	V.G.	Good	Fair	Poor
700	525	450	375	275

Match Rifle

Similar to the Champion rifle, with a thumbhole stock and an adjustable buttplate. It was manufactured between 1937 and 1972.

Exc.	V.G.	Good	Fair	Poor
600	425	350	275	200

FIOCCHI OF AMERICA, INC.

Ozark, Missouri

SEE—Pardini and A. Zoli

Imports the above firearms, and they are listed in their own respective sections.

FIREARMS INTERNATIONAL

Washington, D.C.

SEE—Star and Garcia

Was once the importer of the Star Model D as it was sold in the U.S.A. They also imported various other .25 caliber Colt copies that are not considered collectible and would be valued in the $150-and-under range. For the .22/.410 Bronco, see "Garcia."

FIRESTORM

Argentina

Firestorm .22 LR

A semi-automatic pistol chambered for the .22 Long Rifle cartridge. Ten-round magazine capacity. Matte blue finish or duotone.

NIB	Exc.	V.G.	Good	Fair	Poor
240	185	—	—	—	—

Firestorm .32

Double-action semi-auto chambered for .32 with 10+1 capacity. Blued, 3.5" barrel, 23 oz. Fixed sights and rubber grips. Introduced 2006. MSRP: 275

Firestorm .380

This semi-auto double-action pistol is chambered for the .380 ACP cartridge and fitted with a 3.5" barrel. Fixed three-dot combat sights. Matte blue or duotone finish. Magazine capacity is 7 rounds. Weight is about 23 oz.

NIB	Exc.	V.G.	Good	Fair	Poor
240	185	—	—	—	—

Mini Firestorm 9mm

This 9mm semi-auto double-action pistol is fitted with a 3.5" barrel. White outline drift adjustable target sights. Matte blue finish. Polymer grips. Magazine capacity is 10 rounds. Weight is about 25 oz.

NIB	Exc.	V.G.	Good	Fair	Poor
350	275	—	—	—	—

Mini Firestorm .40 S&W

As above but chambered for the .40 S&W cartridge.

NIB	Exc.	V.G.	Good	Fair	Poor
350	275	—	—	—	—

Firestorm .45 Government

This is a single-action semi-automatic pistol chambered for the .45 ACP cartridge. Fitted with a 5.125" barrel and 3 dot fixed combat sights. Magazine capacity is 7 rounds. Black rubber grips. Matte blue, nickel, or duotone finish. Weight is about 36 oz.

NIB	Exc.	V.G.	Good	Fair	Poor
300	250	—	—	—	—

Compact Firestorm .45 Government

As above but with 4.25" barrel. Weight is about 34 oz.

NIB	Exc.	V.G.	Good	Fair	Poor
300	250	—	—	—	—

Mini Firestorm .45 Government

As above but with 3.14" barrel. Black polymer grips and magazine capacity of 10 rounds. Weight is about 31 oz.

NIB	Exc.	V.G.	Good	Fair	Poor
350	275	—	—	—	—

1911 Mil-Spec Standard Government

1911A1-style single-action semi-auto chambered in .45 ACP; 5.125" barrel, steel frame, 7- or 8-round magazine, steel frame, plastic or wood grips, matte blue or deluxe polished blue finish.

NIB	Exc.	V.G.	Good	Fair	Poor
350	275	—	—	—	—

FLETCHER BIDWELL, LLC

Viroqua, Wisconsin

Spencer 1860 Military Carbine

Introduced in 2001 this is a faithful reproduction of the original Spencer Carbine. It is chambered for the .56-50 black powder cartridge but in centerfire. Fitted with a blued 22" round barrel. Magazine capacity is 7 rounds in butt tube. Bone charcoal case hardened receiver. Walnut stock. Blade front sight with ladder rear sight adjustable to 800 yards. Weight is about 9 lbs. Built in U.S.

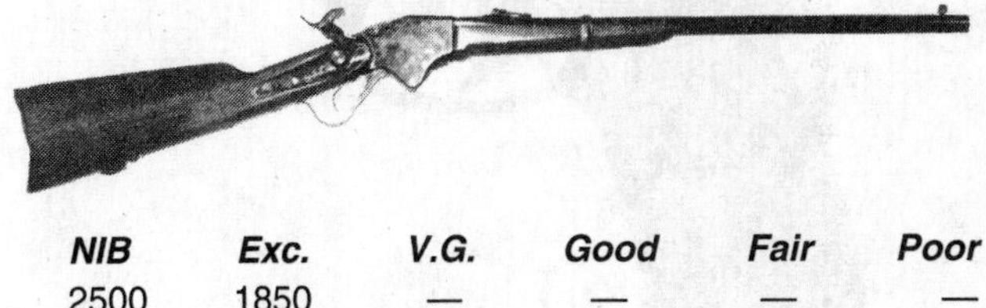

NIB	Exc.	V.G.	Good	Fair	Poor
2500	1850	—	—	—	—

FLORENCE ARMORY

Florence, Guilford Counry, North Carolina

Founded in 1862 as a repair facility to alter sporting arms for military use. Majority of work done by H.C. Lamb & Company. In 1862, Captain Z. Coffin ordered stocks, barrels and locks to assemble newly made rifles. Furniture of these arms varied, either being supplied by Glaze & Company or being the remainders from Searcy & Moore's production. Number made estimated to be in excess of 300 rifles in both .50 and .54 calibers. These arms (particularly the barrels) exhibit characteristics of North Carolina contract pieces.

Exc.	V.G.	Good	Fair	Poor
—	—	25000	10000	4000

FNH USA, INC.

McLean, Virginia

This company is a subsidary of FN Herstal in Belgium. It is essentially the sales and marketing arm for FN in the U.S. market.

PISTOLS

Model Forty-Nine

This pistol is built by FN Manufacturing, Inc. in Columbia, S.C. It has a polymer frame and stainless steel slide. Chambered for 9mm or .40 S&W cartridge. Barrel length is 4.25". Magazine capacity is 16 rounds for law enforcement and 10 rounds for commercial sales. It features a repeatable secure striker trigger system. Offered in stainless steel slide or black coated slide. Weight is about 26 oz. Offered primarly for sale to law enforcement agencies. Introduced in 2000.

NIB	Exc.	V.G.	Good	Fair	Poor
470	375	—	—	—	—

Model FNP-9

Introduced in 2003, this pistol is chambered for the 9mm or .40 S&W cartridge. Fitted with a 4" barrel and featuring a polymer frame. The action is a double-action/single-action design with an ambidextrous manual decocking lever. Fixed sights. Ten-round magazine capacity. Weight is about 25 oz.

NIB	Exc.	V.G.	Good	Fair	Poor
550	425	—	—	—	—

Model HP-SA

This is the famous John Browning design Hi-Power pistol. Chambered for the 9mm or .40 S&W cartridge. Barrel length is 4.6". Magazine capacity is 10 rounds. Weight is around 32 oz. Blued finish.

NIB	Exc.	V.G.	Good	Fair	Poor
750	600	—	—	—	—

Model HP-SA-SFS

Introduced in 2003 this variant of the Hi-Power pistol features a single-action double-action mechanism that allows cocked-and-locked carry with the hammer and slide locked. When the safety is pushed off the hammer is set in the cocked position and is fired single action.

NIB	Exc.	V.G.	Good	Fair	Poor
775	625	—	—	—	—

Model HP-DA/HP-DAO

This model is offered in two different configurations. The first is with double-action/single-action trigger while the second is double-action-only. Chambered for the 9mm cartridge, the pistol is fitted with fixed sights. Magazine capacity is 15 rounds for law enforcement and 10 rounds for commerical sales. Weight is about 31 oz. Intended primarly for law enforcement sales. Introduced in 2000.

NIB	Exc.	V.G.	Good	Fair	Poor
540	425	—	—	—	—

Model HP-DA/HP-DAO Compact

As above but in a smaller and lighter package.

NIB	Exc.	V.G.	Good	Fair	Poor
540	425	—	—	—	—

Model BDA/BDAO Compact

This is a short recoil compact pistol chambered for the 9mm Parabellum cartridge. Fitted with a double-action/single-action trigger or double-action-only trigger. Each configuration has a 10-round magazine capacity. Weight is about 28 oz. Corrosion-resistant finish. Fixed sights.

NIB	Exc.	V.G.	Good	Fair	Poor
800	650	—	—	—	—

SPECIAL POLICE RIFLES (FN SPR)

These rifles are produced at FN manufacturing in the U.S.

FN A1 SPR

Chambered for the .308 7.62x51mm cartridge. Bolt-action. Fitted with a 24" heavy barrel with no sights. Choice of hinged floorplate or detachable box magazine. Stock is McMillan A3 tactical. Weight is about 10.75 lbs.

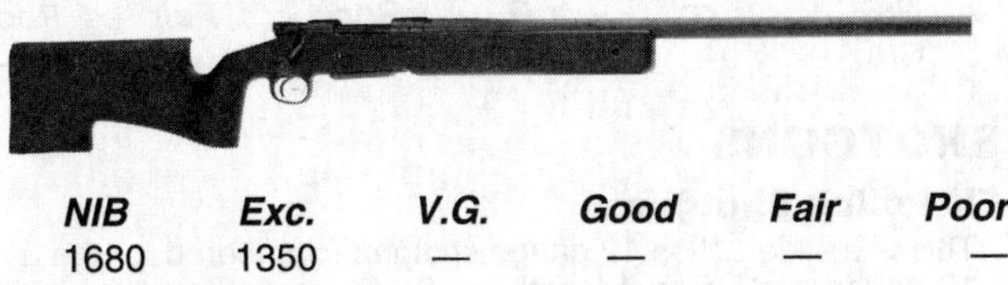

NIB	Exc.	V.G.	Good	Fair	Poor
1680	1350	—	—	—	—

FN A1a SPR

Similar to the above model but fitted with a 20" heavy fluted barrel. McMillan A3 tactical stock. Weight is about 9.75 lbs.

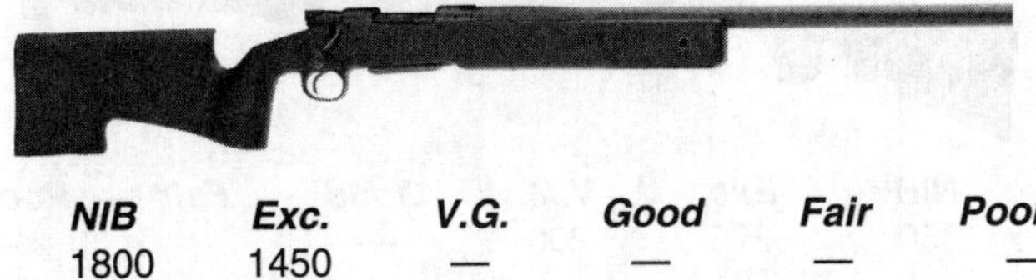

NIB	Exc.	V.G.	Good	Fair	Poor
1800	1450	—	—	—	—

FN A2 SPR

Fitted with a 24" heavy barrel with McMillan A4 tactical stock and Badger Ordinance scope base. Weight is about 10.75 lbs.

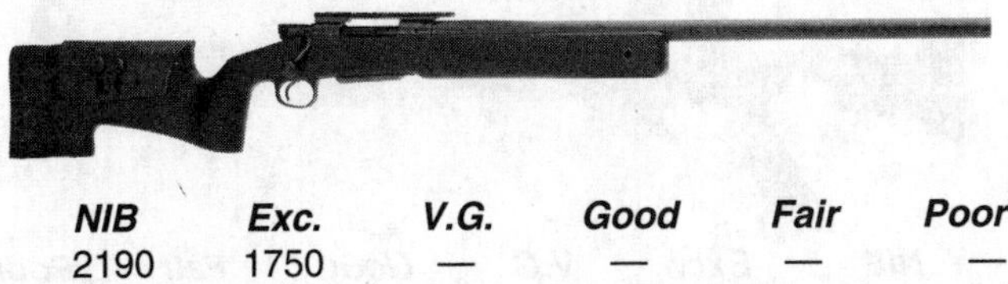

NIB	Exc.	V.G.	Good	Fair	Poor
2190	1750	—	—	—	—

FN A3 SPR

This model has a 24" heavy barrel with McMillan A4 adjustable stock, Badger Ordinance scope base and Badger Ordinance or FN scope rings. Supplied with FNH Parker-Hale type or Harris bipod. Weight is about 10.75 lbs.

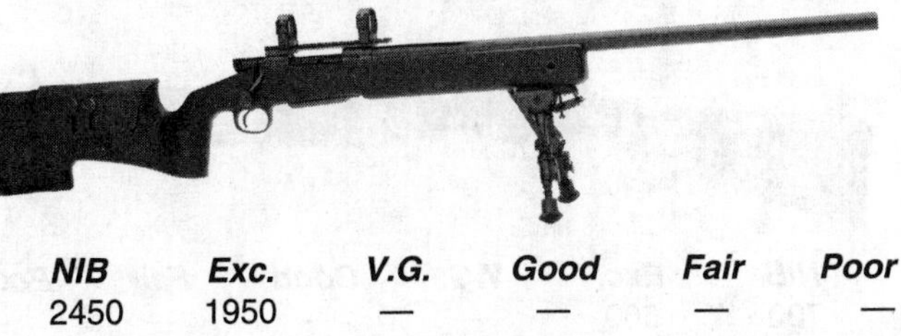

NIB	Exc.	V.G.	Good	Fair	Poor
2450	1950	—	—	—	—

FN A4 SPR

Fitted with a 24" heavy barrel with McMillan A4 adjustable tactical stock. Scope base and rings standard. Choice of several tactical scopes. Bipod. Sling. Drag bag. Kill flash. Tool kit. Cleaning kit. Hard case. Weight is about 10.75 lbs.

NIB	Exc.	V.G.	Good	Fair	Poor
5725	4350	—	—	—	—

NOTE: Price listed does not include scope.

FN A5 SPR

This model has a 20" heavy fluted barrel threaded for a suppressor. Special McMillan tactical stock. The rest of the features are the same as the FN A4 model.

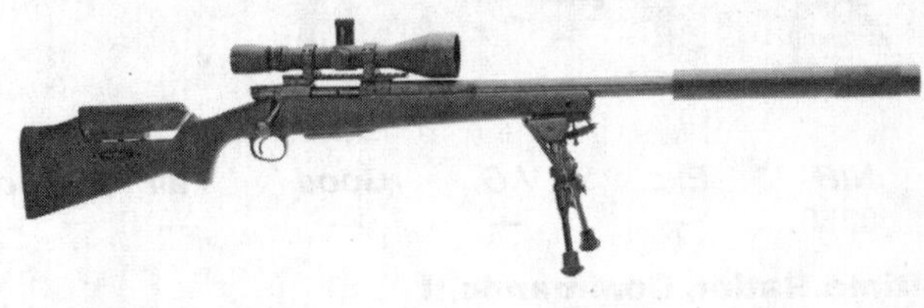

NIB	Exc.	V.G.	Good	Fair	Poor
7600	5750	—	—	—	—

NOTE: Price listed do not include scope.

FN A5a SPR

This model has a 20" heavy fluted barrel threaded for a suppressor. Special SPR McMillan adjustable tactical stock. Weight is about 9.75 lbs.

NIB	Exc.	V.G.	Good	Fair	Poor
2460	1975	—	—	—	—

FN PBR (Patrol Bolt Rifle)

Introduced in 2004 this rifle is chambered for the .308 cartridge. Offered with four different barrel lengths: 18", 20", 22", or 24". Fitted with a two-piece MIL spec M1913 rail. Black Hogue stock. Magazine capacity is 4 rounds. Weight is about 9 lbs.

NIB	Exc.	V.G.	Good	Fair	Poor
N/A	—	—	—	—	—

PGM PRECISION RIFLES

These rifles are made by PGM Precision, a subsidary of FN, in Poisy Cedex, France.

Ultima Ratio Intervention

This bolt-action rifle is chambered for the .308 7.62x51mm cartridge and fitted with a 23.6" ribbed barrel with integral muzzlebrake. Folding bipod. Stock, trigger group, and action are fixed to a rigid metal girder. Stock is adjustable. No sights. Magazine capacity is 5 or 10 rounds. Weight is about 13.25 lbs. depending on configuration.

NIB	Exc.	V.G.	Good	Fair	Poor
7880	—	—	—	—	—

Ultima Ratio Commando I

Similar to the above model but with 18.5" fluted barrel with muzzlebrake. Weight is about 12 lbs.

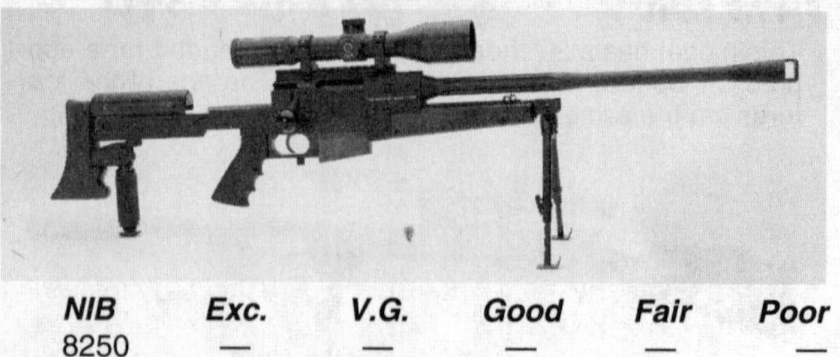

NIB	Exc.	V.G.	Good	Fair	Poor
8250	—	—	—	—	—

Ultima Ration Commando II

Similar to the Commando I but with folding stock.

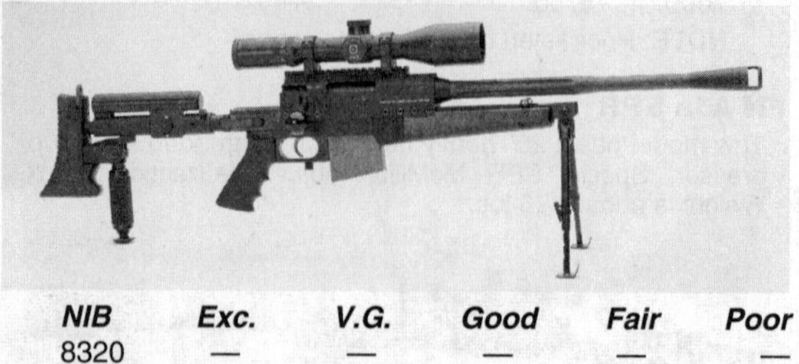

NIB	Exc.	V.G.	Good	Fair	Poor
8320	—	—	—	—	—

FN-Mini-Hecate

Chambered for the .308 cartridge this bolt-action rifle features a free-loading interchangeable 18.5", 19.7", 21.7", or 23.6" match-grade barrel. Collapsible buttstock. Magazine capacity is 10 rounds. Weight is about 14 lbs. Introduced in 2001.

NIB	Exc.	V.G.	Good	Fair	Poor
N/A	—	—	—	—	—

.338 Lapua

Similar to the Mini-Hecate but chambered for the .33 Lapua cartridge and fitted with a 27.2" barrel with integral muzzlebrake. Collapsible buttstock. Weight is about 15 lbs. Magazine capacity is 10 rounds.

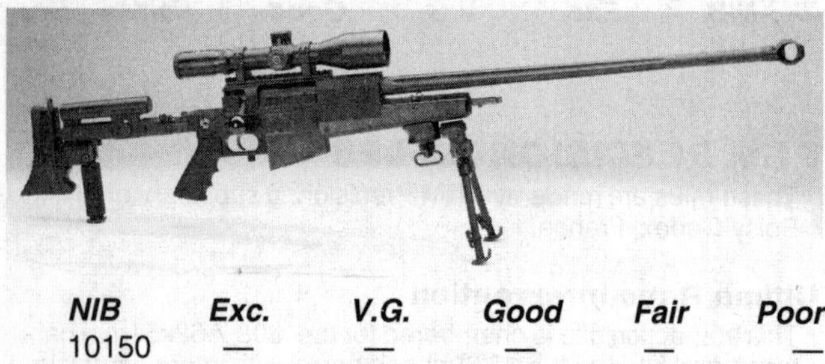

NIB	Exc.	V.G.	Good	Fair	Poor
10150					—

Hecate II

Chambered for the .50 BMG cartridge. Fitted with a 27.6" heavy barrel with integral muzzlebrake. Bipod. Adjustable stock. Magazine capacity is 7 rounds. Weight is about 36 lbs.

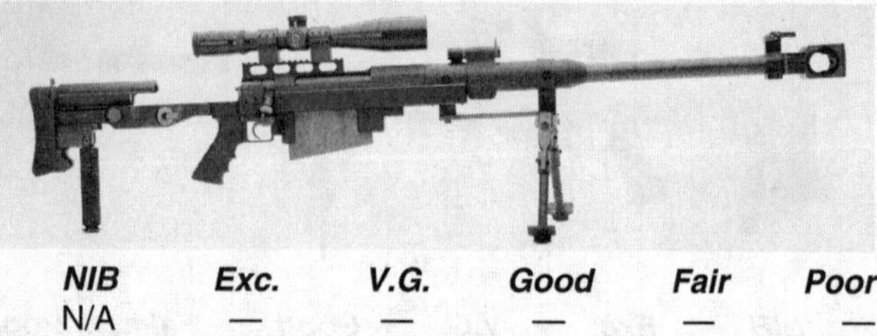

NIB	Exc.	V.G.	Good	Fair	Poor
N/A	—	—	—	—	—

OM .50 Nemesis

Chambered for the .50 caliber Browning cartridge (12.7x99mm) this bolt-action rifle features an adjustable buttstock, bipod, and other characteristics that make it a long range material rifle. Weight is approximately 28 lbs.

NIB	Exc.	V.G.	Good	Fair	Poor
N/A	—	—	—	—	—

SHOTGUNS

FN Police Shotgun

This is a slide-action 12 gauge shotgun chambered for the 3" 12 gauge shell. Barrel length is 18". Magazine capacity is 7 rounds. Black synthetic stock. Corrosion-resistant finish. Weight is about 6.5 lbs.

NIB	Exc.	V.G.	Good	Fair	Poor
350	275	200	—	—	—

FN Tactical Police

Similar to the standard model but with ported barrel and collapsible stock with pistol grip. Weight is about 6.5 lbs.

NIB	Exc.	V.G.	Good	Fair	Poor
650	475	400	—	—	—

FN Self-Loading Police

This shotgun is a gas-operated semi-automatic shotgun fitted with a picatinny rail and short stock. Chambered for the 12 gauge shell. Magazine capacity is 6 rounds. Weight is about 7.75 lbs.

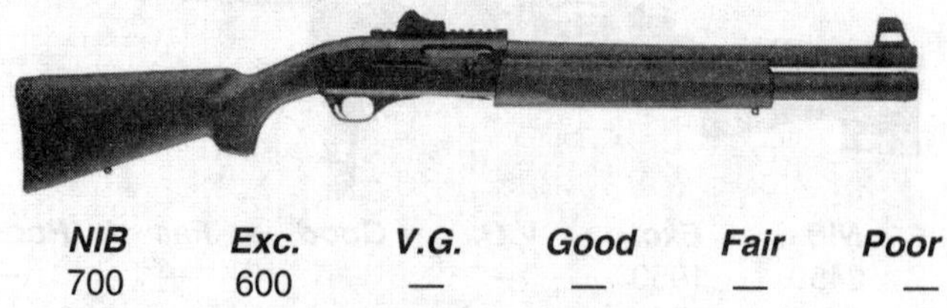

NIB	Exc.	V.G.	Good	Fair	Poor
700	600	—	—	—	—

FOEHL & WEEKS

Philadelphia, Pennsylvania

Columbian

A .32 or .38 caliber revolver marked with the patent date "20 January 1891."

Exc.	V.G.	Good	Fair	Poor
—	350	150	75	50

Columbian Automatic

A .38 caliber revolver with a hinged barrel and cylinder assembly.

Exc.	V.G.	Good	Fair	Poor
—	400	200	100	75

Perfect

As above, with a concealed hammer and also in .32 caliber.

Exc.	V.G.	Good	Fair	Poor
—	400	200	100	75

FOEHL, C.
Philadelphia, Pennsylvania

Foehl Derringer

A .41 caliber percussion single-shot pistol with a 2" barrel, German silver mounts and a walnut stock. The lock marked "C. Foehl."

Exc.	V.G.	Good	Fair	Poor
—	—	1750	750	300

FOGARTY
American Repeating Rifle Co.
Boston, Massachusetts

Fogarty Repeating Rifle and Carbine

A limited number of repeating rifles and carbines based upon Valentine Fogarty's patents were produced between 1866 and 1867. The calibers of these arms varies and the normal barrel lengths are 20" and 28". Blued, casehardened with walnut stocks. The American Repeating Rifle Company was purchased by the Winchester Repeating Arms Company in 1869.

Rifle

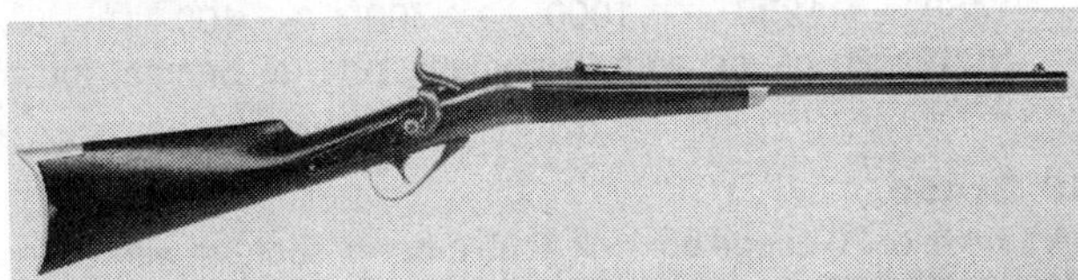

Courtesy Buffalo Bill Historical Center, Cody, Wyoming

Exc.	V.G.	Good	Fair	Poor
—	—	7500	3750	1250

Carbine

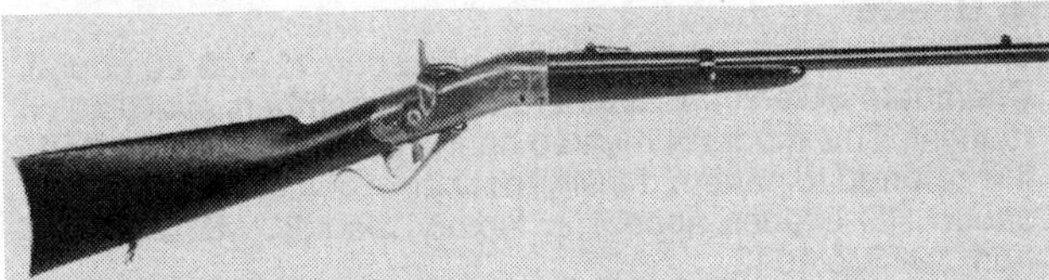

Courtesy Buffalo Bill Historical Center, Cody, Wyoming

Exc.	V.G.	Good	Fair	Poor
—	—	7500	3750	1250

FOLSOM, H.
St. Louis, Missouri

Derringer

A .41 caliber single-shot percussion pocket pistol with a 2.5" barrel, German silver mounts and a walnut stock. The barrel marked "H. Folsom."

Exc.	V.G.	Good	Fair	Poor
—	—	800	350	275

FOLSOM, H&D ARMS CO.

Double-Barrel Shotguns

Large distributor of double and single barrel shotguns produced by Crescent Firearms Co., Norwich, Connecticut. Folsom owned and later sold to Savage Arms Co. the Crescent Firearms Co., Davis Warner Co., and Baker Gun Co. around 1930. For more information see also Crescent Firearms Co.

FOREHAND & WADSWORTH
Worcester, Massachusetts

Established in 1871 and operated under the above name until 1890 when it became the Forehand Arms Company. Hopkins & Allen purchased the company in 1902.

Single-Shot Derringer

A .22 caliber single-shot pocket pistol with a 2" half-octagonal pivoted barrel, spur trigger and nickel- or silver-plated frame. Walnut grips. The barrel marked "Forehand & Wadsworth Worcester."

Exc.	V.G.	Good	Fair	Poor
—	1250	500	250	100

Single-Shot .41 Derringer

As above in .41 caliber with a 2.5" round barrel.

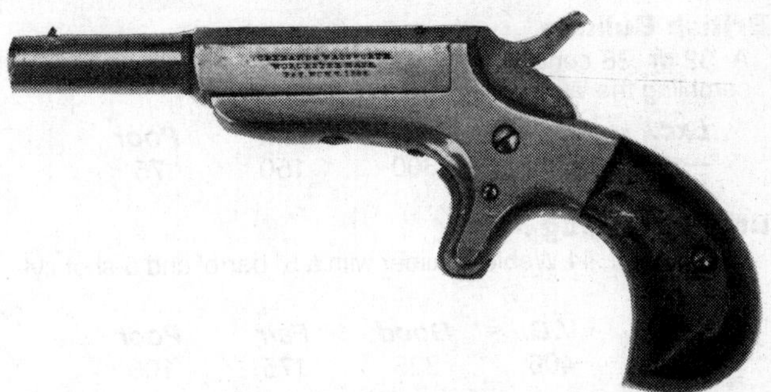

Courtesy Milwaukee Public Museum, Milwaukee, Wisconsin

Exc.	V.G.	Good	Fair	Poor
—	—	850	450	200

Side Hammer .22

A .22 caliber spur trigger revolver with a 2.25" to 4" octagonal barrel and 7-shot cylinder. Blued or nickel-plated with walnut grips.

Exc.	V.G.	Good	Fair	Poor
—	600	450	200	100

Center Hammer

A .32 caliber spur trigger revolver with a 3.5" octagonal barrel and 6-shot cylinder. Blued or nickel-plated with rosewood or walnut grips. The top strap commonly found marked "Terror."

Courtesy Milwaukee Public Museum, Milwaukee, Wisconsin

Exc.	V.G.	Good	Fair	Poor
—	400	300	200	100

Old Model Army Single-Action Revolver

A .44 Russian caliber revolver with a 7.5" round barrel and 6-shot cylinder. The barrel marked "Forehand & Wadsworth, Worchester, Mass. U.S. Patd. Oct. 22, '61, June 27, '71 Oct. 28, '73." Blued with walnut grips. Approximately 250 were manufactured between 1872 and 1878.

Exc.	V.G.	Good	Fair	Poor
—	—	3250	2000	500

New Model Army Single-Action Revolver

Similar to the above, with a 6.5" barrel and half-cock notch on the hammer. Approximately 250 were made between 1878 and 1882.

Exc.	V.G.	Good	Fair	Poor
—	—	3000	2250	500

Double-Action Revolver

A .32 or .38 centerfire or rimfire caliber double-action revolver with a 3.5" barrel and 6- or 7-shot cylinder. The .32 caliber version marked "Forehand & Wadsworth Double-Action," and the .38 caliber "American Bulldog." Manufactured from 1871 to 1890.

Exc.	V.G.	Good	Fair	Poor
400	300	200	100	35

British Bulldog

A .32 or .38 centerfire solid frame double-action revolver resembling the Webley Bulldog.

Exc.	V.G.	Good	Fair	Poor
—	375	300	150	75

British Bulldog .44

As above in .44 Webley caliber with a 5" barrel and 5-shot cylinder.

Exc.	V.G.	Good	Fair	Poor
—	400	325	175	100

Swamp Angel

A .41 caliber single-action revolver with a 3" barrel and 5-shot cylinder. The top strap marked "Swamp Angel."

Exc.	V.G.	Good	Fair	Poor
—	400	275	100	50

Forehand Arms Co. 1898-1902

Perfection Automatic

A .32 or .38 caliber double-action revolver with a hinged barrel and cylinder assembly. Varying barrel lengths. Blued or nickel-plated with hard rubber grips.

Exc.	V.G.	Good	Fair	Poor
—	250	100	75	50

Double-Barrel Shotguns

Good quality hammer and hammerless doubles but few produced until taken over by Hopkins and Allen Firearms Co. Values from $100 to $1,000 depending on grade and condition.

FOWLER, B. JR.

Hartford, Connecticut

Percussion Pistol

A .38 caliber single-shot percussion pistol with a 4" half octagonal barrel, iron frame and maple grips. The barrel marked "B. Fowler, Jr." Manufactured between 1835 and 1838.

Exc.	V.G.	Good	Fair	Poor
—	950	500	300	150

FOX, A. H.

Philadelphia, Pennsylvania

Ansley H. Fox established the Fox Gun Company in Baltimore, Maryland, in 1896. Subsequently, he made arms under the name Philadelphia Gun Company. As of 1905, he operated under the name A.H. Fox. In 1930, this company was purchased by the Savage Arms Company who continued manufacturing all grades of Fox shotguns. As of 1942, the Savage Company only made the plainer grades.

NOTE: Fox Model B double shotguns see Savage Arms Co.

Sterlingworth

A 12, 16, or 20 gauge boxlock double-barrel shotgun with 26", 28", or 30" barrels, double triggers and extractors. Automatic ejectors were also available and would add approximately 30 percent to the values listed. Blued, casehardened with a walnut stock. Manufactured from 1911 to 1946.

Courtesy Nick Niles, Paul Goodwin photo

Exc.	V.G.	Good	Fair	Poor
1250	1000	800	500	275

NOTE: 20 gauge add 50 percent. Add 25 percent for 16 gauge.

Sterlingworth Deluxe

As above, with an ivory bead, recoil pad and optional 32" barrel.

Exc.	V.G.	Good	Fair	Poor
1450	1250	1000	700	400

NOTE: 20 gauge add 50 percent. Add 25 percent for 16 gauge.

SP Grade

A 12, 16, or 20 gauge boxlock double-barrel shotgun with varying length barrels, double triggers and extractors.

Exc.	V.G.	Good	Fair	Poor
1000	850	750	450	225

NOTE: 20 gauge add 35 percent. Automatic ejectors add 15 percent. Add 25 percent for 16 gauge.

HE Grade

Similar to the early A Grade and offered in 12 and 20 gauge. Chambers were 2-1/4" standard with 3" chambers available on request. This model is marked on the barrel "Not Warranted." this referred to pattern density, not barrel quality. Only sixty 20 gauge HE Grades appear in factory records. Manufactured from 1923 to 1942.

Exc.	V.G.	Good	Fair	Poor
2500	2150	1750	1000	650

NOTE: Single-selective trigger add 20 percent. Add 30 percent premium for 20 gauge.

High Grade Guns A-FE

The Fox Company as well as the Savage Arms Company produced a variety of shotguns decorated in varying grades. They were available in 12, 16, and 20 gauge. As the value for these arms depends on the particular features of these arms, prospective purchasers are advised to secure a qualified appraisal prior to acquisition.

NOTE: A 25 percent premium should be added to the grades below for small gauge guns and guns with single selective trigger.

A Grade

Built from 1905 to 1942.

Exc.	V.G.	Good	Fair	Poor
1450	1150	850	600	400

AE Grade (Automatic Ejectors)

Built from 1905 to 1946.

Exc.	V.G.	Good	Fair	Poor
1750	1450	1150	900	700

B Grade
Built from 1905 to 1918.

Exc.	V.G.	Good	Fair	Poor
2400	2100	1600	1100	500

BE Grade
Built from 1905 to 1918.

Exc.	V.G.	Good	Fair	Poor
2800	2500	2000	1500	900

C Grade
Built from 1905 to 1913.

Exc.	V.G.	Good	Fair	Poor
2600	2200	1700	1100	550

CE Grade
Built from 1905 to 1946.

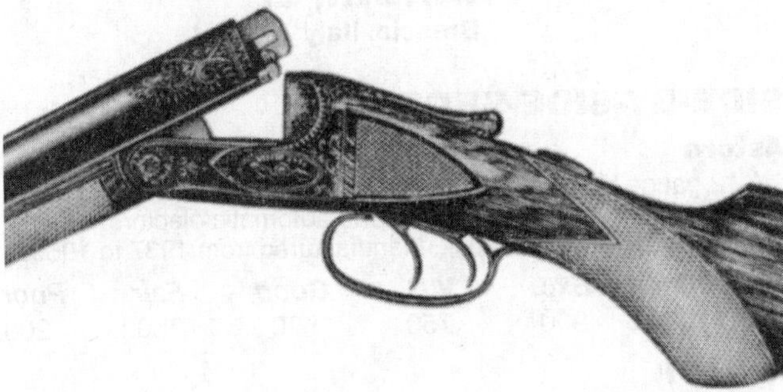

Exc.	V.G.	Good	Fair	Poor
3000	2600	2100	1550	950

XE Grade
Built from 1914 to 1945.

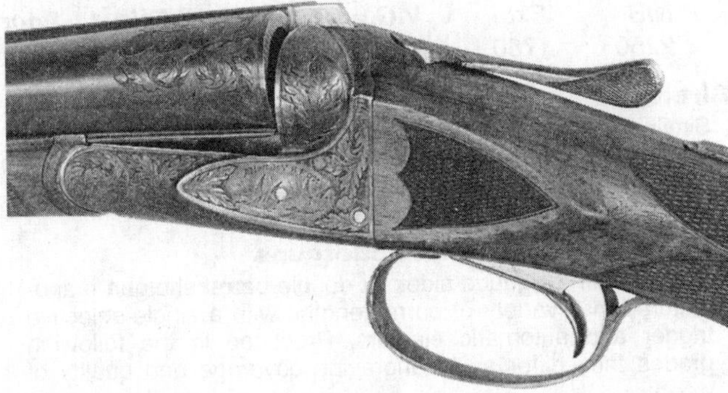

Courtesy William Hammond

Exc.	V.G.	Good	Fair	Poor
5500	5000	3500	1850	1100

D Grade
Built from 1906 to 1913.

Exc.	V.G.	Good	Fair	Poor
8000	7000	4500	2500	1000

DE Grade
Built from 1906 to 1945.

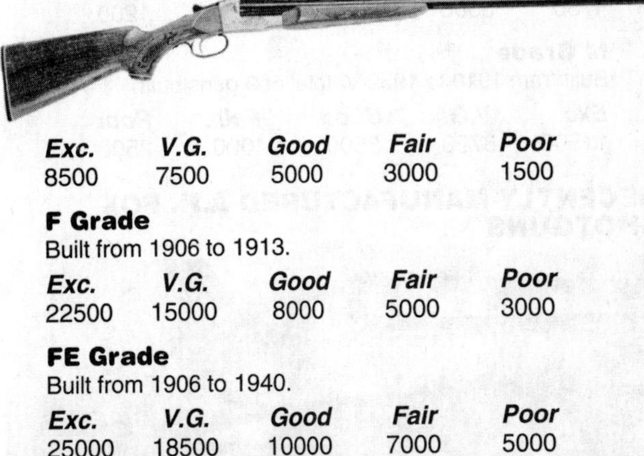

Exc.	V.G.	Good	Fair	Poor
8500	7500	5000	3000	1500

F Grade
Built from 1906 to 1913.

Exc.	V.G.	Good	Fair	Poor
22500	15000	8000	5000	3000

FE Grade
Built from 1906 to 1940.

Exc.	V.G.	Good	Fair	Poor
25000	18500	10000	7000	5000

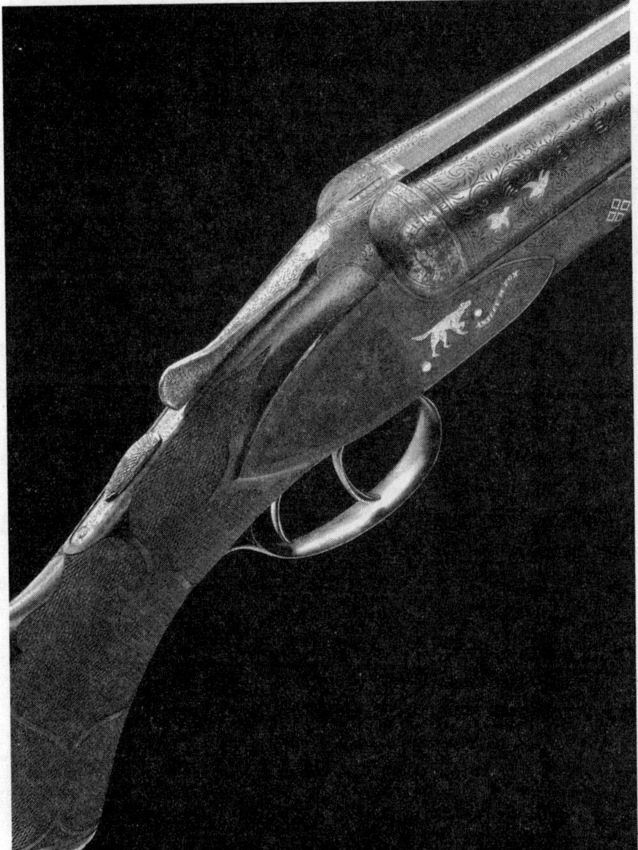

Fox FE Grade Courtesy Bonhams & Butterfields

Single Barrel Trap Guns

A 12 gauge single barrel boxlock shotgun with 30" or 32" ventilated rib barrels and automatic ejector. There were approximately 571 single-barrel trap guns manufactured. Produced in four grades as listed:

J Grade
Built from 1919 to 1936.

Exc.	V.G.	Good	Fair	Poor
2350	1950	1250	950	600

K Grade

Built from 1919 to 1931. Approximately 75 built.

Exc.	V.G.	Good	Fair	Poor
3500	2750	2000	1500	950

L Grade

Built from 1919 to 1931. Approximately 25 built.

Exc.	V.G.	Good	Fair	Poor
4750	3300	2700	1950	1200

M Grade

Built from 1919 to 1932. A total of 9 guns built.

Exc.	V.G.	Good	Fair	Poor
11500	8750	5500	4000	2500

RECENTLY MANUFACTURED A.H. FOX SHOTGUNS

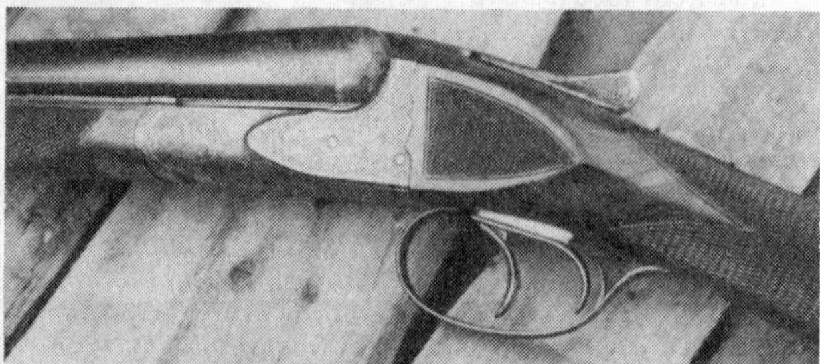

In 1993 the Connecticut Manufacturing Company of New Britain, Connecticut, announced the production of the A.H. Fox shotgun in 20 gauge exclusively. The gun is hand-built and constructed to the same dimensions and standards as the original Fox. The gun is offered in five grades with many standard features and several optional ones as well. Each shotgun is built to order. Because these guns are newly built and have no pricing history, only manufacturer's retail price for the base gun will be given. Extra sets of barrels, single triggers, and other extra costs options will greatly affect price.

CE Grade

Receiver engraved with fine scroll and game scene engraving with Turkish Circassian walnut stock, fine line hand checkering. Choice of full, half, or straight grip with splinter forend. Double triggers, automatic ejectors, automatic safety, choice of chokes, and barrel lengths in 26, 28, and 30 inches.

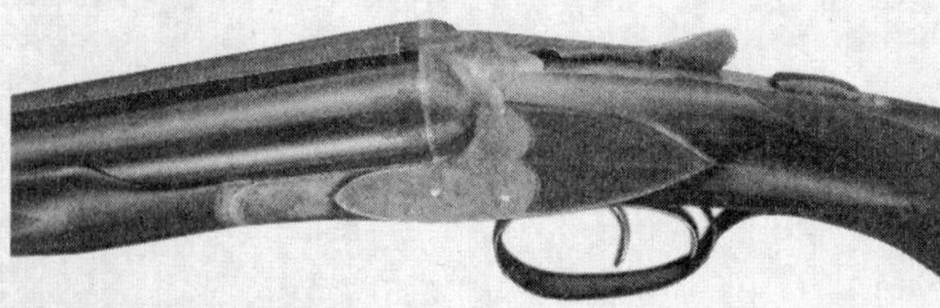

Retail price: $13,500

XE Grade

Same features as above with the addition of chiseled scroll work with engraved game scenes and higher quality Circassian walnut.

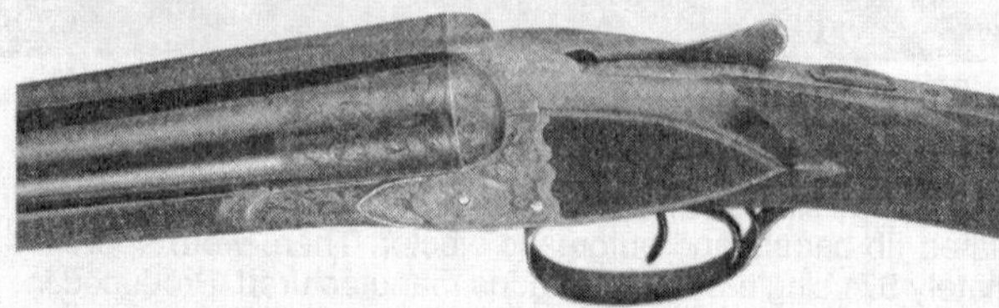

Retail price: $15,500

DE Grade

Same features as above with more intricate and extensive engraving. Even higher quality wood with diamond pattern checkering.

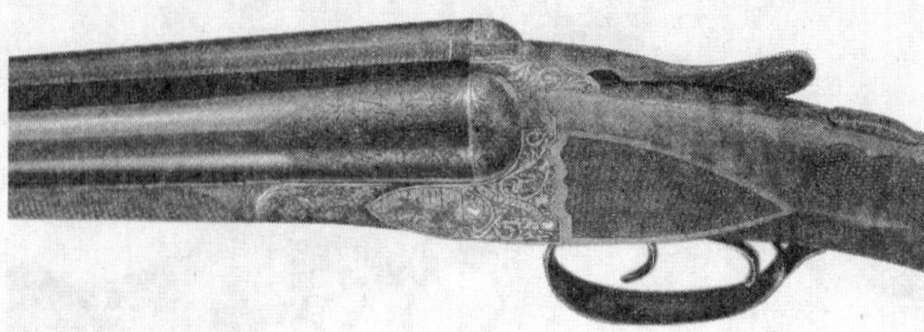

Retail price: $18,000

FE Grade

This grade features gold inlays and distinctive scroll work. Best quality wood with very fine line diamond pattern checkering.

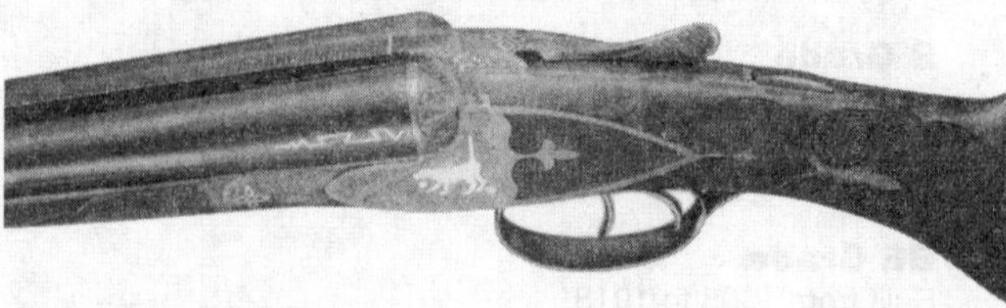

Retail price: $23,000

Exhibition Grade

This is the company's highest grade and features any optional detail the customer desires including custom engraving and exhibition quality wood.

Retail price: $36,500

FRANCHI, L.

Brescia, Italy

SIDE-BY-SIDE-SHOTGUNS

Astore

A 12 gauge boxlock shotgun manufactured in a variety of barrel lengths with double triggers and automatic ejectors. Blued with a straight walnut stock. Manufactured from 1937 to 1960.

NIB	Exc.	V.G.	Good	Fair	Poor
1100	900	750	500	350	200

Astore II

As above, but more finely finished.

NIB	Exc.	V.G.	Good	Fair	Poor
1350	1100	900	700	450	250

Astore 5

As above, but more finely finished.

NIB	Exc.	V.G.	Good	Fair	Poor
2250	1750	1250	950	600	300

Airone

Similar to the Astore. Manufactured during the 1940s.

NIB	Exc.	V.G.	Good	Fair	Poor
1300	1050	950	750	500	250

Sidelock Double-Barrel Shotguns

A 12, 16, or 20 gauge sidelock double-barrel shotgun manufactured in a variety of barrel lengths with a single-selective trigger and automatic ejectors. Produced in the following grades they differ as to engraving coverage and quality of wood:

Condor

NIB	Exc.	V.G.	Good	Fair	Poor
7500	6500	4500	3500	2500	1250

Imperial

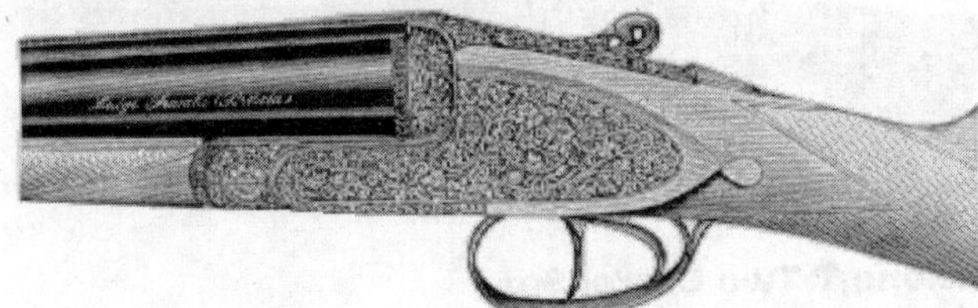

NIB	Exc.	V.G.	Good	Fair	Poor
10000	8500	6000	4500	3250	1500

Imperiales

NIB	Exc.	V.G.	Good	Fair	Poor
10500	9000	6500	5000	3500	1500

No. 5 Imperial Monte Carlo

NIB	Exc.	V.G.	Good	Fair	Poor
15000	12500	9000	7500	5000	2000

No. 11 Imperial Monte Carlo

NIB	Exc.	V.G.	Good	Fair	Poor
16000	13500	10000	8000	5500	2000

Imperial Monte Carlo Extra

NIB	Exc.	V.G.	Good	Fair	Poor
20000	17500	12500	9500	7500	3500

Highlander

Introduced in 2003 this model features either a 12, 20, or 28 gauge gun fitted with 26" barrels and fixed chokes. Select walnut straight grip stock with splinter forend. Coin finished steel receiver. Single trigger. Weight is 6.4 lbs. for 12 gauge; 5.8 lbs. for 20 gauge, and 5.7 lbs. for 28 gauge.

NIB	Exc.	V.G.	Good	Fair	Poor
1800	1300	—	—	—	—

NOTE: Add $150 for 28 gauge.

OVER/UNDER SHOTGUNS

Priti Deluxe Model

A 12 or 20 gauge Over/Under boxlock double-barrel shotgun with 26" or 28" ventilated rib barrels, single trigger and automatic ejectors. Introduced in 1988.

NIB	Exc.	V.G.	Good	Fair	Poor
400	350	300	250	200	150

Falconet

A 12, 16, 20, and 28 gauge as well as .410 bore boxlock double-barrel shotgun with single-selective trigger and automatic ejectors. The receiver was anodized in tan, ebony, or silver finishes. Manufactured from 1968 to 1975.

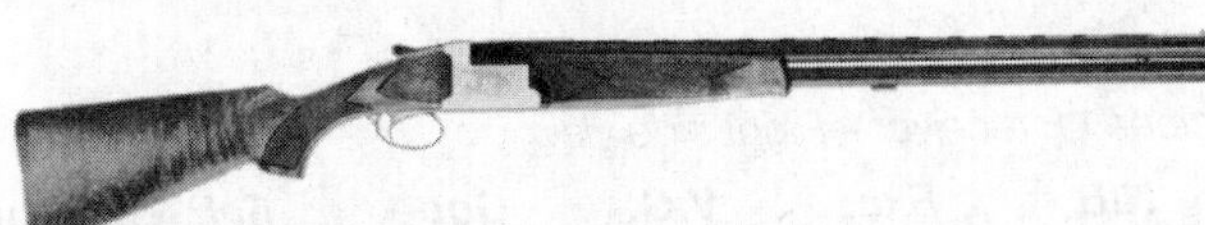

NIB	Exc.	V.G.	Good	Fair	Poor
550	500	425	350	250	200

NOTE: Silver receiver add 10 percent. 28 gauge and .410 add 25 percent.

Falconet Skeet

As above, with a 26" skeet barrel with a wide rib and the receiver casehardened. Manufactured from 1970 to 1974.

NIB	Exc.	V.G.	Good	Fair	Poor
950	850	700	550	450	250

Falconet International Skeet

As above, but more finely finished.

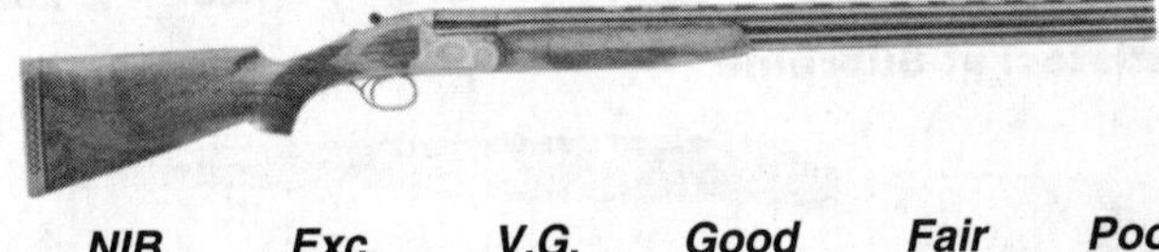

NIB	Exc.	V.G.	Good	Fair	Poor
1000	900	750	600	475	250

Falconet Trap

As above, with a 30" modified and full choke barrel, and trap stock. Manufactured from 1970 to 1974.

NIB	Exc.	V.G.	Good	Fair	Poor
950	850	700	550	450	250

Falconet International Trap

As above, but more finely finished.

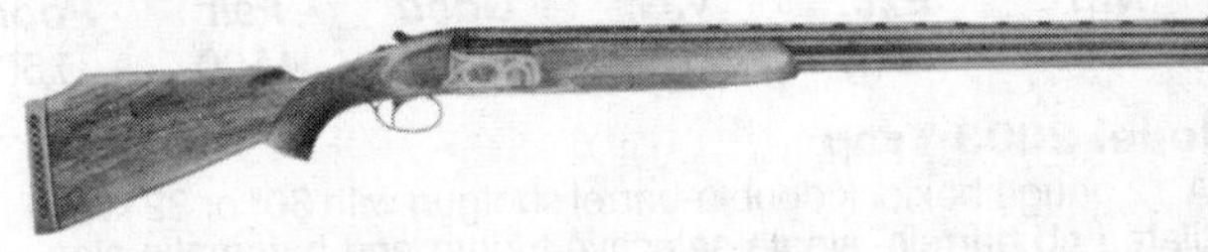

NIB	Exc.	V.G.	Good	Fair	Poor
1000	900	750	600	475	250

Peregrine Model 451

A 12 gauge boxlock double-barrel shotgun with 26" or 28" ventilated rib barrels, alloy receiver, single-selective trigger and automatic ejectors. Manufactured in 1975.

NIB	Exc.	V.G.	Good	Fair	Poor
600	525	450	375	275	200

Peregrine Model 400

As above, with a steel frame.

NIB	Exc.	V.G.	Good	Fair	Poor
650	575	500	400	300	200

Aristocrat

Similar to the above, with 26", 28", or 30" ventilated rib barrels. Manufactured from 1960 to 1969.

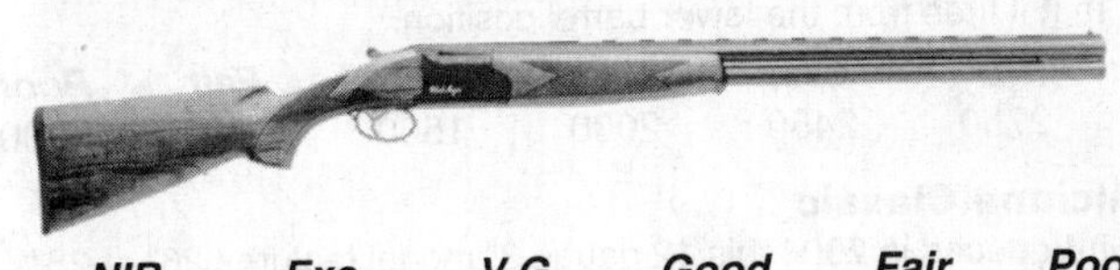

NIB	Exc.	V.G.	Good	Fair	Poor
650	575	500	400	300	200

Aristocrat Magnum

As above, with 3" chambers and 32" full choke barrels.

NIB	Exc.	V.G.	Good	Fair	Poor
650	575	500	400	300	200

Aristocrat Silver King

As above, with a French case hardened receiver, and available in four grades of decoration.

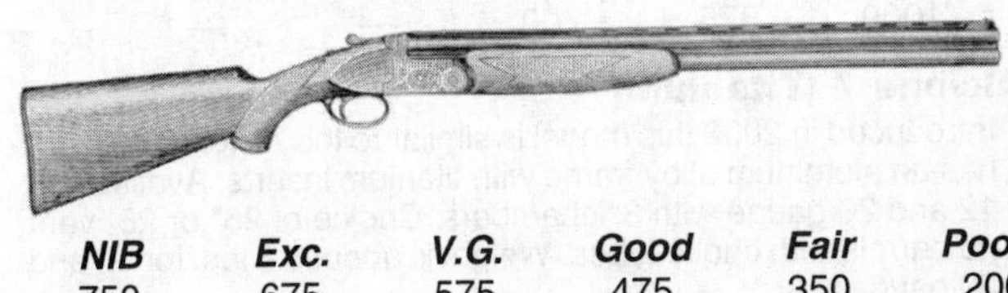

NIB	Exc.	V.G.	Good	Fair	Poor
750	675	575	475	350	200

Aristocrat Deluxe

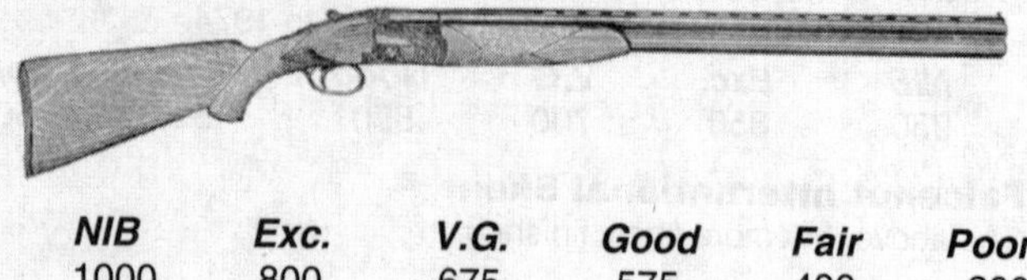

NIB	Exc.	V.G.	Good	Fair	Poor
1000	800	675	575	400	200

Aristocrat Supreme

NIB	Exc.	V.G.	Good	Fair	Poor
1450	1200	850	700	575	250

Aristocrat Imperial

NIB	Exc.	V.G.	Good	Fair	Poor
2750	2250	1750	1250	950	450

Aristocrat Monte Carlo

NIB	Exc.	V.G.	Good	Fair	Poor
3500	3000	2750	2000	1500	750

Model 2003 Trap

A 12 gauge boxlock double-barrel shotgun with 30" or 32" ventilated rib barrels, single-selective trigger and automatic ejectors. Manufactured in 1976.

NIB	Exc.	V.G.	Good	Fair	Poor
1250	1100	800	650	500	250

Model 2004 Trap

A single-barreled version of the Model 2003.

NIB	Exc.	V.G.	Good	Fair	Poor
1250	1100	800	650	500	250

Model 2005 Combination Trap

The Model 2003 with both a single and set of Over/Under barrels.

NIB	Exc.	V.G.	Good	Fair	Poor
2500	2200	1750	1200	950	450

Model 3000 "Undergun"

As above, with a single barrel fitted with a high ventilated rib so that it fires from the lower barrel position.

NIB	Exc.	V.G.	Good	Fair	Poor
2750	2450	2000	1500	1200	600

Alcione Classic

Introduced in 2004 this 12 gauge 3" model features 26" or 28" ventilated rib barrels. Side rib is ventilated. Walnut stock with schnabel forend. Optional 20 gauge barrels. Weight is about 7.5 lbs.

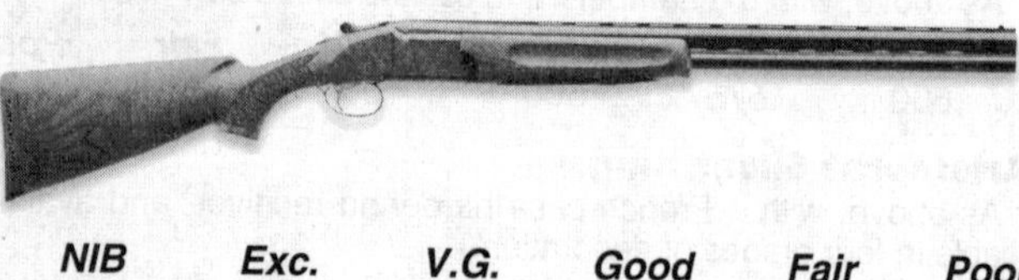

NIB	Exc.	V.G.	Good	Fair	Poor
1000	875	700	—	—	—

Alcione T (Titanium)

Introduced in 2002 this model is similar to the Alcione Field but has an aluminum alloy frame with titanium inserts. Available in 12 and 20 gauge with 3" chambers. Choice of 26" or 28" vent rib barrels with choke tubes. Weight is about 6.8 lbs. for 12 and 20 gauge.

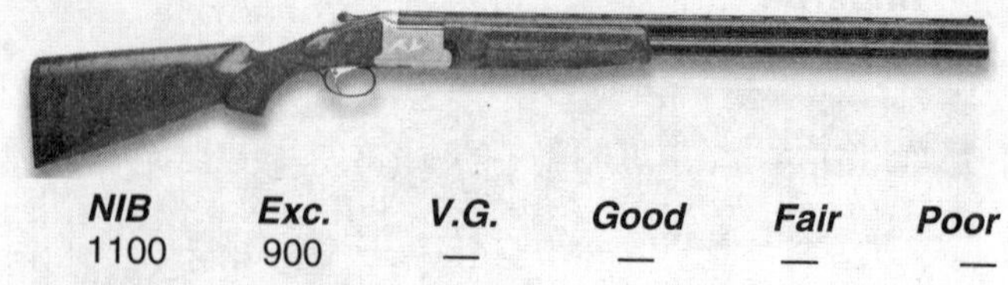

NIB	Exc.	V.G.	Good	Fair	Poor
1100	900	—	—	—	—

Alcione T Two Barrel Set

As above but with a two-barrel set: One 12 gauge 28" and the other is a 20 gauge 26". Introduced in 2004.

NIB	Exc.	V.G.	Good	Fair	Poor
1300	1000	—	—	—	—

Alcione Field Model

A 12 gauge boxlock double-barrel shotgun with 26" or 28" ventilated rib barrels, single-selective trigger and automatic ejectors. Engraved silver receiver. Weight is about 7.5 lbs.

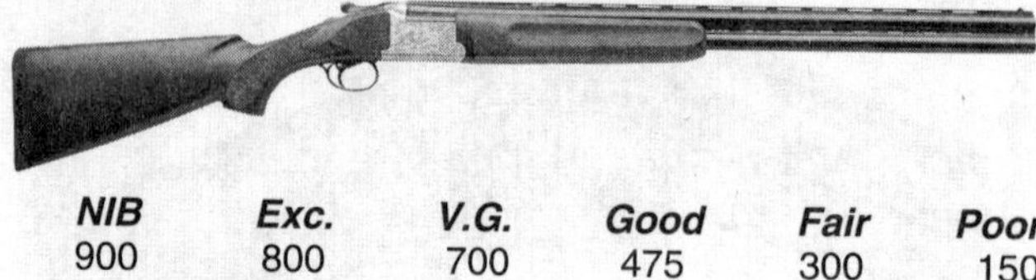

NIB	Exc.	V.G.	Good	Fair	Poor
900	800	700	475	300	150

Alcione Sporting

This over/under gun is designed for sporting clays competition. Fitted with mechanical triggers and ported barrels. Offered in 12 gauge only with 30" barrels. Select walnut stock. Removable sideplates. Weight about 7.5 lbs.

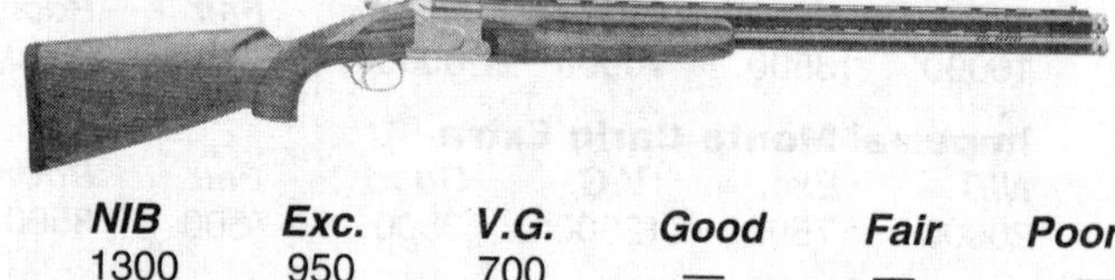

NIB	Exc.	V.G.	Good	Fair	Poor
1300	950	700	—	—	—

Alcione LF

This 12 or 20 gauge model features barrels of 26" and 28" in 12 gauge and 26" in 20 gauge. Both gauges are chambered for 3" shells. Walnut stock. Receiver is aluminum alloy with etched games scenes with gold fill. Weight is about 6.8 lbs.

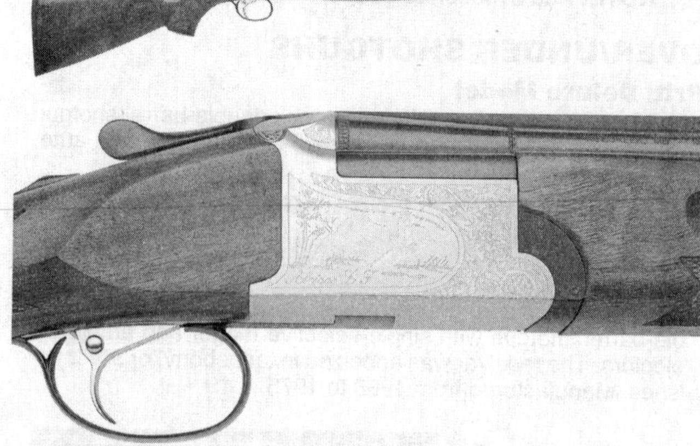

Alcione LF receiver—Right side view

NIB	Exc.	V.G.	Good	Fair	Poor
1000	800	600	—	—	—

Alcione SL Sport

As above, but more finely finished and with a French case-hardened receiver.

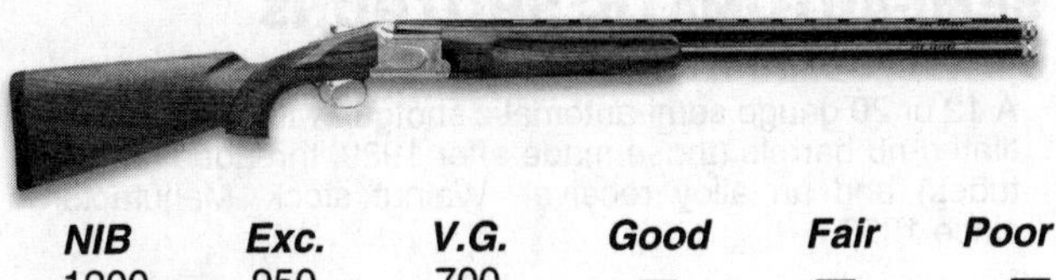

NIB	Exc.	V.G.	Good	Fair	Poor
1200	950	700	—	—	—

Alcione SP

Chambered for the 12 gauge shell and fitted with 28" vent rib barrels with choke tubes. Full slide lock-style side plates with engraving and gold pheasants and mallards. Weight is about 7.5 lbs. Introduced in 2003.

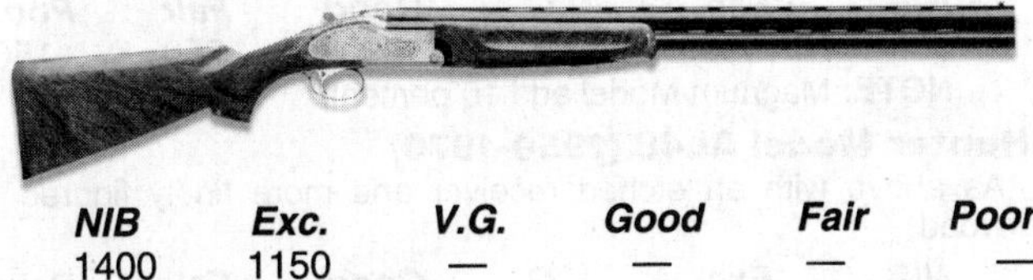

NIB	Exc.	V.G.	Good	Fair	Poor
1400	1150	—	—	—	—

ALCIONE SIDEPLATES

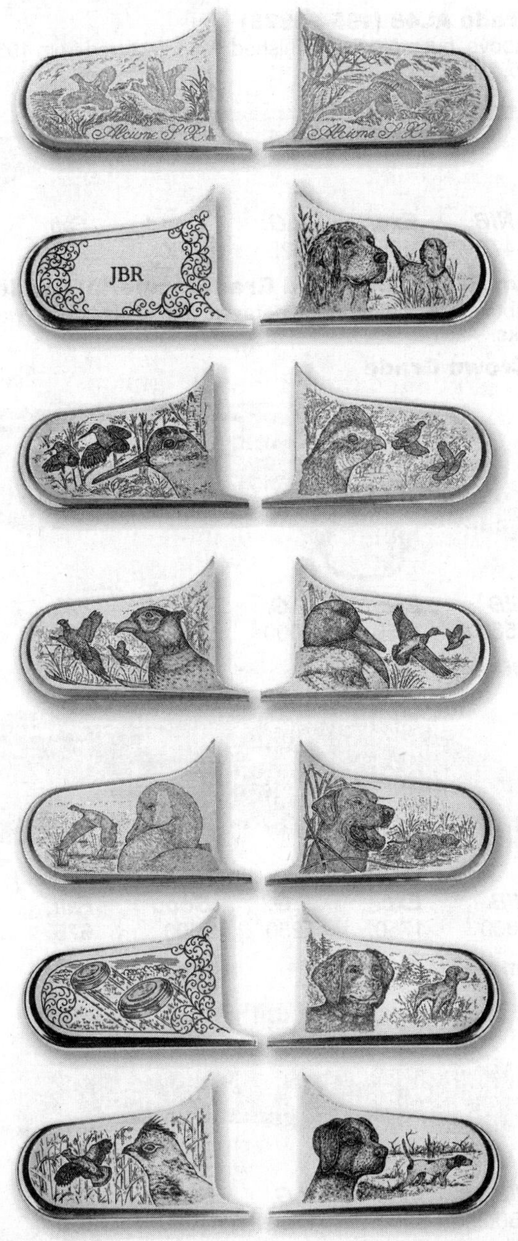

Alcione Classic SX

This 12 gauge 3" model is similar to the Alcione Field SX above but with blued receiver. Available with choice of 26" or 28" vent rib barrels. An extra 12 gauge 30" ported barrel and 20 gauge barrels are also optional. Weight is about 7.5 lbs. Introduced in 2004.

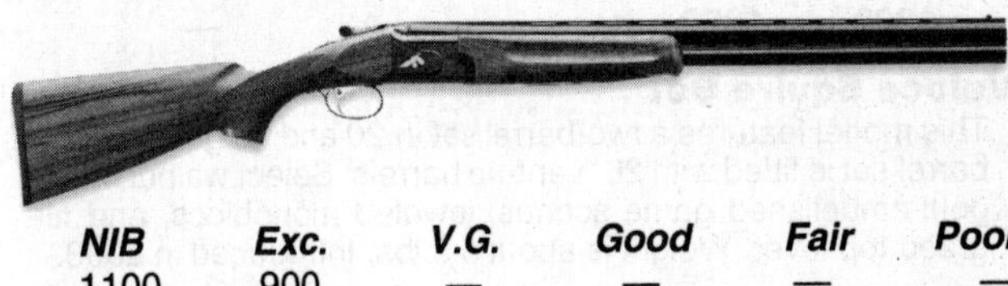

NIB	Exc.	V.G.	Good	Fair	Poor
1100	900	—	—	—	—

Alcione Field SX

This model is fitted with a high grade walnut stock, fine checkering, and engraved receivers with gold filled etched side plates. Offered with 28" or 26" barrels. Weight is about 7.3 lbs.

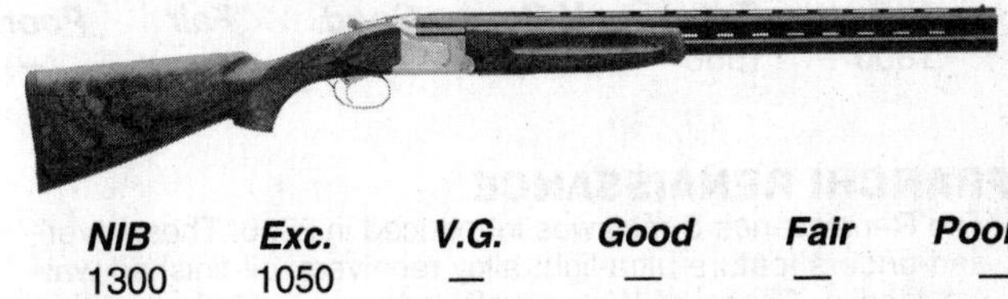

NIB	Exc.	V.G.	Good	Fair	Poor
1300	1050	—	—	—	—

Veloce

Introduced in 2001 this model is chambered for the 20 or 28 gauge only with 26" or 28" barrels for 20 gauge guns and 26" barrels for 28 gauge guns. Aluminum alloy receiver. Engraved side plates with gold filled game scenes. Mechanical trigger. Select walnut stock. Weight of 20 gauge guns is about 5.8 lbs. and 28 gauge guns about 5.5 lbs.

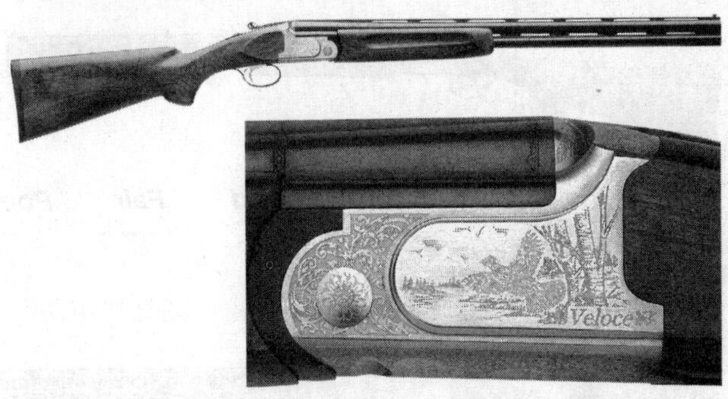

NIB	Exc.	V.G.	Good	Fair	Poor
1000	825	—	—	—	—

Veloce English Stock

Introduced in 2002 this model is similar ot the Veloce but with a straight-grip stock. Offered in 20 and 28 gauge with 26" vent-rib barrels. Choke tubes. Weight is about 5.7 lbs. in 20 gauge and 5.5 lbs. in 28 gauge.

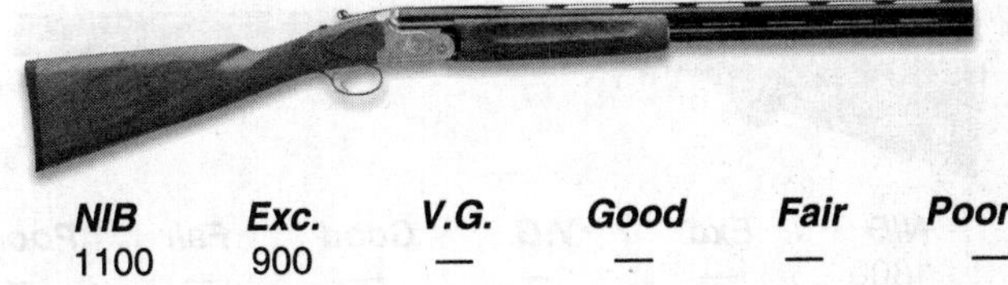

NIB	Exc.	V.G.	Good	Fair	Poor
1100	900	—	—	—	—

Veloce Grade II

This 20 or 28 gauge model features an extra-select-grade walnut stock with gold-filled birds and scroll engraving. The 20 gauge is offered with either a 26" or 28" vent-rib barrel, while the 28 gauge is fitted with a 26" vent-rib barrel. The 20 gauge gun weighs about 5.75 lbs., while the 28 gauge gun weighs about 5.5 lbs.

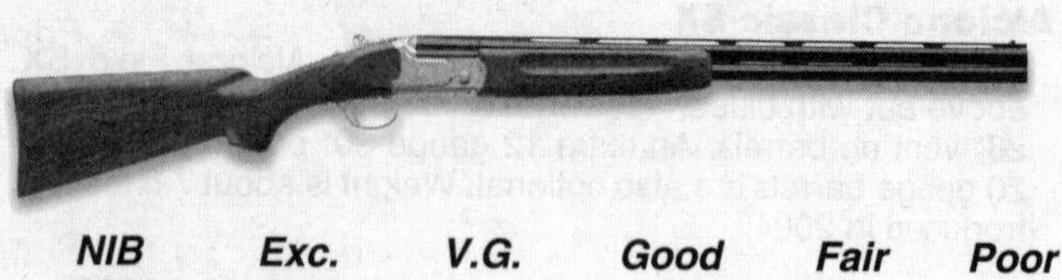

NIB	Exc.	V.G.	Good	Fair	Poor
1300	1050	—	—	—	—

Veloce Squire Set

This model features a two-barrel set in 20 and 28 gauge. Each barrel set is fitted with 26" vent-rib barrels. Select walnut stock, gold-embelished game scenes, jeweled monoblocs, and filigreed top lever. Weight is about 5.5 lbs. Introduced in 2003.

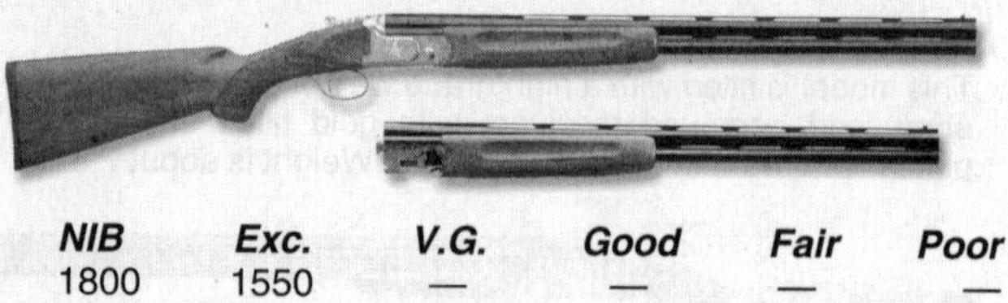

NIB	Exc.	V.G.	Good	Fair	Poor
1800	1550	—	—	—	—

FRANCHI RENAISSANCE

The Renaissance Series was introduced in 2006. These over-and-unders feature ultra-light alloy receivers, oil-finished walnut stocks, Prince of Wales pistol grips, cut checkering and Twin Shock Absorber recoil pads with gel insert. The 3" 12 and 20 gauges have 26" or 28" barrels; the 28 gauge has a 26" barrel. Weights average 6.2 lbs. in 12 gauge, 5.8 lbs. in 20 gauge and 5.5 lbs. in 28 gauge. Add 5 percent to values shown for 28 gauge.

Renaissance Field

Walnut stock with engraved receiver.

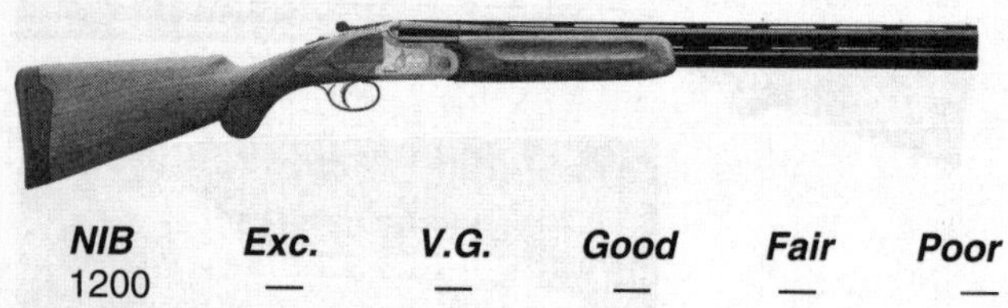

NIB	Exc.	V.G.	Good	Fair	Poor
1200	—	—	—	—	—

Renaissance Classic

A-Grade walnut with gold inlaid receiver.

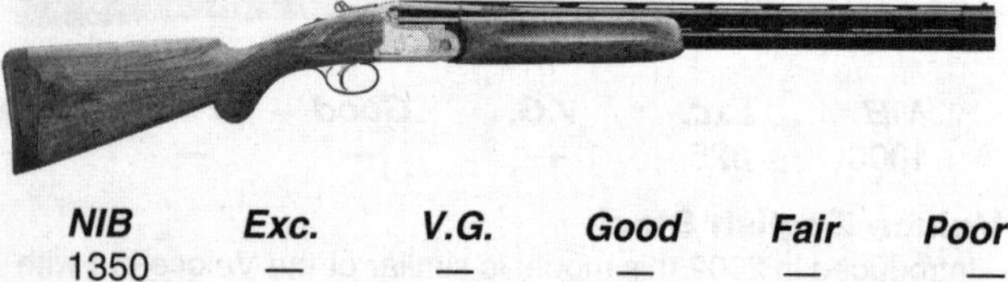

NIB	Exc.	V.G.	Good	Fair	Poor
1350					—

Renaissance Elite

AA-Grade Walnut with gold inlaid receiver.

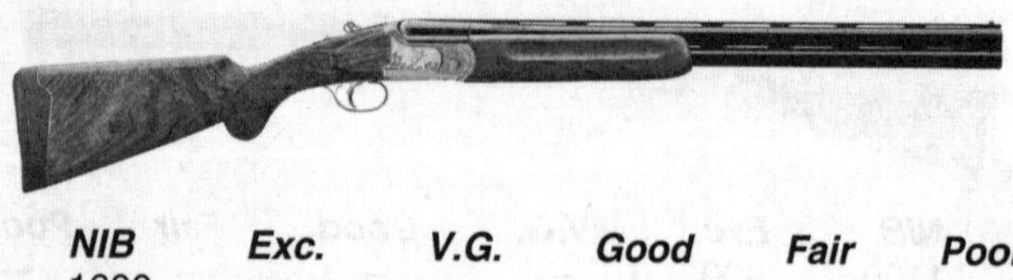

NIB	Exc.	V.G.	Good	Fair	Poor
1600	—	—	—	—	—

Renaissance Sporting

This 3" 12 gauge model was introduced in 2007. It features a 30" barrel, A-Grade walnut stock, engraved receiver with gold inlay and adjustable comb. Weight is about 7.9 lbs.

NIB	Exc.	V.G.	Good	Fair	Poor
1675	—	—	—	—	—

SEMI-AUTOMATIC SHOTGUNS

Standard Model AL48 (1950-1970)

A 12 or 20 gauge semi-automatic shotgun with 24" to 30" ventilated-rib barrels (those made after 1989, threaded for choke tubes) and an alloy receiver. Walnut stock. Manufactured since 1950.

NIB	Exc.	V.G.	Good	Fair	Poor
500	450	350	300	250	150

NOTE: Magnum Model add 10 percent.

Hunter Model AL48 (1950-1970)

As above with an etched receiver and more finely figured wood.

NIB	Exc.	V.G.	Good	Fair	Poor
400	350	300	250	200	150

NOTE: Magnum Model add 10 percent.

Eldorado AL48 (1954-1975)

As above, but more finely finished. Manufactured from 1954 to 1975.

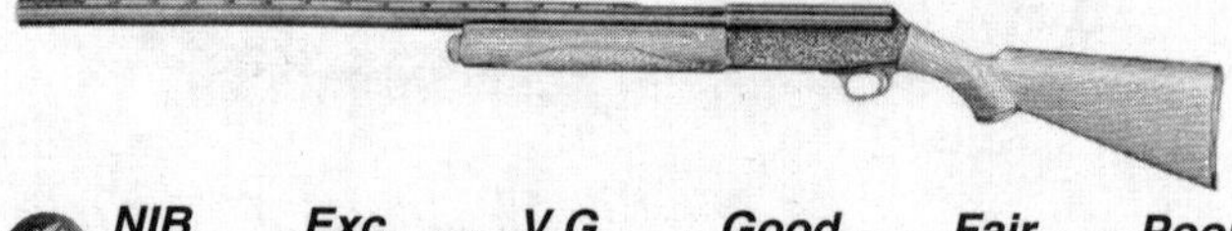

NIB	Exc.	V.G.	Good	Fair	Poor
475	425	325	250	200	150

Crown Grade, Diamond Grade, Imperial Grade

As above, with hand-done engraving and finely figured walnut stocks.

Crown Grade

NIB	Exc.	V.G.	Good	Fair	Poor
1500	1250	1000	700	475	250

Diamond Grade

NIB	Exc.	V.G.	Good	Fair	Poor
2000	1750	1250	900	675	300

Imperial Grade

NIB	Exc.	V.G.	Good	Fair	Poor
2500	2250	1750	1250	950	450

This symbol denotes "Sleepers" with rapidly-rising values and/or significant collector potential.

Model 500

A 12 gauge semi-automatic shotgun with a 28" ventilated-rib barrel and walnut stock. Introduced in 1976.

NIB	Exc.	V.G.	Good	Fair	Poor
350	325	275	200	150	100

NOTE: Deluxe version add 10 percent.

Model 520 "Eldorado Gold"

An engraved and gold-inlaid version of the above.

NIB	Exc.	V.G.	Good	Fair	Poor
1000	850	650	450	300	150

Model 530 Trap

The Model 500 with a 30" or 32" ventilated-rib barrel and trap stock.

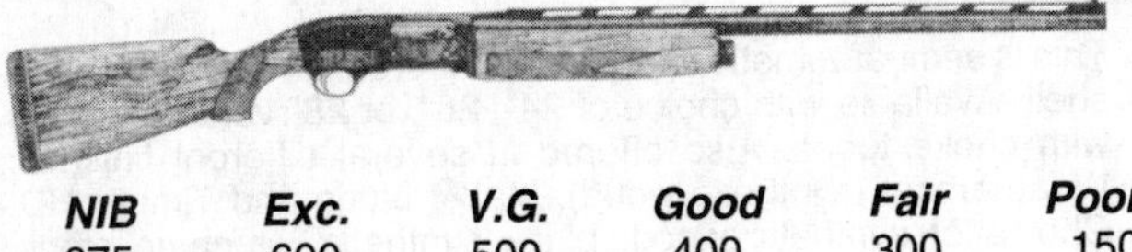

NIB	Exc.	V.G.	Good	Fair	Poor
675	600	500	400	300	150

Prestige Model

A 12 gauge semi-automatic shotgun manufactured in a variety of barrel lengths. After 1989 the barrels threaded for choke tubes. Alloy receiver and walnut stock.

NIB	Exc.	V.G.	Good	Fair	Poor
575	500	425	350	250	150

Elite Model

As above, with an etched receiver and more finely figured stock.

NIB	Exc.	V.G.	Good	Fair	Poor
600	500	425	350	250	150

SPAS12

A 12 gauge slide-action or semi-automatic shotgun with a 21.5" barrel and 9-shot magazine. Anodized, black finish with a composition folding or fixed stock.

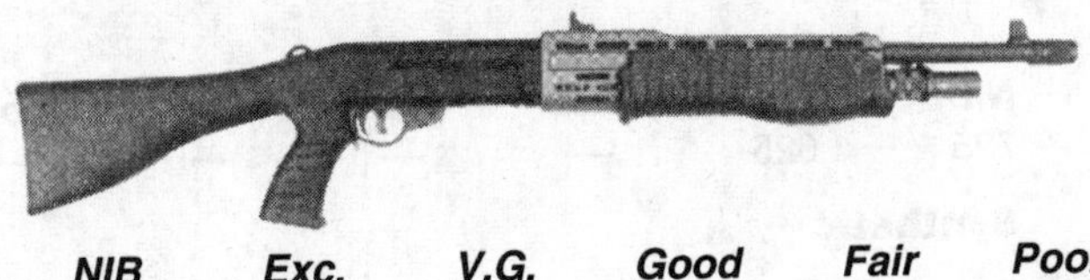

NIB	Exc.	V.G.	Good	Fair	Poor
950	800	600	500	400	300

Black Magic Game Model

A 12 gauge Magnum semi-automatic shotgun with 24" to 28" ventilated rib barrels threaded for choke tubes, gold anodized alloy receiver, blackened barrel and walnut stock. Also available in trap or skeet configuration.

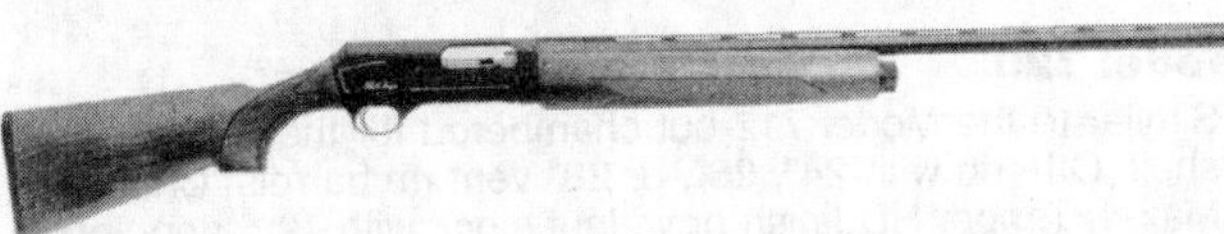

NIB	Exc.	V.G.	Good	Fair	Poor
400	350	275	200	150	100

NOTE: Skeet Model add 10 percent. Trap Model add 15 percent.

Black Magic Hunter

A 12 gauge Magnum double-barrel shotgun with 28" ventilated-rib barrels threaded for choke tubes, single-selective triggers and automatic ejectors. Blued with a walnut stock. Introduced in 1989.

NIB	Exc.	V.G.	Good	Fair	Poor
975	850	650	400	300	150

Black Magic Lightweight Hunter

As above, with 26" barrels and 2.75" chambers.

NIB	Exc.	V.G.	Good	Fair	Poor
975	850	650	400	300	150

Variomax 912

Introduced in 2001 this model is chambered for the 12 gauge 3.5" shell. It is offered with a choice of 24", 26", 28", or 30" barrels with vent-rib. Black synthetic stock. Weight is about 7.6 lbs. Choke tubes. In 2002 a walnut stock was added as an option.

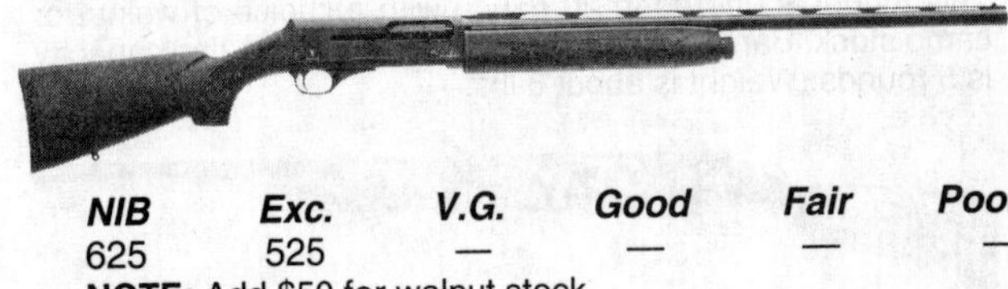

NIB	Exc.	V.G.	Good	Fair	Poor
625	525	—	—	—	—

NOTE: Add $50 for walnut stock.

Variomax 912 Camo

Same as above but with Advantage Timber camo finish.

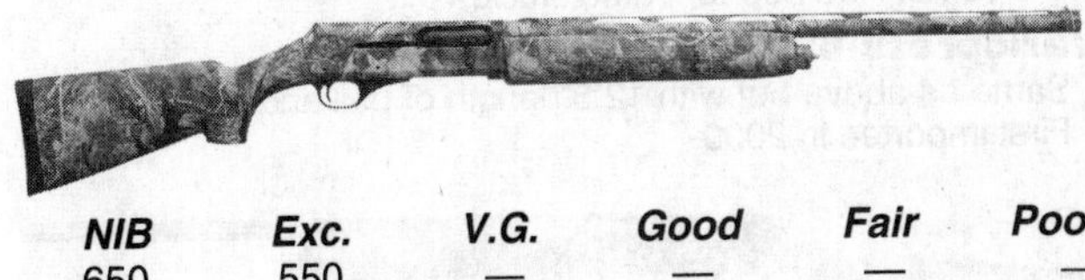

NIB	Exc.	V.G.	Good	Fair	Poor
650	550	—	—	—	—

Variomax 912 SteadyGrip

Introduced in 2005 this model features a extended pistol grip and Advantage H-D camo stock with 24" vent rib barrel and choke tubes. Weight is about 8 lbs.

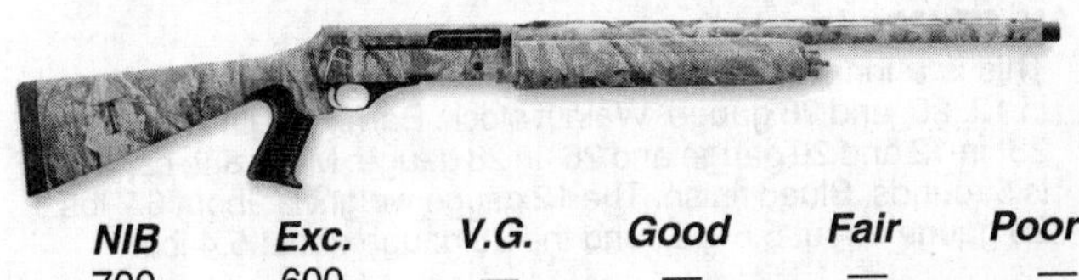

NIB	Exc.	V.G.	Good	Fair	Poor
700	600	—	—	—	—

Variopress 612 Sporting

This is a 12 gauge semi-automatic gas-operated shotgun with 30" ported barrel. Extended choke tubes. Select walnut stock with stock drop kit. Magazine capacity is 5 rounds. Weight is about 7 lbs. First imported in 2000.

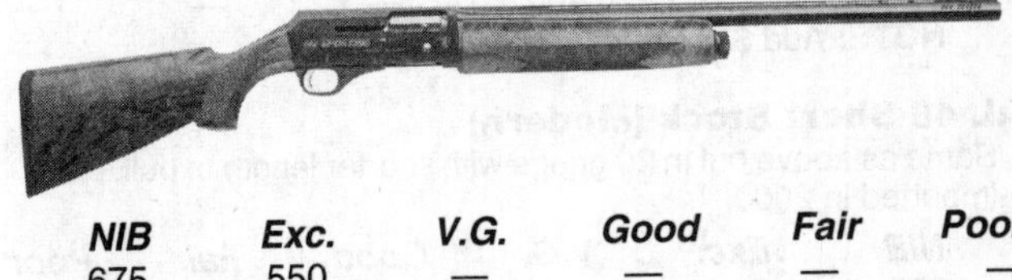

NIB	Exc.	V.G.	Good	Fair	Poor
675	550	—	—	—	—

Variopress 612 Field

This 12 gauge model is offered with barrel lengths from 24" to 28". Stock configurations are walnut, synthetic, or camo. Magazine capacity is 5 rounds. Weight is about 7 lbs. depending on barrel length.

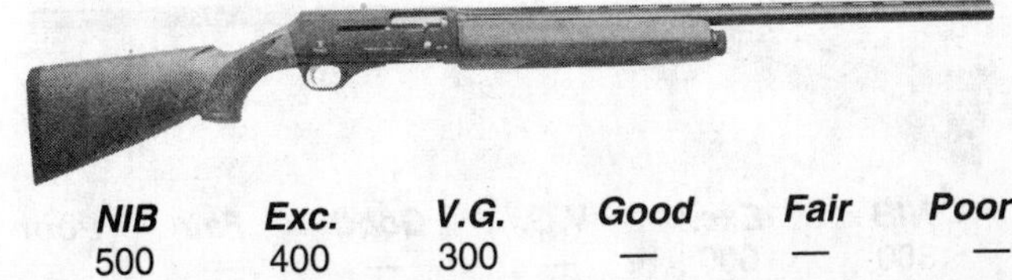

NIB	Exc.	V.G.	Good	Fair	Poor
500	400	300	—	—	—

Variopress 612 Defense

This 12 gauge gun is fitted with an 18.5" barrel and black synthetic stock. Matte black finish. Choke is cylinder. Weight is about 6.5 lbs. Magazine capacity is 5 rounds. First imported in 2000.

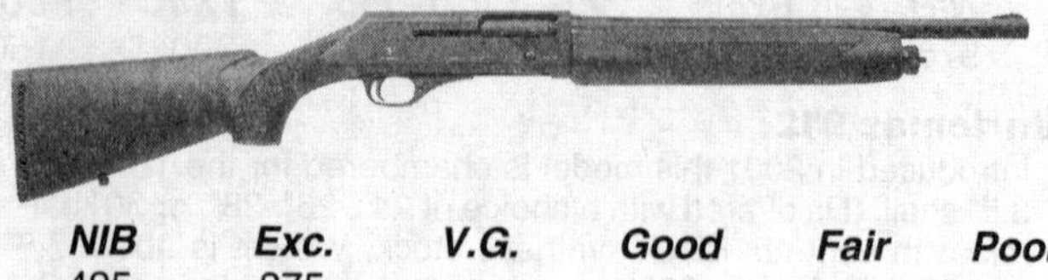

NIB	Exc.	V.G.	Good	Fair	Poor
425	375	—	—	—	—

Variopress 620 Field

This model is offered in 20 gauge with a choice of walnut or camo stock. Barrel lengths from 24" to 28". Magazine capacity is 5 rounds. Weight is about 6 lbs.

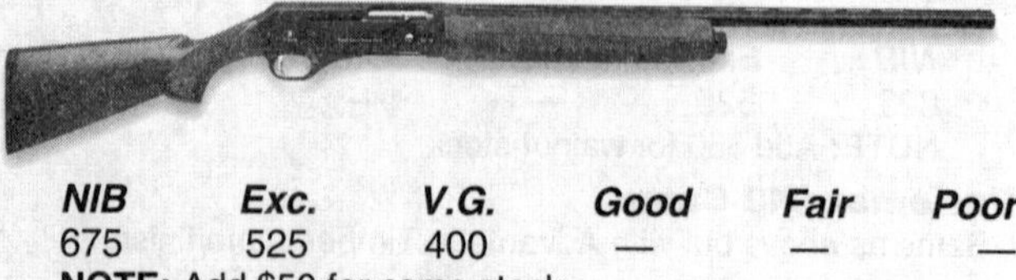

NIB	Exc.	V.G.	Good	Fair	Poor
675	525	400	—	—	—

NOTE: Add $50 for camo stock.

Variopress 620 Short Stock

Same as above but with 12.5" length of pull and walnut stock. First imported in 2000.

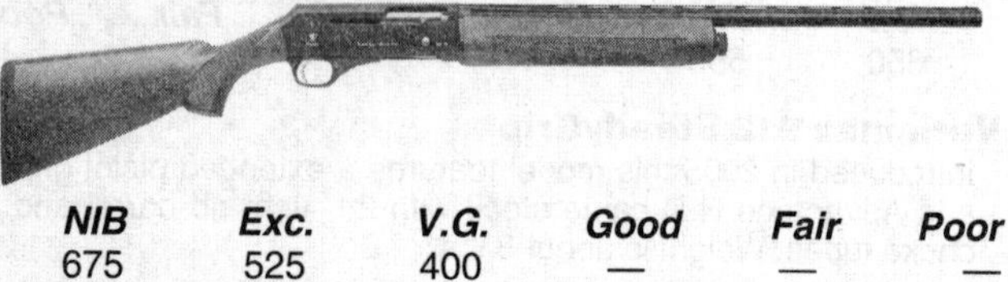

NIB	Exc.	V.G.	Good	Fair	Poor
675	525	400	—	—	—

AL 48 (Modern)

This is a long recoil operated semi-automatic shotgun offered in 12, 20, and 28 gauge. Walnut stock. Barrel lengths are 24" to 28" in 12 and 20 gauge and 26" in 28 gauge. Magazine capacity is 5 rounds. Blued finish. The 12 gauge weight is about 6.7 lbs.; 20 gauge about 5.6 lbs.; and the 28 gauge about 5.4 lbs.

NIB	Exc.	V.G.	Good	Fair	Poor
635	550	400	—	—	—

NOTE: Add $75 for 28 gauge model.

AL 48 Short Stock (Modern)

Same as above but in 20 gauge with shorter length of pull. First imported in 2000.

NIB	Exc.	V.G.	Good	Fair	Poor
635	550	—	—	—	—

AL 48 Deluxe English Stock (Modern)

Similar to the standard AL 48 but with straight grip stock. Offered in 20 and 28 gauge with 26" vent-rib barrel with choke tubes. Weight is about 5.5 lbs. Introduced in 2002.

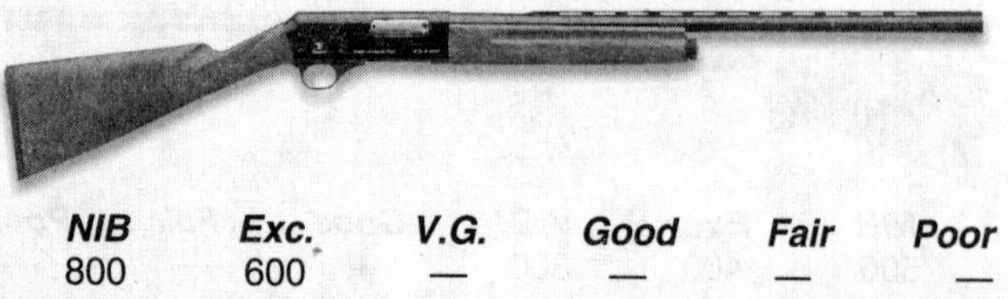

NIB	Exc.	V.G.	Good	Fair	Poor
800	600	—	—	—	—

AL 48 Deluxe (Modern)

This is a deluxe version of the AL 48 that features upgraded walnut stock and a high polish blue finish. Offered in 20 and 28 gauge with 26" barrel. Weight is about 5.5 lbs. First imported in 2000.

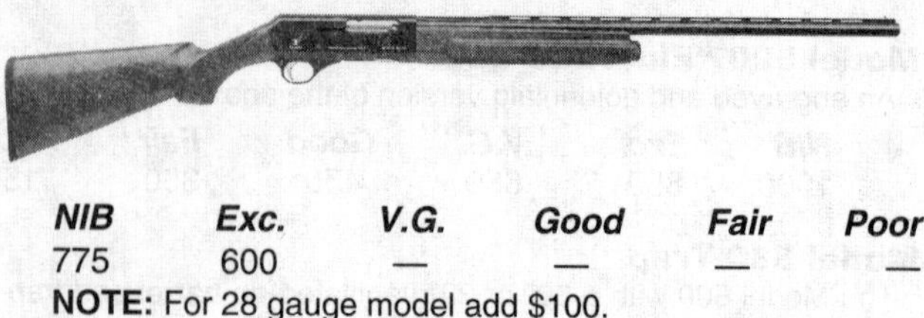

NIB	Exc.	V.G.	Good	Fair	Poor
775	600	—	—	—	—

NOTE: For 28 gauge model add $100.

Model 712

This is semi-automatic shotgun chambered for the 12 gauge 3" shell. Available with choice of 24", 26", or 28" vent rib barrels with choke tubes. Also offered in several different finishes: Weathercoat (synthetic wood), Max-4 camo and Timber HD. Choice of synthetic wood, black synthetic, or camo stock. Weight is about 6.8 lbs. to 7 lbs., depending on stock and barrel length. Introduced in 2004.

Weathercoat

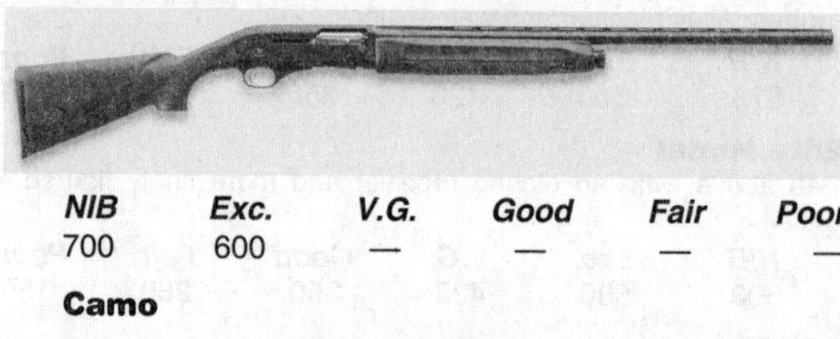

NIB	Exc.	V.G.	Good	Fair	Poor
700	600	—	—	—	—

Camo

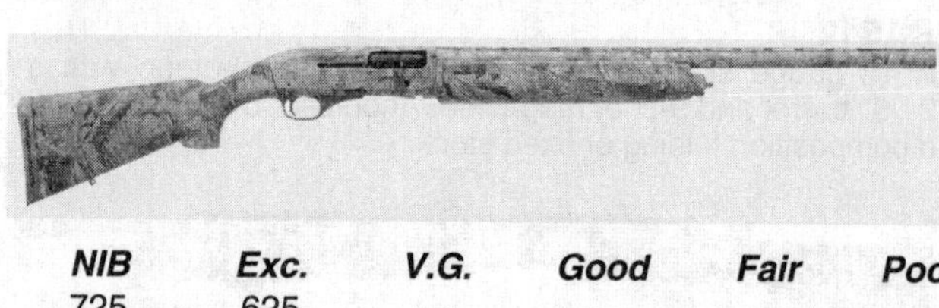

NIB	Exc.	V.G.	Good	Fair	Poor
725	625	—	—	—	—

Synthetic

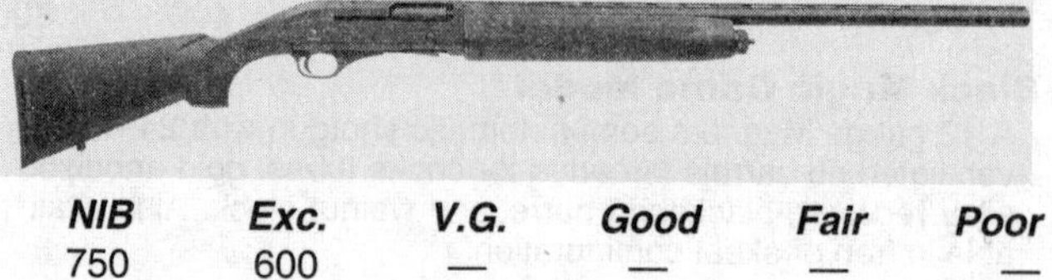

NIB	Exc.	V.G.	Good	Fair	Poor
750	600	—	—	—	—

Model 720

Similar to the Model 712 but chambered for the 20 gauge 3" shell. Offered with 24", 26", or 28" vent rib barrels. Choice of Max-4, Timber HD finish or walnut stock with 12.5" lop. Introduced in 2004.

Camo

NIB	Exc.	V.G.	Good	Fair	Poor
700	600	—	—	—	—

Walnut Short Stock

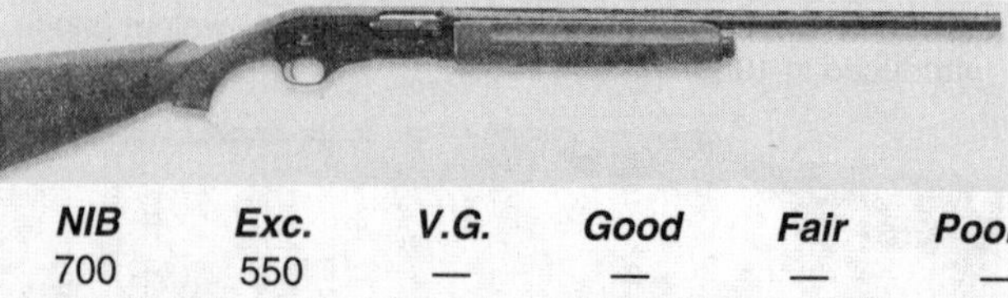

NIB	Exc.	V.G.	Good	Fair	Poor
700	550	—	—	—	—

WeatherCoat

Introduced in 2005 with 28" vent rib barrel. Weight is about 6.2 lbs.

NIB	Exc.	V.G.	Good	Fair	Poor
750	600	—	—	—	—

I-12

Introduced in 2005 this 12 gauge model is offered with 3" chambers and choice of 24", 26", or 28" vent rib barrels. Available with synthetic, walnut, Max-4, or Timber H-D stock. Choke tubes. Weight is about 7.5 lbs. depending on barrel length.

NIB	Exc.	V.G.	Good	Fair	Poor
660	500	—	—	—	—

I-12 White Gold

Similar to Inertia I-12 but with highly figured walnut stock and white gold game bird scene on a satin nickel receiver. Introduced in 2006. Available only with 28" barrel. Weight is about 7.7 lbs.

NIB	Exc.	V.G.	Good	Fair	Poor
1025	—	—	—	—	—

RIFLES

Centennial Semi-Automatic

A .22 caliber semi-automatic rifle with a 21" barrel, adjustable sights, Alloy receiver and walnut stock. Manufactured in 1968 only.

NIB	Exc.	V.G.	Good	Fair	Poor
500	350	300	250	175	125

NOTE: Deluxe Engraved Model add 20 percent.

FRANCOTTE, A.

Liege, Belgium

For pistols and revolvers SEE—AFC.

Jubilee

A 12, 16, 20, and 28 gauge Anson & Deeley boxlock double-barrel shotgun with various barrel lengths and chokes, automatic ejectors, double triggers and walnut stock.

Exc.	V.G.	Good	Fair	Poor
1650	1350	1100	850	450

No. 14

Courtesy William Hammond

Exc.	V.G.	Good	Fair	Poor
2250	1850	1600	1300	650

No. 18

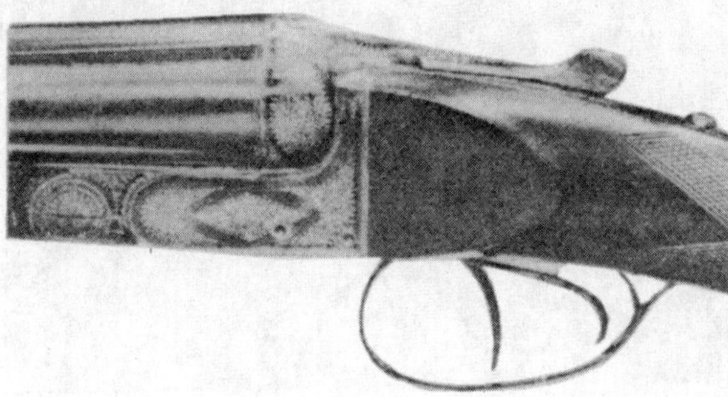

Exc.	V.G.	Good	Fair	Poor
2750	2250	2000	1500	750

No. 20

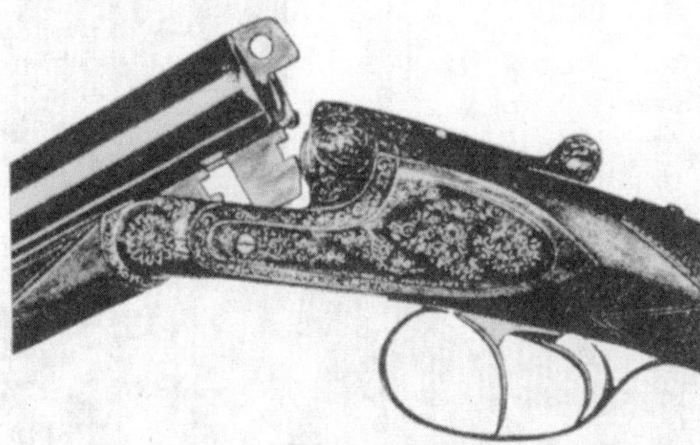

Exc.	V.G.	Good	Fair	Poor
3250	2500	2250	1750	900

No. 25

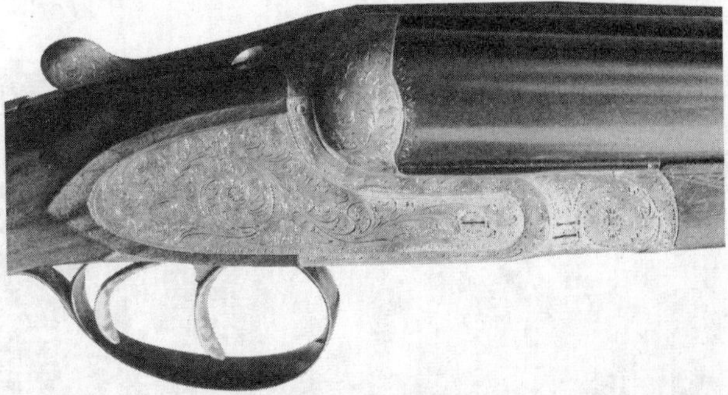

Exc.	V.G.	Good	Fair	Poor
3750	3000	2750	2000	1000

Francotte Engraving Patterns

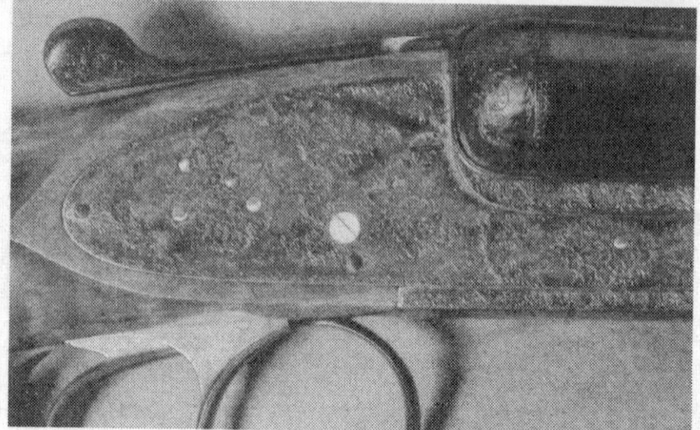

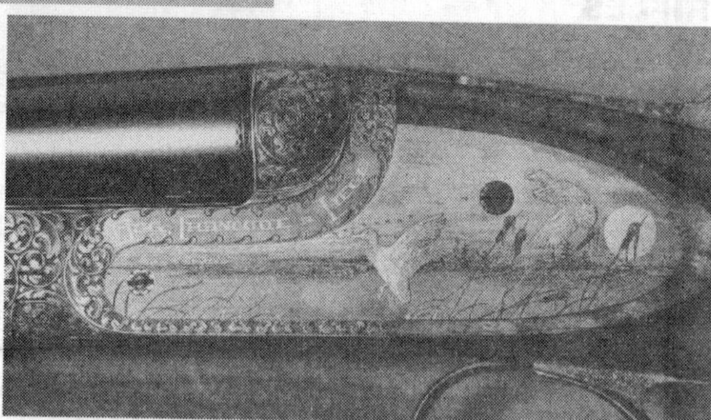

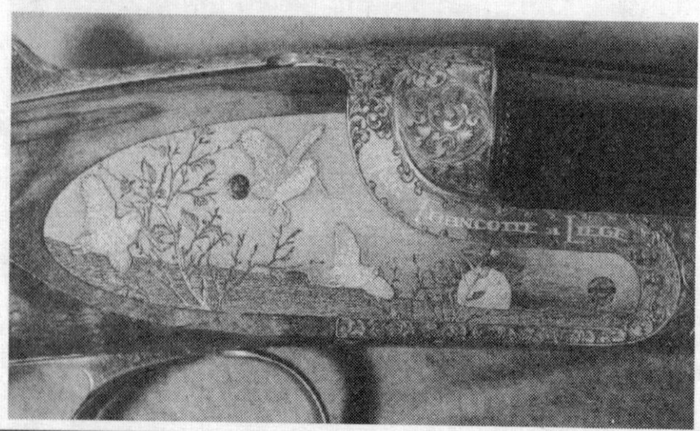

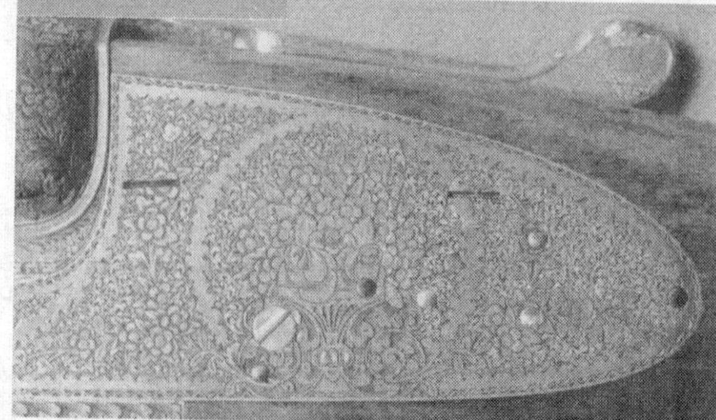

No. 30

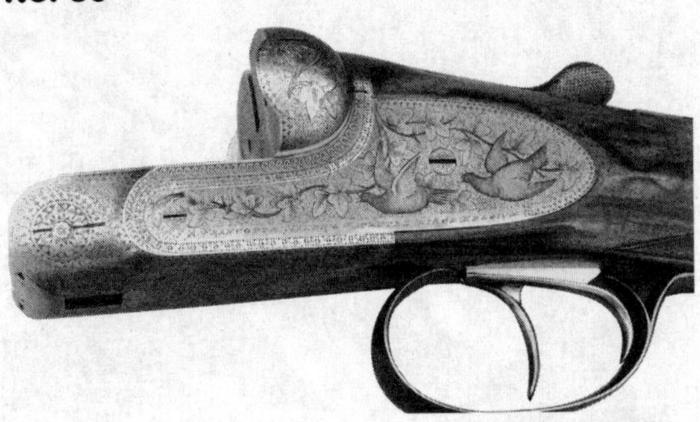

Courtesy William Hammond

Exc.	V.G.	Good	Fair	Poor
4800	4000	3500	3000	1500

Eagle Grade No. 45

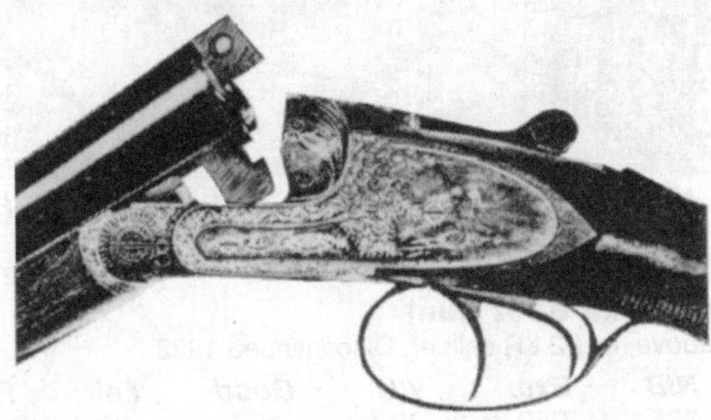

Exc.	V.G.	Good	Fair	Poor
3750	3000	2500	2000	1000

Knockabout

A plain version of the Jubilee Model in 12, 16, 20, and 28 gauge and .410 bore.

Exc.	V.G.	Good	Fair	Poor
1250	1100	850	650	500

NOTE: 20 gauge add 20 percent; 28 gauge add 30 percent; .410 add 40 percent.

Sidelock Side-by-Side

A 12, 16, 20, and 28 gauge and .410 bore sidelock shotgun ordered per customer's specifications. Extensive scroll engraving, deluxe walnut stock and finely checkered. The .410 will bring a premium of from $1,200-$1,500.

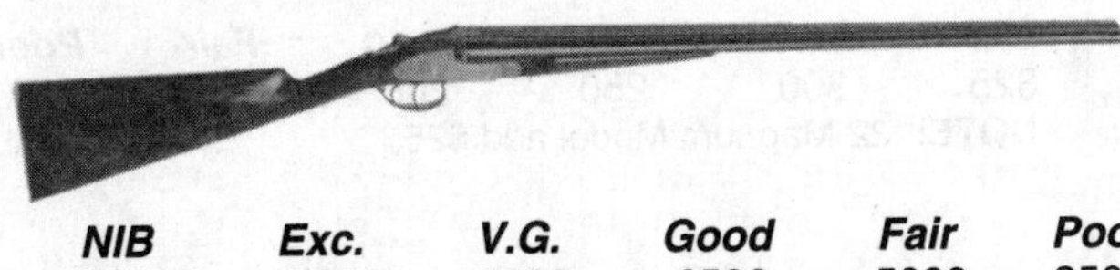

NIB	Exc.	V.G.	Good	Fair	Poor
12650	10000	8000	6500	5000	3500

Deluxe Sidelock Side-by-Side

As above, with gold-inlaid hunting scenes.

NIB	Exc.	V.G.	Good	Fair	Poor
15000	12500	10000	8000	5750	4800

CURRENTLY IMPORTED SHOTGUNS AND RIFLES

Francotte currently imports side-by-side boxlock or sidelock shotguns, double rifles, and single-shot rifles as well as bolt-action rifles into the United States through Armes De Chasse. These shotguns and rifles are all custom built to the customer's specifications. Gauge (including 24 and 32 gauge), caliber, barrel length, engraving, wood type and style are all individually produced. No two are alike. These shotguns and rifles should be individually appraised before the sale. Prices listed are subject to fluctuations in international currency.

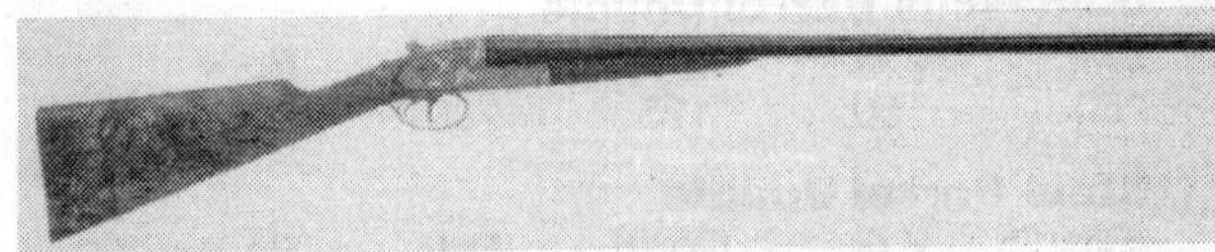

Custom Side-by-Side Shotguns

Available in 12, 16, 20, 28 gauge and .410 bore in either boxlock or sidelock actions. Barrel length, engraving, wood type and style are at the customer's discretion. Retail prices range from:

Basic Boxlock with 27.5" barrels and walnut stock with double triggers in 12, 16, and 20 gauge without engraving—$15,000

Basic Boxlock in 28 gauge or .410 bore without engraving—$11,000

Basic Boxlock with 26.5" or 28" barrels and deluxe walnut stock with scroll engraving, and double triggers in 12, 16, and 20 gauge—$20,000

Basic Boxlock in 28 gauge or .410 bore—$25,000

Prices for 24 and 32 gauge are extra. These prices do not include engraving.

Custom Double Rifles

These custom built double rifles are offered in calibers from 9.3x74R to .470 Nitro Express in boxlock or sidelock actions. Barrel length, engraving, wood type and style are at the customer's discretion. Retail prices range from:

Prices for 24 and 32 gauge are extra. These prices do not include engraving.

Boxlock in 9.3x74R, 8x57JRS and other European calibers-$11,800

Boxlock in.375 H&H and.470 NE—$15,700

Sidelock in 9.3x74R, etc.—$23,700. Sidelock in large calibers—$28,500

Custom Single-Shot Mountain Rifles

These single-shot rifles are offered in rimmed cartridges but rimless cartridge rifles can be built on special request. Barrel length, engraving, wood type and style are at the customer's discretion. Retail prices range from Boxlock in rimmed calibers—Prices start at $10,000. Sidelock in 7x65R and 7mm Rem. Mag.—Prices start at $21,000

Custom Bolt-Action Rifles

These bolt-action rifles utilize a Mauser 98 type action with adjustable trigger. They are offered in calibers from .17 Bee to .505 Gibbs. Barrel lengths are 21" to 24.5", engraving wood type and style are at the customers' discretion. Retail prices range from:

Standard bolt-action calibers: .270, .30-06, 7x64, 8x60S and 9.3x62—Prices start at $5,650

Short-action calibers: .222, .223—Prices start at $7,100

Magnum-action calibers: 7mm Rem. Mag., .300 Win. Mag., .338 Win. Mag., .375 H&H, and .458 Win. Mag.—Prices start at $6,400

African calibers: .416 Rigby, .460 Wby., .505 Gibbs—Prices start at $10,250.

NOTE: Please note that the prices listed are for the basic models. They do not reflect the extensive list of options available on these custom firearms.

FRANKLIN, C. W.

Liege, Belgium

Manufacturer of utilitarian shotguns with either exposed or enclosed hammers. Circa 1900.

Single-Barrel

Exc.	V.G.	Good	Fair	Poor
150	75	50	35	20

Damascus Barrel Double

Exc.	V.G.	Good	Fair	Poor
250	150	125	100	65

Steel Barrel Double

Exc.	V.G.	Good	Fair	Poor
300	175	150	125	90

FRANKONIAJAGD
Favorit, Germany

Favorit Standard

Chambered for various European calibers, this bolt-action rifle has a 24" barrel and set triggers. Blued, with a checkered walnut stock.

Exc.	V.G.	Good	Fair	Poor
400	275	250	175	125

Favorit Deluxe

As above, with a more finely figured stock.

Exc.	V.G.	Good	Fair	Poor
450	300	275	200	150

Safari Model

As above, in Magnum calibers.

Exc.	V.G.	Good	Fair	Poor
650	450	375	275	200

Heeren Rifle

A best quality single-shot rifle with a 26" octagonal barrel, double-set triggers, and adjustable sights. Engraved with hand checkered, high-grade walnut. Blued. Produced in a variety of calibers.

Exc.	V.G.	Good	Fair	Poor
4500	2650	2200	1700	1250

FRASER, DANIEL & SON
Edinburgh, Scotland

This renowned rifle maker was an apprentice of Alexander Henry. Fraser had retail stores at these addresses:

22 Greenside Place	1873-1874
18 Leith Walk	1874-?
4 Leith Street Terrace	?-1916

FRASER F. A. CORP.
Fraser, Michigan

Fraser .25 cal.

A .25 ACP caliber semi-automatic pistol with a 2.25" barrel and 6-round magazine. Stainless steel with black nylon grips. There is a 24 kt. gold-plated model that is worth approximately $100 additional.

NIB	Exc.	V.G.	Good	Fair	Poor
250	175	125	100	50	35

FREEDOM ARMS
Freedom, Wyoming

"Percussion" Mini-Revolver

A .22 caliber spur trigger revolver with 1", 1.75", or 3" barrel lengths, 5-shot cylinder and a bird's-head grip. Stainless steel. A belt buckle is available that houses the pistol for an additional $40.

NIB	Exc.	V.G.	Good	Fair	Poor
250	200	150	125	100	75

Bostonian (aka Boot Gun)

As above, with a 3" barrel, in .22 Magnum. Discontinued 1992.

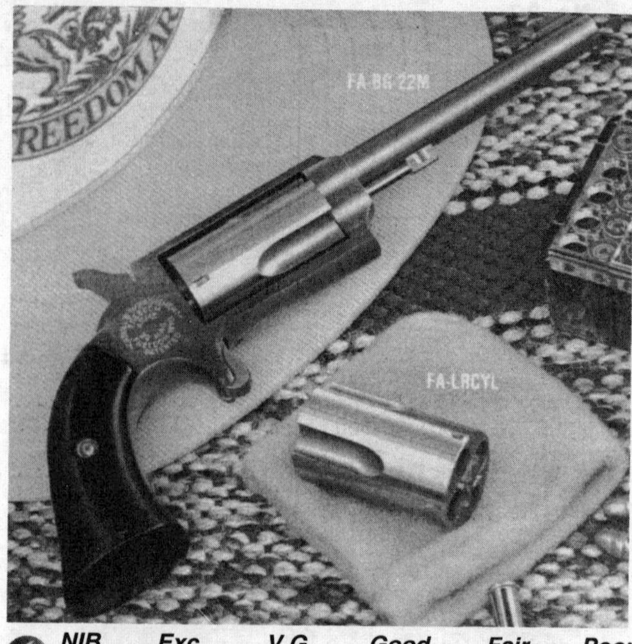

NIB	Exc.	V.G.	Good	Fair	Poor
300	250	200	125	80	60

Patriot (aka Boot Gun)

As above, in .22 LR caliber. Discontinued 1992.

NIB	Exc.	V.G.	Good	Fair	Poor
325	250	200	125	80	60

Minuteman

As above, with a 3" barrel. Discontinued in 1988.

NIB	Exc.	V.G.	Good	Fair	Poor
350	250	200	125	80	60

Ironsides

As above, in .22 Magnum with a 1" or a 1.75" barrel.

NIB	Exc.	V.G.	Good	Fair	Poor
225	200	150	100	80	60

Celebrity

As above, with the belt buckle mount for either .22 or .22 Magnum revolvers.

NIB	Exc.	V.G.	Good	Fair	Poor
325	300	250	200	150	100

NOTE: .22 Magnum Model add $25.

PREMIER AND FIELD GRADE REVOLVERS

Both grades use the same materials and machining tolerances. The difference is in the finish, standard components, and warranty.

The **Premier Grade** has a bright brushed finish, screw adjustable rear sight, laminated hardwood grips, and a limited lifetime warranty.

The **Field Grade** has a matte finish, adjustable rear sight for elevation only, Pachmayr rubber grips, and a one year warranty.

Casull Field Grade Model 83

A .454 Casull Magnum revolver with a 4.75", 6", 7.5", and a 10" barrel and standard fixed sights. Fires a 225-grain bullet. Also offered in .50 AE, .475 Linebaugh, .44 Rem. Mag, .41 Magnum, and .357 Magnum. Adjustable sights available as a $75 option. Matte stainless steel with black rubber Pachmayr grips. Introduced in 1988.

NIB	Exc.	V.G.	Good	Fair	Poor
1525	1100	800	550	—	—

NOTE: Add $75 for .454 Casull, .475 Linebaugh, or .50 AE calibers.

Casull Premier Grade Model 83

A .454 Mag., .44 Rem. Mag., .45 Win. Mag., .475 Linebaugh, and .50 AE, with replaceable forcing and walnut grips. The finish is a brush stainless steel. The adjustable sights are an extra cost option on this model as well. Offered in barrel lengths of 4.75", 6", 7.5", and 10" except for .475 Casull. .55 Wyoming Express added 2006.

NIB	Exc.	V.G.	Good	Fair	Poor
1950	1400	950	700	—	—

NOTE: Extra cylinders are available for these models in .45 Colt, .45 Win. Mag., and .45 ACP. Add $250 to the price of the gun for each cylinder. Add $75 for .454 Casull, .475 Linebaugh, or .50 AE calibers.

Model 97

This revolver is chambered for either the .357 Magnum, .45 Colt, .44 Special, and .22 Long Rifle cartridges. Available in Field or Premier grades. Available with a choice of 4.25", 5.5" or 7.5" barrel. Optional .45 ACP cylinder of .45 Colt and optional .38 Special cylinder for .357 Magnum model.

In 2004 this model was also offered in .17 HMR and .32 H&R Magnum calibers.

NIB	Exc.	V.G.	Good	Fair	Poor
1665	1250	900	600	—	—

NOTE: There are a number of extra-cost options that will affect the price. Some of these options are sights, grips, Mag-Na-Port barrels, slings and trigger overtravel screws. Add $265 for extra .38 Special, .45 ACP cylinder or .22 WMR cylinder. Add $475 for extra fitted .22 Long Rifle match grade cylinder. Add $215 for match grade chambered instead of .22 Long Rifle sport chamber.

Model 353

Chambered for .357 Magnum cartridge with choice of 4.75", 6", 7.5", or 9" barrel length. Adjustable sights. This model designation no longer used; see Model 97.

Field Grade

NIB	Exc.	V.G.	Good	Fair	Poor
1100	900	750	550	400	300

Premier Grade

NIB	Exc.	V.G.	Good	Fair	Poor
1500	1200	900	700	500	300

Signature Edition

As above, with a highly polished finish, rosewood grips, 7.5" barrel only and a fitted case. The serial numbers are DC1-DC2000. (The DC represents Dick Casull, the designer of the firearm.) A total of 2,000 were made.

NIB	Exc.	V.G.	Good	Fair	Poor
2000	1750	1500	1250	900	600

Model 252

This is a stainless steel version of the large frame revolver chambered for the .22 Long Rifle cartridge. Available in 5.12", 7.5", or 10" barrel lengths. Matte finish. This designation no longer used, see Model 97.

Silhouette Class

10" barrel.

NIB	Exc.	V.G.	Good	Fair	Poor
1700	1150	850	600	450	250

NOTE: Optional .22 magnum cylinder available for $250.

Varmint Class

5.12" or 7.5" barrel.

NIB	Exc.	V.G.	Good	Fair	Poor
1700	1150	850	600	450	250

Model 757

Introduced in 1999, this five-shot revolver is chambered for the .475 Linebaugh cartridge. Fitted with adjustable sights and offered in both Field and Premier grades. Choice of 4.75", 6", or 7.5" barrel. This designation no longer used; see Model 83.

Field Grade

NIB	Exc.	V.G.	Good	Fair	Poor
1400	1100	—	—	—	—

Premier Grade

NIB	Exc.	V.G.	Good	Fair	Poor
1800	1450	—	—	—	—

Model 654

This five-shot revolver is chambered for the .41 Magnum cartridge. Adjustable sights. Introduced in 1999. This designation no longer used; see Model 97.

Field Grade

NIB	Exc.	V.G.	Good	Fair	Poor
1325	1050	—	—	—	—

Premier Grade

NIB	Exc.	V.G.	Good	Fair	Poor
1750	1400	—	—	—	—

Model 83 .500 Wyoming Express

Similar to Model 83 but chambered in .500 Wyoming Express. Introduced 2007.

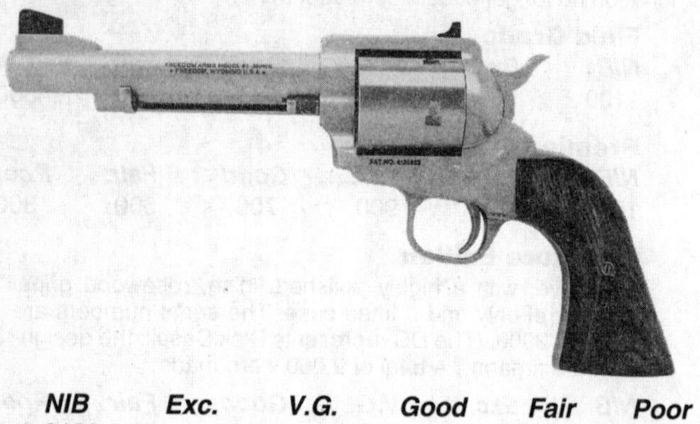

NIB	Exc.	V.G.	Good	Fair	Poor
2120	—	—	—	—	—

FREEMAN, AUSTIN T.

Hoard's Armory
Watertown, New York

Freeman Army Model Revolver

A .44 caliber percussion revolver with a 7.5" round barrel and a 6-shot unfluted cylinder with recessed nipples. Blued, case-hardened rammer and hammer, and walnut grips. The frame is marked "Freeman's Pat. Dec. 9, 1862/Hoard's Armory, Watertown, N.Y." Several thousand were manufactured in 1863 and 1864.

Exc.	V.G.	Good	Fair	Poor
—	—	5000	2000	500

FRENCH MILITARY FIREARMS

(including copies made in Liege, Belgium)
Charleville, St. Etienne, Chatellrault, Mutzig and Tulle Armories

Most of these firearms were the products of five major armories, the old Charleville Armory and St. Etienne works, and the newer armories at Chatellrault, Mutzig, and Tulle. The armory of manufacture was invariably inscribed in script upon the lock, usually preceeded by an abbreviation "Manufactire Roy le de" or M re R le de" until 1848, "M re N le de" from 1848 until 1852, and "M re Imp ale de" after 1852, respectively representing, "The Royal Manufactory at ..." "The National Manufactory at ...," and, "The Imperial Manufactory at ..." In addition to these lock markings, the specific model year was usually marked upon the barrel tang, preceded by an "M." If the model had been altered, a "T" (for "transformed") was added after the date, and if subsequently remodeled, the script ("bis" was added after that (for "again"). Date of manufacture usually appears upon the barrel, and also within the pressed circle surrounding the "touch mark" on the right side of the buttstock. Numerous inspection marks also appear on the metal parts of the gun.

The arms manufactured for the French military were widely copied in Europe's major firearms center, Liege, Belgium. The Liege gun trade, however, was based on the "factory" system. Each specialist, working out of his own cottage, manufactured one type of part on subcontract and delivered it to an assembler. Many of the final assemblers in Liege did not mark their products or did so only with crowned initials. Those that did usually marked their "products" upon the lockplates. Among the better known Liege assemblers' marks during the middle of the 19th century were ANCION & CIE/A LIEGE, A F (A. Francofte), B F (Beuret Freres), C D (probably for Charles Dandoy), D (anchor) C (probably Dejerdine & Co., Demousse & Co., or DeFooz & Co.), D L (DeLoneux) C. DANDOY/A LIEGE, A. & CH DE LONEUX DRISKET & WAROUX, G M (Gulikers Marquinay), V. GULIKERS/A LIEGE, J L (Joseph LeMille), L (anchor) C or L. LAMBIN & CIE/LIEGE, LE MILLE/A LIEGE, P.J. MALHEREBE & CIE/LIEGE, E. MUNSEUR/LIEGE, J.A. PETRY/A LIEGE, G. SCHOPEN/A LEIGE, TANNER & CIE., T. TILKEN/A/LIEGE, AND V P (Vivario- Plombeur). It should be noted, however, that these makers produced not only copies of French arms, but also accepted contracts for arms from other European powers, notably Russia, Spain, the Piedmont, Saxony, and England. Whether marked on the lock or not, all Liege barrels were required to pass a proof of strength, and having done so were marked near their breech with a small tower and the Liege black powder proof, an oval encompassing the letters "E/LG/"(star). The main French firearms produced or copied during the muzzleloading era were:

French M1816 Flintlock Musket (for Infantry/Light Infantry)

Overall length 58-1/8" to 56"; barrel length 42-7/8" to 40-1/2"; caliber .69 This musket is basically the French M1777 musket with minor improvements. Although the French did not subsequently alter this model to percussion, the Kingdom of Wurtemberg obtained several thousand from the Charleville Armory, which were altered to percussion and then rifled and sighted after their own models of 1842 and 1855, the barrel receiving a long-range French-style rear sight after rifling. As many as 2,000 of these may have been imported into the United States in 1862 by Marcellus Hartley.

In flintlock

Exc.	V.G.	Good	Fair	Poor
—	—	3250	1350	700

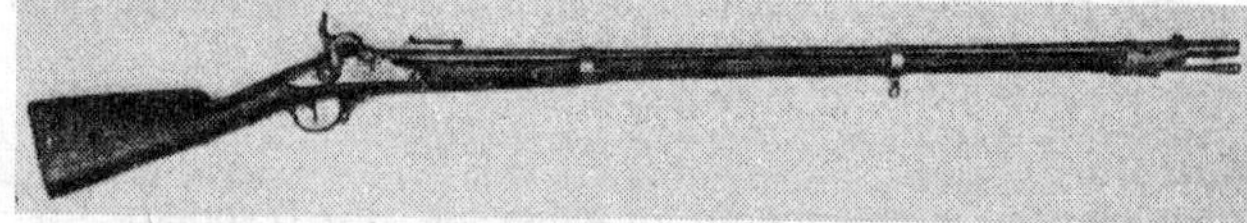

Courtesy Milwaukee Public Museum, Milwaukee, Wisconsin

Altered to percussion, rifled and sighted

Exc.	V.G.	Good	Fair	Poor
—	—	1150	400	275

French M1822 Flintlock Musket (for Infantry/Light Infantry)

Overall length 58" to 55-7/8"; barrel length 42-5/8" to 40-5/8" (40-5/8" for both types if "T bis"); caliber .69 (.71 for rifled versions). The French M1822 musket in either full infantry length or the shorter version for light infantry (voltiguers), set the pattern for most of the muskets subsequently adopted by the European powers during the second quarter of the 19th Century.

In the 1840s many were "transformed," i.e. altered to percussion by adding a convex bolster to the upper right side of the barrel near the breech for a cone and replacing the flintlock battery with a percussion hammer. With the adoption of the Minie ball projectile, it was determined to further upgrade these arms; however, because a new caliber had been adopted, the old barrels were deemed too thin to both enlarge and rifle. Accordingly new barrels were made in .71 caliber. The percussioned version was copied in Liege (by Ancion, Francotte, and Falise & Trapmann) for the Kingdom of Piedmont as its M1844 musket and M1860 rifle musket. These are distinguished by the enlarged tip of the hammer spur, a peculiar rear sight added to the breech and tang, and Liege markings.

In flintlock

Exc.	V.G.	Good	Fair	Poor
—	—	3250	1350	700

Altered to percussion, and rifled

Exc.	V.G.	Good	Fair	Poor
—	—	1150	400	275

French M1822 Cavalry Flintlock Pistol (and "T bis")

Overall length 13-1/4"; barrel length 7-7/8"; caliber .69 (.71 in "T bis"). The M1822 cavalry or horse pistol served as the secondary arm of the French mounted forces, with a pair assigned to each horseman to be kept in saddle holsters astride the pommel of the saddle. Like the M1822 muskets, these were altered ("transformed") to percussion after 1842 in the same manner as the muskets. In 1860, the ordnance department decided to rifle them as well ("transformed again"—hence "Tbis") but this required a new barrel since the adoption of the new caliber (.71) precluded rifling the thin old barrels.

In flintlock

Exc.	V.G.	Good	Fair	Poor
—	—	1750	600	375

In percussion and rifled

Exc.	V.G.	Good	Fair	Poor
—	—	850	450	250

French M1822 Cavalry and Lancer Flintlock Musketoons (and "T")

Overall length 34-5/8"; barrel length 19-5/8"; caliber .69. The main difference between the carbines carried by the cavalry and that of the lancers was the manner of slinging, with the latter having sling rings attached to the upper band and to a projection set into the buttstock. The ramrod was carried separately, consequently there was no inletting of the forestock. After 1842, both types were altered to percussion in the same manner as the M1822 muskets and pistols.

In flintlock

Exc.	V.G.	Good	Fair	Poor
—	—	1750	600	375

In percussion and rifled

Exc.	V.G.	Good	Fair	Poor
—	—	850	450	250

French M1829 Artillery Flintlock Carbine (and "T bis")

Overall length 37-1/4" to 38-1/4" (for "T bis"); barrel length 23-5/8"; caliber .69/.71 (for "T bis"). The carbine for artillerists was similar in configuration to that for the cavalry and lancers, differing primarily in having a ramrod in a channel below the barrel. After 1841, these arms were altered to percussion and after 1846 a bayonet lug with long guide was added to the right side of the barrel to accommodate the French M1847 yatagan saber bayonet. At the same time, a number of these arms were sighted, rifled, and a "tige" (a metal column or pillar) was inserted into the breech of the bore that permitted the arm to fire the Thouvenin projectile. After 1857 new barrels were manufactured that permitted the introduction of the standard Minie projectile of .71 caliber.

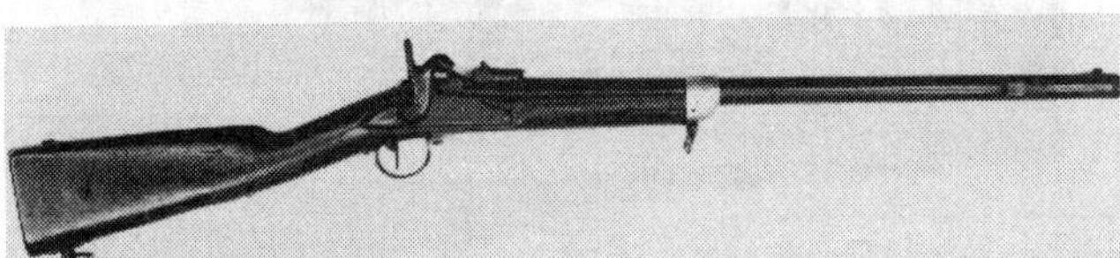

Courtesy Milwaukee Public Museum, Milwaukee, Wisconsin

Exc.	V.G.	Good	Fair	Poor
—	—	1750	600	375

In percussion and rifled

Exc.	V.G.	Good	Fair	Poor
—	—	850	450	250

French M1837 Rifle 4" Carbine a la Poncharra")

Overall length 51-5/8"; barrel length 34-1/4"; caliber .69. The first of the French percussion arms for the general services, the M1837 rifle was designed on the Poncharra system. In this system, a chamber of lesser diameter than the bore was affixed to the barrel. A projectile of the diameter across the lands and its "sabot" was rammed into the barrel, and upon striking the lip of the chamber theoretically expanded into the rifling.

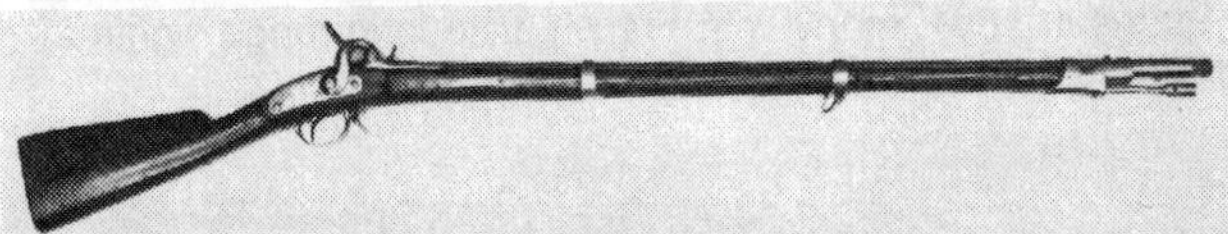

Courtesy Milwaukee Public Museum, Milwaukee, Wisconsin

Exc.	V.G.	Good	Fair	Poor
—	—	2250	950	450

French M1840 Rifle ("Carbine de Munition")

Overall length 48-1/8"; barrel 32-5/8"; caliber .71. After the success of the M1837 carbine, the rifle went into production at the armories at Mutzig and Chatellrault as the M1840 "carbine Tierry" or "carbine de munition." It was modified in 1842. The design was modified by adding a projection to the lower end of the buttplate. Herman Boker of New York City imported 25,000 of the M1840 rifles in 1862, but the slow twist of the rifling caused them to be classified as "4th class" weapons and none were issued.

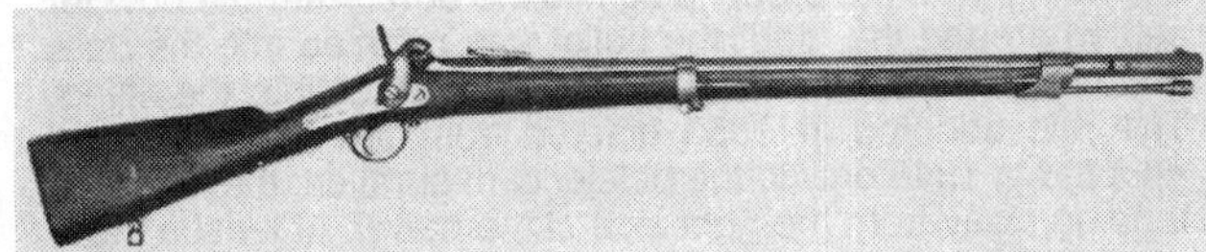

Courtesy Milwaukee Public Museum, Milwaukee, Wisconsin

Exc.	V.G.	Good	Fair	Poor
—	—	1750	600	300

French M1840 and M1842 Percussion Muskets (Infantry/Light Infantry)

Overall length 58-1/4" to 55-1/4"; barrel length 42-5/8" to 40-1/2"; caliber .71. The M1840 and M1842 muskets were the first percussion arms adopted for general infantry service in the French army, both being distinguished by employing back action percussion locks. The M1840 was distinguished from the M1842 by having a screwed in "patent" breech integrating the bolster, while the bolster of the M1842 musket was forged integral to the barrel, both flush with the right side of the barrel. The M1842 musket was later "transformed" to the M1842T by rifling the barrel with four broad grooves. The Belgian gun trade copied the M1842T both with and without the block rear sight that stood on the breechplug tang.

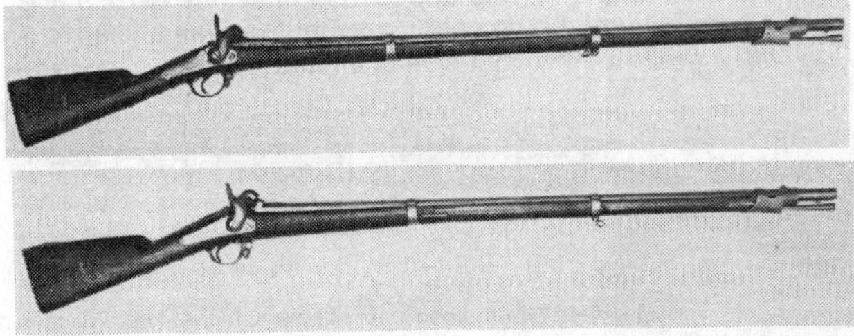

Courtesy Milwaukee Public Museum, Milwaukee, Wisconsin

Exc.	V.G.	Good	Fair	Poor
—	—	1150	500	275

French M1853 Musket, M1853 "T" and M1857 Rifle-Muskets

Overall length 58-1/8" (M1853 infantry musket only) to 55-1/4"; barrels 42-5/8" (M1853 only) to 40-1/2"; caliber .71. In 1853, the M1842 series of arms was modified slightly, the most visible difference being the right face of the bolster, which stands away from the right side of the barrel. After the adoption of the

"Minie ball" as the main projectile of the French army, the new M1857 rifle musket was introduced. It was essentially the same as the M1853 "T" light infantry musket but its bore was rifled with four broad grooves. Subsequent to the adoption of the M1857 rifle musket the M1853 muskets were "transformed," the light infantry muskets simply by rifling them, and the infantry muskets by shortening them to 55-1/4" with 40-1/2" barrels and rifling them. Both types were widely copied by the Belgian gun trade, who exported thousands to the United States in 1861, many with French style long range sights affixed to the barrels.

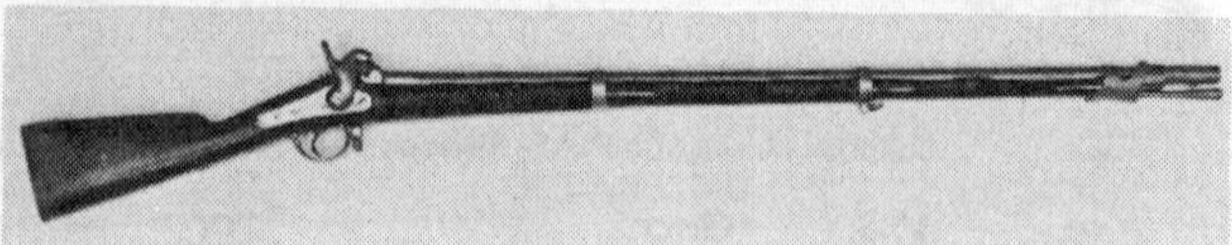

Courtesy Milwaukee Public Museum, Milwaukee, Wisconsin

Exc.	V.G.	Good	Fair	Poor
—	—	1150	500	300

French M1846 and M1853 Rifles ("Carbine a tige")

Overall length 49-1/4"; barrel length 34-1/4"; caliber .71. In 1846 the French abandoned the Delvigne chamber rifles in favor of a different method of compressing the projectile into the rifling, that of M. Thouvenin. In Thouvenin's system, the chamber with a lip was replaced with a metal column or pillar "a tige" extending from the breechplug into the bore. After the powder settled around the "tige" the bullet was rammed into the bore and compressed against the tige to expand it into the rifling. The rifle adopted in 1853 differed from the original model adopted in 1846 only in the bolster configuration, the latter extending away from the right side of the barrel. At least a thousand Belgian made "carbines a tige" were imported into the Confederacy in 1861. Accordingly, Belgian "tige" rifles with proven Southern usage should command a premium over those without such history.

Exc.	V.G.	Good	Fair	Poor
—	—	1750	600	350

French M1853 "T" and M1859 Rifles ("Carbine de Vincennes")

Overall length 49-1/4"; barrel length 34-1/4"; caliber .71. With the adoption of the self expanding "Minie ball" in 1857, the French ordnance soon adopted a rifle which was suitable for it, the M1859 "carbine de Vincennes." Beginning in 1860, the M1853 "tige" rifles were "transformed" by the removal of the pillars from the breechplugs and fitting them with the rear sight leaves of the M1859 rifle. The M1853 "T" and M1859 French rifle was widely copied in Liege, and thousands were exported to the United States during the American Civil War, while most of the French made M1859 rifles reposed in French arsenals. Like the M1840 and M1846 and M1853 rifles, the M1859 rifle took a long yatagan blade saber bayonet that was affixed to a lug with a guide on the right side of the barrel.

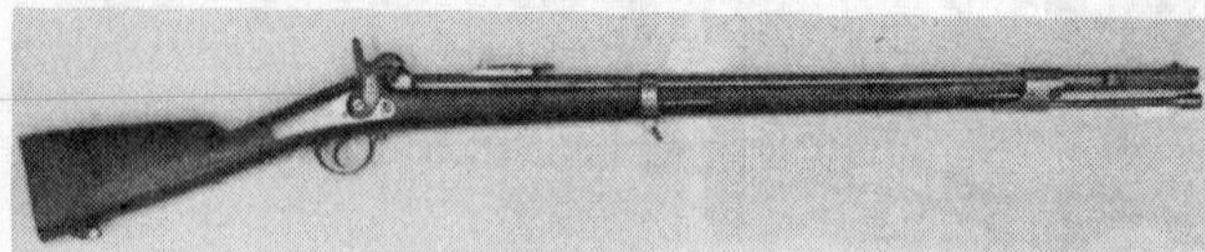

Courtesy Milwaukee Public Museum, Milwaukee, Wisconsin

Exc.	V.G.	Good	Fair	Poor
—	—	1750	650	425

FRENCH STATE

Manufactured by MAS: Etienne, France
SACM: Cholet, France
MAC: Chatellerault, France
MAT: Tulle, France

NOTE: For history, technical data, descriptions, and prices see the *Standard Catalog of Military Firearms* under France.

FRIGON

Clay Center, Kansas

An importer of guns manufactured by Marocchi of Italy.

FT I

A 12 gauge boxlock single-barrel shotgun with a 32" or 34" ventilated rib barrel, full choke, automatic ejector and interchanged stock. Blued. Introduced in 1986.

NIB	Exc.	V.G.	Good	Fair	Poor
950	750	650	550	450	300

FTC

As above, with two sets of barrels (a single ventilated rib trap barrel and a set of Over/Under ventilated rib barrels). In a fitted case. Introduced in 1986.

NIB	Exc.	V.G.	Good	Fair	Poor
1750	1400	1150	800	650	500

FS-4

A four gauge set (12, 20, and 28 gauge and .410 bore). Introduced in 1986.

NIB	Exc.	V.G.	Good	Fair	Poor
2500	2100	1750	1500	1100	750

FROMMER

SEE—FEG (Fegyver Es Gazkeszulekgyar)

FRUHWIRTH

Austria

M1872 Fruhwirth System Rifle

An 11mm bolt-action rifle with a 25" barrel and 6-shot magazine. Blued with a full-length walnut stock.

Exc.	V.G.	Good	Fair	Poor
500	300	250	175	100

FUNK, CHRISTOPH

Suhl, Germany

Christoph Funk began his gun business before 1900. The vast majority of long guns were best quality. Some collectors believe that J.P. Sauer built receivers for Funk but this is not known for certain. Funk produced shotguns, shotgun-rifle combinations, and double rifles. Some were exported to England and the U.S. Most of the U.S. imports are in the more common North American calibers such as .300 Savage, 30-30, 32-20 Winchester, and 12 or 16 gauge. Most are found with only a right-hand extension arm which locks into the receiver, but some higher grades have both extension arms. The quality of these guns is extremely high. Guns were probably not made after 1940. Quality of engraving and caliber determines value. American calibers will command a higher price. Prices listed are for American calibers.

Courtesy Jim Cate

Exc.	V.G.	Good	Fair	Poor
2800	2000	1250	600	400

FURR ARMS

Prescott, Arizona
J. & G. Sale, Inc.
Prescott, Arizona

In addition to producing reproductions of various cannon, this company also manufactured one-tenth to three-quarter scale reproductions of Gatling guns. Prospective purchasers are advised to secure a qualified appraisal prior to acquisition.

FYRBERG, ANDREW

Worcester and Hopkinton, Massachusetts

Double-Barrel Shotguns

Fyrberg did work for Iver Johnson and C.S. Shattuck Co. of Hatfield, Mass. He began producing a hammerless double about 1902, a well designed boxlock with coil mainsprings. An estimated 2,000 were produced at Hopkinton and Worcester, Mass. Some have been made at Meriden, Conn. Sears cataloged the Fyrberg guns in 1902 to about 1908.

Exc.	*V.G.*	*Good*	*Fair*	*Poor*
500	400	300	200	150

Revolvers

A 3"-barreled .32 caliber and a 3.5" .38 caliber revolver with round ribbed barrels and round butts. The grips bear the trademark, "AFCo." This model was most likely made by Iver Johnson for Andrew Fyrburg.

Exc.	*V.G.*	*Good*	*Fair*	*Poor*
200	125	100	75	50

G M
(Gulikers Marquinay of Liege, Belgium)
SEE—French Military Firearms

GABBET-FAIRFAX, H.
Birmingham, England

Mars

Designed by Hugh Gabbet-Fairfax, this semi-automatic pistol was first produced on an experimental basis by Webley & Scott Revolvers in the 1890s. After Webley gave up on the idea an extremely limited number were built by the Mars Automatic Pistol Syndicate, Ltd., 1897 to 1905. The pistol was produced in four calibers; the 8.5mm Mars, 9mm Mars, .45 Mars Short Case, and .45 Mars Long Case. This was the most powerful handgun cartridge of its time and remained so until well after World War II. It is estimated that only about 80 of these pistols were ever produced.

Courtesy James Rankin

Exc.	V.G.	Good	Fair	Poor
30000	22000	15000	8000	6000

NOTE: Webley examples are worth a premium.

GABILONDO Y CIA
SEE—Llama

GABILONDO Y URRESTI
Guernica, Spain
Elgoibar, Spain
SEE—Llama

This Spanish firm was founded in 1904 to produce inexpensive revolvers of the Velo-Dog type. Sometime around 1909 the firm began to manufacture the Radium revolver. In 1914 the company produced a semi-automatic pistol distributed as the Ruby. This pistol soon became the mainstay of the company with orders of 30,000 pistols a month for the French army. With the end of WWI Gabilondo Y Urresti moved to Elgoeibar, Spain. The company produced a Browning 1910 replica pistol until the early 1930s. It was at this point that Gabilondo began to manufacture a Colt Model 1911 copy that became known as the Llama. For information of specific Llama models see the Llama section. The pistols listed reflect the pre-Llama period and are so marked with the trade name of that particular model. The monogram "GC" frequently appears on the grips but not on the slide.

Velo-Dog Revolver

A 6.35mm double-action revolver with a 1.5" barrel, folding trigger and concealed hammer. Blued with walnut grips. Manufactured from 1904 to 1914.

Exc.	V.G.	Good	Fair	Poor
175	125	100	75	50

Radium

A semi-automatic pistol in caliber 7.65mm. Produced both for the commercial and military market in the Ruby style. "Radium" is stamped on the slide as well as the top of each grip plate.

Courtesy James Rankin

Exc.	V.G.	Good	Fair	Poor
225	175	150	100	70

Ruby

A 7.65mm caliber semi-automatic pistol. Discontinued in 1930.

Exc.	V.G.	Good	Fair	Poor
225	175	150	100	75

Bufalo 6.35mm

A semi-automatic pistol in caliber 6.35mm. A copy of the Browning Model 1906 with a squeeze grip safety. Has "Bufalo" stamped on the slide and the Gabilondo logo along with a buffalo's head on each side of the grip plates. Manufactured between 1918 and 1925.

NOTE: The spelling of "Bufalo" is at it appears on the pistol.

Courtesy James Rankin

Exc.	V.G.	Good	Fair	Poor
200	150	125	100	75

Bufalo 7.65mm

A semi-automatic pistol in caliber 7.65mm. Patterned after the Browning Model 1910 with a squeeze grip safety. There were two models, with either a 7-round or a 9-round magazine. The model with the 9-round magazine usually is fitted with wood grips and a lanyard ring. A buffalo's head is inset in each grip plate. Manufactured between 1918 and 1925.

Courtesy James Rankin

Exc.	V.G.	Good	Fair	Poor
225	175	125	100	75

Bufalo 9mmK

A semi-automatic pistol in caliber 9mmK. Nearly the same pistol as the 7.65mm model but fitted with a grip safety. "Bufalo" is stamped on the slide and the Gabilondo logo and buffalo's head are on each grip plate. Manufactured between 1918 and 1925.

Courtesy James Rankin

Exc.	V.G.	Good	Fair	Poor
225	175	125	100	70

Danton 6.35mm

A semi-automatic pistol in caliber 6.35mm. Patterned after the Browning Model 1906 with a grip safety. "Danton" appears on the slide as well as the grips. The Gabilondo logo is on each grip plate. Manufactured between 1925 and 1931.

Courtesy James Rankin

Exc.	V.G.	Good	Fair	Poor
225	175	125	100	75

Danton War Model

A semi-automatic pistol in caliber 7.65mm. Similar to the Bufalo above and it was made with and without a grip safety. It came in two models with 9- and 20-round magazines. Fitted with a lanyard ring. "Danton" stamped on the slide and the grips. The Gabilondo log is on each side of the grip plates. Manufactured between 1925 and 1931.

Courtesy James Rankin

Nine-Round Magazine

Exc.	V.G.	Good	Fair	Poor
250	200	150	100	75

Twenty-Round Magazine

Exc.	V.G.	Good	Fair	Poor
500	300	250	200	100

Perfect

This semi-automatic pistol was chambered for the 6.35mm and 7.65mm cartridges. It was a cheap, low-priced pistol marketed by Mugica. These pistols usually have the word "Perfect" on the grips. The slide may be stamped with the name MUGICA but many are not.

Exc.	V.G.	Good	Fair	Poor
225	175	150	100	75

Plus Ultra

This pistol is chambered for the 7.65mm cartridge and was built from 1925 to 1933. It had a 20-round magazine that gave the pistol an unusual appearance. "Plus Ultra" appears on the slide and the grips. A Gabilondo logo is on each grip plate. Equipped with a lanyard ring.

Courtesy James Rankin

Exc.	V.G.	Good	Fair	Poor
1800	1500	1000	500	250

GALAND, C.F.

Liege, Belgium

Galand, Galand & Sommerville, Galand Perrin

A 7mm, 9mm, and 12mm caliber double-action revolver with a 6-shot cylinder, open frame, a unique ejection system that, by means of rotating a lever downward from the trigger guard, causes the barrel and cylinder to slide forward, leaving the ejector and the spent cases behind. Circa 1870.

Courtesy Bonhams & Butterfields

Exc.	V.G.	Good	Fair	Poor
—	500	275	200	150

Velo-Dog

A 5.5mm Velo-Dog caliber fixed trigger and guard double-action revolver with open-top design. Later models (.22 and 6.35mm caliber) feature folding triggers and no trigger guards.

Exc.	V.G.	Good	Fair	Poor
200	125	100	75	50

Le Novo

As above, with a concealed hammer and in 6.35mm caliber.

Exc.	V.G.	Good	Fair	Poor
225	175	125	100	75

Tue-Tue

A .22 short, 5.5mm Velo-Dog, and 6.35mm caliber double-action revolver with a concealed hammer, folding trigger, and a swing-out cylinder with central extractor. Introduced in 1894.

Exc.	V.G.	Good	Fair	Poor
225	175	150	100	75

GALAND & SOMMERVILLE

Liege, Belgium

SEE—Galand

GALEF

Zabala Hermanos & Antonio Zoli

Spain

Zabala Double

A 10, 12, 16, and 20 caliber boxlock shotgun with a 22" to 30" barrel and various chokes. Hardwood stock. Add 40 percent for 10 gauge.

Exc.	V.G.	Good	Fair	Poor
300	200	150	100	75

Companion

A folding 12 to .410 bore single-shot underlever shotgun with a 28" or 30" barrel.

Exc.	V.G.	Good	Fair	Poor
175	100	75	50	25

Monte Carlo Trap

A 12 gauge underlever single-shot shotgun with a 32" ventilated rib barrel.

Exc.	V.G.	Good	Fair	Poor
225	175	150	100	75

Silver Snipe, Golden Snipe, and Silver Hawk

SEE—Antonio Zoli

GALENA INDUSTRIES INC.

Sturgis, South Dakota

In 1998 Galena Industries purchased the rights to use the AMT trademark and manufacturing rights to many, but not all, AMT designs. For AMT models made by AMT see that section. This company is no longer in business.

AMT Backups

This model features a double-action-only trigger system and is offered in both stainless steel and matte black finish. The small frame .380 Backup weighs 18 oz. with its 2.5" barrel. The large frame Backups are fitted with a 3" barrel and are offered in 9mm, .38 Super, .357 Sig., .40 S&W, .400 CorBon, and .45 ACP. Weights are approximately 23 oz. and magazine capacity is 5 to 6 rounds, depending on caliber.

Galena .380 DAO Backup

Galena .45 ACP DAO Backup

NIB	Exc.	V.G.	Good	Fair	Poor
320	225	175	—	—	—

NOTE: Add $50 for .38 Super, .357 Sig, and .400 CorBon.

Automag II

This semi-automatic pistol is chambered for the .22 WMR cartridge. Offered in 3.38", 4.5", or 6" barrel lengths. Magazine capacity is 9 rounds except for the 3.38" model where capacity is 7 rounds. Weight is about 32 oz.

Automag II with 4.5" barrel

NIB	Exc.	V.G.	Good	Fair	Poor
425	300	250	—	—	—

Automag III

This pistol is chambered for the .30 Carbine cartridge. Barrel length is 6.38" and weight is about 43 oz. Stainless steel finish.

NIB	Exc.	V.G.	Good	Fair	Poor
525	400	325	—	—	—

Automag IV

This model is chambered for the .45 Winchester Magnum cartridge. It is fitted with a 6.5" barrel and has a magazine capacity of 7 rounds. Weight is approximately 46 oz.

NIB	Exc.	V.G.	Good	Fair	Poor
600	450	350	—	—	—

Automag .440 CorBon

This semi-automatic pistol is chambered for the .440 CorBon cartridge and fitted with a 7.5" barrel. Magazine capacity is 5 rounds. Finish is matte black. Weight is about 46 oz. Checkered walnut grips. Introduced in 2000. Special order only.

NIB	Exc.	V.G.	Good	Fair	Poor
900	750	—	—	—	—

Galena Accelerator

This model has a 7" barrel built on a 1911 frame and is chambered for the .400 CorBon. Magazine capacity is 7 rounds. Weight is about 46 oz. Finish is stainless steel.

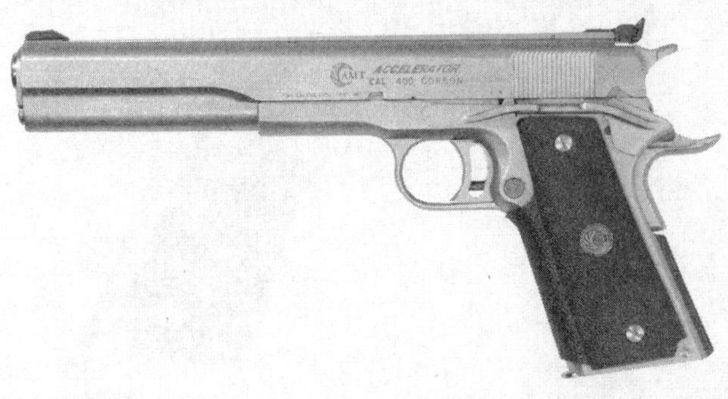

NIB	Exc.	V.G.	Good	Fair	Poor
550	425	350	—	—	—

Galena Hardballer

This pistol is based on the Colt Model 1911 design and is chambered for the .45 ACP cartridge. It is fitted with a 5" barrel and has a magazine capacity of 7 rounds. Finish is stainless steel. Adjustable trigger and beveled magazine well. Also offered chambered for the .40 S&W and .400 CorBon cartridges. Weight is about 38 oz.

NIB	Exc.	V.G.	Good	Fair	Poor
445	325	275	—	—	—

Galena Longslide

This model is chambered for the .45 ACP cartridge and fitted with a 7" barrel. Magazine capacity is 7 rounds with weight about 46 oz. Finish is stainless steel.

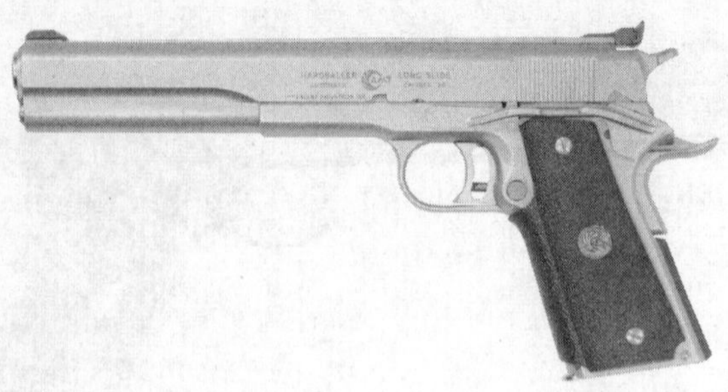

NIB	Exc.	V.G.	Good	Fair	Poor
525	400	325	—	—	—

Galena Commando

The Cammando is chambered for the .40 S&W cartridge and fitted with a 4" barrel. Magazine capacity is 8 rounds. Weight is about 38 oz. Finish is stainless steel.

NIB	Exc.	V.G.	Good	Fair	Poor
425	300	250	—	—	—

GALESI, INDUSTRIA ARMI

Brescia, Italy

Rino Galesi Armi, Collebeato, Italy, manufactured shotguns, revolvers, and automatic pistols. The firm's name changed from Rino Galesi Armi to Industria Armi Galesi, to Rigarmi di Rino Galesi. Their semi-automatic pistols were designated by model year, model number, and a 500 Series. Most models named in the 500 Series came after the firm changed its name to Industria Armi Galesi.

Model 1923

A 6.35mm and 7.65mm caliber semi-automatic pistol. Has a squeeze grip safety and wood grip plates with crest. Model 1923 is stamped on the slide.

Courtesy James Rankin

Exc.	V.G.	Good	Fair	Poor
250	175	125	75	50

Model 1930

A 6.35mm and 7.65mm caliber semi-automatic pistol. A very few were made in 1946 in 9mm parabellum. Based on the 1910 Browning design. Blued with plastic grips. The slide marked "Brevetto Mod. 1930."

Courtesy James Rankin

Exc.	V.G.	Good	Fair	Poor
250	175	100	75	50

9mm Parabellum

Exc.	V.G.	Good	Fair	Poor
600	500	400	300	100

Model 6

Updated Model 1930. Manufactured approximately 1938 to 1948 in calibers; 22 Short, .22 Long, .22 Long Rifle, 6.35mm, 7.65mm, and 9mm Short.

Courtesy James Rankin

Exc.	V.G.	Good	Fair	Poor
350	175	100	75	50

Model 9

Manufactured from approximately 1947 to 1956 in calibers .22 Short, .22 Long, .22 Long Rifle, 6.35mm, 7.65mm, and 9mm Short. Also, listed under the 500 Series.

Courtesy James Rankin

Exc.	V.G.	Good	Fair	Poor
295	175	100	75	50

GALIL
Israel Military Industries
Israel

Model AR

NIB	Exc.	V.G.	Good	Fair	Poor
2800	2400	2000	1500	900	700

Model ARM

NIB	Exc.	V.G.	Good	Fair	Poor
3000	2700	2000	1500	900	700

Sniper Rifle

NIB	Exc.	V.G.	Good	Fair	Poor
8500	7500	6000	4000	3000	2000

Hadar II

NIB	Exc.	V.G.	Good	Fair	Poor
1300	1100	800	650	500	400

GALLAGER
Richardson & Overman
Philadelphia, Pennsylvania

Gallager Carbine
A .50 caliber single-shot percussion carbine with a 22.25" barrel, saddle ring and walnut stock. Blued and case hardened. Approximately 23,000 were made during the Civil War.

Percussion Model
As above, in .56-62 rimfire caliber. Approximately 5,000 of this model were made.

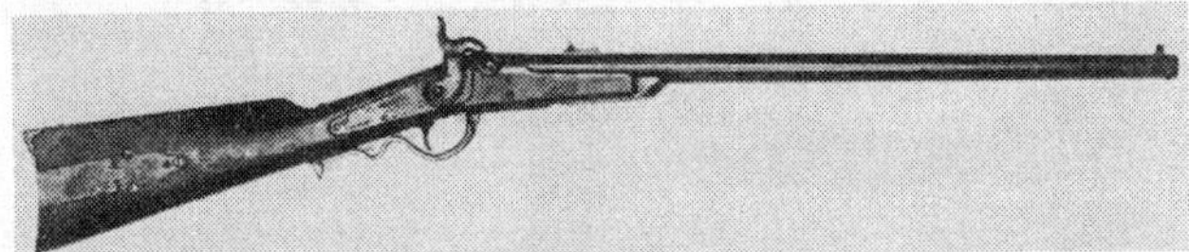

Courtesy Milwaukee Public Museum, Milwaukee, Wisconsin

Exc.	V.G.	Good	Fair	Poor
—	3250	2000	1250	500

Spencer Cartridge Model

Exc.	V.G.	Good	Fair	Poor
—	2750	1500	950	400

GAMBA, RENATO
Gardone V. T., Italy

SIDE-BY-SIDE SHOTGUNS

Hunter Super
A 12 gauge Anson & Deeley boxlock double-barrel shotgun with a variety of barrel lengths and chokes, double triggers and extractors. Engraved and silver-plated.

NIB	Exc.	V.G.	Good	Fair	Poor
1250	900	700	550	450	250

Principessa
A 12 or 20 gauge boxlock shotgun. Engraved, checkered stock.

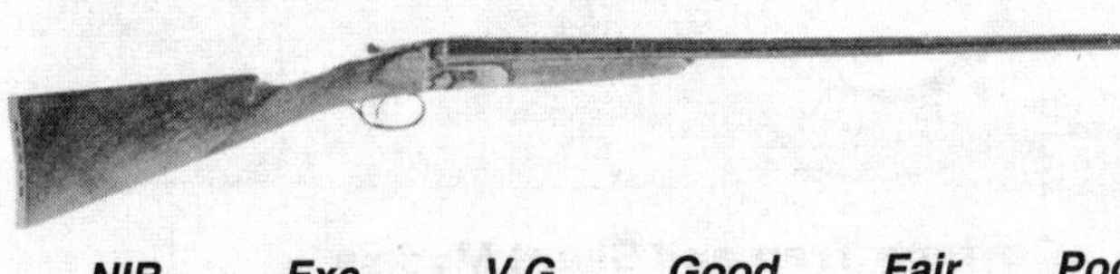

NIB	Exc.	V.G.	Good	Fair	Poor
1850	1250	900	700	500	250

Oxford 90
A 12 or 20 gauge sidelock shotgun with various barrel lengths and chokes, the Purdey locking system, double triggers, and automatic ejectors. Walnut stock.

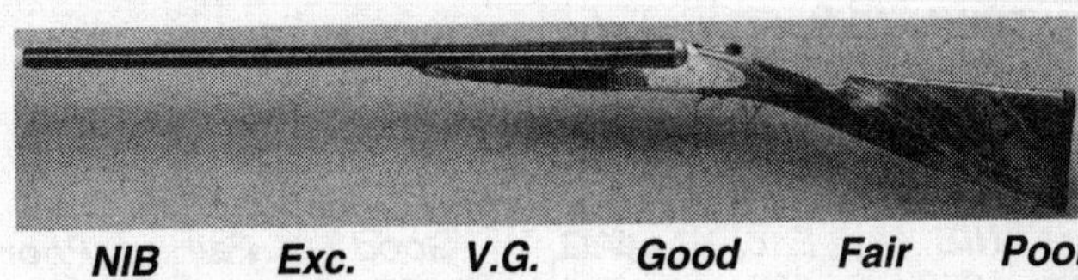

NIB	Exc.	V.G.	Good	Fair	Poor
4250	3250	1700	900	600	300

Oxford Extra
Same as above but with fine engraving.

NIB	Exc.	V.G.	Good	Fair	Poor
5200	4000	2250	1500	900	450

Gamba 624 Prince
Fitted with a Wesley Richards-type frame, select walnut stock, and fine hand engraving. Offered in 12 gauge with 28" barrels.

NIB	Exc.	V.G.	Good	Fair	Poor
4800	3900	2500	1500	850	400

Gamba 624 Extra
Same as above but with deep floral engraving.

NIB	Exc.	V.G.	Good	Fair	Poor
8000	5000	4500	2500	1250	600

London
A 12 or 20 gauge Holland & Holland sidelock shotgun with various barrel lengths and chokes, double- or single-selective trigger, automatic ejectors. Walnut stock.

NIB	Exc.	V.G.	Good	Fair	Poor
7000	5500	4500	2500	1250	700

London Royal
As above with engraved hunting scenes.

NIB	Exc.	V.G.	Good	Fair	Poor
8000	6500	5000	3750	2000	950

Ambassador Gold and Black
A 12 and 20 gauge Holland & Holland sidelock shotgun with various barrel lengths and choke combinations, single-selective trigger, automatic ejectors, and a single gold line engraved on the barrels and the frame. Walnut stocks.

NIB	Exc.	V.G.	Good	Fair	Poor
25000	19000	13500	9500	5000	2500

Ambassador Executive
Gamba's best quality shotgun produced in 12 or 20 gauge to the customer's specifications.

NIB	Exc.	V.G.	Good	Fair	Poor
28000	20000	15000	10000	5000	2500

OVER-AND-UNDER SHOTGUNS

Country Model
A 12 and 20 gauge Over/Under shotgun with 28" or 30" barrels with ventilated rib, double triggers, extractors, and walnut stock.

NIB	Exc.	V.G.	Good	Fair	Poor
650	550	400	300	275	200

Grifone Model
A 12 and 20 gauge Over/Under shotgun with 26", 28", or 30" ventilated-rib barrels, a single-selective trigger, and automatic ejectors. The boxlock action is silver-plated, with walnut stock. Available with screw-in chokes, and this would add 10 percent to the values.

NIB	Exc.	V.G.	Good	Fair	Poor
800	650	550	350	250	200

Europa 2000

A 12 gauge Over/Under shotgun in various barrel lengths and choke combinations, single-selective trigger, and automatic ejectors. Engraved, silver-plated, boxlock action with false sideplates and walnut stock.

NIB	Exc.	V.G.	Good	Fair	Poor
1250	900	700	550	350	250

Grinta Trap and Skeet

A 12 gauge Over/Under shotgun with 26" Skeet or 30" Full choke barrels, a single-selective trigger, automatic ejectors, and some engraving. Walnut stock.

NIB	Exc.	V.G.	Good	Fair	Poor
1350	900	700	550	350	250

Victory Trap and Skeet

As above, but more finely finished.

NIB	Exc.	V.G.	Good	Fair	Poor
1650	1150	850	600	400	250

Edinburg Match

As above, with slightly different engraving patterns.

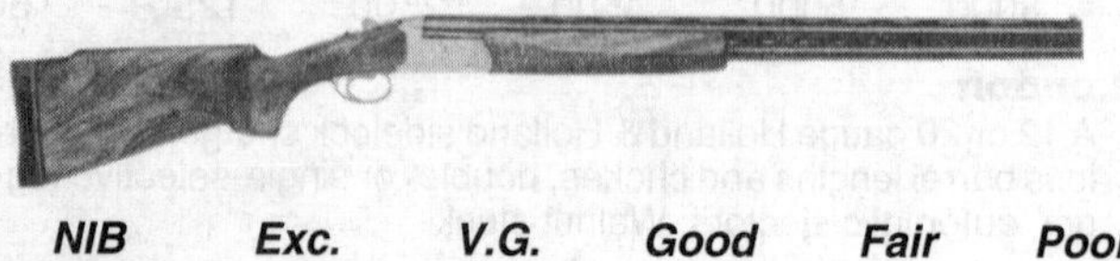

NIB	Exc.	V.G.	Good	Fair	Poor
1250	1000	800	600	400	250

Boyern 88 Combination Gun

A 12 gauge combination Over/Under rifle/shotgun with double triggers, and extractors. Engraved game scenes and coin-finished with walnut stock.

NIB	Exc.	V.G.	Good	Fair	Poor
1250	900	700	500	400	250

DAYTONA SERIES

This is a competition shotgun, first introduced into the US in 1986 as the Type I. The Type I was available in different configurations with the base model selling for about $4,000 until 1991. In 1994 Gamba introduced the Daytona in a wide variety of configurations and grades under a new designation called the Type II. The primary difference was in the location of the stock bolt. Only about 80 Daytona Type II shotguns are allocated to the US per year. They are a high quality shotgun with an excellent reputation. Prices are listed for 12 gauge guns. 20 gauge guns are available on special request.

Daytona Trap

Offered in 12 gauge with 30" or 32" barrels. Select walnut stock with hand checkering. Removable trigger group, improved Boss lock-up, and boxlock receiver.

NIB	Exc.	V.G.	Good	Fair	Poor
5900	4750	3000	2250	1200	600

Daytona Sporting

Available in 12 gauge with 30" barrel with screw-in chokes and single-selective trigger.

NIB	Exc.	V.G.	Good	Fair	Poor
4000	3250	2500	1900	1200	700

Daytona Skeet

Offered in 12 gauge with 29" barrels and single-selective trigger.

NIB	Exc.	V.G.	Good	Fair	Poor
4000	3250	2500	1900	1200	700

Daytona America Trap

Offered in 12 gauge with 30" or 32" barrels, high adjustable rib, adjustable stock, and single trigger.

NIB	Exc.	V.G.	Good	Fair	Poor
4000	3250	2500	1900	1200	700

Daytona Game

Offered in 12 gauge with 28" barrels and single trigger.

NIB	Exc.	V.G.	Good	Fair	Poor
3900	3500	3000	2250	1200	700

NOTE: Add $300 for black frame with gold inlaid names and logo.

Daytona Grade 6 Engraving

Fine English scroll hand engraving edged with gold line work.

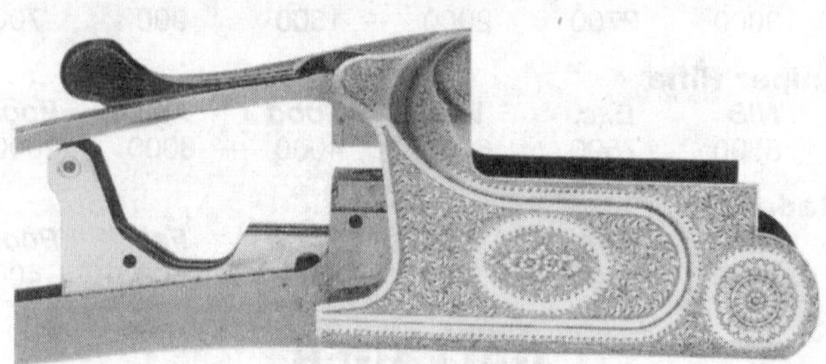

Daytona Trap and Skeet Models

NIB	Exc.	V.G.	Good	Fair	Poor
13000	5000	4000	3000	1500	700

Daytona Sporting Model

NIB	Exc.	V.G.	Good	Fair	Poor
13500	5000	4000	3000	1500	700

Daytona Grade 5 Engraving

Deep relief floral engraving with gold inlaid griffons.

Daytona Trap and Skeet Models

NIB	Exc.	V.G.	Good	Fair	Poor
14000	9000	6500	5000	2500	1200

Daytona Sporting Model

NIB	Exc.	V.G.	Good	Fair	Poor
14500	9000	6500	5000	2500	1200

Daytona Grade 4 Engraving

A flying eagle in a landscape and very fine English scroll by master engravers.

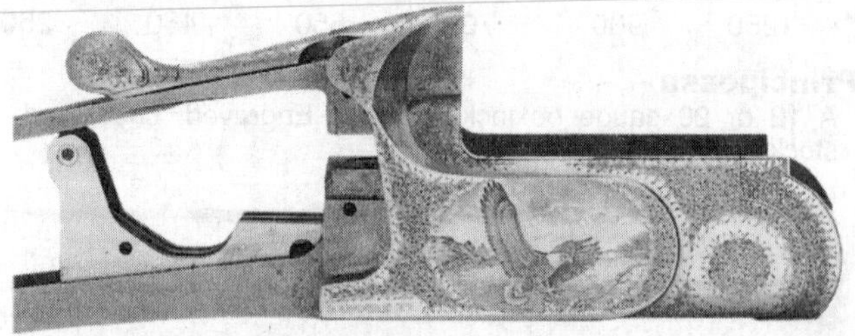

Daytona Trap and Skeet Models

NIB	Exc.	V.G.	Good	Fair	Poor
16250	10000	7500	5500	3000	1500

Daytona Sporting Model

NIB	Exc.	V.G.	Good	Fair	Poor
16750	10000	7500	5500	3000	1500

Daytona SL Grade 3 Engraving

Fitted with sideplates with engraved game scenes and fine English scroll by master engravers.

Daytona Trap and Skeet Models

NIB	Exc.	V.G.	Good	Fair	Poor
18750	15000	11000	7500	3500	1750

Daytona Sporting Model

NIB	Exc.	V.G.	Good	Fair	Poor
19250	11000	9000	6500	3500	1750

Daytona Game

NIB	Exc.	V.G.	Good	Fair	Poor
18750	11000	9000	6500	3500	1750

Daytona SLHH Grade 2 Engraving

Fitted with sideplates and Boss lock-up system, automatic ejectors, figured walnut stock, and fine game scene engraving signed by a master. Offered in 12 gauge with 28" barrels.

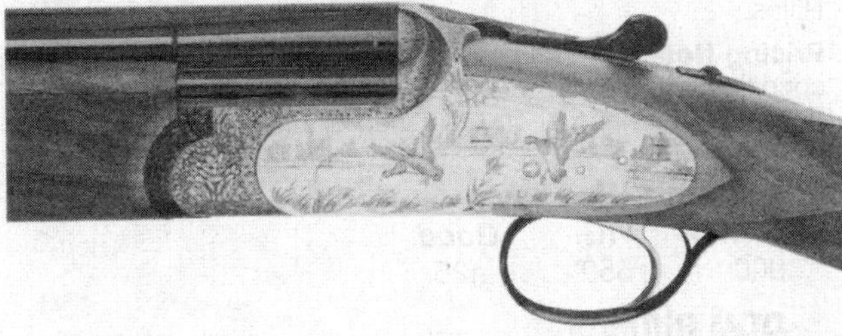

NIB	Exc.	V.G.	Good	Fair	Poor
36250	16000	12500	9500	6000	3000

Daytona SLHH Grade 1 Gold Engraving

Same as above but with gold inlaid game scenes and floral-style engraving signed by master engraver. Offered in 12 gauge with 28" barrels.

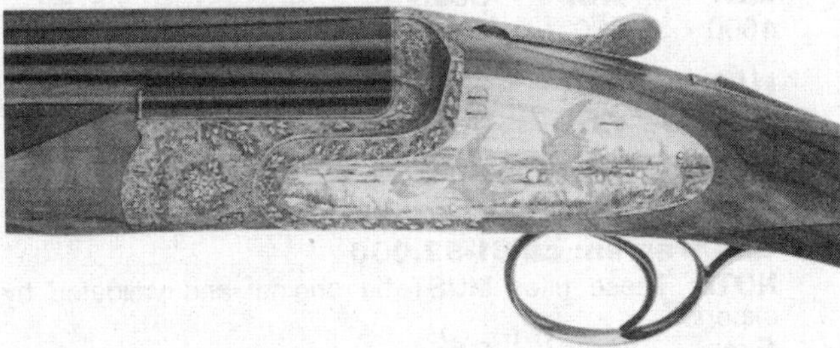

NIB	Exc.	V.G.	Good	Fair	Poor
43500	17000	13000	9500	5500	2500

Daytona SLHH "One of Thousand"

Same as above but game scene is executed at customers direction and is a totally custom ordered gun. Available in all configurations.

NIB	Exc.	V.G.	Good	Fair	Poor
106000	40000	—	—	—	—

Concorde Game Shotguns

This over-and-under model is offered as a slightly less expensive alternative to the Daytona Series guns. The base gun is available with a blued or chromed action. Extra barrel are interchangeable in both 12 and 20 gauges with 28" barrels and single triggers.

NIB	Exc.	V.G.	Good	Fair	Poor
6000	4250	3000	1500	750	450

Concorde Trap

Available in 12 gauge with 30" or 32" barrels with single trigger.

NIB	Exc.	V.G.	Good	Fair	Poor
2250	2000	1500	1000	600	450

Concorde Skeet

Available in 12 gauge with 29" barrels and single trigger.

NIB	Exc.	V.G.	Good	Fair	Poor
6000	4250	3000	1500	750	450

Concorde Sporting

Offered in 12 gauge with 30" barrels, screw-in chokes, and single-selective trigger.

NIB	Exc.	V.G.	Good	Fair	Poor
6100	2900	2000	1500	900	500

Concorde Game Grade 7 Engraving

Game scene engraving with fine English scroll.

NIB	Exc.	V.G.	Good	Fair	Poor
8700	4000	3250	2250	1200	600

Concorde Game Grade 8 Engraving

English scroll engraving.

NIB	Exc.	V.G.	Good	Fair	Poor
6250	3000	2500	1750	1000	500

Concorde 2nd Generation

Similar to the Concorde series but with fixed trigger group. Black or chrome frame. Automatic ejectors. Select walnut stock. Choice of 12 or 20 gauge with 28" or 30" barrels and single trigger. Introduced in 2002.

NIB	Exc.	V.G.	Good	Fair	Poor
6100	4850	—	—	—	—

Le Mans

This model is chambered for the 12 gauge shell and fitted with a choice of 28" or 30" barrels. Automatic ejectors. Single-selective trigger. Five choke tubes. Introduced in 2002.

NIB	Exc.	V.G.	Good	Fair	Poor
1750	1200	—	—	—	—

Hunter II

This 12 gauge model has an alloy frame with reinforced barrel with automatic ejectors. Five choke tubes. Single-selective trigger. Barrel lengths of 26" to 27.5". Introduced in 2002.

NIB	Exc.	V.G.	Good	Fair	Poor
1600	1100	—	—	—	—

RIFLES

Safari Express

A 7x65R, 9.3x74R, or .375 H&H caliber boxlock double-barrel rifle with 25" barrels, open sights, double triggers, automatic ejectors, and a coin-finished scroll engraved receiver. Walnut stock.

NIB	Exc.	V.G.	Good	Fair	Poor
5500	4000	2500	1500	750	350

Mustang

A 5.6x50, 6.5x57R, 7x65R, .222 Rem., .270 Win., or .30-06 caliber sidelock single barrel rifle with double-set triggers, engraved sidelock action and walnut stock.

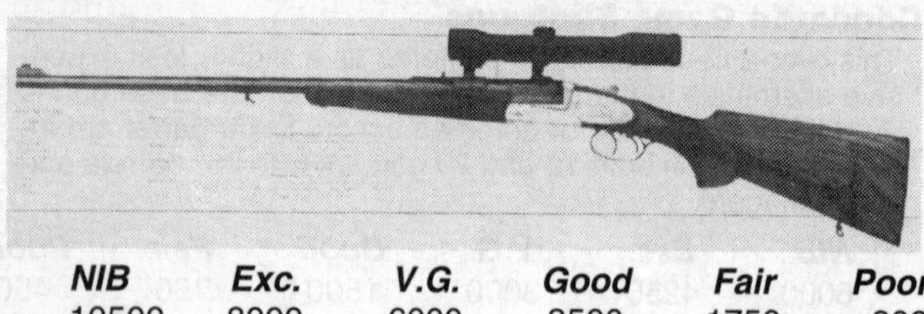

NIB	Exc.	V.G.	Good	Fair	Poor
10500	8000	6000	3500	1750	800

RGZ 1000

7x64, .270 Win., 7mm Rem. Mag., and .300 Win. Mag. caliber Mauser 98 bolt-action with a 20.5" barrel. Walnut pistol grip stock with a cheekpiece.

NIB	Exc.	V.G.	Good	Fair	Poor
1100	900	750	550	400	200

RGX 1000 Express

As above, with double-set triggers and a 23.75" barrel.

NIB	Exc.	V.G.	Good	Fair	Poor
1250	950	750	550	400	200

PISTOLS

SAB G90

A 7.65 Parabellum or 9mm caliber double-action semi-automatic pistol with a 4.75" barrel, and 15-shot magazine. Blued or chrome-plated with walnut grips.

NIB	Exc.	V.G.	Good	Fair	Poor
575	450	350	300	250	175

SAB G91 Compact

As above, with a 3.5" barrel and a 12-shot magazine.

NIB	Exc.	V.G.	Good	Fair	Poor
550	400	325	275	225	150

Trident Fast Action

A .32 S&W or .38 Special caliber double-action revolver with a 2.5" or 3" barrel and 6-shot cylinder. Blued, with walnut grips.

NIB	Exc.	V.G.	Good	Fair	Poor
500	400	300	250	200	150

Trident Super

As above, with a 4" ventilated-rib barrel.

NIB	Exc.	V.G.	Good	Fair	Poor
550	400	325	275	225	150

Trident Match 900

As above, with 6" heavy barrel, adjustable sights and target type, walnut grips.

NIB	Exc.	V.G.	Good	Fair	Poor
850	700	550	400	350	200

GARAND
(U.S. M1 Rifle)
U.S. Rifle, CAL. M1 (Garand)

NOTE: For history, technical data, descriptions, and prices see the *Standard Catalog of Military Firearms* under United States, Rifles.

Pricing Note: Prices listed are for rifles in original, unaltered condition. Rifles also must include sale papers if necessary. For rifles that have been refinished or restored deduct about 50 percent.

Rebuilt Rifle, any manufacture

Exc.	V.G.	Good
900	550	425

DCM Rifles

Exc.	V.G.	Good
850	575	450

Navy Trophy Rifles U.S.N. Crane Depot Rebuild

Exc.	V.G.	Good
1800	1000	900

AMF Rebuild

Exc.	V.G.	Good
1000	900	750

H&R Rebuild

Exc.	V.G.	Good
900	800	700

Springfield Armory Production
Gas trap sn: ca 81-52,000

NOTE: These rifles MUST be original and validated by experts.

Exc.	V.G.	Good
40000	35000	25000

Gas tap/modified to gas port

Exc.	V.G.	Good
5000	3500	2500

Pre-Dec. 7, 1941 gas port production pn sn: ca 410,000

Exc.	V.G.	Good	Fair	Poor
4000	2200	1300	—	—

WWII Production sn: ca 410,000-3,880,000

Exc.	V.G.	Good	Fair	Poor
1400	1100	900	750	500

Post-WWII Production sn: ca 4,200,000-6,099,361

Exc.	V.G.	Good	Fair	Poor
1100	850	650	500	450

Winchester Educational Contract sn: 100,000-100,500

Exc.	V.G.	Good	Fair	Poor
10000	6000	4500	—	—

Winchester sn: 100,501-165,000

Exc.	V.G.	Good	Fair	Poor
6500	4500	3000	—	—

Winchester sn: 1,200,00-1,380,000

Exc.	V.G.	Good	Fair	Poor
5500	4500	2500	—	—

Winchester sn: 2,305,850-2,536,493

Exc.	V.G.	Good	Fair	Poor
3500	2800	1500	—	

Winchester sn: 1,601,150-1,640,000 "WIN-13"

Exc.	V.G.	Good	Fair	Poor
3500	2200	1800	1500	850

Harrington & Richardson Production

Exc.	V.G.	Good	Fair	Poor
1800	1200	900	—	—

International Harvester Production

Exc.	V.G.	Good	Fair	Poor
2200	1500	800	—	—

International Harvester/with Springfield Receiver (postage stamp)

Exc.	V.G.	Good
2800	1500	1000

International Harvester/with Springfield Receiver (arrow head)

Exc.	V.G.	Good
2800	1500	1000

International Harvester/with Springfield Receiver (Gap letter)

Exc.	V.G.	Good
2800	1500	1000

International Harvester/with Harrington & Richardson Receiver

Exc.	V.G.	Good
1900	1200	900

British Garands (Lend Lease)

Exc.	V.G.	Good	Fair	Poor
1300	1200	875	—	—

M1 Garand Cutaway

Exc.	V.G.	Good	Fair	Poor
3000	2500	1000	600	500

NOTE: For examples with documentation add 300 percent.

SCOPE VARIANTS (SNIPER RIFLES)

NOTE: Sniper rifles must have sales or varification papers.

M1C

Exc.	V.G.	Good
10000	8000	5000

MC 1952 (USMC Issue) M1D

Exc.	V.G.	Good
3800	3000	2000

National Match

Type I

Exc.	V.G.	Good
4500	2500	1800

Type II

Exc.	V.G.	Good
3200	2200	1500

GARATE, ANITUA

Eibar, Spain

Charola

A 5.5mm Clement semi-automatic pistol with the magazine located in front of the trigger and with an exposed hammer.

Courtesy James Rankin

Exc.	V.G.	Good	Fair	Poor
1500	1200	750	500	400

Cosmopolite

A .38 caliber copy of the Colt Police Positive. Manufactured from 1920 to 1930.

Exc.	V.G.	Good	Fair	Poor
250	150	125	100	75

El Lunar

Resembling the Colt Police Positive in 8mm Lebel caliber, this revolver was made for the French government in 1915 and 1916.

Exc.	V.G.	Good	Fair	Poor
300	175	150	125	100

G.A.C.

A copy of the Smith & Wesson Military & Police revolver, manufactured between 1930 and 1936, in .32-20 caliber. Marked "G.A.C. Firearms Mfg. Co."

Exc.	V.G.	Good	Fair	Poor
250	150	125	100	75

"Modelo Militar"

A copy of the Smith & Wesson Triple Lock/New Century N-frame revolver chambered in .44 Special. Marked "G.A.C.."

Exc.	V.G.	Good	Fair	Poor
300	250	200	175	75

Express or Danton

A 7.65mm caliber "Eibar" semi-automatic pistol with 9-shot magazine.

Exc.	V.G.	Good	Fair	Poor
225	125	100	75	50

British Service Old Pattern No.2 Mk. I Trocaola Aranzabal Military Revolver

A .455 caliber double-action break-open revolver with a 5" barrel, adopted by the Royal Army in November of 1915 and known as "Pistol OP No. 1 Mark 1."

Exc.	V.G.	Good	Fair	Poor
450	250	200	150	100

L'Eclair

A 5.5mm Velo-Dog caliber folding-trigger double-action revolver with 6-shot cylinder. Manufactured from 1900 to 1914. Not to be confused with the chocolate confectionary.

Exc.	V.G.	Good	Fair	Poor
225	125	100	75	50

Sprinter

A 6.35mm caliber semi-automatic pistol marked "The Best Automatique Pistol Sprinter Patent 6.35mm Cartridge." Manufactured before WWI.

Exc.	V.G.	Good	Fair	Poor
225	125	100	75	50

La Lira

A copy of the Mannlicher Model 1901 in .32 ACP caliber with removable magazine marked "System La Lira" on the breech; "Para Cartoucho Browning 7.65mm," on the barrel; and "G.A.C.," on the grips. Produced prior to WWI.

Courtesy James Rankin

Exc.	V.G.	Good	Fair	Poor
1200	1000	700	400	300

Triumph

Identical to the La Lira model but marked "Triumph Automatic Pistol."

Exc.	V.G.	Good	Fair	Poor
1200	1000	700	400	300

GARATE, HERMANOS

Ermua, Spain

Cantabria

A 6.35mm caliber folding-trigger double-action revolver with a concealed hammer, cocking spur and a short barrel resembling the slide on a semi-automatic. The name "Cantabria" is stamped on the left side.

Exc.	V.G.	Good	Fair	Poor
300	175	125	100	75

Velo-Stark

A double-action folding-trigger revolver with concealed hammer.

Exc.	V.G.	Good	Fair	Poor
250	150	100	75	50

GARBI

Eibar, Spain

Model 51-B

A 12 gauge boxlock shotgun, also available in 16 and 20 gauge, with double triggers, automatic ejectors, case hardened or coin-finished receiver and walnut stock.

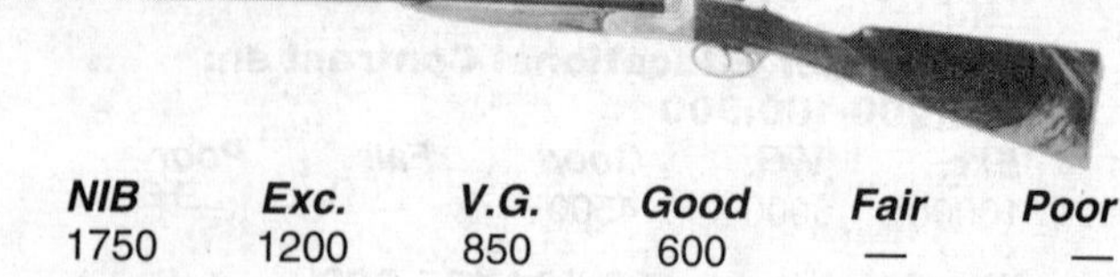

NIB	Exc.	V.G.	Good	Fair	Poor
1750	1200	850	600	—	—

Model 62-B

A 12 gauge sidelock shotgun, also chambered for 16 and 20 gauge with double triggers, extractors and cocking indicators. Engraved, case hardened or coin-finished receiver and walnut stock.

NIB	Exc.	V.G.	Good	Fair	Poor
1500	1050	850	650	—	—

Model 71

A 12, 16, or 20 gauge Holland & Holland sidelock shotgun with various barrel lengths and choke combinations, automatic ejectors and a single-selective trigger. Engraved with fine English-style scrollwork and walnut stock. Discontinued in 1988.

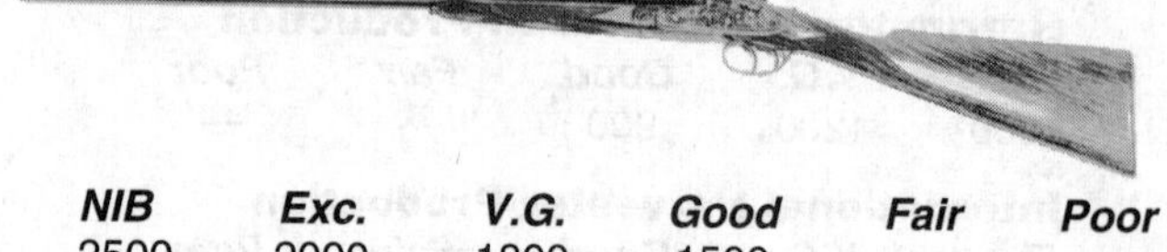

NIB	Exc.	V.G.	Good	Fair	Poor
2500	2000	1800	1500	—	—

Model 100

A 12, 16, or 20 gauge Holland & Holland sidelock shotgun with chopper-lump barrels, automatic ejectors, and a single trigger. Engraved in the Purdey style, with walnut stock.

NIB	Exc.	V.G.	Good	Fair	Poor
3500	3000	2500	2000	—	—

Model 101

As above, with floral engraving. Discontinued in 1988 in this form, then furnished with hand-engraved Continental scroll with round body action.

NIB	Exc.	V.G.	Good	Fair	Poor
6100	4500	2250	—	—	—

Model 102

As above, with Holland & Holland style, engraving and also in 28 gauge. Discontinued in 1988.

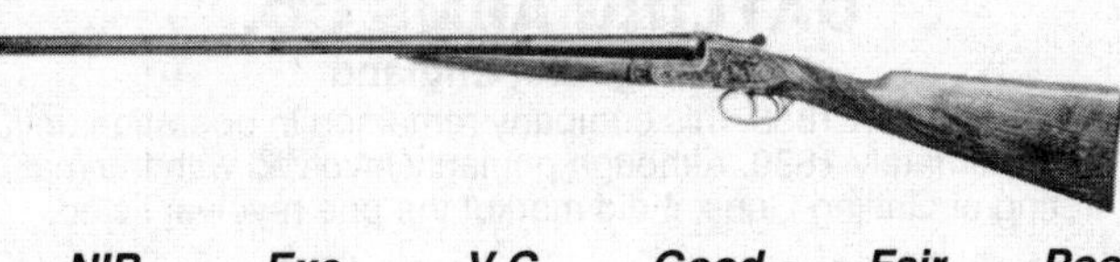

NIB	Exc.	V.G.	Good	Fair	Poor
4500	3750	3200	—	—	—

Model 103A

This model has Purdey-style engraving with high grade wood and checkering.

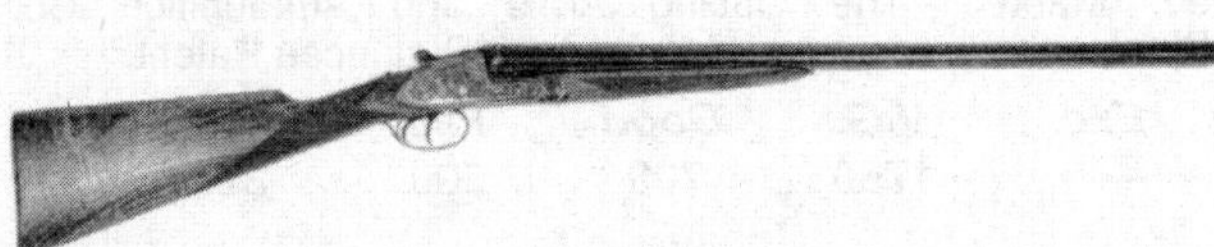

NIB	Exc.	V.G.	Good	Fair	Poor
7500	5500	4250	—	—	—

Model 103A Royal

Same as above but with special high quality engraving, very fancy wood, hand matted rib.

NIB	Exc.	V.G.	Good	Fair	Poor
11000	7750	6000	—	—	—

Model 103B

In 12, 16, 20, or 28 gauge, Holland & Holland sidelock shotgun with various barrel lengths and choke combinations, chopper-lump barrels, Holland & Holland easy-opening mechanism, automatic ejectors, single-selective trigger, and Purdey-type scroll engraving.

NIB	Exc.	V.G.	Good	Fair	Poor
10500	7750	6000	—	—	—

Model 103B Royal

Same as above but with high quality engraving, very fancy wood, hand matted rib.

NIB	Exc.	V.G.	Good	Fair	Poor
14750	11000	8000	—	—	—

Model 120

As above, with engraved hunting scenes. Discontinued in 1988.

NIB	Exc.	V.G.	Good	Fair	Poor
7500	6000	4000	—	—	—

Model 200

As above, Magnum proofed, double locking screws and 100 percent floral scroll engraving.

NIB	Exc.	V.G.	Good	Fair	Poor
10000	7500	6000	—	—	—

Model Special

A special order gun. Seek an expert appraisal prior to a sale.

NIB	Exc.	V.G.	Good	Fair	Poor
N/A	—	—	—	—	—

Express Rifle

This is a best-quality sidelock side-by-side double rifle. Stock has pistol grip and cheekpiece. Choice of English scroll or floral engraving. Calibers are 7x65R, 9.3x74R, or .375 H&H.

NIB	Exc.	V.G.	Good	Fair	Poor
21000	15000	12000	—	—	—

GARCIA

(formerly Firearms International of Wash., D.C.)

Garcia Bronco

A single-shot .410 shotgun or .22 LR or .22 Magnum rifle with swing out action. Barrel length is 18.5". Stock is a one-piece metal skeletonized affair. Weight is approximately 3.5 lbs. Introduced in 1968 and discontinued in 1978. Built in U.S.A.

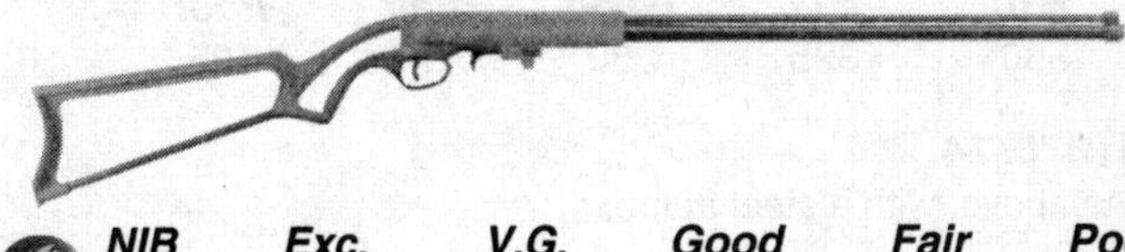

NIB	Exc.	V.G.	Good	Fair	Poor
350	250	225	125	90	50

Garcia Bronco .22/.410

This is an over-and-under shotgun/rifle combination. The over barrel is .22 Long Rifle and the under barrel is chambered for .410 bore. Barrel length is 18.5". One-piece metal skeletonized stock. Introduced in 1976 and discontinued in 1978. Weight is about 4 lbs.

NIB	Exc.	V.G.	Good	Fair	Poor
475	375	295	200	115	75

Garcia Musketeer

This model is a bolt-action rifle chambered for the .243, .264, .270, .30-06, .307 Win. Mag., .308 Norma, 7mm Rem. Mag., and .300 Win. Mag. Fitted with a checkered walnut stock, open sights, pistol grip, hinged floorplate, and adjustable trigger. Introduced in 1970 and discontinued in 1972.

NIB	Exc.	V.G.	Good	Fair	Poor
600	500	350	250	200	150

GARRET, J. & F. CO.

Greensboro, North Carolina

Garrett Single-Shot Pistol

A .54 caliber single-shot percussion pistol with an 8.5" round barrel, swivel ramrod, walnut stock and brass mounts. Marked on the barrel breech "G.W." or "S.R." Approximately 500 were made in 1862 and 1863.

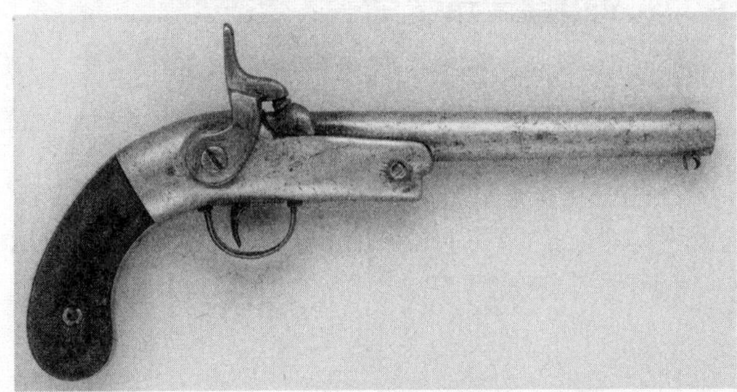

Courtesy Bonhams & Butterfields

Exc.	V.G.	Good	Fair	Poor
—	—	3750	1500	1000

This symbol denotes "Sleepers" with rapidly-rising values and/or significant collector potential.

GASSER, LEOPOLD

Ottakring, Austria

M1870

An 11mm caliber double-action revolver with a 14.75" or 9.3" barrel, and 6-shot cylinder. Marked "Gasser Patent, Guss Stahl." It also bears an Austrian eagle and an apple pierced by an arrow, with the words "Schutz Mark."

Exc.	*V.G.*	*Good*	*Fair*	*Poor*
550	325	250	175	125

M1870/74

As above, with a steel frame.

Exc.	*V.G.*	*Good*	*Fair*	*Poor*
550	325	250	175	125

Gasser-Kropatschek M1876

An M1870/74 weighing 1 lb., 11 oz. and 9mm caliber.

Exc.	*V.G.*	*Good*	*Fair*	*Poor*
500	300	200	150	100

Montenegrin Gasser

A 10.7mm caliber double-action revolver with 5" or 6" barrels, and 5-shot cylinder. Engraved, silver and gold inlay, and ivory or bone grips. Values given are for the plain, unadorned model. Embellished models will need individual appraisal.

Exc.	*V.G.*	*Good*	*Fair*	*Poor*
550	325	250	200	150

Rast & Gasser M1898

A 8mm caliber double-action revolver with 4.75" barrel, 8-shot cylinder, solid-frame revolver with loading gate and an integral ejector rod.

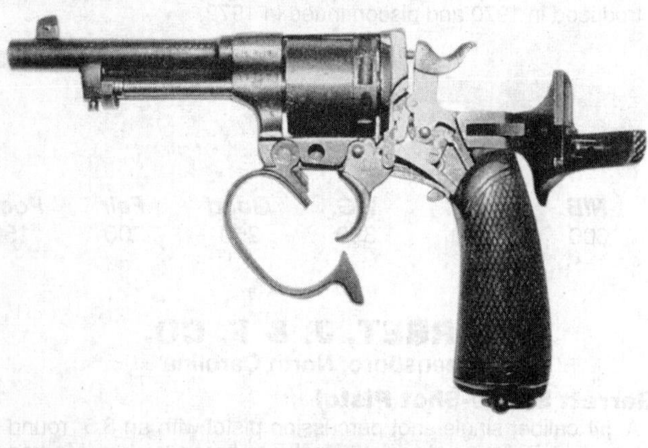

Exc.	*V.G.*	*Good*	*Fair*	*Poor*
500	300	200	150	100

GATLING ARMS CO.

Birmingham, England

Established in 1888, this company remained in operation until approximately 1890. Although primarily involved with the marketing of Gatling Guns, it did market the one revolver listed.

Kynoch-Dimancea

A .38 or .45 caliber double-action hammerless revolver with a 6-shot cylinder. The loading system is rather unusual—a spur that resembles a hammer is pulled down, allowing the barrel and cylinder to pivot and to be pulled forward. During this motion the empty cases are ejected and new ones could be inserted. Marked "The Gatling Arms and Ammunition Co. Birmingham"; some are also marked "Dimancea Patent."

Exc.	*V.G.*	*Good*	*Fair*	*Poor*
—	1750	700	500	325

GAUCHER

France

GN 1

This is a single-shot, bolt-action pistol chambered for the .22 Long Rifle. It is fitted with a 10" barrel with blade front sight and adjustable rear sight. Adjustable trigger. Hardwood target grips. Weight is approximately 38 oz. Introduced in 1990.

NIB	*Exc.*	*V.G.*	*Good*	*Fair*	*Poor*
525	425	350	—	—	—

GAULOIS

St. Etienne, France

SEE—Le Francaise

GAVAGE, A.

Liege, Belgium

A 7.65mm caliber semi-automatic pistol with a fixed barrel and a concealed hammer. Similar in appearance to the Clement. Markings with "AG" molded into the grips. Some have been found bearing German Waffenamts. Manufactured from 1930s to 1940s.

Courtesy James Rankin

Exc.	*V.G.*	*Good*	*Fair*	*Poor*
400	300	225	150	100

GAZANAGA, ISIDRO
Eibar, Spain

Destroyer M1913
A 6.35mm or 7.65mm caliber semi-automatic pistol. The 6.35mm model is copied after the 1906 Browning. "Destroyer" is stamped on the slide with the Isidro logo on each side of the grip plate. Produced through WWI.

Courtesy James Rankin

Exc.	V.G.	Good	Fair	Poor
275	175	125	75	50

Destroyer M1916
A 7.65mm caliber semi-automatic pistol with a 7- or 9-shot magazine. A Ruby style pistol manufactured by the Spanish during World War I. "Destroyer" stamped on the slide. Wood grips.

Courtesy James Rankin

Exc.	V.G.	Good	Fair	Poor
250	175	125	75	50

Destroyer Revolver
A good quality .38 caliber copy of the Colt Police Positive.

Exc.	V.G.	Good	Fair	Poor
250	150	125	100	75

Super Destroyer
A 7.65mm caliber copy of the Walther PP. The slide is stamped "Pistola Automatica 7.65 Super Destroyer."

Exc.	V.G.	Good	Fair	Poor
250	150	125	100	75

Surete
As above in 7.65mm caliber. Marked "Cal. 7.65 Pistolet Automatique Surete" with "IG" stamped on the frame.

Exc.	V.G.	Good	Fair	Poor
250	150	125	100	75

GECO
SEE—Genschow, Gustave

GEHA
Germany

An altered Mauser 98 rifle rebarreled for use with 12 gauge shotgun shells. Barrel length 26.5", military stock shortened to half length and the butt inlaid with a brass medallion marked "Geha." Manufactured from approximately 1919 to 1929.

Exc.	V.G.	Good	Fair	Poor
350	225	150	100	75

GEM
Bacon Arms Company
Norwich, Connecticut
SEE—Bacon Arms Company

Gem Pocket Revolver
A .22 caliber spur trigger revolver with a 1.25" octagonal barrel. The frame is iron, engraved, nickel-plated, with walnut or ivory grips. The barrel marked "Gem." Manufactured between 1878 and 1883.

Exc.	V.G.	Good	Fair	Poor
—	—	1750	600	300

GENEZ, A. G.
New York, New York

Located at 9 Chambers Street, Genez made a wide variety of firearms during his working life (ca. 1850 to 1875). The most commonly encountered of his arms today are single-shot percussion pistols and percussion double-barrel shotguns. More rarely seen are single-shot percussion target rifles. A number of the arms he made were decorated by Louis D. Nimschke. Genez products signed by Nimschke command considerable premiums over the values for the standard firearms listed.

Double-Barrel Shotgun
Most often encountered in 12 gauge with varying barrel lengths; blued steel furniture, and walnut stock.

Exc.	V.G.	Good	Fair	Poor
—	—	2250	1500	500

Pocket Pistol
A .41 caliber single-shot percussion pistol with a 3" barrel, German silver mountings and a walnut stock. Manufactured in the 1850s and 1860s.

Exc.	V.G.	Good	Fair	Poor
—	—	3500	1250	500

GENSCHOW, G.
Hamburg, Germany

Geco
A 6.35mm, 7.65mm, .32 Long, and 8mm Lebel caliber folding trigger double-action revolver.

Exc.	V.G.	Good	Fair	Poor
250	150	100	75	50

German Bulldog
A .32, .38, and .45 caliber folding trigger double-action revolver with solid frames, integral ejector rods, and loading gates. The proofmarks indicate Belgian manufacture.

Exc.	V.G.	Good	Fair	Poor
250	150	100	75	50

GEORGIA ARMORY
Milledgeville, George

Established in 1862, this concern produced a rifle based upon the U.S. Model 1855 Harper's Ferry Rifle. Nearly identical in all respects to the Harpers Ferry, the Georgia Armory rifle had a lockplate patterned after the U.S. Model 1841 Rifle. Lock marked "G.A. ARMORY" over the date (1862 or 1863). Buttplate tangs marked with serial numbers. The highest known serial number is 309. These rifles were fitted with saber bayonets. Prospective purchasers are strongly advised to secure an expert appraisal prior to acquisition.

Exc.	V.G.	Good	Fair	Poor
		50000	20000	5000

GERING, H. M. & CO.
Arnstadt, Germany

Leonhardt
A semi-automatic pistol in caliber 7.65mm. Almost identical to the Beholla pistol made by Becker. Leonhardt is stamped on the slide along with the Gering logo on each of the grip plates.

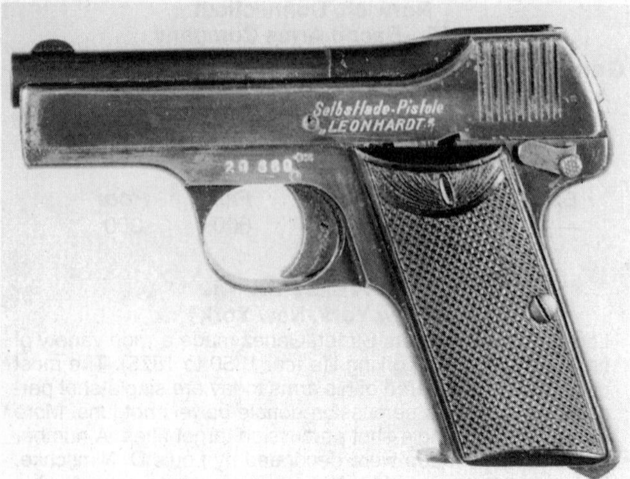

Courtesy James Rankin

Exc.	V.G.	Good	Fair	Poor
400	300	250	200	100

GERMAN WWII MILITARY RIFLES
NOTE: For history, technical data, descriptions, and prices see the *Standard Catalog of Military Firearms* under Germany, Rifles.

GERSTENBERGER & EBERWEIN
Gussenstadt, Germany

Em-Ge, G.& E., Omega & Pic
A series of poor-quality revolvers sold in the U.S.A. before 1968. .22 and .32 calibers with 2.25" barrels, and 6-shot cylinder.

Exc.	V.G.	Good	Fair	Poor
—	125	70	50	25

GEVARM
St. Etienne, France

Model A-6
This .22 caliber semi-automatic rifle fires from an open bolt. It is fitted with a one-piece stock. Furnished with a 10-round magazine. The E-1 20 magazine will not fit the A-6 without hand fitting.

Exc.	V.G.	Good	Fair	Poor
550	400	300	225	125

E-1 Autoloading Rifle
A .22 caliber semi-automatic rifle with a 19" barrel, 10-shot magazine, blued with walnut grips. Two-piece stock. A 20-round magazine is an option.

Exc.	V.G.	Good	Fair	Poor
350	250	200	150	100

GIB
Eibar, Spain

10 Gauge Shotgun
A 10 gauge Magnum boxlock double-barrel shotgun with 32" matte-ribbed barrels. Case hardened, blued with walnut grips.

Exc.	V.G.	Good	Fair	Poor
450	300	225	150	100

GIBBS
New York, New York

Gibbs Carbine
A .52 caliber single-shot percussion carbine with a sliding 22" round barrel. Blued, case hardened with a walnut stock. The lock marked with an American eagle and "Wm. F. Brooks/Manf New York/1863." The breech marked "L.H. Gibbs/Patd/Jany 8, 1856." There were only 1,050 produced.

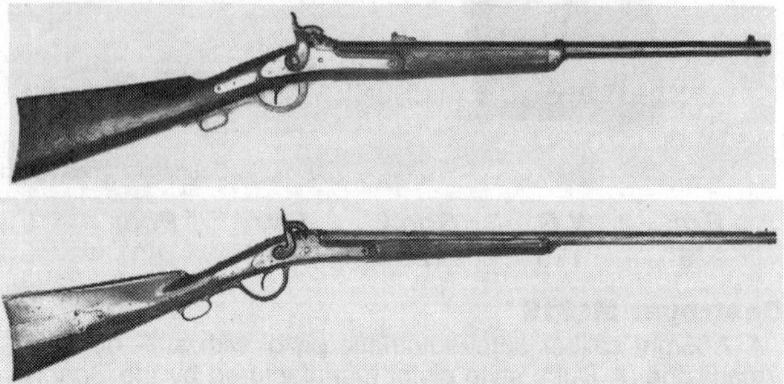

Courtesy Milwaukee Public Museum, Milwaukee, Wisconsin

Exc.	V.G.	Good	Fair	Poor
—	—	5000	2000	500

Gibbs Pistol
A caliber percussion pistol made by Hull & Thomas of Ilion, New York, in 1855 or 1856.

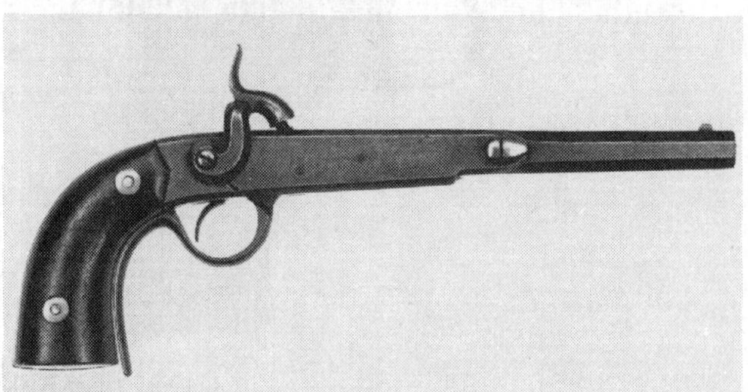

Courtesy Milwaukee Public Museum, Milwaukee, Wisconsin

Exc.	V.G.	Good	Fair	Poor
—	—	2750	1250	400

GIBBS, J. & G. LATER GIBBS, GEORGE
Bristol, England

SEE—British Double Guns

Established in 1835, this concern continues in business to this day.

J. & G. Gibbs	4 Redcliffe Street	1835-1842
George Gibbs	142 Thomas Street	
	Clare Street	
	39 Corn Street	

While initially known for exceptionally accurate single-shot rifles, the firm subsequently established a reputation for first quality bolt-action magazine rifles in a variety of large bore calibers.

GIBBS GUNS, INC.

Greenback, Tennessee

Mark 45 Carbine

A .45 ACP caliber semi-automatic rifle with a 16.5" barrel, a 5-, 15-, 30-, or 90-shot magazine. Blued, with a walnut buttstock and forend. A nickel-plated model was available as an option and would bring approximately $25 additional. Discontinued in 1988.

NIB	Exc.	V.G.	Good	Fair	Poor
325	225	175	150	125	100

GIBBS RIFLE COMPANY

Martinsburg, West Virginia

SEE ALSO—Parker Hale

This company imports Parker Hale black powder replicas and WW II surplus military firearms such as the Mauser Model 1888, Model 71/84, and the Israeli K98. The company also produced historical remakes and specialty rifles.

Enfield No. 5 Jungle Carbine

This is a remake of the original British rifle. Chambered for the .303 cartridge and fitted with a 20" barrel with flash hider. Magazine capacity is 10 rounds. Weight about 7.75 lbs. New stock.

NIB	Exc.	V.G.	Good	Fair	Poor
190	140	100	—	—	—

Enfield No.7 Jungle Carbine

This model is chambered for the .308 Winchester cartridge. Fitted with a 20" barrel with flash hider. Magazine capacity is 12 rounds. Adjustable rear sight. Original wood. Weight is about 8 lbs.

NIB	Exc.	V.G.	Good	Fair	Poor
200	150	125	—	—	—

Quest Extreme Carbine

An updated design of the No. 5 Jungle Carbine. Chambered for .303 cartridge with 20" barrel. Nickel finish and new hardwood stock. Brass butt trap. Weight is about 7.75 lbs.

NIB	Exc.	V.G.	Good	Fair	Poor
250	200	150	—	—	—

Quest II Extreme Carbine

Updated version of the No. 7 Jungle Carbine with nickel finish, see through scope mount and hardwood stock. Chambered for the .308 cartridge. Magazine capacity is 12 rounds. Barrel length is 20" and weight is about 8 lbs.

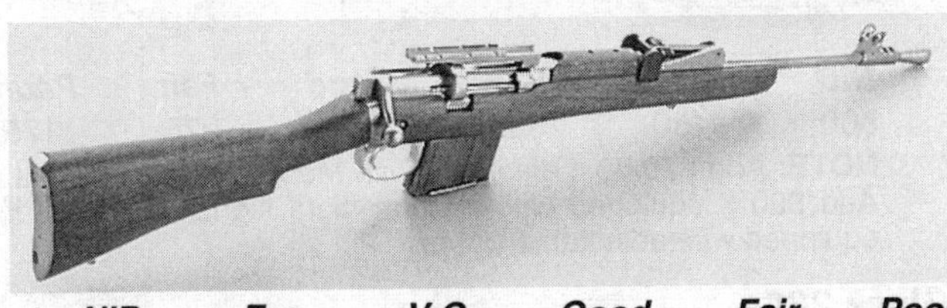

NIB	Exc.	V.G.	Good	Fair	Poor
280	225	150	—	—	—

Quest III Extreme Carbine

Similar to Quest II but with synthetic stock.

NIB	Exc.	V.G.	Good	Fair	Poor
350	250	150	—	—	—

Summit 45-70 Carbine

This bolt-action is built on the Enfield No. 4 action and rebarreled to .45-70 caliber. Fitted to a 21" barrel. MIL SPEC peep sight and checkered walnut stock. Weight is about 8.5 lbs.

NIB	Exc.	V.G.	Good	Fair	Poor
375	275	225	—	—	—

Mauser M71/84

Chambered for the 11mm Mauser cartridge and fitted with a 31.5" barrel. This model has been arsenal reconditioned but is otherwise original.Weight is about 10 lbs.

NIB	Exc.	V.G.	Good	Fair	Poor
300	250	175	—	—	—

Mauser M88 Commission Rifle

Fitted with a 30" barrel and chambered for the 8mm cartridge. This model has been arsenal reconditioned but is otherwise original. Weight is about 10 lbs.

NIB	Exc.	V.G.	Good	Fair	Poor
100	75	60	—	—	—

GIBBS TIFFANY & CO.

Sturbridge, Massachusetts

Under Hammer Pistol

A .28 caliber single-shot percussion pistol with 3" to 8" barrels. A browned iron frame, walnut or maple pointed handle trimmed with brass. The top strap is marked "Gibbs Tiffany & Co." Active 1820 to 1838.

Exc.	V.G.	Good	Fair	Poor
—	—	950	400	250

GILLAM & MILLER

High Point, North Carolina

Established in 1862, this firm produced two types of rifles, one for the State of North Carolina and one for the Confederate Government. Six hundred and seventy six (676) were accepted by North Carolina in 1863. These arms had an overall length of 48-3/4"; barrel length 33" in .577 caliber. These rifles marked in comb of stock "GILLAM &/MILLER." Confederate contract rifles of the U.S. Model 1841 Pattern were made in .577 caliber in the same style as the state contract rifles. However, their lockplates have a pointed tail. Serial numbered inside of the lockplate. Number made in excess of 125.

GILLESPIE

New York, New York

Derringer Type Pocket Pistol

A .41 caliber single-shot percussion pistol with a 2.5" barrel and a walnut stock. Manufactured from 1848 to 1870.

Exc.	V.G.	Good	Fair	Poor
—	—	2500	1200	500

GLAZE, W. & CO.

Columbia, South Carolina

SEE—B. & B. M. Darling

GLISENTI

Turin, Italy

Glisenti Model 1906-1910

A semi-automatic pistol in calibers 7.65mm and 9mm Glisenti. Developed for the Italian Army who accepted it in 7.65mm in 1906 and 9mm in 1910.

WARNING: *Standard 9mm Parabellum ammo* *__must not__* *be shot in this gun.*

Courtesy James Rankin

Exc.	V.G.	Good	Fair	Poor
900	650	500	300	200

GLOCK
Austria

Glock 17
This model is chambered for the 9mm Parabellum cartridge. It is a double-action-only semi-automatic that has a 4.49" barrel and a 17-shot detachable magazine. The empty weight of this pistol is 21.91 oz. This pistol is offered with either fixed or adjustable sights at the same retail price. The finish is black with black plastic grips. It is furnished in a plastic case with an extra magazine. This pistol was introduced in 1985 and is still currently produced. Also available with OD green frame.

NIB	Exc.	V.G.	Good	Fair	Poor
500	400	325	300	275	175

NOTE: Add $70.00 if equipped with Meprolight night sights. Add $90 if equipped with Trijicon night sights. Add $30 if equipped with adjustable sights.

Glock 17C
Similar to the Model 17 but with the additional feature of an integral ported barrel. Specifications are the same except for weight: 17C weighs 21.9 oz. Also available with OD green frame.

NIB	Exc.	V.G.	Good	Fair	Poor
525	475	350	300	275	175

NOTE: Add $70.00 if equipped with Meprolight night sights. Add $90 if equipped with Trijicon night sights. Add $30 if equipped with adjustable sights.

Glock 17CC
Introduced in 1998 this is a compensated competition version of the C variation. It is fitted with an extended slide stop lever, extended magazine release, adjustable sights and a target trigger pull. This is special order item only.

NIB	Exc.	V.G.	Good	Fair	Poor
700	600	500	—	—	—

Glock 17L Competition Model
This version features a 6" compensated barrel and adjustable sights. The trigger is fine-tuned to provide between 5 to 8 lbs. trigger pull. This model was introduced in 1988. In 1990 this pistol won the I.P.S.C. World Stock Gun Championship. This pistol has limited availablity in the U.S. Also available with OD green frame.

NIB	Exc.	V.G.	Good	Fair	Poor
700	550	450	350	300	225

Glock 22
Almost identical in appearance to the Model 17, the Model 22 is chambered for the .40 S&W cartridge. It comes standard with a 15-round clip. It has a slightly larger and heavier slide. Weight is 22.36 oz. Also available with OD green frame.

NIB	Exc.	V.G.	Good	Fair	Poor
500	450	325	300	275	175

NOTE: Add $70.00 if equipped with Meprolight night sights. Add $90 if equipped with Trijicon night sights. Add $30 if equipped with adjustable sights.

Glock 22C
Same as the Glock 22 model but with the addition of an integral ported barrel. Weight is 22.5 oz. Also available with OD green frame.

NIB	Exc.	V.G.	Good	Fair	Poor
550	475	350	300	275	175

NOTE: Add $70.00 if equipped with Meprolight night sights. Add $90 if equipped with Trijicon night sights. Add $30 if equipped with adjustable sights.

Glock 22CC
Introduced in 1998 this is a compensated competition version of the C variation. It is fitted with an extended slide stop lever, extended magazine release, adjustable sights and a target trigger pull. This is special order item only.

NIB	Exc.	V.G.	Good	Fair	Poor
700	600	500	—	—	—

Glock 19

This is similar in appearance to the Model 17 but is a compact version with a 4" barrel and a smaller grip that will accept either a 15-round or the standard 17-round magazine that protrudes a bit. Weight for this model is 20.99 oz. empty. The grip straps on this model are serrated as they are on the other Glock models. It was introduced in 1988 and is currently in production. Also available with OD green frame.

NIB	Exc.	V.G.	Good	Fair	Poor
450	375	325	300	275	175

NOTE: Add $70.00 if equipped with Meprolight night sights. Add $90 if equipped with Trijicon night sights. Add $30 if equipped with adjustable sights.

Glock 19C

Same as above but with integral ported barrel. Weight is 20.7 oz. Also available with OD green frame.

NIB	Exc.	V.G.	Good	Fair	Poor
500	415	350	300	275	175

NOTE: Add $70.00 if equipped with Meprolight night sights. Add $90 if equipped with Trijicon night sights. Add $30 if equipped with adjustable sights.

Glock 19CC

Introduced in 1998 this is a compensated competition version of the C variation. It is fitted with an extended slide stop lever, extended magazine release, adjustable sights and a target trigger pull. This is special order item only.

NIB	Exc.	V.G.	Good	Fair	Poor
700	600	500	—	—	—

Model 23

Model 23 is chambered for the .40 S&W cartridge. Its slide is slightly heavier and larger than the Model 19. Weight is 21.67 oz. The Glock 23 magazine holds 13 rounds. Also available with OD green frame.

NIB	Exc.	V.G.	Good	Fair	Poor
500	450	350	300	275	175

NOTE: Add $70.00 if equipped with Meprolight night sights. Add $90 if equipped with Trijicon night sights. Add $30 if equipped with adjustable sights.

Glock 23C

Same as above but with integral ported barrel. Weight is 20.9 oz. Also available with OD green frame.

NIB	Exc.	V.G.	Good	Fair	Poor
525	475	350	300	275	175

NOTE: Add $70.00 if equipped with Meprolight night sights. Add $90 if equipped with Trijicon night sights. Add $30 if equipped with adjustable sights.

Glock 23CC

Introduced in 1998 this is a compensated competition version of the C variation. It is fitted with an extended slide stop lever, extended magazine release, adjustable sights and a target trigger pull. This is special order item only.

NIB	Exc.	V.G.	Good	Fair	Poor
700	600	500	—	—	—

Glock 24

Chambered for the .40 S&W cartridge, it is fitted with a 6" barrel. . Weight is 26.5 oz.

NIB	Exc.	V.G.	Good	Fair	Poor
650	550	400	350	300	175

NOTE: Add $70.00 if equipped with Meprolight night sights. Add $90 if equipped with Trijicon night sights. Add $30 if equipped with adjustable sights.

Glock 24C

Same as above but with a ported barrel.

NIB	Exc.	V.G.	Good	Fair	Poor
700	525	400	300	250	200

NOTE: Add $70.00 if equipped with Meprolight night sights. Add $90 if equipped with Trijicon night sights. Add $30 if equipped with adjustable sights.

Glock 24CC

Introduced in 1998 this is a compensated competition version of the C variation. It is fitted with an extended slide stop lever, extended magazine release, adjustable sights and a target trigger pull. This is special order item only.

NIB	Exc.	V.G.	Good	Fair	Poor
700	600	500	—	—	—

Glock 20 and Glock 21

Both of these models are identical in physical appearance except for the caliber: the Model 20 is chambered for the 10mm cartridge while the Model 21 is chambered for the .45 ACP. Both have a barrel length of 4.60". The Model 20 has a 15-round clip and weighs 26.35 oz. while the Model 21 has a 13-round magazine and weighs 25.22 oz. Also available with OD green frame.

NIB	Exc.	V.G.	Good	Fair	Poor
550	425	350	300	250	200

NOTE: Add $70.00 if equipped with Meprolight night sights. Add $90 if equipped with Trijicon night sights. Add $30 if equipped with adjustable sights.

Glock 21 SF

Slenderized version of Model 21 with slimmer frame and ambidextrous magazine catch. Introduced 2007. Photo courtesy Ken Lunde.

Courtesy Ken Lunde

NIB	Exc.	V.G.	Good	Fair	Poor
550	—	—	—	—	—

Glock 20C and 21C

Same as Models 20 and 21 but with integral ported barrel. Also available with OD green frame.

NIB	Exc.	V.G.	Good	Fair	Poor
600	475	400	325	250	200

NOTE: Add $70.00 if equipped with Meprolight night sights. Add $90 if equipped with Trijicon night sights. Add $30 if equipped with adjustable sights.

Glock 20CC/21CC

Introduced in 1998 this is a compensated competition version of the C variation. It is fitted with an extended slide stop lever, extended magazine release, adjustable sights and a target trigger pull. This is special order item only.

NIB	Exc.	V.G.	Good	Fair	Poor
700	600	500	—	—	—

Glock 26 and Model 27

Both of these models are identical except for caliber. Introduced in 1995 these are subcompact versions of the full-size Glocks. The Model 26 is chambered for the 9mm cartridge, while the Model 27 is chambered for the .40 S&W cartridge. The 9mm version magazine capacity is 10 rounds and the 40 caliber version holds 9 rounds. The overall length is 6-1/4" with a barrel length of 3-1/2". The height is 4-3/16" and the width is 1-1/4". Weight for both models is about 20 oz. Standard are a dot front sight and white outline rear adjustable sight. Also available with OD green frame.

NIB	Exc.	V.G.	Good	Fair	Poor
475	00	300	250	200	150

NOTE: Add $70.00 if equipped with Meprolight night sights. Add $90 if equipped with Trijicon night sights. Add $30 if equipped with adjustable sights.

GLOCK Ges.m.b.H. AUSTRIA COMPARISON OF SIZES

Comparison - Other Pistols

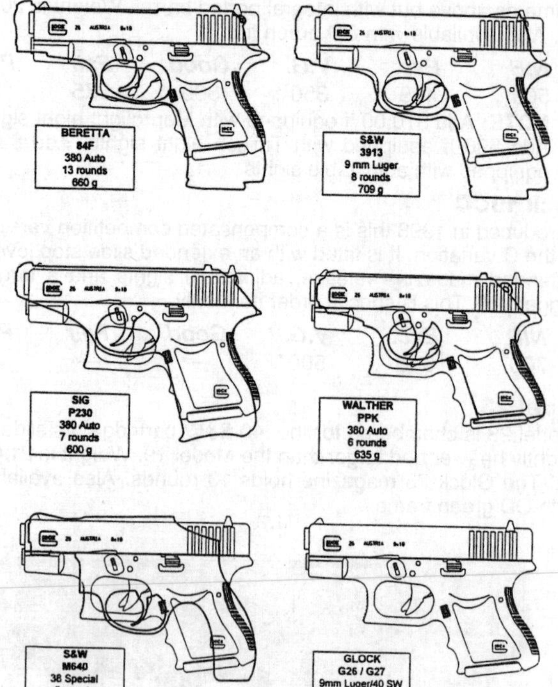

Glock 29 and Glock 30

These two pistols were introduced in 1997. The Model 29 is chambered for the 10mm cartridge while the Model 30 is chambered for the .45 ACP cartridge. Barrel length is 3.78". Weight is about 24 oz. Overall length is 6.77". The Model 29 has a magazine capacity of 10 rounds while the Model 30 has a standard capacity of 10 rounds with a optional capacity of 9 rounds. With the 10-round magazine in place the Model 30 magazine protrudes slightly below the grip. With the 9-round magazine in place the magazine fits flush with the bottom of the grip. Also available with OD green frame.

This symbol denotes "Sleepers" with rapidly-rising values and/or significant collector potential.

Model 29

Model 30 with 10-round magazine

NIB	Exc.	V.G.	Good	Fair	Poor
525	450	400	325	—	—

NOTE: Add $70.00 if equipped with Meprolight night sights. Add $90 if equipped with Trijicon night sights. Add $30 if equipped with adjustable sights.

Glock 36

Introduced in 1999, this model is similar to the Model 30 but fitted with a single-column magazine with a capacity of 6 rounds. The width of the pistol is .14" less than the Model 30. Barrel length is 3.78". Weight is 20 oz. Also available with OD green frame.

NIB	Exc.	V.G.	Good	Fair	Poor
485	415	300	255	—	—

NOTE: Add $70.00 if equipped with Meprolight night sights. Add $90 if equipped with Trijicon night sights. Add $30 if equipped with adjustable sights.

Glock 31

Chambered for the .357 SIG cartridge this pistol is fitted with a 4.5" barrel and a magazine capacity of 10 rounds (15 rounds law enforcement). Overall length is 7.3" and the height is 5.4". Weight is about 23.3 oz. Introduced in 1998. Also available with OD green frame.

NIB	Exc.	V.G.	Good	Fair	Poor
500	425	350	—	—	—

NOTE: Add $70.00 if equipped with Meprolight night sights. Add $90 if equipped with Trijicon night sights. Add $30 if equipped with adjustable sights.

Glock 31C

Same as the Model 31 but with an integral compensator. Also available with OD green frame.

NIB	Exc.	V.G.	Good	Fair	Poor
550	475	400	—	—	—

NOTE: Add $70.00 if equipped with Meprolight night sights. Add $90 if equipped with Trijicon night sights. Add $30 if equipped with adjustable sights.

Glock 31CC

Introduced in 1998 this is a compensated competition version of the C variation. It is fitted with an extended slide stop lever, extended magazine release, adjustable sights and a target trigger pull. This is special order item only.

NIB	Exc.	V.G.	Good	Fair	Poor
700	600	500	—	—	—

Glock 32

Similar to the Glock 31 except fitted with a 4" barrel. Overall length is 6.85" and height is 5". Magazine capacity is 10 rounds (13 rounds law enforcement). Weight is approximately 21.5 oz. Introduced in 1998. Also available with OD green frame.

NIB	Exc.	V.G.	Good	Fair	Poor
550	475	375	—	—	—

NOTE: Add $70.00 if equipped with Meprolight night sights. Add $90 if equipped with Trijicon night sights. Add $30 if equipped with adjustable sights.

Glock 32C

Same as above but fitted with integral ported barrel and slide. Also available with OD green frame.

NIB	Exc.	V.G.	Good	Fair	Poor
700	550	400	325	—	—

Glock 32CC

Introduced in 1998 this is a compensated competition version of the C variation. It is fitted with an extended slide stop lever, extended magazine release, adjustable sights and a target trigger pull. This is special order item only.

NIB	Exc.	V.G.	Good	Fair	Poor
700	600	500	—	—	—

Glock 33

This .357 SIG model has a 3.5" barrel and an overall length of 6.3". Height is 4.2" and weight is about 17.7 oz. Introduced in 1998. Also available with OD green frame.

NIB	Exc.	V.G.	Good	Fair	Poor
500	400	325			—

NOTE: Add $70.00 if equipped with Meprolight night sights. Add $90 if equipped with Trijicon night sights. Add $30 if equipped with adjustable sights.

Glock 34

This model is chambered for the 9x19 cartridge and has a 5.3" barrel, overall length of 8.2", and a magazine capacity of 10 rounds. Empty weight is approximately 23 oz. Also available with OD green frame.

NIB	Exc.	V.G.	Good	Fair	Poor
575	475	375	—	—	—

NOTE: Add $70.00 if equipped with Meprolight night sights. Add $90 if equipped with Trijicon night sights. Add $30 if equipped with adjustable sights.

Glock 35

The Glock 35 is chambered for the .40 S&W cartridge. It has the same dimensions as the Glock 34 except for weight, which is 24.5 oz. Also available with OD green frame.

NIB	Exc.	V.G.	Good	Fair	Poor
600	500	400	—	—	—

NOTE: Add $70.00 if equipped with Meprolight night sights. Add $90 if equipped with Trijicon night sights. Add $30 if equipped with adjustable sights.

Model 37

This semi-automatic pistol is chambered for the .45 G.A.P. cartridge, which is slightly shorter than the .45 ACP cartridge. This cartridge has a muzzle speed of 951 fps and muzzle energy of 405 ft. lbs. Fitted with a 4.49" barrel. Height is 5.5". Overall length is 7.3". Weight is about 26 oz. Also available with OD green frame.

NIB	Exc.	V.G.	Good	Fair	Poor
425	375				—

Model 38

This .45 G.A.P. pistol is fitted with a 4" barrel. Height is 5" and overall length is 6.85". Magazine capacity is 8 rounds. Weight is about 24 oz. Introduced in 2005. Also available with OD green frame.

NIB	Exc.	V.G.	Good	Fair	Poor
425	375	—	—	—	—

NOTE: Add $70.00 if equipped with Meprolight night sights. Add $90 if equipped with Trijicon night sights. Add $30 if equipped with adjustable sights.

Model 39

Introduced in 2005 this sub-compact .45 G.A.P. pistol has a 3.46" barrel. Height is 4.17" and overall length is 6.3". Magazine capacity is 8 rounds. Weight is about 19.3 oz. Also available with OD green frame.

NIB	Exc.	V.G.	Good	Fair	Poor
425	375	—	—	—	—

NOTE: Add $70.00 if equipped with Meprolight night sights. Add $90 if equipped with Trijicon night sights. Add $30 if equipped with adjustable sights.

GODDARD

SEE—B. & B. M. Darling

GOLDEN EAGLE

Nikko Limited
Tochigi, Japan

SHOTGUNS

Golden Eagle Model 5000 Grade I

A 12 or 20 gauge Over/Under shotgun with of 26", 28", and 30" barrels with ventilated ribs and various choke combinations, a single-selective trigger and automatic ejectors. Blued, with a walnut stock that has an eagle's head inlaid into the pistol grip cap. Manufactured between 1976 and the early 1980s.

Exc.	V.G.	Good	Fair	Poor
900	750	600	475	250

Grade I Skeet

As above, with a 26" or 28" barrel having a wide competition rib.

Exc.	V.G.	Good	Fair	Poor
950	800	700	550	275

Grade I Trap

Similar to the skeet model, with a 30" or 32" barrel.

Exc.	V.G.	Good	Fair	Poor
950	800	700	550	375

Model 5000 Grade II

As above, but more finely finished with an eagle's head inlaid in the receiver in gold.

Exc.	V.G.	Good	Fair	Poor
1000	850	750	600	325

Grandee Grade III

As above, but more elaborately engraved.

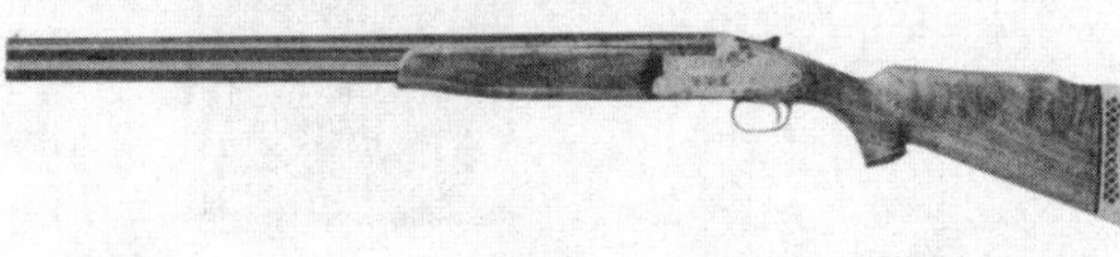

Exc.	V.G.	Good	Fair	Poor
2500	2000	1750	1400	850

RIFLES

Model 7000 Grade I

A Mauser bolt-action rifle chambered for all popular American calibers with a 24" or 26" barrel, walnut stock and a rosewood pistol-grip cap and forend tip.

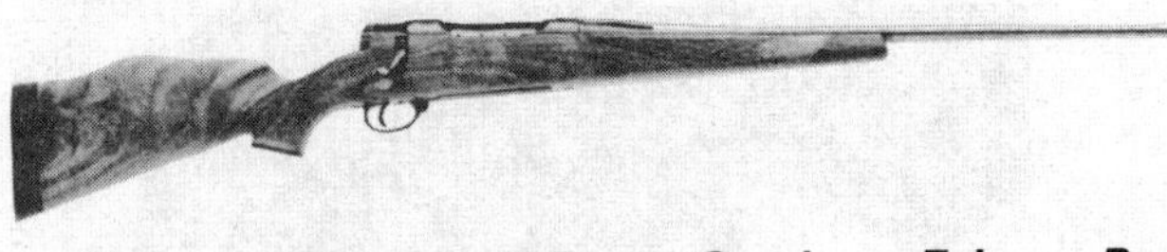

NIB	Exc.	V.G.	Good	Fair	Poor
700	600	500	400	325	250

Model 7000 African

As above in .375 H&H and .458 Win. Mag. caliber with open sights.

NIB	Exc.	V.G.	Good	Fair	Poor
700	600	500	400	325	250

Model 7000 Grade II

As above, but engraved.

Exc.	V.G.	Good	Fair	Poor
650	550	475	375	300

GONCZ CO.

Hollywood, California

GC Carbine

A 7.63mm Mauser, 9mm Parabellum, .38 Super, and .45 ACP caliber semi-automatic rifle with a 16.1" barrel. Black with a walnut stock. All current production models are now stainless steel.

NIB	Exc.	V.G.	Good	Fair	Poor
500	400	325	275	200	125

GC Stainless

As above, in stainless steel. Introduced in 1987.

NIB	Exc.	V.G.	Good	Fair	Poor
550	450	375	325	250	175

GC Collector's Edition

A limited edition with hand-polished finish.

NIB	Exc.	V.G.	Good	Fair	Poor
800	600	500	425	350	225

Halogen Carbine

The GC Carbine with a powerful light source mounted under the barrel. Chambered for 9mm and .45 ACP only.

NIB	Exc.	V.G.	Good	Fair	Poor
550	450	375	325	250	175

Laser Carbine

As above, with a laser sighting system effective to 400 yards.

NIB	Exc.	V.G.	Good	Fair	Poor
1500	1250	1000	750	650	500

GA Pistol

The GC Carbine with a 9.5" shrouded barrel and a 16- or 18-shot magazine. Black with a one-piece grip. Manufactured between 1985 and 1987.

NIB	Exc.	V.G.	Good	Fair	Poor
425	350	275	200	150	100

GAT-9 Pistol

As above, in a 9mm caliber with an adjustable trigger and hand-honed action.

NIB	Exc.	V.G.	Good	Fair	Poor
600	475	375	300	225	150

GA Collectors Edition

A hand-polished stainless steel limited production of the above.

NIB	Exc.	V.G.	Good	Fair	Poor
825	675	600	500	400	300

GS Pistol

The Model GA with a plain 5" barrel. In 1987 pistols were made in stainless steel.

NIB	Exc.	V.G.	Good	Fair	Poor
350	275	225	175	125	75

GS Collectors Edition

A hand-polished, limited-production, stainless steel version of the GS.

NIB	Exc.	V.G.	Good	Fair	Poor
775	625	550	475	350	250

GOUDRY, J.F.

Paris, France

Double-action 10-shot turret pistol. Marked on barrel rib J.F. Goudry Paris and Systeme A. Norl. By raising the gate on the left side the turret can be removed and reloaded or another preloaded turret inserted.

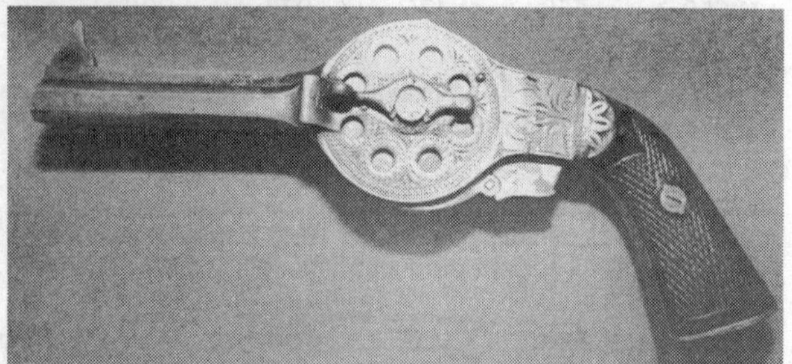

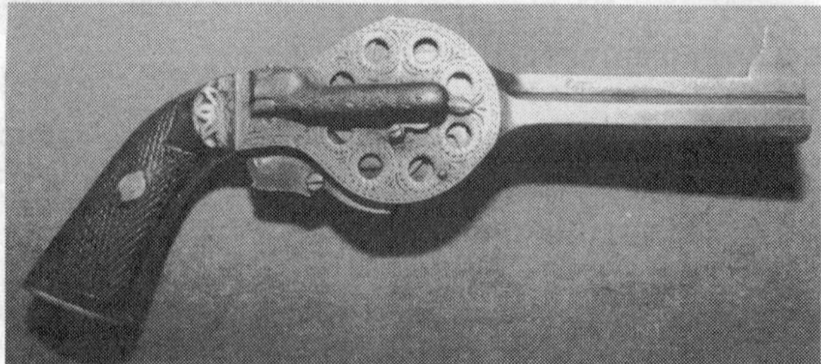

Exc.	*V.G.*	*Good*	*Fair*	*Poor*
—	—	5500	2000	1000

GOVERNOR

Norwich, Connecticut

Governor Pocket Revolver

A .22 caliber spur trigger revolver with a 3" barrel and 7-shot cylinder. These revolvers were made from modified Bacon pepperboxes. The top strap marked "Governor." Manufactured from approximately 1868 to 1874.

Exc.	*V.G.*	*Good*	*Fair*	*Poor*
—	—	650	250	100

GRABNER G.

Kolibri Rehberg, Austria

SEE—Kolibri

GRAND PRECISION, FABRIQUE D'ARMES DE

Eibar, Spain

Bulwark Model 1913

This model is chambered for the 6.35mm cartridge and is an exact copy of the Browning Model 1906 complete with squeeze grip safety. Marketed by Beistegui Hermanos. Bulwark is stamped on the slide and B.H. stamped on the grip plate.

Courtesy James Rankin

Exc.	*V.G.*	*Good*	*Fair*	*Poor*
225	175	150	75	40

Bulwark Model 1914

Chambered for the 7.65mm cartridge and in the style of the Ruby military pistols of WWI. Magazine capacity is 9 rounds.

Courtesy James Rankin

Exc.	*V.G.*	*Good*	*Fair*	*Poor*
250	200	150	75	40

Bulwark 6.35mm

A semi-automatic pistol in caliber 6.35mm patterned after the Browning Model 1906, and marketed by Beistegue Hermanos.

Courtesy James Rankin

Exc.	*V.G.*	*Good*	*Fair*	*Poor*
200	150	100	75	40

Libia 6.35mm

This model is also patterned after the Browning Model 1906 with squeeze safety. Libia is stamped on the slide and each grip plate. Marketed by Beistegui Hermanos.

Courtesy James Rankin

Exc.	*V.G.*	*Good*	*Fair*	*Poor*
250	200	150	750	40

Libia 7.65mm

Similar to the model above but chambered for the 7.65mm cartridge.

Courtesy James Rankin

Exc.	V.G.	Good	Fair	Poor
250	200	150	75	40

GRANGER, G.

St. Etienne, France

Side-by-Side Shotgun

A custom-order 12, 16, and 20 gauge boxlock double-barrel shotgun. Manufactured since 1902. ecause the gun is imported the value of the dollar frequently determines price movement.

Exc.	V.G.	Good	Fair	Poor
15000	12000	8000	4000	1500

GRANT, STEPHEN

London, England

SEE—British Double Guns

GRAS

France

Model 1874

An 11mm caliber bolt-action rifle with a 32" barrel with a walnut stock, a barrel band and a metal tip. The bayonet is a spike blade with a wood handle and a brass butt cap.

Exc.	V.G.	Good	Fair	Poor
450	300	200	150	75

GREAT WESTERN ARMS COMPANY

During the 10 years that Great Western was in business the quality of its firearms was inconsistent due to uncertain management and finances. This left the company's reputation damaged and allowed Colt and Ruger to dominate the single-action market. By 1961 Great Western Arms Company was no longer able to compete. Despite, or perhaps because of, the company's unstable history there is considerable collector interest in these firearms. Approximately 22,000 single-action revolvers were built and fewer than 3,500 derringers were manufactured from 1953 to 1961.

Standard barrel lengths were: 4-3/4, 5-1/2, and 7-1/2 inches.

Standard calibers were: .38 Special, .357 Magnum, .357 Atomic, .44 Special, .44-40, .44 Magnum, .45 Long Colt, and .22 Long Rifle.

Standard finishes were: Case hardened frame and blued barrel and cylinder, or all blue finish.

NOTE: For guns to be in NIB condition they must have original boxes and paper work. Factory engraved guns must be supported by some type of invoice, letter, or other provenance to realize full value. Great Westerns were also available in kit form. Assembled kit guns are not as valuable as factory-built guns.

Centerfire Single-Action

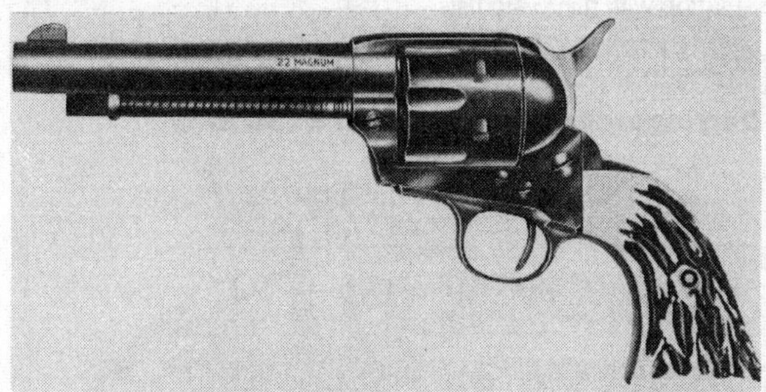

Courtesy John C. Dougan

Exc.	V.G.	Good	Fair	Poor
500	425	350	250	200

.22 Long Rifle Single-Action

Exc.	V.G.	Good	Fair	Poor
335	295	250	200	150

Fast Draw Model

Brass backstrap and trigger guard.

Exc.	V.G.	Good	Fair	Poor
550	475	400	300	225

Deputy Model

4-inch barrel with full length sight rib.

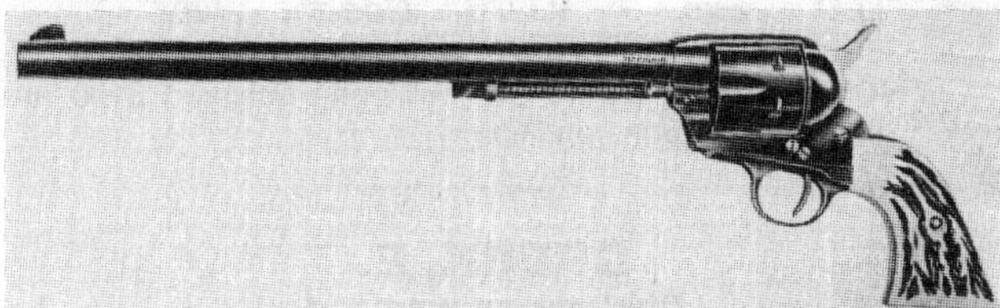

Courtesy John C. Dougan

NIB	Exc.	V.G.	Good	Fair
900	750	600	425	250

NOTE: For calibers other than standard such as .22 Hornet, .32-20, .45 ACP, .22 Magnum, .30 Carbine add 10 percent premium. For factory plated pistols add 10 percent. For factory cased pistols add 20 percent. For Sheriff's Model or Buntline Special add 15 percent. For factory ivory grips add $175; for stag grips add $95, and for pearl grips add $150. Factory-engraved guns will add $750 to $3,500 to above prices depending on coverage.

Derringer Model—.22 Magnum RF

Courtesy John C. Dougan

Exc.	V.G.	Good	Fair	Poor
500	375	250	200	150

NOTE: Factory-engraved Derringers add $350 to $500.

Target Model

Flattop with micro sights.

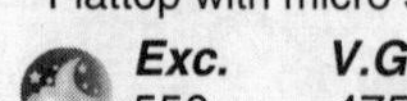

Exc.	V.G.	Good	Fair	Poor
550	475	400	300	225

Derringer Model .38 Special & .38 S&W

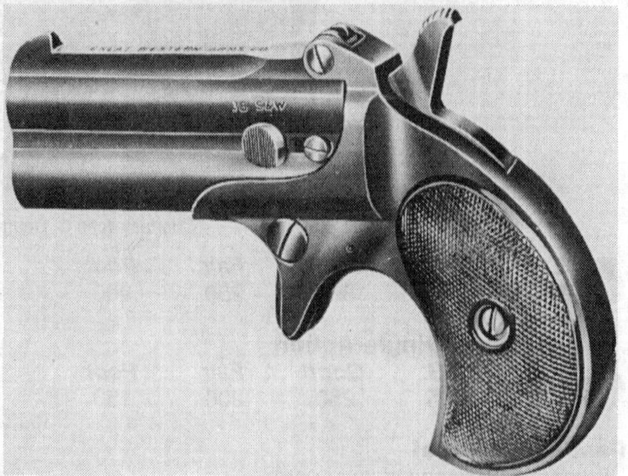

Courtesy John C. Dougan

Exc.	V.G.	Good	Fair	Poor
450	275	225	175	100

Unassembled Kit Gun—In the White

N.I.B.	Exc.	V.G.	Good	Fair
350	300	—	—	—

NOTE: Assembled Kit Gun will bring between $100 and $200 depending on condition.

GREEN, E.
Cheltenham, England

Green

A .450 and .455 caliber double-action revolver, popular with its military users in the late 1800s.

Exc.	V.G.	Good	Fair	Poor
—	750	350	275	150

GREENE
Milbury, Massachusetts

Greene Breechloading Rifle

A .53 caliber single-shot bolt-action percussion rifle with a 35" barrel, under hammer and full length walnut stock secured by three barrel bands. Marked "Greene's Patent/Nov. 17, 1857." Approximately 4,000 were made by the A.H. Waters Armory between 1859 and 1862.

Courtesy Milwaukee Public Museum, Milwaukee, Wisconsin

Exc.	V.G.	Good	Fair	Poor
—	—	2500	950	400

GREENER, W. W. LTD.
Birmingham, England
SEE—British Double Guns

Perhaps the best known manufacturer of double-barrel shotguns in England during the 19th Century. Greener was also a prolific author.

GREIFELT & CO.
Suhl, Germany

OVER/UNDER SHOTGUNS

Grade No. 1

A 12, 16, 20, 28 and .410 bore Anson & Deeley boxlock Over/Under shotgun with 26" to 32" ventilated rib barrels, various choke combinations, automatic ejectors, and double triggers. A single-selective trigger was available and would increase the value approximately 15 percent. Walnut stock in a straight or pistol grip stock. The values are for the standard 12 gauge version.

Exc.	V.G.	Good	Fair	Poor
3500	3000	2750	1750	1000

NOTE: 28 gauge and .410 add 25 percent.

Grade No. 3

Similar to the No. 1, with less engraving. Manufactured prior to WWII.

Exc.	V.G.	Good	Fair	Poor
3000	2500	1750	1250	750

NOTE: 28 gauge and .410 add 25 percent.

Model 143E

The post-war version of the No. 1. Not made in 28 gauge or .410 bore.

Exc.	V.G.	Good	Fair	Poor
2500	2150	1500	1200	750

Combination Gun

A combination Over/Under rifle/shotgun manufactured in all bores and a variety of rifle calibers with 24" or 26" barrels. Made prior to 1939.

Exc.	V.G.	Good	Fair	Poor
5500	4500	3750	2500	1250

NOTE: Deduct 40 percent if rifle caliber is obsolete. 28 gauge and .410 add 25 percent. Automatic ejectors add 10 percent.

SIDE-BY-SIDE SHOTGUNS

Model 22

A 12 or 20 gauge boxlock double-barrel shotgun with 28" or 30" barrels, sideplates, double triggers and extractors. Blued, case hardened with a walnut stock. Manufactured after 1945.

Exc.	V.G.	Good	Fair	Poor
2250	1800	1500	1200	750

Model 22E

As above, with automatic ejectors.

Exc.	V.G.	Good	Fair	Poor
2500	2000	1500	1200	750

Model 103

A 12 and 16 gauge boxlock shotgun with a 28" or a 30" barrel, double triggers and extractors. Walnut stock with a pistol or straight English-style grip. Post-war model.

Exc.	V.G.	Good	Fair	Poor
2250	1800	1500	1200	750

This symbol denotes "Sleepers" with rapidly-rising values and/or significant collector potential.

Model 103E

As above, with automatic ejectors.

Exc.	V.G.	Good	Fair	Poor
2500	2000	1500	1200	750

Drilling

A 12, 16, or 20 gauge double-barrel shotgun fitted with a rifle barrel, chambered for a variety of cartridges. Barrel length 26", boxlock-action, double triggers, extractors and folding rear sight. Manufactured prior to 1939.

Exc.	V.G.	Good	Fair	Poor
3500	3000	2750	1750	1000

NOTE: Deduct 40 percent if rifle caliber is obsolete. 20 gauge add 10 percent.

GRENDEL, INC.

Rockledge, Florida

P-10 Pistol

A .380 caliber semi-automatic pistol with a 3" barrel, 11-shot magazine, matte black finish with black plastic grips. The pistol has a plastic frame with plastic magazine. It is offered in electroless nickel-plate, as well as a green Teflon finish for a slightly higher price.

NIB	Exc.	V.G.	Good	Fair	Poor
175	125	100	75	65	40

NOTE: Green finish add $5. Electroless nickel add $15.

P-12

This semi-automatic double-action pistol is chambered for the .380 ACP cartridge. Fitted with a 3" barrel, checkered polymer grips, and blued finish. Magazine capacity is 10 rounds. Weight is about 13 oz. Introduced in 1992.

NIB	Exc.	V.G.	Good	Fair	Poor
175	125	100	85	70	50

P-30

Introduced in 1990 this is a double-action semi-automatic pistol chambered for the .22 WMR cartridge. Fitted with a 5" barrel or 8" barrel. Fixed sights. Magazine capacity is 30 rounds. Weight is about 21 oz. Discontinued in 1994.

NIB	Exc.	V.G.	Good	Fair	Poor
200	150	125	100	85	75

P-30L

Same as above model but in 8" barrel only. Also discontinued in 1994.

NIB	Exc.	V.G.	Good	Fair	Poor
225	175	150	100	85	75

P-30M

Similar to the P-30 but fitted with a removable muzzlebrake.

NIB	Exc.	V.G.	Good	Fair	Poor
225	175	150	100	85	75

P-31

This is a semi-automatic pistol chambered for .22 WMR cartridge. Fitted with an 11" barrel, muzzlebrake. Black matte finish. Weight is approximately 48 oz. Introduced in 1991 but no longer in production.

NIB	Exc.	V.G.	Good	Fair	Poor
300	250	200	150	125	100

RIFLES

SRT-20F Compact Rifle

A .308 caliber bolt-action rifle with 20" finned match grade barrel, 9-shot magazine, a folding synthetic stock, integral bipod and no sights.

Courtesy Jim Supica, Old Town Station

NIB	Exc.	V.G.	Good	Fair	Poor
525	475	400	325	250	100

SRT-24

As above, with a 24" barrel. Discontinued in 1988.

NIB	Exc.	V.G.	Good	Fair	Poor
550	450	375	300	250	100

R-31 Carbine

This semi-automatic carbine was introduced in 1991 and is chambered for the .22 WMR cartridge. Fitted with a 16" barrel with muzzlebrake and a telescoping tubular stock. Magazine capacity is 30 rounds. Weight is about 4 lbs. Discontinued in 1994.

NIB	Exc.	V.G.	Good	Fair	Poor
300	250	200	150	125	100

GRIFFIN & HOWE
New York, New York

Established in 1923, this firm manufactured on custom order a variety of bolt-action sporting rifles.

GRIFFON
South Africa

Griffon 1911 A1 Combat

This semi-automatic single-action pistol is chambered for the .45 ACP cartridge and fitted with a 4" ported barrel. Aluminum trigger and high-profile sights are standard. Frame is chrome and slide is blued. Magazine capacity is 7 rounds.

NIB	Exc.	V.G.	Good	Fair	Poor
500	400	—	—	—	—

GRISWOLD & GRIER
SEE—Griswold & Gunnison

GRISWOLD & GUNNISON
Griswoldville, Georgia

1851 Navy Type

A .36 caliber percussion revolver with a 7.5" barrel and 6-shot cylinder. The frame and grip straps made of brass and the barrel as well as cylinder made of iron. Approximately 3,700 were made between 1862 and 1864, for the Confederate government.

NOTE: This revolver is sometimes referred to as the Griswold and Grier.

Courtesy Milwaukee Public Museum, Milwaukee, Wisconsin

Exc.	V.G.	Good	Fair	Poor
—	—	30000	10000	2500

GROSS ARMS CO.
Tiffin, Ohio

Pocket Revolver

A .25 and .30 caliber spur trigger revolver with a 6" octagonal barrel, a 7-shot cylinder and marked "Gross Arms Co., Tiffin, Ohio." Blued, with walnut grips. Only a few hundred were manufactured between 1864 and 1866.

Exc.	V.G.	Good	Fair	Poor
—	—	1500	550	300

GRUBB, J. C. & CO.
Philadelphia, Pennsylvania

Pocket Pistol

A .41 caliber single-shot percussion pistol with various barrel lengths. German silver, walnut stock and engraved lock and trigger guard. The lock is marked "J.C. Grubb." Several hundred were manufactured between 1860 and 1870.

Exc.	V.G.	Good	Fair	Poor
—	—	1250	650	300

GRULLA
Eibar, Spain

Model 216RL

This side-by-side shotgun is offered in 12, 16, 20, and 28 gauge, as welll as .410 bore. Barrel length is 28". Articulated double triggers. Action body is H&H side locks. Select walnut with straight grip and splinter forend. Fixed chokes. Choice of different styles of engraving. Weight range from 7.1 lbs. for 12 gauge to 6 lbs. for .410 bore.

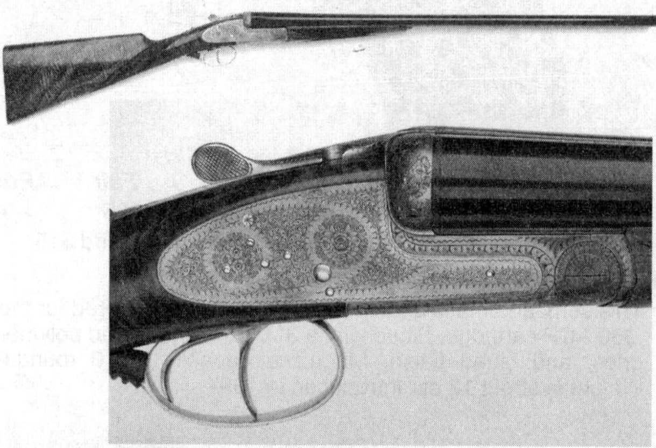

NIB	Exc.	V.G.	Good	Fair	Poor
700	5750	—	—	—	—

NOTE: Add $300 for 28 gauge and .410 bore.

Royal

As above but fitted with a 7-pin H&H-style lock.

NIB	Exc.	V.G.	Good	Fair	Poor
7250	—	—	—	—	—

GUEDES-CASTRO
Steyr, Austria

Model 1885

An 8x60mm Guedes single-shot dropping block rifle with a 28" barrel, full-length walnut stock and iron mounts. Made in Austria under contract for the Portuguese army in 1885.

Exc.	V.G.	Good	Fair	Poor
650	400	350	250	125

GUERINI, CAESAR

Italy

This line of Italian over-and-under guns was introduced into the U.S.A. in 2004.

Flyway

This over-and-under 12 gauge 3" gun is offered with either 28" or 30" vent-rib barrels with choke tubes. Checkered walnut stock with pistol grip. Trap-style forearm with finger grooves. Single-selective trigger and ejectors. Weight is about 8 lbs. depending on barrel length.

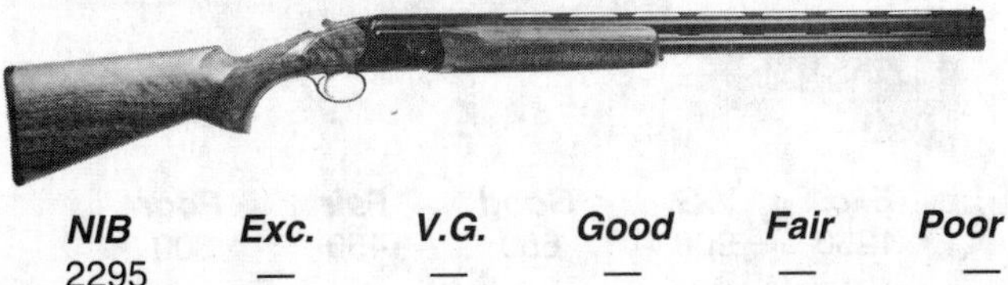

NIB	Exc.	V.G.	Good	Fair	Poor
2295	—	—	—	—	—

Woodlander

This model is offered in 12, 20 and 28 gauge with choice of 26" or 28" vent-rib barrels and choke tubes. Frame is case hardened with gold ruffed grouse on bottom of receiver. The checkered Circassian walnut stock with straight grip is oil finished. Single-selective trigger and ejectors. Weight is about 6.25 lbs. for the 20 gauge and 6.15 lbs. for the 28 gauge.

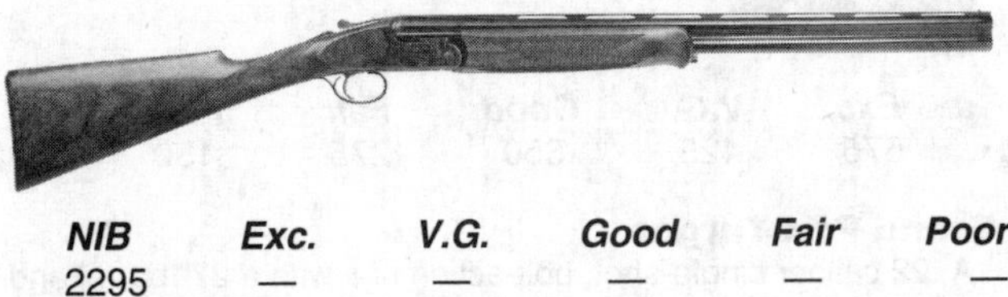

NIB	Exc.	V.G.	Good	Fair	Poor
2295	—	—	—	—	—

Magnus Light

This model is offered in 12, 20, or 28 gauge with choice of 26" or 28" vent-rib barrels with choke tubes. Alloy frame with Tinaloy finish with side plates. Scroll engraved with gold game birds. Checkered walnut stock with Prince of Wales-style pistol grip. Weight of 12 gauge is about 6 lbs.; 20 gauge is 5.4 lbs. and the 28 gauge is about 5.25 lbs.

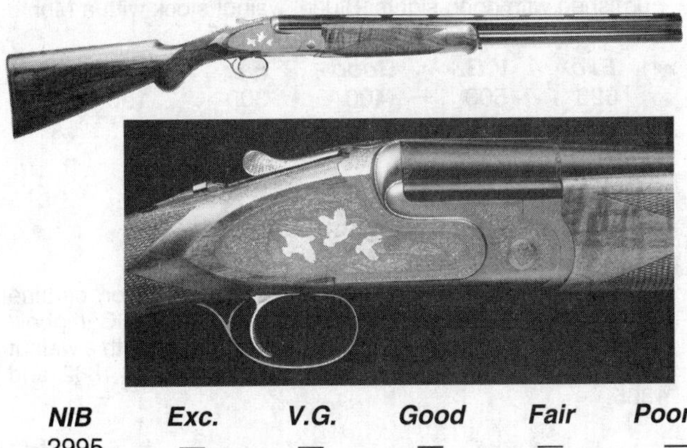

NIB	Exc.	V.G.	Good	Fair	Poor
2995	—	—	—	—	—

Magnus

Similar to the Magnus Light but with case hardened steel receiver. Weight is about 6.75 lbs. for the 12 gauge, 6.5 lbs. for the 20 gauge, and 6.25 lbs. for the 28 gauge.

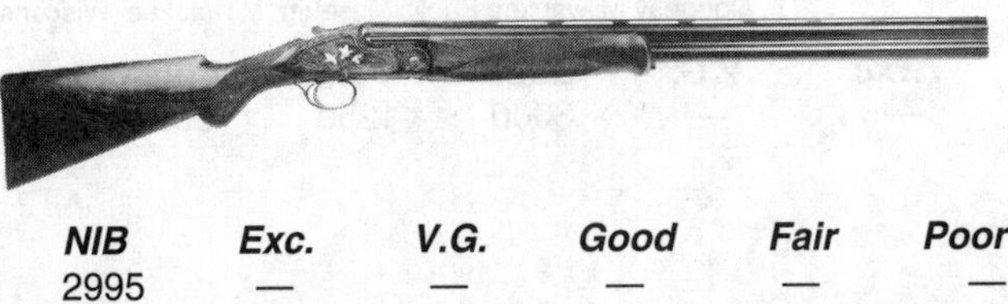

NIB	Exc.	V.G.	Good	Fair	Poor
2995	—	—	—	—	—

Tempio

This over-and-under gun is offered in 12, 20, and 28 gauge with choice of 26" or 28" barrels with choke tubes. Checkered Circassian walnut stock with Prince of Wales-style pistol grip. Alloy receiver is a gray finish of Tinaloy. Engraved with scroll and gold game birds. Single-selective trigger with ejectors. Weight is about 6.8 lbs. for 12 gauge, 6.4 lbs. for 20 gauge, and 6.25 lbs. for the 28 gauge.

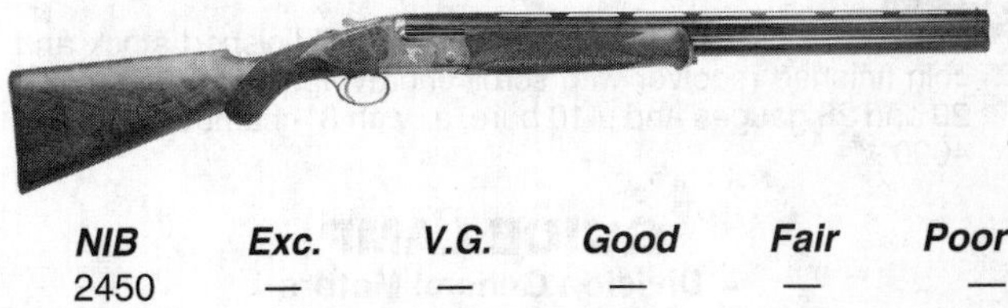

NIB	Exc.	V.G.	Good	Fair	Poor
2450	—	—	—	—	—

Forum/Forum Sporting

This model is offered in 12, 20 and 28 gauge, with choice of 26" or 28" barrels on the Forum and 30", 32", or 34" on the Forum Sporting. Gun has silver receiver with scroll and game scene engraving with side plates.

NIB	Exc.	V.G.	Good	Fair	Poor
6695	—	—	—	—	—

NOTE: Add $300 for Forum Sporting.

Summit Sporting/Summit Limited

Offered in 12, 20, or 28 gauge with choice of 30" or 32" vent-rib barrels with extended choke tubes. Alloy receiver with engraving. Single-selective trigger is adjustable for length of pull. Ejectors. Checkered walnut stock with pistol grip. Weight of 12 gauge is about 8 lbs., the 20 gauge about 7.5 lbs., and the 28 gauge about 7.45 lbs.

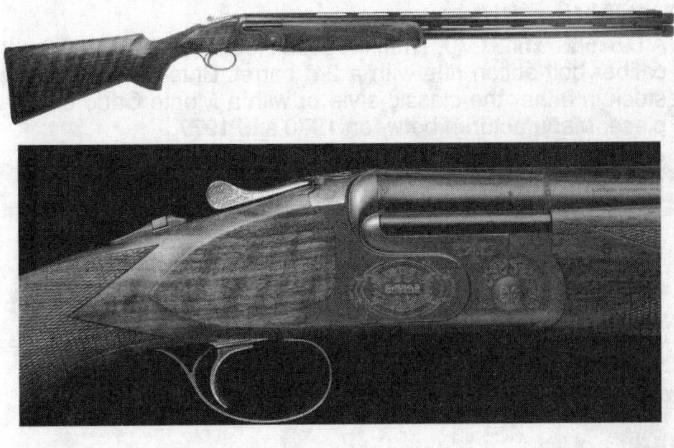

NIB	Exc.	V.G.	Good	Fair	Poor
2650	—	—	—	—	—

NOTE: For Summit Limited add $300.

Magnus Sporting

This model is similar to the Summit but with upgraded wood and sidelock-style receiver with scroll engraving and gold game birds.

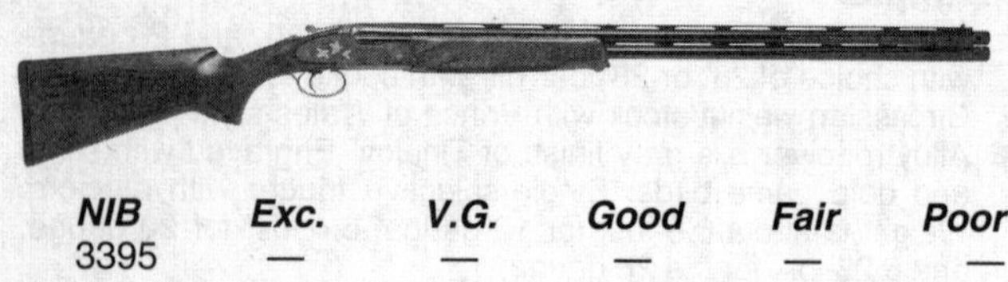

NIB	Exc.	V.G.	Good	Fair	Poor
3395	—	—	—	—	—

Essex

New in 2006, this over-and-under with oil-finished stock and coin finished receiver with scroll engraving is available in 12, 20 and 28 gauges and .410 bore, all with 3" chambers. MSRP: 4000

GUIDE LAMP

Division General Motors
Detroit, Michigan

Liberator

NIB	Exc.	V.G.	Good	Fair	Poor
2500	1200	750	400	300	175

GUION, T. F.

New Orleans, Louisiana

Pocket Pistol

A .41 caliber single-shot percussion pistol with a 2.5" barrel, German silver mountings, and a walnut stock. Manufactured in the 1850s.

Exc.	V.G.	Good	Fair	Poor
—	—	1750	500	275

GULIKERS, V./A LIEGE

SEE—French Military Firearms

GUNWORKS LTD.

Buffalo, New York

Model 9 Derringer

An Over/Under derringer chambered in 9mm, .38 Special, .38 Super, and .357 Magnum caliber with 2.5" barrels, with a spur trigger and Millet sights. Nickel-plate, with walnut grips. Manufacturing ceased in 1986.

Exc.	V.G.	Good	Fair	Poor
150	115	90	75	50

GUSTAF, CARL

Eskilstuna, Sweden

Bolt-Action Rifle

A 6.5x55, 7x64, .270, 7mm Magnum, .308, .30-06, and 9.3x62 caliber bolt-action rifle with a 24" barrel. Blued with a walnut stock in either the classic style or with a Monte Carlo cheekpiece. Manufactured between 1970 and 1977.

Exc.	V.G.	Good	Fair	Poor
650	475	350	275	150

Grade II

As above, with better walnut and a rosewood pistol grip cap and forend tip.

Exc.	V.G.	Good	Fair	Poor
800	600	450	375	175

Grade III

As above, with a high-gloss finish and a finely figured walnut stock.

Exc.	V.G.	Good	Fair	Poor
950	700	550	475	275

Deluxe Bolt-Action

As above, with an engraved floorplate and trigger guard, a Damascened bolt, and a high-grade French walnut stock. Manufactured between 1970 and 1977.

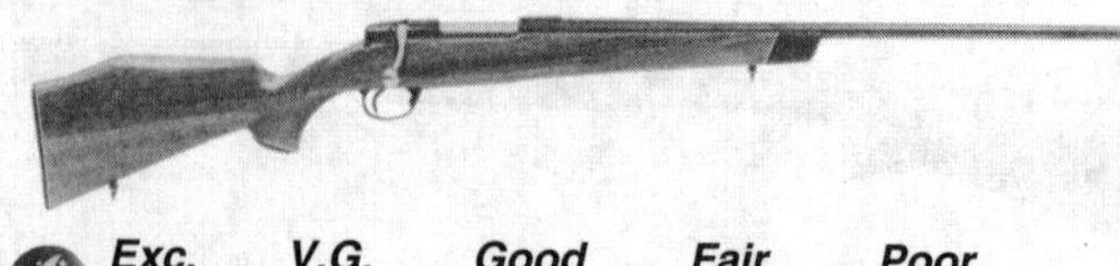

Exc.	V.G.	Good	Fair	Poor
1250	900	650	450	300

Varmint Model

A .222, .22-250, .243, and 6.5x55 caliber bolt-action rifle with 27" barrel and a large bolt knob made of Bakelite. Furnished without open sights and has a heavy target-type stock. Manufactured in 1970 only.

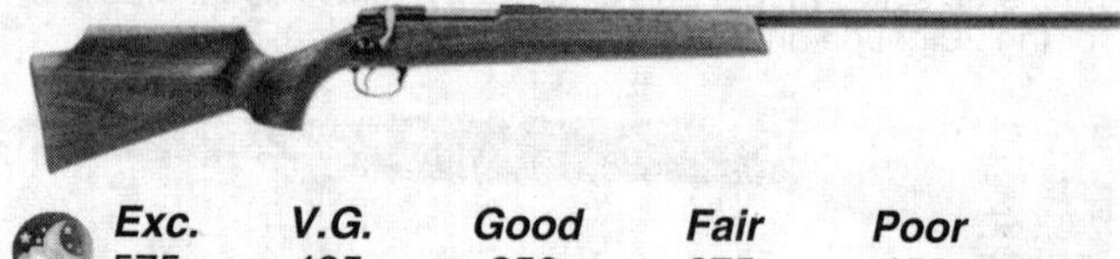

Exc.	V.G.	Good	Fair	Poor
575	425	350	275	150

Grand Prix Target

A .22 caliber single-shot, bolt-action rifle with a 27" barrel and adjustable weights. Furnished without sights and with an adjustable butt target stock. Only manufactured in 1970.

Exc.	V.G.	Good	Fair	Poor
600	475	400	325	175

Model 2000

A 6.5x55, .243, .270, .308, and .30-06 caliber bolt-action rifle with a 60 percent bolt lift and a cold swagged barrel and action. Furnished with open sights. Blued, walnut stock with a Monte Carlo cheekpiece. Manufactured until 1985.

Exc.	V.G.	Good	Fair	Poor
625	500	400	300	150

GWYN & CAMPBELL

Hamilton, Ohio

Union Carbine

A .52 caliber single-shot breech loading percussion carbine with a round/octagonal 20" barrel marked "Gwyn & Campbell/ Patent/1862/ Hamilton,O." Blued, case hardened with a walnut stock. Approximately 8,500 were made between 1862 and 1865.

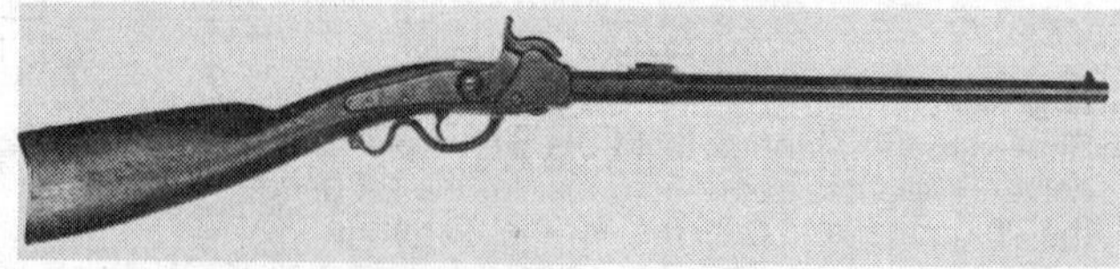

Courtesy Milwaukee Public Museum, Milwaukee, Wisconsin

Exc.	V.G.	Good	Fair	Poor
—	—	3000	1250	500

H.J.S. INDUSTRIES, INC.

Brownsville, Texas

Frontier Four Derringer

A .22 caliber four-barreled pocket pistol with 2.5" sliding barrels, stainless steel frame and barrel grip and walnut grips.

Exc.	V.G.	Good	Fair	Poor
200	150	75	50	25

Lone Star Derringer

A .38 Special caliber single-shot spur trigger pistol with a 2.5" barrel. Stainless steel with wood grips.

Exc.	V.G.	Good	Fair	Poor
200	150	75	50	25

H-S PRECISION, INC.

Rapid City, South Dakota

SPR Sporter Rifle

This bolt-action rifle is offered in both long and short actions with any standard SAAMI caliber. Match grade stainless steel barrel lengths are 22", 24", or 26" with optional muzzlebrake available. Synthetic stock is offered in various colors. Weight is between 7.5 and 7.75 lbs. depending on barrel length. Magazine capacity is 4 rounds for standard calibers and 3 rounds for magnum calibers.

NIB	Exc.	V.G.	Good	Fair	Poor
2175	1600	1200	—	—	—

SPL Lightweight Sporter

Introduced in 2005 this model features a 22", 24", or 26" fluted barrel with choice of short or long action calibers. Detachable magazine. No sights. Pro-series synthetic stock. Weight is under 7 lbs.

NIB	Exc.	V.G.	Good	Fair	Poor
2175	1600	—	—	—	—

PHR Professional Hunter Rifle

This bolt-action rifle is chambered for magnum calibers only and is fitted with 24" or 26" stainless steel match grade fluted barrel (except .416 Rigby). Built in recoil reduced in synthetic stock with choice of colors. Matte black finish. Weight is between 7.75 lbs. and 8.25 depending on barrel length and caliber. Offered in any standard SAAMI caliber. Magazine capacity is 3 rounds.

NIB	Exc.	V.G.	Good	Fair	Poor
2375	1750	1300	—	—	—

BHR Big Game Professional Hunter Rifle

Introduced in 2005 this model has the same features as the PHR series with the addition of adjustable iron sights and specially designed stock. Weight is about 7.75 to 8.25 lbs. depending on caliber and barrel length.

NIB	Exc.	V.G.	Good	Fair	Poor
2375	1750	—	—	—	—

PHL Professional Hunter Lightweight Rifle

This model features a weight of 5.75 lbs. Fitted with a Pro-Series stock and choice of 20" or 22" contoured fluted stock. Matte black teflon finish. Detachable magazine. Chambered for short action calibers. Introduced in 2005.

NIB	Exc.	V.G.	Good	Fair	Poor
2475	1850	—	—	—	—

VAR Varmint Rifle

Offered in long or short action with .17 Rem., 6mm PPC, and .223 Rem. in single-shot. Fitted with match grade stainless steel fluted barrel in 24" or 26" lengths. Also available is a lightweight 20" barrel. Synthetic stock in choice of colors with 20" barrel guns offered with thumbhole stocks. Black matte finish. Weight is between 8 and 8.25 lbs. for standard rifles and 7.5 and 7.75 lbs. for 20" barrel guns. Available in any standard SAAMI caliber.

NIB	Exc.	V.G.	Good	Fair	Poor
2275	1700	1200	—	—	—

Varmint Take-Down Rifle

This take-down bolt-action rifle is offered in a stainless steel long or short action with 24" stainless steel match grade fluted barrel. Matte black finish. Weight is between 8.5 and 9 lbs.

NIB	Exc.	V.G.	Good	Fair	Poor
3500	2500	—	—	—	—

NOTE: Add $1,000 for extra barrel with same head size caliber and $1,200 for extra barrel with different head size caliber.

Professional Hunter Take-Down Rifle

This take-down rifle is offered in magnum and super magnum calibers with 24" fluted stainless steel barrel. Built in recoil reducer. Matte black finish. Weight is between 8.25 and 8.75 lbs.

NIB	Exc.	V.G.	Good	Fair	Poor
3600	2600	—	—	—	—

Varmint Pistol

Bolt-action single-shot pistol chambered for a wide variety of calibers from .17 Rem. to 7mm BR. Fitted with a heavy contour fluted stainless steel match barrel. Synthetic stock with center grip. Matte black finish. Weight is about 5.25 to 5.5 lbs.

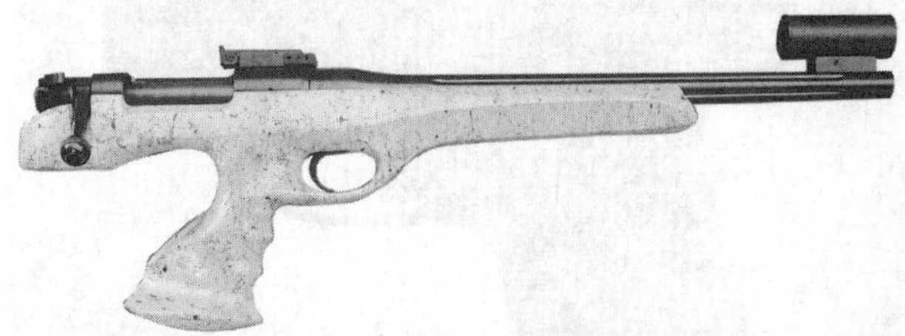

NIB	Exc.	V.G.	Good	Fair	Poor
1250	1000	—	—	—	—

Silhouette Pistol

Same as above but with sporter contoured barrel. Weight is about 4.5 lbs.

NIB	Exc.	V.G.	Good	Fair	Poor
1250	1000	—	—	—	—

HTR Heavy Tactical Rifle

This bolt-action model features a stainless steel long or short action with fluted stainless steel 24" heavy barrel. Stock is synthetic with adjustable cheekpiece and length of pull. Any standard SAAMI caliber is available. Weight is about 10.75 to 11.25 lbs. Matte black finish.

NIB	Exc.	V.G.	Good	Fair	Poor
2400	1750	—	—	—	—

Short Tactical

Chambered for the .308 cartridge and fitted with a 20" fluted barrel with matte teflon finish. Pro-Series tactical stock.

NIB	Exc.	V.G.	Good	Fair	Poor
2375	1750	—	—	—	—

RDR Rapid Deployment Rifle

This is similar ot the model above but with 20" stainlees steel fluted barrel and smaller stock. Thumbhole stock on request. Magazine is 4 rounds. Matte black finish. Offered in any short action SAAMI calibers. Weight is between 7.5 and 7.75 lbs.

NIB	Exc.	V.G.	Good	Fair	Poor
2275	1700	—	—	—	—

TTD Tactical Take-Down System

This take-down rifle is chambered for any standard SAAMI caliber and fitted with a 24" fluted heavy stainless steel barrel. Magazine capacity is 4 rounds for standard calibers and 3 rounds for magnum calibers. Synthetic stock that is adjustable for length of pull and cheekpiece. Matte black finish. Weight is between 11.25 and 11.75 lbs.

NIB	Exc.	V.G.	Good	Fair	Poor
3800	2750	—	—	—	—

HAENEL, C. G.

Suhl, Germany

Established in 1840, this company began to manufacture semi-automatic pistols after Hugo Schmeisser joined the firm in 1921 as its chief engineer.

Model 1

A 6.35mm caliber semi-automatic pistol with a 2.48" barrel, striker-fired, a 6-shot magazine. Weight is approximately 13.5 oz. The left side of the slide is stamped "C.G. Haenel Suhl-Schmeisser Patent." Each grip panel is marked "HS" in an oval.

Exc.	V.G.	Good	Fair	Poor
400	300	225	175	100

Model 2

As above, but shorter (2" barrel) and lighter in weight (12 oz.). "Schmeisser" is molded into the grips.

Courtesy Orvel Reichert

Exc.	V.G.	Good	Fair	Poor
450	325	250	200	125

HAFDASA

Buenos Aires, Argentina

Ballester-Molina

A copy of the Colt Model 1911 semi-automatic pistol differing only in the absence of a grip safety, smaller grip and the finger grooves on the slide. The slide stamped "Pistola Automatica Cal. .45 Fabricado por HAFDASA Patentes Internacional Ballester Molina Industria Argentina" on the slide. Introduced in 1941.

Courtesy James Rankin

Exc.	V.G.	Good	Fair	Poor
475	400	300	225	100

Criolla

A .22 caliber automatic pistol, similar to the Ballester-Molina. Some were sold commercially under the trademark "La Criolla."

Exc.	V.G.	Good	Fair	Poor
1000	800	650	500	250

This symbol denotes "Sleepers" with rapidly-rising values and/or significant collector potential.

Hafdasa

A .22 caliber semi-automatic pistol with a tubular receiver. A true hammerless, striker-fired, with an angled grip. Markings are "HA" on the butt.

Exc.	V.G.	Good	Fair	Poor
400	325	275	200	100

Zonda

As above, but marked "Zonda."

Exc.	V.G.	Good	Fair	Poor
400	325	275	200	100

Rigaud

A semi-automatic copy of the Colt Model 1911 with no grip safety. Caliber is .45 ACP and later .22 LR. Barrel length is 5". Magazine capacity is 7 rounds. The .22 caliber was introduced in 1940.

Courtesy James Rankin

Exc.	V.G.	Good	Fair	Poor
475	400	300	225	100

Campeon

The same as the Ballester-Molina but with a floating chamber to accommodate the .22 LR cartridge. There were three variations of the target model: Sights, trigger, and barrel lengths. The pistol was first introduced in 1941 and produced until 1953.

Courtesy James Rankin

Exc.	V.G.	Good	Fair	Poor
750	550	400	300	200

HAKIM
Egypt

A 7.92x57mm caliber semi-automatic rifle copied from the Swedish Model 42 Ljungman. Manufactured by Maadi Military and Civil Industries Co.

Exc.	V.G.	Good	Fair	Poor
275	225	200	150	100

HAHN, WILLIAM
New York, New York

Pocket Pistol

A .41 caliber single-shot percussion pistol with a 2.5" round barrel, German silver mountings, and a walnut stock. Manufactured in the 1860s and 1870s.

Exc.	V.G.	Good	Fair	Poor
—	—	1500	900	400

HALE, H. J.
Bristol, Connecticut

Under Hammer Pistol

A .31 caliber single-shot, under hammer percussion pistol with a 5" or 6" part-round, part-octagonal barrel and an iron frame with either a pointed or a round walnut butt. Markings read "H.J.Hale/Warranted/Cast Steel." Manufactured during the 1850s.

Exc.	V.G.	Good	Fair	Poor
—	—	850	300	200

HALE & TULLER
Hartford, Connecticut

Under Hammer Pistol

A .44 caliber single-shot under hammer percussion pistol with a 6" tapered round barrel and a pointed walnut grip. Manufactured at the Connecticut State Prison between 1837 and 1840.

Exc.	V.G.	Good	Fair	Poor
—	—	800	300	200

HALL, ALEXANDER
New York, New York

Revolving Rifle

A .58 caliber percussion revolving rifle with a 15-shot open centered cylinder. The frame was made of brass, the barrel and cylinder of iron and the stock of walnut. Manufactured during the 1850s in limited quantities. This is a very rare firearm.

Exc.	V.G.	Good	Fair	Poor
—	—	22500	9500	3000

HALL-NORTH
Middletown, Connecticut

Model 1840 Carbine

This carbine was manufactured by Simeon North and was chambered for .52 caliber percussion. It is a single-shot, breech-loading, smoothbore with a 21" round barrel. It has a full-length stock held on by two barrel bands. There is a ramrod mounted under the barrel, and the mountings are of iron. The lock is case hardened, and the barrel is brown. The stock is walnut. The markings are "US/S. North/Midltn/ Conn." There are two distinct variations, both produced under military contract.

Type 1 Carbine

This model has a squared, right-angled breech lever mounted on the trigger plate. There were 500 of these manufactured in 1840.

Exc.	V.G.	Good	Fair	Poor
—	—	7500	3000	1200

Type 2 Carbine

This variation features a curved, breech-operating lever that is known as a fishtail. There were approximately 6,000 of these manufactured from 1840 to 1843. Some have an 8" bar and ring.

Exc.	V.G.	Good	Fair	Poor
—	—	5000	2000	750

HAMBUSH, JOSEPH
Ferlach, Austria

Boxlock Side-by-Side Shotgun

A custom-order boxlock double-barrel shotgun chambered for all gauges, single-selective or double trigger and automatic ejectors. It features workmanship of a high order, and all specification could vary with the customer's wishes. Engraved with hunting scenes. This is a rare gun and is not often encountered on today's market.

Exc.	*V.G.*	*Good*	*Fair*	*Poor*
1750	1000	800	550	350

NOTE: Pricing is only estimated as not enough are traded to provide accurate values.

Sidelock Side-by-Side Shotgun

Similar to the above, but features a full sidelock-action.

Exc.	*V.G.*	*Good*	*Fair*	*Poor*
3500	2000	1800	1500	1250

HAMILTON RIFLE COMPANY
Plymouth, Michigan

Manufacturer of inexpensive .22 caliber rifles established by Clarence J. Hamilton and his son Coello. The company was established in 1898 in Plymouth, Michigan. The company ceased production in 1945. Over 1 million rifles were produced between 1900 and 1911.

NOTE: Despite the fact that there were many Hamilton rifles sold, most of these little guns were used hard and many did not survive. Hamilton rifles in excellent condition are hardly ever encountered. No prices are quoted for rifles in this condition as few exist. Further information about these rifles is gratefully accepted by the editor.

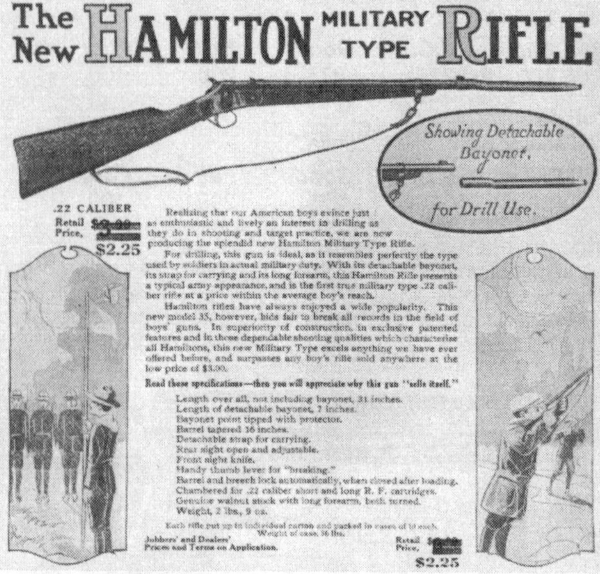

Model 7

The first rifle produced by the company, it was made entirely of castings and stampings. It was nickel plated. Chambered for the .22 Short cartridge with an 8" brass-lined barrel that pivots for loading. The stock was a metal skeleton. Production ceased in 1901 with a total of 44,000 rifles produced.

THE HAMILTON NO. 7

DAN SHIDELER

Probably more people were introduced to the No. 7 by the old *Sears, Roebuck Consumer Guide*—better known simply as the "Wish Book"—than by any other route. On Page 373 of *Sears, Roebuck's Catalog No. 110*, published in Fall 1900, we find the following tucked into 1/16 page in the upper right column:

> "Our $2.00 Rifle—A Rare Bargain, and Perfectly Safe." "Worth $3.50 / No. 34669 / **Our new 22-Caliber Rifle**. Uses 22-caliber short rim fire cartridges, including smokeless. **Is absolutely safe.** Total length, 32 inches. Length of barrel, 8 inches, brass lined, with steel jacket. **The rifling is absolutely perfect,** as fine as the highest priced rifles. Bead front and peep rear sights. All parts interchangeable. Entire rifle nickel plated. We recommend and guarantee these rifles. Our special price **$2.00**."

That two-dollar gun was the Hamilton No. 7.

The Hamilton Rifle Co. might be the least-documented American rifle manufacturer. Information concerning it is usually found in bits and pieces in a wide variety of printed and electronic sources. One of the most helpful resources I have found is a Web site maintained by Jim Ringbauer at home.comcast.net/%7Ejimringbauer/HamiltonRiflesindex.html. I recommend his site highly to anyone who has an interest in Hamilton rifles.

According to Ringbauer, Clarence Hamilton of Plymouth, Mich., founded a windmill manufacturing company—the descriptively named Plymouth Iron Windmill Co.—in 1882. Before the company folded about 16 years later, Hamilton entered a partnership with a buddy of his who had patented an all-metal air rifle. They began producing the air rifle which surprised everyone by becoming more popular than the company's windmills! In 1898, Hamilton sold his share of the windmill concern and the air rifle company. (The latter went on to enduring fame as the Daisy Air Rifle Co.) Hamilton's son Coello, a tool and die maker, joined what was left of his father's business, and the Hamilton Rifle Co. was born.

Clarence Hamilton died two years later, but the company he founded would persist until 1945. The Hamilton Rifle Co. would eventually manufacture 14 models of rimfire rifles. The No. 7 was its first. (I have no idea what happened to Models No. 1 through No. 6. Possibly the numbering system started with the earlier Plymouth air rifles.)

The No. 7 will seem familiar to anyone who's ever handled a Garcia Bronco. The No. 7 had a pivoting 8" barrel that swung to the left for loading, just as the Bronco did. The barrel itself was a nickel-plated, rifled brass tube enclosed in a plated steel jacket, and the extractor was a sliding flange in the chamber that you operated with a thumbnail. It's a simple design, not pretty but darn near foolproof.

In all, 44,700 No. 7s were made from 1899 to 1901, of which Ringbauer estimates about 99.9 percent have since gone to "rifle heaven."

Perhaps that's why it took me 46 years to see my first Hamilton No. 7!

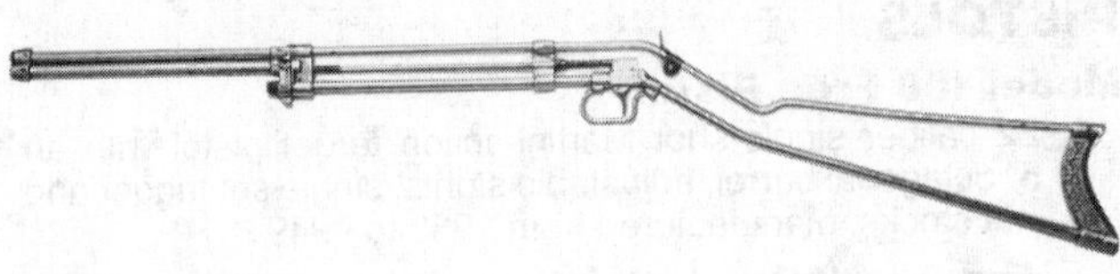

Hamilton Model 7 Courtesy William F. Krause

Exc.	V.G.	Good	Fair	Poor
—	400	250	200	150

Model 11

Similar to the Model 7 but fitted with a board-like walnut stock. There are markings stamped into the buttstock: HAMILTON RIFLES CO., PLYMOUTH, MICH., PAT. PENDING NO.11. The Model 11 was produced from 1900 to 1902 and approximately 22,000 were sold.

Exc.	V.G.	Good	Fair	Poor
—	475	300	200	150

Model 15

Produced from 1901 to 1910 the Model 15 was chambered for the .22 Short with an 8" brass lined barrel. Walnut stock. The design was an under lever single-shot with the loading port under the barrel. The cocking knob is located at the rear of the frame. Blued finish. Approximately 234,000 of these rifles were sold.

Exc.	V.G.	Good	Fair	Poor
—	400	200	150	100

Model 19

This is similar to the Model 15 with a modified loading port and a 12" barrel. A few Model 19s have been seen with 13" barrels. these will bring a premium. Produced from 1903 to 1910 there were about 59,000 of these models sold.

Exc.	V.G.	Good	Fair	Poor
—	475	300	200	150

Model 23

This was the first bolt-action rifle made by the company. The receiver is a steel tube with a loading port in the top where the barrel joins the receiver. The bolt handle is located at the extreme rear of the bolt. The cocking knob must be operated manually. Walnut stock either rounded or flat. Chamber for the .22 Short and .22 Long cartridges. 15" brass lined barrel. Blued finish. Weighs about 3 lbs. Produced from 1905 to 1909. About 25,000 guns were sold.

Exc.	V.G.	Good	Fair	Poor
—	475	300	200	150

Model 27

Single-shot tip-up .22 caliber rifle with stamped steel receiver. Barrel length 16" brass lined or 14-7/8"; overall length 30". First produced in 1906.

Exc.	V.G.	Good	Fair	Poor
—	300	200	150	100

Model 027

As above with a walnut stock. First produced in 1908.

Exc.	V.G.	Good	Fair	Poor
—	300	200	150	100

Model 31

Introduced in 1910 this single-shot rifle is chambered for the .22 Short and Long cartridge. Fitted with a 15-3/4" barrel with brass liner. It is a tip-up design. Blued finish. Weighs about 2.25 lbs.

Exc.	V.G.	Good	Fair	Poor
—	575	400	250	200

Model 35 or Boys' Military Rifle

Single-shot .22 caliber rifle with a full-length oval walnut straight-grip stock and 15-3/4" brass lined barrel. Produced from 1915 to 1918. Sold with a stamped steel bayonet. Few bayonets survive.

Exc.	V.G.	Good	Fair	Poor
—	400	250	150	100

NOTE: Add $100 for bayonet to above prices.

Model 39

This was the only repeating rifle built by the company. It is a hammerless slide-action design with a tubular magazine. Magazine capacity is 15 rounds of .22 Short. Barrel length is 16" with brass liner. Walnut stock with blade front sight. Produced from 1922 to 1930. Weighs about 4 lbs.

Exc.	V.G.	Good	Fair	Poor
—	300	200	150	100

Model 43

This is a bolt-action design with the loading port on the top of the barrel. There is no external cocking knob but the bolt is pulled to the rear when in the locked position. Chambered for the .22 Short and .22 Long cartridges. 15.75" brass lined barrel. Fitted with an oval walnut stock with blade front sight and open non-adjustable rear sight. Weighs about 3 lbs. Built from 1924 to 1932.

Exc.	V.G.	Good	Fair	Poor
—	300	200	150	100

Model 47

This is a bolt-action single-shot rifle with the loading port located on top of the barrel. It was chambered for the .22 Short and Long cartridges. The cocking knob is located at the rear of the bolt handle. Early Model 47 were built with 16" brass lined barrels. Later examples were fitted with 18.25" steel lined barrels. Early guns had an oval buttstock while later guns had a pistol grip stock. Very late guns had an all-steel barrel. Produced from 1927 to 1932.

Exc.	V.G.	Good	Fair	Poor
—	475	300	200	150

Model 51

This was a conventional type bolt-action rifle with the cocking knob located at the rear of the bolt. Two styles of buttstocks were used: a flat style or later an oval shape. This was the first Hamilton rifle chambered for the .22 LR cartridge. Barrel was 20" steel. Finish was blue. Weight was approximately 3.5 lbs. Produced from 1935 to 1941.

Exc.	V.G.	Good	Fair	Poor
—	400	250	200	150

Model 55

This bolt-action rifle was chambered for the .22 Short, Long, and LR cartridges. Fitted with a 20" steel barrel with bead front sight and open adjustable rear sight. Walnut stock. This is the rarest Hamilton rifle. Only one example is known. Produced from late 1941 to early 1942.

NOTE: No price has yet been established.

HAMMERLI, SA
Lenzburg, Switzerland

RIFLES

Model 45 Smallbore Rifle

A .22 caliber bolt-action single-shot, with a 27.5" heavy barrel, an aperture rear and globe target front sight and a match rifle-type thumbhole stock. Manufactured between 1945 and 1957.

Exc.	V.G.	Good	Fair	Poor
725	600	525	425	225

Model 54 Smallbore Rifle

As above, with an adjustable buttplate. Manufactured between 1954 and 1957.

Exc.	V.G.	Good	Fair	Poor
750	625	550	450	250

Model 503 Smallbore Free Rifle

Similar to the Model 54, with a free rifle-style stock.

Exc.	V.G.	Good	Fair	Poor
700	575	500	400	200

Model 506 Smallbore Match Rifle

The later version of the Smallbore target series. Manufactured between 1963 and 1966.

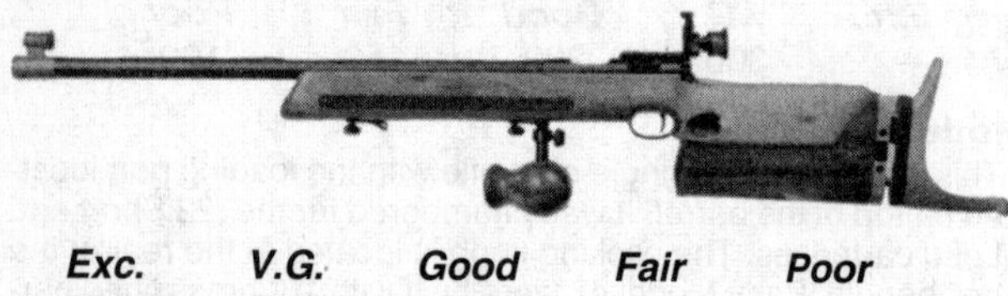

Exc.	V.G.	Good	Fair	Poor
750	725	650	550	350

Olympic 300 Meter

A 7x57, .30-06, or .300 H&H Magnum caliber bolt-action, single-shot, rifle with a 20.5" heavy barrel, an aperture rear, globe target front sight, double-set triggers and a free rifle-type, adjustable thumbhole stock with a wide beavertail forearm and schuetzen-style buttplate. Manufactured between 1945 and 1959.

Exc.	V.G.	Good	Fair	Poor
950	800	650	500	300

Sporting Rifle

A bolt-action, single-shot rifle chambered for many popular calibers (American and European), double-set triggers and a classic-style stock.

Exc.	V.G.	Good	Fair	Poor
700	575	500	400	325

PISTOLS

Model 100 Free Pistol

A .22 caliber single-shot Martini-action target pistol with an 11.5" octagonal barrel, adjustable sights, single set trigger and walnut stocks. Manufactured from 1933 to 1949.

Exc.	V.G.	Good	Fair	Poor
900	725	650	500	300

Model 101

As above, with a heavy round barrel and more sophisticated target sights. A matte-blued finish and was manufactured between 1956 and 1960.

Exc.	V.G.	Good	Fair	Poor
900	725	650	500	300

Model 102

As above, with highly polished blue finish. Manufactured between 1956 and 1960.

Exc.	V.G.	Good	Fair	Poor
900	725	650	500	300

Model 103

Similar to the Model 101, with a lighter-weight octagonal barrel, high-polished blued finish. Manufactured between 1956 and 1960.

Exc.	V.G.	Good	Fair	Poor
1000	825	750	600	400

Model 104

As above, with a lightweight round barrel. Manufactured between 1961 and 1965.

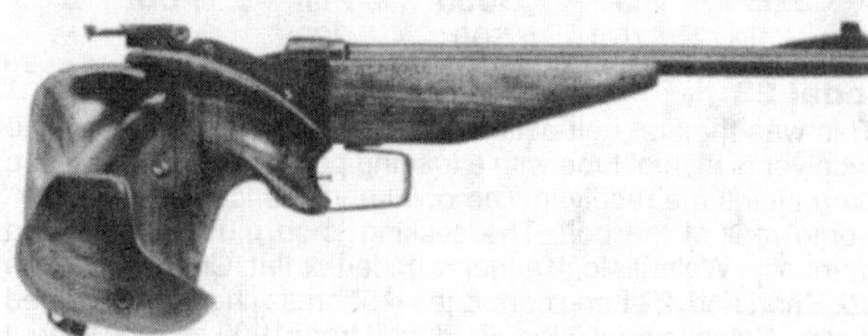

Exc.	V.G.	Good	Fair	Poor
750	625	550	450	300

Model 105

As above, with a redesigned stock and an improved action. Manufactured between 1962 and 1965.

Exc.	V.G.	Good	Fair	Poor
1000	825	750	600	400

Model 106

As above, with an improved trigger.

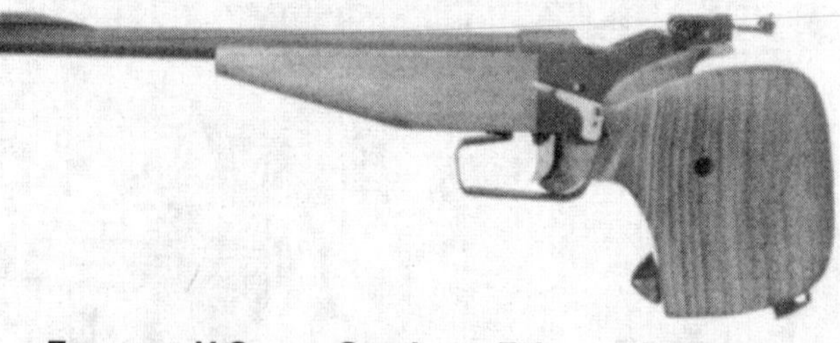

Exc.	V.G.	Good	Fair	Poor
1100	900	750	600	400

Model 107

This variation is fitted with a five-level set trigger. Introduced in 1965 and discontinued in 1971.

Exc.	V.G.	Good	Fair	Poor
750	600	500	300	—

Model 107 Deluxe

As above, but engraved and with a carved stock.

Exc.	V.G.	Good	Fair	Poor
1500	1250	900	800	500

Model 120-1 Free Pistol

A bolt-action, single-shot pistol in .22 LR caliber with a a 9.9" barrel, adjustable target sights, activated for loading and cocking by an alloy lever on the side of the bolt. Blued, with checkered walnut grips.

Exc.	V.G.	Good	Fair	Poor
450	375	300	225	150

Model 120-2

As above with contoured grips.

Exc.	V.G.	Good	Fair	Poor
475	400	325	250	175

Model 120 Heavy Barrel

As above, with a 5.7" heavy barrel.

Exc.	V.G.	Good	Fair	Poor
450	375	300	225	150

Model 150

A single-shot, Martini-action .22 caliber pistol with an 11.25" barrel, adjustable sights, contoured grips and a single-set trigger. Blued with walnut stocks.

Exc.	V.G.	Good	Fair	Poor
1500	1000	—	—	—

Model 152

As above, with an 11.25" barrel, and an electronic release trigger.

Exc.	V.G.	Good	Fair	Poor
1800	1300	—	—	—

International Model 206

A .22 caliber semi-automatic pistol with a 7.5" barrel, an integral muzzlebrake, adjustable sights, and walnut grips. Manufactured between 1962 and 1969.

Exc.	V.G.	Good	Fair	Poor
725	600	475	375	275

International Model 207

As above, with adjustable grips.

Exc.	V.G.	Good	Fair	Poor
750	625	500	400	200

International Model 208

A .22 caliber semi-automatic pistol with a 6" barrel, adjustable sights and an 8-shot magazine, adjustable trigger, and target grips. The barrel is drilled and tapped for the addition of barrel weights. Manufactured between 1966 and 1988.

Exc.	V.G.	Good	Fair	Poor
1850	1550	1250	1000	750

International Model 208 Deluxe

As above, with an engraved receiver, and carved grips. Discontinued in 1988.

Exc.	V.G.	Good	Fair	Poor
3250	2750	2500	2000	1500

International Model 209

A .22 Short caliber semi-automatic pistol with a 4.75" barrel, a muzzlebrake, adjustable target sights, and 5-shot magazine. Blued, with walnut grips. Manufactured between 1966 and 1970.

Exc.	V.G.	Good	Fair	Poor
850	700	600	450	350

International Model 210

As above, with adjustable grips.

Exc.	V.G.	Good	Fair	Poor
850	700	600	450	350

International Model 211

As above, with non-adjustable thumb rest grips.

Exc.	V.G.	Good	Fair	Poor
1850	1550	1250	1000	750

Model 212

A .22 caliber semi-automatic pistol with a 5" barrel, and adjustable sights. Blued with walnut grips.

Exc.	V.G.	Good	Fair	Poor
1400	1275	1000	750	650

Model 230

A .22 Short caliber semi-automatic pistol with a 6.3" barrel, a 5-shot magazine, adjustable sights and walnut grip. Manufactured between 1970 and 1983.

Exc.	V.G.	Good	Fair	Poor
725	600	500	400	200

Model 232

A .22 short caliber semi-automatic pistol with a 5" barrel, adjustable sights, and a 6-shot magazine. Contoured walnut grips. Introduced in 1984.

Exc.	V.G.	Good	Fair	Poor
1300	1000	—	—	—

Model 280

This is the new state-of-the-art target pistol from Hammerli. It features a modular design and has a frame of carbon fiber material. It has a 4.6" barrel with adjustable sights, trigger, and grips. It is chambered for .22 LR or .32 wadcutter. The magazine holds 5 rounds, and the pistol was introduced in 1988.

Exc.	V.G.	Good	Fair	Poor
1800	1500	1350	1000	600

Model SP 20

Introduced in 1998, this pistol has a very low sight line and features a wide variety of special items such as adjustable buffer system, anatomically shaped trigger in various sizes, various receiver colors, change over caliber system from .22 LR to .32 S&W.

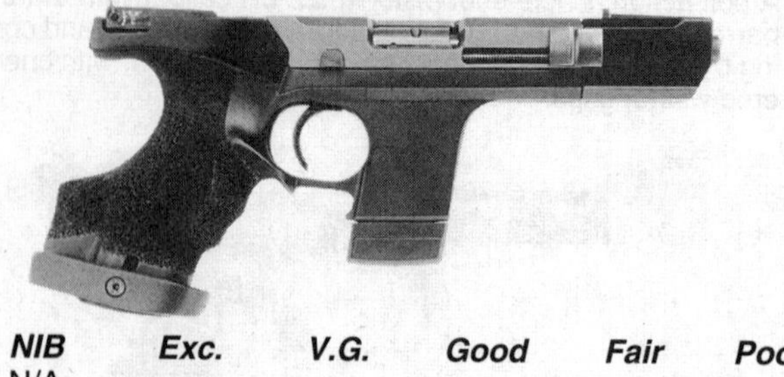

NIB	Exc.	V.G.	Good	Fair	Poor
N/A	—	—	—	—	—

Dakota

A single-action revolver based on the Colt SAA design. It has a solid frame and is loaded through a gate. It is chambered for .22 LR, .357 Magnum, .44-40, and .45 Colt and was offered with barrel lengths of 5", 6", and 7.5". It has a 6-shot cylinder and is blued, with a brass trigger guard and walnut grips.

Exc.	V.G.	Good	Fair	Poor
250	175	125	100	50

Large Calibers

Exc.	V.G.	Good	Fair	Poor
450	350	200	100	50

Super Dakota

Similar to the Dakota but is chambered for .41 and .44 Magnum, with adjustable sights.

Exc.	V.G.	Good	Fair	Poor
475	375	275	150	100

Virginian

Basically a more deluxe version of the Dakota. It is chambered for the .357 and .45 Colt cartridge. The trigger guard and back strap are chrome plated, with the frame case colored and the remainder blued. This model features the "Swissafe" safety system that allows the cylinder axis pin to be locked back to prevent the hammer from falling.

Exc.	V.G.	Good	Fair	Poor
450	350	200	100	50

HAMMERLI-WALTHER

Lenzburg, Switzerland

These target pistols were produced by Hammerli under license from Walther after WWII. This project continued until approximately 1963, when production was ceased.

Olympia Model 200 Type 1952

A .22 caliber semi-automatic pistol with a 7.5" barrel, a 10-shot magazine, adjustable target sights, and a blued with walnut grips. Manufactured between 1952 and 1958.

Exc.	V.G.	Good	Fair	Poor
700	575	475	375	300

This symbol denotes "Sleepers" with rapidly-rising values and/or significant collector potential.

Model 200 Type 1958

As above with an integral muzzlebrake. Manufactured between 1958 and 1963.

Exc.	V.G.	Good	Fair	Poor
750	625	525	425	325

Model 201

A Model 200 Type 1952 with a 9.5" barrel. Manufactured between 1955 and 1957.

Exc.	V.G.	Good	Fair	Poor
700	575	475	375	300

Model 202

Similar to the Model 201, with adjustable walnut grips. Manufactured between 1955 and 1957.

Exc.	V.G.	Good	Fair	Poor
750	625	525	425	325

Model 203

Similar to the Model 200, with the adjustable grips, available with or without a muzzlebrake.

Exc.	V.G.	Good	Fair	Poor
750	625	525	425	325

Model 204

A .22 caliber semi-automatic pistol with a 7.5" barrel, a muzzlebrake, and barrel weights. Manufactured between 1956 and 1963.

Exc.	V.G.	Good	Fair	Poor
800	675	575	475	375

Model 205

As above, with adjustable target grips. Manufactured between 1956 and 1963.

Exc.	V.G.	Good	Fair	Poor
925	775	675	575	450

HAMMOND BULLDOG

Connecticut Arms & Mfg. Co.
Naubuc, Connecticut

Hammond Bulldog

A .44 rimfire single-shot spur trigger pistol with a 4" octagonal barrel that pivots to open. Blued with checkered walnut grips. Manufactured from 1864 to approximately 1867.

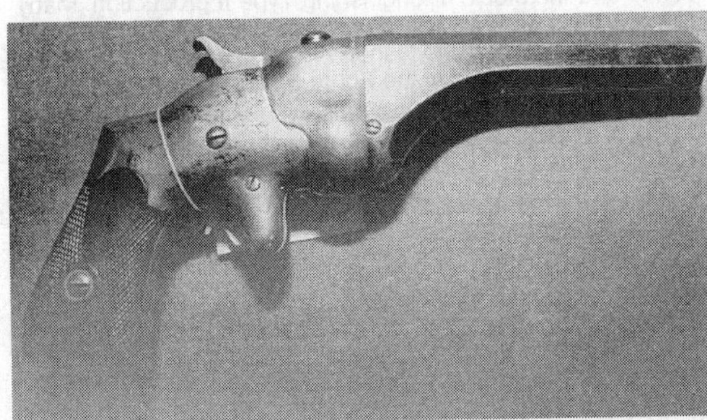

Exc.	V.G.	Good	Fair	Poor
—	1000	500	375	250

HAMMOND, GRANT MFG. CO.

New Haven, Connecticut

Military Automatic Pistol

A .45 ACP caliber semi-automatic pistol with a 6.75" barrel and an 8-shot magazine. Blued, with checkered walnut grips. Marked on the right of the slide "Grant Hammond Mfg. Corp. New Haven, Conn." The left side shows the patent dates. Manufactured in 1917. As all the known specimens of this pistol exhibit differences, it is believed that they were only made as prototypes. The highest serial number known is under 20.

Courtesy Horst Held

Exc.	V.G.	Good	Fair	Poor
TOO RARE TO PRICE				

Grant Hammond 7.65mm Pistol

A semi-automatic pistol in 7.65mm caliber. Has a blow-forward action and a spur hammer.

Courtesy James Rankin

Exc.	V.G.	Good	Fair	Poor
TOO RARE TO PRICE				

H&R 1871, LLC

Gardner, Massachusetts
SEE—Harrington & Richardson

HANKINS, WILLIAM

Philadelphia, Pennsylvania

Pocket Revolver

A .26 caliber spur trigger percussion revolver with a 3" octagonal barrel, and a 5-shot unfluted cylinder. Blued with walnut grips. Approximately 650 were manufactured in 1860 and 1861.

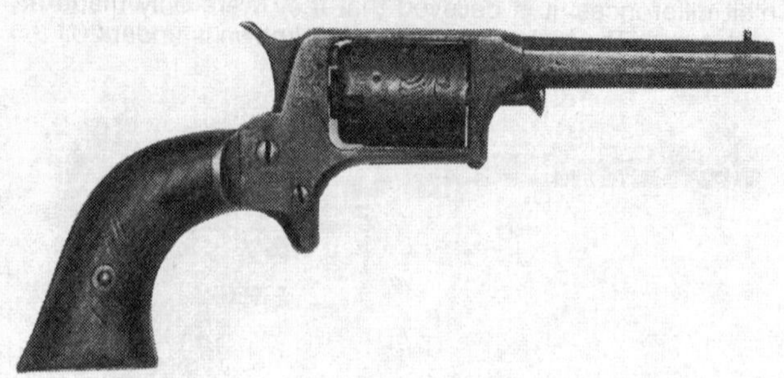

Courtesy Milwaukee Public Museum, Milwaukee, Wisconsin

Exc.	V.G.	Good	Fair	Poor
—	—	2750	1250	500

HANUS, BILL

Newport, Oregon

Bill Hanus Classic

Built in Spain by Ignacio Ugartechea these side-by-side shotguns are offered in 16, 20, 28 gauge, as well as .410 bore. They are fitted with 27" barrel with concave ribs and are choked IC/M. Stock is straight grip with splinter forearm. Double triggers are standard as are automatic ejectors.

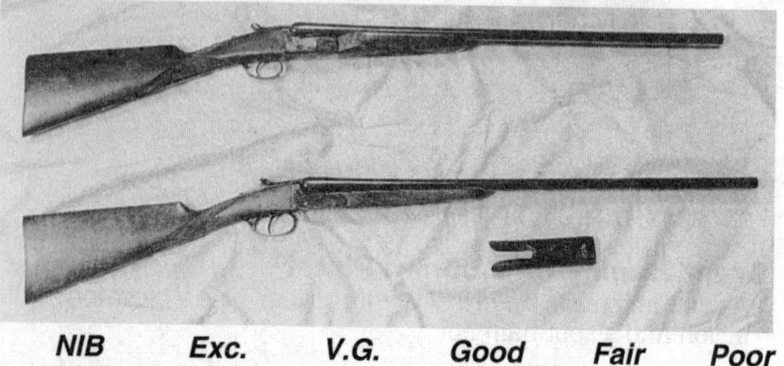

NIB	Exc.	V.G.	Good	Fair	Poor
1600	1250	—	—	—	—

HARPERS FERRY ARMORY MUSKETS AND CARBINES

Harpers Ferry, Virginia

Established at Harpers Ferry, Virginia, in 1798 as the new nation's "Southern Armory," production finally began in 1800 and continued at the "musket works" until the facilities were seized by Virginia state militia in April 1861. With the signing of a contract in 1819 between the government and J.H. Hall, the latter was permitted to construct a separate facility for the production of his patent breechloading rifles, which continued to be known as the "rifle works" after the discontinuation of Hall production until it, too, was seized by Virginia militia in 1861. The machinery of the former was sent to Richmond to be used in the manufacture of the "Richmond rifle musket" while the rifle machinery was sent to Fayetteville, North Carolina, where it was employed in making "Fayetteville rifles."

Harpers Ferry U.S. M1816 Muskets (Types I to III)

Overall length 57-3/4"; barrel length 42"; caliber .69. Markings: on lockplate eagle over "US" forward of cock, "HARPERS/FERRY/(date) on tail. Barrel tang also bears the date, and barrel should show proofmarks on upper left side near breech. The 45605 (type 1) muskets produced at Harpers Ferry from 1817 through 1821 were made with a lower sling swivel that was attached to a separate lug extending from the forward strap of the trigger guard. In 1822, this piece was eliminated and the balance of the production (216,116) officially known as the M1822 musket, incorporated the lower sling swivel directly to the trigger guard bow. Until 1832, these muskets were manufactured with a "browned" barrel to inhibit rusting. The brown barrels of these 107,684 muskets distinguish them as Type II production. The balance of production until 1844 (98,432) were made with bright barrel, distinguishing Type III muskets. Despite the large numbers produced, most were altered to percussion during the 1850s. Most by the "cone-in-barrel" (so called arsenal) method. Many of these were altered again during the American Civil War, usually with a "Patent Breech," and were then rifled and sighted.

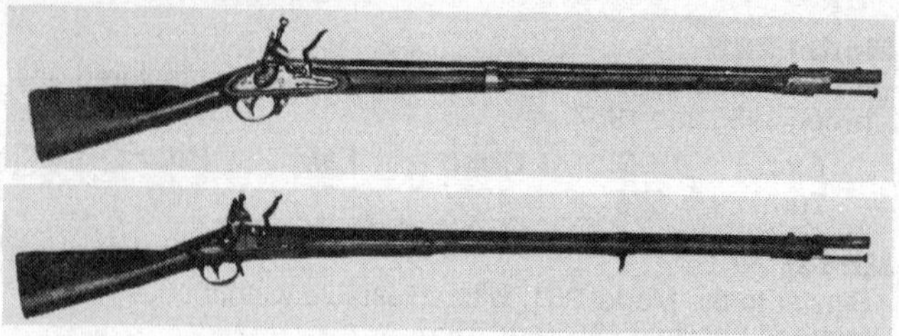

Courtesy Milwaukee Public Museum, Milwaukee, Wisconsin

In flintlock

Exc.	V.G.	Good	Fair	Poor
—	—	4500	2000	500

Altered to percussion

Exc.	V.G.	Good	Fair	Poor
—	—	1200	600	300

NOTE: Add 100 percent for Type III flintlock muskets (Rare).

Harpers Ferry U.S. M1842 Musket

Overall length 57-3/4"; barrel length 42"; caliber .69. Markings: on lockplate, eagle over "US" forward of hammer, "HARPERS/FERRY/(date)" on tail; barrel tang also shows date; upper left quarter of barrel near breech includes proofmarks (an eagle's head, a "V," and a "P") and inspector's initials. Between 1844 and 1855, Harpers Ferry manufactured 106,629 of these smoothbore muskets, many of which were subsequently rifled and sighted; the latter will bring a slight premium.

Exc.	V.G.	Good	Fair	Poor
—	—	3500	1250	400

Harpers Ferry U.S. M1819 Hall Rifle (Types I and II)

Overall length 52-3/4"; barrel (bore) length 32-5/8"; caliber.52. Markings: on top of receiver, either "J.H. HALL/H.FERRY/(date)/U.S." or "J.H. HALL.S./(date)." The 2,000 rifles manufactured between 1824 and 1826 (Type I) are distinguished by having their barrel bands retained by band springs on the right side of the stock. The balance of production (17,680), made between 1828 and 1840, have pins driven through the bands and the stock, distinguishing Type II production. Many of these rifles were altered to percussion just before and in the early months of the American Civil War. Those with evidence of having been altered in the South will command a premium.

In flintlock

Exc.	V.G.	Good	Fair	Poor
—	—	5000	2000	750

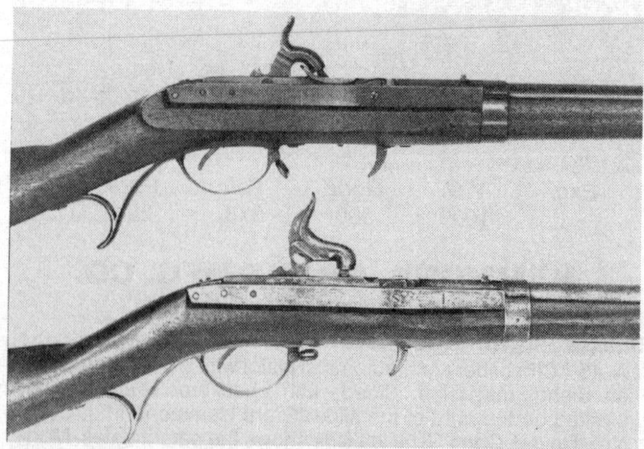

Courtesy Milwaukee Public Museum, Milwaukee, Wisconsin

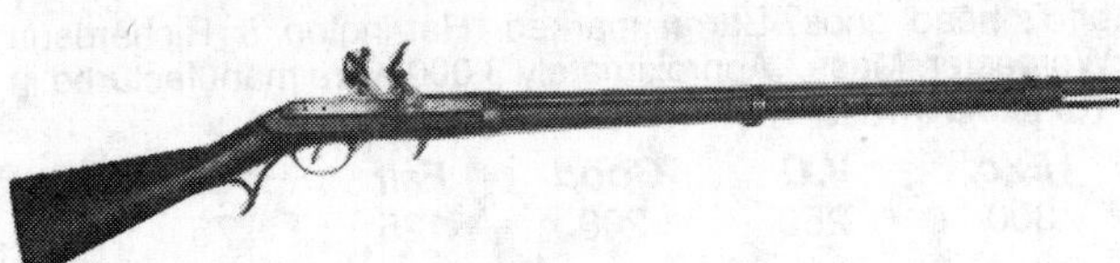

Altered to percussion

Exc.	V.G.	Good	Fair	Poor
—	—	1750	800	400

NOTE: For Type I flintlocks add 250 percent.

Harpers Ferry U.S. M1841 Hall Rifle

Overall length 52-3/4"; barrel (bore) length 32-5/8"; caliber .52. Markings: on top of receiver, either "J.H. HALL/H.FERRY/US/(date)." With the general adoption of the percussion system of ignition, the manufacture of Hall's rifles was changed to conform to the new system, a cone tapped directly into the breechblock substituting for the frizzen and pan, and a hammer replacing the flint cock. The newly made percussion arms also incorporated the newly adopted "fishtail" latch for levering the breechblock. Two-thirds of the 4,213 rifles made were still in storage at the arsenal when it was burned in 1861, enhancing the rarity of the arm.

Exc.	V.G.	Good	Fair	Poor
—	—	5000	2000	650

Harpers Ferry U.S. M1836 Hall Carbine (Types I & II)

Overall length 43"; barrel (bore) length 23"; caliber .64. Markings: on top of receiver, "J.H. HALL/U.S./(date)." To furnish the newly raised 2nd Regiment U.S. Dragoons raised in 1836, Harpers Ferry Armory was directed to construct 1,003 Hall carbines, differing in length and caliber over the M1833 model produced by the North for the 1st Regiment, but were not ready when the unit was sent to Florida. Another 1,017 were made during 1839-1840 with the addition of a tool compartment in the buttstock, distinguishing type II production.

Courtesy Milwaukee Public Museum, Milwaukee, Wisconsin

Exc.	V.G.	Good	Fair	Poor
—	—	4500	1750	650

Harpers Ferry U.S. M1842 Hall Carbine

Overall length 40"; barrel (bore) length 21"; caliber .52. Markings: on top of receiver, "H. FERRY/U S/1842." To meet the needs of the U.S. Dragoons for replacement carbines, Harpers Ferry manufactured 1,001 carbines in 1842, differing only from the North M1840 (Type II—"fishtail lever") carbine by being brass instead of iron mounted.

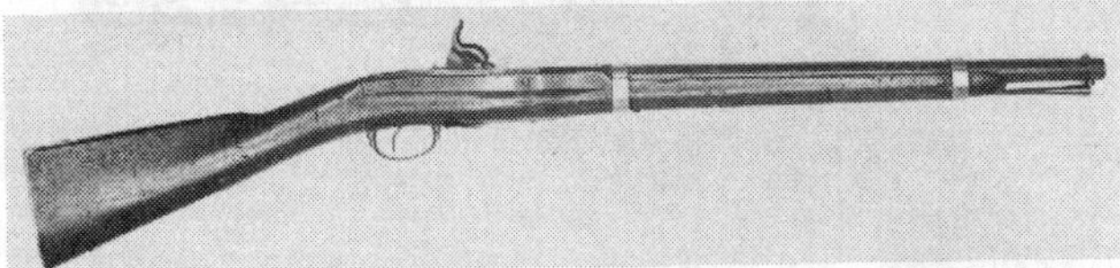

Courtesy Milwaukee Public Museum, Milwaukee, Wisconsin

Exc.	V.G.	Good	Fair	Poor
—	—	9500	4000	1500

Harpers Ferry U.S. M 1841 Muzzleloading Rifle—The "Mississippi Rifle"

Overall length 49"; barrel length 33"; caliber .54 (altered to .58 after 1857). Markings: on lockplate, eagle over "US" forward of hammer; "HARPERS/FERRY/(date)" on tail; date also on tang of breechplug; inspector's initials "AW/P" or "WW/P" and proofmarks (eagle's head, "V" and "P" on upper left side of barrel). With the discontinuance of production of the Hall patent arms, Hall's Rifle Works was transformed into the production of the new U.S. rifle adopted in 1841. From 1846 until 1855 a total of 25,296 were manufactured at Harpers Ferry. Approximately 10,000 of these rifles were subsequently adapted for long range firing and to saber bayonets at Harpers Ferry between 1855 and 1861. The adaptations in chronological order included the adoption of the Snell bayonet and Benton long range "screw" sight, the adoption of a saber bayonet lug with guide and the Benton sight, the adoption of the saber bayonet lug with guide and the Burton "ladder" long range sights, the adoption of the U.S. M1855 (Type 1) rifle sights and bayonet lug (first in .54 and then in .58 caliber), and finally the adoption of the U.S. M1855 (Type II) rifle sights and bayonet lug (in .58 caliber). A few thousand were also adapted to the Colt revolving rifle sights and split ring bayonet adaptor in 1861-1862, but that adaptation was not restricted to Harpers Ferry-made rifles.

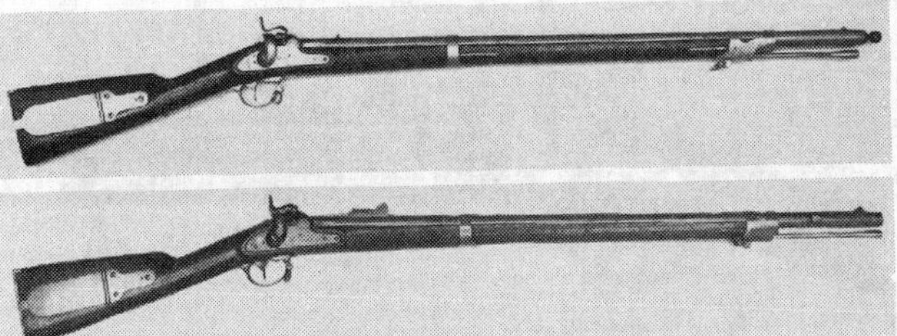

Courtesy Milwaukee Public Museum, Milwaukee, Wisconsin

Exc.	V.G.	Good	Fair	Poor
—	—	5000	2000	750

Harpers Ferry U.S. M1842 Musket

Overall length 57-3/4"; barrel length 42"; caliber .69. Markings: on lockplate, eagle over "US" forward of hammer; "HARPERS/FERRY/(date)" on tail; date also on tang of breechplug; inspector's initials and proofmarks on barrel near breech. Harpers Ferry manufactured a total of 106,629 of these smoothbore muskets between 1844 and 1855. Many of these muskets were subsequently rifled and sighted from 1855 to 1858 or simply rifled during the early years of the American Civil War.

Exc.	V.G.	Good	Fair	Poor
—	—	3500	1750	750

Harpers Ferry U.S. M1855 Rifle-Musket (Type I & II)

Overall length 56"; barrel length 40"; caliber .58. Markings: on lockplate, eagle on Maynard primer door; "US/HARPERS FERRY" forward of hammer; date on tail; date also on top of barrel near breech plus proofmarks (eagle's head, "V," and "P"). Between 1857 and 1858 Harpers Ferry produced 15,071 of these rifles, but many were still unsighted at the end of the fiscal year. This early production (Type I) is distinguished from the later production (1859-1860) by the absence of the iron "patchbox" on the right side of the buttstock, a long range rear sight, and a brass nosecap. The "patchbox" was added in 1859 together with a short base rear sight with leaves graduated to only 300 and 500 yards. The brass nosecaps were gradually phased out during 1859.

Exc.	V.G.	Good	Fair	Poor
—	—	5500	2500	800

Harpers Ferry U.S. M1855 Rifles (Type I & II)

Overall length 49"; barrel length 33"; caliber .58. Markings: on lockplate, eagle on Maynard primer door; "U S/HARPERS FERRY" forward of hammer; date on tail; date also on top of barrel near breech plus proofmarks (eagle's head, "V," and "P"). Designed as the replacement of the U.S. M1841 rifle, production of the U.S. M1855 rifle began at John Hall's old "Harpers Ferry Rifle Works" in 1857. The production of 1857 and 1858 (Type I), numbering only 3,645 rifles, were all brass mounted, bore a long range rear sight on the browned barrel, and bore a "patchbox" inletted for a special crosshair figure "8" detachable front sight, though many were still without their rear sights at the end of the fiscal year due to the intervention of the

Secretary of War. Most of these were never issued and were subsequently destroyed when the arsenal was set afire in April 1861 to prevent the capture of its arms by Virginia forces. The 3,771 rifles produced between 1858 and April 1861 (Type II) were all iron mounted (though a transitional period continued to utilize the brass nosecaps), eliminated the special front sight (permitting the cavity to be enlarged for greased patches), and employed a short base long range rear sight similar to that of the Type II M 1855 rifle musket.

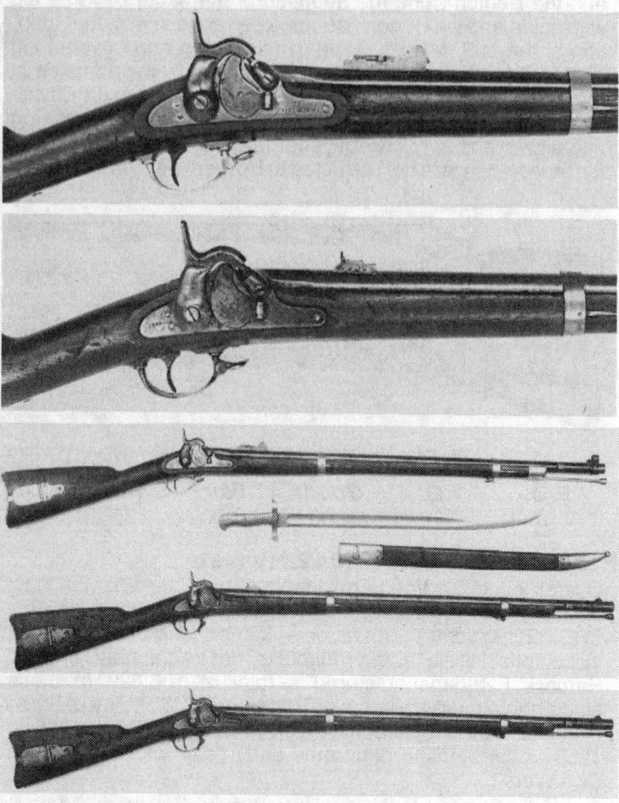

Courtesy Milwaukee Public Museum, Milwaukee, Wisconsin

Type I

Exc.	V.G.	Good	Fair	Poor
—	—	11000	5500	1750

Type II

Exc.	V.G.	Good	Fair	Poor
—	—	6500	3500	1250

HARRINGTON & RICHARDSON, INC.

Worcester, Massachusetts

Established in 1877 by G.H. Harrington and W.A. Richardson. The arms originally produced by this company were marketed under the trade name Aetna. The firm is now located in Gardner, Massachusetts. In November 2000 the Marlin Firearms Company purchased the assets of Harrington & Richardson.

Model No. 1

A .32 or .38 caliber spur-trigger single-action revolver with a 3" octagonal barrel, solid frame, a 7-shot or a 5-shot cylinder, depending on the caliber. Nickel-plated with checkered rubber bird's-head grips. Barrel marked "Harrington & Richardson Worcester, Mass." Approximately 3,000 were manufactured in 1877 and 1878.

Exc.	V.G.	Good	Fair	Poor
300	250	200	125	75

Model 1-1/2

A .32 caliber spur-trigger, single-action revolver with a 2.5" octagonal barrel and a 5-shot cylinder. Nickel-plated, round-butt rubber grips with an "H&R" emblem molded in. Approximately 10,000 were manufactured between 1878 and 1883.

Exc.	V.G.	Good	Fair	Poor
175	150	125	75	50

Model 2-1/2

As above, with a 3.25" barrel and a 7-shot cylinder. Approximately 5,000 were manufactured between 1878 and 1883.

Exc.	V.G.	Good	Fair	Poor
175	150	125	75	50

Model 3-1/2

Similar to the Model 2-1/2 except in .38 rimfire caliber with a 3.5" barrel and a 5-shot cylinder. Approximately 2,500 were manufactured.

Exc.	V.G.	Good	Fair	Poor
200	175	150	100	75

Model 4-1/2

A .41 rimfire caliber spur trigger revolver with a 2.5" barrel and 5-shot cylinder. Approximately 1,000 were manufactured.

Exc.	V.G.	Good	Fair	Poor
250	200	175	125	90

Model 1880

A .32 or .38 S&W centerfire caliber double-action revolver with a 3" round barrel, a solid frame, and a 5- or 6-shot cylinder, depending on the caliber. Nickel-plated with hard rubber grips. Marked "Harrington & Richardson Worchester, Mass." Approximately 4,000 were manufactured between 1880 and 1883.

Exc.	V.G.	Good	Fair	Poor
250	200	175	125	90

The American Double-Action

A .32, .28, or .44 centerfire caliber double-action revolver with a 2.5", 4.5", or 6" round or octagonal barrel, a 5- or 6-shot fluted cylinder, depending on the caliber, and solid frame, nickel-plated, with some blue models noted. The grips are hard rubber. Marked "The American Double Action." Some noted are marked "H&R Bulldog." Approximately 850,000 were manufactured between 1883 and 1940. Add 150 percent for .44.

Exc.	V.G.	Good	Fair	Poor
125	100	85	65	40

The Young America Double-Action

A .22 rimfire or .32 S&W centerfire caliber, double-action revolver, with 2", 4.5", or 6" round or octagonal barrels, solid frame, and a 5- or 7-shot cylinder, depending on the caliber.

Blued or nickel-plated, with hard rubber grips. Marked "Young America Double Action" or "Young America Bulldog." Approximately 1,500,000 were manufactured between 1884 and 1941.

Exc.	*V.G.*	*Good*	*Fair*	*Poor*
125	100	85	65	40

Hunter

A .22 caliber double-action revolver with a 10" octagonal barrel and a 9-shot fluted cylinder. Blued, with checkered walnut grips.

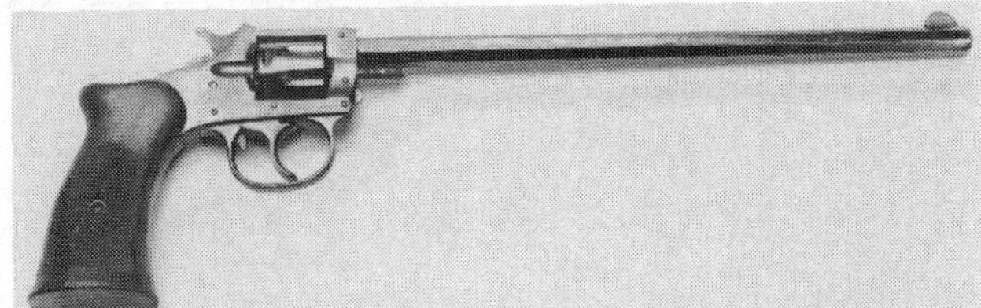

Courtesy Mike Stuckslager

Exc.	*V.G.*	*Good*	*Fair*	*Poor*
400	300	200	150	100

Trapper

As above, with a 6" octagonal barrel and a 7-shot cylinder. Otherwise it is similar to the Hunter.

Courtesy Mike Stuckslager

Exc.	*V.G.*	*Good*	*Fair*	*Poor*
200	150	125	100	75

Self-Loader

A 6.35mm or the 7.65mm semi-automatic pistol with a 2" or 3.5" barrel, a 6- or 8-shot magazine. The larger 7.65 model has a grip safety. Blued or nickel-plated with checkered, hard rubber grips that bear the H&R monogram. The slide is marked, "H&R Self-Loading" with 1907 or 1909 patent dates. Approximately 16,500 were manufactured in 6.35mm between 1912 and 1916 and 34,500 in 7.65mm manufactured between 1916 and 1924. Add 10% for .32.

Courtesy Orvel Reichert

Courtesy Orvel Reichert

Exc.	*V.G.*	*Good*	*Fair*	*Poor*
300	250	200	150	100

First Model Hand Ejector

A .32 or .38 centerfire caliber double-action revolver with a 3.25" ribbed round barrel. This version does not feature the automatic ejection found on later models. Nickel-plated, with hard rubber grips. The company name is marked on the barrel. Approximately 6,000 were manufactured between 1886 and 1888.

Exc.	*V.G.*	*Good*	*Fair*	*Poor*
200	150	125	90	65

Model 1 Double-Action Revolver

A .32, .32 Long, and the .38 S&W caliber double-action revolver with a 3.25" ribbed round barrel, and a 5- or 6-shot cylinder, depending on the caliber. Nickel-plated, with hard rubber grips. Approximately 5,000 were manufactured between 1887 and 1889.

Exc.	*V.G.*	*Good*	*Fair*	*Poor*
175	145	110	80	50

Model 2

Similar to the Model 1, with 2.5", 3.25", 4", 5", or 6" barrels. The grips feature the H&R target logo. There were approximately 1,300,000 manufactured between 1889 and 1940.

Exc.	V.G.	Good	Fair	Poor
125	100	80	65	40

Knife Model

The Model 2 with a 4" ribbed round barrel having a folding 2.25" double-edged knife mounted under the barrel. Blued or nickel-plated. Approximately 2,000 were manufactured between 1901 and 1917.

Exc.	V.G.	Good	Fair	Poor
550	400	350	250	150

Model 922 First Issue

A .22 caliber double-action revolver with a 2.5", 4", or 6" barrel. Blued, with checkered walnut grips.

Exc.	V.G.	Good	Fair	Poor
150	125	100	75	50

Target Model

A .22 LR or .22 rimfire Magnum caliber double-action revolver with 7-shot cylinder, a break-open frame and a 6" barrel with fixed sights. Blued, with checkered walnut grips.

Exc.	V.G.	Good	Fair	Poor
150	125	100	75	50

.22 Special

A .22 LR or the .22 rimfire Magnum double-action, break-open revolver with a 6" barrel and a 7-shot cylinder. Blued, with checkered walnut grips.

Exc.	V.G.	Good	Fair	Poor
175	150	125	90	65

Expert

As above, with a 10" barrel.

Exc.	V.G.	Good	Fair	Poor
150	125	100	75	50

No. 199 Sportsman

A .22 caliber single-action, break-open revolver with a 6" barrel, adjustable target sights and a 9-shot cylinder. Blued, with checkered walnut grips.

Exc.	V.G.	Good	Fair	Poor
275	200	150	100	75

Ultra Sportsman

As above, but more finely finished and with a special, wide target hammer and an improved action.

Exc.	V.G.	Good	Fair	Poor
295	215	175	125	90

Defender

A .38 S&W caliber double-action, break-open revolver with a 4" or 6" barrel and fixed sights. Blued, with plastic grips.

Exc.	V.G.	Good	Fair	Poor
225	175	125	75	50

New Defender

A .22 caliber double-action, break-open revolver with a 2" barrel and a 9-shot cylinder. Blued with checkered, walnut round-butt grips.

Exc.	V.G.	Good	Fair	Poor
225	200	175	125	90

.22 U.S.R.A./Model 195 Single-Shot Match Target Pistol

Also called the Model 195, this pistol underwent nearly constant modifications from its inception in 1928 until production ceased in 1941. Its development was greatly influenced by the United States Revolver Association (USRA), which established certain rules for target pistol shooting. The lack of any H&R-published model chronology for the estimated 3,500 guns manufactured makes model determination by examination complicated; a further difficulty is that H&R supplied newly designed parts to owners of older variations, who would then retrofit their pistols with newer triggers, hammers, sights, and trigger guards. Extracted from the available literature, the parts represent approximately: 14 different stocks and virtually endless custom variations by Walter F. Roper; 5 different trigger guards; 3 different triggers; 2 different hammers; 2 different extractors; 3 barrel lengths (7", 8", 10"); and 3 barrel rib styles. From this array of potential characteristics, at least four distinct variations can be identified.

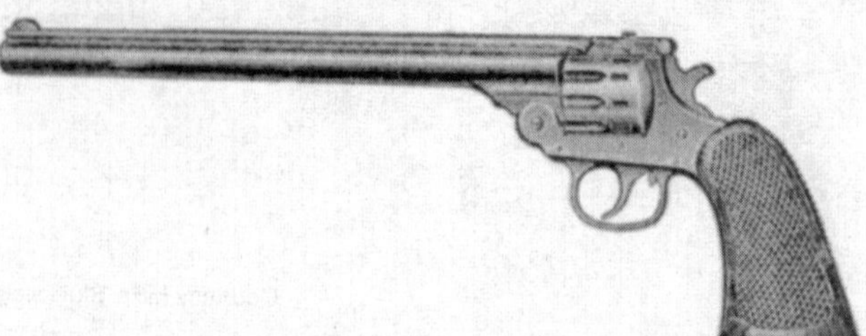

.22 U.S.R.A./Model 195 Pistol, Variations 1 to 3

Exc.	V.G.	Good	Fair	Poor
500	350	325	275	200

.22 U.S.R.A./Model 195 Pistol, Variation 4

Exc.	V.G.	Good	Fair	Poor
550	400	350	325	250

Variation 1, pre-U.S.R.A., 1928-30: Not marked **U.S.R.A.**, and known as the "H&R Single-Shot Pistol." There is no finger rest between the trigger guard and front grip strap; it was advertised with "sawhandle" shape grip copied from the Model 1 or 2 smooth bore H&R Handy-Gun, manufactured with a 10" "hourglass" barrel with a deeply undercut rib. These are the first 500 pistols.

Variation 2, U.S.R.A. Keyhole Barrel, 1930-31: This is the standard "early" model marked **U.S.R.A.**, has a finger rest, and non-sawhandle grips; however, several grip shapes were offered as options. The grip screw goes from rear of grip into threaded hold in back grip strap.

Variation 3, Modified Keyhole Barrel, 1931: Modification of Variation 2 to improve rear sight, barrel catch changed, reduced spent cartridge force by replacing cylindrical extractor with less powerful hinged type, and the hammer cocking spur and finger rest were made wider. The 8" barrel was offered as an option to standard 10" length, and the number of different grip shapes was increased. This is a transition model between "early" Variation 2 and "final" Variation 4 designs.

Variation 4, Tapered Slabside Barrel, 1931-41: New "truncated teardrop" barrel cross section shape; new standard barrel length of 7", with 10" optional; adjustable trigger; new sear; grip screw location was changed to front of grip; and front sight was adjustable for elevation. The trigger design was changed from curved to straight beveled type with relocated cocking surfaces, and the number of grip shapes increased further to 13 types. A front sight protector was supplied as standard equipment, and luggage style case offered as an option. It appears that Variation 4 was introduced around 1931; the 1932 advertisements describe the fully redesigned gun, but picture Variation 2, indicating H&R probably did not re-photograph the new design. The final variation has a special, tight bore .217" in diameter, with bullet seating .03125" (1/32") into rifling, and is among the most accurate of single-shot .22 caliber pistols. The Model 195/U.S.R.A. was relatively expensive, costing approximately $30 in 1932, and increased to slightly more than $36 by the time production ended in 1941, yet was the least expensive of all single-shot .22 target pistols of quality.

Model 504

A .32 H&R Magnum caliber double-action, swing-out cylinder revolver with a 4" or 6" heavy barrel, adjustable sights, and 5-shot cylinder. Blued, with either black plastic or walnut grips.

Smaller version manufactured with a 3" or 4" barrel and a round butt.

Exc.	V.G.	Good	Fair	Poor
300	225	150	90	65

Model 532

As above, but with a cylinder that has to be removed for loading. Manufactured in 1984 and 1985.

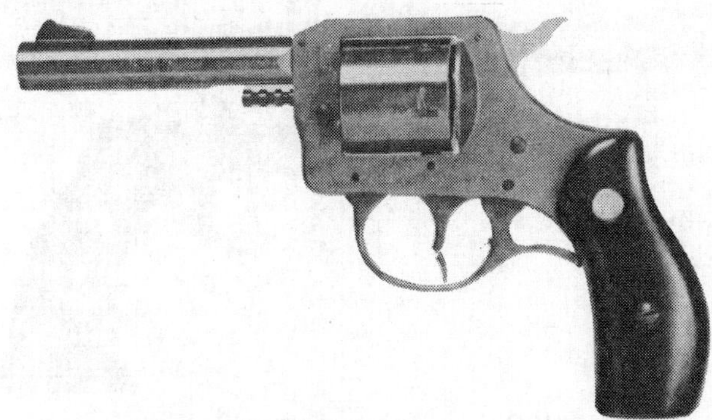

Exc.	V.G.	Good	Fair	Poor
245	150	125	75	50

Model 586

A .32 H&R Magnum caliber double-action revolver with a 4.5", 5.5", 7.5", or 10" barrel, adjustable sights and a 5-shot cylinder. Blued, with either black plastic or walnut grips.

Exc.	V.G.	Good	Fair	Poor
275	175	150	100	75

Model 603

A .22 rimfire Magnum caliber double-action revolver with a 6" flat-sided barrel and swing-out 6-shot cylinder. Blued, with smooth walnut grips.

Exc.	V.G.	Good	Fair	Poor
165	140	110	85	60

Model 604

As above, with a 6", ribbed, heavy barrel.

Exc.	V.G.	Good	Fair	Poor
175	150	125	90	65

Model 622

A .22 caliber solid-frame double-action revolver with a 2.5" or 4" barrel. Blued, with round-butt plastic grips.

Exc.	V.G.	Good	Fair	Poor
100	80	65	50	25

Model 623

As above, but nickel-plated.

Exc.	V.G.	Good	Fair	Poor
125	100	80	60	40

Model 632

As above in .32 centerfire.

Exc.	V.G.	Good	Fair	Poor
110	90	75	60	30

Model 642

As above, in .22 rimfire Magnum.

Exc.	V.G.	Good	Fair	Poor
100	80	65	50	25

Model 649

The Model 622, with a 5.5" or 7.5" barrel.

Exc.	V.G.	Good	Fair	Poor
150	125	100	75	50

Model 650

As above, but nickel-plated.

Exc.	V.G.	Good	Fair	Poor
175	150	125	75	50

Model 660

A .22 caliber solid-frame, Western-style revolver with a 5.5" barrel and is a double-action. Blued, with walnut grips. It is also known as the "Gunfighter."

Exc.	V.G.	Good	Fair	Poor
150	125	100	50	25

Model 666

A .22 or .22 rimfire Magnum caliber double-action revolver with a 6" barrel and a 6-shot cylinder. Blued, with plastic grips. Manufactured between 1976 and 1982.

Exc.	V.G.	Good	Fair	Poor
150	125	100	50	25

Model 676

Similar to the Model 660. Blued, with a case colored frame. It has walnut grips. Manufactured between 1976 and 1982.

Exc.	V.G.	Good	Fair	Poor
175	150	100	75	50

Model 686

Similar to the Model 660 "Gunfighter" with a 4.5", 5.5", 7.5", 10", or 12" barrel.

Exc.	V.G.	Good	Fair	Poor
175	150	125	100	75

Model 732

A .32 caliber double-action, solid-frame revolver with a swing-out cylinder, a 2.5" or 4" barrel and a 6-shot cylinder. Blued, with black plastic grips. Also known as the "Guardsman."

Exc.	V.G.	Good	Fair	Poor
150	125	90	65	45

Model 733

As above, but nickel-plated and a 2.5" barrel.

Exc.	V.G.	Good	Fair	Poor
175	150	100	75	50

Model 900

A .22 caliber solid-frame revolver with a removable cylinder, a 2.5", 4", or 6" barrel and a 9-shot cylinder. Blued, with black plastic grips. Manufactured between 1962 and 1973.

Exc.	V.G.	Good	Fair	Poor
150	125	90	60	40

Model 901

As above, but chrome-plated with white plastic grips. Manufactured in 1962 and 1963 only.

Exc.	V.G.	Good	Fair	Poor
150	125	90	60	40

Model 903

As above, with a swing-out cylinder, a flat-sided, 6" barrel, and a 9-shot cylinder. Blued, with walnut grips.

Exc.	V.G.	Good	Fair	Poor
150	125	90	75	50

Model 904

As above, with a ribbed heavy barrel.

Exc.	V.G.	Good	Fair	Poor
175	150	125	100	50

Model 905

As above, but nickel-plated.

Exc.	V.G.	Good	Fair	Poor
200	175	150	80	65

Model 922 Second Issue

A .22 rimfire caliber solid-frame revolver with a 2.5", 4", or 6" barrel. Blued, with black plastic grips. Manufactured between 1950 and 1982.

Exc.	V.G.	Good	Fair	Poor
100	90	80	60	40

Model 923

As above, but nickel-plated.

Exc.	V.G.	Good	Fair	Poor
110	90	80	60	40

Model 925

A .38 S&W caliber double-action, break-open, hand ejector revolver with a 2.5" barrel, adjustable sights and a 5-shot cylinder. Blued, with a one-piece wraparound grip. Manufactured between 1964 and 1984.

Exc.	V.G.	Good	Fair	Poor
225	175	125	75	50

Model 935

As above, but nickel-plated.

Exc.	V.G.	Good	Fair	Poor
250	200	150	100	50

Model 929

A .22 rimfire solid-frame, swing-out revolver with a 2.5", 4", or 6" barrel and a 9-shot cylinder. Blued, with plastic grips. It is also known as the "Sidekick." Manufactured between 1956 and 1985.

Exc.	V.G.	Good	Fair	Poor
175	150	125	65	45

Model 929 Sidekick—New Model

Reintroduced in 1996 this single- and double-action revolver chambered for the .22 short, long, or LR cartridges. Cylinder holds 9 rounds. Sold with a lockable storage case, nylon holster, and gun oil and gun grease samples. Weighs about 30 oz. Discontinued.

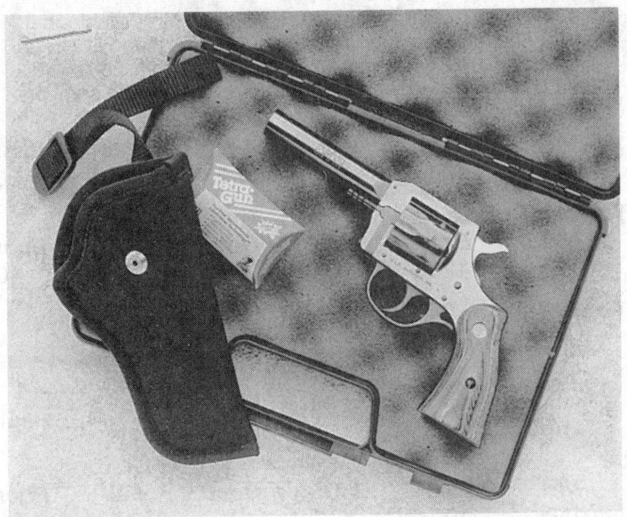

NIB	Exc.	V.G.	Good	Fair	Poor
225	175	150	—	—	—

Model 929 Sidekick Trapper Edition

Same as above but with grey laminate grips and special "NTA" Trapper Edition roll stamp on barrel.

NIB	Exc.	V.G.	Good	Fair	Poor
225	175	150	—	—	—

Model 930

As above, but nickel-plated and not available with a 6" barrel.

Exc.	V.G.	Good	Fair	Poor
200	150	125	65	45

Model 939 Ultra Sidekick

As above, with a ventilated rib, flat sided 6" barrel, adjustable sights, thumb rest grips and features a safety device whereby the pistol could not be fired unless it was unlocked by a furnished key. Manufactured between 1958 and 1982.

Exc.	V.G.	Good	Fair	Poor
225	200	150	75	50

Model 939 Premier

Similar to the above models but fitted with a 6" barrel with sighting rib, adjustable rear sight, hard wood grips, high polished blued finish. Weighs about 36 oz.

NIB	Exc.	V.G.	Good	Fair	Poor
250	225	200	125	75	50

Model 940

A round-barreled version of the above.

Exc.	V.G	Good	Fair	Poor
225	200	125	75	50

Model 949

A .22 caliber double-action, Western-type revolver with a 5.5" barrel with an ejector rod, 9-shot, gate-loaded cylinder and adjustable sights. Blued, with walnut grips. Manufactured between 1960 and 1985.

Exc.	V.G.	Good	Fair	Poor
200	175	150	75	50

Model 949 Western

Similar to the above model this revolver is offered with a choice of 5.5" or 7.5" barrel. Adjustable rear sight, walnut grips, and case colored frame and backstrap with blued cylinder and barrel. Weight is about 36 oz.

NIB	Exc.	V.G.	Good	Fair	Poor
250	200	150	100	75	50

Model 950

As above, but nickel-plated.

Exc.	V.G.	Good	Fair	Poor
250	175	125	75	50

Model 976

As above, with a case-hardened frame.

Exc.	V.G.	Good	Fair	Poor
200	150	100	75	50

Model 999 Sportsman

A .22 rimfire caliber double-action, break-open, self ejecting revolver with a 6"or 4" barrel ventilated rib barrel and windage adjustable sights. Blued, with walnut grips. Weighs about 30 oz. with 4" barrel and 34 oz. with 6" barrel.

Exc.	V.G.	Good	Fair	Poor
300	225	150	100	50

Engraved Model 999

As above, but engraved.

Exc.	V.G.	Good	Fair	Poor
425	350	300	200	125

Amtec 2000

This is a German-designed (Erma) and American-built double-action revolver introduced in 1996. Offered in 2" or 3" barrel and chambered for .38 Special cartridge. Pachmayr composition grips. Cylinder holds 5 rounds. Weight is approximately 25 oz. Discontinued.

NIB	Exc.	V.G.	Good	Fair	Poor
250	200	—	—	—	—

SHOTGUNS

Hammerless Double

A 10 or 12 gauge Anson & Deeley hammerless boxlock double-barrel shotgun with 28", 30", or 32" Damascus barrels in various choke combinations, double triggers and extractors. Engraved, case hardened and walnut stock. Four grades were available. They differ in the amount of engraving and the quality of materials and workmanship utilized. Approximately 3,500 were manufactured between 1882 and 1885.

D Grade

Exc.	V.G.	Good	Fair	Poor
650	550	425	300	175

C Grade

Exc.	V.G.	Good	Fair	Poor
750	650	500	400	275

B Grade

Exc.	V.G.	Good	Fair	Poor
900	750	600	500	350

A Grade

Exc.	V.G.	Good	Fair	Poor
2000	1750	1500	1000	550

Harrich No. 1

A 12 gauge boxlock single barrel shotgun with a 32" or 34", ventilated rib, full-choke barrel and automatic ejector. Engraved, blued with a checkered, walnut stock. Imported between 1971 and 1975.

Exc.	V.G.	Good	Fair	Poor
1750	1500	1150	850	650

Single-Barrel Shotguns

Harrington & Richardson manufactured a series of single-barrel, break-open shotguns between 1908 and 1942. They were chambered for various gauges and had various barrel lengths and chokes. The finishes were blued with walnut stocks. There is little collector interest in these guns and, if in sound condition, are desirable as shooters only. They are the Models 3, 5, 6, 7, 8, and 9, as well as a hinged-frame, folding design.

Exc.	V.G.	Good	Fair	Poor
125	100	85	65	40

Turkey Mag

A single-shot break-open side release gun chambered for the 12 gauge 3-1/2" shell with screw-in Full choke. The hardwood stock has a Mossy Oak finish. Barrel length is 24" with a bead front sight. Weight is about 6 lbs.

NIB	Exc.	V.G.	Good	Fair	Poor
175	150	125	100	75	50

Youth Turkey Gun

Similar in appearance to the Turkey Mag. but on a smaller scale. Chambered for the 20 gauge 3" shell with 22" barrel. Weighs about 5.5 lbs.

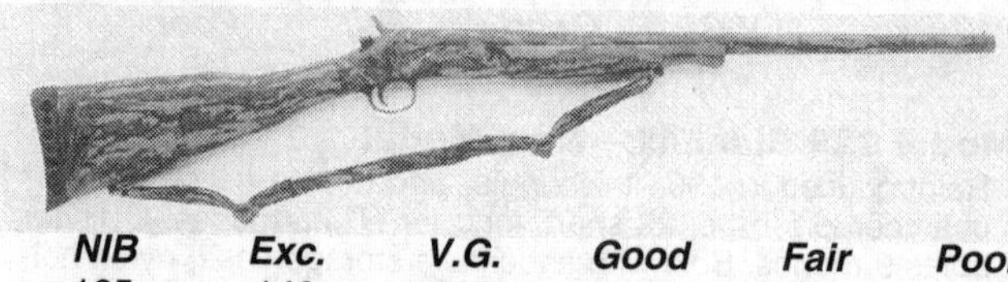

NIB	Exc.	V.G.	Good	Fair	Poor
165	140	115	90	60	40

Topper (New Production)

This is a break-open side release single-shot available in 12 and 20 gauge as well as .410 bore. The 12 gauge is offered with a 28" barrel while the others are fitted with 26" barrels. Blued finish with hardwood stock in black finish with semi-pistol grip. Weight is approximately 6 lbs.

NIB	Exc.	V.G.	Good	Fair	Poor
150	100	80	60	45	30

Topper Deluxe

NIB	Exc.	V.G.	Good	Fair	Poor
170	125	90	70	50	40

Topper Jr. in 20 Gauge and .410 Bore Only

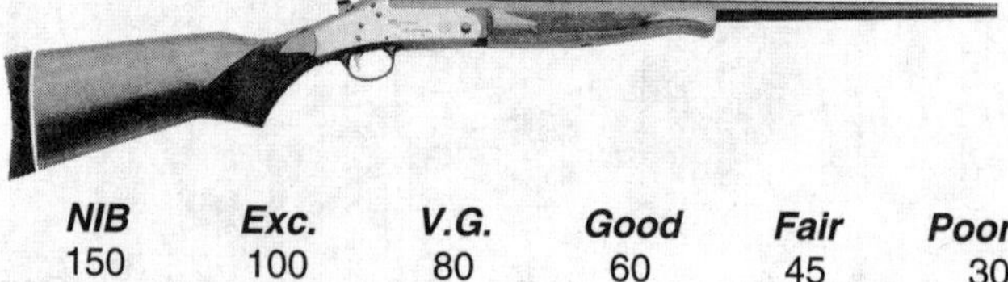

NIB	Exc.	V.G.	Good	Fair	Poor
150	100	80	60	45	30

Topper Jr. Classic

Similar to the Topper Jr. Features a black walnut stock with butt checkering. White line spacer and black recoil pad. Weighs about 7.5 lbs.

NIB	Exc.	V.G.	Good	Fair	Poor
150	100	80	60	45	30

Topper Deluxe Slug

This 12 gauge single-shot has a 24" fully rifled barrel with built-in compensator.

NIB	Exc.	V.G.	Good	Fair	Poor
150	115	90	70	50	40

Topper Deluxe Classic

Introduced in 2004, this 12 gauge 3" single shot gun is fitted with a 28" vent rib barrel with screw-in modified choke. American black walnut stock with pistol grip and ventilated recoil pad. Barrel has black finish while the receiver has a nickel finish. Weight is about 5.5 lbs. In 2005 this model was offerd in 20 gauge.

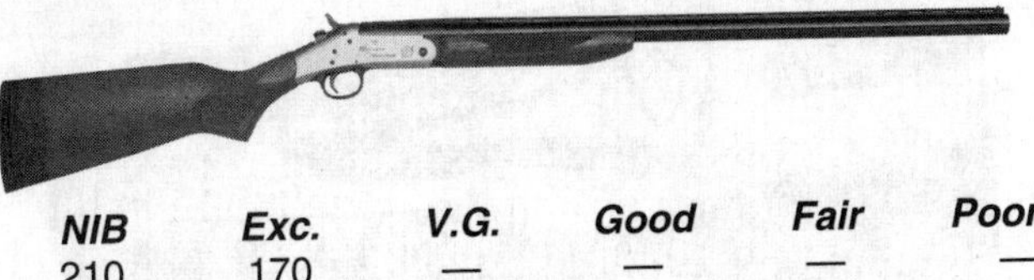

NIB	Exc.	V.G.	Good	Fair	Poor
210	170	—	—	—	—

Tamer

This single-shot gun is chambered for the .410 shell with 3" chamber. It is fitted with a 19-1/2" barrel and had a matte nickel finish. The stock is matte black polymer. Weighs about 6 lbs.

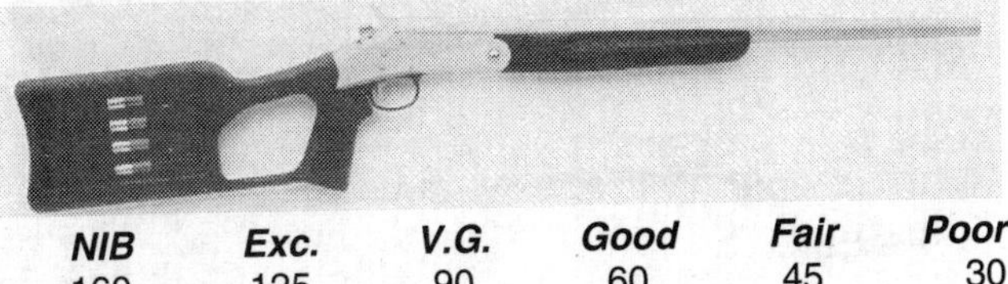

NIB	Exc.	V.G.	Good	Fair	Poor
160	125	90	60	45	30

Ultra Slug Hunter

Introduced in 1995 this model uses a heavy 10 gauge action fitted with a 24" 12 gauge barrel. Weight is about 8 lbs.

NIB	Exc.	V.G.	Good	Fair	Poor
150	115	90	70	50	40

Ultra Slug Hunter Deluxe

20 Gauge

Introduced in 1997 this model is chambered for 20 gauge shells and features a hand checkered camo laminated wood stock. Fitted with a fully rifled heavy slug barrel 24" long.

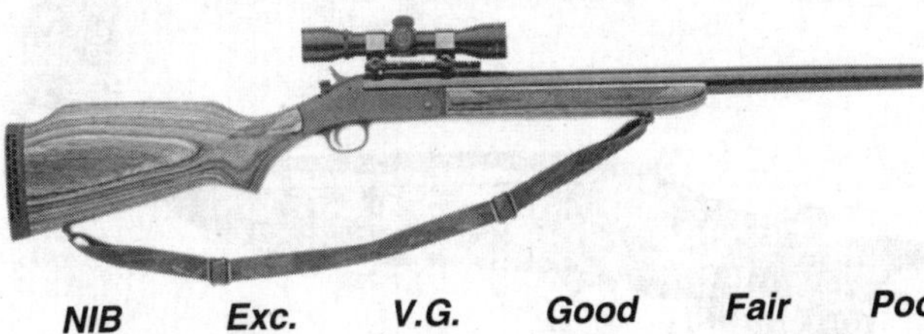

NIB	Exc.	V.G.	Good	Fair	Poor
315	250	200	150	—	—

12 Gauge

Same as above but in 12 gauge with 3" chamber.

NIB	Exc.	V.G.	Good	Fair	Poor
315	250	200	150	—	—

Ultra Slug Youth Model

As above but chambered for 20 gauge shell. Weight is approximately 7 lbs.

NIB	Exc.	V.G.	Good	Fair	Poor
260	200	150	100	60	—

Ultra Slug Hunter Bull Barrel

Same as above but chambered for 20 gauge.

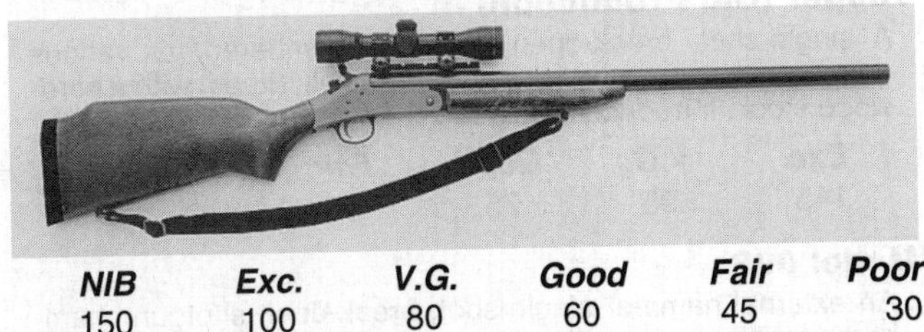

NIB	Exc.	V.G.	Good	Fair	Poor
150	100	80	60	45	30

Ultra Slug Youth Bull Barrel

Same as above but with 22" barrel.

NIB	Exc.	V.G.	Good	Fair	Poor
150	100	80	60	45	30

Camo Laminate Turkey NWTF Edition

Introduced in 1999 this single barrel model features a 12 gauge 3.5" 22" barrel choked Turkey full. Polished receiver has laser engraved NWTF logo. Stock is hand checkered and is hardwood laminate with a green, brown, and black pattern. Ventilated recoil pad and sling swivels and camo sling are standard.

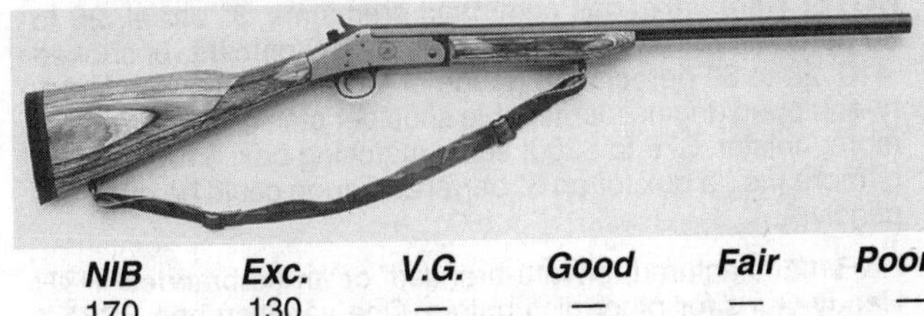

NIB	Exc.	V.G.	Good	Fair	Poor
170	130	—	—	—	—

Camo Laminate Turkey Youth NWTF Edition

Similar to the Camo Turkey above but chambered for 20 gauge with 3" chambers. Stock is laminated hardwood but with special shorter dimensions.

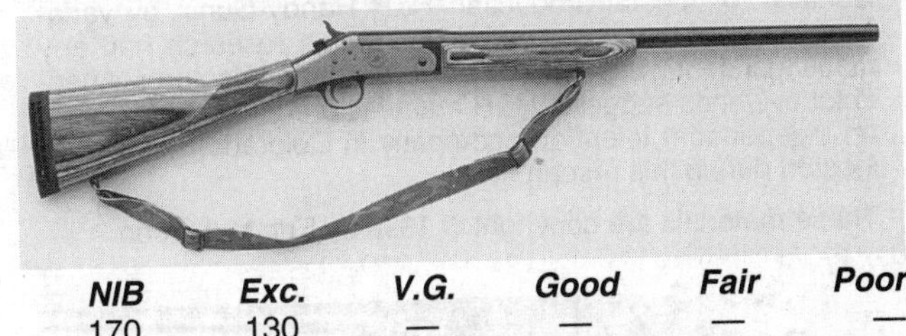

NIB	Exc.	V.G.	Good	Fair	Poor
170	130	—	—	—	—

H&R Handy-Gun (rifled barrel) CURIO OR RELIC

Rifled-barrel H&R Handy-Guns were manufactured about 1930-34, but details of their production are not well documented. In H&R catalogue #19 (copyright 1931) and #20, the .22 and .32-20 are listed as available with blued frame only, 12.25" barrel, with an optional ($1.50) detachable shoulder stock. Whether the .22 W.R.F. version listed on page 83 of the 1932 ***Stoeger's Bible*** was manufactured is unknown. Guns that were originally factory fitted for the shoulder stock (all are extremely rare) have **H.&R. ARMS COMPANY/WORCESTER, MASS.U.S.A./PAT.PENDING** stamped on the bottom of the grip in .125" letters. Production of the rifled-barrel H&R Handy-Gun was halted in 1934 when the Treasury Department classified it as a "firearm" under the NFA, because it was available with a shoulder stock. Any rifled-barrel H&R Handy-Gun is (and always was) exempt from the NFA, if not accompanied by a shoulder stock.

.32-20 W.C.F. serial range mostly from 43851 (?) to 43937 (?)

Exc.	V.G.	Good	Fair	Poor
1400	900	800	700	600

.22 rimfire serial range from 1 (?) to 223 (?)

Exc.	V.G.	Good	Fair	Poor
1200	900	750	650	500

H&R Handy-Gun (smooth bore) NFA, CURIO OR RELIC

The .410 bore or 28 gauge H&R Handy-Gun is a single-shot pistol with an 8" or 12.25" smooth bore barrel, made from 1921 to 1934 by the Harrington & Richardson Arms Co., Worcester, Massachusetts. It shares internal parts with H&R's Model 1915

(No. 5) shotgun, but the Handy-Gun's shorter receiver is designed for a pistol grip, its barrels won't fit the No. 5, and these firearms are serial numbered separately. About 54,000 H&R Handy-Guns were manufactured, nearly all for 2.5" shells. Production was halted after the government ruled the H&R Handy-Gun to be a "firearm" in the "any other weapon" category under the NFA, when its retail price was about $16. An H&R Handy-Gun with an 18" smooth bore barrel is subject to the NFA, but exempt if accompanied by an original (detachable) wire shoulder stock.

.410 bore, Model 2, Types II and III

Exc.	*V.G.*	*Good*	*Fair*	*Poor*
500	375	300	250	175

28 gauge, Model 2, Type I

Exc.	*V.G.*	*Good*	*Fair*	*Poor*
1200	900	700	650	500

NOTE: Rare variations command premiums: 8" barrel, 25 to 50 percent; 18" barrel (rarest), 200 to 300 percent; unchoked .410, 20 to 30 percent; 28 gauge or Model 3 (only) with factory-equipped original detachable shoulder stock, 150 percent or more; holster, $75 to $200; serial matching box, $100 to $200 or more (i.e., a box for an 8" barrel 28 gauge could be quite expensive).

H&R manufactured "private-branded" or "trade-branded" H&R Handy-Guns for other distributors. One variation has **ESSEX GUN WORKS** on the left side of the receiver. Another has **HIBBARD** stamped on the left side, and **MODEL W.H.** stamped on the right; a holster with identical stampings was also available. Most have nickel-plated receivers and are serial numbered within the same ranges as, and have other characteristics identical to, regular-production H&R Handy-Guns, by variation. None of those inspected during this research had any markings identifying H&R as the original manufacturer. Anecdotal evidence suggests H&R manufactured a Handy-Gun for an independent telephone company in Colorado; none were located during this research.

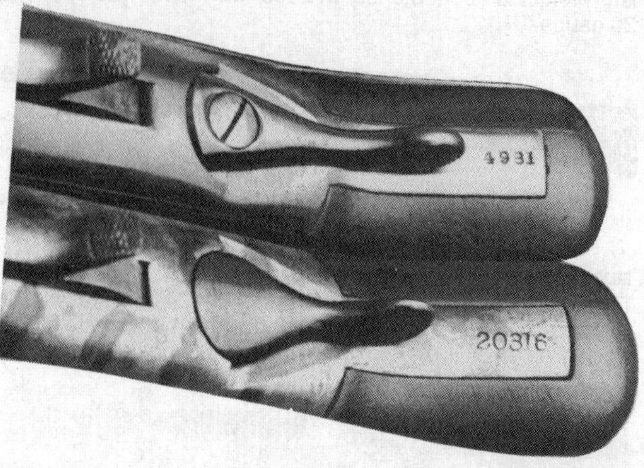

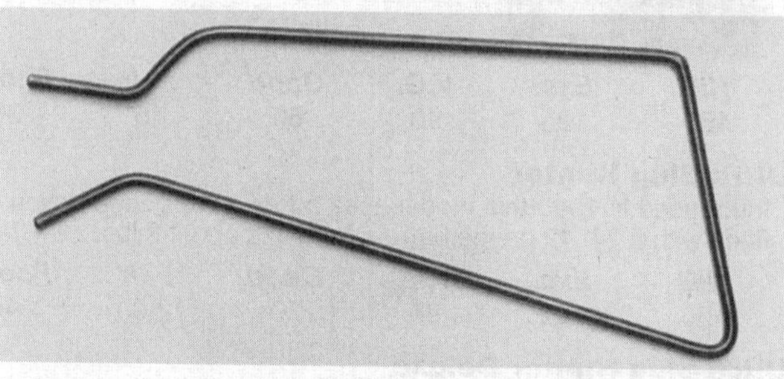

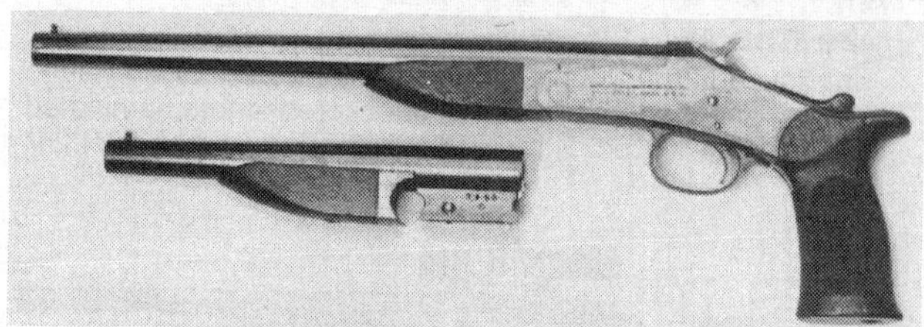

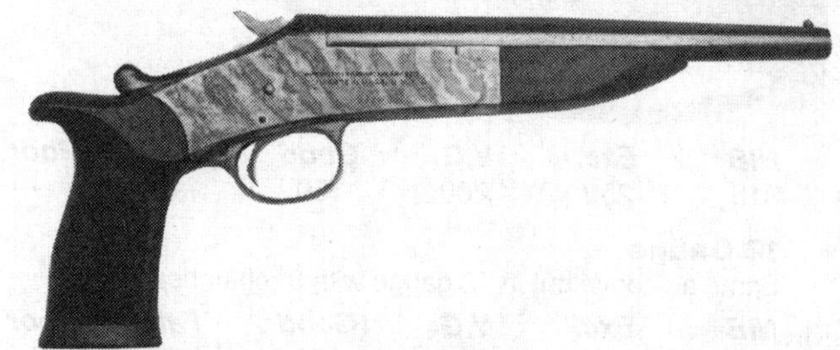

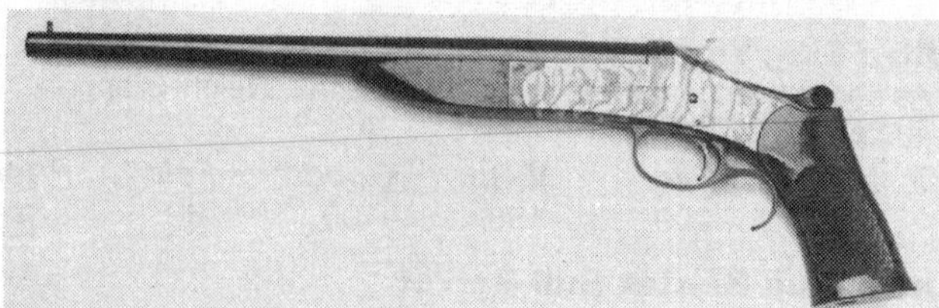

Topper (Old Production)

A single-shot, break-open shotgun chambered for various gauges with various barrel lengths, chokes. Blued, with a hardwood stock. Introduced in 1946.

Exc.	*V.G.*	*Good*	*Fair*	*Poor*
145	95	75	60	40

Model 088

An external hammer single-shot, break-open shotgun chambered for all gauges with various barrel lengths, chokes and an automatic ejector. Blued, with a case colored frame and hardwood stock.

Exc.	*V.G.*	*Good*	*Fair*	*Poor*
80	65	50	40	30

Model 099

As above, but matte, electroless, nickel-plated.

Exc.	*V.G.*	*Good*	*Fair*	*Poor*
110	95	75	60	40

Model 162

A 12 or 20 gauge boxlock single-shotgun with a 24" barrel with rifle sights.

Exc.	*V.G.*	*Good*	*Fair*	*Poor*
125	100	80	65	45

Model 176

A 10-gauge, 3.5" Magnum caliber boxlock single barrel shotgun with a heavyweight 36" barrel and a Full choke. Manufactured between 1977 and 1985.

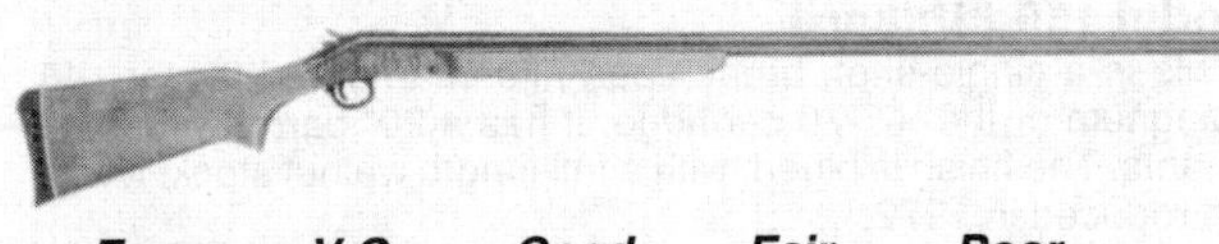

Exc.	*V.G.*	*Good*	*Fair*	*Poor*
125	100	80	65	45

Model 400

A 12, 16, or 20 gauge slide-action shotgun with a 28" Full choke barrel. Blued, with a hardwood stock. Manufactured between 1955 and 1967.

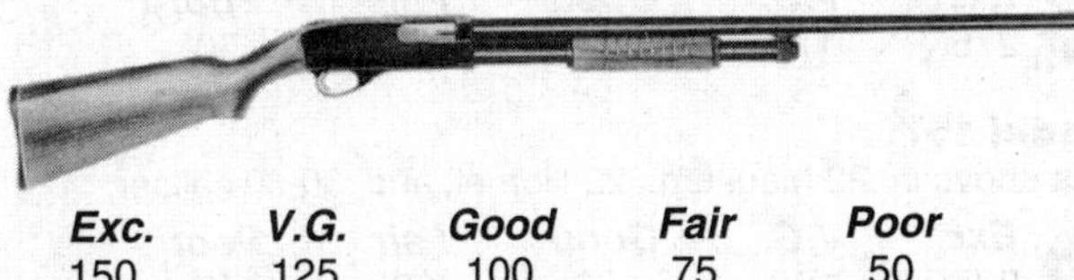

Exc.	*V.G.*	*Good*	*Fair*	*Poor*
150	125	100	75	50

Model 401

As above, with a variable choke device. Manufactured between 1956 and 1963.

Exc.	*V.G.*	*Good*	*Fair*	*Poor*
175	150	125	90	65

Model 402

As above, in a .410 bore. Manufactured between 1959 and 1967.

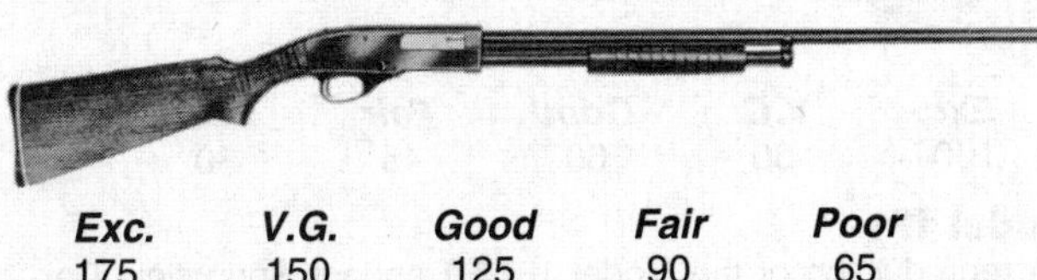

Exc.	*V.G.*	*Good*	*Fair*	*Poor*
175	150	125	90	65

Model 440

A 12, 16, or 20 gauge slide-action shotgun with a 26", 28", or 30" barrel in various chokes. Blued, with a hardwood stock. Manufactured between 1968 and 1973.

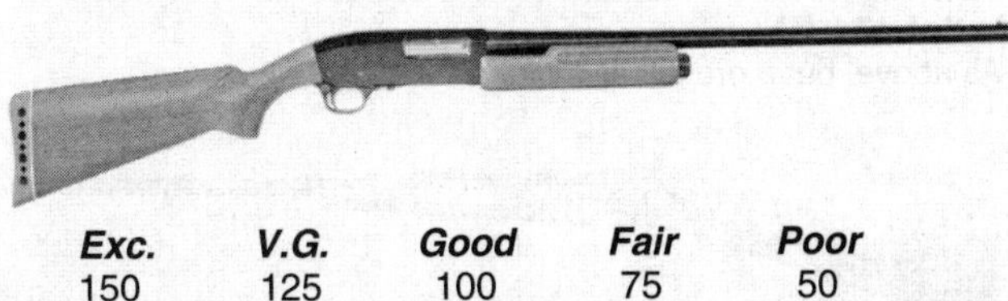

Exc.	*V.G.*	*Good*	*Fair*	*Poor*
150	125	100	75	50

Model 442

As above with a ventilated-rib barrel and a checkered stock. Manufactured between 1969 and 1973.

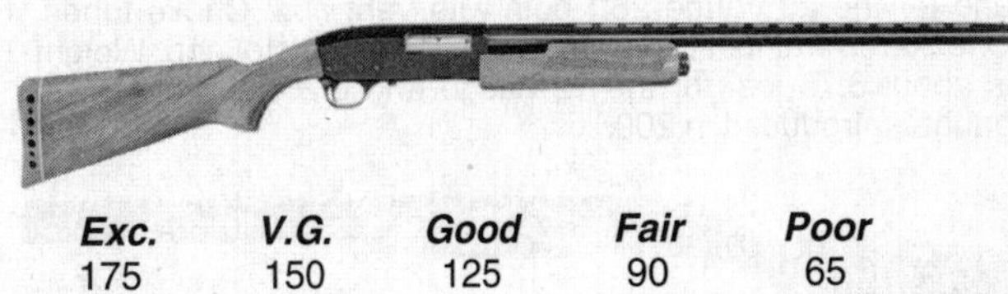

Exc.	*V.G.*	*Good*	*Fair*	*Poor*
175	150	125	90	65

Model 403

A .410 bore semi-automatic shotgun with a 26", Full choke barrel. Blued, with a hardwood stock. Manufactured in 1964.

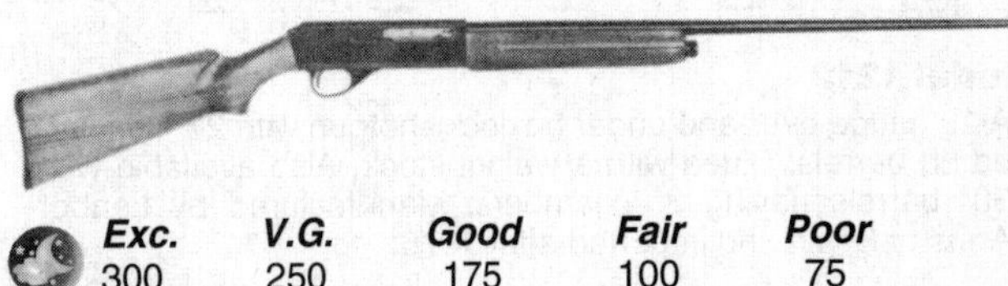

Exc.	*V.G.*	*Good*	*Fair*	*Poor*
300	250	175	100	75

Model 404

A 12, 20, or .410 bore boxlock double-barrel shotgun with 26" or 28" barrels, double triggers and extractors. Blued with a walnut stock. Manufactured by Rossi in Brazil and imported between 1969 and 1972.

Exc.	*V.G.*	*Good*	*Fair*	*Poor*
175	150	125	90	65

Excell Auto 5

Introduced in 2005 this model is chambered for the 12 gauge 3" shell and fitted with a 28" vent rib barrel with choke tubes. Checkered black synthetic stock. Magazine capacity is 5 rounds. Weight is about 7 lbs.

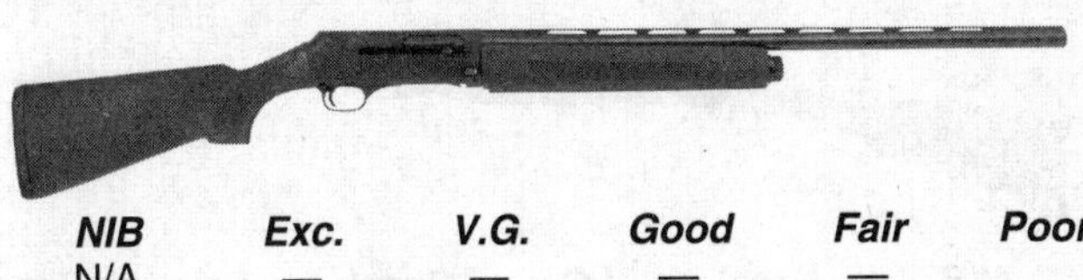

NIB	*Exc.*	*V.G.*	*Good*	*Fair*	*Poor*
N/A	—	—	—	—	

Excell Auto 5 Waterfowl

As above but with Real Tree Advantage Wetlands camo finish. Introduced in 2005.

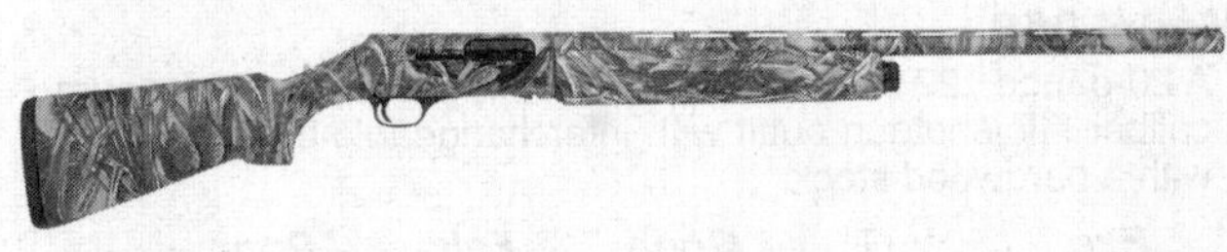

NIB	*Exc.*	*V.G.*	*Good*	*Fair*	*Poor*
N/A	—	—	—	—	

Excell Auto 5 Turkey

This model is fitted with a 22" barrel with choke tubes and fiber optic front sight. Real Tree Advantage Hardwoods camo finish. Weight is 7 lbs. Introduced in 2005.

NIB	*Exc.*	*V.G.*	*Good*	*Fair*	*Poor*
N/A	—	—	—	—	

Excell Auto 5 Combo

This model has a black synthetic stock and two barrels: 28" vent rib with choke tubes, and 24" rifled barrel. Weight is about 7 lbs. depending on barrel length. Introduced in 2005.

NIB	*Exc.*	*V.G.*	*Good*	*Fair*	*Poor*
N/A	—	—	—	—	

Pinnacle

This is an over-and-under gun chambered for the 12 or 20 gauge with 3" chambers. Barrel length for the 12 gauge is 28" and for the 20 gauge 26"; both with vent ribs. Choke tubes. Checkered walnut stock with recoil pad and pistol grip. Weight is about 6.75 lbs. for the 12 gauge and 6.25 lbs. for the 20 gauge. Introduced in 2005.

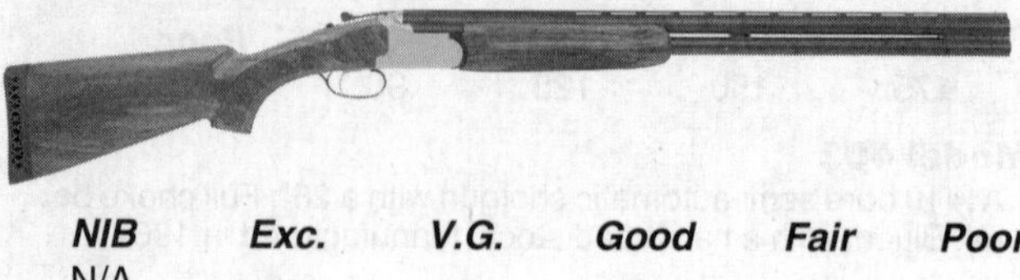

NIB	Exc.	V.G.	Good	Fair	Poor
N/A	—	—	—	—	

Model 1212

A 12 gauge over-and-under boxlock shotgun with 28" ventilated rib barrels. Blued with a walnut stock. Also available with 30" barrels having 3" chambers. Manufactured by Lanber Arms of Spain and imported after 1976.

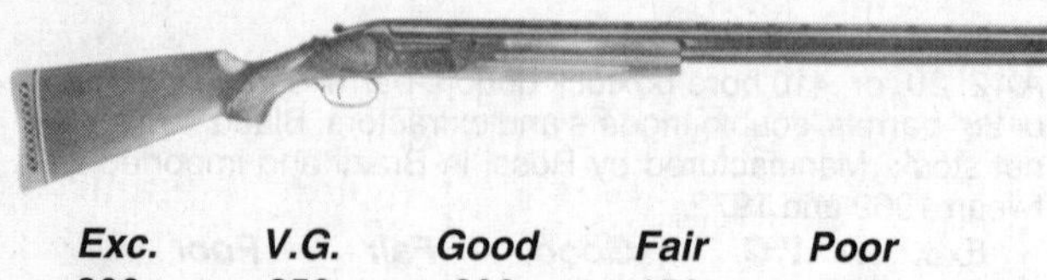

Exc.	V.G.	Good	Fair	Poor
300	250	200	150	100

Long Tom Classic

Introduced in 1996 this limited edition single-barrel shotgun features a case hardened frame with 32" Full choked barrel. Stock is hand-checkered black walnut with crescent buttplate. Chambered for 12 gauge. Weight is about 7.5 lbs.

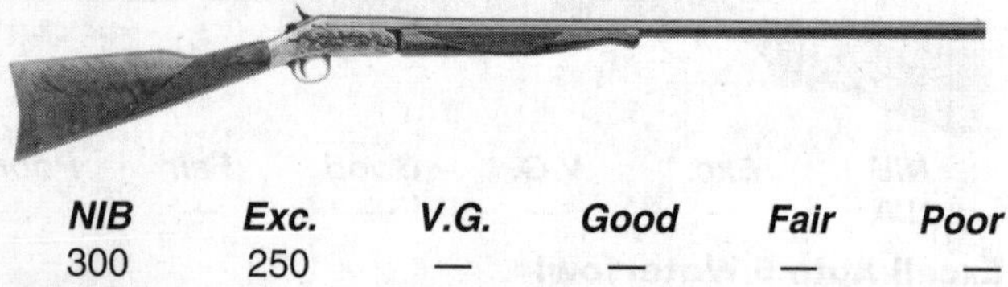

NIB	Exc.	V.G.	Good	Fair	Poor
300	250	—			

RIFLES

Model 058

A 20-gauge, .22 Hornet, .30-30, .357 Magnum, or .44 Magnum caliber rifle/shotgun outfit with interchangeable barrels. Blued with a hardwood stock.

Exc.	V.G.	Good	Fair	Poor
125	100	80	65	40

Model 258

As above, but with a matte, electroless nickel-plate finish.

Exc.	V.G.	Good	Fair	Poor
175	150	125	90	65

Reising Model 60

A .45 ACP caliber semi-automatic rifle with an 18.25" barrel and a 12- or 20-round detachable magazine. Blued, with a walnut stock. It operates on a retarded blowback system and was developed to be used as a police weapon. Manufactured between 1944 and 1946.

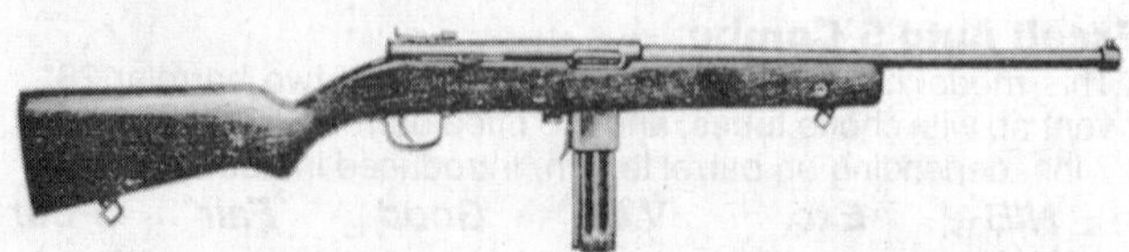

Courtesy Richard M. Kumor, Sr.

Exc.	V.G.	Good	Fair	Poor
1400	1200	500	250	100

Model 65 Military

A .22 LR caliber semi-automatic rifle with a 23" barrel and Redfield peep sights. Blued, with a walnut stock. Manufactured between 1944 and 1956.

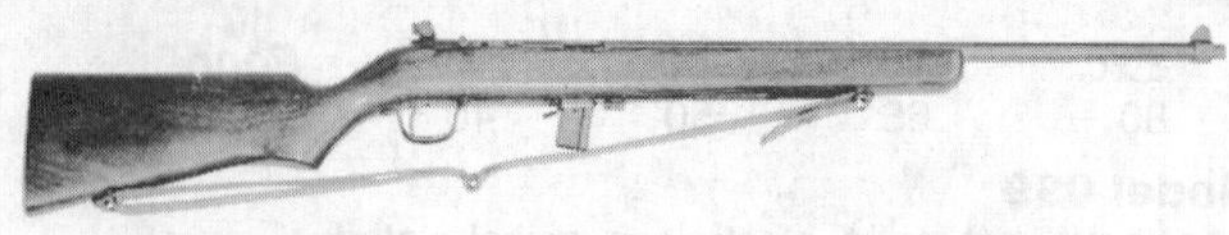

Courtesy Richard M. Kumor, Sr.

Exc.	V.G.	Good	Fair	Poor
350	300	200	125	90

NOTE: Add 100 percent if USMC marked.

Model 150

A .22 LR caliber semi-automatic rifle with a 20" barrel and a 5-shot magazine. Blued, with a walnut stock. Manufactured between 1949 and 1953.

Exc.	V.G.	Good	Fair	Poor
100	80	60	45	30

Model 155 (Shikari)

This is a single-shot, break-open rifle chambered for the .44 Magnum or the .45-70 cartridge. It has a 20" barrel with fixed sights. The finish is blued, with a full-length walnut stock. It was introduced in 1972.

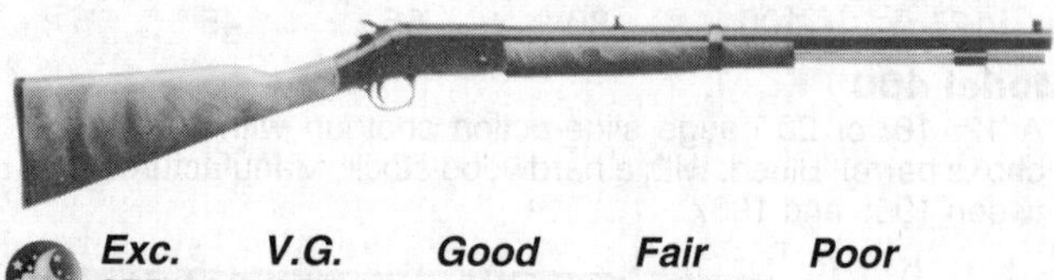

Exc.	V.G.	Good	Fair	Poor
275	175	125	100	50

Model 157

As above in .22 Magnum, .22 Hornet, and .30-30 caliber.

Exc.	V.G.	Good	Fair	Poor
225	150	100	60	40

Model 158

A .357 or .44 Magnum single-shot side lever rifle with a 22" barrel. Blued, case hardened with a walnut stock. Available with an interchangeable 26" 20 gauge barrel. Manufactured prior to 1986.

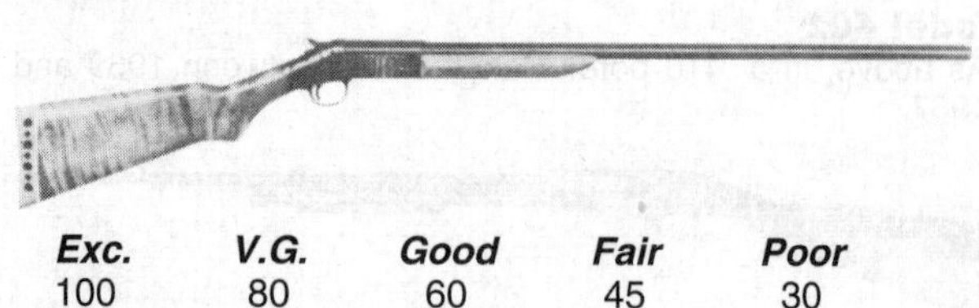

Exc.	V.G.	Good	Fair	Poor
100	80	60	45	30

Model 171

A reproduction of the Model 1873 Trapdoor Springfield Carbine with a 22" barrel. Blued, with a case colored receiver and a walnut stock.

Exc.	V.G.	Good	Fair	Poor
300	250	200	150	100

Model 171-DL

As above, but more finely finished.

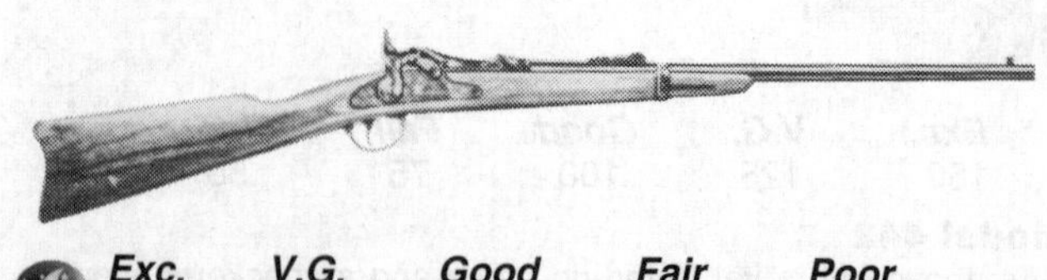

Exc.	V.G.	Good	Fair	Poor
350	300	250	200	125

Model 300 Ultra

A .22-250 up to the .300 Winchester Magnum caliber, bolt-action rifle with a 22" or 24" barrel and without sights. High polished blue, and checkered walnut stock. Manufactured between 1965 and 1978.

Exc.	V.G.	Good	Fair	Poor
450	400	350	275	175

Model 301 Carbine

As above with an 18" barrel and a full-length, Mannlicher-style stock.

Exc.	V.G.	Good	Fair	Poor
450	400	350	275	175

Model 317 Ultra Wildcat

A .17 Rem., .17-223, .222 Rem., and the .223 Rem. caliber short Sako bolt-action rifle with a 20" barrel furnished without sights. Blued, with a checkered walnut stock. Manufactured between 1968 and 1976.

Exc.	V.G.	Good	Fair	Poor
550	400	350	275	175

Handi-Rifle

Break-action single-shot rifle that's been around in one form another since God invented dirt. Side lever release, automatic ejection, hardwood stock, transfer bar passive safety. Available in nearly every conceivable rimfire and centerfire chambering (except the biggest centerfires) and now made under the auspices of Marlin, this rifle is as good a bargain today as it ever was. Some newer models feature factory scopes, bull barrels, thumbhole stocks and other niceties, but they're still Handi-Rifles. Value is generally under $300 even in New or Excellent condition, sometimes remarkably under.

Ultra Varmint Rifle

This single-shot rifle is chambered for the .223 Rem. or the .22-250 cartridge. It is fitted with a 22" heavy barrel. The stock is hand checkered curly maple with Monte Carlo cheekpiece. Comes with no sights but scopes mounts are included. Weighs about 7.5 lbs.

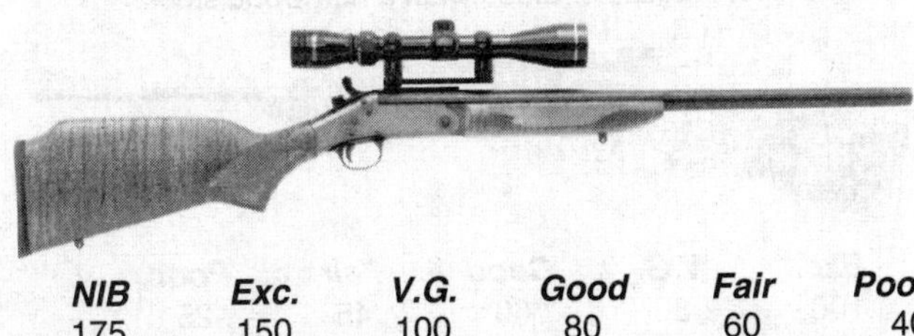

NIB	Exc.	V.G.	Good	Fair	Poor
175	150	100	80	60	40

Ultra Varmint Fluted

Introduced in 2005 this model is chambered for the .204 Ruger, .22-250, or the .223 Rem. cartridge. Fitted with a 24" fluted barrel with no sights. Stock is black synthetic with vertical adjustable adjustment knob, recoil pad, and adjustable bipod mount. Weight is about 7 lbs.

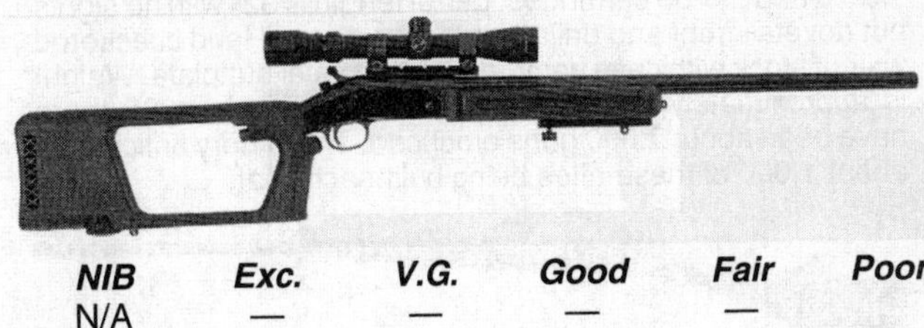

NIB	Exc.	V.G.	Good	Fair	Poor
N/A	—	—	—	—	—

Model 317P

As above, but more finely finished. Manufactured between 1968 and 1976.

Exc.	V.G.	Good	Fair	Poor
550	500	450	375	250

Ultra Rifle—Hunting

Single-shot rifle chambered for .25-06, .308 Win., and .357 Rem. Max. The .25-06 has a 26" barrel, the other two are fitted with 22" barrels. A Cinnamon laminated stock is standard. Weight is about 7 lbs. In 2001 the .450 Marlin cartridge was added.

NIB	Exc.	V.G.	Good	Fair	Poor
225	175	125	100	75	50

Ultra Rifle—Varmint

Same as above but chambered for .223 Rem. with 22" barrel. Laminated stock with checkered pistol grip.

NIB	Exc.	V.G.	Good	Fair	Poor
225	175	125	100	75	50

Ultra .22 Magnum Rifle

Same as above but chambered for the .22 Winchester Magnum. Introduced in 2001.

NIB	Exc.	V.G.	Good	Fair	Poor
225	175	—	—	—	—

Ultra Rifle—Comp

Introduced in 1997 this single-shot rifle features an integral muzzlebrake on the end of the barrel. Available in .270 Win. and .30-06 calibers with 24" barrels. Camo laminated stock.

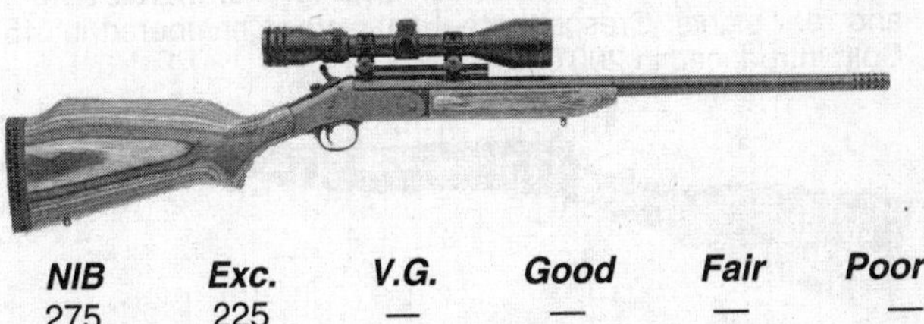

NIB	Exc.	V.G.	Good	Fair	Poor
275	225	—	—	—	—

Ultra Rifle Rocky Mountain Elk Foundation Commemorative

A limited edition single rifle chambered for the .35 Whelen cartridge. Selected laminated stock with Monte Carlo. Barrel length is 26".

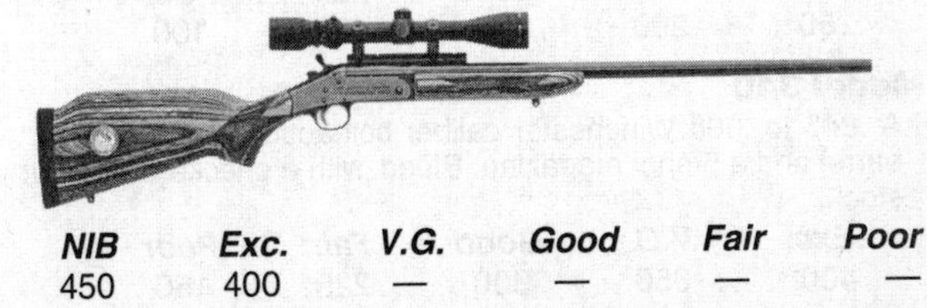

NIB	Exc.	V.G.	Good	Fair	Poor
450	400	—	—	—	—

Buffalo Classic

This rifle was first produced in 1995. It is chambered for the .45-70 and .38-55 cartridges. Barrel length is 32" with no sights but dovetail front and drilled and tapped rear. Hand checkered walnut stock with case colored crescent steel buttplate. Weight is approximately 8 lbs. Since its introduction in 1995 there have been about 2,000 guns produced. The factory anticipates about 1,000 of these rifles being built each year.

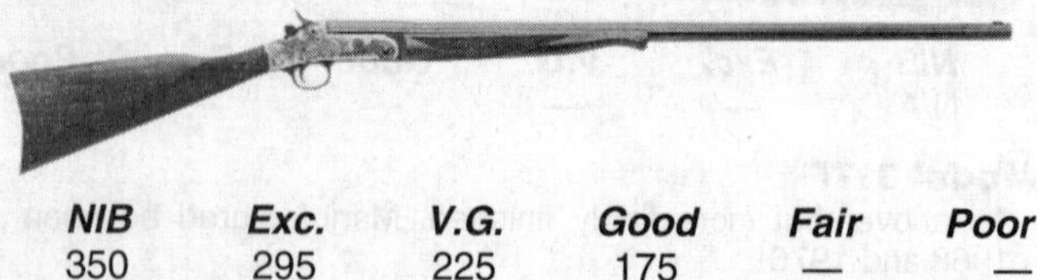

NIB	Exc.	V.G.	Good	Fair	Poor
350	295	225	175	—	—

Wesson & Harrington Brand 125th Anniversary Rifle

Introduced in 1996 this rifle commemorates the 125th anniversary of the partnership. This special rifle is chambered for the .45-70 Government cartridge. The receiver is hand engraved. The barrel length is 32". The stock is American black walnut with crescent steel butt.

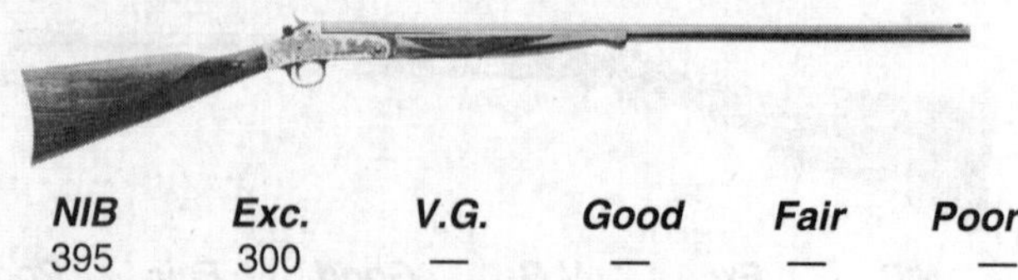

NIB	Exc.	V.G.	Good	Fair	Poor
395	300	—	—	—	—

Ultra Rifle Whitetails Unlimited 1997 Commemorative Edition

Introduced in 1997 and chambered for the .45-70 Govt. cartridge this model features a hand checkered black walnut stock. Special laser engraving on the action and pewter finished medallion inletted into stock. Barrel length is 22".

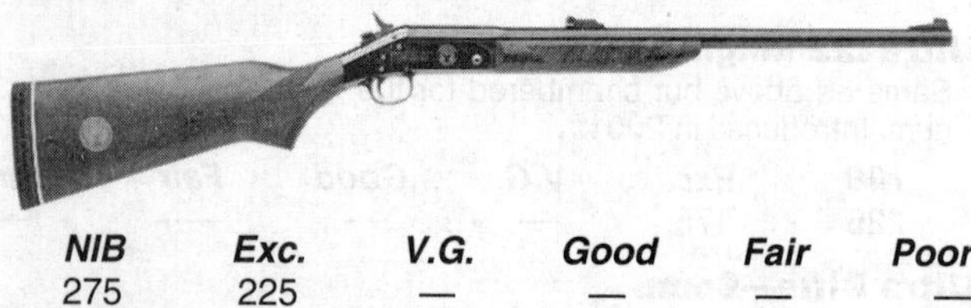

NIB	Exc.	V.G.	Good	Fair	Poor
275	225	—	—	—	—

CR Carbine

Single-shot rifle based on the Handi-Rifle design. Two-piece checkered walnut stock with schnabel forend. Marble's front and rear sights, Crescent steel buttplate. Chambered in .45 Colt. Introduced in 2007.

NIB	Exc.	V.G.	Good	Fair	Poor
375	—	—	—	—	—

Model 333

The Model 300 in 7mm Mag. caliber. Manufactured in 1974.

Exc.	V.G.	Good	Fair	Poor
250	200	175	125	100

Model 340

A .243 to .308 Winchester caliber bolt-action rifle with a 22" barrel and a 5-shot magazine. Blued, with a checkered walnut stock.

Exc.	V.G.	Good	Fair	Poor
400	350	300	225	150

Model 360 Ultra Automatic

A .243 Win. and the .308 Win. caliber semi-automatic rifle with a 22" barrel, adjustable sights and a 3-shot detachable magazine. Blued, with a checkered walnut stock. Manufactured between 1965 and 1978.

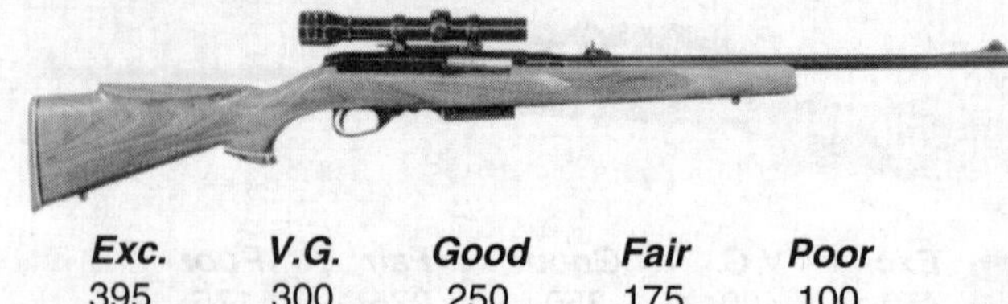

Exc.	V.G.	Good	Fair	Poor
395	300	250	175	100

Model 451 Medalist

A .22 LR caliber bolt-action rifle with a 26" barrel, open sights and a 5-shot detachable magazine. Blued, with a walnut stock. Manufactured between 1948 and 1961.

Exc.	V.G.	Good	Fair	Poor
175	150	125	100	75

Model 700

A .22 rimfire Magnum caliber, semi-automatic rifle with a 22" barrel, adjustable sights and a 5-round, detachable magazine. Blued, with a checkered walnut stock. Manufactured between 1977 and 1985.

Exc.	V.G.	Good	Fair	Poor
225	200	150	125	85

Model 700 DL

As above, with a checkered walnut stock and with a 4X scope. Manufactured until 1985.

Exc.	V.G.	Good	Fair	Poor
300	250	200	150	100

Model 750

A .22 LR bolt-action single-shot rifle with a 22" barrel with sights and a short stock. Blued, and the stock is hardwood.

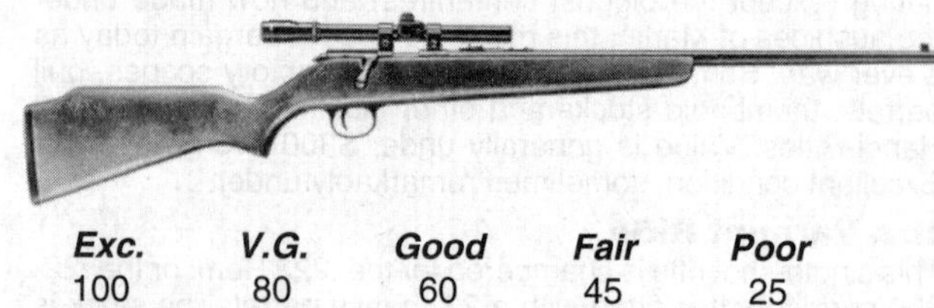

Exc.	V.G.	Good	Fair	Poor
100	80	60	45	25

Model 865

A .22 LR caliber bolt-action rifle with a 22" barrel, open sights and a 5-shot magazine. Blued, with a hardwood stock.

Exc.	V.G.	Good	Fair	Poor
100	80	60	45	25

Model 5200

A .22 LR caliber bolt-action, single-shot rifle with a 28" heavy barrel without sights, and an adjustable trigger. Blued, with a target-type walnut stock.

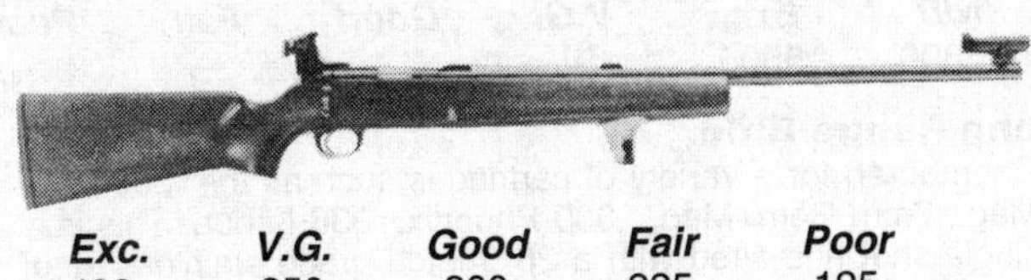

Exc.	V.G.	Good	Fair	Poor
400	350	300	225	125

Model 5200 Sporter

A .22 LR caliber bolt-action rifle with a 24" barrel, adjustable sights and a 5-shot magazine. Blued with a walnut stock. Not manufactured after 1983.

Exc.	V.G.	Good	Fair	Poor
400	350	300	225	125

100th Anniversary Officer's Model

A commemorative replica of the Officer's Model 1873 Trapdoor Springfield Rifle, with a 26" barrel. Engraved, and an anniversary plaque mounted on the stock. Blued, with a case colored receiver and a pewter forend tip. There were 10,000 manufactured in 1971. As with all commemoratives, this model is most desirable when NIB with all supplied material.

NIB	Exc.	V.G.	Good	Fair	Poor
750	550	—	—	—	—

Custer Memorial Issue

A limited production issue commemorating George Armstrong Custer's Battle of the Little Bighorn. Heavily engraved and gold inlaid with a high-grade checkered walnut stock. Furnished in a mahogany display case that included two books dealing with the subject. There were two versions produced—an Officer's Model, of which 25 were issued commemorating the 25 officers that fell with Custer, and another version commemorating the 243 enlisted men who lost their lives at the Little Bighorn. As with all commemoratives, to be collectible they must be NIB with all furnished material.

Officer's Model

25 manufactured.

NIB	Exc.	V.G.	Good	Fair	Poor
1800	—	—	—	—	—

Enlisted Men's Model

243 manufactured.

NIB	Exc.	V.G.	Good	Fair	Poor
1100	850	—	—	—	—

Model 174

A plain copy of the Springfield Model 1873 Carbine in .45-70 caliber with a 22" barrel. Manufactured in 1972.

Exc.	V.G.	Good	Fair	Poor
525	400	325	250	175

Model 178

A copy of the Springfield Model 1873 rifle with a 32" barrel. Manufactured from 1973 to 1984.

Exc.	V.G.	Good	Fair	Poor
525	400	325	250	175

HARRIS GUNWORKS

Phoenix, Arizona

NOTE: There are a wide range of extra costs options for all Harris Gunworks models that in many cases will dramatically affect price.

National Match Rifle

Introduced in 1989 this model features a bolt-action rifle chambered for the 7mm-08 or .308 with 5-round magazine. It is fitted with a 24" stainless steel match grade barrel with Canjar trigger. The stock is fiberglass with adjustable buttplate. Weight is about 11 lbs.

NIB	Exc.	V.G.	Good	Fair	Poor
3500	2750	1750	950	—	—

Model 86 Sniper Rifle

Chambered for .308, .30-06, .300 Win. Mag. with 24" heavy match grade barrel. The stock is a special design McHale fiberglass with textured grip and forearm. Fitted with a recoil pad. Supplied with a bipod. Weight is about 11.25 lbs.

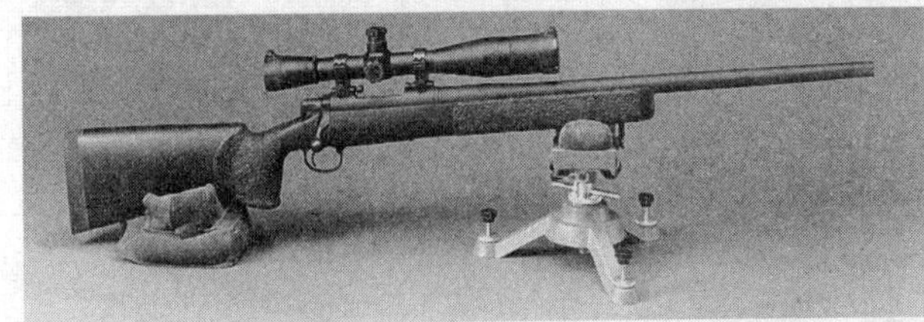

NIB	Exc.	V.G.	Good	Fair	Poor
2700	2100	1600	—	—	—

NOTE: Add $100 for take-down model.

Model 87 Series

These are single-shot rifles chambered for .50 BMG. Fitted with a 29" barrel with muzzlebrake. Fiberglass stock. Introduced in 1987. Weight is approximately 21.5 lbs.

NIB	Exc.	V.G.	Good	Fair	Poor
3700	2900	2000	—	—	—

NOTE: For Model 87R 5-shot repeater add $400. For Model 87 5-shot repeater add $300. For Model 92 Bullpup add $300.

Model 88

These bolt-action .50 BMG rifles are offered in two different configurations. One is fitted with a 20" carbon graphite barrel with add-on recoil arrestor with black teflon finish. The second variation is fitted with a 16.5" stainless steel barrel with integral recoil arrestor. Both rifles weigh about 14 lbs. Titanium action is available for further weight reduction.

NIB	Exc.	V.G.	Good	Fair	Poor
3600	2850	—	—	—	—

Model 89 Sniper Rifle

This bolt-action rifle is chambered for .308 cartridge. Fitted with a 28" barrel. Supplied with a bipod. Stock is fiberglass with adjustable length of pull and fitted with a recoil pad. Weight is about 15.25 lbs.

NIB	Exc.	V.G.	Good	Fair	Poor
2700	2100	1600	—	—	—

Model 93

Bolt-action .50 BMG rifle with folding hinge stock assembly. Furnished with a 10-round or 20-round magazine. Barrel length is 29". Weight is approximately 21 lbs.

Model 93 folding model

NIB	Exc.	V.G.	Good	Fair	Poor
4450	3500	—	—	—	—

Model 95

This is a lightweight variation of the .50 BMG models featuring Titanium and graphite. Supplied with bipod. Barrel length is 29". Weight is approximately 18 lbs.

NIB	Exc.	V.G.	Good	Fair	Poor
5200	4000	—	—	—	—

Model 96

This is a gas-operated semi-automatic .50 BMG sniper rifle. Barrel length is 29". Detachable 5-round magazine. Weight is approximately 25 lbs.

NIB	Exc.	V.G.	Good	Fair	Poor
6800	5500	—	—	—	—

Long Range Rifle

Chambered for a variety of cartridges such as the .300 Win. Mag., 7mm Rem. Mag., .300 Phoenix, .338 Lapua. This is a single-shot rifle fitted with a 26" match grade stainless steel barrel. Fiberglass stock with adjustable buttplate and cheekpiece. Weight is about 14 lbs.

NIB	Exc.	V.G.	Good	Fair	Poor
3600	2850	1500	—	—	—

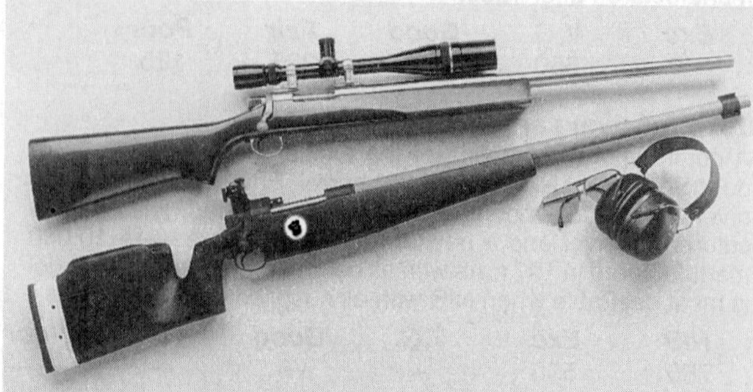

Target/Benchrest Rifle on top and Long Range Rifle on bottom

Target/Benchrest Rifle

Offered in .243, .308, 6mm BR, 6mm PPC, and 6mm Rem. This model is custom built for the customer. Available in both left- and right-hand. Weight is about 11 lbs.

NIB	Exc.	V.G.	Good	Fair	Poor
3000	2500	—	—	—	—

Antietam Sharps Rifle

This is a replica of the Sharps Model 1874 sidehammer introduced in 1994. Chambered for the .40-65 or the .45-70. Choice of 30" or 32" octagon or round barrel. Stock is fancy walnut with either straight, pistol grip, or Creedmoor with schnabel forearm. Many optional sights offered. Weight is about 11.25 lbs.

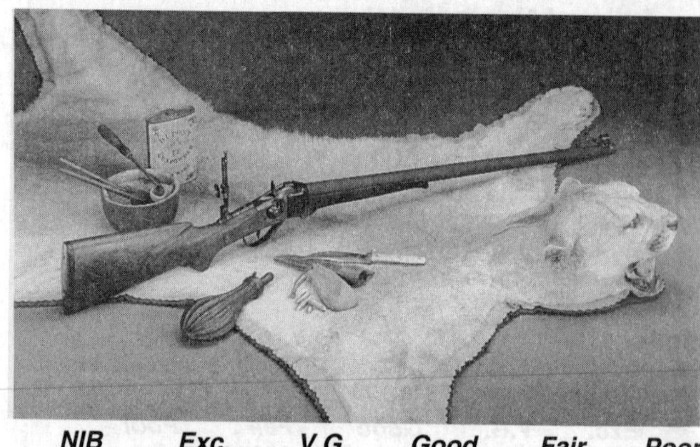

NIB	Exc.	V.G.	Good	Fair	Poor
2400	1850	1200	—	—	—

Signature Classic Sporter

This is a left- or right-handed bolt-action model introduced in 1987 with a choice of calibers from .22-250 to .375 H&H. Barrel lengths are 22", 24", or 26" depending on caliber. Choice of fiberglass stocks in green, beige, brown, or black. A wood stock is optional. Weight is about 7 lbs. for short action calibers.

NIB	Exc.	V.G.	Good	Fair	Poor
2900	2250	1500	—	—	—

Signature Classic Stainless Sporter

Same as above but with barrel and action made from stainless steel. A .416 Rem. Mag is available in this variation also. This model is also available with interchangeable barrels.

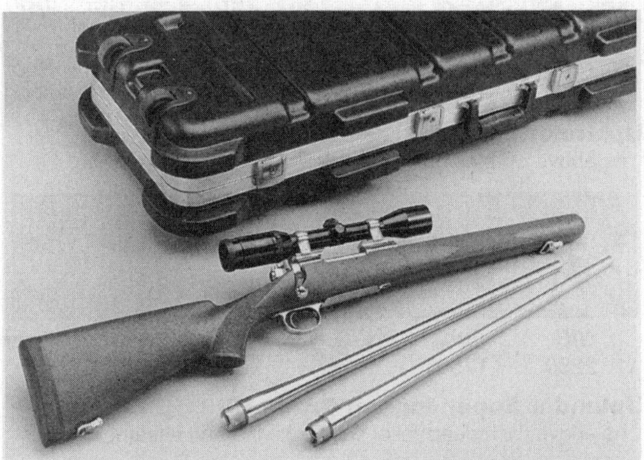

NIB	Exc.	V.G.	Good	Fair	Poor
2700	2000	1500	—	—	—

NOTE: Add $600 for interchangeable barrels.

Signature Super Varminter

Similar to the Classic Sporter except fitted with a heavy contoured barrel, adjustable trigger, and special hand-bedded fiberglass stock. Chambered for .223, .22-250, .220 Swift, .243, 6mm Rem., .25-06, 7mm-08, 7mm BR, .308, .350 Rem. Introduced in 1989.

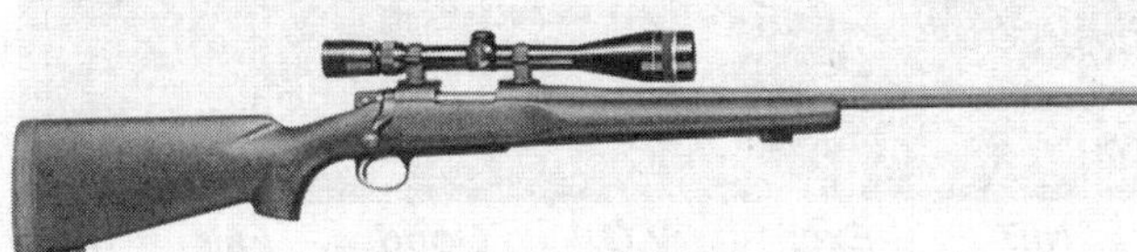

NIB	Exc.	V.G.	Good	Fair	Poor
2700	2000	1500	—	—	—

Signature Alaskan

Similar to the Classic Sporter except fitted with a match grade barrel with single leaf rear sight. Nickel finish. Walnut Monte Carlo stock with cheekpiece and palm swell grip. Chambered for .270 to .375 H&H. Introduced in 1989.

NIB	Exc.	V.G.	Good	Fair	Poor
3800	3000	2000	—	—	—

Signature Titanium Mountain Rifle

Similar to the Classic Sporter except action is made of titanium alloy and barrel of chrome-moly steel. Stock is graphite reinforced fiberglass. Chambered for .270 to .300 Win. Mag. Weight is about 5.5 lbs. Introduced in 1989.

NIB	Exc.	V.G.	Good	Fair	Poor
3300	2600	1750	—	—	—

NOTE: Add $400 for graphite steel barrel.

Sportsman 97

This bolt-action rifle is chambered for a variety of calibers from .270 Win. to .338 Win. The stock is fancy grade walnut, Bastogne, or English. A Talon action is fitted.

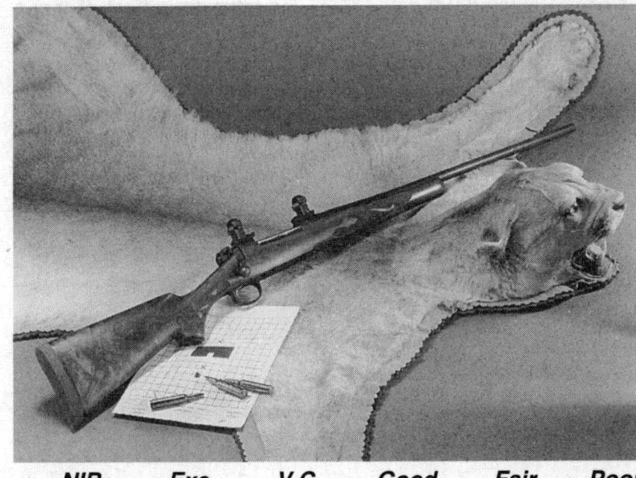

NIB	Exc.	V.G.	Good	Fair	Poor
2800	2250	—	—	—	—

Talon Safari Rifle

This bolt-action rifle is chambered for 16 different calibers from .300 Win. Mag. to .460 Weatherby Mag. The finish is a matte black with fiberglass Safari stock. Weight is between 9 and 10 lbs. depending on caliber.

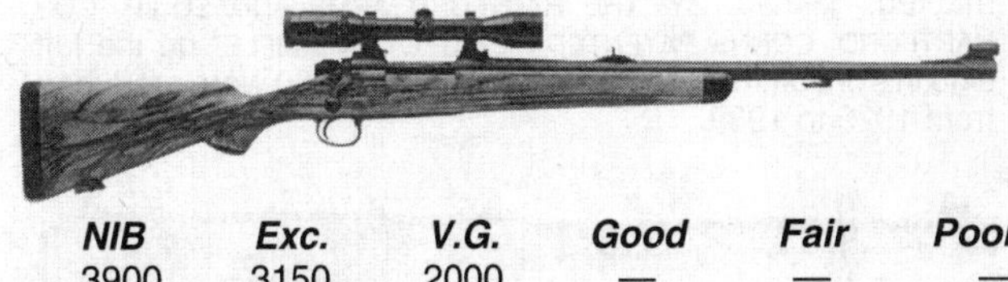

NIB	Exc.	V.G.	Good	Fair	Poor
3900	3150	2000	—	—	—

Talon Sporter Rifle

This bolt-action rifle, introduced in 1991, uses a pre-64 Model 70 type action with cone breech. Barrel and action are stainless steel. Chambered for a wide variety of calibers from .22-250 to .416 Rem. Mag. Choice of walnut or fiberglass stock. Most barrel lengths are 24". Weight is about 7.5 lbs. depending on caliber.

NIB	Exc.	V.G.	Good	Fair	Poor
2900	2500	1750	—	—	—

Double Rifle/Shotgun

This side-by-side gun is offered in .470 NE or .500 NE as well as 12 and 20 gauge guns. Engraved receiver, AAA fancy walnut stocks and 3-leaf express sights are standard. Offered in boxlock and side lock models.

Boxlock

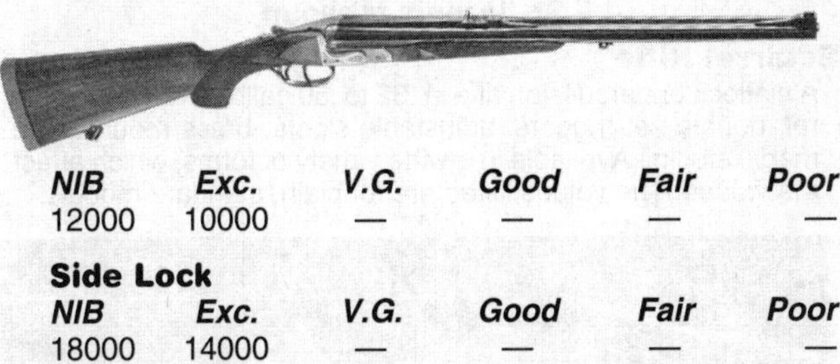

NIB	Exc.	V.G.	Good	Fair	Poor
12000	10000	—	—	—	—

Side Lock

NIB	Exc.	V.G.	Good	Fair	Poor
18000	14000	—	—	—	—

HARTFORD ARMS & EQUIPMENT CO.

Hartford, Connecticut

Established in 1925, this firm was purchased by the High Standard Company in 1932.

Single-Shot Target

A .22 caliber single-shot pistol with a 6.75" round barrel, fixed sights and either walnut or composition grips. The frame marked "Manfd. by the/ Hartford Arms and Equip. Co./ Hartford,

Conn./ Patented .22 cal./ l.r." on the left side in front of ther breach. Although this pistol resembles a semi-automatic, it is in fact a single-shot manually operated pistol.

Add $150 premium for guns in original Hartford Arms box numbered to the gun. Add $250 premium for guns in original High Standard box numbered to the gun.

Courtesy John J. Stimson, Jr.

Exc.	V.G.	Good	Fair	Poor
575	425	310	200	150

Model 1925

Semi-automatic pistol chambered for .22 caliber with 6.75" round barrel, checkered hard black rubber grips or ribbed walnut grips. Magazine capacity is 10 rounds. The frame is marked, "MANFD. BY/ THE HARTFORD ARMS AND EQUIP. CO./ HARTFORD, CONN./ PATENTED/ .22 CAL/LONG RIFLE" on the left side in front of the breach. Approximately 5,000 were produced from 1925 to 1932.

Courtesy John J. Stimson, Jr.

Exc.	V.G.	Good	Fair	Poor
575	450	350	200	150

NOTE: Add $150 premium for guns in original Hartford Arms box numbered to the gun.

HATFIELD RIFLE COMPANY

St. Joseph, Missouri

Squirrel Rifle

A flintlock or percussion rifle in .32 to .50 caliber with a 39" barrel, double set triggers, adjustable sights, brass mounts and maple stocks. Available in a wide variety of forms, which affect the values. The values listed are for plain, standard models.

NIB	Exc.	V.G.	Good	Fair	Poor
550	400	350	300	225	150

SHOTGUNS

Uplander Grade I

A 20 gauge boxlock double-barrel shotgun with a 26" improved cylinder and modified barrel with a matte raised rib, single-selective trigger and automatic ejectors. Case hardened, blued with a deluxe-grade, hand-checkered walnut stock. Introduced in 1987.

NIB	Exc.	V.G.	Good	Fair	Poor
1250	1050	750	600	475	200

Uplander Pigeon Grade II

As above, with scroll engraving with a fitted leather case.

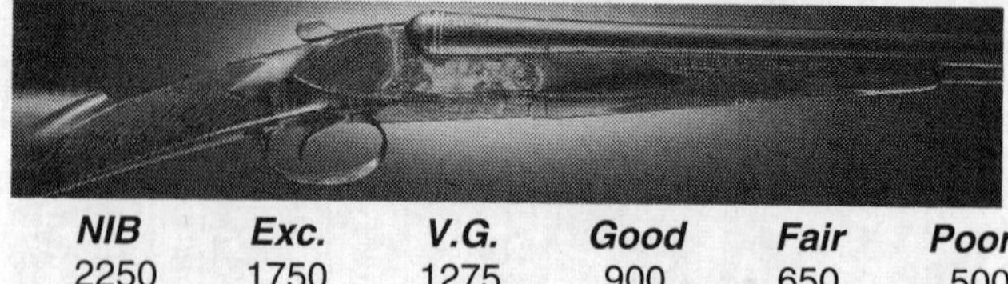

NIB	Exc.	V.G.	Good	Fair	Poor
2250	1750	1275	900	650	500

Uplander Super Pigeon Grade III

As above, with deep-relief cut engraving and a leather case.

NIB	Exc.	V.G.	Good	Fair	Poor
2500	2200	1700	1400	1000	700

Uplander Golden Quail Grade IV

A gold-inlaid version of the above.

NIB	Exc.	V.G.	Good	Fair	Poor
4000	3500	2750	2000	1700	1300

Uplander Woodcock Grade V

As above, with seven 24 kt. gold inlays and best quality engraving. Furnished with a leather case.

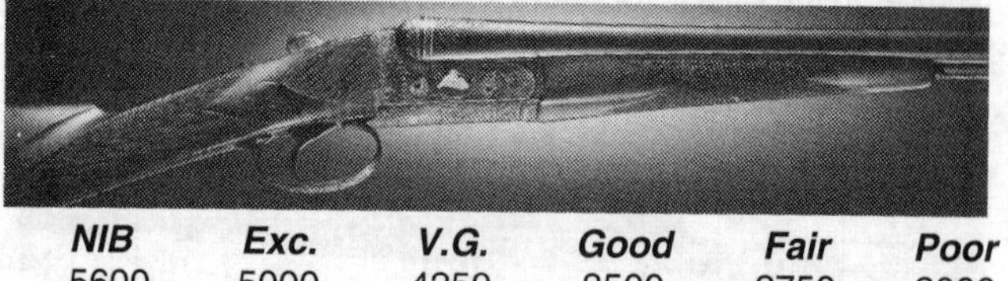

NIB	Exc.	V.G.	Good	Fair	Poor
5600	5000	4250	3500	2750	2000

HAVILAND & GUNN

Ilion, New York

Gallery Pistol

A .17 caliber rimfire single-shot pistol with a 5" barrel. The barrel and frame made of one piece of iron and nickel plated. There are no markings on these pistols whatsoever. Believed to have been made during the 1870s.

Exc.	V.G.	Good	Fair	Poor
—	—	850	350	175

HAWES

Los Angeles, California

An importer of handguns primarily made in Europe

Courier

A .25 caliber, blowback, semi-automatic pocket pistol manufactured by Galesi.

Exc.	V.G.	Good	Fair	Poor
125	100	75	50	25

Diplomat

A .380 ACP pistol with an external hammer.

Exc.	V.G.	Good	Fair	Poor
150	125	100	75	50

Trophy

A J.P. Sauer & Sohn, manufactured revolver with a swing-out cylinder and a 6" barrel. Chambered for the .22 LR and the .38 Special. Has adjustable sights.

Exc.	V.G.	Good	Fair	Poor
250	200	175	125	90

Medalion

As above, with a 3", 4", or 6" barrel and fixed sights.

Exc.	V.G.	Good	Fair	Poor
200	175	125	100	75

MARSHAL SINGLE-ACTION ARMY REVOLVERS

J. P. Sauer also made a Western-styled series for Hawes based in appearance on the Colt Single-Action Army.

Silver City Marshal

A .22 LR or .22 rimfire Magnum caliber single-action revolver with a 5.5" barrel, 6-shot cylinder, and fixed sights.

Exc.	V.G.	Good	Fair	Poor
125	100	75	50	25

Western Marshal

A .357 Magnum, .44 Magnum, .45 Colt, .45 ACP, .44-40, 9mm, .22 LR, and .22 rimfire Magnum single-action revolver with fixed sights. Blued.

Exc.	V.G.	Good	Fair	Poor
175	150	125	100	75

Texas Marshal

As above, but nickel-plated.

Exc.	V.G.	Good	Fair	Poor
185	160	135	100	75

Montana Marshal

The Western Marshal with a brass backstrap and trigger guard.

Exc.	V.G.	Good	Fair	Poor
175	150	125	100	75

Deputy Marshal

A .22 LR and .22 rimfire Magnum single-action revolver with a 5.5" barrel, and 6-shot cylinder.

Exc.	V.G.	Good	Fair	Poor
125	100	75	50	25

Tip-Up Target Pistol

Replica of the Stevens Model 35 .22 LR single-shot. Globe front sight, adjustable rear.

Exc.	V.G.	Good	Fair	Poor
275	200	135	75	35

Chief Marshal

A .357 Magnum, .44 Magnum, and the .45 Colt caliber revolver with a 6.5" barrel, and 6-shot cylinder and adjustable sights. Blued.

Exc.	V.G.	Good	Fair	Poor
175	150	125	100	75

Federal Marshal

A 6-shot single-action revolver in .357 Magnum, .44 Magnum, and the .45 Colt caliber.

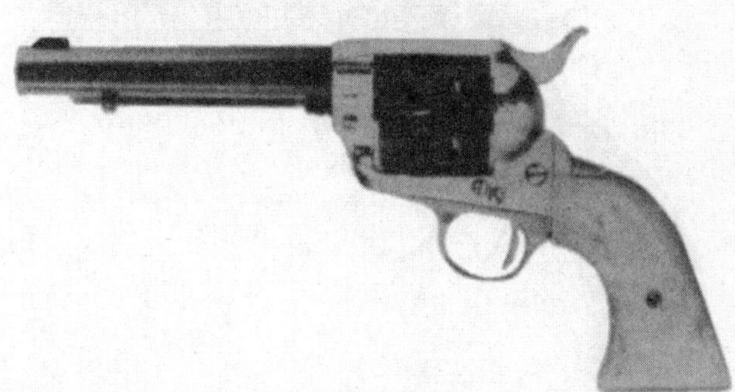

Exc.	V.G.	Good	Fair	Poor
175	150	125	100	75

HAWES & WAGGONER

Philadelphia, Pennsylvania

Pocket Pistol

A .41 caliber single-shot percussion pistol with a 3" barrel, German silver mountings, and a walnut stock. Manufactured in the 1850s.

Exc.	V.G.	Good	Fair	Poor
—	1750	650	350	250

HAWKEN

St. Louis, Missouri

During the early part of the 19th century, Jacob and Samuel Hawken manufactured a variety of flintlock, percussion and cartridge rifles, shotguns and pistols. They are best known, however, for half stock Plains Rifles. Though of a plain nature, these arms were recognized for their accuracy and dependability. Early Hawken rifles will be worth a substantial premium over later examples. Some examples in very good condition may be worth as much as $40,000. Proceed with caution.

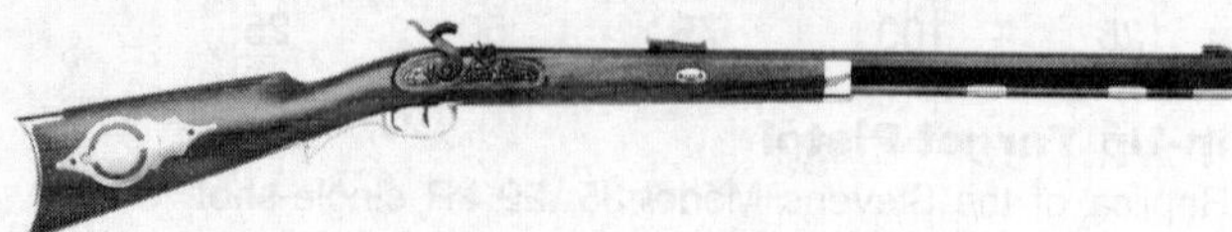

HDH, SA.

Henrion, Dassy & Heuschen
Liege, Belgium

Cobold

A 9.4mm Dutch, 10.6mm German, .38, and .45 caliber double-action five-shot revolver with solid frame, octagonal barrel, and an odd safety catch that locks the cylinder.

Exc.	V.G.	Good	Fair	Poor
375	275	225	150	100

Puppy

A 5.5mm to 7.65mm caliber folding trigger, double-action revolver. Most are "Velo-Dogs."

Exc.	V.G.	Good	Fair	Poor
175	125	100	75	50

Lincoln

A .22 caliber folding trigger, double-action revolver with a solid frame, imitation pearl or ivory grips, and engraving.

Exc.	V.G.	Good	Fair	Poor
175	125	100	75	50

Lincoln-Bossu

A 5.5mm or 6.35mm caliber folding trigger double-action revolver ("Velo-Dog" type) with solid-frame and hammerless.

Exc.	V.G.	Good	Fair	Poor
175	125	100	75	50

Left Wheeler

A Colt Police Positive copy in .32 or .38 caliber. The last revolver HDH manufactured.

Exc.	V.G.	Good	Fair	Poor
200	150	125	100	75

HEAVY EXPRESS INC.

Colorado Springs, Colorado

This company builds custom-built rifles using its proprietary nonbelted cartridges from .260 Heavy Express Magnum to the .416 Heavy Express Magnum. The company's rifles are built on Ruger Model 77 Mark II and Winchester Model 70 Classic actions. Barrels are 4140 chrome-moly blue and 416R stainless steel. Stocks include factory walnut, laminated, or composite designs. The prices listed are for the basic guns. Options are not included and will affect price.

Heavy Express Premier—Ruger M77 Mk II

This rifle is chambered for the .260 HE Mag, .284 HE Mag., or .300 HE Mag. Choice of walnut, laminated, or composite stocks.

NIB	Exc.	V.G.	Good	Fair	Poor
1200	900	—	—	—	—

NOTE: Add $200 for stainless steel.

Heavy Express Monarch—Winchester M70 Classic

Same as above but built on a Winchester M70 Classic action. Choice of stocks.

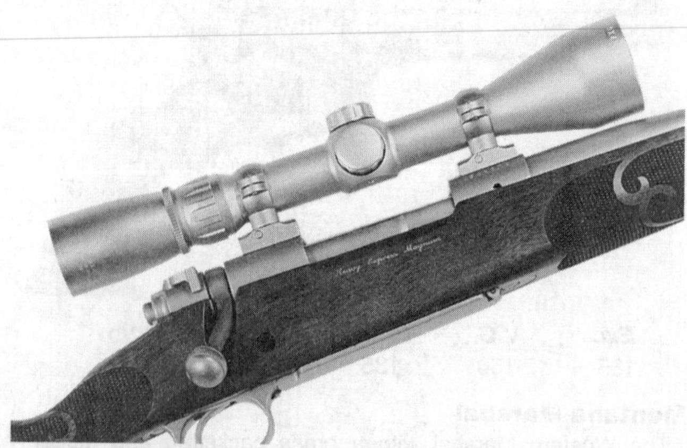

Close-up of Model 70 Classic stainless steel action

NIB	Exc.	V.G.	Good	Fair	Poor
1575	1200	—	—	—	—

NOTE: Add $200 for stainless steel.

Heavy Express Monarch—Ruger 77 MK II

This rifle is built on a Ruger M77 action and is chambered for the .338, .350, .375, .416, and .460 HE Magnum cartridges. Choice of stocks.

NIB	Exc.	V.G.	Good	Fair	Poor
1475	1100	—	—	—	—

NOTE: Add $200 for stainless steel.

Heavy Express Single-Shot—Ruger #1

This rifle is chambered in .300, .338, .350, and .416 HE Magnum cartridges. Choice of stocks.

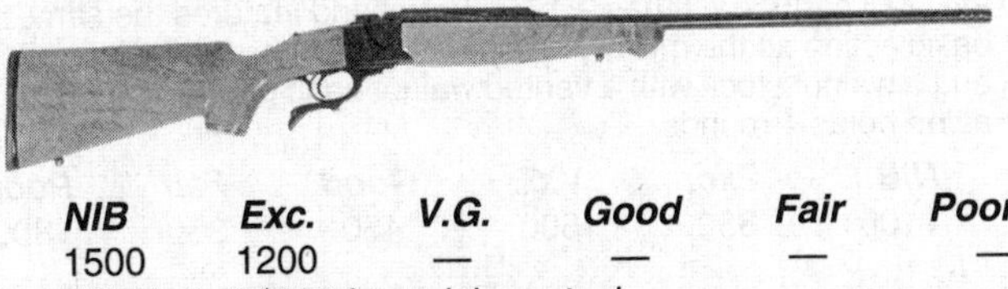

NIB	Exc.	V.G.	Good	Fair	Poor
1500	1200	—	—	—	—

NOTE: Add $200 for stainless steel.

Heavy Express Premier—Winchester M70 Classic

This rifle is built on a Ruger M77 Mk II action in .260 HE Mag., .284 HE Mag., or .300 HE Mag. Choice of stocks.

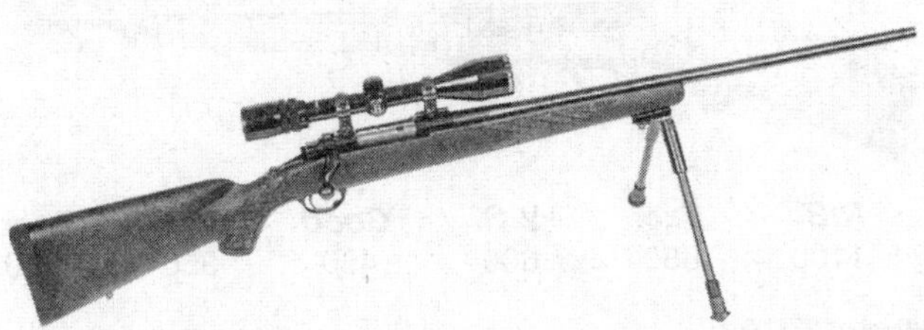

NIB	Exc.	V.G.	Good	Fair	Poor
1300	950	—	—	—	—

NOTE: Add $200 for stainless steel.

HECKLER & KOCH

Oberndorf/Neckar, Germany

At the end of WWII, the French dismantled the Mauser factory as part of their reparations; and the buildings remained idle until 1949, when firearms production was again allowed in Germany. Heckler & Koch was formed as a machine tool enterprise and occupied the vacant Mauser plant. In the early 1950s Edmund Heckler and Theodor Koch began to produce the G3 automatic rifle based on the Spanish CETME design and progressed to machine guns and submachine guns and eventually to the production of commercial civilian rifles and pistols. In 1990 the company got into financial difficulties because of a failed contract bid. In December 1990 the French state consortium GIAT announced the purchase of Heckler and Koch, but a little more than a year later the contract was cancelled. Later in 1991 the company was purchased by Royal Ordnance of Britain. In 2002 the company was sold to a combined group of European investors and long-time company managers.

Model 91 A2

This rifle is recoil-operated, with a delayed-roller lock bolt. It is chambered for the .308 Winchester cartridge and has a 17.7" barrel with military style aperture sights. It is furnished with a 20-round detachable magazine and is finished in matte black with a black plastic stock. Some areas of the country have made its ownership illegal.

NIB	Exc.	V.G.	Good	Fair	Poor
2850	2450	2000	1900	1750	800

Model 91 A3

This model is simply the Model 91 with a retractable metal stock.

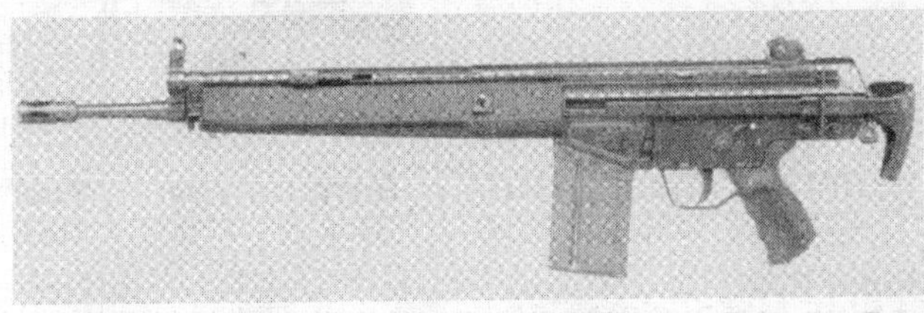

NIB	Exc.	V.G.	Good	Fair	Poor
3100	2650	2250	2100	1950	900

Model 93 A2

This model is similar to the Model 91 except that it is chambered for the .223 cartridge and has a 16.4" barrel. The magazine holds 25 rounds, and the specification are the same as for the Model 91.

NIB	Exc.	V.G.	Good	Fair	Poor
2950	2550	2100	2000	1850	800

Model 93 A3

This is the Model 93 with the retractable metal stock.

NIB	Exc.	V.G.	Good	Fair	Poor
3200	2750	2300	2100	1850	900

Model 94 A2

This is a carbine version chambered for the 9mm Parabellum cartridge, with a 16.5" barrel. It is a smaller-scaled weapon that has a 15-shot magazine.

NIB	Exc.	V.G.	Good	Fair	Poor
4000	3750	3500	3100	2500	1250

Model 94 A3

This model is a variation of the Model 94 with the addition of a retractable metal stock.

NIB	Exc.	V.G.	Good	Fair	Poor
4200	3950	3750	3300	2700	1000

Model 270

This model is chambered for the .22 LR cartridge. It is a sporting-styled rifle with a 16.5" barrel. It is furnished with either a 5- or a 20-round magazine and is blued, with a checkered walnut stock. This rifle was discontinued in 1985.

NIB	Exc.	V.G.	Good	Fair	Poor
600	500	450	350	250	150

Model 300

This model is similar to the Model 270 except that it is chambered for the .22 rimfire Magnum cartridge. It was not imported after 1988.

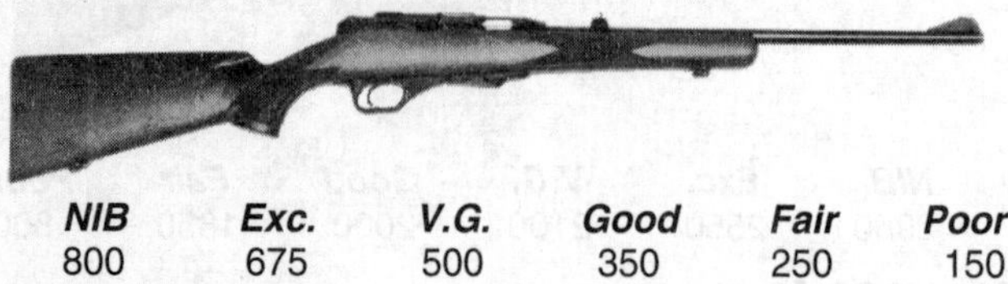

NIB	Exc.	V.G.	Good	Fair	Poor
800	675	500	350	250	150

Model 630

This model is chambered for the .223 and features the same roller-delayed semi-automatic action as found on the paramilitary-type weapons. This is a sporting-style rifle that has a polished blue finish and a checkered walnut stock. The barrel is 17.7" long, and the magazines offered hold either 4 or 10 rounds. Importation was discontinued in 1986.

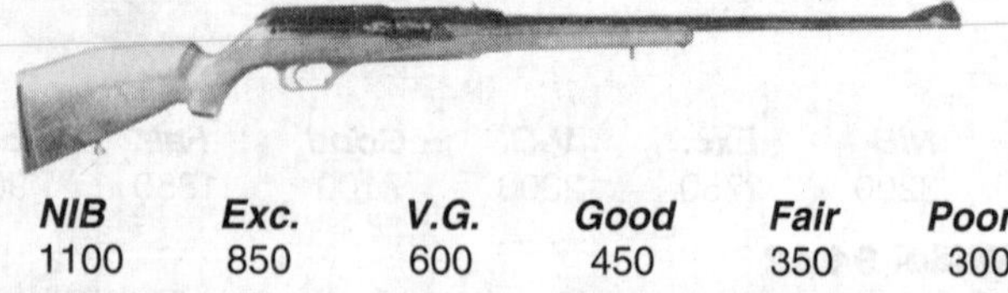

NIB	Exc.	V.G.	Good	Fair	Poor
1100	850	600	450	350	300

Model 770

This model is similar to the Model 630 except that it is chambered for the .308 Winchester cartridge and has 19.7" barrel. It was not imported after 1986.

NIB	Exc.	V.G.	Good	Fair	Poor
1100	950	600	450	350	300

Model 820

This rifle is a falling design and chambered for the .30-06 cartridge. Two of these rifles are known in the U.S., one of which is in the H&K museum.

NIB	Exc.	V.G.	Good	Fair	Poor
3500	3000	—	—	—	—

Model 877

This rifle is a breech loading rifle chambered for .30-06 or .22-250 cartridge. Two of these rifles are known in the U.S., one of which is the H&K museum.

NIB	Exc.	V.G.	Good	Fair	Poor
3500	3000	—	—	—	—

Model 940

This model is essentially the same as the Model 770 except that it is chambered for the .30-06 cartridge. It has a 21" barrel and was not imported after 1986.

NIB	Exc.	V.G.	Good	Fair	Poor
1450	1100	800	600	400	300

Model SL6

This is Heckler & Koch's current sporting rifle chambered for the .223 cartridge. It has a 17.7" barrel and features the same basic action as the military versions. It has a matte black finish and a walnut stock with a vented walnut hand guard. The magazine holds 4 rounds.

NIB	Exc.	V.G.	Good	Fair	Poor
1100	850	600	450	350	300

Model SL7

This model is similar to the SL6 except that it is chambered for the .308 Winchester cartridge and has a 3-round magazine.

NIB	Exc.	V.G.	Good	Fair	Poor
1100	850	600	450	350	300

Model SR9

This model was introduced into the U.S. market after the federal government prohibited the importation of H&K's other semi-automatic rifles. The SR9 is similar to the HK91 but has been certified by the BATF as a sporting rifle. This model features a special thumb hole stock made of Kevlar reinforced fiberglass. The action is a delayed-roller locked bolt semi-automatic design chambered for the .308 Winchester cartridge. The barrel is 19.7" in length and features adjustable rear sight with hooded front sight. The rifle weighs 10.9 lbs.

NIB	Exc.	V.G.	Good	Fair	Poor
2000	1700	1400	1000	700	500

Model SR9 (T) Target

Similar to the standard model SR9 but with the addition of a special MSG90 adjustable buttstock, PSG-1 trigger group, and a PSG-1 contoured hand grip. Rifle weighs 10.6 lbs.

NIB	Exc.	V.G.	Good	Fair	Poor
3000	2800	2200	1650	1050	800

Model SR9 (TC) Target Competition

Similar to the Model SR9 (T) but with the addition of the PSG-1 adjustable buttstock. Rifle weighs 10.9 lbs.

NIB	Exc.	V.G.	Good	Fair	Poor
3300	3000	2300	1950	1100	900

BASR Model

This is a bolt-action rifle chambered for various popular calibers. It has a stainless steel barrel and was essentially custom built to the customer's specifications. The stock is of Kevlar. This model is quite rare because only 100 were manufactured in 1968.

Exc.	V.G.	Good	Fair	Poor
1750	1200	900	650	400

PSG-1

This rifle is a high precision sniping rifle that features the delayed-roller semi-automatic action. It is chambered for the .308 Winchester cartridge and has a 5-shot magazine. Barrel length is 25.6". It is furnished with a complete array of accessories including a 6x42-power illuminated Hensoldt scope. Rifle weighs 17.8 lbs.

NIB	Exc.	V.G.	Good	Fair	Poor
14500	12500	9000	7500	6000	4000

Model SL8-1

This is a new generation .223 rifle modeled after the military Model G36 and introduced in 2000. It is built of carbon fiber polymer and is gas operated. Thumbhole stock with cheekpiece. Barrel length is 20.8". Magazine capacity is 10 rounds. Adjustable sights. Weight is approximately 8.6 lbs.

NIB	Exc.	V.G.	Good	Fair	Poor
1600	1200	—	—	—	—

SLB 2000

Introduced in 2001 this gas-operated semi-automatic rifle is chamberd for the .30-06 cartridge. The receiver is built of lightweight alloy. The barrel is 16.7" in length and will accept interchangeable barrels at some future date. Oil finished walnut stock. Open sights with both barrel and receiver drilled and tapped for scope mounts. Magazine capacity is 2, 5, or 10 rounds. Weight is about 7.25 lbs.

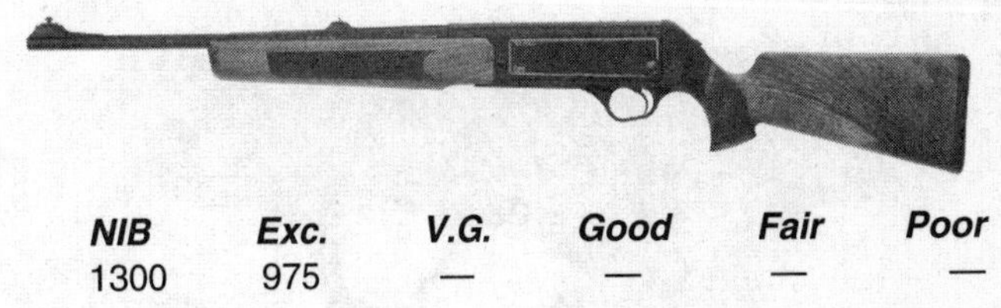

NIB	Exc.	V.G.	Good	Fair	Poor
1300	975	—	—	—	—

Model USC

Introduced in 2000 this semi-automatic blowback carbine is derived from H&K's UMP submachine gun. Chambered for the .45 ACP cartridge and fitted with a 16" barrel. Skeltonized stock. Accessory rail on top of receiver. Adjustable sights. Magazine capacity is 10 rounds. Weight is approximately 6 lbs.

NIB	Exc.	V.G.	Good	Fair	Poor
1200	900	—	—	—	—

PISTOLS

HK4

This is a blowback-operated semi-automatic pistol based on the Mauser HSc design. It is chambered for .22 LR, .25 ACP, .32 ACP, and .380. These calibers were easily converted by switching the barrels, recoil springs and magazines. The rimfire model could be changed by rotating the breechface. The conversion kits were available for all calibers. The barrel is 3" long; and the finish is blued, with molded plastic thumb rest grips. This pistol was sold from 1968-1973 as the Harrington & Richardson HK4 and is so marked. It was completely discontinued in 1984.

.22 Caliber or .380 Caliber

Exc.	V.G.	Good	Fair	Poor
475	350	250	200	100

.25 Caliber or .32 Caliber

Exc.	V.G.	Good	Fair	Poor
350	300	250	200	100

Conversion Units

Exc.	V.G.	Good	Fair	Poor
150	125	90	60	30

P9

This is a single-action, delayed-blowback semi-automatic pistol chambered for 9mm or 7.65mm Parabellum. The action is based on the G-3 rifle mechanism. The barrel is 4" in length, and the pistol has an internal hammer and a thumb-operated hammer drop and decocking lever. There is also a manual safety and a loaded-chamber indicator. The finish is Parkerized, and the grips are molded plastic and well contoured. It has fixed sights. This model was manufactured between 1977 and 1984. This model is rarer than the P9S model.

NIB	Exc.	V.G.	Good	Fair	Poor
800	650	500	400	300	200

P9S

This model is similar to the Model P9 except that the action features a double-action capability and it is chambered for the .45 ACP and the 9mm Parabellum with a 5.5" barrel. This model was also manufactured between 1977 and 1984.

NIB	Exc.	V.G.	Good	Fair	Poor
800	650	500	400	300	200

P9S Target Model

This version is similar to the Model P9S chambered for the 9mm or .45 ACP cartridges, with adjustable sights, and an adjustable trigger. It was discontinued in 1984.

NIB	Exc.	V.G.	Good	Fair	Poor
1100	850	700	600	500	300

P9S Competition

Similar to the P9S target but with the addition of barrel weights and special competition grips.

NIB	Exc.	V.G.	Good	Fair	Poor
2000	1500	1200	—	—	—

VP 70Z

This is a blowback-operated semi-automatic chambered for the 9mm Parabellum cartridge. It is striker-fired and double-action-only. The barrel is 4.5" long, and the double-column magazine holds 18 rounds. The finish is blued, and the receiver and grip are molded from plastic. This model was discontinued in 1984.

NIB	Exc.	V.G.	Good	Fair	Poor
550	450	350	300	250	200

P7 PSP

This was the first of the squeeze-cocked H&K pistols. It is a single-action semi-automatic that is placed in the firing position by pressure on the front of the grip strap. This moves the striker into battery; and firing is then accomplished by a single action pressure on the trigger, releasing the grip strap cocking device and decocking the mechanism. This particular model does not have the extended finger guard on the trigger and also does not have an ambidextrous safety. It was discontinued in 1984.

NIB	Exc.	V.G.	Good	Fair	Poor
800	700	600	500	400	200

P7 K3

This is the "Squeeze Cocker" chambered for either the .380 or .22 LR caliber. It has a recoil buffer that is oil-filled and a 3.8" barrel. The magazine holds 8 rounds. This model was introduced in 1988.

NIB	Exc.	V.G.	Good	Fair	Poor
1000	900	750	650	500	300

.22 Caliber Conversion Kit

This unit will convert the P7 K3 to fire the .22 LR cartridge.

NIB	Exc.	V.G.	Good	Fair	Poor
575	400	350	300	150	75

.32 ACP Caliber Conversion Kit

NIB	Exc.	V.G.	Good	Fair	Poor
200	175	150	100	75	50

P7 M8

This is the 8-shot newer version of the "squeeze cocker." It has the heat-shield finger guard and the ambidextrous safety. It has a 4" barrel and a 3-dot sight system. The finish is matte blue or nickel with stippled black plastic grips. This model is no longer in production.

NIB	Exc.	V.G.	Good	Fair	Poor
1500	1200	900	700	500	300

NOTE: For night sights, introduced in 1993, add $100.

P7 M10

A new addition to the P7 series in 1993, this variation is chambered for the .40 S&W cartridge. Magazine holds 10 rounds and the finish is available in either blue or nickel. Pistol weighs 2.69 lbs.

NIB	Exc.	V.G.	Good	Fair	Poor
1200	1000	800	650	500	300

NOTE: For night sights add $100.

P7 M13

This version is similar to the P7 M8 except that it has a double column 13-shot magazine.

NIB	Exc.	V.G.	Good	Fair	Poor
1300	1000	800	650	500	300

NOTE: For night sights add $100.

SP89

Introduced in the early 1990s, this is a large frame semi-automatic pistol chambered for the 9mm cartridge. It features a 15-round magazine and a square notch rear sight with a hooded front sight. The pistol has a 4.5" barrel and is 13" overall. It weighs 4.4 lbs. In August 1993 this model was no longer imported due to a ban on assault pistols.

NIB	Exc.	V.G.	Good	Fair	Poor
4000	3600	3200	2500	1800	1000

USP SERIES

NOTE: Late in 1999 H&K began shipping its USPs and Mark 23s with an internal locking system. This lock-out is installed in the grip and blocks the movement of the hammer, trigger, and slide. It is operated with a two pronged key, supplied with the pistol. This system is in addition to the traditional trigger lock that is sold with each H&K firearm. In 2001 the stainless steel version of these pistols was discontinued.

In 2005 H&K offered a limited edition run of colr frame variations for the USP line. These colors are Desert tan, green and gray.

Gray: USP 45 and USP 40 Compact

Green: USP 45, USP 40, USP 40 Compact, and USP 45 Tactical.

Desert Tan: USP 45, USP 40, USP 40 Compact, and USP 45 Tactical and Mark 23.

Retail prices are the same for these color variations as the standtd black frame pistols.

USP 40

Introduced in 1993 this new semi-automatic H&K pistol features a new design that incorporates a short recoil modified Browning action. Chambered for the .40 S&W cartridge this model has a 4.13" barrel and a magazine capacity of 13 rounds. Stainless steel model introduced in 1996. It weighs 1.74 lbs. Available in seven different variations from traditional double-action to double-action-only and various safety locations and styles. These variants are numbered by H&K are listed.

1. DA/SA with safe position and control lever on left side of frame.
2. DA/SA with safe position and control lever on right side of frame.
3. DA/SA without safe position and decocking lever on left side of frame.
4. DA/SA without safe position and decocking lever on left side of frame.
5. DA only with safe position and safety lever on left side of frame.
6. DA only with safe position and safety lever on right side of frame.
7. DA only without control lever.
9. DA/SA with safe position and safety lever on left side of frame.
10. DA/SA with safety lever on the right side of frame.

From top to bottom is the USP 45, the USP 40, and the USP 40 Compact

NIB	Exc.	V.G.	Good	Fair	Poor
770	600	450	300	250	—

NOTE: For stainless steel model add $45.

USP 9

Same as the USP 40 but chambered for the 9mm cartridge. Magazine holds 16 rounds and pistol weighs 1.66 lbs. This model also has the choice of seven variations as listed above for the USP 40. New for 1993.

NIB	Exc.	V.G.	Good	Fair	Poor
770	600	450	300	250	—

NOTE: For stainless steel model add $45.

USP 9SD

This variation of the USP 9 is fitted with target sights to see over an optional sound suppressor. The barrel is threaded left-hand and does not have an O-ring and does not require a thread cap. Introduced in 2004.

NIB	Exc.	V.G.	Good	Fair	Poor
940	725	—	—	—	—

USP 45

Introduced in 1995 this version is slightly larger than the 9mm and .40 S&W models. Barrel length is 4.41" and overall length is 7.87". Weight is 1.9 lbs. The USP 45 is available in the same variants as the other USP models. Magazine capacity is 12 rounds.

H&K Stainless Steel Model

NIB	Exc.	V.G.	Good	Fair	Poor
840	625	450	350	250	—

NOTE: For stainless steel model add $45.

USP 9 Compact

Introduced in 1997 this 9mm model is a smaller version of the full size USP 9. There are some internal differences due to size. Barrel length is 3.58". Overall length is 6.81". Magazine capacity is 10 rounds. Weight is approximately 26 oz. Also available with stainless steel slide. Add $45 to NIB price.

NIB	Exc.	V.G.	Good	Fair	Poor
800	600	450	300	200	150

USP 40 Compact

Same as 9mm Compact model but chambered for .40 S&W cartridge. Weight is about 27 oz. All other dimensions are the same.

NIB	Exc.	V.G.	Good	Fair	Poor
800	600	450	300	200	150

USP Compact LEM (Law Enforcement Modification)

This model, introduced in 2002, is identical to the USP Compact .40 S&W Variant 7, but with a double-action-only trigger with a special trigger mechanism. The mechanism improves the double-action trigger performance and reduces the weight of pull to between 7.5 and 8.5 lbs. Offered in blued finish.

NIB	Exc.	V.G.	Good	Fair	Poor
820	650	—	—	—	—

USP 45 Match

Introduced in 1997 this model is a match grade variation of the USP. It is chambered for the .45 ACP cartridge. Fitted with a 6.02" barrel with barrel weight assembly. Adjustable rear sight and target front sight. Adjustable trigger stop. Blued finish. Weight is approximately 38 oz. Also available in a stainless steel version.

NIB	Exc.	V.G.	Good	Fair	Poor
1370	1100	—	—	—	—

NOTE: Add $60 for stainless steel.

USP 45 Compact

Introduced in 1997 this pistol is chambered for the .45 ACP cartridge. It has a 3.8" barrel and an overall length of 7.1". It weighs approximately 28 oz. Magazine capacity is 8 rounds.

NIB	Exc.	V.G.	Good	Fair	Poor
875	650	500	350	250	—

USP 45 Compact Tactical

Blued semi-auto .45 ACP. Double-action with 4.46" barrel, 8-round capacity. 27.5 oz. Polymer grip. MSRP: 1115

USP .357 Compact

Introduced in mid-1998 this pistol is built on the same frame as the .40 S&W Compact but chambered for the .357 Sig cartridge. Magazine capacity is 10 rounds. Weight is about 28 oz.

NIB	Exc.	V.G.	Good	Fair	Poor
800	600	450	300	200	150

USP 45 Tactical

This pistol was introduced in 1998. It is an enhanced version of the USP 45. It is fitted with a 4.9" threaded barrel with adjustable high profile target sights. Overall length is 8.6" and weight is approximately 36 oz. Magazine capacity is 10 rounds. Availability limited to between 1,000 and 2,500 pistols.

NIB	Exc.	V.G.	Good	Fair	Poor
1115	850	625	425	300	175

USP 45 Expert

Introduced in the fall of 1998, this .45 ACP pistol is fitted with a 5.2" barrel and slide and 10-round magazine. Overall length is 8.7" and height is 1.87". Weight is approximately 30 oz. Adjustable low-profile sights. Limited availability of between 1,000 and 2,500 pistols. In 2003 this model was also offered chambered for the 9mm and the .40 S&W cartridge.

NIB	Exc.	V.G.	Good	Fair	Poor
1355	1000	—	—	—	—

NOTE: H&K price reduction in 2005.

USP Elite

Introduced in 2003 this model features a 6.2" barrel chambered for the 9mm or .45 ACP cartridge. Fitted with a match trigger, adjustable trigger stop, adjustable micrometer rear target sights, extended floorplate and loaded chamber indicator. Weight is about 30 oz. empty. Magazine capacity is 10 rounds.

NIB	Exc.	V.G.	Good	Fair	Poor
1355	1000	—	—	—	—

NOTE: H&K price reduction in 2005.

USP 45 50th Anniversary Commemorative

Limited to 1,000 pistols this pistol features a high polish blue with 50th anniversary logo engraved in gold and silver. Supplied with custom-made wooden box with commemorative coin. Introduced in 2000.

NIB	Exc.	V.G.	Good	Fair	Poor
1000	—	—	—	—	—

P2000 GPM

Introduced in 2003 this model is similar to the USP compact LEM pistol but with several modular features, such as interchangeable back straps, ambidextrous slide release, and short trigger reset distance. Chambered for the 9mm or .40 S&W cartridge and fitted with a 3.62" barrel. Fixed sights. Magazine capacity is 12 rounds for the .40S&W and .357 SIG, and 13 rounds for the 9mm. Weight is about 22 oz.

NIB	Exc.	V.G.	Good	Fair	Poor
890	675	—	—	—	—

NOTE: Add $30 for magazine disconnect.

P2000 SK

This semi-auto double-action pistol is a subcompact version of the P2000. It is chambered for the 9mm or .40 S&W cartridge as well as the .357 SIG .It has a 2.5" barrel with an overall length of 6.4". Magazine capacity is 10 rounds for 9mm, 12 rounds for the .357 SIG, and 9 rounds for the .40 S&W. Weight is about 21 oz. Introduced in 2004.

NIB	Exc.	V.G.	Good	Fair	Poor
930	700	—	—	—	—

USP ACCESSORIES

The items listed are factory options for the USP pistol and may be encountered when a sale is contemplated. We have listed the retail price of the factory item.

Tritium Sights

MSRP—$95.00

Mark II UTL (Universal Tactical Light)

MSRP—$267.00

Quik-Comp

MSRP—$184.00 (Discontinued 1997)

Optical Sight/Scope Mount

MSRP—$221.00

Optical sight/scope mount and Quik-Comp

Mark 23

Very similar to the H&K's US government contract pistol developed for special Operation Units. Chambered for the .45 ACP and fitted with a 5.87" barrel, this pistol has a polymer frame with steel slide. Magazine capacity is 10 rounds on civilian models and 12 rounds on law enforcement models. Barrel is threaded for noise suppressor. Weight is about 42 oz. Limited availability in fall 1996 to about 2,000 pistols.

NIB	Exc.	V.G.	Good	Fair	Poor
2410	1750	1250	—	—	—

Mk 23 Suppressor

This unit can be fitted to the threaded barrel of the MK 23 and be compensated for point of aim. With water the dB sound reduction is 33-35dB. Produced by Knight Armament Corp. of Vero Beach, FL. This suppressor, with a different piston assembly, can be fitted to the USP Tactical.

NOTE: Suppressors require a Class III transfer tax. All NFA rules apply to the sale or purchase of these suppressors.

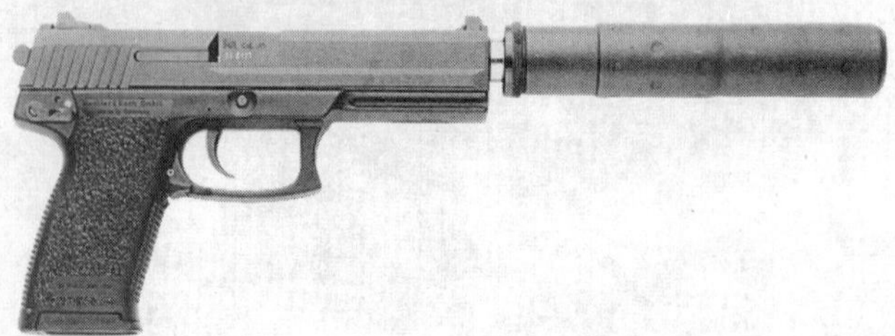

NIB	Exc.	V.G.	Good	Fair	Poor
1350	—	—	—	—	—

HEINZELMANN, C.E.

Plochipnam Neckar, Germany

Heim

A 6.35mm semi-automatic pistol with a 2" barrel. Detachable magazine holds 6 rounds. Weight is approximately 11 oz. Manufactured during the 1930s and marked on the frame "C.E. Heinzelmann Plochingen A.N. Patent Heim-6.35."

Exc.	V.G.	Good	Fair	Poor
800	675	550	400	200

HEISER, CARL

SEE—Austrian Military Firearms

HELFRICHT

Zella-Mehlis, Germany

Model 3 Pocket Pistol

A 6.35mm semi-automatic pistol with a 2" barrel and 6-shot magazine. Weight is about 11 oz. Blued with checkererd black plastic grips having the monogram "KH" cast in them. These pistols have no external sights.

Courtesy James Rankin

Exc.	V.G.	Good	Fair	Poor
500	400	300	200	100

Model 4 Pocket Pistol

A semi-automatic pistol in caliber 6.35mm. It has checkered black plastic grips with the "KH" logo on each grip.

Courtesy James Rankin

Exc.	V.G.	Good	Fair	Poor
400	300	200	150	100

HELLIS, CHARLES

London, England

SEE—British Double Guns

HENRION & DASSY

Liege, Belgium

Semi-Automatic

A 6.35mm semi-automatic pistol with a 2.5" barrel and 5-shot magazine. Blued with black plastic grips. Marked "H&D."

Exc.	V.G.	Good	Fair	Poor
600	500	450	375	275

HENRY

SEE—Winchester

HENRY, ALEXANDER

Edinburgh, Scotland

Noted for both the rifling system he developed and the falling block single-shot rifles he made, Alexander Henry conducted business at these locations:

12 South Street, Andrew Street	1853-1858
8 South Street, Andrew Street	1858-1862
12 South Street, Andrew Street	1862-1871
12 and 14 South Street, Andrew Street	1871-1875
12 South Street, Andrew Street	1875-1895
18 Frederick Street	1895-1911
22 Frederick Street	1911-

Single-Shot Rifle

A high-grade single-shot that features a true falling-block action that is activated by a side lever on the action. It was available in the popular European cartridges of the era, and the barrel length varies from 22" to 28" in length. This rifle exhibits fine quality materials and workmanship. The select-grade walnut stock and schnabel forend are hand checkered. The finish of the rifle is scroll-engraved and blued. This company manufactured firearms from 1869 until 1895.

Exc.	V.G.	Good	Fair	Poor
—	—	3500	1250	400

Double Rifle

A side-by-side, double-barreled Express Rifle chambered for the .500/450 Black Powder Express cartridge. It has Damascus barrels and double triggers. This gun is hammerless and features ornate scroll engraving as well as a high-grade hand checkered walnut stock and forend. It was furnished with a fitted leather case and accessories. This rifle was manufactured in the 1890s.

Exc.	V.G.	Good	Fair	Poor
—	6000	3500	1250	600

HENRY REPEATING ARMS COMPANY

Brooklyn, New York

Henry Lever-Action

Chambered for the .22 LR, Long, and Short cartridges It is fitted with a 18.25" barrel and weighs 5.5 lbs. Magazine capacity is 15 for the .22 LR cartridge. Rear sight is adjustable and the front sight is hooded.

NIB	Exc.	V.G.	Good	Fair	Poor
280	175	125	—	—	—

Henry Carbine

Similar to the above model but with an overall length of 34". It features a large loop lever.

NIB	Exc.	V.G.	Good	Fair	Poor
290	175	125	—	—	—

Henry Youth Model

Similar to the carbine model above but with an overall length of 33".

NIB	Exc.	V.G.	Good	Fair	Poor
280	175	125	—	—	—

Henry Lever-Action .22 Magnum

Fitted with a 19.5" barrel with a tubular magazine capacity of 11 rounds. Checkered deluxe walnut stock. Weight is about 5.5 lbs.

NIB	Exc.	V.G.	Good	Fair	Poor
410	300	250	—	—	—

Henry Lever Action Frontier Model

Similar to Henry Lever Action but with 20-inch octagon barrel. Chambered in .22 WMR and .17HMR. Introduced 2006. MSRP: 350

Henry Golden Boy

This lever-action rifle is chambered for the .22 LR, Short, or Long cartridges as well as the .22 WRM cartridge in a seperate model. Fitted with a brass receiver and 20" octagon barrel. Walnut stock. Weight is about 6.75 lbs.

NIB	Exc.	V.G.	Good	Fair	Poor
410	300	250	—	—	—

NOTE: Add $70 for .22 WRM model or .17 HMR. Add $20 for large loop lever. Add $600 for hand-engraved model.

Henry Golden Boy Deluxe

Chambered for the .22 Long Rifle cartridge and fitted with a 20" octagon barrel. Fancy walnut stock. Deeply engraved receiver.

NIB	Exc.	V.G.	Good	Fair	Poor
1200	—	—	—	—	—

Henry Deluxe Engraved Golden Boy Magnum

Similar to Golden Boy Deluxe but chambered in .22 WMR. Features deluxe deep-cut German-style engraving on receiver. Introduced 2006. MSRP: 1325

Henry Varmint Express

This lever-action rifle is chambered for the .17 HMR cartridge and fitted with a 20" round barrel. Checkered American walnut stock. Scope mount included. Magazine capacity is 11 rounds. Weight is about 5.75 lbs.

NIB	Exc.	V.G.	Good	Fair	Poor
475	350	—	—	—	—

Henry Big Boy

This lever-action model is chambered for the .44 Magnum or .45 Colt cartridge. Octagonal barrel is 20". Magazine capacity is 10 rounds. American walnut stock with straight grip. Weight is about 8.7 lbs. .357 Magnum added 1006.

NIB	Exc.	V.G.	Good	Fair	Poor
775	575	—	—	—	—

Henry Big Boy Deluxe Engraved .44 Magnum

Similar to Henry Big Boy but with deluxe deep-cut German-style engraving on receiver. Introduced 2006.

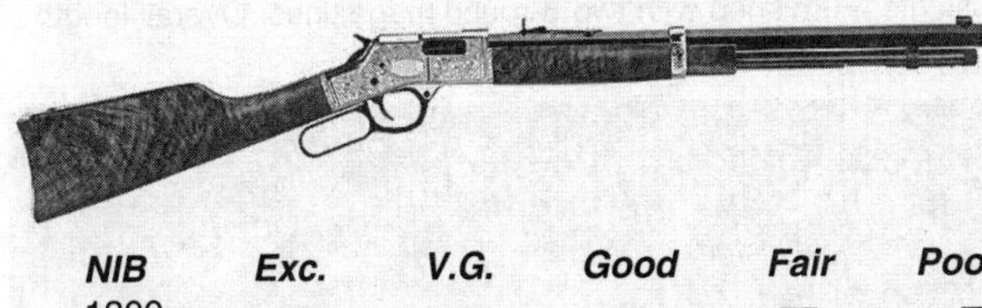

NIB	Exc.	V.G.	Good	Fair	Poor
1300	—	—	—	—	—

Big Boy .44 Magnum "Wildlife Edition"

Similar to Big Boy .44 Magnum but with forend and buttstock laser-engraved with whitetail deer scenes. Introduced in 2007.

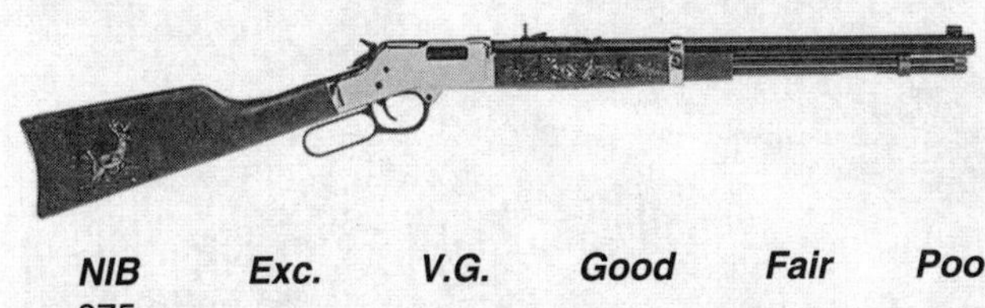

NIB	Exc.	V.G.	Good	Fair	Poor
875	—	—	—	—	—

Big Boy .45 Colt "Cowboy Edition"

Similar to Big Boy .45 Colt but with forend and buttstock laser-engraved with Old West scenes. Introduced in 2007.

NIB	Exc.	V.G.	Good	Fair	Poor
900	—	—	—	—	—

Henry Pump-Action Rifle

Introduced in 1999 this .22 caliber is fitted with a 18.25" barrel and chambered for the .22 LR cartridge. Walnut stock and adjustable rear sight. Weight is approximately 5.5 lbs.

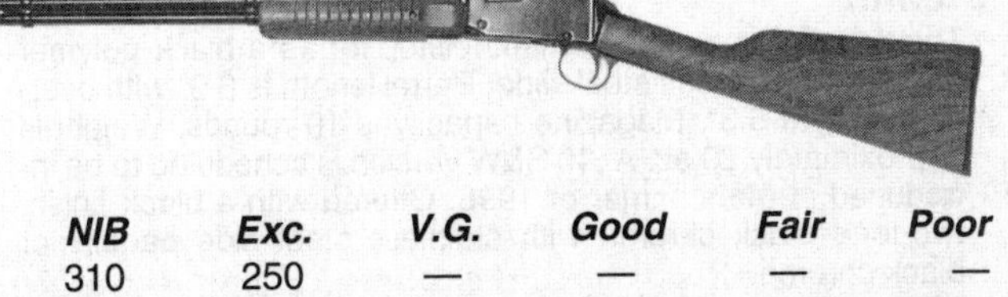

NIB	Exc.	V.G.	Good	Fair	Poor
310	250	—	—	—	—

Henry Pump Action .22 Octagon Rifle

Similar to Henry Pump-Action Rifle but with 20-inch octagon barrel. Introduced 2006. Add 10 percent for .22 WMR.

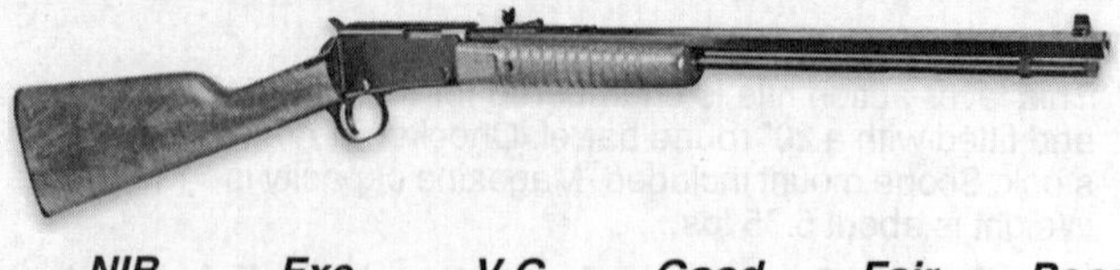

NIB	Exc.	V.G.	Good	Fair	Poor
425	315	—	—	—	—

Henry Mini Bolt

This single-shot bolt-action .22 caliber rifle is designed for young shooters. Barrel length is 16.25". Overall length is 30.25" Stainless steel barrel and receiver. Adjustable sights. Weight is about 3.25 lbs.

NIB	Exc.	V.G.	Good	Fair	Poor
205	160	—	—	—	—

Henry U.S. Survival Rifle

This model is an improved version of the AR-7 .22 caliber survival rifle issued to the Air Force. It is a breakdown design and features a waterproof stock, a steel-lined barrel and adjustable sights. Furnished with two 8-round magazines. Overall length when broken down is 16.5".

NIB	Exc.	V.G.	Good	Fair	Poor
205	160	100	—	—	—

Henry Acu-Bolt

Chambered for the .22 LR, .22 WMR, or the .17 HMR cartridges and fitted with a 20" barrel. Fiberglass stock. Scope mounts. Weight is about 4.25 lbs.

NIB	Exc.	V.G.	Good	Fair	Poor
335	260	—	—	—	—

HERITAGE MANUFACTURING, INC.

Opa Locka, Florida

Stealth

This is a 9mm semi-automatic pistol. It has a black polymer frame with stainless steel slide. Barrel length is 3.9" with overall length at 6.3". Magazine capacity is 10 rounds. Weight is approximately 20 oz. A .40 S&W version is scheduled to be introduced in the summer of 1996. Offered with a black finish, two-tone black chrome with stainless steel side panels, or black chrome.

NIB	Exc.	V.G.	Good	Fair	Poor
300	225	175	150	125	100

Model H25S

A semi-automatic pistol chambered for the .25 ACP cartridge. Barrel length is 2.25" and overall length is 4.58". Weight is about 13.5 oz. Frame mounted safety. Single-action-only. Available in blue or nickel.

NIB	Exc.	V.G.	Good	Fair	Poor
150	125	100	85	65	50

Sentry

This is a double-action revolver chambered for the .38 Special. Cylinder holds 6 rounds. Barrel length is 2". Weight is about 23 oz. Blue or nickel finish.

NIB	Exc.	V.G.	Good	Fair	Poor
130	100	85	65	50	30

Rough Rider

Single-action revolver chambered for the .22 caliber cartridges. Barrel lengths are 4.75", 6.5", and 9". Cylinder holds 6 rounds. Weight is about 34 oz. Available in blue or nickel finish.

NIB	Exc.	V.G.	Good	Fair	Poor
200	150	120	75	50	30

With Combination Cylinder—.22 Mag.

NIB	Exc.	V.G.	Good	Fair	Poor
190	150	120	75	50	30

With Bird's-Head Grip & Combo Cylinder

NIB	Exc.	V.G.	Good	Fair	Poor
190	150	120	75	50	30

Rough Rider .17 HMR

Introduced in 2004.

NIB	Exc.	V.G.	Good	Fair	Poor
240	190	—	—	—	—

Rough Rider .32

Six-shot revolver chambered for .32 H&R Magnum centerfire (interchangeably .32 S&W, .32 S&W Long). Black satin finish. Offered with 3.5", 4.75" or 6.5" barrels. 35 oz. (6.5" bbl.). 11.785" LOA.) Fixed sights. Bird's head grip available. MSRP: 230

Rough Rider Big-Bore Series

Six-shot, steel-frame revolver chambered for .357, .44-40 or .45 Long Colt. Barrel lengths 4.75", 5.5" or 7.5". 36 oz. Fixed sights. MSRP: 380 (blued), 390 (case hardened), 420 (nickel finish), 500 stainless

HEROLD

Franz Jaeger
Suhl, Germany

Bolt-Action Rifle

A .22 Hornet bolt-action sporting rifle with a 24" ribbed barrel, adjustable sights, double set triggers and walnut stock. Imported by Charles Daly and Stoeger Arms prior to WWII.

Exc.	V.G.	Good	Fair	Poor
1500	850	600	400	250

HERTER'S

Waseca, Minnesota

An importer and retailer of European-made firearms. Active until approximately 1980.

REVOLVERS

Guide

A .22 caliber double-action swing-out cylinder revolver with a 6" barrel and 6-shot cylinder. Blued with walnut grips.

Exc.	V.G.	Good	Fair	Poor
125	95	70	45	30

Power-Mag Revolver

A .357 Magnum, .401 Herter Power Mag, and .44 Magnum caliber single-action revolver with a 4" or 6" barrel and 6-shot cylinder. Blued, with walnut grips.

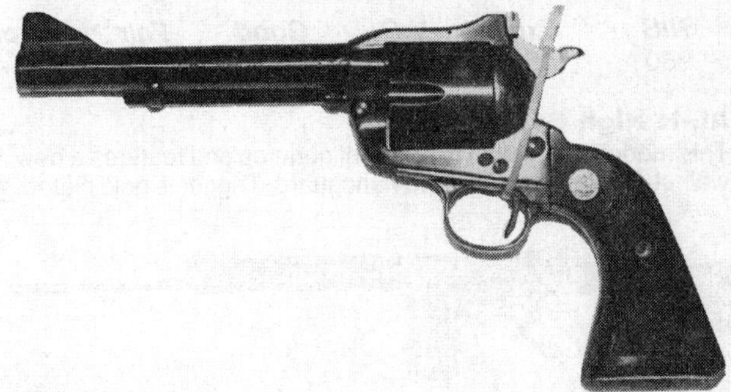

Exc.	V.G.	Good	Fair	Poor
400	325	200	125	75

Western

As above, in .22 caliber.

Exc.	V.G.	Good	Fair	Poor
200	150	125	75	50

RIFLES

J-9 or U-9 Hunter

Mauser-action sporting rifles manufactured in England (J-9) and Yugoslavia (U-9), with 24" barrels and Monte Carlo-style walnut stocks.

Exc.	V.G.	Good	Fair	Poor
225	185	135	100	75

J-9 or U-9 Presentation or Supreme

As above, with checkering and sling swivels.

Exc.	V.G.	Good	Fair	Poor
250	225	200	150	100

HESSE ARMS

Inver Grove Heights, Minnesota

FAL-H RIFLES

All FAL-H rifles include these features: military spec internal parts, new or as new barrel, military finish, post ban legal muzzlebrake, one magazine, new metric pattern Type 3 receiver, adjustable gas system, refinished or new pistol grip, hard case, carry handle, sling, and manual. All rifles chambered for .308 Winchester cartridge. Additional calibers in .22-250 and .243 are also available. Weights are from 8.5 to 14 lbs. depending on model.

FALO Tactical Rifle

This model features a free floating handguard assembly.

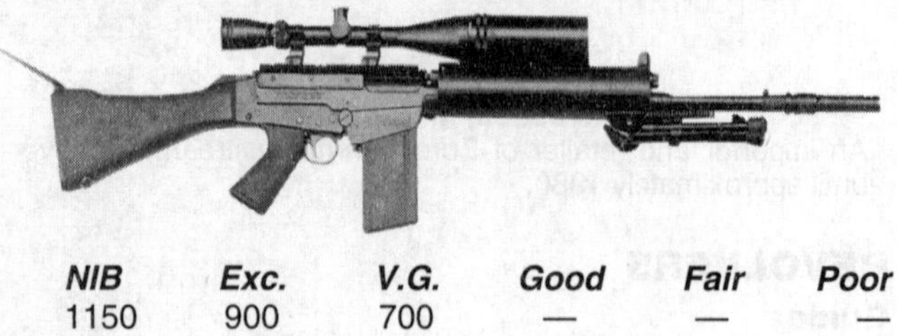

NIB	Exc.	V.G.	Good	Fair	Poor
1150	900	700	—	—	—

FALO Heavy Barrel

This model features a heavy barrel and is based on the Israeli FALO rifle.

NIB	Exc.	V.G.	Good	Fair	Poor
950	750	600	—	—	—

FAL-H High Grade

This model is available in any configuration and features a new walnut stock, pistol grip, and handguard. Trigger is gold plated.

NIB	Exc.	V.G.	Good	Fair	Poor
1350	1050	850	—	—	—

FAL-H Standard Grade

This is standard model that is similar in appearance to the original FAL.

NIB	Exc.	V.G.	Good	Fair	Poor
950	750	600	—	—	—

FAL-H Congo Rifle

This model features a 16" barrel.

NIB	Exc.	V.G.	Good	Fair	Poor
1000	800	650	—	—	—

FALO Congo Rifle

Similar to the model above but fitted with a 16" heavy barrel.

NIB	Exc.	V.G.	Good	Fair	Poor
1000	800	650	—	—	—

HAR-15 RIFLES

All of the HAR-15 rifles have these features: military spec internal parts, heavy match grade barrels, post ban legal muzzle-brake, A2 upper receiver, A2 round handguards with heat shields, A2 stock, A2 lower receiver. Each rifle comes with hard case, manual, and sling. Rifles are chambered for .223 Remington but can be chambered in other calibers as well. These are: .17 Rem. add $145, 9mm NATO add $85, 6mm PPC add $145, 6mmx45 add $95, .300 Fireball add $195, 7.62x39 add $45.

Omega Match

Fitted with a 1" diameter stainless steel barrel, adjustable match trigger, E2 stock, flat top receiver, free floating handguard.

NIB	Exc.	V.G.	Good	Fair	Poor
1000	800	650	—	—	—

HAR-15A2 Standard Rifle

This model has all of the standard features offered for HAR-15 rifles.

NIB	Exc.	V.G.	Good	Fair	Poor
725	575	475	—	—	—

HAR-15A2 National Match

This model is fitted with special bolt carrier, adjustable match trigger. Designed as Match grade rifle.

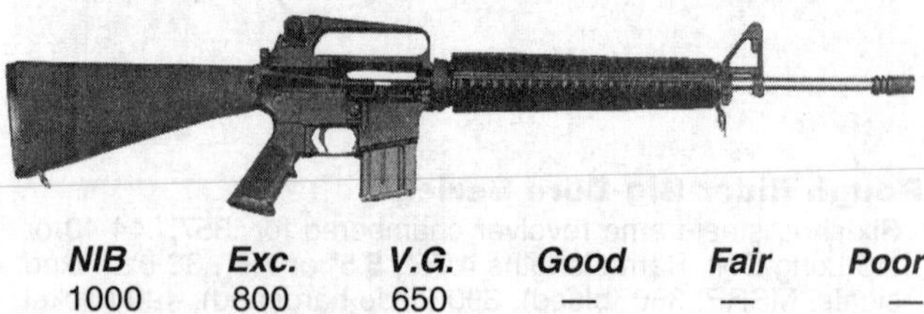

NIB	Exc.	V.G.	Good	Fair	Poor
1000	800	650	—	—	—

HAR-15A2 Bull Gun

This model is fitted with a 1" stainless steel barrel with special front sight base.

NIB	Exc.	V.G.	Good	Fair	Poor
775	600	475	—	—	—

HAR-15A2 Dispatcher

Fitted with a 16" barrel with full length handguard.

NIB	Exc.	V.G.	Good	Fair	Poor
725	575	450	—	—	—

HAR-15A2 Carbine

Fitted with a 16" heavy barrel and a non-collapsing stock with short handguard.

NIB	Exc.	V.G.	Good	Fair	Poor
725	575	475	—	—	—

H-22 RIFLES

All H-22 rifles include these features: new internal parts interchangeable with Ruger 10/22 rifle, heavy stainless steel barrel with match chamber, stainless steel receiver, laminated stock, hard case, magazine, and manual. All rifle are chambered for .22 LR. For an additional $250 charge any H-22 rifle can be converted to .22 Magnum. Weight of these rifles is approximately 7 lbs.

H-22 Tigershark

Special forearm and skeleton stock with heavy fluted barrel. Special trigger pack with over travel screw and glass bedded stock.

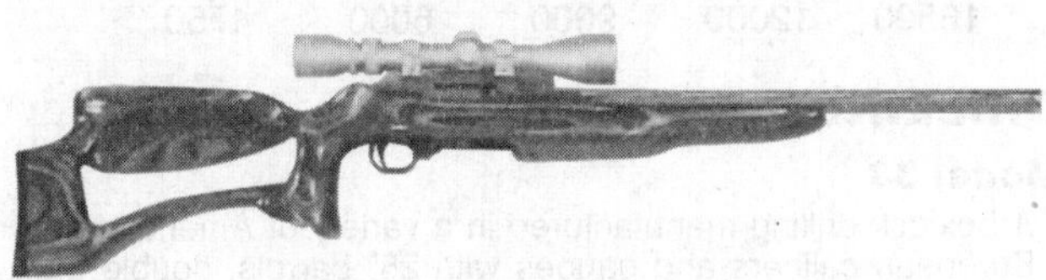

NIB	Exc.	V.G.	Good	Fair	Poor
800	650	525	—	—	—

H-22 Competition Rifle

This model features a gloss finished laminated competition thumbhole stock.

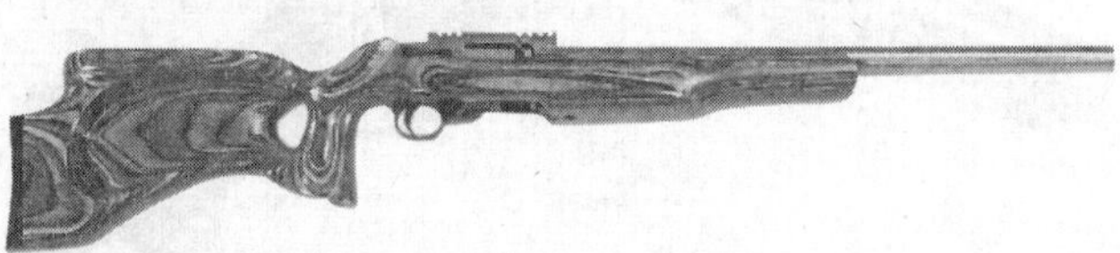

NIB	Exc.	V.G.	Good	Fair	Poor
550	450	350	—	—	—

H-22 Wildcat

This model has a screwed-in heavy barrel and a special laminated stock.

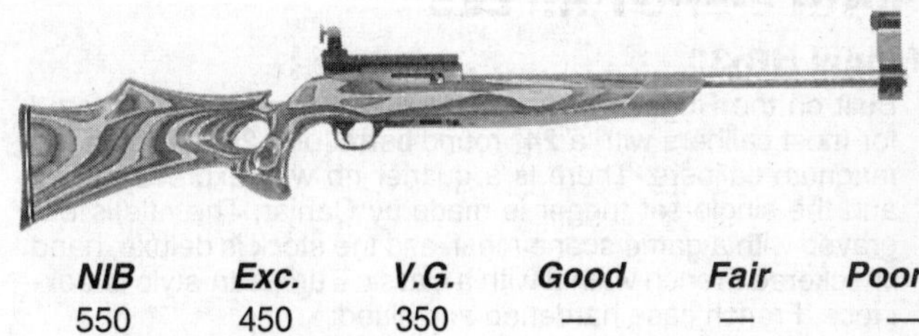

NIB	Exc.	V.G.	Good	Fair	Poor
550	450	350	—	—	—

H-22 Standard Rifle

Has all the standard features of the H-22 rifle including a buttstock with cheekpiece.

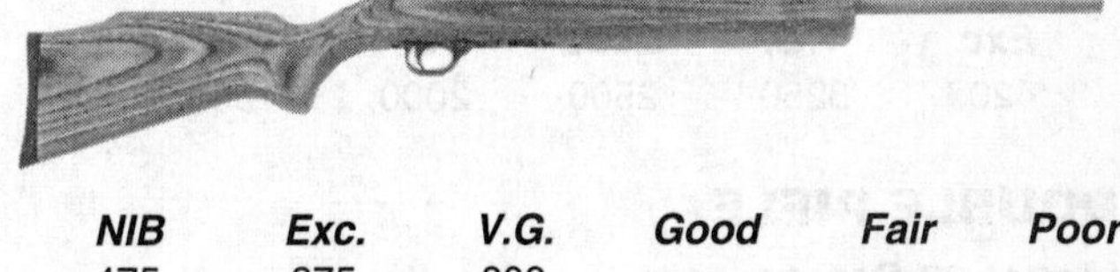

NIB	Exc.	V.G.	Good	Fair	Poor
475	375	300	—	—	—

M14-H Standard Rifle

This is a semi-automatic version of the M14 rifle chambered for the .308 cartridge. It is fitted with a new receiver, walnut stock or synthetic stock. Each rifle is sold with a sling, annual, and 10-round magazine and an extra original M145 stock.

NIB	Exc.	V.G.	Good	Fair	Poor
1000	800	650	—	—	—

M14-H Brush Rifle

This model has the same features as the standard rifle but with an 18" barrel.

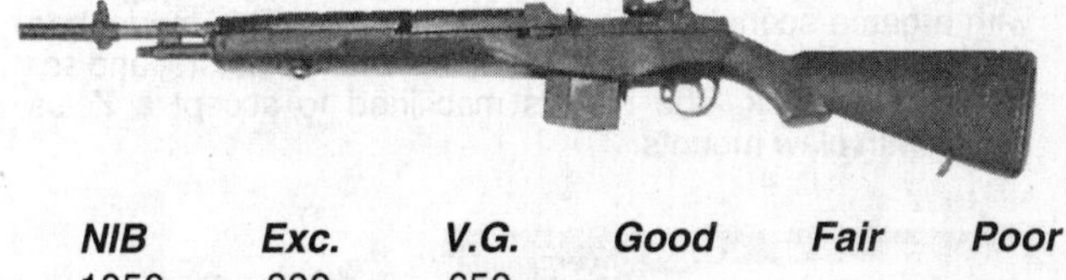

NIB	Exc.	V.G.	Good	Fair	Poor
1050	800	650	—	—	—

Hesse Model 47 Rifle

This is a copy of the AK-47 and it is chambered for the 7.63x39 cartridge. It is also available in .223 caliber.

NIB	Exc.	V.G.	Good	Fair	Poor
600	475	375	—	—	—

HEYM, F. W.

Suhl, Germany

Established in 1865 in Suhl, Germany, this company was reestablished after WWII in Munnerstadt. The company remained there until 1996 when it moved back to a suburb of Suhl. Post-war arms were originally imported by Paul Jaeger of Grand Junction, Tennessee.

SINGLE-SHOT RIFLES

Model HR-30

Built on the Ruger No. 1 falling-block-action and chambered for most calibers with a 24" round barrel or a 26" barrel in the magnum calibers. There is a quarter rib with express sights, and the single-set trigger is made by Canjar. The rifle is engraved with a game scene motif, and the stock is deluxe, hand checkered French walnut with a classic European-style cheekpiece. French case hardened and blued.

Exc.	V.G.	Good	Fair	Poor
4000	2900	2250	1750	1250

Model HR-38

As above, with an octagonal barrel.

Exc.	V.G.	Good	Fair	Poor
4200	3250	2500	2000	1500

DOUBLE RIFLE

Model 22 Safety

An over-and-under combination rifle/shotgun chambered for 16 or 20 gauge over .22 Hornet, .22 WMR, .222 Remington, .222 Remington Magnum, .223, 5.6x50Rmm, 6.5x57Rmm, and 7x57Rmm with 24" barrels. Boxlock action with a single trigger, automatic ejectors, and automatic decocking mechanism. French case hardening, blued with a walnut stock.

Exc.	V.G.	Good	Fair	Poor
2500	2000	1750	1200	900

Model 77B/55B Over-and-Under Rifle

An over-and-under rifle manufactured in a variety of calibers with 25" barrels having open sights: and a boxlock-action with Kersten double cross bolts. The action is heavily engraved with a game scene motif and is silver plated. This model has double triggers, cocking indicators, automatic ejectors, and select walnut stock. The barrels machined to accept a Zeiss scope with claw mounts.

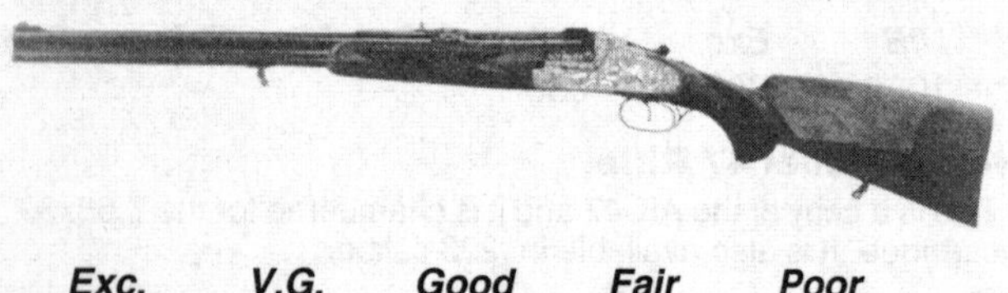

Exc.	V.G.	Good	Fair	Poor
5000	4500	4000	3250	2500

Model 55BSS

As above with sidelocks.

Exc.	V.G.	Good	Fair	Poor
9500	8500	7500	5000	3500

Model 55BF/77BF

Similar to the Model 55B, except one barrel is rifled and the other smooth in 12, 16, or 20 gauge.

Exc.	V.G.	Good	Fair	Poor
5000	4500	4000	3250	2500

Model 55BFSS

As above, with sidelocks.

Exc.	V.G	Good	Fair	Poor
9500	8500	7500	5000	3500

Model 88 B

A large bore double-barrel boxlock rifle with 24" barrels, automatic ejectors, double triggers, and select walnut stock.

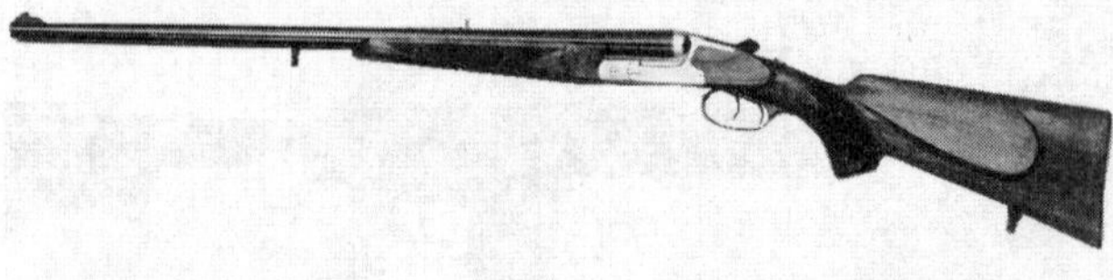

Exc.	V.G.	Good	Fair	Poor
9500	8750	7750	5500	4000

Model 88 BSS

As above with sidelocks.

Exc.	V.G.	Good	Fair	Poor
14000	12500	9500	6500	5250

Model 88 Safari

As above, but chambered for .375 Holland & Holland, .458 Winchester Magnum, .470, or .500 Nitro Express calibers with 25" barrels.

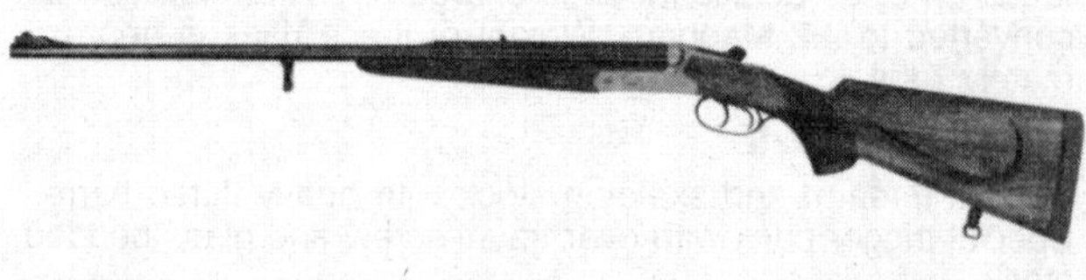

Exc.	V.G.	Good	Fair	Poor
13500	12000	9000	6000	4750

DRILLINGS

Model 33

A boxlock drilling manufactured in a variety of American and European calibers and gauges with 25" barrels, double triggers and extractors. Case hardened, blued with a walnut stock.

Exc.	V.G.	Good	Fair	Poor
6000	5000	4250	2750	2000

Model 33 Deluxe

Same as above but with game scene engraving.

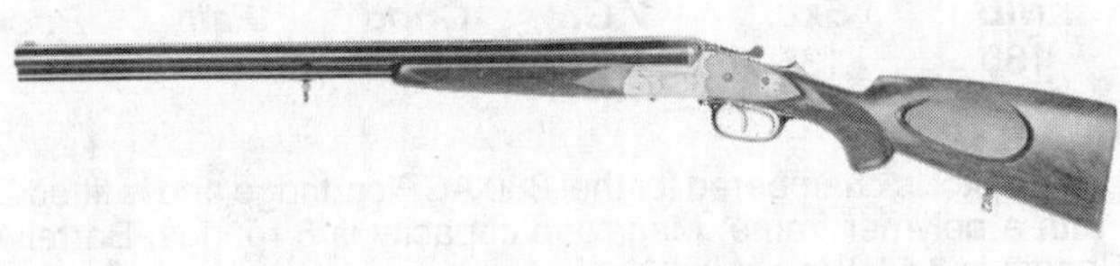

Exc.	V.G.	Good	Fair	Poor
7500	6000	4750	3500	2500

Model 37

Similar to the Model 33 Standard but with full sidelocks.

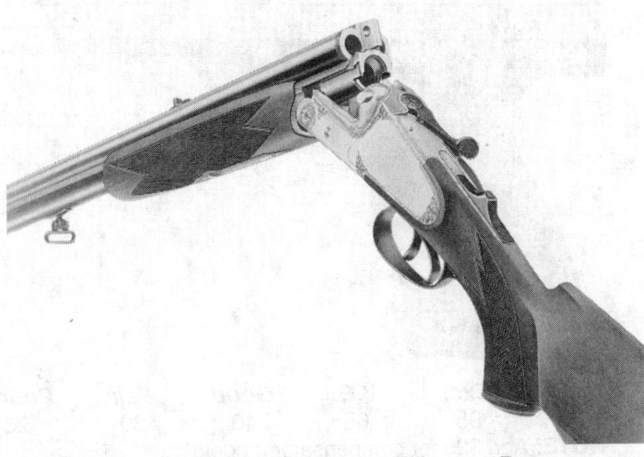

Exc.	V.G.	Good	Fair	Poor
12500	10000	7500	5000	2500

Model 37 Deluxe

Similar to the above Model 37 but with hand engraved scroll work and fancy walnut stock.

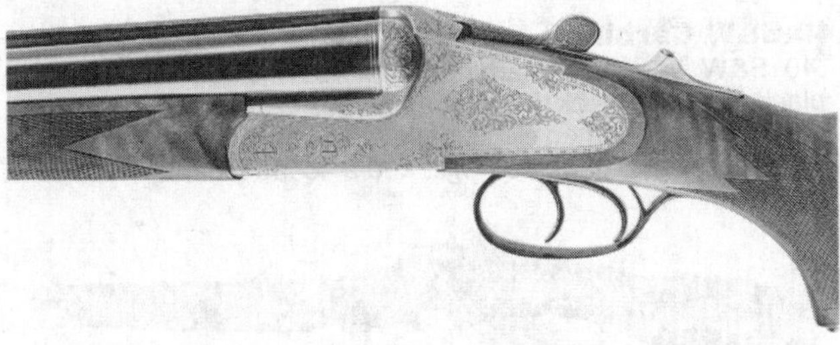

Exc.	V.G.	Good	Fair	Poor
15000	12000	8500	6000	3000

BOLT-ACTION RIFLES

Model SR-20

A Mauser-action sporting rifle manufactured in a variety of calibers with 21", 24", or 26" barrels, open sights, adjustable trigger or set trigger. Blued with a walnut stock.

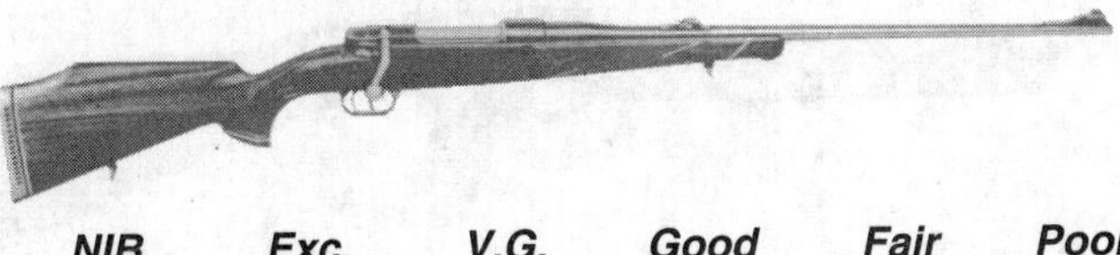

NIB	Exc.	V.G.	Good	Fair	Poor
1450	1250	950	750	600	450

Model SR-20 Alpine

As above with a 20" barrel and Mannlicher stock. Introduced in 1989.

NIB	Exc.	V.G.	Good	Fair	Poor
2650	2250	1750	1250	850	600

SR-20 Classic Safari

As above, but chambered for .404 Jeffries, .425 Express, and the .458 Winchester Magnum with a 24" barrel having express sights. Introduced in 1989.

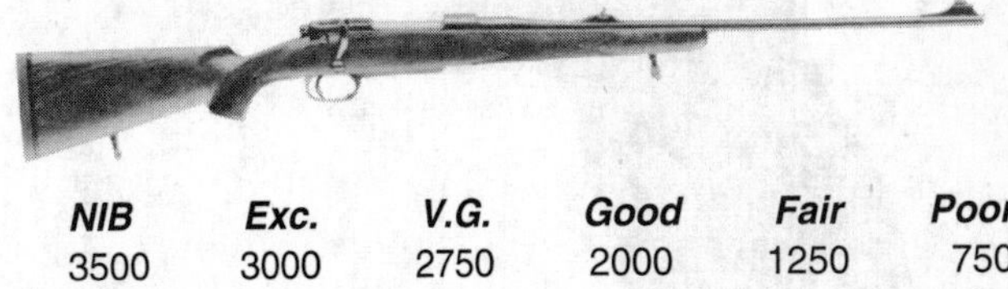

NIB	Exc.	V.G.	Good	Fair	Poor
3500	3000	2750	2000	1250	750

SR-20 Classic Sportsman

This model features a round barrel without sights. Chambered for many calibers from .243 to .375 H&H. Introduced in 1988. Add $100 for Magnum calibers.

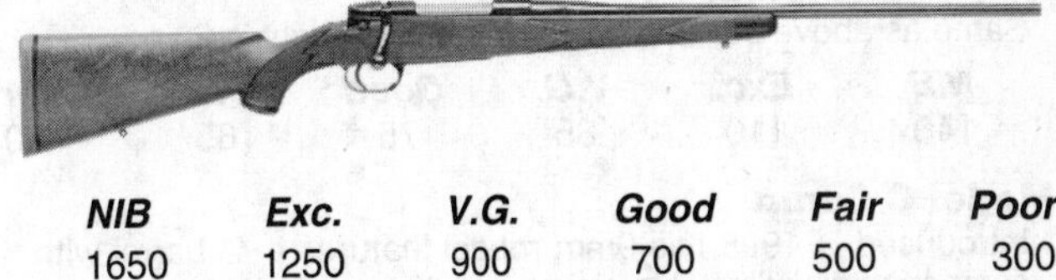

NIB	Exc.	V.G.	Good	Fair	Poor
1650	1250	900	700	500	300

SR-20 Trophy

Similar to the above Classic Sportsman model but with German bead ramp sight and open quarter rib rear sight. Select walnut stock with oil finish. Octagonal barrel and rosewood grip cap.

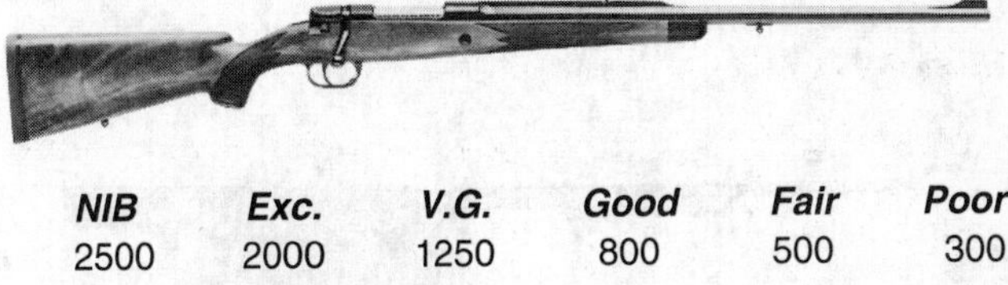

NIB	Exc.	V.G.	Good	Fair	Poor
2500	2000	1250	800	500	300

Heym Magnum Express

This bolt-action rifle is chambered for .338 Lapua, .375 H&H, .416 Rigby, .500 Nitro Express, .500 A-Square, and a few were built in .600 Nitro Express. Fitted with a 24" barrel. Adjustable front sight, three leaf rear express sight. Select hand checkered European walnut stock, and many other special features. Introduced in 1989.

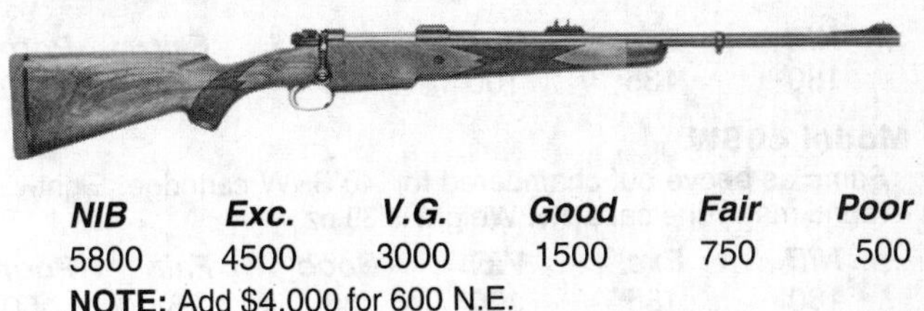

NIB	Exc.	V.G.	Good	Fair	Poor
5800	4500	3000	1500	750	500

NOTE: Add $4,000 for 600 N.E.

HI-POINT FIREARMS

MKS Supply
Dayton, Ohio

Model C

This is a 9mm single-action compact semi-automatic pistol with a 3.5" barrel. Magazine capacity is 8 rounds. Black or chrome finish. Weight is 32 oz.

NIB	Exc.	V.G.	Good	Fair	Poor
125	100	85	75	65	50

Model C Polymer

Same as above but with polymer frame. Weight is 28 oz.

NIB	Exc.	V.G.	Good	Fair	Poor
140	110	85	75	65	50

Model C Comp

Introduced in 1998 this 9mm model features a 4" barrel with compensator, adjustable sights and 10-round magazine.

NIB	Exc.	V.G.	Good	Fair	Poor
170	130	—	—	—	—

Model JH

All steel construction chambered for .45 ACP with 4.5" barrel. Magazine capacity is 7 rounds. Weight is 39 oz.

NIB	Exc.	V.G.	Good	Fair	Poor
180	135	100	85	75	50

Model 40SW

Same as above but chambered for .40 S&W cartridge. Eight-round magazine capacity. Weight is 39 oz.

NIB	Exc.	V.G.	Good	Fair	Poor
180	135	100	85	75	50

Model .45 Polymer

This model has a polymer frame and 4.5" barrel chambered for the .45 ACP cartridge. Magazine capacity is 9 rounds. Weight is about 32 oz.

NIB	Exc.	V.G.	Good	Fair	Poor
180	135	—	—	—	—

Model .40 Polymer

As above but chambered for the .40 S&W cartridge with a magazine capacity of 10 rounds. Weight is about 32 oz.

NIB	Exc.	V.G.	Good	Fair	Poor
180	135	—	—	—	—

Model CF

This pistol is chambered for the .380 ACP cartridge and is fitted with a polymer frame. Magazine capacity is 8 rounds. Barrel length is 3.5". Weight is 29 oz.

NIB	Exc.	V.G.	Good	Fair	Poor
120	95	65	40	30	25

NOTE: Add $25 for compensator model.

.380 ACP Compensated

Semi-auto with fully-adjustable 3-dot sights, muzzle compensator, 4" barrel, 31 oz, polymer frame. Two magazines: one 10-round, one 8-round. Add 50 percent for laser sight.

NIB	Exc.	V.G.	Good	Fair	Poor
150	125	100	85	75	50

.40 S&W Carbine

.40 S&W semi-auto carbine. Features include all-weather, black, polymer stock, 10 shot maazine, 17.5-inch barrel, sling swivels, grip mounted clip release, quick on & off thumb safety, rear peep sight, 32.5-inch OAL and a scope mount.

NIB	Exc.	V.G.	Good	Fair	Poor
275	200	150	100	75	50

Model 995 Carbine

Similar to .40 S&W Carbine but chambered for 9mm Parabellum.

NIB	Exc.	V.G.	Good	Fair	Poor
285	210	160	110	75	50

HIGGINS, J. C.

Chicago, Illinois

The Sears, Roebuck & Company of Chicago used the trade name J.C. Higgins on the firearms and other sporting goods it sold between 1946 and 1962. Arms bearing this tradename were manufactured by a variety of American gunmakers. See High Standard, Mossberg, etc.

HIGH STANDARD MANUFACTURING CORPORATION

New Haven, Hamden, and East Hartford, Connecticut

The High Standard Manufacturing Company was established in 1926, by Carl Swebilius and Gustave Beck to produce drills and machine tools. In 1932, the firm purchased the Hartford Arms & Equipment Company (q.v.) and began the manufacture of the latter's Model 1925 semi-automatic pistol as the Hi-Standard Model "B."

Throughout the High Standard Manufacturing Corporation's business life, its products were highly regarded for both their design and quality. While the company was originally located in New Haven, during WWII High Standard operated plants in New Haven and Hamden. After the war the operations were consolidated in Hamden. In 1968 the company was sold to the Leisure Group, Inc. The Leisure Group sold High Standard to High Standard, Inc. in January 1978. A final move was made to East Hartford, Connecticut, in 1977 where it remained until the doors closed in late 1984. In the spring of 1993 the High Standard Manufacturing Co, Inc. of Houston, Texas, acquired the company assets and trademarks as well as the .22 Target Pistols. These original assets were transfered from Connecticut to Houston, Texas, in July 1993. The first shipments of Houston manufactured pistols began in March 1994. Prices listed here are separated for both the Connecticut and Houston models. Collectors will pay a premium for the Connecticut pistols.

Model descriptions, photos, and prices by John J. Stimson, Jr.

LETTER MODELS

Model B

A .22 LR caliber semi-automatic pistol with either a 4.5" or a 6.75" round barrel and a 10-shot magazine. Blued; came with checkered hard rubber grips (later production versions have checkered grips impressed with the High Standard monogram). Introduced 1932, with serial numbers beginning at 5000. Early production utilized Hartford parts. Approximately 65,000 made. Add $75 premium for Type-I-B takedown. Add a $75 premium for early models with Hartford Arms front sight, safety, and takedown levers. Box with papers add premium of 15 percent.C&R eligible. Most guns are found in serial number ranges from 5,000 to about 95,894 and 148198 to about 151021.

Exc.	*V.G.*	*Good*	*Fair*	*Poor*
500	300	175	125	90

Model B-US

A version of the Model B with slight contour modifications to the back of the frame. Approximately 14,000 were made for the U.S. government in 1942-1943. Most are marked "PROPERTY OF U.S." On the top of the barrel and on the right side of the frame. Monogrammed hard rubber grips. Most guns are found in serial number range 92344 to about 111631.

Exc.	*V.G.*	*Good*	*Fair*	*Poor*
800	520	375	175	125

NOTE: Box with papers add premium of 20 percent.

Model C

Like the Model B except in .22 Short. Introduced 1936; approximately 4,700 made. Both plain and monogrammed hard rubber grips. Available with either a 4.5" or a 6.75" round barrel.

Exc.	*V.G.*	*Good*	*Fair*	*Poor*
825	450	300	225	150

NOTE: Add $75 premium for I-A takedown. Add $175 premuim for I-B takedown. Box with papers add premium of 15 percent.

Model A

Similar to the Model B but with checkered walnut grips over an extended grip and an adjustable sight. Introduced 1938; approximately 7,300 made. Available with either a 4.5" or a 6.75" round barrel. The same light barrel as the model B.

Exc.	*V.G.*	*Good*	*Fair*	*Poor*
675	450	300	175	125

NOTE: Add $175 premium for I-B takedown. Box with papers add premium of 15 percent.

Model D

Similar to a Model A but with a heavier weight barrel. (The middle weight barrel.) Available with either a 4.5" or a 6.75" barrel and optional checkered walnut grips. Introduced 1938; approximately 2,500 made.

Exc.	*V.G.*	*Good*	*Fair*	*Poor*
835	490	310	200	130

NOTE: C-R. Add $175 premium for I-B takedown. Box with papers add premium of 15 percent.

Model E

Like the Model D but with a still heavier weight barrel (the heavy weight barrel). Available with either a 4.5" or a 6.75" barrel. Checkered walnut grips with thumb rest. Introduced 1938; approximately 2,600 made.

Exc.	V.G.	Good	Fair	Poor
1025	725	500	250	140

NOTE: Add $175 for I-B takedown. Box with papers add premium of 18 percent.

Model S

Not a production model. Like the model B but with a smooth bore. Nine registered as Model S. Additional five with Model C slides are registered, Model C/S. Note ivory bead front sight. Others may exist but only 14 are registered with BATF. Manufactured in 1939 and 1940. Values for both variations are equal. 6.75" barrels. C-R.

NOTE: Serial numbers for registered samples.

Model S: 48142; 48143; 48144; 48145; 48146; 59474; 59458; 59459

Model C/S: 59279; 59460; 59469; 59473; 59478

Exc.	V.G.	Good	Fair	Poor
4750	3500	2800	—	—

Hammer Letter Models

Second models made. Like the letter models with external hammers.

Model H-B, Type 1 Pre-War

Like the Model B but with exposed hammer. Introduced 1940; approximately 2,100 made.

Exc.	V.G.	Good	Fair	Poor
725	425	275	175	125

NOTE: Box with papers add premium of 15 percent.

Model H-B, Type 2 Post-War

Post-war variation has an external safety. Approximately 25,000 made.

Exc.	V.G.	Good	Fair	Poor
550	375	225	150	100

NOTE: Box with papers add premium of 15 percent.

Model H-A

Like the Model A but with exposed hammer. Introduced 1940; approximately 1,040 made.

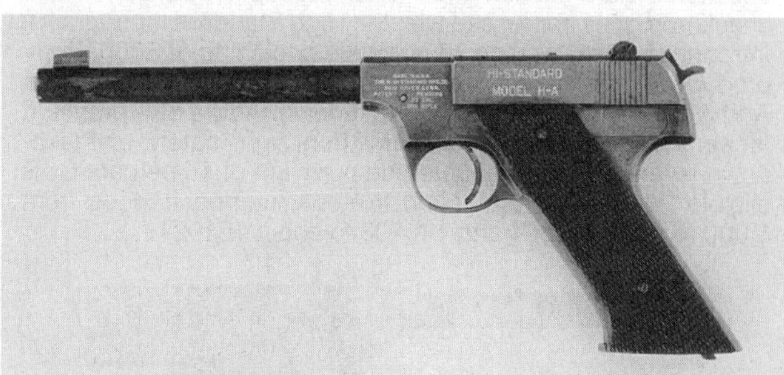

Exc.	V.G.	Good	Fair	Poor
1025	625	400	200	125

NOTE: Box with papers add premium of 15 percent.

Model H-D

Like the Model D but with exposed hammer. Introduced 1940; approximately 6,900 made.

Model H-D with 6.75" barrel

Exc.	V.G.	Good	Fair	Poor
1100	575	400	175	125

NOTE: Box with papers add premium of 15 percent.

Model H-E

Like the Model E but with exposed hammer. Introduced 1940; approximately 2,100 made.

Exc.	V.G.	Good	Fair	Poor
1770	1035	700	275	150

NOTE: Box with papers add premium of 15 percent.

Model USA—Model HD

Similar to the Model HD but 4.5" barrel only. Had fixed sights, checkered black hard rubber grips and an external safety. Early models blued; later model Parkerized. Introduced 1943; approximately 44,000 produced for the U.S. government.

Exc.	V.G.	Good	Fair	Poor
725	575	400	200	125

NOTE: Box with papers add premium of 20 percent.

Model USA—Model HD-MS

A silenced variation of the USA Model HD. Approximately 2,000 produced for the OSS during 1944 and 1945. 6.75" shrouded barrel. Early models blued; later model Parkerized. Only a few registered with BATF for civilian ownership.

Exc.	V.G.	Good	Fair	Poor
6000	5000	—	—	—

Model H-D Military

Similar to the HD but with external safety. Early production had checkered plastic grips; later production changed to checkered walnut. Introduced 1945; approximately 150,000 produced.

Exc.	V.G.	Good	Fair	Poor
525	360	230	175	125

NOTE: Box with papers add premium of 15 percent.

Lever Letter Models

Third design models which incorporate interchangeable barrels with a lever takedown.

G-.380

A .380 caliber semi-automatic pistol with a 5" barrel and 6-shot magazine. Blues with checkered plastic grips. Fixed sights. Introduced 1947, discontinued 1950; approximately 7,400 made. High Standard's only production centerfire pistol.

Exc.	V.G.	Good	Fair	Poor
550	350	245	150	115

NOTE: Box with papers add premium of 10 percent.

G-B

Similar characteristics with the Model B but with interchangeable 4.5" or 6.75" barrels. Sold with either barrel or as a combination with both barrels. Fixed sights. Blued with monogrammed plastic grips. Last short frame model produced. Introduced 1949, discontinued 1950; approximately 4,900 produced.

Exc.	V.G.	Good	Fair	Poor
550	325	225	135	100

NOTE: Box with papers add premium of 15 percent. Add $225 premium for factory combination.

G-D

Similar characteristics with the Model D but with interchangeable 4.5" or 6.75" barrels. Sold with either barrel or as a combination with both barrels. Adjustable sights. Blued with checkered walnut grips. Optional checkered thumb rest walnut grips. Introduced 1949, discontinued 1950; approximately 3,300 produced.

Exc.	V.G.	Good	Fair	Poor
875	675	400	175	125

NOTE: Add $325 premium for factory combination, $50 premium for factory target grips. Box with papers add premium of 15 percent.

G-E

Similar characteristics with the Model E but with interchangeable 4.5" or 6.75" barrels. Sold with either barrel or as a combination with both barrels. Adjustable sights. Blued with checkered thumb rest walnut grips. Introduced 1949, discontinued 1950; approximately 2,900 produced.

Exc.	V.G.	Good	Fair	Poor
1275	800	450	225	135

NOTE: Add $375 premium for factory combination. Box with papers add premium of 15 percent.

Olympic (commonly called "G-O")

New gun design for competitive shooting in .22 short caliber. 4.5" or 6.75" barrels. Sold with either barrel or as a combination with both barrels. Grooved front and back straps on frame. Adjustable sights. Blued with checkered thumb rest walnut grips. Introduced 1949, discontinued 1950; approximately 1,200 produced. This model uses a special curved magazine. A few guns will utilize a straight-back magazine. The majority of these Olympics use the curved magazine with a humped back.

Exc.	V.G.	Good	Fair	Poor
1500	875	550	225	125

NOTE: Add $375 premium for factory combination. Box with papers add premium of 15 percent. Add $300 for the straight magazine variation.

LEVER NAME MODELS

Fourth design models evolving from the lever letter series designs with slight changes.

Supermatic

.22 LR caliber pistol with 10-shot magazine. Heavy round barrel, blued finish; adjustable sights and brown plastic thumb rest grips. Grooved front and back straps on frame. Available with 4.5" or 6.75" barrels or combination with both barrels. Ribbed barrels and provisions for weights. A 2 oz. and a 3 oz. weight were provided with this model, as was a filler strip for when the weights were not used.

Exc.	V.G.	Good	Fair	Poor
650	440	320	175	135

NOTE: Add $250 for factory combination. Box with papers add premium of 15 percent.

Olympic

.22 Short caliber pistol with 10-shot magazine. Heavy round barrel, blued finish, adjustable sights and brown plastic thumb rest grips. Grooved front and back straps on frame. Available with 4.5" or 6.75" barrels or combination with both barrels. Ribbed barrels and provisions for weights. Weights of 2 oz. and 3 oz. were provided with this model, as was a filler strip for when the weights were not used.

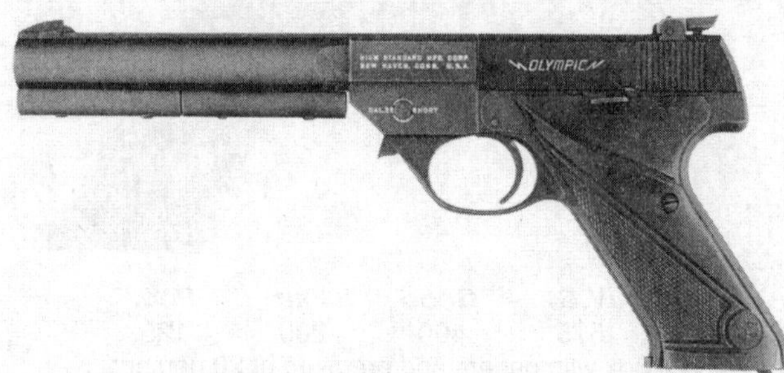

Exc.	V.G.	Good	Fair	Poor
950	675	500	225	150

NOTE: Add $250 for factory combination. Box with papers add premium of 15 percent.

Field King

.22 LR caliber pistol with 10-shot magazine. Heavy round barrel, blued finish, adjustable sights and brown plastic thumb rest grips. Available with 4.5" or 6.75" barrels or combination with both barrels. No rib on barrels or provisions for weights.

Exc.	V.G.	Good	Fair	Poor
575	380	250	150	125

NOTE: Add $225 premium for factory combination. Box with papers add premium of 15 percent.

Sport King

.22 caliber pistol with 10-shot magazine. Lightweight round barrel, blued finish, fixed sights and brown plastic thumb rest grips. Available with 4.5" or 6.75" barrels or combination with both barrels. Early models did not have a slide holdback when the magazine was empty. Early variation without holdback was produced in about twice the quantity as the later models incorporating this feature.

Exc.	V.G.	Good	Fair	Poor
375	275	200	140	110

NOTE: Add $200 premium for factory combination. Box with papers add premium of 15 percent. Add a $25 premium for guns with holdback feature.

100 SERIES MODELS

Fifth design models evolving from the lever name series designs. This series introduced the small pushbutton barrel release takedown and deletes the shrouded breach.

Supermatic S-100

Like the lever takedown Supermatic but with new takedown. Available with 4.5", 6.75", or a combination with both barrel lengths. Grooved front and back straps on frame. This model produced briefly in 1954. Weights of 2 oz. and 3 oz. were provided with this model, as was a filler strip for when the weights were not used.

Exc.	V.G.	Good	Fair	Poor
775	550	350	150	125

NOTE: Add $250 for factory combination. Box with papers add premium of 15 percent.

Olympic O-100

Like the lever takedown Olympic but with new takedown. Available with 4.5", 6.75", or a combination with both barrel lengths. Grooved front and back straps on frame. This model produced briefly in 1954. Weights of 2 oz. and 3 oz. were provided with this model, as was a filler strip for when the weights were not used.

Exc.	V.G.	Good	Fair	Poor
1100	625	425	225	135

NOTE: Add $250 for factory combination. Box with papers add premium of 15 percent.

Field King FK-100

Like the lever takedown Field King but with new takedown. Available with 4.5", 6.75", or a combination with both barrel lengths. This model produced briefly in 1954.

Exc.	V.G.	Good	Fair	Poor
675	450	350	160	125

NOTE: Add $225 premium for factory combination. Box with papers add premium of 15 percent.

Sport King SK-100

Like the lever takedown Sport King but with new takedown. Available with 4.5", 6.75", or a combination with both barrel lengths. This model produced 1954 to 1957. In late 1958 Col. Rex Applegate imported about 300 of these pistols into Mexico. These guns are marked with his compay's name "ARMAMEX." Marked "ARMAMEX, MEXICO" on the right side of the barrel and "SPORT KING/CAL .22 L.R." on the left side of the barrel. Serial numbers around 870,084-870,383. Note that the Applegate guns were made after the 102 series was in production. Armamex catalog number 1910.

Exc.	V.G.	Good	Fair	Poor
375	225	175	120	100

NOTE: Add $200 premium for factory combination. Add $250 premium for Armamex version. Box with papers add premium of 10 percent.

Sport King Lightweight SK-100

Aluminum frame like Flite King LW-100 but in .22 LR caliber. Produced 1956 to 1964. Also available nickel plated 1957 to 1960.

Exc.	V.G.	Good	Fair	Poor
475	275	175	120	100

NOTE: Add $150 premium for nickel finish, $200 premium for factory combination. Box with papers add premium of 12 percent.

Flite King LW-100

.22 Short caliber semi-automatic pistol with 10-shot magazine. Blued finish with black anodized aluminum frame and slide. Brown plastic checkered thumb rest grips. Fixed sights. Available with 4.5", 6.75", or a combination with both barrel lengths. This model produced 1954 to 1957.

Exc.	V.G.	Good	Fair	Poor
500	360	260	130	100

NOTE: Add $200 for factory combination. Box with papers add premium of 12 percent.

Dura-Matic M-100

.22 LR caliber semi-automatic pistol with 10-shot magazine. Striker-fired, fixed sights, blued finish, brown checkered plastic one-piece grip. Takedown by thumb nut. Available with 4.5", 6.5", or a combination with both barrel lengths. This model produced briefly in 1954.

Exc.	V.G.	Good	Fair	Poor
325	200	150	125	95

NOTE: Add $150 premium for factory combination. Box with papers add premium of 12 percent.

101 SERIES MODELS

Sixth design models evolving from the 100 series. This series continued the small pushbutton barrel release takedown.

Olympic O-101

A .22 Short caliber semi-automatic pistol with a 10-shot magazine. Heavy round barrel, blued finish, adjustable sights and brown plastic thumb rest grips. Grooved front and back straps on frame. Available with 4.5", 6.75", or a combination with both barrel lengths. The 6.75" barrel incorporates a muzzlebrake with one slot on either side of the front sight.

Exc.	V.G.	Good	Fair	Poor
875	550	400	175	175

NOTE: Add $250 premium for factory combination. Box with papers add premium of 13 percent.

Supermatic S-101

A .22 LR caliber semi-automatic pistol with a 10-shot magazine. Heavy round barrel, blued finish, adjustable sights and brown plastic thumb rest grips. Grooved front and back straps on frame. Available with 4.5", 6.75", or a combination with both barrel lengths. The 6.75" barrel incorporates a muzzlebrake with one slot on either side of the front sight. Also produced with U.S. marking for the military.

Exc.	V.G.	Good	Fair	Poor
700	425	325	175	130

NOTE: Add $250 premium for factory combination. Box with papers add premium of 13 percent.

Field King FK-101

A .22 LR caliber semi-automatic pistol with a 10-shot magazine. Heavy round barrel, blued finish, adjustable sights and brown plastic thumb rest grips. Available with 4.5", 6.75", or a combination with both barrel lengths.

Exc.	V.G.	Good	Fair	Poor
575	435	325	160	125

NOTE: Add $225 premium for factory combination. Box with papers add premium of 15 percent.

Dura-Matic M-101

Like the Dura-matic M-100 with slightly different locking method for thumb nut takedown. Produced 1954 to 1970.

Later appeared renamed "Plinker" M-101 in 1971 to 1973. Plinker not available with both barrel combinations. A slightly modified version was sold by Sears Roebuck & Co. as the J. C. Higgins M-80.

Exc.	V.G.	Good	Fair	Poor
300	200	125	100	80

NOTE: Add $150 premium for factory combination. Box with papers add premium of 10 percent.

Conversion Kits

These kits convert .22 LR to .22 Short and include a barrel, an aluminum slide, and magazine for .22 Short to .22 LR in which case the slide is steel. Prices are for the kit in original factory boxes.

NOTE: First advertised for 101 Series guns. Later, versions were produced for lever takedown guns. Catalog numbers unknown for conversion kits for lever takedown guns.

Exc.	V.G.
500	375

102 & 103 SERIES MODELS

The 102 Series was a major design change incorporating a new frame with a large pushbutton takedown release. Also new was a superb adjustable sight. There is little difference between the two series.

Supermatic Trophy

A .22 LR caliber semi-automatic pistol with a 10-shot magazine. A tapered barrel with an enlarged register at the muzzle end to hold a removable muzzlebrake. Super polished blue finish; adjustable sights; 2 and 3 oz. adjustable weights and checkered walnut thumb rest grips. Grooved front and back straps on frame. Available with 6.75", 8" or 10" barrels. Occasionally sold as a combination including two barrels. Premiums for 10" barrels and combinations in original boxes. 5.5" bull barrel available in 103s after April 1962, 7.25" fluted barrels available in 103s after April 1963.

Exc.	*V.G.*	*Good*	*Fair*	*Poor*
1000	700	475	175	120

NOTE: Add $125 premium for 8" barrel and $225 premium for 10" barrel. Box with papers add premium of 12 percent. Occasionally found with the optional light oak case, which will command a premium of about 14 percent.

Supermatic Citation

Like the Supermatic Trophy with checkered plastic grips. Blued finish without the trophy's super polished finish. Grooved front and back straps on frame. 5.5" bull barrel available in 103s after April 1962. Also produced with U.S. marking for the military.

Exc.	*V.G.*	*Good*	*Fair*	*Poor*
675	450	340	150	120

NOTE: Add $100 premium for 8" barrel and $200 premium for 10" barrel. Box with papers add premium of 12 percent. Occasionally found with optional light oak case, which will command a premium of about 18 percent.

Supermatic Tournament

A .22 LR caliber semi-automatic pistol with a 10-shot magazine. Barrels are round and tapered. Blued finish, adjustable sights and checkered plastic grips. Available with 4.5", 6.75", or a combination with both barrels. Combinations available in 102 Series only. 5.5" bull barrel replaced the 4.5" barrel in early 1962. Also produced with **U.S.** marking for the military.

Exc.	*V.G.*	*Good*	*Fair*	*Poor*
590	425	250	140	110

NOTE: Add $200 premium for factory combination. Box with papers add premium of 12 percent.

Olympic

A .22 Short caliber version of the Supermatic Citation. Early models marked "Olympic Citation," changed to "Olympic" only in 1960. Grooved front and back straps on frame. 6.75", 8" and 10" barrels produced. 5.5" bull barrel available on later 103 production.

Exc.	*V.G.*	*Good*	*Fair*	*Poor*
1050	550	330	150	120

NOTE: Add $125 premium for 8" barrel and $225 premium for 10" barrel and $150 premium for "Olympic Citation" marked guns. Box with papers add premium of 12 percent.

Olympic ISU

Like an Olympic but only available with a 6.75" barrel with integral muzzlebrake. Grooved front and back straps on frame.

Exc.	*V.G.*	*Good*	*Fair*	*Poor*
1050	600	325	150	120

NOTE: Box with papers add premium of 12 percent.

Olympic Trophy ISU

An Olympic ISU with a Supermatic Trophy finish. Grooved front and back straps on frame. Produced in the 103 Series only. Fewer than 500 produced.

Exc.	*V.G.*	*Good*	*Fair*	*Poor*
2100	700	340	150	120

NOTE: Box with papers add premium of 10 percent.

Sharpshooter

A .22 LR caliber semi-automatic pistol with a 10-shot magazine. 5.5" bull barrel, blued finish, adjustable sights, checkered plastic grips. Some produced with Model 103-marked slides. Although the 103-marked guns have 1969 and later serial numbers they were shipped after the introduction of the Sharpshooter in 1971 and were probably converted from unsold Sport Kings. No premium for 103-marked. Variation without series marked on slide is the most plentiful. Produced 1971 to 1977.

Exc.	V.G.	Good	Fair	Poor
450	290	240	140	110

NOTE: Box with papers add premium of 15 percent.

Sport King

A .22 LR caliber semi-automatic pistol with a 10-shot magazine. Barrels are lightweight, round, and tapered. Blued finish; fixed sights and checkered plastic grips. Available with 4.5", 6.75", or a combination with both barrel lengths. Produced 1957 to 1970 and 1974 to 1977. Also available 1974 to 1977 with nickel finish. $100 premium for nickel finish and $200 premium for factory combination. **NOTE:** Box with papers add premium of 10 percent.

Flite King

A .22 Short caliber version of the Sport King Models 102 and 103. Note these models have steel frames.

Exc.	V.G.	Good	Fair	Poor
425	325	240	135	100

NOTE: Add $200 premium for factory combination. Box with papers add premium of 12 percent.

Conversion Kits

These kits convert .22 LR to .22 Short and include a barrel, an aluminum slide, and magazine. Prices are for kits in original boxes.

Exc.	V.G.
800-600	500

104 SERIES MODELS

The last of the slant grip gun designs. The early production marked "Model 104." Later production is unmarked.

Supermatic Trophy

A .22 LR caliber semi-automatic pistol with a 10-shot magazine. Super polished blue finish; adjustable sights; 2 and 3 oz. adjustable weights, checkered walnut thumb rest grips. Grooved front and back straps on frame. Available with 5.5" bull or 7.25" fluted barrels. Both barrels accept the removable muzzlebrake.

Exc.	V.G.	Good	Fair	Poor
990	580	375	160	110

NOTE: Add $150 premium for high polish blue finish. Box with papers add premium of 12 percent.

Supermatic Citation

A .22 LR caliber semi-automatic pistol with a 10-shot magazine. Blue finish; adjustable sights; 2 and 3 oz. adjustable weights, checkered walnut thumb rest grips. Grooved front and back straps on frame.

Exc.	V.G.	Good	Fair	Poor
650	450	300	125	110

NOTE: Box with papers add premium of 12 percent.

Olympic

Like the 103 Series 8" barrel models.

Exc.	V.G.	Good	Fair	Poor
1050	580	325	160	110

NOTE: Box with papers add premium of 12 percent.

Olympic ISU

Like the 103 model. 6.75" barrel with integral brake. 5.5" version introduced in 1964. Catalogs and price list refer to the 9295 as both Olympic and Olympic ISU. It met the ISU regulations and included a removable muzzlebrake and weights.

Exc.	V.G.	Good	Fair	Poor
1000	580	325	160	110

NOTE: Box with papers add premium of 12 percent.

Victor

A .22 LR caliber semi-automatic pistol with a 10-shot magazine. 4.5" and 5.5" slab-sided barrels with either ventilated or solid ribs. The adjustable sights are integral with the rib. Blue finish, barrel tapped for weight, checkered walnut thumb rest grips. Grooved front and back straps on frame. Probably fewer than 600 of these slant grip Victors in all configurations. Probably fewer than 40 each of the 4.5" guns. Trigger is adjustable for both pull and over-travel. Most guns in serial number range above 2401xxx with a few in the ML serial number series. Note the early vent rib barrels were steel and later ones aluminum without a change in catalog numbers. BEWARE—fakes exist.

Victor with 4.5" solid-rib barrel

 *This symbol denotes "Sleepers" with rapidly-rising values and/or significant collector potential.*

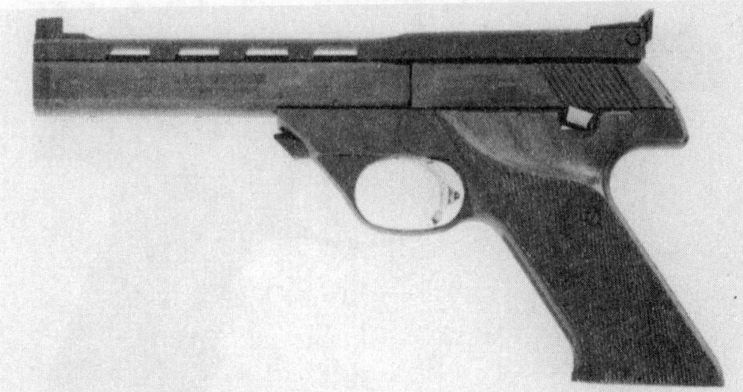

Victor with 5.5" vent rib barrel

Exc.	V.G.	Good	Fair	Poor
2500	1400	550	375	250

NOTE: Add $75 premium for steel rib, $200 premium for solid rib, and $200 premium for 4.5" barrel. Box with papers add premium of 15 percent.

106 SERIES MODELS

Referred to as military models, this series was designed to provide the same grip angles and feel of the Colt military model 1911. This design was introduced in 1965 and continued through most of 1968.

Supermatic Trophy

Like the 104 Series Supermatic Trophy with the new military frame. Stippled front and back straps on frame.

Exc.	V.G.	Good	Fair	Poor
900	560	375	175	120

NOTE: Add $100 premium for high polish blue finish, $200 premium for guns with boxes and accessories if factory records verify model numbers. Box with papers add premium of 12 percent.

Supermatic Citation

Like the 104 Series Supermatic Citation with the new military frame. Stippled front and back straps on frame.

Exc.	V.G.	Good	Fair	Poor
600	425	275	175	120

NOTE: Add $150 premium for guns with boxes and accessories if factory records verify model numbers. Box with papers add premium of 12 percent.

Supermatic Tournament

Like the 104 Series Supermatic Tournament with the new military frame. Stippled front and back straps on frame.

Exc.	V.G.	Good	Fair	Poor
550	325	225	150	120

NOTE: Add $125 premium for guns with boxes and accessories if factory records verify model numbers. Box with papers add premium of 12 percent.

Olympic

Listed in catalog but not in shipping records. Catalog number 9235 for 5.5" barrel.

WARNING: There is no evidence that this model was actually produced.

Olympic ISU

Like the 104 Series Olympic ISU with the new military frame. Stippled front and back straps on frame.

Exc.	V.G.	Good	Fair	Poor
950	575	350	175	120

NOTE: Add $200 premium for guns with boxes and accessories if factory records verify model numbers. Box with papers add premium of 12 percent.

107 SERIES MODELS

The evolutionary successor to the 106 Series. This series had the frame redesigned to eliminate the plugging of the spring hole produced with the old tooling. During the time of this series production, the MILITARY marking on the frame was removed and then later reappeared near the end of the end of the traditional serial number series. The MILITARY marking is absent from the guns with the ML prefixed serial numbers. There is no premium associated with these variations.

Supermatic Trophy

Like the 106 Series Supermatic Trophy.

Exc.	V.G.	Good	Fair	Poor
850	500	325	175	120

NOTE: Box with papers add premium of 12 percent.

Supermatic Trophy 1972 Commemorative

A limited edition of the 107 Supermatic Trophy with 1000 planned. "T" prefix on serial numbers from 0000 to 999. Engraved, right side of slide has the five gold ring Olympic logo. Offered with lined presentation case. Only 107 guns listed in the shipping records, plus one frame. A couple of prototypes believed to exist in the regular serial number series. Prices are for guns in original presentation cases. C-R. One fully engraved gun known to exist.

NOTE: One fully engraved gun is known.

NIB	Exc.	V.G.	Good	Fair	Poor
5500	4000	—	—	—	—

Supermatic Citation

Like the 106 Series Supermatic Citation.

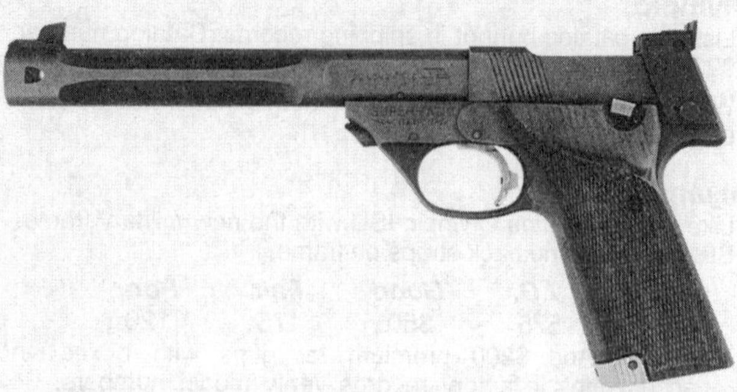

Exc.	V.G.	Good	Fair	Poor
575	375	275	200	110

NOTE: Box with papers add premium of 12 percent.

Supermatic Tournament

Like the 106 Series Supermatic Tournament. Smooth front and back straps on frame.

Exc.	V.G.	Good	Fair	Poor
495	325	275	160	110

NOTE: Box with papers add premium of 12 percent.

Olympic ISU

Like the 106 Series Olympic ISU.

Exc.	V.G.	Good	Fair	Poor
1000	600	475	200	110

NOTE: Box with papers add premium of 12 percent.

Olympic ISU 1980 Commemorative

A limited edition of the 107 Olympic ISU with 1,000 produced. "USA" prefix on serial numbers from 0001 to 1000. Engraved, right side of slide has the five gold ring Olympic logo. Offered with lined presentation case.

Exc.	V.G.	Good	Fair	Poor
1250	775	475	275	175

NOTE: Prices are for guns with box, papers, and presentation case; otherwise deduct $250 for guns in excellent condition.

Sport King

Like the 103 Series Sport King with the military frame.

Exc.	V.G.	Good	Fair	Poor
295	200	175	140	100

NOTE: Box with papers add premium of 12 percent.

Victor

A .22 LR caliber semi-automatic pistol with a 10-shot magazine. 4.5" and 5.5" slab-sided barrels with either ventilated or solid ribs. The adjustable sights are integral with the rib. Blue finish, barrel tapped for weight, checkered walnut thumb rest grips. Stippled front and back straps on frame. Early ventilated ribs were steel; aluminum replaced the steel on later ventilated ribs. Still later a clearance groove was added for spent shell ejection behind the barrel. Early models marked THE VICTOR on the left side of the barrel; later guns marked simply VICTOR on the left side of the frame. A few transition guns marked in both locations.

Exc.	V.G.	Good	Fair	Poor
700	450	300	175	120

NOTE: Add $125 premium for steel ribs, $125 premium for solid rib guns, premium for 4.5" barreled guns, $140 premium for Hamden guns (7-digit serial numbers and ML prefix serial numbers below ML 25,000). Box with papers add premium of 12 percent.

Sharpshooter

Like the 103 Series Sharpshooter with the military frame.

Exc.	*V.G.*	*Good*	*Fair*	*Poor*
400	275	200	150	110

NOTE: Box with papers add premium of 12 percent.

Survival Kit

An electroless nickel Sharpshooter with 5.5" barrel in a canvas carrying case with an extra electroless nickel magazine.

Exc.	*V.G.*	*Good*	*Fair*	*Poor*
625	425	250	150	110

NOTE: Deduct $100 for guns without the case and $65 for guns without the extra magazine for guns in excellent condition.

10-X

A .22 LR caliber semi-automatic pistol with a 10-shot magazine. Matte blue finish, adjustable sights, checkered walnut thumb rest grips painted black. Stippled front and back straps on frame. Available with 5.5" bull barrel. Assembled by a master gunsmith. Gunsmith's initials stamped in frame under left grip panel. Produced in 1981.

Exc.	*V.G.*	*Good*	*Fair*	*Poor*
2400	1400	800	300	125

NOTE: Prices are for guns with box and papers including test target. Otherwise deduct $175.

SH SERIES MODELS

The final design produced by High Standard. A change in takedown from the large pushbutton introduced with the 102 Series and continuing through the 107 Series, to a hex socket head cap screw takedown.

Supermatic Trophy

Like the 107 Supermatic Trophy with a new takedown.

Exc.	*V.G.*	*Good*	*Fair*	*Poor*
550	325	250	150	120

NOTE: Box with papers add premium of 10 percent.

Supermatic Citation

Like the 107 Supermatic Citation with a new takedown.

Exc.	*V.G.*	*Good*	*Fair*	*Poor*
475	315	225	150	120

NOTE: Box with papers add premium of 10 percent.

Citation II

A new gun like the Supermatic Citation but with the barrel slabbed on the sides like the Victor and smooth front and back straps on frame. 5.5" and 7.25" barrels available. Blued finish,adjustable sights. Electroless nickel version utilized in some survival kits.

Exc.	*V.G.*	*Good*	*Fair*	*Poor*
425	300	225	140	110

NOTE: Box with papers add premium of 10 percent.

Sport King

Like the 107 Sport King with a new takedown. Electroless nickel finish also available.

Exc.	V.G.	Good	Fair	Poor
265	200	150	120	90

NOTE: Box with papers add premium of 10 percent.

Victor

Like the 107 Victor with a new takedown. Only available with 5.5" barrel.

Exc.	V.G.	Good	Fair	Poor
500	300	225	150	110

NOTE: Box with papers add premium of 10 percent.

Sharpshooter

Like the 107 Sharpshooter with a new takedown. Electroless nickel version utilized in some survival kits.

Exc.	V.G.	Good	Fair	Poor
325	225	175	140	100

NOTE: Box with papers add premium of 10 percent.

10-X

Like the 107 10-X with a new takedown. Also available with 7.25" fluted barrel and a 5.5" ribbed barrel like a Victor.

Exc.	V.G.	Good	Fair	Poor
2100	1300	775	300	125

NOTE: Prices are for guns with box and papers including test target. Otherwise deduct $150. Add $500 premium for 7.25" barrel, $1,000 for ribbed barrel like Victor.

Survival Kit

Either an electroless nickel Sharpshooter or electroless nickel Citation II with 5.5" barrel in a canvas carrying case with an extra electroless nickel magazine. Two different fabrics utilized during production.

Exc.	V.G.	Good	Fair	Poor
625	425	250	175	110

NOTE: Deduct $100 for guns without the case and $65 for guns without the extra magazine for guns in excellent condition.

Conversion Kits for Military Frame Guns

These kits convert .22 LR to .22 Short and include a barrel, an aluminum slide, and 2 magazines.

Exc.	V.G.
550	350

NOTE: Prices are for kits in original boxes.

CURRENTLY MANUFACTURED HOUSTON MODELS

Supermatic Citation

Chambered for the .22 LR and fitted with a 5.5" barrel. Matte blue or Parkerized finish. Weight is about 44 oz.

NIB	Exc.	V.G.	Good	Fair	Poor
425	325	275	225	175	100

Supermatic Citation MS

Designed for metallic silhouette shooting and introduced in 1996. Fitted with a 10" barrel. Weight is approximately 49 oz.

NIB	Exc.	V.G.	Good	Fair	Poor
675	575	425	350	250	125

Supermatic Tournament

Chambered for .22 LR and fitted with a 5.5" barrel. Matte blue finish. Weight is approximately 44 oz.

NIB	Exc.	V.G.	Good	Fair	Poor
400	325	250	200	175	100

Supermatic Trophy

Offered with 5.5" or 7.25" barrels and chambered for .22 LR Adjustable trigger, barrel weights, gold-plated trigger, safety, slide stop and magazine catch. Matte blue or Parkerized finish. Weight is about 45 oz.

NIB	Exc.	V.G.	Good	Fair	Poor
500	425	350	250	150	100

Olympic Model

Chambered for .22 Short and fitted with a 5.5" bull barrel. Blued finish. Weight is approximately 44 oz.

NIB	Exc.	V.G.	Good	Fair	Poor
525	425	300	250	200	100

Olympic ISU

Similar to the previous model but fitted with a 6.75" barrel with internal stabilizer. Magazine capacity is 5 rounds. Checkered walnut grips. Weight is approximately 45 oz. This model was discontinued in 1995.

NIB	Exc.	V.G.	Good	Fair	Poor
500	400	350	300	200	150

Olympic Rapid Fire

Introduced in 1996. Chambered for the .22 Short cartridge with a 4" barrel, integral muzzlebrake and forward mounted compensator. Special grips. Weight is about 46 oz.

NIB	Exc.	V.G.	Good	Fair	Poor
1995	1550	1200	900	600	—

Sport King

Chambered for .22 LR and fitted with a 4.5" or 6.75" barrel. Adjustable rear sight. Weight is about 44 oz.

NIB	Exc.	V.G.	Good	Fair	Poor
350	300	225	150	100	80

Victor

With 4.5" barrel and blue or Parkerized finish.

NIB	Exc.	V.G.	Good	Fair	Poor
525	425	350	300	200	125

10-X

Fitted with 5.5" barrel. Weight is about 44 oz.

NIB	Exc.	V.G.	Good	Fair	Poor
850	700	550	450	350	200

10-X—Shea model

Fitted with a 4.5" or 5.5" barrel. Limited to 150 pistols per year.

NIB	Exc.	V.G.	Good	Fair	Poor
1100	850	700	500	350	200

HIGH STANDARD DERRINGERS

A .22 caliber or .22 Magnum caliber Over/Under double-action-only derringer with 3.50" barrels. They are found with three different types of markings:

Type 1 Markings are found on early models which are marked "HI-STANDARD" / "DERRINGER" and have the EAGLE logo on the left side of the barrel. These models were marked "D-100" for the .22 caliber and "DM-101" for the .22 Magnum on the left side of the barrel. Date range 1962 to about 1967.

Type 2 Markings are found on later models were marked "HI-STANDARD" / "DERRINGER" and had the TRIGGER logo. The early .22 caliber models were marked D-100 and the later .22 caliber models beginning about 1969 were marked D-101 on the left side of the barrel. The .22 Magnum models were marked DM-101on the left side of the barrel. Date range 1967 to about 1970.

Type 3 Markings are found on the latest models were marked simply "DERRINGER" without HI STANDARD, or either logo. These models were also marked D-101 for the .22 caliber and DM-101 for the .22 Magnum on the left side of the barrel. Date Blue, white or black grips

Blued finish, white or Black Grips, 1962-1984

Exc.	V.G.	Good	Fair	Poor
250	185	140	80	65

Nickel Finish black grips, introduced 1970

Exc.	V.G.	Good	Fair	Poor
250	185	140	80	65

Electroless Nickel Finish with checkered walnut grips

Exc.	V.G.	Good	Fair	Poor
275	190	145	80	65

SILVER-PLATED DERRINGER

A .22 Magnum derringer with a presentation case. Faux black mother of pearl grips. 501 made. Serial numbers SP 0 through SP 500. Produced in 1981.

Exc.	V.G.	Good	Fair	Poor
500	275	175	90	75

GOLD-PLATED DERRINGERS

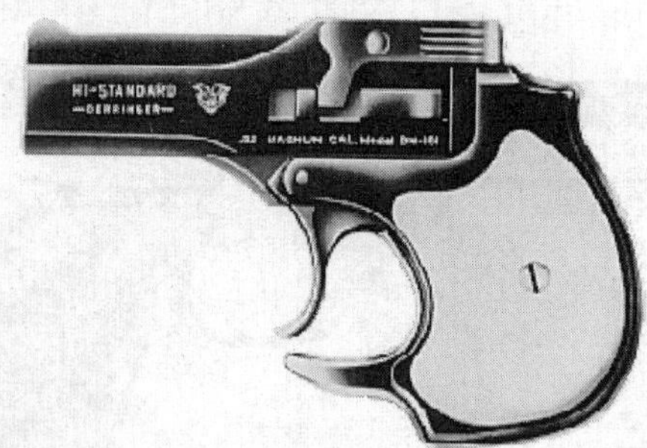

Exc.	V.G.	Good	Fair	Poor
450	300	200	100	80

NOTE: Prices are for GP serial number guns with presentation case. $100 premium for DM prefix guns in Exc. condition with presentation case. $150 premium for 1960s gold guns in Exc. condition with presentation cases.

HIGH STANDARD REVOLVERS

POLICE-STYLE REVOLVERS

The revolvers begin with the R-100 design series and continue through the R-109 design series. Later steel-framed Sentinels carry no design series markings. The changes of design series designations indicate design changes to the guns. The only R-105 known to date is a private label gun made for Sears. The design series designations and the associated catalog numbers listed are the best estimates at the time of publication.

Earliest Sentinels in 1955 were in a seperate serial number series from 1 through approximately 45000. Then they were included in serial number series common to all handguns. In 1974 they were again put in a seperate serial number series with an S prefix: S101 through S79946. Many of the later guns had a V suffix which indicated the gun was visually imperfect but guaranteed to work properly.

Sentinel aluminum frames

A 9-shot single-action or double-action revolver with swing-out cylinder for .22 Short, Long, or LR cartridges. Fixed sights. The Sentinel snub 2.375" barrel model had a bobbed hammer from its introduction until 1960. Beginning in 1961 this changed to a standard spur hammer with no change in the catalog number. Beginning with R-102 series the ejector had a spring return. Available in configurations listed.

High Standard private-labeled the aluminum-framed Sentinels for both Sears and Weatern Auto.

From 1957 through 1962 High Standard offered the 2.375" snub-barreled Sentinel in three different color anodized frames. These guns had nickel-plated cylinders, triggers, and hammers. The grips were round-butt ivory-colored plastic.

Exc.	V.G.	Good	Fair	Poor
180	105	85	70	45

NOTE: Add $20 premium for nickel. Deduct $15 for early models without spring return ejector.

Gold

Exc.	V.G.	Good	Fair	Poor
475	240	170	80	55

NOTE: Add $20 for R-102 marked guns.

Turquoise

Exc.	V.G.	Good	Fair	Poor
500	250	170	80	55

NOTE: Add $20 for R-102 marked guns.

Pink

Exc.	V.G.	Good	Fair	Poor
500	250	170	80	55

NOTE: Add $20 for R-102 marked guns.

The Sentinel Imperial

Has two-piece walnut square-butt grips, ramp front and adjustable rear sights.

Exc.	V.G.	Good	Fair	Poor
210	145	110	75	50

NOTE: Add $15 premium for nickel.

The Sentinel Deluxe

Has two-piece walnut square-butt grips and fixed sights.

Exc.	V.G.	Good	Fair	Poor
200	130	95	75	50

NOTE: Add $20 premium for nickel.

The Sentinel Snub

Has a 2.375" barrel with round-butt grips.

Exc.	V.G.	Good	Fair	Poor
200	120	100	75	50

NOTE: Add $20 premium for nickel.

Sentinel Steel Frames

This model is like the Mark I sentinels without the Mark I markings. Offered as a combination with cylinders for .22 LR and .22 Win. Mag. Prices are for guns with both cylinders.

Exc.	V.G.	Good	Fair	Poor
260	220	205	80	55

NOTE: Add $25 premium for adjustable sights. Deduct $50 for guns with only one cylinder.

Kit Gun

A 9-shot single-action or double-action revolver with swing-out cylinder for .22 Short, Long, or LR cartridges. Blue finish, aluminum frame, 4.0" barrel, and adjustable sights. Wood round-butt grips.

Exc.	V.G.	Good	Fair	Poor
215	130	110	80	55

Sentinel Mark I

A 9-shot single-action or double-action revolver with swing-out cylinder for .22 Short, Long, or LR cartridges. Steel frame, and fixed sights. Available with blue and nickel finishes in 2", 3", and 4" barrels. Adjustable sights available on 3" and 4" barreled guns only. Wood square-butt grips.

Exc.	V.G.	Good	Fair	Poor
225	165	120	80	55

NOTE: Add $25 premium for adjustable sights. Add $25 for nickel.

Sentinel Mark IV

Like the Mark I above except in .22 Magnum.

Exc.	V.G.	Good	Fair	Poor
235	175	130	80	55

NOTE: Add $25 premium for nickel. $25 premium for adjustable sights.

Sentinel Mark II

A .357 Magnum single-action or double-action 6-shot revolver with swing-out cylinder. Blue finish, steel frame, fixed sights. Produced by Dan Wesson for High Standard Sold 1974 through 1975.

Exc.	V.G.	Good	Fair	Poor
265	190	150	90	60

Sentinel Mark III

Like the Mark II above except with adjustable sights. Sold 1974 through 1975.

Exc.	V.G.	Good	Fair	Poor
300	205	165	90	60

Camp Gun

A nine-shot single-action or double-action revolver with swing-out cylinder for .22 Short, Long, or LR cartridges or for.22 mag. Also available as a combination with both cylinders. Blue finished steel frame, adjustable sights.

Exc.	V.G.	Good	Fair	Poor
220	160	120	80	55

NOTE: Add $50 premium for combination with both cylinders.

Power Plus

A five-shot single-action or double-action revolver with swing-out cylinder for .38 Special cartridges. Blue finished steel frame. Only 177 guns produced. "Serial numbers between PG 1010 and PG 1273.

Exc.	V.G.	Good	Fair	Poor
550	375	250	110	70

Crusader

A .44 Magnum or .45 Colt caliber double-action swing-out cylinder revolver with a unique geared action. Adjustable sights. 6-shot cylinder. The first 51 guns had the long barrels, special engraving, a gold crusader figure on the side plate, and an anniversary rollmark to commemorate High Standard's 50th anniversary.

Exc.	V.G.	Good	Fair	Poor
1350	900	700	—	—

NOTE: Prices for serial numbers 0 through 50 with the 8.375" barrels.

Exc.	V.G.	Good	Fair	Poor
725	475	380	—	—

NOTE: Prices for serial numbers 51 through 500 with the 6.5" barrels.

WESTERN-STYLE REVOLVERS

The Western-style revolvers begin with the W-100 design series and continue through the W-106 design series. Later steel-framed Sentinels carry no design series markings. The changes of design series designations indicate design changes to the guns. The design series designations and the associated catalog numbers which are listed are the best estimates at the time of publication.

High Standard private labeled the aluminum-framed Western-style revolvers for both Sears and Western Auto.

Double Nine with Aluminum Frame

A 9-shot single-action or double-action revolver for .22 Short, Long, or LR cartridges for all aluminum frame guns. One model has grip straps and trigger guard with gold plating contrasting with the blue frame.

Exc.	V.G.	Good	Fair	Poor
200	135	100	80	55

NOTE: Add Add $25 premium for nickel.

Double Nines with Steel Frame

Available as .22 S / L / LR, .22 mag, or a combination with both cylinders.

Exc.	V.G.	Good	Fair	Poor
260	180	130	90	60

NOTE: Add $45 premium for combination models $20 premium for nickel.

Longhorn

A 9-shot single-action or double-action revolver for .22 Short, Long, or LR cartridges for all aluminum frame guns. Blue finish, fixed sights, and square-butt grips. One model has grip straps and trigger guard with gold plating contrasting with the blue frame. A Sears version exists.

Exc.	V.G.	Good	Fair	Poor
190	150	125	95	75

Longhorns with Steel Frame

Guns available as .22 S / L / LR, .22 mag., or a combination with both cylinders.

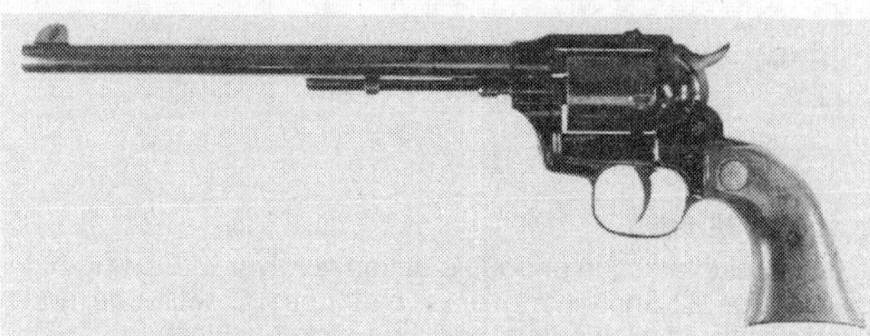

Exc.	V.G.	Good	Fair	Poor
240	170	125	100	75

NOTE: Add $45 premium for combination models, and a $25 premium for adjustable sights.

Marshall

A nine-shot single-action or double-action revolver for .22 Short, Long, or LR cartridges. Blue finish. Aluminum frame, 5.5" barrel, fixed sights and square-butt stag style plastic grips. Offered in a special promotion package with a holster, trigger lock and spray can of G-96 gun scrubber. Price is for gun only. Add $40 premium if box, papers and accessories are present and in excellent condition.

Exc.	V.G.	Good	Fair	Poor
200	135	110	80	55

Posse

A nine-shot single-action or double-action revolver for .22 Short, Long, or LR cartridges. Blue finish with brass colored grip straps and trigger guard. Aluminum frame, 3.5" barrel, fixed sights and square-butt walnut grips.

Exc.	V.G.	Good	Fair	Poor
200	140	90	70	55

Natchez

A 9-shot single-action or double-action revolver for .22 Short, Long, or LR cartridges. Aluminum frame, 4.5" barrel, fixed sights and bird's-head-style ivory-colored plastic grips.

Pistol Serial Numbers by Date

By John Stimson©

Year	Regular Serial Numbers	Year	Regular Serial Numbers	Year	Regular Serial Numbers	Year	Regular Serial Numbers
1932	5102	1943	115423	1954	475186	1965	1507541
1933	6567	1944	135659	1955	508613	1966	1610707
1934	8313	1945	145817	1956	652405	1967	1853513
1935	11651	1946	174194	1957	776129	1968	2030404
1936	18751	1947	233402	1958	913111	1969	2172356
1937	30026	1948	301349	1959	1044802	1970	2232503
1938	39430	1949	325953	1960	1147641	1971	2282293
1939	50619	1950	335693	1961	1224652	1972	2356207
1940	70715	1951	356899	1962	1285049	1973	2424175
1941	91986	1952	408862	1963	1353764		
1942	104520	1953	442984	1964	1418870		

Year	Regular Serial Numbers	G prefix 5-digit	G prefix 6-digit	ML prefix 5-digit	MLG prefix 5-digit	SH prefix 5-digit
1974	2469497 3000000 (1)					
1975	2500810 (2)	G 01001 (4) G 04566		ML 01001 (9) ML 06747		
1976	2500811 (3)	G 13757		ML 23056 (10)		
1977		G 18298 (5)	G 160000 (8) G 162590	EH 0001 (11) ML 25000 (12) ML 29708 (13)		
1978		G 19299 to G 19319 (6) & G 20000 to G 20223 (7)		ML 29708 (14) ML 29721 & ML 30000 (15) ML 41270		
1979				ML 63483		
1980				ML 81629	MLG 20224 MLG 20408 (18)	
1981				ML 86641 (16) ML 90000 (17)		SH 10001 (19) SH 18446
1982						SH 25964
1983						SH 31558
1984						SH 34034 (20)

(1) 3000000. This 9211 Victor shipped 1 March 1974

(2) Last gun in regular series shipping in 1975. This 9247 Supermatic Trophy shipped 29 August 1975

(3) Last serial number in regular series excluding the special Victory S/N 2000000. This 9329 Double Nine shipped 26 October 1976

(4) First G prefix guns to assembly 8 July 1975, packed 14 July 1975, shipments began 21 July 1975

(5) Last? Leisure Group G prefix 12 August 1977

(6) G 19299 — G 19319 are all 9201 Sport Kings 20 guns all shipped March 1978

(7) First High Standard Inc.: G20000-G20105 (103 guns) are all 9244 Supermatic Citations

G20,106-G20223 (116 guns) are all 9201 Sport Kings. All guns shipped March, April and May 1978

(8) G 6-digit are all 9200 or 9201 Sport Kings. Note right most digit is always a zero so the serial number increments by 10's not 1's

(9) First ML prefix serial number. To production 22 July 1975, packed 25 July 1975, shipped 25 July 1975. Note records shot ML prefix from ML 01001 to ML 01099 and ML prefix from ML 10000 on. This needs to be verified by observation of actual guns.

(10) Last Hamden ML prefix 14 December 1976

(11) EH 00001 9217. First East Hartford Gun 16 June 1977

(12) First East Hartford ML prefix pistol. First shipments of ML prefix guns 17 June 1977

(13) Last Leisure Grup ML prefix 12 December 1977

(14) First pistols with ML prefix made for High Standard Inc. Mixed production dates between 2 February 1978 and 9 November 1978 with one gun manufactured 16 February 1980

(15) First pistols with ML prefix made for High Standard Inc. 21 March 1978

(16) Last regular ML prefix gun 15 September 1981

(17) Gun is a single with no other listed on the page

(18) MLG prefix are all 9259 Sport Kings. 123 guns. All shipped May 1980

(19) First SH serial number shipped 22 May 1981

(20) Last SH gun 25 June 1984. Last observed shipment 28 July 1984. Last SH serial number SH 34075. Frames only SH 34000-SH 34075.

Note overlap with serial numbers of shipped guns. Frames to G. W. Elliott 13 November 1984.

Leisure Group sold High Standard division to High Standard Inc. in 1978

Exc.	V.G.	Good	Fair	Poor
395	290	200	125	60

Hombre

A nine shot single-action or double-action revolver for .22 Short, Long, or LR cartridges. Blue or nickel finish. Aluminum frame, 4" barrel, fixed sights and square-butt walnut grips.

Exc.	V.G.	Good	Fair	Poor
200	130	90	70	50

NOTE: Add $20 premium for nickel.

Durango

A nine-shot single- or double-action revolver for .22 Short, Long, or LR cartridges. Blue or nickel finish. Aluminum or steel frame, 4.5" or 5.5" barrel, fixed or adjustable sights and square-butt walnut grips. Two models have their grip straps and trigger guard with contrasting plating to the blue frame.

Exc.	V.G.	Good	Fair	Poor
200	140	95	70	50

NOTE: Add $20 premium for nickel. Add $25 premium for steel frame and $25 premium for adjustable sights.

The Gun/High Sierra

A 9-shot single- or double-action revolver for .22 Short, Long, or LR cartridges. Also available as a combination model with a second cylinder in .22 Mag. Blued finish with gold plated grip straps and trigger guard. Steel frame, 7" octagonal barrel, fixed or adjustable sights and square-butt walnut grips. This revolver was introduced as "The Gun" in the February 1973 price list and the name was changed to "High Sierra" by November 1973 price list. Note that early "The Gun" had neither "High Sierra" markings nor any other name.

Exc.	V.G.	Good	Fair	Poor
315	220	150	95	60

NOTE: Add $60 premium for presentation case. Add $55 premium for combination models. Add $25 for adjustable sights.

BLACKPOWDER REVOLVERS

These guns were a series of .36 caliber cap-and-ball revolvers that began production in 1974 and ran through 1976. These are reproductions of the Confederate copies of the Colt Model 1851 Navy. Note most Confederate copies of the Colt had round barrels, not octagonal as found on Colts. The frames were made by High Standard and the balance of the parts by Uberti. The guns were assembled and finished by High Standard.

Griswold & Gunnison

Blued finish with a brass frame. Six-shot single-action. Commemorative gun came wtih a pine presentation case and a brass belt plate depicting the Georgia state seal.

Exc.	V.G.	Good
480	235	175

NOTE: Price is for gun in case with accessories. Deduct $100 for gun only in Exc. condition.

Leech & Rigdon

Blued finish with a steel frame. Six-shot single-action. Commemorative gun came with a presentation case and a reproduction of a Civil War belt buckle.

Exc.	V.G.	Good
470	235	175

NOTE: Price is for gun in case with accessories. Deduct $100 for gun only in Exc. condition.

Schneider & Glassick

Blued finish with a steel frame. Six-shot single-action. Commemorative gun came with a presentation case and a modern version of a Confederate "D" guard Bowie knife.

Exc.	V.G.	Good
450	235	175

Bicentennial 1776-1976

Blued finish with a steel frame. Six-shot single-action. Guns came with two versions of presentation case. One case is pine, marked High Standard and the trigger logo is on the lid with a powder flask and silver dollar-sized medallion inside. The other is a brown leatherette covered case with American Bicentennial 1776-1976 and contains a pewter Bicentennial belt buckle.

Exc.	V.G.	Good
450	235	175

Special Presentation Bicentennial

100 guns were available in presentation cases with "US" serial number prefixes. Serial numbers US 11 through US 50 are in walnut presentation cases with purple fitted lining and a pewter Bicentennial belt buckle. The top of the case is marked "Limited Edition / American Bicentennial / 1776 – 1976." The guns are engraved on the frame, cylinder barrel, loading lever, and hammer. Catalog number 9339 has a steel frame with a round barrel and catalog number 9340 has a brass frame with an octagonal barrel.

Exc.	V.G.	Good
900	700	400

HIGH STANDARD SHOTGUNS

High Standard began making shotguns for Sears Roebuck in the late 1940s. In 1960 High Standard began marketing shotguns under its own name and the approximately 200 models in the listings are derived from the High Standard catalogs and price lists of the 1960s and 1970s. Additionally, there are more than 150 catalog numbers not listed that represent models with High Standard markings, but with special roll marking or other features which High Standard produced for several large distributors. A redesign of the shotgun line occurred with new models introduced in 1966. In 1973 High Standard introduced their new "Trophy Line" of shotguns and this marked a change in catalog numbers from the number beginning with the numeral 8 to the number beginning with the numeral 6. At this time the previous catalog numbers were referred to as the "Regular Line." Some Regular Line guns were catalogued in 1973 but this was the last year for them except the Police models. The 12 gauge pumps in the Trophy Line were guns which had interchangeable barrels. Serial numbers began appearing on the High Standard shotguns during mid to late 1967. Beginning about 1958 many of these shotguns had a two-letter date code. These private label guns are NOT listed in this data.

Additionally, there are more than 150 catalog numbers not listed here, which represent models with High Standard markings but with special roll markings or other features which High Standard produced for several large distributors. Many of these distributors specials had their own model names which included: Point Right, Pointer, Birdwing, NATO Pintail, Model 200 (J.C. Penney 12 gauge semi-auto), Sport Deluxe, and others still unknown. These distributor label guns are not listed in this data.

The choke markings used by High Standard are: * Full, ** Modified, *** Improved Cylinder, and **** Skeet Bore. Cylinder Bore has no mark.

SEMI-AUTOMATIC SHOTGUNS

Supermatic Field

Gas-operated semi-automatic shotgun. Blued finish, plain pistol-grip walnut stock and forearm. 4-round magazine capacity. Supermatic Field models were superceded by models in the Supermatic Deluxe group beginning in 1966. The 12 gauge guns have 2-3/4" chambers while the 20 gauge guns have 3" chambers.

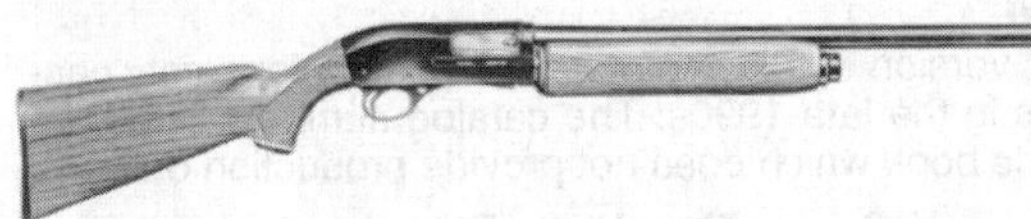

Exc.	V.G.	Good	Fair	Poor
225	175	150	100	75

NOTE: Slight premium for 20 gauge.

Supermatic Special

Like the Supermatic Field except with 27" barrel with six-position click-stop adjustable choke. Supermatic Special models were superceded by models in the Supermatic Deluxe group beginning in 1966. The 12 gauge guns have 2-3/4" chambers

Exc.	V.G.	Good	Fair	Poor
225	180	150	100	75

Supermatic Deluxe

Gas-operated semi-automatic shotgun. Blued finish, Checkered pistol grip walnut stock and forearm. Four-round magazine capacity. The adjustable choke had 6 click-stop positions. Recoil pad beginning 1966. The 12 gauge guns have 2-3/4" chambers while the 20 gauge guns have 3" chambers.

Exc.	V.G.	Good	Fair	Poor
265	185	150	100	75

NOTE: Add $20 premium for vent rib versions.

Supermatic Citation

Same as Trophy except without ventilated rib. Six click-stop adjustable choke. Catalog number 8220 has a compensator integral with the adjustable choke. The 12 gauge guns have 2-3/4" chambers.

Exc.	V.G.	Good	Fair	Poor
240	195	160	100	75

Supermatic Trophy

Gas-operated semi-automatic shotgun. Blued finish, checkered walnut stock and forend. 4-round magazine capacity. Six click-stop adjustable choke. Catalog number 8230 has a compensator integral with the adjustable choke. The 12 gauge guns have 2-3/4" chambers while the 20 gauge guns have 3" chambers.

Exc.	V.G.	Good	Fair	Poor
250	200	165	100	75

Supermatic Duck

Gas-operated semi-automatic shotgun chambered for 3" magnum and suitable for all 2-3/4" shells. Blued finish. Checkered pistol-grip walnut stock and forearm. Magazine capacity: five 2-3/4" shells, four 3" shells. Recoil pad.

Exc.	V.G.	Good	Fair	Poor
285	195	145	100	75

NOTE: Add $20 premium for vent rib versions.

Supermatic Deer Gun

Like Supermatic Deluxe with rifle sight. Recoil pad. Receiver tapped for peep sight on catalog number 8246. The 12 gauge guns have 2-3/4" chambers.

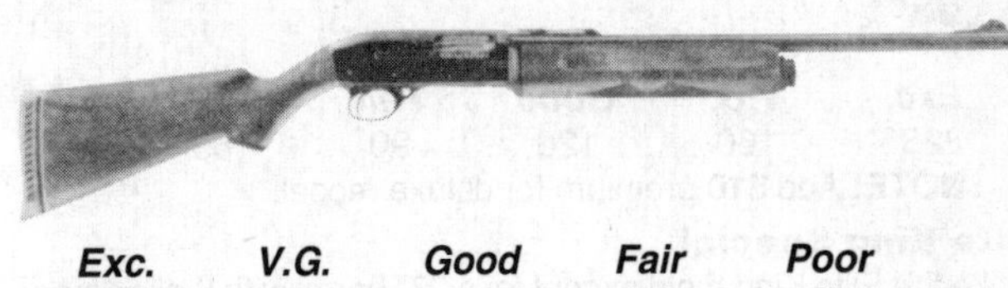

Exc.	V.G.	Good	Fair	Poor
245	180	150	100	75

Supermatic Skeet

Same features as Supermatic Deluxe except select American walnut stock and forearm and no recoil pad. The 12 gauge guns have 2-3/4" chambers while the 20 gauge guns have 3" chambers.

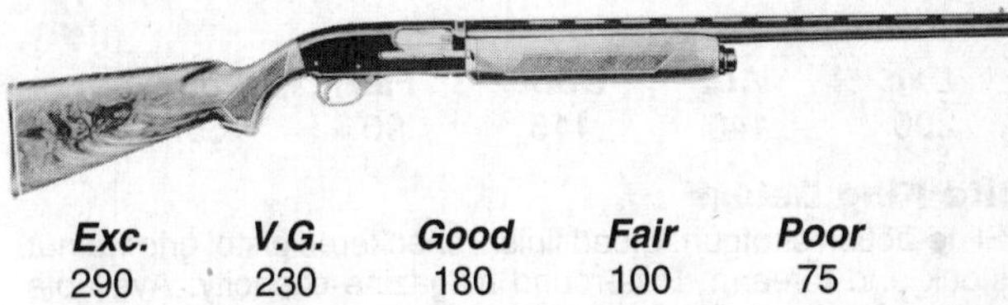

Exc.	V.G.	Good	Fair	Poor
290	230	180	100	75

Supermatic Trap

Same features as Supermatic Deluxe except select American walnut stock and forearm. Recoil pad. Catalog number 8266 is the Executive Trap model with Fajen Monte Carlo stock. The 12 gauge guns have 2-3/4" chambers.

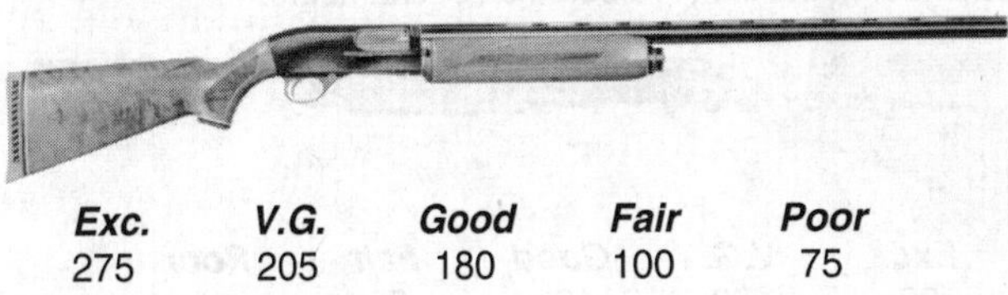

Exc.	V.G.	Good	Fair	Poor
275	205	180	100	75

PUMP SHOTGUNS

Flite King Field

Slide-action shotgun. Blued finish, plain pistol grip walnut stock and forearm. Catalog number 8450, magazine capacity: five 2-1/2" shells, four 3" shells. The 12 gauge guns have 2-3/4" chambers while the 20 gauge guns have 3" chambers.

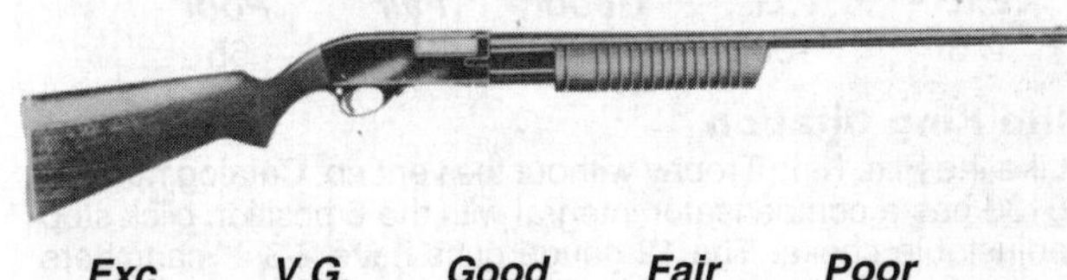

Exc.	V.G.	Good	Fair	Poor
200	140	115	90	65

NOTE: Add 50 percent for .410 bore.

Flite King Brush

Like the Flite King Field except has adjustable rifle sights. Receiver is tapped for the Williams sight and provision exist for sling swivels. Deluxe models have Williams receiver sight, a leather sling with swivels, and a recoil pad. The 12 gauge guns have 2-3/4" chambers.

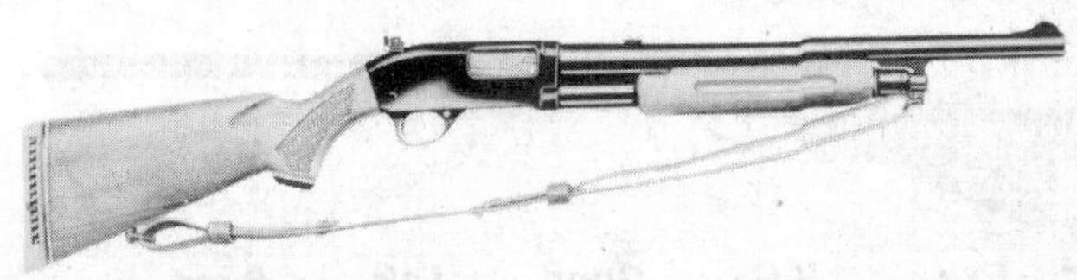

Flite King Brush Deluxe

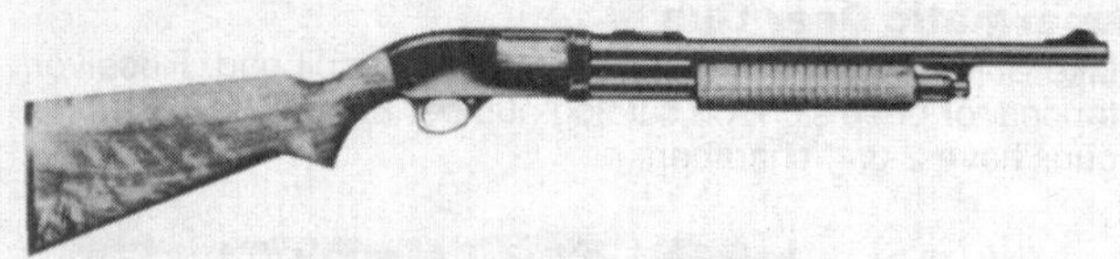

Exc.	V.G.	Good	Fair	Poor
225	160	120	90	65

NOTE: Add $10 premium for deluxe model.

Flite King Special

Like the Flite King Field except for a 27" barrel with 6-click-stop adjustable choke. The 12 gauge guns have 2-3/4" chambers while the 20 gauge guns have 3" chambers.

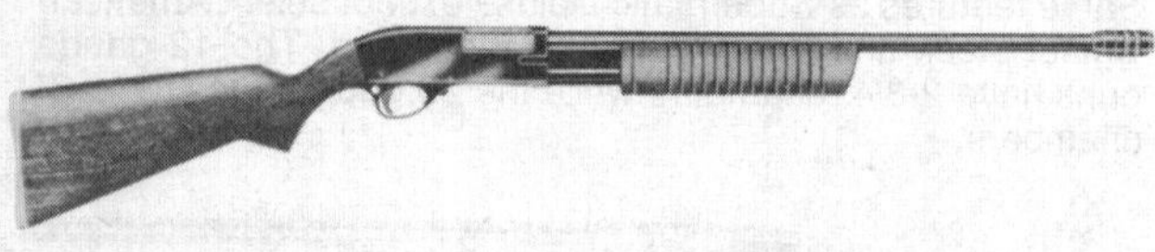

Exc.	V.G.	Good	Fair	Poor
200	140	115	90	65

Flite King Deluxe

Slide-action shotgun. Blued finish, checkered pistol grip walnut stock and forearm. Five-round magazine capacity. Available with and without a vent rib. 8411 and 6411 were the boys "Converta Pump" sold with two stocks: one youth size and one full size. The adjustable choke had six click-stop positions. Recoil pad beginning 1966 except .410 models.The 12 gauge guns have 2-3/4" chambers, the 16 gauge has 2-3/4" chambers, the 20 gauge guns have 3" chambers, the 28 gauge has 2-3/4" chambers, and the .410 bore has 3" chambers.

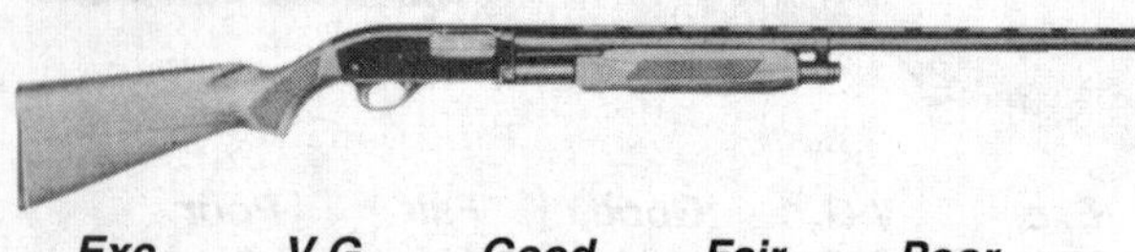

Exc.	V.G.	Good	Fair	Poor
205	150	120	95	65

NOTE: Add $20 for vent rib.

Model 200

An economy 12 gauge pump shotgun sold as part of a promotional package beginning in 1971. The package included the Model 200, a zippered gun case, a plastic trigger lock, and G-96 gun lubricant. Prices are for gun alone. Add $30 for gun with complete promotional package.

Exc.	V.G.	Good	Fair	Poor
175	130	105	90	65

Flite King Citation

Like the Flite King Trophy without the vent rib. Catalog number 8130 has a compensator integral with the 6 position click stop adjustable choke. The 12 gauge guns have 2-3/4" chambers while the 16 gauge guns have 2-3/4" chambers as well.

Exc.	V.G.	Good	Fair	Poor
205	160	120	100	75

Flite King Trophy

Slide-action shotgun. Blued finish, checkered pistol grip walnut stock and forearm. Five-round magazine capacity. Ventilated rib. Catalog number 8140 has a compensator integral with the adjustable choke. The 12 gauge guns have 2-3/4" chambers while the 20 gauge guns have 3" chambers.

Exc.	V.G.	Good	Fair	Poor
215	170	130	100	75

Flite King Skeet

Same features as Flite King Deluxe except select American walnut stock and forearm and no recoil pad. The 12 gauge guns have 2-3/4" chambers, the 20 gauge guns have 3" chambers, the 28 gauge has 2-3/4" chambers, and the .410 bore has 3" chambers.

Exc.	V.G.	Good	Fair	Poor
290	200	150	100	75

Flite King Trap

Same features as Flite King Deluxe except select American walnut stock and forearm. Recoil pad. 8166 is the Executive Trap model with Fajen Monte Carlo stock. Catalog number 6165 is a model with provisions for interchangeable barrels. The 12 gauge guns have 2-3/4" chambers.

Exc.	V.G.	Good	Fair	Poor
275	185	150	100	75

NOTE: Add $25 for Fajen Monte Carlo stock.

BOLT-ACTION

Model 514

The Sears version of this shotgun was recalled for safety considerations in the late 1990s. The catalog numbers listed are from a parts book which does not provide production dates.

Exc.	V.G.	Good	Fair	Poor
135	85	60	—	—

POLICE SHOTGUNS

Semi-Automatic

A gas-operated semi-automatic 12 gauge shotgun. Plain oiled pistol grip walnut stock and forearm. Magazine capacity is four. Recoil pad.

Exc.	V.G.	Good	Fair	Poor
250	170	130	100	75

Model 10-A

A gas-operated semi-automatic 12 gauge shotgun in bullpup configuration with pistol grip. Integral carrying handle and integral flashlight on top of gun. Magazine capacity is four.

Exc.	V.G.	Good	Fair	Poor
775	625	475	325	225

Model 10-B

A gas-operated semi-automatic 12 gauge shotgun in bullpup configuration with pistol grip. Fitted with a integral folding carrying handle and mounting provisions for a flashlight. Magazine capacity is four. Carrying case catalog number 50284 and attachable flashlight catalog number 50285 sold optionally.

Exc.	V.G.	Good	Fair	Poor
695	595	450	350	250

NOTE: Prices are for gun without flashlight. Add $125 if gun has a flashlight.

Pump

A slide-action 12 gauge shotgun. Plain pistol-grip oiled walnut stock and forearm—changed from walnut to stained and lacquered birch in the mid 1970s. 8111/8113 magazine capacity six. 8104/8129 magazine capacity five. A 1963 flyer mentions the #8105 Flite King Brush 20" and the #8107 Flite King Deluxe 20" as riot guns. The data on the #8105 and #8107 is listed under Flite King Brush.

Exc.	V.G.	Good	Fair	Poor
230	160	125	100	75

IMPORTED SHOTGUNS

Supermatic Shadow Automatic

A gas-operated semi-automatic shotgun in 12 and 20 gauge, interchangeable barrels. Checkered walnut stock and forearm. Special "airflow" rib. Imported from Nikko in Japan.

Exc.	V.G.	Good	Fair	Poor
395	280	200	130	100

Supermatic Shadow Indy Over-and-Under

A boxlock over-and-under 12 gauge shotgun with selective auto ejectors and single trigger. Receiver is fully engraved. Skipline checkered walnut stock with pistol grip. Ventilated forearm. Recoil pad. Special "airflow" rib. Imported from Nikko in Japan.

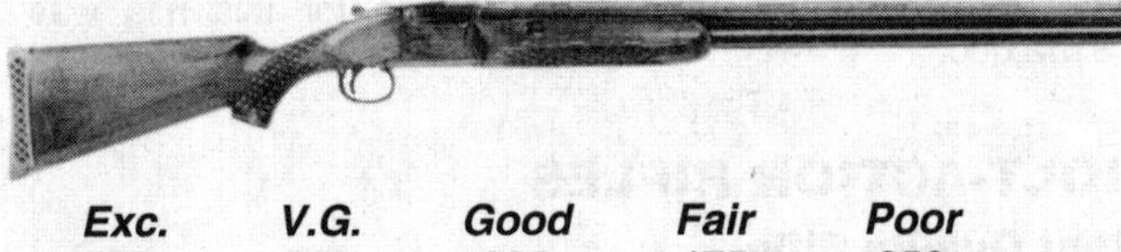

Exc.	V.G.	Good	Fair	Poor
860	730	625	475	350

Supermatic Shadow Seven Over-and-Under

Like the Shadow Indy but with a standard size vent rib, conventional forearm, no recoil pad, standard checkering, and less engraving. Imported from Nikko in Japan.

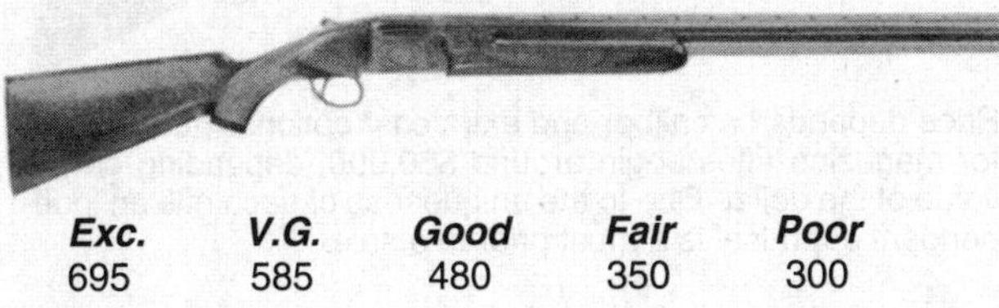

Exc.	V.G.	Good	Fair	Poor
695	585	480	350	300

RIFLES

RIMFIRE PUMP

Sport King/Flite King

A .22 caliber slide-action rifle capable of using S / L / LR ammunition interchangeably. 24" barrel, open sights, and a tubular magazine. Magazine capacity 21 S, 17 L or 15 LR. Monte

Exc.	V.G.	Good	Fair	Poor
175	110	80	65	45

RIMFIRE SEMI-AUTO

Sport King Field

A .22 caliber semi-auto rifle capable of using S / L / LR ammunition interchangeably. 22.25" barrel, open sights, and a tubular magazine. Magazine capacity 21 S, 17 L, or 15 LR. Walnut stock.

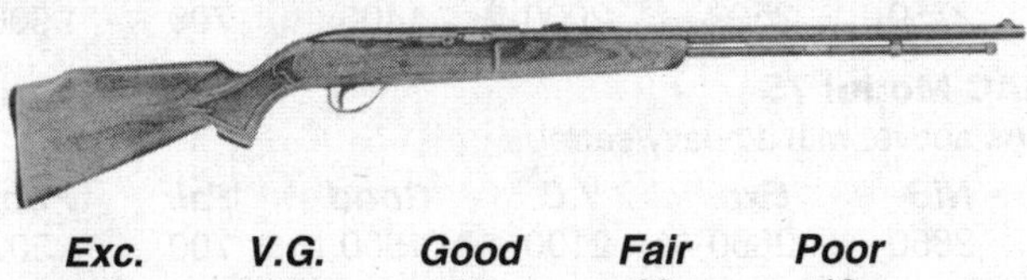

Exc.	V.G.	Good	Fair	Poor
165	95	70	60	40

Sport King Special

Like the Sport King Field except Monte Carlo walnut stock with pistol grip.

Exc.	V.G.	Good	Fair	Poor
185	130	100	60	40

Sport King Deluxe/Sport King

The Sport King Special with a new name. Catalog number 6005 is also the same gun but called just Sport King. A promotional package was offered that included the Sport King rifle, a zippered gun case, a plastic trigger lock, and G-96 gun lubricant. This package was catalog number 8007.

Exc.	V.G.	Good	Fair	Poor
215	145	110	80	50

NOTE: Add a 10 percent premium for complete 8007 package in original box.

Sport King Carbine

A .22 carbine semi-automatic rifle capable of using S / L / LR ammunition interchangeably. 18.25" barrel, open sights, and a tubular magazine. Magazine capacity 17 S, 14 L, or 12 LR. Straight grip walnut stock with barrel band and sling.

Exc.	V.G.	Good	Fair	Poor
195	145	110	80	50

CENTERFIRE

Hi-Power Field Grade

A .270 or .30-06 caliber bolt-action rifle with a 22" barrel, open sights and a 4-shot magazine. Blued with a walnut stock.

Exc.	V.G.	Good	Fair	Poor
350	265	225	150	100

Hi-Power Deluxe

Like the Field Grade except has a Monte Carlo-style stock.

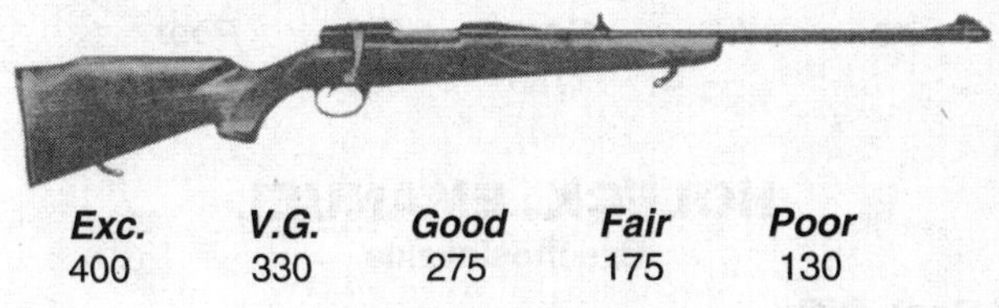

Exc.	V.G.	Good	Fair	Poor
400	330	275	175	130

HILL, W.J.

Birmingham, England

Hill's Self-Extracting Revolver

A .32 caliber double-action folding trigger revolver with a 3.75" barrel and 6-shot cylinder. Marked "Hill's Patent Self Extractor." Blued with walnut grips.

Exc.	V.G.	Good	Fair	Poor
—	900	400	250	150

HILLIARD, D. H.

Cornish, New Hampshire

Under Hammer Pistol

A .34 caliber under hammer percussion pistol with varying barrel lengths. Blued with walnut grips. Active 1842 to 1877.

Exc.	V.G.	Good	Fair	Poor
—	—	800	350	200

HINO-KOMURA

Tokyo, Japan

A 7.65mm or 8mm Nambu semi-automatic pistol manufactured in limited quantities between 1905 and 1912. The operation of this pistol involves pulling the muzzle forward until the slide engages a catch on the trigger assembly. Pulling the trigger at this point allows the barrel to move back and engage the cartridge nose into the chamber. Squeezing the grip safety then allows the barrel to slam back into the fixed firing pin on the breechblock. Prospective purchasers are advised to secure a qualified appraisal prior to acquisition.

Exc.	V.G.	Good	Fair	Poor
3500	3250	2750	2000	1000

HODGKINS, D. C. & SONS

Macon, Georgia

SEE—Bilharz, Hall & Co.

HOFER, P.

Feriach, Austria

A gunmaker specializing in double-barrel rifles made strictly to custom order. Prospective purchasers should secure a qualified appraisal prior to acquisition.

HOFFMAN, LOUIS

Vicksburg, Mississippi

Pocket Pistol

A .41 caliber percussion pocket pistol with a 3" barrel, German silver mounts and walnut stock. Active 1857 to 1886.

Exc.	*V.G.*	*Good*	*Fair*	*Poor*
—	—	750	450	200

HOLDEN, C. B.

Worcester, Massachusetts

Open Frame Rifle

A .44 rimfire single-shot rifle with a 28" barrel, open sights, silver plated bronze frame and walnut stock. The barrel marked "C.B. Holden Worcester-Mass." Produced in limited quantities during the mid-1860s.

Exc.	*V.G.*	*Good*	*Fair*	*Poor*
—	—	1750	600	300

HOLECK, EMANUEL

Czechoslovakia

Holeck Rifle

Chambered for the .276 cartridge this semi-automatic rifle was submitted for testing for U.S. military trials in the 1920s. Barrel length is 21.5" with upper portion slotted for operating handle. Rotating dial at barrel band. Rarely encountered.

Exc.	*V.G.*	*Good*	*Fair*	*Poor*
3900	—	—	—	—

NOTE: Thanks to Jim Supica for the research found in his *Old Town Station Dispatch,* in which one of these rifles was offered for sale.

HOLLAND & HOLLAND, LTD.

London, England

SEE—British Double Guns

Established in 1835, Holland & Holland has manufactured a wide variety of shotguns and rifles during its existence. The greater part of these arms were made to custom order and, therefore, prospective purchasers are advised to secure a qualified appraisal prior to acquisition.

DOUBLE RIFLES

No. 2 Grade Double Rifle

A sidelock double-barrel rifle produced in a variety of calibers with 24" barrels, double triggers, automatic ejectors and express sights. Obsolete cartridges could be worth less.

Exc.	*V.G.*	*Good*	*Fair*	*Poor*
15000	12500	8500	7000	4000

Royal Side-by-Side Rifle

Price depends on caliber.

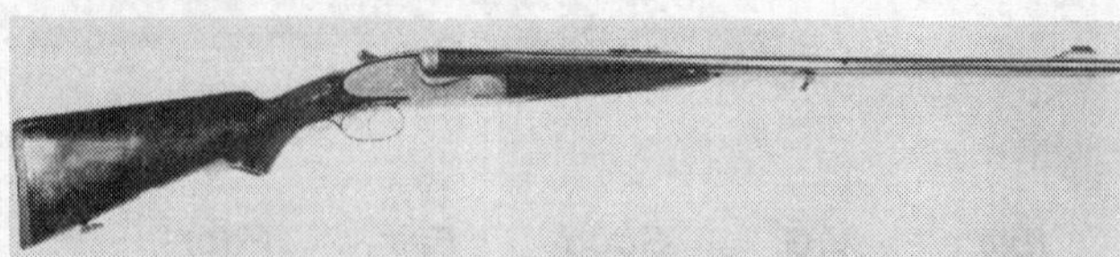

Prices start at $90,000 and go to $115,000 for .600 Nitro Express. Each rifle is unique. An independent appraisal is a must for this gun.

H&H .700 Bore Side-by-Side Rifle

A .700 Holland & Holland double-barrel rifle with a weight of approximately 18 lbs. Currently manufactured. Because of the uniqueness of the piece, buyers should seek qualified appraisal. The last known quoted retail price for this rifle was $152,000.

BOLT-ACTION RIFLES

Best Quality Rifle

A bolt-action rifle produced in calibers up to .375 Holland & Holland with a 24" barrel, express sights and 4-shot magazine.

Price depends on caliber and extra cost options. Retail prices for magazine rifles begin around $30,000, depending on the value of the dollar. Due to the uniqueness of each rifle an independent appraisal is a must prior to a sale.

HOLLIS & SONS

SEE—English Military Firearms

HOLLOWAY ARMS CO.

Ft. Worth, Texas

HAC Model 7

A 7.62x54mm semi-automatic rifle with a 20" barrel, adjustable sights, integral telescope mount and 20-shot magazine. Black anodized finish with folding stock. No longer in production.

NIB	*Exc.*	*V.G.*	*Good*	*Fair*	*Poor*
2500	2000	1750	1200	600	500

HAC Model 7C

As above, with a 16" barrel.

NIB	*Exc.*	*V.G.*	*Good*	*Fair*	*Poor*
2750	2500	2000	1400	700	500

HAC Model 7S

As above, with a heavy barrel.

NIB	*Exc.*	*V.G.*	*Good*	*Fair*	*Poor*
2850	2650	2100	1500	700	500

HOLMES FIREARMS

Wheeler, Arkansas

MP-22

A .22 caliber semi-automatic pistol with a 6" barrel and alloy receiver. Anodized black finish with a walnut grip. Manufactured in 1985.

NIB	*Exc.*	*V.G.*	*Good*	*Fair*	*Poor*
425	325	250	200	150	100

MP-83

Similar to the above, but in 9mm or .45 caliber. Manufactured in 1985.

NIB	Exc.	V.G.	Good	Fair	Poor
550	425	325	250	200	125

NOTE: Several of the Holmes pistols have been declared machine guns by the BATF because of their easy conversion to full automatic. Make sure before purchase that a Class III license is not required.

HOOD F. A. CO.

Norwich, Connecticut

A manufacturer of spur trigger .22 or .32 caliber revolvers with varying length barrels and finishes. Many of these revolvers are found stamped only with trade names. This type of handgun is often referred to as a suicide special to denote its poor quality and lack of reliability.

Exc.	V.G.	Good	Fair	Poor
—	200	100	75	50

HOPKINS & ALLEN

Norwich, Connecticut

***ALSO SEE*—Bacon Arms Co. & Merwin Hulbert & Co.**

Established in 1868, this company produced a variety of spur trigger revolvers in .22, .32, .38, or .41 caliber often marked with trade names such as: Acme, Blue Jacket, Captain Jack, Chichester, Defender, Dictator, Hopkins & Allen, Imperial Arms Co., Monarch, Mountain Eagle, Ranger, Tower's Police Safety, Universal and XL.

Some of these revolvers are hinged-frame, double-action break-opens with round-ribbed barrels of various lengths. Blued or nickel-plated, with checkered plastic grips.

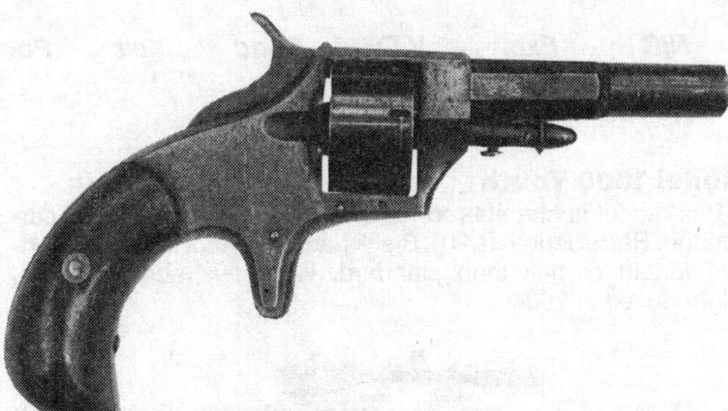

Courtesy Milwaukee Public Museum, Milwaukee, Wisconsin

Exc.	V.G.	Good	Fair	Poor
—	—	400	175	75

Dictator

A .36 caliber percussion or .38 rimfire single-action revolver with a 4" barrel and 5-shot cylinder. Blued with walnut grips. The barrel marked "Dictator." Approximately 6,000 percussion revolvers were made and 5,000 rimfire.

Exc.	V.G.	Good	Fair	Poor
—	—	850	375	100

Falling Block Rifle

A .22 to .38-55 caliber single-shot rifle with a 24", 26", or 28" octagonal barrel. Blued with a walnut stock. Manufactured between 1888 and 1892.

Exc.	V.G.	Good	Fair	Poor
—	900	400	200	100

Schuetzen Rifle

A .22 or .25-20 caliber single-shot rifle with a 26" octagonal barrel, double-set trigger and a Schuetzen-type buttplate. Blued with a walnut stock.

Exc.	V.G.	Good	Fair	Poor
—	2250	950	500	200

Navy Revolver

A .38 caliber rimfire single-action revolver with a 6.5" barrel marked, "Hopkins & Allen Mfg. Co., Pat. Mar. 28, 71, Apr. 27, 75" and a 6-shot cylinder. The top strap marked "XL Navy." Blued or nickel-plated with walnut grips. Several hundred were made between 1878 and 1882.

Exc.	V.G.	Good	Fair	Poor
—	—	1500	600	175

Army Revolver

As above, in .44 rimfire with a 4.5", 6", or 7.5" barrel. The top strap marked "XL No. 8." Several hundred were manufactured between 1878 and 1882.

Exc.	V.G.	Good	Fair	Poor
—	—	2250	850	350

Derringer

A .22 caliber single-shot pistol with a hinged 1.75" barrel that pivots downwards for loading. Blued or nickel-plated with walnut, ivory, or pearl grips. The frame marked, "Hopkins & Allen Arms Co., Norwich, Conn. U.S.A." Several hundred were manufactured in the 1880s and 1890s.

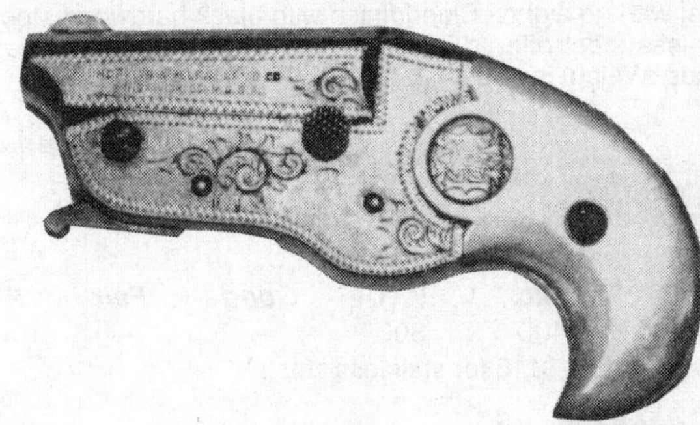

Exc.	V.G.	Good	Fair	Poor
—	2250	850	300	

Double-Barrel Shotguns

Hopkins & Allen also made good quality single and double-barrel shotguns in large numbers. Many were sold under private brand names such as Seminole and King Nitro. Both hammer and hammerless versions were offered. Values vary from $100 to $1,000 depending on model and condition.

HORSLEY, THOMAS

York, England

SEE—British Double Guns

HOTCHKISS

Winchester Arms Co.

New Haven, Connecticut

HOWA MACHINE COMPANY

Japan

This company manufactured bolt-action rifles for Smith & Wesson until 1985 and then for Mossberg in 1986 and 1987. From

1988 to 2000 Howa firearms were imported by Interarms of Alexandria, Virginia. These rifles are now imported by Legacy Sports of Alexandria, Virginia.

Model 1500 Hunter

A .22-250, .223, .243, .270, 7mm Remington Magnum .308, .30-06, .300 Win. Mag., and .338 Winchester Magnum caliber bolt-action sporting rifle with a 22" or 24" barrel and 3- or 5-shot magazine. Blued or stainless steel with a checkered walnut stock. In 2002 this rifle was offered with black polymer stock. Weight is approximately 7.6 lbs.

NIB	Exc.	V.G.	Good	Fair	Poor
575	450	325	225	175	100

NOTE: Add $70 for stainless steel.

Model 1500 Mountain

Introduced in 2004 this bolt-action model is chambered for the .243, .308, or 7mm-08 cartridges. Fitted with a 20" contoured barrel with no sights. Blued finish with black hardwood stock. Stainless steel offered in .308 only. Magazine capacity is 5 rounds. Weight is about 6.4 lbs.

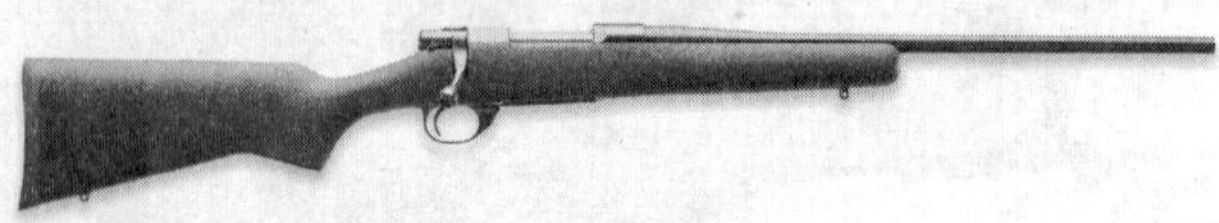

NIB	Exc.	V.G.	Good	Fair	Poor
540	400	300	—	—	—

NOTE: Add $115 for stainless steel.

Model 1500 Trophy

As above, but with more finely figured walnut stocks and checkering. Introduced in 1988. No longer imported.

NIB	Exc.	V.G.	Good	Fair	Poor
500	400	300	250	200	150

Model 1500 Varmint

As above, in .22-250 or .223 caliber with a 24" heavy barrel. Choice of walnut or synthetic stock, in blue or stainless. Weight is about 9.3 lbs. Introduced in 1988.

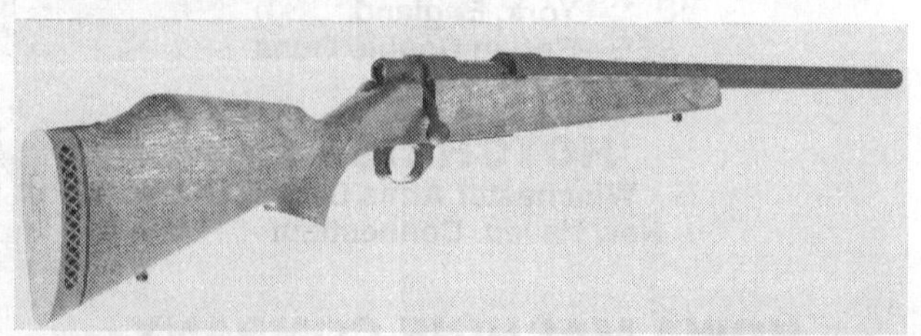

NIB	Exc.	V.G.	Good	Fair	Poor
545	400	300	225	200	150

NOTE: Add $70 for stainless steel and $20 for walnut stock.

Model 1500 Varmint Supreme

This model features a stainless steel barrel chambered for the .223, .22-250, .308, and .243 with no sights. Choice of black synthetic, or laminated stock with Monte Carlo comb.

NIB	Exc.	V.G.	Good	Fair	Poor
710	550	—	—	—	—

NOTE: Add $110 for thumbhole stock.

Model 1500 Lightning Rifle

Introduced in 1993, this model has a black composite checkered stock with schnabel forend. The buttstock is Monte Carlo. Choice of blue or stainless steel. Offered in .223, .22-250, .243, .270, .308, .30-06, 7mm Rem. Mag., .300 and .338 Win. Mag. Weighs about 7.5 lbs.

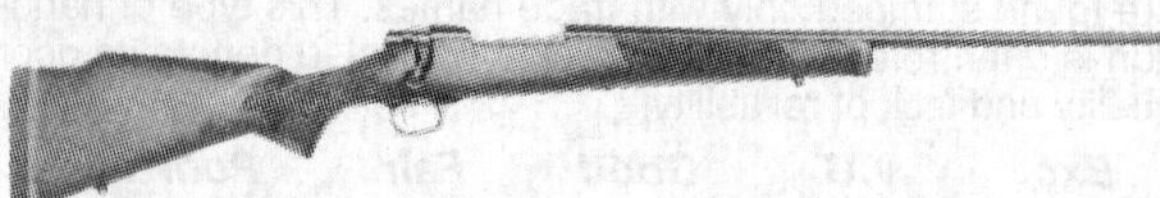

NIB	Exc.	V.G.	Good	Fair	Poor
500	375	275	200	150	150

NOTE: Add $70 for stainless steel.

Model 1500 JRS Classic

Offered in blue or stainless steel with laminated stock, these rifles are chambered for the .223 through .338 Win. Mag calibers. Barrel length is 22" or 24", depending on caliber. Weight is about 8 lbs.

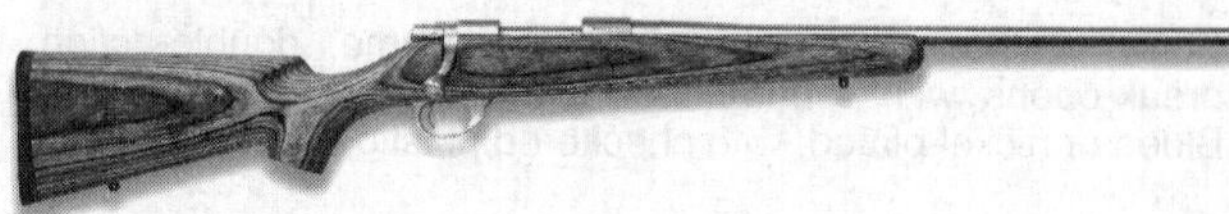

NIB	Exc.	V.G.	Good	Fair	Poor
645	475	—	—	—	—

NOTE: Add $70 for stainless steel.

Model 1500 Youth

This model is chambered for the .243, .308, or 7mm-08 cartridge. Barrel length is 20". Black hardwood stock with 1" shorter length of pull than standard. Weight is about 6.3 lbs. Introduced in 2004.

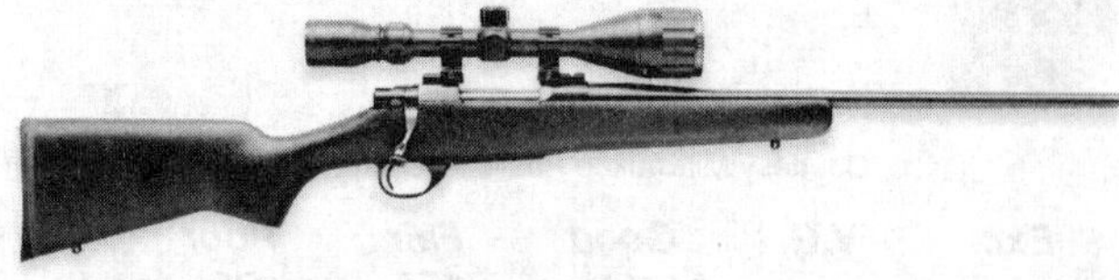

NIB	Exc.	V.G.	Good	Fair	Poor
540	400	—	—	—	—

NOTE: Add $115 for stainless steel .308 version.

Model 1500 Thumbhole Sporter

As above but with thumbhole stock. Weight is about 8.25 lbs.

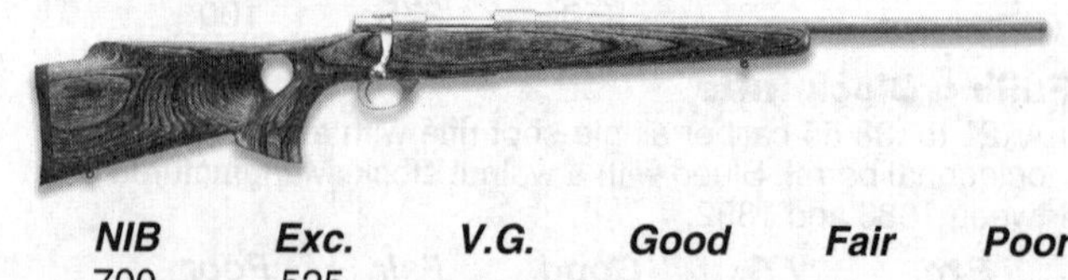

NIB	Exc.	V.G.	Good	Fair	Poor
700	525	—	—	—	—

NOTE: Add $70 for stainless steel.

Model 1500 Custom

Chambered for the .300 WSM or .300 Win. Magnum cartridge this rifle is fitted with a 22" or 24" barrel, depending on caliber.

Polymer or laminated stock. Weight is around 8 lbs. Blued or stainless steel.

NIB	Exc.	V.G.	Good	Fair	Poor
850	700	—	—	—	—

NOTE: Add $70 for stainless steel.

Realtree Camo Rifle

Introduced in 1993, this bolt-action model features a composite stock and a 22" barrel. Both the metal and stock finish are a brown leaf pattern. The receiver is a mono-block system. The floorplate is hinged and the magazine holds 5 rounds. The receiver is drilled and tapped for scope mounts. Fitted with a sling swivel and recoil pad. Offered in .30-06 and .270 calibers. Weighs 8 lbs.

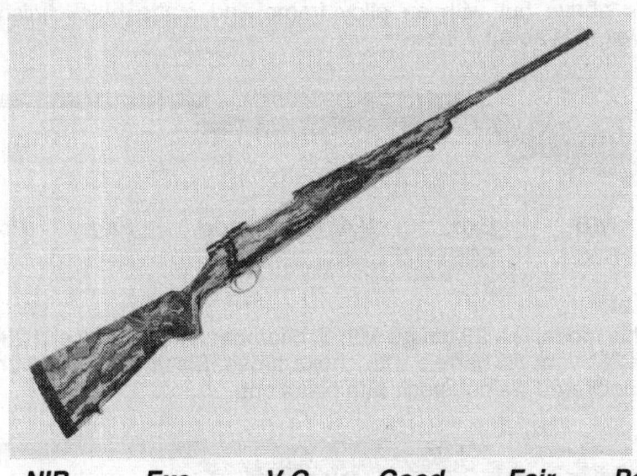

NIB	Exc.	V.G.	Good	Fair	Poor
545	400	300	225	200	150

Texas Safari Rifle

Chambered for the .270 Win. or .300 Win. Magnum cartridge, this rifle is modified by gunsmith Bill Wiseman. Blue Teflon finish and 22" or 24" barrel depending on caliber. Laminated stock. Weight is about 7.8 lbs.

NIB	Exc.	V.G.	Good	Fair	Poor
1500	1200	—	—	—	—

Model 1500 PCS (Police Counter Sniper)

This bolt-action is offered in .308 Winchester and fitted with a 24" heavy barrel. Magazine capacity is 5 rounds. Available in blue or stainless steel and walnut or synthetic stock. Weight is approximately 9.3 lbs.

NIB	Exc.	V.G.	Good	Fair	Poor
450	350	300	250	—	—

HOWARD-WHITNEY

New Haven, Connecticut

SEE—Whitney Arms Co.

HUGLU

Turkey

SIDE-BY-SIDE

Bobwhite

Offered in 12, 20, 28 gauge as well as .410 bore with 26" or 28" barrel with choke tubes. The .410 bore has fixed chokes. Double triggers with no auto ejectors. Manual safety. Box lock receiver with silver finish. Walnut stock with round knob pistol grip and splinter schnabel forend.

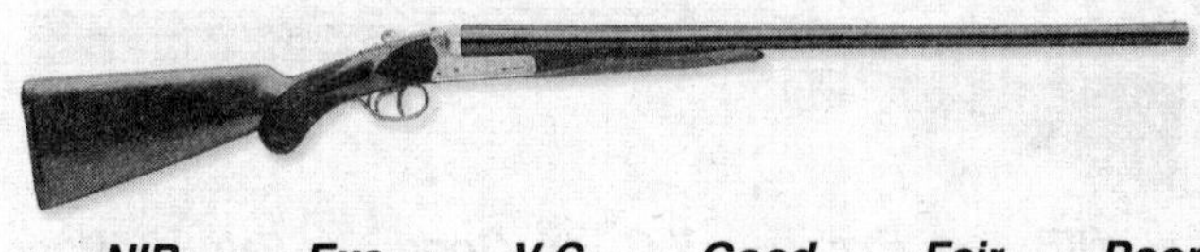

NIB	Exc.	V.G.	Good	Fair	Poor
700	550	—	—	—	—

NOTE: Add $200 for 28 gauge or .410 models.

Ringneck

Similar to the Bobwhite but with single trigger and case colored frame with side plates. Choice of round knob pistol grip or straight grip. Forend is beavertail schnabel.

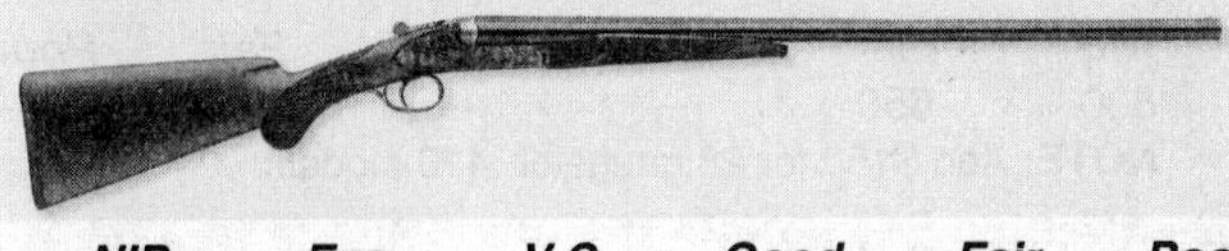

NIB	Exc.	V.G.	Good	Fair	Poor
1000	750	—	—	—	—

NOTE: Add $200 for 28 gauge or .410 models.

OVER-AND-UNDER

Woodcock

This gun is available in 12, 20, or 28 gauge as well as .410 bore. Choice of 26" or 28" vent rib barrels with choke tubes, except for fixed chokes on the .410. Single trigger. No auto ejectors. Manual safety. Receiver finish is case colored. Checkered walnut stock with round knob pistol grip and schnabel forend.

NIB	Exc.	V.G.	Good	Fair	Poor
1050	825	—	—	—	—

NOTE: Add $150 for 28 gauge or .410 models.

Woodcock Deluxe

As above but in 12 gauge with auto ejectors and side plates.

NIB	Exc.	V.G.	Good	Fair	Poor
1200	900	—	—	—	—

Redhead

Available in 12, 20, 28, and .410. Choice of 26" or 28" vent rib barrels with choke tubes, except for .410 with fixed chokes. The 20 gauge is also offered with 24" barrels. Single trigger, no auto ejectors, and manual safety. Boxlock receiver with silver finish. Checkered walnut stock with round knob pistol grip and schnabel forearm.

NIB	Exc.	V.G.	Good	Fair	Poor
800	650	—	—	—	—

NOTE: Add $150 for 28 gauge or .410 models.

Redhead Deluxe

As above but in 12 and 20 gauge only with 26" or 28" barrels. Auto ejectors.

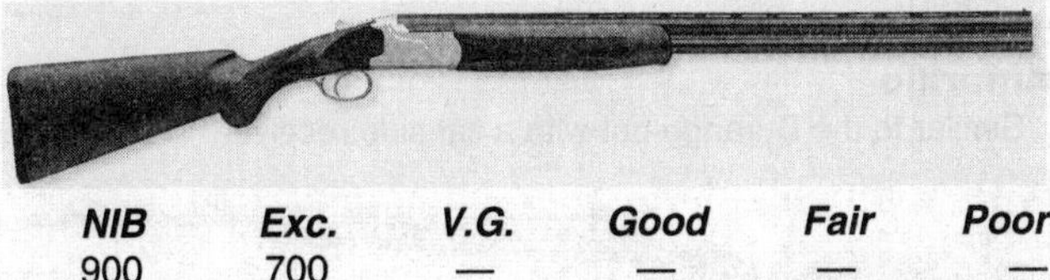

NIB	Exc.	V.G.	Good	Fair	Poor
900	700	—	—	—	—

Mallard

This 12 or 20 gauge gun is fitted with 28" vent rib barrels with choke tubes. Double triggers and no auto ejectors. Silver receiver. Checkered walnut stock with round knob pistol grip and schnabel forend.

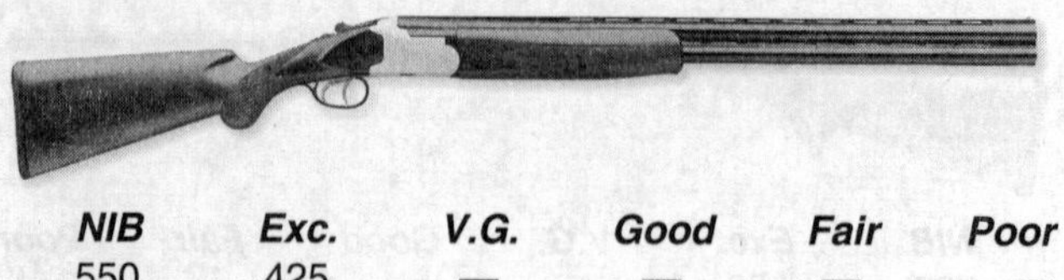

NIB	Exc.	V.G.	Good	Fair	Poor
550	425	—	—	—	—

Canvasback

This gun is available in 12, 20, 28, and .410 bore. Choice of 26" or 28" vent rib barrels with choke tubes, except for the .410 with fixed chokes. Single trigger with no auto ejectors and manual safety. Black boxlock receiver. Checkered walnut stock with round knob pistol grip and schnabel forend.

NIB	Exc.	V.G.	Good	Fair	Poor
800	650	—	—	—	—

NOTE: Add $150 for 28 gauge or .410 models.

Canvasback Deluxe

As above but in 12 and 20 gauge only with auto ejectors.

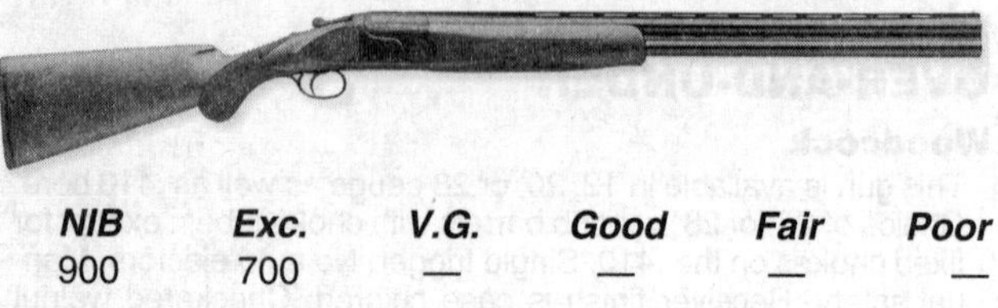

NIB	Exc.	V.G.	Good	Fair	Poor
900	700	—	—	—	—

COWBOY & SINGLE-SHOT

Cottontail

This is a single-barrel shotgun in 12 or 20 gauge as well as .410 bore with choice of 24" or 28" barrels. Modified choke. No auto ejectors. Silver receiver with blued barrel. Checkered walnut stock with pistol grip.

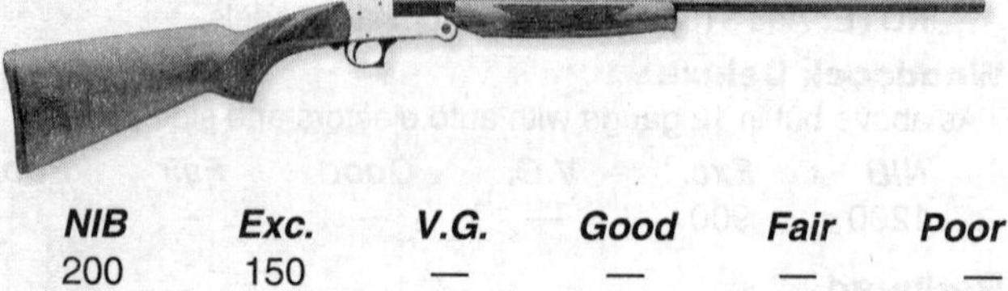

NIB	Exc.	V.G.	Good	Fair	Poor
200	150	—	—	—	—

Durango

This side-by-side shotgun is chambered for the 12 or 20 gauge with single trigger and choke tubes. Barrel lengths are 20". No auto ejectors. The boxlock receiver is case colored. Checkered walnut grips with round knob pistol grip and schnabel forend.

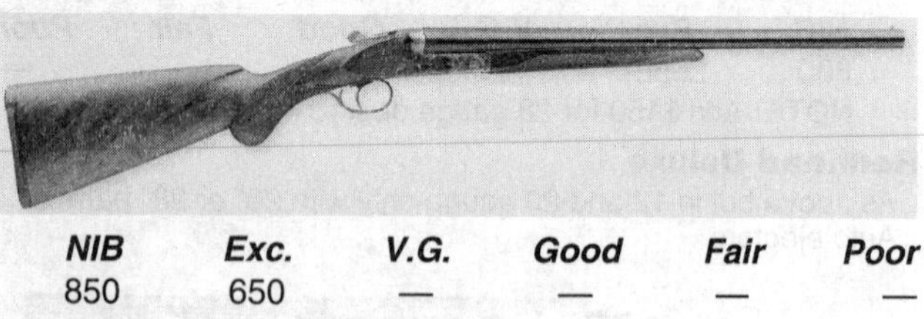

NIB	Exc.	V.G.	Good	Fair	Poor
850	650	—	—	—	—

Amarillo

Similar to the Durango but with a flat-side receiver.

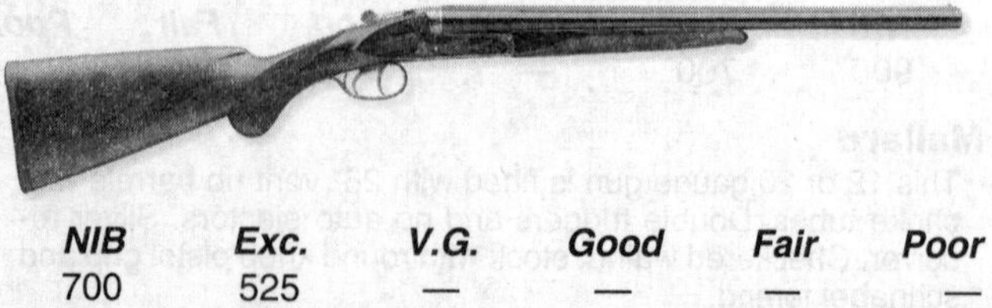

NIB	Exc.	V.G.	Good	Fair	Poor
700	525	—	—	—	—

SEMI-AUTOMATIC

Sharptail

This 12 gauge 3" gun is fitted with a choice of 26" or 28" vent rib barrels with choke tubes. Black receiver. Checkered walnut stock with pistol grip. Weight is about 7.3 lbs.

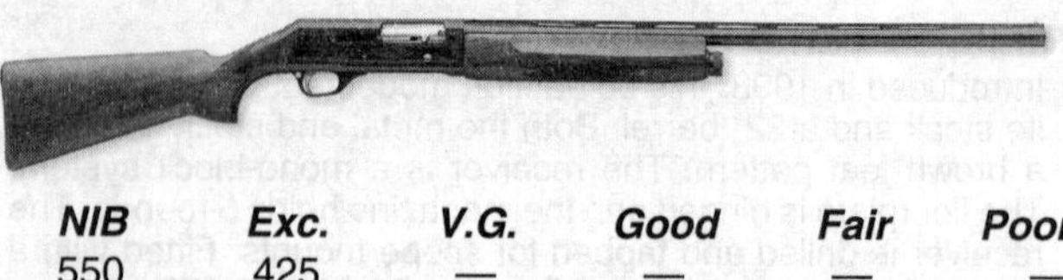

NIB	Exc.	V.G.	Good	Fair	Poor
550	425	—	—	—	—

Canadian

As above but with an alloy frame and matte black finish. Weight is about 7 lbs.

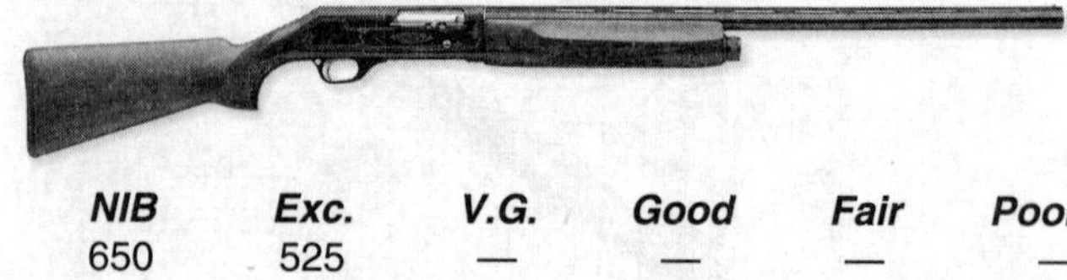

NIB	Exc.	V.G.	Good	Fair	Poor
650	525	—	—	—	—

Teal

This model is a 20 gauge with 3" chambers and a choice of 26" or 28" vent rib barrels with choke tubes. Black alloy receiver. Checkered walnut stock with pistol grip.

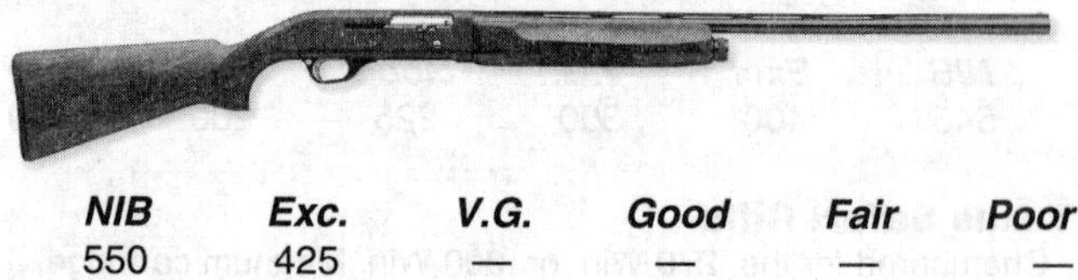

NIB	Exc.	V.G.	Good	Fair	Poor
550	425	—	—	—	—

COMPETITION GUNS

Vandalia Trap

This 12 gauge trap gun is offered with either a single barrel/double barrel combo; single barrel only, or double barrel only. Five choke tubes. Engraved silver receiver. Checkered walnut stock with pistol grip and adjustable comb.

NIB	Exc.	V.G.	Good	Fair	Poor
1900	1400	—	—	—	—

NOTE: For Combo model add $300.

English Sporter

This is a sporting clays model chambered for the 12 gauge shell and fitted with a 30" barrel with ten choke tubes. Black receiver. Adjustable comb with checkered walnut stock with pistol grip.

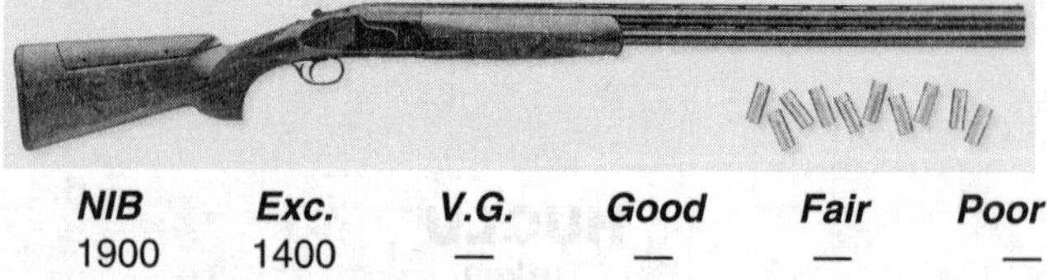

NIB	Exc.	V.G.	Good	Fair	Poor
1900	1400	—	—	—	—

CUSTOM GRADES

Custom Grade II

This is a custom-built side-by-side gun in the customer's choice of gauge. Engraved case colored receiver with side plates. Choice of barrel lengths. Select walnut stock with hand checkering and round knob pistol grip.

NIB	Exc.	V.G.	Good	Fair	Poor
2200	1600	—	—	—	—

Custom Grade IV

This custom-built side-by-side features a silver scroll engraved receiver with side plates. Straight grip stock. Choice of bore and barrel lengths.

NIB	Exc.	V.G.	Good	Fair	Poor
2800	1900	—	—	—	—

Custom Grade IV with Upgrade

This is a over-and-under gun with extra fancy walnut stock and elaborately engraved silver receiver. Choice of gauge and barrel lengths.

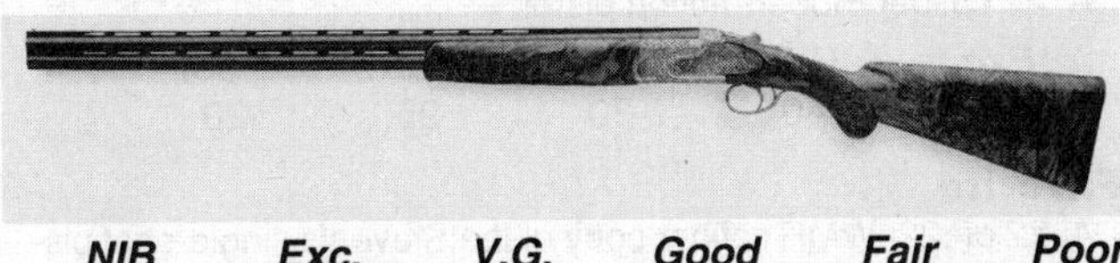

NIB	Exc.	V.G.	Good	Fair	Poor
N/A	—	—	—	—	—

Custom Grade VI

This is the highest grade offered with the finest walnut stock and engraving.

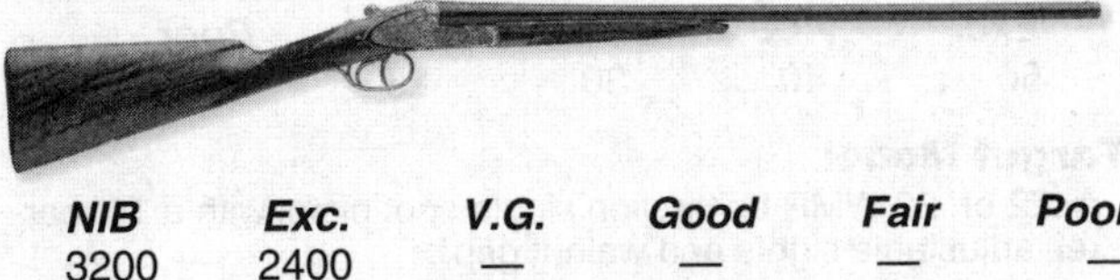

NIB	Exc.	V.G.	Good	Fair	Poor
3200	2400			—	—

HUNGARY

SA-85M

This is pre-ban semi-automatic copy of the AKM rifle. Chambered for the 7.62x39mm cartridge. Fixed or folding stock.

NIB	Exc.	V.G.	Good	Fair	Poor
1800	1600	1200	850	600	500

HUNT

New Haven, Connecticut

SEE—Winchester Repeating Arms Co.

HUNTER ARMS CO.

Fulton, New York

SEE—L. C. Smith

HUSQVARNA

Husqvarna, Sweden

PISTOLS

Model 1907

This pistol is a copy of the FN Browning Model 1903 made for the Swedish Army. It is identical in every way to the FN model. Many were converted to the .380 caliber and imported into the U.S.

Courtesy Orvel Reichert

Exc.	V.G.	Good	Fair	Poor
350	250	200	150	100

NOTE: If converted to .380 caliber reduce values by 50 percent.

Lahti

A 9mm caliber semi-automatic pistol with a 5.5" barrel and 8-shot magazine. Designed by Aino Lahti and adopted as the standard Swedish sidearm in 1940.

Exc.	V.G.	Good	Fair	Poor
425	350	275	225	150

BOLT-ACTION RIFLES

Hi-Power

A bolt-action sporting rifle manufactured in a variety of calibers with a 24" barrel, open sights and beechwood stock. Manufactured between 1946 and 1951.

Exc.	V.G.	Good	Fair	Poor
400	300	275	200	150

Model 1100 Deluxe

As above, with a walnut stock. Manufactured between 1952 and 1956.

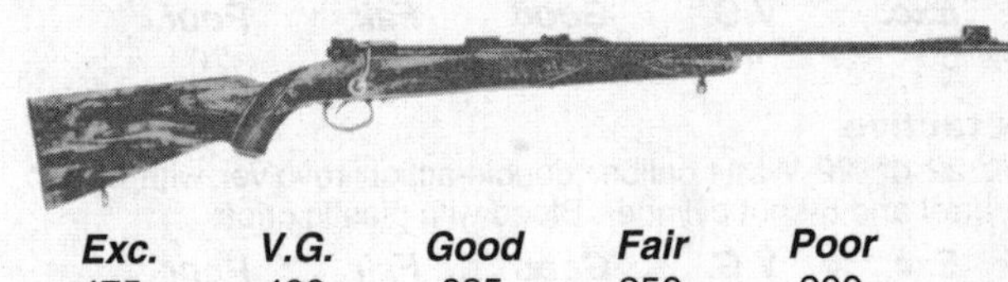

Exc.	V.G.	Good	Fair	Poor
475	400	325	250	200

Model 1000 Super Grade

As above, with a Monte Carlo-style stock. Manufactured between 1952 and 1956.

Exc.	V.G.	Good	Fair	Poor
475	400	325	250	200

Model 3100 Crown Grade

A bolt-action sporting rifle manufactured in a variety of calibers with a 24" barrel, walnut stock with a black composition forend tip and pistol grip cap. Manufactured between 1954 and 1972.

Exc.	V.G.	Good	Fair	Poor
575	475	350	300	200

Model 4100 Lightweight

As above, with a schnabel forend tip. Manufactured between 1954 and 1972.

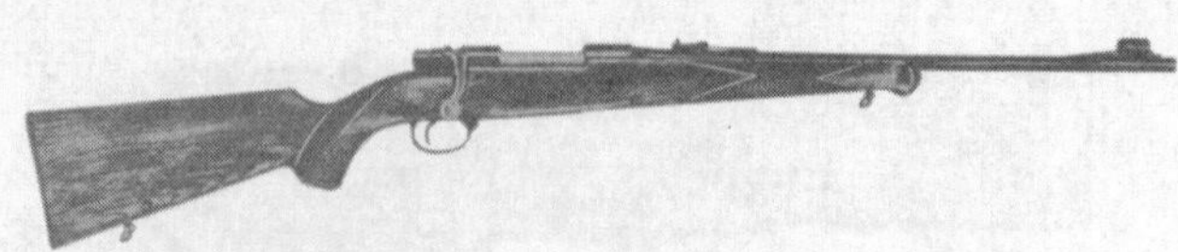

Exc.	V.G.	Good	Fair	Poor
575	475	350	300	200

Model 456

As above, with a full length Mannlicher-style stock. Manufactured between 1959 and 1970.

Exc.	V.G.	Good	Fair	Poor
425	350	300	250	200

Model 6000

The Model 4100 with express folding sights and a finely figured walnut stock. Manufactured between 1968 and 1970.

Exc.	V.G.	Good	Fair	Poor
600	500	400	300	200

Model 9000 Crown Grade

A bolt-action sporting rifle manufactured in a variety of calibers with a 23.5" barrel, open sights, adjustable trigger and walnut stock. Manufactured in 1971 and 1972.

Exc.	V.G.	Good	Fair	Poor
500	425	350	300	250

Model 8000 Imperial Grade

As above, with an engraved magazine floor plate, machine jeweled bolt and finely figured walnut stock. Manufactured in 1971 and 1972.

Exc.	V.G.	Good	Fair	Poor
675	550	475	400	300

HY-HUNTER, INC.

Burbank, California

Chicago Cub

A .22 caliber folding trigger double-action revolver with a 2" barrel and 6-shot cylinder.

Exc.	V.G.	Good	Fair	Poor
50	40	30	25	20

Detective

A .22 or .22 WMR caliber double-action revolver with a 2.5" barrel and 6-shot cylinder. Blued with plastic grips.

Exc.	V.G.	Good	Fair	Poor
65	50	40	30	25

Frontier Six Shooter

A .22 or .22 WMR caliber single-action revolver with a 6-shot cylinder.

Exc.	V.G.	Good	Fair	Poor
75	65	50	40	30

Frontier Six Shooter

As above, in .357 Magnum, .44 Magnum or .45 Colt.

Exc.	V.G.	Good	Fair	Poor
125	100	85	75	50

Maxim

A .25 caliber semi-automatic pistol with a 2" barrel and 5-shot magazine.

Exc.	V.G.	Good	Fair	Poor
75	65	50	40	30

Military

A .22, .32 or .380 caliber double-action semi-automatic pistol with a 4" barrel and 6-shot magazine.

Exc.	V.G.	Good	Fair	Poor
100	80	60	50	40

Stingray

A .25 caliber semi-automatic pistol with a 2.5" barrel and 5-shot magazine.

Exc.	V.G.	Good	Fair	Poor
75	65	50	40	30

Panzer

A .22 caliber semi-automatic pistol with a 4" barrel and 7-shot magazine.

Exc.	V.G.	Good	Fair	Poor
75	65	50	40	30

Stuka

Similar to the above.

Exc.	V.G.	Good	Fair	Poor
75	65	50	40	30

Automatic Derringer

A .22 caliber over-and-under pocket pistol patterned after the Remington Double Derringer.

Exc.	V.G.	Good	Fair	Poor
50	40	30	25	20

Accurate Ace

A .22 caliber Flobert-action pistol.

Exc.	V.G.	Good	Fair	Poor
50	40	30	25	20

Favorite

A .22 or .22 WMR caliber copy of the Steven's single-shot pistol with a 6" barrel and nickel-plated frame.

Exc.	V.G.	Good	Fair	Poor
100	80	70	50	25

Gold Rush Derringer

A .22 caliber spur trigger single-shot pistol with a 2.5" barrel.

Exc.	V.G.	Good	Fair	Poor
50	40	30	25	20

Target Model

A .22 or .22 WMR bolt-action single-shot pistol with a 10" barrel, adjustable sights and walnut grip.

Exc.	V.G.	Good	Fair	Poor
50	40	30	25	20

HYDE & SHATTUCK

Hatfield, Massachusetts

Queen Derringer

A .22 caliber spur trigger single-shot pistol with a 2.5" half octagonal barrel. Blued or nickel-plated with walnut grips. The barrel normally marked "Queen," but sometimes "Hyde & Shattuck." Manufactured between 1876 and 1879.

Exc.	V.G.	Good	Fair	Poor
—	—	450	300	150

HYPER

Jenks, Oklahoma

Single-Shot Rifle

A custom made falling block-action single-shot rifle manufactured in a variety of calibers, barrel lengths, barrel types, and stock styles. Manufactured until 1984.

Exc.	V.G.	Good	Fair	Poor
2500	2000	1750	1450	800

I.G.I.
Itaiguns International
Zingone de Tressano, Italy

Domino SP602

A .22 caliber semi-automatic target pistol with a 6" barrel and 5-shot magazine (that is inserted into the action from the top), adjustable trigger and customized grips.

Exc.	V.G.	Good	Fair	Poor
900	700	600	450	250

Domino OP601

As above, but in .22 short caliber.

Exc.	V.G.	Good	Fair	Poor
900	700	600	450	250

IAB
Industria Armi Bresciane
Brescia, Italy

Imported by Puccinelli & Company of San Anselmo, California, and by Sporting Arms International of Indianola, Mississippi.

S-300

A 12 gauge boxlock single-barrel trap gun with 30" or 32" barrels having a wide ventilated rib and walnut trap-style stock.

Exc.	V.G.	Good	Fair	Poor
1500	1250	1000	850	450

C-300 Combo

A 12 gauge over-and-under boxlock double-barrel shotgun with 30" or 32" barrels, single-selective trigger, automatic ejectors, trap-style walnut stock, accompanied by two extra single barrels.

Exc.	V.G.	Good	Fair	Poor
2750	2250	1850	1500	800

C-300 Super Combo

As above, but more finely finished.

Exc.	V.G.	Good	Fair	Poor
3500	2750	2250	1750	900

IAI-AMERICAN LEGENDS
Houston, Texas

RIFLES

M-888 M1 Carbine

A re-creation of the U.S. M1 Carbine in .30 caliber. Barrel length is 18". Weight is about 5.5 lbs. Uses surplus magazines of 15 to 30 rounds. Comes with 10-round magazine. Options of wooden or metal handguard and walnut or birchwood stock.

NIB	Exc.	V.G.	Good	Fair	Poor
450	350	—	—	—	—

M-333 M1 Garand

Remanufactured to GI specifications. Fitted with 24" barrel and GI wood stock. Eight-round capacity. Parkerized finish. Weight is about 9.5 lbs.

NIB	Exc.	V.G.	Good	Fair	Poor
700	600	—	—	—	—

PISTOLS

M-2000

This is a Government model .45 ACP pistol fitted with a 5" barrel and 7-round magazine. Fixed sights. Wood grips. Parkerized finish. Weight is about 38 oz.

NIB	Exc.	V.G.	Good	Fair	Poor
475	350	—	—	—	—

M-999

Similar to the above model but with rubber-style combat grips, extended slide stop, safety, and magazine release. Fixed sights. Offered with stainless steel slide and blued frame or all stainless steel. Supplied with 7-round magazine. Weight is about 38 oz.

NIB	Exc.	V.G.	Good	Fair	Poor
475	350	—	—	—	—

NOTE: Add $25 for stainless steel frame.

M-777

Same as M-999 but fitted with 4.25" barrel. Weight is about 36 oz.

NIB	Exc.	V.G.	Good	Fair	Poor
475	350	—	—	—	—

NOTE: Add $25 for stainless steel frame.

M-6000

This .45 ACP pistol is fitted with a 5" barrel, plastic grips, extended slide stop, safety, and magazine release. Safety is ambidextrous. Magazine capacity is 8 rounds. Fixed sights. Weight is about 38 oz.

NIB	Exc.	V.G.	Good	Fair	Poor
400	300	—	—	—	—

M-5000

This model is similar to the M-6000 but fitted with a 4.25" barrel. Weight is about 36 oz.

NIB	Exc.	V.G.	Good	Fair	Poor
400	300	—	—	—	—

IAR
San Juan Capistrano, California

An importer of Italian made reproduction pistol and rifles. For a complete listing see ***Uberti.***

IGA
Veranopolis, Brazil

Single-Barrel Shotgun

A 12 or 20 gauge or .410 bore single barrel shotgun with an exposed hammer, 28" barrel and hardwood stock.

NIB	Exc.	V.G.	Good	Fair	Poor
150	90	75	50	40	30

Single-Barrel Shotgun Youth Model

Offered in 20 gauge and .410 bore this model features a 22" barrel and shorter than standard buttstock. Weighs 5 lbs.

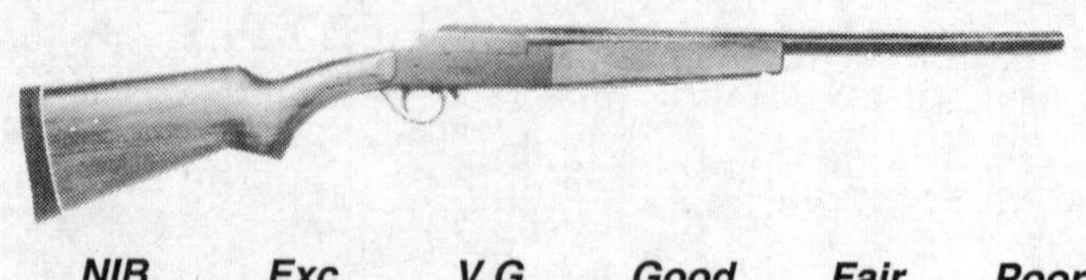

NIB	Exc.	V.G.	Good	Fair	Poor
150	100	80	60	50	35

Coach Gun

A 12 and 20 gauge as well as .410 bore boxlock double-barrel shotgun with 20" barrels, double triggers and extractors. Blued with a hardwood stock.

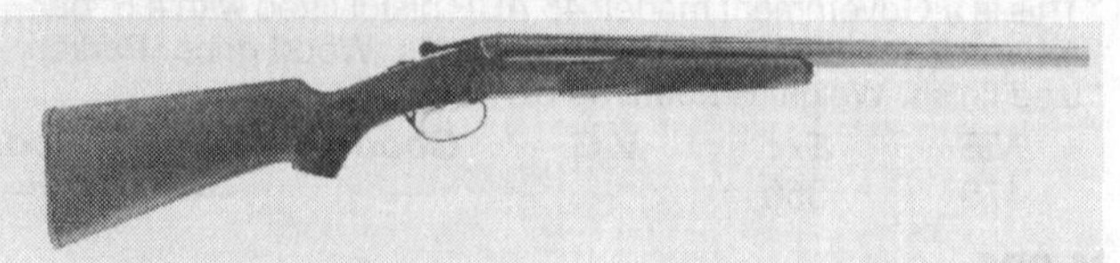

NIB	Exc.	V.G.	Good	Fair	Poor
425	325	250	150	100	75

NOTE: Add $50 for nickel finish. Add $60 for engraved butt stock.

Standard Side-by-Side Uplander Model

Offered in 12, 20, 28 gauge, and .410 bore with 26" and 28" barrels. Checkered hardwood stock with pistol grip or straight grip in 20 gauge only. Weighs 6.75 lbs.

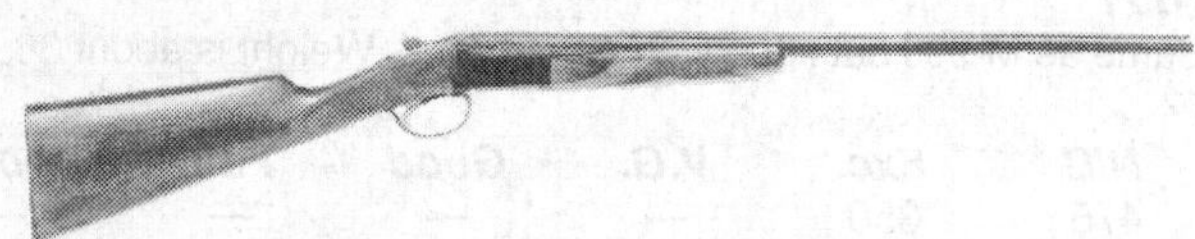

NIB	Exc.	V.G.	Good	Fair	Poor
425	325	250	150	100	75

NOTE: Add $40 for choke tubes.

Uplander Youth Model

Same as above but offered in .410 bore with 24" barrel or 20 gauge with 24" barrels. Shorter length of pull. Recoil pad standard.

NIB	Exc.	V.G.	Good	Fair	Poor
450	325	250	150	100	75

Uplander Supreme

Introduced in 2000 this model features a high grade walnut stock with checkering, single-selective trigger, choke tubes, and automatic ejectors. Offered in 12 and 20 gauge with 26" or 28" barrels. Chambered for 3" shells. Soft rubber recoil pad standard.

NIB	Exc.	V.G.	Good	Fair	Poor
600	450	—	—	—	—

Standard Over-and-Under Condor I

This model is offered in 12 or 20 gauge with 26" or 28" barrels. Fitted with extractors and single trigger. Choke tubes are standard. Checkered hardwood stock with pistol grip and recoil pad. Weighs 8 lbs.

NIB	Exc.	V.G.	Good	Fair	Poor
300	250	225	200	150	100

Condor II

Same as above but with double triggers and plastic buttplate.

NIB	Exc.	V.G.	Good	Fair	Poor
275	225	200	150	100	75

Condor Supreme Deluxe

This model is similar to the standard Condor model but has a high grade walnut stock, hand checkering, recoil pad, single-selective trigger, and automatic ejectors. Offered in 12 and 20 gauge with 26" or 28" vent rib barrels. Chambered for 3" shells. Choke tubes standard. First offered in 2000.

NIB	Exc.	V.G.	Good	Fair	Poor
550	400	—	—	—	—

Deluxe Over-and-Under ERA 2000

Offered in 12 gauge only with 26" or 28" barrels. Fitted with single trigger and extractors. Choke tubes are standard. Barrels are chrome lined and stock is hand checkered.

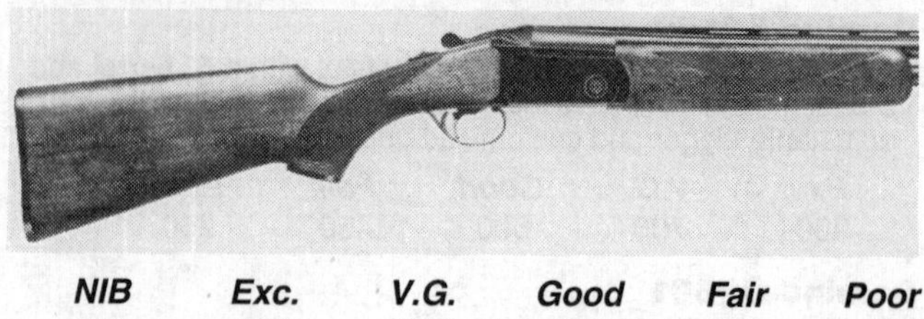

NIB	Exc.	V.G.	Good	Fair	Poor
400	325	275	225	175	125

INDIAN ARMS CORP.

Detroit, Michigan

Indian Arms .380

A .380 caliber semi-automatic pistol with a 3.25" barrel and 6-shot magazine. Made of stainless steel and finished either in the white or blued with walnut grips. Manufactured from 1975 to 1977.

Exc.	V.G.	Good	Fair	Poor
375	300	225	150	100

INDUSTRIA ARMI GALESI

Brescia, Italy

SEE—Galesi

INGLIS, JOHN & COMPANY

Toronto, Canada

NOTE: For history, technical data, descriptions, and prices see the *Standard Catalog of Military Firearms* under Canada, Handguns.

INGRAM

Military Armament Corp.
Atlanta, Georgia

MAC 10

A 9mm or .45 caliber open-bolt semi-automatic pistol with a 5.75" barrel and 32-shot magazine. Anodized with plastic grips. Discontinued.

NIB	Exc.	V.G.	Good	Fair	Poor
900	700	500	375	250	175

NOTE: Accessory kit (barrel extension and extra magazine) add 20 percent.

MAC 10AI

As above, but firing from a closed bolt. Add 300 percent for earlier open-bolt model.

NIB	Exc.	V.G.	Good	Fair	Poor
450	350	250	200	150	100

NOTE: Accessory kit add 20 percent.

MAC 11

As above in a smaller version and chambered for the 9mm cartridge. Add 300 percent for earlier open-bolt model.

NIB	Exc.	V.G.	Good	Fair	Poor
400	300	200	150	100	50

NOTE: Accessory kit add 20 percent.

INTERARMS
WORLD CLASS SPORTING ARMS

INTERARMS

Alexandria, Virginia

An importer of arms made by Howa Machine, Star and Walther. This firm is no longer in business.

RIFLES

Mark X Viscount

Bolt-action sporting rifle made in a variety of calibers with a 24" barrel, open sights, adjustable trigger and magazine holding either 3 or 5 cartridges. Manufactured in Yugoslavia. Blued with a walnut stock.

NIB	Exc.	V.G.	Good	Fair	Poor
450	300	250	200	175	125

Mark X Lightweight

As above, with a 20" barrel and composition stock. Introduced in 1988.

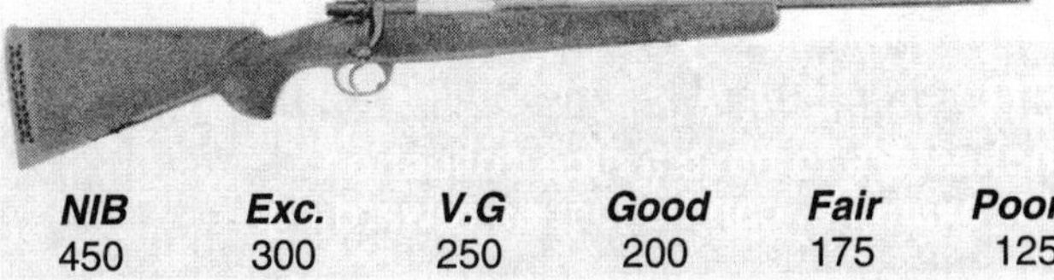

NIB	Exc.	V.G	Good	Fair	Poor
450	300	250	200	175	125

Mini Mark X

As above, with a short action in .223 caliber only with a 20" barrel, open sights, adjustable trigger and 5-shot magazine. Introduced in 1987.

NIB	Exc.	V.G.	Good	Fair	Poor
450	300	250	200	175	125

Mark X American Field

As above, with a finely figured walnut stock, ebony forend tip, pistol grip cap, sling swivels and recoil pad. Introduced in 1984.

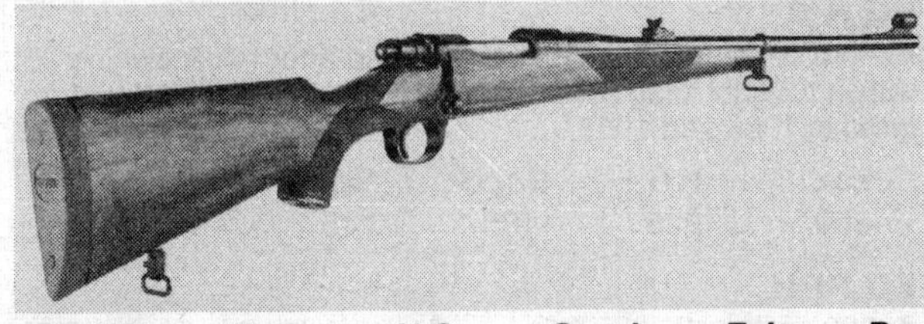

NIB	Exc.	V.G.	Good	Fair	Poor
525	400	350	300	250	175

Whitworth Express Rifle

A .375 Holland & Holland or .458 Winchester Magnum bolt-action sporting rifle with a 24" barrel, express sights and 3-shot magazine. Blued with a walnut stock. Introduced in 1974.

NIB	Exc.	V.G.	Good	Fair	Poor
750	550	450	350	250	200

Whitworth Mannlicher Carbine

A .243, .270, 7x57mm, .308, and the .30-06 caliber bolt-action rifle with a 20" barrel, open sights, sling swivels and a full length stock. Manufactured between 1984 and 1987.

Exc.	V.G.	Good	Fair	Poor
550	400	350	250	200

Cavalier

A bolt-action sporting rifle made in a variety of calibers with a modern styled stock having a rollover cheekpiece. Discontinued.

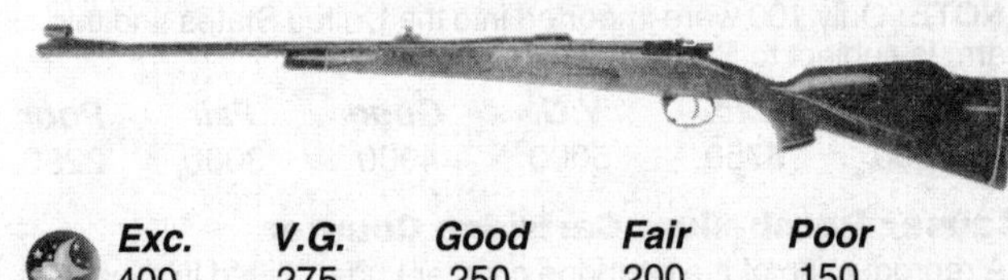

Exc.	V.G.	Good	Fair	Poor
400	275	250	200	150

Mannlicher Carbine

As above, with a 20" barrel and full length stock. Discontinued.

Exc.	V.G.	Good	Fair	Poor
400	275	250	200	150

Continental Carbine

As above, with double set triggers. Discontinued.

Exc.	V.G.	Good	Fair	Poor
425	300	250	200	150

Alaskan Model

Similar to the Mark X, in .375 Holland & Holland or .458 Winchester Magnum with a 24" barrel. Discontinued in 1985.

Exc.	V.G.	Good	Fair	Poor
525	400	350	300	200

22-ATD

A .22 caliber semi-automatic rifle with a 19.4" barrel, open sights, and 11-shot magazine. Blued with a hardwood stock. Manufactured by Norinco. Introduced in 1987.

NIB	Exc.	V.G.	Good	Fair	Poor
175	100	80	60	50	40

HANDGUNS

Helwan Brigadier

A 9mm semi-automatic pistol with a 4.5" barrel, fixed sights, and 8-shot magazine. Blued with plastic grips. Introduced in 1988.

NIB	Exc.	V.G.	Good	Fair	Poor
350	225	200	175	125	100

FEG R-9

A 9mm semi-automatic pistol patterned after the Browning 35 with a 13-shot magazine. Blued with walnut grips. Manufactured in 1986 and 1987.

Exc.	V.G.	Good	Fair	Poor
350	225	185	145	100

FEG PPH

A .380 caliber double-action semi-automatic pistol with a 3.5" barrel and 6-shot magazine. Blued with plastic grips.

Exc.	V.G.	Good	Fair	Poor
300	175	150	125	100

Mark II AP

A copy of the Walther PP. Chambered for the .380 ACP or .22 LR cartridge.

NIB	Exc.	V.G.	Good	Fair	Poor
300	175	125	100	—	—

Mark II APK

A copy of the Walther PPK. Chambered for the .380 ACP cartridge only.

NIB	Exc.	V.G.	Good	Fair	Poor
300	175	125	100	—	—

Mauser Parabellum Karabiner

A 9mm caliber semi-automatic carbine with an 11.75" barrel and detachable shoulder stock. Fitted in a leather case.

NOTE: Only 100 were imported into the United States and this arm is subject to BATF registration.

NIB	Exc.	V.G.	Good	Fair	Poor
6500	5750	5000	4000	3000	2250

Mauser Parabellum Cartridge Counter

A reproduction of the cartridge counter Luger. Fitted in a leather case with only 100 units imported into the United States.

NIB	Exc.	V.G.	Good	Fair	Poor
4000	3000	2500	2000	1500	1000

Virginian Dragoon

A .44 Magnum single-action revolver with a 6", 7.5", 8.75", or 12" barrel, adjustable sights and 6-shot cylinder. Originally made in Switzerland and then in the U.S.A. Discontinued in 1984. Add 20 percent for Swiss manufacture.

Exc.	V.G.	Good	Fair	Poor
275	200	125	100	75

Stainless Dragoon

As above, in stainless steel.

Exc.	V.G.	Good	Fair	Poor
300	225	150	125	100

Virginian .22 Convertible

As above, in .22 caliber with a 5.5" barrel.

Exc.	V.G.	Good	Fair	Poor
250	150	125	100	75

Virginian Stainless .22 Convertible

As above, in stainless steel.

Exc.	V.G.	Good	Fair	Poor
275	175	150	100	80

INTERDYNAMICS OF AMERICA

Miami, Florida

KG-9

A 9mm caliber semi-automatic pistol with a 3" barrel and 36-shot magazine. Manufactured from 1981 and 1983.

Exc.	V.G.	Good	Fair	Poor
800	650	575	500	300

KG-99

As above, with a barrel shroud. Manufactured from 1981 and 1984.

Exc.	V.G.	Good	Fair	Poor
300	225	175	125	100

KG-99 Stainless

As above, in stainless steel. Manufactured in 1984.

Exc.	V.G.	Good	Fair	Poor
350	275	225	150	125

KG-99M

A more compact version of the above. Manufactured in 1984.

Exc.	V.G.	Good	Fair	Poor
250	200	150	125	100

REMINDER

You don't have to specialize in Colts and Winchesters to have a nice collection. Collecting Marlin or Mossberg .22 semi-autos, for example, can be just as rewarding.

This symbol denotes "Sleepers" with rapidly-rising values and/or significant collector potential.

INTRATEC USA, INC.

Miami, Florida

TEC-9

A 9mm caliber semi-automatic pistol with a 5" shrouded barrel and 36-shot magazine. Introduced in 1985.

NIB	Exc.	V.G.	Good	Fair	Poor
350	200	175	150	125	100

TEC-9C

As above, with a 16" barrel and a folding stock. Manufactured in 1987.

Exc.	V.G.	Good	Fair	Poor
325	225	200	150	100

TEC-9M

As above, with a 3" barrel and 20-shot magazine. Also made in stainless steel.

NIB	Exc.	V.G.	Good	Fair	Poor
325	200	175	150	100	75

TEC-22 "Scorpion"

Similar to the above, but in .22 caliber with a 4" barrel and 30-shot magazine.

NIB	Exc.	V.G.	Good	Fair	Poor
275	150	125	100	75	50

TEC-38

A .38 caliber over-and-under double-action derringer with 3" barrels. Manufactured between 1986 and 1988.

Exc.	V.G.	Good	Fair	Poor
175	100	80	65	45

IRVING, W.

New York, New York

Single-Shot Derringer

A .22 caliber spur trigger single-shot pistol with a 2.75" half octagonal barrel. Silver plated brass frame, blued barrel and rosewood grips. The barrel marked "W. Irving." Manufactured in the 1860s. The .32 caliber variation has a 3" barrel and is worth approximately 40 percent more than the values listed.

Exc.	V.G.	Good	Fair	Poor
—	—	900	300	125

POCKET REVOLVER

1st Model

A .31 caliber spur trigger percussion revolver with a 3" octagonal barrel, 6-shot cylinder and brass frame. The barrel marked "W. Irving." Approximately 50 were made between 1858 and 1862.

Exc.	V.G.	Good	Fair	Poor
—	—	2000	750	250

2nd Model

A .31 caliber percussion revolver with a 4.5" round barrel, loading lever and either brass or iron frame. The barrel marked "Address W. Irving. 20 Cliff St. N.Y." Approximately 600 manufactured with a brass frame and 1,500 with a frame of iron. The brass-frame version will bring a premium of about 35 percent.

Exc.	V.G.	Good	Fair	Poor
—	—	1150	400	200

IRWINDALE ARMS, INC.

Irwindale, California

SEE—AMT

ISRAELI MILITARY INDUSTRIES

Israel

Civilian firearms manufactured by this firm have been and are being retailed by Action Arms Limited, Magnum Research, and Mossberg.

ITHACA GUN CO.

Ithaca, New York

This material was supplied by Walter C. Snyder and is copyrighted in his name. Used with the author's permission.

The Ithaca Gun Company was founded by William Henry Baker, John VanNatta, and Dwight McIntyre. Gun production started during the latter half of 1883 at an industrial site located on Fall Creek, Ithaca, New York. Leroy Smith joined the company by 1885 and George Livermore joined the firm in 1887. By 1894 the company was under the exclusive control of Leroy Smith and George Livermore. Many of the company's assets were purchased by the Ithaca Acquisition Corporation in 1987 and moved to King Ferry, New York, where it operated until May, 1996. Now dba Ithaca Guns USA LLC of Upper Sandusky, Ohio.

HAMMER MODELS

Ithaca Baker Model

The first model produced by the company was designed by W.H. Baker and was manufactured from 1883 through 1887. It was offered in six grades; Quality A ($35) through Quality F ($200) in either 10 or 12 gauge. All Ithaca-produced Baker models had exposed hammers. Grades above Quality B are seldom encountered and an expert appraisal is recommended.

Quality A

Courtesy Walter C. Snyder

Exc.	V.G.	Good	Fair	Poor
900	500	300	200	100

Quality B

Exc.	V.G.	Good	Fair	Poor
1200	700	350	200	100

New Ithaca Gun

The New Ithaca Gun was introduced in 1888 and discontinued during 1915. Like its predecessor, it was introduced in the same seven grades, Quality A through Quality F. Later, the Quality F was discontinued. By 1900, a "condensed steel" barreled model, named Quality X, was introduced. The New Ithaca Gun was produced in gauges 10, 12, and 16, and very rarely, 20. Lower grade models carried the logo, "New Ithaca Gun," usually within a banner, on each side of the frame. Like its predecessor, grades above Quality B are seldom encountered, and an expert appraisal is recommended. Sixteen gauge guns command a 30 percent price premium. The extremely rare 20 gauge model requires an expert appraisal.

Quality A

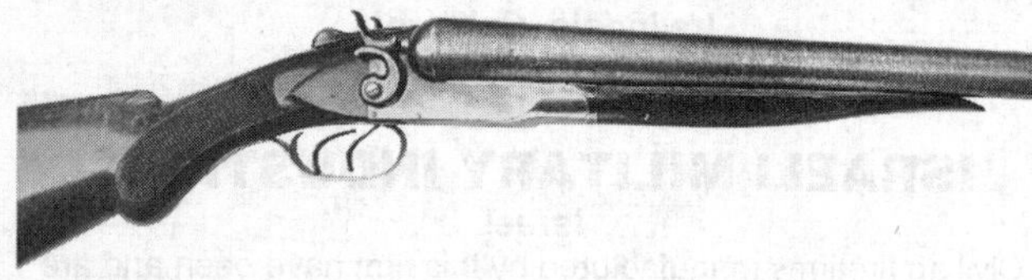

Courtesy Walter C. Snyder

Exc.	V.G.	Good	Fair	Poor
1000	700	250	150	100

Quality AA

Exc.	V.G.	Good	Fair	Poor
1000	700	300	150	100

Quality B

Exc.	V.G.	Good	Fair	Poor
1200	800	400	200	100

Quality X

Exc.	V.G.	Good	Fair	Poor
1200	800	400	200	100

NOTE: Sixteen gauge guns command a 30 percent premium. The extremely rare 20 gauge model requires an expert appraisal.

The "New Double Bolted Hammer Gun"

During 1915, the Ithaca Gun Company replaced the New Ithaca Gun with a model it referred to as "our new model two bolt hammer gun." The new hammer gun had coil springs powering the external hammers. The "two bolt" lock up was accomplished by a bottom bolt and by the top lever engagement with the rear nub of the rib extension. Lower grade models were marked on both sides of the frame with a setter dog and the logo, "Ithaca Gun Co." The 1915 catalog is the last year hammer guns were advertised but the old records indicate a few were sold as late as 1919.

Grades offered were X, A, AA, B, C, D, and E. The 1915 catalogue advertised a price of $29 for an A Quality model and $150 for the elaborately engraved Quality E. All grades were available in 10, 12, and 16 gauges. Like the New Ithaca Gun, grades above Quality B are seldom encountered, and an expert appraisal is recommended. Sixteen gauge guns command a 30 percent price premium. The extremely rare 20 gauge model requires an expert appraisal.

Quality A

Exc.	V.G.	Good	Fair	Poor
1200	800	300	200	100

Quality AA

Exc.	V.G.	Good	Fair	Poor
1500	1000	400	200	100

Quality B

Exc.	V.G.	Good	Fair	Poor
1500	1000	400	200	100

Quality X

Exc.	V.G.	Good	Fair	Poor
1500	1000	450	200	100

HAMMERLESS MODELS

The first hammerless Ithaca gun was introduced in 1888. All Ithaca double guns were discontinued in 1948.

The gauge and grade can usually be found on the left front corner of the water table of the frame, the serial number is usually found on the right side of the same water table, on the barrel flats, and on the forend iron.

Crass Model

The Crass Model, named after Ithaca's Frederick Crass who designed it, was introduced in 1888. It was offered in Quality 1 through Quality 7. The Quality 1P, a model with no engraving, was introduced in 1898. The Crass Model underwent three major frame redesigns before it was discontinued during 1901. The gun was available in 10, 12, and 16 gauge. Automatic ejectors were introduced in 1893 and were available in any quality gun at extra cost.

NOTE: Sixteen gauge guns will command a 20 percent price premium. Guns above Quality 4 are seldom encountered, and an expert appraisal is necessary. For automatic ejectors add $250. The serial number range for the Crass Model is approximately 7000 to 50000.

Quality 1

Exc.	V.G.	Good	Fair	Poor
800	500	350	200	100

Quality 1-1/2

Exc.	V.G.	Good	Fair	Poor
800	500	350	200	100

Quality 1P

Exc.	V.G.	Good	Fair	Poor
800	500	350	200	100

Quality 2

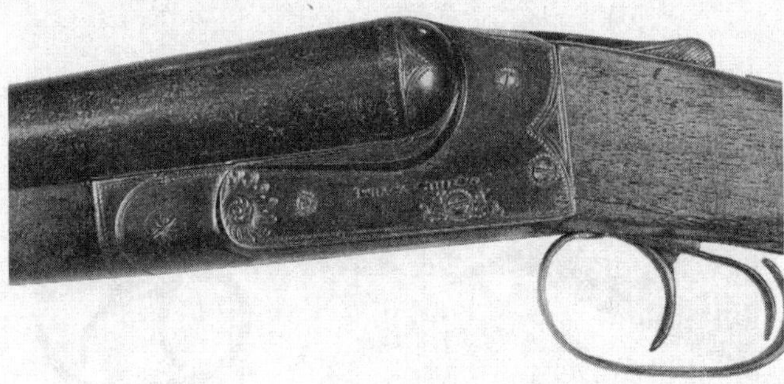
Courtesy Walter C. Snyder

Exc.	V.G.	Good	Fair	Poor
1200	800	550	200	100

Quality 3

Exc.	V.G.	Good	Fair	Poor
1700	1200	700	300	100

Quality 4

Exc.	V.G.	Good	Fair	Poor
2000	1750	1000	300	100

Lewis Model

Chester Lewis, an Ithaca Gun employee, was credited with the design of the gun that now bears his name. The gun was bolted through the rib extension in addition to the traditional under bolt. The model was available from 1901 through 1906, and was offered in Qualities 1 through 7. It was made in 10, 12, and 16 gauge, and after 1906, 20 gauge. Automatic ejectors were offered at added cost.

Qualities offered: 1, 1 Special, 1-1/2, 2, 3, 4, 5, 6, 7. The 1 Special had Nitro Steel barrels.

NOTE: Automatic ejectors add about $250 to grades below Quality 4. The serial number range for the Lewis Model is approximately 55000 to 123600.

Quality 1

Exc.	V.G.	Good	Fair	Poor
800	500	300	150	100

Quality 1 Special

Courtesy Walter C. Snyder

Exc.	V.G.	Good	Fair	Poor
800	500	300	150	100

Quality 1-1/2

Exc.	V.G.	Good	Fair	Poor
850	550	300	150	100

Quality 2

Exc.	V.G.	Good	Fair	Poor
1000	600	400	200	100

Quality 3

Exc.	V.G.	Good	Fair	Poor
1700	1400	800	400	100

Quality 4

Exc.	V.G.	Good	Fair	Poor
2500	2200	1800	400	100

Quality 5

Exc.	V.G.	Good	Fair	Poor
3500	3000	2000	700	300

Quality 6

Exc.	V.G.	Good	Fair	Poor
6000	4500	3000	700	300

Quality 7

Exc.	V.G.	Good	Fair	Poor
6000	4500	3000	700	300

Minier Model

The Minier Model, named after Ithaca's David Minier, was introduced in 1906 and was available through 1908. It was offered in Qualities Field through 7 and any grade could be ordered with ejectors. The Minier Model was the first Ithaca gun to use coil springs to power the internal hammers. This model was triple bolted, e.g., two fastenings at the rib extension and the under bolt. Gauges 10, 12, 16, and 20 were offered.

Grades offered: Field, 1, 1 Special, 1-1/2, 2, 3, 4, 5, 6, 7.

NOTE: Automatic ejectors add $250 to guns below Quality 4. The serial number range for the Minier Model is approximately 130000 to 151000.

Field Grade

Exc.	V.G.	Good	Fair	Poor
1000	500	300	150	100

Quality 1

Exc.	V.G.	Good	Fair	Poor
1000	500	300	150	100

Quality 1 Special

Exc.	V.G.	Good	Fair	Poor
1000	500	300	150	100

Quality 1-1/2

Exc.	V.G.	Good	Fair	Poor
1000	550	300	150	100

Quality 2

Exc.	V.G.	Good	Fair	Poor
1200	600	400	200	100

Quality 3

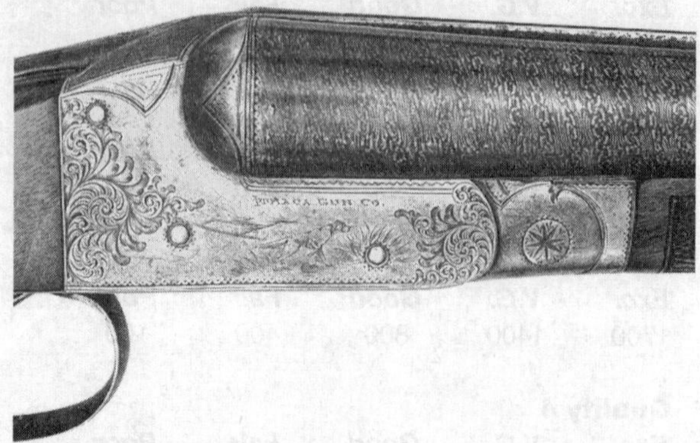

Quality 3 Minier Model Courtesy Walter C. Snyder

Exc.	V.G.	Good	Fair	Poor
2000	1000	500	400	100

Quality 4

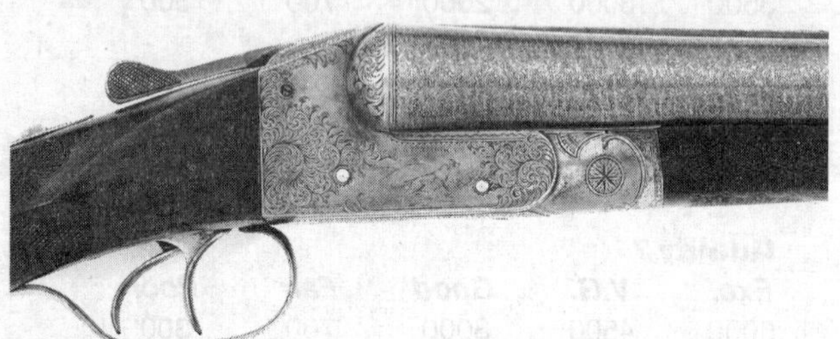

Quality 4 Minier Model Courtesy Amoskeag Auction Company

Exc.	V.G.	Good	Fair	Poor
2500	1200	800	400	100

Quality 5

Exc.	V.G.	Good	Fair	Poor
3500	2500	1500	700	300

Quality 6

Exc.	V.G.	Good	Fair	Poor
5000	4000	1500	700	300

Quality 7

Exc.	V.G.	Good	Fair	Poor
6500	4000	1500	700	300

Flues Model

The Flues Model Ithaca gun was built on a three-piece lock mechanism invented and patented by Emil Flues. Introduced in 1908, it remained in production through 1926 when it was replaced by the Ithaca New Double. It was offered in gauges 10, 12, 16, 20, and 28, and enjoyed the longest production life of any Ithaca double gun. Several grades were offered beginning with the Field grade and ending with the Sousa Special. The Flues Model had the same bolting system as used on the Minier Model. Any grade could have been ordered with automatic ejectors at extra cost. A single-selective trigger made by the Infallible Trigger company was offered after 1914 and was the first single trigger offered from the company.

Qualities offered were: Field, 1, 1 Special, 1-1/2, 2, 3, 4, 5, 6, 7, and Sousa.

NOTE: Add $200 for factory-ordered single trigger, add $200 for automatic ejectors on grades lower than Grade 4. Small gauges command a price premium. A 20 gauge gun may command up to a 50 percent price premium; a 28 gauge field grade perhaps as much as 200 percent. The serial number range for the Flues is approximately 175000 to 399000. Expert appraisals are recommended on higher-grade, small-gauge models as they are seldom encountered.

Field Grade

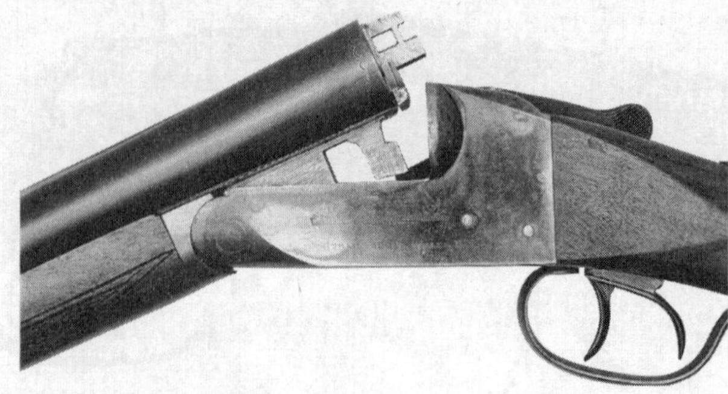

Flues Model Field Grade Courtesy Walter C. Snyder

Exc.	V.G.	Good	Fair	Poor
1000	600	300	150	100

Grade 1

Exc.	V.G.	Good	Fair	Poor
1000	750	400	150	100

Grade 1 Special

Exc.	V.G.	Good	Fair	Poor
1000	750	400	150	100

Grade 1-1/2

Exc.	V.G.	Good	Fair	Poor
1100	750	400	150	100

Grade 2

Exc.	V.G.	Good	Fair	Poor
1200	800	400	200	100

Grade 3

Exc.	V.G.	Good	Fair	Poor
2000	1500	800	300	100

Grade 4

Exc.	V.G.	Good	Fair	Poor
2000	1600	1200	300	100

Grade 5

Exc.	V.G.	Good	Fair	Poor
2500	2000	1500	500	200

Grade 6

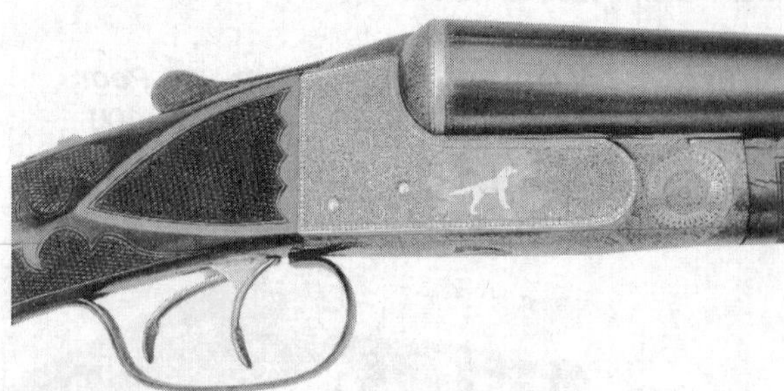

Courtesy Walter C. Snyder

Exc.	V.G.	Good	Fair	Poor
10000	5000	2500	1000	300

Grade 7

Exc.	V.G.	Good	Fair	Poor
9000	4500	2000	1000	300

Sousa

Exc.	V.G.	Good	Fair	Poor
15000	10000	6000	3000	N/A

The New Ithaca Double

The New Ithaca Double, commonly referred to as the NID, was manufactured from 1926 to 1948. It has the distinction of being the last double gun manufactured by the factory. The NID was bolted by a single rotary top bolt and was considered of all Ithaca double guns manufactured up to that time. External cocking indicators were standard on all NID models until about 1934, when they were eliminated from the design. Selective and non-selective single triggers and automatic ejectors were optional at additional costs. A special variation of the NID was introduced in 1932 to accommodate 10 gauge 3-1/2" magnum ammunition and was named, appropriately, the Magnum 10. All NID were available in grades Field, 1, 2, 3, 4, 5, 7, and Sousa (renamed the $1,000 grade after 1936). Gauges Magnum 10, standard 10, 12, 16, 20, 28, and .410 bore were offered.

NOTE: Like most collectible double guns, the smaller gauges command a price premium over the 12 gauge model. A 16 gauge field grade may command a 25 percent price premium, a 20 gauge field grade may command up to a 50 percent price premium, and the 28 gauge, and .410 caliber field-grade models perhaps as much as 250-300 percent. It is recommended that an expert opinion be sought for the valuation of high-grade, small-gauge models. Of late, the Magnum 10 gauge model also commands a price premium. Few of these guns trade, and the advice of an expert appraiser is suggested.

Non-selective single trigger add $150. Single-selective trigger add $250. Ventilated rib add $300. Automatic ejectors for grade below Grade 4 add $300. Beavertail forearm add $200. Monte Carlo buttstock add $300.

Field Grade

Exc.	V.G.	Good	Fair	Poor
1000	700	350	150	100

Grade 1

Exc.	V.G.	Good	Fair	Poor
1250	750	400	200	100

Grade 2

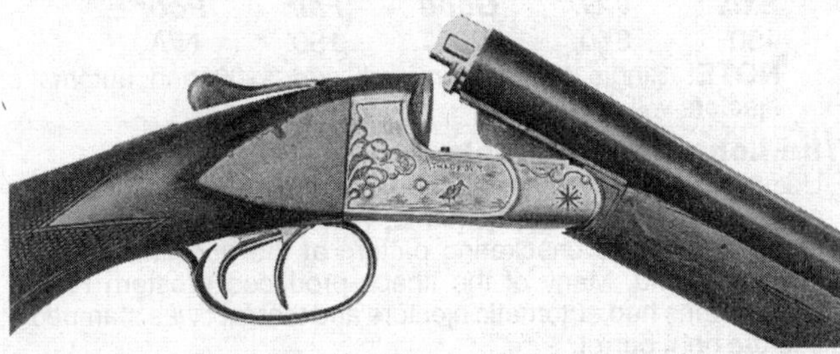

Courtesy Walter C. Snyder

Exc.	V.G.	Good	Fair	Poor
1500	800	650	300	100

Grade 3

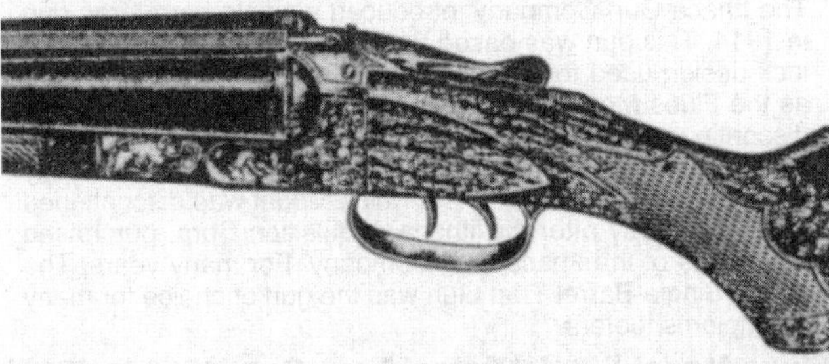

Exc.	V.G.	Good	Fair	Poor
2500	1500	1000	400	100

Grade 4

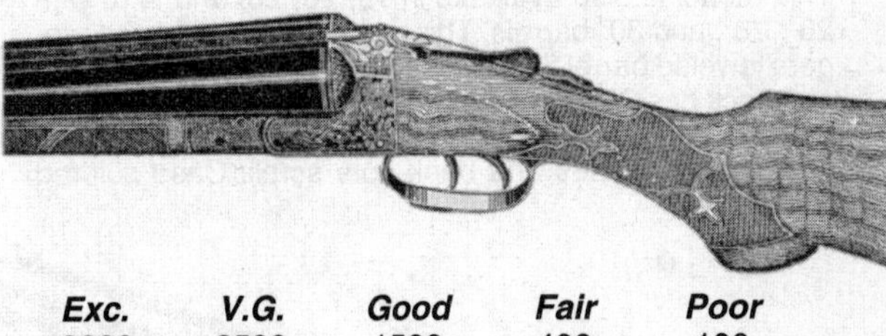

Exc.	V.G.	Good	Fair	Poor
3000	2500	1500	400	100

Grade 5

Grade 5 NID Courtesy Walter C. Snyder

Exc.	V.G.	Good	Fair	Poor
4000	3200	2000	700	200

Grade 7

Exc.	V.G.	Good	Fair	Poor
10000	7000	4000	1000	300

Sousa Grade

Exc.	V.G.	Good	Fair	Poor
20000	10000	6000	3000	500

THE NEW ITHACA DOUBLE (MODERN-1999)

Reborn in 1999 under the company name Ithaca Classic Doubles of Victor, New York, the reintroduction of the NID will begin with serial number 470000. The last recorded production number from the Ithaca factory for NID was 469999. Only about 50 guns will be produced per year.

Special Field Grade

This side-by-side double is offered in 16, 20, 28, and .410 bore with a choice of matted rib barrel lengths of 26", 28", or 30". Ivory bead front sight. The action is case colored with light line border engraving. The stock is feather crotch black walnut with 22 lpi checkering. Choice of pistol or straight grip. Double trigger is standard. Weight in 20 gauge is about 5 lbs. 14 oz. 28 gauge is about 5 lbs. 8 oz., and .410 bore weighs about 5 lbs. 5 oz.

NIB	Exc.	V.G.	Good	Fair	Poor
6000	4750	—	—	—	—

Grade 4E

This model is also available in 16, 20, 28, and .410 with 26", 28", and 30" barrels. This model has gold plated triggers jeweled barrel flats and hand tuned locks. Black walnut stock has 28 lpi checkering with a fleur-de-lis pattern. Pistol or straight grip stock. Action is hand engraved with three game scenes and bank note scroll. Case colored frame.

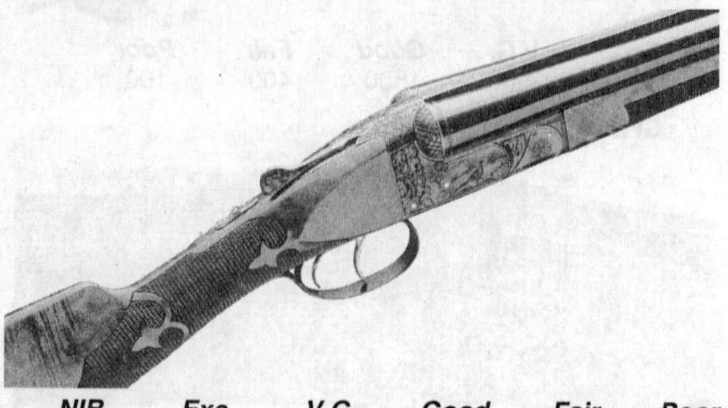

NIB	Exc.	V.G.	Good	Fair	Poor
8000	6000	—	—	—	—

Grade 7E

This model has all of the gauges and barrel lengths of the above guns. Action is hand engraved with gold two tone inlays. Exhibition grade black walnut stock with elaborate patterns. Custom built dimensions.

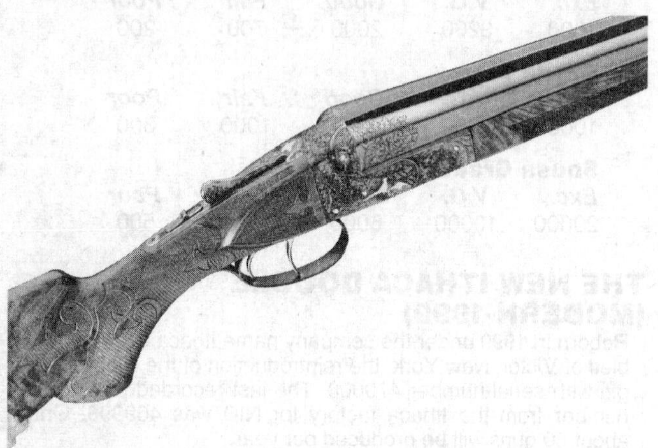

NIB	Exc.	V.G.	Good	Fair	Poor
11000	8750	—	—	—	—

Sousa Grade

This model, available in the same gauges and barrel lengths as the above guns is stocked with presentation grade black walnut, hand carved with 32 lpi checkering. The action is hand engraved with bank note scroll and gold inlays. The entire gun is hand fitted and polished. Extremely limited availability. Special order only.

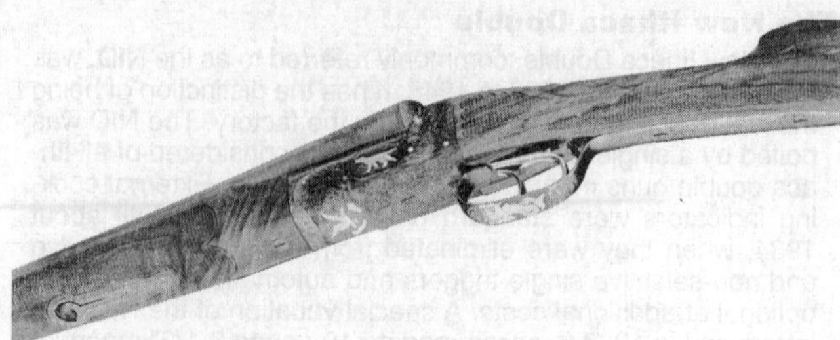

The famous Sousa mermaid in raised gold inlay

NIB	Exc.	V.G.	Good	Fair	Poor
18000	—	—	—	—	—

LEFEVER ARMS COMPANY, INC.

During 1921, Ithaca Gun, under the name "The Lefever Arms Company, Inc." introduced a line of lower-cost, boxlock guns. See the Lefever Arms Company section of this book for prices concerning those guns.

WESTERN ARMS CORPORATION

During 1929 the Ithaca Gun Company created the Western Arms Corporation, which introduced a new, low-cost double gun. That new double gun was named The Long Range Double and it was produced in 12, 16, and 20 gauges, and .410 caliber. Twenty gauge guns often command a 20 percent premium, a .410 caliber can command up to a 250 percent premium. This model was last made at the start of World War II.

The Long Range Double

The Long Range Double had walnut stocks that were not checkered.

Exc.	V.G.	Good	Fair	Poor
450	350	200	150	N/A

NOTE: Single trigger guns will add $100 and automatic ejectors will add $200.

The Long Range Double Deluxe

Usually made exclusively for the Montgomery Ward Company and sold by them under the name, Western Field Deluxe. This model had a line checkering pattern at the grip and on the splinter forend. Many of the Ithaca produced Western Field Deluxe guns had automatic ejectors and that fact was stamped into the right barrel.

Exc.	V.G.	Good	Fair	Poor
450	350	300	150	N/A

NOTE: Single triggers add $100. Automatic ejectors add $200.

ITHACA SINGLE-BARREL TRAP GUNS

The Ithaca Gun Company introduced a single-barrel trap gun in 1914. This gun was based upon the Emil Flues three piece lock design used for the double gun and has become known as the Flues Model Single-Barrel Trap. The Flues Model was discontinued during 1922 and was replaced that year by a model designed by Ithaca's Frank Knickerbocker, commonly referred to as the "Knick." The Knick Model was discontinued in 1988, shortly after the Ithaca Acquisition Corp. purchased the assets of the Ithaca Gun Company. For many years, The Ithaca Single-Barrel Trap Gun was the gun of choice for many champion shooters.

Flues Model Single-Barrel Trap Gun (1914 to 1922)

The Flues Model trap gun was introduced in 1914 and offered in Grades 4, 5, 6, and 7. A lower cost Victory grade was introduced in 1919 and the highest cost variety, the Sousa Special was introduced in 1918. All Flues model trap guns were made within the same serial number sequence as the double guns but do have the letter "T" for Trap following the serial number. All Flues Models with the exception of the Victory Grade were produced with an automatic ejector. A rubber anti-recoil pad was an option. Guns having a pre-1916 engraving pattern will command the highest prices.

Courtesy Walter C. Snyder

Victory Grade

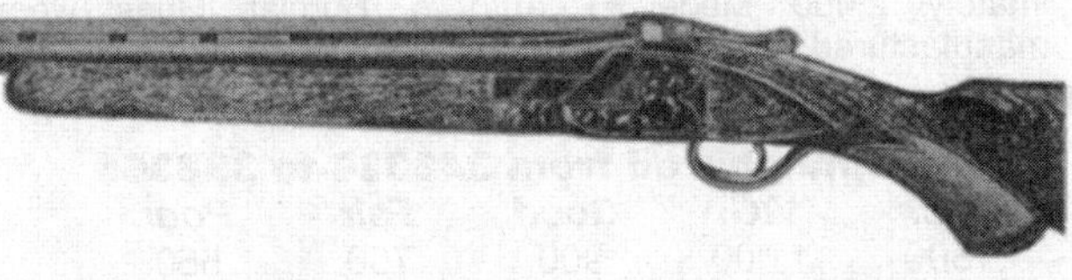

Exc.	V.G.	Good	Fair	Poor
1200	800	650	300	N/A

Grade 4E

Exc.	V.G.	Good	Fair	Poor
2200	1800	1250	400	N/A

Grade 5E

Grade 5E Flues Model Courtesy Walter C. Snyder

Exc.	V.G.	Good	Fair	Poor
4000	3000	2500	600	N/A

Grade 6E

Exc.	V.G.	Good	Fair	Poor
6000	5000	3000	800	N/A

Grade 7E

Exc.	V.G.	Good	Fair	Poor
8000	6000	4000	1000	N/A

Sousa Grade

Exc.	V.G.	Good	Fair	Poor
15000	10000	8000	2000	N/A

Knick Model Single-Barrel Trap

The Knick Model trap gun was introduced during 1922 and was based on a design credited to Frank Knickerbocker. The design was simple and very serviceable, had been in continues production until 1988 when it was discontinued. The model was available in Victory, 4, 5, 7, and Sousa Special Grades. The Sousa was replaced by the $1,000 Grade in about 1936, which was replaced by the $2,000 Grade by 1952, the $2,500 Grade by 1960, the $3,000 Grade by 1965, the $5,000 Grade by 1974, and finally, the Dollar Grade in the early 1980s as the cost of production increased. All Knick models were produced with an automatic ejector and a rubber anti-recoil pad.

Victory Grade

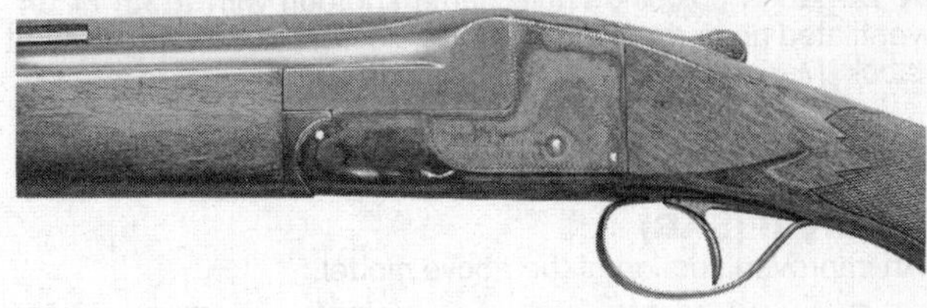

Courtesy William Hammond

NIB	Exc.	V.G.	Good	Fair	Poor
2000	1200	800	650	300	N/A

Grade 4E

Courtesy C. Hadley Smith

NIB	Exc.	V.G.	Good	Fair	Poor
3000	2200	1800	1000	500	N/A

Grade 5E

NIB	Exc.	V.G.	Good	Fair	Poor
5000	4000	3000	2500	800	N/A

Grade 7E

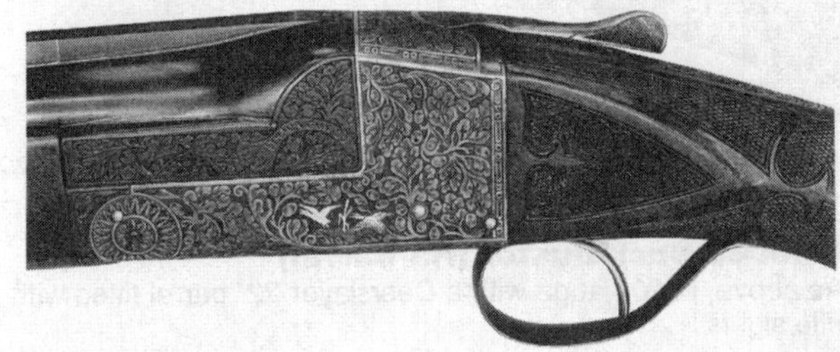

Grade 7 Knick Model Courtesy Walter C. Snyder

NIB	Exc.	V.G.	Good	Fair	Poor
8000	5000	4000	3000	1000	N/A

Sousa Grade

NIB	Exc.	V.G.	Good	Fair	Poor
17000	10000	6000	4000	N/A	N/A

$1,000 to $2,500 Grades

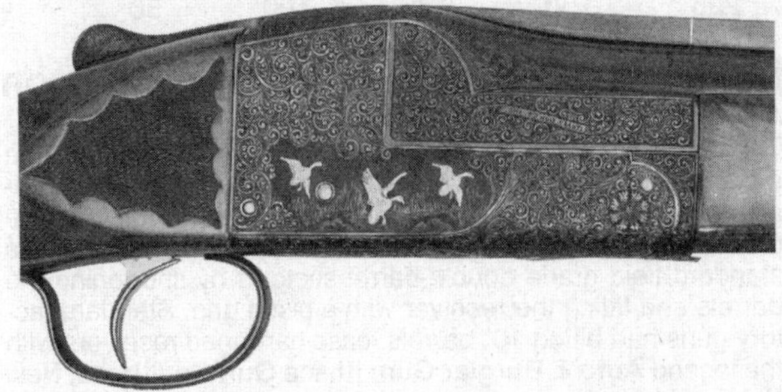

$2,000 Grade Knick Model Courtesy Walter C. Snyder

NIB	Exc.	V.G.	Good	Fair	Poor
15000	12000	8000	6000	2000	N/A

$3,000 through the Dollar Grade

NIB	Exc.	V.G.	Good	Fair	Poor
12000	10000	6000	5000	2000	N/A

Century Grade Trap (SKB)

A 12 gauge boxlock single barrel shotgun with a 32" or 34" ventilated rib barrel and automatic ejector. Blued with a walnut stock. Manufactured by SKB during the 1970s.

Exc.	V.G.	Good	Fair	Poor
700	500	450	350	300

Century II (SKB)

An improved version of the above model.

Exc.	V.G.	Good	Fair	Poor
750	550	500	400	350

Model 66—1963-1978

A 12, 20 or .410 bore lever action single-shot shotgun with a 24" barrel. Blued with a walnut stock. The 20 gauge and .410 bore command a 50 percent price premium.

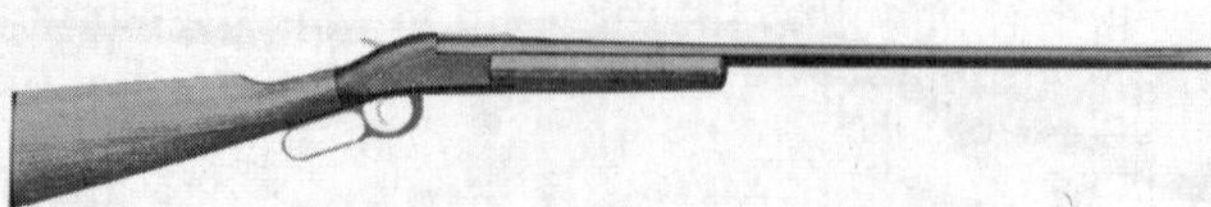

Courtesy C. Hadley Smith

NIB	Exc.	V.G.	Good	Fair	Poor
175	150	125	75	50	—

Model 66 Youth Grade

A special gun offered for the youth market in 20 gauge and .410 bore.

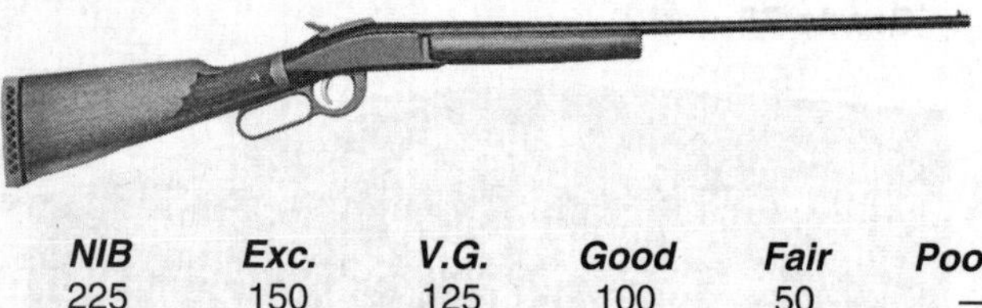

NIB	Exc.	V.G.	Good	Fair	Poor
225	150	125	100	50	—

Model 66 Buck Buster (RS Barrel)

As above, in 20 gauge with a Deerslayer 22" barrel fitted with rifle sights.

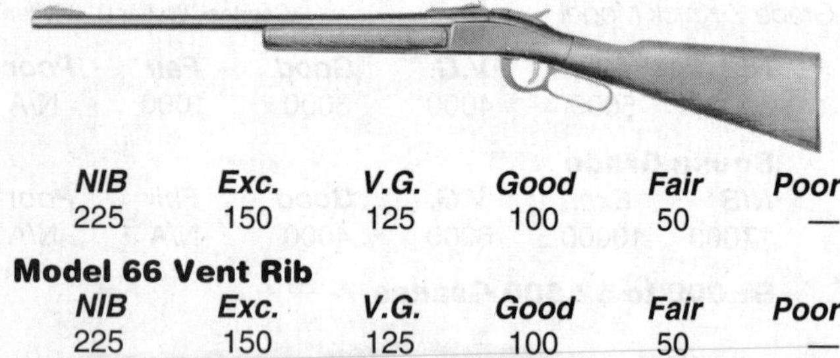

NIB	Exc.	V.G.	Good	Fair	Poor
225	150	125	100	50	—

Model 66 Vent Rib

NIB	Exc.	V.G.	Good	Fair	Poor
225	150	125	100	50	—

ITHACA AUTO & BURGLAR GUN NFA, CURIO OR RELIC

The Ithaca Auto & Burglar Gun is a double-barreled 20 gauge smooth bore pistol manufactured by Ithaca Gun Company, Ithaca, New York, from 1922 to 1934. Total production was approximately 4,500. They were made by modifying Ithaca's standard field grade double-barrel shotgun by shortening the barrels and fitting the receiver with a pistol grip. Standard factory guns had blued 10" barrels, case hardened receivers with the legend **Auto & Burglar Gun/ Ithaca Gun Co./Ithaca, New York**, and the figure of a pointing dog stamped on each side. The barrel length on 21 guns inspected varied to 10.25" (typically in increments divisible by .125"), apparently from inexact factory quality control. Ithaca set a $37.50 retail price when the gun was in production, but some dealers sold it for $40 or more. Production was halted when the government ruled the Ithaca Auto & Burglar Gun to be a "firearm" in the "any other weapon" category under the National Firearms Act (NFA) of 1934.

There are two variations, termed Model A and Model B. Model A utilizes the so-called Flues frame (named after Emil Flues, who designed it in 1908), and its distinctive grip has a curving butt and a large spur. Model A is designed for 2.5" shells, and is not considered safe to fire using modern ammunition. Approximately 2,500 Model A Auto & Burglar Guns were manufactured from 1922 to 1925, when the Flues model was discontinued.

Model B utilizes the so-called N.I.D. frame (short for New Ithaca Double), introduced in 1926 and discontinued in 1948. The N.I.D. is designed for modern ammunition and 2.75" shells, has cocking indicators, and a different pistol grip that is perpendicular to the barrel and which lacks the distinctive spur. Some Model Bs have been observed with rosettes or "stars" engraved in each side of the receiver; their significance is unknown at this time, but they probably are decorations. Approximately 2,000 Model B Auto & Burglar Guns were manufactured from 1926 to 1934.

Model A

Serial numbered from 343336 to 398365

Exc.	V.G.	Good	Fair	Poor
1500	1,000	900	750	550

Model B

Serial numbered from 425000 to 464699

Exc.	V.G.	Good	Fair	Poor
1300	950	750	550	450

NOTE: Nonstandard or special order guns command premiums of 100 percent or more. Original holsters (marked Auto and Burglar Gun/MADE BY/ITHACA GUN CO./ITHACA, N.Y.) are extremely rare and worth $300 to $500 or more.

ITHACA MODEL 37 REPEATER

The Ithaca Model 37 Repeater was introduced in 1937 in 12 gauge, 1938 in 16 gauge, and in 1939 in 20 gauge. It underwent very few design changes throughout its long life which ended 1987 when the Ithaca Acquisition Corp. acquired the assets of the Ithaca Gun Company during 1987 and renamed the gun the Model 87. The name has recently been changed again to the M37 after the assets of the Ithaca Acquisition Corp. were purchased in May of 1996 by the Ithaca Gun Company, LLC. All Model 37 guns were chambered only for 2-3/4" ammunition until 1983, when the Magnum with 3" chamber was introduced to some configurations. Most Model 37 guns had blued metal and walnut stocks with the exception of the Model 37 Field Grade series which had matte finished metal and Birch stocks. Sixteen gauge guns were discontinued in 1973. Ithaca Gun closed in April, 2005, but reopened in 2006 as Ithaca Guns USA of Upper Sandusky, Ohio.

NOTE: Twenty gauge guns made before 1968 will generally command a price premium.

Model 37/Standard Grade—1937-1983

Guns made before 1968 will enjoy a 15 percent price premium; those made before World War II, a 30 percent price premium.

Courtesy C. Hadley Smith

Exc.	V.G.	Good	Fair	Poor
350	200	175	125	75

Model 37S/Skeet Grade—1937-1953

Guns made before World War II will enjoy a 50 percent price premium.

Exc.	V.G.	Good	Fair	Poor
600	400	350	250	100

This symbol denotes "Sleepers" with rapidly-rising values and/or significant collector potential.

Model 37T/Trap—1937-1953

Guns made before World War II will enjoy a 50 percent price premium.

Exc.	V.G.	Good	Fair	Poor
600	400	350	250	100

Model 37T/Target—1954-1961

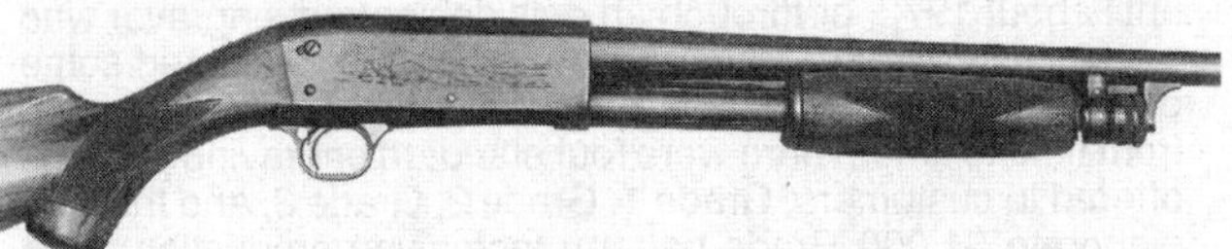

Exc.	V.G.	Good	Fair	Poor
600	400	350	250	100

Model 37R/Solid Rib—1940-1967

Guns made before World War II will enjoy a 50 percent price premium.

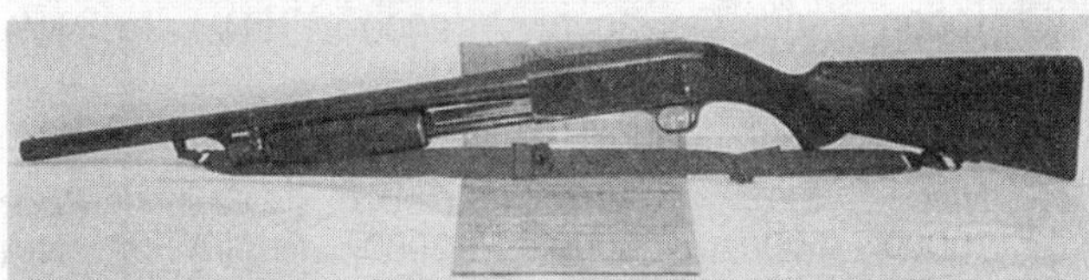

Courtesy Walter C. Snyder

Exc.	V.G.	Good	Fair	Poor
400	275	225	200	75

Model 37 Military Marked (WWII)

This is one of the scarcest military shotguns. It was built in three different configurations; 30" barrel, 20" barrel, and 20" barrel with handguard and bayonet lug (Trench Gun). A scarce shotgun, proceed with caution.

Model 37 with 20" barrel and release papers

Courtesy Richard M. Kumor, Sr.

Exc.	V.G.	Good	Fair	Poor
2000	1800	1500	—	—

NOTE: Add $200 for government release papers and 150 percent for Trench Gun configuration.

Model 37RD/Deluxe Solid Rib—1954-1962

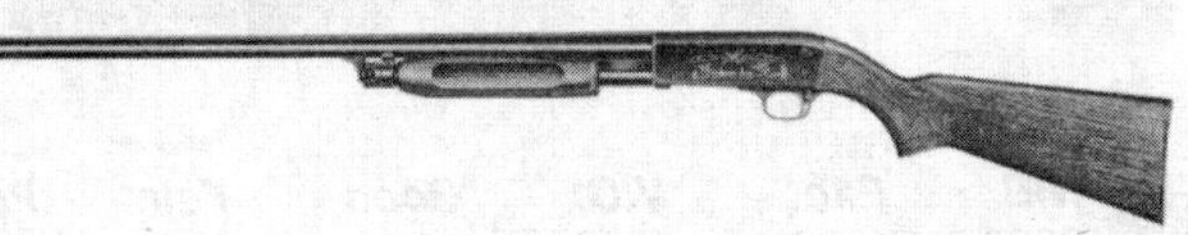

Courtesy C. Hadley Smith

Exc.	V.G.	Good	Fair	Poor
500	375	300	200	100

Model 37 Deerslayer—1959-1987

All Deerslayer models made before 1968 will enjoy a 10 percent to 20 percent price premium.

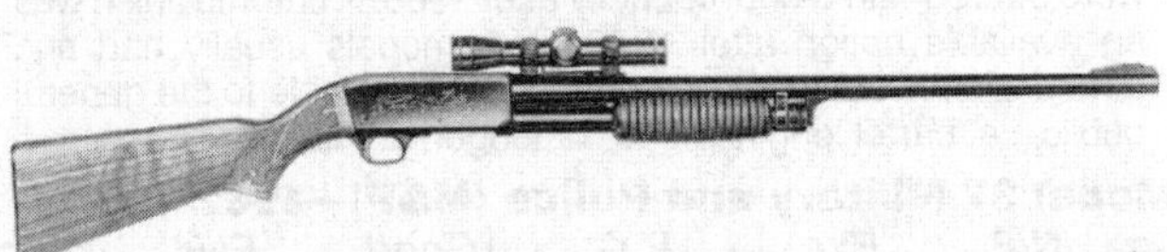

Courtesy C. Hadley Smith

Exc.	V.G.	Good	Fair	Poor
300	250	200	125	75

Model 37 Deluxe Deerslayer—1959-1971

Exc.	V.G.	Good	Fair	Poor
300	250	225	125	75

Model 37 Super Deluxe Deerslayer—1959-1987

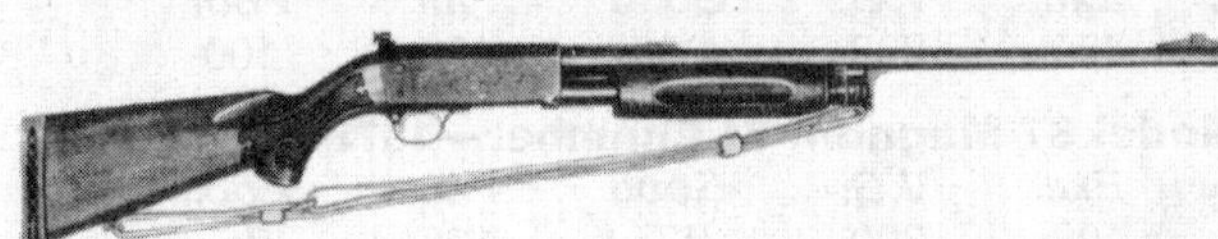

Courtesy C. Hadley Smith

Exc.	V.G.	Good	Fair	Poor
450	325	275	200	100

Model 37 Supreme Grade—1967-1987

Exc.	V.G.	Good	Fair	Poor
700	450	350	200	100

Model 37 Field Grade Standard—1983-1985

Exc.	V.G.	Good	Fair	Poor
350	200	150	125	75

Model 37 Field Grade Vent—1983-1986

Exc.	V.G.	Good	Fair	Poor
350	250	200	125	75

Model 37 Basic Featherlight—1979-1983

Manufactured in 12 gauge only.

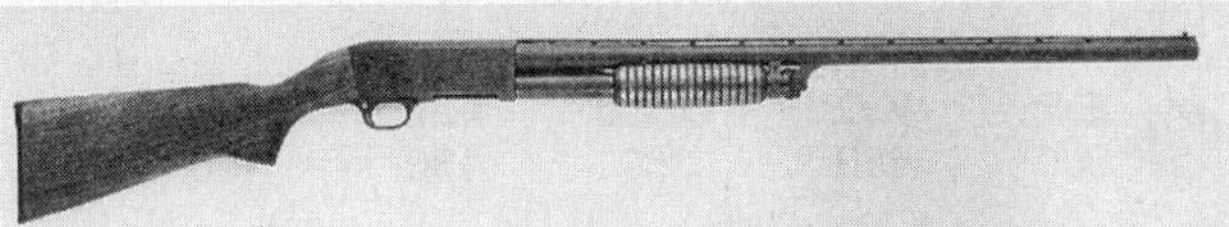

Courtesy Walter C. Snyder

Exc.	V.G.	Good	Fair	Poor
300	250	200	125	75

Model 37V/Vent Rib—1961-1983

Guns made before 1968 will enjoy a 10 percent to 20 percent price premium.

Exc.	V.G.	Good	Fair	Poor
350	300	175	150	75

Model 37RV/Deluxe Vent Rib—1961-1966

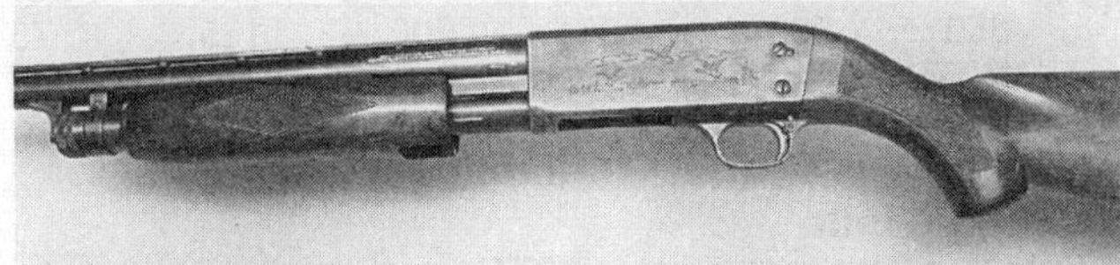

Courtesy Walter C. Snyder

Exc.	V.G.	Good	Fair	Poor
750	500	300	200	75

Model 37D/Deluxe—1955-1977

Guns made before 1968 will enjoy a 10 percent to 20 percent price premium.

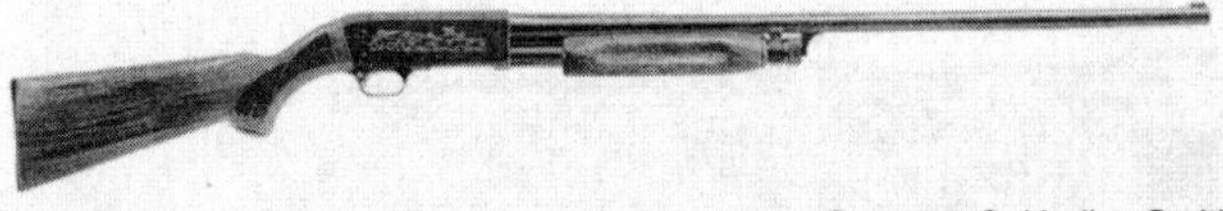

Courtesy C. Hadley Smith

Exc.	V.G.	Good	Fair	Poor
400	250	175	125	75

Model 37DV/Deluxe Vent Rib—1961-1987

Guns made before 1968 will enjoy a 10 percent to 20 percent price premium.

Exc.	V.G.	Good	Fair	Poor
450	300	200	150	100

Model 37 Magnum 3" Chamber—1978-1987

Exc.	V.G.	Good	Fair	Poor
400	300	225	125	75

Model 37 Field Grade Magnum—1984-1987

Exc.	V.G.	Good	Fair	Poor
300	225	175	125	75

Model 37 UltraLight—1978 to 1987

The UltraLight had an aluminum alloy frame and trigger plate. The barrels are marked Ultra Featherlight and the serial number is prefaced with the mark, "ULT." Both the 12 and 20 gauges were offered.

Exc.	V.G.	Good	Fair	Poor
475	400	300	150	100

Model 37 English UltraLight—1982-1987

This gun is the same as the Model 37 UltraLight, but has an English-style straight grip stock.

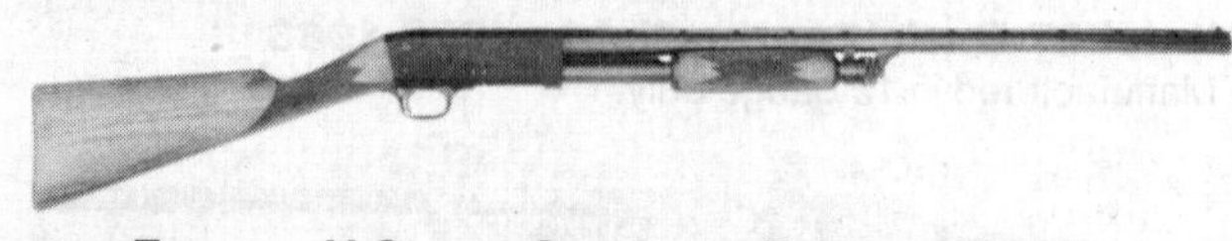

Exc.	V.G.	Good	Fair	Poor
500	450	350	150	100

Model 37 Camo

Introduced in 1985, this model is available with either a green or brown camouflage finish and was offered only in 12 gauge.

Exc.	V.G.	Good	Fair	Poor
350	300	200	150	100

Model 37 Bicentennial

A special model produced during 1976 to commemorate the 200 year anniversary of the United States. The gun came with a full-length trunk-style hard case and a pewter belt buckle number to the gun. The serial number was prefaced with "U.S.A."

NIB	Exc.	V.G.	Good	Fair	Poor
650	500	300	200	125	75

NOTE: Subtract 35 percent if the original case and belt buckle are missing.

Model 37 Ducks Unlimited Commemorative, Auction Grade

Special edition made during 1977. Serial number sequence was 40-DU0001 to 40-DU1125.

NIB	Exc.	V.G.	Good	Fair	Poor
650	400	300	150	100	75

Model 37 Ducks Unlimited Commemorative, Trade Grade

Special edition made during 1977. Lower grade version of the Auction Grade. Serial number preceded with the mark, DU37040.

NIB	Exc.	V.G.	Good	Fair	Poor
450	400	350	200	N/A	N/A

Model 37 2500 Series Centennial

A commemorative Model 37 12 gauge shotgun with silver-plated receiver and press checkered stocks. Manufactured in 1984.

NIB	Exc.	V.G.	Good	Fair	Poor
800	500	300	150	100	75

Model 37 Presentation Series Centennial

A commemorative Mode 37 12 gauge with a gold-plated receiver and high grade hand checkered stocks. It was manufactured during 1980, but is still available as of August 1997.

NIB	Exc.	V.G.	Good	Fair	Poor
1500	800	500	150	100	—

HI-GRADE ITHACA MODEL 37 GUNS

The Ithaca Gun company offered custom engraving services either from its in-house engraver, one of which was retained until about 1972, or through an outside contract engraver who was usually William Mains. Many customers requested some degree of custom work and guns with various patterns turn up from time to time. There were four standard engraving patterns offered to customers, Grade 1, Grade 2, Grade 3, and the very elaborate $1,000 Grade pattern. Increasing production costs forced the $1,000 Grade to become the $2,000 Grade, the $2,500, and finally the $3,000 Grade over the years.

NOTE: All factory engraved Model 37 guns are rare and require an expert appraiser to determine an accurate value.

$1,000 Grade

The Model 37 with an engraved receiver, gold inlays, and a well-figured walnut stock. Manufactured between 1940 and 1942.

NIB	Exc.	V.G.	Good	Fair	Poor
10000	5000	3000	2000	N/A	N/A

$2,000 Grade

Manufactured from 1946 to 1957.

NIB	Exc.	V.G.	Good	Fair	Poor
10000	5000	3000	2000	N/A	N/A

$3,000 Grade

As above. Manufactured from 1958 to 1967.

NIB	Exc.	V.G.	Good	Fair	Poor
8000	4000	2500	1500	N/A	N/A

Model 37 Law Enforcement Weapons

The Ithaca Gun Company entered the law enforcement market in 1962 when it introduced the Model 37 Military and Police (M&P) and the Model 37DS Police special (DSPS). The M&P Model was styled after the riot guns made for various military contracts. The DSPS was styled after the Ithaca Deerslayer. Both models were offered with 8-shot capacity after 1968. A chrome finish was an available option after 1976. Both models usually had ring turned slide handles. Only those models available to the general public, i.e. barrel lengths of 18" or longer, are listed.

Model 37 Military and Police (M&P)—1962-1986

NIB	Exc.	V.G.	Good	Fair	Poor
350	300	250	200	125	75

NOTE: Add 20 percent for an 8-shot model in NIB or EXC. condition, and add an additional 15 percent for chrome plated models in similar condition.

 *This symbol denotes "Sleepers" with rapidly-rising values and/or significant collector potential.*

Model 37 DS Police Special—1962-1986

NIB	Exc.	V.G.	Good	Fair	Poor
400	350	250	200	125	75

NOTE: Add 20 percent for an 8-shot model in NIB or EXC. condition, and add an additional 15 percent for chrome plated models in similar condition.

ITHACA MODEL 87 REPEATER

During 1987 many of the assets of the bankrupt Ithaca Gun Company were purchased by the Ithaca Acquisition Corporation. Manufacture of the Model 37 was resumed that summer after the gun was renamed the Model 87. Many of the Models offered by the old company were continued. All Model 87 field guns were produced with ventilated ribs. All Deerslayer models continued the rifle sights used on the Model 37 guns.

Model 87 Basic—1989-1994

Early models had birch stocks, later production had walnut stocks. All had ring turned slide handles.

NIB	Exc.	V.G.	Good	Fair	Poor
350	300	250	175	125	75

Model 87 Magnum

A 12 or 20 gauge Magnum slide action shotgun with a 25" barrel fitted with screw-in choke tubes and a ventilated rib that is similar to the Model 37. Blued with a walnut stock.

NIB	Exc.	V.G.	Good	Fair	Poor
400	350	300	225	150	100

The Model 87 was manufactured in the styles listed as of 1989:

Model 87 Field Grade—1987-1990

Stocks were walnut with pressed checkering.

NIB	Exc.	V.G.	Good	Fair	Poor
325	250	200	175	125	75

Model 87 Camo—1987-1994

NIB	Exc.	V.G.	Good	Fair	Poor
300	250	200	175	125	75

Model 87 Turkey Gun—1987-1996

Courtesy C. Hadley Smith

NIB	Exc.	V.G.	Good	Fair	Poor
325	250	200	175	125	75

Model 87 Deluxe—1987-1996

The buttstocks and slide handle were walnut with a machine cut checkered pattern.

Courtesy C. Hadley Smith

NIB	Exc.	V.G.	Good	Fair	Poor
375	300	250	200	125	75

Model 87 Ultralite—1987-1990

All IAC manufactured Ultralite guns carry the old Model 37 serial number.

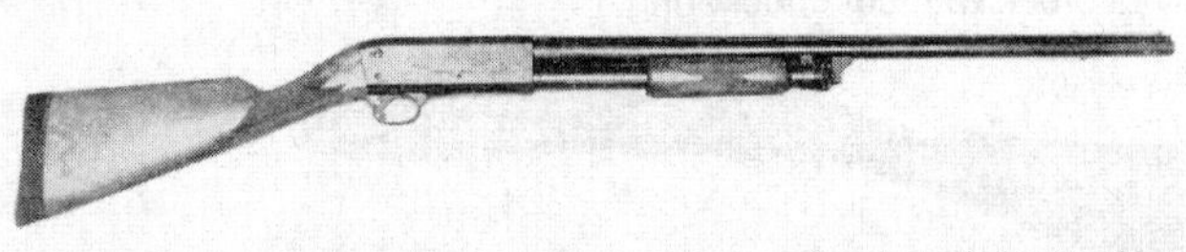

Courtesy C. Hadley Smith

NIB	Exc.	V.G.	Good	Fair	Poor
500	350	250	175	125	75

Model 87 English—1993-1996

Hand-checkered walnut stocks. The slide handle was styled after the pre-war Model 37 slide handle.

NIB	Exc.	V.G.	Good	Fair	Poor
400	350	250	175	125	75

Model 87 Ultralite Deluxe

NIB	Exc.	V.G.	Good	Fair	Poor
400	350	300	250	125	75

Model 87 Supreme Grade—1987-1996

High grade walnut stocks with hand checkering. Metal had extra fine polish and finish.

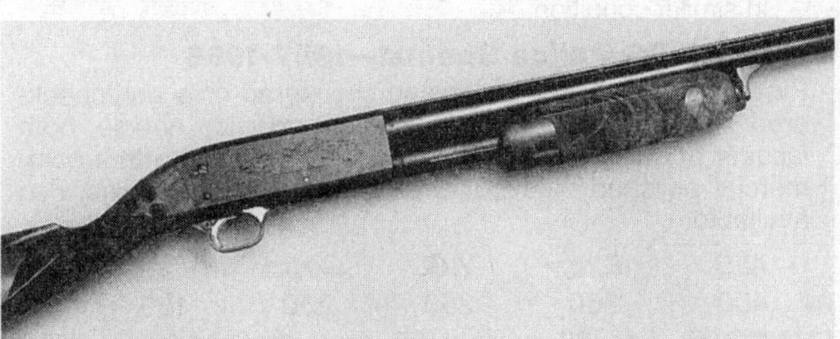

Courtesy C. Hadley Smith

NIB	Exc.	V.G.	Good	Fair	Poor
1000	700	500	—	—	—

Model 87 Deerslayer Basic—1989-1996

Walnut, oil finish butt and slide handle stocks. Slide handle was classic ring turned style.

NIB	Exc.	V.G.	Good	Fair	Poor
300	275	250	200	125	75

Model 87 Deerslayer—1989-1996

It was sometimes advertised as the Model 87 Deerslayer Field. Buttstock and slide handle were walnut and usually had a pressed checkered pattern. The slide handle was the beavertail style.

Courtesy C. Hadley Smith

NIB	Exc.	V.G.	Good	Fair	Poor
350	300	250	200	125	75

Model 87 Deluxe Deerslayer—1989-1996

Butt stock and slide handle were walnut with a machine-cut checkering pattern. The slide handle was beavertail.

NIB	Exc.	V.G.	Good	Fair	Poor
400	350	250	200	125	75

Model 87 Deerslayer II—1988-1996

This model had a fixed rifle barrel and a Monte Carlo buttstock. A small number of guns were specially made with a fast twist barrel to handle Brenneke ammunition and are marked "BRENNEKE" on the receiver.

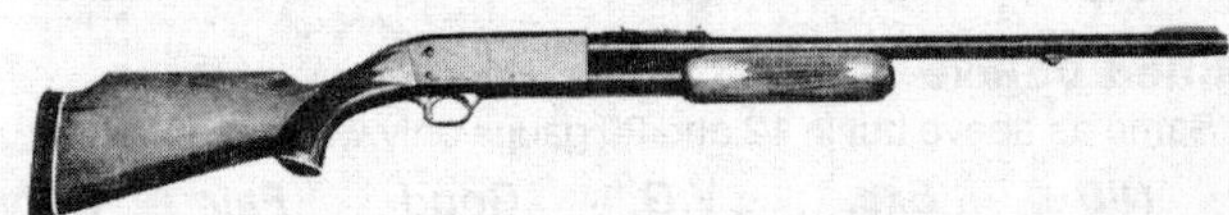

Courtesy C. Hadley Smith

NIB	Exc.	V.G.	Good	Fair	Poor
550	450	350	200	125	75

NOTE: Brenneke-marked guns will command a 30 percent price premium.

Model 87 Home Protection and Law Enforcement Models

The Ithaca Acquisition Corporation continued production of many of the law enforcement firearms produced by the Ithaca Gun Company. Only those models available to the general public are listed.

Model 87 Military & Police—1987-1996

Generally produced with a non-checkered walnut buttstock and a ring turned slide handle, both of which were oil finished. Add 20 percent for an 8-shot model in NIB or excellent condition.

NIB	Exc.	V.G.	Good	Fair	Poor
350	300	250	200	125	75

NOTE: Add an additional 15 percent for chrome plated models in similar condition.

Model 87 DS Police Special—1987-1996

Produced with either a pressed checkered or a non-checkered walnut buttstock, and a ring-turned slide handle, both lacquer finished. The metal was usually finished with a commercial polished blue but a chrome-plated finish was also available.

NIB	Exc.	V.G.	Good	Fair	Poor
400	350	250	200	125	75

NOTE: Add 20 percent for an 8-shot model in NIB or excellent condition, and add an additional 15 percent for a chrome plated models in similar condition.

NEW MODEL 37

During 1996, the assets of the bankrupt Ithaca Acquisition Corporation were purchased by a new company named the Ithaca Gun Company, LLC. One of the first public actions of the new firm was to rename the Model 87 the Model 37, before resuming production later that year, the serial number of the new Model 37 is prefaced with the letter "M." A used market for the new Model 37 has not been established at this time. Suggested retail prices for each model currently produced are listed.

In 2001 a Legacy Edition upgrade featuring a laser carved handwritten message in the stock was available for an additional $125.

Model 37 Deerslayer II

This model is offered in both 12 and 20 gauge. Fitted with either 20" or 25" barrels with rifled bores. These barrel are fixed to the receiver. Magazine capacity is 5 rounds. Walnut stock. Weight is approximately 7 lbs. In 2001 a 16 gauge version with fixed rifled barrel was offered.

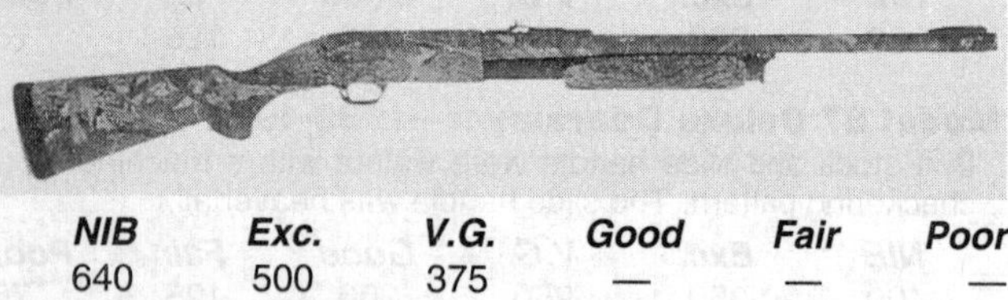

NIB	Exc.	V.G.	Good	Fair	Poor
640	500	375	—	—	—

Smooth Bore Deluxe

Offered in 12, 16, or 20 gauge with interchangeable barrels in 20" or 25" with smoothbore for deer. Walnut stock. Magazine capacity is 5 rounds. Weight is approximately 6.75 lbs.

NIB	Exc.	V.G.	Good	Fair	Poor
675	400	350	—	—	—

Rifled Deluxe

Same as above but in 12 and 20 gauge only with rifled barrels.

NIB	Exc.	V.G.	Good	Fair	Poor
675	400	350	—	—	—

Model 37 Deluxe Field

This model is offered in 12, 16, and 20 gauge with interchangeable vent rib barrels of 26", 28", or 30" (12 gauge only). Walnut stock. Magazine capacity is 5 rounds. Weight is about 7 lbs.

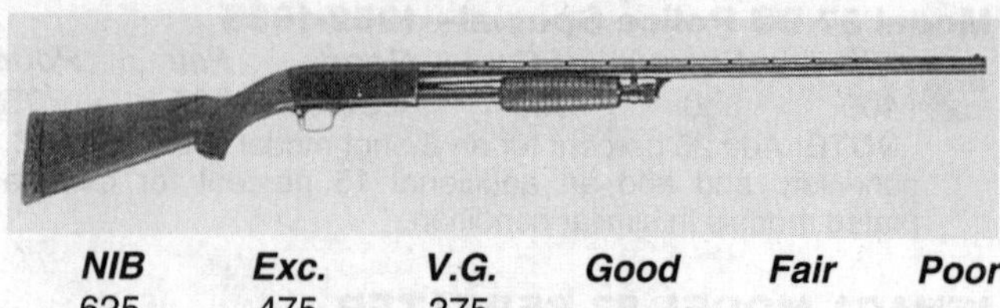

NIB	Exc.	V.G.	Good	Fair	Poor
625	475	375	—	—	—

Model 37 Deluxe Field English Style

This model is offered in 20 gauge only with 24", 26", or 28" vent rib barrels. Walnut stock. Weight is about 7 lbs. Magazine capacity is 5 rounds.

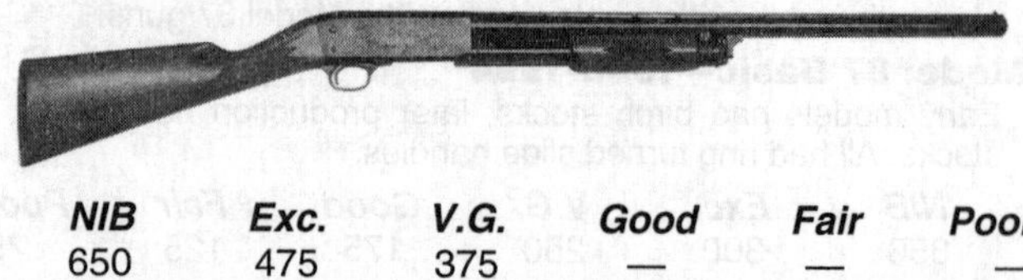

NIB	Exc.	V.G.	Good	Fair	Poor
650	475	375	—	—	—

Model 37 Ultra Featherlight Grouse Special

Based on the Classic Model 37 with bottom ejection this model features an aluminum receiver and 24" vent rib barrel with choke tubes. Straight grip stock of American black walnut.

NIB	Exc.	V.G.	Good	Fair	Poor
650	525	—	—	—	—

Model 37 Ultra Featherlight Youth

Similar to the above model but with a 22" barrel and 12.75" length of pull buttstock with ventilated recoil pad.

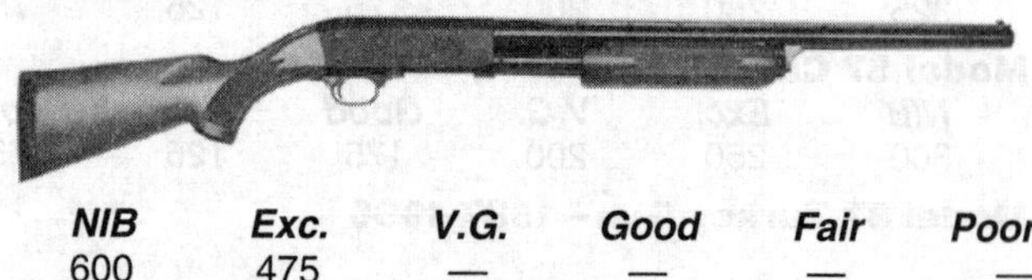

NIB	Exc.	V.G.	Good	Fair	Poor
600	475	—	—	—	—

Model 37 Sporting Clays

This model features a choice of 24", 26", or 28" wide vent rib barrels with Briley choke tubes. Receiver has an antiqued finish with scroll engraving and high grade American black walnut.

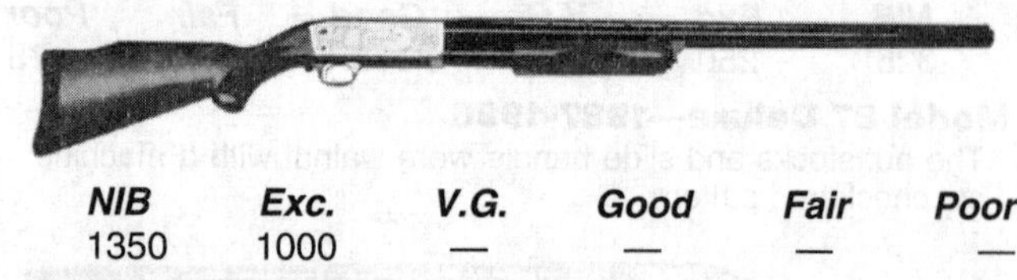

NIB	Exc.	V.G.	Good	Fair	Poor
1350	1000	—	—	—	—

Model 37 Trap

This model has similar features as the sporting clays but with 30" wide vent rib barrel.

NIB	Exc.	V.G.	Good	Fair	Poor
1350	1000	—	—	—	—

Model 37 Women's Endowment Shotgun

Offered in 16 or 20 gauge with straight grip stock and a length of pull designed for the woman's height of 5'5". American walnut stock with cut checkering.

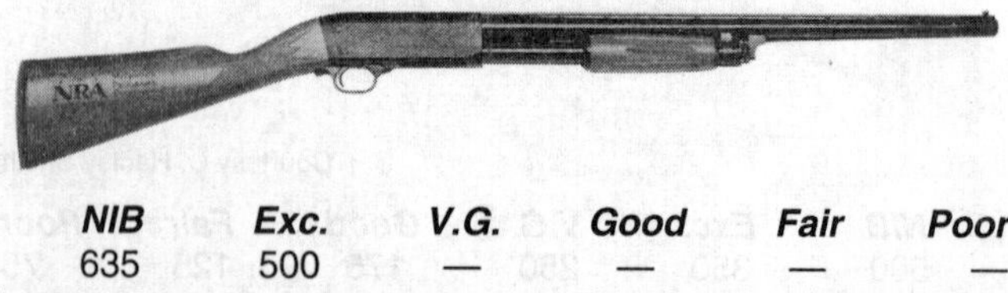

NIB	Exc.	V.G.	Good	Fair	Poor
635	500	—	—	—	—

Model 37 Turkeyslayer

This model is offered in 12 gauge with 22" Full choke barrel. Choice of 22" ported barrel. Also, a 20 gauge youth model is offered with 22" barrel. Camo stock is standard. Weight is about 7 lbs.

NIB	Exc.	V.G.	Good	Fair	Poor
600	475	375	—	—	—

NOTE: Add $15 for ported barrel option.

Model 37 Waterfowler

Available in 12 gauge only with 28" steel shot barrel. Camo pattern stock. Weight is about 7 lbs. Magazine capacity is 5 rounds.

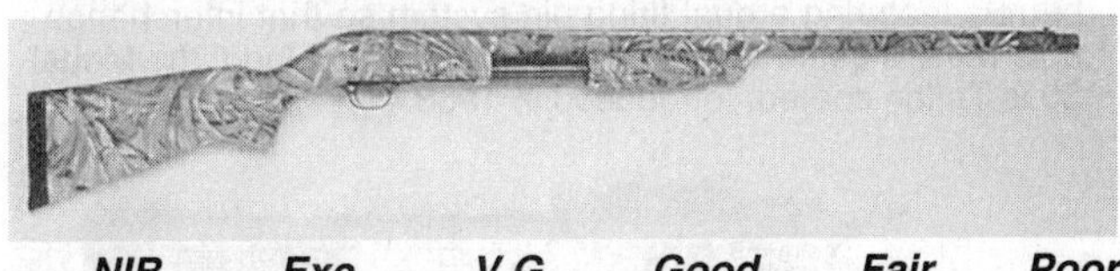

NIB	Exc.	V.G.	Good	Fair	Poor
595	475	375	—	—	—

Model 37 New Classic

Available in 12, 20, or 16 gauge with hand checkered walnut stock with choice of pistol grip or straight grip and high polish bolt and other component parts. Sunburst recoil pad. Interchangeable vent rib barrels in either 26" or 28". Weight is about 7 lbs.

NIB	Exc.	V.G.	Good	Fair	Poor
810	625	—	—	—	—

MODEL 51 SERIES

A 12 or 20 gauge semi-automatic shotgun with 26", 28", or 30" ventilated rib barrels. Blued with a walnut stock. Manufactured from 1970 to 1985 as listed.

Model 51A Standard

Plain barrel.

Courtesy C. Hadley Smith

Exc.	V.G.	Good	Fair	Poor
275	225	200	150	75

NOTE: Vent rib add $100.

Model 51A Magnum

3" chamber.

Exc.	V.G.	Good	Fair	Poor
300	250	225	175	75

NOTE: Vent rib add $100.

Model 51A Waterfowler

Matte finished.

Exc.	V.G.	Good	Fair	Poor
425	375	325	250	75

Model 51A Deerslayer

Courtesy C. Hadley Smith

Exc.	V.G.	Good	Fair	Poor
325	275	225	150	75

Model 51A Turkey Gun

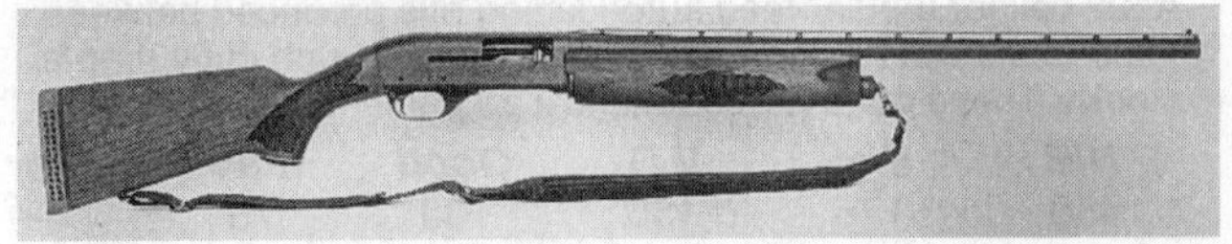

Courtesy C. Hadley Smith

Exc.	V.G.	Good	Fair	Poor
325	275	225	150	75

Model 51 Supreme Trap

Exc.	V.G.	Good	Fair	Poor
425	375	325	250	75

Model 51 Supreme Skeet

Exc.	V.G.	Good	Fair	Poor
450	400	350	275	200

Model 51 Ducks Unlimited Commemorative

NIB	Exc.	V.G.	Good	Fair	Poor
475	400	375	325	275	200

Model 51 Presentation

Engraved receiver.

NIB	Exc.	V.G.	Good	Fair	Poor
1500	1250	1000	750	500	N/A

Mag-10 Series

A 10 gauge Magnum semi-automatic shotgun manufactured in a variety of barrel lengths, styles and finishes. Manufactured from 1975 to 1986 as listed.

Standard Grade

Exc.	V.G.	Good	Fair	Poor
750	700	650	300	250

Standard Vent Rib Grade

Exc.	V.G.	Good	Fair	Poor
850	775	700	550	250

Deluxe Vent Rib Grade

Exc.	V.G.	Good	Fair	Poor
1000	850	775	600	250

Supreme Grade

Exc.	V.G.	Good	Fair	Poor
1200	1050	850	700	250

Roadblocker—Military and Police Model

Exc.	V.G.	Good	Fair	Poor
650	575	500	400	200

Presentation Grade

Engraved, gold-inlaid, 200 made.

NIB	Exc.	V.G.	Good	Fair	Poor
1875	1500	1100	900	750	300

National Wild Turkey Federation

1985 manufacture.

NIB	Exc.	V.G.	Good	Fair	Poor
850	700	600	550	450	350

Shotguns manufactured by Perazzi and Japanese firms that were marketed by Ithaca are listed under the respective manufacturer's name.

RIFLES

Model X5-C

A .22 caliber semi-automatic rifle with a 7-shot magazine. A 10-shot magazine was available as an extra cost option. Blued with a walnut stock. Manufactured between 1958 and 1964.

NIB	Exc.	V.G.	Good	Fair	Poor
400	200	150	100	75	—

Model X5T Lightning

A .22 caliber tubular feed auto-loading rifle produced between 1959 and 1963. Some models were stocked with curly maple stocks. These guns will command a 25 percent price premium.

NIB	Exc.	V.G.	Good	Fair	Poor
450	175	150	100	75	—

Model X-15 Lightning

Similar to the above, but manufactured between 1964 and 1966.

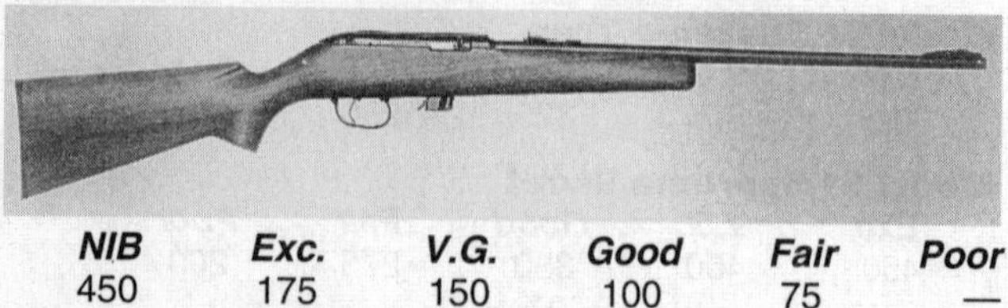

NIB	Exc.	V.G.	Good	Fair	Poor
450	175	150	100	75	—

Model 49 Saddlegun—1961-1979

A .22 caliber lever action single-shot rifle with an 18.5" barrel, fixed sights, alloy receiver and hardwood stock. It was offered chambered for the .22 Magnum in 1962.

Courtesy C. Hadley Smith

NIB	Exc.	V.G.	Good	Fair	Poor
350	200	125	100	50	—

Model 49 Saddlegun Deluxe Grade

Fitted with gold plated trigger, hammer, and equipped with sling and sling swivels.

NIB	Exc.	V.G.	Good	Fair	Poor
450	250	150	100	50	—

Model 49 Saddlegun Presentation Grade

High grade wood and engraved frame.

NIB	Exc.	V.G.	Good	Fair	Poor
550	300	250	200	50	—

Model 49R—1968-1971

A lever action .22 caliber tubular feed repeater. Magazine capacity is 15 LR cartridges.

NIB	Exc.	V.G.	Good	Fair	Poor
350	250	200	150	50	—

Model 72 Saddlegun—1973-1979

A .22 or .22 Magnum caliber lever action rifle with an 18.5" barrel, tubular magazine, open sights and walnut stock. Made by Erma in Germany.

NIB	Exc.	V.G.	Good	Fair	Poor
375	275	225	200	100	—

LSA-55 or 65 Series

A bolt-action sporting rifle manufactured in a variety of calibers and barrel lengths by Tikka of Finland. Imported between 1969 and 1977 in the models listed.

LSA-55 Standard

Exc.	V.G.	Good	Fair	Poor
500	350	300	250	175

LSA-55 Deluxe

Exc.	V.G.	Good	Fair	Poor
600	375	325	275	200

LSA-55 Varmint Heavy Barrel

Exc.	V.G.	Good	Fair	Poor
600	400	350	300	225

LSA-65 Long Action

Exc.	V.G.	Good	Fair	Poor
500	350	300	250	175

LSA-65 Deluxe

Exc.	V.G.	Good	Fair	Poor
600	375	325	275	200

LSA-55 Turkey Gun

A 12 gauge by .222 Remington caliber over-and-under combination rifle/shotgun with 24.5" barrels, single trigger, exposed hammer and walnut stock. Manufactured in Finland by Tikka between 1970 and 1981.

Exc.	V.G.	Good	Fair	Poor
850	700	450	350	275

X-Caliber

A .22 to .44 Magnum caliber single-shot pistol with 10" or 15" barrels featuring a dual firing pin system so that interchangeable barrels could be used. The Model 20 is blued, the Model 30 is Teflon coated. Introduced in 1988.

NIB	Exc.	V.G.	Good	Fair	Poor
425	350	300	225	175	125

IVER JOHNSON ARMS, INC.

Middlesex, New Jersey

SEE—AMAC

Established in 1883 in Fitchburg, Massachusetts, this company has produced a wide variety of firearms during its existence.

Trade Name Revolvers

A series of spur trigger revolvers were made by Iver Johnson bearing only the trade names such as Encore, Eclipse, Favorite, Tycoon, and Eagle. In general, the value for these revolvers are listed.

Exc.	V.G.	Good	Fair	Poor
250	170	120	95	65

Safety Automatic Double-Action

A .22, .32 CF, or .38 CF caliber double-action revolver produced in a variety of barrel lengths with or without exposed hammers. Manufactured between 1893 and 1950.

Exc.	V.G.	Good	Fair	Poor
250	170	120	95	65

This symbol denotes "Sleepers" with rapidly-rising values and/or significant collector potential.

Model 1900

A .22 to .38 caliber double-action revolver with a 2.5", 4.5", or 6" barrel. Blued or nickel-plated with rubber grips and no cartridge ejecting system. Manufactured between 1900 and 1947.

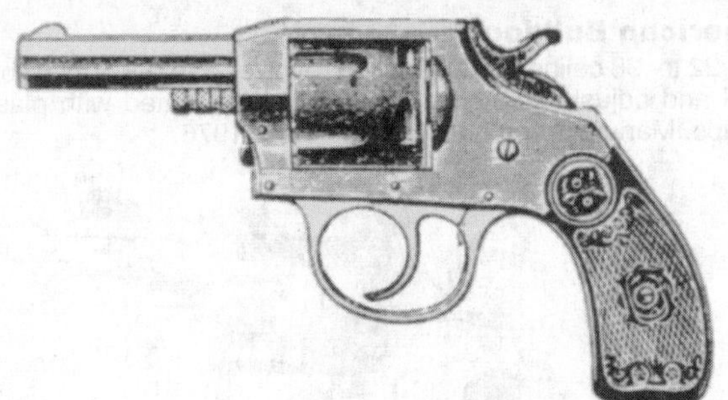

Exc.	V.G.	Good	Fair	Poor
250	170	120	95	65

Safety Cycle Automatic

Similar to the Safety Automatic with a 2" barrel.

Exc.	V.G.	Good	Fair	Poor
250	170	120	95	65

Petite

A .22 Short caliber double-action folding trigger revolver with a 1" barrel and 7-shot cylinder. Nickel-plated with rubber grips. Introduced in 1909.

Exc.	V.G.	Good	Fair	Poor
350	250	200	150	100

Supershot Sealed 8

A .22 caliber double-action revolver with a 6" barrel and counterbored 8-shot cylinder. Blued with rubber grips. Manufactured from 1919 to 1957.

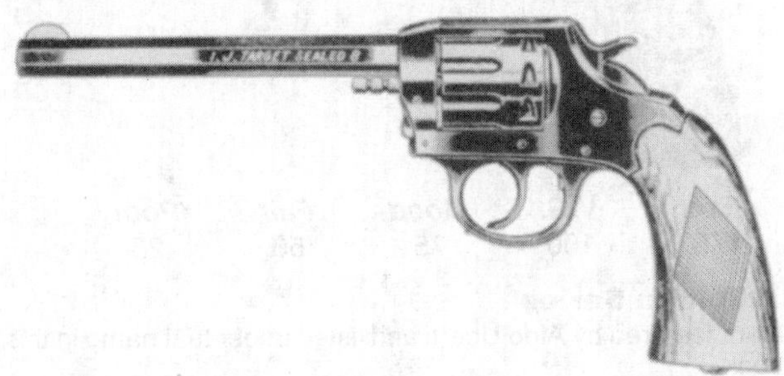

Exc.	V.G.	Good	Fair	Poor
250	170	120	95	65

Protector Sealed 8

As above, with a 2.5" barrel.

Exc.	V.G.	Good	Fair	Poor
250	170	120	95	65

Supershot 9

Similar to the Supershot Sealed 8 with a 9-shot uncounterbored cylinder. Manufactured between 1929 and 1949.

Exc.	V.G.	Good	Fair	Poor
250	170	120	95	65

Trigger Cocker Single-Action

A .22 caliber single-action revolver with a 6" barrel and 8-shot counterbored cylinder. Blued with walnut grips. Manufactured between 1940 and 1947.

Exc.	V.G.	Good	Fair	Poor
200	125	100	50	25

.22 Target Single-Action

As above, with adjustable sights and adjustable grips. Manufactured between 1938 and 1948.

Exc.	V.G.	Good	Fair	Poor
250	190	150	125	65

Model 844

A .22 caliber double-action revolver with a 4.5" or 6" barrel, adjustable sights, and an 8-shot cylinder. Manufactured in the 1950s.

Exc.	V.G.	Good	Fair	Poor
225	140	100	80	40

Model 855

As above, but single-action with a 6" barrel. Manufactured in the 1950s.

Exc.	V.G.	Good	Fair	Poor
225	140	100	80	40

Model 55A Sportsmen Target

A .22 caliber single-action revolver with a 4.75" or 6" barrel, fixed sights and 8-shot cylinder. Blued with walnut grips.

Exc.	V.G.	Good	Fair	Poor
200	125	100	75	35

Model 55S-A Cadet

A .22 to .38 caliber single-action revolver with a 2.5" barrel and fixed sights. Blued with plastic grips. Introduced in 1955.

Exc.	V.G.	Good	Fair	Poor
250	170	120	95	65

Model 57A Target

As above, with a 4.5" or 6" barrel and adjustable sights. Manufactured between 1955 and 1975.

Exc.	V.G.	Good	Fair	Poor
175	110	85	60	35

Model 66 Trailsman

A .22 caliber double-action revolver with a 6" barrel, adjustable sights, and 8-shot cylinder. Blued with walnut grips. Manufactured between 1958 and 1975.

Exc.	V.G.	Good	Fair	Poor
125	75	65	50	25

Model 67 Viking

As above, with a safety hammer.

Exc.	V.G.	Good	Fair	Poor
125	75	65	50	25

Model 67S Viking Snub

Same as above but fitted with 2" barrel.

Exc.	V.G.	Good	Fair	Poor
125	75	65	50	25

Model 50

A .22 or .22 Magnum single-action revolver with a 4.75" or 6" barrel, 8-shot cylinder and either fixed or adjustable sights. Also known as the Sidewinder. Manufactured between 1961 and 1975.

Exc.	V.G.	Good	Fair	Poor
125	75	65	50	25

American Bulldog

A .22 to .38 caliber double-action revolver with a 2.5" or 4" barrel and adjustable sights. Blued or nickel-plated with plastic grips. Manufactured between 1974 and 1976.

Exc.	V.G.	Good	Fair	Poor
175	100	75	50	25

Rookie

A .38 caliber revolver with a 4" barrel and 5-shot cylinder. Blued or nickel-plated with plastic grips.

Exc.	V.G.	Good	Fair	Poor
175	100	75	50	25

Cattleman Series

Manufactured by Aldo Uberti and listed under that name in this book.

Model X300 Pony

A .380 semi-automatic pistol with a 3" barrel and 6-shot magazine. Blued with plastic grips. Introduced in 1975.

Exc.	V.G.	Good	Fair	Poor
275	195	165	135	85

Trailsman

A .22 caliber semi-automatic pistol with a 4.5" or 6" barrel and 10-shot magazine. Blued with plastic or walnut grips.

Exc.	V.G.	Good	Fair	Poor
275	195	165	135	85

TP22/TP25 Pistol

A .22 or .25 ACP caliber double-action semi-automatic pistol with a 2.8" barrel and 7-shot magazine. Blued or nickel-plated with plastic grips.

Exc.	V.G.	Good	Fair	Poor
275	195	165	135	85

RIFLES

Model X

Bolt action .22 caliber single-shot rifle fitted with 22" barrel with open sights, pistol grip. Manufactured between 1927 and 1932.

Exc.	V.G.	Good	Fair	Poor
175	110	90	70	40

Model XA

As above but with Lyman receiver sight, swivels, leather strap, and ivory bead. Manufactured between 1927 and 1932.

Exc.	V.G.	Good	Fair	Poor
325	225	175	130	80

Model 2X

Fitted with a 24" heavy barrel and adjustable sights. Manufactured between 1932 and 1955.

Exc.	V.G.	Good	Fair	Poor
400	300	250	150	100

Li'L Champ

Chambered for the .22 LR cartridge this is a bolt-action single-shot rifle that weighs about 3 lbs.

Exc.	V.G.	Good	Fair	Poor
125	85	70	50	30

Long Range Rifle

This is a single-shot bolt-action rifle chambered for the .50 caliber Browning cartridge. Fitted with a 29" fluted barrel and adjustable trigger. Bipod. Comes supplied with a 20 power Leopold scope. Limited production. Weight is about 36 lbs. Manufactured between 1988 and 1993.

Exc.	V.G.	Good	Fair	Poor
4600	4000	3000	2500	1000

JJ 9mm Carbine

This is a copy of the U.S. military M1. Blued finish and hardwood stock. Magazine is 20 rounds. Chambered for the 9mm cartridge. Built between 1985 and 1986.

Exc.	V.G.	Good	Fair	Poor
300	200	150	100	80

NOTE: Add 10 percent for folding stock. Deduct 5 percent for plastic stock.

Delta-786 Carbine

Similar to the M1 carbine but in 9mm only. Matte finish. Manufactured in 1989.

Exc.	V.G.	Good	Fair	Poor
650	550	400	300	150

Carbine .30 Caliber

Similar to the M1 carbine and chambered for the .30 carbine cartridge. Offered in various stock configurations. Built from 1985 to 1986 and again in 1988 to 1993.

Exc.	V.G.	Good	Fair	Poor
400	285	215	150	100

NOTE: For paratrooper model add $50, for Johnson 5.7mm caliber deduct $75, no premium for stainless steel.

U.S. Carbine .22 Caliber

Same as above but chambered for the .22 LR or .22 Magnum cartridge. Built in 1985 and 1986 and again in 1988. Fitted with 15-round magazine.

Exc.	V.G.	Good	Fair	Poor
225	145	125	85	50

Slide Action Targetmaster

Chambered for the .22 LR or .22 Magnum cartridge this rifle has a 15-round tubular magazine. Manufactured between 1985 and 1988 and again in 1990.

Exc.	V.G.	Good	Fair	Poor
250	170	125	100	50

Wagonmaster Model EW .22 HBL Lever Action

Chambered for the .22 LR or .22 Magnum cartridge and fitted with a hardwood stock. Blued finish. Grooved scope mounts. Built in 1985 and 1986 and again between 1988 and 1990.

Exc.	V.G.	Good	Fair	Poor
250	175	130	100	50

Model IJ .22 HB Semi-Automatic (Trail Blazer)

Chambered for .22 LR only with 10-round magazine. Manufactured in 1985 only.

Exc.	V.G.	Good	Fair	Poor
225	130	100	60	40

SHOTGUNS

Champion

A single barrel shotgun manufactured in a variety of gauges as well as .44 or .45 caliber with 26" to 32" barrels, external hammers, and automatic ejectors. Blued with a walnut stock. Manufactured between 1909 and 1956.

Exc.	V.G.	Good	Fair	Poor
175	100	75	50	25

Matted Rib Grade

As above, in 12, 16, or 20 gauge with a matte rib barrel. Manufactured between 1909 and 1948.

Exc.	V.G.	Good	Fair	Poor
200	125	100	75	50

Trap Grade

As above, in 12 gauge with a 32" ventilated rib barrel. Manufactured between 1909 and 1942.

Exc.	V.G.	Good	Fair	Poor
425	300	250	175	100

Hercules Grade

A boxlock double-barrel shotgun manufactured in a variety of gauges with 26" to 32" barrels, double triggers and extractors. Blued with a walnut stock.

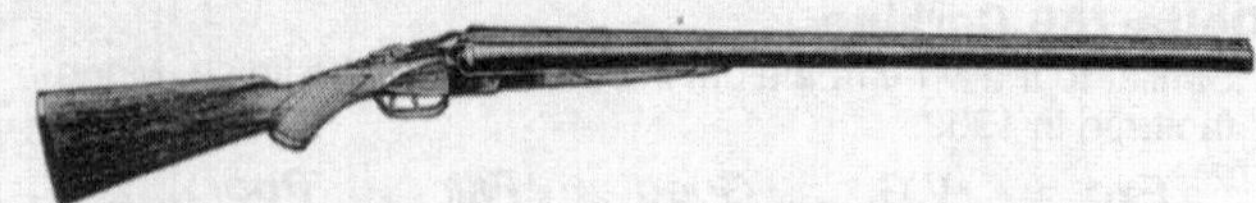

Exc.	V.G.	Good	Fair	Poor
1250	950	700	500	350

NOTE: Add premium for these features:

Single trigger—50 percent	Ejectors—50 percent
28 gauge—200 percent	.410 bore—150 percent
20 gauge—75 percent	16 gauge—20 percent
Engraving—200 percent	Vent rib—25 percent

Skeeter Model

As above, but more finely finished. Discontinued in 1946.

Exc.	V.G.	Good	Fair	Poor
2000	1500	1000	750	500

NOTE: Add premium for these features:

Single trigger—50 percent	Ejectors—50 percent
28 gauge—200 percent	.410 bore—150 percent
20 gauge—75 percent	16 gauge—20 percent
Engraving—200 percent	Vent rib—25 percent

Super Trap

A 12 gauge boxlock double barrel shotgun with a 32" full choked barrels, and extractors. Discontinued in 1942.

Exc.	V.G.	Good	Fair	Poor
2500	1900	1350	850	350

NOTE: Add 50 percent for Miller single selective trigger and 35 percent for non-selective single trigger.

Silver Shadow

A 12 gauge boxlock over-and-under shotgun with a 26" or 28" ventilated rib barrels, double triggers and extractors. Blued with a walnut stock. Manufactured in Italy and imported by Iver Johnson.

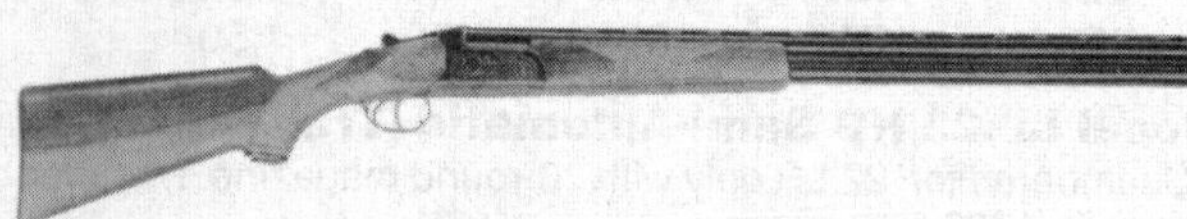

Exc.	V.G.	Good	Fair	Poor
550	400	350	300	200

NOTE: Also available with a single trigger, which would increase the values listed by approximately 25 percent.

THE "NEW" IVER-JOHNSON BRAND (2006)

The Iver Johnson name resurfaced in 2006 in connection with a line of firearms based in Rockledge, Florida.)

Frontier Four Derringer

Four-barrel, stainless .22 LR single-action derringer with unique rotating firing pin. Based on old Sharps derringer. 5.5 oz. Introduced 2006.

NIB	Exc.	V.G.	Good	Fair
175	—	—	—	—

EAGLE TARGET SERIES

1911 .45

All-steel 7+1 capacity 1911 .45 ACP with 5" Government or 4.5" Commander barrel. Adjustable white outline rear sight. Adjustable trigger. Polished blue. Introduced 2006. MSRP: 650

1911 .22 LR

Aluminum slide and frame, 15+1 capacity 1911 .22 LR with 5" Government or 4.5" Commander barrel. 19 oz. Adjustable white outline rear sight. Adjustable trigger. Blued or stainless. Introduced 2006. MSRP: 600

RAVEN SERIES

1911 .45

All-steel 7+1 capacity 1911 .45 ACP with 5" Government or 4.5" Commander barrel. Fixed sights. Matte blue, Parkerized or two-tone. Introduced 2006. MSRP: 525

1911 .22 LR

Aluminum slide and frame, 15+1 capacity 1911 in .22 LR with 5" Government or 4.5" Commander barrel. 19 oz. Fixed sights. Matte blued or stainless two-tone finish. Introduced 2006. MSRP: 550

IXL

New York, New York

Pocket Revolver

A .31 caliber double-action percussion revolver with a 4" octagonal barrel and 6-shot cylinder. Blued with walnut grips. The barrel marked "IXL N.York." Approximately 750 were made without hammer spurs and 150 with side mounted hammers during the 1850s.

Exc.	V.G.	Good	Fair	Poor
—	—	1250	600	300

Navy Revolver

As above in .36 caliber. Approximately 100 were made with both center and side mounted hammers during the 1850s.

Courtesy Milwaukee Public Museum, Milwaukee, Wisconsin

Exc.	V.G.	Good	Fair	Poor
—	—	3250	1400	500

JACQUESMART, JULES
Liege, Belgium

Le Monobloc

A 6.35mm semi-automatic pistol with a 2" barrel and 6-shot magazine. The slide marked "Le Monobloc/Pistolet Automatique/Brevefte." Blued with composition grips. Production ceased in 1914.

Courtesy James Rankin

Exc.	V.G.	Good	Fair	Poor
550	450	350	200	100

JACQUITH, ELIJAH
Brattleboro, Vermont

Revolving Under Hammer Rifle

An extremely rare .40 caliber percussion revolving rifle with a 34" round-octagonal barrel and 8-shot cylinder. It is believed that approximately 25 of these rifles were made in 1838 and 1839. The barrel marked "E. Jaquith Brattleboro. Vt." Prospective purchasers should secure a qualified appraisal prior to acquisition.

Exc.	V.G.	Good	Fair	Poor
—	—	15000	6500	2000

JAGER WAFFENFABIK
Suhl, Germany

Jager Semi-Automatic Pistol

A 7.65mm caliber semi-automatic pistol with a 3" barrel and 7-shot magazine. Largely made from steel stampings. Weight is approximately 23 oz. Blued with plastic grips. The slide marked "Jager-Pistole DRP Angem." Approximately 5,500 were made prior to 1914.

Courtesy Richard M. Kumor, Sr.

Exc.	V.G.	Good	Fair	Poor
450	350	300	175	100

NOTE: Add 50 percent for Imperial proofed examples.

JAPANESE STATE MILITARY WEAPONS
Japan

NOTE: For history, technical data, descriptions, and prices see the *Standard Catalog of Military Firearms* under Japan.

JEFFERY, W. J. & CO. LTD.
London, England

This company produced high quality shotguns and rifles. Their products have been used by wealthy sportsmen for many years. They produced guns under their own banner and also as contractors for other distributors. They made the guns sold by the Army & Navy Department Store in London. Guns of this type were basically custom-ordered and as such are extremely hard to evaluate on a general basis. We supply estimated values for standard models.

SHOTGUNS

SEE—British Double Guns

RIFLES

Single-Shot

Built on the Farquharson Falling Block action and was chambered for many calibers up to the .600 Nitro Express. This was also a custom-order gun, and the barrel length was optional. There are usually folding express sights, and the finish is usually blued with a select, hand-checkered walnut stock. These were high quality firearms, and the values would be determined, for the most part, by the options and embellishments on the particular specimen. Individual appraisal is definitely advised. The caliber in which a rifle is chambered will also have an effect on the value. Obsolete calibers bring less, and the larger express calibers bring more.

Exc.	V.G.	Good	Fair	Poor
4500	3250	2500	1750	900

Boxlock Double Rifle

A boxlock chambered for many different calibers. It can be found with either a top or underlever action and has folding express sights. The stock and forearm are select, hand-checkered walnut, and the finish is usually blue. This was a custom-order proposition, and values can be affected by many variables such as caliber, options, and embellishment. Damascus barreled hammerguns are worth approximately 50 percent less.

Exc.	V.G.	Good	Fair	Poor
8000	6500	4500	3500	2500

Sidelock Double Rifle

Has detachable sidelocks and otherwise is comparable to the boxlock version.

Exc.	V.G.	Good	Fair	Poor
12500	10000	7500	5000	4000

JENISON, J. & CO.

Southbridge, Connecticut

Under Hammer Pistol

A .28 caliber single-shot under hammer percussion pistol with a 4" half-octagonal barrel marked "J.Jenison & Co./Southbridge, Mass." Blued with a maple or oak grip. Manufactured during the 1850s.

Exc.	V.G.	Good	Fair	Poor
—	—	1150	500	200

JENKS CARBINE

Manufacturer—N. P. Ames
Springfield, Massachusetts

Jenks "Mule Ear Carbine"

A .54 caliber percussion side hammer carbine with a 24.5" round barrel and full length stock secured by two barrel bands. The lock case hardened, the barrel browned and the furniture of brass. The lock marked "N.P.Ames/Springfield/Mass." The barrel stamped "Wm.Jenks/USN" followed by the inspector's initials. The buttstock carries an inspector's cartouche. Approximately 4,250 were made between 1841 and 1846. Some were marked "USR" for the "U.S. Revenue Cutter Service," and these would bring approximately an 80 percent premium over the values listed. However, prospective purchasers should secure a qualified appraisal prior to acquisition.

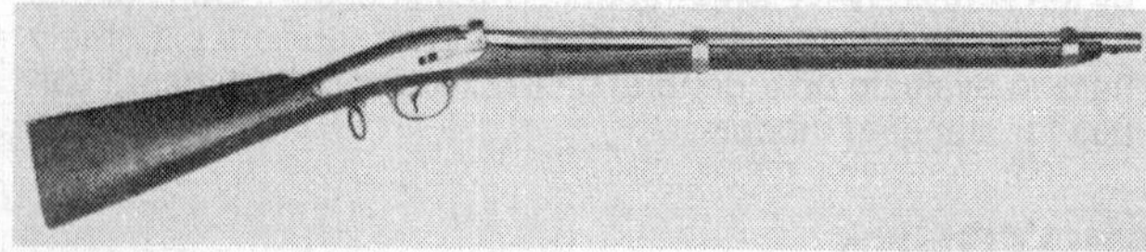

Courtesy Milwaukee Public Museum, Milwaukee, Wisconsin

Exc.	V.G.	Good	Fair	Poor
—	—	3750	1500	600

Jenks Navy Rifle

As above, with a 30" round barrel and full-length stock secured by three barrel bands. Approximately 1,000 were made for the U.S. Navy in 1841.

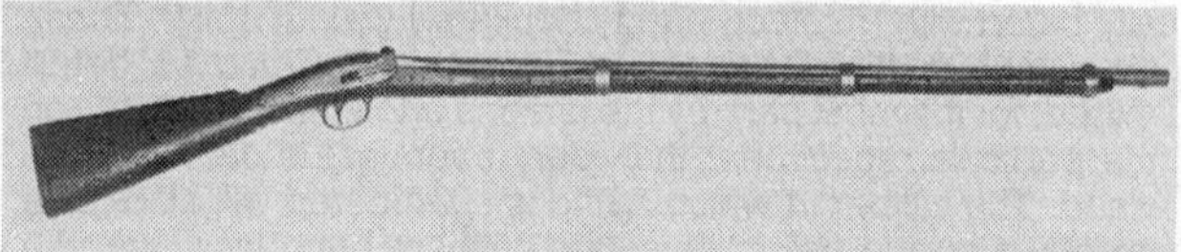

Courtesy Milwaukee Public Museum, Milwaukee, Wisconsin

Exc.	V.G.	Good	Fair	Poor
—	—	4250	1750	750

JENKS-HERKIMER

New York
Manufacturer—E. Remington & Son

Jenks Carbine

Identical to the Jenks Carbine listed in the previous entry except that the barrel length is 24.25" and the lock is fitted with a Maynard tape primer. The lock marked "Remington's/Herkimer/N.Y." The barrel is marked "W. Jenks/USN/RC/P/Cast Steel." Approximately 1,000 of these carbines manufactured circa 1846.

Exc.	V.G.	Good	Fair	Poor
—	—	4250	1750	750

JENKS-MERRILL

Baltimore, Maryland

An alteration of the Jenks Carbine listed previously to a breech loading system developed by J.H. Merrill. The conventional sidelock marked "J. H. Merrill Balto./Pat. July 1858." The breech retains the mark "Wm.Jenks/USN." Approximately 300 were altered between 1858 and 1860.

Exc.	V.G.	Good	Fair	Poor
—	—	7500	3000	950

JENNINGS

Manufacturer—Robbins & Lawrence
Windsor, Vermont
SEE—Winchester Repeating Arms

JENNINGS F. A., INC.

Carson City, Nevada

Distributors of arms manufactured by Calwestco in Chino, California, and Bryco Firearms in Carson City, Nevada.

J-22

A .22 caliber semi-automatic pistol with a 2.5" barrel and 6-shot magazine. Aluminum, finished in bright chrome, Teflon, or satin nickel with plastic or wood grips.

Exc.	V.G.	Good	Fair	Poor
90	65	50	35	25

Bryco Model 25

A .25 caliber semi-automatic pistol with a 2.5" barrel and 6-shot magazine. Constructed and finished as above.

Exc.	V.G.	Good	Fair	Poor
90	75	65	50	35

Bryco Model 38

A .22, .32, or .380 semi-automatic pistol with a 2.8" barrel and 6-shot magazine. Constructed and finished as above.

Exc.	V.G.	Good	Fair	Poor
90	75	65	50	35

Bryco Model 48

Similar to the above, with a redesigned trigger guard with a squared forward section. Introduced in 1988.

Exc.	V.G.	Good	Fair	Poor
90	75	65	50	35

JERICHO

Israeli Military Industries, Israel

Jericho

A 9mm or .41 Action Express double-action semi-automatic pistol with a 4.72" barrel, polygonal rifling, ambidextrous safety and fixed sights. Blued with plastic grips. No longer imported.

Exc.	V.G.	Good	Fair	Poor
500	400	350	300	200

JIEFFCO

Liege, Belgium

SEE—Robar et Cie

JOHNSON AUTOMATIC RIFLE

Cranston Arms Co.

Providence, Rhode Island

NOTE: For history, photos, technical data, descriptions, and prices see the *Standard Catalog of Military Firearms.*

JOHNSON, STAN, BYE & CO.

Worcester, Massachusetts

Established in 1871 by Martin Bye and Iver Johnson. This company primarily manufactured inexpensive pistols. In 1883 Johnson assumed full control of the company and renamed it the Iver Johnson Arms Company.

Defender, Eagle, Encore, Eureka, Favorite, Lion, Smoker, and Tycoon

A .22, .32, .38, or .44 caliber spur trigger revolver manufactured with various barrel lengths and normally nickel-plated. The barrel marked with one of the above trade names.

Exc.	V.G.	Good	Fair	Poor
—	500	200	75	25

Eclipse

A .22 caliber spur trigger single-shot pistol with a 1.5" barrel. Blued with walnut grips.

Exc.	V.G.	Good	Fair	Poor
—	250	100	50	25

American Bulldog

A .22, .32, or .38 caliber double-action revolver with a 3" barrel. Blued or nickel-plated with walnut or composition grips.

Exc.	V.G.	Good	Fair	Poor
—	250	100	50	25

JOSEF JESCHER

SEE—Austrian Military Firearms

JOSLYN

Milbury, Massachusetts

Manufacturer—A.H. Waters

Model 1855 Carbine

A .54 caliber breech loading single-shot percussion carbine with a 22.5" barrel secured to the forend by one barrel band. Blued, case hardened with brass mounts. The lock marked "A.H.Waters & Co./Milbury, Mass.," and the patent dates stamped on the breech lever. Approximately 1,000 manufactured in 1855 and 1856.

Exc.	V.G.	Good	Fair	Poor
—	—	4750	2000	950

Model 1855 Rifle

Similar to the above, in .58 caliber with a 38" barrel secured by three barrel bands. Several hundred were made in 1856.

Exc.	V.G.	Good	Fair	Poor
—	—	7500	3250	1100

JOSLYN

Springfield, Massachusetts

Manufacturer—Springfield Armory

Joslyn Breechloading Rifle

The first mass-produced, true breechloading cartridge firearm manufactured in a national armory. The actions were supplied by the Joslyn Firearms Company, and the rifles were chambered for the .56-50 rimfire cartridge. This rifle has a 35.5" round barrel and a full-length stock that is held on by three barrel bands. The lock is marked "U.S./Springfield" with "1864" at the back. The barrel is marked "B. F. Joslyn's Patent/ Oct. 8th, 1861 / June 24th, 1862." There were approximately 3,000 of these manufactured circa 1865. They were probably issued to Union forces, but it is unknown if they saw action before the end of the Civil War.

Exc.	V.G.	Good	Fair	Poor
—	—	2250	950	500

.50-70 Alteration

Approximately 1,600 Joslyn rifles were rechambered to fire the .50-70 centerfire cartridge. The conversion consisted of re-chambering and drilling a new firing pin hole after the rimfire pin was sealed. There was no specific serial number range in which these conversions were done. Most of these weapons were eventually converted to smoothbores and sold in Africa. The original military specimens are extremely scarce.

Exc.	V.G.	Good	Fair	Poor
—	—	2500	1500	750

JOSLYN FIREARMS COMPANY

Stonington, Connecticut

Model 1862 Carbine

A .52 rimfire breechloading single-shot carbine with a 22" round barrel secured by one barrel band. Blued, case hardened with brass mounts. The lock marked "Joslyn Firearms Co./Stonington/Conn.," and the patent date marked on the barrel. The trigger plate is 8" long, and the upper tang measures 4.5". Approximately 4,000 manufactured in 1862.

Courtesy Milwaukee Public Museum, Milwaukee, Wisconsin

Exc.	V.G.	Good	Fair	Poor
—	—	3250	1250	400

Model 1864 Carbine

As above, with case hardened iron mounts, a 7" trigger plate and 2" upper tang. Approximately 12,000 were made in 1864 and 1865.

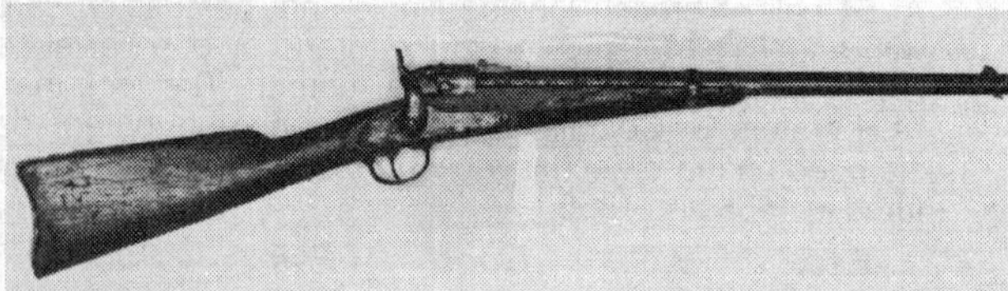

Courtesy Milwaukee Public Museum, Milwaukee, Wisconsin

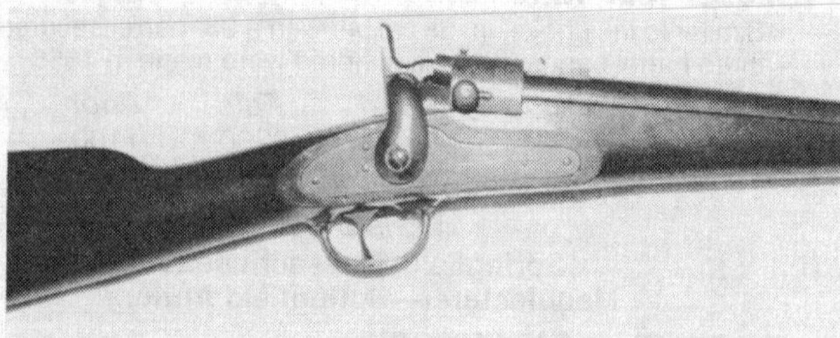

Exc.	V.G.	Good	Fair	Poor
—	—	3000	1000	400

Army Model Revolver

A .44 caliber side hammer percussion revolver with an 8" octagonal barrel and 5-shot cylinder. Blued, case hardened with walnut grips. The barrel marked "B. F. Joslyn/Patd. May 4, 1858." Martially marked examples are worth a premium of approximately 25 percent over the values listed.

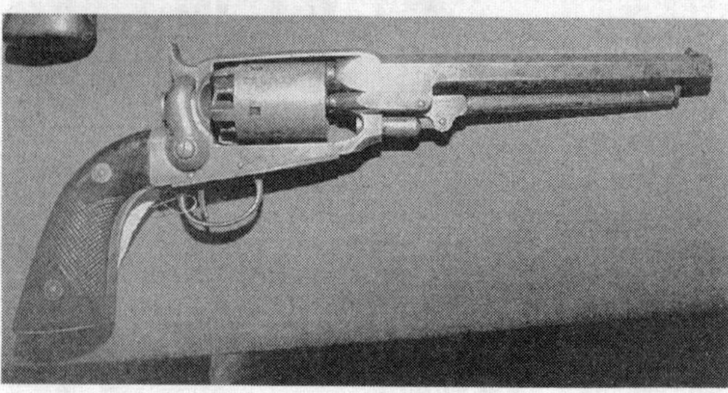

First Model

With a brass trigger guard and iron butt cap. Approximately 500 made in 1861.

Exc.	V.G.	Good	Fair	Poor
—	—	4750	2000	650

Second Model

Fitted with an iron trigger guard and without a butt cap. Approximately 2,500 were made in 1861 and 1862.

Exc.	V.G.	Good	Fair	Poor
—	—	4250	1600	500

JURRAS, LEE

Prescott, Arizona

SEE—Auto Mag

While Jurras is best known for manufacturing the last model of the Auto Mag, he also produced the pistol listed sold by J. & G. Sales in Prescott, Arizona.

Howdah Pistol

A .375, .416, .460, .475, .500, and .577 caliber single-shot pistol with a 12" barrel, adjustable sights and Nitex finish, built on a Thompson/Center Contender frame.

Exc.	V.G.	Good	Fair	Poor
1500	1000	800	650	500

JUSTICE, P. S.

Philadelphia, Pennsylvania

Percussion Rifle

A .58 caliber percussion rifle with a 35" round barrel secured by two barrel bands, browned barrel, polished lock and brass furniture. The lock marked "P.S. Justice/Philada." Approximately 2,500 were manufactured in 1861.

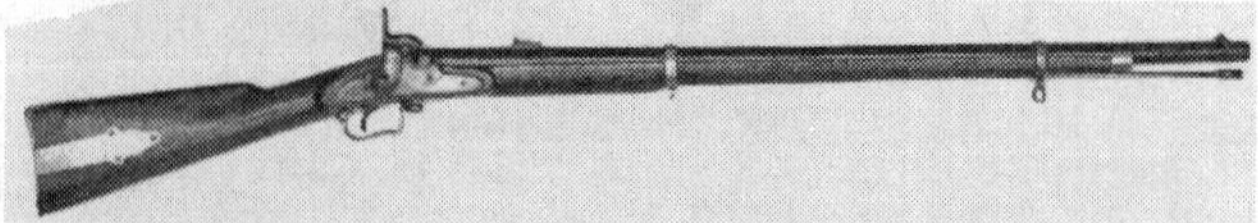

Courtesy Milwaukee Public Museum, Milwaukee, Wisconsin

Exc.	V.G.	Good	Fair	Poor
—	—	1750	800	450

This symbol denotes "Sleepers" with rapidly-rising values and/or significant collector potential.

K.F.C.
Japan

E-1 Trap or Skeet Over-and-Under
A 12 gauge boxlock double-barrel shotgun with 26" or 30" barrels, competition rib, single-selective trigger, and automatic ejectors. Engraved, blued with a walnut stock. Manufactured until 1986.

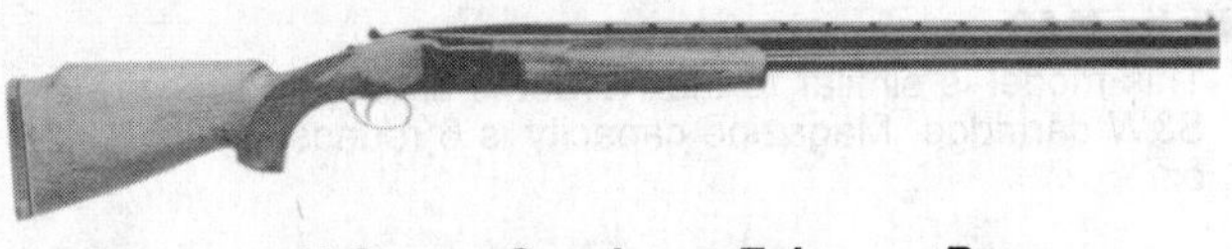

Exc.	V.G.	Good	Fair	Poor
950	800	700	500	300

E-2 Trap or Skeet Over-and-Under
As above, but more finely finished.

Exc.	V.G.	Good	Fair	Poor
1400	1250	1000	750	350

Field Grade Over-and-Under
As above, with a narrow rib and 26" or 28" barrels. Discontinued in 1986.

Exc.	V.G.	Good	Fair	Poor
650	575	500	400	275

Model 250
A 12 gauge semi-automatic shotgun with 26", 28", or 30" barrels fitted for choke tubes. Matte blued with a walnut stock. Manufactured from 1980 to 1986.

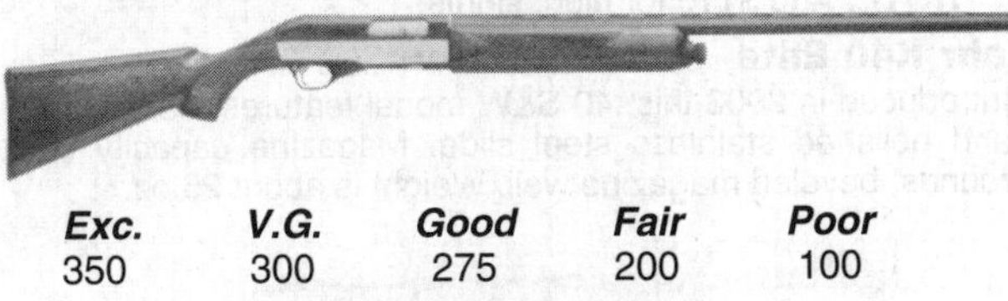

Exc.	V.G.	Good	Fair	Poor
350	300	275	200	100

KAHR ARMS
Blauvelt, New York

Kahr K9
This is a semi-automatic pistol chambered for the 9mm cartridge. It is a ultra-compact size. The barrel length is 3.5" and the overall length is 6". The width at the slide is .9". The magazine capacity is 7 rounds. Available in blue or electroless nickel finish. Weight is 25 oz.

NIB	Exc.	V.G.	Good	Fair	Poor
550	425	325	250	150	—

NOTE: Add $30 for blackened stainless steel slide; $130 for night sights.

Kahr Lady K9
Same as above but with lightened recoil spring.

NIB	Exc.	V.G.	Good	Fair	Poor
500	375	300	225	125	—

Kahr K9 Elite
Introduced in 2003 this 9mm model features a 3.5" barrel and polished stainless steel slide. Magazine capacity is 7 rounds. Weight is about 25 oz.

NIB	Exc.	V.G.	Good	Fair	Poor
575	425	350	275	—	—

NOTE: Add $110 for night sights.

Kahr MK9 Elite
Introduced in 2003 this 9mm model features a 3" barrel and polished stainless steel slide. Magazine capacity is 7 rounds. Weight is about 24 oz.

NIB	Exc.	V.G.	Good	Fair	Poor
575	425	350	275	—	—

NOTE: Add $110 for night sights.

Kahr P9 Compact Polymer
Introduced in 1999 this 9mm model features a 3.5" barrel with double-action-only trigger. Black polymer frame with stainless steel slide. Overall length is 6", height is 4.5". Weight is about 18 oz. Magazine capacity is 7 rounds.

NIB	Exc.	V.G.	Good	Fair	Poor
575	475	325	250	—	—

Kahr K9 Compact Polymer Covert
Same as the model above but with 1/2" shorter grip frame. Weight is about 17 oz. Magazine capacity is 6 rounds. Introduced in 1999.

NIB	Exc.	V.G.	Good	Fair	Poor
575	475	325	250	—	—

Kahr TP9
Introduced in 2004 this 9mm model features a black polymer frame with matte stainless steel slide. Fitted with a 4" barrel. Weight is about 20 oz.

NIB	Exc.	V.G.	Good	Fair	Poor
500	400	300	225	—	—

NOTE: Add $130 for Novak night sights.

TP40

Double-action-only semi-auto pistol chambered in .40 S&W. Black polymer frame, matte stainless slide, 4" barrel, textured polymer grips, 6- or 7-round capacity depending on magazine. Drift-adjustable white bar-dot sights or Novak two-dot tritium sights. Introduced 2006.

NIB	Exc.	V.G.	Good	Fair	Poor
500	—	—	—	—	—

Kahr PM9

This 9mm model is fitted with a 3" barrel with blackened stainless steel slide and black polymer frame. Magazine capacity is 6 rounds. Weight is about 16 oz. Introduced in 2004.

NIB	Exc.	V.G.	Good	Fair	Poor
735	550	300	—	—	—

NOTE: Add $110 for night sights.

Kahr PM9 Micro

Fitted with a 3" barrel and chambered for the 9mm cartridge this pistol weighs about 16 oz. Polymer frame and stainless steel slide. Introduced in 2002.

NIB	Exc.	V.G.	Good	Fair	Poor
500	400	300	—	—	—

Kahr K40

This model is similar to the K9 but is chambered for the .40 S&W cartridge. Magazine capacity is 6 rounds. Weight is 26 oz.

NIB	Exc.	V.G.	Good	Fair	Poor
550	450	350	—	—	—

NOTE: Add $110 for night sights.

Kahr K40 Elite

Introduced in 2003 this .40 S&W model features a 3.5" barrel and polished stainless steel slide. Magazine capacity is 6 rounds, beveled magazine well. Weight is about 26 oz.

NIB	Exc.	V.G.	Good	Fair	Poor
600	500	375	—	—	—

NOTE: For night sights add $110. For nickel finish add $70. For black titanium finish add $100. For the K40 stainless steel version add $50. Add $50 for Elite models.

Kahr K40 Covert

Similar to the K40 with a 1/2" shorter grip frame and flush fitting 5-round magazine. Barrel length is 3.5". Weight is about 25 oz. Finish is matte stainless steel.

NIB	Exc.	V.G.	Good	Fair	Poor
600	500	375	—	—	—

Kahr MK40

This .40 S&W model is fitted with a 3" barrel. Its overall length is 5.4" and height is 4". Finish is matte stainless steel. Magazine capacity is 5 rounds. Uses same magazines as K40 Covert. Introduced in 1999.

NIB	Exc.	V.G.	Good	Fair	Poor
600	475	375	250	—	—

Kahr MK40 Elite

Introduced in 2003 this .40 S&W model features a 3" barrel and polished stainless steel slide. Magazine capacity is 5 rounds, beveled magazine well. Weight is about 25 oz.

NIB	Exc.	V.G.	Good	Fair	Poor
780	625	525	—	—	—

NOTE: Add $110 for night sights.

Kahr P40

Similar to the P9 but chambered for the .40 S&W cartridge. Fitted with a 3.5" match grade barrel and matte stainless steel slide and black polymer frame. Supplied with two 6-round stainless steel magazines. Weight is approximately 19 oz. Introduced in 2001.

NIB	Exc.	V.G.	Good	Fair	Poor
600	500	375	—	—	—

Kahr P45

Introduced in 2005 this polymer frame stainless steel slide model is chambered for the .45 ACP cartridge. Barrel length is 3.5". Fixed sights. Magazine capacity is 6 rounds. Height of pistol is 4.8". Overall length is 6.3". Slide width is 1". Weight is about 18.5 oz.

NIB	Exc.	V.G.	Good	Fair	Poor
600	500	375	—	—	—

NOTE: Add $105 for night sights.

Kahr MK9

This is a 9mm model with double-action-only trigger. Barrel length is 3". Overall length is 5.5" and height is 4". Weight is approximately 22 oz. One 6-round magazine and one 7-round magazine with grip extension standard. This model is fitted with a specially designed trigger for shorter trigger stroke.

NIB	Exc.	V.G.	Good	Fair	Poor
425	300	225	200	—	—

NOTE: Add $150 for two-tone finish, add $50 for Elite stainless steel finish.

Kahr CW9

This 9mm model, introduced in 2005, features a 3.5" barrel, polymer frame, and stainless steel slide. Magazine capacity is 7 rounds. Height of pistol is 4.5". Overall length is 6". Slide width is .9".

NIB	Exc.	V.G.	Good	Fair	Poor
375	300	225	200	—	—

CW40

Semi-auto with textured polymer grip chambered for .40 S&W and 6+1 capacity. Double-action with 3.6" barrel, 16.8 oz. Adjustable rear sights. Introduced 2006.

NIB	Exc.	V.G.	Good	Fair	Poor
400	—	—	—	—	—

Wilson Combat Kahr Pistols

Offered in both the K9 and K40 models this is a customized pistol by Wilson's Gun Shop. It features hard chrome frame, black slide, 30 lpi checkering on front strap, beveled magazine well and several other special features. Initial production for the K40 is 50 pistols and for the K9 25 pistols.

NIB	Exc.	V.G.	Good	Fair	Poor
1300	1050	—	—	—	—

Model 1911PKZ

This model uses the Auto-Ordnance 1911 pistols re-engineered by Kahr Arms. This model includes a Parkerized finish, lanyard loop and U.S. Army roll mark of the slide. Seven-round magazine standard. Introduced in 2001.

NIB	Exc.	V.G.	Good	Fair	Poor
475	375	250	—	—	—

Model 1911 Standard

This model features a blued finish, plastic grips with Thompson medallion and bullet logo on the slide. Seven-round magazine. Introduced in 2001.

NIB	Exc.	V.G.	Good	Fair	Poor
400	300	225	—	—	—

Model 1911C

Similar to the Standard Model but with a 4.25" barrel.

NIB	Exc.	V.G.	Good	Fair	Poor
500	400	—	—	—	—

Model 1911WGS Deluxe

This model has a blued finish, rubber wrap-around grips with Thompson medallion, high profile white dot sights, and Thompson bullet logo on the slide. Seven-round magazine. Introduced in 2001.

NIB	Exc.	V.G.	Good	Fair	Poor
575	475	425	—	—	—

KASSNAR IMPORTS, INC.

Harrisburg, Pennsylvania

Currently, the firearms listed are imported by this company.

Standard Over-and-Under

A 12, 20, 28 or .410 bore boxlock double-barrel shotgun with 26" or 28" barrels, ventilated ribs, single trigger and extractors. Blued with a walnut stock.

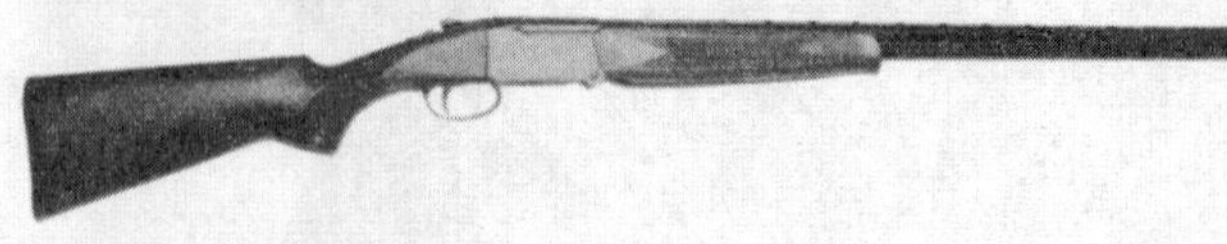

NIB	Exc.	V.G.	Good	Fair	Poor
350	275	225	200	150	100

Deluxe Over-and-Under

As above, with a more finely figured stock.

NIB	Exc.	V.G.	Good	Fair	Poor
400	325	250	225	175	100

Standard Side-by-Side

A 20, 28 or .410 bore boxlock folding double-barrel shotgun with 26" barrels, double triggers and extractors. Blued with a walnut stock.

NIB	Exc.	V.G.	Good	Fair	Poor
250	200	175	150	100	75

Deluxe Side-by-Side

As above, in .410 bore only and with more finely figured wood.

NIB	Exc.	V.G.	Good	Fair	Poor
300	250	200	175	125	75

KBI, INC.

Harrisburg, Pennsylvania

PSP-25

A .25 caliber semi-automatic pistol with a 2" barrel manufactured in Charlottesville, Virginia, under license from Fabrique Nationale. Introduced in 1989.

NIB	Exc.	V.G.	Good	Fair
250	200	175	150	100

KDF, INC.

Kleinguenther Distinctive Firearms

Seguin, Texas

The former importer of Voere and Mauser rifles into the U.S.

Condor

A 12 gauge boxlock over-and-under shotgun with 28" barrels with ventilated ribs, single-selective trigger and automatic ejectors. Blued with a walnut stock. Manufactured in Italy.

Exc.	V.G.	Good	Fair	Poor
700	600	525	375	275

Brescia

A 12 gauge boxlock double-barrel shotgun with 28" barrels, double triggers and extractors. Blued with a walnut stock. Manufactured in Italy.

Exc.	V.G.	Good	Fair	Poor
400	325	300	200	125

K-14 Insta Fire Rifle

A bolt-action sporting rifle manufactured in a variety of calibers with 24" or 26" barrels furnished without sights. Blued with a Monte Carlo-style walnut stock.

Exc.	V.G.	Good	Fair	Poor
650	550	450	325	250

K-15

Similar to the above, with a 60-degree bolt angle and an accurized barrel guaranteed to fire a .5" group at 100 yards. Manufactured with a variety of optional features.

Exc.	V.G.	Good	Fair	Poor
1150	850	750	550	300

K-15 Pro-Hunter

As above, matte blued or electroless nickel-plated with a fiberglass stock.

Exc.	V.G.	Good	Fair	Poor
1400	1250	1000	700	500

K-15 Swat Rifle

A 7.62x54mm caliber bolt-action rifle with a 24" or 26" barrel furnished without sights, 4-shot magazine and Parkerized finish. Walnut stock.

Exc.	V.G.	Good	Fair	Poor
1500	1300	1100	800	550

K-15 Dangerous Game

As above, in .411 KDF caliber.

Exc.	V.G.	Good	Fair	Poor
2000	1600	1300	1000	700

K-16

A bolt-action sporting rifle manufactured in a variety of calibers with a 24" or 26" barrel furnished without sights, single stage adjustable trigger, accurized barrel and Dupont Rynite stock. Produced with a variety of optional features.

Exc.	V.G.	Good	Fair	Poor
775	675	500	400	200

Titan Menor

A .222 or .223 caliber bolt-action rifle with a 24" or 26" barrel furnished without sights and Monte Carlo-style or standard schnabel tipped walnut stock. Blued.

Exc.	V.G.	Good	Fair	Poor
700	600	550	400	200

Titan II Standard

As above, with a mid-sized action.

Exc.	V.G.	Good	Fair	Poor
950	800	700	500	250

Titan II Magnum

As above, with a long action. Discontinued in 1988.

Exc.	V.G.	Good	Fair	Poor
1150	850	750	550	250

Titan .411 KDF Mag.

As above, in .411 KDF with a 26" barrel having an integral muzzlebrake. Blued or electroless nickel-plated with a walnut stock. Discontinued in 1988.

Exc.	V.G.	Good	Fair	Poor
1200	1050	850	650	350

K-22

A .22 caliber bolt-action rifle with a 21" free floating barrel furnished without sights, adjustable trigger, and 5-shot magazine. Also known as the Mauser 201.

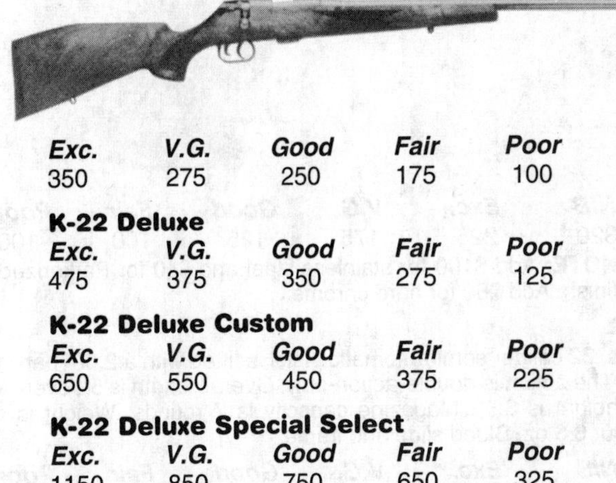

Exc.	V.G.	Good	Fair	Poor
350	275	250	175	100

K-22 Deluxe

Exc.	V.G.	Good	Fair	Poor
475	375	350	275	125

K-22 Deluxe Custom

Exc.	V.G.	Good	Fair	Poor
650	550	450	375	225

K-22 Deluxe Special Select

Exc.	V.G.	Good	Fair	Poor
1150	850	750	650	325

Model 2005

A .22 caliber semi-automatic rifle with a 19.5" barrel, open sights, and 5-shot magazine. Blued with a walnut stock. Also available in a deluxe model. Imported in 1986.

NIB	Exc.	V.G.	Good	Fair	Poor
150	100	80	60	40	30

Model 2107

A .22 or .22 Magnum caliber bolt-action rifle with a 19.5" barrel, open sights, and 5-shot magazine. Blued with a walnut stock.

Exc.	V.G.	Good	Fair	Poor
200	150	125	100	75

Model 2112

The deluxe version of the Model 2107.

Exc.	V.G.	Good	Fair	Poor
300	200	175	125	90

KEBERST INTERNATIONAL

Kendall International
Paris, Kentucky

Keberst Model 1A

A .338 Lapua Magnum, .338-416 Rigby, and the .338-06 caliber bolt-action rifle with a 24" barrel having an integral muzzlebrake, and fitted with a 3-9 power Leupold telescope. Matte blued with a camouflaged composition stock. Manufactured in 1987 and 1988.

Exc.	V.G.	Good	Fair	Poor
3750	3000	2500	1800	900

KEL-TEC CNC INDUSTRIES

Cocoa, Florida

P-11

This is a semi-automatic pistol chambered for the 9mm cartridge. It is double-action-only with a barrel length of 3.1".

Overall length is 5.6". Weight is 14 oz. Magazine capacity is 10 rounds. Standard model has blued slide with black grip. Stainless steel and Parkerized finish are offered as well.

NIB	Exc.	V.G.	Good	Fair	Poor
320	225	175	125	100	100

NOTE: Add $100 for stainless steel and $40 for Parkerized finish. Add $60 for hard chrome.

P-32

This .32 caliber semi-automatic pistol is fitted with a 2.68" barrel. The action is double-action-only. Overall length is 5", overall height is 3.5". Magazine capacity is 7 rounds. Weight is about 6.6 oz. Blued slide and frame.

NIB	Exc.	V.G.	Good	Fair	Poor
305	225	175	125	100	100

NOTE: Add $40 for Parkerized finish. Add $60 for hard chrome.

P-3AT

This model is chambered for the .380 cartridge and fitted with a 2.75" barrel. Blued finish. Magazine capacity is 6 rounds. Weight is about 7.3 oz.

NIB	Exc.	V.G.	Good	Fair	Poor
310	225	175	125	100	100

NOTE: Add $40 for Parkerized finish and $60 for hard chrome finish.

P-40

This model is similar to the P-11 but chambered for the .40 S&W cartridge. Barrel length is 3.3". Magazine capacity is 9 rounds. Weight is approximately 16 oz. Blued finish.

NIB	Exc.	V.G.	Good	Fair	Poor
320	225	175	125	100	100

NOTE: Add $40 for Parkerized finish. Add $60 for hard chrome.

SUB-2000 Rifle

Introduced in 1996 this is a semi-automatic rifle chambered for the 9mm or .40 S&W cartridge. The barrel length is 16.1". The rifle can be folded closed with an overall length of 16". Weight is approximately 4.6 lbs. Different grip assembly can be fitted to this rifle allowing for the use of different magazines.

NIB	Exc.	V.G.	Good	Fair	Poor
375	295	175	125	—	—

SU-16

This semi-automatic gas operated rifle is chambered for the .223 cartridge. It is fitted with an 18" barrel. This rifle has several unique features: the forend folds down to form a bipod, the stock can store spare magazines and the rifle folds into two parts for carry. Weight is about 5 lbs. SU-16A, 18.5-inch barrel; SU-16B, 16-inch lightweight barrel; SU-16C, 16-inch barrel, folding stock; SU-16CA, 16-inch standard barrel and standard stock.

NIB	Exc.	V.G.	Good	Fair	Poor
500	375	275	150	—	—

PLR-16

A 5.56 mm NATO gas-operated, semi-automatic AR-15-style long-range pistol. Windage-adjustable rear sight. Picatinny rail. Muzzle threaded for muzzle-brake. 9.2" barrel, 51 oz. 10-round or M-16 magazine. Blued finish, polymer construction. Introduced 2006.

NIB	Exc.	V.G.	Good	Fair	Poor
500	—	—	—	—	—

RFB Rifle

Bullpup semi-auto rifle with 32", 24" or 18" barrel, black laminated stock, third swivel for bipod. Forward ejection; takes FAL-type magazines. Chambered in .308 Winchester. Introduced in 2007. Price shown is for sporter.

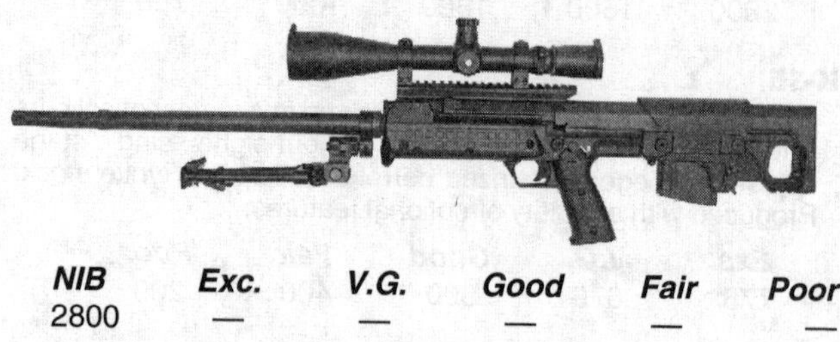

NIB	Exc.	V.G.	Good	Fair	Poor
2800	—	—	—	—	—

KEMPER, SHRIVER & COMPANY

Nashville, Tennessee

Delivered rifles made from sporting arm parts to the Ordnance Department at Nashville from December 1861 to March 1862. In all 150 arms were assembled. Overall length 48-1/2"; octagonal barrels shortened 33" and bored to .48 caliber; some fitted with saber bayonet lugs; stocks of military with brass furniture.

Exc.	V.G.	Good	Fair	Poor
—	—	4500	2000	1500

KENDALL, INTERNATIONAL

Paris, Kentucky

SEE—Keberst International

KENDALL, NICANOR
Windsor, Vermont

Under Hammer Pistol
A .31 to .41 caliber under hammer percussion pistol with 4" to 10" octagonal/round barrels marked "N.Kendall/Windsor,Vt." Browned or blued with brass mounts and maple grips. Manufactured in the 1850s.

Exc.	*V.G.*	*Good*	*Fair*	*Poor*
—	—	1750	600	200

KENO
Unknown

Derringer
A .22 caliber single-shot spur trigger pistol with a 2.5" barrel, brass frame, and walnut grips. The barrel blued or nickel-plated and marked "Keno."

Exc.	*V.G.*	*Good*	*Fair*	*Poor*
—	—	500	175	100

KERR
London, England

Kerr Revolver
A .44 caliber double-action percussion revolver with a 5.5" barrel and 6-shot cylinder. Blued with walnut grips. The frame marked "Kerr's Patent 648"; and "London Armoury Bermondsey."

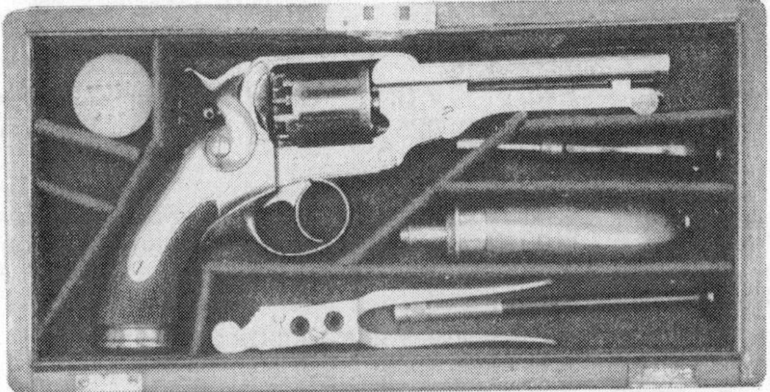

Courtesy Bonhams & Butterfields, San Francisco, California

Exc.	*V.G.*	*Good*	*Fair*	*Poor*
—	3250	1250	600	300

KERR
SEE—English Military Firearms

KESSLER ARMS CORPORATION
Silver Creek, New York

Bolt-Action Shotgun
A 12, 16, or 20 gauge shotgun with 26" or 28" barrels. Blued with a walnut stock. Manufactured between 1951 and 1953.

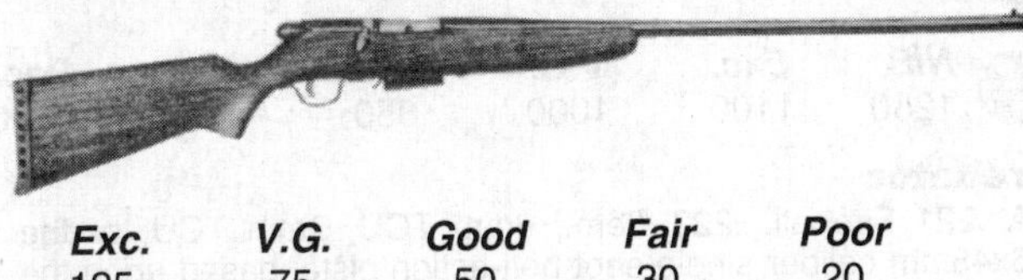

Exc.	*V.G.*	*Good*	*Fair*	*Poor*
125	75	50	30	20

Levermatic Shotgun
A 12, 16, or 20 gauge lever-action shotgun with a 26" or 28" barrel. Blued with a walnut stock. Manufactured between 1951 and 1953.

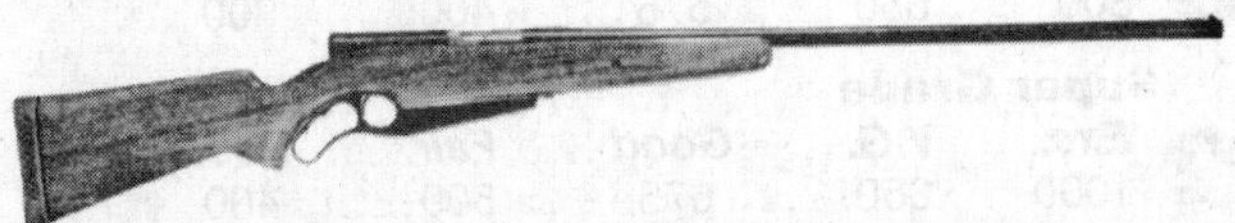

Exc.	*V.G.*	*Good*	*Fair*	*Poor*
300	275	200	150	75

KETTNER, EDWARD
Suhl, Germany

Drilling
This is a high-quality three-barreled firearm chambered for 12x12 gauge or 16x16 gauge over various metric rifle cartridges. The barrels are 25" in length and feature ejectors, selective triggers, and pop-up rifle sights that appear when the rifle barrel is selected. This gun is deep-relief engraved in the German style and has a high-grade checkered walnut stock. It was manufactured between 1922 and 1939.

Exc.	*V.G.*	*Good*	*Fair*	*Poor*
—	3000	1750	950	500

KIMBALL ARMS COMPANY
Detroit, Michigan

Semi-Automatic Pistol
A .30 carbine caliber semi-automatic pistol with a 3.5" or 5" barrel. Blued with plastic grips. Also believed to have been made in .22 Hornet and .357 Magnum, though few legitimate examples have been seen. Manufactured from 1955 to 1958. Approximately 238 were made.

Courtesy James Rankin

Exc.	*V.G.*	*Good*	*Fair*	*Poor*
2500	2000	1500	1000	800

KIMBER MFG., INC.
Yonkers, New York

Kimber of Oregon was established in April 1979 by Greg and Jack Warne. The company produced high quality rimfire and centerfire rifles until going out of business in early 1991. Kimber produced approximately 60,000 rifles during its operation. In April 1993, Greg Warne opened Kimber of America in Clackamas, Oregon. This new company presently manufactures the same high-quality rifles built on an improved Model 82 Sporter action and stock, but in rimfire only. In 1995 the company expanded its product line to include centerfire rifles as well as a 1911 .45 ACP semi-automatic pistol line. In 1997 manufacturing operations were consolidated in the New York pistol factory and the two factories in Oregon were closed.

DISCONTINUED MODELS

Model 82 Classic
A .22, .22 Magnum, or .22 Hornet bolt-action rifle with a 22" barrel furnished without sights and 4- or 5-shot magazine. Blued with a walnut stock. Discontinued in 1988.

Exc.	*V.G.*	*Good*	*Fair*	*Poor*
700	600	550	450	350

NOTE: For Model 82 Series rifles in .22 Magnum caliber add 10 percent. For rifles chambered for .22 Hornet add 15 percent.

This symbol denotes "Sleepers" with rapidly-rising values and/or significant collector potential.

Cascade Model

As above, with a Monte Carlo-style stock.

Exc.	V.G.	Good	Fair	Poor
750	650	600	500	400

Custom Classic Model

As above, in .218 Bee or .25-20.

Exc.	V.G.	Good	Fair	Poor
800	725	650	400	300

Mini Classic

The Model 82 with an 18" barrel. Manufactured in 1988.

Exc.	V.G.	Good	Fair	Poor
600	550	475	400	300

Deluxe Grade

Similar to the Custom Classic. Introduced in 1989.

NIB	Exc.	V.G.	Good	Fair	Poor
1000	850	650	550	450	350

Model 82A Government

A .22 caliber bolt-action rifle with a 25" heavy barrel fitted with telescope mounts. Matte blued with a walnut stock. Introduced in 1987.

NIB	Exc.	V.G.	Good	Fair	Poor
675	550	450	375	300	200

Continental

Similar to the Custom Classic with a 20" barrel, open sights, and full length Mannlicher-style stock. Introduced in 1987.

NIB	Exc.	V.G.	Good	Fair	Poor
850	750	650	500	400	300

Super Continental

As above, but more finely finished. Discontinued in 1988.

NIB	Exc.	V.G.	Good	Fair	Poor
1200	1100	1000	750	600	300

Super America

The Model 82 but more finely finished. Discontinued in 1988.

NIB	Exc.	V.G.	Good	Fair	Poor
1500	1200	950	850	650	500

Super Grade

As above, introduced in 1989.

NIB	Exc.	V.G.	Good	Fair	Poor
1200	1000	900	750	600	475

Centennial

A commemorative rifle moderately engraved including a special match barrel, skeleton buttplate, hand-selected walnut stock, and light engraving. Issued to commemorate the 100th anniversary of the .22 LR cartridge. One hundred were manufactured in 1987.

NIB	Exc.	V.G.	Good	Fair	Poor
2500	2250	2000	1750	1500	1150

Brownell

In 1986, 500 commemorative rifles were produced in honor of Leonard Brownell, featuring a high-grade, Mannlicher-style, full-length walnut stock.

NIB	Exc.	V.G.	Good	Fair	Poor
1500	1250	1000	800	600	500

MODEL 84 SERIES—DISCONTINUED MODELS

A bolt-action rifle manufactured in a variety of smallbore calibers with a 22" or 24" barrel and 5-shot magazine. Blued with a walnut stock. Variations are listed.

Classic Model

NIB	Exc.	V.G.	Good	Fair	Poor
700	650	600	400	250	200

Custom Classic Model

NIB	Exc.	V.G.	Good	Fair	Poor
900	800	700	500	350	200

Deluxe Grade Sporter

NIB	Exc.	V.G.	Good	Fair	Poor
1200	1000	850	750	500	250

Continental

NIB	Exc.	V.G.	Good	Fair	Poor
975	900	800	700	500	250

Super Continental

NIB	Exc.	V.G.	Good	Fair	Poor
1300	1100	850	700	575	250

Super America

NIB	Exc.	V.G.	Good	Fair	Poor
1500	1000	925	825	600	300

Super Grade

NIB	Exc.	V.G.	Good	Fair	Poor
1250	1100	1000	850	650	300

Ultra Varmint

As above, with a 24" stainless steel barrel and laminated birch wood stock. Introduced in 1989.

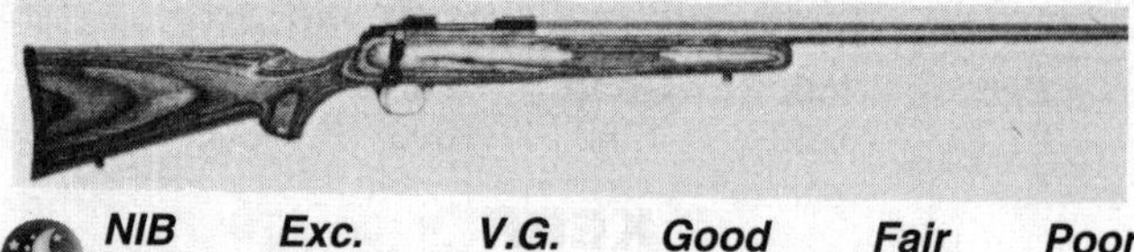

NIB	Exc.	V.G.	Good	Fair	Poor
1150	1000	900	750	550	250

Super Varmint

As above with a walnut stock. Introduced in 1989.

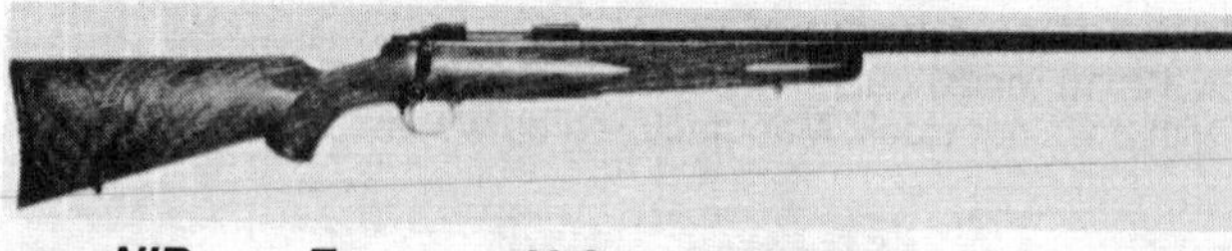

NIB	Exc.	V.G.	Good	Fair	Poor
1250	1100	1000	850	650	300

Predator

A .221 Fireball, .223 Rem., 6mm TCU, 7mm TCU, or the 6x45mm caliber single-shot bolt-action pistol based upon the Model 84 action with a 14.75" barrel adopted for a telescope. Blued with a walnut stock and available in two grades as listed. Manufactured in 1987 and 1988 only.

Hunter Grade

Exc.	V.G.	Good	Fair	Poor
800	650	575	400	300

Super Grade

Exc.	V.G.	Good	Fair	Poor
1000	850	675	500	400

MODEL 89 SERIES/BGR (BIG GAME RIFLES)

A bolt-action sporting rifle produced in .270 Winchester to .375 Holland & Holland caliber with a 22" or 24" barrel. Blued with a walnut stock. The variations of this model are listed.

Classic Model

NIB	Exc.	V.G.	Good	Fair	Poor
800	650	550	400	300	200

Custom Classic Model

NIB	Exc.	V.G.	Good	Fair	Poor
1000	850	650	450	350	250

Deluxe Grade

NIB	Exc.	V.G.	Good	Fair	Poor
1400	1150	900	650	450	250

Super America

NIB	Exc.	V.G.	Good	Fair	Poor
1800	1250	900	700	500	250

Super Grade

NIB	Exc.	V.G.	Good	Fair	Poor
1800	1250	900	700	500	250

MODEL 82C SERIES

NOTE: In 1998 the Model 82C series rifles went out of production.

Model 82C Classic

Bolt-action rifle chambered for the .22 LR cartridge. Receiver drilled and tapped for sights. Fitted with a 22" barrel. Detachable magazine holds 4 rounds. Stock is plain with standard grade Claro Walnut. Checkering is 18 lines to the inch with 4 point side panel pattern. Red rubber butt pad and polished steel pistol grip cap are standard. Weight is approximately 6-1/2 lbs.

NIB	Exc.	V.G.	Good	Fair	Poor
900	650	500	400	—	—

Model 82C Super America

Same as above but fitted with AAA fancy grade Claro Walnut with ebony tip and beaded cheekpiece. Hand checkering is 22 lpi in a full-coverage pattern. Steel buttplate and steel pistol grip cap are standard.

NIB	Exc.	V.G.	Good	Fair	Poor
1475	1100	750	450	—	—

Model 82C Custom Match

This bolt-action .22 caliber has a 22" barrel. The stock is AA French walnut with full coverage checkering. Finish is rust blued. Weight is about 6.75 lbs.

NIB	Exc.	V.G.	Good	Fair	Poor
2000	1600	950	700	—	—

Model 82C Custom Shop SuperAmerica (Basic)

Same as above but furnished with a number of special order options that greatly affect the value. Seek an independent appraisal before the sale. Prices begin at $1,650.00.

Model 82C Stainless Classic Limited Edition

Introduced in 1996 this limited edition Model 82C is chambered for the .22 long rifle cartridge The stainless steel barrel is 22" long. A 4-shot magazine is included. Production limited to about 600 rifles.

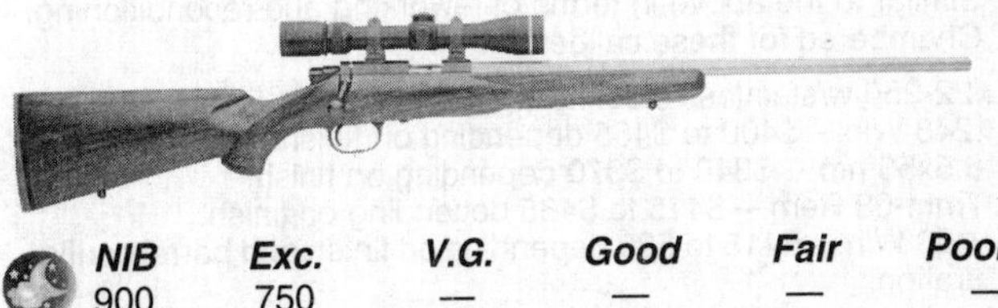

NIB	Exc.	V.G.	Good	Fair	Poor
900	750	—	—	—	—

Model 82C SVT (Short Varmint/Target)

First introduced in 1996 this .22 caliber rifle is a single-shot. It is fitted with an 18" stainless steel fluted barrel. The walnut stock is a target style with no checkering. Weight is about 7.5 lbs.

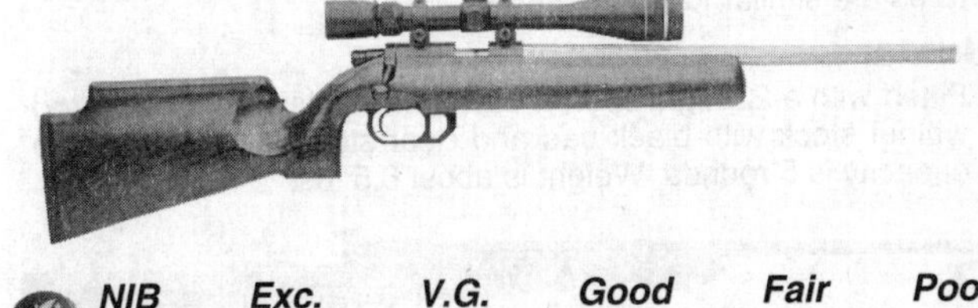

NIB	Exc.	V.G.	Good	Fair	Poor
900	700	500	400	—	—

Model 82C HS (Hunter Silhouette)

Introduced in 1997 this model features a 24" half-fluted barrel. Chambered for .22 Long Rifle cartridge. Stock is American walnut with high comb. Trigger is fully adjustable. Four-round magazine is standard. Weight is about 7 lbs.

NIB	Exc.	V.G.	Good	Fair	Poor
750	600	500	—	—	—

MODEL 84C SERIES

NOTE: In 1998 the Model 84C series rifle went out of production.

Model 84C Single-Shot Varmint

Chambered for the .17 Rem. or .223 Rem. cartridge this rifle is fitted with a 25" stainless steel fluted barrel. Claro walnut stock with varmint-style forearm. Weight is approximately 7.5 lbs.

NIB	Exc.	V.G.	Good	Fair	Poor
1000	750	600	500	400	200

Sporterized Model 98 Swedish Mausers

These are reconditioned and reworked Mausers that are fitted with new match grade stainless steel fluted barrels in 24" or 26" depending on caliber. The stock is new synthetic checkered. Chambered in .257 Roberts, .270 Win., .280 Rem., .30-06, 7mm Rem. Mag, .300 Win. Mag., .338 Win. Mag., and the .220 Swift with a 25" barrel.

This symbol denotes "Sleepers" with rapidly-rising values and/or significant collector potential.

Suggested retail price is $535 for standard calibers and $560 for Magnums.

Sporterized Model 96 Swedish Mausers

Similar to the above in terms of reworking and reconditioning. Chambered for these calibers:

.22-250 w/stainless steel heavy barrel fluted—Retail $500.
.243 Win.—$400 to $465 depending on finish.
6.5x55mm—$340 to $370 depending on finish.
7mm-08 Rem.—$415 to $465 depending on finish.
.308 Win.—$415 to 520 depending on finish and barrel configuration.

CURRENT PRODUCTION MODELS

17 SERIES

This series of .17 Mach 2 rifles was introduced in 2005. Features are similar to the 22 Series.

Hunter

Fitted with a 22" light sporter barrel with no sights. Checkered walnut stock with black pad and clear stock finish. Magazine capacity is 5 rounds. Weight is about 6.5 lbs.

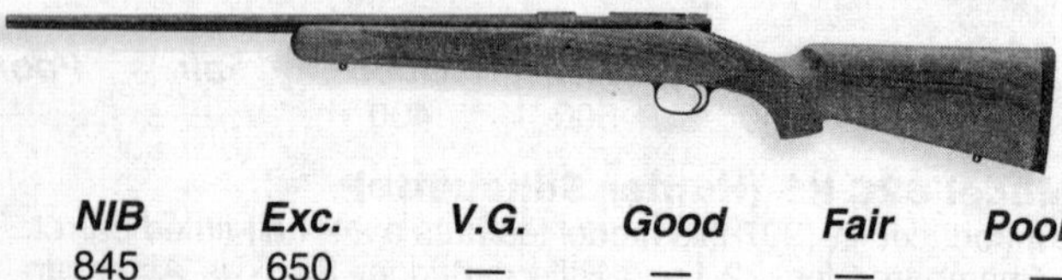

NIB	Exc.	V.G.	Good	Fair	Poor
845	650	—	—	—	—

SVT (Short Varmint/Target)

This model is fitted with a 18.25" stainless steel bull fluted barrel with no sights. Checkered walnut stock with black pad and oil finish. Magazine capacity is 5 rounds. Weight is about 7.9 lbs.

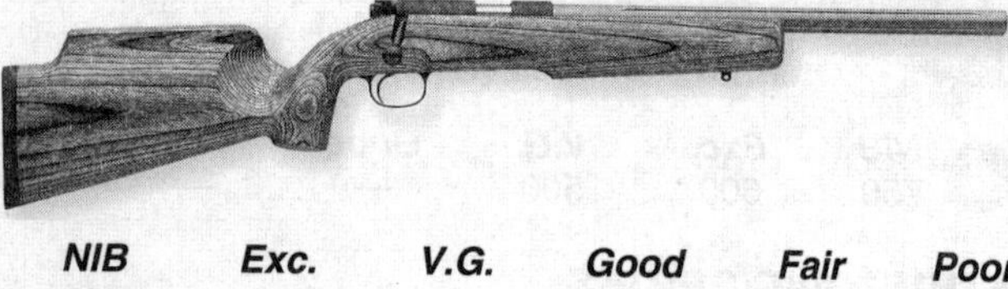

NIB	Exc.	V.G.	Good	Fair	Poor
1055	800	—	—	—	—

Pro Varmint

This model features a 20" stainless steel heavy sporter fluted barrel with no sights. Stock is gray laminate with oil finish and no checkering. Magazine capacity is 5 rounds. Weight is about 6.75 lbs.

NIB	Exc.	V.G.	Good	Fair	Poor
1160	875	—	—	—	—

Classic Varmint

Fitted with a 20" heavy sporter fluted barrel with no sights. Checkered walnut stock with oil finish. Magazine capacity is 5 rounds. Weight is about 6.5 lbs.

NIB	Exc.	V.G.	Good	Fair	Poor
1055	850	—	—	—	—

22 SERIES

In 1999 Kimber introduced a new line of bolt-action .22 caliber rimfire rifles. First deliveries were made early in 2000. This series is built on a totally new design from bolt, to magazine, to barrel. All rifles in this series have a 5-round magazine capacity. This line replaces the Model 82-C series of rifles.

Classic

This .22 caliber rifle is fitted with a 22" barrel with fully adjustble trigger. Stock is A grade Claro walnut with 18 lpi checkering. Fitted with a Model 70 style safety. Blued finish. Weight is about 6.5 lbs.

NIB	Exc.	V.G.	Good	Fair	Poor
1085	850	—	—	—	—

Custom Classic

Fitted with a 22" barrel, ebony forend tip, hand-rubbed oil finish, and 24 lpi checkering, This rifle was introduced in 2003. Weight is about 6.5 lbs.

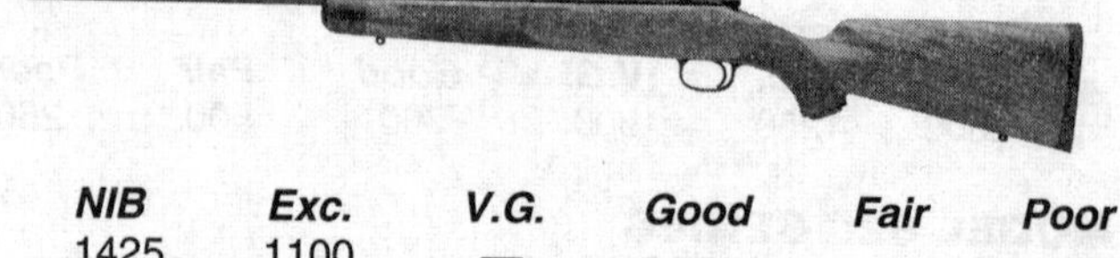

NIB	Exc.	V.G.	Good	Fair	Poor
1425	1100	—	—	—	—

SuperAmerica

This model features a 22" barrel with fully adjustable trigger. Stock is AAA grade Claro walnut with 22 lpi wrap-around checkering and ebony forend tip. Black recoil pad. Weight is about 6.5 lbs.

NIB	Exc.	V.G.	Good	Fair	Poor
1760	1400	—	—	—	—

SVT (Short Varmint/Target)

Fitted with an 18" fluted stainless steel barrel and gray laminated wood stock with high target comb. This model weighs about 7.5 lbs. In 2004 this model was also offered in the .17 Mach 2 caliber.

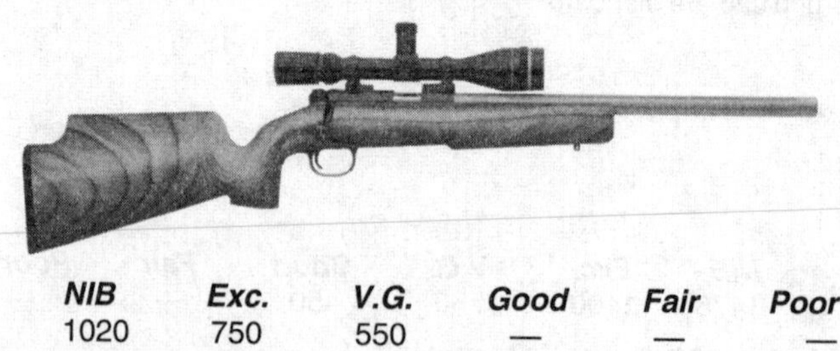

NIB	Exc.	V.G.	Good	Fair	Poor
1020	750	550	—	—	—

Classic Varmint

Introduced in 2003, this model features a 20" barrel with hand-rubbed oil finish and 20 lpi checkering. Weight is about 6.5 lbs. In 2004 this model is also available in the .17 Mach 2 caliber.

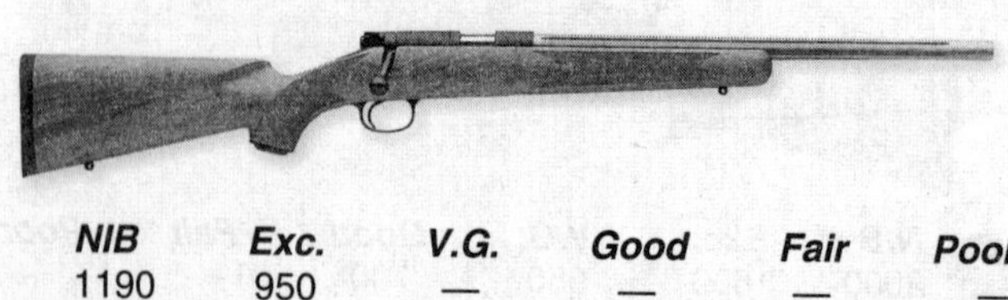

NIB	Exc.	V.G.	Good	Fair	Poor
1190	950	—	—	—	—

Pro Varmint

This model features a heavy fluted 20" stainless steel barrel and a gray laminated stock. No sights. Magazine capacity is 5 rounds. Weight is about 6.75 lbs. Introduced in 2004. This model is also available in .17 Mach 2 caliber.

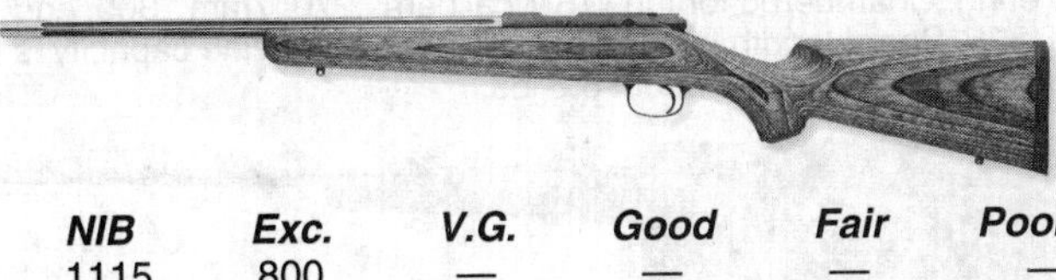

NIB	Exc.	V.G.	Good	Fair	Poor
1115	800	—	—	—	—

HS (Hunter Silhouette)

This model is fitted with a 24" medium sporter match grade barrel with match chambered and half fluting. Walnut stock with 18 lpi checkering and Monte Carlo comb. Weight is about 7 lbs.

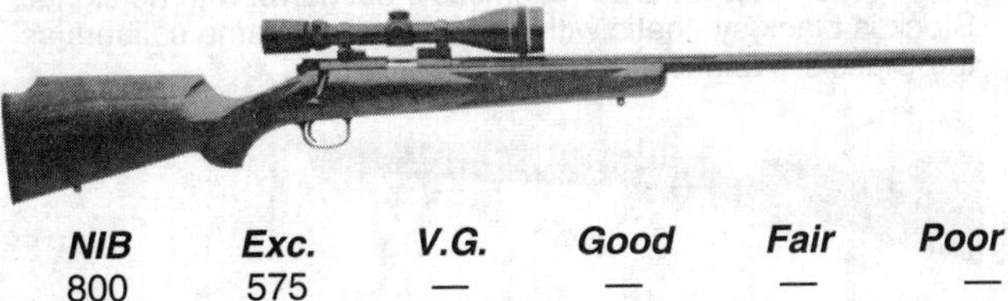

NIB	Exc.	V.G.	Good	Fair	Poor
800	575	—	—	—	—

Youth

Introduced in 2002 this .22 caliber rifle is fitted with a 18.5" barrel. Checkered Claro walnut stock with 12.25" length of pull. Weight is about 5.25 lbs.

NIB	Exc.	V.G.	Good	Fair	Poor
740	575	—	—	—	—

Hunter

This is a lower-priced version of the Classic.

NIB	Exc.	V.G.	Good	Fair	Poor
675	500	—	—	—	—

Custom Match Limited Edition

Introduced in 2004 this is a limited edition of 300 rifles. This rifle features a checkered French walnut stock of AAA wood and several custom features. Serial numbered from KAN25001-KAN25300.

NIB	Exc.	V.G.	Good	Fair	Poor
2850	—	—	—	—	—

MODEL 84M SERIES

Model 84M Classic

Introduced in 2001 this centerfire bolt-action rifle is chambered for the .243 Win., .260 Rem., 7mm-08 Rem., and the .308 Win. In 2005 this model was offered chambered for the .22-250 cartridge. Fitted with a 22" light sporter match grade barrel Claro walnut stock with 20 lpi checkering and satin wood finish. Matted blue finish. Fitted with a 1" Pachmayr Decelerator recoil pad. Weight is about 5.75 lbs.

NIB	Exc.	V.G.	Good	Fair	Poor
895	700	—	—	—	—

Model 84M Montana

This model is essentially a stainless steel version of the Model 84M Classic with a black synthetic stock. Weight is about 5.25 lbs. Introduced in 2003.

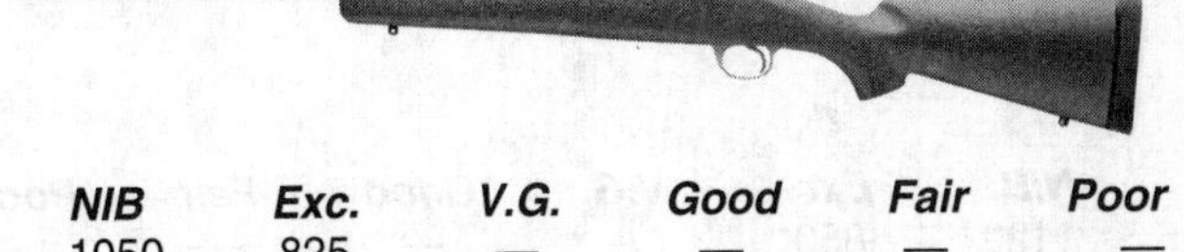

NIB	Exc.	V.G.	Good	Fair	Poor
1050	825	—	—	—	—

Model 84M SuperAmerica

This model was first offered in 2003 and is available in .243, .260 Rem., 7mm-08 Rem., and .308 Win. Fitted with a 22" barrel. In 2005 this model was offered chambered for the .223 cartridge. Stock is select walnut with 24 lines-to-the-inch checkering and fitted with an ebony forend tip, cheekpiece, and hand-rubbed oil finish. Weight is approximately 5.75 lbs. depending on caliber. Magazine capacity is 5 rounds.

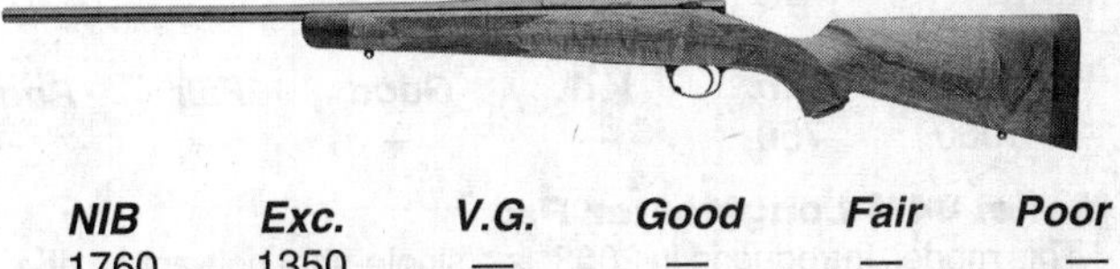

NIB	Exc.	V.G.	Good	Fair	Poor
1760	1350	—	—	—	—

Model 84M Pro Varmint

This rifle is chambered for the .22-250 Win. cartridge and fitted with a 24" stainless steel fluted barrel with no sights. In 2005 offered in 204 Ruger and .223 calibers. Gray laminted stock. Magazine capacity is 5 rounds. Weight is 7.25 lbs. Introduced in 2004.

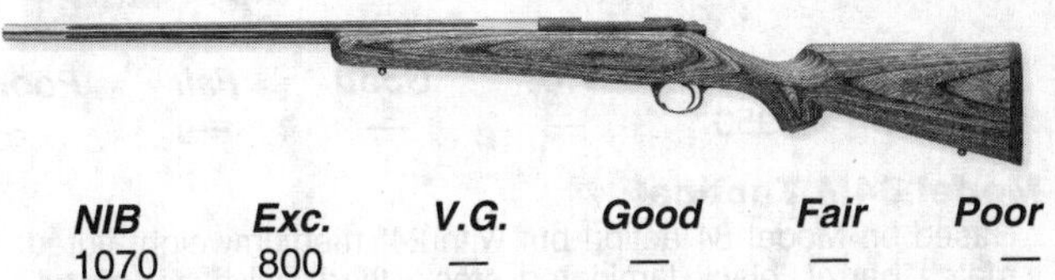

NIB	Exc.	V.G.	Good	Fair	Poor
1070	800	—	—	—	—

Model 84M Varmint

Similar to the Classic but fitted with a stainless steel 26" match grade barrel. Chambered for the .22-250 Rem. cartridge. In 2005 offered in the .204 Ruger caliber. Fitted with a .5" solid recoil pad. Weight is approximately 7.4 lbs.

NIB	Exc.	V.G.	Good	Fair	Poor
780	625	—	—	—	—

Model 84M SVT

Stocked in gray laminate with Monte Carlo comb. Barrel length is 18.25" in stainless steel and fluted. Chambered for the .223 cartridge. Magazine capacity is 5 rounds. Weight is about 8.3 lbs.

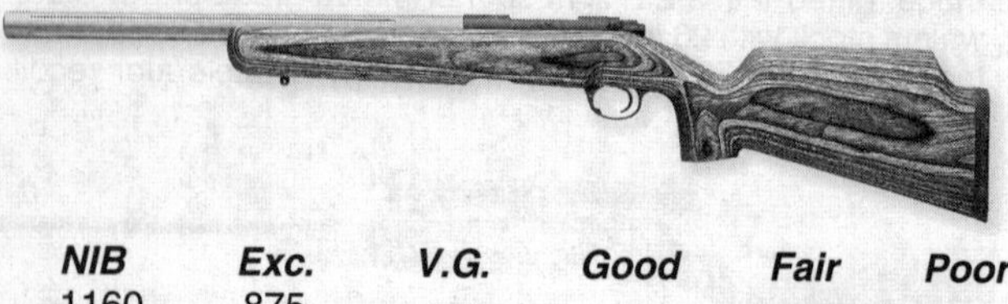

NIB	Exc.	V.G.	Good	Fair	Poor
1160	875	—	—	—	—

Model 84M LongMaster VT

This bolt-action rifle is chambered for the .22-250 cartridge and is fitted with a 26" fluted stainless steel match grade barrel. Special laminated target stock. Weight is about 10 lbs. No sights. Introduced in 2002.

NIB	Exc.	V.G.	Good	Fair	Poor
1120	850	—	—	—	—

Model 84M LongMaster Classic

Same features as the Model 84M Classic but with 24" fluted stainless steel barrel chambered for the .308 Win. cartridge. In 2005 offered in .223 caliber. Checkered walnut stock. Weight is about 7.25 lbs. Introduced in 2002.

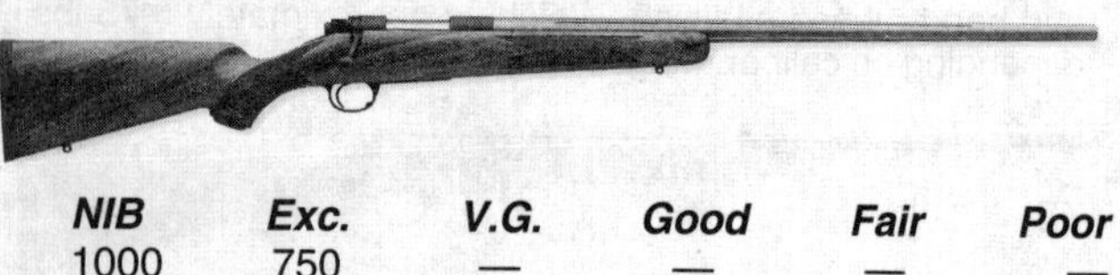

NIB	Exc.	V.G.	Good	Fair	Poor
1000	750	—	—	—	—

Model 84M LongMaster Pro

This model, introduced in 2003, is a single-shot bolt-action rifle fitted with a 24" fluted heavy barrel chambered for the .308 Win. or .22-250 cartridge. Fitted with a synthetic benchrest stock. Weight is about 7.25 lbs.

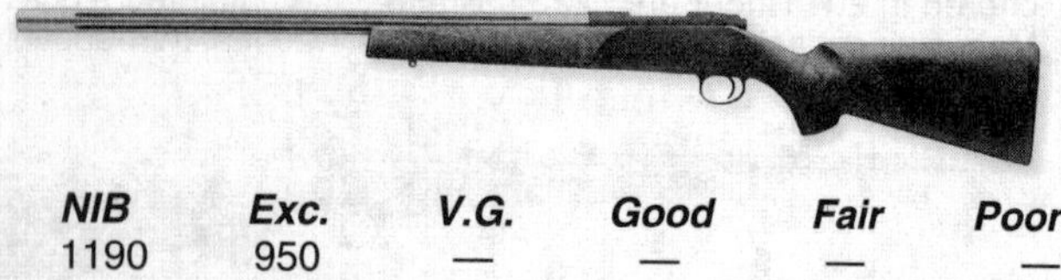

NIB	Exc.	V.G.	Good	Fair	Poor
1190	950	—	—	—	—

Model 84M Tactical

Based on Model 84 action but with 24" mediumweight fluted match barrel, black laminated stock, third swivel for bipod. Chambered in .308 Winchester. Introduced in 2007.

NIB	Exc.	V.G.	Good	Fair	Poor
1025	—	—	—	—	—

MODEL 8400 SERIES

This series was introduced in 2003 and features the smallest action size compatible with the WSM family of cartridges.

Model 8400 Classic

This model is fitted with a select walnut stock with 20 lpi checkering. Chambered for the WSM calibers: .270, 7mm, .300, and .325. Barrel length is 24" with no sights. Magazine capacity is 3 rounds. Weight is about 6.6 lbs.

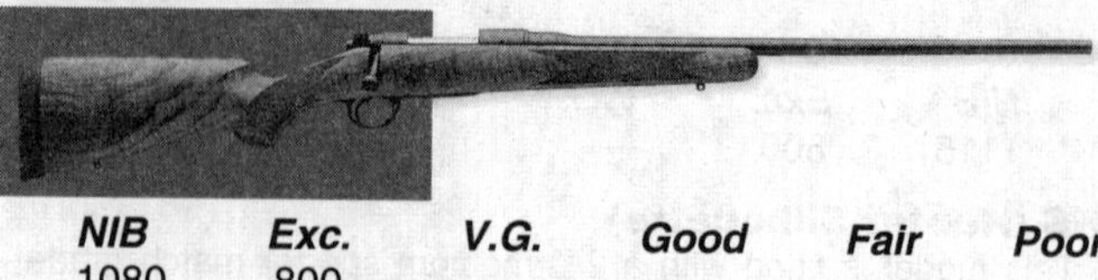

NIB	Exc.	V.G.	Good	Fair	Poor
1080	800	—	—	—	—

NOTE: Add $140 for French walnut.

Model 8400 Montana

This model features a 24" stainless steel barrel with no sights. Stock is black synthetic with no checkering. Same calibers as the Classic. Weight is about 6.25 lbs.

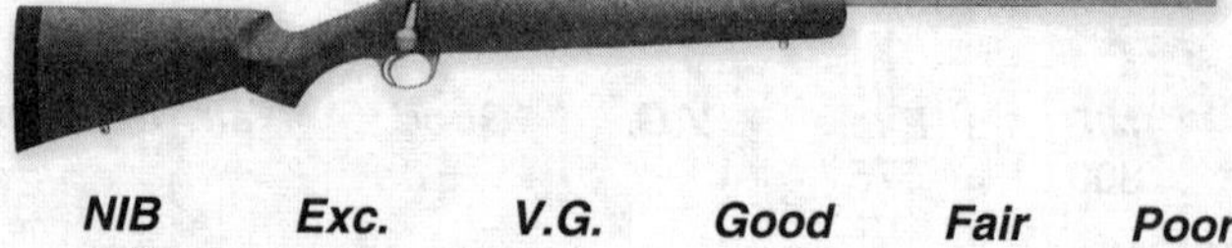

NIB	Exc.	V.G.	Good	Fair	Poor
1220	925	—	—	—	—

Model 8400 SuperAmerica

This model is fitted with a AAA walnut stock with 24 lpi checkering. Cheekpiece and ebony forend tip are standard. Barrel length is 24" with no sights and chambered for the same calibers as the Classic. Weight is about 6.6 lbs.

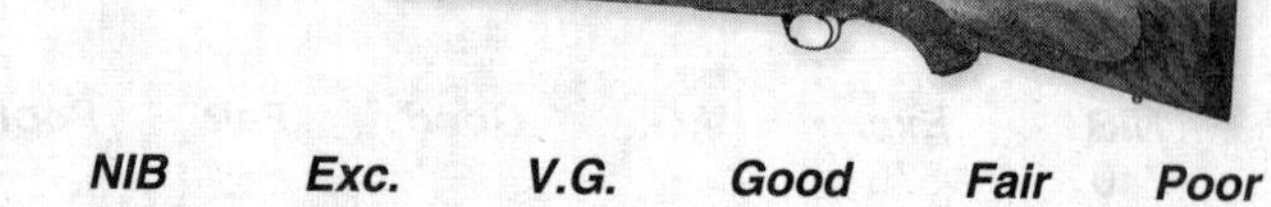

NIB	Exc.	V.G.	Good	Fair	Poor
2020	1500	—	—	—	—

8400 Classic Select Grade

Similar to 8400 Classic but with hand-rubbed, oil-finished select stock of Claro or French walnut. Introduced 2006.

NIB	Exc.	V.G.	Good	Fair	Poor
1700	—	—	—	—	—

Model 8400 Tactical

24" heavyweight match barrel, stippled black McMillan stock, third swivel for bipod. Chambered in .308 Winchester. Introduced in 2007.

NIB	Exc.	V.G.	Good	Fair	Poor
1500	—	—	—	—	—

Model 8400 Advanced Tactical

Similar to Model 8400 Tactical but with KimPro II Dark Earth finish, fully-adjustable stock and hard case. Introduced in 2007.

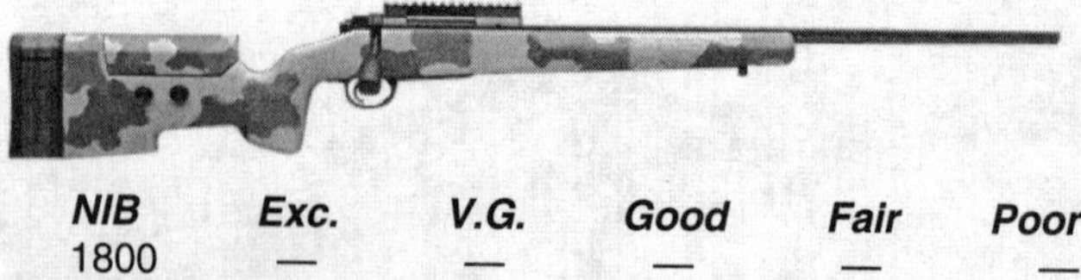

NIB	Exc.	V.G.	Good	Fair	Poor
1800	—	—	—	—	—

AUGUSTA SHOTGUNS

These shotguns are made in Italy for Kimber. Based on a Boss-type action, each model is fitted with H-Viz sights and Pachmayr Decelerator recoil pads. Back bored. Single-selective trigger and automatic ejectors. Introduced in 2002.

Augusta Sporting

Chambered for the 12 gauge shell and fitted with a choice of barrel lengths from 28.5" to 32". Checkered walnut stock with pistol grip and schnabel forearm. Blued finish with silver frame. Weight is about 7.75 lbs.

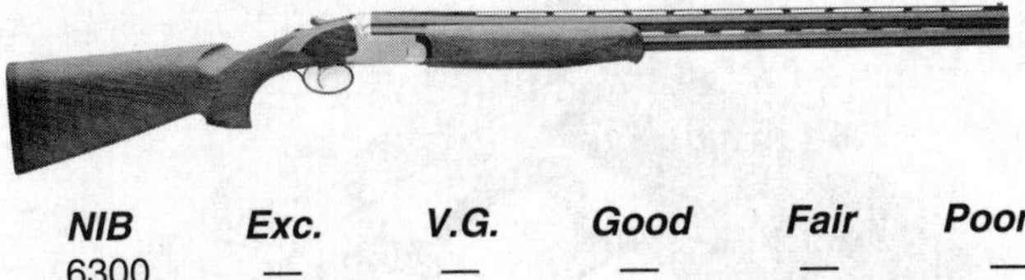

NIB	Exc.	V.G.	Good	Fair	Poor
6300	—	—	—	—	—

Augusta Field

Also chambered for the 12 gauge shell and choice of barrel lengths from 26" to 27.5". Checkered with pistol grip and beavertail forearm. Weight is about 7 lbs.

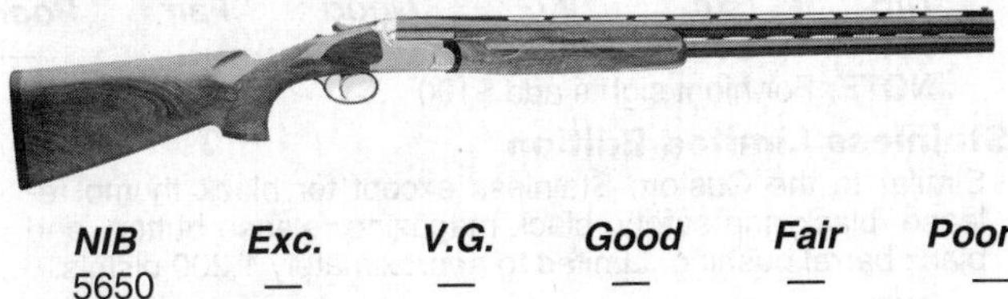

NIB	Exc.	V.G.	Good	Fair	Poor
5650	—	—	—	—	—

Augusta Trap

This 12-gauge model is offered in barrel lengths from 30" to 34". Beavertail forearm. Wide ramped ventilated rib. Weight is about 7.75 lbs.

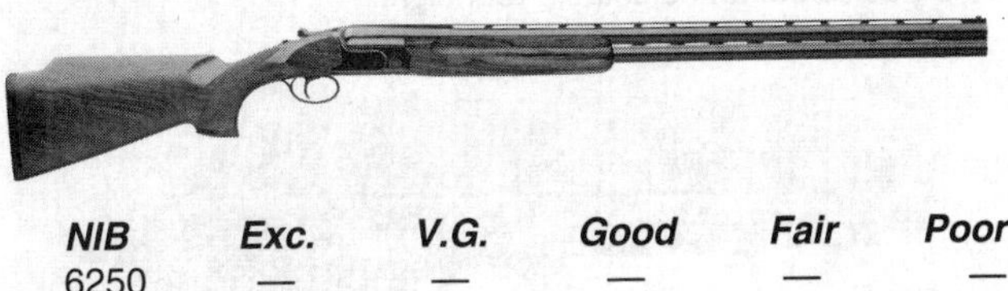

NIB	Exc.	V.G.	Good	Fair	Poor
6250	—	—	—	—	—

Augusta Skeet

This 12-gauge gun has a choice of 26" or 27.5" barrels. Barrels are fitted with an 11mm flat rib. Checkered walnut stock with beavertail forearm. Weight is about 7.5 lbs.

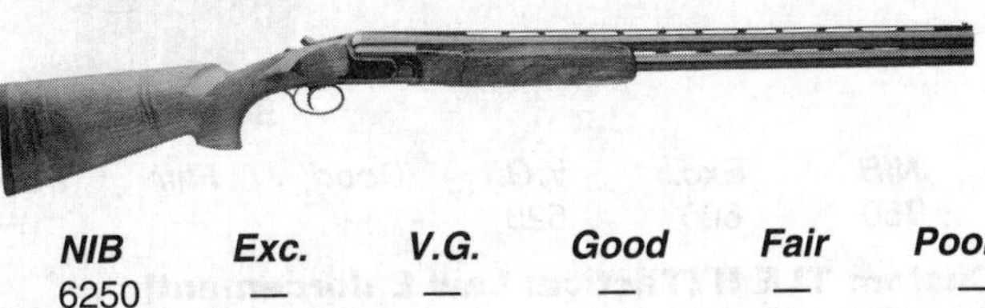

NIB	Exc.	V.G.	Good	Fair	Poor
6250	—	—	—	—	—

VALIER SHOTGUNS

These side-by-side guns were introduced into the Kimber line in 2005.

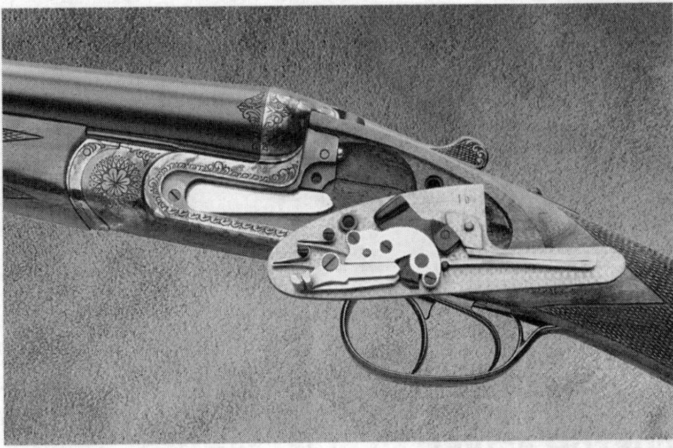

Grade I

A lightweight, properly-scaled side-by-side in 16- and 20-gauge. Double triggers and extractors. Choked IC and Mod. Color case-hardened receiver, straight stock and splinter forend. Hand checkered wood at 24 lpi. Chambered for 2.75" shells in 16 gauge and 3" shells in 20 gauge.

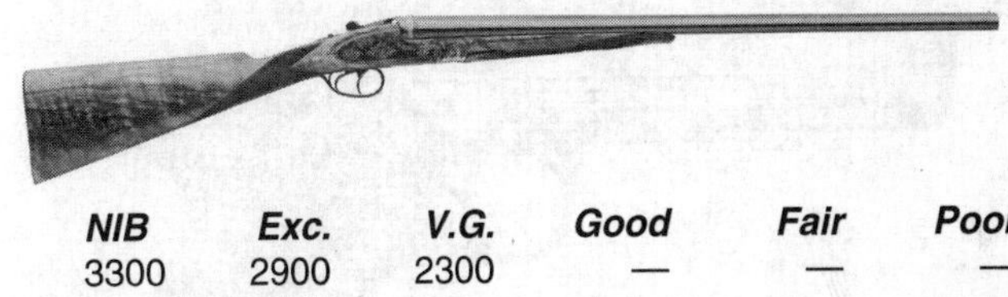

NIB	Exc.	V.G.	Good	Fair	Poor
3300	2900	2300	—	—	—

Grade II

Similar to Valier Grade I but with higher grade wood and choice of color case, blued or bone charcoal receiver in 20 gauge; bone charcoal only in 16 gauge. Automatic ejectors.

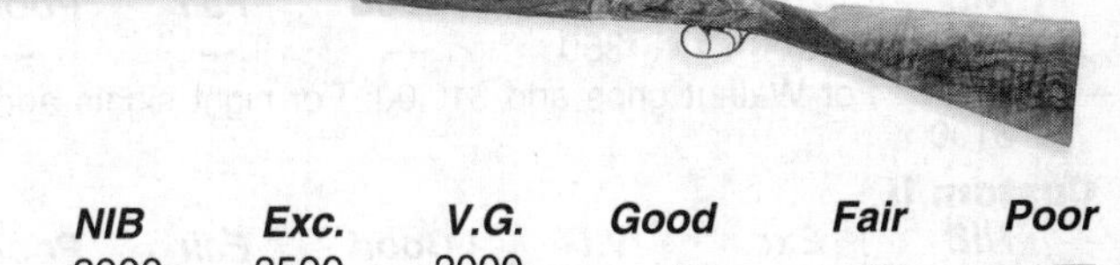

NIB	Exc.	V.G.	Good	Fair	Poor
3900	3500	2000	—	—	—

Marias Grade I

This single-trigger sidelock over-and-under features scroll hand engraving and bone charcoal case colors with 24 lpi checkered wood. Grade I is available with 28" barrels and Prince of Wales stock in 12 and 20 gauge. Chambered for 3" shells. Automatic ejectors. Comes with 5 choke tubes.

NIB	Exc.	V.G.	Good	Fair	Poor
4600	—	—	—	—	—

Marias Grade II

Similar to Marias Grade I but with higher grade wood. Available in 12 gauge with PW stock or 20 gauge with PW or straight stock in 26", 28" or 30" barrels.

NIB	Exc.	V.G.	Good	Fair	Poor
5000	—	—	—	—	—

CLASSIC .45 PISTOLS

First introduced in 1996 this is a quality built American-made 1911 designed by Chip McCormick for Kimber.

NOTE: In 2001 Kimber phased in a new safety system on its pistols: the Kimber firing pin safety. Models with this new firing pin safety will bear the designation "II" as part of their model name.

CUSTOM SERIES

Custom

Barrel length is 5" with black oxide finish fixed sights. Black synthetic grips. Magazine capacity is 8 rounds. Weight is about 38 oz.

NIB	Exc.	V.G.	Good	Fair	Poor
650	500	350	—	—	—

NOTE: For Walnut grips add $10.00. For night sights add $100.

Custom II

NIB	Exc.	V.G.	Good	Fair	Poor
765	575	—	—	—	—

Custom Heritage Edition

Chambered for .45 ACP cartridge and fitted with a 5" barrel. Magazine capacity is 7 rounds. Checkered front strap, ambidextrous thumb safety, aluminum trigger, hand checkered rosewood grips, special edition markings on slide. Sights are low-profile fixed. Weight is about 38 oz. Introduced in 2000.

NIB	Exc.	V.G.	Good	Fair	Poor
1065	850	—	—	—	—

Custom Stainless

As above but in stainless steel.

NIB	Exc.	V.G.	Good	Fair	Poor
750	500	425	—	—	—

NOTE: For night sights add $100.

Stainless Limited Edition

Similar to the Custom Stainless except for black thumb release, black grip safety, black magazine release button, and black barrel bushing. Limited to approximately 1,200 pistols.

NIB	Exc.	V.G.	Good	Fair	Poor
800	600	525	—	—	—

Custom Target

The Custom Target has the same features as the Custom with the addition of an adjustable rear sight.

NIB	Exc.	V.G.	Good	Fair	Poor
750	600	525	—	—	—

Custom TLE II (Tactical Law Enforcement)

Introduced in 2003 this model features Meprolight three-dot night sights and 30 lpi checkering on the front strap. Magazine capacity is 7 rounds. Weight is about 38 oz.

NIB	Exc.	V.G.	Good	Fair	Poor
920	700	—	—	—	—

NOTE: In 2004 a stainless steel version was offered. Add $135 for this model.

Custom TLE/RL II

This model is similar ot the TLE with the addition of an integral tactical rail. Weight is about 39 oz. Introduced in 2004.

NIB	Exc.	V.G.	Good	Fair	Poor
1050	825	—	—	—	—

Stainless II

Chambered for the .45 ACP or .40 S&W cartridge and fitted with a 5" barrel with fixed low profile sights. Both frame and slide are satin stainless steel. Magazine capacity for the .45 ACP is 7 rounds and 8 rounds for the .40 S&W. Weight is about 38 oz.

NIB	Exc.	V.G.	Good	Fair	Poor
865	650	—	—	—	—

Stainless II (polished)

As above but chambererd for the .38 Super cartridge. Frame and slide are polished stainless steel. Magazine capacity is 9 rounds. Weight is about 38 oz. Introduced in 2005.

NIB	Exc.	V.G.	Good	Fair	Poor
1040	825	—	—	—	—

Stainless Target II

Chambered for the .45 ACP or .38 Super cartridge with a slide and frame machined from stainless steel. Weight is 38 oz.

NIB	Exc.	V.G.	Good	Fair	Poor
980	750	600	—	—	—

Stainless Target II 9mm/10mm

As above but chambererd for the 9mm or 10mm cartridge. The 9mm pistol has a magazine capacity of 9 rounds and the 10mm has a magazine capacity of 8 rounds. Both of these pistols are produced on a one-run basis only with production in the low hundreds. Introduced in 2003.

NIB	Exc.	V.G.	Good	Fair	Poor
1065	825	—	—	—	—

Stainless Target II (polished)

As above but chambered for the .38 Super cartridge. Frame and slide are polished stainless steel. Magazine capacity is 9 rounds. Weight is about 38 oz. Introduced in 2005.

NIB	Exc.	V.G.	Good	Fair	Poor
1110	850	—	—	—	—

Stainless Target Limited Edition

Similar to the Stainless Target but with black thumb safety, black grip safety, black slide release, and black barrel bushing. This model is limited to approximately 700 pistols. Introduced in 1998.

NIB	Exc.	V.G.	Good	Fair	Poor
825	650	—	—	—	—

Custom Royal

This has all the features of the Custom plus a high polish blue finish, hand checkered walnut grips, and long guide rod.

NIB	Exc.	V.G.	Good	Fair	Poor
775	625	525	—	—	—

Custom Royal II

NIB	Exc.	V.G.	Good	Fair	Poor
910	700	—	—	—	—

Custom TLE/RL II Special Edition

This .45 ACP pistol is fitted with a 5" barrel with fixed night sights. Steel frame and slide with tactical accessory rail on frame. Black rubber grips. Black matte finish. Magazine capacity is 7 rounds. Weight is about 38 oz. Introduced in 2003.

NIB	Exc.	V.G.	Good	Fair	Poor
1030	825	—	—	—	—

Warrior

This model, introduced in 2005, is chambered for the .45 ACP cartridge and fitted with a 5" barrel with night sights. Grips are Kimber G-10 Tactical with lanyard loop. Accessory rail on frame. KimPro finish. Magazine capacity is 7 rounds. Weight is about 39 oz.

NIB	Exc.	V.G.	Good	Fair	Poor
1260	950	—	—	—	—

Desert Warrior

This model is similar to the Warrior but with a desert tan finish and lighter tan G10 tactical grips.

NIB	Exc.	V.G.	Good	Fair	Poor
1280	950	—	—	—	—

25TH ANNIVERSARY LIMITED EDITIONS

Anniversary Custom

Introduced in 2004 this is a limited edition of 1,911 pistol. Chambered for the .45 ACP cartridge. Select walnut grips. Serial numbered: KAPC0001-KAPC1911.

NIB	Exc.	V.G.	Good	Fair	Poor
930	750	—	—	—	—

Anniversary Gold Match

This .45 ACP pistol is limited to 500 pistols. Serial numbered KAPG0001-KAPG0500.

NIB	Exc.	V.G.	Good	Fair	Poor
1370	—	—	—	—	—

Anniversary Match Pair Custom

This is a matched pair of Custom pistols in .45 ACP. Matching serial numbers and presentation case. Limited to 250 pairs.

NIB	Exc.	V.G.	Good	Fair	Poor
2620	—	—	—	—	—

GOLD MATCH SERIES

Gold Match

All of the features of the Custom Royal plus BoMar adjustable sights, fancy checkered diamond grips.

NIB	Exc.	V.G.	Good	Fair	Poor
975	775	600	—	—	—

Gold Match II

NIB	Exc.	V.G.	Good	Fair	Poor
1205	900	—	—	—	—

Stainless Gold Match

Similar to the Gold Match except slide and frame are stainless steel. Introduced in 1998.

NIB	Exc.	V.G.	Good	Fair	Poor
1150	900	—	—	—	—

Gold Team Match II

Introduced in 2003 this .45 ACP 5" barrel model features a stainless steel slide and frame along with a Kimber Tactical

Extractor with loaded chamber indicator. Front strap is checkered 30 lpi and the grips are red, white, and blue USA Shooting Team logo. Weight is about 38 oz.

NIB	Exc.	V.G.	Good	Fair	Poor
1310	975	—	—	—	—

Team Match II .38 Super

As above but without external extractor. Limited production run. Introduced in 2003.

NIB	Exc.	V.G.	Good	Fair	Poor
1375	1075	—	—	—	—

TEN II SERIES

In 2002 the Polymer series pistols were upgraded to the Ten II series with the addition of a firing pin block safety, a Kimber-made frame of improved dimensions, and an external extractor. The orginial Polymer pistol magazines of 10 and 14 rounds will interchange with the newer Ten II Series pistols.

Polymer

This model features a polymer frame with a matte black oxide slide. Sights are McCormick low profile. Barrel length is 5" and overall length is 8.75". Weight is about 34 oz. Magazine is 14 rounds. One 14-round magazine is supplied with gun when new.

NIB	Exc.	V.G.	Good	Fair	Poor
850	675	550	—	—	—

Polymer Stainless

Similar to the Polymer model but with a stainless steel slide. Weight is the same as the Polymer model; 34 oz.

NIB	Exc.	V.G.	Good	Fair	Poor
925	750	600	—	—	—

Polymer Target

Introduced in 1998 this pistol has a matte black oxide slide with adjustable sights. Magazine is 14 rounds. Weight is about 34 oz.

NIB	Exc.	V.G.	Good	Fair	Poor
950	750	—	—	—	—

Polymer Stainless Target

Same as above but with stainless steel slide. Introduced in 1998.

NIB	Exc.	V.G.	Good	Fair	Poor
1025	825	650	—	—	—

Polymer Pro Carry Stainless

Chambered for the .45 ACP cartridge with a 4" barrel. McCormick Low Profile sights. Stainless steel slide with black polymer frame. Weight is about 32 oz. Magazine capacity is 14 rounds. Introduced in 1999.

NIB	Exc.	V.G.	Good	Fair	Poor
800	600	—	—	—	—

Polymer Stainless Gold Match

This model is similar to the Polymer Gold Match with the addition of a stainless steel slide. This model is also chambered for several calibers: .45 ACP, .40 S&W, 9mm, and .38 Super. Weight is about 34 oz.

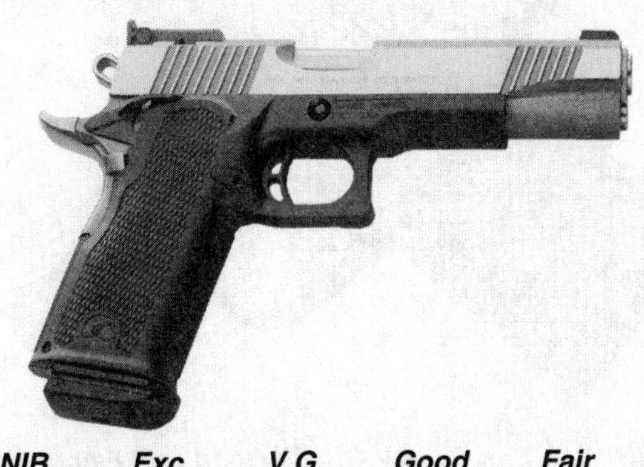

NIB	Exc.	V.G.	Good	Fair	Poor
1070	800	—	—	—	—

Pro Carry Ten II

This .45 ACP model features a 4" bull barrel with no barrel bushing. Stainess steel slide. Weight is about 28 oz.

NIB	Exc.	V.G.	Good	Fair	Poor
800	600	—	—	—	—

Ultra Ten II

Introduced in 2001 this pistol is chambered for the .45 ACP cartridge and fitted with a 3" barrel. Stainless steel slide and black Polymer frame. Supplied with 10-round magazine. McCormick low-profile sights. Weight is about 24 oz.

NIB	Exc.	V.G.	Good	Fair	Poor
790	625	—	—	—	—

Ultra Ten CDP II

Introduced in 2003 this model features night sights and rounded edges. Fitted with a 3" bull barrel. Chambered for the .45 ACP. Weight is about 24 oz.

NIB	Exc.	V.G.	Good	Fair	Poor
925	725	—	—	—	—

Gold Match Ten II

This .45 ACP 5" barrel model has all of the standard features of the Gold Match with a black Polymer frame and blued steel slide. Magazine capacity is 14 rounds. Weight is approximately 34 oz.

NIB	Exc.	V.G.	Good	Fair	Poor
1070	825	—	—	—	—

BP Ten II

This .45 ACP pistol has a 5" barrel and a 10-round magazine capacity. Steel slide with polymer frame. Fixed sights. Black matte finish. Weight is about 30 oz. Introduced in 2003.

NIB	Exc.	V.G.	Good	Fair	Poor
640	500	—	—	—	—

Pro BP Ten II

As above but with 4" barrel. Weight is about 31 oz. Introduced in 2003.

NIB	Exc.	V.G.	Good	Fair	Poor
640	500	—	—	—	—

This symbol denotes "Sleepers" with rapidly-rising values and/or significant collector potential.

COMPACT SERIES

Compact

These steel frame and slide pistols are fitted with a 4" bull barrel and shortened grip (.4" shorter than full size). Offered in .45 ACP. Finish is matte black oxide. Grips are black synthetic. Overall length is 7.7". Weight is about 43 oz. Introduced in 1998.

NIB	Exc.	V.G.	Good	Fair	Poor
675	550	—	—	—	—

Compact Aluminum

This model has the same appearance as the Compact but with an aluminum frame. Matte black finish. Weight is approximately 28 oz. Introduced in 1998.

NIB	Exc.	V.G.	Good	Fair	Poor
675	550	450	—	—	—

Compact Stainless

Same as the Compact model but with a stainless steel slide and frame. Offered in both .45 ACP and .40 S&W. Introduced in 1998.

NIB	Exc.	V.G.	Good	Fair	Poor
775	625	475	—	—	—

Compact Stainless II

NIB	Exc.	V.G.	Good	Fair	Poor
905	675	—	—	—	—

Compact Stainless Aluminum

Offered in both .45 ACP and .40 S&W this model features a 4" barrel with stainless steel slide and aluminum frame. Weight is about 28 oz.

NIB	Exc.	V.G.	Good	Fair	Poor
750	600	475	—	—	—

NOTE: Add $25 for .40 S&W models.

PRO CARRY

Pro Carry II

Introduced in 1998 this .45 ACP or .40 S&W model features a full-size aluminum frame and 4" slide and bull barrel. Other features are match grade trigger, beveled magazine well, full-length guide rod, low-profile combat sights, and 7-round magazine. Finish is matte black oxide. Weight is approximately 28 oz. In 2005 this model was offered in 9mm.

NIB	Exc.	V.G.	Good	Fair	Poor
800	600	—	—	—	—

Pro Carry II Night Sights

As above but fitted with night sights.

NIB	Exc.	V.G.	Good	Fair	Poor
900	675	—	—	—	—

Pro Carry Stainless

Same as above but with stainless steel slide.

NIB	Exc.	V.G.	Good	Fair	Poor
850	675	—	—	—	—

Pro Carry Stainless Night Sights

As above but fitted with night sights.

NIB	Exc.	V.G.	Good	Fair	Poor
950	750	—	—	—	—

Pro TLE/RL II

Introduced in 2005 this model features a 45 ACP with 4" barrel with night sights. Slide and frame are steel with a steel finish. Accessory rail on frame. Magazine capacity is 7 rounds. Weight is about 36 oz.

NIB	Exc.	V.G.	Good	Fair	Poor
1070	800	—	—	—	—

Stainless Pro TLE/RL II

As above but with stainless steel frame and slide. Introduced in 2005.

NIB	Exc.	V.G.	Good	Fair	Poor
1220	900	—	—	—	—

ULTRA CARRY II SERIES

Ultra Carry

This model is chambered for the .45 ACP or .40 S&W cartridge. It is fitted with a 3" barrel with McCormick low profile sights. Grips are black synthetic. Magazine capacity is 7 rounds. Weight is about 25 oz. Black oxide finish. Introduced in 1999.

NIB	Exc.	V.G.	Good	Fair	Poor
765	600	—	—	—	—

NOTE: Add $100 for night sights.

Ultra Carry II

NIB	Exc.	V.G.	Good	Fair	Poor
790	600	—	—	—	—

Ultra Carry Stainless

Same as above but with stainless steel slide.

NIB	Exc.	V.G.	Good	Fair	Poor
840	650	—	—	—	—

NOTE: Add $25 for .40 S&W model. Add $100 for night sights.

Ultra Carry Stainless II

NIB	Exc.	V.G.	Good	Fair	Poor
875	675	—	—	—	—

CUSTOM SHOP PISTOLS

Royal Carry

This is a limited edition of 600 pistols. Chambered for .45 ACP and fitted with a 4" barrel with night sights. Hand checkered rosewood grips. Steel slide and aluminum frame. High polish blue finish. Magazine capacity is 7 rounds. Weight is approximately 28 oz. Introduced in 1998.

NIB	Exc.	V.G.	Good	Fair	Poor
900	725	575	—	—	—

Elite Carry

Introduced in 1998 this custom shop pistol is limited to 1,200 pistols. Chambered for .45 ACP with a 4" barrel with night sights. Frame is aluminum with black oxide finish. Slide is steel with stainless steel finish. Ambidextrous extended thumb safety, checkered front strap, match trigger, and hand checkered rosewood grips. Magazine capacity is 7 rounds. Weight is about 28 oz.

NIB	Exc.	V.G.	Good	Fair	Poor
900	700	500	—	—	—

Gold Guardian

This limited edition custom shop pistol is limited to 300 pistols. Chambered for .45 ACP and fitted with a 5" barrel with fixed night sights. Stainless steel slide and frame. Ambidextrous extended thumb safety, match grade barrel, extended magazine well, match trigger, and special markings and serial number. Magazine capacity is 8 rounds and weight is about 38 oz. Introduced in 1998.

NIB	Exc.	V.G.	Good	Fair	Poor
1350	—	—	—	—	—

Combat Carry

This 4" barrel pistol is chambered for the .45 ACP or .40 S&W cartridge. Many custom features. Special markings. Stainless steel slide and blued frame. Night sights standard. Weight is approximately 28 oz. Introduced in 1999.

NIB	Exc.	V.G.	Good	Fair	Poor
1025	800	—	—	—	—

Gold Combat

This full-size pistol is chambered for the .45 ACP cartridge. Many custom features. Night sights standard. Special markings. Weight is about 38 oz. Blued slide and frame. Introduced in 1999.

NIB	Exc.	V.G.	Good	Fair	Poor
1680	1250	925	—	—	—

Gold Combat II

NIB	Exc.	V.G.	Good	Fair	Poor
1730	1300	925	—	—	—

Gold Combat Stainless

Same as the model above but with stainless steel slide.

NIB	Exc.	V.G.	Good	Fair	Poor
1625	1200	—	—	—	—

Gold Combat II

NIB	Exc.	V.G.	Good	Fair	Poor
1675	1250	—	—	—	—

Super Match

This is Kimber's most accurate .45 ACP pistol. Fitted with a 5" barrel and many special features. Adjustable sights. Weight is about 38 oz. Stainless steel slide and frame with two-tone finish. Introduced in 1999.

NIB	Exc.	V.G.	Good	Fair	Poor
1925	1500	900	—	—	—

Super Match II

NIB	Exc.	V.G.	Good	Fair	Poor
1985	1550	900	—	—	—

LTP II

Designed for limited pistol competition. Fitted with external extractor, flat top serrated slide with adjustable sights, and extended and beveled magazine well. Fitted with a 5" barrel with tungsten guide rod. Ten-round magazine. Front strap has 20 lpi checkering. Weight is about 38 oz.

NIB	Exc.	V.G.	Good	Fair	Poor
2035	1500	900	—	—	—

LTP II

NIB	Exc.	V.G.	Good	Fair	Poor
2100	1575	—	—	—	—

Raptor II

Introduced in 2005 this .45 ACP model features a 5" barrel with night sights. Blued finished. This model also has scale serrations on front strap and slide along with scaled zebra wood grips. Magazine capacity is 8 rounds. Weight is about 38 oz.

NIB	Exc.	V.G.	Good	Fair	Poor
1215	925	—	—	—	—

Pro Raptor II

Similar to the Raptor II except for a 4" barrel. Weight is about 35 oz. Introduced in 2005.

NIB	Exc.	V.G.	Good	Fair	Poor
1100	825	—	—	—	—

Grand Raptor

This is a .45 ACP pistol with 5" match grade stainless steel barrel with adjustable night sights, black aluminum trigger, and rosewood grips. The slide serrations are lizard scale. Stainless steel frame. The slide is matte black and engraved with the Custom Shop logo.

NIB	Exc.	V.G.	Good	Fair	Poor
1395	1050	—	—	—	—

Ultra Raptor II

This .45 ACP model features a 3" ramped match grade bushingless bull barrel. Fixed night sights. Ambidextrous thumb safety. Lizard scale slide serrations. Introduced in 2005.

NIB	Exc.	V.G.	Good	Fair	Poor
1100	825	—	—	—	—

Ultra RCP II

Introduced in 2003 this pistol features a 3" barrel, aluminum frame, sight rail, and a 26 oz. weight. Chambered for the .45 ACP cartridge. Magazine capacity is 7 rounds. No longer in production.

NIB	Exc.	V.G.	Good	Fair	Poor
1290	1000	—	—	—	—

Gold Combat RL II

Similar to the above model but with premium trigger, KimPro finish, and rosewood grips. Magazine capacity is 8 rounds. Weight is about 38 oz. Introduced in 2003.

NIB	Exc.	V.G.	Good	Fair	Poor
1750	1400	—	—	—	—

Gold Combat RL II

NIB	Exc.	V.G.	Good	Fair	Poor
1775	1325	—	—	—	—

Target Match

A limited edition of 1,000 pistols chambered for the .45 ACP cartridge. Matte black frame with adjustable sights. Match grade barrel and chamber. Solid aluminum trigger. Checkered front strap and underside of trigger guard. Special serial numbers: KTM0001-KTM1000. Introduced in 2005.

NIB	Exc.	V.G.	Good	Fair	Poor
1335	1000	—	—	—	—

SuperAmerica

Billed as Kimber's ultimate top-of-the-line custom 1911. Polished/matte blue finish, scroll engraving, mammoth ivory grips, presentation case with matching sheath knife. Introduced 2007.

NIB	Exc.	V.G.	Good	Fair	Poor
3000	—	—	—	—	—

CDP SERIES (CUSTOM DEFENSE PACKAGE)

Ultra CDP

This custom shop model features a 3" barrel, night sights, hand checkered rosewood grips, numerous custom features. Finish is stainless steel slide and matte black frame. Chambered for .45 ACP cartridge. Magazine capacity is 6 rounds. Weight is about 25 oz. Introduced in 2000.

NIB	Exc.	V.G.	Good	Fair	Poor
1140	900	—	—	—	—

Ultra CDP II

NIB	Exc.	V.G.	Good	Fair	Poor
1175	900	—	—	—	—

Compact CDP

This model, introduced in 2000, features a 4" bull barrel, night sights, hand checkered rosewood grips, and other custom features. Stainless steel slide and matte black frame. Chambered for .45 ACP cartridge. Magazine capacity is 6 rounds. Weight is about 28 oz.

NIB	Exc.	V.G.	Good	Fair	Poor
1140	900	—	—	—	—

Compact CDP II

NIB	Exc.	V.G.	Good	Fair	Poor
1175	900	—	—	—	—

Pro CDP

This model is similar to the Compact CDP but with a full length grip. Magazine capacity is 7 rounds and weight is about 28 oz. Introduced in 2000.

NIB	Exc.	V.G.	Good	Fair	Poor
1140	900	—	—	—	—

Pro CDP II

NIB	Exc.	V.G.	Good	Fair	Poor
1175	900	—	—	—	—

Custom CDP

This .45 ACP full-size pistol is fitted with a 5" match grade barrel and stainless steel slide with front and rear beveled serrations. Matte black steel frame with checkered rosewood grips. Night sights standard. Introduced in 2001.

NIB	Exc.	V.G.	Good	Fair	Poor
1140	900	—	—	—	—

Custom CDP II

NIB	Exc.	V.G.	Good	Fair	Poor
1175	900	—	—	—	—

ECLIPSE II SERIES

Eclipse Custom II

Chambered for the .45 ACP cartridge and fitted with a 5" barrel with match-grade bushing. Fixed night sights. Magazine capacity is 8 rounds. Weight is about 38 oz. Introduced in 2002. In 2005 this model was offered in 10mm.

NIB	Exc.	V.G.	Good	Fair	Poor
1105	850	—	—	—	—

NOTE: Add $110 for 10mm model.

Eclipse Target II

Similar to the Eclipse Custom II with the addition of adjustable night sights. Introduced in 2002.

NIB	Exc.	V.G.	Good	Fair	Poor
1190	950	—	—	—	—

Eclipse Ultra II

This .45 ACP pistol with a 3" barrel has a slide machined from a stainless steel forging. Frontstrap checkering. Fixed night sights. Magazine capacity is 7 rounds. Weight is about 34 oz. Introduced in 2002.

NIB	Exc.	V.G.	Good	Fair	Poor
1085	850	—	—	—	—

Eclipse Pro II

This model is similar to the Eclipse Ultra II but features a full-length grip frame and a 4" barrel. Fixed night sights. Introduced in 2002.

NIB	Exc.	V.G.	Good	Fair	Poor
1085	850	—	—	—	—

Eclipse Pro Target II

Similar to the Eclipse Pro but fitted with adjustable night sights. Introduced in 2002.

NIB	Exc.	V.G.	Good	Fair	Poor
1190	950	—	—	—	—

TEN II SERIES

Ultra Ten II

This .45 ACP model features a polymer frame with stainless steel slide and 3" barrel. Low-profile fixed sights. Magazine capacity is 10 rounds. Weight is 24 oz. Introduced in 2002.

NIB	Exc.	V.G.	Good	Fair	Poor
850	650	—	—	—	—

Pro Carry Ten II

Similar to the Ultra Ten II but is fitted with a 4" bull barrel and a full-length frame. Weight is about 32 oz. Low-profile fixed sights. Introduced in 2002.

NIB	Exc.	V.G.	Good	Fair	Poor
800	625	—	—	—	—

Stainless Ten II

This .45 ACP pistol is fitted with a 5" barrel. Fixed sights. Magazine capacity is 10 rounds.Weight is about 34 oz. Introduced in 2002.

NIB	Exc.	V.G.	Good	Fair	Poor
785	600	—	—	—	—

BP Ten II

This .45 ACP pistol has a black polymer frame and a 5" barrel. Slide is black with fixed low-profile sights. Magazine capacity is 10 rounds. Weight is about 34 oz. Introduced in 2004.

NIB	Exc.	V.G.	Good	Fair	Poor
630	475	—	—	—	—

Pro BP Ten II

Similar to the BP Ten II except for a 4" bull barrel. Weight is about 32 oz. Introduced in 2004.

NIB	Exc.	V.G.	Good	Fair	Poor
785	600	—	—	—	—

Gold Match Ten II

This .45 ACP 5" stainless steel barrel model features an adjustable sight, front and rear slide serrations, and polished flats. Magazine capacity is 10 rounds and weight is about 34 oz. Introduced in 2002.

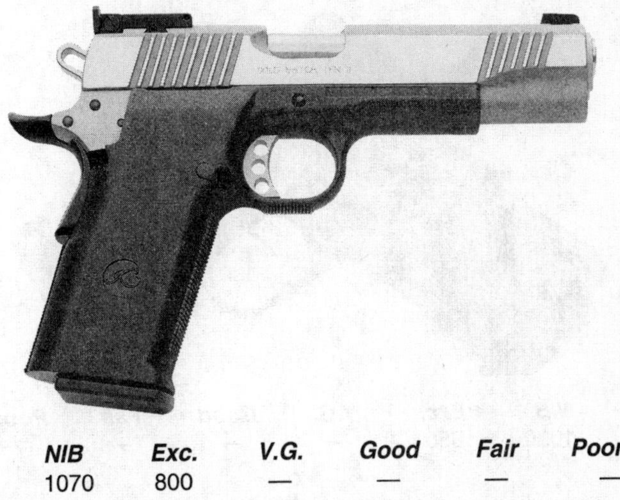

NIB	Exc.	V.G.	Good	Fair	Poor
1070	800	—	—	—	—

TACTICAL SERIES

This series of pistols was introduced in 2003. Each pistol has 30 lpi checkering on the front strap and under the trigger guard, Meprolight three dot night sights, an extended and beveled magazine well, magazines with extended bumper pads, laminated grips, and match grade barrel and chamber.

Tactical Custom II

Chambered for the .45 ACP cartridge and fitted with a 5" barrel. Magazine capacity is 7 rounds. Weight is about 31 oz.

NIB	Exc.	V.G.	Good	Fair	Poor
1090	850	—	—	—	—

Tactical Pro II

This model is fitted with a 4" barrel. Weight is about 28 oz.

NIB	Exc.	V.G.	Good	Fair	Poor
1090	850	—	—	—	—

Tactical Ultra II

This model is fitted with a 3" barrel. Weight is about 25 oz.

NIB	Exc.	V.G.	Good	Fair	Poor
1090	850	—	—	—	—

COVERT SERIES

Custom Covert II

1911-style semi-auto carry gun chambered in .45 ACP. Aluminum frame, steel slide. Frame finished in Desert Tan; slide finished in matte black. Five-inch barrel with 3-dot sights. Introduced in 2007.

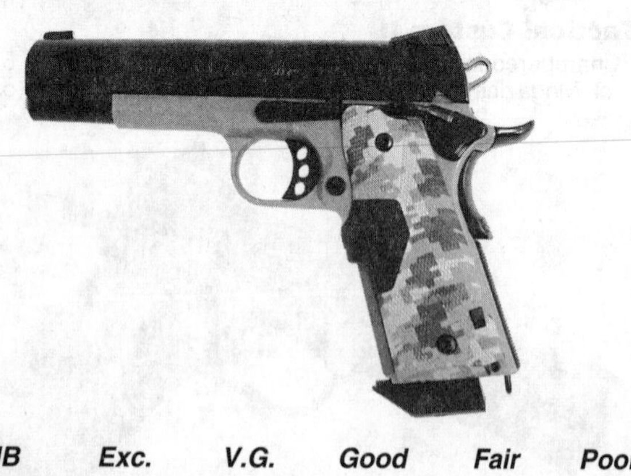

NIB	Exc.	V.G.	Good	Fair	Poor
—	—	—	—	—	—

Pro Covert II

Similar to Custom Covert II but with four-inch barrel. Introduced in 2007.

NIB	Exc.	V.G.	Good	Fair	Poor
—	—	—	—	—	—

Ultra Covert II

Similar to Pro Covert II but with three-inch barrel. Introduced 2007.

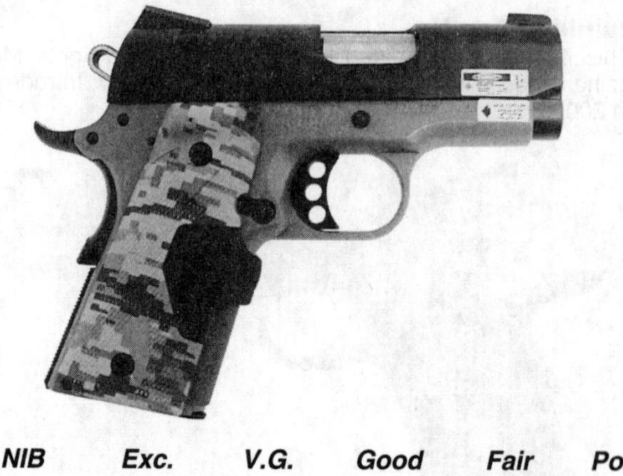

NIB	Exc.	V.G.	Good	Fair	Poor
—	—	—	—	—	—

KPD 40

Kimber Pro Defense double-action .40 S&W semi-auto. Comes with two 12-round magazines for 12+1 capacity. 4.1" barrel, 25 oz. Fixed white dot sights. Introduced 2006. MSRP: 545

AEGIS SERIES

Pro Aegis II

1911-style semi-auto carry gun chambered in 9mm Parabellum. Aluminum frame, steel slide. Frame finished in matte aluminum; slide finished in matte black. Four-inch bull barrel with 3-dot sights. Introduced in 2007.

NIB	Exc.	V.G.	Good	Fair	Poor
900	—	—	—	—	—

Custom Aegis II

Full-size 1911-style semi-auto carry gun chambered in 9mm Parabellum. Aluminum frame, steel slide. Frame finished in matte aluminum; slide finished in matte black. Five-inch bull barrel with 3-dot sights. Introduced in 2007.

NIB	Exc.	V.G.	Good	Fair	Poor
950	—	—	—	—	—

Ultra Aegis II

Similar to Pro Aegis II but with four-inch barrel. Introduced in 2007.

NIB	Exc.	V.G.	Good	Fair	Poor
900	—	—	—	—	—

RIMFIRE SERIES

Rimfire Custom

Introduced in 2003 this .22 caliber pistol features a 5" barrel with fixed sights and 10-round magazine. Matte black or silver anodized finish. Weight is about 23 oz.

NIB	Exc.	V.G.	Good	Fair	Poor
N/A	—	—	—	—	—

Rimfire Target

As above but fitted with adjustable sights. In 2004 this model was also available in .17 Mach 2 caliber.

NIB	Exc.	V.G.	Good	Fair	Poor
775	575	—	—	—	—

Rimfire Super

This model was introduced in 2004 and features a serrated flat top slide with flutes in the upper corners, an ambidextrous thumb safety, an alimunum trigger, and two-tone finish. Weight is about 23 oz.

NIB	Exc.	V.G.	Good	Fair	Poor
1090	800	—	—	—	—

.22 LR Conversion Kit

Introduced in 1998 this Kimber kit features a complete upper assembly: slide, barrel, guide rod, shock buffer, and 10-round magazine. Finish is satin silver or satin blue. Will fit all Kimber 1911 .45 ACP models. In 2005 this kit was also offered for the .17 Mach 2 cartridge conversion.

NIB	Exc.	V.G.	Good	Fair	Poor
300	250	—	—	—	—

KIMBER OF AMERICA

Yonkers, New York

SEE—Kimber Mfg., Inc.

NOTE: Firearms marked "Kimber of America" or "Kimber, Yonkers, NY" will be found under Kimber Mfg., Inc.

KIMBER OF OREGON, INC.

Clackamas, Oregon

SEE—Kimber Mfg., Inc

NOTE: Firearms marked "Kimber, Clackamas, Oregon" will be found under Kimber Mfg., Inc. Usually firearms produced in the Oregon facility were stamped in this manner.

KING PIN

Unknown

Derringer

A .22 caliber spur trigger brass constructed single-shot pistol with a 2.5" barrel and walnut grips. Believed to have been made during the 1880s.

Exc.	V.G.	Good	Fair	Poor
—	—	600	200	100

KIRRIKALE, ENDUSTRISI

Ankara, Turkey

Kirrikale Pistol

A 7.65 or 9mm short caliber semi-automatic pistol with a 3.5" barrel and 6-shot magazine. Blued with plastic grips. The slide marked "MKE"; and "Kirrikale Tufek Fb Cal.—." Imported by Firearms Center in Victoria, Texas, and also by Mandall Shooting Supplies. This was an unauthorized copy of the Walther PP that was imported into the U.S. briefly.

NIB	Exc.	V.G.	Good	Fair	Poor
450	350	275	225	150	100

KLIPZIG & COMPANY

San Francisco, California

Pocket Pistol

A .41 caliber single-shot percussion pistol with a 2.5" barrel, German silver mounts and walnut stocks. Manufactured during the 1850s and early 1860s.

Exc.	V.G.	Good	Fair	Poor
—	—	1500	900	400

KNICKERBOCKER

Made by Crescent Fire Arms Co.

Knickerbocker Pistol NFA

The Knickerbocker is a 14" double-barreled 20 gauge smooth bore pistol manufactured by Crescent Fire Arms Co. of Norwich, Connecticut. On the basis of its hammerless design and the dates of production of similarly designed firearms by Crescent, the Knickerbocker was probably manufactured sometime during the early 1900s. The receiver is case hardened, and the barrels are nickel-plated. The right side of the receiver is stamped **AMERICAN GUN CO./ NEW YORK U S A**; the left side is stamped **KNICKERBOCKER**. It probably was intended for law enforcement and/or defensive purposes, and manufactured using the same techniques used to produce the Ithaca Auto & Burglar Gun. The receiver is fitted with a checkered pistol grip resembling that of the Model 1 and Model 2 smooth bore H&R Handy-Gun. The only known specimen of the Knickerbocker bears serial number 200114. The Knickerbocker was classified as an "any other weapon" under the NFA in 1934 because it was originally designed as "a so-called shotgun with a pistol grip" and because it is concealable (see Treasury Department ruling S.T. 772, dated August 6, 1934). Its rarity precludes being able to reliably estimate its value at this time.

Double-Barrel Shotgun

Knickerbocker was a popular Dutch name for a New Yorker and was used as a brand on many hammerless sidelock doubles made by Crescent Firearms Co. Valued from $100 to $700 depending on model and condition,

KNIGHT RIFLES

Centerville, Iowa

This company was started in 1985 by Tony Knight. The company produces in-line blackpowder muzzleloading rifles and a complete line of accessories

Disc Magnum

Available in .50 caliber with a choice of blued or stainless steel 24"" or 26" barrel. Adjustable rear sight. Checkered stock with palm swell and rubber recoil pad. Stock also offered in black or camo. Adjustable trigger. Weight is approximately 8 lbs.

NIB	Exc.	V.G.	Good	Fair	Poor
450	350	300	250	200	150

NOTE: Add $50 for camo finish, $70 for stainless steel.

Bighorn Magnum

Available in .50 caliber with choice of 22" or 26" blued or stainless steel barrel. Adjustable rear sight. Checkered stock with rubber recoil pad. Stock also offered in black or camo. Adjustable trigger. Weight is about 7.7 lbs.

NIB	Exc.	V.G.	Good	Fair	Poor
325	250	200	175	150	100

NOTE: Add $50 for camo finish, $70 for stainless steel.

T-Bolt Magnum

Available in .50 caliber with choice of blue or stainless steel 22" or 26" barrel. Adjustable rear sight. Composite stock with rubber recoil pad. Stock also available in camo. Adjustable trigger. Weight is about 8 lbs.

NIB	Exc.	V.G.	Good	Fair	Poor
400	325	275	225	150	100

NOTE: Add $50 for camo finish, $70 for stainless steel.

LK-93 Wolverine

Available in .50 or .54 caliber with a choice of 22" blued or stainless steel barrel. Adjustable rear sight. Composite skeleton or thumbhole stock. Stock also available in black or camo. Adjustable trigger. Weight is about 6.5 lbs.

NIB	Exc.	V.G.	Good	Fair	Poor
265	200	150	100	75	—

NOTE: Add $50 for camo finish, $70 for stainless steel, $40 for thumbhole stock.

LK-93 Wolverine Youth

Same as model above but with shorter length of pull. Offered in black stock only.

NIB	Exc.	V.G.	Good	Fair	Poor
275	225	175	125	100	75

American Knight

Available in .50 caliber with 22" blued barrel. Adjustable rear sight. Black composite stock. Non-adjustable trigger. Weight is approximately 6.3 lbs.

NIB	Exc.	V.G.	Good	Fair	Poor
200	150	100	75	—	—

MK-85 Hunter

This model is offered in .50 or .54 caliber with blued finish and walnut stock.

NIB	Exc.	V.G.	Good	Fair	Poor
550	450	375	325	250	200

MK-85 Predator

This is a stainless steel version of the Hunter model. Offered with composite stock or various camo finishes.

NIB	Exc.	V.G.	Good	Fair	Poor
650	525	450	300	250	200

NOTE: Add $50 for camo finish.

MK-85 Stalker

This model is offered in .50 or .54 caliber with a variety of stock options. Standard stock is composite. Blued finish.

NIB	Exc.	V.G.	Good	Fair	Poor
565	450	375	325	250	200

NOTE: Add $50 for camo finish.

MK-85 Knight Hawk

This model is offered in .50 or .54 caliber with black composite stock and stainless steel.

NIB	Exc.	V.G.	Good	Fair	Poor
750	600	500	400	300	200

MK-86 Shotgun

Available in 12 gauge with 24" extra full choked barrel. Black composite stock with blued finish.

NIB	Exc.	V.G.	Good	Fair	Poor
600	475	375	250	200	150

HK-94 Hawkeye Pistol

This is a .50 caliber pistol fitted with a 12" barrel and an overall length of 20" and a weight of 52 oz. Offered in stainless steel or blued finish. First offered in 1993 and discontinued in 1998.

NIB	Exc.	V.G.	Good	Fair	Poor
400	300	250	200	150	100

NOTE: Add $70 for stainless steel.

Knight Rolling Block Rifle

Rolling-block blackpowder rifle similar in design to the old Remington rolling block design. 209 primer ignition, .50 caliber barrel rifled for sabots. Finishes include blued/composite, stainless/camo, and all-camo. Introduced in 2007.

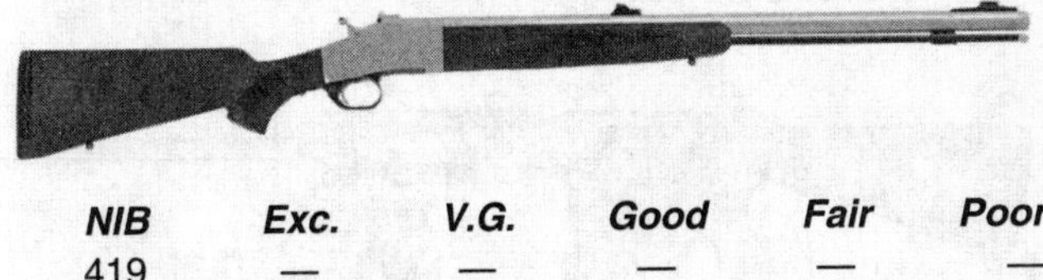

NIB	Exc.	V.G.	Good	Fair	Poor
419	—	—	—	—	—

Knight Long Range Hunter

.45-, .50- or .52-caliber bolt-action muzzleloader with 27" fluted stainless barrel. Said to shoot 4" 3-shot groups at 200 yards. Laminated stock. Introduced in 2007.

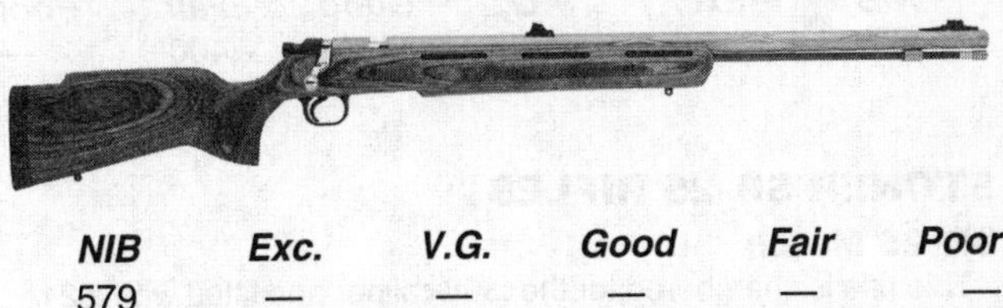

NIB	Exc.	V.G.	Good	Fair	Poor
579	—	—	—	—	—

KNIGHT'S MANUFACTURING CO.

Vero Beach, Florida

STONER SR-15 RIFLES

SR-15 Match

Chambered for .223 Win. and fitted with a target contour 20" free floating barrel. Two-stage match trigger. Flat top receiver. No sights. Weight is approximately 7.9 lbs.

NIB	Exc.	V.G.	Good	Fair	Poor
1850	1400	1050	750	500	—

SR-15 M-5 Rifle

This .223 is fitted with a 20" standard weight barrel with two-stage target trigger. Handguard employs RAS accessory system. Fitted with flip-up low profile rear sight. Weight is about 7.6 lbs.

NIB	Exc.	V.G.	Good	Fair	Poor
1700	1250	950	700	400	—

SR-15 E3 URX Carbine

Similar to SR-15 M5 but with 16-inch barrel, telescoping buttstock and vertical forend grip. Introduced 2006. MSRP: 2063

SR-15 M-4 Carbine

This model also includes the RAS system and has a flip-up rear sight. Two-stage target trigger and 16" lightweight barrel. Weight is about 6.8 lbs.

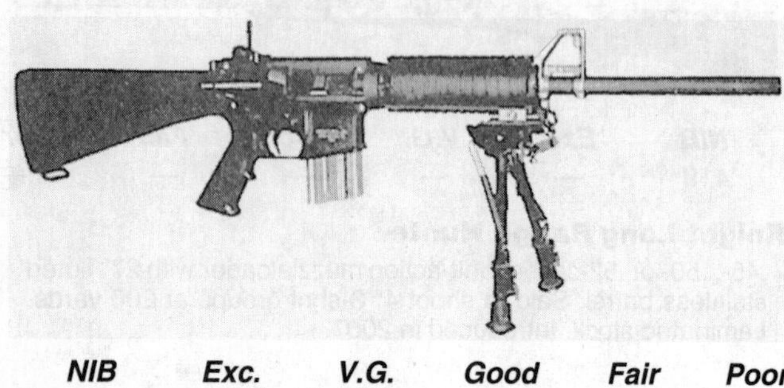

NIB	Exc.	V.G.	Good	Fair	Poor
1700	1250	950	700	400	—

STONER SR-25 RIFLES

SR-25 Match

This rifle is chambered for the .308 caliber and fitted with a 24" target contour free floating barrel. Special rifling and twist rate. No sights. Weight is about 10.75 lbs.

NIB	Exc.	V.G.	Good	Fair	Poor
3495	2600	1850	950	—	—

SR-25 Lightweight Match

This .308 rifle is fitted with a 20" free floating barrel. No sights. Weight is about 9.5 lbs.

NIB	Exc.	V.G.	Good	Fair	Poor
2995	2250	1500	900	—	—

SR-25 Stoner Carbine

Fitted with a 16" free floating barrel and special short non-slip handguard. Weight is about 7.75 lbs.

NIB	Exc.	V.G.	Good	Fair	Poor
2995	2250	1500	900	—	—

SR-25 Competition Match

This rifle is chambered for either .308 or .260 cartridge and has a 26" match barrel. Fitted with a special forearm which rotates in 15 degree increments. Trigger is adjustable two-stage with extended trigger guard. Special bolt stop and charging handle. Adjustable buttstock. This model may be fitted with several extra costs options that will affect price.

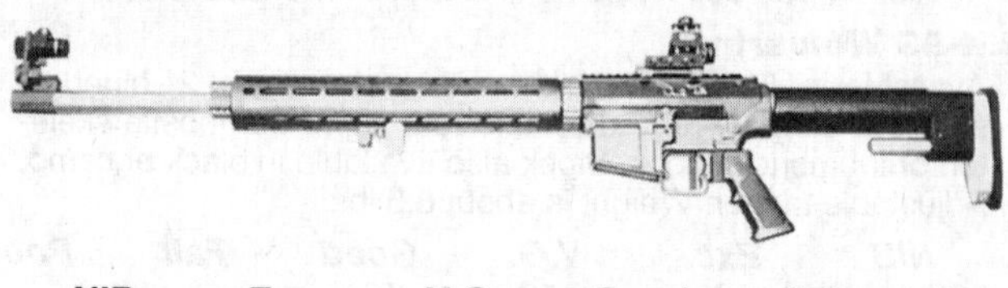

NIB	Exc.	V.G.	Good	Fair	Poor
6000	4750	3000	—	—	—

SR-25 Mk11 Mod 0 Match Rifle

Introduced in 2004 this rifle features a heavy 20" free floating target grade barrel.

NIB	Exc.	V.G.	Good	Fair	Poor
5295	3900	—	—	—	—

SR-50 Rifle

This is a semi-automatic rifle chambered for the .50 BMG cartridge. Magazine feed. Weight is approximately 31 lbs.

NIB	Exc.	V.G.	Good	Fair	Poor
7000	5500	4000	—	—	—

KOHOUT & SPOLECNOST

Kdyne, Czechoslovakia

Mars

A 6.35 or 7.65mm caliber semi-automatic pistol, the larger caliber having a grip safety. Blued with plastic grips impressed with the word "Mars." The slide marked "Mars 7.65 (or 6.35) Kohout & Spol. Kdyne." Manufactured between 1928 and 1945.

Exc.	V.G.	Good	Fair	Poor
350	250	200	150	100

Niva, PZK

Similar to the above in 6.35mm caliber.

Exc.	V.G.	Good	Fair	Poor
350	250	200	150	100

KOLB, HENRY M.

Philadelphia, Pennsylvania

The revolvers listed were manufactured by Henry Kolb and Charles Foehl until 1912 when R.F. Sedgely replaced Foehl. Manufacture continued until approximately 1938.

Baby Hammerless

A .22 caliber folding-trigger double-action revolver with an enclosed hammer and 5-shot cylinder.

Exc.	*V.G.*	*Good*	*Fair*	*Poor*
—	200	150	100	50

New Baby Hammerless

Similar to the above, with a hinged barrel to facilitate loading.

Exc.	*V.G.*	*Good*	*Fair*	*Poor*
—	200	150	100	50

KOLIBRI

Frederich Pfannl
Rehberg, Austria

2.7mm

A 2.7mm semi-automatic pistol with a 7-round magazine. F.P. trademark are on the grips as well as the Kolibri name at the bottom of the grips. A single cartridge may be worth as much as $75!

Courtesy James Rankin

Exc.	*V.G.*	*Good*	*Fair*	*Poor*
1500	1250	850	600	400

3mm

A 3mm semi-automatic pistol with a 6-round magazine. The 3mm version is the rarer of the two Kolibri pistols. The F.P. trademark is on the grips.

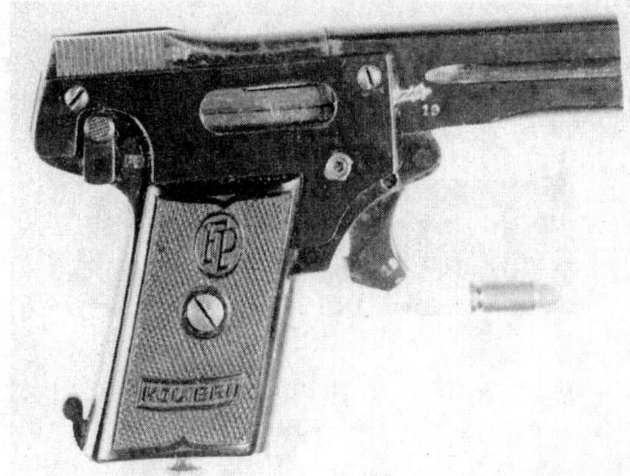

Courtesy James Rankin

Exc.	*V.G.*	*Good*	*Fair*	*Poor*
2500	2000	1500	1000	600

KOMMER, THEODOR WAFFENFABRIK

Zella Mehlis, Germany

Model 1

A 6.35mm semi-automatic pistol with an 8-shot magazine. Blued with plastic grips. Kommer name is both on the slide and the frame with T.K. trademark on the grips. Manufactured during the 1920s.

Courtesy James Rankin

Exc.	*V.G.*	*Good*	*Fair*	*Poor*
300	250	200	150	90

Model 2

A 6.35mm semi-automatic pistol with a 6-round magazine similar to the Model 1906 Browning. Barrel length is 2". Weight is about 13 oz. The Kommer name is on the slide. The late TH.K. trademark is on the grips. Manufactured in the 1930s.

Courtesy James Rankin

Exc.	*V.G.*	*Good*	*Fair*	*Poor*
300	250	200	150	90

Model 3

A 6.35mm semi-automatic pistol with a 9-round magazine.The Kommer name is on the slide and the TH.K. trademark is on the grips. Same as the Model 2 with extended grips straps for longer magazine.

Courtesy James Rankin

Exc.	V.G.	Good	Fair	Poor
300	250	200	150	90

Model 4

A 7.65mm caliber semi-automatic pistol with a 7-shot magazine and without a grip safety. Similar to the FN Model 1901. Barrel length is 3". Weight is about 20 oz. The slide marked "Waffenfabrik Kommer Zella Mehlis Kal. 7.65." Manufactured between 1936 and 1940.

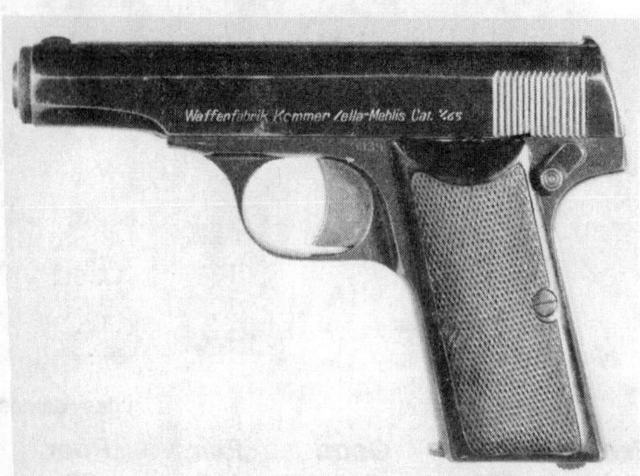

Courtesy James Rankin

Exc.	V.G.	Good	Fair	Poor
375	325	275	175	100

KONGSBERG
Norway

Thumbhole Sporter

Introduced in 1993, this bolt-action rifle is chambered of the .22-250 and .308 Win. cartridges. It is fitted with a 23" heavy barrel. The stock is American walnut with stippled thumbhole grip and wide forend. Cheekpiece is adjustable for height. Weight is about 8.5 lbs. Available in both right- and left-hand configurations.

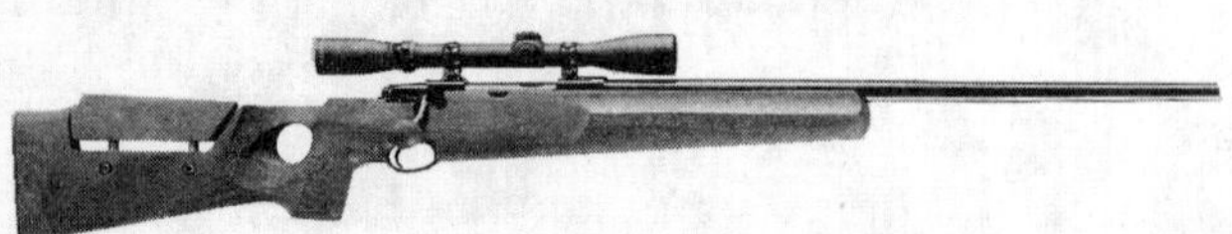

NIB	Exc.	V.G.	Good	Fair	Poor
1575	1250	900	—	—	—

NOTE: Add 10 percent for left-hand model.

Classic Rifle

This model was also introduced in 1993 and is chambered for a wide variety of calibers from .22-250 to .338 Win. Mag. Fitted with a 23" barrel for standard calibers and a 26" barrel for magnum calibers. European walnut stock with straight comb. Hand checkered. Open sights. Weight is about 7.5 lbs. depending on caliber. Offered in both left- and right-hand configurations.

NIB	Exc.	V.G.	Good	Fair	Poor
995	800	650	—	—	—

NOTE: Add 10 percent for left-hand models and 10 percent for magnum calibers.

KORRIPHILIA
Germany

HSP

A 7.65mm Luger, .38 Special, 9mm Police, 9mm Luger, 9mm Steyr, 10mm ACP, and the .45 ACP caliber double-action semi-automatic pistol with a 4" barrel made of stainless steel.

NIB	Exc.	V.G.	Good	Fair	Poor
7500	6000	—	—	—	—

HSP—Single-Action Only

NIB	Exc.	V.G.	Good	Fair	Poor
7500	6000	—	—	—	—

Odin's Eye

Essentially the same model as above in the same calibers with choice of barrel lengths of 4" or 5". Frame and slide are made of Damascus steel.

NIB	Exc.	V.G.	Good	Fair	Poor
14000	10000	—	—	—	—

KORTH
Germany

Korth started business in Ratzegurg, Germany, in 1954.

Semi-Automatic Pistol

A 9mm caliber double-action semi-automatic pistol with a 4" barrel, adjustable sights and 13-shot magazine. Other calibers are offered such as .40 S&W, .357 SIG, and 9x21. Optional 5" barrel is also offered. Weight is about 44 oz. Matte or polished blue with walnut grips. Introduced in 1985.

NIB	Exc.	V.G.	Good	Fair	Poor
7000	5000	3750	2750	1300	650

Combat Revolver

A .22 LR, .22 Magnum, .357 Magnum, and 9mm caliber revolver with a 3", 4", 5.25", or 6" barrel and 6-shot cylinder. The barrels and cylinders are interchangeable, matte or polished blue with walnut grips.

NIB	Exc.	V.G.	Good	Fair	Poor
5000	3900	3000	1750	1150	700

Match Revolver

Built in the same calibers as the Combat revolver with a choice of 5.25" or 6" barrel. Adjustable rear sight with adjustable sight notch widths. Machined trigger shoe. Grips are adjustable match grips with oiled walnut and matte finish.

NIB	Exc.	V.G.	Good	Fair	Poor
6250	5000	—	—	—	—

KRAG JORGENSEN

Springfield, Massachusetts

NOTE: For history, technical data, descriptions, and prices see the *Standard Catalog of Military Firearms* under United States, Norway, Denmark, Rifles

KRAUSER, ALFRED

Zella Mehlis, Germany

Helfricht or Helkra

A 6.35mm semi-automatic pistol with a 2" barrel. Produced in four models, the fourth with an enclosed barrel. Blued with composition grips. Manufactured from 1921 to 1929.

Exc.	V.G.	Good	Fair	Poor
475	400	350	250	150

KRICO

Stuttgart, West Germany

Sporting Rifle

A .22 Hornet or .222 caliber bolt-action rifle with 22", 24", or 26" barrels, single or double set trigger, adjustable sights and a 4-shot magazine. Blued with a walnut stock. Manufactured between 1956 and 1962.

Exc.	V.G.	Good	Fair	Poor
650	550	475	375	275

Sporting Carbine

As above, with a 20" barrel and full length stock.

Exc.	V.G.	Good	Fair	Poor
675	575	500	400	300

Varmint Special Rifle

The Sporting Rifle with a heavier barrel.

Exc.	V.G.	Good	Fair	Poor
650	550	475	375	275

Model 300

A .22 caliber bolt-action rifle with a 23.5" barrel, 5-shot magazine and grooved receiver. Blued with a walnut stock. Imported prior to 1989.

Exc.	V.G.	Good	Fair	Poor
700	600	550	400	300

Model 302 and 304

Variations of the above. Discontinued in 1986.

Exc.	V.G.	Good	Fair	Poor
700	600	550	400	300

Model 311 Smallbore

A .22 caliber bolt-action rifle with a 22" barrel, double set triggers, adjustable sights and a 5- or 10-shot magazine. Blued with walnut stock. Not imported after 1988.

Exc.	V.G.	Good	Fair	Poor
325	275	225	150	100

Model 320

As above, with a 19.5" barrel and full length stock. Discontinued in 1988.

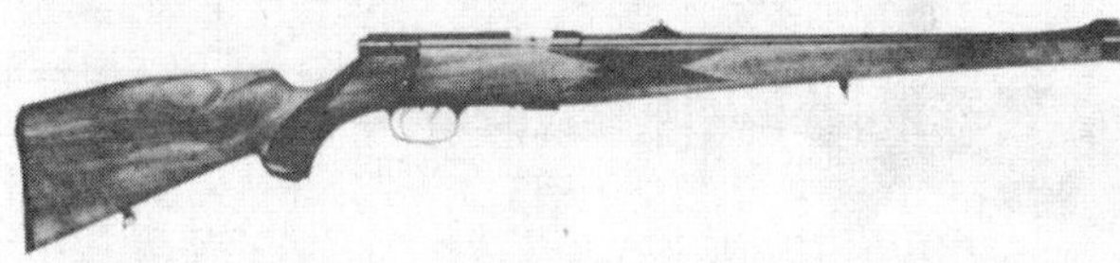

Exc.	V.G	Good	Fair	Poor
700	600	550	400	300

Model 340

A .22 caliber bolt-action rifle with a 21" heavy barrel furnished without sights, adjustable trigger and 5-shot magazine. Blued with a walnut stock. Not imported after 1988.

Exc.	V.G.	Good	Fair	Poor
750	625	575	425	325

Model 340 Mini-Sniper

As above, but matte finished, barrel fitted with a muzzlebrake and stock with a raised cheekpiece as well as ventilated hand guard.

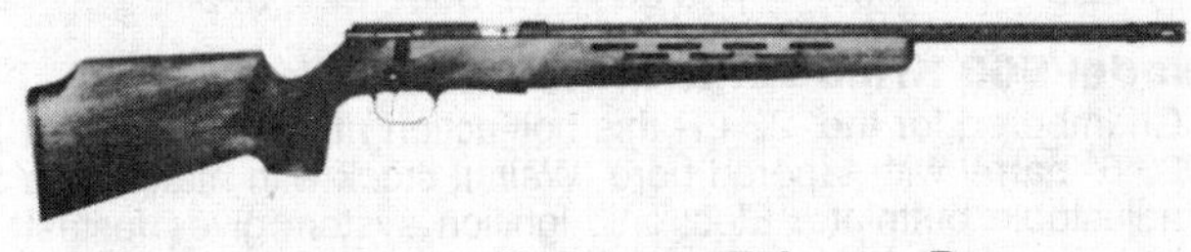

Exc.	V.G.	Good	Fair	Poor
1000	850	750	500	400

Model 340 Kricotronic

The Model 340 fitted with an electronic trigger. Not imported after 1988.

Exc.	V.G.	Good	Fair	Poor
1250	1000	850	600	500

Model 360S Biathlon Rifle

Introduced in 1991 this model features a .22 Long Rifle straight pull bolt-action with 5-round magazine and fitted with a 21.25" barrel. Walnut stock with high comb and adjustable buttplate. Fully adjustable match peep sight. Fitted with 17 oz. match trigger. Weight is approximately 9.25 lbs.

NIB	Exc.	V.G.	Good	Fair	Poor
1600	1350	850	—	—	—

Model 360S2 Biathlon Rifle

Same as above but fitted with a black epoxy finished walnut stock with pistol grip. Weight is 9 lbs.

NIB	Exc.	V.G.	Good	Fair	Poor
1500	1250	800	—	—	—

Model 400 Match

Chambered for the .22 LR or the .22 Hornet this bolt-action rifle is fitted with a heavy match 23" barrel and a 5-round magazine. The match-style stock is of European walnut. Fitted with a double set of match triggers. Weight is about 8.8 lbs.

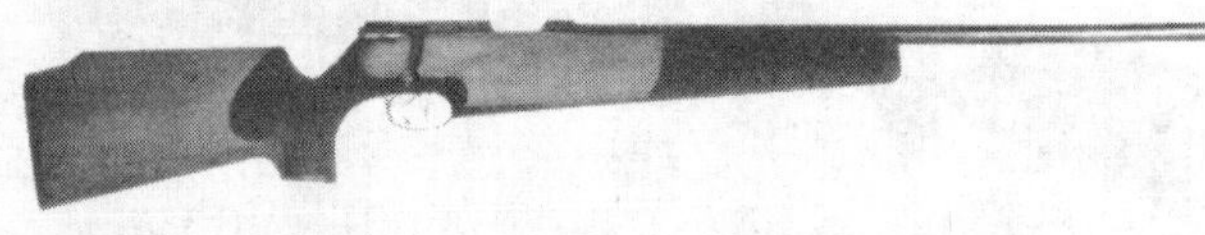

NIB	Exc.	V.G.	Good	Fair	Poor
900	775	650	500	300	150

Model 400 Sporter

A .22 Hornet caliber bolt-action rifle with a 23.5" barrel, open sights and 5-shot magazine. Blued with a walnut stock. Not imported after 1988.

Exc.	V.G.	Good	Fair	Poor
750	625	550	425	325

Model 420

As above, with a 19.5" barrel, double set triggers, and a full-length stock. Discontinued in 1988.

Exc.	V.G.	Good	Fair	Poor
900	750	675	500	400

Model 440

Similar to the Model 340. Not imported after 1988.

Exc.	V.G	Good	Fair	Poor
950	800	700	500	375

Model 500 Kricotronic Match Rifle

Chambered for the .22 LR this bolt-action rifle is fitted with a 23.6" barrel with tapered bore. Walnut stock with match-type adjustable buttplate. Electronic ignition system gives fastest lock time. Weight is approximately 9.4 lbs.

NIB	Exc.	V.G.	Good	Fair	Poor
3900	3000	—	—	—	—

Model 600 Sporter

A .17 Remington to .308 Winchester caliber bolt-action rifle with a 23.5" barrel, open sights and 3-shot magazine. Blued with a walnut stock. Not imported after 1988.

Exc.	V.G.	Good	Fair	Poor
1150	950	875	700	575

Model 600 Sniper Rifle

This bolt-action rifle is chambered for the .222, .223, .22-250, .243, and 308. It is fitted with a 25.6" heavy barrel with flack hider. The stock is walnut with adjustable rubber buttplate. Magazine holds 4 rounds. Weight is about 9.2 lbs.

NIB	Exc.	V.G.	Good	Fair	Poor
2600	2000	1500	—	—	—

Model 600 Match Rifle

Chambered for the same calibers as the 600 Sniper with the addition of the 5.6x50 Mag. Fitted with a 23.6" barrel. The match stock is vented in forearm for cooling. Wood is walnut with cheekpiece. Weight is approximately 8.8 lbs.

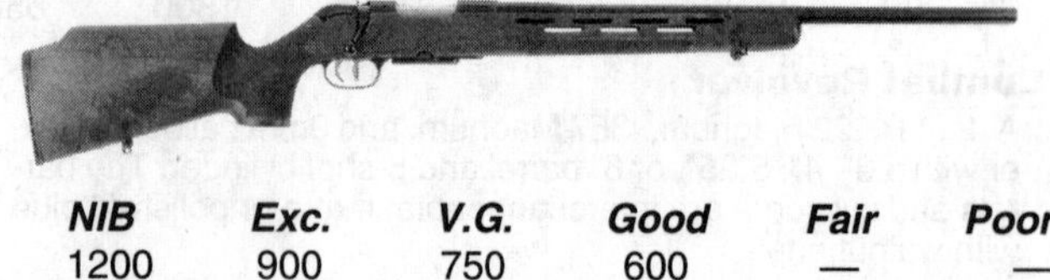

NIB	Exc.	V.G.	Good	Fair	Poor
1200	900	750	600	—	—

Model 620

As above, with a 20.5" barrel, double set triggers, and full-length stock.

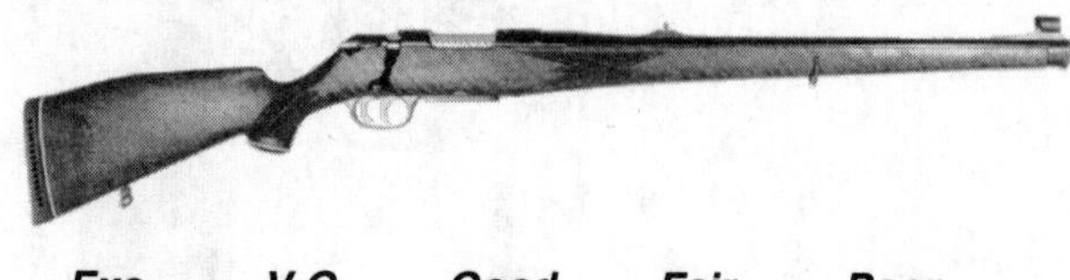

Exc.	V.G.	Good	Fair	Poor
1200	1000	900	750	600

Model 640 Varmint Rifle

Similar to the above, in .22-250, .222 or .223 caliber with a 23.5" heavy barrel. Not imported after 1988.

Exc.	V.G.	Good	Fair	Poor
1250	1025	925	775	625

Model 640 Sniper Rifle

As above, but matte finished. Discontinued in 1988.

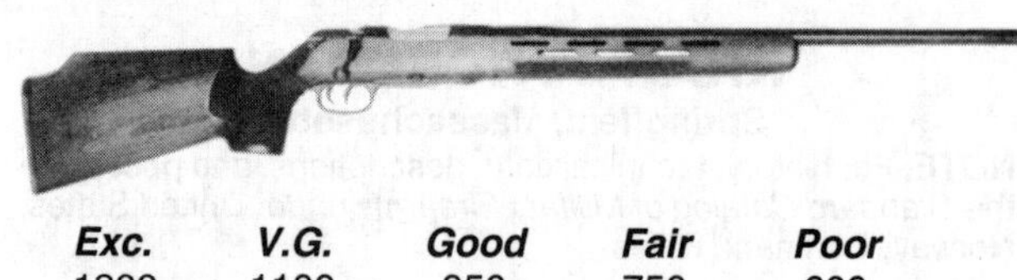

Exc.	V.G.	Good	Fair	Poor
1300	1100	950	750	600

Model 640 Deluxe Sniper Rifle

As above, in .223 or .308 caliber with a 23" barrel, stippled stock, and adjustable trigger. Not imported after 1988.

Exc.	V.G.	Good	Fair	Poor
1500	1250	1000	750	650

Model 700 Sporter

A .270 or .30-06 caliber bolt-action rifle with a 23.5" barrel, open sights, single set trigger, and 3-shot magazine. Blued with a walnut stock. Discontinued in 1988.

Exc.	V.G.	Good	Fair	Poor
1050	850	750	600	500

Model 720

As above, with a 20.5" barrel, double set triggers, and full-length stock. Discontinued in 1988.

Exc.	V.G.	Good	Fair	Poor
1050	850	750	600	500

Model 720 Limited Edition

As above, in .270 caliber only with gold-plated furniture and gold highlighted engraving. Not imported after 1988.

Exc.	V.G.	Good	Fair	Poor
2500	2000	1750	1400	900

KRIDER, J. H.

Philadelphia, Pennsylvania

Pocket Pistol

A .41 caliber percussion pocket pistol with a 3" barrel, German silver furniture and walnut stock. The barrel marked "Krider Phila." Manufactured during the 1850s and 1860s.

Exc.	V.G.	Good	Fair	Poor
—	—	1500	700	300

Militia Rifle

A .58 caliber percussion rifle with a 39" barrel and full length stock secured by two barrel bands. The barrel is browned, the lock marked "Krider." Case hardened and furniture of brass. Several hundred were manufactured in 1861.

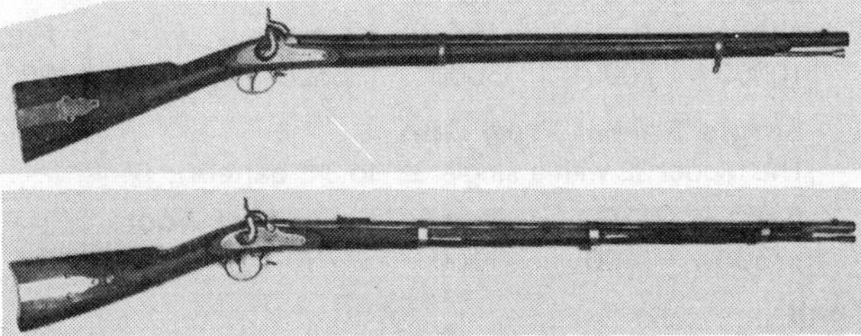

Courtesy Milwaukee Public Museum, Milwaukee, Wisconsin

Exc.	V.G.	Good	Fair	Poor
—	—	4250	2000	750

KRIEGHOFF, HEINRICH, GUN CO.

Ulm, Germany

NOTE: Krieghoff-manufactured Lugers are listed in the Luger section.

DRILLINGS AND COMBINATION GUNS

Plus Model

A three-barrel combination rifle/shotgun produced in a variety of gauges and calibers with 25" barrels, double triggers, and automatic ejectors. Blued with a walnut stock. Introduced in 1988.

NIB	Exc.	V.G.	Good	Fair	Poor
6000	4750	3750	—	—	—

Trumpf Model

A combination rifle/shotgun produced in a variety of calibers and gauges with 25" barrels and double triggers. Blued with a walnut stock.

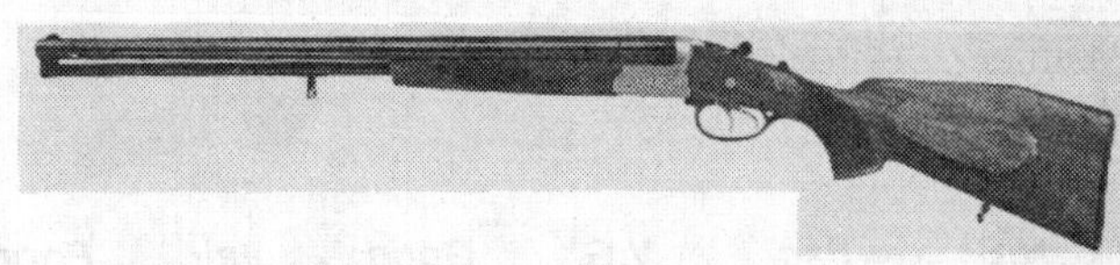

NIB	Exc.	V.G.	Good	Fair	Poor
10000	7000	4750	—	—	—

Trumpf Dural

As above, lightweight boxlock with a Duraluminum frame.

NIB	Exc.	V.G.	Good	Fair	Poor
10000	7000	4750	—	—	—

NOTE: For single trigger add $1,850. For free-floating barrel add $450.

Neptun Model

A combination over-and-under rifle/shotgun with sidelocks produced in a variety of gauges and calibers. Engraved, blued with a walnut stock.

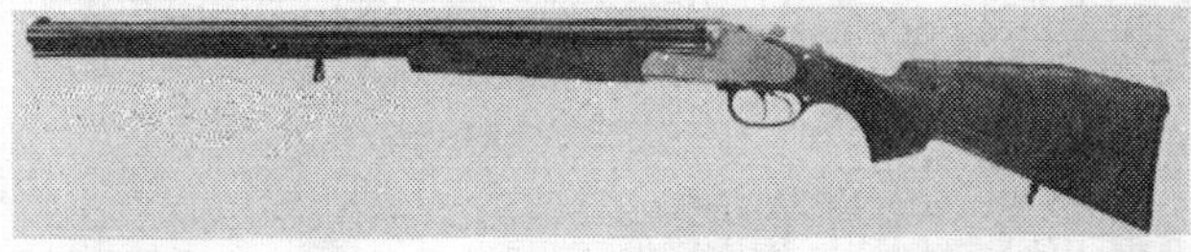

NIB	Exc.	V.G.	Good	Fair	Poor
16500	12500	9500	—	—	—

Neptun Dural

As above, lightweight boxlock with a Duraluminum frame.

NIB	Exc.	V.G.	Good	Fair	Poor
16500	12500	9500	—	—	—

Neptun Primus Model

The Neptun with relief engraving and detachable sidelocks.

NIB	Exc.	V.G.	Good	Fair	Poor
24500	18500	12500	—	—	—

Neptun Primus Dural

As above, lightweight sidelock with a Duraluminum frame.

NIB	Exc.	V.G.	Good	Fair	Poor
24500	18500	12500	—	—	—

DOUBLE RIFLES

Teck Over-and-Under

A boxlock over-and-under rifle manufactured in a variety of calibers with 25" barrels, double triggers, extractors, and express sights. Blued with a walnut stock.

NIB	Exc.	V.G.	Good	Fair	Poor
10500	7500	6000	—	—	—

NOTE: For .458 Win. Mag add $1,500.

Ulm Model

As above, with sidelocks.

NIB	Exc.	V.G.	Good	Fair	Poor
17900	14000	10000	—	—	—

Ulm Primus

As above, with detachable sidelocks.

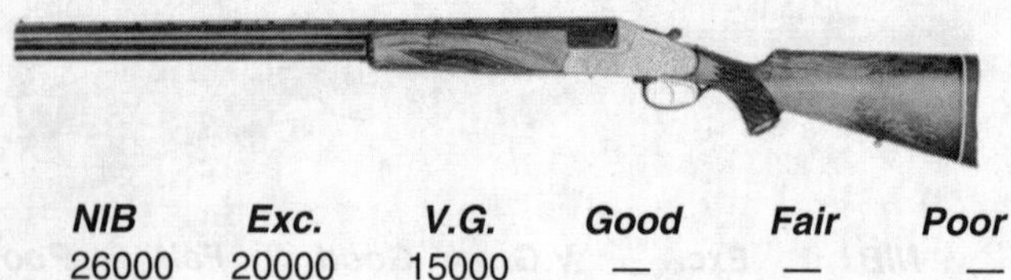

NIB	Exc.	V.G.	Good	Fair	Poor
26000	20000	15000	—	—	—

Ultra

This boxlock over-and-under rifle is offered with several different options such as same caliber rifle barrels or different caliber rifle barrels. Built on a 20 gauge frame with game scene engraving. Weights are depending on calibers and combinations of calibers but are between 6.5 lbs. and 8 lbs.

NIB	Exc.	V.G.	Good	Fair	Poor
6900	5500	4000	—	—	—

Classic

This is a side-by-side rifle with sideplates. Offered in 7x65R to 9.3x74R calibers with an optional interchangeable 20 gauge shotgun barrel. Single trigger. Choice of standard stock with cheekpiece or classic Bavaria style. Weight is approximately 7.25 to 8 lbs. depending on calibers.

Classic with sideplates

NIB	Exc.	V.G.	Good	Fair	Poor
7850	6250	—	—	—	—

Classic Big Five

Similar to the Classic but chambered for .375 H&H, .375 NE, .458 Win. Mag., .416 Rigby, .470 NE, and .500 NE 3". Double trigger with hinged front trigger. Weighs approximately 9.25 to 10 lbs. depending on caliber. Interchangeable barrel are optional.

NIB	Exc.	V.G.	Good	Fair	Poor
9400	7500	—	—	—	—

NOTE: There are many optional engraving patterns available for these double rifles that may affect price. Consult an expert prior to a sale.

SHOTGUNS

Model 32 Standard

A 12, 20, 28 or .410 bore boxlock over-and-under shotgun with 26.5" to 32" barrels, single-selective trigger and automatic ejectors. Blued with a walnut stock. Discontinued in 1980.

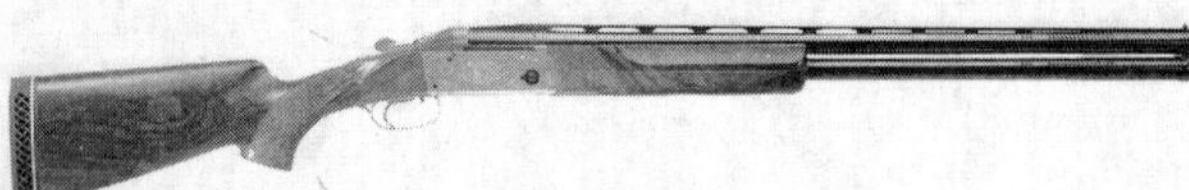

Exc.	V.G.	Good	Fair	Poor
2000	1750	1500	1000	750

NOTE: 28 gauge or .410 two barrel set add 50 percent. Four-barrel Skeet set add 100 percent.

San Remo Grade

Exc.	V.G.	Good	Fair	Poor
3250	2500	1750	1250	1000

Monte Carlo Grade

Exc.	V.G.	Good	Fair	Poor
4750	3500	2500	1500	1250

Crown Grade

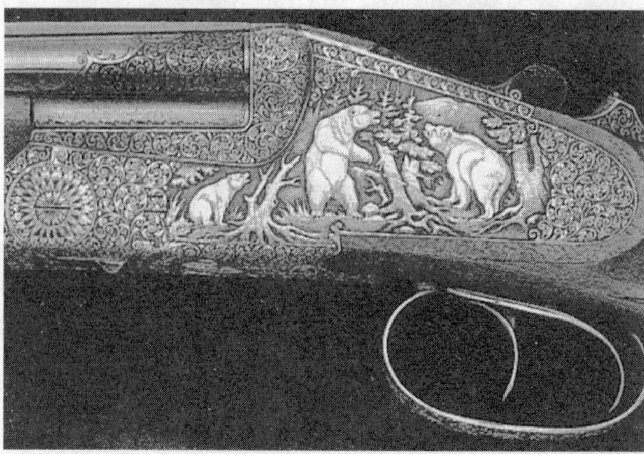

Courtesy Bonhams & Butterfields

Exc.	V.G.	Good	Fair	Poor
7000	5000	3000	2000	1500

Super Crown Grade

NIB	Exc.	V.G.	Good	Fair	Poor
10000	7000	5000	3500	2500	2000

Single Barrel Trap Gun

The Model 32 with a single 32" to 34" barrel.

Exc.	V.G.	Good	Fair	Poor
1750	1400	1100	750	600

Teck

Similar to the Teck double rifle but offered in 12 and 16 gauge.

NIB	Exc.	V.G.	Good	Fair	Poor
7750	6250	—	—	—	—

Teck Dural

Same as above but with lightweight aluminum frame.

NIB	Exc.	V.G.	Good	Fair	Poor
7750	6250	—	—	—	—

Ulm

This sidelock over-and-under is offered in both 12 and 16 gauge.

NIB	Exc.	V.G.	Good	Fair	Poor
14500	11000	—	—	—	—

Ulm Dural

This is a lightweight version of the above model.

NIB	Exc.	V.G.	Good	Fair	Poor
14500	11000	—	—	—	—

Ulm Primus

This is a deluxe version of the Ulm series with sidelocks and extensive engraving.

NIB	Exc.	V.G.	Good	Fair	Poor
22800	17500	—	—	—	—

Ulm Primus Dural

This is a lightweight version of the above model.

NIB	Exc.	V.G.	Good	Fair	Poor
22800	17500	—	—	—	—

Ultra

This is a lightweight over-and-under gun offered in 12 or 20 gauge.

NIB	Exc.	V.G.	Good	Fair	Poor
5000	4000	3000	—	—	—

KS-5 Single Barrel Trap

This model is a boxlock 12 gauge only trap gun with 32" or 34" ventilated tapered rib barrel and case hardened frame with a satin gray finish. The barrel features an adjustable point of impact and is offered with screw-in choke tubes. Weight is approximately 8.6 lbs.

NIB	Exc.	V.G.	Good	Fair	Poor
2850	2250	1750	1500	1250	800

KS-5 Special

Same as above but furnished with adjustable rib and adjustable comb.

NIB	Exc.	V.G.	Good	Fair	Poor
3500	3000	2500	2000	1500	1000

KS-80 Trap

This is a boxlock 12 gauge shotgun built to trap dimensions. This model is offered in many variations. Available in over-and-under trap with choice of 30" or 32" vent tapered step rib barrels. Also a single barrel is offered in 32" or 34" tapered step rib lengths. These single barrels are adjustable for point of impact. A top single barrel is available as well in 34" length. Trap combos are offered also. All barrels are offered with or without choke tubes. The checkered walnut stock is offered in Monte Carlo or straight trap dimensions. Trap guns weigh approximately 8.75 lbs. Prices listed are for Standard Grade.

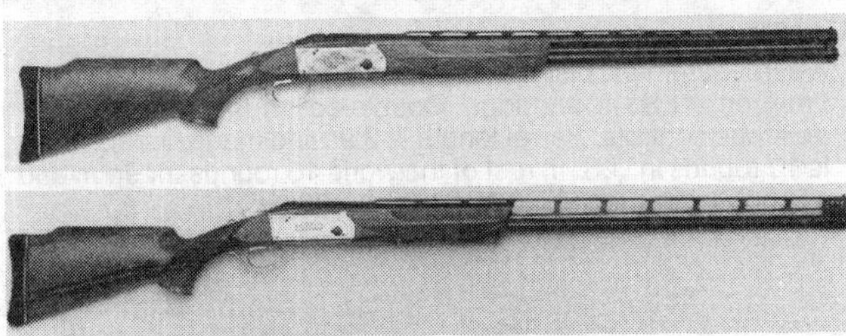

Over-and-Under Trap

NIB	Exc.	V.G.	Good	Fair	Poor
5400	4900	4000	3500	2000	1000

Unsingle Trap

NIB	Exc.	V.G.	Good	Fair	Poor
5800	5300	4500	4000	2250	1250

Top Single Trap

NIB	Exc.	V.G.	Good	Fair	Poor
7500	6500	5000	4000	3000	1500

Trap Combos

NIB	Exc.	V.G.	Good	Fair	Poor
8200	7000	6000	4000	3000	1500

NOTE: Bavaria Grade add 70 percent. Danube Grade add 100 percent. Gold Target Grade add 200 percent.

K-80 Sporting Clays

The frame is the same as the trap model with the addition of a lightweight alloy model and is available in 12 gauge only. Barrel lengths for standard weight model are 28", 30", or 32" with tapered flat rib. The lightweight model is offered with 28" or 30" flat rib barrels. Select European walnut stock with hand checkering and supplied with a #3 Sporting stock with schnabel forearm. The standard weight model weighs about 8.25 lbs. while the lightweight model weighs 7.75 lbs. Prices listed are for the Standard Grade.

NIB	Exc.	V.G.	Good	Fair	Poor
5800	5250	4500	3000	2000	1000

NOTE: Bavaria Grade add 70 percent. Danube Grade add 100 percent. Gold Target Grade add 200 percent.

K-80 Skeet

This model is offered in a number of variations. The standard weight skeet with 28" or 30" tapered or parallel ribs, lightweight skeet with 28" or 30" tapered or parallel ribs, International skeet with 28" parallel broadway rib, and the 4 barrel skeet set in 12, 20, and 28 gauge as well as .410 bore with 8mm rib. Stock is hand-checkered select European walnut with a choice of several skeet dimensions. Prices listed are for Standard Grade.

Standard Weight Skeet

NIB	Exc.	V.G.	Good	Fair	Poor
5000	4500	3500	2500	1750	1250

Lightweight Skeet

NIB	Exc.	V.G.	Good	Fair	Poor
5000	4500	3500	2500	1750	1250

International Skeet

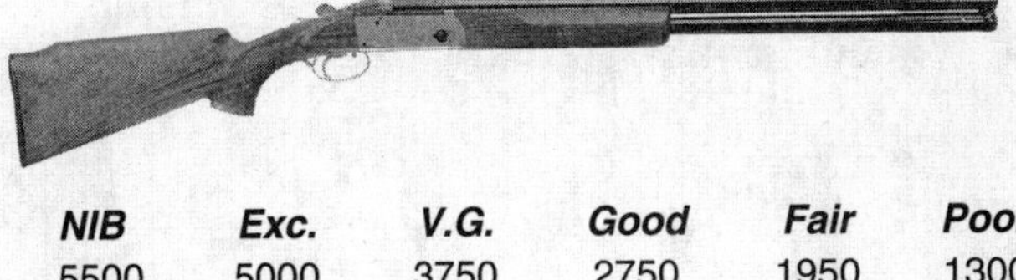

NIB	Exc.	V.G.	Good	Fair	Poor
5500	5000	3750	2750	1950	1300

4 Barrel Set

NIB	Exc.	V.G.	Good	Fair	Poor
11250	8000	6000	4000	3000	2000

NOTE: Bavaria Grade add 70 percent. Danube Grade add 100 percent. Gold Target Grade add 200 percent. Optional Engravings available by special order on NIB or Exc. conditions guns: Parcours add $1500. Parcours Special add $2800. Super Scroll add $1100. Gold Super Scroll add $2900. Custom Bavaria $4700 over Bavaria Grade price.

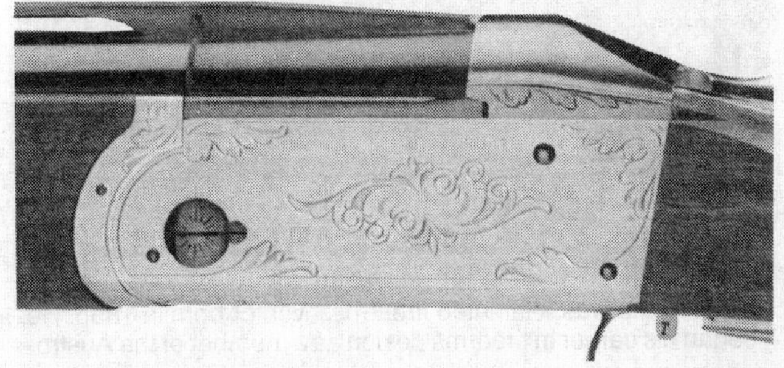

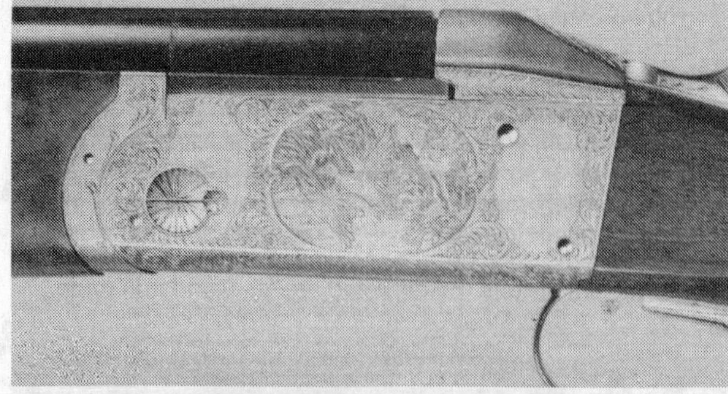

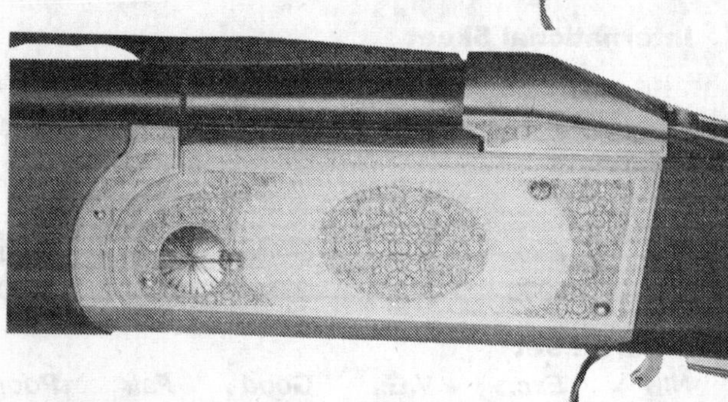

KRNKA, KAREL

Vienna, Austria

Karel Krnka was a talented firearms inventor born in 1858. He began his career in firearms design as a member of the Austro-Hungarian army. He made many improvements to their service rifle design. After he left the military, he took the job of head engineer with the ill-fated and short-lived "Gatling Gun Company." This company ceased operations in 1890, and then Krnka went to work for the patent office and remained there for a few years. In 1898 he became foreman of the Roth Cartridge Company and worked with Roth on firearms designs until the death of Roth in 1909. After this he became associated with the Hertenberger Cartridge Company; and finally in 1922 he moved to Czechoslovakia, where he became a firearms designer for the firm of C.Z. He remained at this post until his death in 1926. He recorded his first firearm patent in 1888 for a mechanical repeater with a ring trigger. His best known innovations are the internal butt magazine that is loaded by means of a stripper clip and the rotating locked bolt with internal firing pin. These designs were never actually turned into a mass-marketed pistol but were major contributions in the development of a practical semi-automatic pistol design.

Model 1892

Exc.	V.G.	Good	Fair	Poor
—	7500	5000	2000	950

KROPATSCHEK

Steyr-Werke
Steyr, Austria

Model 1878

An 11mm caliber bolt-action rifle with a 32" barrel, full length stock secured by three barrel bands, and 7-shot magazine. Finished in the white with a walnut stock.

Exc.	V.G.	Good	Fair	Poor
—	400	200	125	75

KSN INDUSTRIES

Israel

Golan

A semi-automatic pistol, introduced in 1996, chambered for the 9mm or .40 S&W cartridge. Double-action trigger with ambidextrous controls. Barrel length is 3.9" and magazine capacity is 10 rounds in U.S. In rest of the world 15 rounds for 9mm and 11 rounds for the .40 S&W. Weight is 29 oz.

NIB	Exc.	V.G.	Good	Fair	Poor
650	525	400	325	—	—

Kareen MK II

This single-action semi-automatic pistol is chambered for the 9mm cartridge. The barrel length is 4.5". Ambidextrous safety and rubber grips. Steel slide and frame. Weight is about 34 oz.

NIB	Exc.	V.G.	Good	Fair	Poor
400	325	250	200	150	100

Kareen MK II-Compact

Same as above but fitted with a 3.9" barrel. Weight is about 32 oz.

NIB	Exc.	V.G.	Good	Fair	Poor
500	400	300	250	200	150

GAL

Same as the full size Kareen but chambered for the .45 ACP cartridge.

NIB	Exc.	V.G.	Good	Fair	Poor
400	325	250	200	150	100

KUFAHL, G. L.

Sommerda, Germany

Kufahl Needle-Fire Revolver

Designed and patented in Britain in 1852 by G.L. Kufahl, who tried unsuccessfully to interest a British company in producing it. He then went to the firm of Rheinmettal Dreyse, where a needle-fire gun was produced in 1838. This company manufactured his design. This revolver was chambered for a unique, totally consumed .30 caliber "cartridge." A lead projectile had the ignition percussion cap affixed to its base, with the propellant powder in the rear. The firing pin had to be long enough to penetrate the powder charge and hit the percussion cap. This does not sound efficient, but realize that these were the days before cartridges. This revolver has a 3.2" barrel and an unfluted cylinder that holds six shots. It is not bored all the way through but is loaded from the front. The finish is blued, with a modicum of simple engraving and checkered wood grips that protrude all the way over the trigger. The markings are "Fv.V. Dreyse Sommerda."

Exc.	V.G.	Good	Fair	Poor
—	2500	1250	600	400

KYNOCH GUN FACTORY

Birmingham, England

Established by George Kynoch in approximately 1886, this company ceased operation in 1890.

Early Double Trigger Revolver

A .45 caliber double trigger revolver with a 6" barrel, 6-shot cylinder and enclosed hammer. Blued with walnut grips. Manufactured in 1885.

Exc.	V.G.	Good	Fair	Poor
—	1250	600	450	350

Late Double Trigger Revolver

Similar to the above, but in .32, .38, or .45 caliber with the cocking trigger enclosed within the trigger guard. Approximately 600 of these revolvers were made between 1896 and 1890.

Exc.	V.G.	Good	Fair	Poor
—	1500	700	550	450

L

LAGRESE
Paris, France

Lagrese Revolver

A large ornate revolver chambered for the .43 rimfire cartridge. It has a 6.25" barrel and a 6-shot fluted cylinder. This revolver has no top strap; and the frame, as well as the grip straps, are cast in one piece with the barrel screwed into the frame. It is loaded through a gate and has double-action lockwork. The outstanding feature about this well-made revolver is its extremely ornate appearance. There are more sweeps and curves than could be imagined. It is engraved and blued, with well-figured curved walnut grips. It is marked "Lagrese Bte a Paris" and was manufactured in the late 1860s.

Exc.	V.G.	Good	Fair	Poor
—	—	2500	1150	800

LAHTI
Finland

SEE—Husqvarna

Lahti

This is a commercial version of the Finnish L-35 9mm pistol. These late pistols have the barrel and trigger guard design of the L-35 but the barrel extension of the Swedish M40. Produced in the late 1950s.

Late Commercial Lahti with "Valmet" stamped on top.

Courtesy J.B. Wood

Exc.	V.G.	Good	Fair	Poor
1250	1000	800	550	300

LAKELANDER
Gulfport, Mississippi

Model 389 Premium

This bolt action rifle is chambered for .270 Win., .308 Win., and .30-06 calibers. It is fitted with a 22" lightweight barrel. The stock is oil finished walnut with diamond checkering. Rosewood forend cap, black recoil pad, and Monte Carlo buttstock. Weight is approximately 7.6 lbs. Introduced in 1997.

NIB	Exc.	V.G.	Good	Fair	Poor
1600	1250	850	—	—	—

Model 389 Classic

Similar to the Premium grade rifle above but offered with traditional stock and checkering and less fancy walnut stock. Weight is approximately 7.3 lbs. Introduced in 1997.

NIB	Exc.	V.G.	Good	Fair	Poor
1650	1300	900	—	—	—

Model 389 Match-Maker

This bolt action is chambered for the .308 cartridge and is fitted with a 21.7" barrel. The stock is target style with adjustable chin support with benchrest-style buttpad. Weight is approximately 8.4 lbs. Introduced in 1997.

NIB	Exc.	V.G.	Good	Fair	Poor
2050	1650	1250	—	—	—

NOTE: Add $50 for magnum calibers.

LAMB, H. C. & CO.
Jamestown, North Carolina

Muzzle Loading Rifle

Chambered for .58 caliber and utilizes the percussion ignition system. It has a 33" barrel and a full-length oak stock held on by two barrel bands. There is a ramrod mounted under the barrel that is made of iron. All other trim is brass, and there is a bayonet lug at the muzzle. This rifle was made for the Confederacy; and the workmanship was crude, as it was on most CSA weapons. The stock is marked "H.C.Lamb & Co., N.C." There were supposedly 10,000 rifles ordered, but actually there were approximately 250 manufactured between 1861 and 1863. The rarity of the guns of the Confederacy gives them a great deal of collector appeal.

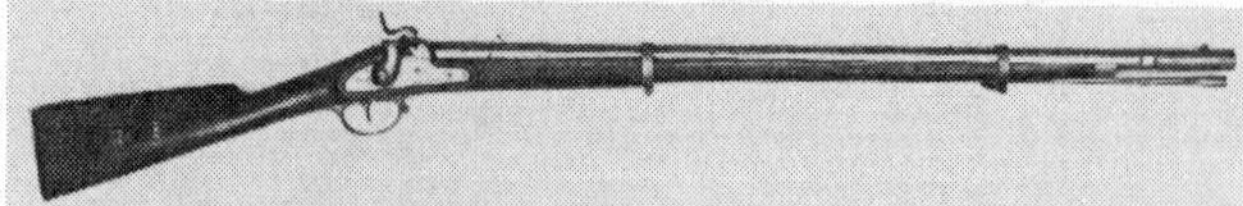

Courtesy Milwaukee Public Museum, Milwaukee, Wisconsin

Exc.	V.G.	Good	Fair	Poor
—	—	30000	10000	2500

LAMES
Chiavari, Italy

Skeet or Trap Grade

An over-and-under shotgun chambered for 12 gauge with either 26" skeet-and-skeet barrels or 30" or 32" full-choked barrels. It has a competition-style wide vent rib and automatic ejectors. The trigger is single-selective, and the finish is blued. The trap gun has a Monte Carlo stock of checkered walnut. Both models feature recoil pads.

Exc.	V.G.	Good	Fair	Poor
600	500	450	350	200

California Trap Grade

This over-and-under is similar to the standard trap model, with separated barrels. All other features are the same.

Exc.	V.G.	Good	Fair	Poor
700	600	550	450	225

Field Grade

Similar in design to the standard trap model, with 3" chambers and barrel lengths of 26", 28", or 30" and a field dimensioned stock. It features various choke combinations and was also available with the separated barrels of the California Trap for an additional 20 percent in cost.

Exc.	V.G.	Good	Fair	Poor
400	350	300	225	150

LANBER ARMAS S.A.

Vizcaya, Spain

Model 844 ST

A 12-gauge over-and-under shotgun with 26" or 28" vent rib barrels. The chokes vary, and the gun features a single-selective trigger, extractors, and an engraved receiver with a blued finish and a walnut stock. This gun was manufactured until 1986.

Exc.	V.G.	Good	Fair	Poor
425	350	300	250	175

Model 844 MST

Similar to the Model 844 ST except that it is chambered for 3" Magnum and has 30" Full and Modified choked barrels.

Exc.	V.G.	Good	Fair	Poor
425	350	300	250	175

Model 844 EST

Similar to the others, but it features automatic ejectors.

Exc.	V.G.	Good	Fair	Poor
475	400	350	300	200

Model 844 EST CHR

Has automatic ejectors and double triggers. All other features are the same as the EST.

Exc.	V.G.	Good	Fair	Poor
450	375	325	275	175

Model 2004 LCH

An over-and-under chambered for 12 gauge and features 28" vent rib barrels with screw-in choke tubes. It has a single-selective trigger, automatic ejectors, and an engraved boxlock action that is matte finished, with a hand-checkered walnut stock. This model was also discontinued in 1986.

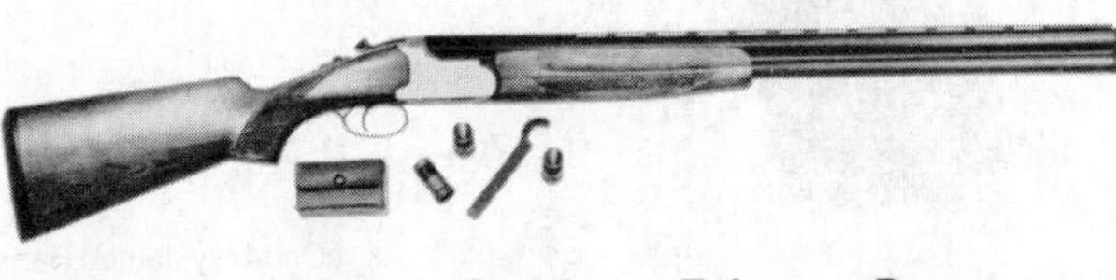

Exc.	V.G.	Good	Fair	Poor
775	650	550	475	375

Model 2008 LCH and Model 2009 LCH

The trap and skeet versions of the series. The basic differences are in the barrel lengths and the stock dimensions.

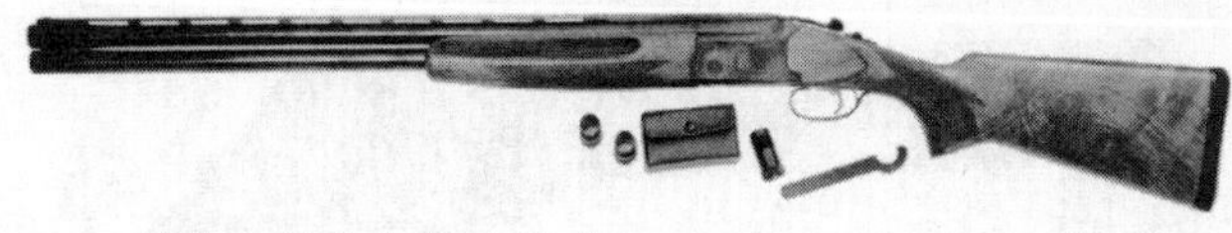

Model 2008 LCH

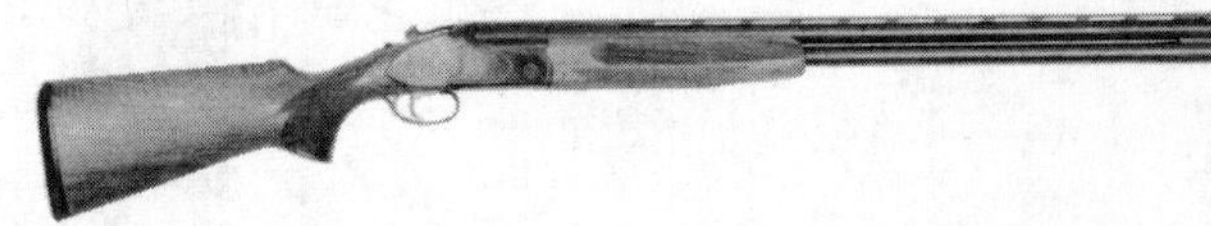

Model 2009 LCH

Exc.	V.G.	Good	Fair	Poor
900	750	650	575	475

LANCASTER, CHARLES

London, England

SEE—British Double Guns

4 Barreled Pistol

A unique pistol for several reasons. It is chambered for the .476 rimfire cartridge and has four 6.25" barrels. The bore has a slightly twisted oval pattern that imparts a spin to the bullet. The barrels are hinged at the bottom and break downward for loading. It is a double-action type lockwork with a long, difficult trigger pull. The pistol is well made; and the caliber, suitably heavy to insure stopping power. The primary goal was military; and it was successful, seeing action in the Sudan campaigns of 1882 and 1885. This powerful weapon was also popular with big game hunters as a backup sidearm. The finish is blued, with checkered walnut grips. It is marked "Charles Lancaster (Patent) 151 New Bond St. London." This model was introduced in 1881. There are smaller-caliber versions of this pistol with shorter barrels. They are not as well known as the large-caliber version, and the values would be similar as their rarity would be balanced by the desirability of the large bore models.

Exc.	V.G.	Good	Fair	Poor
—	3950	2500	1000	750

2 Barreled Pistol

Similar to the 4 barreled version, with only two superposed barrels chambered for a variety of calibers from .320 to .577. It was also chambered for the 20 gauge and .410 bore shotshell. The advantage to the 2 barreled pistol is that it is lighter and better balanced. The 2 barrel is less common than the 4 barrel version.

Courtesy James Rankin

Exc.	V.G.	Good	Fair	Poor
—	3000	2000	900	600

4 Barreled Shotgun

This company also produced a shotgun in the 4 barrel configuration. It is chambered for 12 or 16 gauge and has 28" barrels. The gun is, as one would imagine, quite heavy and poorly balanced; and it was not a great success.

Exc.	V.G.	Good	Fair	Poor
—	300	2000	900	600

Bolt Action Rifle

A high-grade sporting rifle chambered for various different calibers. The barrel is 24" in length; and the finish is blued with a classic-styled, hand-checkered walnut stock. This rifle was discontinued in 1936.

Exc.	V.G.	Good	Fair	Poor
1750	1000	800	550	400

LANG, J.

London, England

SEE—British Double Guns

Percussion Pistol

Chambered for .60 caliber percussion. It is a single-barreled, muzzle-loading pistol with a 3.25" barrel. This is essentially a defensive weapon that was well made, with Damascus barrels and an ornate engraved hammer and frame.

Exc.	V.G.	Good	Fair	Poor
—	—	4500	2750	1000

Gas Seal Revolver

Chambered for the .42 caliber percussion and has a 4.75" barrel. The unfluted cylinder holds 6 shots and is spring-loaded to be forced into the barrel when cocked, in order to obtain the "Gas Seal" feature desired. This revolver was well made and finished. It is lightly engraved, with a case-colored cylinder and a blued barrel and frame. The grips are finely checkered walnut, and the markings are "J.Lang 22 Cockspur St. London." This type of firearm was the forerunner of later designs such as the Russian Nagant. This revolver was manufactured in the 1850s.

Exc.	V.G.	Good	Fair	Poor
—	2750	1250	900	550

LANGENHAN, FRIEDRICH

Zella Mehlis, Germany

Langenhan Army Model

A blowback-operated semi-automatic pistol chambered for the 7.65mm Auto Pistol cartridge. It has a 4" barrel and a detachable magazine that holds 8 rounds. Weight is about 24 oz. The pistol was made with a separate breechblock that is held into the slide by a screw. This feature doomed this pistol to eventual failure as when this screw became worn, it could loosen when firing and allow the breechblock to pivot upwards—and the slide would then be propelled rearward and into the face of the shooter. This pistol was produced with wood grips.

Courtesy James Rankin

Exc.	V.G.	Good	Fair	Poor
375	300	250	175	100

Langenhan Open Model

A semi-automatic pistol that is similar to the Army Model with some minor variations, and an open window in the frame. Checkered hard rubber grips with "FL" logo on each side.

Courtesy James Rankin

Exc.	V.G.	Good	Fair	Poor
400	325	275	200	100

Langenhan Closed Model

Similar to the Open Model with closed frame and other minor variations.

Courtesy James Rankin

Exc.	V.G.	Good	Fair	Poor
400	325	275	200	100

Model 2

A blowback-operated semi-automatic pistol chambered for the 6.35mm cartridge. It has a 3" barrel and an 8-round detachable magazine. Weight is about 18 oz. The pistol fires by means of a concealed hammer, and the breechblock is separate from the rest of the slide and is held in place by a heavy crossbolt. The finish is blued, and the grips are molded checkered black plastic with the monogram "F.L." at the top. The slide is marked "Langenhan 6.35." This model was manufactured between 1921 and 1936.

Courtesy James Rankin

Exc.	V.G.	Good	Fair	Poor
375	300	250	200	100

Model 3

Similar to the Model 2 except that it is somewhat smaller. The barrel is 2.25" in length, and the butt is only large enough to house a 5-round detachable magazine. Weight is about 17 oz. The markings are the same with the addition of "Model 111" on the slide. This model was also manufactured until 1936.

Exc.	V.G.	Good	Fair	Poor
325	275	250	200	150

LAR MFG. CO.

West Jordan, Utah

Grizzly Mark I

A .357 Magnum, .45 ACP, 10mm, or .45 Winchester Magnum semi-automatic pistol with a 5.4", 6.5", 8", or 10" barrel, Millett sights, ambidextrous safety and 7-shot magazine. Parkerized, blued, or hard-chrome plated with rubber grips. Available with cartridge conversion units, telescope mounts, or a compensator. Weight is approximately 48 oz. Introduced in 1984.

NIB	Exc.	V.G.	Good	Fair	Poor
1200	950	750	600	400	200

Grizzly Mark II

As above, with fixed sights and without the ambidextrous safety. Manufactured in 1986.

Exc.	V.G.	Good	Fair	Poor
1100	850	575	375	300

Grizzly Mark IV

Similar to the Mark I but chambered for the .44 Magnum cartridge. Barrel length is 5.4" or 6.5". Choice of blue or Parkerized finish.

NIB	Exc.	V.G.	Good	Fair	Poor
1500	1100	775	500	400	200

Grizzly Mark V

Same as above model but chambered for .50 AE cartridge. Empty weight is 56 oz. Add $200 for nickel finish.

NIB	Exc.	V.G.	Good	Fair	Poor
1750	1150	800	550	425	200

Grizzly State Pistol

This is a limited edition of 50 Grizzly pistols with serial numbers that match the order in which each state was admitted into the union. Each pistol features the state outline, the state seal, and the name of the state engraved in gold. Supplied with a cherry wood fitted case with glass top. Chambered for .45 Win. Mag cartridge.

NIB	Exc.	V.G.	Good	Fair	Poor
3000	—	—	—	—	—

Grizzly 50 Big Boar

A single-shot breech loading rifle chambered for the .50 caliber BMG cartridge. The barrel is 36" in length and the rifle weighs approximately 30 lbs.

NIB	Exc.	V.G.	Good	Fair	Poor
1800	1300	1050	800	550	300

NOTE: Add $100 for Parkerized finish. Add $250 for nickel frame, and $350 for full nickel finish.

LASALLE
France

Slide-Action Shotgun

Chambered for 12 or 20 gauge and is offered with a 26", 28", or 30" barrel with improved-cylinder, modified, or full chokes. The receiver is alloy, anodized blue and the vent rib barrel is blued. The stock is checkered walnut.

Exc.	V.G.	Good	Fair	Poor
275	225	200	150	100

Semi-Automatic Shotgun

A gas-operated semi-automatic shotgun chambered for 12 gauge only, with the same barrel length and choke combinations as are available on the slide-action model. The receiver is also alloy, and the stock is checkered walnut.

Exc.	V.G.	Good	Fair	Poor
350	275	225	175	100

LASERAIM ARMS
Little Rock, Arkansas

Series I

Offered in 10mm or .45 ACP this single-action semi-automatic pistol is fitted with a 6" barrel with compensator. Adjustable rear sight. Stainless steel frame and barrel with matte black Teflon finish. Introduced in 1993. Magazine capacity for 10mm is 8 rounds and 7 rounds for .45 ACP. Weight is about 46 oz.

NIB	Exc.	V.G.	Good	Fair	Poor
550	475	400	—	—	—

Series II

This is similar to the Series I except this model has no compensator. It is fitted with a 5" barrel and stainless steel finish. A compact version has a 3-3/8" barrel. Introduced in 1993. Weight is 43 oz. for 5" barrel and 37 oz. for compact version.

NIB	Exc.	V.G.	Good	Fair	Poor
350	300	250	—	—	—

Series III

This model is similar to the Series II except it is offered with 5" barrel only with a dual port compensator. Introduced in 1994. Weight is about 43 oz.

NIB	Exc.	V.G.	Good	Fair	Poor
500	400	300	—	—	—

LAURONA
Eibar, Spain

The list of models listed was compilied by Thomas E. Barker of Galaxy Imports, Ltd., Inc.

Model 67

The first over-and-under Laurona chambered for 12 gauge only with double triggers and 28" vent rib barrels with extractors. The boxlock action and barrels are blued, and the stock is checkered walnut in 20 lpi skip line checkering.

Exc.	V.G.	Good	Fair	Poor
300	200	100	75	50

Model 71

Similar to the Model 67 with minor cosmetic changes and improvements to facilitate ease of manufacturing. Receiver is bright chromed with roll engraving depicting dogs on the right side and birds on the left. This model was imported and sold by Sears & Robuck in about 1973 and 1974. The earlier models had traditional solid center ribbed blued barrels, the later models having black chrome finished solid ribbed barrels.

Exc.	V.G.	Good	Fair	Poor
300	200	100	75	50

MODEL 82

Similar to the Model 71 with auto-ejectors. Chambered for 12 gauge only. All barrels separated without center rib with Black Chrome finish and hard chrome bores with long forcing cones in chambers. Firing pins changed to traditional round type. Many internal parts improved for reliability. Checkering changed from skip diamond to standard 20 lpi. In most respects the 82 Models are representative of present-day Laurona over-and-under shotguns and will share most internal parts.

Model 82 Game

Barrels are 28" with 2-3/4" or 3" chambers, long forcing cones, hard chrome bores, 5mm rib, and chokes ****/**(IC/IM) or ***/*(M/F). Finish on barrels is black chrome with nickel receiver with Louis XVI style engraving. Tulip forend, field-style stock with plastic buttplate. Weighs approximately 7 lbs.

Exc.	V.G.	Good	Fair	Poor
350	250	150	125	100

Model 82 Super Game

Similar to the Model 82 Game except with more elaborate and very delicate engraving

Exc.	V.G.	Good	Fair	Poor
350	250	150	125	100

Model 82 Trap Combi

Similar to the Model 82 Game except for 28" or 29" barrels. The rib is 8mm. The Trap stock is fitted with a rubber recoil pad. Weight is about 7.4 lbs.

Exc.	V.G.	Good	Fair	Poor
450	400	350	300	200

Model 82 Trap Competition

Similar to the Model 82 Trap Combi except for the 13mm aluminum rib with long white sight. Engraving consist of motifs on sides of receiver. Beavertail fluted forend and Monte Carlo Trap stock with black rubber special Trap recoil pad. Weight is approximately 8 lbs.

Exc.	V.G.	Good	Fair	Poor
500	400	300	250	200

Model 82 Super Trap (U only)

Similar to the Model 82 Trap Competition except for special trap Pachmayr recoil pad with imitation leather face. Engraving very delicate fine scroll. Weight is 7 lbs., 12 oz.

Exc.	V.G.	Good	Fair	Poor
575	475	350	300	250

Model 82 Super Skeet

Similar to the Model 82 Super Trap except fitted with 28" barrels choked sheet with field-style buttstock with plastic buttplate. Weight is approximately 7 lbs.

Exc.	V.G.	Good	Fair	Poor
500	400	300	250	200

Model 82 Pigeon Competition

Similar to the Model 82 Trap Competition except fitted with 28" barrels. Recoil pad is special competition-style Pachmayr with imitation leather face. Weight is about 7 lbs., 13 oz.

Exc.	V.G.	Good	Fair	Poor
550	450	350	300	250

Model 82 Super Pigeon

Similar to the Model 82 Super Trap except fitted with 28" barrels. Weight is approximately 7 lbs., 9 oz.

Exc.	V.G.	Good	Fair	Poor
575	475	350	300	250

NOTE: The Super Models listed have nickel-finish receivers featuring delicate fine scroll engraving with black chrome relief. All barrels have a very durable rust-resistant black chrome finish.

Model 84S Super Game

Similar to the Model 82 Super Game except for the new single-selective trigger which is designated by "S" in the model number. Chambered for the 12 gauge 3" magnum with 28" barrels with 8mm rib. Weight is approximately 7 lbs.

Exc.	V.G.	Good	Fair	Poor
500	400	350	200	100

NOTE: The Super Game models listed were available with an extra set of 20 gauge multi-choke barrels in 26" or 28". Add $400 to ***Exc.*** value for these barrels. For models with cast-on stocks for left-hand shooters add $50 to ***Exc.*** value.

Model 83MG Super Game

Similar to the Model 82 Super Game except this model was the advent of Laurona's new multi-choke. **CAUTION!** The Laurona multi-choke is not compatible with any other brand of screw-in chokes because of the black chrome plating on the metric threads. Do not attempt to interchange with other guns. Barrel for this model in 12 gauge are 28" in length and for the 20 gauge 26" or 28". Both are chambered for the 3" shell. Rib is 8mm. Weight is about 7 lbs.

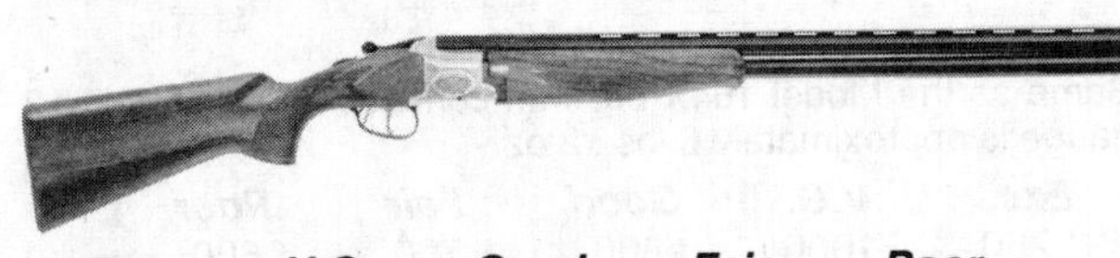

Exc.	V.G.	Good	Fair	Poor
500	400	350	200	100

Model 85MS Super Game

Similar to the Model 83MG Super Game except for the single-selective trigger. Chambered for the 12 or 20 gauge 3" Magnum. Weight is about 7 lbs.

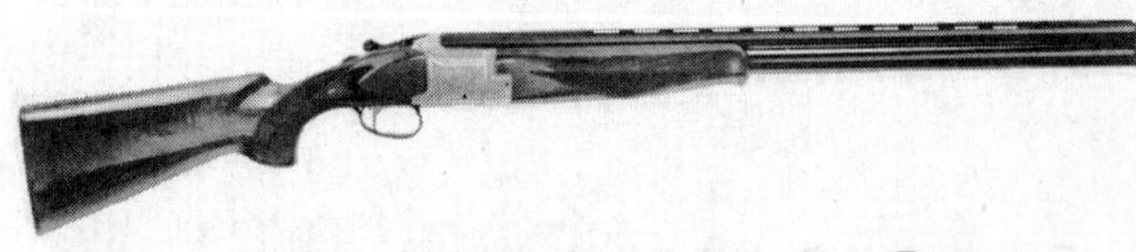

Exc.	V.G.	Good	Fair	Poor
700	650	450	250	200

Model 84S Super Trap

Single-selective trigger with 29" barrels. Chambered for 2-3/4" shells with long forcing cones. The aluminum rib is 13mm wide. Auto ejectors. Receiver is nickel plated with fine scroll engraving with black chrome relief. Beavertail forearm and choice of Monte Carlo or standard Trap stock. Weight is about 7 lbs., 12 oz.

Exc.	V.G.	Good	Fair	Poor
800	750	550	350	250

Model 85MS Super Trap

Similar to the Model 82S Super Trap except multi-choke in bottom barrel with fixed choke on top barrel. Weight is about 7 lbs., 12 oz.

Exc.	V.G.	Good	Fair	Poor
900	825	700	500	300

Model 85MS Super Pigeon

Similar to the Model 85MS Super Trap except with 28" barrels with fixed IM choke on top barrel and multi-choke on bottom barrel. Intended for live bird competition. Weight is about 7 lbs., 4 oz.

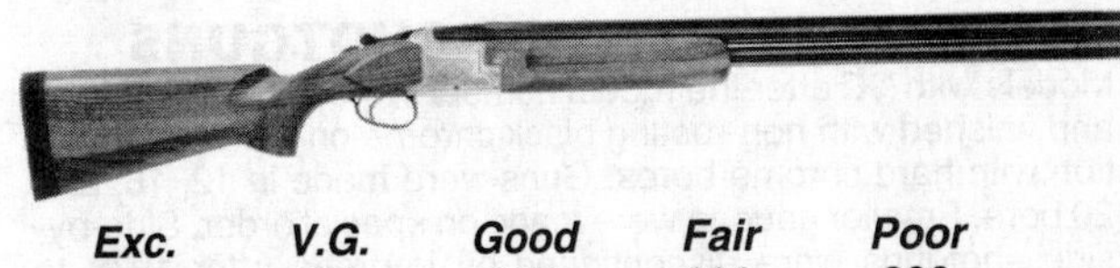

Exc.	V.G.	Good	Fair	Poor
950	900	800	600	300

Model 85MS Special Sporting

Similar to the Model 85MS Super Pigeon except for field-style buttstock with plastic buttplate. Intended for upland game. Weight is approximately 7 lbs., 4 oz.

Exc.	V.G.	Good	Fair	Poor
950	900	800	600	300

Model 84S SuperSkeet

Similar to the Model 85MS Special Sporting except choked skeet and skeet. Weight is approximately 7 lbs.

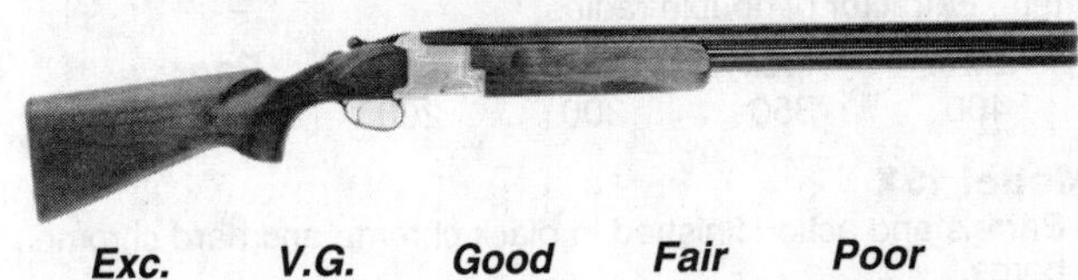

Exc.	V.G.	Good	Fair	Poor
950	900	800	600	300

LAURONA OVER-AND-UNDER MODELS SILHOUETTE 300

These guns are basically the same as the Super series above with these exceptions: They are readily identified by the white and black chrome stripped receiver with the model engraved on the side of the receiver. Barrels are multi-choked on both bores and have 11mm steel ribs. **NOTE:** Two types of chokes were used. Some guns came with knurl head-type as in the Super models and others were made with the flush invector style. A later option for ease of changing chokes is the knurl long choke, which is a flush-type with a knurl head added. Both later type chokes, the flush and the knurl long-type, can be used in the early multi-choke models with some extension showing.

Silhouette 300 Trap

This model has barrels 29" with 2-3/4" chambers and long forcing cones with hard chrome bores and 11mm rib. Beavertail forearm and straight comb trap stock fitted with a ventilated black rubber recoil pad are standard. Weight is approximately 8 lbs.

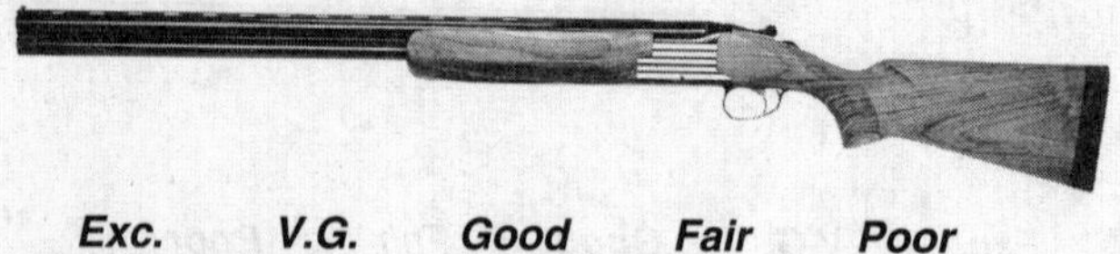

Exc.	V.G.	Good	Fair	Poor
750	500	300	200	100

Silhouette 300 Sporting Clays

Similar to the Model 300 Trap except with 28" barrels. Some guns came with 3" chambers. The buttstock is field style with plastic buttplate or hard rubber sporting clays pad. Weight is about 8 lbs.

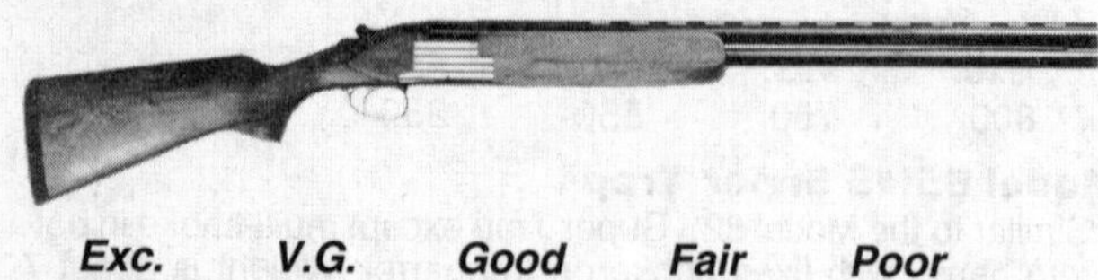

Exc.	V.G.	Good	Fair	Poor
750	500	300	200	100

Silhouette 300 Ultra Magnum

Similar to the Model 300 Sporting Clays except with 3-1/2" chamber in 12 gauge for waterfowl hunting. . Weight is about 7 lbs., 8 oz.

Exc.	V.G.	Good	Fair	Poor
850	600	450	275	150

LAURONA SIDE-BY-SIDE SHOTGUNS

Models with "X" after the model number were made after 1975 and finished with non-rusting black chrome on barrels and action with hard chrome bores. Guns were made in 12, 16, and 20 bore. Smaller gauges were made on special order. Side-by-side shotguns were discontinued by Laurona after 1978 to concentrate on the over-and-under market.

Model 11

Boxlock action with triple Greener-type round crossbolt. Independent firing pins bushed into the face of the action. Barrels of "Bellota" steel. Made in 12, 16, and 20 gauge.

Exc.	V.G.	Good	Fair	Poor
400	350	300	200	150

Model 13

Similar to the Model 11 except with Purdey-type bolting system. Extractor of double radius.

Exc.	V.G.	Good	Fair	Poor
400	350	300	200	150

Model 13X

Barrels and action finished in black chrome and hard chrome bores.

Exc.	V.G.	Good	Fair	Poor
500	400	300	250	200

Model 13E

Similar to the Model 13 except with automatic ejectors.

Exc.	V.G.	Good	Fair	Poor
500	400	300	250	200

Model 13XE

Similar to the Model 13E except black chrome finish and hard chrome bores.

Exc.	V.G.	Good	Fair	Poor
600	500	400	350	300

Model 15 Economic Pluma

Similar to the Model 13 except first model has hard chrome bores.

Exc.	V.G.	Good	Fair	Poor
450	400	300	250	200

Model 15X

Similar to the Model 15 except black chrome finish and hard chrome bores.

Exc.	V.G.	Good	Fair	Poor
500	400	300	250	200

Model 15E Economic Pluma

Similar to the Model 15 except with automatic ejectors.

Exc.	V.G.	Good	Fair	Poor
550	450	350	300	250

Model 15XE

Similar to the Model 15E except black chrome finish and hard chrome bores.

Exc.	V.G.	Good	Fair	Poor
600	500	400	350	300

Model 52 Pluma

Boxlock action with back of action scalloped and artistically engraved in fine English-style scroll. Churchill rib and double radius extractor. Hard chrome bores. Weight is about 6 lbs.

Exc.	V.G.	Good	Fair	Poor
750	650	500	400	350

Model 52E Pluma

Similar to the Model 52 except with automatic ejectors. Weight is approximately 6 lbs., 2 oz.

Exc.	V.G.	Good	Fair	Poor
850	750	600	500	450

LAURONA SIDE-BY-SIDE SIDELOCKS

Model 103

Blued sidelock with some light border engraving. Triple Purdey-type bolting system. Extractor of double radius. Barrels of special "Bellota" steel with hard chrome bores. Made in 12, 16, and 20 gauge.

Exc.	V.G.	Good	Fair	Poor
900	800	700	500	400

Model 103E

Similar to the Model 103 except with automatic ejectors.

Exc.	V.G.	Good	Fair	Poor
1000	800	700	600	500

Model 104X

Case-colored sidelocks with Purdey-type bolting system. Extractor with double radius. Fine double safety sidelocks. Gas relief vents. Articulated trigger. Hard chrome bores. Demi-block barrels of special "Bellota" steel. Black chrome barrels. Produced in 12, 16, and 20 gauge with smaller bores available on special order.

Exc.	V.G.	Good	Fair	Poor
1200	1000	800	700	600

Model 104XE

Same as Model 104X but with Holland automatic selective ejectors.

Exc.	V.G.	Good	Fair	Poor
1350	1100	900	800	700

Model 105X Feather

Same as the Model 104X but with concave rib. Weight in 12 gauge is approximately 6 lbs., 2 oz.

Exc.	V.G.	Good	Fair	Poor
1250	1000	800	700	600

Model 105XE Feather

Same as Model 105X but with Holland automatic selective ejectors.

Exc.	V.G.	Good	Fair	Poor
1400	1250	1000	800	750

Model 502 Feather

Fine sidelock with Purdey-type bolting system. Very fine double safety sidelocks, hand detachable. Gas relief vents. Holland automatic selective ejectors. Articulated trigger. Inside hard chromed demi-block barrels of special "Bellota" steel. Outside Black Chrome finish. Fine English-style scroll engraving. Marble gray or Laurona Imperial finish. Churchill or concave type rib. Weight: 12 gauge is approximately 6.25 lbs. Offered in 12, 16, and 20 gauge.

Exc.	V.G.	Good	Fair	Poor
2200	1800	1600	1500	1400

Model 801 Deluxe

Same as the Model 502 Feather but engraving is a true deluxe Renaissance style. Fully handmade with Imperial finish. First grade walnut stock and forearm.

Exc.	V.G.	Good	Fair	Poor
4400	4000	3750	2750	2250

Model 802 Eagle

Same as the Model 801 Deluxe except highly artistic base relief hand engraving of hunting scenes.

Exc.	V.G.	Good	Fair	Poor
5000	4500	4000	3500	3250

LAW ENFORCEMENT ORDNANCE CORP.

Ridgeway, Pennsylvania

Striker 12

A semi-automatic shotgun designed for self-defense. It is chambered for 12 gauge and has an 18.25" cylinder bored barrel. The unique feature about this gun is its 12-round drum magazine. The barrel is shrouded, and the stock folds. A fixed-stock model is also available. This gun was introduced primarily as a law enforcement tool, and the original models had 12" barrels and were legal for law enforcement agencies and Class 3 licensed individuals only. This shotgun is no longer imported into the U.S. This shotgun is now classified as a Class III weapon and subject to restrictions of the B.A.T.F. Be certain that the particular shotgun is transferable before purchase. If there are any questions contact B.A.T.F. before purchase.

Striker 12 shotguns in excellent condition may sell for as much as $1500.

LAZZERONI ARMS COMPANY

Tucson, Arizona

Model 2000 ST-F

This model, as with all Lazzeroni models, is chambered for the company's own proprietary calibers. The 6.17 (.243) Spitfire, 6.53 (.257) Scramjet, 6.71 (.264) Phantom, 7.21 (.284) Tomahawk, 7.82 (.308) Patriot, and the 8.59 (.338) Galaxy. Fitted with a 27" match grade barrel with fully adjustable trigger, and removable muzzlebrake. Conventional fiberglass stock.

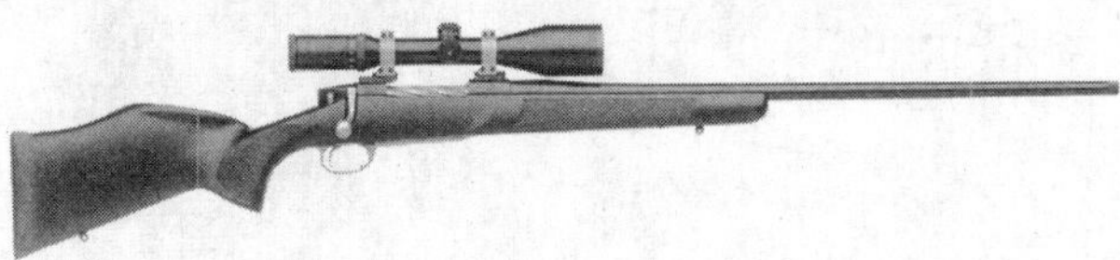

NIB	Exc.	V.G.	Good	Fair	Poor
3700	3000	2200	—	—	—

Model 2000 ST-W

As above but fitted with a conventional black wood laminate stock. No longer offered.

NIB	Exc.	V.G.	Good	Fair	Poor
4800	3900	2700	—	—	—

Model 2000ST-FW

As above but fitted with a conventional fiberglass stock and an additional black wood laminate stock. No longer offered.

NIB	Exc.	V.G.	Good	Fair	Poor
5300	4250	3000	—	—	—

Model 2000ST-28

This model is a 28" barrel variation of the Model 2000 ST chambered for the 7.82 Warbird cartridge. Introduced in 1999.

NIB	Exc.	V.G.	Good	Fair	Poor
5300	4250	3000	—	—	—

Model 2000SLR

This model has a 28" extra-heavy fluted barrel with conventional fiberglass stock. Chambered for the 6.53 Scramjet, 7.21 Firehawk, and the 7.82 Warbird.

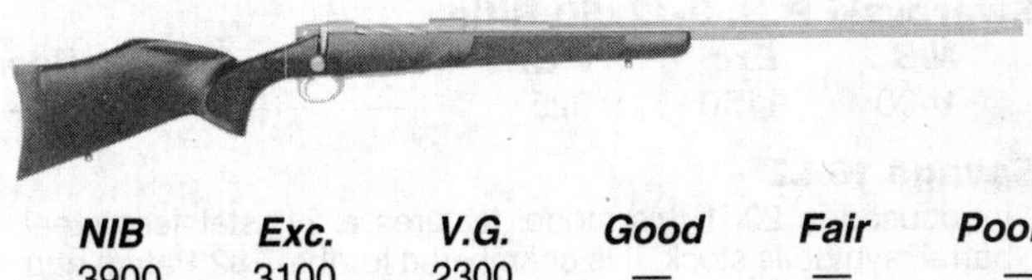

NIB	Exc.	V.G.	Good	Fair	Poor
3900	3100	2300	—	—	—

Model 2000SP-F

This model is fitted with a 23" match grade and Lazzeroni thumbhole fiberglass stock. Chambered for all Lazzeroni calibers.

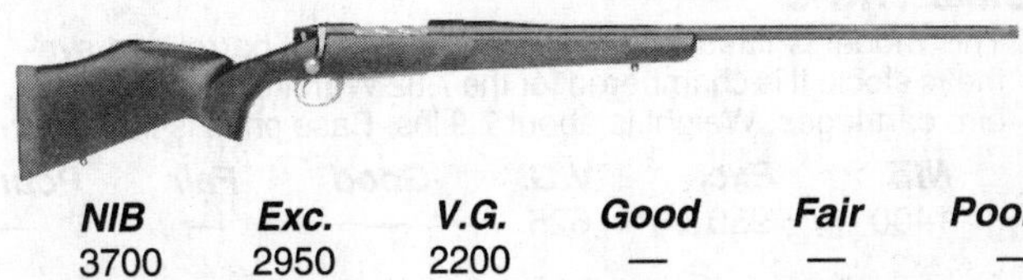

NIB	Exc.	V.G.	Good	Fair	Poor
3700	2950	2200	—	—	—

Model 2000SP-W

Same as above but with black wood laminate thumbhole stock. No longer offered.

NIB	Exc.	V.G.	Good	Fair	Poor
4800	3850	2500	—	—	—

Model 2000SP-FW

Same as above model but supplied with two stocks: a thumbhole fiberglass stock and a black wood laminate stock. No longer offered.

NIB	Exc.	V.G.	Good	Fair	Poor
5300	4250	3000	—	—	—

Model 2000SA

Designed as a lightweight mountain rifle. Chambered for .308, .284, or .338 propriety calibers. Barrel length is 24" and fluted except for .338 caliber. Offered in both right- and left-hand models. Stock has Monte Carlo cheekpiece. Weight is approximately 6.8 lbs.

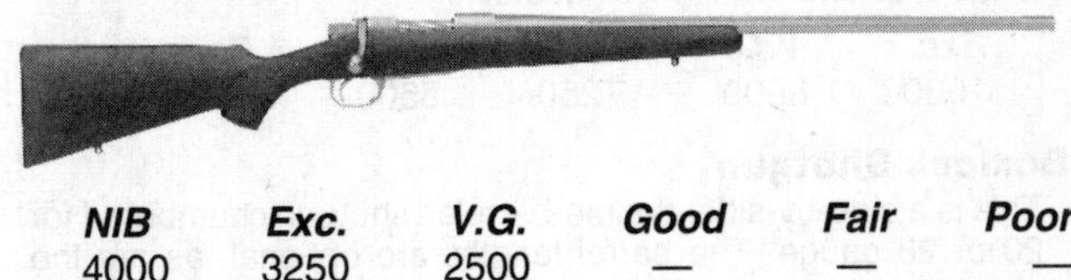

NIB	Exc.	V.G.	Good	Fair	Poor
4000	3250	2500	—	—	—

Model 2000DG

Offered in Saturn and Meteor calibers only and fitted with a 24" barrel this rifle weight about 10 lbs. Fibergrain stock finish, removable muzzlebrake, and threaded muzzle protector are standard.

NIB	Exc.	V.G.	Good	Fair	Poor
4400	3500	2700	—	—	—

Model 700ST

This rifle is built around a modified Remington 700 action and fitted with a 26" barrel. Chambered for all Lazzeroni long action calibers except Saturn and Meteor. Weight is about 8 lbs. synthetic stock.

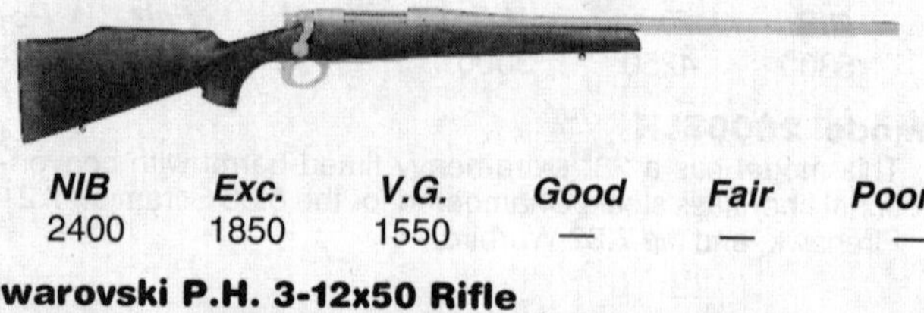

NIB	Exc.	V.G.	Good	Fair	Poor
2400	1850	1550	—	—	—

Swarovski P.H. 3-12x50 Rifle

NIB	Exc.	V.G.	Good	Fair	Poor
1400	1150	925	—	—	—

Savage 16 LZ

Introduced in 2001 this model features a 24" stainless steel barrel, synthetic stock. It is chambered for the 7.82 Patriot and 7.21 Tomahawk cartridges. Weight is approximately 6.8 lbs. Base price is listed.

NIB	Exc.	V.G.	Good	Fair	Poor
900	775	500	—	—	—

Sako TRG-S

This model is fitted with a 26" stainless steel barrel and synthetic stock. It is chambered for the 7.82 Warbird and 7.21 Firebird cartridges. Weight is about 7.9 lbs. Base price is listed.

NIB	Exc.	V.G.	Good	Fair	Poor
1400	950	625	—	—	—

LE FORGERON

Liege, Belgium

Model 6020 Double Rifle

A boxlock-actioned side-by-side rifle that is chambered for the 9.3x74R cartridge. It has 25" barrels with double triggers and automatic ejectors. The finish is blued, and the pistol grip stock is checkered walnut.

Exc.	V.G.	Good	Fair	Poor
5500	4500	4000	3000	1250

Model 6040

Simply the Model 6020 with false sideplates. All other specifications are the same.

Exc.	V.G.	Good	Fair	Poor
6250	5200	4500	3500	1500

Model 6030

A double rifle that has a true sidelock action and is engraved. It has a deluxe French walnut stock.

Exc.	V.G.	Good	Fair	Poor
10000	8000	7250	5500	2000

Boxlock Shotgun

This is a side-by-side, double-barreled shotgun chambered for 20 or 28 gauge. The barrel lengths are optional, as are the choke combinations. This gun has a single-selective trigger and automatic ejectors. It is engraved and blued, with a deluxe French walnut stock.

Exc.	V.G.	Good	Fair	Poor
5000	4000	3250	2250	1000

NOTE: False sideplates add 20 percent.

Sidelock Shotgun

Has similar specifications to the boxlock except that it has a true sidelock action and is generally more deluxe in materials and workmanship.

Exc.	V.G.	Good	Fair	Poor
11500	10500	8500	6500	2500

LE FRANCAIS

St. Etienne, France

Francais D'Armes et Cycles de St. Etienne

SEE ALSO—Manufrance

Gaulois

An 8mm palm pistol designed by Brun-Latrige and manufactured by Le Francais. Furnished with a 5-round magazine.

Courtesy James Rankin

Exc.	V.G.	Good	Fair	Poor
—	950	550	400	300

Le Francais Model 28 (Type Armee)

A unique pistol chambered for the 9mm Browning cartridge. It is a large pistol, with a 5" barrel that was hinged with a tip-up breech. This is a blowback-operated semi-automatic pistol that has no extractor. The empty cases are blown out of the breech by gas pressure. The one feature about this pistol that is desirable is that it is possible to tip the barrel breech forward like a shotgun and load cartridges singly, while holding the contents of the magazine in reserve. This weapon has fixed sights and a blued finish, with checkered walnut grips. It was manufactured in 1928.

Courtesy James Rankin

Exc.	V.G.	Good	Fair	Poor
1250	950	750	500	200

Police Model (Type Policeman)

A blowback-operated, double-action semi-automatic that is chambered for the .25 ACP cartridge. It has a 3.5" barrel and a 7-round magazine. It has the same hinged barrel feature of the Model 28 and is blued, with fixed sights and Ebonite grips. This model was manufactured 1913 to 1914.

Courtesy James Rankin

Exc.	V.G.	Good	Fair	Poor
800	650	450	300	150

Officer's Model (Pocket Model)

May also be referred to a "Staff Model." Also a blowback-operated semi-automatic chambered for the .25 ACP cartridge. It has a 2.5" barrel and a concealed hammer. It has fixed sights and the finish is blued. The grips are Ebonite. This model was manufactured between 1914 and 1938 in two variations: early and second type.

Early variation Pocket Courtesy James Rankin

Second variation Pocket Courtesy James Rankin

Exc.	V.G.	Good	Fair	Poor
300	250	200	150	100

Target Model (Type Champion)

Chambered for 6.35mm cartridge and fitted with a 6" barrel. Extended magazine base is for grip purchase, not additional cartridges.

Courtesy James Rankin

Exc.	V.G.	Good	Fair	Poor
900	700	550	400	275

LE MAT
Paris, France

LeMat

Has a somewhat unique background that makes it a bit controversial among collectors. It is a foreign-made firearm manufactured in Paris, France, as well as in Birmingham, England. It was designed and patented by an American, Jean Alexander Le Mat of New Orleans, Louisiana; and it was purchased for use by the Confederate States of America and used in the Civil War. This is a curious firearm as it is a huge weapon that has two barrels. The top 6.5" barrel is chambered for .42 caliber percussion and is supplied by a 9-shot unfluted cylinder that revolves on a 5", .63 caliber, smoothbore barrel that doubles as the cylinder axis pin. These two barrels are held together by a front and a rear ring. The rear sight is a notch in the nose of the hammer, and there is an attached ramrod on the side of the top barrel. The weapon is marked "Lemat and Girards Patent, London." The finish is blued, with checkered walnut grips. There were fewer than 3,000 manufactured, of which approximately one-half were purchased by the Confederate States of America. They were made between 1856 and 1865.

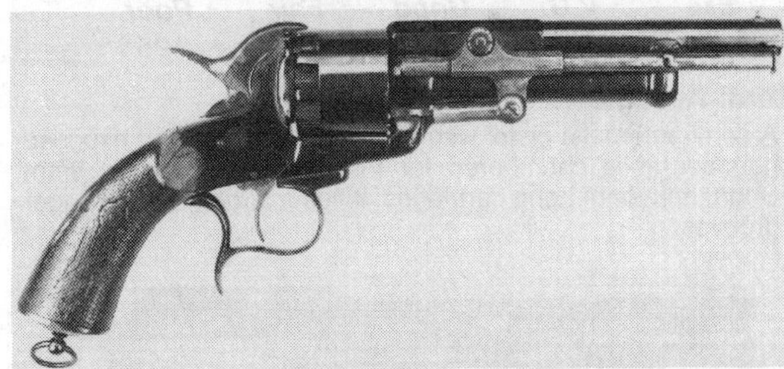

Courtesy Milwaukee Public Museum, Milwaukee, Wisconsin

Exc.	V.G.	Good	Fair	Poor
—	25000	10000	5000	1750

Baby LeMat

Similar in appearance (though a good deal smaller in size) to the standard model pistol. It is chambered for .32 caliber percussion and has a 4.25" top barrel and a .41 caliber smoothbore lower barrel. The cylinder is unfluted and holds 9 shots. The barrel is marked "Systeme Le Mat Bte s.g.d.g. Paris." It has British proofmarks and is blued, with checkered walnut grips. This is the scarcest model Le Mat, as there were only an estimated 100 manufactured and used by the Confederate States of America in the Civil War.

Exc.	V.G.	Good	Fair	Poor
—	—	20000	9500	3000

LeMat Revolving Carbine

Chambered for the centerfire, rimfire cartridges, or percussion. Barrel are half round half octagon and 20" in length. Chambered for a variaty of calibers but in percussion usually .42 caliber with a .62 caliber soothbore lower barrel.

Courtesy Little John's Auction Service, Inc., Paul Goodwin photo

Exc.	V.G.	Good	Fair	Poor
—	—	20000	9500	3000

REMINDER

The difference between "New in Box" and "Excellent" can be enormous to the "condition collector": as much as 50 percent of the gun's value, in some cases.

LE PAGE SA.

Liege, Belgium

Pinfire Revolver

This company was in the business of revolver manufacture in the 1850s, producing a .40 caliber pinfire revolver that was similar to the Lefauchaux and other pinfires of the day. The barrel lengths vary, and the unfluted cylinder holds 6 shots. These pistols are double-action and are sometimes found with ornate, but somewhat crude engraving. The finish is blued, with wood grips. The quality of these weapons is fair. They were serviceable; but the ammunition created somewhat of a problem, as it is rather fragile and difficult to handle with the protruding primer pin to contend with.

Exc.	V.G.	Good	Fair	Poor
—	750	300	200	125

Semi-Automatic Pistol

A semi-automatic pistol with an open top slide, and exposed hammer. It is chambered for the 6.35mm, 7.65mm, 9mm Short, and 9mm Long cartridges. It has a large grip with finger grooves.

Courtesy James Rankin

Exc.	V.G.	Good	Fair	Poor
850	650	500	300	200

Pocket Pistol

A semi-automatic pistol in caliber 6.35mm. Checkered hard rubber grips with crossed sword and pistol logo of Le Page on each side of the grip.

Courtesy James Rankin

Exc.	V.G.	Good	Fair	Poor
300	250	200	150	75

LEBEAU COURALLY

Liege, Belgium

This company has been in business since 1865 and has made more guns for royalty than any other gun company in the world. The prices listed are for guns without engraving. There are other extra-cost options that will affect price.

Boxlock Side-by-Side

NIB	Exc.	V.G.	Good	Fair	Poor
23000	17500	—	—	—	—

NOTE: Add $3,000 to $8,400 for engraving.

Sidelock Side-by-Side

NIB	Exc.	V.G.	Good	Fair	Poor
47000	35000	—	—	—	—

NOTE: Add $3,600 to $20,000 for engraving.

Over-and-Under Boss-Verees

NIB	Exc.	V.G.	Good	Fair	Poor
81000	55000	—	—	—	—

NOTE: Add $6,000 to $20,000 for engraving.

Express Rifle

NIB	Exc.	V.G.	Good	Fair	Poor
51000	37500	—	—	—	—

NOTE: Add $3,600 to $20,000 for engraving, and $2,250 for .470 NE caliber.

LEBEL

French State

NOTE: For history, technical data, descriptions, and prices see the *Standard Catalog of Military Firearms* under France.

LEE FIREARMS CO.

Milwaukee, Wisconsin

Lee Single-Shot Carbine

A rare single-shot break-open carbine that pivots to the right side for loading. It is chambered for the .44 rimfire cartridge and has a 21.5" barrel with a hammer mounted in the center of the frame. The carbine has a walnut buttstock but no forearm and is marked "Lee's Firearms Co. Milwaukee, Wisc." There were approximately 450 manufactured between 1863 and 1865. There are few surviving examples, and one should be wary of fakes.

Courtesy Milwaukee Public Museum, Milwaukee, Wisconsin

Exc.	V.G.	Good	Fair	Poor
—	—	5000	2000	900

Lee Sporting Rifle

Similar to the military carbine except that it has a longer octagonal barrel. The barrel length was varied, and there were more of these manufactured. The survival rate appears to have been better than for the carbine model.

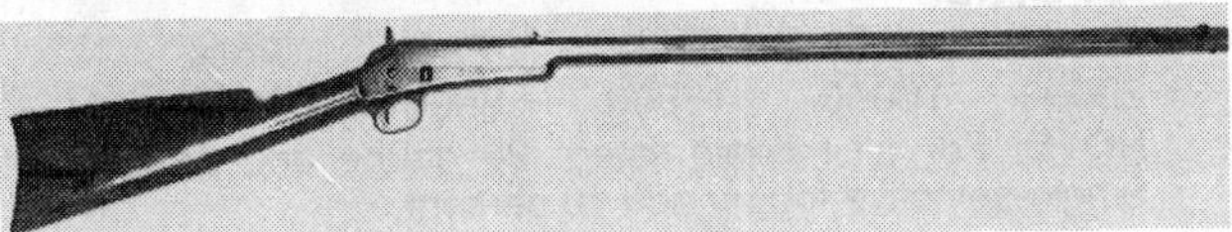
Courtesy Milwaukee Public Museum, Milwaukee, Wisconsin

Exc.	V.G.	Good	Fair	Poor
—	—	1250	600	300

LEE-ENFIELD

Middlesex, England

NOTE: For history, technical data, descriptions, and prices see the *Standard Catalog of Military Firearms* under Great Britain.

LEE-METFORD

Great Britain

NOTE: For history, technical data, descriptions, and prices see the *Standard Catalog of Military Firearms* under Great Britain.

LEECH & RIGDON

Greensboro, Georgia

Leech & Rigdon Revolver

This Confederate revolver was patterned after the 1851 Colt Navy. It is chambered for .36 caliber percussion and has a 6-shot unfluted cylinder. The 7.5" barrel is part-octagonal and has a loading lever beneath it. The frame is open-topped; and the finish is blued, with brass grip straps and walnut one-piece grips. The barrel is marked "Leech & Rigdon CSA." There were approximately 1,500 revolvers manufactured in 1863 and 1864. These were all contracted for by the Confederacy and are considered to be a prime acquisition for collectors. Be wary of fakes, and trust in qualified independent appraisals only.

Courtesy Jim and Caroline Cerny

Exc.	V.G.	Good	Fair	Poor
—	—	25000	10000	2500

LEFAUCHAUX, CASIMER & EUGENE

Paris, France

Pinfire Revolver

The pinfire ignition system was invented by Casimir Lefauchaux in 1828 but was not widely used until the 1850s. It consists of a smooth rimless case that contains the powder charge and a percussion cap. A pin protrudes from the side of this case at the rear and when struck by the hammer is driven into the cap, thereby igniting the charge and firing the weapon. The pistols for this cartridge are slotted at the end of the cylinder to allow the pins to protrude and be struck by the downward blow of the hammer. This particular revolver is chambered for .43 caliber and has a 5.25" barrel. The cylinder holds 6 shots; and the finish is blued, with checkered walnut grips. This revolver was manufactured after 1865 and was selected for service by the French military.

Exc.	V.G.	Good	Fair	Poor
—	—	575	250	125

LEFEVER ARMS CO.

Syracuse, New York

Founded by Dan Lefever, who was a pioneer in the field of breech-loading firearms. This company was founded in 1884, with Lefever as the president. He was referred to as "Uncle Dan" within the firearms industry. He was responsible for many improvements in the double-barrel shotgun design. He developed the automatic hammerless system in the late 1880s. He also developed a compensating action that allowed simple adjustments to compensate for action wear. In 1901 he was forced out of the company and organized another company—the D.M. Lefever, Sons & Company—also in Syracuse. Dan Lefever died in 1906, and his new company went out of business. The original company was acquired by Ithaca in 1916. They continued to produce Lefever guns until 1948.

Sideplated Shotgun

A double-barrel, side-by-side shotgun chambered for 10, 12, 16, or 20 gauge. It was offered with 26", 28", 30", or 32" barrels with various choke combinations. The barrels are either Damascus or fluid steel. Damascus guns have become collectible and in better condition—very good to excellent—can bring nearly the same price as the fluid-steel guns. It features a fractional sidelock because the hammers were mounted in the frame and the sears and cocking indicators were mounted on the sideplates. After serial number 25,000, the entire locking mechanism was frame mounted and only the cocking indicators remained on the side plates. Double triggers are standard. The finish is blued, with a checkered walnut stock. There are a number of variations that differ in the amount of ornamentation and the quality of materials and workmanship utilized in their construction. Automatic ejectors are represented by the letter "E" after the respective grade designation. This shotgun was manufactured between 1885 and 1919. We strongly recommend that a qualified appraisal be secured if a transaction is contemplated.

There was also an Optimus Grade and a Thousand Dollar Grade offered. These are extremely high-grade, heavily ornamented firearms inlaid with precious metals. They are extremely rare, and evaluating them on a general basis is impossible.

H Grade

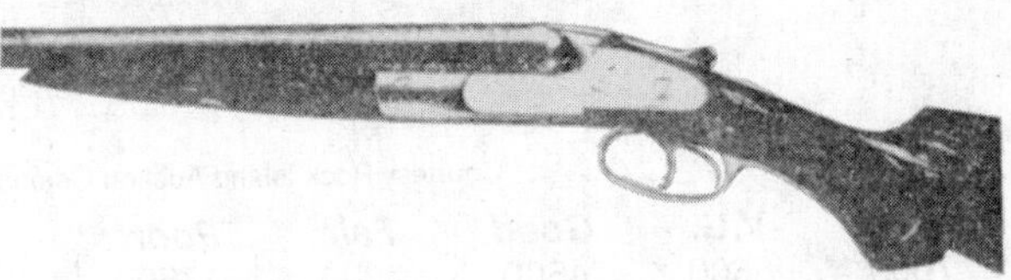

Exc.	V.G.	Good	Fair	Poor
1400	1100	850	550	350

HE Grade

Exc.	V.G.	Good	Fair	Poor
2200	1750	1450	900	650

G Grade

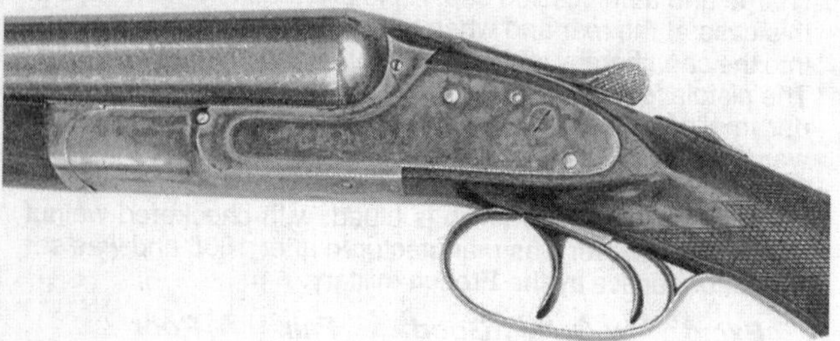

Exc.	V.G.	Good	Fair	Poor
1700	1350	1100	700	425

GE Grade

Exc.	V.G.	Good	Fair	Poor
2600	2000	1700	1000	650

F Grade

Exc.	V.G.	Good	Fair	Poor
2200	1750	1450	900	650

FE Grade

Exc.	V.G.	Good	Fair	Poor
3200	2500	2100	1300	800

E Grade

Exc.	V.G.	Good	Fair	Poor
3500	2800	2300	1400	900

EE Grade

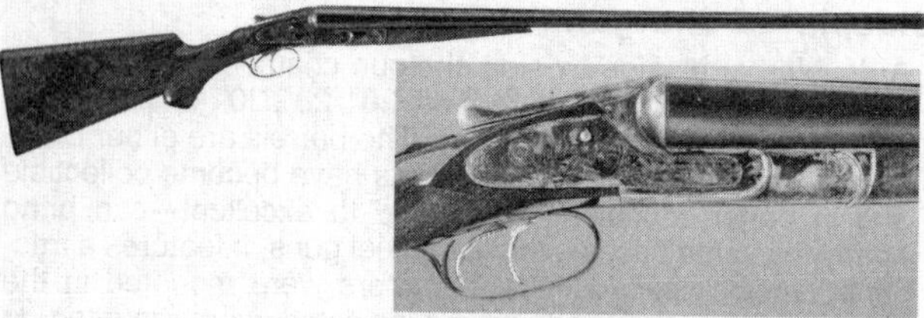

Courtesy Rock Island Auction Company

Exc.	V.G.	Good	Fair	Poor
4600	3700	3000	1850	1150

D Grade

Exc.	V.G.	Good	Fair	Poor
4500	3500	2900	1800	1100

DS Grade

Exc.	V.G.	Good	Fair	Poor
1250	1000	800	500	300

DE Grade

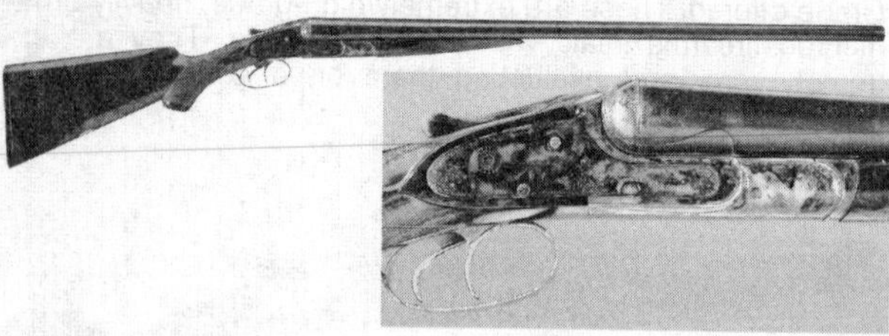

Courtesy Rock Island Auction Company

Exc.	V.G.	Good	Fair	Poor
7000	5600	4500	2800	1750

DSE Grade

Exc.	V.G.	Good	Fair	Poor
1750	1400	1150	700	500

C Grade

Exc.	V.G.	Good	Fair	Poor
6000	4800	4000	2400	1500

CE Grade

Exc.	V.G.	Good	Fair	Poor
8500	6800	5500	3400	2100

B Grade

Exc.	V.G.	Good	Fair	Poor
8000	6400	5200	3200	2000

BE Grade

Exc.	V.G.	Good	Fair	Poor
10000	8000	6500	4000	2500

A Grade

Exc.	V.G.	Good	Fair	Poor
15000	12000	10000	6000	3700

AA Grade

Exc.	V.G.	Good	Fair	Poor
20000	16000	13000	8000	5000

NOTE: For all models listed: 20 gauge add 25 percent. Single-selective trigger add 10 percent.

LEFEVER ARMS COMPANY, INC. (ITHACA)

During 1916, the Ithaca Gun company purchased the gunmaking assets of the Syracuse, New York based, Lefever Arms Company. Between then and World War I, they continued to manufacture the same sideplate gun that had been made in Syracuse until about 1919 when they were discontinued. Prices for those guns are listed above. During 1921, Ithaca Gun Company, under the name the Lefever Arms Company, Inc., introduced a line of lower costs, boxlock guns. Eventually, six different models were produced. Ithaca's Lefever guns were produced in 12, 16, and 20 gauges, and in .410 bore. Twenty gauge guns often command a price premium of 50 percent; a .410 bore gun may command up to a 200 percent premium.

Nitro Special

A side-by-side, double-barrel shotgun chambered for 12, 16, or 20 gauge, as well as .410. The barrels were offered in lengths of 26" to 32" with various choke combinations. It features a boxlock action with double triggers and extractors standard. The finish is blued, with a case-colored receiver and a checkered walnut stock. This model was manufactured between 1921 and 1948 and, incredible as it may seem, its price at introduction was $29.

Exc.	V.G.	Good	Fair	Poor
600	400	250	200	—

NOTE: Single-selective trigger add $100. Automatic ejectors add $200.

Long Range Single-Barrel Trap and Field (Model 2)

Manufactured from 1927 to 1947, the Model 2 was a single-barrel gun with no rib. Like the Nitro Special, it had walnut stocks that were line cut checkered at the grip area of the buttstock and on the forend.

Exc.	V.G.	Good	Fair	Poor
500	300	200	100	—

Single-Barrel Trap Ventilated Rib (Model 3)

Manufactured from 1927 to 1942, the Model 3 was a single-barrel gun with the same ventilated rib that was used on the "Knick" trap gun. The walnut stocks had line cut checkering at the grip area of the buttstock and on the forend.

Exc.	V.G.	Good	Fair	Poor
1200	500	250	100	—

Double-Barrel Ventilated Rib Trap (Model 4)

Manufactured during 1929 but catalogued until 1939, the Model 4 was a double-barrel gun with a ventilated rib barrel. The walnut stocks had line cut checkering at the grip area of the buttstock and on the beavertail forend. Only about 200 units were produced.

Exc.	V.G.	Good	Fair	Poor
2000	1200	1000	700	—

This symbol denotes "Sleepers" with rapidly-rising values and/or significant collector potential.

A Grade (Model 5)

Manufactured from 1936 to 1939, the A Grade was a double-barreled gun. The walnut stocks had pointed checkering cut at the grip area of the buttstock and on the splinter forend. A line engraving outlined its nicely sculptured frame.

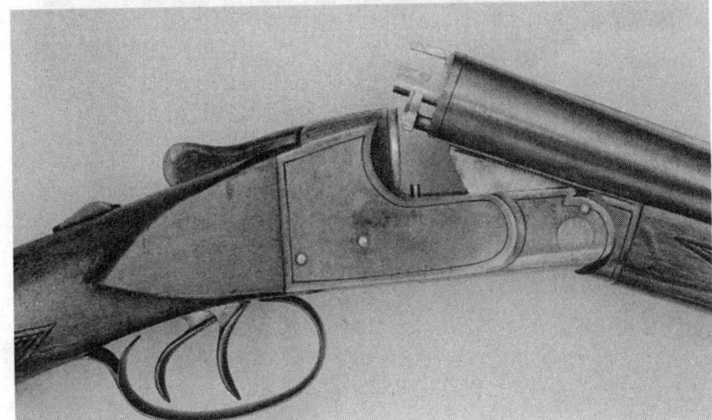

Photo by Walter C. Snyder

Exc.	V.G.	Good	Fair	Poor
900	600	400	300	—

NOTE: Single trigger add $200, automatic ejectors add $200, beavertail forend add $300.

Skeet Special (Model 6)

Manufactured from 1936 to 1939, the A Grade was a double-barreled gun. The walnut stocks had pointed checkering cut at the grip area of the buttstock and on the beavertail forend. A beavertail forend, single trigger, automatic ejectors, a recoil pad, and ivory center and front sight were standard. The frame was sculptured and line engraved like the Model 5.

Exc.	V.G.	Good	Fair	Poor
1500	1200	1000	400	—

LEFEVER, D. M., SONS & COMPANY

Syracuse, New York

"Uncle Dan" Lefever founded the Lefever Arms Company in 1884. In 1901 he was forced out of his company and founded the D.M. Lefever, Sons & Company. He continued to produce high-grade, side-by-side shotguns, but of a totally new boxlock design. There were approximately 1,200 shotguns of all variations produced during this period, making them extremely rare and difficult to evaluate on a general basis. We list the models and average values but strongly suggest securing qualified appraisal if a transaction is contemplated.

Lefever Double-Barrel Shotgun

A side-by-side, double-barrel shotgun chambered for 12, 16, or 20 gauge. It was offered with various-length barrels and choke combinations that were made to order. It features double triggers and automatic ejectors. A single-selective trigger was available as an option. The finish is blued, with a checkered walnut stock. The individual grades differ in the amount of ornamentation and the general quality of the materials and workmanship utilized in their construction. This model was discontinued in 1906.

There are an "Optimus" and an "Uncle Dan" grade, which are top-of-the-line models, that features extremely high quality in materials and workmanship and a great deal of ornamentation. This firearm is extremely rare and seldom found in today's market. It is impossible to evaluate it on a general basis.

O Excelsior Grade—Extractors

Exc.	V.G.	Good	Fair	Poor
2500	2000	1650	950	700

Excelsior Grade—Auto Ejectors

Exc.	V.G.	Good	Fair	Poor
3000	2500	2000	1250	900

F Grade, No. 9

Exc.	V.G.	Good	Fair	Poor
3000	2750	2250	1500	1100

E Grade, No. 8

Exc.	V.G.	Good	Fair	Poor
4000	3500	3000	2400	1700

D Grade, No. 7

Exc.	V.G.	Good	Fair	Poor
4500	3900	3400	2750	2000

C Grade, No. 6

Exc.	V.G.	Good	Fair	Poor
5000	4500	3750	3000	2500

B Grade, No. 5

Exc.	V.G.	Good	Fair	Poor
6500	5750	4800	3500	3000

AA Grade, No. 4

Exc.	V.G.	Good	Fair	Poor
9000	7800	6500	4200	2750

NOTE: For all models listed: 20 gauge add 50 percent. Single-selective trigger add 25 percent.

LEMAN, H. E.

Lancaster, Pennsylvania

Leman Militia Rifle

A .58 caliber percussion muzzleloader that has a 33" round barrel. The stock is full-length and is held on by two barrel bands. There is a ramrod mounted under the barrel. The trim is brass; and the barrel is browned, with a case-colored lock. The lock is marked "H.E.Leman/Lancaster, Pa." There were approximately 500 manufactured between 1860 and 1864. They are believed to have been used by the Pennsylvania State Militia in the Civil War.

Courtesy Milwaukee Public Museum, Milwaukee, Wisconsin

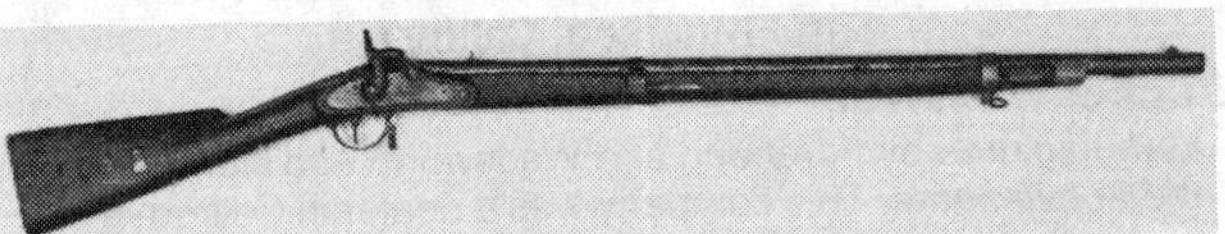

Courtesy Milwaukee Public Museum, Milwaukee, Wisconsin

Exc.	V.G.	Good	Fair	Poor
—	—	4250	2000	750

LEONARD, G.

Charlestown, Massachusetts

Pepperbox

A .31-caliber, four-barreled pepperbox with a concealed hammer. The barrels are 3.25" in length. There is a ring trigger used to cock the weapon, while a smaller trigger located outside the ring is used to fire the weapon. The barrels on this pistol do not revolve. There is a revolving striker inside the frame that turns to fire each chamber. The barrels must be removed for loading and capping purposes. The frame is iron and blued, with engraving. The rounded grips are walnut. The barrel is stamped "G. Leonard Jr. Charlestown." There were fewer than 200 manufactured in 1849 and 1850.

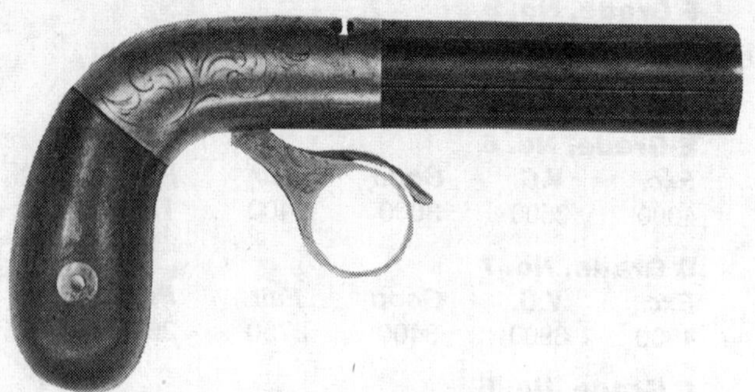

Exc.	V.G.	Good	Fair	Poor
—	—	1500	650	300

LES, INC.
Skokie, Illinois

Rogak P-18
A 9mm caliber double-action semi-automatic pistol with a 5.5" barrel and 18-shot magazine. Stainless steel. Discontinued.

Exc.	V.G.	Good	Fair	Poor
350	300	275	200	150

LEWIS, G.E.
Halesowen, England
SEE—British Double Guns

LIDDLE & KAEDING
San Francisco, California

Pocket Revolver
Manufactured by Forehand and Wadsworth and stamped with the above name. This company was a dealer in California and had nothing whatever to do with the production of this revolver. It is chambered for the .32 rimfire cartridge and has a 3.25" octagonal barrel and a 5-shot fluted cylinder. The frame is iron; and the finish is blued, with walnut grips. There were a few hundred manufactured between 1880 and 1886. The dealer's name is marked on the top strap.

Exc.	V.G.	Good	Fair	Poor
—	—	450	200	75

LIEGEOISE D ARMES
Liege, Belgium

Side-by-Side Boxlock Shotgun
This double-barreled gun is chambered for 12 and 20 gauge. The barrels are 28" or 30" in length, and the choke combinations are varied. It has a single trigger and automatic ejectors. The action is moderately engraved; and the finish is blued, with a checkered walnut stock.

Exc.	V.G.	Good	Fair	Poor
900	700	500	400	200

Liegeoise Pistol
A semi-automatic pistol in 6.35mm caliber.

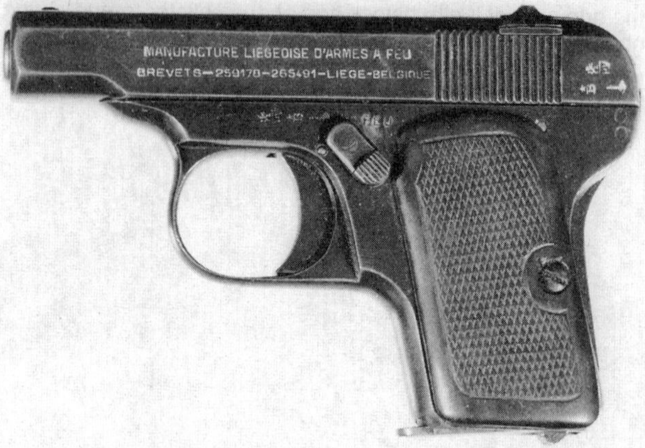

Courtesy James Rankin

Exc.	V.G.	Good	Fair	Poor
250	200	175	125	75

LIGNOSE
Suhl, Germany

In 1921, Bergmann Industriewerke was incorporated into Aktiengesellschaft Lignose, Berlin, with a manufacturing division in Suhl.

Liliput Model I
Manufactured in caliber 6.35mm during the 1920s.

Exc.	V.G.	Good	Fair	Poor
400	300	200	150	100

Lignose Model 2
The Pocket Model in 6.35mm caliber.

Courtesy James Rankin

Exc.	V.G.	Good	Fair	Poor
450	400	350	250	150

Lignose Model 3
The same as the Model 2 but with a 9-round magazine capacity.

Exc.	V.G.	Good	Fair	Poor
750	650	500	400	250

Einhand Model 2A
This unique design resembled the Swiss Chylewski. It allows the shooter to cock and fire this blowback-operated semi-automatic pistol with one hand (Einhand). It is chambered for the 6.35mm cartridge and has a 2" barrel. The magazine holds 6 shots, and the finish is blued, with molded horn grips marked "Lignose." The trigger guard on this pistol has a reverse curve that fits the finger, and it moves backward to cock the slide.

The short-grip model without the Einhard feature was the Model 2; the long grip model without the Einhand was the Model 3. The first 9,000 to 10,000 examples (all four variations serial numbered in the same series) were marketed under the Bergmann name; only later Lignose. It was manufactured in the early 1920s by the Bergman Company, but the firm was merged with Lignose under whose name it was produced.

Courtesy James Rankin

Exc.	V.G.	Good	Fair	Poor
750	650	500	400	250

Einhand Model 3A

Similar to the Model 2A, with a longer grip that houses a 9-shot magazine. All other specifications are the same as the Model 2A.

Courtesy Orvel Reichert

Exc.	V.G.	Good	Fair	Poor
850	700	650	500	300

LILLIPUT

SEE—Menz

LINDE A.

Memphis, Tennessee

Pocket Pistol

This company manufactured a small, concealable firearm patterned after the Henry Deringer Philadelphia-type pistol. It is chambered for .41 caliber percussion and has a 2.5" barrel, German silver mountings, and a walnut stock. It was manufactured in the 1850s.

Exc.	V.G.	Good	Fair	Poor
—	—	1750	700	300

LINDSAY, JOHN P.

Naugatuck, Connecticut
Union Knife Company

The Union Knife Company manufactured the Lindsay 2-shot pistols for the inventor, John P. Lindsay. There are three separate and distinct models listed.

2 Shot Belt Pistol

An oddity. It is a single-barreled, .41 caliber percussion pistol with a double chamber that contains two powder charges and projectiles that are simultaneously fired by two separate hammers. The hammers are released by a single trigger that allows them to fall in the proper sequence. The 5.5" octagonal barrel is contoured into a radical stepped-down shape, and there is a spur trigger. The frame is brass and has scroll engraving. The barrel is blued and is marked "Lindsay's Young America."There were estimated to be fewer than 100 manufactured between 1860 and 1862.

Exc.	V.G.	Good	Fair	Poor
—	—	3750	1250	700

2 Shot Pocket Pistol

A smaller version of the Belt Pistol. It is chambered for the same caliber but has a 4" barrel. There were approximately 200 manufactured between 1860 and 1862.

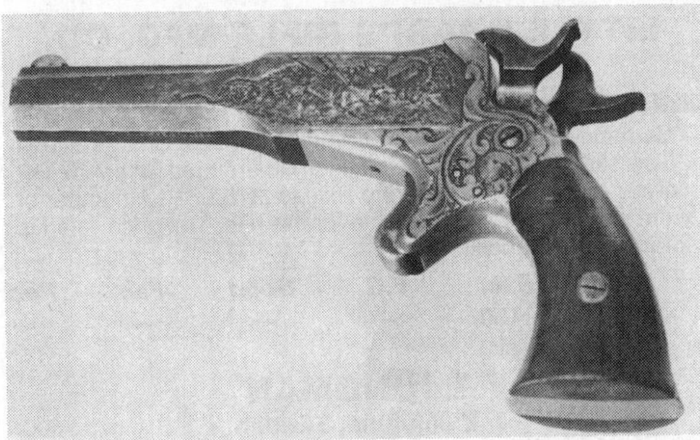

Courtesy W. P. Hallstein III and son Chip

Exc.	V.G.	Good	Fair	Poor
—	—	2750	1000	400

2 Shot Martial Pistol

A large version of the Lindsay design. It is chambered for .45 caliber smoothbore and has an 8.5" part-round, part-octagonal barrel. In other respects it is similar to the smaller models. The inventor tried to sell this pistol to the government but was unsuccessful. It was estimated that there were 100 manufactured between 1860 and 1862.

Exc.	V.G.	Good	Fair	Poor
—	—	4750	2000	700

LINS, A. F.
Philadelphia, Pennsylvania

Pocket Pistol
Chambered for .41 caliber percussion and a copy of the Henry Deringer pistol. It has a 3" barrel and a walnut stock and is marked "A. Fred. Lins. Philada." This pistol was manufactured between 1855 and 1860.

Exc.	V.G.	Good	Fair	Poor
—	—	1750	800	350

Rifled Musket
A single-shot, muzzleloading, percussion rifle chambered for .58 caliber. It has a 39" barrel and a full-length walnut stock held on by three barrel bands. There is an iron ramrod mounted under the barrel. The mountings are iron, and there is a bayonet lug combined with the front sight. The lock is marked "A. Fred. Lins/Philada." This is a rare weapon that was used by Union forces in the Civil War. There were approximately 200 manufactured in 1861 and 1862.

Courtesy Milwaukee Public Museum, Milwaukee, Wisconsin

Exc.	V.G.	Good	Fair	Poor
—	—	4500	1750	750

LITTLE SHARPS RIFLE MFG. CO.
Big Sandy, Montana

Little Sharps Rifle
This hand-built reproduction of the single-shot Sharps rifle is 20 percent smaller than the original. Chambered for a wide variety of calibers from .22 Long Rifle to .375 LSR. A number of extra cost options are available for this rifle. The price listed is for the basic model.

NIB	Exc.	V.G.	Good	Fair	Poor
3250	2750	—	—	—	—

LJUNGMAN
Eskilstuna, Sweden
Carl Gustav

NOTE: For history, technical data, descriptions, and prices see the *Standard Catalog of Military Firearms,* under Sweden.

LJUTIC INDUSTRIES
Yakima, Washington

Bi-Matic Semi-Automatic
A custom-built, gas-operated, semi-automatic shotgun that is known for its low level of felt recoil. It is chambered for 12 gauge and has 26" to 32" barrels choked for either skeet or trap. The stock specifications are to the customer's order. There are options available that affect the value, so we recommend an individual appraisal.

Exc.	V.G.	Good	Fair	Poor
2000	1500	1000	800	400

Dynatrap Single-Barrel
A single-shot trap gun chambered for 12 gauge. It has a 33" vent rib full-choke barrel and features a push-button opener and a manual extractor. The stock is made to trap specifications. There are many options that affect the value.

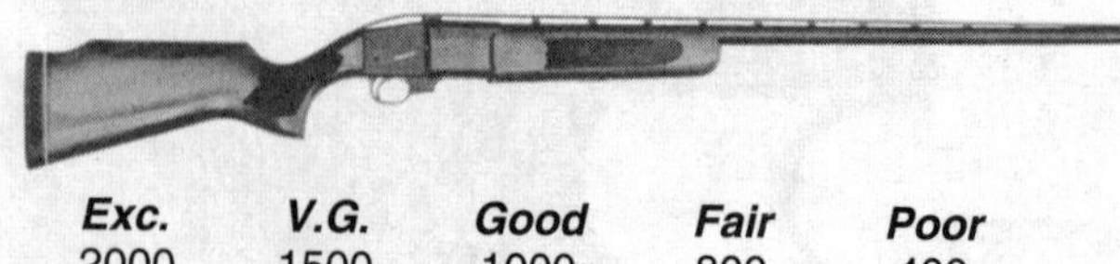

Exc.	V.G.	Good	Fair	Poor
2000	1500	1000	800	400

Model X-73 Single-Barrel
Similar features to the Dynatrap, with a high competition rib. Appraisal is recommended.

Exc.	V.G.	Good	Fair	Poor
2500	2000	1500	950	500

Mono Gun Single-Barrel
Chambered for 12 gauge and has a 34" vent rib barrel. It is essentially a custom-order proposition that is available with a standard, as well as a release, trigger. There are many value-affecting options available.

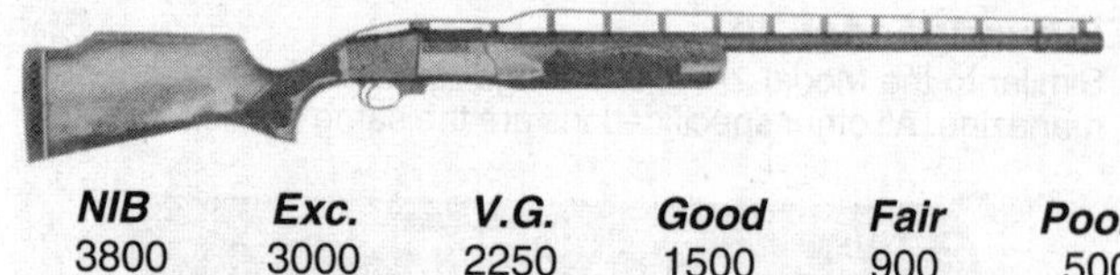

NIB	Exc.	V.G.	Good	Fair	Poor
3800	3000	2250	1500	900	500

LTX Model
A deluxe version of the Mono Gun with a 33" medium-height vent rib and a high-grade walnut stock with fine hand checkering. Options raise values drastically.

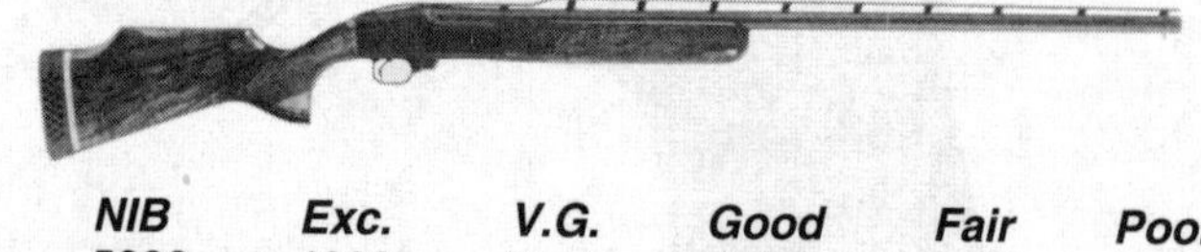

NIB	Exc.	V.G.	Good	Fair	Poor
5000	4000	3000	1500	900	500

Space Gun
A unique single-barrel gun chambered for 12 gauge, with trap choking. It has a stock and forearm that reminds one of a crutch in appearance but which allows the shooter to have in-line control with little felt recoil. The barrel, forearm, and stock are all on one line. There is a recoil pad and a high ventilated rib.

NIB	Exc.	V.G.	Good	Fair	Poor
3750	3000	2250	1500	900	500

Bi-Gun Over-and-Under
An over-and-under double chambered for 12 gauge. It has 30" or 32" vent ribbed barrels that are separated. The choking is to trap specifications, and the stock is deluxe hand-checkered walnut.

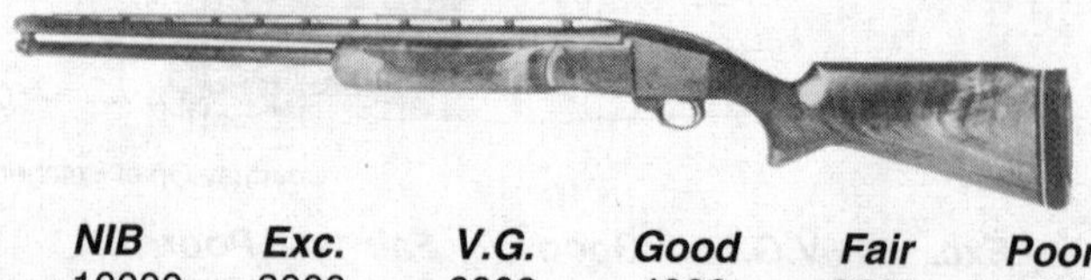

NIB	Exc.	V.G.	Good	Fair	Poor
10000	8000	6000	4000	2000	1000

Bi-Gun Combo

The over-and-under Bi-Gun supplied with a high ribbed single-barrel in addition to the separated over-and-under barrels. It is furnished in a fitted case, and the walnut is of exhibition grade.

NIB	Exc.	V.G.	Good	Fair	Poor
17000	13000	7000	4000	2000	1000

LM-6 Super Deluxe

This is a custom-built over-and-under gun made to the customer's specifications. Available in 12 gauge with barrel lengths from 28" to 34". All other specifications are custom. Expert appraisal recommended prior to sale.

NIB	Exc.	V.G.	Good	Fair	Poor
18000	13500	8000	—	—	—

NOTE: Extra single-barrel add $7,000.

LLAMA

Manufactured by
Gabilondo y Cia
Vitoria, Spain

This is the same firm that was founded in 1904 and produced several inexpensive revolvers and pistols prior to 1931. In 1931 the company began to produce a semi-automatic pistol based on the Colt Model 1911. They were of high quality and have been sold around the world. After the Spanish civil war the company moved its facilities to Vitoria, Spain, where it continued to build handguns under the Llama trade name. In the 1980s the firm introduced a new line of pistols that were more modern in design and function. The Llama pistol is still produced today. For Llama pistols built prior to 1936 the slide marking reads: "GABILONDO Y CIA ELOEIBAR (ESPANA) CAL 9MM/.380IN LLAMA." For pistols built after 1936 the slide marking reads: "LLAMA GABILONDO Y CIA ELOEIBAR (ESPANA) CAL 9MM .380." Current production Llama pistols will show a slide marking with either "LLAMA CAL..." or "GABILONDO Y CIA VITORIA (ESPANA)" and the Llama logo. "Llama" is now a trade name for handguns manufactured by Bersa of Argentina.

LLAMA AUTOMATICS

Model I-A

This is a 7.65mm blowback design introduced in 1933. Magazine capacity is 7 rounds. The barrel was 3.62", overall length 6.3", and weight about 19 oz.

Exc.	V.G.	Good	Fair	Poor
225	175	125	100	75

Model II

Chambered for the 9mm Short introduced in the same year. Identical to the Model I. Discontinued in 1936.

Exc.	V.G.	Good	Fair	Poor
250	200	150	125	100

Model III

An improved version of the Model II. Introduced in 1936 and discontinued in 1954.

Exc.	V.G.	Good	Fair	Poor
275	225	175	125	100

Model III-A

Similar to the Model III, chambered for the .380 ACP, but with the addition of the Colt-type grip safety. Introduced in 1955. Weight is about 23 oz.

Exc.	V.G.	Good	Fair	Poor
250	200	150	125	100

Model IV

Chambered for the 9mm Largo or .380 ACP. Is not fitted with a grip safety. Introduced in 1931, it is the first of the Llama designs.

Exc.	V.G.	Good	Fair	Poor
275	225	175	125	100

Model V

The same as the Model IV but was intended for export to the United States and is stamped "made in Spain" on the slide.

Exc.	V.G.	Good	Fair	Poor
250	200	150	100	75

Model VI

Chambered for the 9mm Short and without a grip safety.

Exc.	V.G.	Good	Fair	Poor
250	200	150	100	75

Model VII

This model was introduced in 1932 and manufactured until 1954. It is chambered for the .38 Super Auto cartridge. It does not have a grip safety.

Exc.	V.G.	Good	Fair	Poor
275	225	175	125	100

Model VIII

This model was introduced in 1955 and is chambered for the .45 ACP, .38 Super, or 9mm Largo. It is fitted with a grip safety. Barrel length is 5", overall length is 8.5", and weight is about 38 oz. Magazine capacity is 7 rounds.

Exc.	V.G.	Good	Fair	Poor
300	250	175	125	100

NOTE: For the .38 Super cartridge add $25.

Model IX

Chambered for the 7.65mm Para, 9mm Largo, or .45 ACP, this model has a locked breech with no grip safety. Built from 1936 to 1954.

Exc.	V.G.	Good	Fair	Poor
325	275	200	150	100

Model IX-A

This version of the Model IX is fitted with a grip safety. Current production models are chambered for the .45 ACP only. Weighs about 30 oz. with 5" barrel.

Exc.	V.G.	Good	Fair	Poor
275	225	150	125	100

Model IX-B

This version of the Model IX series is chambered in .45 ACP. It is fitted with an extended slide release, black plastic grips, and target-type hammer. Offered in blue or satin chrome finish.

NIB	Exc.	V.G.	Good	Fair	Poor
350	300	250	175	125	100

Model IX-C

This is the current large-frame version of the Model IX. It is chambered for the .45 ACP and is fitted with a 5.125" barrel. Blade front sight with adjustable rear sight. Magazine capacity is 10 rounds. Weight is approximately 41 oz.

NIB	Exc.	V.G.	Good	Fair	Poor
350	300	250	200	150	100

Model IX-D

This model is a compact frame version with a 4.25" barrel and chambered for the .45 ACP cartridge. Stocks are black rubber. Fixed front sight with adjustable rear. Introduced in 1995. Magazine capacity is 10 rounds. Weight is about 39 oz.

NIB	Exc.	V.G.	Good	Fair	Poor
350	300	—	—	—	—

Model X

First produced in 1935, this model is chambered for the 7.65mm cartridge. It has no grip safety.

Exc.	V.G.	Good	Fair	Poor
250	200	150	100	75

Model X-A

This version is similar to the Model X but with a grip safety. Produced from 1954 to the present.

Exc.	V.G.	Good	Fair	Poor
250	200	150	100	75

Model XI

Chambered for the 9mm Parabellum cartridge this model is different from previous models with a longer curved butt, ring hammer, and vertically grooved walnut grips. Magazine capacity is 9 rounds. Barrel length is 5". Discontinued in 1954.

Exc.	V.G.	Good	Fair	Poor
300	250	200	150	100

Model XI-B

(Currently imported by Century International Arms Co.) Similar to the Model XI but with a spur hammer and shorter barrel. Currently in production.

NIB	Exc.	V.G.	Good	Fair	Poor
250	200	150	125	100	75

Model XII-B

This model is chambered for the .40 S&W cartridge. It has a compact frame. Currently in production.

NIB	Exc.	V.G.	Good	Fair	Poor
325	275	225	175	125	100

Model XV

Chambered for the .22 Long Rifle this model is marked "Especial." It is fitted with a grip safety and comes in several finishes and with different grip styles. The barrel length is 3.6", the overall length is 6.5", and the weight is about 17 oz.

Exc.	V.G.	Good	Fair	Poor
225	175	150	125	100

Model XVI

This is a deluxe version of the Model XV with engraving, ventilated rib, and adjustable sights.

Exc.	V.G.	Good	Fair	Poor
350	275	200	150	100

Model XVII

This model is chambered for the .22 Short. It is small version of the Model XV with a finger-shaped grip.

Exc.	V.G.	Good	Fair	Poor
300	250	175	125	100

Model XVIII

Introduced in 1998 this model is chambered for the .25 ACP cartridge and offered with gold or chrome finish and stag grips.

Exc.	V.G.	Good	Fair	Poor
300	225	175	150	125

Model Omni

This pistol is chambered for the .45 ACP or 9mm cartridge and fitted with a 4.25" barrel. Blued finish. Adjustable rear sight. Magazine capacity is 7 rounds for the .45 ACP and 13 rounds for the 9mm. Weight is approximately 40 oz. Produced between 1984 and 1986.

Courtesy J.B. Wood

Courtesy J.B. Wood

NIB	Exc.	V.G.	Good	Fair	Poor
395	300	250	150	125	100

Model Max-I

Introduced in 1995 this 1911 design single-action model features a choice of 9mm or .45 ACP chambers with a 4.25" barrel or a 5.125" barrel. Black rubber grips with blade front sight and adjustable rear sight. Weight is 34 oz. for compact model and 36 oz. for Government model.

NIB	Exc.	V.G.	Good	Fair	Poor
300	250	200	150	—	—

NOTE: For compact model add $25. For duo-tone model add $25.

Model Mini-Max

This version is chambered for the 9mm, .40 S&W, or .45 ACP. Furnished with a 6-round magazine. Barrel length is 3.5". Checkered rubber grips. Introduced in 1996. Weight is about 35 oz. Choice of blue, duo-tone, satin chrome, or stainless steel.

NIB	Exc.	V.G.	Good	Fair	Poor
325	275	225	150	—	—

NOTE: Add $40 for satin chrome finish. Add $60 for stainless. Add $20 for duo-tone finish.

Mini-Max Sub Compact

This semi-automatic is chambered for the 9mm, .40 S&W, or .45 ACP cartridge. It is fitted with a 3.14" barrel with an overall length of 6.5" and a height of 4.5". Skeletonized combat-style hammer. Grips are black polymer. Weight is about 31 oz. Introduced in 1999.

NIB	Exc.	V.G.	Good	Fair	Poor
325	250	200	—	—	—

NOTE: Add $40 for satin chrome finish. Add $60 for stainless. Add $20 for duo-tone finish.

Mini-Max Sub Compact

Chambered for the .45 ACP cartridge, this is a single-action pistol. Fitted with a 3.14" barrel with steel frame and black polymer grips. Magazine capacity is 10 rounds. Overall length is 6.5" and overall height is 4.5". Weight is about 31 oz. Matte blue, chrome or duo-tone finish.

NIB	Exc.	V.G.	Good	Fair	Poor
360	290	—	—	—	—

NOTE: Add $15 for chrome finish and $10 for duo-tone finish.

Model Max-I with Compensator

Similar to the Max-I with the addition of a compensator. This model introduced in 1996. Weight is about 42 oz.

NIB	Exc.	V.G.	Good	Fair	Poor
450	400	—	—	—	—

Micro-Max

This pistol is chambered for the .32 ACP or .380 cartridge. It operates on a straight blowback system with a single-action trigger. Black polymer grips. Barrel length is 3.6". Overall length is 6.5" and height is 4.37". Weight is approximately 23 oz. Introduced in 1999.

NIB	Exc.	V.G.	Good	Fair	Poor
275	200	150	125	100	—

NOTE: Add $20 for satin chrome finish.

Model 82

This is a large-frame double-action semi-automatic pistol. It features plastic grips, ambidextrous safety, 3-dot sights. The barrel length is 4.25" and overall length is 8". Weight is approximately 39 oz. Choice of blue or satin chrome finish.

NIB	Exc.	V.G.	Good	Fair	Poor
650	500	350	250	150	100

Model 87 Competition

Chambered for the 9mm cartridge and fitted with a integral muzzle compensator. Has a number of competition features such as beveled magazine well and oversize safety and magazine release. Magazine capacity is 14 rounds. Offered between 1989 and 1993.

NIB	Exc.	V.G.	Good	Fair	Poor
1000	825	650	525	—	—

Llama Compact Frame Semi-Automatic

A 9mm or the .45 ACP caliber semi-automatic pistol with a 4.25" barrel and either a 7- or 9-shot detachable magazine. Blued. Introduced in 1986.

NIB	Exc.	V.G.	Good	Fair	Poor
250	225	175	125	100	75

Llama Small Frame Semi-Automatic

A .22, .32 ACP, and the .380 ACP caliber semi-automatic pistol with a 3-11/16" barrel and 7-shot detachable magazine. Either blued or satin chrome finished.

NIB	Exc.	V.G.	Good	Fair	Poor
225	175	150	125	100	75

NOTE: Add $75 for satin chrome finish.

Llama Large Frame Semi-Automatic

A 9mm, .38 Super or .45 ACP caliber semi-automatic pistol with a 5.25" barrel and either a 7- or 9-shot detachable magazine, depending on the caliber. Blued or satin chrome.

NIB	Exc.	V.G.	Good	Fair	Poor
250	225	175	125	100	75

NOTE: Add $125 for satin chrome finish.

Mugica

Eibar gun dealer Jose Mugica sold Llama pistols under his private trade name. They are marked "mugica-ebir-spain" on the slide. These pistols do not seem to have any additional value over and above their respective Llama models. For the sake of clarification the Mugica models are listed with their Llama counterparts:

Mugica Model 101	Llama Model X
Mugica Model 101-G	Llama Model X-A
Mugica Model 105	Llama Model III
Mugica Model 105-G	Llama Model III-A
Mugica Model 110	Llama Model VII
Mugica Model 110-G	Llama Model VIII
Mugica Model 120	Llama Model XI

Tauler

In an arrangement similar to Mugica a gun dealer in Madrid sold Llama pistols under his own brand name. Most of these pistols were sold in the early 1930s to police and other government officials. The most common Llama models were Models I to VIII. Slide inscriptions were in English and had the name Tauler in them. No additional value is attached to this private trademark.

REVOLVERS

Ruby Extra Models

These revolvers were produced in the 1950s and were copies of Smith & Wessons. They were marked "RUBY EXTRA" on the left side of the frame. At the top of the grips was a Ruby medallion. The barrel address is stamped: gabilondo y cia elgoeibar espana. The Ruby Extra Models represent the company's attempts to produce and sell a low-cost revolver.

Model XII

This model is chambered for the .38 Long cartridge and is fitted with a 5" barrel and a squared butt.

Exc.	V.G.	Good	Fair	Poor
200	150	125	100	75

Model XIII

(Currently imported by Century International Arms Co.) Chambered for the .38 Special, this revolver has a round butt with 4" or 6" ventilated rib barrel. The 6" barreled gun was fitted with adjustable sights and target grips.

Exc.	V.G.	Good	Fair	Poor
225	175	150	125	100

Model XIV

Offered in .22 LR or .32 caliber, this model was available in a wide choice of barrel lengths and sights.

Exc.	V.G.	Good	Fair	Poor
200	150	125	100	75

Model XXII Olimpico

This model was designed as a .38 Special target revolver. It features an adjustable anatomic grip, adjustable rear sight, ventilated rib barrel, and a web that joins the barrel to the ejector shroud.

Exc.	V.G.	Good	Fair	Poor
275	225	150	125	100

Model XXIX Olimpico

This is the Model XXI I chambered for the .22 LR.

Exc.	V.G.	Good	Fair	Poor
250	200	150	125	100

Model XXVI

Chambered for the .22 LR, it features traditional grips and shrouded ejector rod.

Exc.	V.G.	Good	Fair	Poor
175	150	125	100	75

Model XXVII

Similar to the model above but fitted with a 2" barrel and chambered for the .32 Long cartridge.

Exc.	V.G.	Good	Fair	Poor
175	150	125	100	75

Model XXVIII

This model is chambered for the .22 LR and is fitted with a 6" barrel. It has a ramp front sight and adjustable rear sight.

Exc.	V.G.	Good	Fair	Poor
200	175	150	100	75

Model XXXII Olimpico

This model is a .32 target revolver with an unusual cylinder and frame design.

Exc.	V.G.	Good	Fair	Poor
275	225	150	125	100

Llama Martial

A .22 or the .38 Special caliber double-action revolver with a 6-round swingout cylinder, a 4" or 6" barrel and adjustable sights. Blued, with checkered hardwood grips. Manufactured between 1969 and 1976.

Exc.	V.G.	Good	Fair	Poor
275	225	200	150	125

NOTE: Add $25 for engraved chrome, $50 for engraved blue, and 600 percent for gold model.

Llama Comanche I

This .22 caliber revolver is fitted with a 6" barrel and has a 9 shot cylinder. Rubber grips with adjustable sights. Choice of blue or stainless steel. Weight is about 39 oz.

NIB	Exc.	V.G.	Good	Fair	Poor
240	175	125	100	75	50

Llama Comanche II

As above, in .38 Special caliber with 6 shot cylinder. Choice of 3" or 4" barrel. Rubber grips and adjustable sights. Blue or stainless steel. Weight is about 30 oz.

NIB	Exc.	V.G.	Good	Fair	Poor
225	175	125	100	75	50

Llama Comanche III

As above, in .357 Magnum with a 3", 4", 6", barrel and adjustable sights. Rubber grips. Blue or stainless steel. Weight is about 30 oz. for 3" or 4" barrel guns and 39 oz. for 6" gun. Introduced in 1975.

NIB	Exc.	V.G.	Good	Fair	Poor
275	225	175	125	100	75

NOTE: Add 20 percent for satin chrome finish.

Llama Super Comanche

As above, in .357 or .44 Magnum with a 10" ventilated rib barrel and adjustable sights. Blued, with walnut grips. Weight is about 47 oz.

NIB	Exc.	V.G.	Good	Fair	Poor
325	250	200	150	100	75

LOEWE, LUDWIG & CO.

Berlin, Germany

SEE—Borchardt

During the 1870s and 1880s this firm manufactured a close copy of the Smith & Wesson Russian Model for the Russian government. They are marked "Ludwig Loewe Berlin" on the top of the barrel.

Loewe Smith & Wesson Russian Revolver

Exc.	V.G.	Good	Fair	Poor
—	400	200	125	75

LOHNER, C.
Philadelphia, Pennsylvania

Pocket Pistol
A .44 caliber single-shot percussion pistol with a 5" barrel, German silver mounts and walnut grip. The barrel marked "C. Lohner." Manufactured during the 1850s.

Exc.	*V.G.*	*Good*	*Fair*	*Poor*
—	—	1250	550	250

LOMBARD, H. C. & CO.
Springfield, Massachusetts

Pocket Pistol
A .22 caliber single-shot spur trigger pistol with a 3.5" octagonal barrel. The frame is silver plated, barrel blued and grips are of walnut. Barrel marked "H.C. Lombard & Co. Springfield, Mass."

Exc.	*V.G.*	*Good*	*Fair*	*Poor*
—	—	450	200	100

LONDON ARMOURY COMPANY
London

This firm was established in 1856, by Robert Adams. In addition to marketing revolvers based upon Adams' designs, the London Armoury Company were major retailers of other arms, particularly Enfield Pattern 53 Percussion Rifles. During the 1870s, the London Armoury distributed Colt pistols. During its business life, the London Armoury Company was located at these addresses:

Henry Street	1857-1863
36 King William Street	1864-1868
54 King William Street	1868-1883
118 Queen Victoria Street	1884-1886
114 Queen Victoria Street	1887-1905
1 Lawrence Pounty Hill	1905-1910
31 Bury Street, St. James	1910-1939
10 Ryder Street, St. James	1940-1950

Although the firm continued in business after 1950, its operations were restricted to the trade of used arms.

LONE STAR RIFLE COMPANY
Conroe, Texas

This company builds custom blackpowder rifles. They are built on the rolling block design and are offered in two basic configurations. There are a wide number of options that will affect the price of these rifles.

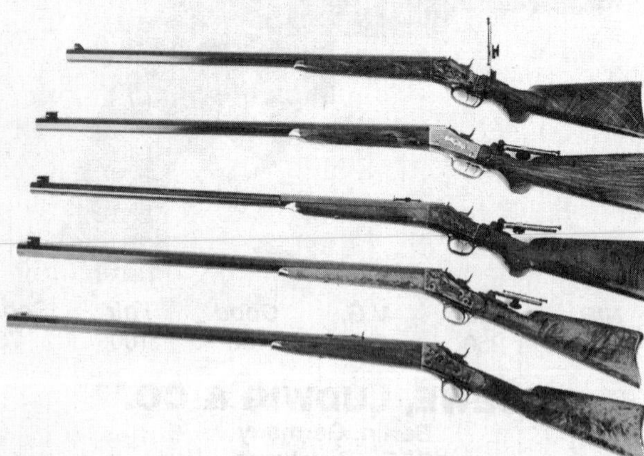

Sporting Rifle
This is a basic configuration that features a straight grip stock with semi-crescent butt. Offered in a wide variety of calibers from .32-40 to .50-90. Barrel lengths, barrel configurations, wood, triggers, sights, engraving, finishes, hammers, and accessories will greatly affect the final price.

Basic retail price: $1,995.

Target Rifle
This is a basic configuration that features a straight grip stock with semi-crescent butt. Offered in a wide variety of calibers from .32-40 to .50-90. Barrel lengths, barrel configurations, wood, triggers, sights, engraving, finishes, hammers, and accessories will greatly affect the final price.

Basic retail price: $1,995.

LORCIN ENGINEERING CO., INC.
Mira Loma, California

NOTE: This company was in business from 1989 to 1999.

Model L-25
A .25 caliber semi-automatic pistol with a 2.5" barrel and 7-shot magazine. Weight is 14.5 oz. Overall length is 4.8". Introduced in 1989.

NIB	*Exc.*	*V.G.*	*Good*	*Fair*	*Poor*
75	60	50	40	30	20

Model LT-25
Same as above but with aluminum alloy frame. Introduced in 1989.

NIB	*Exc.*	*V.G.*	*Good*	*Fair*	*Poor*
100	75	60	50	40	30

Model L-22
Chambered for the .22 LR cartridge with a 2.5" barrel. Magazine capacity is 9 rounds. Introduced in 1989. Weight is 16 oz.

NIB	*Exc.*	*V.G.*	*Good*	*Fair*	*Poor*
90	65	55	45	35	25

Model L-380
This semi-automatic pistol is chambered for the .380 ACP cartridge. Barrel length is 3.5" with a magazine capacity of 7 rounds. Introduced in 1992. Weight is about 23 oz.

NIB	*Exc.*	*V.G.*	*Good*	*Fair*	*Poor*
120	95	80	50	40	30

Model I-380 10th Anniversary
Same as above but frame and slide are plated in 24 karat gold. Limited edition model.

NIB	*Exc.*	*V.G.*	*Good*	*Fair*	*Poor*
150	—	—	—	—	—

Model L-32

Same as above but chambered for the .32 ACP cartridge. Introduced in 1992

NIB	Exc.	V.G.	Good	Fair	Poor
100	80	70	50	40	30

Model LH-380

This semi-automatic pistol is chambered for the .380 ACP cartridge. The barrel length is 4.5" and the magazine capacity is 10 rounds. Offered in black, satin or bright chrome finishes.

NIB	Exc.	V.G.	Good	Fair	Poor
150	125	100	75	60	50

Model L-9mm

Same as above but chambered for 9mm cartridge. Weight is 36 oz.

NIB	Exc.	V.G.	Good	Fair	Poor
150	125	100	75	60	50

Derringer

This over-and-under pistol is chambered for the .38 Special, .357 Magnum, and .45 ACP. Barrel length is 3.5". Overall length is 6.5".

NIB	Exc.	V.G.	Good	Fair	Poor
140	120	95	65	50	40

LOWELL ARMS CO.

SEE—Rollin White Arms Co.

LOWER, J. P.

SEE—Slotter & Co.

LUGERS

Various Manufacturers

Just before the turn of the 20th century, Georg Luger redesigned the Borchardt semi-automatic pistol so that its mainspring was housed in the rear of the grip. The resulting pistol was to prove extremely successful and his name has become synonymous with the pistol despite the fact his name never appeared on it.

These companies manufactured Luger pattern pistols at various times.

1. DWM - Deutsch Waffen und Munitions - Karlsruhe, Germany
2. The Royal Arsenal of Erfurt Germany
3. Simson & Company - Suhl, Germany
4. Mauser - Oberndorf, Germany
5. Vickers Ltd. - England
6. Waffenfabrik Bern - Bern, Switzerland
7. Heinrich Krieghoff - Suhl, Germany

Those interested in these pistols are advised to read the various books written about the marque which are listed in the bibliography at the close of this book.

DEUTSCH WAFFEN UND MUNITIONS

1899/1900 Swiss Test Model

4.75" barrel, 7.65mm caliber. The Swiss Cross in Sunburst is stamped over the chamber. The serial range runs to three digits. With fewer than 100 manufactured and only one known to exist, it is one of the rarest of the Lugers and the first true Luger that was produced. This model is far too rare to estimate an accurate value.

1900 Swiss Contract

4.75" barrel, 7.65mm caliber. The Swiss Cross in Sunburst is stamped over the chamber. The military serial number range is 2001-5000; the commercial range, 01-21250. There were approximately 2,000 commercial and 3,000 military models manufactured.

Swiss Cross & Sunburst Courtesy Gale Morgan

Exc.	V.G.	Good	Fair	Poor
6000	4700	2000	1500	1000

NOTE: Wide trigger add 20 percent.

1900 Commercial

4.75" barrel, 7.65mm caliber. The area above the chamber is blank. The serial range is 01-19000, and there were approximately 5,500 manufactured for commercial sale in Germany or other countries. Some have "Germany" stamped on the frame. These pistols were imported into the U.S., and some were even stamped after blueing.

Courtesy Gale Morgan

Exc.	V.G.	Good	Fair	Poor
5000	3700	2000	1000	650

1900 American Eagle

4.75" barrel, 7.65mm caliber. The American Eagle crest is stamped over the chamber. The serial range is between 2000-200000, and there were approximately 11,000-12,000 commercial models marked "Germany" and 1,000 military test models without the commercial import stamp. The serial numbers of this military lot have been estimated at between 6100-7100.

Exc.	V.G.	Good	Fair	Poor
4500	3200	1500	850	600

1900 Bulgarian Contract

An old model, 1900 Type, with no stock lug. It has a 4.75" barrel and is chambered for the 7.65mm cartridge. The Bulgarian crest is stamped over the chamber, and the safety is marked in Bulgarian letters. The serial range is 20000-21000, with 1,000 manufactured. This is a military test model and is quite rare as most were rebarreled to 9mm during the time they were used. Even with the 9mm versions, approximately 10 are known to exist. It was the only variation to feature a marked safety before 1904.

Courtesy Gale Morgan

Exc.	V.G.	Good	Fair	Poor
12000	8000	4000	2500	1800

1900 Carbine

11.75" barrel, 7.65mm caliber. The carbines have a gracefully contoured and finely checkered walnut forearm and detachable shoulder stock. The rear sight on this extremely rare variation is a five-position sliding model located on the rear link. The area above the chamber is blank. The serial range is three digits or under, and this may have been a prototype as less than 100 were produced. This model is far too rare to estimate an accurate value.

1902 Prototype

6" barrel, 7.65mm caliber. The serial numbers are in the 10000 range with a capital B, and the chamber is blank. The 6" barrel is of a heavy contour, and there were less than 10 manufactured. The rarity of this variation precludes estimating value.

1902 Carbine

11.75" barrel, 7.65mm caliber. The sight has four positions and is silver-soldered to the barrel. A stock and forearm were sold with this weapon. The serial range was 21000-22100 and 23500-24900. There were approximately 2,500 manufactured for commercial sale in and out of Germany. Many were imported into the United States, but none here have been noted with the "Germany" export stamp.

Courtesy Gale Morgan

Exc.	V.G.	Good	Fair	Poor
14500	10000	6000	3500	2500

NOTE: With stock add 50 percent.

1902 Commercial—"Fat Barrel"

Thick 4" barrel, 9mm caliber. The area above the chamber is blank. It is chambered for the 9mm cartridge, and the serial numbers fall within the 22300-22400 and the 22900-23500 range. There were approximately 600 manufactured, and the greater part of those noted were marked "Germany" for export purposes.

Exc.	V.G.	Good	Fair	Poor
12000	9000	6000	4000	1500

1902 American Eagle

As above, with an American Eagle stamped over the chamber. It is chambered for the 9mm cartridge, and the serial numbers fall within the 22100-22300 and the 22450-22900 range. This model was solely intended for export sales in the U.S.A., and all are marked "Germany" on the frame. There were approximately 700 manufactured.

Exc.	V.G.	Good	Fair	Poor
11000	9000	5500	3750	1300

1902 American Eagle Cartridge Counter

As above, with a "Powell Indicating Device" added to the left grip. A slotted magazine with a numbered window that allows visual access to the number of cartridges remaining. There were 50 Lugers altered in this way at the request of the U.S. Board of Ordnance, for U.S. Army evaluation. The serial numbers are 22401-22450. Be especially wary of fakes!

Exc.	V.G.	Good	Fair	Poor
30000	25000	16000	6000	3500

1902 Presentation Carbine

11.75" barrel, 7.65mm caliber. These carbines have the initials of the owner gold-inlaid above the chamber. They are furnished with a checkered walnut stock and forearm. Only four have been noted in the 9000C serial number range. They have the initials "GL" for Georg Luger on the back of the rear toggle. They are too rare to estimate value.

1902/06 Carbine (Transitional)

11.75" barrel, 7.65mm caliber. Assembled from Model 1902 parts with a new toggle assembly. They have the four-position sliding sight, silver-soldered to the barrel, and a checkered walnut stock and forearm. There were approximately 100 manufactured in the 23600 serial number range.

Exc.	V.G.	Good	Fair	Poor
15000	10000	8000	5000	3000

NOTE: With stock add 25 percent.

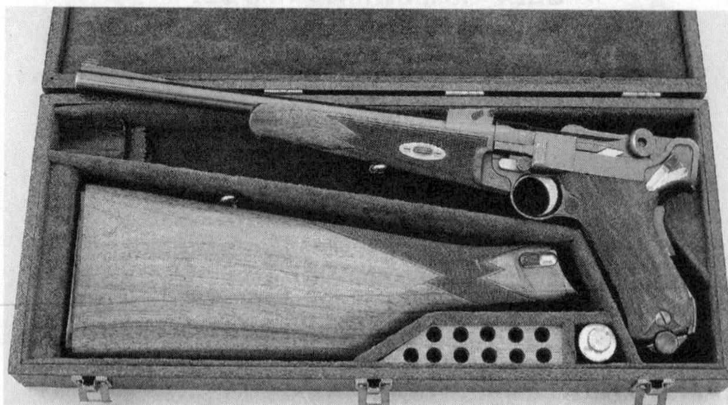

Paul Goodwin photo

1903 Commercial

4" barrel, 7.65mm caliber. The chamber area is blank. There were approximately 50 manufactured for export to France, serial numbered 25000-25050. The extractor on this model is marked "CHARGE."

Exc.	V.G.	Good	Fair	Poor
12000	9000	5000	3200	2500

1904 Navy

6" thick barrel, 9mm caliber. The chamber area is blank, and the extractor is marked "Geladen." The safety is marked "Gesichert." There were approximately 1,500 manufactured in the one- to four-digit serial range, for military sales to the German Navy. The toggle has a "lock" comparable to 1900 types.

Exc.	V.G.	Good	Fair	Poor
40000	30000	16000	6000	4500

1906 Navy Commercial

This is a new model, 1906 Type, with stock lug. It has a 6" barrel and is chambered for the 9mm cartridge. The chamber is blank, and the extractor is marked "Geladen." The safety is marked "Gesichert," and some have the "Germany" export stamp. The proper magazine has a wood bottom with concentric circles on the sides. There were approximately 2,500 manufactured in the 25050-65000 serial range. They were produced for commercial sales in and outside of Germany.

Exc.	V.G.	Good	Fair	Poor
6500	4500	2700	1500	1000

1906 Commercial

4" barrel, 9mm caliber. The extractor is marked "Geladen," and the area of the frame under the safety in its lower position is polished and not blued. The chamber is blank. There were approximately 4,000 manufactured for commercial sales. Some have the "Germany" export stamp. The serial range is 26500-68000.

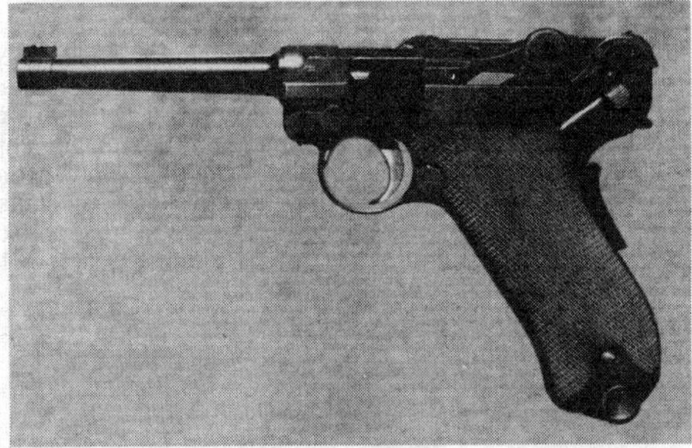

Courtesy Orvel Reichert

Exc.	V.G.	Good	Fair	Poor
3500	2500	1000	800	600

1906 Commercial (Marked Safety)

As above, with the area of the frame under the safety in its lowest position is marked "Gesichert" and the barrel is 4.75" in length and chambered for the 7.65mm cartridge. There were approximately 750 manufactured, serial numbered 25050-26800.

Exc.	V.G.	Good	Fair	Poor
4500	4000	2000	800	600

1906 American Eagle

4" barrel, 9mm caliber. The chamber area has the American Eagle stamped upon it. The extractor is marked "Loaded," and the frame under the safety at its lowest point is polished and not blued. This model has no stock lug. There were approximately 3,000 manufactured for commercial sale in the U.S.A. in the serial range 25800-69000.

Exc.	V.G.	Good	Fair	Poor
3700	2500	1200	700	500

NOTE: Add 10 percent premium for "CAL. 9MM" mag.

1906 American Eagle (Marked Safety)

4.75" barrel, 7.65mm caliber. The frame under the safety at its lowest point is marked "Gesichert." There were approximately 750 manufactured in the 25100-26500 serial number range.

Courtesy Gale Morgan

Exc.	V.G.	Good	Fair	Poor
4500	3500	1500	1200	800

1906 American Eagle 4.75" Barrel

As above but with polished bright safety area. Approximately 8,000 manufactured in the 26500-69000 serial range.

Exc.	V.G.	Good	Fair	Poor
4500	3000	1100	700	450

1906 U.S. Army Test Luger .45 Caliber

5" barrel, .45 ACP caliber. Sent to the United States for testing in 1907. The chamber is blank; the extractor is marked "Loaded," and the frame is polished under the safety lever. The trigger on this model has an odd hook at the bottom. Only five of these pistols were manufactured. **Buyer Caution:** Perfect copies of this pistol are currently being produced.

1906 Swiss Commercial

4.75" barrel, 7.65mm caliber. The Swiss Cross in Sunburst appears over the chamber. The extractor is marked "Geladen," and the frame under the safety is polished. There is no stock lug, and the proofmarks are commercial. There were approximately 1,000 manufactured in the 35000-55000 serial number range.

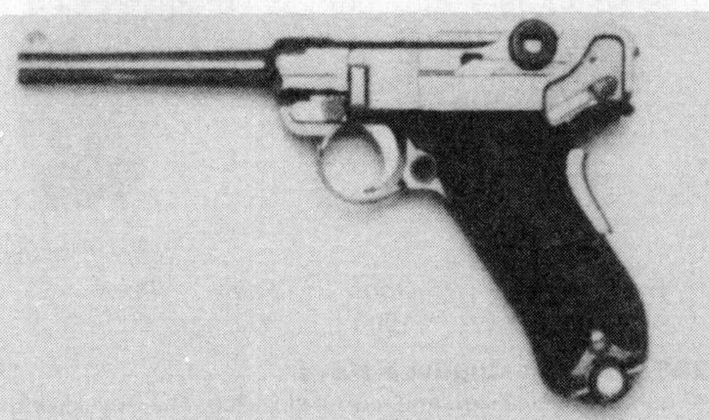

Courtesy Bonhams & Butterfields, San Francisco, California

Exc.	V.G.	Good	Fair	Poor
5300	4200	2500	1400	800

1906 Swiss Military

As the Swiss Commercial, except with military proofmarks.

Exc.	V.G.	Good	Fair	Poor
5000	3300	2200	900	700

1906 Swiss Police Cross in Shield

As above, with a shield replacing the sunburst on the chamber marking. There were 10,215 of both models combined. They are in the 5000-15215 serial number range.

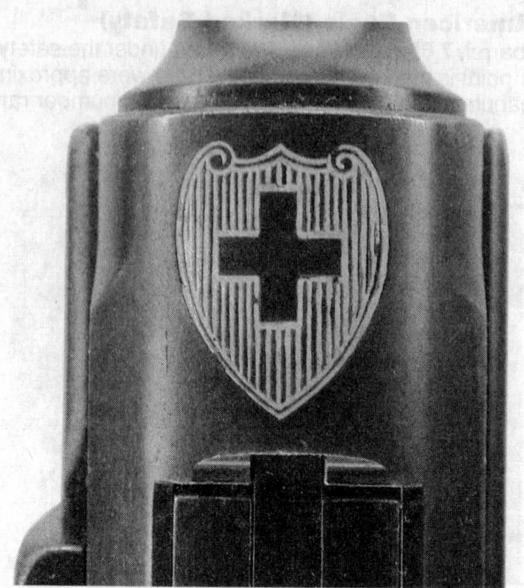
Courtesy Gale Morgan

Exc.	V.G.	Good	Fair	Poor
4700	3700	2000	1000	700

1906 Dutch Contract

4" barrel, 9mm caliber. It has no stock lug, and the chamber is blank. The extractor is marked "Geleden" on both sides, and the safety is marked "RUST" with a curved upward pointing arrow. This pistol was manufactured for military sales to the Netherlands, and a date will be found on the barrel of most examples encountered. The Dutch refinished their pistols on a regular basis and marked the date on the barrels. There were approximately 4,000 manufactured, serial numbered between 1 and 4000.

Courtesy Gale Morgan

Exc.	V.G.	Good	Fair	Poor
4200	3000	1500	800	600

1906 Royal Portuguese Navy

4" barrel, 9mm caliber, and has no stock lug. The Royal Portuguese Naval crest, an anchor under a crown, is stamped above the chamber. The extractor is marked "CARREGADA" on the left side. The frame under the safety is polished. There were approximately 1,000 manufactured with one- to four-digit serial numbers.

Exc.	V.G.	Good	Fair	Poor
12000	9000	6500	4000	2500

1906 Royal Portuguese Army (M2)

4.75" barrel, 7.65mm caliber. It has no stock lug. The chamber area has the Royal Portuguese crest of Mannuel II stamped upon it. The extractor is marked "CARREGADA." There were approximately 5,000 manufactured, with one- to four-digit serial numbers.

Portugese "M2"

Courtesy Gale Morgan

Exc.	V.G.	Good	Fair	Poor
3500	2700	1200	600	500

1906 Republic of Portugal Navy

4" barrel, 9mm caliber. It has no stock lug, and the extractor was marked "CARREGADA." This model was made after 1910, when Portugal had become a republic. The anchor on the chamber is under the letters "R.P." There were approximately 1,000 manufactured, with one- to four-digit serial numbers.

Exc.	V.G.	Good	Fair	Poor
11000	9000	5500	2500	1500

1906 Brazilian Contract

4.75" barrel, 7.65mm caliber. It has no stock lug, and chamber area is blank. The extractor is marked "CARREGADA," and the frame under the safety is polished. There were approximately 5,000 manufactured for military sales to Brazil.

Exc.	V.G.	Good	Fair	Poor
3000	2400	1100	750	450

1906 Bulgarian Contract

4.75" barrel, 7.65mm caliber. It has no stock lug, and the extractor and safety are marked in cyrillic letters. The Bulgarian crest is stamped above the chamber. Nearly all of the examples located have the barrels replaced with 4" 9mm units. This was done after the later 1908 model was adopted. Some were refurbished during the Nazi era, and these pistols bear Waffenamts and usually mismatched parts. There were approximately 1,500 manufactured, with serial numbers of one- to four-digits.

Exc.	V.G.	Good	Fair	Poor
9500	7000	5000	3500	1500

1906 Russian Contract

4" barrel, 9mm caliber. It has no stock lug, and the extractor and safety are marked with cyrillic letters. Crossed Nagant rifles are stamped over the chamber. There were approximately 1,000 manufactured, with one- to four-digit serial numbers; but few survive. This is an extremely rare variation, and caution should be exercised if purchase is contemplated.

Courtesy Gale Morgan

Exc.	V.G.	Good	Fair	Poor
14000	12000	6500	4000	2500

1906 Navy 1st Issue

6" barrel, 9mm caliber. The safety and extractor are both marked in German, and the chamber area is blank. There is a stock lug, and the unique two-position sliding Navy sight is mounted on the rear toggle link. There were approximately 12,000 manufactured for the German Navy, with serial numbers of one- to five-digits. The wooden magazine bottom features concentric rings.

Courtesy Gale Morgan

Exc.	V.G.	Good	Fair	Poor
8000	6000	4000	1500	950

NOTE: Many of these pistols had their safety changed so that they were "safe" in the lower position. Known as "1st issue altered." Value at approximately 20 percent less.

1906 Navy 2nd Issue

As above, but manufactured to be safe in the lower position. Approximately 11,000 2nd Issue Navies manufactured, with one- to five-digit serial numbers—some with an "a" or "b" suffix. They were produced for sale to the German Navy.

Courtesy Gale Morgan

Exc.	V.G.	Good	Fair	Poor
6500	4000	2500	1200	700

1908 Commercial

4" barrel, 9mm caliber. It has no stock lug, and the chamber area is blank. The extractor and the safety are both marked in German, and many examples are marked with the "Germany" export stamp. There were approximately 9,000 manufactured in the 39000-71500 serial number range.

Exc.	V.G.	Good	Fair	Poor
3500	2000	750	600	450

1908 Navy Commercial

6" barrel, 9mm caliber. It has a stock lug, no grip safety, and the characteristic two-position sliding sight mounted on the rear toggle link. The chamber area is blank, and the safety and extractor are both marked. The "Germany" export stamp appears on some examples. There were approximately 1,500 manufactured, in the 44000-50000 serial number range.

Exc.	V.G.	Good	Fair	Poor
5600	4700	2500	1750	1250

1908 Navy

As above, with the "Crown M" military proof. They may or may not have the concentric rings on the magazine bottom. There were approximately 40,000 manufactured, with one- to five-digit serial numbers with an "a" or "b" suffix. These Lugers are quite scarce as many were destroyed during and after WWI.

Exc.	V.G.	Good	Fair	Poor
4200	3200	2000	1100	800

1914 Navy

Similar to the above, but stamped with the dates from 1914-1918 above the chamber. Most noted are dated 1916-1918. There were approximately 30,000 manufactured, with one- to five-digit serial numbers with an "a" or "b" suffix. They are scarce as many were destroyed as a result of WWI.

Buyer Caution: Many counterfeit pistols reported.

Exc.	V.G.	Good	Fair	Poor
5000	3000	1580	950	700

1908 Military 1st Issue

4" barrel, 9mm caliber. It has no stock lug, and the extractor and safety are both marked in German. The chamber is blank. There were approximately 20,000 manufactured, with one- to five-digit serial numbers—some with an "a" suffix.

Exc.	V.G.	Good	Fair	Poor
1800	1200	600	500	350

1908 Military Dated Chamber (1910-1913)

As above, with the date of manufacture stamped on the chamber.

Exc.	V.G.	Good	Fair	Poor
1500	1000	600	500	350

1914 Military

As above, with a stock lug.

Exc.	V.G.	Good	Fair	Poor
1400	900	650	500	350

NOTE: Add 50 percent to a 1914 dated chamber ***without*** a stock lug.

1913 Commercial

As above, with a grip safety. Approximately 1,000 manufactured, with serial numbers 71000-72000; but few have been noted, and it is considered to be quite rare.

Exc.	V.G.	Good	Fair	Poor
2800	1700	1300	850	600

1914 Artillery

8" barrel, 9mm caliber. It features a nine-position adjustable sight that has a base that is an integral part of the barrel. This model has a stock lug and was furnished with a military-style flat board stock and holster rig (see Accessories). The chamber is dated from 1914-1918, and the safety and extractor are both marked. This model was developed for artillery and machine gun crews; and many thousands were manufactured, with one- to five-digit serial numbers—some have letter suffixes. This model is quite desirable from a collector's standpoint and is rarer than its production figures would indicate. After the war many were destroyed as the allies deemed them more insidious than other models, for some reason.

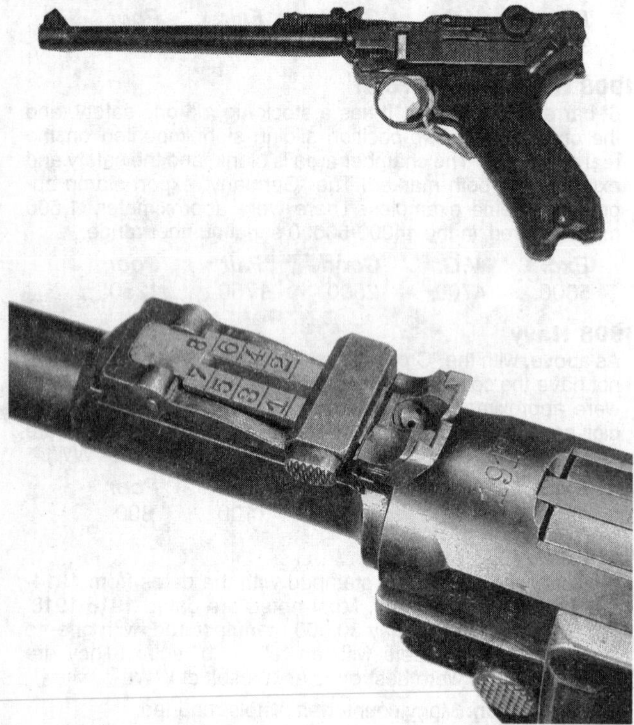

Courtesy Gale Morgan

Exc.	V.G.	Good	Fair	Poor
3000	2000	1300	900	600

NOTE: For models stamped with 1914 date add 75 percent.

DWM Double Dated

4" barrel, 9mm cartridge. The date 1920 or 1921 is stamped over the original chamber date of 1910-1918, creating the double-date nomenclature. These are arsenal-reworked WWI military pistols and were then issued to the German military and/or police units within the provisions of the Treaty of Versailles. Many thousands of these Lugers were produced.

Exc.	V.G.	Good	Fair	Poor
1300	800	550	400	300

1920 Police Rework

As above, except that the original manufacture date was removed before the rework date was stamped. There were many thousands of these produced.

Exc.	V.G.	Good	Fair	Poor
800	650	500	350	300

1920 Commercial

Similar to the above, with 3.5" to 6" barrels in 7.65mm or 9mm and marked "Germany" or "Made in Germany" for export. Others are unmarked and were produced for commercial sale inside Germany. Some of these pistols are military reworks with the markings and the proofmarks removed; others were newly manufactured. The extractors and safety are both marked, and the chamber is blank. The serial number range is one to five digits, and letter suffixes often appear.

Exc.	V.G.	Good	Fair	Poor
1700	1200	600	450	350

NOTE: Add 15 percent for 9mm.

1920 Commercial Navy

6" barrel, 9mm caliber. Some have a stock lug; others have been noted without. The chamber area is generally blank, but some have been found with 1914-1918 dates stamped upon them. These were reworked by DWM from Military Navy Lugers after WWI for commercial sales. They are marked "Germany" or "Made in Germany" and were sold by Stoeger Arms, among others. The extractor and safety are both marked, and the unique Navy sight is on the rear toggle link. No one knows exactly how many were produced, but they are quite scarce.

Exc.	V.G.	Good	Fair	Poor
6000	3000	1600	1100	850

1920 Commercial Artillery

8" barrel, 9mm caliber. Erfurt-manufactured pistols, as well as DWM-manufactured pistols, were reworked in this manner. The export markings "Germany" or "Made in Germany" are found on most examples. The number produced is not known, but examples are quite scarce.

Exc.	V.G.	Good	Fair	Poor
3500	2300	1100	700	450

1920 Long Barrel Commercial

10" to 24" barrels, 7.65mm or 9mm caliber. The extractor and safety are both marked, and an artillery model rear sight is used. This model was often built to a customer's specifications. They are rare, and the number manufactured is not known.

Exc.	V.G.	Good	Fair	Poor
3000	2000	1500	1000	800

1920 Carbine

11.75" barrel, 7.65mm caliber. The chamber is blank, and the extractor is marked either "Geleden" or "Loaded." The safety is not-marked. The carbine has a checkered walnut forearm and stock, and most have the "Germany" or "Made in Germany" export stamp. There were few of these carbines manufactured for commercial sales in and outside of Germany.

Exc.	V.G.	Good	Fair	Poor
9000	6000	5000	2500	1500

NOTE: With stock add 25 percent.

1920 Navy Carbine

Assembled from surplus Navy parts with the distinctive two position, sliding navy sight on the rear toggle link. Most are marked with the export stamp and have the naval military proofmarks still in evidence. The safety and extractor are marked, and rarely one is found chambered for the 9mm cartridge. Few were manufactured.

Exc.	V.G.	Good	Fair	Poor
6250	5000	3000	1800	900

1920 Swiss Commercial

3.5"-6" barrels, 7.65mm or 9mm caliber. The Swiss Cross in Sunburst is stamped over the chamber, and the extractor is marked "Geladen." The frame under the safety is polished. There were a few thousand produced, with serial numbers in the one- to five-digit range, sometimes with a letter suffix.

Exc.	V.G.	Good	Fair	Poor
4500	3000	1600	1000	800

1923 Stoeger Commercial

3.5" to 24" barrels, 7.65mm or 9mm caliber. There is a stock lug. The chamber area is either blank or has the American Eagle stamped on it. The export stamp and "A.F.Stoeger Inc. New York" is found on the right side of the receiver. The extractor and safety are marked in German or English. This was the model that Stoeger registered with the U.S. Patent office to secure the Luger name, and some examples will be so marked. There were less than 1,000 manufactured, with one- to five-digit serial numbers without a letter suffix. Individual appraisal must be secured on barrel lengths above 6". Be wary as fakes have been noted. The values given here are for the shorter barreled models.

Courtesy Gale Morgan

Exc.	V.G.	Good	Fair	Poor
5000	4000	1800	1000	700

NOTE: For barrel lengths over 8" add 25 percent.

Abercrombie & Fitch Commercial 100

Swiss Lugers were made for commercial sale in the United States by "Abercrombie & Fitch Co. New York. Made in Switzerland."—in either one or two lines—is stamped on the top of the barrel. The barrel is 4.75" in length, and there were 49 chambered for 9mm and 51 chambered for the 7.65mm cartridge. This pistol has a grip safety and no stock lug. The Swiss Cross in Sunburst is stamped over the chamber. The extractor is marked, but the safety area is polished. The serial range is four digits—some with a letter suffix. This is a rare and desirable Luger. Be careful of fakes on models of this type and rarity.

Exc.	V.G.	Good	Fair	Poor
12000	9000	5000	3000	2000

1923 Commercial

7-1/2" barrel, 7.65mm caliber. It has a stock lug, and the chamber area is blank. The extractor and safety are both marked in German. These pistols were manufactured for commercial sales in and outside of Germany. There were approximately 18,000 produced, with serial numbers in the 73500-96000 range.

Exc.	V.G.	Good	Fair	Poor
1600	1200	800	600	450

1923 Commercial Safe & Loaded

As above, except that the extractor and safety are marked in English "Safe" & "Loaded." There were approximately 7,000 manufactured in the 73500-96000 serial number range.

Courtesy Gale Morgan

Exc.	V.G.	Good	Fair	Poor
2700	1800	1000	800	500

1923 Dutch Commercial & Military

4" barrel, 9mm caliber. It has a stock lug, and the chamber area is blank. The extractor is marked in German, and the safety is marked "RUST" with a downward pointing arrow. This model was sold commercially and to the military in the Netherlands. There were approximately 1,000 manufactured in the one- to three-digit serial range, with no letter suffix.

Exc.	V.G.	Good	Fair	Poor
3500	2400	1000	850	550

Royal Dutch Air Force

4" barrel, 9mm caliber. Marked with the Mauser Oberndorf proofmark and serial numbered in the 10000 to 14000 range. The safety marked "RUST."

Exc.	V.G.	Good	Fair	Poor
4000	2500	1000	800	550

VICKERS LTD.

1906 Vickers Dutch

4" barrel, 9mm caliber. There is no stock lug, and it uses a grip safety. The chamber is blank, and the extractor is marked "Geleden." "Vickers Ltd." is stamped on the front toggle link. The safety is marked "RUST" with an upward pointing arrow. Examples have been found with an additional date as late as 1933 stamped on the barrel. These dates indicate arsenal refinishing and in no way detract from the value of this variation. Arsenal reworks are matte-finished, and the originals are a higher-polished rust blue. There were approximately 10,000 manufactured in the 1-10100 serial-number range.

Exc.	V.G.	Good	Fair	Poor
3500	2800	1800	1200	750

ERFURT ROYAL ARSENAL

1908 Erfurt

4" barrel, 9mm caliber. It has no stock lug; and the year of manufacture, from 1910-1913, is stamped above the chamber. The extractor and safety are both marked in German, and "ERFURT" under a crown is stamped on the front toggle link. There were many thousands produced as Germany was involved in WWI. They are found in the one- to five-digit serial range, sometimes with a letter suffix.

Exc.	V.G.	Good	Fair	Poor
1500	950	600	400	350

1914 Erfurt Military

4" barrel, 9mm caliber. It has a stock lug and the date of manufacture over the chamber, 1914-1918. The extractor and safety are both marked in German, and the front link is marked "ERFURT" under a crown. The finish on this model is rough; and as the war progressed in 1917 and 1918, the finish got worse. There were many thousands produced with one- to five-digit serial numbers, some with letter suffixes.

Exc.	V.G.	Good	Fair	Poor
1000	800	600	400	350

1914 Erfurt Artillery

8" barrel, 9mm caliber. It has a stock lug and was issued with a flat board-type stock and other accessories which will be covered in the section of this book dealing with same. The sight is a nine-position adjustable model. The chamber is dated 1914-1918, and the extractor and safety are both marked in German. "ERFURT" under a crown is stamped on the front toggle link. There were a great many manufactured with one- to five-digit serial numbers, some with a letter suffix. This model is similar to the DWM Artillery except that the finish is not as fine.

Exc.	V.G.	Good	Fair	Poor
2900	1700	1100	800	600

NOTE: Add 50 percent for 1914 dated chamber.

Double Date Erfurt

4" barrel, 9mm caliber. The area above the chamber has two dates: the original 1910-1918, and the date of rework, 1920 or 1921. The extractor and safety are both marked in German, and this model can be found with or without a stock lug. "ERFURT" under a crown is stamped on the front toggle link. Police or military unit markings are found on the front of the grip straps more often than not. There were thousands of these produced by DWM as well as Erfurt.

Exc.	V.G.	Good	Fair	Poor
750	600	500	400	350

WAFFENFABRIK BERN

See separate section on Bern.

SIMSON & CO. SUHL, GERMANY

Simson & Co. Rework

4" barrels, 7.65 or 9mm caliber. The chamber is blank, but some examples are dated 1917 or 1918. The forward toggle link is stamped "SIMSON & CO. Suhl." The extractor and safety are marked in German. Most examples have stock lugs; some have been noted without them. The only difference between military models and commercial models is the proofmarks.

Exc.	V.G.	Good	Fair	Poor
2000	1300	900	600	500

Simson Grip Safety Rework

4" barrel, 9mm caliber and a grip safety was added. There is a stock lug. The chamber area is blank; the extractor is marked but the safety is not. There were only a few of these commercial reworks manufactured, and caution should be taken to avoid fakes.

Exc.	V.G.	Good	Fair	Poor
3200	2200	1500	850	550

Simson Dated Military

4" barrel, 9mm caliber. There is a stock lug, and the year of manufacture from 1925-1928 is stamped above the chamber. The extractor and the safety are both marked in German. The checkered walnut grips of Simson-made Lugers are noticeably thicker than others. This is an extremely rare variation. Approximately 2,000 were manufactured with one- to three-digit serial numbers, and few seem to have survived.

Exc.	V.G.	Good	Fair	Poor
3200	2200	1800	900	650

Simson S Code

4" barrel, 9mm caliber. The forward toggle link is stamped with a Gothic S. It has a stock lug, and the area above the chamber is blank. The extractor and the safety are both marked. The grips are also thicker. There were approximately 12,000 manufactured with one- to five-digit serial numbers—some with the letter "a" suffix. This pistol is quite rare on today's market.

Exc.	V.G.	Good	Fair	Poor
4200	3000	1500	1000	750

EARLY NAZI ERA REWORKS MAUSER

Produced between 1930 and 1933, and normally marked with Waffenamt markings.

Deaths Head Rework

4" barrel, 9mm caliber. It has a stock lug; and a skull and crossbones are stamped, in addition to the date of manufacture, on the chamber area. This date was from 1914-1918. The extractor and safety are both marked. The Waffenamt proof is present. It is thought that this variation was produced for the 1930-1933 era "SS" division of the Nazi Party. Mixed serial numbers are encountered on this model and do not lower the value. This is a rare Luger on today's market, and caution should be exercised if purchase is contemplated.

Exc.	V.G.	Good	Fair	Poor
2500	1500	950	600	450

Kadetten Institute Rework

4" barrel, 9mm caliber. It has a stock lug, and the chamber area is stamped "K.I." above the date 1933. This stood for Cadets Institute, an early "SA" and "SS" officers' training school. The extractor and safety are both marked, and the Waffenamt is present. There were only a few hundred reworked, and the variation is quite scarce. Be wary of fakes.

Exc.	V.G.	Good	Fair	Poor
3200	2500	1100	800	600

Mauser Unmarked Rework

4" barrel, 9mm caliber. The entire weapon is void of identifying markings. There is extensive refurbishing, removal of all markings, rebarreling, etc. The stock lug is present, and the extractor and safety are marked. The Waffenamt proofmark is on the right side of the receiver. The number manufactured is not known.

Exc.	V.G.	Good	Fair	Poor
1450	1000	850	600	450

MAUSER MANUFACTURED LUGERS 1930-1942 DWM

Mauser Oberndorf

4" barrel, 9mm caliber. It has a stock lug, blank chamber area and a marked extractor and safety. This is an early example of

This symbol denotes "Sleepers" with rapidly-rising values and/or significant collector potential.

Mauser Luger, and the front toggle link is still marked DWM as leftover parts were intermixed with new Mauser parts in the production of this pistol. This is one of the first Lugers to be finished with the "Salt" blue process. There were approximately 500 manufactured with one- to four-digit serial numbers with the letter "v" suffix. This is a rare variation.

Exc.	V.G.	Good	Fair	Poor
5000	3200	2000	1500	900

1934/06 Swiss Commercial Mauser

4.75" barrel, 7.65mm caliber. There is no stock lug, but it has a grip safety. The Swiss Cross in Sunburst is stamped above the chamber. The extractor and safety are marked in German. The front toggle link is marked with the Mauser banner. There were approximately 200 manufactured for commercial sale in Switzerland. This variation is very well finished, and the serial numbers are all four digits with a "v" suffix.

Exc.	V.G.	Good	Fair	Poor
7500	5500	4000	1800	1000

1935/06 Portuguese "GNR"

4.75" barrel, 7.65mm caliber. It has no stock lug but has a grip safety. The chamber is marked "GNR," representing the Republic National Guard. The extractor is marked "Carregada"; and the safety, "Seguranca." The Mauser banner is stamped on the front toggle link. There were exactly 564 manufactured according to the original contract records that the Portuguese government made public. They all have four-digit serial numbers with a "v" suffix.

Exc.	V.G.	Good	Fair	Poor
4000	2800	1800	900	750

1934 Mauser Commercial

4" barrel, 7.65mm or 9mm caliber. It has a stock lug, and the chamber area is blank. The extractor and the safety are marked. The Mauser banner is stamped on the front toggle link. The finish on this pistol was very good, and the grips are either checkered walnut or black plastic on the later models. There were a few thousand manufactured for commercial sales in and outside of Germany.

Exc.	V.G.	Good	Fair	Poor
3500	3000	1650	1100	700

S/42 K Date

4" barrel, 9mm caliber. It has a stock lug, and the extractor and safety are marked. This was the first Luger that utilized codes to represent maker and date of manufacture. The front toggle link is marked S/42 in either Gothic or script; this was the code for Mauser. The chamber area is stamped with the letter "K," the code for 1934, the year of manufacture. Approximately 10,500 were manufactured with one- to five-digit serial numbers—some with letter suffixes.

Exc.	V.G.	Good	Fair	Poor
7500	5000	2200	1200	1000

S/42 G Date

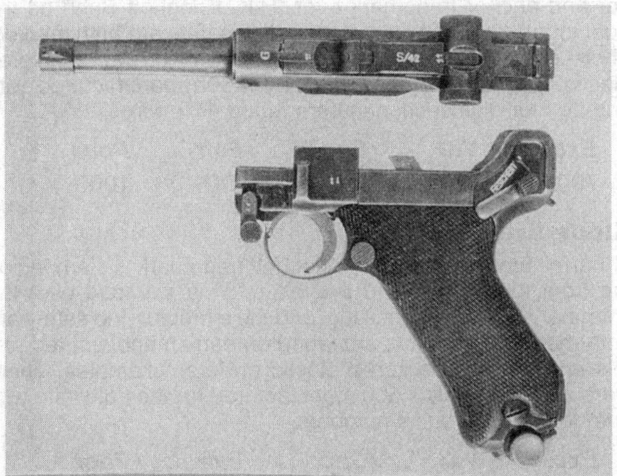

Courtesy Orvel Reichert

As above, with the chamber stamped "G," the code for the year 1935. The Gothic lettering was eliminated, and there were many thousands of this model produced.

Exc.	V.G.	Good	Fair	Poor
2800	2000	1000	650	450

Dated Chamber S/42

4" barrel, 9mm caliber. The chamber area is dated 1936-1940, and there is a stock lug. The extractor and safety are marked. In 1937 the rust blue process was eliminated entirely, and all subsequent pistols were salt blued. There were many thousands manufactured with one- to five-digit serial numbers—some with the letter suffix.

Exc.	V.G.	Good	Fair	Poor
1600	1100	750	500	400

NOTE: Rarest variation is early 1937 with rust blued and strawed parts, add 20 percent.

S/42 Commercial Contract

4" barrel, 9mm caliber. It has a stock lug, and the chamber area is dated. It has a marked extractor and safety. The unusual feature is that, although this was a commercial pistol, the front toggle link is stamped S/42, which was the military code for Mauser. There were only a few hundred manufactured, so perhaps the toggles were left over from previous military production runs. The serial number range is four digits with the letter "v."

Exc.	V.G.	Good	Fair	Poor
2800	2000	1000	750	450

Code 42 Dated Chamber

4" barrel, 9mm caliber. The new German code for Mauser, the number 42, is stamped on the front toggle link. There is a stock lug. The chamber area is dated 1939 or 1940. There were at least 50,000 manufactured with one- to five-digit serial numbers; some have letter suffixes.

Exc.	V.G.	Good	Fair	Poor
1500	850	650	400	350

41/42 Code

As above, except that the date of manufacture is represented by the final two digits (e.g. 41 for 1941). There were approximately 20,000 manufactured with the one- to five-digit serial number range.

Exc.	V.G.	Good	Fair	Poor
1600	1350	900	700	500

byf Code

As above, with the "byf" code stamp on the toggle link. The year of manufacture, either 41 or 42, is stamped on the chamber. This model was also made with black plastic, as well as walnut grips. There were many thousands produced with the one- to five-digit serial numbers—some with a letter suffix.

Exc.	V.G.	Good	Fair	Poor
1500	950	750	450	350

Persian Contract 4"

4" barrel, 9mm caliber. It has a stock lug, and the Persian crest is stamped over the chamber. All identifying markings on this variation—including extractor, safety and toggle—are marked in Farsi, the Persian alphabet. There were 1,000 manufactured. The serial numbers are also in Farsi.

Exc.	V.G.	Good	Fair	Poor
6500	5000	3500	2500	2000

Persian Contract Artillery

As above, with an 8" barrel and nine-position adjustable sight on the barrel. This model is supplied with a flat board stock. There were 1,000 manufactured and sold to Persia.

Exc.	V.G.	Good	Fair	Poor
5500	3000	1800	1300	1000

1934/06 Dated Commercial

4.75" barrel, 7.65mm caliber. It has a grip safety but no stock lug. The year of manufacture, from 1937-1942, is stamped above the chamber, and the Mauser banner is stamped on the front link. The extractor is marked, but the safety is not. There were approximately 1,000 manufactured with one- to three-digit serial numbers—some with the letter suffix.

Exc.	V.G.	Good	Fair	Poor
3000	2200	1400	900	500

1934 Mauser Dutch Contract

4" barrel, 9mm caliber. The year of manufacture, 1936-1940, is stamped above the chamber. The extractor is marked "Geladen," and the safety is marked "RUST" with a downward pointing arrow. The Mauser banner is stamped on the front toggle link. This was a military contract sale, and approximately 1,000 were manufactured with four-digit serial numbers with a letter "v" suffix.

Exc.	V.G.	Good	Fair	Poor
3500	3000	2000	1100	850

1934 Mauser Swedish Contract

4.75" barrel, 9mm or 7.65mm caliber. The chamber is dated 1938 or 1939. The extractor and safety are both marked in German, and there is a stock lug. The front toggle link is stamped with the Mauser banner. There were only 275 dated 1938 and 25 dated 1939 in 9mm. There were only 30 chambered for 7.65mm dated 1939. The serial number range is four digits with the letter "v" suffix.

Exc.	V.G.	Good	Fair	Poor
4300	3000	2000	1500	700

1934 Mauser Swedish Commercial

4" barrel, 7.65mm caliber. 1940 is stamped over the chamber; "Kal. 7.65" is stamped on the left side of the barrel. The extractor and safety are both marked, and the Mauser banner is stamped on the front toggle link. There is a stock lug. This model is rare as there were only a few hundred manufactured with four digit serial numbers with the letter "w" suffix.

Exc.	V.G.	Good	Fair	Poor
3000	2000	1200	850	600

1934 Mauser German Contract

4" barrel, 9mm caliber. The chamber is dated 1939-1942, and the front toggle link is stamped with the Mauser banner. There is a stock lug, and the extractor and safety are both marked. The grips are either walnut or black plastic. There were several thousand manufactured with one- to five-digit serial numbers—some with letter suffixes. They were purchased for issue to police or paramilitary units.

Exc.	V.G.	Good	Fair	Poor
2800	2300	1500	800	550

Austrian Bundes Heer (Federal Army)

4" barrel, 9mm caliber. The chamber is blank, and there is a stock lug. The extractor and safety are marked in German, and the Austrian Federal Army Proof is stamped on the left side of the frame above the trigger guard. There were approximately 200 manufactured with four-digit serial numbers and no letter suffix.

Exc.	V.G.	Good	Fair	Poor
2500	1850	1200	700	500

Mauser 2 Digit Date

4" barrel, 9mm caliber. The last two digits of the year of manufacture—41 or 42—are stamped over the chamber. There is a stock lug, and the Mauser banner is on the front toggle link. The extractor and safety are both marked, and the proofmarks were commercial. Grips are either walnut or black plastic. There were approximately 2,000 manufactured for sale to Nazi political groups. They have one- to five-digit serial numbers; some have the letter suffix.

Exc.	V.G.	Good	Fair	Poor
2800	2200	1500	900	650

Ku Luger (Prefix or suffix)

A 4" barrel, 9mm Luger probably manufactured by Mauser for the German Luftwaffe in the early 1940s. The serial number (on the left side receiver area) has a "Ku" prefix or suffix. Total production is estimated at 5000 pieces.

Courtesy Gale Morgan

Exc.	V.G.	Good	Fair	Poor
3000	1800	1200	900	550

KRIEGHOFF MANUFACTURED LUGERS

1923 DWM/Krieghoff Commercial

4" barrel, 7.65mm or 9mm caliber. The chamber is dated 1921 or left blank. There is a stock lug. The front toggle is marked DWM, as they manufactured this Luger to be sold by Krieghoff. "Krieghoff Suhl" is stamped on the back above the lanyard loop. The second "F" in Krieghoff was defective, and all specimens have this distinctive die strike. The safety and extractor are marked in German. There were only a few hundred manufactured with four-digit serial numbers with the letter "i" suffix.

Exc.	V.G.	Good	Fair	Poor
3000	2000	950	650	500

DWM/Krieghoff Commercial

As above, but marked "Heinrich Krieghoff Waffenfabrik Suhl" on the right side of the frame. Some examples have the "Germany" export stamp. There were several hundred manufactured with four-digit serial numbers with a letter suffix.

Exc.	V.G.	Good	Fair	Poor
3500	2850	2000	950	800

Krieghoff Commercial Inscribed Side Frame

4" or 6" barrel, 7.65mm or 9mm caliber. 1,000 were marked "Heinrich Krieghoff Waffenfabrik Suhl" on the right side of the frame, and 500 were devoid of this marking. All have the dagger and anchor trademark over "H.K. Krieghoff Suhl" on the front toggle link. The extractor and the safety are both marked. There is a stock lug, and the grips are of brown checkered plastic. There were approximately 1,500 manufactured with one- to four-digit serial numbers with a "P" prefix.

Exc.	V.G.	Good	Fair	Poor
7000	5000	3000	2000	1000

S Code Krieghoff

4" barrel, 9mm caliber. The Krieghoff trademark is stamped on the front toggle link, and the letter "S" is stamped over the chamber. There is a stock lug, and the extractor and safety are both marked. The grips are wood on early manufactured pistols and brown checkered plastic on later examples. There were approximately 4,500 manufactured for the Luftwaffe with one- to four-digit serial numbers.

Exc.	V.G.	Good	Fair	Poor
6000	4300	2000	950	750

A Commercial Krieghoff Luger in 9mm sold at auction for $10,925. Matching numbers. Condition is 99 percent blue, 92 percent straw colors and excellent grips.
Rock Island Auction Company

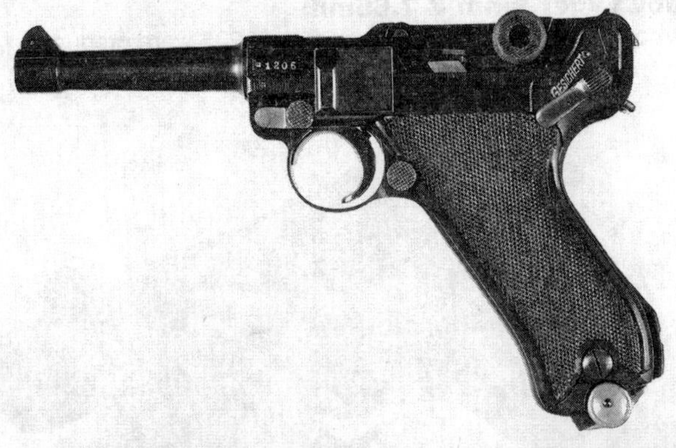

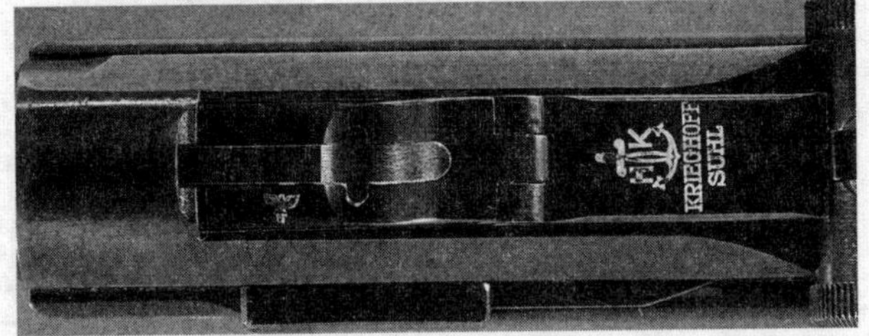

Grip Safety Krieghoff

4" barrel, 9mm caliber. The chamber area is blank, and the front toggle link is stamped with the Krieghoff trademark. There is a stock lug and a grip safety. The extractor is marked "Geleden," and the safety is marked "FEUER" (fire) in the lower position. The grips are checkered brown plastic. This is a rare Luger, and the number produced is not known.

Exc.	V.G.	Good	Fair	Poor
6500	4000	2800	1400	900

36 Date Krieghoff

4" barrel, 9mm caliber. It has a stock lug and the Krieghoff trademark on the front toggle link. The safety and extractor are marked, and the grips are brown plastic. The two-digit year of manufacture, 36, is stamped over the chamber. There were approximately 700 produced in the 3800-4500 serial number range.

Exc.	V.G.	Good	Fair	Poor
4500	3850	2200	1200	950

4 Digit Dated Krieghoff

As above, with the date of production, 1936-1945, stamped above the chamber. There were approximately 9,000 manufactured within the 4500-14000 serial number range.

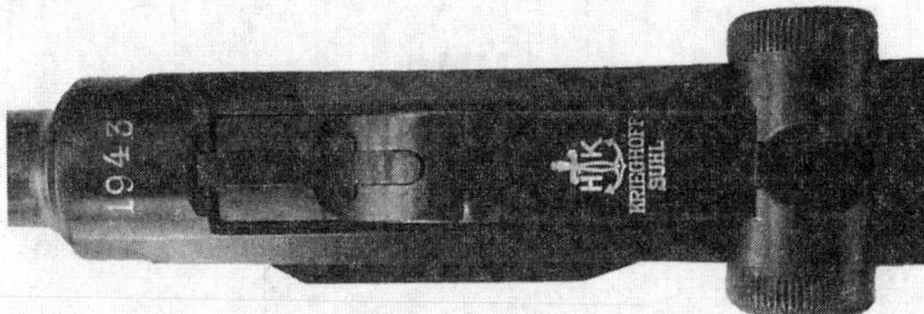

Courtesy Gale Morgan

Exc.	V.G.	Good	Fair	Poor
4000	3000	1850	950	750

NOTE: Later years add 20-35 percent premium.

2nd Series Krieghoff Commercial

4" barrel, 9mm caliber. There is a stock lug, and the Krieghoff trademark is stamped on the front link. The chamber area is blank, and the extractor and safety are marked. There were approximately 500 manufactured for commercial sales inside Germany. The date of manufacture is estimated at 1939-1940, as this variation has the dark finish that results from blueing without polishing the surface, which was done during these years. The grips are coarsely checkered black plastic. The serial number range is one to three digits with a "P" prefix.

Exc.	V.G.	Good	Fair	Poor
4300	3000	2000	1300	800

Post-war Krieghoff

4" barrel, 9mm caliber. There is a stock lug, and the chamber area is blank. The extractor and safety are marked, and the serial numbers in the one- to three-digit range are unusually large—about 3/16ths of an inch. There were 300 of these post-war Lugers produced for the occupation forces. They were assembled from leftover parts, and only 150 have the Krieghoff trademark on the front toggle link—the second 150 have blank links.

Exc.	V.G.	Good	Fair	Poor
3500	2000	1000	750	650

Krieghoff Post-war Commercial

As above, in 7.65mm caliber and the extractor not marked. Approximately 200 manufactured with standard-sized two- or three-digit serial numbers. They were supposedly sold to the occupation forces in the PX stores.

Exc.	V.G.	Good	Fair	Poor
3000	2000	1000	700	550

LUGER ACCESSORIES

Detachable Carbine Stocks

Approximately 13" in length, with a sling swivel and horn buttplate.

Exc.	V.G.	Good	Fair	Poor
4500	3500	1500	700	500

Artillery Stock with Holster

The artillery stock is of a flat board style approximately 13.75" in length. There is a holster and magazine pouches with straps attached. This is a desirable addition to the Artillery Luger.

Exc.	V.G.	Good	Fair	Poor
1500	1000	500	400	300

Navy Stock without Holster

As above, but 12.75" in length with a metal disc inlaid on the left side.

Exc.	V.G.	Good	Fair	Poor
3700	2000	1000	500	400

NOTE: With holster add 100 percent.

Ideal Stock/Holster with Grips

A telescoping metal tube stock with an attached leather holster. It is used in conjunction with a metal-backed set of plain grips that correspond to the metal hooks on the stock and allow attachment. This Ideal Stock is U.S. patented and is so marked.

Exc.	V.G.	Good	Fair	Poor
2000	1400	1000	700	450

Drum Magazine 1st Issue

A 32-round, snail-like affair that is used with the Artillery Luger. It is also used with an adapter in the German 9mm submachine gun. The 1st Issue has a telescoping tube that is used to wind the spring. There is a dust cover that protects the interior from dirt.

Exc.	V.G.	Good	Fair	Poor
1500	800	600	350	300

Drum Magazine 2nd Issue

As above, with a folding spring winding lever.

Exc.	V.G.	Good	Fair	Poor
1300	700	500	350	300

Drum Magazine Loading Tool

This tool is slipped over the magazine and allows the spring to be compressed so that cartridges could be inserted.

Exc.	V.G.	Good	Fair	Poor
800	550	500	300	200

Drum Magazine Unloading Tool

The origin of this tool is unknown and caution should be exercised prior to purchase.

Drum Carrying Case

The same caveat as above applies.

Exc.	V.G.	Good	Fair	Poor
250	200	125	100	50

Holsters

Produced in a wide variety of styles.

Exc.	V.G.	Good	Fair	Poor
450	300	150	60	50

LATE PRODUCTION MAUSER LUGERS MANUFACTURED DURING THE 1970S

P.08 Interarms

4" or 6" barrel, 7.65mm or 9mm caliber.

NIB	Exc.	V.G.	Good	Fair	Poor
1200	750	500	400	350	300

Swiss Eagle Interarms

Swiss-style straight front grip strap and the American Eagle crest over the chamber. It is chambered for 7.65mm or 9mm and is offered with a 4" or 6" barrel.

NIB	Exc.	V.G.	Good	Fair	Poor
700	550	450	350	325	300

Cartridge Counter

Chambered for 9mm cartridge and fitted with a slotted grip to show cartridge count in magazine.

NIB	Exc.	V.G.	Good	Fair	Poor
2000	1600	—	—	—	—

Commemorative Bulgarian

The Bulgarian crest is stamped over the chamber. There were only 100 produced.

NIB	Exc.	V.G.	Good	Fair	Poor
2000	1600	—	—	—	—

Commemorative Russian

Crossed Nagant rifles are stamped over the chamber. There were 100 produced.

NIB	Exc.	V.G.	Good	Fair	Poor
2000	1600	—	—	—	—

Modern Production Carbine

This splendid reproduction was produced on a limited basis. The workmanship is excellent, and the carbine and stock are furnished in a case.

NIB	Exc.	V.G.	Good	Fair	Poor
6000	4500	4000	3200	2500	2000

JOHN MARTZ CUSTOM LUGERS

Martz Luger Carbine

16" barrel. Approximately 88 were manufactured.

Mint	Exc.	V.G	Good	Fair	Poor
8700	7000	4500	—	—	—

.45 ACP

6" barrel, .45 ACP caliber. Assembled from two Luger pistols that were split and welded together. 85 manufactured.

Mint	Exc.	V.G.	Good	Fair	Poor
5500	4000	3000	—	—	—

Baby Luger 9mm & 7.65mm

A compact Luger pistol. Approximately 205 were produced.

Courtesy Gale Morgan

Mint	Exc.	V.G.	Good	Fair	Poor
3500	2500	1500	1000	—	—

Baby Luger .380 ACP

As above, in .380 caliber. Approximately 7 were manufactured.

Courtesy Gale Morgan

Mint	Exc.	V.G.	Good	Fair	Poor
7000	6000	4000	—	—	—

LUNA

Zella-Mehlis, Germany

Model 200 Free Pistol

A .22 caliber Martini action single-shot pistol with an 11" barrel, adjustable sights, and walnut grips. Manufactured prior to WWII.

Exc.	V.G.	Good	Fair	Poor
1150	850	700	500	300

Model 300 Free Pistol

This model is a single-shot target pistol chambered for .22 Short cartridge. Fitted with an 11" barrel, set trigger, walnut stocks and forearm with adjustable palm rest. Built from about 1929 to 1939

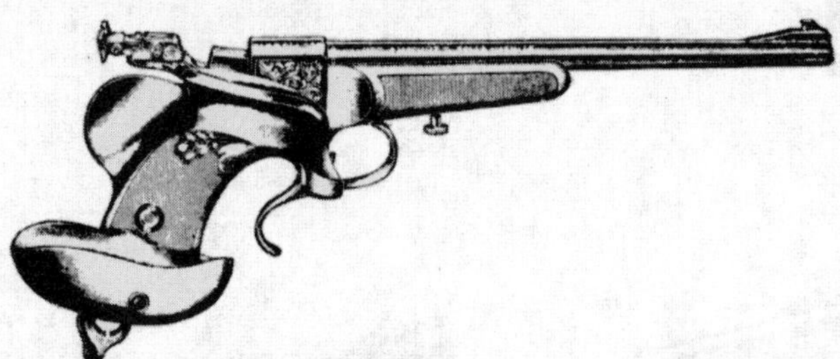

Exc.	V.G.	Good	Fair	Poor
950	750	650	400	300

Target Rifle

A .22 or .22 Hornet caliber Martini action single-shot rifle with a 20" barrel, adjustable sights, and walnut stock. Manufactured prior to WWII.

Exc.	V.G.	Good	Fair	Poor
1000	850	650	500	250

LYMAN

Middletown, Connecticut

Lyman In-Line

Introduced in 1998 this in-line muzzleloader is offered in either .50 or .54 caliber. Fitted with a 22" barrel. Hardwood stock. Add $80 for stainless steel version.

NIB	Exc.	V.G.	Good	Fair	Poor
300	250	200	—	—	—

Deerstalker Rifle

Available in either .50 or .54 caliber percussion or flintlock. Fitted with a 24" barrel and hardwood stock. A stainless steel version is also offered for an additional $80.

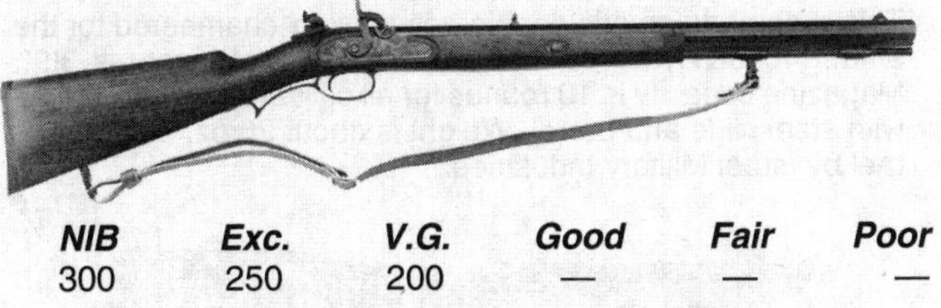

NIB	Exc.	V.G.	Good	Fair	Poor
300	250	200	—	—	—

Deerstalker Carbine

Same as above but with 21" barrel. Offered in .50 caliber only.

NIB	Exc.	V.G.	Good	Fair	Poor
325	275	225	—	—	—

Great Plains Rifle

This rifle is offered in .50 or .54 caliber flint or percussion. Barrel length is 32". Hardwood stock.

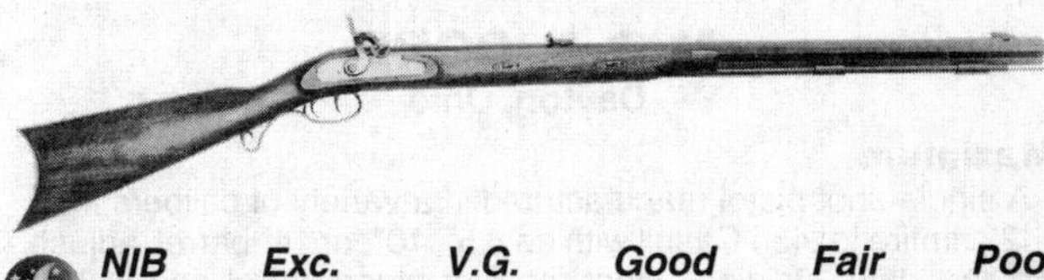

NIB	Exc.	V.G.	Good	Fair	Poor
425	350	300	—	—	—

NOTE: Add $25 for flintlock version and $10 for left-hand rifles. Early models in Excellent condition are showing significant collector potential.

Trade Rifle

This rifle is offered in either .50 or .54 caliber with 28" octagonal barrel and hardwood stock. Polished brass furniture. Add $25 for flintlock rifle.

NIB	Exc.	V.G.	Good	Fair	Poor
300	250	200	—	—	—

Plains Pistol

Available in .50 or .54 caliber percussion.

NIB	Exc.	V.G.	Good	Fair	Poor
225	175	150	—	—	—

M.O.A. CORP.
Dayton, Ohio

Maximum

A single-shot pistol manufactured in a variety of calibers from .22 rimfire to .454 Casull with an 8.5", 10", or 14" barrel, adjustable sights, stainless steel receiver blued barrel and walnut grip. Introduced in 1986.

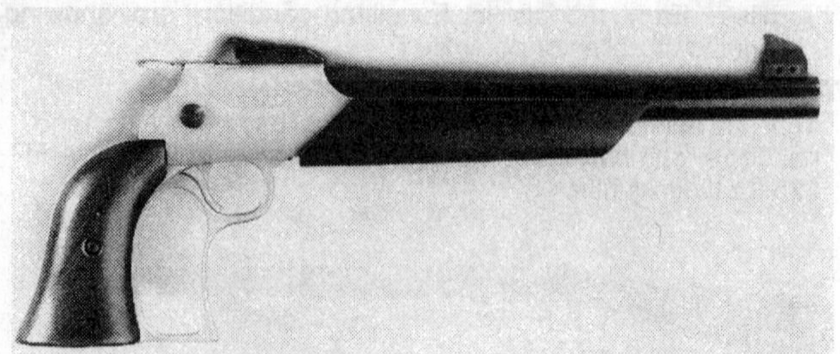

NIB	Exc.	V.G.	Good	Fair	Poor
800	600	475	325	250	—

NOTE: Add 100 percent for stainless steel barrel.

Carbine

As above with an 18" barrel. Discontinued.

NIB	Exc.	V.G.	Good	Fair	Poor
1000	675	525	350	275	—

MAB
SEE—Bayonne

MAC
SEE—Ingram

MAS
St. Etienne, France
Manufacture d'Armes de St. Etienne

NOTE: For history, technical data, descriptions, and prices see the *Standard Catalog of Military Firearms* under France.

MACNAUGHTON & SON
Edinburg, Scotland; Carrizo Springs, Texas
SEE—British Double Guns

MADSEN
Copenhagen, Denmark

Model 47

Exc.	V.G.	Good	Fair	Poor
500	425	300	—	—

NOTE: Add $75 for rifles with numbered matching bayonet.

MAGNUM RESEARCH, INC.
SEE ALSO—Desert Eagle

BFR (Long Cylinder)

This is a single-action revolver with a long cylinder chambered for .22 Hrnet, .30-30, .475/.480, .444, .45-70, .460 S&W, and .45 LC/.410 with 7.5" or 10" barrel and .444 Marlin with 10" barrel. Fitted with adjustable sights and stainless steel finish. Weight is about 4 lbs. with 7.5" barrel. Introduced in 1998.

NIB	Exc.	V.G.	Good	Fair	Poor
800	675	500	—	—	—

BFR Little Max (Short Cylinder)

This single-action revolver has a standard cylinder chambered for the .454 Casull (6.5", 7.5", or 10" barrel), .45 Long Colt (6.5" or 7.5" barrel), .22 Hornet (7.5" barrel), or .50 A.E (7.5" barrel). Weight is about 3.5 lbs. with 7.5" barrel. Introduced in 1998. Discontinued.

NIB	Exc.	V.G.	Good	Fair	Poor
800	675	500	—	—	—

IMI SP-21

This is semi-automatic double-action pistol chambered for the 9mm, .40 S&W, or .45 ACP cartridge. Barrel length is 3.9". Magazine capacity is 10 rounds for all calibers. Polymer frame with steel slide and barrel. Weight is about 26 oz. Made in Israel by Israel Military Industries.

Flashlight not included

NIB	Exc.	V.G.	Good	Fair	Poor
500	400	—	—	—	—

MAKAROV
Former Soviet Union, Warsaw Pact Nations, and China

NOTE: For history, technical data, descriptions, and prices see the *Standard Catalog of Military Firearms*under Russia.

MALIN, F. E.

London, England

Boxlock and sidelock shotguns made by Malin were imported into the United States for a number of years. As these arms were all essentially built to specific customer's requirements, standard values cannot be provided. Prospective purchasers are advised to secure a qualified appraisal prior to acquisition.

Boxlock

Features an Anson & Deeley action and high-grade walnut. All other specification were on a custom-order basis. This gun should definitely be individually appraised as values will fluctuate greatly with options.

Basic Model

NIB	Exc.	V.G.	Good	Fair	Poor
4000	3500	3000	2500	1850	1000

NOTE: Estimated value only.

Sidelock

Features a Holland & Holland-type detachable sidelock action, and all other features (as on the boxlock) were on a custom-order basis. This model should also be appraised individually.

Basic Model

NIB	Exc.	V.G.	Good	Fair	Poor
5500	5000	4250	3000	2500	1250

NOTE: Estimated value only.

MALTBY, HENLEY AND CO.

New York, New York

Spencer Safety Hammerless Revolver

A .32 caliber double-action revolver with a 3" barrel and 5-shot cylinder. The frame and barrel made of brass and the cylinder of steel. The barrel marked "Spencer Safety Hammerless Pat. Jan. 24, 1888 & Oct. 29, 1889." Several thousand were manufactured during in the 1890s.

Courtesy Mike Stuckslager

Exc.	V.G.	Good	Fair	Poor
—	500	225	125	75

MANHATTAN FIREARMS COMPANY

Norwich, Connecticut
Newark, New Jersey

Bar Hammer Pistol

A .31, .34, or .36 caliber single-shot percussion pistol with a 2" or 4" barrel. The hammer marked "Manhattan F.A. Mfg. Co. New York." Blued with walnut grips. Approximately 1,500 were made during the 1850s.

Exc.	V.G.	Good	Fair	Poor
—	—	550	250	150

Shotgun Hammer Pistol

A .36 caliber bar hammer single-shot percussion pistol with a 5.5" half octagonal barrel marked as above. Blued with walnut grips. Approximately 500 were made.

Exc.	V.G.	Good	Fair	Poor
—	—	600	250	150

Pepperbox

A .28 or .31 caliber double-action percussion pepperbox with 3", 4", or 5" barrels and 5- or 6-shot barrel groups. Blued, case hardened with walnut grips. Marked as above and also "Cast Steel." The major variations of this pistol are as follows:

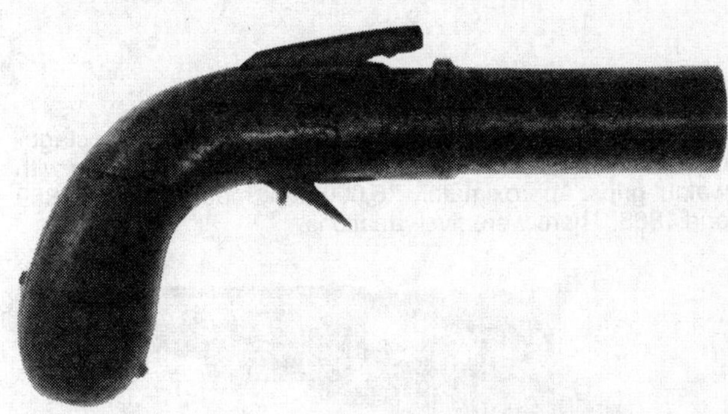

Courtesy Milwaukee Public Museum, Milwaukee, Wisconsin

Three-shot with 3" Barrel

Manually rotated barrels.

Exc.	V.G.	Good	Fair	Poor
—	—	850	450	250

Five-shot with 3", 4", 5" Barrel

Automatically rotated barrels.

Exc.	V.G.	Good	Fair	Poor
—	—	850	450	250

Six-shot with 3" or 4" Barrel

Automatic rotation.

Exc.	V.G.	Good	Fair	Poor
—	—	850	450	250

Six-shot with 5" Barrel

Automatic rotation.

Exc.	V.G.	Good	Fair	Poor
—	—	1200	550	350

Pocket Revolver

A .31 caliber percussion revolver with a 4", 5", or 6" barrel and either 5-shot or 6-shot cylinder. Blued, case hardened with walnut grips. The barrel marked, "Manhattan Firearms/Manufg. Co. New York" on the 5-shot model, serial numbers from 1 to approximately 1,000, and "Manhattan Firearms Mfg. Co. New York" on the 6-shot model. The frame marked "December 27, 1859."

Courtesy Milwaukee Public Museum, Milwaukee, Wisconsin

First Model—Five-Shot

Exc.	V.G.	Good	Fair	Poor
—	—	900	400	150

Second Model—Six-Shot

Exc.	V.G.	Good	Fair	Poor
—	—	900	400	150

London Pistol Company

As above, but marked "London Pistol Company." Approximately 200 manufactured between 1859 and 1861.

Exc.	V.G.	Good	Fair	Poor
—	—	1150	450	150

.36 Caliber Percussion Revolver

A .36 caliber percussion revolver with a 4", 5", or 6.5" octagonal barrel and 5- or 6-shot cylinder. Blued, case hardened with walnut grips. Approximately 78,000 were made between 1859 and 1868. There were five variations.

Courtesy Milwaukee Public Museum, Milwaukee, Wisconsin

Model I

A 5-shot cylinder marked "Manhattan Firearms Mfg. Co. New York." The serial numbers from 1 through 4200.

Exc.	V.G.	Good	Fair	Poor
—	—	1250	500	250

NOTE: The 6" barreled version would be worth a 15 percent premium.

Model II

As above with the 1859 patent date marked on the barrel. The serial range is 4200 to 14500.

Exc.	V.G.	Good	Fair	Poor
—	—	1200	500	200

Model III

A 5-shot cylinder and marked, "Manhattan Firearms Co. Newark NJ," together with the 1859 patent date. The serial numbers are from 14500 to 45200.

Exc.	V.G.	Good	Fair	Poor
—	—	1100	400	150

Model IV

As above, with a modified recoil shield and the patent date March 8, 1864, added to the barrel inscription. Serial numbers from 45200 to 69200.

Exc.	V.G.	Good	Fair	Poor
—	—	1100	400	150

Model V

As above, with a 6-shot cylinder and numbered 1 to approximately 9000.

Exc.	V.G.	Good	Fair	Poor
—	—	1200	500	200

.22 Caliber Pocket Revolver

A .22 caliber spur trigger revolver with a 3" barrel and 7-shot cylinder. Blued, silver plated with walnut or rosewood grips. Approximately 17,000 were made during the 1860s.

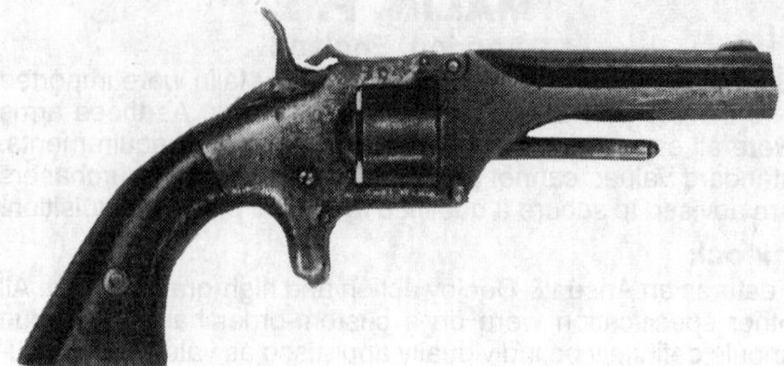

Courtesy Milwaukee Public Museum, Milwaukee, Wisconsin

Exc.	V.G.	Good	Fair	Poor
—	—	550	250	100

Manhattan-American Standard Hero

A .34 caliber single-shot percussion pistol with a 2" or 3" round barrel that unscrews for loading. Blued, brass frame with walnut grips. Marked "A.S.T. Co./HERO." Made by the American Standard Tool Company, Manhattan's successor. Approximately 30,000 manufactured between 1868 and 1873.

Manhattan Manufactured

Marked, "HERO/M.F.A.Co." Approximately 5,000 were produced.

Exc.	V.G.	Good	Fair	Poor
—	—	550	250	100

American Standard Manufactured

Approximately 25,000 were produced.

Exc.	V.G.	Good	Fair	Poor
—	—	500	225	100

MANN, FRITZ

Suhl, Germany

6.35mm Pocket Pistol

A 6.35mm caliber semi-automatic pistol with a 1.65" barrel and 5-shot magazine. Blued with plastic grips having the name "Mann" cast in them. This pistol, which weighs only 9 oz., is one of the smallest semi-automatic pistols ever manufactured. Made between 1920 and 1922.

Exc.	V.G.	Good	Fair	Poor
395	295	200	150	100

7.65mm Pocket Pistol

A 7.65mm or 9mm short semi-automatic pistol with a 2.35" barrel and 5-shot magazine. Blued with plastic grips that have the name "Mann" cast in them. Manufactured between 1924 and 1929.

Exc.	V.G.	Good	Fair	Poor
375	275	200	150	100

MANNLICHER PISTOL

Steyr, Austria

SEE—Steyr

MANNLICHER SCHOENAUER

Steyr, Austria

NOTE: For military models and their history, technical data, descriptions, and prices see the *Standard Catalog of Military Firearms* under Austria-Hungary. For currently imported Mannlicher models, see Steyr.

Model 1903 Carbine

A 6.5x54mm caliber bolt-action rifle with a 17.7" barrel. Rotary magazine capacity is 5 rounds. Folding rear leaf sight, double set triggers, and full-length walnut stock. Discontinued prior to WWII.

Exc.	V.G.	Good	Fair	Poor
1500	1200	1000	750	550

Model 1905 Carbine

As above but chambered for the 9x56mm cartridge. Discontinued prior to WWII.

Exc.	V.G.	Good	Fair	Poor
1500	1200	1000	750	550

Model 1908 Carbine

As above but chambered for the 7x57mm or 8x56mm cartridge. Discontinued prior to WWII.

Exc.	V.G.	Good	Fair	Poor
1500	1200	1000	750	550

Model 1910 Carbine

As above but chambered for the 9.5x57mm cartridge. Discontinued prior to WWII.

Exc.	V.G.	Good	Fair	Poor
1300	1050	900	700	500

Model 1924 Carbine

As above but chambered for the .30-06 cartridge. Discontinued prior to WWII.

Exc.	V.G.	Good	Fair	Poor
2750	2250	1750	1000	550

High Velocity Rifle

As above, but in 7x64mm Brenneke, .30-06, 8x60Smm Magnum, 9.3x62mm, and the 10.75x68mm caliber with a 23.5" barrel and folding leaf sight. Half-length walnut stock. Discontinued prior to WWII.

Exc.	V.G.	Good	Fair	Poor
2750	2250	1750	1000	550

NOTE: Takedown Model add 75 percent.

Model 1950

A .257 Roberts, .270 Winchester, and the .30-06 caliber bolt-action rifle with a 24" barrel and 5-shot rotary magazine. Blued with a half length walnut stock. Manufactured between 1950 and 1952.

Exc.	V.G.	Good	Fair	Poor
1250	1000	800	650	450

Model 1950 Carbine

As above, with a 20" barrel and a full-length stock.

Exc.	V.G.	Good	Fair	Poor
1300	1050	900	700	350

Model 1950 6.5 Carbine

As above, in 6.5x54mm Mannlicher Schoenauer caliber with a 18.5" barrel and full-length stock.

Exc.	V.G.	Good	Fair	Poor
1500	1100	850	650	300

Model 1952

Similar to the above, with a turned back bold handle. Manufactured between 1952 and 1956.

Exc.	V.G.	Good	Fair	Poor
1500	1200	1000	750	600

Model 1952 Carbine

Similar to the Model 1950 carbine, but additionally in 7x57mm caliber. Manufactured between 1952 and 1956.

Exc.	V.G.	Good	Fair	Poor
1500	1200	1000	750	600

Model 1952 6.5mm Carbine

As above, in 6.5x54mm Mannlicher Schoenauer caliber with an 18.5" barrel. Manufactured between 1952 and 1956.

Exc.	V.G.	Good	Fair	Poor
1500	1100	850	650	300

Model 1956 Rifle

A .243 or .30-06 caliber bolt-action rifle with a 22" barrel and Monte Carlo-style stock. Manufactured between 1956 and 1960.

Exc.	V.G.	Good	Fair	Poor
1250	1100	900	700	600

Model 1956 Carbine

As above, with a 20" barrel and full-length stock. Manufactured between 1956 and 1960.

Exc.	V.G.	Good	Fair	Poor
1450	1100	900	700	600

Model 1961 MCA Rifle

As above, but modified for easier use with a telescopic sight.

Exc.	V.G.	Good	Fair	Poor
1350	1200	1000	800	650

Model 1961 MCA Carbine

As above, with a 20" barrel and half-length stock.

Exc.	V.G.	Good	Fair	Poor
1450	1250	1100	700	600

Model M72 LM Rifle

Fitted with a 23" fluted barrel, double set or single trigger and full-length stock. Manufactured between 1972 and 1980.

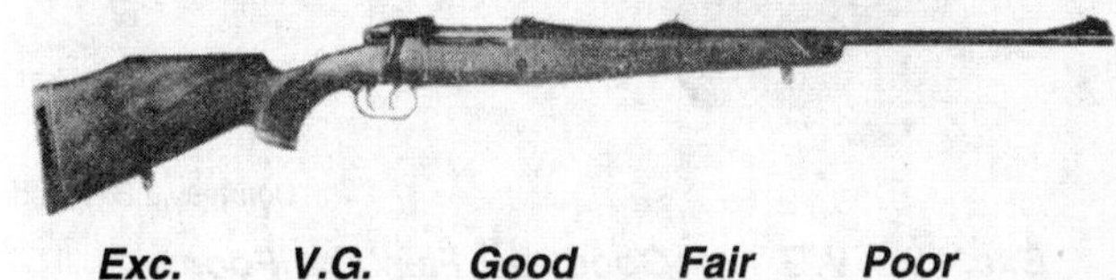

Exc.	V.G.	Good	Fair	Poor
1150	950	700	550	450

MANUFRANCE

St. Etienne, France

SEE—Le Francais

Auto Stand

A .22 caliber semi-automatic pistol manufactured by Pyrenees and sold by Manufrance under the trade name Auto Stand.

Exc.	V.G.	Good	Fair	Poor
250	225	200	150	100

Buffalo Stand

A .22 caliber bolt-action pistol with a 12" barrel and adjustable sights. Blued with a walnut stock. Manufactured prior to 1914.

Exc.	V.G.	Good	Fair	Poor
250	225	200	150	100

Le Agent

An 8mm caliber double-action revolver with a 5" barrel. Blued with walnut grips.

Exc.	V.G.	Good	Fair	Poor
200	100	175	150	75

Le Colonial

As above, with an enclosed hammer.

Exc.	V.G.	Good	Fair	Poor
200	175	150	100	75

LeFrancais

A semi-automatic pistol chambered for the 7.65mm cartridge. Built on the blowback design. The 7.65mm pistols were first built in 1950 and production stopped in 1959. Very few of these pistols are in the U.S.

Courtesy J.B. Wood

Exc.	V.G.	Good	Fair	Poor
500	400	300	200	100

MANURHIN

Saint-Bonnet-le-Chateau, France

This company manufactured the Walther PP and PPK models under license and these are marked "Manufacture de Machines du Haut-Rhin" on the left front of the slide and "Lic Excl. Walther" on the left rear. These arms were imported into the U.S.A. in the early 1950s by Thalson Import Company of San Francisco, California, and later by Interarms. The latter are marked "Mark 11" and "Made in France."

NEW PRODUCTION

Manurhin is now owned by Chapuis Armes.

Model 73 Defense Revolver

A .38 Special or .357 Magnum caliber double-action swing-out cylinder revolver with a 2.5", 3", or 4" barrel having fixed sights. Blued with walnut grips.

NIB	Exc.	V.G.	Good	Fair	Poor
1150	1000	850	750	500	350

Model 73 Gendarmerie

As above, with a 5.5", 6", or 8" long barrel and adjustable sights.

NIB	Exc.	V.G.	Good	Fair	Poor
1250	1100	900	800	550	400

Model 73 Sport

Similar to the above, with a shortened lock time and target-style adjustable sights.

NIB	Exc.	V.G.	Good	Fair	Poor
1250	1100	900	800	550	400

Model 73 Convertible

As above, with interchangeable .22, .32, or .38 caliber barrels and cylinders.

NIB	Exc.	V.G.	Good	Fair	Poor
2250	1850	1600	1400	950	750

Model 73 Silhouette

Similar to the Model 73 Sport, but in .22 to .357 Magnum caliber with a 10" or 10.75" shrouded barrel and formfitting walnut grips.

NIB	Exc.	V.G.	Good	Fair	Poor
1200	1050	850	750	500	350

Model PP

Similar to the Walther Model PP, with a revised safety. Discontinued.

Exc.	V.G.	Good	Fair	Poor
400	350	300	225	150

Model PPK/S

Similar to the Walther Model PPK/S, with a revised safety. Discontinued.

Exc.	V.G.	Good	Fair	Poor
400	350	300	225	150

Model PP Sports

This is a target version of the PP chambered for the .22 caliber shell. Available in various barrel lengths. Discontinued.

Exc.	V.G.	Good	Fair	Poor
400	350	300	225	150

MARATHON PRODUCTS, INC.

Santa Barbara, California

.22 First Shot

A .22 caliber single-shot bolt-action rifle with a 16.5" barrel and overall length of 31". Blued with a walnut stock. Manufactured between 1985 and 1987.

Exc.	V.G.	Good	Fair	Poor
75	55	45	30	25

.22 Super Shot

As above, with a 24" barrel. Manufactured between 1985 and 1987.

Exc.	V.G.	Good	Fair	Poor
75	55	45	30	25

.22 Hot Shot Pistol

A .22 caliber bolt-action pistol with a 14.5" barrel. Blued with a walnut stock. Manufactured in 1986 and 1987.

Exc.	V.G.	Good	Fair	Poor
75	55	45	30	25

Centerfire Rifle

A bolt-action sporting rifle manufactured in a variety of calibers with a 24" barrel, open sights, adjustable trigger and 5-shot magazine. Blued with a walnut stock. Manufactured in 1985 and 1986.

Exc.	V.G.	Good	Fair	Poor
325	250	200	150	125

MARBLE'S ARMS & MFG. CO.

Gladstone, Michigan

Marble's Game Getter Gun NFA, CURIO OR RELIC

The Game Getter has 12", 15", or 18" separated over-and-under rifled/smooth bore barrels in .22/.44 or .22/.410, a manually pivoted hammer striker to select the upper or lower barrel, an attached folding steel skeleton stock, and is intended to be fired from the shoulder. The tip-up barrels are opened by pulling back the trigger guard. Two versions, Model 1908 and Model 1921, indicating their first years of production, were made. Both apparently were designed by Webster L. Marble (1854-1930), and manufactured by Marble Safety Axe Co. of Gladstone, Michigan, which became Marble's Arms & Mfg. Co. in 1911.

Marble's suspended sales of the Game Getter in the United States after the Treasury Department ruled it was a "firearm" under the NFA, but continued sales abroad. Its retail price in 1934 was about $24 (12" or 15" barrels) to $26 (18" barrels). The Bureau of Internal Revenue removed the 18" barrel variation from the NFA in a Letter Ruling dated March 1, 1939. Today, the 12" and 15" barrel variations are controlled under the NFA in the "any other weapon" category. If the shoulder stock is removed from a 12", 15", or 18" barreled Game Getter, however, ATF has ruled it to be an NFA "firearm" subject to a $200 transfer tax.

Model 1908

Serial numbered from A to M; then 001 to 10000.

Exc.	V.G.	Good	Fair	Poor
1500	900	750	550	425

Model 1921

Serial numbered from 10001 to 20076.

Exc.	V.G.	Good	Fair	Poor
900	750	550	450	375

NOTE: Boxed guns (wooden box, Model 1908; cardboard box, Model 1921) with accessories, or 18" barrel variations, nonstandard calibers (.25-20, .32-20, .38-40, etc.) command premiums of 50 to 200 percent or more; an original holster is $75 to $150. Two new-in-box Model 1908 with 15" and 18" barrels sold for $2,700 and $3,600, respectively, in 1994. An original wooden Model 1908 box alone may sell for $500 to $900. All 18" barrel variations are rare.

The Model 1908 was available in two variations. Model 1908A has a flexible rear tang sight, and the Model 1908B has a filler block. Some confusion about the serial numbering exists because some Marbles factory representatives gave out incorrect information during the 1960s and 1970s. According to some letters from this period on Marble's factory letterhead, serial numbers began with number 700 and ended with 9999. Original factory records, however, disclose that the Model 1908 was first shipped from the factory in 1909, and serial numbered with letters from A through M, before beginning numerically with serial number 001 through 10000, when production ended in May, 1914. Serial number 001 was shipped from the factory on March 3, 1909, and the last Model 1908 was shipped on May 22, 1918.

The markings on the Model 1908 are:

Type I (serial 1 to about 4000
Type II (about serial 4000 to 9999)

LEFT SIDE:

MANUFACTURED BY THE	MANUFACTURED BY THE
MARBLE SAFETY AXE CO.	MARBLE SAFETY AXE CO.
GLADSTONE, MICH. U.S.A.	GLADSTONE, MICH. U.S.A.
MARBLE ARMS & MFG. CO.	SUCCESSOR

RIGHT SIDE:

Calibers 22 & 44	*Calibers 22 & 44*
Patent Allowed	***Patent Allowed***

Each of the markings on the right side is enclosed within an elongated circle.

OTHER CHARACTERISTICS: Separate flat buttplate attached with two screws up to approximately serial number 1200; afterwards, a flattened buttplate was integrally formed from the same round steel used to form the skeleton stock. Early stocks have drop adjustment with a knurled collar 3/8" diameter by 13/16" long; at approximately serial number 2500, the collar was changed to 1/2" by 5/8" long. The hammer spur is curved down up to approximately serial number 2,000, then the curve at hammer is up.

The Model 1908 was originally designed for .22 short, long or LR and .44 shot and ball ammunition, but the most satisfactory load was the long-cased .44-40 that held the shot in place with a disk and mouth crimp. The 1915 Marble's catalog stated the Model 1908 was available for use with the 2" .410 shotgun shell; chambering is slightly different from that of the .44-40, but is seldom encountered.

Production of the Model 1908 was not resumed because of World War I. To meet the continuing demand for this extremely popular firearm, Marble's produced an entirely new gun in 1921. The grip, folding stock (made from cold-rolled sheet metal and nickel-plated), and other features were redesigned. The serial number range for the Model 1921 is 10001 (shipped in October 1921) to 20076. Most production of the Model 1921 apparently ended around the time of World War II; however, factory records disclose that Marble's was exporting 15" barrel Model 1921s into Canada in 1955, where their registration was not required at that time. Marble's also assembled approximately 200 Model 1921s from parts circa 1960-61, and sold them (without the holster) for $200 each.

The Model 1921 was originally designed from the 2" .410 shotgun shell, but Marble's changed the extractor marking on some guns to 2-1/2" or 2 1/2" to indicate factory rechambering for the 2.5" shell, which has been reported to have started in 1924. However, the change to a 2-1/2" chamber may not have been uniform, because both 2" and 2-1/2" marked guns have been observed in low (14000) and high (19000) serial number ranges. The lowest serial number with 2" marking observed so far is 14601. The range from approximately 14500 to 17000 have plastic rather than walnut grips, a single-bladed rear sight rather than multiple-blade, and blued rather than case-hardened hammer. Outside this range, only 19288 has the 2" marking; and number 19692 is marked 2-1/2". No Model 1921 Game Getters are known to have been factory chambered for the 3" .410 shell.

The markings on the Model 1921 are:

LEFT SIDE:
MARBLE'S
Game Getter Gun
Marble Arms & Mfg.Co.
Gladstone, Mich.U.S.A.

RIGHT SIDE: ***UPPER BARREL 22 S.L. LR.&N.R.A***
LOWER BARREL .44GG & .410 2"

OTHER CHARACTERISTICS: Other barrel markings for the Model 1921 in .410 are ***.410 2-1/2"*** and ***.410 2-1/2"***; the latter appears in the serial number range from approximately 15000 to 16600, and in the low 19000 range. Plastic grips were used in the serial range from approximately 14600 to 17000.

The Model 1921 was originally designed for the 2" .410 shotgun shell, but Marble's changed the extractor marking on some guns to **2-1/2"** or **2-1/2"** to indicate factory rechambering for the 2.5" shell, apparently on a random or special-order basis (both 2" and 2-1/2" marked guns have been observed in low (14000) and high (19000) serial number ranges). The lowest serial number with 2?" marking observed so far is 14601. The range from approximately 14500 to 17000 have plastic rather than walnut grips, single-bladed rear sight rather than multiple-blades, and blued rather than case hardened hammer. Outside this range, only 19288 has the 2?" marking; number 19692 is marked **2-1/2"**. No Model 1921 Game Getters are known to have been factory chambered for the 3" .410 shell.

Marble's Game Getter Pistol and other special-order or experimental Game Getters NFA, CURIO OR RELIC

Contemporary articles and advertisements in *Hunter-Trader-Trapper*, and some early Marble's catalogs, state that a small number of Model 1908 Game Getters were originally manufactured (with rifled barrels) for .25-20, .32-20, and.38-40 cartridges. An illustrated advertisement in a 1910 issue of *Hunter-Trapper-Trader* states that 12", 15" and 18" barrel Game Getters were available for delivery in .25-20, .32-20 and .38-40, and that these firearms were designed as over-and-under rifles with rifled barrels. An article in the October 1913 issue of *Outdoor Life* states that Marble's was manufacturing a Game Getter pistol, with 10" barrels, and that any barrel length could be ordered.

Original factory records have confirmed the manufacture of the foregoing Game Getters, and clarified their designs. All original guns are thus correctly classified as experimental or special-order guns, and all are extremely rare. Factory records disclose that about 20 each of the Model 1908 were manufactured with .22/25-20 and .22/.32-20 over-and-under rifled barrels, but the barrel lengths are not specified. No .22/.38-40 Model 1908 Game Getters are listed in the factory records, but that may not have precluded a later factory alteration to that configuration. It is important to note that any Model 1908 Game Getter with over-and-under rifled barrels less than 18" in length is currently subject to registration under the NFA as a short barreled rifle, with a $200 transfer tax. Under current law, if these firearms are not registered they are contraband and cannot be legally owned unless ATF administratively removes them from the NFA as collector's items.

Factory records disclose that eight Model 1908 Game Getter pistols were manufactured, and all were shipped to a Minneapolis hardware store. Two specimens have been located: serial number 3810, with a 8" .22/.44 smooth bore barrel, and serial number 3837, with a 10" .22/.44 smooth bore barrel. Inspection of serial numbers 3810 and 3837 (including removal of the grips) reveal they were never fitted with shoulder stocks, because the portion of the frame which would have accommodated the stock was never machined out to receive one. Under current law, an original Marble's Game Getter pistol is subject to registration under the NFA as an "Any Other Weapon" with a $5 transfer tax. According to very incomplete factory records, a relatively small number—about a dozen—Model 1921 Game Getters were manufactured with .22/.38-40 rifled barrels, but the barrel lengths are not specified. It is possible that other factory-original configurations exist, such as .22/.25-20 and others.

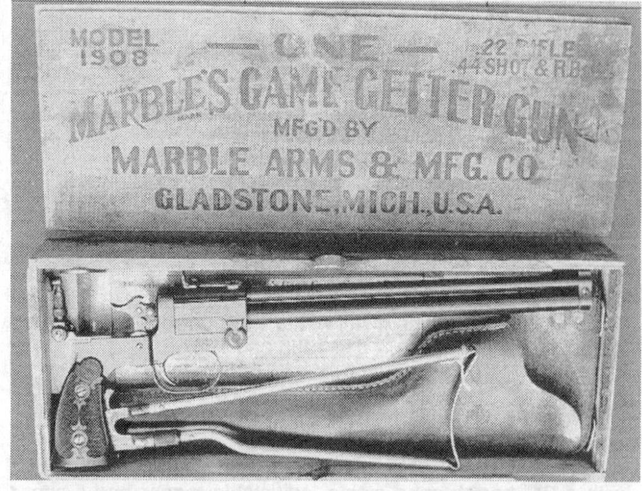

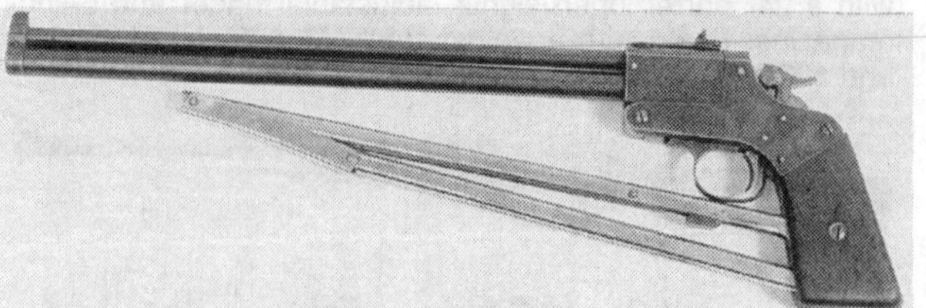

MARGOLIN

Tula, Soviet State Arsenal

Model MT Sports

This is a semi-automatic .22 caliber pistol with no barrel weights and is not threaded for a compensator. Barrel length is 7.5". Furnished with a black plastic case with spare magazine and repair parts. Discontinued.

Courtesy Orvel Reichert

Exc.	*V.G.*	*Good*	*Fair*	*Poor*
600	500	400	300	200

REMINDER

The prices given in this book are designed as a guide, not a quote. This is an important distinction because prices for firearms vary with the time of the year and geographical location.

Model MTS-1

A .22 short semi-automatic pistol with a 5.9" barrel having an integral muzzle brake (7.4" overall), adjustable walnut grips and a 6-shot magazine. Normally, accompanied by a wooden case with cleaning accessories. Discontinued.

Courtesy Orvel Reichert

Exc.	*V.G.*	*Good*	*Fair*	*Poor*
800	700	600	450	350

Model MTS-2

As above, in .22 LR with a 5.9" barrel. Discontinued.

Exc.	*V.G.*	*Good*	*Fair*	*Poor*
800	700	600	450	350

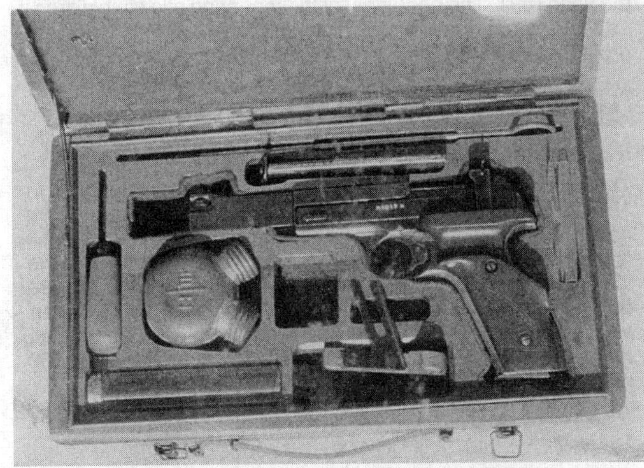

An unusual Margolin .22 caliber Olympic Model with wrap around square barrel weights and wooden case.

Courtesy Orvel Reichert

MARIETTE BREVETTE

Liege, Belgium

A number of European manufacturers produced percussion pepperbox pistols based upon a patent issued to Mariette during the 1840s and 1850s. These pistols have detachable barrels that are loaded at the breech, double-action ring triggers, and internally mounted hammers. They are normally blued and foliate engraved.

6 Barrel Pepperbox

Exc.	*V.G.*	*Good*	*Fair*	*Poor*
—	—	2000	900	400

4 Barrel Pepperbox

Exc.	*V.G.*	*Good*	*Fair*	*Poor*
—	—	2000	900	400

MARLIN FIREARMS CO.

New Haven, Connecticut

Ballard Rifles

Established by John Mahlon Marlin in 1863. Marlin manufactured pistols until 1875 when he began production of Ballard rifles. In 1881 he made his first lever-action repeating rifle for which his company became famous.

The Marlin Firearms Company has the distinction of being the oldest family owned firearms company in the United States.

The Ballard single-shot rifle was invented by C.H. Ballard of Worcester, Massachusetts. It was patented in 1861. The first of the Ballard rifles was manufactured by the Ball and Williams Co. of Worchester, Massachusetts. In 1866 Merwin and Bray purchased the firm, calling it Merrimack Arms Company, and operated until 1869, when they sold it to the Brown Manufacturing Company of New York City. This venture took a decidedly negative turn, and in 1873 mortgage foreclosure forced the sale to Schoverling and Daly of New York City. These gentlemen were arms dealers, not manufacturers, so they entered into an agreement with John M. Marlin to produce the Ballard rifle. The rifles produced during this period are regarded as some of the finest single-shots ever made, and the venture finally became successful. In 1881 the business became incorporated as the Marlin Firearms Company, and the Ballard was produced under this banner until it was discontinued around the year 1891. The popularity of the repeating rifle simply eroded the demand for the fine single-shot until it was no longer a profitable venture.

BALL & WILLIAMS BALLARDS

First Model

This model was the first Ballard produced. It was introduced in 1861 and was offered with a 24" or 28" octagonal barrel. The frame is case colored, and the barrel is blued. The walnut stock is varnished. The major identifying feature of this model is the inside extractor. This was the only Ballard that had this feature before Marlin began to manufacture the rifle in 1875. The barrel is stamped "Ball & Williams/Worchester, Mass." and "Ballards Patent/Nov. 5, 1861." There were approximately 100 manufactured and serial numbered from 1-100.

Exc.	*V.G.*	*Good*	*Fair*	*Poor*
—	—	2500	900	400

Military Rifle

There is not enough known about these rifles and probably never will be. They were chambered most frequently for the .44 and .54 rimfire cartridges and feature the outside tangs and extractors. They were offered with a 30" round barrel and full-length forearm. There are three barrel bands and sling swivels. The government ordered only 35 of these for use in the Civil War; and if one was to be definitely authenticated as a genuine martial specimen, it would be quite valuable. Many of these rifles were marked "Kentucky" on top of the receiver because the militia of that state armed its men with the Ballard rifles and carbines. This marking was a sales aid used by the company and does not indicate militia ownership. The amount manufactured is not known. Barrel markings are as on the First Model.

Exc.	*V.G.*	*Good*	*Fair*	*Poor*
—	—	1850	750	300

Civil War Military Carbine

This model has a 22" part-round, part-octagonal barrel and is chambered for the .44 rimfire cartridge. It has the outside tang and extractor. The stock and forearm are walnut with a barrel band sling swivel. The buttstock bears an oval cartouche surrounding the inspector's marks, "MM." These letters also appear stamped on major metal parts. There were 1,509 ordered by the government for use in the Civil War. The barrel was marked the same as the rifle.

Exc.	*V.G.*	*Good*	*Fair*	*Poor*
—	—	3750	1500	500

Sporting Rifle

This model is chambered for the .32, .38, and .44 rimfire cartridges. The octagonal barrel is 24", 26", or 28" in length and is blued. The frame is case colored. The stock and forearm are varnished walnut, and there is a knob that protrudes in front of the frame to operate the outside manual extractor. There is a crescent buttplate standard. There were approximately 6,500 manufactured, and barrel markings are the same as on the First Model.

Exc.	*V.G.*	*Good*	*Fair*	*Poor*
—	—	1250	500	200

Sporting Carbine

This model is similar in appearance to the Sporting Rifle with a 22" part-round, part-octagonal barrel. It is chambered for the .44 and .54 caliber cartridge, and the sling swivel is found on a barrel band in the front. The knob on the bottom activates the outside extractor. There have been some encountered with "Kentucky" stamped on the top, but this does not affect the value. The markings are the same as on the previous models. There are no production figures available, but some estimate approximately 2,000 were manufactured.

Exc.	*V.G.*	*Good*	*Fair*	*Poor*
—	—	1750	600	250

Dual Ignition System

This system allows the use of the rimfire cartridge or percussion method by simply turning the striker on the hammer from one position to the other. This model features a percussion nipple mounted on the breechblock, and the hammer is marked "Patented Jan. 5, 1864." The patent was held by Merwin and Bray. This swivel system is usually found on the sporting models and would increase the value of the weapon by 20 percent.

MERRIMACK ARMS CO. AND BROWN MANUFACTURING CO.

The values for the Ballard rifles manufactured by these two firms are the same, and the specifications are similar. The identifying difference is in the markings, "Merrimack Arms & Mfg. Co./Newburyport Mass." or "Brown Mfg. Co. Newburyport, Mass." Merrimack produced approximately 3,000 of these rifles between 1867 and 1869 serial numbered in the 18000-20000 range. Brown produced approximately 1,800 between 1869 and 1873 in the 20000-22000 serial number range.

Sporting Rifle

This model was produced in .22 (rare), .32, .38, .44, .46, and .52 caliber rimfire or percussion, as most encountered featured the dual ignition system and had the nipple in the breechblock. They have either a round or octagonal barrel in 24", 26", or 28" lengths. The appearance and finish is similar to the Ball & Williams rifles; and the major difference is the inside tang. The extractor was still outside mounted and manually activated. Exact production breakdown is unknown. There is no premium for the dual ignition system on these later guns.

Exc.	*V.G.*	*Good*	*Fair*	*Poor*
—	—	1150	450	200

Sporting Carbine

This model is quite similar in appearance to the Sporting Rifle, with a 22" part-round, part-octagonal barrel.

Exc.	*V.G.*	*Good*	*Fair*	*Poor*
—	—	1250	550	300

Military Rifle

The Military Rifle is similar to the sporting version except that it has a 30" round barrel and full-length forearm with three barrel bands. It is chambered for the .44 and .52 caliber rimfire or percussion with the dual ignition system.

Exc.	*V.G.*	*Good*	*Fair*	*Poor*
—	—	1500	650	300

Shotgun

This model is similar to the Sporting Rifle in appearance but is chambered for 24 gauge, with a 30" round barrel. There is a groove milled in the top of the frame to use as a sight. The buttplate is shotgun-style instead of the usual crescent shape.

Exc.	*V.G.*	*Good*	*Fair*	*Poor*
—	—	800	350	200

MARLIN-BALLARD RIFLES

Commencing in 1875 the Ballard single-shot rifle was made by John Marlin for Schoverling and Daly. In 1881 the business was incorporated and became the Marlin Firearms Co. All the Ballards made from then until 1891, when they were discontinued, were produced under this banner. The only real difference in the rifles manufactured during these periods was in the markings. The earlier rifles are stamped "J.M. Marlin New Haven. Conn. U.S.A./Ballards Patent. Nov. 5, 1861"; and the post-1881 models are stamped "Marlin Firearms Co. New Haven Ct. U.S.A./Patented Feb. 9, 1875/Ballards Patent Nov. 5, 1861." The major difference between Marlin-made Ballards and the earlier models is the inside tang and the internal extractor on the Marlin-made rifles. All of the Marlin-made Ballards have an octagonal frame top, and the Marlin Firearms Co. models have grooved receiver sides. The standard finish on all these later rifles is case colored frames and blued octagonal or part-round, part-octagonal barrels. There are many variations in these rifles as to types of sights, stock, engraving, and other special order features-such as barrel lengths, weights, and contours. These rifles must be considered individually and competently appraised. There is also the fact that many of these Ballards have been rebarreled and rechambered over the years, as they were known for their shooting ability and were used quite extensively. This can seriously affect the value in a negative manner unless it can be authenticated that the work was done by the likes of Harry Pope or George Schoyen and other noted and respected gunsmiths of that era. This can add considerably to the value of the rifle. One must approach this model with caution and learn all that can be learned before purchasing.

Ballard Hunters Rifle

This model resembles the earlier Brown Manufacturing Company rifles, and it utilizes many leftover parts acquired by Marlin. It is chambered for the .32, .38, and .44 rimfire and centerfire and features John Marlin's unique reversible firing pin that allows the same gun to use both rimfire and centerfire ammunition simply by rotating the firing pin in the breechblock. This model still had the external ejector and bears the J.M. Marlin markings. There were approximately 500 manufactured in the 1 to 500 serial range. They were produced in 1875 and 1876.

Exc.	V.G.	Good	Fair	Poor
—	—	2750	950	400

Ballard No. 1 Hunters Rifle

This model bears the early J.M. Marlin marking only, as it was manufactured from 1876 until 1880 and was discontinued before the incorporation. It has a 26", 28", and 30" barrel and is chambered for the .44 rimfire or centerfire cartridge. It has the reversible firing pin and also the new internal extractor. Production figures are not available, but the serial number range is between 500 and 4000.

Exc.	V.G.	Good	Fair	Poor
—	—	3000	1000	400

Ballard No. 1-1/2 Hunters Rifle

This model is similar to the No. 1 except that it is chambered for the .45-70, .40-63, and the .40-65 cartridges and does not have the reversible firing pin. The barrel length is 30" and 32". It was manufactured between 1879 and 1883. This model is found with both early and later markings.

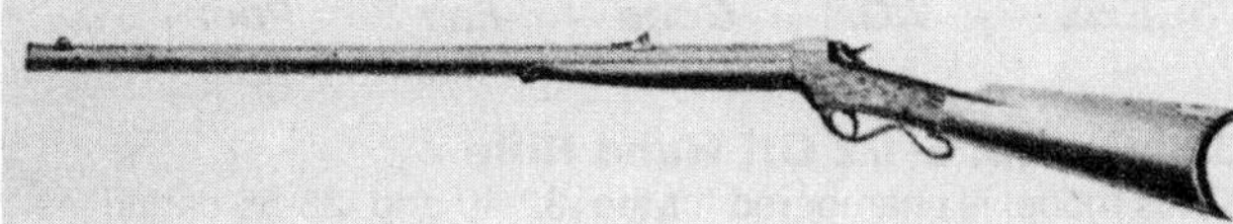

Photo by Lt. Col. William S. Brophy from *Marlin Firearms* with permission

Exc.	V.G.	Good	Fair	Poor
—	—	3750	1500	500

Ballard No. 1-3/4 "Far West" Hunters Rifle

This model was made by J. M. Marlin only and is similar to the 1-1/2, the difference being the addition of double-set triggers and a ring on the opening lever. It was manufactured in 1880 and 1881.

Exc.	V.G.	Good	Fair	Poor
—	—	4750	2000	600

Ballard No. 2 Sporting Rifle

This model is chambered for the .32, .38 rimfire or centerfire cartridges, and the .44 centerfire. It has the reversible firing pin and was offered in 26", 28", and 30" barrel lengths. This model features "Rocky Mountain" sights and was manufactured between 1876 and 1891. It is found with both early and late markings.

Courtesy Milwaukee Public Museum, Milwaukee, Wisconsin

Exc.	V.G.	Good	Fair	Poor
—	—	2000	650	200

Ballard No. 3 Gallery Rifle

This model is similar to the No. 2 rifle but is chambered for the .22 rimfire cartridge and has a manually operated external extractor. The sights are the same; and a 24" barrel was offered in addition to the 26", 28", and 30". This rifle was manufactured between 1876 and 1891.

Exc.	V.G.	Good	Fair	Poor
—	—	2000	650	200

Ballard No. 3F Gallery Rifle

This is a deluxe version of the No. 3. It has a pistol-grip stock, a nickel-plated Schutzen-style buttplate, and an opening lever like a repeating rifle. It features a 26" octagonal barrel and an oil-finished stock. It was manufactured in the late 1880s and is quite scarce in today's market.

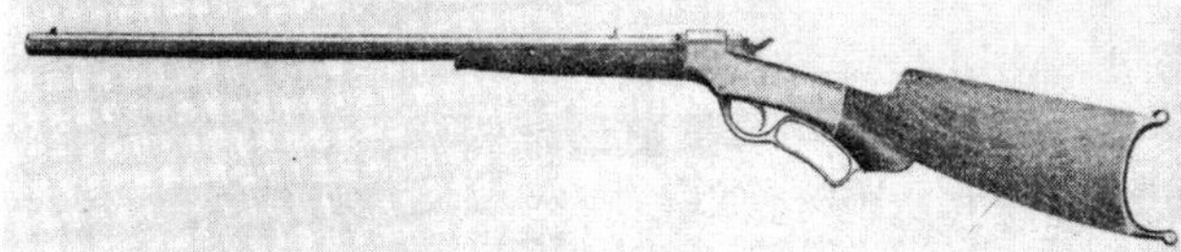

Photo by Lt. Col. William S. Brophy from *Marlin Firearms* with permission

Exc.	V.G.	Good	Fair	Poor
—	—	4250	1750	500

Ballard No. 4 Perfection Rifle

This model is chambered for a number of centerfire calibers from .32-40 to .50-70. The barrel lengths are from 26" to 30", and the sights are of the "Rocky Mountain" type. This model was manufactured between 1876 and 1891.

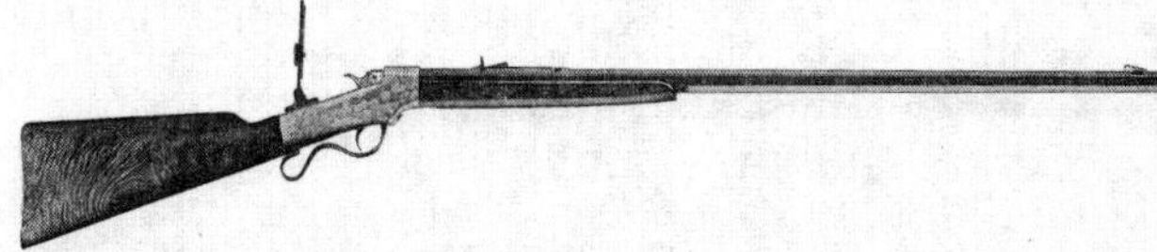

Courtesy Rock Island Auction Company

Exc.	V.G.	Good	Fair	Poor
—	—	4250	1750	500

Ballard No. 3-1/2 Target Rifle

This model is similar to the No. 4 Perfection Rifle except that it has a checkered stock with a shotgun-style buttplate, a 30" barrel, and a tang peep sight with globe front sight. It was chambered for the .40-65 cartridge and was manufactured from 1880-1882.

Exc.	V.G.	Good	Fair	Poor
—	—	4250	1750	500

Ballard No. 4-1/2 Mid Range Rifle

This model is also a variation of the No. 4 Perfection model. It has a higher-grade checkered stock with a shotgun buttplate. It has a 30" part-round, part-octagonal barrel and is chambered for the .38-40, .40-65, and the .45-70 cartridges. It features a Vernier tang peep sight and a globe front sight. It was manufactured between 1878 and 1882.

Exc.	V.G.	Good	Fair	Poor
—	—	4500	2000	500

Ballard No. 4-1/2 A-1 Mid Range Target Rifle

This is a deluxe version of the No. 4-1/2" rifle. It features scroll engraving on the frame with "Ballard A-1" on the left and "Mid-Range" on the right. It is chambered for the .38-50 and the .40-65 cartridge and has a high-grade checkered stock with a horn forend tip. The sights are the highest-grade Vernier tang sight and a spirit lever front sight. The shotgun or rifle-style butt was optional. This model was manufactured between 1878 and 1880.

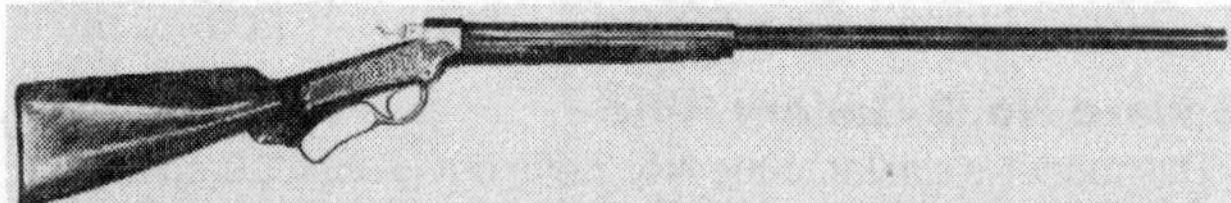

Courtesy Milwaukee Public Museum, Milwaukee, Wisconsin

Exc.	V.G.	Good	Fair	Poor
—	—	7250	3500	750

Ballard No. 5 Pacific Rifle

This model has a 30" or 32" medium to heavyweight barrel, with a ramrod mounted underneath. It is chambered for many different calibers from .38-50 to .50-70. This model features "Rocky Mountain" sights, a crescent butt, double-set triggers, and a ring-style opening lever. It was manufactured between 1876 and 1891.

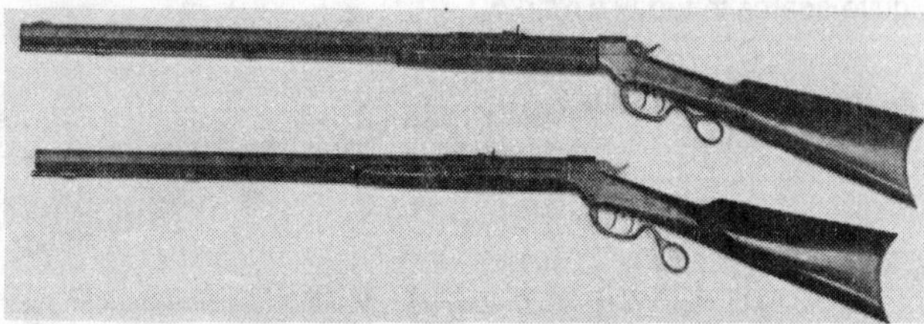

Courtesy Milwaukee Public Museum, Milwaukee, Wisconsin

Exc.	V.G.	Good	Fair	Poor
—	—	4750	2000	500

Ballard No. 5-1/2 Montana Rifle

This model is similar to the Pacific Rifle, with an extra heavy-weight barrel, and is chambered for the .45 Sharps cartridge only. It features a checkered steel shotgun-style buttplate. It was manufactured from 1882-1884 and has the late markings only.

Courtesy Milwaukee Public Museum, Milwaukee, Wisconsin

Exc.	V.G.	Good	Fair	Poor
—	—	10000	5500	1250

Ballard No. 6 Schuetzen Off Hand Rifle

This model has a 30" or 32" octagonal barrel and is chambered for the .40-65, .44-75, and the .38-50 cartridges. The stock is of select walnut in the high-combed Schuetzen style. The buttplate is nickel-plated, and the receiver is not engraved. The sights are Vernier tang type on the rear and a spirit lever front. The triggers are double set, and the opening lever has a ring and a spur. This model is marked J.M. Marlin only and was manufactured between 1876 and 1880.

Exc.	V.G.	Good	Fair	Poor
—	—	6500	2500	500

Ballard No. 6 Schuetzen Rifle

This model is similar to the Off Hand model but was produced by the later Marlin Firearms Company and was so marked. It is a more deluxe version with checkered stock, horn forend tip, and a fully engraved receiver. This model was chambered for the .32-40 and the .38-55 cartridges and was manufactured between 1881 and 1891.

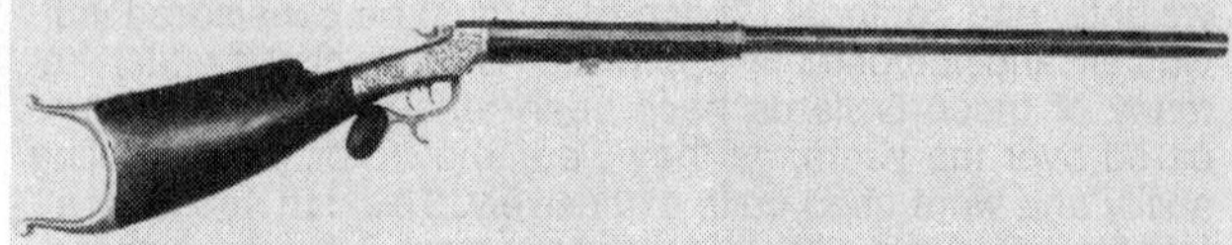

Courtesy Milwaukee Public Museum, Milwaukee, Wisconsin

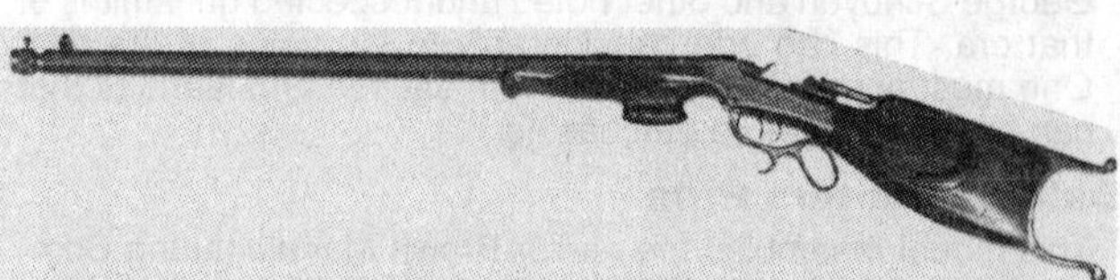

Courtesy Milwaukee Public Museum, Milwaukee, Wisconsin

Exc.	V.G.	Good	Fair	Poor
—	—	8500	4500	1250

Ballard No. 6-1/2 Off Hand Mid Range Rifle

This model is chambered for the .40-54 Everlasting cartridge only. It has a 28" or 30" part-round, part-octagonal barrel, a Schuetzen-style stock, and a plain non-engraved receiver. It was manufactured between 1880 and 1882.

Exc.	V.G.	Good	Fair	Poor
—	—	5500	2500	500

Ballard No. 6-1/2 Rigby Off Hand Mid Range Rifle

This model is chambered for the .38-50 and the .40-65 cartridges. It features the Rigby ribbed-style barrel in 26" and 28" lengths, with Vernier rear and globe front sights and a high grade, checkered walnut, Schuetzen-style stock with horn forend tip, and pistol-grip cap. The buttplate is nickel-plated, and the opening lever is of the ring type with a single trigger and extensively engraved receiver. This model was manufactured from 1880 to 1882.

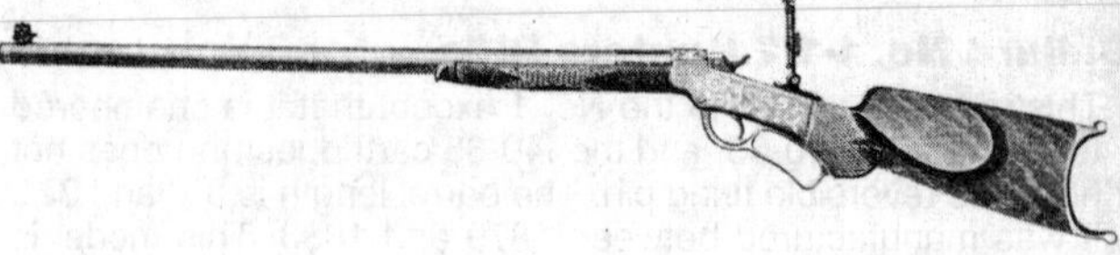

Photo by Lt. Col. William S. Brophy from *Marlin Firearms* with permission

Exc.	V.G.	Good	Fair	Poor
—	—	9000	5500	1250

Ballard No. 6-1/2 Off Hand Rifle

This model is chambered for the .32-40 and .38-55 cartridges and features barrel lengths of 28" and 30". It has a checkered, high-grade walnut, Schuetzen-style stock with nickel-plated buttplate. The forend tip and pistol-grip cap are of horn, and the receiver is engraved. This model has a single trigger, full-ring opening lever, Vernier tang rear sight, and spirit lever front

A Ballard Schuetzen rifle sold at auction for $34,500. Engraved action. Chambered for the .32-40 and fitted wtih a heavy 31-inch octagon barrel by H.M. Pope. Double set triggers. Schuetzeen buttplate, palm rest. Supplied with shooting kit with accessories. Condition is 98 percent barrel blue. Some case colors. Excellent stock.
Rock Island Auction Company

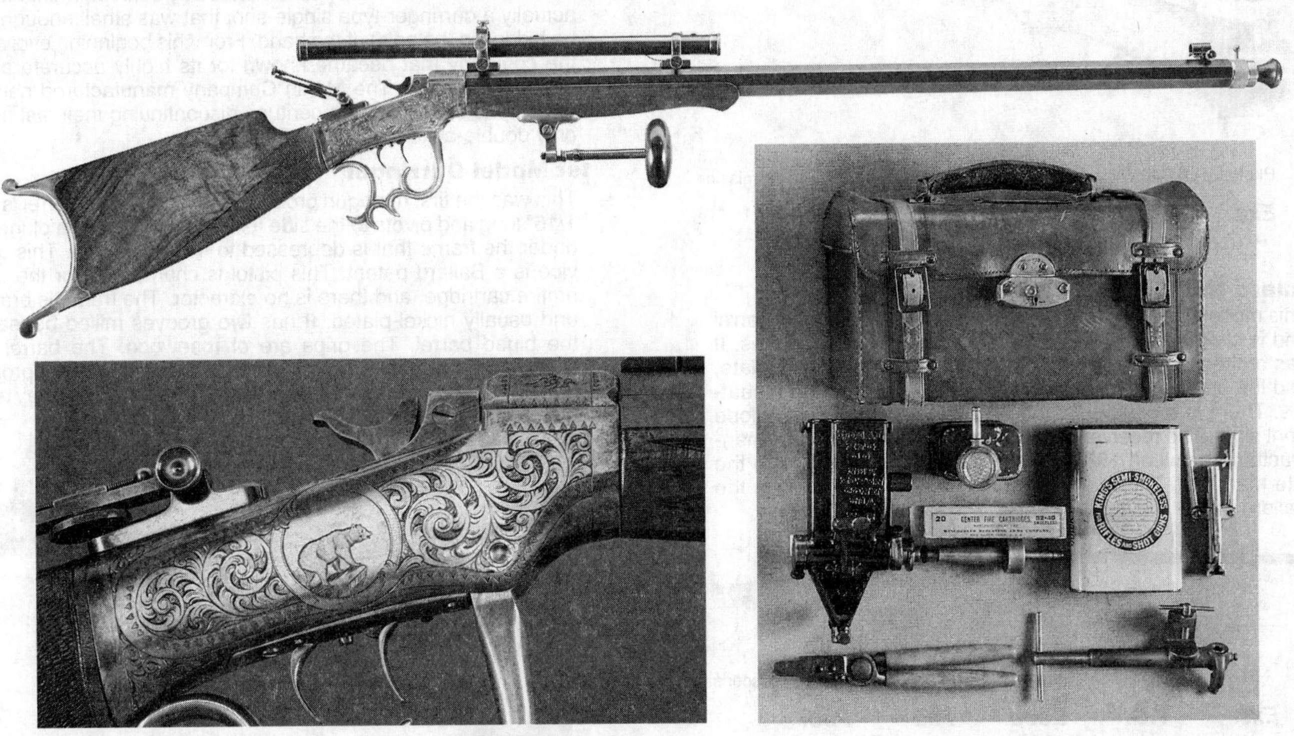

sight. The 6-1/2 Off Hand was made by the Marlin Firearms Company between 1883 and 1891 and is found with the later markings only.

Exc.	*V.G.*	*Good*	*Fair*	*Poor*
—	—	9000	5500	1250

Ballard No. 7 "Creedmore A-1" Long Range Rifle

This model is commonly chambered for the .44-100 or the .45100 cartridges. It has a 34" part-round, part-octagonal barrel and a high grade checkered pistol-grip stock, with a horn forend tip and shotgun-style butt. The sights are a special 1,300-yard Vernier tang rear and a spirit level front. There is another sight base on the heel of the stock for mounting the rear sight for ultra long-range shooting. The opening lever is similar to a repeating rifle, and a single trigger is featured. The receiver is engraved and marked "Ballard A-1" on the left and "Long Range" on the right. This model was manufactured between 1876 and 1886 and is found with both early and late markings.

Courtesy Milwaukee Public Museum, Milwaukee, Wisconsin

Exc.	*V.G.*	*Good*	*Fair*	*Poor*
—	—	9000	5500	1250

Ballard No. 7 Long Range Rifle

This model is similar to the "Creedmore A-1" but is slightly less deluxe. The engraving is less elaborate, and the lettering on the receiver is absent. This model was manufactured between 1883 and 1890 and is found with the later markings only.

Photo by Lt. Col. William S. Brophy from *Marlin Firearms* with permission

Exc.	*V.G.*	*Good*	*Fair*	*Poor*
—	—	8000	4500	850

Ballard No. 7A-1 Long Range Rifle

This model is a higher grade version of the "Creedmore A-l," with fancier walnut and a checkered straight stock. Better sights and deluxe engraving are also featured. This model was manufactured between 1879 and 1883 and is found with both markings.

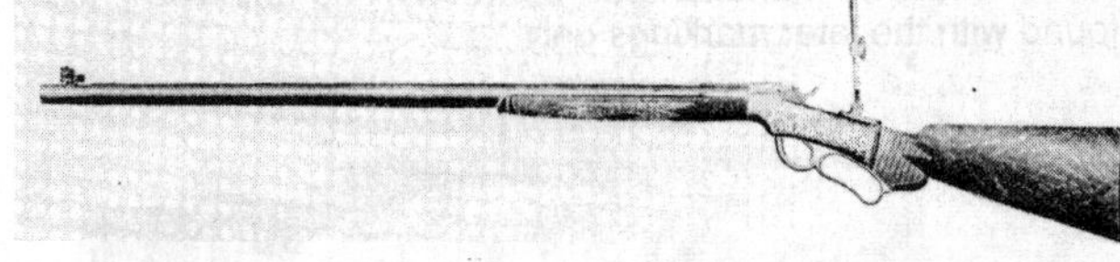

Photo by Lt. Col. William S. Brophy from *Marlin Firearms* with permission

Exc.	*V.G.*	*Good*	*Fair*	*Poor*
—	—	9000	5500	1250

Ballard No. 7A-1 Extra Grade Long Range Rifle

This is the highest grade version of the No. 7 rifles. It features a 34" "Rigby"-type ribbed, round barrel. This was usually a special-order rifle with most features to customer specifications. The model was manufactured in limited numbers between 1879 and 1883. It is found with both markings.

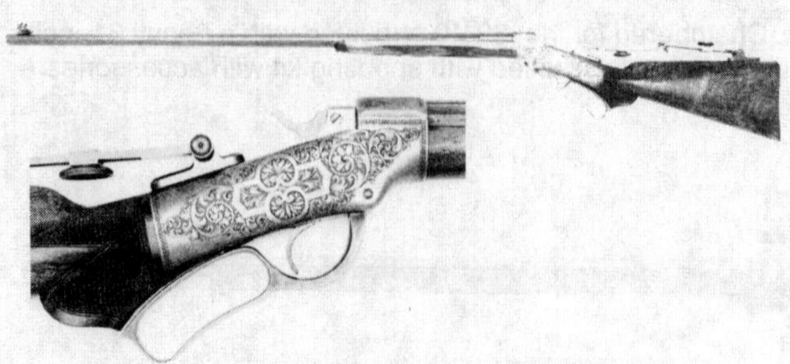

Photo by Lt. Col. William S. Brophy from *Marlin Firearms* with permission

Exc.	V.G.	Good	Fair	Poor
—	—	11500	6500	1500

Ballard No. 8 Union Hill Rifle

This model has a 28" and 30" part-round, part-octagonal barrel and is chambered for the .32-40 and the .38-55 cartridges. It has a checkered pistol-grip stock with nickel-plated buttplate; and the opening lever is fully enclosed ring, as on the repeaters. There is a double-set trigger and a tang peep with globe front sight. The receiver is not engraved. This model was manufactured between 1884 and 1890 and is found only with the late markings. This was one of the most popular rifles in the Ballard line.

Courtesy Milwaukee Public Museum, Milwaukee, Wisconsin

Exc.	V.G.	Good	Fair	Poor
—	—	4250	1750	500

Ballard No. 9 Union Hill Rifle

This model is similar to the No. 8 except that it features a single trigger and better sights. It was manufactured between 1884 and 1891 and has the later markings only.

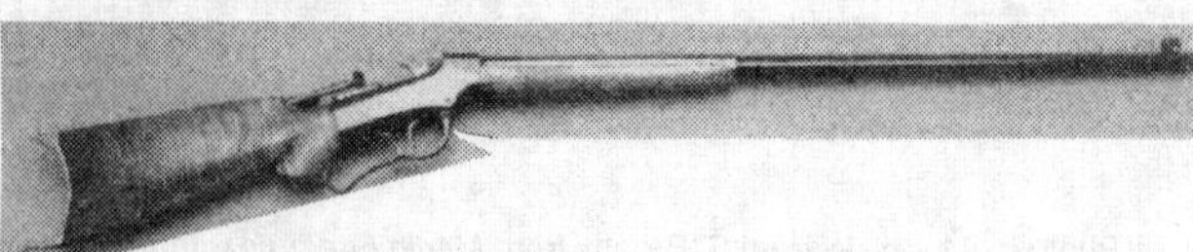

Courtesy Bonhams & Butterfields, San Francisco, California

Exc.	V.G.	Good	Fair	Poor
—	—	4250	1750	500

Ballard No. 10 Schuetzen Junior Rifle

This model is simply a heavier barreled version of the No. 9. The barrel is 32" long, and the checkered pistol-grip stock is of the off-hand style. The rear sight is a Vernier Mid Range model, and the front sight is a spirit-level type. This was a popular model that was manufactured between 1885 and 1891. It is found with the later markings only.

Courtesy Amoskeag Auction Company

Exc.	V.G.	Good	Fair	Poor
—	—	4750	2000	650

MARLIN HANDGUNS

The first firearm that was manufactured by John M. Marlin was actually a derringer-type single-shot that was small enough to be hidden in the palm of the hand. From this beginning evolved the company that became known for its highly accurate and dependable rifles. The Marlin Company manufactured handguns up to the turn of the century, discontinuing their last and only double-action model in 1899.

1st Model Derringer

This was the first handgun produced by Marlin. The barrel is 2-1/16" long and pivots to the side for loading. There is a plunger under the frame that is depressed to free the barrel. This device is a Ballard patent. This pistol is chambered for the .22 rimfire cartridge, and there is no extractor. The frame is brass and usually nickel-plated. It has two grooves milled beneath the blued barrel. The grips are of rosewood. The barrel is stamped "J.M. Marlin, New Haven, Ct." There were approximately 2,000 manufactured between 1863 and 1867. They are quite scarce on today's market.

Courtesy Milwaukee Public Museum, Milwaukee, Wisconsin

Exc.	V.G.	Good	Fair	Poor
—	—	750	300	100

Victor Model Derringer

This model is similar in appearance to the "O.K." Model but is larger in size and is chambered for the .38-caliber rimfire cartridge. The barrel is 2-11/16" long; and there was, for the first time, an extractor. The finish and function were unchanged. The right side of the barrel is stamped "J.M. Marlin/New Haven, Ct./Pat. April 5.1870." "Victor" is stamped on the top of the barrel. There were approximately 4,000 manufactured between 1870 and 1881.

Exc.	V.G.	Good	Fair	Poor
—	—	1250	500	150

O.K. Model Derringer

The O.K. Model is chambered for .22, .30, and .32 rimfire cartridges. The barrel is 2-1/8" or 3-1/8" on the .32. There is no extractor, and it functions as the 1st Model. The frame is plated brass with flat sides, and the barrel is found either blued or nickel-plated. The grips are rosewood. The markings are the same as on the 1st Model but are located on the right side of the barrel. The top of the barrel is marked "O.K." There were approximately 5,000 manufactured between 1863 and 1870.

REMINDER

An "N/A" or "—" instead of a price indicates that pricing is not available for that gun in that condition, or that sales for that particular model are so few that a reliable price cannot be given.

Photo by Lt. Col. William S. Brophy from *Marlin Firearms* with permission

Exc.	V.G.	Good	Fair	Poor
—	—	750	300	100

Nevermiss Model Derringer

This model was made in three different sizes chambered for the .22, .32, and .41 rimfire cartridges. The barrel is 2.5" long and swings sideways for loading. The frame is plated brass, and the barrels are either blued or nickel-plated. The grips are rosewood. The frame is grooved under the barrels as on the 1st model. There is an extractor on this model. The barrel markings are the same as on the "Victor," with the top of the barrel marked "Nevermiss." There were approximately 5,000 manufactured between 1870 and 1881.

.22 Caliber Model

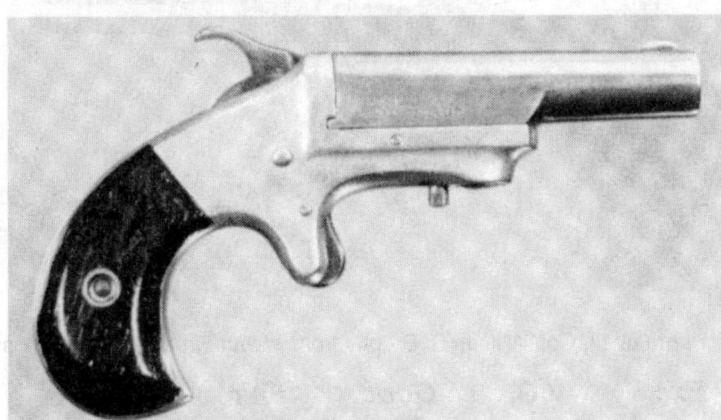

Photo by Lt. Col. William S. Brophy from *Marlin Firearms* with permission

Exc.	V.G.	Good	Fair	Poor
—	—	1150	500	100

.32 Caliber Model

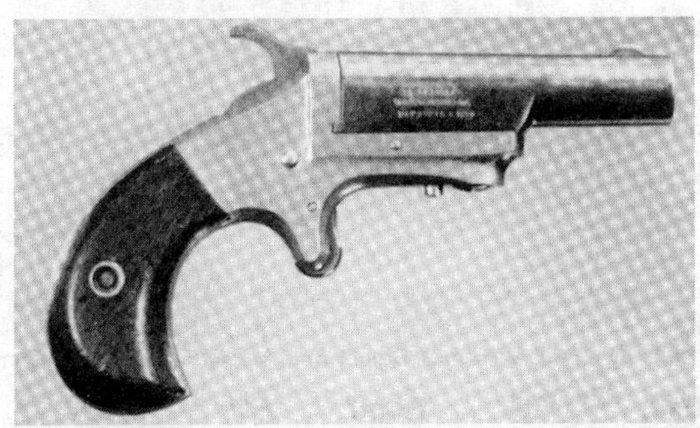

Photo by Lt. Col. William S. Brophy from *Marlin Firearms* with permission

Exc.	V.G.	Good	Fair	Poor
—	—	750	350	100

.41 Caliber Model

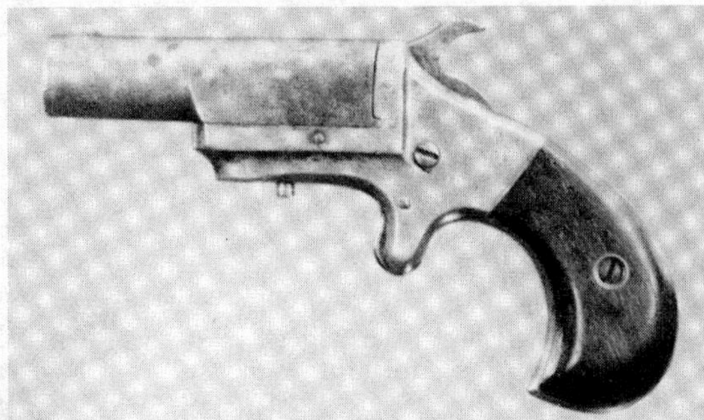

Photo by Lt. Col. William S. Brophy from *Marlin Firearms* with permission

Exc.	V.G.	Good	Fair	Poor
—	—	2500	1000	400

Stonewall Model Derringer

This model is identical to the .41-caliber "Nevermiss," but the top of the barrel is marked "Stonewall." It is rarely encountered.

Photo by Lt. Col. William S. Brophy from *Marlin Firearms* with permission

Exc.	V.G.	Good	Fair	Poor
—	—	4250	2000	750

O.K. Pocket Revolver

This is a solid-frame, spur-trigger, single-action revolver chambered for the .22 rimfire short. The round barrel is 2.25", and the 7-shot cylinder is unfluted. The frame is nickel-plated brass with a blue or nickel-plated barrel, and the bird's-head grips are rosewood. The cylinder pin is removable and is used to knock the empty cases out of the cylinder. The top of the barrel is marked "O.K." and "J.M. Marlin. New Haven, Conn. U.S.A." There were approximately 1,500 manufactured between 1870 and 1875.

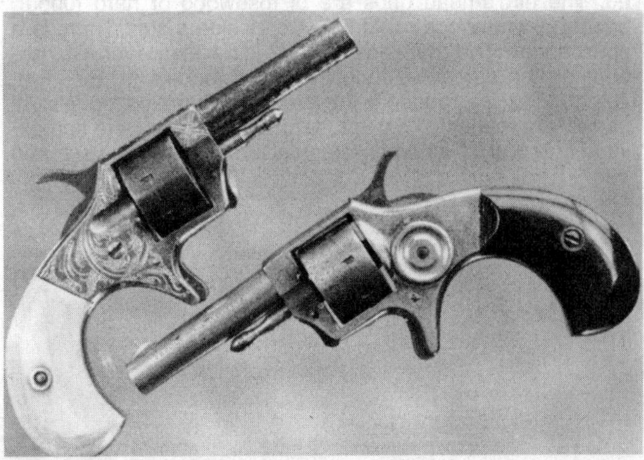

Photo by Lt. Col. William S. Brophy from *Marlin Firearms* with permission

Exc.	V.G.	Good	Fair	Poor
—	—	550	200	75

Little Joker Revolver

This model is similar in appearance to the "O.K." Model except that it features engraving and ivory or pearl grips. There were approximately 500 manufactured between 1871 and 1873.

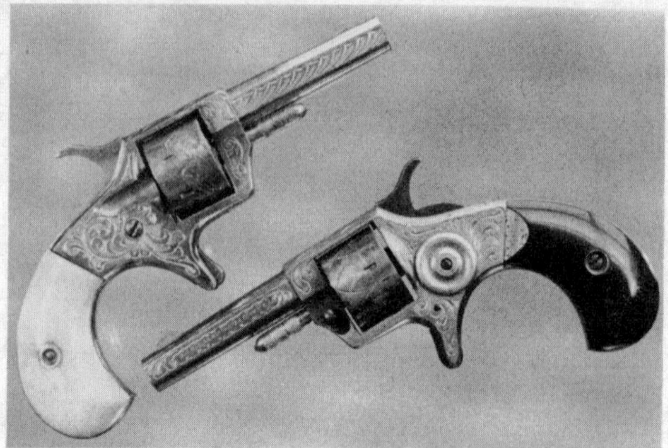

Photo by Lt. Col. William S. Brophy from Marlin Firearms with permission

Exc.	V.G.	Good	Fair	Poor
—	—	800	350	125

J. M. MARLIN STANDARD POCKET REVOLVERS

In 1872 Marlin began production of its Smith & Wesson look-alike. The Manhattan Firearms Company had developed a copy of the Model 1 S&W .22 cartridge revolver. In 1868 the company ceased business, and the revolvers were produced by the American Standard Tool Company until their dissolution in 1873. In 1872 Marlin had entered into an agreement with this company to manufacture these revolvers, which were no longer protected by the Rollin White patent after 1869. The Marlin revolvers are similar to those made by American Standard, the only real difference being that Marlin grips are of the bird's-head round configuration. A contoured grip frame and a patented pawl spring mechanism is utilized on the Marlin revolvers.

Marlin XXX Standard 1872 Pocket Revolver

This is the first in the series of four Standard model revolvers. It is chambered for the .30 caliber rimfire. The earlier model has an octagonal 3-1/8" barrel; and the later, a round 3" barrel. There are round and octagonal barrel variations (with unfluted cylinder) and round barrel variations (with short and long fluted cylinders). All of the barrels are ribbed and tip up for loading. They have plated brass frames, and the barrels are nickel-plated. The bird's-head grips are of rosewood or hard rubber, bearing the monogram "M.F.A. Co." inside a star. There is a spur trigger. The markings "J.M. Marlin-New Haven Ct." appear on the earlier octagonal barreled models. "U.S.A. Pat. July 1. 1873" was added to the later round barreled models. All barrels are marked "XXX Standard 1872." There were approximately 5,000 of all types manufactured between 1872 and 1887.

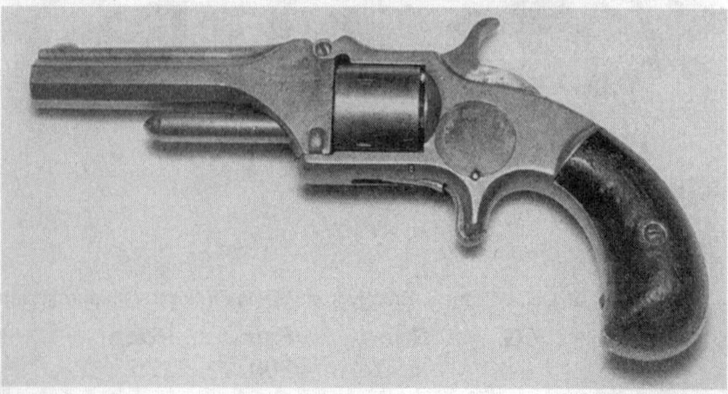

Octagon Barrel—Early Variation

Exc.	V.G.	Good	Fair	Poor
—	—	500	300	75

Round Barrel—Non-Fluted Cylinder

Exc.	V.G.	Good	Fair	Poor
—	—	400	275	75

Round Barrel—Short Fluted Cylinder

Exc.	V.G.	Good	Fair	Poor
—	—	350	200	75

Round Barrel—Long Fluted Cylinder

Exc.	V.G.	Good	Fair	Poor
—	—	450	150	75

Marlin XX Standard 1873 Pocket Revolver

This model is similar in appearance to the XXX 1872 model except that it is chambered for the .22 long rimfire and is marked "XX Standard 1873." There are three basic variations: the early octagonal barrel model with non-fluted cylinder, the round barrel model with non-fluted cylinder, and the round barrel with fluted cylinder. Function and features are the same as described for the "XXX Standard 1872" model. There were approximately 5,000 manufactured between 1873 and 1887.

Early Octagon Barrel Model

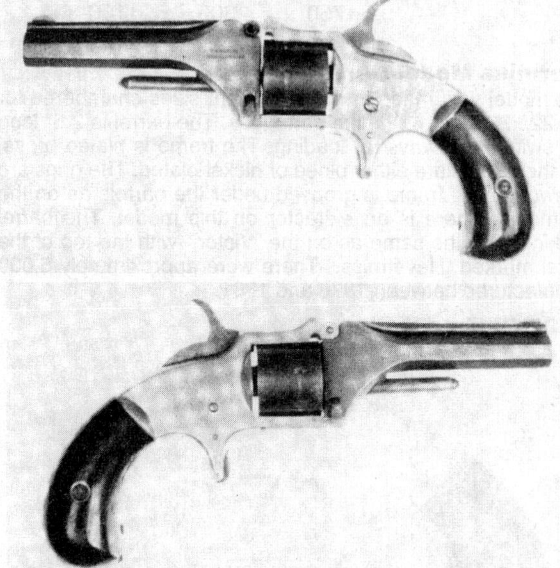

Photo by Lt. Col. William S. Brophy from *Marlin Firearms* with permission

Exc.	V.G.	Good	Fair	Poor
—	—	600	200	100

Round Barrel—Fluted Cylinder

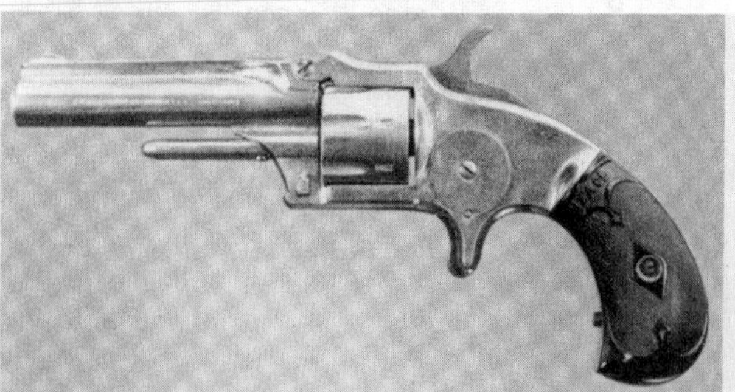

Photo by Lt. Col. William S. Brophy from *Marlin Firearms* with permission

Exc.	V.G.	Good	Fair	Poor
—	—	500	200	75

Round Barrel—Non-Fluted Cylinder

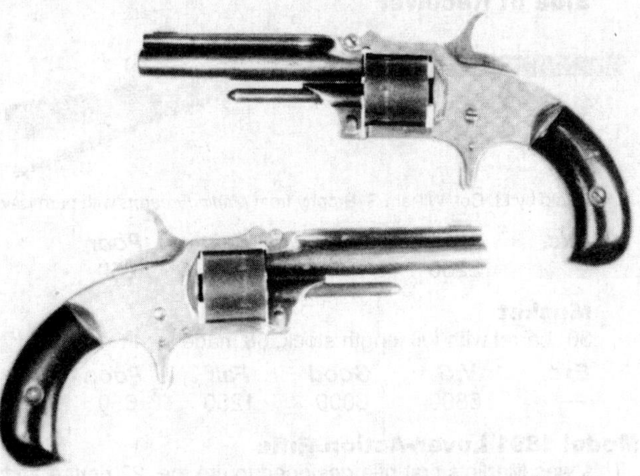

Photo by Lt. Col. William S. Brophy from *Marlin Firearms* with permission

Exc.	V.G.	Good	Fair	Poor
		650	400	100

Marlin No. 32 Standard 1875 Pocket Revolver

This model is also similar in appearance to the "XXX Standard 1872" model except that it is chambered for the .32 rimfire cartridge. The 3" barrel is round with a rib, and the 5-shot cylinder is fluted and is in two different lengths to accommodate either the .32 Short or Long cartridge. The finish, function, and most markings are the same as on previous models with the exception of the barrel top marking "No. 32 Standard 1875." There were approximately 8,000 manufactured between 1875 and 1887.

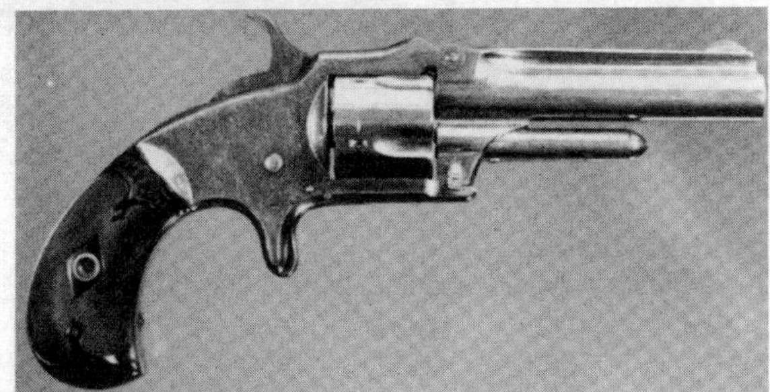

Photo by Lt. Col. William S. Brophy from *Marlin Firearms* with permission

Exc.	V.G.	Good	Fair	Poor
—	—	450	200	75

Marlin 38 Standard 1878 Pocket Revolver

This model is different than its predecessors in that it features a steel frame and flat bottom butt, with hard rubber monogram grips. There was still a spur trigger, and the 3.25" ribbed round barrel still tipped up for loading. This model is chambered for the .38 centerfire cartridge. The finish is full nickel plate, and the top of the barrel is marked "38 Standard 1878." There were approximately 9,000 manufactured between 1878 and 1887.

Photo by Lt. Col. William S. Brophy from *Marlin Firearms* with permission

Exc.	V.G.	Good	Fair	Poor
—	—	600	250	75

Marlin 1887 Double-Action Revolver

This is the last handgun that Marlin produced and the only double-action. It is chambered for the .32 or the .38 caliber centerfire cartridges and is of the break-open auto-ejector type. The fluted cylinder holds 6 shots in .32 and 5 shots in .38 caliber. The round ribbed barrel is 3.25" in length, and the frame is made of steel. The standard finish is nickel-plated with a blued trigger guard. Many full-blued examples have been noted. The round butt grips are hard rubber, and the top of the barrel is marked "Marlin Firearms Co. New Haven Conn. U.S.A./Patented Aug. 9 1887." There were approximately 15,000 manufactured between 1887 and 1899.

Photo by Lt. Col. William S. Brophy from *Marlin Firearms* with permission

Exc.	V.G.	Good	Fair	Poor
—	—	500	200	75

EARLY PRODUCTION MARLIN RIFLES

Model 1881 Lever-Action Rifle

This was the first of the Marlin lever-action rifles and has always been regarded as a high quality rifle. It is capable of handling the large calibers and was well received by the shooting public. The rifle is chambered for the .32-40, .38-55, .40-60, .45-70, and the .45-85. The 24", 28", or 30" octagonal barrel is standard. Round barrels were offered and are scarce today. There is a tubular magazine beneath the barrel, and the rear sight is the buckhorn type with a blade on the front. This model ejects its empty cartridges from the top. The finish is blued, with a case colored hammer, lever, and buttplate. The walnut stock is varnished. There were approximately 20,000 manufactured between 1881 and 1892 but this is not easy to ascertain, as the factory records on Marlin rifles are quite incomplete.

Courtesy Bonhams & Butterfields, San Francisco, California

Courtesy Bonhams & Butterfields, San Francisco, California

Exc.	V.G.	Good	Fair	Poor
—	3500	2000	750	300

Lightweight Model

Thinner frame, lever, and barrel .32-40 and .38-55 caliber only-24" and 28" Barrel

Exc.	V.G.	Good	Fair	Poor
—	3000	1750	600	300

NOTE: Add 200-300 percent premium for 1st Models prior to serial number 600. Add 15 percent premium for .45-70 caliber.

Model 1888 Lever-Action Rifle

This model is chambered for the .32-20, .38-40, and the .44-40 cartridges. This is a shorter action that was designed (chiefly by Lewis Hepburn) to handle the pistol cartridges for which it was chambered. The standard barrel was octagonal, but round barrels were available as special-order items. This is a top ejecting action. It has a buckhorn rear and a blade front sight. The finish is blued with a case colored hammer, lever, and buttplate. The walnut stock is varnished. There were approximately 4,800 manufactured in 1888 and 1889. As with most of these fine old rifles, many special-order options were available that affect today's market value. Individual appraisal would be necessary for these special models, to ascertain both value and authenticity.

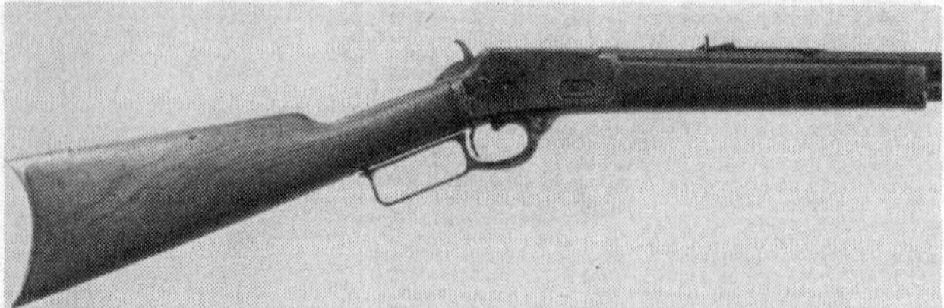

Exc.	V.G.	Good	Fair	Poor
—	3500	2500	600	350

NOTE: Add 40 percent premium for half octagon barrel. Add 20 percent premium for round barrel.

Model 1889 Lever-Action Rifle

This was Marlin's first side-eject, solid-top rifle. It is chambered for .25-20, .32-20, .38-40, and the .44-40 cartridges. It features either octagonal or round barrels in lengths from 24" to 32" with buckhorn rear and blade front sights. The finish is blued with a case colored hammer, lever, and buttplate. The plain walnut stock is varnished. The barrel is stamped "Marlin Fire-Arms Co. New Haven Ct. U.S.A./Patented Oct.11 1887 April 2.1889." This model features a lever latch, and many options were offered. Again one must urge individual appraisal on such variations. Values fluctuate greatly due to some seemingly insignificant variation. There were approximately 55,000 manufactured between 1889 and 1899.

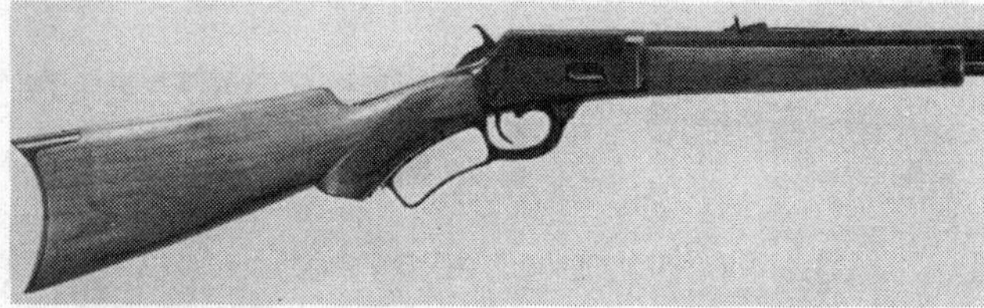

Production Model

24" barrel.

Exc.	V.G.	Good	Fair	Poor
—	1500	1000	450	150

Short Carbine

15" barrel. 327 produced.

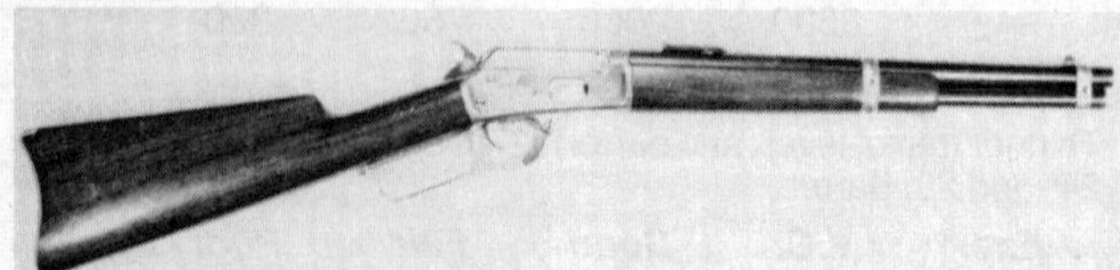

Photo by Lt. Col. William S. Brophy from *Marlin Firearms* with permission

Exc.	V.G.	Good	Fair	Poor
—	5000	2250	1000	500

Carbine 20" Barrel and Saddle Ring on Left Side of Receiver

Photo by Lt. Col. William S. Brophy from *Marlin Firearms* with permission

Exc.	V.G.	Good	Fair	Poor
—	2250	1250	500	250

Musket

30" barrel with full-length stock, 68 made in .44-40.

Exc.	V.G.	Good	Fair	Poor
—	6500	3000	1250	650

Model 1891 Lever-Action Rifle

This was Marlin's first rifle designed to fire the .22 rimfire and the first repeating rifle to accept the .22 Short, Long, and LR cartridges interchangeably. It was also chambered for the .32 rimfire and centerfire. The 24" octagonal barrel is standard, with a buckhorn rear and blade front sight. The finish is blued with a case colored hammer, lever, and buttplate. The stock is plain walnut. The first variation is marked "Marlin Fire-Arms Co. New Haven, Ct. U.S.A./Pat'd Nov.19.1878.April 2.1889. Aug.12 1890" on the barrel, with the solid-topped frame marked "Marlin Safety." The second variation was marked the same with "March 1,1892" added. There were approximately 18,650 manufactured between 1891 and 1897.

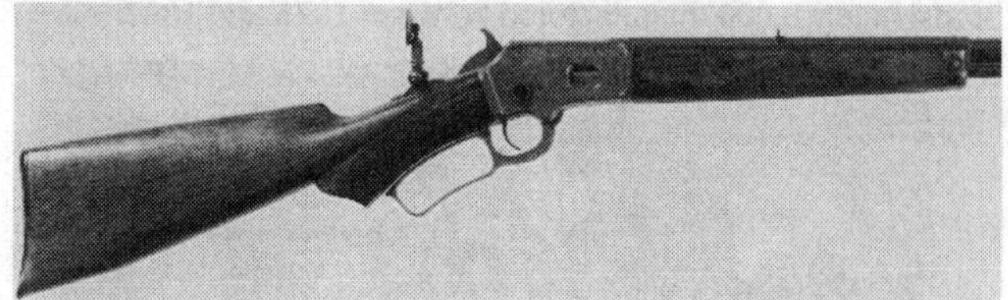

1st Variation

.22 rimfire only, side loading, appr. 5,000.

Exc.	V.G.	Good	Fair	Poor
—	2500	1000	550	300

2nd Variation

.22 and .32 rimfire, .32 centerfire, tube loading, Model 1891 on later model tangs (3rd variation).

Exc.	V.G.	Good	Fair	Poor
—	1500	500	300	150

NOTE: Add 20 percent for .22 rifle with "1891" stamped on tang. Deduct 50 percent for .32 caliber.

Model 1892 Lever-Action Rifle

This is basically an improved version of the Model 1891 and is similar to the second variation of the 1891. The only notable exceptions were the tang marking "Model 1892" and "Model 92" on later models. The .22 rimfire was scarce in the Model 1892. There were approximately 45,000 manufactured between 1895 and 1916. There were many options, and these special-order guns must be individually appraised to ascertain value and authenticity.

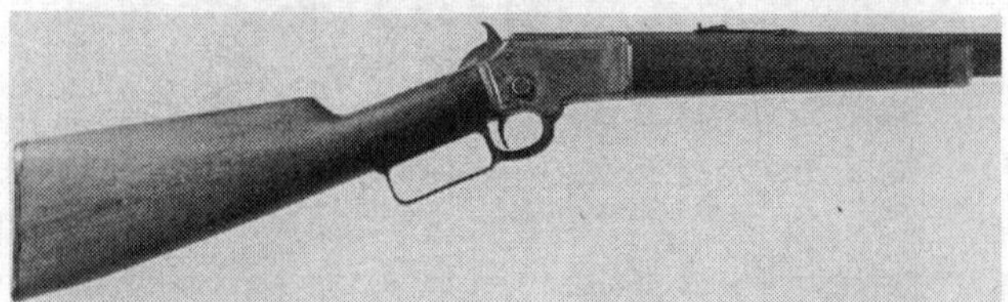

Exc.	V.G.	Good	Fair	Poor
—	1250	400	250	150

NOTE: Antique (pre-1898) add 20 percent.

.32 Rimfire and Centerfire

Exc.	V.G.	Good	Fair	Poor
—	850	350	150	100

Model 1893 Lever-Action Rifle

This model was the first rifle Marlin designed for the then new smokeless powder cartridges. It is chambered for the .25-36, .30-30, .32 Special, .32-40, and the .38-55. It was offered standard with either a round or octagonal barrel, in lengths of 24" to 32". Buckhorn rear and blade front sights were also standard. The receiver, lever, hammer, and buttplate are case colored, and the rest is blued. The stock is varnished walnut.

As with all of these early Marlins, many options were offered and, when encountered, will drastically alter the value of the particular rifle. For this reason we supply the values for the basic model and urge securing competent appraisal on non-standard specimens. The barrel on earlier guns is marked "Marlin FireArms Co. New Haven, Ct.U.S.A./ Patented Oct.11. 1887.April 2.1889.Aug.1.1893." In 1919 the markings were changed to "The Marlin Firearms Corporation/ New Haven, Conn.U.S.A.Patented." The rifles manufactured after 1904 are marked "Special Smokeless Steel" on the left side of the barrel. The upper tang is marked "Model 1893" on early guns; and "Model 93," on later specimens. There were approximately 900,000 manufactured between 1893 and 1935. Factory records are incomplete on the Model 1893.

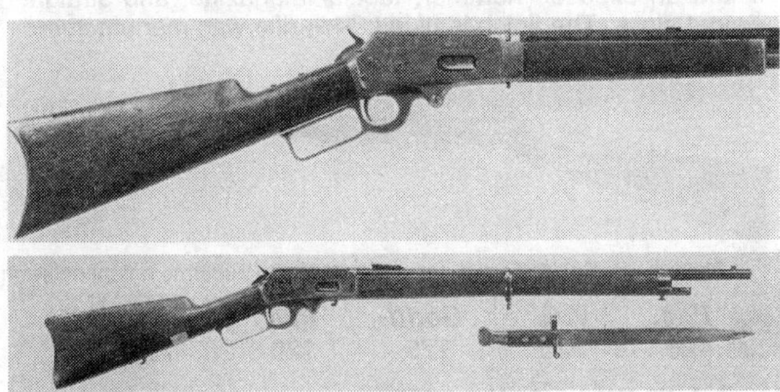

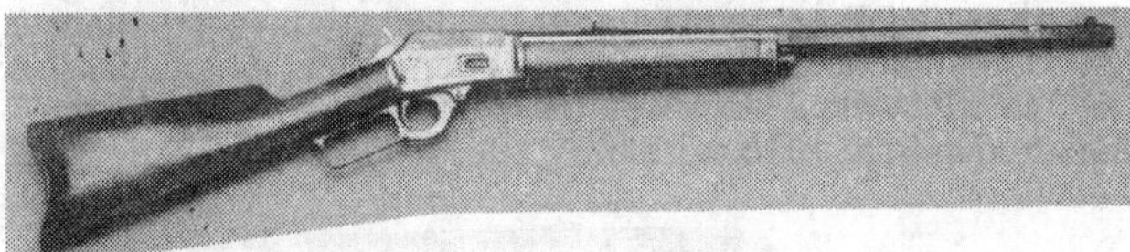

Antique Production (Pre-1898)

Courtesy Bonhams & Butterfields, San Francisco, California

Exc.	V.G.	Good	Fair	Poor
2250	1000	650	450	275

Modern Production 1899-1935

Exc.	V.G.	Good	Fair	Poor
1750	850	550	350	225

NOTE: Add 100 percent premium for musket. Deduct 50 percent for B model with blued receiver.

Model 1894 Lever-Action Rifle

This model is similar to the Model 1893, with a shorter action. It is chambered for the .25-20, .32-20, .38-40, and the .44-40. 24" to 32" round or octagonal barrels with full-length magazine tubes are standard, as are buckhorn rear and blade front sights. The finish is case colored receiver, lever, hammer, and buttplate, with the rest blued. The walnut stock is varnished. The first versions were marked "Marlin Fire-Arms Co., New Haven, Ct.U.S.A./Patented Oct.11, 1887. April 2,1889." The top of the frame is marked "Marlin Safety," and the model designation is not stamped on the tang. These early rifles were chambered for .38-40 and .44-40 only. The later rifles added the patent date "Aug. 1, 1893"; and "Model 1894" was stamped on the tang. On the latest versions this was shortened to "Model 94." There were approximately 250,000 manufactured between 1894 and 1935. This model was also produced with a great many options. Individual appraisal should be secured when confronted with these features.

Antique Production (Pre-1898)

Exc.	V.G.	Good	Fair	Poor
1700	1000	650	450	275

Modern Production (1899-1935)

Exc.	V.G.	Good	Fair	Poor
1600	850	550	350	225

NOTE: Add 100 percent premium for musket. Add 25 percent premium for saddle ring carbine. Add 30 percent premium for "Baby" carbine.

Model 1895 Lever-Action Rifle

This is a large rifle designed to fire the larger hunting cartridges. It is chambered for the .33 W.C.F., .38-56, .40-65, .40-70, .40-83, .45-70, and the .45-90. It came standard with round or octagonal barrels from 26" to 32" in length. A bull-length magazine tube was also standard, as were buckhorn rear and blade front sights. The finish is case colored receiver, lever, and hammer; the rest is blued with a varnished walnut stock. The barrel markings are the same as the Model 1894, and the top tang is marked "Model 1895." After 1896 "Special Smokeless Steel" was stamped on the barrel. There were also many options available for this model, and they have a big effect on the value. There were approximately 18,000 manufactured between 1895 and 1917.

Antique Production (Pre-1898)

Exc.	V.G.	Good	Fair	Poor
3500	2750	2000	1250	600

Modern Production (1899-1917)

Exc.	V.G.	Good	Fair	Poor
2400	1500	875	650	500

Model 1895M Guide Gun

This lever-action model is chambered for the .450 Marlin cartridge and is fitted with a 18.5" barrel. Adjustable rear sight. Blued finish is sandblasted receiver top. Checkered walnut stock is Mar-Shield finish. Weight is about 7 lbs.

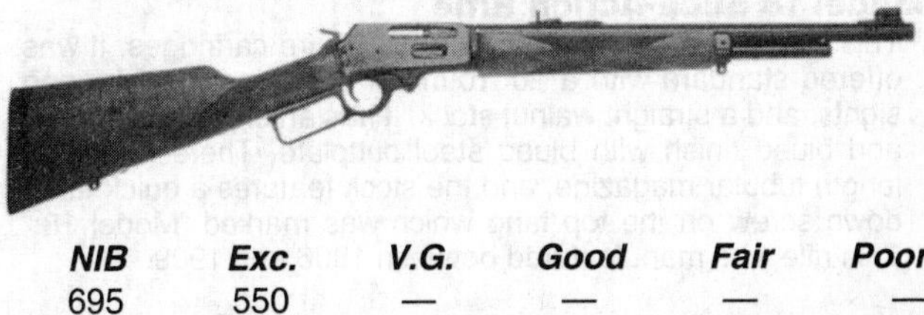

NIB	Exc.	V.G.	Good	Fair	Poor
695	550	—	—	—	—

Model 1895MR

Similar to the Model 1895M but fitted with a 22" barrel and chambered for the .450 Marlin cartridge. Walnut stock has pistol-grip with ventilated recoil pad. Adjustable rear sight. Weight is about 7.5 lbs. Introduced in 2003.

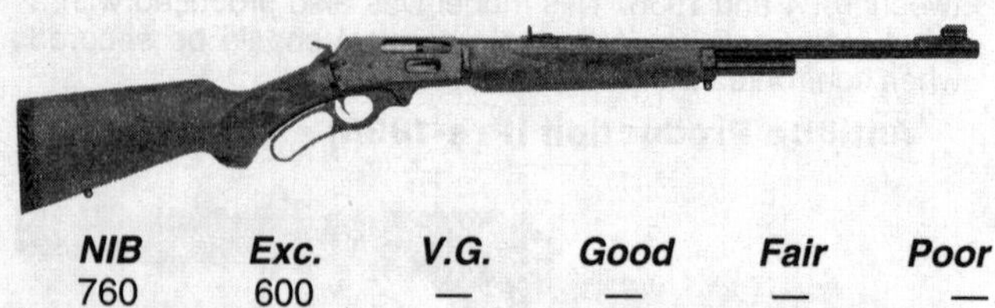

NIB	Exc.	V.G.	Good	Fair	Poor
760	600	—	—	—	—

Model 1895 Century Limited

Introduced in 1995 to commemorate the 100th anniversary of the Marlin Model 1895, as well as the 125th anniversary of the Marlin Company. The rifle is chambered for the .45-70 Government cartridge. It features a 24" half round/half octagon barrel, a crescent buttplate, semi-fancy American black walnut stock. and French greyed engraved receiver. Production limited to 2,500 guns.

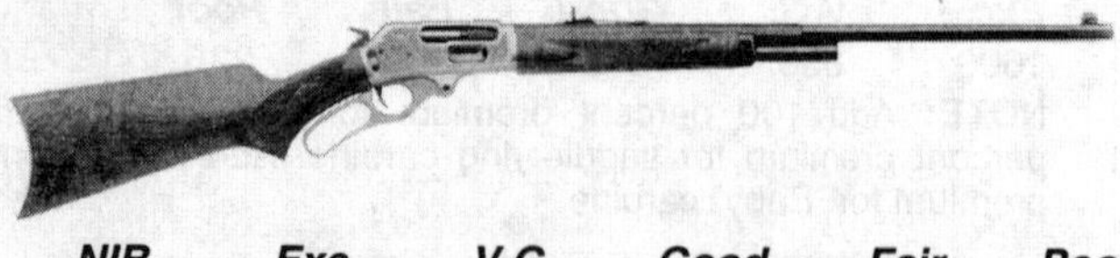

NIB	Exc.	V.G.	Good	Fair	Poor
800	650	500	350	275	200

Model 1897 Lever-Action Rifle

This model is an improved version of the Model 1892. It was chambered for the .22 rimfire only and came standard with a 24", 26", or 28" round, octagonal, or part-round, part-octagonal barrel. The standard sights are buckhorn rear and blade front, and all were manufactured as takedown rifles. They have case colored receiver, lever, and hammer. The rest is blued, and the walnut stock is varnished. There were approximately 125,000 manufactured between 1897 and 1917. In 1922 production was begun with the designation changed to Model 39 which is produced to this day. There were also options offered with this rifle that have great effect on the value; take this into consideration and seek qualified appraisal.

Standard Production Rifle

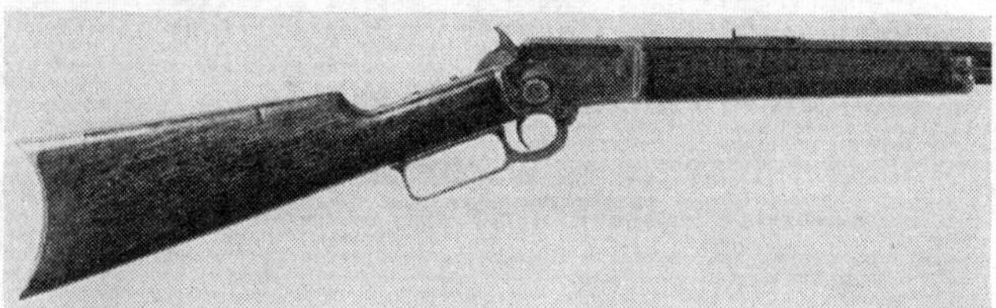

Exc.	V.G.	Good	Fair	Poor
1500	1000	650	350	200

NOTE: For first year production antique add 40 percent.

Deluxe Rifle

Checkering and fancy pistol-grip stock.

Exc.	V.G.	Good	Fair	Poor
2500	1500	850	500	300

MODERN PRODUCTION MARLIN RIFLES

Model 18 Slide-Action Rifle

This model is chambered for the .22 rimfire cartridges. It was offered standard with a 20" round or octagonal barrel, open sights, and a straight walnut stock. It has an exposed hammer and blued finish with blued steel buttplate. There is a half-length tubular magazine, and the stock features a quick takedown screw on the top tang which was marked "Model 18." This rifle was manufactured between 1906 and 1909.

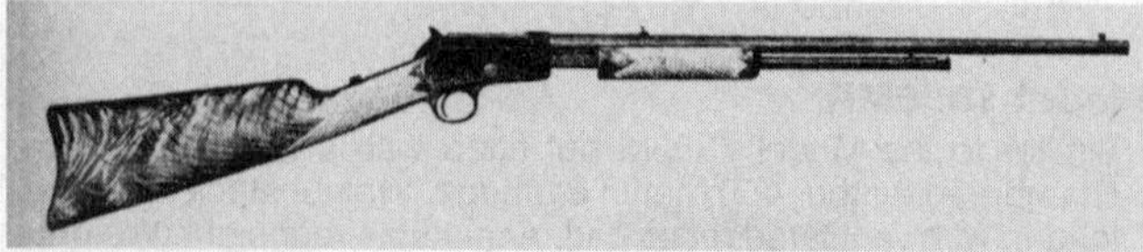

Photo by Lt. Col. William S. Brophy from Marlin Firearms with permission

Exc.	V.G.	Good	Fair	Poor
500	350	200	150	80

Model 20 Slide-Action Rifle

The Model 20 was chambered for the .22 rimfire cartridges and was offered standard with a 24" octagonal barrel and open sight, with an exposed hammer. This rifle was only made as a "Takedown" receiver model and is blued, with a straight walnut stock. It was manufactured between 1907 and 1922.

Exc.	V.G.	Good	Fair	Poor
425	325	200	125	75

Model 25 Slide-Action Rifle

This model was chambered for the .22 Short only and was not a commercial success. The 23" round or octagonal barrel is standard, as are open sights. It is called a takedown model, but only the stock is removable—the receiver does not separate. It has an exposed hammer, tubular magazine, and straight walnut stock. The finish is blued. This rifle was manufactured in 1909 and 1910.

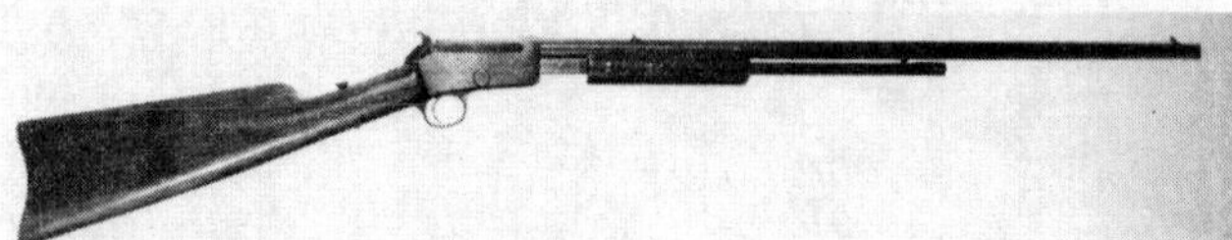

Photo by Lt. Col. William S. Brophy from Marlin Firearms with permission

Exc.	V.G.	Good	Fair	Poor
425	325	175	120	75

Model 27 Slide-Action Rifle

This is a centerfire rifle chambered for the .25-20 and .32-20 cartridges. Also chambered for the .25 caliber rimfire cartridge. It features a 24" octagonal barrel with two-thirds-length magazine tube that holds 7 shots. It has open sights, a blued finish, and straight walnut stock with crescent buttplate. It was manufactured in from 1910 to 1916.

Exc.	V.G.	Good	Fair	Poor
500	400	275	175	100

NOTE: Deduct 20 percent for rifles chambered for the .25 rimfire.

Model 27S Slide-Action Rifle

The Model 27S is similar to the Model 27 but with a sliding button on the right side of the receiver that permitted the gun to be opened while a cartridge was in the chamber. It was offered with a round (1913) or octagonal 24" barrel. The .25 rimfire cartridge was added in 1913 to those already available. This model was introduced in 1910 and was manufactured until 1932.

Exc.	V.G.	Good	Fair	Poor
375	300	175	100	70

This symbol denotes "Sleepers" with rapidly-rising values and/or significant collector potential.

Model 29 Slide-Action Rifle

This model is identical to the Model 20 with a 23" round barrel and smooth walnut forend instead of a grooved one as found on the Model 20. It was manufactured between 1913 and 1916.

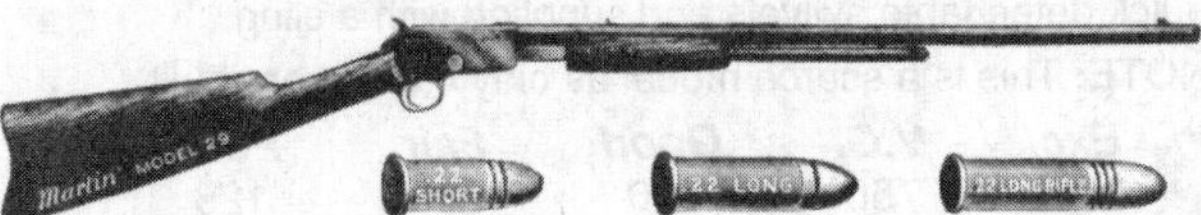

Photo by Lt. Col. William S. Brophy from *Marlin Firearms* with permission

Exc.	V.G.	Good	Fair	Poor
375	300	185	120	80

Model 32 Slide-Action Rifle

This model was the first of the hammerless slide-action rifles. It is chambered for the .22 rimfire and has a 24" octagonal barrel and half-length magazine tube. The Model 32 is a take-down rifle with adjustable sights and features "Ballard" rifling. It is blued, with a pistol-grip walnut stock. The advent of WWI and the need for Marlin to produce military arms cut short the production of this model. It was manufactured in 1914 and 1915 only.

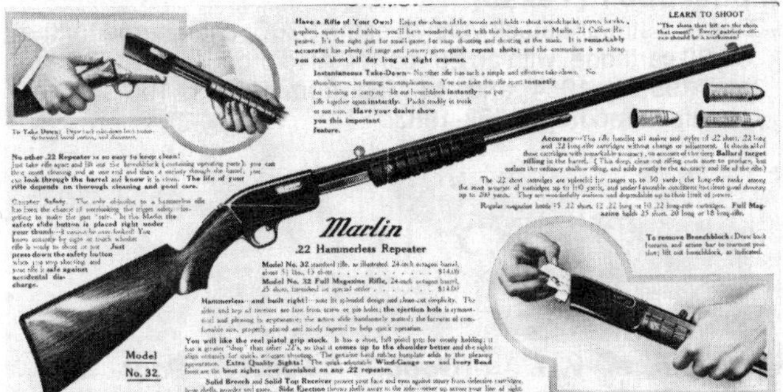

Photo by Lt. Col. William S. Brophy from *Marlin Firearms* with permission

Exc.	V.G.	Good	Fair	Poor
600	425	275	150	100

Model 37 Slide-Action Rifle

This model is the same as the Model 29 with a 24" round barrel and full-length magazine tube. It was manufactured between 1913 and 1916.

Photo by Lt. Col. William S. Brophy from *Marlin Firearms* with permission

Exc.	V.G.	Good	Fair	Poor
350	300	250	150	100

Model 38 Slide-Action Rifle

This was the hammerless model introduced after the end of WWI to replace the Model 32. It is similar in appearance but features a Rocky Mountain adjustable rear and an ivory bead front sight instead of the distinctive round Swebilius sight on the Model 32. The Model 38 was manufactured between 1920 and 1930.

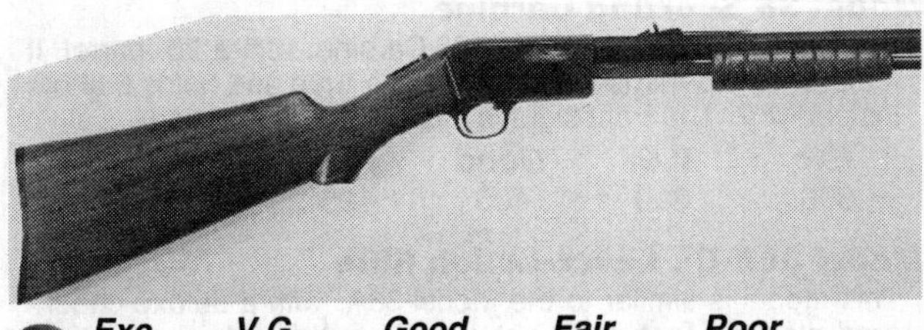

Exc.	V.G.	Good	Fair	Poor
500	400	300	175	115

Model 40 Slide-Action Rifle

This model is identical to the Model 27S centerfire rifle except that the barrel is marked "Marlin-Rockwell." The top tang is stamped "Marlin/Mod. 40." This is a rare model, and not many marked in this manner have been noted.

Exc.	V.G.	Good	Fair	Poor
700	575	375	225	150

Model 47 Slide-Action Rifle

This model is similar to the Model 20, with a 23" round barrel and an improved magazine tube. The Model 47 has a case colored receiver and a checkered buttstock. This model was not offered for sale nor was it listed in Marlin's catalog but was offered free of charge to anyone purchasing four shares of Marlin stock for $100. One other fact about this model is that it was the first Marlin to be case colored with the new cyanide method; this created a tiger-striped pattern that is peculiar to the Model 47 Rifle.

Exc.	V.G.	Good	Fair	Poor
750	600	400	250	160

Model 1936 Lever-Action Rifle or Carbine

This model is a direct descendant of the Model 1893. It is chambered for the .30-30 and the .32 Special cartridge. The stock is streamlined with a pistol grip added and a 20" round barrel. A barrel band and improved sights are utilized. It has a 7-shot tube magazine and a semi-beavertail forearm. The receiver, lever, and hammer are case colored; and the rest is blued. This model was manufactured between 1936 and 1948. It was designated the Model 36 in 1937.

1st Variation (early 1936)

This variation has a slight "fish-belly" forearm, long tang, case colored receiver, lever, and hammer, with no serial number prefix. These are rare.

Exc.	V.G.	Good	Fair	Poor
1200	850	400	175	125

2nd Variation (late 1936-1947)

This variation has thicker forearm, short tang, and "B" serial number prefix.

Exc.	V.G.	Good	Fair	Poor
1000	650	300	150	100

Model 36 Lever-Action Rifle or Carbine (1937-1948)

First and Second variations both have case colored receiver and "C" serial number prefix. Second variation tapped for receiver sight.

Exc.	V.G.	Good	Fair	Poor
800	600	400	195	125

Third Variation—Blued Receiver

Exc.	V.G.	Good	Fair	Poor
600	400	300	175	100

Model 36 Sporting Carbine

This model is similar to the 1936 Carbine, with a 20" barrel. It features a two-thirds-length magazine tube and holds 6 shots instead of 7. The front sight is a ramp sight with hood.

Exc.	V.G.	Good	Fair	Poor
800	600	400	195	125

Model 36A-DL Lever-Action Rifle

This model is similar to the Model 36A, with a deluxe checkered stock. It features sight swivels and is furnished with a leather sling.

Exc.	V.G.	Good	Fair	Poor
800	650	400	225	150

Model 336

Information and prices on the Model 336 were provided by Doug Murray, author and publisher of *The 336* (1983).

Model 336 Carbine (R.C. Regular Carbine)

This model was introduced in 1948 and was an improved version of the Model 36. It features a new-type round bolt, chrome-plated with improved extractor and redesigned cartridge carrier that improved feeding. It is chambered for the .30-30 and the .32 Special cartridges and has a 20" tapered round barrel with Ballard-type rifling. The finish is blued, with the receiver top matted to reduce reflections. The pistol-grip stock and semi-beavertail forend are of American walnut. It features Rocky Mountain-style rear and bead front sights, and the hammer is lowered to facilitate scope mounting.

Exc.	V.G.	Good	Fair	Poor
375	250	175	125	100

Model 336C

The same as the Model 336 Carbine. In 1951 the catalog model designation was changed. In 1952 the .35 Remington cartridge was added to the line. In 1963 the .32 Special was discontinued.

Exc.	V.G.	Good	Fair	Poor
375	250	175	125	100

Model 336A

This model is similar to the 336C, with a 24" barrel and steel forend tip instead of a barrel band. The magazine tube is two-thirds-length and holds 6 shots. This model was introduced in 1948 and built until 1962. It was reintroduced in 1973 and discontinued in 1980. In 1950 the .35 Rem. was introduced, and in 1960 the .32 Special was discontinued.

Exc.	V.G.	Good	Fair	Poor
350	275	200	150	125

Model 336ADL

This model differs from the Model 336A by having a deluxe wood checkered stock and forend, quick detachable swivels, better grade finish, and a sling.

Exc.	V.G.	Good	Fair	Poor
650	500	300	150	125

Model 336SC (Sporting Carbine)

This is basically a 336A with forend tip and two-thirds magazine but has a 20" barrel instead of the 24" found on the 336A.

Exc.	V.G.	Good	Fair	Poor
400	300	200	150	100

Model 336SD (Sporting Deluxe Carbine)

This is the 336 SC in a deluxe checkered stock version, with quick detachable swivels and supplied with a sling.

NOTE: This is a scarce model as only 4,392 were built.

Exc.	V.G.	Good	Fair	Poor
1000	750	400	200	125

Model 336 MicroGroove Zipper

This model was advertised as a fast-handling, lever-action carbine chambered for the .219 Zipper cartridges flat trajectory, varmint-type round. It has a 20" heavy barrel, which was the feature that doomed it to failure as this was too short to coax the maximum performance and accuracy from the cartridge. The "MicroGroove" rifling that was used did not yield long barrel life; and the model survived from 1955 through 1959, when it was discontinued. It is externally similar to the 336 SC.

Exc.	V.G.	Good	Fair	Poor
900	550	350	200	150

NOTE: First few thousand zippers made in standard weight barrels, not heavy weight. These are scarce and found in the "M" prefix code number. Add 100 percent.

Model 336T (Texan)

This is a straight-stock version of the 336C, chambered for the .30-30 cartridge, with an 20" barrel. Also produced in .35 Rem. from 1953 to 1964, and .44 Mag. from 1965 to 1967. It was manufactured from 1953-1983.

Exc.	V.G.	Good	Fair	Poor
425	350	250	175	100

Model 336DT

A deluxe-stock version of the "Texan," with the map of Texas and a longhorn carved on the butt. It was manufactured between 1962 and 1964. Calibers are .30-30 and .35 Rem.

Exc.	V.G.	Good	Fair	Poor
475	360	225	175	125

Model 336 "Marauder"

This is simply a 336T with a 16.25" barrel and a slimmer forend. It is chambered for either the .30-30 or .35 Remington cartridges, has a gold trigger, and is drilled and tapped for both scope mounts and receiver sights. It was manufactured in 1963 and 1964.

Exc.	V.G.	Good	Fair	Poor
675	550	300	150	100

Model 336 .44 Magnum

This is the 336 "Marauder" with a 20" MicroGroove barrel chambered for the .44 Magnum cartridge. It holds 10 shots and was introduced in 1963.

Exc.	V.G.	Good	Fair	Poor
550	350	250	150	100

Model 336 "Centennial"

In 1970 a 100th year medallion was embedded into the buttstock of the 336 Carbines, the 336 Texan, and the 444 Rifle.

Exc.	V.G.	Good	Fair	Poor
400	300	250	200	150

1970 100th Year Commemorative Matched Pair

This is a deluxe octagonal barreled .30-30 with an engraved receiver and deluxe wood with an inlaid medallion, accompanied by a matching Model 339 .22 rimfire rifle. They are numbered the same and are furnished in a deluxe luggage case.

 *This symbol denotes "Sleepers" with rapidly-rising values and/or significant collector potential.*

There were 1,000 sets manufactured in 1970. These are commemoratives, and as such it should be noted that collectors usually will only show interest if they are new and uncocked in the original packaging. All accessories and brochures should be included for them to be worth top dollar. Once a commemorative has been used, it has no more value than as a shooter.

NIB	Exc.	V.G.	Good	Fair	Poor
1800	1400	900	600	400	300

Model 336 "Zane Grey Century"

This model was introduced in 1972, the 100th anniversary of the birth of Zane Grey, the famous Western author. This model has a 22" octagonal barrel chambered for the .30-30. The stock is high grade walnut and features a brass buttplate and pistol-grip cap. A Zane Grey medallion is inlaid into the receiver. There were 10,000 manufactured in 1972. This is a commemorative rifle and must be new in the box to generate the top collector appeal.

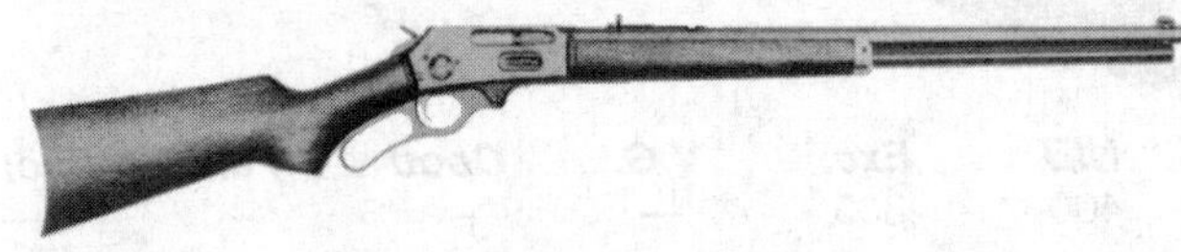

NIB	Exc.	V.G.	Good	Fair	Poor
600	425	275	200	150	100

Model 336 Octagon

This model was introduced to utilize the octagonal barrel making equipment that was on hand from the manufacture of the commemoratives. It is essentially a 336T with a 22" tapered octagonal barrel chambered for .30-30 only. It features a full-length magazine tube, slim forend with steel cap, and a classic-style hard rubber buttplate. The walnut stock is straight, and the lever is square. The finish, including the trigger, is blued. This model was made in 1973 only.

NIB	Exc.	V.G.	Good	Fair	Poor
600	500	325	175	150	100

Model 336ER (Extra Range)

This model was introduced in 1983 and was advertised as being chambered for the .307 Winchester and the .356 Winchester cartridges. The .307 was never produced. The .356 Winchester was supposed to add new capabilities to this classic rifle, but it never caught on with the shooting public and was discontinued in 1986 after only 2,441 Model ERs were manufactured. It has a 20" barrel and 5-shot tube magazine.

Exc.	V.G.	Good	Fair	Poor
800	550	300	250	150

Model 336CS

This is the current carbine model of this line. It has a hammer-block safety and is chambered for the .30-30, .35 Remington, and until 1988 the .375 Winchester. The barrel is 20", and the magazine tube holds 6 shots. The pistol-grip stock and semi-beavertail forearm are American walnut. This model has been manufactured since 1984. The 1983 model was known as the 336C and had no hammer-block safety. Weight is approximately 7 lbs.

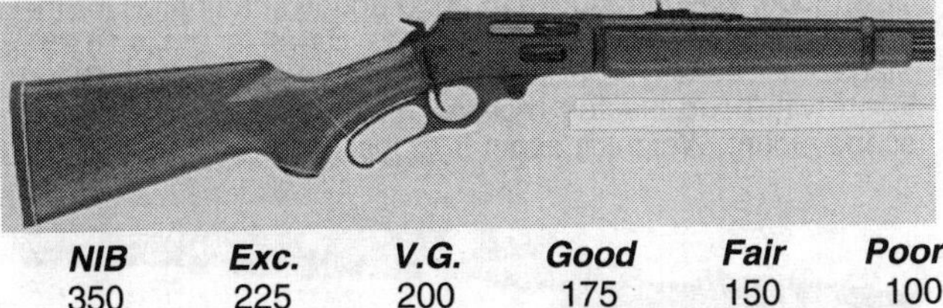

NIB	Exc.	V.G.	Good	Fair	Poor
350	225	200	175	150	100

Model 336LTS

This is the latest version of the old "Marauder" carbine. It was dubbed the LTS or "Lightweight" model instead of the Marauder as it was feared that the latter designation would be inappropriate in today's society. The model features a 16.5" barrel with full-length tube magazine that holds 5 shots. The walnut stock has a straight grip, and there is a barrel band on the forearm. The butt has a rubber rifle pad. This model was introduced in 1988.

NIB	Exc.	V.G.	Good	Fair	Poor
450	300	250	200	150	100

Model 336 Cowboy

This model is similar to the Model 336 CS. It is available in both .30-30 and .38-55 calibers. It is fitted with 24" tapered octagon barrel. Rear sight is Marble buckhorn. Tubular magazine holds 6 rounds. Straight grip walnut stock has a hard rubber buttplate. Weight is about 7.5 lbs. First introduced in 1999.

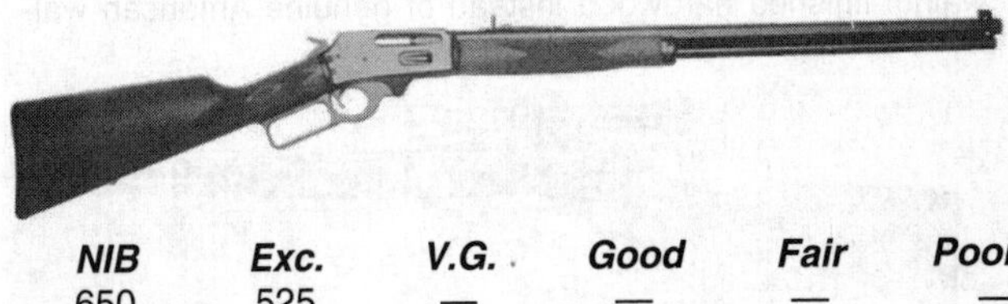

NIB	Exc.	V.G.	Good	Fair	Poor
650	525	—	—	—	—

Model 336M

Introduced in 2000, this model is chambered for the .30-30 cartridge. It features a stainless steel receiver and barrel; all other parts are nickel plated. Barrel length is 20". Magazine capacity is 6 rounds. Checkered walnut stock has a Mar-Shield finish. Rubber buttpad. Weight is about 7 lbs.

NIB	Exc.	V.G.	Good	Fair	Poor
N/A	—	—	—	—	—

Model 336CC

Chambered for the .30-30 cartridge and fitted with a 20" barrel this model features a Mossy Oak Break-Up camo finish. Adjustable rear sight. Weight is about 7 lbs. Introduced in 2001.

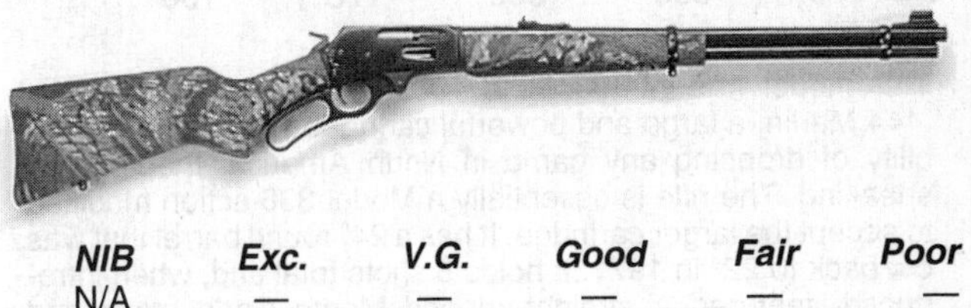

NIB	Exc.	V.G.	Good	Fair	Poor
N/A	—	—	—	—	—

Model 336Y "Spike Horn"

Chambered for the .30-30 cartridge and fitted with a 16.5" barrel, this rifle features a checkered walnut stock with pistol grip. Magazine capacity is 5 rounds. Adjustable rear sight. Weight is about 6.5 lbs. Introduced in 2003.

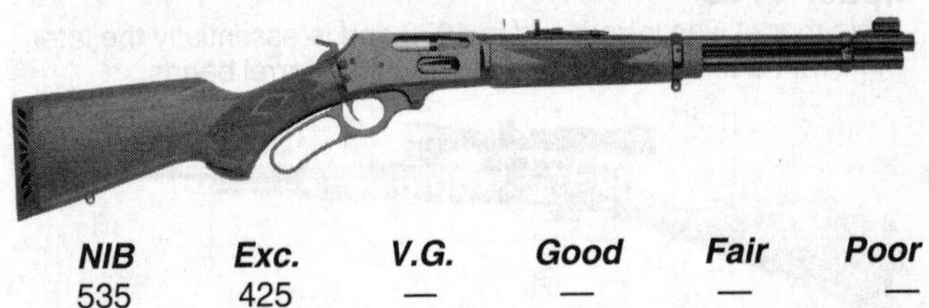

NIB	Exc.	V.G.	Good	Fair	Poor
535	425	—	—	—	—

Model 336XLR

Lever-action chambered in 30/30, with 5-shot tubular magazine, 24-inch stainless steel barrel, along with stainless steel receiver, trigger, trigger guard plate, magazine tube, loading gate, and lever. Full pistol grip, swivel studs, and Ballard-type rifling precision fluted bolt. Features solid top receiver with side-ejection, adjustable folding semi-buckhorn rear sight,

This symbol denotes "Sleepers" with rapidly-rising values and/or significant collector potential. 

ramp front sight, tapped for scope mount. Designed for Hornady LEVERevolution cartridges. Introduced 2006.

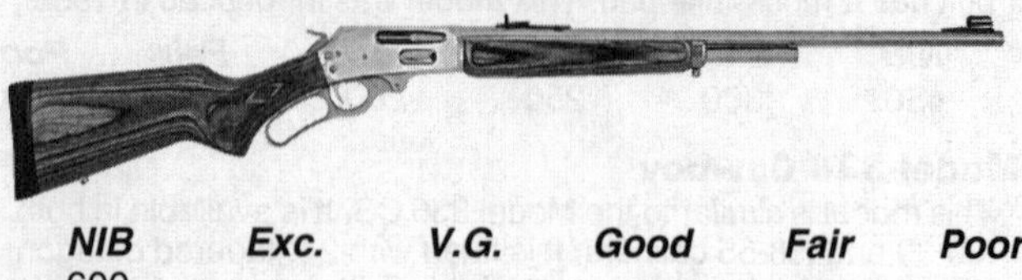

NIB	Exc.	V.G.	Good	Fair	Poor
600	—	—	—	—	—

Model 30AS

This model is similar to the 336 CS, but the stock is made of walnut-finished hardwood instead of genuine American walnut. It is chambered for .30-30 only.

Marlin 30AS with scope

NIB	Exc.	V.G.	Good	Fair	Poor
285	250	200	175	125	100

Model 375 Lever-Action

This model was introduced in 1980. It has a 20" MicroGroove barrel and is chambered for the .375 Winchester cartridge. This should have been a popular rifle; but perhaps because of difficulty in obtaining ammunition, it was not a commercial success. Its appearance is much the same as the Model 336, with walnut pistol stock and steel forend tip. This model was discontinued in 1983 after 16,315 were manufactured.

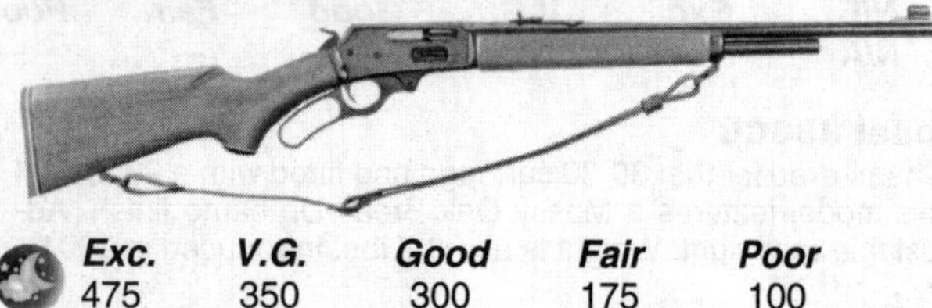

Exc.	V.G.	Good	Fair	Poor
475	350	300	175	100

Model 444 Lever-Action

This model was introduced in 1965. It is chambered for the .444 Marlin, a large and powerful cartridge that has the capability of dropping any game in North America, theoretically speaking. The rifle is essentially a Model 336 action modified to accept the larger cartridge. It has a 24" round barrel that was cut back to 22" in 1971. It holds 5 shots total and, when introduced, featured a straight-gripped Monte Carlo stock and semi-beavertail forend with barrel band. Another band holds the two-thirds-length magazine tube in place. In 1971 the stock was changed to a pistol grip without the Monte Carlo comb.

Exc.	V.G.	Good	Fair	Poor
450	300	175	125	100

Model 444S

This model was introduced in 1972 and is essentially the later 444 with a steel forend tip instead of the barrel bands.

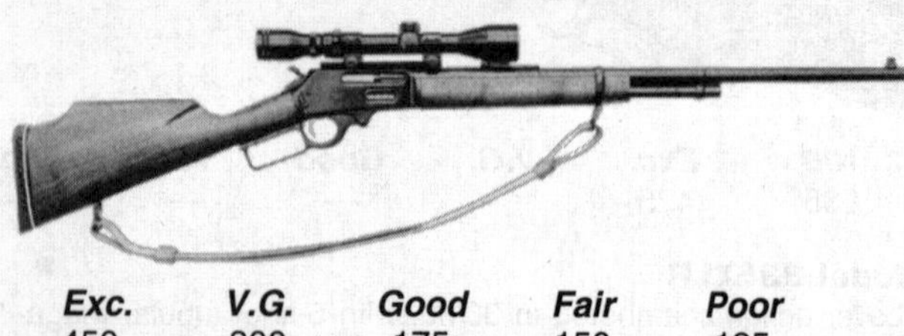

Exc.	V.G.	Good	Fair	Poor
450	300	175	150	125

Model 444SS

In 1984 the company added a crossbolt hammer-block safety to the 444 S and redesignated it the 444 SS. This Model is currently in production.

NIB	Exc.	V.G.	Good	Fair	Poor
395	300	225	175	150	125

Model 444P Outfitter

Introduced in 1999 this model is chambered for the .444 Marlin cartridge. It is fitted with a 18.5" ported barrel. Tubular magazine capacity is 5 rounds. Walnut stock with straight grip and ventilated recoil pad standard. Weight is approximately 6.75 lbs.

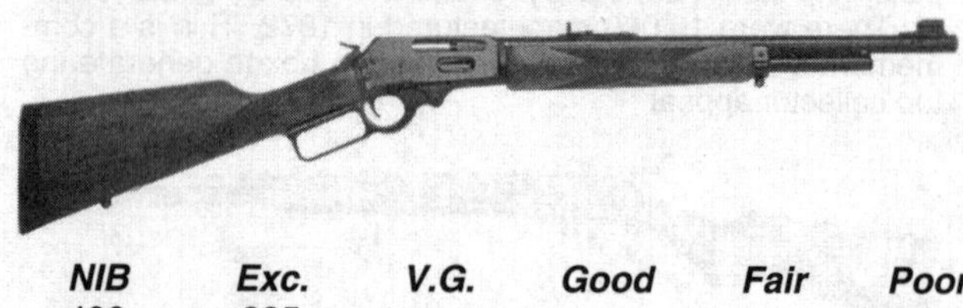

NIB	Exc.	V.G.	Good	Fair	Poor
400	335	—	—	—	—

Model 444XLR

Similar to Model 1895XLR but chambered in .444 Marlin.Introduced 2006.

NIB	Exc.	V.G.	Good	Fair	Poor
600	—	—	—	—	—

Model 1894 Lever-Action

The production of the Model 336 in .44 Magnum was a frustrating experience as the action was simply too long for a short pistol case. In 1969 Marlin reintroduced the Model 1894 chambered for the .44 Magnum cartridge. The barrel is 20", and the full-length magazine tube holds 10 rounds. It features an adjustable rear and a ramp-type front sight. The finish is blued, with a matted receiver top. The walnut stock has a straight grip; and the forend, a barrel band. From 1969 to 1971 there was a brass saddle ring.

NIB	Exc.	V.G.	Good	Fair	Poor
450	375	300	200	150	100

Model 1894 Octagon Barrel

This is basically the same as the Model 1894, with a 20" octagonal barrel and a steel forend tip instead of the barrel band. There were 2,957 manufactured in 1973 only.

Exc.	V.G.	Good	Fair	Poor
475	375	275	200	100

Model 1894 Sporter

This variation has a 20" round barrel, half-length magazine tube that holds 6 shots, and a hard rubber classic-style buttplate. Only 1,398 were manufactured in 1973.

NIB	Exc.	V.G.	Good	Fair	Poor
475	325	250	175	125	100

Model 1894P

This model was introduced in 2000 and is chambered for the .44 Magnum or .44 Special cartridges. Barrel length is 16.25". Magazine capacity is 8 rounds. Adjustable rear sight. Blued finish with bead blasted receiver top. Drilled and tapped for scope mount. Weight is about 5.75 lbs.

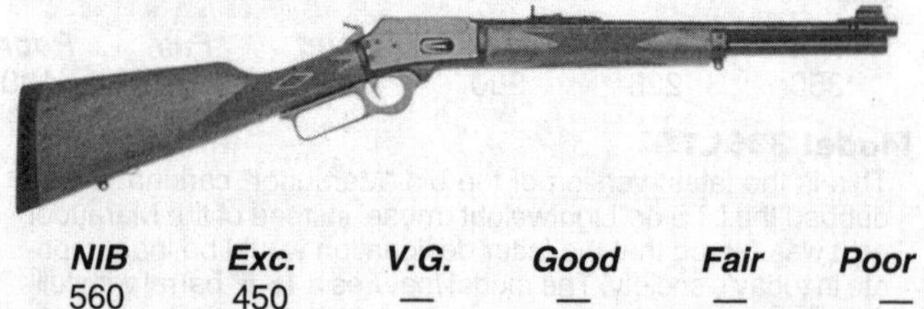

NIB	Exc.	V.G.	Good	Fair	Poor
560	450	—	—	—	—

This symbol denotes "Sleepers" with rapidly-rising values and/or significant collector potential.

Model 1894CS Lever-Action

This model is chambered for the .38 Special and .357 Magnum cartridges. It features an 18.5" round barrel, with full-length magazine tube and two barrel bands. It holds 9 shots and has a walnut straight-grip stock. This model was manufactured between 1969 and 1984. In 1984 a hammer-block crossbolt safety was added, and the model number was changed to 1894 CS. All other specifications remained the same.

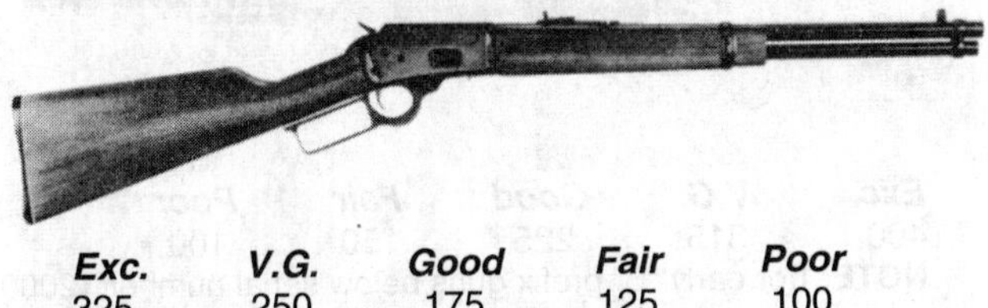

Exc.	V.G.	Good	Fair	Poor
325	250	175	125	100

Model 1894M Lever-Action Rifle

This model is similar to the other 1894 rifles except that it is chambered for the .22 Magnum cartridge and features an outside loading tube magazine that holds 11 shots. The barrel is 20" long, and there is a steel forend tip instead of a barrel band.

NOTE: It is important to note that this model will not function properly with any cartridge except the .22 Magnum and that injury could result from attempting to chamber and fire the shorter .22 LR. This model was manufactured between 1983 and 1988 and was only produced with the crossbolt safety.

Exc.	V.G.	Good	Fair	Poor
375	325	275	200	100

Model 1894S Lever-Action Rifle

This model was introduced in 1984. It is chambered for the .41 Magnum and the .44 Special/.44 Magnum cartridges. In 1988 the .45 Colt chambering was offered. This model has a 20" barrel and a straight-grip stock. The forend has a steel cap. This model is currently produced and features the hammer-block safety.

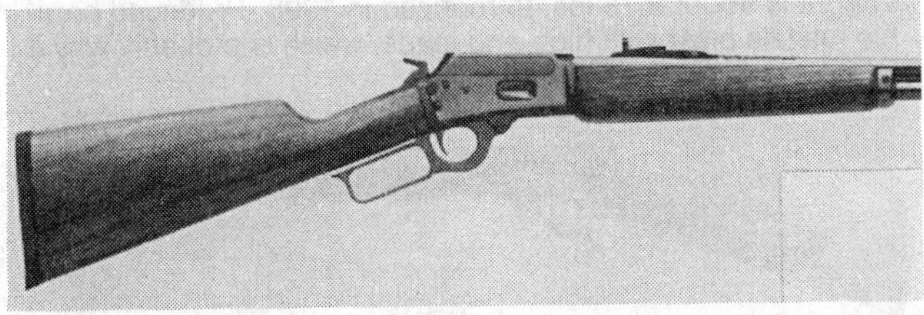

NIB	Exc.	V.G.	Good	Fair	Poor
450	375	275	225	175	125

Model 1894CL (Classic) Lever-Action Rifle

This model was introduced in 1988 and is the same basic rifle chambered for the old .25-20 and .32-20 cartridges. The rifle is also chambered for the .218 Bee cartridge. The barrel is 22", and the half-length magazine tube holds 6 shots. The walnut stock has no white spacers and has a black buttplate. Discontinued in 1993.

NOTE: Collector interest has been growing in this model since it was discontinued in 1993.

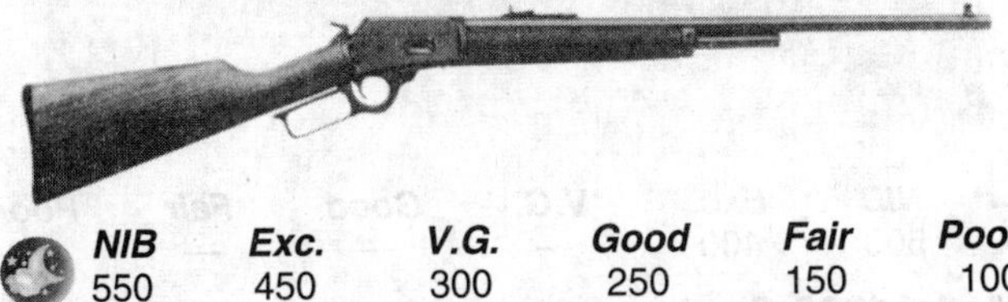

NIB	Exc.	V.G.	Good	Fair	Poor
550	450	300	250	150	100

Model 1894CL (Classic) New

Reintroduced in 2005 this model is chambered for the .32-20 cartridge and fitted with a 22" barrel with open sights. Tubular magazine capacity is 6 rounds. Checkered straight grip walnut stock. Weight is about 6 lbs.

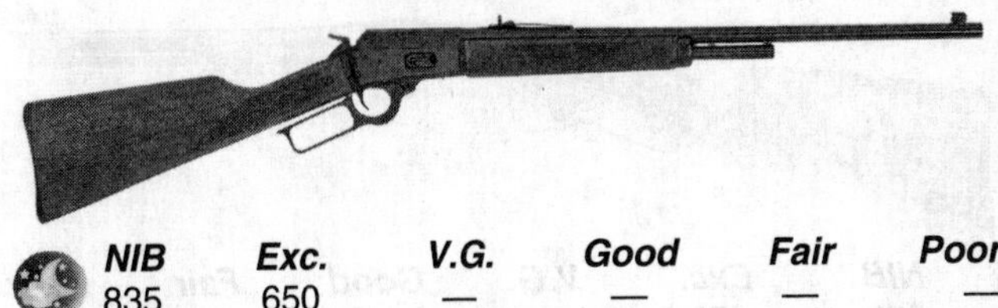

NIB	Exc.	V.G.	Good	Fair	Poor
835	650	—	—	—	—

Model 1894 Century Limited

An anniversary edition of the Marlin Model 1894 is limited to 2,500 rifles chambered in .44-40 caliber. Frame engraved and case colored. It is fitted with a 24" octagon barrel with 10-round magazine tube. The stock is semi-fancy walnut with straight grip and cut checkering with brass crescent buttplate.

NIB	Exc.	V.G.	Good	Fair	Poor
950	700	425	—	—	—

Model 1894 Century Limited Employee Edition

Same as above but limited to 100 rifles. The gun has a finer grade wood and the Marlin Man on the Horse logo is inlaid in gold on the right side of the receiver.

NIB	Exc.	V.G.	Good	Fair	Poor
1500	825	—	—	—	—

Model 1894 Cowboy

Introduced in 1996 this lever-action rifle features a 24" tapered octagon barrel with a 10-round tubular magazine. It is chambered for the .45 Long Colt, a popular cartridge for "Cowboy Action Shooting." Straight-grip checkered stock with blued steel forearm cap. Weight is approximately 7.5 lbs.

NIB	Exc.	V.G.	Good	Fair	Poor
600	450	300	—	—	—

Model 1894 Cowboy 32

As above but chambered for the .32 H&R Magnum cartridge. Introduced in 2004.

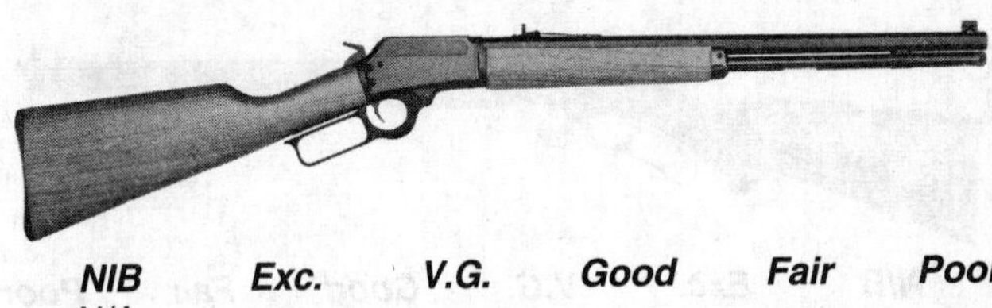

NIB	Exc.	V.G.	Good	Fair	Poor
N/A	—	—	—	—	—

Model 1894 Cowboy II

Introduced in 1997 and is the same as the Model 1894 Cowboy but is chambered for several cartridges. Available in .44-40, .357 Mag., .38 Special, and .44 Mag/.44 Special.

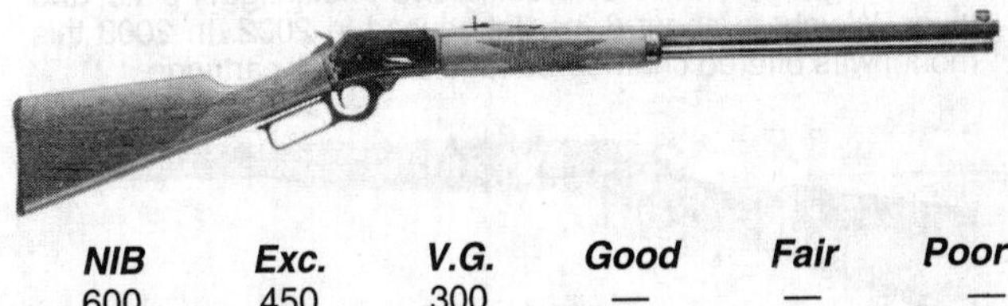

NIB	Exc.	V.G.	Good	Fair	Poor
600	450	300	—	—	—

Model 1894CP

This model is chambered for the .375 Magnum cartridge and fitted with a 16.25" ported barrel. Tubular magazine holds 8 rounds. Checkered American black walnut stock. Adjustable semi-buckhorn rear sight. Receiver drilled and tapped for scope mount. Weight is about 5.75 lbs. Introduced in 2001.

NIB	Exc.	V.G.	Good	Fair	Poor
560	450	—	—	—	—

Model 1894SS

This lever-action rifle is chambered for the .44 Magnum and .44 Special cartridges. Fitted with a 20" barrel with 10-round magazine. Stainless steel barrel and receiver. Checkered walnut stock with straight grip. Rubber buttpad. Weight is about 6 lbs. Introduced in 2002.

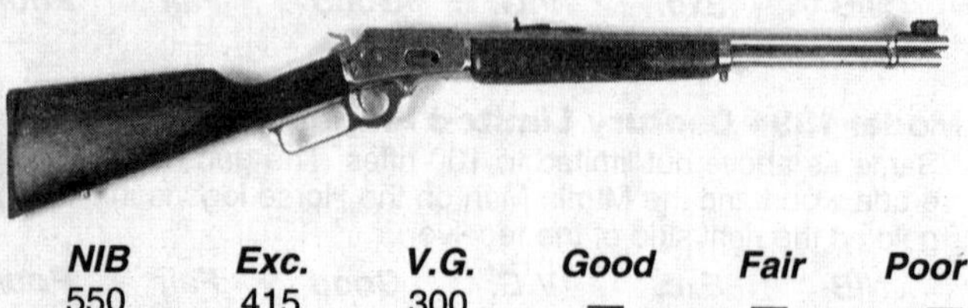

NIB	Exc.	V.G.	Good	Fair	Poor
550	415	300	—	—	—

Model 1894PG

Introduced in 2003, this lever-action model is chambered for the .44 Rem. Mag cartridge and fitted with a 20" barrel. Checkered walnut stock with pistol grip. Magazine capacity is 10 rounds. Adjustable rear sight. Blued finish. Weight is about 6.5 lbs.

NIB	Exc.	V.G.	Good	Fair	Poor
525	400	—	—	—	—

Model 1894FG

This lever-action model is chambered for the .41 Rem. Magnum cartridge and fitted with a 20" barrel. Checkered walnut stock with pistol grip. Magazine capacity is 10 rounds. Weight is about 6.5 lbs. Introduced in 2003.

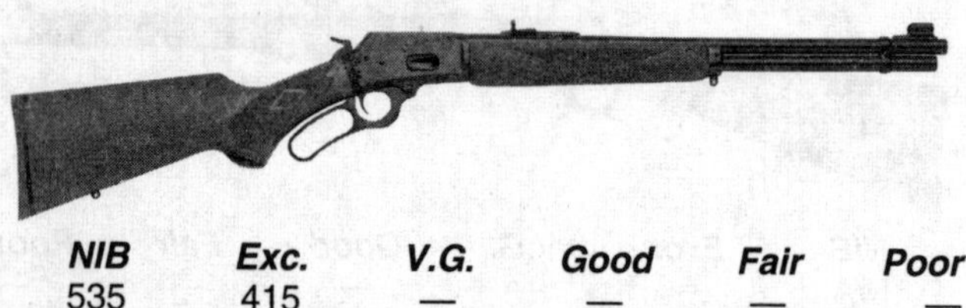

NIB	Exc.	V.G.	Good	Fair	Poor
535	415	—	—	—	—

Model 1894 Cowboy Competition

Fitted with a 20" barrel and chambered for the .38 Special cartridge, this rifle is designed for Cowboy Action Shooting. Special hand-tuned parts. Magazine capacity is 10 rounds. Walnut stock with straight grip. Case colored receiver, bolt, trigger plate, and lever. Weight is about 6 lbs. Introduced in 2002. In 2003 this model was offered chambered for the .45 Colt cartridge.

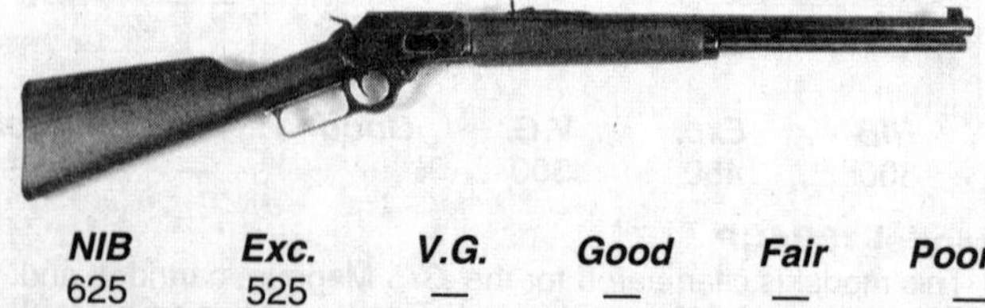

NIB	Exc.	V.G.	Good	Fair	Poor
625	525	—	—	—	—

Model 1895 and 1895SS Lever-Action

The model 1895 was reintroduced on the Model 336 action that had been modified to handle the .45-70 cartridge. This was done to capitalize on the nostalgia wave that descended on the country in the early 1970s. This model features a 22" round barrel with a two-thirds-length magazine tube that holds 4 shots. The walnut stock had a straight grip until the Model 1895 S was released in 1980, when a pistol-grip stock was used. In 1983 the Model 1895 SS with the crossbolt hammer-block safety was added; it is currently produced in this configuration.

Exc.	V.G.	Good	Fair	Poor
400	315	225	150	100

NOTE: For early "B" prefix guns below serial number 12000 add 25 percent.

Model 1895 Century Limited

Chambered for the .45-70 cartridge this model features a 4-shot tubular magazine, 24" half round/half octagon barrel, semi-fancy walnut stock with pistol grip. The receiver is French greyed and engraved with the Marlin Man on one side and two bears on the other. Weight is about 7.5 lbs.

NIB	Exc.	V.G.	Good	Fair	Poor
995	750	—	—	—	—

Model 1895 Century Limited Employee Edition

Similar to the above model but limited to 100 rifles. The company logo is inlaid in gold on the right side and the left side has two cow elk and a bull elk.

NIB	Exc.	V.G.	Good	Fair	Poor
1450	—	—	—	—	—

Model 1895G

This model is chambered for the .45-70 Government cartridge. It has a 18.5" ported barrel. Straight grip walnut stock with cut checkering and ventilated recoil pad. Adjustable rear sight. Weight is about 6.75 lbs. Introduced in 1998. Produced horrible muzzle blast with high-end loads, which is probably why it was discontinued.

NIB	Exc.	V.G.	Good	Fair	Poor
450	350	—	—	—	—

Model 1895GS

Introduced in 2001, this .45-70 rifle is fitted with a 18.5" ported barrel with 4-round magazine. Stainless steel receiver and barrel. American black walnut stock with cut checkering and ventilated recoil pad. Adjustable rear semi-buckhorn sight. Weight is about 7 lbs.

NIB	Exc.	V.G.	Good	Fair	Poor
500	400	—	—	—	—

Model 1895 Cowboy

This rifle is chambered for the .45-70 cartridge and fitted with a 26" tapered octagon barrel. Tubular magazine has a 9-round capacity. Adjustable semi-buckhorn rear sight. American black stock with cut checkering. Hard rubber butt. Weight is about 8 lbs. Introduced in 2001.

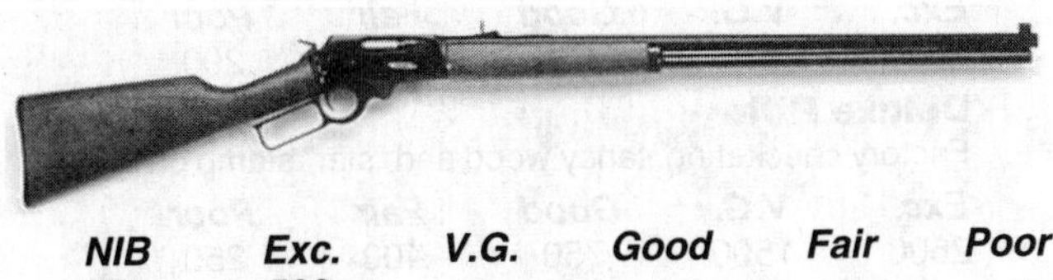

NIB	Exc.	V.G.	Good	Fair	Poor
650	500	—	—	—	—

Model 1895RL

This lever-action model, introduced in 2004, features an 18.5" barrel chambered for the .480 Ruger or .475 Linebaugh. Checkered American black walnut stock with pistol grip. Ventilated recoil pad. Adjustable rear sight. Magazine capacity is 6 rounds for the .480 Ruger and 5 rounds for the .475 Linebaugh. Weight is about 7 lbs.

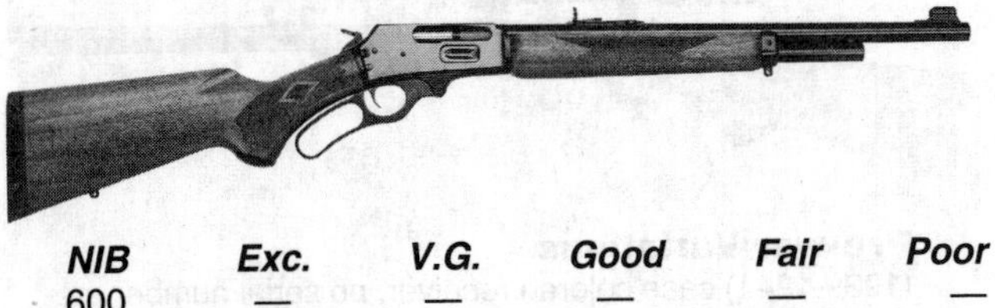

NIB	Exc.	V.G.	Good	Fair	Poor
600	—	—	—	—	—

Model 1895XLR

Lever-action chambered in .45-70 Government or .450 Marlin with a 4-shot tubular magazine, 24-inch stainless steel barrel, along with stainless steel receiver, trigger, trigger guard plate, magazine tube, loading gate, and lever. Full pistol grip, swivel studs, and Ballard-type rifling precision fluted bolt. Features solid top receiver with side-ejection, adjustable folding semi-buckhorn rear sight, ramp front sight, tapped for scope mount. Designed for Hornady LEVERevolution cartridges. Introduced 2006.

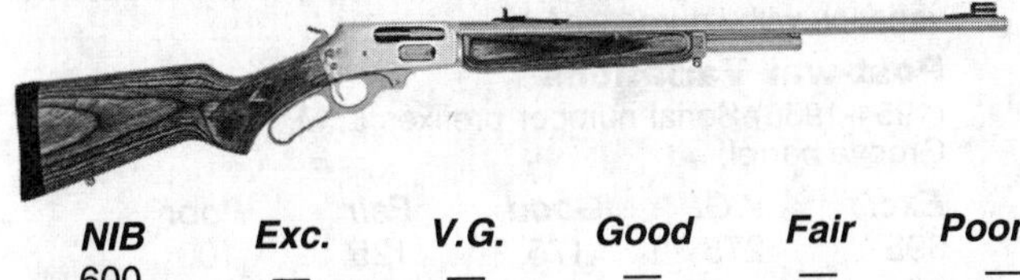

NIB	Exc.	V.G.	Good	Fair	Poor
600	—	—	—	—	—

Model 1895MXLR

Similar to Model 1895XLR but chambered in .450 Marlin. Introduced 2006.

NIB	Exc.	V.G.	Good	Fair	Poor
600	—	—	—	—	—

Model 308MXLR

Similar to the Model 1895MXLR but chambered in the proprietary .308 Marlin Express cartridge.

NIB	Exc.	V.G.	Good	Fair	Poor
650	—	—	—	—	—

Model 308MX

Similar to the Model 308MXLR but with blued receiver and barrel.

NIB	Exc.	V.G.	Good	Fair	Poor
615	—	—	—	—	—

Model 1897 Century Limited

Introduced in 1997 this model is chambered for the .22 caliber cartridge and commemorates the 100th anniversary of the Model 1897. It is fitted with a 24" half round/half octagon barrel with adjustable Marble rear sight and Marble front sight with brass bead. Blued receiver is engraved and gold inlayed with semi-fancy walnut stock and hard rubber buttplate. Weight is about 6.5 lbs.

NIB	Exc.	V.G.	Good	Fair	Poor
750	600	—	—	—	—

Model 1897 Century Limited Employee Edition

Similar to the model above but with additional gold engraving on the lever. Limited to 100 rifles.

NIB	Exc.	V.G.	Good	Fair	Poor
1300	—	—	—	—	—

Model 1897 Cowboy

This .22 caliber lever-action rifle is fitted with a 24" tapered octagon barrel with adjustable Marble buckhorn sight and Marble front sight with brass bead. Full-length tubular magazine holds 26 Shorts, 21 Longs, and 19 LR cartridges. Walnut straight grip stock with hard rubber buttplate. Weight is 7.5 lbs. Introduced in 1999.

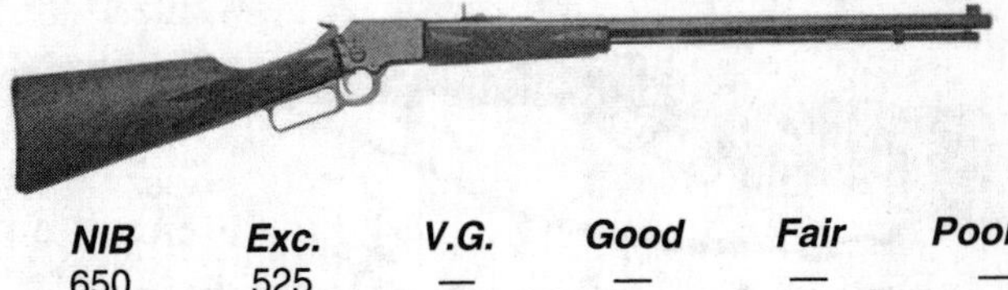

NIB	Exc.	V.G.	Good	Fair	Poor
650	525	—	—	—	—

Model 1897 Annie Oakley

Introduced in 1998 this .22 caliber model features an 18.5" tapered octagon barrel, adjustable Marble rear sight and Marble front sight. The blued receiver is roll engraved with gold signature. Stock is straight grip with blued end cap and hard rubber buttplate. Weight is approximately 5.5 lbs.

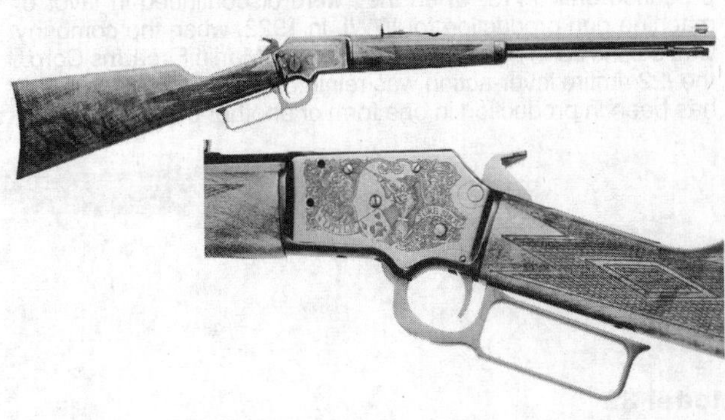

NIB	Exc.	V.G.	Good	Fair	Poor
700	600	400	—	—	—

Model 1897 Texan

Chambered for the .22 caliber cartridge and fitted with a 20" octagon barrel, this rifle has a walnut stock with straight grip. Magazine capacity is 14 to 21 cartridges depending on type. Weight is about 6 lbs. Introduced in 2002.

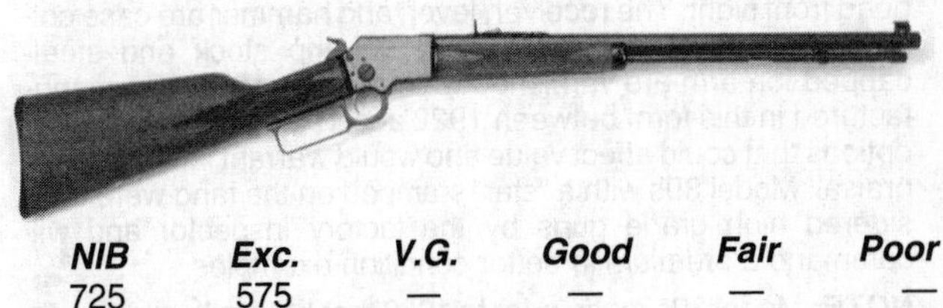

NIB	Exc.	V.G.	Good	Fair	Poor
725	575	—	—	—	—

Marlin Glenfield Lever-Action Rifles

The Glenfield line of rifles was designed to be sold in large outlet chain stores and were simply cheaper versions that were to be sold for less money. The rifles functioned fine, but birch was used instead of walnut and pressed checkering instead of handcut. These rifles were manufactured under the Glenfield name between 1964 and 1983. There are five models of Lever-Action Glenfields: the 36G, 30, 30A, 30 GT, and the 30 AS. They are chambered for the .30-30 cartridge, and the basic differences are slight and, in most cases, merely cosmetic. They are good, serviceable rifles but have little or no collector interest or investment potential.

NIB	Exc.	V.G.	Good	Fair	Poor
150	125	100	90	75	50

Model 30AW

This lever-action rifle is chambered for the .30-30 cartridge. It has a 20" barrel and 6-round magazine tube. The stock is walnut finished birch with pistol-grip cap and hard rubber buttplate. Introduced in 1998.

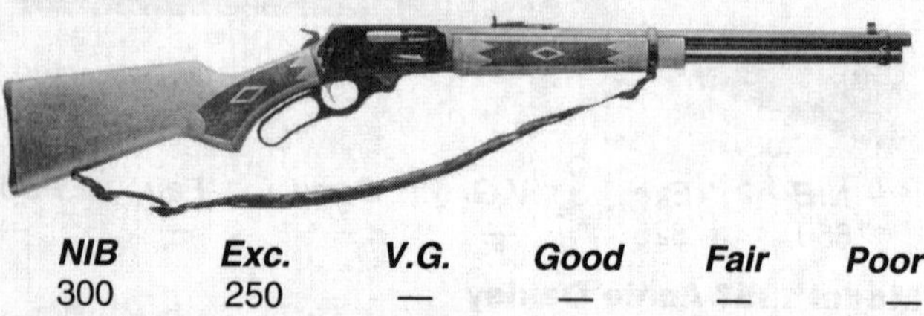

NIB	Exc.	V.G.	Good	Fair	Poor
300	250	—	—	—	—

Model 39 Lever-Action Rifle

This model originally evolved from the Model 1891 invented by L.L. Hepburn. The 1891 rifle became the 1892 and eventually developed into the takedown Model 1897. The latter two were produced until 1915, when they were discontinued in favor of machine gun production for WWI. In 1922, when the company was sold to John Moran and became the Marlin Firearms Corp., the .22 rimfire lever-action was reintroduced as the Model 39. It has been in production in one form or another ever since.

Model 39

As it was introduced in 1922, the Model 39 was chambered for the .22 rimfire and had a 24" octagonal barrel and a takedown receiver. It has a full-length magazine tube which holds 25 Shorts, 20 Longs, or 18 LR cartridges. Most Model 39s had a spring-loaded button outer magazine tube release. Very early variations had the Model '97 type knurled latch release. As the Model 39As were being phased in around 1939 many have the more modern removable inner magazine tube. It has a solid top frame and side ejection, a Rocky Mountain rear, and ivory bead front sight. The receiver, lever, and hammer are case colored; the barrel is blued. The pistol-grip stock and steel-capped forearm are varnished walnut. This model was manufactured in this form between 1922 and 1938 with a number of options that could affect value and would warrant individual appraisal. Model 39s with a "star" stamped on the tang were considered high grade guns by the factory inspector and will command a premium in better condition examples.

NOTE: Model 39s made prior to 1932 that have either no prefix or the prefix S on the serial number should not be used with high-speed ammunition. The prefix HS indicates the improved bolt that is safe for this ammunition.

Standard Rifle

Exc.	V.G.	Good	Fair	Poor
1500	850	475	300	200

Deluxe Rifle

Factory checkering, fancy wood and "star" stamp on tang.

Exc.	V.G.	Good	Fair	Poor
2500	1500	750	400	250

Model 39A Lever-Action Rifle

This is an improved version of the Model 39. It has a heavier, tapered round barrel and semi-beavertail forearm and a redesigned pistol-grip stock. The rubber buttplate was replaced by one of a synthetic fiber; otherwise, specifications were similar to the Model 39. This model was manufactured from 1939 to 1960. Several variations are listed.

Pre-war Variations

(1939-1941) case colored receiver, no serial number prefix (1939) or "B" prefix (1940-1941).

Exc.	V.G.	Good	Fair	Poor
1200	800	450	250	150

Post-war Variations

(1945-1953) Serial number prefixes up to letter "K." Ballard-type deep rifling

Exc.	V.G.	Good	Fair	Poor
500	375	275	150	100

NOTE: Add 20 percent premium of C prefix 1st post-war variation with figured wood.

Post-war Variations

(1954-1956) Serial number prefixes L, M, N, with Micro-Groove barrel.

Exc.	V.G.	Good	Fair	Poor
395	275	175	125	100

"Golden 39A's"

(1954-1963) Gold trigger, MicroGroove rifling. Serial number prefixes L through W.

Exc.	V.G.	Good	Fair	Poor
395	275	175	125	100

Model 39A Mountie

This is basically a carbine version of the Model 39A. It features a 20" tapered round barrel, straight-grip walnut stock, and slimmed-down forearm. It was manufactured between 1953 and 1960.

1st Variation

K prefix and 24" barrel, fat forearm.

Exc.	V.G.	Good	Fair	Poor
600	450	300	—	—

NOTE: Add 20 percent for slim forearm.

Standard

Exc.	V.G.	Good	Fair	Poor
275	225	175	125	100

Model 39A 1960 Presentation Model

Released in 1960, this was Marlin's 90th Anniversary model. It is similar to the 39A but has a chrome-plated barrel and receiver with a high grade, checkered walnut stock and forend. There is a squirrel carved on the right side of the buttstock. There were 500 produced in 1960. This is a commemorative and as such will be desirable to collectors only if NIB with all boxes and papers with which it was originally sold. Once used, it becomes a shooter and is not easily sold.

NIB	Exc.	V.G.	Good	Fair	Poor
1200	900	500	300	175	125

Model 39M Mountie 1960 Presentation Model

This is the carbine version of the 90th Anniversary model. This is the same as the 39A with a 20" barrel and straight-grip stock. There were 500 of this model manufactured in 1960.

NIB	Exc.	V.G.	Good	Fair	Poor
1200	900	500	300	175	125

Model 39ADL Lever-Action Rifle

This model is the same as the 90th Anniversary issue except that it is blued instead of chrome-plated. There were 3,306 manufactured between 1960 and 1963.

NIB	Exc.	V.G.	Good	Fair	Poor
1000	850	500	300	175	125

Model Golden 39A Lever-Action Rifle

This model is similar to the 39A, with a gold-plated trigger and sling swivels. It was manufactured between 1960 and 1983.

Exc.	V.G.	Good	Fair	Poor
200	175	150	100	75

Model 39 Carbine

This is a slimmer, lighter version of the Model 39A. It features a slimmer forend and thinner barrel. There were 12,140 manufactured between 1963 and 1967.

Exc.	V.G.	Good	Fair	Poor
175	150	125	90	60

Model 39 Century Limited

The introduction of this model marked the 100th Anniversary of the Marlin Company. This model features a 20" octagonal barrel with semi-buckhorn rear and brass blade front sight. The stock is fancy walnut, with a straight grip and a brass forend tip and buttplate. There is a medallion inlaid into the right side of the receiver and a brass plate on the stock. There were 34,197 manufactured in 1970. As a commemorative this model needs to be as it came from the factory to command collector interest.

NIB	Exc.	V.G.	Good	Fair	Poor
350	250	200	150	125	100

Model 39A Article II

This model commemorated the National Rifle Association's 100th Anniversary in 1971. It has a 24" octagonal barrel, high grade walnut pistol-grip stock, and brass forend tip and buttplate. The right side of the receiver has the NRA's Second Amendment "Right to Keep and Bear Arms" medallion inlaid. There were 6,244 of these .22 rifles manufactured in 1971.

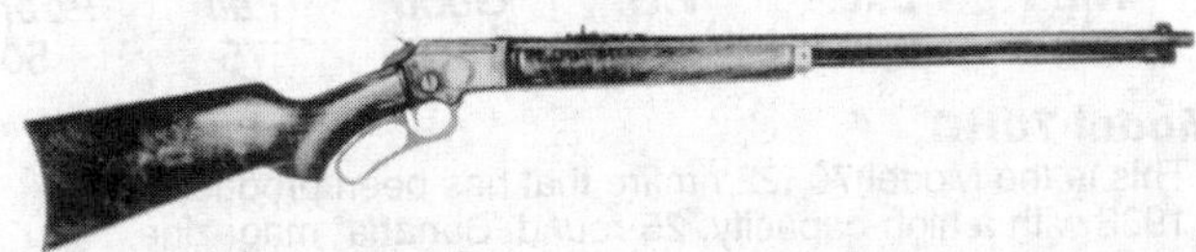

NIB	Exc.	V.G.	Good	Fair	Poor
450	350	200	150	125	100

Model 39M Article II

This model is the same as the Model 39A Article II except that it is a carbine version with a 20" octagonal barrel and a straight grip stock. There were 3,824 manufactured in 1971. As commemoratives NIB condition is essential to collector interest.

NIB	Exc.	V.G.	Good	Fair	Poor
450	350	200	150	125	100

Model 39A Octagon

This model was produced because the company had the machinery and some leftover barrels from the two commemorative models produced in 1970 and 1971. This was a regular production run that was meant to be used and was not a special issue. It has a 24", tapered octagonal barrel and is chambered for the .22 rimfire cartridges. It has a pistol-grip walnut stock, with steel forend tip. There were 2,551 manufactured in 1972 and 1973. This was not a commercially successful model, and it was discontinued for that reason.

NIB	Exc.	V.G.	Good	Fair	Poor
750	600	400	250	200	175

Model 39M Octagon

This is the 20", octagonal barreled carbine version with a straight-grip stock. There were 2,140 manufactured in 1973.

NIB	Exc.	V.G.	Good	Fair	Poor
750	600	400	250	200	175

Model 39D Lever-Action Rifle

This is essentially the Model 39M carbine, 20" barrel version with a pistol-grip stock. It was manufactured in 1971 and reintroduced in 1973.The 1971 version has white line spacers and pistol-grip caps. The 1973 version has neither of these features.

Exc.	V.G.	Good	Fair	Poor
275	200	125	75	50

Model 39AS Lever-Action Rifle

This is the current production model of this extremely popular .22 rifle. It features the hammer-block crossbolt safety and sling swivel studs. It is similar in appearance to its predecessors and still boasts a genuine walnut pistol-grip stock and the same quality fit and finish we have come to expect from Marlin.

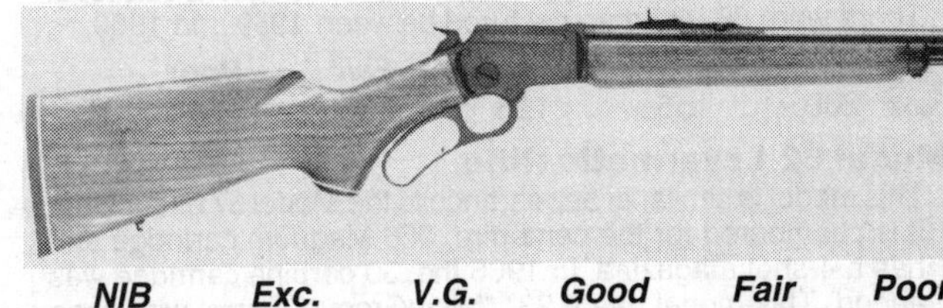

NIB	Exc.	V.G.	Good	Fair	Poor
340	275	225	200	150	100

Model 39TDS Lever-Action Rifle

This is another current production model. It is similar to the Model 39AS, with a 20" carbine barrel and straight-grip stock. It replaced the Model 39M and was introduced in 1988.

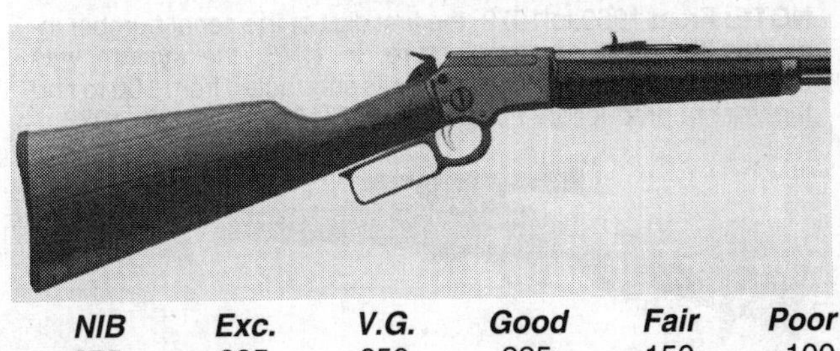

NIB	Exc.	V.G.	Good	Fair	Poor
375	325	250	225	150	100

Model 39AWL

This is a limited edition of 2,000 rifles distributed solely through Wal-Mart. Fitted with a 24.5" octagon barrel, select checkered walnut stock, gold filled engraving, and stamped "Wildlife For Tomorrow."

NIB	Exc.	V.G.	Good	Fair	Poor
700	500	—	—	—	—

Model 56 Levermatic Rifle

This is a streamlined version of the lever-action. It features a short lever throw and a one-piece walnut stock. The 22" barrel is round and is chambered for the .22 rimfire cartridges. There is a 7-shot detachable magazine, open sights, and a gold-plated trigger. The receiver on this model was made of aluminum after 1956. There were 31,523 manufactured between 1955 and 1964.

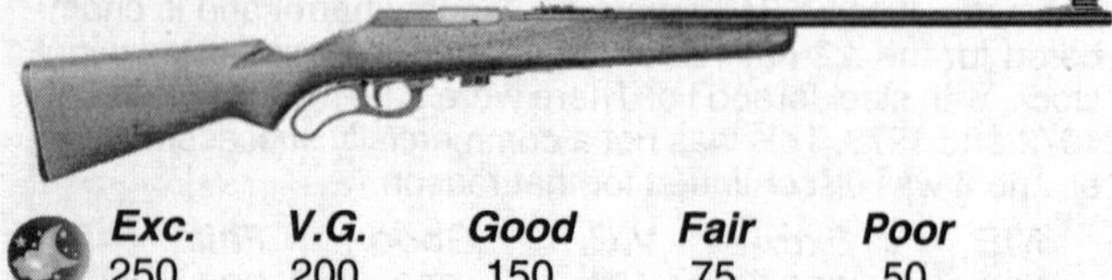

Exc.	V.G.	Good	Fair	Poor
250	200	150	75	50

Model 56 "Clipper King" Levermatic

This is the same as the Model 56 except that it is specially packaged and comes with a 4X .22 scope. The name "Clipper King" is stamped on the barrel, and the buttplate is red hard rubber. There were only 152 of these manufactured in 1959.

Exc.	V.G.	Good	Fair	Poor
275	225	175	100	75

Model 57 Levermatic Rifle

This model is similar to the Model 56, with a tube magazine and Monte Carlo stock. In 1960 Marlin went back to a steel receiver on this model. There were 34,628 manufactured from 1959 to 1965.

Exc.	V.G.	Good	Fair	Poor
225	175	150	75	50

Model 57M Levermatic Rifle

This is the Model 57 chambered for the .22 Magnum cartridge. There were 66,889 manufactured between 1959 and 1969.

Exc.	V.G.	Good	Fair	Poor
200	155	125	100	75

Model 62 Levermatic Rifle

This model is similar in appearance to the Model 57 except that it is chambered for the centerfire .256 Magnum cartridge and has a 4-shot magazine. In 1966 the .30 carbine cartridge was added. This model has a 23" "MicroGroove" barrel with open sights and a walnut one-piece stock. The first 4,000 Model 62s were shipped without serial numbers in violation of federal law. The company recalled the rifles for numbering; and, to this day, the owner of a centerfire Model 62 can return the rifle for numbering. There were 15,714 manufactured between 1963 and 1969. Add 15 percent for .256.

NOTE: From 1969 to 1972, the first digit of the serial number indicates the year of manufacture. In 1973, the system was changed by having the first two digits subtracted from 100 to find the year of production. For example: 2717793=100-27=1973.

Exc.	V.G.	Good	Fair	Poor
450	375	250	175	100

BOLT-ACTIONS

The Marlin Firearms Company produced a great many bolt-action rifles, both single-shot and repeaters, starting in 1930 and continuing today. These rifles were low-priced and designed primarily as utility rifles. They also manufactured many autoloaders of the same type during these years. The Glenfield name will also be found on these models, as many were produced to be marketed by the large chain outlets. These rifles have no collectible value of which I am aware, and they often sell for under $100 in today's market. This list is for reference purposes.

Single Shot		Repeater	
Model 65	1935-37	Model 80	1935-59
Model 65E	1935-37	Model 80E	1935-39
Model 100	1935-59	Model 81	1939
Model 100S	1937-38	Model 81E	1939
Model 101	1941-77	Model 81DL	1939
Model 101 DL	1941-45	Model 80B	1940
Model 100 SB	1941	Model 80BE	1940
Model 101	1959	Model 81B	1940
Model 122	1962-65	Model 81BE	1940
		Model 80 CSB	1941
		Model 80DL	1941-64
		Model 80C	1941-71
		Model 980	1966-71
		Model 780	1971-88
		Model 781	1971-88
		Model 782	1971-88
		Model 783	1971-88
		Model 880	1988-Pres.
		Model 881	1988-Pres.
		Model 882	1988-Pres.
		Model 883	1988-Pres.

AUTOLOADERS

Model 50	1931-34	Model 98	1950-61
Model 50E	1931-34	Model 99	1959-61
Model A-1	1935-46	Model 99C	1962-78
Model A-1 E	1935-46	Model 99G	1960-65
Model A-1C	1940-46	Model DL	1960-65
Model A-1 DL	1940-46	Model 60	1960-Pres.
Model 88-C	1947-56	Model 49	1968-71
Model 88-DL	1953-56	Model 49DL	1971-78
Model 89-C	1950-61	Model 990	1979-87
Model 89-DL	1950-61	Model 995	1979-Pres.

Model 70P "Papoose"

This model is quite unique in that it is a total package concept. It is a semi-automatic takedown carbine chambered for the .22 rimfire family of cartridges. It has a 16.25" barrel and a 7-shot detachable magazine. It is supplied with 4X scope and bright red case that will float if dropped overboard. The stock is walnut-finished birch, with a pistol grip and rubber buttplate. It was introduced in 1986.

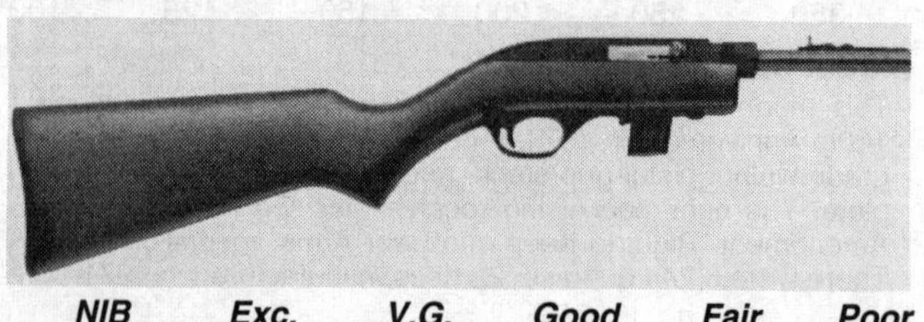

NIB	Exc.	V.G.	Good	Fair	Poor
160	140	110	85	75	50

Model 70HC

This is the Model 70 .22 rimfire that has been produced since 1983 with a high-capacity, 25-round "Banana" magazine.

 *This symbol denotes "Sleepers" with rapidly-rising values and/or significant collector potential.*

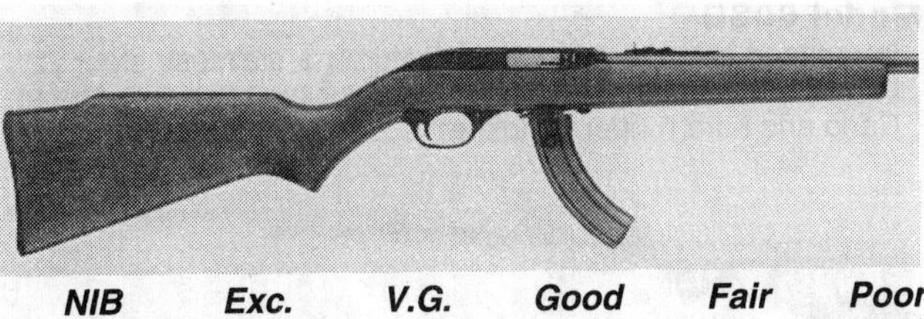

NIB	Exc.	V.G.	Good	Fair	Poor
160	140	110	85	75	50

Model 70PSS

Same as Model 70P above but furnished with a 10-round magazine and finished in stainless steel with synthetic stock. Automatic last shot bolt hold-open.

NIB	Exc.	V.G.	Good	Fair	Poor
180	150	125	100	85	60

Model 9 Camp Carbine

This model has a 16.5" barrel and is chambered for the 9mm Parabellum pistol cartridge. It has a 12- or 20-shot detachable magazine, walnut-finished hardwood pistol-grip stock, and a sandblasted matte-blued finish. There are open sights, and the receiver is drilled and tapped for scope mounting. This model was introduced in 1985.

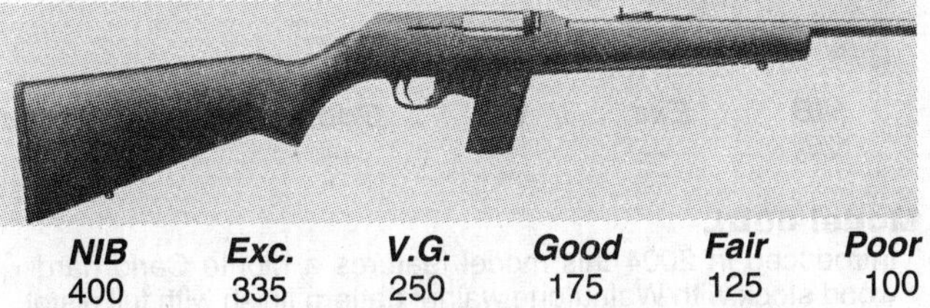

NIB	Exc.	V.G.	Good	Fair	Poor
400	335	250	175	125	100

Model 9N

Similar to the Model 9mm Carbine but furnished with nickel-plated metal parts.

NIB	Exc.	V.G.	Good	Fair	Poor
450	350	225	175	125	100

Model 45 Camp Carbine

This is the same as the 9mm version but is chambered for the .45 ACP cartridge and has a 7-shot detachable magazine.

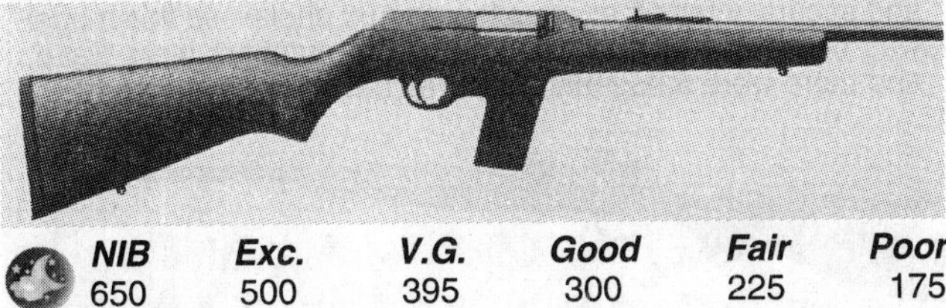

NIB	Exc.	V.G.	Good	Fair	Poor
650	500	395	300	225	175

Model 922M

First offered in 1993 this model is a semi-automatic .22 Win. Magnum Rimfire rifle. It features a 7-shot clip, 20.5" Micro-Grove barrel. The receiver is sandblasted and drilled and tapped for scope mounting. Monte Carlo black walnut stock with rubber rifle buff pad. Adjustable rear sight and ramp front sight with hood. Rifle weighs 6.5 lbs.

NIB	Exc.	V.G.	Good	Fair	Poor
425	325	225	150	125	110

The year of manufacture of Marlin modern production rifles made between 1946 and 1968 can be determined by the letter prefix on the serial number.

The prefixes are as follows:

1946–C	1951–H	1956–N	1961–U	1966–AB
1947–D	1952–J	1957–P	1962–V	1967–AC
1948–E	1953–K	1958–R	1963–W	1968–AD
1949–F	1954–L	1959–S	1964–Y, Z	

Model 995

Semi-automatic .22 LR only rifle features a 7-shot clip, 18" MicroGroove barrel. Receiver is grooved for scope mount and receiver has a serrated non-glare top. Adjustable sights. Monte Carlo American black walnut stock with checkered pistol grip and forearm. White buttplate spacer is standard. Rifle weighs 5 lbs. Introduced in 1979 and still in production.

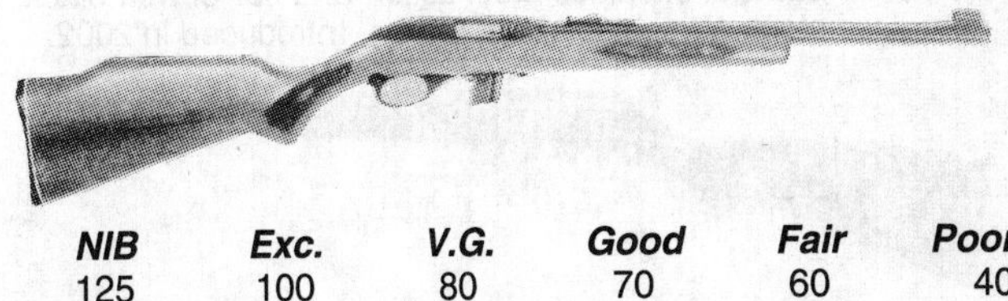

NIB	Exc.	V.G.	Good	Fair	Poor
125	100	80	70	60	40

Model 995SS

Same as above but with stainless steel finish and black fiberglass stock. Introduced in 1995.

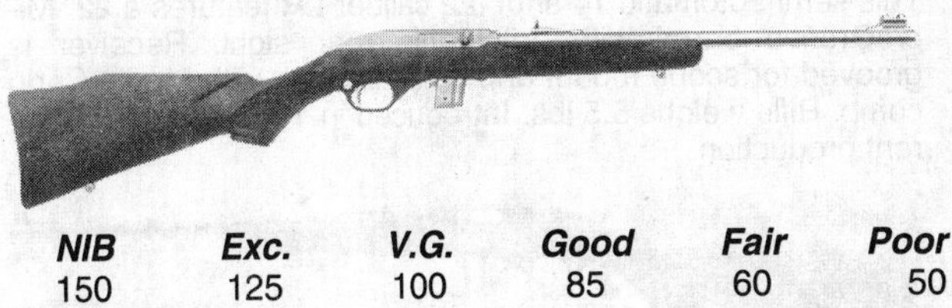

NIB	Exc.	V.G.	Good	Fair	Poor
150	125	100	85	60	50

Model 990L

This semi-automatic .22 LR Marlin features a tubular 14-round magazine with 22" MicroGrove barrel. The trigger is gold plated. The receiver is grooved for a scope mount while the stock is a two-tone brown birch Monte Carlo. Rubber rifle buttpad is standard. Rifle weighs 5.75 lbs.

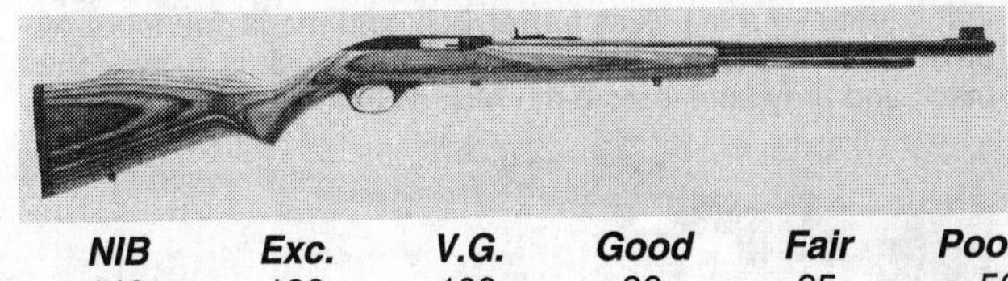

NIB	Exc.	V.G.	Good	Fair	Poor
140	120	100	80	65	50

Model 7000

This model was first offered in 1997 and is a semi-automatic .22 caliber rifle with 18" heavy barrel. Magazine holds 10 rounds. Black synthetic stock with Monte Carlo comb and molded checkering. Receiver grooved for scope mount. No sights included. Weight about 6 lbs.

NIB	Exc.	V.G.	Good	Fair	Poor
200	150	125	100	—	—

Model 7000T

This target rifle is fitted with an 18" barrel with recessed muzzle. No sights. The stock is laminated red, white, and blue with pistol grip. Serrated rubber buttplate is adjustable for length of pull, height, and angle. Weight is about 7.5 lbs. Introduced in 1999.

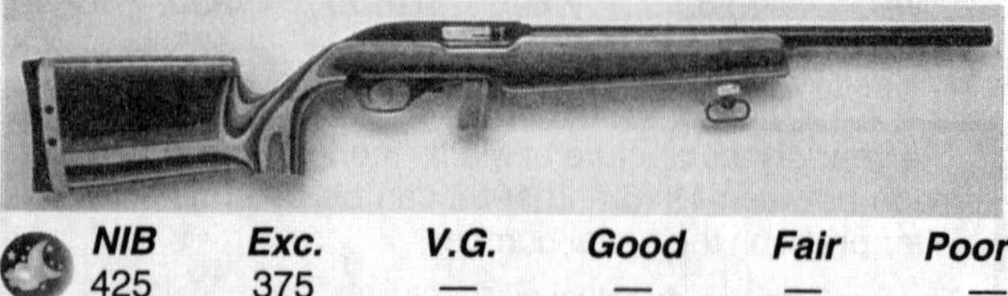

NIB	Exc.	V.G.	Good	Fair	Poor
425	375	—	—	—	—

Model 795

Similar to the model above but with an 18" standard weight barrel. Weight is about 5 lbs. Also available with 4X scope.

NIB	Exc.	V.G.	Good	Fair	Poor
150	115	—	—	—	—

NOTE: Add $5 for scope.

Model 795SS

As above but with stainless steel action and barrel with black fiberglass stock. Weight is about 4.5 lbs. Introduced in 2002.

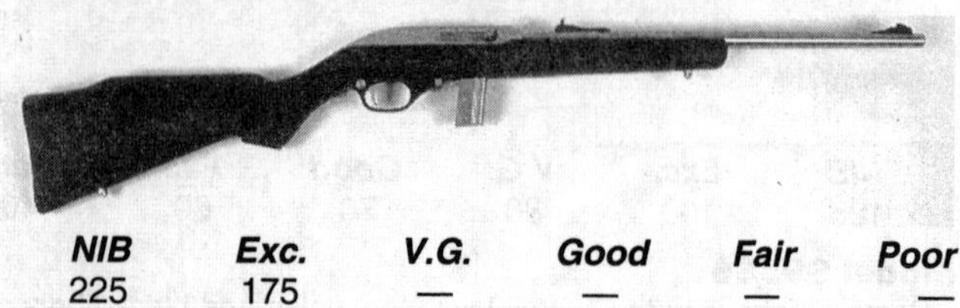

NIB	Exc.	V.G.	Good	Fair	Poor
225	175	—	—	—	—

Model 60

This semi-automatic 14-shot .22 caliber LR features a 22" MicroGroove barrel with adjustable rear sight. Receiver is grooved for scope mount and stock is birch with Monte Carlo comb. Rifle weighs 5.5 lbs. Introduced in 1960 and still in current production.

NIB	Exc.	V.G.	Good	Fair	Poor
100	85	70	60	50	40

Model 60SS

Introduced in 1993 this model is similar to the Model 60 except that it features a stainless barrel, bolt, and magazine tube. All other metal parts are nickel plated. The stock is a two-tone black and gray laminated birch Monte Carlo.

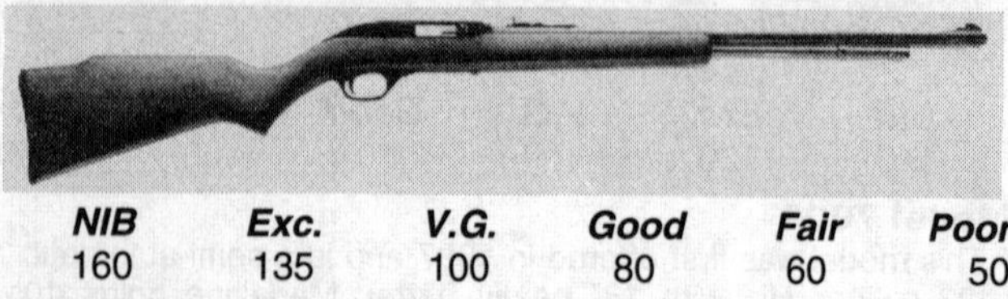

NIB	Exc.	V.G.	Good	Fair	Poor
160	135	100	80	60	50

Model 60SN

Similar to Model 60SS but with black synthetic stock with molded checkering and swivel studs. Introduced in 2007.

NIB	Exc.	V.G.	Good	Fair	Poor
215	—	—	—	—	—

Model 60SB

Introduced in 1998 this model features a stainless steel 22" barrel, bolt and magazine tube. The stock is birch with Monte Carlo and hard rubber buttplate.

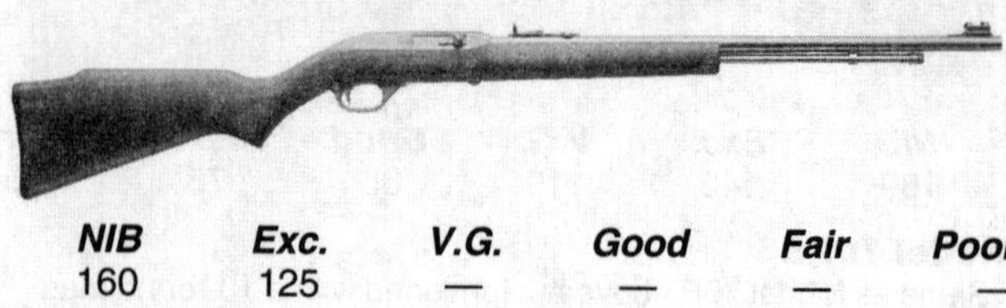

NIB	Exc.	V.G.	Good	Fair	Poor
160	125	—	—	—	—

Model 60SSK

Similar to the Model 60SB with the addition of a black synthetic Monte Carlo stock with checkering.

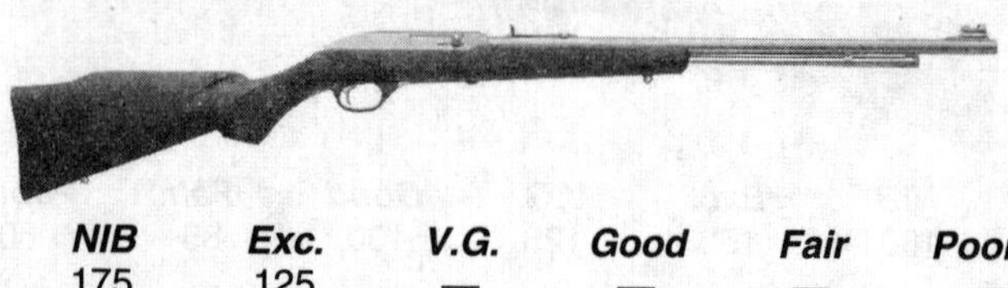

NIB	Exc.	V.G.	Good	Fair	Poor
175	125	—	—	—	—

Model 60C

Similar to the Model 60 but with Mossy Oak Break-Up camo finish. Introduced in 2000.

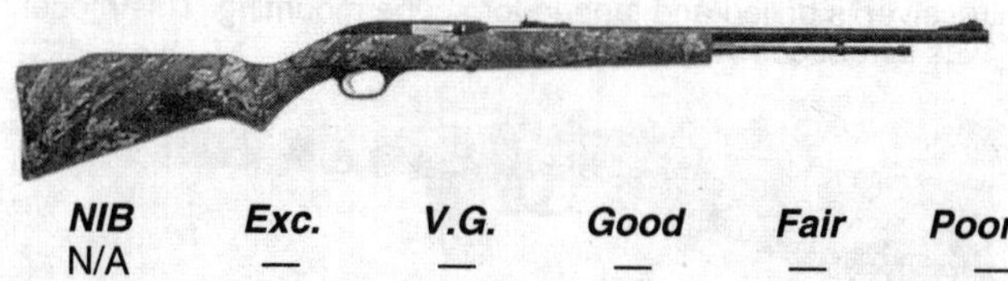

NIB	Exc.	V.G.	Good	Fair	Poor
N/A	—	—	—	—	—

Model 60DL

Introduced in 2004 this model features a Monte Carlo hardwood stock with Walnutone walnut pattern finish with full pistol grip. Weight is about 5.5 lbs.

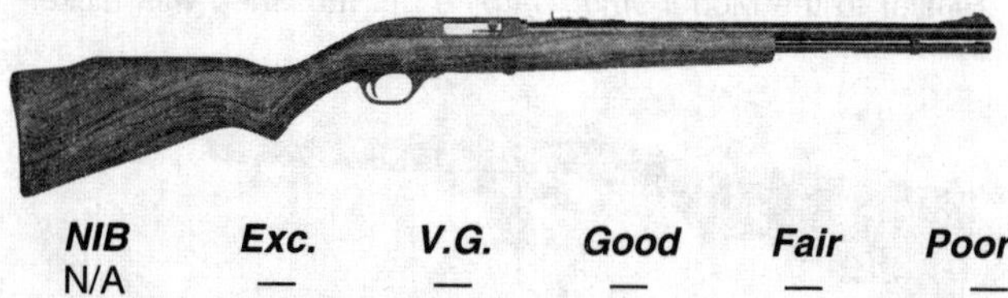

NIB	Exc.	V.G.	Good	Fair	Poor
N/A	—	—	—	—	—

Model 322 Bolt-Action Rifle

This model is chambered for the .222 cartridge and has a 24" medium-weight barrel with MicroGroove rifling. It has a checkered walnut pistol-grip stock. The magazine holds 4 shots, and the adjustable trigger and sights are Sako products. The Sako receiver is fitted for Sako scope mounting bases. The MicroGroove rifling in the barrel was not successful for this caliber, and accuracy fell off after as few as 500 shots—so this model was dropped and replaced. The serial numbers were Sako, and there were 5,859 manufactured between 1954 and 1959.

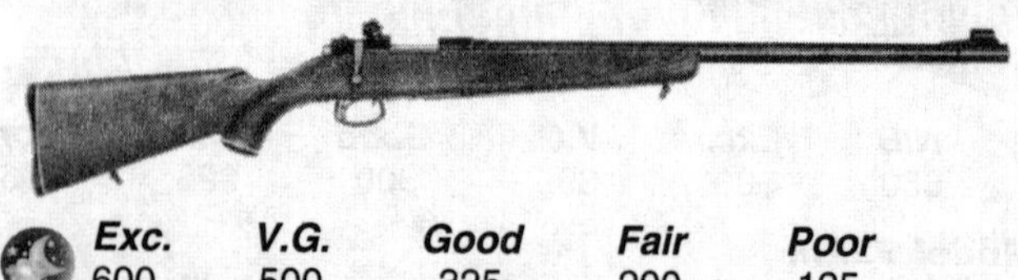

Exc.	V.G.	Good	Fair	Poor
600	500	325	200	125

Model 422 Bolt-Action Rifle

This model is the successor to the Model 322. It is simply the same rifle fitted with a 24", featherweight, stainless steel barrel and named the "Varmint King." The stock features a Monte

Carlo stock with a cheekpiece. There were only 354 manufactured between 1956 and 1958.

Exc.	V.G.	Good	Fair	Poor
675	600	375	275	175

Model 455 Bolt-Action Rifle

This model is built on the Fabrique Nationale Belgian Mauser action. It is chambered for the .308 and the .30-06 cartridges. It has a stainless steel barrel made by Marlin and has a 5-shot magazine. It has a Bishop checkered walnut stock with detachable sling swivels and a leather sling. The rear sight is a Lyman 48, and the front is a ramp type with a detachable hood. The receiver is drilled and tapped for scope mounts. The trigger is an adjustable Sako unit. There were 1,079 manufactured in .3006 and only 59 in .308 between 1955 and 1959.

Exc.	V.G.	Good	Fair	Poor
600	500	325	200	125

Model 880SS

Introduced in 1994 this .22 caliber rifle features a synthetic stock and a stainless steel receiver and barrel. The barrel is 22" long and a 7-shot magazine is standard. Discontinued in 2004.

NIB	Exc.	V.G.	Good	Fair	Poor
225	175	150	125	75	60

Model 2000

This is a bolt-action single-shot target rifle chambered for the .22 LR. The barrel is a 22" long MicroGroove design with match chamber and recessed muzzle. The rear sight is a fully adjustable target peep sight with a hooded front sight supplied with 10 aperture inserts. The stock is a Marlin blue fiberglass/Kevlar material with adjustable buttplate. There is an aluminum forearm rail with forearm stop and quick detachable swivel. Rifle weighs 8 lbs. Discontinued.

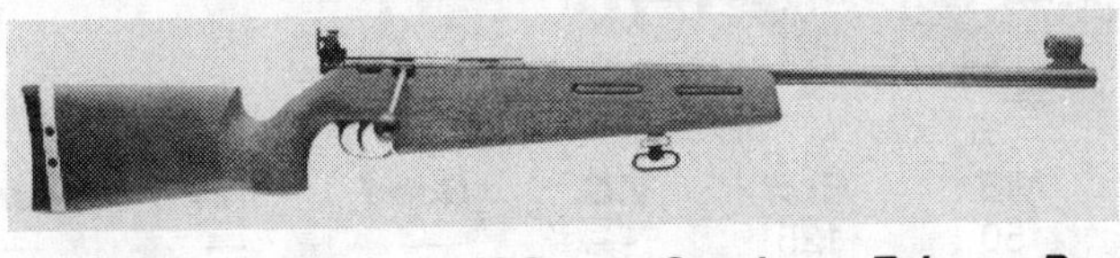

NIB	Exc.	V.G.	Good	Fair	Poor
400	375	250	200	150	125

Model 2000A

This is a 1996 version of the Model 2000 introduced in 1994 that features an adjustable comb and an ambidextrous pistol grip. A Marlin logo is molded into the side of the buttstock. Weighs approximately 8-1/2 lbs. Discontinued.

NIB	Exc.	V.G.	Good	Fair	Poor
425	325	250	200	—	—

Model 2000L

Introduced in 1996 this version of the Model 2000 features a black/grey laminated stock. It is fitted with a heavy 22" barrel with a match chamber. Fitted with a two-stage target trigger and a rubber buttplate that is adjustable for length of pull, height and angle. Weight is about 8 lbs. Discontinued.

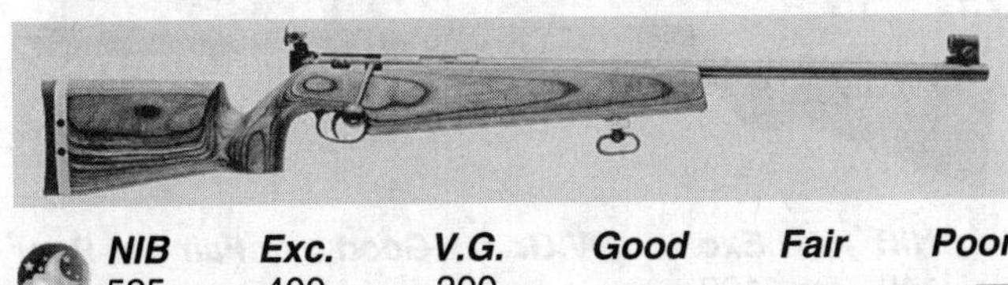

NIB	Exc.	V.G.	Good	Fair	Poor
525	400	300	—	—	—

Model 880

This is a bolt-action clip-fed rifle chambered for the .22 LR caliber. The clip is a 7-shot magazine. The MicroGroove barrel is 22" and has adjustable folding rear sight and ramp front sight with hood. Rifle weighs 5.5 lbs. and was introduced in 1988. Discontinued in 2004.

NIB	Exc.	V.G.	Good	Fair	Poor
160	135	110	90	75	50

Model 880SQ

Similar to the Model 880 but fitted with a 22" heavy barrel and no sights. Introduced in 1996. Weight is approximately 7 lbs. Discontinued in 2004.

NIB	Exc.	V.G.	Good	Fair	Poor
285	225	200	—	—	—

Model 881

Bolt-action .22 caliber rifle has a tubular magazine that holds 25 Shorts, 19 longs, and 17 LR. A 22" MicroGroove barrel has adjustable folding rear sight and ramp front sight with hood. Stock is black walnut with Monte Carlo and a rubber rifle buttpad with sling swivels. Rifle weighs 6 lbs. First offered in 1988. Discontinued in 2004.

NIB	Exc.	V.G.	Good	Fair	Poor
175	150	125	100	80	60

Model 882SS

This bolt-action magazine rifle is chambered for the .22 Magnum cartridge. It has a stainless steel barrel and action with black synthetic stock. It has Marlin "Fire Sights" installed. Introduced in 1998. Discontinued in 2004.

NIB	Exc.	V.G.	Good	Fair	Poor
225	175	—	—	—	—

Model 25N

A Marlin promotional model. Bolt-action rifle chambered for the .22 LR only. Seven-shot clip magazine with a 22" MicroGroove barrel. Receiver grooved for scope mount. Walnut finished birch stock. Gun weighs 5.5 lbs.

NIB	Exc.	V.G.	Good	Fair	Poor
100	90	80	70	50	40

Model 25NC

Similar to the model above but with Mossy Oak Break-Up camo finish. Introduced in 2000.

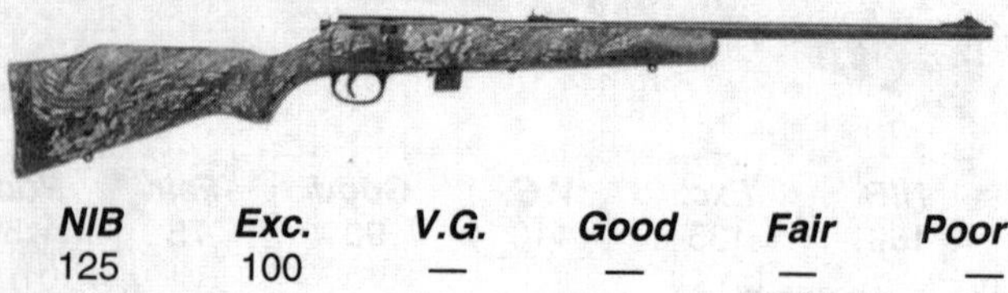

NIB	Exc.	V.G.	Good	Fair	Poor
125	100	—	—	—	—

Model 25MN

Same as above but chambered for the .22 Win. Magnum Rimfire cartridge. Gun weighs 6 lbs.

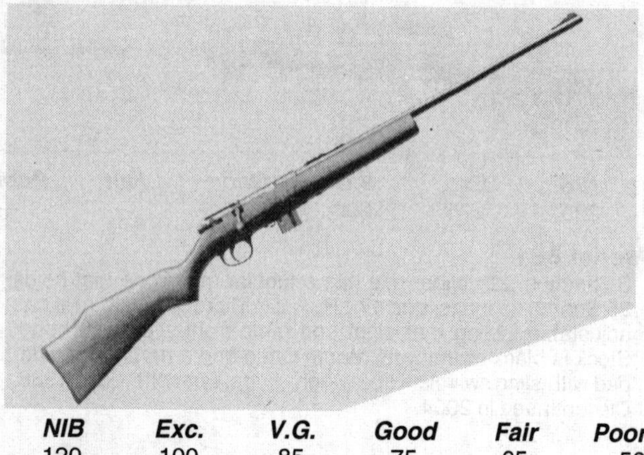

NIB	Exc.	V.G.	Good	Fair	Poor
120	100	85	75	65	50

Model 25MNC

Similar to the above model but with Mossy Oak Break-Up camo finish. Weight is about 6 lbs. Introduced in 2001.

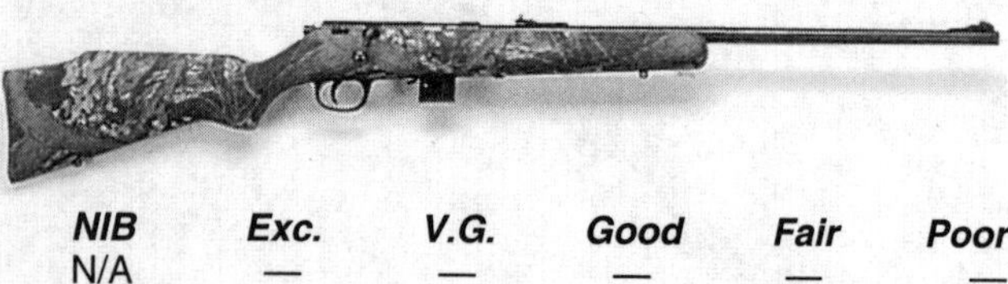

NIB	Exc.	V.G.	Good	Fair	Poor
N/A	—	—	—	—	—

Model 17V

Introduced in 2002 this bolt-action rifle is chambered for the .17 Hornady Magnum Rimfire cartridge. Fitted with a 22" heavy barrel. Hardwood stock. No sights. Magazine capacity is 7-round detachable magazine. Weight is about 6 lbs.

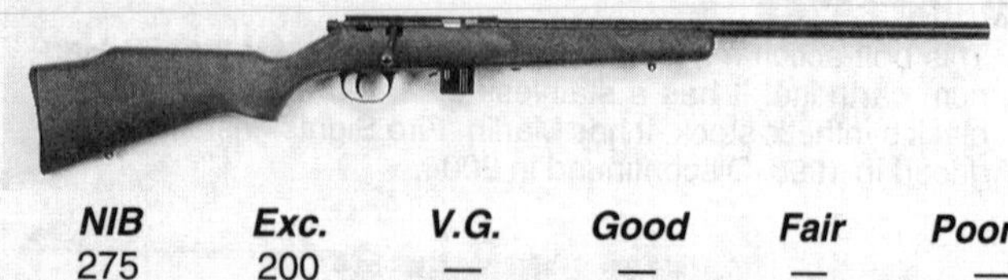

NIB	Exc.	V.G.	Good	Fair	Poor
275	200	—	—	—	—

Model 17VS

As above but with stainless steel barrel and action and laminated stock. Weight is about 7 lbs.

NIB	Exc.	V.G.	Good	Fair	Poor
390	300	—	—	—	—

Model 15YN

A Marlin promotional model referred to as the "Little Buckaroo." A bolt-action .22 caliber single-shot rifle for the beginner. Features a MicroGroove 16.25" barrel adjustable rear sight and receiver grooved for scope mount. Birch stock. Rifle weighs 4.25 lbs.

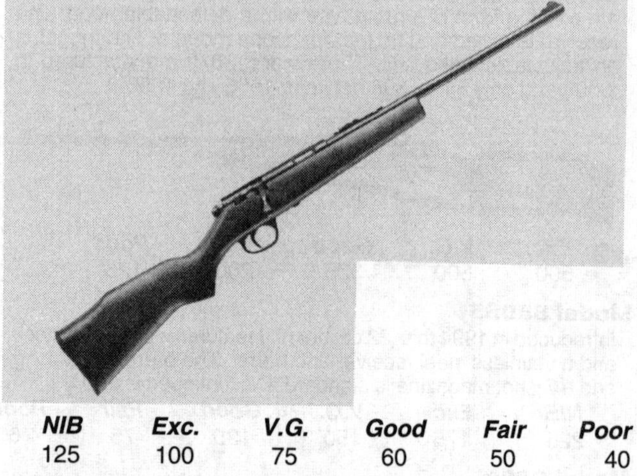

NIB	Exc.	V.G.	Good	Fair	Poor
125	100	75	60	50	40

Model 15N

This bolt-action rifle is chambered for all three .22 caliber rimfire cartridges. It is fitted with an adjustable rear sight. It has a full size birch interchangeable with the Model 15YN. Weight is about 4.25 lbs. Introduced in 1998.

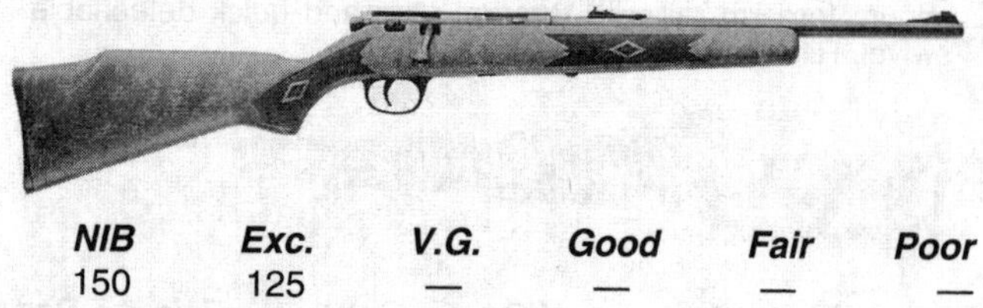

NIB	Exc.	V.G.	Good	Fair	Poor
150	125	—	—	—	—

Model 15YS (Youth)

This is single-shot bolt-action rifle with a shorter-than-standard length of pull. Barrel length is 16.25". Hardwood stock. Weight is about 4.25 lbs. Introduced in 2002.

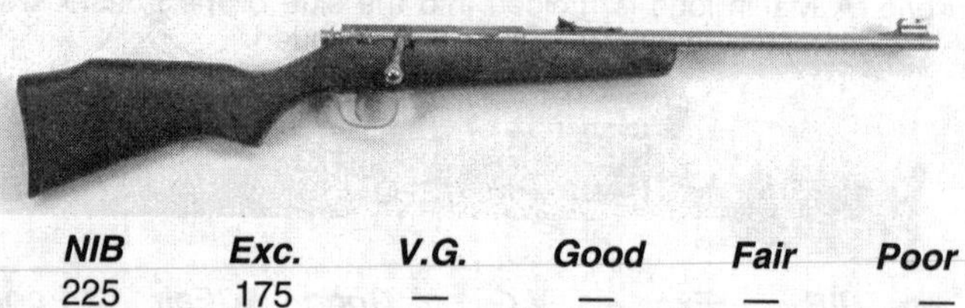

NIB	Exc.	V.G.	Good	Fair	Poor
225	175	—	—	—	—

Model 81TS

This is a bolt-action rifle chambered for the .22 Short, Long, and LR cartridges. It is fitted with a 22" barrel and has a tubular magazine. It comes with a black Monte Carlo synthetic stock and adjustable rear sight. Weight is about 6 lbs. Introduced in 1998. Discontinued in 2004.

NIB	Exc.	V.G.	Good	Fair	Poor
140	100	—	—	—	—

Model 882

Bolt-action rifle chambered for .22 Win. Magnum Rimfire cartridge. A 7-shot clip is standard. A MicroGroove 22" barrel with adjustable rear sight and ramp front sight with hood. Receiver grooved for scope mount. Black walnut stock with Monte Carlo and rubber rifle butt. Rifle weighs 6 lbs. Introduced in 1988 and still in production. Discontinued in 2004.

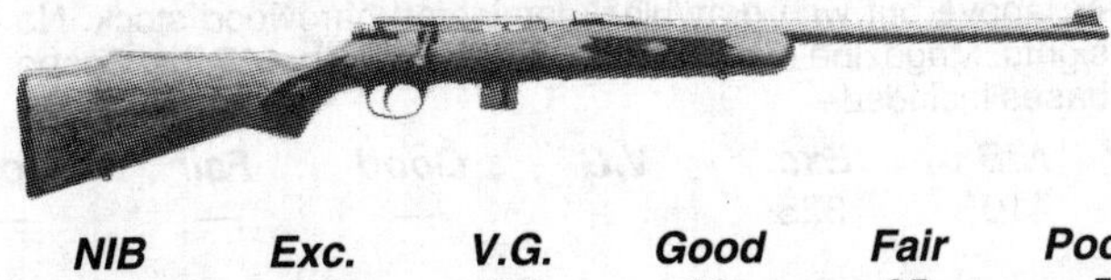

NIB	Exc.	V.G.	Good	Fair	Poor
150	125	100	80	65	50

Model 882L

Same as above but furnished with a two-tone brown hardwood Monte Carlo stock. Rifle weighs 6.25 lbs. Discontinued in 2004.

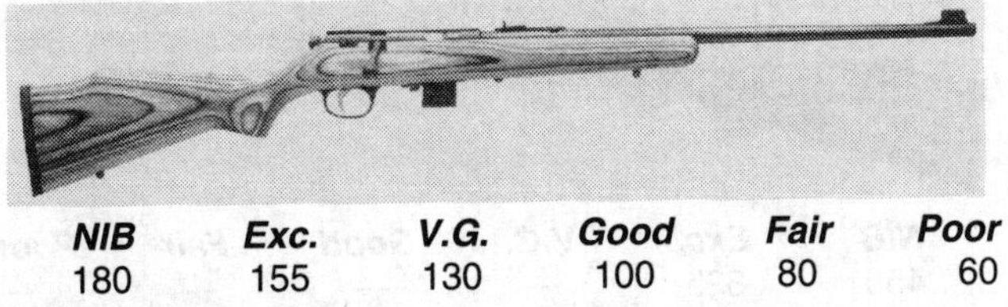

NIB	Exc.	V.G.	Good	Fair	Poor
180	155	130	100	80	60

Model 882SS

Same as above but furnished in stainless steel. With black fiberglass stock. Introduced in 1995. Discontinued in 2004.

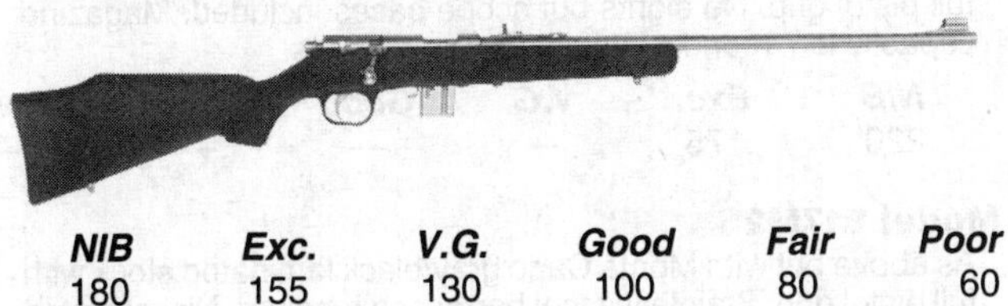

NIB	Exc.	V.G.	Good	Fair	Poor
180	155	130	100	80	60

Model 882SSV

This variation of the Model 882, introduced in 1997, is all in stainless steel and chambered for the .22 WMR cartridge. It is fitted with a nickel plated 7-round magazine and 22" barrel. The stock is black synthetic with molded checkering. Receiver is grooved for scope mount. 1" brushed aluminum scope ring mounts included. Weighs about 7 lbs. Discontinued in 2004.

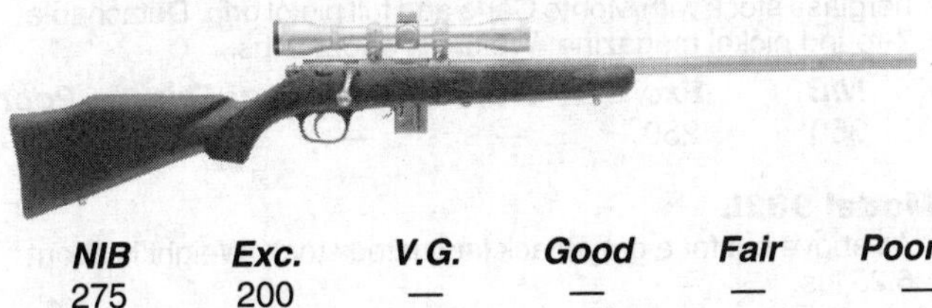

NIB	Exc.	V.G.	Good	Fair	Poor
275	200	—	—	—	—

Model 83TS

Chambered for the .22 Win. Mag cartridge and fitted with a 22" barrel with 12-round tubular magazine. Adjustable rear sight. Bolt-action with synthetic stock. Weight is about 6 lbs. Introduced in 2001. Discontinued in 2004.

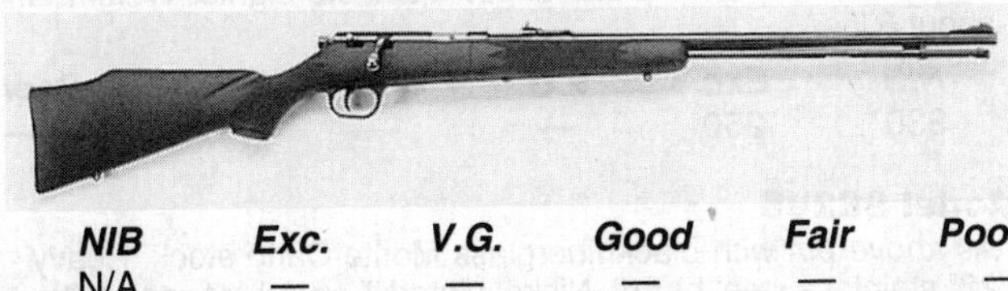

NIB	Exc.	V.G.	Good	Fair	Poor
N/A	—	—	—	—	—

Model 883

Bolt-action rifle chambered for .22 Win. Magnum cartridge with 12-shot tubular magazine. Furnished with a 22" MicroGroove barrel and adjustable rear sight, ramp front sight with hood. Checkered American black walnut stock with Monte Carlo. Rifle weighs 6 lbs. Introduced in 1988. Discontinued in 2004.

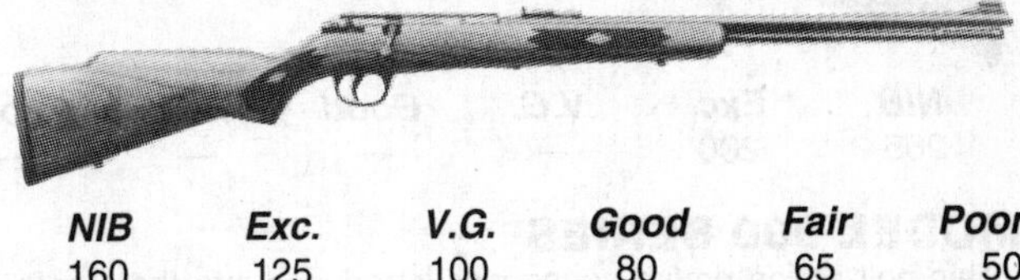

NIB	Exc.	V.G.	Good	Fair	Poor
160	125	100	80	65	50

Model 883N

Same as above but furnished with stainless steel barrel, receiver, front breech bolt, and striker. All other metal parts, except for sights, are nickel plated. Discontinued in 2004.

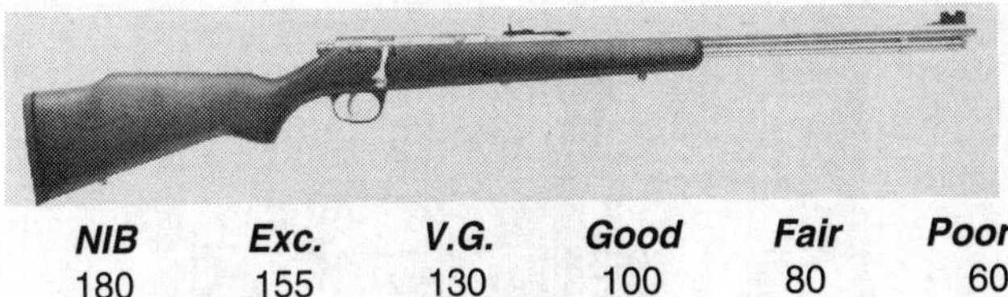

NIB	Exc.	V.G.	Good	Fair	Poor
180	155	130	100	80	60

Model 883SS

Introduced in 1993 this model is similar to the Model 883 but with all metal parts in stainless steel or nickel and the stock is a two-tone brown birch Monte Carlo that is not checkered. Discontinued in 2004.

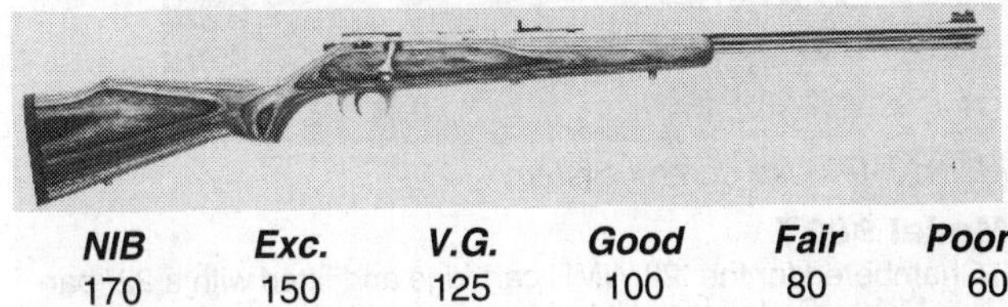

NIB	Exc.	V.G.	Good	Fair	Poor
170	150	125	100	80	60

Model MR-7

Introduced in 1996, this was an American made bolt-action centerfire rifle of a totally new design. Chambered for the .25-06 (first offered in 1997), .243, .270 Win. .280, .308, or .30-06 cartridges it is fitted with a 22" barrel. It has an American black walnut stock and a 4-shot detachable box magazine. Offered with or without sights. Weight is approximately 7.5 lbs. Discontinued.

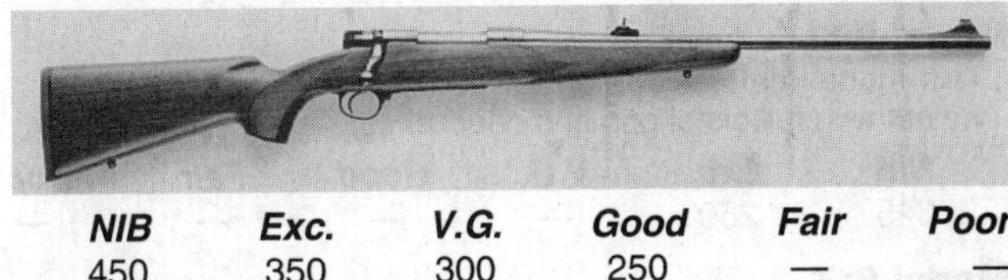

NIB	Exc.	V.G.	Good	Fair	Poor
450	350	300	250	—	—

Model MR-7B

Similar to the MR-7 but fitted with a 4-round blind magazine and birch stock. Offered in .30-06 or .270 with or without sights. Introduced in 1998. Discontinued.

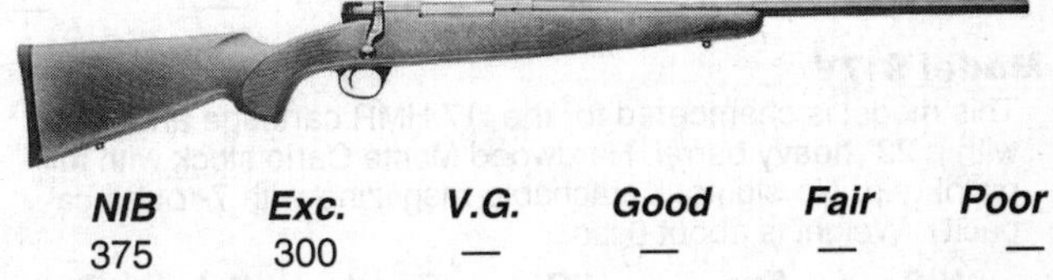

NIB	Exc.	V.G.	Good	Fair	Poor
375	300	—	—	—	—

Model 717M2

Introduced in 2005 this semi-automatic model is chambered for the .17 Mach 2 cartridge. Laminated hardwood stock with Monte Carlo comb. Fitted with an 18" barrel with iron sights. Magazine capacity is 7 rounds. Weight is about 5 lbs.

NIB	Exc.	V.G.	Good	Fair	Poor
265	200	—	—	—	—

MODEL 900 SERIES

This bolt action rimfire series was introduced into the Marlin line in 2004 and features a T-900 fire control system. This is a trigger and safety system that features a wide serrated trigger and improved trigger pull. The safety activitation is also improved. The 900 series also features drilled and tapped receivers on all models.

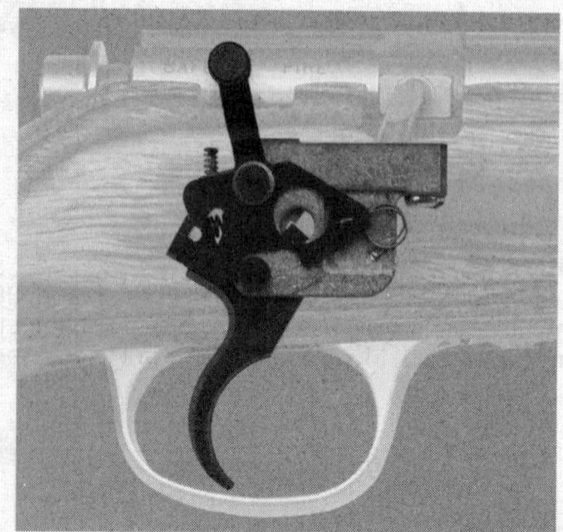

Marlin T-900 fire control system

Model 983T

Chambered for the .22 WMR cartridge and fitted with a 22" barrel. Monte Carlo black fiberglass stock with checkering. Adjustable sights. Tubular 12-round magazine. Weight is about 6 lbs.

NIB	Exc.	V.G.	Good	Fair	Poor
265	200	—	—	—	—

Model 983S

As above but with laminated two-tone stock.

NIB	Exc.	V.G.	Good	Fair	Poor
365	275	—	—	—	—

Model 983

This model features a Monte Carlo stock of American black walnut with full pistol grip and checkering.

NIB	Exc.	V.G.	Good	Fair	Poor
345	250	—	—	—	—

Model 917

Bolt-action rifle chambered in 17 Hornady Mag. Rimfire; 7-shot clip magazine; fiberglass-filled synthetic stock with full pistol grip; swivel studs and molded-in checkering. Adjustable open rear sight, ramp front. 22-inch barrel. Introduced 2006.

NIB	Exc.	V.G.	Good	Fair	Poor
345	—	—	—	—	—

Model 917V

This model is chambered for the .17 HMR cartridge and fitted with a 22" heavy barrel. Hardwood Monte Carlo stock with full pistol grip. No sights. Detachable magazine with 7-round capacity. Weight is about 6 lbs.

NIB	Exc.	V.G.	Good	Fair	Poor
275	225	—	—	—	—

Model 917VR

Similar to Model 917 but with fiberglass-filled synthetic stock. Introduced 2006. MSRP: 269

Model 917VS

As above but with gray/black laminated hardwood stock. No sights. Magazine is nickel plated. Weight is about 7 lbs. Scope bases included.

NIB	Exc.	V.G.	Good	Fair	Poor
410	325	—	—	—	—

Model 917VSF

Chambered for the .17 HMR cartridge and fitted with a 22" heavy stainless steel fluted barrel with no sights. Nickel magazine capacity is 7 rounds. Laminated gray stock with Monte Carlo comb. Weight is about 6.75 lbs. Introduced in 2005.

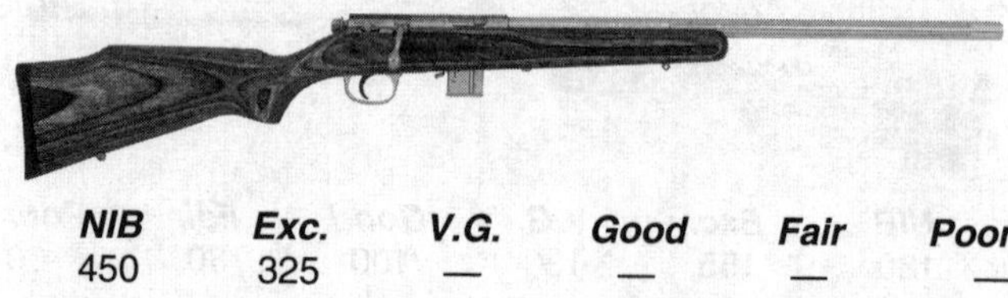

NIB	Exc.	V.G.	Good	Fair	Poor
450	325	—	—	—	—

Model 917M2

This model is chambered for the .17 Mach 2 cartridge and fitted with a 22" heavy barrel. Monte Carlo hardwood stock with full pistol grip. No sights but scope bases included. Magazine capacity is 7 rounds. Weight is about 5.5 lbs.

NIB	Exc.	V.G.	Good	Fair	Poor
220	175	—	—	—	—

Model 917M2S

As above but with Monte Carlo gray/black laminated stock with full pistol grip. Stainless steel barrel and receiver. Nickel plated magazine.

NIB	Exc.	V.G.	Good	Fair	Poor
N/A	—	—	—	—	—

Model 982S

This model is chambered for the .22 WMR cartridge and fitted with a 22" stainless steel barrel with adjustable sights. Black fiberglass stock with Monte Carlo and full pistol grip. Detachable 7-round nickel magazine. Weight is about 6 lbs.

NIB	Exc.	V.G.	Good	Fair	Poor
350	250	—	—	—	—

Model 982L

As above but for a gray/black laminated stock. Weight is about 6.25 lbs.

NIB	Exc.	V.G.	Good	Fair	Poor
N/A	—	—	—	—	—

Model 982

As above but with American black walnut checkered stock with Monte Carlo and full pistol grip. Adjustable sights. Weight is about 6 lbs.

NIB	Exc.	V.G.	Good	Fair	Poor
330	250	—	—	—	—

Model 982VS

As above but with black fiberglass Monte Carlo stock. Heavy 22" stainless steel barrel. Nickel plated 7-round magazine. No sights. Weight is about 7 lbs.

NIB	Exc.	V.G.	Good	Fair	Poor
345	260	—	—	—	—

Model 925M

As above but with hardwood stock and full pistol grip. Fitted with 22" standard weight barrel. Adjustable sights. Weight is about 6 lbs.

NIB	Exc.	V.G.	Good	Fair	Poor
250	200	—	—	—	—

Model 925MC

As above but with Monte Carlo stock with Mossy Oak Break-up camo stock. Weight is about 6 lbs.

NIB	Exc.	V.G.	Good	Fair	Poor
285	225	—	—	—	—

Model 980V

This model is chambered for the .22 LR cartridge and fitted with a 22" heavy barrel. Black fiberglass stock with Monte Carlo and full pistol grip. No sights. Magazine capacity is 7 rounds. Weight is about 7 lbs.

NIB	Exc.	V.G.	Good	Fair	Poor
270	—	—	—	—	—

Model 980S

As above but with standard weight 22" barrel and 7-round nickel plated magazine. Adjustable sights. Weight is about 6 lbs.

NIB	Exc.	V.G.	Good	Fair	Poor
250	—	—	—	—	—

Model 980S-CF

As above but with carbon fiber stock. Introduced in 2007.

NIB	Exc.	V.G.	Good	Fair	Poor
275	—	—	—	—	—

Model 981T

This model is chambered to handle interchangeably the .22 Short, Long, or LR cartridges in a tubular magazine. Black Monte Carlo fiberglass stock with full pistol grip. Adjustable sights. Fitted with a standard weight 22" barrel. Weight is about 6 lbs.

NIB	Exc.	V.G.	Good	Fair	Poor
270	200	—	—	—	—

Model 925

This model is chambered for the .22 LR cartridge and fitted with a 22" standard weight barrel with adjustable sights. Monte Carlo hardwood stock with full pistol grip. Seven-round magazine. Weight is about 5.5 lbs.

NIB	Exc.	V.G.	Good	Fair	Poor
225	175	—	—	—	—

Model 925C

As above but with Monte Carlo hardwood stock with Mossy Oak Break-up camo pattern. Adjustable sights.

NIB	Exc.	V.G.	Good	Fair	Poor
335	250	—	—	—	—

MARLIN SHOTGUNS

Model 1898 Slide-Action Shotgun

This model was made in 12 gauge, with an exposed hammer. It has a takedown receiver and walnut pistol-grip stock and forend.

There is a 5-shot tube magazine, and the barrel lengths are from 26" and 32". They were manufactured between 1898 and 1905.

Grade A

This variation has a 38", 30", or 32" barrel, is Full choke, and is the plainest grade.

Photo by Lt. Col. William S. Brophy from *Marlin Firearms* with permission

Exc.	V.G.	Good	Fair	Poor
375	325	225	125	75

Grade A Brush or Riot

This is the same shotgun with a 26" cylinder-bore barrel.

Exc.	V.G.	Good	Fair	Poor
425	375	250	150	100

Grade B

This is the same as the Grade A with a special smokeless steel barrel and a checkered stock.

Exc.	V.G.	Good	Fair	Poor
575	450	250	150	100

Grade C

This is a more deluxe version with engraving and fancier wood.

Exc.	V.G.	Good	Fair	Poor
1050	750	450	275	125

Grade D

This variation has a Damascus barrel and the greatest amount of engraving.

Exc.	V.G.	Good	Fair	Poor
2000	1300	800	400	250

Model 16 Slide-Action Shotgun

This model is exactly the same as the Model 1898 except that it is chambered for 16 gauge only. The four grades are the same also. They were manufactured between 1903 and 1910.

Grade A

Exc.	V.G.	Good	Fair	Poor
400	350	300	250	150

Grade B

Exc.	V.G.	Good	Fair	Poor
550	450	300	200	100

Grade C

Exc.	V.G.	Good	Fair	Poor
1000	750	400	300	150

Grade D

Exc.	V.G.	Good	Fair	Poor
2000	1300	800	425	250

Model 17 Slide-Action Shotgun

This model is an exposed-hammer gun with a solid frame and a straight-grip stock. It is chambered for 12 gauge, with a 30" or 32" barrel. The Model 17 was manufactured between 1906 and 1908.

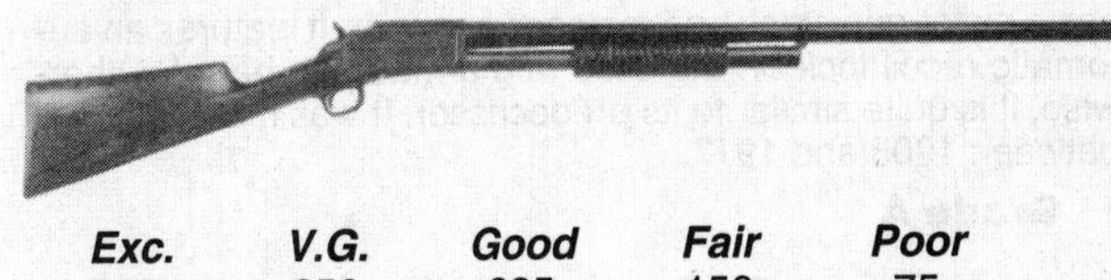

Exc.	V.G.	Good	Fair	Poor
425	350	225	150	75

Model 17 Brush Gun

This variation is similar to the standard Model 17, with a 26" cylinder-bore barrel.

Exc.	V.G.	Good	Fair	Poor
450	375	300	200	100

Model 17 Riot Gun

This variation has a 20" cylinder-bore barrel.

Exc.	V.G.	Good	Fair	Poor
450	350	225	150	75

Model 19 Slide-Action Shotgun

This is a takedown gun, chambered for 12 gauge. It is basically an improved and lightened version of the Model 1898. It is available in the same four grades. It was manufactured in 1906 and 1907.

Grade A

Exc.	V.G.	Good	Fair	Poor
400	350	200	150	100

Grade B

Exc.	V.G.	Good	Fair	Poor
500	450	400	350	225

Grade C

Exc.	V.G.	Good	Fair	Poor
650	575	500	425	300

Grade D

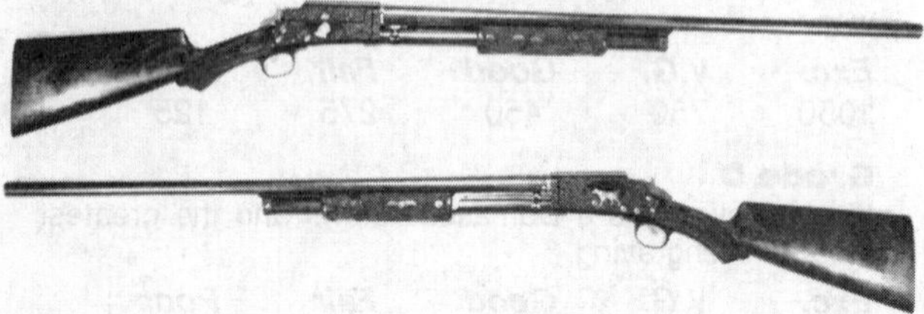

Photo by Lt. Col. William S. Brophy from *Marlin Firearms* with permission

Exc.	V.G.	Good	Fair	Poor
1750	1400	950	400	200

Model 21 "Trap" Slide-Action Shotgun

This model is basically the same as the Model 19 with a straight-grip stock. The 1907 catalog listed it as a Trap model. This model was manufactured in 1907 and 1908. The four grades are similar to the previous models.

Grade A

Exc.	V.G.	Good	Fair	Poor
400	350	250	200	100

Grade B

Exc.	V.G.	Good	Fair	Poor
500	450	300	200	100

Grade C

Exc.	V.G.	Good	Fair	Poor
650	575	450	350	200

Grade D

Exc.	V.G.	Good	Fair	Poor
1400	1200	1000	700	550

Model 24 Slide-Action Shotgun

This model is actually an improved version of the Model 21. It has a pistol-grip stock and exposed hammer. It features an automatic recoil lock on the slide and a matte rib barrel. Otherwise, it is quite similar to its predecessor. It was manufactured between 1908 and 1917.

Grade A

Photo by Lt. Col. William S. Brophy from *Marlin Firearms* with permission

Exc.	V.G.	Good	Fair	Poor
375	300	250	150	100

Grade B

Exc.	V.G.	Good	Fair	Poor
500	450	400	350	225

Grade C

Exc.	V.G.	Good	Fair	Poor
650	575	500	425	300

Grade D

Exc.	V.G.	Good	Fair	Poor
1400	1200	850	600	400

Marlin "Trap Gun"

This model is unique in that it has no numerical designation and is simply known as the "Trap Gun." It is a takedown gun with interchangeable barrels from 16" to 32". It has a straight-grip buttstock and is quite similar in appearance to the Model 24. It was manufactured between 1909 and 1912.

Exc.	V.G.	Good	Fair	Poor
450	400	350	250	175

Model 26 Slide-Action Shotgun

This model is similar to the Model 24 Grade A, with a solid frame. It has 30" or 32" barrels.

Exc.	V.G.	Good	Fair	Poor
425	350	275	125	100

Model 26 Brush Gun

This model has a 26" cylinder-bored barrel.

Exc.	V.G.	Good	Fair	Poor
450	375	300	150	125

Model 26 Riot Gun

This variation has a 20" cylinder-bored barrel.

Exc.	V.G.	Good	Fair	Poor
400	350	275	125	75

Model 28 Hammerless Slide-Action Shotgun

This model was the first of the Marlin hammerless shotguns. It is a takedown 12 gauge, with barrels from 26" to 32" in length. The stock has a pistol grip, and it comes in four grades like its predecessors. The Model 28 was manufactured between 1913 and 1922.

Grade A

Exc.	V.G.	Good	Fair	Poor
300	235	140	100	70

Grade B

Exc.	V.G.	Good	Fair	Poor
500	450	400	350	225

Grade C

Exc.	V.G.	Good	Fair	Poor
650	575	500	425	300

Grade D

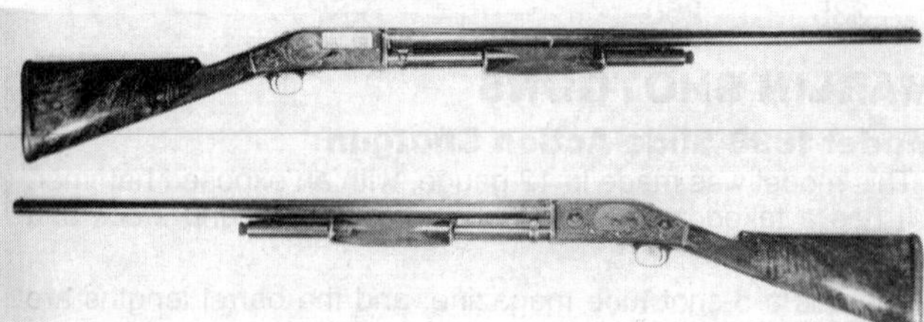

Photo by Lt. Col. William S. Brophy from *Marlin Firearms* with permission

Exc.	V.G.	Good	Fair	Poor
1700	1200	800	600	300

Model 28TS Trap Gun

This variation is the same as the Model 28 with a 30" Full choke barrel with matte rib and a high-comb straight grip stock. It was manufactured in 1915.

Exc.	V.G.	Good	Fair	Poor
425	375	300	200	100

Model 28T Trap Gun

This variation is the deluxe model, similar to the Model 28TS, with engraving, high-grade walnut, and hand checkering. It was manufactured in 1915.

Exc.	V.G.	Good	Fair	Poor
600	525	450	250	150

Model 30 Slide-Action Shotgun

This model is an improved version of the Model 16, 16 gauge shotgun. Its features are similar, with the addition of the improved takedown system and the automatic recoil lock on the slide. This model was manufactured between 1910 and 1914.

Grade A

Exc.	V.G.	Good	Fair	Poor
450	375	300	200	100

Grade B

Exc.	V.G.	Good	Fair	Poor
500	450	400	200	100

Grade C

Exc.	V.G.	Good	Fair	Poor
650	575	500	250	150

Grade D

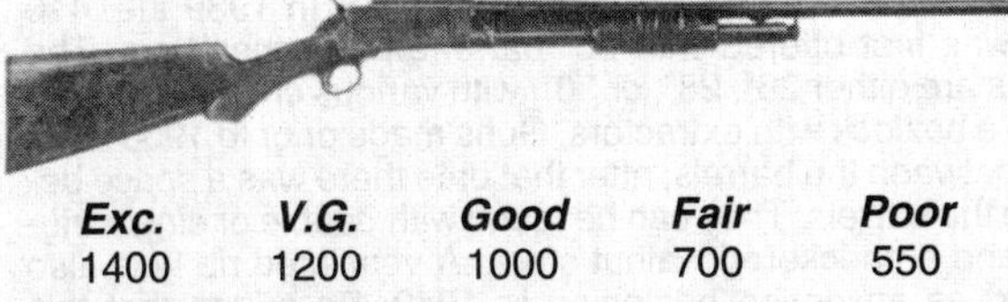

Exc.	V.G.	Good	Fair	Poor
1400	1200	1000	700	550

Model 30 Field Grade

This model is similar to the Model 30 Grade B, with a 25" modified-choke barrel and a straight-grip stock. It was manufactured in 1913 and 1914.

Exc.	V.G.	Good	Fair	Poor
350	275	200	150	100

Model 31 Slide-Action Shotgun

This model is a smaller version of the Model 28 hammerless takedown shotgun, chambered for 16 and 20 gauge. It was produced with barrel lengths of 26" and 28" and was available in the usual four grades, with various different chokes. This model was manufactured between 1915 and 1922.

Grade A

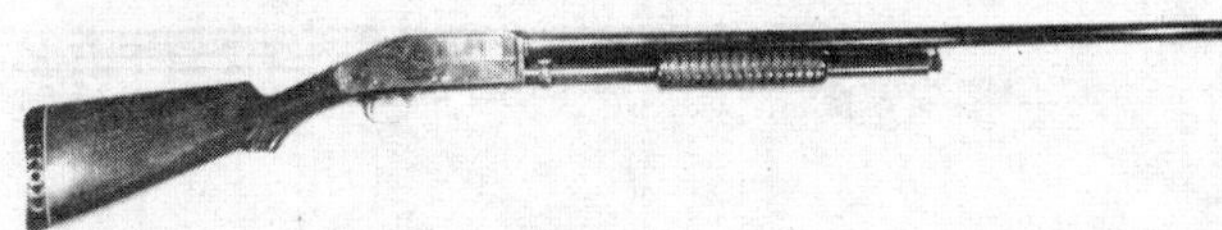

Photo by Lt. Col. William S. Brophy from *Marlin Firearms* with permission

Exc.	V.G.	Good	Fair	Poor
400	350	300	150	100

Grade B

Exc.	V.G.	Good	Fair	Poor
500	450	400	250	150

Grade C

Exc.	V.G.	Good	Fair	Poor
650	575	500	300	150

Grade D

Exc.	V.G.	Good	Fair	Poor
1400	1200	1000	600	300

Model 42/42A Slide-Action Shotgun

This model was originally listed as the Model 42; but in the second year of production, the designation was changed to 42/A for no more apparent reason than standardization of models. This model is similar to the Model 24 except that the barrel markings are different. It is still an exposed hammer takedown gun chambered for 12 gauge. It was manufactured between 1922 and 1933.

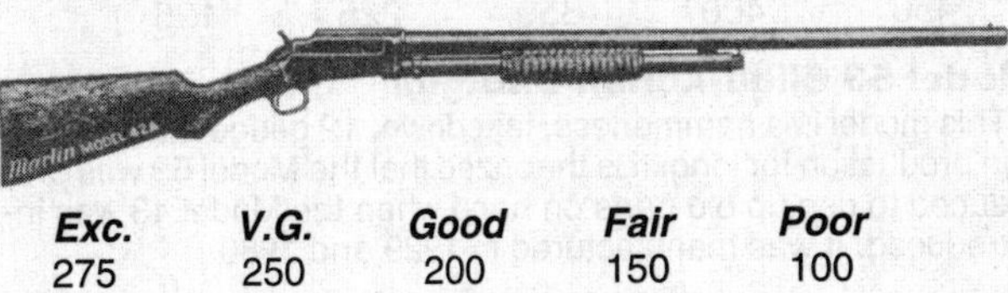

Exc.	V.G.	Good	Fair	Poor
275	250	200	150	100

Model 43A Slide-Action Shotgun

This hammerless model was quite similar to the Model 28, with different markings and less attention to finishing detail. It was manufactured between 1923 and 1930.

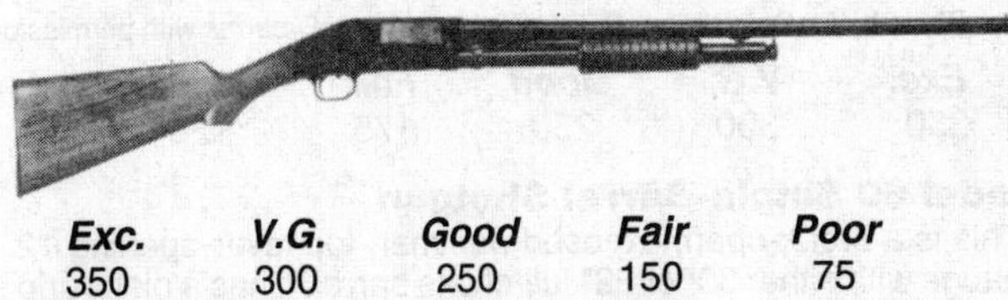

Exc.	V.G.	Good	Fair	Poor
350	300	250	150	75

Model 43T Slide-Action Shotgun

This model is the same as the Model 43A takedown hammerless with a 30" or 32" matte rib barrel. The straight-grip stock is of high grade walnut, with a non-gloss oil finish and fitted recoil paid. This model was manufactured between 1922 and 1930.

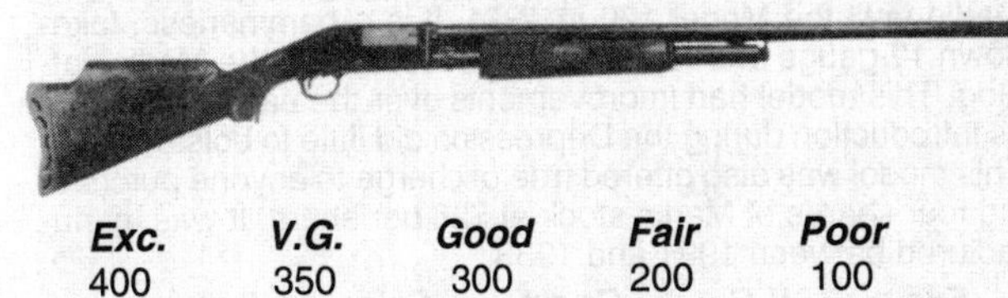

Exc.	V.G.	Good	Fair	Poor
400	350	300	200	100

Model 43TS Slide-Action Shotgun

This is a custom-order version of the Model 43T, the same in all respects except that the stock could be ordered to any specifications the shooter desired. It was manufactured between 1922 and 1930.

Exc.	V.G.	Good	Fair	Poor
600	550	500	250	150

Model 44A Slide-Action Shotgun

This model is similar to the Model 31 and was advertised as its successor. It is a hammerless takedown chambered for the 20 gauge. It features an improved bolt opening device located in the trigger guard area instead of at the top of the receiver and has a shorter 4-shot magazine tube. The model was manufactured from 1922 until 1933.

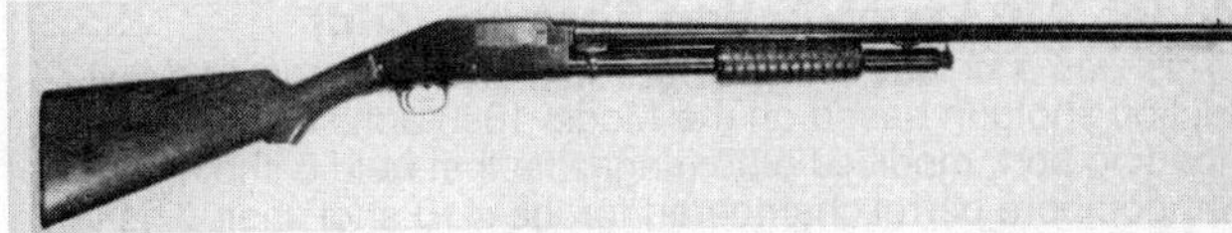

Photo by Lt. Col. William S. Brophy from *Marlin Firearms* with permission

Exc.	V.G.	Good	Fair	Poor
375	325	275	150	100

Model 44S Slide-Action Shotgun

This model is similar to the Model 44A, with a higher grade walnut stock that featured hand-cut checkering.

Exc.	V.G.	Good	Fair	Poor
500	400	300	200	100

Model 49 Slide-Action Shotgun

This model is a 12-gauge, exposed-hammer takedown that combines features of the Model 42 and the Model 24. It is basically a lower-priced model that was never listed in the Marlin catalog. This model was part of Frank Kenna's money-raising program—anyone who purchased four shares of stock for $25 per share was given one, free of charge. This model was manufactured between 1925 and 1928.

Exc.	V.G.	Good	Fair	Poor
450	400	350	225	125

Model 53 Slide-Action Shotgun

This model is a hammerless, takedown, 12 gauge that was not in production for long. It is theorized that the Model 53 was produced to use up old parts on hand when the Model 43 was introduced. It was manufactured in 1929 and 1980.

Photo by Lt. Col. William S. Brophy from *Marlin Firearms* with permission

Exc.	V.G.	Good	Fair	Poor
350	300	250	175	125

Model 60 Single-Barrel Shotgun

This is a break-open, exposed-hammer, top lever-opening 12 gauge with either 30" or 32" full-choke barrel. It has a pistol grip stock. There were approximately 60 manufactured in 1923.

Exc.	V.G.	Good	Fair	Poor
200	175	150	100	70

Model 63 Slide-Action Shotgun

This was the last of the slide-action shotguns produced by Marlin until the Model 120 in 1971. It is a hammerless, takedown 12 gauge and replaced the Model 43A in the Marlin catalog. This model had improvements over the earlier guns, but its introduction during the Depression did little to bolster sales. This model was also offered free of charge to anyone purchasing four shares of Marlin stock at $25 per share. It was manufactured between 1931 and 1933.

Exc.	V.G.	Good	Fair	Poor
350	300	250	175	125

Model 63T Slide-Action Shotgun

This is the trap-grade version of the Model 63. It has a better grade hand-checkered stock, with a fitted recoil pad and oil finish. It was manufactured between 1931 and 1933.

Exc.	V.G.	Good	Fair	Poor
375	325	275	150	100

Model 63TS Slide-Action Shotgun

This variation is the same as the Model 63T except that the stock dimensions were custom-made to the customer's specifications. It was manufactured between 1931 and 1933.

Exc.	V.G.	Good	Fair	Poor
400	350	300	200	100

Model .410 Lever-Action Shotgun (Old)

This was a unique venture for the Marlin Company—a lever-action shotgun based on the Model 1893 action with a longer loading port, modified tube magazine that held 5 shots, and a smoothbore barrel chambered for the .410 shot shell. The finish of this gun is blued, with a walnut pistol grip stock and grooved beavertail forend. It has a hard rubber rifle-type buttplate. The model was available with either a 22" or 26" full-choke barrel. This gun was also part of the stock purchase plan and was given free of charge to anyone purchasing four shares at $25 per share. It was also cataloged for sale and was manufactured between 1929 and 1932.

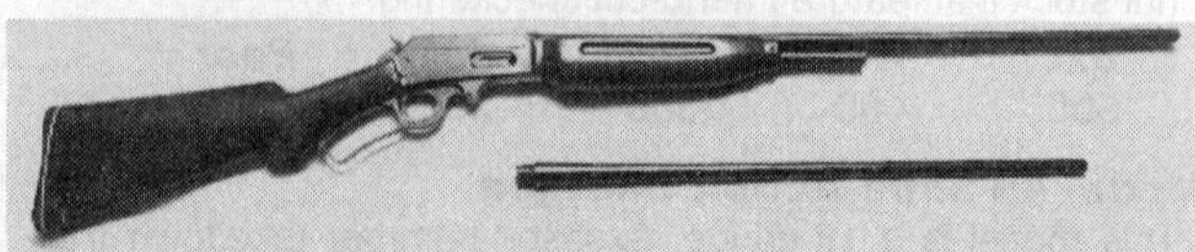

Courtesy Mike Stuckslager

Exc.	V.G.	Good	Fair	Poor
1450	1000	650	500	200

Model .410 Deluxe

This variation was never cataloged and is essentially the same as the standard version with a hand-checkered stock. The forend does not have the grooves found on the standard model. Be wary of fakes!

Exc.	V.G.	Good	Fair	Poor
2200	1200	800	400	200

Model .410 (New)

A lever-action shotgun chambered for the 2.5-inch .410 shotshell. Checkered walnut stock, fluorescent front sight. Based on the Model 336 action. Discontinued.

NIB	Exc.	V.G.	Good	Fair
850	625	—	—	—

Model 90 Over-and-Under Shotgun

This gun was produced in response to a request from Sears Roebuck that Marlin should manufacture an over-and-under shotgun for Sears to market in their stores. The guns produced for Sears have the prefix 103 in their serial numbers and were marked "Ranger" before WWII and "J.C. Higgins" after the war. Prior to 1945 they were not marked Marlin; after that date Sears requested that the company stamp their name on the guns. They were also produced as the Marlin Model 90 during the same period and were chambered for 12, 16, and 20 gauge, as well as .410 bore. The 16 and 20 gauge guns were first offered in 1937 with 26" or 28" barrels. In 1939 the .410 bore was first offered with 26" barrel and 3" chambers. The barrels are either 26", 28", or 30", with various chokes. The action is a boxlock with extractors. Guns made prior to 1950 were solid between the barrels; after that date there was a space between the barrels. They can be found with double or single triggers and a checkered walnut stock. A ventilated rib was also offered as an option beginning in 1949. Be aware that this model was also available as a combination gun in .22 LR/.410, .22 Hornet/.410, and .218 Bee/.410. There were approximately 34,000 Model 90s manufactured between 1937 and 1963.

EDITOR'S NOTE: Collectors should be aware that this model has a receiver of malleable iron. It will not blue by the usual bluing methods. The barrels and ribs are soft soldered and cannot take hot bluing. Use caution.

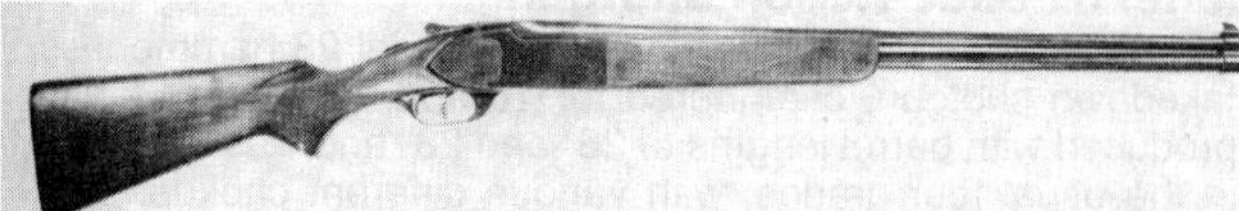

Photo by Lt. Col. William S. Brophy from *Marlin Firearms* with permission

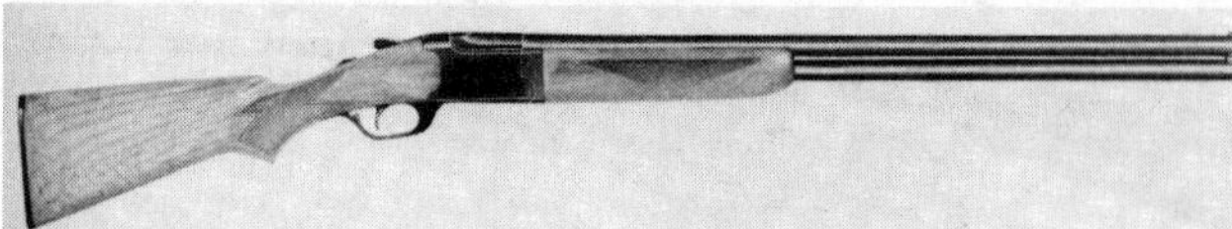

Marlin Model 90 Combination Gun

Photo by Lt. Col. William S. Brophy from *Marlin Firearms* with permission

Marlin Model 90 .410 bore

Photo by Lt. Col. William S. Brophy from *Marlin Firearms* with permission

Exc.	V.G.	Good	Fair	Poor
500	425	350	275	200

NOTE: Single trigger add 15 percent. Add 25 percent for 20 gauge guns and 125 percent for .410 bores. Add a 150 percent premium for combination guns. There are other rare gauge and barrel combinations that may affect value.

Premier Mark I Slide-Action Shotgun

This model was made by Manufrance and called the LaSalle. Marlin was able to purchase them without the barrels at a good enough price for them to barrel and market them under their own name. This model is 12 gauge only, with an alloy receiver and seven interchangeable barrels in 26"-30" lengths and various chokes. The plain stock is French walnut. The biggest problem with this gun is that the light weight (six pounds) produced severe recoil, and it was less than enjoyable to shoot. This model was in production from 1959 through 1963, with approximately 13,700 sold.

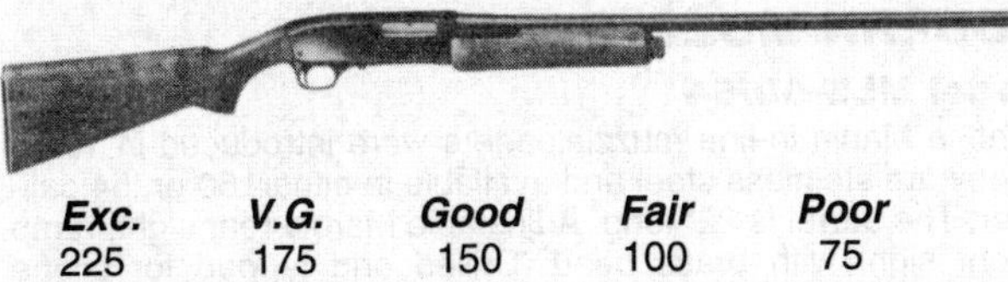

Exc.	V.G.	Good	Fair	Poor
225	175	150	100	75

Premier Mark II

This model is similar to the Mark I, with light engraving and a checkered stock.

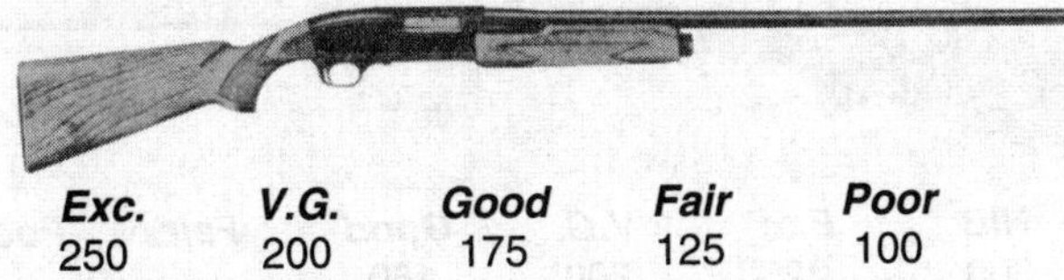

Exc.	V.G.	Good	Fair	Poor
250	200	175	125	100

Premier Mark IV

This model is similar to the Mark II, with more engraving on the receiver.

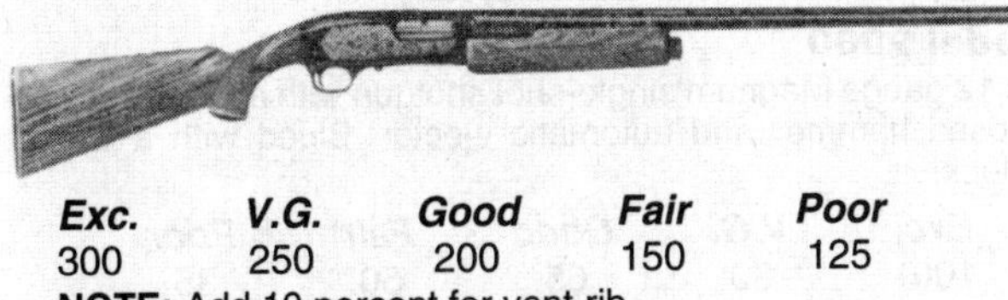

Exc.	V.G.	Good	Fair	Poor
300	250	200	150	125

NOTE: Add 10 percent for vent rib.

Model 120 Slide-Action Shotgun

This model was styled to resemble the Winchester Model 12 and was advertised as an all steel and walnut shotgun. It was offered with interchangeable barrels from 26" to 40", and various chokes were available. The checkered stock is of walnut, with a fitted recoil pad. The tube magazine holds 5 shots, 4 in 3". There was a Trap Model available (1973-1975), as well as a slug gun (1974-1984). This model was manufactured between 1971 and 1985.

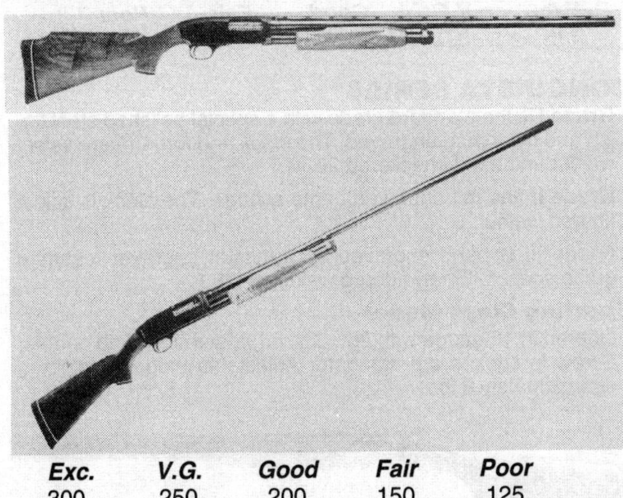

Exc.	V.G.	Good	Fair	Poor
300	250	200	150	125

Model 778 Slide-Action Shotgun (Glenfield)

This model is similar to the Model 120, with a walnut finished hardwood stock instead of walnut, and the Glenfield name stamped on it. It was manufactured between 1979 and 1984.

Exc.	V.G.	Good	Fair	Poor
225	175	150	125	100

Model 50DL

This bolt-action 12 gauge shotgun is available with a 28" modified barrel, black synthetic stock. Ventilated recoil pad is standard. Brass bead front sight. Weight is approximately 7.5 lbs.

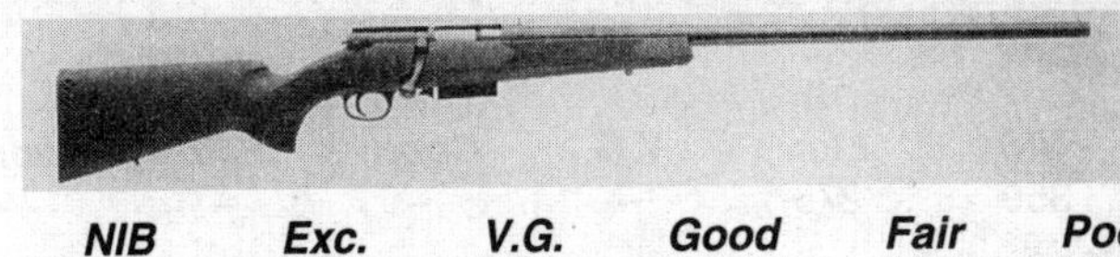

NIB	Exc.	V.G.	Good	Fair	Poor
300	275	225	150	125	100

Model 55 Bolt-Action Shotgun

This model is chambered for 12, 16, and 20 gauge, with Full or adjustable choke and barrels of 26" or 28". It is a bolt-action with 2-shot box magazine. The pistol grip stock is plain. This model was manufactured between 1950 and 1965.

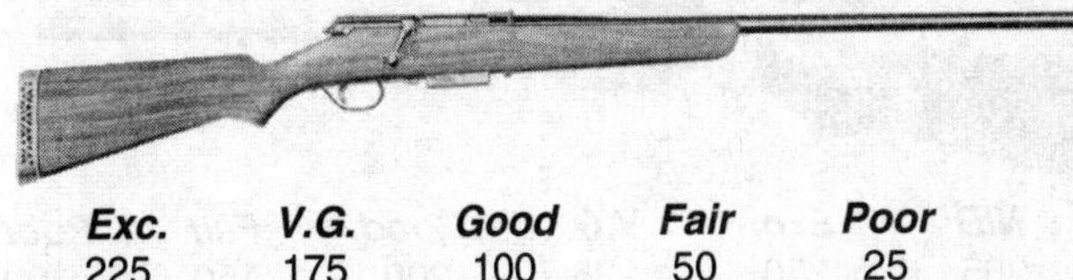

Exc.	V.G.	Good	Fair	Poor
225	175	100	50	25

Model 55 Swamp Gun

This is simply the Model 55 with a 3" Magnum, 20" barrel and an adjustable choke. It was manufactured between 1963 and 1965.

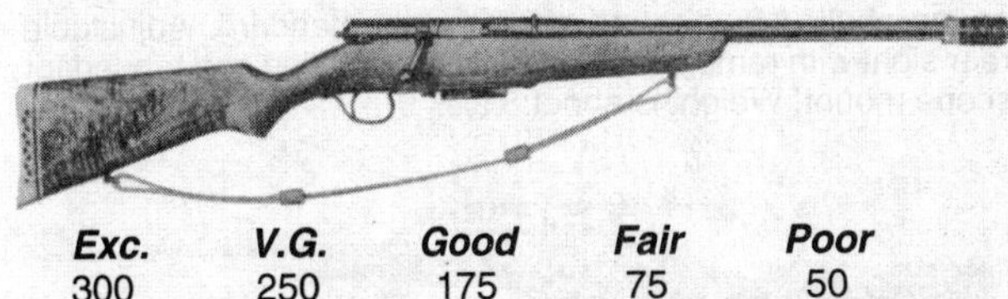

Exc.	V.G.	Good	Fair	Poor
300	250	175	75	50

Model 55 Goose Gun

This is the Model 55 with a 3" chambered, 36" Full choke barrel and a recoil pad and sling. It was introduced in 1962.

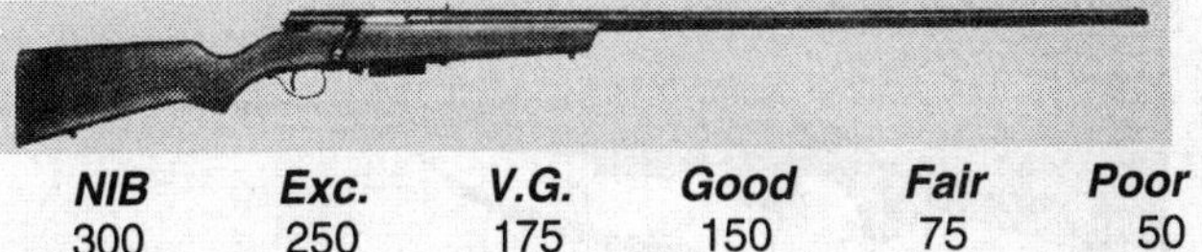

NIB	Exc.	V.G.	Good	Fair	Poor
300	250	175	150	75	50

Model 55S Slug Gun

This is the Model 55 with a 24" cylinder-bore barrel and rifle sights. It was manufactured between 1974 and 1983.

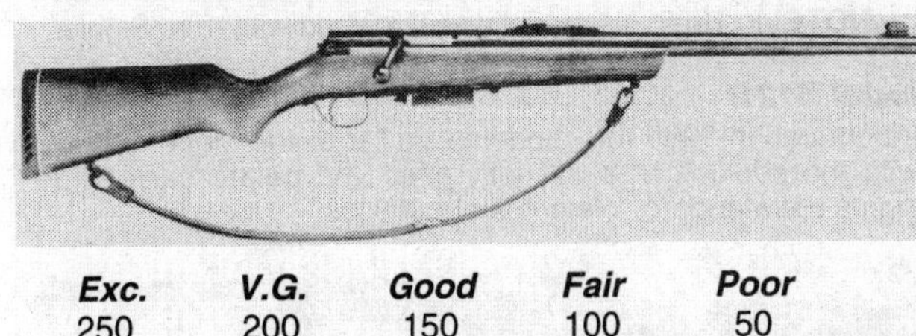

Exc.	V.G.	Good	Fair	Poor
250	200	150	100	50

Model 5510 Bolt-Action Shotgun

This model is chambered for the 3.5" 10 gauge. It has a 34" Full choke barrel and a recoil pad and sling. It was manufactured between 1976 and 1985.

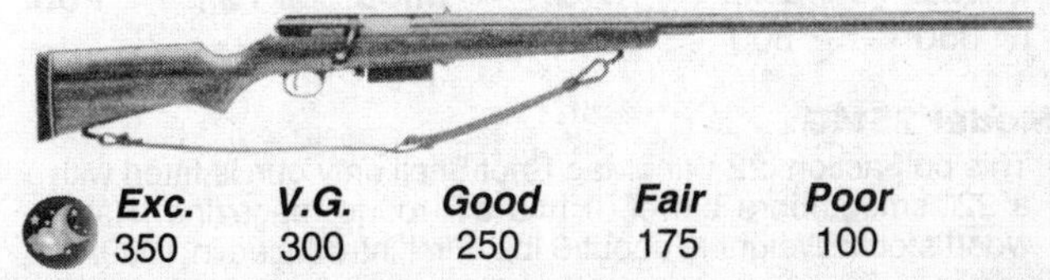

Exc.	V.G.	Good	Fair	Poor
350	300	250	175	100

Model 55GDL

This bolt-action shotgun is fitted with a 36" full choke barrel and reinforced black synthetic stock. Magazine holds two rounds. Ventilated recoil pad is standard. First introduced in 1997. Weight is about 8 lbs.

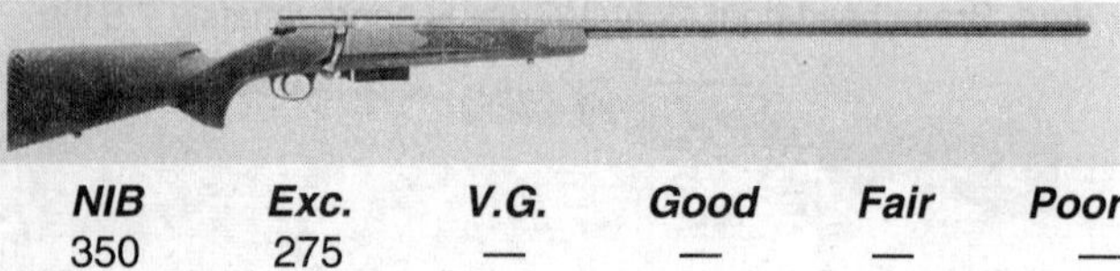

NIB	Exc.	V.G.	Good	Fair	Poor
350	275	—	—	—	—

Model 512 Slugmaster

Introduced in 1994 this bolt-action shotgun features a rifled 21" barrel. It is equipped with a two-shot detachable magazine and a ventilated recoil pad. A special scope is also provided. Weight is approximately 8 lbs.

NIB	Exc.	V.G.	Good	Fair	Poor
285	250	225	200	150	100

Model 512DL Slugmaster

Introduced in 1997 this bolt-action model features a black synthetic stock with a fully rifled 21" barrel chambered for the 12 gauge shell. A two-round magazine is standard. Adjustable rear sight with ramp front sight. Receiver drilled and tapped for scope mount. Weight is about 8 lbs.

Model 512 DL with Fire Sights

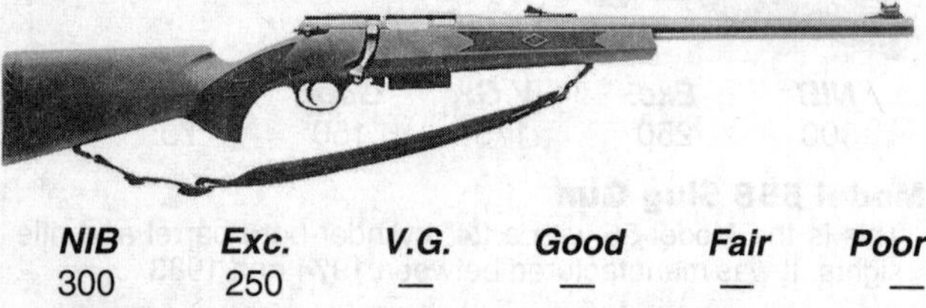

NIB	Exc.	V.G.	Good	Fair	Poor
300	250	—	—	—	—

NOTE: In 1998 this model was furnished with "Fire Sights."

Model 512P

Introduced in 1999 this model is similar to the Model 512 DL with the addition of a 21" fully rifled and ported barrel. Fire sights are standard. Weight is about 8 lbs.

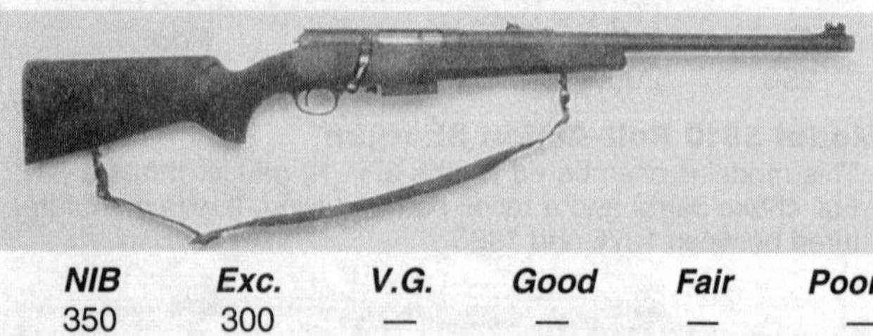

NIB	Exc.	V.G.	Good	Fair	Poor
350	300	—	—	—	—

Model 25MG

This bolt-action .22 Win. Mag Shot Shell only gun is fitted with a 22" smoothbore barrel. It has a 7-round magazine. Hardwood stock. Weight is about 6 lbs. First introduced in 1999.

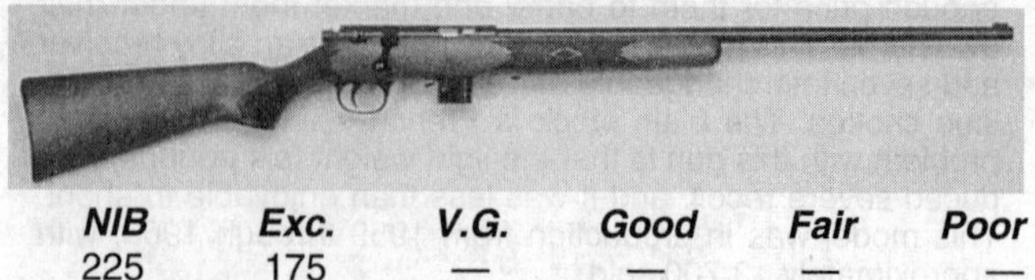

NIB	Exc.	V.G.	Good	Fair	Poor
225	175	—	—	—	—

MODERN MUZZLELOADERS

Model MLS-50/54

These Marlin in-line muzzleloaders were introduced in 1997. They are stainless steel and available in either .50 or .54 caliber. The barrel is 22" long. Adjustable Marble rear sight, ramp front sight with brass bead. Drilled and tapped for scope mount. Black synthetic stock with molded in checkering. Weight is about 7 lbs. Discontinued, and not particularly easy to take down for cleaning.

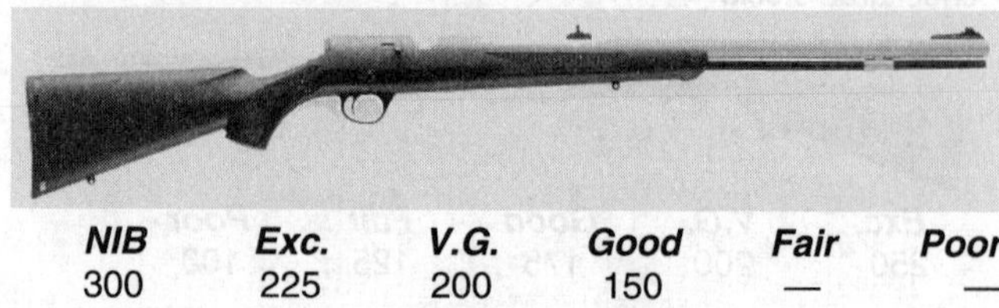

NIB	Exc.	V.G.	Good	Fair	Poor
300	225	200	150	—	—

MAROCCHI ARMI

Brescia, Italy

Model 2000

A 12 gauge Magnum single-shot shotgun with a 28" barrel, exposed hammer and automatic ejector. Blued with a walnut stock.

Exc.	V.G.	Good	Fair	Poor
100	80	65	50	35

Field Master I

A 12 gauge over-and-under shotgun with 26" or 28" ventilated rib barrels fitted for choke tubes, single trigger and automatic ejectors. Blued, French case hardened with a walnut stock.

Exc.	V.G.	Good	Fair	Poor
400	350	300	200	150

Field Master II

As above, with a single-selective trigger.

Exc.	V.G.	Good	Fair	Poor
425	375	325	225	175

CONQUISTA SERIES

Grade I is the standard grade with a special polished steel finish and machined engraved. The stock and forearm are select walnut and hand checkered 20 lpi.

Grade II has roll engraved game scenes. The stock is select figured walnut.

Grade III is hand engraved by a master engraver featuring game scenes. Finely figured walnut stock.

Sporting Clays Model

Offered in 12 gauge with 28", 30", or 32" ventilated rib barrels. Screw in chokes are standard. Adjustable trigger. Weight is approximately 8 lbs.

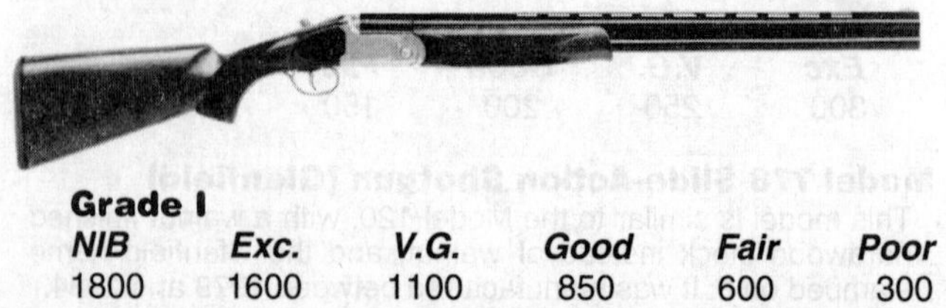

Grade I

NIB	Exc.	V.G.	Good	Fair	Poor
1800	1600	1100	850	600	300

Grade II

NIB	Exc.	V.G.	Good	Fair	Poor
2200	1800	1400	950	700	350

Grade III

NIB	Exc.	V.G.	Good	Fair	Poor
3200	2750	1750	1150	800	400

Sporting Light

Same as above but slightly smaller dimensions. Available in 28" or 30" barrel length. Weight is about 7.5 lbs.

Grade I

NIB	Exc.	V.G.	Good	Fair	Poor
1900	1600	1100	850	600	300

Sporting Clays Left-Hand Model

Same as Sporting Clays Model but designed for the left-handed shooter.

Grade I

NIB	Exc.	V.G.	Good	Fair	Poor
1900	1600	1100	850	600	300

Lady Sport Model

Offered in 12 gauge only with choice of 28" or 30" vent rib barrels. Slightly smaller dimensions for women. Weight 7.75 lbs.

Grade I

NIB	Exc.	V.G.	Good	Fair	Poor
1900	1600	1100	850	600	300

Spectrum Grade—Colored Frame

NIB	Exc.	V.G.	Good	Fair	Poor
1975	1650	1150	850	600	300

Lady Sport Left-Handed

Same as above but for left-handed shooters.

Grade I

NIB	Exc.	V.G.	Good	Fair	Poor
1975	1650	1150	850	600	300

Spectrum Left-Handed

NIB	Exc.	V.G.	Good	Fair	Poor
2025	1700	1175	850	600	300

Trap Model

Built for the competition shooter this model features a choice of 30" or 32" vent rib barrels. Trap dimension stock. Weight approximately 8.25 lbs.

Grade I

NIB	Exc.	V.G.	Good	Fair	Poor
1875	1650	1150	850	600	300

Grade II

NIB	Exc.	V.G.	Good	Fair	Poor
2275	1850	1450	1000	750	350

Grade III

NIB	Exc.	V.G.	Good	Fair	Poor
3250	2600	1850	1500	800	400

Skeet Model

This model is designed for the competition shooter. Only a 28" vent rib barrel is offered as standard. Skeet dimension stock. Skeet chokes. Weight is approximately 7.75 lbs.

Grade I

NIB	Exc.	V.G.	Good	Fair	Poor
1875	1650	1150	850	600	300

Grade II

NIB	Exc.	V.G.	Good	Fair	Poor
2275	1850	1450	1000	750	350

Grade III

NIB	Exc.	V.G.	Good	Fair	Poor
3250	2600	1850	1500	800	400

Classic Doubles Model 92

Offered in 12 gauge only with 30" vent rib barrels. Adjustable trigger. Walnut stock with 18 lpi checkering. Weight is approximately 8.12 lbs.

NIB	Exc.	V.G.	Good	Fair	Poor
1500	1250	800	600	500	250

Model 99 Grade I

This over-and-under gun features a silver-grayed receiver, boxlock action with single-selective trigger, pistol-grip stock and schnabel forearm. Sporting models are offered with 28", 30", or 32" barrels. Trap models are offered with 30" or 32" barrels, and skeet models with 28" or 30" barrels. All barrels are supplied with five extended choke tubes.

NIB	Exc.	V.G.	Good	Fair	Poor
2995	2250	—	—	—	—

Model 99 Grade III

This model has all of the above features in addition to five flush-mounted choke tubes and silver game scene engraved receiver.

NIB	Exc.	V.G.	Good	Fair	Poor
4595	3400	—	—	—	—

MARS

SEE—Gabbet-Fairfax or Bergmann

MARSTON, S.W.

New York, New York

Double-Action Pepperbox

A .31 caliber double-action percussion pepperbox with a 5" barrel group and ring trigger. Blued with walnut grips. Manufactured between 1850 and 1855.

Exc.	V.G.	Good	Fair	Poor
—	—	1750	750	250

2 Barrel Pistol

A .31 or .36 revolving barrel 2-shot pistol with a ring trigger. The barrel marked "J.Cohn & S.W.Marston-New York." Blued, brass frame with walnut grips. Manufactured during the 1850s.

Exc.	V.G.	Good	Fair	Poor
—	—	2250	1000	350

MARSTON, W. W. & CO.

New York, New York

W.W. Marston & Company manufactured a variety of firearms some of which are marked only with the trade names: Union Arms Company, Phoenix Armory, Western Arms Company, Washington Arms Company, Sprague and Marston, and Marston and Knox.

Pocket Revolver

A .31 caliber percussion revolver with a 3.25" to 7.5" barrel and 6-shot cylinder. Blued with walnut grips. Approximately 13,000 were manufactured between 1857 and 1862.

Exc.	V.G.	Good	Fair	Poor
—	—	900	400	200

Navy Revolver

A .36 caliber percussion revolver with a 7.5" or 8.5" octagonal barrel and 6-shot cylinder. Blued with walnut grips. Manufactured between 1857 and 1862.

Exc.	V.G.	Good	Fair	Poor
—	—	2750	1200	400

Double-Action Single-Shot Pistol

A .31 or .36 caliber bar hammer percussion pistol with a 2.5" or 5" half octagonal barrel. Blued with walnut grips. Manufactured during the 1850s.

Exc.	V.G.	Good	Fair	Poor
—	—	500	200	100

Single-Action Pistol

A .31 or .36 caliber percussion pistol with a 4" or 6" barrel. Blued with walnut grips. Manufactured during the 1860s.

Exc.	V.G.	Good	Fair	Poor
—	—	550	225	100

Breech Loading Pistol

A .36 caliber breech loading percussion pistol with a 4" to 8.5" half octagonal barrel and either a brass or iron frame. Blued, case hardened with walnut grips. Approximately 1,000 were manufactured in the 1850s.

Courtesy Milwaukee Public Museum, Milwaukee, Wisconsin

Brass Frame

Exc.	V.G.	Good	Fair	Poor
—	—	3250	1500	500

Iron Frame

Exc.	V.G.	Good	Fair	Poor
—	—	2750	1000	300

Double-Action Pepperbox

A .31 caliber double-action 6-shot percussion pepperbox with 4" or 5" barrel groups and a bar hammer. Blued, case hardened with walnut grips. Manufactured during the 1850s.

Courtesy Milwaukee Public Museum, Milwaukee, Wisconsin

Exc.	V.G.	Good	Fair	Poor
—	—	2250	950	300

3 Barreled Derringer

A .22 caliber 3-barreled spur-trigger pocket pistol with a sliding knife blade mounted on the left side of the 3" barrel group. Blued, silver-plated with walnut grips. The barrel marked "Wm. W. Marston/New York City." Approximately 1,500 were manufactured between 1858 and 1864.

Knife Bladed Model

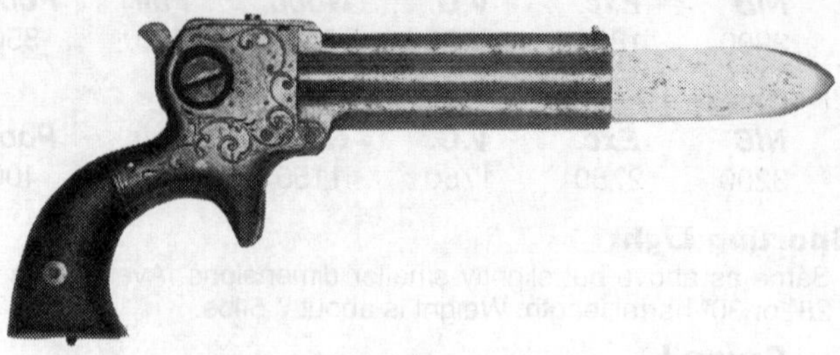

Courtesy Milwaukee Public Museum, Milwaukee, Wisconsin

Exc.	V.G.	Good	Fair	Poor
—	—	3750	1500	400

Model Without Knife

Courtesy Milwaukee Public Museum, Milwaukee, Wisconsin

Exc.	V.G.	Good	Fair	Poor
—	—	1750	700	200

.32 Caliber 3 Barrel Derringer

Similar to the above, but in .32 caliber with either 3" or 4" barrels and not fitted with a knife blade. Approximately 3,000 were manufactured between 1864 and 1872.

Courtesy Milwaukee Public Museum, Milwaukee, Wisconsin

Exc.	V.G.	Good	Fair	Poor
—	—	2750	750	200

MASQUELIER S. A.

Liege, Belgium

Carpathe

A .243, .270, .7x57mm, 7x65Rmm, or .30-06 caliber single-shot rifle with a 24" barrel, adjustable trigger and adjustable sights. Blued, with an engraved receiver and walnut stock. Imported until 1986.

Exc.	V.G.	Good	Fair	Poor
3500	2750	1950	1250	750

Express

A .270, .30-06, 8x57JRSmm, or 9.3x74Rmm caliber over-and-under double-barrel rifle with 24" barrels, single-selective trigger and automatic ejectors. Blued, engraved with a walnut stock. Not imported after 1986.

Exc.	V.G.	Good	Fair	Poor
3500	2750	1950	1250	750

Ardennes

As above, but made on custom order only. Discontinued in 1986.

Exc.	V.G.	Good	Fair	Poor
6500	5250	3750	2500	1000

Boxlock Side-by-Side Shotgun

A 12 gauge boxlock double-barrel shotgun manufactured in a variety of barrel lengths with a single-selective trigger and automatic ejectors. Blued with a walnut stock. Imported prior to 1987.

Exc.	V.G.	Good	Fair	Poor
4500	3250	2500	1500	850

Sidelock Side-by-Side Shotgun

Similar to the above, but with detachable sidelocks and finely engraved. Imported prior to 1987.

Exc.	V.G.	Good	Fair	Poor
13000	10500	7000	5000	1750

MASSACHUSETTS ARMS CO.

Chicopee Falls, Massachusetts

Wesson & Leavitt Dragoon

A .40 caliber percussion revolver with a 7" round barrel, 6-shot cylinder and side-mounted hammer. Blued, case hardened with walnut grips. Approximately 800 were manufactured in 1850 and 1851.

Early Model with 6" Barrel

Approximately 30 made.

Exc.	V.G.	Good	Fair	Poor
—	—	6000	2500	750

Fully Marked 7" Barrel Standard Model

Exc.	V.G.	Good	Fair	Poor
—	—	5500	2000	650

Wesson & Leavitt Belt Revolver

A .31 caliber percussion revolver with a 3" to 7" round barrel and 6-shot cylinder. Similar in appearance to the above. Approximately 1,000 were manufactured in 1850 and 1851.

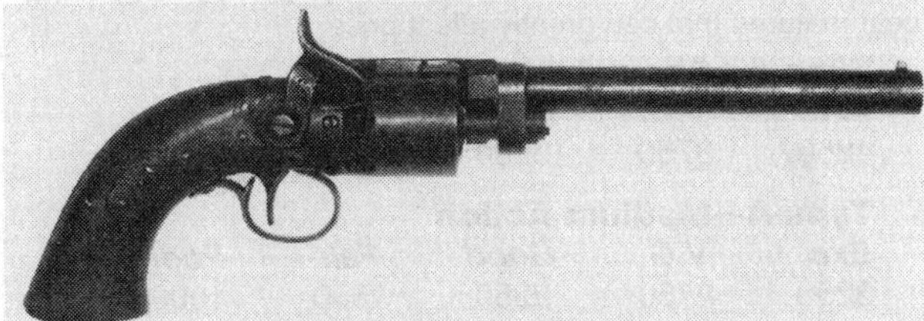

Courtesy Milwaukee Public Museum, Milwaukee, Wisconsin

Exc.	V.G.	Good	Fair	Poor
—	—	1750	700	250

Maynard Primed Belt Revolver

Similar to the above, with a Maynard tape primer. Approximately 1,000 were manufactured between 1851 and 1857.

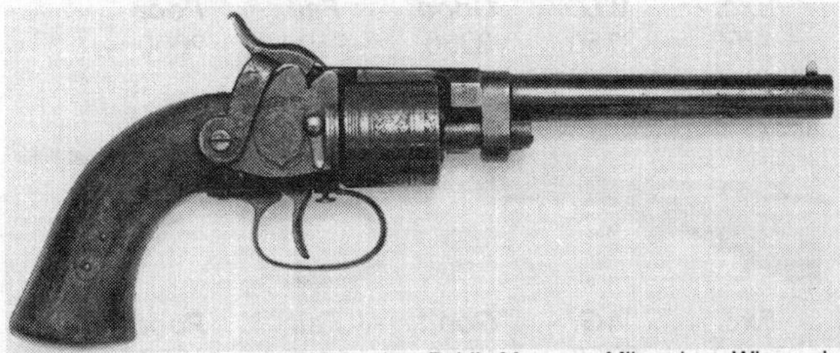

Courtesy Milwaukee Public Museum, Milwaukee, Wisconsin

Exc.	V.G.	Good	Fair	Poor
—	—	2500	800	250

Maynard Primed Pocket Revolver

Similar to the above, but in .28 or .30 caliber with 2.5" to 3.5" octagonal or round barrels. Approximately 3,000 were made between 1851 and 1860.

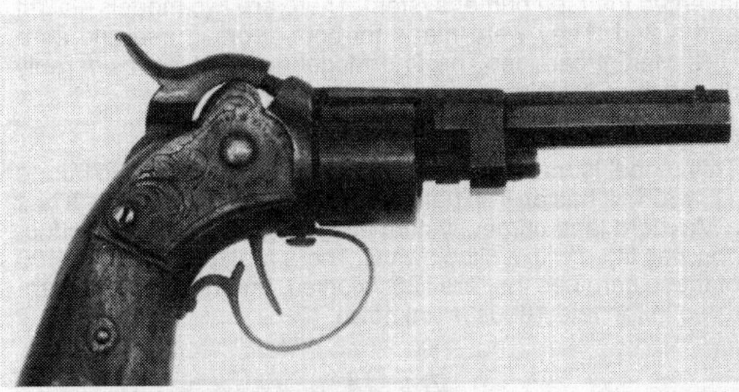

Courtesy Milwaukee Public Museum, Milwaukee, Wisconsin

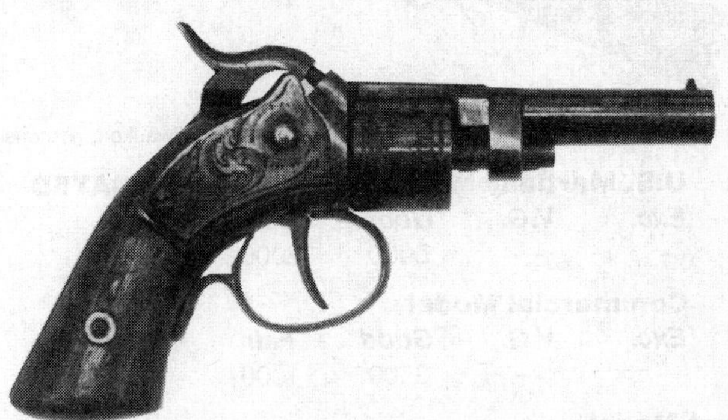

Courtesy Milwaukee Public Museum, Milwaukee, Wisconsin

Exc.	V.G.	Good	Fair	Poor
—	—	1250	550	200

Adams Patent Navy Revolver

As above, in .36 caliber with a 6" octagonal barrel. Approximately 600 of the 1,000 made were purchased by the U.S. government.

Courtesy Milwaukee Public Museum, Milwaukee, Wisconsin

Exc.	V.G.	Good	Fair	Poor
—	—	2250	750	300

NOTE: Those bearing inspection marks will bring approximately a 20 percent premium over the values listed.

Single-Shot Pocket Pistol

A .31 caliber single-shot percussion pistol with a 2.5" to 3.5" half octagonal barrel and a Maynard tape primer. The barrel marked "Mass. Arms Co/Chicopee Falls" and the primer door "Maynard's Patent Sept. 22, 1845." Blued, case hardened with walnut grips. Manufactured in the 1850s.

Exc.	V.G.	Good	Fair	Poor
—	—	2500	850	300

Maynard Carbine

This is a single-shot breechloader chambered for .35 or.50 caliber percussion. The barrel is round and 20" in length. The trigger guard is the lever that pivots the barrel in break-open fashion when it is lowered. The finish is blued, with a case colored frame. The buttstock is walnut, and there is no forend. This carbine was designed by the same Maynard who invented the tape primer system. There are two models—a 1st and a 2nd. They were made for both sporting use and as a U.S. Martial carbine. The 2nd Model was used considerably during the Civil War.

1st Model

This model is marked "Maynard Patentee/May 27, 1851/June 17, 1856." It has an iron patchbox and a curved buttplate. It has a Maynard tape primer system and a tang sight. Later production was fitted with a sling swivel. There are approximately 400 of these carbines that are U.S. marked, but the total manufactured in the late 1850s is unknown.

Courtesy Milwaukee Public Museum, Milwaukee, Wisconsin

U.S. Martially Marked and AUTHENTICATED

Exc.	V.G.	Good	Fair	Poor
—	—	5000	2000	500

Commercial Model

Exc.	V.G.	Good	Fair	Poor
—	—	3500	1000	350

2nd Model

This model is chambered for .50 caliber only and does not have the tape primer system or the tang sight. There is no patchbox, and the buttplate is not as curved as on the 1st Model. It is marked "Manufactured By/Mass. Arms Co./Chicopee Falls." There were approximately 20,000 manufactured between 1860 and 1865. This model was used by Union forces during the Civil War.

Courtesy Milwaukee Public Museum, Milwaukee, Wisconsin

Exc.	V.G.	Good	Fair	Poor
—	—	2750	1200	450

Maynard Patent Sporting Rifles

Sporting rifles bearing the designations Model 1865, 1873 and 1882 were manufactured in a wide variety of calibers, gauges, stock styles, finishes, and options. As these features affect the values of individual arms considerably, it is recommended that prospective purchasers are advised to secure a qualified appraisal prior to acquisition.

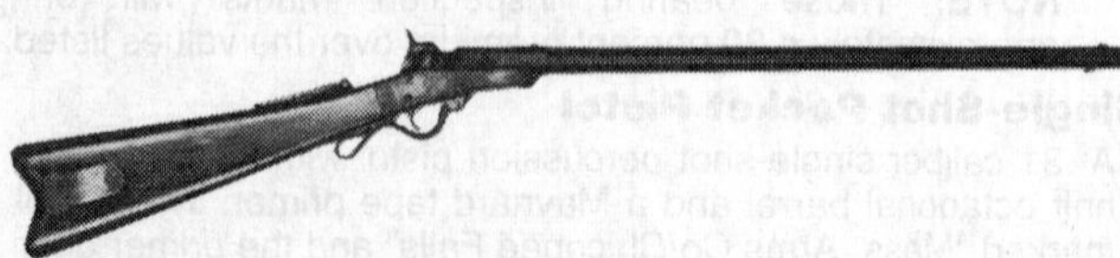

Courtesy Milwaukee Public Museum, Milwaukee, Wisconsin

Exc.	V.G.	Good	Fair	Poor
—	—	1500	600	200

MATEBA ARMS

Italy

AutoRevolver

Introduced in 2000 this revolver is chambered for the .357 magnum or .44 Magnum with 4", 6", or 8" barrel. The gun features a single-action trigger that has a reciprocating cylinder that fires from the bottom chamber rather than the top. The firing of the gun cocks the hammer and cycles the action for the next round. Available with or without compensator. Offered in blue or nickel finish. Extra barrels available.

NIB	Exc.	V.G.	Good	Fair	Poor
1200	875	675	—	—	—

NOTE: Guns without compensator deduct $80. For nickel finish add $50. For extra barrel add $140.

AutoRevolver Carbine

Similar in principle to handgun but with18" barrel and walnut buttstock, pistol grip and forend.

NIB	Exc.	V.G.	Good	Fair	Poor
1500	—	—	—	—	—

MATRA MANURHIN DEFENSE

Mulhouse, France

SEE—Manurhin

MAUSER WERKE

Oberndorf-am-Neckar, Germany

Established in 1869 by Peter and Wilhelm Mauser, this company came under the effective control of Ludwig Loewe and Company of Berlin in 1887. In 1896 the latter company was reorganized under the name *Deutsches Waffen und Munition* or as it is better known, DWM.

NOTE: For historical information, technical details, and photos and prices see the *Standard Catalog of Military Firearms.*

EARLY SPORTING RIFLES

A wide variety of commercial Model 98 Sporting Rifles were made, most of which had 23.5" ribbed barrels, open sights, 5-shot magazines, single or double set triggers, and either full or semi-pistol grip stocks.

NOTE: While the values listed are representative, it is suggested that prospective purchasers secure a qualified appraisal prior to acquisition. Mauser rifles almost always have extra cost features that can greatly affect price.

Type A—Short Action

Exc.	V.G.	Good	Fair	Poor
4250	3750	3200	1850	1200

Type A—Medium Action

Exc.	V.G.	Good	Fair	Poor
3250	2750	2250	1600	1000

Type A—Long Action

Exc.	V.G.	Good	Fair	Poor
4250	3750	3250	2500	2000

Type B

Exc.	V.G.	Good	Fair	Poor
3250	2750	2200	1400	1050

Type K

21.65" barrel.

Exc.	V.G.	Good	Fair	Poor
4250	3750	3200	2250	1000

Type M

Full-length stock, spoon bolt handle.

Exc.	V.G.	Good	Fair	Poor
4250	3750	3000	1750	1100

Type S

Full-length stock, no forend cap.

Exc.	V.G.	Good	Fair	Poor
4250	3750	3000	1750	1100

MODEL 1896 "BROOMHANDLE MAUSER PISTOL"

Manufactured from 1896 to 1939, the Model 1896 Pistol was produced in a wide variety of styles as listed. It is recommended that those considering the purchase of any of the models listed should consult Breathed & Schroeder's *System Mauser* (Chicago 1967) as it provides detailed descriptions and photographs of the various models.

PRICING NOTE: Prices listed are for the pistol only. A correct, matching stock/holster will add approximately 40 percent to value of each category. Non-matching stock/holster will add between $350 and $600 to prices.

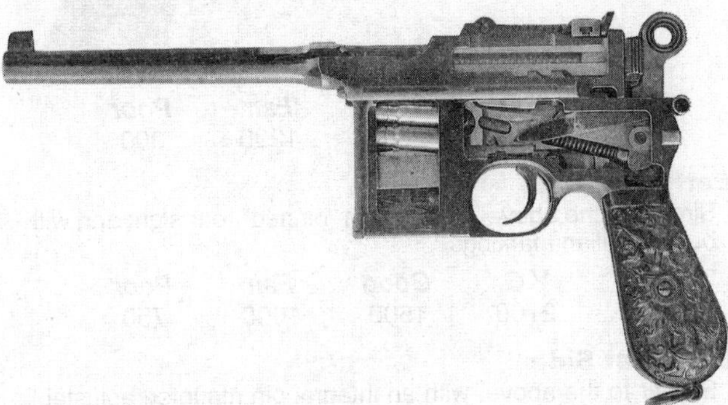

Large Ring Cutaway Courtesy Gale Morgan

"BUYER BEWARE" ALERT by Gale Morgan: As noted in previous editions of the *Standard Catalog of Firearms,* over the past several years large quantities of "Broomhandle" Mausers and Astra "copies" have been imported into the United States. Generally these are in poor or fair condition and have been offered for sale in the $125 to $300 price range, primarily as shooters or parts guns. During recent years, a cottage industry has sprung up where these very common pistols have been "converted" to "rare, exotic, near mint, original" specimens selling well into the four figure price range. I have personallly seen English Crest, the U.S. Great Seal, unheard-of European dealers, aristocratic Coats-of-Arms, and Middle East Medallions beautifully photo-etched into the magazine wells and rear panels of some really common wartime commercials with price tags that have been elevated to $2,500 plus. They are quite eye-catching and if they are sold as customized/modified Mausers, the seller can price the piece at whatever the market will bear. However, if sold as a factory original—BUYER BEWARE.

Six-Shot Step-Barrel Cone Hammer

A 7.63mm semi-automatic pistol with a 5.5" barrel, fixed rear sight and checkered walnut grips. Marked "Ruecklauf Pistole System Mauser, Oberndorf am/Neckar 1896." Very few were manufactured. Too rare to price.

Twenty-Shot Step-Barrel Cone Hammer

As above, with a 20-shot extended magazine and tangent rear sight. Engraved "SYSTEM MAUSER" on top of chamber. Too rare to price.

System Mauser 10-Shot Cone Hammer

As above, with either fixed or tangent rear sight. Step barrel (pictured) is very rare as is tapered barrel. Magazine capacity 10 rounds.

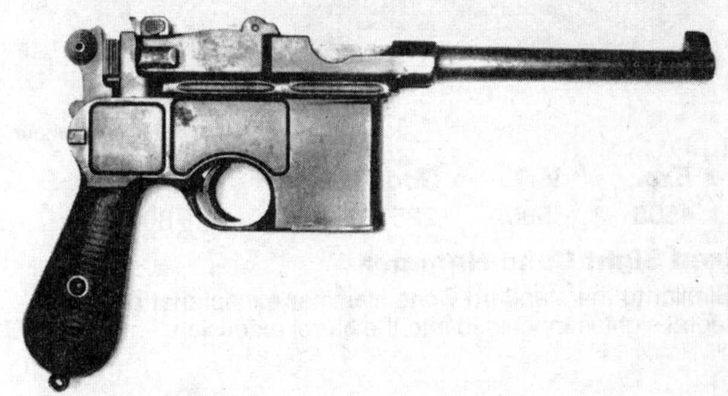

Courtesy Joe Schroeder

Exc.	V.G.	Good	Fair	Poor
17000	13000	10000	8000	7000

Six-Shot Standard Cone Hammer

Similar to the above but with no step in the barrel, 6-shot magazine and marked "Waffenfabrik Mauser, Oberndorf A/N" over the chamber. May have fixed or, rarely, tangent rear sight.

Courtesy Joe Schroeder

Exc.	V.G.	Good	Fair	Poor
12000	9000	6750	4500	3000

Twenty-Shot Cone Hammer

As above, with an extended magazine holding 20 cartridges. May have panels or flat sides.

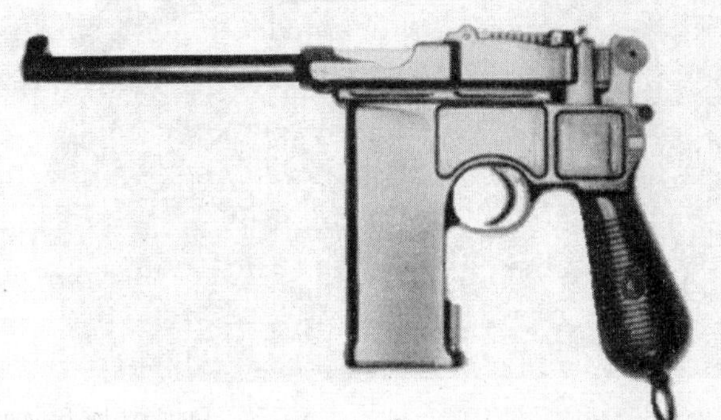

Courtesy Joe Schroeder

Exc.	V.G.	Good	Fair	Poor
30000	25000	15000	10000	7000

Standard Cone Hammer

As above, with a 10-shot magazine and 23-groove grips.

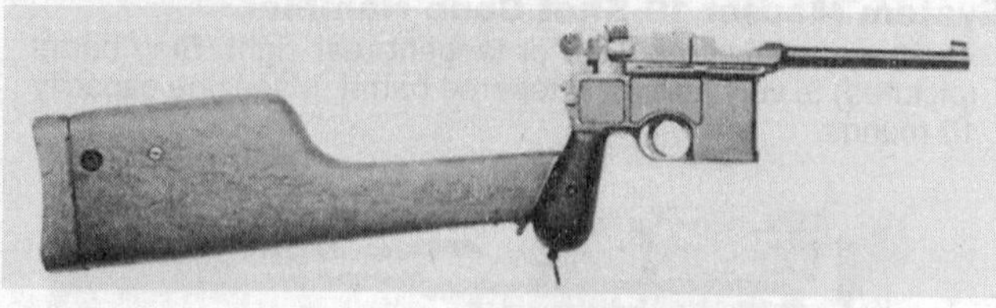

Courtesy Rock Island Auction Company

Exc.	V.G.	Good	Fair	Poor
4500	3500	2250	1400	800

Fixed Sight Cone Hammer

Similar to the standard Cone Hammer except that a fixed, integral sight is machined into the barrel extension.

Courtesy Joe Schroeder

Exc.	V.G.	Good	Fair	Poor
5500	3500	2500	1500	1000

Turkish Contract Cone Hammer

As above, but sight marked in Farsi and bearing the crest of Sultan Abdul-Hamid II on the frame. Approximately 1,000 were made.

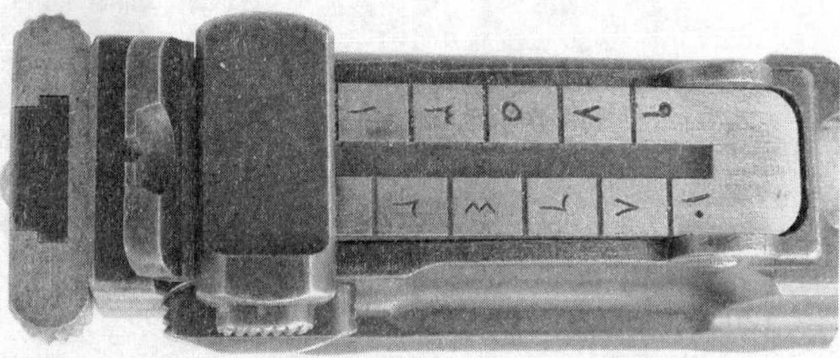

Courtesy Gale Morgan

Courtesy Joe Schroeder

Exc.	V.G.	Good	Fair	Poor
12000	8000	6500	3000	2000

Early Transitional Large Ring Hammer

This variation has the same characteristics of the "Standard Cone Hammer" except the hammer has a larger, open ring.

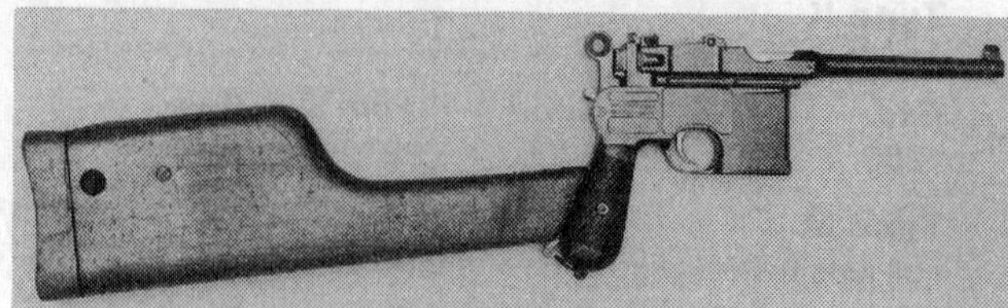

Courtesy Wallis & Wallis, Lewes, Sussex, England

Exc.	V.G.	Good	Fair	Poor
3500	2800	2500	1150	800

Model 1899 Flat Side—Italian Contract

Similar to the above, with a 5.5" barrel, adjustable rear sight and the frame sides milled flat. Left flat of chamber marked with "DV" proof. Approximately 5,000 were manufactured in 1899.

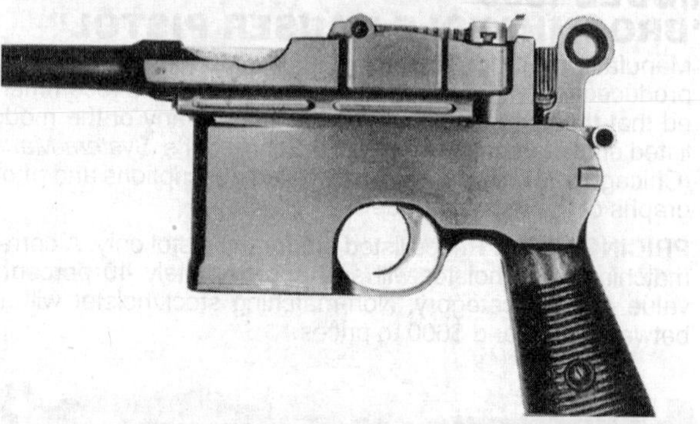

Courtesy Joe Schroeder

Exc.	V.G.	Good	Fair	Poor
4500	3500	2000	1200	900

Early Flat Side

Similar to the above, except with "pinned" rear sight and without the Italian markings.

Exc.	V.G.	Good	Fair	Poor
3000	2700	1500	1000	750

Late Flat Side

Similar to the above, with an integral pin mounted adjustable rear sight and often marked with dealer's names such as "Von Lengerke & Detmold, New York."

Exc.	V.G.	Good	Fair	Poor
2700	2200	1500	1000	750

Flat Side Bolo

Similar to the above, but with a 3.9" barrel, fixed sights, and checkered walnut grips. Very rare.

Exc.	V.G.	Good	Fair	Poor
7500	6000	4000	3000	2000

Early Large Ring Hammer Bolo

As above, with a milled frame, adjustable rear sight, and grooved wood or hard rubber grips cast with a floral pattern. 10-shot magazine.

Exc.	V.G.	Good	Fair	Poor
4700	3700	2000	1500	1000

Shallow-Milled Panel Model

Full size. Similar to the above, with a 5.5" barrel and either 23-groove walnut or checkered hard rubber grips. Shallow frame panels.

Exc.	V.G.	Good	Fair	Poor
3800	2700	1000	750	500

Deep-Milled Panel Model

As above, with deeper milled panels on the sides of the receiver.

Exc.	V.G.	Good	Fair	Poor
3500	2000	1500	1000	750

Late Large Ring Hammer Bolo

Similar to the Early Large Ring Hammer Bolo, but with the late style adjustable rear sight.

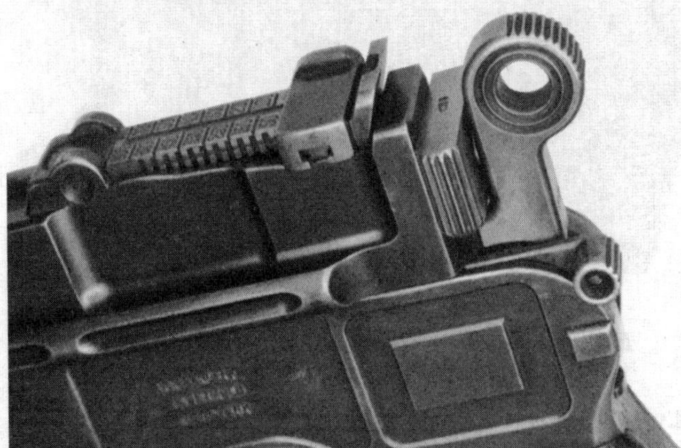

Courtesy Joe Schroeder

Exc.	V.G.	Good	Fair	Poor
3000	2500	1500	1000	750

Six-Shot Large Ring Bolo

Similar to the above Large Ring Bolo but with six-shot magazine. This model may be equipped with either fixed or tangent sights.

Courtesy James Rankin

Exc.	V.G.	Good	Fair	Poor
8700	6500	5000	3000	1800

Early Small Ring Hammer Model, Transitional

The Model 96 with an early long extractor, a hammer with a small-diameter hole, and a 5.5" barrel. The grips have 34 grooves.

Courtesy Joe Schroeder

Exc.	V.G.	Good	Fair	Poor
3200	2000	1500	1000	500

Early Small Ring Hammer Bolo Model

As above, with a 3.9" barrel and wood or hard rubber grips cast with a floral pattern. Serial numbers in the 40,000 range.

Exc.	V.G.	Good	Fair	Poor
4000	3000	2000	1500	600

Six-Shot Small Ring Hammer Model

As above, with 27-groove walnut grips.

Exc.	V.G.	Good	Fair	Poor
7200	5000	3000	1800	1000

Standard Pre-war Commercial

A Model 96 with a 5.5" barrel, late-style adjustable rear sight and either 34-groove walnut grips or checkered hard rubber grips. Often found with dealers markings such as "Von Lengerke & Detmold."

Courtesy Joe Schroeder

Exc.	V.G.	Good	Fair	Poor
2500	1800	1200	650	300

9mm Export Model

As above, in 9mm Mauser with 34-groove walnut grips.

Exc.	V.G.	Good	Fair	Poor
3250	2250	1500	1000	700

Mauser Banner Model

Standard pre-war features except chamber stamped with the Mauser Banner trademark and 32-groove walnut grips. Approximately 10,000 were manufactured.

Courtesy Joe Schroeder

Exc.	V.G.	Good	Fair	Poor
4000	3200	2300	1100	600

Persian Contract

Persian rampant lion on left rear panel. Prospective purchasers should secure a qualified appraisal prior to acquisition. Serial numbers in the 154000 range.

Exc.	V.G.	Good	Fair	Poor
4200	3500	2250	1400	1000

Standard Wartime Commercial

Identical to the pre-war Commercial Model 96, except that it has 30 groove walnut grips and the rear of the hammer is stamped "NS" for new safety. Many also bear German or Austrian military acceptance proofs.

Courtesy Gale Morgan

Exc.	V.G.	Good	Fair	Poor
1700	1100	800	500	350

9mm Parabellum Military Contract

As above, in 9mm Parabellum caliber with 24 groove grips, stamped with a large **"9"** filled with red paint.

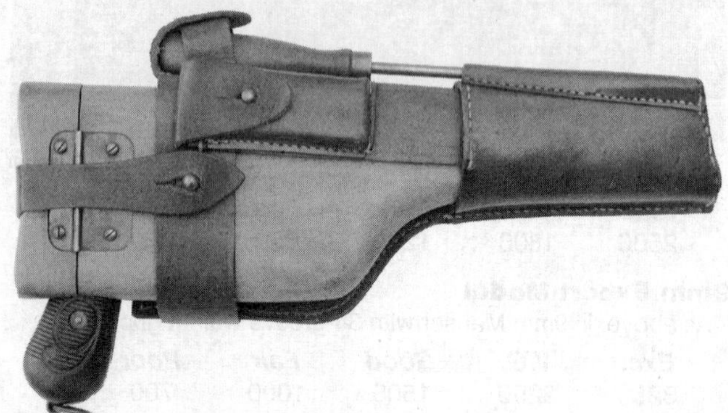
Mauser 9mm Military Contract "Red 9" rig Courtesy Gale Morgan

Exc.	V.G.	Good	Fair	Poor
3200	2000	1000	700	450

1920 Rework

A Model 96 modified to a barrel length of 3.9" and in 7.63mm Mauser or 9mm Parabellum caliber. Often encountered with police markings.

Courtesy Bonhams & Butterfields, San Francisco, California

Courtesy Joe Schroeder

Exc.	V.G.	Good	Fair	Poor
1500	1000	500	400	350

Luger Barreled 1920 Rework

Similar to the above, but fitted with a Luger barrel of 4" in length. 23 groove walnut grips and of 9mm caliber.

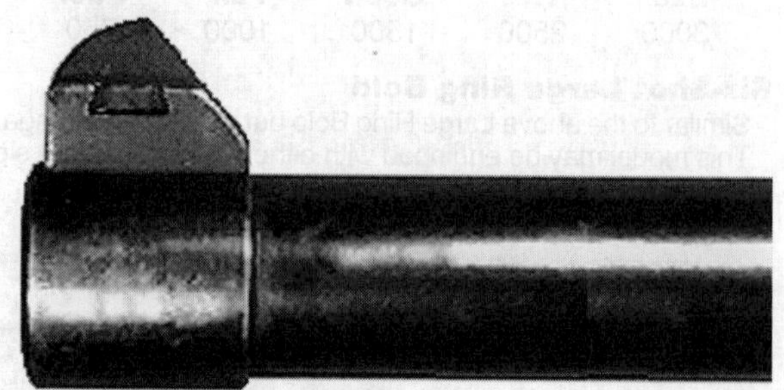
Courtesy Gale Morgan

Exc.	V.G.	Good	Fair	Poor
2000	1200	700	500	450

Early Post-war Bolo Model

A Model 96 in 7.63mm caliber with a 3.9" barrel, adjustable rear sight and 22-groove walnut grips.

Exc.	V.G.	Good	Fair	Poor
2400	1300	600	400	200

Late Post-war Bolo Model

As above, with the Mauser Banner trademark stamped on the left rear panel.

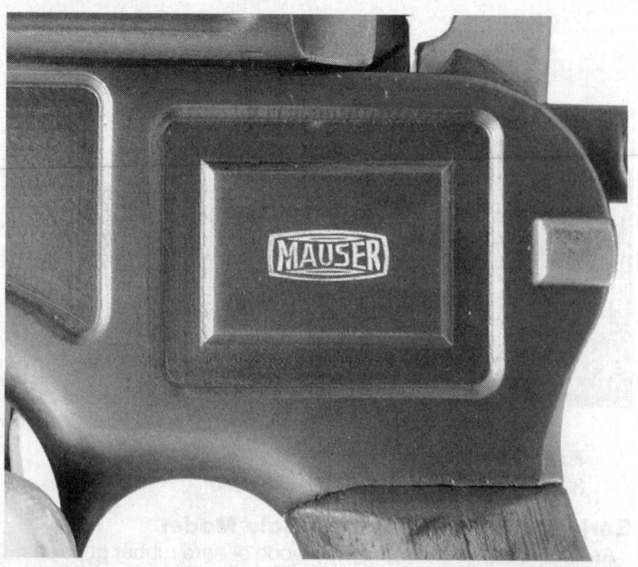

Courtesy Gale Morgan

Courtesy James Rankin

Exc.	V.G.	Good	Fair	Poor
2200	1200	700	400	200

French Gendarme Model

A standard Model 96 fitted with a 3.9" barrel and checkered hard rubber grips. Although reputed to have been made under a French contract, no record of that has been found to date.

Courtesy James Rankin

Exc.	V.G.	Good	Fair	Poor
3700	2500	1000	600	350

Early Model 1930

A 7.63mm caliber Model 96 with a 5.2" stepped barrel, grooved side rails, 12-groove walnut grips and late-style safety.

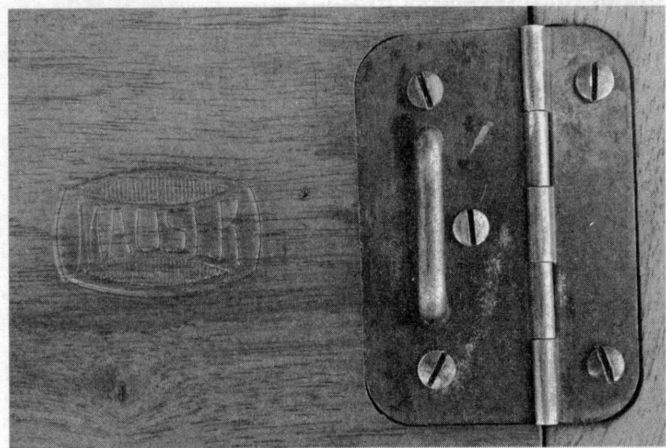

Courtesy Gale Morgan

Exc.	V.G.	Good	Fair	Poor
2400	1800	1200	800	500

Late Model 1930

Similar to the above, except for solid receiver rails.

Exc.	V.G.	Good	Fair	Poor
2700	2000	1200	800	400

Model 1930 Removable Magazine

Similar to the above, but with a detachable magazine. Prospective purchasers should secure a qualified appraisal prior to acquisition. Too rare to price.

CARBINE MODELS

Cone Hammer Flat Side Carbine

A 7.63mm caliber carbine with an 11.75" barrel, early adjustable sight, flat frame and detachable buttstock. Prospective purchasers should secure a qualified appraisal prior to acquisition. Too rare to price. **NOTE:** Watch for fakes.

Large Ring Hammer Transitional Carbine

Similar to the above, with milled frame panels. Prospective purchasers should secure a qualified appraisal prior to acquisition.

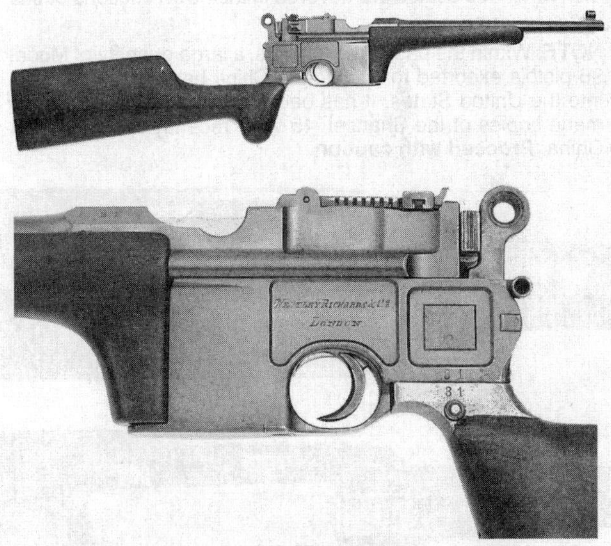

Exc.	V.G.	Good	Fair	Poor
25000	18000	11000	5000	3000

Large Ring Hammer Flatside Carbine

Similar to the above, with a 14.5" barrel. Prospective purchasers should secure a qualified appraisal prior to acquisition.

Exc.	V.G.	Good	Fair	Poor
22000	17000	10000	5000	3000

Small Ring Hammer Carbine

Similar to the above, with the hammer having a smaller diameter hole at its tip. Prospective purchasers should secure a qualified appraisal prior to acquisition. Some late carbines were chambered for the 9mm export.

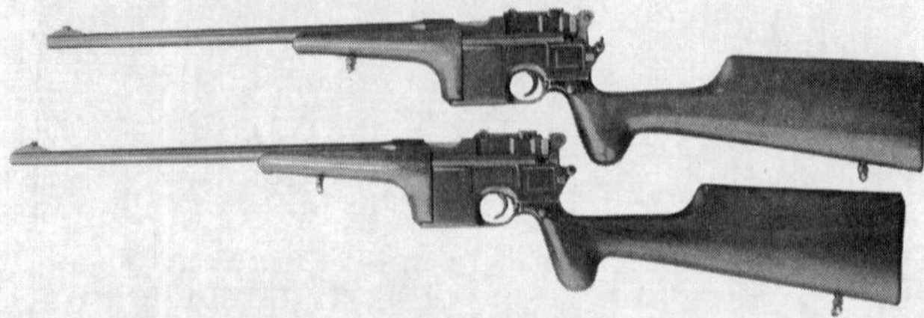

Small Ring Hammer Carbine with serial numbers 1035 and 1045, the highest known manufactured by Mauser

Courtesy Gale Morgan

Exc.	V.G	Good	Fair	Poor
23000	18000	15000	6000	4000

CHINESE COPIES

Chinese Marked, Handmade Copies

Crude copies of the Model 96 and unsafe to fire.

Exc.	V.G.	Good	Fair	Poor
500	400	350	250	175

Taku-Naval Dockyard Model

Approximately 6,000 copies of the Model 96 were made at the Taku-Naval Dockyard in several variations, both flat and paneled sides.

Exc.	V.G.	Good	Fair	Poor
3500	1500	1000	600	400

Shansei Arsenal Model

Approximately 8,000 Model 96 pistols were manufactured in .45 ACP caliber.

Copies of the Model 96 were made by Unceta (Astra) and Zulaica y Cia (Royal) and marketed by the firm of Beistegui Hermanos. These copies are covered in their own sections of this text.

NOTE: Within the past several years, a large quantity of Model 96 pistols exported to or made in China have been imported into the United States. It has been reported that some *newly* made copies of the Shansei .45 were recently exported from China. **Proceed with caution.**

Shansei Panel Marking

Courtesy Gale Morgan

Exc.	V.G.	Good	Fair	Poor
5000	3500	2250	1500	1300

MAUSER POCKET PISTOLS

Model 1910

A 6.35mm (.25 ACP) caliber pistol with a 3" barrel, 9-shot magazine and either a checkered walnut or (scarce) hard rubber wraparound grip. Early examples (below serial 60,000 or so) have a pivoting takedown latch above the trigger guard and are identified as "Sidelatch" models by collectors. Later production Models 1910s are often identified as the Model 1910/14. Manufactured from 1910 to 1934.

Sidelatch Model

Exc.	V.G.	Good	Fair	Poor
700	500	300	200	150

Later Production (Model 1910/14)

Exc.	V.G.	Good	Fair	Poor
450	275	200	150	100

Model 1914

A larger version of the Model 1910, chambered for 7.65mm Browning (.32 ACP) with a 3.5" or (rarely) 4.5" barrel. Very early examples up to serial 2500 or so had an odd hump on the slide and are called "Humpbacks" by collectors; these bring a considerable premium. Model 1914s with police or military markings bring a small premium. Manufactured between 1914 and 1934.

Model 1914 "Humpback"

Exc.	V.G.	Good	Fair	Poor
3500	2000	1500	800	400

REMINDER

You don't have to specialize in Colts and Winchesters to have a nice collection. Collecting Marlin or Mossberg .22 semi-autos, for example, can be just as rewarding.

Model 1914 (later)

Exc.	*V.G.*	*Good*	*Fair*	*Poor*
475	300	200	150	100

Model 1912/14

While Mauser's pocket pistols were very successful on the commercial market, Mauser was also trying to develop a larger caliber pistol for military use. The most successful of these was the Model 1912/14, though only about 200 were ever made. A few of these did reach the commercial market, and it's likely the pistol would have continued in production had WWI not broken out. Higher serial numbered guns were slotted for a Model 1896-style holster stock, and a few of these also had tangent sights.

Exc.	*V.G.*	*Good*	*Fair*	*Poor*
29000	17000	11000	8000	4000

NOTE: Add 25 percent for shoulder stock.

Model WTP I

This was Mauser's first post-WWI new design and first vest pocket pistol, with a 2.5" barrel and 6-shot magazine capacity. Grips were plastic wraparound, with one, two or three grip screws depending on production period. Production ended in the late 1930s, when the WTP II was introduced.

Exc.	*V.G.*	*Good*	*Fair*	*Poor*
600	300	250	175	125

Model WTP II

The WTP II was a much more compact design that its predecessor, with a 2" barrel and separate grip panels instead of Mauser's usual wraparound grip. Production was limited by the outbreak of WWII, so the WTP II is much scarcer than the WTP I. Under French occupation at least several hundred WTP IIs were assembled and sold; these can be identified by their very low electric penciled serial numbers and lack of German proofing, and bring a slight premium over the pre-war German manufactured pistols.

Courtesy Gale Morgan

Exc.	*V.G.*	*Good*	*Fair*	*Poor*
650	450	325	250	175

Model 1934

In response to competition from Walther and others, in 1934 Mauser spruced up its aging 1910/14 and 1914 pistols with a new high-polish finish and form-fitting swept back grips. Nickel finish was also offered, but is very rare (50 percent premium, but beware of renickeled blued guns). The 7.65mm pistols became popular with both the military and police, but those so marked can bring a considerable premium.

Courtesy Orvel Reichert

Courtesy Gale Morgan

6.35mm

Exc.	V.G.	Good	Fair	Poor
525	325	250	200	125

7.65mm Commercial

Exc.	V.G.	Good	Fair	Poor
450	325	250	200	125

7.65mm Eagle L proofed

Exc.	V.G.	Good	Fair	Poor
675	450	300	250	150

7.56mm Large Eagle over M (Navy)

Exc.	V.G.	Good	Fair	Poor
1200	750	450	300	200

MODEL HSC

The HSc was a totally new design, chambered for 7.65mm Browning and featuring double-action lockwork and a partially concealed external hammer. Introduced just as WWII broke out, the HSc was produced through the war for both commercial sale and military use. Serials started at 700,000, and the first 1500 or so had the grip screws located near the bottom of the grip and bring a large premium. Finish deteriorated as the war progressed, and some HSc pistols were even produced under French occupation after the war ended.

Courtesy Orvel Reichert

NOTE: Add 20 percent for Waffenamt markings, and 50 percent for Navy marked front straps.

Low Grip Screw Model

As above, with screws that attach the grip located near the bottom of the grip. Highly-polished blue, checkered walnut grips and the early address without the lines and has the Eagle N proof. Some have been observed with Nazi Kriegsmarine markings. Approximately 2,000 were manufactured.

Exc.	V.G.	Good	Fair	Poor
6000	4500	1800	750	650

Early Commercial Model

A highly polished blued finish, checkered walnut grips, the standard Mauser address on the slide, and the Eagle N proofmark. The floorplate of the magazine stamped with the Mauser Banner.

Exc.	V.G.	Good	Fair	Poor
650	500	350	175	125

Transition Model

As above, but not as highly finished.

Exc.	V.G.	Good	Fair	Poor
525	400	300	150	100

Early Nazi Army Model

Courtesy Orvel Reichert

Exc.	V.G.	Good	Fair	Poor
650	550	400	200	125

Late Nazi Army Model

Exc.	V.G.	Good	Fair	Poor
450	375	250	150	100

Early Nazi Navy Model

Exc.	V.G.	Good	Fair	Poor
1000	800	550	400	300

Wartime Nazi Navy Model

Exc.	V.G.	Good	Fair	Poor
800	600	500	400	200

Early Nazi Police Model

Exc.	V.G.	Good	Fair	Poor
600	500	425	250	175

Wartime Nazi Police Model

Exc.	V.G.	Good	Fair	Poor
500	400	350	250	175

Wartime Commercial Model

As above, without acceptance markings on the trigger guard.

Exc.	V.G.	Good	Fair	Poor
425	350	300	200	125

French Manufactured Model

Blued or Parkerized with walnut or plastic grips and the trigger guard marked on the left side with the monogram "MR."

Exc.	V.G.	Good	Fair	Poor
375	275	225	150	100

Model HSc Post-war Production

In the late 1960s Mauser resumed production of the HSc in both 7.65mm and 9mm Browning short (.380). Five thousand post-war HSc pistols were specially marked with an American eagle, and bring a slight premium over standard marked pistols. In the 1980s Mauser licensed HSc production to Gamba in Italy, which produced an enlarged frame version of the HSc with a double-column magazine. In both German and Italian production, .380s bring about a 20 percent premium over .32s.

Mauser Production (.32)

Exc.	V.G.	Good	Fair	Poor
325	250	200	175	125

This symbol denotes "Sleepers" with rapidly-rising values and/or significant collector potential.

Gamba Production

In recent years Mauser has licensed several firms other than Gamba to produce pistols bearing the Mauser trademark, such as a Browning Hi Power knockoff made in Hungary. In 1999 Mauser was bought by SIG-Sauer, and a new large caliber Mauser pistol was announced.

Exc.	V.G.	Good	Fair	Poor
250	200	175	150	100

MAUSER RIFLES & PISTOLS—RECENT PRODUCTION

NOTE: In February 1999 SIGARMS announced the acquisition of the Mauser line of small arms. With the acquisition, SIG assumes the rights to the Mauser name and will integrate the Mauser product line into SIGARMS' line of small arms.

Model 2000

A .270, .308, or the .30-06 caliber bolt-action rifle with a 24" barrel, open sights and a 5-shot magazine. Blued, with a checkered walnut stock. Manufactured between 1969 and 1971 by Heym.

Exc.	V.G.	Good	Fair	Poor
350	300	250	200	150

Model 3000

As above, with a 22" barrel, no sights and Monte Carlo-style stock. Manufactured from 1971 to 1974 by Heym.

Exc.	V.G.	Good	Fair	Poor
450	400	350	300	250

Model 3000 Magnum

As above, in 7mm Rem. Mag., .300 Win. Mag. and the .375 H&H Mag. caliber with a 26" barrel and a 3-shot integral magazine. Blued, with a checkered walnut stock. Produced by Heym.

Exc.	V.G.	Good	Fair	Poor
500	450	400	350	300

Model 4000

Similar to the Model 3000, but in .222 or .223 caliber with folding open sights. Produced by Heym.

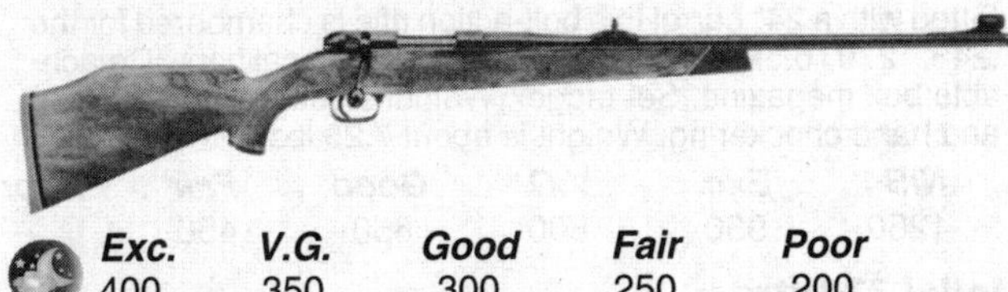

Exc.	V.G.	Good	Fair	Poor
400	350	300	250	200

Model 225

A .243 to. 300 Weatherby Magnum caliber bolt-action rifle with a 24" or 26" barrel, no sights, adjustable trigger or 3- or 5-shot magazine. Blued with a walnut stock.

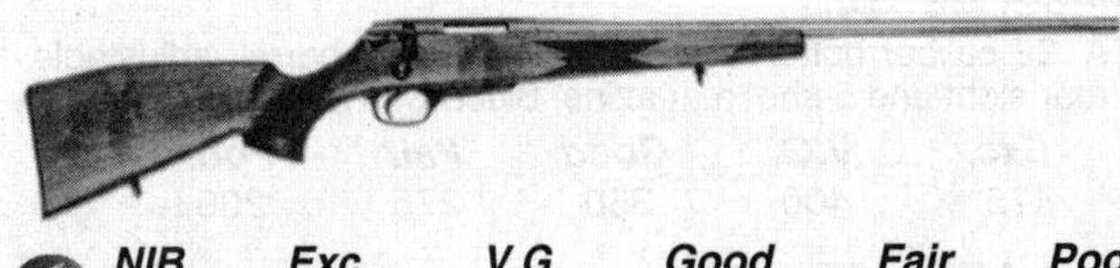

NIB	Exc.	V.G.	Good	Fair	Poor
1400	1250	1000	750	600	500

Model ES340

A .22 caliber single-shot bolt-action rifle with a 25.5" barrel, open sights, and walnut stock. Manufactured before WWII.

Exc.	V.G.	Good	Fair	Poor
300	250	225	175	125

Model DSM34

Similar to the above, with a 25" barrel and full-length walnut stock. Manufactured prior to WWII.

Exc.	V.G.	Good	Fair	Poor
325	275	250	200	150

Model MS420B

Similar to the above, with a 25" barrel and 5-shot magazine. Manufactured before WWII.

Exc.	V.G.	Good	Fair	Poor
375	325	300	275	200

Model ES350

A .22 caliber single-shot bolt-action rifle with a 27.5" barrel and checkered pistol grip walnut stock. Manufactured before WWII.

Exc.	V.G.	Good	Fair	Poor
450	400	375	350	275

Model M410

Similar to the above, with a 23.5" barrel and 5-shot magazine. Manufactured before WWII.

Exc.	V.G.	Good	Fair	Poor
375	325	300	275	200

Model M420

As above, with a 25.5" barrel.

Exc.	V.G.	Good	Fair	Poor
375	325	300	275	200

Model EN310

A .22 caliber single-shot bolt-action rifle with a 19.75" barrel, open sights, and plain walnut stock. Manufactured before WWII.

Exc.	V.G.	Good	Fair	Poor
250	225	200	150	100

Model EL320

As above, with a 23.5" barrel and checkered walnut stock.

Exc.	V.G.	Good	Fair	Poor
275	250	225	175	125

Model KKW

A .22 caliber single-shot bolt-action rifle with a 26" barrel, ladder rear sight and full-length walnut stock. Manufactured prior to WWII.

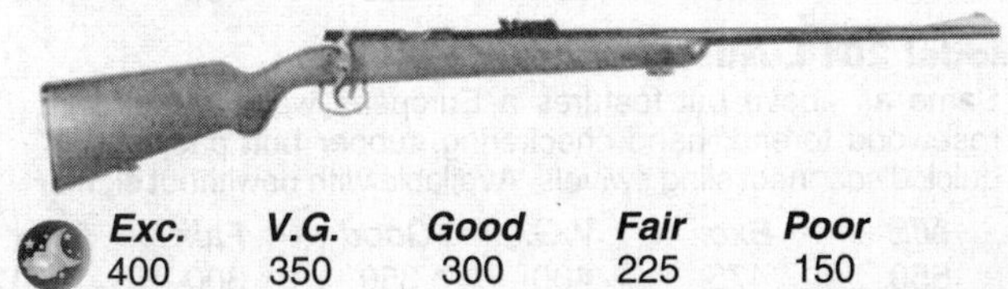

Exc.	V.G.	Good	Fair	Poor
400	350	300	225	150

Model MS350B

A .22 caliber bolt-action rifle with a 26.75" barrel, adjustable rear sight and 5-shot magazine. Blued with a walnut stock.

Exc.	V.G.	Good	Fair	Poor
475	400	350	275	200

Model ES340B

Similar to the above, but in single-shot form.

Exc.	V.G.	Good	Fair	Poor
375	300	250	175	100

Model MM410BN

A .22 caliber bolt-action rifle with a 23.5" barrel, adjustable sights, and 5-shot magazine. Blued with a walnut stock.

Exc.	V.G.	Good	Fair	Poor
400	350	300	200	125

Model MS420B

As above, with a 26.75" barrel and target-style stock.

Exc.	V.G.	Good	Fair	Poor
400	350	300	200	125

Model 107

This is a bolt-action rifle chambered for the .22 LR. Barrel length is 21.6" and box magazine has a 5-shot capacity. The beechwood checkered Monte Carlo stock is full size with pistol grip, plastic buttplate. The rear sight is adjustable. Metal finish is blue. Weighs about 5 lbs.

NIB	Exc.	V.G.	Good	Fair	Poor
265	225	180	150	125	100

Model 201 Standard

This model features a 21" medium heavy free-floating barrel. The receiver accepts all rail mounts and is also drilled and tapped for scope mount. Magazine capacity is 5-shot. Chambered for. 22 LR or .22 WMR cartridge. The beechwood stock is hand checkered with plastic buttplate. The Monte Carlo stock is fitted with cheekpiece. Weighs about 6.5 lbs.

NIB	Exc.	V.G.	Good	Fair	Poor
400	325	250	200	150	100

Model 201 Luxus

Same as above but features a European walnut stock with rosewood forend, hand checkering, rubber butt pad, and 1" quick disconnect sling swivels. Available with or without sights.

NIB	Exc.	V.G.	Good	Fair	Poor
550	475	400	350	300	200

Model 66 Standard

This is a centerfire bolt-action rifle fitted with a European Walnut hand-checkered oil finish stock. Stock is half stock design. Rosewood forends and pistol grip caps are standard. Fitted with rubber recoil pad and 1" quick disconnect sling swivels. Barrels are interchangeable on this model. Barrels with standard calibers is 24" and approximate weight is 7.5 lbs. Standard calibers are: .243 Win., .270, .308, .30-06, 5.6x57, 6.5x57, 7.64, and 9.3x62.

NIB	Exc.	V.G.	Good	Fair	Poor
1400	1150	850	700	550	350

Model 66 Magnum

Same as above but chambered for 7mm Rem. Mag., .300 and .338 Win. Mag., 6.5x68, 8x86S, 9.3x64. Fitted with a 26" barrel and weighs about 7.9 lbs.

NIB	Exc.	V.G.	Good	Fair	Poor
1500	1250	950	800	600	400

Model 66 Safari

Same as above but chambered for .375 H&H and .458 Win. Mag. Fitted with a 26" barrel and weighs about 9.3 lbs.

NIB	Exc.	V.G.	Good	Fair	Poor
1650	1400	1100	850	650	400

Model 66 Stuzen

Same as the Standard Model 66 but fitted with a full stock. Barrel length is 21" and calibers are same as Standard. Weighs about 7.5 lbs.

NIB	Exc.	V.G.	Good	Fair	Poor
1500	1250	950	800	600	400

IDF Mauser Rifle Model 66SP

This is a bolt-action rifle chambered for the .308 Win. cartridge. Adjustable trigger for pull and travel. Barrel length is 27". Specially designed stock has broad forend and a thumb hole pistol grip. Cheekpiece is adjustable as is the recoil pad. Supplied with case. This rifle is military issue. Fewer than 100 imported into the U.S. by Springfield Armory.

NIB	Exc.	V.G.	Good	Fair	Poor
2200	1750	—	—	—	—

Model 77

Fitted with a 24" barrel this bolt-action rifle is chambered for the .243, .270, 6.5x57, 7x64, .308, and .30-06 calibers. Detachable box magazine. Set trigger. Walnut stock with cheekpiece and hand checkering. Weight is about 7.25 lbs.

NIB	Exc.	V.G.	Good	Fair	Poor
1250	950	800	650	450	—

Model 77 Ultra

This model is fitted with a 20" barrel and chambered for the 6.5x57, 7x64, and .30-06 calibers. Weight is about 7.5 lbs.

NIB	Exc.	V.G.	Good	Fair	Poor
1250	950	800	650	450	—

Model 77 Mannlicher

Similar to the Ultra Model but with a full-length Mannlicher stock. Set trigger. Weight is about 7.5 lbs.

NIB	Exc.	V.G.	Good	Fair	Poor
1250	950	800	650	450	—

Model 77 Big Game

Chambered for the .375 H&H Magnum cartridge and fitted with a 26" barrel. Weight is about 8.5 lbs.

NIB	Exc.	V.G.	Good	Fair	Poor
1400	1100	900	750	500	—

Model 86 SR

Introduced in 1993 this bolt-action .308 is sometimes referred to as the Specialty Rifle. Fitted with a laminated wood and special match thumbhole stock or fiberglass stock with adjustable cheekpiece. Stock has rail in forearm and an adjustable recoil pad. Magazine capacity is 9 rounds. Finish is a non-glare blue. The barrel length with muzzlebrake is 28.8". Many special features are found on this rifle from adjustable trigger weight to silent safety. Mauser offers many options on this rifle as well that will affect the price. Weight is approximately 11 lbs.

NIB	Exc.	V.G.	Good	Fair	Poor
3300	2950	2500	1750	1250	750

Model 93 SR

Introduced in 1996 this is a tactical semi-automatic rifle chambered for the .300 Win. Mag. or the .338 Lapua cartridge. Barrel length is 25.5" with an overall length of 48.4". Barrel is fitted with a muzzlebrake. Magazine capacity is 6 rounds for .300 and 5 rounds for .338 caliber. Weight is approximately 13 lbs.

NIB	Exc.	V.G.	Good	Fair	Poor
1900	—	—	—	—	—

Model 96

This bolt-action rifle is chambered for the .25-06, .270 Win., 7x64, .308, or .30-06 cartridge. It is fitted with a 22" barrel (24" Magnum calibers) and has a 5-round top loading magazine. Receiver is drilled and tapped. Checkered walnut stock. No sights. Approximately weight is 6.25 lbs.

NIB	Exc.	V.G.	Good	Fair	Poor
500	400	300	200	125	100

Model 98 (SIG Arms)

Built in Germany this bolt-action rifle features a select walnut stock with oil finish. Express rear sight and single stage trigger. Chambered for the .416 Rigby, .450 Dakota, .458 Lott, and .500 Jeffry. Weight is approximately 8.8 lbs.

NIB	Exc.	V.G.	Good	Fair	Poor
9500	—	—	—	—	—

NOTE: Add $1,000 for .500 Jeffry.

Model 99 Standard

This model is a bolt-action centerfire sporting rifle. It is offered with two stock designs: a classic with straight oil finish stock or high luster with cheekpiece and schnabel forend and Monte Carlo with rosewood forend tip and pistol grip cap. Chambered for standard calibers: .243, .25-06, .270, .308, .30-06, 5.6x57, 6.5x57, 7x57, 7x64. Barrel length is 24". Weight about 8 lbs.

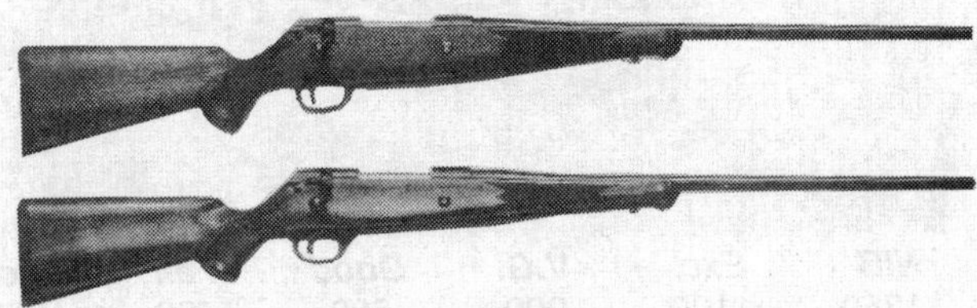

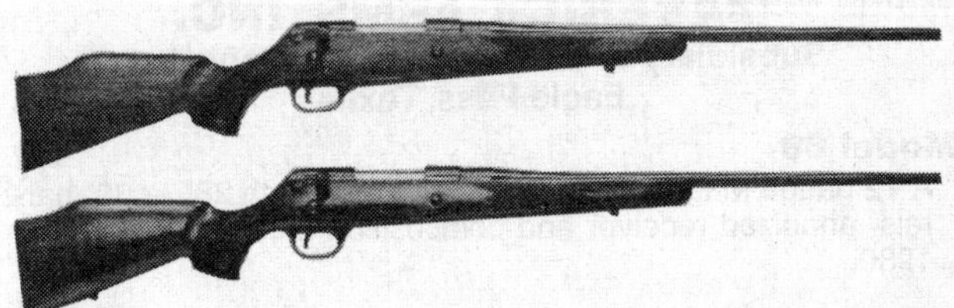

NIB	Exc.	V.G.	Good	Fair	Poor
900	700	600	500	400	300

Model 99 Magnum

Same as above but chambered for magnum calibers: 7mm Rem. Mag., .257 Wby., .270 Wby., .300 Wby., .300 and .338 Win. Mag., 8x68S, and 9.3x64. Fitted with 26" barrel. Weighs about 8 lbs.

NIB	Exc.	V.G.	Good	Fair	Poor
950	750	650	550	400	300

Model 80 SA

This single-action semi-automatic pistol is based on the Browning Hi-Power design. Chambered for the 9mm Parabellum cartridge it has a barrel length of 4.66" and a magazine capacity of 14 rounds. Weighs approximately 35 oz.

NIB	Exc.	V.G.	Good	Fair	Poor
300	275	225	175	125	100

Model Compact DA

Same as above but double-action trigger and shorter barrel: 4.13". Weighs approximately 33 oz.

NIB	Exc.	V.G.	Good	Fair	Poor
340	320	250	175	125	100

Model 90 DA

Similar to the Model 80 but with a double-action trigger.

NIB	Exc.	V.G.	Good	Fair	Poor
310	285	235	175	125	100

Model M2 (Imported by SIGARMS)

Introduced in 2000 this pistol is chambered for the .45 ACP, .40 S&W, or .357 SIG cartridges. It has an aluminum alloy frame and steel slide. The action is an enclosed hammerless striker-fired design. Barrel length is 3.5". Fixed sights. Weight is about 29 oz. Magazine capacity for .45 ACP is 8 rounds, for .40 S&W and .357 SIG capacity is 10 rounds.

NIB	Exc.	V.G.	Good	Fair	Poor
475	400	—	—	—	—

MAVERICK ARMS, INC.

Subsidiary of O. F. Mossberg & Sons, Inc.
Eagle Pass, Texas

Model 88

A 12 gauge Magnum slide-action shotgun with 28" or 30" barrels, anodized receiver and composition stock. Introduced in 1989.

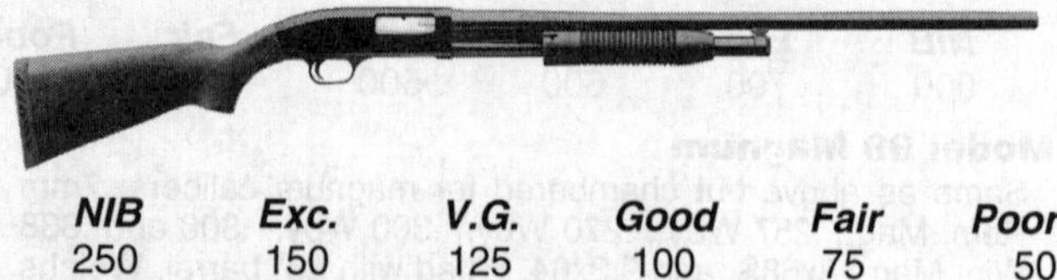

NIB	Exc.	V.G.	Good	Fair	Poor
250	150	125	100	75	50

Model 88 Slug Pump Shotgun

A 12-gauge Magnum pump-action shotgun with an interchangeable Cylinder-bore barrel. Black synthetic stock and forearm, blued metal finish, 6-shot magazine. Add $20 for rifled 24" barrel with adjustable rifle sights.

NIB	Exc.	V.G.	Good	Fair	Poor
295	200	100	—	—	—

Model 88 Six-Shot Security Model

A 12-gauge Magnum pump-action shotgun with a 6-shot magazine and an interchangeable 18-1/2" Cylinder-bore fixed choke barrel. A rugged black synthetic stock and forearm, blued metal finish and brass front sight bead are also included. Add 5 percent for Eight-Shot Security Model with 20" Cylinder-bore fixed choke barrel. Add 10 percent for heat shield.

NIB	Exc.	V.G.	Good	Fair	Poor
325	200	100	—	—	—

MAYNARD/PERRY

Keen, Walker & Co.
Danville, Virginia

Brass Framed Carbine

Overall length 40"; barrel length 22.5"; caliber .54. Browned, blued barrel, brass frame and walnut stock. Manufactured in 1861 and 1862. Fewer than 300 produced. Prospective purchasers are advised to secure a qualified appraisal prior to acquisition.

Exc.	V.G.	Good	Fair	Poor
—	—	30000	12500	—

M. B. ASSOCIATES-GYROJET

San Ramon, California

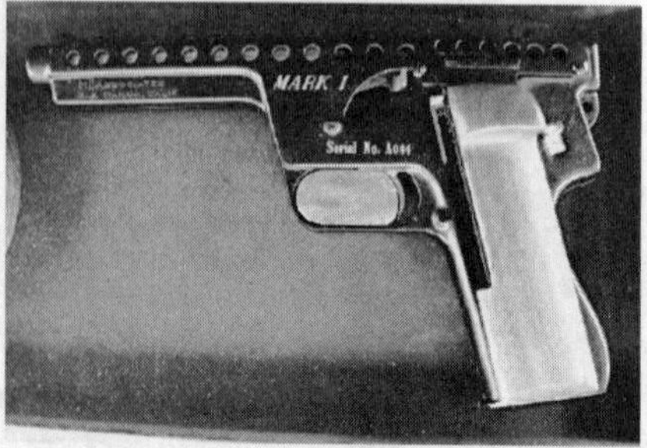

Established in 1960 by R. Maynard and Art Biehl, M. B. Associates produced the Gyrojet pistols and carbines from 1962 to 1970. Basically a hand held rocket launcher, shooting a 12mm or 13mm spin stablized rocket cartridge, composed of four-part solid rocket fuel. The nose of the round was forced rearward onto a stationary firing pin, igniting the fuel, expelling the round and recocking for the next shot. These were not very accurate and led to MBA's demise. Ammunition typically sells for $35 per round or more. *Dave Rachwal.*

Mark I Model A

13mm pistol, cased with a Goddard commemorative medal and 10 dummy rounds, black anodized finish, with walnut grips.

Exc.	V.G.	Good	Fair	Poor
2195	1500	1200	900	500

Mark I Model B

13mm pistol, cased with the commemorative Goddard medal and 10 dummy rounds, black with walnut grips or antique nickel with pearlite grips.

Exc.	V.G.	Good	Fair	Poor
1895	1695	1000	600	300

Mark I Model B

13mm pistol, cardboard box, black anodized with walnut grips usually. This model was produced in many variations and finishes.

Exc.	V.G.	Good	Fair	Poor
995	800	650	400	200

Mark II Model C

12mm pistol, black anodized with walnut grips. This was manufactured for the 12mm round to conform with the 1968 gun control act, because 13mm is 51 cal. and 12mm is 49 cal.

Exc.	V.G.	Good	Fair	Poor
995	800	650	400	200

Mark I Model A Carbine

13mm, black anodized finish with walnut stock and carrying handle.

Exc.	V.G.	Good	Fair	Poor
2495	2195	1700	1000	600

Mark I Model B Carbine

13mm, antique nickel finish with walnut stock. This was the sporter carbine and had a flared muzzle and sleek lines.

Exc.	V.G.	Good	Fair	Poor
1495	800	900	400	200

McMILLAN, G. & CO. INC.

Phoenix, Arizona

Competition Model

A custom order bolt-action rifle in .308, 7mm-08, and the .300 Winchester Magnum caliber with the barrel length, stock type, and dimensions to the customer's specifications. Introduced in 1988.

NIB	Exc.	V.G.	Good	Fair	Poor
1700	1500	1150	800	600	300

Model 86 Sniper's Rifle

A custom order rifle in .308 Winchester or the .300 Winchester Magnum calibers with a synthetic stock and a choice of scope systems. Introduced in 1988.

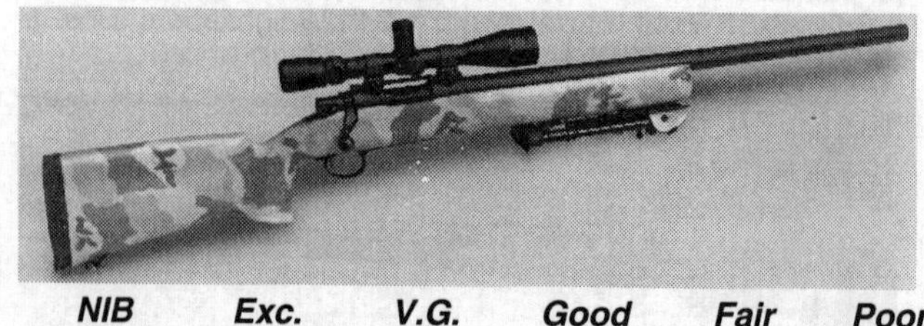

NIB	Exc.	V.G.	Good	Fair	Poor
1350	1100	900	600	400	200

Model 86 System

As above, with the Ultra scope, mounting system, bipod, and fitted case. Introduced in 1988.

NIB	Exc.	V.G.	Good	Fair	Poor
2150	1850	1500	1100	550	250

Model 87 Long Range Snipers Rifle

A large stainless steel, single-shot bolt-action rifle in .50 BMG caliber featuring a 29" barrel with an integral muzzlebrake. Camouflaged synthetic stock. Weight 21 lbs. Accurate to 1,500 meters. Introduced in 1988.

NIB	Exc.	V.G.	Good	Fair	Poor
2700	2200	1800	1200	600	250

Model 87 System

As above, with a bipod and a 20X Ultra scope, mounting system, and a fitted case. Introduced in 1988.

NIB	Exc.	V.G.	Good	Fair	Poor
3350	2700	2100	1500	900	400

Signature Model

A bolt-action sporting rifle manufactured in a variety of calibers up to .375 Holland & Holland with a 22" or 24" stainless barrel, composition stock and either 3- or 4-shot magazine. Introduced in 1988.

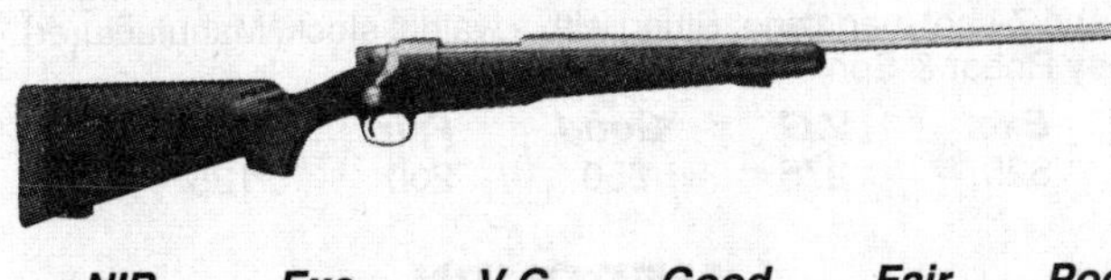

NIB	Exc.	V.G.	Good	Fair	Poor
2200	1750	1250	800	600	300

Signature Stainless

Same as model above but barrel and action made of stainless steel. Fiberglass stock. Left- or right-hand model. The .416 Rigby is also offered in this configuration. Introduced in 1990.

NIB	Exc.	V.G.	Good	Fair	Poor
2200	1750	1250	800	600	300

Signature Alaskan

This model, introduced in 1989, is offered in .270 .280 Rem., .30-06, 7mm Rem. Mag., .300 Win. Mag., .300 Wby. Mag., .358 Win. Mag., .340 Wby. Mag., .375 H&H. Match grade barrel from 22" to 26" in length. Single leaf rear sight and barrel band front sight.

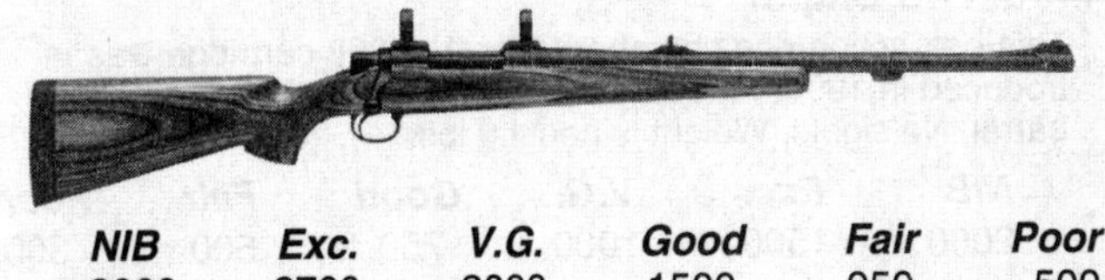

NIB	Exc.	V.G.	Good	Fair	Poor
3000	2700	2000	1500	950	500

Signature Titanium Mountain

Offered in calibers from .270 Win. to 7mm Rem. Mag. Match grade barrel is produced from titanium. Stock is graphite. Weight is about 6.5 lbs.

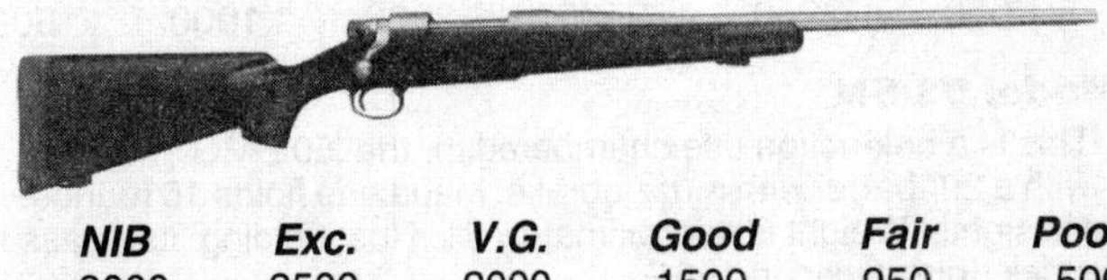

NIB	Exc.	V.G.	Good	Fair	Poor
3000	2500	2000	1500	950	500

Signature Varminter

Available in calibers such as .223, .22-250, .220 Swift, .243, 6mm Rem., .25-06, 7mm-08, .308. Barrel lengths from 22" to 26". Heavy barrel configuration with hand bedded fiberglass stock. Field bipod is standard. Introduced in 1989.

NIB	Exc.	V.G.	Good	Fair	Poor
2500	2000	1500	900	600	400

Talon Safari

Bolt-action rifle offered in various calibers from .300 Win. Mag. to .458 Win. Mag. Stainless steel barrel is 24". Four-round magazine. Fiberglass stock. Introduced in 1989. Weight is approximately 10 lbs.

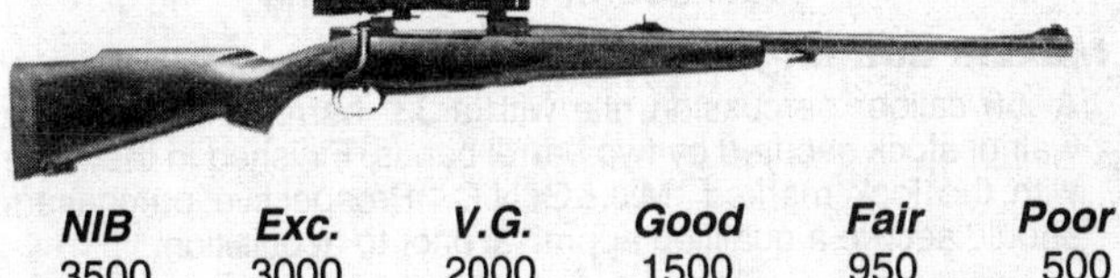

NIB	Exc.	V.G.	Good	Fair	Poor
3500	3000	2000	1500	950	500

Talon Sporter

Offered in calibers from .25-06 to .416 Rem. Mag. 24" barrel with no sights. Built on a pre-1964 Winchester Model 70 action. Choice of walnut or fiberglass stock. Weight is about 7.5 lbs.

NIB	Exc.	V.G.	Good	Fair	Poor
2500	2000	1750	1250	600	250

Model 300 Phoenix Long Range Rifle

Introduced in 1992 and chambered for the .300 Phoenix cartridge. Fitted with a 28" barrel with no sights. Fiberglass stock. Weight is approximately 12.5 lbs.

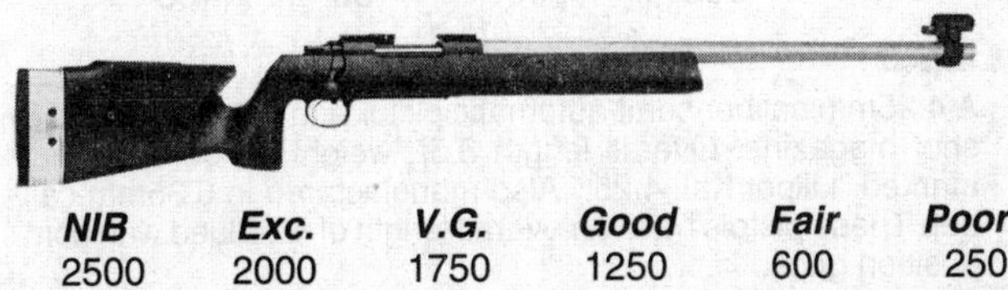

NIB	Exc.	V.G.	Good	Fair	Poor
2500	2000	1750	1250	600	250

Model 40 Sniper

This bolt-action rifle chambered for the .308 cartridge was introduced in 1990. Fitted with a 24" match grade heavy weight barrel. No sights. Weight is about 9 lbs.

NIB	Exc.	V.G.	Good	Fair	Poor
2000	1500	1000	750	500	300

Model 92 Bullpup

This is a single-shot rifle chambered for the .50 caliber BMG. Fitted with a 26" barrel and no sights. Fiberglass bullpup stock. First introduced in 1995.

NIB	Exc.	V.G.	Good	Fair	Poor
4000	3250	2500	2000	1000	500

Model 93 SN

This is a bolt-action rifle chambered for the .50 BMG and fitted with a 29" barrel with muzzlebrake. Magazine holds 10 rounds. No sights. Weight is approximately 21.5 lbs. Folding fiberglass stock. Introduced in 1995.

NIB	Exc.	V.G.	Good	Fair	Poor
4250	3750	3000	2250	1250	750

MEAD & ADRIANCE

St. Louis, Missouri

This company retailed a variety of single-shot percussion pistols most of which were manufactured by Ethan Allen of Grafton, Massachusetts. In general, the value for pistols marked "Mead & Adriance" are listed.

Exc.	V.G.	Good	Fair	Poor
—	—	1500	500	250

MEIJA

SEE—Japan State

MENDENHALL, JONES & GARDNER

Greensboro, North Carolina

Muzzle Loading Rifle

A .58 caliber percussion rifle with a 33" barrel and full-length walnut stock secured by two barrel bands. Finished in the white with the lock marked "M.J.&G.,N.C." Prospective purchasers should secure a qualified appraisal prior to acquisition.

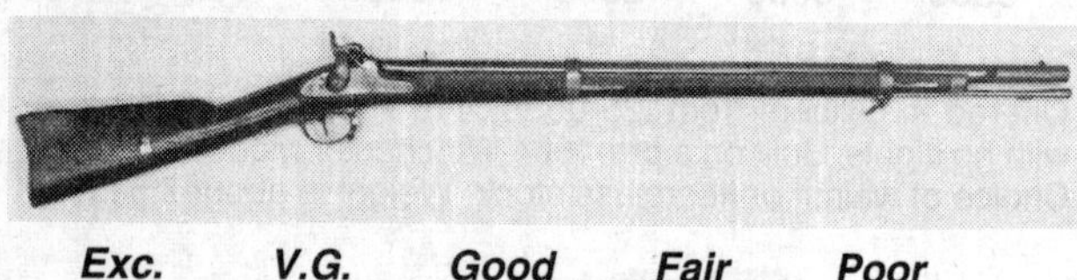

Exc.	V.G.	Good	Fair	Poor
—	—	30000	12500	—

MENZ, AUGUST

Suhl, Germany

Established prior to WWI to manufacture Beholla pistols, this company was purchased by Lignose in 1937.

Menta

Identical to the Beholla, which is listed separately.

Exc.	V.G.	Good	Fair	Poor
350	250	200	150	100

Liliput

A 4.25mm caliber semi-automatic pistol with a 2" barrel and 6-shot magazine. Overall length 3.5", weight 10 oz. The slide marked "Liliput Kal. 4.25." Also manufactured in 6.35mm caliber. These pistols have an overall length of 4". Blued with composition grips.

Exc.	V.G.	Good	Fair	Poor
800	600	450	300	200

Menz Model II

As above in 7.65mm caliber.

Exc.	V.G.	Good	Fair	Poor
400	300	250	200	125

Menz VP Model

Similar to the Model 2, but in 6.35mm caliber with a 2.35" barrel, 6-shot magazine and fitted with a cocking indicator.

Exc.	V.G.	Good	Fair	Poor
400	300	250	200	125

Model III

A total redesign. It has a closed-top slide, and the quality is much better than the previous Menz pistols. It has a fixed barrel and is similar to the Model 1910 Browning with an exposed hammer. This model was produced until 1937.

Exc.	V.G.	Good	Fair	Poor
450	350	300	250	150

MERCURY

Liege, Belgium

Model 622 VP

A .22 caliber semi-automatic rifle with a 20" barrel, open sights and 7-shot magazine. Blued with a walnut stock. Manufactured by Robar & Son.

Exc.	V.G.	Good	Fair	Poor
325	275	250	200	125

MERCURY

Eibar, Spain

Double-Barreled Shotgun

A 10, 12, or 20 gauge Magnum boxlock double-barrel shotgun with 28" or 32" barrels, double triggers and extractors. Blued with a walnut stock.

Exc.	V.G.	Good	Fair	Poor
325	250	225	175	125

NOTE: 10 gauge add 25 percent.

MERIDEN FIREARMS CO.

Meriden, Connecticut

Pocket Pistol

A .32 or .38 caliber double-action revolver manufactured in a variety of barrel lengths and with either an exposed or enclosed hammer. Nickel-plated with rubber grips. The barrel marked "Meriden Firearms Co. Meriden, Conn. USA." Manufactured between 1895 and 1915.

Exc.	V.G.	Good	Fair	Poor
—	400	150	75	50

 *This symbol denotes "Sleepers" with rapidly-rising values and/or significant collector potential.*

Double-Barrel Shotguns

From 1905-1918 Meriden Fire Arms Co. successor to A.J. Aubrey, made 12, 16, and 20 gauge sidelock double-barrel shotguns. These were better quality hammer and hammerless side-by-sides fitted with twist, laminated, Damascus, and steel barrels in grades A to G. Some of these guns were beautifully engraved by the same artisans who worked for Parker Bros. and other Connecticut gunmakers. Prices in 1910 ranged from $40 to $250 but they represented great value for the money as they were superior to the popular Crescent guns which they closely resembled. Current values depend on model, grade, gauge, and condition. It is difficult to find examples in excellent condition as these were sold by Sears to customers who put them to hard use. In good condition their current values range from $250 for plain Janes to $3,500 or more for the top grades, of which few specimens are known.

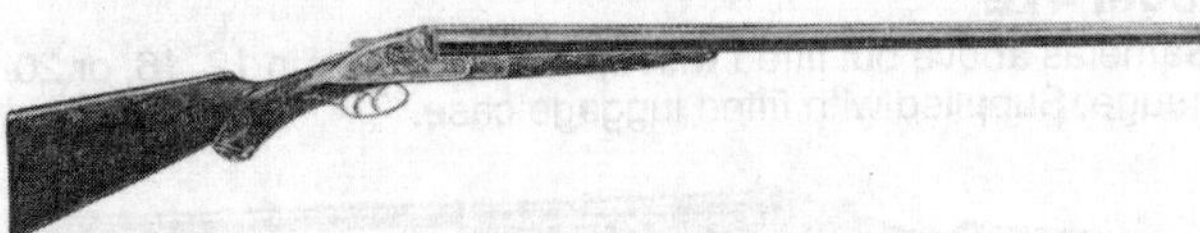

Single-Barrel Shotguns and Rifles

Meriden Fire Arms Co. also made many single-barrel shotguns and rifles whose current values are determined by growing collector interest and condition.

MERKEL, GEBRUDER

Suhl, Germany

An Introduction to Merkel Brother's Guns by Dan Sheil

Merkel Brothers shotgun and rifle makers began production around the turn of the century in Suhl, Germany. Merkel made a number of different models but the company was most well known for its over-and-under shotgun. It also made bolt-action rifles, side-by-side double express rifles, falling block single-shot rifles, side-by-side shotguns, drillings, and just about anything in the way of firearms its customers desired.

Perhaps the company's greatest productive era fell between the end of World War I and the 1950s. During the 1930s most of the live pigeon shoots were won with Merkel shotguns. However, there seems to be a difference of opinion about when Merkel built its best quality guns. This is not an easy question to answer. Most shooters and collectors feel that pre-World War II guns are the best examples of Merkel craftsmanship. But, in my opinion, some of the finest Merkels I have seen were produced immediately after World War II. Outstanding examples of Merkel's quality continue to appear up to the construction of the Berlin Wall in 1961.

Another area of controversy is the high grade Merkel 300 series shotgun. Many have compared this gun to the Italian and British makers and believe it is a mass produced gun. This is not the case because all Merkel shotguns are handcrafted and as far as I know barrels will not interchange unless they are supplied with the gun from the factory. While the 100 and 200 series guns may be mass produced, the 300 series is not, and that is easy to determine by looking at the serial number together with the date stamped on the barrel. Very few 300 series guns were produced in a given period.

In terms of durability, strength, and reliability, there is not an over-and-under shotgun that is built as strong as the Merkel. It has two Kersten style locking lugs on the upper barrel that fit into the face of the receiver while the bottom has two under lugs that give the gun a rugged four position locking system. I don't think I have ever heard of a Merkel being sent back to the gunmaker or a gunsmith to have the frame tightened. It just is not necessary; the guns will not shoot loose.

With respect to value, the Merkel over-and-under guns have been sleepers in the gun industry for a number of years. Until recently they have not brought the price that they deserve. I am specifically talking about the 300 series; the 303 Luxus and the 304. Generally speaking all of the special order Merkel over-and-under shotguns have done well. I think the shooting public will begin to recognize the quality and craftsmanship built into every one of these fine guns.

One last comment regarding special order Merkels and the company's reputation for building just about anything the customer wanted. It is impossible to cover all of the variations that the company produced in its long history, but the buyer should be aware that he may encounter some different and uncataloged Merkels along the way.

In August 1993 Merkel Brothers declared bankruptcy. The assets of the company were reportedly purchased by Steyr. GSI, Inc. Trussville, Alabama currently imports Merkel guns.

NOTE: Merkel is now owned by Heckler & Koch.

Editor's Comment: The Merkel gun prices listed are based on either one or two factors. First, they are no longer in production or second that the guns were built prior to the Berlin Wall, which generally bring a premium. An additional factor was introduced in 1994 when the factory began to use an alpha numeric serial number system. This new system dates the guns from 1994. The prices listed for new Merkels are influenced by the value of the dollar to the German Mark.

SIDE-BY-SIDE SHOTGUNS

Model 8

This model has a self-cocking Deeley boxlock action side-by-side with cocking indicators. The locking mechanism is a Greener cross-bolt with double-barrel locking lug. Triggers are single-selective or double. The safety is automatic and tang mounted. This model has an extractor. Offered in 12 and 16 gauge with 28" solid rib barrels or 20 gauge with 26.75" barrels. Available with straight or pistol grip oil-finished walnut stock. Receiver is case colored with light scroll engraving. The 12 and 16 gauge guns weigh about 6.8 lbs. while the 20 gauge weighs approximately 6 lbs.

NIB	*Exc.*	*V.G.*	*Good*	*Fair*	*Poor*
1000	800	700	600	500	400

Model 117/117E

Offered in 12 and 16 gauge with various barrel lengths, this model featured a boxlock action with double triggers and extractors. Ejectors were available under the "E" designation. The boxlock action body was scrupled at the rear with fine line scroll engraving.

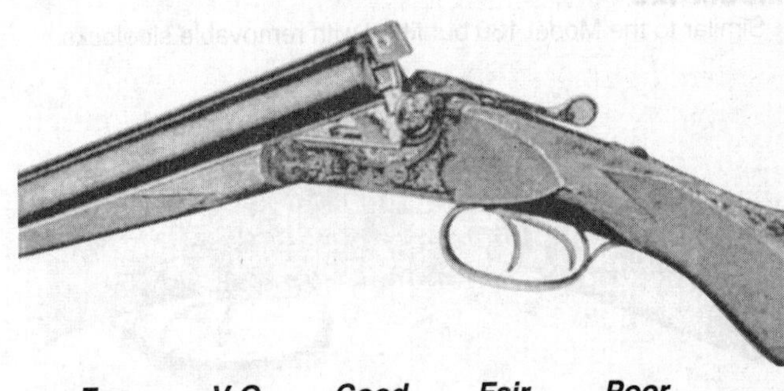

Exc.	*V.G.*	*Good*	*Fair*	*Poor*
5000	3500	1500	1000	500

Model 118/118E

Also offered in 12 and 16 gauge this model is similar to above model with slightly more engraving and better wood. This model also has some engraving coverage on the breech end of the barrels.

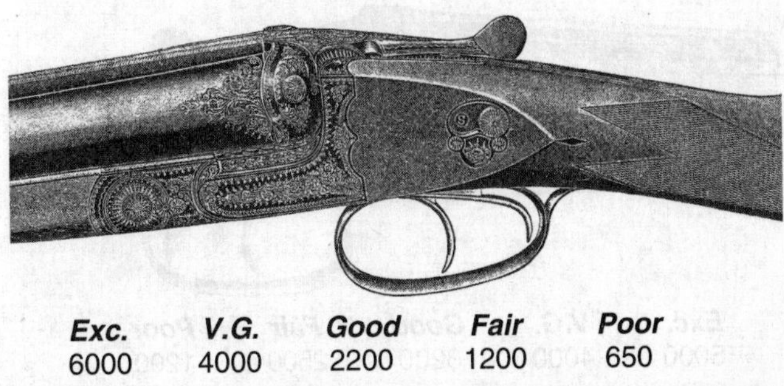

Exc.	*V.G.*	*Good*	*Fair*	*Poor*
6000	4000	2200	1200	650

Model 124/125

Similar to the above models but supplied with extractors for the Model 124 and ejectors for the Model 125. Both models have more engraving coverage with game scenes. Finer checkering and fancy wood is seen on this model.

Model 124

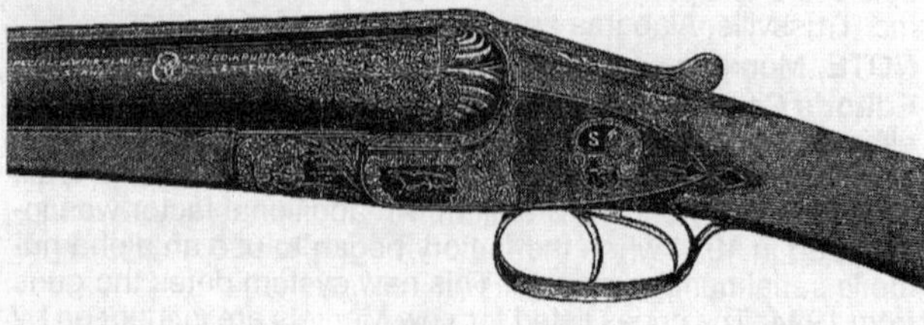

Exc.	V.G.	Good	Fair	Poor
4500	3500	2000	1500	700

Model 125

Exc.	V.G.	Good	Fair	Poor
5000	3750	3000	2000	1000

Model 130

This was one of Merkel's highest side-by-side shotguns. It featured a sidelock action, extra fancy wood, fine line checkering, and full coverage game scene engraving.

Exc.	V.G.	Good	Fair	Poor
15000	12000	7500	4500	—

Model 126

Similar to the Model 130 but fitted with removable sidelocks.

Exc.	V.G.	Good	Fair	Poor
15000	12000	7500	4500	—

Model 170

This model was offered in 12 gauge only with automatic ejectors. The boxlock action was engraved with fine full coverage scroll.

Exc.	V.G.	Good	Fair	Poor
5000	4000	3200	2500	1200

Model 127

This model was Merkel's finest side-by-side shotgun. The sidelock action featured full coverage fine line scroll engraving of the best quality.

Exc.	V.G.	Good	Fair	Poor
21000	16000	12000	6000	—

Model 47E

Same as above but fitted with ejectors. Offered in 12, 16, or 20 gauge. Supplied with fitted luggage case.

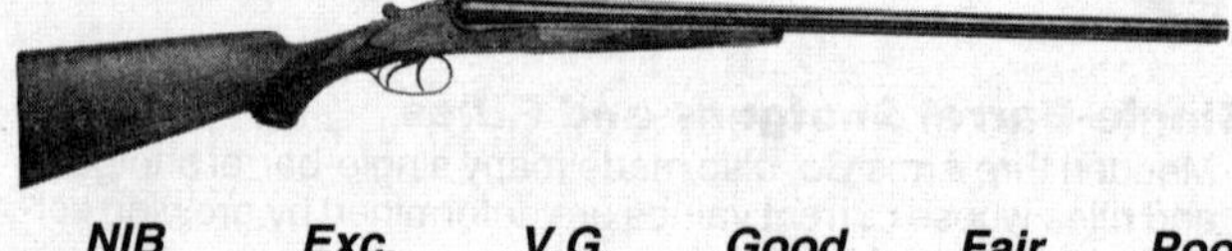

NIB	Exc.	V.G.	Good	Fair	Poor
3995	2900	1900	1200	—	—

Model 147

Same as Model 8 but with silver grayed receiver with fine engraved hunting scenes, engraved border, and screws. This model has been discontinued.

NIB	Exc.	V.G.	Good	Fair	Poor
2900	2500	1750	1100	600	400

Model 147E

Same as above but fitted with ejectors. Offered in 12, 16, 20, or 28 gauge. Supplied with fitted luggage case.

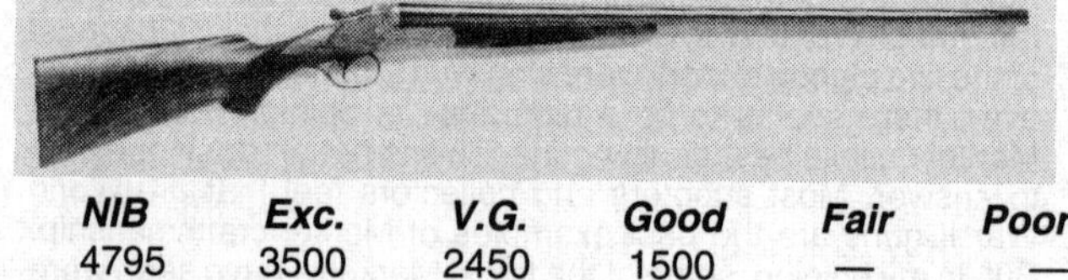

NIB	Exc.	V.G.	Good	Fair	Poor
4795	3500	2450	1500	—	—

Model 147EL

Similar to the Model 147E but with fancy walnut stock. Supplied with fitted luggage case.

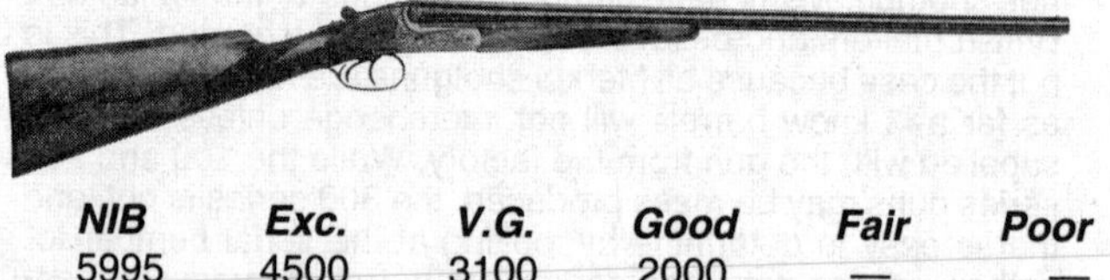

NIB	Exc.	V.G.	Good	Fair	Poor
5995	4500	3100	2000	—	—

Model 122

This model features the same specifications as the above models but has false sideplates. This model is fitted with ejectors and the receiver is silver grayed with fine engraved hunting scenes on false sideplates, engraved border, and screws.

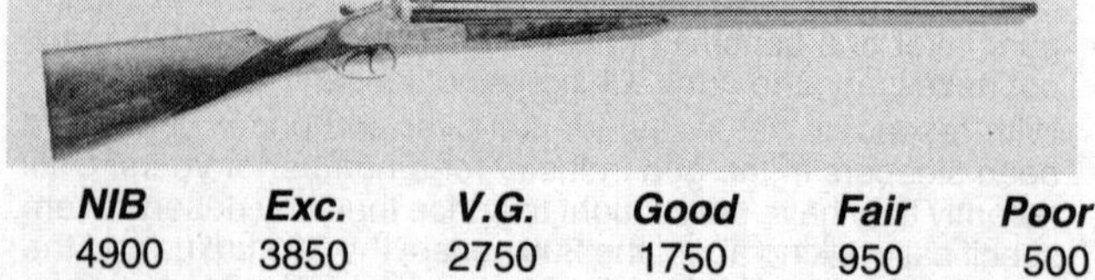

NIB	Exc.	V.G.	Good	Fair	Poor
4900	3850	2750	1750	950	500

Model 47SL

Same as above but with scroll engraving in place of hunting scenes.

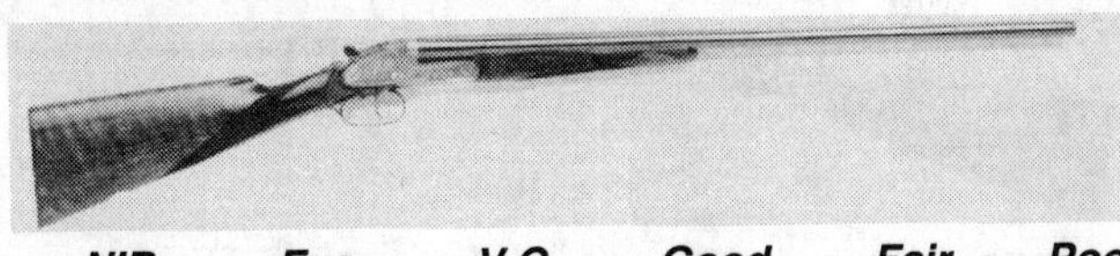

NIB	Exc.	V.G.	Good	Fair	Poor
7495	5500	4000	2750	1750	850

Model 147SL

This model features true Holland and Holland-style sidelocks with cocking indicators. Gauge and barrel lengths are as above. Stock is fancy walnut. However, 20 gauge gun weighs 6.4 lbs., 28 gauge gun weighs about 6.1 lbs.

NIB	Exc.	V.G.	Good	Fair	Poor
9395	7000	5000	3500	2250	1000

Model 147SSL

Similar to the Model 147SL but fitted with removable side plates. Fancy walnut stock. Supplied with fitted luggage case.

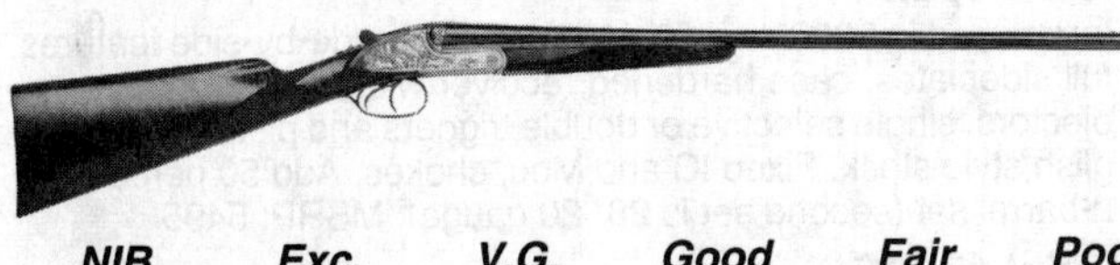

NIB	Exc.	V.G.	Good	Fair	Poor
7950	5900	4750	3000	—	—

Models 247S/347S

These models are the same as the Model 147S with the exception of the types of engraving.

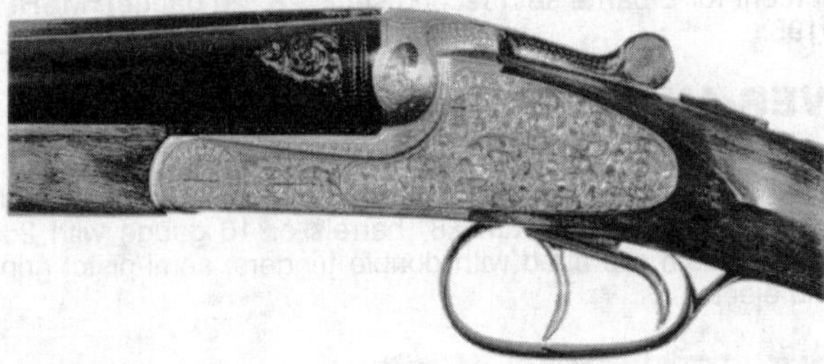

Model 247S

Large scroll engraving.

NIB	Exc.	V.G.	Good	Fair	Poor
7000	5250	4000	2500	—	—

Model 347S

Medium scroll engraving.

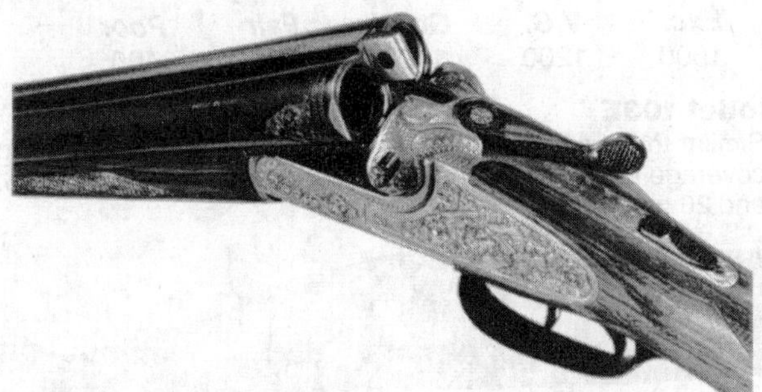

NIB	Exc.	V.G.	Good	Fair	Poor
6500	5500	4500	3500	2250	1500

Model 447SL

Small scroll engraving.

NIB	Exc.	V.G.	Good	Fair	Poor
9000	6750	5250	4000	—	—

NOTE: For wood upgrade add $1,200. For custom stock dimensions add $ 1,400. For left-hand stocks add $900.

Model 280

This is a boxlock gun chambered for the 28 gauge shell and fitted with 28" barrels choked Improved Cylinder and Modified. Double triggers with ejectors. Straight-grip walnut stock. Scroll engraving with case colored receiver. Weight is about 5.2 lbs.

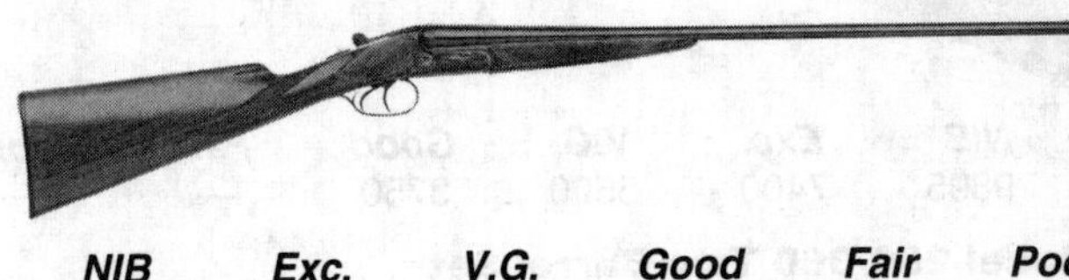

NIB	Exc.	V.G.	Good	Fair	Poor
4395	3250	2400	—	—	—

Model 280EL

This model features an Anson & Deely boxlock action with engraved hunting scenes on a silver-grayed action. Double triggers. Fancy walnut with straight grip stock. Offered in 28 gauge with 28" barrels. Fitted luggage case standard. Weight is about 5.2 lbs. First imported in 2000.

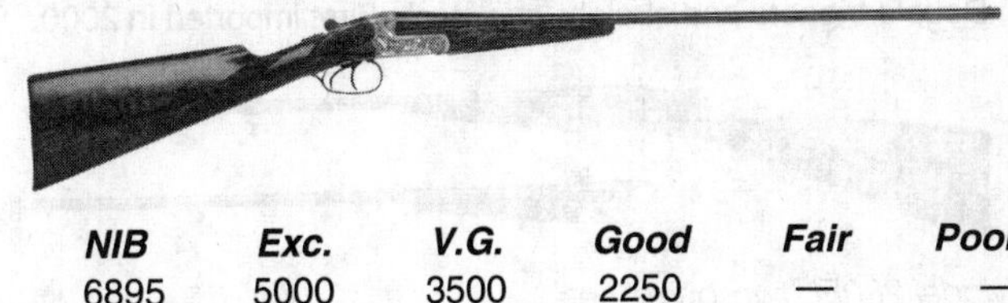

NIB	Exc.	V.G.	Good	Fair	Poor
6895	5000	3500	2250	—	—

Model 280SL

Similar to the Model 280EL, but with English-style scroll engraving on H&H style sidelocks with choice of pistol-grip or straight-grip fancy walnut stock. Fitted luggage case standard. First imported in 2000.

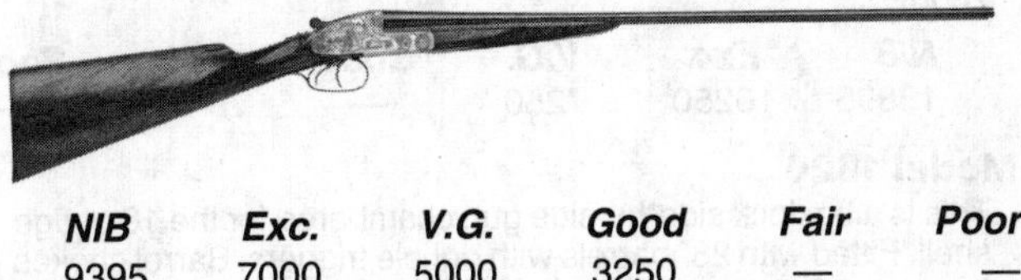

NIB	Exc.	V.G.	Good	Fair	Poor
9395	7000	5000	3250	—	—

Model 360

This boxlock model is the same as the Model 280 but chambered for the .410 bore. Straight grip walnut stock. Scroll engraving on case colored receiver. Barrel is 28" choke Modified and Full. Weight is about 5.2 lbs.

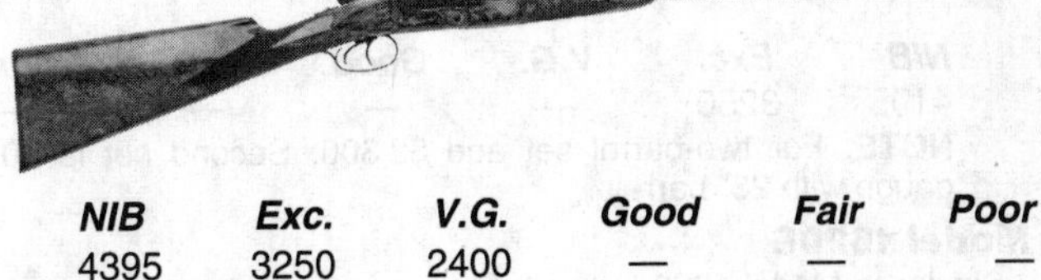

NIB	Exc.	V.G.	Good	Fair	Poor
4395	3250	2400	—	—	—

Model 360EL

This model is the same as the Model 280EL but chambered for the .410 shell and fitted with 28" barrels. Fancy walnut and fitted case. Weight is about 5.5 lbs. First imported in 2000.

NIB	Exc.	V.G.	Good	Fair	Poor
6895	5100	3750	2500	—	—

Model 360SL

Same as the Model 360EL but with English-style scroll engraving on H&H style sidelocks and choice of pistol grip or straight grip stock. First imported in 2000.

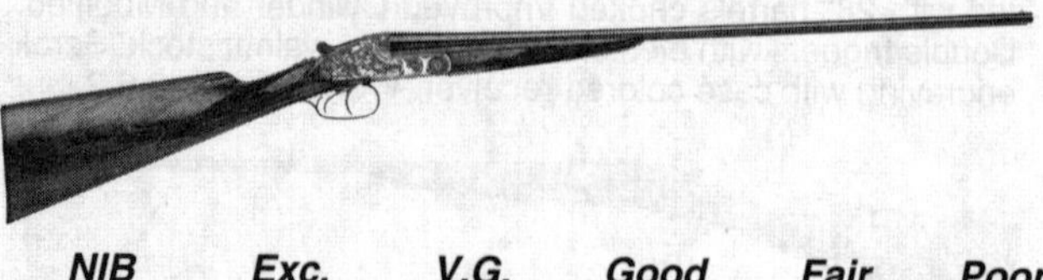

NIB	Exc.	V.G.	Good	Fair	Poor
9895	7400	5500	3750	—	—

Model 280/360 Two Barrel Set

This set consists of a 28 gauge 28" barrel and a .410 bore 28" barrel with scroll engraving and oil finish walnut stock. Double triggers and straight grip stock.

NIB	Exc.	V.G.	Good	Fair	Poor
9895	7400	5500	3750	—	—

Model 280/360EL Two Barrel Set

This set consists of a 28 gauge 28" barrel and a .410 bore 28" barrel with engraved hunting scenes and fancy walnut stock. Double triggers and straight-grip stock. First imported in 2000.

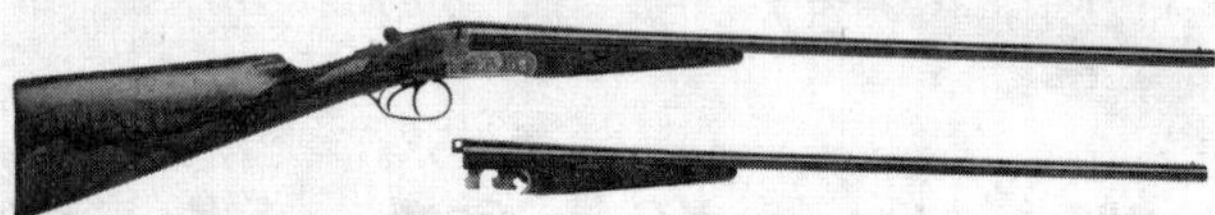

Model 280EL two-barrel set

NIB	Exc.	V.G.	Good	Fair	Poor
9895	7400	5500	3750	—	—

Model 280/360SL Two Barrel Set

Same as above but with English-style scroll engraving and choice of pistol-grip or straight-grip stock. First imported in 2000.

NIB	Exc.	V.G.	Good	Fair	Poor
13895	10250	7250	—	—	—

Model 1620

This is a boxlock side-by-side gun chambered for the 16 gauge shell. Fitted with 28" barrels with double triggers. Barrel chokes Improved Cylinder and Modified. Ejectors. Straight-grip walnut stock with oil finish. Case colored receiver finish. Light scroll engraving. Fitted luggage case. Weight is about 6.1 lbs.

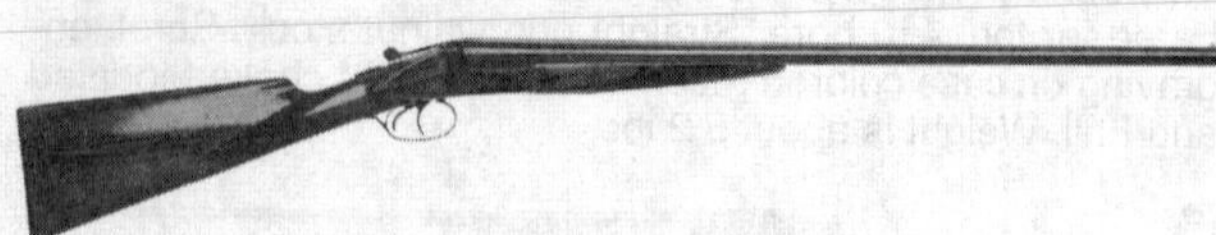

NIB	Exc.	V.G.	Good	Fair	Poor
4195	3250	—	—	—	—

NOTE: For two-barrel set add $2,300. Second set is 20 gauge with 28" barrels.

Model 1620E

Similar to Model 1620 but with fine engraved hunting scenes on silver-grayed receiver. MSRP: 5195

Model 1620EL

As above but with high-grade walnut straight-grip stock and deeply engraved hunting scenes.

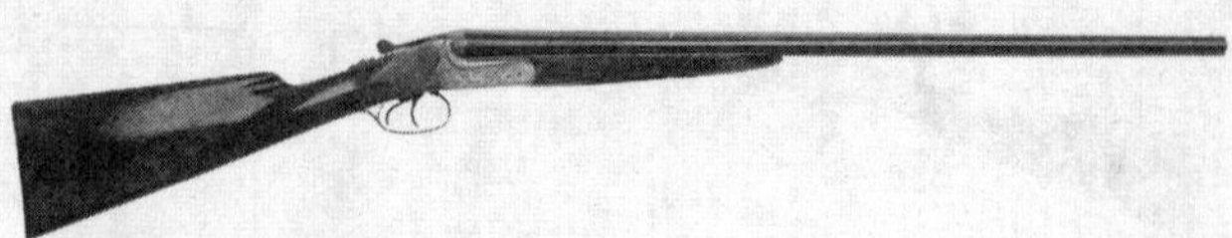

NIB	Exc.	V.G.	Good	Fair	Poor
6895	5100	3500	—	—	—

NOTE: For two-barrel set add $2,900. Second set is 20 gauge with 28" barrels.

Model 1620SL

Similar to the 1620 models above but with grayed sidelocks with deeply engraved hunting scenes. High-grade walnut stock with oil finish. Weight is 6.6 lbs.

NIB	Exc.	V.G.	Good	Fair	Poor
9895	7500	5500	3750	—	—

NOTE: For two-barrel set add $3,800. Second set is 20 gauge with 28" barrels.

Model 1622

Introduced in 2006, this 16-gauge boxlock side-by-side features full sideplates, case hardened receiver with cocking indicators, ejectors, single selective or double triggers and pistol grip or English style stock. Fixed IC and Mod. chokes. Add 50 percent for 2-barrel set (second set is 28" 20 gauge). MSRP: 5495

Model 1622E

Similar to 1622 but with fine engraved hunting scenes on silver-grayed receiver. MSRP: 6895

Model 1622EL

Similar to Model 1622E but with luxury grade wood. Add 30 percent for 2-barrel set (second set is 28" 20 gauge). MSRP: 9195

OVER-AND-UNDER SHOTGUNS

Model 102E

This was Merkel's standard over-and-under boxlock model. Offered in 12 gauge with 28" barrels or 16 gauge with 26" barrels. Both are fitted with double triggers, semi-pistol grip, and ejectors.

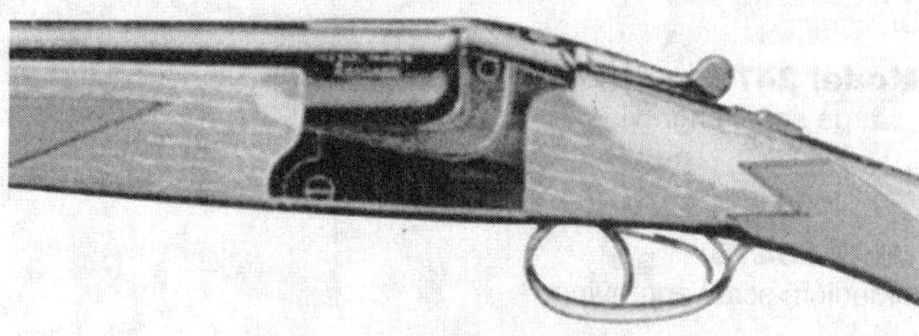

Exc.	V.G.	Good	Fair	Poor
1600	1200	1000	650	400

Model 103E

Similar to the standard but with more English scroll engraving coverage and better wood. This model was offered in 12, 16, and 20 gauge.

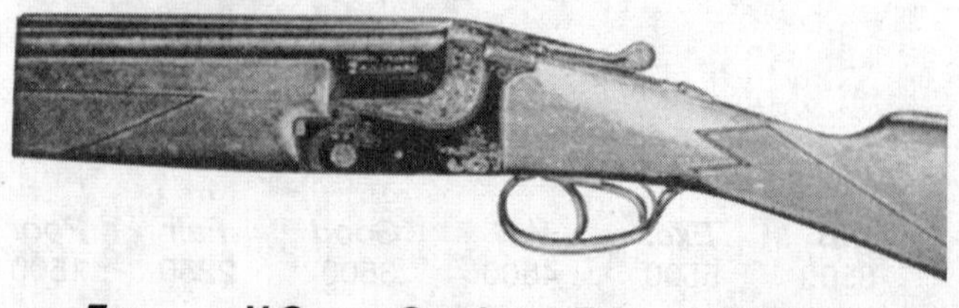

Exc.	V.G.	Good	Fair	Poor
2200	1500	1200	950	600

Model 204E

This model is essentially a Model 203E with finer engraving. This model was discontinued prior to 1939.

Exc.	V.G.	Good	Fair	Poor
6000	4500	3000	2200	1750

Model 301E

This is a boxlock model with scalloped action chambered for the 12, 16, 20, 24, 28, and 32 gauge. The engraving is an English scroll and the trigger guard is horn. Double triggers and pistol grip are standard. This model was produced prior to 1939.

Exc.	V.G.	Good	Fair	Poor
4500	4000	2500	2000	1850

Model 302E

Similar to the Model 301E but fitted with side plates. The full-coverage engraving features game scenes. This model produced prior to WWII.

Exc.	V.G.	Good	Fair	Poor
12000	10000	7500	4000	2000

Model 303 Luxus

This over-and-under Merkel is custom built to the customer's specifications. Each gun is unique and should be appraised by a knowledgeable individual who is familiar with quality European shotguns. Prices for this model start at $20,000.

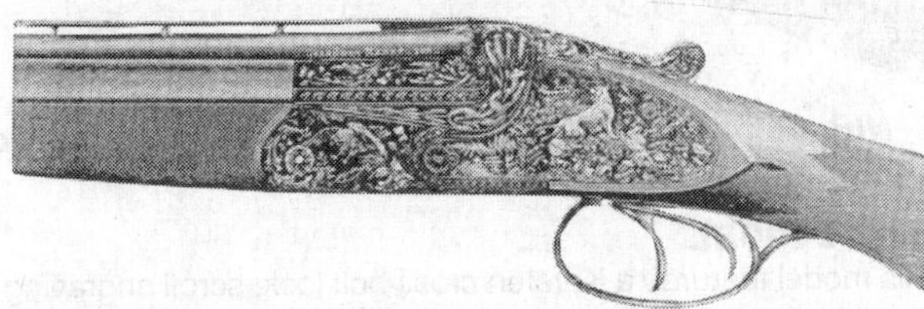

Model 304E

This pre-war model was the highest grade in Merkel's over-and-under shotgun line. A sidelock gun with full coverage scroll engraving of the highest quality. Fine line checkering and extra fancy wood make this gun difficult to appraise due to its rarity. A qualified appraisal before a sale is highly recommended.

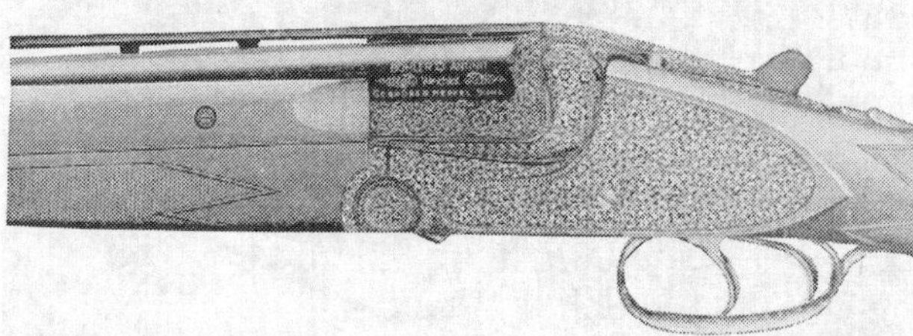

Model 400E

A higher grade over-and-under fitted with Kersten crossbolt, finer engraving, and fancy wood. Merkel offered this grade in 12, 16, 20, 24, 28, and 32 gauge with choice of barrel lengths. This model was produced prior to 1939.

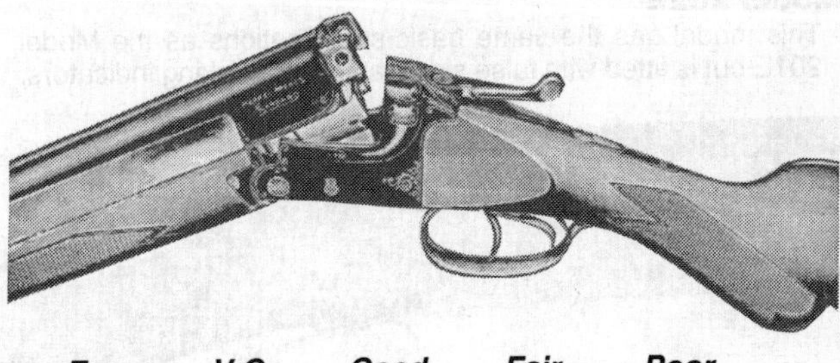

Exc.	V.G.	Good	Fair	Poor
1800	1300	1000	600	400

Model 401E

Similar to the model above but with full coverage game scene engraving.

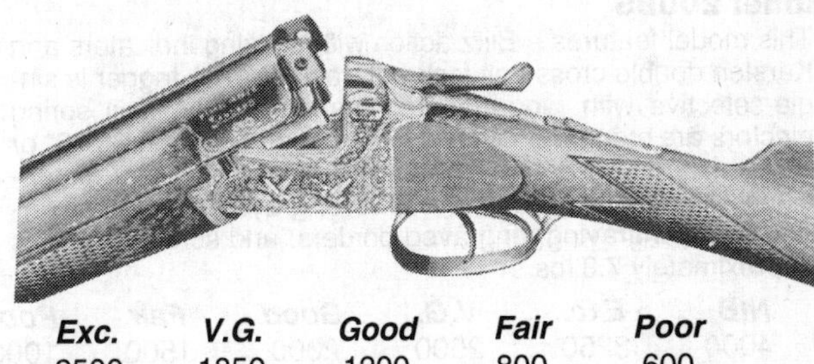

Exc.	V.G.	Good	Fair	Poor
2500	1850	1200	800	600

Model 200E

The action on this model is a self cocking Blitz where the hammers are attached to the trigger plates. The locking mechanism is a Kersten double cross bolt lock with release. Trigger may be either single-selective or double. The manual safety is mounted on the tang. Fitted with coil spring ejectors. Offered in 12 and 16 gauge with 28" solid rib barrels or 20 gauge with 26.75" barrels. The oil-finished stock is offered with straight or pistol grip. The receiver is case colored with engraved border and screws. The 12 gauge weighs 7 lbs., the 16 gauge 6.8 lbs., and the 20 gauge 6.4 lbs.

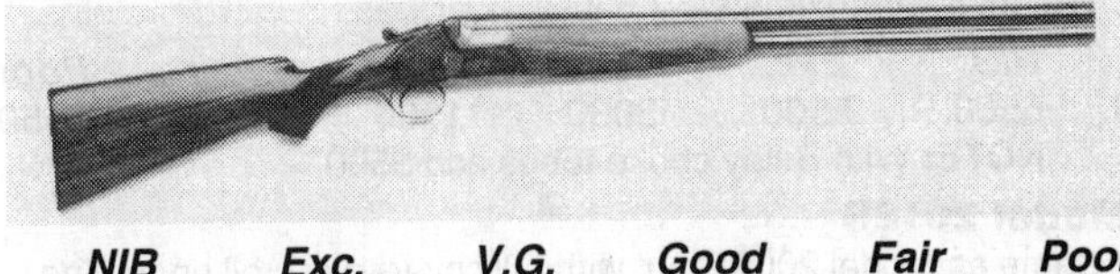

NIB	Exc.	V.G.	Good	Fair	Poor
2700	2000	1500	1000	800	500

Model 201E

Same as Model 200E but with silver grayed receiver with fine engraved hunting scenes, engraved border, and screws.

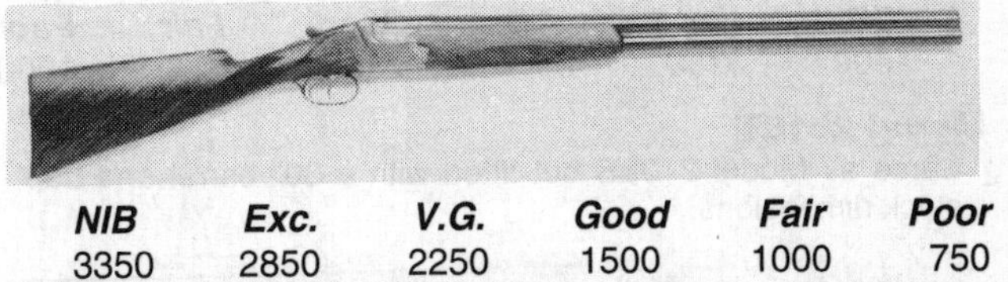

NIB	Exc.	V.G.	Good	Fair	Poor
3350	2850	2250	1500	1000	750

REMINDER
"A well regulated militia being necessary to the security of a free State, the right of the People to keep and bear arms shall not be infringed."

Model 202E

This model has the same basic specifications as the Model 201E but is fitted with false side plates with cocking indicators.

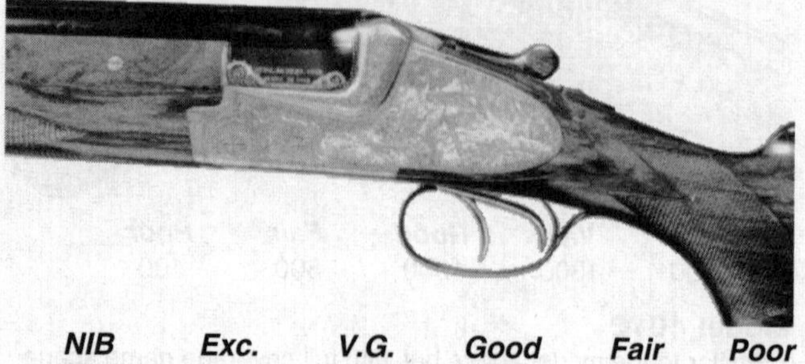

NIB	Exc.	V.G.	Good	Fair	Poor
6500	5000	3500	2500	1500	1000

Model 200ES

This model features a Blitz action with cocking indicators and Kersten double cross bolt lock with release. The trigger is single-selective with tang-mounted manual safety. Coil spring ejectors are standard. Offered in 12 gauge only with 26.75" or 28" ventilated rib barrel. The walnut stock has skeet dimensions with pistol grip. Receiver is silver grayed with 112 coverage scroll engraving, engraved borders, and screws. Weighs approximately 7.3 lbs.

NIB	Exc.	V.G.	Good	Fair	Poor
4000	3250	2500	2000	1500	1000

Model 200ET

Same as Model 200ES, but in a trap configuration. The ventilated rib barrel length offered is 30".

NIB	Exc.	V.G.	Good	Fair	Poor
4250	3500	2750	2250	1750	1000

Model 200SC (Sporting Clays)

Introduced in 1995 this model is offered in 12 gauge only with 3" chambers and 30" barrels with ventilated rib. It is fitted with a single-selective trigger adjustable for length of pull. It has a special walnut oil finished stock with 26 lpi checkering. Pistol grip and Pachmayr Sporting Clays recoil pad is standard. Weight is approximately 7.6 lbs.

NIB	Exc.	V.G.	Good	Fair	Poor
6500	5500	3000	1500	900	450

NOTE: With Briley choke tubes add $500.

Model 201ES

Same as Model 200SC but with full coverage scroll engraving.

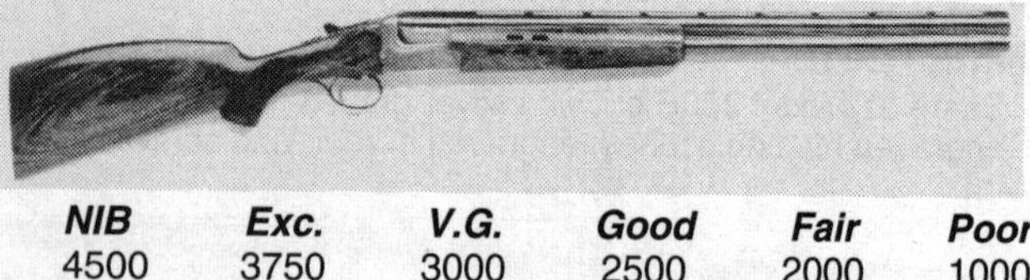

NIB	Exc.	V.G.	Good	Fair	Poor
4500	3750	3000	2500	2000	1000

Model 201ET

Same as Model 210ES but fitted with a 30" barrel and trap stock dimensions.

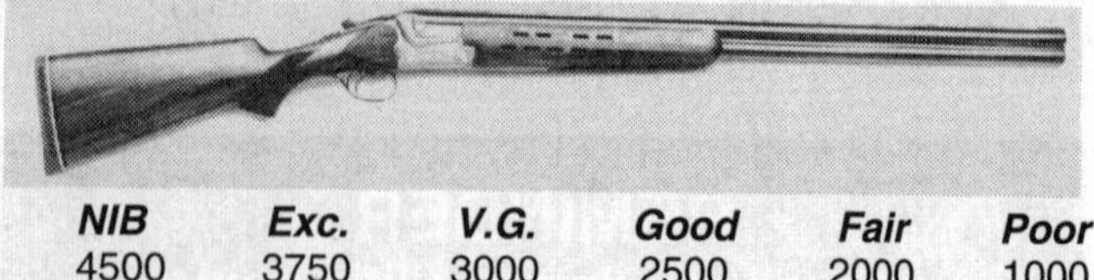

NIB	Exc.	V.G.	Good	Fair	Poor
4500	3750	3000	2500	2000	1000

Model 203E

This model has true Holland & Holland-style sidelocks with cocking indicators. These sideplates are removable with cranked screw. The gauge selection and barrel are the same as those listed above. The silver grayed receiver has English-style large scroll engraving. This model has been discontinued.

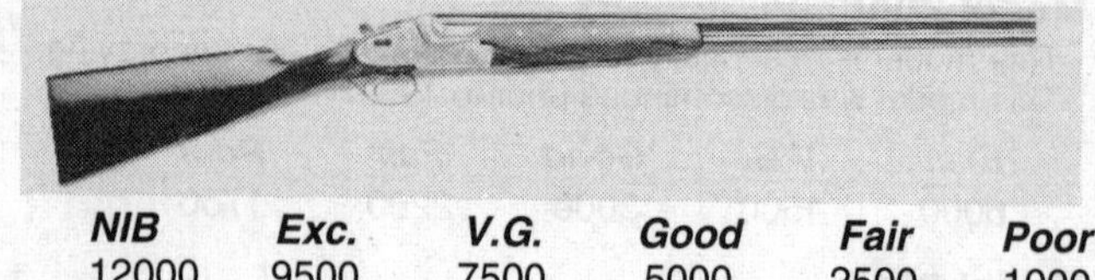

NIB	Exc.	V.G.	Good	Fair	Poor
12000	9500	7500	5000	2500	1000

Model 303E

Same as Model 203E but with detachable sidelock plates with integral retracting hook. The Model 303E also has medium scroll work engraving and Holland & Holland-type ejectors.

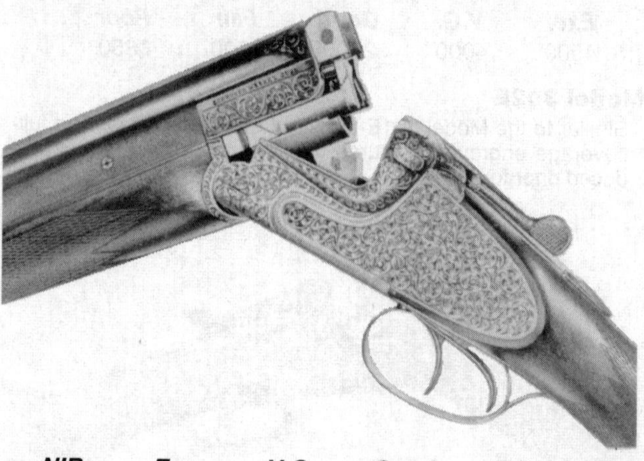

NIB	Exc.	V.G.	Good	Fair	Poor
17000	15000	12000	7500	5000	2500

Model 303EL

This model features H&H-style sidelocks that are quick detachable without tools. Receiver is engraved with hunting scenes. Offered in 12, 20 and 28 gauge. Double triggers and fancy wanut stock with pistol or straight grip. Weight for 12 gauge is about 7 lbs, for the 20 gauge about 6.4 lbs, and for the 28 gauge about 6.4 lbs. Fitted luggage case standard.

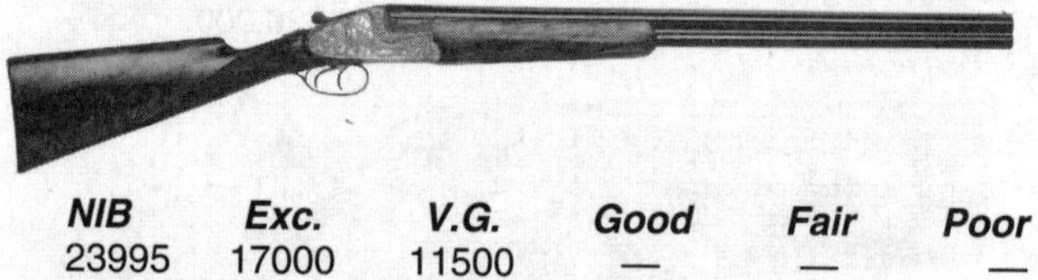

NIB	Exc.	V.G.	Good	Fair	Poor
23995	17000	11500	—	—	—

Model 2000EL

This model features a Kersten cross bolt lock, scroll engraving on a silver grayed receiver and a modified Anson & Deely boxlock action. This gun is offered in 12, 20, or 28 gauge with ejectors, single-selective or double triggers, fancy wood, and choice of pistol or straight grip stock. Weight is about 7 lbs. for 12 gauge, 6.4 lbs. for 20 gauge, and 6.4 lbs. for 28 gauge.

NIB	Exc.	V.G.	Good	Fair	Poor
6495	4750	3250	2200	1500	750

Model 2000EL Sporter

Similar to the above model but fitted with 30" barrels on the 12 gauge, and 28" barrels on the 20 and 28 gauge.

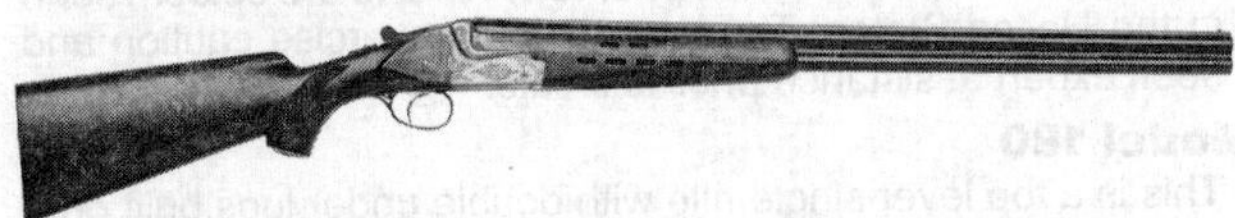

NIB	Exc.	V.G.	Good	Fair	Poor
6495	4750	3250	2200	1500	750

Model 2000CL

Introduced in 2005 this model is chambered for the 12, 20, or 28 gauge with 28" barrels choked improved cylinder and modified. Scroll engraved receiver with case colors. Single selective trigger with auto ejectors. High grade wood with semi-pistol grip and straight grip.

NIB	Exc.	V.G.	Good	Fair	Poor
6995	5250	—	—	—	—

Model 2000CL Sporter

As above but with 30" barrel for the 12 gauge with vent rib and 28" barrels with solid rib for the 20 and 28 gauge guns. Pistol grip stock. Introduced in 2005.

NIB	Exc.	V.G.	Good	Fair	Poor
7495	5500	—	—	—	—

NOTE: Deduct $500 for 20 and 28 gauge models.

Model 2001EL

Similar to the Model 2000 but with finely engraved hunting scenes. This model is offered in 28 gauge as well as 12 and 20 gauge.

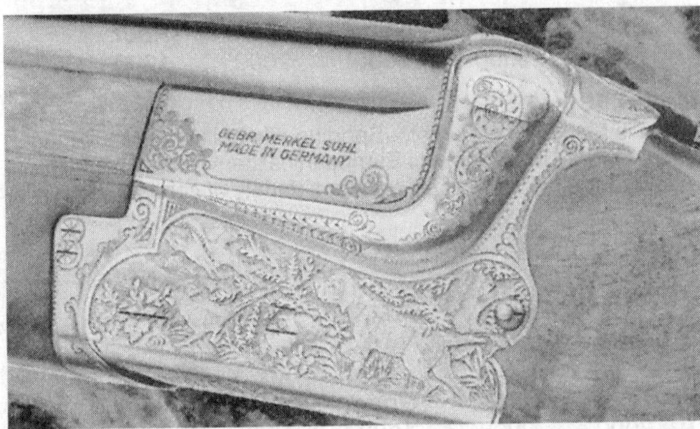

NIB	Exc.	V.G.	Good	Fair	Poor
8695	6500	4500	2900	2000	1000

Model 2001EL Sporter

Same as above but with 30" barrels for 12 gauge, 28" barrels for 20 and 28 gauge.

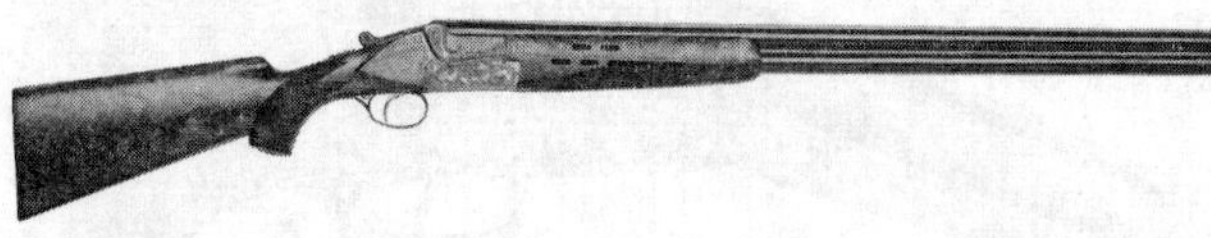

NIB	Exc.	V.G.	Good	Fair	Poor
9195	6750	4750	3250	2000	1000

Model 2002EL

This model features finely engraved hunting scenes with arabesque style. Offered in 12, 20 and 28 gauges.

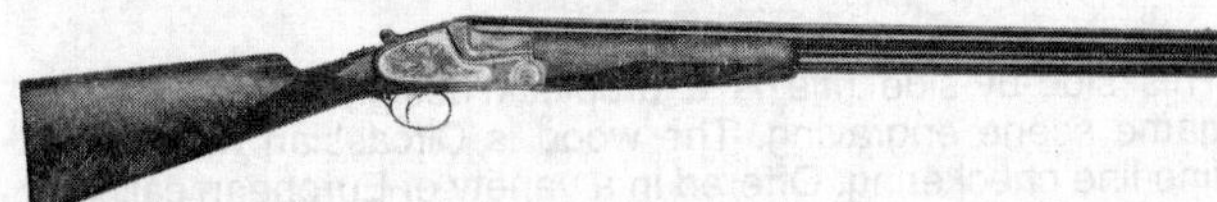

NIB	Exc.	V.G.	Good	Fair	Poor
10000	8000	6000	4000	—	—

Model 2016EL

This is a 16 gauge gun with 28" barrels and single non-selective trigger and ejectors. Fixed chokes. Checkered walnut stock with semi-pistol grip. Scroll engraving on the case colored receiver. Weight is about 6.6 lbs.

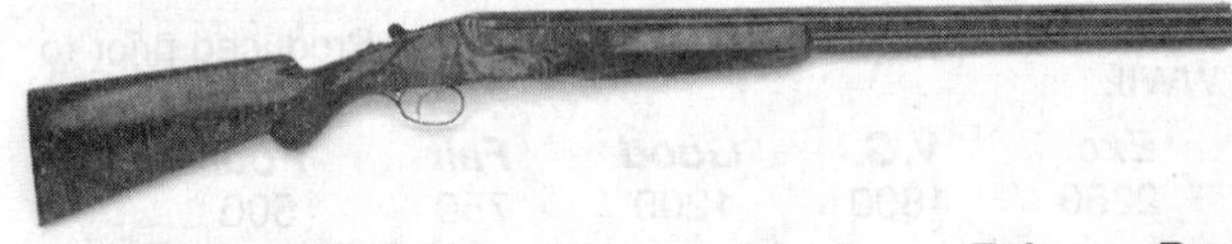

NIB	Exc.	V.G.	Good	Fair	Poor
6495	5000	—	—	—	—

Model 2016EL Two Barrel Set

As above but with extra set of 20 gauge 28" barrels with fixed chokes.n

NIB	Exc.	V.G.	Good	Fair	Poor
9695	7200	—	—	—	—

Model 2116EL

This 16 gauge model is similar to the above but with game scene engraving on the case colored receiver.

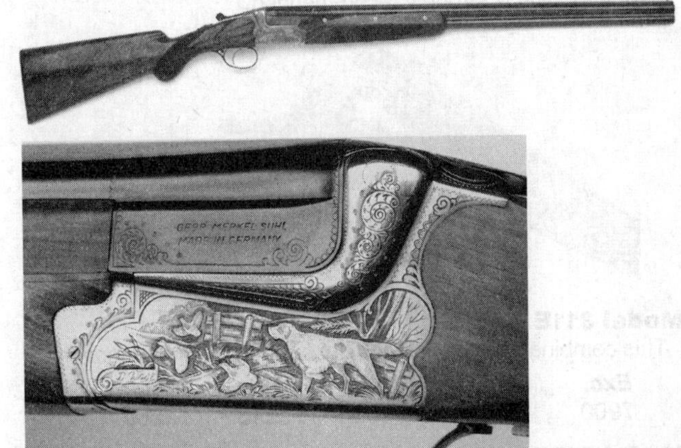

NIB	Exc.	V.G.	Good	Fair	Poor
8295	6200	—	—	—	—

MERKEL SHOTGUN CHOKE DESIGNATIONS		
Choke ID	**Description**	**Percentage**
1/1	Full Choke	70 to 75 (at 40 yds)
3/4	Imp. Modified	65 to 70
1/2	Modified	60 to 65
1/4	Quarter Choke	55 to 60
VZ	Imp. Cylinder	45 to 50
S	Skeet Choke	70 to 75 (at 25 yds)

Model 2116EL Two Barrel Set

As above with extra set of 20 gauge 28" barrels with fixed chokes.

NIB	Exc.	V.G.	Good	Fair	Poor
11495	8500	—	—	—	—

RIFLE/SHOTGUN COMBINATION GUNS

Model 410E

Merkel's base boxlock model with ejectors. Produced prior to WWII.

Exc.	V.G.	Good	Fair	Poor
2250	1800	1200	750	500

Model 411 E

Similar to the above but with the addition of a small coverage of scroll engraving.

Exc.	V.G.	Good	Fair	Poor
2500	2000	1500	1000	600

Model 300

A boxlock hammerless four barrel shotgun/rifle combination. The shotgun barrels were 12, 16, or 20 gauge, while the top rifle barrel was .22 rimfire with the bottom rifle barrel .30-30 or .25-35. Probably any combination of rifle and shotgun could be used as this was a special order gun. Very rare. An independent appraisal is strongly recommended.

Model 311E

This combination gun has additional English scroll engraving.

Exc.	V.G.	Good	Fair	Poor
7900	6500	5000	2250	1250

Model 312E

This model is fitted with sideplates and game scene engraving.

Exc.	V.G.	Good	Fair	Poor
9500	8150	6600	4000	2000

Model 313E

This model has sidelocks with fine, full coverage scroll engraving. An expert appraisal is recommended due to this model's rarity and unique features.

Exc.	V.G.	Good	Fair	Poor
11500	10500	8000	4000	2000

Model 314E

This sidelock model is also rare and unique. An expert appraisal is recommended prior to a sale. Extra barrels will frequently be seen with this model.

SINGLE-SHOT AND BOLT-ACTION RIFLES

Merkel built special single-shot rifles and bolt-action rifles. These guns were produced prior to WWII and are seldom seen in the United States. The buyer should exercise caution and seek expert assistance prior to a sale.

Model 180

This is a top lever single rifle with double under lugs built on a boxlock action. The stock is 3/4 with pistol grip. Commonly referred to as a stalking rifle. Offered in a variety of European calibers. A rare Merkel.

Exc.	V.G.	Good	Fair	Poor
3000	2100	1500	1000	500

Model 183

This top lever model features a Holland & Holland-type sidelock action with the sidelock on the left side and the removable side plate on the right side. Fitted with a straight-grip stock and full-length forearm with sling swivels, fine line checkering, and fancy wood. A rare rifle.

Exc.	V.G.	Good	Fair	Poor
7500	5000	3500	2000	1200

Model 190

This is Merkel's version of a Sporting rifle built on a Mauser action. Offered in a variety of European calibers. These were special order rifles and will be seen in a variety of configurations.

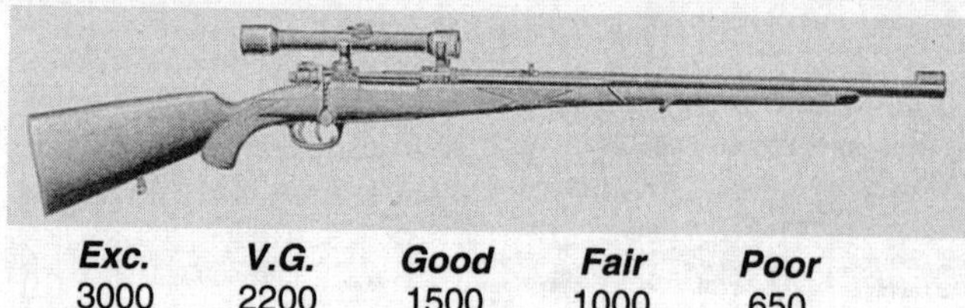

Exc.	V.G.	Good	Fair	Poor
3000	2200	1500	1000	650

DOUBLE RIFLES—COMBINATION GUNS—DRILLINGS

Side-by-Side Double Rifles Model 128E

This side-by-side rifle is a droplock design with scroll and game scene engraving. The wood is Circassian walnut with fine line checkering. Offered in a variety of European calibers.

Because of the rarity and uniqueness of each rifle a qualified appraisal should be sought prior to a sale.

Model 132E

Similar to the Model 128E but with full coverage scroll engraving and fancy wood. This model also should have an expert appraisal done prior to a sale.

Model 140-1

This model features a Greener cross bolt, scroll engraving with case hardened receiver. Extractors and double triggers with pistol grip stock are standard. Offered in a wide variety of European and American calibers.

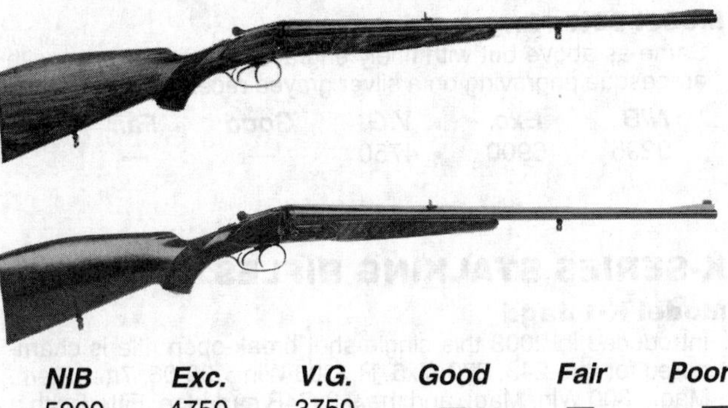

NIB	Exc.	V.G.	Good	Fair	Poor
5900	4750	3750	—	—	—

Model 140-1.1

Same as above model but with finely engraved hunting scenes.

NIB	Exc.	V.G.	Good	Fair	Poor
6800	5500	4000	—	—	—

Model 140-2

This double rifle has an Anson & Deely boxlock action. Double triggers. Barrel length is 23.6". Chambered for .375 H&H, .416 Rigby, and the .470 NE. Pistol grip stock with cheekpiece on oil finish walnut. Weight is about 10.7 lbs. depending on caliber.

NIB	Exc.	V.G.	Good	Fair	Poor
10595	7500	5250	—	—	—

Model 140-2.1

This model is similar to the one above but is engraved with African game scenes.

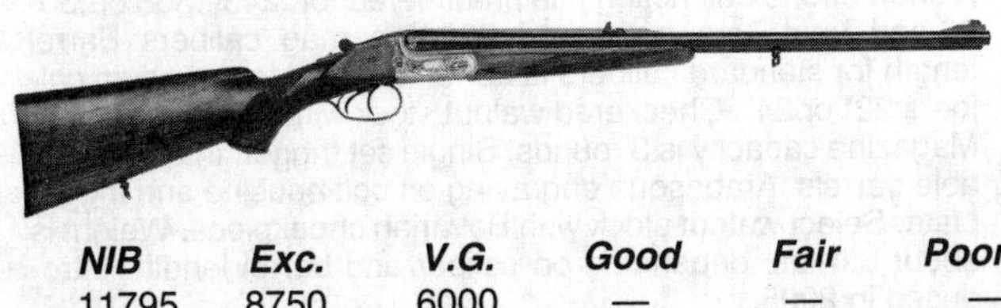

NIB	Exc.	V.G.	Good	Fair	Poor
11795	8750	6000	—	—	—

Model 150-1

This model features an arabesque engraving on a silver greyed receiver. Extractors, double triggers, and pistol grip are standard.

NIB	Exc.	V.G.	Good	Fair	Poor
7500	6000	4750	—	—	—

Model 150-1.1

Same as above model but with finely engraved hunting scenes.

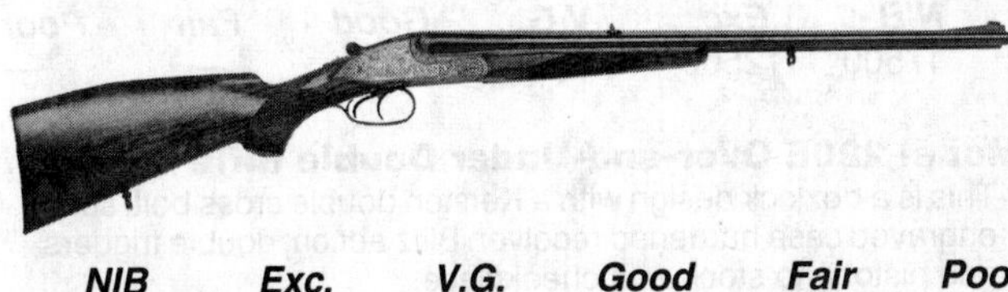

NIB	Exc.	V.G.	Good	Fair	Poor
8700	7000	5500	—	—	—

Model 160S Luxus Double Rifle

This double rifle is part of the Luxus series and features on the highest quality sidelock action, wood, and fittings. It is offered in .222 Rem., 5.6x5OR Mag., .243, 6.5x57R, 7x57, 7x65, .3006, .30R Blaser, 8x57IRS, 8x57RS, .308 Win., and 9.3x74R. Weighs approximately 8 lbs. An expert appraisal should be sought prior to a sale due to the unique nature of this model.

NIB	Exc.	V.G.	Good	Fair	Poor
13300	10500	—	—	—	—

Model 160S-2.1

Same as above but with finely engraved hunting scenes. Chambered for the .470 Nitro Express. Weight is about 11 lbs.

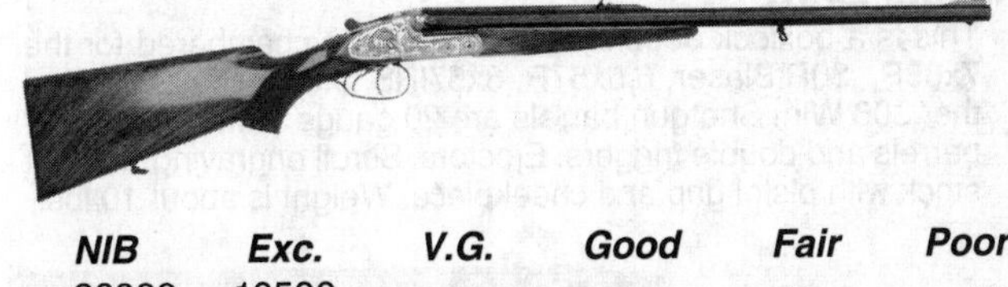

NIB	Exc.	V.G.	Good	Fair	Poor
26000	19500	—	—	—	—

Model 211E Rifle/Shotgun Combination

This over-and-under model features a gray metal boxlock action with hunting scenes. The top barrel is available in 12, 16, or 20 gauge and the bottom barrel is offered in .22 Hornet, 5.6R Mag., 5.6R, .222 Rem., .243 Win., 6.5x55, 6.5x57R, 7x57R, 7x65R, .30-06, 8x57IRS, 9.3x74R, and .375 H&H Mag. The barrel has a solid rib and the trigger is single-selective. The select walnut stock is hand checkered. Weight is about 7 lbs.

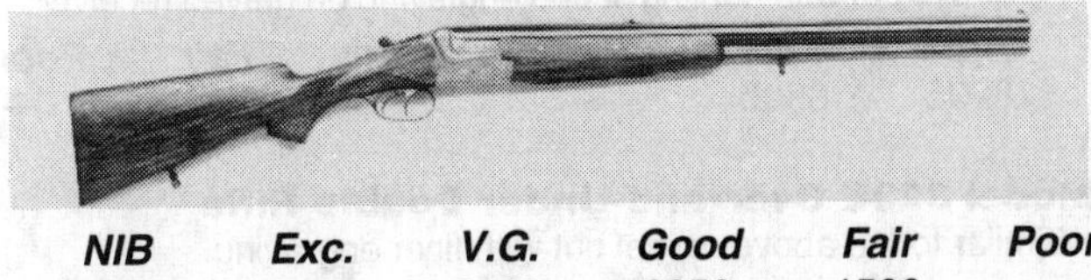

NIB	Exc.	V.G.	Good	Fair	Poor
6000	4500	3500	2250	1500	—

Model 210E Rifle/Shotgun Combination

Same as above model but features a scroll engraved case hardened receiver. This model has been discontinued.

NIB	Exc.	V.G.	Good	Fair	Poor
6200	5000	4000	2750	1200	700

Model 211E Rifle/Shotgun Combination

Similar to the above model but with finely engraved hunting scenes.

NIB	Exc.	V.G.	Good	Fair	Poor
7500	6000	4500	3000	1500	—

Model 213E Rifle/Shotgun Combination

This combination gun features sidelocks with English style large scroll engraving on a silver grayed receiver. Also is fitted with double triggers and pistol grip with cheekpiece.

NIB	Exc.	V.G.	Good	Fair	Poor
11500	9500	7500	5500	—	—

Model 313E Rifle/Shotgun Combination

Same as above model but with finer scroll engraving and fancy wood.

NIB	Exc.	V.G.	Good	Fair	Poor
17500	12500	7500	6500	—	—

Model 220E Over-and-Under Double Rifle

This is a boxlock design with a Kersten double cross bolt, scroll engraved case hardened receiver, Blitz action, double triggers, and pistol-grip stock with cheekpiece.

NIB	Exc.	V.G.	Good	Fair	Poor
8500	6000	4500	3800	—	—

Model 221E Over-and-Under Double Rifle

Similar to the model above but with game scene engraving on a silver grayed receiver.

NIB	Exc.	V.G.	Good	Fair	Poor
10900	8500	5750	—	—	—

Model 223E Over-and-Under Double Rifle

This model is fitted with sidelocks and features English-style arabesque engraving in large scrolls on silver grayed receiver.

NIB	Exc.	V.G.	Good	Fair	Poor
14500	12500	10000	—	—	—

Model 240-1

This is a boxlock double rifle and shotgun chambered for the 7x65R, .30R Blaser, 6.5x57R, 8x57IRS, 9.3x74R, .30-06, and the .308 Win. Shotgun barrels are 20 gauge. Fitted with 23.6" barrels and double triggers. Ejectors. Scroll engraving. Walnut stock with pistol grip and cheekpiece. Weight is about 10 lbs.

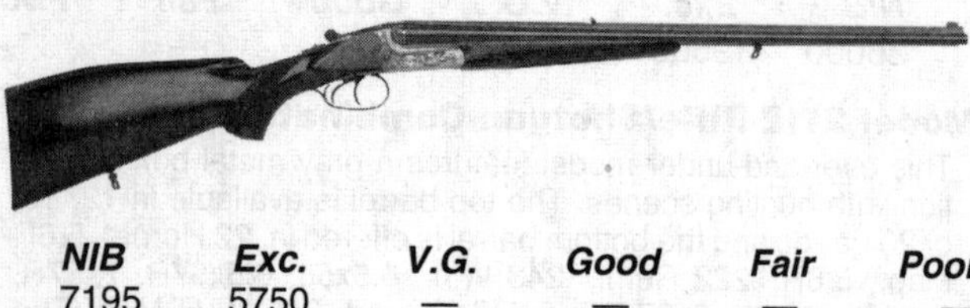

NIB	Exc.	V.G.	Good	Fair	Poor
7195	5750	—	—	—	—

Model 240-1.1

As above but with hunting scene engraving on grayed receiver.

NIB	Exc.	V.G.	Good	Fair	Poor
8295	6500	—	—	—	—

Model 323E Over-and-Under Double Rifle

Similar to the above model but with finer engraving.

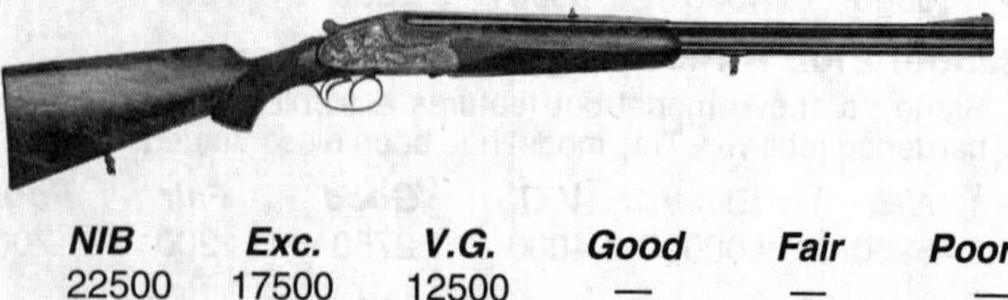

NIB	Exc.	V.G.	Good	Fair	Poor
22500	17500	12500	—	—	—

Model 95K Drilling

This model is a three-barrel shotgun/rifle combination. The top two barrels are chambered for 12, 16, or 20 gauge and the bottom barrel is available in rifle calibers from .22 Hornet to .375 H&H Mag. The action is a boxlock design with scroll engraving on borders and screws. The stock is select grade walnut with raised comb, pistol grip with cap, cheekpiece, and plastic buttplate. Weighs about 7.7 lbs. This model has been discontinued.

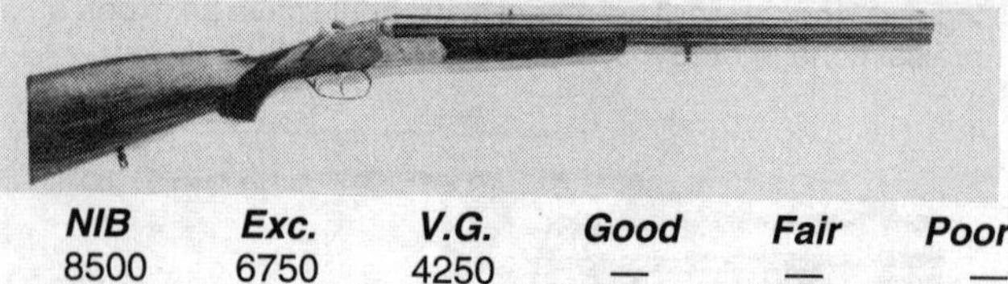

NIB	Exc.	V.G.	Good	Fair	Poor
8500	6750	4250	—	—	—

Model 96K

Similar to the above model but with scroll engraving on a case hardened frame.

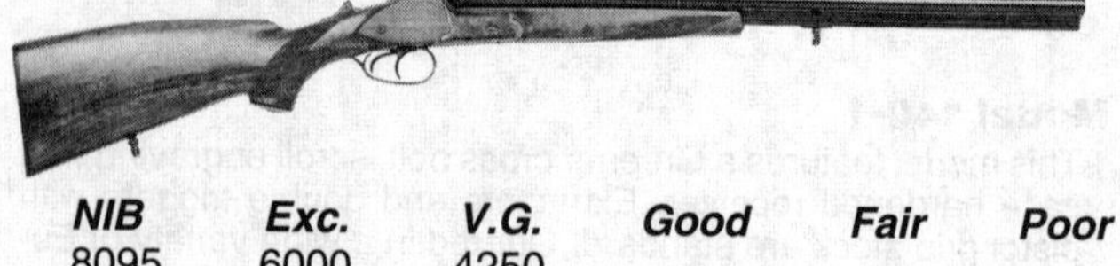

NIB	Exc.	V.G.	Good	Fair	Poor
8095	6000	4250	—	—	—

Model 96K—Engraved

Same as above but with finely engraved hunting scenes with arabesque engraving on a silver grayed receiver.

NIB	Exc.	V.G.	Good	Fair	Poor
9295	6900	4750	—	—	—

K-SERIES STALKING RIFLES

Model K-1 Jagd

Introduced in 2003 this single-shot break-open rifle is chambered for the .243, 270, 7x57R, .308 Win., .30-06, 7mm Rem. Mag., .300 Win. Mag., and the 9.3x74R cartridge. Fitted with a 23.6" barrel. Hunting scene engraving. Weight is about 5.4 lbs.

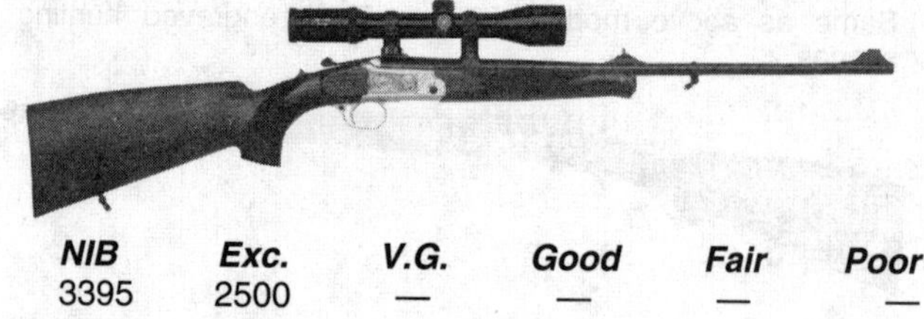

NIB	Exc.	V.G.	Good	Fair	Poor
3395	2500	—	—	—	—

BOLT ACTION RIFLES

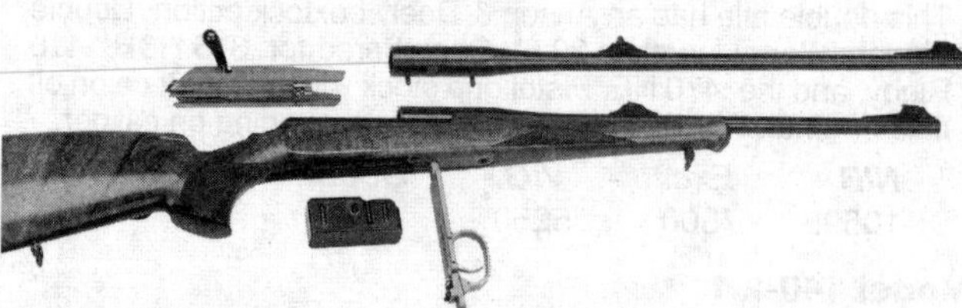

KR-1 Premium

A short stroke bolt action rifle chambered for .243, .308 or .30-06 and 7mm Rem. mag., and .300 Win. mag. calibers. Barrel length for standard calibers is 20" or 22", and for magnum calibers 22" or 24". Checkered walnut stock with hog-back comb. Magazine capacity is 3 rounds. Single set trigger. Interchangeable barrels. Arabesque engraving on bolt housing and trigger plate. Select walnut stock with Bavarian cheekpiece. Weight is about 6.4 lbs. depending on caliber and barrel length. Introduced in 2005.

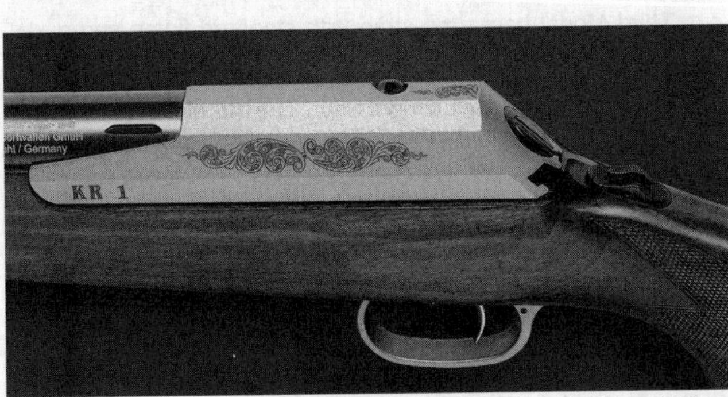

NIB	Exc.	V.G.	Good	Fair	Poor
3195	—	—	—	—	—

NOTE: Add $200 for magnum calibers.

KR-1 Weimar

As above but with rounded bolt housing with hand chiselled engraving with game scenes. Trigger and lock bolt head are gold titanium nitride plated. Select walnut stock with rosewood forearm tip and Bavarian double fold cheekpiece. Introduced in 2005.

NIB	Exc.	V.G.	Good	Fair	Poor
9995	—	—	—	—	—

NOTE: Add $200 for magnum calibers.

MERRILL
Fullerton, California

Sportsman

A single-shot pistol manufactured in a variety of calibers with either a 9" or 12" octagonal barrel having a wide ventilated rib, adjustable sights, and integral telescope mounts. Blued with walnut grips.

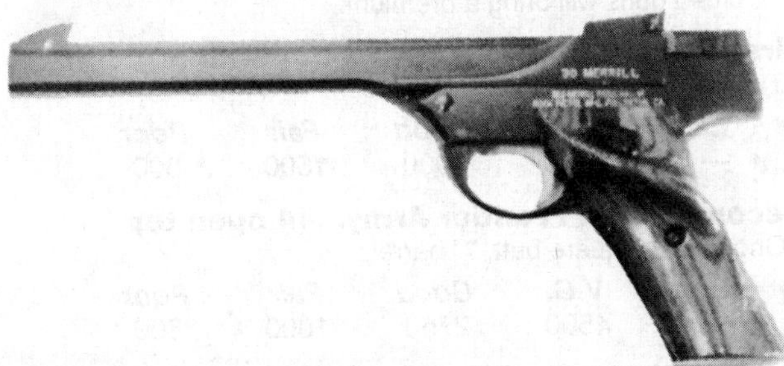

Exc.	V.G.	Good	Fair	Poor
300	275	225	175	125

NOTE: Interchangeable barrels add $75. Wrist support add $25.

MERRILL, JAMES H.
Baltimore, Maryland

Merrill Rifle

A single-shot breechloading rifle that is chambered for .54 caliber and utilizes the percussion ignition system. The breech opens for loading by lifting and pulling back on a lever. The barrel is 33" in length, and there is a full-length walnut stock held on by two barrel bands. The mountings and patch box are brass; and the lock is case colored, with a browned barrel. The lock is marked "J.H. Merrill Balto./Pat. July 1858." There are military acceptance marks on the stock. There were approximately 775 of these rifles manufactured and purchased by the government for use during the Civil War. They were made in 1864 and 1865.

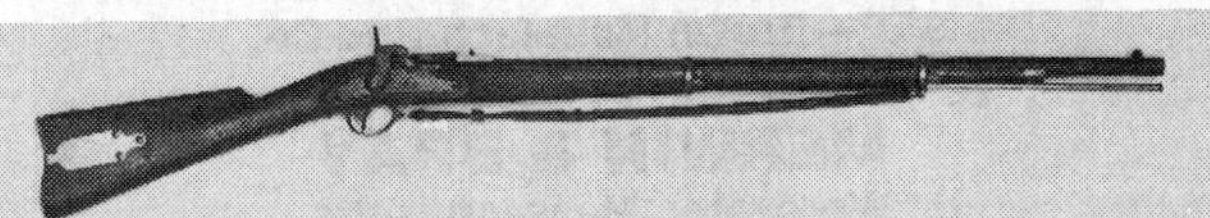

Courtesy Milwaukee Public Museum, Milwaukee, Wisconsin

Exc.	V.G.	Good	Fair	Poor
—	—	5250	2250	750

Merrill Carbine

Similar in appearance to the rifle except that the barrel length is 22" and the stock is only half-length with one barrel band. There are some variations that are quite subtle in appearance but which have a considerable effect on values. We recommend that an independent appraisal be secured. The values given are for the standard 1st and 2nd Types. There were approximately 15,000 total manufactured, and most were used in the Civil War.

1st Type

No eagle stamped on the lock, and the breech lever is flat.

Courtesy Milwaukee Public Museum, Milwaukee, Wisconsin

Exc.	V.G.	Good	Fair	Poor
—	—	3750	1500	500

2nd Type

An eagle stamped on the lock, and the stock has no patch box. The breech lever has a round tip.

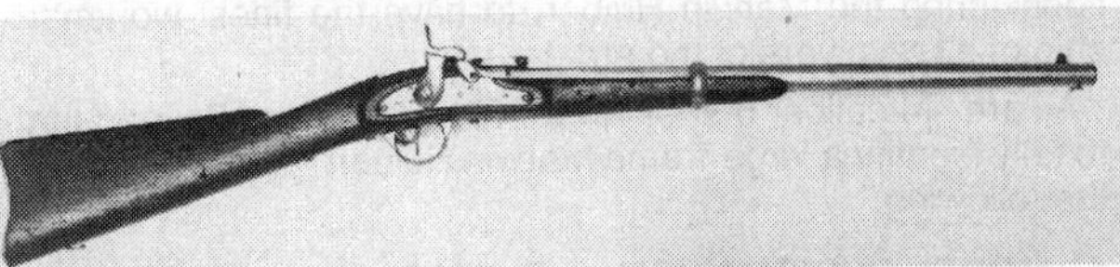

Courtesy Milwaukee Public Museum, Milwaukee, Wisconsin

Exc.	V.G.	Good	Fair	Poor
—	—	4250	1750	700

MERRILL, LATROBE & THOMAS

S. Remington—Maker
Ilion, New York

Carbine

A .58 caliber breech loading percussion carbine with an overall length of 38" and barrel length of 21". The lock marked "S. Remington/ Ilion, N.Y." and the barrel "Merrill, Latrobe & Thomas/Baltimore, Md./Patent Applied For." Approximately 170 were made in 1855.

Exc.	*V.G.*	*Good*	*Fair*	*Poor*
—	—	35000	12500	—

MERRIMACK ARMS

SEE—Brown Manufacturing Co.

MERWIN & BRAY

Worcester, Massachusetts

This company marketed a number of firearms produced by various manufacturers under their own name.

Merwin & Bray Pocket Pistol

A .32 caliber spur trigger single-shot pistol with a 3.5" barrel. Blued, silver-plated with walnut grips. The barrel marked "Merwin & Bray New York."

Exc.	*V.G.*	*Good*	*Fair*	*Poor*
—	—	300	150	75

MERWIN HULBERT & CO.

New York, New York

By Jim Supica, Pres., Old Town Station, Ltd.

Merwin Hulbert & Co., New York City. Founder Joseph Merwin had previously been involved in Merwin & Bray. Merwin Hulbert & Co. or its principals were also involved in Phoenix Rifle, Evans Rifle Company, American Cartridge Company, and Hopkins & Allen of Norwich, CT. Most Merwin Hulbert revolvers will be marked with the Hopkins & Allen name, in addition to Merwin Hulbert. They were made for a fairly brief period, with most production apparently taking place during the 1870s & early 1880s.

There has been some confusion over a classification system for MH revolvers. The system adopted here is based on the distinctions listed in Art Phelps' book, *The Story of Merwin Hulbert & Co. Firearms*. We believe this is the first time the Phelps system has been adapted to a list format.

LARGE-FRAME MERWIN HULBERT SIXGUNS

There has been a marked increase in interest in Merwin Hulbert & Co. over the past decade, with many coming to recognize them as one of the pre-eminent makers of large-frame revolvers used in the American West. Total production of large-frame revolvers has been estimated at a few thousand by some sources. However, the frequency with which they are encountered suggests possibly greater production.

MH used a unique system of opening, loading & unloading their revolvers which was supposed to allow selective ejection of spent shells, leaving remaining cartridges in place. A latch on the bottom of the frame is pushed toward the rear of the gun, and the barrel and cylinder are rotated to the right (clockwise, as viewed from the rear of the revolver) 90 degrees. The barrel and cylinder are then pulled forward, far enough to allow empty brass to fall free. This system required exceptional quality machining, and some modern authorities are on record as considering the Merwin Hulbert to have the finest workmanship of all revolvers of the era.

All are .44 caliber 6-shot large-frame revolvers. Beyond that, to fully identify a large-frame Merwin Hulbert, you must specify the following:

1. **MODEL DESIGNATION** — First Model has an open top and scoop flutes, round barrel, and two small screws above the trigger guard. Second Model is similar to the first, except with only one screw above the trigger guard. Third Model has a top-strap with standard flutes and a round barrel. Fourth Model is similar to the third, except that it has a ribbed barrel. The open-top 1st and 2nd Models seem to be more sought after. The 4th Model is rare, and will bring a premium from a serious Merwin collector.
2. **FRONTIER ARMY or POCKET ARMY** — Frontier Army models have a square butt, and were made in 1st through 4th models. Pocket Army models have a bird's-head butt with a pointed extension with lanyard hole, and are found in 2nd or 3rd Model configuration. Generally, the Frontier Army will bring more than the Pocket Army.
3. **SINGLE-ACTION or DOUBLE-ACTION** — The topstrap models, 3rd and 4th, were manufactured in both single-action and double-action. The single-action models tend to bring more.
4. **BARREL LENGTH** — Standard barrel length on the Frontier Army 1st, 2nd, & 3rd Models is 7", with a 5-1/2" barrel common on the 4th Model. Standard barrel length on the Pocket Army was a more "pocket-sized" 3-1/2". However, somewhat ironically, bird's-head butt models marked "Pocket Army" were also produced with full length 7" barrels. Generally, these longer barrels will bring a bit more than the shorter ones.
5. **CALIBER** — Most common is .44-40 (designated "Winchester Calibre 1873"). Merwins were also chambered for .44 Merwin Hulbert (somewhat similar to the S&W .44 American cartridge), and .44 Russian. The less common calibers may bring a small premium from serious Merwin collectors.
6. **FOREIGN COPIES** — The Merwin Hulbert design was relatively widely copied during the period of use, particularly in Spain. It seems that much of this production may have gone to Mexico, and some found their way to the U.S. Although these Spanish copies may bear markings such as "System Merwin Hulbert" or other usage of the words "Merwin Hulbert," they generally will not be found with the Hopkins & Allen marking. Spanish firms making Merwin copies included Orbea Hermanos and Anitua y Charola. These Spanish copies may bring half or less of what an original Merwin will bring, and it can sometimes take a fairly experienced eye to tell the difference.
7. **ENGRAVING** — Special order engraving was available, and it was usually executed in a distinctive and colorful "punch dot" style, which has come to be associated with Merwins (although it is occasionally encountered on other makes of firearms). For a long time, this style was somewhat dismissed as a bit crude and lacking in artistry. However, a new appreciation of Merwin engraving has emerged, and factory engraved pieces will bring a significant premium. Often, a panel scene depicts an animal, object, or landmark. These panel scenes have an almost "folk art" quality to them, and will enhance the value further. Engraved Merwins are sometimes encountered with the engraving filled with colored enamel, quite rare, and, if original, this will bring a further premium.
8. **FINISH** — The vast majority were nickel plated. Original blued guns will bring a premium.

First Model Frontier Army, .44 open top

Two screws, square butt, 7" barrel.

Exc.	*V.G.*	*Good*	*Fair*	*Poor*
—	5500	3000	1500	500

Second Model Frontier Army, .44 open top

One screw, square butt, 7" barrel.

Exc.	*V.G.*	*Good*	*Fair*	*Poor*
—	4500	2750	1000	500

Second Model Pocket Army, .44 open top

Bird's-head butt. 3-1/2" barrel standard, 7" will bring a premium.

Exc.	*V.G.*	*Good*	*Fair*	*Poor*
—	3500	2000	700	400

 *This symbol denotes "Sleepers" with rapidly-rising values and/or significant collector potential.*

Top: Open Top Pocket Army. Bottom: Topstrap Double-Action Pocket Army Courtesy Supica's Old Town Station

Third Model Frontier Army, Single-Action, .44, topstrap

Square butt, 7" barrel.

Exc.	V.G.	Good	Fair	Poor
—	3750	2250	800	450

Third Model Frontier Army, Double-Action, .44, topstrap

Square butt, 7" barrel.

Exc.	V.G.	Good	Fair	Poor
—	3250	1750	700	400

Third Model Pocket Army, Single-Action, .44 topstrap

Bird's-head butt. 3-1/2" barrel standard, 7" will bring a premium.

Exc.	V.G.	Good	Fair	Poor
—	3250	1750	700	400

Third Model Pocket Army, Double-Action, .44, topstrap

Bird's-head butt. 3-1/2" barrel standard, 7" will bring a premium.

Exc.	V.G.	Good	Fair	Poor
—	3000	1600	650	400

An Exhibition Grade Merwin Hulbert Single Action Army sold at auction for $30,937.50. Fitted with a 7" barrel and chambered for the .44 caliber cartridge. Nickel plated finish with gold plated cylinder. Ivory grips. Condition is 99 percent plating.

Greg Martin Auctions

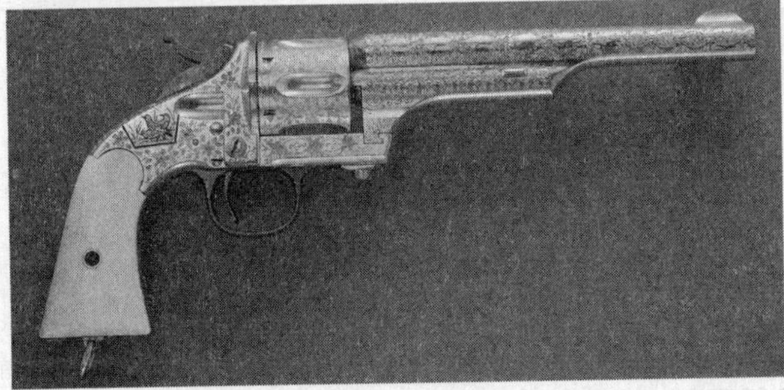

Fourth Model Frontier Army, Single-Action, .44, topstrap

Ribbed barrel, scarce. 5-1/2" barrel seems to be most common, also offered in 7" and 3-1/2".

Exc.	V.G.	Good	Fair	Poor
—	5000	2750	800	550

Fourth Model Frontier Army, Double-Action, .44, topstrap

Ribbed barrel. Barrel lengths as above.

Exc.	V.G.	Good	Fair	Poor
—	4750	2500	750	550

SMALL FRAME MERWIN HULBERT POCKET REVOLVERS

Top: Single-Action Pocket Revolver. Bottom: Double-Action Pocket Revolver Courtesy Supica's Old Town Station

The .32 & .38 centerfire revolvers were manufactured with the unique Merwin Hulbert twist-open system, like the large frame revolvers. They were often advertised as chambered for the .32 MH & Co. or .38 MH & Co. cartridges, but it appears as if these cartridges may have been essentially the same as the .32 S&W and .38 S&W rounds. Of course, the Merwin Hulbert revolvers were manufactured for the original lower pressure black-powder loadings of these cartridges. Saw-handled grip frames were standard, although some were manufactured with the distinctive Pocket Army type pointed "skullcrusher" bird's-head grip frames, and these will generally bring a premium. Most common barrel length for most models is 3-1/2", with 5-1/2" barrels somewhat scarcer in most models, and 2-3/4" barrels quite scarce and worth a premium. A number of police departments purchased small frame Merwin Hulbert revolvers in the late 19th century. Department marked guns will bring a premium.

Terminology alert—note that the .44 caliber "Pocket Army" model is a large-frame, and is listed in the section above.

The .22 Merwin Hulbert revolver is the only one not to use the MH twist-open system. It is, instead, a tip-up revolver closely resembling the S&W Model One.

First Pocket Model Single-Action

Spur-trigger, cylinder pin exposed at front of frame, round loading aperture in recoil shield (no loading gate), five-shot .38, scarce.

Exc.	V.G.	Good	Fair	Poor
—	1250	800	300	175

Second Pocket Model Single-Action

Spur-trigger, cylinder pin exposed, sliding loading gate, five-shot .38.

Exc.	V.G.	Good	Fair	Poor
—	1000	650	285	150

Third Pocket Model Single-Action Spur-Trigger

Enclosed cylinder pin, sliding loading gate, five-shot .38.

Exc.	V.G.	Good	Fair	Poor
—	950	600	225	125

Third Pocket Model Single-Action w/Trigger Guard

Five-shot .38.

Exc.	V.G.	Good	Fair	Poor
—	1000	675	285	150

Double-Action Pocket Model, medium frame

Usually .38 five shot. Scarce .32 seven shot will bring a 25 percent to 50 percent premium. Patent marked folding hammer spur will bring a small premium.

Exc.	V.G.	Good	Fair	Poor
—	900	900	225	150

Double-Action Pocket Model, small frame

.32 cal. five shot. Patent marked folding hammer spur will bring a small premium.

Exc.	V.G.	Good	Fair	Poor
—	800	550	185	125

Tip-up .22 Spur-Trigger

.22 rimfire, a S&W patent infringement, looks similar to S&W Mod. One Third Issue. Scarce. "Made by Merwin Hulbert & Co. for Smith & Wesson" marking will bring a small premium.

Exc.	V.G.	Good	Fair	Poor
—	1000	650	275	175

Merwin Hulbert Rifles

Very similar in design to Hopkins & Allen single-shot breech loaders. Advertised in .22 and .32 rimfire, as well as .32 WCF, .38 WCF, and .44 WCF. May have been offered in .32-40 and .38-55 chamberings. A 20 ga. shotgun barrel was offered separately for these rifles. Features included set trigger, rebounding hammer, pistol grip stock, & takedown. Seldom encountered, the Merwin Hulbert name on these should bring a premium over standard Hopkins & Allen single-shot rifles. A small frame "Merwin Hulbert & Co's. Junior" rifle was also offered, chambered for .22 rimfire.

METROPOLITAN ARMS CO.

New York, New York

Established in February 1864, this company manufactured copies of the Colt Model 1851 and 1861 Navy Revolvers, as well as copies of the Colt Model 1862 Police Revolver. Two of the firm's principle officers were Samuel and William Syms (formerly of Blunt & Syms) and it is believed that they were responsible for production. Curiously, although most Metropolitan pistols were produced during the 1864 to 1866 period, the company itself was not dissolved until 1920.

1851 Navy Revolver

A .36 caliber percussion revolver with a 7.5" octagonal barrel and 6-shot cylinder. Blued, case hardened with walnut grips. The barrel marked "Metropolitan Arms Co. New York." Approximately 6,000 of these revolvers were made during the 1860s. Those bearing H.E. Dimick markings are worth considerably more than the standard marked examples.

Standard Navy Model

Exc.	V.G.	Good	Fair	Poor
—	—	3750	1250	500

H.E. Dimick Navy Model

Exc.	V.G.	Good	Fair	Poor
—	—	7250	2750	850

1861 Navy Revolver

A .36 caliber percussion revolver with a 7.5" round barrel and 6-shot cylinder. The loading lever of the rack-and-pinion type. Blued, case hardened with walnut grips. The barrel marked "Metropolitan Arms Co. New York." Approximately 50 were made in 1864 and 1865.

Exc.	V.G.	Good	Fair	Poor
—	—	7250	3000	950

Police Revolver

A .36 caliber percussion revolver with either 4.5", 5.5" or 6.5" round barrels and a fluted 5-shot cylinder. Blued, case hardened with walnut grips. The barrel normally marked "Metropolitan Arms Co. New York," although examples have been noted without any markings. Approximately 2,750 were made between 1864 and 1866.

Exc.	V.G.	Good	Fair	Poor
—	—	1500	600	250

MIIDA

Japan

Marubeni America Corp.

Model 612

A 12 gauge boxlock over-and-under shotgun with 26" or 28" ventilated rib barrels, single-selective trigger and automatic ejectors. Blued with a walnut stock. Imported between 1972 and 1974.

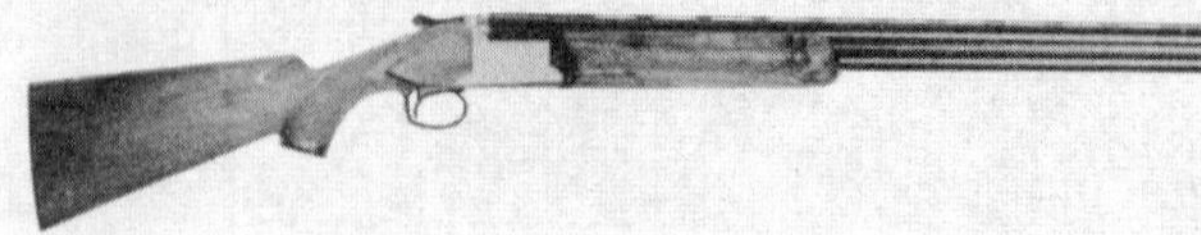

Exc.	V.G.	Good	Fair	Poor
900	750	600	400	250

Model 612 Skeet

As above, with 27" Skeet choked barrels and some engraving. Imported between 1972 and 1974.

Exc.	V.G.	Good	Fair	Poor
900	750	600	400	250

Model 2100 Skeet

Similar to the Model 612 but with more engraving coverage.

Exc.	V.G.	Good	Fair	Poor
950	800	650	450	300

Model 2200 Trap or Skeet

As above, with either 30" trap or 27" skeet bored barrels and more finely engraved. Imported between 1972 and 1974.

Exc.	V.G.	Good	Fair	Poor
1100	850	700	450	300

Model 2300 Trap or Skeet

A more finely finished Model 2200. Imported from 1972 until 1974.

Exc.	V.G.	Good	Fair	Poor
1200	900	750	500	300

Model GRT Trap or GRS Skeet

A 12 gauge boxlock shotgun fitted with false sideplates, 27" skeet or 29" Full choked barrels, single-selective trigger and automatic ejector. Imported between 1972 and 1974.

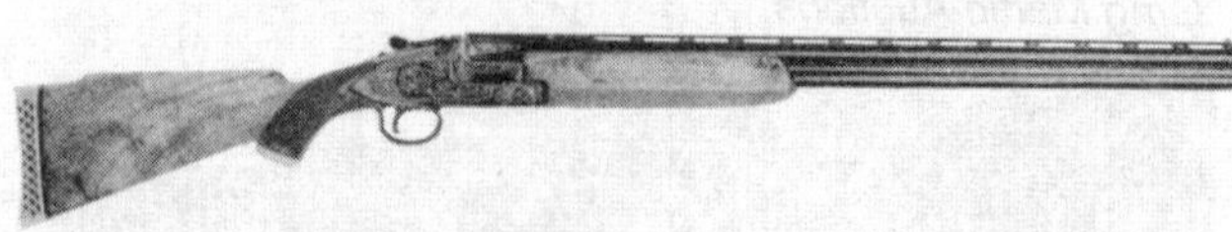

Exc.	V.G.	Good	Fair	Poor
2250	1850	1250	800	500

MILLER ARMS

Sturgis, South Dakota

NOTE: There are a large number of extra costs options avialable for these rifles. Consult the company or an expert prior to a sale.

Standard Rifle

This is single shot falling block rifle. Fitted with a 26" round barrel chambered for centerfire cartridges up to .375 caliber. Stock is checkered XXX walnut with pistol grip. Quarter rib scope base. Weight depends on caliber.

NIB	Exc.	V.G.	Good	Fair	Poor
4500	3500	—	—	—	—

Low Boy

This model features a 24" half round/half octagon barrel. All other features as above.

NIB	Exc.	V.G.	Good	Fair	Poor
5000	4000	—	—	—	—

Model F

This model is similar to the standard rifle with the addition of a 26" octagon barrel with tang sight and globe front sight. All calibers to .45-110.

NIB	Exc.	V.G.	Good	Fair	Poor
6000	4750	—	—	—	—

MILTECH

Los Altos, California

This company has been in business for 19 years and rebuilds and refinishes selected military firearms. All firearms are thoroughly inspected for safety and are considered safe to shoot. All firearms have their original receivers and markings. These rifles are not stamped with the Miltech name but do have a unique Miltech pine crate serial numbered to the gun as standard. The company will verify that it did the rebuild if asked. All guns come with manual, sling, and other selected accessories depending on model.

German Mauser Model 98k

NIB	Exc.	V.G.	Good	Fair	Poor
1025	—	—	—	—	—

M1 Garand

NIB	Exc.	V.G.	Good	Fair	Poor
1475	—	—	—	—	—

NOTE: For International Harvester and Winchester add $125.

M1D Garand

NIB	Exc.	V.G.	Good	Fair	Poor
2495	—	—	—	—	—

M1 Carbine

NIB	Exc.	V.G.	Good	Fair	Poor
1025	—	—	—	—	—

NOTE: For Rockola and Winchester add $100.

Model 1941 Johnson

NIB	Exc.	V.G.	Good	Fair	Poor
3000+	—	—	—	—	—

Model 1903 Springfield

NIB	Exc.	V.G.	Good	Fair	Poor
1095	—	—	—	—	—

Model 1903A3 Springfield

NIB	Exc.	V.G.	Good	Fair	Poor
1025	—	—	—	—	—

Model 1903 Mark I Springfield

NIB	Exc.	V.G.	Good	Fair	Poor
1195	—	—	—	—	—

Model 1917 U.S. Enfield

NIB	Exc.	V.G.	Good	Fair	Poor
1025	—	—	—	—	—

MINNEAPOLIS F. A. CO.

Minneapolis, Minnesota

Palm Pistol

A .32 caliber radial cylinder pistol with a 1.75" barrel manufactured by the Ames Manufacturing Company (see the Ames entry). Nickel-plated with hard rubber grips. The sideplates marked "Minneapolis Firearms Co." and "The Protector." Several thousand were sold during the 1890s.

Exc.	V.G.	Good	Fair	Poor
—	2250	850	350	100

MIROKU B. C.

Miroku, Japan

Firearms produced by this manufacturer have been imported and marketed by a variety of companies such as Charles Daly, Browning, Winchester, and SKB.

MITCHELL ARMS, INC.

Santa Ana, California

An importer and distributor of foreign-made firearms, this company is no longer in business. However, some Mitchell models were available under Brolin Arms through 1998. Brolin Arms was no longer in business as of 1999.

This company also imported Yugoslavian-manufactured semi-automatic AK-47 rifles in 7.62x39mm, as well as 7.62x54mm.

M-16

A .22 rimfire copy of the Colt AR-15. Introduced in 1987.

NIB	Exc.	V.G.	Good	Fair	Poor
325	250	150	125	100	75

MAS

A .22 or .22 Magnum caliber copy of the French MAS Bullpup Service Rifle. Introduced in 1987.

NIB	Exc.	V.G.	Good	Fair	Poor
400	325	200	150	125	100

Galil

A .22 or .22 Magnum caliber copy of the Galil rifle. Introduced in 1987.

NIB	Exc.	V.G.	Good	Fair	Poor
500	400	300	150	125	100

AK-22

A .22 or .22 Magnum caliber copy of the AK-47 rifle. Introduced in 1985.

NIB	Exc.	V.G.	Good	Fair	Poor
400	300	250	125	100	75

PPSH-30/50

A .22 or .22 Magnum caliber copy of the PPSH Submachine gun.

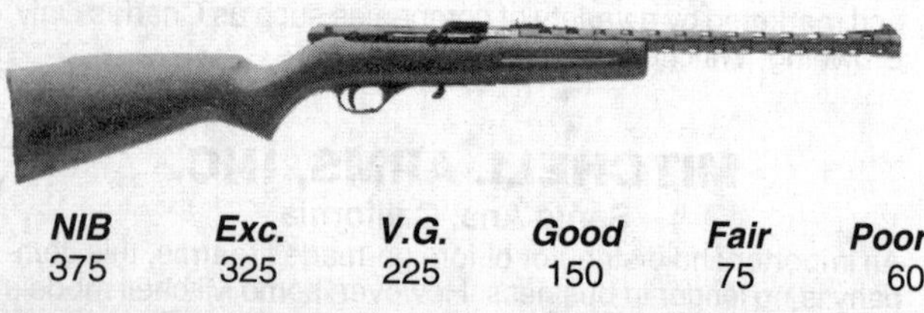

NIB	Exc.	V.G.	Good	Fair	Poor
375	325	225	150	75	60

REMINDER

You don't have to specialize in Colts or Winchesters to have a nice collection. Collecting Marlin or Mossberg .22 semi-autos, for example, can be just as rewarding.

HANDGUNS

Trophy II

A semi-automatic pistol chambered for the .22 LR cartridge. Offered in either 7-1/4" fluted or 5-1/2" bull barrel. Barrels are interchangeable. Trigger is adjustable for weight and pull. Walnut grips with thumb rest are standard.

NIB	Exc.	V.G.	Good	Fair	Poor
400	325	275	200	150	100

Citation II

Similar to the Trophy II but with a matte satin finish.

NIB	Exc.	V.G.	Good	Fair	Poor
375	300	250	200	150	100

Sharpshooter II

This is a stainless steel target pistol with 5-1/2" bull barrel to which barrel weights can be added. Fully adjustable rear sight and checkered walnut grips are standard.

NIB	Exc.	V.G.	Good	Fair	Poor
325	275	225	200	150	100

Olympic I.S.U.

This competition pistol features a 6-3/4" barrel with integral stabilizer. Rear sight is adjustable as is the trigger. Barrel weights are adjustable as well as removable.

NIB	Exc.	V.G.	Good	Fair	Poor
525	475	400	300	200	100

Victor II

This .22 caliber pistol is built from stainless steel and has interchangeable barrels in 4-1/2" or 5-1/2" lengths. Barrels have full length ventilated ribs, checkered walnut grips with thumb rest. Gold plated trigger is adjustable.

NIB	Exc.	V.G.	Good	Fair	Poor
450	375	325	250	175	125

Victor II with Weaver Rib

NIB	Exc.	V.G.	Good	Fair	Poor
525	450	375	275	175	125

High Standard Collectors' Association Special Editions

Limited run of Mitchell's version of the High Standard pistol with special roll marking on the slide "High Standard / Collectors Association / Special Edition" and a special serial number series with a HSCA prefix. Manufactured by Pastucek Industries, Fort Worth, Texas.

Trophy II

5.5" barrel. See standard Mitchell guns for rest of description.

NIB	Exc.
420	325

Victor II

4.5" barrel. See standard Mitchell guns for rest of description.

NIB	Exc.
450	325

Citation II

7.25" barrel. See standard Mitchell guns for rest of description.

NIB	Exc.
400	300

Three Gun Set

Includes Trophy II, Olympic ISU, and Victor II. Eleven sets manufactured.

NIB	Exc.
1400	1100

Six Gun Set

Includes 5.5" Trophy II, 6.75" Olympic II, and 4.5" Victor II, Sharpshooter II, Citation II, and 4.5" Sport King II. Nineteen sets manufactured.

NIB	Exc.
2450	1975

Skorpion

A .32 caliber semi-automatic pistol with a 4.75" barrel and either 20- or 30-shot magazine. Blued with plastic grips. Imported from Yugoslavia in 1987 and 1988 only.

Exc.	V.G.	Good	Fair	Poor
600	500	425	350	175

Spectre

A 9mm caliber semi-automatic pistol with an 8" shrouded barrel and either 30- or 50-shot magazine. Blued with plastic grips. Also produced with an 18" barrel and folding buttstock. Imported from Yugoslavia in 1987 and 1988.

Exc.	V.G.	Good	Fair	Poor
600	500	425	350	175

MITCHELL'S MAUSERS

Fountain Valley, California

Black Arrow

This is a .50 caliber bolt-action rifle with 5-round box magazine. Fitted with a recoil compensator. Iron sights. Bipod.

NIB	Exc.	V.G.	Good	Fair	Poor
6500	5000	—	—	—	—

Centurion Revolver

This is a double-action revolver with either a 4" or 6" barrel. Chambered for the .357 Magnum cartridge. Blued or stainless steel.

NIB	Exc.	V.G.	Good	Fair	Poor
695	550	—	—	—	—

Valkyrie Revolver

This revolver is chambered for the .44 magnum cartridge and has a choice of 4" or 6" barrel. Blued or stainless steel.

NIB	Exc.	V.G.	Good	Fair	Poor
895	700	—	—	—	—

Gold Series '03 Pistol

Chambered for the 9mm, .40 S&W, or .45 ACP cartridge. Built on the model 1911 Government Model. Blued or stainless steel.

NIB	Exc.	V.G.	Good	Fair	Poor
795	600	—	—	—	—

Escalade

This is a slide-action shotgun chambered for the 12 gauge shell. Fitted with a choice of 18.5" barrel, 28" vent rib barrel, or 22" barrel with Turkey choke. Turkish walnut stock. Blued.

NIB	Exc.	V.G.	Good	Fair	Poor
395	325	—	—	—	—

Sabre

This is a semi-automatic 12 gauge shotgun with choice of 22" vent rib barrel or 28" vent rib barrel. Blued.

NIB	Exc.	V.G.	Good	Fair	Poor
495	400	—	—	—	—

Mauser M98 Basic

This bolt-action rifle is fitted with a Mauser 98 action and offered in most standard hunting calibers.

NIB	Exc.	V.G.	Good	Fair	Poor
7900	6000	—	—	—	—

NOTE: For magnum calibers add $2,000.

Mauser M98 Varmint

As above but chambered for .22-250 or .220 Swift.

NIB	Exc.	V.G.	Good	Fair	Poor
8900	7000	—	—	—	—

Mauser M98 African/Alaskan

Chambered for heavy calibers up to .500 Jeffries.

NIB	Exc.	V.G.	Good	Fair	Poor
12000	9000	—	—	—	—

MK ARMS, INC.

Irvine, California

K 760

A 9mm caliber semi-automatic carbine with a 16" shrouded barrel, fixed sights, and 14-, 24- or 36-shot magazine. Parkerized with a folding stock. Introduced in 1983.

NIB	Exc.	V.G.	Good	Fair	Poor
500	450	375	300	250	125

MKE

Ankara, Turkey

Kirrikale

A 7.65 or 9mm short semi-automatic pistol with a 4" barrel and 7-shot magazine. It is an unauthorized copy of the Walther PP. Blued with plastic grips.

NIB	Exc.	V.G.	Good	Fair	Poor
400	350	275	225	150	100

MODESTO SANTOS CIA.

Eibar, Spain

Action, Corrientes, and M.S.

A 6.35mm or 7.65mm caliber semi-automatic pistol of low quality marked on the slide "Pistolet Automatique Model 1920." Blued with composition grips having the monogram "M.S." cast in them. Manufactured between 1920 and 1935.

Exc.	V.G.	Good	Fair	Poor
200	125	100	75	50

MONDRAGON

Mexico City, Mexico

Firearms designed by Manuel Mondragon were produced on an experimental basis first at St. Chamond Arsenal in France and later at SIG in Neuhausen, Switzerland. The latter company was responsible for the manufacture of the two known production models; the Model 1890 and 1908.

The Model 1890 Mondragon semi-automatic rifle holds the distinction of being the first self-loading rifle to be issued to any armed forces.

Courtesy Rock Island Auction Company

Exc.	V.G.	Good	Fair	Poor
6000	4000	2000	1000	750

MONTENEGRAN-GASSER

SEE—Gasser, Leopold

MOORE-ENFIELD

SEE—English Military Firearms

MOORES PATENT FIREARMS CO.

Brooklyn, New York

In 1866 this company became known as the National Arms Company.

No. 1 Derringer

A .41 caliber spur trigger all metal pistol with a 2.5" barrel. Blued or silver-plated. Approximately 10,000 were manufactured between 1860 and 1865. This model was also marketed as the No. 1 Derringer by the Colt Company after they purchased the National Arms Company in 1870.

Courtesy Milwaukee Public Museum, Milwaukee, Wisconsin

1st Variation Marked "Patent Applied For"

Exc.	V.G.	Good	Fair	Poor
—	—	2500	1100	400

2nd Variation Marked "D. Moore Patented Feb. 19 1861"

Exc.	V.G.	Good	Fair	Poor
—	—	1500	700	250

Standard Model Marked "Moore's Pat F.A. Co."

Exc.	V.G.	Good	Fair	Poor
—	—	850	350	150

National Arms Co. Production

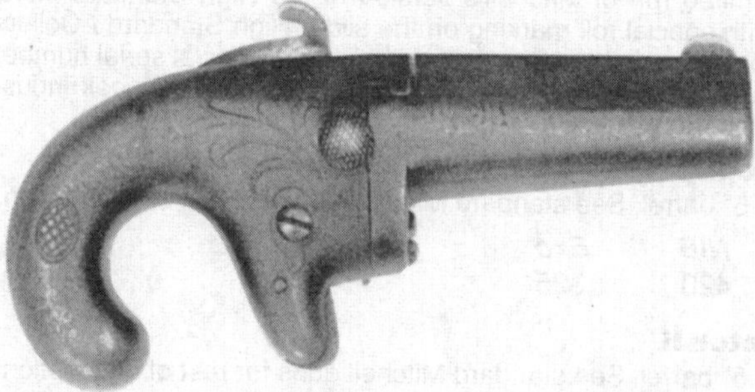

Courtesy Milwaukee Public Museum, Milwaukee, Wisconsin

Exc.	V.G.	Good	Fair	Poor
—	—	800	350	150

Iron Model

Exc.	V.G.	Good	Fair	Poor
—	—	1000	500	250

Pocket Revolver

A .32 teat fire caliber spur trigger revolver with a round 3.25" barrel and 6-shot cylinder. Blued or silver plated with walnut grips. Approximately 30,000 were manufactured between 1864 and 1870.

Exc.	V.G.	Good	Fair	Poor
—	—	500	250	100

Belt Revolver

A .32 rimfire caliber revolver with a 4", 5", or 6" octagonal barrel and 7-shot cylinder. The barrel and cylinder blued, the brass frame sometimes silver-plated with walnut grips. The barrel marked "D. Moore Patent Sept. 18, 1860." Several thousand were manufactured between 1861 and 1863.

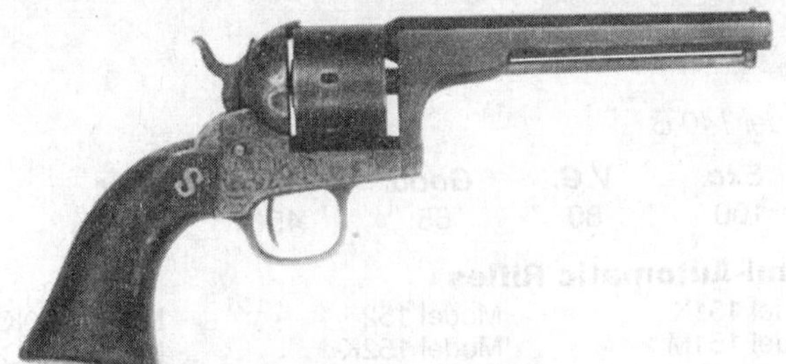

Courtesy Milwaukee Public Museum, Milwaukee, Wisconsin

Belt Revolver and holster belonging to Capt. Henry Kellogg, Illinois 33rd during American Civil War Courtesy Rudolph R. Massenzi

Exc.	V.G.	Good	Fair	Poor
—	—	950	350	150

MORGAN & CLAPP
New Haven, Connecticut

Single-Shot Pocket Pistol
A .22 or .23 caliber spur trigger single-shot pistol with a 3.5" octagonal barrel. Blued, silver-plated frame with walnut grips. The barrel marked "Morgan & Clapp New Haven." Active 1864 to 1867.

Exc.	V.G.	Good	Fair	Poor
—	—	600	250	100

MORINI
Italy

C-80 Standard
A .22 caliber single-shot pistol with a free floating 10" barrel, match sights, adjustable frame, and adjustable grips. Discontinued in 1989.

Exc.	V.G.	Good	Fair	Poor
900	800	675	550	250

CM-80 Super Competition
As above, with a trigger adjustable from 5 to 120 grams pressure, Plexiglass front sight and a polished finish. Discontinued in 1989.

Exc.	V.G.	Good	Fair	Poor
1000	900	750	650	300

Model 84E Free Pistol
Introduced in 1995 this competition pistol features an 11.4" barrel chambered for the .22 LR. It is a single-shot. Adjustable sights with adjustable electronic trigger. Weight is about 44 oz.

NIB	Exc.	V.G.	Good	Fair	Poor
1450	1150	900	700	500	—

MORRONE
Hope Valley, Rhode Island
SEE—Rhode Island Arms Company

MORSE
Greenville, South Carolina
State Armory

Morse Carbine
Overall length 40"; barrel length 2"; caliber .50 (other calibers are known to have been made on an experimental basis). The round barrel is blued, the frame is of brass and the stock is of either walnut or beechwood. Approximately 1,000 were manufactured during the Civil War.

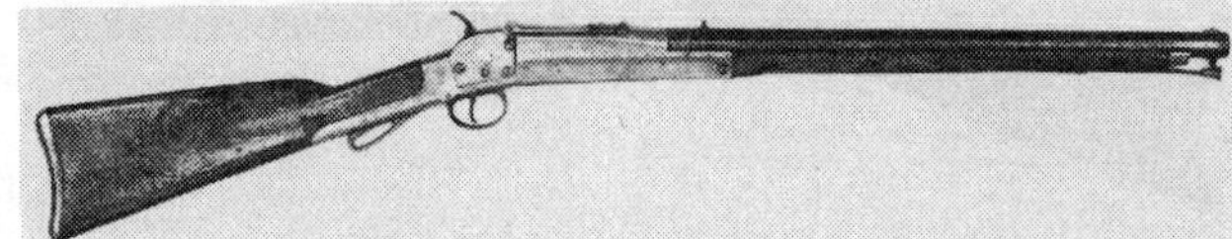

Courtesy Milwaukee Public Museum, Milwaukee, Wisconsin

Courtesy Milwaukee Public Museum, Milwaukee, Wisconsin

Exc.	V.G.	Good	Fair	Poor
—	—	20000	7500	1500

MOSIN-NAGANT
Russia

NOTE: For history, technical data, descriptions, and prices see the *Standard Catalog of Military Firearms.*

MOSSBERG, O. F. & SONS, INC.
North Haven, Connecticut

Founded by Oscar F. Mossberg in 1892 at Fitchburg, Massachusetts, this company for a time was located at Chicopee Falls, Massachusetts, and since 1919 has been in North Haven, Connecticut. It is the oldest family-owned firearms manufacturer in America.

Brownie
A .22 caliber four-barreled pocket pistol with a revolving firing pin. This pistol resembles a semi-automatic. Manufactured from 1906 to approximately 1940.

Exc.	V.G.	Good	Fair	Poor
450	325	300	225	150

RIFLES

Model K Rifle

A .22 caliber slide-action rifle with a 22" barrel, tubular magazine, internal hammer and takedown system. Blued with a walnut stock. Discontinued in 1931.

Exc.	V.G.	Good	Fair	Poor
175	150	125	75	50

Model M Rifle

As above, with a 24" octagonal barrel. Manufactured from 1928 and 1931.

Exc.	V.G.	Good	Fair	Poor
175	150	125	75	50

Model L Rifle

A .22 caliber Martini-style single-shot takedown rifle with a 24" barrel. Manufactured from 1927 to 1932.

Exc.	V.G.	Good	Fair	Poor
450	325	250	175	100

Beginning in 1930, the Mossberg company manufactured a variety of utilitarian single-shot and repeating bolt-action rifles. Later they introduced a similar line of semi-automatic rifles. As these arms were intended for extensive use and were low-priced, the values for them may be categorized as listed.

Bolt-Action Rifles

Model 10	Model 25	Model 340M
Model 14	Model 25A	Model 341
Model 140B	Model 26B	Model 342K
Model 140K	Model 26C	Model 346B
Model 142A	Model 30	Model 346K
Model 142K	Model 320B	Model 352K
Model 144	Model 320K	Model 450
Model 144LS	Model 321K	Model 432
Model 146B	Model 340B	Model 50
Model 20	Model 340K	Model 51
		Model 51M

Model 140 B

Exc.	V.G.	Good	Fair	Poor
100	80	65	45	20

Semi-Automatic Rifles

Model 151K	Model 152	Model 350K
Model 151M	Model 152K	Model 351C
	Model 351K	

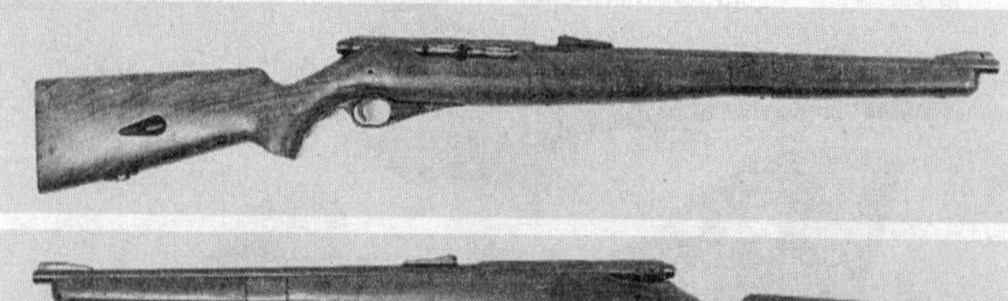

Exc.	V.G.	Good	Fair	Poor
125	100	80	60	40

Model 400 Palomino

A .22 caliber lever-action rifle with a 22" barrel, open sights and tubular magazine. Also made with an 18.5" barrel. Blued with a walnut stock. Manufactured from 1959 to 1964.

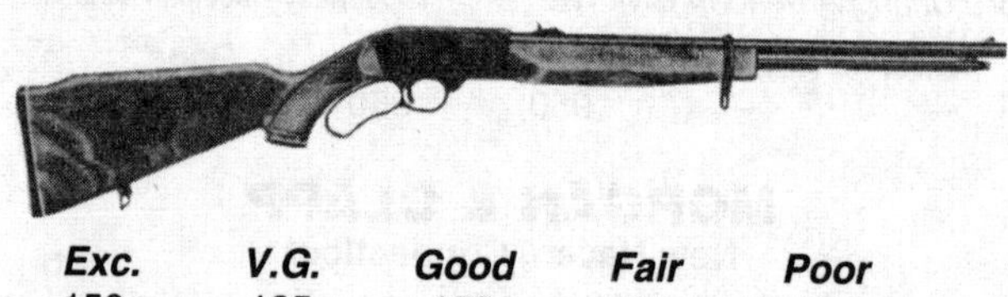

Exc.	V.G.	Good	Fair	Poor
150	125	100	75	50

Model 702 Plinkster

Introduced in 2004 this 22 caliber semi-automatic rifle is fitted with a 18" barrel with adjustable sights. Detachable 10-round magazine. Blued finish and choice of black synthetic stock or Mossy Oak Break-Up camo pattern. Weight is about 4 lbs. Also available as scope package (add 10 percent) and with tiger maple or carbon fiber stock and chromed barrel and receiver.

NIB	Exc.	V.G.	Good	Fair	Poor
130	100	80	—	—	—

Model 702 International Plinkster

This model features a 21" chrome barrel with iron sights. Black synthetic stock. Weight is about 4.5 lbs.

NIB	Exc.	V.G.	Good	Fair	Poor
145	115	—	—	—	—

This symbol denotes "Sleepers" with rapidly-rising values and/or significant collector potential.

Model 100 ATR (All-Terrain Rifle)

Introduced in 2005, this bolt action rifle is chambered for the .270 or .30-06 calibers. Fitted with a 22" barrel with no sights. Choice of black synthetic, synthetic walnut, or camo stock. Matte blue or all-weather finish. Weight is about 7 lbs. .243, 308. Also available as 3X9 scope package (add 10 percent).

NIB	Exc.	V.G.	Good	Fair	Poor
345	275	—	—	—	—

NOTE: Add $40 for all-weather finish.

100 ATR Super Bantam

Similar to Model 100 ATR but chambered only in .243 and .308. No sights. Synthetic black stock adjustable for length of pull. Introduced in 2007.

NIB	Exc.	V.G.	Good	Fair	Poor
300	—	—	—	—	—

Model 800

A bolt-action rifle manufactured in a variety of calibers with a 22" barrel and folding leaf rear sight. Blued with a walnut stock. Introduced in 1967.

Exc.	V.G.	Good	Fair	Poor
225	200	150	100	75

Model 800D

As above, with a comb stock, rosewood forend tip and pistol grip cap. Manufactured from 1970 to 1973.

Exc.	V.G.	Good	Fair	Poor
300	250	200	150	100

Model 800V

As above, with a 24" heavy barrel not fitted with sights. Introduced in 1968.

Exc.	V.G.	Good	Fair	Poor
225	200	150	100	75

Model 800M

As above, with a Mannlicher-style stock.

Exc.	V.G.	Good	Fair	Poor
275	250	200	150	100

Model 800SM

As above, with a 4X scope.

Exc.	V.G.	Good	Fair	Poor
300	275	225	150	100

Model 802 Plinkster Bolt Action

Bolt-action rifle chambered in .22 LR with 18-inch steel barrel and black synthetic stock with schnabel. Also available with 4X scope package (add 10 percent). Introduced 2006.

NIB	Exc.	V.G.	Good	Fair	Poor
150	—	—	—	—	—

817 Plinkster Rifle

Similar to Model 802 Plinkster but chambered in .17 HMR. Introduced in 2007.

NIB	Exc.	V.G.	Good	Fair	Poor
165	—	—	—	—	—

Model 810

A .270 to .338 Winchester Magnum caliber bolt-action rifle with a 22" or 24" barrel fitted with a folding rear sight. Blued with a Monte Carlo-style stock. Introduced in 1970.

Exc.	V.G.	Good	Fair	Poor
275	250	200	150	100

Model 472C

A .30-30 or. 35 Remington Caliber lever-action rifle with a 20" barrel, open sights, and tubular magazine. Blued with a walnut stock. Introduced in 1972.

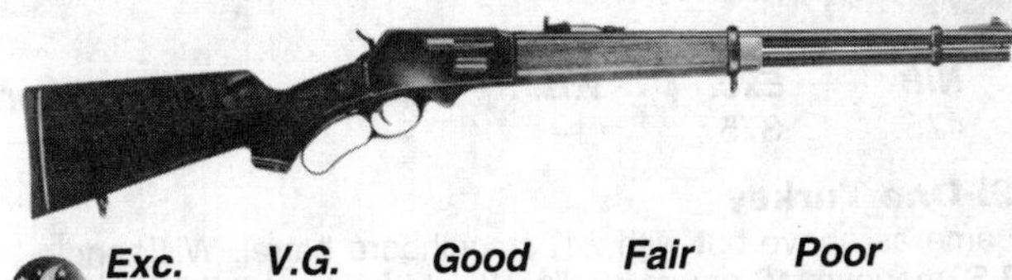

Exc.	V.G.	Good	Fair	Poor
250	195	150	100	75

Model 472P

As above, with a pistol grip stock and not fitted with a saddle ring.

Exc.	V.G.	Good	Fair	Poor
250	195	150	100	75

Model 472 One in Five Thousand

As above, with an etched receiver, brass buttplate, saddle ring and barrel band. A total of 5,000 were made in 1974.

Exc.	V.G.	Good	Fair	Poor
400	350	300	200	150

Model 479 PCA

Similar to the Model 472C in .30-30 caliber with a 20" barrel. Blued with a walnut stock.

Exc.	V.G.	Good	Fair	Poor
250	195	150	100	75

Model 479 RR

As above, with a gold-plated trigger and barrel band as well as "Roy Rogers" signature. A total of 5,000 were made in 1983.

Exc.	V.G.	Good	Fair	Poor
325	250	200	150	100

SSi-One Sporter

Introduced in 2000 this is a single-shot rifle chambered for the .223, .243, 270 Win., .308, and .30-06 cartridges. Fitted with a 24" barrel without sights. Matte blue finish. Checkered walnut stock. Weight is about 8 lbs. Interchangeable barrels including 12 gauge.

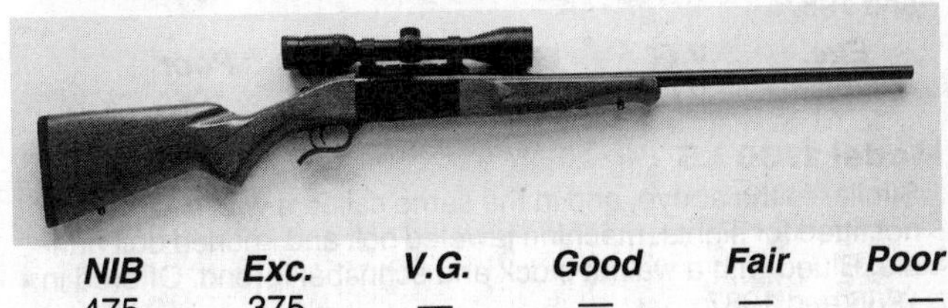

NIB	Exc.	V.G.	Good	Fair	Poor
475	375	—	—	—	—

SSi-One Varmint

Similar to the above model but fitted with a 24" bull barrel chambered for the .22-250 cartridge. Walnut stock. Weight is about 10 lbs. Introduced in 2000. Interchangeable barrels.

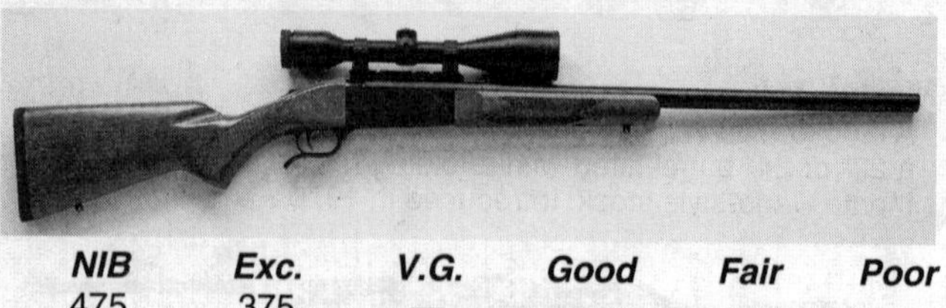

NIB	Exc.	V.G.	Good	Fair	Poor
475	375	—	—	—	—

SSi-One Slug

This model is similar to the other SSi-One guns but is fitted with a 24" fully rifled 12 gauge barrel. Walnut stock. Weight is about 8 lbs. Interchangeable barrels. Introduced in 2000.

NIB	Exc.	V.G.	Good	Fair	Poor
475	375	—	—	—	—

SSi-One Turkey

Same as above but with 24" smoothbore barrel. Will handle 3.5" magnum 12 gauge shells. Weight is about 7.5 lbs. Introduced in 2001.

NIB	Exc.	V.G.	Good	Fair	Poor
475	375	—	—	—	—

MODEL 1500 SERIES

A .223 to .338 Winchester Magnum bolt-action rifle with a 22" or 24" barrel, 5- or 6-shot magazine and various sights. Blued with a hardwood or walnut stock. Manufactured by Howa in Japan and also known as the Smith & Wesson Model 1500. Offered in 1986 and 1987.

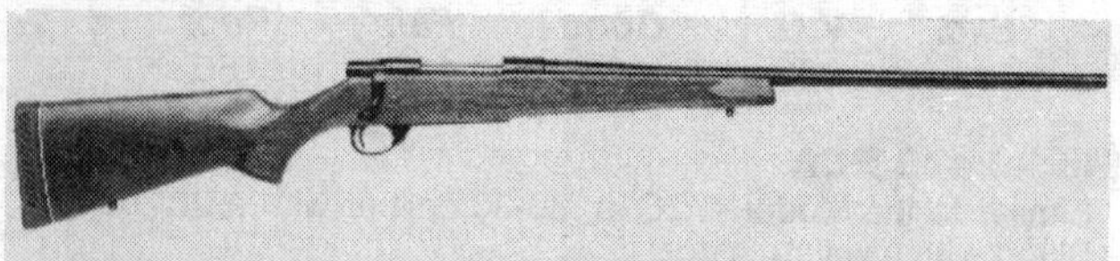

Model 1500 Mountaineer Grade I

Exc.	V.G.	Good	Fair	Poor
350	250	225	150	125

Model 1500 Mountaineer Grade II

Exc.	V.G.	Good	Fair	Poor
325	275	250	175	125

Model 1500 Varmint

24" heavy barrel.

Exc.	V.G.	Good	Fair	Poor
350	300	275	200	150

Model 1550

As above, but in .243, .270 or .30-06 caliber. Offered in 1986 and 1987.

Exc.	V.G.	Good	Fair	Poor
325	275	250	175	125

Model 1700 LS

Similar to the above, and in the same calibers with a 22" barrel not fitted for sights, machine jeweled bolt and knurled bolt handle. Blued with a walnut stock and schnabel forend. Offered in 1986 and 1987.

Exc.	V.G.	Good	Fair	Poor
400	350	275	200	150

4x4 Rifle

Bolt-action centerfire rifle chambered in .25-06, .270, .30-06, 7mm Rem Mag, .300 Win Mag, .338 Win Mag. Barrel length 22" (iron sight) or 24" (sightless). Detachable box magazine, two-position safety. Walnut, laminated or black synthetic stock with lightening cutouts in butt and forend. Scope package also available. Introduced in 2007.

NIB	Exc.	V.G.	Good	Fair	Poor
749	—	—	—	—	—

SHOTGUNS

Mossberg manufactured a variety of shotguns that were sold at low to moderate prices. The values for these arms are approximately all the same.

Bolt-Action Shotguns

Model 173	Model 190D	Model 390K
Model 173Y	Model 190K	Model 390T
Model 183D	Model 195D	Model 395K
Model 183K	Model 195K	Model 395S
Model 183T	Model 385K	Model 395T
Model 185D	Model 385T	Model 73
Model 185K		

Model 190D

Exc.	V.G.	Good	Fair	Poor
90	65	50	40	25

Model 695

Introduced in 1969 this bolt-action shotgun is chambered for the 12 gauge shell. Barrel length is 22" with either a rifled bore or plain bore. Finish is matte blue. In 1997 this model was offered with a 22" plain ported barrel with rifled bore. Magazine capacity is 3 rounds. Weight is about 7.5 lbs.

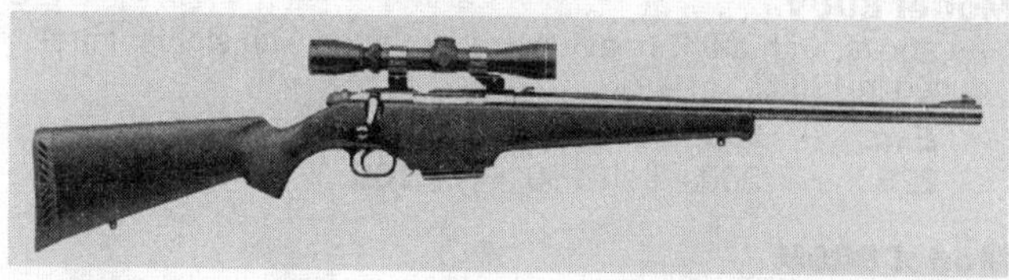

NIB	Exc.	V.G.	Good	Fair	Poor
275	225	175	150	125	100

Model 695 Camo

Introduced in 2000 this model is the same as the standard Model 695 with the addition of Woodlands camo finish.

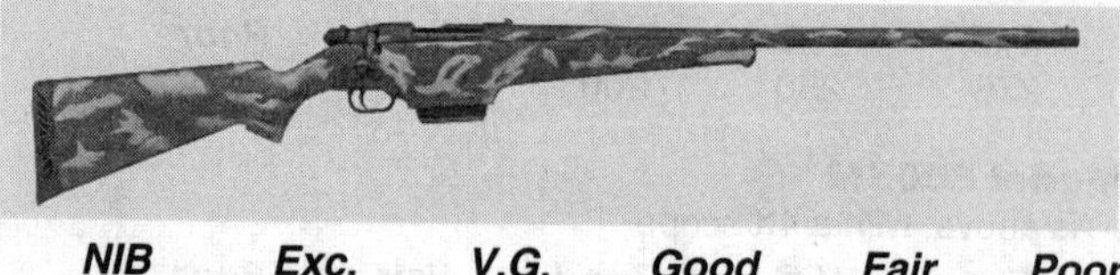

NIB	Exc.	V.G.	Good	Fair	Poor
N/A	—	—	—	—	—

Model 200K

A 12 gauge slide-action shotgun with a 28" barrel and Mossberg select choke. Blued with a composition slide handle and walnut stock. Manufactured from 1955 to 1959.

Exc.	V.G.	Good	Fair	Poor
150	125	100	75	50

This symbol denotes "Sleepers" with rapidly-rising values and/or significant collector potential.

MODEL 500 SERIES

A 12, 20 or .410 bore slide-action shotgun manufactured in a variety of barrel lengths and styles, as listed.

Model 500 Regal

Exc.	V.G.	Good	Fair	Poor
250	200	150	100	75

Model 500 Field Grade

NIB	Exc.	V.G.	Good	Fair	Poor
285	250	200	150	100	75

Model 500 Steel Shot

Chrome bore.

Exc.	V.G.	Good	Fair	Poor
300	250	200	125	100

Model 500 Slugster

Crown grade, iron sights.

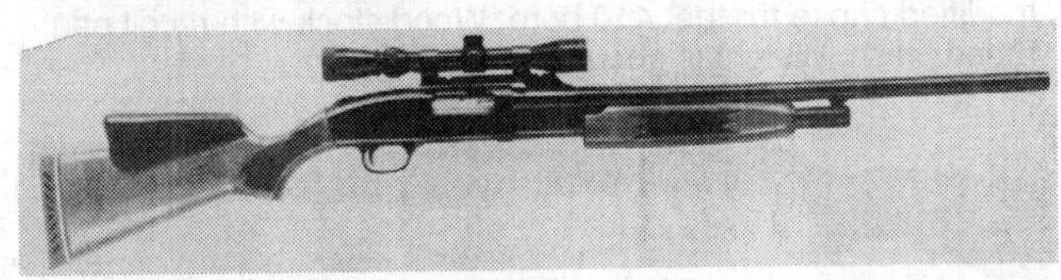

Exc.	V.G.	Good	Fair	Poor
275	250	200	150	100

Model 500 Camper

18.5" barrel, camo case.

Exc.	V.G.	Good	Fair	Poor
295	275	225	175	125

Model 500 Hi-Rib Trap

Exc.	V.G.	Good	Fair	Poor
275	250	200	150	100

Model 500 Super Grade

Exc.	V.G.	Good	Fair	Poor
200	175	150	100	75

Model 500 Pigeon Grade

Exc.	V.G.	Good	Fair	Poor
375	300	250	200	125

Model 500 Pigeon Grade Trap

Exc.	V.G.	Good	Fair	Poor
450	375	300	250	175

Model 500 Persuader

Riot gun, 18.5" barrel.

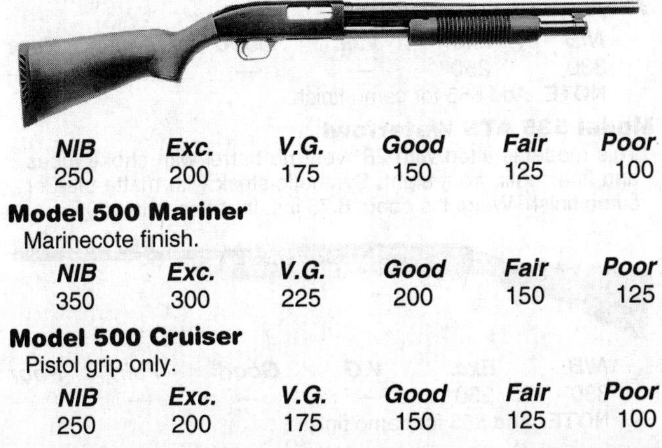

NIB	Exc.	V.G.	Good	Fair	Poor
250	200	175	150	125	100

Model 500 Mariner

Marinecote finish.

NIB	Exc.	V.G.	Good	Fair	Poor
350	300	225	200	150	125

Model 500 Cruiser

Pistol grip only.

NIB	Exc.	V.G.	Good	Fair	Poor
250	200	175	150	125	100

Model 500 Muzzleloader Combo

NIB	Exc.	V.G.	Good	Fair	Poor
350	325	275	225	200	150

Model 500 Bantam

Introduced in 1996 this model is slightly smaller overall than the full-size guns. Chambered for the 20 gauge shell it is fitted with a 22" shotgun barrel or 24" rifled vent rib barrel. Walnut stock. Weight is about 6.9 lbs.

NIB	Exc.	V.G.	Good	Fair	Poor
275	225	200	150	125	100

Model 500 Super Bantam Field

Introduced in 2005 this model features a 20 gauge 3" chamber with 22" ventilated rib barrel with choke tubes. Blued finish. Synthetic stock with adjustabe length of pull. Weight is about 5.25 lbs.

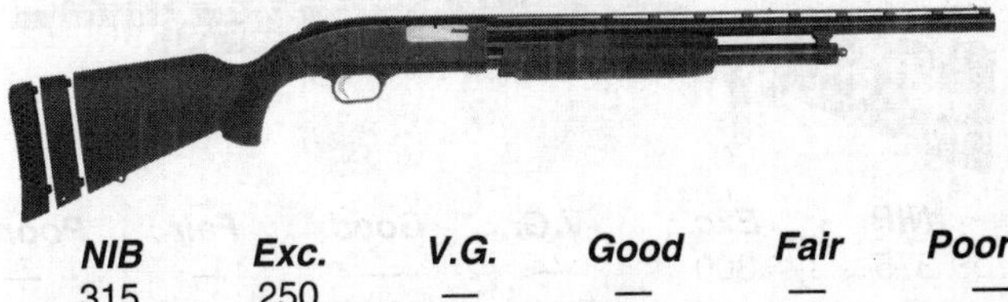

NIB	Exc.	V.G.	Good	Fair	Poor
315	250	—	—	—	—

Model 500 Super Bantam Turkey

This 20 gauge 3" model has a 22" vent rib ported barrel with extra full choke. Synthetic camo stock. Adjustable stock for lop. Weight is about 5.25 lbs. Introduced in 2005.

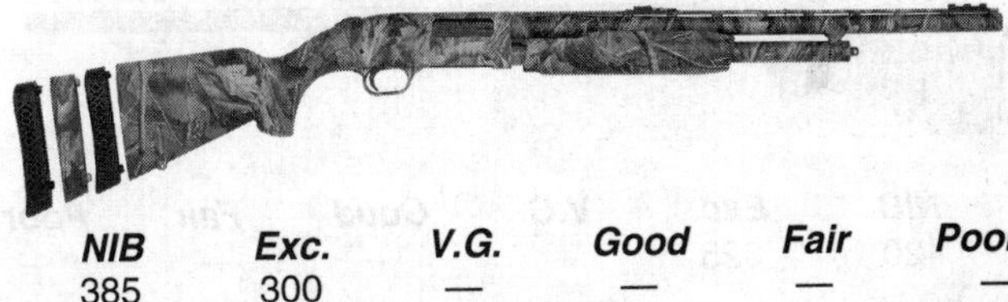

NIB	Exc.	V.G.	Good	Fair	Poor
385	300	—	—	—	—

Model 500 Super Bantam Slug

This 20 gauge model features a full rifled 24" ported barrel with adjustable sights. Synthetic stock with blue or camo finish. Weight is about 5.25 lbs. Introduced in 2005.

NIB	Exc.	V.G.	Good	Fair	Poor
365	300	—	—	—	—

Model 500 Super Bantam Combo

This model introduced in 2005, features a 22" vent rib barrel with choke tubes and a 24" fully rifled ported barrel. Camo finish with adjustable lop synthetic stock. Weight is about 5.25 lbs.

NIB	Exc.	V.G.	Good	Fair	Poor
405	325	—	—	—	—

Model 500 Bullpup

A 12 gauge slide-action Bullpup shotgun with an 18.5" or 20" shrouded barrel. Matte black finish with a composition stock. Introduced in 1986. Discontinued.

NIB	Exc.	V.G.	Good	Fair	Poor
525	400	300	250	150	100

Model 500 Slug Gun Viking Grade

Introduced in 1996 this model is a 12 gauge gun with 24" rifled barrel with iron sights and green synthetic stock. **NOTE:** In 1997 Mossberg introduced ported barrels on some of its slug models. These ported barrels will be seen on rifled barrels only.

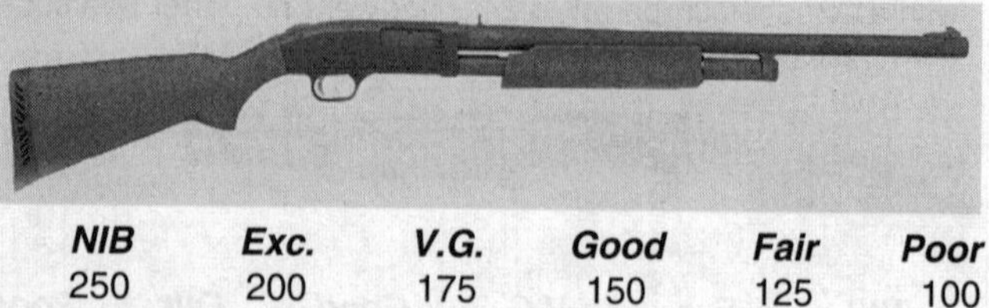

NIB	Exc.	V.G.	Good	Fair	Poor
250	200	175	150	125	100

Model 500 Grand Slam Turkey

This 12 or 20 gauge 3" gun was introduced in 2004. Offered with a 20" vent rib barrel with adjustable fiber optic sights and ported Extra Full choke tube. Available in Real Tree Hardwood or Mossy Oak Break-Up camo pattern. Weight is about 7 lbs. for the 12 gauge gun and about 6.75 lbs. for the 20 gauge.

NIB	Exc.	V.G.	Good	Fair	Poor
375	300	—	—	—	—

Model 500 Flyway Series

Introduced in 2005 this model is a 12 gauge 3.5" gun with 28" vent rib barrel with fiber optic front sight. Choke tubes. Advantage camo synthetic stock. Weight is about 7.5 lbs.

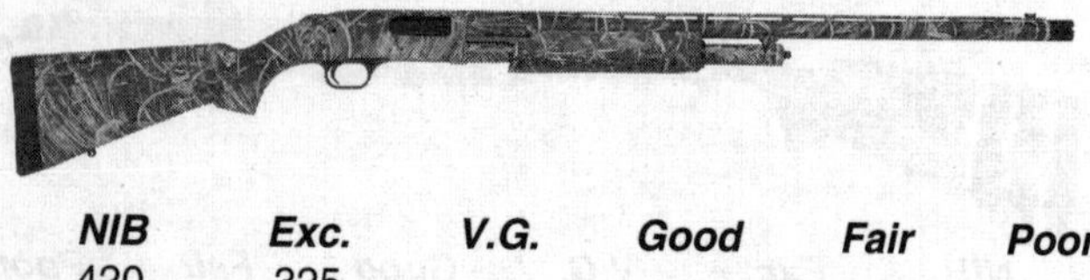

NIB	Exc.	V.G.	Good	Fair	Poor
420	325	—	—	—	—

Model 500 Combo

The 500 series has a total of nine combination sets available to choose from. They are a combination of shotgun barrels and rifled barrels for different hunting applications they are offered in both 12 and 20 gauge sets of the same gauge only.

NIB	Exc.	V.G.	Good	Fair	Poor
400	325	275	225	175	125

Model 500 USA

Introduced in 1997 this model is similar to the military model. It has a Parkerized finish with heavy-duty sling swivels. Fitted with a plain 20" barrel choked Cylinder. Stock is black synthetic. Magazine capacity is 6 rounds. Weight is about 7.2 lbs.

NIB	Exc.	V.G.	Good	Fair	Poor
250	200	175	150	125	100

Model 500 HS (Home Security)

This shotgun is chambered for the .410 shell and fitted with an 18.5" barrel. Five-round magazine capacity. Synthetic stock and blue finish. **NOTE:** In 1999 Mossberg offered a .50 muzzleloader 24" fully rifled barrel that will fit directly onto any six-shot Model 500.

NIB	Exc.	V.G.	Good	Fair	Poor
250	200	175	150	125	100

Porting on most 500 series and 835 series vent rib and slug barrels

Model 505 Youth

Offered in 20 gauge or .410 bore this model is fitted with a 20" vent rib barrel with choke tubes for the 20 gauge and fixed modified choke for the .410 bore. Wood stock with recoil pad. Blued finish. Weight is about 5.25 lbs.

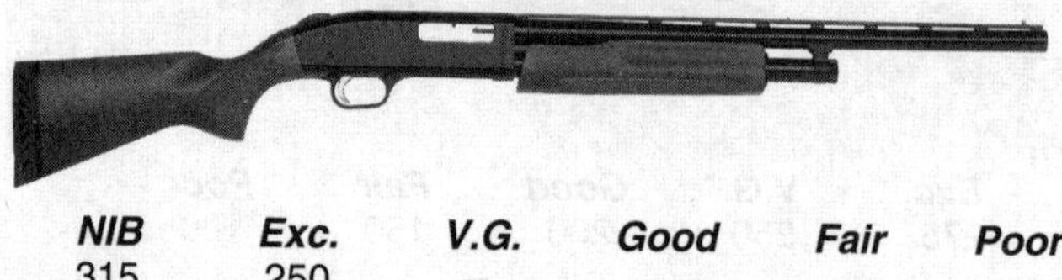

NIB	Exc.	V.G.	Good	Fair	Poor
315	250	—	—	—	—

Model 535 ATS (All Terrain Shotgun) Field

Introduced in 2005 this 12 gauge 3.5" model features a 28" vent rib barrel with choke tubes. Blued finish with checkered wood stock with pistol grip. Weight is about 6.75 lbs.

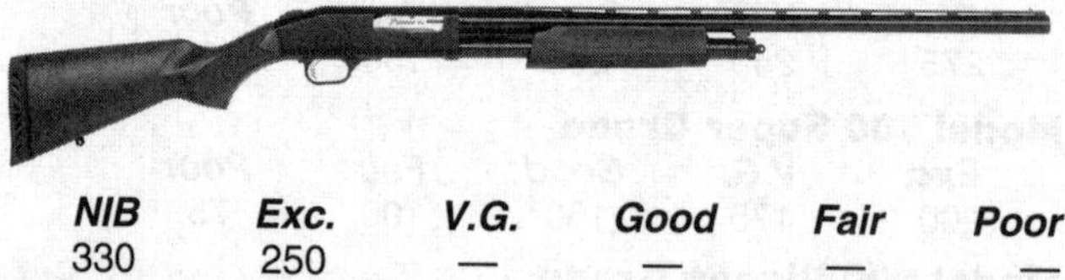

NIB	Exc.	V.G.	Good	Fair	Poor
330	250	—	—	—	—

Model 535 ATS Turkey

As above but with 22" vent rib barrel with extra full choke and fiber optic front sight. Synthetic stock with matte blue or camo finsh. Weight is about 6.5 lbs. Introduced in 2005.

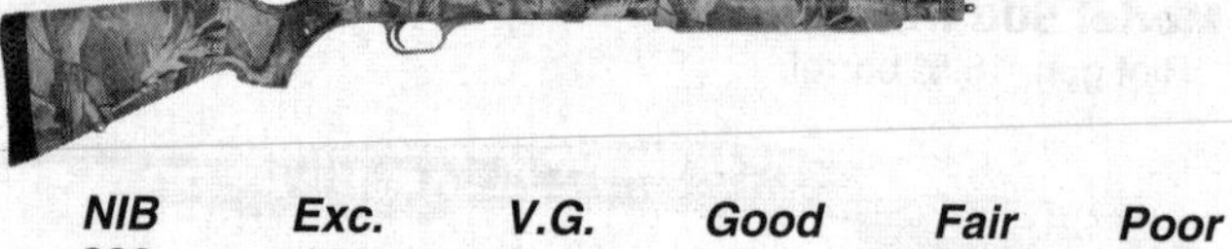

NIB	Exc.	V.G.	Good	Fair	Poor
330	250	—	—	—	—

NOTE: Add $55 for camo finish.

Model 535 ATS Waterfowl

This model is fitted with 28" vent rib barrel with choke tubes and fiber optic front sight. Synthetic stock with matte blue or camo finish. Weight is about 6.75 lbs. Introduced in 2005.

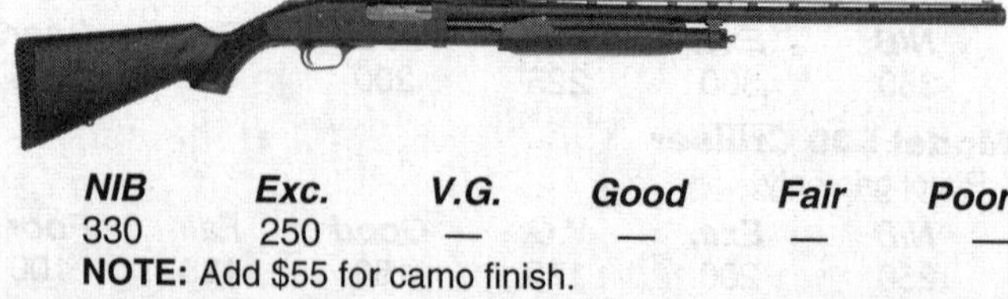

NIB	Exc.	V.G.	Good	Fair	Poor
330	250	—	—	—	—

NOTE: Add $55 for camo finish.

Remington's family of "Nylon" rifles (1959-1989) comprises many of today's hottest firearms collectibles. We hope you enjoy this sampling, provided courtesy of Mr. Jim Stark.

Above: *Nylon 76 (MB) "Trailrider," the only lever action repeater Remington ever produced. Note the extremely short lever throw.*

Top: *Nylon 76 (MB) "Trailrider": Lever action, .22 LR only, 14-rd. tubular magazine. Blued metal parts, Mohawk brown stock with white trim. Approximately 25,300 produced from 1962-1964.*

Bottom: *Nylon 76 (not catalogued): Lever action, .22 LR only, 14-rd. tubular magazine. Blued metal parts, black stock with white trim. Production numbers for this model do not exist.*

Nylon 66 (BD) "Black Diamond." Semi-auto, .22 LR only, 14-rd. tubular magazine. Blued metal parts with a black stock having black diamonds on the balance of trim in white. Approximately 56,000 produced from 1962-1983.

Above: *BC GR-8 "Black Beauty" receiver cover stamped with manufacturer's and importer's identification as required by BATF.*

Brazilian import, manufactured by CBC (Cia Brazileire Cartouchos, Santo Andre, Brazil, SA). This "nylon" rifle is an almost identical copy of the Remington Nylon 66. It was sometimes marketed as the model GR-8 "Black Beauty." Internal parts are not interchangeable. It was imported by several different companies.

Top: *Nylon "Apache 77": Manufactured exclusively for K-Mart from 1987-1989. Metal parts are coated with a matte black sprayed-on finish; the stock is a swirled green, orange and black. It is fed through a 10-rd. box magazine made of plastic; magazines are marked "77." Not to be confused with the 66 (SG) Seneca green or the 77 (MB) Mohawk.*

Bottom: *Nylon 66 (AB) "Apache Black": Semi-auto, .22 LR only, 14-rd. tubular magazine. Chrome plated metal parts, black stock with white trim. Approximately 220,000 produced from 1962-1983.*

Below: *Nylon 66 (AB) "Apache Black" lifetime warranty sticker. The conventional wisdom is that all factory replacement stickers were lost or destroyed.*

Middle: *Nylon 66 (GS) "Gallery Special": Semi-auto, .22 Short only, 20-rd. tubular magazine. Specially equipped for the shooting galleries with a shell deflector and a counter chain retainer. Blued metal parts, Mohawk brown stock with white trim. Approximately 6500 produced from 1961-1981.*

Nylon 66 (GS) "Gallery Special" shell deflector.

Nylon 66 (GS) "Gallery Special" counter chain retainer. It secured the rifle to the countertop in a shooting gallery.

Nylon 66 (GS) "Gallery Special" barrel marking: "22 SHORT".

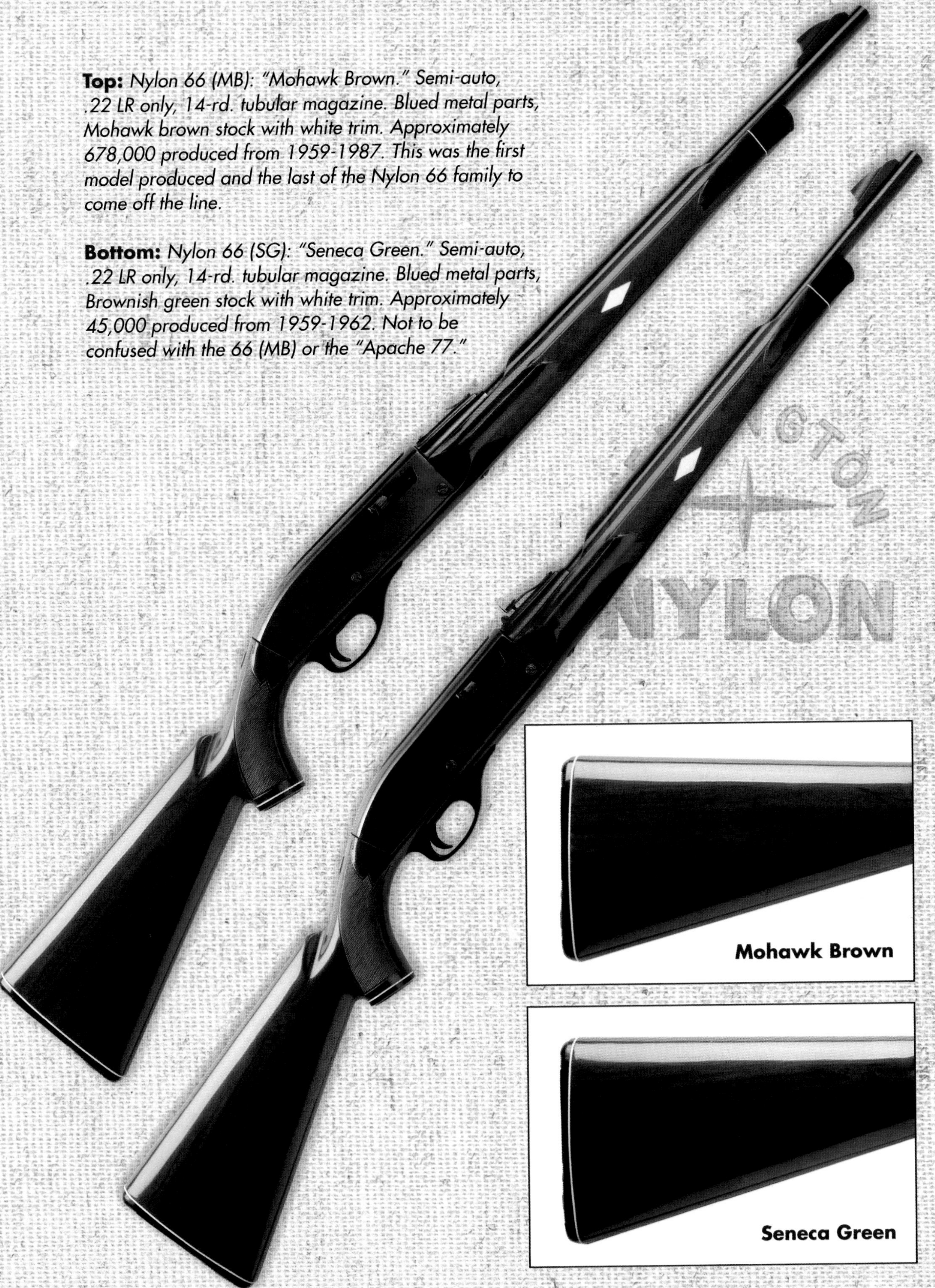

Top: *Nylon 66 (MB): "Mohawk Brown." Semi-auto, .22 LR only, 14-rd. tubular magazine. Blued metal parts, Mohawk brown stock with white trim. Approximately 678,000 produced from 1959-1987. This was the first model produced and the last of the Nylon 66 family to come off the line.*

Bottom: *Nylon 66 (SG): "Seneca Green." Semi-auto, .22 LR only, 14-rd. tubular magazine. Blued metal parts, Brownish green stock with white trim. Approximately 45,000 produced from 1959-1962. Not to be confused with the 66 (MB) or the "Apache 77."*

Top: Nylon "Mohawk 10C:": Semi-auto, .22 LR only, 10-rd. box magazine made of plastic. Magazines are marked "10C." Blued metal parts; Mohawk brown stock with white trim. Approximately 128,000 produced from 1972-1978.

Bottom: Nylon 77: Semi-auto, .22 LR only, 5-rd. box magazine made of plastic. ORIGINAL magazines are NOT marked. Aftermarket magazines are available, marked "77." Blued metal parts, Mohawk brown stock with white trim. Approximately 15,300 produced in 1972. This model was discontinued after the one year of production and brought back out in late 1972 as the Nylon 10C with a higher capacity (10-rd.) magazine.

Nylon Remington semi-automatic magazines made of plastic. Shown are both 5- and 10-rounders for the Models 77, the 10C, and the "Apache 77."

Below: *Nylon 10: Bolt action, single shot, .22 S, L, or LR ammunition, silver spoon-shaped bolt handle. Blued metal parts, Mohawk brown stock with white trim. Shown with 19-5/8" barrel. Also available in 24" barrel length, in both rifled and smoothbore configurations. Smoothbore was for .22 shot shells. Approximately 10,700 produced from 1962-1964. Approximately 2000 in smoothbore, an estimated 200 of those in the 24" barrel length. Smoothbore barrels are marked "smoothbore." Safety engages upon cocking.*

Above: *Nylon 11: Bolt action , 22 S, L, or LR ammunition fed from a metallic box magazine having a capacity of 6 or 10 rounds, silver spoon-shaped bolt handle. Blued metal parts, Mohawk brown stock with white trim. Shown with 19-5/8" barrel. Approximately 22,500 produced from 1962-1964.*

Above: *Nylon 12s in 19-5/8″ and 24″ barrel lengths. Note tubular magazine feed ports.*

Right: *Nylon 12: Bolt action, 22 S, L, or LR ammunition fed through a tube under the barrel, silver spoon-shaped bolt handle. Blued metal parts, Mohawk brown stock with white trim. Shown with 24″ barrel. Production numbers for this barrel length are not available.*

Left: *Nylon 12: Bolt action, 22 S,L, or LR ammunition fed through a tube under the barrel, silver spoon-shaped bolt handle. Blued metal parts, Mohawk brown stock with white trim. Shown with 19-5/8″ barrel. Also available in 24″ barrel configuration. Approximately 27,600 produced from 1962-1964.*

Above: *Gold-filled, embossed receiver cover of Nylon 66 (AN) "150th Anniversary."*

Left: Nylon 66 (AN): "150th Anniversary" commemorative edition. Blued metal parts, Mohawk brown stock with white trim, 22 LR only. Distinguished by the 150th Anniversary stamping on the left side of the receiver cover. Approximately 4000 produced in 1966 only.

Right: Nylon 66 (BI): "Bicentennial" commemorative edition. Blued metal parts, Mohawk brown stock with white trim, .22 LR ONLY. Distinguished by the Eagle and "1776 /1976" stamping on the left side of the receiver cover. Approximately 10,000 produced in 1976 only.

Below: Gold-filled, embossed receiver cover of Nylon 66 (BI) "Bicentennial."

GRIP CAPS

Each of the Remington Nylon rifles is simple to identify. The model number is on the grip cap. The Brazilian " Black Beauty" grip cap is unmarked.

Nylon 76

Nylon 66

Brazilian "Black Beauty"

Nylon 77

Nylon Apache 77

Nylon Mohawk 10 C

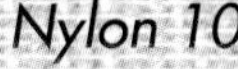
Nylon 10

Nylon 11

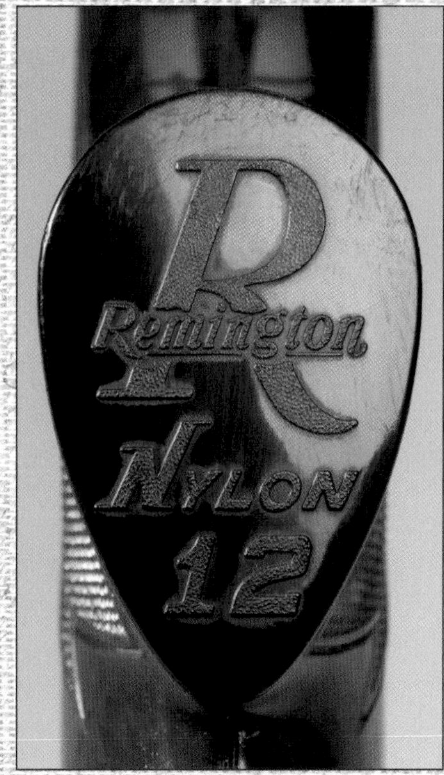

Nylon 12

SIGHT SCREWS

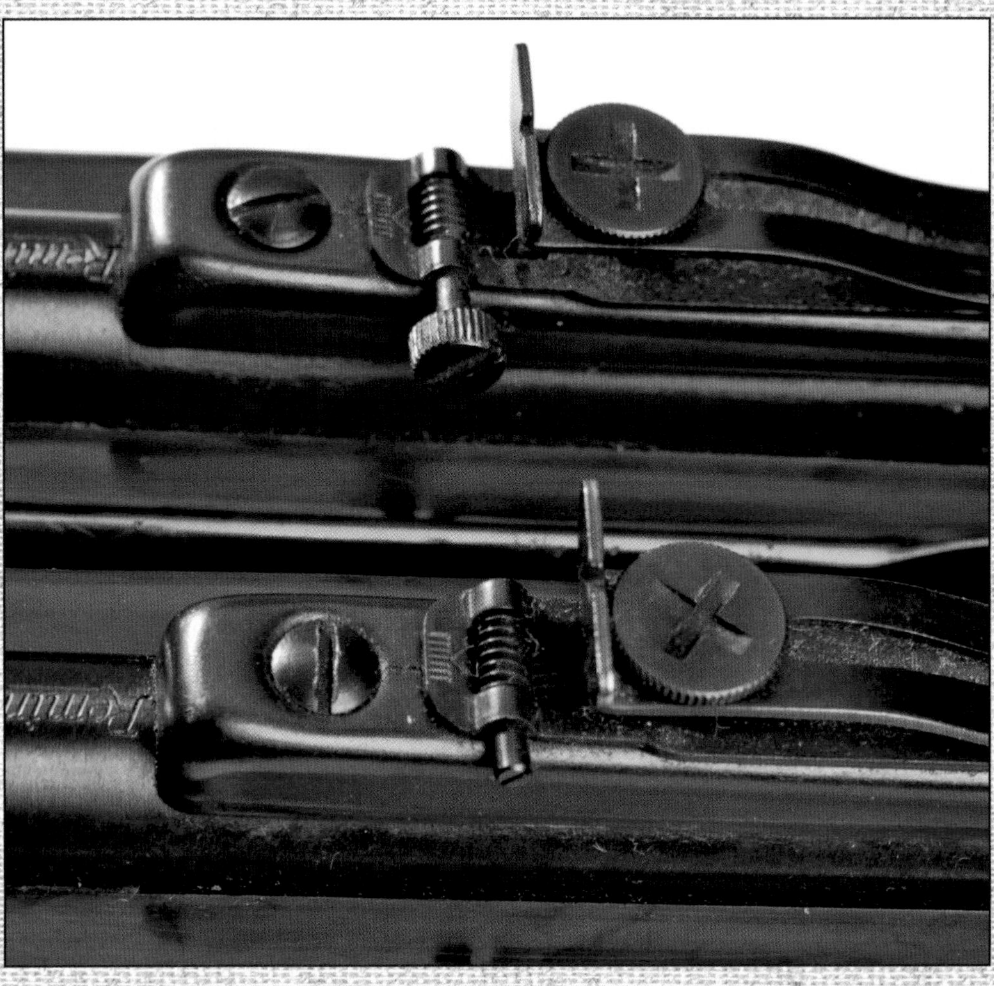

Left: *Rear sight windage screws, large and small. The large one was most susceptible to damage as it allowed more torque to be applied to the rather tiny shaft.*

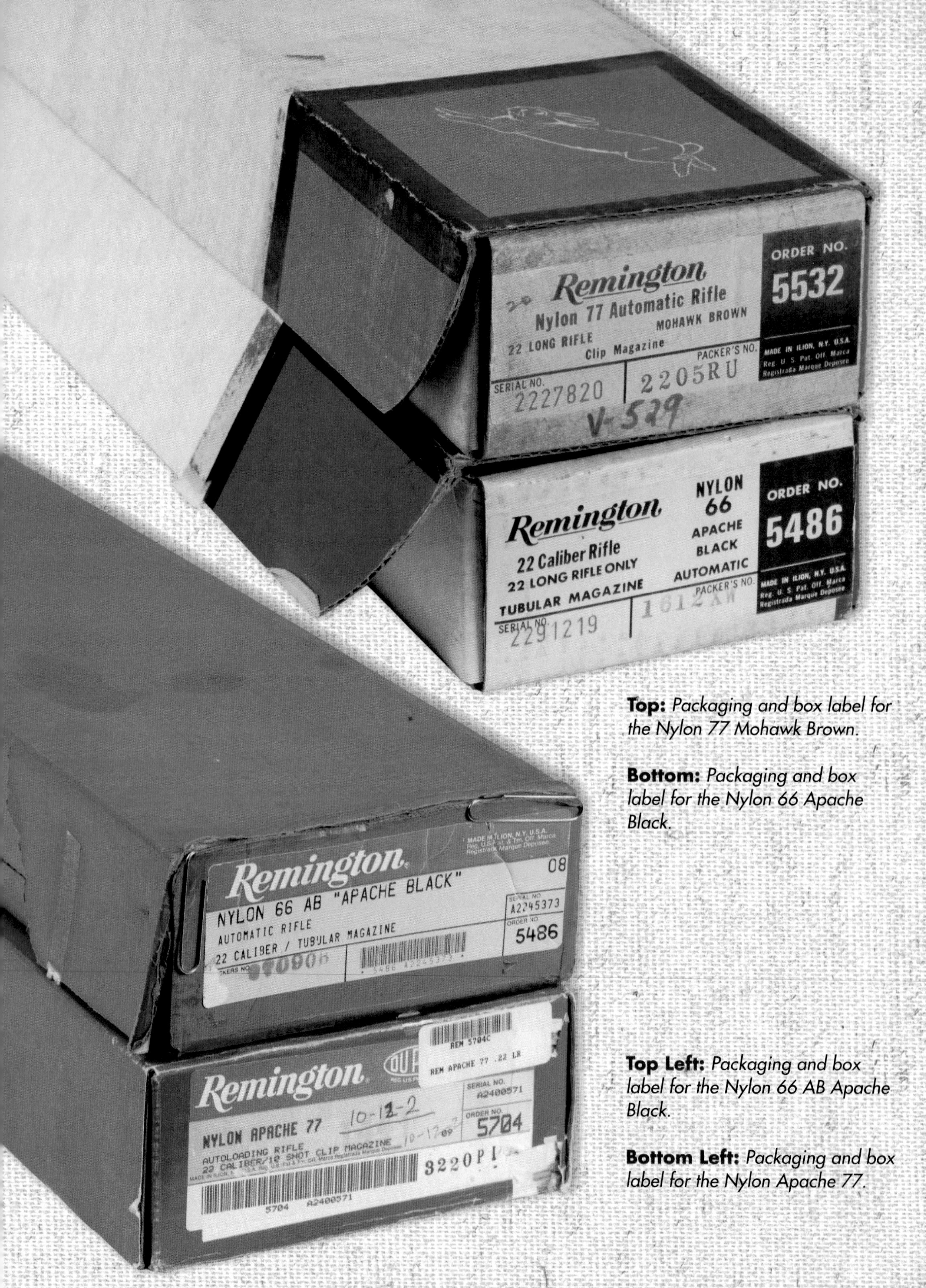

Top: *Packaging and box label for the Nylon 77 Mohawk Brown.*

Bottom: *Packaging and box label for the Nylon 66 Apache Black.*

Top Left: *Packaging and box label for the Nylon 66 AB Apache Black.*

Bottom Left: *Packaging and box label for the Nylon Apache 77.*

Nylon "Apache 77"; K-Mart retail packaging.

Nylon 66 (AB) "Apache Black"; retail packaging.

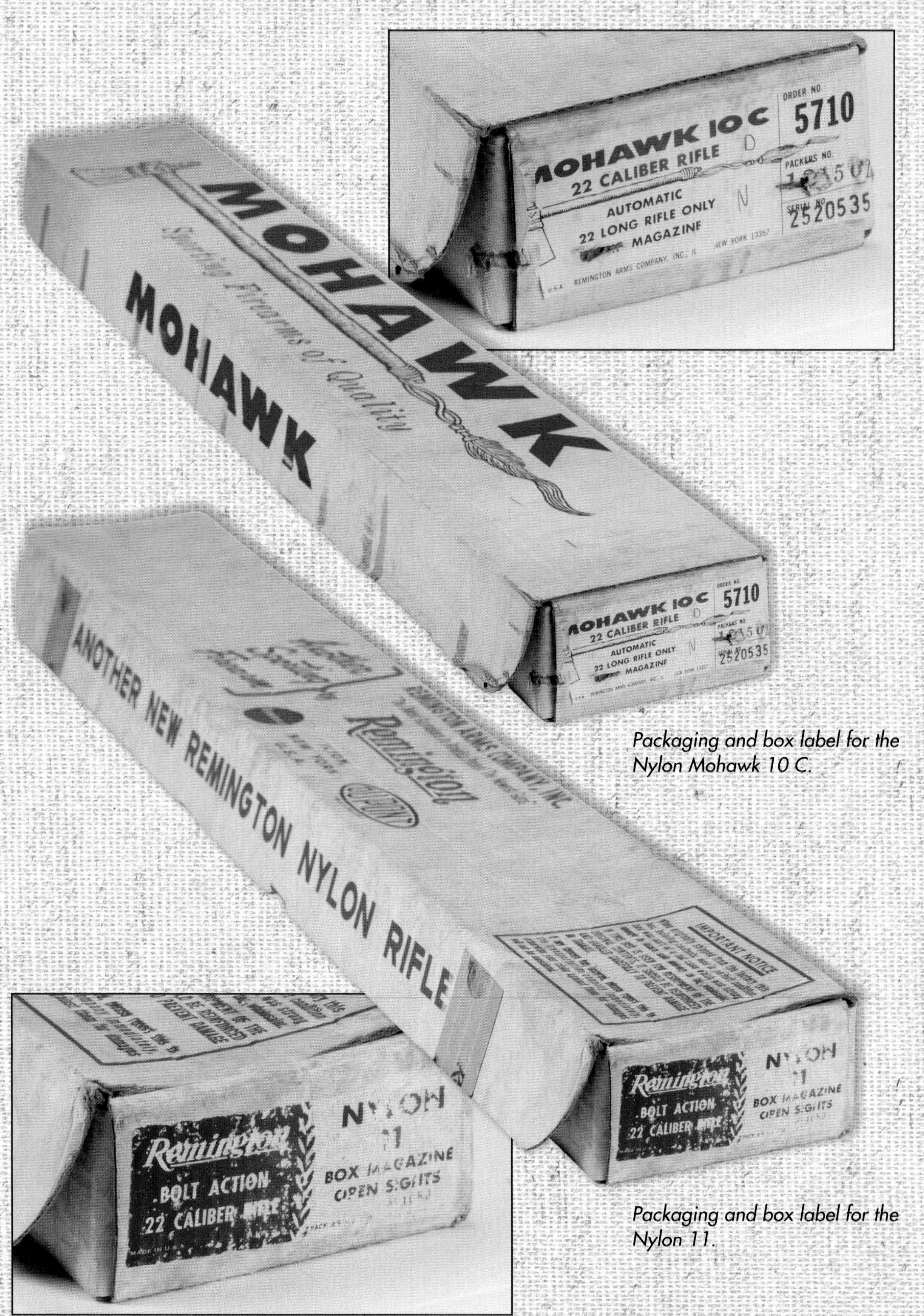

Packaging and box label for the Nylon Mohawk 10 C.

Packaging and box label for the Nylon 11.

Model 535 ATS Slugster

Fitted with a fully rifled 24" vent rib barrel with adjustable sights. Choice of matte blue or camo finish and synthetic stock. Weight is about 7 lbs.

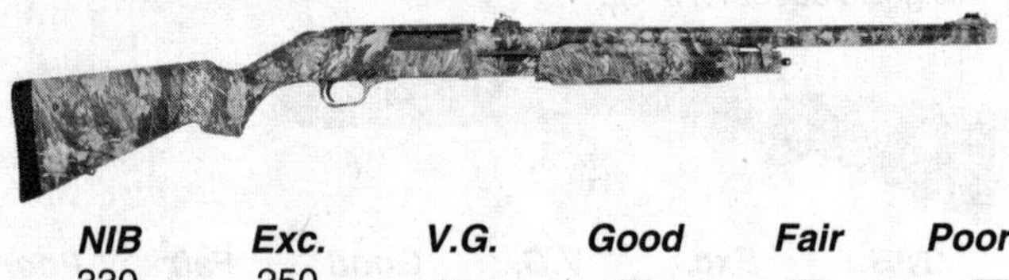

NIB	Exc.	V.G.	Good	Fair	Poor
330	250	—	—	—	—

Model 535 ATS Combos

This set is offered in several different configurations: Field/Deer, 28" and 24"; Turkey/Deer, 22" and 24"; and Turkey/Slug/Waterfowl, 22" and 28". Weights are from 6.5 to 7 lbs. depending on barrel length. Introduced in 2005.

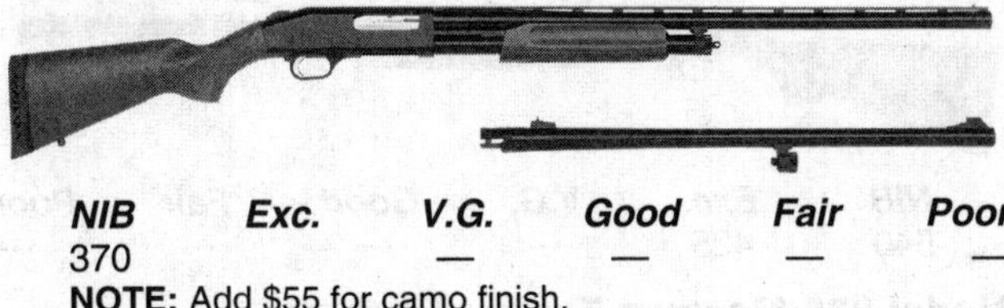

NIB	Exc.	V.G.	Good	Fair	Poor
370	—	—	—	—	—

NOTE: Add $55 for camo finish.

MODEL 590 SERIES

Model 590 Special Purpose

Fitted with a 20" shrouded barrel, bayonet lug, Parkerized or blued finish. Speed feed stock and ghost ring sights. Introduced in 1987. Weight is about 7.25 lbs.

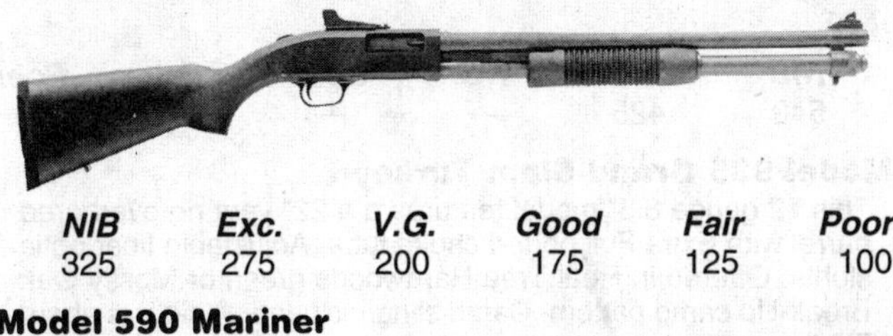

NIB	Exc.	V.G.	Good	Fair	Poor
325	275	200	175	125	100

Model 590 Mariner

Marinecote finish.

NIB	Exc.	V.G.	Good	Fair	Poor
425	350	275	225	150	100

Model 590 Bullpup

The Model 500 with a 20" barrel and 9-shot magazine. Introduced in 1989.

NIB	Exc.	V.G.	Good	Fair	Poor
475	400	325	250	200	125

Model 590DA

This 12 gauge model, introduced in 2000, features a 6-round tubular magazine and an 18.5" barrel. Choice of plain bead sight or ghost ring sights. Choke is fixed Modified. Weight is about 7 lbs. A 14" barreled model is also offered but NFA rules apply.

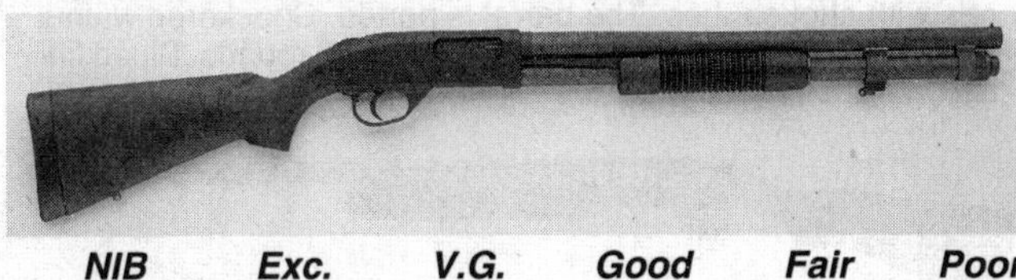

NIB	Exc.	V.G.	Good	Fair	Poor
500	400	—	—	—	—

NOTE: Add $50 for Ghost Ring sights.

MODEL 835 SERIES

Model 835 Ulti-Mag

A 12 gauge Magnum slide-action shotgun with a choice of 24" or 28" ventilated rib barrel fitted for choke tubes, 6-shot magazine and either composition camo or walnut stock. Barrel is ported. Introduced in 1988. In 1998 this model was offered with Shadow Grass camo pattern on both stock and barrel. In 1999 this model was offered with Woodland camo. Weight is 7.3 to 7.7 lbs. In 2000 this model was offered with Realtree Hardwoods camo finish.

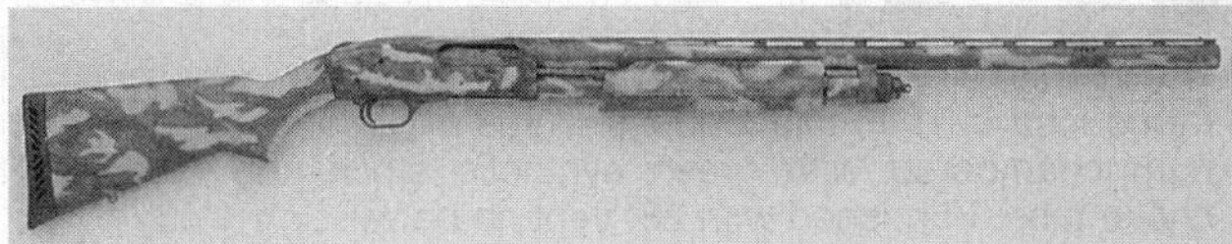

Shadow Grass Camo pattern

Woodland Camo

NIB	Exc.	V.G.	Good	Fair	Poor
425	350	275	225	150	100

Model 835 Ulti-Mag Crown Grade

The Crown Grade features checkered walnut stock with fluted comb. It is chambered for the 12 gauge with 3.5" chamber. Offered in 24" or 28" vent rib barrels with blued or camo finish. Weight is about 7.3 to 7.7 lbs.

NIB	Exc.	V.G.	Good	Fair	Poor
350	275	225	200	150	100

Model 835 Ulti-Mag Crown Grade Combo Model

Same as above but offered with both a 28" vent rib barrel and a 24" rifled barrel with iron sights.

NIB	Exc.	V.G.	Good	Fair	Poor
400	350	300	250	200	100

Model 835 Ulti-Mag Grand Slam Turkey

Introduced in 2004 this 12 gauge 3.5" model features a 20" vent rib overbored barrel with Extra Full ported choke tube. Magazine capacity is 6 rounds for 2.75" shells, 5 rounds for 3", and 4 rounds for 3.5" shells. Adjustable fiber optic sights. Available in Real Tree Hardwoods camo or Mossy Oak Break-Up. Weight is about 7.25 lbs.

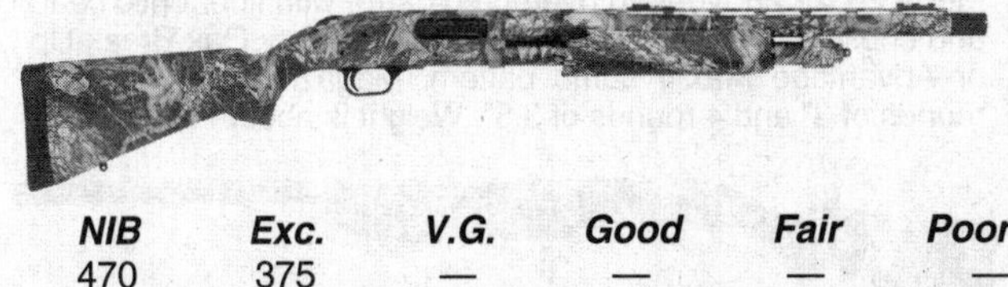

NIB	Exc.	V.G.	Good	Fair	Poor
470	375	—	—	—	—

Model 835 Ulti-Mag Thumbhole Turkey

New in 2006, this dedicated pump-action 12 gauge turkey gun features a thumbhole stock and overbored barrel. Chambered for 3.5 inch shells. X-Factor ported choke tube. Barrel is 20 inches and has adjustable fiber-optic front and rear sights. Weight is about 7.75 lbs. Available in Mossy Oak New Break-Up camo or Realtree Hardwoods Green camo. MSRP: 475

Model 835 Ulti-Mag Tactical Turkey

Same as above but with extended pistol grip stock that is adjustable for length of pull from 10.75" to 14.5". MSRP: 475

Model 835 Ulti-Mag Viking Grade

Introduced in 1996 this model features a 12 gauge 3.5" magnum chambered with green synthetic stock and Modified choke tube. Furnished with 28" vent rib barrel.

NIB	Exc.	V.G.	Good	Fair	Poor
300	250	200	175	125	100

Model 835 Wild Turkey Federation

As above, with a Wild Turkey Federation medallion inlaid in the stock. Introduced in 1989.

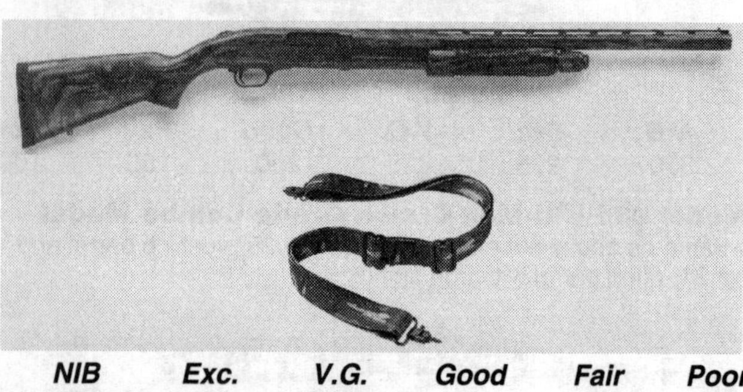

NIB	Exc.	V.G.	Good	Fair	Poor
475	400	325	250	200	125

Model 835 American Field

This 12 gauge model has a checkered walnut stock, 28" ventilated rib barrel with Modified choke tube. Weight is about 7.7 lbs.

NIB	Exc.	V.G.	Good	Fair	Poor
300	275	225	200	150	100

MODEL 935 MAGNUM SERIES

The 935 Magnum series of guns was introduced in 2004.

Model 935 Magnum Waterfowl Camo

This 12 gauge 3.5" semi-automatic shotgun is available with either a 26" or 28" vent rib overbored barrel with fiber optic bead and choke tubes. Offered with choice of Mossy Oak Break-Up or Advantage Max-4 camo pattern. Magazine capacity is 5 rounds of 3" and 4 rounds of 3.5". Weight is about 7.75 lbs.

NIB	Exc.	V.G.	Good	Fair	Poor
645	500	—	—	—	—

Model 935 Magnum Turkey Camo

This 12 gauge 3.5" model features a 24" vent rib overbored barrel with adjustable fiber optic sights. Ultra Full choke tube. Offered in Mossy Oak Break-Up or Hardwoods HD-Green. Weight is about 7.75 lbs.

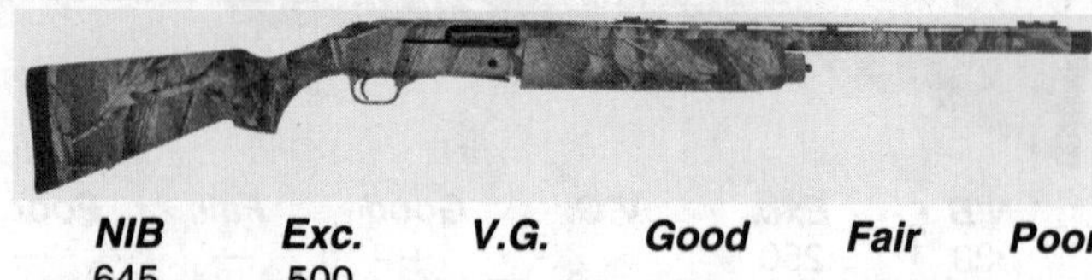

NIB	Exc.	V.G.	Good	Fair	Poor
645	500	—	—	—	—

Model 935 Magnum Waterfowl Synthetic

This 12 gauge 3.5" gun features a choice of 26" or 28" vent rib overbored barrel with choke tubes. Fiber optic bead. Matte black finish with black synthetic stock. Weight is about 7.75 lbs.

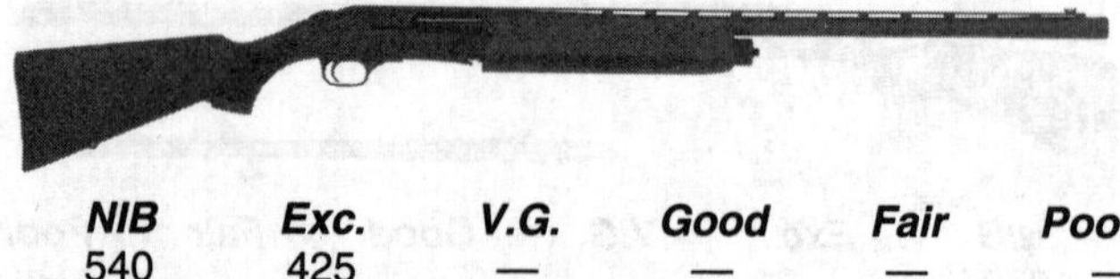

NIB	Exc.	V.G.	Good	Fair	Poor
540	425	—	—	—	—

Model 935 Magnum Turkey Synthetic

As above but with 24" vent rib overbored barrel with Ultra Full choke tube. Weight is about 7.75 lbs.

NIB	Exc.	V.G.	Good	Fair	Poor
540	425	—	—	—	—

Model 935 Grand Slam Turkey

This 12 gauge 3.5" model features a a 22" vent rib overbored barrel with Extra Full ported choke tube. Adjustable fiber optic sights. Offered in Real Tree Hardwoods green or Mossy Oak Break-Up camo pattern. Camo sling included. Weight is about 7.5 lbs.

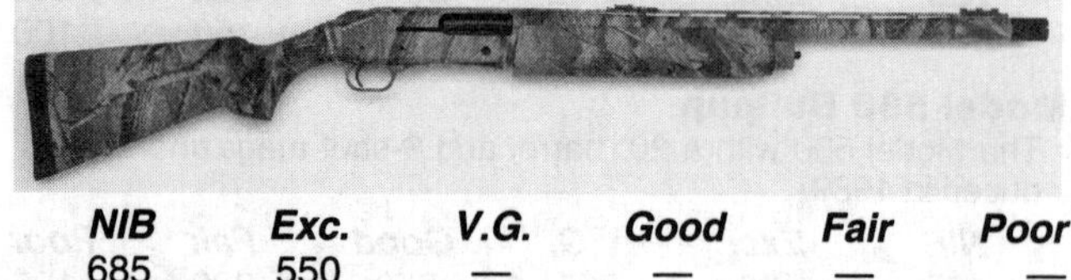

NIB	Exc.	V.G.	Good	Fair	Poor
685	550	—	—	—	—

MODEL 930 SERIES

This is a 12 gauge 3" chamber semi-automatic shotgun series introduced in 2005.

Model 930 Field

This 12 gauge 3" gun is fitted with either 26" or 28" vent rib barrels with choke tubes. The barrel is ported. Checkered walnut stock with recoil pad. Magazine capacity is 5 rounds. Blued finish. Weight is about 7.75 lbs.

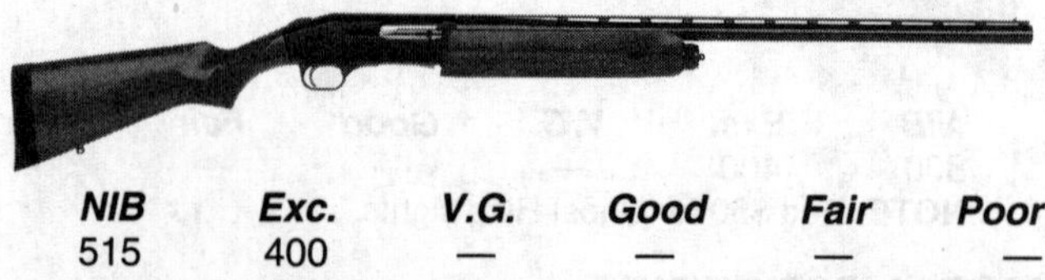

NIB	Exc.	V.G.	Good	Fair	Poor
515	400	—	—	—	—

Model 930 Turkey

Fitted with a synthetic stock and 24" vent rib ported barrel. Chokes are extra full extended tubes. Offered with matte blue finish or camo finish. Weight is about 7.5 lbs.

NIB	Exc.	V.G.	Good	Fair	Poor
500	400	—	—	—	—

NOTE: Add $100 for camo finish.

Model 930 Waterfowl

This model is fitted with a 28" vent rin ported barrel with choke tubes. Choice of matte blue or camo finish. Weight is about 7.75 lbs.

NIB	Exc.	V.G.	Good	Fair	Poor
500	400	—	—	—	—

NOTE: Add $100 for camo finish.

Model 930 Slugster

This model features a 24" vent rib ported barrel with choice of plain or Monte Carlo synthetic stock. Matte blue or camo finish. Weight is about 7.5 lbs.

NIB	Exc.	V.G.	Good	Fair	Poor
515	400	—	—	—	—

NOTE: Add $100 for camo finish.

Model 3000

A 12 or 20 gauge slide-action shotgun manufactured in a variety of barrel lengths and styles. Blued with a walnut stock. Also known as the Smith & Wesson Model 3000.

Exc.	V.G.	Good	Fair	Poor
325	250	175	125	75

Model 3000 Waterfowler

As above, but matte finished, fitted with sling swivels and accompanied by a camouflage sling. Produced in 1986.

Exc.	V.G.	Good	Fair	Poor
350	275	200	150	100

Model 3000 Law Enforcement

As above, with an 18.5" or 20" cylinder-bore barrel. Manufactured in 1986 and 1987.

Exc.	V.G.	Good	Fair	Poor
325	250	175	125	75

Model 1000

A 12 or 20 gauge semi-automatic shotgun manufactured in a variety of barrel lengths and styles, the receiver of an aluminum alloy and blued. Also known as the Smith & Wesson Model 1000. Offered in 1986 and 1987.

Exc.	V.G.	Good	Fair	Poor
300	250	200	150	100

Model 1000 Slug

As above, with a 22" barrel fitted with rifle sights. Offered in 1986 and 1987.

Exc.	V.G.	Good	Fair	Poor
325	250	200	125	100

MODEL 1000 SUPER SERIES

As above, with a steel receiver and a self-regulating gas system that allows the use of either standard or Magnum shells.

Exc.	V.G.	Good	Fair	Poor
375	300	250	150	100

Model 1000 Super Waterfowler

Matte finish.

Exc.	V.G.	Good	Fair	Poor
375	300	250	150	100

Model 1000 Super Slug

Rifle sights.

Exc.	V.G.	Good	Fair	Poor
375	300	250	150	100

Model 1000 Super Trap

30" high rib barrel.

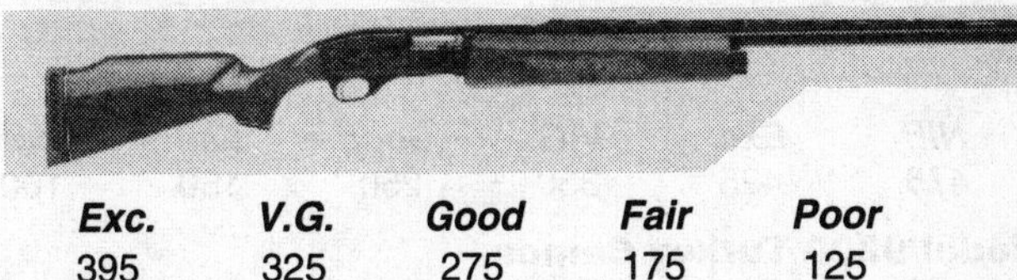

Exc.	V.G.	Good	Fair	Poor
395	325	275	175	125

Model 1000 Super Skeet

25" barrel.

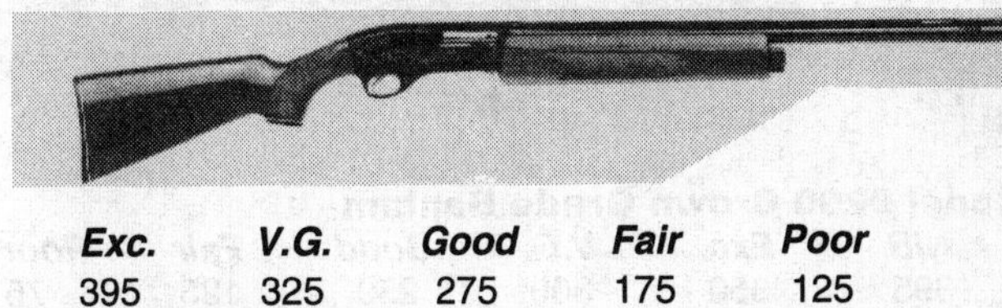

Exc.	V.G.	Good	Fair	Poor
395	325	275	175	125

Model 5500 MKI I

A 12 gauge semi-automatic shotgun supplied with either a 26" barrel for 2.75" shells or a 28" barrel for 3" shells. Blued with a walnut stock. Introduced in 1989.

NIB	Exc.	V.G.	Good	Fair	Poor
300	235	200	175	150	125

MODEL 9200 SERIES

This model has a variety of configurations. It is a 12 gauge semi-automatic with a choice of walnut stock or camo synthetic stock. Barrel lengths are from 22" to 28". Weights range from 7 to 7.7 lbs.

Model 9200 Viking Grade

NIB	Exc.	V.G.	Good	Fair	Poor
350	300	275	200	100	75

Mossy Oak Shadow Branch Camo

Model 9200 USST Crown Grade

NIB	Exc.	V.G.	Good	Fair	Poor
400	350	300	200	100	75

Model 9200 Combos

NIB	Exc.	V.G.	Good	Fair	Poor
475	425	350	250	150	100

Model 9200 Special Hunter

28" vent rib barrel with synthetic stock.

NIB	Exc.	V.G.	Good	Fair	Poor
475	425	350	250	150	100

Model 9200 Deer Combo

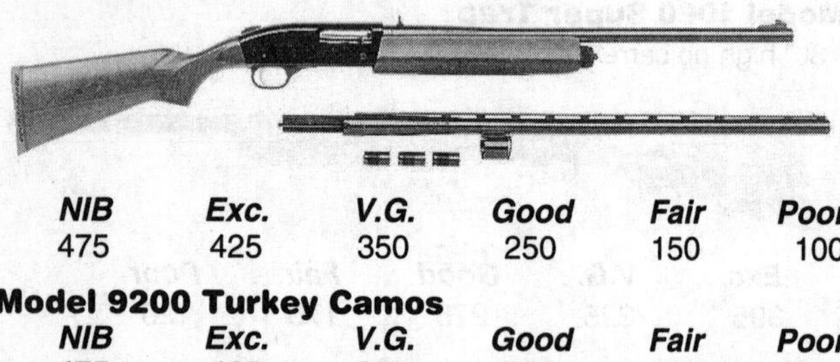

NIB	Exc.	V.G.	Good	Fair	Poor
475	425	350	250	150	100

Model 9200 Turkey Camos

NIB	Exc.	V.G.	Good	Fair	Poor
475	425	350	250	150	100

Model 9200 Crown Grade Bantam

NIB	Exc.	V.G.	Good	Fair	Poor
395	350	300	250	125	75

Model 9200 Jungle Gun

This is a 12 gauge auto loader fitted with a plain 18.5" barrel with bead sight. Barrel choked Cylinder. Chambers are 2-3/4". Magazine capacity is 5 rounds. Parkerized finish. Synthetic stock.

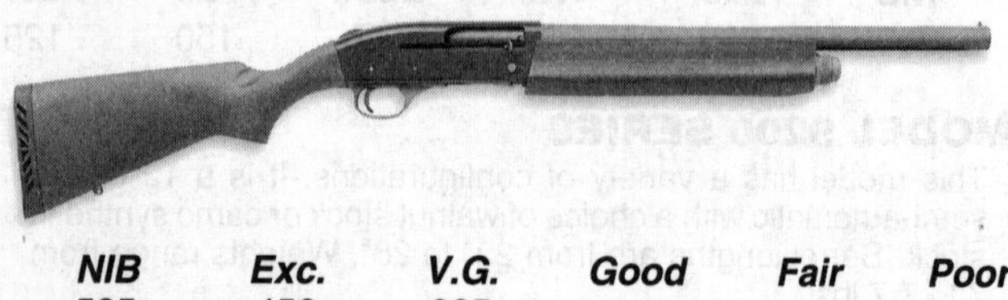

NIB	Exc.	V.G.	Good	Fair	Poor
525	450	325	—	—	—

RESERVE SERIES

Introduced in 2005 this is an over-and-under gun in 12, 20, 28 gauge as well as .410 bore. Made in Turkey.

Silver Reserve Field

Offered in 12 gauge with 28" vent rib barrels, 20 gauge with 26" or 28" vent rib barrels, 28 gauge with 26" vent rib barrels, .410 with 26" vent rib barrels. All gauge have choke tubes except for the .410 with fixed chokes. Steel silvered receiver with scroll engraving and game senes in gold. Checkered walnut stock with recoil pad. Single trigger. Weight is from 6 lbs. to 7.7 lbs. depending on gauge. Add 20 percent for 28 and .410.

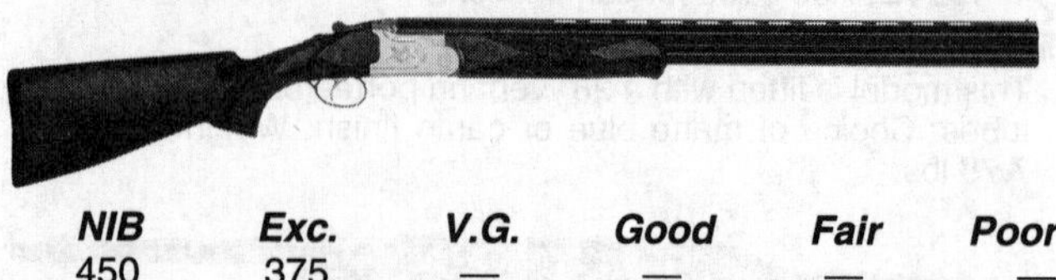

NIB	Exc.	V.G.	Good	Fair	Poor
450	375	—	—	—	—

Silver Reserve Sporting

As above but in 12 gauge only with 28" vent 10mm rib barrels with choke tubes and ported barrels. Weight is about 7.7 lbs.

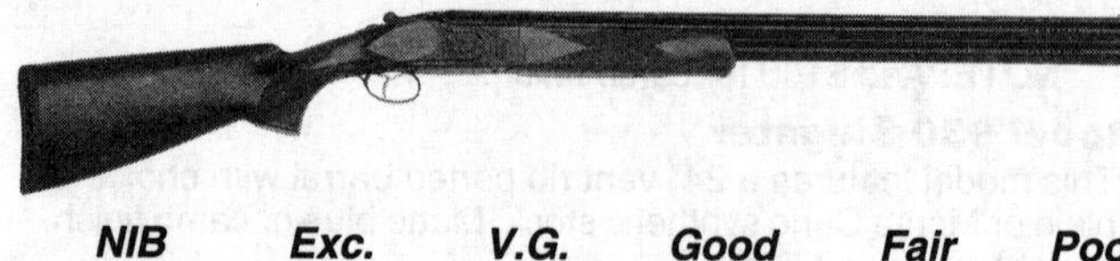

NIB	Exc.	V.G.	Good	Fair	Poor
485	375	—	—	—	—

Onyx Reserve Sporting

Similar to Silver Reserve Sporting but with blued receiver.

NIB	Exc.	V.G.	Good	Fair	Poor
450	350	—	—	—	—

MOUNTAIN ARMS

Ozark, Missouri

Wildcat

Similar to Rau Arms Wildcat (*q.v.*) but with plastic stock inserts. A takedown model was offered as well. Estimated 6,243 produced 1971-1978. The first several thousand bore the Rau Arms label.

NIB	Exc.	V.G.	Good	Fair	Poor
225	175	125	100	65	35

MOUNTAIN RIFLES, INC.

Palmer, Alaska

Mountaineer

This bolt-action rifle, introduced in 1997, is built on a Remington action with Model 70 style bolt release. A factory muzzlebrake is installed with open sights. A Timney trigger is standard. Stock is fiberglass. Finish is Parkerized. This model is chambered for many different calibers, from .223 Rem. to .416 Rem., including Dakota and Weatherby cartridges. Weight starts at about 6 lbs. and is dependent on caliber. There are several options that will affect price. A left-hand model is offered as an option.

NIB	Exc.	V.G.	Good	Fair	Poor
2195	1750	—	—	—	—

Super Mountaineer

Similar to the Mountaineer model but the bolt is fluted and hollow. Barrel is match grade stainless steel with muzzlebrake. Kevlar/Graphite stock. Wide variety of calibers. Weight starts at about 4.25 lbs. depending on caliber.

NIB	Exc.	V.G.	Good	Fair	Poor
2895	2350	—	—	—	—

Pro Mountaineer

This model is built on a Winchester Model 70 action. Premium match grade barrel with muzzlebrake. Model 70 trigger. Stainless steel matte finish. Kevlar/Graphite stock. Wide variety of calibers. Weight starts at about 6 lbs.

NIB	Exc.	V.G.	Good	Fair	Poor
2895	2350	—	—	—	—

Pro Safari

This model is built on an MRI action with controlled feed. Premium match grade barrel. Timney trigger. Matte blue finish. Exhibition grade walnut stock with custom bottom metal. Weight starts at about 7 lbs. depending on caliber. Caliber from .223 to .458 Lott.

NIB	Exc.	V.G.	Good	Fair	Poor
4495	3500	—	—	—	—

Ultra Mountaineer

Built on an MRI action with premium match grade barrel and muzzlebrake. Timney trigger. Parkerized finish. Kevlar/Graphite stock. Calibers from .223 to .505 Gibbs. Weight begins at 5 lbs. depending on caliber.

NIB	Exc.	V.G.	Good	Fair	Poor
2995	2500	—	—	—	—

NOTE: Add $500 for Rigby-length calibers.

MUGICA, JOSE

Eibar, Spain

SEE—Llama

A trade name found on Llama pistols that were manufactured by Gabilondo.

MURATA

SEE—Japan State

MURFEESBORO ARMORY

Murfeesboro, Tennessee

Established in 1861 by William Ledbetter. Made copies of U.S. Model 1841 Rifle complete with patchbox and double strapped nose cap. Barrel bands pinned to stock. Between 270 and 390 made from October of 1861 through March of 1862. Overall length 48-3/4"; barrel length 33"; .54 caliber. Unmarked except for serial number on various parts including the barrel.

Exc.	V.G.	Good	Fair	Poor
—	—	15000	6000	2000

MURRAY, J. P.

Columbus, Georgia

Percussion Rifle

A .58 caliber percussion rifle with a 33" barrel, full stock and brass mounts. Also made with a 23.5" to 24" barrel as a carbine. The lock marked "J.P. Murray/Columbus Ga." Several hundred were manufactured between 1862 and 1864.

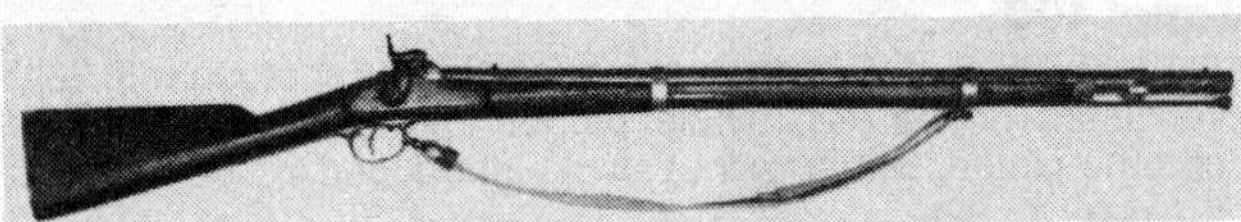

Courtesy Milwaukee Public Museum, Milwaukee, Wisconsin

Exc.	V.G.	Good	Fair	Poor
—	—	30000	12500	1500

MURPHY & O'CONNEL

New York, New York

Pocket Pistol

A .41 caliber single-shot percussion pocket pistol with a 3" barrel, German silver mounts and a walnut stock. Manufactured during the 1850s.

Exc.	V.G.	Good	Fair	Poor
—	—	2750	1000	450

MUSGRAVE

Republic of South Africa

RSA NR I Single-Shot Target Rifle

A .308 caliber single-shot bolt-action rifle with a 26" barrel, match sights, adjustable trigger and target-style stock. Made of walnut. Manufactured between 1971 and 1976.

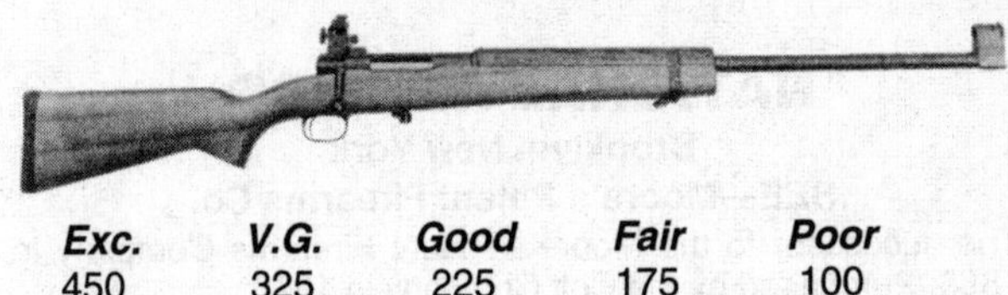

Exc.	V.G.	Good	Fair	Poor
450	325	225	175	100

Valiant NR6

A .243, .270, .308, .30-06, and 7mm Remington Magnum caliber bolt-action sporting rifle with a 24" barrel, open sights and English-style stock. Imported from 1971 to 1976.

Exc.	V.G.	Good	Fair	Poor
350	250	200	150	100

Premier NR5

As above, with a 26" barrel and pistol-grip Monte Carlo-style stock. Discontinued in 1976.

Exc.	V.G.	Good	Fair	Poor
500	400	250	200	100

MUSKETEER RIFLES

Firearms International

Washington, D.C.

Sporter

A .243 to .300 Winchester Magnum caliber bolt-action rifle with a 24" barrel without sights, and Monte Carlo-style stock. Imported between 1963 and 1972.

Exc.	V.G.	Good	Fair	Poor
375	300	200	175	100

Deluxe Sporter

As above, with an adjustable trigger and more finely figured walnut stock.

Exc.	V.G.	Good	Fair	Poor
425	350	250	200	100

Carbine

The Sporter with a 20" barrel.

Exc.	V.G.	Good	Fair	Poor
375	300	200	175	100

N

NAGANT, EMILE & LEON

Liege, Belgium

NOTE: For history, technical data, descriptions, photos, and prices see the *Standard Catalog of MIlitary Firearms.*

NAMBU

SEE—Japan State

NATIONAL ARMS CO.

Brooklyn, New York

SEE—Moore's Patent Firearms Co.

The successor to the Moore's Patent Firearms Company in 1865. Purchased by the Colt Company in 1870.

Large Frame Teat-Fire Revolver

A .45 teat fire caliber revolver with a 7.5" barrel and 6-shot cylinder. Blued or silver-plated with walnut grips. The barrel marked "National Arms Co. Brooklyn." The exact number of these revolvers made is unknown, but it is estimated to be fewer than 30.

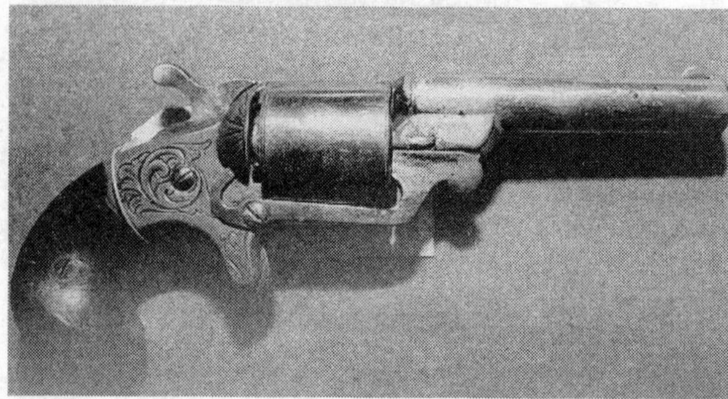

Exc.	V.G.	Good	Fair	Poor
—	—	13500	5500	850

No. 2 Derringer

A .41 caliber spur trigger pocket pistol with a 2.5" barrel. Blued or silver-plated with walnut grips. Later manufactured by the Colt Company as their No. 2 Derringer.

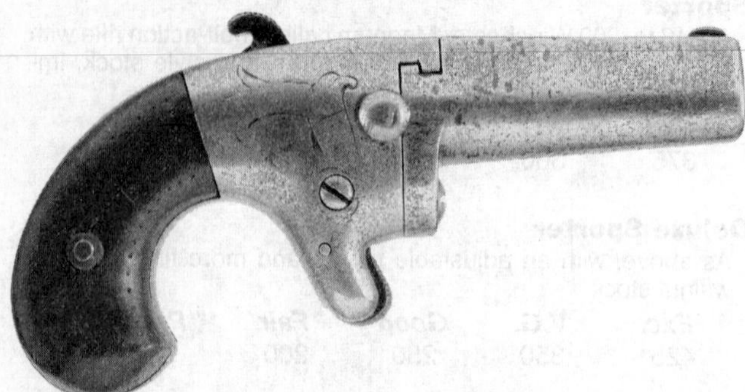

Courtesy Rock Island Auction Company

Exc.	V.G.	Good	Fair	Poor
—	—	1150	500	150

NAVY ARMS COMPANY

Ridgefield, New Jersey

Not a manufacturer but an importer. Founded in 1957 by Val Forgett to enhance the shooting of blackpowder firearms without destroying the originals. The first replica was the Colt 1851 Navy. Thus, the name of the new company, "Navy Arms." In the early 1980s Navy Arms began importing surplus firearms from European countries. Navy Arms continues to offer both blackpowder replicas and foreign imports. For a short period of time the company imported double-barrel shotguns. This was discontinued in 1990. Most if not all of the guns listed below are also to be found under the manufacturers' names as well as those of other importers.

SHOTGUNS

Model 83

A 12 or 20 gauge Magnum Over/Under shotgun manufactured in a variety of barrel lengths and styles with double triggers and extractors. Blued, engraved, with a walnut stock. Introduced in 1985.

NIB	Exc.	V.G.	Good	Fair	Poor
400	300	275	200	175	100

Model 93

As above, with automatic ejectors.

NIB	Exc.	V.G.	Good	Fair	Poor
475	400	300	250	200	100

Model 95

As above, with a single trigger and screw-in choke tubes.

NIB	Exc.	V.G.	Good	Fair	Poor
550	450	350	250	200	100

Model 96 Sportsman

As above, in 12 gauge only with a gold-plated receiver.

NIB	Exc.	V.G.	Good	Fair	Poor
600	475	350	300	225	150

Model 100

A 12, 20, 28 or .410 bore Over/Under boxlock shotgun with 26" ventilated rib barrels, single trigger and extractors. Blued, chrome-plated, with a walnut stock. Introduced in 1989.

NIB	Exc.	V.G.	Good	Fair	Poor
350	250	200	150	100	75

Model 100 Side-by-Side

A 12 or 20 gauge Magnum boxlock double-barrel shotgun with 27.5" barrels, double triggers and extractors. Blued with a walnut stock. Imported between 1985 and 1987.

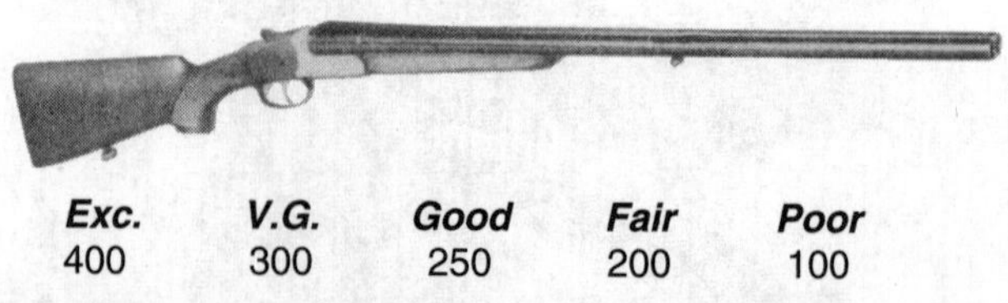

Exc.	V.G.	Good	Fair	Poor
400	300	250	200	100

Model 150

As above, with automatic ejectors.

Exc.	V.G.	Good	Fair	Poor
450	350	300	225	125

Model 105

A 12, 20 or .410 bore folding single barrel shotgun with a 26" or 28" barrel, chrome-plated engraved receiver, blued barrel and hardwood stock. Introduced in 1985.

NIB	Exc.	V.G.	Good	Fair	Poor
100	80	75	65	50	35

Model 105 Deluxe

As above, with vent rib barrel and a checkered walnut stock.

NIB	Exc.	V.G.	Good	Fair	Poor
120	100	85	75	60	45

REPLICA LONG GUNS

Harpers Ferry Flint Rifle

This model is a copy of the 1803 rifle in the original .54 caliber. It features a rust blued 35" barrel. Weight is 8.5 lbs.

NIB	Exc.	V.G.	Good	Fair	Poor
600	475	350	300	200	100

Harpers Ferry "Journey of Discovery" Rifle

Similar to the Harpers Ferry Flint Rifle above but with oil finished walnut stock, brass fittings brass patchbox engraved "Lewis and Clark 'Journey of Discovery';1803 to 1806." Introduced in 2003.

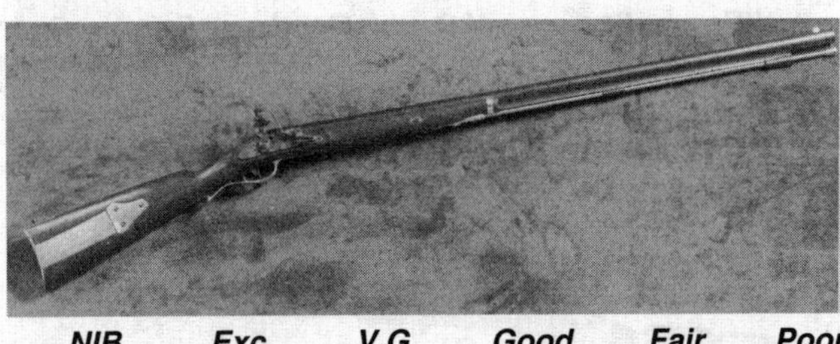

NIB	Exc.	V.G.	Good	Fair	Poor
765	600	—	—	—	—

Brown Bess Musket

This replica is a copy of the second model used between 1760 and 1776. Bright finish on metal and one-piece walnut stock with polished brass locks. Barrel is 42" and weight is 9.5 lbs.

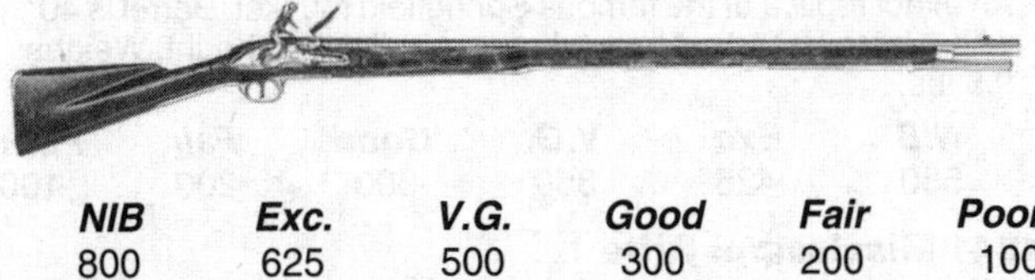

NIB	Exc.	V.G.	Good	Fair	Poor
800	625	500	300	200	100

Brown Bess Carbine

Same as above but fitted with a 30" barrel. Weighs 7.75 lbs.

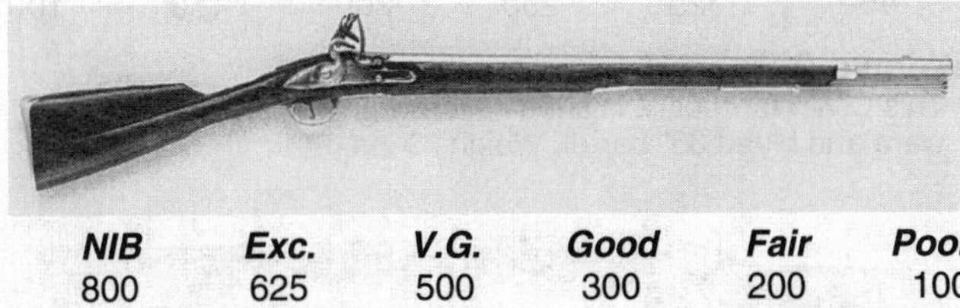

NIB	Exc.	V.G.	Good	Fair	Poor
800	625	500	300	200	100

1777 Charleville Musket

Copy of French flintlock in .69 caliber. Fittings are steel with brass front sight and brass flashpan. Barrel length is 44.625" and weight is about 8.75 lbs.

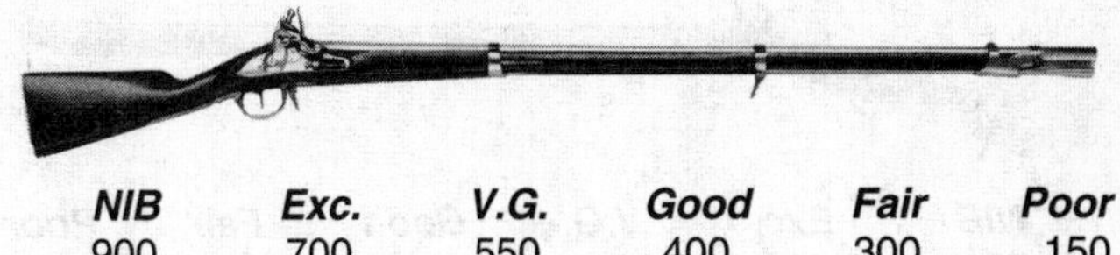

NIB	Exc.	V.G.	Good	Fair	Poor
900	700	550	400	300	150

1777 Standard Charleville Musket

Same as above with polished steel barrel and select walnut stock.

NIB	Exc.	V.G.	Good	Fair	Poor
900	700	550	400	300	150

1816 M.T. Wickham Musket

Furnished in .69 caliber with steel ramrod with button head. Brass flashpan and walnut stock are standard.

NIB	Exc.	V.G.	Good	Fair	Poor
600	550	450	350	250	200

1808 Springfield Musket

This model is a U.S. copy of the 1763 Charleville musket with 1808 Springfield markings. Barrel length is 44" and weight is 8.75 lbs.

NIB	Exc.	V.G.	Good	Fair	Poor
950	800	600	400	200	100

Pennsylvania Long Rifle

This model is offered in either percussion or flintlock ignition and is offered in a choice of .32 caliber or .45 caliber. It has an octagonal 40.5" rust blued barrel, polished lock, double set triggers, and brass furniture on a walnut stock. Weighs 7.5 lbs.

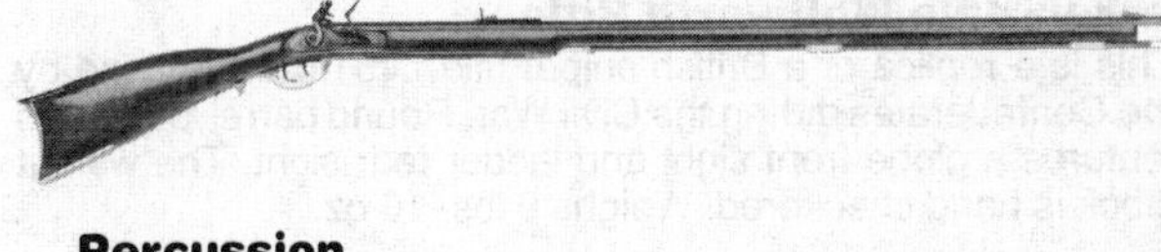

Percussion

NIB	Exc.	V.G.	Good	Fair	Poor
450	375	250	200	150	100

Flintlock

NIB	Exc.	V.G.	Good	Fair	Poor
475	400	275	225	150	100

Kentucky Rifle

Offered in either percussion or flintlock ignition it has a blue steel barrel, case colored lockplate, and a polished brass patch box inletted into a walnut stock. The barrel length is 35" and the rifle is available in .45 oz. 50 caliber. Weight is 6 lbs. 14 oz.

Percussion

NIB	Exc.	V.G.	Good	Fair	Poor
475	325	200	150	100	75

Flintlock

NIB	Exc.	V.G.	Good	Fair	Poor
495	335	225	150	100	75

Mortimer Flintlock Rifle

Offered in .54 caliber with rust blued barrel, walnut stock with cheekpiece and checkered straight grip. It also has a external safety and sling swivels. Barrel length is 36" and weight is 9 lbs. Optional shotgun barrel. Made by Pedersoli.

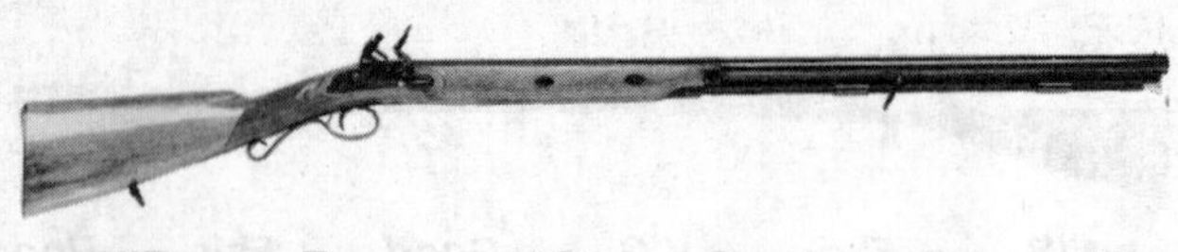

NIB	Exc.	V.G.	Good	Fair	Poor
750	600	500	450	350	150

NOTE: Optional shotgun barrel add $240.

Tryon Creedmoor Rifle

This .45 caliber model features a heavy blued 33" octagonal barrel, hooded front sight, adjustable tang sight, double set triggers, sling swivels, and a walnut stock. Weighs about 9.5 lbs.

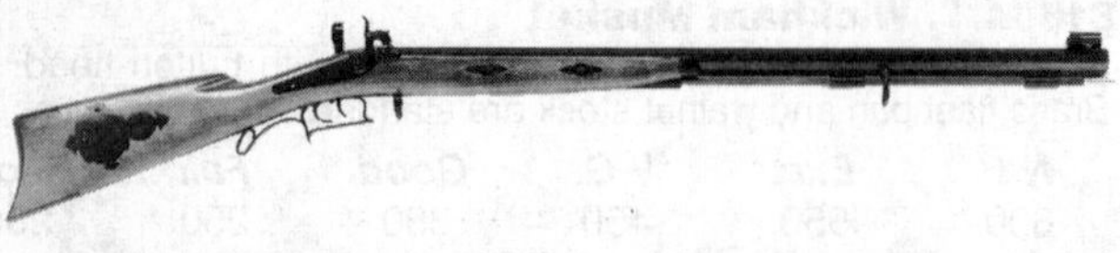

NIB	Exc.	V.G.	Good	Fair	Poor
600	525	450	400	300	150

Standard Tryon Rifle

Same as above but without target sights.

NIB	Exc.	V.G.	Good	Fair	Poor
500	350	300	250	200	100

Deluxe Tryon Rifle

Same as above but with polished and engraved lock and patch box.

NIB	Exc.	V.G.	Good	Fair	Poor
525	375	325	250	200	100

Parker-Hale Whitworth Rifle

This is a replica of a British sniper rifle, .451 caliber, used by the Confederates during the Civil War. Round barrel is 36" and features a globe front sight and ladder rear sight. The walnut stock is hand checkered. Weighs 9 lbs. 10 oz.

NIB	Exc.	V.G.	Good	Fair	Poor
850	675	600	450	300	150

NOTE: Limited edition telescope add $150.

Parker-Hale Volunteer Rifle

A .451 caliber rifle with hand checkered walnut stock. Fitted with 32" barrel with globe front sight and ladder rear sight. Weighs 9.5 lbs.

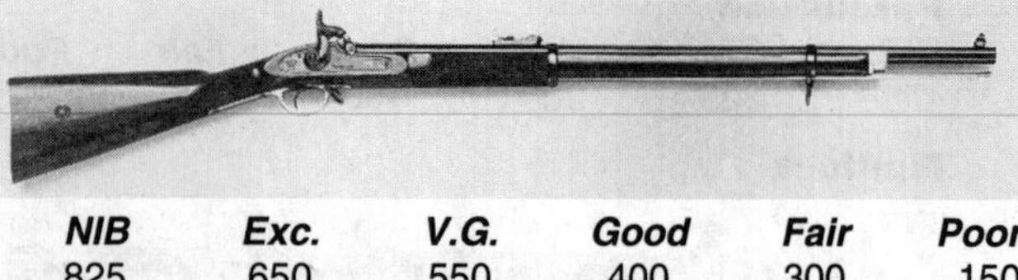

NIB	Exc.	V.G.	Good	Fair	Poor
825	650	550	400	300	150

Parker-Hale 3 Band Volunteer Rifle

Same basic specifications as Whitworth rifle but furnished with Alexander Henry rifling.

NIB	Exc.	V.G.	Good	Fair	Poor
750	650	600	400	250	50

Rigby Target Rifle

The 1880s replica is chambered for the .451 caliber. It is fitted with adjustable front sight and vernier tang sight. The lock, breech plug, trigger guard, buttplate, and escutcheons are case colored. Barrel length is 32" and weight is 7 lbs. 12 oz.

NIB	Exc.	V.G.	Good	Fair	Poor
700	500	450	300	200	100

1861 Springfield Rifle

This .58 caliber replica is fitted with an 1855-style hammer. Barrel length is 40" and weight is 10 lbs. 4 oz.

NIB	Exc.	V.G.	Good	Fair	Poor
550	425	350	300	200	100

Model 1873 Springfield Officer's Trapdoor

This model features a single set trigger, case colored breechblock, deluxe walnut stock, adjustable rear peep sight with Beech front sight. Chambered for the .45-70 cartridge and fitted with a 26" round barrel. Weight is about 8 lbs. Introduced in 2003.

NIB	Exc.	V.G.	Good	Fair	Poor
900	750	495	—	—	—

1862 C.S. Richmond Rifle

This Confederate rifle is .58 caliber and is a faithful reproduction of those produced at the Richmond Armory. Barrel length is 40". Weighs 10 lbs. 4 oz.

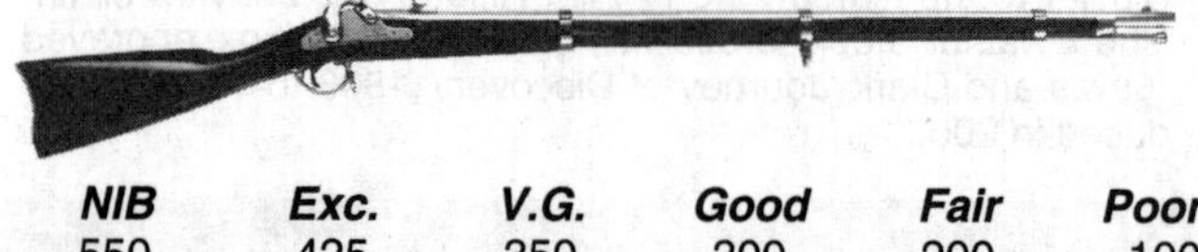

NIB	Exc.	V.G.	Good	Fair	Poor
550	425	350	300	200	100

J.P. Murray Carbine

This Confederate cavalry .58 caliber carbine has a case colored lock and brass furniture on a walnut stock. Barrel length is 23.5" and weight is 8 lbs. 5 oz.

NIB	Exc.	V.G.	Good	Fair	Poor
495	325	250	200	150	100

1863 Springfield Rifle

An exact replica of the famous Springfield Musket. Barrel is 40" with 3 barrel bands. All metal parts are finished bright. Weighs 9.5 lbs.

NIB	Exc.	V.G.	Good	Fair	Poor
550	425	350	300	200	100

1841 Mississippi Rifle

Also known as the "Yager" rifle; offered in either .54 or .58 caliber. Barrel length is 33" and weighs 9.5 lbs.

NIB	Exc.	V.G.	Good	Fair	Poor
450	325	250	200	150	100

Zouave Rifle

This Civil War replica is a .58 caliber with polished brass hardware and blued 33" barrel. Weighs 9 lbs.

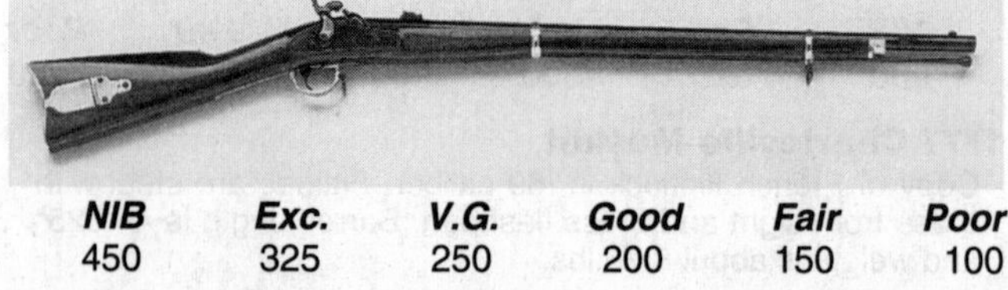

NIB	Exc.	V.G.	Good	Fair	Poor
450	325	250	200	150	100

Parker-Hale 1861 Musketoon

Made by Gibbs Rifle Company using 130-year-old gauges for reference. This .577 caliber replica features a 24" barrel with folding ladder military sight. The stock is walnut and the lock is case colored. All furniture is polished brass. Weighs 7.5 lbs.

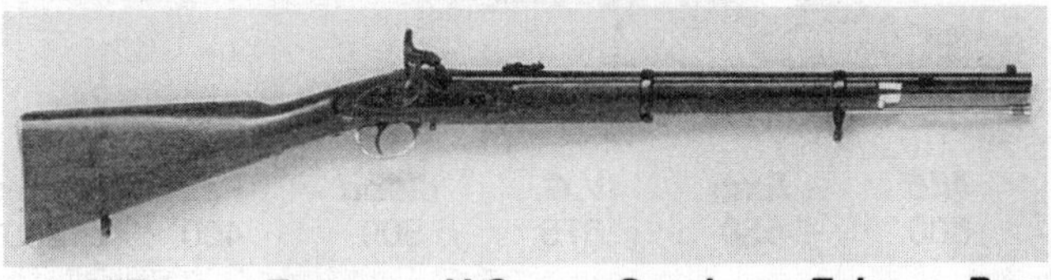

NIB	Exc.	V.G.	Good	Fair	Poor
400	325	250	200	150	100

Navy Arms Musketoon

Same as above but manufactured in Italy.

NIB	Exc.	V.G.	Good	Fair	Poor
400	325	250	200	150	100

Parker-Hale 1858 Two Band Musket

This .577 caliber model is based on the 1858 Enfield naval pattern. Fitted with a military sight graduated to 1,100 yards. Case colored lock and walnut stock with brass fittings. Barrel length is 33" and weighs 8.5 lbs.

NIB	Exc.	V.G.	Good	Fair	Poor
550	425	350	300	200	100

Navy Arms 1858 Two Band Musket

Same as above but built in Italy.

NIB	Exc.	V.G.	Good	Fair	Poor
450	325	250	200	150	100

Parker-Hale Three Band Musket

This replica is based on the design produced between 1853 and 1863. The rear sight is based on an 1853 model graduated to 900 yards. Is fitted with a case colored lock and walnut stock with brass furniture. Barrel is 39" and weighs 9 lbs.

NIB	Exc.	V.G.	Good	Fair	Poor
600	475	400	300	200	100

Navy Arms Three Band Musket

Same as above but produced in Italy.

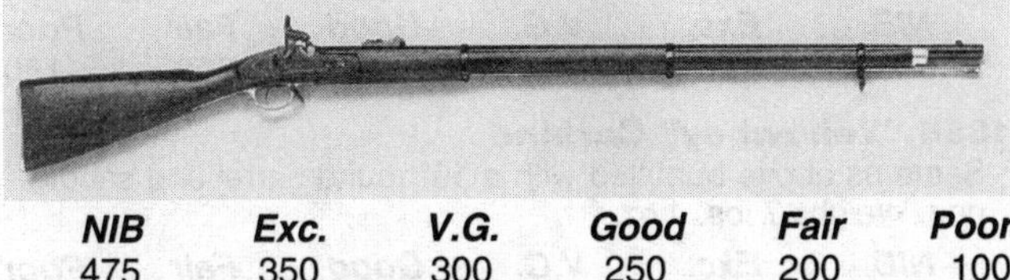

NIB	Exc.	V.G.	Good	Fair	Poor
475	350	300	250	200	100

Navy Arms Revolving Carbine

Fitted with a 20" barrel and chambered for the .357 Magnum, .44-40, or .45 Colt cartridge. This model has a revolving 6-shot cylinder. Straight-grip stock with brass buttplate and trigger guard. The action is based on the Remington Model 1874 revolver. Introduced in 1968 and discontinued in 1984.

NIB	Exc.	V.G.	Good	Fair	Poor
600	500	400	300	200	100

1859 Sharps Infantry Rifle

This is a .54 caliber copy of the three band Sharps. Barrel length is 30". Case hardened receiver and patch box. Blued barrel and walnut stock. Weight is about 8.5 lbs.

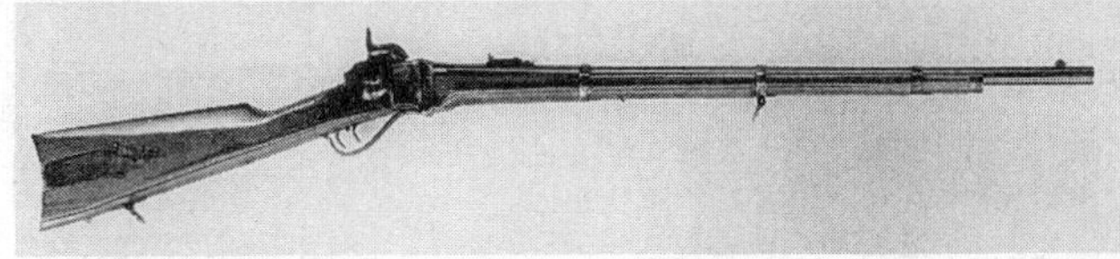

NIB	Exc.	V.G.	Good	Fair	Poor
1000	800	600	400	300	150

1859 Berdan Sharps Rifle

Similar to the 1859 Sharps above but with double set triggers.

NIB	Exc.	V.G.	Good	Fair	Poor
1075	850	650	450	325	150

1873 Sharps No. 2 Creedmore

Chambered for the .45-70 cartridge and fitted with a 30" round barrel. Polished nickel receiver. Target-grade rear tang sight and front globe sight with inserts. Checkered walnut stock with pistol grip. Weight is about 10 lbs. Introduced in 2002.

NIB	Exc.	V.G.	Good	Fair	Poor
1325	1000	—	—	—	—

Sharps #2 Silhouette Rifle

This model is identical to the standard No. 2 above but with a full octagon barrel. Weight is about 10.5 lbs. Introduced in 2003.

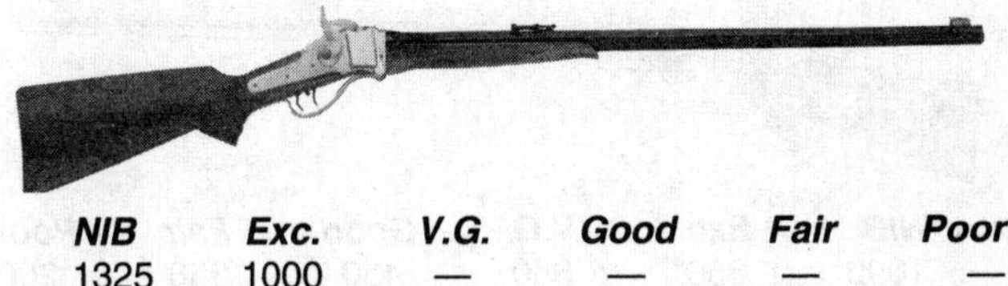

NIB	Exc.	V.G.	Good	Fair	Poor
1325	1000	—	—	—	—

Sharps #2 Sporting Rifle

Same as the No. 2 standard rifle but with case colored receiver. Introduced in 2003.

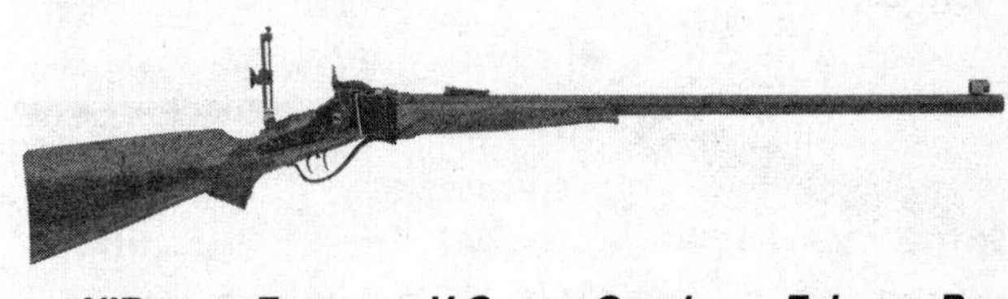

NIB	Exc.	V.G.	Good	Fair	Poor
1325	1000	—	—	—	—

1873 Sharps Quigley

This model is chambered for the .45-70 cartridge and fitted with a heavy 34" octagon barrel. Case hardened receiver with military patchbox. Open sights. Weight is about 13 lbs. Introduced in 2002.

NIB	Exc.	V.G.	Good	Fair	Poor
1390	1100	—	—	—	—

1874 Sharps Infantry Rifle

This model is fitted with a 30" round barrel and chambered for the .45-70 cartridge. Blued barrel with case hardened receiver. Walnut stock with 3 barrel bands. Weight is about 8.5 lbs.

NIB	Exc.	V.G.	Good	Fair	Poor
1050	750	550	—	—	—

1874 Sharps Sniper Rifle

Same as 1874 Infantry rifle but with double set triggers.

NIB	Exc.	V.G.	Good	Fair	Poor
1100	800	600	—	—	—

Sharps Cavalry Carbine

A breech-loading .54 caliber carbine with 22" blued barrel. Military-style sights, walnut stocks, and saddle bar with ring are standard. Weighs 7 lbs. 12 oz.

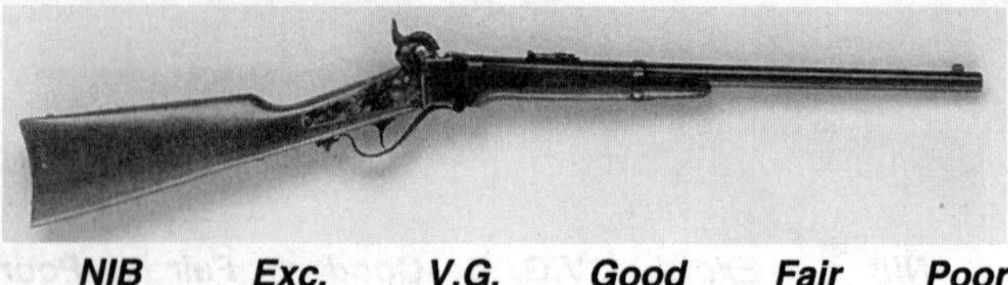

NIB	Exc.	V.G.	Good	Fair	Poor
925	550	500	400	300	150

Sharps Cavalry Carbine Cartridge Model

Same as above but chambered for the .45-70 Government cartridge.

NIB	Exc.	V.G.	Good	Fair	Poor
925	550	500	400	300	150

1874 Sharps Plains Rifle

This model features a case colored receiver, blued barrel, and checkered walnut stock. Offered in .44-70 or .54 caliber percussion. Barrel length is 28.5". Weight is 8 lbs. 10 oz.

NIB	Exc.	V.G.	Good	Fair	Poor
1050	800	600	400	300	150

1874 Sharps Sporting Rifle

Similar to the above model but features a full pistol grip, 32" medium weight octagonal barrel, double set triggers, and case colored frame. Weight is about 10.75 lbs.

NIB	Exc.	V.G.	Good	Fair	Poor
1090	850	650	450	350	200

1874 Sharps Buffalo Rifle

Chambered for the .45-70 or .45-90 and fitted with a 28" heavy octagon barrel. Buttstock is checkered. Weight is approximately 12 lbs.

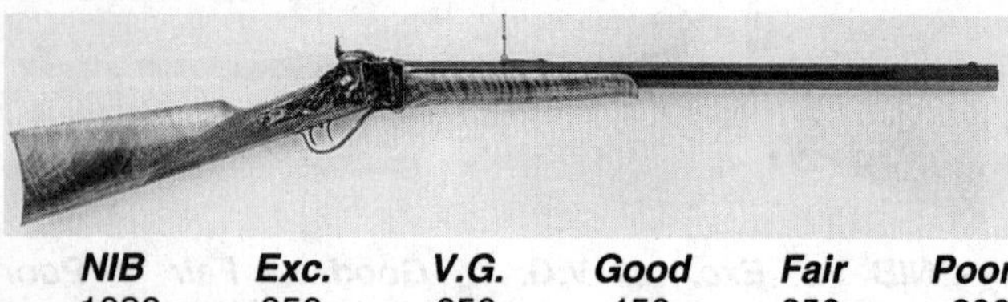

NIB	Exc.	V.G.	Good	Fair	Poor
1090	850	650	450	350	200

1874 Sharps No. 3 Long Range Rifle

Built by Pedersoli this rifle is fitted with a 34" medium weight octagon barrel, globe target front sight and match grade rear tang sight. Double set trigger. Case hardened frame. Walnut stock. Weight is about 11 lbs.

NIB	Exc.	V.G.	Good	Fair	Poor
1725	1250	900	—	—	—

1873 Winchester Rifle

This replica features a case colored receiver, blued octagon 24" barrel, and walnut stocks. Offered in either .44-40 or .45 Long Colt. Weighs about 8 lbs. 4 oz.

NIB	Exc.	V.G.	Good	Fair	Poor
900	725	600	500	400	200

1873 Winchester Carbine

Same specifications as rifle above but fitted with a 19" round barrel, blued receiver, and saddle ring. Weighs 7 lbs. 4 oz.

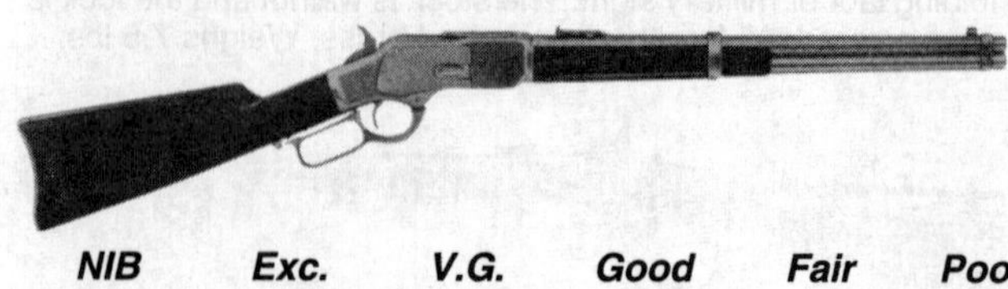

NIB	Exc.	V.G.	Good	Fair	Poor
800	650	575	500	400	200

1873 Winchester Sporting Rifle

This model features a 24.25" octagonal barrel, case colored receiver, and checkered pistol grip. Offered in .44-40 or. 45 Long Colt. Weighs about 8 lbs. 14 oz.

NIB	Exc.	V.G.	Good	Fair	Poor
950	750	650	525	400	200

1873 Sporting Long Range Rifle

Similar to the Sporting Rifle above but chambered for the .44-40 cartridge and fitted with a 30" octagon barrel. Long-range rear tang sight. Weight is about 7.5 lbs. Introduced in 2002.

NIB	Exc.	V.G.	Good	Fair	Poor
1075	850	—	—	—	—

1873 Border Model

Introduced in 2000 this model features a 20" blued octagon barrel with buckhorn rear sight. Magazine capacity is 10 rounds. Checkered pistol-grip stock is walnut with oil finish. Chambered for the .357 Mag., .44-40, or .45 Colt cartridge.

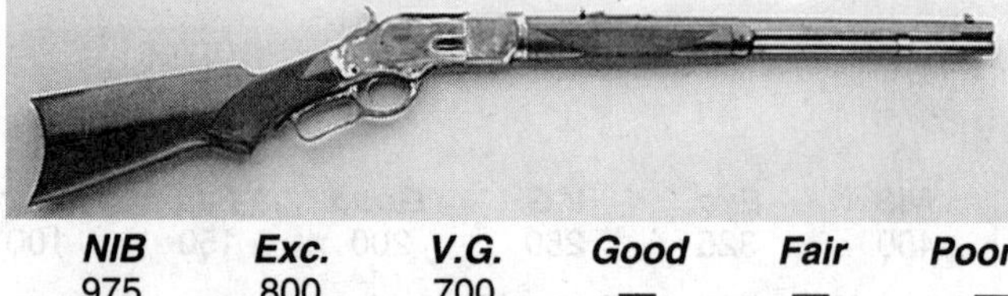

NIB	Exc.	V.G.	Good	Fair	Poor
975	800	700	—	—	—

1866 "Yellowboy" Rifle

This model features a brass receiver, 24" octagon barrel, and walnut stocks. Weighs 8.5 lbs.

NIB	Exc.	V.G.	Good	Fair	Poor
675	525	450	400	300	150

1866 "Yellowboy" Carbine

Same as above but fitted with a 19" round barrel and saddle ring. Weighs 7 lbs. 4 oz.

NIB	Exc.	V.G.	Good	Fair	Poor
675	525	450	400	300	150

1866 "Yellowboy" Short Rifle

Introduced in 2000 this model features a 20" barrel with buckhorn rear sight. Walnut stock with oil finish. Receiver is yellow brass. Chambered for the .38 Special, .44-40, or .45 Colt cartridge. Magazine capacity is 10 rounds.

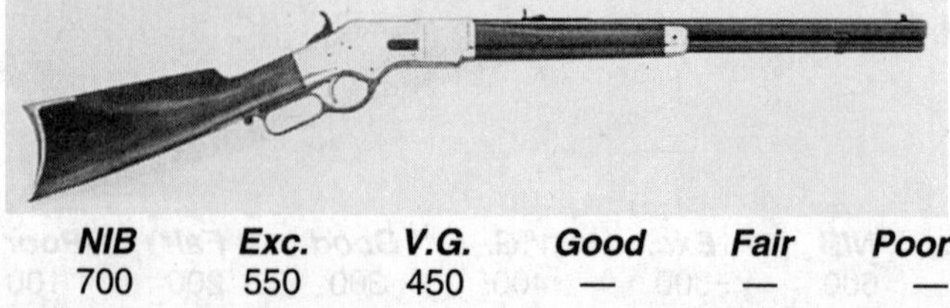

NIB	Exc.	V.G.	Good	Fair	Poor
700	550	450	—	—	—

Iron Frame Henry

This is a replica of the famous and rare .44-40 Iron Frame Henry that features a case colored frame. Barrel length is 24" and rifle weighs 9 lbs.

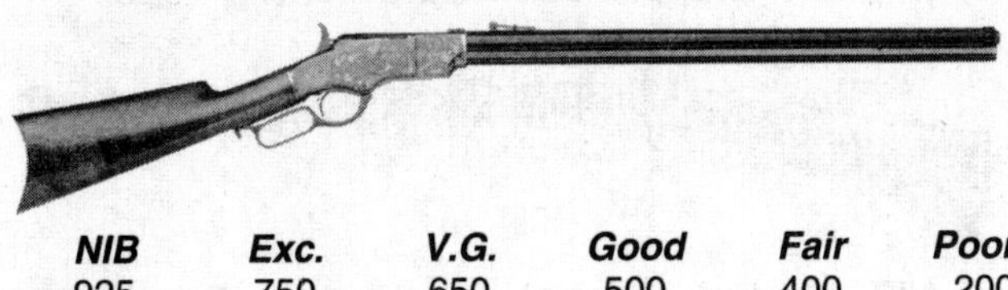

NIB	Exc.	V.G.	Good	Fair	Poor
925	750	650	500	400	200

Blued Iron Frame Henry

Same as above but furnished with a highly polished blued receiver.

NIB	Exc.	V.G.	Good	Fair	Poor
925	750	650	500	400	200

Military Henry

Based on the brass frame military version of the Henry rifle this model is furnished with sling swivels mounted on the left side. The buttplate is fitted with a trap door. Caliber is .44-40 and barrel length is 24". Weighs 9 lbs. 4 oz.

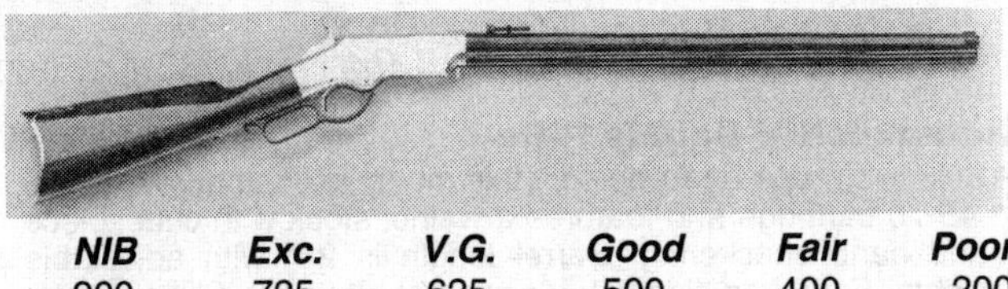

NIB	Exc.	V.G.	Good	Fair	Poor
900	725	625	500	400	200

Henry Carbine

This is the brass frame carbine version and features a 22" barrel. Chambered for the .44-40 cartridge. Weighs 8 lbs. 12 oz.

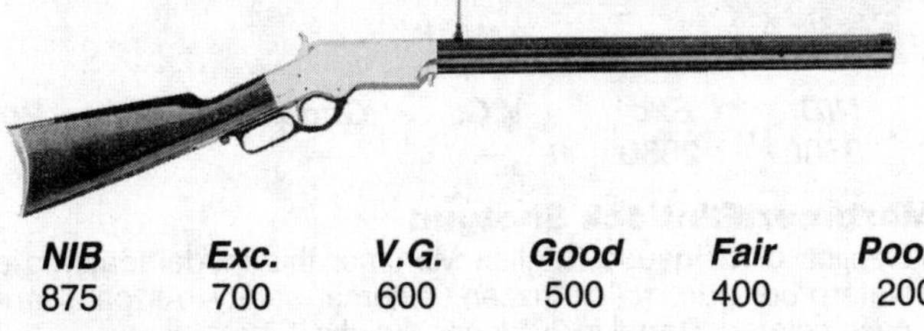

NIB	Exc.	V.G.	Good	Fair	Poor
875	700	600	500	400	200

Henry Trapper

This replica is not based on an actual Henry. Fitted with a unique 16.5" barrel, this brass frame model weighs 7 lbs. 7 oz. Chambered for the .44-40 cartridge.

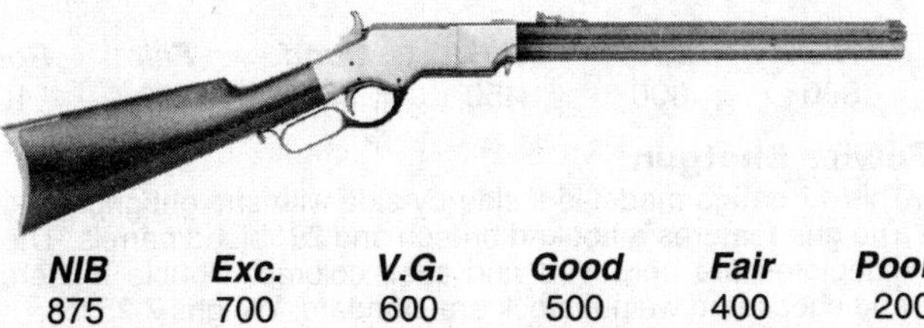

NIB	Exc.	V.G.	Good	Fair	Poor
875	700	600	500	400	200

1892 Rifle

This lever-action rifle is chambered for the .357 Mag., .44-40, .45 Colt, or .32-20 cartridge. Octagon barrel is 24.25". Walnut stock, crescent butt and blued or case colored receiver. Weight is about 6.25 lbs.

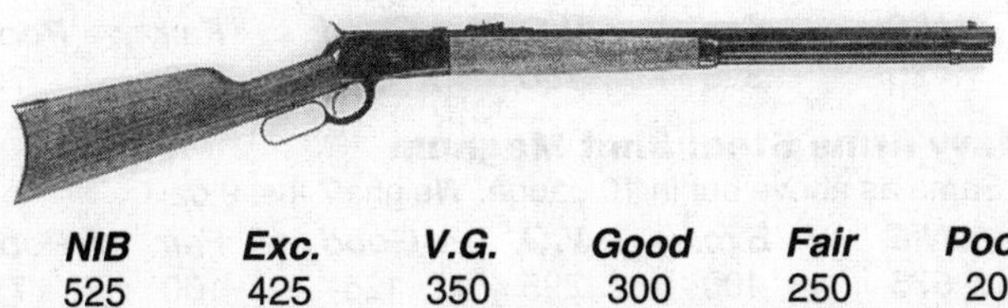

NIB	Exc.	V.G.	Good	Fair	Poor
525	425	350	300	250	200

1892 Short Rifle

Same as above but with 20" octagon barrel. Weight is about 6.25 lbs.

NIB	Exc.	V.G.	Good	Fair	Poor
525	425	350	300	250	200

1892 Carbine

Similar to the short rifle but fitted with a 20" round barrel and saddle ring on left side of receiver. Weight is about 5.75 lbs.

NIB	Exc.	V.G.	Good	Fair	Poor
450	350	300	250	200	150

1892 Brass Frame Carbine

Same as above but with polished brass receiver.

NIB	Exc.	V.G.	Good	Fair	Poor
450	350	300	250	200	150

1892 Brass Frame Rifle

This model is the same as the rifle but with polished brass receiver.

NIB	Exc.	V.G.	Good	Fair	Poor
525	425	350	300	250	200

No. 2 Creedmoor Target Rifle

This is a reproduction of the Remington No. 2 Creedmoor. It features a case colored receiver, tapered 30" octagonal barrel, hooded front sight, Creedmoor tang sight, and walnut stock with checkered pistol grip. Furnished in .45-70 Government. Weighs 9 lbs.

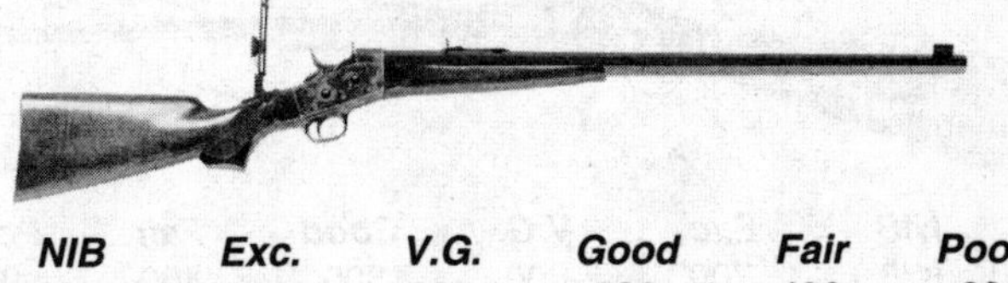

NIB	Exc.	V.G.	Good	Fair	Poor
900	725	625	500	400	200

Rolling Block Buffalo Rifle

This rifle is a replica of the Remington Buffalo rifle. It is fitted with a 26" or 30" octagonal or half octagonal barrel, case colored receiver, blade front sight, notch rear sight, brass trigger guard, with walnut stocks. Tang is drilled and tapped for tang sight.

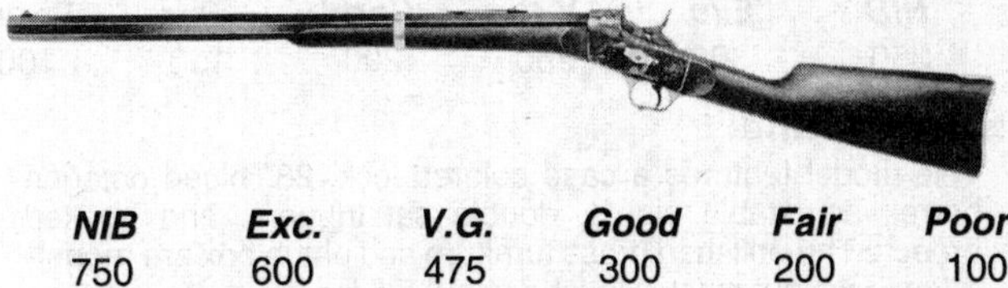

NIB	Exc.	V.G.	Good	Fair	Poor
750	600	475	300	200	100

Half Octagon Barrel Model

NIB	Exc.	V.G.	Good	Fair	Poor
750	600	475	300	200	100

"John Bodine" Rolling Block Rifle

Chambered for the .45-70 cartridge and fitted with a 30" octagon barrel. Double set triggers. Match-grade rear tang sight. Weight is about 12 lbs. Introduced in 2002.

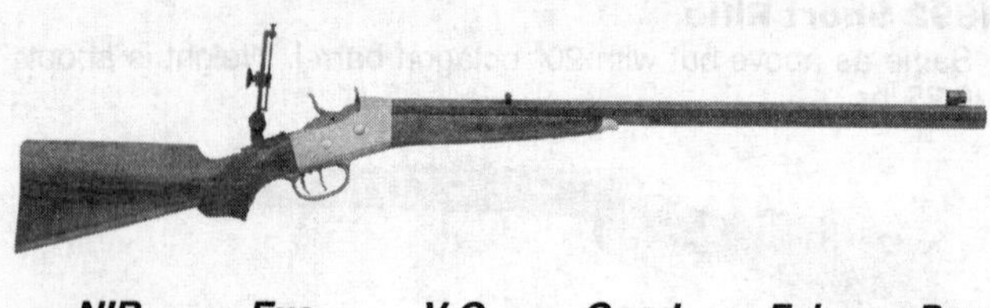

NIB	Exc.	V.G.	Good	Fair	Poor
1375	1050	—	—	—	—

1885 High Wall

Chambered for the .45-70 cartridge this rifle is fitted with a 30" medium heavy octagon barrel. Case colored receiver, target sights and walnut stocks. Also available with 28" round barrel.

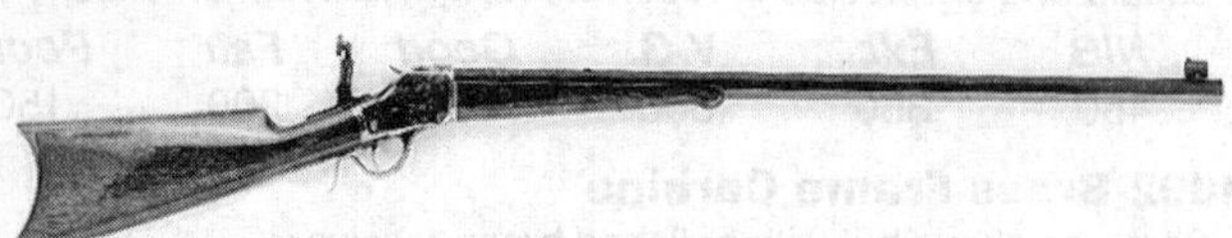

NIB	Exc.	V.G.	Good	Fair	Poor
900	725	600	500	400	200

NOTE: Reduce price by $100 for Buckhorn sights and $60 for 28" barrel.

1873 Springfield Infantry Rifle

A copy of the Trapdoor Springfield. Chambered for .45-70 and fitted with a 32.5" barrel. Walnut stock and case hardened breechlock. Weight is approximately 8.25 lbs.

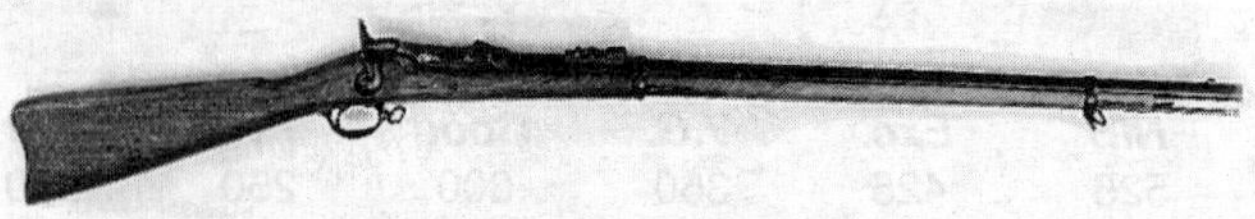

NIB	Exc.	V.G.	Good	Fair	Poor
975	800	600	500	400	200

1873 Springfield Cavalry Carbine

Same as above but with 22" barrel. Weight is about 7 lbs.

NIB	Exc.	V.G.	Good	Fair	Poor
875	700	600	500	400	200

Ithaca/Navy Hawken Rifle

Offered in either .50 or. 54 caliber percussion. Features a 31.5" rust blued octagon barrel. The percussion lockplate is case colored, while the rest of the hardware is blued with the exception of the nose cap and escutcheons. Weighs about 9 lbs. 13 oz.

NIB	Exc.	V.G.	Good	Fair	Poor
350	300	250	200	150	100

Hawken Rifle

This model features a case colored lock, 28" blued octagon barrel, adjustable sights, double set triggers, and hooked breech. The polished brass furniture and patch box are mounted on a walnut stock. Weighs about 8.5 lbs.

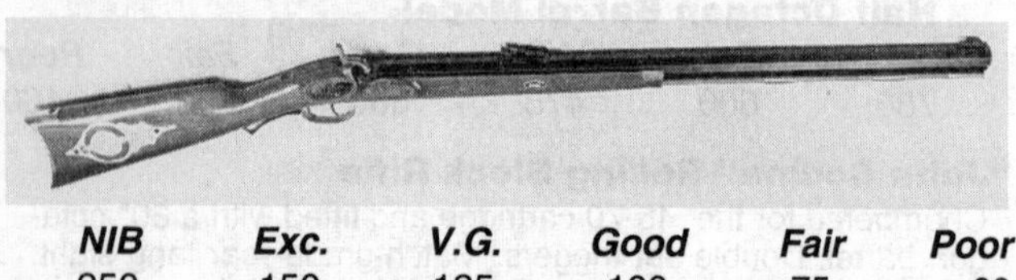

NIB	Exc.	V.G.	Good	Fair	Poor
250	150	125	100	75	60

Hawken Hunter Rifle

Offered in .50, .54, or .58 caliber, this model features blued hardware, adjustable sights, case colored lock, and hooked breech. The walnut stock is hand checkered with a cheekpiece. Rubber recoil pad is standard. Barrel length is 28".

NIB	Exc.	V.G.	Good	Fair	Poor
240	190	150	100	75	60

Hawken Hunter Carbine

Same as above but fitted with a 22.5" barrel. Weighs about 6 lbs. 12 oz.

NIB	Exc.	V.G.	Good	Fair	Poor
240	190	150	100	75	60

Kodiak MKIV Double Rifle

Built in Europe by Pedersoli, this model is chambered for the .45-70 cartridge and features a walnut stock with cheekpiece and hand checkering. Barrel length is 24" with adjustable sights. Engraved sideplates are polished bright. Sling swivels standard. Weighs 10.2 lbs.

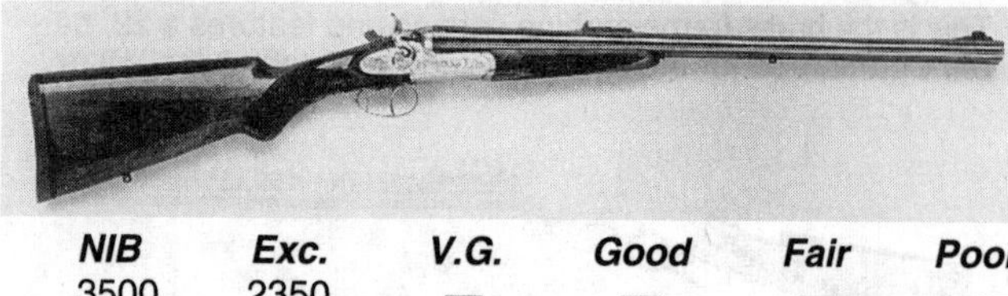

NIB	Exc.	V.G.	Good	Fair	Poor
3500	2350	—	—	—	—

Mortimer Flintlock Shotgun

Replica of 12 gauge English Mortimer this model features a waterproof pan, roller frizzen, external safety. All parts are case colored. Barrel is 36" long. Weighs 7 lbs.

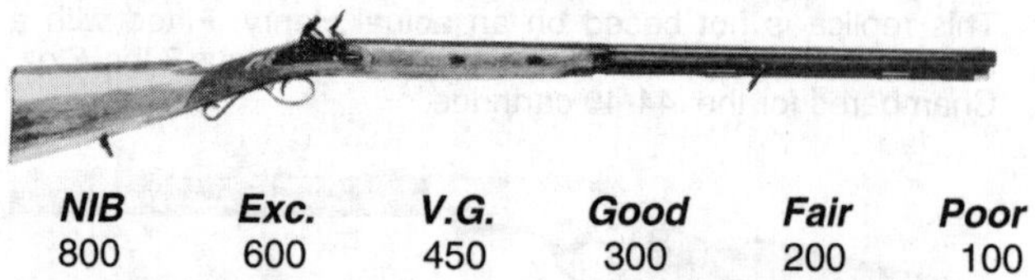

NIB	Exc.	V.G.	Good	Fair	Poor
800	600	450	300	200	100

Fowler Shotgun

This 12 gauge model is a side-by-side with straight gripstock. The gun features a hooked breech and 28" blued barrels. The sideplates are engraved and case colored. Double triggers and checkered walnut stock are standard. Weighs 7.25 lbs.

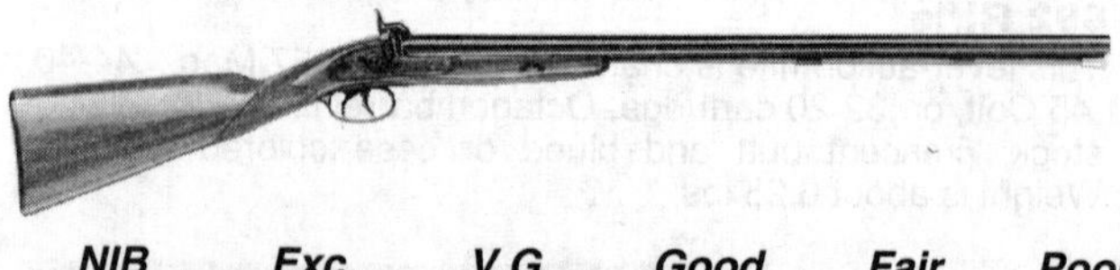

NIB	Exc.	V.G.	Good	Fair	Poor
425	325	150	125	100	75

Navy Arms Steel Shot Magnum

Same as above but in 10 gauge. Weighs 7 lbs. 9 oz.

NIB	Exc.	V.G.	Good	Fair	Poor
575	400	295	125	100	75

T&T Shotgun

This turkey and trap model has a straight grip stock and 28" barrel choked Full and Full. Locks are case colored and engraved. Walnut stock is checkered. Weighs 7.5 lbs.

NIB	Exc.	V.G.	Good	Fair	Poor
550	395	300	250	200	100

Japanese Matchlock

This model is a .50 caliber with 41" barrels. Weighs 8.5 lbs.

NIB	Exc.	V.G.	Good	Fair	Poor
800	550	300	200	100	75

HANDGUNS

Le Page Pistol

This .44 caliber percussion pistol has a 10.25" tapered octagon barrel, adjustable single set trigger. The lock, trigger guard, and buttcap are engraved. The walnut stocks are hand checkered. Weighs 36 oz.

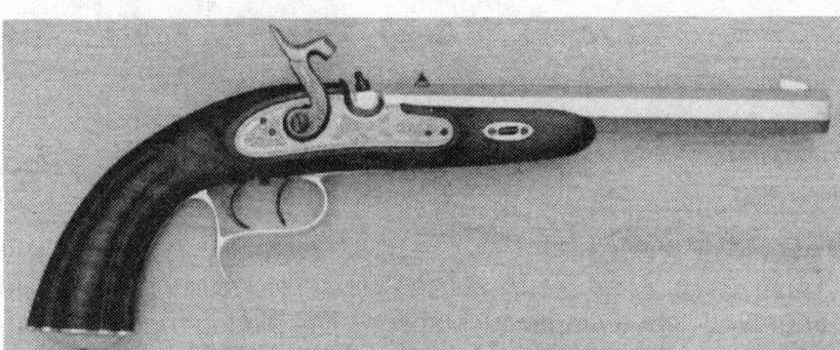

NIB	Exc.	V.G.	Good	Fair	Poor
400	350	300	250	200	100

Single Cased Set

NIB	Exc.	V.G.	Good	Fair	Poor
580	530	475	400	300	150

Double Cased Set

NIB	Exc.	V.G.	Good	Fair	Poor
995	875	750	600	400	200

Le Page Flintlock

Same as above but with flintlock ignition. Weighs 41 oz.

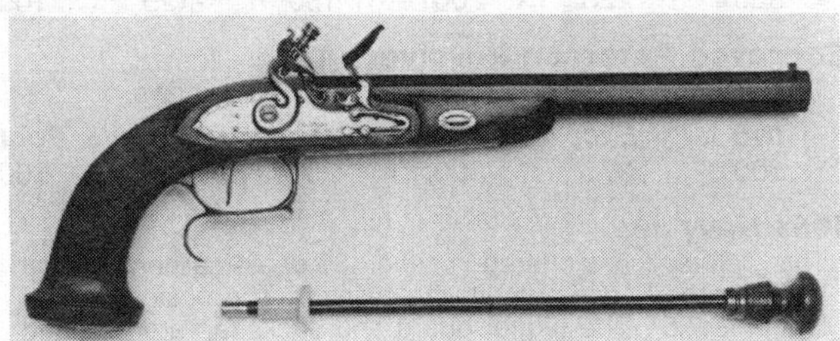

NIB	Exc.	V.G.	Good	Fair	Poor
470	425	350	250	150	100

Le Page Smoothbore Flintlock Pistol

Same as above but with a smooth bore.

NIB	Exc.	V.G.	Good	Fair	Poor
470	425	350	250	150	100

Single Cased Set

NIB	Exc.	V.G.	Good	Fair	Poor
650	600	500	400	300	150

Double Cased Set

NIB	Exc.	V.G.	Good	Fair	Poor
995	875	750	600	400	200

Kentucky Pistol

A percussion replica of a pistol developed in the 1840s. It has a 10.125" blued barrel, case colored lock, brass furniture and trigger guard with walnut stock. Weighs 32 oz.

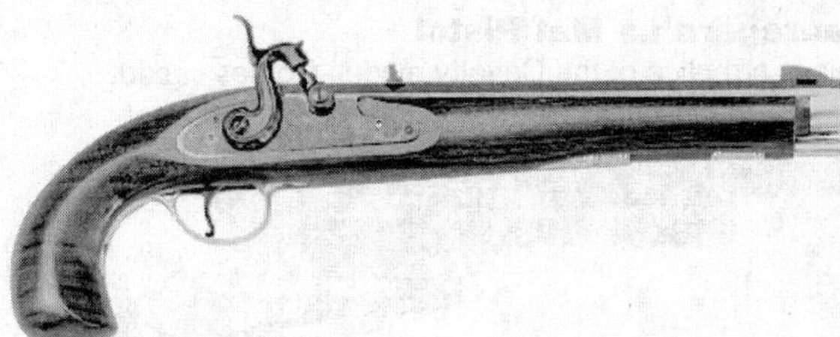

NIB	Exc.	V.G.	Good	Fair	Poor
225	175	150	100	85	60

Single Cased Set

NIB	Exc.	V.G.	Good	Fair	Poor
350	275	225	175	125	75

Double Cased Set

NIB	Exc.	V.G.	Good	Fair	Poor
550	450	350	250	150	100

Kentucky Flintlock Pistol

Same as above but with flintlock ignition.

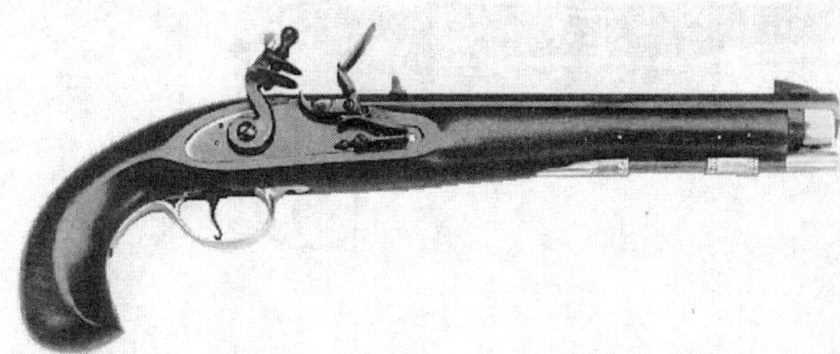

NIB	Exc.	V.G.	Good	Fair	Poor
225	175	150	100	75	60

Single Cased Set

NIB	Exc.	V.G.	Good	Fair	Poor
350	275	225	175	125	75

Double Cased Set

NIB	Exc.	V.G.	Good	Fair	Poor
550	450	350	275	175	100

Harpers Ferry Pistol

This pistol has a .58 caliber rifled 10" barrel. Case hardened lock and walnut stock. Weight is approximately 39 oz.

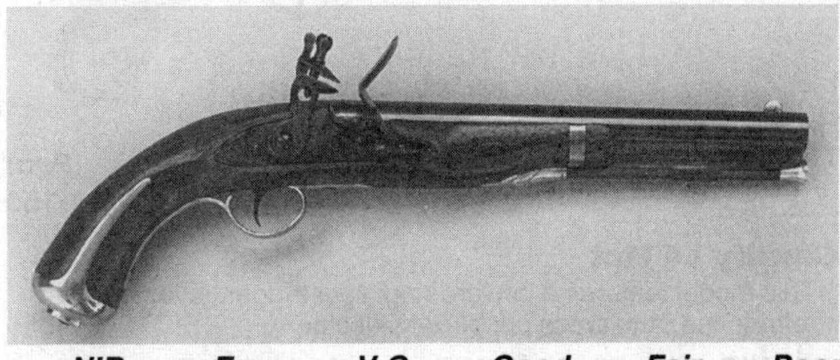

NIB	Exc.	V.G.	Good	Fair	Poor
300	250	200	150	100	75

Single Cased Set

NIB	Exc.	V.G.	Good	Fair	Poor
350	275	225	175	125	100

18th Georgia Le Mat Pistol

This 9-shot .44 caliber percussion revolver has a 7.625" blued barrel and engraved cylinder. An engraved banner on the left side of the frame reads "DEO VINDICE." Hammer and trigger are case colored. Stocks are checkered walnut. Comes with Le Mat mould and velvet draped French fitted case. Weighs 55 oz.

NIB	Exc.	V.G.	Good	Fair	Poor
795	625	500	400	300	150

Beauregard Le Mat Pistol

This is a replica of the Cavalry model. Comes cased.

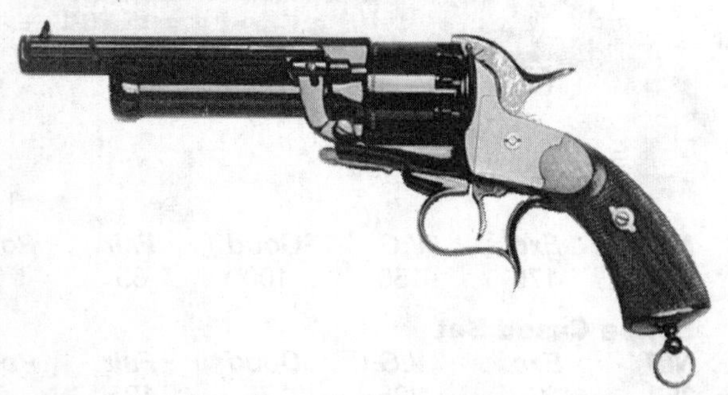

NIB	Exc.	V.G.	Good	Fair	Poor
1000	800	650	550	350	200

Navy Le Mat

This model features a knurled pin barrel release and spur barrel selector.

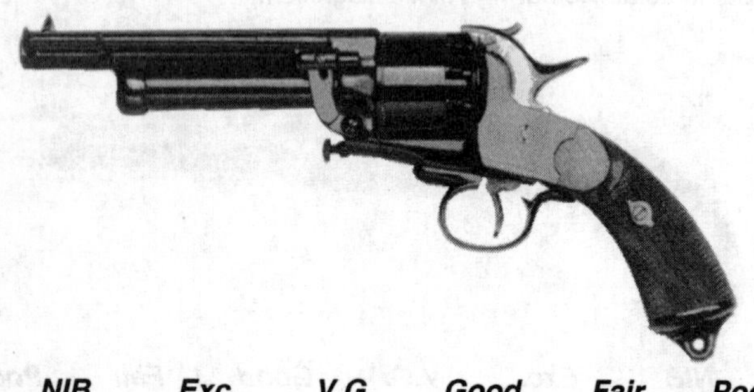

NIB	Exc.	V.G.	Good	Fair	Poor
595	450	400	350	300	150

Army Le Mat

This model features a knurled pin barrel release and cross pin barrel selector.

NIB	Exc.	V.G.	Good	Fair	Poor
595	450	400	350	300	150

Cavalry Le Mat

This model features a lanyard ring, spur trigger, lever type barrel release, and cross pin barrel selector.

NIB	Exc.	V.G.	Good	Fair	Poor
595	450	400	350	300	150

Starr Double-Action Model 1858 Army

This model is a double-action revolver chambered for .44 caliber. Fitted with a 6" barrel. Blued finish. Weight is about 48 oz.

NIB	Exc.	V.G.	Good	Fair	Poor
350	250	200	—	—	—

Starr Single-Action Model 1863 Army

This model is fitted with an 8" barrel and is chambered for .44 caliber. Blued finish and walnut stock. Weight is about 48 oz.

NIB	Exc.	V.G.	Good	Fair	Poor
350	250	200	—	—	—

1862 New Model Police

This replica is based on the Colt .36 caliber pocket pistol of the same name. It features a half fluted and re-dated cylinder, case colored frame and loading gate, and a polished brass trigger guard and backstrap. Barrel length is 5.5" and pistol weigh 26 oz.

NIB	Exc.	V.G.	Good	Fair	Poor
290	225	175	150	100	75

1862 New Model Book-Style Cased Set

NIB	Exc.	V.G.	Good	Fair	Poor
350	250	200	150	100	75

Paterson Revolver

This replica is the five-shot .36 caliber. The cylinder is scroll engraved with a stagecoach scene. The hidden trigger drops down when the hammer is cocked. Barrel is 9" and the pistol weighs 43 oz.

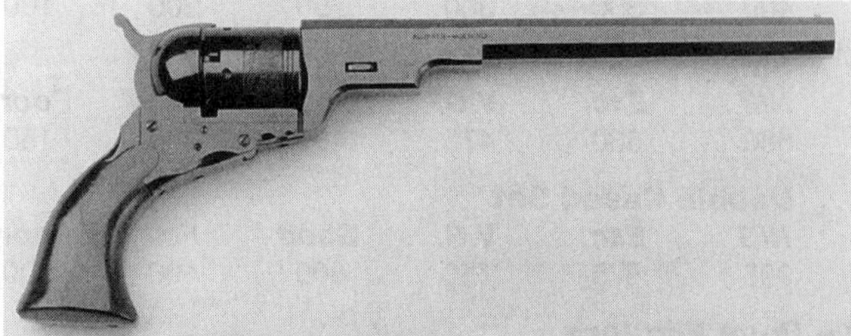

NIB	Exc.	V.G.	Good	Fair	Poor
325	225	200	150	125	100

Engraved Paterson Revolver

This model features hand engraving with silver inlays.

NIB	Exc.	V.G.	Good	Fair	Poor
500	375	300	250	200	100

1851 Navy

This Colt replica is offered in either .36 or .44 caliber. A naval battle scene is engraved in the cylinder. The octagon barrel length is 7.5". The trigger guard and backstrap are polished brass. The walnut grips are hand rubbed. Weighs 32 oz.

NIB	Exc.	V.G.	Good	Fair	Poor
150	125	100	75	50	40

Single Cased Set

NIB	Exc.	V.G.	Good	Fair	Poor
275	225	175	125	100	60

Double Cased Set

NIB	Exc.	V.G.	Good	Fair	Poor
450	350	300	250	200	100

NOTE: Optional shoulder stock add $100.

1851 Navy Conversion

This is a replica of the Colt 1851 Navy cartridge conversion. Offered in 38 Special or .38 Long Colt with choice of 5.5" or 7.5" barrels. Weight is about 40 oz.

NIB	Exc.	V.G.	Good	Fair	Poor
350	275	225	—	—	—

Augusta 1851 Navy Pistol

Available with either 5" or 7.5" barrel. Engraved with "A" coverage.

NIB	Exc.	V.G.	Good	Fair	Poor
300	250	200	150	100	75

Model 1851 Navy Frontiersman

Introduced in 2003 this revolver features a 5" .36 caliber barrel. The receiver, loading lever and hammer are case colored while the barrel and cylinder are charcoal blued. Fitted with a German silver backstrap and walnut grips.

NIB	Exc.	V.G.	Good	Fair	Poor
N/A	—	—	—	—	—

Reb Model 1860 Pistol

This is a replica of the Confederate Griswold and Gunnison revolver. It features a blued round 7.5" barrel, brass frame, trigger guard and backstrap. Offered in .36 or .44 caliber. Weighs 44 oz.

NIB	Exc.	V.G.	Good	Fair	Poor
100	80	70	60	50	35

Reb 1860 Sheriff's Model

Same as above but fitted with a 5" barrel. Weighs 40 oz.

NIB	Exc.	V.G.	Good	Fair	Poor
100	80	70	60	50	35

1847 Walker Dragoon

This is a replica of the rare Colt .44 caliber revolver. The barrel and cylinder are blued while the frame and loading lever are case colored. Barrel length is 9" and pistol weighs 75 oz.

NIB	Exc.	V.G.	Good	Fair	Poor
275	225	175	150	125	100

Single Cased Set

NIB	Exc.	V.G.	Good	Fair	Poor
400	325	275	250	200	100

Single Deluxe Cased Set

NIB	Exc.	V.G.	Good	Fair	Poor
525	425	350	300	200	100

1860 Army Pistol

This .44 caliber model features a case colored frame and loading lever with blued barrel, cylinder, and backstrap. The trigger guard is brass. The cylinder is engraved with a battle scene. Barrel is 8" and pistol weighs 41 oz.

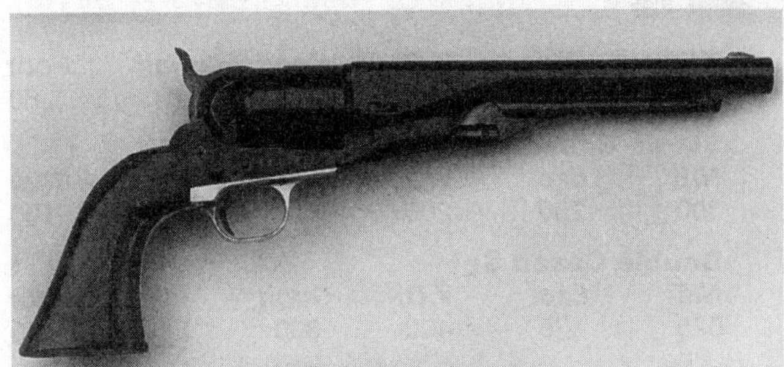

NIB	Exc.	V.G.	Good	Fair	Poor
175	150	125	100	75	45

Single Cased Set

NIB	Exc.	V.G.	Good	Fair	Poor
300	250	200	150	100	75

Double Cased Set

NIB	Exc.	V.G.	Good	Fair	Poor
490	400	325	250	200	100

1860 Army Conversion

Chambered for the .38 Special or .38 Long Colt this model is fitted with either a 5.5" or 7.5" barrel. Blued finish. Walnut grips. Weight is about 40 oz.

NIB	Exc.	V.G.	Good	Fair	Poor
350	275	225	—	—	—

1858 New Model Remington-Style Pistol

This replica has a solid frame, as did the original. The frame and 8" barrel are blued, while the trigger guard is brass. Walnut grips are standard. Weighs 40 oz.

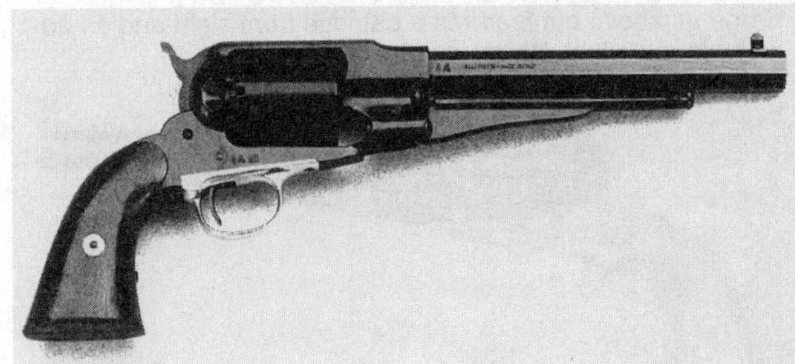

NIB	Exc.	V.G.	Good	Fair	Poor
170	125	100	75	60	45

Single Cased Set

NIB	Exc.	V.G.	Good	Fair	Poor
290	225	175	125	100	75

Double Cased Set

NIB	Exc.	V.G.	Good	Fair	Poor
475	375	300	250	200	100

Stainless Steel 1858 New Model Army

Same as above but in stainless steel. Weighs 40 oz.

NIB	Exc.	V.G.	Good	Fair	Poor
220	180	150	125	100	80

Single Cased Set

NIB	Exc.	V.G.	Good	Fair	Poor
300	250	200	150	125	100

Double Cased Set

NIB	Exc.	V.G.	Good	Fair	Poor
525	475	400	300	200	150

Brass Framed 1858 New Model Army

This version features a highly polished brass frame. Barrel length is 7.75".

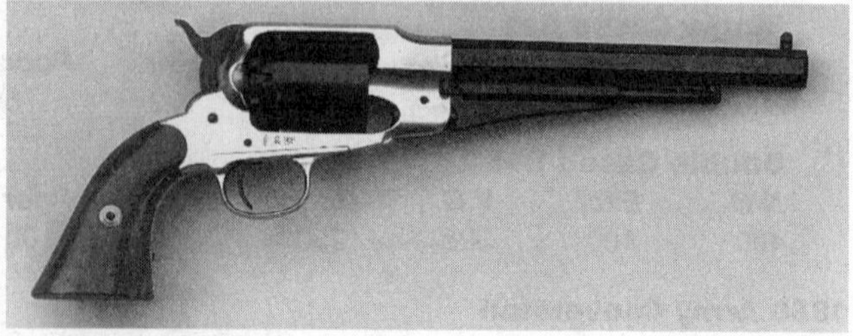

NIB	Exc.	V.G.	Good	Fair	Poor
125	100	80	60	50	35

Single Cased Set

NIB	Exc.	V.G.	Good	Fair	Poor
250	200	150	100	75	60

Double Cased Set

NIB	Exc.	V.G.	Good	Fair	Poor
395	325	300	250	200	100

1858 Target Model

Same as above but features a patridge front sight and an adjustable rear sight. Barrel length is 8".

NIB	Exc.	V.G.	Good	Fair	Poor
175	150	125	100	75	50

Deluxe 1858 New Model Army

This replica is built to the exact dimensions as the original. The barrel is 8" with adjustable front sight. The trigger guard is silver plated. The action is tuned for competition. Weighs 46 oz.

NIB	Exc.	V.G.	Good	Fair	Poor
400	325	250	200	150	100

Spiller and Burr Pistol

This is a .36 caliber pistol with 7" blued octagon barrel. The frame is brass with walnut grips. Weighs 40 oz.

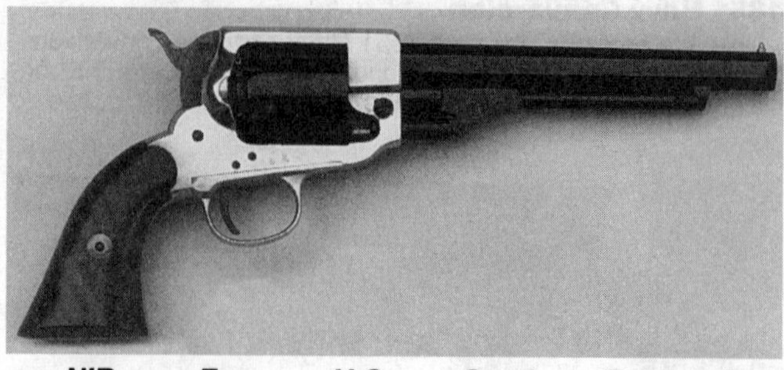

NIB	Exc.	V.G.	Good	Fair	Poor
140	100	80	65	50	40

Single Cased Set

NIB	Exc.	V.G.	Good	Fair	Poor
250	200	150	100	75	60

Double Cased Set

NIB	Exc.	V.G.	Good	Fair	Poor
425	350	300	250	200	100

Rogers and Spencer

This model features a 7.5" barrel with blued frame and barrel. Offered in .44 caliber. Walnut grips. Weighs 48 oz.

NIB	Exc.	V.G.	Good	Fair	Poor
240	200	150	100	75	50

"London Gray" Rogers and Spencer Pistol

Same as above but with a burnished satin chrome finish.

NIB	Exc.	V.G.	Good	Fair	Poor
240	200	150	125	100	80

Rogers and Spencer Target Model

Same as standard model but fitted with adjustable target sights.

NIB	Exc.	V.G.	Good	Fair	Poor
275	225	175	125	100	80

1861 Navy Conversion

Replica of the cartridge conversion of the 1861 Navy. Chambered for .38 Special or .38 Long Colt. Fitted with either a 5.5" or 7.5" barrel. Weight is about 40 oz.

NIB	Exc.	V.G.	Good	Fair	Poor
350	275	225	—	—	—

1872 Colt Open Top

This model features a 5.5" or 7.5" barrel with case hardened frame, blued barrel and cylinder, and silver-plated brass trigger guard and backstrap. Walnut grips. Chambered for .38 caliber cartridge. Weight is about 40 oz.

NIB	Exc.	V.G.	Good	Fair	Poor
490	375	225	—	—	—

1873 Colt-Style Single-Action Army

This replica features a case colored frame and hammer with blued round barrel in 3", 4.75", 5.5", or 7.5" lengths. Trigger guard and cylinder are blued. Offered in .44-40, .45 Long Colt, .357 Magnum, and .32-20.

NIB	Exc.	V.G.	Good	Fair	Poor
390	325	275	200	150	100

Model 1873 SAA Stainless Gunfighter

Introduced in 2003 this model is the same as the standard 1873, but features all stainless steel construction. Offered in .45 Colt and .357 Magnum caliber with choice of 4.75", 5.5", or 7.5" barrel. Weight is about 45 oz. depending on barrel length.

NIB	Exc.	V.G.	Good	Fair	Poor
510	400	—	—	—	—

Economy Model 1873 S.A.A.

Same as above but with brass trigger guard and backstrap.

NIB	Exc.	V.G.	Good	Fair	Poor
275	250	200	150	125	100

Nickel 1873 S.A.A.

NIB	Exc.	V.G.	Good	Fair	Poor
500	400	300	225	150	100

1873 U.S. Cavalry Model

This .45 Long Colt model features U.S. arsenal stampings, case colored frame, and walnut grips. Barrel length is 7.5" and pistol weighs 45 oz.

NIB	Exc.	V.G.	Good	Fair	Poor
390	325	275	200	150	100

1873 Pinched Frame Model

This is a replica of the "pinched" frame 1873 with "U" shape rear sight notch. Chambered for .45 Colt with 7.5" barrel.

NIB	Exc.	V.G.	Good	Fair	Poor
400	325	275	225	—	—

1873 Flat Top Target

This model features a windage adjustable rear sight on a flat top frame and a spring loaded front sight. Barrel length is 7.5". Offered in .45 Colt. Weight is about 40 oz. Introduced in 1998.

NIB	Exc.	V.G.	Good	Fair	Poor
425	350	—	—	—	—

Deputy Single-Action Army

Similar to the Model 1873 but with a bird's-head grip. Barrel lengths are 3", 3.5", 4", and 4.75". Chambered for .44-40 and .45 Colt.

NIB	Exc.	V.G.	Good	Fair	Poor
400	300	250	200	—	—

Shootist Model S.A.A.

This model is a reproduction of the Colt 1873. Parts are interchangeable with the originals. Blued barrel, cylinder, trigger guard, and backstrap. Case hardened frame and hammer. Walnut grips. Offered in 4.75", 5.5", and 7.5" barrel lengths. Chambered for .357 Magnum, .44-40, or .45 Colt.

NIB	Exc.	V.G.	Good	Fair	Poor
375	275	225	—	—	—

Scout Small Frame Revolver

This model is identical to the Colt 1872 SAA but with smaller dimensions. Offered in .38 Special with choice of 4.75" or 5.5" barrel. Weight is about 30 oz. Introduced in 2003.

NIB	Exc.	V.G.	Good	Fair	Poor
415	325	—	—	—	—

Deluxe 1873 Colt Revolver

This model is chambered for the .32-20 cartridge and features bright charcoal blue with case colored frame and hammer. Walnut grips. Fitted with a 5.5" barrel. Limited production. Weight is about 41 oz.

NIB	Exc.	V.G.	Good	Fair	Poor
435	350	—	—	—	—

Bisley Model

This model features the famous Bisley grip. Barrel length is 4.75", 5.5", and 7.5". Chambered for .44-40 or .45 Colt.

This symbol denotes "Sleepers" with rapidly-rising values and/or significant collector potential.

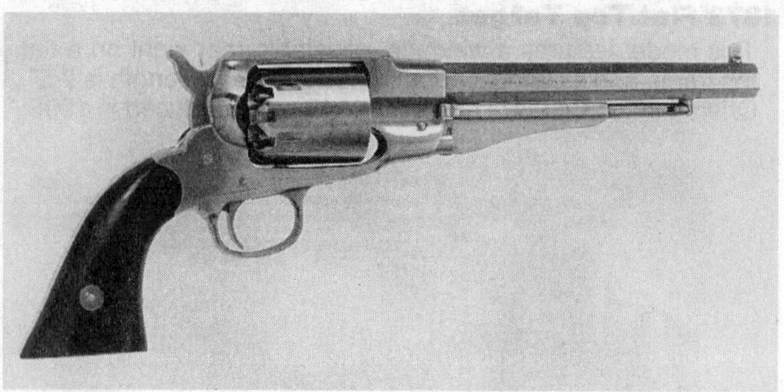

NIB	Exc.	V.G.	Good	Fair	Poor
425	300	250	200	—	—

Bisley Flat Top Target

Similar to the Bisley but with 7.5" barrel with flat top frame with adjustable front sight and windage adjustable rear sight. Chambered for .44-40 or .45 Colt. Weight is about 40 oz.

NIB	Exc.	V.G.	Good	Fair	Poor
450	350	250	200	—	—

1895 U.S. Artillery Model

Same as Cavalry Model but fitted with a 5.5" barrel. Weighs 42 oz.

NIB	Exc.	V.G.	Good	Fair	Poor
475	375	300	250	200	100

1875 Remington-Style Revolver

The frame is case colored while all other parts are blued except for brass trigger guard. Available in .44-40 or .45 Long Colt. Furnished with walnut grips. Barrel length is 7.5". Weighs 41 oz.

NIB	Exc.	V.G.	Good	Fair	Poor
425	350	300	250	200	100

1890 Remington-Style Revolver

This is a modified version of the 1875 model that is also offered in .44-40 or .45 Long Colt. The web under the barrel has been eliminated. It has blued 5.5" steel barrel and frame. Lanyard loop is on bottom of walnut grips. Weighs 39 oz.

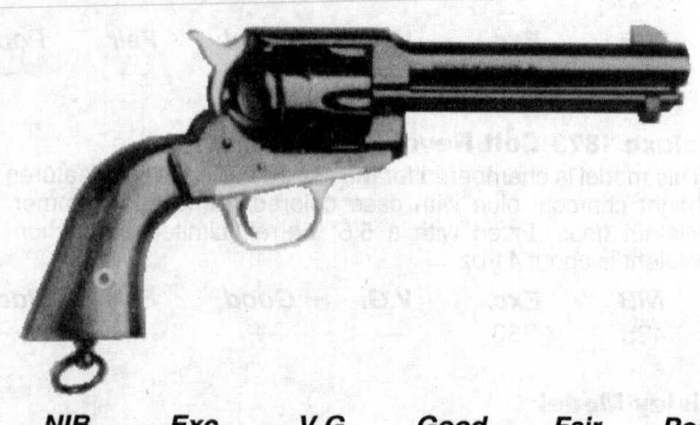

NIB	Exc.	V.G.	Good	Fair	Poor
445	350	300	250	200	100

TOP BREAK REVOLVERS

Model 1875 Schofield—Wells Fargo 5" barrel

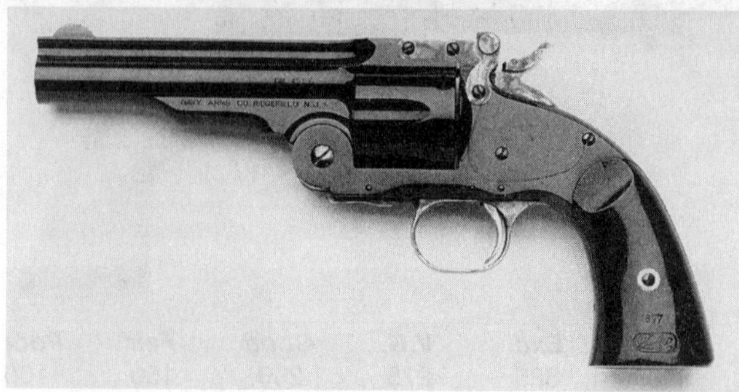

NIB	Exc.	V.G.	Good	Fair	Poor
650	525	450	350	200	100

Model 1875 Schofield—Cavalry 7" barrel

A reproduction of the S&W Model 3 top break revolver in either .44-40 or .45 Long Colt. The Cavalry model has a 7" barrel while the Wells Fargo model has a 5" barrel. Weight is about 39 oz.

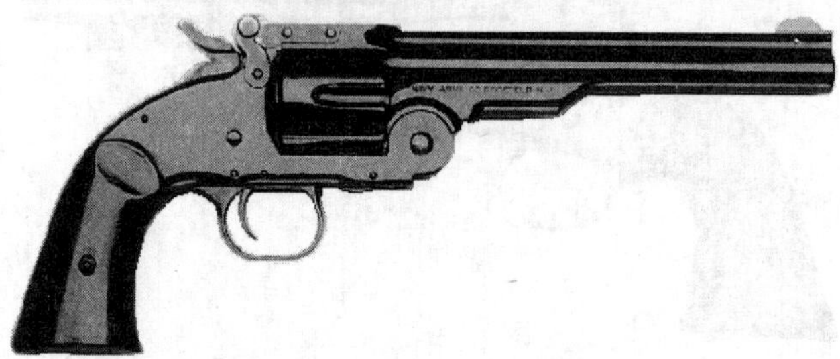

NIB	Exc.	V.G.	Good	Fair	Poor
650	525	450	350	200	100

Model 1875 Schofield—Deluxe

This model has a charcoal blue finish with gold inlays and "A" style hand engraving. Available in either the Cavalry or Wells Fargo model. Special order only.

NIB	Exc.	V.G.	Good	Fair	Poor
925	—	—	—	—	—

Model 1875 Schofield—B Engraved

Available In Cavalry or Wells Fargo Model. This grade is "B" style engraved with 35 percent coverage. Special order only.

NIB	Exc.	V.G.	Good	Fair	Poor
1000	—	—	—	—	—

Model 1875 Schofield—C Engraved

This model is available in Cavalry or Wells Fargo with "C" style engraving with 50 percent coverage. Special order only.

NIB	Exc.	V.G.	Good	Fair	Poor
1150	—	—	—	—	—

Model 1875 Schofield Founder's Model

Introduced in 2003 to honor Val Forgett, Sr. and Aldo Uberti. This revolver features a charcoal blued barrel and cylinder with color case hardened receiver, backstrap, trigger guard and trigger. Grip are white ivory polymer. Limited production with special serial number prefix of "VF."

NIB	Exc.	V.G.	Good	Fair	Poor
780	625	—	—	—	—

Model 1875 Schofield—Hideout

This is a short-barrel variation of the Schofield. It is fitted with a 3.5" barrel and chambered for the .44-40 or .45 Colt cartridge. Weight is about 38 oz.

NIB	Exc.	V.G.	Good	Fair	Poor
650	550	—	—	—	—

New Model Russian

Built around the single-action Smith & Wesson Model 3, this revolver is chambered for the .44 Russian cartridge. It is fitted with a 6.5" barrel. Case colored spur trigger guard, latch and hammer. Blued frame, barrel and cylinder. Walnut grips. Weight is about 40 oz. Introduced in 1999.

NIB	Exc.	V.G.	Good	Fair	Poor
650	550	—	—	—	—

MILITARY SURPLUS ARMS

SKS Type 56 w/Scope Rail

This semi-automatic gas operated rifle is chambered for the 7.62x39 cartridge. It has a 10-round clip. This model is fitted with a scope rail on the left side of the receiver. Barrel length is 20.5". Weight is 8 lbs.

NIB	Exc.	V.G.	Good	Fair	Poor
120	100	75	60	50	35

Standard SKS Type 56

Same as above without the scope rail.

NIB	Exc.	V.G.	Good	Fair	Poor
115	95	75	60	50	35

With Scope and Bipod

As above but fitted with a 2.75 power Type 89 scope and RPK style folding bipod.

NIB	Exc.	V.G.	Good	Fair	Poor
280	250	200	150	125	100

SKS "Cowboy's Companion" Carbine

Barrel length on this version is 16.5". Weighs 7 lbs. 8 oz.

NIB	Exc.	V.G.	Good	Fair	Poor
135	110	85	70	60	40

Military Version

This is the military version of the "Cowboy's Companion" fitted with a short cruciform folding bayonet.

NIB	Exc.	V.G.	Good	Fair	Poor
145	120	90	75	60	40

SKS "Hunter" Carbine

This model has a checkered composite Monte Carlo stock with full length pull. Comes with 5-round magazine.

NIB	Exc.	V.G.	Good	Fair	Poor
195	175	150	125	100	75

TT-Olympia Pistol

This is a reproduction of the Walther target pistol. Chambered for .22 LR. Barrel length is 4.625" and pistol weighs 27 oz.

NIB	Exc.	V.G.	Good	Fair	Poor
225	200	150	125	100	—

TU-90 Pistol

This model is based on the Tokagypt pistol. It features a wraparound grip with thumb rest. Barrel length is 4.5" and pistol weighs 30 oz.

NIB	Exc.	V.G.	Good	Fair	Poor
250	190	115	75	50	40

TU-KKW Training Rifle

Based on the 98 Mauser and chambered for the .22 LR cartridge. It is fitted with military sights, bayonet lug, cleaning rod and take down disc. Comes with detachable 5-round box magazine. Barrel length is 26" and weighs 8 lbs.

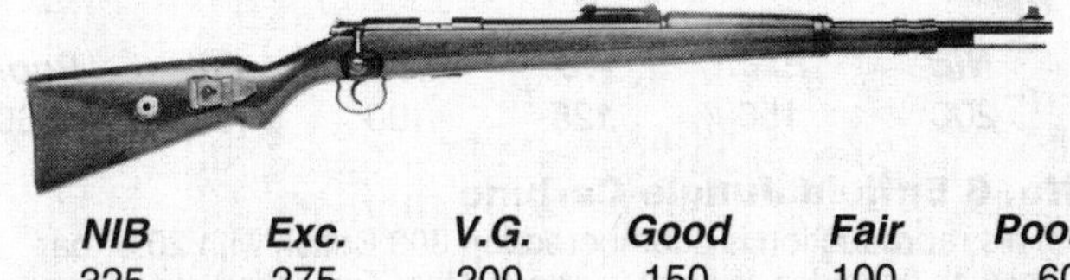

NIB	Exc.	V.G.	Good	Fair	Poor
325	275	200	150	100	60

TU-KKW Sniper Trainer

Same as above but fitted with a 2.75 power Type 89 scope and quick detachable mounting system.

NIB	Exc.	V.G.	Good	Fair	Poor
375	325	275	200	150	100

TU-33/40 Carbine

This model is based on the WWII Mauser G 33/40 mountain carbine. Chambered for the .22 LR or 7.62x39 cartridge. Barrel length is 20.75" and weighs 7.5 lbs.

NIB	Exc.	V.G.	Good	Fair	Poor
325	275	200	150	100	

JW-15 Rifle

This model is a bolt-action design based on the BRNO Model 5 action. Chambered for the .22 LR it features adjustable sights, sling swivels, an detachable 5-round magazine. The top of the receiver is dovetailed for easy scope mounting. Barrel is 24" long and rifle weighs 5 lbs. 12 oz.

NIB	Exc.	V.G.	Good	Fair	Poor
100	80	70	60	50	35

Martini Target Rifle

A .444 or .45-70 caliber single-shot Martini-action rifle with a 26" or 30" octagonal barrel, tang sight, and walnut stock. Offered between 1972 and 1984.

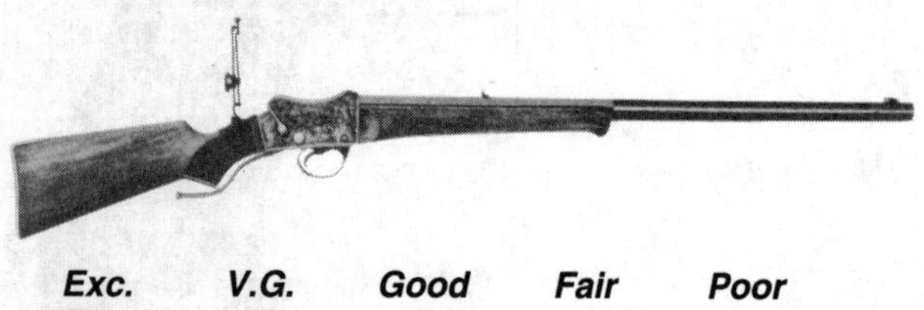

Exc.	V.G.	Good	Fair	Poor
475	425	350	275	175

Parker-Hale Sniper Rifle

SEE—Parker-Hale.

RPKS-74

A 5.56mm or 7.62x39mm caliber semi-automatic rifle with a 19" barrel patterned after the Russian AK series rifles.

No. 5 Enfield Jungle Carbine

This replica is chambered for .303 British cartridge and fitted with cupped buttplate and flashider. Barrel length is 20.5". Magazine capacity is 10 rounds. Weight is approximately 7 lbs.

NIB	Exc.	V.G.	Good	Fair	Poor
200	150	125	100	80	60

No. 6 Enfield Jungle Carbine

This reproduction is chambered for .303 British with 20.5" barrel with flashider. Weight is about 7 lbs. Ten-round magazine.

NIB	Exc.	V.G.	Good	Fair	Poor
250	180	150	125	100	80

Ishapore 2A No. 1 MK III Rifle

This is a refinished rifle with 25" barrel and chambered for .308 Win. cartridge. Magazine capacity is 12 rounds. Weight is about 9.3 lbs.

NIB	Exc.	V.G.	Good	Fair	Poor
225	150	125	100	80	60

2A Tanker Carbine

This is a replica with a short 20" barrel. Chambered for .308 Win. Magazine capacity is 12 rounds. Weight is approximately 8.7 lbs.

NIB	Exc.	V.G.	Good	Fair	Poor
250	180	150	125	100	80

MK III Tanker Carbine

Similar to the above model but chambered for the .303 British cartridge. Magazine capacity is 10 rounds.

NIB	Exc.	V.G.	Good	Fair	Poor
250	180	150	125	100	80

Lithgow No. 1 MK III Rifle

These rifles are in unissued condition. Barrel length is 25". Chambered for .303 British cartridge. Magazine capacity is 10 rounds. Weight is about 9 lbs.

NIB	Exc.	V.G.	Good	Fair	Poor
250	200	150	125	100	75

No. 1 MK III Enfield Rifle

These rifles are standard MK III S.M.L.E. rifles that have been refinished. Barrel length is 25.25". Magazine capacity is 10 rounds of .303 British. Weight is about 9 lbs.

NIB	Exc.	V.G.	Good	Fair	Poor
225	180	150	125	100	80

No. 4 Tanker Carbine

This is a cut-down version of the No. 4 MK I Enfield. Barrel length is 20.5". Chambered for .303 with magazine capacity of 10 rounds. Weight is approximately 8.2 lbs.

NIB	Exc.	V.G.	Good	Fair	Poor
250	180	150	125	100	80

No. 4 MK I Enfield Rifle

This is a reconditioned rifle. Barrel length is 25". Magazine capacity is 10 rounds of .303 British. Weight is about 8.6 lbs.

NIB	Exc.	V.G.	Good	Fair	Poor
250	195	100	80	60	—

Savage No. 4 MK I Rifle

Chambered for .303 British cartridge with 25" barrel. Stocks are unissued. Magazine capacity is 10 rounds. Weight is approximately 8.7 lbs.

NIB	Exc.	V.G.	Good	Fair	Poor
250	180	150	125	100	80

Luger

A .22 caliber semi-automatic pistol with a 4", 6", or 8" barrel, fixed sights, and 10-shot magazine. Blued with walnut grips. Manufactured in the U.S.A. in 1986 and 1987.

Exc.	V.G.	Good	Fair	Poor
175	150	125	100	75

Grand Prix Silhouette Pistol

A .30-30, .44 Magnum, 7mm Special, and .45-70 caliber single-shot pistol with a 13.75" barrel, adjustable sights, and an aluminum, heat-disbursing rib. Matte-blued, walnut grips and forearm. Manufactured in 1985.

Exc.	V.G.	Good	Fair	Poor
325	275	225	175	125

NEAL, W.

Bangor, Maine

Under Hammer Pistol

A .31 caliber under hammer percussion pistol with 5" to 8" barrels, iron frame and walnut grip. The barrel marked "Wm. Neal/Bangor, Me."

Exc.	V.G.	Good	Fair	Poor
—	—	950	400	150

NEPPERHAN FIREARMS CO.

Yonkers, New York

Pocket Revolver

A .31 caliber percussion revolver with 3.5" to 6" barrels and a 5-shot cylinder. Blued, case hardened with walnut grips. The barrel marked "Nepperhan/Fire Arms Co" and on some additionally "Yonkers New York." The latter are worth a slight premium over the values listed. Approximately 5,000 were made during the 1860s.

Exc.	V.G.	Good	Fair	Poor
—	—	900	350	200

NESIKA BAY PRECISION, INC.

Sturgis, South Dakota

Hunting Rifles

Offered in a number of different calibers with several stock options to choose from. All rifles are fitted with adjustable trigger.

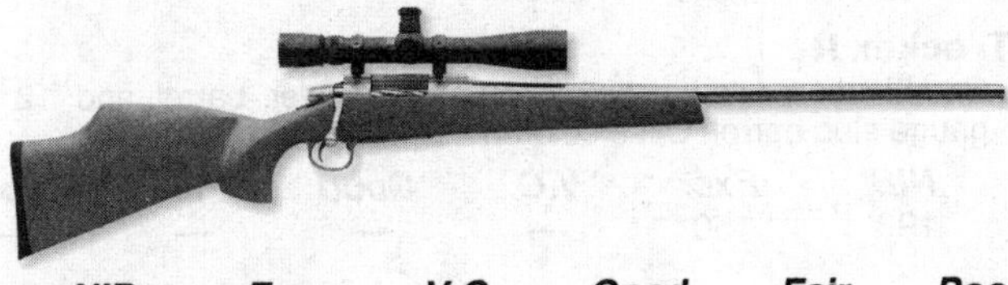

NIB	Exc.	V.G.	Good	Fair	Poor
3700	2900	—	—	—	—

Varmint Rifles

Offered in a variety of calibers and barrel lengths and weights. Single shot or repeater.

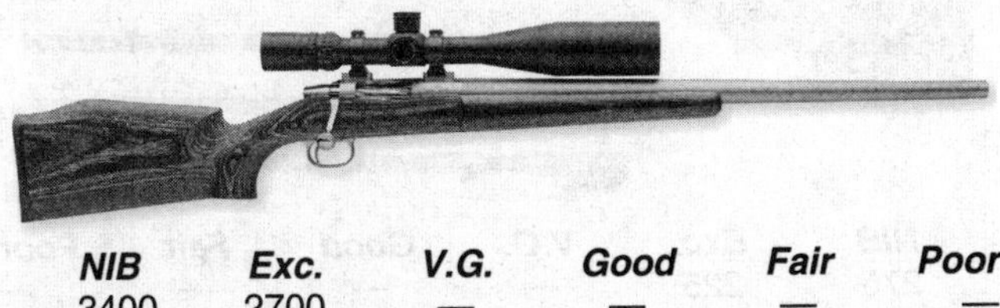

NIB	Exc.	V.G.	Good	Fair	Poor
3400	2700	—	—	—	—

Urban Tactical Rifle

Chambered for the .308 cartridge and fitted with a 20" fluted barrel. Detachable box magazine. Weight is about 10 lbs.

NIB	Exc.	V.G.	Good	Fair	Poor
5040	4000	—	—	—	—

NOTE: For .300 win. Mag add $100.

Heavy Tactical Rifle

As above but with heavyweight receiver and barrel (24" to 28") with heavy stock. Weight is about 14 lbs.

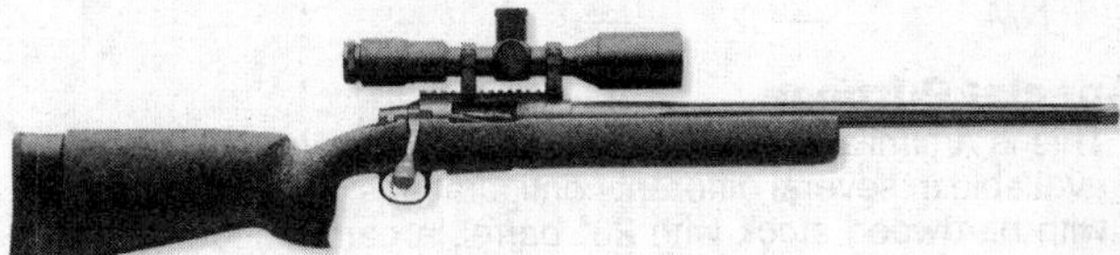

NIB	Exc.	V.G.	Good	Fair	Poor
5200	4200	—	—	—	—

NOTE: For .300 Win. Mag add $100.

NEW ENGLAND FIREARMS CO.

Gardner, Massachusetts

New England Firearms Company is now owned by Marlin.

Model R22

Magnum or .32 H&R Magnum double-action revolver with a 2.5", 4", or 6" barrel and either a 6- or 9-shot cylinder. Blued or nickel-plated with walnut grips. Introduced in 1988.

NIB	Exc.	V.G.	Good	Fair	Poor
110	95	80	70	60	40

Pardner

A 12, 16, 20 or .410 bore single-shot shotgun with a 24", 26", or 28" barrel. Blued with a walnut stock. Introduced in 1987.

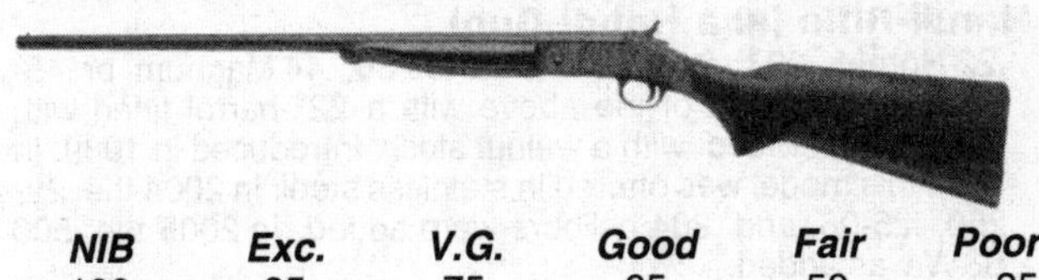

NIB	Exc.	V.G.	Good	Fair	Poor
100	85	75	65	50	35

Pardner Youth

Similar to the above model but offered only in 20 and 28 gauge as well as .410 bore. Fitted with a 26" barrel. Weight is between 5 and 6 lbs.

NIB	Exc.	V.G.	Good	Fair	Poor
100	85	75	65	50	35

Pardner Pump

Introduced in 2004 this 12 gauge 3" shotgun is fitted with a 28" vent rib barrel. Plain American walnut or synthetic stock with grooved forearm. Modified choke tubes. Weight is about 7.5 lbs.

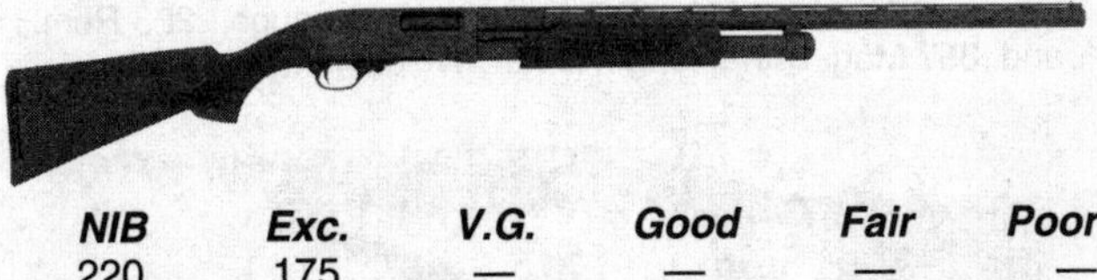

NIB	Exc.	V.G.	Good	Fair	Poor
220	175	—	—	—	—

Pardner Pump Turkey

This model is chambered for the 12 gauge 3" shell and fitted with 22" barrel with turkey choke tube. Magazine capacity is 5 rounds. Weight is about 7.5 lbs. Introduced in 2005.

NIB	Exc.	V.G.	Good	Fair	Poor
N/A	—	—	—	—	

Pardner Pump Combo

Introduced in 2005 this model features two 12 gauge 3" barrels. One 28" with vent rib and choke tubes, and the other 22" rifled slug barrel. Walnut stock. Weight is about 7.5 lbs. depending on barrel length.

NIB	Exc.	V.G.	Good	Fair	Poor
N/A	—	—	—	—	

Special Purpose

This is a similar model but it is offered only in 10 gauge. It is available in several different configurations: A 10 gauge model with hardwood stock with 28" barrel, a camo model with 28" barrel, a camo model with 32" barrel choked Modified, and a black matte finish model with 24" barrel with screw-in turkey Full choke. Weight is about 9.5 lbs.

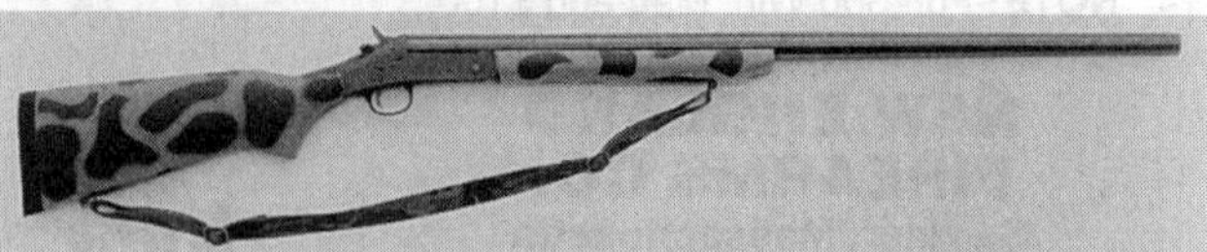

Special Purpose Waterfowl Model

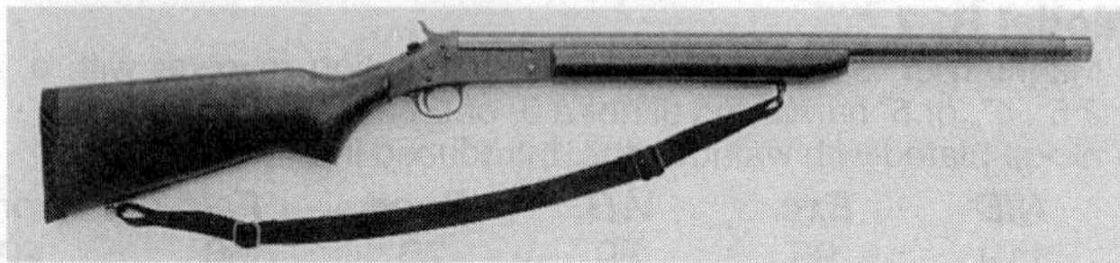

Special Purpose Turkey Gun

NIB	Exc.	V.G.	Good	Fair	Poor
250	175	125	100	75	50

Handi-Rifle (aka Handi-Gun)

.22 Hornet, .223, .243, .270, .280, .30-30, .44 Magnum, or .45-70 caliber version of the above with a 22" barrel fitted with open sights. Blued, with a walnut stock. Introduced in 1989. In 2003 this model was offered in stainless steel. In 2004 the .22-250, .25-06, and .204 calibers were added. In 2005 the .500 S&W was added.

NIB	Exc.	V.G.	Good	Fair	Poor
275	200	150	125	100	75

Survivor

Based on a single-shot break-action design this rifle or shotgun is fitted with a synthetic stock with integral storage compartments. Offered in .410/.45 Colt, 12 and 20 gauge, .223 Rem., and .357 Mag. Barrel length is 22". Weight is about 6 lbs.

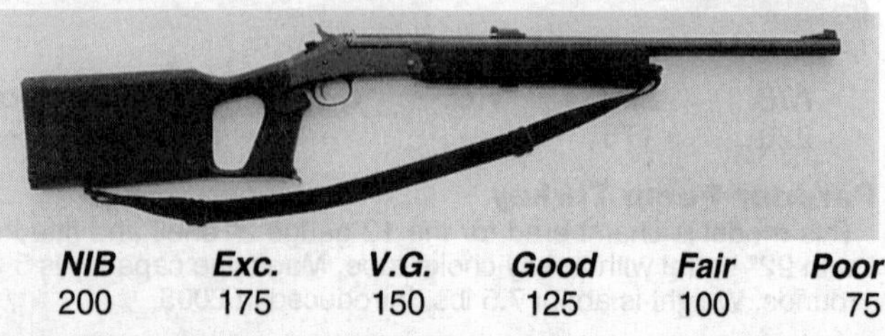

NIB	Exc.	V.G.	Good	Fair	Poor
200	175	150	125	100	75

Tracker

This single-shot break-open shotgun is offered in both 12 and 20 gauge with rifled barrel or cylinder bore barrel. Both are 24" in length. Equipped with adjustable rifle sights. Weight is about 6 lbs.

NIB	Exc.	V.G.	Good	Fair	Poor
150	125	100	75	60	50

Super Light Rifles

This single-shot rifle is chambered for the .22 Hornet or .223 Rem. It is fitted with a 20" light weight barrel. Choice of scope mount and no sights or adjustable rear sight and ramp front sight. Black polymer stock with semi-beavertail forend. Weight is about 5.5 lbs.

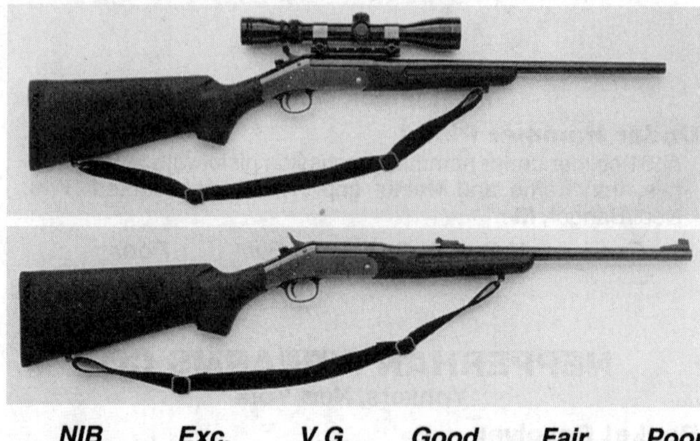

NIB	Exc.	V.G.	Good	Fair	Poor
175	125	100	75	60	50

Huntsman

This is a blackpowder gun with break-open action hardwood pistol-grip stock. Fitted with a 24" barrel. Chambered for .50 or .45 caliber slug. Recoil pad. Weight is about 6.5 lbs. Introduced in 2002.

In 2003 this model was offered in stainless steel.

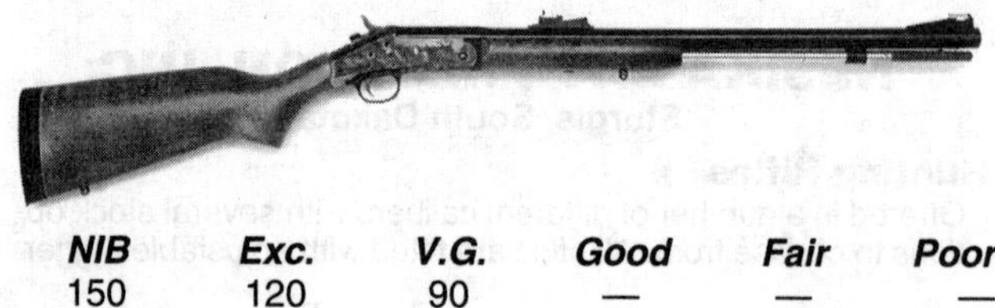

NIB	Exc.	V.G.	Good	Fair	Poor
150	120	90	—	—	—

Tracker II

Combination two-barrel set of blackpowder barrel and 12 gauge slug barrel. Case colored frame. Hardwood stock.

NIB	Exc.	V.G.	Good	Fair	Poor
190	150	—	—	—	—

Handi-Rifle Combo

Combination two-barrel set of .50 blackpowder barrel and .243 Win. barrel. Hardwood stock. No iron sights.

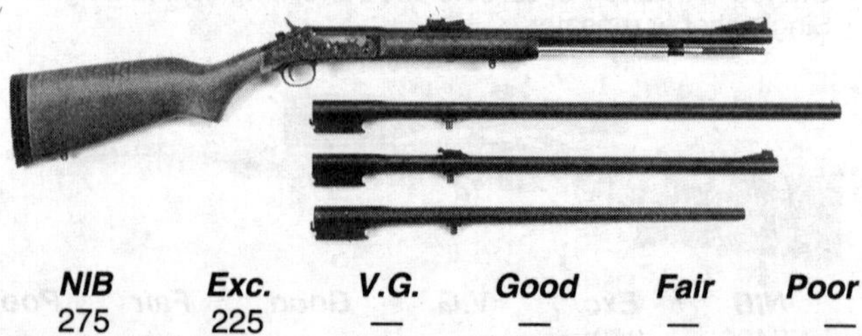

NIB	Exc.	V.G.	Good	Fair	Poor
275	225	—	—	—	—

Sportster

This is a single shot .22 caliber short, LR and .22 WMR rifle with a 20" barrel. No iron sights. Black polymer Monte Carlo stock with matte black metal finish. Scope mount rail. Weight is about 5.5 lbs.

NIB	Exc.	V.G.	Good	Fair	Poor
150	120	—	—	—	—

Sportster Youth

As above but with no Monte Carlo. Weight is about 5.25 lbs.

NIB	Exc.	V.G.	Good	Fair	Poor
150	120	—	—	—	—

Sportster .17 HMR

This single-shot model is chambered for the .17 HMR cartridge and fitted with a 22" heavy varmint barrel. No iron sights. Black polymer Monte Carlo stock with matte black metal finish. Weight is about 7 lbs.

NIB	Exc.	V.G.	Good	Fair	Poor
180	140	—	—	—	—

Sportster .17 M2

As above but chambered for the .17 Mach2 cartridge. Introduced in 2005.

NIB	Exc.	V.G.	Good	Fair	Poor
180	140	—	—	—	—

Sportster SL

This is a semi-automatic rifle chambered for the .22 LR cartridge. Fitted with a 19" barrel. Walnut finished hardwood stock with Monte Carlo and pistol grip. Adjustable sights. Ten-round magazine. Weight is about 5.5 lbs. Introduced in 2004.

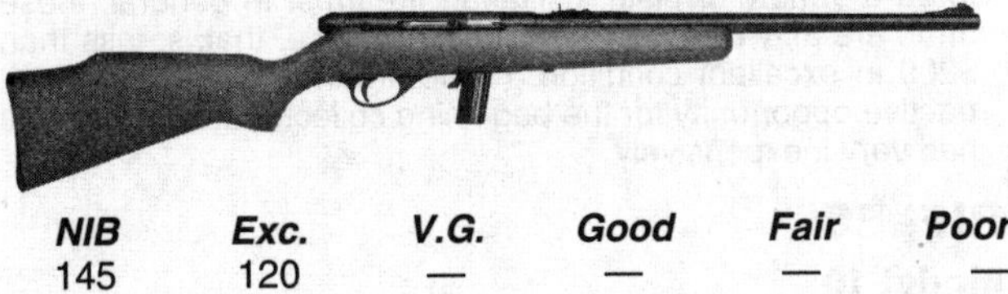

NIB	Exc.	V.G.	Good	Fair	Poor
145	120	—	—	—	—

Sportster Versa-Pack

This is a two-barrel set with a 22" .410 barrel and the other a 20" .22 caliber barrel. Hardwood stock with straight grip. Iron sights. Weight about 5.5 lbs.

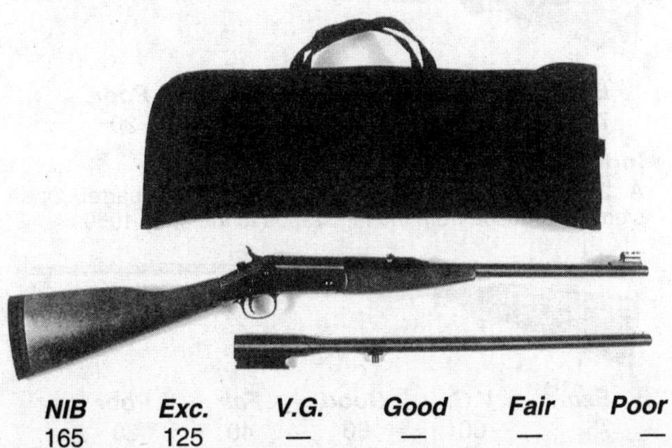

NIB	Exc.	V.G.	Good	Fair	Poor
165	125	—	—	—	—

Sidekick Muzzleloader

Introduced in 2004 this model features a break-open action with side lever release chambered for the .50 caliber ball. Barrel length is 24" or 26". American hardwood stock with pistol grip and recoil pad. Black matte finish or stainless steel. Adjustable fiber optic sights. Weight is about 6.5 lbs.

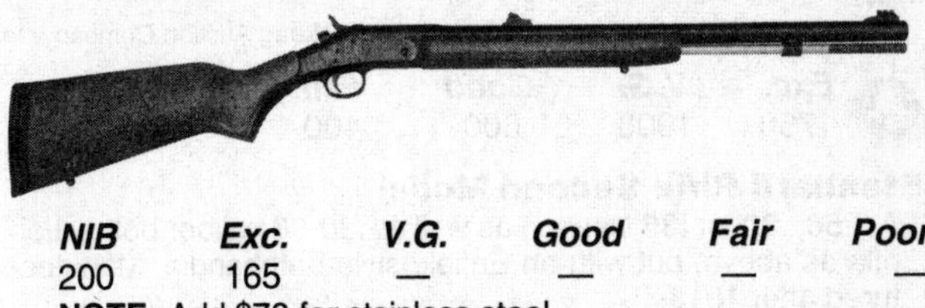

NIB	Exc.	V.G.	Good	Fair	Poor
200	165	—	—	—	—

NOTE: Add $70 for stainless steel.

NEWBURY ARMS CO.

Catskill, New York
Albany, New York

Pocket Pistol

A .25 caliber spur trigger pocket pistol with a 4" octagonal barrel. Blued, silver-plated with walnut grips.

Exc.	V.G.	Good	Fair	Poor
—	—	1950	800	200

Pocket Revolver

A .26 caliber double-action percussion revolver with a 5" barrel and C-shaped exposed trigger. Blued with an iron or brass frame and walnut grips. The barrel marked "Newbury Arms Co. Albany." Produced in limited numbers between 1855 and 1860. Prospective purchasers are advised to secure a qualified appraisal prior to acquisition.

Exc.	V.G.	Good	Fair	Poor
—	—	6250	2750	750

NEWCOMB, H. G.

Natchez, Mississippi

Pocket Pistol

A .41 caliber percussion pocket pistol with a 2.5" barrel, German silver mounts and a walnut stock. Manufactured in the 1850s.

Exc.	V.G.	Good	Fair	Poor
—	—	1850	700	250

NEWTON ARMS CO.

Buffalo, New York

Also known as the Buffalo Newton Rifle Company and the Charles Newton Rifle Company. In operation from 1913 to 1932.

NOTE: Any of the rifles listed chambered for a Newton caliber will bring a premium over standard calibers of about 25 percent.

Newton-Mauser Rifle

A .256 Newton caliber bolt-action rifle with a 24" barrel and double set triggers. Blued with a walnut stock. Manufactured circa 1914.

Exc.	V.G.	Good	Fair	Poor
2000	1400	850	500	—

Standard Rifle First Type

A .22, .256, .280, .30, .33, and .35 Newton as well as .30-06 caliber bolt-action rifle with a 24" barrel, open or aperture sights and double set triggers. Blued with a walnut stock. Manufactured between 1916 and 1918.

Courtesy Amoskeag Auction Company, Inc.

Exc.	V.G.	Good	Fair	Poor
1750	1000	600	400	—

Standard Rifle Second Model

A .256, .30, or .35 Newton as well as .30-06 caliber bolt-action rifle as above, but with an Enfield-style bolt handle. Manufactured after 1918.

Exc.	V.G.	Good	Fair	Poor
1750	1000	600	400	—

Buffalo Newton Rifle

As above, but marked "Buffalo Newton Rifle Company."

Exc.	V.G.	Good	Fair	Poor
1750	1000	600	400	—

NICHOLS & CHILDS

Conway, Massachusetts

Percussion Belt Revolver

A .34 caliber percussion revolver with a 6" round barrel and 6-shot cylinder. Blued or browned with walnut grips. It is estimated that fewer than 25 were made in 1838. Prospective purchasers are advised to secure a qualified appraisal prior to acquisition.

Exc.	V.G.	Good	Fair	Poor
—	—	10500	4500	1250

Revolving Percussion Rifle

A .36 or .40 caliber percussion rifle with a 22", 26", or 30" barrel and a 5-, 6-, 7- or 9-shot cylinder. Blued or browned with a walnut stock with a patch box. It is believed that approximately 150 were made between 1838 and 1840. Prospective purchasers are advised to secure a qualified appraisal prior to acquisition.

Exc.	V.G.	Good	Fair	Poor
—	—	15000	6000	2000

NIGHTHAWK CUSTOM

Berryville, Arkansas

Custom Talon

1911-style semi-auto with 5" or 4.25" barrel and fixed or adjustable sights. Several other barrel lengths/finishes available. MSRP: 2300

Custom Predator

1911-style semi-auto with 5" barrel or 4.25" and fixed or adjustable sights. Several other barrel lengths/finishes available. MSRP: 2700

GRP

Global Response Pistol. 1911-style semi-auto with 5" or 4.25" barrel and fixed or adjustable sights. Several other barrel lengths/finishes available. MSRP: 2395

NOBLE

Haydenville, Massachusetts

In business between 1946 and 1971, this company manufactured a variety of plain, utilitarian firearms. In general, these arms are all worth approximately the same, that is, less than $200 in excellent condition. Noble firearms represent an attractive opportunity for the beginning collector as most can be had very inexpensively.

RIFLES

Model 10

A .22 caliber bolt-action single rifle with a 24" barrel. Pistol grip stock with no checkering. Open sights. Produced in the late 1950s.

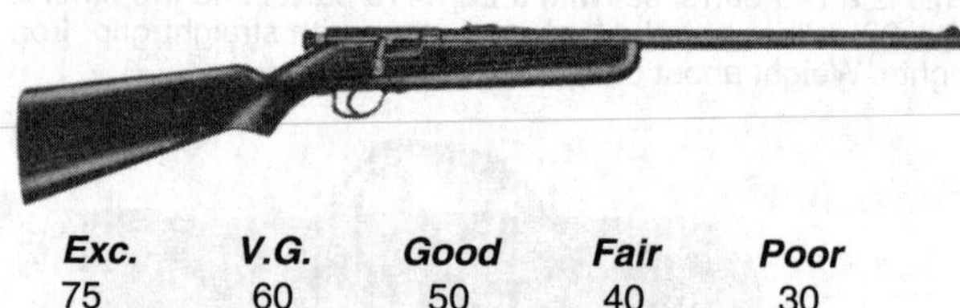

Exc.	V.G.	Good	Fair	Poor
75	60	50	40	30

Model 20

A .22 caliber bolt-action rifle fitted with a 22" barrel. Open sights. Produced from the late 1950s to the early 1960s.

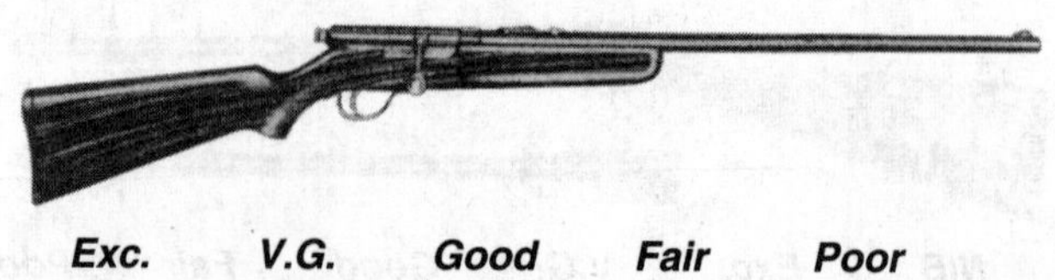

Exc.	V.G.	Good	Fair	Poor
75	60	50	40	30

Model 33

This is a .22 caliber slide-action rifle fitted with a 24" barrel and tubular magazine and Tenite stock. Produced from the late 1940s to the early 1950s.

Exc.	V.G.	Good	Fair	Poor
80	70	60	50	40

Model 33A

Same as above but fitted with a wood stock.

Exc.	V.G.	Good	Fair	Poor
75	60	50	40	30

Model 222

This is a single-shot bolt-action rifle chambered for the .22 caliber cartridge. Plain pistol-grip stock.

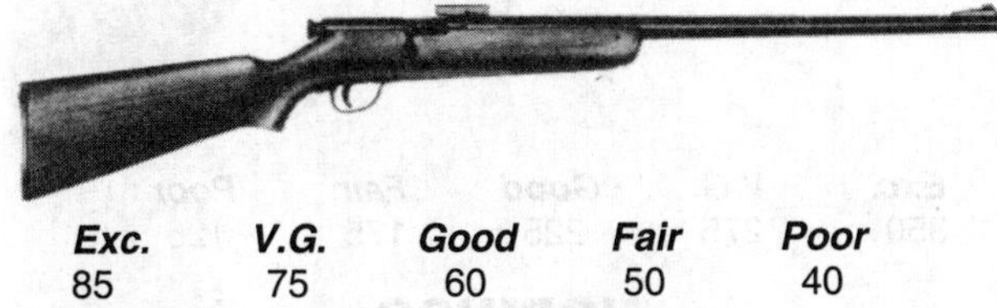

Exc.	V.G.	Good	Fair	Poor
85	75	60	50	40

Model 236

A .22 caliber slide-action rifle with a 24" barrel and tubular magazine. Plain pistol-grip stock and groved slide handle.

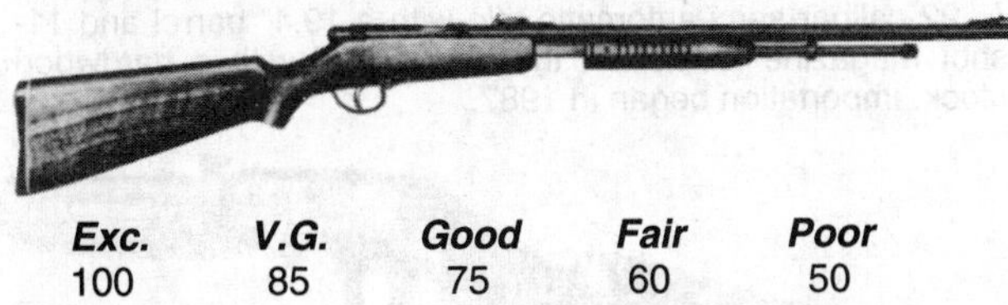

Exc.	V.G.	Good	Fair	Poor
100	85	75	60	50

Model 275

A .22 caliber lever-action rifle with tubular magazine. Fitted with a 24" barrel. The plain stock has a semi-pistol grip.

Exc.	V.G.	Good	Fair	Poor
125	100	80	60	50

SHOTGUNS

Model 40

This is a hammerless slide-action shotgun chambered for the 12 gauge shell. It is fitted with a tubular magazine and 28" barrel with multi choke. Plain pistol stock with grooved slide handle.

Exc.	V.G.	Good	Fair	Poor
125	100	85	70	50

Model 50

Same as above but without the multi choke.

Exc.	V.G.	Good	Fair	Poor
115	90	80	65	50

Model 60

A hammerless slide-action shotgun in 12 or 16 gauge with tubular magazine and fitted with a 28" barrel with adjustable choke. Plain pistol grip stock with grooved slide handle.

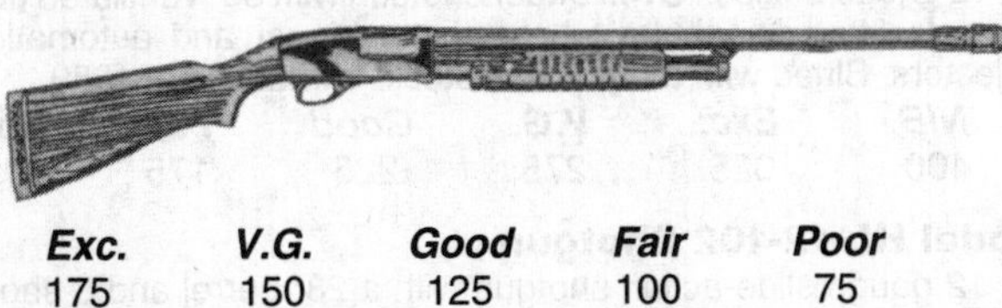

Exc.	V.G.	Good	Fair	Poor
175	150	125	100	75

Model 65

Same as above but without adjustable choke.

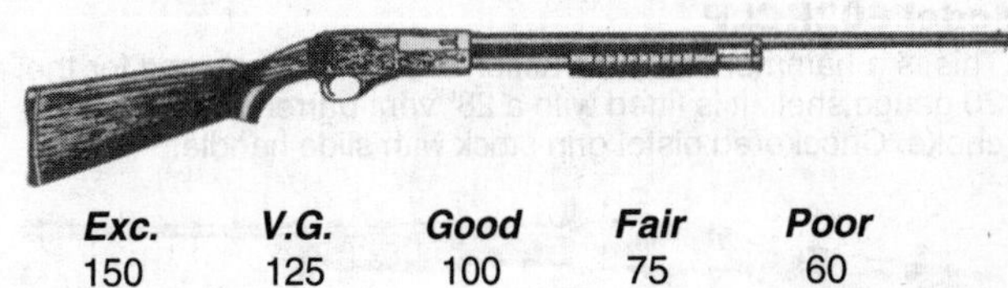

Exc.	V.G.	Good	Fair	Poor
150	125	100	75	60

Model 66CLP

Offered in 12 or 16 gauge this slide-action shotgun is fitted with a 28" plain barrel and a keyed lock fire control system.

Exc.	V.G.	Good	Fair	Poor
160	140	110	85	70

Model 66RCLP

Similar to above but fitted with a 28" vent rib barrel and checkered pistol-grip stock. Adjustable choke is standard.

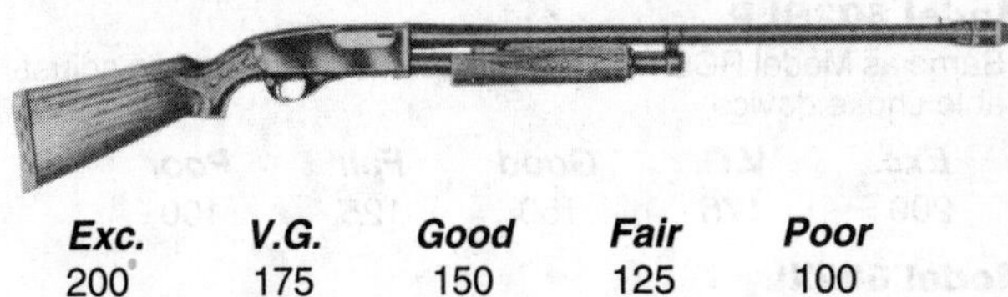

Exc.	V.G.	Good	Fair	Poor
200	175	150	125	100

Model 66 RLP

Same as above but without adjustable choke.

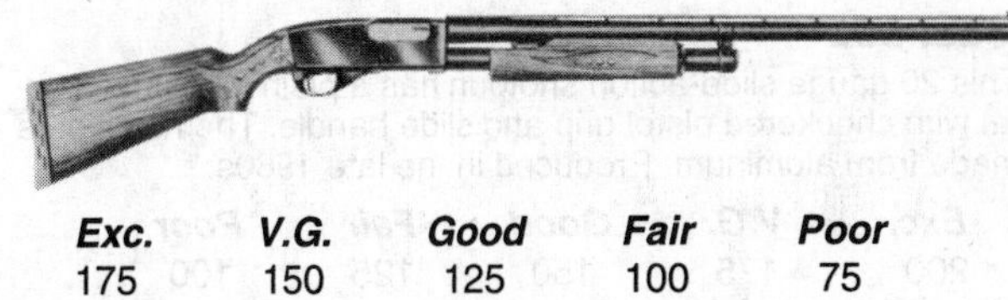

Exc.	V.G.	Good	Fair	Poor
175	150	125	100	75

Model 66XL

Similar to the above models but with plain barrel, and checkering only on the slide handle.

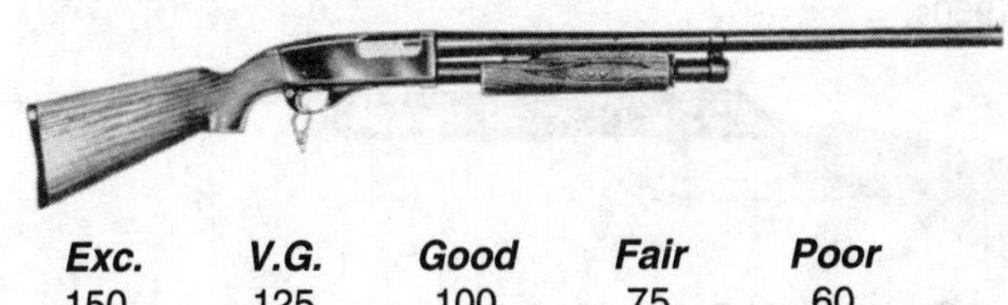

Exc.	V.G.	Good	Fair	Poor
150	125	100	75	60

Model 70CLP

Similar to the Model 66 series but offered in .410 bore with 26" barrel and adjustable choke. Both the buttstock and slide handle are checkered.

Exc.	V.G.	Good	Fair	Poor
175	150	125	100	75

Model 70RCLP

This variation is fitted with a 26" ventilated rib barrel.

Exc.	V.G.	Good	Fair	Poor
200	175	150	125	100

Model 70RLP

This model has a vent rib barrel and no adjustable choke.

Exc.	V.G.	Good	Fair	Poor
175	150	125	100	75

Model 70XL

This version has no adjustable choke but is fitted with a 26" vent rib barrel. Stock is checked.

Exc.	V.G.	Good	Fair	Poor
125	100	80	70	60

Model 602RCLP

This is a hammerless slide-action shotgun chambered for the 20 gauge shell. It is fitted with a 28" vent barrel and adjustable choke. Checkered pistol grip stock with slide handle.

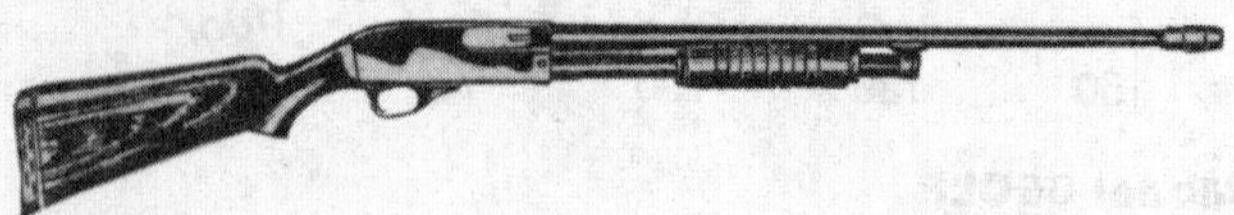

Exc.	V.G.	Good	Fair	Poor
225	200	175	125	100

Model 602CLP

Same as above but with plain barrel.

Exc.	V.G.	Good	Fair	Poor
175	150	125	100	75

Model 602RLP

Same as Model RCLP except without the addition of an adjustable choke device.

Exc.	V.G.	Good	Fair	Poor
200	175	150	125	100

Model 602XL

Same as above but with only the slide handle checkered.

Exc.	V.G.	Good	Fair	Poor
150	125	100	75	60

Model 662

This 20 gauge slide-action shotgun has a plain aluminum barrel with checkered pistol grip and slide handle. The receiver is made from aluminum. Produced in the late 1960s.

Exc.	V.G.	Good	Fair	Poor
200	175	150	125	100

Model 80

This model is a semi-automatic inertia-operated shotgun chambered for the .410 shell. It is fitted with a 26" barrel, plain pistol stock with slotted forearm. Produced in the early to mid 1960s.

Exc.	V.G.	Good	Fair	Poor
250	200	150	125	100

Model 166L

This is a 12 gauge slide-action shotgun with a key lock system. It is fitted with a 24" barrel bored for rifled slug. Lyman peep rear sight with post front sight. Checkered pistol and slide handle.

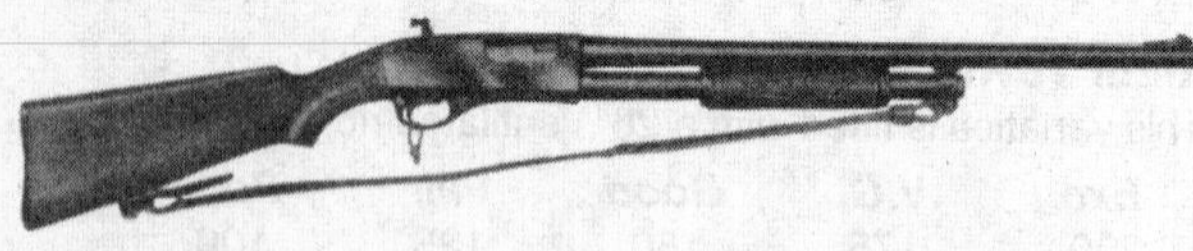

Exc.	V.G.	Good	Fair	Poor
250	200	150	125	100

Model 420

This shotgun is a box lock design side-by-side with double triggers and offered in 12, 16, 20 gauge, as well as .410 bore. Barrel lengths are 28" for all gauges except .410 where it is 26". Lightly engraved frame. Checkered walnut stock and splinter forearm.

Exc.	V.G.	Good	Fair	Poor
300	250	200	150	100

Model 450E

This model is similar to the Model 420 with the addition of automatic ejectors and not offered in .410 bore. Checkered pistol grip stock with beavertail forearm. Produced in the late 1960s.

Exc.	V.G.	Good	Fair	Poor
350	275	225	175	125

NORINCO

Peoples Republic of China
China North Industries Corp.

ATD .22

A .22 caliber semi-automatic rifle with a 19.4" barrel and 11-shot magazine located in the butt. Blued with a hardwood stock. Importation began in 1987.

NIB	Exc.	V.G.	Good	Fair	Poor
200	150	125	100	75	50

EM-321

A .22 caliber slide-action rifle with a 19.5" barrel and 10-shot tubular magazine. Blued with a hardwood stock. Introduced in 1989.

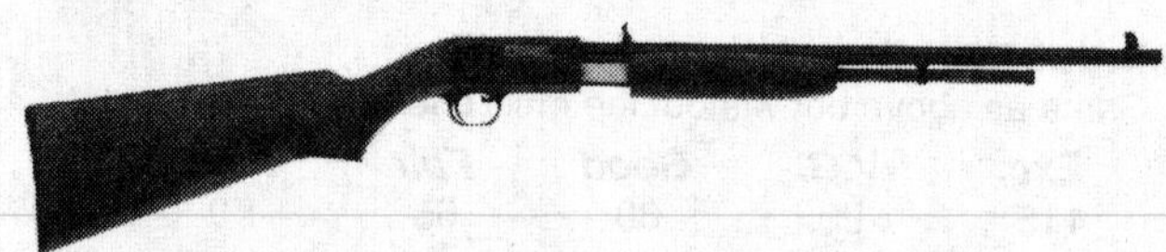

NIB	Exc.	V.G.	Good	Fair	Poor
150	100	85	75	65	50

Model HL-12-203 Shotgun

A 12 gauge boxlock Over/Under shotgun with 30" ventilated rib barrels fitted for choke tubes, single trigger and automatic ejectors. Blued with a hardwood stock. Introduced in 1989.

NIB	Exc.	V.G.	Good	Fair	Poor
400	325	275	225	175	125

Model HL-12-102 Shotgun

A 12 gauge slide-action shotgun with a 28" barrel and 3-shot magazine. Blued with a hardwood stock. Introduced in 1989.

NIB	Exc.	V.G.	Good	Fair	Poor
275	225	200	175	125	100

Model 97 Hammer Pump

Similar in appearance to the Winchester Model 1897 shotgun. Fitted with a 20" barrel with cylinder choke. Hardwood stock.

NIB	Exc.	V.G.	Good	Fair	Poor
375	275	—	—	—	—

Model 213 Pistol

A copy of the Browning P-35 semi-automatic pistol. Sold in 1988 only.

Exc.	V.G.	Good	Fair	Poor
250	200	150	100	75

Type 59 Makarov

A .380 or 9mm Makarov caliber double-action semi-automatic pistol with a 3.5" barrel and 8-shot magazine. Blued with plastic grips.

Exc.	V.G.	Good	Fair	Poor
275	250	225	175	125

Type 54-1 Tokarev

A 7.62x25mm caliber semi-automatic pistol with a 4.6" barrel, fixed sights, and 8-shot magazine. Blued with plastic grips. Imported in 1989.

Exc.	V.G.	Good	Fair	Poor
300	250	200	100	80

1911 A1

Steel-framed clone of the 1911 .45 A1 semi-auto. Very popular with competition shooters as a platform for custom guns. No longer imported.

Exc.	V.G.	Good	Fair	Poor
400	350	200	100	80

SKS Rifle

A 7.62x39mm caliber semi-automatic rifle with a 20.5" barrel, folding bayonet and either a 10-shot fixed magazine or 30-shot detachable magazine. Blued with a hardwood stock. Importation began in 1988.

Exc.	V.G.	Good	Fair	Poor
200	175	125	75	50

Type 84S AK

Similar to the AKS service rifle, in 5.56mm caliber with a 16" barrel and 30-shot magazine.

NIB	Exc.	V.G.	Good	Fair	Poor
900	800	700	—	—	—

Type 84S-1

As above, with an underfolding metal stock.

NIB	Exc.	V.G.	Good	Fair	Poor
1050	900	750	—	—	—

Type 84S-3

As above, with a composition stock.

NIB	Exc.	V.G.	Good	Fair	Poor
1000	850	700	—	—	—

Type 84S-5

As above, with a stock that folds to the side and without a bayonet.

Type 81S

A semi-automatic copy of the AK47.

Type 81S-1

As above, with a folding stock.

NORTH AMERICAN ARMS

Provo, Utah

Mini-Revolver

A .22 or .22 Magnum caliber spur trigger revolver with a 1" or 2.5" barrel and 5-shot cylinder. Stainless steel with plastic or laminated rosewood grips. Introduced in 1975 and made in the styles listed.

Standard Rimfire Version

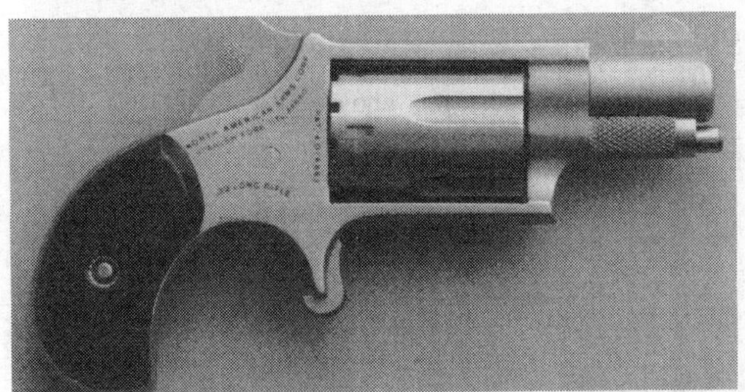

NIB	Exc.	V.G.	Fair	Poor
175	125	110	85	60

2 Cylinder Magnum Convertible Version

NIB	Exc.	V.G.	Fair	Poor
225	175	150	125	100

Viper Belt Buckle Version

NIB	Exc.	V.G.	Fair	Poor
175	140	120	100	75

Magnum Version

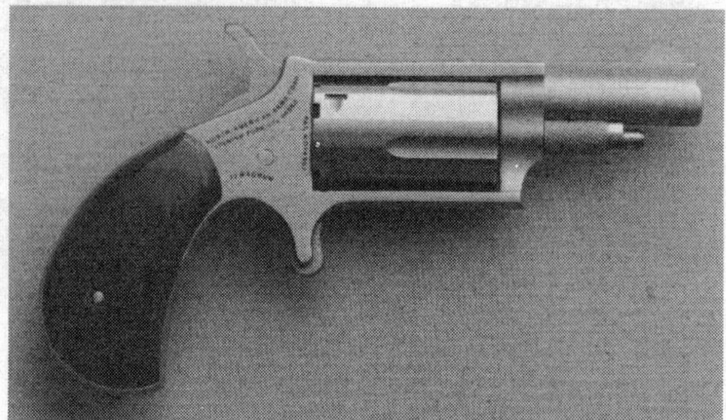

NIB	Exc.	V.G.	Fair	Poor
190	150	125	100	75

Standard 3 Gun Set

NIB	Exc.	V.G.	Fair	Poor
725	575	400	300	225

Deluxe 3 Gun Set

NIB	Exc.	V.G.	Fair	Poor
800	650	475	375	275

Cased .22 Magnum

NIB	Exc.	V.G.	Fair	Poor
350	250	200	150	125

Companion

This is a .22 caliber cap-and-ball mini revolver. It has a 1.125" barrel. Overall length is 4.6" and weight is about 5 oz.

NIB	Exc.	V.G.	Good	Fair	Poor
140	125	100	75	50	35

Super Companion

Same as above but with longer cylinder. It has a 1.62" barrel and weighs about 7 oz.

NIB	Exc.	V.G.	Good	Fair	Poor
160	140	100	75	50	35

Black Widow

This is a five-shot fixed-sight revolver with oversize black rubber grips with a 2" or 4" barrel. Chambered for .22 LR or .22 Win. Mag. Stainless steel. Weight is approximately 8.8 oz.

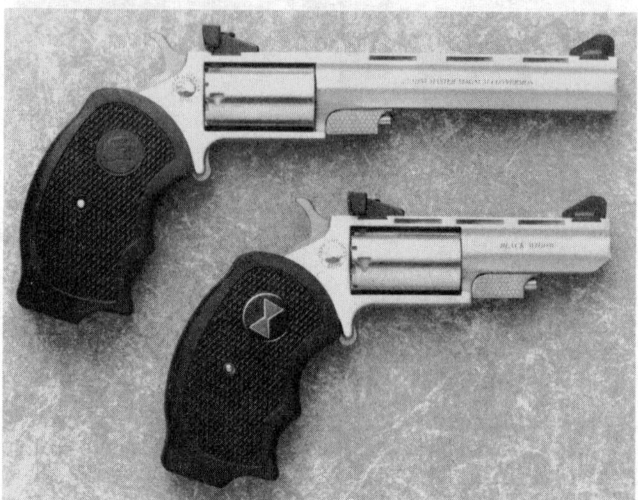

NIB	Exc.	V.G.	Good	Fair	Poor
250	200	150	100	75	50

NOTE: Add $20 for adjustable sights.

Mini-Master

This model is similar to the Black Widow with a 2" or 4" barrel. This model also gives a choice of either .22 LR or .22 Win. Mag. Stainless steel. Weight is approximately 10.7 oz.

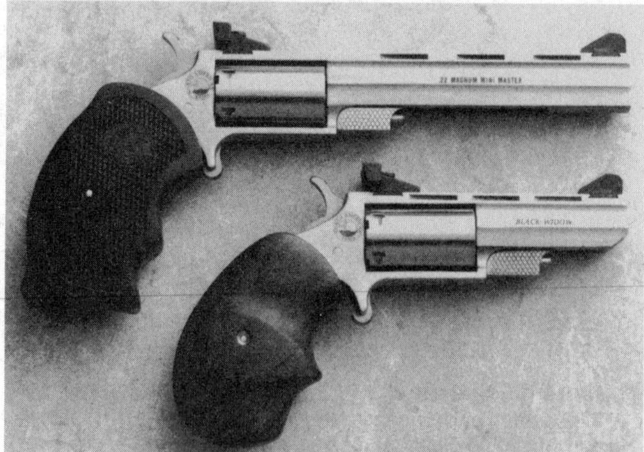

NIB	Exc.	V.G.	Good	Fair	Poor
280	225	175	125	100	75

NOTE: Add $20 for adjustable sights.

Single-Action Revolver

A polished stainless steel single-action revolver chambered for the .45 Winchester Magnum and the .450 Magnum Express cartridge. It has a 7.5" barrel and a 5-shot cylinder. There is a transfer bar safety, and the grips are walnut. This model was discontinued in 1988.

Exc.	V.G.	Good	Fair	Poor
850	775	650	500	400

Guardian

This is a semi-automatic double-action-only pocket pistol chambered in .32 ACP, .32 NAA or .25 NAA. Magazine capacity is 6 rounds and the barrel length is 2.2". Overall length of the pistol is 4.4" and weight empty is 13.5 oz. Introduced in 1998.

NIB	Exc.	V.G.	Good	Fair	Poor
400	300	225	175	—	—

Guardian .380

Similar to the above model but chambered for the .380 cartridge. Barrel length is 2.5". Magazine capacity is 6 rounds. Weight is about 19 oz.

NIB	Exc.	V.G.	Good	Fair	Poor
450	350	—	—	—	—

NORTH AMERICAN ARMS CORP.

Toronto, Canada

Brigadier

A .45 ACP caliber semi-automatic pistol with a 5" barrel, 8-shot magazine and alloy frame. Weight 4.5 lbs. Produced in limited quantity between 1948 and 1951. Prospective purchasers are advised to secure a qualified appraisal prior to acquisition.

Exc.	V.G.	Good	Fair	Poor
1250	1000	800	600	500

NORTH AMERICAN SAFARI EXPRESS

Liege, Belgium

SEE—Francotte

A trade name used by Francotte on their double rifles imported and distributed by Armes De Chasse of Chads Ford, Pennsylvania.

NORTH & COUCH

New York, New York

Animal Trap Gun

A .28 or. 30 caliber percussion pepperbox with either a 1.75" or 2.12" barrel group and a hammer made with or without a spur. Marked "North & Couch, Middletown, Conn." or "North & Couch New York." Manufactured during the 1860s.

Disk Hammer Model

Exc.	V.G.	Good	Fair	Poor
—	—	1850	700	300

Spur Hammer Model

Exc.	V.G.	Good	Fair	Poor
—	—	2750	900	350

NORTON ARMS CO.

Mt. Clemens, Michigan

SEE—Budischowsky

This firm manufactured Budischowsky Model TP-70 semi-automatic pistols prior to 1979. After that date, these arms were made by the American Arms and Ammunition Company. The values for both manufacturers' products are listed.

Exc.	V.G.	Good	Fair	Poor
350	275	200	125	100

NOSLER CUSTOM

Bend, Oregon

NoslerCustom Model 48 Sporter

Bolt-action centerfire rifle chambered in .270 Winchester Short Magnum. 24" barrel, round top receiver, onyx gray composite stock. Introduced 2007. Price shown includes scope.

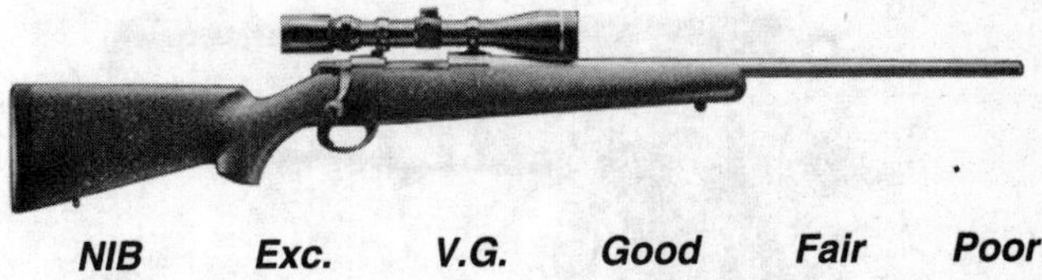

NIB	Exc.	V.G.	Good	Fair	Poor
2495	—	—	—	—	—

NORWICH PISTOL CO.

Norwich, Connecticut

Established in 1875 by the New York retailer Maltby, Curtis & Company, this firm manufactured a wide variety of inexpensive spur trigger revolvers that were sold under these trade names: America, Bulldozer, Challenge, Chieftain, Crescent, Defiance, Hartford Arms, Maltby Henley, Metropolitan Police, Nonpariel, Norwich Arms, Parole, Patriot, Pinafore, Prairie King, Protector, Spy, True Blue, U.M.C. Winfield Arms.

The company ceased operations in 1881. The value for any of its arms listed is approximate.

Exc.	V.G.	Good	Fair	Poor
—	475	200	75	50

NOWLIN MANUFACTURING COMPANY

Claremore, Oklahoma

Match Classic

This 1911 pistol has a wide range of features. It can be chambered in 9mm, .38 Super, 9x23, .40 S&W, and .45 ACP. It has a 5" barrel, adjustable trigger, checkered main spring housing, hardwood grips, front and rear cocking serrations. The price listed is for the basic pistols. Options will greatly affect price.

NIB	Exc.	V.G.	Good	Fair	Poor
1295	1050	800	—	—	—

Compact Carry

This pistol is similar to the Match Classic with the exception of a 4" barrel on a full-size frame. Again options will greatly affect price.

NIB	Exc.	V.G.	Good	Fair	Poor
1395	1100	875	—	—	—

Match Master

These hand-built pistols offered a choice of S.T.I., Caspian Hi-Cap, or Nowlin STD Gov't frames. Available in 9mm, 9x23, .38 Super, .40 S&W, and .45 ACP. Many special features are included in standard pistol and many extra cost options are available.

NIB	Exc.	V.G.	Good	Fair	Poor
2195	1750	1200	—	—	—

NOTE: Add $140 for hard chrome finish.

This symbol denotes "Sleepers" with rapidly-rising values and/or significant collector potential.

O.D.I.

Midland Park, New Jersey

Viking

A .45 caliber double-action semi-automatic pistol with a 5" barrel and 7-shot magazine. Stainless steel with teak grips. Manufactured in 1981 and 1982.

NIB	Exc.	V.G.	Good	Fair	Poor
525	425	365	300	200	100

Viking Combat

As above, with a 4.24" barrel.

NIB	Exc.	V.G.	Good	Fair	Poor
525	425	365	300	200	100

O.K.

Unknown

SEE—Marlin

O'CONNELL, DAVID

New York, New York

Pocket Pistol

A .41 caliber percussion pocket pistol with a 2.5" barrel, German silver mounts, and walnut stock. Manufactured during the 1850s.

Exc.	V.G.	Good	Fair	Poor
—	—	2750	950	300

O'DELL, STEPHEN

Natchez, Mississippi

Pocket Pistol

A .34 to .44 caliber percussion pocket pistol with a 2" to 4" barrel, German silver mounts and walnut stock. Manufactured during the 1850s.

Exc.	V.G.	Good	Fair	Poor
—	—	6000	2500	950

OBREGON

Mexico City, Mexico

This is a .45 caliber semi-automatic pistol with a 5" barrel. Similar to the Colt M1911A1 but with a combination side and safety latch on the left side of the frame. The breech is locked by rotating the barrel, instead of the Browning swinging link. This unusual locking system results in a tubular front end appearance to the pistol. Originally designed for the Mexican military it was not adopted as such and only about 1,000 pistols were produced and sold commercially. The pistol is 8.5" overall and weighs about 40 ozs. The magazine holds seven cartridges. This is a rare pistol; an independent appraisal is suggested prior to sale.

Exc.	V.G.	Good	Fair	Poor
4500	2500	1250	750	400

OHIO ORDNANCE INC.

Chardon, Ohio

Model 1918A3 Self-Loading Rifle

This rifle is a semi-automatic version of the famed Browning Automatic Rifle. It is chambered for the .30-06 cartridge and has a 20-round magazine. It was introduced in this configuration in 1996.

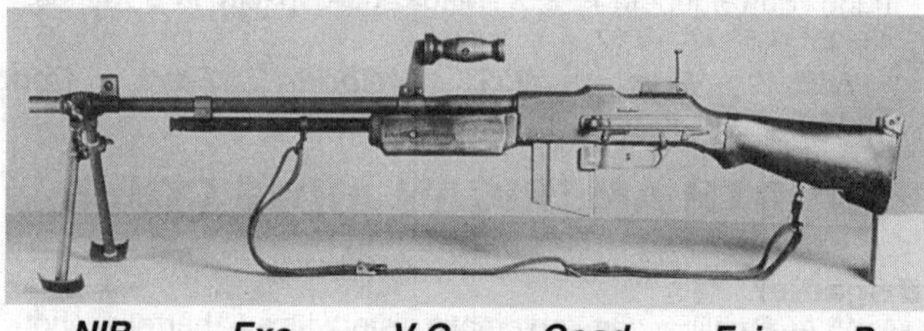

NIB	Exc.	V.G.	Good	Fair	Poor
4000	—	—	—	—	—

Colt Browning Water Cooled Gun

Introduced in 2001, this is a semi-automatic version of the famous Browning Model 1917 belt-fed machine gun. This model features a .30-06 or 7.65 Argentine caliber belt-fed gun with tripod, wooden ammo box, water hose, water can, and one 250 cloth belt.

NIB	Exc.	V.G.	Good	Fair	Poor
3700	—	—	—	—	—

NOTE: Add $200 for .308 or 8mm caliber guns.

1919A4

Semi-auto version of the air-cooled, belt-fed .30-caliber 1919 machine gun. Chambered for .308/7.62 NATO.

NIB	Exc.	V.G.	Good	Fair	Poor
2750	—	—	—	—	—

OJANGUREN Y VIDOSA

Eibar, Spain

This typical Eibar company produced mediocre firearms from the early 1920s and was forced out of business during the Spanish Civil War.

Apache (Model 1920)

A typical Eibar Browning copy that is chambered for the 6.35mm cartridge. It is of the typical low quality associated with most Spanish arms of this era. The slide is marked "Pistole Browning Automatica Cal. 6.35 Apache." The finish is blued, and the plastic grips have a head with a beret and the word "Apache" molded into them.

Courtesy James Rankin

Exc.	V.G.	Good	Fair	Poor
200	150	100	75	50

Apache (Model 1920)

As above but chambered for the 7.65mm cartridge

Courtesy James Rankin

Exc.	V.G.	Good	Fair	Poor
275	225	190	100	75

Ojanguren

The trade name this company used to cover the line of revolvers they produced in the 1930s. They produced two in .32 caliber and two chambered for the .38 Special cartridge. They are similar in appearance and have barrel lengths of either 3" or 6". The finishes are blued, and they have plastic grips. One of the .38 caliber models—the "Legitimo Tanque"—is a reasonably well-made gun that was popular with the Spanish target shooters. These guns have little collector value, little practical value and are all priced alike.

Exc.	V.G.	Good	Fair	Poor
175	125	100	75	50

Tanque

A blowback-operated semi-automatic chambered for the 6.35mm cartridge. It has a 1.5" barrel and is actually an original design, which was rarely found on Eibar guns of this period. It has an oddly shaped slide, and the barrel is retained by means of a screw in the front of the frame. It has a 6-shot magazine, and the slide is marked "6.35 Tanque Patent." The plastic grips have a tank molded into them and the word "Tanque," as well as the letters "O&V."

Exc.	V.G.	Good	Fair	Poor
175	125	100	75	50

OLD WEST GUN CO.

Houston, Texas

SEE—Cimarron Arms

An importer of reproduction firearms primarily manufactured by Aldo Uberti of Italy. In 1987 this company purchased the inventory of Allen Firearms and subsequently changed their name to Cimarron Arms.

OLYMPIC ARMS, INC.

Olympia, Washington

PISTOLS

Black Widow

A .45 caliber semi-automatic pistol with a 3.9" barrel and 6-shot magazine. Nickel-plated with ivory Micarta grips with a spider engraved on them.

NIB	Exc.	V.G.	Good	Fair	Poor
700	575	450	350	300	200

Enforcer

A .45 caliber semi-automatic pistol with a 3.8" barrel and 6-shot magazine. Parkerized, anodized or nickel-plated with rubber grips. Weight is approximately 36 oz.

NIB	Exc.	V.G.	Good	Fair	Poor
650	500	400	350	300	200

Match Master

As above, with a 5" barrel and 7-shot magazine. Weight is about 40 oz.

NIB	Exc.	V.G.	Good	Fair	Poor
650	500	400	350	300	200

Match Master 6"

Same as above but with 6" barrel and slide. Weight is approximately 44 oz.

NIB	Exc.	V.G.	Good	Fair	Poor
675	550	400	350	300	200

Cohort

Fitted with a 4" bull barrel with a full size frame. Magazine capacity is 7 rounds. Weight is about 38 oz.

NIB	Exc.	V.G.	Good	Fair	Poor
675	550	400	350	300	200

Safari G.I.

This model is built on a Match Master frame with 5" barrel with fixed sights. Finish is flat black Parkerized. Checkered walnut grips.

NIB	Exc.	V.G.	Good	Fair	Poor
550	450	400	—	—	—

Schuetzen Pistol Works Big Deuce

This model is made in Olympic Arms specialty shop called Schuetzen Pistol Works. Marked "Schuetzen Pistol Works" on the slide and "Safari Arms" on the frame. Introduced in 1995. This semi-automatic pistol is chambered for the .45 ACP cartridge and fitted with a 6" barrel, smooth walnut grips, and a number of other custom features. Magazine capacity is 7 rounds. Weight is approximately 40 oz. Black slide with stainless steel frame.

NIB	Exc.	V.G.	Good	Fair	Poor
950	800	700	500	—	—

Schuetzen Pistol Works Crest

Similar to the above model with the same markings. This version features a .45 ACP pistol with 4.5", 5", or 5.5" barrel Checkered walnut grips. Offered in both right- and left-hand configurations. Stainless steel finish. Introduced in 1993. Weight is about 39 oz. depending on barrel length.

NIB	Exc.	V.G.	Good	Fair	Poor
700	600	500	—	—	—

NOTE: Left-hand model will bring a small premium.

Schuetzen Pistol Works Griffon

Similar to the above specialty models. This version is fitted with a 5" barrel and smooth walnut grips. Magazine capacity is 10 rounds. Stainless steel finish. Numerous custom features. Introduced in 1995.

NIB	Exc.	V.G.	Good	Fair	Poor
N/A	—	—	—	—	—

Schuetzen Pistol Works Carrier

Special built model along the lines of the Detonics Score Master with adjustable sights.

NIB	Exc.	V.G.	Good	Fair	Poor
750	600	—	—	—	—

Black-Tac

Semi-auto .45 ACP pistol treated with "black-tac" process – advantages of hard chrome without its drawbacks such as embrittlement.

NIB	Exc.	V.G.	Good	Fair	Poor
800	700	—	—	—	—

Constable

Semi-auto pistol chambered for .45 ACP with 4" barrel, 5.75" sight radius, 7+1 capacity, 35 oz. Introduced 2006.

NIB	Exc.	V.G.	Good	Fair	Poor
900	750	—	—	—	—

Custom Street Deuce

Semi-auto chambered for .45 ACP with 5.2" bull barrel, 7" sight radius, 7+1 capacity, 38 oz. Many options. Introduced 2006. MSRP: 1299

Custom Journeyman

Semi-auto chambered for .45 ACP with 4" bull barrel, 6" sight radius, 6+1 capacity, 35 oz. Many options. Introduced 2006.

NIB	Exc.	V.G.	Good	Fair	Poor
1050	800	—	—	—	—

Trail Boss

Semi-auto pistol in the Westerner line chambered for .45 ACP. 6" barrel, 8" sight radius, 7+1 capacity, 43 oz. Introduced 2006.

NIB	Exc.	V.G.	Good	Fair	Poor
900	750	—	—	—	—

Westerner

Semi-auto pistol chambered for .45 ACP with 5" barrel, 7" sight radius, 7+1 capacity, 39 oz. Introduced 2006.

NIB	Exc.	V.G.	Good	Fair	Poor
800	700	—	500	400	200

Model OA-93-PT

Similar to OA-93-CAR but with F8R handguard with vertical grip, post-ban muzzle brake, and detachable stock.

NIB	Exc.	V.G.	Good	Fair	Poor
950	700	—	—	—	—

Wolverine

Polymer-frame, vent-rib replica of the old "ray gun" .22 Whitney Wolverine semi-auto pistol. Cool, baby!

NIB	Exc.	V.G.	Good	Fair	Poor
275	225	—	—	—	—

RIFLES

SGW Ultra Match (PCR-1)

A match grade copy of the AR-15 with a 20" or 24" barrel and not fitted with a carrying handle. Weight is about 10 lbs.

NIB	Exc.	V.G.	Good	Fair	Poor
800	700	600	500	400	200

Model PCR-2

Similar to the above model but fitted with a 16" match grade barrel, post front and E2 rear sight. Weight is approximately 8.2 lbs.

NIB	Exc.	V.G.	Good	Fair	Poor
825	725	625	525	425	225

Model PCR-3

Same as above model but with forged T-12 upper receiver.

NIB	Exc.	V.G.	Good	Fair	Poor
825	725	625	525	425	225

Model PCR-4

This version is fitted with a 20" steel barrel with post front sight and A-1 style rear sight. Weight is approximately 8.5 lbs.

NIB	Exc.	V.G.	Good	Fair	Poor
725	575	450	350	250	150

Model PCR-5

Similar to the above but fitted with a 16" barrel. Weight is about 7 lbs.

NIB	Exc.	V.G.	Good	Fair	Poor
700	550	400	300	200	100

Model PCR-6

This AR-15 style rifle is chambered for the 7.62x39 Russian short caliber. It is fitted with a 16" barrel with a post front sight and a A-1 style rear sight. Weight is about 7 lbs.

NIB	Exc.	V.G.	Good	Fair	Poor
700	550	400	300	200	100

Model PCR-7 "Eliminator"

This model is a shortened version of the PCR-4. It is fitted with a 16" barrel, A2 handguard, A2 stock, and an A2 pistol grip. Weight is about 7.6 lbs.

NIB	Exc.	V.G.	Good	Fair	Poor
725	575	450	350	250	150

Model PCR-Service Match

This .223 caliber rifle has a 20" stainless steel match barrel. It is fitted with a post front sight and a E-2 style rear sight. Weight is about 8.7 lbs.

NIB	Exc.	V.G.	Good	Fair	Poor
825	725	625	525	425	225

Ultra CSR Tactical Rifle

This is a bolt-action rifle chambered for the .308 Winchester cartridge. Barrel length is 26". Magazine capacity is 5 rounds. Tactical-style stock is black synthetic with aluminum bedding block. Comes complete with scope rings and Harris bipod in a hardcase. Weight is approximately 9.4 lbs.

NIB	Exc.	V.G.	Good	Fair	Poor
1050	800	—	—	—	—

Model CAR-97

Chambered for the .223 cartridge or optional 9mm, .40 S&W, or .45 ACP pistol cartridges. Fitted with a 16" barrel and non-collapsible CAR-style stock. Overall length is 34". Weight is about 7 lbs.

NIB	Exc.	V.G.	Good	Fair	Poor
800	650	550	—	—	—

NOTE: Add $50 for pistol cartridge conversion.

Model OA-96

This model has a 6" barrel with pistol grip only, no buttstock. The 30-round magazine is pinned and cannot be detached. Break-open-action allows loading with stripper clips. Overall length is 15.75". Weight is about 4.2 lbs. BATF approved.

NIB	Exc.	V.G.	Good	Fair	Poor
900	700	600	—	—	—

Model OA-93 TG

Similar to the OA-96 but with a vertical grip. Barrel length is 7.5". Pistol grip only, no buttstock. Chambered for .223 cartridge. Weight is about 5 lbs. Overall length is 18.5". Classified by the BATF as any other weapon and subject to all NFA regulations. This weapon can only be purchased through a Class III dealer.

NIB	Exc.	V.G.	Good	Fair	Poor
800	650	550	—	—	—

Model OA-98

Similar to the OA-93 but with lightning holes on the grip, mount, magazine. Fitted with a 6" barrel with no vertical grip. Weight is about 3 lbs. No buttstock.

NIB	Exc.	V.G.	Good	Fair	Poor
800	650	550	—	—	—

UM-1P

Gas-operated .223 semi-auto target rifle based on AR-15 chassis. Features include 24-inch stainless steel bull barrel, anodized finish, pistol grip with bottom swell, Picatinny rail, Harris bipod, and competition trigger.

NIB	Exc.	V.G.	Good	Fair	Poor
1200	950	800	—	—	—

UM-1

Similar to UM-1P but with 20-inch stainless steel bull barrel, standard pistol grip, no bipod.

NIB	Exc.	V.G.	Good	Fair	Poor
900	750	600	—	—	—

SM-1P

Tricked-out AR-15 in .223 with 20-inch stainless steel barrel, free-floating sleeve handguard, carry handle upper or Picatinny rail flattop, pneumatic recoil buffer, Bob Jones interchangeable sight system, competition trigger, and Maxhard receivers.

NIB	Exc.	V.G.	Good	Fair	Poor
1200	950	800	—	—	—

SM-1

Similar to SM-1P but with standard receivers, trigger and sights. No pneumatic recoil buffer.

NIB	Exc.	V.G.	Good	Fair	Poor
900	750	600	—	—	—

ML-1

Similar to SM-1 but with 16-inch barrel with flash hider, 6-position collapsible buttstock and free-floating aluminum tube handguard.

NIB	Exc.	V.G.	Good	Fair	Poor
900	750	600	—	—	—

ML-2

Similar to ML-1 but with flat-top upper receiver with Picatinny rails, standard buttstock and bull barrel.

NIB	Exc.	V.G.	Good	Fair	Poor
800	650	500	—	—	—

Model K8

Similar to ML-2 but with 20-inch barrel and extended aluminum tube handguard.

NIB	Exc.	V.G.	Good	Fair	Poor
700	550	400	—	—	—

Model K8-MAG

Similar to K8 but with 24-inch bull barrel and chambered in .223 WSM, .243 WSM or .25 WSM.

NIB	Exc.	V.G.	Good	Fair	Poor
900	750	600	—	—	—

K3B

Features include 16-inch chrome-moly barrel with flash-hide-fully adjustable rear sight, 6-position collapsible buttstock and carbine-length handguard.

NIB	Exc.	V.G.	Good	Fair	Poor
700	550	400	—	—	—

K3B-M4

Similar to K3B but with M4S fiberite handguard with heatshield and 32.25-inch overall length.

NIB	Exc.	V.G.	Good	Fair	Poor
700	550	400	—	—	—

K3B-CAR

Similar to K3B but with 30.5-inch overall length.

NIB	Exc.	V.G.	Good	Fair	Poor
700	550	400	—	—	—

K3B-FAR

Similar to K3B but with Featherweight barrel and weight of 5.84 lbs.

NIB	Exc.	V.G.	Good	Fair	Poor
700	550	400	—	—	—

K4B

Similar to K3B but with 20-inch barrel and rifle-length fiberite handguard.

NIB	Exc.	V.G.	Good	Fair	Poor
700	550	400	—	—	—

K4B-A4

Similar to K4B but with ventilated FIRSH rifle-length handguard.

NIB	Exc.	V.G.	Good	Fair	Poor
750	600	450	—	—	—

LTF

Features include 16-inch chrome-mol barrel, free-floating FIRSH handguard with Picatinny rails, ACE FX skeleton stock, ERGO pistol grip and multiple-aperture flipup sight system.

NIB	Exc.	V.G.	Good	Fair	Poor
1000	850	700	—	—	—

LT-M4

Similar to LTF but with 16-inch stainless steel barrel.

NIB	Exc.	V.G.	Good	Fair	Poor
1000	850	700	—	—	—

K16

Similar to K8 but with 16-inch bull chrome-moly barrel.

NIB	Exc.	V.G.	Good	Fair	Poor
600	500	400	—	—	—

GI-16

Basic AR-15-inspired semi-auto rifle chambered in .223. 16-inch chrome-moly barrel with flash-hider, 6-position collapsible buttstock, carbine-length handguard and rear sight adjustable for windage only.

NIB	Exc.	V.G.	Good	Fair	Poor
700	500	400	—	—	—

Plinker Plus

Similar to GI-16 but with standard buttstock.

NIB	Exc.	V.G.	Good	Fair	Poor
650	550	350	—	—	—

Plinker Plus 20

Similar to Plinker Plus but with 20-inch barrel and rifle-length handguard.

NIB	Exc.	V.G.	Good	Fair	Poor
650	550	350	—	—	—

K7 Eliminator

Similar to K4B but with 16-inch barrel with extended handguard and sight radius of 20-inch-barreled models.

NIB	Exc.	V.G.	Good	Fair	Poor
700	500	400	—	—	—

K30

Similar to GI-16 but chambered in .30 Carbine. Includes mag well insert to accept military-spec magazines.

NIB	Exc.	V.G.	Good	Fair	Poor
750	600	400	—	—	—

K9/K10/K40/K45

Similar to K30 but chambered, respectively, for 9mm Parabellum, 10mm, .40 S&W and .45ACP. Models use converted surplus military magazines.

NIB	Exc.	V.G.	Good	Fair	Poor
700	500	400	—	—	—

K9-GL/K40-GL

Similar to K9 and K40 but accept standard Glock pistol magazines.

NIB	Exc.	V.G.	Good	Fair	Poor
800	700	600	—	—	—

OA-93-CAR

Features include OA-93 FT recoil-reducing upper, 16-inch chrome-moly barrel with Phantom flash hider, and side-folding buttstock.

NIB	Exc.	V.G.	Good	Fair	Poor
900	700	600	—	—	—

Model OA-93-PT

Similar to OA-93-CAR but with F8R handguard with vertical grip, post-ban muzzle brake, and detachable stock.

NIB	Exc.	V.G.	Good	Fair	Poor
900	700	600	—	—	—

OMEGA

Harrisburg, Pennsylvania
Importer—Kassnar

Over-and-Under Shotgun

A 12, 20, 28 or .410 bore boxlock over-and-under shotgun with 26" or 28" ventilated rib barrels, single trigger and extractors. Blued with a walnut stock.

Exc.	V.G.	Good	Fair	Poor
450	300	200	150	125

Side-by-Side Double Barreled Shotgun

A 20, 28 or .410 bore boxlock double-barrel shotgun with 26" barrels, double triggers and extractors. Blued with a hardwood stock.

Exc.	V.G.	Good	Fair	Poor
350	250	150	100	75

Single Barreled Shotgun

A 12, 20 or .410 bore single barrel shotgun manufactured in a variety of barrel lengths and fitted with an extractor. Blued with a hardwood stock.

Exc.	V.G.	Good	Fair	Poor
125	85	65	50	35

OMEGA

Elbar, Spain
SEE—Armero Especialistas

OMEGA

Geneseo, Illinois
Springfield Armory

Omega Pistol

A high-grade target-type pistol that is patterned after the Colt Model 1911 pistol, with marked improvements. It is chambered for the .38 Super, 10mm, and the .45 ACP cartridges. The barrel is either 5" or 6" in length and has polygonal rifling. The barrels are furnished either ported or plain and feature a lockup system that eliminates the barrel link and bushing associated with the normal Browning design. This pistol has a dual extractor system, adjustable sights, and Pachmayr grips. It was introduced in 1987.

NIB	Exc.	V.G.	Good	Fair	Poor
850	700	600	500	400	200

OMEGA FIREARMS CO.
Flower Mound, Texas

Bolt-Action Rifle

A .25-06 to .358 Norma Magnum bolt-action rifle with a 22" or 24" barrel, octagonal bolt, adjustable trigger and rotary magazine. Blued with a two-piece walnut or laminated stock. Discontinued circa 1975.

Exc.	V.G.	Good	Fair	Poor
750	600	500	400	200

OPUS SPORTING ARMS, INC.
Long Beach, California

Opus One

A .243, .270, or .30-06 caliber bolt-action rifle with a 24" barrel, well figured walnut stock and an ebony pistol grip cap as well as forend tip. Built on a Model 70 Winchester action. Manufactured in 1987 and 1988.

Exc.	V.G.	Good	Fair	Poor
2250	1600	1150	700	350

Opus Two

As above, in 7mm Remington Magnum and .300 Winchester Magnum.

Exc.	V.G.	Good	Fair	Poor
2500	1750	1250	750	350

Opus Three

As above, in .375 Holland & Holland and .458 Winchester Magnum.

Exc.	V.G.	Good	Fair	Poor
3000	2000	1500	900	500

ORBEA & CIA
Eibar, Spain

Pocket Pistol

A 6.35mm semi-automatic pistol with a 2.5" barrel. Blued with plastic grips. The slide marked "Orbea y Cia Eibar Espana Pistola Automatica Cal. 6.35." Manufactured from approximately 1918 to 1936.

Exc.	V.G.	Good	Fair	Poor
175	150	125	75	50

ORTGIES, HEINRICH & CO.
Erfurt, Germany

Ortgies Pistol

A 6.35mm or 7.65mm semi-automatic pistol with a 2.75" or 3.25" barrel. Blued with walnut grips. The slide marked "Ortgies & Co. Erfurt." After 1921, these pistols were manufactured by Deutsche Werke.

Exc.	V.G.	Good	Fair	Poor
550	300	175	125	85

ORVIS
Dallas, Texas

An importer and retailer of sporting goods including foreign manufactured firearms.

OSBORN, S.
Canton, Connecticut

Under Hammer Pistol

A .34 caliber under hammer percussion pistol with a 7" half octagonal barrel, brass mounts and a walnut grip. The barrel marked "S. Osborn/Canton, Conn."

Exc.	V.G.	Good	Fair	Poor
—	—	550	250	125

OSGOOD GUN WORKS
Norwich, Connecticut

Duplex Revolver

A .22 caliber spur trigger revolver with two super-imposed barrels, the upper most of .22 caliber and the lower a .32 caliber. The cylinder with eight .22 chambers. The hammer fitted with a moveable firing pin so that the pistol can be used either as a revolver or as a single shot with a .32 caliber barrel. Blued or nickel-plated with hard rubber grips. The barrel marked "Osgood Gun Works-Norwich Conn." and "Duplex." An unknown quantity were manufactured during the 1880s.

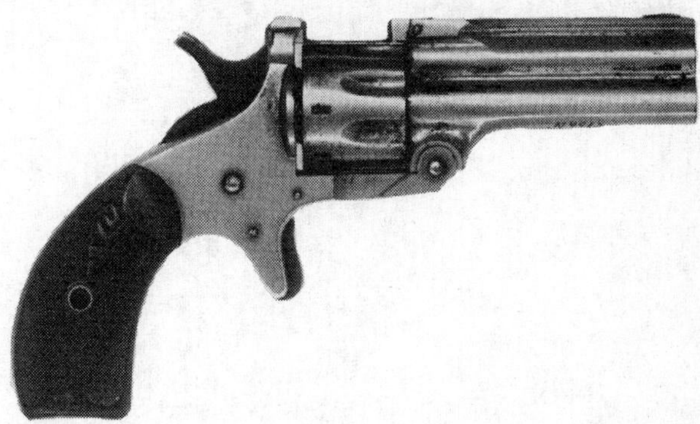

Courtesy Milwaukee Public Museum, Milwaukee, Wisconsin

Exc.	V.G.	Good	Fair	Poor
—	1350	800	350	100

OVERTON, JOHN
Nashville, Tennessee

Formerly armorer at Harpers Ferry Armory. He delivered 81 rifles copying the U.S. Model 1841 but with a saber bayonet lug on the right side of the barrel. Unmarked externally but are serial numbered internally. Overall length ca. 48-3/4"; barrel length 33"; .54 caliber.

Prospective purchasers are strongly advised to secure an expert appraisal prior to acquisition.

Exc.	V.G.	Good	Fair	Poor
—	—	12500	5000	2000

OWA
Osterreiche Werke Anstalt
Vienna, Austria

OWA Pocket Pistol

A 6.35mm semi-automatic pistol with a 2" barrel. Unmarked except for "OWA" logo cast in the grips. Blued with plastic grips. Manufactured between 1920 and 1925.

Courtesy Orvel Reichert

Exc.	V.G.	Good	Fair	Poor
300	200	175	100	75

P.38

THE GERMAN WWII SERVICE PISTOL

NOTE: For history, technical data, descriptions, photos, and prices, see the *Standard Catalog of Military Firearms*.

WALTHER COMMERCIAL

The Commercial version of the P.38 is identified by commercial proofmarks of a crown over N or an eagle over N. Production started at around serial number 1000 and went through serial number 26659. This was the first of the commercial pistols and was a high-quality, well made gun with a complete inscription on the left slide. A few of these early pistols were equipped with checkered wooden grips. The quality decreased as the war progressed. There are many variations of these commercial models and values can range up to more than $30,000. It is suggested that these pistols be appraised and evaluated by an expert. For post-war Walther P.38 pistols see the Walther section.

A few of the Walther Commercial Model variations are listed.

MOD HP

H Prefix w/rectangular firing pin

Exc.	V.G.	Good	Fair	Poor
3200	2000	950	750	450

Early w/High Gloss Blue

Exc.	V.G.	Good	Fair	Poor
3000	1750	750	600	400

.30 caliber, extremely rare

Exc.	V.G.	Good	Fair	Poor
28000	—	—		

Early w/High Gloss Blue & Alloy Frame

Exc.	V.G.	Good	Fair	Poor
10000	6500	3500	2000	1000

Croatian contract, 100 built, 6 known

Exc.	V.G.	Good	Fair	Poor
10000	—			—

Late w/Military Blue Finish

Exc.	V.G.	Good	Fair	Poor
2000	1400	750	550	350

NOTE: Add $500 for "Eagle/359" on right side.

MOD P38—Late with Military Blue

1800 produced.

Exc.	V.G.	Good	Fair	Poor
2700	1750	750	600	400

"ac45" Zero Series

1200 made.

Exc.	V.G.	Good	Fair	Poor
2800	1750	750	600	400

WALTHER MILITARY

ZERO SERIES

First Issue

Exc.	V.G.	Good	Fair	Poor
8500	5500	3500	2500	1500

Second Issue

Exc.	V.G.	Good	Fair	Poor
7000	4500	3250	2000	1000

Third Issue

Exc.	V.G.	Good	Fair	Poor
3500	2200	1250	800	500

480 CODE

Exc.	V.G.	Good	Fair	Poor
8500	5500	3000	1750	1000

"AC" CODES

This variation follows the 480 code.

"ac" (no date)

Exc.	V.G.	Good	Fair	Poor
9500	6000	4250	2800	2000

"AC40"

Added

Exc.	V.G.	Good	Fair	Poor
3800	2500	1750	1000	600

Standard

Exc.	V.G.	Good	Fair	Poor
2500	1200	950	700	500

"AC41"

1st Variation

Exc.	V.G.	Good	Fair	Poor
2200	1100	700	500	350

2nd Variation

Exc.	V.G.	Good	Fair	Poor
1500	750	600	450	300

3rd Variation

Exc.	V.G.	Good	Fair	Poor
1300	600	475	400	300

"AC42"

1st Variation

Exc.	V.G.	Good	Fair	Poor
1300	550	400	350	275

2nd Variation

Exc.	V.G.	Good	Fair	Poor
1100	500	400	300	250

"AC43"

1st Variation

Exc.	V.G.	Good	Fair	Poor
900	450	300	250	200

2nd Variation

Exc.	V.G.	Good	Fair	Poor
550	350	300	250	200

Single Line Slide

Exc.	V.G.	Good	Fair	Poor
1200	550	450	350	250

"AC44"

Exc.	V.G.	Good	Fair	Poor
800	450	300	250	200

NOTE: Add $300 for FN frame (Eagle/140).

"AC45"

1st Variation

Exc.	V.G.	Good	Fair	Poor
800	450	300	250	200

2nd Variation

Exc.	V.G.	Good	Fair	Poor
950	500	325	300	250

3rd Variation

Exc.	V.G.	Good	Fair	Poor
750	400	300	250	200

NOTE: Add $200 for pistols with Czech barrels; barrel code "fnh."

MAUSER MILITARY

"byf42"

Exc.	V.G.	Good	Fair	Poor
2200	1200	700	500	300

"byf43"

Exc.	V.G.	Good	Fair	Poor
950	550	300	250	200

"byf44"

Exc.	V.G.	Good	Fair	Poor
950	550	300	250	200

NOTE: Add $100 for dual tone finish that is a combination of blue and gray components.

AC43/44—FN slide

Exc.	V.G.	Good	Fair	Poor
2200	1200	725	550	400

"SVW45"

German Proofed

Exc.	V.G.	Good	Fair	Poor
2200	1200	725	550	400

French Proofed

Exc.	V.G.	Good	Fair	Poor
650	400	300	250	200

"svw46"—French Proofed

Exc.	V.G.	Good	Fair	Poor
800	500	400	350	300

MAUSER "POLICE" P.38

"byf/43"

Exc.	V.G.	Good	Fair	Poor
2500	1700	1200	800	500

"byf/44"

Exc.	V.G.	Good	Fair	Poor
2500	1700	1200	800	500

"ac/43"

Exc.	V.G.	Good	Fair	Poor
5000	3500	2000	1250	800

"ac/44"

Exc.	V.G.	Good	Fair	Poor
5000	3500	2000	1250	800

"svw/45"

Exc.	V.G.	Good	Fair	Poor
6000	4500	2500	1600	1000

SPREEWERKE MILITARY

"cyq"

Eagle /211 on frame

2 known.

Exc.	V.G.	Good	Fair	Poor
5000	—	—	—	—

1st Variation

Exc.	V.G.	Good	Fair	Poor
1400	1000	750	600	500

Standard Variation

Exc.	V.G.	Good	Fair	Poor
800	400	275	250	200

NOTE: If "A" or "B" prefix add $250.

Zero Series

Exc.	V.G.	Good	Fair	Poor
1250	550	400	350	275

NOTE: Add $250 for AC43 or AC44 marked "FN" slide.

POST-WAR PISTOLS

Standard Slides

Exc.	V.G.	Good	Fair	Poor
400	250	200	175	150

Single Line Code (Rare)

Exc.	V.G.	Good	Fair	Poor
1000	550	350	250	200

Manurhin

Exc.	V.G.	Good	Fair	Poor
400	300	200	175	150

P.A.F.

Pretoria Small Arms Factory
Pretoria, South Africa

P.A.F. Junior

A .22 or .25 caliber semi-automatic pistol with a 2" barrel and 6-shot magazine. Blued with plastic grips. Slide marked "Junior Verwaardig in Suid Afrika Made in South Africa." Manufactured during the 1950s.

Exc.	V.G.	Good	Fair	Poor
275	175	125	100	70

P.S.M.G. GUN CO.

Arlington, Massachusetts

Six-In-One Supreme

A .22 LR, .30 Luger, .38 Super, .38 Special, 9mm, and the .45 ACP caliber semi-automatic pistol with interchangeable 3.5", 5", or 7.5" barrels, and adjustable sights. Blued or satin nickel-plated. Introduced in 1988. Conversion kits are valued at $450 per unit.

NIB	Exc.	V.G.	Good	Fair	Poor
900	700	550	450	300	150

PAGE-LEWIS ARMS CO.

Chicopee Falls, Massachusetts

Model A Target

A .22 caliber single-shot lever-action rifle with a 20" barrel and open sights. Blued with a walnut stock. Manufactured from 1920 to 1926.

Exc.	V.G.	Good	Fair	Poor
300	225	175	125	100

Model B Sharpshooter

As above, with a 24" barrel and longer forend.

Exc.	V.G.	Good	Fair	Poor
300	225	175	125	100

Model C Olympic

As above, with a 24" barrel and improved sights.

Exc.	V.G.	Good	Fair	Poor
375	275	200	150	100

Challenge Model 49

Single shot .22 LR boy's rifle, manufactured c. 1925-1930. Stamped on top of barrel "Page Lewis Arms Co., Chicopee Falls, Mass USA/22 LR" Model 49. 22" long barrel, fixed front and rear sights.

Exc.	V.G.	Good	Fair	Poor
150	100	75	50	35

PALMER

Windsor, Vermont
E. G. Lamson & Co.

Palmer Bolt-Action Carbine

A .50 caliber single-shot bolt-action carbine with a 20" round barrel, walnut half stock and full sidelock. Blued and case hardened. The receiver marked "Wm. Palmer / Patent / Dec.22, 1863" and the lock "G.Lamson & Co./ Windsor, Vt." Approximately 1,000 were made in 1865.

Exc.	V.G.	Good	Fair	Poor
—	3250	1500	700	250

PANTHER ARMS

SEE—DPMS

PAPE, W.R.

Newcastle-Upon-Tyne, England
SEE—British Double Guns

Para®

PARA-ORDNANCE MFG. INC.

Scarborough, Ontario, Canada

NOTE: In the descriptions for models listed, figures in parentheses refer to pre- and post-ban magazine capacities.

Model P14.45

Similar in appearance to the Colt Government model this .45 ACP semi-automatic pistol features a 5" barrel, flared ejection port, combat style hammer beveled magazine well and a 13-round magazine capacity. Overall length is 8.5" and weight is 40 oz. for steel and stainless steel version and 31 oz. for alloy frame model. Finish is black except for stainless steel model.

NIB	Exc.	V.G.	Good	Fair	Poor
695	500	500	400	300	200

NOTE: Add $50 for steel frame, $45 for stainless steel, and $30 for duo-tone.

Model P14.45 Limited

Similar to the above model but with extra features such as full length recoil guide, beavertail grip safety, adjustable rear sight, competition hammer, lowered ejection port, front and rear slide serrations, and trigger overtravel stop. Match grade barrel. Choice of black carbon steel or stainless steel finish. Weight is about 40 oz.

NIB	Exc.	V.G.	Good	Fair	Poor
750	575	550	375	—	—

Model P14.45 LDA/P14.45 LDA Stainless

This model is essentially the same as the P14.45 but with a double-action trigger. Offered in black carbon steel only. Weight is about 40 oz. First introduced in 1999.

NIB	Exc.	V.G.	Good	Fair	Poor
700	500	400	350	—	—

NOTE: Add $50 for stainless steel.

Model P16.40

This is essentially the same as the Model 14.45 except that it is chambered for the .40 S&W cartridge. The magazine capacity is 15 rounds.

NIB	Exc.	V.G.	Good	Fair	Poor
700	500	400	400	300	200

NOTE: Add $50 for steel frame, $45 for stainless steel, and $30 for duo-tone.

Model P16.40 Limited

Similar to the above model but with extra features such as full length recoil guide, beavertail grip safety, adjustable rear sight, competition hammer, lowered ejection port, front and rear slide serrations, and trigger overtravel stop. Match grade barrel. Black carbon steel finish.

NIB	Exc.	V.G.	Good	Fair	Poor
750	575	550	375	—	—

Model P16.40 LDA

This model is a double-action version of the P16.40 in black carbon steel only. First offered in 1999.

NIB	Exc.	V.G.	Good	Fair	Poor
600	500	400	300	—	—

Model P13.45

Introduced in 1994 this .45 ACP model features a 4-1/4" barrel with a 13-round magazine. The grip is 1/4" longer than the 12.45 model. Offered in light alloy, carbon, or stainless steel. Overall length is 7-3/4" and the height is 5-1/4". Weight is about 36 oz. in steel version and 28 oz. in alloy version.

NIB	Exc.	V.G.	Good	Fair	Poor
600	450	350	300	—	—

NOTE: Add $50 for steel frame, $45 for stainless steel, and $30 for duo-tone.

Model 13.45/P12.45 Limited

Similar to the above model but with extra features such as full length recoil guide, beavertail grip safety, adjustable rear sight, competition hammer, lowered ejection port, front and rear slide serrations, and trigger overtravel stop. Match grade barrel. Black carbon steel finish.

P13.45

P12.45

NIB	Exc.	V.G.	Good	Fair	Poor
750	575	550	375	—	—

Model P12.45 LDA/P12.45 LDA

This model is fitted with a 3.5" barrel and has a magazine capacity of 12 rounds. It features a double-action trigger. Finish is black. Weight is about 34 oz. Introduced in 2000.

NIB	Exc.	V.G.	Good	Fair	Poor
600	450	350	300	—	—

NOTE: Add $50 for stainless steel.

Model P12.45/P12.40

Similar to the Model P14 but in a smaller package. Introduced in 1993. Has all the same features as the Model P14 but has a magazine capacity of 11 rounds. Also available in alloy, steel, or stainless steel this model weighs 24 oz. in alloy model and 33 oz. in steel models. The P12.40 is the same model but chambered for .40 S&W cartridge.

NIB	Exc.	V.G.	Good	Fair	Poor
600	450	350	300	—	—

NOTE: Add $50 for steel frame, $45 for stainless steel, and $30 for duo-tone.

Model P10.45/P10.40/P10.9

Introduced in 1996 this model is the smallest semi-auto .45 ACP in production. Overall length is 6.5" with height of 4.5". Magazine capacity is 10 rounds. Barrel length is 3.5". Offered in stainless steel, duo-tone, or black alloy finish. Also offered chambered for .40 S&W cartridge and the 9mm cartridge. Weight is about 31 oz. for stainless and 24 oz. for alloy model.

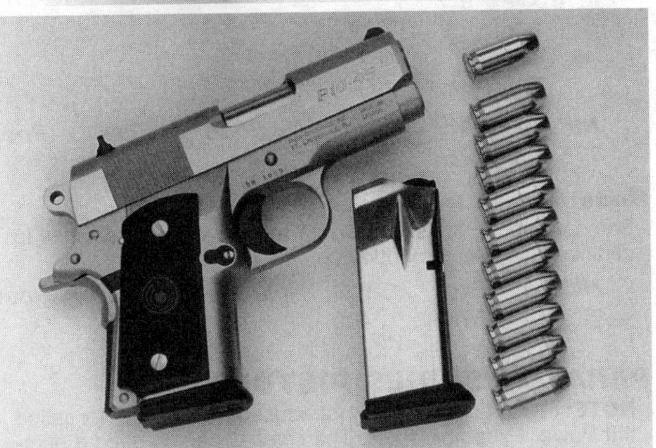

NIB	Exc.	V.G.	Good	Fair	Poor
600	450	350	300	—	—

NOTE: Add $50 for steel frame, $45 for stainless steel, and $30 for duo-tone.

Model P10.45 Limited

Similar to the above model but with extra features such as full length recoil guide, beavertail grip safety, adjustable rear sight, competition hammer, lowered ejection port, front and rear slide serrations, and trigger overtravel stop. Match grade barrel. Black carbon steel finish.

NIB	Exc.	V.G.	Good	Fair	Poor
650	500	400	300	—	—

Model P18.9

This pistol is chambered for the 9mm cartridge and is fitted with a 5" barrel. Finish is stainless steel. Rear sight is adjustable; dovetail front sight. Magazine capacity is 18 rounds (10 rounds for US and Canada). Weight is approximately 40 oz.

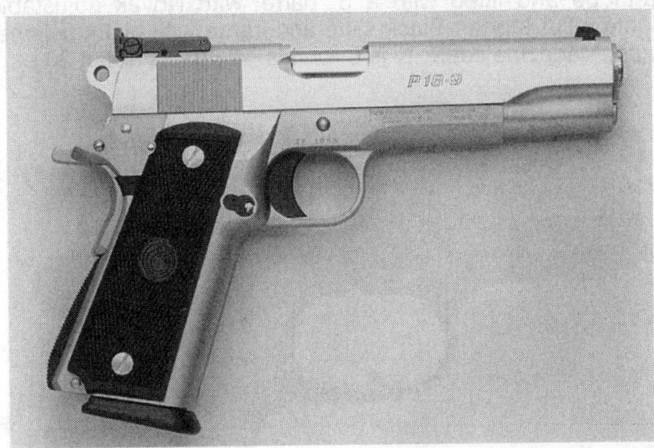

NIB	Exc.	V.G.	Good	Fair	Poor
775	625	500	350	—	—

Model P18.9 LDA

This is a double-action version of the P18-9. Offered in black carbon steel only. Introduced in 1999.

NIB	Exc.	V.G.	Good	Fair	Poor
775	625	500	350	—	—

Model C7.45 LDA (Para Companion)

This .45 ACP pistol is fitted with a 3.5" barrel. Stainless steel slide and frame. Low profile fixed sights. Magazine is 7 rounds. Weight is about 32 oz.

NIB	Exc.	V.G.	Good	Fair	Poor
600	450	350	300	—	—

Model C6.45 LDA (Para Carry)

Similar to the model above but with 3" barrel and 6-round magazine. Weight is about 30 oz.

NIB	Exc.	V.G.	Good	Fair	Poor
750	575	550	375	—	—

Model Stealth Carry

This model, introduced in 2005, is chambered for the .45 ACP cartridge and fitted with a 3" barrel with Novak adjustable sights. LDA trigger. Black slide and frame with black polymer grips. Magazine capacity is 6 rounds. Weight is about 30 oz.

NIB	Exc.	V.G.	Good	Fair	Poor
850	600	—	—	—	—

Model Para CCW

Introduced in 2003 this .45 ACP model features a 4.25" barrel with stainless steel receiver and frame. Magazine capacity is 7 rounds. Fitted with the LDA trigger system. Weight is about 34 oz.

NIB	Exc.	V.G.	Good	Fair	Poor
775	575	400	—	—	—

Model Para Companion Carry Option

This model is similar to the CCW above but it is fitted with a 3.5" barrel. Weight is about 32 oz. Introduced in 2003.

NIB	Exc.	V.G.	Good	Fair	Poor
775	575	400	—	—	—

Model Tac-Four

This .45 ACP model features the LDA trigger system. It is fitted with a 4.25" barrel and has a stainless steel slide and frame. Early models shipped with two pre-ban 13-round magazines. Later models will ship with two 10-round magazines. Weight is about 36 oz. Introduced in 2003.

NIB	Exc.	V.G.	Good	Fair	Poor
775	575	400	—	—	—

Model Tac-Four LE

Same as above but shipped with two 13-round magazines to certified law enforcement only.

NIB	Exc.	V.G.	Good	Fair	Poor
775	575	400	—	—	—

PARA PXT SERIES PISTOLS

NOTE: In 2004 the company introduced a new extractor called the Power Extractor (PXT). The company also added a number of new finishes and features for its PXT line. All Para pistols have integral ramp barrels that are of match grade quality. All pistols have full-length guide rod, match trigger, flared ejection port, extended slide lock safety, beavertail grip safety, cocobolo stocks with gold medallion and high-visibility, low-mount, dovetail, three-dot sights.

Para has introduced five finishes:

1. Sterling—All stainless steel, black slide with polished sides.
2. Stealth—Black slide, black frame with black fire controls.
3. Black Watch—Black slide, green frame with green fire controls on hi-cap models, and black controls on single- stack models.
4. Regal—Black slide, black frame with stainless steel fire controls.
5. Spec Ops—Green slide, green frame with black fire controls.

SINGLE ACTION, SINGLE STACK MODELS

Model OPS

Chambered for the .45 ACP cartridge and fitted with a 3.5" barrel. Stainless steel receiver. Magazine capacity is 7 rounds. Weight is about 32 oz.

NIB	Exc.	V.G.	Good	Fair	Poor
965	750	625	—	—	—

Model LTC

This .45 ACP pistol has a 4.25" ramped match barrel with steel receiver and Regal finish. Fixed 3-dot sights. Cocobolo wood grips with gold medallion. Magazine capacity is 7 rounds. Weight is about 37 oz.

NIB	Exc.	V.G.	Good	Fair	Poor
750	600	450	—	—	—

Model LTC Alloy

As above but with alloy frame. Weight is about 28 oz.

NIB	Exc.	V.G.	Good	Fair	Poor
750	600	450	—	—	—

Model LTC Stainless

Same as the Model LTC but with stainless steel frame and slide. Weight is about 35 oz. Introduced in 2005.

NIB	Exc.	V.G.	Good	Fair	Poor
985	725	575	—	—	—

Model Hawg 9

Chambered for the .45 ACP cartridge and fitted with a 3" ramped barrel. Alloy receiver and steel slide. Fixed 3-dot sights. Black polymer stocks with black slide, black frame and stainless steel fire controls. Weight is about 24 oz. Introduced in 2005.

NIB	Exc.	V.G.	Good	Fair	Poor
550	450	350	—	—	—

Model OPS

This .45 ACP pistol is fitted with a 3.5" barrel. It has a stainless steel frame and slide. Low mount fixed sights. Cocobolo grips. Magazine capacity is 7 rounds. Weight is about 32 oz. Introduced in 2005.

NIB	Exc.	V.G.	Good	Fair	Poor
600	525	—	—	—	—

Model 1911

This .45 ACP model has a 5" barrel with steel receiver and Regal finish. Magazine capacity is 7 rounds. Weight is about 39 oz.

NIB	Exc.	V.G.	Good	Fair	Poor
550	400	350	—	—	—

1911 SSP

7+1 capacity .45 ACP 1911-style semi-auto with 5" barrel. 39 oz. Competition triggers and hammers. Fixed sights. Cocobolo grip panels.

NIB	Exc.	V.G.	Good	Fair	Poor
650	500	350	—	—	—

HIGH CAPACITY, SINGLE ACTION MODELS

Warthog

Introduced in 2004 this .45 ACP pistol is fitted with a 3" barrel. The receiver is alloy. Black slide and frame with stainless steel fire controls. Overall length is 6.5". Height is 4.5". Magazine capacity is 10 rounds. Weight is about 24 oz. In 2005 this model was also chambered for the 9mm cartridge.

NIB	Exc.	V.G.	Good	Fair	Poor
625	500	400	300	—	—

Stealth Warthog

Chambered for the .45 ACP cartridge and fitted with a 3" ramped barrel. Black alloy slide with black frame and black fire controls. Tritium night sights. Extended slide lock, beavertail grip and firing pin. Weight is about 24 oz. Introduced in 2004.

NIB	Exc.	V.G.	Good	Fair	Poor
675	575	—	—	—	—

Slim Hawg

A .45 ACP pistol with 6+1 capacity. Single-stack, single-action 1911. Barrel 3", 30 oz. Stainless construction, checkered wood grips. Fixed, 3-dot sights. Introduced 2006.

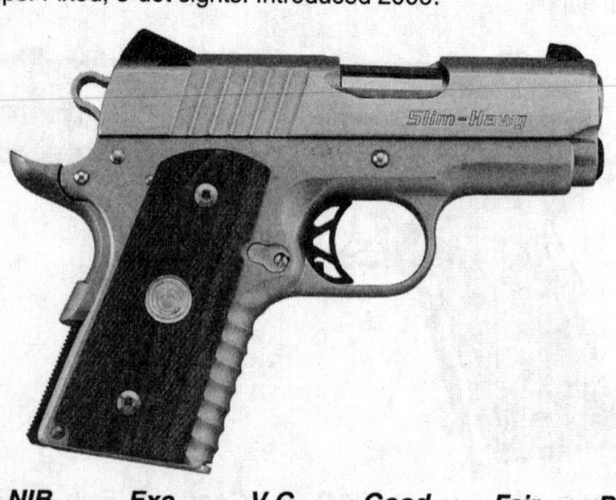

NIB	Exc.	V.G.	Good	Fair	Poor
675	575	—	—	—	—

Stainless Warthog

Stainless .45 ACP with 10+1 capacity. Single-stack, single-action 1911. Barrel 3", 31 oz. Fixed, 3-dot sights and plastic grips. Introduced 2006.

NIB	Exc.	V.G.	Good	Fair	Poor
675	575	—	—	—	—

Lite Hawg 9

Double-stack, 12+1 single-action 9mm in non-reflective black finish. Barrel 3", 31.5 oz and capacity. Fixed, 3-dot sights. Introduced 2006.

NIB	Exc.	V.G.	Good	Fair	Poor
675	575				

P12.45

This .45 ACP model is fitted with a 3.5" barrel and has a stainless steel receiver with stainless finish. Magazine capacity is 10 (12) rounds. Weight is about 34 oz.

NIB	Exc.	V.G.	Good	Fair	Poor
525	425	300	—	—	—

P13.45

This .45 ACP pistol has a 4.25" barrel with stainless steel receiver and Spec Ops finish. Magazine capacity is 10 (13) rounds. Weight is about 36 oz.

NIB	Exc.	V.G.	Good	Fair	Poor
600	500	350	—	—	—

Midnight Blue P14-45

Double-stack, 14+1 single-action 45 ACP in non-reflective black. 5" barrel, fixed, 3-dot sights and black plastic grips. Introduced 2006.

NIB	Exc.	V.G.	Good	Fair	Poor
600	500	350		—	—

Hi-Cap LTC

Introduced in 2005 this model is chambered for the .45 ACP cartridge and fitted with a 4.25" barrel with low mount fixed sights. Green frame, green slide with black fire controls. Black polymer grips. Magazine capacity is 14 rounds. Weight is about 37 oz.

NIB	Exc.	V.G.	Good	Fair	Poor
575	425	300	—	—	—

Stealth P14.45

This .45 ACP model is fitted with a 5" barrel and has a steel receiver with Stealth finish. Magazine capacity is 10 (14) rounds. Weight is about 40 oz.

NIB	Exc.	V.G.	Good	Fair	Poor
700	575	—	—	—	—

P14.45

As above but with stainless steel receiver and finish.

NIB	Exc.	V.G.	Good	Fair	Poor
725	600	—	—	—	—

P18.45

This model is chambered for the 9mm Parabellum cartridge and fitted with a 5" barrel. The receiver is stainless steel with stainless steel finish. Magazine is 10 (18) rounds. Weight is about 40 oz.

NIB	Exc.	V.G.	Good	Fair	Poor
800	675	—	—	—	—

HIGH CAPACITY, SINGLE ACTION, LIMITED MODELS

S12.45 Limited

This .45 ACP pistol has a 3.5" barrel with stainless steel receiver and Sterling finish. Magazine capacity is 10 (12) rounds. Weight is about 34 oz. Introduced in 2005.

NIB	Exc.	V.G.	Good	Fair	Poor
1105	850	—	—	—	—

S13.45 Limited

A .45 ACP pistol with 4.25" barrel. Stainless steel receiver and Sterling finish. Spurless hammer. Magazine capacity is 10 (13) rounds. Weight is about 36 oz.

NIB	Exc.	V.G.	Good	Fair	Poor
800	650	—	—	—	—

Stealth S14.45 Limited

This .45 ACP pistol is fitted with a 5" barrel and has a steel receiver with Stealth finish. Magazine capacity is 10 (14) rounds. Weight is about 40 oz.

NIB	Exc.	V.G.	Good	Fair	Poor
800	650	—	—	—	—

S14.45 Limited

As above but with stainless steel receiver and Sterling finish.

NIB	Exc.	V.G.	Good	Fair	Poor
900	695	—	—	—	—

Stealth S16.40 Limited

This pistol is chambered for the .40 S&W cartridge and fitted with a 5" barrel. Receiver is steel with Stealth finish. Magazine capacity is 10 (16) rounds. Weight is about 40 oz.

NIB	Exc.	V.G.	Good	Fair	Poor
900	695	—	—	—	—

S16.40 Limited

As above but with stainless steel receiver and Sterling finish.

NIB	Exc.	V.G.	Good	Fair	Poor
900	695	—	—	—	—

Todd Jarrett .40 USPSA

A limited edition 16+1 (or 10+1) .40 S&W custom competition pistol with adjustable rear sight and fiber optic front sight. 5" barrel, 40 oz., covert non-reflective black or sterling.

NIB	Exc.	V.G.	Good	Fair	Poor
1250	—	—	—	—	—

Todd Jarrett .45 USPSA

Limited edition 8+1 .45 ACP caliber custom competition pistol with adjustable rear sight and fiber optic front sight. 5" barrel, 39 oz.; covert non-reflective black or stainless finish.

NIB	Exc.	V.G.	Good	Fair	Poor
1250	—	—	—	—	—

LDA, DOUBLE ACTION, SINGLE STACK, CARRY OPTION

Carry Model

This .45 ACP model has a 3" barrel and stainless steel receiver with stainless finish. Magazine capacity is 6 rounds. Weight is about 30 oz.

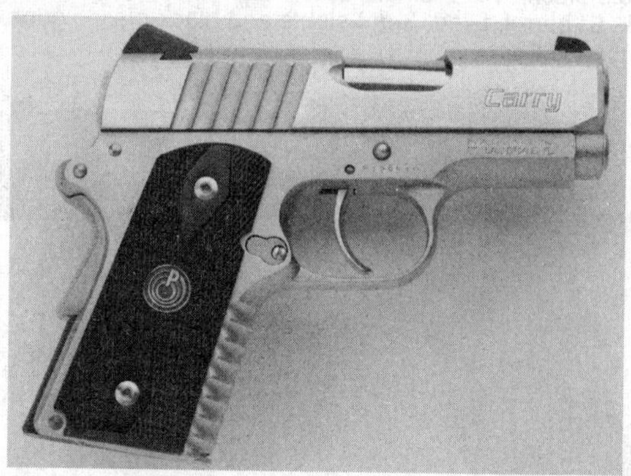

NIB	Exc.	V.G.	Good	Fair	Poor
750	600	—	—	—	—

Stealth Carry

Similar to the model above but with Stealth finish and Novak adjustable sights.

NIB	Exc.	V.G.	Good	Fair	Poor
800	625	—	—	—	—

CCO (Companion Carry Option)

This .45 ACP model is fitted with a 3.5" barrel. The receiver is stainless steel with a stainless finish. Magazine capacity is 7 rounds. Weight is about 32 oz.

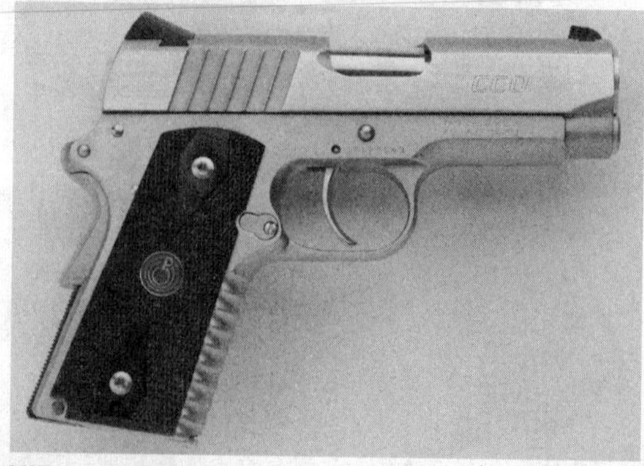

NIB	Exc.	V.G.	Good	Fair	Poor
750	600	—	—	—	—

CCW

Similar to the model above but fitted with a 4.45" barrel. Weight is about 34 oz.

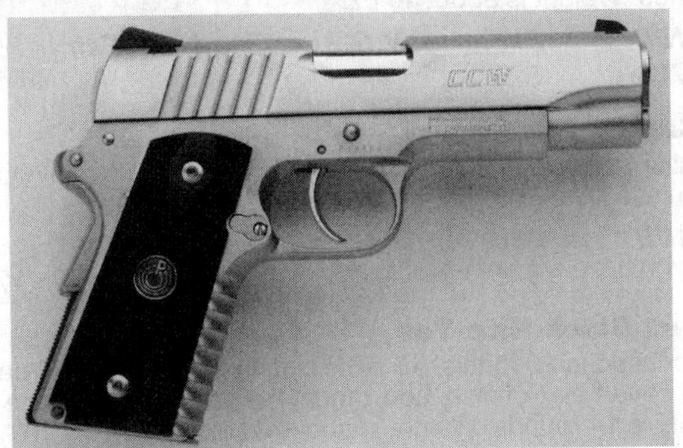

NIB	Exc.	V.G.	Good	Fair	Poor
750	600	—	—	—	—

DOUBLE ACTION ONLY, SINGLE STACK MODELS

Black Watch Companion

This .45 ACP pistol is fitted with a 3.5" barrel. Receiver is stainless steel with black watch finish. Magazine capacity is 7 rounds. Weight is about 32 oz.

NIB	Exc.	V.G.	Good	Fair	Poor
750	575	—	—	—	—

TAC-S

Chambered for the .45 ACP cartridge with a 4.45" barrel. Steel receiver and Spec Ops finish. Magazine capacity is 7 rounds. Weight is about 35 oz.

NIB	Exc.	V.G.	Good	Fair	Poor
700	525	—	—	—	—

Black Watch SSP

This .45 ACP pistol has a 5" barrel with steel receiver and Black Watch finish. Fixed 3-dot sights. Match trigger. Cocobolo wood grip with gold medallion. Magazine capacity is 7 rounds. Weight is about 39 oz.

NIB	Exc.	V.G.	Good	Fair	Poor
700	525	—	—	—	—

SSP

Similar to the model above but with stainless steel reciever and stainless finish.

NIB	Exc.	V.G.	Good	Fair	Poor
750	575	—	—	—	—

LDA, DOUBLE ACTION, SINGLE STACK, LIMITED MODELS

Stealth Limited

This .45 ACP pistol has a 5" barrel with adjustable sights. Receiver is steel with Stealth finish. Magazine capacity is 7 rounds. Weight is about 40 oz.

NIB	Exc.	V.G.	Good	Fair	Poor
800	650	—	—	—	—

Limited

This .45 ACP model has a 5" barrel and stainless steel receiver with Sterling finish. Magazine capacity is 7 rounds. Weight is about 40 oz. Adjustable sights.

NIB	Exc.	V.G.	Good	Fair	Poor
875	700	—	—	—	—

LDA, DOUBLE ACTION, HIGH CAPACITY, CARRY OPTION SERIES

Carry 12

This is a 45 ACP pistol with a 3.5" barrel fitted with night sights. Receiver is stainless steel with a stainless finish. Magazine capacity is 10 (12) rounds. Weight is about 34 oz.

NIB	Exc.	V.G.	Good	Fair	Poor
800	650	—	—	—	—

Tac-Four

This .45 ACP model is fitted with a 4.35" barrel. Stainless steel receiver with Spec Ops finish. Magazine capacity is 10 (13) rounds. Sight are 3-dot. Weight is about 36 oz.

NIB	Exc.	V.G.	Good	Fair	Poor
750	575	—	—	—	—

Tac-Five

Light double-action 9mm with 18+1 capacity. 5" barrel, 37.5 oz., stainless finish, adjustable rear sight, plastic grips.

NIB	Exc.	V.G.	Good	Fair	Poor
650	—	—	—	—	—

LDA, DOUBLE ACTION, HIGH CAPACITY MODELS

Stealth Hi-Cap .45

This .45 ACP pistol has a 5" barrel with steel receiver and Stealth finish. Spurless hammer. sights are 3-dot. Magazine capacity is 10 (14) rounds. Weight is about 40 oz.

NIB	Exc.	V.G.	Good	Fair	Poor
700	525	—	—	—	—

Hi-Cap .45

Similar to the model above but with stainless steel receiver and stainless finish.

NIB	Exc.	V.G.	Good	Fair	Poor
750	575	—	—	—	—

Colonel

This .45 ACP pistol is fitted with a 4.25" barrel with low mount fixed sights. The slide and frame are green with black fire controls. Black polymer grips. Magazine capacity is 14 rounds. Weight is about 37 oz. Introduced in 2005.

NIB	Exc.	V.G.	Good	Fair	Poor
725	550	—	—	—	—

Hi-Cap .40

This model is chambered for the .40 S&W cartridge and fitted with a 5" barrel with 3-dot sights. Stainless steel receiver with stainless finish. Magazine capacity is 10 (16) rounds. Weight is about 40 oz.

NIB	Exc.	V.G.	Good	Fair	Poor
650	500	—	—	—	—

Stealth Hi-Cap 9

This 9mm pistol is fitted with a 5" barrel with 3-dot sights and steel receiver with Stealth finish. Magazine capacity is 10 (18) rounds. Weight is about 40 oz.

NIB	Exc.	V.G.	Good	Fair	Poor
700	525	—	—	—	—

Hi-Cap 9

Similar to the model above but for stainless steel receiver and stainless finish.

NIB	Exc.	V.G.	Good	Fair	Poor
750	575	—	—	—	—

Covert Black Nite-Tac

Introduced in 2005 this .45 ACP pistol is fitted with a 5" barrel with covert black finish. Low mount fixed sights. Magazine capacity is 14 rounds. Weight is about 40 oz.

NIB	Exc.	V.G.	Good	Fair	Poor
775	—	—	—	—	—

Nite-Tac

As above but with stainless steel frame and slide. Introduced in 2005.

NIB	Exc.	V.G.	Good	Fair	Poor
700	575	—	—	—	

Nite-Tac .40

A .40 S&W 16+1 capacity double-action duty pistol with fixed sights. 5" barrel, 40 oz., stainless finish.

NIB	Exc.	V.G.	Good	Fair	Poor
775	—	—	—	—	—

Nite-Tac 9

A 9mm 18+1 double-action duty pistol with fixed sights. 5" barrel, 40 oz., stainless finish.

NIB	Exc.	V.G.	Good	Fair	Poor
775	—	—	—	—	—

LDA, DOUBLE ACTION, HIGH CAPACITY, LIMITED

Hi-Cap Limited .40

This .40 S&W pistol has a 5" barrel with 3-dot sights and a stainless steel receiver with Sterling finish. Magazine capacity is 10 (16) rounds. Weight is about 40 oz.

NIB	Exc.	V.G.	Good	Fair	Poor
875	725	—	—	—	—

Stealth Hi-Cap Limited 9

This model is chambered for the 9mm cartridge and fitted with a 5" barrel with 3-dot sights. The receiver is steel with Stealth finish. Magazine capacity is 10 (18) rounds. Weight is about 40 oz.

NIB	Exc.	V.G.	Good	Fair	Poor
800	675	—	—	—	—

Hi-Cap Limited 9

As above but with stainless steel receiver and Sterling finish.

NIB	Exc.	V.G.	Good	Fair	Poor
875	725	—	—	—	—

Stealth Hi-Cap Ltd .45

This .45 ACP pistol has a 5" barrel with 3-dot sights and spurless hammer. Receiver is steel with Stealth finish. Magazine capacity is 10 (14) rounds. Weight is about 40 oz.

NIB	Exc.	V.G.	Good	Fair	Poor
800	650	—	—	—	—

Hi-Cap Limited .45

This model is similar to the one above but with stainless steel receiver and Sterling finish.

NIB	Exc.	V.G.	Good	Fair	Poor
875	700	—	—	—	—

PARDINI

Italy

Standard Target Pistol

A .22 caliber semi-automatic pistol with a 4.7" barrel, adjustable rear sight and adjustable trigger. Blued with two sizes of walnut grips, one suitable for use by ladies. Introduced in 1986.

NIB	Exc.	V.G.	Good	Fair	Poor
950	800	700	600	500	250

Rapidfire Pistol

Similar to the above, in .22 short with an alloy bolt, 4.6" barrel and enclosed grip. Weight is about 43 oz. Introduced in 1995.

NIB	Exc.	V.G.	Good	Fair	Poor
950	800	700	600	500	250

Centerfire Pistol

Similar to the standard model, but in .32 Smith & Wesson caliber. Introduced in 1986.

NIB	Exc.	V.G.	Good	Fair	Poor
950	800	700	600	500	250

Free Pistol

A .22 caliber single-shot pistol with a 9.8" barrel, adjustable sights and adjustable grip. Furnished with barrel weights. Weight is about 35 oz. Introduced in 1995.

NIB	Exc.	V.G.	Good	Fair	Poor
950	800	700	600	500	250

PARKER

Springfield, Massachusetts

4-Shot Pistol

A .33 caliber percussion pistol with a 4" half-octagonal barrel and a 4-shot sliding chamber. Marked "Albert Parker/Patent Secured/Springfield, Mass." Original finish unknown with walnut grips. Prospective purchasers are advised to secure a qualified appraisal prior to acquisition.

Exc.	V.G.	Good	Fair	Poor
—	—	13500	6000	2000

PARKER BROS.

Meriden, Connecticut

Perhaps the best known of all American shotgun manufacturers. Established by Charles Parker shortly after the Civil War, this company has produced a wide variety of shotguns in a number of different styles over the years. In the early 1930s the company was purchased by Remington Arms Company.

WARNING NOTE: Parker shotguns are among the most collectible of American-made shotguns. Both the beginning and the veteran collector should be aware that originality and condition are absolutely critical in establishing such high values for these shotguns. There are numerous upgraded and refinished guns that are represented as original. Beware that such misrepresentations exist because refinished and upgraded Parker guns should sell for as much as 50 to 75 percent below the price of an original gun. Extreme caution should be exercised and we would recommend that an expert be consulted. Even the most advanced collectors may benefit from such consultations. Also, the prices indicated for guns in excellent condition may fluctuate drastically, especially in high grade or small bore guns, due to their extreme rarity.

In addition, uncommon extras such as single triggers, ventilated ribs, beavertail forearms, straight-grip stocks, and skeleton steel buttplates may add substantial value to an individual gun. Extra sets of factory barrels that were installed at the time of delivery will add an average of a 30 percent premium. This premium will increase with grade and gauge; the higher the grade and smaller the gauge the higher the premium.

NOTE: Letters of authenticity are available. These letters are a must in order for any Parker gun to attain maximum value. Contact: the Exec. Secetary Parker Gun Collectors Association, 8825 Bud Smith Road, Wake Forest, SC 27587. FAX: 919-554-8120. The letter is $25 for members of the PCGA and $40 for non-members.

Editor's Comment: We now have reliable information on the production totals of Parker gauges and grades. This information comes from the book; *The Parker Story* by Gunther, Mullins, Parker, Price, and Cote (1998). **These totals reflect guns built with modern steel barrels *only*** and are based on factory records. It is the editor's opinion that while production statistics are interesting it is the relative number of guns produced in each grade and bore that are the most significant.

VH

A 12, 16, 20, 28 or .410 bore boxlock double-barrel shotgun manufactured in a variety of barrel lengths with double triggers and extractors. Blued, case hardened receiver with a walnut stock. Only 2,297 guns had single triggers. Only 3,983 guns had straight grip stocks.

*Approximately 78,659 were made: 10 gauge—20, 12 gauge—51,901, 16 gauge—14,446, 20 gauge—10,406, 28 gauge—1,417, .410 bore—469.

NOTE: Also made with automatic ejectors and known as the Model VHE. The E suffix was used on all models to denote automatic ejectors.

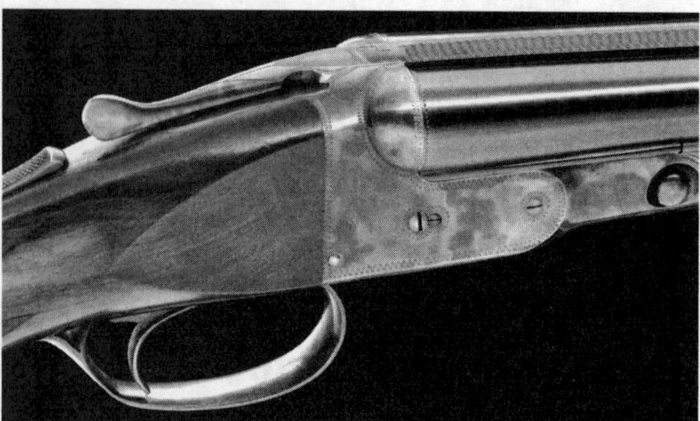

Courtesy Bonhams & Butterfields

Exc.	*V.G.*	*Good*	*Fair*	*Poor*
3500	1800	1500	1000	700

NOTE: VHE add 40 percent, 20 gauge add 60 percent, 28 gauge add 500 percent, .410 add 500 percent.

PH

Similar to the above, but with a small amount of scroll engraving. slightly better grade of walnut.

*Approximately 1,339 were made: 10 gauge—798, 12 gauge—839, 16 gauge—208, 20 gauge—204, 28 gauge—only 5, .410 bore—only 4.

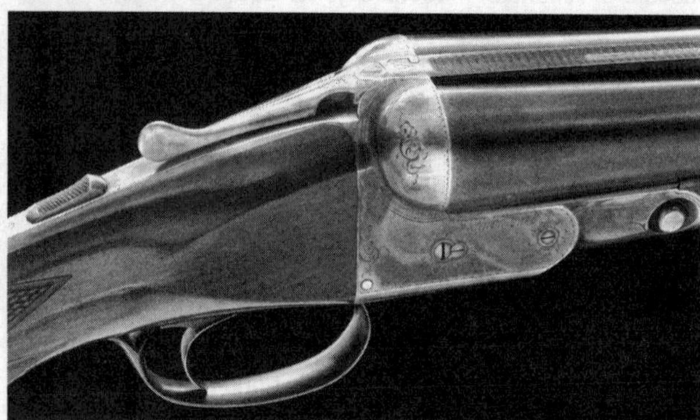

Courtesy Bonhams & Butterfields

Exc.	*V.G.*	*Good*	*Fair*	*Poor*
3500	2200	1700	1200	900

NOTE: PHE add 40 percent, 20 gauge add 45 percent, 28 gauge add 500 percent.

GH

Similar to the above, with a modest amount of scroll and game scene engraving and the barrels marked "Parker Special Steel." Only about 430 G grades were built with straight grip stocks.

*Approximately 4,291 were made: 8 gauge—11, 10 gauge—63, 12 gauge—2,501, 16 gauge—607, 20 gauge—990, 28 gauge—91, .410 bore—28.

Exc.	*V.G.*	*Good*	*Fair*	*Poor*
3900	2700	2200	1400	1000

NOTE: GHE add 35 percent, 16 gauge add 15 percent, 20 gauge add 40 percent, 28 gauge add 500 percent, .410 add 500 percent.

DH

As above, but more finely finished. Engraving coverage more profuse. Most modern D grade guns were fitted with Titanic barrels. Only about 280 were built with Parker single triggers, and only about 280 were built with ventilated ribs.

*Approximately 9,346 were made: 8 gauge—10, 10 gauge—45, 12 gauge—6,330, 16 gauge—1,178, 20 gauge—1,536, 28 gauge—187, .410 bore—60.

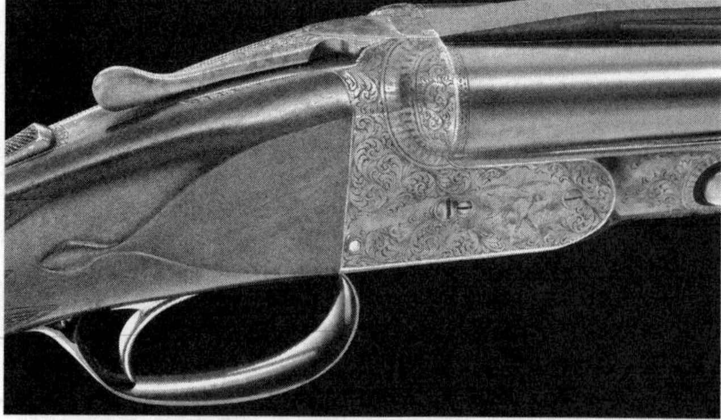

Courtesy Bonhams & Butterfields

Exc.	*V.G.*	*Good*	*Fair*	*Poor*
6500	5000	4000	2000	1500

NOTE: DHE add 35 percent, 16 gauge add 10 percent, 20 gauge add 40 percent, 28 gauge add 500 percent, .410 add 500 percent.

CH

As above, with more scroll and game scene engraving coverage. Marked with Acme steel barrels. Only about 93 C grades had straight-grip stocks.

*Approximately 697 were made: 8 gauge—only 2, 10 gauge—only 9, 12 gauge—410, 16 gauge—105, 20 gauge—149, 28 gauge—only 16, .410 bore—only 6.

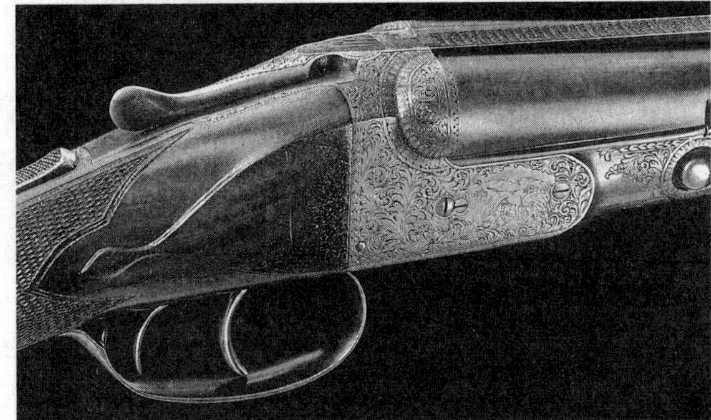

Exc.	*V.G.*	*Good*	*Fair*	*Poor*
7750	5600	4300	2500	2000

NOTE: CHE add 35 percent, 16 gauge add 10 percent, 20 gauge add 40 percent, 28 gauge add 400 percent, .410 add 700 percent.

BH

As above, but offered in a variety of different styles of engraved decoration. Only about 66 guns had straight-grip stocks, 29 had beavertail forends, 20 were built with vent ribs, and 57 had single triggers.

*Approximately 512 were made: 10 gauge—only 2, 12 gauge—317, 16 gauge—71, 20 gauge—109, 28 gauge—13.

NOTE: Prospective purchasers are advised to secure a qualified appraisal prior to acquisition.

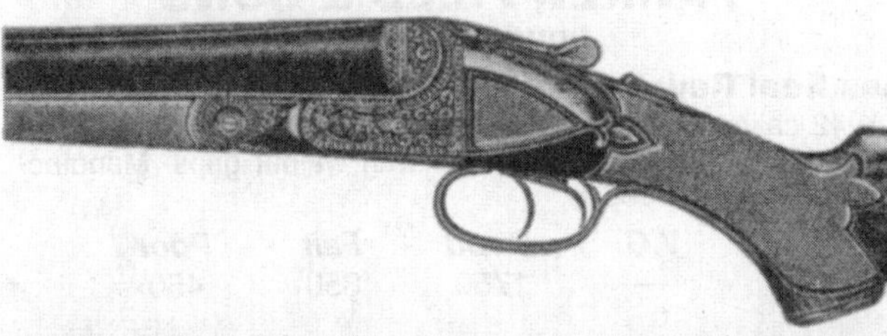

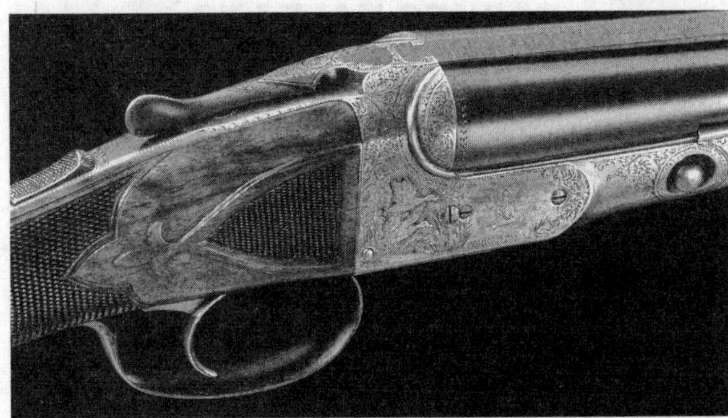

Exc.	*V.G.*	*Good*	*Fair*	*Poor*
10000	7500	5000	3300	2500

NOTE: BHE add 35 percent, 16 gauge add 15 percent, 20 gauge add 50 percent, 28 gauge add 450 percent.

AH

As above, but highly engraved with finely figured walnut stocks. Most had Acme steel barrels. About 42 A grade guns were built with straight grip stocks.

*Approximately 167 were made: 10 gauge—only 1, 12 gauge—92, 16 gauge—23, 20 gauge—44, 28 gauge—only 6, .410 bore— only 1.

NOTE: Due to the rarity of this grade prospective purchasers are advised to secure a qualified appraisal prior to acquisition.

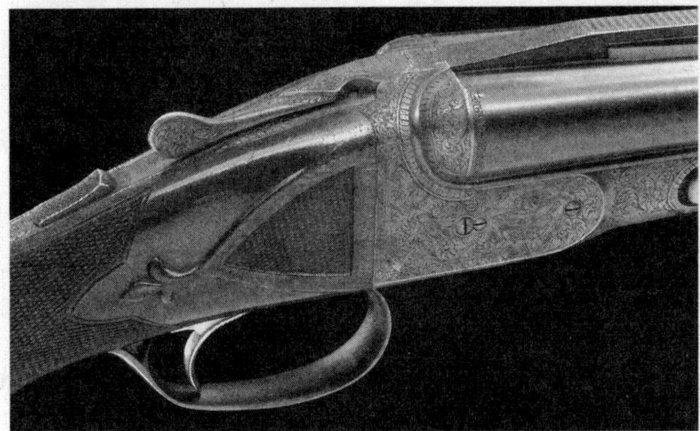

Courtesy Bonhams & Butterfields

Exc.	*V.G.*	*Good*	*Fair*	*Poor*
18500	13000	10000	8000	5000

NOTE: AHE add 30 percent, 16 gauge add 25 percent, 20 gauge add 75 percent, 28 gauge add 450 percent, .410 add 600 percent.

AAH

As above, with either Whitworth or Peerless barrels and not made in .410 bore. The engraving is more extensive and of the first quality. Only one AA grade has a ventilated rib, ten were built with single trigger and 95 had straight grip stocks.

*Approximately 238 were made: 10 gauge—only 2, 12 gauge—185, 16 gauge—19, 20 gauge—27, 28 gauge—only 5.

NOTE: Due to the rarity of this grade prospective purchasers are advised to secure a qualified appraisal prior to acquisition.

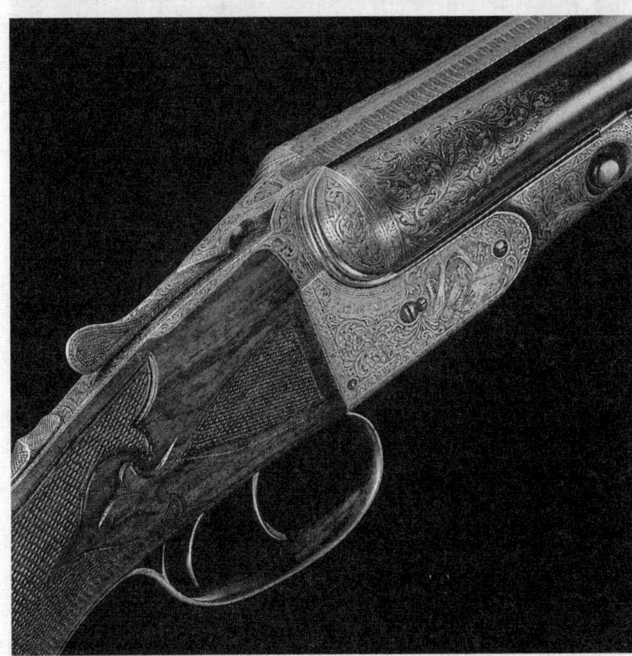

Exc.	*V.G.*	*Good*	*Fair*	*Poor*
35000	25000	18000	10000	7000

NOTE: AAHE add 30 percent, 16 gauge add 35 percent, 20 gauge add 75 percent, 28 gauge add 250 percent.

A-1 Special

As above, but made strictly on special order and not manufactured in .410 bore. Two A-1 Specials were built with ventilated rib, 7 had single triggers, 3 had beavertail forends, and 24 were built with straight-grip stocks.

*Approximately 79 were made: 12 gauge—55, 16 gauge—only 6, 20 gauge—11, and 28 gauge—only 7.

NOTE: Due to the extreme rarity of this grade prospective purchasers are advised to secure a qualified appraisal prior to acquisition.

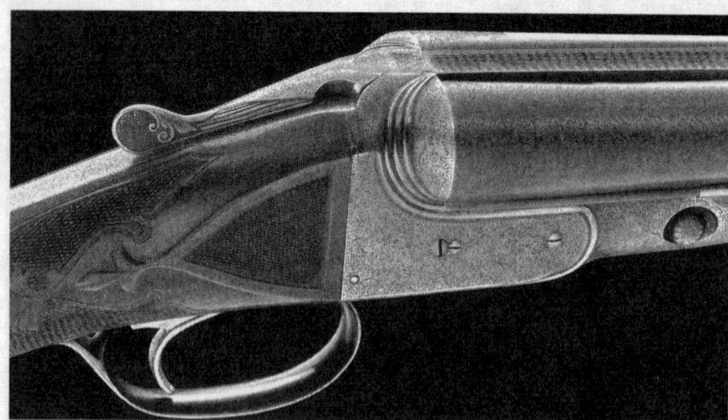

Courtesy Bonhams & Butterfields

Exc.	V.G.	Good	Fair	Poor
65000	55000	42000	30000	20000

NOTE: 16 gauge add 35 percent, 20 gauge add 75 percent, 28 gauge add 400 percent.

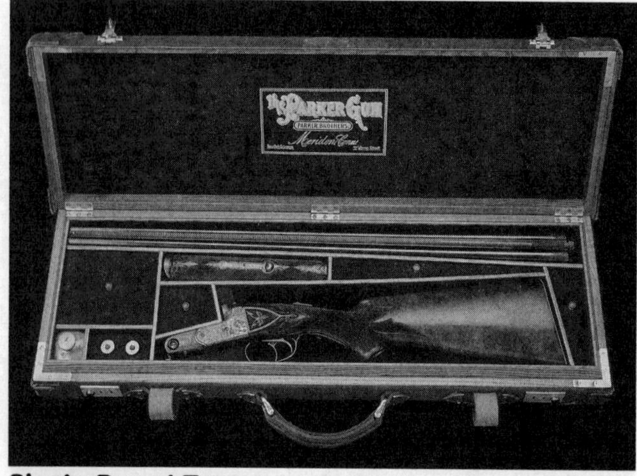

Single-Barrel Trap

A 12 gauge single-shot shotgun with a 30", 32", or 34" barrel, automatic ejector and walnut stock. Produced in a variety of grades as listed. Prospective purchasers are advised to secure a qualified appraisal prior to acquisition.

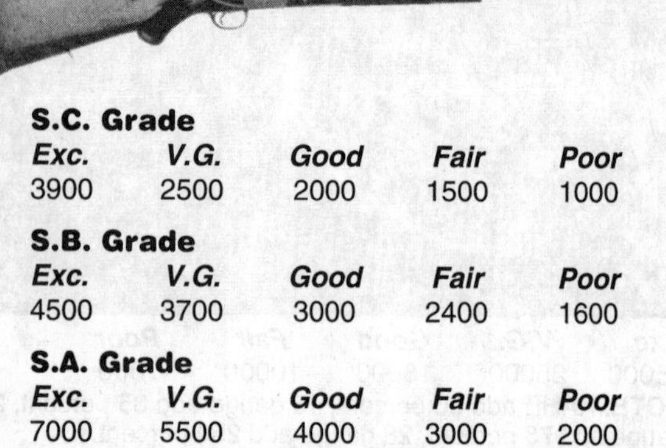

S.C. Grade

Exc.	V.G.	Good	Fair	Poor
3900	2500	2000	1500	1000

S.B. Grade

Exc.	V.G.	Good	Fair	Poor
4500	3700	3000	2400	1600

S.A. Grade

Exc.	V.G.	Good	Fair	Poor
7000	5500	4000	3000	2000

S.A.A. Grade

Exc.	V.G.	Good	Fair	Poor
12000	7000	5500	3800	2400

S.A-1 Special Grade

Exc.	V.G.	Good	Fair	Poor
20000	12000	8000	6000	4000

Under Lifter Hammer Gun

A side hammer double-barrel shotgun manufactured in a variety of gauges with the barrel release located in front of the triggerguards. Damascus barrels, case hardened locks, blued furniture with walnut stocks. Manufactured during the 1870s and later.

Exc.	V.G.	Good	Fair	Poor
6000	3200	1500	800	600

Trojan

A 12, 16, or 20 gauge boxlock double-barrel shotgun manufactured in a variety of barrel lengths with double triggers and extractors. Only 27 Trojans were built with single triggers. Blued, case hardened receiver with a walnut stock.

*Approximately 33,000 were made: 12 gauge—21,977, 16 gauge—6,573, 20 gauge—5450, 28 gauge—None.

Exc.	V.G.	Good	Fair	Poor
2400	1500	1000	800	600

NOTE: 20 gauge add 40 percent.

PARKER FIELD & SONS

SEE—English Military Firearms

PARKER FIELD & SONS

London, England

Gas Seal Revolver

A .42 caliber percussion revolver with a 6" barrel and 6-shot cylinder. Blued, case hardened with walnut grips. Manufactured during the 1860s.

Exc.	V.G.	Good	Fair	Poor
—	—	1750	850	450

PARKER-HALE LTD.

Birmingham, England

S&W Victory Conversion

A .22 caliber double-action revolver with a 4" barrel and 6-shot cylinder. Blued with walnut grips. An alteration of the Smith & Wesson Victor model.

Exc.	V.G.	Good	Fair	Poor
275	200	150	100	75

Model 1200

A .22-250 to .300 Winchester Magnum bolt-action rifle with a 24" barrel and open sights. Blued, with walnut stock.

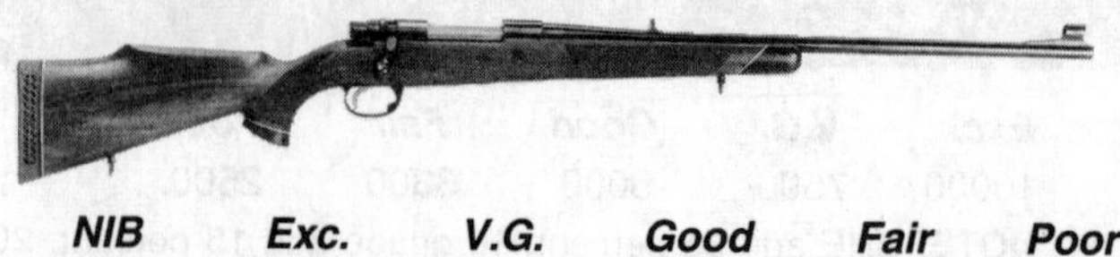

NIB	Exc.	V.G.	Good	Fair	Poor
700	550	450	400	350	250

Model 1100 Lightweight

As above, with a 22" barrel and 4-shot magazine. Introduced in 1985.

NIB	Exc.	V.G.	Good	Fair	Poor
600	475	400	300	250	200

Model 81 Classic

A .22-250 to 7mm Remington Magnum bolt-action rifle with a 24" barrel and open sights. Blued with a walnut stock. Introduced in 1985.

NIB	Exc.	V.G.	Good	Fair	Poor
875	750	600	500	400	350

Model 81 African

As above, but in .375 Holland & Holland caliber. Introduced in 1986.

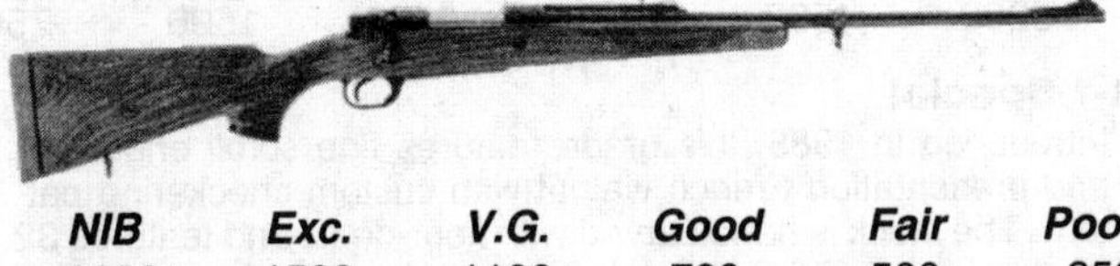

NIB	Exc.	V.G.	Good	Fair	Poor
2000	1500	1100	700	500	350

Model 84 Target

Similar to the Model 81, but in .308 caliber with adjustable rear sights and an adjustable cheekpiece.

NIB	Exc.	V.G.	Good	Fair	Poor
1500	1000	800	600	450	250

Model 85 Sniper

As above, with a telescope and bipod.

NIB	Exc.	V.G.	Good	Fair	Poor
3750	3000	2500	—	—	—

Model 640E Shotgun

A 12, 16, or 20 gauge boxlock double-barrel shotgun manufactured in a variety of barrel lengths with double triggers and extractors. Blued, French case hardened with a walnut stock. Introduced in 1986.

NIB	Exc.	V.G.	Good	Fair	Poor
575	450	400	300	250	200

Model 640A

As above, with a pistol grip, beavertail forend, and single trigger. Introduced in 1986.

NIB	Exc.	V.G.	Good	Fair	Poor
675	550	500	400	300	200

Model 645E

As above, but more finely finished and engraved.

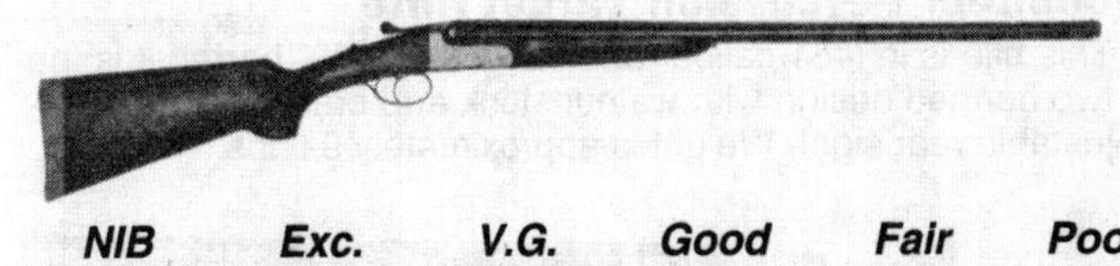

NIB	Exc.	V.G.	Good	Fair	Poor
700	550	500	400	300	200

Model 670E

A sidelock double-barrel shotgun made on special order. Introduced in 1986.

NIB	Exc.	V.G.	Good	Fair	Poor
3000	2500	1850	1200	750	400

Model 680E—XXV

As above, with case hardened lockplates and 25" barrels.

NIB	Exc.	V.G.	Good	Fair	Poor
3000	2500	1850	1200	750	400

BLACKPOWDER REPRODUCTIONS

Imported by Gibbs Rifle Company

1853 Enfield Rifle Musket

This is a three band version in .577 caliber. Barrel length is 39". Rear sight graduated to 900 yards. Weight about 9 lbs.

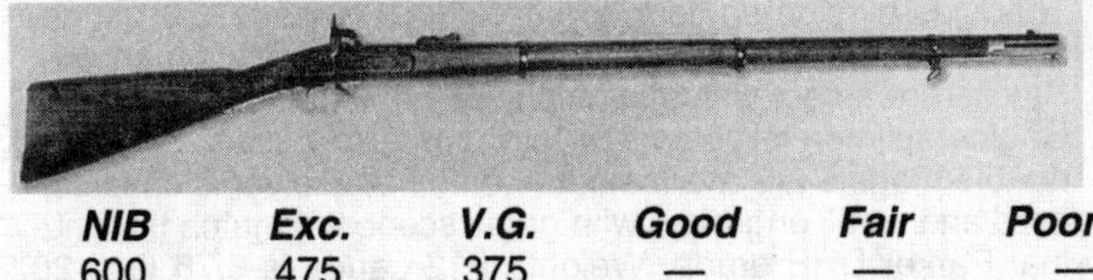

NIB	Exc.	V.G.	Good	Fair	Poor
600	475	375	—	—	—

1858 Enfield Naval Pattern Rifle

This is the Naval version with two bands in .577 caliber. Barrel length is 33". Walnut stock with brass furniture. Rear sight adjustable to 1100 yards. Weight is approximately 8.5 lbs.

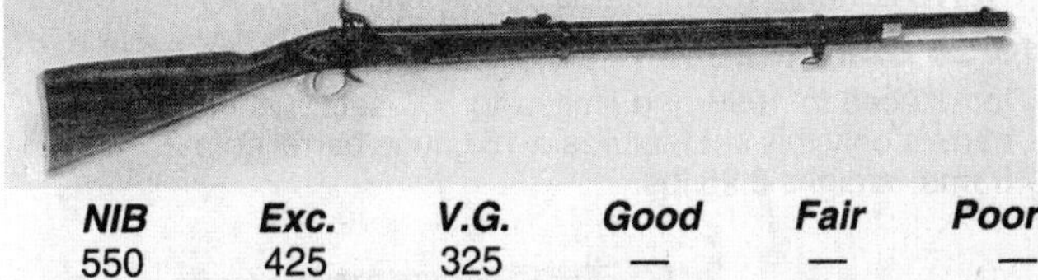

NIB	Exc.	V.G.	Good	Fair	Poor
550	425	325	—	—	—

1861 Enfield Artillery Carbine Musketoon

This is the Artillery version in .577 caliber with 24" barrel. Walnut stock with brass furniture. Rear sight adjustable to 600 yards. Weight is about 7.5 lbs.

NIB	Exc.	V.G.	Good	Fair	Poor
475	375	300	—	—	—

Whitworth Military Target Rifle

This model is in .451 caliber. Barrel length is 36". Weight is about 9.9 lbs.

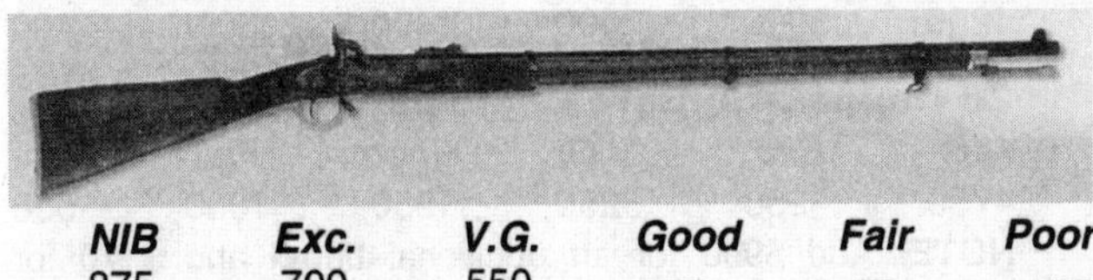

NIB	Exc.	V.G.	Good	Fair	Poor
875	700	550	—	—	—

Whitworth Sniping Rifle

Same as above but with brass scope and mounts.

NIB	Exc.	V.G.	Good	Fair	Poor
1400	1050	800	—	—	—

Volunteer Percussion Target Rifle

This rifle is in .451 caliber and fitted with a 33" barrel. It is the two banned design with walnut stock and brass furniture. Adjustable rear sight. Weight is approximately 9.5 lbs.

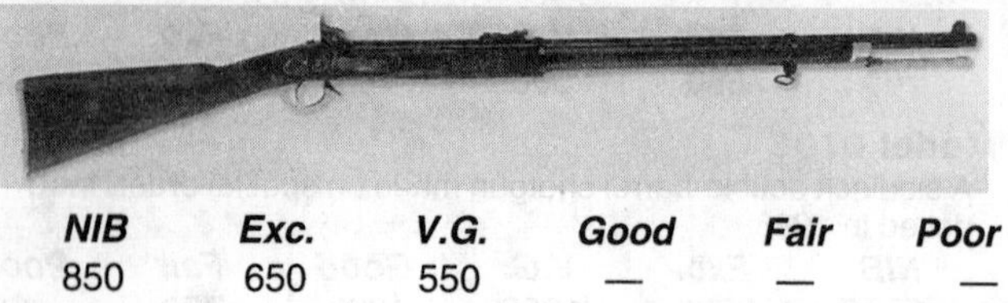

NIB	Exc.	V.G.	Good	Fair	Poor
850	650	550	—	—	—

PARKER REPRODUCTIONS

Japan

This company had exact reproductions of Parker D, DHE, B and A-1 Special shotguns made in Japan. They are of the finest quality and workmanship. The styles of engraving and features of these shotguns correspond exactly to the original Parker Arms.

D-Grade

This side-by-side shotgun is offered in 12 gauge, 20 gauge, and 28 gauge. Barrel lengths are 26" or 28" with sold matte rib. Stocks are select walnut with choice of pistol or straight grip. Choice splinter or beavertail forearms are offered. Single or double triggers are available as well. The receiver is case colored and scroll engraved with game scenes to match the original Parker DHE grade. Weight of 12 gauge is 6.75 lbs., 20 gauge is 6.5 lbs., and 28 gauge weighs 5.3 lbs.

12 or 20 Gauge

NIB	Exc.	V.G.	Good	Fair	Poor
3800	2800	1950	1200	750	400

NOTE: For 28 gauge add 10 percent.

16/20 Combination

Introduced in 1993 and limited to 500 sets. Offered with 28" barrels only this set features a 16 gauge barrel on a 20 gauge frame. Weighs 6.25 lbs.

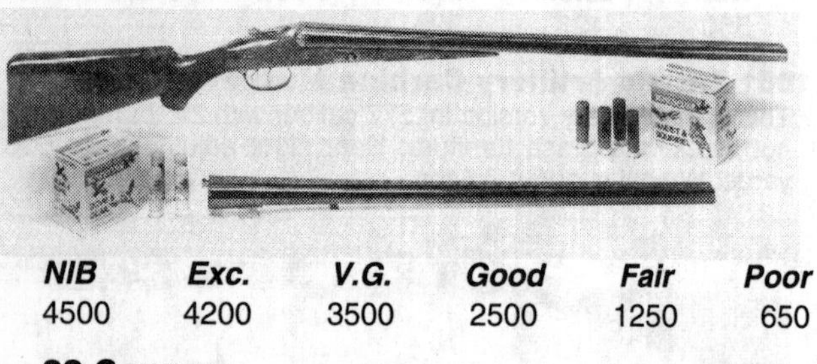

NIB	Exc.	V.G.	Good	Fair	Poor
4500	4200	3500	2500	1250	650

28 Gauge

NIB	Exc.	V.G.	Good	Fair	Poor
4250	3000	2000	1400	800	400

28 Gauge/.410 Bore Combination

NIB	Exc.	V.G.	Good	Fair	Poor
4750	4250	3250	1950	1000	550

NOTE: Add $990 for an additional barrel and $170 for beavertail forearm. For the D Grade, three-barrel sets are offered in 16/20/20 combinations for an additional $2300.

DHE Grade Steel-Shot Special

Offered in 12 gauge only with 28" barrels. Fitted with 3" chambers and special chrome lined barrels. Weighs 7 lbs.

NIB	Exc.	V.G	Good	Fair	Poor
3800	2750	2000	1200	700	400

B-Grade Limited Edition

This model features engraving similar to the original Parker BHE Grade. Fancy walnut stocks with fine line checkering was standard. It was offered in 12 gauge, 20 gauge, and 28 gauge. A 28 gauge/.410 bore combination was also offered. Only 100 shotguns in this grade were produced in 1989.

NIB	Exc.	V.G.	Good	Fair	Poor
4500	3650	2900	1750	900	450

28 Gauge/.410 Bore Combination

NIB	Exc.	V.G.	Good	Fair	Poor
5000	4500	3500	2500	1500	750

A-1 Special

Introduced in 1988, this grade features fine scroll engraving and presentation French walnut with custom checkering pattern. The stock is hand carved with fleur-de-lis and features 32 lpi checkering. The grip cap is rosewood and gold or gold initial plate on straight grip guns. Gold wire is used on the breech end on the barrels. Serial numbers are in gold relief as is the word "SAFE" and "L" and "R" on models with selective single trigger. Barrels flats and frame water table is jeweled. This grade is offered in 12, 20, and 28 gauge with a few early guns sold with 28 gauge/.410 bore combinations. Furnished with English-style oak-and-leather case with canvas and leather cover, engraved snap caps, and engraved oil bottle.

12 or 20 Gauge

NIB	Exc.	V.G.	Good	Fair	Poor
9500	8000	5000	4000	2500	1000

28 Gauge

NIB	Exc.	V.G.	Good	Fair	Poor
10500	8500	6000	5000	3000	1000

A-1 Special Custom Engraved

This model is a custom A-1 Special hand-engraved to each individual customer's specifications. Only a limited number of these shotguns will be built. Initial price in 1989 was $10,500. It is strongly recommended that the prospective purchaser acquire an appraisal prior to the sale due to the unique features of each gun.

PEABODY

Providence, Rhode Island
Providence Tool Company

NOTE: For historical information, photos, and data on Peabody military rifles see the *Standard Catalog of Military Firearms.*

Peabody Rifle and Carbine

A .43 Spanish, .443, .45 Peabody, .45-70, .50 or .50-70 caliber single-shot rifle with a 33" or 20" (carbine) barrel and either a full-length or half stock. The receiver marked "Peabody's Patent July 22, 1862 / Mannf'd by Providence Tool Co. Prov. R.I." Blued, with a walnut stock. Produced in large quantities during the 1860s and 1870s.

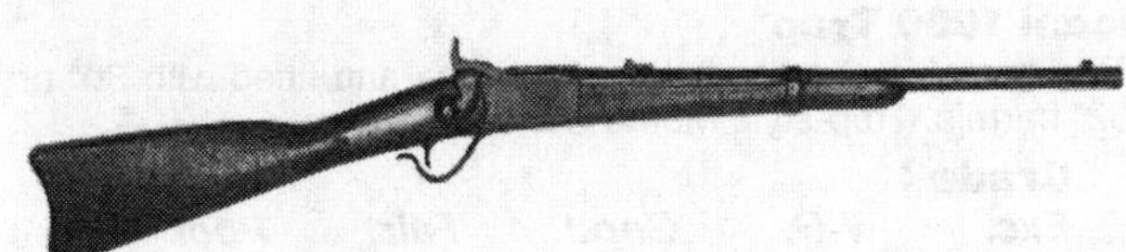
Courtesy Milwaukee Public Museum, Milwaukee, Wisconsin

Exc.	V.G.	Good	Fair	Poor
—	1700	750	300	100

Sporting Rifle

As above, in a sporting configuration with either 26" or 28" barrels. The frame marked, "Peabody's Patent, July 22, 1862 / Manf'd by Providence Tool Co., Prov. R.I." Blued, case hardened with a walnut stock. Manufactured from approximately 1866 to 1875.

Exc.	V.G.	Good	Fair	Poor
—	5000	2750	1000	400

PEABODY-MARTINI SPORTING RIFLES

NOTE: For historical information, photos, and data on Peabody-Martini military rifles see the *Standard Catalog of Military Firearms.*

Creedmoor

A .40-90 or .44-100 caliber Martini-action single-shot rifle with a 32" round/octagonal barrel, butt-mounted vernier rear sight, combination wind gauge and spirit level front sight. The receiver marked, "Peabody & Martini Patents" and the barrel "Manufactured by the Providence Tool Co. Providence R.I. U.S.A." Blued, case hardened with a walnut stock.

Courtesy Milwaukee Public Museum, Milwaukee, Wisconsin

Exc.	V.G.	Good	Fair	Poor
—	7500	3500	1500	550

Creedmoor Mid-Range

Similar to the above, but in .40-70 or .40-90 caliber with a 28" round/octagonal barrel, vernier tang sight and wind gauge front sight. Blued, case hardened with a walnut stock.

Exc.	V.G.	Good	Fair	Poor
—	6000	3250	1250	400

What Cheer

The Creedmoor without a pistol grip.

Exc.	V.G.	Good	Fair	Poor
—	6000	3250	1250	400

What Cheer Mid-Range

The Mid-Range Creedmoor without a pistol grip.

Exc.	V.G.	Good	Fair	Poor
—	5000	2750	1000	300

Kill Deer

A .45-70 caliber single-shot Martini-action rifle with 28" or 30" round/octagonal barrels, adjustable tang rear sight and globe front sights. Blued, case hardened with a walnut stock.

Exc.	V.G.	Good	Fair	Poor
—	7500	4250	1500	500

PEAVY, A. J.

South Montville, Maine

Knife-Pistol

A .22 caliber single-shot knife pistol constructed of steel and brass with a folding trigger. The sideplates marked "A.J. Peavy Pat. Sept. 5, '65 & Mar. 27, '66." Produced between 1866 and 1870.

Exc.	V.G.	Good	Fair	Poor
—	—	4250	1750	500

PECARE & SMITH

New York, New York

Pepperbox

A .28 caliber 4-shot or 1-shot percussion pepperbox with a folding trigger and 4" barrel group. The barrel group enclosed within an iron casing. Blued, silver-plated frame with walnut grips. The barrel casing marked "Pecare & Smith." Manufactured during the 1840s and early 1850s.

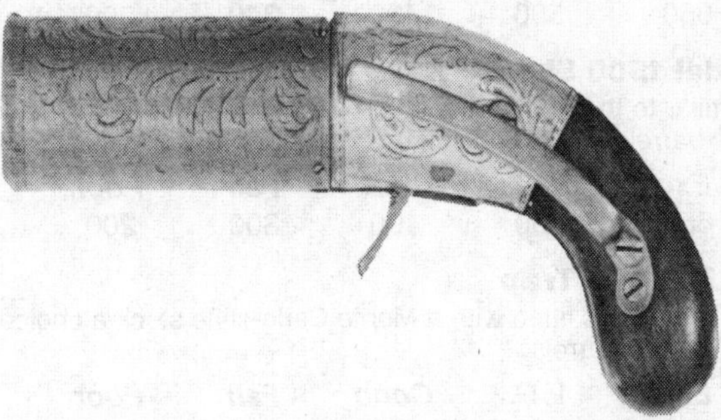

Exc.	V.G.	Good	Fair	Poor
—	—	2750	1150	350

Ten-Shot Pepperbox (rare)

Exc.	V.G.	Good	Fair	Poor
—	—	6000	2500	600

PEDERSEN, JOHN D.

Denver, Colorado & Jackson, Wyoming

Pedersen Rifle

Exc.	V.G.	Good	Fair	Poor
12500	7500	—	—	—

Pedersen Carbine

Exc.	V.G.	Good	Fair	Poor
15000	8500	—	—	—

PEDERSEN CUSTOM GUNS

North Haven, Connecticut

A division of the O.F. Mossberg Company operated between 1973 and 1975.

Model 4000 Shotgun

The Mossberg Model 500 slide-action shotgun in 12, 20 or .410 bore with 26", 28", or 30" ventilated rib barrels. Blued, engraved with a walnut stock. Manufactured in 1975.

Exc.	V.G.	Good	Fair	Poor
400	350	250	200	100

Model 4000 Trap

Chambered for 12 gauge only with 30" Full choke barrel. Monte Carlo stock with factory recoil pad.

Exc.	V.G.	Good	Fair	Poor
450	400	300	200	100

Model 4500

As above, but with a reduced amount of engraving.

Exc.	V.G.	Good	Fair	Poor
375	325	225	175	100

Model 4500 Trap

Same as the Model 4000 Trap but with less engraving.

Exc.	V.G.	Good	Fair	Poor
400	350	250	200	100

Model 1500

A 12 gauge Magnum over-and-under shotgun with 26", 28", or 30" ventilated rib barrels, single-selective trigger and automatic ejectors. Blued with a walnut stock. Weight is about 7.5 lbs. depending on barrel length. Manufactured between 1973 and 1975.

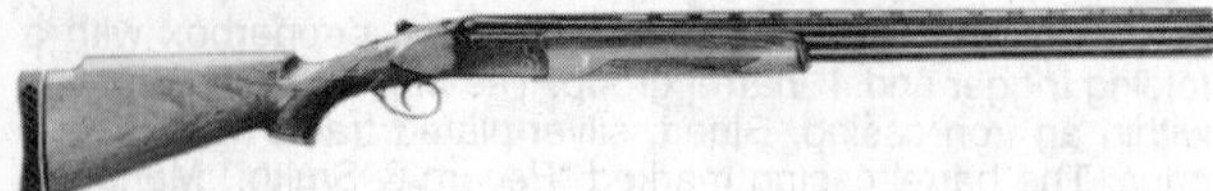

Exc.	V.G.	Good	Fair	Poor
650	500	400	300	200

Model 1500 Skeet

Similar to the above model but fitted with a skeet-style stock, 27" barrels and skeet chokes.

Exc.	V.G.	Good	Fair	Poor
650	500	400	300	200

Model 1500 Trap

This model is fitted with a Monte Carlo-style stock a choice of 30" or 32" barrels.

Exc.	V.G.	Good	Fair	Poor
650	500	400	300	200

Model 1000

As above, but manufactured in two grades of decoration. Manufactured between 1973 and 1975.

Grade I

Exc.	V.G.	Good	Fair	Poor
1750	1250	800	500	—

Grade II

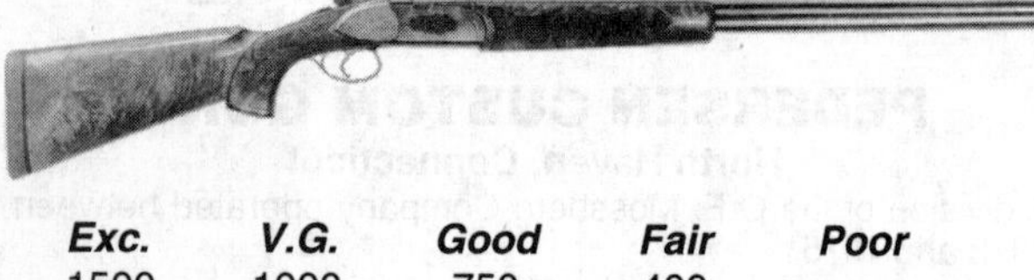

Exc.	V.G.	Good	Fair	Poor
1500	1000	750	400	—

Model 1000 Magnum

This model is chambered for the 12 gauge 3" shell and fitted with 30" barrels.

Grade I

Exc.	V.G.	Good	Fair	Poor
1600	1200	800	500	

Grade II

Exc.	V.G.	Good	Fair	Poor
1400	1100	750	400	—

Model 1000 Skeet

Offered in 12 gauge only with 26" or 28" barrels. Skeet-style stock and skeet chokes.

Grade I

Exc.	V.G.	Good	Fair	Poor
1750	1250	800	400	—

Grade II

Exc.	V.G.	Good	Fair	Poor
1500	1000	750	400	—

Model 1000 Trap

This model is chambered for 12 gauge and fitted with 30" or 32" barrels. Trap-style Monte Carlo stock.

Grade I

Exc.	V.G.	Good	Fair	Poor
1600	1200	800	500	—

Grade II

Exc.	V.G.	Good	Fair	Poor
1400	1100	750	400	—

Model 2000

A 12 or 20 gauge boxlock double-barrel shotgun with 26", 28", or 30" barrels, single-selective trigger and automatic ejectors. Produced in two grades of decoration. Manufactured in 1973 and 1974.

Grade I

Exc.	V.G.	Good	Fair	Poor
2000	1500	1000	600	—

Grade II

Exc.	V.G.	Good	Fair	Poor
1750	1250	800	400	—

Model 2500

A 12 or 20 gauge boxlock double-barrel shotgun with 26" or 28" barrels, double triggers and automatic ejectors. Blued with a walnut stock.

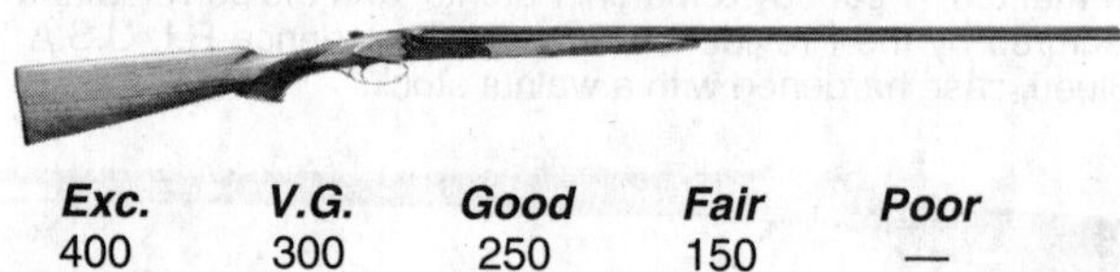

Exc.	V.G.	Good	Fair	Poor
400	300	250	150	—

Model 3000

A Mossberg Model 810 bolt-action rifle manufactured in .270 to .338 Winchester Magnum caliber with a 22" or 24" barrel with open sights. Produced in three grades.

Grade III—Plain

Exc.	V.G.	Good	Fair	Poor
450	400	350	150	—

Grade II

Exc.	V.G.	Good	Fair	Poor
525	425	350	150	—

Grade I

Exc.	V.G.	Good	Fair	Poor
800	650	500	200	—

Model 4700

The Mossberg Model 472 lever-action in .30-30 or .35 Remington caliber with a 24" barrel and 5-shot tubular magazine. Blued with a walnut stock.

Exc.	V.G.	Good	Fair	Poor
350	275	225	125	100

PEDERSOLI, DAVIDE

Brescia, Italy

Davide Pedersoli & C. was founded in 1957 by the late Davide Pedersoli. In the nearly half-century since, Pedersoli has established itself as a manufacturer of extremely high-quality replica and modern firearms. Pedersoli products are frequently marked with the importer's or retailer's name (e.g., Dixie Gun Works or Cabela's) rather than the Pedersoli brand, usually at widely varying discounts. Many muzzleloading rifles and pistols are available in kit form at reduced prices.

HANDGUNS

Mang In Graz Pistol

Recreation of single-shot percussion pistol made c. 1850 by Martin Mang. .38 or .44 caliber. Add 10 percent for target model, 20 percent for deluxe.

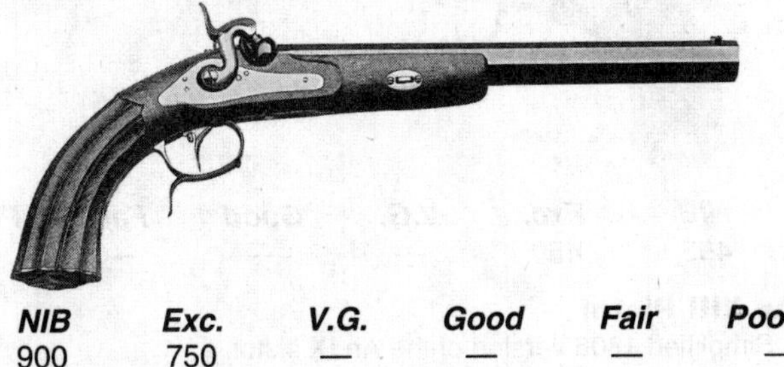

NIB	Exc.	V.G.	Good	Fair	Poor
900	750	—	—	—	—

Kuchenreuter Pistol

Recreation of single-shot percussion pistol made c. 1854 by Bartholomaus Kuchenreuter of Steinweg, Germany. .38 or .44 caliber. Add 20 percent for deluxe.

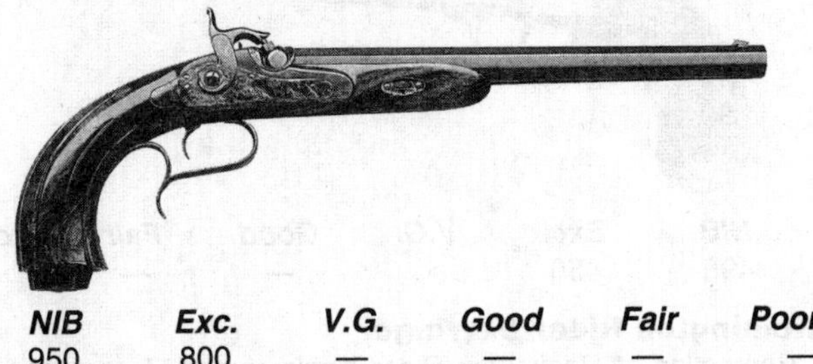

NIB	Exc.	V.G.	Good	Fair	Poor
950	800	—	—	—	—

Mortimer Pistol

Recreation of single-shot pistol first made c. 1810 by H. W Mortimer & Son of London. .44 caliber, smooth or rifled barrel. Percussion and flint versions available. Add 10 percent for Match model, 20 percent for deluxe.

NIB	Exc.	V.G.	Good	Fair	Poor
750	675	525	—	—	—

LePage Dueller

Recreation of single-shot duelling pistol made by Henry LePage c. 1840. Percussion and flint versions available. .31, .36 or .44 caliber. Add 20 percent for deluxe.

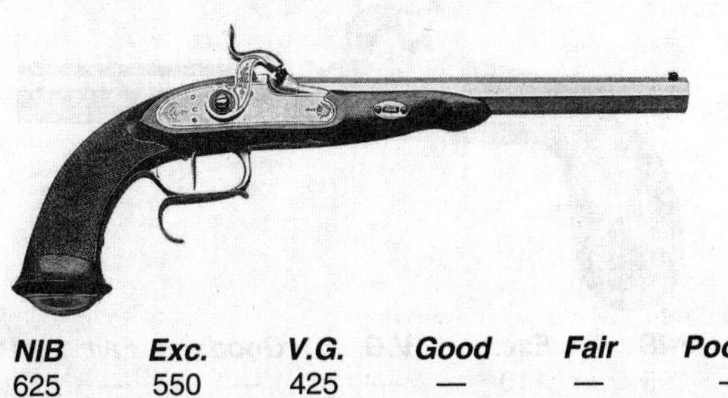

NIB	Exc.	V.G.	Good	Fair	Poor
625	550	425	—	—	—

Charles Moore Duelling Pistol

Recreation of single-shot duelling pistol made by Charles Moore of London c. 1800. Percussion and flint versions available. .36 or .44 caliber. Add 10 percent for target model.

NIB	Exc.	V.G.	Good	Fair	Poor
425	375	325	—	—	—

Carleton Underhammer Pistol

Recreation of saw-handled underhammer percussion pistol c. 1850. .36 caliber.

NIB	Exc.	V.G.	Good	Fair	Poor
575	500	400	—	—	—

Remington Pattern Target Revolver

Replica of Remington "1858-style" .44-caliber percussion revolver.

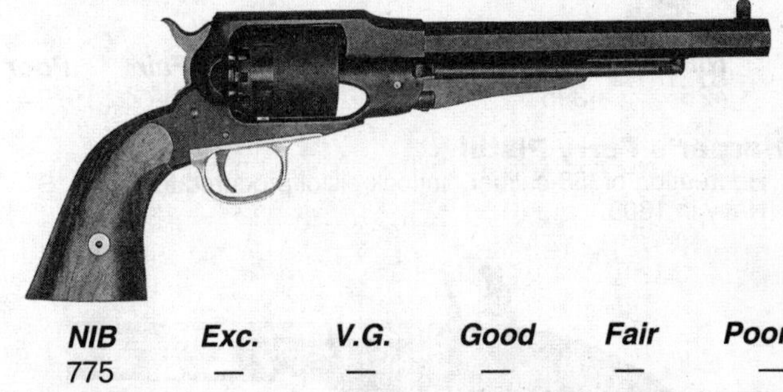

NIB	Exc.	V.G.	Good	Fair	Poor
775	—	—	—	—	—

Rogers & Spencer Target Percussion Target Revolver

Replica of the .44-caliber Rogers and Spencer revolver that didn't quite make it in time for the Civil War.

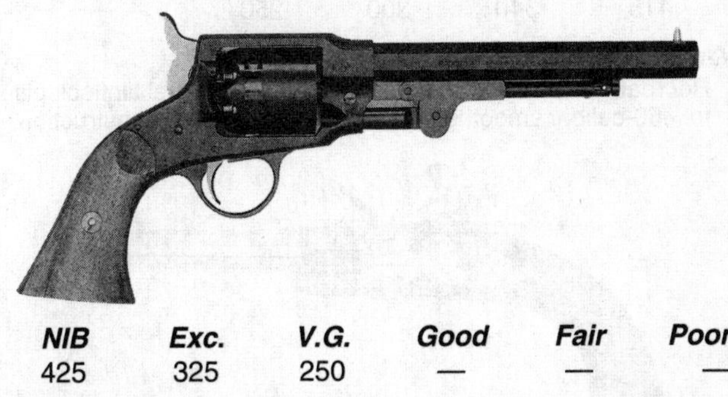

NIB	Exc.	V.G.	Good	Fair	Poor
425	325	250	—	—	—

Kentucky Pistol

Recreation of single-shot pistol of American colonial era. Flint and percussion versions available. .45, .50 and .54 caliber. Add 50 percent for "Silver Star" models.

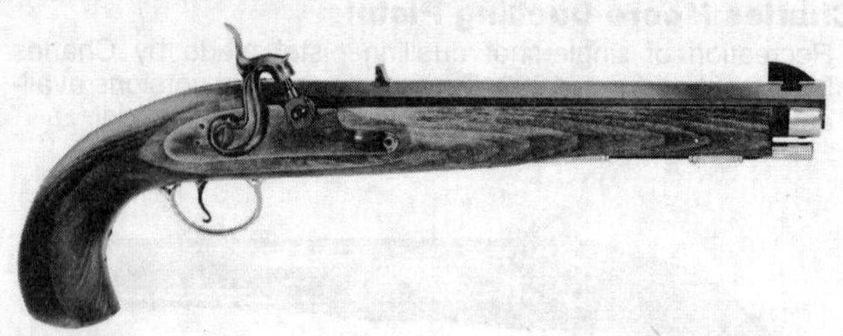

NIB	Exc.	V.G.	Good	Fair	Poor
275	250	225	—	—	—

Bounty Pistol

Similar to Kentucky Pistol standard version but with 16" barrel. .45 or .50 caliber only.

NIB	Exc.	V.G.	Good	Fair	Poor
350	300	275	—	—	—

Navy Moll Pistol

Similar to Kentucky pistol but with brass trim. Flint and percussion versions available. .45 caliber.

NIB	Exc.	V.G.	Good	Fair	Poor
425	395	—	—	—	—

Harper's Ferry Pistol

Recreation of .58-caliber flintlock pistol procured for the U. S. Navy in 1806.

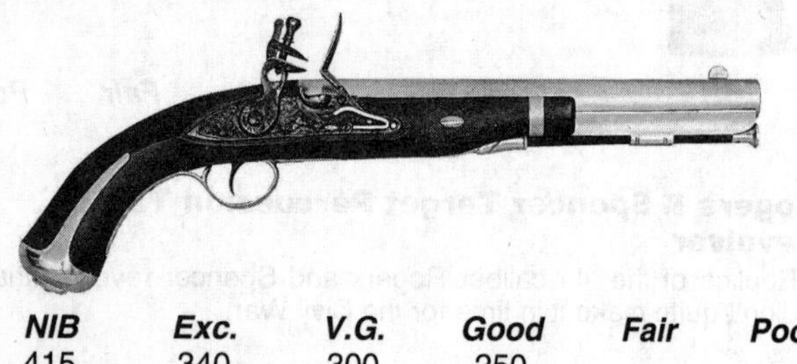

NIB	Exc.	V.G.	Good	Fair	Poor
415	340	300	250	—	—

Queen Anne Pistol

Recreation of English 17th-century cannon-barrel flintlock pistol. .50-caliber smoothbore barrel. Steel or brass construction.

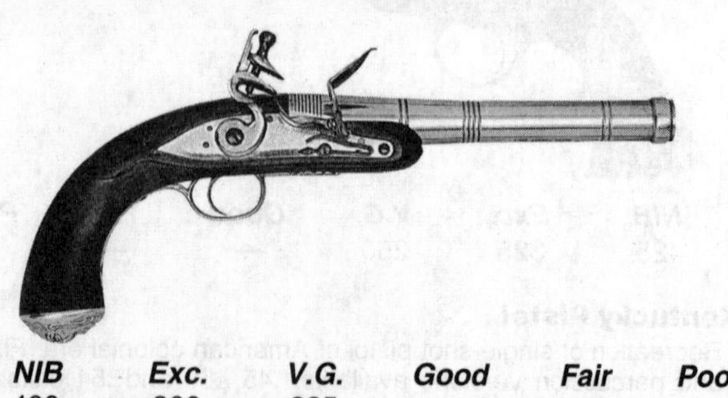

NIB	Exc.	V.G.	Good	Fair	Poor
400	300	225	—	—	—

An IX Pistol

Recreation of .69-caliber Napoleonic flintlock cavalry pistol of 1803. Brass trim.

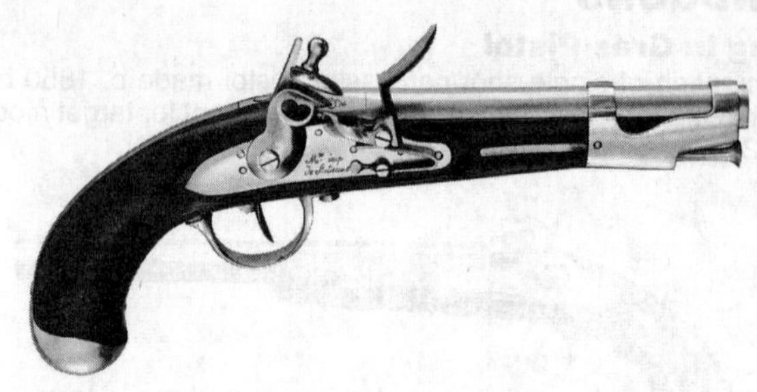

NIB	Exc.	V.G.	Good	Fair	Poor
495	450	—	—	—	—

An XIII Pistol

Simplified 1806 version of the An IX pistol.

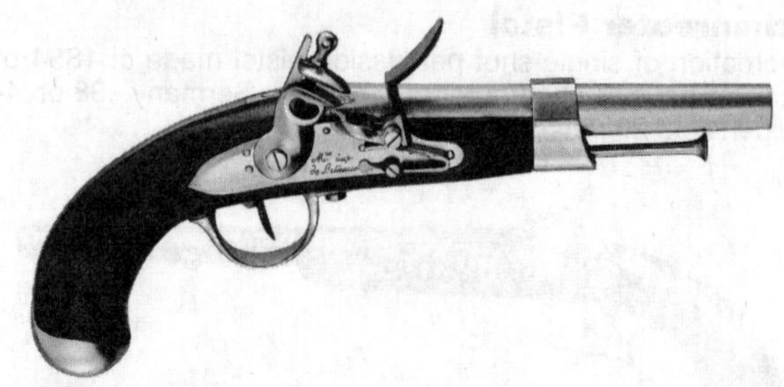

NIB	Exc.	V.G.	Good	Fair	Poor
495	450	—	—	—	—

Remington Rider Derringer

Recreation of Remington Rider single-shot .177 percussion parlor pistol. Available in the white or with casehardened, gold-toned or engraved/silvered finish. Pricing for basic model.

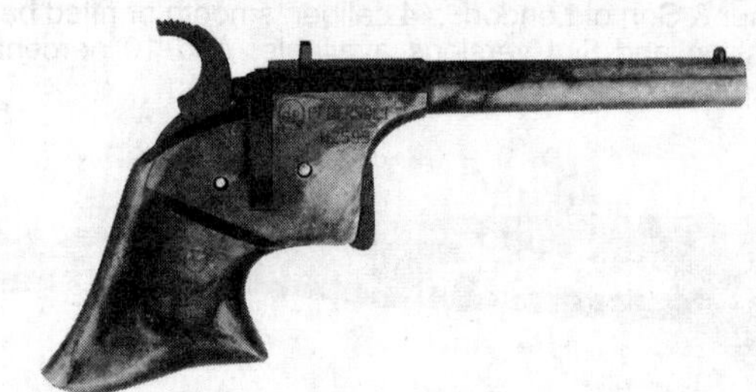

NIB	Exc.	V.G.	Good	Fair	Poor
300	—	—	—	—	—

Derringer Liegi

Recreation of c. 1850 screw-barrel percussion pocket pistol with folding trigger and bag grip. .44 caliber. Add 10 percent for engraved model.

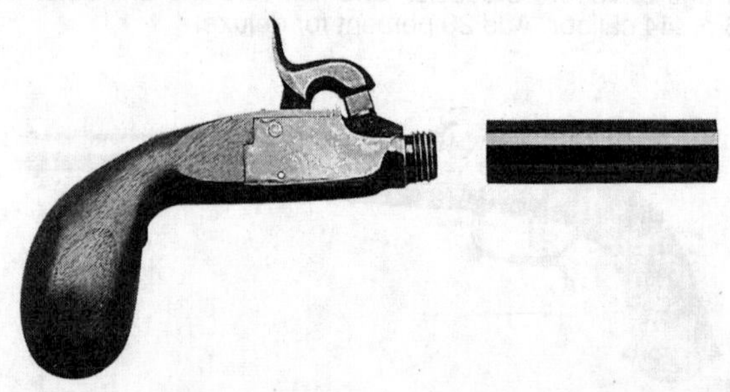

NIB	Exc.	V.G.	Good	Fair	Poor
195	110	—	—	—	—

Zimmer Pistol

Recreation of c. 1850 single-shot percussion parlor pistol. .177 caliber; fluted grip with butt cap. Discontinued.

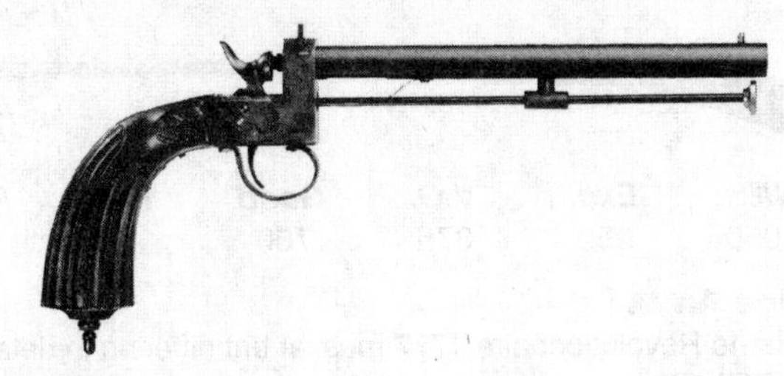

NIB	Exc.	V.G.	Good	Fair	Poor
380	350	—	—	—	—

Saloon Pistol

Recreation of c. 1850 single-shot percussion parlor pistol. .36 or .177 caliber. Discontinued.

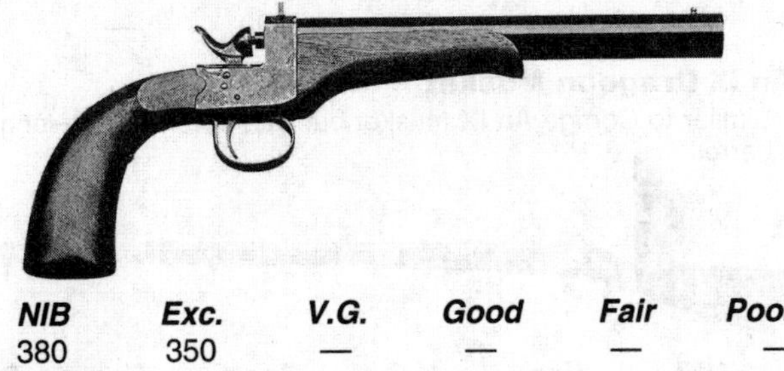

NIB	Exc.	V.G.	Good	Fair	Poor
380	350	—	—	—	—

RIFLES

Swivel-Breech Rifle

Muzzlerloading over-under rotating percussion rifle in .45, .50, or .54 caliber. Browned barrel, walnut stock. Discontinued.

NIB	Exc.	V.G.	Good	Fair	Poor
700	625	500	—	—	—

Bristlen A. Morges Target Rifle

Recreation of 1850-vintage percussion target rifle made by Marc Bristlen of Morges, Switzerland. Schuetzen-style buttplate, double triggers, false muzzle. Shoots .35- or .45-caliber elongated conical. Add 20 percent for deluxe model.

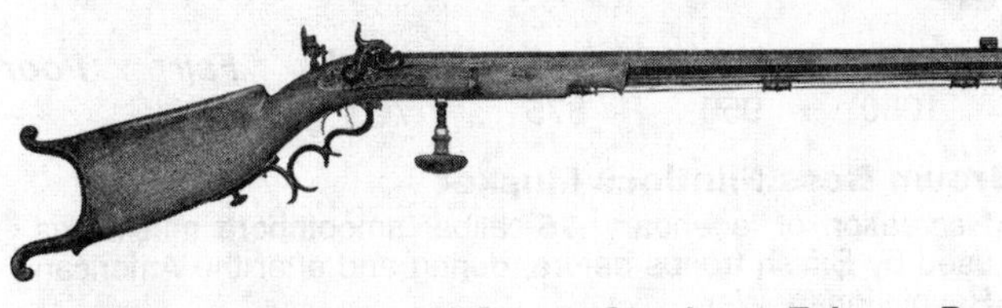

NIB	Exc.	V.G.	Good	Fair	Poor
900	600	—	—	—	

Waadtlander Target Rifle

Similar to Bristel A. Morges target rifle but rifled for .45-caliber round ball. Add 20 percent for deluxe version.

NIB	Exc.	V.G.	Good	Fair	Poor
900	600	—	—	—	—

Swiss Rifle

Similar to Waadtlander Target Rifle but in flintlock with 29.5" barrel.

NIB	Exc.	V.G.	Good	Fair	Poor
1000	700	500	—	—	—

Wurttemberg Mauser

Replica of 1857 Mauser military percussion rifle made from 1857 to 1856. Shoots .54 Minie ball. Designed for 100m target shooting.

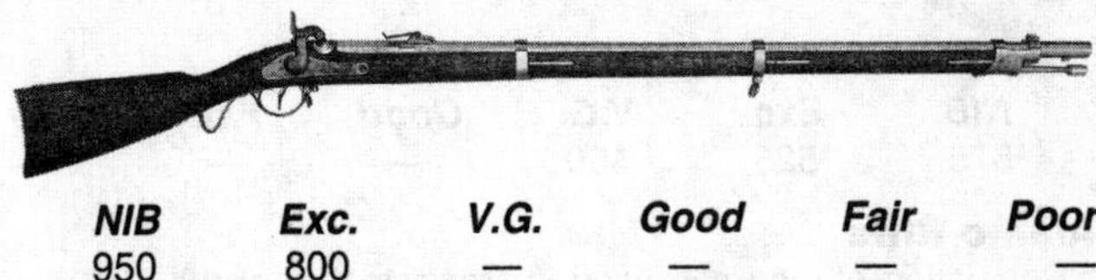

NIB	Exc.	V.G.	Good	Fair	Poor
950	800	—	—	—	—

Gibbs Rifle

Recreation of the 1865-vintage long-range percussion rifle made by George Gibbs of London. Shoots elongated .40- or .45-caliber conicals.

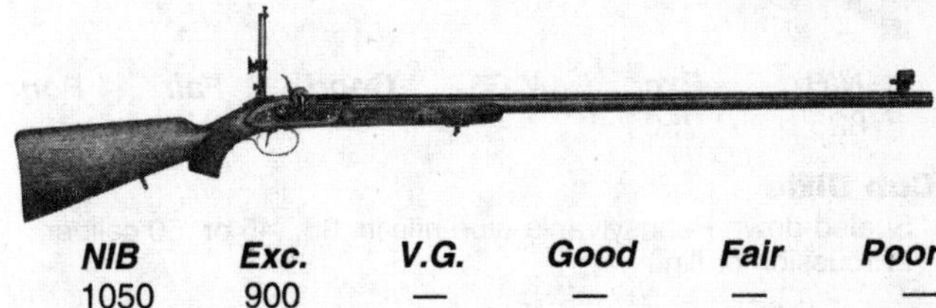

NIB	Exc.	V.G.	Good	Fair	Poor
1050	900	—	—	—	—

Tryon Rifle

Recreation of noteworthy American percussion plains rifle c. 1850. .45-, .50-, or .54-caliber. Add 10 percent for Creedmore model; 20 percent for deluxe target model.

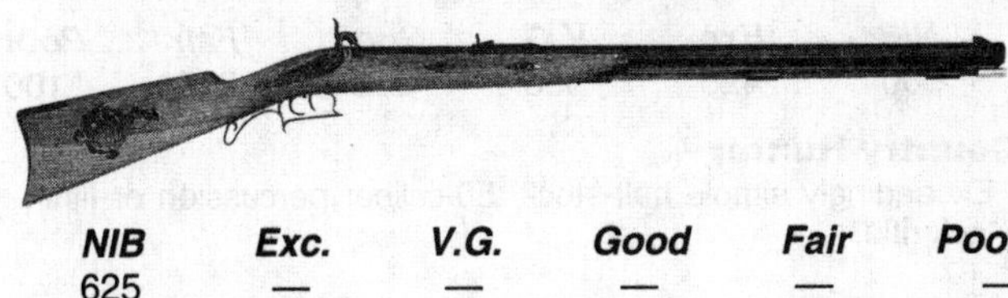

NIB	Exc.	V.G.	Good	Fair	Poor
625	—	—	—	—	—

Mortimer Rifle

Recreation of arms made c. 1850 by H. W Mortimer & Son of London. Percussion and flint versions available. Various configurations including Whitworth, Vetterli, and 12-ga. fowler.

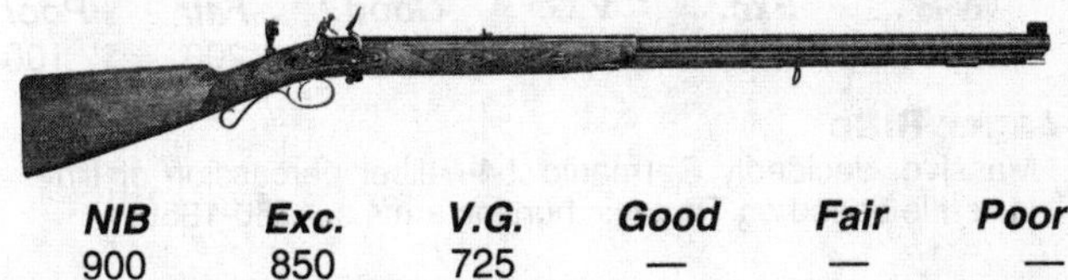

NIB	Exc.	V.G.	Good	Fair	Poor
900	850	725	—	—	—

Indian Trade Musket

Recreation of 18th-century flintlock smoothbore fusil as typified by colonial and early 19th-century trading companies.

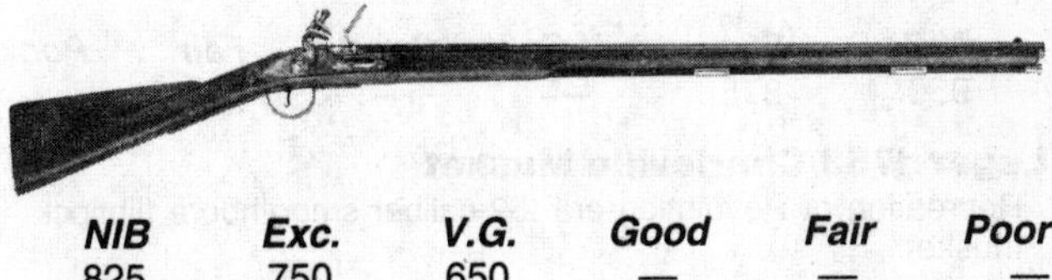

NIB	Exc.	V.G.	Good	Fair	Poor
825	750	650	—	—	—

Frontier Rifle

Recreation of typical American hunting rifle c. 1800 - 1840. .32-, .36-, .45-, .50- and .54-caliber versions available in flintlock and percussion. Various barrel lengths.

NIB	Exc.	V.G.	Good	Fair	Poor
575	525	450	—	—	—

Kentucky Rifle

Recreation of Pennsylvania-style rifle c. 1800. .32-, .45- and .50-caliber percussion or flintlock. Add 35 percent for "Silver Star" model.

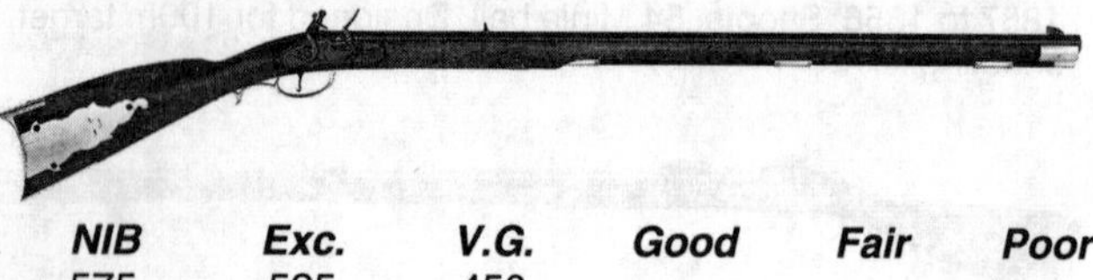

NIB	Exc.	V.G.	Good	Fair	Poor
575	525	450	—	—	—

Alamo Rifle

Recreation of long rifle used in Mexican War of the 1840s. Double triggers; .32-, .45- or .50-caliber.

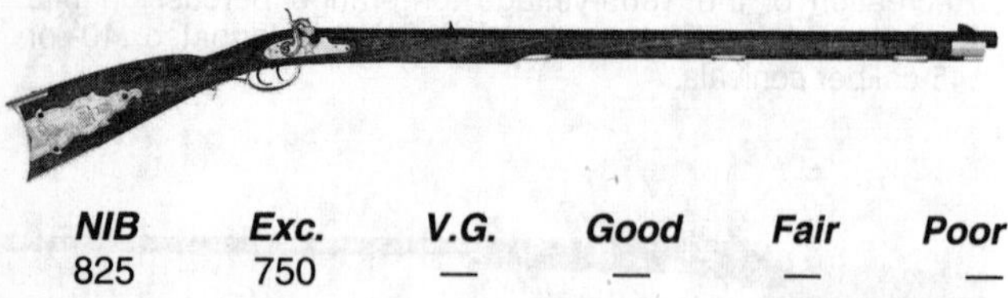

NIB	Exc.	V.G.	Good	Fair	Poor
825	750	—	—	—	—

Cub Dixie

Scaled-down Pennsylvania-type rifle in .36, .45 or .50 caliber. Percussion or flint.

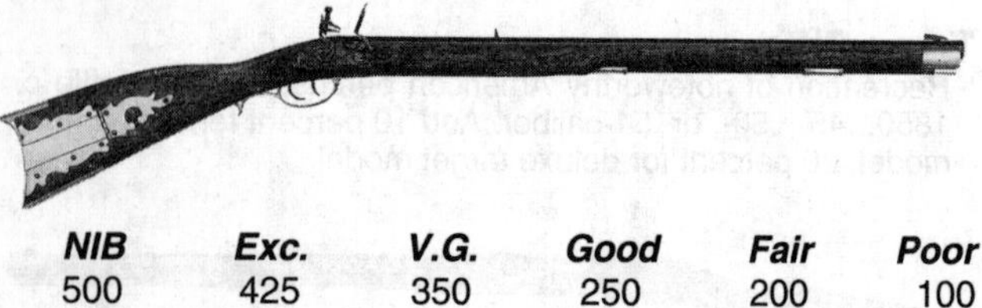

NIB	Exc.	V.G.	Good	Fair	Poor
500	425	350	250	200	100

Country Hunter

Exceedingly simple half-stock .50-caliber percussion or flintlock rifle.

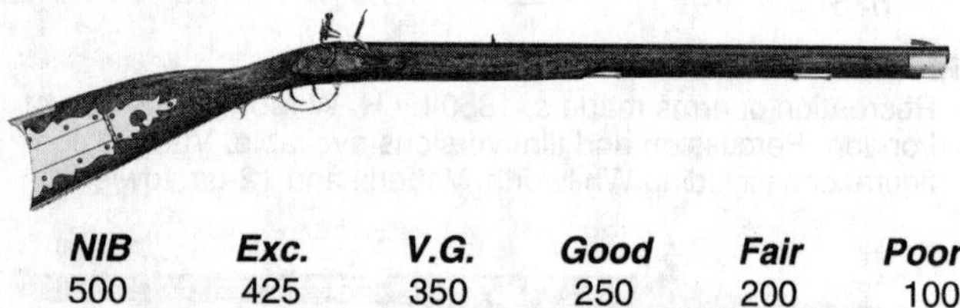

NIB	Exc.	V.G.	Good	Fair	Poor
500	425	350	250	200	100

Jager Rifle

Massive, decidedly Germanic .54-caliber percussion or flintlock rifle based on Teutonic hunting arms c. 1750-1850.

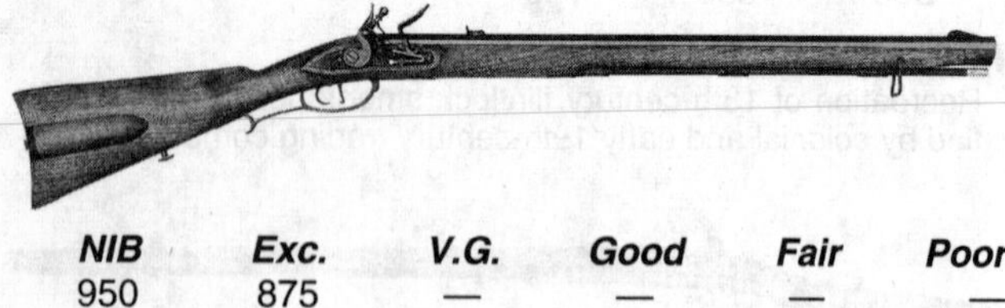

NIB	Exc.	V.G.	Good	Fair	Poor
950	875	—	—	—	—

Leger 1763 Charleville Musket

Recreation of Revolution-era .69-caliber smoothbore flintlock musket.

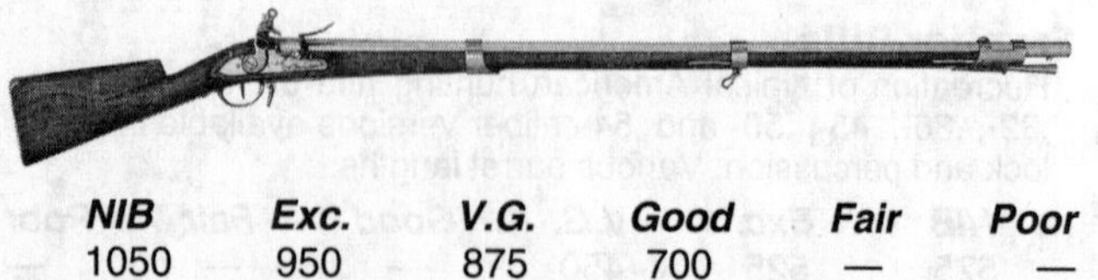

NIB	Exc.	V.G.	Good	Fair	Poor
1050	950	875	700	—	—

Revolutionnaire 1777 Musket

Similar to Charleville musket but in detail patterned after muskets used in French Revolution.

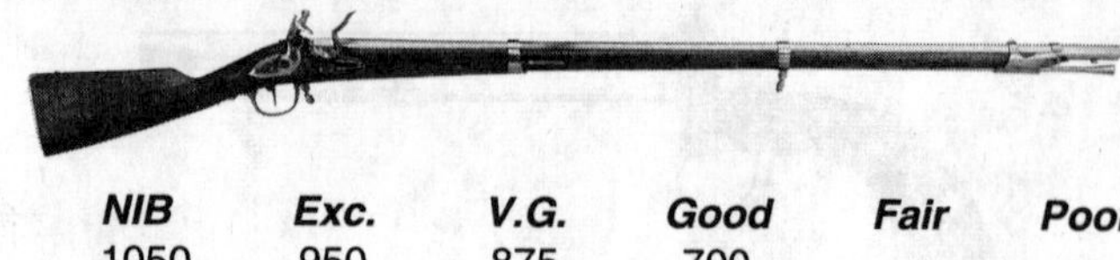

NIB	Exc.	V.G.	Good	Fair	Poor
1050	950	875	700	—	—

Corrige An IX

Similar to Revolutionnaire 1777 musket but differing in details of frizzen, etc.

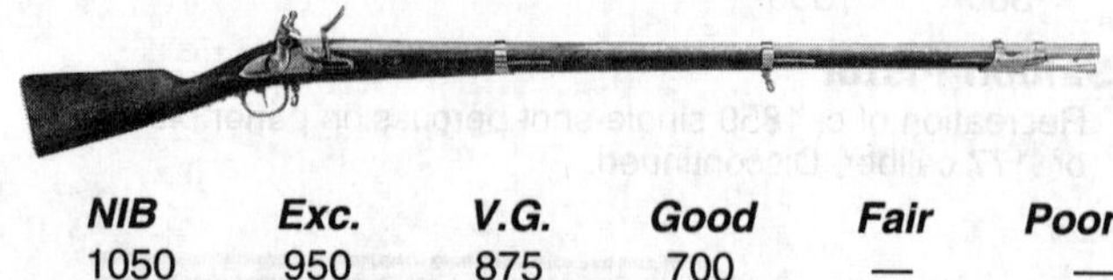

NIB	Exc.	V.G.	Good	Fair	Poor
1050	950	875	700	—	—

An IX Dragoon Musket

Similar to Corrige An IX musket but with 40.5" cavalry-length barrel.

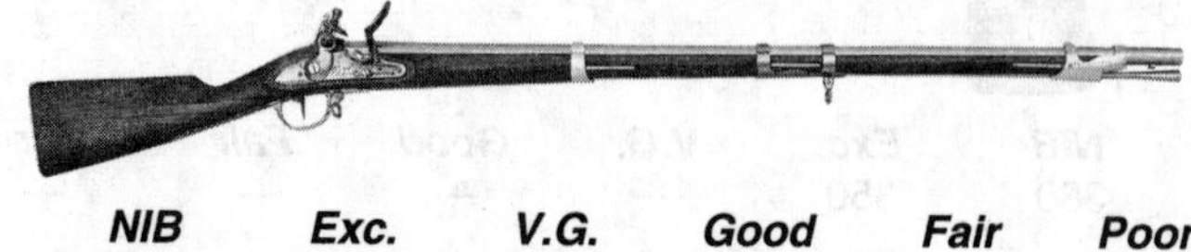

NIB	Exc.	V.G.	Good	Fair	Poor
1050	950	875	700	—	—

Austrian 1798 Flintlock Musket

Similar to 1777 musket but with Austrian modifications in barel bands, bayonet mount, etc.

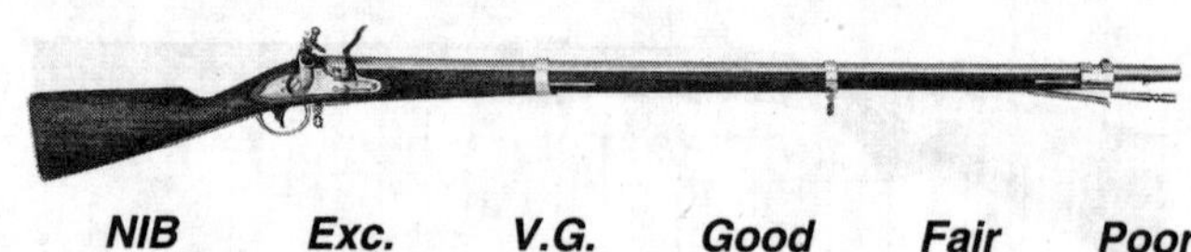

NIB	Exc.	V.G.	Good	Fair	Poor
1050	950	875	700	—	—

Prussian 1809 Flintlock Musket

Similar to French 1777 musket but in .75 caliber with "Potsdam" markings.

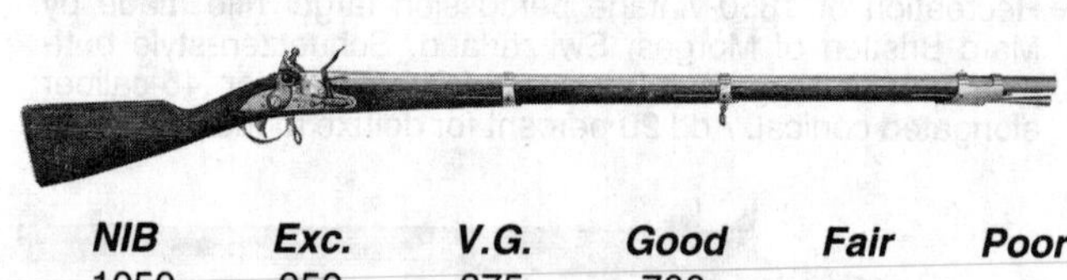

NIB	Exc.	V.G.	Good	Fair	Poor
1050	950	875	700	—	—

Brown Bess Flintlock Musket

Recreation of legendary .75-caliber smoothbore musket as used by British troops before, during and after the American Revolutionary War.

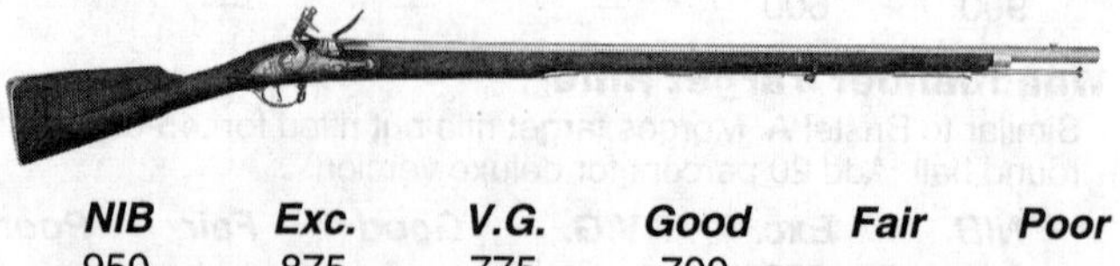

NIB	Exc.	V.G.	Good	Fair	Poor
950	875	775	700	—	—

Springfield 1795 Musket

Recreation of America's first indigenous military arm. .69-caliber smoothbore.

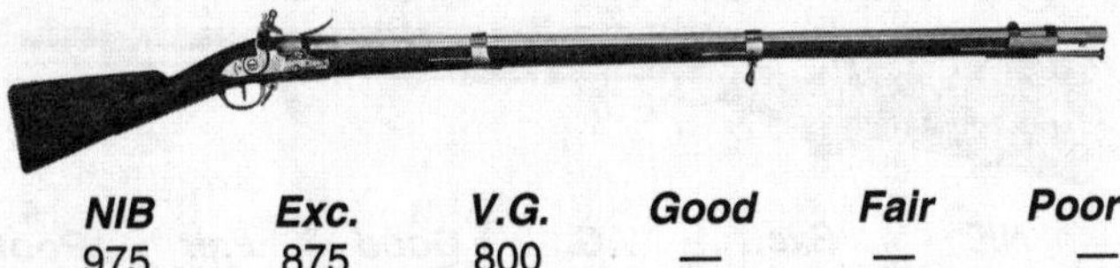

NIB	Exc.	V.G.	Good	Fair	Poor
975	875	800	—	—	—

Harper's Ferry 1816 Musket

Recreation of U.S. martial .69-caliber smoothbore flintlock musket.

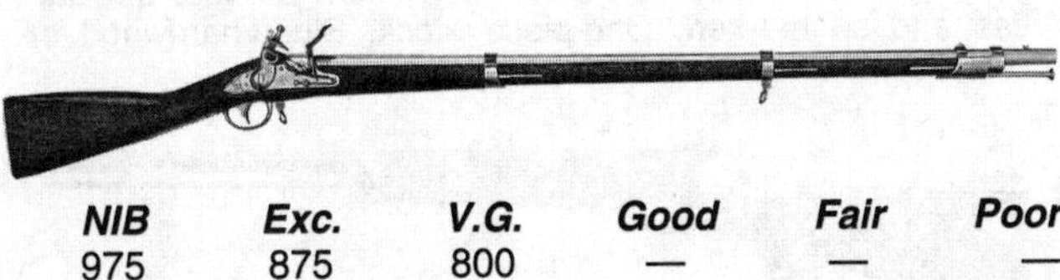

NIB	Exc.	V.G.	Good	Fair	Poor
975	875	800	—	—	—

Rocky Mountain Hawken

Faithful recreation of legendary plains rifle. .54 caliber.

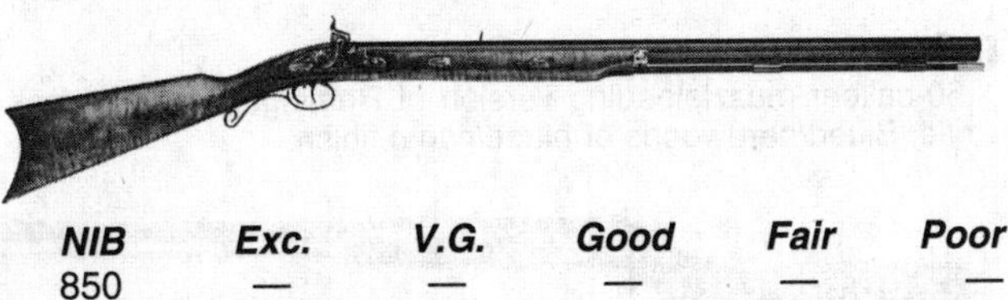

NIB	Exc.	V.G.	Good	Fair	Poor
850	—	—	—	—	—

Springfield 1861 Rifle

Recreation of .58-caliber percussion rifle as used in American Civil War.

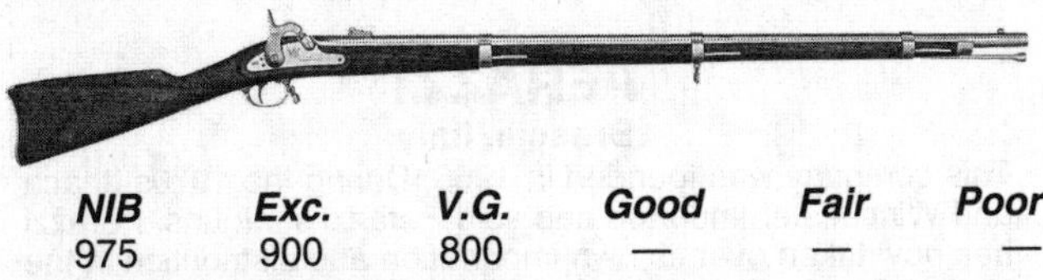

NIB	Exc.	V.G.	Good	Fair	Poor
975	900	800	—	—	—

Kodiak Combination Gun

Percussion side-by-side rifle/shotgun combination gun with 12-ga. smoothbore barrel and .50-, .54- and .58-caliber rifled barrel.

NIB	Exc.	V.G.	Good	Fair	Poor
900	800	700	—	—	—

Kodiak Double Rifle

Side-by-side double percussion rifle in .50, .54, .58 and .72 caliber. Sights regulated to 75 yards.

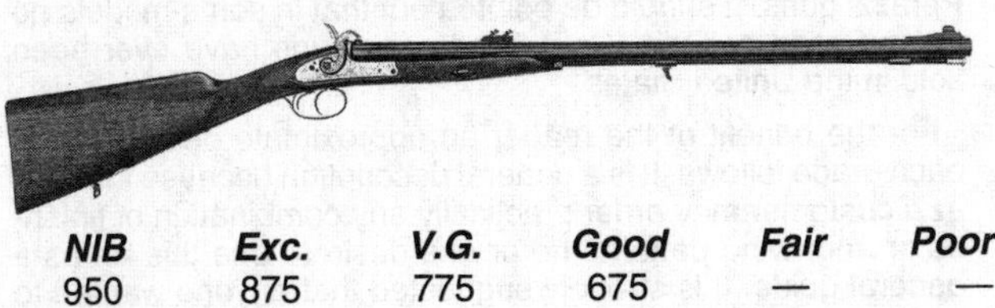

NIB	Exc.	V.G.	Good	Fair	Poor
950	875	775	675	—	—

Rolling Block Rifle

Replica of famous Remington rolling block single-shot rifle 1867 – c. 1890. Various centerfire chamberings and configurations including Baby carbine. Prices shown are for standard version in .45-70.

NIB	Exc.	V.G.	Good	Fair	Poor
800	725	625	—	—	—

1859 Sharps Cavalry Carbine

Replica of Sharps percussion carbine with 22" barrel, patchbox and elvator sight; .54 caliber. Also available as Infantry Rifle with 30" barrel.

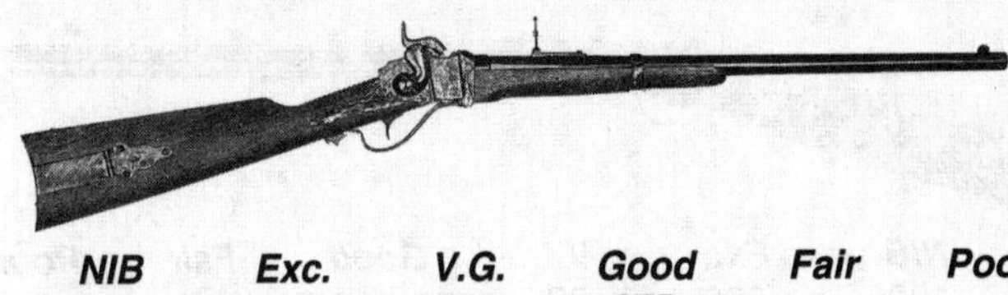

NIB	Exc.	V.G.	Good	Fair	Poor
895	825	775	675	—	—

1862 Robinson Confederate Sharps

Similar to 1859 Sharps carbine but with different barrel band, receiver details, and rear sight.

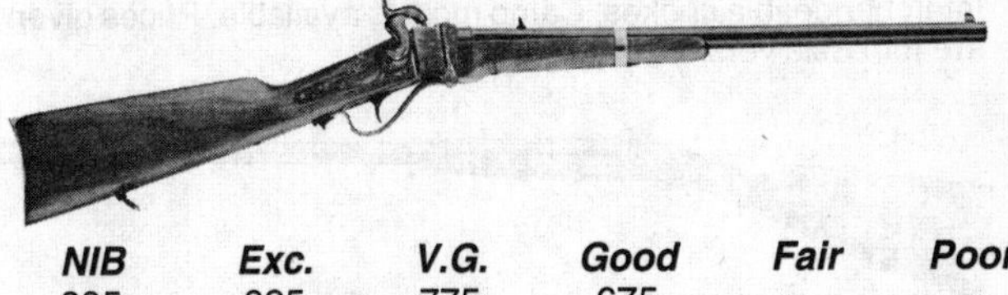

NIB	Exc.	V.G.	Good	Fair	Poor
895	825	775	675	—	—

Sharps 1863 Sporting Rifle

Replica of Sharps sporting rifle with 32" barrel, set trigger and sculpted forend; .45 or .54 caliber. .45 version rifled for elongated conicals.

NIB	Exc.	V.G.	Good	Fair	Poor
1000	900	825	—	—	—

1874 Sharps

High-quality replica of first Sharps chambered for metallic cartridges. Chamberings include .45-70, .45-90, .45-110, .45-120, .50-70 and .50-90. Several variations available including Sporting Standard Sporting, Cavalry Rifle, Cavalry Carbine, Sporting Deluxe, Sporting Extra Deluxe, Silhouette Standard, Silhouette Deluxe, Boss, Business Rifle, Buffalo, Billy Dixon, Long Range, Quigley, Creedmore #2 and Competition Standard. Prices given are for Standard Sporting model.

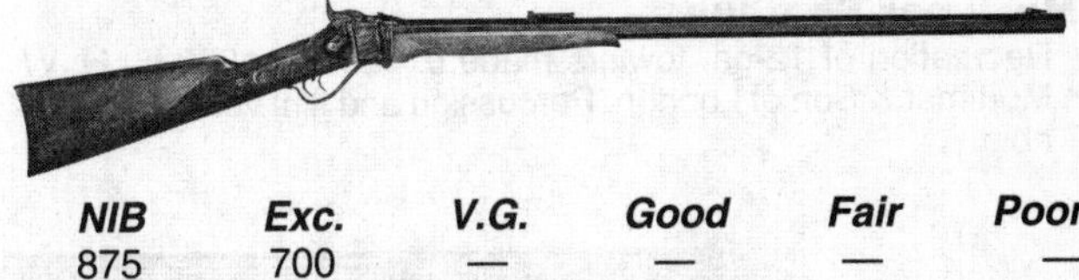

NIB	Exc.	V.G.	Good	Fair	Poor
875	700	—	—	—	—

1873 Trapdoor Springfield

Replica of famous single-shot cartridge rifle chambered in .45-70. Several variations available including Standard Rifle, Standard Carbine, Officer's Model and Long Range Model. Add 30 percent for Deluxe models. Prices given are for Standard Rifle.

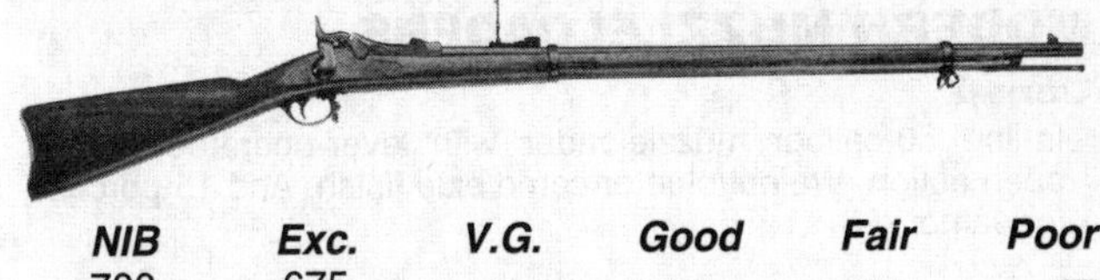

NIB	Exc.	V.G.	Good	Fair	Poor
700	675	—	—	—	—

Kodiak Mark IV Express Rifle

Side-by-side double rifle chambered for .45-70 cartridge.

NIB	Exc.	V.G.	Good	Fair	Poor
2400	1850	1500	—	—	—

Pedersoli Lightning Rifle

Updated replica of Model 1883 Colt Lightning Magazine Rifle. Pump action with magazine disconnector. Chambered for .44-40 and .45 Colt.

NIB	Exc.	V.G.	Good	Fair	Poor
1000	900	825	—	—	—

SHOTGUNS

Double Percussion Shotgun

Side-by-side muzzleloading shotgun in 20, 12 and 10 gauge. Interchangeable chokes. Camo models available. Prices given are for basic version in 12 ga.

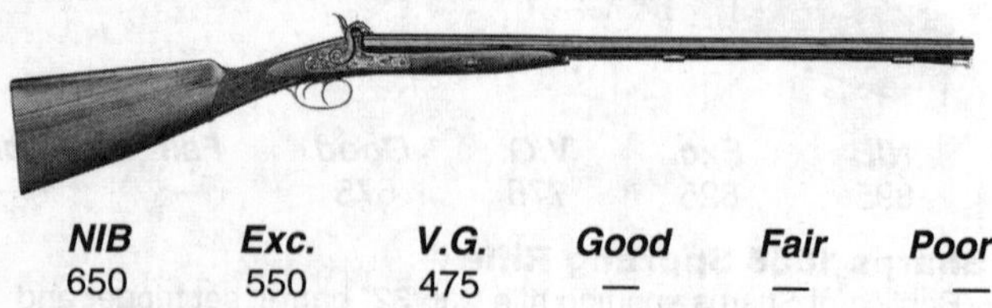

NIB	Exc.	V.G.	Good	Fair	Poor
650	550	475	—	—	—

Coach Shotgun

Side-by-side 12-ga. percussion shotgun with 20" barrels. Discontinued.

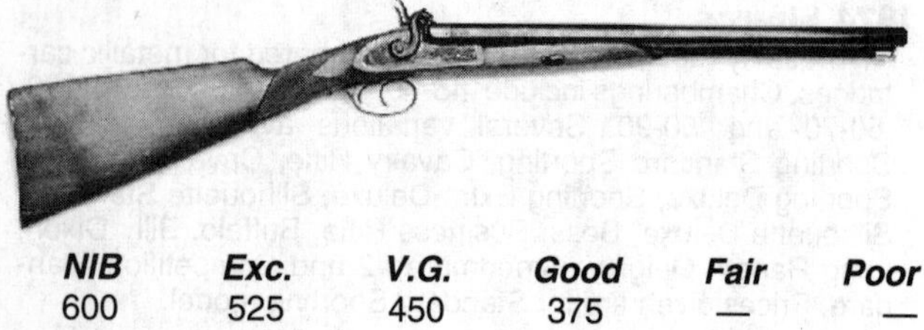

NIB	Exc.	V.G.	Good	Fair	Poor
600	525	450	375	—	—

Mortimer Shotgun

Recreation of 12-ga. fowlers made c. 1830 to 1850 by H. W Mortimer & Son of London. Percussion and flint versions available.

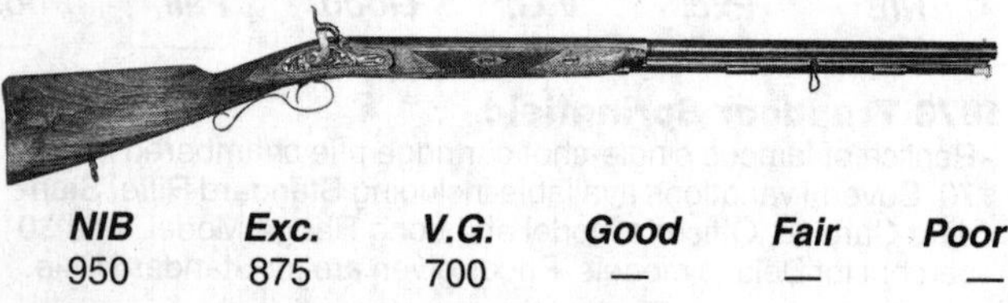

NIB	Exc.	V.G.	Good	Fair	Poor
950	875	700	—	—	—

MODERN MUZZLELOADERS

Denali

In-line 50-caliber muzzleloader with lever-operated break-open action. Walnut/blue or camo/blue finish. Add 15 percent for camo.

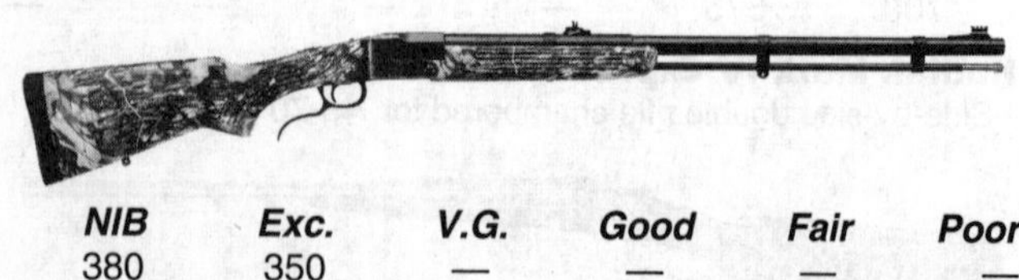

NIB	Exc.	V.G.	Good	Fair	Poor
380	350	—	—	—	—

Brutus 94

Inline .50-caliber muzzleloader. Blued/composite, blued/synthetic or stainless/blued/walnut finish. Add 15 percent for camo.

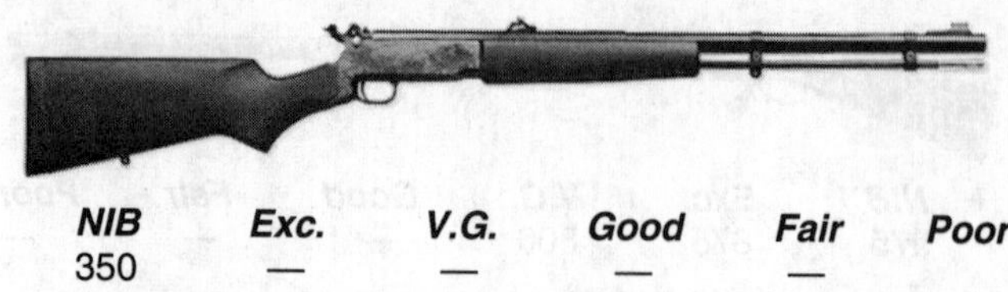

NIB	Exc.	V.G.	Good	Fair	Poor
350	—	—	—		

Brutus Ovation

Inline .50-caliber muzzleloader with interchangeable barrels. Developed in cooperation with Mid-Western Outdoor Specialties and so marked. One-piece stock. Blued/hardwood or blued/camo finish. Add 15 percent for camo.

NIB	Exc.	V.G.	Good	Fair	Poor
350	—	—	—	—	

Rolling Block Percussion Rifle

.50-caliber muzzleloading version of Remington rolling block rifle. Blued/hardwoods or blued/camo finish.

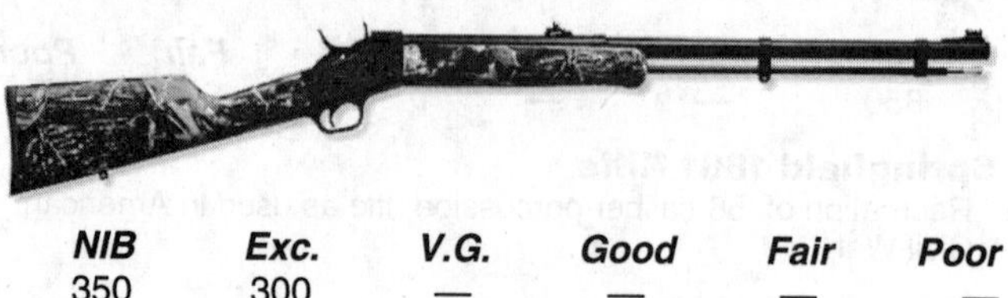

NIB	Exc.	V.G.	Good	Fair	Poor
350	300	—	—	—	—

PERAZZI

Brescia, Italy

This company was founded in 1965. During the 1970s Ithaca and Winchester imported and sold Perazzi shotguns. Perazzi has now taken over its own importation and distribution in the United States with the creation of Perazzi USA, Inc. Many shooters consider the Perazzi to be the finest currently produced shotgun in the world.

Perazzi has an extensive variety of models to choose from. In addition, each model may be available in different grades. These grades are based on the type of finish, engraving, and wood quality. The vast majority of Perazzi shotguns that are sold in this country are Standard Grade guns. According to Perazzi USA, these Standard Grade guns account for approximately 98 percent of North American sales. Therefore, it is unlikely that the shooter or collector will encounter high-grade Perazzi guns. It should be pointed out that in some models no Extra Grade or Extra Gold Grade shotguns have ever been sold in the United States.

For the benefit of the reader an approximate description of each grade follows. It is a general description because the Perazzi customer may order practically any combination of finishes or engraving patterns he or she desires. Use this list as a general guide. It is strongly suggested that anyone wanted to know more about Perazzi guns buy a copy of Karl Lippard's book, *Perazzi Shotguns*. He can be reached at P.O. Box 60719, Colorado Springs, CO, 719-444-0786.

PRICING NOTE: Because of the difficulty in pricing grades above the SCO Grade because of their rarity and custom configurations these grades are not priced.

OUT-OF-PRODUCTION SHOTGUNS

NOTE: Very high premiums on early SCO and higher grades.

COMP1-SB TRAP

This model is a single barrel trap gun in 12 gauge only with 32" or 34" vent rib barrel.

Standard Grade

NIB	Exc.	V.G.	Good	Fair	Poor
2750	2250	1500	1000	750	500

COMP1-TRAP

This is an over-and-under version of the above model.

Standard Grade

NIB	Exc.	V.G.	Good	Fair	Poor
3500	2750	2000	1500	900	500

Light Game Model

Offered in 12 gauge with a 27.5" vent rib barrel. Trigger group is not detachable. Produced between 1972 and 1974.

Standard Grade

NIB	Exc.	V.G.	Good	Fair	Poor
3000	2250	1750	—	—	—

NOTE: Deduct 25 percent for skeet chokes.

MT-6 Model

This model was offered in 12 gauge with a tapered vent rib. The trigger group was not removable. Discontinued in 1983.

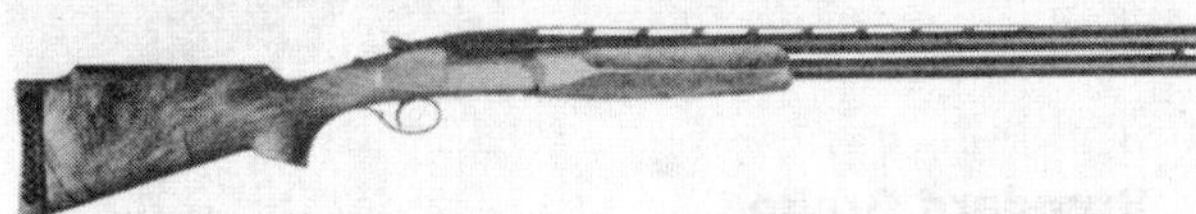

Standard Grade

NIB	Exc.	V.G.	Good	Fair	Poor
2500	2000	1500	—	—	—

NOTE: Deduct 20 percent for 27.375" barrels.

MX3

This model was discontinued in 1988 and was available in 12 gauge only for single barrel Trap, over-and-under trap, combination trap, skeet, and sporting configurations.

Standard Grade

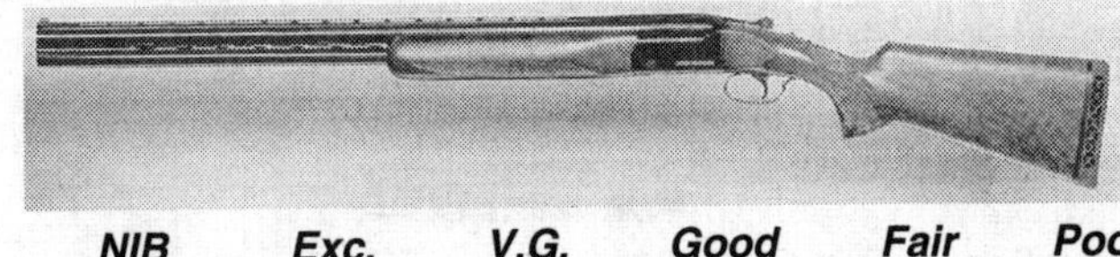

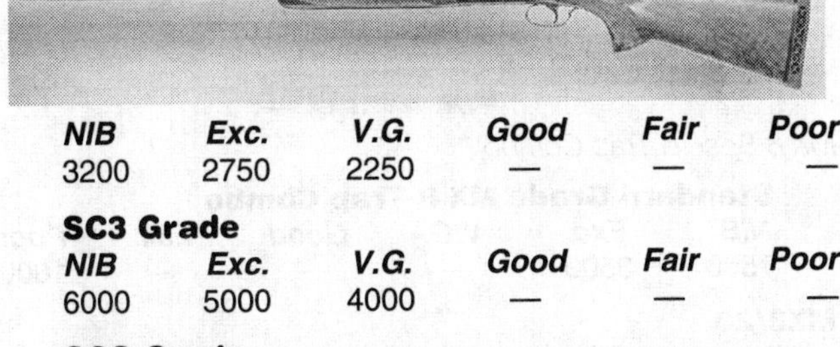

NIB	Exc.	V.G.	Good	Fair	Poor
3200	2750	2250	—	—	—

SC3 Grade

NIB	Exc.	V.G.	Good	Fair	Poor
6000	5000	4000	—	—	—

SCO Grade

NIB	Exc.	V.G.	Good	Fair	Poor
8000	6500	5500	4000	2500	1000

Gold Grade

NIB	Exc.	V.G.	Good	Fair	Poor
10000	8500	7000	5000	2700	1200

NOTE: Add 50 percent to above prices for Combination Trap Guns.

Grand American Special

This model was introduced in 1988 and features a high ramped rib similar to the MX3 model. The forend was grooved. Discontinued in 1991. It was offered in single barrel trap, combination trap, and over-and-under trap configurations.

Standard Grade

NIB	Exc.	V.G.	Good	Fair	Poor
5250	4250	3500	3000	1500	700

SC3 Grade

NIB	Exc.	V.G.	Good	Fair	Poor
6500	5250	4500	4000	1700	900

SCO Grade

NIB	Exc.	V.G.	Good	Fair	Poor
8000	6500	5500	5000	2000	1000

Gold Grade

NIB	Exc.	V.G.	Good	Fair	Poor
10000	7500	6000	—	—	—

SCO Grade w/Sideplates

NIB	Exc.	V.G.	Good	Fair	Poor
13500	10000	7500	—	—	—

Gold Grade w/Sideplates

NIB	Exc.	V.G.	Good	Fair	Poor
15000	12000	8500	—	—	—

Extra Grade

NIB	Exc.	V.G.	Good	Fair	Poor
17000	—	—	—	—	—

Extra Gold Grade

NIB	Exc.	V.G.	Good	Fair	Poor
23000	—	—	—	—	—

NOTE: The Extra Grade and Extra Gold Grade have not been imported into the US.

SHO Model

NOTE: This over-and-under sidelock model is available in 12 gauge only in both Type 1 and Type 2 configurations. Type 1 does not have rebounding firing pins and is worth approximately 50 percent less than Type 2 models that are fitted with rebounding firing pins. There are no parts available in this country or at the factory for Type 1 guns. An expert appraisal is recommended for this model due to its unique features.

The SHO model features a silver finish with fine scroll engraving with game scenes to customer's specifications. Select walnut stock built to customer's dimensions with fine line checkering. A custom built shotgun. Special order only. An expert appraisal is recommended for this model due to its unique features.

DHO Model

This is a side-by-side shotgun offered in 12 gauge only. It has full sidelocks and a silver receiver finish with scroll and game scene engraving of the same quality as the SHO Model. Fancy walnut stock with fine line checkering. An expert appraisal is recommended for this model due to its unique features.

NOTE: There are no replacement parts available for the model.

DHO Extra Gold

Available in any gauge and barrel length combination. Only the finest presentation walnut and checkering. A totally custom built shotgun. Special order only. An expert appraisal is recommended for this model due to its unique features.

NOTE: There are no replacement parts available for this model.

CURRENT PRODUCTION SHOTGUNS

MX9

Introduced in 1993 this model features removable inserts on rib to adjust point of impact and a walnut stock with adjustable comb. Offered in 12 gauge with 32" or 34" barrel with screw-in chokes in Trap configuration and single barrels in Trap/Combo models. A competition version is also offered with unique vent rib inserts to correct for point of impact.The trigger group is removable. Available in several different grades of ornamentation.

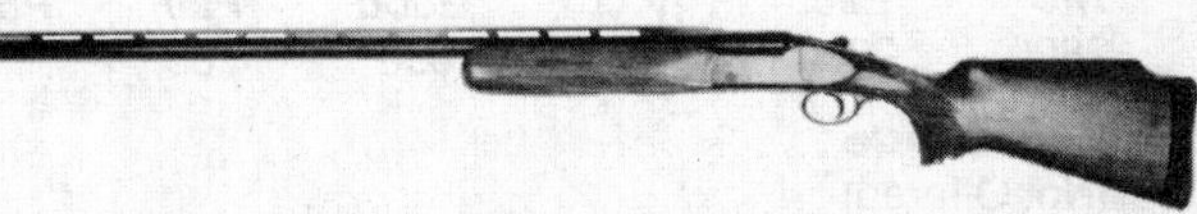

Standard Grade

NIB	Exc.	V.G.	Good	Fair	Poor
5500	4000	2500	1800	1250	—

SC3 Grade

NIB	Exc.	V.G.	Good	Fair	Poor
11500	6000	5000	3000	2000	—

SCO Grade

NIB	Exc.	V.G.	Good	Fair	Poor
18000	8000	7000	3500	2000	—

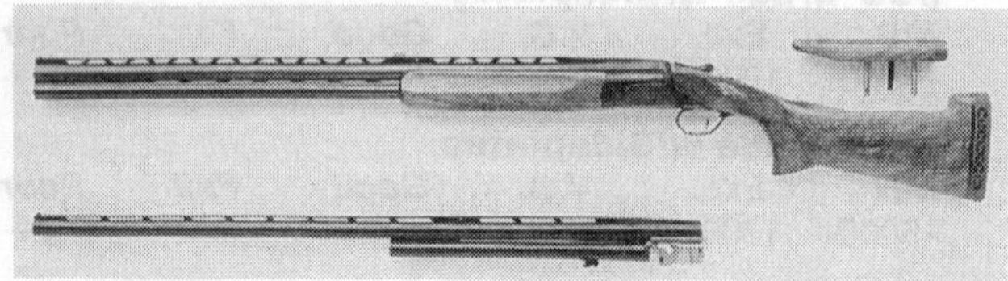

MX9 Trap Combo Model

Standard Grade Trap Combo MX 9

NIB	Exc.	V.G.	Good	Fair	Poor
8000	6500	—	—	—	—

MX10

This model was introduced in 1993. Its Single Barrel Trap models feature a different method of rib height and pattern adjustment. This model also has an adjustable stock. Available in 12 gauge with 32" or 34" barrels. Trap/Combo models are offered in 12 gauge with 29.5" or 31.5" over-and-under barrels with 32" or 34" single barrel. Chokes are fixed. Competition models are offered in 12 gauge and 20 gauge with choice of 29.5" or 31.5" barrel for 12 gauge and 29.5" barrel for 20 gauge. The ventilated rib height is adjustable as is the comb position on the stock. Trigger is removable.

Standard Grade

NIB	Exc.	V.G.	Good	Fair	Poor
6000	4750	—	—	—	—

SC3 Grade

NIB	Exc.	V.G.	Good	Fair	Poor
7500	5500	—	—	—	—

SCO Grade

NIB	Exc.	V.G.	Good	Fair	Poor
9000	7000	—	—	—	—

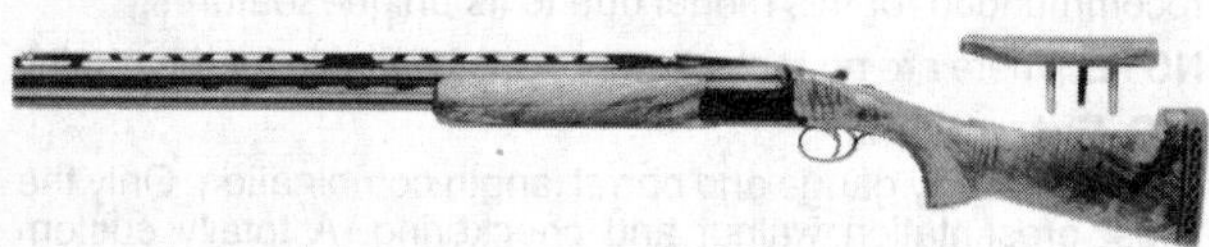

MX 10 Competition model

Standard Grade Combo Model

NIB	Exc.	V.G.	Good	Fair	Poor
10000	7500	—	—	—	—

TM I Special

This basic single barrel Perazzi Trap model is offered in 12 gauge with 32" or 34" barrel. Trigger is adjustable.

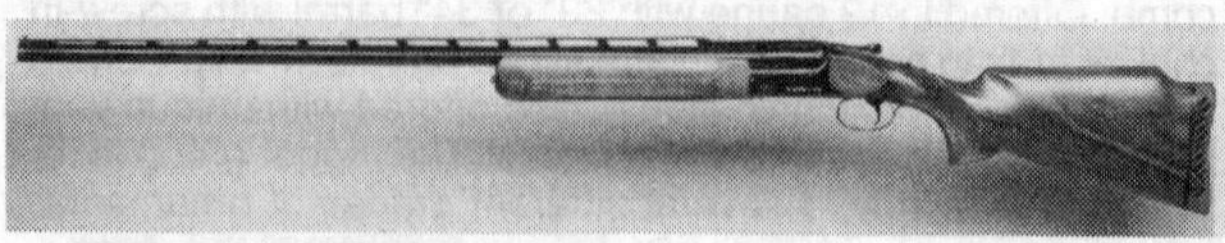

Standard Grade

NIB	Exc.	V.G.	Good	Fair	Poor
2800	2000	1250	850	700	—

SC3 Grade
(Not Offered)

TMX Special

Similar to TM I Special with select walnut.

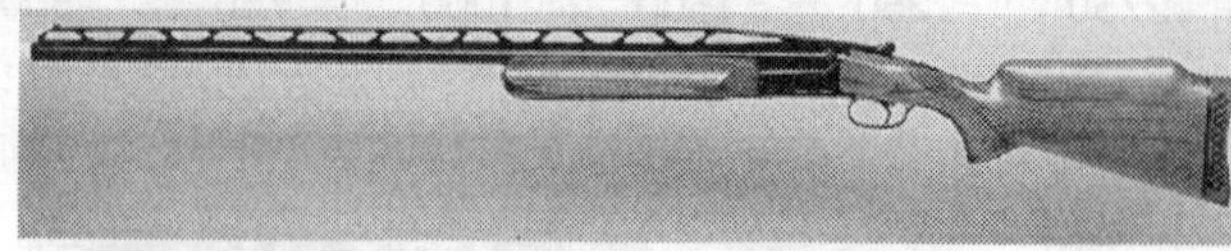

Standard Grade

NIB	Exc.	V.G.	Good	Fair	Poor
3250	2400	1700	900	750	—

SC3 Grade
(Not Offered)

SCO Grade

NIB	Exc.	V.G.	Good	Fair	Poor
13500	7000	6000	5000	2500	2000

MX8 Special

This model features a low contour vent rib, adjustable trigger, and grooved forend.

NOTE: Some SCO engraving patterns on early models have sold in the $30,000 to $45,000 price range. depending on the engraver. Get an expert appraisal. Beware of counterfeits.

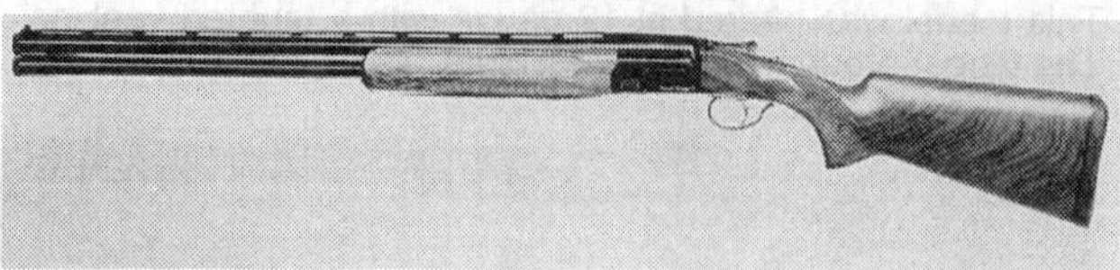

Standard Grade

NIB	Exc.	V.G.	Good	Fair	Poor
5500	4000	—	—	—	1000

SC3 Grade

NIB	Exc.	V.G.	Good	Fair	Poor
7500	5500	3800	—	—	—

SCO Grade

NIB	Exc.	V.G.	Good	Fair	Poor
10000	7500	5500	—	—	—

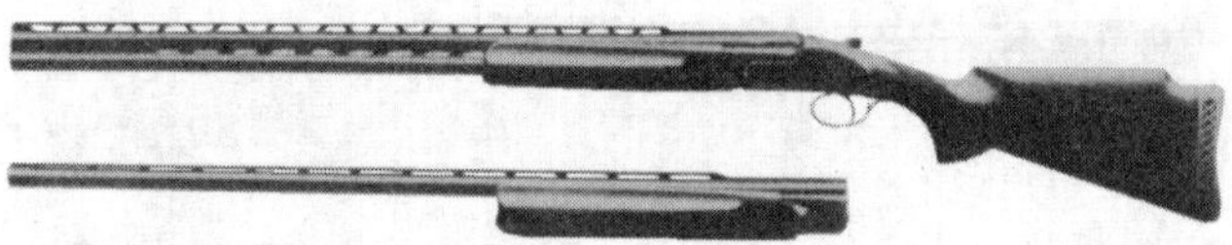

MX 8 Special Trap Combo

Standard Grade MX 8 Trap Combo

NIB	Exc.	V.G.	Good	Fair	Poor
7500	3500	—	—	—	1000

MX8/20

This model was first introduced in 1993. It features a removable trigger group. Available in 20 gauge only with choice of 27.5", 28.375", 29.5" flat ventilated rib barrels. Choice of fixed or screw-in chokes on sporting model. Stock is custom made to customer's dimensions with beavertail forend.

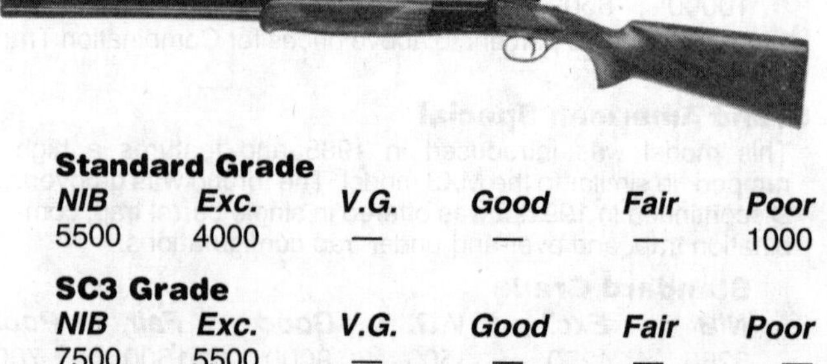

Standard Grade

NIB	Exc.	V.G.	Good	Fair	Poor
5500	4000	—	—	—	1000

SC3 Grade

NIB	Exc.	V.G.	Good	Fair	Poor
7500	5500	—	—	—	—

SCO Grade

NIB	Exc.	V.G.	Good	Fair	Poor
10000	7500	—	—	—	—

MX8/20-8/20C

Introduced in 1993 and offered in 20 gauge with 26" or 27.625" vent rib barrels. The trigger group on this model is removable. The stock is a high-grade walnut custom made to customers' specifications. The forend is round. The MX8/20 is supplied with fixed chokes while the MX8/20C has 5 screw-in choke tubes. Add $400 for MX8/20C values.

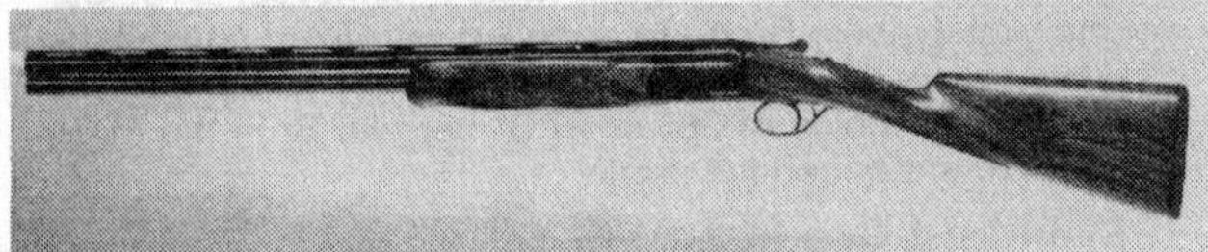

Standard Grade

NIB	Exc.	V.G.	Good	Fair	Poor
6000	4500	—	—	—	1000

SC3 Grade

NIB	Exc.	V.G.	Good	Fair	Poor
8000	6000	—	—	—	—

SCO Grade

NIB	Exc.	V.G.	Good	Fair	Poor
11500	8500	—	—	—	—

MX7

Introduced in 1993. This an over-and-under trap model that is offered in 12 gauge with 29.5" or 31.5" over-and-under barrels with either 32" or 34" single barrel. This model has a non-renewable trigger group feathering fixed coil spring trigger mechanism. The trigger is selective and works in conjunction with the safety catch. The vent rib is ramped on the Combo Trap model. The walnut is custom made to the customer's dimensions.

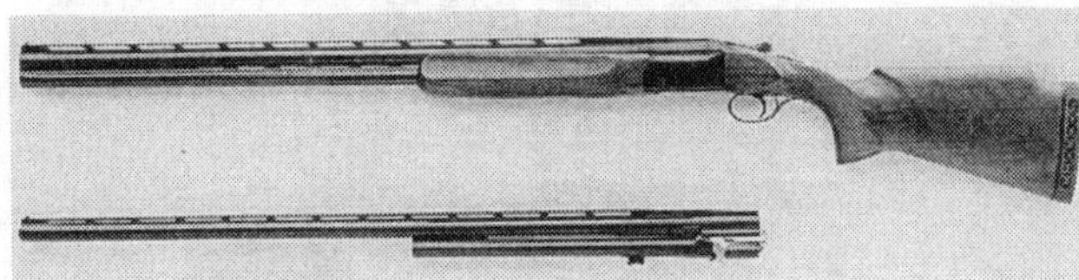

Standard Grade

NIB	Exc.	V.G.	Good	Fair	Poor
4500	3200	—	—	—	750

MX7C

Introduced in 1993 this model is offered in 12 gauge with a non-renewable trigger group. It has a coil spring mechanism, fully selective in conjunction with the safety. Offered in 27.5", 29.5", or 31.5" flat vent rib barrels. Screw-in chokes are standard. Walnut stock is custom made to customer's dimensions. The forend is beavertail.

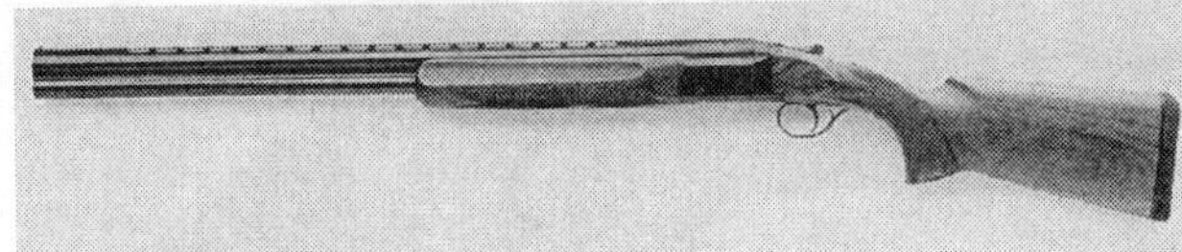

Standard Grade

NIB	Exc.	V.G.	Good	Fair	Poor
5000	3500	—	—	—	750

DB81 Special

This model, offered in 12 guage only, features a high ramped ventilated rib. Trigger is adjustable with internal selector. Barrel length are 29.5" or 31.5".Add $1,000 for two forends and two triggers for Trap/Combo models.

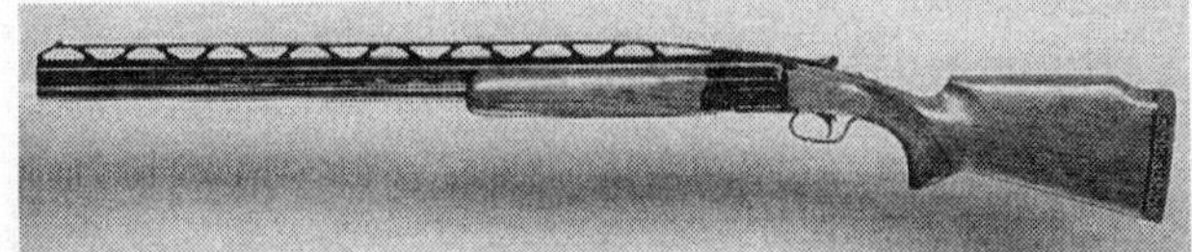

Standard Grade

NIB	Exc.	V.G.	Good	Fair	Poor
8700	6500	—	—	—	1000

SC3 Grade

NIB	Exc.	V.G.	Good	Fair	Poor
11000	8000	—	—	—	—

SCO Grade

NIB	Exc.	V.G.	Good	Fair	Poor
17500	12500	—	—	—	—

COMPETITION MODELS

Competition versions are over-and-under shotguns in trap, skeet, pigeon, and sporting models. Stock dimensions are based on the particular model chosen. Trap models feature trap stock dimensions and forearm designed for that purpose. The other models also have their own particular specifications. However, prices are based on a common style referred to by Perazzi as Competition. Thus, all models within this group are priced the same regardless of specific type.

Mirage Special

This model features an adjustable trigger and is available in 12 gauge with choice of 27.5", 28.375", 29.5", or 31.5" ventilated rib barrels.

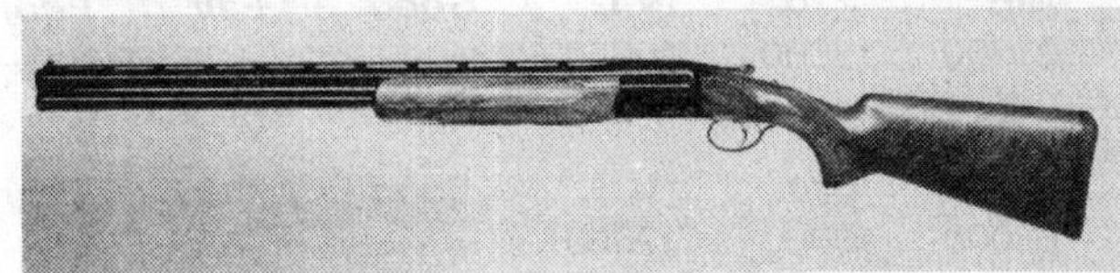

Standard Grade

NIB	Exc.	V.G.	Good	Fair	Poor
6100	4250	—	—	—	1000

Mirage Special Sporting

Similar to the Mirage Special listed above, but with external trigger selection and screw-in chokes. Offered in 12 gauge only with choice of 27.5", 28.375", or 29.5" vent rib barrels.

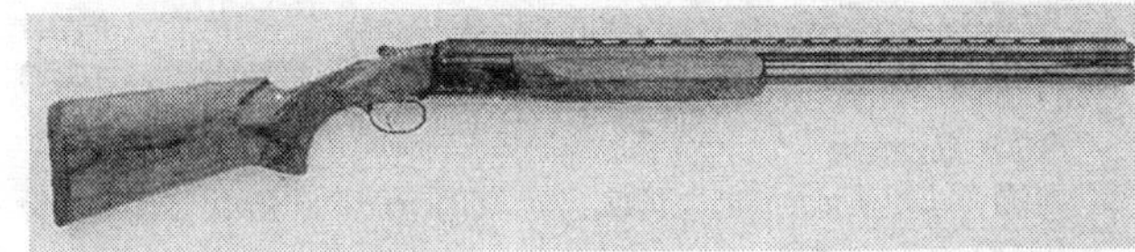

Standard Grade

NIB	Exc.	V.G.	Good	Fair	Poor
4500	3250	—	—	—	1000

Mirage Special Sporting Classic

This model features the same basic specifications as the Mirage Special Sporting with the addition of a scroll border on the receiver and triggerguard. The wood is of slightly higher quality. Offered in 12 gauge only with 27.5", 28.375", or 29.5" vent rib barrels.

Standard Grade

NIB	Exc.	V.G.	Good	Fair	Poor
4500	3250	—	—	—	1000

Mirage MX8

Standard Grade

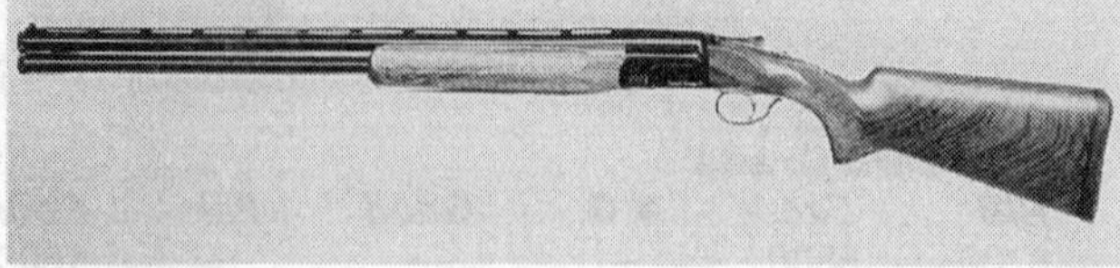

NIB	Exc.	V.G.	Good	Fair	Poor
5800	4250	—	—	—	1000

SCO Model

This model is similar to the MX8 but offered only in 12 gauge with barrel length from 27.5" to 31.5". The trigger is adjustable instead of removable.

SCO Grade

NIB	Exc.	V.G.	Good	Fair	Poor
10500	6000	—	—	—	1500

Mirage Special 4-Gauge Set

Similar to the Mirage Special in appearance and specifications but fitted with four barrel sets with 27.62" barrels in 12, 20, 28 gauge, and .410 bore. For 28.37" barrels add $2,000 and for 29.5" barrels add $3,000.

Standard Grade

NIB	Exc.	V.G.	Good	Fair	Poor
14000	10000	7000	—	—	1500

SC3 Grade

NIB	Exc.	V.G.	Good	Fair	Poor
21000	15000	10000	—	—	—

SCO Grade

NIB	Exc.	V.G.	Good	Fair	Poor
28000	19000	12500	—	—	—

MX12/12C

Offered in 12 gauge only with 26.75" or 27.5" vent rib barrels. The single-selective trigger is nonrefillable. The walnut stock is fitted with a schnabel forend and the receiver has a light-scroll engraved border. The MX12 is supplied with fixed chokes while the MX12C is fitted with 5 screw-in choke tubes. Add $400 to MX12 prices to get MX12C values.

Standard Grade

NIB	Exc.	V.G.	Good	Fair	Poor
4500	3250	—	—	—	1000

SC3 Grade

NIB	Exc.	V.G.	Good	Fair	Poor
6500	4750	—	—	—	—

SCO Grade

NIB	Exc.	V.G.	Good	Fair	Poor
10000	7000	—	—	—	—

MX20/20C

This model is offered in 20 gauge. It features a nonremovable trigger group. The frame is smaller than 12 gauge. Offered with 26" or 27.5" vent rib barrels. The MX20 has fixed chokes while the MX20C is supplied with 5 screw-in choke tubes. Add $400 to MX20 prices to get MX20C values.

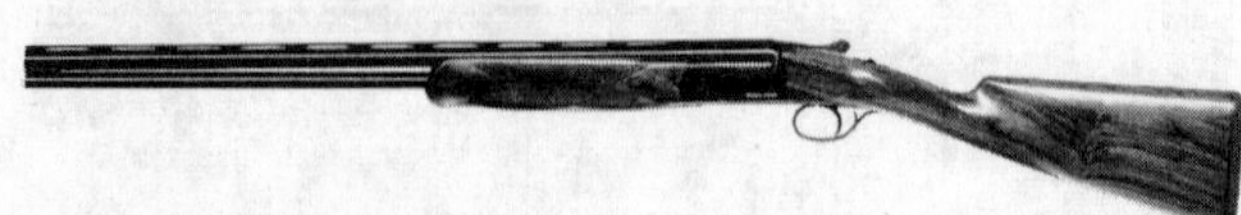

Standard Grade

NIB	Exc.	V.G.	Good	Fair	Poor
4500	3250	—	—	—	1000

SC3 Grade

NIB	Exc.	V.G.	Good	Fair	Poor
6500	4750	—	—	—	1000

SCO Grade

NIB	Exc.	V.G.	Good	Fair	Poor
10500	7000	—	—	—	—

MX28 and MX410

Introduced in 1993 these two models feature a nonremovable trigger group and a special small frame for each. The MX28, .28 gauge, weighs about 5.5 lbs. while the MX410, .410 bore, weighs slightly less. Both are supplied with fixed chokes, flat ribs, custom made stocks, and round forends. Each model is offered with a choice of 26" or 27.5" barrels. Both the MX28 and MX410 are priced the same.

Standard Grade

NIB	Exc.	V.G.	Good	Fair	Poor
8500	6250	—	—	—	1500

SC3 Grade

(Not Available)

SCO Grade

NIB	Exc.	V.G.	Good	Fair	Poor
13000	9500	—	—	—	2000

PERRY & GODDARD

Renwick Arms Co.
New York, New York

Derringer

A .44 caliber single-shot spur trigger pistol with a 2" octagonal barrel. Blued or silver-plated with walnut or gutta-percha grips. The barrel may be swiveled so that either end can serve as the chamber and is marked "Double Header/ E.S. Renwick." Produced in limited quantities during the 1860s.

Exc.	V.G.	Good	Fair	Poor
—	—	19500	8500	1500

PERRY PATENT FIREARMS CO.

Newark, New Jersey

Perry Single-Shot Pistol

A .52 caliber breech-loading percussion pistol with a 6" round barrel. Blued with walnut grips. The barrel marked "Perry Patent Firearms Co./Newark, N.J." Approximately 200 were made between 1854 and 1856 in two styles.

1st Type

Long, contoured trigger guard, opening lever.

Exc.	V.G.	Good	Fair	Poor
—	—	4500	1750	500

2nd Type

S curved shorter trigger guard and an automatic primer feed that protrudes from the butt.

Exc.	V.G.	Good	Fair	Poor
—	—	4250	1500	500

Perry Carbine

A .54 caliber breech-loading percussion carbine with a 20.75" barrel and half-length walnut stock secured by one barrel band. Blued with a case hardened lock. Approximately 200 were made.

Courtesy Milwaukee Public Museum, Milwaukee, Wisconsin

Exc.	V.G.	Good	Fair	Poor
—	—	7500	3250	1000

PERUGINI & VISINI

Brescia, Italy

Arms by this maker were imported by W.L. Moore of Westlake Village, California.

Liberty Model

A side-by-side 12, 20, 28 and .410 gauge shotgun with 28" barrels. Anson & Deeley action with a double Purdy lock. Blued overall with checkered walnut stock.

NIB	Exc.	V.G.	Good	Fair	Poor
5000	4000	3500	2500	1250	750

Classic Model

A 12 or 20 gauge double-barrel shotgun with a Holland & Holland-style sidelock and a double Purdy lock. The barrels are 28" in length. Single trigger and automatic ejectors. The sidelocks and mounts and engraved and blued. Well figured and checkered walnut stock.

NIB	Exc.	V.G.	Good	Fair	Poor
11000	8500	6500	4000	2000	1000

Bolt-Action Rifle

A Mauser-type bolt-action rifle available in a variety of chamberings, with 24" or 26" barrels. Sights not furnished. Well figured checkered walnut stock.

NIB	Exc.	V.G.	Good	Fair	Poor
4000	3250	2500	1500	900	500

Deluxe Bolt-Action Rifle

As above with first quality walnut stocks and a case.

NIB	Exc.	V.G.	Good	Fair	Poor
4500	3750	3000	1500	1000	600

Eagle Single-Shot

An Anson & Deeley single-shot rifle fitted with either 24" or 26" barrels, open sights, automatic ejector and adjustable trigger. Stock of checkered walnut.

NIB	Exc.	V.G.	Good	Fair	Poor
5000	4000	3000	1500	1000	600

Boxlock Express Rifle

An Anson & Deeley action double-barrel rifle chambered for .444 Marlin or 9.3x74R cartridges. The barrel length is 24" and is fitted with express sights. Double triggers and automatic ejectors. Receiver case hardened and the barrels as well as mounts blued. Checkered walnut stock.

NIB	Exc.	V.G.	Good	Fair	Poor
3250	2500	1750	1200	900	500

Magnum Over-and-Under

An Anson & Deeley action over-and-under rifle available .375 Holland & Holland and .458 Winchester Magnum. The barrels are 24" in length and fitted with express sights. Double triggers and automatic ejectors. Receiver and barrels blued, the stock of checkered walnut.

NIB	Exc.	V.G.	Good	Fair	Poor
5500	4250	3000	2000	1500	750

Super Express Rifle

A Holland & Holland-style sidelock double-barrel rifle. Having 24" barrels fitted with express sights. Available in a variety of chamberings. The receiver and sidelocks are either case hardened or finished in the bright and fully engraved. Checkered walnut stock.

NIB	Exc.	V.G.	Good	Fair	Poor
9500	8000	6500	4000	2000	950

Victoria Side-by-Side Rifle

Similar to the Boxlock Express Rifle but chambered for .30-06, 7x65R, or 9.3x74R cartridges. Either 24" or 26" barrels were available. Double triggers and automatic ejectors. Blued with minimal engraving. Stock of checkered walnut.

NIB	Exc.	V.G.	Good	Fair	Poor
6500	5250	4000	3000	1500	750

Selous Side-by-Side Rifle

First quality double-barrel express rifle with 24" or 26" barrels. Fully detachable Holland & Holland-style sidelocks, double triggers and automatic ejectors. Fully engraved with well figured checkered walnut stocks.

NIB	Exc.	V.G.	Good	Fair	Poor
22500	17500	12500	6000	3000	1500

PETTINGILL C. S.

New Haven, Connecticut
Rogers, Spencer & Co.
Willowvale, New York

Pocket Revolver

A hammerless, double-action .31 caliber percussion revolver having a 4" octagonal barrel. The frame of brass or iron. Blued barrel, the grips of oil finished walnut. The First and Second Models are marked "Pettingill's Patent 1856" as well as "T.K. Austin." The Third Model is marked "Pettengill Patent 1856," and "Raymond and Robitaille Patented 1858." Approximately 400 were manufactured in the late 1850s and early 1860s.

1st Model

Brass frame.

Exc.	V.G.	Good	Fair	Poor
—	—	2500	1000	400

2nd Model

Iron frame.

Exc.	V.G.	Good	Fair	Poor
—	—	1500	600	200

3rd Model

Iron frame and improved action.

Exc.	V.G.	Good	Fair	Poor
—	—	1250	400	200

Navy Revolver

As above but in .34 caliber with a 4.5" barrel and a 6-shot cylinder. The frame of iron, blued overall, and the grips of walnut. This model is marked "Pettengill's Patent 1856" and "Raymond & Robitaille Patented 1858." Approximately 900 were manufactured in the late 1850s and early 1860s.

Courtesy Milwaukee Public Museum, Milwaukee, Wisconsin

Exc.	V.G.	Good	Fair	Poor
—	—	1750	700	250

Army Model Revolver

As above but of .44 caliber and fitted with a 7.5" barrel. The frame of iron that is case hardened, the octagonal barrel blued, the grips of oil finished walnut. Early production models are marked as the Navy models, while later production examples are marked "Petingill's Patent 1856, pat'd July 22, 1856 and July 27, 1858." Some examples will be found with government inspector's marks and are worth approximately 25 percent more. It is believed that 3,400 were made in the 1860s.

Courtesy Milwaukee Public Museum, Milwaukee, Wisconsin

Exc.	V.G.	Good	Fair	Poor
—	—	4500	1500	500

PFANNL, FRANCOIS

Krems, Austria

Erika

A 4.25mm semi-automatic pistol with a hinged barrel assembly. The barrel either 1.5" or 2.25" in length. The grips are marked "Erika." Approximately 3,500 made between 1912 and 1926.

Exc.	V.G.	Good	Fair	Poor
1000	800	600	500	300

PGM PRECISION

France

Model PGM

This is a highly sophisticated semi-automatic rifle designed and built on a modular component system. Barrel change is fast and available calibers are .308 Win., .300 Savage, 7mm-08, .243, and .22-250. Match grade barrel length is 23.4". Fully adjustable trigger and buttstock with adjustable bipod. Five-round magazine is standard. Weight is approximately 13 lbs.

NIB	Exc.	V.G.	Good	Fair	Poor
8900	7000	5000	—	—	—

PHILLIPS & RODGERS INC.

Huntsville, Texas

Medusa Model 47

Introduced in 1996 this unique multi-caliber revolver is designed to chamber, fire, and extract almost any cartridge using 9mm, .357, or .38 cartridges—a total of about 25 different calibers. The barrel lengths are 2.5", 3", 4", 5", or 6". Rubber grips and interchangeable front sights. Finish is matte blue. Rarely if ever encountered.Disccontinued.

NIB	Exc.	V.G.	Good	Fair	Poor
900	700	550	450	—	—

Ruger 50 Conversion

This conversion, executed on a new revolver, converts a .44 Magnum Ruger into a .50 Action Express. Stainless steel or blue with 5-shot cylinder. Barrel length is 6.5".

NIB	Exc.	V.G.	Good	Fair	Poor
1000	800	550	450	—	—

Wilderness Explorer

This bolt-action rifle was introduced in 1997 and features an 18" match grade barrel. The bolt face and barrel are quick change so four calibers can be used in the same rifle. Synthetic stock. Chambered for .22 Hornet, .218 Bee, .44 Magnum, and .50 AE calibers. Weight is approximately 5.5 lbs.

NIB	Exc.	V.G.	Good	Fair	Poor
N/A	—	—	—	—	—

PHOENIX

Lowell, Massachusetts

Pocket Pistol

A rare .25 ACP semi-automatic pistol with a 2.25" barrel and 6-round magazine. Receiver and slide are blued, the grips are of hard rubber. Manufactured during the 1920s.

Exc.	V.G.	Good	Fair	Poor
950	700	350	200	100

PHOENIX ARMS

Ontario, California

HP22

A pocket-size semi-automatic pistol chambered for the .22 Long Rifle cartridge. Barrel length is 3". Magazine capacity is 11 rounds. Offered in bright chrome or polished blue finish with black checkered grips. Top of gun is fitted with vent rib. Overall length is 4.1" and weight is about 20 oz.

NIB	Exc.	V.G.	Good	Fair	Poor
100	75	60	40	30	20

HP25

This model is the same as above but chambered for the .25 ACP cartridge. Magazine capacity is 10 rounds.

NIB	Exc.	V.G.	Good	Fair	Poor
100	75	60	40	30	20

HP22/HP25 Target

A conversion kit to convert the HP22/HP25 into a target pistol. Kit includes extended vent rib barrel and a convertible 10-round magazine. Finish is either blue or nickel.

NIB	Exc.	V.G.	Good	Fair	Poor
125	100	75	60	—	—

Raven

A small pocket-size semi-automatic pistol chambered for the .25 ACP cartridge. Magazine capacity is 6 rounds. Barrel length is 2.4" with fixed sights. Offered in 3 finishes: bright chrome, satin nickel, or polished blue. Grips are either ivory, pink pearl, or black. Overall length is 4.8" and weight is approximately 15 oz.

NIB	Exc.	V.G.	Good	Fair	Poor
80	65	50	40	20	20

PHOENIX ARMS CO.

Liege, Belgium

SEE—Robar and de Kirkhave

PICKERT, FRIEDRICH

Arminius Waffenfabrik

Zella-Mehlis, Germany

This firm produced revolvers bearing the trade name "Arminius." The revolvers manufactured by Pickert of the double-action type, with or without exposed hammers. Some models are fitted with ejectors, while others have removable cylinders. Calibers and barrel lengths vary. After WWII, the trade name was acquired by Hermann Wiehauch.

Arminius 7.65mm

A five-shot concealed hammer revolver in 7.65mm caliber. The Arminius head is on the grips.

Courtesy James Rankin

Exc.	V.G.	Good	Fair	Poor
350	225	175	125	90

Arminius Single-Shot Target Pistol

A single-shot target pistol chambered for the 22 caliber cartridge. Some of these were built under the name PICKERT. The Arminius name is seen on the frame.

Courtesy James Rankin

Exc.	V.G.	Good	Fair	Poor
900	700	600	400	300

Pickert Revolver

Similar to the Arminius revolver but with a half-round, half-octagon barrel. Chambered for the 7.54mm cartridge.

Courtesy James Rankin

Exc.	V.G.	Good	Fair	Poor
275	225	175	150	100

PIEPER, HENRI & NICOLAS

Liege, Belgium

Originally founded by Henri Pieper in 1859, the company was reorganized in 1898 when his son, Nicolas, assumed control. The firm is perhaps best known for a series of semi-automatic pistols that are listed below, but Pieper also manufactured a bewildering variety of drillings, combination guns, cape guns, rook rifles, salon rifles and even volley guns. These guns must be evaluated on their own merits, and their value is strictly a function of what the market will bear.

Pieper Model 1907

A 6.35 or 7.65mm semi-automatic pistol featuring a hinged barrel assembly 2.5" in length. Receiver and barrel are blued, the grips are of hard rubber with the firm's trademark cast in them. The Model 1907 variation does not have a hinged barrel assembly. The Model 1908 is also known as the "Basculant," and the Model 1918 as the "Demontant."

Courtesy Orvel Reichert

Exc.	V.G.	Good	Fair	Poor
250	150	125	100	75

Model 1908/Basculant

This is a tipping barrel pistol chambered for the 6.35mm Auto cartridge. Similar in appearance to the Model 1907 this model had several improvements. The front end of the barrel was retained by a pivot bolt and the recoil spring rod had a hook that engaged the lug on the slide.

Courtesy Orvel Reichert

Exc.	V.G.	Good	Fair	Poor
275	175	150	125	100

Pieper Bayard Revolver

In competition with the Nagant gas seal revolver, Henri Pieper developed a superior design. Revolvers of this type have 5" barrels and are chambered for 8mm cartridges. The first model of this revolver had an automatic ejection system, while the second version utilized a swing-out cylinder. Standard finish is blued, with checkered hard rubber grips.

Exc.	V.G.	Good	Fair	Poor
350	250	200	150	100

Legia

This model was patterned after that of the Browning, and is chambered for the 6.35mm cartridge. The standard magazine holds 6 cartridges but a 10-round magazine was also available.

Exc.	V.G.	Good	Fair	Poor
250	150	125	100	75

Bayard

A 6.35, 7.65 or 9mm short semi-automatic pistol with a 2.5" barrel. Standard magazine capacity 6 rounds. The slide is stamped "Anciens Etablissement Pieper Liege, Belgium."

Exc.	V.G.	Good	Fair	Poor
250	150	125	100	75

PILSEN, ZBROVKA
Pilsen, Czechoslovakia

Pocket Pistol

Essentially a Model 1910 Browning semi-automatic pistol without a grip safety, this pistol was of 7.65mm caliber and had a 3.5" barrel with a 6-round magazine. The slide is marked "Akciova Spolecnost drive Skodovny zavody Zbrovka Plzen." Standard finish is blued, the grips of hard rubber. Manufactured during the 1920s.

Exc.	V.G.	Good	Fair	Poor
300	200	150	125	100

PIOTTI
Brescia, Italy

This Italian gunmaking firm is located in Gardone Val Trompia in the province of Brescia. Its shotguns are hand crafted and limited to a few each year. Each gun is made to individual specifications. Many consider them one of the best double shotguns made in the world today. Actions are either Anson & Deeley boxlock or Holland & Holland sidelock. Several features are offered on these shotguns at no additional cost: type of stock and forearm, barrel length and chokes, rib, action shape and finish.

Other features are considered extra cost options and will affect the value of the gun. There are: single triggers, detachable sidelocks, automatic safety, recoil pads, upgraded wood, engraving, and multi-gauge sets. With the exception of a few grades Piotti guns are available in 10, 12, 16, 20, and 28 gauge, as well as .410 bore. Depending on gauge barrel lengths are from 25" to 32".

Model Piuma (BSEE)

This model is the firm's standard boxlock offering. Available in 12 gauge to .410 bore it features ejectors and a scalloped frame. Fine scroll and rosette engraving is standard.

NOTE: Around serial number 9000, or 1989, Piotti began building the Model BSEE to the same standards as the King Model. Therefore, guns below serial number 9000 deduct about 40 percent from prices listed.

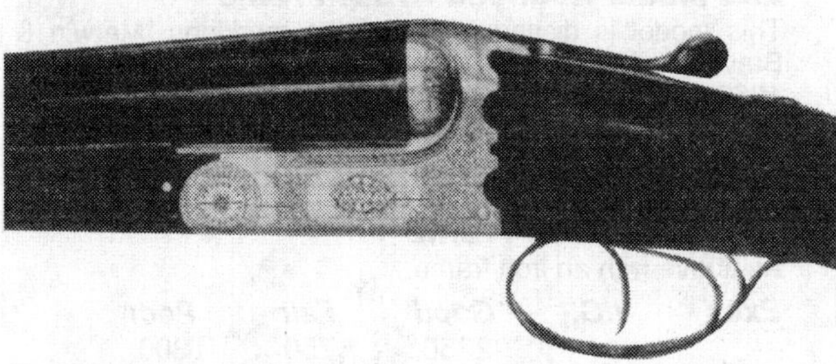

NIB	Exc.	V.G.	Good	Fair	Poor
14250	10500	7500	—	—	—

Westlake Model

This was Piotti's second quality model. It features a case colored receiver with gold line work. Offered in 12, 16, and 20 gauge. Discontinued in 1989.

NIB	Exc.	V.G.	Good	Fair	Poor
8500	6250	4750	—	—	—

Over-and-Under Gun

This model features King 2 engraving which has a light border scroll with 10 percent coverage. Custom engraving patterns available at extra charge.

NIB	Exc.	V.G.	Good	Fair	Poor
44750	33500	—	—	—	—

Model King No. I

This model features a sidelock with fine line scroll engraving with full coverage. A gold crown is inlaid on the top lever prior to 1989. H&H or Purdey-style engraving. Select walnut with hand checkering is standard. Chambered from 10 gauge to .410 bore.

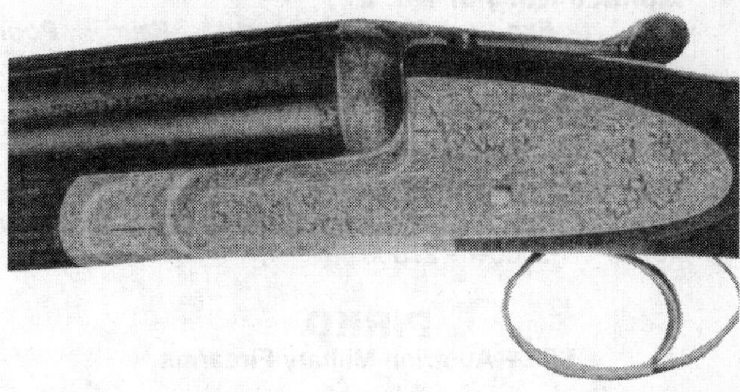

NIB	Exc.	V.G.	Good	Fair	Poor
26750	20000	15000	—	—	—

Monte Carlo Model

This model was a less expensive version of the King Model. It had H&H or Purdey-style engraving. It was discontinued in 1989 and was upgraded and became part of the King Model. This occured around serial number 9000.

NIB	Exc.	V.G.	Good	Fair	Poor
14000	10000	7000	—	—	—

Model King Extra

This model is similar to the King No. 1 but with the addition of a number of engraving styles from English to game scenes with gold inlays. Because of the wide variety of engraving patterns offered on this model it is advisable to secure a qualified appraisal before purchase.

Model Lunik

This model is fitted with Holland & Holland sidelocks. Engraving is Renaissance-style relief cut scroll engraving. A gold crown is inlaid on the top lever. Offered in gauges from 10 to .410 bore.

NIB	Exc.	V.G.	Good	Fair	Poor
28600	21000	16000	—	—	—

Model Monaco

This sidelock model features all of the best that Piotti has to offer and extra attention is paid to hand work and fitting. Only the finest European hardwoods are used. Available in 10 gauge to 410 bore. Offered with three different types of engraving designated No. 1, No. 2, and No. 4.

Monaco No. 1 or No. 2

NIB	Exc.	V.G.	Good	Fair	Poor
35500	26500	20000	—	—	—

Monaco No. 3

NIB	Exc.	V.G.	Good	Fair	Poor
38500	28500	22500	—	—	—

Monaco No. 4

NIB	Exc.	V.G.	Good	Fair	Poor
46750	35000	27500	—	—	—

PIRKO

SEE—Austrian Military Firearms

PLAINFIELD MACHINE CO.

Dunelien, New Jersey

Super Enforcer

A cut-down version of the U.S. M1 Carbine with a 12" barrel and pistol grip. The finish is blued and stocks are walnut.

Exc.	V.G.	Good	Fair	Poor
500	375	275	175	100

M1 Carbine

A commercial reproduction of the U.S. M1 Carbine. The finish is blued. Walnut stock.

Exc.	V.G.	Good	Fair	Poor
350	225	150	100	75

MI Paratrooper Carbine

As above with a telescoping wire buttstock and walnut forend.

Exc.	V.G.	Good	Fair	Poor
400	275	200	125	100

PLAINFIELD ORDNANCE CO.

Middlesex, New Jersey

Model 71

A stainless steel .22 caliber semi-automatic pistol with a 10-shot magazine and 1" barrel. Also available in .25 ACP and conversion kits were available.

Conversion Kit

Exc.	V.G.	Good	Fair	Poor
50	40	30	25	20

.22 or .25 Caliber Pistol

Exc.	V.G.	Good	Fair	Poor
175	125	100	75	50

Model 72

As above except with an alloy frame.

Exc.	V.G.	Good	Fair	Poor
175	125	100	75	50

PLANT'S MANUFACTURING CO.

New Haven, Connecticut

Army Model Revolver

A large single-action revolver chambered for a .42 caliber cup-primed cartridge that loads from the front of the cylinder. Barrel length 6" and of octagonal form with a rib. The frame is made of either brass or iron. Finish is blued, with walnut or rosewood grips. Interchangeable percussion cylinders also were made for these revolvers. If present, the values would be increased approximately 30 percent. This revolver was marketed by Merwin & Bray, and there were approximately 1,500 of the 1st and 2nd Models manufactured and 10,000 of the 3rd Model in the 1860s.

1st Model Brass Frame

Marked "Plant's Mfg. Co. New Haven, Ct." on the barrel, "M & B" on the side of the frame, and "Patented July 12, 1859" on the cylinder. Approximately 100 manufactured.

Exc.	V.G.	Good	Fair	Poor
—	—	2500	950	300

1st Model Iron Frame

As above with an iron frame. Approximately 500 made.

Exc.	V.G.	Good	Fair	Poor
—	—	2500	950	300

2nd Model Rounded Brass Frame

This model is distinguished by the markings "Merwin & Bray, New York" on the frame and the patent date "July 21, 1863". Approximately 300 made.

Exc.	V.G.	Good	Fair	Poor
—	—	3250	1250	400

2nd Model Iron Frame

As above with an iron frame.

Exc.	V.G.	Good	Fair	Poor
—	—	2250	750	300

3rd Model

As above with a flat brass frame.

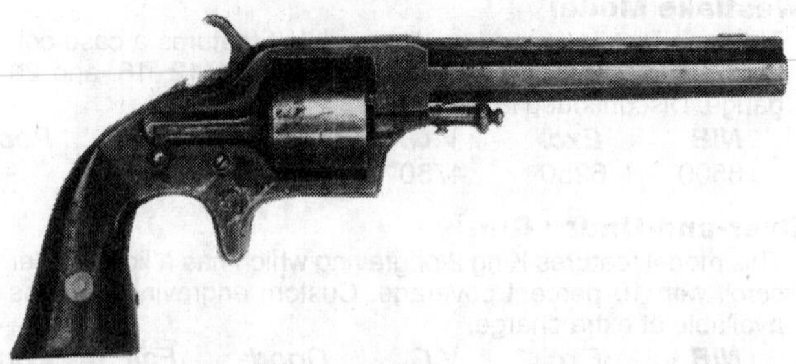

Courtesy Milwaukee Public Museum, Milwaukee, Wisconsin

Exc.	V.G.	Good	Fair	Poor
—	—	1150	400	150

Pocket Revolver

Similar to the Army model described above except chambered for .30 caliber cartridges. Barrel length 3.5", five-shot cylinder.

The frame normally silver plated, barrel and cylinder blued and the grips of rosewood or walnut. This model is encountered with a variety of retailer's markings: Eagle Arms Co., New York, "Reynolds, Plant & Hotchkiss, New Haven, Ct.," and Merwin & Bray Firearms Co., N.Y." Approximately 20,000 were made.

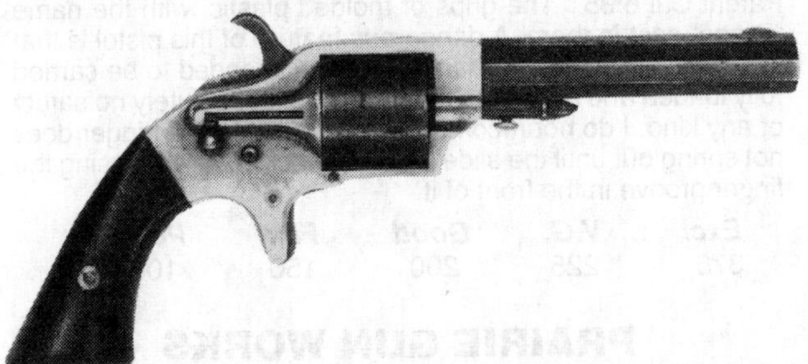

Courtesy Milwaukee Public Museum, Milwaukee, Wisconsin

Exc.	*V.G.*	*Good*	*Fair*	*Poor*
—	—	550	250	100

POINTER

Hopkins & Allen
Norwich, Connecticut

Single-Shot Derringer

An unmarked Hopkins & Allen single-shot pistol stamped "Pointer" on the barrel. Barrel length 2.75", caliber .22, frame of nickel-plated brass. The barrel swings sideways for loading. Bird's-head walnut grips. It is believed that about 2,500 were made between 1870 and 1890.

Exc.	*V.G.*	*Good*	*Fair*	*Poor*
—	—	650	250	100

POLY-TECHNOLOGIES, INC.

China

SKS

A semi-automatic rifle chambered for the 7.62x39mm cartridge with a 20.5" barrel and 10-shot fixed magazine. Based on the Soviet Siminov carbine. Finish is blued, and the stock and hand guard are made of a Chinese hardwood.

NIB	*Exc.*	*V.G.*	*Good*	*Fair*	*Poor*
150	100	80	70	50	35

AKS-762

A semi-automatic version of the Chinese-type 56 Assault rifle chambered for the 7.62x39mm cartridge with a 16.5" barrel. Furnished with a 20-round magazine and a Chinese bayonet. The finish is blued, and the stock is hardwood.

NIB	*Exc.*	*V.G.*	*Good*	*Fair*	*Poor*
800	700	550	400	300	200

NOTE: For folding stock model add $250.

AK-47/S

Chambered for the 7.62x39 cartridge.

NIB	*Exc.*	*V.G.*	*Good*	*Fair*	*Poor*
1650	1400	1100	750	600	400

NOTE: For folding stock model add $350. With a Soviet-style bayonet add $15.

M-14/S

A reproduction of the U.S. M14 rifle chambered for the 7.62mm cartridge with a 22" barrel and 20-round magazine. Finish is blued and the stock is of hardwood.

NIB	*Exc.*	*V.G.*	*Good*	*Fair*	*Poor*
600	400	300	200	150	100

POND, LUCIUS, W.

Worchester, Massachusetts

Pocket Revolver

A single-action, spur trigger .32 caliber revolver with octagonal barrels of 4", 5", or 6" length. The barrel top strap and cylinder pivot upwards for loading. Made with either brass or iron frames. A screwdriver is fitted in the butt. As these revolvers were an infringement of Rollin White's patent, they were discontinued. Some revolvers are to be found with the inscription "Manuf'd. for Smith & Wesson Pat'd. April 5, 1855." These examples are worth approximately 20 percent more than the values listed.

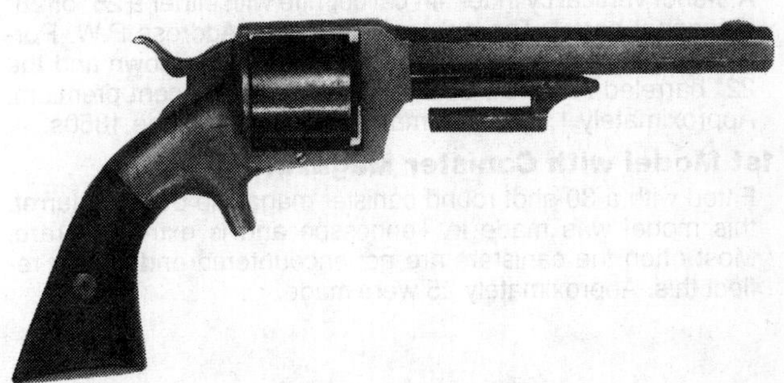

Courtesy Milwaukee Public Museum, Milwaukee, Wisconsin

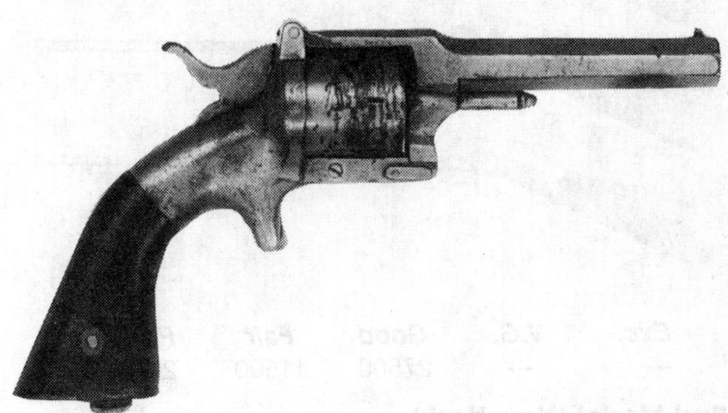

Courtesy Milwaukee Public Museum, Milwaukee, Wisconsin

Brass Framed Revolver

Exc.	*V.G.*	*Good*	*Fair*	*Poor*
—		800	350	100

Iron Framed Revolver

Exc.	*V.G.*	*Good*	*Fair*	*Poor*
—	—	700	300	75

Separate Chamber Revolver

To avoid the Rollin White patent, this revolver is chambered for .22 or .32 caliber rimfire cartridges that fit into separate steel chamber inserts that can be removed from the front of the cylinder for loading. The .22 caliber version has a 3.5" octagonal barrel with a 7-round unfluted cylinder; the .32 caliber version has a 4", 5", or 6" octagonal barrel and 6-shot unfluted cylinder. Frames are of silver-plated brass; and the barrels and cylinders are blued. Grips of walnut. Standard markings include "L.W. Pond, Worcester, Mass." and patent dates. Approximately 2,000 manufactured in .22 caliber and 5,000 in .32 caliber between 1863 and 1870.

.22 Caliber Version

Exc.	*V.G.*	*Good*	*Fair*	*Poor*
—	—	1250	500	150

.32 Caliber Version

Exc.	*V.G.*	*Good*	*Fair*	*Poor*
—	—	1250	500	150

PORTER, P. W.
New York, New York

Turret Revolver

An extremely rare 9-shot vertical cylinder .41 caliber percussion revolver with a 5.25" round barrel. The trigger guard is also a lever that turns the cylinder and cocks the hammer. An automatic primer system is also fitted to this revolver. Manufactured during the 1850s in an unknown quantity.

Exc.	V.G.	Good	Fair	Poor
—	—	18000	8000	100

Turret Rifle

A 9-shot vertical cylinder .44 caliber rifle with either a 26" or 28" octagonal barrel. The only markings are "Address P.W. Porter/New York." Four variations of this rifle are known and the 22" barreled carbine would command a 25 percent premium. Approximately 1,250 were manufactured during the 1850s.

1st Model with Canister Magazine

Fitted with a 30-shot round canister magazine over the turret, this model was made in Tennessee and is extremely rare. Most often the canisters are not encountered and values reflect this. Approximately 25 were made.

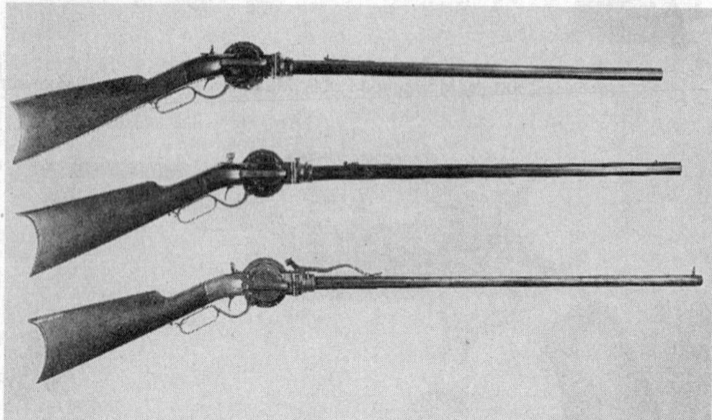

Exc.	V.G.	Good	Fair	Poor
—	—	27500	11500	2000

2nd Model (New York)

Exc.	V.G.	Good	Fair	Poor
—	—	10500	4750	1000

3rd Model (New York)

This model has a screw-off cover over the magazine.

Exc.	V.G.	Good	Fair	Poor
—	—	9500	4750	1000

4th Model (New York)

As above but without an automatic primer magazine and the nipples are exposed.

Exc.	V.G.	Good	Fair	Poor
—	—	8000	3750	750

POWELL, W. & SON LTD.
Birmingham, England

SEE—British Double Guns

PRAGA, ZBROVKA
Prague, Czechoslovakia

Established in 1918 by A. Novotny, this company ceased operations in 1926.

VZ2L

A 7.65mm semi-automatic pistol patterned after the Model 1910 Browning, but without a grip safety. Barrel length 3.5", magazine capacity 6 rounds, grips of wood. The slide is marked "Zbrojowka Praga Praha."

Exc.	V.G.	Good	Fair	Poor
400	250	200	150	100

Praga 1921

A 6.35mm semi-automatic pistol with a slide of stamped steel cut with a finger groove at the front. Folding trigger. The barrel 2" in length. The slide is marked "Zbrojowka Praga Praha Patent Cal 6.35." The grips of molded plastic, with the name "Praga" cast in them. A dangerous feature of this pistol is that it is striker-fired with no hammer and is intended to be carried fully loaded and cocked in the pocket with absolutely no safety of any kind. I do not recommend this. The folding trigger does not spring out until the slide is drawn back slightly by using the finger groove in the front of it.

Exc.	V.G.	Good	Fair	Poor
375	225	200	150	100

PRAIRIE GUN WORKS
Winnipeg, Manitoba, Canada

M-15

This is a lightweight mountain rifle chambered for .22-250, 6mm-284, .25-284, 6.5-284, 7mm-08, .308 Win., and most short calibers. Built on a Remington 700 action with 20" lightweight barrel. Stock is Kevlar and comes in either green, black or gray. Barrel length is usually 20". Weight is approximately 4.75 lbs.

NIB	Exc.	V.G.	Good	Fair	Poor
1750	1350	—	—	—	—

M-18

Similar to the above model but chambered for long action calibers and fitted with barrel lengths from 22" to 24". Weight is approximately 5.25 lbs.

NIB	Exc.	V.G.	Good	Fair	Poor
1750	1350	—	—	—	—

PRANDELLI & GASPARINI
Brescia, Italy

Boxlock Side-by-Side Shotgun

A good quality double-barrel 12 or 20 gauge shotgun with 26" or 28" barrels. Single-selective trigger, automatic ejectors and an Anson & Deeley action. Blued, stock of select walnut.

Exc.	V.G.	Good	Fair	Poor
1500	1150	900	700	450

Sidelock Side-by-Side Shotgun

Similar to the above, but with full sidelocks.

Exc.	V.G.	Good	Fair	Poor
2500	2150	1500	900	500

Boxlock Over-and-Under Shotgun

An over-and-under double-barrel 12 or 20 gauge shotgun with 26" or 28" barrels, single triggers and automatic ejectors. Blued, with select walnut stock.

Exc.	V.G.	Good	Fair	Poor
1750	1250	950	700	350

Sidelock Over-and-Under Shotgun

As above with full sidelocks.

Exc.	V.G.	Good	Fair	Poor
3000	2500	1800	950	450

PRATT, GEORGE
Middletown, Connecticut

Trap Gun

A doubled-barreled, stationary burglar alarm or animal trap gun that is chambered for .38 caliber centerfire. The barrel is 4" in length, and all of the components are made of cast iron with a galvanized finish. Barrels and action are mounted on a round base, which can turn 360 degrees. The patent date

 *This symbol denotes "Sleepers" with rapidly-rising values and/or significant collector potential.*

"Dec. 18, 1883" is marked on the gun. Many were manufactured between 1880 and the early 1890s.

Exc.	V.G.	Good	Fair	Poor
—	—	750	400	150

PRATT, H.

Roxbury, Massachusetts

Under Hammer Pistol

A .31 caliber percussion single-shot pistol with an 8.5" octagonal barrel. The frame marked "H. Pratt's/ Patent." Manufactured during the 1850s.

Exc.	V.G.	Good	Fair	Poor
—	—	1200	600	200

PRECISION SMALL ARMS

Beverly Hills, California

PSA-25

This is a semi-automatic pistol chambered for the .25 ACP. The barrel length is 2.13". Magazine capacity is 6 rounds. The frame and slide is steel alloy. Weight is 9.5 oz. Overall length is 4.11". Grips are black polymer. Standard finish is black oxide.

NIB	Exc.	V.G.	Good	Fair	Poor
225	175	150	125	100	75

NOTE: For brushed chrome finish add $50 and for stainless steel add $75.

Featherweight Model

Same as above, but with aluminum frame and chrome slide with gold-plated trigger.

NIB	Exc.	V.G.	Good	Fair	Poor
400	300	250	200	150	100

Diplomat Model

Black oxide with gold highlights and ivory grips.

NIB	Exc.	V.G.	Good	Fair	Poor
625	500	400	—	—	—

Montreaux Model

Gold plated with ivory grips.

NIB	Exc.	V.G.	Good	Fair	Poor
700	550	400	—	—	—

Renaissance Model

Same as above but with hand engraved steel frame and slide. Antique stain chrome finish.

NIB	Exc.	V.G.	Good	Fair	Poor
1250	900	600	450	—	—

Imperiale

Inlaid gold filigree over blue with scrimshawed ivory grips.

NIB	Exc.	V.G.	Good	Fair	Poor
3750	2750	—	—	—	—

PREMIER

Italy and Spain

A trade name used by various retailers on shotguns manufactured in Italy and Spain that were imported during the late 1950s and early 1960s.

Regent Side-by-Side Shotgun

A double-barrel shotgun with 26" to 30" barrels available in all standard gauges. Receiver blued, stock of walnut. Normally found with a pistol grip and beavertail forend.

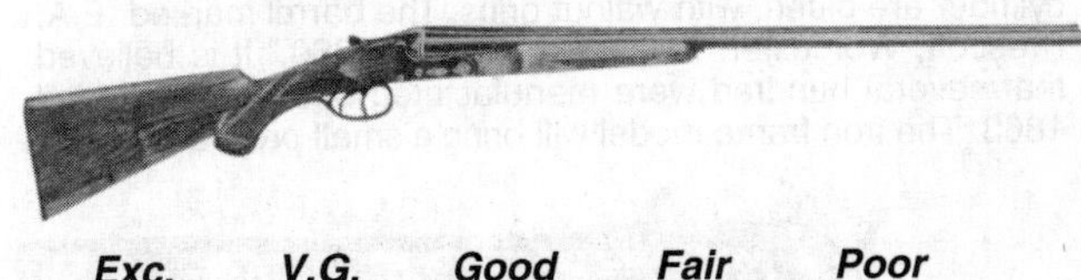

Exc.	V.G.	Good	Fair	Poor
450	250	200	150	100

Regent Magnum

As above but chambered for the 3.5" 10 gauge Magnum cartridge. Barrels 32" in length and choked Full and Full.

Exc.	V.G.	Good	Fair	Poor
500	300	250	200	150

Brush King

Identical to the Regent Model except that it is fitted with 22" Modified and Improved Cylinder barrels and a straight-grip English-style stock.

Exc.	V.G.	Good	Fair	Poor
500	375	250	200	150

Ambassador Model

A more ornate version of the Regent Model.

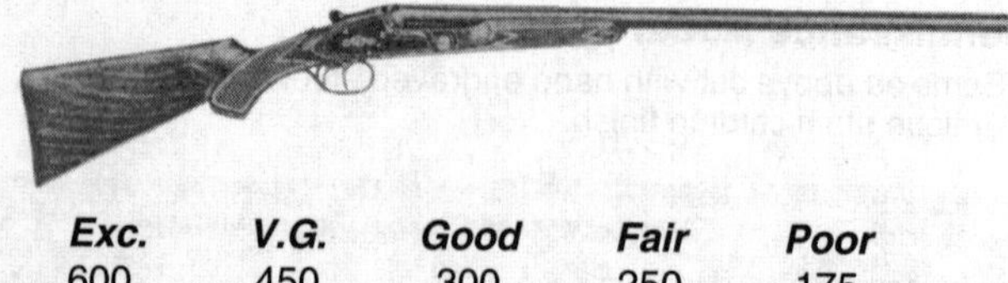

Exc.	V.G.	Good	Fair	Poor
600	450	300	250	175

Presentation Custom Grade

A custom-order shotgun with game scenes as well as gold and silver inlays.

Exc.	V.G.	Good	Fair	Poor
2500	1750	1250	850	400

PRESCOTT, E. A.

Worcester, Massachusetts

Percussion Pocket Revolver

A .31 caliber percussion spur trigger revolver with either 4" or 4.25" octagonal barrel and a 6-shot cylinder. The frame of brass, and the grips of walnut. It is believed that approximately 100 were manufactured during 1860 and 1861.

Exc.	V.G.	Good	Fair	Poor
—	—	2250	950	200

Pocket Revolver

A .22 or .32 spur trigger revolver with a barrel of either 3" or 4" length. The .22 caliber version has a 7-shot cylinder and the .32 caliber version a 6-shot cylinder. The standard markings are "E.A. Prescott Worchester Mass. Pat. Oct. 2, 1860." Approximately 1,000 were manufactured between 1862 and 1867.

Exc.	V.G.	Good	Fair	Poor
—	—	750	300	100

Navy Revolver

A single-action revolver fitted with a conventional trigger, chambered for .38 rimfire cartridges with a 7.25" octagonal barrel. The unfluted cylinder holds 6 shots. The frame is of either silver-plated brass or blued iron; and the barrel and the cylinder are blued, with walnut grips. The barrel marked "E.A. Prescott, Worcester, Mass. Pat. Oct. 2, 1860." It is believed that several hundred were manufactured between 1861 and 1863. The iron frame model will bring a small premium.

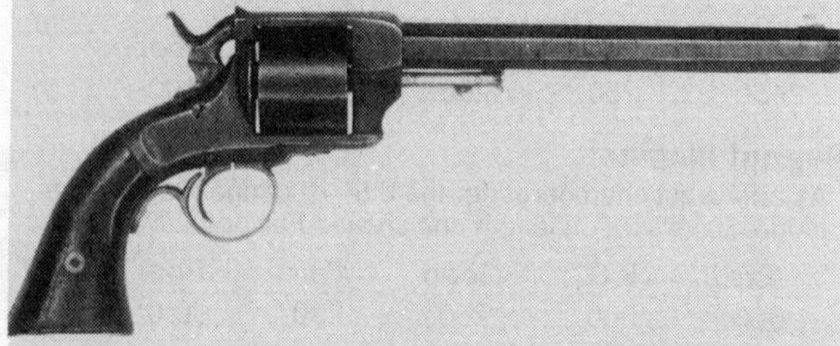

Courtesy Milwaukee Public Museum, Milwaukee, Wisconsin

Exc.	V.G.	Good	Fair	Poor
—	—	1250	500	200

Army Revolver

Similar in appearance to the Navy model but with a larger frame. Chambered for .44 caliber rimfire cartridge. Fitted with a 9" octagon barrel with extractor rod and loading gate on right side of frame. Very rare.

Exc.	V.G.	Good	Fair	Poor
—	—	18000	8000	—

Belt Revolver

Although similar in appearance to early Smith & Wesson revolvers, the Prescott has a solid frame. Available in either .22 or .32 caliber, the .22 caliber model has a 3" barrel and the .32 caliber a 5.75" barrel. Markings are identical found on the Pocket Revolver. Approximately 300 were manufactured between 1861 and 1863.

Exc.	V.G.	Good	Fair	Poor
—	—	750	300	100

PRETORIA

Pretoria, South Africa

SEE—P.A.F.

PRINZ

Germany

Grade 1 Bolt-Action Rifle

A high quality bolt-action rifle chambered for the .243, .30-06, .308, 7mm Remington Magnum or the .300 Winchester Magnum cartridges. Barrel length 24", double-set triggers available. Finish is blued, stock is of oil-finished select walnut. Introduced in 1989.

NIB	Exc.	V.G.	Good	Fair	Poor
750	550	400	300	225	150

Grade 2 Bolt-Action Rifle

As above with a rosewood forend tip and pistol grip cap.

NIB	Exc.	V.G.	Good	Fair	Poor
950	700	525	375	250	150

Tip Up Rifle

A high quality single-shot rifle available in a variety of American cartridges. Barrel length 24" and not furnished with sights. Finish blued, stock of select walnut.

NIB	Exc.	V.G.	Good	Fair	Poor
2500	1850	1300	800	550	300

Model 85 "Princess"

A combination 12 gauge shotgun and rifle with 24" or 26" barrels, double triggers, and automatic ejectors. Finish blued, stock of select walnut.

NIB	Exc.	V.G.	Good	Fair	Poor
1750	1250	900	650	500	300

PRITCHETT, POTTS & HUNT

SEE—English Military Firearms

PROFESSIONAL ORDNANCE, INC.

Ontario, California

NOTE: This company has been purchased by Bushmaster.

Carbon-15 Pistol—Type 97

Introduced in 1996 this semi-automatic pistol is built on a carbon fiber upper and lower receiver. Chambered for the 5.56 cartridge it has a 7.25" fluted stainless steel barrel. Ghost ring sights are standard. Magazine is AR-15 compatible. Quick detach compensator. Furnished with a 10-round magazine. Weight is approximately 46 oz.

NOTE: This pistol has several options which will affect value.

NIB	Exc.	V.G.	Good	Fair	Poor
825	600	450	325	—	—

Carbon-15 Rifle—Type 97

Similar to the above model but fitted with a 16" barrel, quick detachable buttstock, quick detach compensator, Weaver type mounting base. Overall length is 35". Weight is about 3.9 lbs.

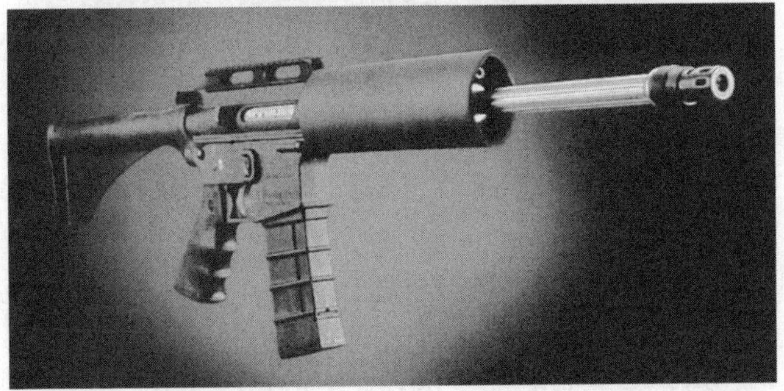

NIB	Exc.	V.G.	Good	Fair	Poor
850	625	500	400	—	—

Carbon-15 Rifle—Type 97S

Introduced in 2000 this rifle incorporated several new features. Its foregrip is double walled and insulated with a sheet of ultra-lightweight amumina silica ceramic fiber. The recoil buffer has been increased in size by 30 percent for less recoil. A new ambidextrous safety has been added, and a new multi carry silent sling with Hogue grip is standard. Weight is approximately 4.3 lbs.

NIB	Exc.	V.G.	Good	Fair	Poor
1285	950	700	550	—	—

Carbon-15 Pistol—Type 21

Introduced in 1999 this model features a light profile stainless steel 7.25" barrel. Ghost ring sights are standard. Optional recoil compensator. A 30-round magazine is standard until supplies are exhausted. Weight is about 40 oz.

NIB	Exc.	V.G.	Good	Fair	Poor
800	600	450	325	—	—

Carbon-15 Rifle—Type 21

This model is fitted with a 16" light profile stainless steel barrel. Quick detachable stock, weaver mounting base. Introduced in 1999. Weight is approximately 3.9 lbs.

NIB	Exc.	V.G.	Good	Fair	Poor
988	750	600	500	—	—

PROTECTION

Unknown

Protection Pocket Revolver

A .28 caliber percussion spur-trigger revolver with a 3.25" octagonal barrel and 6-shot cylinder roll engraved with a police arrest scene. The frame of brass and grips of walnut. The cylinder is marked "Protection." Approximately 1,000 were manufactured during the late 1850s and early 1860s.

1st Model

Roll engraved cylinder.

Exc.	V.G.	Good	Fair	Poor
—	—	1150	450	100

2nd Model

Plain cylinder above serial no. 650.

Exc.	V.G.	Good	Fair	Poor
—	—	950	350	100

PTK INTERNATIONAL, INC.

Atlanta, Georgia

SEE—Poly-Technologies

PULASKI ARMORY

Pulaski, Tennessee

Founded in 1861, this firm produced rifles for the State of Tennessee. Overall length 48-1/2" to 49-1/2"; round barrels 32-1/2" to 33-1/4"; caliber .54. Resemble U.S. Model 1841 Rifles except without patchbox. Had single screw sporting locks with diamond-shaped ferrules. Usually marked on barrel "PULASKI T. C.S.A. 61." Production estimated to be about 300.

Exc.	V.G.	Good	Fair	Poor
—	—	10000	5000	1500

PUMA (Rossi)

Model 92 Rifle

This model is a copy of the Winchester lever-action rifle. It is fitted with a 24" octagon barrel and chambered for the .44 Magnum, .357 Magnum, or .45 Colt cartridge. Offered in a variety of finishes such as stainless steel, blued, blued and brass, and blued and case colored. Fitted with a cresent butt and hardwood stock.

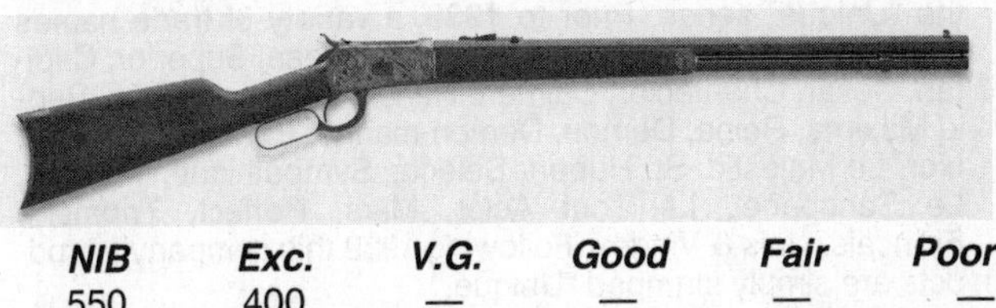

NIB	Exc.	V.G.	Good	Fair	Poor
550	400	—	—	—	—

NOTE: Add $50 for stainless steel

Model 92 Carbine

This model is also available with a 20" round barrel chambered as above and also in .454 Casull and .480 Ruger. Fitted with a shotgun butt.

NIB	Exc.	V.G.	Good	Fair	Poor
450	330	—	—	—	—

NOTE: Add $50 for stainless steel.

Model 92 Trapper

Introduced in 2004 this model features a 16" barrel with large-loop lever and saddle ring. Available in all of the calibers noted above.

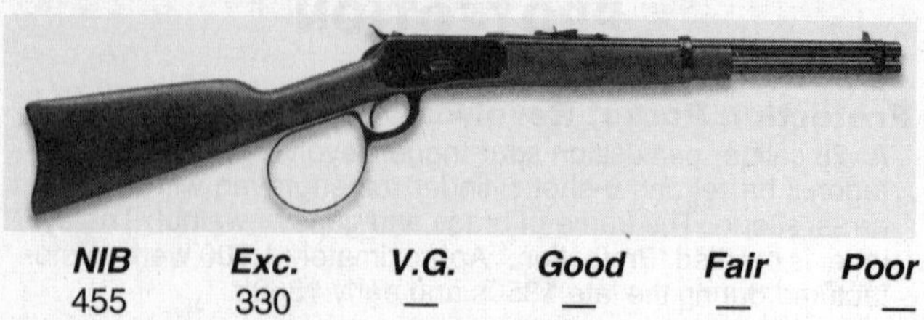

NIB	Exc.	V.G.	Good	Fair	Poor
455	330	—	—	—	—

PURDEY, J. & SONS LTD.
London, England
SEE ALSO—British Double Guns

Perhaps the finest manufacturer of shotguns, double-barrel and bolt-action rifles in the world. Virtually all their products are made on special order and it is impossible to establish general values for their products. Prospective purchasers are advised to seek qualified guidance prior to the acquisition of any arms made by this maker. The prices listed are for standard guns as of 1999 with no extras.

Hammerless Ejector Side-by-Side Game Gun
Available in 12, 16, 20, 28, and .410 bore. Engraved sidelocks.

NIB	Exc.	V.G.	Good	Fair	Poor
48000	—	—	—	—	—

NOTE: For 28 and .410 bore guns add an additional $3,000.

Hammerless Ejector Over-and-Under Gun
This gun is offered in 12, 16, 20, 28, and .410 bore with sidelocks.

NIB	Exc.	V.G.	Good	Fair	Poor
61000	—	—	—	—	—

NOTE: For 28 and .410 bore guns add an additional $3,500.

Double-Barreled Rifle
A side-by-side double rifle with sidelocks. It can be built in any caliber. Prices listed are for new guns in various bore sizes:

.300 bore—$77,000 .375 bore—$77,500
.470 bore—$80,500 .577 bore—$90,000
.600 bore—$92,000

PYRENEES
Hendaye, France

Founded in 1923 and still in operation today, this company has produced a variety of models. The most popular of which was the "Unique" series. Prior to 1939, a variety of trade names were marked on their products such as these: Superior, Capitan, Cesar, Chantecler, Chimere Renoir, Colonial, Prima, Rapid Maxima, Reina, Demon, Demon-marine, Ebac, Elite, Gallia, Ixor, Le Majestic, St. Hubert, Selecta, Sympathique, Touriste, Le Sanspariel, Le Tout Acier, Mars, Perfect, Triomphe Francais, Unis & Vindex. Following 1939 this company's products are simply stamped "Unique."

Model 10 Unique
A 6.35mm semi-automatic pistol similar to the Model 1906 Browning. The slide is marked "Le Veritable Pistolet Francais Unique." Introduced in 1923.

Exc.	V.G.	Good	Fair	Poor
250	175	150	100	75

Model 11
As above with a grip safety and loaded chamber indicator.

Exc.	V.G.	Good	Fair	Poor
275	200	175	125	100

Model 12
As above but without the loaded chamber indicator.

Exc.	V.G.	Good	Fair	Poor
250	175	150	100	75

Model 13
As above with a 7-shot magazine.

Exc.	V.G.	Good	Fair	Poor
250	175	150	100	75

Model 14
As above with a 9-shot magazine.

Exc.	V.G.	Good	Fair	Poor
250	175	150	100	75

Model 15
As above but in 7.65mm caliber. Introduced in 1923.

Exc.	V.G.	Good	Fair	Poor
250	175	150	100	75

Model 16
As above with a 7-shot magazine.

Courtesy Orvel Reichert

Exc.	V.G.	Good	Fair	Poor
250	175	150	100	75

Model 17
As above with a 9-shot magazine.

Courtesy Orvel Reichert

Exc.	V.G.	Good	Fair	Poor
300	250	200	150	100

Model 18

A 7.65mm caliber semi-automatic pistol patterned after the Model 1920 Browning but without a grip safety.

Exc.	*V.G.*	*Good*	*Fair*	*Poor*
250	175	150	100	75

Model 19

As above with a 7-shot magazine.

Exc.	*V.G.*	*Good*	*Fair*	*Poor*
250	175	150	100	75

Model 20

As above but with a 9-shot magazine.

Exc.	*V.G.*	*Good*	*Fair*	*Poor*
275	200	175	125	100

Model 21

As above except chambered for the 9mm short cartridge.

Exc.	*V.G.*	*Good*	*Fair*	*Poor*
275	200	175	125	100

NOTE: During World War II production at this company was taken over by the Nazis. Consequently, the various models listed above will be found with German inspection marks. These arms are worth approximately 25 percent more than the values listed.

POST-WAR UNIQUE

Model BCF66

A 9mm short semi-automatic pistol with a 3.5" barrel, open top slide and external hammer. The slide marked "Armes Unique Hendaye BP France." Blued finish blued, plastic grips.

Exc.	*V.G.*	*Good*	*Fair*	*Poor*
250	175	150	125	100

Model C

Virtually identical to the Model 17 listed above. The slide marked "7.65 Court 9 coups Unique." Blued finish, plastic grips with the trademark "PF" in a circle cast into them.

Exc.	*V.G.*	*Good*	*Fair*	*Poor*
225	150	125	100	75

Model F

Identical to the Model C except chambered for 9mm Short cartridges. Magazine capacity 8 rounds.

Exc.	*V.G.*	*Good*	*Fair*	*Poor*
250	175	150	125	100

Model D

A .22 caliber semi-automatic pistol with barrels ranging from 4" to 7.5" in length. The 7.5" barreled version is fitted with a muzzlebrake. Magazine capacity 10 rounds. Finish blued, plastic grips.

Exc.	*V.G.*	*Good*	*Fair*	*Poor*
250	175	150	125	100

Model DES/VO

Identical to the Model D but chambered for .22 Short cartridges.

Exc.	*V.G.*	*Good*	*Fair*	*Poor*
250	175	150	125	100

Model L

Similar to the Model D except chambered for .22, .32 ACP, and 9mm Short cartridges. Available with either a steel or alloy frame.

Exc.	*V.G.*	*Good*	*Fair*	*Poor*
275	225	200	150	125

Model Des 69

As above with better quality sights, special trigger and improved grips.

Exc.	*V.G.*	*Good*	*Fair*	*Poor*
300	250	200	175	125

Model 2000

Courtesy John J. Stimson, Jr.

NIB	*Exc.*	*V.G.*	*Good*	*Fair*	*Poor*
1250	950	—	—	—	—

QUACKENBUSH
Herkimer, New York

Quackenbush Safety Cartridge Rifle
A single-shot, takedown boy's rifle chambered for .22 rimfire cartridges in either .22 Short or .22 Long. Barrel length 18". Weight was about 4.5 lbs. All metal parts nickel-plated. The breech swings to the side for loading. Stock of walnut. Manufactured between 1886 and about 1920. Approximately 50,000 were produced. Quackenbush also made nickel-plated nutcrackers. Who'd'a thought?

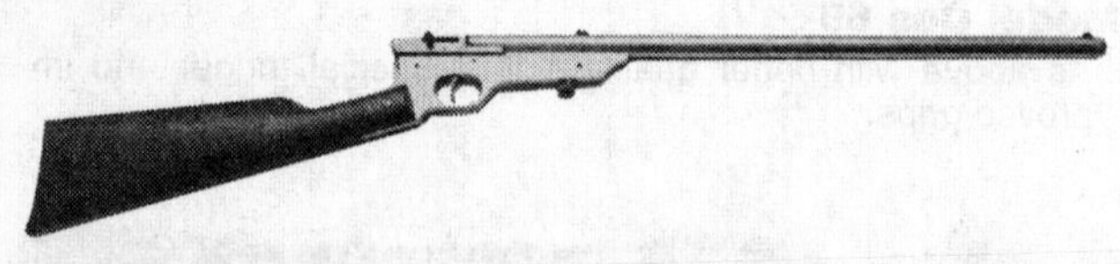

Courtesy Mike Stuckslager

Exc.	V.G.	Good	Fair	Poor
—	900	500	200	100

Junior Safety Rifle
Same as above but with skeleton stock. Built between 1893 and 1920. About 7,000 guns were manufactured. Weight was about 4 lbs.

Exc.	V.G.	Good	Fair	Poor
—	950	600	200	100

Bicycle Rifle
Chambered for the .22 cartridge, this rifle was fitted with a 12" barrel. Skeleton wire pistol grip.

Exc.	V.G.	Good	Fair	Poor
—	1200	750	350	150

QUINABAUG MFG. CO.
Southridge, Massachusetts

Under Hammer Pistol
A .31 caliber percussion under hammer pistol with barrels from 3" to 8" in length. Frame of blued iron, the grips of walnut or maple. The top of the frame is marked "Quinabaug Rifle M'g Co. Southbridge, Mass." The barrels are normally marked "E. Hutchings & Co. Agents." Manufactured during the 1850s.

Exc.	V.G.	Good	Fair	Poor
—	—	1250	550	200

R

R. G. INDUSTRIES
Miami, Florida
Rohm Gmbh
Sontheim/Brenz, Germany

An importer of inexpensive handguns of dubious quality that ceased operations in 1986.

RG-25
A .25 caliber semi-automatic pistol available with either a blued or chrome-plated finish.

Exc.	V.G.	Good	Fair	Poor
75	65	50	35	25

RG-16
A double-barrel .22 caliber chrome-plated derringer.

Exc.	V.G.	Good	Fair	Poor
75	65	50	35	25

RG-17
As above except chambered for. 38 Special cartridge.

Exc.	V.G.	Good	Fair	Poor
75	70	60	50	25

RG-14
A .22 caliber double-action revolver with a 4" barrel and 6-shot cylinder. Blued finish, plastic grips.

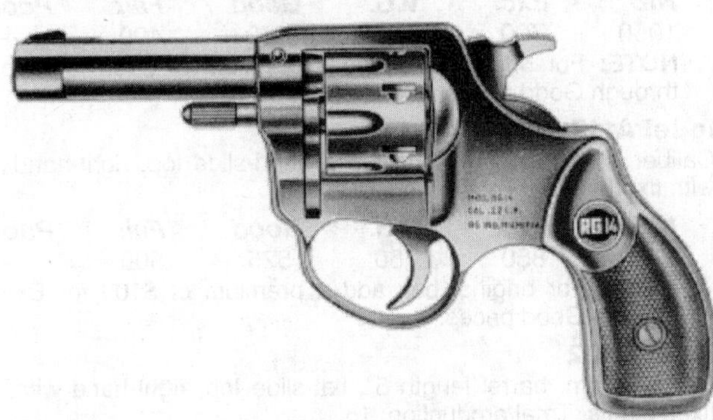

Exc.	V.G.	Good	Fair	Poor
75	70	60	50	25

RG-30
A .22 LR or Magnum double-action revolver. Blued finish, plastic grips.

Exc.	V.G.	Good	Fair	Poor
75	65	50	35	25

RG-40
A .38 Special double-action revolver with swing-out cylinder. Blued finish, plastic grips.

Exc.	V.G.	Good	Fair	Poor
75	70	60	50	25

RG-57
A .357 or .44 Magnum double-action revolver with 6-shot cylinder. Blued finish, checkered wood grips.

Exc.	V.G.	Good	Fair	Poor
150	100	80	65	50

RG-63
A .22 caliber double-action revolver resembling a Colt Model 1873.

Exc.	V.G.	Good	Fair	Poor
90	70	50	35	25

RG-66
A .22 or .22 Magnum single-action revolver patterned after the Colt Model 1873.

Exc.	V.G.	Good	Fair	Poor
90	70	50	35	25

RG-66T
As above with adjustable sights.

Exc.	V.G.	Good	Fair	Poor
90	70	50	35	25

RG-74

A .22 caliber double-action revolver with swing-out cylinder.

Exc.	V.G.	Good	Fair	Poor
75	65	55	45	35

RG-88

A .357 Magnum double-action revolver with swing-out cylinder.

Exc.	V.G.	Good	Fair	Poor
75	65	55	45	40

R.E.

Valencia, Spain

The initials "R.E." stand for "Republica Espana." This copy of the Spanish Army Model 1921, also known as the Astra 400, was produced between 1936 and 1939 during the Spanish Civil War by the Republican forces. This variation can be identified by the "RE" monogram on the butt and the absence of any manufacturer's stampings.

Exc.	V.G.	Good	Fair	Poor
350	250	200	150	100

RADOM

Radom, Poland

NOTE: For history, technical data, descriptions, photos, and prices see the *Standard Catalog of Military Firearms*.

VIS-35 Reissue

This is an exact copy of the original VIS-35 pistol. Limited to 100 pistols with fewer than that number imported into the U.S. The importer, "Dalvar of USA" is stamped on the barrel.

NIB	Exc.	V.G.	Good	Fair	Poor
2300	—	—	—	—	—

RANDALL FIREARMS CO.

Sun Valley, California

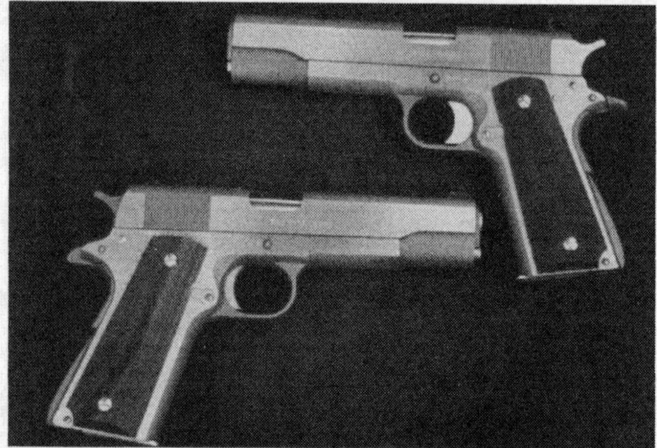

Randall matched set, serial-number RFOO010C. Made for the TV series 'Magnum PI." (Photo by Steve Comus)

NOTE: Randall prototypes can be identified by a "T" prefix. Add 50 percent to the price for this variety. For serial numbers under 2000 add $100 to $150.

Randall Documentation & Collectors Club: Research letters on original Randall Letterhead are available at a cost of $30 each postpaid (Randal pistols only). Readers and collectors interested in joining the Randall Firearms/Pistol Collectors Association contact the Randall Historian, Rick Kennerknecht at:

P.O. Box 1180, Mills, Wyoming 82644-1180
Web: www.Randall45.com
Email: Historian@Randal45.com
Phone: 877-464-0180
U.S. Fax: 419-464-0180; Euro-Fax:44-(0870) 131-2598

Model A111

Caliber is .45 Auto, barrel length 5", round-slide top, right-hand with fixed sights. Total production: 3,431.

NIB	Exc.	V.G.	Good	Fair	Poor
995	600	500	400	350	—

NOTE: For original box add a premium of $100 for Exc. through Good prices.

Model A121

Caliber is .45 Auto, barrel length 5", flat-slide top, right-hand with fixed sights. Total production: 1,067.

NIB	Exc.	V.G.	Good	Fair	Poor
800	685	500	425	375	—

NOTE: For original box add a premium of $100 for Exc. through Good prices.

Model A131

Caliber is .45 Auto, barrel length 5", flat-slide top, right-hand with Millet sights. Total production: 2,083.

Randall A131/SO in. 451 Detonics Magnum with Randall memorabilia. (Photo by Larry Gray)

NIB	Exc.	V.G.	Good	Fair	Poor
1050	700	600	450	400	—

NOTE: For original box add a premium of $100 for Exc. through Good prices.

Model A112

Caliber is 9mm, barrel length 5", round-slide top, right-hand with fixed sights. Total production: 301.

NIB	Exc.	V.G.	Good	Fair	Poor
1250	850	750	575	500	—

NOTE: For original box add a premium of $100 for Exc. through Good prices.

Model A122

Caliber 9mm. barrel length 5", flat-slide top, right-hand with fixed sights. Total production: 18.

NIB	Exc.	V.G.	Good	Fair	Poor
1775	1465	1245	1100	840	735

NOTE: For original box add a premium of $100 for Exc. through Good prices.

Model A211

Caliber .45 Auto, barrel length 4-1/4", round-slide top, right-hand with fixed sights. Total production: 922.

NIB	Exc.	V.G.	Good	Fair	Poor
1075	715	600	450	400	—

NOTE: For original box add a premium of $100 for Exc. through Good prices.

Model A231

Caliber .45 Auto, barrel length 4-1/4", flat-slide top, right-hand with Millet sights. Total production: 574.

NIB	Exc.	V.G.	Good	Fair	Poor
1200	825	700	525	450	—

NOTE: For original box add a premium of $100 for Exc. through Good prices.

This symbol denotes "Sleepers" with rapidly-rising values and/or significant collector potential.

Model A212

Caliber 9mm, barrel length 4-1/4", round-slide top, right-hand with fixed sights. Total production: 76.

NIB	Exc.	V.G.	Good	Fair	Poor
1325	915	800	605	525	—

NOTE: For original box add a premium of $100 for Exc. through Good prices.

Model A232

Caliber 9mm. barrel length 4-1/4", flat-slide top, right-hand with Millet sights. Total production: 5.

NIB	Exc.	V.G.
2075	1400	—

NOTE: For original box add a premium of $100 for Exc. through Good prices.

Model A311

Caliber .45 Auto, barrel length 4-1/4", round-slide top, right-hand with fixed sights. Total production: 361.

A311B black oxide LeMay special order by **Soldier of Fortune** *magazine for field testing in El Salvador. (Photo by Steve Comus)*

NIB	Exc.	V.G.	Good	Fair	Poor
1550	1075	950	710	605	—

NOTE: For original box add a premium of $100 for Exc. through Good prices.

Model A331 Curtis LeMay

Caliber .45 Auto, barrel length 4-1/4", flat-slide top, right-hand with Millet sights. Total production: 293.

NIB	Exc.	V.G.	Good	Fair	Poor
1675	1175	1000	840	735	—

Model A312

Caliber 9mm. barrel length 4-1/4", round-slide top, right-hand with fixed sights. Total production: 2.

NIB	Exc.	V.G.	Good	Fair	Poor
3525	2995	—	—	—	—

NOTE: For original box add a premium of $100 for Exc. through Good prices.

Model A332

Caliber 9mm. barrel length 4-1/4", flat-slide top, right-hand with Millet sights. Total production: 9.

NIB	Exc.	V.G.	Good	Fair	Poor
2000	1625	—	—	—	—

NOTE: For original box add a premium of $100 for Exc. through Good prices.

Model B111

Caliber .45 Auto, barrel length 5", round-slide top, left-hand with fixed sights. Total production: 297.

NIB	Exc.	V.G.	Good	Fair	Poor
1775	1200	1100	840	735	—

NOTE: For original box add a premium of $100 for Exc. through Good prices.

Model B121

Caliber .45 Auto, barrel length 5", flat-slide top, left-hand with fixed sights. Total production: 110.

NIB	Exc.	V.G.	Good	Fair	Poor
2075	1450	1300	920	815	—

NOTE: For original box add a premium of $100 for Exc. through Good prices.

Model B122

Caliber 9mm. barrel length 5", flat-slide top, left-hand with fixed sights. Total production: 2.

NIB	Exc.	V.G.	Good	Fair	Poor
3950	3450	—	—	—	—

Model B123

Caliber .38 Super, barrel length 5", flat-slide top, left-hand with fixed sights. Total production: 2.

NIB	Exc.	V.G.	Good	Fair	Poor
3950	3450	—	—	—	—

Model B131

Caliber .45 Auto, barrel length 5", flat-slide top, left-hand with Millet sights. Total production: 225.

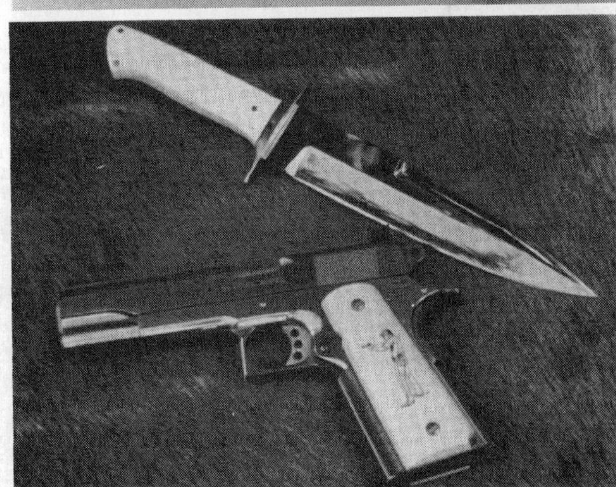

B131/SO left-hand service model with custom Chuck Stapel knife. (Photo by Steve Comus)

NIB	Exc.	V.G.	Good	Fair	Poor
1950	1200	920	815	—	—

NOTE: For original box add a premium of $100 for Exc. through Good prices.

Model B311

Caliber .45 Auto, barrel length 4-1/4", round-slide top, left-hand with fixed sights. Total production: 52.

Randall left-hand B311 with original box. Few left-hand Randalls were shipped in boxes. Most were shipped in Randall pistol rugs. (Photo by Steve Comus)

NIB	Exc.	V.G.	Good	Fair	Poor
2075	1450	1300	1000	850	—

NOTE: For original box add a premium of $100 for Exc. through Good prices.

Model B312

Caliber 9mm. barrel length 4-1/4", round-slide top, left-hand with fixed sights. Total production: 9.

Randall B312 left-hand 9mm LeMay, one of the most sought-after of the B-series guns. Only nine were manufactured. (Photo by Steve Comus)

Randall B312 with factory 45 ACP conversion unit. Only one of these factory units were made. (Photo by Steve Comus)

NIB	Exc.	V.G.	Good	Fair	Poor
3525	2550	2300	1340	1100	

NOTE: For original box add a premium of $100 for Exc. through Good prices.

Model B331

Caliber .45 Auto, barrel length 4-1/4", flat-slide top, left-hand with Millet sights. Total production: 45.

NIB	Exc.	V.G.	Good	Fair	Poor
2325	1650	1500	—	—	—

NOTE: For original box add a premium of $100 for Exc. through Good prices.

Model C311

Caliber .45 Auto, barrel length 4-1/4", round-slide top, right-hand with fixed sights. Total production: 1.

NIB
3950

Model C332

Caliber 9mm. barrel length 4-1/4", flat-slide top, right-hand with Millet sights. Total production: 4.

NIB	Exc.	V.G.	Good
1800	1575	1350	1200

Model B321 SET

Serial number REK I.

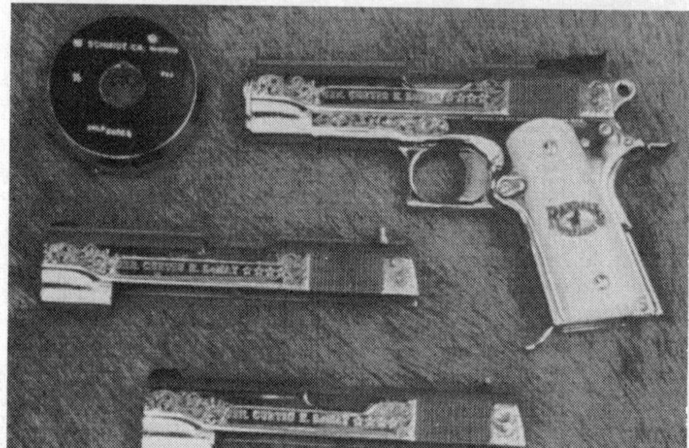

B321 set with gold-plated LeMay roll mark die. (Photo by Steve Comus)

Randall B321 of the B321 set, serial-number REK1. (Photo by Steve Comus)

NIB
23000

Model A111/111 Matched Set

Serial numbers RFOOOOOC, RFOO001C, RFOO010-C, RFOO024C.

NIB
8600

 *This symbol denotes "Sleepers" with rapidly-rising values and/or significant collector potential.*

Austrian Randall

Total production: 5.

Close-up view of Austrian proof marks. (Photo by Christopher Todd)

Four of the five Austrian Randalls. Each of these A111s bear cartouches from an Austrian proof house. These Randalls were proofed for the Austrian government for law enforcement evaluation. (Photo by Christopher Todd)

NIB
3000

NOTE: Prototypes with "T" serial numbers add 50 percent. For serial numbers under 2000 add $200 to $300. With factory box add $100 for A111, A121, and A131. Add $200 for all other right-hand models and $300 for all left-hand models.

RANDALL MAGAZINES

.45 LeMay—Right-Hand

NIB	Exc.	V.G.	Good	Fair	Poor
100	90	80	80	—	—

.45 LeMay—Dogleg Right-Hand

NIB	Exc.	V.G.	Good	Fair	Poor
80	70	70	70	—	—

.45 LeMay—Left-Hand

NIB	Exc.	V.G.	Good	Fair	Poor
150	130	125	125	—	—

.45 LeMay—Dogleg Left-Hand

NIB	Exc.	V.G.	Good	Fair	Poor
140	130	120	120	—	—

.45 Service—Right-Hand

NIB	Exc.	V.G.	Good	Fair	Poor
60	45	40	40	—	—

.45 Service—Left-Hand

NIB	Exc.	V.G.	Good	Fair	Poor
125	115	100	100	—	—

9mm Service—Right-Hand

NIB	Exc.	V.G.	Good	Fair	Poor
125	115	100	100	—	—

9mm Service—Left-Hand

NIB	Exc.	V.G.	Good	Fair	Poor
200	175	150	150	—	—

RANGER ARMS, INC.

Gainesville, Texas

Statesman

A bolt-action rifle produced in various calibers with a 22" barrel, no sights, and a checkered walnut stock. Standard finish blued. Manufactured in the early 1970s.

Exc.	V.G.	Good	Fair	Poor
350	250	200	150	100

Statesman Magnum

As above, but chambered for magnum calibers and with a 24" barrel.

Exc.	V.G.	Good	Fair	Poor
400	300	250	200	100

Senator

As above with a better finish.

Exc.	V.G.	Good	Fair	Poor
450	350	300	250	125

Senator Magnum

As above chambered for magnum cartridges.

Exc.	V.G.	Good	Fair	Poor
450	350	300	250	125

Governor

As above with better walnut and finer lined checkering.

Exc.	V.G.	Good	Fair	Poor
500	400	350	250	125

Governor Magnum

As above chambered for magnum cartridges.

Exc.	V.G.	Good	Fair	Poor
500	400	350	250	125

RAPTOR ARMS CO.

Alexandria, Virginia

Raptor Bolt-Action Rifle

Introduced in 1997 and chambered for the .270, .30-06, .243, .25-06, and .308 calibers. Fitted with a 22" barrel and black synthetic checkered stock with recoil pad. Adjustable trigger. Weight is about 7.5 lbs.

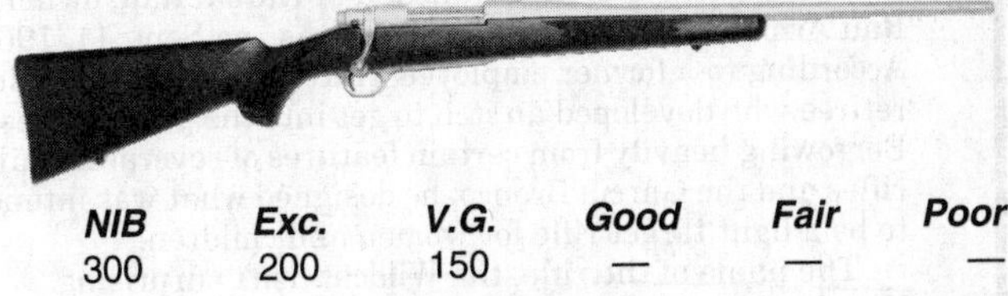

NIB	Exc.	V.G.	Good	Fair	Poor
300	200	150	—	—	—

RASHID

Egypt

Rashid Carbine

A gas-operated 7.62x39mm caliber semi-automatic carbine with a 20.5" barrel and 10-round integral magazine. Fitted with a folded bayonet similar to that found on the Russian SKS. Blued finish and hardwood stock. This rifle is based upon the Swedish Ljungman.

Courtesy Richard M. Kumor, Sr.

Exc.	V.G.	Good	Fair	Poor
450	375	300	150	100

RAST & GASSER

SEE—Gasser

RAU ARMS CORP.

El Dorado, Kansas

Wildcat

Single-shot pivoting-barrel .22 rimfore rifle with skeletonized stock with walnut or mahogany inset. Forend acts as extractor. Similar in overall look to FIE/Garcia Bronco. Mfd. 1969-1970 with c.2500-3000 produced. Later produced by Mountain Arms (*q.v.*).

Wildcat Model 500

Blued with walnut stock insert.

NIB	Exc.	V.G.	Good	Fair	Poor
300	200	150	100	75	45

Wildcat Model 600 Deluxe

Chrome finish with mahogany stock insert.

NIB	Exc.	V.G.	Good	Fair	Poor
325	225	175	125	95	50

RAVELL

Barcelona, Spain

Maxim Double Rifle

A Holland & Holland-styled sidelock double-barrel rifle available in either .375 Holland & Holland or 9.3x74R with 23" barrels having express sights. Double triggers and automatic ejectors. The sidelocks and mounts engraved, stock of well figured walnut normally fitted with a recoil pad.

NIB	Exc.	V.G.	Good	Fair	Poor
4500	3500	2750	1850	1250	850

RAVEN ARMS

Industry, California

P-25

A .25 caliber semi-automatic pistol with a 2.75" barrel and 6-round magazine. Available with a blued, chrome or nickel-plated finish and walnut grips. Manufacture ceased in 1984.

THE RAU WILDCAT

DAN SHIDELER

Up near the top of any list of America's Forgotten Firearms must be the Rau Wildcat.

The Rau Wildcat was kind of an upscale version of the increasingly collectible Garcia Bronco single-shot rifle and shared the Bronco's skeleton stock, slabby little receiver and pivoting barrel extension. But hanging beneath the Wildcat's barrel is a corncob forend that looks for all the world like an old Winchester .22 pump handle. It's not, of course; it's simply the operating handle for the extractor.

The Wildcat differs in a few key respects from the Bronco. For one thing, its skeletonized buttstock is made of heavy-gauge wire, not a zinc casting, and it's filled with a boardlike, walnut-stained panel. Whereas the Garcia's cocking handle looked like a second trigger, the Wildcat's was a more conventional serrated knob on the right side of the receiver. And, unlike the Bronco—in which you unlocked the action by pulling back on the trigger-like handle—the Wildcat's barrel was locked shut simply by a spring-loaded ball detent.

The Wildcat was the brainchild of Harold Rau, owner of Rau Arms, founded in El Dorado, Kans., on Sept. 11, 1969. According to a former employee, Harold Rau was a Florida retiree who developed an itch to get into the gun business. Borrowing heavily from certain features of several Hamilton rifles and the Garcia Bronco, he designed what was intended to be a light target rifle for women and children.

The name of the rifle, the Wildcat, isn't surprising. Kansas State University, home of the Wildcats, is only about 100 miles from El Dorado. The Wildcat came in two models: the Wildcat 500 (blued with walnut stock) and the Model 600 Deluxe (with a chrome-plated wire and mahogany stock). The actions and receivers were actually built in Oklahoma City, Okla., with final assembly taking place in El Dorado. The finished guns sold for around $20 for the standard version and a few bucks more for the deluxe.

It isn't clear how many Wildcats were made; mine is No. 547. Known serial numbers range close to 3,000. Model 500s had an "A" prefix, Model 600s a "D" prefix. Harold Rau planned on building a .22 revolver, too, but it never got past the prototype stage.

Rau backed out of the business in August 1970, selling the company to Precision Industries (also known as Mountain Arms) of Ozark, Missouri. Rau Arms was formally delisted as a Kansas corporation on Dec. 15, 1970, and the factory in El Dorado was emptied out sometime in 1971. Precision Industries/Mountain Arms apparently continued producing Wildcats under the Rau Arms name from 1971 to 1975, at which time the rifle became known as the Mountain Arms Wildcat.

Mountain Arms seems not to have been a well-documented enterprise, but thanks to our friends at the U.S. Bureau of Alcohol, Tobacco, Firearms and Explosives, we can tell precisely how many Mountain Arms Wildcats were made before the company fizzled out in 1978. They built 496 in 1975, 1,782 in 1976, hit a high of 3,649 in 1977 and finished up with 316 in 1978, for a total of 6,243 Mountain Arms Wildcats.

Mountain Arms introduced several changes to the Wildcat, including a takedown model and plastic stock inserts. Production seems to have been a rather hit-or-miss affair, at least as the company was dwindling down, because some Mountain Arms Wildcats have been reported as being new in the box but missing stock inserts or other parts.

Few Wildcats—Rau Arms or Mountain Arms varieties—enter the used gun market, so it's a bit difficult to assign value to them. Pristine Rau Arms specimens have brought as much as $350 at auction, but that's largely a matter of finding the right buyer. It's safe to say, however, that Wildcats are prime sleepers. After all, 1500 percent appreciation ain't half-bad, even adjusted for inflation!

Exc.	V.G.	Good	Fair	Poor
75	65	50	35	25

MP-25

As above with a die-cast frame and imitation ivory grips.

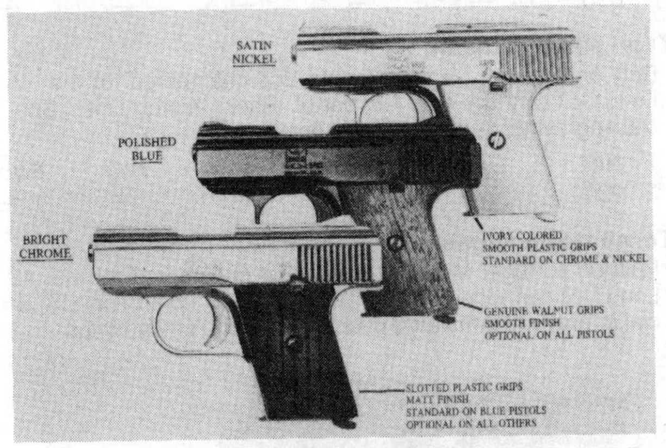

NIB	Exc.	V.G.	Good	Fair	Poor
75	65	55	45	35	25

READ & WATSON

Danville, Virginia

During 1862 and 1863, Read & Watson produced approximately 900 altered Hall rifles for the State of Virginia. These arms were made from Hall rifles issued to the state prior to the Civil War. The original breech loading mechanisms were removed and a brass breech piece or receiver was secured in their place. New buttstocks were fitted and the original Hall furniture was reused. Carbines have an overall length of 42-1/8"; barrel length of 26" and are of .52 caliber. Position and style of serial numbers varies.

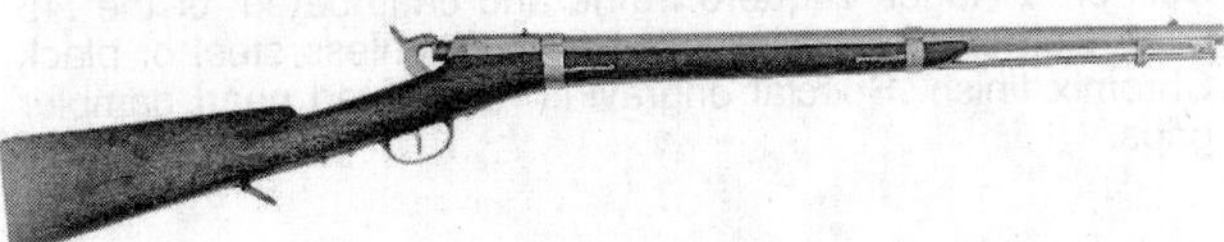

Exc.	V.G.	Good	Fair	Poor
—	—	15000	6500	1000

RECORD-MATCH ANSCHUTZ

Zelia-Mehlis, Germany

Model 210 Free Pistol

A single-shot .22 caliber target pistol using a Martini falling block action. Barrel length 11", set trigger, and adjustable sights. Blued finish with checkered walnut grips and forend. Manufactured during the 1930s.

Exc.	V.G.	Good	Fair	Poor
1250	1000	850	750	400

Model 210A

As above with a lightweight alloy frame.

Exc.	V.G.	Good	Fair	Poor
1200	950	800	700	350

Model 200 Free Pistol

As above without a set trigger.

Exc.	V.G.	Good	Fair	Poor
950	850	750	550	300

REEDER, GARY CUSTOM GUNS

Flagstaff, Arizona

This company offers complete guns as listed below. It also offers custom options built on customer guns as well. An extensive number of custom options is available on any of these models. Prices listed below reflect the standard for that particular model. Retail prices only are listed below due to lack of active secondary market for these limited edition guns. Reeder is a custom manufacturer, or restylist, working primarily with Ruger frames. Only a representative sampling of his works is presented here.

Black Widow

Chambered for the .44 magnum cartridge and fitted with a 4.625" barrel with black Chromix finish. Round butt with Black Cape Buffalo grips. Engraved with Black Widow on each side of the cylinder. Built on a Ruger Super Blackhawk.

NIB	Exc.	V.G.	Good	Fair	Poor
995	—	—	—	—	—

Black Widow II

Similar to the Black Widow but chambered for the .45 Long Colt cartridge. Barrel length is 4.5".

NIB	Exc.	V.G.	Good	Fair	Poor
995	—	—	—	—	—

Arizona Ranger Classic

Built on a Ruger Vaquero this model is chambered for the .45 Long Colt cartridge and fitted with a choice of a 4.5", 5.5", or 7.5" barrel. Blue or stainless steel finish. Special engraving with Stag grips.

NIB	Exc.	V.G.	Good	Fair	Poor
995	—	—	—	—	—

Badlands Classic

Built on a Ruger Vaquero and chambered for the .45 Long Colt cartridge with an extra .45 ACP cylinder. Fitted with a 4.5" barrel. Special engraving. Pearl grips.

NIB	Exc.	V.G.	Good	Fair	Poor
1095	—	—	—	—	—

Cowboy Classic

Built on a Ruger Vaquero and chambered for the .45 Long Colt with a 6.75" barrel. Stainless steel or black Chromix finish. Ivory polymer or pearlite grips. Special engraving.

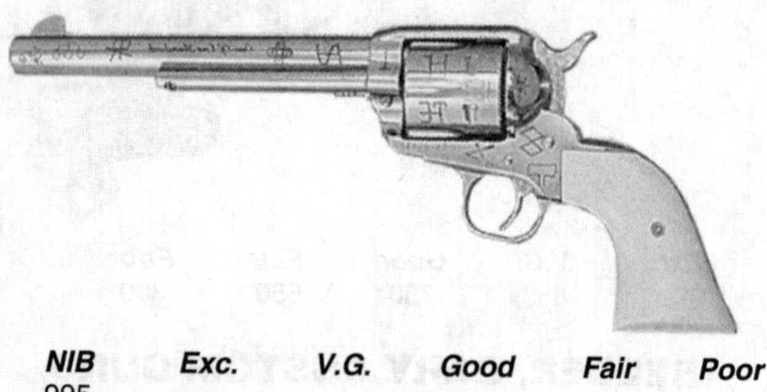

NIB	Exc.	V.G.	Good	Fair	Poor
995	—	—	—	—	—

Cowtown Classic

Built on a Ruger Vaquero and chambered for the .45 Long Colt with 7.5" barrel. Special engraving. Walnut grips.

NIB	Exc.	V.G.	Good	Fair	Poor
995	—	—	—	—	—

Gamblers Classic

Built on a Ruger Vaquero and chambered for the .45 Long Colt with a 2.5" barrel. Stainless steel or black Chromix finish. Choice of black or white pearl grips. No ejector rod. Special engraving.

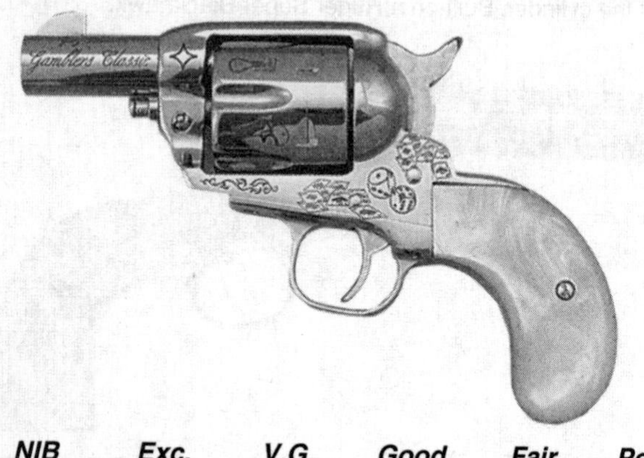

NIB	Exc.	V.G.	Good	Fair	Poor
995	—	—	—	—	—

Lone Star Classic

Built on a Ruger Vaquero and chambered for the .45 Long Colt cartridge with 7.5" barrel. Stainless steel finish. Special engraving and walnut grips with five notches.

NIB	Exc.	V.G.	Good	Fair	Poor
995	—	—	—	—	—

Long Rider Classic

Built on a Ruger Vaquero and chambered for the .45 Long Colt cartridge with 4.5", 5.5", or 7.5" barrel. Special engraving with black Chromix finish. Gunfighter grip with simulated pearl or ivory.

NIB	Exc.	V.G.	Good	Fair	Poor
995	—	—	—	—	—

Texas Ranger Classic

Built on a Ruger Vaquero frame and chambered for the .45 Long Colt cartridge with 4.5", 5.5", or 7.5" barrel. Stainless steel finish. Special engraving. Simulated pearl gunfighter grips.

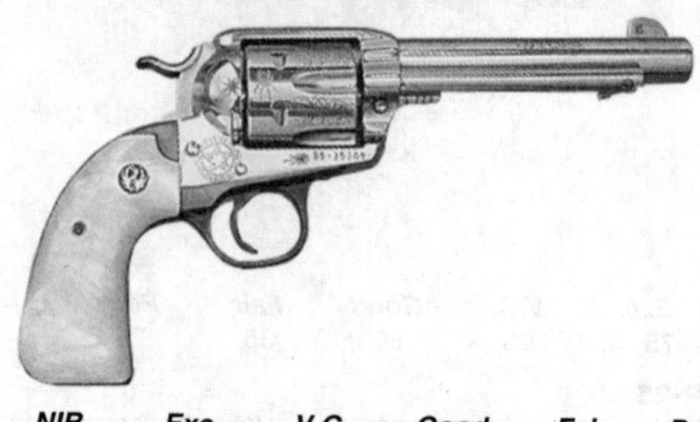

NIB	Exc.	V.G.	Good	Fair	Poor
995	—	—	—	—	—

Trail Rider Classic

Built on a Ruger Vaquero frame and chambered for the .45 Long Colt cartridge with 7.5" barrel. Black Chromix finish. Special engraving. Simulated pearl grips.

NIB	Exc.	V.G.	Good	Fair	Poor
995	—	—	—	—	—

Tombstone Classic

Built on a Ruger Vaquero frame and chambered for the .45 Long Colt cartridge with 3.5" barrel. Black Chromix finish. Special engraving. Simulated pearl or ivory bird's-head grips.

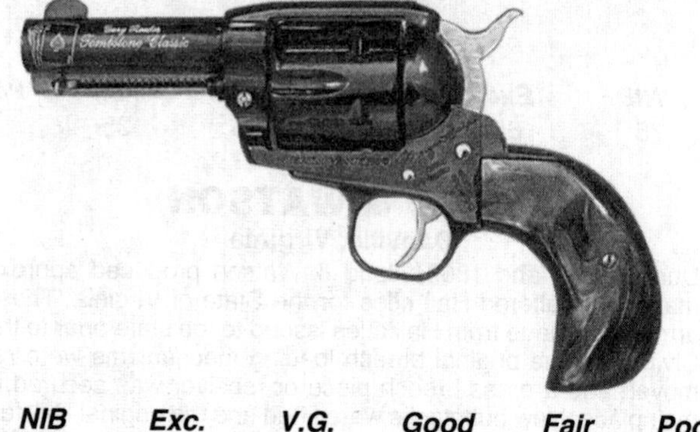

NIB	Exc.	V.G.	Good	Fair	Poor
995	—	—	—	—	—

Doc Holliday Classic

Built on a Ruger Vaquero frame and chambered for the .45 Long Colt cartridge with 3.5" barrel. Stainless steel or black Chromix finish. Special engraving. Simulated pearl gambler grips.

NIB	Exc.	V.G.	Good	Fair	Poor
995	—	—	—	—	—

Night Rider

Built on a Ruger Vaquero frame and chambered for the .44-40 cartridge with 7.5" barrel. Black Chromix finish. Special engraving. Stag grips.

NIB	Exc.	V.G.	Good	Fair	Poor
995	—	—	—	—	—

Ultimate Vaquero

Built on a Ruger Vaquero frame and chambered for the .45 Long Colt cartridge with 4" barrel. Stainless steel or black Chromix finish. Special engraving. Simulated pearl gambler grips.

NIB	Exc.	V.G.	Good	Fair	Poor
995	—	—	—	—	—

Ultimate Bisley

Built on a Ruger Vaquero frame and chambered for the .45 Long Colt or .44 magnum cartridge with 4.5", 5.5", 6.5", or 7.5" barrel. Black Chromix finish. Special engraving. Simulated pearl or ivory Bisley grips.

NIB	Exc.	V.G.	Good	Fair	Poor
1095	—	—	—	—	—

Long Colt Hunter

Built on a Ruger Blackhawk frame and chambered for the .45 Long Colt cartridge with 5.5" or 7.5" barrel. Stainless steel finish. Adjustable rear sight with gold bead front sight. Special engraving. Ebony grips.

NIB	Exc.	V.G.	Good	Fair	Poor
995	—	—	—	—	—

Long Colt Hunter II

Built on a Ruger Redhawk frame and chambered for the .45 Long Colt or .44 Magnum cartridge with 5" barrel. Stainless steel finish. Special engraving. Wooden gunfighter grips.

NIB	Exc.	V.G.	Good	Fair	Poor
995	—	—	—	—	—

African Hunter

Built on a Ruger Bisley or Super Blackhawk frame and chambered for the .475 or .500 Linebaugh cartridge with 6" barrel. Available with or without muzzlebrake. Adjustable rear sight and interchangeable front sights. Stainless steel or black Chromix finish. Special engraving. Ebony grips.

NIB	Exc.	V.G.	Good	Fair	Poor
1195	—	—	—	—	—

Ultimate 41

Built on a Ruger Blackhawk frame and chambered for the .41 magnum or .41 GNR cartridge with 4.5", 5.5", or 7.5" barrel. Unfluted cylinder. Stainless steel finish. Adjustable rear sights. Special engraving. Ebony grips.

NIB	Exc.	V.G.	Good	Fair	Poor
1295	—	—	—	—	—

Coyote Classic

Built on a Ruger frame and chambered for the .22 Hornet, .22 K Hornet, .218 Bee, .218 Mashburn Bee, .17 Ackley Bee, .17 Ackley Hornet, .256 Winchester, and .25-20 with 8" barrel. Adjustable rear sight and drilled and tapped for scope mount. Black Chromix or stainless steel finish. Special engraving. Laminated cherry grips.

NIB	Exc.	V.G.	Good	Fair	Poor
995	—	—	—	—	—

Classic Hunter

Built on a Ruger Vaquero frame and chambered for the .475 Linebaugh cartridge with heavy 6" barrel. Black Chromix finish. Special engraving. Laminated ironwood, cherry, or walnut gunfighter grips.

NIB	Exc.	V.G.	Good	Fair	Poor
1295	—	—	—	—	—

Alaskan Grizzly

Built on a Ruger Vaquero frame and chambered for the .475 or .500 Linebaugh cartridge with customer's choice of barrel.

Black Chromix or stainless steel finish. Special engraving. Horn or black laminated gunfighter grips.

NIB	Exc.	V.G.	Good	Fair	Poor
1195	—	—	—	—	—

Ultimate Back Up 2

Built on a Ruger Blackhawk or Super Blackhawk frame and chambered for the .475 or .500 Linebaugh cartridge with 3.5" ported barrel. Stainless steel finish. Special engraving. Laminated wood or Buffalo horn grips.

NIB	Exc.	V.G.	Good	Fair	Poor
1295	—	—	—	—	—

Montana Hunter

Built on a Ruger Blackhawk or Super Blackhawk frame and chambered for the .45 Long Colt or .44 Magnum cartridge with customer's choice of barrel. Stainless steel finish. Special engraving. Laminated gunfighter grips.

NIB	Exc.	V.G.	Good	Fair	Poor
995	—	—	—	—	—

Alaskan Survivalist

Built on a Ruger Redhawk frame and chambered for the .45 Long Colt or .44 Magnum cartridge with 3" barrel. Adjustable rear sight. Stainless steel finish. Special engraving. Ebony round butt grips.

NIB	Exc.	V.G.	Good	Fair	Poor
995	—	—	—	—	—

American Hunter

Built on a Winchester Model 94 big bore frame and chambered for the .444 Marlin cartridge. Black Chromix finish. Ghost ring rear sight. Special engraving. Checkering walnut stock.

NIB	Exc.	V.G.	Good	Fair	Poor
995	—	—	—	—	—

Alaskan Classic

Built on a Marlin Model 1895 frame and chambered for the .45-70 cartridge. Barrel length is 16.5". Black Chromix finish. Ghost ring rear sight. Special engraving. Checkering walnut stock.

NIB	Exc.	V.G.	Good	Fair	Poor
1195	—	—	—	—	—

Buffalo Hunter

Built on a Marlin Model 1895 frame and chambered for the .475 GNR cartridge. Barrel length is 18". Full length magazine tube. Black Chromix finish. Peep rear sight. Special engraving. Checkering walnut stock.

NIB	Exc.	V.G.	Good	Fair	Poor
1250	—	—	—	—	—

Kodiak Hunter

Built on a Contender frame and chambered for the .50 Action Express or .454 Casull cartridge. Barrel length is 10". Black Chromix finish. Adjustable rear sight with barrel band front sight. Special engraving. Walnut grips.

NIB	Exc.	V.G.	Good	Fair	Poor
995	—	—	—	—	—

Ultimate Encore

Built on a Thompson/Center frame and chambered for a variety of big bore cartridges. Fitted with a 15" barrel with muzzle-brake. Black Chromix finish. Ghost ring rear sight. Special engraving.

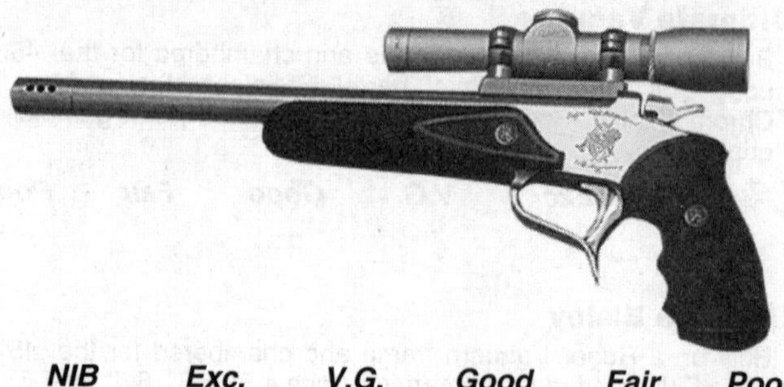

NIB	Exc.	V.G.	Good	Fair	Poor
995	—	—	—	—	—

Ultimate 44

Built on the customer's Ruger Hunter this model features an extra long five-shot cylinder, Bisley hammer and trigger, special grip frame with laminated cherry grips, Magna-Ported barrel, sling swivels, and action job. Game scene engraving.

NIB	Exc.	V.G.	Good	Fair	Poor
1395	—	—	—	—	—

Southern Comfort

Built on the customer's Blackhawk or Super Blackhawk Ruger this revolver features a five-shot cylinder chambered for the .454 Casull cartridge, tear drop hammer, special set back trigger, special grip frame, and light engraving. Barrel length to the customer's choice.

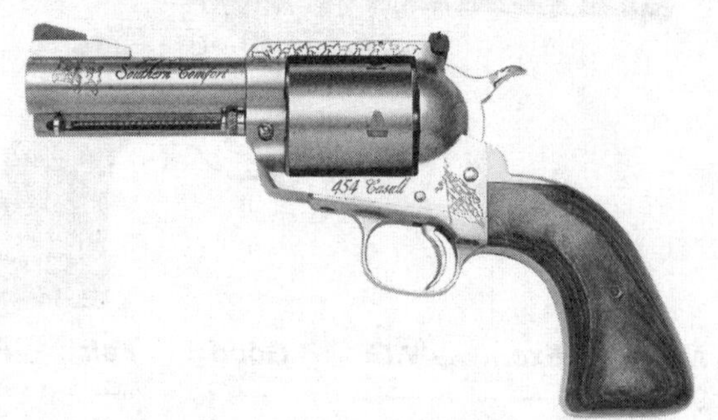

NIB	Exc.	V.G.	Good	Fair	Poor
1295	—	—	—	—	—

Professional Hunter

This model features a number of special features from an extended frame to a five-shot cylinder. Choice of calibers from .224 GNR to .500 Maximum. Fitted with a 8" barrel with heavy taper. Limited production.

NIB	Exc.	V.G.	Good	Fair	Poor
2395	—	—	—	—	—

Ultimate 480

This model is built on the customer's Ruger Blackhawk or Super Blackhawk and is chambered for the .480 cartridge. Cylinder has five rounds, heavy barrel to customer's length, special grip. Blued or stainless steel.

NIB	Exc.	V.G.	Good	Fair	Poor
1195	—	—	—	—	—

Ultimate 500

This model is chambered for the .500 S&W cartridge. Fitted with a heavy five-shot cylinder and barrel length of customer's choice. Black or ivory Micarta grips. Engraved games scenes and other special features.

NIB	Exc.	V.G.	Good	Fair	Poor
2495	—	—	—	—	—

Classic 45

This model is chambered for the .45 Colt, .45 ACP, or .45 Schofield cartridge without full moon clips. It is fitted with a six-shot unfluted cylinder. Special set back trigger, Bisley hammer, Super Blackhawk or Blackhawk stainless steel frame, and other special features.

NIB	Exc.	V.G.	Good	Fair	Poor
1295	—	—	—	—	—

Big 5 Classic

This single-shot rifle is built on the customer's Ruger No. 1 rifle. Chambered for the .500 Jeffery cartridge. Fitted with a heavy barrel to customer's length and muzzlebrake. Tuned action. Buttstock weight added. Game scene engraved.

NIB	Exc.	V.G.	Good	Fair	Poor
1995	—	—	—	—	—

The BMF

This model features a 4" barrel chambered for the .500 Maximum cartridge and Magna-Ported. Bisley grip. Satin stainless steel finish with black Micarta grips. Game scene engraved.

NIB	Exc.	V.G.	Good	Fair	Poor
2395	—	—	—	—	—

Double Duce

This Ruger Single Six revolver is fitted with an eight-shot cylinder and 8" barrel for the .22 WMR cartridge. Longer grip frame with red cherry grips. Game scene engraved.

NIB	Exc.	V.G.	Good	Fair	Poor
1195	—	—	—	—	—

Ultimate Black Widow

This model, built on the customer's Blackhawk, Bisley, or Super Blackhawk Ruger, is chambered for the .475 or .500 Linebaugh. Heavy duty five-shot cylinder. Barrel length to customer's choice. Bisley grip with black Micarta grips. Black Chromix finish.

NIB	Exc.	V.G.	Good	Fair	Poor
1395	—	—	—		

REFORM

Suhl, Germany

August Schuler

Reform Pistol

A 6.35 or .25 ACP four barreled double-action pistol constructed so that the barrel unit rises upward when the trigger is pulled. It superficially resembles a semi-automatic pistol. Blued with hard rubber grips. Manufactured between 1906 and about 1913.

Exc.	V.G.	Good	Fair	Poor
900	675	450	275	175

REICHS REVOLVER

Germany

Model 1879

Exc.	V.G.	Good	Fair	Poor
600	500	375	250	175

Model 1883

Exc.	V.G.	Good	Fair	Poor
500	400	325	225	150

REID, JAMES

New York, New York

Model 1 Revolver

A spur trigger .22 caliber revolver with a 3.5" octagonal barrel and 7-shot unfluted cylinder. Blued with walnut grips. The barrel marked "J. Reid, New York." Approximately 500 were manufactured between 1862 and 1865.

Exc.	V.G.	Good	Fair	Poor
—	—	850	350	100

Model 2 Revolver

As above but in .32 caliber, the barrel marked "Address W.P. Irving, 20 Cliff Street. N.Y." or "James P. Fitch. N.Y." Approximately 1,300 were manufactured between 1862 and 1865.

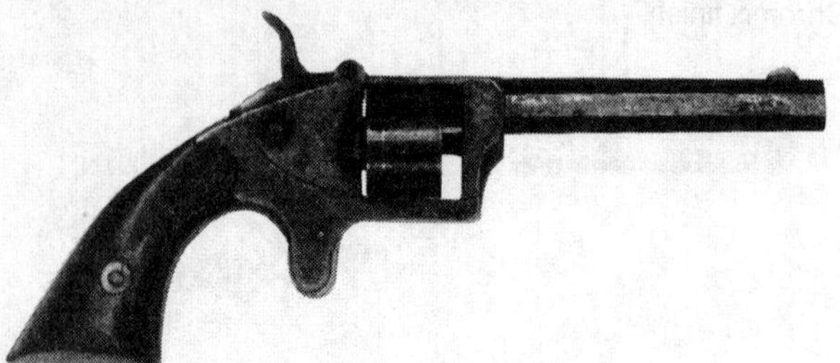

Exc.	V.G.	Good	Fair	Poor
—	—	850	350	100

Model 3 Revolver

Similar to the above, but with the grip angle sharpened. Chambered for the .32 rimfire cartridge with a 4.75" barrel. The cylinder chambers are threaded so that percussion nipples can be inserted. The barrel is marked "J. Reid N.Y. City." Approximately 300 were made between 1862 and 1865.

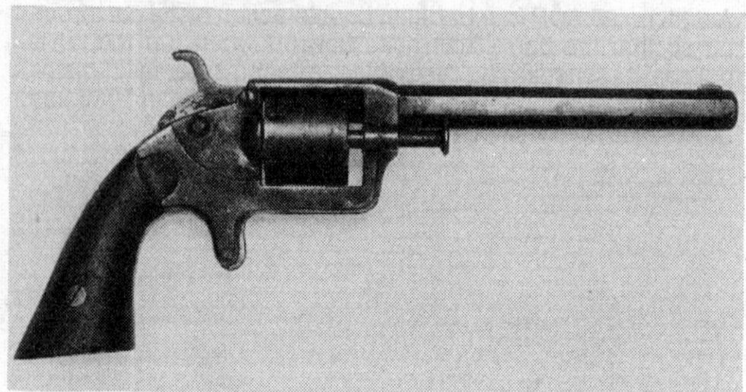

Exc.	V.G.	Good	Fair	Poor
—	—	1250	500	200

Model 4 Revolver

As above with barrel lengths varying from 3.75" to 8". Approximately 1,600 were manufactured between 1862 and 1865.

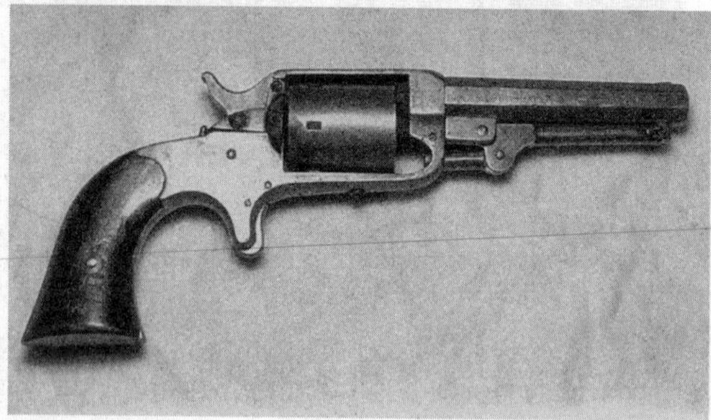

Exc.	V.G.	Good	Fair	Poor
—	—	1250	500	200

"My Friend" Knuckle Duster

A 7-shot .22 caliber revolver constructed entirely of metal and without a barrel. The frame of silver-plated brass or blued iron and marked "My Friend Patd. Dec. 26, 1865." The grip is formed with a finger hole so that the pistol can be used as a set of brass knuckles.

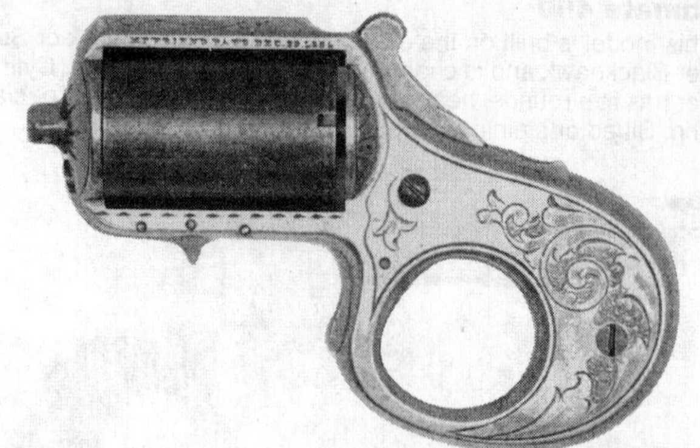

Courtesy W.P. Hallstein III and son Chip

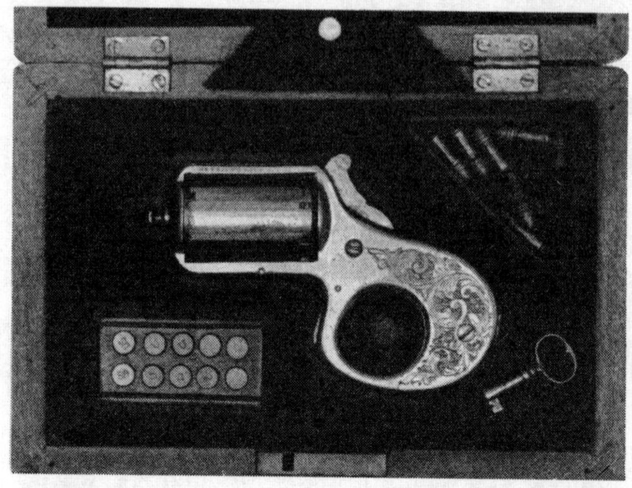

Courtesy W.P. Hallstein III and son Chip

Brass Frame

Exc.	V.G.	Good	Fair	Poor
—	1200	800	500	200

Iron Frame

Exc.	V.G.	Good	Fair	Poor
—	2250	800	500	250

.32 Caliber Knuckle Duster

As above but .32 caliber. Approximately 3,400 were manufactured between 1869 and 1884.

Brass Frame

Exc.	V.G.	Good	Fair	Poor
—	1500	800	600	200

Iron Frame

Exc.	V.G.	Good	Fair	Poor
—	2250	1300	800	250

.41 Caliber Knuckle Duster

As above but .41 caliber and marked "J. Reid's Derringer." Approximately 300 were manufactured between 1875 and 1878.

Exc.	V.G.	Good	Fair	Poor
—	15000	9000	6500	1500

Model No. 1 Knuckle Duster

As above with a 3" barrel. Approximately 350 were made between 1875 and 1880.

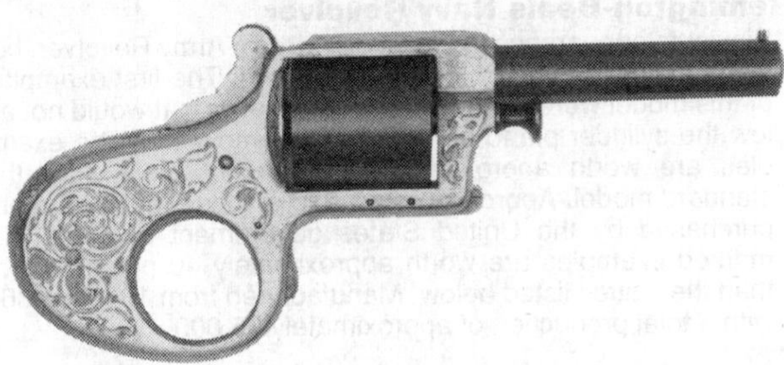

Courtesy W.P. Hallstein III and son Chip

Exc.	V.G.	Good	Fair	Poor
—	2750	1300	850	250

Model No. 2 Knuckle Duster

As above with a 1.75" barrel. Approximately 150 were made between 1875 and 1880.

Exc.	V.G.	Good	Fair	Poor
—	3000	1700	1250	500

Model No. 3 Derringer

A .41 caliber revolver with a 3" octagonal barrel and 5-shot fluted cylinder. The frame silver-plated and the barrel as well as cylinder blued. Approximately 75 were made between 1880 and 1884.

Exc.	V.G.	Good	Fair	Poor
—	2500	1200	950	350

Model No. 4 Derringer

As above but with a brass frame and walnut grips and marked "Reid's Extra." Approximately 200 were made during 1883 and 1884.

Exc.	V.G.	Good	Fair	Poor
—	1500	1000	700	250

New Model Knuckle Duster

Similar to the Model 2 with a 2" barrel and 5-shot cylinder. The barrel marked "Reid's New Model .32 My Friend." Approximately 150 were made in 1884.

Exc.	V.G.	Good	Fair	Poor
—	1500	1050	650	250

REISING ARMS CO.

Hartford, Connecticut

Standard Model

A .22 caliber semi-automatic pistol with a hinged 6.5" barrel and 10-round magazine. Standard finish is blued, however, nickel-plated versions are known. The slide marked with the company's name and patent dates. Bakelite grips impressed with a bear's head and the motto "Reising, It's A Bear." Manufactured in both New York City and Hartford, during the 1920s. **CAUTION: High-velocity ammunition should not be used in these pistols.**

Courtesy John J. Stimson, Jr.

New York Manufacture

Exc.	V.G.	Good	Fair	Poor
500	400	300	200	100

Hartford Manufacture

Exc.	V.G.	Good	Fair	Poor
450	350	275	175	100

Remington. COUNTRY

REMINGTON ARMS COMPANY, INC.

Madison, North Carolina

Founded in 1816 by Eliphalet Remington, this company has the distinction of being the oldest firearms manufacturing firm in the United States. Since 1856 it has been known by four different names: between 1856 and 1888, E. Remington & Sons; 1888-1910, Remington Arms Company; 1910-1925, Remington Arms U.M.C. Company (Union Metallic Cartridge Company); and 1925 to the present, Remington Arms Company.

1st Model Remington-Beals Revolver

A .31 caliber 5-shot percussion revolver with a 3" octagonal barrel. The cylinder turning mechanism is mounted on the left outside frame. Blued, case hardened, silver-plated, brass trigger guard and gutta-percha grips. The barrel marked, "F. Beal's Patent, June 24, '56 & May 26, '57" and the frame, "Remington's Ilion, N.Y." Approximately 5,000 were manufactured in 1857 and 1858.

Courtesy Milwaukee Public Museum, Milwaukee, Wisconsin

Exc.	V.G.	Good	Fair	Poor
—	1000	600	300	150

2nd Model Remington-Beals Revolver

A spur trigger .31 caliber 5-shot percussion revolver with a 3" octagonal barrel. Blued, case hardened with a squared gutta-percha grip. The barrel marked, "Beals Patent 1856 & 57, Manufactured by Remingtons Ilion, N.Y." Approximately 1,000 were manufactured between 1858 and 1860.

Exc.	V.G.	Good	Fair	Poor
—	8000	3000	1000	300

3rd Model Remington-Beals Revolver

A .31 caliber 5-shot percussion revolver with a 4" octagonal barrel. A loading lever mounted beneath the barrel. Blued, case hardened with gutta-percha grips. The barrel marked, "Beals Pat. 1856, 57, 58 and also "Manufactured by Remingtons, Ilion, N.Y." Approximately 1,500 were manufactured in 1859 and 1860.

Courtesy Milwaukee Public Museum, Milwaukee, Wisconsin

Exc.	V.G.	Good	Fair	Poor
—	2000	1250	500	200

Remington-Rider Revolver

A double-action .31 caliber percussion revolver with a 3" barrel and 5-shot cylinder. Most of these revolvers were blued but a few were nickel-plated, case hardened with gutta-percha grips. This model is also encountered altered to .32 rimfire. The barrel marked, "Manufactured by Remingtons, Ilion, N.Y., Riders Pt. Aug. 17, 1858, May 3, 1859." Approximately 20,000 were manufactured between 1860 and 1873.

Exc.	V.G.	Good	Fair	Poor
—	1150	500	200	100

NOTE: The cartridge variation is worth approximately 20 percent less than the original percussion version.

Remington-Beals Army Revolver

A .44 caliber percussion revolver with an 8" barrel and 6-shot cylinder. Blued, case hardened with walnut grips. The barrel marked "Beals Patent Sept. 14, 1858 Manufactured by Remington's Ilion, New York." Approximately 2,500 were manufactured between 1860 and 1862.

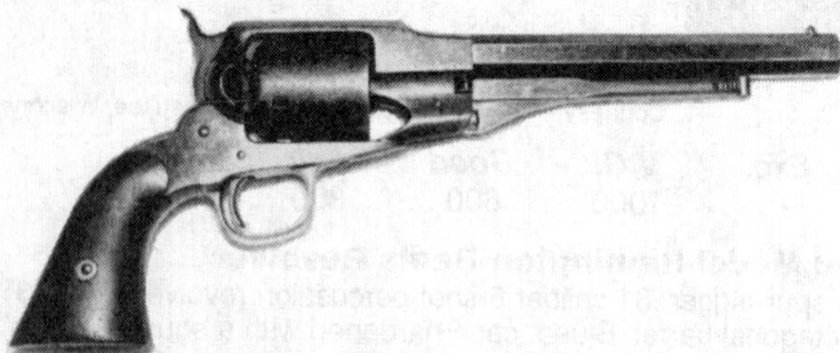

Exc.	V.G.	Good	Fair	Poor
—	3750	1500	500	200

NOTE: A martially marked example is extremely rare and would be worth approximately 35 percent additional.

Remington-Beals Navy Revolver

Similar in appearance to Remington-Beals Army Revolver, but in .36 caliber with a 7.5" octagonal barrel. The first examples of this model were fitted with a loading lever that would not allow the cylinder pin to be completely removed. These examples are worth approximately 80 percent more than the standard model. Approximately 1,000 of these revolvers were purchased by the United States government and martially marked examples are worth approximately 40 percent more than the values listed below. Manufactured from 1860 to 1862 with a total production of approximately 15,000.

Courtesy Wallis & Wallis, Lewes, Sussex, England

Exc.	V.G.	Good	Fair	Poor
—	2500	1000	400	200

1861 Army Revolver

A .44 caliber percussion revolver with an 8" octagonal barrel and 6-shot cylinder. The loading lever is cut with a slot so that the cylinder pin can be drawn forward without the lever being lowered. Blued, case hardened with walnut grips. The barrel marked "Patented Dec. 17, 1861 Manufactured by Remington's, Ilion, N.Y." Some examples were converted to .46 caliber rimfire cartridge, and would be worth approximately 25 percent more than the original, martially marked, standard percussion model. Approximately 12,000 were manufactured in 1862. This model is also known as the "Old Army Model."

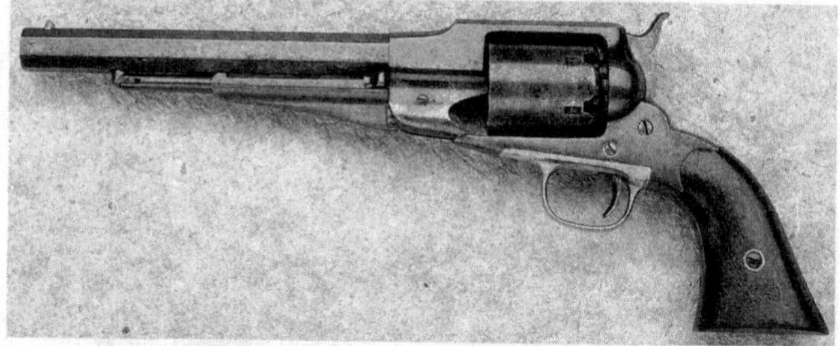

Paul Goodwin photo

Exc.	V.G.	Good	Fair	Poor
—	2500	1000	500	200

1861 Navy Revolver

As above, but .36 caliber with a 7.25" octagonal barrel. Blued, case hardened with walnut grips. This model is also found altered to .38 metallic cartridge. Cartridge examples are worth approximately 35 percent less than the percussion versions. Approximately 8,000 were manufactured in 1862.

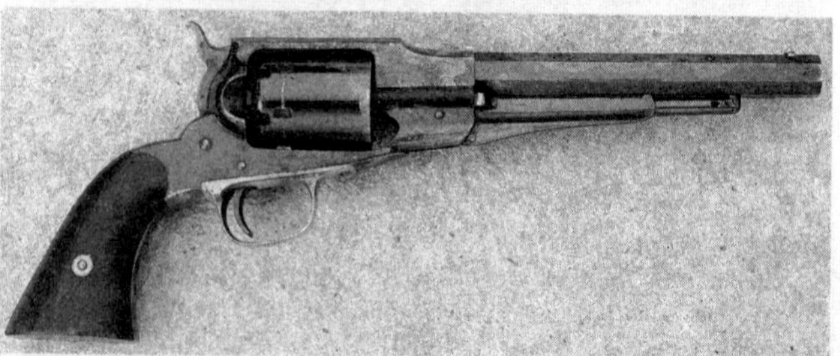

Paul Goodwin photo

Exc.	V.G.	Good	Fair	Poor
—	2250	800	600	400

NOTE: Add 25 percent for martial.

New Model Army Revolver

A .44 caliber 6-shot percussion revolver with an 8" octagonal barrel. Blued, case hardened with walnut grips. The barrel marked "Patented Sept. 14, 1858 E. Remington & Sons, Ilion, New York, U.S.A. New Model." Approximately 132,000 were made between 1863 and 1873.

Standard Model—Military Version

Exc.	V.G.	Good	Fair	Poor
—	2500	1600	1000	400

Civilian Model—No Government Inspector's Markings

Exc.	V.G.	Good	Fair	Poor
—	2000	1250	800	400

.44 or .46 Cartridge Conversion

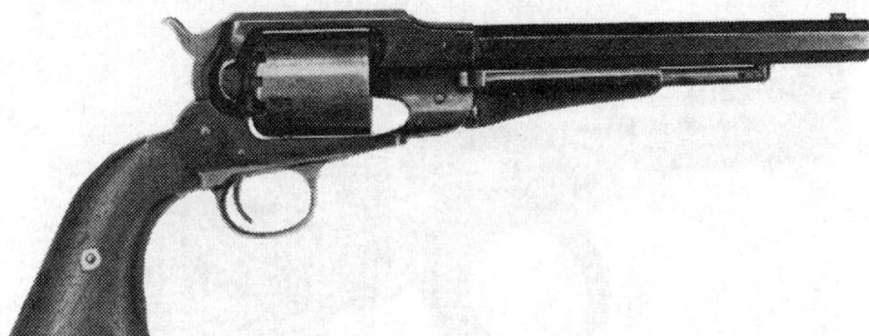

Courtesy Milwaukee Public Museum, Milwaukee, Wisconsin

Exc.	V.G.	Good	Fair	Poor
—	2000	1250	800	400

New Model Navy Revolver

As above, but .36 caliber with a 7.23" octagonal barrel. Approximately 22,000 were made between 1863 and 1875.

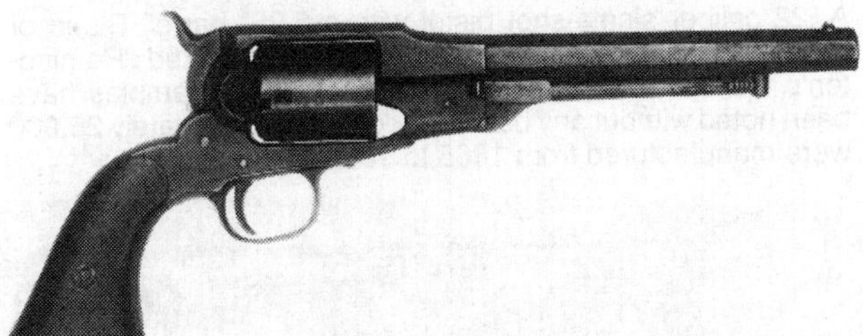

Courtesy Milwaukee Public Museum, Milwaukee, Wisconsin

Military Version

Exc.	V.G.	Good	Fair	Poor
3250	1200	900	500	200

Civilian Version

Exc.	V.G.	Good	Fair	Poor
2500	1000	700	400	150

.38 Cartridge Conversion—1873 to 1888

Exc.	V.G.	Good	Fair	Poor
2000	1300	800	400	150

New Model Single-Action Belt Revolver

As above, but with a 6.5" barrel. Blued or nickel-plated, case hardened with walnut grips. This model is sometimes encountered altered to .38 cartridge. Cartridge examples are worth approximately 25 percent less than the values listed below. Approximately 3,000 were made between 1863 and 1873.

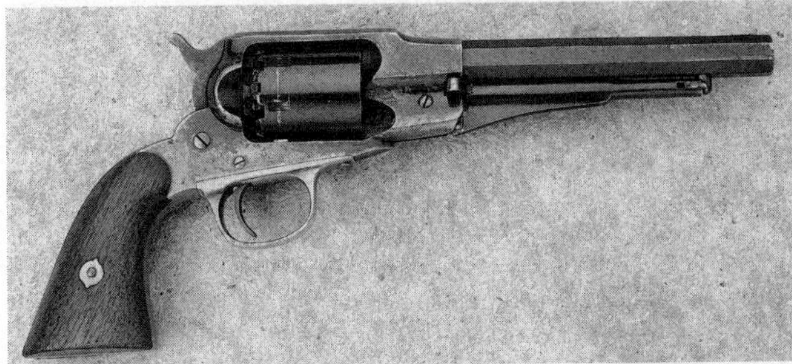

Paul Goodwin photo

Exc.	V.G.	Good	Fair	Poor
—	1800	800	400	200

NOTE: Blued models will command a premium.

Remington-Rider Double-Action Belt Revolver

A double-action .36 caliber percussion revolver with a 6.5" octagonal barrel marked, "Manufactured by Remington's, Ilion, N.Y. Rider's Pt. Aug. 17, 1858, May 3, 1859." Blued or nickel-plated, case hardened with walnut grips. This model is also found altered to cartridge and such examples would be worth approximately 20 percent less than the values listed below. Several hundred of this model were made with fluted cylinders and are worth a premium of about 25 percent. Approximately 5,000 were made between 1863 and 1873.

Courtesy Milwaukee Public Museum, Milwaukee, Wisconsin

Exc.	V.G.	Good	Fair	Poor
—	2500	1000	400	200

New Model Police Revolver

A .36 caliber percussion revolver with octagonal barrels ranging from 3.5" to 6.5" and with a 5-shot cylinder. Blued or nickel-plated, case hardened with walnut grips. This model is also found altered to cartridge and such examples would be worth approximately 20 percent less than the values listed below. Approximately 18,000 were manufactured between 1863 and 1873.

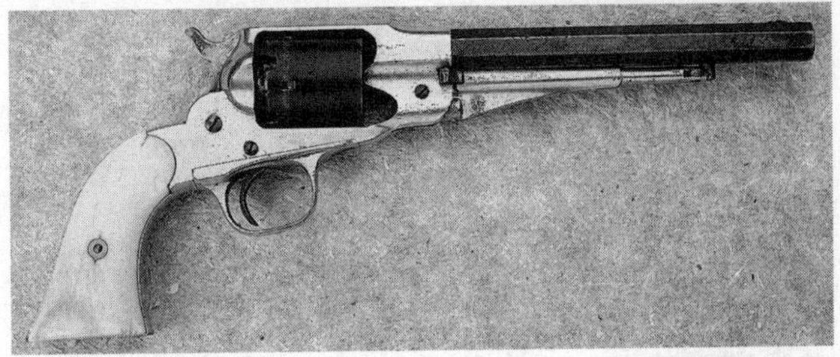

Paul Goodwin photo

Exc.	V.G.	Good	Fair	Poor
—	1400	800	300	150

NOTE: Blued models will command a premium.

New Model Pocket Revolver

A .31 caliber spur trigger percussion revolver with octagonal barrels ranging from 3" to 4.5" in length and a 5-shot cylinder. Blued or nickel-plated, case hardened, walnut grips. The barrel marked, "Patented Sept. 14, 1858, March 17, 1863 E. Remington & Sons, Ilion, New York U.S.A. New Model." Approximately 25,000 were manufactured between 1863 and 1873.

1st Version

Brass frame and trigger.

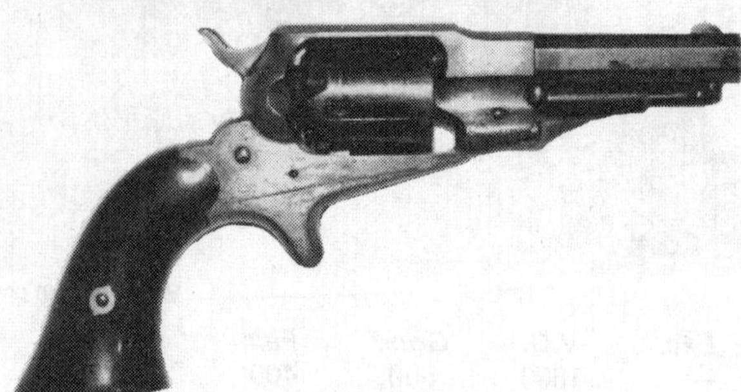

Exc.	V.G.	Good	Fair	Poor
—	2500	1200	500	200

2nd Version

Iron frame, brass trigger.

Exc.	V.G.	Good	Fair	Poor
—	1200	800	400	200

3rd Version

Iron frame, iron trigger.

Exc.	V.G.	Good	Fair	Poor
—	1000	800	400	200

.32 Cartridge Conversion

Exc.	V.G.	Good	Fair	Poor
—	1000	800	400	200

NOTE: Add 15 percent for blued models.

Remington-Rider Derringer

A small, silver-plated brass single-shot .17 caliber percussion pistol with a 3" round barrel. The barrel marked, "Rider's Pt. Sept. 13, 1859." Approximately 1,000 were manufactured between 1860 and 1863. Beware of fakes.

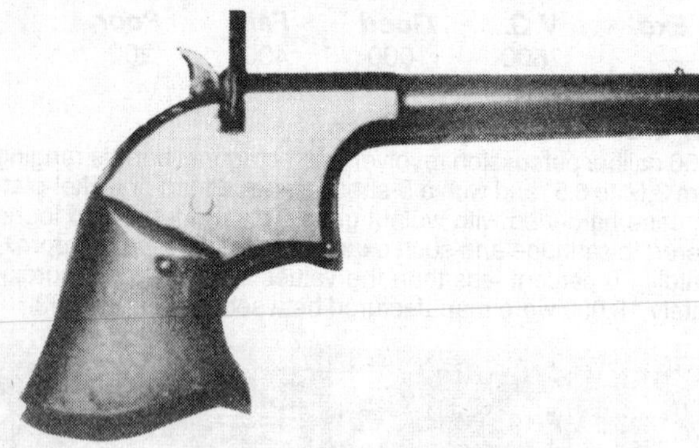

Exc.	V.G.	Good	Fair	Poor
—	6250	3000	900	300

Zig-Zag Derringer

A 6-shot .22 caliber revolving barrel pocket pistol with barrels 3.25" in length. The barrels are cut with zigzag grooves, which are part of the revolving mechanism. The trigger is formed as a ring that when moved forward and rearward turns the barrels and cocks the internal hammer. The barrel group marked "Elliot's Patent Aug. 17, 1858 May 29, 1860" as well as "Manufactured by Remington's Ilion, N.Y." Approximately 1,000 were manufactured in 1861 and 1862.

Paul Goodwin photo

Exc.	V.G.	Good	Fair	Poor
—	3250	1500	600	300

Remington-Elliot Derringer

A 5-shot .22 or 4-shot .32 caliber pepperbox pistol with a revolving firing pin. Blued or nickel-plated with hard rubber grips. The barrel group marked "Manufactured by E. Remington & Sons, Ilion, N.Y. Elliot's Patents May 19, 1860 - Oct.1, 1861." Approximately 25,000 were manufactured between 1863 and 1888.

5-shot .22 caliber

Exc.	V.G.	Good	Fair	Poor
—	1100	650	400	150

4-shot .32 caliber

Courtesy W.P. Hallstein III and son Chip

Exc.	V.G.	Good	Fair	Poor
—	950	550	400	150

Vest Pocket Pistol

A .22 caliber single-shot pistol with a 3.25" barrel. Blued or nickel-plated with walnut grips. The barrel marked "Remington's Ilion, N.Y. Patent Oct. 1, 1861." Early examples have been noted without any barrel markings. Approximately 25,000 were manufactured from 1865 to 1888.

Paul Goodwin photo

Exc.	V.G.	Good	Fair	Poor
—	800	400	200	100

NOTE: Add a 35 percent premium for blued models.

Large-Bore Vest Pocket Pistol

As above, but in .30, .32, or .41 caliber with barrel lengths of either 3.5" or 4". Blued or nickel-plated with walnut or rosewood grips. The barrel markings as above except for the addition of the patent date, November 15, 1864. The smaller caliber versions are worth approximately 20 percent more than the .41 caliber. Approximately 10,000 were made from 1865 to 1888.

Exc.	V.G.	Good	Fair	Poor
—	1250	600	300	150

NOTE: Add a 35 percent premium for blued models.

Remington-Elliot Single-Shot Derringer

A .41 caliber single-shot pistol with a 2.5" round barrel. Blued or nickel-plated with walnut, ivory, or pearl grips. The barrel marked "Remingtons, Ilion, N.Y. Elliot Pat. Aug. 27, 1867." Approximately 10,000 were manufactured between 1867 and 1888.

Exc.	V.G.	Good	Fair	Poor
—	1500	700	350	125

NOTE: Add a 35 percent premium for blued models.

Remington Over-and-Under Derringer

A double-barrel .41 caliber pocket pistol with 3" round barrels that pivot upward for loading. There is a lock bar to release the barrels on the right side of the frame. The firing pin raises and lowers automatically to fire each respective barrel. It has a spur trigger and bird's-head grip. The finish is either blued or nickel-plated; and it is featured with walnut, rosewood, or checkered hard rubber grips. Examples with factory pearl or ivory grips would be worth a small premium. Approximately 150,000 were manufactured between 1866 and 1935.

Early Type I

Manufactured without an extractor, this type is marked "E." Remington & Sons, Ilion, N.Y." on one side and "Elliot's Patent Dec. 12, 1865" on the other side of the barrel rib. Only a few hundred were manufactured in 1866.

Exc.	V.G.	Good	Fair	Poor
—	2250	800	400	200

NOTE: Add a 25 percent premium for blued models.

Type I Mid-Production

As above, but fitted with an extractor. Manufactured in the late 1860s.

Exc.	V.G.	Good	Fair	Poor
—	2500	1000	500	250

NOTE: Add a 25 percent premium for blued models.

Type I Late Production

Fitted with an automatic extractor and marked on the top of the barrel rib. Manufactured from the late 1860s to 1888.

Exc.	V.G.	Good	Fair	Poor
—	2000	900	400	200

NOTE: Add a 25 percent premium for blued models.

Type II

Marked "Remington Arms Co., Ilion, N.Y." on the barrel rib. Manufactured between 1888 and 1911.

Exc.	V.G.	Good	Fair	Poor
—	1750	800	400	200

NOTE: Add a 25 percent premium for blued models.

Type III

Marked "Remington Arms - U.M.C. Co., Ilion, N.Y." on the barrel rib. Manufactured between 1912 and 1935.

Exc.	V.G.	Good	Fair	Poor
—	1600	800	400	200

NOTE: For Type III models, blue or nickel prices are the same.

Remington-Rider Magazine Pistol

A 5-shot .32 caliber magazine pistol with a spur trigger and 3" octagonal barrel. The magazine is located beneath the barrel and can be loaded from the front. Blued, nickel-plated or case hardened with walnut, pearl, or ivory grips. The barrel marked "E. Remington & Sons, Ilion, N.Y. Riders Pat. Aug. 15, 1871." Approximately 10,000 were manufactured between 1871 and 1888.

Courtesy William F. Krause

Exc.	V.G.	Good	Fair	Poor
—	1800	750	300	150

NOTE: For blued finish add a 50 percent premium.

Model 1865 Navy Rolling Block Pistol

A spur trigger single-shot rolling block .50 caliber rimfire cartridge pistol with an 8.5" round barrel. Blued, case hardened with walnut grips and forend. The barrel marked "Remingtons, Ilion N.Y. U.S.A. Pat. May 3d Nov. 15th, 1864 April 17th, 1866." Examples bearing military inspection marks are worth approximately 25 percent more than the values listed below. Examples are also to be found altered to centerfire cartridge and these are worth approximately 10 percent less than the values listed below. Approximately 6,500 were manufactured between 1866 and 1870.

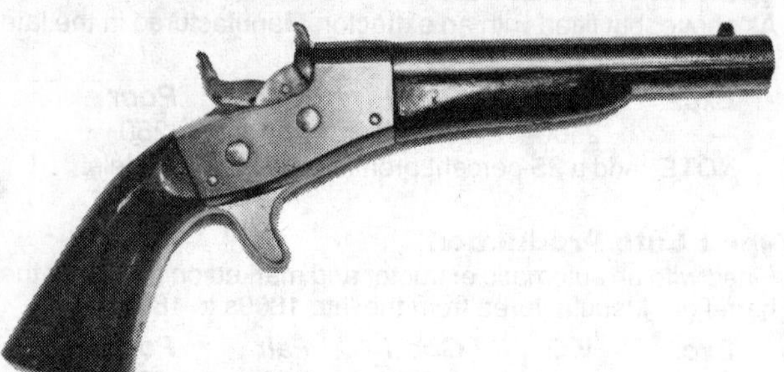

Exc.	V.G.	Good	Fair	Poor
—	2000	1000	600	400

Model 1867 Navy Rolling Block Pistol

A .50 caliber single-shot rolling block pistol with a 7" round barrel. Blued, case hardened with walnut grips and forend. The majority of these pistols were purchased by the United States government and civilian examples without inspection marks are worth approximately 30 percent more than the values listed.

Exc.	V.G.	Good	Fair	Poor
—	1500	800	600	200

Model 1871 Army Rolling Block Pistol

A .50 caliber rolling block single-shot pistol with an 8" round barrel. Blued, case hardened with walnut grips and forend. The distinguishing feature of this model is that it has a rearward extension at the top of the grip and a squared butt. Approximately 6,000 were made between 1872 and 1888. Engraved ivory-stocked versions, as pictured below, will bring considerable premiums.

Exc.	V.G.	Good	Fair	Poor
—	—	1400	800	400

Remington-Smoot No. 1 Revolver

A .30 caliber spur trigger revolver with a 2.75" octagonal barrel and 5-shot fluted cylinder. Blued or nickel-plated with walnut or hard rubber grips. The barrel rib is marked, "E. Remington & Sons, Ilion, N.Y. Pat. W. S. Smoot Oct. 21, 1873." Examples dating from the beginning of production are found with a revolving recoil shield. Such examples would command approximately a 300 percent premium over the values listed.

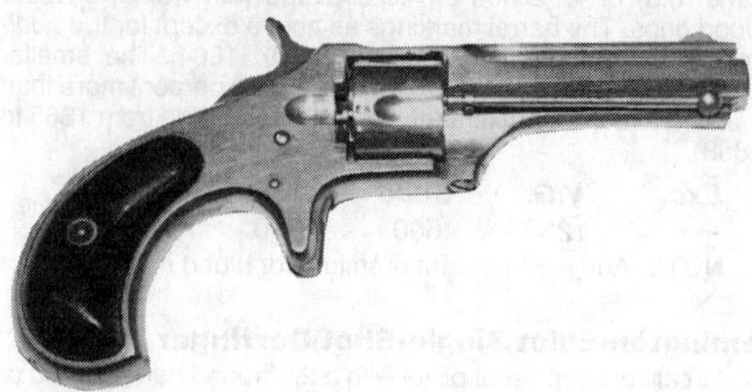

Exc.	V.G.	Good	Fair	Poor
—	1500	1000	600	250

NOTE: For blued finish add a 50 percent premium.

Remington-Smoot No. 2 Revolver

As above, except in .32 caliber; approximately 20,000 were made between 1878 and 1888.

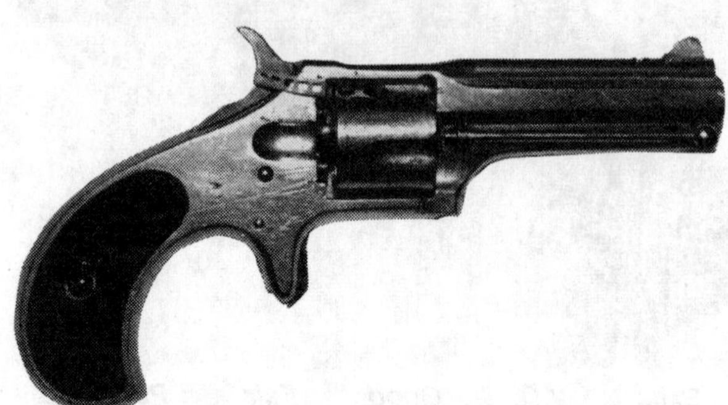

Exc.	V.G.	Good	Fair	Poor
—	800	550	250	100

NOTE: For blued finish add a 50 percent premium.

Remington-Smoot No. 3 Revolver

Two variations of this spur trigger .38 caliber revolver exist. One with a rounded grip and no barrel rib, the other with a squared back, squared butt grip with a barrel rib. Centerfire versions are also known and they are worth approximately 10 percent more than the values listed below. Blued or nickel-plated with hard rubber grips. Approximately 25,000 were made between 1878 and 1888.

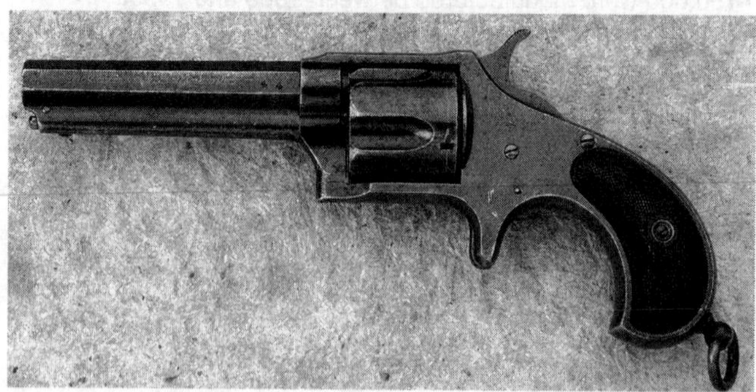

Paul Goodwin photo

Exc.	V.G.	Good	Fair	Poor
—	600	500	300	100

NOTE: For blued finish add a 50 percent premium.

No. 4 Revolver

A .38 or .41 caliber spur trigger revolver with a 2.5" barrel and no ejector rod. Blued or nickel-plated with hard rubber grips. The barrel marked "E. Remington & Sons, Ilion, N.Y." Approximately 10,000 were manufactured between 1877 and 1888.

Paul Goodwin photo

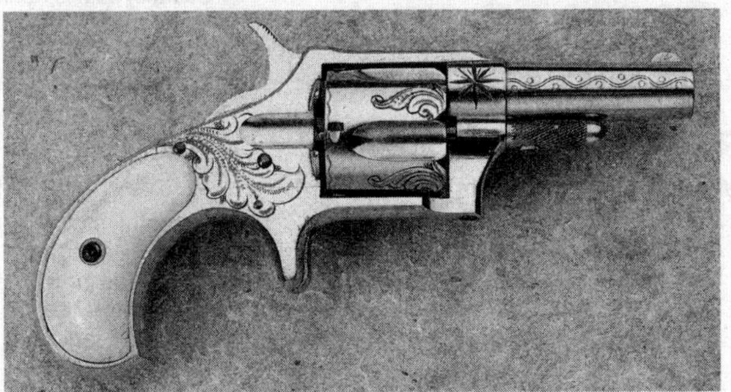

Paul Goodwin photo

Exc.	V.G.	Good	Fair	Poor
—	700	450	200	100

NOTE: For blued finish add a 50 percent premium.

Remington Iroquois Revolver

A .22 caliber spur trigger revolver with a 2.25" barrel and 7-shot cylinder. Blued or nickel-plated with hard rubber grips. The barrel marked "Remington, Ilion, N.Y." and "Iroquois." Some examples of this model will be found without the Remington markings. Approximately 10,000 were manufactured between 1878 and 1888.

Exc.	V.G.	Good	Fair	Poor
—	900	750	350	150

NOTE: For blued finish add a 50 percent premium.

Model 1875 Single-Action Army

A .44 Remington or .44-40 or .45 caliber single-action revolver with a 7.5" barrel. Blued or nickel-plated, case hardened with walnut grips. Some examples are to be found fitted with a lanyard ring at the butt. The barrel marked "E. Remington & Sons Ilion, N.Y. U.S.A." Approximately 25,000 were manufactured between 1875 and 1889.

Courtesy Milwaukee Public Museum, Milwaukee, Wisconsin

Exc.	V.G.	Good	Fair	Poor
—	3250	2200	1500	600

NOTE: Blued version add 40 percent.

Model 1890 Single-Action Army

A .44-40 caliber single-action revolver with a 5.5" or 7.5" barrel and 6-shot cylinder. Blued or nickel-plated with hard rubber grips bearing the monogram "RA" at the top. The barrel marked "Remington Arms Co., Ilion, N.Y." Approximately 2,000 were made between 1891 and 1894. Beware of fakes.

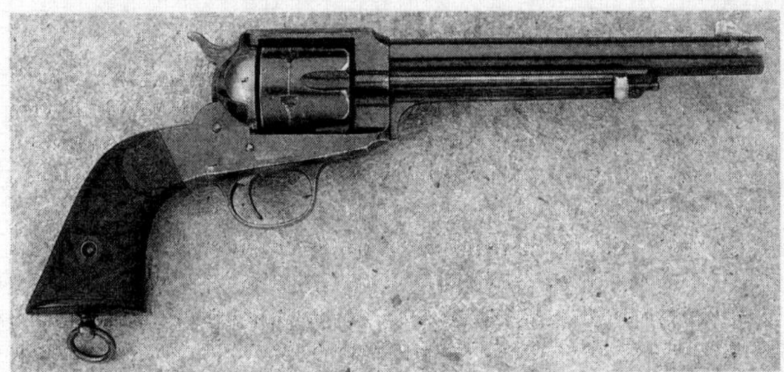

Paul Goodwin photo

Exc.	V.G.	Good	Fair	Poor	
—	9000	4500	2000	900	450

NOTE: Blued version add 40 percent.

Model 1891 Target Rolling Block Pistol

A .22, .25 Stevens, or .32 S&W caliber single-shot rolling block pistol with a 10" half octagonal barrel fitted with target sights. Blued, case hardened with walnut grips and forend. The barrel marked "Remington Arms Co. Ilion, N.Y.," and the frame "Remingtons Ilion N.Y. U.S.A. Pat. May 3 Nov. 15, 1864 April 17, 1866 P S." This is an extremely rare pistol, with slightly more than 100 manufactured between 1892 and 1898. Prospective purchasers are advised to secure a qualified appraisal prior to acquisition.

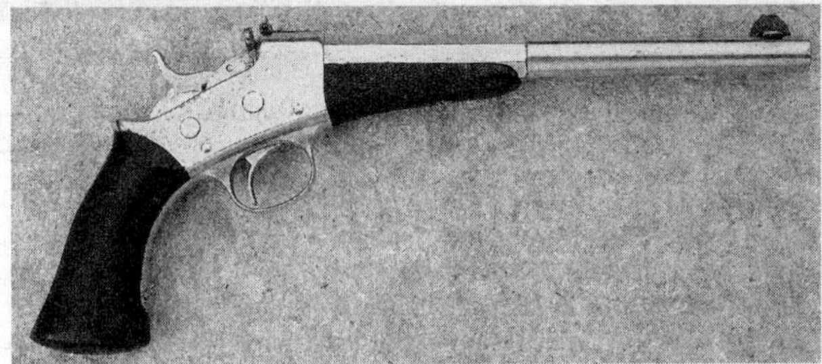

Paul Goodwin photo

Exc.	V.G.	Good	Fair	Poor
—	—	2500	1100	500

Model 1901 Target Rolling Block

As above, with the exception that the bridge block thumb piece has been moved out of the line of sight and the rear sight is mounted on the frame instead of the barrel. Approximately 735 were made between 1901 and 1909. Prospective purchasers are advised to secure a qualified appraisal prior to acquisition.

Paul Goodwin photo

Exc.	V.G.	Good	Fair	Poor
—	—	2500	1100	500

Mark III Signal Pistol

A 10 gauge spur trigger flare pistol with a 9" round barrel. The frame of brass and the barrel of iron finished matte black with walnut grips. The barrel marked "The Remington Arms - Union Metallic Cartridge Co., Inc. Mark III, Remington Bridgeport

This symbol denotes "Sleepers" with rapidly-rising values and/or significant collector potential. 

Works Bridgeport, Connecticut U.S.A." Approximately 25,000 were manufactured between 1915 and 1918.

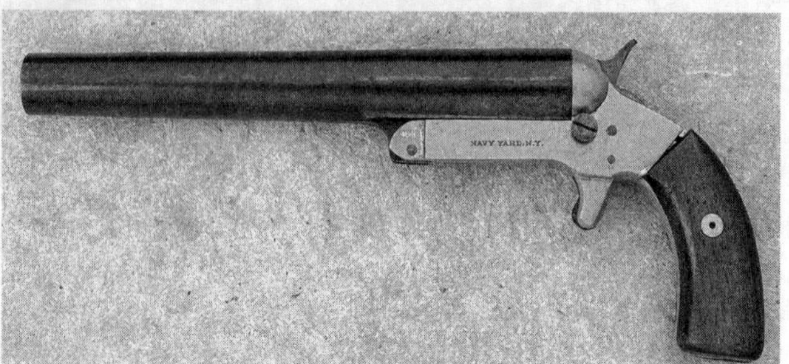

Paul Goodwin photo

Exc.	V.G.	Good	Fair	Poor
—	650	325	75	55

Remington 1911 and 1911A1

See the Colt section of this book for pistols of this type.

IMPORTANT PRICING INFORMATION

Generally a collectible gun MUST have ALL original parts and original finish.

Model 51

A .32 or .380 caliber semi-automatic pistol with a 3.5" barrel and magazines capable of holding either 7 or 8 cartridges depending on the caliber. Blued with hard rubber grips having the legend "Remington UMC" in a circle at the top. The slide marked "The Remington Arms - Union Metallic Cartridge Co., Inc. Remington Ilion Wks. Ilion, N.Y. U.S.A. Pedersen's Patents Pending." Later versions carried a 1920 and a 1921 patent date. The early examples have nine grooves on the slide; later models have 15 grooves with the frame marked "Remington Trademark." Early variations are worth approximately 10 percent more than the values listed below and .32 caliber examples are worth approximately 25 percent additional. Approximately 65,000 were manufactured between 1918 and 1934.

Courtesy Orvel Reichert

Exc.	V.G.	Good	Fair	Poor
—	500	350	125	75

Model 53

Built in 1917 in .45 ACP for the U.S. government test. Similar to the Model 51 except for size and an external hammer. Tested by the US Army and Navy. Overall length is 8.25", weight is about 35 oz., and magazine capacity is 7 rounds.

Courtesy James Rankin

Exc.	V.G.	Good	Fair	Poor
Too Rare To Price				

RIFLES

Model 1841 "Mississippi Rifle"

A .54 caliber percussion rifle with a 33" barrel and full stock secured by two barrel bands. The lock (marked Remington's Herkimer N.Y.) is case hardened, the barrel browned and the furniture of brass. The stock is fitted with a brass patch box on the right side. Approximately 20,000 were made between 1846 and 1855.

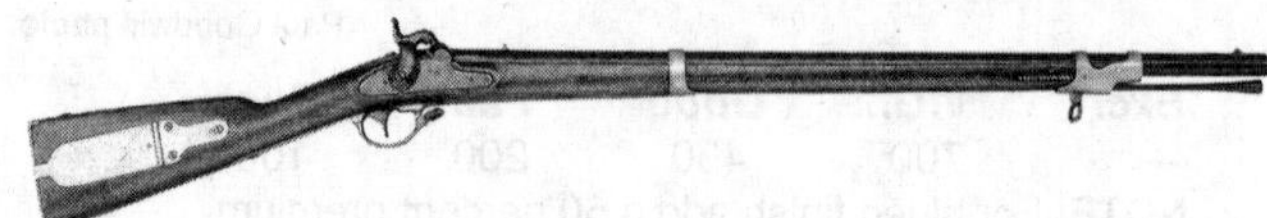
Paul Goodwin photo

Exc.	V.G.	Good	Fair	Poor
—	4750	1750	750	400

Model 1861 U.S. Rifle Musket

A .58 caliber percussion rifle with a 40" barrel and full length stock secured by three barrel bands. The lock marked "Remington's Ilion, N.Y." Finished in the white with a walnut stock. Approximately 40,000 were made between 1864 and 1866.

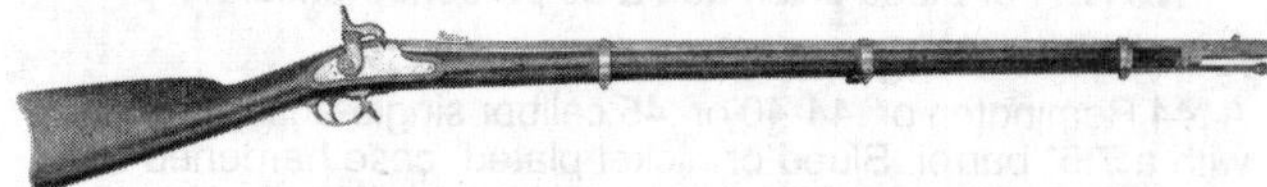
Paul Goodwin photo

Exc.	V.G.	Good	Fair	Poor
—	3000	1250	500	200

Model 1863 Zouave Rifle

A .58 caliber percussion rifle with a 33" barrel and full length stock secured by two barrel bands. The lock case hardened and marked "Remington's Ilion N.Y.," the barrel blued and the furniture of brass. Approximately 12,500 were manufactured between 1862 and 1865.

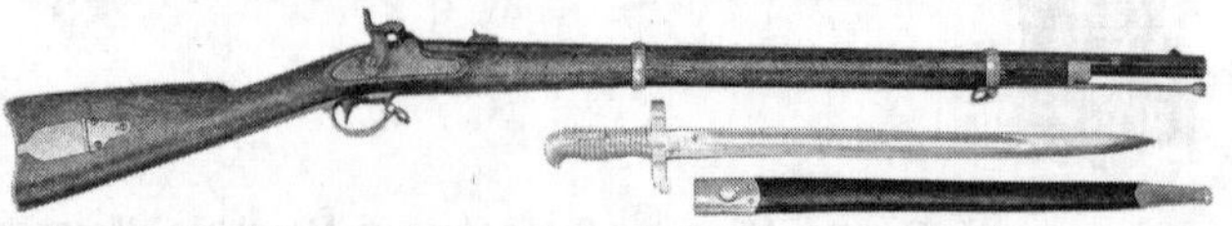
Paul Goodwin photo

Exc.	V.G.	Good	Fair	Poor
—	—	4250	1500	500

Breech-Loading Carbine

A .46 or .50 rimfire single-shot rolling block carbine with a 20" barrel. Blued, case hardened with a walnut stock. The tang marked "Remington's Ilion, N.Y. Pat. Dec. 23, 1863 May 3 &

Nov. 16, 1864." The .50 caliber version is worth approximately 15 percent more than the .46 caliber. Approximately 15,000 .50-caliber variations were made, most of which were sold to France. Approximately 5,000 carbines were made in .46 caliber. Manufactured from 1864 to 1866.

Paul Goodwin photo

Exc.	V.G.	Good	Fair	Poor
—	3750	1500	500	200

Revolving Rifle

A .36 or. 44 caliber revolving rifle with either 24" or 28" octagonal barrels with a 6-shot cylinder. The trigger guard formed with a scrolled finger extension at the rear. Blued, case hardened with a walnut stock. These rifles are also encountered altered to cartridge and would be worth approximately 20 percent less than the percussion values listed below. The barrel marked "Patented Sept. 14, 1858 E. Remington & Sons, Ilion, New York, U.S.A. New Model." The .44 caliber model will bring a premium of about 15 percent and is rare. Approximately 1,000 were manufactured between 1866 and 1879.

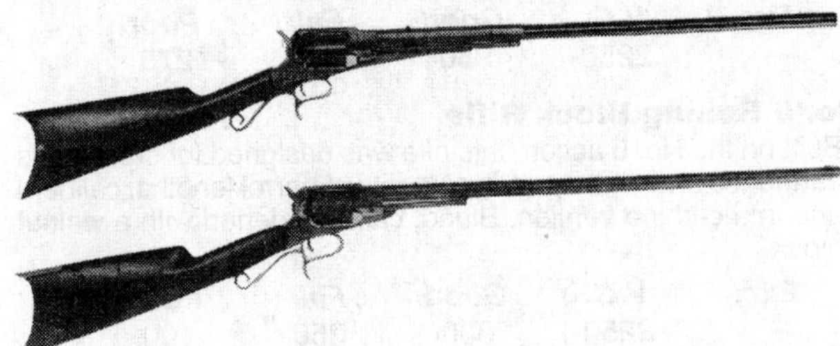

Courtesy Buffalo Bill Historical Center, Cody, Wyoming

Courtesy Milwaukee Public Museum, Milwaukee, Wisconsin

Exc.	V.G.	Good	Fair	Poor
—	5000	2000	500	300

Remington-Beals Rifle

A .32 or .38 caliber sliding barrel single-shot rifle with octagonal barrels of 24", 26", or 28" length. The barrel can be moved forward by lowering the trigger guard/lever. This model is to be found with either frames made of brass or iron, the latter being worth approximately 20 percent more than the values listed below. Walnut stock. The barrel marked "Beals Patent June 28, 1864 Jan. 30, 1866 E. Remington & Sons, Ilion, New York." Approximately 800 were manufactured between 1866 and 1888. A few examples are known to have been factory engraved. Prospective purchasers are advised to secure a qualified appraisal prior to acquisition.

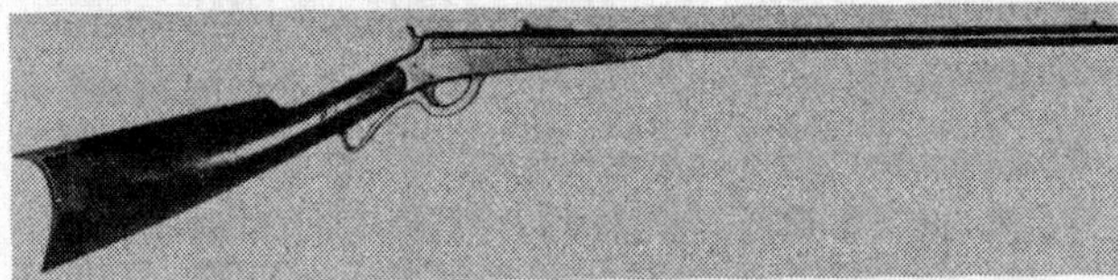

Courtesy Milwaukee Public Museum, Milwaukee, Wisconsin

Exc.	V.G.	Good	Fair	Poor
—	—	950	400	150

U.S. Navy Rolling Block Carbine

Exc.	V.G.	Good	Fair	Poor
—	—	2750	1000	350

Model 1867 Navy Cadet Rifle

Paul Goodwin photo

Exc.	V.G.	Good	Fair	Poor
—	2750	1400	700	350

Rolling Block Military Rifles

Exc.	V.G.	Good	Fair	Poor
—	900	750	400	100

NO. 1 ROLLING BLOCK SPORTING RIFLE

Standard No. 1 Sporting Rifle

A single-shot rolling block rifle produced in a variety of calibers from .40-50 to .50-70 centerfire as well as .44 and .46 rimfire. Standard barrel lengths were either 28" or 30" and of octagonal form.

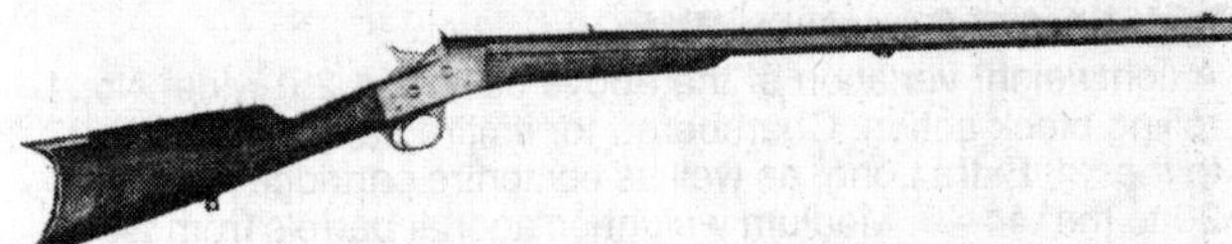

Courtesy Milwaukee Public Museum, Milwaukee, Wisconsin

Exc.	V.G.	Good	Fair	Poor
—	—	3750	1500	500

Long-Range Creedmoor Rifle

A .44-90, .44-100, or .44-105 caliber rolling block rifle with a 34" half-octagonal barrel, long-range vernier tang sights and globe front sights. Blued, case hardened with a walnut stock and a checkered pistol grip. This rifle was available with a number of optional features and a qualified appraisal should be secured if those features are in doubt. Produced from 1873 to 1890.

Courtesy Bonhams & Butterfields, San Francisco, California

Exc.	V.G.	Good	Fair	Poor
—	7500	3750	1500	500

Mid-Range Target Rifle

As above, except chambered for .40-70, .44-77, .45-70, or .50-70 caliber with 28" or 30" half-octagonal barrels. Produced from 1875 to 1890.

Exc.	V.G.	Good	Fair	Poor
—	5000	2000	750	300

Short-Range Rifle

As above, chambered for cartridges between .38 and .44 caliber with 26" or 30" round or octagonal barrels. Open rear sight with beach front sight. The walnut stock is checkered. Produced from 1875 to 1890.

Exc.	V.G.	Good	Fair	Poor
—	4000	1750	600	250

Black Hills Rifle

As above, in .45-60 caliber with a 28" round barrel fitted with open sights and a plain straight grip stock. Produced from 1877 to 1882.

Exc.	V.G.	Good	Fair	Poor
—	4000	2000	850	300

Shotgun

As above, in 16 gauge with either a 30" or 32" Damascus or fluid steel barrels. Produced from 1870 to 1892.

Exc.	V.G.	Good	Fair	Poor
—	1000	500	250	100

Baby Carbine

As above, with a 20" thin round barrel chambered for the .44-40 cartridge and fitted with a saddle ring on the left side of the frame. Blued, case hardened with a walnut stock and a carbine buttplate. Manufactured from 1892 to 1902.

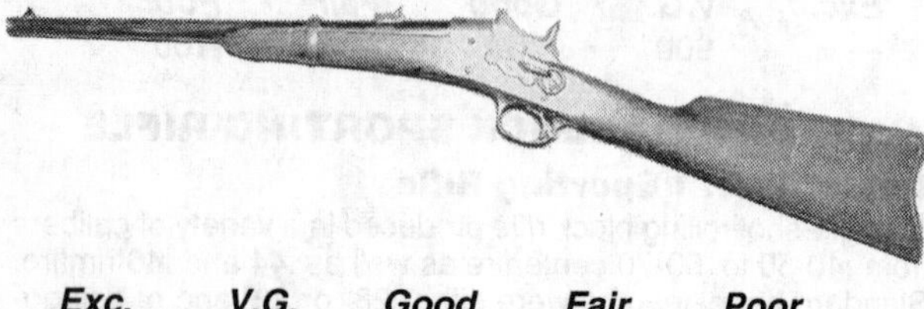

Exc.	V.G.	Good	Fair	Poor
—	3250	1250	600	200

Model 1-1/2 Sporting Rifle

A lightweight variation of the above using a 1.25" wide, No. 1 rolling block action. Chambered for rimfire cartridges from .22 to the .38 Extra Long, as well as centerfire cartridges from .32-20 to the .44-40. Medium weight octagonal barrels from 24" to 28" in length, with open rear and a blade-type front sight. Blued, case hardened with a walnut stock. There were several thousand manufactured between 1888 and 1897.

Paul Goodwin photo

Exc.	V.G.	Good	Fair	Poor
—	2000	950	400	100

Model 2 Sporting Rifle

As above, using a No. 2 action and chambered for various cartridges from .22 to .38 caliber with 24" or 26" octagonal barrels. Blued, case hardened with a walnut stock. This model was produced with a number of optional features that affect its value. Prospective purchasers are advised to secure a qualified appraisal prior to acquisition. Manufactured from 1873 to 1910.

Paul Goodwin photo

Exc.	V.G.	Good	Fair	Poor
—	1500	600	250	100

No. 4 Rolling Block Rifle

Built on the lightweight No. 4 action, this rifle was available in .22, .25 Stevens, or .32 caliber, with either a 22.5" or 24" octagonal barrel. Blued, case hardened with a walnut stock. A takedown version was also made and these are worth approximately 10 percent more than the values listed. Approximately 50,000 were made between 1890 and 1933.

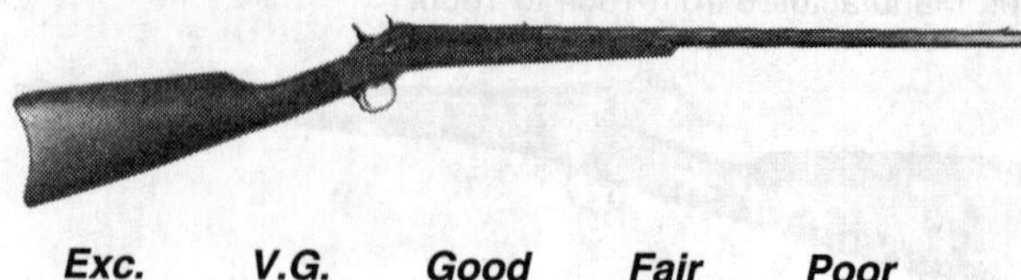

Exc.	V.G.	Good	Fair	Poor
900	700	400	200	75

Model No. 4 S Military Rifle

At the request of the United States Boy Scouts in 1913, the Remington Company designed a military style rifle having a 28" barrel and full length forend secured by one barrel band. A short upper hand guard was also fitted and a bayonet stud is to be found at the muzzle. In 1915 the designation of this model was changed from "Boy Scout" to "Military Model." Approximately 15,000 were made between 1913 and 1923.

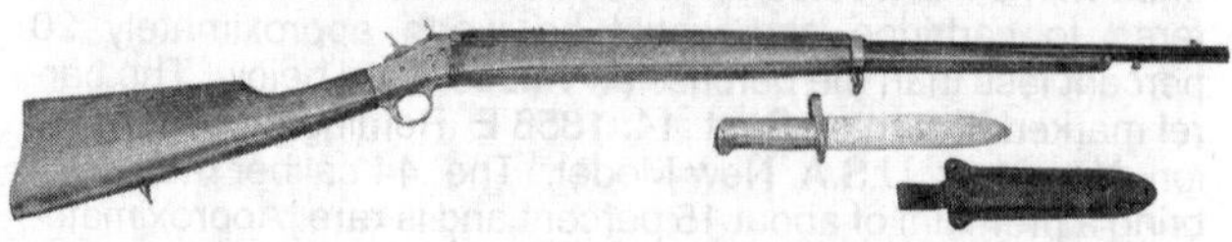

Paul Goodwin photo

Exc.	V.G.	Good	Fair	Poor
—	2250	950	400	275

No. 5 Rolling Block Rifle

Built on the No. 5 action, this rifle was designed for smokeless cartridges and was made in a variety of barrel lengths, calibers and in a carbine version. Blued, case hardened with a walnut stock.

Exc.	V.G.	Good	Fair	Poor
—	2250	800	350	100

No. 5 Sporting or Target Rifle

Chambered for the .30-30, .303 British, 7mm, .30 U.S., .32-40, .32 U.S., and the .38-55 cartridges. This rifle was offered with 28" or 30" round barrels and features a plain, straight-grip stock with a half-length forend. It has open rear sights and was available with double-set triggers that would add approximately 10 percent to the value. It was manufactured between 1898 and 1905.

Exc.	V.G.	Good	Fair	Poor
—	5750	2250	850	300

Model 1897

A 7x57mm and .30 U.S. caliber full stock rolling block rifle. The Model 1902 is of identical form except that it was fitted with an automatic ejector. Manufactured from 1897 to 1902.

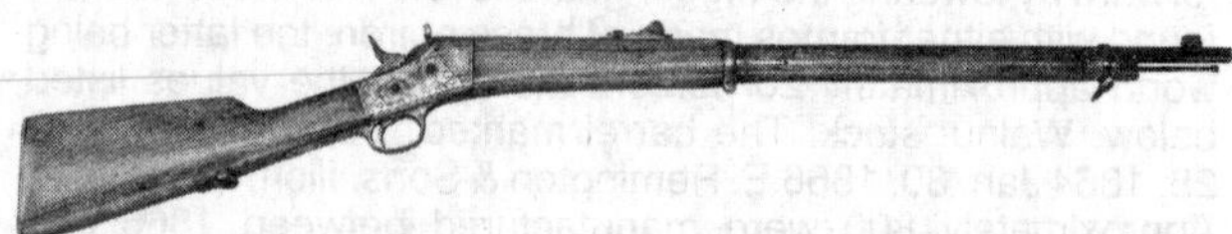

Paul Goodwin photo

Exc.	V.G.	Good	Fair	Poor
—	1250	550	250	100

Carbine

As above, fitted with a 20" round barrel and a half-length forend secured by one barrel band.

Exc.	V.G.	Good	Fair	Poor
—	1750	750	350	100

No. 6 Rolling Block Rifle

A lightweight, small rifle designed expressly to be used by young boys. It is chambered for the .22 rimfire cartridge, as well as the .32 Short or Long. It was also produced with a smoothbore barrel to be used with shot cartridges. The round barrel is 20" in length. It has a takedown action with a barrel held on by a knurled knob underneath the frame. It is a lightweight rolling block, with a thin operating knob on the breech. The finish is blued overall. Early models featured a case-colored frame, and these versions would be worth approximately 10 percent additional. It has a straight-grip walnut stock with a small forearm. Over 250,000 manufactured between 1902 and 1903.

Paul Goodwin photo

Exc.	V.G.	Good	Fair	Poor
750	475	300	100	75

No. 7 Rolling Block Rifle

Readily identifiable by its accentuated checked pistol grip, this model was available in .22 or .25-10 Stevens caliber with 24", 26", or 28" half octagonal barrels. Fitted with a tang mounted aperture rear sight. Blued, case hardened with a walnut stock. Approximately 1,000 were made between 1903 and 1911.

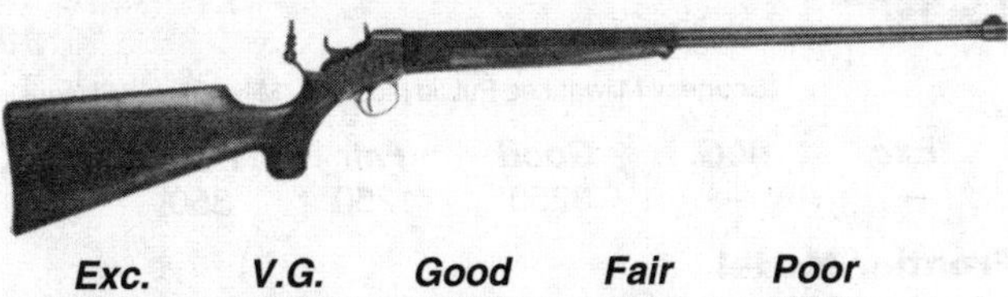

Exc.	V.G.	Good	Fair	Poor
6500	2500	1400	750	300

Remington-Hepburn No. 3 Rifle

A lever activated falling block single-shot rifle designed by Lewis Hepburn available in a variety of calibers from .22 Winchester centerfire to .50-90 Sharps with octagonal or round barrels of 26", 28", or 30" length. Blued, case hardened with a walnut stock. This model was available with a variety of optional features that affect the value considerably. Prospective purchasers are advised to secure a qualified appraisal prior to acquisition. Approximately 10,000 were made between 1883 and 1907.

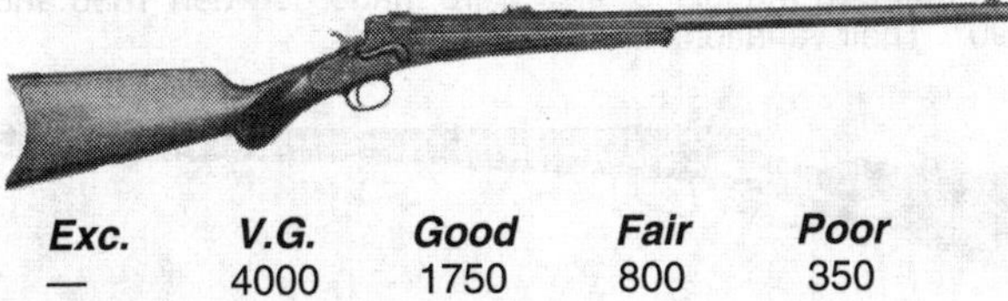

Exc.	V.G.	Good	Fair	Poor
—	4000	1750	800	350

No. 3 Match Rifle

As above, but fitted with a high comb buttstock and a nickel-plated Schuetzen buttplate. Manufactured in various calibers from .25-20 Stevens to .40-65 with 30" half octagonal barrels. This model was made in two versions: “A Quality” with a plain stock, tang mounted rear sight and a Beach front sight, and; “B Quality” with a checkered walnut stock having a cheek rest, checkered forend, vernier rear sight and a combination wind gauge and spirit level front sight. Double set triggers were also available and these would add approximately 10 percent to the values listed below. Approximately 1,000 were made between 1883 and 1907.

A Quality

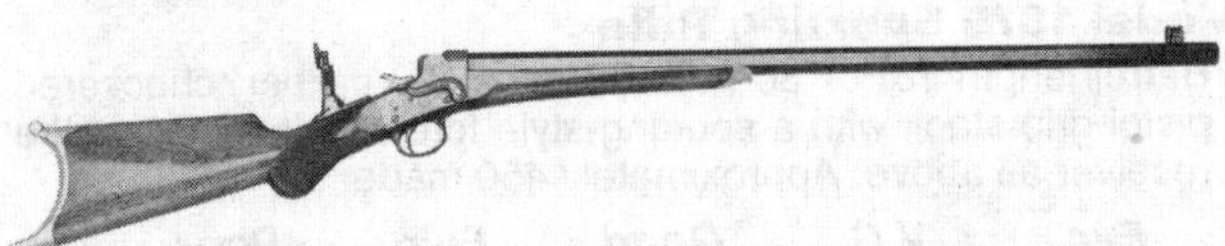

Paul Goodwin photo

Exc.	V.G.	Good	Fair	Poor
—	4500	2000	800	350

B Quality

Paul Goodwin photo

Exc.	V.G.	Good	Fair	Poor
—	5500	2500	1200	500

No. 3 Long-Range Creedmoor Rifle

As above, in .44 caliber with a 32" or 34" half-octagonal barrel, long-range vernier rear sight, combination wind gauge and spirit level front sight, deluxe checkered walnut stock and a rubber shotgun buttplate. Produced with a number of optional features that affect the value. Prospective purchasers are advised to secure a qualified appraisal prior to acquisition. Manufactured from 1880 to 1907.

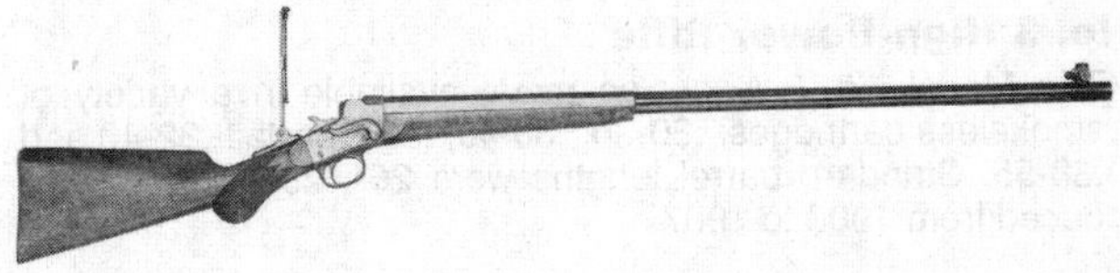

Paul Goodwin photo

Exc.	V.G.	Good	Fair	Poor
—	7500	3500	1250	500

No. 3 Mid-Range Creedmoor Rifle

As above, but chambered for the .40-65 cartridge and fitted with a 28" barrel.

Exc.	V.G.	Good	Fair	Poor
—	5000	2250	950	350

No. 3 Long-Range Military Rifle

This is a rare variation that is chambered for the .44-20 Remington cartridge. It has a round 34" barrel and a full-length forearm held on by two barrel bands. The finish is blued and case-colored, and the stock is walnut. There are two basic versions. The plain grade has an uncheckered, straight-grip stock with military-type sights. There is also a fancy grade that features a high-grade, checkered, pistol-grip stock with a full-length, checkered forend, vernier tang sight, and wind gauge, spirit lever front sight. There were a few manufactured in the 1880s.

Paul Goodwin photo

Plain Grade

Exc.	V.G.	Good	Fair	Poor
—	4500	2500	1200	400

Fancy Grade

Exc.	V.G.	Good	Fair	Poor
—	7500	3750	1500	600

No. 3 Schuetzen Match Rifle

As above, with the exception that instead of the side lever, the action is raised or lowered by means of the lever on the trigger guard. Chambered for various popular cartridges and offered with a 30" or 32" part-octagonal, heavy barrel. It features a vernier tang sight with a hooded front sight. It was standard with double-set triggers and a palm rest. The finish is blued and

case-colored, with a high-grade checkered walnut stock and forend. It has an ornate, Swiss-type Schuetzen buttplate and is also known as the "Walker-Hepburn Rifle." There were two versions available. One, a standard breechloader with the Remington Walker-marked barrel; and the other, a muzzleloading variation that was fitted with a removable false muzzle. This version was supplied with a brass bullet starter and other accessories. Prospective purchasers are advised to secure a qualified appraisal prior to acquisition.

Breechloading Version

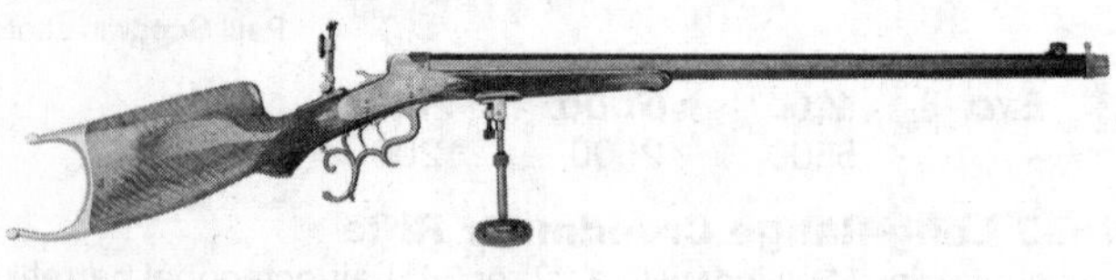

Exc.	V.G.	Good	Fair	Poor
—	27500	12500	3500	900

Muzzleloading Version

Exc.	V.G.	Good	Fair	Poor
—	42500	17500	5000	1500

No. 3 High-Power Rifle

The Model No. 3 was also made available in a variety of smokeless cartridges: .30-30, .30-40, .32 Special, .32-40 and .38-55. Standard barrel lengths were 26", 28", or 30". Produced from 1900 to 1907.

Exc.	V.G.	Good	Fair	Poor
4000	2500	1750	650	250

Remington-Keene Magazine Rifle

A bolt-action rifle chambered for the .40, .43, and .45-70 centerfire cartridges with 22", 24.5", 29.25", or 32.5" barrels. It is readily identifiable by the exposed hammer at the end of the bolt. Blued, case hardened hammer and furniture, with a walnut stock. The receiver marked "E. Remington & Sons, Ilion, N.Y." together with the patent dates 1874, 1876, and 1877. The magazine on this rifle was located beneath the barrel and the receiver is fitted with a cut-off so that the rifle could be used as a single-shot. Approximately 5,000 rifles were made between 1880 and 1888 in the variations listed.

Sporting Rifle

24.5" barrel.

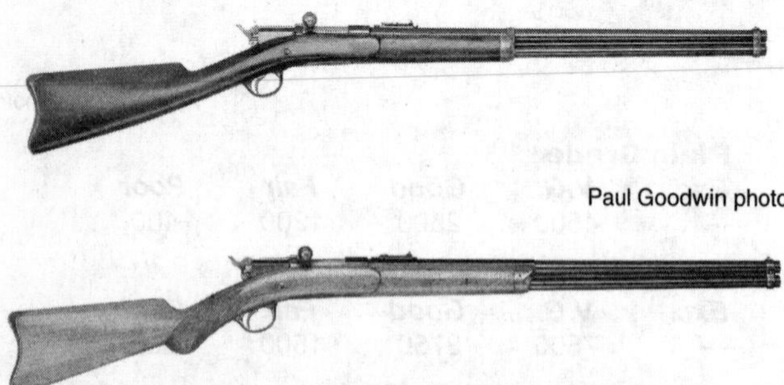

Paul Goodwin photo

Remington-Keene Repeating Sporting Rifle Fancy Grade

Paul Goodwin photo

Exc.	V.G.	Good	Fair	Poor
—	2000	750	350	150

Army Rifle

Barrel length 32.5" with a full-length stock secured by two barrel bands.

Courtesy Milwaukee Public Museum, Milwaukee, Wisconsin

Exc.	V.G.	Good	Fair	Poor
—	—	3500	950	450

Navy Rifle

As above, with a 29.25" barrel.

Exc.	V.G.	Good	Fair	Poor
—	—	4500	1750	450

Carbine

As above, with a 22" barrel and a half-length forend secured by one barrel band.

Courtesy Milwaukee Public Museum, Milwaukee, Wisconsin

Exc.	V.G.	Good	Fair	Poor
—	—	3250	1250	350

Frontier Model

As above, with a 24" barrel and half-length forend secured by one barrel band. Those purchased by the United States Department of the Interior for arming the Indian Police are marked "U.S.I.D." on the receiver.

Exc.	V.G.	Good	Fair	Poor
—	—	5250	2500	850

Remington-Lee Magazine Rifle

Designed by James Paris Lee, rifles of this type were originally manufactured by the Sharps Rifle Company in 1880. The Remington Company began production of this model in 1881 after the Sharps Company ceased operations. Approximately 100,000 Lee magazine rifles were made between 1880 and 1907. Their variations are listed.

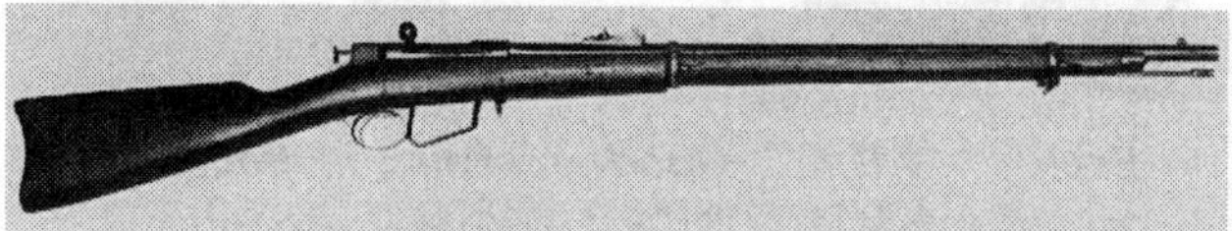

Courtesy Milwaukee Public Museum, Milwaukee, Wisconsin

Model 1879 Sharps Mfg.

Barrel length 28" with a full-length stock secured by two barrel bands. The barrel marked "Sharps Rifle Co. Bridgeport, Conn." and "Old Reliable" in a rectangular cartouche. Approximately 300 were made prior to 1881.

Exc.	V.G.	Good	Fair	Poor
—	—	4750	2000	600

Model 1879 U.S. Navy Model

Exc.	V.G.	Good	Fair	Poor
—	—	2250	750	250

Model 1879 Sporting Rifle

Barrel length 28" or 30", .45-70 or .45-90 caliber, checkered pistol-grip stock with a sporting-style forend. Markings on the receiver as above. Approximately 450 made.

Exc.	V.G.	Good	Fair	Poor
—	—	1750	700	250

Model 1879 Military Rifle

Identical to the Navy model, except chambered for the .43 Spanish cartridge. A limited number were also produced in .45-70 caliber. The Spanish versions are worth approximately 25 percent less than the values listed below. Approximately 1,000 were made. The majority of these rifles were made for export.

Exc.	V.G.	Good	Fair	Poor
—	—	1250	500	150

Model 1882 Army Contract

Exc.	V.G.	Good	Fair	Poor
—	—	2000	750	300

Model 1885 Navy Contract

Exc.	V.G.	Good	Fair	Poor
—	—	2000	750	300

Model 1882 & 1885 Military Rifles

Barrel length 32", full-length stock secured by two barrel bands, chambered for .42 Russian, .43 Spanish, .45 Gardner or .45-70 cartridges. The values for those rifles not in .45-70 caliber would be approximately 25 percent less than those listed. Approximately 10,000 Model 1882 rifles were made and 60,000 Model 1885 rifles. The two models can be differentiated by the fact that the cocking piece on the bolt of the Model 1885 is larger. The majority of these rifles were made for foreign contracts and commercial sales.

Exc.	V.G.	Good	Fair	Poor
—	—	950	400	150

Model 1882 & 1885 Sporting Rifle

As above, chambered for .45-70 and .45-90 caliber with 26" or 30" octagonal barrels and walnut sporting stocks. Approximately 200 were made.

Exc.	V.G.	Good	Fair	Poor
—	—	1750	750	200

Model 1882 & 1885 Carbine

As above, with a 24" barrel and a half-length forend secured by one barrel band. Prospective purchasers are advised to secure a qualified appraisal prior to acquisition.

Exc.	V.G.	Good	Fair	Poor
—	—	1750	750	200

Model 1899

Designed for use with smokeless and rimless cartridges, this model is marked on the receiver "Remington Arms Co. Ilion, N.Y. Patented Aug. 26th 1884 Sept. 9th 1884 March 17th 1885 Jan 18th 1887." Produced from 1889 to 1907 in the variations listed.

Military Rifle

Exc.	V.G.	Good	Fair	Poor
—	1250	500	200	100

Military Carbine

Exc.	V.G.	Good	Fair	Poor
—	1750	700	300	100

Sporting Rifle

As above, with a 24", 26", or 28" round or octagonal barrel and a half-length sporting stock with a checkered pistol grip. Approximately 7,000 were manufactured.

Exc.	V.G.	Good	Fair	Poor
—	1250	500	200	100

Remington Lebel Bolt-Action Rifle

Exc.	V.G.	Good	Fair	Poor
—	750	450	150	100

Remington Mosin-Nagant Bolt-Action Rifle

Exc.	V.G.	Good	Fair	Poor
—	600	300	100	75

U.S. Model 1917 Magazine Rifle

Exc.	V.G.	Good	Fair	Poor
—	1250	600	150	100

Remington-Whitmore Model 1874

A sidelock double-barrel shotgun, combination shotgun/rifle or double-barrel rifle with 28" or 30" fluid steel barrels. Also available with Damascus barrels. The barrels released by pushing forward the top lever. Blued, case hardened with a straight or semi-pistol grip walnut stock. The barrels marked "A. E. Whitmore's Patent Aug. 8, 1871, April 16, 1872." The rib between the barrels is marked "E. Remington & Sons, Ilion, N.Y." Several thousand were manufactured between 1874 and 1882.

Shotgun

Exc.	V.G.	Good	Fair	Poor
—	1750	650	250	100

Combination Gun (Rare)

Exc.	V.G.	Good	Fair	Poor
—	4250	1750	750	300

Double Rifle

Prospective purchasers are advised to secure a qualified appraisal prior to acquisition. Very rare.

Exc.	V.G.	Good	Fair	Poor
—	9000	4250	1500	500

Model 1882 Shotgun

A sidelock double-barrel 10 or 12 gauge shotgun with 28" or 30" fluid steel or Damascus barrels. Blued, case hardened with a checkered pistol grip stock and hard rubber buttplate. The barrels are marked "E. Remington & Sons, Ilion, N.Y." and the lock is marked "Remington Arms Co." This model has a conventional top lever that moves to the side. Offered with optional engraving, and such models should be individually appraised. Approximately 7,500 were manufactured between 1882 and 1889.

Exc.	V.G.	Good	Fair	Poor
—	1750	750	300	100

Model 1883 through 1889 Shotgun

A sidelock 10, 12, or 16 gauge double-barrel shotgun with fluid steel or Damascus barrels 28" to 32" in length. The models 1883, 1885, 1887, and 1889 are all somewhat alike, varying only in the form of their hammers and internal mechanisms. Blued, case hardened, checkered pistol-grip stock with a grip cap. Available in a variety of styles including highly engraved models that should be individually appraised. Approximately 30,000 were made between 1883 and 1909.

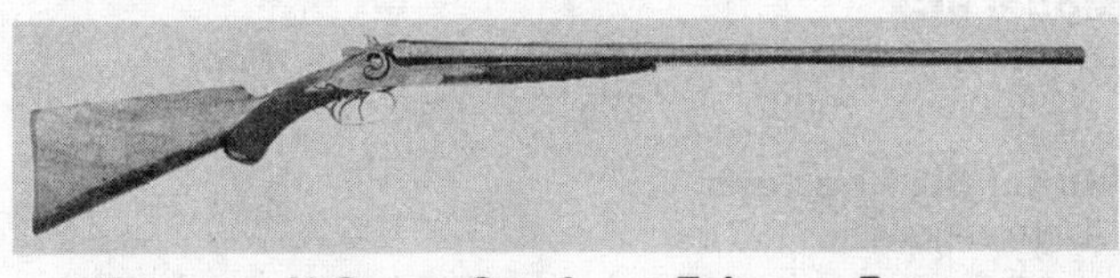

Exc.	V.G.	Good	Fair	Poor
—	1750	750	300	100

Model 1893 (No. 9)

Single-barrel hammer gun in 10, 12, 16, 20, 24, and 28 gauge. Barrel lengths from 28" to 34". Case colored frame with hard rubber buttplate.

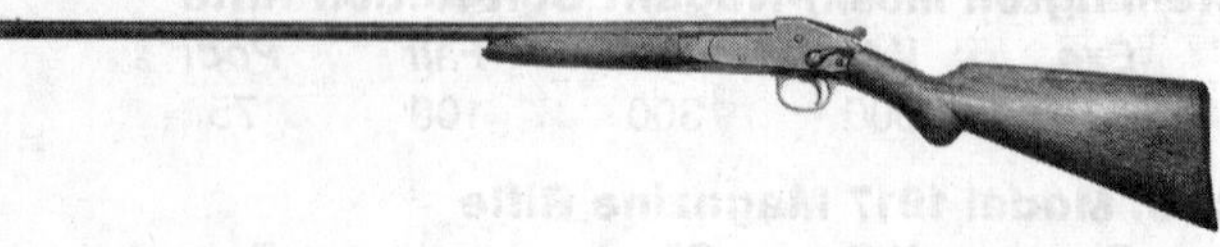

Courtesy William F. Krause

Exc.	V.G.	Good	Fair	Poor
—	—	600	250	100

Hammerless Shotgun Model 1894

A boxlock 10, 12, or 16 gauge double shotgun with fluid steel or Damascus barrels 26" to 32" in length. Blued, case hardened with a pistol-grip stock. Available in a variety of styles and it is advised that highly engraved examples should be individually appraised.

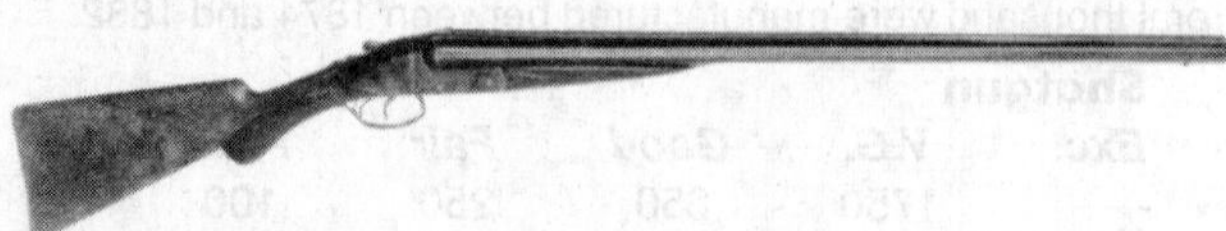

Exc.	V.G.	Good	Fair	Poor
—	1750	750	300	100

NOTE: Fluid steel barrels add 25 percent premium.

Model 1900 Shotgun

As above, in 12 and 16 gauge only. The same cautions apply to highly engraved examples.

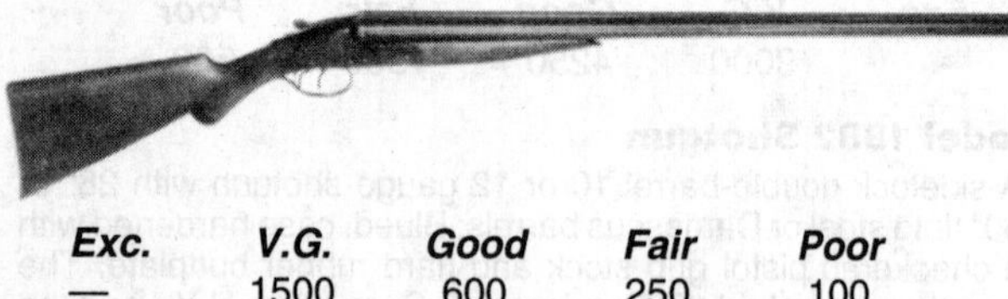

Exc.	V.G.	Good	Fair	Poor
—	1500	600	250	100

Model 8

A .25, .30, .32, or .35 Remington semi-automatic rifle featuring a 22" barrel with open sights. The barrel is covered by a full-length tube that encloses the recoil spring. Blued with walnut stock. Approximately 60,000 were made between 1906 and 1936 in the styles listed. Add 85 percent for .25 Remington.

Standard Grade

Courtesy Remington Arms

Exc.	V.G.	Good	Fair	Poor
550	400	250	175	125

Model 8A

Checkered stock.

Exc.	V.G.	Good	Fair	Poor
700	450	350	225	150

Model 8C

Exc.	V.G.	Good	Fair	Poor
800	500	375	300	200

Model 8D Peerless

Light engraving.

Exc.	V.G.	Good	Fair	Poor
1500	850	500	400	300

Model 8E Expert

Exc.	V.G.	Good	Fair	Poor
1750	1200	900	600	450

Model 8F Premier

Heavily engraved.

Paul Goodwin photo

Exc.	V.G.	Good	Fair	Poor
2250	1475	1000	750	550

Model 81 Woodsmaster

An improved variation of the Model 8, chambered for the same calibers as well as the .300 Savage cartridge. Produced from 1936 to 1950 in the styles listed. Add 300 percent for police model with detachable magazine.

Standard Grade

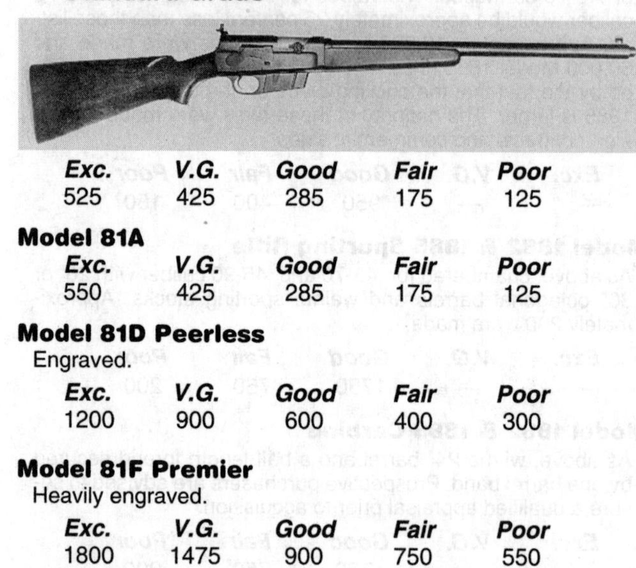

Exc.	V.G.	Good	Fair	Poor
525	425	285	175	125

Model 81A

Exc.	V.G.	Good	Fair	Poor
550	425	285	175	125

Model 81D Peerless

Engraved.

Exc.	V.G.	Good	Fair	Poor
1200	900	600	400	300

Model 81F Premier

Heavily engraved.

Exc.	V.G.	Good	Fair	Poor
1800	1475	900	750	550

Model 12 or 12 A

A .22 caliber slide-action rifle with a 22" round or octagonal barrel having open sights. Blued with a walnut stock. Manufactured from 1909 to 1936 in the styles listed.

Model 12A

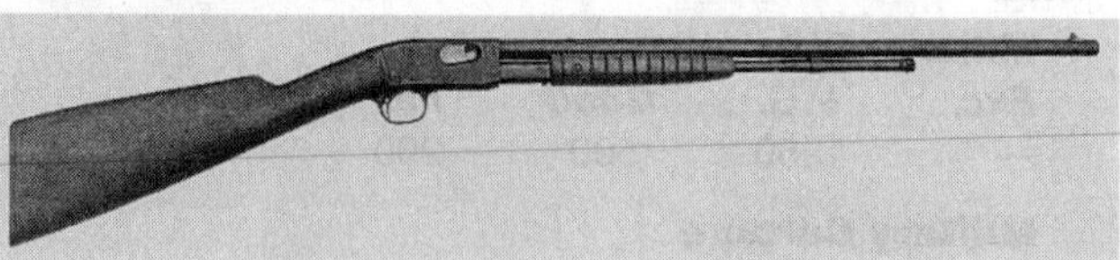

Courtesy Remington Arms

Exc.	V.G.	Good	Fair	Poor
550	375	300	225	150

Model 12B

.22 Short, Gallery Model.

Exc.	V.G.	Good	Fair	Poor
550	375	300	225	150

Model 12C

24" octagon barrel.

Exc.	V.G.	Good	Fair	Poor
500	425	350	250	175

Model 12C N.R.A. Target

Limited production.

Exc.	V.G.	Good	Fair	Poor
750	550	450	250	200

Model 12CS

.22 Remington Special.

Exc.	V.G.	Good	Fair	Poor
500	400	325	250	175

Model 12D Peerless

Light engraving.

Exc.	V.G.	Good	Fair	Poor
2250	1750	1200	1000	500

Model 12E Expert

Exc.	V.G.	Good	Fair	Poor
2500	2250	1750	1200	800

Model 12F Premier

Heavily engraved.

Paul Goodwin photo

Exc.	V.G.	Good	Fair	Poor
3000	2250	1850	1200	800

Model 121 and/or 121A

A .22 caliber slide-action rifle with a 24" round barrel. Blued with a walnut stock. Manufactured from 1936 to 1954 in the styles listed.

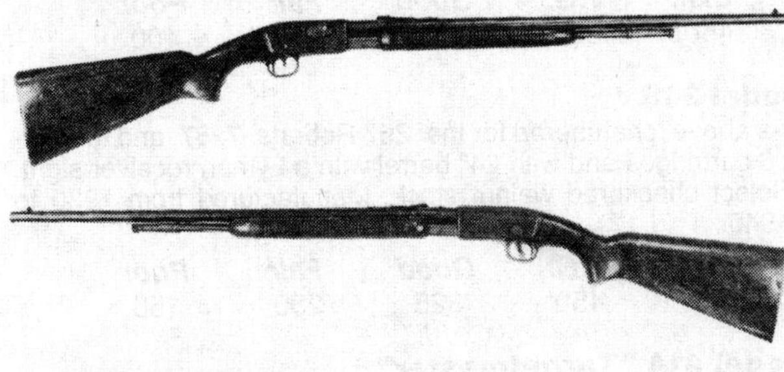

Standard Grade

Exc.	V.G.	Good	Fair	Poor
495	350	225	175	100

Model 121D Peerless

Engraved.

Exc.	V.G.	Good	Fair	Poor
2250	2000	1250	1000	750

Model 121F Premier

Heavily engraved.

Exc.	V.G.	Good	Fair	Poor
3250	2500	1750	1200	1000

Model 121S

.22 WRF.

Exc.	V.G.	Good	Fair	Poor
850	700	400	350	250

Model 121SB—Smoothbore

There are four different variations of this smoothbore rifle. Seek expert advice before a sale.

Exc.	V.G.	Good	Fair	Poor
600	450	350	250	200

Model 14 or 14A

A .25, .30, .32 or .35 Remington caliber slide-action rifle with a 22" round barrel and open sights. Blued, plain walnut stock. Manufactured from 1912 to 1936. Add 85 percent for .25 Remington.

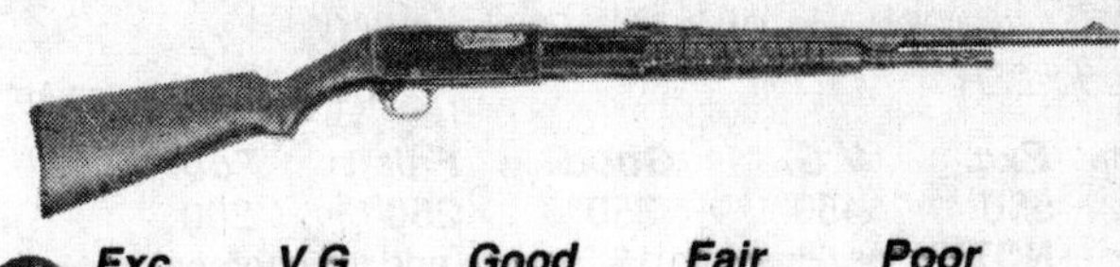

Exc.	V.G.	Good	Fair	Poor
425	300	225	150	100

Model 14R

As above, with an 18.5" barrel.

Exc.	V.G.	Good	Fair	Poor
500	400	300	250	175

Model 14-1/2

As above, except chambered for the .38-40 or .44-40 cartridge with a 22.5" barrel. A carbine with an 18.5" barrel known as the Model 14-1/2R, would be worth approximately 10 percent more than the values listed. Manufactured from 1912 to 1922.

Exc.	V.G.	Good	Fair	Poor
1100	750	500	350	250

Model 16

A .22 caliber semi-automatic rifle with a 22" barrel and open sights. Blued with a walnut stock. Later production examples were known as the Model 16A. Manufactured from 1914 to 1928.

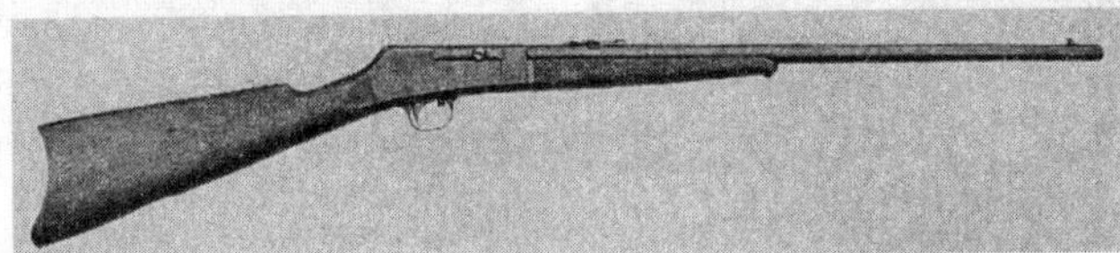

Courtesy Remington Arms

Exc.	V.G.	Good	Fair	Poor
400	350	250	125	75

Model 141

A .30, .32, or .35 Remington caliber slide-action rifle with a 24" barrel having open sights. Blued with a plain walnut stock. Later production versions of this rifle were known as the Model 141A. Manufactured from 1936 to 1950.

Courtesy Remington Arms

Exc.	V.G.	Good	Fair	Poor
500	400	300	250	175

Model 25

A .25-20 or .32-20 caliber slide-action rifle with a 24" barrel having open sights. Blued with a walnut stock. Later production examples were known as the Model 25A and a carbine version with an 18" barrel as the Model 25R. Manufactured from 1923 to 1936.

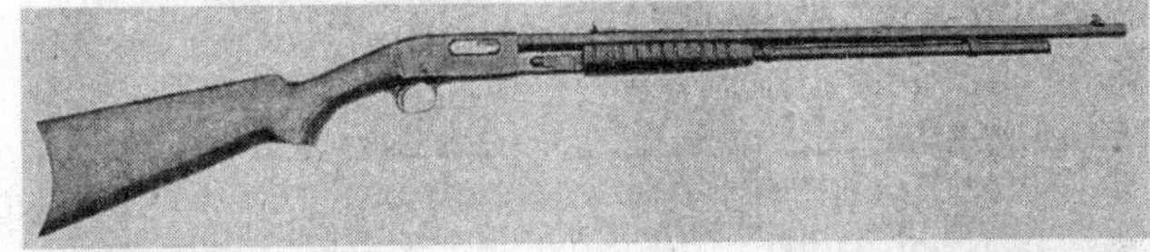

Model 25 Courtesy Remington Arms

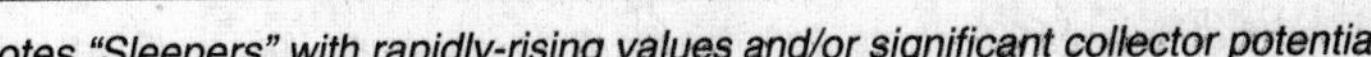

This symbol denotes "Sleepers" with rapidly-rising values and/or significant collector potential.

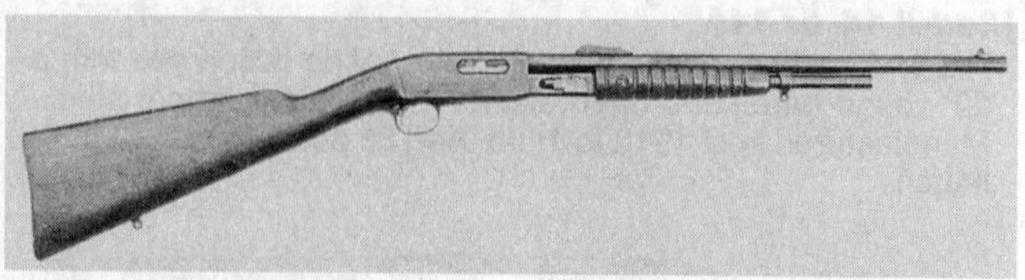

Model 25R Courtesy Remington Arms

Exc.	V.G.	Good	Fair	Poor
550	450	350	250	200

NOTE: For rifles with 18" barrels add 100 percent.

Model 24

Designed by John M. Browning, this semi-automatic rifle is of .22 caliber with a 19" barrel and open sights. Blued with a walnut pistol grip stock. Later production versions were known as the Model 24A. Produced from 1922 to 1935.

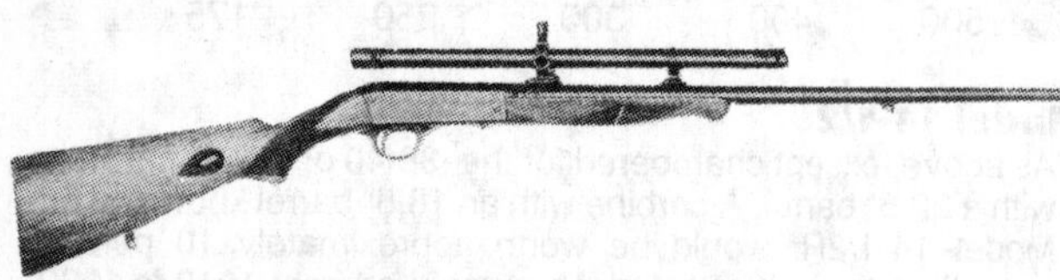

Courtesy Wallis & Wallis, Lewes, Sussex, England

Exc.	V.G.	Good	Fair	Poor
400	350	250	150	100

Model 241 Speedmaster

A .22 caliber takedown semi-automatic rifle with a 24" barrel and open sights. Blued with a walnut stock. Later production versions were known as the Model 241A. Approximately 56,000 were made between 1935 and 1949 in the styles listed.

Model 241

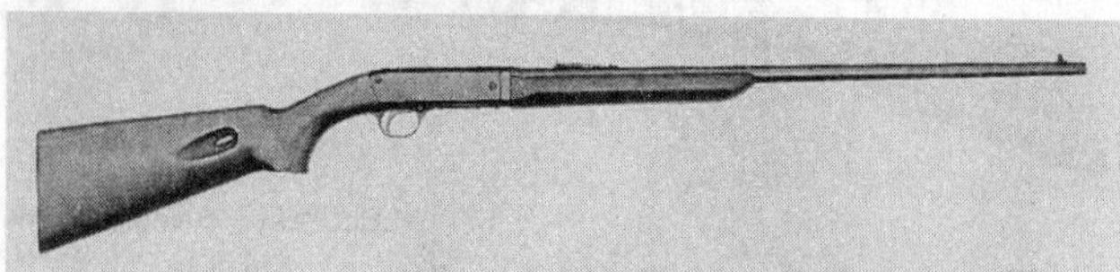

Courtesy Remington Arms

Exc.	V.G.	Good	Fair	Poor
450	350	250	200	150

Model 241D Peerless

Engraved.

Exc.	V.G.	Good	Fair	Poor
2500	2000	1500	1000	600

Model 241E Expert

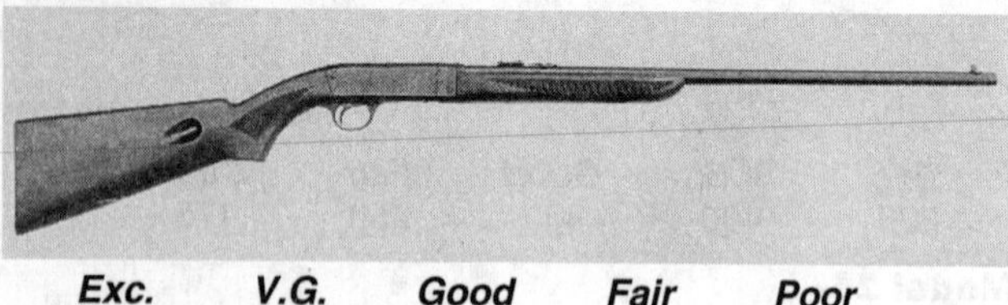

Exc.	V.G.	Good	Fair	Poor
2750	2250	1700	1000	500

Model 241F Premier

Heavily engraved.

Exc.	V.G.	Good	Fair	Poor
3250	2500	2100	1500	1000

Model 550A

A .22 Short, Long, or LR caliber semi-automatic rifle with a 24" barrel and open sights. Blued with a walnut pistol-grip stock. Approximately 220,000 were made between 1941 and 1971.

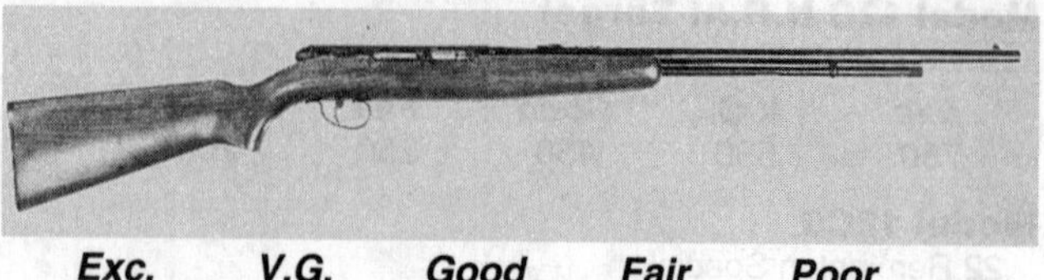

Exc.	V.G.	Good	Fair	Poor
200	175	150	100	75

Model 550P

As above, with an aperture rear sight.

Exc.	V.G.	Good	Fair	Poor
225	200	175	125	100

Model 55-2G

As above, except fitted with a shell deflector and a screw eye for securing it to a shooting gallery counter.

Exc.	V.G.	Good	Fair	Poor
200	175	150	100	75

Model 30A

A sporting rifle using the U.S. Model 1917 Enfield bolt-action chambered for various Remington cartridges as well as the 7x57mm and .30-06 cartridges. Barrel length 22". Checkered walnut stock. A carbine model fitted with a 20" barrel was known as the Model 30R. Manufactured from 1921 to 1940.

Courtesy Remington Arms

Exc.	V.G.	Good	Fair	Poor
450	350	250	175	100

Model 30S

As above, chambered for the .257 Roberts, 7x57, and the .30-06 cartridges and with 24" barrel with a Lyman receiver sight. Select checkered walnut stock. Manufactured from 1930 to 1940.

Exc.	V.G.	Good	Fair	Poor
550	450	325	250	150

Model 41A "Targetmaster"

This is a bolt-action rimfire rifle chambered for the .22 caliber Short, Long, LR. It is fitted with a 27" barrel with an open rear sight and bead front sight. The pistol-grip stock is plain. It was produced from 1936 to 1940.

Exc.	V.G.	Good	Fair	Poor
150	125	85	70	50

Model 41AS

Same as above but chambered for the .22 Remington Special or .22 WRF cartridge.

Exc.	V.G.	Good	Fair	Poor
175	150	125	100	75

Model 41P

Same as Model 41A with the addition of a rear peep sight and hooded front sight.

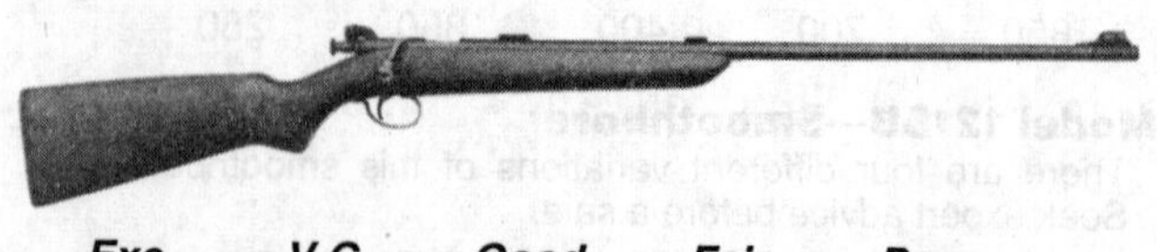

Exc.	V.G.	Good	Fair	Poor
135	115	90	70	50

This symbol denotes "Sleepers" with rapidly-rising values and/or significant collector potential.

Model 41SB

Same as Model 41A except for use with .22 shot cartridge. Barrel is smoothbore.

Exc.	V.G.	Good	Fair	Poor
250	200	150	100	75

NOTE: Smoothbore Models add 50 percent.

From 1930 to 1970 the Remington Company produced a variety of single-shot and repeating .22 caliber rifles. The values for these are much the same, consequently, they are listed for reference only.

Model 33	Model 510 X
Model 33 NRA	Model 511 A
Model 34	Model 511 P
Model 34 NRA	Model 511 X
Model 341 A	Model 512 A
Model 341 P	Model 512 P
Model 341 SB	Model 512 X
Model 510	Model 514
Model 510 P	Model 514 P
Model 510 SB	Model 514 BC

Model 510 Courtesy Remington Arms

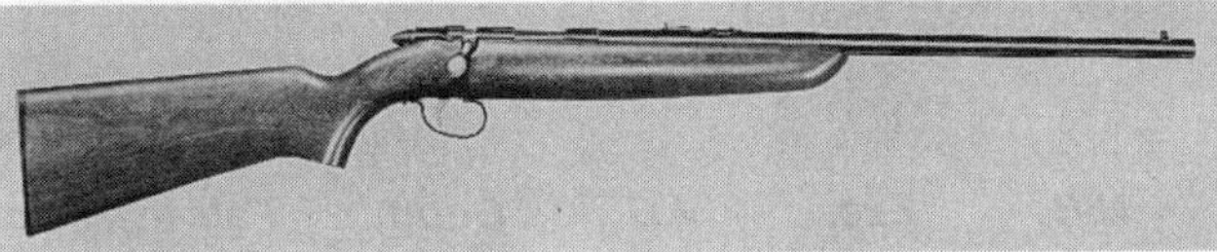

Model 510 Carbine Courtesy Remington Arms

Exc.	V.G.	Good	Fair	Poor
125	100	75	50	25

Model 37

A .22 caliber bolt-action magazine target rifle with a heavy 28" barrel featuring target-sights and telescope bases. Blued with a walnut target style stock. Manufactured from 1937 to 1940.

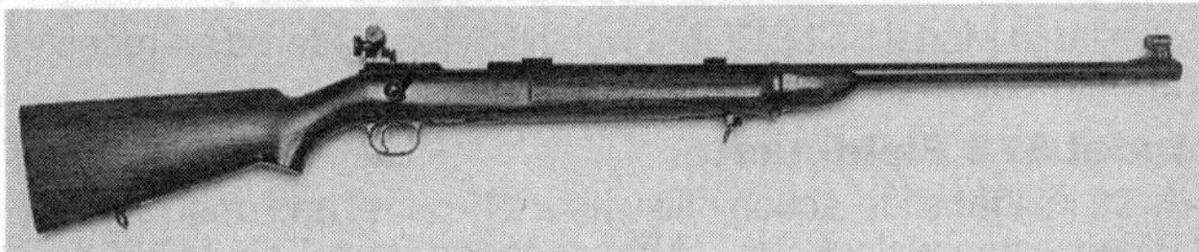

Courtesy Remington Arms

Exc.	V.G.	Good	Fair	Poor
600	500	400	300	250

Model 37-1940

As above, with an improved lock, trigger pull and redesigned stock. Manufactured from 1940 to 1954.

Courtesy Remington Arms

Exc.	V.G.	Good	Fair	Poor
650	525	400	300	200

Model 504

Introduced in 2004 this .22 caliber bolt action rifle is fitted with a 20" barrel with no sights. American walnut stock with checkering and pistol grip. Satin blue metal finish. Six round flush mounted detachable magazine. Receiver is drilled and tapped for scope mounts. Weight is about 6 lbs. Discontinued 2006.

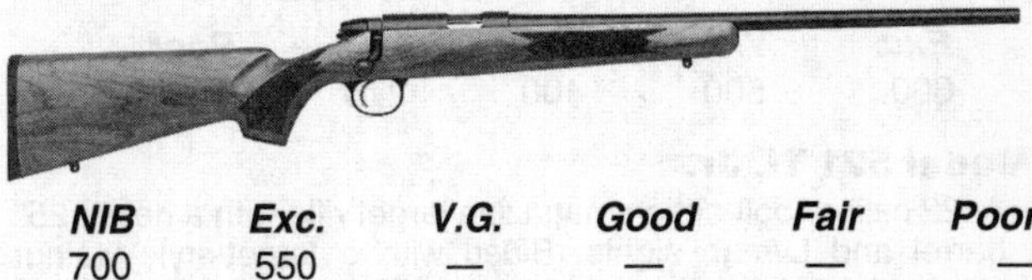

NIB	Exc.	V.G.	Good	Fair	Poor
700	550	—	—	—	—

Model 504 Custom

Introduced in 2005 this model features a fancy walnut stock.

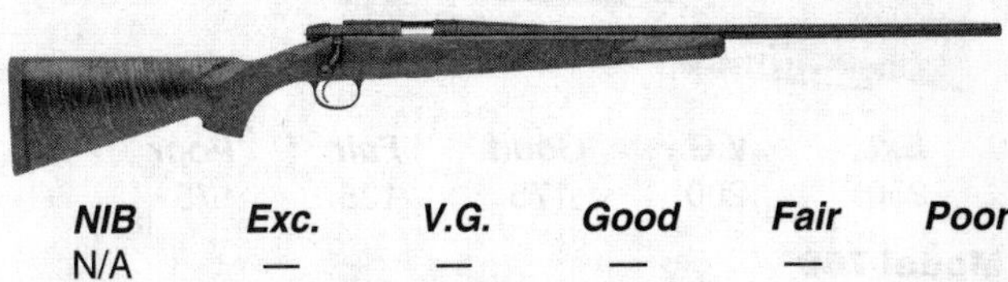

NIB	Exc.	V.G.	Good	Fair	Poor
N/A	—	—	—	—	—

Model 504-T LS HB

Introduced in 2005 this model features a 20" heavy barrel with blued finish. Chambered for the .22 Long Rifle or the .17 HMR cartridge. Brown laminate stock with Monte Carlo comb. Weight is about 8.5 lbs.

NIB	Exc.	V.G.	Good	Fair	Poor
825	—	—	—	—	—

Model 547

High-quality magazine-fed .17 or .22 rimfire sporter with walnut stock, crowned muzzle, tuned rigger and other goodies. Suspiciously similar to the defunct Model 504. A dealer exclusive for 2007.

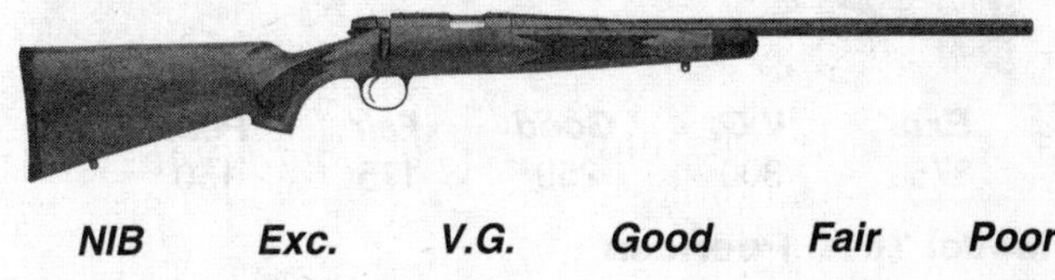

NIB	Exc.	V.G.	Good	Fair	Poor
—	—	—	—	—	—

Model 511 Scoremaster

A .22 caliber bolt-action magazine sporting rifle with a 22" barrel. Blued with a walnut stock.

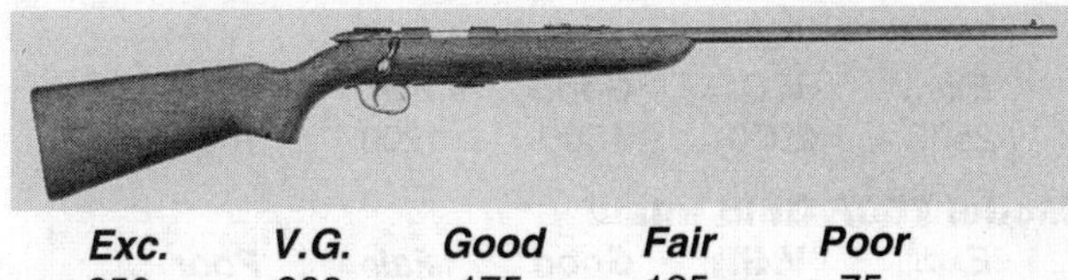

Exc.	V.G.	Good	Fair	Poor
250	200	175	125	75

Model 513 TR Matchmaster

A .22 caliber bolt-action magazine target rifle with a heavy 27" barrel and Redfield aperture rear sight. Blued with a target-style walnut stock. Manufactured from 1940 to 1969.

Exc.	V.G.	Good	Fair	Poor
350	300	200	150	100

Model 513 S

As above, with Marble sights and a checkered walnut sporting-style stock. Manufactured from 1941 to 1956.

Exc.	V.G.	Good	Fair	Poor
600	500	400	275	225

Model 521 TL Jr.

A .22 caliber bolt-action magazine target rifle with a heavy 25" barrel and Lyman sights. Blued with a target-style walnut stock. Manufactured from 1947 to 1969.

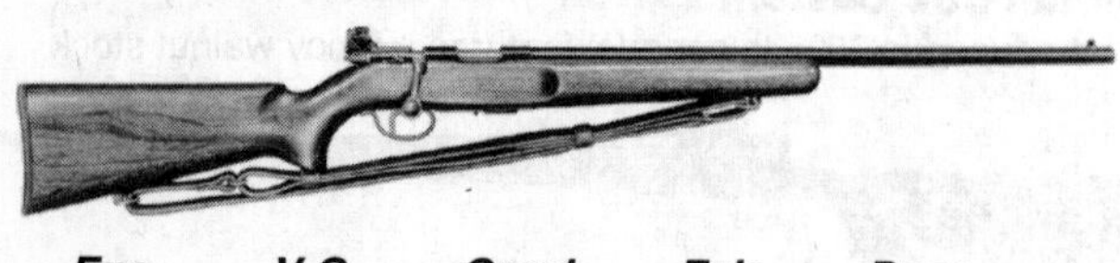

Exc.	V.G.	Good	Fair	Poor
250	200	175	125	75

Model 760

A slide-action sporting rifle chambered for various popular centerfire cartridges from the .222 up to the .35 Remington cartridge, with a 22" round barrel and open sights. It features a detachable box magazine. Blued with a checkered, walnut, pistol-grip stock. Manufactured between 1952 and 1982. Examples of this rifle chambered for the .222, .223, .244, and the .257 Roberts are worth a premium over other calibers. Prospective purchasers are advised to secure a qualified appraisal prior to acquisition. This model was produced in the styles listed.

Standard Model

Exc.	V.G.	Good	Fair	Poor
275	200	175	125	100

Model 760 Carbine

18.5" barrel.

Exc.	V.G.	Good	Fair	Poor
375	300	250	175	150

Model 760D Peerless

Engraved.

Exc.	V.G.	Good	Fair	Poor
1000	850	650	550	450

Model 760F Premier

Game scene engraved.

Exc.	V.G.	Good	Fair	Poor
2500	2000	1500	1200	1000

Model 760F Gold Inlaid

Exc.	V.G.	Good	Fair	Poor
5000	4000	3000	2200	1750

Model 760 Bicentennial

1976 only.

Exc.	V.G.	Good	Fair	Poor
350	300	250	175	100

Model 760 ADL

Exc.	V.G.	Good	Fair	Poor
275	225	175	125	75

Model 760 BDL

Basketweave checkering.

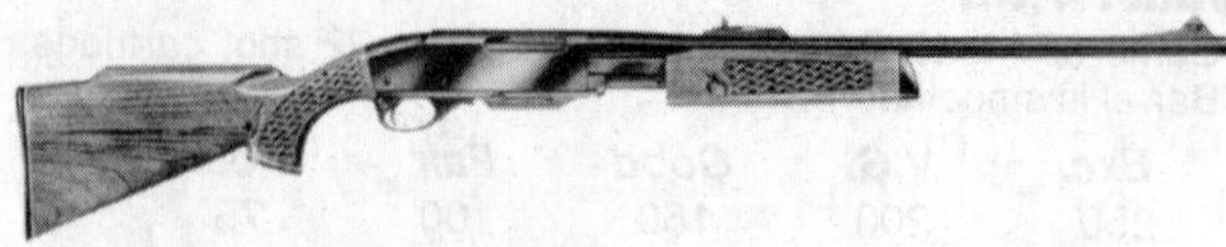

Exc.	V.G.	Good	Fair	Poor
300	250	200	150	100

Model 552A Speedmaster

A .22 caliber semi-automatic rifle with a 23" barrel and open sights. Blued with a pistol grip walnut stock. Manufactured from 1959 to 1988.

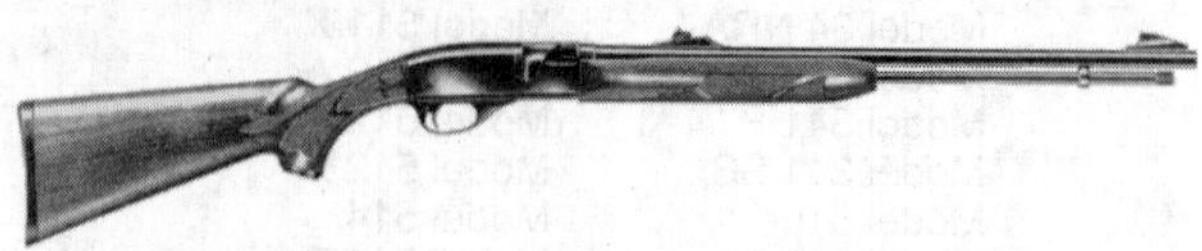

Exc.	V.G.	Good	Fair	Poor
150	125	100	75	50

Model 552 BDL

As above, with a more fully figured stock and impressed checkering. Introduced in 1966.

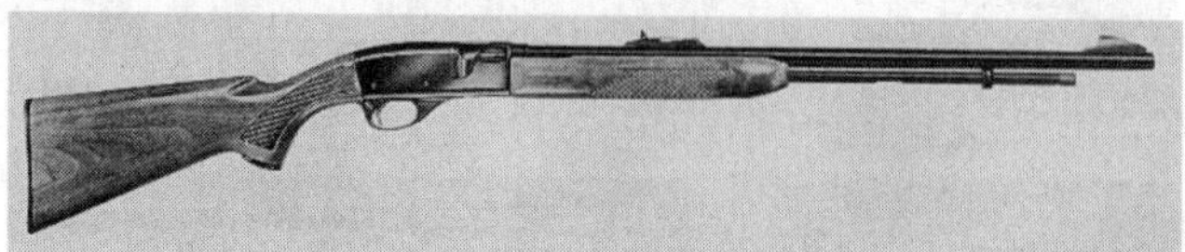

Courtesy Remington Arms

NIB	Exc.	V.G.	Good	Fair	Poor
410	300	225	150	100	75

Model 552 BDL Deluxe Speedmaster NRA Edition

Introduced in 2005 this model features a walnut stock with checkering and high gloss finish. Blued receiver and barrel with NRA logos etched on both sides of the receiver.

NIB	Exc.	V.G.	Good	Fair	Poor
520	400	—	—	—	—

Model 552 NRA Edition Speedmaster

Similar to Model 552 BDL but with NRA logo lasered on receiver. Introduced 2006. MSRP: 575

Model 572 Fieldmaster

A .22 caliber slide-action rifle with a 21" barrel and open sights. Blued with a walnut stock. Manufactured from 1955 to 1988.

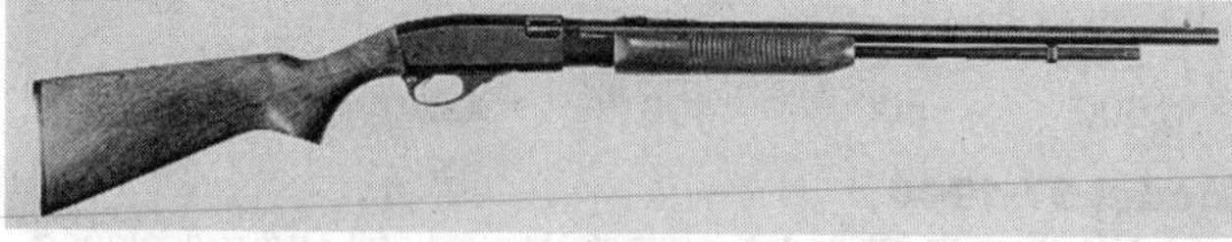

Courtesy Remington Arms

Exc.	V.G.	Good	Fair	Poor
150	125	100	75	50

Model 572 BDL

As above, but with a more fully figured walnut stock with impressed checkering. Introduced in 1966.

NIB	Exc.	V.G.	Good	Fair	Poor
425	300	225	150	110	85

Model 572SB

This is the same as the Model 572 but it has a smoothbore barrel and is chambered for the .22 LR cartridge.

NIB	Exc.	V.G.	Good	Fair	Poor
250	175	125	100	75	60

Model 572 BDL Smoothbore

Similar to Model 572 but with unrifled barrel for use with shot cartridges. Introduced as a special production item in 2007.

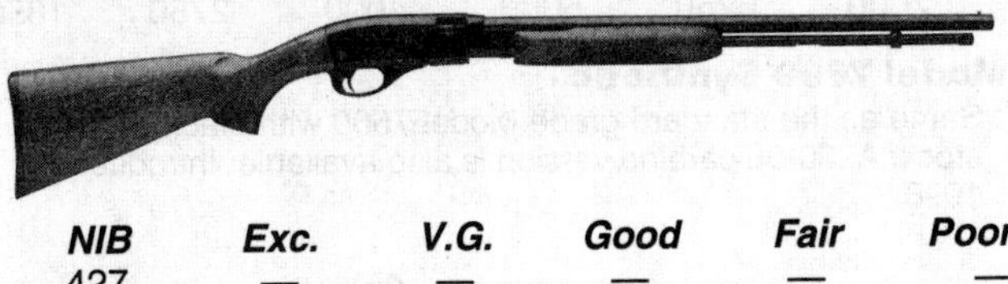

NIB	Exc.	V.G.	Good	Fair	Poor
427	—	—	—	—	—

Model 580

A .22 caliber single-shot bolt-action rifle with a 24" barrel, open sights and a Monte Carlo-style stock. Blued. Manufactured from 1968 to 1978.

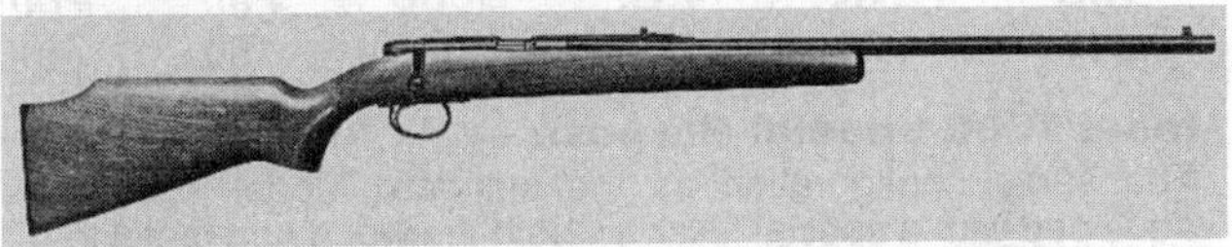

Courtesy Remington Arms

Exc.	V.G.	Good	Fair	Poor
150	100	75	50	25

Model 580 BR

Same as above but with 1" shorter buttstock.

NIB	Exc.	V.G.	Good	Fair	Poor
130	100	75	60	50	40

Model 580SB

This is the same as the Model 580 except with a smoothbore barrel for .22 LR cartridges.

NIB	Exc.	V.G.	Good	Fair	Poor
200	125	100	75	60	50

Model 581

A .22 caliber bolt-action magazine rifle, blued with a 24" barrel and walnut stock. Manufactured from 1967 to 1983.

Exc.	V.G.	Good	Fair	Poor
175	125	100	75	50

Model 581 Left-Hand

Same as above but built for a left-handed shooter.

NIB	Exc.	V.G.	Good	Fair	Poor
200	150	100	75	60	50

Model 581-S

As above, fitted with a 5-round detachable magazine. Introduced in 1986.

Exc.	V.G.	Good	Fair	Poor
225	165	145	110	85

Model 582

As above, fitted with a tubular magazine in place of the detachable box magazine. Manufactured from 1967 to 1983.

Courtesy Remington Arms

Exc.	V.G.	Good	Fair	Poor
175	125	100	75	50

Model 591

A 5mm rimfire Magnum bolt-action rifle with a 24" barrel and Monte Carlo-style stock. Approximately 20,000 were made between 1970 and 1973.

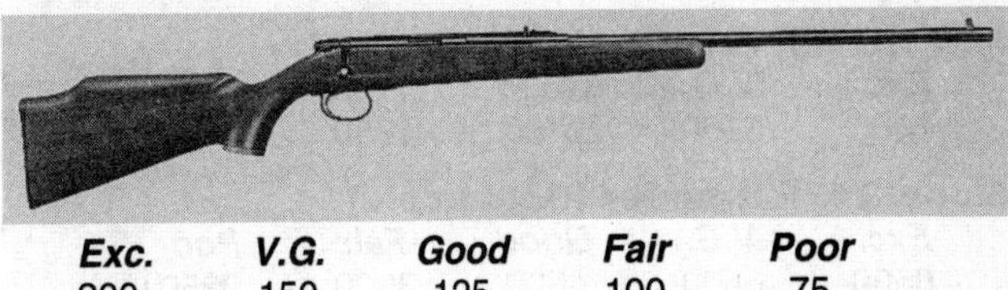

Exc.	V.G.	Good	Fair	Poor
200	150	125	100	75

Model 592

As above, with a tubular magazine. Approximately 7,000 were made.

Exc.	V.G.	Good	Fair	Poor
350	250	200	150	100

Model 740

A .308 or .30-06 semi-automatic rifle with a 22" barrel and detachable box magazine. Blued with a plain walnut stock. Also available with an 18.5" barrel that would be worth approximately 10 percent more than the values listed below. Manufactured from 1955 to 1960.

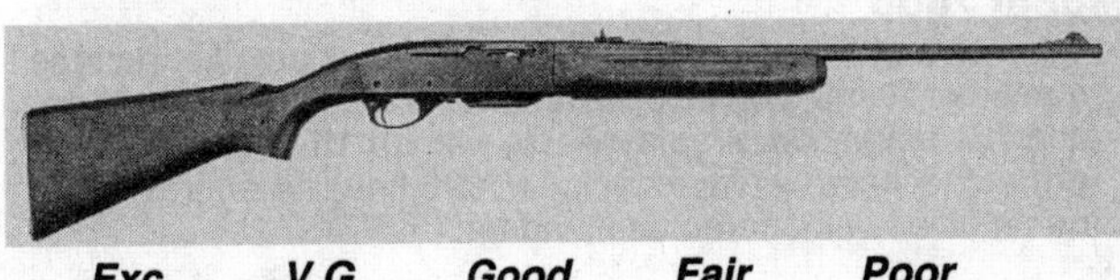

Exc.	V.G.	Good	Fair	Poor
300	225	200	150	100

Model 740 ADL

As above, with a checkered walnut stock with a pistol grip.

Exc.	V.G.	Good	Fair	Poor
350	250	225	150	100

Model 740 BDL

As above, with a more finely figured walnut stock.

Exc.	V.G.	Good	Fair	Poor
350	275	250	150	100

Model 742

A 6mm Remington, .243, .280, .30-06, or .308 caliber semi-automatic rifle with a 22" barrel and 4-shot magazine. Also available with an 18" barrel in calibers .308 and .30-06 that are worth approximately 10 percent more than the values listed below. Blued with a checkered walnut stock. Manufactured from 1960 to 1980.

Courtesy Remington Arms

Exc.	V.G.	Good	Fair	Poor
350	275	250	150	100

Model 742 BDL

As above, with a Monte Carlo-style stock and basketweave checkering.

Standard Grade

Exc.	V.G.	Good	Fair	Poor
375	275	225	175	125

Model 742D Peerless

Engraved.

Exc.	V.G.	Good	Fair	Poor
2100	1750	1500	1150	800

Model 742F Premier (Game Scene)

Exc.	V.G.	Good	Fair	Poor
4000	3500	2750	1850	1300

Model 742F Premier (Gold Inlaid)

Exc.	V.G.	Good	Fair	Poor
6500	5500	4000	3000	2250

Model 742 Bicentennial

Mfg. 1976 only.

Exc.	V.G.	Good	Fair	Poor
340	300	250	175	125

Model 76 Sportsman

A .30-06 slide-action rifle with a 22" barrel and 4-shot magazine. Blued with walnut stock. Manufactured from 1985 to 1987.

Exc.	V.G.	Good	Fair	Poor
325	225	175	125	75

Model 7600

A variation of the above, chambered for a variety of cartridges from 6mm Remington to .35 Whelen with a 22" barrel and a detachable magazine. Also available with an 18.5" barrel. Blued with a checkered walnut stock. In 1996 fine line engraving on the receiver was offered as standard.

Model 7600 with new engraving Courtesy Remington Arms

Close-up of new engraving on Model 7600

Courtesy Remington Arms

Standard Grade

NIB	Exc.	V.G.	Good	Fair	Poor
615	450	325	225	150	100

Model 7600D Peerless

Engraved.

NIB	Exc.	V.G.	Good	Fair	Poor
2250	1800	1400	1200	950	750

Model 7600F Premier

Game scene engraved.

NIB	Exc.	V.G.	Good	Fair	Poor
4750	4000	3500	2750	1850	1250

Model 7600 Premier

Gold inlaid.

NIB	Exc.	V.G.	Good	Fair	Poor
7000	6250	5000	4000	2750	1850

Model 7600 Synthetic

Same as the standard grade Model 7600 with black synthetic stock. A .30-06 carbine version is also available. Introduced in 1998.

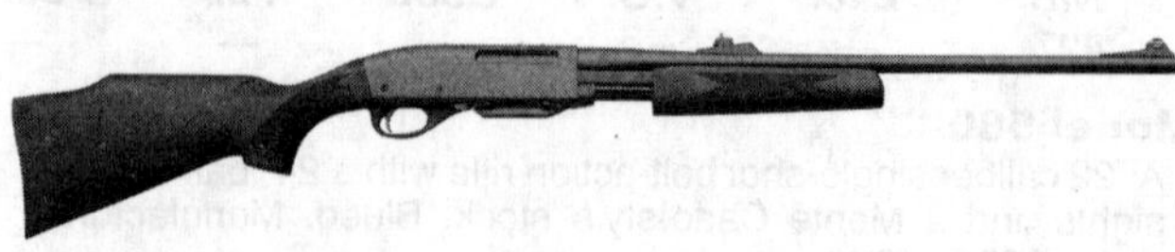

NIB	Exc.	V.G.	Good	Fair	Poor
510	375	275	200	150	100

Model 7600 Special Purpose

The same configuration as the standard Model 7600 but equipped with a special finish on both the wood and metal that is nonreflective. First offered in 1993.

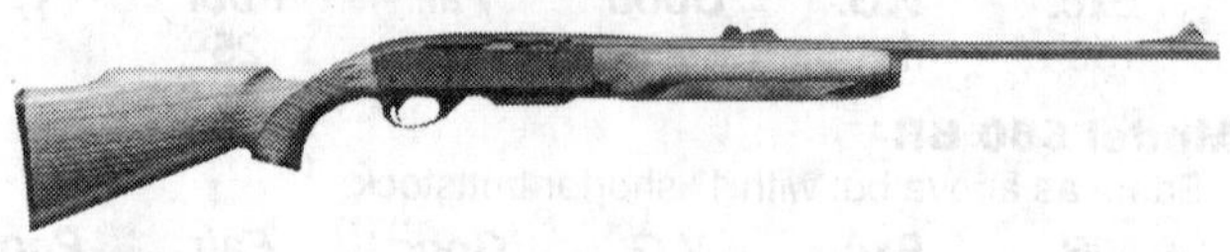

NIB	Exc.	V.G.	Good	Fair	Poor
500	375	275	200	150	100

Model 7600P Patrol Rifle

Introduced in 2002 this rifle is chambered for the .308 cartridge. It is fitted with a 16.5" barrel. Synthetic stock with matte black finish. Parkerized finish on metal. Wilson Combat rear ghost-ring sights with AO front sight. Weight is about 7 lbs.

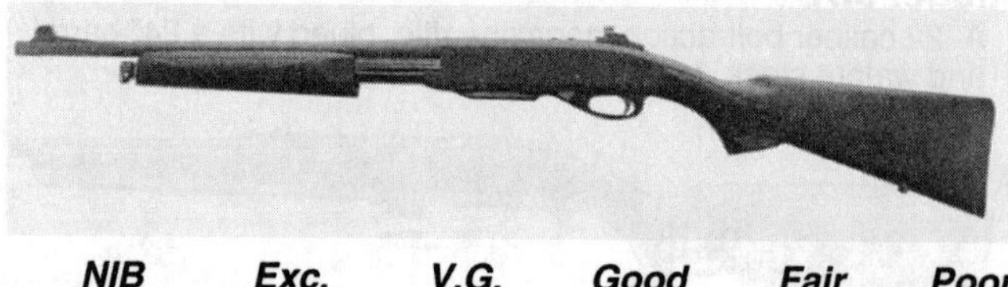

NIB	Exc.	V.G.	Good	Fair	Poor
500	375	—	—	—	—

Model 7600 Buckmasters ADF (American Deer Foundation)

Introduced in 1997 and built only for that year this model is chambered for the .30-06 cartridge and is a limited edition item. Fitted with a 22" barrel and special fine line engraved receiver.

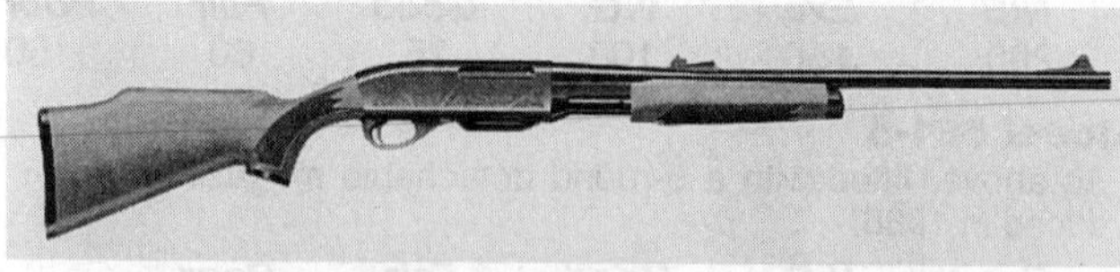

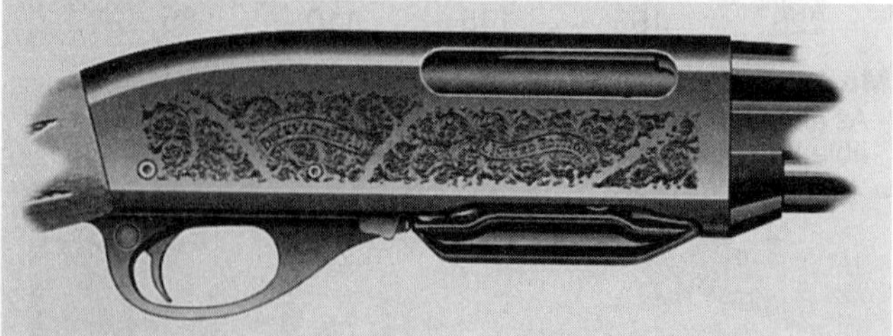

Close-up detail on engraving for Model 7600

NIB	Exc.	V.G.	Good	Fair	Poor
600	450	—	—	—	—

Model 7600 Custom Grade

This Custom Shop model is available in three levels of engraving, gold inlay, wood grade and finish, metal work finish, recoil pad/buttplate, and dimensions. Each gun should be individually appraised prior to a sale.

D Grade

NIB	Exc.	V.G.	Good	Fair	Poor
2600	—	—	—	—	—

F Grade

NIB	Exc.	V.G.	Good	Fair	Poor
5375	—	—	—	—	—

F Grade with Gold Inlay

NIB	Exc.	V.G.	Good	Fair	Poor
8050	—	—	—	—	—

Model Six

A centerfire slide-action rifle with a 22" barrel and a 4-shot detachable magazine. Blued with a walnut stock. Manufactured from 1981 to 1987.

Exc.	V.G.	Good	Fair	Poor
450	350	275	200	125

Model 7615 Tactical Pump Carbine

Pump-action rifle based on Model 7600 action and chambered in .223 Remington with 16-1/2" barrel. Folding synthetic stock. Introduced in 2007.

NIB	Exc.	V.G.	Good	Fair	Poor
600	—	—	—	—	—

Model 7615 Special Purpose Synthetic

Similar to Model 7615 Tactical but with fixed stock and picatinny rail. A dealer exclusive for 2007.

NIB	Exc.	V.G.	Good	Fair	Poor
625	—	—	—	—	—

Model 7615 Camo Hunter

Similar to Model 7615 Tactical but with fixed buttstock and entirely camo-finished except for action parts and trigger guard assembly. Introduced in 2007.

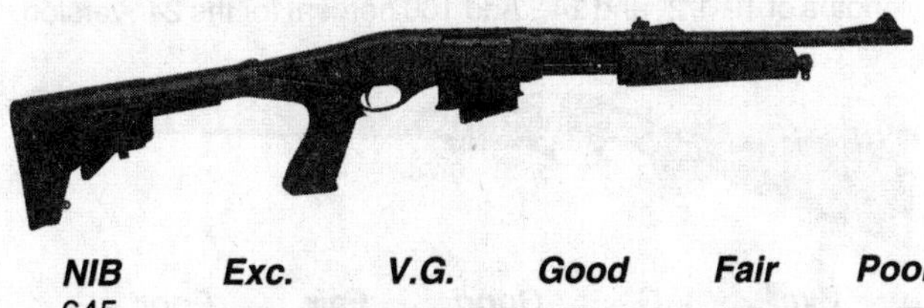

NIB	Exc.	V.G.	Good	Fair	Poor
645	—	—	—	—	—

Model 7615 Ranch Carbine

Similar to Model 7615 Tactical but with fixed buttstock, walnut buttstock and forend, and 18-1/2" barrel. No iron sights but drilled and tapped for scope mounts. Introduced in 2007.

NIB	Exc.	V.G.	Good	Fair	Poor
630	—	—	—	—	—

Model 74 Sportsman

A .30-06 caliber semi-automatic rifle with a 22" barrel and a 4-shot detachable magazine. Blued with a walnut stock. Manufactured from 1985 to 1987.

Exc.	V.G.	Good	Fair	Poor
350	250	175	125	75

Model Four

As above, with a select Monte Carlo-style stock. Manufactured from 1982 to 1987.

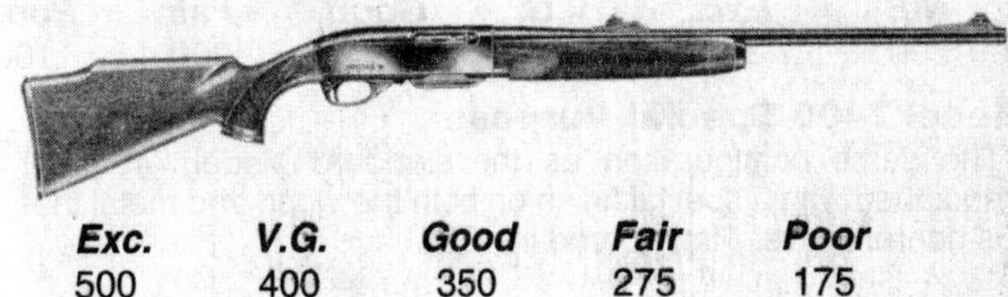

Exc.	V.G.	Good	Fair	Poor
500	400	350	275	175

Model 7400

This is a semi-automatic rifle with a 22" barrel. It is chambered for the .243, .270, .280, .30-06, .308, and the .35 Whelen. Blued with a checkered walnut stock. Average weight is about 7.5 lbs. Introduced in 1982. In 1996 this model was offered with fine line engraving on the receiver as standard.

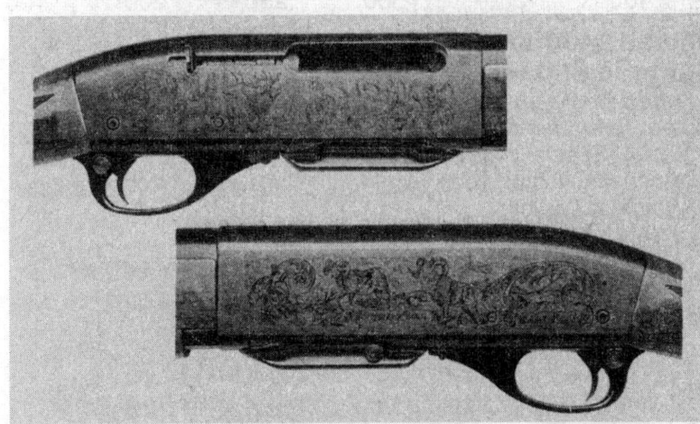

Close-up detail on engraving for Model 7400

Courtesy Remington Arms

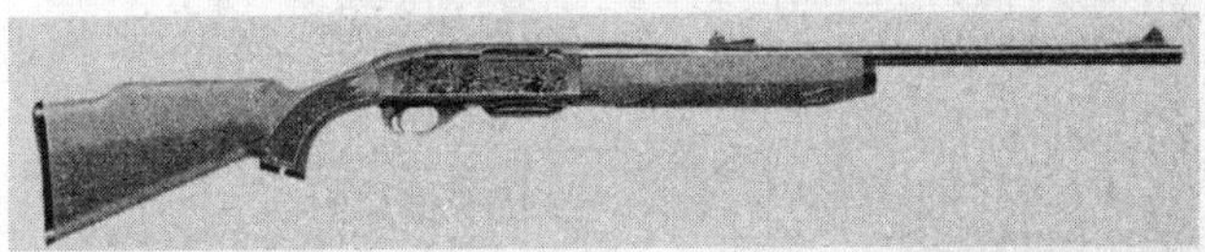

Model 7400 with new engraving Courtesy Remington Arms

NIB	Exc.	V.G.	Good	Fair	Poor
650	475	350	250	200	100

Model 7400 Synthetic

Similar to the Model 7400 with black nonreflective synthetic stock. A .30-06 carbine is also offered. Introduced in 1998.

NIB	Exc.	V.G.	Good	Fair	Poor
550	400	300	200	150	100

Model 7400 Weathermaster

Introduced in 2003 this semi-automatic model features a weather-resistant black synthetic stock and matte nickel-plated receiver, barrel, and magazine. Barrel length is 22" with iron sights. Chambered for the .30-06 or .270 Win. cartridges. Weight is about 7.5 lbs.

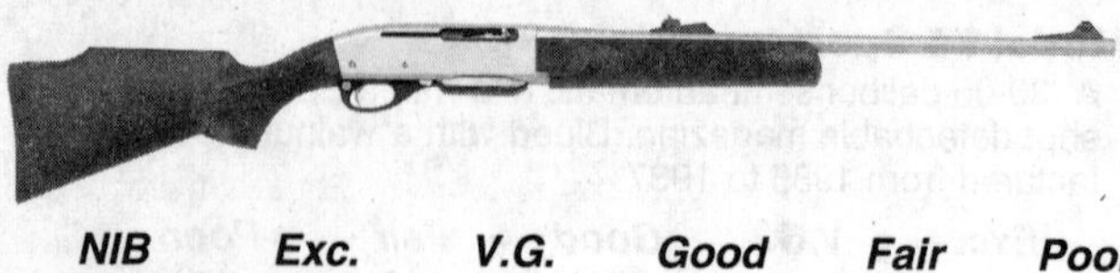

NIB	Exc.	V.G.	Good	Fair	Poor
650	500	—	—	—	—

Model 7400 Carbine

Same as above but with 18.5" barrel and chambered for the .30-06 cartridge.

NIB	Exc.	V.G.	Good	Fair	Poor
500	375	300	250	200	100

Model 7400 Special Purpose

The same configuration as the standard Model 7400 but equipped with a special finish on both the wood and metal that is nonreflective. First offered in 1993.

NIB	Exc.	V.G.	Good	Fair	Poor
450	350	300	250	200	100

Model 7400 Buckmasters ADF (American Deer Foundation)

Introduced in 1997, and built only in that year this model is limited. Chambered for the .30-06 cartridge and fitted with a 22" barrel. Special fine line engraving and polished blue finish. American walnut stock with Monte Carlo and cut checkering. Weight is 7.5 lbs.

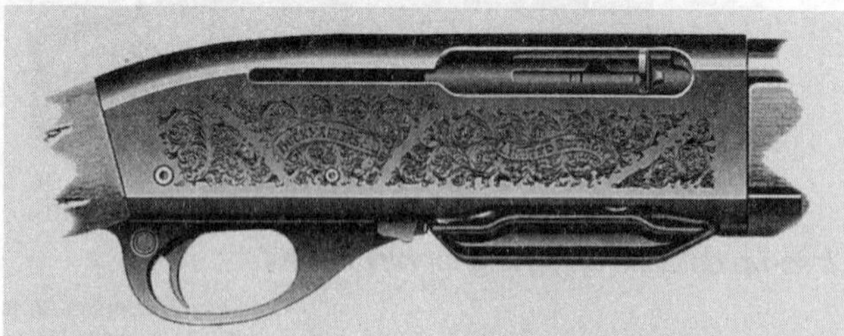

Close-up detail on engraving for Model 7400 Buckmasters ADF

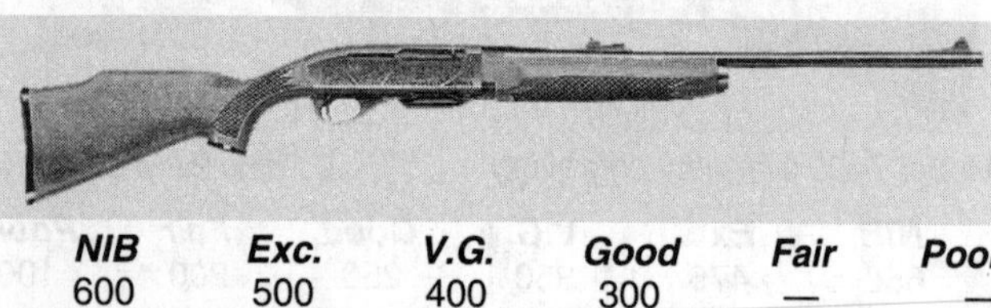

NIB	Exc.	V.G.	Good	Fair	Poor
600	500	400	300	—	—

Model 7400 Custom Grade

This Custom Shop model is available in three levels of engraving, gold inlay, wood grade and finish, metal work finish, recoil pad/buttplate, and dimensions. Each gun should be individually appraised prior to a sale.

D Grade

NIB	Exc.	V.G.	Good	Fair	Poor
2600	—	—	—	—	—

F Grade

NIB	Exc.	V.G.	Good	Fair	Poor
5375	—	—	—	—	—

F Grade with Gold Inlay

NIB	Exc.	V.G.	Good	Fair	Poor
8050	—	—	—	—	—

Model 750 Woodsmaster

Wood-stocked version of Model 7400 semi-auto. Rifle version has 22" barrel; carbine has 18.5" barrel. Introduced 2006.

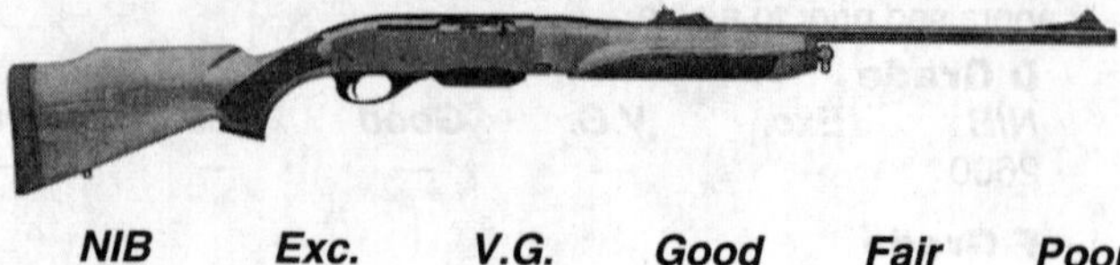

NIB	Exc.	V.G.	Good	Fair	Poor
650	—	—	—	—	—

Model 750 Synthetic

Similar to Model 750 Woodsmaster but with black synthetic stock and forend. Introduced in 2007.

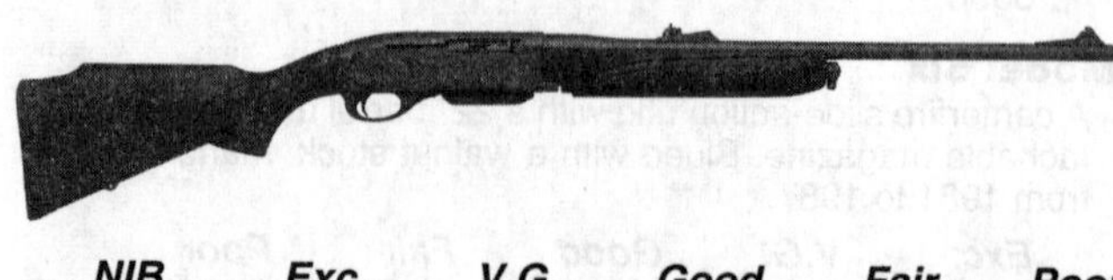

NIB	Exc.	V.G.	Good	Fair	Poor
625	—	—	—	—	—

Model 10

Bolt action single shot. Approximately 10,700 (approx. 2000 smoothbore and only 200 of those with 24" barrel) produced from 1962-1964. Mohawk brown nylon stock with white accents, chrome spoon style bolt handle, safety engages upon cocking, .22 short, long, and long rifle. This model is available in both rifled and smoothbore versions (smoothbore barrels are marked "smoothbore" and in barrel lengths of 19-1/2" and 24". Add 100 percent+ for the 24" versions. Add 100 percent+ for NIB.

Courtesy Remington Arms

	Exc.	V.G.	Good	Fair	Poor
10	700	600	500	300	200
10 (SB)	1000	800	700	500	450

Model 11

Bolt action repeater, 6- or 10-round metal box magazine. Approximately 22,500 produced from 1962-1964. Mohawk brown nylon stock with white accents, chrome spoon style bolt handle, manual right side safety. .22 short, long or long rifle. Barrel lengths of 19-1/2" and 24". Add 100 percent for the 24" version.

Exc.	V.G.	Good	Fair	Poor
475	375	300	275	175

Model 12

Bolt action repeater, 14 round external tubular magazine under the barrel. Approximately 27,600 produced from 1962-1964. Mohawk brown nylon stock with white accents, chrome spoon style bolt handle, manual right side safety. .22 short, long or long rifle. Barrel lengths of 19-1/2" and 24". Add 100 percent for 24" version.

Exc.	V.G.	Good	Fair	Poor
475	375	300	275	175

Model 66

Semi-automatic, 19-1/2" barrel, 14 round tubular magazine, fed through the buttplate. In excess of 1,000,000 produced from 1959-1987. Seven different variations of style and color were sold. Non-serialized prior to the 1968 gun control act of 1968. An "A" prefix was added to the serialization in 1977. Add 100 percent+ for NIB.

66 (MB) "Mohawk" Brown

Blued metal parts, dark chocolate brown stock with white accents, .22 LR ONLY. 1959-1987. Approx. 678,000.

66 (SG) "Seneca" Green

Blued metal parts, dark olive green stock (often confused with MB in artificial light) with white accents, .22 LR ONLY, 1959-1962. Approx. 45,000.

66 (AB) "Apache" Black

Bright chrome plated metal parts, black stock with white accents, .22 LR ONLY.1962-1983. Approx. 220,000.

66 (BD) "Black Diamond"

Blued metal parts, black stock with black diamonds in the forend. The remainder of accents are white, .22 LR ONLY, 1978-1987. Approx. 56,000.

66 (GS) "Gallery Special"

Blued metal parts, Dark brown stock with white accents. Barrel marked .22 SHORT. Distinguished by shell deflector over ejection port and a loop on the forend for the counter chain. 1961-1981. Approx. 6500.

66 (AN) "150th Anniversary Rifle"

Blued metal parts, dark brown stock with white accents, .22 LR ONLY. Distinguished by 150th Anniversary stamping on the left side of the receiver cover. 1966 ONLY. Approx. 4000.

66 (BI) "Bicentennial Rifle"

Blued metal parts, dark brown stock with white accents, .22 LR ONLY. Distinguished by the eagle and 1776/1976 stamping on the left side of the receiver cover. 1976 ONLY. Approx. 10,000.

	Exc.	V.G.	Good	Fair	Poor
66 (MB)	250	175	150	125	100
66 (SG)	550	450	325	275	175
66 (AB)	300	250	200	150	125
66 (BD)	325	300	225	175	150
66 (GS)	1200	950	700	450	300
66 (AN)	850	650	450	300	250
66 (BI)	750	500	325	275	200

NOTE: One should expect 100 percent+ premium for new in the box examples.

Model 66 Bicentennial Commemorative

As above, but with a 1976 commemorative inscription on the barrel. Manufactured in 1976.

Exc.	V.G.	Good	Fair	Poor
375	275	200	125	75

Model 76

Lever action repeater. The only lever action Remington ever produced. 19-1/2" barrel, 14 round tubular magazine, fed through the buttplate. Produced from 1962-1964 in three different variations. Add 100 percent+ for NIB.

76 (MB) "Trailrider"

Blued metal parts, dark brown stocks with white accents. Approximately 25,300 produced.

76 (AB) "Trailrider"

Bright chrome metal parts, black stock with white accents. Approximately 1600 produced.

76 (not cataloged)

Blued metal parts, black stock with white accents. Production numbers do not exist.

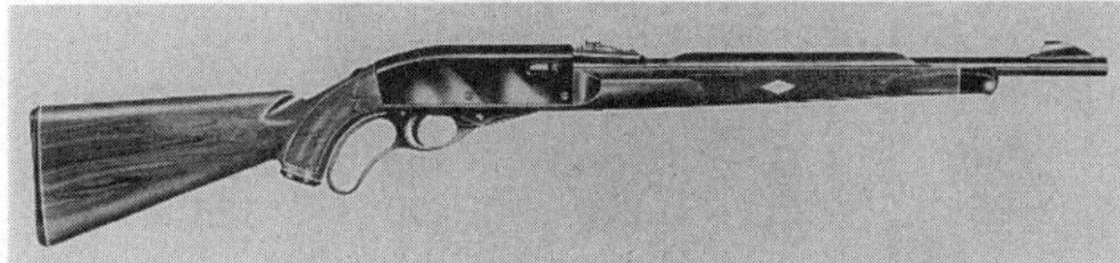

Courtesy Remington Arms

	Exc.	V.G.	Good	Fair	Poor
76 (MB)	1700	600	500	375	250
76 (AB)	2000	800	700	500	400
76 (Not cataloged)	1800	675	600	400	300

Model 77

Known as the 77 (MB): Semi-automatic,19-1/2" barrel, 5 round plastic box magazine. Blued metal parts, dark brown stock with white accents. .22 LR ONLY. 1970-1971. Approx. 15,300 produced. This model was replaced by the Model 10C in 1972. Add 100 percent for NIB.

Exc.	V.G.	Good	Fair	Poor
500	375	300	200	150

Model 10C

Known as the 10C. An identical copy of the 77 (MB), except that the box magazine capacity was increased to 10 rounds. 1972-1978. Approx. 128,000 produced. Add 50 percent for NIB.

Exc.	V.G.	Good	Fair	Poor
325	275	225	175	100

Model 77 Apache

Known as the "APACHE 77." Semi-automatic, 19-1/2" barrel, 10 round plastic box magazine. Metal parts coated with a black "teflon-like" finish, bright green stock with swirls of orange brown and black (highly variable), not to be confused with the 66 (SG). This rifle was contracted as an "exclusive" run, marketed by K-Mart. The number manufactured is hazy, but estimates run from 54,000 to over 100,000. Produced from 1987-1989. Add 100 percent for NIB.

Exc.	V.G.	Good	Fair	Poor
350	250	200	140	120

Model 522 Viper

Introduced in 1993 the Model 522 Viper is a new Remington .22 rimfire caliber semi-automatic design. The black stock is made from synthetic resin, while the receiver is made from a synthetic as well. It features a 20" barrel and a 10-shot detachable clip. The rifle weighs 4.6 lbs.

This symbol denotes "Sleepers" with rapidly-rising values and/or significant collector potential. 

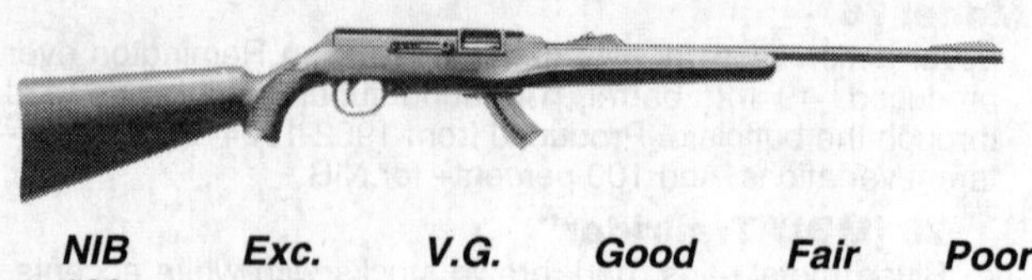

NIB	Exc.	V.G.	Good	Fair	Poor
160	120	100	80	60	40

Model 541 S Custom

A .22 caliber bolt-action magazine rifle with a 24" barrel. Blued with a scroll engraved receiver, and checkered walnut stock having a rosewood pistol grip cap and forend tip. Manufactured from 1972 to 1984.

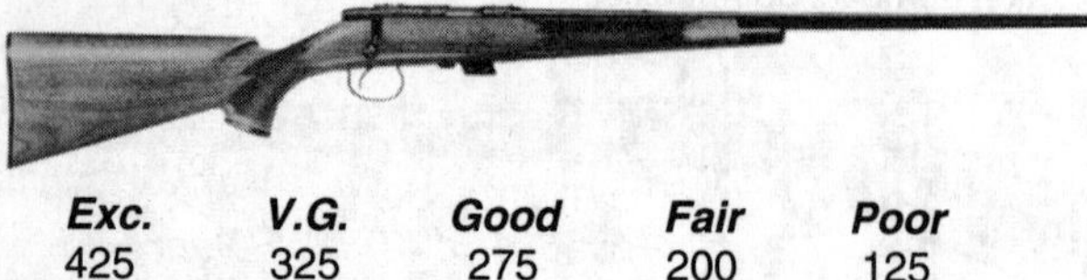

Exc.	V.G.	Good	Fair	Poor
425	325	275	200	125

Model 541T

As above, drilled and tapped for telescopic sights. Introduced in 1986.

NIB	Exc.	V.G.	Good	Fair	Poor
375	275	200	175	125	75

Model 541T Heavy Barrel

This model is the same as the standard 541-T with the exception of a 24" heavy barrel. First introduced in 1993.

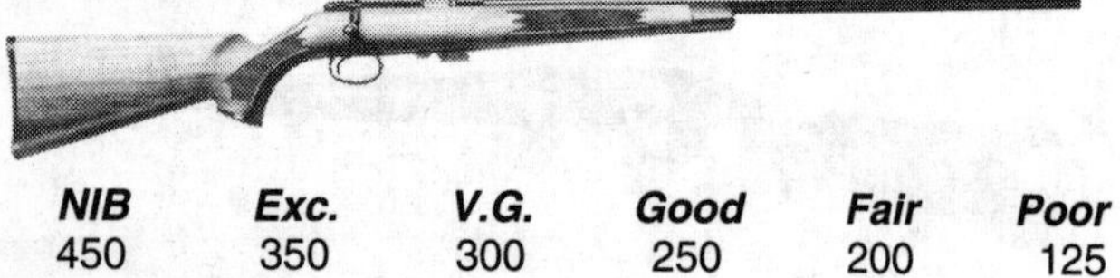

NIB	Exc.	V.G.	Good	Fair	Poor
450	350	300	250	200	125

Model 597

Introduced in 1997 this automatic .22 LR rimfire rifle features a carbon steel barrel with alloy receiver. All metal has a nonreflective matte black finish. Stock is dark gray synthetic. Barrel length is 20" and weight is approximately 5.5 lbs.

NIB	Exc.	V.G.	Good	Fair	Poor
225	150	100	70	50	—

Model 597 Sporter

Introduced in 1998 this version of the Model 597 has a blued finish with a hardwood stock with beavertail-style forearm. Magazine capacity is 10 rounds.

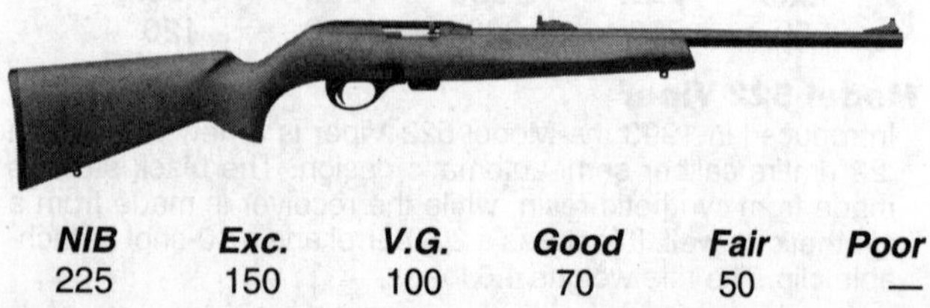

NIB	Exc.	V.G.	Good	Fair	Poor
225	150	100	70	50	—

Model 597 Stainless Sporter

Same as the Model 597SS but fitted with a hardwood stock. Introduced in 2000.

NIB	Exc.	V.G.	Good	Fair	Poor
275	200	150	100	75	—

Model 597 LSS

This version of the Model 597 is similar to the above but with the addition of a laminated stock and stainless steel finish.

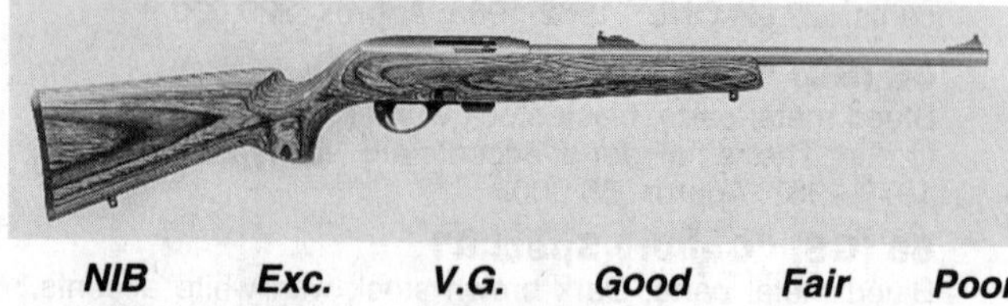

NIB	Exc.	V.G.	Good	Fair	Poor
300	225	175	—	—	—

Model 597 SS

This version is also chambered for the .22 LR and has a stainless steel barrel on an alloy receiver. The stock is gray synthetic with beavertail style forearm. Magazine capacity is 10 rounds. Weight is about 5.5 lbs. Introduced in 1998.

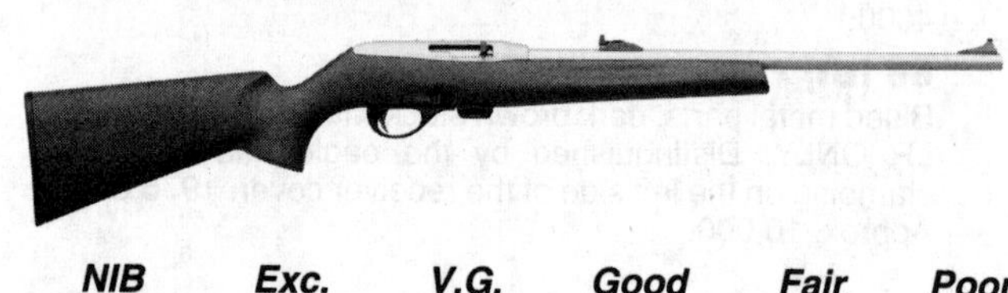

NIB	Exc.	V.G.	Good	Fair	Poor
240	175	125	100	—	—

Model 597 HB

Introduced in 2001 this model features a 20" carbon steel heavy barrel chambered for the .22 LR cartridge. Fitted with a brown laminated stock. No sights. Weight is about 6 lbs.

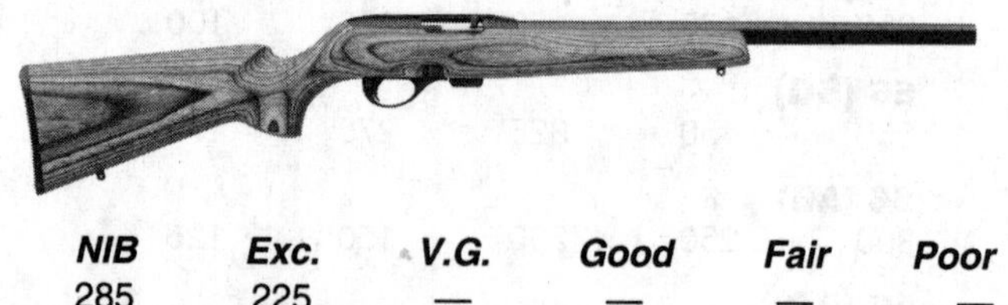

NIB	Exc.	V.G.	Good	Fair	Poor
285	225	—	—	—	—

Model 597 HB Magnum

Same as model above but chambered for the .22 Winchester Magnum cartridge. Introduced in 2001.

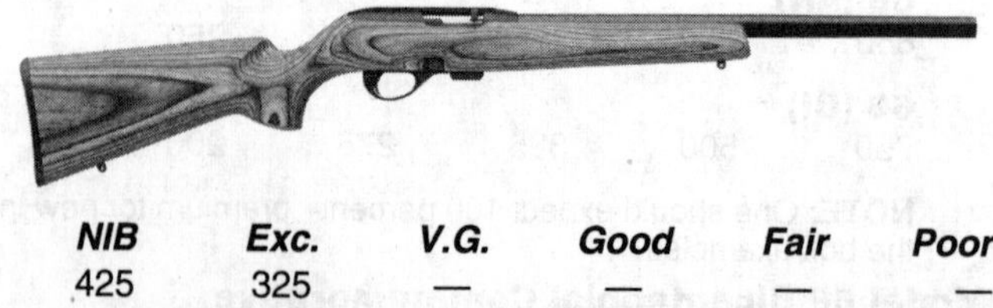

NIB	Exc.	V.G.	Good	Fair	Poor
425	325	—	—	—	—

Model 597 Magnum

This model features a 20" carbon steel barrel, alloy receiver, and black synthetic stock. It is chambered for the .22 Win. Magnum cartridge. Weight is approximately 6 lbs.

NIB	Exc.	V.G.	Good	Fair	Poor
350	250	—	—	—	—

Model 597 Magnum LS

Chambered for the .22 Magnum. The receiver and barrel are blued with a gray laminated hardwood stock with beavertail-style forearm. Magazine capacity is 10 rounds. Introduced in 1998. In 2003 this model was also offered chambered for the .17 HMR cartridge.

NIB	Exc.	V.G.	Good	Fair	Poor
375	275	—	—	—	—

Model 597 Custom Target

This model is available on special order from the Custom Shop. It is chambered for the .22 LR cartridge and has a 20" stainless steel heavy target barrel without sights. The stock is a green, laminated-wood target style with pistol grip. Trigger is custom tuned. Weight is approximately 7.5 lbs. Introduced in 1998.

NIB	Exc.	V.G.	Good	Fair	Poor
600	475	—	—	—	—

Model 597 Custom Target Magnum

Similar to the model above but chambered for the .22 Win. Mag. Weight is approximately 8 lbs. Introduced in 1998. This is special order item only.

NIB	Exc.	V.G.	Good	Fair	Poor
750	600	—	—	—	—

Model 597 LSS

Similar to Model 597 but with laminated stock, stainless barrel and 3-9X scope. Dealer exclusive for 2007.

NIB	Exc.	V.G.	Good	Fair	Poor
275	—	—	—	—	—

Model 597 Synthetic Scope Combo

"Package rifle" similar to Model 597 but with 3-9X scope included. Introduced in 2007.

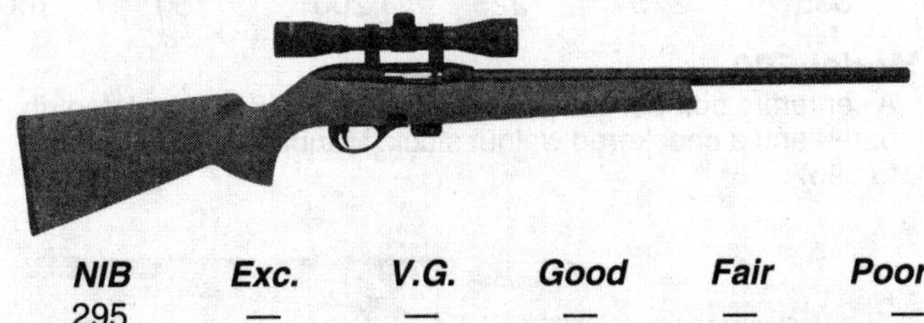

NIB	Exc.	V.G.	Good	Fair	Poor
295	—	—	—	—	—

Model 5

.22 rimfire bolt-action sporter. Calibers: .22 LR or .22 WMR; five-shot detachable magazine. Barrel: 22" blued with iron sights; receiver blued for scope mounts. Stock: laminated walnut with QD swivels. Add 5 percent for .22 WMR. Introduced 2006. MSRP: 348

Model 40X-BR

A .22 caliber single-shot bolt-action rifle with a heavy 28" barrel fitted with Redfield Olympic sights or telescopic sight bases. Blued with a walnut target style stock having a hard rubber butt-plate. Manufactured from 1955 to 1964.

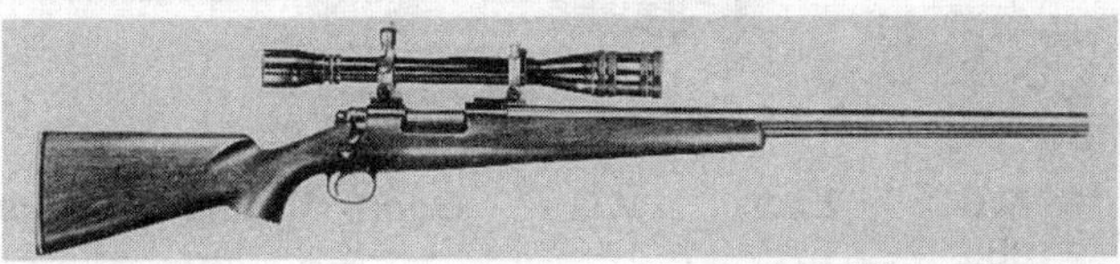

Courtesy Remington Arms

Exc.	V.G.	Good	Fair	Poor
500	400	325	250	150

Model 40X Sporter

As above, with a 24" barrel, 5-shot magazine and a walnut sporting style stock. Less than 700 were made between 1969 and 1980.

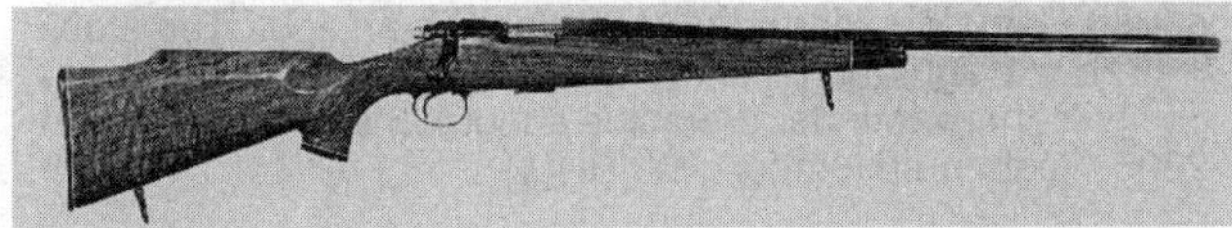

Courtesy Remington Arms

Exc.	V.G.	Good	Fair	Poor
2500	1500	1000	750	500

Model 40X Centerfire

As above, chambered for .22, .22 Magnum, .308, or .30-06 centerfire cartridges. Manufactured from 1961 to 1964.

Exc.	V.G.	Good	Fair	Poor
550	450	350	300	200

Model 40XB Stainless

This model is built in the Custom Shop and features stainless steel barrel, receiver, and bolt. The receiver is drilled and tapped and fitted with a 27-1/4" heavy target barrel. The trigger is fully adjustable. There is a choice of walnut stock or synthetic stock. Starting in 1998 this model was offered with a special laminated thumbhole stock. Offered in calibers from .222 to .300 Win. Mag. This rifle is built to order. Retail prices range from $1,200 to $1,500 depending on configuration and finish.

Model 40-XB with laminated thumbhole stock

Model 40XB BR

This is a bench rest Custom Shop version of the above model. This rifle has a 22" stainless heavy barrel chambered for the .22 LR. Adjustable trigger. Built to order. Retail prices begin around $1,350.

Model 40XB Tactical Rifle

First offered in 2003 this bolt-action rifle features a Teflon coated stainless steel 27.25" barrel chambered for the .308 Win. cartridge. Fitted with a H.S. Precision tactical stock with vertical pistol grip. Remington 40-X trigger. Retail prices $2,100.

Model 40XR KS Sporter

This Custom Shop version is also chambered for the .22 LR and is fitted with a 24" barrel. Fully adjustable trigger. This model is also built to special order and prices begin around $1,350.

Model XR-100 Rangemaster

Introduced in 2005 this model features a 26" barrel chambered for the .204 Ruger, .223, or .22-250 calibers. Black laminate stock with thumbhole and vented forearm. Adjustable trigger. Blued finish. Weight is about 9.12 lbs.

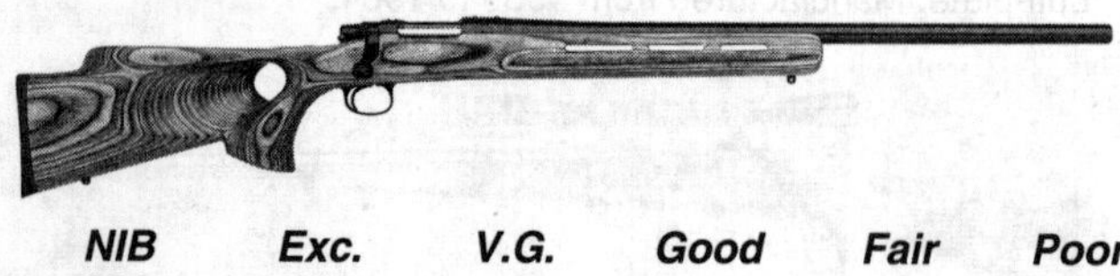

NIB	Exc.	V.G.	Good	Fair	Poor
880	675	—	—	—	—

Model XC

This is a Custom Shop position rifle with 24" stainless steel heavy barrel chambered for .223 Rem. and .308 Win. cartridges. Kevlar stock with palm rail. Weight is approximately 11 lbs. Prices begin around $1,550.

Model 673 Guide Rifle

Introduced in 2003 this bolt-action rifle features a 22" vent rib barrel chambered for the 6.5 mm Rem. Mag, .308, .300 RUM, or.350 Rem. Mag cartridge. Adjustable rear sight. The stock is dark and light tan laminate with checkering. Magazine capacity is three rounds. Weight is about 7.5 lbs. Discontinued 2006. Slight premium for .300 RUM.

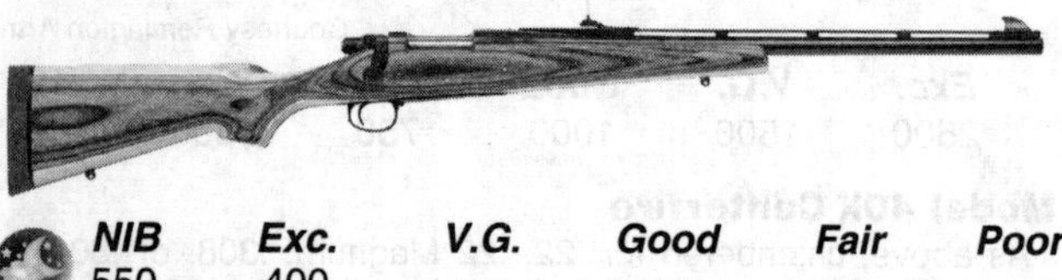

NIB	Exc.	V.G.	Good	Fair	Poor
550	400	—	—	—	—

Model 720A

A .257 Roberts, .270, or .30-06 bolt-action sporting rifle with a 22" barrel and a 5-shot integral magazine. Blued with a checkered walnut stock. Approximately 2,500 were manufactured in 1941.

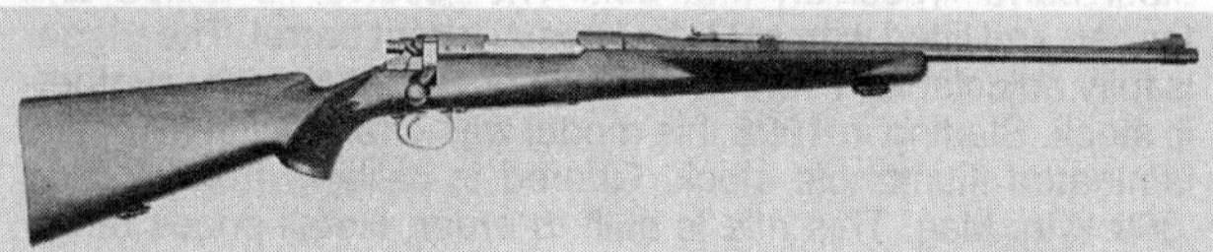

Courtesy Remington Arms

Exc.	V.G.	Good	Fair	Poor
1250	1000	800	600	475

Model 721

A .264 Magnum, .270, or .30-06 bolt-action rifle with a 24" barrel and a 4-shot magazine. Blued with a plain walnut stock. Manufactured from 1948 to 1962.

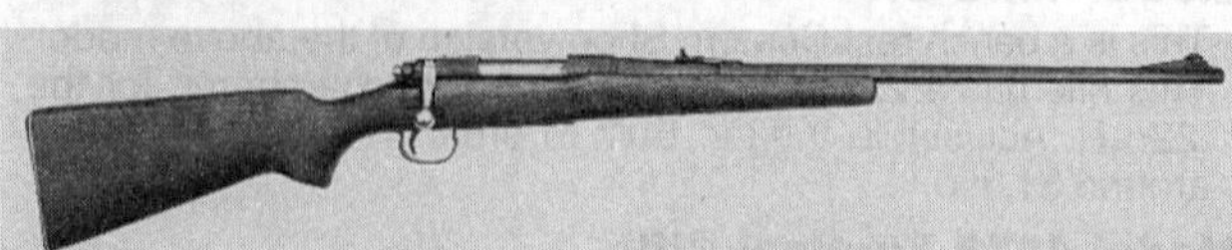

Courtesy Remington Arms

Standard Version

Exc.	V.G.	Good	Fair	Poor
450	350	200	150	100

Model 721 ADL

Exc.	V.G.	Good	Fair	Poor
475	375	250	200	125

Model 721 BDL

Select stock.

Exc.	V.G.	Good	Fair	Poor
450	375	300	250	150

Model 721A Magnum

.300 H&H.

Exc.	V.G.	Good	Fair	Poor
550	400	350	275	150

Model 722 BDL

As above, with a shorter action chambered for .222 Remington cartridge. Manufactured from 1948 to 1962.

NIB	Exc.	V.G.	Good	Fair	Poor
500	375	300	200	150	100

Model 725 ADL

A centerfire bolt-action sporting rifle with a 22" barrel, 4-shot magazine and Monte Carlo-style stock. The .222 caliber version was produced in limited quantities and should be individually appraised. Manufactured from 1958 to 1961.

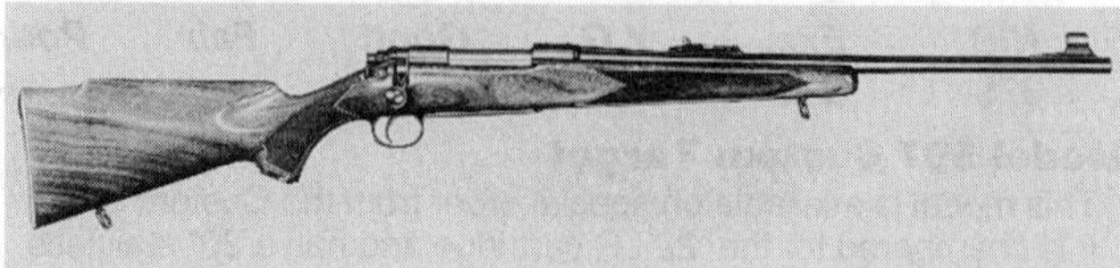

Courtesy Remington Arms

Exc.	V.G.	Good	Fair	Poor
1000	525	275	225	150

Model 725 Kodiak

A .375 Holland & Holland Magnum or .458 Winchester Magnum, bolt-action sporting rifle with a 26" barrel, muzzlebrake, open sights and 3-shot magazine. Blued with a checkered walnut stock. Manufactured in 1961.

Exc.	V.G.	Good	Fair	Poor
1200	700	550	400	300

Model 78 Sportsman

A centerfire bolt-action sporting rifle with a 22" barrel and 4-shot magazine. Blued with a walnut stock. Introduced in 1985.

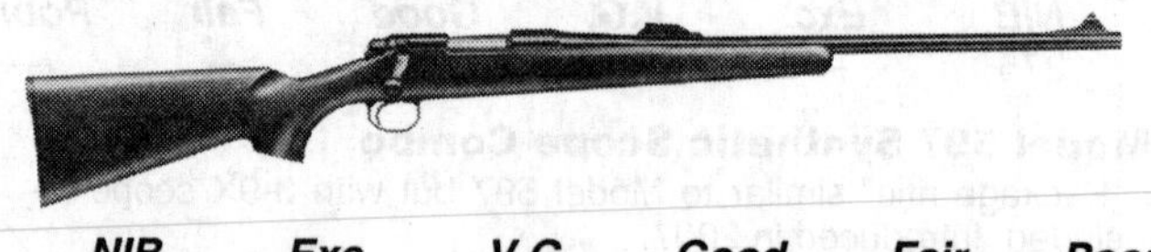

NIB	Exc.	V.G.	Good	Fair	Poor
335	275	225	200	150	100

Model 600

A centerfire bolt-action sporting rifle with an 18.5" ventilated rib barrel and a checkered walnut stock. Manufactured from 1964 to 1967.

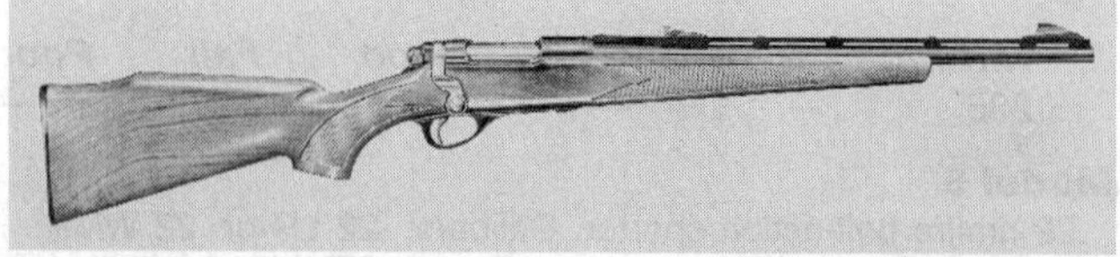

Courtesy Remington Arms

Exc.	V.G.	Good	Fair	Poor
550	450	350	225	150

This symbol denotes "Sleepers" with rapidly-rising values and/or significant collector potential.

Model 600 Mohawk

As above, but with a plain barrel and chambered only for the .222 Remington, .243 Winchester or .308 Winchester cartridges. Manufactured from 1971 to 1979.

Exc.	V.G.	Good	Fair	Poor
600	375	225	175	125

Model 600 Magnum

As above, chambered for the 6.5mm Remington Magnum and .350 Remington Magnum cartridges. Stock of laminated walnut and beechwood. Manufactured from 1965 to 1967.

Exc.	V.G.	Good	Fair	Poor
1000	750	600	450	200

Model 660

An improved version of the Model 600. Manufactured from 1968 to 1971.

Exc.	V.G.	Good	Fair	Poor
550	425	350	250	200

Model 660 Magnum

As above, but chambered for either the 6.5mm Remington Magnum or .350 Remington Magnum cartridges and fitted with a laminated stock.

Exc.	V.G.	Good	Fair	Poor
1000	750	600	450	200

MODEL 700 SERIES

NOTE #1: In 1996 Remington added fine-line engraving to its Model 700 line. All Model 700 BDL rifles will have this new engraving on them at no extra charge.

NOTE #2: In 1999 Remington introduced a new cartridge, the .300 Remington Ultra Magnum. It will be offered in these production models: Model 700 BDL, Model 700 BDL SS, Model 700 LSS, Model 700 LSS LH, Model 700 Sendero SF. Custom shop rifles are: Model 700 APR, Model 700 AWR, Model 700 Custom KS Mountain Rifle, Model 700 Custom KS Stainless Mountain Rifle. In 2000 the company added the .338 Ultra Magnum cartridge.

Model 700 ADL

A centerfire bolt-action sporting rifle with either a 22" or 24" barrel, open sights and a 4-shot magazine. Blued with a checkered Monte Carlo-style walnut stock. Introduced in 1962. In 1998 this model was available in .223 Rem. and .300 Win. Mag.

NIB	Exc.	V.G.	Good	Fair	Poor
425	325	250	200	150	100

Model 700 ADL Synthetic

This model features a black matte metal finish with 22" barrel or 24" on Magnums. The synthetic stock is black with checkering, recoil pad, and sling swivel studs. Receiver is drilled and tapped for scope. Offered in .243, .270, .30-06 and 7mm Rem. Mag. In 1998 this model was available in .223 Rem. and .300 Win. Mag.

Courtesy Remington Arms

NIB	Exc.	V.G.	Good	Fair	Poor
350	300	250	200	150	100

Model 700 ADL Synthetic Youth

Introduced in 1998 this model has a shortened synthetic stock with a 13" lop. Offered in .243 and .308 calibers.

NIB	Exc.	V.G.	Good	Fair	Poor
400	300	250	200	150	100

Model 700 BDL

Same as above, with a hinged floorplate, hand cut checkering, black forend tip and pistol grip cap. Offered in a wide variety of calibers from the .17 Rem. to the .338 Rem. Ultra Mag. Weights are between 7.25 lbs. to 7.62 lbs. depending on caliber and barrel length.

Courtesy Remington Arms

NIB	Exc.	V.G.	Good	Fair	Poor
715	525	400	275	225	150

Model 700 BDL LH (Left-Hand)

This model is also offered in selected calibers for left-hand shooters. They are: .270 Win., 7mm Rem. Mag., .30-06, and .300 Rem. Ultra Mag.

NIB	Exc.	V.G.	Good	Fair	Poor
715	525	400	300	—	—

Model 700 BDL (DM)

Same as above but introduced in 1995 with detachable magazine.

NIB	Exc.	V.G.	Good	Fair	Poor
715	525	400	300	225	150

Model 700 BDL LSS

This is a Model 700, introduced in 1996, with a synthetic stock and stainless steel bolt, floor plate, trigger guard, and sling swivels. The action and barrel are stainless steel as well. In 1997 the .260 Rem. cartridge was also available.

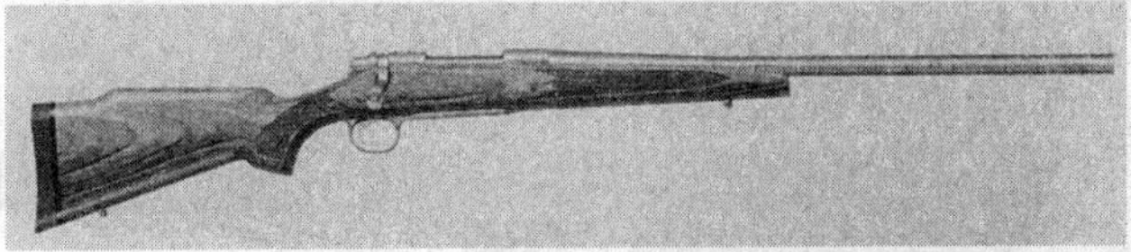

Courtesy Remington Arms

NIB	Exc.	V.G.	Good	Fair	Poor
600	475	400	350	300	200

Model 700 BDL SS DM—Magnum Rifle

Introduced in 1996 this Model 700 version is fitted with a factory installed muzzlebrake on its Magnum calibers: 7mm Rem. Mag., .300 Win. Mag., .300 Wthby. Mag., and the .338 Win. Mag. and the .338 Rem. Ultra Mag. Weight is approximately 7.5 lbs. In 1997 the 7mm STW cartridge was added to this model.

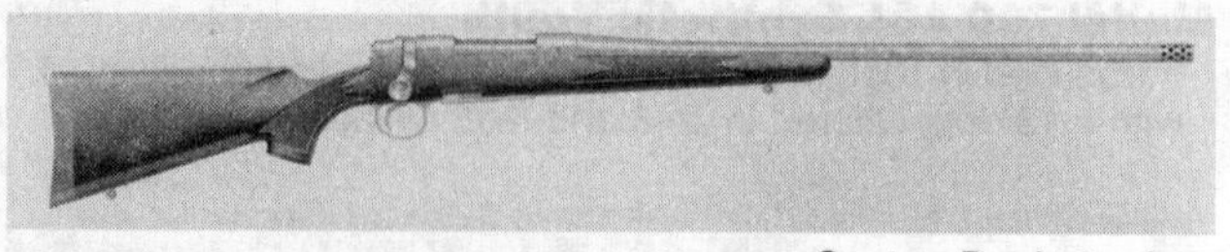

Courtesy Remington Arms

NIB	Exc.	V.G.	Good	Fair	Poor
675	500	400	300	200	150

Model 700 BDL SS Short Action

Fitted with stainless steel 24" and chambered for the 7mm Rem. Ultra Mag. and the .300 Rem. Ultra Mag. Black synthetic stock. No sights. Weight is about 7.325 lbs. Introduced in 2003.

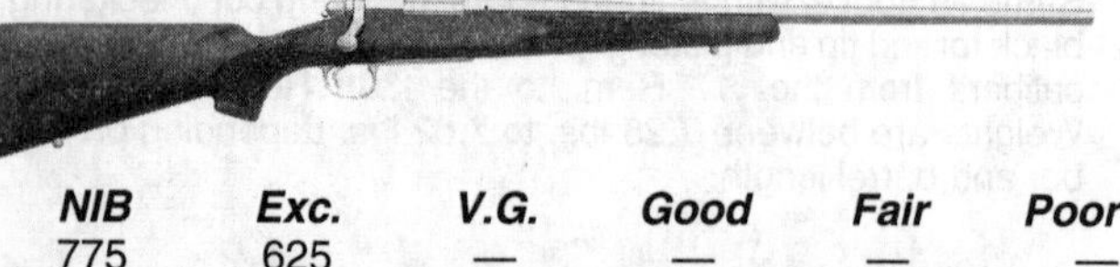

NIB	Exc.	V.G.	Good	Fair	Poor
775	625	—	—	—	—

Model 700 BDL SS Camo Special Edition (RMEF)

This is a special edition rifle for the Rocky Mountain Elk Foundation. Fitted with a 24" barrel and chambered for the .300 Rem. Ultra Mag cartridge. Camo stock with stainless steel receiver and barrel. Weight is about 7.5 lbs. Introduced in 2001. In 2002 the 7mm Rem. Ultra Mag chambering was added for one year only. In 2003 the .300 Rem. Ultra Mag was offered.

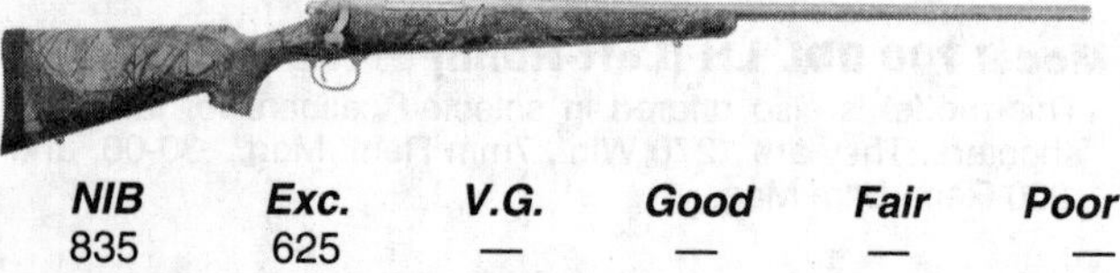

NIB	Exc.	V.G.	Good	Fair	Poor
835	625	—	—	—	—

Model 700 EtronX

Introduced in 2000 this rifle features a new technology that electronically discharges the round resulting in nearly instant ignition. LED located on top of the grip that shows safe or fire and chamber status. There is also a low battery indicator and malfunction indicators as well. The rifle is fitted with a 26" stainless steel fluted barrel. The stock is fiberglass and graphite reinforced with Kevlar. Chambers are .220 Swift, .22-250 Rem., and .243 Win. cartridges. Average weight is about 8.88 lbs. The gun was a flopperoo.

NIB	Exc.	V.G.	Good	Fair	Poor
1950	1500	—	—	—	—

Model 700 Sendero

This Model 700 configuration is chambered for the .25-06, .270, 7mm Rem. Mag., .300 Win. Mag. It is fitted with a synthetic stock and a 26" heavy barrel.

NIB	Exc.	V.G.	Good	Fair	Poor
600	475	400	300	200	150

Model 700 Sendero SF

Introduced in 1996 this model features a stainless steel fluted barrel. It has a synthetic stock with full length bedding. It weighs about 8.5 lbs. Chambered for same calibers as the standard Sendero above except for the .270. In 1997 the 7mm STW cartridge was made available for this model. In 2003 the 7mm Rem. Ultra Mag. and the .300 Rem. Ultra Mag. were added calibers.

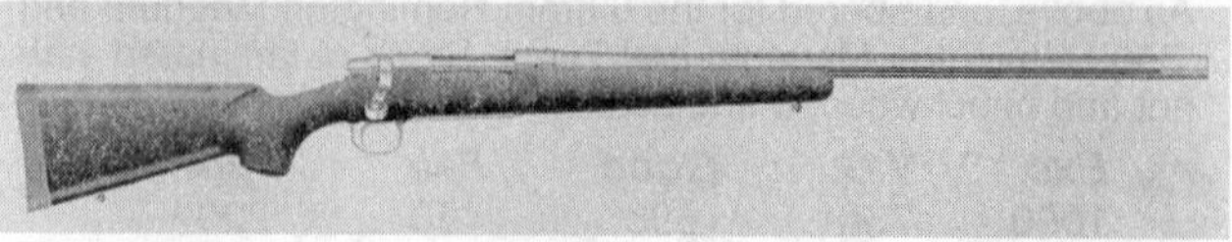

Courtesy Remington Arms

NIB	Exc.	V.G.	Good	Fair	Poor
1015	800	600	450	350	200

Model 700 Sendero SF-II

Similar to Sendero SF but with HS Precision synthetic stock. Chambered in .264 WM, 7mm RM, 7mm RUM, .300 WM, and .300 RUM. Introduced 2006. MSRP: 1128

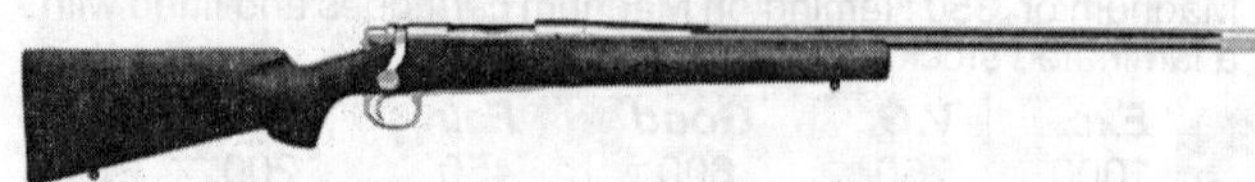

Model 700 Sendero Composite

Introduced in 1999, this model features a composite barrel of graphite fiber with a stainless steel liner. Stock is synthetic. Calibers available are .25-06, 7mm STW, and .300 Win. Mag. Barrel length is 26". Weight is just under 8 lbs.

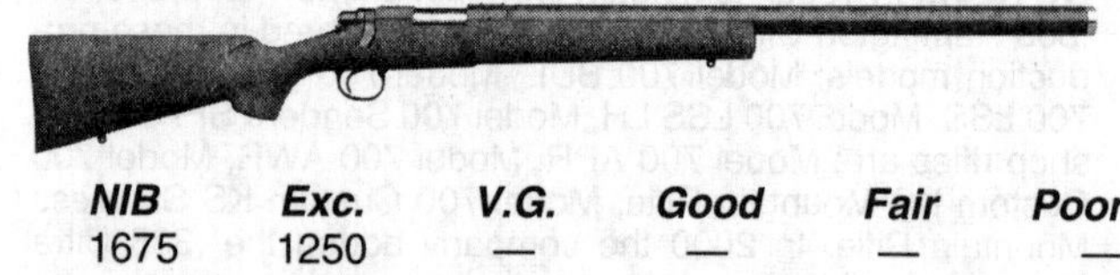

NIB	Exc.	V.G.	Good	Fair	Poor
1675	1250	—	—	—	—

Model 700 Mountain Rifle

As above, with a tapered 22" lightweight barrel, blued with checkered walnut stock. Introduced in 1986.

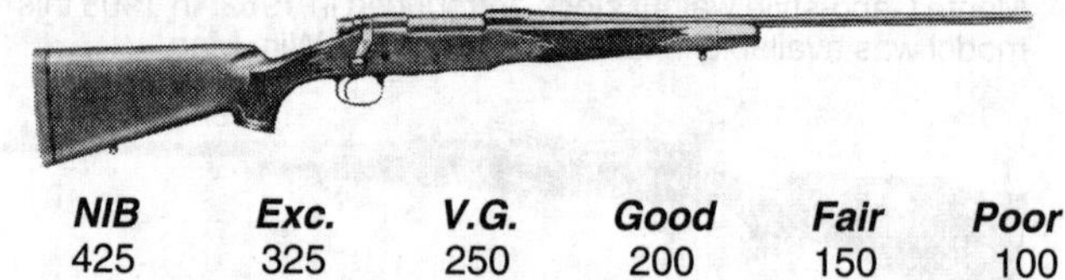

NIB	Exc.	V.G.	Good	Fair	Poor
425	325	250	200	150	100

Model 700KS Mountain Rifle

As above, with a lightweight Kevlar stock. Introduced in 1986.

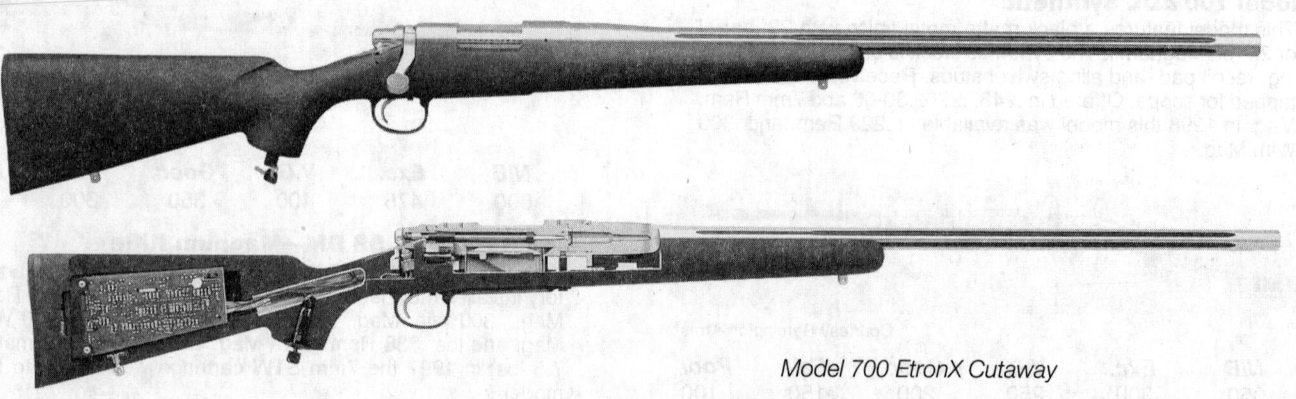

Model 700 EtronX Cutaway

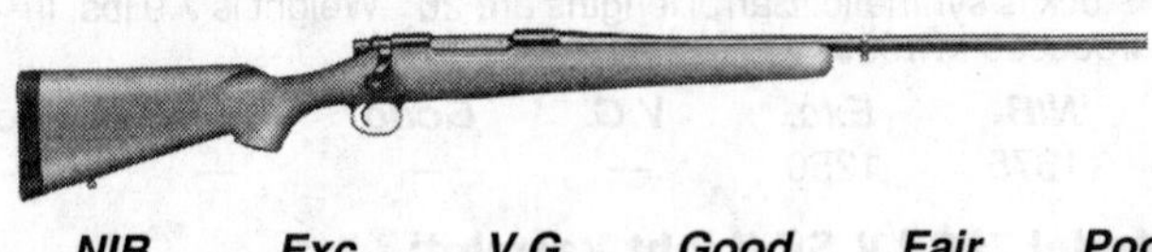

NIB	Exc.	V.G.	Good	Fair	Poor
750	700	600	500	400	300

Model 700 Mountain Rifle (DM)

Same as standard Mountain Rifle but introduced in 1995 with detachable magazine. In 1998 this model was available in .260 Rem. caliber.

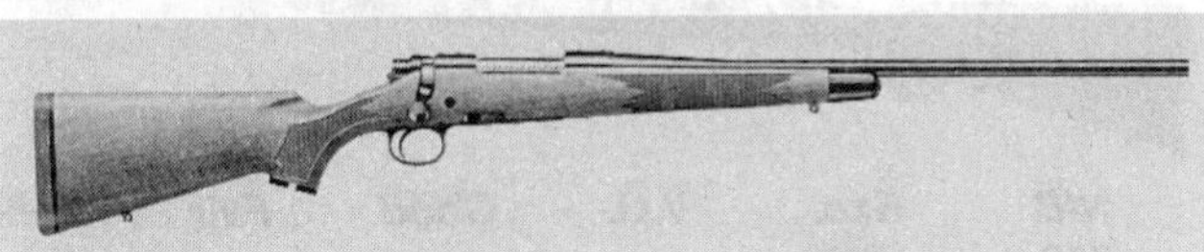

Courtesy Remington Arms

NIB	Exc.	V.G.	Good	Fair	Poor
780	575	425	300	250	175

Model 700 Safari Grade

As the Model 700BDL chambered for 8mm Remington Magnum, .375 Holland & Holland, .416 Remington Magnum or .458 Winchester Magnum cartridges, 24" barrel and 3-shot magazine. Blued with a finely figured walnut checkered stock. The Model KS Safari Grade was fitted with a Kevlar stock and would be worth approximately 20 percent more than the values listed. Introduced in 1962.

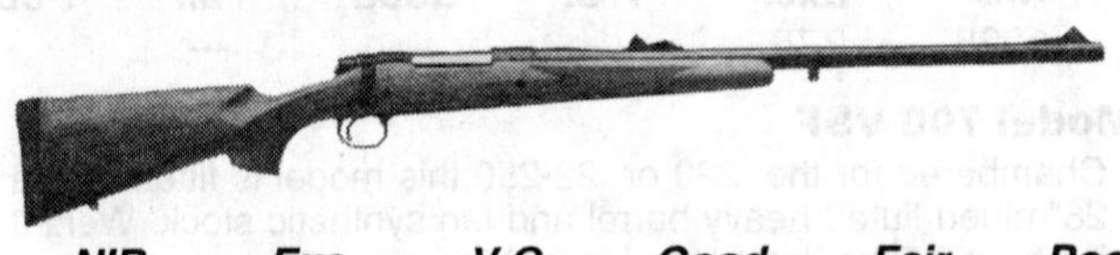

NIB	Exc.	V.G.	Good	Fair	Poor
875	750	600	500	400	300

Model 700 RS

As above, chambered for the .270 Winchester, .280 Remington, or .30-06 cartridges, 22" barrel and 4-shot magazine. Blued with a DuPont Rynite stock. Manufactured during 1987 and 1988.

Exc.	V.G.	Good	Fair	Poor
550	425	350	250	150

Model 700 FS

As above, with a Kevlar stock.

Exc.	V.G.	Good	Fair	Poor
550	475	400	300	200

Model 700 BDL European

Available for the first time in 1993, this model features an oil finish stock with Monte Carlo comb and raised cheekpiece. The checkering is fine line. In addition the rifle has a hinged floorplate, sling swivel studs, hooded ramp front sight, and adjustable rear sight. Offered in these calibers: .243, .207, .280, 7mm-08, 7mm Mag. .30-06, and .308.

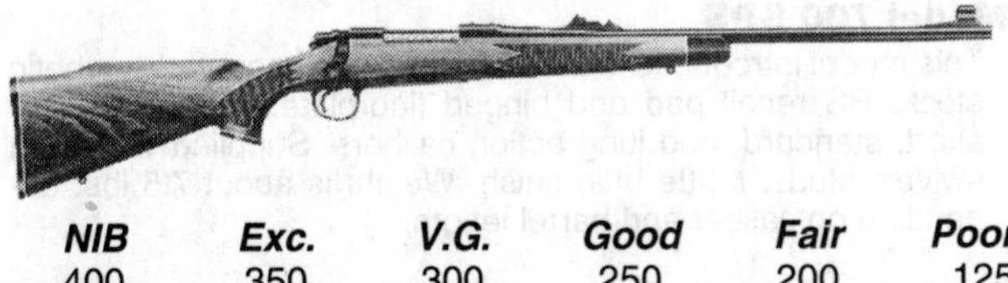

NIB	Exc.	V.G.	Good	Fair	Poor
400	350	300	250	200	125

Model 700 BDL Stainless Synthetic

Offered in 1993 this model features a stainless steel receiver, barrel, and bolt. Synthetic stock has straight comb, raised cheekpiece, and hinged floor plate. Metal is finished in a black matte nonreflective finish. Available in 14 calibers from .223 to .338 Win. Mag. All barrel lengths regardless of caliber are 24".

NIB	Exc.	V.G.	Good	Fair	Poor
550	450	350	300	200	150

Model 700 BDL Stainless Synthetic (DM)

Same as above but introduced in 1995 with detachable magazine.

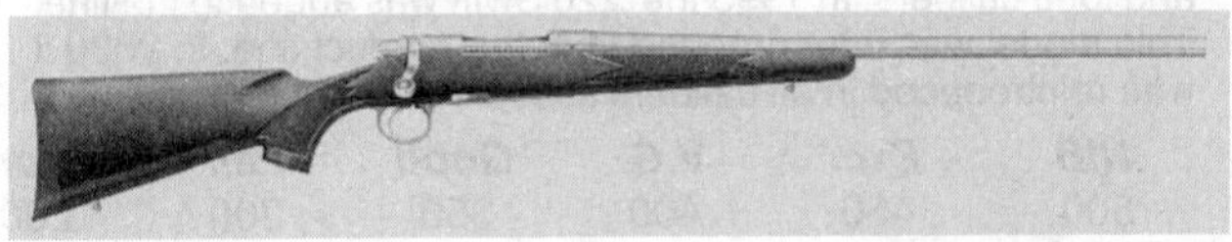

Courtesy Remington Arms

NIB	Exc.	V.G.	Good	Fair	Poor
575	475	350	300	200	150

Model 700 CDL

This model was introduced in 2004 and features a classic-style checkered walnut stock with black forend tip and grip cap. Hinged floor plate. Chambered for the .243, .270, 7mm-08, 7mm Rem. Mag., 7mm Rem. Ultra Mag, .30-06, .300 Win. Mag, and .300 Rem. Ultra Mag. Standard calibers are fitted with a 24" barrel while magnum calibers have a 26" barrel. Weight is about 7.5 lbs. depending on caliber.

NIB	Exc.	V.G.	Good	Fair	Poor
740	550	—	—	—	—

Model 700 CDL SF LTD.

Similar to Model 700 CDL but with engraved floorplate and stainless, fluted barrel. Chambered in .30-06 and .17 Remington Fireball. 2006 "Centennial" model commemorates the centennial of the .30-06 cartridge and was introduced in 2006 for one year only.

NIB	Exc.	V.G.	Good	Fair	Poor
1100	—	—	—	—	—

Model 700 Mountain Rifle Stainless Synthetic

This model is the same as the Mountain Rifle but with stainless steel receiver, bolt, and barrel. Offered in .25-06 Rem., .270, .280, and .30-06. All calibers are supplied with a 22" barrel. In 1998 this model was available in .260 Rem. caliber.

NIB	Exc.	V.G.	Good	Fair	Poor
830	600	450	300	225	150

Model 700 LSS Mountain Rifle

This model, introduced in 1999, is fitted with a two-tone laminated stock with black forend tip and cheekpiece. Stainless steel barrel and action. Offered in .260 Remington, 7mm-08 Rem., .270 Win., and .30-06. Barrel length is 22". Weight is approximately 6.5 lbs.

NIB	Exc.	V.G.	Good	Fair	Poor
830	625	450	300	—	—

Model 700 Titanium

Introduced in 2001 this model features a titanium receiver drilled and tapped for scope mounts. Fitted with a 22" stainless steel barrel chambered for both long and short calibers. Synthetic stock. Weight is approximately 5.25 lbs. In 2002 the .308 Win. chambering was added.

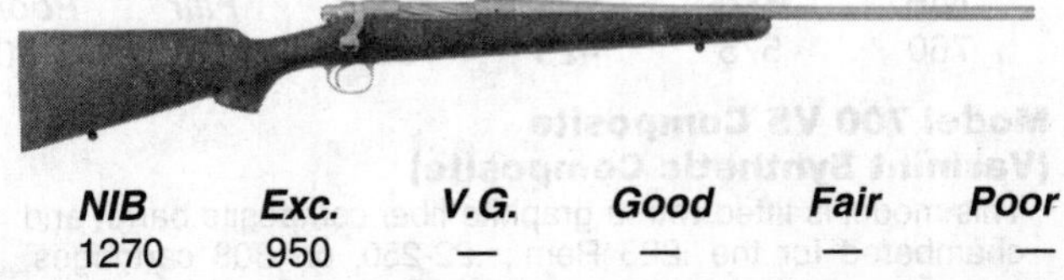

NIB	Exc.	V.G.	Good	Fair	Poor
1270	950	—	—	—	—

Model 700 Varmint Special Synthetic

The stock on this model is reinforced with DuPont Kevlar, fiberglass, and graphite. Rifle is offered with a heavy barrel and all metal has a fine matte black finish. The barrel rest on a machined aircraft-grade aluminum bedding stock. The receiver is drilled and tapped for scope mounts. Offered in .22-250, .223, and .308 calibers. In 1993 the .220 Swift was added to the line. This model was later dropped from the product line. In 2000 it was reintroduced in all calibers above but the .220 Swift.

NIB	Exc.	V.G.	Good	Fair	Poor
500	450	400	350	300	200

Model 700 VS SF (Varmint Synthetic Stainless Fluted)

Introduced in 1994 this model features a stainless steel barrel, receiver and action. It is fitted with a 26" heavy varmint barrel that has a spherical concave crown contour. Six flutes reduce barrel weight and help cooling. A synthetic stock made from fiberglass reinforced with graphite is standard. The stock is dark gray. Offered in .223, .220 Swift, .22-250, and .308 calibers. The .243 Win. cartridge was added to this model in 1997. The rifle weighs about 8-3/8 lbs. In 1998 the barrel was fluted and ported.

Model 700 VS SF-P fluted and ported barrel

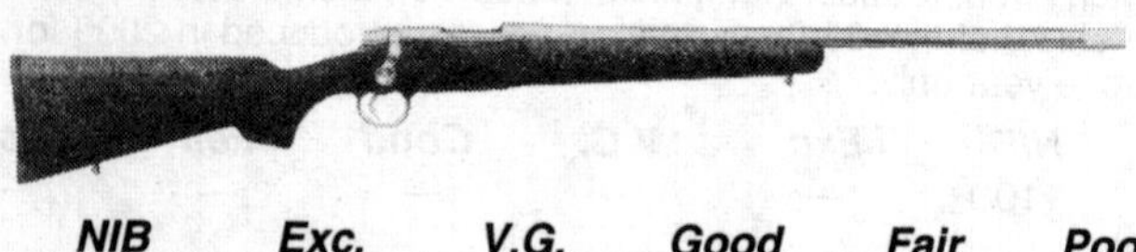

NIB	Exc.	V.G.	Good	Fair	Poor
800	650	500	400	300	200

Model 700 Varmint Special Wood

Same as above but furnished with walnut stock and offered in these calibers: .222, .22-250, .223, 6mm, .243, 7mm-08, and .308.

NIB	Exc.	V.G.	Good	Fair	Poor
450	400	350	300	250	150

Model 700 Varmint Laminated Stock (VLS)

Same as above but furnished with special laminated stock. Introduced in 1995.The 7mm-08 Rem. cartridge was added to this model in 1997. In 1998 a beavertail forend was added to this model, as well as the .260 Rem and the 6mm Rem. calibers.

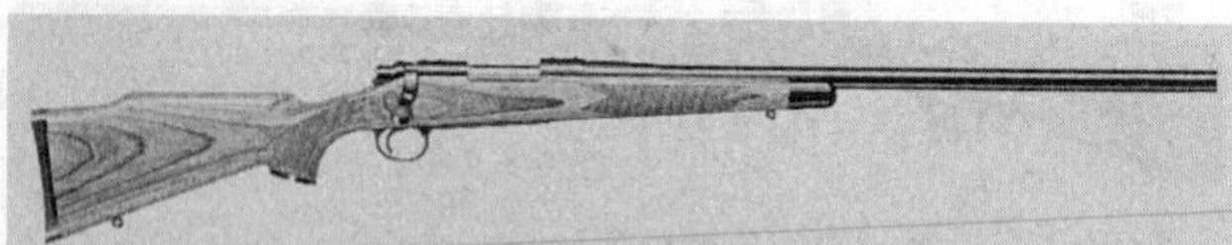

Courtesy Remington Arms

Model 700 VLS with beavertail forearm

NIB	Exc.	V.G.	Good	Fair	Poor
760	575	425	300	250	150

Model 700 VS Composite (Varmint Synthetic Composite)

This model is fitted with a graphite fiber composite barrel and chambered for the .223 Rem., .22-250, or .308 cartridges. Stock is synthetic. Barrel lengths are 26". Weight is 7.9 lbs. Introduced in 1999.

NIB	Exc.	V.G.	Good	Fair	Poor
1675	1250	—	—	—	—

Model 700 LV SF (Light Varmint)

This model, introduced in 2004, features a black synthetic stock with 22" stainless steel fluted barrel. Chambered for the .17 Rem, .221 Rem Fireball, .223, and .22-250. Weight is about 6.75 lbs.

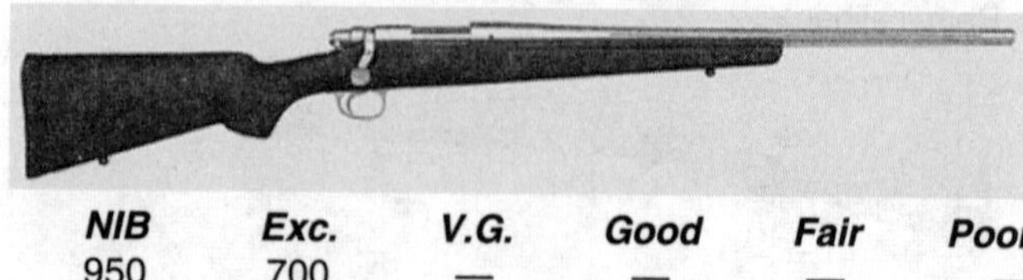

NIB	Exc.	V.G.	Good	Fair	Poor
950	700	—	—	—	—

Model 700 VS SF II

Introduced in 2005 this model features a varmint synthetic stock with stainless steel action and stainless fluted barrel chambered for the .204 Ruger, .220 Swift, 223, and .22-250. Barrel length is 26". Weight is about 8.5 lbs.

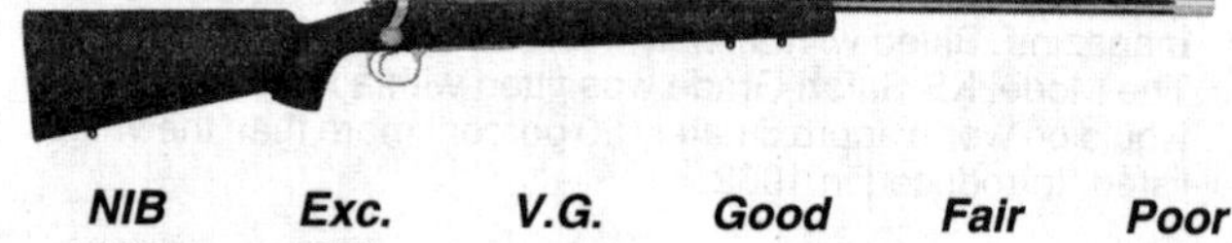

NIB	Exc.	V.G.	Good	Fair	Poor
1025	775	—	—	—	—

Model 700 VSF

Chambered for the .223 or .22-250 this model is fitted with a 26" blued fluted heavy barrel and tan synthetic stock. Weight is about 8.5 lbs. Introduced in 2005.

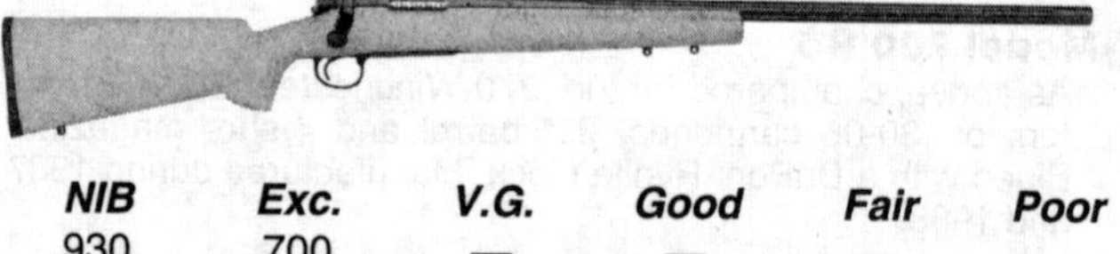

NIB	Exc.	V.G.	Good	Fair	Poor
930	700	—	—	—	—

Model 700 LSS LH (Laminated Stock SS Left-Hand)

Introduced in 1998 this model features a stainless steel barreled action with satin finish. Stock is similar to the BDL style with Monte Carlo comb and cheekpiece with hinged floor plate. Barrel is 24" with no sights. Offered in .270, .30-06, 7mm Rem. Mag, and .300 Win. Mag.

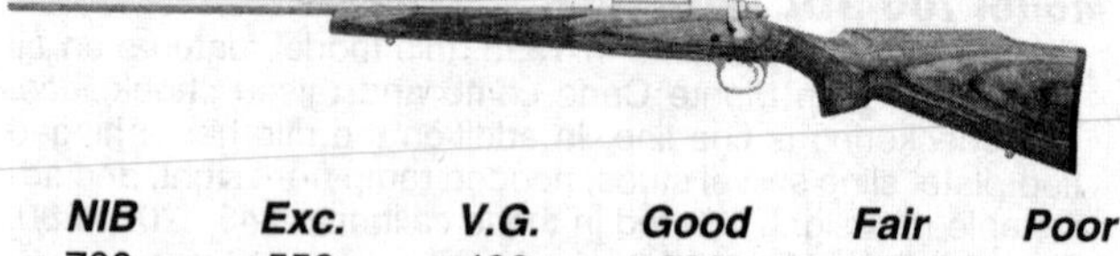

NIB	Exc.	V.G.	Good	Fair	Poor
700	550	400	300	250	150

Model 700 SPS

This model introduced in 2005, features an improved synthetic stock, RS recoil pad and hinged floorplate. Chambered for short, standard, and long action calibers. Supplied with sling swivels studs. Matte blue finish. Weight is about 7.5 lbs. depending on caliber and barrel length.

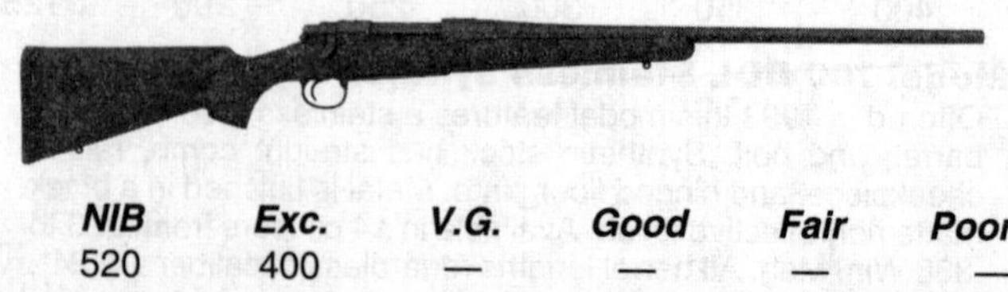

NIB	Exc.	V.G.	Good	Fair	Poor
520	400	—	—	—	—

Model 700 SPS Stainless

As above but with matte stainless steel barrel and action. No Ultra magnum calibers offered in this configuration. Introduced in 2005.

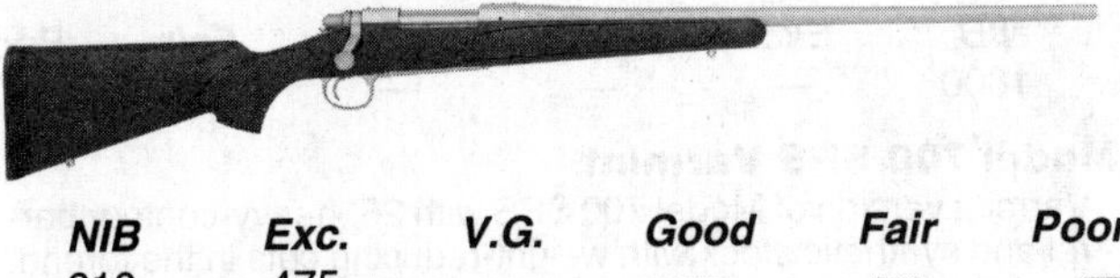

NIB	Exc.	V.G.	Good	Fair	Poor
610	475	—	—	—	—

Model 700 SPS DM

This model is the same as the Model SPS but with detachable magazine. Matte blue finish. Introduced in 2005.

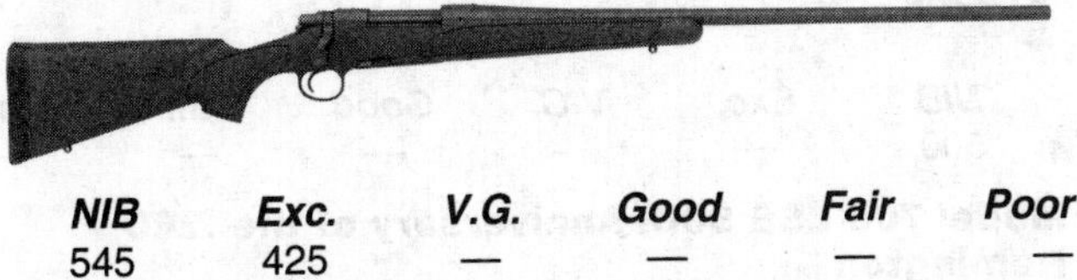

NIB	Exc.	V.G.	Good	Fair	Poor
545	425	—	—	—	—

Model 700 SPS Youth

Offered in both long and short action calibers this model features barrel lengths of 20" and 22" depending on caliber. Weight is about 7 lbs. Introduced in 2005.

NIB	Exc.	V.G.	Good	Fair	Poor
520	400	—	—	—	—

Model 700 XCR

Introduced in 2005 this model features a stainless steel action and barrel with synthetic stock, rubber grip and forearm panels. Hinged floorplate. RS recoil pad. Chambered for the .270 Win., .280 Rem., 7mm Ultra Mag., .30-06, .300 WSM, and the .300 Win. Mag. cartridges. Barrel lengths are 24" and 26" depending on caliber. Weight is around 7.5 lbs. depending on caliber.

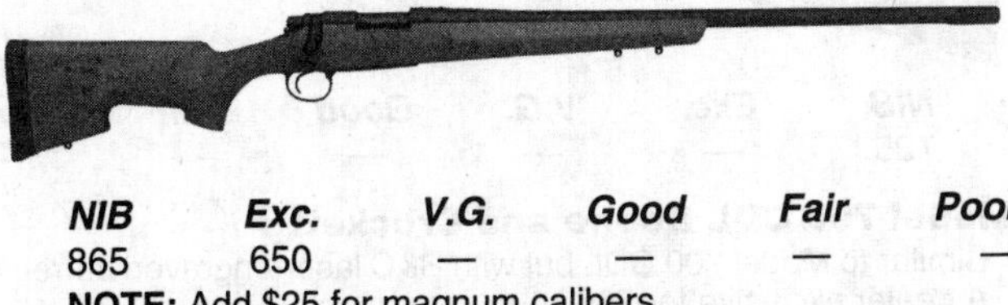

NIB	Exc.	V.G.	Good	Fair	Poor
865	650	—	—	—	—

NOTE: Add $25 for magnum calibers.

Model 700 XCR (Rocky Mountain Elk Foundation)

As above but with camo stock, engraved floorplate and 7mm Rem. Mag. caliber. Introduced in 2005.

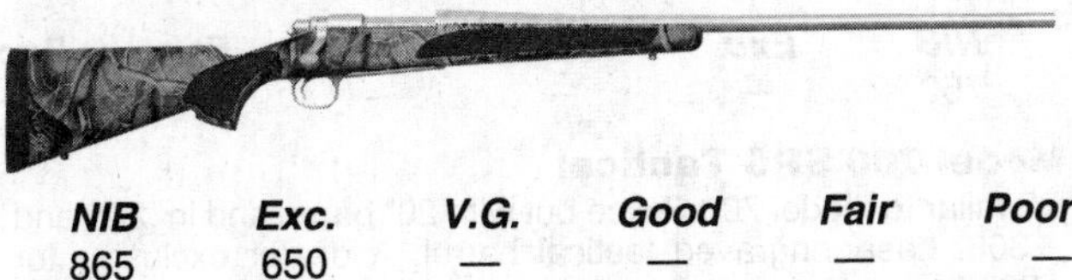

NIB	Exc.	V.G.	Good	Fair	Poor
865	650	—	—	—	—

Model 700 Classic

This limited edition model is furnished with a straight comb, satin finished walnut stock, sling swivel studs, and hinged magazine floorplate. The series began in 1981 and each year Remington has offered the Model 700 Classic in a special chambering.

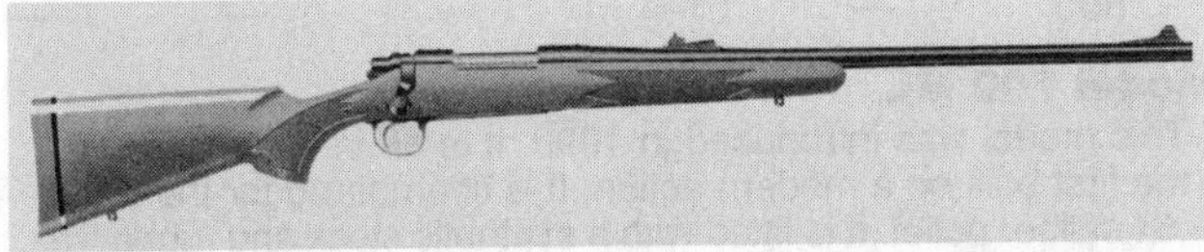

Courtesy Remington Arms

A list of chamberings by year.

1981—7MM Mauser
1982—.257 Roberts
1983—.300 H&H Mag.
1984—.250-3000
1985—.350 Rem. Mag.
1986—.264 Win. Mag.
1987—.338 Win. Mag.
1988—.35 Whelen
1989—.300 Wthby. Mag.
1990—.25-06 Rem.
1991—7mm Wthby. Mag.
1992—.220 Swift
1993—.222 Rem.
1994—6.5X55 Swedish
1995—.300 Win. Mag.
1996—.375 H&H Mag.
1997—.280 Rem.
1998—8mm Rem. Mag.
1999—.17 Remington
2000—.223 Remington
2001—7mm-08
2002—.221 Rem. Fireball
2003—.300 Savage
2004—
2005—.308 Winchester

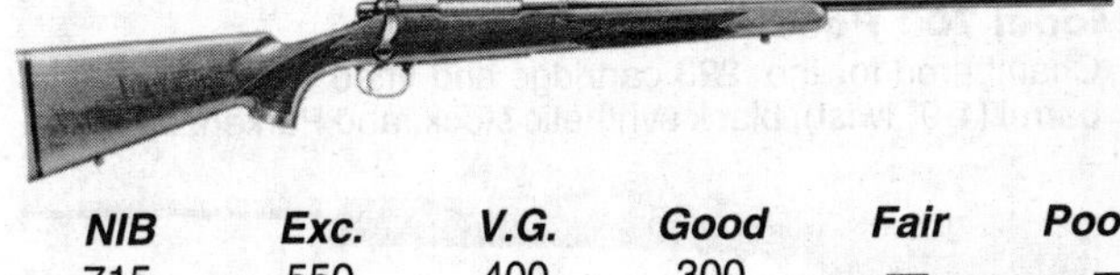

NIB	Exc.	V.G.	Good	Fair	Poor
715	550	400	300	—	—

Model 700 Custom

A special order rifle available in either American, English, or California walnut. Stock can be fitted to customer's own dimensions. Engraving is available as is a large selection of calibers. Model 700 Custom rifles should be priced individually and an appraisal should be obtained.

Model 700 Custom "C" Grade

Introduced in 2003 this Custom Shop bolt-action rifle is fitted with fancy walnut with Monte Carlo stock and rosewood forend tip and grip cap. Offered in all standard calibers. Barrel length is 24" for all calibers except Ultra Mags. which are 26". Retail price of $1,730.

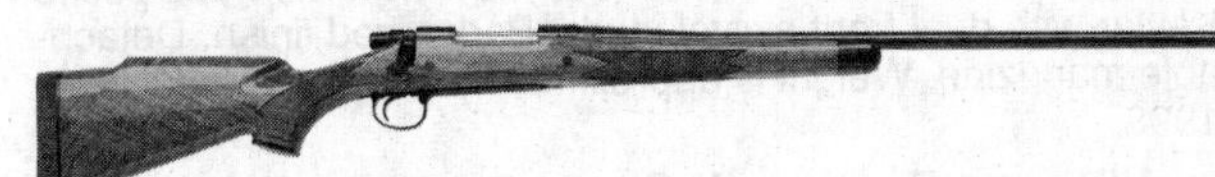

Model 700 AWR (Alaskan Wilderness Rifle)

This model is built in the Custom Shop and features a blind magazine and stainless steel components on a black matte synthetic stock. Fitted with a 24" barrel, all metal parts are finished in a black satin. Offered in .300 Weatherby Magnum, 7mm Rem. Mag., .300 Win. Mag., .338, and .375 calibers. In 1998 the 7mm STW was added as an additional caliber to this model. Weighs about 6-3/4 lbs. Built to order with a retail price of $1,200 in 1995.

Model 700 APR (African Plains Rifle)

This Custom Shop model features a hinged floorplate, a 26" barrel, and blue metal finish. The stock is a laminated Monte Carlo style with cheekpiece and is fitted with black rubber recoil pad. Offered in same calibers as Model 700 AWR. Weighs about 7-3/4 lbs. Retail price in 1995 is $1,500 on a special order basis.

Model 700 ABG (African Big Game)

This Custom Shop rifle is fitted with a laminated stock, matte finished receiver and barrel, and 3-round detachable magazine. Chambered for the .375 Rem. Ultra Mag, .375 H&H, .416 Rem. Mag, and .458 Win. Mag. Introduced in 2001. Many extra cost options are offered for Custom Shop firearms. Retail prices in 2001 for this rifle begin at $1,727.

Model 700 Safari KS Stainless

A new addition to the Remington line in 1993, the Safari KS Stainless has a special reinforced Kevlar stock in a nonreflective gray finish. Checkering is 18 lines to the inch. Offered in these calibers: .375 H&H Mag., .416 Rem. Mag., and the .458 Win. Mag.

NIB	Exc.	V.G.	Good	Fair	Poor
500	450	400	350	300	150

Model 700 Police

Chambered for the .223 cartridge and fitted with a 26" heavy barrel (1-9" twist), black synthetic stock, and Parkerized finish.

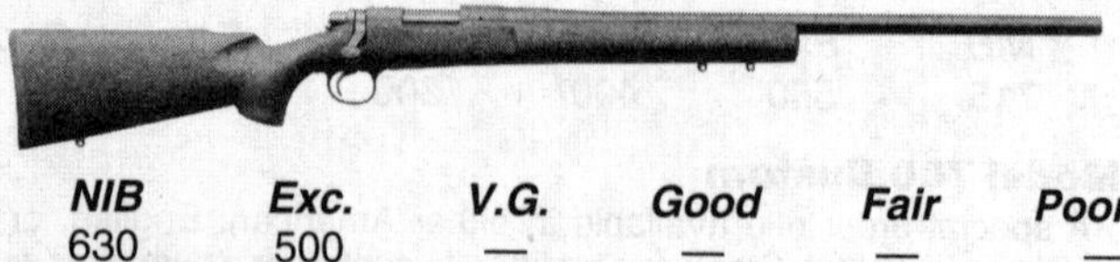

NIB	Exc.	V.G.	Good	Fair	Poor
630	500	—	—	—	—

Model 700 Police DM

Same as above but chambered for .308 Win. (1-12" twist) or .300 Win. Mag (1-10" twist). Detachable magazine standard.

NIB	Exc.	V.G.	Good	Fair	Poor
670	525	—	—	—	—

NOTE: Add $20 for .300 Win. Mag model.

Model 700 Police Lightweight Tactical

This model is chambered for the .308 Win. cartridge and fitted with a 20" fluted barrel (1-12" twist). Stock is slim composite Kevlar with dual front swivel studs. Parkerized finish. Detachable magazine. Weight is approximately 7.5 lbs. Introduced in 1998.

NIB	Exc.	V.G.	Good	Fair	Poor
700	550	—	—	—	—

Model 700 XCR Tactical Long Range Rifle

Chambered in .223 Rem., .300 WM and .338 WM; 26" crowned stainless varmint contour barrel; olive drab Bell & Carlson synthetic stock. Coated overall with TriNyte Corrosion Control finish. Introduced in 2007.

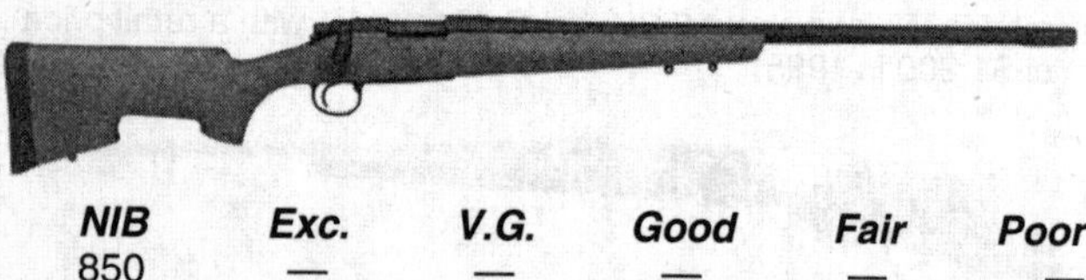

NIB	Exc.	V.G.	Good	Fair	Poor
850	—	—	—	—	—

Model 700 SPS Buckmasters Edition

Similar to Model 700 SPS but with engraved floorplate and camo stock. Also available in Youth model chambered in .243 only. Introduced in 2007.

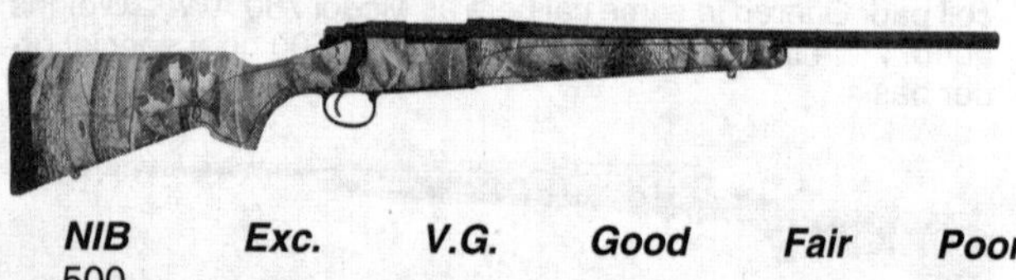

NIB	Exc.	V.G.	Good	Fair	Poor
500	—	—	—	—	—

Model 700 Alaskan Ti

Lightweight (6.25 lbs.) version of Model 700 with titanium receiver, 24" fluted stainless barrel and Bell & Carlson synthetic stock. Chambered in a variety of long, short, and super-short cartridges. Introduced in 2007.

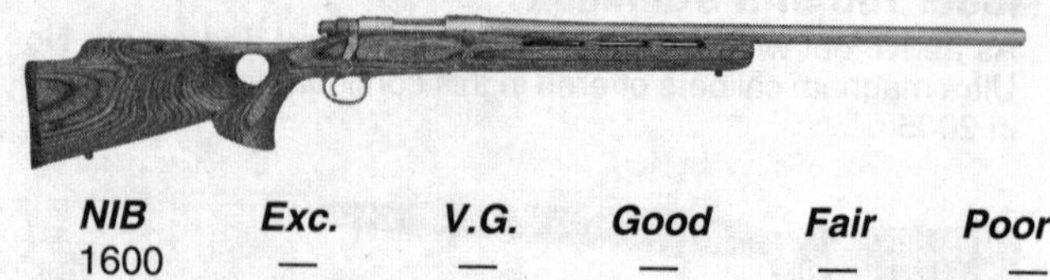

NIB	Exc.	V.G.	Good	Fair	Poor
1600	—	—	—	—	—

Model 700 SPS Varmint

Varmint version of Model 700 SPS with 26" heavy-contour barrel and synthetic stock with weight-reducing cuts in the forend. Available in a variety of chamberings from .17 Remington Fireball to .308 Winchester. Introduced in 2007.

NIB	Exc.	V.G.	Good	Fair	Poor
500	—	—	—	—	—

Model 700 LSS 50th Anniversary of the .280 Remington

Similar to Model 700 LSS but in .280 Remington. A dealer exclusive for 2007.

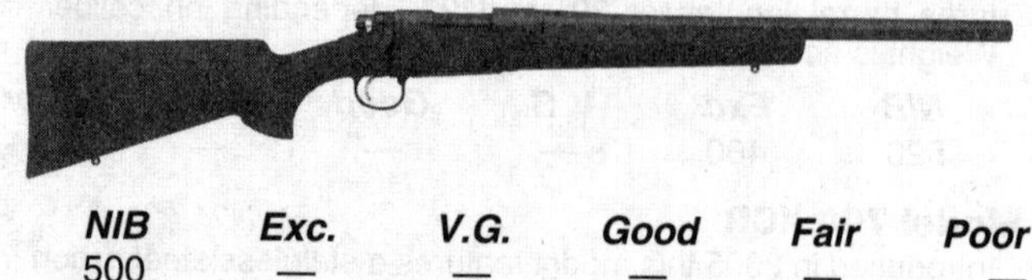

NIB	Exc.	V.G.	Good	Fair	Poor
500	—	—	—	—	—

Model 700 VL SS Thumbhole

Similar to Model 700 VS Composite but with brown laminated thumbhole stock and stainless steel barrel. Introduced in 2007.

NIB	Exc.	V.G.	Good	Fair	Poor
725	—	—	—	—	—

Model 700 CDL Boone and Crockett

Similar to Model 700 CDL but with B&C laser-engraved barrel. A dealer exclusive for 2007.

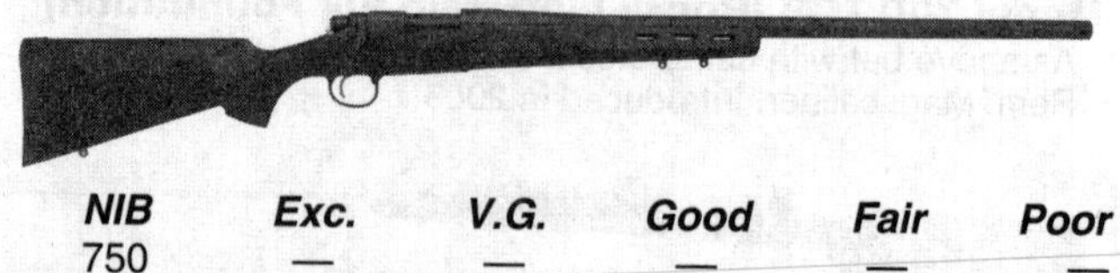

NIB	Exc.	V.G.	Good	Fair	Poor
750	—	—	—	—	—

Model 700 SPS Tactical

Similar to Model 700 Police but with 20" barrel and in .223 and .308. Laser-engraved tactical barrel. A dealer exclusive for 2007.

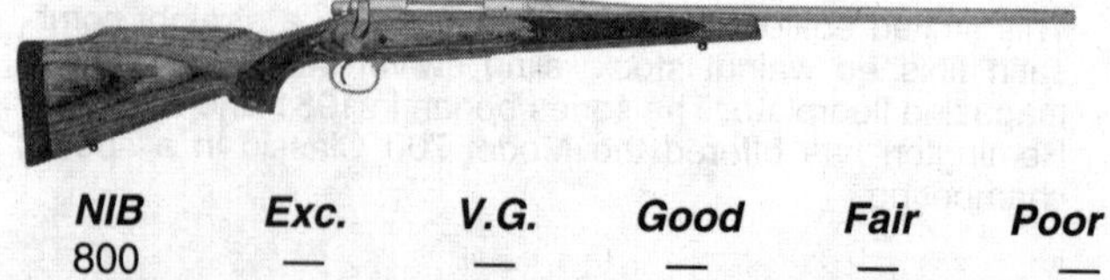

NIB	Exc.	V.G.	Good	Fair	Poor
800	—	—	—	—	—

Model 700 ML

This model was introduced in 1996. It is an in-line design and the first built on a modern action. It is chambered for the .50 or .54 caliber bullet. It is fitted with a synthetic stock and rubber recoil pad. The barrel length is 24" and the approximate weight is

7.75 lbs. A camo stock option was added to this model in 1997. Discontinued 2006.

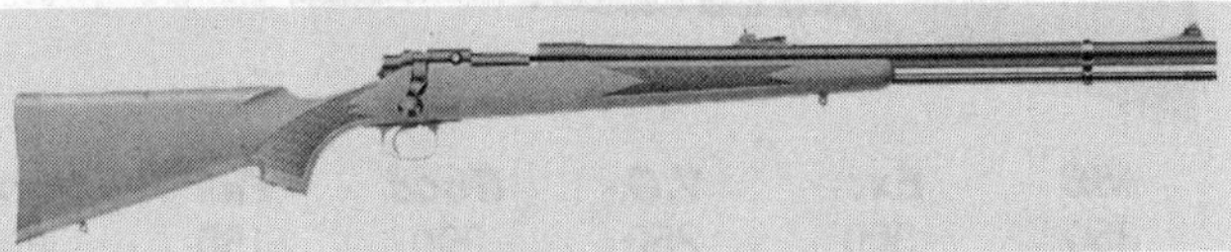

Courtesy Remington Arms

Remington Model 700 ML Camo

NIB	Exc.	V.G.	Good	Fair	Poor
350	250	200	150	100	75

Model 700 ML Custom

Introduced in 1997 this new model is similar to the above model but features a satin metal finish and gray laminated thumbhole stock with roll-over cheekpiece.

NIB	Exc.	V.G.	Good	Fair	Poor
775	650	—	—	—	—

Model 700 MLS

Same as above but with stainless steel barrel and action.

Courtesy Remington Arms

Remington Model 700 MLS Camo

NIB	Exc.	V.G.	Good	Fair	Poor
400	300	250	200	150	100

Model 700 MLS Custom

Similar to the above model but with a satin stainless steel finish and a two-toned gray laminated thumbhole stock with roll-over cheekpiece. Introduced in 1997.

NIB	Exc.	V.G.	Good	Fair	Poor
875	725	—	—	—	—

Model 700 ML Youth

This model is similar to the Model ML with a shortened stock with 13" lop with a rubber recoil pad.

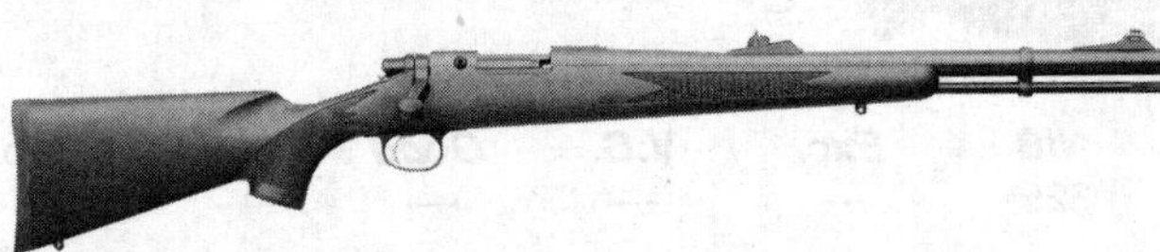

NIB	Exc.	V.G.	Good	Fair	Poor
370	300	250	200	150	100

Genesis Muzzleloaders

Fixed-breech hammer-fired muzzleloaders manufactured in a variety of configurations. Imported. Value is generally less than $225.

Model 700 Tactical Weapons System

This set is designed for law enforcement use and features a Model 700 Police chambered for the .308 Win. cartridge, a 24" barrel (1-12" twist), and detachable magazine. Also furnished with a Leupold VARI X III scope with rings and base, and a Harris 1A2 bipod, sling, lens covers, and case.

NIB	Exc.	V.G.	Good	Fair	Poor
N/A	—	—	—	—	—

Model 710

Introduced in 2001 this rifle is chambered for the .270 Win. or .30-06 cartridge. Fitted with a 22" barrel and dark gray synthetic stock. Detachable box magazine. Supplied with pre-mounted Bushnell Sharpshooter 3-9x scope. Barrel finish is ordnance gray steel with a matte finish. Weight is about 7.12 lbs. In 2004 the 7mm Rem. Mag. and .300 Win Mag chamberings were added. In 2005 the receiver was extruded solid steel. Calibers: .243, 7mm RM, .300 WM.

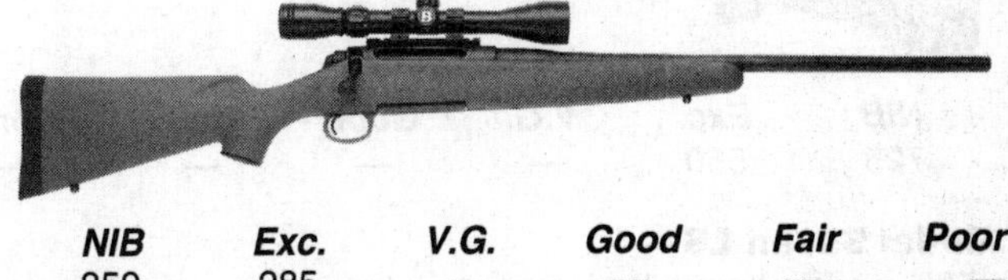

NIB	Exc.	V.G.	Good	Fair	Poor
359	285	—	—	—	—

Model 710 Youth

Similar to Model 710 but with 20" barrel and 39.5" overall length. Chambered in .243 Win. Introduced 2006. MSRP: 426

Model 788

A centerfire bolt-action sporting rifle with either a 22" or 24" barrel and a plain walnut stock. An 18" barrel carbine was also manufactured and is worth approximately 10 percent more than the values listed below. Manufactured from 1967 to 1983.

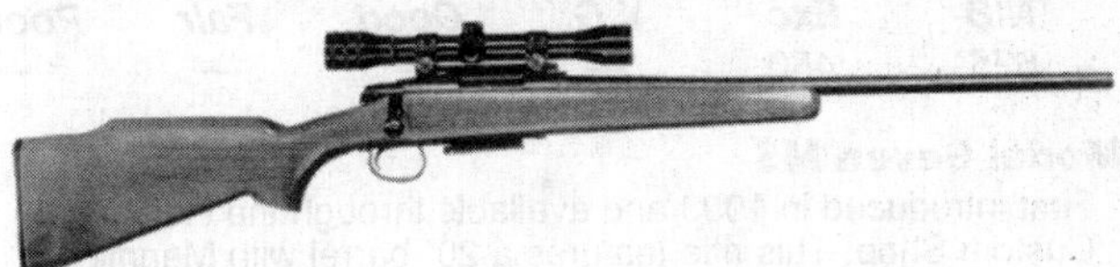

Exc.	V.G.	Good	Fair	Poor
500	425	375	300	250

NOTE: Add a 30 percent premium for .44 Magnum, 25 percent for .30-30, and 20 percent premium for 7mm-08 caliber. Add 40 percent premium for left-hand models in 6mm and .308.

Model Seven

A centerfire bolt-action sporting rifle with an 18.5" barrel and 4- or 5-shot magazine. Blued with a checkered walnut stock. Chambered for .223 Rem., .243 Rem., 7mm-08 Rem., .308 Win., and for 1997 the .260 Rem. cartridge. Introduced into the Remington product line in 1982.

NIB	Exc.	V.G.	Good	Fair	Poor
450	400	325	275	200	100

Model Seven FS

As above with a Kevlar stock. Introduced in 1987.

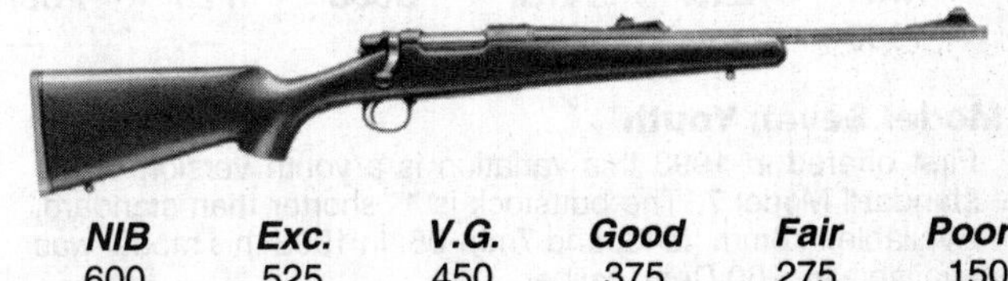

NIB	Exc.	V.G.	Good	Fair	Poor
600	525	450	375	275	150

Model Seven SS (Stainless Synthetic)

Introduced in 1994 this model features a stainless steel barrel, receiver, and bolt with a matte finish. It is fitted with a 20" barrel, and a hinged floorplate. The synthetic stock is textured black. Available in .243, 7mm-08, and .308. In 1997 the .260 Rem. cartridge was also offered. Weight approximately 6.25 lbs.

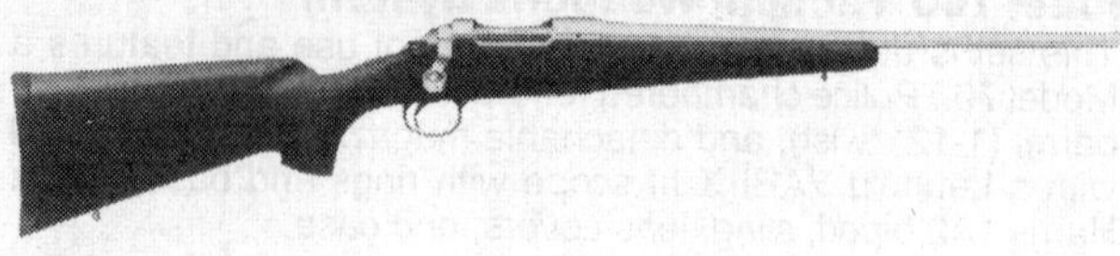

NIB	Exc.	V.G.	Good	Fair	Poor
475	400	350	300	200	150

Model Seven LSS

This model has a stainless steel barrel and action but is fitted with a satin finished laminated stock. Chambered for .22-250, .243, and 7mm-08 Rem. Weight is about 6.5 lbs. Introduced in 2000.

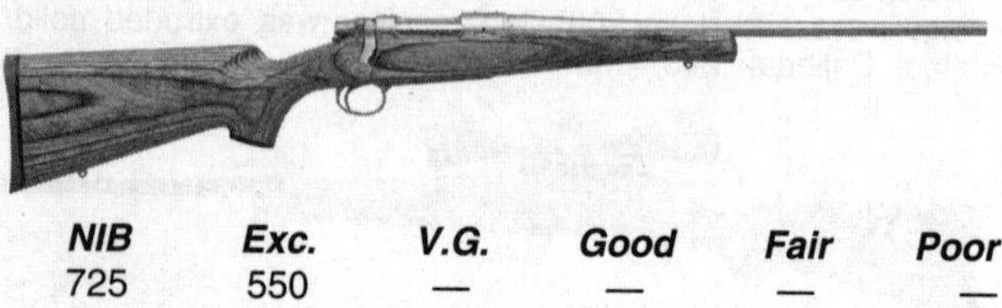

NIB	Exc.	V.G.	Good	Fair	Poor
725	550	—	—	—	—

Model Seven LS

This model offers a laminated stock but with a carbon steel blued barrel. Offered in five calibers: .22-250, .243, .260 Rem., 8mm-08 Rem., and .308 Win. Weight is about 6.5 lbs. Introduced in 2000.

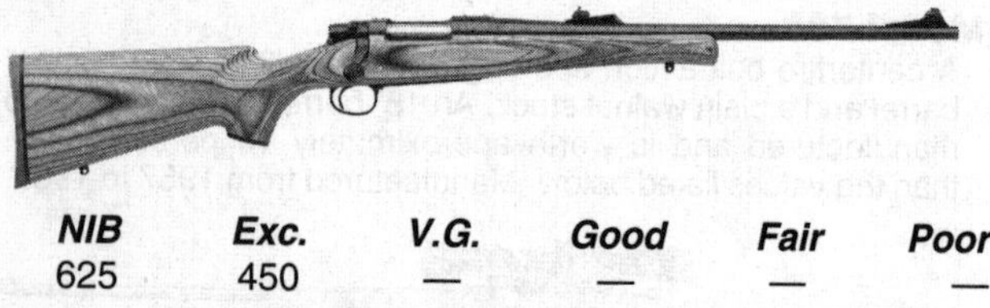

NIB	Exc.	V.G.	Good	Fair	Poor
625	450	—	—	—	—

Model Seven MS

First introduced in 1993 and available through the Remington Custom Shop. This rifle features a 20" barrel with Mannlicher stock made from select grain wood and laminated for strength. Available in calibers for .270 Rem. to .308. In 1998 this model was available in .260 Rem. caliber.

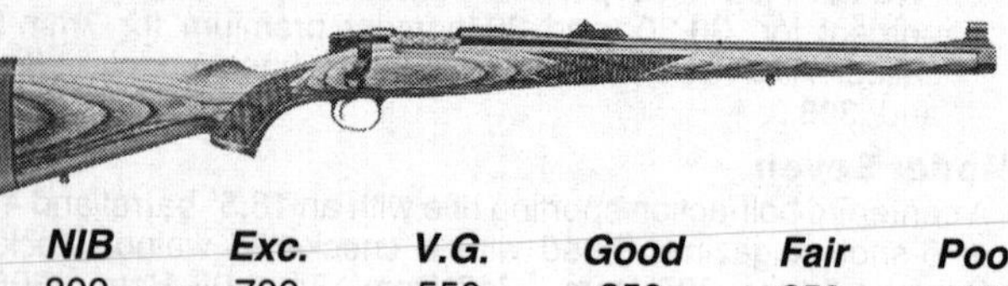

NIB	Exc.	V.G.	Good	Fair	Poor
800	700	550	350	250	150

Model Seven AWR

This Custom Shop model features a black synthetic stock and is chambered for short action calibers including the 6.7mm SPC. Fitted with a 22" barrel. Blued finish. Weight is about 6.125 lbs. Introduced in 2005.

NIB	Exc.	V.G.	Good	Fair	Poor
1000	—	—	—	—	—

Model Seven Youth

First offered in 1993 this variation is a youth version of the standard Model 7. The buttstock is 1" shorter than standard. Available in 6mm, .243, and 7mm-08. In 1998 this model was available in .260 Rem. caliber.

NIB	Exc.	V.G.	Good	Fair	Poor
350	300	250	200	150	100

Model Seven CDL

Similar to Model Seven but with satin walnut.satin blue finish, sightless barrel, and Limbsaver recoil pad. Introduced 2006. MSRP: 829

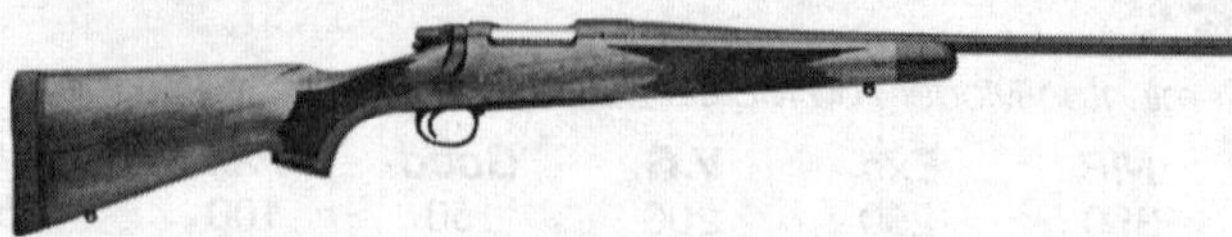

Model Seven XCR Camo

Similar to Model Seven LSS but with camo stock, fluted barrel and weather-resistant coating. Chambered in .243, 7mm-08, .308, .270 WSM and .300 WSM. Introduced in 2007.

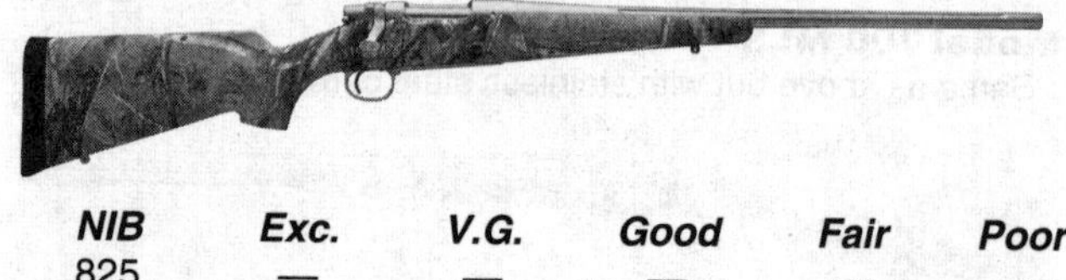

NIB	Exc.	V.G.	Good	Fair	Poor
825	—	—	—	—	—

Model 770

Package rifle similar to Model 710 but with redesigned bolt assembly and magazine catch. Chambered in .243, .270, 7mm-08, .308, .30-06, and .300 WM. Also available in Youth model chambered in .243 only. Introduced in 2007.

NIB	Exc.	V.G.	Good	Fair	Poor
400	—	—	—	—	—

Model 770 Youth

Similar to Model 770 but with shorter stock and barrel.

NIB	Exc.	V.G.	Good	Fair	Poor
365	—	—	—	—	—

Model 715 Sportsman

Similar to Model 770. A dealer exclusive for 2007.

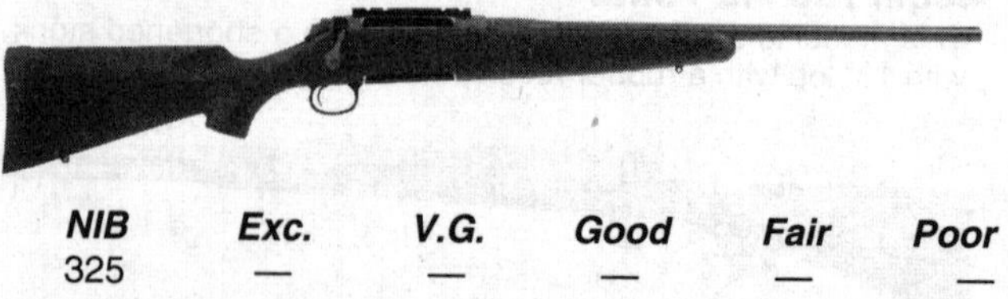

NIB	Exc.	V.G.	Good	Fair	Poor
325	—	—	—	—	—

Model 798

Long-action sporting rifle built on reworked 98 Mauser action. Calibers: .243, .308, .30-06, .270, .300 WM, .375 H&H, .458 WM. Barrel: 22" or 24" blued sightless. Stock: Brown laminated with recoil pad. Claw extractor, 2-position safety, hinged floorplate. Add 10 percent for Magnum chamberings; add 40 percent for .375 and .458. Introduced 2006.

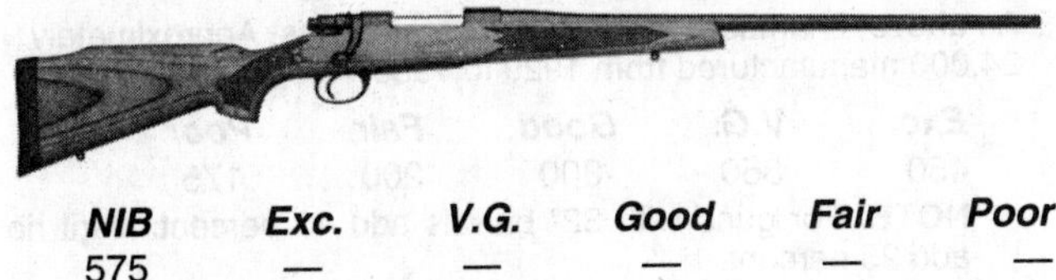

NIB	Exc.	V.G.	Good	Fair	Poor
575	—	—	—	—	—

Model 798 Stainless Laminate

Similar to Model 798 but with laminated stock and stainless barrel. Chambered in .243, .25-06, .270, .30-06, 7mm Mag, .300 WM and .375 H&H Mag. Introduced in 2007.

NIB	Exc.	V.G.	Good	Fair	Poor
695	—	—	—	—	—

Model 799

Similar to Model 798 but short-action without recoil pad. Calibers: .22 Hornet, .222 Remington, .22-250, .223, 762X39. Introduced 2006.

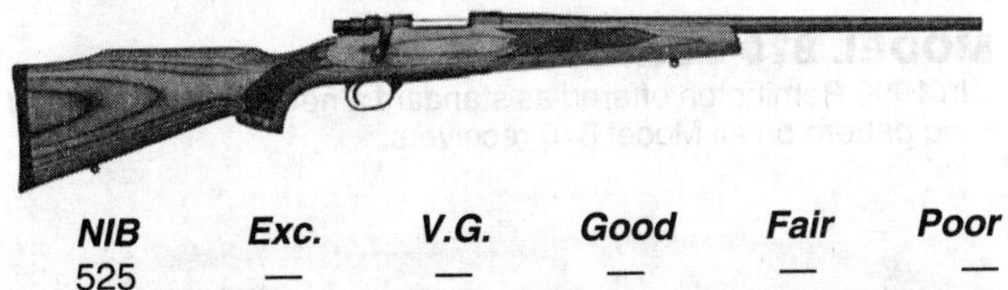

NIB	Exc.	V.G.	Good	Fair	Poor
525	—	—	—	—	—

Model 1816 Commemorative Flint Lock Rifle

Introduced in 1995. It features a 39", .50 caliber octagonal barrel. Stock is hand finished extra fancy curly maple. Built for one year only. Special order only.

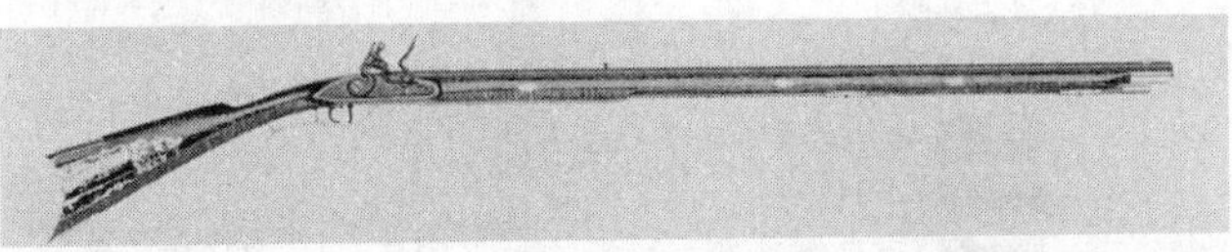

Courtesy Remington Arms

NIB	Exc.	V.G.	Good	Fair	Poor
1800	1200	850	700	500	300

Remington No. 1 Rolling Block Mid-Range

This classic rifle was reintroduced into the Remington line in 1997 and features a 30" half octagon, half-round barrel chambered for the .45-70 Govt. cartridge. Designed for use with black powder and lead cast bullets. The receiver is case colored. All barrel, receiver, and metalwork markings match the original rifle. Rear tang-mounted vernier sight and front globe sight with interchangeable inserts. A single set trigger is standard. Steel buttplate. Weight is approximately 9.75 lbs.

NIB	Exc.	V.G.	Good	Fair	Poor
2200	—	—	—	—	—

Remington Mid-Range Sporter Rolling Block

Introduced in 1998 this model features a 30" round barrel with pistol grip sporter stock. Adjustable rear sight. Chambered for .30-30, .444 Marlin, and .45-70 Govt. A number of extra cost options are available for this model including barrels, sights, fancy wood, etc. Prices listed below are for standard model.

NIB	Exc.	V.G.	Good	Fair	Poor
1275	1000	—	—	—	—

Model SPR18 Single Shot Rifle

A break-action rifle with silvertone receiver and fluted barrel. Calibers: .223, .243, .270, .30-06, .308. Weight: 6-3/4 lbs. Imported; introduced 2005.

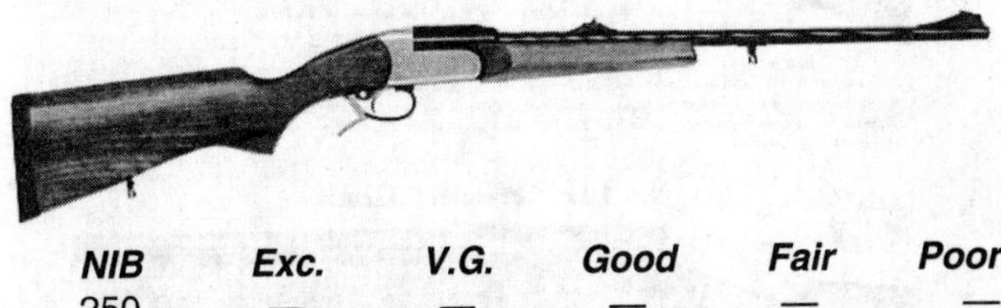

NIB	Exc.	V.G.	Good	Fair	Poor
250	—	—	—	—	—

Model SPR22 Double Rifle

Lever-operated break-action SXS double rifle in .30-06 and .45-70. Double triggers, tang safety. Barrels can be regulated via jackscrew. Imported; introduced 2005. Not widely sitibuted in USA, if at all.

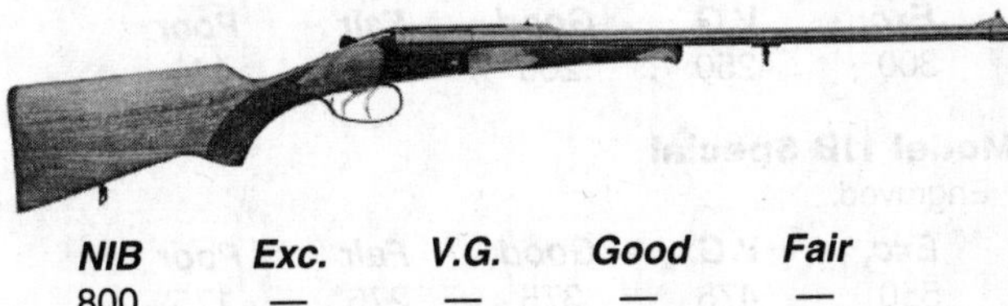

NIB	Exc.	V.G.	Good	Fair
800	—	—	—	—

Model SPR94 Combo Gun

Over/under rifle shotgun. Combinations: .410/.22 rimfire, .410/.17HMR, .41o/.22WMR, 12-ga./.223, 12-ga./.30-06, 12-ga./.308. Double triggers, tang safety. Imported; introduced 2005.

NIB	Exc.	V.G.	Good	Fair
400	—	—	—	—

Model 412

Compact single-shot chambered for .22 LR. 19.5" blued barrel, hardwood stock. Introduced 2006.

NIB	Exc.	V.G.	Good	Fair
125	—	—	—	—

SHOTGUNS

Model 10A

A 12, 16, or 20 gauge slide-action shotgun with barrels ranging from 26" to 32". Takedown, blued with a plain walnut stock. Manufactured from 1907 to 1929.

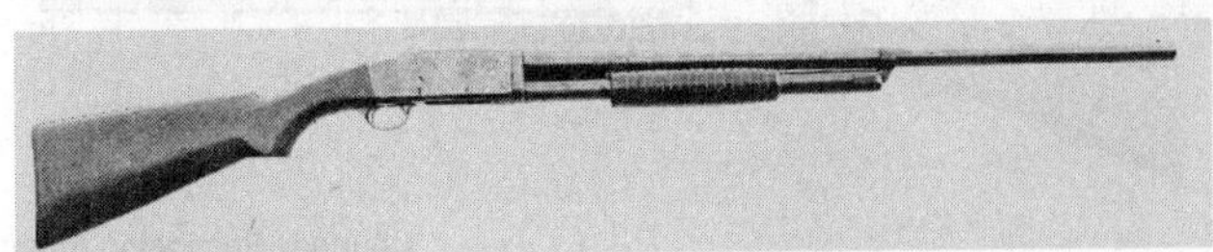

Courtesy Remington Arms

Exc.	V.G.	Good	Fair	Poor
375	300	250	200	100

Model 11

A 12, 16, or 20 gauge semi-automatic shotgun with barrels ranging in length from 26" to 32". Designed by John M. Browning and produced under license from Fabrique Nationale. Blued with a checkered walnut stock. Approximately 300,000 were made from 1911 to 1948. Solid rib or vent rib add 30 percent to listed values.

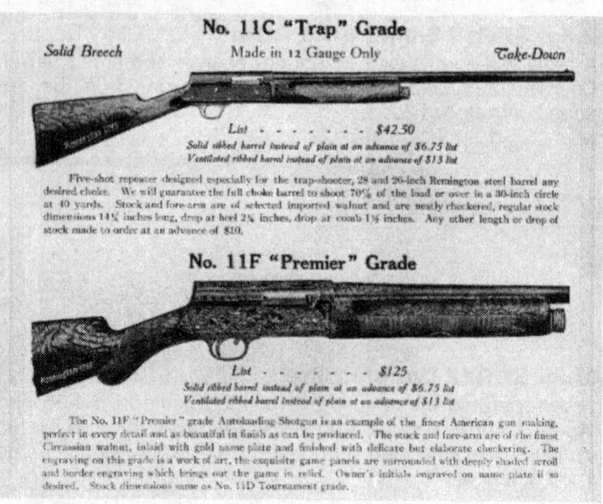

No. 11C "Trap" Grade

Solid Breech Made in 12 Gauge Only *Take-Down*

List - - - - - - - - $42.50

Solid ribbed barrel instead of plain at an advance of $6.75 list
Ventilated ribbed barrel instead of plain at an advance of $13 list

Five-shot repeater designed especially for the trap-shooter, 28 and 26-inch Remington steel barrel any desired choke. We will guarantee the full choke barrel to shoot 70% of the load or over in a 30-inch circle at 40 yards. Stock and fore-arm are of selected imported walnut and are neatly checkered, regular stock dimensions 14¼ inches long, drop at heel 2¼ inches, drop at comb 1½ inches. Any other length or drop of stock made to order at an advance of $10.

No. 11F "Premier" Grade

List - - - - - - - - $125

Solid ribbed barrel instead of plain at an advance of $6.75 list
Ventilated ribbed barrel instead of plain at an advance of $13 list

The No. 11F "Premier" grade Autoloading Shotgun is an example of the finest American gun making, perfect in every detail and as beautiful in finish as can be produced. The stock and fore-arm are of the finest Circassian walnut, inlaid with gold name plate and finished with delicate but elaborate checkering. The engraving on this grade is a work of art, the exquisite game panels are surrounded with deeply shaded scroll and border engraving which brings out the game in relief. Owner's initials engraved on name plate if so desired. Stock dimensions same as No. 11D Tournament grade.

Exc.	V.G.	Good	Fair	Poor
300	250	200	150	100

Model 11B Special

Engraved.

Exc.	V.G.	Good	Fair	Poor
550	475	375	275	175

Model 11D Tournament

Exc.	V.G.	Good	Fair	Poor
850	750	650	450	300

Model 11E Expert

Engraved.

Exc.	V.G.	Good	Fair	Poor
1300	1150	1000	650	450

Model 11F Premier

Heavily engraved.

Exc.	V.G.	Good	Fair	Poor
2250	1900	1600	1150	600

Model 11R

20" barrel riot gun.

Exc.	V.G.	Good	Fair	Poor
350	300	250	175	100

Model 17

A 20 gauge slide-action shotgun with barrels ranging in length from 26" to 32". Takedown, blued with a plain walnut stock. Approximately 48,000 were made from 1917 to 1933.

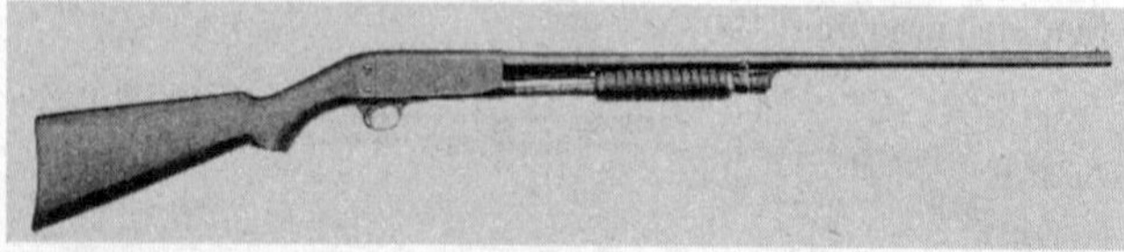

Courtesy Remington Arms

Exc.	V.G.	Good	Fair	Poor
350	300	250	175	100

NOTE: Vent rib add 25 percent.

Model 29

As above, chambered for 12 gauge cartridges. Approximately 24,000 manufactured from 1929 to 1933.

Exc.	V.G.	Good	Fair	Poor
450	350	300	200	175

NOTE: For guns with 32" barrels add 40 percent. Vent rib add 25 percent.

Model 31

A 12, 16, or 20 gauge slide-action shotgun with barrels ranging in length from 26" to 32" and a magazine capacity of either 2 or 4 rounds. Takedown, blued with a walnut stock. Approximately 160,000 were made from 1931 to 1949.

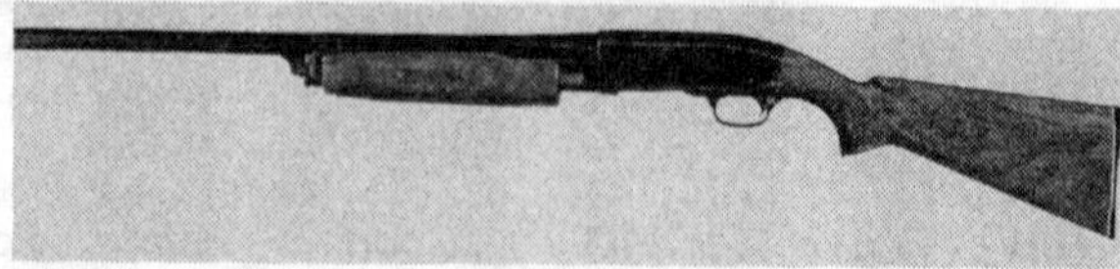

Exc.	V.G.	Good	Fair	Poor
400	325	275	200	125

NOTE: For guns with 32" barrel add 50 percent. For early models with checkered stocks add 40 percent. Solid rib or vent rib add 25 percent. For early banded barrels add 25 percent.

MODEL 870 SERIES

In 1996 Remington offered as standard a new fine line engraving pattern on all Model 870 receivers.

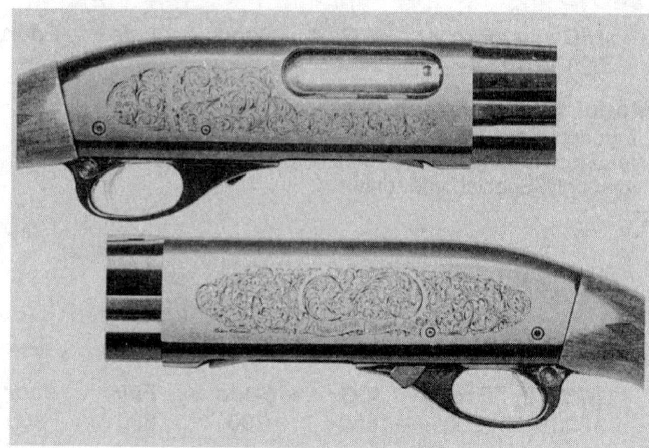

Close-up detail of new engraving on the Model 870

Courtesy Remington Arms

Model 870 Wingmaster

A 12, 16, or 20 gauge slide-action shotgun with 26", 28", or 30" barrels and a 5-shot tubular magazine. Blued with a plain walnut stock. Manufactured from 1950 to 1963.

Exc.	V.G.	Good	Fair	Poor
250	225	200	150	100

NOTE: Vent rib add 10 percent.

Model 870 Field Wingmaster

As above, with a checkered walnut stock and screw-in choke tubes. Introduced in 1964. In 1980 the 16 gauge was dropped as an offering.

NIB	Exc.	V.G.	Good	Fair	Poor
550	450	300	225	150	100

Model 870 Field Wingmaster 16 Gauge

In 2002 the 16 gauge was reintroduced into the Wingmaster line. Offered with 26" or 28" vent rib barrel with choke tubes. Walnut stock with blued finish. Weight is about 7 lbs. Offered in 16 gauge in other configurations listed.

NIB	Exc.	V.G.	Good	Fair	Poor
575	450	—	—	—	—

Model 870 Wingmaster NRA Edition

This is a 12 gauge 3" gun with a 28" vent rib barrel with choke tubes. Walnut stock with checkering. Blued receiver with NRA logos on both sides. Introduced in 2005.

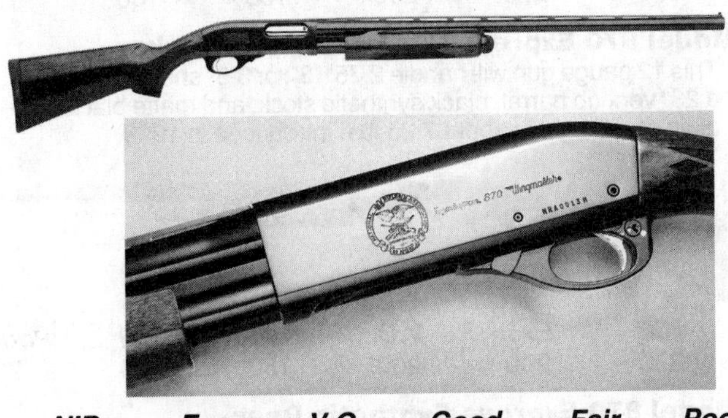

NIB	Exc.	V.G.	Good	Fair	Poor
500	375	—	—	—	—

Model 870 Wingmaster Jr.

Introduced in 2005 this model features a 20 gauge gun with 18.75" vent rib barrel with choke tubes. Checkered walnut stock with recoil pad. Blued finish. Weight is about 6 lbs.

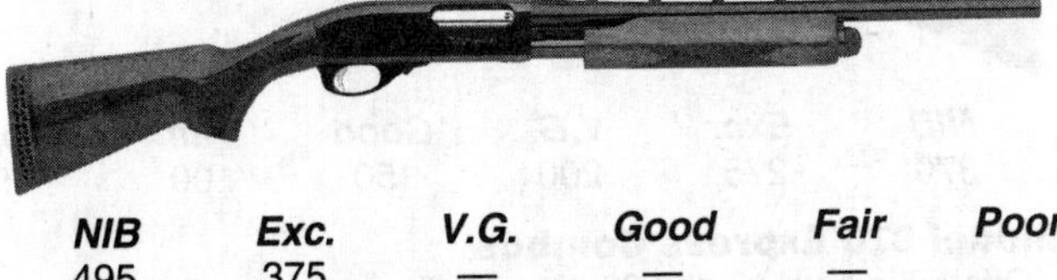

NIB	Exc.	V.G.	Good	Fair	Poor
495	375	—	—	—	—

Model 870 Field Wingmaster Small Bores

Introduced in 1999 this model is now offered in both 28 gauge and .410 bore. Checkered walnut stock. High polish blue finish. Both guns are fitted with 25" barrels. The 28 gauge has Rem chokes while the .410 comes with fixed Modified chokes. Weight is approximately 6 lbs. Price listed is for the .410 bore.

Wingmaster 28 gauge

NIB	Exc.	V.G.	Good	Fair	Poor
600	450	—	—	—	—

NOTE: Add $50 for 28 gauge gun.

Model 870 Magnum

As above, chambered for 12 or 20 gauge 3" Magnum shells. Introduced in 1964. Choke tubes introduced in 1987.

NIB	Exc.	V.G.	Good	Fair	Poor
450	395	300	225	150	100

Model 870 Express

As above, for 3", 12 gauge shells with a 28" ventilated rib and one choke tube. Parkerized with a matte finished stock. Introduced in 1987.

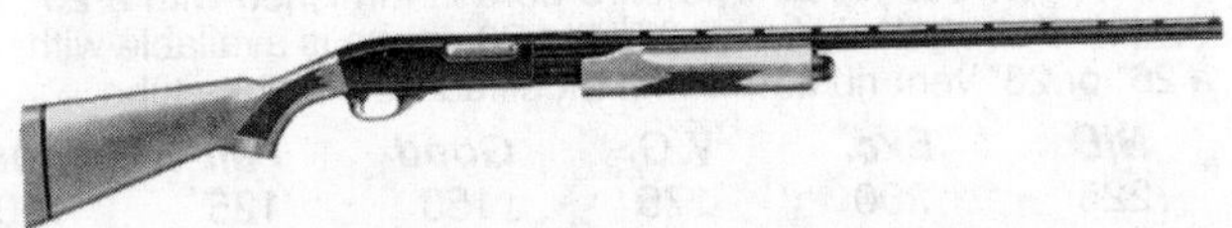

NIB	Exc.	V.G.	Good	Fair	Poor
330	250	200	150	100	75

Model 870 Express Synthetic

NIB	Exc.	V.G.	Good	Fair	Poor
330	250	200	—	—	—

Model 870 Express Synthetic Youth

NIB	Exc.	V.G.	Good	Fair	Poor
300	250	—	—	—	—

Model 870 Express Jr. NWTF Edition

This 20 gauge model is fitted with a 18.75" vent rib barrel with choke tubes. Synthetic stock has a camo finish. Metal is matte black. Weight is about 6 lbs. Introduced in 2005.

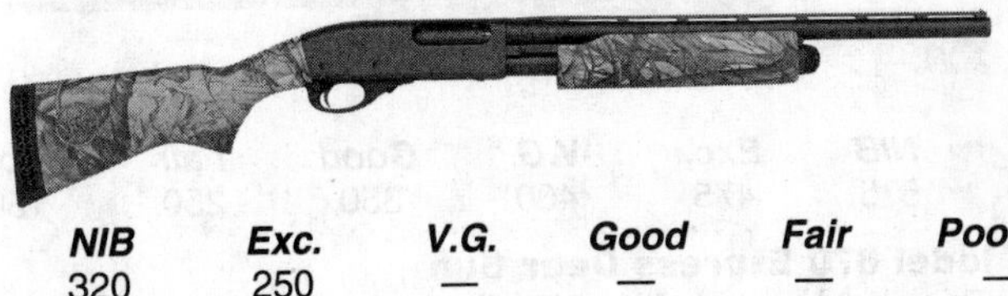

NIB	Exc.	V.G.	Good	Fair	Poor
320	250	—	—	—	—

Model 870 Express Super Magnum

Introduced in 1998, this 870 is similar to the 870 Express but is chambered for 3.5" 12 gauge. Offered in walnut stock with blued 28" barrel, matte black synthetic with 26" or 28" barrel or various camo finishes. Also available as a combo with extra 20" rifled deer barrel. Add $100 for camo. Add 20 percent for combo with deer barrel. Introduced in 1998.

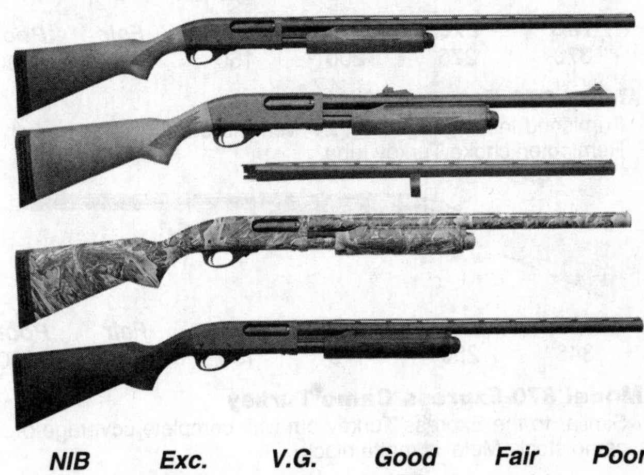

NIB	Exc.	V.G.	Good	Fair	Poor
425	330	225	175	—	—

Model 870 Express Super Magnum Fall Flight

Chambered for the 12 gauge with either 2.75", 3", or 3.5" shells. Fitted with a 30" vent rib barrel with choke tubes. Finish is Skyline Fall Flight camo. Weight is about 7.75 lbs. Introduced in 2005.

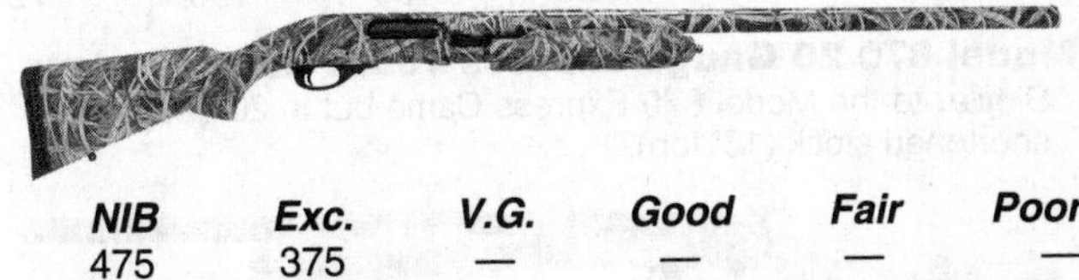

NIB	Exc.	V.G.	Good	Fair	Poor
475	375	—	—	—	—

Model 870TA Trap

As above, with a competition ventilated rib and checkered stock. Produced in 12 gauge only. Discontinued in 1986.

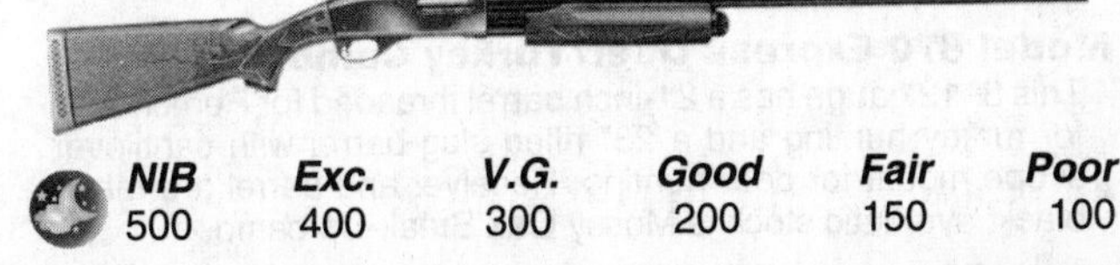

NIB	Exc.	V.G.	Good	Fair	Poor
500	400	300	200	150	100

Model 870TB Trap

As above, with a 28" or 30" Full choke, ventilated rib barrel and a trap-style walnut stock. Manufactured from 1950 to 1981.

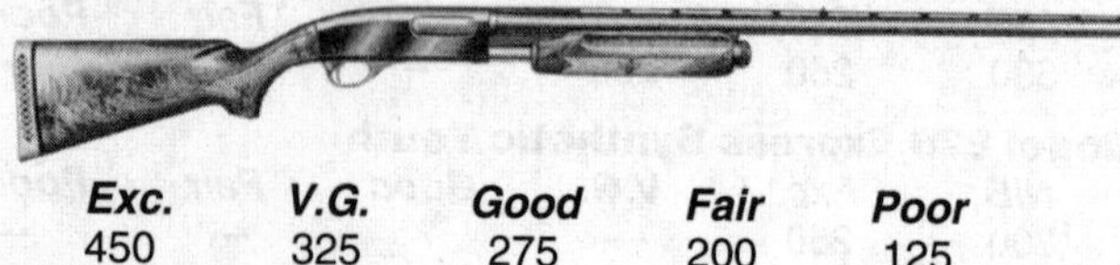

Exc.	V.G.	Good	Fair	Poor
450	325	275	200	125

Model 870TC Trap

As above, with a finely figured walnut stock and screw-in choke tubes.

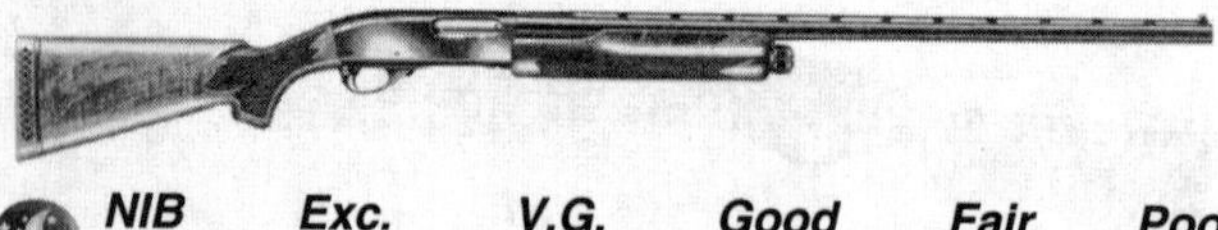

NIB	Exc.	V.G.	Good	Fair	Poor
575	475	400	350	250	150

Model 870 Express Deer Gun

This model is fitted with a 20" fully rifled barrel, iron sights, and Monte Carlo stock. Also offered with a 20" IC rifle sighted barrel. Available in 12 gauge only.

NIB	Exc.	V.G.	Good	Fair	Poor
370	275	200	150	125	100

Model 870 Express Turkey

Furnished in 12 gauge with 21" vent rib barrel with extra-full Remington choke Turkey tube.

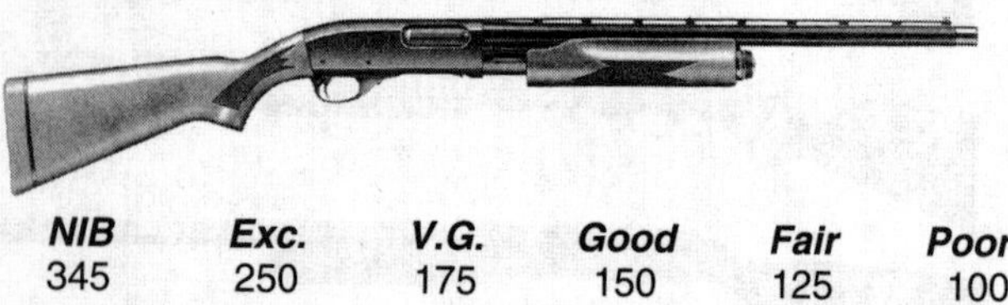

NIB	Exc.	V.G.	Good	Fair	Poor
345	250	175	150	125	100

Model 870 Express Camo Turkey

Similar to the Express Turkey but with complete coverage of camo stock. Metal is matte black.

NIB	Exc.	V.G.	Good	Fair	Poor
400	300	225	150	100	75

Model 870 20 Gauge Express Youth Camo Turkey

Similar to the Model 870 Express Camo but in 20 gauge with shortened stock (13" lop).

NIB	Exc.	V.G.	Good	Fair	Poor
400	300	225	150	100	75

Model 870 Express Deer/Turkey Combo

This 3" 12 gauge has a 21-inch barrel threaded for Remchokes for turkey hunting and a 23" rifled slug barrel with cantilever scope mount for deer hunting. Receiver and barrel are matte black; synthetic stock is Mossy Oak Break-Up camo.

NIB	Exc.	V.G.	Good	Fair	Poor
632	—	—	—	—	—

Model 870 Express Left-Hand

Left-hand version of the Express model fitted with a 28" vent rib barrel and checkered hardwood stock. Black matte finish.

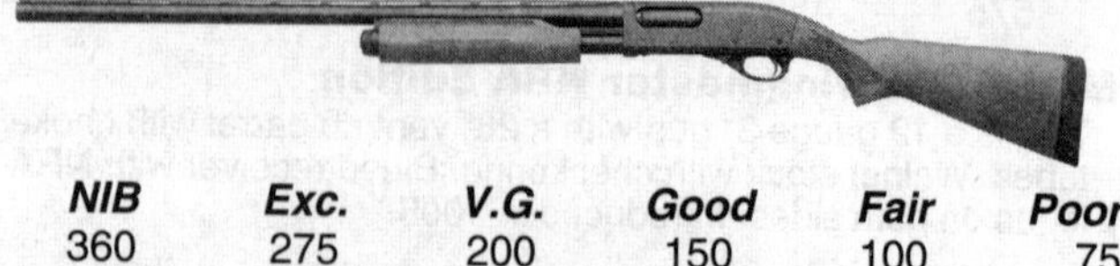

NIB	Exc.	V.G.	Good	Fair	Poor
360	275	200	150	100	75

Model 870 Express Super Magnum Turkey

This 12 gauge gun will handle 2.75", 3", or 3.5" shells. Fitted with a 23" vent rib barrel, black synthetic stock, and matte black metal finish. Weight is about 7.25 lbs. Introduced in 1999.

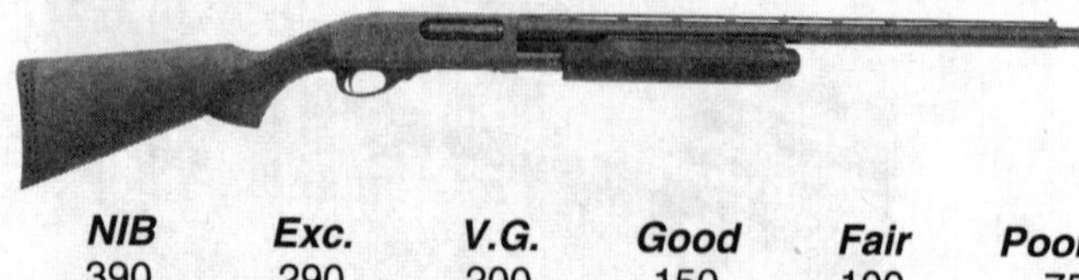

NIB	Exc.	V.G.	Good	Fair	Poor
390	290	200	150	100	75

Model 870 Express Synthetic Deer

This model is fitted with a 20" fully rifled barrel with adjustable rifle sights. Black synthetic stock with Monte Carlo comb and matte black finish. Weight is about 7 lbs. Introduced in 1999.

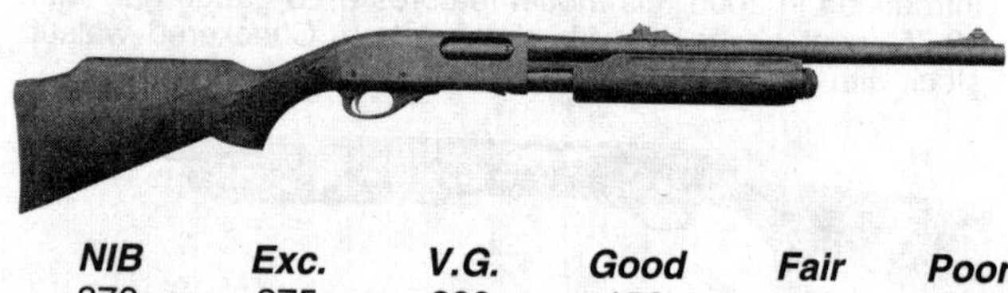

NIB	Exc.	V.G.	Good	Fair	Poor
370	275	200	150	100	75

Model 870 Express Combos

Offered in both 12 and 20 gauge with a 26" vent rib modified barrel and a 20" fully rifled deer barrel.

NIB	Exc.	V.G.	Good	Fair	Poor
450	325	250	200	150	100

Model 870 Express HD (Home Defense)

Introduced in 1995 this model features an 18" 12 gauge barrel with cylinder barrel with front bead sight. Weight approximately 7.25 lb.

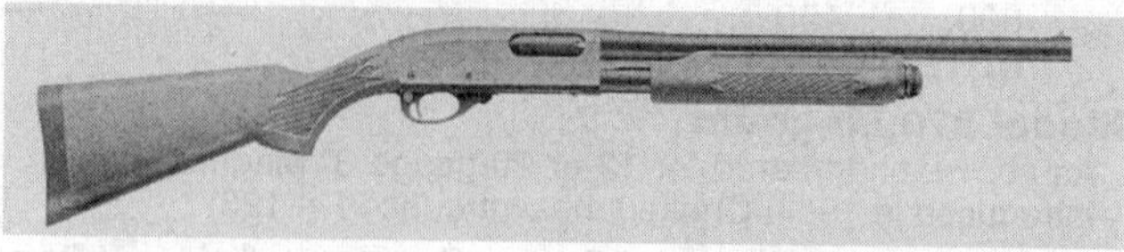

Courtesy Remington Arms

NIB	Exc.	V.G.	Good	Fair	Poor
345	250	175	150	125	100

Model 870 Express Small Game

Offered in 20 gauge or .410, this model has a nonreflective metal and wood finish. The .410 bore is furnished with a 25" vent rib Full choke barrel, while the 20 gauge is available with a 26" or 28" vent rib barrel with Modified Rem. choke tube.

NIB	Exc.	V.G.	Good	Fair	Poor
225	200	175	150	125	100

This symbol denotes "Sleepers" with rapidly-rising values and/or significant collector potential.

Model 870 Express Youth Gun

Available in 20 gauge only, this shotgun is built for children. It has a 13" length of pull, a 21" vent rib barrel, and is sold with a Modified Rem. choke tube.

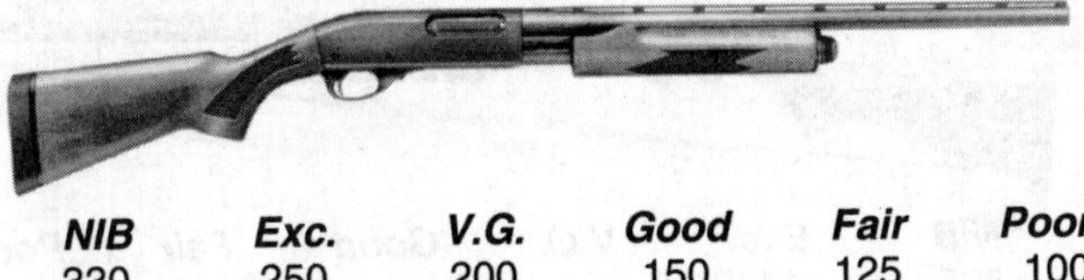

NIB	Exc.	V.G.	Good	Fair	Poor
330	250	200	150	125	100

Model 870 Classic Trap

Introduced in 2000 this model features special fine line engraving with gold inlays. Stock is select walnut with Monte Carlo comb. Barrel length is 30" with a contoured vent rib. Ventilated recoil pad with white-line spacers. Choke tubes. Weight is about 8 lbs.

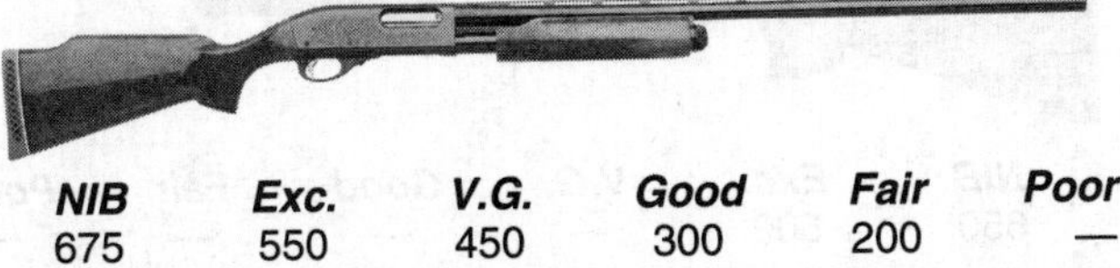

NIB	Exc.	V.G.	Good	Fair	Poor
675	550	450	300	200	—

Model 870 Special Field

This Remington pump-action shotgun is available in either 12 or 20 gauge and features an English-style straight grip stock, 21" vent rib barrel and slim shortened slide handle. In 12 gauge the gun weighs 7 lbs. and in 20 gauge it weighs 6.25 lbs. Comes with a set of Remington choke tubes.

NIB	Exc.	V.G.	Good	Fair	Poor
550	450	300	250	150	100

Model 870 Brushmaster Deer Gun

This 12 gauge slide-action shotgun is fitted with a 20" Remington choke plain barrel and Monte Carlo stock. Available for either left-hand or right-hand shooters.

NIB	Exc.	V.G.	Good	Fair	Poor
350	300	250	200	150	100

Model 870 Rifle Deer Gun

This new 20 gauge model was introduced in 1994 and features a fully rifled 20" barrel. It has a new scope rail design that is more rigid. The finish is blue and the Monte Carlo stock is walnut. Is equipped with recoil pad and checkering.

Close-up of new engraving detail on Model 870 Deer Gun

Courtesy Remington Arms

NIB	Exc.	V.G.	Good	Fair	Poor
450	400	350	300	200	100

Model 870 SPS-T Youth Turkey Camo

This shotgun is finished in Mossy Oak Break-Up and chambered for the 12 gauge shell. Fitted with a 20" Super Full choke. Weight is about 7.125 lbs. Introduced in 2001.

NIB	Exc.	V.G.	Good	Fair	Poor
565	450	—	—	—	—

Model 870 Express Youth Turkey Camo

Similar to the model above but chambered for the 20 gauge shell and finished with Realtree Camo. Weight is about 6 lbs.

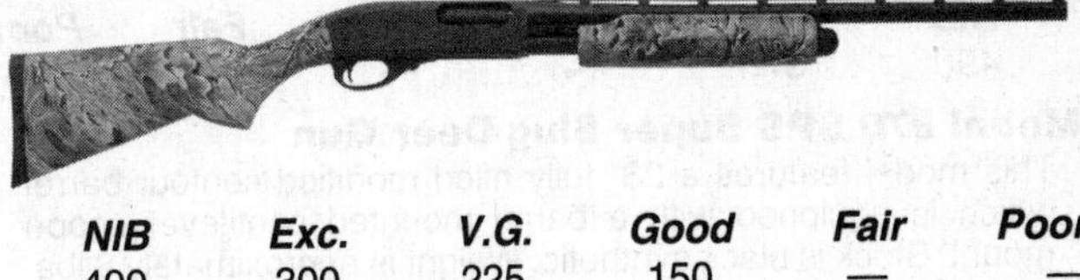

NIB	Exc.	V.G.	Good	Fair	Poor
400	300	225	150	—	—

Model 870 Youth Deer Gun

Chambered for the 20 gauge shell and fitted with a 21" full choked barrel. Realtree Camo finish. Magazine capacity is 4 rounds. Weight is about 6 lbs.

NIB	Exc.	V.G.	Good	Fair	Poor
330	250	200	150	125	100

Model 870 Security

Offered in 12 gauge only this personal protection shotgun has an 18.5" Cylinder-choked plain barrel with front bead sight.

NIB	Exc.	V.G.	Good	Fair	Poor
330	250	200	150	125	100

Model 870 SPS-Camo

Offered in 12 gauge only and a choice of 26" or 28" vent rib barrel with Rem. choke tubes. The wood and metal are finished in a brown camo color. Introduced in 2001.

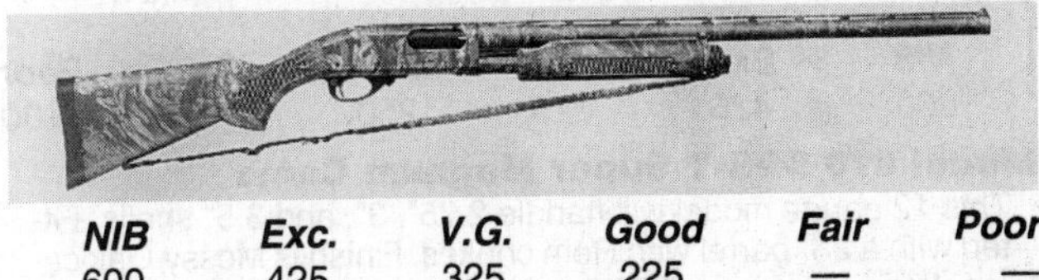

NIB	Exc.	V.G.	Good	Fair	Poor
600	425	325	225	—	—

Model 870 SPS Super Magnum Camo

This model is chambered for 12 gauge shells with chambers that will handle both 3" magnum and 3.5" magnum shells as well as all 2.75" shells. Barrel is 23" with ventilated rib and Rem. chokes. Finish is Mossy Oak camo. Weight is about 7.25 lbs. Introduced in 1999.

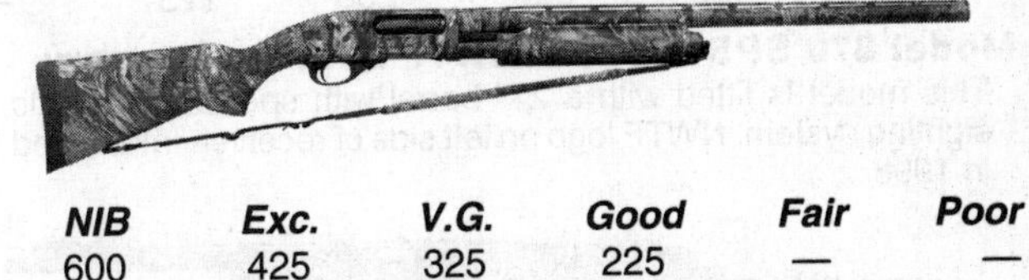

NIB	Exc.	V.G.	Good	Fair	Poor
600	425	325	225	—	—

Model 870 SPS-BG Camo

Available for the first time in 1993 this model features a 12 gauge 20" plain barrel with IC and Turkey Super Full Rem. choke tubes. The wood and metal are finished in a brown camo color.

This symbol denotes "Sleepers" with rapidly-rising values and/or significant collector potential.

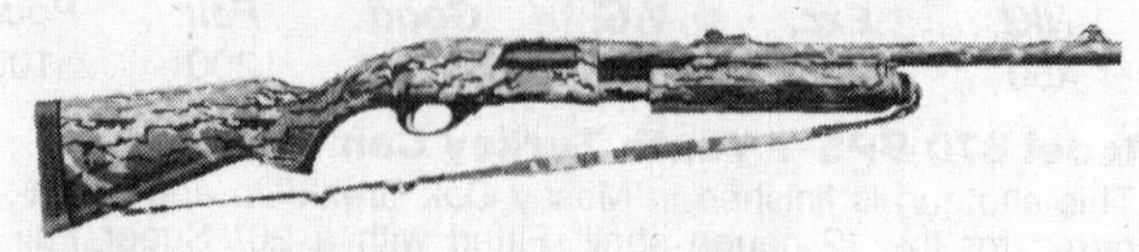

NIB	Exc.	V.G.	Good	Fair	Poor
400	300	225	175	125	100

Model 870 SPS Fully Rifled Deer Gun

This 20 gauge model features an 18.5" fully rifled heavy barrel with no sights. Receiver has a cantilever scope mount. Black synthetic stock. Black matte finish. Weight is about 8 lbs. Magazine capacity is 4 rounds. Introduced in 2004.

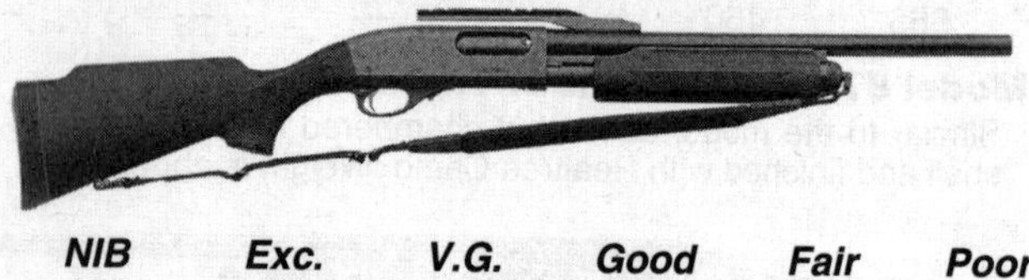

NIB	Exc.	V.G.	Good	Fair	Poor
490	375	—	—	—	—

Model 870 SPS Super Slug Deer Gun

This model features a 23" fully rifled modified contour barrel which is equipped with a barrel mounted cantilever scope mount. Stock is black synthetic. Weight is approximately 8 lbs. Introduced in 1999.

NIB	Exc.	V.G.	Good	Fair	Poor
600	425	325	250	175	100

Model 870 SPS-T Camo

Same as above with the exception of a 21" vent rib barrel with IC and Turkey Super Full Rem. choke tubes. Both wood and metal are finished in a green camo color.

NIB	Exc.	V.G.	Good	Fair	Poor
600	425	325	250	175	100

Model 870 SPS-T Super Magnum Camo

This 12 gauge model will handle 2.75", 3", and 3.5" shells. Fitted with a 23" barrel with Rem chokes. Finish is Mossy Oak camo. Weight is about 7.25 lbs. Introduced in 1999.

NIB	Exc.	V.G.	Good	Fair	Poor
615	425	325	250	175	—

Model 870 SPS-T Camo NWTF 25th Anniversary

This model is fitted with a 21" barrel with special fiber optic sighting system. NWTF logo on left side of receiver. Introduced in 1998.

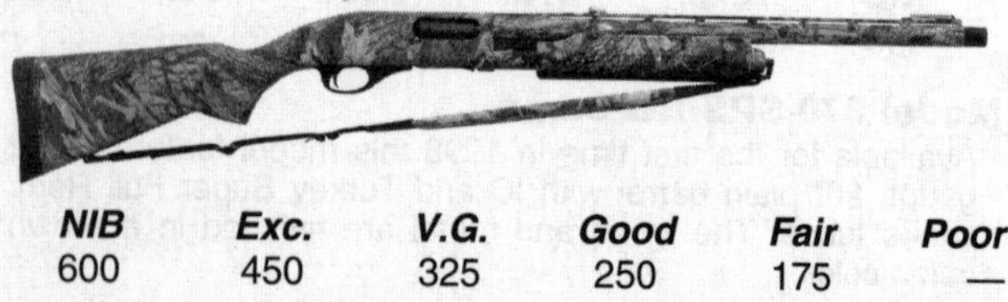

NIB	Exc.	V.G.	Good	Fair	Poor
600	450	325	250	175	—

Model 870 SPS-T Camo

Chambered for the 20 gauge 3" shell and fitted with a 20" barrel with full choke. Stock is Mossy Oak camo. Fiber optic front sight. Weight is about 6 lbs. Introduced in 2003.

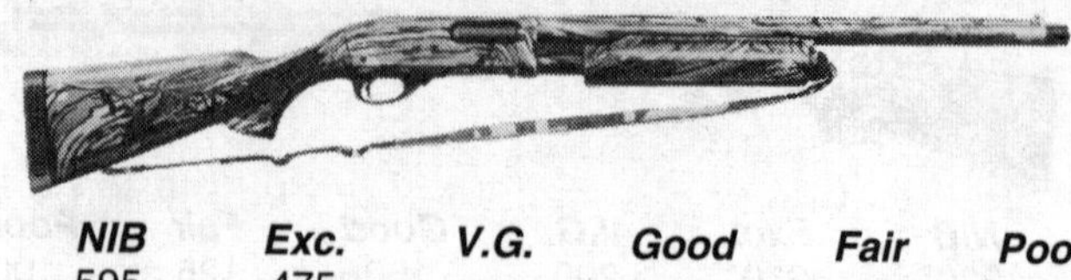

NIB	Exc.	V.G.	Good	Fair	Poor
595	475	—	—	—	—

Model 870 SP-T Super Magnum Thumbhole

This 12 gauge 3.5" gun is fitted with a 23" barrel with choke tubes. Mossy Oak Obsession finish. Open sights with fiber-optic front sight. Weight is about 8 lbs. Introduced in 2005.

NIB	Exc.	V.G.	Good	Fair	Poor
650	500	—	—	—	—

Model 870 Dale Earnhardt Limited Edition

This is a 12 gauge with a 28" vent rib barrel with choke tubes. Checkered walnut stock. The receiver is engraved with Earnhardt's likeness and gold signature. High polish blue finish. Weight is about 8 lbs. Introduced in 2005.

NIB	Exc.	V.G.	Good	Fair	Poor
820	625	—	—	—	—

Model 870 Marine Magnum

This 12 gauge shotgun has a nickel finish on the inside and outside of the receiver and barrel. Synthetic stock is checkered. The 18" barrel is bored cylinder and is fitted with a 7-round magazine. Sling swivel studs are standard.

NIB	Exc.	V.G.	Good	Fair	Poor
560	325	275	225	175	125

Model 870 SPS

Offered in 12 gauge only with synthetic stock and black matte finish. The barrel is either 26" or 28" with ventilated rib and Rem. choke tubes.

NIB	Exc.	V.G.	Good	Fair	Poor
325	275	225	175	125	100

Model 870 SPS-Deer

Available with a 20" rifle with plain barrel, this 12 gauge shotgun has a black synthetic stock and black matte finish. First introduced in 1993.

NIB	Exc.	V.G.	Good	Fair	Poor
300	250	225	175	125	100

Model 870 SPS-T

This 12 gauge model comes standard with a 21" vent rib barrel, Rem. choke tubes in IC and Turkey Super Full, black synthetic stock, and black matte finish.

NIB	Exc.	V.G.	Good	Fair	Poor
300	250	225	175	125	100

Model 870 Police

This model comes in a wide variety (21) of 12 gauge configurations. Fitted with barrel from 14" (Class III), 18", or 20". Most with Parkerized finish, although some variations have blued finish. Wood stock, folding stock, Speedfeed stock, or synthetic stock. Rifle or bead sights, and some configurations with

Ghost-ring and tritium night sights. Some variations have 7- or 8-round magazine extensions depending on barrel length.

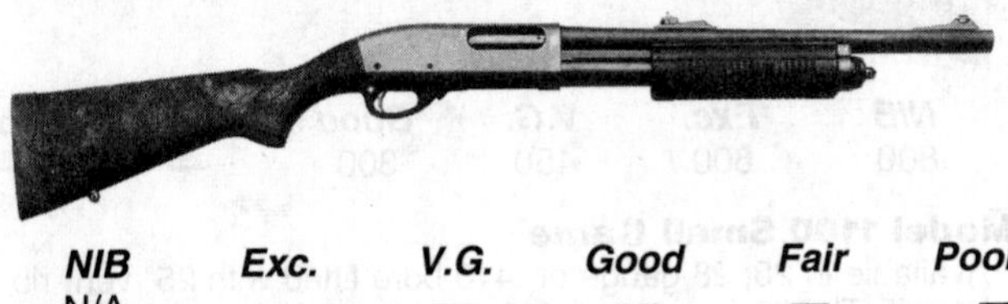

NIB	Exc.	V.G.	Good	Fair	Poor
N/A	—	—	—	—	—

Model 870 Tac-2 SpecOps Stock

Tactical 3" 12 gauge is available with a Knoxx pistol-grip or folding stock. Barrel is 18" with fixed Cylinder choke. Magazine capacity is 6 shells. Weight is 7 lbs.

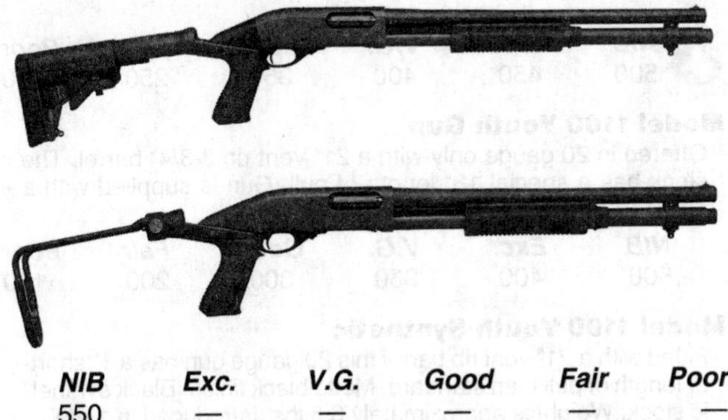

NIB	Exc.	V.G.	Good	Fair	Poor
550	—	—	—	—	—

Model 870 Tac-3 Speedfeed IV

Tactical 3" 12 gauge with pistol-grip stock and 20" barrel. Extended 7-round magazine. Weight is 7.5 lbs.

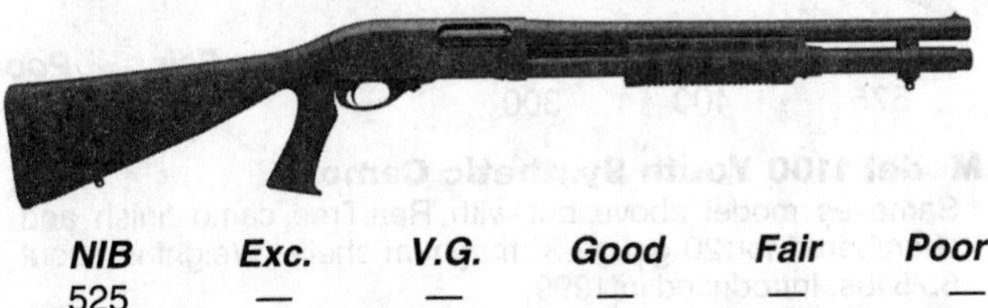

NIB	Exc.	V.G.	Good	Fair	Poor
525	—	—	—	—	—

Model 870 Tac-3 Folder

As above but with Knoxx Spec-Ops folding stock. Weight is 7 lbs.

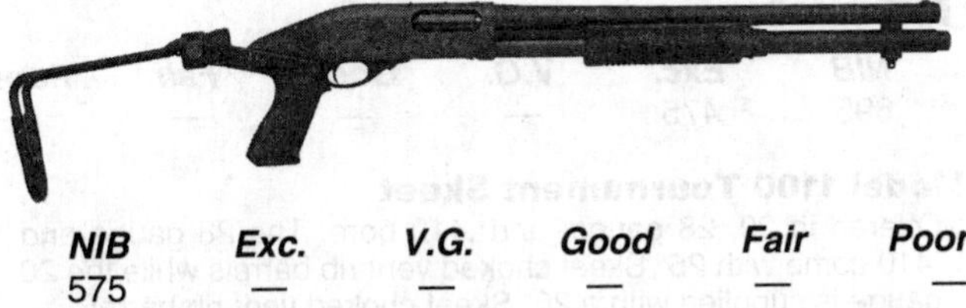

NIB	Exc.	V.G.	Good	Fair	Poor
575	—	—	—	—	—

Model 870 Custom Grade

This Custom Shop model is available in three levels of engraving, gold inlay, wood grade and finish, metal work finish, recoil pad/buttplate, and dimensions.

D Grade

NIB	Exc.	V.G.	Good	Fair	Poor
2600	—	—	—	—	—

F Grade

NIB	Exc.	V.G.	Good	Fair	Poor
5375	—	—	—	—	—

F Grade with Gold Inlay

NIB	Exc.	V.G.	Good	Fair	Poor
8050	—	—	—	—	—

Model 870 SP-T Thumbhole

Introduced in 2005, this 3.5" 12 gauge is designed specifically for turkey hunting with full coverage in Mossy Oak Obsession camo and thumbhole stock. The 23" barrel features fiber-optic adjustable rifle sights and is drilled and tapped for scope mounting. Includes R3 recoil pad, sling, swivels and turkey super full choke tube. MSRP: 600

Model 870 SPS-T Super Mag

Similar to Model 870 SP-T Thumbhole but with pistol-grip stock and vent-rib barrel.

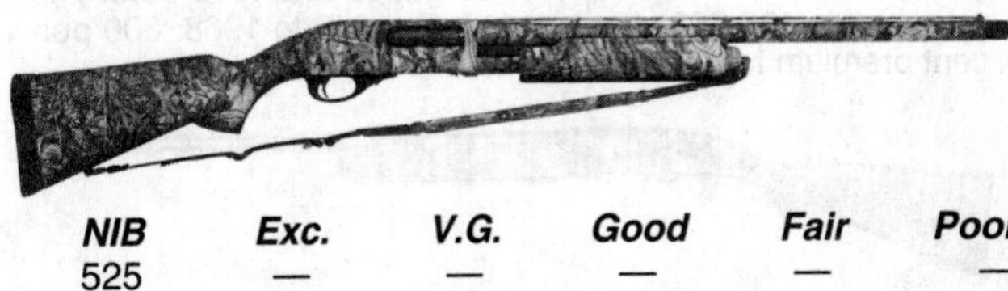

NIB	Exc.	V.G.	Good	Fair	Poor
525	—	—	—	—	—

Model 870 SPS-T/20

This 20-gauge turkey gun features a 3" chamber, 23" vent rib barrel, R3 recoil pad and full coverage in Mossy Oak New Break-Up camo. Drilled and tapped for scope mount.

NIB	Exc.	V.G.	Good	Fair	Poor
400	300	—	—	—	—

Model 870 Special Purpose Thumbhole

Laminated stock 12 gauge slug gun with 3" chamber and 23" fully rifled cantilever barrel.

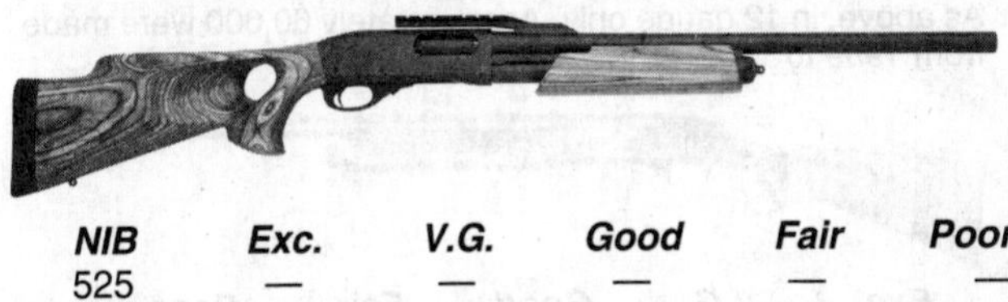

NIB	Exc.	V.G.	Good	Fair	Poor
525	—	—	—	—	—

Model 870 XCS Marine Magnum

New in 2007, this weather-resistant 870 is a 3" 12 gauge with full black TriNyte coverage, 18" fixed Cylinder barrel and 7 round capacity. Weight is 7.5 lbs.

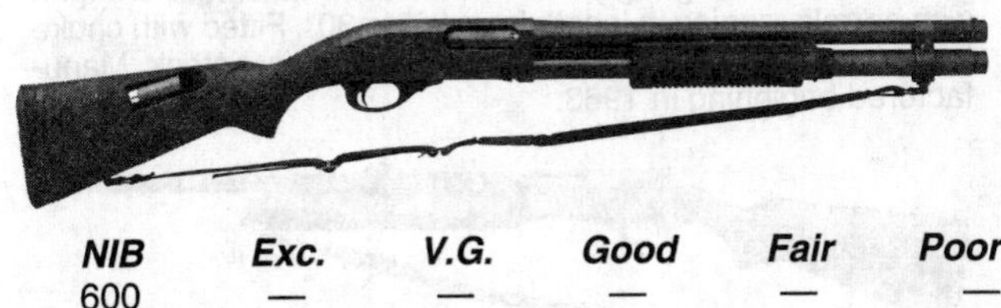

NIB	Exc.	V.G.	Good	Fair	Poor
600	—	—	—	—	—

Model 870 SPS MAX Gobbler

This dedicated turkey gun is a 3.5" 12 gauge featuring a length-adjustable Knoxx SpecOps stock, 23" barrel, fiber-optic rifle sights, Super Full turkey choke tube and full coverage in Realtree APG camo. Drilled and tapped for Weaver style mount. Weight is 8 lbs.

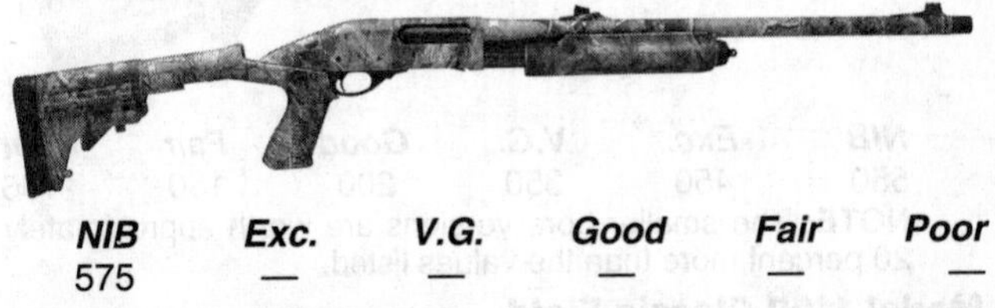

NIB	Exc.	V.G.	Good	Fair	Poor
575	—	—	—	—	—

Model 48 Sportsman

A 12, 16, or 20 gauge semi-automatic shotgun with 26", 28", or 32" barrels and a 3-shot tubular magazine. Blued with a checkered walnut stock. Approximately 275,000 were made from 1949 to 1959.

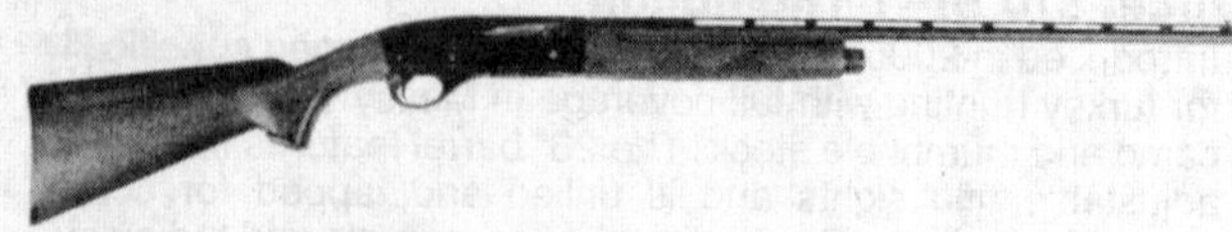

Exc.	V.G.	Good	Fair	Poor
325	300	250	175	100

NOTE: Vent rib add 20 percent.

Model 11-48

As above, with the addition of 28 gauge and .410 bore. Approximately 425,000 were made from 1949 to 1968. 300 percent premium for 28 ga.

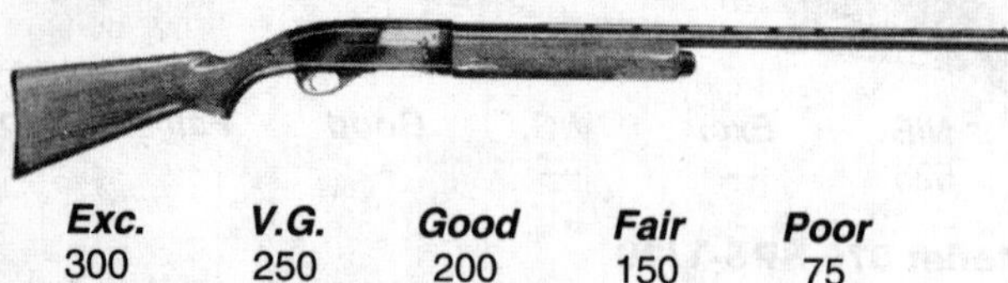

Exc.	V.G.	Good	Fair	Poor
300	250	200	150	75

Model 58 Sportsman

A 12, 16, or 20 gauge semi-automatic shotgun with 26", 28", or 30" barrels and a 3-shot tubular magazine. The receiver is scroll engraved and blued. Checkered walnut stock. Approximately 270,000 were made from 1956 to 1963.

Exc.	V.G.	Good	Fair	Poor
300	250	200	150	75

Model 878 Automaster

As above, in 12 gauge only. Approximately 60,000 were made from 1959 to 1962.

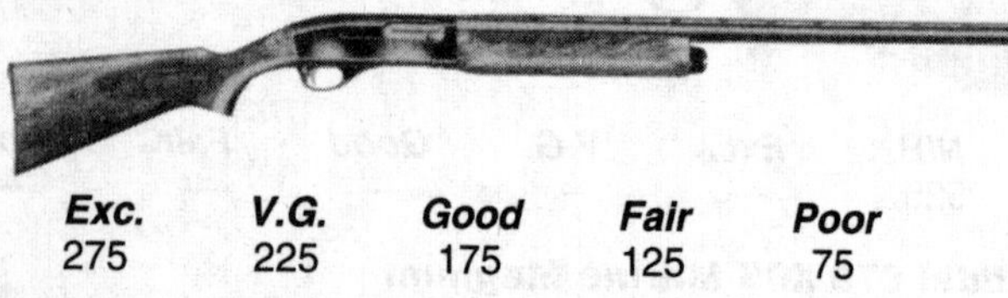

Exc.	V.G.	Good	Fair	Poor
275	225	175	125	75

MODEL 1100 SERIES

A 12, 16, 20 or 28 gauge or .410 bore semi-automatic shotgun with barrels ranging in length from 26" to 30". Fitted with choke tubes after 1987. Blued with a checkered walnut stock. Manufactured beginning in 1963.

NIB	Exc.	V.G.	Good	Fair	Poor
550	450	350	200	150	100

NOTE: The smaller bore versions are worth approximately 20 percent more than the values listed.

Model 1100 Classic Field

Introduced in 2003 this shotgun is chambered for the 16 gauge shell and fitted with a choice of 26" or 28" vent rib barrel with Remington choke tubes. Checkered walnut stock with pistol grip. High polish blue finish. Magazine capacity is four rounds. Weight is about 7 to 7.25 lbs. depending on barrel length.

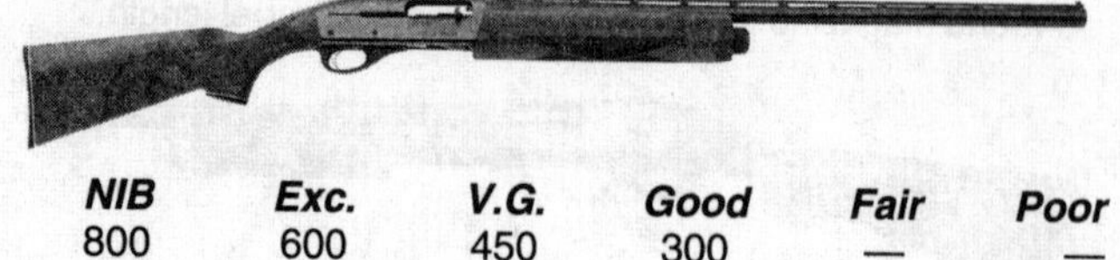

NIB	Exc.	V.G.	Good	Fair	Poor
800	600	450	300	—	—

Model 1100 Small Game

Available in 20, 28 gauge or .410 bore fitted with 25" vent rib barrels. The 28 gauge and .410 have fixed chokes while the 20 gauge has Rem. choke tubes.

NIB	Exc.	V.G.	Good	Fair	Poor
500	450	400	350	250	150

Model 1100 Youth Gun

Offered in 20 gauge only with a 21" vent rib 2-3/4" barrel. The stock has a special 13" length of pull. Gun is supplied with a set of Rem. choke tubes.

NIB	Exc.	V.G.	Good	Fair	Poor
600	400	350	300	200	150

Model 1100 Youth Synthetic

Fitted with a 21" vent rib barrel this 20 gauge gun has a 1" shorter length of pull than standard. Matte black finish. Black synthetic stock. Weight is approximately 6.5 lbs. Introduced in 1999.

NIB	Exc.	V.G.	Good	Fair	Poor
575	400	300	—	—	—

Model 1100 Youth Synthetic Camo

Same as model above but with RealTree camo finish and chambered for 20 gauge 3" magnum shells. Weight is about 6.75 lbs. Introduced in 1999.

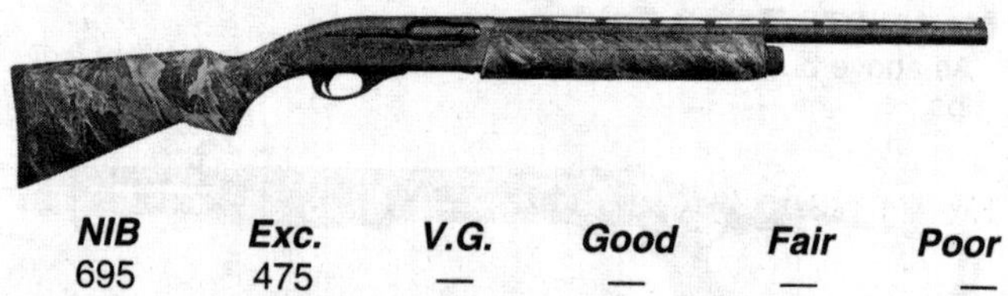

NIB	Exc.	V.G.	Good	Fair	Poor
695	475	—	—	—	—

Model 1100 Tournament Skeet

Offered in 20, 28 gauge, and .410 bore. The 28 gauge and .410 come with 25" Skeet choked vent rib barrels while the 20 gauge is supplied with a 26" Skeet choked vent rib barrel.

Courtesy Remington Arms

NIB	Exc.	V.G.	Good	Fair	Poor
800	650	500	400	250	150

Model 1100 Tournament Skeet, 12 Gauge

Introduced in 2003 this model is fitted with a 26" light contour vent rib barrel. Stock is semi-fancy walnut. Receiver is rolled-marked "TOURNAMENT SKEET." Supplied with extended choke tubes and gold-plated trigger. Weight is about 7.75 lbs.

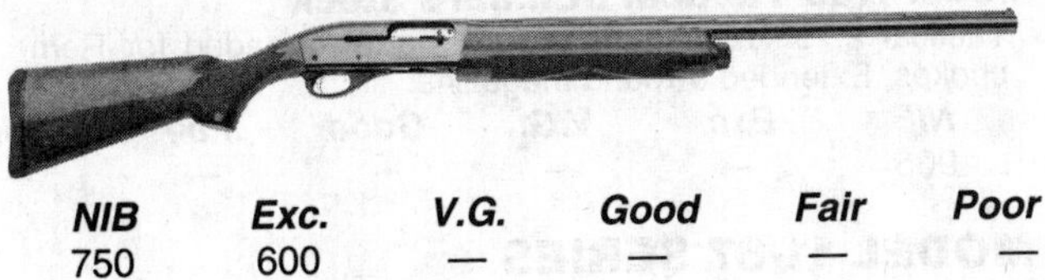

NIB	Exc.	V.G.	Good	Fair	Poor
750	600	—	—	—	—

Model 1100 Classic Trap

This model features a 30" low-profile vent rib barrel. The stock is semi-fancy walnut with Monte Carlo comb and ventilated recoil pad. Receiver has fine line engraving with gold inlays and the trigger is gold. Weight is about 8.25 lbs.

NIB	Exc.	V.G.	Good	Fair	Poor
700	600	—	—	—	—

Model 1100 Sporting 12

Introduced in 2000 this 12 gauge model features a 28" low profile vent rib barrel. Stock is walnut with cut checkering and Sporting Clays-style recoil pad. Gold trigger and fine line engraving on the receiver. Weight is about 8 lbs.

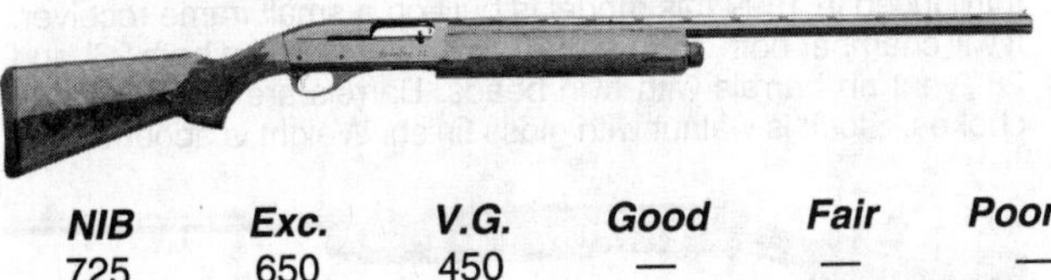

NIB	Exc.	V.G.	Good	Fair	Poor
725	650	450	—	—	—

Model 1100 Sporting 20

This model has a high grade walnut stock with glass finish and recoil pad. It is fitted with a 28" barrel with target sights. Interchangeable chokes. Introduced in 1998.

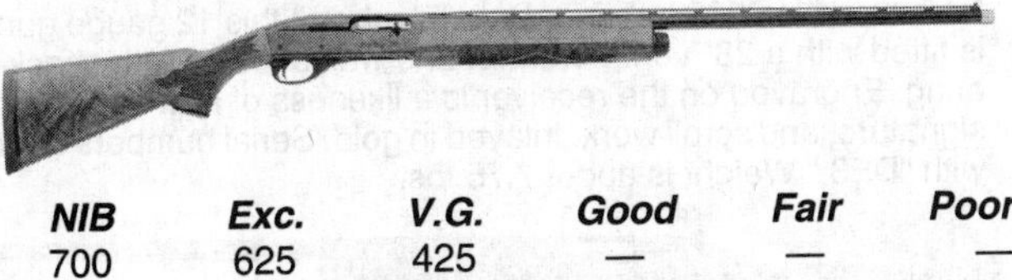

NIB	Exc.	V.G.	Good	Fair	Poor
700	625	425	—	—	—

Model 1100 Sporting 28

Introduced in 1996 this version is chambered for the 28 gauge shell. It is fitted with interchangeable chokes and a 25" vent rib barrel. The stock is walnut with Tournament grade checkering and recoil pad.

Courtesy Remington Arms

NIB	Exc.	V.G.	Good	Fair	Poor
825	650	475	—	—	—

Model 1100 Competition Master

Introduced in 2003 this model features a 12 gauge gun chambered for the 2.75" shell. Fitted with a 22" vent rib barrel with Remington chokes and fiber optic front sight. Has a gray synthetic stock with matte black finish on receiver and barrel. Magazine extension has eight-round capacity. Receiver mounted ammo carrier for seven extra shells. Weight is about 8 lbs. Designed for practical shooting competition.

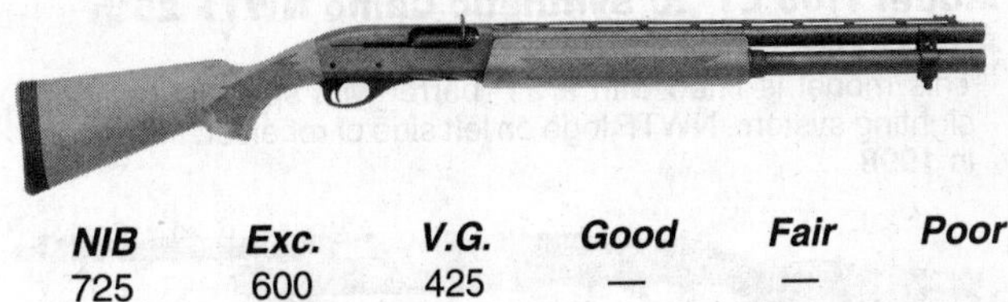

NIB	Exc.	V.G.	Good	Fair	Poor
725	600	425	—	—	—

Model 1100 Competition

Introduced in 2005 this model is chambered for the 12 gauge shells with 2.75" chamber. Fitted with a 30" target style barrel with 10mm vent rib. Extended choke tubes. Receiver is nickel plated. Stock is semi-fancy American walnut with checkering and high gloss finish. Adjustable comb offered as option. Weight is about 8 lbs.

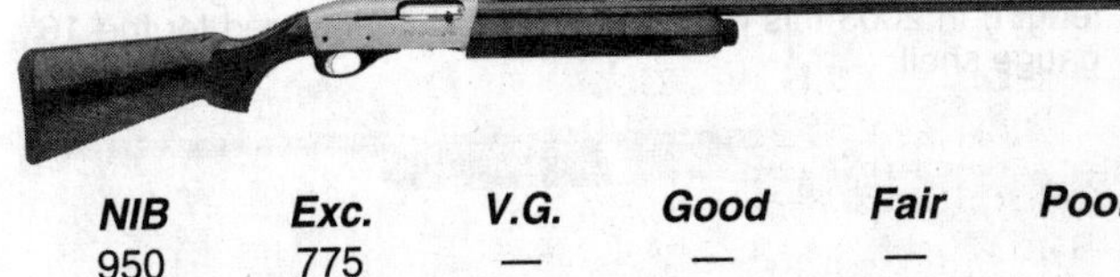

NIB	Exc.	V.G.	Good	Fair	Poor
950	775	—	—	—	—

NOTE: Add $175 for adjustable comb model.

Model 1100 LT-20

This 20 gauge model features a choice of 26" or 28" vent rib barrels with Rem choke tubes. It has a blue finish and walnut Monte Carlo stock. Recoil pad and cut checkering are standard. Weight is 6.75 to 7 lbs. depending on barrel length.

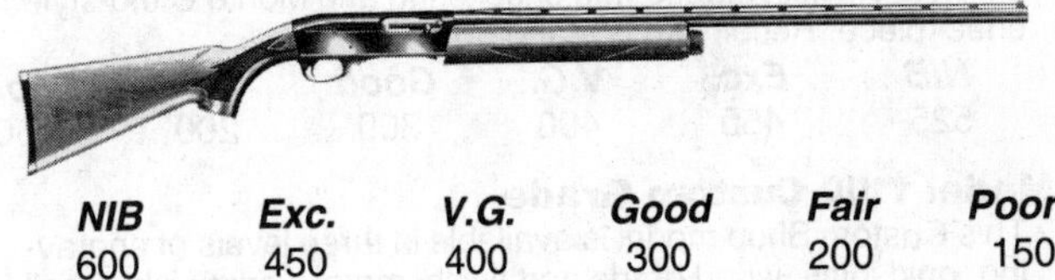

NIB	Exc.	V.G.	Good	Fair	Poor
600	450	400	300	200	150

Model 1100 LT-20 Deer Gun

Same as above but fitted with a 21" barrel with adjustable sights and an improved cylinder choke. Satin finish with American walnut stock. Weight is approximately 6.5 lbs.

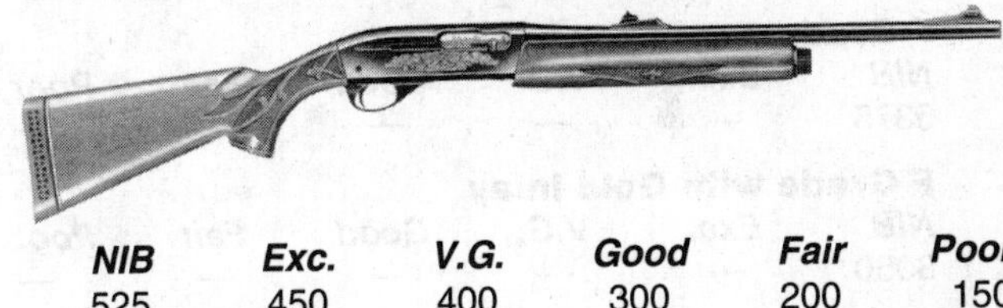

NIB	Exc.	V.G.	Good	Fair	Poor
525	450	400	300	200	150

Model 1100 LT-20 Synthetic

Same as above but fitted with a synthetic stock with recoil pad.

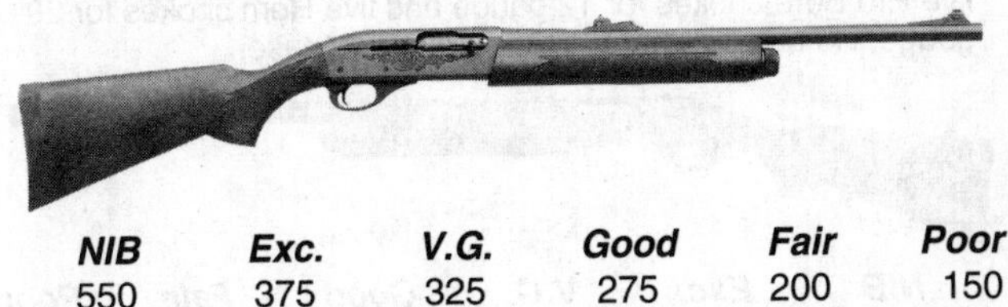

NIB	Exc.	V.G.	Good	Fair	Poor
550	375	325	275	200	150

Model 1100 LT-20 Magnum

This 20 gauge Model 1100 is chambered for the 3" 20 gauge shell. It is fitted with a 28" vent rib barrel with interchangeable chokes. Checkered walnut stock. Weight is about 7 lbs.

NIB	Exc.	V.G.	Good	Fair	Poor
575	395	400	300	200	150

Model 1100 LT-20 Synthetic Camo NWTF 25th Anniversary

This model is fitted with a 21" barrel with special fiber optic sighting system. NWTF logo on left side of receiver. Introduced in 1998.

NIB	Exc.	V.G.	Good	Fair	Poor
650	525	—	—	—	—

Model 1100 Synthetic

Introduced in 1995 this model is furnished with a black synthetic stock with black matte metal finish. Available in both 12 and 20 gauge. Weight is about 6.75 to 7 lbs. depending on barrel length. In 2003 this model was offered chambered for the 16 gauge shell.

Courtesy Remington Arms

NIB	Exc.	V.G.	Good	Fair	Poor
550	450	350	250	200	100

Model 1100 Synthetic Deer Gun

Same as above but fitted with a 21" fully rifled barrel with cantilever rail for scope mounting. Furnished with 2-3/4" chamber. Stock is black synthetic with checkering and Monte Carlo-style cheekpiece. Recoil pad is standard.

NIB	Exc.	V.G.	Good	Fair	Poor
525	450	400	300	200	150

Model 1100 Custom Grade

This Custom Shop model is available in three levels of engraving, gold inlay, wood grade and finish, metal work finish, recoil pad/buttplate, and dimensions. Each gun should be individually appraised prior to a sale.

D Grade

NIB	Exc.	V.G.	Good	Fair	Poor
2600	—	—	—	—	—

F Grade

NIB	Exc.	V.G.	Good	Fair	Poor
5375	—	—	—	—	—

F Grade with Gold Inlay

NIB	Exc.	V.G.	Good	Fair	Poor
8050	—	—	—	—	—

Model 1100 G3

Introduced in 2006, this updated 1100 features a Realwood high gloss semi-fancy stock and forend. Available in 12 and 20 gauges with 26" or 28" barrel and chambered for 3" shells. Includes five Pro Bore chokes for 12 gauge and five Rem chokes for 20 gauge, R3 recoil pad and high-grade travel case.

NIB	Exc.	V.G.	Good	Fair	Poor
825	600	450	300	—	—

Model 1100 Tactical Speedfeed IV

All-black 2.75" 12 gauge has an 18" barrel with fixed Improved Cylinder choke and Speedfeed IV stock. Extended 6-round magazine. Weight is 7.5 lbs.

NIB	Exc.	V.G.	Good	Fair	Poor
839	—	—	—	—	—

Model 1100 Tactical Standard Stock

Tactical 2.75" 12 gauge has 22" barrel threaded for Remchokes. Extended 8-round magazine.

NIB	Exc.	V.G.	Good	Fair	Poor
905	—	—	—	—	—

MODEL 11-87 SERIES

Model 11-87 Premier

A 3", 12 gauge semi-automatic shotgun with 26" to 32" ventilated rib barrels having screw-in choke tubes. Blued with a checkered walnut stock. Weight is approximately 7.75 lbs. Introduced in 1987. In 1999 this model was offered in a left-hand version.

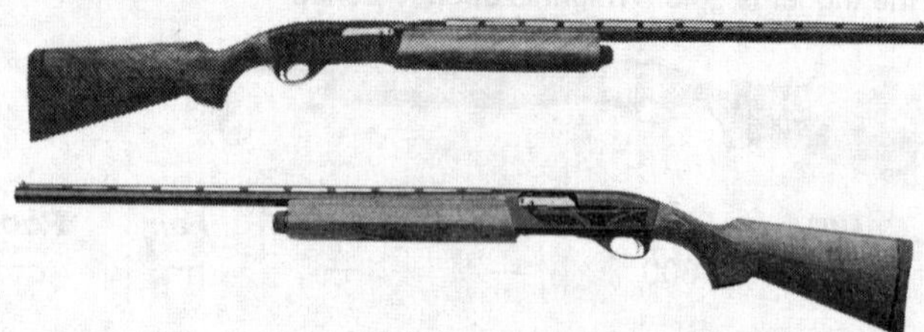

Model 11-87 Premier left-hand model

NIB	Exc.	V.G.	Good	Fair	Poor
700	600	450	300	200	150

Model 11-87 Premier 20 Gauge

Introduced in 1999 this model is built on a small frame receiver. It will chamber both 2.75" and 3" shells. Available in both 26" and 28" vent rib barrels with twin beads. Barrels are built for Rem. chokes. Stock is walnut with gloss finish. Weight is about 7 lbs.

NIB	Exc.	V.G.	Good	Fair	Poor
675	575	425	300	—	—

Model 11-87 Dale Earnhardt Tribute

Introduced in 2003 to honor Dale Earnhardt this 12 gauge gun is fitted with a 28" vent rib barrel and walnut stock with checkering. Engraved on the receiver is a likeness of Earnhardt, his signature, and scroll work. Inlayed in gold. Serial numbers start with "DE3." Weight is about 7.75 lbs.

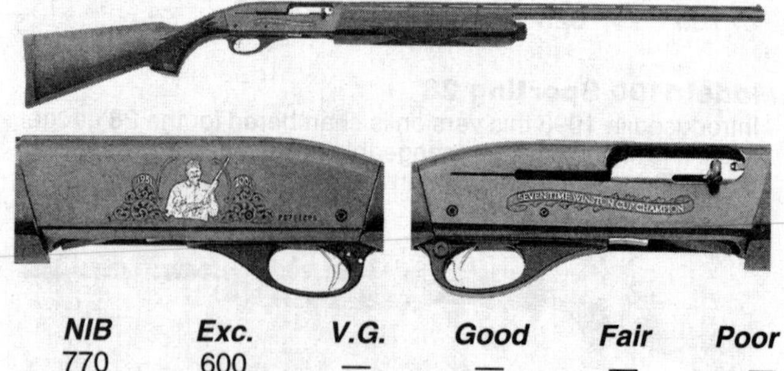

NIB	Exc.	V.G.	Good	Fair	Poor
770	600	—	—	—	—

Model 11-87 Upland Special

This model is offered in 12 or 20 gauge with 23" barrel with twin bead sights. Chambered for 3" shells. Stock is walnut with straight grip. Choke tubes standard. Weight is about 7.25 for 12 gauge and 6.5 lbs. for 20 gauge. Introduced in 2000.

NIB	Exc.	V.G.	Good	Fair	Poor
725	600	450	300	—	—

Model 11-87 Premier Cantilever Scope Mount Deer Gun

This semi-automatic model has a Monte Carlo stock and the option of a barrel-mounted scope (not included). Optional with a fully rifled barrel 21" long with a 1-in-35" twist. Also available in a 21" nonrifled barrel with Rifled and IC Rem. choke tubes. Available in 12 gauge only. Sling swivel studs and camo are standard.

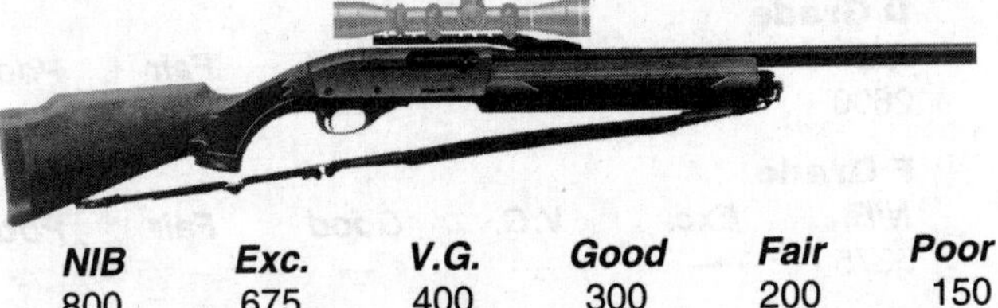

NIB	Exc.	V.G.	Good	Fair	Poor
800	675	400	300	200	150

Model 11-87 Premier Trap

Available in either right- or left-hand models. Is available with either a straight or Monte Carlo comb, 2.75" chamber, 30" vent rib overbored barrel and special Rem. Trap choke tubes. This model is set up to handle 12 gauge target loads only.

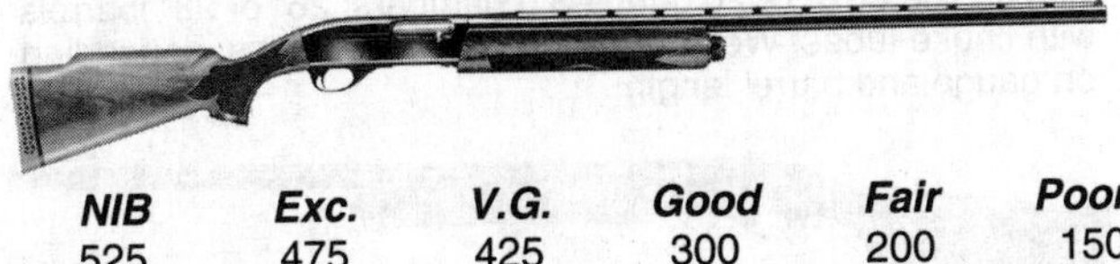

NIB	Exc.	V.G.	Good	Fair	Poor
525	475	425	300	200	150

Model 11-87 Premier SC (Sporting Clays)

This model features a special target stock with a 3.16" length of pull longer than standard and 1/4" higher at the heel. The butt pad is radiused at the heel and rounded at the toe. The receiver top, barrel, and rib have a fine matte finish on the blueing. The vent rib is a medium wide 8mm with stainless steel mid bead and a Bradley-style front bead sight. Gun is supplied new with these Rem. choke tubes: Skeet, Improved Skeet, Improved Cylinder, Modified, and Full. Supplied from the factory with a two-barrel custom fitted hard case.

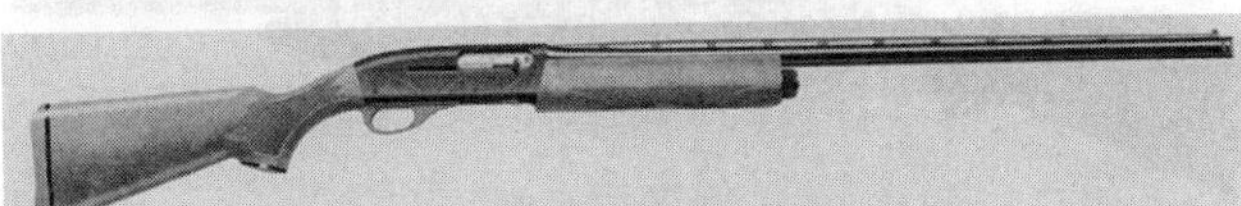

Model 11-87 Sporting Clays with new engraving

Courtesy Remington Arms

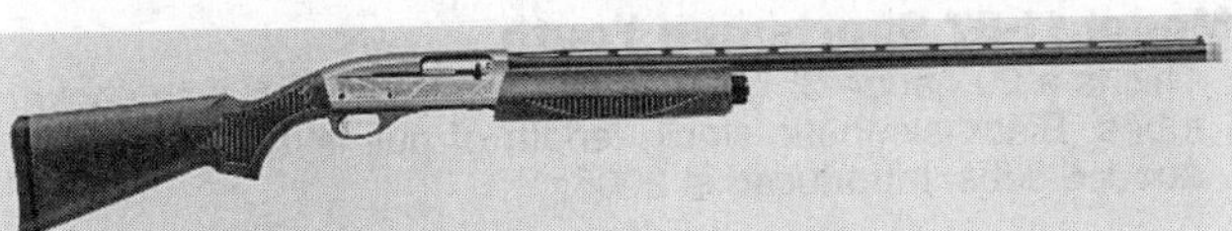

Remington Model 11-87 Sporting Clays with nickel-plated receiver and ported barrel

NIB	Exc.	V.G.	Good	Fair	Poor
750	600	450	350	200	150

Model 11-87 SC NP (Sporting Clays Nickel-Plated)

Same as above but with nickel-plated receiver.

NIB	Exc.	V.G.	Good	Fair	Poor
800	650	500	400	300	200

Model 11-87 SPS-BG Camo

This 12 gauge model is fitted with a rifle sighted 21" barrel with a brown camo finish on the stock and metal parts. Introduced in 1993.

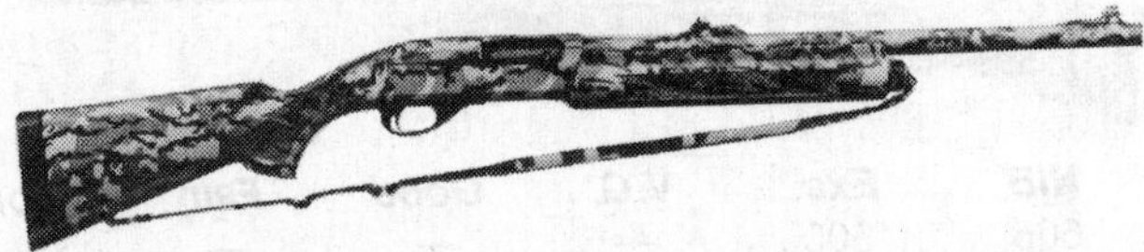

NIB	Exc.	V.G.	Good	Fair	Poor
525	475	425	300	200	150

Model 11-87 SPS-T Camo

Same as above but supplied with a 21" vent rib barrel with IC and Turkey Super Full Rem. choke tubes. Camo finish is green. Introduced in 1993.

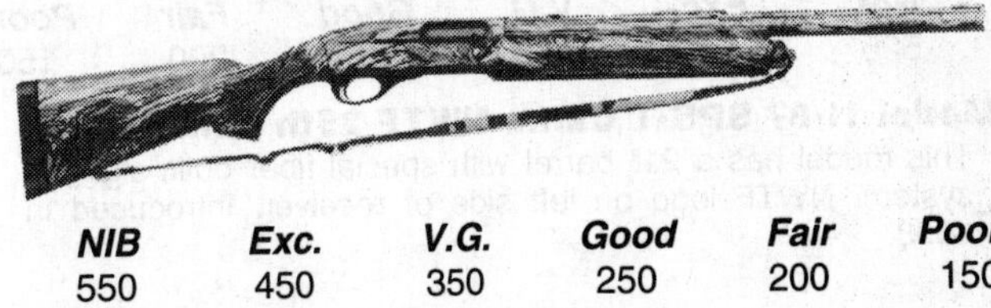

NIB	Exc.	V.G.	Good	Fair	Poor
550	450	350	250	200	150

Model 11-87 SPS

This 12 gauge model is furnished with a 26" or 28" vent rib barrel with IC, Mod., and Full Rem. choke tubes. The stock is a black synthetic material and the metal is finished in a black matte. In 1997 a camo version of this model was introduced.

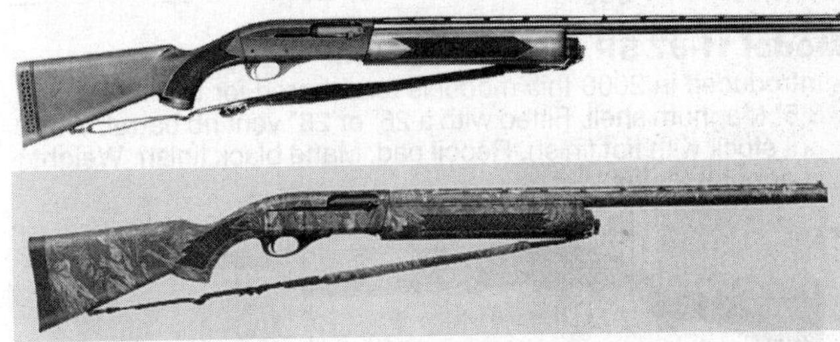

Remington Model 11-87 SPS Camo

NIB	Exc.	V.G.	Good	Fair	Poor
450	400	300	250	200	150

Model 11-87 SPS-Deer

The same as above but fitted with a 21" rifled, sighted barrel. First introduced in 1993.

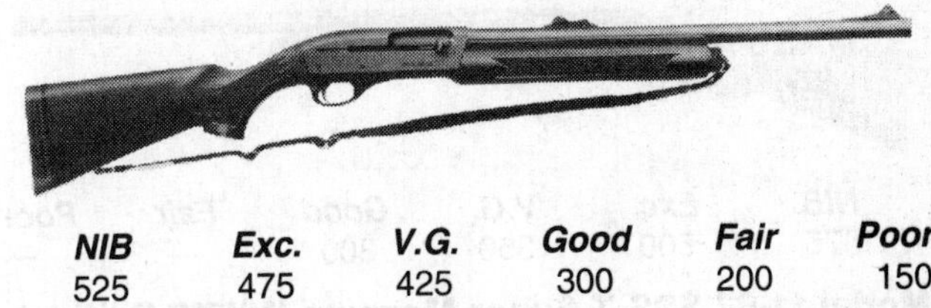

NIB	Exc.	V.G.	Good	Fair	Poor
525	475	425	300	200	150

Model 11-87 Waterfowl

This 12 gauge gun is fitted with a 28" vent rib barrel with choke tubes and Hi-Viz sights. Camo pattern is Mossy Oak Shadowgrass. Weight is about 8.25 lbs. Introduced in 2004.

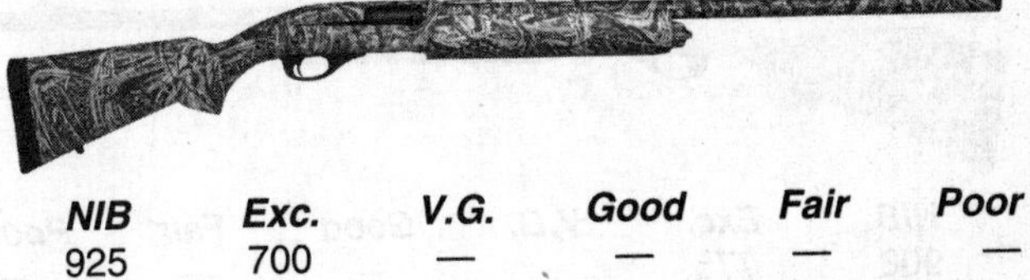

NIB	Exc.	V.G.	Good	Fair	Poor
925	700	—	—	—	—

Model 11-87 SPS-T

Same as above but fitted with a 21" vent rib barrel with IC and Turkey Super Full Rem. choke tubes. In 1997 a camo version of this model was introduced.

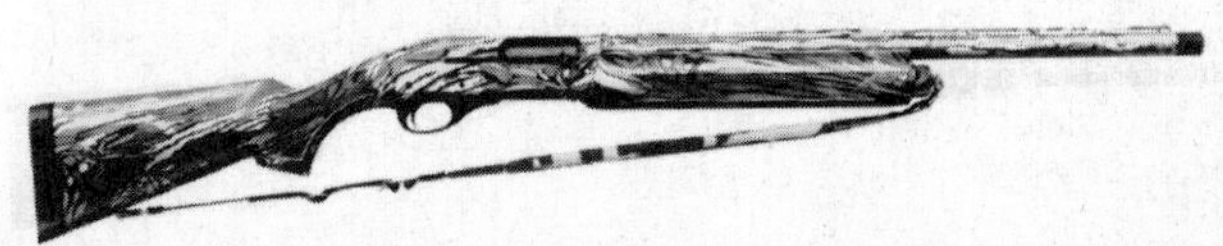

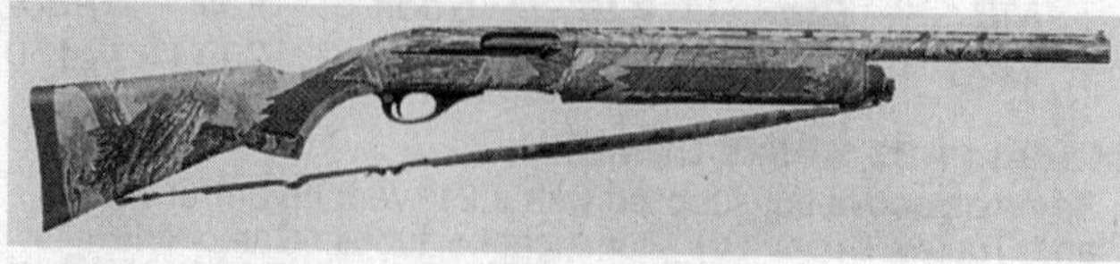

Remington Model 11-87 SPS-T Camo

NIB	Exc.	V.G.	Good	Fair	Poor
525	475	425	300	200	150

Model 11-87 SPS-T Camo NWTF 25th Anniversary

This model has a 21" barrel with special fiber optic sighting system. NWTF logo on left side of receiver. Introduced in 1998.

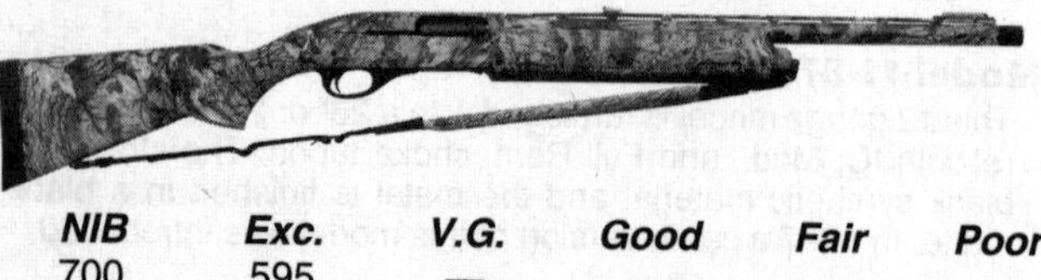

NIB	Exc.	V.G.	Good	Fair	Poor
700	595	—	—	—	—

Model 11-87 SP Super Magnum

Introduced in 2000 this model is chambered for the 12 gauge 3.5" Magnum shell. Fitted with a 26" or 28" vent rib barrel. Walnut stock with flat finish. Recoil pad. Matte black finish. Weight is about 8.25 lbs.

NIB	Exc.	V.G.	Good	Fair	Poor
675	500	350	300	—	—

Model 11-87 SPS Super Magnum

Same as above but with a black synthetic stock. Introduced in 2000. Weight is about 8.25 lbs.

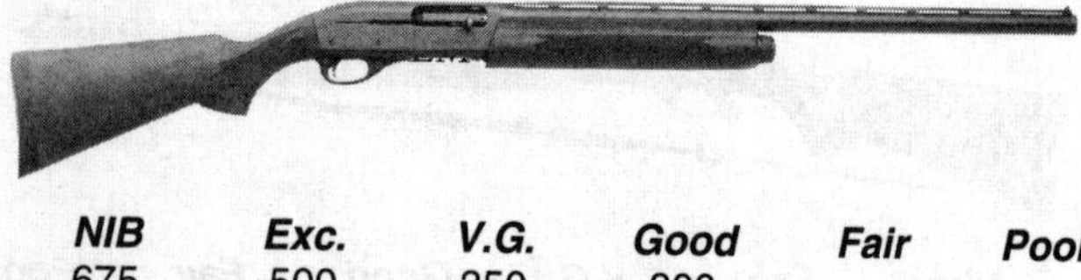

NIB	Exc.	V.G.	Good	Fair	Poor
675	500	350	300	—	—

Model 11-87 SPS-T Super Magnum (NWTF Edition)

Introduced in 2005 this model features a 12 gauge 3.5" chamber with 23" barrel with choke tubes and iron sights. Mossy Oak Obsession camo stock with Monte Carlo comb. Weight is about 8 lbs.

NIB	Exc.	V.G.	Good	Fair	Poor
900	775	—	—	—	—

Model 11-87 Police

Offered chambered for 12 gauge shells, this model features a synthetic stock, 18" barrel with bead, rifle, or Ghost Ring sights, and 7-shot magazine extension.

NIB	Exc.	V.G.	Good	Fair	Poor
650	575	—	—	—	—

NOTE: Add $20 for rifle sights and $60 for Ghost Ring sights.

Model 11-87 Custom Grade

This Custom Shop model is available in three levels of engraving, gold inlay, wood grade and finish, metal work finish, recoil pad/buttplate, and dimensions.

D Grade

NIB	Exc.	V.G.	Good	Fair	Poor
2600	—	—	—	—	—

F Grade

NIB	Exc.	V.G.	Good	Fair	Poor
5375	—	—	—	—	—

F Grade with Gold Inlay

NIB	Exc.	V.G.	Good	Fair	Poor
8050	—	—	—	—	—

Model 11-87 Sportsman Synthetic

Introduced in 2005, this model features a black synthetic stock with choice of 12 or 20 gauge 3" chambers; 26" or 28" ibarrels with choke tubes. Weight is about 7.75 to 8.25 lbs. depending on gauge and barrel length.

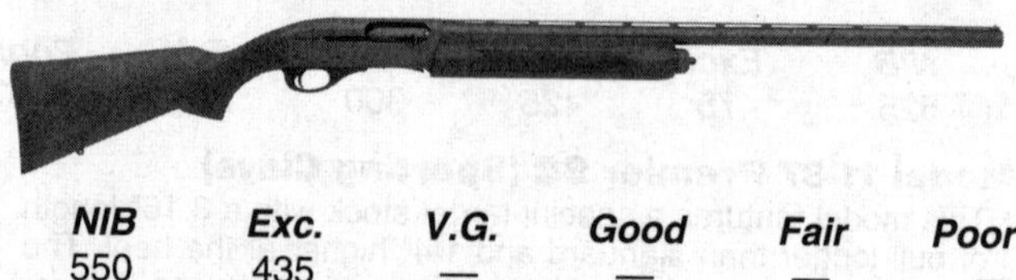

NIB	Exc.	V.G.	Good	Fair	Poor
550	435	—	—	—	—

Model 11-87 Sportsman Rifled

This is a 12 gauge 3" gun with 21" rifled barrel with cantilever scope mount. Black synthetic stock with black metal finish. Weight is about 8.5 lbs. Introduced in 2005.

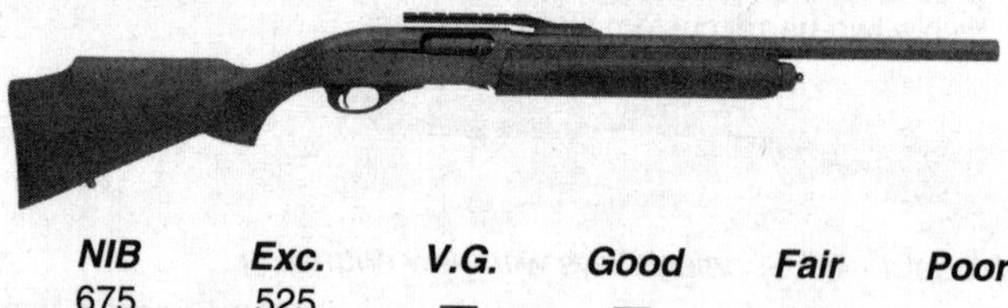

NIB	Exc.	V.G.	Good	Fair	Poor
675	525	—	—	—	—

Model 11-87 Sportsman Youth

This is a 20 gauge 3" gun with 21" vent rib barrel with choke tubes. Black synthetic stock, length of pull is 13". Weight is about 6.5 lbs. Introduced in 2005.

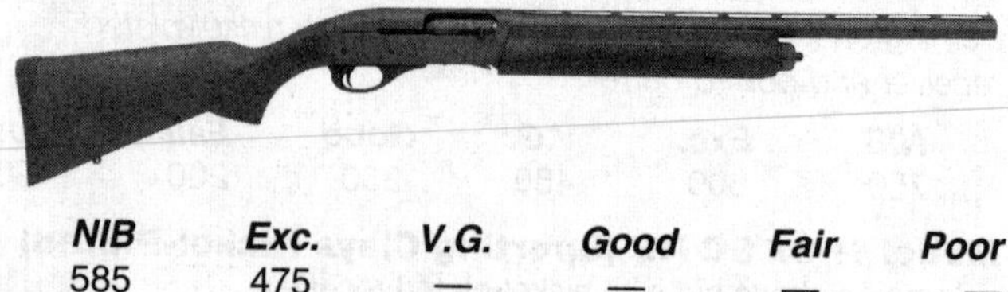

NIB	Exc.	V.G.	Good	Fair	Poor
585	475	—	—	—	—

Model 11-87 Sportsman NRA Edition

This 12 gauge, 3" model is fitted with a 28" vent rib barrel with choke tubes. Synthetic stock with Mossy Oak New Break-Up camo. NRA logo on the left side of the matte black receiver. Introduced in 2005.

NIB	Exc.	V.G.	Good	Fair	Poor
665	500	—	—	—	—

Model 11-87 SP Thumbhole

Laminated, thumbhole-stock 12 gauge slug gun with 3" chamber and 21" fully rifled cantilever barrel.

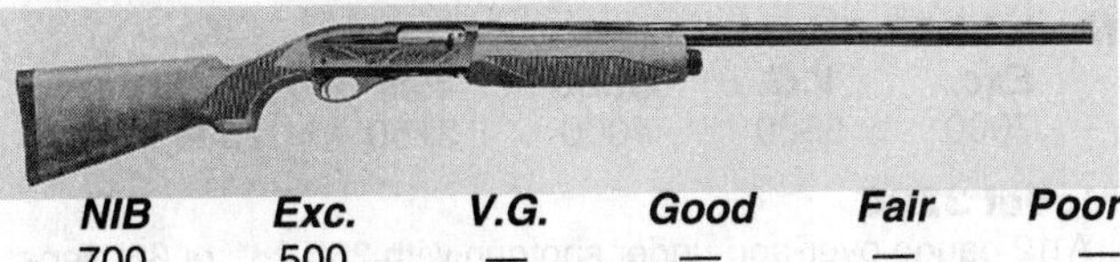

NIB	Exc.	V.G.	Good	Fair	Poor
700	500	—	—	—	—

Model 11-87 SPS-T Super Magnum

Similar to Model 11-87 SP Thumbhole but with pistol-grip stock and vent rib barrel.

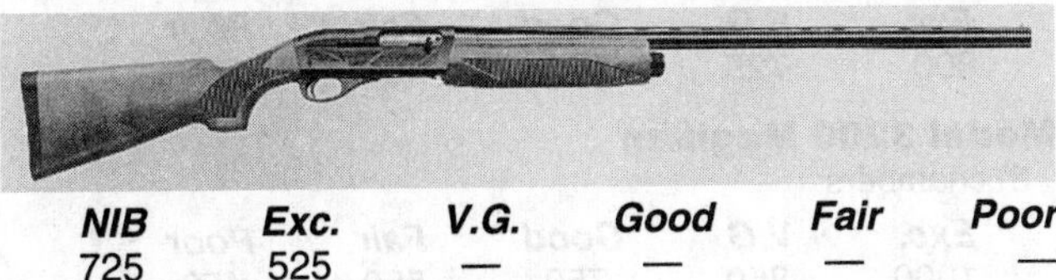

NIB	Exc.	V.G.	Good	Fair	Poor
725	525	—	—	—	—

Model 11-87 SP-T Thumbhole

This 12 gauge with 3.5" chamber is made specifically for turkey hunting. Camouflaged in Mossy Oak Obsession with an R3 recoil pad and thumbhole stock. The 23" barrel has fiber-optic adjustable rifle sights and is drilled and tapped for scope mounting. Includes a turkey super full choke tube and sling/swivels. Introduced 2006. M

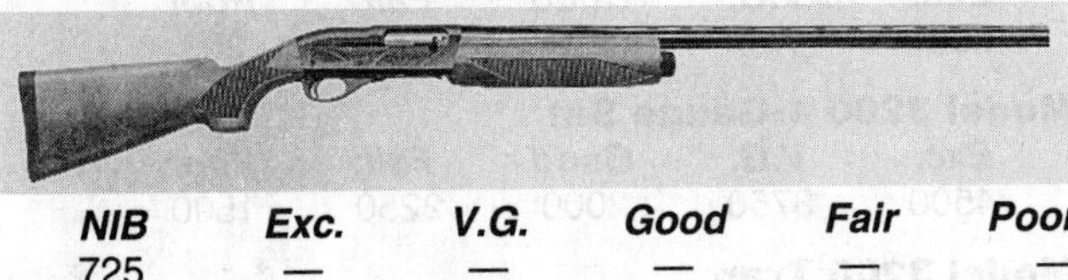

NIB	Exc.	V.G.	Good	Fair	Poor
725	—	—	—	—	—

Model 11-87 Sportsman Camo

New in 2007, the camo version of the Sportsman comes in 12 and 20 gauge with 26" or 28" barrel. Finished in Mossy Oak Break-Up camo.

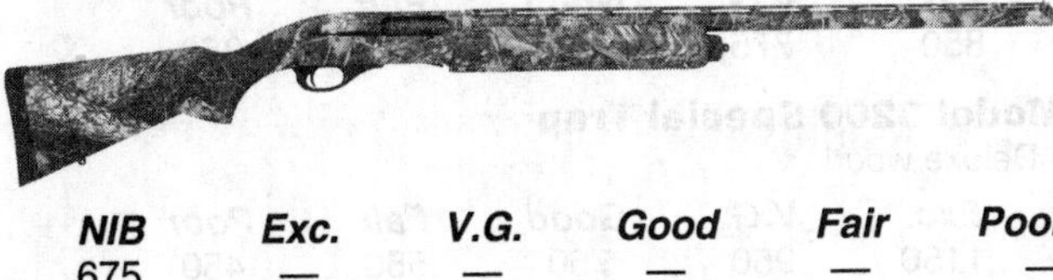

NIB	Exc.	V.G.	Good	Fair	Poor
675	—	—	—	—	—

Model 11-87 Sportsman Camo Rifled

Camo 12 gauge slug gun with 21" barrel and cantilever scope mount.

NIB	Exc.	V.G.	Good	Fair	Poor
695	—	—	—	—	—

Model 11-87 Sportsman Camo Youth

Youth model in 20 gauge with shorter length of pull was introduced in 2007. Weight is about 6.5 lbs.

NIB	Exc.	V.G.	Good	Fair	Poor
625	—	—	—	—	—

Model 11-87 SPS Super Magnum Waterfowl

This 3.5" 12 gauge is finished in Mossy Oak Duck Blind camo. It has a 30" barrel and includes three chokes. Weight is 8.25 lbs.

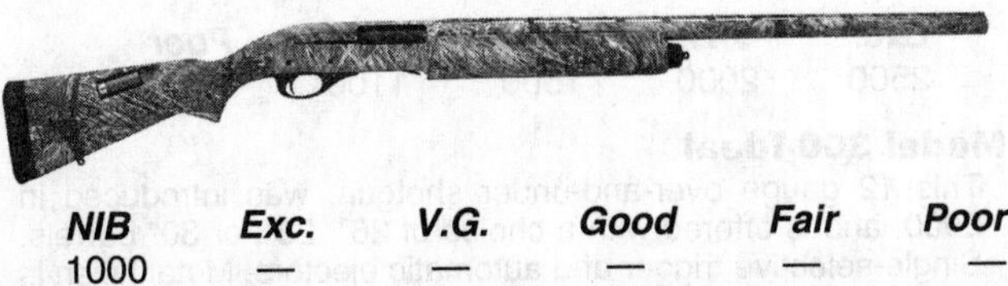

NIB	Exc.	V.G.	Good	Fair	Poor
1000	—	—	—	—	—

Model 11-96 Euro Lightweight

Introduced in 1996 this model is based on the Model 11-87 action. Two vent rib barrel lengths are offered: 26" and 28" supplied with three Rem chokes. Fine line engraving on the receiver and checkered Claro walnut stocks are standard. Blued finish. Weight is approximately 7 lbs.

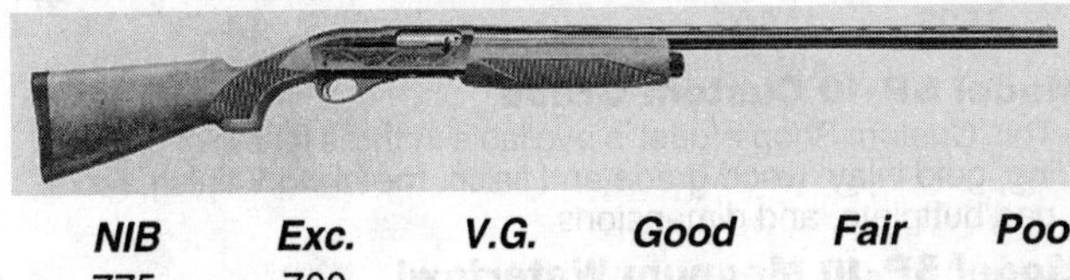

NIB	Exc.	V.G.	Good	Fair	Poor
775	700	—	—	—	—

Model SP-10

A 3.5", 10 gauge semi-automatic shotgun with 26" or 30" ventilated rib barrels having screw-in choke tubes. Matte blued with a checkered walnut stock.

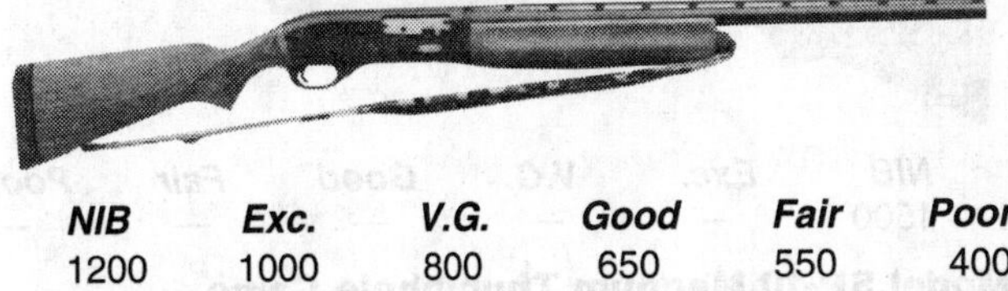

NIB	Exc.	V.G.	Good	Fair	Poor
1200	1000	800	650	550	400

Model SP-10 Magnum Camo

A new model introduced in 1993, this 10 gauge semi-automatic is designed for the turkey or deer hunter. Available with either 26" or 30" vent rib barrel or a 22" deer barrel. An additional barrel option is a 23" vent rib barrel with a camo finish. All barrels are fitted with Remington choke tubes.

NIB	Exc.	V.G.	Good	Fair	Poor
1350	800	700	500	350	200

Model SP-10 Magnum Camo NWTF 25th Anniversary

This model has a special fiber optic sighting system. The "NWTF" logo is on the left side of the receiver. Barrel length is 23". Introduced in 1998.

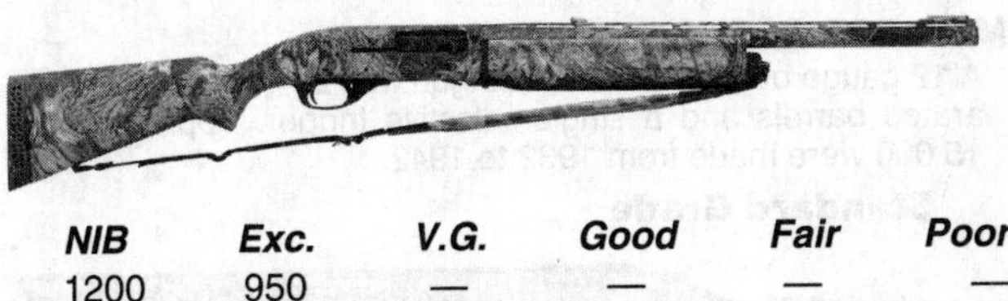

NIB	Exc.	V.G.	Good	Fair	Poor
1200	950	—	—	—	—

Model SP-10 Synthetic

This model features a black synthetic stock with 26" barrel chambered for 10 gauge shells. Matte black metal finish. Choke tubes standard. Introduced in 2000. Weight is about 10 lbs.

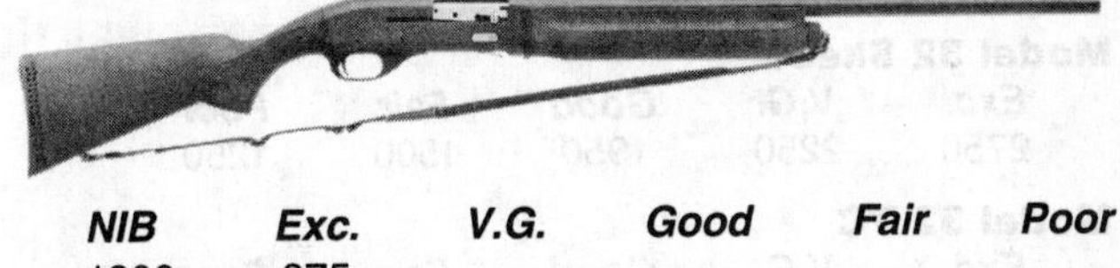

NIB	Exc.	V.G.	Good	Fair	Poor
1300	875	—	—	—	—

Model SP-10 RC/VT

This 10 gauge gun was introduced in 2005 and is fitted with a 26" vent rib barrel with choke tubes. Mossy Oak Obsession finish. Weight is about 10.75 lbs.

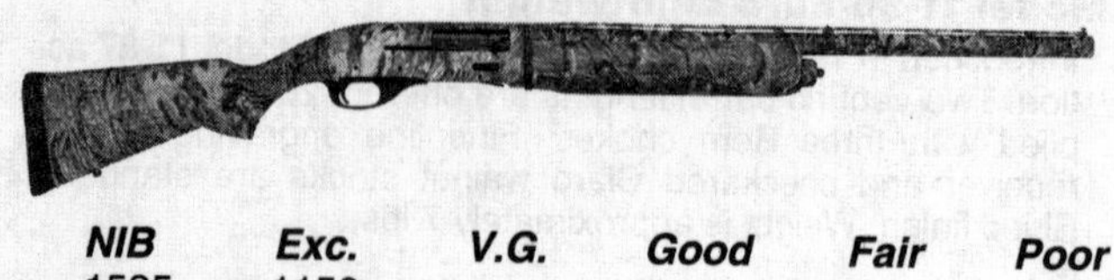

NIB	Exc.	V.G.	Good	Fair	Poor
1525	1150	—	—	—	—

Model SP-10 Custom Grade

This Custom Shop model is available in three levels of engraving, gold inlay, wood grade and finish, metal work finish, recoil pad/buttplate, and dimensions.

Model SP-10 Magnum Waterfowl

New in 2007, this waterfowl-specific model is a synthetic-stock 3.5" 10 gauge with Mossy Oak Duck Blind camo finish and 26" barrel. Includes three Briley ported choke tubes. Weight is about 10.9 lbs.

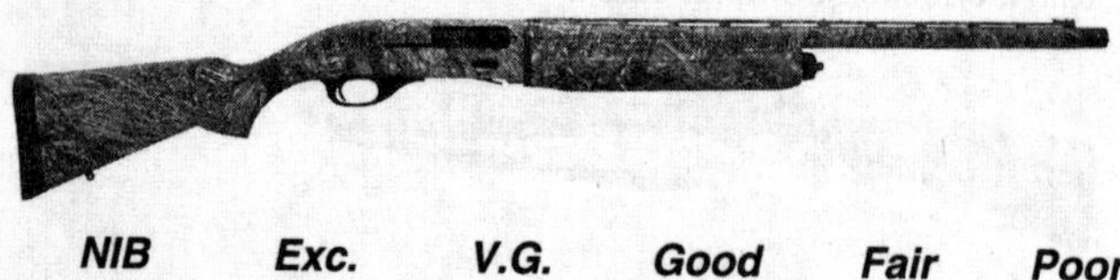

NIB	Exc.	V.G.	Good	Fair	Poor
1500	—	—	—	—	—

Model SP-10 Magnum Thumbhole Camo

Special turkey model features a synthetic thumbhole stock and complete Mossy Oak Obsession camo finish. Barrel is 23". Briley ported turkey choke included. Weight is 10.9 lbs.

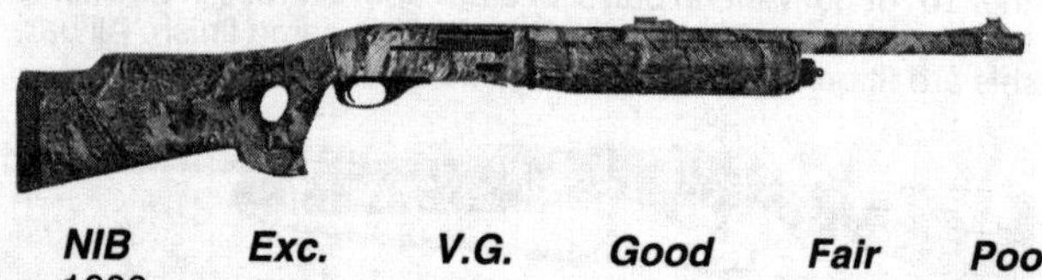

NIB	Exc.	V.G.	Good	Fair	Poor
1600	—	—	—	—	—

Model 105CTi

New in 2006, this ultralight gas-operated 12 gauge autoloader features advanced recoil reduction and bottom feed and ejection. Available with 26" or 28" barrel. Satin finish walnut stock. Chambered for 3" shells. Includes three Pro Bore chokes. Weighs about 7 lbs.

NIB	Exc.	V.G.	Good	Fair	Poor
980	—	—	—	—	—

Model 32

A 12 gauge over-and-under shotgun with 26", 28", or 30" separated barrels and a single-selective trigger. Approximately 15,000 were made from 1932 to 1942.

Standard Grade

Exc.	V.G.	Good	Fair	Poor
2200	1900	1600	1250	1000

NOTE: Solid or vent rib add 10 percent.

Model 32 Skeet

Exc.	V.G.	Good	Fair	Poor
2750	2250	1950	1500	1250

Model 32 TC

Exc.	V.G.	Good	Fair	Poor
2750	2500	2250	1750	1450

Model 32D

Exc.	V.G.	Good	Fair	Poor
3500	3000	2500	2000	1650

Model 32E Expert

Exc.	V.G.	Good	Fair	Poor
4500	3500	3000	2500	2000

Model 32F Premier

Exc.	V.G.	Good	Fair	Poor
7000	5500	4000	3250	2500

Model 3200

A 12 gauge over-and-under shotgun with 26", 28", or 30" separated ventilated rib barrels, single-selective trigger, and automatic ejector. Blued with a checkered walnut stock. Manufactured from 1972 to 1984.

Field Grade

Exc.	V.G.	Good	Fair	Poor
800	725	600	450	300

Model 3200 Magnum

3" chambers.

Exc.	V.G.	Good	Fair	Poor
1000	850	750	550	450

Model 3200 Skeet

Exc.	V.G.	Good	Fair	Poor
800	725	600	450	300

Model 3200 4-Gauge Set

Exc.	V.G.	Good	Fair	Poor
4500	3750	3000	2250	1500

Model 3200 Trap

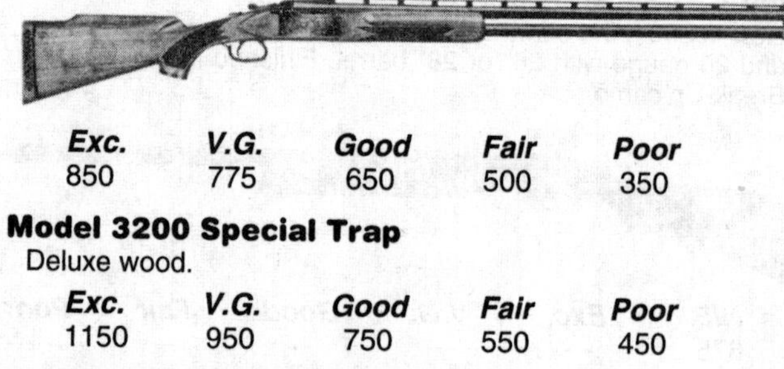

Exc.	V.G.	Good	Fair	Poor
850	775	650	500	350

Model 3200 Special Trap

Deluxe wood.

Exc.	V.G.	Good	Fair	Poor
1150	950	750	550	450

Model 3200 Competition Trap

Engraved.

Exc.	V.G.	Good	Fair	Poor
1750	1200	850	650	550

Model 3200 Premier

Heavily engraved.

Exc.	V.G.	Good	Fair	Poor
2250	2000	1750	1500	1000

Model 3200 "One of One Thousand"

1,000 produced.

Exc.	V.G.	Good	Fair	Poor
2500	2000	1500	1100	500

Model 300 Ideal

This 12 gauge over-and-under shotgun, was introduced in 2000, and is offered with a choice of 26", 28", or 30" barrels. Single-selective trigger and automatic ejectors. Metal finish is blue. Stock is walnut with semi-gloss finish. Solid black recoil pad. Weight is about 7.62 lbs. for 28" barrels. Dropped from production in 2001.

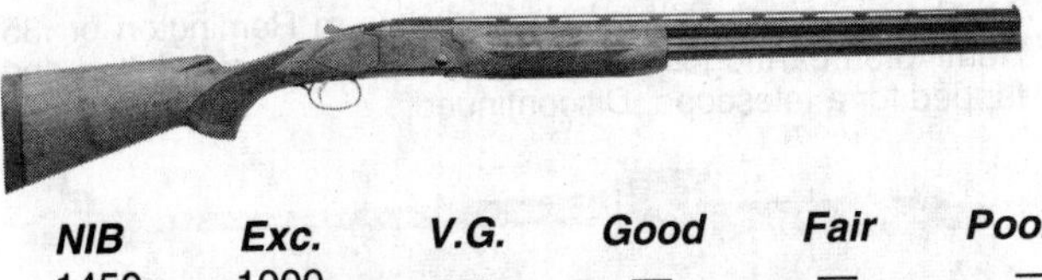

NIB	Exc.	V.G.	Good	Fair	Poor
1450	1000	—	—	—	—

Model 90-T Single-Barrel Trap

Offered in 12 gauge only, this single-barrel Trap shotgun is fitted with either a 32" or 34" overbored Full choke barrel.

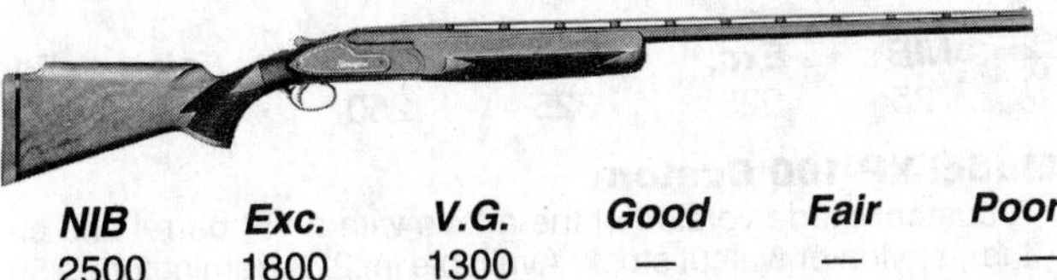

NIB	Exc.	V.G.	Good	Fair	Poor
2500	1800	1300	—	—	—

Model 90-T Single-Barrel Trap (High Rib)

The same shotgun as described above with the exception of an adjustable high rib for shooters who prefer a more open target picture and higher head position.

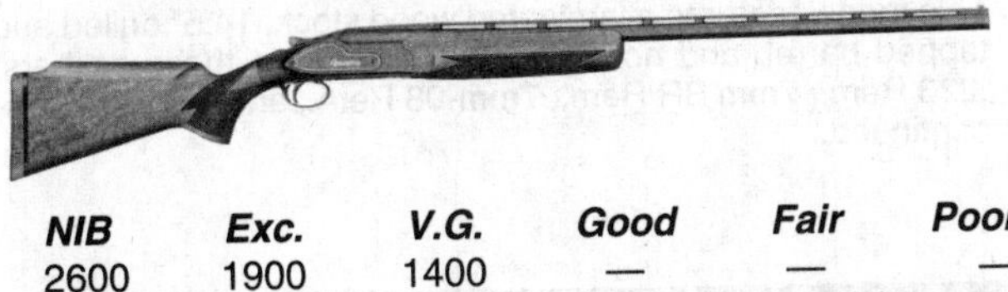

NIB	Exc.	V.G.	Good	Fair	Poor
2600	1900	1400	—	—	—

Model 332

A reintroduction, in 2002, of the famous Remington Model 32 this model features a mechanical set trigger, automatic ejectors with a choice of vent rib barrel lengths in 26", 28", and 30". Checkered walnut stock. Black oxide metal finish. Chambered for the 12 gauge with 3" chambers. Weight is about 7.75 lbs. depending on barrel length.

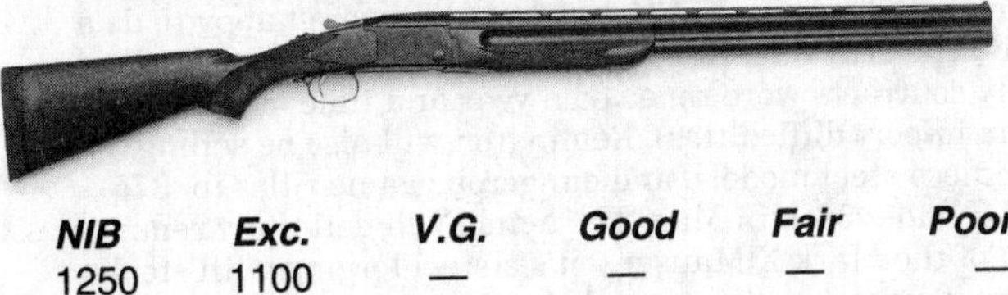

NIB	Exc.	V.G.	Good	Fair	Poor
1250	1100	—	—	—	—

Remington Peerless

Introduced in 1993, this new Remington over-and-under shotgun is offered in 12 gauge only. Available in 26", 28", and 30" vent rib barrel lengths and fitted with Remington choke tubes (IC, M, F). The sideplates are removable and the stock is American walnut. Production stopped in 1998.

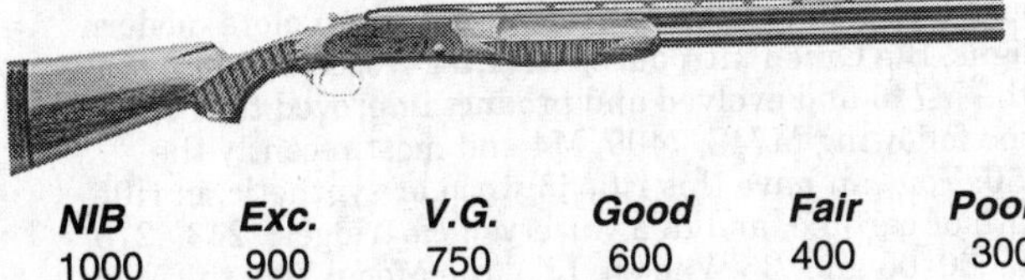

NIB	Exc.	V.G.	Good	Fair	Poor
1000	900	750	600	400	300

Model 396 Sporting

Introduced in 1996 this over-and-under shotgun is designed for sporting clays shooting. It is offered in 12 gauge only with 30" barrels. Chokes are interchangeable Rem. choke system. Fancy American stock with satin finish. Scroll engraving on the receiver and blue finish. Weight is about 8 lbs.

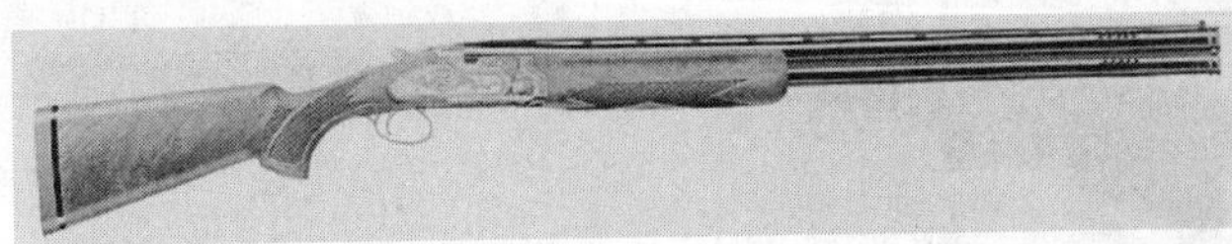

Courtesy Remington Arms

NIB	Exc.	V.G.	Good	Fair	Poor
2150	1700	1150	—	—	—

Model 396 Skeet

Same but with a choice of 28" or 30" barrels.

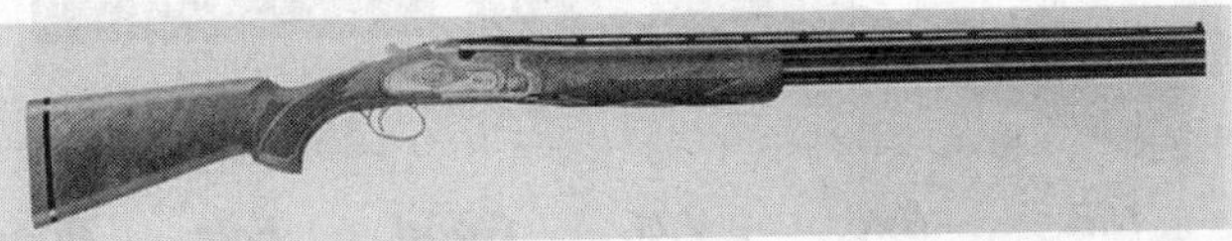

Courtesy Remington Arms

NIB	Exc.	V.G.	Good	Fair	Poor
1975	1500	950	—	—	—

Model 396 Custom Grade

This Custom Shop model is available in three levels of engraving, gold inlay, wood grade and finish, metal work finish, recoil pad/buttplate, and dimensions. Each gun should be individually appraised prior to a sale.

PREMIER SERIES O/U

Introduced in 2006, the Italian-made over-and-unders in the Premier Series feature premium figured walnut stocks, Schnabel forends, ProBore chokes, 3" chambers (2.75" in 28 gauge) and include a hardside case.

Premier STS Competition

This 12 gauge with 28", 30" or 32" overbored barrels has an engraved, nickel-plated receiver and high-gloss finished stock. Weight is about 7.8 lbs. Add 15 percent for adjustable-stock model.

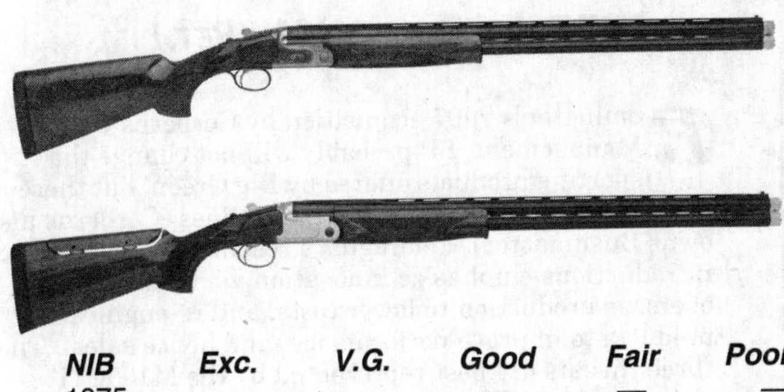

NIB	Exc.	V.G.	Good	Fair	Poor
1975	—	—	—	—	—

Premier Field Grade

Available in 12, 20 and 28 gauges with satin finish and nickel receiver. Available with 26" or 28" barrels. Includes three flush chokes. Weight is about 6.5 lbs. for 20 and 28 gauges and 7.5 lbs. for 12 gauge.

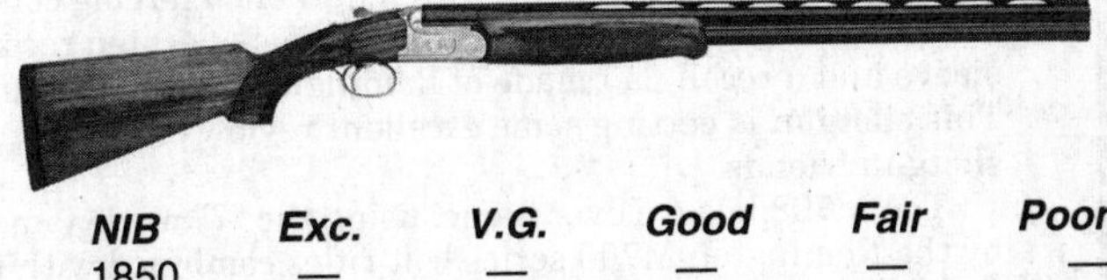

NIB	Exc.	V.G.	Good	Fair	Poor
1850	—	—	—	—	—

Premier Upland Grade

As above but with oil finish stock and case colored receiver with gold game bird scene.

NIB	Exc.	V.G.	Good	Fair	Poor
1150	—	—	—	—	—

Premier RGS

This special Conservation Gun of the Year in 2007 for the Ruffed Grouse Society is a 20 gauge with 26" barrels, satin oil finished stock and satin black oxide receiver. Includes five choke tubes. Weight is 6.5 lbs.

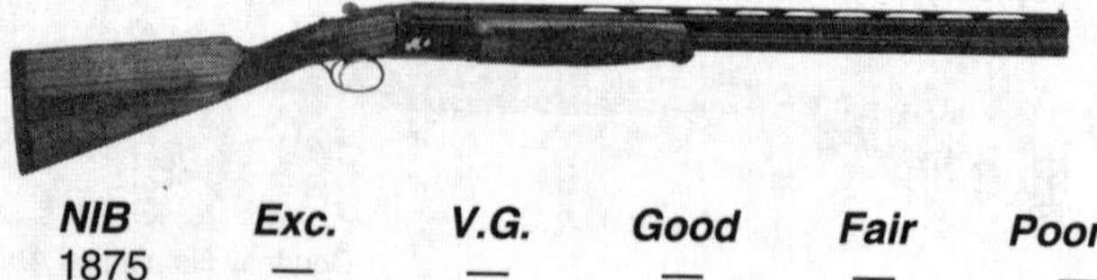

NIB	Exc.	V.G.	Good	Fair	Poor
1875	—	—	—	—	—

Model XP-100

A .221 Remington Fireball or .223 Remington caliber bolt-action single-shot pistol with a 14.5" ventilated rib barrel and adjustable sights. Blued with a nylon stock. Introduced in 1963. Discontinued.

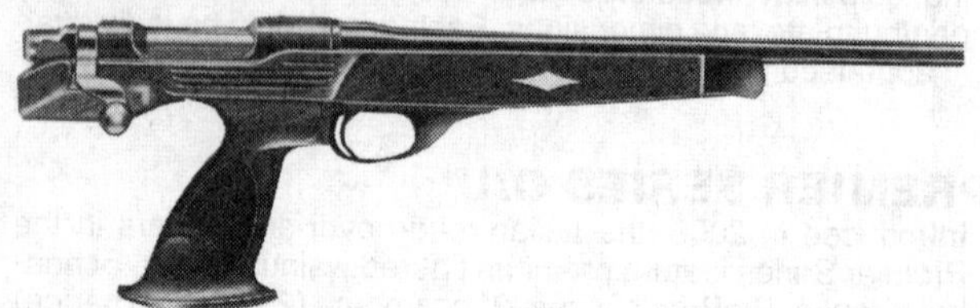

NIB	Exc.	V.G.	Good	Fair	Poor
800	600	375	300	225	175

Model XP-100 Silhouette

As above, chambered for either the 7mm Remington or .35 Remington cartridges and fitted with a 15" barrel drilled and tapped for a telescope. Discontinued.

NIB	Exc.	V.G.	Good	Fair	Poor
725	525	325	250	200	125

Model XP-100 Custom

A custom-made version of the above with a 15" barrel and either a nylon or walnut stock. Available in .223 Remington, .250 Savage, 6mm Benchrest, 7mm Benchrest, 7mm-08, or .35 Remington calibers. Introduced in 1986. Discontinued.

NIB	Exc.	V.G.	Good	Fair	Poor
950	800	650	550	425	300

Model XP-100 Hunter

This model features a laminated wood stock, 14.5" drilled and tapped barrel, and no sights. It is offered in these calibers: .223 Rem., 7mm BR Rem., 7mm-08 Rem., and .35 Rem. Discontinued.

IT'S NOT BUSINESS AS USUAL AT REMINGTON

LCDR JIM DODD, USN (RET.)

Remington's 2007 acquisition by Cerberus Capital Management, LP probably will not change the sporting products offered by Big Green, but there may be changes in their law enforcement lines (Cerberus also owns Bushmaster). Remington's recent firearms product introductions emphasize innovation via technology, overseas production to lower costs, and re-engineering products to improve performance (and hence sales). Those three thrusts are best represented by the M105CTi shotgun, the M798 bolt-action rifle and the M750 Woodsmaster semi-automatic rifle.

Remington continues its titanium technology insertion in the M105CTi shotgun, this time combining a titanium receiver with a carbon fiber shell. This gas gun also features several recoil reducing features so you won't be beaten to death by a 7-lb. 12-gauge gun. The recoil reduction features include an over-bored barrel with lengthened forcing cone, a rate-reduction gas operation system, a gas-operated recoil sleeve and a recoil pad made of Remington's R3 material. This shotgun is getting some excellent reviews from my shotgun friends.

The M798 has a clever name, using the "7" made famous by the Remington M700 series bolt rifles combined with the "98" of Mauser rifle fame. These actions and barrels are commercial Mauser designs built by Zastava Arms in Serbia, and stocked by Remington here, reportedly with Rutland-supplied laminated stocks. Of note is the fact that these rifles are the first controlled-round feed actions in the Remington line since the pre-WWII M720. Zastava used to provide these rifles to Charles Daly but were happy to do a five-year deal with Remington inasmuch as their Charles Daly contracts were renewed a year at a time (and suffered from import difficulties). Remington will also be selling stainless steel models, and dangerous game rifles in .375 H&H and .458 Win Mag. The action will definitely remind you of the Mark X Mauser – it's a steel forging with steel bottom metal and the typical Mauser commercial trigger and safety. It gave me thoughts of the custom rifles that could built from that basic action. Zastava also made left-hand versions, and Remington is lefty-friendly so I expect to see LH in the specs before long.

Remington began its semi-auto rifle product line with the Browning-/Loomis-designed Model 8 in 1906, and the Loomis-designed Model 81 in 1936. These rifles used proprietary Remington cartridges. Moving to more modern designs, Big Green introduced the first Woodsmaster in 1955 as the M740 and evolved and product improved that design in the following M742, 7400, M4 and most recently the M750. You can have this rifle in wood or synthetic, in rifle length or carbine, and in a variety of cartridges: .243, .270, .308, .30-'06 and .35 Whelen. Like the Model 740, the Model 750 is a traditionally-styled gas-operated guns.

Remington sees itself as a sporting goods company, not just the gunmaker we have known for so long. Take a look at those other product lines in their catalog or at www.remington.com.

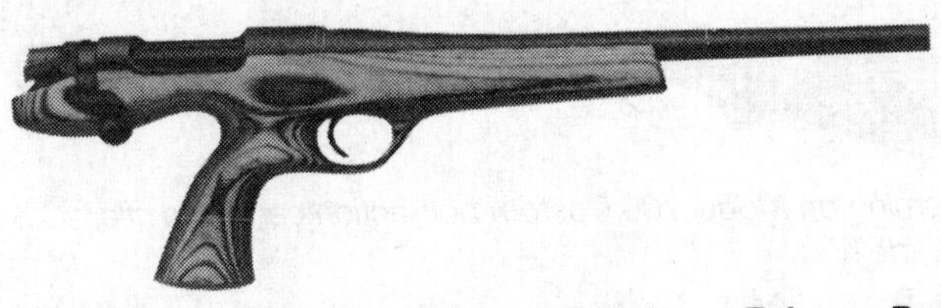

NIB	Exc.	V.G.	Good	Fair	Poor
800	675	375	300	250	175

Model XP-100R Repeater

Introduced in 1998, this model is chambered for the 9.22-250, .223, .260, and .35 Rem. cartridges. It is fitted with a 14.5" barrel that is drilled and tapped for sights.The receiver is drilled and tapped for scope mounts. Fiberglass stock. Weight is approximately 4.5 lbs. Manufacturered 1998. Discontinued.

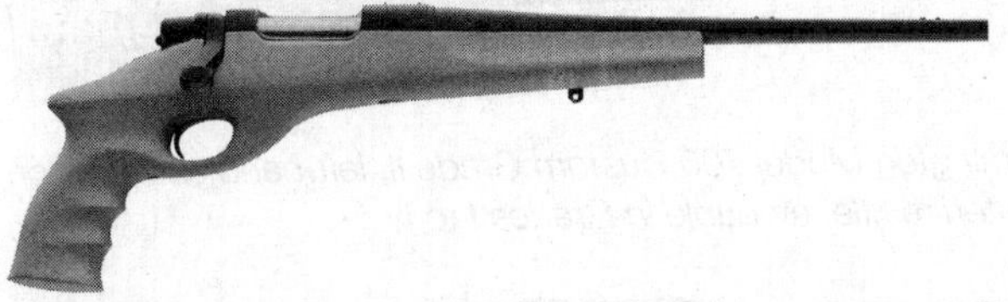

NIB	Exc.	V.G.	Good	Fair	Poor
750	600	400	—	—	—

SPARTAN GUNWORKS BY REMINGTON

This line of imported firearms was introduced into the Remington line in 2004. No longer a separate brand.

Model SPR 210

This is a side-by-side gun with single-selective trigger and auto ejectors. The box lock receiver is nickel and is fitted with 26" or 28" barrels with choke tubes in 12 and 20 gauge, and fixed chokes in 28 and .410 bore. This model is also offered with 20" barrel with choke tubes and blued receiver. Checkered walnut stock with recoil pad. Weight is about 6.75 lbs. depending on gauge and barrel length.

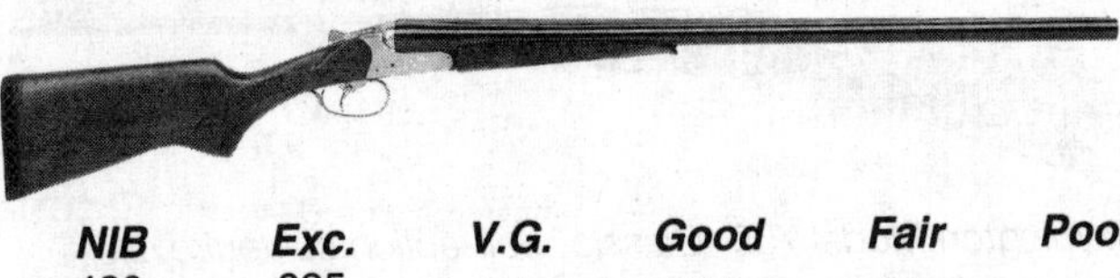

NIB	Exc.	V.G.	Good	Fair	Poor
420	325	—	—	—	

NOTE: Add $30 for 28 and .410 bore models.

Model SPR 220

This is a double trigger model with 20" barrels with choke tubes. Extractors. Nickel or blued receiver. Walnut stock with recoil pad. Weight is about 6.25 lbs.

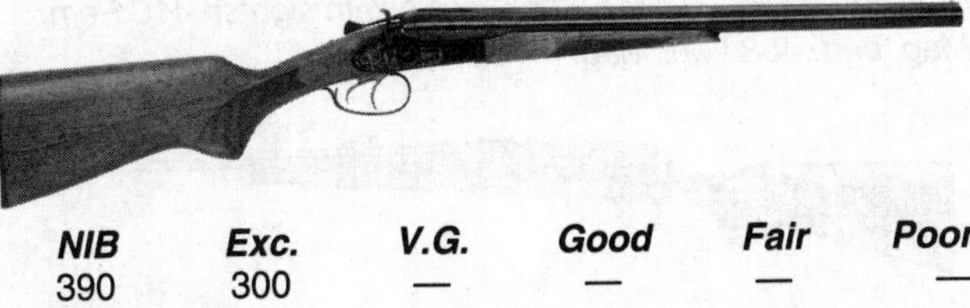

NIB	Exc.	V.G.	Good	Fair	Poor
390	300	—	—	—	—

Model SPR 310

This model is an over-and-under gun chambered for the 12, 20, 28, and .410 bore. Choice of 26" or 28" vent rib barrels with choke tubes or 26" barrels for the 28 and .410. Single selective trigger and auto ejectors. Checkered walnut stock with recoil pad. Weight is about 7.5 lbs.

NIB	Exc.	V.G.	Good	Fair	Poor
515	400	—	—	—	—

Model SPR 310S

This model is chambered for the 12 and 20 gauge 3" shell and is fitted with 29.5" (12 gauge) or 28.5" (20 gauge) ported barrels with choke tubes. Checked walnut stock with recoil pad. Weight is about 7.5 lbs.

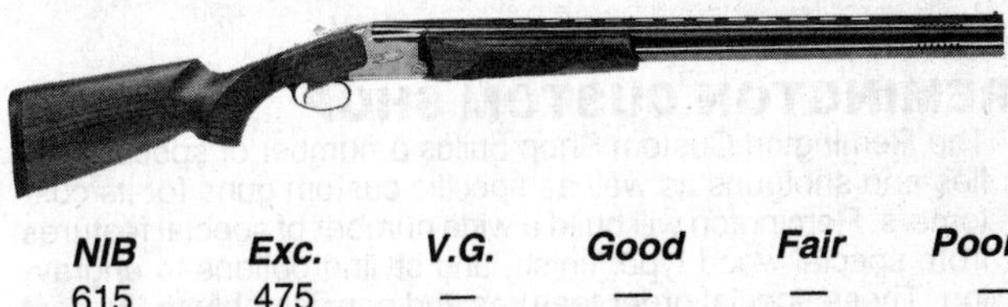

NIB	Exc.	V.G.	Good	Fair	Poor
615	475	—	—	—	—

Model SPR 100/Sporting

This is a single shot gun chambered for the 12, 20 , or .410 bore and fitted with 29.5" (12 gauge), 28.5" (20 gauge), or 26" (.410) barrel. Single trigger with ejectors or extractors. A youth model is also offered with 24" barrel chambered for the .410 bore. Checkered walnut stock with recoil pad. Weight is about 6.25 lbs.

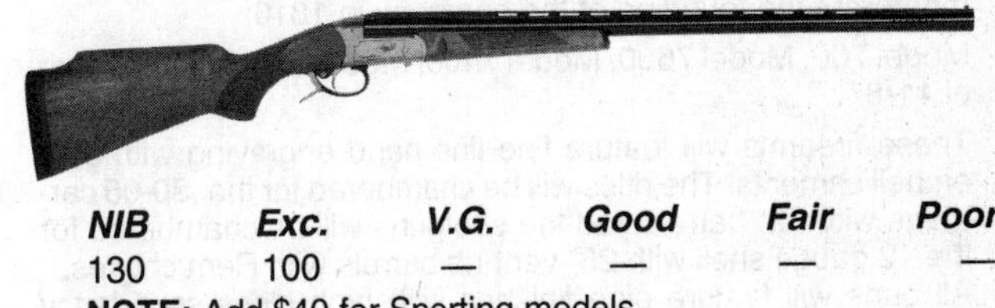

NIB	Exc.	V.G.	Good	Fair	Poor
130	100	—	—	—	—

NOTE: Add $40 for Sporting models.

Model SPR 18

This is a single shot rifle chambered for the .223, .243, .270, or .30-06 calibers. Nickel receiver. Fitted with a 23.5" barrel with iron sights. Checkered walnut stock with recoil pad. Weight is about 6.75 lbs.

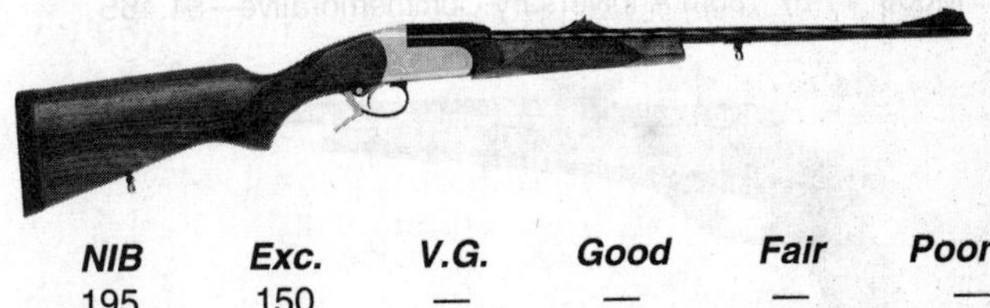

NIB	Exc.	V.G.	Good	Fair	Poor
195	150	—	—	—	—

Model SPR 22

This model is a side-by-side double rifle chambered for the .30-06 or .45-70 calibers and fitted with 23.5" barrels. Blued receiver and checkered walnut stock with recoil pad. Weight is about 7.5 lbs.

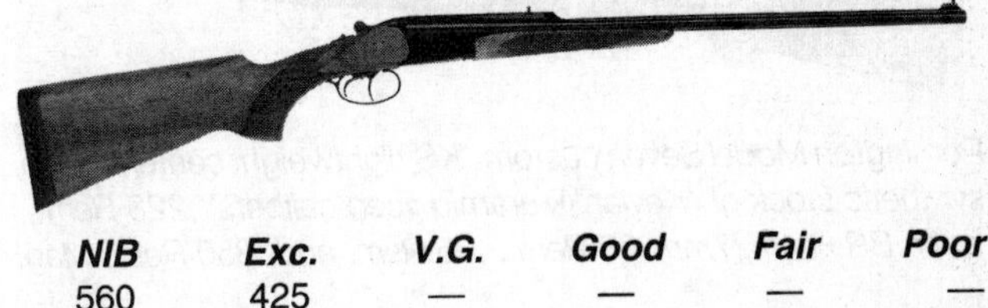

NIB	Exc.	V.G.	Good	Fair	Poor
560	425	—	—	—	—

Model SPR 94

This model features and under-and-under rifle/shotgun combination. Chambered for the .410/17HMR, .410/.22WMR, 12/.223, 12/.30-06, or 12/.308. Fitted with a 24" barrel with iron sights. Checkered walnut stock with recoil pad. Blued receiver. Weight is about 8 lbs. depending on combination.

NIB	Exc.	V.G.	Good	Fair	Poor
235	180	—	—	—	—

NOTE: Add $280 for centerfire models.

REMINGTON CUSTOM SHOP

The Remington Custom Shop builds a number of speciality rifles and shotguns as well as specific custom guns for its customers. Remington will build a wide number of special features from special wood type, finish, and styling options to engraving. These special order features add considerably to the cost of a gun and will affect its price. The Custom Shop can be reached at 1-800-243-9700 for current prices and availability.

REMINGTON 180TH ANNIVERSARY LIMITED EDITION RIFLES AND SHOTGUNS

Remington manufactured 180 each of these firearms to commemorate the founding of the company in 1816:

Model 700, Model 7600, Model 7400, Model 870, and the Model 11-87.

These firearms will feature fine line hand engraving with gold embellishments. The rifles will be chambered for the .30-06 cartridge with 22" barrels and the shotguns will be chambered for the 12 gauge shell with 26" vent rib barrels with Rem chokes. All guns will feature blue finishes with high gloss semi-fancy walnut stocks. If sold in a five-gun set each will have matching serial numbers. The suggested retail price for the five-gun set is $6,925. Individual guns will carry these suggested retail prices:

Model 700 180th Anniversary Commemorative—$1,372
Model 7400 180th Anniversary Commemorative—$1,372
Model 7600 180th Anniversary Commemorative—$1,332
Model 870 180th Anniversary Commemorative—$1,305
Model 11-87 180th Anniversary Commemorative—$1,465

Remington XP-100R custom pistol bolt-action centerfire repeater (with synthetic stock of "Kevlar" ®); Calibers: .223 Rem. (without sights), 7mm-08 Rem. and .35 Rem. (as shown)

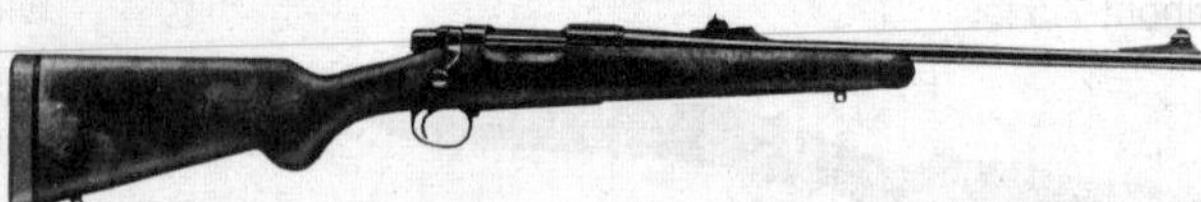

Remington Model Seven custom "KS" lightweight centerfire rifle, synthetic stock of "Kevlar"® aramid fiber; calibers: .223 Rem., 7mm BR Rem., 7mm-08 Rem., .35 Rem. and .350 Rem. Mag.

Remington Model 700 "AS" bolt-action centerfire rifle with synthetic stock

Remington Model 700 Custom bolt-action centerfire rifle, Grade IV

Remington Model 700 Custom bolt-action centerfire rifle, Grade III

Remington Model 700 Custom Grade II, left-hand short action centerfire rifle, available in Grades I to IV

Remington Model 700 custom bolt-action centerfire rifle, Grade II

Remington Model 700 Custom bolt-action centerfire rifle, Grade I

Remington Model 700 "Classic" bolt-action centerfire rifle, limited edition — .25-06 Rem.

Remington Model 700 Safari Classic with sights: .416 Rem. Mag. and .458 Win. Mag.

Remington Model 700 Safari KS, synthetic stock of "Kevlar"® aramid fiber; Calibers: 8mm Rem. Mag., .375 H&H Mag. 416 Rem. Mag and .458 Win. Mag.

Remington Model 870 D tournament grade pump-action shotgun

This symbol denotes "Sleepers" with rapidly-rising values and/or significant collector potential.

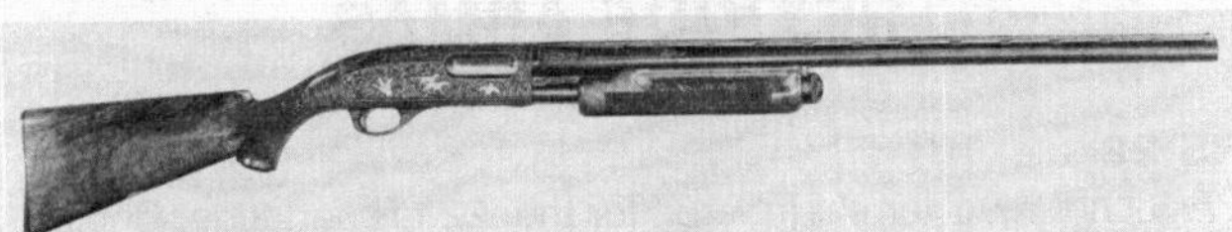

Remington Model 870 F pump-action shotgun, premier grade with gold inlay

Remington Model 1100 D tournament grade 12 gauge, 5 shot

Remington Model 1100 F autoloading shotgun, premier grade with gold inlay

RENETTE, GASTINNE

Paris, France

SHOTGUNS

Model 105

An Anson & Deeley action 12 or 20 gauge double-barrel shotgun available in a variety of barrel lengths, with double triggers and automatic ejectors. Blued, case hardened with a checkered walnut stock.

Exc.	V.G.	Good	Fair	Poor
2000	1600	1250	900	500

Model 98

As above, except more finely finished.

Exc.	V.G.	Good	Fair	Poor
2750	2250	1750	1400	750

Model 202

A 12 or 20 gauge sidelock double-barrel shotgun made only on custom order. French case hardened and blued with a checkered walnut stock.

Exc.	V.G.	Good	Fair	Poor
4500	3500	2500	1750	950

Model 353

A custom manufactured double-barrel shotgun with detachable sidelocks. Highly finished.

Exc.	V.G.	Good	Fair	Poor
18000	15000	9500	4250	1500

RIFLES

Type G Rifle

A .30-06, 9.3x74R, or .375 Holland & Holland double-barrel rifle with 24" barrels, express sights, double triggers and automatic ejectors. Engraved, blued with a checkered walnut stock.

Exc.	V.G.	Good	Fair	Poor
2750	1850	1500	1150	650

Type R Deluxe

As above, engraved with hunting scenes and with a more finely figured walnut stock.

Exc.	V.G.	Good	Fair	Poor
3500	2750	1750	1450	750

Type PT President

As above, inlaid in gold with extremely well figured walnut stock.

Exc.	V.G.	Good	Fair	Poor
4000	3250	2250	1750	950

Mauser Bolt-Action

A custom-made bolt-action rifle built on a Mauser action. Choice of calibers and stock styles. Base price listed.

Exc.	V.G.	Good	Fair	Poor
5750	4500	3250	1500	750

Deluxe Mauser Bolt-Action

Same as above but with fancy wood and other options.

Exc.	V.G.	Good	Fair	Poor
10000	7000	4500	3250	1250

RENWICK ARMS CO.

SEE—Perry & Goddard

REPUBLIC ARMS, INC.

Chino, California

This company was in business from 1997 to 2001. The Republic Patriot pistol may still be available from Cobra Enterpises.

Republic Patriot

This is a double-action-only .45 ACP caliber pistol with a 3" barrel and fixed sights. Black polymer frame with checkered grips and stainless steel slide. Magazine capacity is 6 rounds. Weight is about 20 oz. Introduced in 1997.

NIB	Exc.	V.G.	Good	Fair	Poor
325	250	200	—	—	—

RAP 440

This pistol is chambered for the .40 S&W or 9mm cartridges. It is double-action/single-action operation. Fitted with a 3-3/4" barrel, it has a magazine capacity of 7 rounds. Grips are two-piece black plastic. Weight is approximately 32 oz. Sights are three dot with fixed ramp front and windage adjustable rear. Introduced in 1998. Imported by TSF of Fairfax, Virginia.

NIB	Exc.	V.G.	Good	Fair	Poor
545	450	—	—	—	—

RETOLAZA HERMANOS

Eibar, Spain

Brompetier

A folding trigger 6.35mm or 7.65mm caliber double-action revolver with a 2.5" barrel and a safety mounted on the left side of the frame. Manufactured until 1915.

Exc.	V.G.	Good	Fair	Poor
200	100	85	70	45

Gallus or Titan

A 6.35mm semi-automatic pistol normally marked "Gallus" or "Titan." Blued with plastic grips.

Exc.	V.G.	Good	Fair	Poor
200	125	100	75	50

Liberty, Military, Retolaza, or Paramount

A 6.35mm or 7.65mm semi-automatic pistol with a 3" barrel and 8-shot magazine. The slide marked with any of the trade names listed above.

Exc.	V.G.	Good	Fair	Poor
200	125	100	75	50

Puppy

A folding trigger .22 caliber double-action revolver with a 5-shot cylinder. The trade name "Puppy" stamped on the barrel.

Exc.	V.G.	Good	Fair	Poor
150	100	75	50	25

Stosel

A 6.35mm semi-automatic pistol marked on the slide "Automatic Pistol Stosel No. 1 Patent." Blued with plastic grips.

Exc.	V.G.	Good	Fair	Poor
200	125	100	75	50

Titanic

A 6.35mm semi-automatic pistol with a 2.5" barrel, the slide marked "1913 Model Automatic Pistol Titanic Eibar." Blued with plastic grips.

Exc.	V.G.	Good	Fair	Poor
200	125	100	75	50

REUNIES

Liege, Belgium

Dictator

A 6.35mm semi-automatic pistol with a 1.5" barrel, 5-shot magazine and the name "Dictator" together with the company's details stamped on the slide. This pistol features a bolt of tubular form, the front end of which is hollow and encloses the barrel breech. Manufactured from 1909 to approximately 1925.

Exc.	V.G.	Good	Fair	Poor
250	150	125	100	75

Texas Ranger or Cowboy Ranger

Patterned after the Colt Model 1873 revolver. This pistol is of .38 Special caliber and has a 5.5" barrel. The barrel is marked with the company's details and either the legend "Cowboy Ranger" or "Texas Ranger." Manufactured from 1922 to 1931.

Exc.	V.G.	Good	Fair	Poor
350	200	100	75	50

REUTH, F.

Hartford, Connecticut

Animal Trap Gun

A cast iron .28 to .50 caliber percussion trap gun with either single or double-barrels 3.5" or 5" in length. This firearm fires a barbed arrow and is triggered by a cord attached to an animal trap or bait. The barrels marked "F. Reuth's Patent, May 12, 1857." Several hundred were made between 1858 and 1862.

Exc.	V.G.	Good	Fair	Poor
—	—	1500	500	150

NOTE: The single-barrel model is more common than the double-barrel and is worth approximately 20 percent less.

REXIODE ARMAS

Argentina

RS 22

A 9-shot revolver chambered for the .22 LR cartridge. Choice of blued or stainless steel frame. Fixed or adjustable sights. Barrel lengths are 4" or 6". Fitted with rubber grips.

NIB	Exc.	V.G.	Good	Fair	Poor
235	175	—	—	—	—

NOTE: Add $30 for stainless steel.

RS 22M

Same as above but chambered for the .22 Win. mag cartridge.

NIB	Exc.	V.G.	Good	Fair	Poor
235	175	—	—	—	—

NOTE: Add $30 for stainless steel.

RJ 22

This revolver is chambered for the .22 LR cartridge and fitted with a 3", 4", or 6" barrel. Checkered walnut grips or synthetic grips. Adjustable rear sight. Blued finish. Melting point is 716 degrees F.

NIB	Exc.	V.G.	Good	Fair	Poor
165	125	100	75	50	—

RJ 38

Same as above but chambered for .38 Special cartridge.

NIB	Exc.	V.G.	Good	Fair	Poor
165	125	—	—	—	—

RS 357

Same as above but chambered for the .357 magnum cartridge and offered with 3", 4", or 6" barrels.

NIB	Exc.	V.G.	Good	Fair	Poor
235	175	—	—	—	—

NOTE: Add $30 for stainless steel.

Outfitter Single-Shot

This is a break down single pistol chambered for the .45 Colt/.410 .22 LR or .22 Win. mag. Blued 10" barrel with synthetic grip. Weight is about 43 oz.

NIB	Exc.	V.G.	Good	Fair	Poor
200	150	—	—	—	—

Outfitter Single-Shot Compact

Same as above but with 6" barrel in .22 Win. Mag or .45 Colt/.410.

NIB	Exc.	V.G.	Good	Fair	Poor
200	150	—	—	—	—

RHEINMETALL
Sommerda, Germany

Dreyse 6.35mm Model 1907

A 6.35mm semi-automatic pistol with a 2" barrel, manual safety and 6-shot magazine. Weight is about 14 oz. The slide marked "Dreyse." Blued with hard rubber grips having the trademark "RFM" molded in them. The patent for this design was issued in 1909 to Louis Schmeisser.

Courtesy James Rankin

Exc.	V.G.	Good	Fair	Poor
400	250	200	150	100

Dreyse 7.65mm Model 1907

As above, but chambered for the 7.65mm cartridge, with a 3.6" barrel and a 7-shot magazine. Weight is about 25 oz. Blued with horn grips.

Courtesy Orvel Reichert

Exc.	V.G.	Good	Fair	Poor
300	200	150	125	75

Dreyse 9mm

As above, but chambered for the 9mm cartridge with a 5" barrel and an 8-shot magazine. Weight is about 37 oz. The slide marked "Rheinische Mettallwaaren Und Maschinenfabrik, Sommerda." Blued with hard rubber grips. Manufactured prior to 1916 and in small numbers.

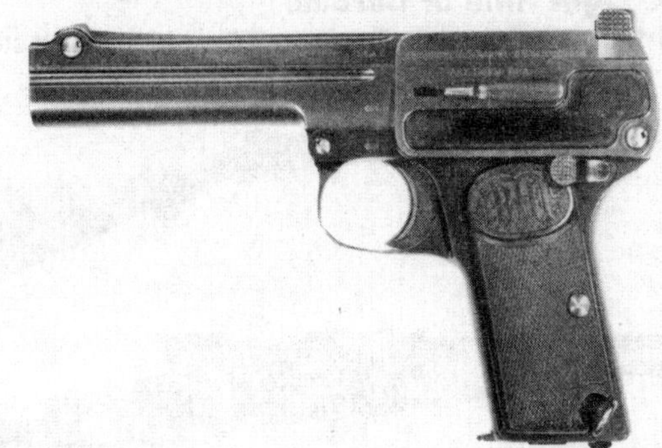

Courtesy James Rankin

Exc.	V.G.	Good	Fair	Poor
4500	3750	2500	1500	750

Rheinmetall 32

A 7.65mm semi-automatic pistol with a 3.65" barrel and an 8-shot magazine. The slide marked "Rheinmetall ABT. Sommerda." Blued with walnut grips. Overall length is 6.5" and weight is about 23.5 oz. Production of this pistol began in 1920.

Courtesy James Rankin

Exc.	V.G.	Good	Fair	Poor
350	225	175	125	90

Rheinmetall 9mm

This is a 9mm version of the Rheinmetall and was built in 1935 to compete with the 9mm Parabellum German military pistols of that time. It was unsuccessful.

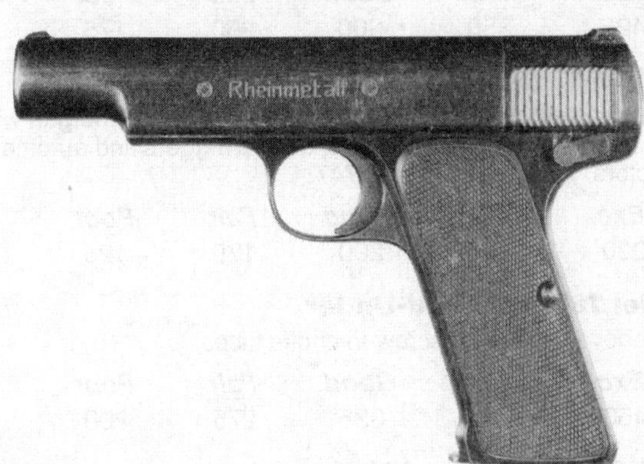

Courtesy James Rankin

Exc.	V.G.	Good	Fair	Poor
Too Rare To Price				

Dreyse Light Rifle or Carbine

Model 1907 in caliber 7.65 Browning. Fitted with a fixed stock and 6-round magazine.

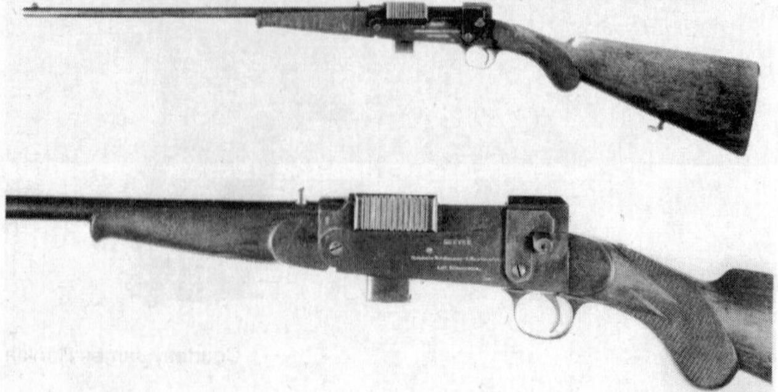

Courtesy James Rankin

Exc.	V.G.	Good	Fair	Poor
1200	900	800	500	300

RHODE ISLAND ARMS CO.
Hope Valley, Rhode Island

Morrone

A 12 or 20 gauge over-and-under boxlock shotgun with 26" or 28" barrels, single trigger and automatic ejectors. Blued with either a straight or pistol grip walnut checkered stock. 450 were made in 12 gauge and 50 in 20 gauge. Manufactured from 1949 to 1953.

Exc.	V.G.	Good	Fair	Poor
1500	1000	750	600	350

RICHLAND ARMS CO.
Blissfield, Michigan

This company, which ceased operation in 1986, imported a variety of Spanish-made shotguns.

Model 41 Ultra Over-and-Under

A 20, 28, or .410 bore double-barrel shotgun with 26" or 28" ventilated rib barrels, single nonselective trigger and automatic ejectors. French case hardened receiver and checkered walnut stock.

Exc.	V.G.	Good	Fair	Poor
300	250	200	150	100

Model 747 Over-and-Under

As above, in 20 gauge only with a single-selective trigger.

Exc.	V.G.	Good	Fair	Poor
425	350	300	250	175

Model 757 Over-and-Under

A Greener-style boxlock 12 gauge double-barrel shotgun with 26" or 28" ventilated rib barrels, double triggers and automatic ejectors. Finished as Model 747.

Exc.	V.G.	Good	Fair	Poor
300	250	200	175	125

Model 787 Over-and-Under

As above, fitted with screw-in choke tubes.

Exc.	V.G.	Good	Fair	Poor
450	375	325	275	200

Model 808 Over-and-Under

A 12 gauge double-barrel shotgun with 26", 28" or 30" ventilated rib barrels, single trigger and automatic ejectors. Blued with checkered walnut stock. Manufactured in Italy from 1963 to 1968.

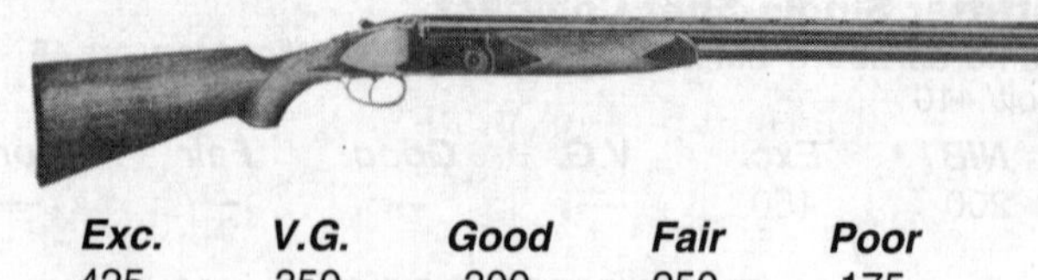

Exc.	V.G.	Good	Fair	Poor
425	350	300	250	175

Model 80 LS

A 12, 20 or .410 bore single-barrel shotgun with 26" or 28" barrels. Blued with checkered walnut stock.

Exc.	V.G.	Good	Fair	Poor
175	125	100	80	60

Model 200

An Anson & Deeley-style 12, 16, 20, 28 or .410 bore double-barrel shotgun with 22", 26" or 28" barrels, double triggers, and automatic ejectors. Blued with a checkered walnut stock.

Exc.	V.G.	Good	Fair	Poor
350	300	250	200	125

Model 202

As above, with an extra set of interchangeable barrels. Imported from 1963 to 1985.

Exc.	V.G.	Good	Fair	Poor
325	275	225	175	100

Model 711 Magnum

As above, chambered for 3" shells and fitted with 30" or 32" barrels.

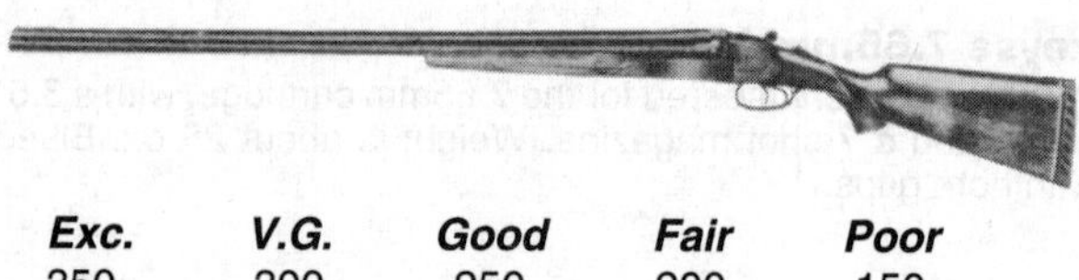

Exc.	V.G.	Good	Fair	Poor
350	300	250	200	150

Model 707 Deluxe

As above, more finely finished and fitted with well figured walnut stocks.

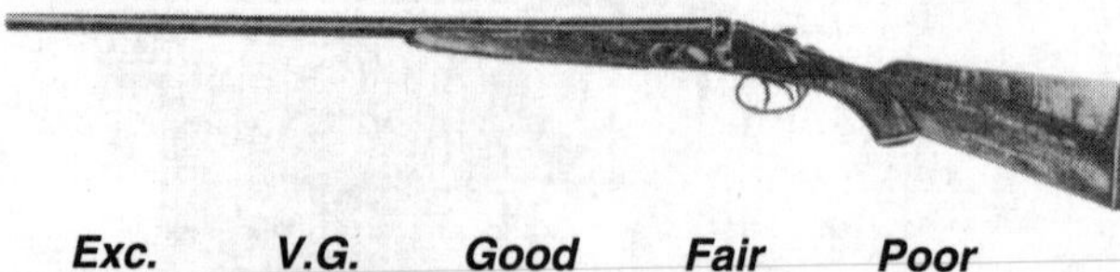

Exc.	V.G.	Good	Fair	Poor
350	300	250	200	150

RICHMOND ARMORY
Richmond, Virginia

Carbine

This weapon was manufactured for use by the Confederate States of America and is extremely collectible. This muzzle-loading carbine is chambered for .58 caliber percussion and has a 25" round barrel and a full-length stock that is held on by two barrel bands. It was manufactured from parts that were captured at the Harper's Ferry Armory in 1861. The locks are marked "Richmond, VA" and dated from 1861 to 1865. There are sling swivels in front of the trigger guard and on the front barrel band; a third swivel is on the underside of the buttstock. The quantity manufactured is not known. They were made between 1861 and 1865.

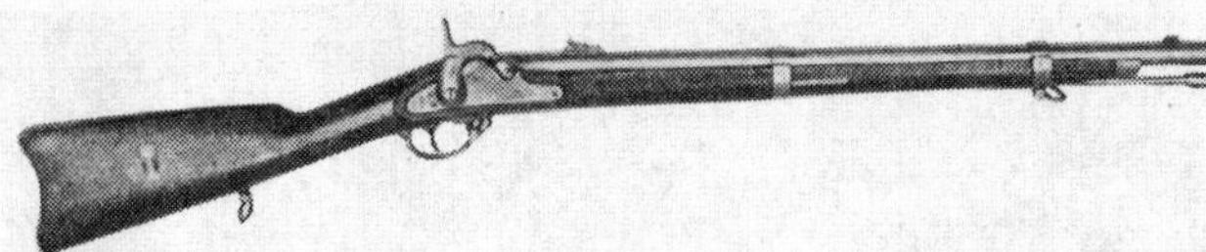

Courtesy Milwaukee Public Museum, Milwaukee, Wisconsin

Exc.	V.G.	Good	Fair	Poor
—	—	20000	7500	1000

Musketoon

This weapon is similar to the carbine except that the barrel is 30" in length and the front sight is also the bayonet lug. There is no sling swivel on the buttstock. This weapon was also manufactured between 1861 and 1865.

Exc.	V.G.	Good	Fair	Poor
—	—	17500	7000	1000

Rifled Musket

This model is also similar to the Carbine, with a 40" barrel and a full-length stock held on by three barrel bands. The front sling swivel is on the middle barrel band instead of on the front band. The Rifled Musket was also manufactured between 1861 and 1865.

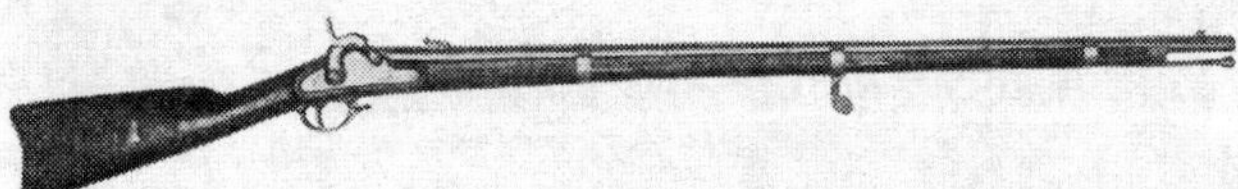

Courtesy Milwaukee Public Museum, Milwaukee, Wisconsin

Exc.	V.G.	Good	Fair	Poor
—	—	20000	7500	1000

RIEDL RIFLE CO.

Westminster, California

Single-Shot Rifle

This company produced custom order dropping block single-shot rifles in a variety of calibers and barrel lengths. Rifles were normally fitted only with telescopic or target sight bases. Blued with a checkered walnut stock.

Exc.	V.G.	Good	Fair	Poor
500	450	400	300	225

RIFLESMITH INC.

Sheridan, Montana

SEE—Axtell Rifle Co.

RIGBY, JOHN & CO., LTD.

London, England

SEE—British Double Guns

This company was established in the early 19th century and has produced a variety of shotguns and rifles over the years. Many of the arms produced by this company were custom ordered.

RIFLES

Magazine Rifle

Utilizing a Mauser action, this rifle is available in a number of calibers, barrel lengths and with either a 3- or 5-shot magazine. Blued checkered walnut stock.

Courtesy Faintich Auction Service, Paul Goodwin photo

NIB	Exc.	V.G.	Good	Fair	Poor
6500	4750	3000	2250	1250	—

Large Bore Magazine Rifle

Utilizing a Bruno square bridge Mauser action, this rifle is chambered for .375 Holland & Holland, .404 Gibbs, .416 Rigby, .458 Winchester Magnum and .505 Gibbs cartridges. Barrel lengths vary from 2" to 24" and a 4-shot magazine is standard.

NIB	Exc.	V.G.	Good	Fair	Poor
7500	5000	3750	2500	1000	—

Single-Shot Rifle

Utilizing a Farquharson dropping block action, this rifle is chambered for a variety of cartridges and has a 24" barrel. The receiver finely engraved and blued. Stock of well figured walnut.

Exc.	V.G.	Good	Fair	Poor
8000	7000	5500	2500	—

Third Quality Boxlock Double Rifle

A double-barrel rifle chambered for cartridges from .275 Magnum to .577 Nitro Express with a 24" to 28" barrel fitted with express sights. Double triggers and automatic ejectors. Blued with light engraving and a checkered walnut stock.

Exc.	V.G.	Good	Fair	Poor
12500	10500	8500	4000	—

Second Quality Boxlock Double Rifle

As above, but more finely engraved and with better quality walnut stocks.

Exc.	V.G.	Good	Fair	Poor
16000	14000	10500	5000	—

Best Quality Sidelock Double Rifle

As above, but fitted with full sidelocks, with best bouquet engraving and finely figured walnut stocks.

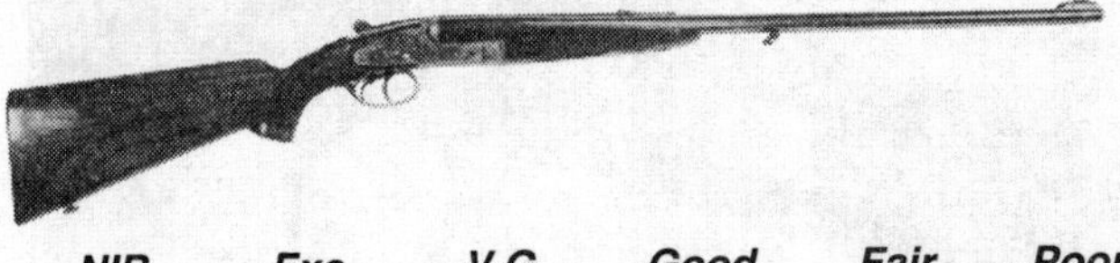

NIB	Exc.	V.G.	Good	Fair	Poor
35000	30000	25000	20000	10000	—

RIGDON, ANSLEY & CO.

Augusta, Georgia

1851 Colt Navy Type

A .36 caliber percussion revolver with a 7.5" barrel and 6-shot cylinder. Blued with walnut grips. Initial production examples marked "Augusta, GA. C.S.A." and later models "C.S.A." Approximately 1,000 were manufactured in 1864 and 1865.

Courtesy Milwaukee Public Museum, Milwaukee, Wisconsin

Early Production Model

Exc.	V.G.	Good	Fair	Poor
—	—	55000	25000	2000

Standard Production Model

Exc.	V.G.	Good	Fair	Poor
—	—	45000	17500	1500

RIPOMANTI, GUY

St. Etienne, France

Side-by-Side Shotgun

A high-grade shotgun offered on a strictly made-to-order basis. There is a boxlock model that begins at $8,500 and a sidelock that is priced from $22,500. These prices rise depending on the options and embellishments desired. These guns are rarely seen on the used-gun market.

Side-by-Side Double Rifles

Extremely high-grade and basically made to order. They are rarely encountered on today's market. They have been imported since 1988. They range in price from $11,000 up.

Over-and-Under Double Rifle

A boxlock action over-and-under chambered for the 9.3x74R cartridge. The barrels are 23.5" in length and have express sights. There are double triggers and automatic ejectors. This model is highly engraved and features a high-grade, hand-checkered walnut stock.

NIB	Exc.	V.G.	Good	Fair	Poor
7000	5750	4750	4000	3000	2250

RIVERSIDE ARMS CO.

Chicopee Falls, Massachusetts

SEE ALSO—Stevens

Double-Barrel Shotguns

Brand name used by J. Stevens Arms Co. on many good quality double-barrel shotguns. Value depends on model, gauge, and condition. From $100 to $1,600. See also Stevens.

Courtesy William Hammond

RIZZINI, BATTISTA

Bresica, Italy

NOTE: There are a number of extra cost options for Rizzini guns that can greatly affect price. Extra barrels and upgraded wood are such options.

SHOTGUNS

Aurum Light

This over-and-under model features a choice of 24.5" to 27.5". Vent rib barrel. Figured oil finish walnut stock with hand checkering and pistol grip. Game scene engraved receiver. Auto ejectors and single-selective trigger. Weight is about 6 lbs.

Courtesy William Larkin Moore & Co.

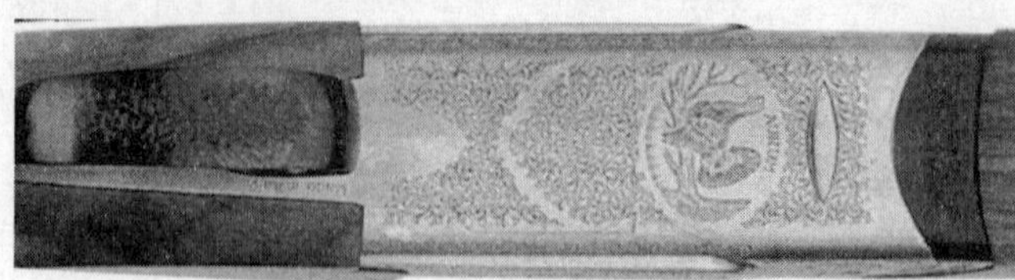

Courtesy William Larkin Moore & Co.

NIB	Exc.	V.G.	Good	Fair	Poor
2250	1650	1250	—	—	—

Artemis

This model features engraved sideplates with game scenes. Offered in 12, 16, 20, 28 gauge as well as .410 bore. Barrel lengths from 24" to 27.5". Auto ejectors and single-selective trigger. Figured walnut stock with hand checkering and pistol grip. Weight is about 6 lbs.

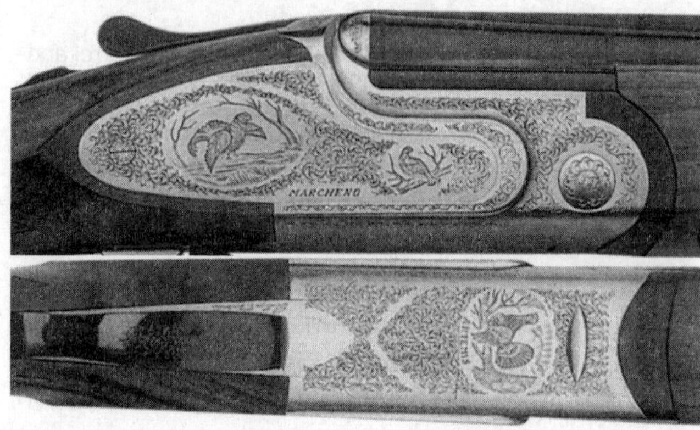

Courtesy William Larkin Moore & Co.

NIB	Exc.	V.G.	Good	Fair	Poor
2375	1750	1250	—		

Artemis Deluxe

Similar to the standard Artemis with the addition of gold inlaid game scenes and fancy walnut stock. Cased.

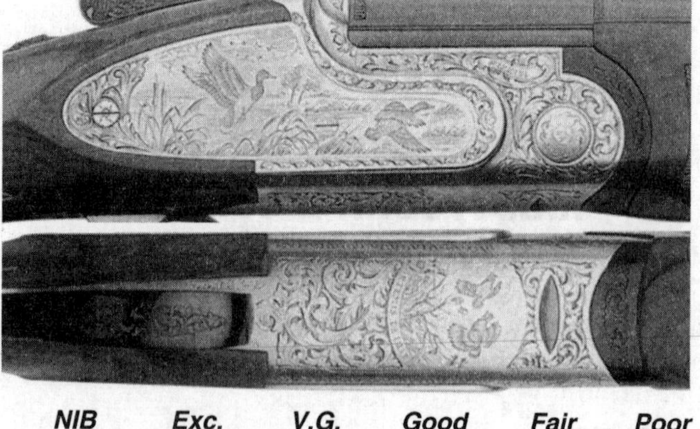

NIB	Exc.	V.G.	Good	Fair	Poor
4675	3500	2750	—	—	—

Artemis EL

This model features sideplates with hand engraved English scroll and game scenes. Extra fancy walnut stock. Cased.

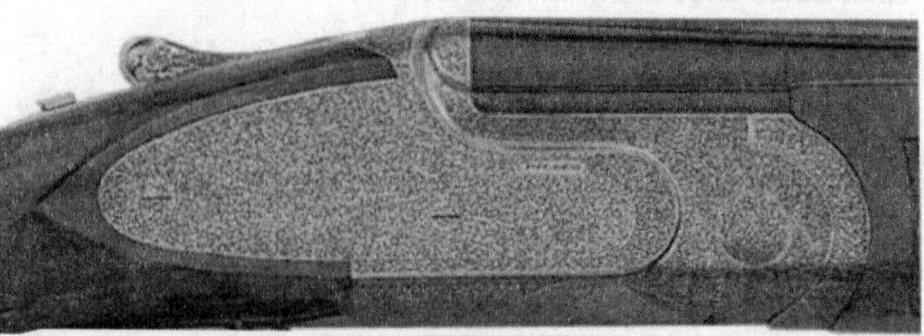

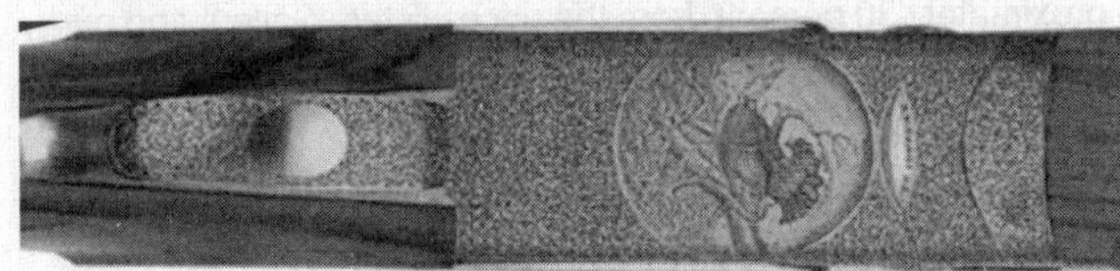

NIB	Exc.	V.G.	Good	Fair	Poor
15600	11500	9000	—	—	—

Upland EL

NIB	Exc.	V.G.	Good	Fair	Poor
3600	2700	2000	—	—	—

S780 Emel

This boxlock model is offered in 12, 16, 20, 28, or .410. Barrel lengths from 24" to 27.5". Hand engraved receiver with game scenes. Auto ejectors and single-selective trigger. Fancy walnut stock with hand checkering. Leather case. Weight for 12 gauge is about 6.8 lbs. and the smaller gauges about 6 lbs.

NIB	Exc.	V.G.	Good	Fair	Poor
10300	7750	6000	—	—	—

REMINDER
The figures listed in this book reflect relative values, not prices. Only the buyer and seller can determine price.

S782 Emel

This model is similar to the S792 but with the addition of hand engraved gold inlaid game scenes.

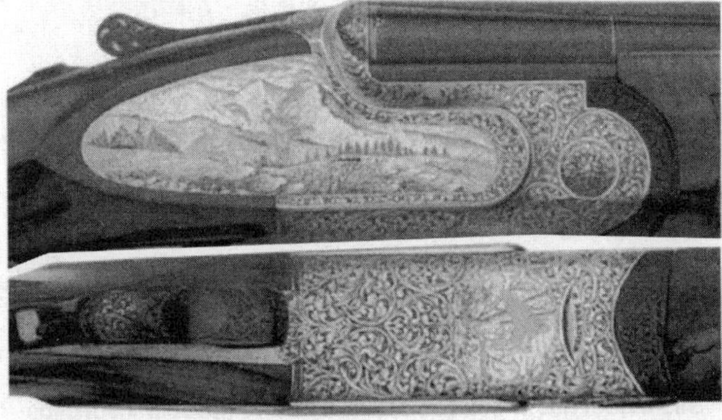

NIB	Exc.	V.G.	Good	Fair	Poor
12250	9200	7200	—	—	—

S790 Emel

This model is similar to the S780 with the exception of the engraving pattern. This model has a thistle-leaf style pattern.

NIB	Exc.	V.G.	Good	Fair	Poor
10250	7750	6000	—	—	—

S792 Emel

This model features sideplates engraved with English scroll and game scenes. Extra select walnut stock. Available in 12, 16, 20, 28, and .410 with barrel lengths from 24" to 27.5".

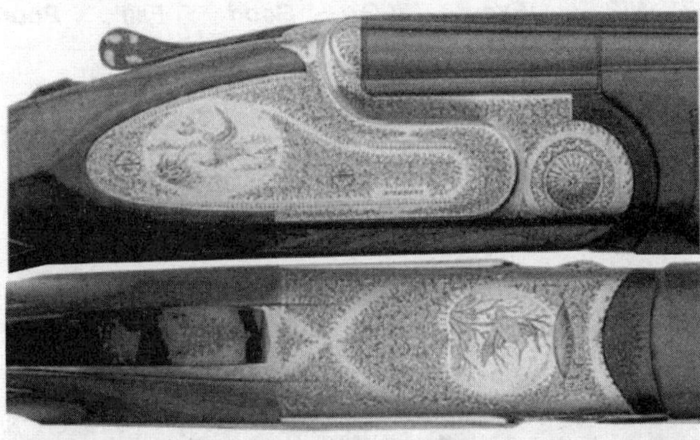

NIB	Exc.	V.G.	Good	Fair	Poor
9750	7250	5500	—	—	—

Premier Sporting

This model is offered in 12 or 20 gauge with choice of barrel lengths from 27.5" to 31.5". Blued boxlock action with auto ejectors and single-selective trigger. Select walnut stock with hand checkering and oil finish. Pistol grip stock and beavertail forend. Weight is about 7.5 lbs.

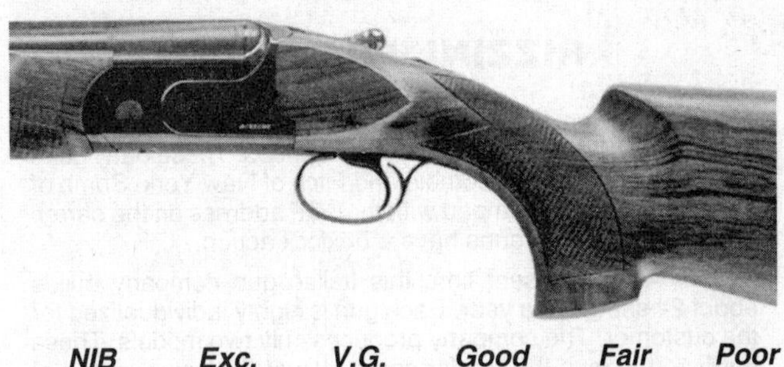

NIB	Exc.	V.G.	Good	Fair	Poor
2750	2100	1600	—	—	—

Sporting EL

NIB	Exc.	V.G.	Good	Fair	Poor
3750	2800	2200	—	—	—

S790 EL Sporting

This model is offered in 12 gauge only and choice of barrel from 27.5" to 31.5". Boxlock action with chrome plate. Auto ejectors and single-selective trigger. Pistol grip stock with fancy walnut. Weight is about 7.5 lbs.

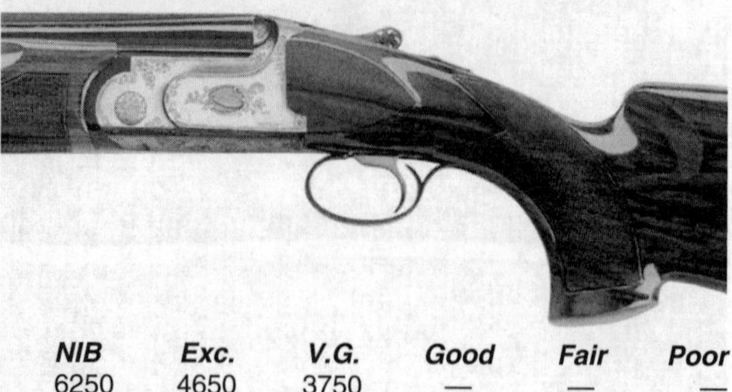

NIB	Exc.	V.G.	Good	Fair	Poor
6250	4650	3750	—	—	—

EXPRESS RIFLES

Express 90 L

This over-and-under rifle is chambered for the 7x65R, 8x57JRS, 9.3x74R, .30-06, .308 Win., and .444 Marlin. Barrel length is 16". Boxlock action with case colored receiver. Auto ejectors and single trigger. Pistol-grip walnut stock with Bavarian cheekpiece. Hand checkered and oil finish stock. Weight is about 8 lbs.

NIB	Exc.	V.G.	Good	Fair	Poor
4600	3250	2500	—	—	—

Express 92 EL

Same calibers as above model but with sideplates engraved with English scroll and game scenes. Extra select walnut stock with pistol grip and round cheekpiece.

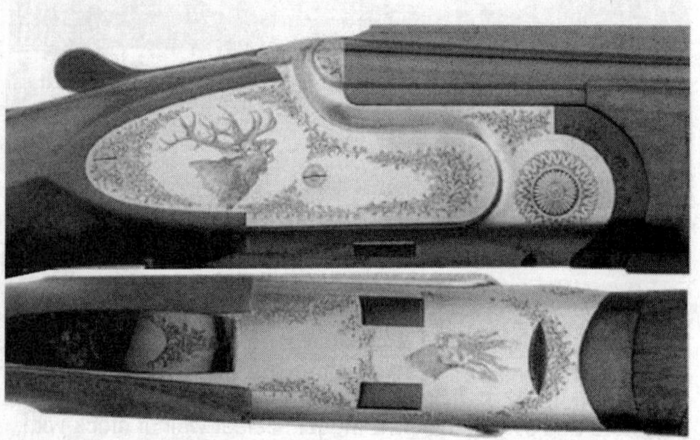

NIB	Exc.	V.G.	Good	Fair	Poor
9750	7250	5750	—	—	—

RIZZINI, FRATELLI

Brescia, Italy

Early guns were manufactured with Antonio Zoli. As a result, these were off-the-shelf guns of lower prices. These early guns were imported by Abercombie and Fitch of New York. Some of these guns will be stamped with the A&F address on the barrel. These side-by-side guns have a boxlock action.

NOTE: At the present time this Italian gun company builds about 24 shotguns a year. Each gun is highly individualized for the customer. The company produces only two models. These are listed to give the reader some idea of the value of one of these models. None of these models includes the cost of engraving and multi barrel set and multi gauge sets are extra.

Rizzini models with serial numbers above #1709 have their own patented action and the prices listed reflect that action. Guns listed have a H&H style action and should deduct approximately 30 percent from the prices listed. Sellers and purchasers should note the the R-1 and R-2 models are some of the finest shotguns produced in the world.

Lusso Grade

12 gauge

NIB	Exc.	V.G.	Good	Fair	Poor
1200	850	700	600	400	200

20 gauge

NIB	Exc.	V.G.	Good	Fair	Poor
1700	1250	800	600	500	250

28 gauge and .410 bore

NIB	Exc.	V.G.	Good	Fair	Poor
2000	1600	1250	800	600	300

Extra Lusso Grade—Scalloped receiver

12 gauge

NIB	Exc.	V.G.	Good	Fair	Poor
2800	2150	1750	1200	800	400

20 gauge

NIB	Exc.	V.G.	Good	Fair	Poor
3450	2600	2000	1500	1150	600

28 gauge

NIB	Exc.	V.G.	Good	Fair	Poor
3850	2900	2250	1750	1300	700

.410 bore

NIB	Exc.	V.G.	Good	Fair	Poor
4250	3250	2400	1800	1350	750

Model R-1

Available in 12 to .410 bore with choice of barrels from 25" to 30". Choice of single or double trigger, pistol or straight grip, rib, barrel length and chokes are standard items on this model. This model features a Holland & Holland sidelock action.

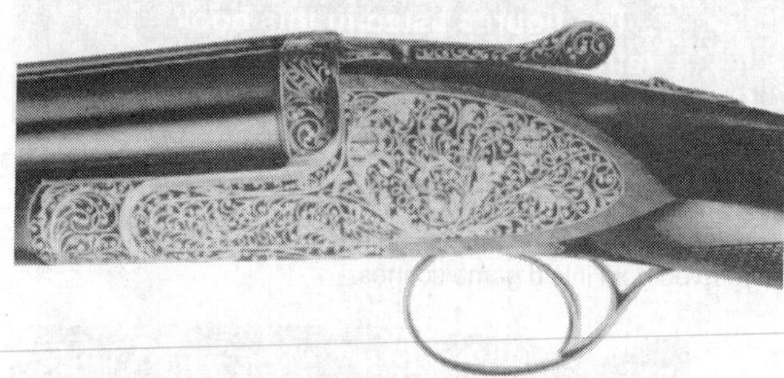

12, 16, or 20 gauge

NIB	Exc.	V.G.	Good	Fair	Poor
45000	34000	19000	—	—	—

28 gauge or .410 bore

NIB	Exc.	V.G.	Good	Fair	Poor
46000	34500	22000	—	—	—

Model R-2

This model has a boxlock action and a removable inspection plate on the bottom of the frame. The stock and forearm is fitted with Turkish Circassian walnut. Offered in 12 gauge to .410 bore.

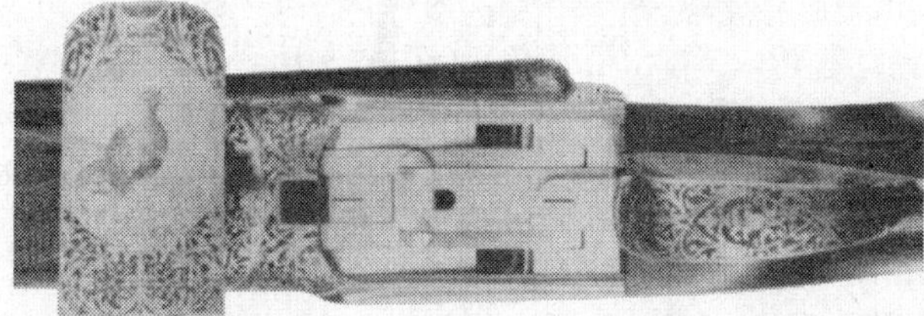

NIB	Exc.	V.G.	Good	Fair	Poor
15000	12000	8500	—	—	—

NOTE: Engraving extras for above models will add $8,700 for English scroll pattern and $22,000 for Fracassi style engraving. Other types of engraving are offered and it is advisable to secure a qualified appraisal of an engraved Rizzini before purchase. Extra set of barrels in same gauge add 15 percent.

ROBAR AND de KIRKHAVE

Liege, Belgium

Model 1909-1910

A 6.35mm or 7.65mm caliber semi-automatic pistol with a 3" barrel. The barrel is located under the recoil spring housing. The slide is marked "Pistolet Automatique Jieffeco Depose Brevete SGDG." Blued with plastic grips. Manufactured from 1910 to 1914. Copy of Browning Model 1900.

Courtesy James Rankin

Exc.	V.G.	Good	Fair	Poor
500	400	300	200	100

Model 1911

A semi-automatic pistol in caliber 6.35mm. Same as the Model 1909-1910. Slide serrations have been added at the muzzle.

Courtesy James Rankin

Exc.	V.G.	Good	Fair	Poor
500	400	300	200	100

Model 1912

A semi-automatic pistol in caliber 7.65mm. Similar to the Model 1909-1910. Slide serrations have been added at the muzzle.

Courtesy James Rankin

Exc.	V.G.	Good	Fair	Poor
500	400	300	200	100

Melior Model 1907

A semi-automatic pistol in calibers 6.35mm and 7.65mm. Barrel is located under the recoil spring housing.

Courtesy James Rankin

Exc.	V.G.	Good	Fair	Poor
500	400	300	200	100

Melior Model 1913-1914

A semi-automatic pistol in caliber 6.35mm and 7.65mm. Same as the Model 1907 but with slide serrations at the muzzle.

Exc.	V.G.	Good	Fair	Poor
500	400	300	200	100

Melior Pocket Model

A semi-automatic pistol in 6.35mm caliber. It is nearly identical to the Jieffeco's made by the same company, Robar. It was manufactured in the 1920s and imported into the U.S. by Phoenix Arms Company, Mass. The Phoenix name appears on the pistol. The model resembles the FN Browning Model 1910.

Courtesy James Rankin

Exc.	V.G.	Good	Fair	Poor
350	250	175	125	75

REMINDER

An "N/A" or "—" instead of a price indicates that pricing for that gun in that condition is not available, or that sales for that particular model are so few that a reliable price cannot be given.

Melior Vest Pocket Model

A semi-automatic pistol in caliber 6.35mm with open-top slide. Blue finish with black checkered rubber grips with Robar logo "ROC" on each grip.

Courtesy James Rankin

Exc.	V.G.	Good	Fair	Poor
300	250	200	150	100

Melior Model .22 Long Rifle

A semi-automatic pistol chambered for the .22 LR cartridge. Very similar in appearance to the Pocket Model, but with no squeeze grip safety.

Courtesy James Rankin

Exc.	V.G.	Good	Fair	Poor
500	400	300	200	100

Melior Model .22 Target

A semi-automatic in .22 LR caliber. Barrel is detachable so that various lengths may be used. A knurled nut at the front of the slide allows for barrel changes.

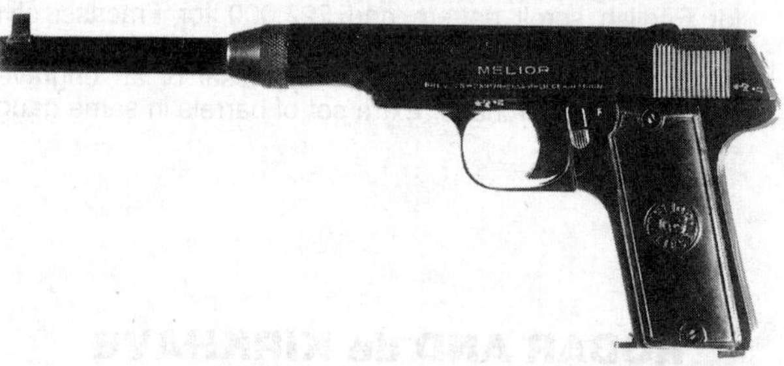

Courtesy James Rankin

Exc.	V.G.	Good	Fair	Poor
500	400	300	200	100

New Model Jieffeco (7.65mm)

In the 1920s Robar and de Kirkhave introduced a New Model Jieffeco, similar to the FN Browning Model 1910. As this time the right to import the Jieffeco into the U.S. was arranged with Davis Warner Arms Corp., New York, whose company name was used on the pistol. The model is a semi-automatic pistol in caliber 7.65mm. On the slide is "Pistolet Automatique Jieffeco Repose."

Courtesy James Rankin

Exc.	V.G.	Good	Fair	Poor
350	250	175	125	75

New Model Jieffeco (6.35mm)

In the 1920s Robar and de Kirkhave introduced a New Model Jieffeco, similar to the FN Browning Model 1910. As this time the right to import the Jieffeco into the U.S. was arranged with Davis Warner Arms Corp., New York, whose company name was used on the pistol. The model is a semi-automatic pistol in caliber 7.65mm. On the slide is "Pistolet Automatique Jieffeco Made in Liege, Belgium. Davis Warmer Arms Corporation, New York."

Courtesy James Rankin

Exc.	V.G.	Good	Fair	Poor
350	250	175	125	75

Mercury

As above, in .22 caliber and imported by Tradewinds of Tacoma, Washington. The slide marked "Mercury Made in Belgium." Blue or nickel-plated. Manufactured from 1946 to 1958.

Exc.	V.G.	Good	Fair	Poor
200	150	125	100	75

ROBAR COMPANIES

Phoenix, Arizona

This company has been building precision rifles, shotguns, and pistol since 1983.

Robar Patriot Tactical Shotgun

Built on a Remington Model 870 this model features an 18" barrel, express sights, seamless extended magazine tube, sidesaddle shell carrier, Wolff springs, etc. as well as Roguard/NP3 finish.

NIB	Exc.	V.G.	Good	Fair	Poor
765	600	—	—	—	—

Robar Spec Ops Tactical Shotgun

Similar to the model above but fitted with tactical ghost ring night sights, tactical safety, and tactical sling.

NIB	Exc.	V.G.	Good	Fair	Poor
990	800	—	—	—	—

Robar Elite Tactical Shotgun

This model features a number of special options such as Robar choke with forcing cone, modified bolt, Pachmayr pad, etc.

NIB	Exc.	V.G.	Good	Fair	Poor
1700	1350	—	—	—	—

Robar MK I Tactical Rifle

This model is built on a Remington Model 700 action with a 24" heavy factory barrel. Chambered for the .308 or .223 cartridge. Fitted with a gray Choate Ultimate sniper stock, Robar bipod, and adjustable trigger. Roguard/MP3 finish.

NIB	Exc.	V.G.	Good	Fair	Poor
1720	1350	—	—	—	—

Robar MK II Tactical Rifle

As above but chambered for the .308 cartridge only. Special trigger job and special hand finish of internal parts and chamber.

NIB	Exc.	V.G.	Good	Fair	Poor
2635	2150	—	—	—	—

Robar SR60 Precision Rifle

This model is a fully accurized Remington Mdeol 700 action with bench rest quality barrel and chamber. Custom stock with hand bedding and pillars. Choice of .308 with 20" or 24" barrel and .223 with 24" barrel.

NIB	Exc.	V.G.	Good	Fair	Poor
2960	2400	—	—	—	—

ROBBINS & LAWRENCE

Windsor, Vermont

Pepperbox

A .28 or .31 caliber percussion 5 barrel pistol with the barrel groups measuring 3.5" or 4.5" in length. Ring trigger, blued iron frame with simple scroll engraving and browned barrels, which are marked "Robbins & Lawrence Co. Windsor, VT. Patent. 1849." The barrel groups for this pistol were made in two types: fluted in both calibers, and ribbed in .31 caliber only. Approximately 7,000 were made between 1851 and 1854.

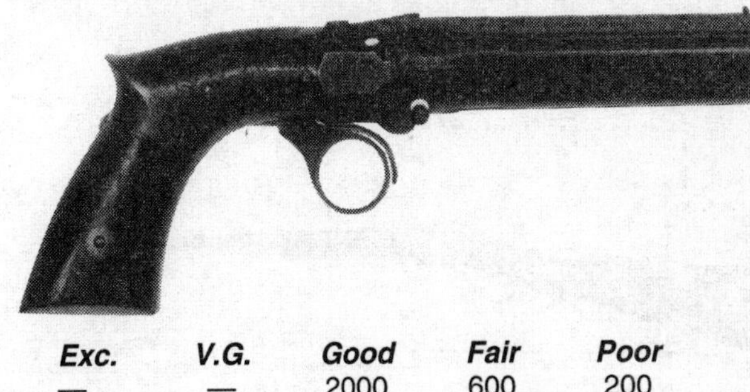

Exc.	V.G.	Good	Fair	Poor
—	—	2000	600	200

ROBERTSON

Philadelphia, Pennsylvania

Pocket Pistol

A .41 caliber single-shot percussion derringer with barrels ranging in length from 3" to 4.5". The barrel marked "Robertson, Phila."

Exc.	V.G.	Good	Fair	Poor
—	—	1500	600	200

ROBINSON ARMAMENT CO.

Salt Lake City, Utah

Super VEPR

This semi-automatic rifle is made in Russia and is chambered for the .308, .223, or 7.62x39mm cartridge. Uses an RPK-type receiver. Chrome lined 21.65" barrel. Walnut thumbhole stock. Black oxide finish. Weight is about 8.5 lbs.

NIB	Exc.	V.G.	Good	Fair	Poor
600	475	—	—	—	—

M-96 Expeditonary Rifle

Chambered for the .223 or 7.62x39mm cartridge. Can use either AK or AR magazines. With quick-change barrel. Adjustable gas operating system. Can interchange calibers without tools. Built in the U.S.A.

NIB	Exc.	V.G.	Good	Fair	Poor
1500	1250	—	—	—	—

M-96 Carbine

As above but with shorter barrel.

NIB	Exc.	V.G.	Good	Fair	Poor
1600	1250	—	—	—	—

M-96 Top Fed

This model has the same specifications as the rifle but with the magazine fitted to the top of the receiver.

NIB	Exc.	V.G.	Good	Fair	Poor
1800	1450	—	—	—	—

ROBINSON, ORVIL

SEE—Adirondack Arms Company

ROBINSON, S.C.

Richmond, Virginia

From December of 1862 through March 1 of 1863, S.C. Robinson produced copies of the Sharps carbine. These arms had an overall length of 38-1/2", with .52 caliber barrels 21-1/2" long. The lockplates were marked "S.C. ROBINSON/ARMS MANUFACTORY/RICHMOND VA/1862" along with the serial number. The barrels were marked forward of the rear sight "S.C. ROBINSON/ARMS MANUFACTORY," as well as "RICHMOND VA/1862" to the rear of the sight. Total number made estimated to be slightly more than 1,900.

In March of 1863, the Robinson factory was taken over by the Confederate States Government. Carbines produced after that date are only stamped with the serial number on their lockplates and "RICHMOND VA" on their barrels. Total number made in excess of 3,400.

Robinson Sharps

Exc.	V.G.	Good	Fair	Poor
—	—	27500	8500	1500

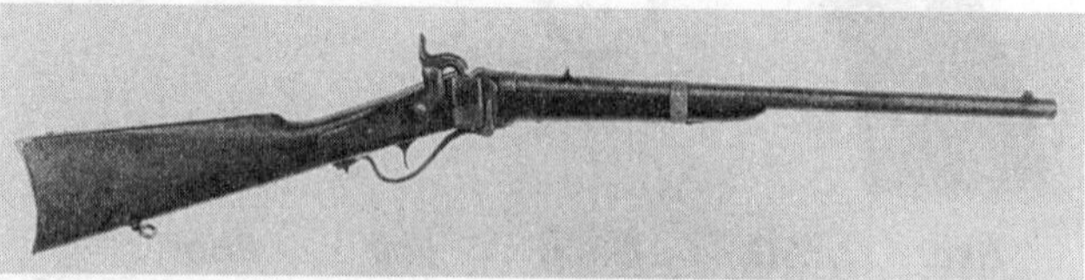

Confederate Sharps

Exc.	V.G.	Good	Fair	Poor
—	—	25000	7500	1500

ROCK ISLAND ARMORY (TRADE NAME OF ARMSCOR)

Pahrump, Nevada

Importer of various centerfire semi-auto pistols manufactured in the Philippines and based on 1911 and CZ designs. All of these pistols typically retail for under $500 new, with used values ranging from 50-75 percent of that, depending on condition.

ROCK RIVER ARMS, INC.

Colona, Illinois

NOTE: This company builds Model 1911-style pistols with a number of custom features and offer many options and upgrades. Consult the company or an expert prior to a sale.

PISTOLS

Elite Commando

Built on a National Match frame with 4" National Match slide with double serrations and lowered ejection port (5" barrel optional). Front strap is 30 lpi. Night sights standard. Aluminum trigger and many more customs features. Checkered cocobolo grips. Guaranteed 2.5" groups at 50 yards. Chambered for the .45 ACP cartridge.

NIB	Exc.	V.G.	Good	Fair	Poor
1725	1300	950	—	—	—

Standard Match

Many of the same features as the above model without the night sights. Also chambered for the .45 ACP cartridge.

NIB	Exc.	V.G.	Good	Fair	Poor
1025	750	—	—	—	—

National Match Hardball

Similar features as above models but with adjustable rear Bomar sight with dovetail front sight. Chambered for .45 ACP cartridge.

NIB	Exc.	V.G.	Good	Fair	Poor
1490	1100	825	—	—	—

REMINDER
You don't have to specialize in Colts and Winchesters to have a nice collection. Collecting Marlin or Mossberg .22 semi-autos, for example, can be just as rewarding.

Bullseye Wadcutter

This model features Rock River slide scope mount. Guaranteed to shoot 1.5" groups at 50 yards. Chambered for .45 ACP.

NIB	Exc.	V.G.	Good	Fair	Poor
1655	1250	925	—	—	—

Basic Limited Match

Similar to the Bullseye Wadcutter but with Bomar adjustable rear sight and dovetail front sights. Chambered for the .45 ACP.

NIB	Exc.	V.G.	Good	Fair	Poor
1700	1300	950	—	—	—

Limited Match

This match pistol comes standard with many custom features. Guaranteed to shoot 1.5" groups at 50 yards. Chambered for the .45 ACP.

NIB	Exc.	V.G.	Good	Fair	Poor
2065	1550	1150	—	—	—

Hi-Cap Basic Limited

This model gives the customer the choice of STI, SVI, Para-Ordnance, or Entréprise frames. Many special features. Chambered for the .45 ACP.

NIB	Exc.	V.G.	Good	Fair	Poor
1895	1500	—	—	—	—

NOTE: Add $200 for Para-Ordnance or Entréprise frames.

Ultimate Match Achiever

This is an IPSC-style pistol with scope and three port muzzle compensator with many special features. Chambered for the .38 Super cartridge.

NIB	Exc.	V.G.	Good	Fair	Poor
2250	1750	—	—	—	—

Match Master Steel

This is a Bianchi-style pistol with scope and three port muzzle-brake. Chambered fo the .38 Super Cartridge.

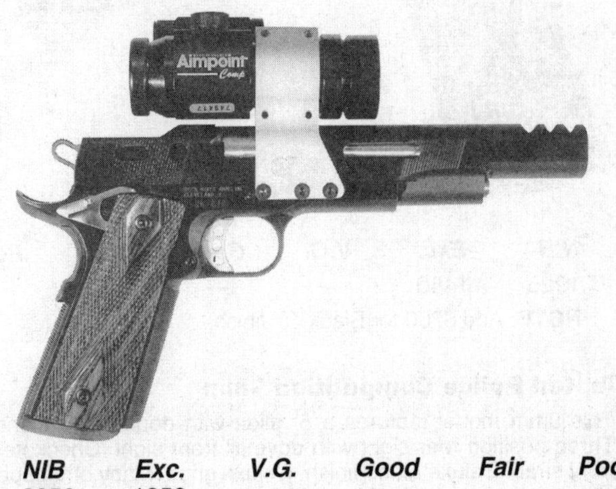

NIB	Exc.	V.G.	Good	Fair	Poor
2350	1850	—	—	—	—

Basic Carry

Introduced in 2005 this .45 ACP model features a 5" match barrel. Checkered front strap, lowered and flared ejection port, Novak rear sight, dehorned for carry, and rosewood grips. Many other special features.

NIB	Exc.	V.G.	Good	Fair	Poor
1525	1150	—	—	—	—

Pro Carry

Similar to Basic Carry but with 4.25", 5" or 6" barrel and choice of Heinie or Novak tritium sights and polished finish; guaranteed to shoot 2.5" group at 50 yards with select ammunition. Other options available.

NIB	Exc.	V.G.	Good	Fair	Poor
1795	—	—	—	—	—

Tactical Pistol

This .45 ACP pistol is fitted with a 5" slide with front serrations and match grade barrel. Heine or Novak rear sight, checkerd front strap, tactical mag catch and safety. Dehorned for carry. Rosewood grips. Introduced in 2005.

NIB	Exc.	V.G.	Good	Fair	Poor
1925	1450	—	—	—	—

NOTE: Add $200 for Black "T" finish.

Limited Police Competition 9mm

This 9mm model features a 5" slide with double serrations. Three position rear sight with dovetail front sight. Checkered front strap. Deluxe blued finish. Deluxe grips. Many other special features. Introduced in 2005.

NIB	Exc.	V.G.	Good	Fair	Poor
2310	1750	—	—	—	—

NOTE: Add $200 for Black "T" finish.

Unlimited Police Competition 9mm

Similar to the above but with additional special features such as a 6" slide. Introduced in 2005.

NIB	Exc.	V.G.	Good	Fair	Poor
2310	1750	—	—	—	—

NOTE: Add $200 for Black "T" finish.

RIFLES

CAR A2

These are AR-15-style rifles chambered for the .223 cartridge. Fitted with a 16" barrel with CAR handguards. Two stage trigger. Choice of A2 or non-collapsible buttstock. Choice of black or green furniture. Weight is about 7 lbs.

NIB	Exc.	V.G.	Good	Fair	Poor
925	750	—	—	—	—

NOTE: Add $25 for non-collapsible buttstock.

CAR A2M

Same as above but with mid-length handguard.

NIB	Exc.	V.G.	Good	Fair	Poor
925	750	—	—	—	—

NOTE: Add $25 for non-collapsible buttstock.

CAR A4

Similar to the models above but with flattop receiver and CAR handguard.

NIB	Exc.	V.G.	Good	Fair	Poor
890	725	—	—	—	—

NOTE: Add $25 for non-collapsible buttstock.

CAR A4M

Flattop receiver with mid-length handguard.

NIB	Exc.	V.G.	Good	Fair	Poor
890	725	—	—	—	—

NOTE: Add $25 for non-collapsible buttstock.

Standard A2

The AR-15-style rifle is fitted with a 20" barrel and chambered for the .223 cartridge. Two stage trigger. Fixed stock and full-length hand guard. Weight is about 8.2 lbs.

NIB	Exc.	V.G.	Good	Fair	Poor
925	750	—	—	—	—

National Match A2

This model features a .22 Wylde chamber with a 20" Wilson air-gauged match stainless steel barrel. A2 receiver. Two stage trigger. Free float high tempeture thermo mold handguard. Match sights. Weight is about 9.7 lbs.

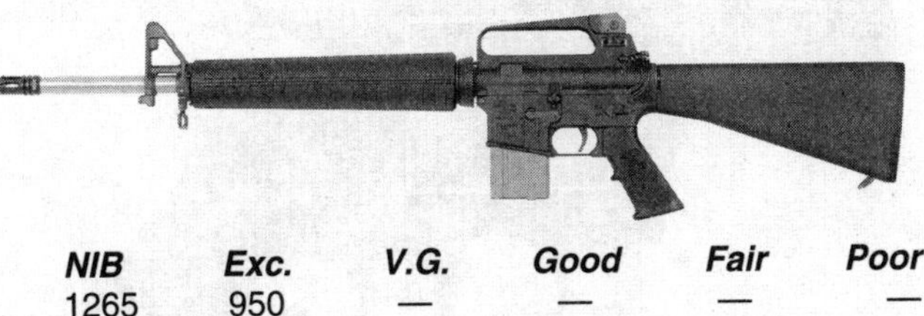

NIB	Exc.	V.G.	Good	Fair	Poor
1265	950	—	—	—	—

Standard A4 Flattop

Same as Standard A2 but with flattop receiver.

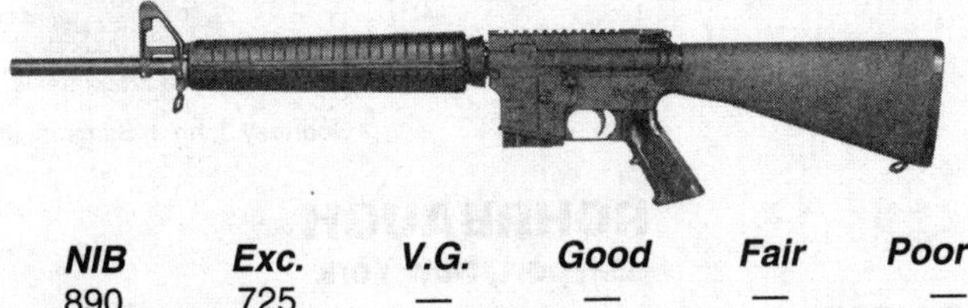

NIB	Exc.	V.G.	Good	Fair	Poor
890	725	—	—	—	—

Varmint Rifle

This flattop model is fitted with a 24" stainless steel barrel without sights. Chambered for the .223 cartridge. Fixed stock. Two-stage trigger. Weight is about 9.5 lbs.

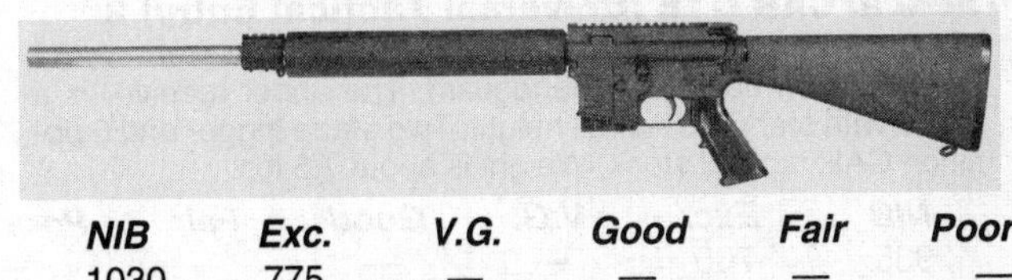

NIB	Exc.	V.G.	Good	Fair	Poor
1030	775	—	—	—	—

Varmint EOP (Elevated Optical Platform)

Chambered for the .223 with a Wylde chamber and fitted with a Wilson air-gauged bull stainless steel barrel. Choice of 16", 18", 20", and 24" barrel lengths. Free float aluminum handguard. National Match two stage trigger. Weight is about 8.2 lbs with 16" barrel and 10 lbs with 24" barrel.

NIB	Exc.	V.G.	Good	Fair	Poor
1025	775	—	—	—	—

NOTE: Add $10 for each barrel lenth for 16".

NM A2-DCM Legal

Fitted with a 20" stainless steel barrel with National Match sleeve and specially selected upper and lower to ensure tight fit. Special high temp handguards. Two-stage trigger. National Match sights. Weight is about 9 lbs.

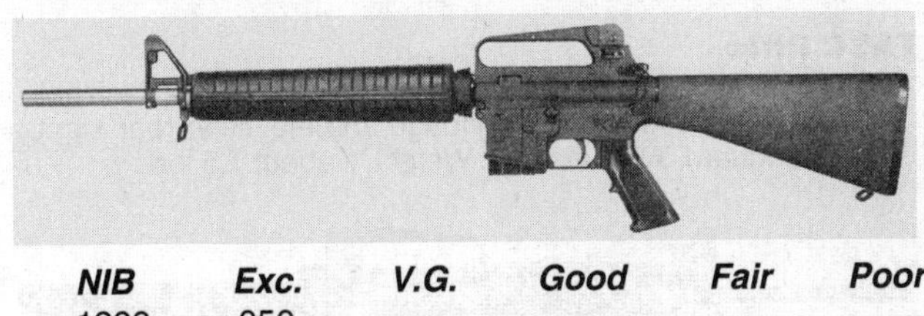

NIB	Exc.	V.G.	Good	Fair	Poor
1200	950	—	—	—	—

Government Model

Chambered for the .223 cartridge and fitted with a 16" Wilson chrome barrel with A2 flash hider. Nation Match two stage trigger. A4 upper receiver. Flip-up rear sight. EOTech M951 light syatem. Surefire M73 Quad Rail handguard, and 6 position tactical CAR stock. Weight is about 8.2 lbs.

NIB	Exc.	V.G.	Good	Fair	Poor
2250	1700	—	—	—	—

Tactical CAR A4

This .223 caliber rifle has a 16" Wilson chrome barrel with A2 flash hider. A4 upper receiver with detachable carry handle. Two stage National Match trigger. R-4 handguard. Six position tactical CAR stock. Weight is about 7.5 lbs.

NIB	Exc.	V.G.	Good	Fair	Poor
950	700	—	—	—	—

Elite CAR A4

As above but with mid-length handguard. Weight is about 7.7 lbs.

NIB	Exc.	V.G.	Good	Fair	Poor
950	700	—	—	—	—

Tactical CAR UTE (Universal Tactical Entry) 2

This .223 caliber rifle has a 16" Wilson chrome barrel with A2 flash hider. It has a R-2 handguard. The upper receiver is a UTE2 with standard A4 rail height. Two stage trigger and 6 position CAR tactical stock. Weight is about 7.5 lbs.

NIB	Exc.	V.G.	Good	Fair	Poor
935	700	—	—	—	—

Elite CAR UTE 2

As above but with mid-length handguard. Weight is about 7.7 lbs.

NIB	Exc.	V.G.	Good	Fair	Poor
935	700	—	—	—	—

Entry Tactical

This .223 model features a 16" Wilson chrome barrel with a R-4 profile. A4 upper receiver with detachable carry handle. National Match two stage trigger. Six position tactical CAR stock. R-4 handguard. Weight is about 7.5 lbs.

NIB	Exc.	V.G.	Good	Fair	Poor
950	700	—	—	—	—

TASC Rifle

This rifle features a 16" Wilson chrome barrel with A2 flash hider. A2 upper receiver with windage and elevation rear sight. R-4 handguard. A2 buttstock. Weight is about 7.5 lbs.

NIB	Exc.	V.G.	Good	Fair	Poor
890	700	—	—	—	—

ROGERS & SPENCER

Utica, New York

Army Revolver

A .44 caliber 6-shot percussion revolver with a 7.5" octagonal barrel. The barrel marked "Rogers & Spencer/Utica, N.Y." Blued, case hardened hammer with walnut grips bearing the inspector's mark "RPB." Approximately 5,800 were made between 1863 and 1865.

Courtesy Milwaukee Public Museum, Milwaukee, Wisconsin

Exc.	V.G.	Good	Fair	Poor
—	2200	1250	550	250

ROGUE RIFLE COMPANY

Prospect, Oregon

SEE—Chipmunk Rifles

ROGUE RIVER RIFLEWORKS

Paso Robles, California

Boxlock Double Rifle

These rifles are custom fitted and available in any barrel length or caliber from .22 Hornet to .577 NE. Anson & Deeley boxlocks. Choice of finish, forend, engraving, wood, and various other options. Each rifle should be appraised individually before a sale. Prices listed are for basic rifle with no extras.

NIB	Exc.	V.G.	Good	Fair	Poor
12500	9000	—	—	—	—

Sidelock Double Rifle

These rifles are custom fitted and available in any barrel length or caliber from .22 Hornet to .577 NE. Holland & Holland pattern sidelocks. Choice of finish, forend, engraving, wood, and various other options. Each rifle should be appraised individually before a sale. Prices listed are for basic rifle with no extras.

NIB	Exc.	V.G.	Good	Fair	Poor
18500	12500	—	—	—	—

ROHM GMBH

Sonthein/Brenz, Germany

This firm produced a variety of revolvers marked with various trade names that were imported into the United States prior to 1968. Essentially, they are of three types: 1) solid-frame, gate-loading models; 2) solid-frame, swingout-cylinder revolvers; and 3) solid-frame, swingout-cylinder revolvers. They are of low quality and little collector interest.

Courtesy John J. Stimson, Jr.

ROHRBAUGH

Bayport, New York

R9/R9S

Introduced in 2004 this is a very small 9mm pistol. Offered with or without sights. Magazine capacity is 6 rounds. Barrel length is 2.9". Height is 3.7", length is 5.2", slide width is .812", and weight is about 12.8 oz.

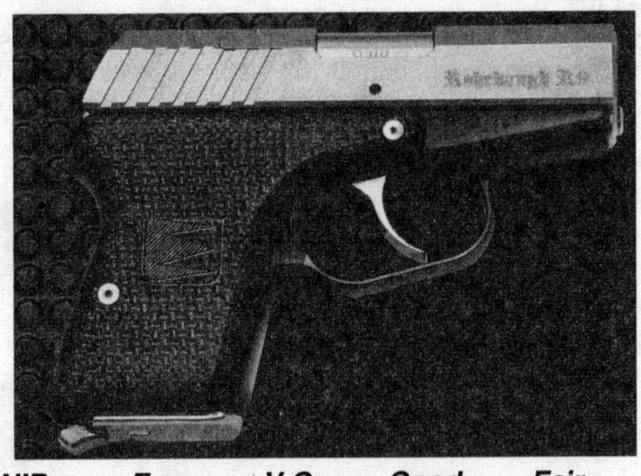

NIB	Exc.	V.G.	Good	Fair	Poor
945	—	—	—	—	—

ROMERWERKE
Suhl, Germany

Romer
A .22 caliber semi-automatic pistol with a 2.5" or 6.5" barrel and 7-shot magazine. The barrels are interchangeable and marked "Kal. .22 Long Rifle," the slide marked "Romerwerke Suhl." Blued, with plastic grips. Manufactured between 1924 and 1926.

Exc.	V.G.	Good	Fair	Poor
550	450	400	300	225

RONGE, J. B.
Liege, Belgium

Bulldog
A .32, .380, or .45 caliber double-action revolver with a 3" barrel. Unmarked except for the monogram "RF" on the grips. Various trade names have been noted on these revolvers and are believed to have been applied by retailers. Manufactured from 1880 to 1910.

Exc.	V.G.	Good	Fair	Poor
200	150	100	75	50

ROSS RIFLE CO.
Quebec, Canada

Designed in 1896 by Sir Charles Ross, this straight pull rifle was manufactured in a variety of styles. Due to problems with the bolt design, it never proved popular and was discontinued in 1915.

Mark I
Barrel length 28", .303 caliber with a "Harris Controlled Platform Magazine" that can be depressed by an external lever to facilitate loading.

Courtesy Buffalo Bill Historical Center, Cody, Wyoming

Exc.	V.G.	Good	Fair	Poor
500	350	250	150	100

Mark I Carbine
As above, with a 22" barrel.

Exc.	V.G.	Good	Fair	Poor
450	300	250	200	150

Mark 2
As above, with a modified rear sight.

Exc.	V.G.	Good	Fair	Poor
500	350	250	150	100

Mark 3
Introduced in 1910 with improved lockwork and stripper clip guides.

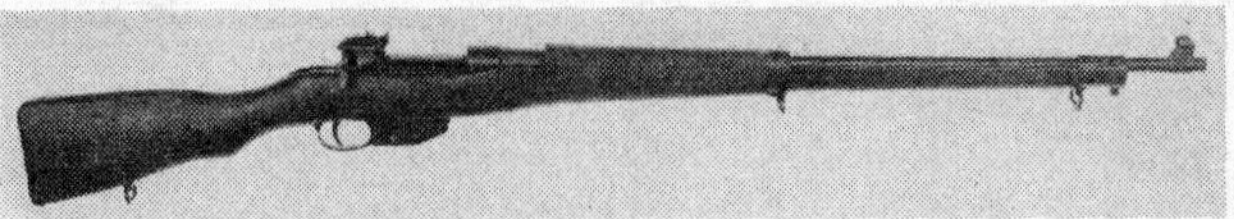

Courtesy Buffalo Bill Historical Center, Cody, Wyoming

Exc.	V.G.	Good	Fair	Poor
1200	875	675	375	175

Mark 3B
As above, with a magazine cut-off.

Exc.	V.G.	Good	Fair	Poor
450	300	250	200	150

Sporting Rifle
A .280 Ross or .303 caliber straight pole sporting rifle with a 24" barrel and open sights. Blued with a checkered walnut stock.

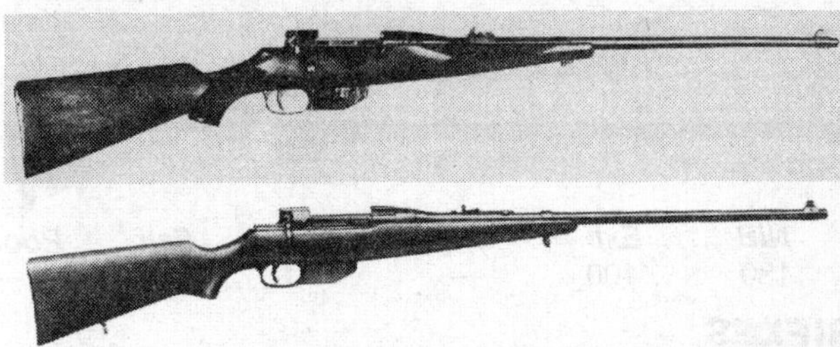

Courtesy Buffalo Bill Historical Center, Cody, Wyoming

Exc.	V.G.	Good	Fair	Poor
775	550	300	150	125

ROSSI, AMADEO
São Leopoldo

NOTE: Rossi handguns are manufactured under license by Taurus.

SHOTGUNS

Overland Shotgun
An exposed hammer sidelock 12, 20 or .410 bore double-barrel shotgun with 26" or 28" barrels and double triggers. Manual extractors. Blued with a walnut stock. Discontinued in 1988.

NIB	Exc.	V.G.	Good	Fair	Poor
250	225	200	150	100	75

Squire Shotgun
A 12, 20 or .410 bore double-barrel shotgun with 20", 26", or 28" barrels, double triggers and manual ejectors. Blued with a walnut stock.

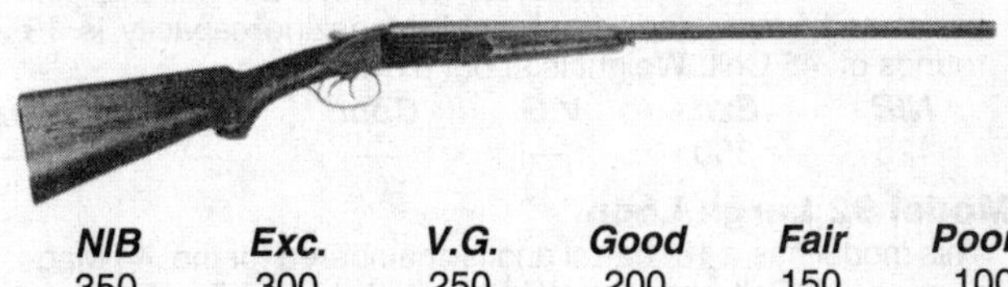

NIB	Exc.	V.G.	Good	Fair	Poor
350	300	250	200	150	100

Field Grade Shotgun
This is a single-shot tip-open gun with oil-finish hardwood stock, low profile hammer, and pistol grip. No checkering. Of-

fered in 12 and 20 gauge, as well as .410 bore. Barrel length is 28". Weight is about 5.25 lbs. for 12 and 20 gauge and 4 lbs. for the .410 bore.

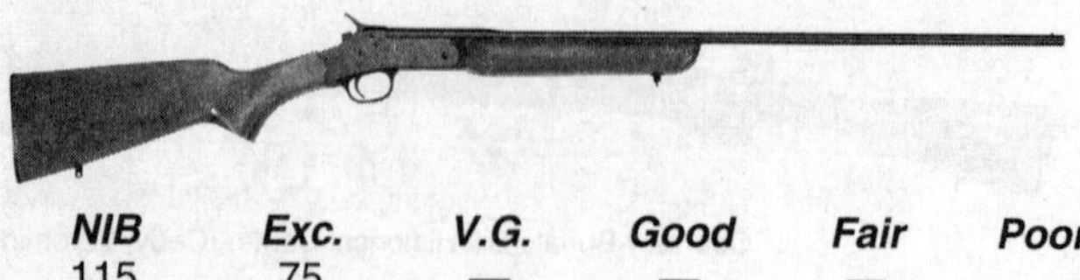

NIB	Exc.	V.G.	Good	Fair	Poor
115	75	—	—	—	—

Youth Model Shotgun

Same as above but with shorter length of pull and 22" barrel. Offered in 20 gauge and .410 bore only. Weight for 20 gauge is about 5 lbs. and 3.75 lbs. for the .410 bore.

NIB	Exc.	V.G.	Good	Fair	Poor
115	75	—	—	—	—

Match Pair Combo Guns

This model matches a single-barrel shotgun with a .22 LR barrel. Offered in 12/.22, 20/.22, and .410/.22. Adjustable sights on the rifle barrel. Blued finish.

NIB	Exc.	V.G.	Good	Fair	Poor
130	100	—	—	—	—

RIFLES

Model 92

A copy of the Winchester Model 1892, chambered for .357 Magnum, .44 Magnum or .44-40 with either a 16" or 20" barrel. Blued with a walnut stock. The engraved version of this model is worth approximately 20 percent more than the values listed.

NIB	Exc.	V.G.	Good	Fair	Poor
300	225	175	150	100	75

NOTE: Add $50 for a 20" stainless steel version introduced in 1997.

Model 92 Rifle

Introduced in 1997 this model is fitted with a 24" half octagon barrel and brass blade front sight. Magazine capacity is 13 rounds of .45 Colt. Weight is about 6.8 lbs.

NIB	Exc.	V.G.	Good	Fair	Poor
425	350	—	—	—	—

Model 92 Large Loop

This model has a 16" barrel and is chambered for the .44 Magnum or .45 Colt cartridge. Weight is about 5.5 lbs. Finish is blue. Introduced in 1997.

NIB	Exc.	V.G.	Good	Fair	Poor
350	250	—	—	—	—

Model 62

A copy of the Winchester Model 1890 rifle with either 16.5" or 23" round or octagonal barrels. Blued or stainless steel with a walnut stock.

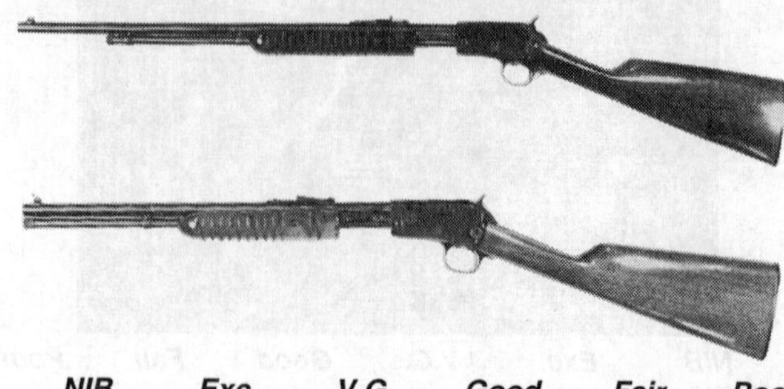

NIB	Exc.	V.G.	Good	Fair	Poor
200	175	150	125	100	75

Model 59

As above, in .22 Magnum caliber.

NIB	Exc.	V.G.	Good	Fair	Poor
210	175	150	125	100	75

Model 65

Similar to the Model 92, but chambered for either the .44 Special or .44 Magnum cartridge. Barrel length 20". Blued with a walnut stock. Introduced in 1989.

NIB	Exc.	V.G.	Good	Fair	Poor
300	250	200	175	150	125

Single-Shot Rifle

Offered in a variety of configurations and chambered for the .22 LR, .22 Magnum, .357 Magnum, .44 Magnum, .45 Colt, .223 Rem., and .243 calibers. Fitted with 23" barrel with wood stock and choice of matte blue or stainless steel finish. Weight varies from 4.75 lbs. to 6.25 lbs. depending on caliber.

NIB	Exc.	V.G.	Good	Fair	Poor
225	175	125	100	—	—

NOTE: For stainless steel add $30, for .357 and .44 add $10. For .223 or .243 add $30.

Single Shot Rifle—Heavy Barrel

Chambered for the .223, .243, and .22-250. This rifle is fitted with a 23" heavy barrel with plain wood stock. Matte blue finish. Weight is about 7 lbs. introduced in 2005.

NIB	Exc.	V.G.	Good	Fair	Poor
230	175	—	—	—	—

Muzzleloading Rifle

This rifle has a .50 caliber bore and is fitted with a 23" barrel. Hardwood stock with recoil pad. Weight is about 6.3 lbs. Introduced in 2003. Blue or stainless steel.

NIB	Exc.	V.G.	Good	Fair	Poor
165	130	—	—	—	—

NOTE: For matte stainless steel finish add $35.

Muzzleloader Matched Pair

This is a .50 caliber muzzleloader with an extra 20 gauge or .243 or .270 barrel. All matched pairs come with blued finish. Price listed is for 20 gauge barrel.

NIB	Exc.	V.G.	Good	Fair	Poor
210	170	—	—	—	—

NOTE: For .243 add $40 and for .270 add $150.

Rossi Blued Synthetic Matched Pair

Single-shot combo outfit consisting of interchangeable rifle and shotgun barrels. Synthetic stock, blued barrel and receiver. Combinations include 12 or 20 ga./.22LR, .22 WMR, .17 HMR, .223, .243, .270, .308, .30-06 and .410/.22 LR or .410/.17 HMR. Youth and full-size versions available. MSRP: 225

Rossi Stainless Synthetic Matched Pair

Single-shot combo outfit consisting of interchangeable rifle and shotgun barrels. Synthetic stock, stainless barrel and receiver. Combinations include 12 or 20 ga./.22LR, .22 WMR, .17 HMR, .223, .243, .270, .308, .30-06 and .410/.22 LR or .410/.17 HMR. Youth and full-size versions available. MSRP: 225

HANDGUNS

Model 51

A .22 caliber double-action revolver with a 6" barrel, adjustable sights and a 6-shot cylinder. Blued with walnut grips. Imported prior to 1986.

Exc.	V.G.	Good	Fair	Poor
125	100	75	50	40

Model 511 Sportsman

As above, with a 4" barrel and made of stainless steel with walnut grips. Introduced in 1986.

NIB	Exc.	V.G.	Good	Fair	Poor
225	200	150	125	100	75

Model 461

This is a 6-round revolver chambered for the .357 Magnum cartridge. Fitted with a 2" barrel. Rubber grips and blued finish. Weight is about 26 oz.

NIB	Exc.	V.G.	Good	Fair	Poor
300	225	—	—	—	—

Model 462

Same as above but with stainless steel finish.

NIB	Exc.	V.G.	Good	Fair	Poor
350	275	—	—	—	—

Model 68S

This new version was introduced in 1993 and features a shrouded ejector rod and fixed sights. Chambered for the .38 Special cartridge, it is offered with either 2" or 3" barrel. Grips wood or rubber. Finish is blue or nickel. Weighs about 23 oz.

NIB	Exc.	V.G.	Good	Fair	Poor
175	150	125	100	75	60

Model 69

As above, in .32 Smith & Wesson caliber with a 3" barrel and 6-shot cylinder. Imported prior to 1986.

Exc.	V.G.	Good	Fair	Poor
125	100	75	50	40

Model 70

As above, in .22 caliber with a 3" barrel and 6-shot cylinder. Imported prior to 1986.

Exc.	V.G.	Good	Fair	Poor
125	100	75	50	40

Model 84

A stainless steel, .38 Special caliber double-action revolver with ribbed 3" or 4" barrel. Blued with walnut grips. Imported in 1985 and 1986.

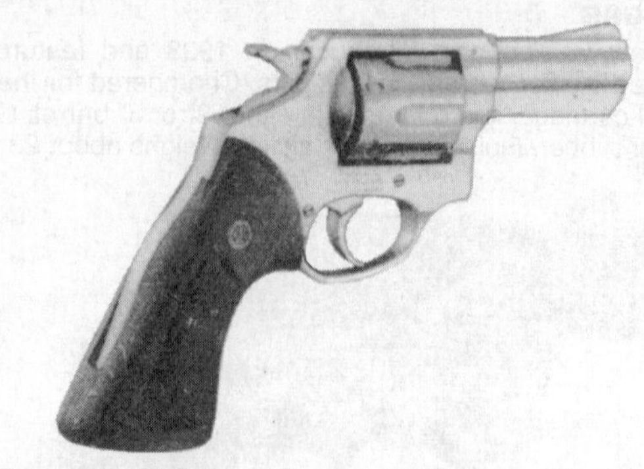

Exc.	V.G.	Good	Fair	Poor
175	150	125	100	75

Model 851

As above, with either a 3" or 4" ventilated rib barrel and adjustable sights.

NIB	Exc.	V.G.	Good	Fair	Poor
200	175	150	125	100	75

Model 68

A .38 Special double-action revolver with a 2" or 3" barrel and 5-shot cylinder. Blued or nickel-plated with walnut grips.

NIB	Exc.	V.G.	Good	Fair	Poor
185	150	125	100	75	50

Model 31

A .38 Special caliber double-action revolver with a 4" barrel and 5-shot cylinder. Blued or nickel-plated with walnut grips. Imported prior to 1986.

Exc.	V.G.	Good	Fair	Poor
125	100	75	50	40

Model 677

This model was first introduced in 1997 and is chambered for the .357 Magnum cartridge. It has a matte blue finish with 2" barrel and black rubber grips. Weight is about 26 oz.

NIB	Exc.	V.G.	Good	Fair	Poor
250	200	—	—	—	—

Model 88S

Introduced in 1993 this improved model has the same features of the Model 68 with the addition of a stainless finish. It is chambered for the .38 Special cartridge and is fitted with either a 2" or 3" barrel. Available with either wood or rubber grips. Cylinder holds 5 cartridges. Weighs approximately 22 oz.

NIB	Exc.	V.G.	Good	Fair	Poor
200	175	150	125	100	75

Model 351

This revolver is chambered for the .38 Special +P cartridge. Fitted with a 2" barrel and rubber grips. 5 round cylinder. Blued finish. Weight is about 24 oz.

NIB	Exc.	V.G.	Good	Fair	Poor
250	200	—	—	—	—

Model 352

Same as above but with stainless steel finish.

NIB	Exc.	V.G.	Good	Fair	Poor
300	225	—	—	—	—

Model 951

A .38 Special caliber double-action revolver with a 3" or 4" ventilated rib barrel and 6-shot cylinder. Blued with walnut grips. Introduced in 1985.

NIB	Exc.	V.G.	Good	Fair	Poor
200	175	150	125	100	75

Model 971

As above, in .357 Magnum caliber with a solid ribbed 4" barrel and enclosed ejector rod. Adjustable sights. Blued with walnut grips. Introduced in 1988.

NIB	Exc.	V.G.	Good	Fair	Poor
225	175	150	125	100	75

Model 971 Comp

Introduced in 1993. Similar to the Model 971 with the addition of a compensator on a 3.25" barrel. Overall length is 9" and weight is 32 oz. Chambered for .357 Magnum cartridge.

NIB	Exc.	V.G.	Good	Fair	Poor
200	175	150	125	100	75

Model 971 Stainless

As above, but constructed of stainless steel with checkered black rubber grips. Introduced in 1989.

NIB	Exc.	V.G.	Good	Fair	Poor
225	200	150	125	100	75

Model 972

Revolver; 6-shot polished stainless double-action .357 Magnum. Adjustable rear sight and red insert on front sight. 6" barrel, rubber grip, 35 oz. Uses Taurus security system. Introduced 2006. MSRP: 410

Model 877

Introduced in 1996 this 6-shot revolver is chambered for the .357 magnum cartridge. It is fitted with a 2" heavy barrel. Stainless steel with black rubber grips. Weight is about 26 oz.

NIB	Exc.	V.G.	Good	Fair	Poor
275	200	175	150	100	80

Model 89

As above, in .32 Smith & Wesson caliber with a 3" barrel.

NIB	Exc.	V.G.	Good	Fair	Poor
200	175	150	125	100	75

Model 971 VRC (vented rib compensator)

Introduced in 1996 this variation features a choice of a 6", 4", or 2.5" vent rib barrel with integral compensator. Stainless steel with black rubber grips. Weight is from 30 oz. to 39 oz. depending on barrel length.

NIB	Exc.	V.G.	Good	Fair	Poor
300	250	200	175	150	100

Model 988 Cyclops

Introduced in 1997 this model is chambered for the .357 Magnum cartridge and is fitted with four recessed compensator ports on each side of the muzzle. Offered in 8" or 6" barrel lengths this six-shot double-action revolver weighs about 44 ozs. for the 6" model and 51 ozs. for the 8" model. Stainless steel finish.

Cyclops with scope mounted

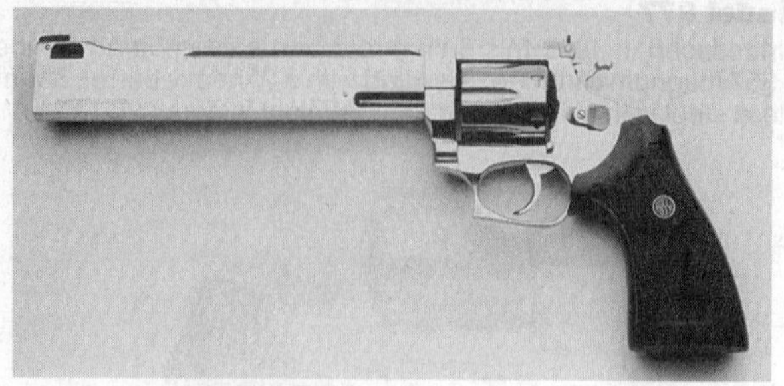

NIB	Exc.	V.G.	Good	Fair	Poor
425	350	—	—	—	—

Model 720

This double-action revolver is chambered for the .44 Special and features a five-round cylinder and 3" barrel. Overall length is 8" and weight is about 27.5 oz. Finish is stainless steel.

NIB	Exc.	V.G.	Good	Fair	Poor
250	200	175	150	125	100

ROTH-SAUER

SEE—J. P. Sauer & Son

ROTH-STEYR

Austria-Hungary
SEE—Steyr

ROTTME, TH.

SEE—Austrian Military Firearms

ROTTWEIL

Rottweil, West Germany

Model 650

A 12 gauge over-and-under shotgun with 28" ventilated rib barrels, screw-in choke tubes, single-selective trigger, and automatic ejectors. The receiver is engraved and case hardened. Checkered stock of well figured walnut. Imported prior to 1987.

Exc.	V.G.	Good	Fair	Poor
700	550	400	300	150

Model 72

A 12 gauge over-and-under shotgun with 28" ventilated rib barrels, screw-in choke tubes, single-selective trigger and automatic ejectors. Blued with a well figured checkered walnut stock. Imported prior to 1988.

Exc.	V.G.	Good	Fair	Poor
1750	1200	750	500	250

Model 72 American Skeet

As above, with a 26.75" ventilated rib barrel, single-selective trigger, and automatic ejectors. The receiver is also engraved. Imported prior to 1988.

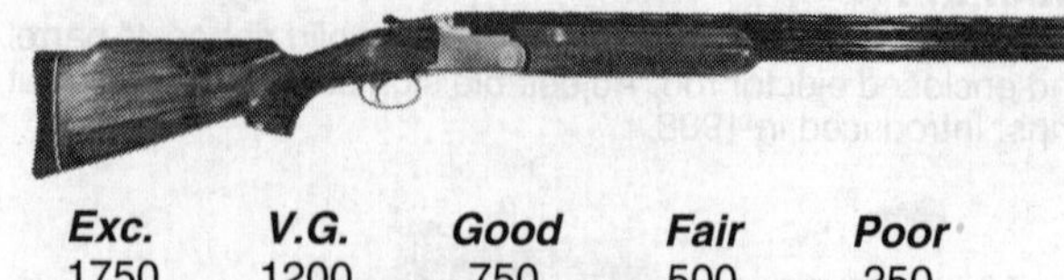

Exc.	V.G.	Good	Fair	Poor
1750	1200	750	500	250

Model 72 Adjustable American Trap

As above, with a 34" ventilated rib barrel, adjustable to point of impact. Imported prior to 1987.

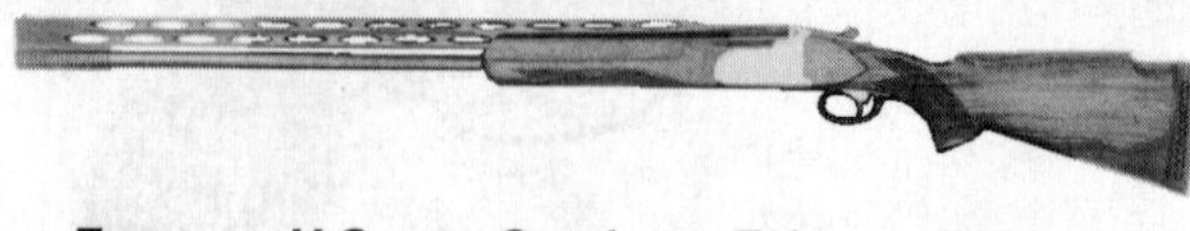

Exc.	V.G.	Good	Fair	Poor
1500	1000	600	300	150

Model 72 American Trap

As above, without the barrel being adjustable to the point of impact.

Exc.	V.G.	Good	Fair	Poor
1750	1200	750	500	250

Model 72 International Skeet

As above, with 26.75" ventilated rib barrels choked Skeet. Imported prior to 1988.

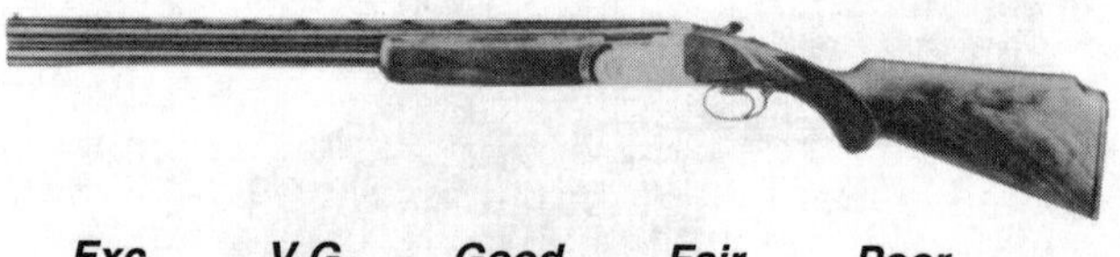

Exc.	V.G.	Good	Fair	Poor
1750	1200	750	500	250

Model 72 International Trap

As above, with 30" high ventilated rib barrels that are choked Improved Modified and Full. Imported prior to 1988.

Exc.	V.G.	Good	Fair	Poor
1750	1200	750	500	250

ROYAL AMERICAN SHOTGUNS

Woodland Hills, California

Model 100

A 12 or 20 gauge over-and-under shotgun with 26", 28", or 30" ventilated rib barrels, double triggers and extractors. Blued with a walnut stock. Imported from 1985 to 1987.

Exc.	V.G.	Good	Fair	Poor
450	300	250	175	150

Model 100AE

As above, with a single trigger and automatic ejectors.

Exc.	V.G.	Good	Fair	Poor
550	375	275	200	175

Model 600

A 12, 20, 28 or. 410 bore double-barrel shotgun with 25", 26", 28", or 30" ventilated rib barrels, double triggers and extractors. Blued with a walnut stock. Imported from 1985 to 1987.

Exc.	V.G.	Good	Fair	Poor
500	325	275	200	175

Model 800

A 28 or .410 bore detachable sidelock double-barrel shotgun with 24", 26", or 28" barrels, double triggers and automatic ejectors. Blued, French case hardened with an English-style walnut stock. Imported from 1985 to 1987.

Exc.	V.G.	Good	Fair	Poor
1250	800	600	475	400

RUBY ARMS COMPANY

Guernica, Spain

Ruby

A 6.35mm or 7.35mm caliber semi-automatic pistol with a 3.5" barrel and 6-shot magazine. The slide marked "Ruby." Blued with plastic grips.

Exc.	V.G.	Good	Fair	Poor
200	150	100	75	50

RUGER

SEE—Sturm, Ruger Co.

RUPERTUS, JACOB

Philadelphia, Pennsylvania

Navy Revolver

This model is equally as rare as the Army model. It is chambered for .36 caliber percussion. Otherwise it is quite similar in appearance to the Army model. There were approximately 12 manufactured in 1859. Both of these revolvers were manufactured for test purposes and were not well-received by the military, so further production was not accomplished.

Exc.	V.G.	Good	Fair	Poor
—	—	10500	5000	1250

Pocket Model Revolver

This is a smaller version of the Army and Navy model, chambered for .25 caliber percussion. It has no loading lever and has a 3-1/8" octagonal barrel. There were approximately 12 manufactured in 1859.

Exc.	V.G.	Good	Fair	Poor
—	—	7500	3250	950

Double-Barrel Pocket Pistol

A .22 caliber double-barrel pistol with 3" round barrels and a spur trigger. The hammer fitted with a sliding firing pin. Blued with walnut grips.

Exc.	V.G.	Good	Fair	Poor
—	—	1750	750	200

Army Revolver

This is an extremely rare revolver chambered for .44 caliber percussion. It has a 7.25" octagon barrel with an integral loading lever that pivots to the side instead of downward. The hammer is mounted on the side, and there is a pellet priming device located on the backstrap. There is only one nipple on the breech that lines up with the top of the cylinder. The cylinder is unfluted and holds 6-shots. The finish is blued, with walnut grips; and the frame is marked "Patented April 19, 1859." There were less than 12 manufactured in 1859. It would behoove one to secure a qualified independent appraisal if a transaction were contemplated.

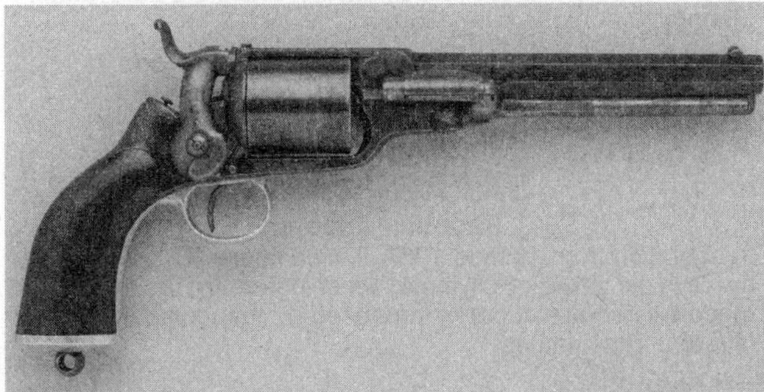

Courtesy Greg Martin Auctions

Exc.	V.G.	Good	Fair	Poor
—	—	10500	5000	1500

Single-Shot Pocket Pistol

A .22, .32, .38, or .41 rimfire single-shot pistol with half-octagonal barrels, ranging in length from 3" to 5". The barrel marked "Rupertus Pat'd. Pistol Mfg. Co. Philadelphia." Blued with walnut grips. Approximately 3,000 were made from 1870 to 1885.

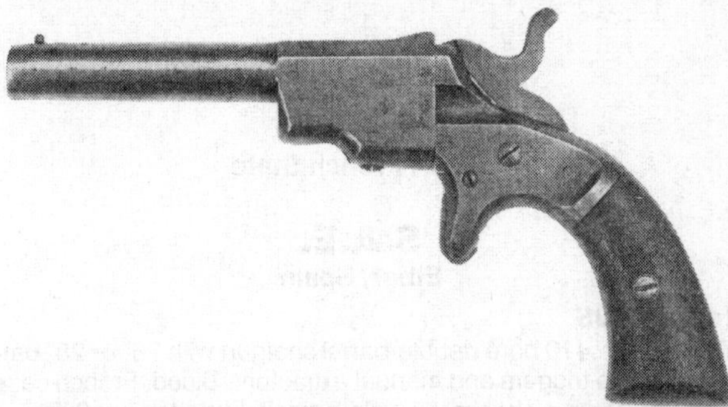

Exc.	V.G.	Good	Fair	Poor
—	—	500	200	75

NOTE: The .41 caliber variety is worth approximately 200 percent more than the values listed.

Spur Trigger Revolver

A .22 caliber spur trigger revolver with a 2.75" round barrel and unfluted cylinder. The top strap marked "Empire Pat. Nov. 21, 71." Blued or nickel-plated with walnut grips. A .41 caliber spur trigger revolver with a 2-7/8" round barrel and a 5-shot fluted cylinder. Blued or nickel-plated with walnut grips. The top strap marked "Empire 41" and the barrel "J. Rupertus Phila. Pa." Manufactured during the 1870s and 1880s.

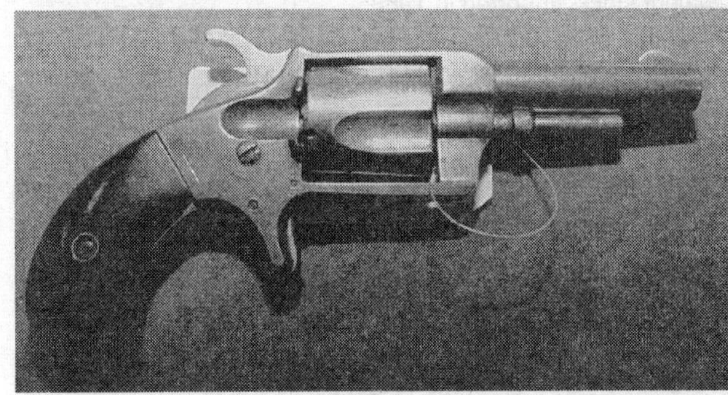

Exc.	V.G.	Good	Fair	Poor
—	—	400	150	75

NOTE: The .41 caliber variety is worth approximately 25 percent more than the values listed.

RWS

Nurenberg, Germany
Dynamit Nobel

Model 820 S

A .22 caliber target rifle with 24" heavy barrel and adjustable aperture sights. The trigger is fully adjustable. Three-position adjustable match stock with stippled pistol grip and forend. Discontinued in 1986.

NIB	Exc.	V.G.	Good	Fair	Poor
1250	800	700	550	450	250

Model 820 SF

As above with a heavier barrel. Discontinued in 1986.

NIB	Exc.	V.G.	Good	Fair	Poor
1000	800	600	500	400	250

Model 820 K

Offhand "Running Boar" model of the above with a lighter barrel. Furnished without sights. Discontinued in 1986.

NIB	Exc.	V.G.	Good	Fair	Poor
950	750	600	500	400	250

S.A.C.M.

SEE—French State

S.A.E.

Eibar, Spain

Model 210S

A 12, 20 or .410 bore double-barrel shotgun with 26" or 28" barrels, double triggers and manual extractors. Blued, French case hardened with a checkered walnut stock. Imported in 1988.

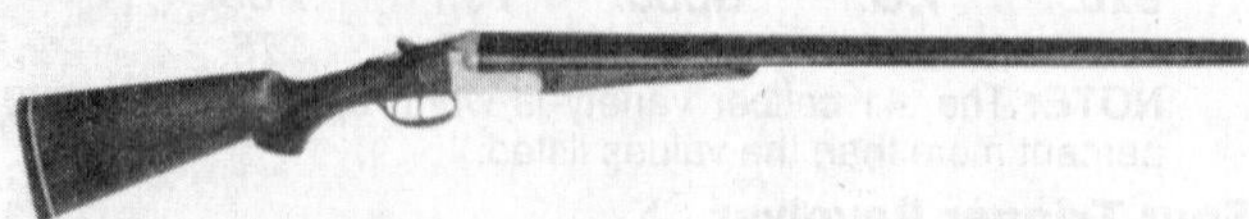

Exc.	V.G.	Good	Fair	Poor
425	375	300	225	150

Model 340X

A Holland & Holland-style sidelock 10 or 20 gauge double-barrel shotgun with 26" barrels, double triggers and automatic ejectors. Blued, case hardened with a checkered English style walnut stock. Imported in 1988.

Exc.	V.G.	Good	Fair	Poor
800	650	500	400	200

Model 209E

As above, with the exception that it was also chambered for .410 bore cartridges, and was more finely engraved. Imported in 1988.

Exc.	V.G.	Good	Fair	Poor
1000	800	700	550	250

Model 70

A 12 or 20 gauge over-and-under shotgun with 26" ventilated rib barrels screw-in choke tubes, single trigger and automatic ejectors. The modestly engraved receiver is either blued or French case hardened. Stock of finely figured walnut. Imported in 1988.

Exc.	V.G.	Good	Fair	Poor
450	300	250	200	100

Model 66C

A 12 gauge over-and-under shotgun with 26" or 30" ventilated rib barrels choked for skeet or trap, single trigger and automatic ejectors. The boxlock action fitted with false sideplates, which are engraved and gold inlaid. Blued with a checkered Monte Carlo-style stock and a beavertail forearm. Imported in 1988.

Exc.	V.G.	Good	Fair	Poor
1000	800	700	575	300

S.E.A.M.

Eibar, Spain

This retailer sold a number of pistols produced by the firm of Urizar prior to 1935.

Praga

A 7.65 caliber semi-automatic pistol marked "Praga Cal 7.65" on the slide. Blued with plastic grips impressed with the trademark S.E.A.M.

Exc.	V.G.	Good	Fair	Poor
200	150	125	90	65

S.E.A.M.

A 6.35mm semi-automatic pistol with a 2" barrel. The slide marked "Fabrica de Armas SEAM." Blued with black plastic grips, having the trademark "SEAM" cast into them.

Exc.	V.G.	Good	Fair	Poor
200	150	125	90	65

Silesia

As above, but of 7.65mm caliber with a 3" barrel and having the word "Silesia" stamped on the slide.

Exc.	V.G.	Good	Fair	Poor
200	150	125	90	65

S.W.D., INC.

Atlanta, Georgia

Cobray M-11

A 9mm semi-automatic pistol with a 32-round magazine. Parkerized finish.

Exc.	V.G.	Good	Fair	Poor
300	200	175	125	100

M-11 Carbine

As above, with a 16.25" barrel enclosed in a shroud and fitted with a telescoping wire stock.

Exc.	V.G.	Good	Fair	Poor
325	225	200	150	125

Terminator

A 12 or 20 gauge single-shot shotgun with an 18" cylinder bored barrel. Parkerized finish.

Exc.	V.G.	Good	Fair	Poor
100	80	70	60	50

SABATTI

SEE—European American Armory

SACKET, D. D.

Westfield, Massachusetts

Under Hammer Pistol

A .34 or .36 single-shot percussion pistol with a half octagonal 3" or 4" barrel marked "D. D. Sacket/Westfield/Cast Steel." Manufactured during the 1850s.

Exc.	V.G.	Good	Fair	Poor
—	—	1100	500	150

SAFARI ARMS

Phoenix, Arizona

In operation from 1978 to 1987, this company was purchased by Olympic Arms of Olympia, Washington, in 1987 and the models listed are currently produced by that company under different trade names.

Enforcer

A .45 caliber semi-automatic pistol with a 3.9" barrel and 5-shot magazine. Patterned after the Colt Model 1911. Blued, Armaloy, electroless nickel-plate or Parkerized finish with checkered walnut or neoprene grips.

This symbol denotes "Sleepers" with rapidly-rising values and/or significant collector potential.

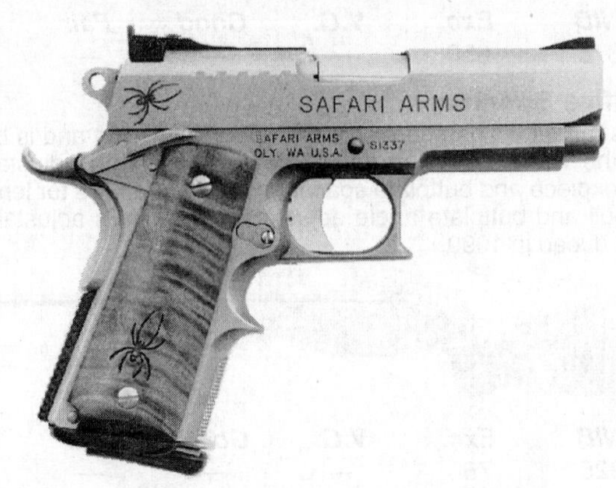

NIB	Exc.	V.G.	Good	Fair	Poor
700	600	500	400	350	150

Match Master

As above, with a 5" barrel.

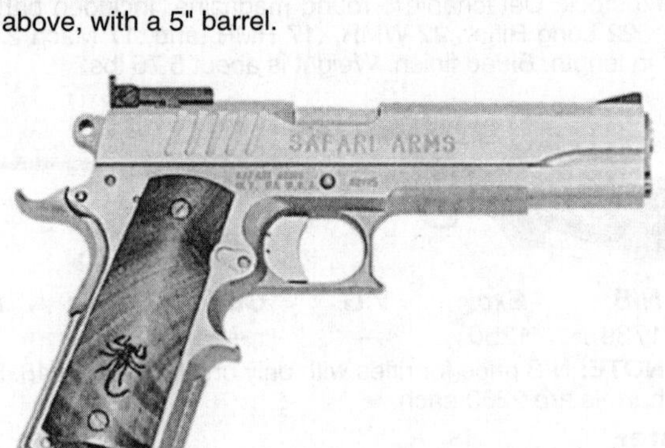

NIB	Exc.	V.G.	Good	Fair	Poor
700	600	500	400	350	150

Black Widow

As above, with ivory Micarta grips etched with a black widow.

NIB	Exc.	V.G.	Good	Fair	Poor
700	600	500	400	350	150

Model 81

As above, without the grip etching. Also offered in .38 caliber.

NIB	Exc.	V.G.	Good	Fair	Poor
800	700	600	500	400	200

Model 81L

As above, with a 6" barrel.

NIB	Exc.	V.G.	Good	Fair	Poor
850	750	650	550	450	200

Ultimate Unlimited

A bolt-action single-shot pistol with a 15" barrel chambered for variety of cartridges. Blued with a laminated stock.

NIB	Exc.	V.G.	Good	Fair	Poor
850	750	650	550	450	200

Survivor I Conversion Unit

A conversion unit lifted to the Model 1911 frame that alters that pistol to a bolt-action carbine. Barrel length 16.25", caliber .223, folding stock.

NIB	Exc.	V.G.	Good	Fair	Poor
300	275	250	200	150	100

Counter Sniper Rifle

A .308 caliber bolt-action target rifle with a heavy 26" barrel and 20-round detachable magazine. Matte blued with a colored composite stock.

NIB	Exc.	V.G.	Good	Fair	Poor
1200	1050	850	650	450	200

SAKO

Riihimaki, Finland

NOTE: Arms produced by this company prior to 1972 are worth approximately 25 percent more than arms of the same type produced thereafter. Prices for fair and poor condition reflect the worth of the action.

In 2000 Beretta Holding Co. purchased Sako and distributes the product line through Beretta U.S.A.

Standard Sporter

A bolt-action magazine rifle produced in a wide variety of calibers with varying barrel lengths, etc. Blued with checkered walnut stocks.

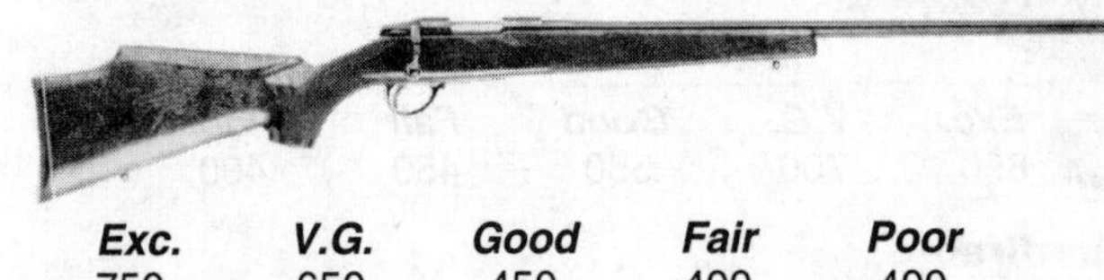

Exc.	V.G.	Good	Fair	Poor
750	650	450	400	400

Deluxe Model

As above, with an engraved floorplate and checkered Monte Carlo-style stock featuring a rosewood pistol grip cap and forend tip.

Exc.	V.G.	Good	Fair	Poor
900	750	600	450	400

Finnbear

As above, with a long action available in a variety of large bore calibers. Fitted with a 20" or 23.5" barrel. Blued with a checkered stock. For .458 Winchester Magnum (only 20 produced), values double.

Exc.	V.G.	Good	Fair	Poor
750	650	550	400	400

Forester

As above, with a shorter action suitable for use with intermediate cartridges.

Exc.	V.G.	Good	Fair	Poor
750	650	550	400	400

Vixen

As above, with a short action.

Exc.	V.G.	Good	Fair	Poor
750	650	550	400	400

This symbol denotes "Sleepers" with rapidly-rising values and/or significant collector potential.

FN Action

Manufactured from 1950 to 1957, this model utilized a Fabrique Nationale manufactured receiver and was chambered for .270 Winchester and .30-06 cartridges. Otherwise, as above.

Exc.	V.G.	Good	Fair	Poor
600	500	400	400	400

FN Magnum Action

As above, with a long action for .300 and .375 Holland & Holland.

Exc.	V.G.	Good	Fair	Poor
650	600	500	400	400

Anniversary Model

A 7mm Remington Magnum bolt-action rifle with a 24" barrel. Blued, checkered walnut stock. A total of 1,000 were manufactured. As with any commemorative firearm, this model should be NIB to realize its full resale potential.

NIB	Exc.	V.G.	Good	Fair	Poor
2500	850	750	450	400	400

Finnwolf

A 4-shot lever-action rifle produced in .243 and .308 calibers. Blued, checkered walnut stock. Manufactured from 1962 to 1974.

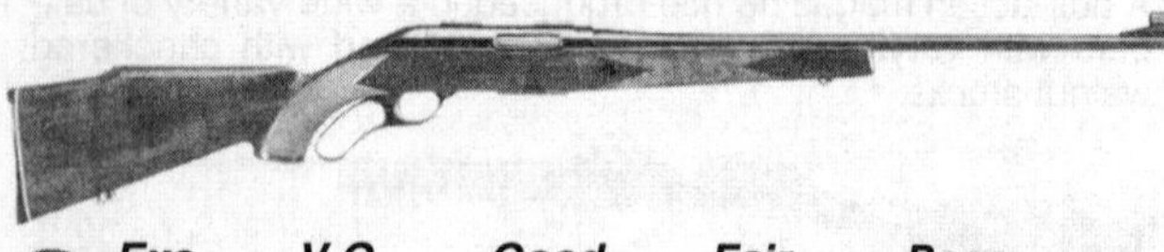

Exc.	V.G.	Good	Fair	Poor
850	700	550	450	400

Finnfire

This bolt-action rifle is chambered for the .22 long rifle cartridge. It is fitted with a 22" barrel with choice of iron sights or no sights, and a European walnut stock. A 5-shot detachable magazine is standard. Weight is about 5.25 lbs.

Courtesy Stoeger

NIB	Exc.	V.G.	Good	Fair	Poor
750	600	450	400	400	400

Finnfire Heavy Barrel

Same as above but fitted with a heavy barrel.

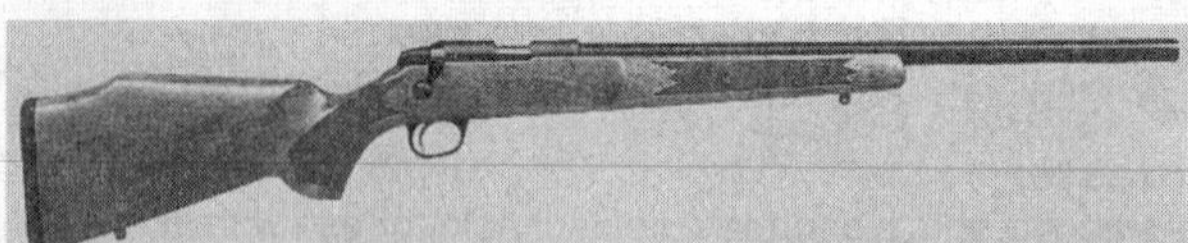

Courtesy Stoeger

NIB	Exc.	V.G.	Good	Fair	Poor
850	675	500	400	400	400

Finnfire Hunter

Introduced in 2000 this bolt-action model is chambered for the .22 LR cartridge. It is fitted with a 22" barrel and a Sako 75 style select walnut stock. Weight is about 5.75 lbs.

NIB	Exc.	V.G.	Good	Fair	Poor
875	650	—	—	—	—

Finnfire Sporter

This model is chambered for the .22 LR cartridge and is built on the P94S action. It has a walnut stock with adjustable cheekpiece and buttplate spacer system that allows for length of pull and buttplate angle adjustment. Trigger is adjustable. Introduced in 1999.

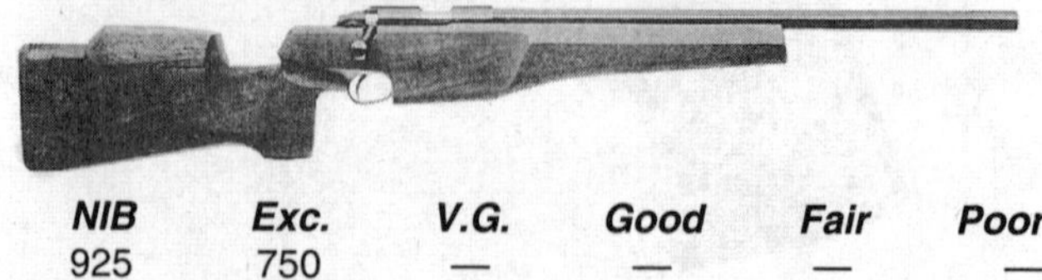

NIB	Exc.	V.G.	Good	Fair	Poor
925	750	—	—	—	—

Sako Quad Combo

Introduced in 2005 this bolt action rifle features four interchangeable barrels in four different rimfire calibers. Black synthetic stock. Detachable 5-round magazine. Included barrels are: .22 Long Rifle, .22 WMR, .17 HMR, and .17 Mach 2. All 22" in length. Blued finish. Weight is about 5.75 lbs.

NIB	Exc.	V.G.	Good	Fair	Poor
1739	1250	—	—	—	—

NOTE: NIB price for rifles with only one barrel is $948. Extra barrels are $260 each.

Hunter

This model is offered in three action lengths: short, medium, and long. In the short action the calibers available are .17 Rem., .222, .223 in 21.25" barrel. In medium action the calibers are: .22-250, .243, .308, and 7mm-08 in 21.75" barrel. The long action calibers are: .25-06, .270 Win., .280 Rem., .30-06 for 22" barrel length. In 24" barrel the long action calibers are: 7mm Rem. Mag., .300 Win. and .300 Wby. Mag., .338 and .375 Win. Mag., and .416 Rem. Mag. In 1996 the .270 Wthby Mag., 7mm Wthby Mag., and the .340 Wthby was added to the long action calibers. Available in left-handed version for all but short action calibers. Adjustable trigger is standard. Checkered European walnut stock. Weight for short action is 6.25 lbs., for medium action 6.5 lbs., and long action calibers 7.75 to 8.25 depending on caliber.

Medium Action

NIB	Exc.	V.G.	Good	Fair	Poor
795	600	500	400	400	400

Short Action

Add 10 percent to Medium Action prices for .222 Rem. and .223 Rem. For .17 Rem. add 20 percent to Medium Action prices.

Long Action

NIB	Exc.	V.G.	Good	Fair	Poor
795	600	500	400	400	400

NOTE: For long action calibers in .300 and .338 Win. Mag. add 10 percent. For .375 H&H Mag. add 20 percent. For .416 Rem. Mag. add 25 percent.

Carbine

As above, with an 18.5" barrel. Produced with either a medium or long-length action.

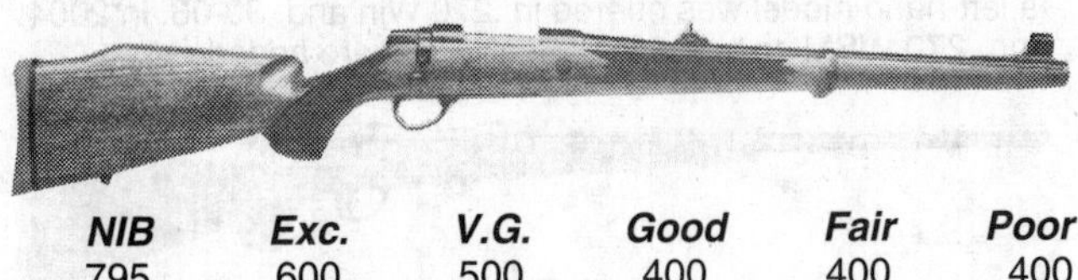

NIB	Exc.	V.G.	Good	Fair	Poor
795	600	500	400	400	400

Long Range Hunting Rifle

Similar to the long action Hunter but fitted with a 26" fluted barrel. Chambered for the .25-06, .270 Win., 7mm Rem. Mag., and .300 Win. Mag. Introduced in 1996.

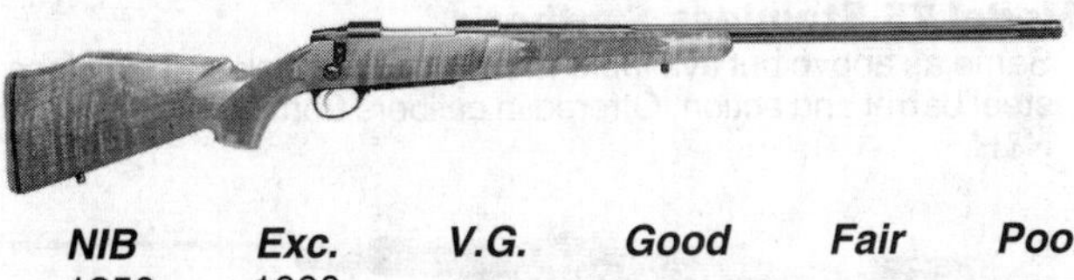

NIB	Exc.	V.G.	Good	Fair	Poor
1250	1000	—	—	—	—

Laminated Model

This model features a laminated checkered hardwood stock made up of 36 layers. Solid recoil pad is standard as are quick detachable sling swivels. Available in both medium and long action calibers. Medium action calibers are: .22-250, .243, .308, and 7mm-08 with 21.75" barrel and weight of 6.5 lbs. Long action calibers are: .25-06, .270, .280, .30-06 with 22" barrel and weight of 7.75 lbs. Offered with 24" barrels are: 7mm Rem. Mag., .300 and .338 Win. Mag., and .375 H&H; weight is 7.75 lbs.

Medium Action

NIB	Exc.	V.G.	Good	Fair	Poor
950	750	600	500	400	400

Long Action

NIB	Exc.	V.G.	Good	Fair	Poor
950	750	600	500	400	400

NOTE: For long action calibers in .300 and .338 Win. Mag. add 10 percent. For.375 H&H Mag. add 20 percent. For .416 Rem. Mag. add 25 percent.

FiberClass

This model features a black plain fiberglass stock. Offered in long action calibers only. The .25-06, .270, .280, and .30-06 are fitted with 22" barrels and weigh 7.25 lbs. The 7mm Rem. Mag., .300 Win. Mag., .338 Win. Mag., and .375 H&H are fitted with 24" barrel and weigh 7.25 lbs. The .416 Rem. Mag. has a 24" barrel and weighs 8 lbs.

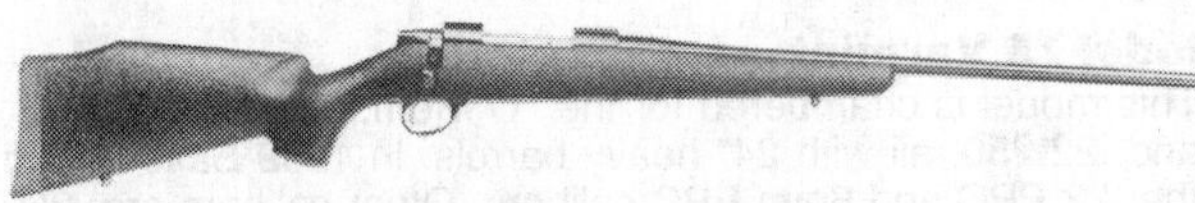

NIB	Exc.	V.G.	Good	Fair	Poor
1050	800	600	500	400	400

NOTE: For long action calibers in .300 and .338 Win. Mag. add 10 percent. For .375 H&H Mag. add 20 percent. For .416 Rem. Mag. add 25 percent.

FiberClass Carbine

As above, with a fiberglass stock.

NIB	Exc.	V.G.	Good	Fair	Poor
1050	800	600	500	400	400

Carbine

This model features a Mannlicher-style stock with a two-piece forearm. It has a checkered walnut stock with oil finish. It is offered in both medium and short actions, all with 18.5" barrels. In medium action the .243 and .308 are available and weigh 6 lbs. The long action calibers are: .270, and .30-06, weighing 7.25 lbs.; and the .338 Win. Mag. and .375 H&H, weighing 7.75 lbs.

Medium Action

NIB	Exc.	V.G.	Good	Fair	Poor
900	700	500	400	400	400

Long Action

NIB	Exc.	V.G.	Good	Fair	Poor
900	700	500	400	400	400

NOTE: For long action calibers in .338 Win. Mag. add 10 percent. For .375 H&H Mag. add 20 percent.

Varmint-Heavy Barrel

The checkered walnut stock on this model features an extra wide beavertail forearm with oil finish. Offered in both short and medium action, all are fitted with a 23" heavy barrel weighing 8.5 lbs. Short action calibers are .17 Rem., .222, and .223. Medium action calibers are: .22-250, .243, .308, and 7mm-08.

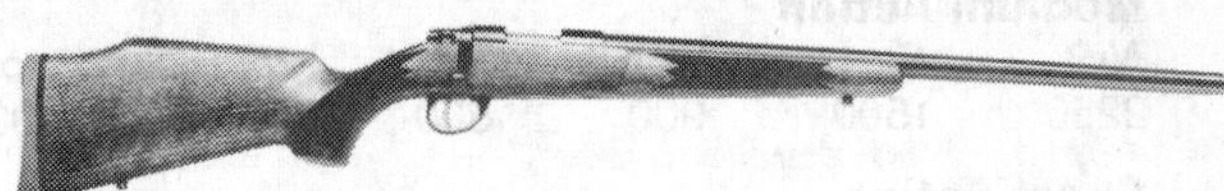

Short Action

NIB	Exc.	V.G.	Good	Fair	Poor
875	700	500	400	400	400

NOTE: Add 10 percent for .222 and .223 Rem. Add 20 percent for .17 Rem. to above prices.

Medium Action

NIB	Exc.	V.G.	Good	Fair	Poor
875	700	500	400	400	400

PPC Bench Rest/Varmint

Similar to the Varmint but single-shot. Fitted with 23.75" barrel and weighs 8.75 lbs. Available in short action special calibers .22 PPC and 6mm PPC.

NIB	Exc.	V.G.	Good	Fair	Poor
1050	800	600	400	400	400

Classic Grade

Hand-checkered select walnut stock with matte lacquer finish is featured on this grade. Offered in medium and long action. Long action rifles are offered in left-hand model. The medium action caliber is .243 Win. with a 21.75" barrel and weight of 6 lbs. The long action calibers are: .270, .30-06, and 7mm Rem. Mag. with 24" barrels. Long action calibers weigh about 7.5 lbs.

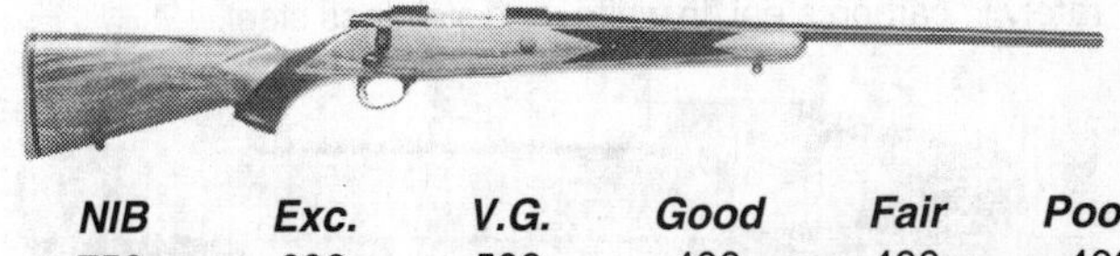

NIB	Exc.	V.G.	Good	Fair	Poor
750	600	500	400	400	400

Deluxe Grade

This grade features a high grade European walnut stock with hand cut basket weave checkering. The forend tip and grip are fitted with rosewood. English-style recoil pad is standard. Long action models are offered in left-hand configuration. As with the Hunter model short, medium, and long action are available in the same calibers, barrel lengths and weights as the Hunter.

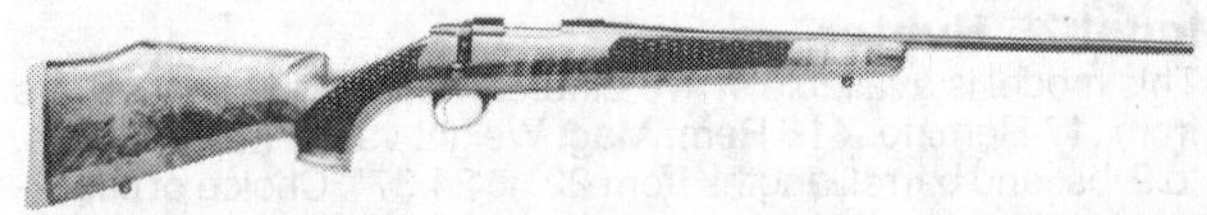

Medium Action

NIB	Exc.	V.G.	Good	Fair	Poor
1100	900	650	500	400	400

Short Action

Add 10 percent to above prices for .222 and .223 Rem. Add 20 percent for .17 Rem.

Long Action

NIB	Exc.	V.G.	Good	Fair	Poor
1100	900	650	500	400	400

NOTE: For long action calibers in .300 and .338 Win. Mag. add 10 percent. For .375 H&H Mag. add 20 percent. For .416 Rem. Mag. add 25 percent. For left-hand models add $100.

Super Grade/Super Deluxe

Similar to Deluxe Grade but offered with fancy walnut stock with oak-leaf carving. Floor plate and trigger guard are engraved. Pistol grip cap has inlaid silver plate. Offered in same actions and calibers as Hunter and Deluxe Grades.

Medium Action

NIB	Exc.	V.G.	Good	Fair	Poor
2250	1500	900	600	400	400

Short Action

Add 10 percent to above prices for .222 and .223 Rem.

Long Action

NIB	Exc.	V.G.	Good	Fair	Poor
2250	1500	900	600	400	400

NOTE: For long action calibers in .300 and .338 Win. Mag. add 10 percent. For .375 H&H Mag. add 20 percent. For .416 Rem. Mag. add 25 percent.

Safari Grade

As above, chambered for .300 Winchester Magnum, .338 Winchester Magnum, or .375 Holland & Holland cartridges.

NIB	Exc.	V.G.	Good	Fair	Poor
2250	1500	900	800	400	400

MODEL 75 SERIES

This model was introduced in March 1997. It is based on a new design by Sako. Each of the five different action sizes is manufactured for a specific range of calibers. Its action, barrel, and stocks are all redesigned components. It is offered in a variety of configurations and calibers. Sako actions are offered separately in carbon steel, in white, and stainless steel.

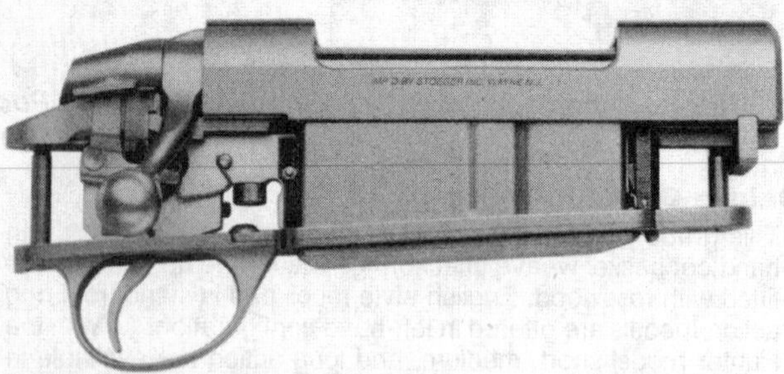

Sako 75 action

Model 75 Hunter

This model is available in five different action sizes for calibers from .17 Rem. to .416 Rem. Mag. Weight varies from 6.37 lbs. to 9 lbs. and barrel lengths from 22" to 24.37". Choice of checkered walnut stock or black synthetic stock. All Hunter models are sold without sights as standard but open sights are an option. Magazine is detachable except for .300 Rem. Ultra Mag and the .416 Rem. Mag. Single set trigger is an option. In 2003 a left-hand model was offered in .270 Win and .30-06. In 2004 the .270 WSM and .300 WSM calibers were added.

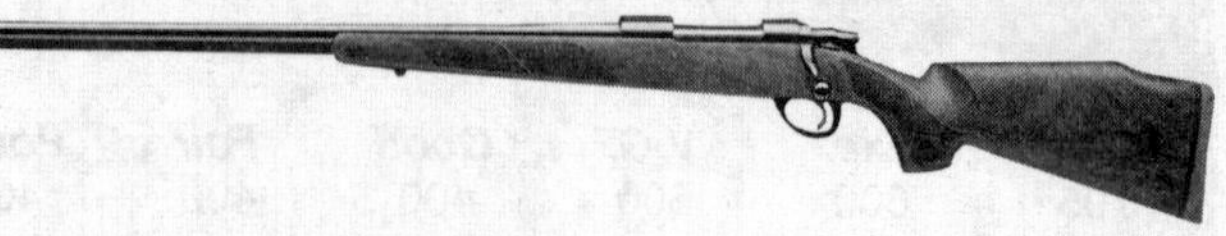

Sako Model 75 left-hand rifle

NIB	Exc.	V.G.	Good	Fair	Poor
1419	1050	700	500	400	400

NOTE: Add $30 for long action calibers from .270 to .416.

Model 75 Stainless Synthetic

Same as above but available with synthetic stock and stainless steel barrel and action. Offered in calibers from .22-250 to .375 H&H.

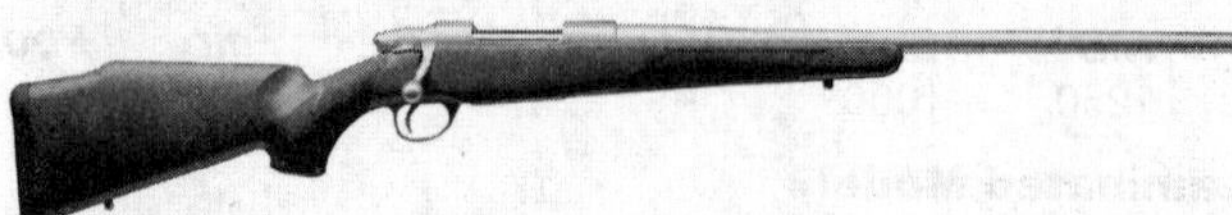

NIB	Exc.	V.G.	Good	Fair	Poor
1499	1100	750	600	400	400

NOTE: Add $30 for long action calibers.

Model 75 Deluxe

This model features all of the elements of the Hunter model with the addition of special checkering on select walnut stock with special black finish. All models have a hinged floor plate. In 2004 the .270 WSM and .300 WSM calibers were added. Weight is about 7.75 lbs.

NIB	Exc.	V.G.	Good	Fair	Poor
2044	1500	1050	800	500	400

NOTE: Add $100 for long action calibers.

Model 75 Big Game Deluxe

This model is similar to the M75 Deluxe except that it is chambered for the .416 Rem. Magnum cartridge and fitted with iron sights.

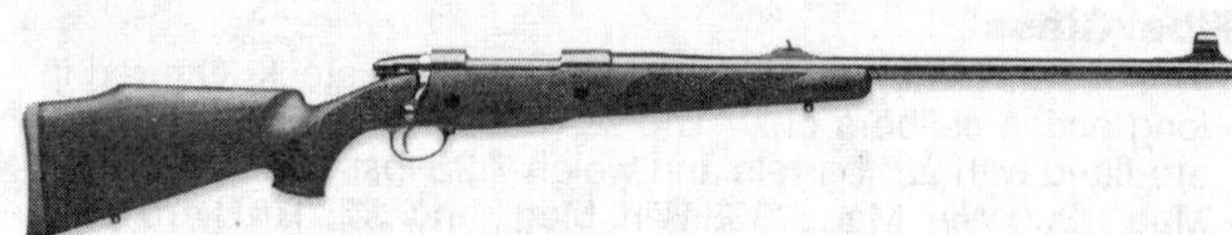

NIB	Exc.	V.G.	Good	Fair	Poor
2000	1600	—	—	—	—

Model 75 Varmint

This model is chambered for the .17 Rem., .222 Rem., .223, and .22-250, all with 24" heavy barrels. In 1999 Sako added the .22 PPC and 6mm PPC calibers. Other calibers are .260 Remington, .308, and .204 Ruger. It weighs about 8.4 lbs. Walnut stock.

NIB	Exc.	V.G.	Good	Fair	Poor
1250	950	750	600	450	400

Model 75 Varmint Set Trigger

As above but with a single set trigger. Introduced in 2005

NIB	Exc.	V.G.	Good	Fair	Poor
1684	1250	—	—	—	—

Model 75 Varmint Stainless

Introduced in 1999 this model is similar to the Varmint 75 but with stainless steel barrel. Magazine is detachable but can be loaded through the ejection port. Trigger is adjustable. Offered in all of the calibers as the standard Model 75 Varmint. Weights vary from about 8 lbs. to 8.6 lbs. The stock is laminated.

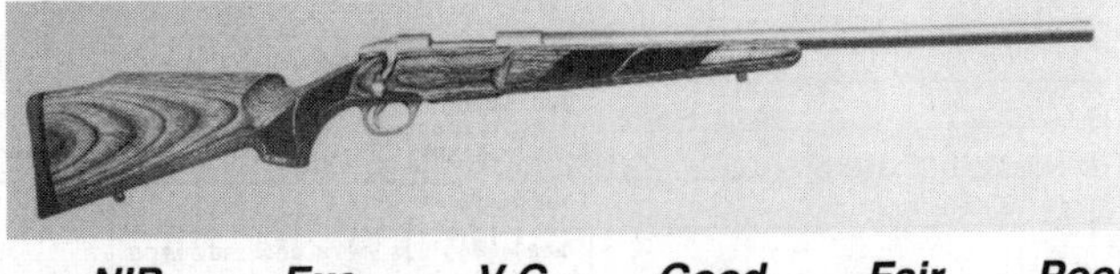

NIB	Exc.	V.G.	Good	Fair	Poor
1475	1150	—	—	—	—

Model 75 Varmint Stainless Set Trigger

As above but with stainless steel barrel and receiver and laminated stock. Weight is about 9 lbs. Introduced in 2005.

NIB	Exc.	V.G.	Good	Fair	Poor
1959	1400	—	—	—	—

Model 75 Finnlight

Introduced in 2001 this bolt-action rifle features short, medium, and long action calibers with stainless steel barrel lengths from 20.25" to 22.5" depending on caliber. Barrels are fluted. Synthetic stock. Weight is about 6.5 lbs. depending on caliber. In 2003 this model was offered in .300 WSM caliber.

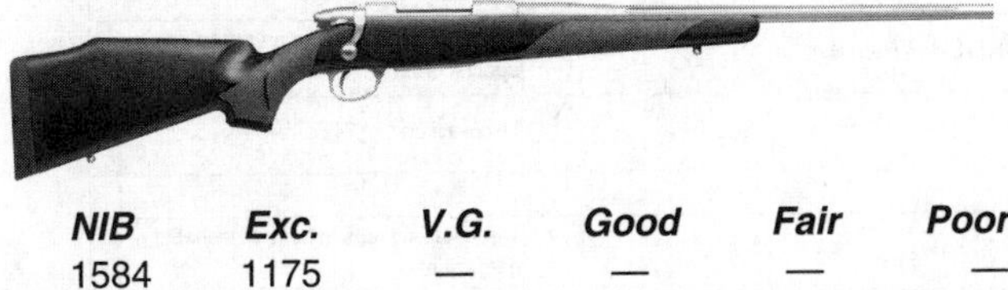

NIB	Exc.	V.G.	Good	Fair	Poor
1584	1175	—	—	—	—

Model 75 Grey Wolf

This bolt action rifle is chambered for a wide variety of calibers from .223 to 7mm WSM. Stainless steel barrel is either 22.5" or 24.3" depending on caliber without sights. The gray stock is laminated and checkered. Rubber recoil pad. Detachable magazine. Weight is about 7.75 lbs. depending on caliber. Introduced in 2005.

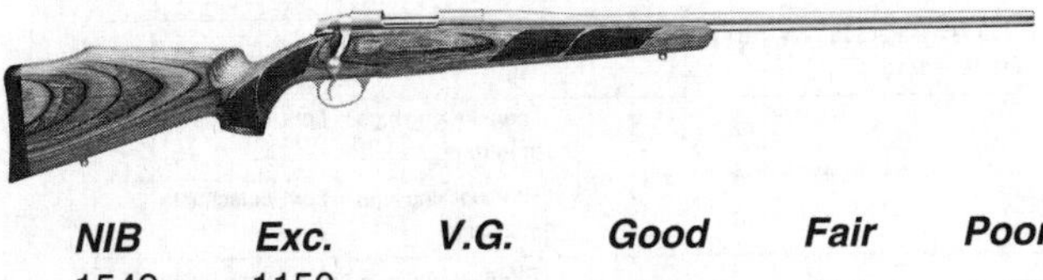

NIB	Exc.	V.G.	Good	Fair	Poor
1549	1150	—	—	—	—

Model 75 Custom Deluxe

Introduced in 2003 this model features an oil-finished premium-grade walnut stock with special fine-line checkering pattern. Factory recoil pad. Chambered for the .270 Win or .30-06 cartridges.

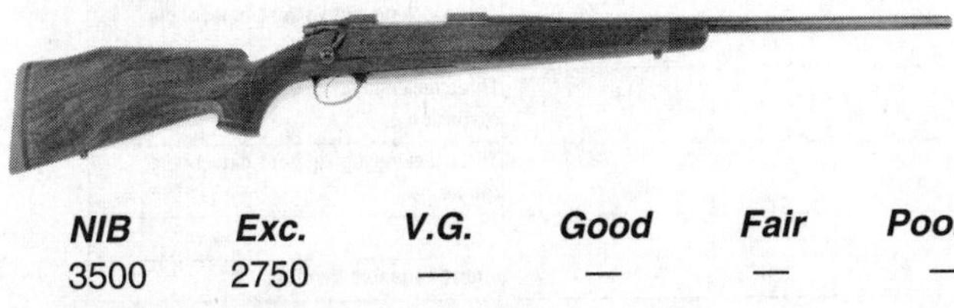

NIB	Exc.	V.G.	Good	Fair	Poor
3500	2750	—	—	—	—

Model 75 Custom Single Shot

Introduced in 2004 this single-shot model is chambered for the .308 cartridge and fitted with a 23.625" heavy fluted stainless steel barrel with no sights. Checkered laminated stock with beavertail forearm. Weight is about 9 lbs.

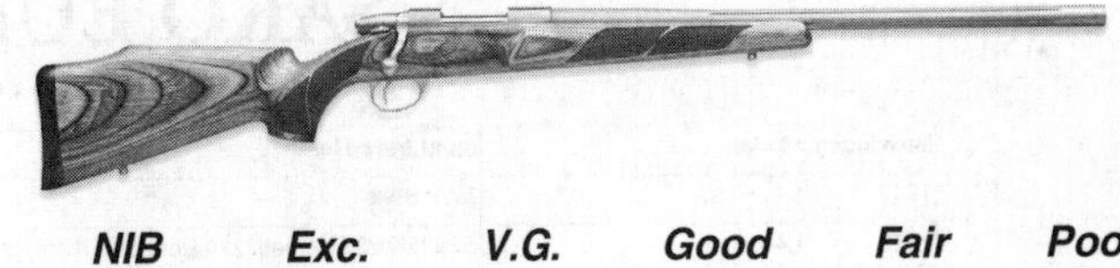

NIB	Exc.	V.G.	Good	Fair	Poor
3448	2500	—	—	—	—

Model 75 Super Deluxe

This is a special order rifle. Advise obtaining an expert opinion before a sale. Prices listed are for the base rifle.

NIB	Exc.	V.G.	Good	Fair	Poor
3400	2400	1850	—	—	—

Model 78

A .22 or .22 Hornet bolt-action rifle with a 22" barrel. Blued with a checkered walnut stock. Discontinued in 1986.

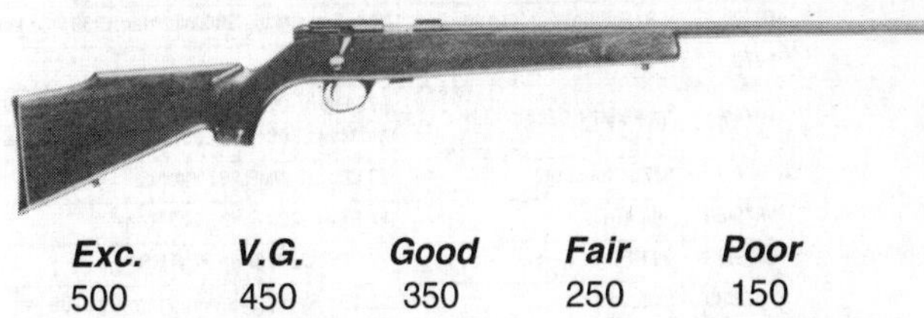

Exc.	V.G.	Good	Fair	Poor
500	450	350	250	150

Model 2700 Finnsport

A .270 to .300 Winchester Magnum bolt-action rifle with a 22" barrel. Blued, checkered walnut stock. Discontinued in 1985.

Exc.	V.G.	Good	Fair	Poor
600	500	400	400	400

Safari 80th Anniversary Model

This is a limited edition rifle. Built on the Sako 75 magnum long action and chambered for the .375 H&H cartridge. Match grade heavy barrel. Select grade walnut stock with straight comb and ebony forend tip. Quarter rib. Equipped with Swarovski PV-1 1.25x24 scope. Engraved floor plate. Supplied with hand-made leather case with cleaning accessories. Limited to 80 rifles worldwide. Serial numbers 200101 to 200180.

NIB	Exc.	V.G.	Good	Fair	Poor
15950	—	—	—	—	—

Sako 85 Hunter

Bolt-action centerfire rifle chambered in short and long calibers ranging from .223 Remington to .375 H&H Mag. Controlled round feeding, checkered walnut stock, satin blued sightless 22-7/16", 22-7/8", or 24-3/8" barrel. Introduced in 2007.

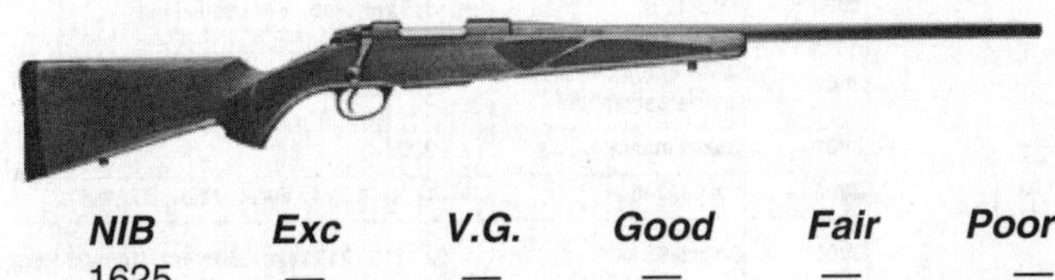

NIB	Exc	V.G.	Good	Fair	Poor
1625	—	—	—	—	—

Sako 85 Stainless Synthetic

Similar to Sako 85 Hunter but with stainless steel reciver and barrel. Introduced 2007.

SAKO EUROPEAN MODELS

courtesy Wikipedia

Introduced	Model	Chambered for	Comments
1942	L42	7x33 Sako	
1946	L46	5.6x35R, .22 Hornet, .218 Bee, .222 Rem, .222 Rem Mag, .25-20 Win, 7x33 Sako, .32-20 Win	Detachable magazine
1954?	P54/P54T	.22LR	
195?	M98	.270Win, .30-06, .300H&H, 8x60, 9.3x62, .375H&H, ?	FN M98 action, Sako stock and barrel
1957	L57	.243 Win, .244 Rem, .308 Win	Fixed magazine
1959	L579 Forester	.22-250, .243 Win, .308 Win	Fixed magazine
1961	L461 Vixen	.17 Rem, .222 Rem, .222 Rem Mag, .223 Rem?, 7x33 Sako?	Fixed magazine
1961	L61R Finnbear	.264 Win, .270 Win, 30-06	Three locking lugs: Two in front and one on the rear end of the bolt
1961	L61R Finnbear Magnum	7mm Rem Mag, .300 Win Mag, .300 H&H, .338 Win Mag, .375 H&H	Three locking lugs: Two in front and one on the rear end of the bolt
1963	VL63 Finnwolf	.243 Win, .244 Rem, .308 Win, .358 Win	Lever-action
1972	L61R Finnbear	.25-06 Rem, 6.5x55, .270 Win, 7x64, .30-06, 9,3x62	Two locking lugs in front
1972	L61R Finnbear Magnum	7mm Rem Mag, .300 Win Mag, .338 Win Mag, .375 H&H	Two locking lugs in front
1972	P72 Finnscout	.22LR	
1974?	Sako M74 Super	.222 Rem, .223 Rem, .22-250, .243 Win, .308 Win, .25-06, .270 Win, .30-06, .264 Mag, 7mm Rem Mag, .300 Win Mag, .300 H&H, .338 Win Mag, .375 H&H	
1978	M78 Finnscout	.22 LR, .22 WMR, .22 Hornet	
1979/80	AI/L461	.17 Rem, .222 Rem, .223 Rem	Also available as single-shot action
1979/80?	AI PPC	.22 PPC USA, 6mm PPC USA	Also available as single-shot action
1979/80	AII/L579	.22-250 Rem, .243 Win, 7mm-08, .308 Win	Also available as single-shot action
1979/80	AIII		early version of the AV, short tang
1979/80	AIV		
1979/80	AV/L61R	.25-06 Rem, 6.5x55, .270 Win, 7x64, .30-06, 9,3x62	Long tang
1979/80	AV Mag/L61R Magnum	7mm Rem Mag, .300 Win Mag, .300 Wby, .338 Win Mag, .375 H&H, .416 Rem Mag	.458 Win Mag has been produced on special order
1982?	VL63 Finnwolf Sako Collectors Association	.243 Win, .308 Win	Lever-action
1988	M579 SM (Super Match)	.308 Win	
1989	TRG-21	.308 Win	Three locking lugs in front, detachable magazine
1989	TRG-41	.300 Win Mag?, .338 Lapua Mag	Three locking lugs in front, detachable magazine
1992?	M591 Left hand	.22-250, .243 Win, 7mm-08 Rem, .308 Win	
1993	S491	.17 Rem, .222 Rem, .223 Rem, .22 PPC USA, 6mm PPC USA	
1993	M591	.22-250, .243 Win, 7mm-08 Rem, .308 Win	
1993	L691	.25-06, 6.5x55, .270 Win, 7x64, .280 Rem, .30-06, 9.3x62	
1993	L691 Mag	.270 Wby, 7mm Rem Mag, 7mm Wby, .300 Win Mag, .300 Wby, .338 Win Mag, .340 Wby, .375 H&H, .416 Rem Mag	
1995?	M995 TRG-S	.25-06, 6.5x55, .270 Win, .280 Rem, 7x64, .308 Win, .30-06, 9.3x62	
1995?	M995 TRG-S Magnum	.270 Wby, 7mm Rem Mag, 7mm Wby, 7mm STW, 7.21 Firebird, .300 Win Mag, .300 Wby, 7.82 Warbird, .30-378 Wby, .338 Win Mag, .340 Wby, .338 Lapua Mag, .375 H&H, .416 Rem Mag	
1997	Sako M75 I	.222 Rem, .223 Rem	Three locking lugs in front, detachable magazine
1997	Sako M75 II	.22 PPC USA, 6mm PPC USA	Three locking lugs in front, detachable magazine
1997	Sako M75 III	.22-250, .243 Win, .260 Rem, 7mm-08 Rem, .308 Win	Three locking lugs in front, detachable magazine
1997	Sako M75 SM	.270 WSM, .300WSM	Three locking lugs in front, detachable magazine
1997	Sako M75 IV	.25-06, 6.5x55, .270 Win, 7x64, .30-06, 9.3x62, 9.3x66 Sako	Three locking lugs in front, detachable magazine
1997	Sako M75 V	7mm Rem Mag, .300 Win Mag, .375 H&H, .416 Rem Mag	Three locking lugs in front, detachable magazine
1999	TRG-22	.308 Win	Three locking lugs in front, detachable magazine
1999	TRG-42	.300 Win Mag, .338 Lapua Mag	Three locking lugs in front, detachable magazine
2001	Sako M75 V Safari anniversary model	.375 H&H	Three locking lugs in front, detachable magazine
2001?	Sako Finnfire	.22LR	
2006?	Sako Quad	.17 Mach 2, .17 HMR, .22LR, .22 WMR	Interchangeable barrels
2006	Sako M85 S	.22-250, .243 Win, .260 Rem, 7mm-08 Rem, .308 Win, .338 Federal	Three locking lugs in front, detachable magazine
2006	Sako M85 SM	.270 WSM, 7mm WSM, .300 WSM	Three locking lugs in front, detachable magazine
2006	Sako M85 M	.25-06, 6.5x55, .270 Win, 7x64, .30-06, 9.3x62, 9.3x66 Sako	Three locking lugs in front, detachable magazine

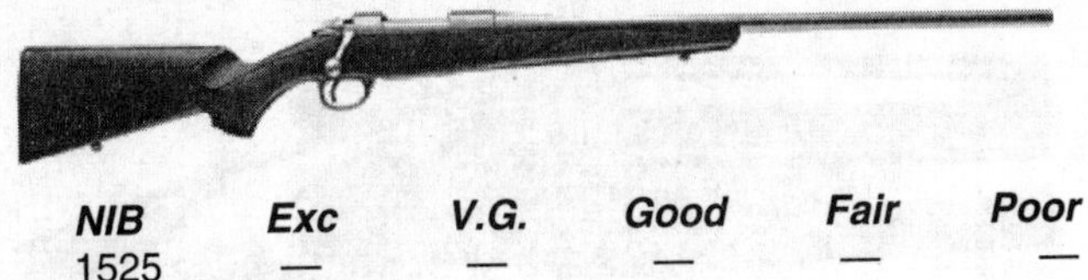

NIB	Exc	V.G.	Good	Fair	Poor
1525	—	—	—	—	—

Sako 85 Finnlight

Similar to Sako 85 Stainless Synthetic but with recoil pad and ultra-lightweight synthetic stock. Chambered in long and short cartridges ranging from .243 to .300 Win Mag. Introduced 2007.

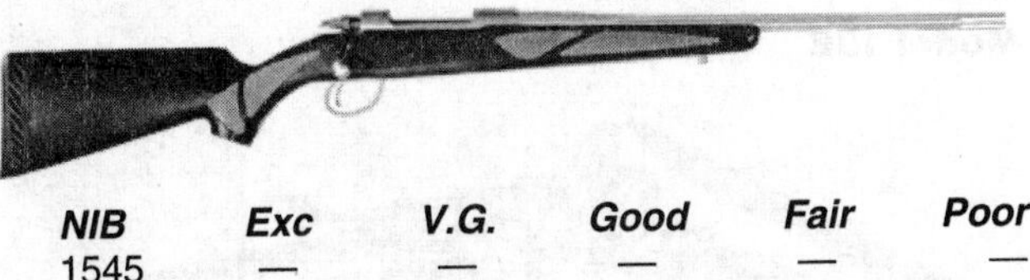

NIB	Exc	V.G.	Good	Fair	Poor
1545	—	—	—	—	—

Sako 85 Varmint

Similar to Sako 85 Hunter but with recoil pad and 7.5-oz. set trigger. Chambered in .204 Ruger, .243, .22-250 or .308. Introduced 2007.

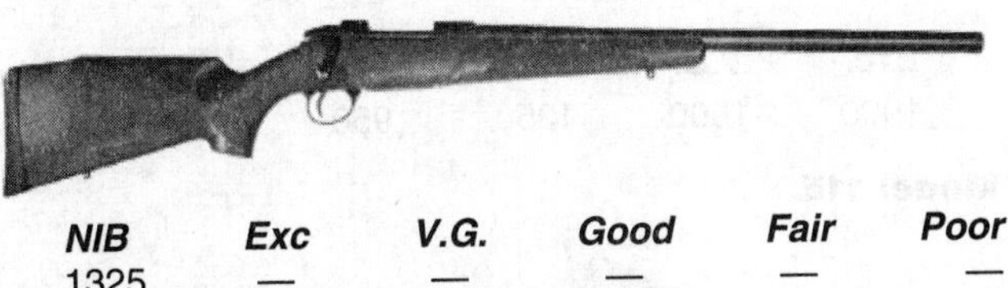

NIB	Exc	V.G.	Good	Fair	Poor
1325	—	—	—	—	—

Sako 85 Laminated SS Varmint

Similar to Sako 85 Varmint but with laminated stock and stainless steel barrel. Introduced 2007.

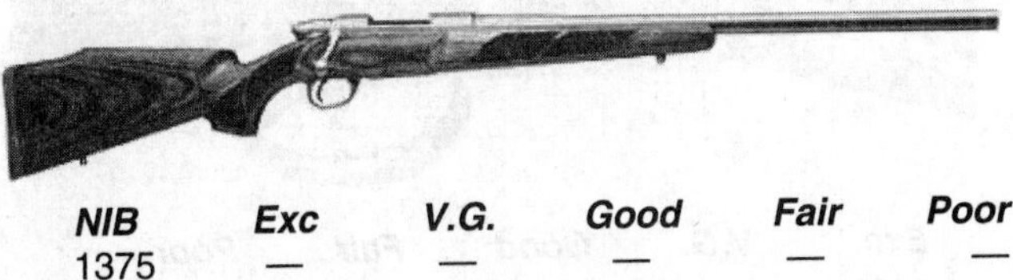

NIB	Exc	V.G.	Good	Fair	Poor
1375	—	—	—	—	—

TRG-S

This model features a unique cold-forged receiver. The stock is a special reinforced polyurethane Monte Carlo without checkering. The recoil pad has spacer for adjustable length of pull. The trigger is adjustable and the detachable magazine holds 5 rounds. Offered in a variety of calibers from .243 to .375 H&H. Non-Magnum calibers are fitted with a 22" barrel and weigh 7.75 lbs. and magnum calibers are fitted with a 24" barrel and also weigh 7.75 lbs. In 1996 the .270 Wthby Mag., 7mm Wthby Mag., the .340 Wthby Mag., as well as the 6.5x55S, were added.

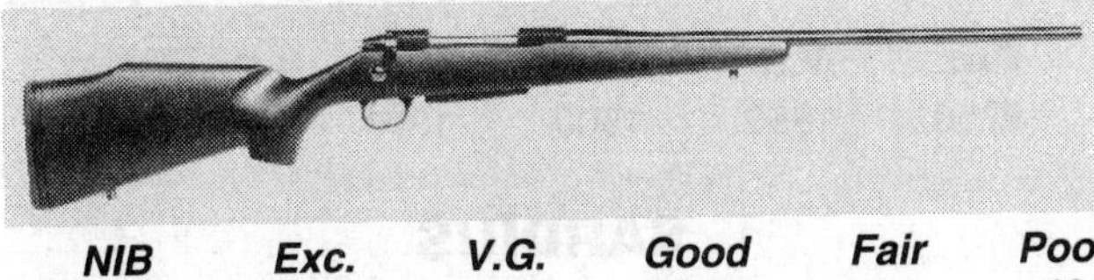

NIB	Exc.	V.G.	Good	Fair	Poor
800	650	500	450	400	400

TRG-21

The receiver is similar to the TRG-S but the polyurethane stock features a unique design. Chambered for the .308 cartridge. The trigger is adjustable for length and two-stage pull and also for horizontal or vertical pitch. This model also has several options that would affect the price; muzzlebrake, one-piece scope mount, bipod, quick detachable sling swivels, and military nylon sling. The rifle is offered in .308 Win. only. It is fitted with a 25.75" barrel and weighs 10.5 lbs.

NIB	Exc.	V.G.	Good	Fair	Poor
3500	2750	1850	—	—	—

TRG-22

This model is similar to the TRG-21 but meets the exact specifications to comply with the Finish military requirements. Chambered for the .308 cartridge. Introduced in 2000. Offered in both green and black finish. Weight is about 10.25 lbs.

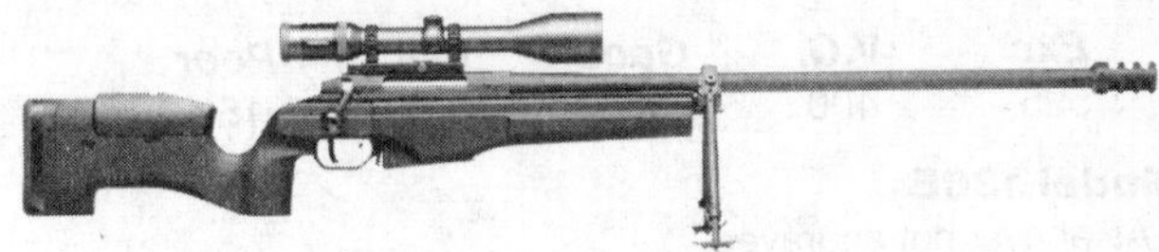

NIB	Exc.	V.G.	Good	Fair	Poor
3589	2650	—	—	—	—

NOTE: Add $2,250 for folding stock version.

TRG-41

Exactly the same as the TRG-21 except chambered for the .338 Lapua Magnum cartridge.

NIB	Exc.	V.G.	Good	Fair	Poor
4350	3500	2500	1500	—	—

TRG-42

This model is similar to the TRG-41 but meets the exact specifications to comply with the Finish military requirements. Chambered for the .338 Lapua or .300 Win. Mag cartridge. Introduced in 2000. Weight is about 11.25 lbs.

NIB	Exc.	V.G.	Good	Fair	Poor
4000	3000	—	—	—	—

SAM, INC.

Special Service Arms Mfg., Inc.
Reston, Virginia

Model 88 Crossfire

A semi-automatic combination 12 gauge/.308 caliber shotgun/rifle, with a 7-shot shotgun magazine and 20-shot rifle magazine. Barrel length 20", matte black finish with a composition stock. This weapon can be fired in either mode by means of a selector switch mounted on the receiver.

NIB	Exc.	V.G.	Good	Fair	Poor
1900	1500	—	—	—	—

SAMCO GLOBAL ARMS, INC.

Miami, Florida

This firm imports a variety of military surplus firearms that under current law are marked with the importer's name.

SARASQUETA, FELIX

Eibar, Spain

Merke

A 12 gauge over-and-under double-barrel shotgun with 22" or 27" ribbed and separated barrels, nonselective trigger and manual extractors. Blued, checkered walnut stock. Imported in 1986 only.

Exc.	V.G.	Good	Fair	Poor
350	225	200	150	100

SARASQUETA, J. J.
Eibar, Spain

Model 107E
A 12, 16, or 20 gauge boxlock double-barrel shotgun with a variety of barrel lengths, double triggers and automatic ejectors. Blued with a checkered walnut stock. Discontinued in 1984.

Exc.	V.G.	Good	Fair	Poor
425	300	275	225	100

Model 119E
As above, with a more finely figured walnut stock.

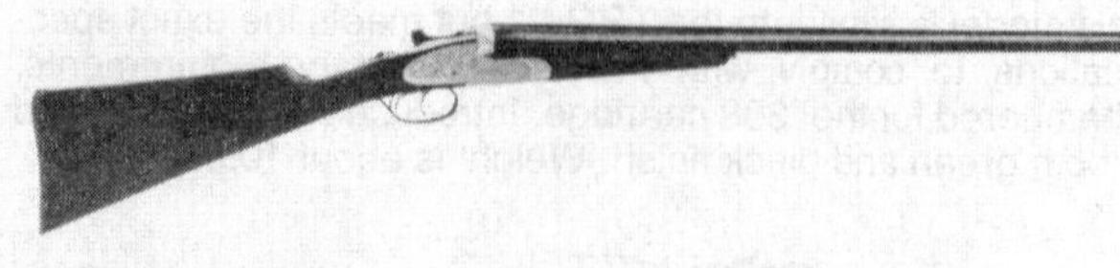

Exc.	V.G.	Good	Fair	Poor
525	400	375	325	150

Model 130E
As above, but engraved.

Exc.	V.G.	Good	Fair	Poor
950	700	600	450	250

Model 131E
As above, with considerably more engraving.

Exc.	V.G.	Good	Fair	Poor
1350	900	800	650	350

Model 1882 E LUXE
As above, with a single-selective trigger and gold inlays. A silver inlaid version is sold for approximately 10 percent less.

Exc.	V.G.	Good	Fair	Poor
1750	1250	900	650	350

SARASQUETA, VICTOR
Eibar, Spain

Model 3
A 12, 16, or 20 gauge boxlock or sidelock double-barrel shotgun available in a variety of barrel lengths, with double triggers and automatic ejectors. Blued with a checkered straight stock. The sidelock version is worth approximately 20 percent more than the values listed. The basic Model 3 was offered in a variety of grades featuring different amounts of engraving and better quality wood. These shotguns are listed under the model designations of 4 to 12E.

Exc.	V.G.	Good	Fair	Poor
650	500	450	350	300

Model 4

Exc.	V.G.	Good	Fair	Poor
675	550	475	400	300

Model 4E (Auto-ejectors)

Exc.	V.G.	Good	Fair	Poor
750	625	550	450	350

Model 203

Exc.	V.G.	Good	Fair	Poor
700	600	525	425	325

Model 203E

Exc.	V.G.	Good	Fair	Poor
800	650	575	475	375

Model 6E

Exc.	V.G.	Good	Fair	Poor
900	750	625	525	425

Model 7E

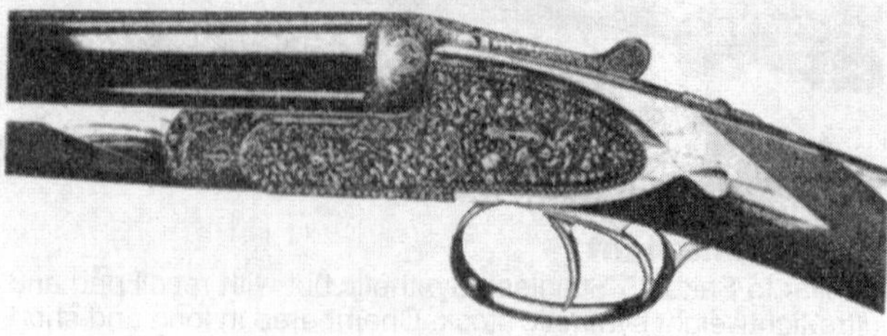

Exc.	V.G.	Good	Fair	Poor
950	800	675	575	475

Model 10E

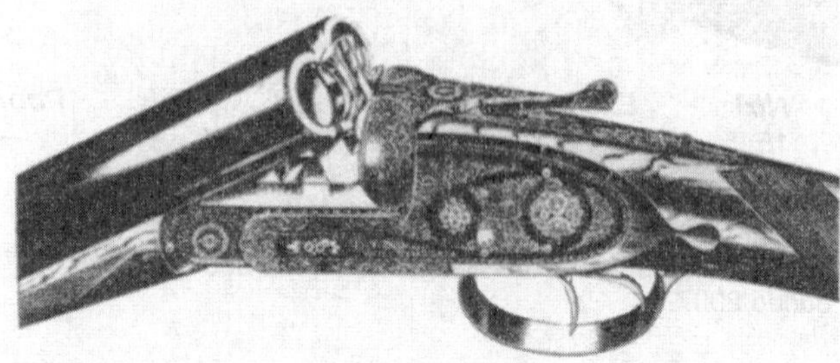

Exc.	V.G.	Good	Fair	Poor
1900	1500	1250	950	750

Model 11E

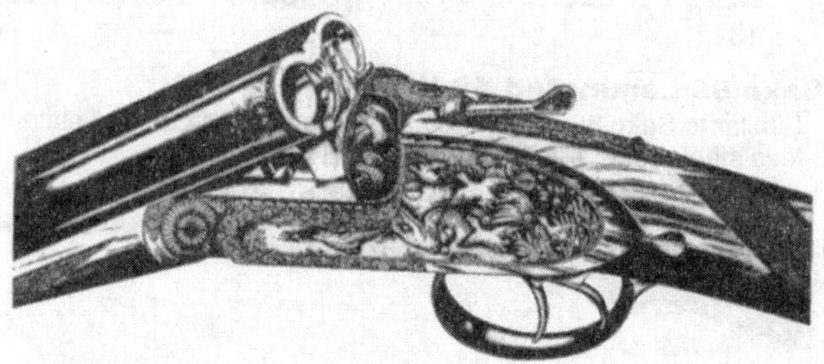

Exc.	V.G.	Good	Fair	Poor
2100	1600	1350	1150	850

Model 12E

Exc.	V.G.	Good	Fair	Poor
2750	1850	1500	1300	1000

SARDIUS
Israel

SD-9
A 9mm double-action semi-automatic pistol with a 3" barrel and 6-shot magazine. Matte black finish with composition grips. Imported since 1988.

NIB	Exc.	V.G.	Good	Fair	Poor
425	300	250	200	150	100

SARSILMAZ
Mercan/Istanbul, Turkey

Professional
CZ-75-style compensated semi-auto in white chrome finish chambered for 9mm. Single-action with adjustable trigger, laser engraving. 16 or 18 round capacity. 42.3 oz.; 5.1" barrel. MSRP: 437

K2
CZ-75-style double-action semi-auto in white chrome or blued. Chambered for 9mm. 16 or 18 round capacity. 35.3 oz.; 4.6" barrel. Plastic grips.

Exc.	V.G.	Good	Fair	Poor
300	—	—	—	—

Kama Sport
CZ-75-style semi-auto 9mm in white chrome or blued. Double-action with 3.9" compensated barrel, laser engraving. 15+1 or 17+1 capacity. 35.4 oz. Plastic grips.

Exc.	V.G.	Good	Fair	Poor
325	—	—	—	—

Kama
CZ-75-style semi-auto 9mm in white chrome or blued. Double-action with 4.3" compensated barrel, laser engraving. 15+1 or 17+1 capacity. 35.4 oz.; 7.7". Plastic grips.

Exc.	V.G.	Good	Fair	Poor
300	—	—	—	—

Kilinc 2000 Mega
CZ-75-style semi-auto 9mm in white chrome or blued. Double-action with 4.7" barrel. 16 or 18 capacity. 35 oz. Plastic grips. Fixed sights.

Exc.	V.G.	Good	Fair	Poor
200	—	—	—	—

Kilinc 2000 Light
CZ-75-style semi-auto 9mm in white chrome, blued or camo. Double-action with 4.7" barrel, laser engraving. 15+1 or 17+1 capacity. 35.4 oz. Plastic grips.

Exc.	V.G.	Good	Fair	Poor
200	—	—	—	—

Hancer 2000/2000 Light
CZ-75-style semi-auto 9mm in white chrome or blued. Double-action with 3.9" barrel, laser engraving. 13+1 capacity. 33.5 oz. (25.4 oz. Light model). Plastic grips.

Exc.	V.G.	Good	Fair	Poor
200	—	—	—	—

Bernardelli
CZ-75-style double-action semi-auto in 9mm. Black/white or blued finish. The 15+1 model has a 4.7" barrel, 27 oz., Plastic grips. The 13+1 model has a 3.9" barrel; 26.7 oz. Plastic grips, fixed sights.

Exc.	V.G.	Good	Fair	Poor
225	—	—	—	—

SAUER, J. P. & SON
Suhl and Eckernfoerde, Germany

This is the oldest firearms manufacturing firm in Germany. It was founded in 1751 in Suhl. During this period the company produced high quality handguns and long guns. In 1938 it introduced a new double-action semi-automatic pistol, the Sauer 38H. This pistol had the first decocking lever ever used on a mass produced pistol. In 1951 the company relocated to Eckernfoerde where it continued to produced high quality forearms.

NOTE: The Model 90 Supreme and Model 202 are currently imported by SIGARMS Inc.

Bolt-Action Rifle
A Mauser action sporting rifle chambered for a variety of cartridges with either a 22" or 24" barrel featuring a raised rib. Double set triggers, express sights, blued with a checkered walnut stock. Manufactured prior to WWII.

Exc.	V.G.	Good	Fair	Poor
700	600	500	400	300

Model 200
A bolt-action rifle chambered for a variety of cartridges with short or medium length actions, 24" barrels, set trigger, 4-round magazine. Blued, checkered walnut stock. Discontinued 1987.

Extra barrels add $235.

NIB	Exc.	V.G.	Good	Fair	Poor
850	650	550	500	425	350

Model 200 Lightweight
As above, with an alloy receiver. Discontinued in 1987.

Exc.	V.G.	Good	Fair	Poor
600	500	400	325	250

Model 200 Lux
As above, with a finely figured walnut stock, rosewood pistol grip cap and forend tip, gold-plated trigger and a machine jewelled bolt. Imported prior to 1988.

Exc.	V.G.	Good	Fair	Poor
700	600	550	475	400

Model 200 Carbon Fiber
The Model 200 fitted with a carbon composition stock. Imported in 1987 and 1988.

Exc.	V.G.	Good	Fair	Poor
800	750	650	500	400

Model 202 Supreme
This is a bolt-action rifle with a barrel change feature. It is fitted with an adjustable two-stage trigger, quick-change fluted barrel, black rubber recoil pad, and removable box magazine. The stock is select American claro walnut with high gloss finish and rosewood forend and grip cap. Buttstock has a Monte Carlo comb and cheekpiece. It is offered in .243, .270, .308, and .30-06. Barrel length for these calibers is 23.6". Weight for these calibers is about 7.7 lbs. In the Supreme Magnum series it is available in 7mm magnum, .300 Win. Mag., and .375 H&H Mag. Barrel for these magnum calibers is 26". Weight for these caliber is 8.4 lbs.

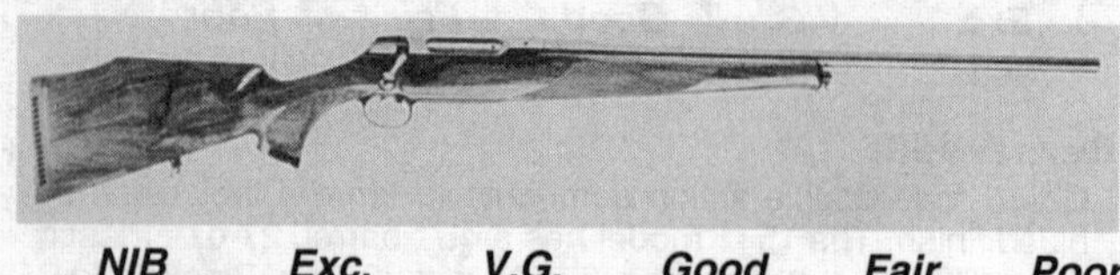

NIB	Exc.	V.G.	Good	Fair	Poor
2000	1650	1200	950	—	—

Model 202 Takedown

This model is a true takedown. Introduced in 2003 this rifle is chambered for the .300 Win. Mag and the .375 H&H; other calibers will be offered in the future. Fancy Turkish walnut stock with Monte Carlo and rosewood forend tip. Base price listed.

NIB	Exc.	V.G.	Good	Fair	Poor
5000	3750	2900	—	—	—

Model S202 Wolverine

Similar to the Model 202 Supreme above but with 25.6" barrel, beavertail forend and adjustable cheekpiece. Chambered in various varmint calibers.

Exc.	V.G.	Good	Fair	Poor
2000	—	—	—	—

Model S202 Highland

Similar to the Model 202 Supreme above but with 20" barrel, schnabel forend and easily-detachable buttstock. Chambered in .308 Winchester and various European cartridges.

Exc.	V.G.	Good	Fair	Poor
2000	—	—	—	—

Model S202 Forest

A carbine-style version of the Model 202 Highland above intended specifically for drive hunts. Has standard forend and 25.6" barrel and is chambered in various varmint calibers.

Exc.	V.G.	Good	Fair	Poor
2000	—	—	—	—

Model S202 Hardwood

Similar to the Model 202 Highland above but, oddly enough, with a synthetic stock with orange inserts. Chambered in .308 Winchester and various European cartridges.

Exc.	V.G.	Good	Fair	Poor
2000	—	—	—	—

Model S202 Match

Target version of the Model 202 with 26.8" match barrel, wide forend. Chambered in .300 Winchester Magnum and 6.5x55 Swedish.

Exc.	V.G.	Good	Fair	Poor
2000	—	—	—	—

Model S202 Outback

Similar to the Model 202 Hardwood above but withlightweight construction and plain black synthetic stock

Exc.	V.G.	Good	Fair	Poor
2000	—	—	—	—

Model S202 Team Sauer

Classically-styled sporter version of Model 202 with heavy medium or magnum-weight barrel and walnut Monte Carlo stock. Chambered in various European and American long-action cartridges from 6.5x55 Swedish up to .300 Winchester Magnum.

Exc.	V.G.	Good	Fair	Poor
1550	—	—	—	—

Model 90

A bolt-action rifle produced in a number of calibers in all action lengths with 23" or 26" barrels, with a detachable magazine. Blued with a checkered walnut stock.

Exc.	V.G.	Good	Fair	Poor
800	700	600	450	400

Model 90 Stutzen

As above, with a full-length Mannlicher-style stock. Imported prior to 1990.

Exc.	V.G.	Good	Fair	Poor
825	725	625	475	425

Model 90 Safari

The Model 90 made for use with the .458 Winchester Magnum cartridge and fitted with a 24" barrel. Imported from 1986 to 1988.

Exc.	V.G.	Good	Fair	Poor
1250	1100	950	750	600

NOTE: The Model 90 Series of bolt-action rifles was available in a deluxe version that differed with the grade of workmanship and materials utilized. This deluxe series would be worth approximately 60 percent additional. There were optional engraved models; these should be individually appraised.

Model 90 Supreme

Similar to the above, with a gold-plated trigger, machine jewelled bolt and finely figured checkered walnut stock. Introduced in 1987.

NIB	Exc.	V.G.	Good	Fair	Poor
1500	1250	1100	950	750	650

SSG-3000

NIB	Exc.	V.G.	Good	Fair	Poor
8800	8000	—	—	—	—

SG 550 Sniper

NIB	Exc.	V.G.	Good	Fair	Poor
14200	12500	10700	—	—	—

NOTE: For other current Sauer rifles see SIGARMS.

SHOTGUN/RIFLE COMBINATIONS

Luftwaffe Survival Drilling

A double-barrel 12 gauge by 9.3x74R combination shotgun/rifle with 28" barrels. Blued with a checkered walnut stock and marked with Nazi inspection. Stampings on the stock and barrel breech. Normally, furnished with an aluminum case.

Exc.	V.G.	Good	Fair	Poor
12000	8500	6000	3250	—

NOTE: Add 50 percent to prices for case.

Model 3000 Drilling

This model was chambered for a variety of gauges and calibers and is built upon a boxlock action with a Greener crossbolt. The action is lightly engraved. Blued, checkered walnut stock.

NIB	Exc.	V.G.	Good	Fair	Poor
5500	3700	2750	2000	1500	1250

Model 54 Combo

A combination rifle/shotgun chambered for a variety of gauges and calibers with an action as above. Discontinued in 1986.

Exc.	V.G.	Good	Fair	Poor
2200	2000	1750	1400	1200

SHOTGUNS

Model 60

A 12, 16 or 20 gauge double-barrel boxlock shotgun produced in a variety of barrel lengths with double triggers and manual extractors. Blued with checkered walnut stock. Produced prior to WWII.

Exc.	V.G.	Good	Fair	Poor
700	625	550	400	300

Royal Model

A 12 or 20 gauge boxlock double-barrel shotgun with 26", 28", or 30" barrels, single-selective triggers with automatic ejectors. The frame is scalloped, blued with a checkered walnut stock. Manufactured from 1955 to 1977.

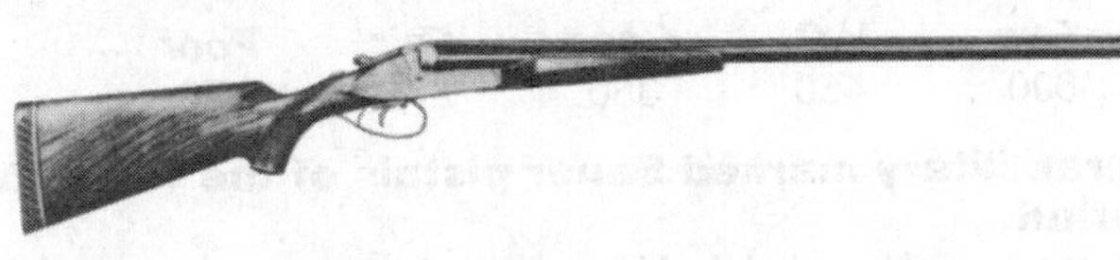

Exc.	V.G.	Good	Fair	Poor
1500	1250	1000	750	500

Grade I Artemis

A 12 gauge sidelock double-barrel shotgun with 28" barrels, single-selective trigger and automatic ejector. Engraved, blued with checkered walnut stock. Manufactured from 1966 to 1977.

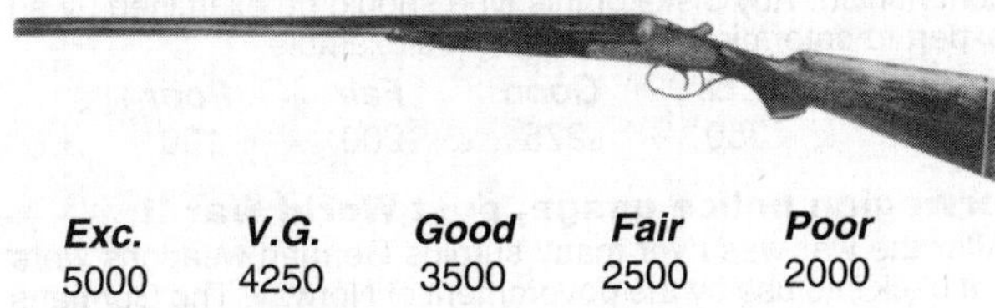

Exc.	V.G.	Good	Fair	Poor
5000	4250	3500	2500	2000

Grade II Artemis

As above, but more finely finished.

Exc.	V.G.	Good	Fair	Poor
6500	5750	4750	3500	3000

Model 66

A 12 gauge sidelock double-barrel shotgun with a 26", 28", or 30" barrel, single-selective trigger and automatic ejectors. Blued, checkered walnut stock. This model was produced in three different grades that have different degrees of engraving. Produced from 1966 to 1975.

Grade I

Exc.	V.G.	Good	Fair	Poor
2000	1800	1500	1150	800

Grade II

Exc.	V.G.	Good	Fair	Poor
3000	2800	2500	2150	1800

Grade III

Exc.	V.G.	Good	Fair	Poor
3750	3500	2850	2500	2000

PISTOLS

Written and compiled by our very good friend Jim Cate.

Roth-Sauer Model

The very first automatic pistol produced by J.P. Sauer & Son and designed by Karl Krinka for George Roth. It is available only in 7.65 Roth-Sauer caliber. It is a locked breech design, beautifully finished and extremely well made. Later this design was modified and became the Roth-Steyr military pistol which was adopted by Austria in 1907. A difficult-to-find pistol.

Exc.	V.G.	Good	Fair	Poor
2250	1500	900	500	300

Sauer Model 1913

First Series, which incorporates an extra safety button on the left side of the frame near the trigger and the rear sight is simply a milled recess in the cocking knob itself. The serial number range runs from 1 to approximately 4750 and this first series is found only in 7.65mm caliber. All were for commercial sales as far as can be determined. Some were tested by various militaries, no doubt.

A.European variation—all slide legends are in the German language

B.English Export variation—slide legends are marked, J.P. Sauer & Son, Suhl - Prussia, "Sauer's Patent" Pat'd May 20 1912

Both were sold in thick paper cartons or boxes with the color being a reddish purple with gold colored letters, etc. Examples of the very early European variation are found with the English language brochure or manual as well as an extra magazine, cleaning brush and grease container. These were shipped to England or the U.S. prior to Sauer producing the English Export variation.

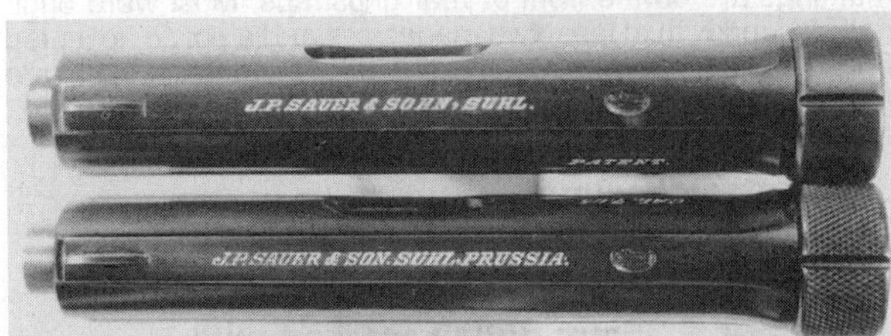

A. European variation:

Exc.	V.G.	Good	Fair	Poor
1100	900	650	400	250

B. English Export variation:

Exc.	V.G.	Good	Fair	Poor
1450	1150	800	500	300

Original box with accessories and manual: Add $500 if complete and in very good to excellent condition.

SECOND SERIES

Extra safety button eliminated, rear sight acts as cocking knob retainer.

Commercial variation

Normal European/German slide markings are normally found; however it has been called to my attention that there are English Export pistols in this SECOND SERIES which have the English markings on the slide which are similar to those found on the FIRST SERIES of the Model 1913. This is applicable to both the 7.65mm and 6.35mm model pistols. These are exceptional scarce pistols and should command at least a 50 percent premium, perhaps more due to their rarity. This commercial variation had factory manuals printed in English, Spanish and German which came with the cardboard boxed pistols. With the original Sauer box accessories and manual: Add $300 if in very good to excellent condition.

Caliber 7.65mm variation

Exc.	V.G.	Good	Fair	Poor
450	375	300	250	100

Caliber 7.65 variation with all words in English (i.e Son, Prussia, etc.)

Exc.	V.G.	Good	Fair	Poor
800	575	450	300	200

Police variations

These will be of the standard German Commercial configuration but nearly always having the Zusatzsicherung (additional safety) added to the pistol. This safety is found between the regular safety lever and the top of the left grip. Police used both calibers, 7.65mm and 6.35mm but the 7.65 was predominant. After the early part of the 1930s the 6.35 was not available to police departments. Thus the 6.35mm police marked Sauer is rather scarce in relation to the 7.65mm caliber. A few in 7.65mm are dated 1920 on the left side of the frame and were used by auxiliary policemen in Bavaria. Normal police property markings are on the front or rear gripstraps. Most were originally issued with at least two magazines and a police accepted holster. The mags were usually numbered and the holsters are found with and without pistol numbers.

Caliber 6.35mm police marked but without Zusatzsicherung

Exc.	V.G.	Good	Fair	Poor
500	350	275	200	75

Caliber 6.35mm police marked with Zusatzsicherung

Exc.	V.G.	Good	Fair	Poor
550	375	275	200	75

Caliber 7.65mm police marked without Zusatzsicherung

Exc.	V.G.	Good	Fair	Poor
575	325	275	175	125

Caliber 7.65mm police marked with Zusatzsicherung

Exc.	V.G.	Good	Fair	Poor
500	350	275	175	125

NOTE: Add 10 percent for one correctly numbered magazine, or 20 percent if found with both correctly numbered magazines. Add 30 percent if found with correct holster and magazines.

R.F.V. (Reich Finanz Verwaltung)

This Sauer variation is rarely found in any condition. The R.F.V. markings and property number could be 1 to 4 digits. This variation is found in both calibers and were used by the Reich's Customs and Finance department personnel.

Caliber 6.35mm R.F.V. marked pistols

Exc.	V.G.	Good	Fair	Poor
800	650	500	350	250

Caliber 7.65mm R.F.V. marked pistols

Exc.	V.G.	Good	Fair	Poor
750	600	400	300	200

Imperial Military variations

These were normal German commercial variations of the time period having either the Imperial Eagle acceptance marking applied on the front of the trigger guard and having the small Imperial Army inspector's acceptance marking (crown over a scriptic letter) on the right side of the frame close to the Nitro proof; or having just the Imperial Army inspector's marking alone. Usually these pistols are found in the 40000 to 85000 range. However, the quantity actually Imperial Military accepted is quite low even though thousands were privately purchased by the officer corps. There are examples in 6.35mm which are Imperial Military accepted but these are very scarce.

Caliber 7.65mm Imperial Military accepted pistols

Exc.	V.G.	Good	Fair	Poor
600	450	350	275	150

Paramilitary marked Sauer pistols of the 1925-35 period

A very few of the Model 1913 pistols will have been marked by paramilitary groups or organizations of this period. Usually this marking is no more than a series of numbers above another series of numbers, such as 23 over 12. These are found usually on the left side of the frame next to the left grip. Most of these numbers are indicative of property numbers assigned to a particular pistols belonging to a particular SA Group, Stahlhelm, or a rightwing organization such as the Red Front (early communist). Any pistol of this type should be examined by an expert to determine if it is an original example.

Exc.	V.G.	Good	Fair	Poor
500	350	275	200	100

Norwegian police usage, post World War II

After the war was over many surplus German weapons were put back into use by the government of Norway. The Germans had occupied this country and large numbers of weapons remained when the fighting ended. This included a large number of surplus Sauer pistols being utilized by the police (POLITI) forces. Most of the Sauers that were used by the Politi which have been imported into the U.S. have been the Model 1913; however there were a number of the Model 1930 pistols which reached our country as well. All examples, regardless of the model, have the word POLITI stamped on the slide as well as a rampant lion on a shield under a crown marking. Following this is the property number and this number is also stamped into the left side of the frame. Most saw much usage during the post-war period. All are in 7.65mm caliber.

Exc.	V.G.	Good	Fair	Poor
350	300	200	150	100

Model 1913/19 in 6.35mm

This particular pistol must be divided into three (3) subvariations. This variation appears to be in a serial number range of its own. The first subvariation appears to run from 1 to 40000. It is highly doubtful if this quantity was manufactured. The second subvariation incorporates a Zusatzsicherung or Additional Safety which can be seen between the normal safety lever and the top of the left grip. It locked the trigger bar when in use. This second range appears to run from approximately serial number 40000 to 51000 which probably was continuous in the number produced. Lastly, the third subvariation examples were manufactured during or after 1926. The trigger guard has a different shape; the slide has a greater area of vertical milled finger grooves; the added Additional safety (Zusatzsicherung) now acts as the hold open device as well. These are found up to approximately 57000. Then a few examples of the first subvariation are found from 57000 up to about 62500. This was, no doubt, usage of remaining parts.

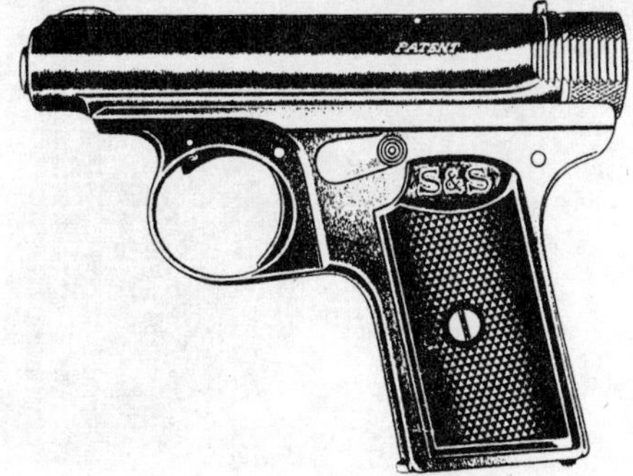

Caliber 6.35mm first subvariation

Exc.	V.G.	Good	Fair	Poor
400	300	250	150	75

Caliber 6.35mm second subvariation

Exc.	V.G.	Good	Fair	Poor
425	350	250	150	75

Caliber 6.35mm third subvariation

Exc.	V.G.	Good	Fair	Poor
550	375	300	200	100

Caliber 6.35mm English export variation

(all words in English; i.e. Son, Prussia, etc.); very rare, only one example known.

Exc.	V.G.	Good	Fair	Poor
1000	700	500	300	200

NOTE: Any commercial pistol could be special ordered with a factory nickel finish, special grip material (pearl, wood, etc.) as well as different types of engraving. It would be in your best interest to have these pistols examined by an expert.

1926 EXPORT MODEL

This variation's name comes from actual Sauer factory records found in the Suhl Archive. It is an interim pistol produced during the 1926 to early 1929 period. It is found only in the 7.65mm caliber. This was an advancement of the normal 1913 design which included changes in (1) the safety lever's design that became a slide hold open device as well, (2) shape of the frame was altered in that the trigger guard became more streamlined and the rear of the frame was shortened, and serrations were added to the slide as well as the cocking knob. These are found in the 162000 to 169000 range in relatively small clusters. Two to four thousand are presumed to have been manufactured. A scarce Sauer pistol! To date, none have been seen in nickel.

Exc.	V.G.	Good	Fair	Poor
750	625	475	300	150

W.T.M.-Westentaschen Model—Vest Pocket Model

Several variations of vest pocket pistols were manufactured. The first was called a Model 1920 by the Sauer firm. We usually refer to it as the Model 1924. This pistol, as well as all other W.T.M. examples, were designed to carry in your pocket. They are quite small in size and are found only in the 6.35mm or .25 ACP caliber. Later on in 1928 an updated version became available and was referred to a the Model 1928. These differed in internal parts design, slide configuration and the bottom of the grip was marked, "Cal.6.35.28." The last version appeared in 1933 and still utilized the same grips but the trigger and some other small parts differed. All three were available in blue or nickel finish, as well as engraving and fancy grip material. A very few of the Model 1933 had stainless steel (NIROSTA marked) barrels.

Model 1920

Serrations on the front and rear of the slide.

Exc.	V.G.	Good	Fair	Poor
550	450	300	200	75

Model 1928

"Cal. 6.35.28" on the black Bakelite grips.

Exc.	V.G.	Good	Fair	Poor
500	450	300	185	75

Model 1933

Different type of trigger and found in the 253000 to early 254000 serial number range.

Exc.	V.G.	Good	Fair	Poor
700	575	400	275	150

NOTE: Add $200 for factory nickel, $250 for factory engraving, $250 for exotic grip material, $500 for factory paper box with cleaning brush, extra magazine and brochure, $750 in original factory imitation leather covered metal presentation case with accessories, $500 for NIROSTA marked stainless barrel.

MODEL 1930 VARIATIONS

Dutch models

These different types of Dutch pistols will have JOH MUNTS - AMSTERDAM on the left side of the slide. The grips are usually a mottled gray color. Sauer manufactured different pistols for the Dutch police, Navy, Army, Department of Finance, S.M.N. (Steam Ships Netherlands) and possibly other agencies.

Dutch Police

First variation manufactured w/o adjustable front sight and w/o lanyard loop.

Exc.	V.G.	Good	Fair	Poor
650	450	350	250	125

Amsterdam Police

Manufactured w/o adjustable sight but having a lanyard loop.

Exc.	V.G.	Good	Fair	Poor
700	500	350	250	125

Navy

Made without adjustable sight and having the Anchor & Crown marked on the rear gripstrap.

Exc.	V.G.	Good	Fair	Poor
800	500	375	250	125

S.M.N.

Found with and w/o adjustable front sights, no lanyard loop, S.M.N. marked horizontally near bottom of rear gripstrap

Exc.	V.G.	Good	Fair	Poor
1000	700	375	225	100

Department of Finance

Found with and w/o adjustable front sight, no lanyard loop, DF over date-1933-on rear grip strap

Exc.	V.G.	Good	Fair	Poor
850	700	385	250	150

NOTE: Accessories: cleaning rod, brush, aluminum oil bottle and manuals, add accordingly.

1930 Commercial Model

These pistols were for sale in Germany and other countries through normal commercial outlets. A very few are factory nickeled, engraved or both; some are with the NIROSTA marked barrels and a very few were made in Duralumin or Dural. The standard caliber was 7.65mm hut a very limited number were made in .22 LR (.22 Long). Standard grip material is black Bakelite. Most of the regular pistols were purchased by military officers, some went to paramilitary groups, such as the SA.

Standard Commercial

Exc.	V.G.	Good	Fair	Poor
600	450	300	200	125

Standard Commercial with NIROSTA marked barrel, 7.65mm

Exc.	V.G.	Good	Fair	Poor
900	600	350	275	150

Standard Commercial in .22 LR (.22 Long)

Exc.	V.G.	Good	Fair	Poor
2500	1850	600	375	300

Duralumin (rural) Variation, 7.65mm

Exc.	V.G.	Good	Fair	Poor
3500	2750	2000	1200	450

NOTE: For any variation listed add $100 for nickel finish; $500 for engraving; $600 for both nickel and engraving; with nickel, engraving, and with a fancy grip material (pearl or ebony, etc.) $750.

BEHORDEN MODEL

The Behorden (Authority) Model is different from the Model 1930 in that it has a trigger safety and a loaded indicator provided.

Behorden Commercial

These are normally found with a high polished blued finish. It was available with a nickel finish, engraving, or both, as well as fancy grip material and a NIROSTA marked barrel. The regular caliber is 7.65mm, but a very few are know in .22 LR that are probably prototype pistols.

Exc.	V.G.	Good	Fair	Poor
675	550	400	350	200

NOTE: Add $100 for nickel finish, $250 for engraving, $350 for both, $500 with nickel, engraving, and a fancy grip material; $500 for NIROSTA marked stainless barrel. Add 200 percent for .22 caliber.

Late Behorden Commercial

These are actually Model 1930 pistols found in the 220000 to 223000 serial number range which do not have the trigger safety and/or the indicator pin.

Exc.	V.G.	Good	Fair	Poor
600	450	300	200	125

Duralumin Model (Dural)

The frame and slide are made of the Duralumin material. These are rare pistols!

Blue Anodized Variation

Found with and w/o NIROSTA marked barrels.

Exc.	V.G.	Good	Fair	Poor
4000	3500	2500	1500	850

NOTE: Add $250 for the stainless barrel.

Nonanodized Variation

Found with and w/o NIROSTA marked barrels.

Exc.	V.G.	Good	Fair	Poor
4000	3500	2500	1500	850

NOTE: Add $250 for the stainless barrel.

Presentation Examples of Anodized and Nonanodized Variations

Please consult an expert for pricing.

Police Models

Examples will be found with police acceptance on the left side of the trigger guard and in a few cases on the front or rear grip straps. Black Bakelite grips are standard.

Sunburst K Police Acceptance

Nonadjustable front sight (a round blade).

Exc.	V.G.	Good	Fair	Poor
600	500	350	275	200

Sunburst K Police Acceptance

Adjustable front sight.

Exc.	V.G.	Good	Fair	Poor
750	625	450	300	225

Diamond in Sunburst Police Acceptance

All known are with the adjustable front sight.

Exc.	V.G.	Good	Fair	Poor
950	750	500	300	225

Grip Strap Marked Variations

(Having abbreviations of a city and the property number of the pistol on the grip strap.) Very few of these are known. Examples are S.Mg. 52, Sch. 78, etc.

Exc.	V.G.	Good	Fair	Poor
750	550	375	250	150

MODEL 36/37

These very few pistols are all prototype Sauer pistols which preceded the Model 38. They are in the 210,000 range. Please consult an expert to determine value! EXTREMELY RARE.

MODEL 38 AND 38-H (H MODEL) VARIATIONS

Model 38

This pistol started at 260000. It is Crown N Nitro proofed, has a cocking/decocking lever, and a loaded indicator pin, and is double-action. It has a high polish blue; is in 7.65m/m (the standard production pistol); is found without the thumbsafety on the slide; with a pinned mag release. VERY RARE.

One Line Slide Legend Variation (inned magazine release button - no screw)

Crown N proofs.Approximately 250 produced. Extremely rare!

Exc.	V.G.	Good	Fair	Poor
4000	3000	2000	600	300

Two Line Slide Legend Variation (pinned magazine release button - no screw)

C/N proofs, blued, with pinned magazine release (about 850 produced) VERY RARE.

Exc.	V.G.	Good	Fair	Poor
1900	1500	1000	500	275

NOTE: Add $250 for factory nickel; $350 for factory chrome; $1000 for engraving; $500 for NIROSTA marked barrel.

Two Line Slide Legend Variation (magazine release button)

C/N proofs, blued, magazine release button retained by a screw. RARE.

Exc.	V.G.	Good	Fair	Poor
1300	950	600	400	275

NOTE: Add $250 for factory nickel; $350 for factory chrome; $1000 for engraving; $500 for NIROSTA marked barrel.

This symbol denotes "Sleepers" with rapidly-rising values and/or significant collector potential. 

SA der NSDAP Gruppe Thuringen Marked Variation

Blued, C/N proofs, with magazine release button held by a screw. VERY RARE.

Exc.	V.G.	Good	Fair	Poor
3800	2500	1000	500	275

Model 38 pistols converted to H Models by Sauer factory.

Currently there are fewer than 30 known examples in collections. The thumbsafety levers were added. Unique milling on the left side of the slide determines these pistols in the 262xxx, 263xxx and 264xxx ranges. This includes SA der NSDAP Gruppe Thüringen marked pistols.

Exc.	V.G.	Good	Fair	Poor
1800	1200	850	450	—

Model 38-H or H Model

This model has a thumbsafety on the slide, Crown N Nitro proof, high polish blued finish, a cocking/decocking lever, double-action, and is found in 7.65m/m caliber as the standard production pistol. This model is found only with the two line slide legend or logo. Type 1, variation 2.

Standard Commercial Variation

Exc.	V.G.	Good	Fair	Poor
950	800	500	300	175

NOTE: Add $100 for factory nickel (factory chromed has not been identified); $1000 for factory engraving; $250 for exotic grip material; $500 for NIROSTA marked stainless barrel.

SA der NSDAP Gruppe Thuringia Variation

Same as Standard. above except having SA markings on slide, with blued finish, VERY RARE.

Exc.	V.G.	Good	Fair	Poor
3500	2500	1000	500	200

NOTE: Add $1,500 for SA marked Akah holster in excellent condition.

L.M. Model

(Leicht Model-lightweight model); frame and slide made of DURAL (Duralumin), in the 264800 range, with thumb safety, and regular black Bakelite grips. EXTREMELY RARE.

Exc.	V.G.	Good	Fair	Poor
5000	3850	2500	1500	850

Flash Light Model

Only four known examples of this variation. Battery flash light attached by four screws to the pistol. Carried by the *SS* night partol at the Reich's chancellory in Berlin. No specific markings, but known serial numbers are 266814, 266842, 266845.

Exc.	V.G.	Good	Fair	Poor
Too Rare To Price				

Police Accepted Variation

Found with Police Eagle C acceptance on left trigger guard and having Crown N proofs. RARE.

Exc.	V.G.	Good	Fair	Poor
1100	900	500	300	175

TYPE TWO MODEL 38-H (H MODEL)

There are no Model 38 pistols in the Type Two description, only the H Model with thumbsafety. These begin at serial number 269100 and have the Eagle N Nitro proofs, with a blued high polish finish and black Bakelite grips. The normal caliber is 7.65mm.

A. H Model

Standard Commercial

Exc.	V.G.	Good	Fair	Poor
750	550	475	300	200

NOTE: Add $1500 for boxed examples complete with factory manual, clean ring rod, all accessories, extra magazine, etc. $250 for factory nickel, $350 for factory chrome, $1000 for factory engraving.

.22 Caliber Variation

Slide and magazines are marked CAL. .22 LANG. (Some with steel frame and slides; some with Dural frames and slides.) Found in 269900 range. Very Rare.

Exc.	V.G.	Good	Fair	Poor
5500	4000	2500	400	250

Jager Model

A special order pistol in .22 caliber which is similar in appearance to Walther's 1936 Jagerschafts pistol. Very rare.

Exc.	V.G.	Good	Fair	Poor
4500	3000	1800	800	400

Police Eagle C and Eagle F Acceptance Variations

These are the first Eagle N (post January 1940) police accepted pistols are found in the 270000 to 276000 ranges.

Exc.	V.G.	Good	Fair	Poor
750	500	400	325	200

NOTE: Add 25 percent for E/F.

German Military Variation

This is the first official military accepted range of 2,000 pistols. It is in a range found between 271000 to 273000. Two Eagle 37 military acceptance marks are found on the trigger guard.

Exc.	V.G.	Good	Fair	Poor
1500	1000	700	475	300

Second Military Variation

These pistols are found with the high polish finish but have only one Eagle 37 acceptance marks. The letter H is found on all small parts.

Exc.	V.G.	Good	Fair	Poor
750	500	350	275	175

Police Eagle C Acceptance

This variation includes the remainder of the high polish blued police accepted pistols.

Exc.	V.G.	Good	Fair	Poor
675	550	350	275	175

NOTE: Add $50 for matching magazine, $200 for both matching mags and correct police holster; $300 for both matching mags and correct matching numbered, police accepted and dated holster.

TYPE THREE 38-H MODEL (H MODEL)

This terminology is used because of the change of the exterior finish of the Sauer pistols. Due to the urgency of the war, the order was received to not polish the exterior surfaces of the pistols as had been done previously. There was also a change in the formulation of the grip's material. Later in this range there will be found stamped parts, zinc triggers and magazine bottoms, etc. used to increase the pistol's production. Type Three has a full slide legend.

A. H Model

Military Accepted

One Eagle 37 Waffenamt mark.

Exc.	V.G.	Good	Fair	Poor
550	450	350	275	150

Commercial

Only Eagle N Nitro proof marks.

Exc.	V.G.	Good	Fair	Poor
450	400	350	250	150

NOTE: See Type Two Commercial info, prices apply here also.

Police Accepted with the Police Eagle C Acceptance

Exc.	V.G.	Good	Fair	Poor
550	450	350	250	150

NOTE: See Type Two Police info, prices apply here also.

TYPE FOUR 38-H MODEL (H MODEL)

This is a continuation of the pistol as described in Type Three except the J.P. Sauer & Sohn, Suhl legend is dropped from the slide and only CAL. 7.65 is found on the left side. The word PATENT may or may not appear on the right side. Many are found with a zinc trigger.

A. H Model

Military Accepted

One Eagle 37 Waffenamt mark.

Exc.	V.G.	Good	Fair	Poor
500	450	350	275	150

Commercial

Having only the Eagle N Nitro proofs.

Exc.	V.G.	Good	Fair	Poor
450	400	350	250	150

NOTE: See Type Two Commercial info, prices apply here also.

Police Accepted with the Police Eagle C Acceptance

Exc.	V.G.	Good	Fair	Poor
500	450	350	275	150

NOTE: See Type Two Price info, prices apply here also.

Eigentum NSDAP SA Gruppe Alpenland Slide Marked Pistols

These unique pistols are found in the 456000 and 457000 serial number ranges. They have thumb safety levers on the slides.

Exc.	V.G.	Good	Fair	Poor
3850	2500	1000	450	250

NSDAP SA Gruppe Alpenland Slide Marked Pistols

These unique pistols are found in the 465000 serial number range. They have thumbsafety levers on the slide.

Exc.	V.G.	Good	Fair	Poor
3850	2500	1000	450	250

Himmler Presentation Pistols

These desirable pistols have a high polish finish with DEM SCHARFSCHUTZEN - H. HIMMLER on the left side of the slide (with no other markings), and J.P. SAUER & SOHN over CAL.7,65 on the right side (opposite of normal). These pistols came in imitation leather cover metal cases with cloth interiors having a cleaning brush, extra magazine and cartridges. Very rare pistols! Extremely rare if cased!

Exc.	V.G.	Good	Fair	Poor
28500	21000	10000	3500	1000

Model 38

To speed up production even more, the thumbsafety (Handsicherung-Hammer safety) was eliminated. The side continues to be marked only with CAL. 7,65. The frame's serial number changes from the right side to the left side at 472000 with overlaps up to 489000.

Military Accepted

One Eagle 37 Waffenamt mark.

Exc.	V.G.	Good	Fair	Poor
450	400	350	250	175

Commercial

Only the Eagle N Nitro proofs.

Exc.	V.G.	Good	Fair	Poor
575	475	350	250	175

NOTE: See Type Two Commercial info, prices apply here also.

Police Accepted with the Police Eagle C Acceptance

Exc.	V.G.	Good	Fair	Poor
575	450	400	300	200

Police Accepted with the Police Eagle F Acceptance

Exc.	V.G.	Good	Fair	Poor
475	400	350	250	175

NOTE: See Type Two Police info, prices apply here also.

TYPE FIVE MODEL 38 & H MODEL PISTOLS

There are two different basic variations of the Type Five Sauer pistols. Either may or may not have a thumbsafety lever on the slide. The main criteria is whether the frame is factory numbered as per normal and follows the chronological sequence of those pistols in the preceding model. After the frames were used which were already numbered and finished upon the arrival of the U.S. Army, the last variation came about. Neither variation has any Nitro proof marks.

First Variation

Factory numbered sequential frames starting on or near serial number 506800. Slides and breech blocks may or may not match.

Exc.	V.G.	Good	Fair	Poor
475	350	275	225	100

Second Variation

Started with serial number 1; made from mostly rejected parts, generally have notched trigger guards, may or may not be blued, no Nitro proofs, slides may or may not have factory legends, etc. Approximately 300 assembled. Definitely rare Sauer pistols!

Exc.	V.G.	Good	Fair	Poor
750	500	300	200	100

NOTE: There are some pistols which have post-war Russian Crown N Nitro proofs. The Russians assembled or refurbished a very few pistols after the U.S. Army left this section after the war. Several have been found with newly made barrels in 7.65mm with a C/N proof. A hard to find Sauer!

SAVAGE ARMS CORPORATION

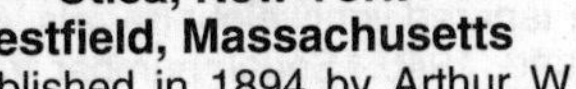

Utica, New York
Westfield, Massachusetts

Established in 1894 by Arthur W. Savage, this company has manufactured a wide variety of firearms, of which its Model 99 is the best known. By 1915, Savage Arms was manufacturing centerfire and rimfire rifles, pistols, and ammunition. During World War I the company produced the Lewis machine guns. In 1920 Savage purchased J. Stevens Arms Company which was associated with Harry Pope, the famous barrel maker. Later in the decade the company acquired the Page Lewis Company, Davis-Warner, Crescent Firearms, and A.H. Fox. At one time Savage was the largest firearms manufacturing company in the free world. During World War II Savage/Stevens produced military small arms and machine guns. In 1947 the Sporting Arms division moved to Chicopee Falls, Mass., where it was incorporated into Stevens Arms Company. In 1960 the entire operation was moved to Westfield, Mass.

Model 1895

A .303 Savage caliber lever-action rifle with a 26" or 30" barrel and 5-shot rotary magazine. Identifiable by the hole in the breechbolt. The barrel marked "Savage Repeating Arms Co. Utica, N.Y. U.S.A. Pat. Feb. 7, 1893, July 25, 1893. CAL. .303." Blued with a walnut stock. Approximately 8,000 were manufactured between 1895 and 1899.

Courtesy Rock Island Auction Company

Exc.	V.G.	Good	Fair	Poor
3000	2000	1200	600	200

NOTE: 22" or 30" barrel add 10 percent.

Model 1899-A 22" Barrel Short Rifle

Chambered for .303, .30-30, .25-35, .32-40, .38-55. Serial number range from 10000 to 220000. Produced from 1899 to 1922. Same cocking indicator as the 1899-A rifle.

Exc.	V.G.	Good	Fair	Poor
1200	900	600	300	100

NOTE: Add 50 percent for .25-35, .32-40, and .38-55 calibers.

Model 1899-A 26" Round Barrel Rifle

A .25-35, .30-30, .303 Savage, .32-40 or .38-55, .300 Savage caliber lever-action rifle with 26" barrel marked "Savage Arms Company, Utica, N.Y. Pat. Feb. 7, 1893, July 25.'93, Oct.3.'99 .CAL.30." Manufactured between 1899 and 1926/27. Blued with a walnut stock. Serial number range 10000 to 300000. Block cocking indicator on bolt to s/n 90000 then changed to pin indicator on tang.

Courtesy Rock Island Auction Company

Exc.	V.G.	Good	Fair	Poor
1200	800	500	250	100

NOTE: Add 50 percent for .25-35, .32-40, and .38-55 calibers.

Model 1899-B 26" Octagon Barrel Rifle

In calibers .303, .30-30, .25-35, .32-40, .38-55. Manufactured between 1899 and 1915. Serial number range 10000 to 175000. Same cocking indicator as 1899-A rifle.

Courtesy Rock Island Auction Company

Exc.	V.G.	Good	Fair	Poor
1600	1100	700	350	150

NOTE: Add 50 percent for .25-35, .32-40, and .38-55 calibers.

Model 1899-C 26" Half Octagon Barrel Rifle

In calibers .303, .30-30, .25-35, .32-40, .38-55. Manufactured between 1899 and 1915. Serial number range 10000 to 175000. Same cocking indicator as 1899-A rifle.

Courtesy Rock Island Auction Company

Exc.	V.G.	Good	Fair	Poor
2000	1500	1000	400	150

NOTE: Add 50 percent for .25-35, .32-40, and .38-55 calibers.

Model 1899-D Military Musket

Chambered for .303 Savage only with 28" barrel. Fitted with full military stocks. Produced from 1899 to 1915. Several hundred produced for Canadian Home Guard during WWI. These will have rack number on buttplate.

Exc.	V.G.	Good	Fair	Poor
4500	3000	1500	700	300

Model 1899-F Saddle Ring Carbine

Fitted with 20" barrel only in calibers .303, .30-30, .25-35, .32-40, .38-55. Built from 1899 to 1919 in serial number range 19000 to 200000. Same cocking indicator as 1899-A rifle. Earliest style with barrel band is rarest variation.

Courtesy Rock Island Auction Company

Exc.	V.G.	Good	Fair	Poor
1500	900	500	300	100

NOTE: Add 100 percent for .25-35, .32-40, and .38-55 calibers. Add 200 percent for barrel band carbine.

Model 1899-CD Deluxe Rifle

In calibers .303, .30-30, .25-35, .32-40, .38-55. Serial number range 50000 to 175000. Built from 1905 to 1917. Same cocking indicator as the 1899-A rifle. The standard Deluxe 1899 rifle with 26" round, octagon, or half octagon barrel with pistol grip stock and checkering. Takedown barrel or short 22" barrel.

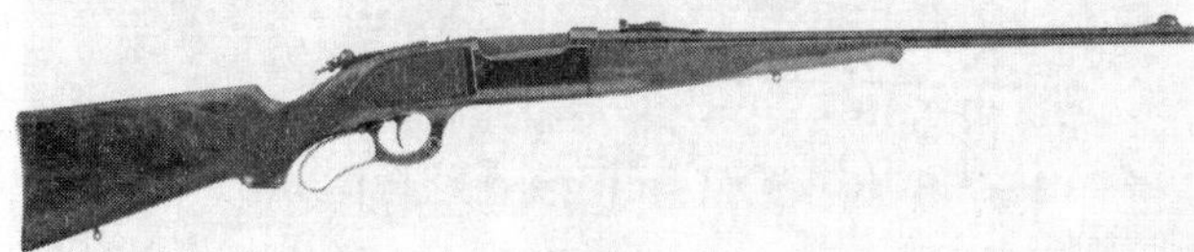

Courtesy Rock Island Auction Company

Exc.	V.G.	Good	Fair	Poor
3000	2000	1500	600	250

NOTE: Add 30 percent for .25-35, .32-40, and .38-55 calibers.

Model 1899-H Featherweight Rifle

Chambered for .303, .30-30, .25-35, and .22 HP Savage in 20" barrel. Serial number range 50000 to 220000. Built from 1905 to 1919. The revolutionary .22 HP cartridge was introduced in this model in 1912. Most 1899-Hs are found with takedown barrels.

Paul Goodwin photo

Exc.	V.G.	Good	Fair	Poor
1600	1200	600	300	100

NOTE: Add 50 percent for .25-35, add 25 percent for .22HP.

Model 1899 .250-3000 Savage Rifle

This deluxe Model 1899 was developed to introduce the Charles Newton designed .250-3000 Savage cartridge. Fitted with a 22" featherweight takedown barrel, pistol grip, checkered perch belly stock, unique checkered trigger. Built from 1914 to 1921 in the 146500 to 237500 serial number range.

Exc.	V.G.	Good	Fair	Poor
2500	2000	800	350	100

Model 99-B 26"/24" Standard Weight Takedown

Chambered for .303, .30-30, and .300 Savage. Serial number range 200000 to 344000. Produced from 1920 to 1934. In 1926 a new 24" barrel with ramp front sight was introduced.

Exc.	V.G.	Good	Fair	Poor
900	700	400	300	100

Model 99-C 22" Standard Weight Short Rifle

Chambered for .303, .30-30, and .300 Savage. Serial number range 238000 to 290000. Built from 1922 to 1926. This model looks like a shortened 26" rifle but with a heavily crowned muzzle.

Exc.	V.G.	Good	Fair	Poor
800	600	400	200	100

Model 99-D 22" Standard Weight Takedown Rifle

Chambered for .303, .30-30, and .300 Savage. Serial number range 238000 to 290000. Built from 1922 to 1926. Same heavily crowned muzzle as 99-C.

Exc.	V.G.	Good	Fair	Poor
900	700	400	200	100

Model 99-E Lightweight Rifle

Chambered for .22 HP, .30-30, .303, .250-3000, and .300 Savage. Manufactured between 1922 and 1934. Serial number range 238000 to 344000. In 1926 new ramp front sight introduced.

Courtesy Rock Island Auction Company

Exc.	V.G.	Good	Fair	Poor
1200	800	500	300	100

NOTE: Add 25 percent for .22 Hi Power and .250-3000 calibers.

Model 99-F Lightweight Takedown Rifle

As above, but in lightweight takedown barrels in 20", 22", and 24". Chambered for .22 HP, .30-30, .303, .250-3000, and .300 Savage.These barrels were tapered lightweight barrels. Manufactured between 1920 and 1940. Serial number range 200000 to 398000. In 1926 new ramp front sight introduced. Early versions look similar to Model 1899-H featherweight. In 1938 checkered stocks offered this option is rare.

Exc.	V.G.	Good	Fair	Poor
1400	1000	600	300	100

NOTE: Add 50 percent for .22 HP, and .250-3000. Add 75 percent for 1938 checkered stocks.

Model 99-G Deluxe Takedown Pistol Grip Rifle

Calibers and barrel lengths as above, with a pistol grip checkered stock. Manufactured between 1922 and 1941. Serial number range 238000 to 407000. No takedown Model 99s made after 1941.

Courtesy Rock Island Auction Company

Exc.	V.G.	Good	Fair	Poor
1800	1200	700	300	100

NOTE: Add 50 percent for .22 Hi Power and 25 percent for .250-3000

Model 99-H Carbine/Barrel Band Carbine

Fitted with 20" or 22" barrels and chambered for .30-30, .303, .250-3000, and .300 Savage. serial number range 220000 to 400000. Built between 1923 and 1940. Distinctive plain stocks with no flat pads on side of buttstock. Curved carbine style butt-plate. In 1931 barrel band added to forend, then commonly called the "barrel band carbine." In 1935 flat pads added to buttstock sides. Also front ramp sight added.

Courtesy Rock Island Auction Company

Exc.	V.G.	Good	Fair	Poor
1000	600	300	200	100

NOTE: Add 50 percent for 1935 barrel band carbine. Add 25 percent for .250-3000, and .300 Savage.

Combination Cased Set .300 Savage/.410 Barrel

Fitted with 22" or 24" barrels with .410 barrels and .300 Savage in Model 99-F, 99-G, or 99-K configuration. In black fitted case. Serial number range 240000 to 350000. built from 1922 to 1934. Be aware that the barrel address on the .410 barrel matches that on the rifle barrel and that the .410 barrel takes up correctly on the receiver, and that the case fits the .410 barrel and receiver.

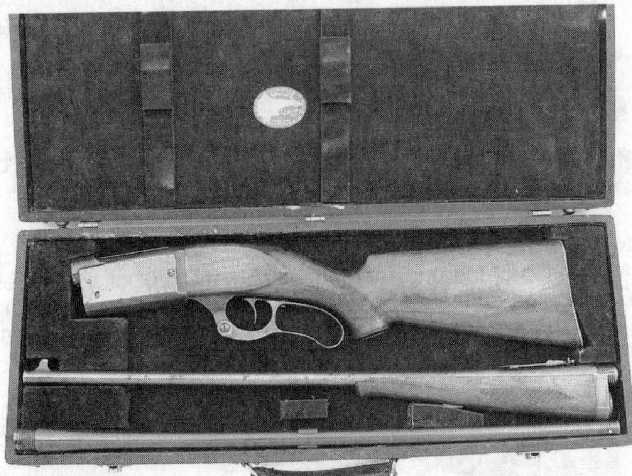

Courtesy Amoskeag Auction Company

Exc.	V.G.	Good	Fair	Poor
4000	2500	1500	800	300

Model 99-A 24" Featherweight Rifle

Fitted with a 24" barrel with new 1926 ramp front sight. Chambered for .303, .30-30, or .300 Savage. Serial number range 290000 to 370000. Built from 1926 to 1937. Buttplate is older 1899 crescent style.

Exc.	V.G.	Good	Fair	Poor
600	500	400	250	75

Model 99-K Deluxe Engraved Rifle

The premier Savage Model 99 with an engraved receiver. Fitted with a checkered pistol grip stock of select American walnut, and a takedown frame. Hand honed and hand fitted. Chambered for .22 HP, .30-30, .303, .250-3000, and .300 Savage. Fitted with 22" or 24" barrels. Serial number range 285000 to 398000. Manufactured between 1926 and 1940.

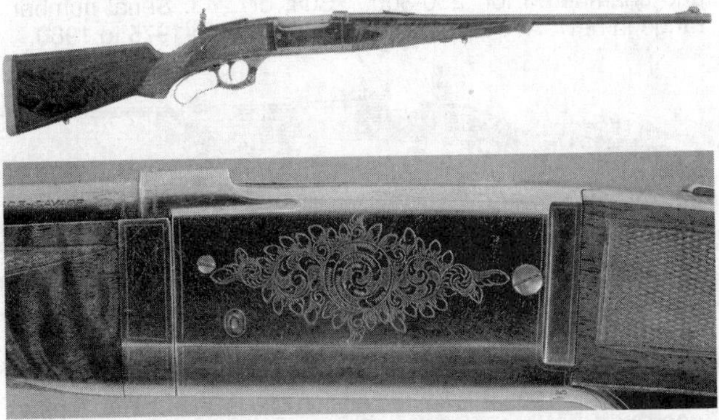

Courtesy Rock Island Auction Company

Exc.	V.G.	Good	Fair	Poor
3000	2500	1400	600	200

NOTE: Add 30 percent for .22 caliber Hi Power. Some of these models found with cased set with .410 barrel. Add $700 for V.G. case and barrels.

Model 99-R Heavy Stocked Rifle

This model features a heavy pistol grip checkered stock with rounded forend tip. Fitted with a 22" or 24" barrel and chambered for .250-3000, .303, .300 Savage, .308, .243, and .358 calibers. Serial number range 340000 to 1060000. Manufactured between 1932 and 1960.

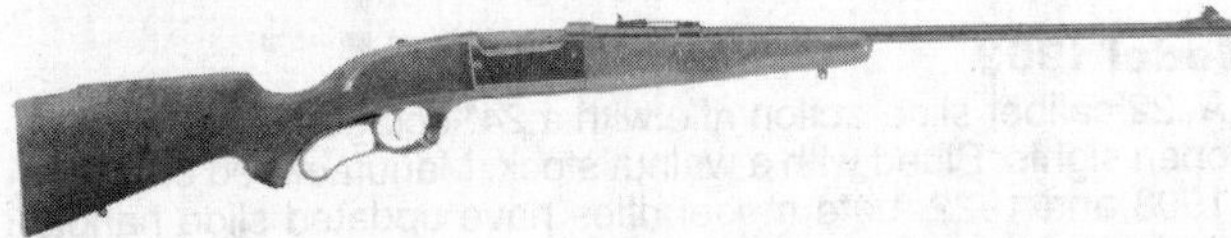

Courtesy Rock Island Auction Company

Exc.	V.G.	Good	Fair	Poor
1000	600	350	200	75

NOTE: Add 50 percent for .358 and 100 percent for rare uncataloged .30-30. Approximately 10 made for A.F. Stoeger of N.Y.C. for N.Y. State Police in 1935 in serial number range 348600. Most of these are found with Redfield No. 102 side peep sight and 1/4" rack number stamped in stock below pistol grip.

Model 99-RS Special Sights

As above, with a Lyman aperture rear tang sight. In 1940 this was changed to a Redfield micrometer tang sight. This was the first model fitted with Savage quick release sling swivels. No .30-30 calibers made in this model. Manufactured between 1932 and 1942.

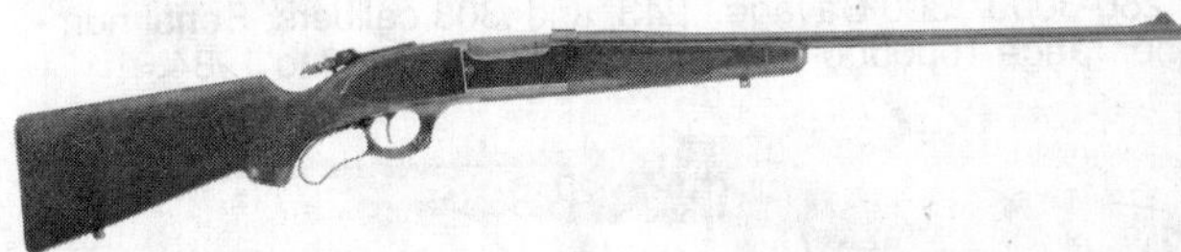

Courtesy Rock Island Auction Company

Exc.	V.G.	Good	Fair	Poor
1200	800	500	350	200

NOTE: Add 50 percent for .358.

Model 99-EG Standard Weight Rifle

Produced with plain uncheckered pistol grip stock until 1940. Available in .22 Hi Power, .250 Savage, .30-30, .303 Savage. .300 Savage, .308, .243, and .358. Serial number range 350000 to 1060000. Manufactured between 1935 and 1960.

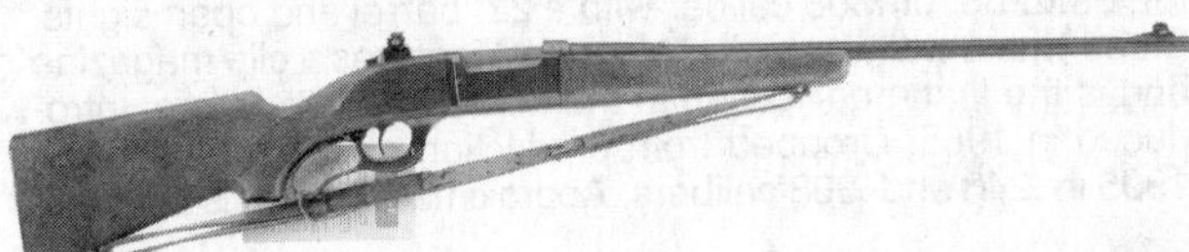

Courtesy Rock Island Auction Company

Exc.	V.G.	Good	Fair	Poor
700	500	300	200	75

NOTE: For pre-1940 uncheckered stocks add 20 percent. Add 100 percent for rifles chambered for .22 Hi Power and .358

Model 99-T Deluxe Featherweight Rifle

This is the classic short barrel deluxe Model 99 with semi-beavertail forend and distinct long checkering pattern. Fitted with 20" or 22" barrels and chambered for .250-3000, .30-30, .303, .22 HP, or .300 Savage. Serial number range 350000 to 400000. Manufactured between 1935 and 1940.

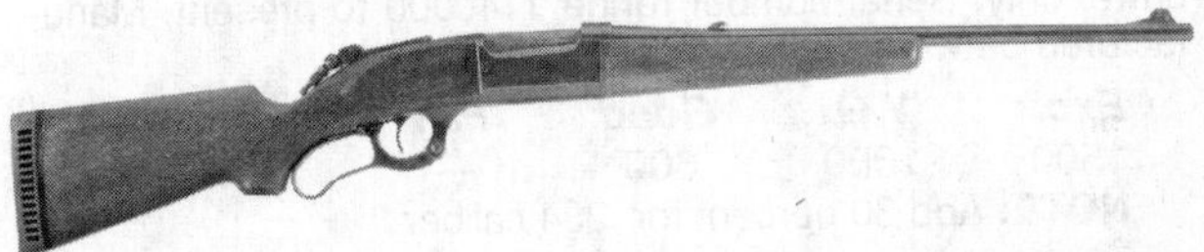

Courtesy Rock Island Auction Company

Exc.	V.G.	Good	Fair	Poor
1500	1000	700	350	100

NOTE: Add 100 percent for .22 Hi Power caliber, 20 percent for .250-3000.

Model 99-F Featherweight Rifle

The first Savage made with the model designation visible on the outside. Located at the rear on the right side of the barrel. A true featherweight with slender 22" barrel, lightweight stocks with butt end hollowed out. Chambered for .250-3000, .300 Savage, .308, .243, .284, and .358 calibers. Serial number range 755000 to present. Built from 1955 to 1973.

Exc.	V.G.	Good	Fair	Poor
900	600	400	250	75

NOTE: Add 100 percent for .284 and .358 calibers, add 50 percent for .243 and .250-3000 Savage.

Model 99-DL Deluxe Monte Carlo Rifle

A deluxe version of the Model 99EG. Available in .243, .250 Savage, .300 Savage, .284, .358, and .308 calibers with a Monte Carlo-style stock. Serial number range 1000000 to present. Manufactured between 1960 and 1973.

Exc.	V.G.	Good	Fair	Poor
500	350	250	150	50

NOTE: Add 75 percent for .358 and .284 calibers.

Model 99-E Economy Rifle

The ugly duckling of the Savage line. The Model 99-E lacked many of the standard features such as left side cartridge counter, tang sight holes, walnut stocks, and capped pistol grip. Fitted with 20", 22", or 24" barrels and chambered for .250-3000, .300 Savage, .243, and .308 calibers. Serial number range 1000000 to present. Built from 1960 to 1984.

Exc.	V.G.	Good	Fair	Poor
450	375	275	150	50

NOTE: The Model 99-E was the last original rotary magazine Model 99 when production discontinued in 1984.

Model 99-C Clip Magazine Rifle

The recent production model in .22-250, .243, .284 Winchester, 7mm-08, or .308 caliber with a 22" barrel and open sights. Blued with a walnut stock. This model features a clip magazine and is the first modification in the Model 99 in 66 years. Introduced in 1965. Dropped from production and reintroduced in 1995 in .243 and .308 calibers. Approximate weight is 7.75 lbs.

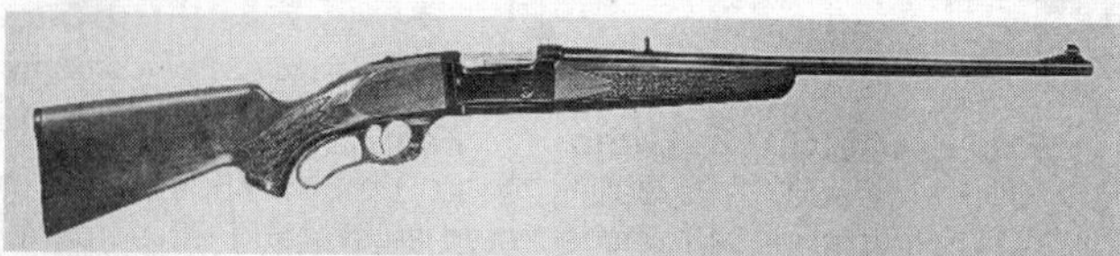

NIB	Exc.	V.G.	Good	Fair	Poor
550	350	300	250	150	50

NOTE: Add 100 percent for .22-250, .284, and 7mm-08.

Model 99-DE Citation Grade Rifle

A premier Savage with an engraved receiver with nickel-like finish and impressed checkering on select walnut stocks. Marked 99-M. Offered in .243, .284, and .308 calibers with 22" barrel only. Serial number range 1140000 to present. Manufactured between 1965 and 1970.

Exc.	V.G.	Good	Fair	Poor
1500	1000	600	—	—

NOTE: Add 30 percent for .284 caliber.

Model 99-PE Presentation Grade Rifle

This model is a presentation grade Model 99 with an engraved receiver as well as a hand-checkered finely figured walnut stock. Mountain lion on right side of receiver and elk on left side. Chambered for .243, .284, and .308 caliber with 22" barrel. Serial number range 1140000 to present. Manufactured between 1965 and 1970.

Exc.	V.G.	Good	Fair	Poor
2000	1500	800	—	—

NOTE: Add 30 percent for .284 caliber.

Model 1895 Anniversary Edition

A .308 caliber reproduction of the Model 1895 with a 24" octagonal barrel, engraved receiver and walnut stock with a schnabel forend. Brass crescent buttplate, brass medallion inlaid in stock. There were 9,999 manufactured in 1970.

NIB	Exc.	V.G.	Good	Fair	Poor
550	300	250	200	—	—

Model 99A Saddle Gun

A variation of the original Model 99A with a 20" or 22" barrel. Chambered for the .243, .250 Savage, .300 Savage, .308, and .375. Serial number range in new "A" series on left side. Manufactured between 1971 and 1982.

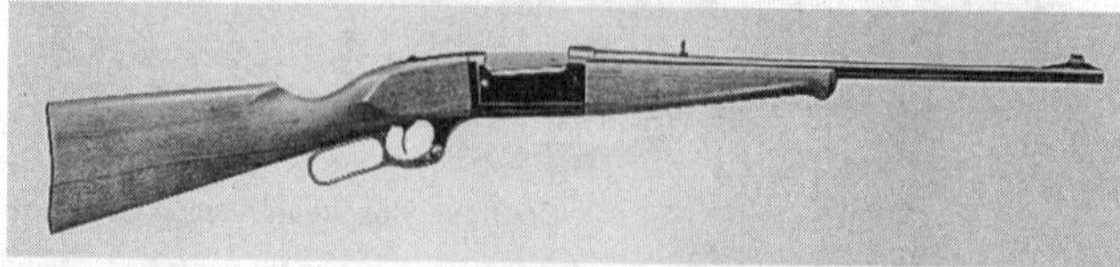

NIB	Exc.	V.G.	Good	Fair	Poor
900	600	300	250	—	—

NOTE: Add 25 percent for .375 caliber.

Model 99-.358 and 99-.375 Brush Guns

Similar to the Model 99-A straight grip saddle gun, but in .358 and .375 Win. (1980) calibers. Has plain grooved forend, rubber recoil pad. Serial number range in the "A" series on left side. Built from 1977 to 1980.

NIB	Exc.	V.G.	Good	Fair	Poor
700	500	300	250	—	—

NOTE: Add 25 percent for .358 Win. caliber.

Model 99-CD Deluxe Clip Model

The North American classic rifle with distinct stocks of checkered walnut with long grooved forend, deep shaped pistol grip, and Monte Carlo stock with cheekpiece. Fitted with 22" barrel and chambered for .250-3000, .308, or .243. Serial number range in new "A" series on left side. Built from 1975 to 1980.

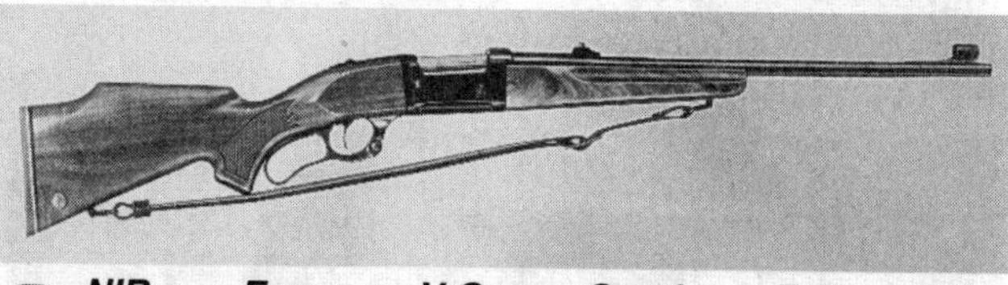

NIB	Exc.	V.G.	Good	Fair	Poor
800	650	400	300	—	—

Model 99CE (Centennial Edition)

Introduced in 1995 this limited edition rifle is chambered for the .300 Savage cartridge. Limited to 1,000 rifles with serial numbers from AS0001 to AS1000. Engraved receiver with gold inlays. Select American walnut stock with Monte Carlo comb.

Courtesy Savage Arms

NIB	Exc.	V.G.	Good	Fair	Poor
1600	1300	900	750	500	250

Model 1903

A .22 caliber slide-action rifle with a 24" octagon barrel having open sights. Blued with a walnut stock. Manufactured between 1903 and 1922. Late model rifles have updated slide handle and pistol-grip stock in same style as Model 1914.

This symbol denotes "Sleepers" with rapidly-rising values and/or significant collector potential.

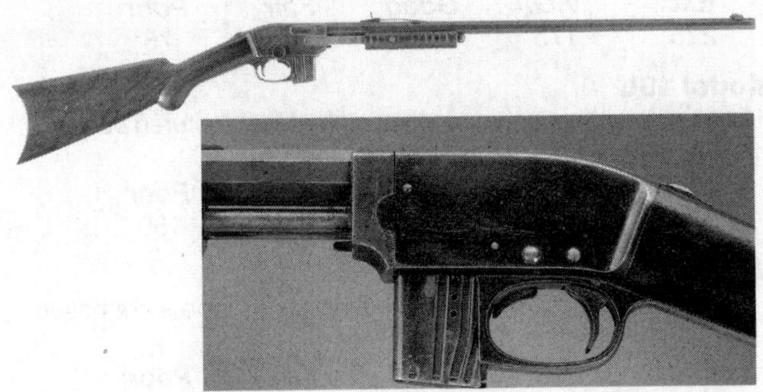

Courtesy Rock Island Auction Company

Exc.	V.G.	Good	Fair	Poor
250	200	150	100	75

Model 1903 Gallery Model

Same general specifications as Model 1903 except for a mechanical counter attached to record shots fired.

Exc.	V.G.	Good	Fair	Poor
350	275	200	150	100

Model 1903 Factory Engraved Models

NOTE: These models are seldom seen. Secure a qualified appraisal prior to a sale.

Grade EF

Grade "B" checkering, fancy English walnut stock, Savage 22B front sights, and 21B rear sight.

Exc.	V.G.	Good	Fair	Poor
N/A	—	—	—	—

Expert Grade

Fancy American walnut stock, Grade "A" engraving, Grade "B" checkering, and standard sights.

Exc.	V.G.	Good	Fair	Poor
N/A	—	—	—	—

Grade GH

Plain American walnut stock, Grade "A" checkering, 22B front sight, and 21B rear sight.

Exc.	V.G.	Good	Fair	Poor
N/A	—	—	—	—

Gold Medal Grade

Plain American walnut stock, animal ornamentation on receiver, Grade "A" checkering, and standard sights.

Exc.	V.G.	Good	Fair	Poor
N/A	—	—	—	—

Model 1909

As above, with a 20" barrel. Manufactured between 1909 and 1915.

Exc.	V.G.	Good	Fair	Poor
250	200	150	100	75

Model 1911

Produced from 1911 to 1915 in .22 short only. Bolt-action repeater. American walnut stock. Shotgun steel buttplate, bead front sight with adjustable open rear sight. Tubular magazine is loaded through buttstock and has capacity of 20 rounds. Weight is approximately 4 lbs.

Exc.	V.G.	Good	Fair	Poor
275	225	175	125	100

Model 1912

A .22 caliber semi-automatic rifle with a 20" barrel, open sights and in takedown form. Magazine capacity is 7 rounds. Blued with a walnut stock. Manufactured between 1912 and 1916. Weight is about 4.5 lbs.

Exc.	V.G.	Good	Fair	Poor
350	300	200	125	90

Model 6

Similar to the above, with a 24" barrel and tubular magazine. The walnut stock checkered prior to 1938 and plain after 1965.

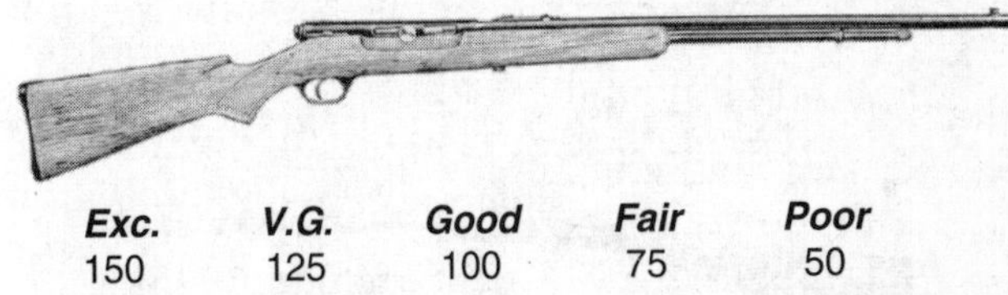

Exc.	V.G.	Good	Fair	Poor
150	125	100	75	50

Model 7

As above, with a detachable magazine. Manufactured between 1938 and 1954.

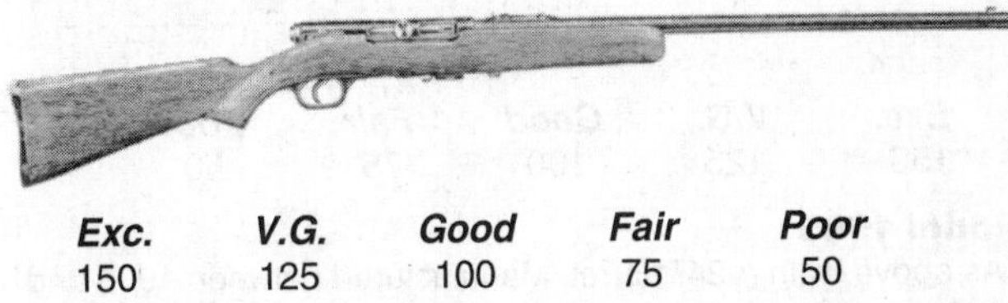

Exc.	V.G.	Good	Fair	Poor
150	125	100	75	50

Model 1914

As above, with a 24" octagonal barrel. Manufactured between 1914 and 1926.

Courtesy Rock Island Auction Company

Exc.	V.G.	Good	Fair	Poor
275	225	175	125	100

Model 25

A .22 caliber slide-action rifle with a 24" octagonal barrel, open sights and tubular magazine. Blued with a plain walnut stock. Manufactured between 1925 and 1929.

Exc.	V.G.	Good	Fair	Poor
350	300	250	200	125

Model 29

Similar to above but with a 22" octagonal barrel, later changed to round on post-war rifles, and a checkered walnut stock, later changed to plain on post-war rifles. Manufactured between 1929 and 1967.

Exc.	V.G.	Good	Fair	Poor
300	250	200	150	100

Model 170

A .30-30 or .35 Remington caliber slide-action rifle with a 22" barrel and 3-shot tubular magazine. Blued with a walnut stock. Manufactured between 1970 and 1981.

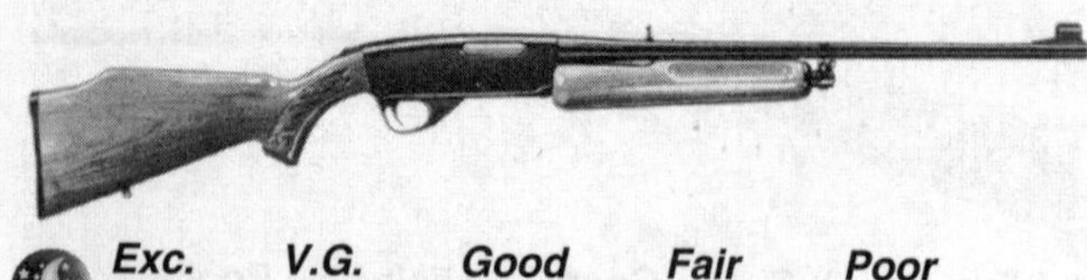

Exc.	V.G.	Good	Fair	Poor
375	300	250	175	100

Model 1904
A .22 caliber single-shot bolt-action rifle with an 18" barrel and walnut stock. Manufactured between 1904 and 1931. After 1915 this model became known as the Model 04.

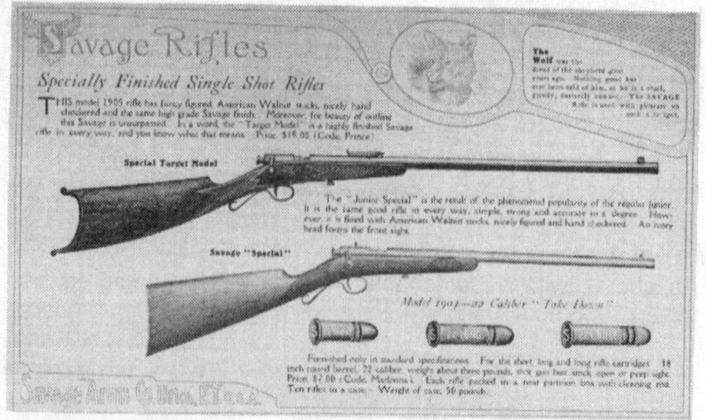

Exc.	V.G.	Good	Fair	Poor
150	125	100	75	50

Model 1905
As above, with a 24" barrel. Manufactured between 1905 and 1919.

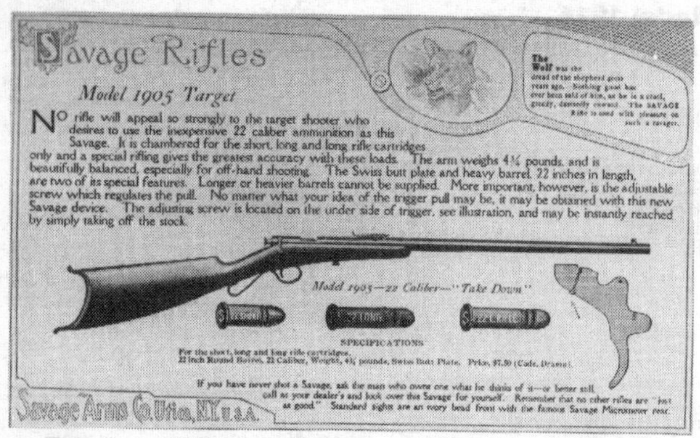

Exc.	V.G.	Good	Fair	Poor
150	125	100	75	50

Model 1905 Style "B"
Same as the Model 1905 target but with shotgun buttplate.

Exc.	V.G.	Good	Fair	Poor
175	150	100	75	50

Model 1905 Special Target Rifle
This model is the same as the Model 1905 Target Rifle except for hand checkered fancy American walnut stock.

Exc.	V.G.	Good	Fair	Poor
350	250	200	150	100

Model 19 NRA
A .22 caliber bolt-action rifle with a 25" barrel, detachable magazine and full-length military-style stock. Approximately 50,000 were manufactured total between 1919 and 1937.

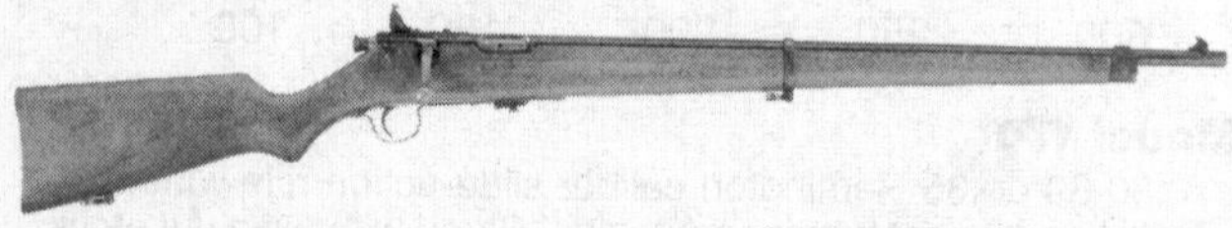
Courtesy Rock Island Auction Company

Exc.	V.G.	Good	Fair	Poor
225	175	150	100	75

Model 19L
As above, with a Lyman receiver sight. Manufactured between 1933 and 1942.

Exc.	V.G.	Good	Fair	Poor
350	300	250	200	150

Model 19M
As above, with a 28" barrel fitted with telescope sight bases. Manufactured between 1933 and 1942.

Exc.	V.G	Good	Fair	Poor
350	300	250	200	150

Model 19H
The Model 19 chambered for .22 Hornet. Manufactured between 1933 and 1942.

Exc.	V.G.	Good	Fair	Poor
500	450	350	300	200

Model 3
A .22 caliber single-shot bolt-action rifle with a 24" barrel, open sights and walnut stock. Manufactured between 1933 and 1952.

Courtesy Rock Island Auction Company

Exc.	V.G.	Good	Fair	Poor
100	80	60	50	35

Model 4
Similar to the above, with a 24" barrel and 5-shot magazine. Produced from 1932 to 1964.

Exc.	V.G.	Good	Fair	Poor
125	100	80	60	50

Model 4M
As above, in .22 Magnum. Produced from 1932 to 1964.

Exc.	V.G.	Good	Fair	Poor
125	100	80	60	50

Model 5
The Model 4 with a tubular magazine. Manufactured between 1933 and 1964.

Exc.	V.G.	Good	Fair	Poor
125	100	80	60	50

Model 1920
A .250-3000 or .300 Savage caliber bolt-action rifle with a 22" or 24" barrel, open sights and 5-shot magazine. Blued, with a walnut stock and schnabel forend. Manufactured between 1920 and 1929. An improved version of this rifle was introduced in 1926 that was heavier and had a Lyman #54 peep sight.

Exc.	V.G.	Good	Fair	Poor
350	300	250	175	125

Model 1922

This model is a variation of the Model 19 NRA with a sporting-style stock and schnabel forend. Fitted with a 23" round barrel it was chambered for the .22 caliber cartridge. This model superceded the Model 23 and looks like a Model 23 sporter. Introduced in 1922 and discontinued in 1923. VERY RARE.

Exc.	V.G.	Good	Fair	Poor
750	600	500	—	—

Model 23A

This bolt-action .22 LR rifle was introduced in 1923 and features a 5-round detachable box magazine and 23" barrel with open sights. The large loading port on the left side of the receiver permitted easy single-shot loading. The stock was plain with pistol grip and a schnabel forend. A varnish wood finish was applied to this model. Production stopped in 1933.

Exc.	V.G.	Good	Fair	Poor
250	200	150	125	100

Model 23AA

This was an improved version of the Model 23A introduced in 1933. It features better speed lock, redesigned stock with oil finish. The receiver was tapped for No. 15 Savage extension peep sight. The rifle weighs approximately 6 lbs. Production ceased in 1942.

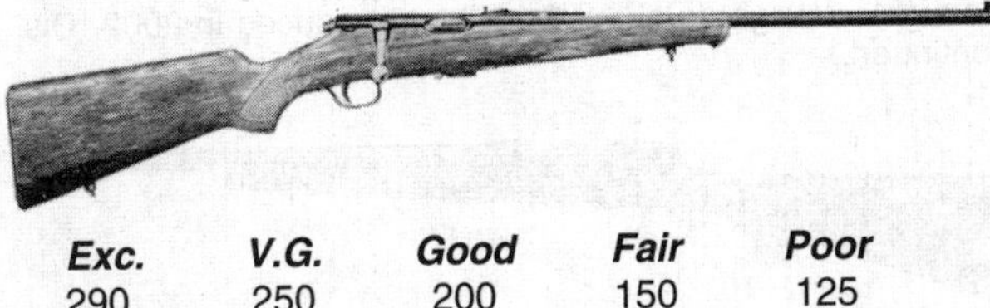

Exc.	V.G.	Good	Fair	Poor
290	250	200	150	125

Model 23B

Similar to the Model 23A except chambered for the .25-20 cartridge. Barrel length was 25" and forearm was a full 1.5" wide beavertail. Receiver was tapped for peep sight and magazine capacity was 4 rounds. Production on the Model 23B was from 1923 to 1940.

Exc.	V.G.	Good	Fair	Poor
250	200	150	125	100

Model 23C

The same configuration as the Model 23B with the exception of the caliber .32-20. Manufactured from 1923 to 1946.

Exc.	V.G.	Good	Fair	Poor
250	200	150	125	100

Model 23D

The same configuration as the Model 23B but chambered for the .22 Hornet cartridge. Manufactured from 1932 to 1948.

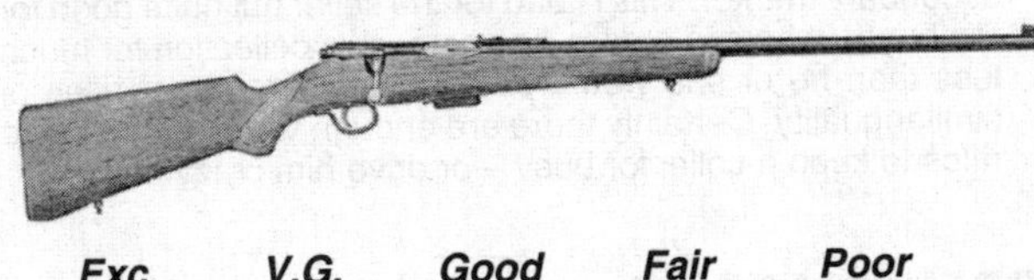

Exc.	V.G.	Good	Fair	Poor
325	300	250	200	150

Model 40

Similar to the above but in .250-3000, .300 Savage, .30-30, and .30-06 caliber. Manufactured between 1928 and 1940.

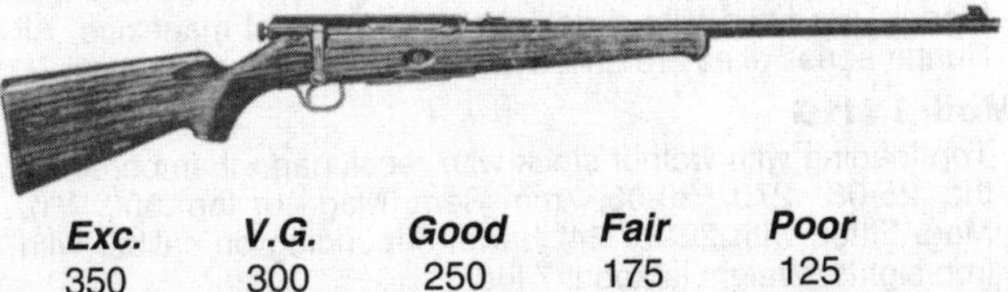

Exc.	V.G.	Good	Fair	Poor
350	300	250	175	125

Model 40 Varmint Hunter

This model, introduced in 2004, is chambered for the .22 Hornet or .223 Rem. cartridge. Fitted with a 24" heavy barrel with no sights. Laminated stock with wide beavertail forearm. Blued. Single shot. Weight is about 7.75 lbs.

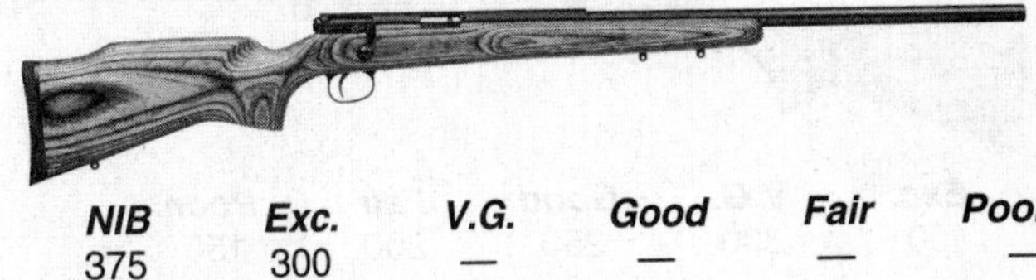

NIB	Exc.	V.G.	Good	Fair	Poor
375	300	—	—	—	—

NOTE: Add $30 for .223 Rem. model.

Model 45 Super

As above, with a Lyman receiver sight and checkered walnut stock. Manufactured between 1928 and 1940.

Exc.	V.G.	Good	Fair	Poor
400	350	300	200	150

Model 35

A .22 caliber bolt-action rifle with a 22" barrel, open sights and 5-shot magazine. Blued with a Monte Carlo-style hardwood stock.

Exc.	V.G.	Good	Fair	Poor
100	80	70	50	35

Model 46

As above with a tubular magazine. Manufactured between 1969 and 1973.

Exc.	V.G.	Good	Fair	Poor
100	80	70	50	35

Model 340

A .22 Hornet, .222 Remington, .223, or .30-30 caliber bolt-action rifle with a 22" or 24" barrel, open sights and 4- or 5-shot magazine. Blued, with a plain walnut stock. Manufactured between 1950 and 1985.

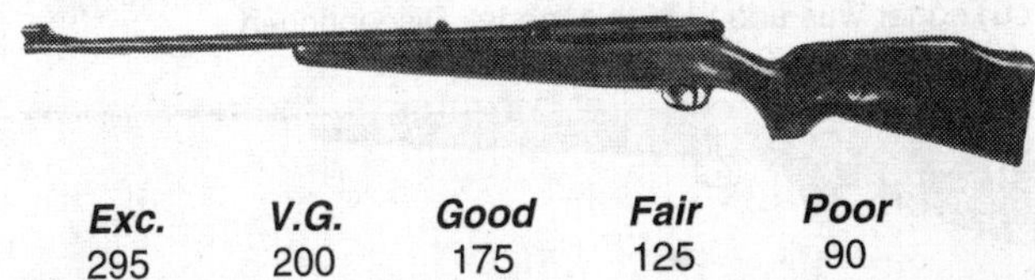

Exc.	V.G.	Good	Fair	Poor
295	200	175	125	90

Model 342

As above, but in .22 Hornet caliber. Manufactured between 1950 and 1955.

Exc.	V.G.	Good	Fair	Poor
295	200	175	125	90

MODEL 110 SERIES

Model 110 Sporter

A bolt-action rifle manufactured in a variety of calibers with a 22" barrel, open sights and 4-shot magazine. Blued with a walnut stock. Manufactured between 1958 and 1963.

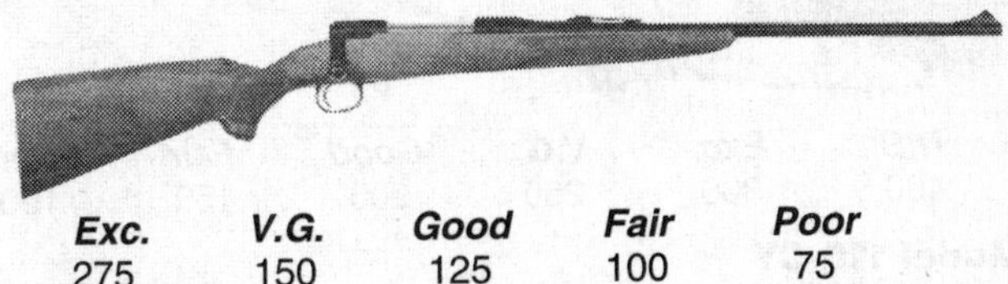

Exc.	V.G.	Good	Fair	Poor
275	150	125	100	75

Model 110-M

Similar to the above, in 7mm Magnum to .338 Winchester Magnum. Manufactured between 1963 and 1969.

Exc.	V.G.	Good	Fair	Poor
325	225	175	150	100

Model 110-D

Similar to the Model 110 in .22-250 to .338 Winchester Magnum caliber with a detachable magazine. Manufactured between 1966 and 1988.

Exc.	V.G.	Good	Fair	Poor
400	300	250	200	150

Model 110-P Premier Grade

As above, with a finely figured walnut stock, rosewood forend tip and pistol grip cap. Manufactured between 1964 and 1970.

Exc.	V.G.	Good	Fair	Poor
500	375	325	250	200

Model 110-PE

As above, with an engraved receiver, magazine floorplate and trigger guard. Manufactured between 1968 and 1970.

Exc.	V.G.	Good	Fair	Poor
950	700	500	400	300

NOTE: Current production Model 110-F are made in the styles listed.

Model 110-F

DuPont Rynite stock and sights. Discontinued.

NIB	Exc.	V.G.	Good	Fair	Poor
450	400	350	300	250	200

Model 110-FX

As above without sights. Discontinued.

NIB	Exc.	V.G.	Good	Fair	Poor
400	350	300	250	200	150

Model 110-FP

Composite stock and 24" heavy barrel. In 2003 the Savage AccuTrigger was added to this model. Discontinued.

NIB	Exc.	V.G.	Good	Fair	Poor
600	450	325	225	150	150

Model 110-G

Checkered hardwood stock and sights. Discontinued.

NIB	Exc.	V.G.	Good	Fair	Poor
425	325	275	225	175	125

Model 110-GX

As above without sights. Discontinued.

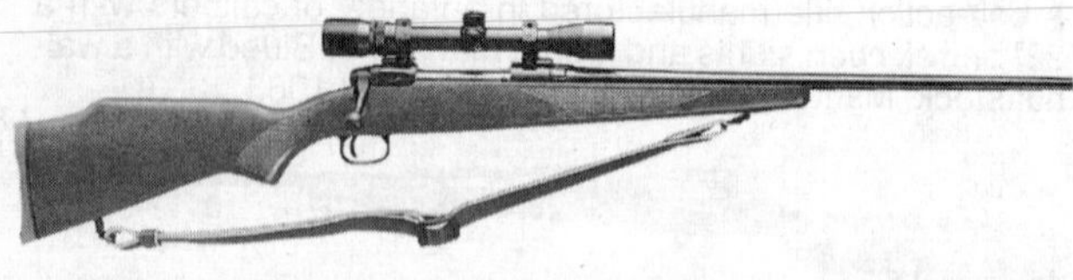

NIB	Exc.	V.G.	Good	Fair	Poor
400	300	250	200	150	100

Model 110-CY

A compact version of the Model 110 series. Shorter length of pull on walnut stock and 22" barrel. Overall length is 42-1/2". Weight is about 6-1/2 lbs. Chambered in .223, .243, .270, .300 Savage, and .308 calibers. Discontinued.

NIB	Exc.	V.G.	Good	Fair	Poor
400	300	250	200	150	100

Model 110FP Tactical

Offered in calibers from .223 Rem. to .300 Win. Mag this bolt-action rifle has a 24" heavy barrel with recessed muzzle. The synthetic stock is black as are all other surfaces. Available in both right- and left-hand versions. Weight is approximately 8.5 lbs. Discontinued.

NIB	Exc.	V.G.	Good	Fair	Poor
600	450	325	225	150	150

Model 110FP Duty

Introduced in 2002 this model is chambered for the .308 cartridge and features a 24" free-floating barrel with open sights. Black synthetic stock. Third swivel stud for bipod. Matte blue finish. Magazine capacity is 4 rounds. Weight is about 8.5 lbs. Discontinued.

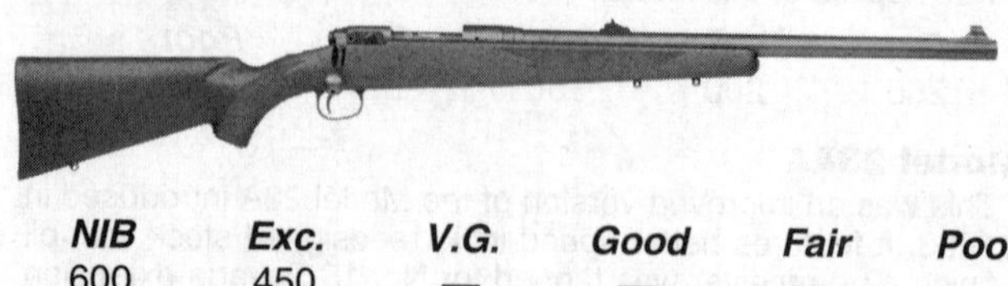

NIB	Exc.	V.G.	Good	Fair	Poor
600	450	—	—	—	—

Model 110FP-LE1

Similar to the Model 110FP-Duty (.308) but with a 20" barrel. No sights. Weight is about 8.25 lbs. Introduced in 2002. Discontinued.

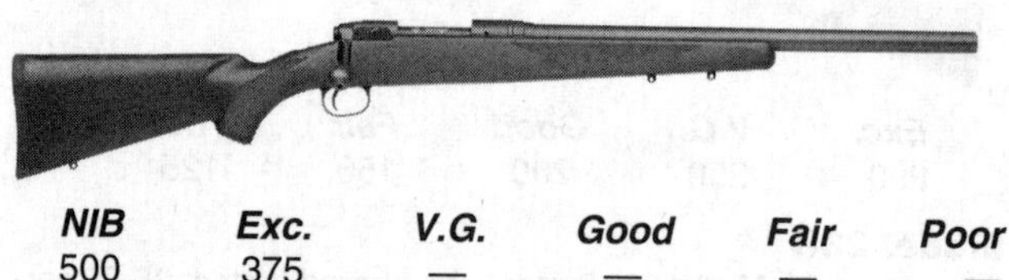

NIB	Exc.	V.G.	Good	Fair	Poor
500	375	—	—	—	—

Model 110FP-LE2

Same as the model above but fitted with a 26" barrel. Weight is about 8.75 lbs. Introduced in 2002. Discontinued.

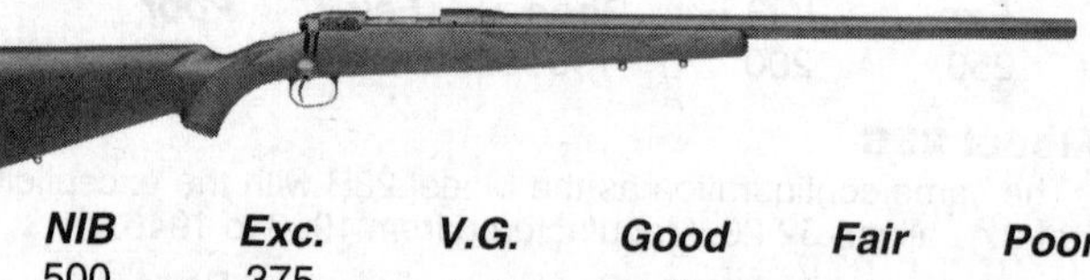

NIB	Exc.	V.G.	Good	Fair	Poor
500	375	—	—	—	—

NOTE: The following section deals primarily with modern Savage bolt-action centerfire rifles in which the barrel is attached to the receiver by means of a threaded collet. For some reason that the editor is unable to determine, these excellent, accurate rifles tend not to bring high prices on the secondary market. This is bad for the seller but quite good for the buyer, who can amass an impressive collection for much less than he or she would pay for other brands of rifles of similar quality. Certainly there are enough variations of these rifles to keep a collector busy – or drive him crazy.

MODEL 111 SERIES

Model 111 Classic Hunter Series

All models under this series are fitted with a classic American-designed straight comb stock with pistol grip. Chambered in 13 different calibers from .223 Rem. to the .338 Win. Mag. Weights vary with caliber and stock type but range from 6-3/8 to 7 lbs. Models are fitted with a detachable or internal magazine. All Hunter series rifles are drilled and tapped for scope mounts.

Model 111G

Top loading with walnut stock with recoil pad. chambered for the .25-06, .270, .30-06, 7mm Rem. Mag., or the .300 Win. Mag. Fitted with 22" or 24" barrel depending on caliber with iron sights. Weight is about 7 lbs.

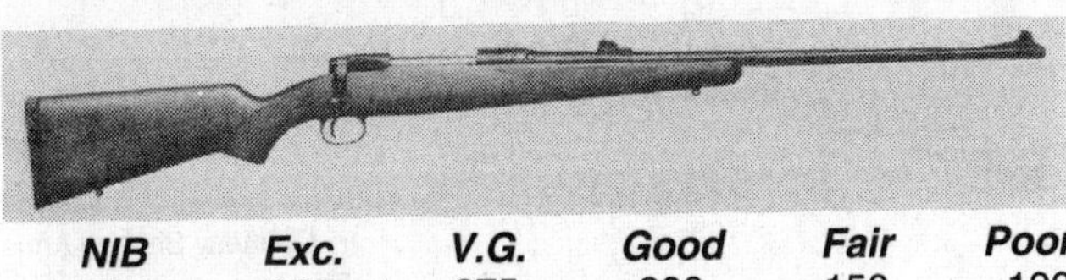

NIB	Exc.	V.G.	Good	Fair	Poor
495	375	275	200	150	100

Model 111GCNS

This is a long action model as above with 22" or 24" barrel depending on caliber with no sights. Introduced in 2005.

NIB	Exc.	V.G.	Good	Fair	Poor
515	400	—	—	—	—

Model 111GC

Detachable magazine with walnut stock and recoil pad. Discontinued.

Savage Model 111 GC

NIB	Exc.	V.G.	Good	Fair	Poor
450	350	300	250	200	150

Model 111GL

Same as the Model 111G model but with left hand action.

NIB	Exc.	V.G.	Good	Fair	Poor
485	350	250	200	150	100

Model 111F

Top loading with graphite stock. Chambered for the .25-06, .270, .30-06, 7mm Rem. Mag., .300 Win. Mag., and the .338 Win. Mag. cartridges. Fitted with either a 22" or 24" barrel depending on caliber with iron sights. Black synthetic stock. Weight is about 6.75 lbs. depending on caliber.

NIB	Exc.	V.G.	Good	Fair	Poor
485	350	250	200	150	100

Model 111FL

As above but with left hand action.

NIB	Exc.	V.G.	Good	Fair	Poor
485	350	250	200	150	100

Model 111FC

Detachable magazine with graphite stock. Discontinued.

NIB	Exc.	V.G.	Good	Fair	Poor
450	350	300	250	200	150

Model 111FCNS

Introduced in 2005 this model is chambered for the .25-06, .270, .30-06, 7mm Rem. Mag., .300 Win. Mag., and the .338 Win. Mag calibers. Fitted with 22" or 24" barrel with no sights. Black synthetic stock. Weight is about 6.75 lbs. depending on caliber.

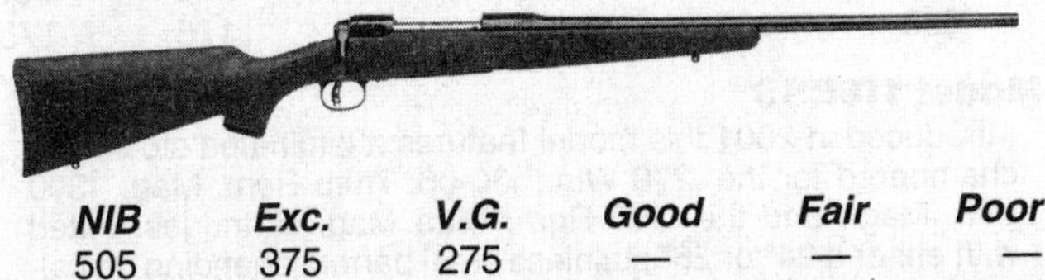

NIB	Exc.	V.G.	Good	Fair	Poor
505	375	275	—	—	—

Model 111FXP3

Top loading with graphite stock and 3x9 scope, rings, and bases, and sling.

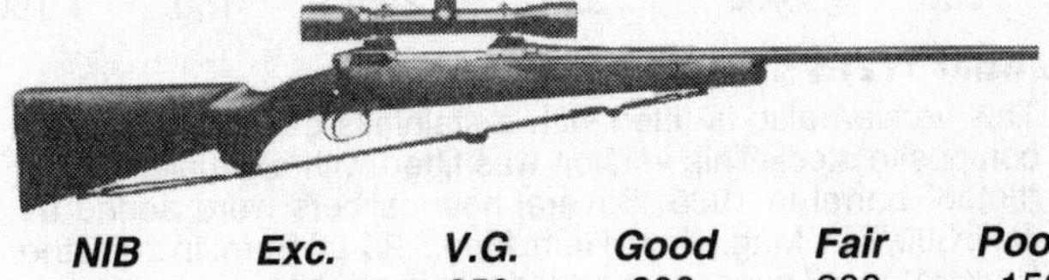

NIB	Exc.	V.G.	Good	Fair	Poor
515	400	350	300	200	150

Model 111FCXP3

Same as above but detachable magazine.

NIB	Exc.	V.G.	Good	Fair	Poor
515	400	350	300	200	150

Model 111FAK

Blued steel barrel, composite stock, muzzlebrake. Discontinued.

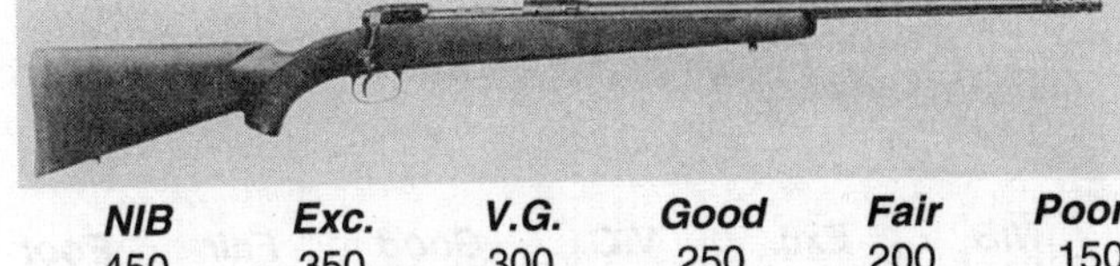

NIB	Exc.	V.G.	Good	Fair	Poor
450	350	300	250	200	150

MODEL 112 SERIES

Model 112BT / 112BT-S (Long Action)

Introduced for the first time in 1994 this model is a competition grade rifle. Chambered for the .223 Rem. and the .308 Win. it features a 26" heavy stainless steel barrel fitted to an alloy steel receiver. In 1995 the .300 Win. Magnum was added to the line referred to as the Model 112BT-S. The barrel finish is black. The stock is laminated with ambidextrous palm swell and adjustable cheek rest. Weight is about 11 lbs.

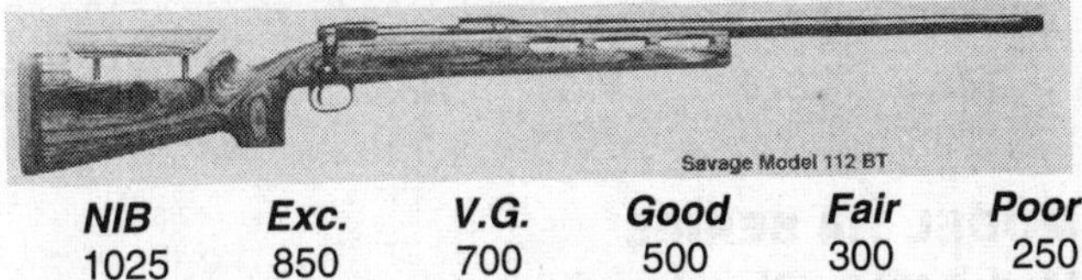

Savage Model 112 BT

NIB	Exc.	V.G.	Good	Fair	Poor
1025	850	700	500	300	250

Model 112 Series Varmint Rifles

This series of varmint rifles features 26" barrels. Offered with either composite or laminated wood stocks all Model 112s are top loading and all are drilled and tapped for scope mounting. Available in .223, .22-250, and .220 Swift the BV configuration weighs about 10-1/2 lbs. while the FV configuration weighs about 9 lbs.

Model 112BVSS (Long Action)

This model has a laminated wood stock with high comb and ambidextrous palm swell. It is fitted with a stainless steel barrel, bolt and trigger guard. In 1996 the .300 Win. Mag., 7mm Rem. Mag., .308 Win., .30-06, and .25-06 was added to this model.

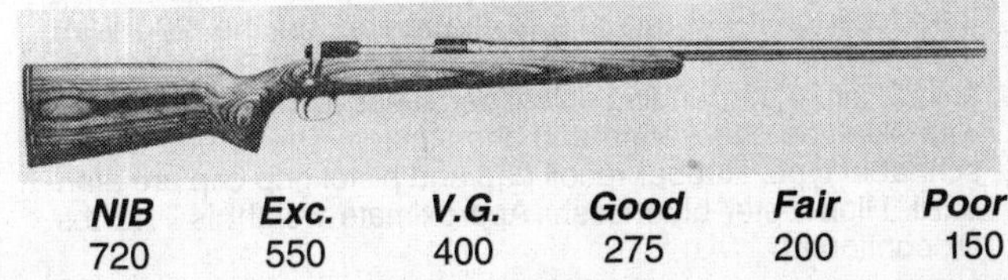

NIB	Exc.	V.G.	Good	Fair	Poor
720	550	400	275	200	150

Model 112BVSS-S

Same as above but single-shot.

NIB	Exc.	V.G.	Good	Fair	Poor
600	450	325	225	150	150

Model 112FVSS

This version also is fitted with a stainless steel barrel and a composite stock This version was fitted with a stainless steel "fluted" barrel in 1995. Several new calibers were added as well: 300 Win. Mag., 7mm Rem. Mag., .25-06 Rem. In 2003 the Savage AccuTrigger was added to this model.

NIB	Exc.	V.G.	Good	Fair	Poor
475	400	350	300	200	150

Model 112FVSS-S

This is a single-shot version of the above model.

NIB	Exc.	V.G.	Good	Fair	Poor
475	400	350	300	200	150

Model 112FV

This is similar to the model above but with a blued barrel.

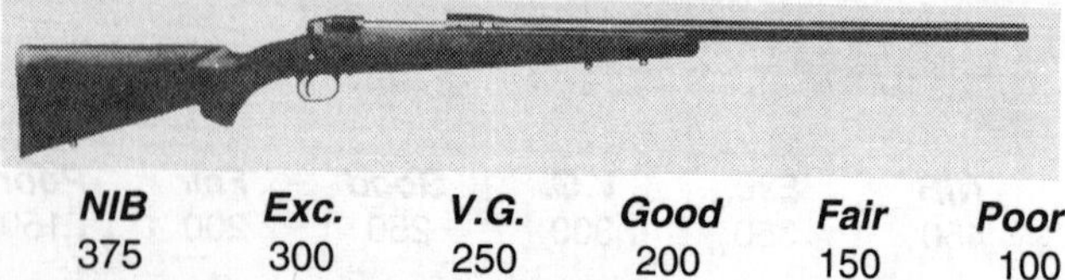

NIB	Exc.	V.G.	Good	Fair	Poor
375	300	250	200	150	100

Model 112BT—Competition Grade

This model was introduced in 1996. It is a competition rifle. It features a 26" blackened stainless steel barrel and custom target style laminated stock with adjustable cheek rest. Chambered for .223 or .308 cartridges. Weight is approximately 11 lbs. The barrel is pillar bedded.

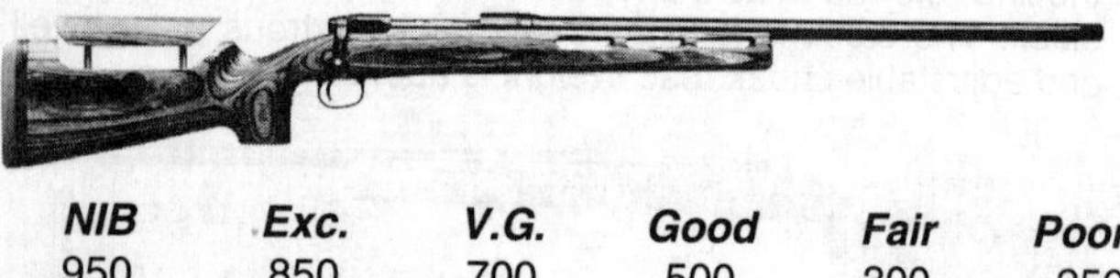

NIB	Exc.	V.G.	Good	Fair	Poor
950	850	700	500	300	250

MODEL 114 SERIES

Model 114C—Classic

This model, introduced in 2000, features a select grade oil finished walnut stock with cut checkering. No sights. Chambered for .270 and .30-06 with 22" barrel, and 7mm Mag. and .300 Win. Mag with 24" barrel.

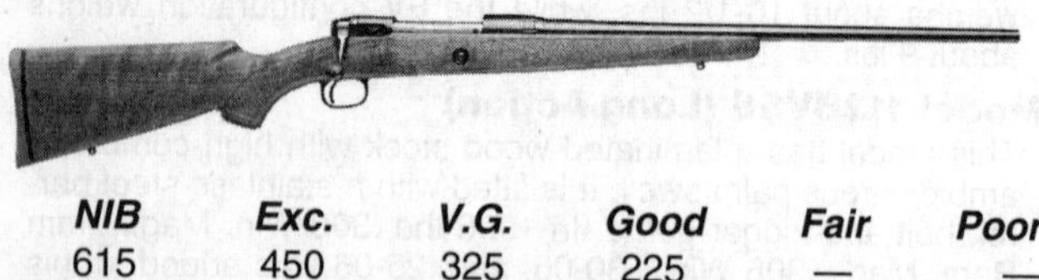

NIB	Exc.	V.G.	Good	Fair	Poor
615	450	325	225	—	—

Model 114CE—Classic European

Introduced in 1996 this rifle is chambered for the .270 Win., .30-06, 7mm Rem. Mag., and .300 Win. Mag. Barrel lengths are 22" or 24" depending on caliber. It has an oil-finished stock with skip line checkering and cheekpiece. The forend tip is a schnabel type. Rubber recoil pad and pistol grip cap are standard. High luster blue finish. Approximate weight is 7.12 lbs. Discontinued.

Courtesy Savage Arms

NIB	Exc.	V.G.	Good	Fair	Poor
550	475	400	350	300	150

Model 114CU

This model has a select grade walnut oil finished stock. The finish is a high polish blue and the bolt has a laser etched Savage logo. A detachable magazine is standard. The receiver is drilled and tapped for a scope mount. Offered in .270, .30-06, 7mm Rem. Mag., and .300 Win. Mag. Weights are about 7-1/8 lbs. Discontinued.

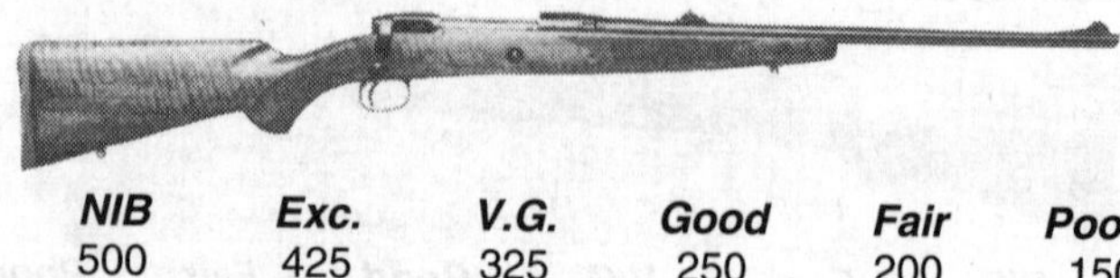

NIB	Exc.	V.G.	Good	Fair	Poor
500	425	325	250	200	150

Model 114U—Ultra

Introduced in 1999 this model features a high gloss walnut stock with custom checkering. Blued finish is high luster with a laser-etched Savage logo on the bolt body. Chambered for the .270 Win., .30-06, 7mm-08 Rem., and .300 Win. Mag cartridges. Barrel length is 22" and 24" depending on caliber. Weight is about 7 lbs.

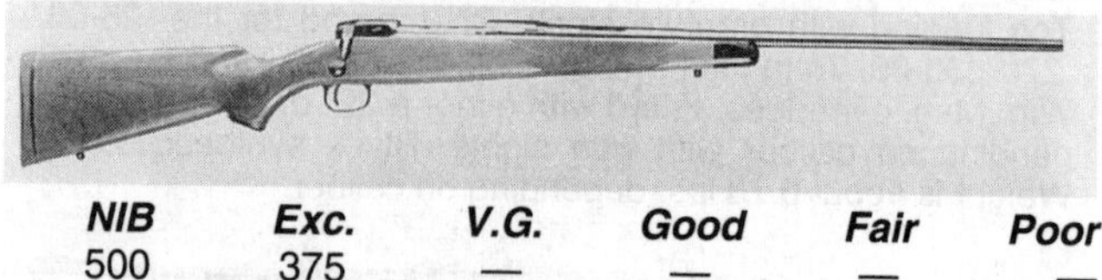

NIB	Exc.	V.G.	Good	Fair	Poor
500	375	—	—	—	—

MODEL 116 SERIES

This series of rifles feature graphite stocks and stainless steel barreled actions. An adjustable muzzlebrake is also included. All rifles in the 116 series are drilled and tapped for scope mounts.

Model 116FCSAK (Long Action)

Features a detachable box magazine. The 22" barrel is fluted. Offered in .270, .30-06, 7mm Rem. Mag., .300 Win. Mag., and .338 Win. Mag. Weighs about 6-1/2 lbs.

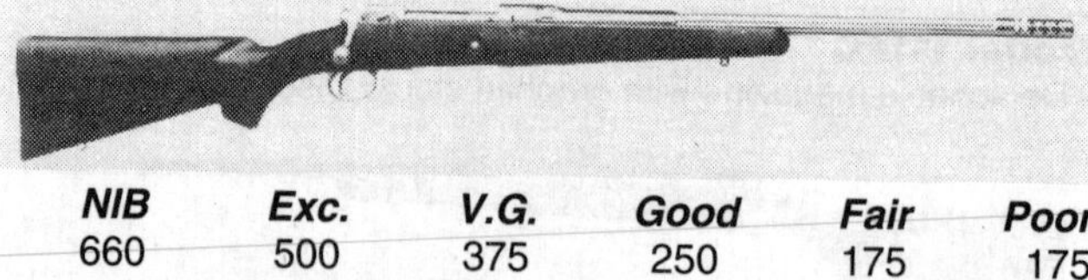

NIB	Exc.	V.G.	Good	Fair	Poor
660	500	375	250	175	175

Model 116FSAK (Long Action)

Same as model above but with on-off choice for muzzlebrake given to shooter. AccuTrigger added in 2004.

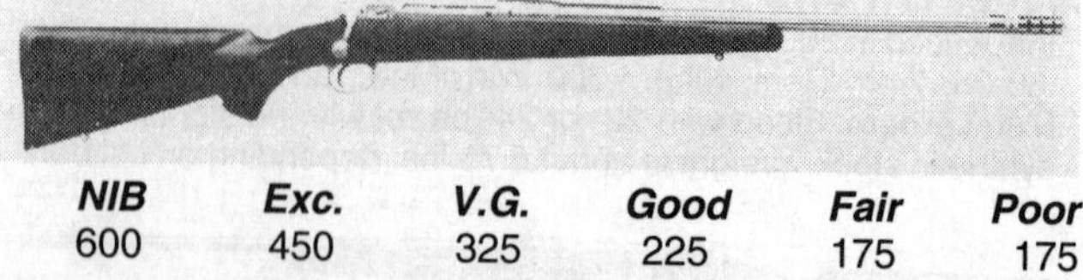

NIB	Exc.	V.G.	Good	Fair	Poor
600	450	325	225	175	175

Model 116BSS

Introduced in 2001 this model features a laminated stock. It is chambered for the .270 Win., .30-06, 7mm Rem. Mag., .300 Win. Mag., and the .300 Rem. Ultra Mag. cartridges. Fitted with either a 24" or 26" stainless steel barrel depending on caliber. No sights. Weight is about 7.5 lbs. depending on caliber.Discontinued.

NIB	Exc.	V.G.	Good	Fair	Poor
625	500	260	—	—	—

Model 116FSS (Long Action)

This is the standard configuration for the 116 series. This model features a top-loading action with 22" or 24" barrel depending on caliber. There is no muzzlebrake fitted to this model. Weight is approximately 6-3/4 lbs. Offered in 7 calibers from .223 to .338 Win. Mag. AccuTrigger added in 2004.

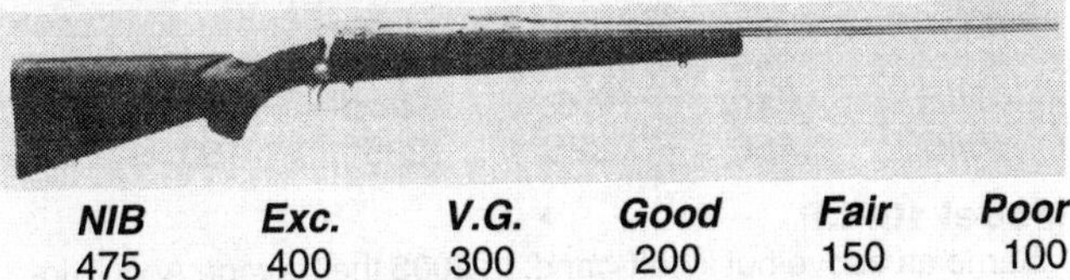

NIB	Exc.	V.G.	Good	Fair	Poor
475	400	300	200	150	100

Model 116FCS

Same as above but with stainless steel removable box magazine.

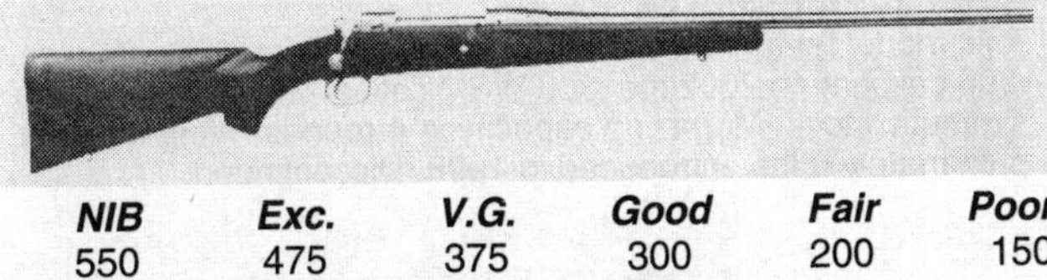

NIB	Exc.	V.G.	Good	Fair	Poor
550	475	375	300	200	150

Model 116FSK—Kodiak (Long Action)

This model features a top loading action with a 22" barrel with muzzlebrake. Weight is approximately 7.25 lbs.

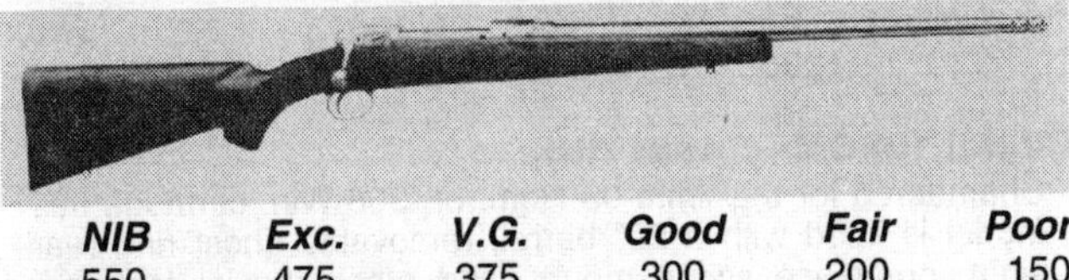

NIB	Exc.	V.G.	Good	Fair	Poor
550	475	375	300	200	150

Model 116SE—Safari Express

Introduced in 1994 this rifle features select grade walnut stock with ebony tip and deluxe checkering. Barrel and action are stainless steel with adjustable muzzlebrake. Offered in .300 Win. Mag., .338 Win. Mag., and .458 calibers. In 1995 the .425 Express cartridge was added. In 2000 this model had a stainless steel action and barrel. Weight is approximately 8-1/2 lbs. Discontinued.

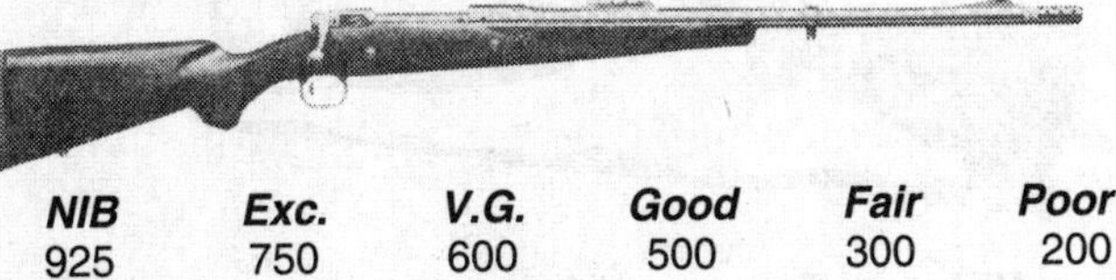

NIB	Exc.	V.G.	Good	Fair	Poor
925	750	600	500	300	200

Model 116US

Introduced in 1995 this model features a stainless steel action and barrel with a high gloss American walnut stock with ebony tip and custom checkering. Offered in .270 Win., .30-06, 7mm Rem. Mag., and .300 Win. Mag. Barrel is 22" on the two smaller calibers and 24" on the magnum calibers. Discontinued.

NIB	Exc.	V.G.	Good	Fair	Poor
600	500	400	300	250	200

MODEL 12 SERIES VARMINT

Introduced in 1998 this series features a short action heavy barrel line of rifles designed for long-range shooting.

Model 12BVSS

This model features a 26" fluted stainless steel barrel with recessed crown and a brown laminated stock with beavertail forend. Chambered for .223, .22-250, and .308. Magazine capacity is 4 rounds. Weight is approximately 9.5 lbs. Introduced in 1998. In 2003 the Savage AccuTrigger was added to this model.

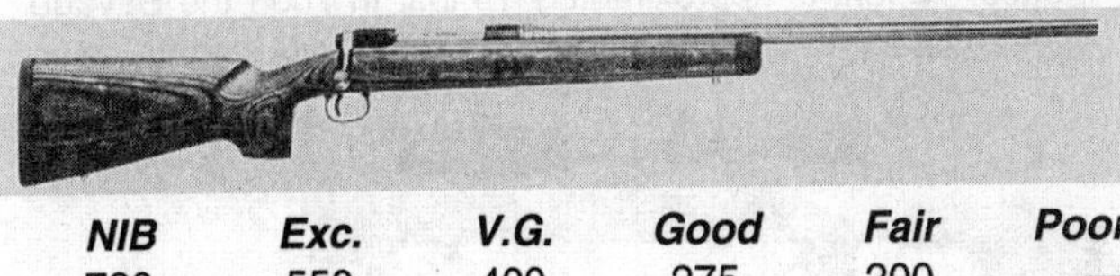

NIB	Exc.	V.G.	Good	Fair	Poor
720	550	400	275	200	—

Model 12BVSS-S

Same as above but in a single-shot version chambered for .223 and .22-250. Weight is 9 lbs. In 2003 the Savage AccuTrigger was added to this model.

NIB	Exc.	V.G.	Good	Fair	Poor
720	550	400	275	200	—

Model 12BVSS-SXP

Introduced in 2003 this single-shot model is chambered for the .223 Rem. or .22-250 Rem. cartridge. Fitted with a 26" stainless steel fluted barrel. Savage AccuTrigger. Stock is a target-style heavy prone laminate. Weight is about 12 lbs.

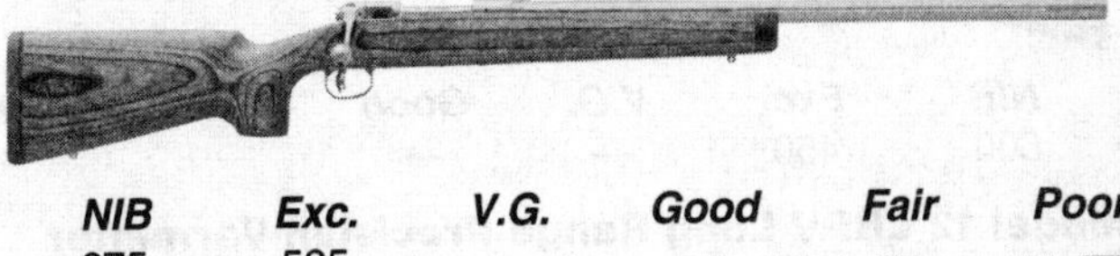

NIB	Exc.	V.G.	Good	Fair	Poor
675	525	—	—	—	—

Model 12FVSS

This model has a 26" stainless steel fluted barrel and a synthetic stock. Offered in .223, .22-250, and .308 calibers. Weight is about 9 lbs. Introduced in 1998. A left-hand version is also offered. In 2003 the Savage AccuTrigger was added to this model.

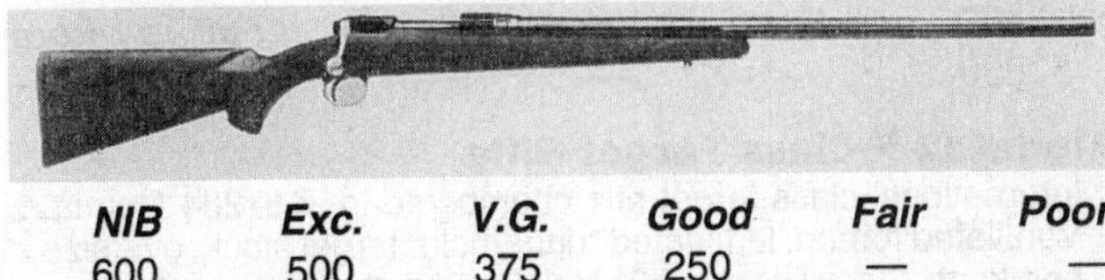

NIB	Exc.	V.G.	Good	Fair	Poor
600	500	375	250	—	—

Model 12FVSS-S

Same as above but in a single-shot configuration chambered for .223 or .22-250. Weight is about 9 lbs. In 2003 the Savage AccuTrigger was added to this model. Discontinued.

NIB	Exc.	V.G.	Good	Fair	Poor
550	450	—	—	—	—

Model 12FV (Short Action)

This model is similar to the other 12 Series rifles but with blued actions and 26" barrels that are nonfluted. Synthetic stock. Chambered for .223 or .22-250. Weight is about 9 lbs. Introduced in 1998. Offered in a left-hand model. In 2003 the Savage AccuTrigger was added to this model.

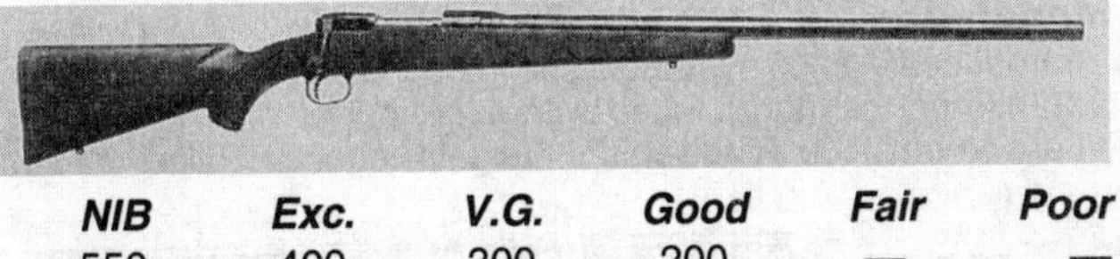

NIB	Exc.	V.G.	Good	Fair	Poor
550	400	300	200	—	—

Model 12FLV

As above but with left hand action. Introduced in 2005.

NIB	Exc.	V.G.	Good	Fair	Poor
550	400	—	—	—	—

Model 12VSS—Varminter (Short Action)

Introduced in 2000 this model features a Choate adjustable black synthetic stock. A heavy fluted stainless steel barrel. Box magazine holds 4 rounds. Chambered for .223 or .22-250 cartridges. Weight is approximately 15 lbs. In 2003 the Savage AccuTrigger was added to this model.

NIB	Exc.	V.G.	Good	Fair	Poor
700	525	375	—	—	—

Model 12 Varminter Low Profile

Introduced in 2004 this model is chambered for the .223 Rem. or .22-250 cartridge and fitted with a 26" heavy fluted stainless steel barrel with no sights. Low-profile laminated stock with extra wide beavertail forearm. Adjustable trigger. Available as a repeater or single shot. Weight is about 10 lbs.

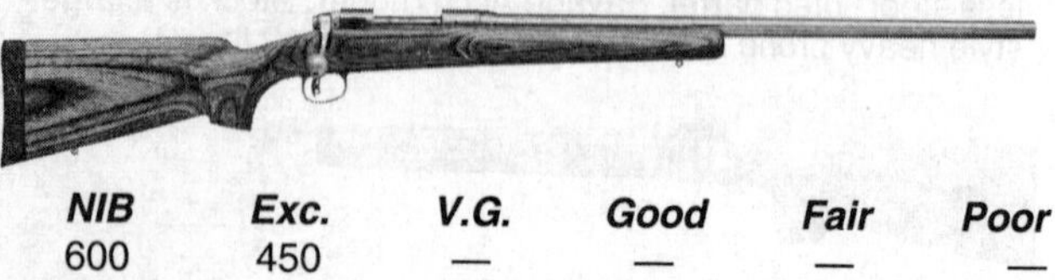

NIB	Exc.	V.G.	Good	Fair	Poor
600	450	—	—	—	—

Model 12 LRPV Long Range Precision Varminter

Similar to Model 12 FVSS but with 30" stainless bull barrel and various accurizing refinements. Chamberd in .204 Ruger, .223 Remington and .22-250. Introduced in 2007.

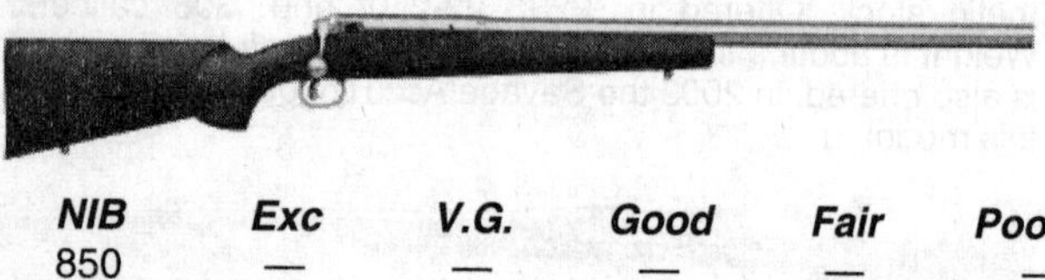

NIB	Exc	V.G.	Good	Fair	Poor
850	—	—	—	—	—

Model 12 F-Class Target Rifle

International-class target rifle chambered in .6.5x284 Norma. Ventilated forend, laminated "underhold" target stock, oversize bolt knob, AccuTrigger, 30" stainless barrel. Also available in Model 12F/TR version with conventional buttstock and elevated cheekpiece. Introduced in 2007.

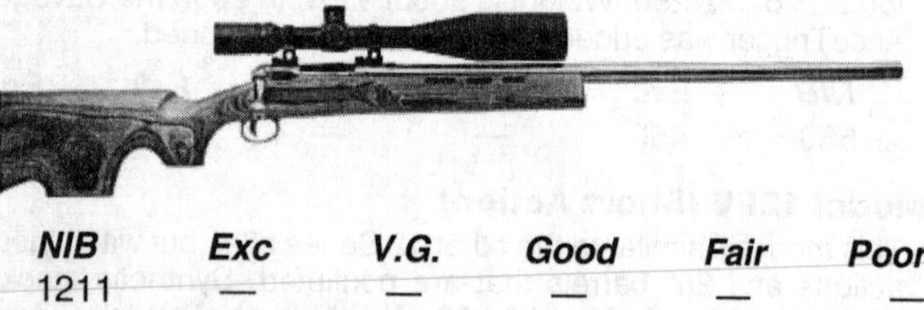

NIB	Exc	V.G.	Good	Fair	Poor
1211	—	—	—	—	—

MODEL 40 VARMINT HUNTER

Model 40

Introduced in 2005 this single shot model is chambererd for the .22 Hornet cartridge. Fitted with a 24" barrel with no sights. Laminated stock. Blued finish. Weight is about 7.75 lbs.

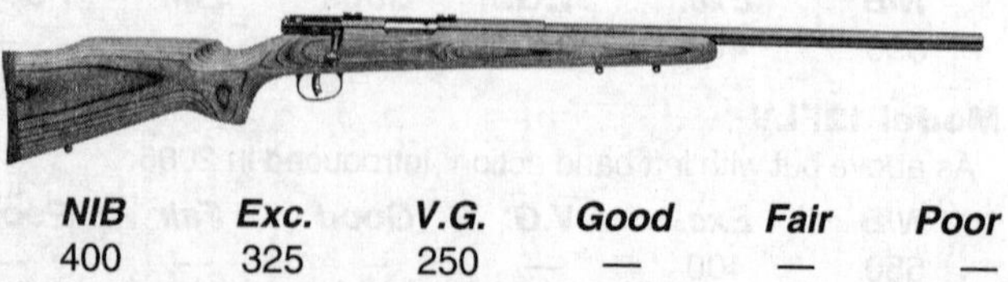

NIB	Exc.	V.G.	Good	Fair	Poor
400	325	250	—	—	—

MODEL 10 SERIES

Model 10FP—Tactical (Short Action)

This is a short action model chambered for the .223 or .308 calibers. Fitted with a 24" barrel. Black synthetic stock. Drilled and tapped for scope mount. Weight is approximately 8 lbs. Introduced in 1998. In 2003 the Savage AccuTrigger was added to this model.

NIB	Exc.	V.G.	Good	Fair	Poor
545	450	325	225	150	—

Model 10FLP

Same as above but in left-hand. In 2003 the Savage AccuTrigger was added to this model.

NIB	Exc.	V.G.	Good	Fair	Poor
550	450	325	225	150	—

Model 10FM—Sierra

This model features a 20" barrel chambered for .223, .243, or .308 calibers. In 2002 the .300 WSM caliber was added. Black synthetic stock. Magazine capacity is 4 rounds. Weight is approximately 6 lbs. Introduced in 1998. Discontinued.

NIB	Exc.	V.G.	Good	Fair	Poor
450	350	—	—	—	—

Model 10FCM—Scout Rifle

Chambered for the 7mm-08 Rem. or .308 Win. cartridge this model is fitted with a 20" barrel, removable ghost ring rear sight, one-piece scope mount, and other special features. Weight is about 6.2 lbs. Introduced in 1999. Discontinued in 2005 but reintroduced in 2007.

NIB	Exc.	V.G.	Good	Fair	Poor
500	400	—	—	—	—

Model 10FCM—Sierra

Introduced in 2005 this model features a 20" light barrel with detachable magazine. Chambered for the .243, 7mm-08 Rem., .308, .270, and .300 WSM calibers. Black synthetic stock. Weight is about 6.25 lbs.

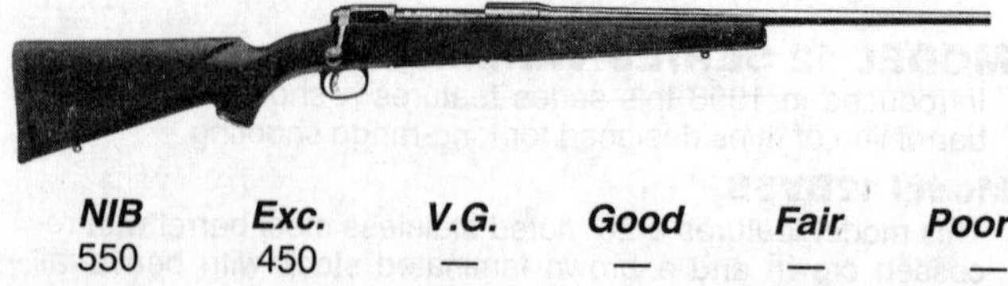

NIB	Exc.	V.G.	Good	Fair	Poor
550	450	—	—	—	—

Model 10GY Youth

This model is similar to the Model 10FM but features a shortened hardwood stock. It is fitted with a 22" barrel and has open sights. It is chambered for .223, .243, or .308 calibers. Weight is about 6.25 lbs. Introduced in 1998.

NIB	Exc.	V.G.	Good	Fair	Poor
450	325	225	165	—	

Model 10 Predator Hunter

Similar to Model 110FCM but with overall camo finish, 22" medium-contour barrel, and AccuTrigger. Chambered in .204 Ruger, .22-250 and .223. Introduced in 2007.

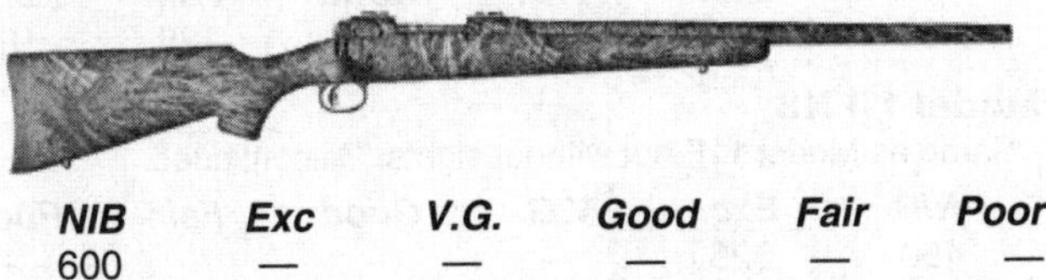

NIB	Exc	V.G.	Good	Fair	Poor
600	—	—	—	—	—

LAW INFORCEMENT SERIES

Model 10FP-LE1

Chambered for the .308 Win. cartridge and fitted with a 20" heavy barrel with no sights. Black synthetic stock. AccuTrigger. Weight is about 8.25 lbs. Introduced in 2003.

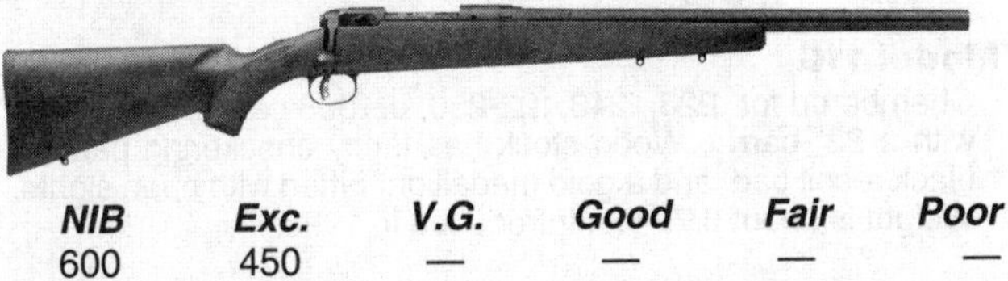

NIB	Exc.	V.G.	Good	Fair	Poor
600	450	—	—	—	—

Model 10FP-LE1A

As above but chambered for the .223 Rem. cartridge as well as the .308. Black synthetic Choate adjustable stock with accessory rail. Weight is about 10.75 lbs. Introduced in 2003.

NIB	Exc.	V.G.	Good	Fair	Poor
730	550	—	—	—	—

Model 10FP-LE2B

This bolt action model is chambered for the .308 Win. cartridge and fitted with a McMillan fiberglass tactical stock. Barrel is 26" with no sights. AccuTrigger. Matte blue finish. Weight is about 10 lbs. Introduced in 2003.

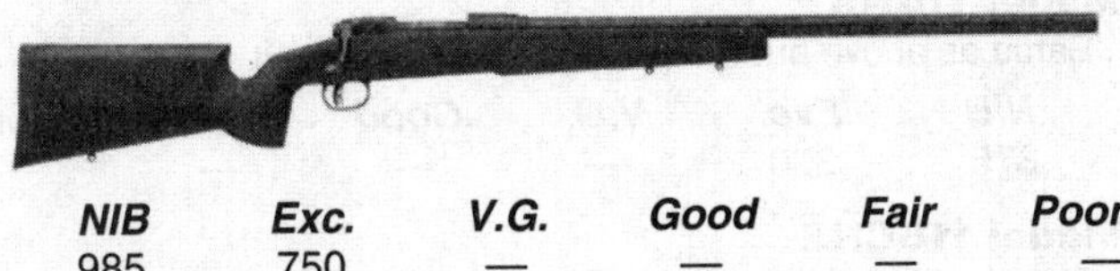

NIB	Exc.	V.G.	Good	Fair	Poor
985	750	—	—	—	—

Model 10FP-LE2

Introduced in 2003 this model features a 26" barrel chambered for the .308 Win. cartridge and fitted with a black synthetic stock. AccuTrigger. Weight is about 8.75 lbs.

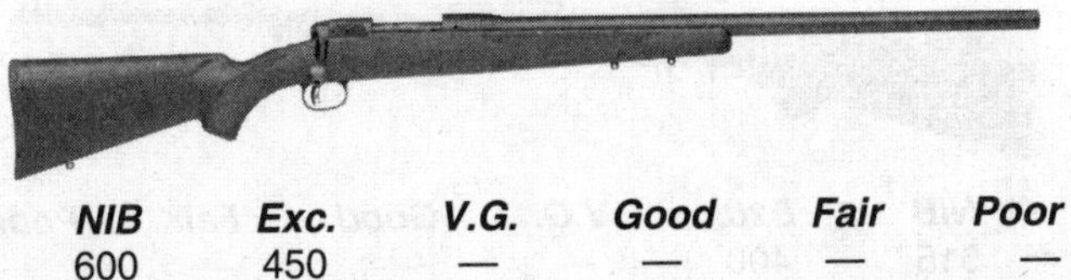

NIB	Exc.	V.G.	Good	Fair	Poor
600	450	—	—	—	—

Model 10FP-LE2A

This model is chambered for the .223 or .308 cartridge and fitted with a 26" heavy barrel with no sights. Black synthetic Choate adjustable stock with accessory rail. Weight is about 11.25 lbs. Introduced in 2003.

NIB	Exc.	V.G.	Good	Fair	Poor
730	550	—	—	—	—

Model 10FPXP-LEA

This item is a package of both rifle and scope with accessories. Features a Model 10FP with 26" barrel and black synthetic stock, Leupold 3.5-10x40 black matte scope with Mil Dot, scope covers and one-piece base. Harris bipod and heavy duty aluminum case. Rifle weighs about 10.5 lbs. Introduced in 2003.

NIB	Exc.	V.G.	Good	Fair	Poor
1950	1450	1100	—	—	—

Model 10FPXP-LE

As above but with Choate adjustable stock with accessory rail. Rifle weighs about 11.25 lbs. Introduced in 2003.

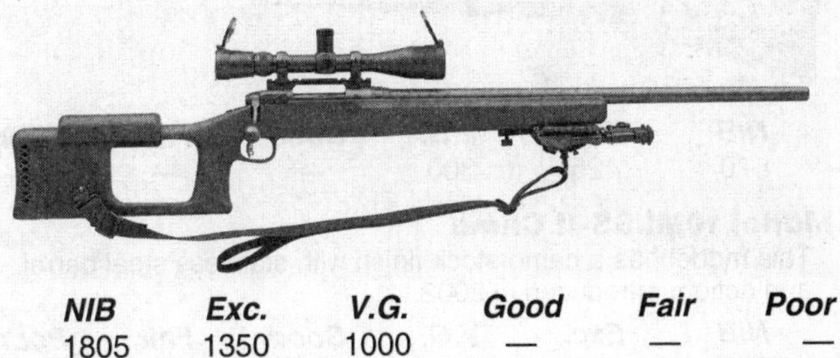

NIB	Exc.	V.G.	Good	Fair	Poor
1805	1350	1000	—	—	—

Model 10FCP-HS Precision

Similar to Model 110FP-LE1 but with one-piece HS Precision synthetic target stock and detachable box magazine. Introduced in 2007.

NIB	Exc	V.G.	Good	Fair	Poor
700	—	—	—	—	—

Model 10FCP Choate

Similar to Model 10FP-LE1 but with Choate synthetic stock. Introduced in 2007.

NIB	Exc	V.G.	Good	Fair	Poor
765	—	—	—	—	—

Model 10FCP McMillan

Similar to Model 10FP-LE1 but with synthetic McMillan precision stock. Introduced in 2007.

NIB	Exc	V.G.	Good	Fair	Poor
900	—	—	—	—	—

Model 10FPXP-HS Precision

Similar to Model 10FPXP-LEA but with HS Precision Tactical Stock. Introduced 2006.

NIB	Exc.	V.G.	Good	Fair	Poor
1725	—	—	—	—	—

Model 10FP-HS

Similar to Model 10FP-LE1 but with HS Precision Tactical stock. Introduced 2006.

NIB	Exc.	V.G.	Good	Fair	Poor
725	—	—	—	—	—

MODEL 10 SERIES MUZZLELOADER

Model 10ML-II

This model is fitted with a .50 caliber 24" barrel with adjustable sights. Synthetic stock. Blued finish. Weight is about 7.75 lbs.

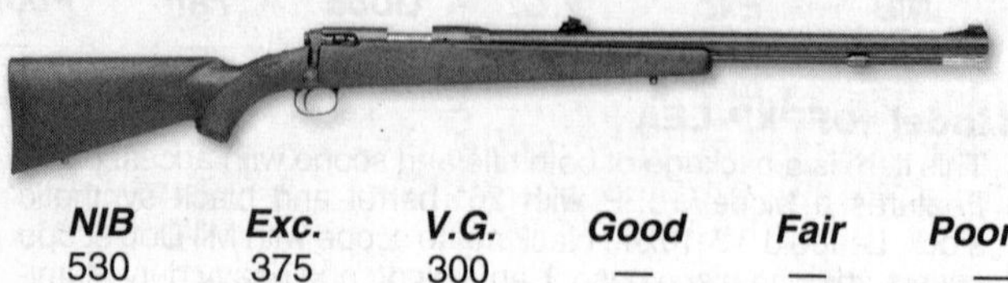

NIB	Exc.	V.G.	Good	Fair	Poor
530	375	300	—	—	—

Model 10MLSS-II

As above in stainless steel.

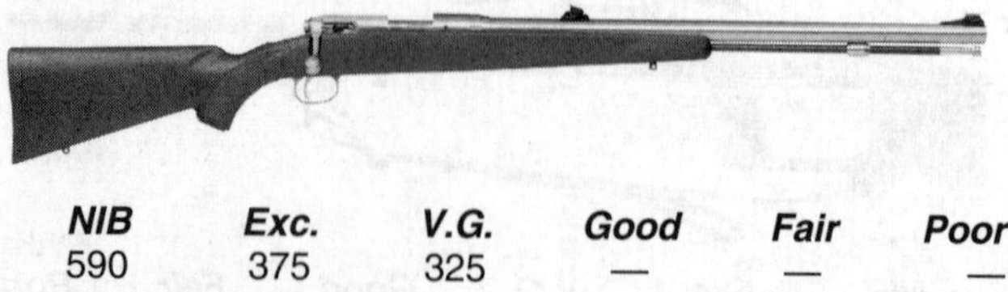

NIB	Exc.	V.G.	Good	Fair	Poor
590	375	325	—	—	—

Model 10ML-II Camo

This model, introduced in 2002, has a camo stock finish with blued barrel and action.

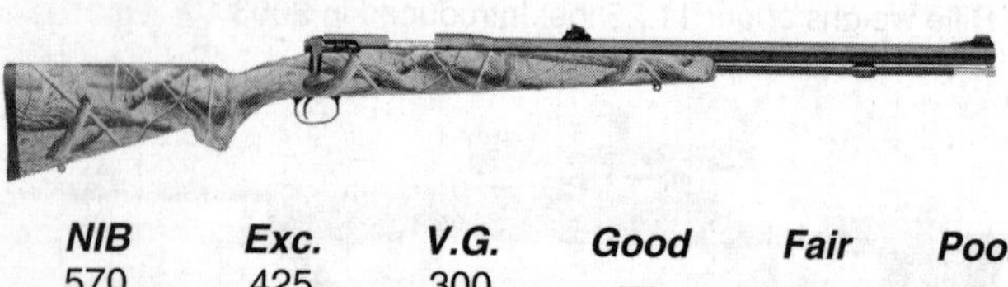

NIB	Exc.	V.G.	Good	Fair	Poor
570	425	300	—	—	—

Model 10MLSS-II Camo

This model has a camo stock finish with stainless steel barrel and action. Introduced in 2002.

NIB	Exc.	V.G.	Good	Fair	Poor
625	475	350	—	—	—

Model 10MLBSS-II

This model features a brown laminate stock with stainless steel action and barrel. Weight is 8.75 lbs. Introduced in 2002.

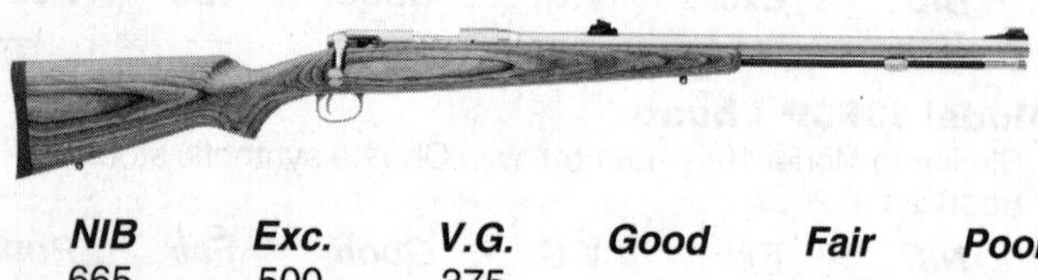

NIB	Exc.	V.G.	Good	Fair	Poor
665	500	375	—	—	—

Model 10ML-IIXP

Introduced in 2002 this model has a blued action and barrel with a synthetic stock. Fitted with a 3-9x40mm scope. Weight is 9.25 lbs.

NIB	Exc.	V.G.	Good	Fair	Poor
570	425	300	—	—	—

Model 10MLSS-IIXP

Same as above but with stainless steel barrel and action.

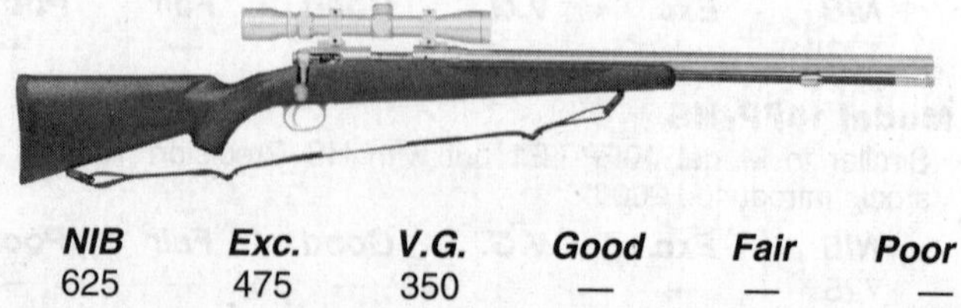

NIB	Exc.	V.G.	Good	Fair	Poor
625	475	350	—	—	—

MODEL 11 SERIES

Model 11F

This model features a short action chambered for the .223, .22-250, .243, or .308 calibers. Barrel lengths are 22" with open sights. Black synthetic stock. Weight is approximately 6.75 lbs. Introduced in 1998.

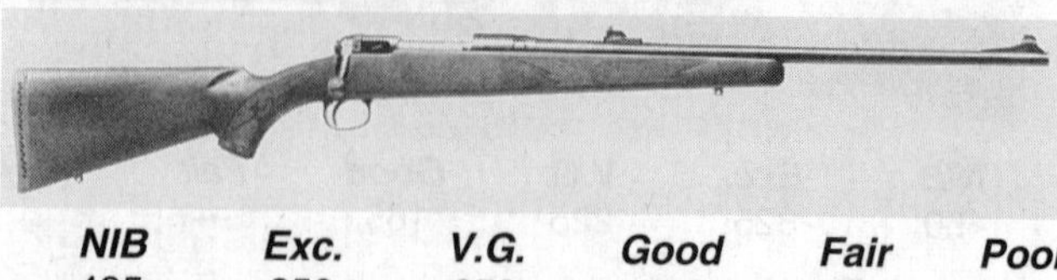

NIB	Exc.	V.G.	Good	Fair	Poor
485	350	250	175	125	

Model 11FL

Same as above but with left-hand action.

NIB	Exc.	V.G.	Good	Fair	Poor
485	350	250	175	125	125

Model 11FNS

Same as Model 11F but without sights. Discontinued.

NIB	Exc.	V.G.	Good	Fair	Poor
450	325	—	—	—	—

Model 11FCNS

Introduced in 2005 this model is chambered for the .22-250, .243, 7mm-08, .308, .270 WSM, .7mm WSN, and the .300 WSM cartridges. Barrel length is 22" or 24" depending on caliber without sights. Detachable box magazine. Black synthetic stock. Weight is about 6.5 lbs. depending on caliber.

NIB	Exc.	V.G.	Good	Fair	Poor
505	375	—	—	—	—

Model 11G

Chambered for .223, .243, .22-250, or .308 calibers and fitted with a 22" barrel. Wood stock has fancy checkering pattern, black recoil pad, and a gold medallion. Fitted with open sights. Weight is about 6.75 lbs. Introduced in 1998.

NIB	Exc.	V.G.	Good	Fair	Poor
375	300	—	—	—	—

Model 11GL

Same as above but with left-hand action.

NIB	Exc.	V.G.	Good	Fair	Poor
375	300	—			—

Model 11GNS

Same as above but without sights. Discontinued.

NIB	Exc.	V.G.	Good	Fair	Poor
375	300	—	—	—	—

Model 11GCNS

This model, introduced in 2005, is chambered for the .22-250, .243, 7mm-08, .308, .270 WSM, 7mm WSM, and the .300 WSM cartridges. Fitted with a 22" or 24" barrel depending on caliber without sights. Checkered walnut stock. Detachable box magazine. Weight is about 6.75 lbs. depending on caliber.

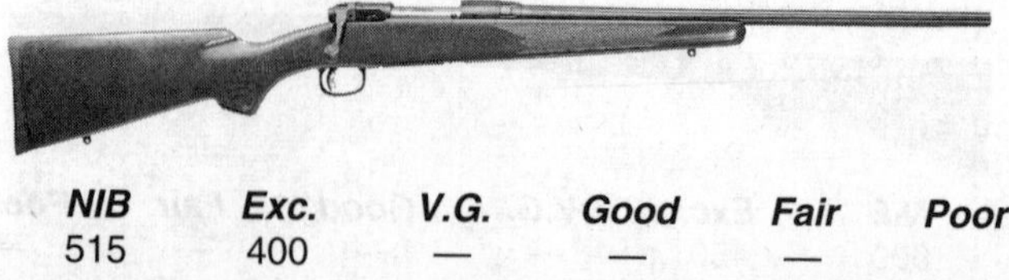

NIB	Exc.	V.G.	Good	Fair	Poor
515	400	—	—	—	

MODEL 16 SERIES

Model 16FSS

This is a short action with a top-loading design and a magazine capacity of 4 rounds. Chambered for the .223, .243, or .308 calibers. Fitted with a 22" stainless steel barrel. Black synthetic stock. Introduced in 1998.

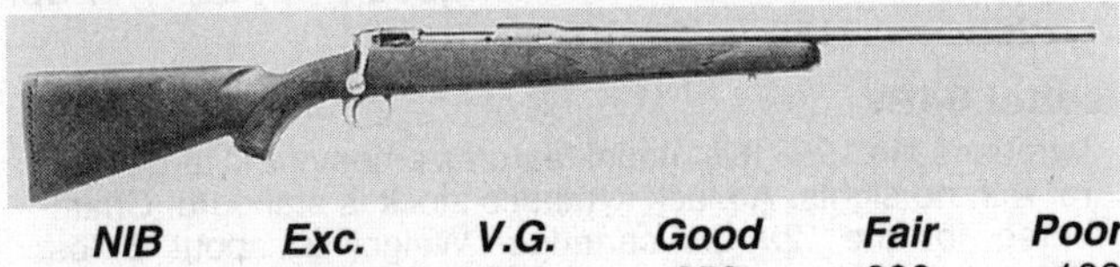

NIB	Exc.	V.G.	Good	Fair	Poor
550	425	325	250	200	100

Model 16FLSS

Same as above but with left-hand action.

NIB	Exc.	V.G.	Good	Fair	Poor
550	425	325	250	200	100

Model 11FLHSS Weather Warrior

Similar to Model 16FSS but in left-hand version. Introduced in 2007.

NIB	Exc	V.G.	Good	Fair	Poor
600	—	—	—	—	—

Model 16FCSAK

Introduced in 2005 this model is chambered for the .243, 7mm-08 Rem., .308, .270 WSM, 7mm WSM, and the .300 WSM cartridges. Fitted with a 22" or 24" barrel depending on caliber. Detachable box magazine. Black synthetic stock. Weights are between 7.75 and 7.25 lbs. depending on caliber.

NIB	Exc.	V.G.	Good	Fair	Poor
660	500	—	—	—	

Model 16FCSS

This model is chambered for the .22-250, .243, 7mm-08 Rem., .308, .270 WSM, 7mm WSM, and the .300 WSM cartridges. Fitted with a 22" or 24" depending on caliber. Detachable box magazine. Black synthetic stock. Weight is about 6.5 lbs. depending on caliber. Introduced in 2005.

NIB	Exc.	V.G.	Good	Fair	Poor
570	425	—	—	—	—

Model 16BSS

Introduced in 2002 this model features a shot action chambered for the 7mm RSUM, .300 RSUM, and the .300 WSM cartridges. Fitted with a 24" stainless steel barrel drilled and tapped for scope mounts. Laminated stock with cut checkering. Weight is about 7.75 lbs. Discontinued.

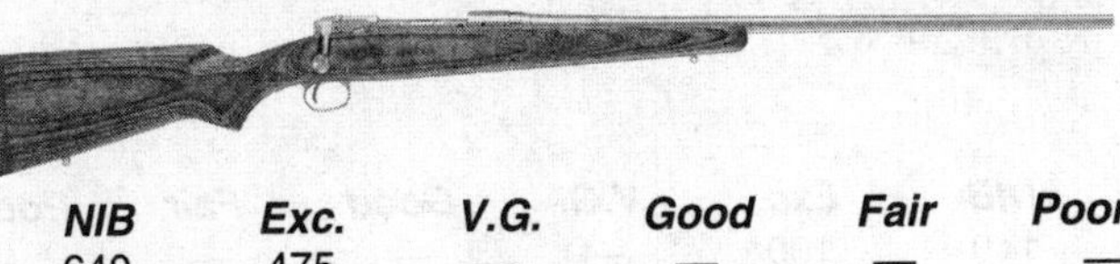

NIB	Exc.	V.G.	Good	Fair	Poor
640	475	—	—	—	—

Long Range Precision Varminter

Single-shot bolt action chambered in .204 Ruger, .223 or .22-250. Features include AccuTrigger and oversized bolt handle. Composite stock, sightless stainless steel fluted barrel. Weight: 11.25 lbs. Introduced 2006. about 6.5 lbs. depending on caliber. Introduced in 2005.

NIB	Exc.	V.G.	Good	Fair	Poor
900	—	—	—	—	—

Model 112 Varmint, Low Profile

Long-action bolt rifle chambered for .25-06 (4) and .300 WM (3). Stock: Brown laminated with recoil pad. Barrel: 26-inch sightless stainless steel bull. Weight: 11.25 lbs.

NIB	Exc.	V.G.	Good	Fair	Poor
600	—	—	—	—	—

Model 116FHSAK

Similar to 166FSAK but with hinged floorplate. Introduced 2006.

NIB	Exc.	V.G.	Good	Fair	Poor
600	—	—	—	—	—

Model 16FHSAK

Similar to Model 116FHSAK but short-action only. Introduced 2006.

NIB	Exc.	V.G.	Good	Fair	Poor
600	—	—	—	—	—

Model 16FHSS

Similar to Model 16FSS but with hinged floorplate. Introduced 2006.

NIB	Exc.	V.G.	Good	Fair	Poor
600	—	—	—	—	—

Model 116FHSS

Similar to Model 116FSS but with hinged floorplate. Introduced 2006.

NIB	Exc.	V.G.	Good	Fair	Poor
600	—	—	—	—	—

Model 14 Classic

Short-action chambered for .22-250, .243, .270 WSM, 7mm-08, .300 WSM and .308. Barrel: 22-inch or 24-inch polished blue without sights. Stock: Select lacquered walnut with contrasting forend. Introduced 2006.

NIB	Exc.	V.G.	Good	Fair	Poor
600	—	—	—	—	—

Model 114 Classic

Similar to Model 14 Classic but long-action chambered for .270, 7mm RM and .300 WM. Introduced 2006.

NIB	Exc.	V.G.	Good	Fair	Poor
620	—	—	—	—	—

Model 14 Euro Classic

Similar to Model 14 Classic but with iron sights. Introduced 2006.

NIB	Exc.	V.G.	Good	Fair	Poor
620	—	—	—	—	—

Model 114 Euro Classic

Similar to Model 114 Classic but with iron sights. Introduced 2006.

NIB	Exc.	V.G.	Good	Fair	Poor
620	—	—	—	—	—

Model 11FYCAK

Short-action youth model chambered in .243, 7mm-08, and .308. Barrel: 22-inch blued with muzzlebrake, no sights. Stock: Black composite. Weight 6.5 lbs.; 41.5-inch overall length. Introduced 2006.

NIB	Exc.	V.G.	Good	Fair	Poor
515	—	—	—	—	—

Model 111FYCAK

Similar to Model 11FYCAK but long-action chambered for .25-06, .270 and .30-06. Introduced 2006.

NIB	Exc.	V.G.	Good	Fair	Poor
515	—	—	—	—	—

Model 111FHNS

Similar to Model 111FCNS but with hinged floorplate. Introduced 2006.

NIB	Exc.	V.G.	Good	Fair	Poor
515	—	—	—	—	—

Model 11FHNS

Similar to Model 11FCNS but with hinged floorplate. Introduced 2006.

NIB	Exc.	V.G.	Good	Fair	Poor
515	—	—	—	—	—

Model 11FCXP3

Similar to Model 111FCXP3 but in short-action. Introduced 2006.

NIB	Exc.	V.G.	Good	Fair	Poor
400	—	—	—	—	—

Model 11FYCXP3

Similar to Model 11FCXP3 but in youth version chambered in .243 Win.

NIB	Exc.	V.G.	Good	Fair	Poor
400	—	—	—	—	—

RIMFIRE RIFLES

Note: As of 2006, virtually all Savage rimfire rifles (with the exception of the 30G and semi-autos) were equipped with Accu-Trigger as a standard feature.

Model 60

A .22 caliber semi-automatic rifle with a 20" barrel, open sights, and tubular magazine. Blued with a Monte Carlo-style walnut stock. Manufactured between 1969 and 1972.

Exc.	V.G.	Good	Fair	Poor
100	80	70	50	35

Model 64G

Introduced in 1996 this semi-automatic .22 long rifle has a 20.25" barrel and 10-shot detachable magazine. The finish is blue and the stock has a Monte Carlo with checkered pistol grip. Bead front sight with adjustable open rear sight is standard. Weight is about 5.5 lbs.

NIB	Exc.	V.G.	Good	Fair	Poor
160	125	90	60	50	40

Model 64GXP

As above but with unmounted 4x15mm scope.

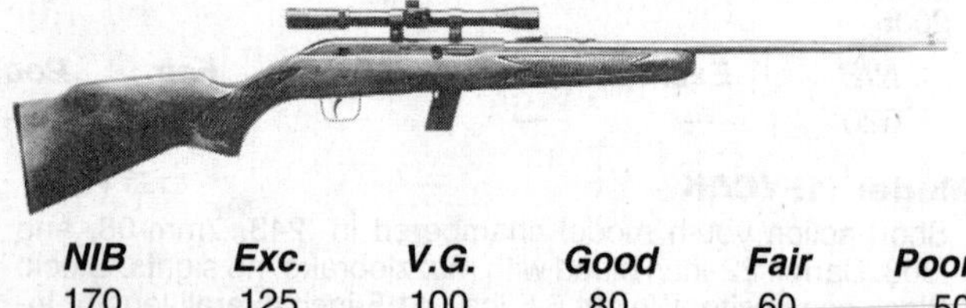

NIB	Exc.	V.G.	Good	Fair	Poor
170	125	100	80	60	50

Model 64F

Introduced in 1997 this model features a black synthetic stock with blue finish. Chambered for .22 LR and fitted with a 20.25" barrel. Weight is approximately 5.5 lbs.

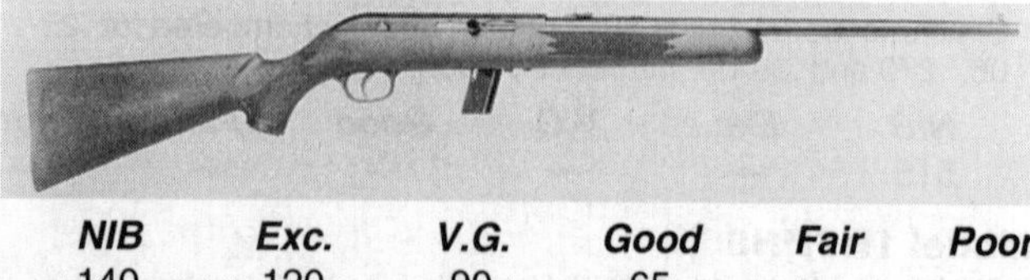

NIB	Exc.	V.G.	Good	Fair	Poor
140	120	90	65	—	—

Model 64FSS

Similar to the model above but with stainless steel action and barrel. Introduced in 2002.

NIB	Exc.	V.G.	Good	Fair	Poor
200	150	110	75	—	—

Model 64FV

Introduced in 1998 this model features a heavy 21" target barrel with no sights. A black synthetic stock is standard. Chambered for the .22 LR cartridge. Weight is about 6 lbs. Discontinued.

NIB	Exc.	V.G.	Good	Fair	Poor
150	125	—	—	—	—

Model 64FVXP

Similar to Model 64FV but with scope package. Introduced 2006.

NIB	Exc.	V.G.	Good	Fair	Poor
190	—	—	—	—	—

Model 64FVSS

Similar to the Model FV but with stainless steel action and barrel. Introduced in 2002. Discontinued

NIB	Exc.	V.G.	Good	Fair	Poor
225	175	—	—	—	—

Model 64FXP

This is a package model that offers a .22 LR gun with 20.25" barrel with detachable 10-round magazine. It comes with a 4x15mm scope as well as open sights. Introduced in 1998. Weight is about 5.25 lbs.

NIB	Exc.	V.G.	Good	Fair	Poor
140	100	—	—	—	—

Model 88

As above, with a hardwood stock. Manufactured between 1969 and 1972.

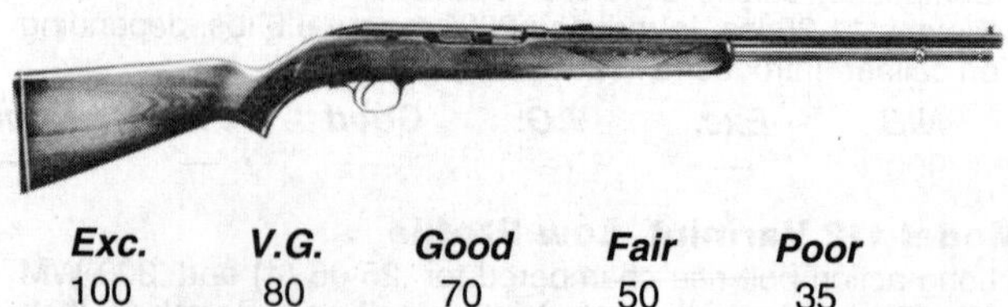

Exc.	V.G.	Good	Fair	Poor
100	80	70	50	35

Model 90 Carbine

As above, with a 16.5" barrel and carbine-style stock. The forend is secured to the barrel by a barrel band. Discontinued.

This symbol denotes "Sleepers" with rapidly-rising values and/or significant collector potential.

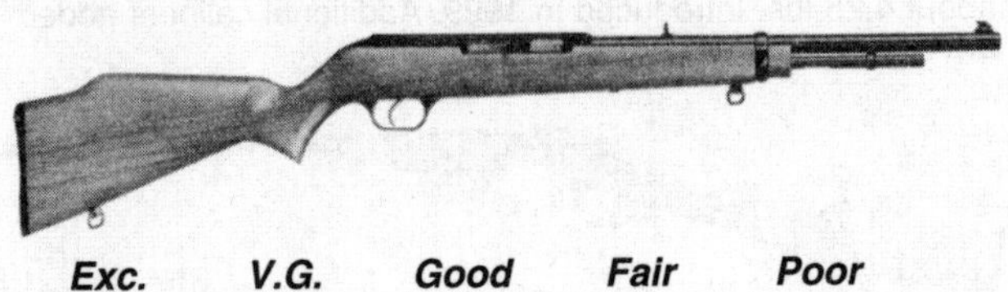

Exc.	V.G.	Good	Fair	Poor
100	80	70	50	35

Model 93G

Introduced in 1996 this model is a bolt-action repeating rifle chambered for the .22 WMR cartridge. It is fitted with a 20.75" barrel with 5-shot magazine. It has a walnut-stained hardwood stock with cut checkering. Open sights standard. Weight is about 5.75 lbs. In 2001 this model was offered in a left-hand version (Model 93GL). AccuTrigger introduced 2006.

NIB	Exc.	V.G.	Good	Fair	Poor
195	150	100	75	60	50

Model 93-FS

This .22 WMR model features a stainless steel finish with a 20.75" barrel and black synthetic stock. Five-round magazine. Front bead sight and sporting rear sight. Introduced in 1997. Weight is about 5.5 lbs. Discontinued.

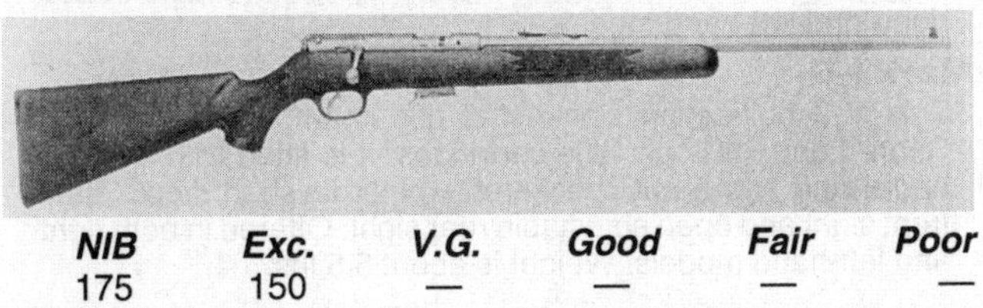

NIB	Exc.	V.G.	Good	Fair	Poor
175	150	—	—	—	—

Model 93FVSS

This model features a 21" heavy barrel chambered for the .22 WMR cartridge, recessed target muzzle and stainless steel barreled action. Equipped with black synthetic stock. Magazine capacity is 5 rounds. Weight is about 6 lbs. Introduced in 1998.

NIB	Exc.	V.G.	Good	Fair	Poor
275	200	150	100	70	—

Model 93BTVS

Similar to Model 93FVSS but with laminated thumbhole stock. Introduced in 2007.

NIB	Exc	V.G.	Good	Fair	Poor
395	—	—	—	—	—

Model 93F

Similar to the above model but with blued finish and a synthetic stock with open sights. Weight is approximately 5 lbs. Introduced in 1998.

NIB	Exc.	V.G.	Good	Fair	Poor
185	125	95	65	—	—

Model 93R17-F

This bolt-action rifle is chambered for the .17 HMR cartridge and fitted with a 20.75" barrel with no sights. Black synthetic stock. Magazine capacity is 5 rounds. Blued finish. Weight is about 5 lbs. Introduced in 2003.

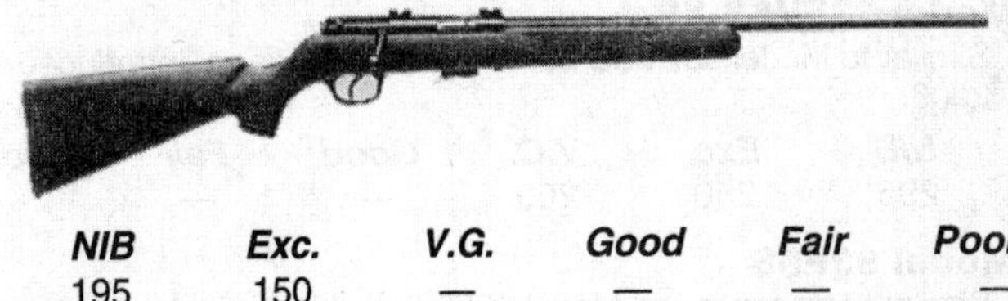

NIB	Exc.	V.G.	Good	Fair	Poor
195	150	—	—	—	—

Model 93R17-BVSS

Similar to the above model but with 21" stainless steel barrel with no sights and laminated hardwood stock. Weight is about 6 lbs. Introduced in 2003.

NIB	Exc.	V.G.	Good	Fair	Poor
325	250	190	125	—	—

Model 93R17-FSS

This .17 HMR caliber rifle has a 20.75" stainless steel barrel with no sights and black synthetic stock. Weight is about 5 lbs. Introduced in 2003.

NIB	Exc.	V.G.	Good	Fair	Poor
240	180	130	—	—	—

Model 93R17-Camo

As above but with Realtree Hardwoods camo stock. Weight is about 5 lbs. Introduced in 2003.

NIB	Exc.	V.G.	Good	Fair	Poor
225	170	125	—	—	—

Model 93R17-FVSS

As above but with 21" stainless steel heavy barrel. Weight is about 6 lbs. Introduced in 2003.

NIB	Exc.	V.G.	Good	Fair	Poor
275	210	150	—	—	—

Model 93R17-GV

This .17 HMR model has a walnut finished hardwood checkered stock and 21" heavy barrel with no sights. Blued finish. Weight is about 6 lbs. Introduced in 2003. A left-hand model is also available.

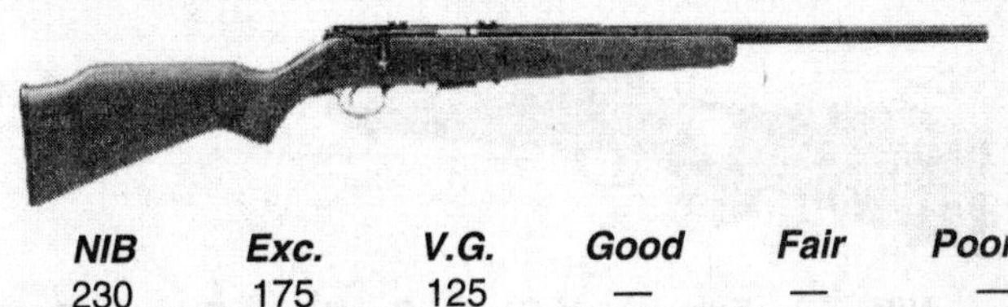

NIB	Exc.	V.G.	Good	Fair	Poor
230	175	125	—	—	—

Model 93R17-GVXP

Similar to Model 93R17-GV but with scope package. Introduced 2006.

NIB	Exc.	V.G.	Good	Fair	Poor
250	200	175	—	—	—

Model 93R17-FXP

Similar to Model 93R17-F but with scope package. Introduced 2006.

NIB	Exc.	V.G.	Good	Fair	Poor
250	200	175	—	—	—

Model 93FVSS-XP

Similar to Model 93FVSS but with scope package. Introduced 2006.

NIB	Exc.	V.G.	Good	Fair	Poor
295	250	200	—	—	—

Model 93FSS

Similar to discontinued Model 93FS but with no sights and AccuTrigger. Introduced 2006.

NIB	Exc.	V.G.	Good	Fair	Poor
250	200	175	—	—	—

Model 93FV

Similar to Model 93F but with AccuTrigger. Introduced 2006.

NIB	Exc.	V.G.	Good	Fair	Poor
230	200	175	—	—	—

Model 93R17-BTVS

Similar to Model 93R17-BVSS but with laminated thumbhole stock. Introduced 2006.

NIB	Exc.	V.G.	Good	Fair	Poor
350	295	245	—	—	—

Model 93R17-BV

Similar to Model 93R17-GV but with brown laminated stock with wide beavertail forend. Introduced 2006.

NIB	Exc.	V.G.	Good	Fair	Poor
350	295	245	—	—	—

Model 93R17 Classic

Similar to Model 93R17 but with sporter-weight barrel and oil-finished premium walnut stock. AccuTrigger. Introduced in 2007.

NIB	Exc	V.G.	Good	Fair	Poor
350	—	—	—	—	—

Model CUB-G (Mini-Youth)

Introduced in 2003 this single-shot bolt-action rifle is chambered for the .22 caliber cartridge. Barrel length is 16" and the walnut-stained hardwood stock is proportionally scaled down. Weight is about 3.3 lbs. In 2005 this model was offered in .17 HM2.

NIB	Exc.	V.G.	Good	Fair	Poor
155	125	—	—	—	—

Model CUB-T

Similar to Model CUB-G but with laminated thumbhole stock. Introduced in 2007.

NIB	Exc	V.G.	Good	Fair	Poor
235	—	—	—	—	—

Model 30G "Stevens Favorite"

Based on the Stevens Favorite model, this lever-action single-shot .22 caliber rifle is fitted with a 21" half octagonal barrel. Walnut stock with schnabel forend. Blued finish. Weight is about 4.25 lbs. Introduced in 1999. Additional calibers added are .22 WMR and .22 Hornet.

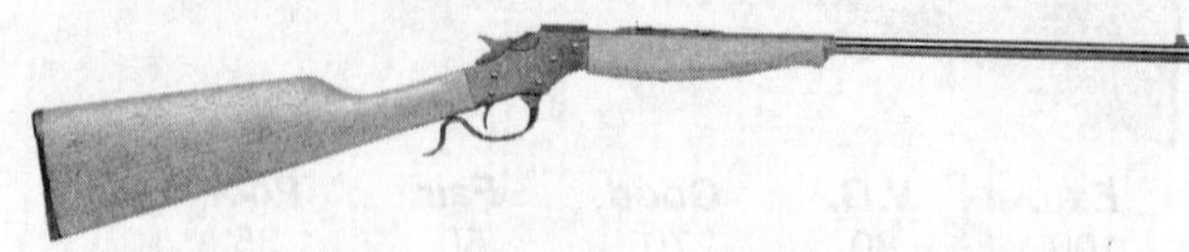

NIB	Exc.	V.G.	Good	Fair	Poor
230	175	125	95	65	—

NOTE: Add $35 for .22WMR and $60 for .22 Hornet.

Model 30G "Favorite" Takedown

Introduced in 2004 this model has a takedown feature. Offered in .17 HMR and .22 LR. The .17 HMR is fitted with a 21" full octagon barrel with sights and scope base included. The .22 LR model is fitted with a 21" half octagon barrel with sights.

NIB	Exc.	V.G.	Good	Fair	Poor
250	175	125	—	—	—

NOTE: Add $65 for .17 HMR model.

MARK I & II SERIES

Introduced in 1996 this series of .22 caliber rifles feature both single-shot and repeating models. They are available in both right- and left-hand models.

Mark I-G

This is a bolt-action single-shot rifle chambered for the .22 Short, Long, or Long Rifle cartridges. It is fitted with a 20.75" barrel and has a cut checkered walnut finished stock. Bead front sight and open adjustable rear sight. Offered in both right- and left-hand models. Weight is about 5.5 lbs.

NIB	Exc.	V.G.	Good	Fair	Poor
150	100	80	70	60	50

Model Mark I-FVT

Similar to Model Mark I-G but with synthetic stock, rear peep sight and hooded front sight. Introduced 2006.

NIB	Exc	V.G.	Good	Fair	Poor
300	—	—	—	—	—

Mark I-GY (Youth Model)

Same as above but fitted with a 19" barrel and shorter buttstock. Weight is about 5 lbs.

NIB	Exc.	V.G.	Good	Fair	Poor
150	100	80	70	60	50

Mark I-GSB

This version of the Mark I is a smoothbore model made for .22 caliber shot cartridges. Barrel length is 20.75" and weight is about 5.5 lbs.

NIB	Exc.	V.G.	Good	Fair	Poor
150	100	80	70	60	50

Mark II-G

This model is a bolt-action repeater with 10-shot magazine. It is chambered for the .22 LR cartridge. Checkered walnut finished stock. Open sights. Barrel length is 20.75". Offered in both right- and left-hand versions. Weight is approximately 5.5 lbs.

NIB	Exc.	V.G.	Good	Fair	Poor
170	125	90	70	60	50

Mark II-GY (Youth Model)

Same as above but with 19" barrel and shorter stock.

NIB	Exc.	V.G.	Good	Fair	Poor
170	125	90	70	60	50

Mark II-GXP

Same as the Mark II-G model but includes an unmounted 4x15mm scope. Discontinued.

NIB	Exc.	V.G.	Good	Fair	Poor
130	100	80	70	60	50

Mark II-FSS

This is a stainless steel .22 caliber rifle with 20.75" barrel and 10-round magazine. Receiver is dovetailed for scope mounting. Stock is black synthetic. Weight is about 5 lbs.

NIB	Exc.	V.G.	Good	Fair	Poor
210	150	110	—	—	—

Mark II-LV

This .22 caliber is fitted with a 21" heavy barrel. It has a laminated hardwood stock with cut checkering. Blue finish and 10-round magazine. Weight is approximately 6.5 lbs. Introduced in 1997. Discontinued.

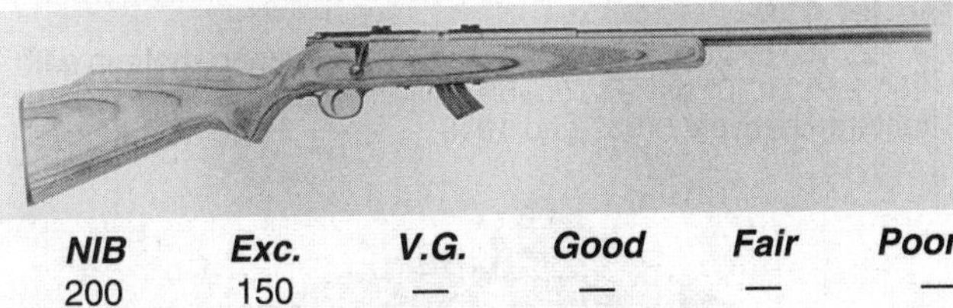

NIB	Exc.	V.G.	Good	Fair	Poor
200	150	—	—	—	—

Mark II-F

This model has the standard Mark II barreled action with a black synthetic stock. Detachable 10-round magazine is standard. Weight is about 5 lbs. Introduced in 1998. .17 Hornady Mach 2 added in 2006.

NIB	Exc.	V.G.	Good	Fair	Poor
150	110	80	70	—	—

Mark II-FXP

Similar to the Mark II-F but with a 4x15mm scope. Weight is approximately 5.25 lbs. First offered in 1998.

NIB	Exc.	V.G.	Good	Fair	Poor
155	110	80	70	—	—

Model Mark II Camo

Similar to Model Mark II-F but with forest camo synthetic stock. Introduced 2006.

NIB	Exc	V.G.	Good	Fair	Poor
200	165	—	—	—	—

Mark II-FV

Introduced in 1998 this model features a 21" heavy barrel with blue alloy steel receiver. Stock is black synthetic. Magazine capacity is 5-round detachable magazine. Weight is about 6 lbs. .17 Hornady Mach 2 added in 2006.

NIB	Exc.	V.G.	Good	Fair	Poor
215	150	110	80	60	—

Model Mark II-FVXP

Similar to Model Mark II-FV but with scope package. Introduced 2006.

NIB	Exc	V.G.	Good	Fair	Poor
250	—	—	—	—	—

Model Mark II-FVT

Similar to Model Mark II-FV but with rear peep sight and hooded front sight. Introduced 2006.

NIB	Exc	V.G.	Good	Fair	Poor
315	—	—	—	—	—

Model Mark II-BV

This model features a 21-inch stainless steel bull barrel without sights and a brown laminate stock. Chambered in .22 LR. Introduced 2006.

NIB	Exc	V.G.	Good	Fair	Poor
275	—	—	—	—	—

Model Mark II Classic

Similar to Mark II-FV but with sporter-weight barrel and oil-finished premium walnut stock. AccuTrigger. Introduced in 2007.

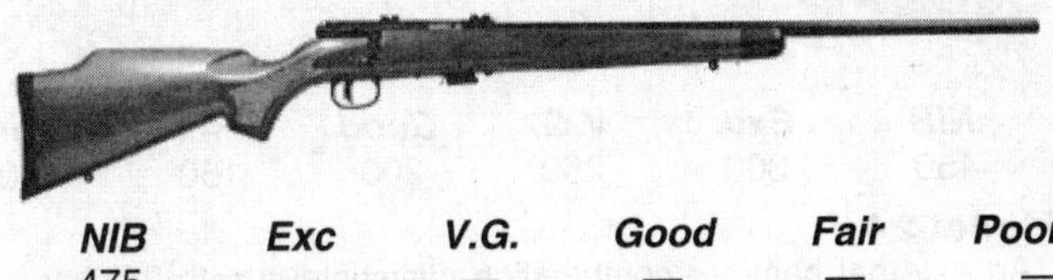

NIB	Exc	V.G.	Good	Fair	Poor
475	—	—	—	—	—

Model Mark II BTVS

Similar to Model Mark II BV with with brown laminated thumbhole stock. Introduced in 2007.

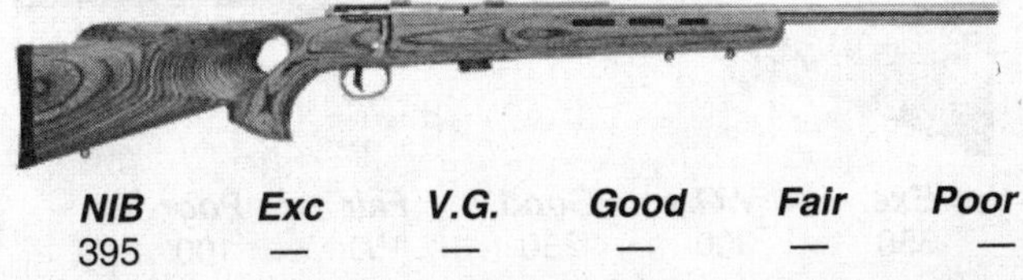

NIB	Exc	V.G.	Good	Fair	Poor
395	—	—	—	—	—

MODEL 900 SERIES

First offered in 1996 this series consists of .22 caliber rimfire target rifles in various configurations. All are available in both right- or left-hand versions.

Model 900B—Biathlon

This rifle features a hardwood stock with 5-round magazine, carrying and shooting rails, butt hook, and hand stop. The barrel length is 21" and comes with a snow cover. Receiver sight are peep variety and the front sight has 7 aperture inserts as standard. Weight is about 8.25 lbs.

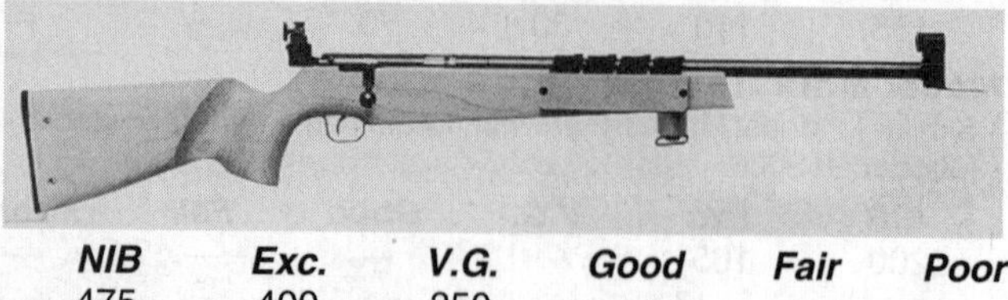

NIB	Exc.	V.G.	Good	Fair	Poor
475	400	350	—	—	—

Model 900 TR—Target

This model has a one-piece hardwood stock with shooting rail and hand stop. Rear sight is adjustable peep and front sight has 7 aperture inserts. Barrel length is 25". Five-shot magazine is standard. Weight is about 8 lbs.

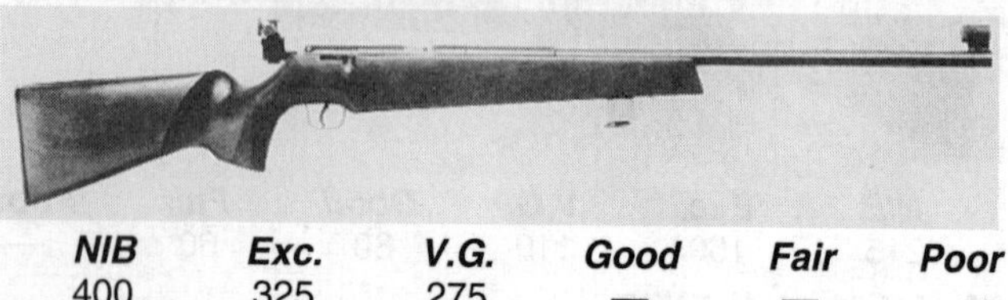

NIB	Exc.	V.G.	Good	Fair	Poor
400	325	275	—	—	—

Model 900S—Silhouette

This version features a 21" heavy barrel with recessed target style crown. Fitted with a one-piece silhouette-style stock with high comb and satin walnut finish. Receiver is drilled and tapped for scope mount. Weight is about 8 lbs.

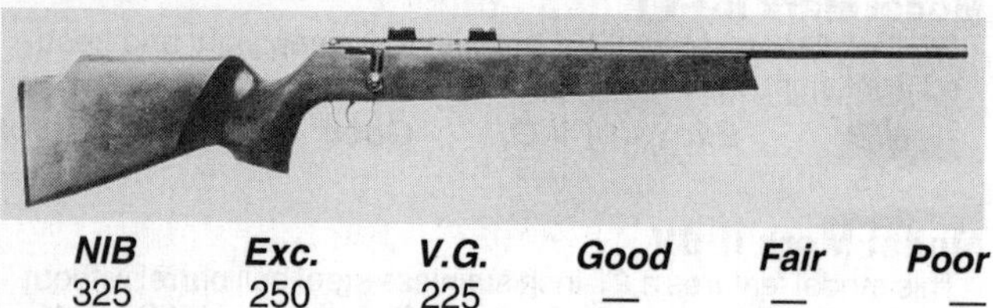

NIB	Exc.	V.G.	Good	Fair	Poor
325	250	225	—	—	—

Model 210F

Introduced in 1996 this bolt-action shotgun has a 24" rifled barrel for slugs. It is chambered for the 3" 12 gauge shell. No sights. Magazine holds 2 rounds. Weight is about 7.5 lbs.

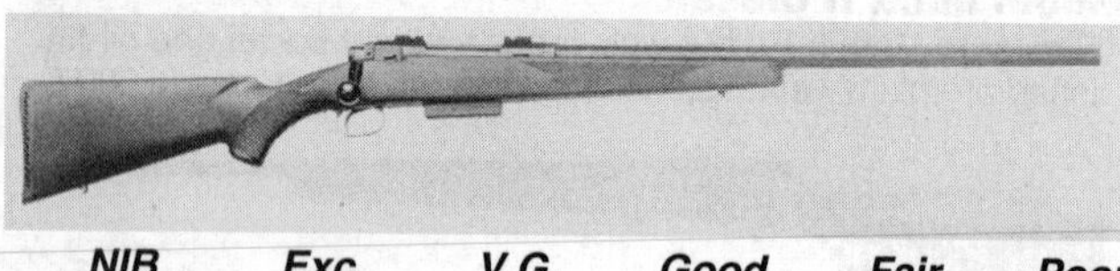

NIB	Exc.	V.G.	Good	Fair	Poor
450	300	250	200	150	100

Model 24

An external hammer combination rifle/shotgun with 24" barrels. Blued with a walnut stock. Manufactured from 1950 to 1965 in a variety of styles. The standard chambering was .22 by .410. Add 20 percent for centerfire chamberings.

Exc.	V.G.	Good	Fair	Poor
350	300	250	150	100

Model 24S

20 gauge.

Exc.	V.G.	Good	Fair	Poor
350	300	250	150	100

Model 24MS

.22 Rimfire Magnum.

Exc.	V.G.	Good	Fair	Poor
375	325	275	175	125

Model 24DL

Satin chrome with checkered stock.

Exc.	V.G.	Good	Fair	Poor
350	325	225	175	125

Model 24 Field—Lightweight Version

Exc.	V.G.	Good	Fair	Poor
350	300	250	150	100

Model 24C

Nickel finish.

Exc.	V.G.	Good	Fair	Poor
375	325	275	175	125

Model 24VS

.357 Magnum or .357 Maximum/20 gauge, nickel finish.

Exc.	V.G.	Good	Fair	Poor
675	575	400	250	175

Model 24F

DuPont Rynite stock.

NIB	Exc.	V.G.	Good	Fair	Poor
500	400	325	250	150	100

Model 2400

A combination 12 gauge by .222 or .308 caliber over-and-under rifle/shotgun with 23.5" barrels and a Monte Carlo-style stock. Made by Valmet and imported between 1975 and 1980.

Exc.	V.G.	Good	Fair	Poor
600	525	450	350	275

SAVAGE SHOTGUNS

Model 411 Upland Sporter

SEE—Stevens.

Model 420

A 12, 16, or 20 gauge boxlock over-and-under shotgun with 26", 28", or 30" barrels, double triggers and extractors. Manufactured between 1937 and 1943.

Courtesy Nick Niles, Paul Goodwin photo

Exc.	V.G.	Good	Fair	Poor
500	400	300	200	150

This symbol denotes "Sleepers" with rapidly-rising values and/or significant collector potential.

Model 420 with Single Trigger

Exc.	V.G.	Good	Fair	Poor
500	400	300	200	150

Model 430

As above, with a checkered walnut stock and solid barrel rib. Produced from 1937 to 1943.

Courtesy Nick Niles, Paul Goodwin photo

Exc.	V.G.	Good	Fair	Poor
550	450	350	200	150

Model 430 with Single Trigger

Exc.	V.G.	Good	Fair	Poor
600	450	300	200	150

Model 320

This is a side-by-side model.

Exc.	V.G.	Good	Fair	Poor
800	650	500	400	300

Model 412

.410 bore adapter.

Exc.	V.G.	Good	Fair	Poor
80	60	50	40	30

Model 412F

.410 bore adapter.

Exc.	V.G.	Good	Fair	Poor
50	45	40	35	25

Model 220

A 12, 16, 20 or .410 bore boxlock single barrel shotgun with 26" to 32" barrels. Blued with a walnut stock. Manufactured between 1938 and 1965.

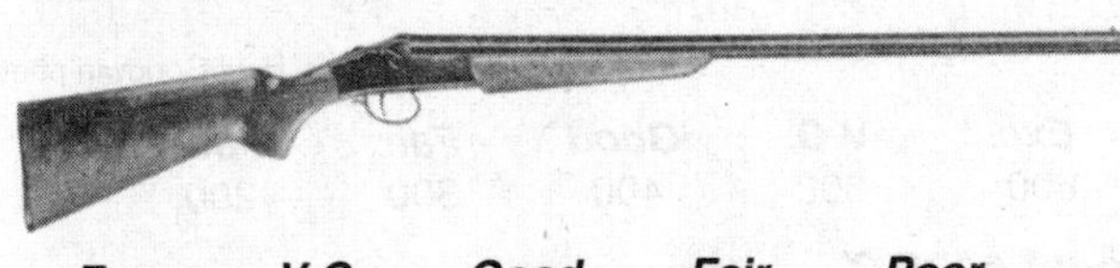

Exc.	V.G.	Good	Fair	Poor
100	80	70	50	35

Model 210F Slug Warrior

A bolt-action 12 gauge gun with 24" barrel. Black synthetic stock with checkering. Blue finish. Weight is about 7.5 lbs. Magazine capacity is 2 rounds.

NIB	Exc.	V.G.	Good	Fair	Poor
475	350	275	—	—	

Model 210F Slug Warrior Camo

As above but with camo stock.

NIB	Exc.	V.G.	Good	Fair	Poor
513	400	325	—	—	—

Model 210FT

Introduced in 1997 this is a 12 gauge bolt-action shotgun with a camouflage finish. Chambered for 3" shells and fitted with a 24" barrel. 2-round magazine. Approximate weight is 7.5 lbs. Drilled and tapped for scope mounting.

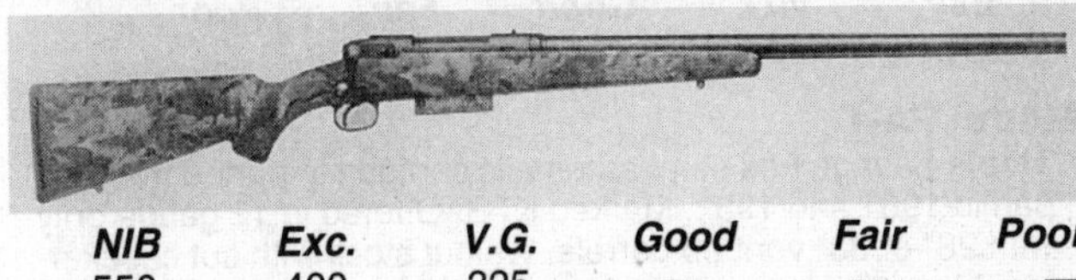

NIB	Exc.	V.G.	Good	Fair	Poor
550	400	325			—

Model 720

A 12 or 16 gauge semi-automatic shotgun with 26" to 32" barrels. Blued with a walnut stock. Manufactured between 1930 and 1949.

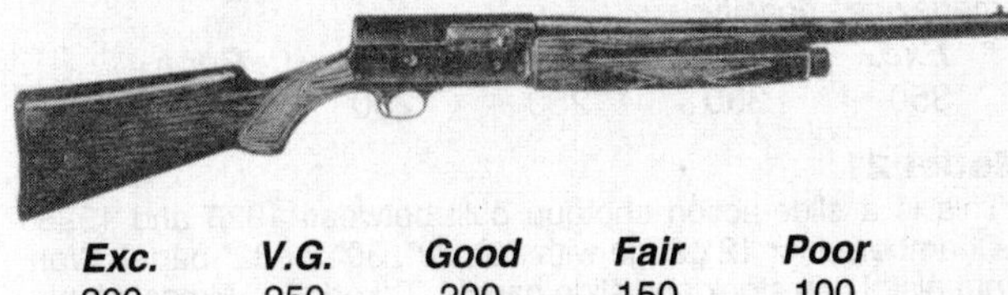

Exc.	V.G.	Good	Fair	Poor
300	250	200	150	100

Model 726 Upland Sporter

As above, with a 2-shot magazine. Manufactured between 1931 and 1949.

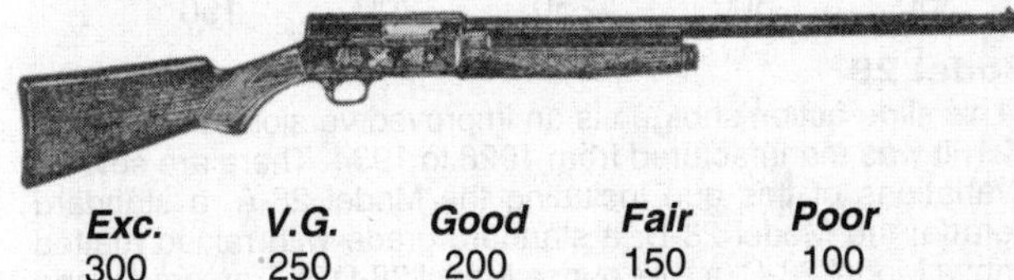

Exc.	V.G.	Good	Fair	Poor
300	250	200	150	100

Model 740C Skeet

The Model 726 with a 24.5" barrel featuring a Cutts compensator and skeet-style stock. Manufactured between 1936 and 1949.

Exc.	V.G.	Good	Fair	Poor
300	250	200	150	100

Model 745

The Model 720 in 12 gauge with an alloy receiver and 28" barrel. Manufactured between 1940 and 1949.

Exc.	V.G.	Good	Fair	Poor
275	225	175	125	75

Model 755

A 12 or 16 gauge semi-automatic shotgun with 26" to 30" barrels. Blued with a walnut stock. Also available with Savage Super Choke. Manufactured between 1949 and 1958.

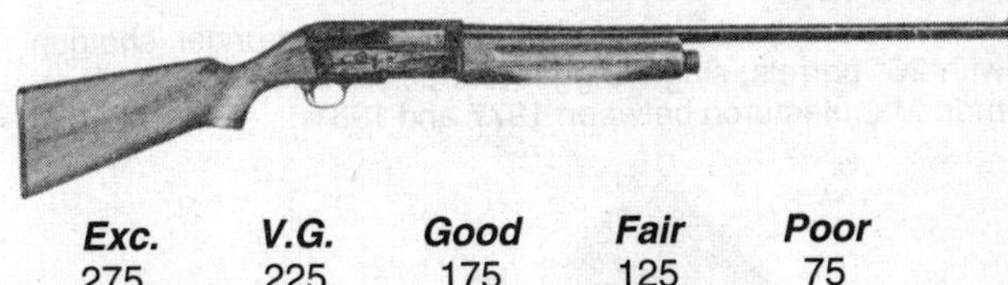

Exc.	V.G.	Good	Fair	Poor
275	225	175	125	75

Model 775

As above, with an alloy receiver. Manufactured between 1950 and 1966.

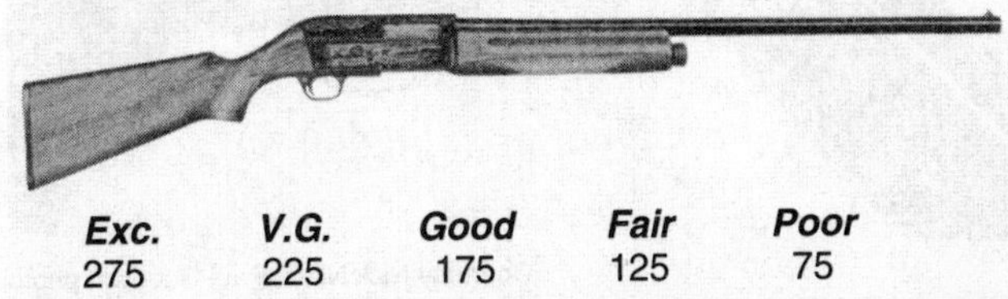

Exc.	V.G.	Good	Fair	Poor
275	225	175	125	75

Model 750

A 12 gauge semi-automatic shotgun with a 26" or 28" barrel. The Model 750SC fitted with the Savage Super Choke and the Model 750AC with a Poly Choke. Blued with a walnut stock. Manufactured between 1960 and 1967.

Exc.	V.G.	Good	Fair	Poor
275	225	175	125	75

Model FA-1

This is Savage Fox semi-automatic shotgun imported from Japan in 1981 and 1982. Marked KTG. Offered in 12 gauge only with 28" or 30" vent rib barrels. Walnut stock with cut checkering. Magazine capacity is 4 rounds. Weight is about 7.5 lbs.

Exc.	V.G.	Good	Fair	Poor
350	300	250	200	150

Model FP-1

Similar to the above model but with 3" chambers and a 5-round magazine capacity.

Exc.	V.G.	Good	Fair	Poor
350	300	250	200	150

Model 21

This is a slide-action shotgun built between 1920 and 1928. Chambered for 12 gauge with 26", 28", 30", or 32" barrel. Walnut pistol grip stock and slide handle. Takedown. Almost identical to the famous Winchester Model 12. Offered in a number of different configurations including standard grade, Trap grade, Tournament grade, and Riot Model. About 13,000 were built.

Exc.	V.G.	Good	Fair	Poor
350	300	250	200	150

Model 28

This slide-action shotgun is an improved version of the Model 21. It was manufactured from 1928 to 1934. There are several variations of this gun including the Model 28-A, a standard grade; the Model 28-B, a standard grade with raised matted rib; a Model 28-C, a Riot gun; a Model 28-D, a Trap grade; and in 1931 a Model 28-3, an improved version with checkering and roll marked game scenes on the receiver.

Exc.	V.G.	Good	Fair	Poor
375	325	275	200	150

Model 30

A 12, 16, 20 or .410 bore slide-action shotgun with 26" to 30" ventilated rib barrels. Blued with a walnut stock. Manufactured between 1958 and 1978.

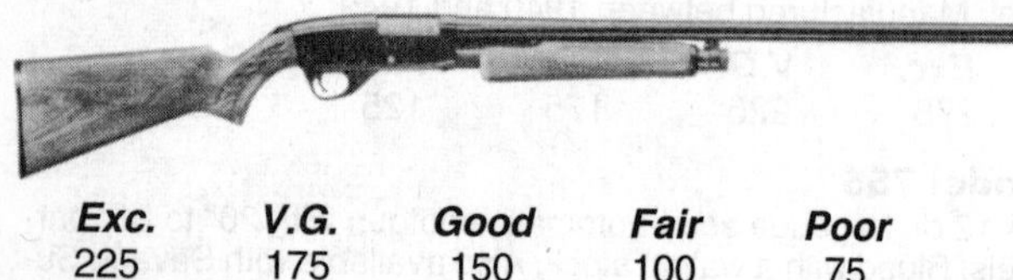

Exc.	V.G.	Good	Fair	Poor
225	175	150	100	75

Model 242

A .410 bore boxlock double-barrel over-and-under shotgun with 26" barrels, single trigger, extractors and exposed hammer. Manufactured between 1977 and 1981.

Courtesy Nick Niles, Paul Goodwin photo

Exc.	V.G.	Good	Fair	Poor
375	300	250	200	150

Model 550

A 12 or 20 gauge boxlock side-by-side double-barrel shotgun with 26", 28", or 30" barrels, single triggers and automatic ejectors. Blued with a hardwood stock. Manufactured between 1971 and 1973. Barrels were built by Valmet.

Courtesy Nick Niles, Paul Goodwin photo

Exc.	V.G.	Good	Fair	Poor
500	400	300	200	150

Model 440

An Italian made 12 or 20 gauge boxlock over-and-under shotgun with 26", 28", or 30" ventilated rib barrels, single-selective trigger and extractors. Blued with a walnut stock. Manufactured between 1968 and 1972.

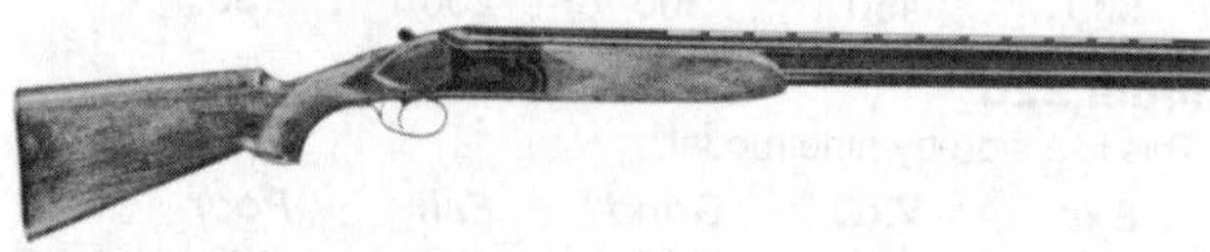

Exc.	V.G.	Good	Fair	Poor
600	500	400	300	200

Model 440A

Courtesy Nick Niles, Paul Goodwin photo

Exc.	V.G.	Good	Fair	Poor
600	500	400	300	200

Model 440B-T

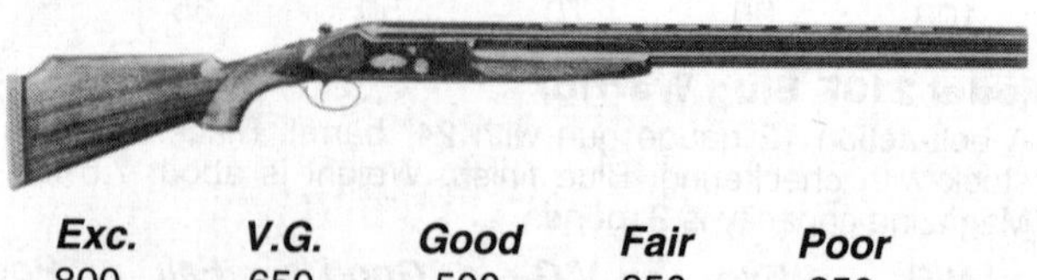

Exc.	V.G.	Good	Fair	Poor
800	650	500	350	250

Model 444 Deluxe

As above, with a more finely figured stock and automatic ejectors. Imported between 1969 and 1972.

Exc.	V.G.	Good	Fair	Poor
550	475	400	300	225

Model 444

Exc.	*V.G.*	*Good*	*Fair*	*Poor*
600	500	400	300	200

Model 444B

Exc.	*V.G.*	*Good*	*Fair*	*Poor*
700	550	400	300	250

Model 440T

A 12 gauge Model 440 with 30" barrels and a trap-style stock. Imported between 1969 and 1972.

Exc.	*V.G.*	*Good*	*Fair*	*Poor*
600	500	400	300	200

Model 330

A Valmet manufactured 12 or 20 gauge over-and-under shotgun with 26", 28", or 30" barrels, single-selective trigger and extractors. Blued with a walnut stock. Imported between 1970 and 1978.

Courtesy Nick Niles, Paul Goodwin photo

Exc.	*V.G.*	*Good*	*Fair*	*Poor*
800	650	500	350	250

Model 333

As above, with a ventilated rib and automatic ejectors. Imported between 1973 and 1980.

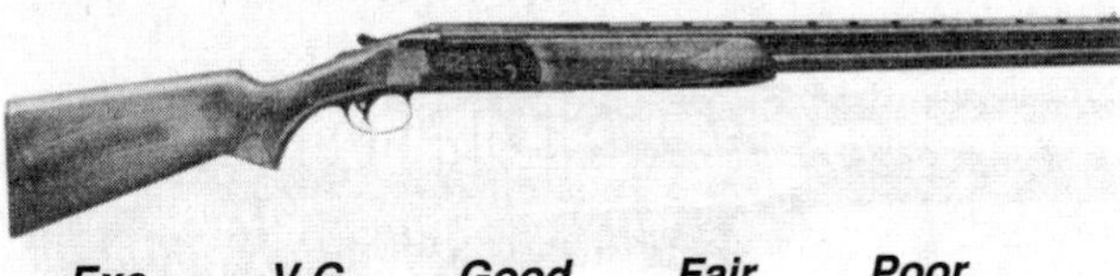

Exc.	*V.G.*	*Good*	*Fair*	*Poor*
700	550	400	300	200

Model 333T

As above, with a 30" barrel and trap-style stock. Imported between 1972 and 1980.

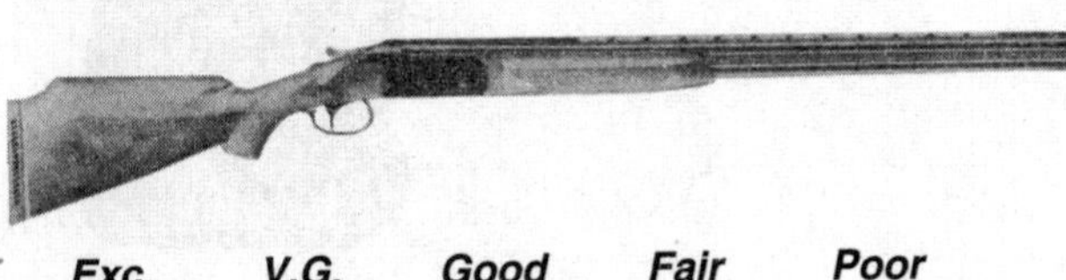

Exc.	*V.G.*	*Good*	*Fair*	*Poor*
800	650	500	350	250

Model 312 Field Over-and-Under

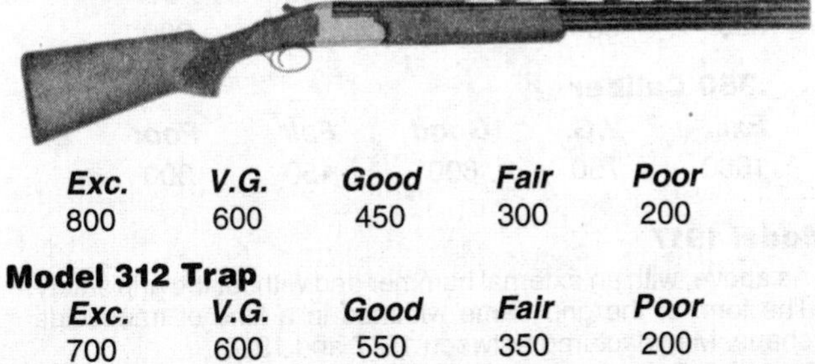

Exc.	*V.G.*	*Good*	*Fair*	*Poor*
800	600	450	300	200

Model 312 Trap

Exc.	*V.G.*	*Good*	*Fair*	*Poor*
700	600	550	350	200

Model 312 Sporting Clay

Exc.	*V.G.*	*Good*	*Fair*	*Poor*
800	600	450	300	200

Model 320 Field

Exc.	*V.G.*	*Good*	*Fair*	*Poor*
800	600	450	300	200

(SAVAGE) FOX B MODELS

The Fox Model B was introduced about 1939 by Savage for the hunter who wanted better fit and finish than offered by the Stevens brand Model 530. It was made in many variations until 1988.

Fox Model B—Utica, NY

NIB	*Exc.*	*V.G.*	*Good*	*Fair*	*Poor*
1000	800	600	450	400	350

Fox Model B—Chicopee Falls, Mass. (later Westfield, Mass.)

Courtesy Nick Niles, Paul Goodwin photo

NIB	*Exc.*	*V.G.*	*Good*	*Fair*	*Poor*
800	750	500	400	350	300

Fox Model B—Single Trigger

NIB	*Exc.*	*V.G.*	*Good*	*Fair*	*Poor*
900	800	600	500	400	300

Fox Model BDL

NIB	*Exc.*	*V.G.*	*Good*	*Fair*	*Poor*
1000	800	700	600	400	350

Fox Model BDE

Courtesy Nick Niles, Paul Goodwin photo

NIB	*Exc.*	*V.G.*	*Good*	*Fair*	*Poor*
1000	800	700	600	400	350

Fox Model BST

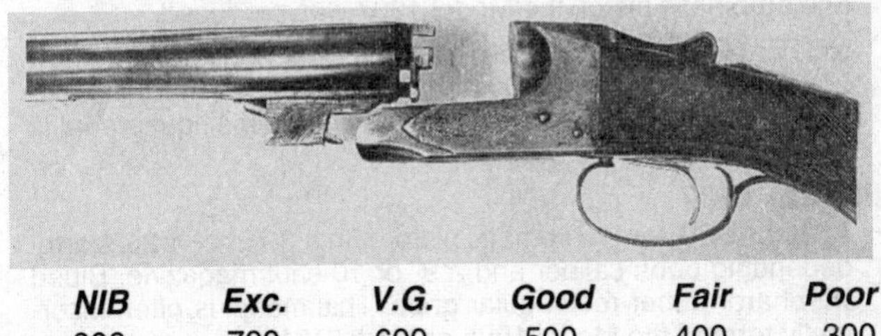

NIB	*Exc.*	*V.G.*	*Good*	*Fair*	*Poor*
800	700	600	500	400	300

Fox Model BSE

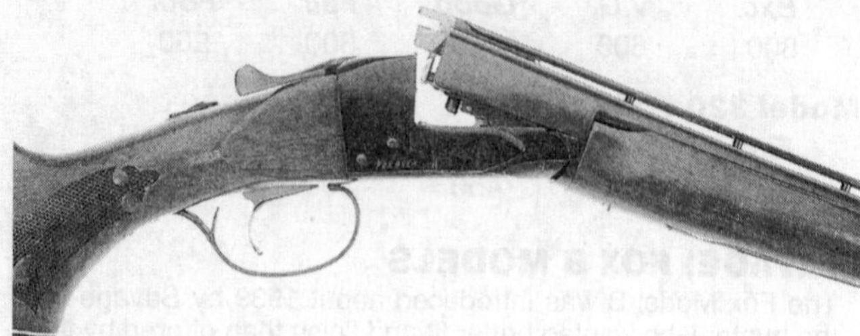

Courtesy Nick Niles, Paul Goodwin photo

NIB	Exc.	V.G.	Good	Fair	Poor
1000	750	650	550	450	350

Fox Model BE

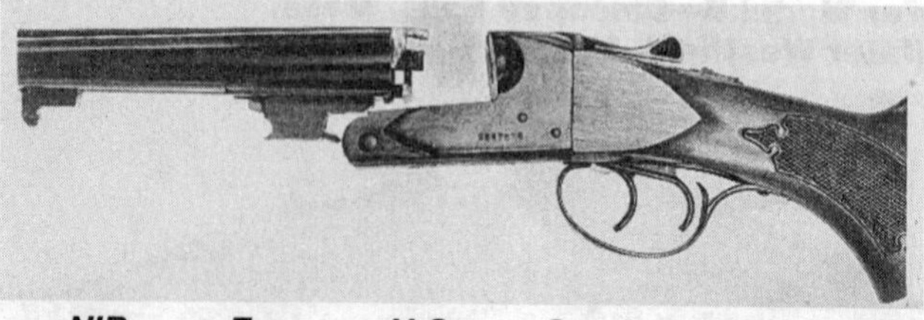

NIB	Exc.	V.G.	Good	Fair	Poor
1000	800	600	450	400	350

Milano

This Italian-made over-and-under is available in 12, 20 and 28 gauges and .410-bore on frames scaled to match, all with 28" barrels and 3" chambers. Single selective trigger. Three choke tubes (fixed IC and Mod. on .410-bore). Automatic ejectors.

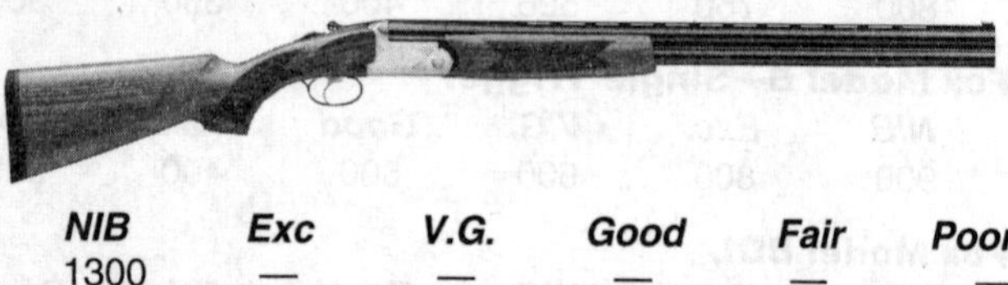

NIB	Exc	V.G.	Good	Fair	Poor
1300	—	—	—	—	—

REMINDER

The difference between "New in Box" and "Excellent" can be enormous to the "condition collector": as much as 50 percent of the gun's value in some cases.

PISTOLS

Elbert Searle was granted a patent on an automatic pistol which utilized the bullet's torque to twist the barrel into a locking position with the slide. The patent also featured a double-row staggered magazine which increased the capacity over ordinary pistols. The patent was sold to Savage and the first Savage automatic pistol, the Model 1907 was produced.

NOTE: Savage automatic pistols with the original cardboard box will bring between $50 and $100 premium. If the instruction pamphlet, cleaning brush, or other advertising material is present the price will escalate.

Model 1907

A .32 or .380 semi-automatic pistol with a 3.75" or 4.25" barrel depending upon caliber and a 9- or 10-shot magazine. Blued with hard rubber rectangular grips. This model is often incorrectly termed the Model 1905 or Model 1910.

Courtesy Bailey Brower, Jr., Copyright 2005, Bailey Brower, Jr.

Exc.	V.G.	Good	Fair	Poor
300	250	200	125	75

NOTE: The .380 caliber model is worth approximately 30 percent more than the values listed.

Model 1907 Portugese Contract

Similar to the commerical guns but with a lanyard ring same as the French contract model. Original Portugese pistols will have the Portugese Crest on the grips. Only about 1,150 of these pistols were produced. Very rare. Proceed with caution.

Exc.	V.G.	Good	Fair	Poor
1500	1000	750	600	300

Model 1915

Similar to the above, except fitted with a grip safety and with an internal hammer. Approximately 6,500 pistols were produced in .32 caliber and 3,900 in the .380 caliber. Manufactured between 1915 and 1917. The rarest of the Savage automatic pistols.

Courtesy Orvel Reichert

.32 Caliber

Exc.	V.G.	Good	Fair	Poor
650	550	400	300	200

.380 Caliber

Exc.	V.G.	Good	Fair	Poor
1000	750	600	450	300

Model 1917

As above, with an external hammer and without the grip safety. The form of the grip frame widened in a kind of trapezoidal shape. Manufactured between 1917 and 1928.

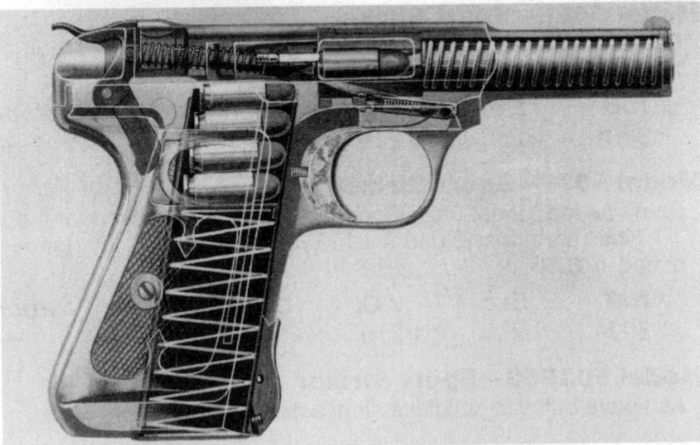

Courtesy Bailey Brower, Jr., Copyright 2005, Bailey Brower, Jr.

Exc.	V.G.	Good	Fair	Poor
275	225	175	100	75

Model 1917 with watch fob for salesmen samples,

Courtesy Bailey Brower, Jr., Copyright 2005, Bailey Brower, Jr.

Model 6.35mm

A small number of .25 caliber Savage pistols were manufactured between 1915 and 1919. Perhaps less than 25 were built. There are two major variations of this pistol. First, is the wide or 10-serrations grip, and second the 27-serrations grip variation. This change occured around 1917. Magazine capacity was 6 to 7 rounds. Very rare.

Courtesy James Rankin

Courtesy Bailey Brower, Jr., Copyright 2005, Bailey Brower, Jr.

Exc.	V.G.	Good	Fair	Poor
8000	7000	4000	2500	1000

Model 1907 Test Pistol

Manufactured in 1907 in .45 ACP this pistol was tested in the U.S. Army trials. About 290 pistols were produced for these trials. Double-stack magazine held 8 rounds.

Courtesy Bailey Brower, Jr.

Exc.	V.G.	Good	Fair	Poor
12500	10000	9500	6000	4000

Model 1910 Test Pistol

This was a modified Model 1907 with a heavier slide that was not concave like the Model 1907. There were a total of 9 Model 1910s built.

Exc.	V.G.	Good	Fair	Poor

Too Rare To Price

Model 1911 Test Pistol

This example was completely modified with a longer and thinner grip. Checkered wood grips were attached by friction instead of screws, the slide release was modified, a full grip safety was added, and a heavier serrated hammer (cocking lever) was added. Four of these pistols were built. Serial #1 has never been located.

Courtesy James Rankin

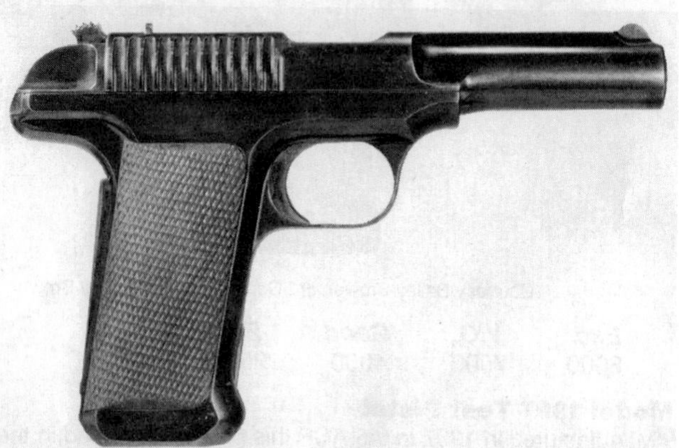

Courtesy Bailey Brower, Jr., Copyright 2005, Bailey Brower, Jr.

Exc.	V.G.	Good	Fair	Poor
Too Rare To Price				

Model 101

.22 caliber single-shot pistol resembling a revolver with a 5.5" barrel. Blued with hardwood grips. This pistol was made in Chicopee Falls or Westfield, Mass. Manufactured between 1960 and 1968.

Exc.	V.G.	Good	Fair	Poor
175	150	125	90	75

500 HANDGUN SERIES

Introduced in 1998 this line of short action handguns feature a left-hand bolt and a right-hand ejection. All are fitted with an internal box magazine, composite stock and 14" barrel.

Model 501F—Sport Striker

This handgun is fitted with a left-hand bolt and 10" free floating barrel. Detachable clip holds 10 rounds of .22 LR cartridges. Drilled and tapped for scope mount. Weight is about 4 lbs. Introduced in 2000.

NIB	Exc.	V.G.	Good	Fair	Poor
250	200	175	125	—	—

Model 501FXP

Introduced in 2002 this model is similar to the one above but fitted with a 1.25-4x28mm scope with soft case.

NIB	Exc.	V.G.	Good	Fair	Poor
300	250	210	—	—	—

Model 502F—Sport Striker

Same as above but chambered for .22 WMR cartridge. Magazine capacity is 5 rounds. Introduced in 2000.

NIB	Exc.	V.G.	Good	Fair	Poor
300	250	210	—	—	—

Model 503F—Sport Striker

Same as the Model 502F-Sport Striker but chambered for the .17 HMR cartridge. Blued finish. Weight is about 4 lbs. Introduced in 2003.

NIB	Exc.	V.G.	Good	Fair	Poor
300	250	210	—	—	—

Model 503FSS—Sport Striker

As above but with stainless steel action and barrel.

NIB	Exc.	V.G.	Good	Fair	Poor
320	250	—	—	—	—

Model 510F Striker

Blued barrel action and chambered for .22-250, .243, or .308 calibers. Weight is approximately 5 lbs.

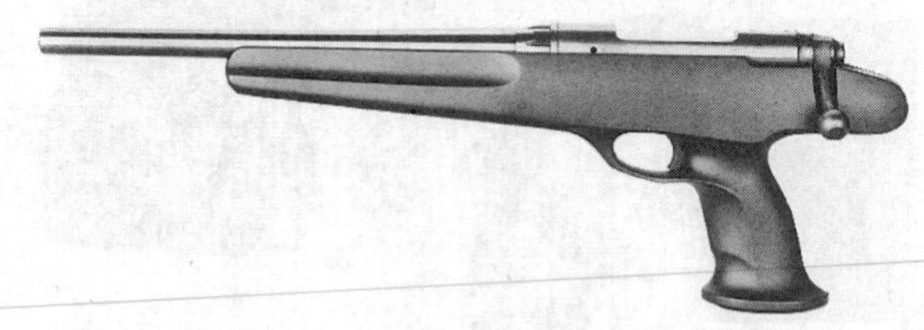

NIB	Exc.	V.G.	Good	Fair	Poor
400	325	—	—	—	—

Model 516FSS

Similar to the model above but with stainless steel barreled action.

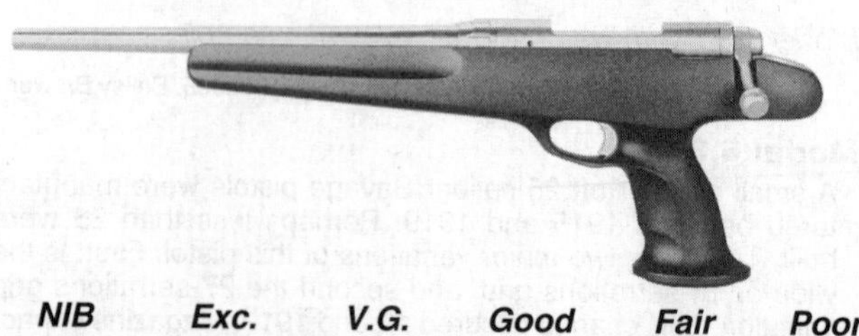

NIB	Exc.	V.G.	Good	Fair	Poor
450	350	—	—	—	—

Model 516FSAK

Features a stainless steel barreled action with adjustable muzzlebrake.

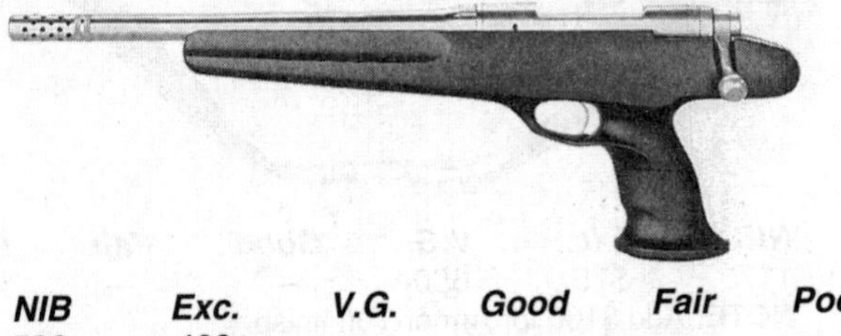

NIB	Exc.	V.G.	Good	Fair	Poor
500	400	—	—	—	—

Model 516FSAK Camo

As above but with Realtree Hardwood camo stock. Chambered for the .300 WSM cartridge. Weight is about 5.5 lbs. Introduced in 2002.

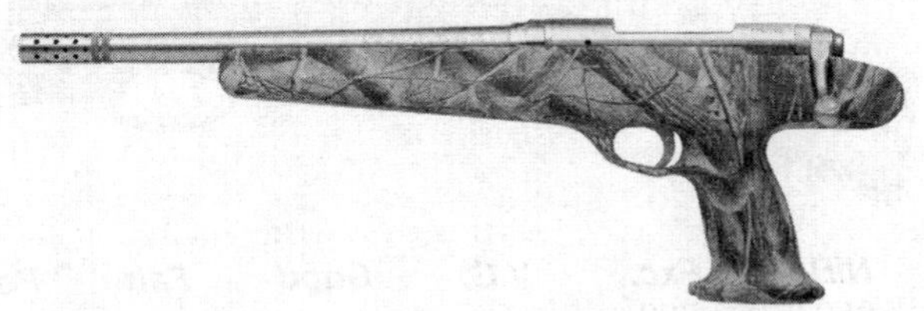

NIB	Exc.	V.G.	Good	Fair	Poor
585	450	—	—	—	—

Model 516BSS

Fitted with a laminated thumbhole stock, left-hand bolt for right-hand ejection, 14" barrel. This model is chambered for the .223, .243, 7mm-08 Rem., .260 Rem., and .308 Win. calibers. Magazine capacity is 2 rounds. Weight is about 5 lbs. Introduced in 1999.

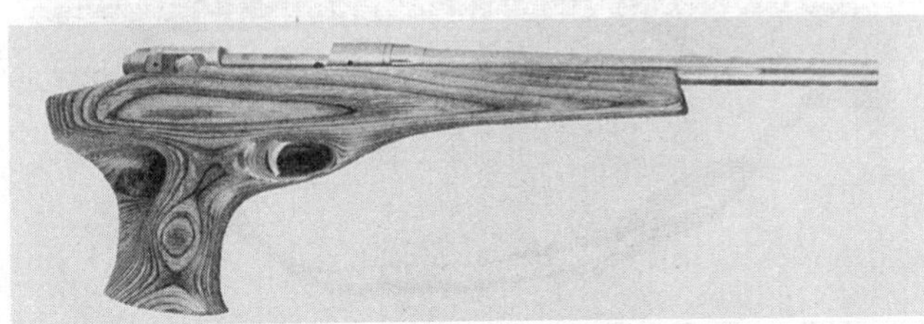

NIB	Exc.	V.G.	Good	Fair	Poor
550	450	—	—	—	—

Model 516BSAK

Similar to the model above but chambered for the .223 or .22-250 cartridges. The 14" barrel is fitted with an adjustable muzzlebrake. Introduced in 1999.

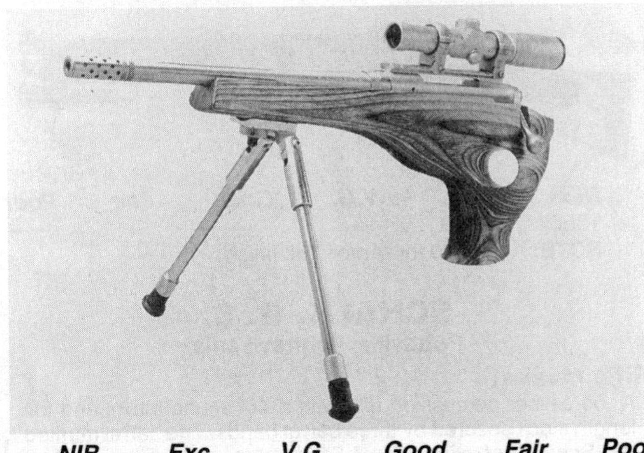

NIB	Exc.	V.G.	Good	Fair	Poor
600	475	—	—	—	—

SAVAGE & NORTH

Middletown, Connecticut

Figure 8 Revolver

A .36 caliber percussion revolver with a 7" octagonal barrel and 6-shot cylinder. The barrel marked "E. Savage, Middletown. CT./H.S. North. Patented June 17, 1856." The four models of this revolver are: (1) With a rounded brass frame, and the mouths of the chamber fitting into the end of the barrel breech; (2) with a rounded iron frame and a modified loading lever that is marked "H.S. North, Patented April 6, 1858"; (3) with a flat-sided brass frame having a round recoil shield; (4) with an iron frame. Approximately 400 of these revolvers were manufactured between 1856 and 1859.

First Model

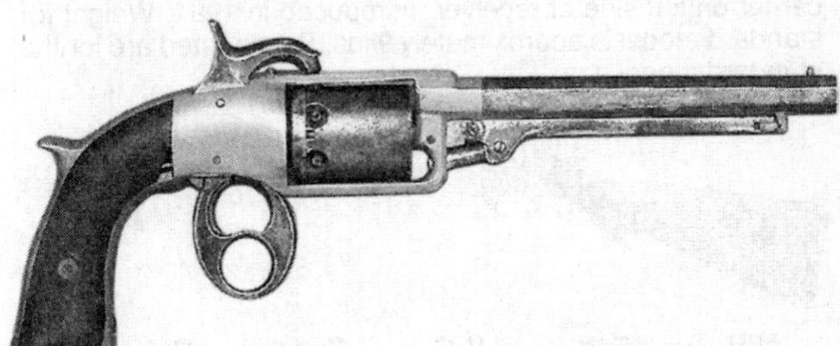

First Model Figure 8 Revolver Courtesy Bonhams & Butterfields

Exc.	V.G.	Good	Fair	Poor
—	—	15000	6500	1500

Second Model

Exc.	V.G.	Good	Fair	Poor
—	—	9000	3500	850

Third Model

Exc.	V.G.	Good	Fair	Poor
—	—	9000	3500	850

Fourth Model

Exc.	V.G.	Good	Fair	Poor
—	—	10000	4000	1000

SAVAGE REVOLVING FIREARMS CO.

Middletown, Connecticut

Navy Revolver

A .36 caliber double-action percussion revolver with a 7" octagonal barrel and 6-shot cylinder. The frame marked "Savage R.F.A. Co./H.S. North Patented June 17, 1856/Jan. 18, 1859, May 15, 1860." Approximately 20,000 were manufactured between 1861 and 1865, of which about 12,000 were purchased by the U.S. Government.

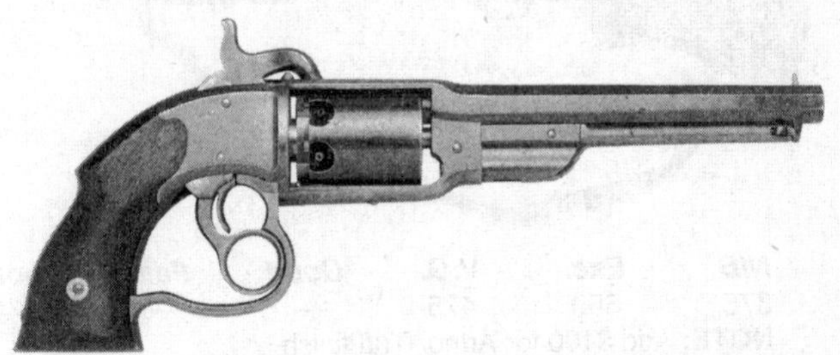

Courtesy Greg Martin Auctions

Exc.	V.G.	Good	Fair	Poor
—	—	4250	1750	700

SCATTERGUN TECHNOLOGIES

Formerly—Nashville, Tennessee
Berryville, Arkansas

NOTE: In 1999 Scattergun Technologies was purchased by Wilson Combat and became a division of Wilson Combat. As of that date Wilson Combat Scattergun Technologies firearms will have the Berryville, Arkansas, address stamped on the receiver.

TR-870

This model is based on the Remington Model 870 slide-action shotgun. It is offered in a wide variety of configurations with different features. The standard model is fitted with an 18" barrel and chambered for the 12 gauge shell. The stock is composite with recoil pad. Tactical forend has flashlight built in. Ghost Ring rear sight. Front sight has tritium insert. Six-round shell carrier on left side of receiver. Introduced in 1991. Weight for standard model is approximately 9 lbs. Prices listed are for the standard model.

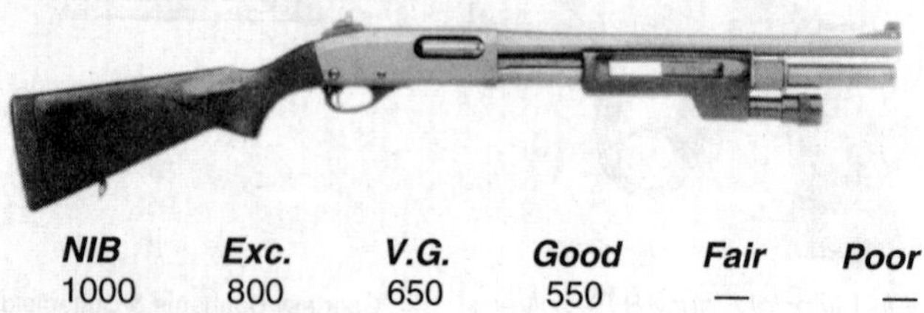

NIB	Exc.	V.G.	Good	Fair	Poor
1000	800	650	550	—	—

WILSON COMBAT CURRENT PRODUCTION MODELS

Standard Model

Based on the Remington 12 gauge 3" 870 Magnum this model is fitted with an 18" barrel with cylinder bore. Adjustable Ghost Ring rear sight with tritium front sight. Seven-round extended magazine. Side saddle shell carrier. Synthetic stock. Tactical sling is standard. Parkerized finish. Fitted with a SURE-FIRE tactical light.

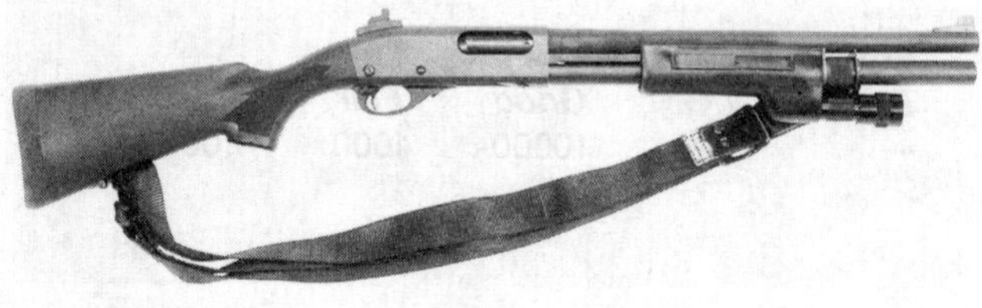

NIB	Exc.	V.G.	Good	Fair	Poor
1150	850	625	—	—	—

NOTE: Add $100 for Armor-Tuff finish.

Border Patrol Model

Similar to the standard model but without the tactical light. A 14" barrel is offered on this model but all NFA rules apply to the purchase of a short barrel shotgun.

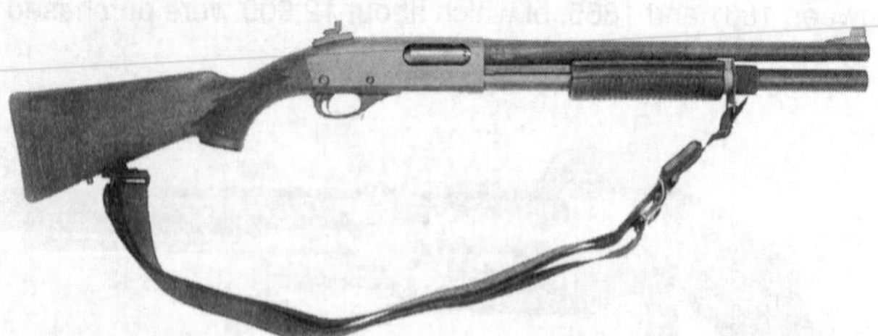

NIB	Exc.	V.G.	Good	Fair	Poor
875	650	475	—	—	—

NOTE: Add $100 for Armor-Tuff finish.

Professional Model

This model features all of the standard model components but it is fitted with a 14" barrel. Magazine capacity is 6 rounds. All NFA rules apply to purchase of short barrel shotgun.

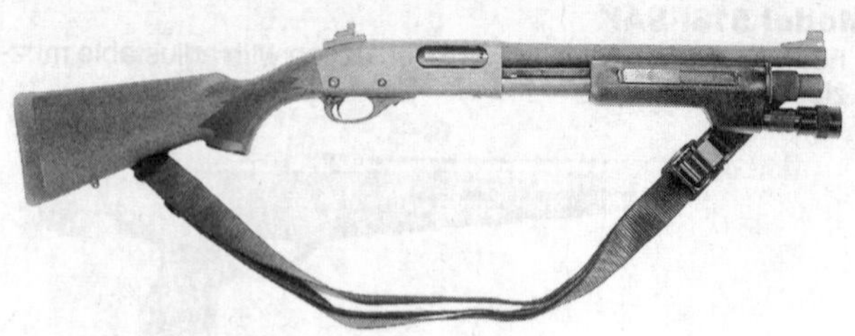

NIB	Exc.	V.G.	Good	Fair	Poor
1175	875	650	—	—	—

NOTE: Add $100 for Armor-Tuff finish.

Entry Model

This model has all the features of the standard model but is fitted with a 12.5" barrel. Magazine capacity is 5 rounds. All NFA rules apply to the purchase of a short barrel shotgun.

NIB	Exc.	V.G.	Good	Fair	Poor
950	700	—	—	—	—

NOTE: Add $100 for Armor-Tuff finish.

K-9 Model

This model is built on a Remington 12 gauge 3" 1187 Magnum semi-automatic. Fitted with Ghost Ring rear sights and tritium front sight. Extended magazine holds 7 rounds. Barrel is 18". Synthetic stock with side saddle shell carrier. Parkerized finish.

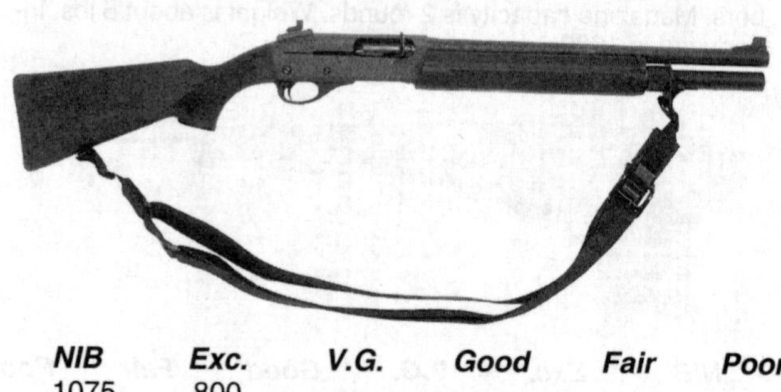

NIB	Exc.	V.G.	Good	Fair	Poor
1075	800	—	—	—	—

NOTE: Add $100 for Armor-Tuff finish.

SWAT Model

Similar to the K-9 model but fitted with a tactical light and 14" barrel. All NFA rules apply to the purchase of a short barrel shotgun.

NIB	Exc.	V.G.	Good	Fair	Poor
1350	1000	—	—	—	—

NOTE: Add $100 for Armor-Tuff finish.

SCHALK, G. S.

Pottsville, Pennsylvania

Rifle Musket

A .58 caliber percussion rifle with a 40" round barrel and full length stock secured by three barrel bands. The barrel marked "G. Schalk Poftsville 1861." Finished in white with a walnut stock. Approximately 100 were manufactured.

Courtesy Milwaukee Public Museum, Milwaukee, Wisconsin

Exc.	V.G.	Good	Fair	Poor
—	—	6250	3000	750

SCHALL & CO.

New Haven, Connecticut

Manufactured the Fiala repeating pistol for Fiala. Later, after Fiala's bankruptcy, Schall provided parts, repair service, and produced repeating pistols with the Schall name. Marketed by Schall between about 1930 and 1935.

Repeating Pistol

A .22 caliber pistol with 10-shot magazine. Tapered 7.5" barrel with fixed sights and blued finish. Rear sight is much simpler than those on the Fiala. Grips are wood with ribs running lengthwise. Typically marked "SCHALL & CO./NEW HAVEN, CONN USA" but guns exist with no markings.

Courtesy Dr. Jon Miller

Exc.	V.G.	Good	Fair	Poor
500	425	325	190	170

SCHMIDT, HERBERT

Ostheim, West Germany

Model 11, Liberty 11, and Eig Model E-8

A .22 caliber double-action revolver with a 2.5" barrel and 6-shot cylinder. Blued with plastic grips.

Exc.	V.G.	Good	Fair	Poor
125	80	60	40	25

Model 11 Target

As above, with a 5.5" barrel and adjustable sights.

Exc.	V.G.	Good	Fair	Poor
150	120	75	45	30

Frontier Model or Texas Scout

.22 caliber revolver with a 5" barrel and 6-shot cylinder. Blued with plastic grips.

Exc.	V.G.	Good	Fair	Poor
125	80	60	40	25

SCHMIDT, E. & COMPANY

Houston, Texas

Pocket Pistol

A .45 caliber percussion single-shot pistol with a 2.5" barrel, German silver mounts and walnut stock. The barrel marked "E. Schmidt & Co. Houston." Manufactured between 1866 and 1870.

Exc.	V.G.	Good	Fair	Poor
—	—	8250	4000	1000

SCHMIDT-RUBIN

Neuhausen, Switzerland

NOTE: For history, technical data, descriptions, and photos see the *Standard Catalog of Military Firearms* under Switzerland.

SCHNEIDER & CO.

Memphis, Tennessee

Pocket Pistol

A .41 caliber single-shot percussion pocket pistol with a 3.5" octagonal barrel, iron or German silver mounts and a walnut stock. The lock marked "Schneider & Co./Memphis, Tenn." Manufactured 1859 and 1860.

Exc.	V.G.	Good	Fair	Poor
—	—	4500	1850	650

SCHNEIDER & GLASSICK

Memphis, Tennessee

Pocket Pistols

A .41 caliber percussion pocket pistol with a 2.5" barrel, German silver mounts and walnut stock. The barrel marked "Schneider & Glassick, Memphis, Tenn." Manufactured 1860 to 1862.

Exc.	V.G.	Good	Fair	Poor
—	—	4750	2250	800

SCHOUBOE

SEE—Dansk Rekylriffel Syndikat

SCHUERMAN ARMS, LTD.

Scottsdale, Arizona

Model SA40

Introduced in 2004 this bolt-action rifle is chambered for a wide variety of calibers from short action to long magnum. Offered in both right-hand and left-hand models. Barrel lengths from 20" to 26" in stainless steel. No sights. Stock is laminated fiberglass sporter style.

NIB	Exc.	V.G.	Good	Fair	Poor
3200	2400	—	—	—	—

NOTE: There are a number of extra costs options that may be ordered with this model. These options will affect price.

SCHULER, AUGUST

Suhl, Germany

Reform

A 6.35mm caliber four-barreled pocket pistol with 2.5" barrels. The barrel unit rises as the trigger is pulled. Blued with walnut or hard rubber grips. Manufactured between 1907 and 1914.

Exc.	V.G.	Good	Fair	Poor
850	750	650	450	300

SCHULTZ & LARSEN

Ofterup, Denmark

Model 47 Match Rifle

A .22 caliber single-shot bolt-action rifle with a 28" barrel, adjustable sights and adjustable trigger. Blued with an ISU-style stock.

Exc.	V.G.	Good	Fair	Poor
800	650	550	400	250

Model 61 Match Rifle

As above, but fitted with a palm rest.

Exc.	V.G.	Good	Fair	Poor
1000	850	750	600	300

Model 62 Match Rifle

Similar to the above, but manufactured for centerfire cartridges.

Exc.	V.G.	Good	Fair	Poor
1250	900	750	650	350

Model 54 Free Rifle

Similar to the above, with a 27" barrel and ISU stock.

Exc.	V.G.	Good	Fair	Poor
950	800	700	550	300

Model 68 DL

A .22-250 to .458 Winchester Magnum bolt-action rifle with a 24" barrel, adjustable trigger and well figured walnut stock.

Exc.	V.G.	Good	Fair	Poor
850	700	600	450	200

SCHWARZLOSE, ANDREAS

Berlin, Germany

Military Model 1898 (Standart)

A 7.63x25mm Borchardt or 7.63x25mm Mauser caliber semi-automatic pistol with a 6.5" barrel, rotary locked bolt, 7-shot magazine and adjustable rear sight. Weight is about 28 oz. Blued with walnut grips. The pistol was neither a commercial or military success, and fewer than 500 were made.

Exc.	V.G.	Good	Fair	Poor
—	—	9000	5000	3000

SEARS, ROEBUCK & CO. BRAND

Chicago, Illinois

Double-Barrel Shotguns

Between 1892 and 1988 the world's largest mail order house carried a huge inventory of sporting doubleguns including any foreign and domestic brands whose makers did not object to Sears' famous price discounts. To increase sales volume, however, Sears also created its own brands which they supported with innovative design, extravagant advertising claims, unbeatable pricing and excellent quality control. These doubles, like many other firearms products handled by Sears, were listed in its very detailed semiannual catalog from about 1892, when the company first offered doubleguns, until about 1988 when social and political pressures made the company stop handling firearms.

Sears marketing people gave birth to and successfully exploited many house and private brands which we no longer associate with Sears at all. In fact, many of these brands clearly rollmarked on guns are now unfamiliar to many collectors. Frequently seen and important in the market segment which many might describe as affordable doubles are some of the most often seen Sears trade names or brands. Listed in chronological order: T. Barker, S.R. & Co., Triumph, Thomas Barker, Sam Holt, Chicago Long Range Wonder, American Bar Lock, Meriden Fire Arms Co., Norwich, A. J. Arbrey Gun Co., New England, Gladiator, Berkshire, Ranger, Eastern Arms Co., J.C. Higgins, Sears, and Ted Williams. These guns were of good quality but sold at bargain prices which gave them tremendous appeal. They were made for Sears to Sears' specifications by a number of American firms and a few foreign ones as well, all of which produced excellent shotguns under their own names. Among the best-known American companies were J. Stevens, Savage Arms, A.H. Fox, High Standard, N.R. Davis, Crescent Firearms, Ithaca, A. Fyrberg, Colton Mfg. Co., Marlin, Hunter Gun Co., Baker Gun Co., and probably a few others. Among the foreign makers were AYA, H. Pieper, Janssen, SKB, Rossi, CBC, and A. Zoli.

Sears customers were not aware of this but they did trust Sears name and bought many millions of these shotguns over the nearly 100 years that Sears was in the business. Today these guns are becoming recognized as interesting and valuable collectibles in their own special niche. Their values range from $100 to $3,500 or more depending on make, model, decoration, if any, and relative rarity.

SEAVER, E.R.

New York, New York

Pocket Pistol

A .41 caliber percussion pocket pistol with a 2.5" barrel, German silver mounts and a walnut stock.

Exc.	V.G.	Good	Fair	Poor
—	—	1750	900	400

SECURITY INDUSTRIES

Little Ferry, New Jersey

Model PSS

A .38 Special double-action revolver with a 2" barrel, fixed sights and 5-shot cylinder. Stainless steel with walnut grips. Manufactured between 1973 and 1978.

Exc.	V.G.	Good	Fair	Poor
250	150	125	100	75

Model PM357

As above, with a 2.5" barrel and in .357 Magnum caliber. Manufactured between 1975 and 1978.

Exc.	V.G.	Good	Fair	Poor
300	200	175	150	100

Model PPM357

As above, with a 2" barrel and a hammer without a finger spur. Manufactured between 1975 and 1978.

Exc.	V.G.	Good	Fair	Poor
300	200	175	150	100

SEDCO INDUSTRIES, INC.

Lake Elsinore, California

This company was in business from 1988 to 1990.

Model SP22

A .22 caliber semi-automatic pistol with a 2.5" barrel. Blackened or nickel-plated with plastic grips. Introduced in 1989.

NIB	Exc.	V.G.	Good	Fair	Poor
125	90	65	50	35	25

SEDERE, TH.

SEE—Austrian Military Firearms

SEDGELY, R. F., INC.

Philadelphia, Pennsylvania

R.F. Sedgely produced specialized bolt-action rifles using the Model 1903 Springfield action. As these arms were for the most part custom order pieces, it is impossible to provide standardized values. It should be noted that his prime engraver was Rudolph J. Kornbrath.

Sedgely also made a .22 caliber hammerless pistol. **SEE—KOLB.**

SEECAMP, L. W. CO., INC.

Milford, Connecticut

LWS .25 ACP Model

A .25 caliber semi-automatic pistol with a 2" barrel, fixed sights and 7-shot magazine. Stainless steel with plastic grips. Approximately 5,000 were manufactured between 1982 and 1985.

NIB	Exc.	V.G.	Good	Fair	Poor
500	400	300	200	150	100

LWS .32 ACP Model

A .32 caliber double-action semi-automatic pistol with a 2" barrel and 6-shot magazine. Matte or polished stainless steel with plastic grips.

NIB	Exc.	V.G.	Good	Fair	Poor
450	400	350	300	200	150

Matched Pair

A matched set of the above, with identical serial numbers. A total of 200 sets were made prior to 1968.

Exc.	V.G.	Good	Fair	Poor
900	800	700	500	350

LWS .380 Model

Same as the .32 caliber but chambered for the .380 cartridge. Essential the same weight and dimensions as the .32 caliber pistol. Introduced in 1999.

NIB	Exc.	V.G.	Good	Fair	Poor
900	650	—	—	—	—

SEMMERLING

Waco, Texas

SEE—American Derringer Corporation

SERBU FIREARMS

Tampa, Florida

BFG-50 Rifle

This is .50 caliber single-shot bolt-action rifle fitted with a 29.5" barrel. Also offered with 36" barrel. Parkerized finish. Weight is about 22 lbs.

NIB	Exc.	V.G.	Good	Fair	Poor
2195	1600	—	—	—	—

BFG-50 Carbine

As above but fitted with a 22" barrel. Weight is about 17 lbs.

NIB	Exc.	V.G.	Good	Fair	Poor
2195	1600	—	—	—	—

BFG-50A

This model is a gas operated semi-automatic takedown rifle with a 25" barrel. Parkerized finish. Magazine capacity is 10 rounds. Weight is about 25 lbs.

NIB	Exc.	V.G.	Good	Fair	Poor
N/A	—	—	—	—	—

SHARPS, C. ARMS CO.

Big Timber, Montana

This company was founded in 1975 in Richland, Washington, and moved to Big Timber, Montana, in 1980. It also produced custom-built rifles included the Model 1877 Sharps and others to individual customer specifications. The models listed are standard production models without extras.

Model 1874 Sharps Hartford Sporting Rifle

Chambered for a number of popular blackpowder calibers and fitted with either a 26", 28", or 30" tapered octagon barrel, double set triggers. American walnut stock with Hartford semi cresent steel butt. Silver nose cap. Case colored receiver with blued barrel. Optional sights. Weight depending on barrel length is about 10 lbs.

NIB	Exc.	V.G.	Good	Fair	Poor
1775	1350	—	—	—	—

Model 1874 Bridgeport Sporting Rifle

As above but with Bridgeport checkered steel butt. Schnabel-style forend.

NIB	Exc.	V.G.	Good	Fair	Poor
1495	1125	—	—	—	—

Model 1875 Carbine—Hunters Rifle

Offered in a variety of calibers from .38-55 to .50-70. Fitted with a choice of tapered round military-style barrels of lengths from 22", 24", or 26". Full buckhorn and silver blade sights. Semi-cresent military-style butt with slender forend. Case colored receiver and blued barrel. Double set triggers.

NIB	Exc.	V.G.	Good	Fair	Poor
1620	1200	—	—	—	—

Model 1874 Boss Gun

This model features engraved receiver, XXX fancy walnut, 34" #1 heavy tapered octagon barrel, long range tang sight, buckhorn rear sight, globe with post front sight, and Hartford nose cap. Calibers offered from .38-55 to .50-100. Weight is about 13.5 lbs. with 34" #1 barrel.

NIB	Exc.	V.G.	Good	Fair	Poor
4395	3250	—	—	—	—

NOTE: For Grade II add $750, for Grade III add $1,500.

Model 1875 Target & Sporting Rifle

Offered in a variety of calibers this rifle is fitted with a 30" heavy tapered round barrel. American walnut stock with pistol grip. Case colored receiver with blued barrel. Single trigger. Price listed is without sights.

NIB	Exc.	V.G.	Good	Fair	Poor
1190	900	—	—	—	—

Model 1875 Classic Rifle

This model features a receiver with octagon top and with tapered octagon barrel lengths from 26" to 30". American walnut stock with straight grip and crescent butt. Single trigger. German steel nose cap. Case colored receiver with blued barrel. Weight is about 9.5 lbs. with 30" barrel. Priced without sights.

NIB	Exc.	V.G.	Good	Fair	Poor
1385	1025	—	—	—	—

Model 1885 High Wall Sporting Rifle

Offered with choice of .26", 28", or 30" tapered octagon barrel. Calibers are from .22 to .45-120. Single trigger. American walnut stock with straight grip and oil finish. Checkered steel butt plate. Schnabel forend. Priced without sights. Weight is about 9.25 lbs. with 30" barrel.

NIB	Exc.	V.G.	Good	Fair	Poor
1350	1000	—	—	—	—

Model 1885 High Wall Classic Rifle

As above but with crescent butt. Stock with cheek rest and silver inlay in forend.

NIB	Exc.	V.G.	Good	Fair	Poor
1550	1150	—	—	—	—

SHARPS RIFLE MANUFACTURING COMPANY

Hartford, Connecticut

The first Sharps rifles to be manufactured were made by A.S. Nippes of Mill Creek, Pennsylvania. Later they were made by Robbins & Lawrence of Windsor, Vermont. It was not until 1855 that Sharps established his own factory in Hartford, Connecticut. After his death in 1874, the company was reorganized as the Sharps Rifle Company and remained in Hartford until 1876 when it moved to Bridgeport, Connecticut. It effectively ceased operations in 1880.

The following descriptions are just a brief guide and are by no means exhaustive.

Model 1849

A breechloading .44 caliber percussion rifle with a 30" barrel having a wooden cleaning rod mounted beneath it. The breech is activated by the trigger guard lever, and there is an automatic disk-type capping device on the right side of the receiver. The finish is blued and case colored. The stock is walnut with a brass patch box, buttplate, and forend cap. It is marked "Sharps Patent 1848." There were approximately 200 manufactured in 1849 and 1850 by the A.S. Nippes Company.

Exc.	V.G.	Good	Fair	Poor
—	—	18000	7500	1500

Model 1850

As above, with a Maynard priming mechanism mounted on the breech. Marked "Sharps Patent 1848" on the breech and the barrel "Manufactured by A.S. Nippes Mill Creek, Pa." The priming device marked "Maynard Patent 1845." There were approximately 200 manufactured in 1850. This model is also known as the 2nd Model Sharps.

Exc.	V.G.	Good	Fair	Poor
—	—	15000	6000	1200

Model 1851 Carbine

A single-shot breechloading percussion rifle in .36, .44, or .52 caliber with a 21.75" barrel and Maynard tape priming device. Blued and case hardened with a walnut stock and forearm held on by a single barrel band. The buttplate and barrel band are brass, and the military versions feature a brass patch box. The tang marked "C. Sharps Patent 1848," the barrel "Robbins & Lawrence," and the priming device "Edward Maynard Patentee 1845." Approximately 1,800 carbines and 180 rifles were manufactured by Robbins & Lawrence in Windsor, Vermont, in 1851.

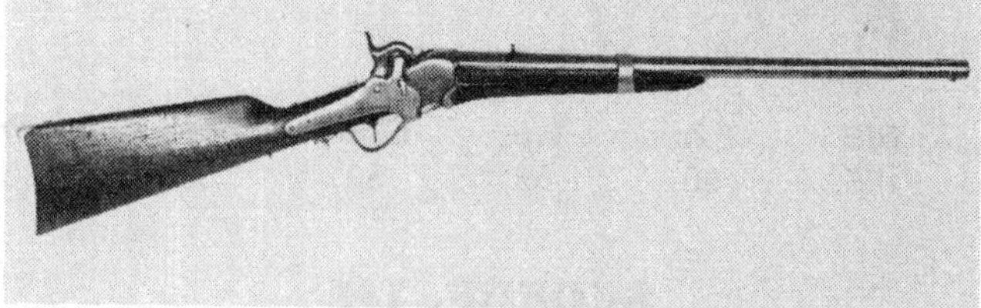

Courtesy Milwaukee Public Museum, Milwaukee, Wisconsin

Exc.	V.G.	Good	Fair	Poor
—	—	9500	4250	1000

NOTE: Those bearing U.S. inspection marks are worth approximately 75 percent more than the values listed.

Model 1852

Similar to the above, but with Sharps' Patent Pellet Primer. The barrel marked "Sharps Rifle Manufg. Co. Hartford, Conn." Blued, case hardened, brass furniture and a walnut stock. Manufactured in carbine, rifle, sporting rifle and shotgun form. Approximately 4,600 carbines and 600 rifles were made between 1853 and 1855.

Military Carbine

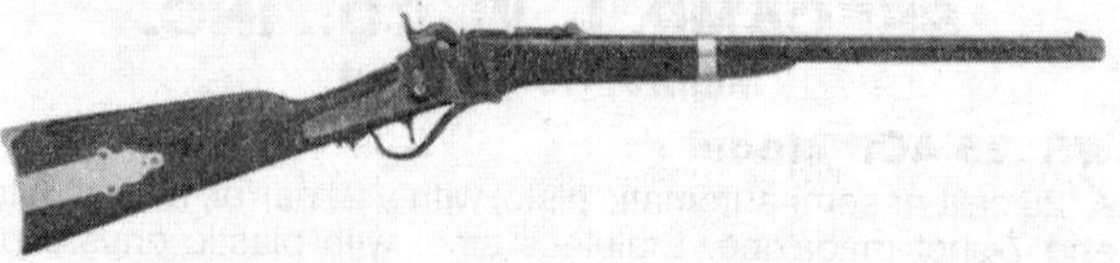

Courtesy Bonhams & Butterfields

Exc.	V.G.	Good	Fair	Poor
—	—	6750	3000	750

Military Rifle

27" barrel, bayonet lug.

Exc.	V.G.	Good	Fair	Poor
—	—	9750	4000	1000

Sporting Rifle

Exc.	V.G.	Good	Fair	Poor
—	—	4250	1750	500

Shotgun

Exc.	V.G.	Good	Fair	Poor
—	—	3250	1250	500

Model 1853

As above, but without the spring retainer for the lever hinge being mounted in the forestock. Approximately 10,500 carbines and 3,000 rifles were made between 1854 and 1858.

Military Carbine

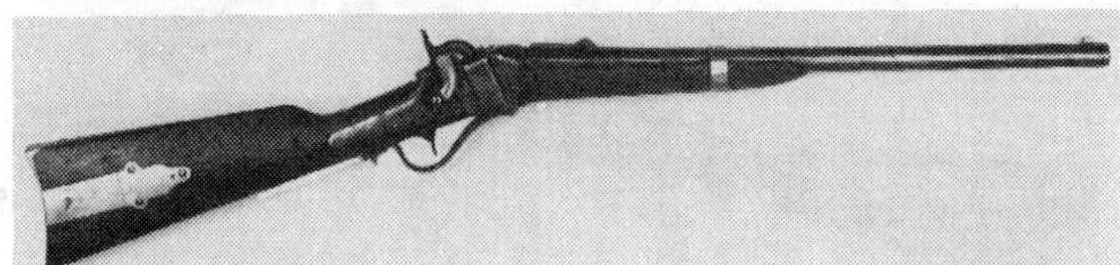

Courtesy Milwaukee Public Museum, Milwaukee, Wisconsin

Exc.	V.G.	Good	Fair	Poor
—	—	6250	2750	750

Military Rifle

Exc.	V.G.	Good	Fair	Poor
—	—	9500	4000	1000

Sporting Rifle

Courtesy Bonhams & Butterfields

Exc.	V.G.	Good	Fair	Poor
—	—	2750	1250	450

Shotgun

Courtesy Bonhams & Butterfields

Exc.	V.G.	Good	Fair	Poor
—	—	2500	1000	450

Model 1855

As above, in .52 caliber and fitted with a Maynard tape primer that is marked "Edward Maynard Patentee 1845." Approximately 700 were made between 1855 and 1856.

Exc.	V.G.	Good	Fair	Poor
—	—	10500	4250	1000

Model 1855 U.S. Navy Rifle

As above, with a 28" barrel, full-length stock and bearing U.S. Navy inspection marks. Approximately 260 were made in 1855.

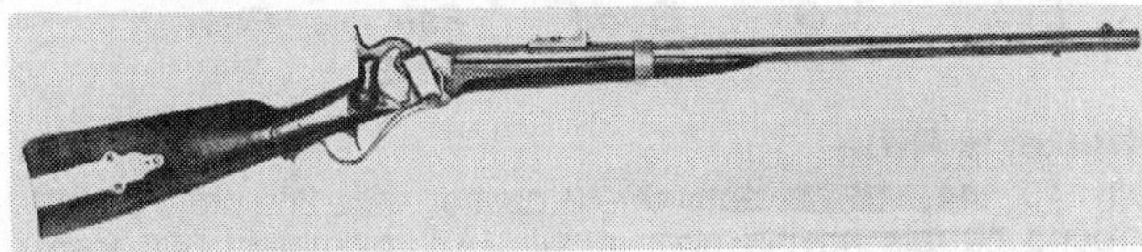

Courtesy Milwaukee Public Museum, Milwaukee, Wisconsin

Exc.	V.G.	Good	Fair	Poor
—	—	10500	4000	1000

Model 1855 British Carbine

The Model 1855 with British inspection marks. Approximately 6,800 were made between 1855 and 1857.

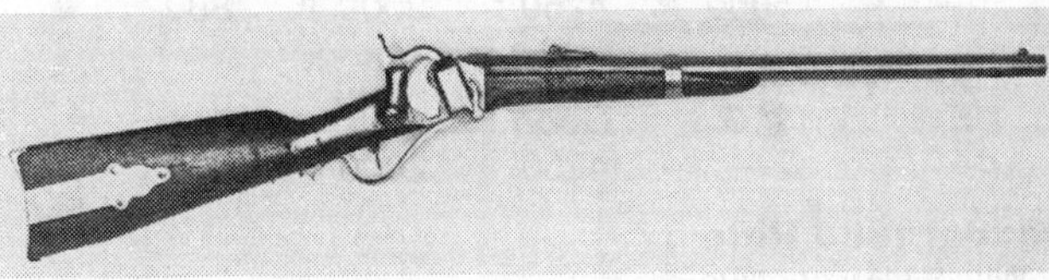

Courtesy Milwaukee Public Museum, Milwaukee, Wisconsin

Exc.	V.G.	Good	Fair	Poor
—	—	6250	3000	850

SHARPS STRAIGHT BREECH MODELS

Similar to the above models, but with the breech opening cut on an almost vertical angle.

Model 1859 Carbine

22" Barrel, Brass Mountings

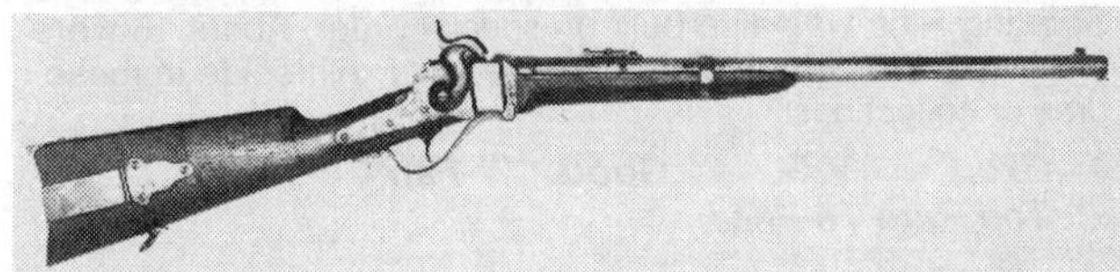

Courtesy Milwaukee Public Museum, Milwaukee, Wisconsin

Exc.	V.G.	Good	Fair	Poor
—	—	6250	2500	500

Iron Mountings

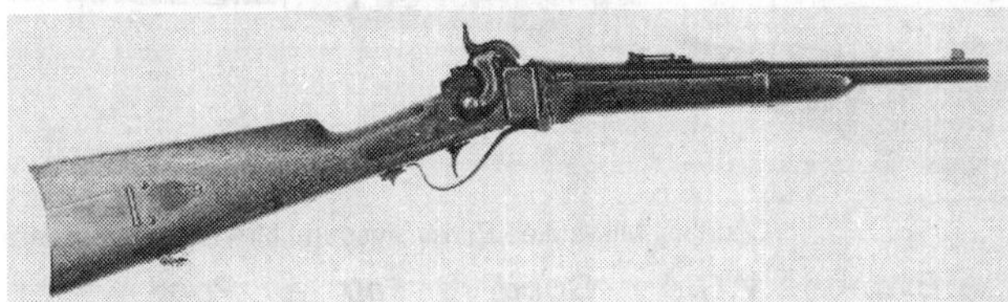

Courtesy Milwaukee Public Museum, Milwaukee, Wisconsin

Exc.	V.G.	Good	Fair	Poor
—	—	3250	1500	500

Model 1863 Carbine

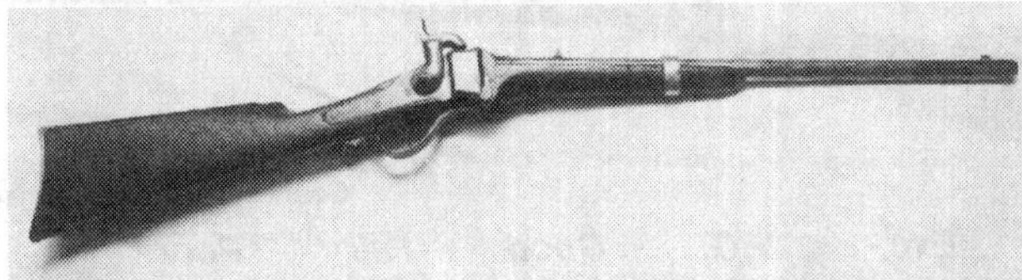

Courtesy Mike Stuckslager

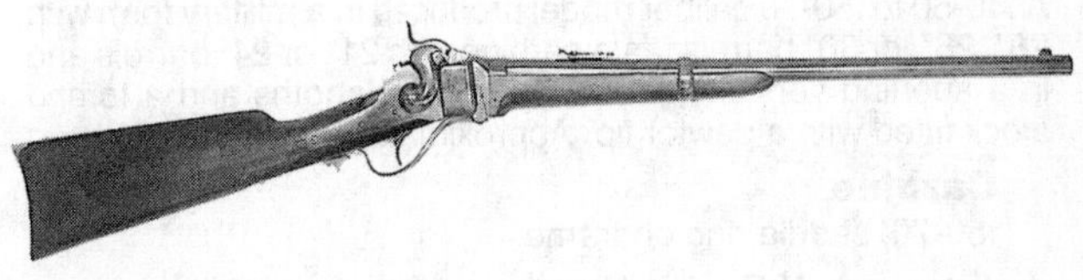

Exc.	V.G.	Good	Fair	Poor
—	—	3250	1500	500

Model 1865 Carbine

Exc.	V.G.	Good	Fair	Poor
—	4000	3750	1750	500

Model 1859 Rifle

30" Barrel

Exc.	V.G.	Good	Fair	Poor
—	5000	4250	2000	800

36" Barrel

Exc.	V.G.	Good	Fair	Poor
—	—	4250	2000	800

Model 1863 Rifle

Without bayonet lug.

Exc.	V.G.	Good	Fair	Poor
—	—	3750	1500	500

Model 1865 Rifle

Without bayonet lug.

Exc.	V.G.	Good	Fair	Poor
—	—	3250	1000	500

Sporting Rifle

As above, with octagonal barrels, set triggers and finely figured walnut stocks. The Model 1853 Sporting rifle was built as a special order. About 32 were produced. The Model 1863 Sporting Rifle was also built on special order. About 16 were produced. No two of this model are alike. All reside in museums or collections.

Exc.	V.G.	Good	Fair	Poor
Too Rare To Price				

Coffee-Mill Model

Some Sharps' carbines were fitted with coffee-mill style grinding devices set into their buttstocks. **CAUTION**: These arms are exceptionally rare and extreme caution should be exercised prior to purchase. Fakes exist.

Courtesy Milwaukee Public Museum, Milwaukee, Wisconsin

Exc.	V.G.	Good	Fair	Poor
—	—	42500	15000	—

Metallic Cartridge Conversions

In 1867 approximately 32,000 Model 1859, 1863 and 1865 Sharps were altered to .52-70 rimfire and centerfire caliber.

Courtesy Mike Stuckslager

Exc.	V.G.	Good	Fair	Poor
—	—	4250	2000	600

Model 1869

A .40-50 to .50-70 caliber model produced in a military form with 26", 28", or 30" barrels; as a carbine with 21" or 24" barrels and in a sporting version with various barrel lengths and a forend stock fitted with a pewter tip. Approximately 650 were made.

Carbine

.50-70, saddle ring on frame.

Exc.	V.G.	Good	Fair	Poor
—	—	4250	1750	500

Military Rifle

.50-70, 30" barrel with three barrel bands.

Exc.	V.G.	Good	Fair	Poor
—	—	5250	2000	800

Sporting Rifle

26" barrel, .44-77 and .50-70.

Exc.	V.G.	Good	Fair	Poor
—	—	6500	3000	950

Model 1870 Springfield Altered

Chambered for .50-70 caliber and fitted with a 35.5" barrel with two barrel bands, walnut stock, case hardened lock and breechlock. Buttplate stamped "US." Also built for Army trials with 22" barrel converted to centerfire.

First Type

Most common, straight breech.

Courtesy Bonhams & Butterfields

Exc.	V.G.	Good	Fair	Poor
—	—	3750	1750	500

Second Type

Model 1874 action, serial #1 to 300.

Exc.	V.G.	Good	Fair	Poor
—	—	6000	2750	750

Carbine

22" barrel converted to centerfire.

Exc.	V.G.	Good	Fair	Poor
—	—	8250	5000	1250

MODEL 1874

This model was manufactured in a variety of calibers, barrel lengths, and stock styles. The barrel markings are of three forms: initially, "Sharps Rifle Manufg. Co. Hartford, Conn."; then, "Sharps Rifle Co. Hartford, Conn."; and finally "Sharps Rifle Co. Bridgeport, Conn." As of 1876 "Old Reliable" was stamped on the barrels. This marking is usually found on Bridgeport-marked rifles only. The major styles of this model are listed.

Military Carbine

.50-70, 21" barrel (460 made).

Exc.	V.G.	Good	Fair	Poor
—	—	5500	2750	750

Military Rifle

In .45-70 and .50-70 centerfire caliber with a 30" barrel and full-length forend secured by three barrel bands. Approximately 1,800 made.

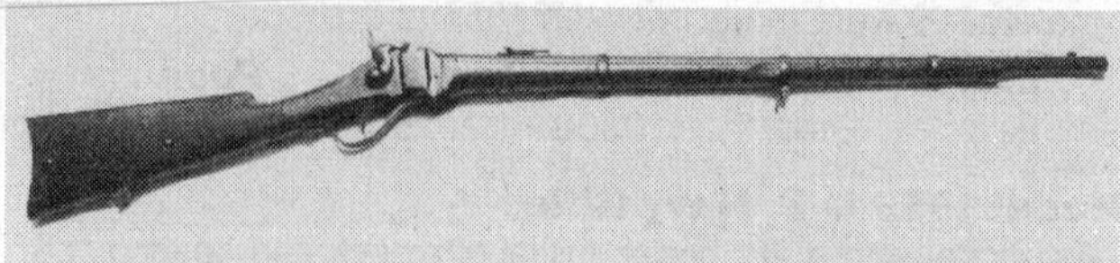

Courtesy Dennis Callender

Exc.	V.G.	Good	Fair	Poor
—	—	5000	2250	750

Hunter's Rifle

In .40, .44, .45-70, and .50-70 caliber with 26", 28", or 30" round barrels having open sights. Approximately 600 were manufactured.

Exc.	V.G.	Good	Fair	Poor
—	—	6250	2750	800

Business Rifle

In .40-70 and .45-75 Sharps caliber with a 26", 28", or 30" round barrel, adjustable sights and double-set triggers. Approximately 1,600 manufactured.

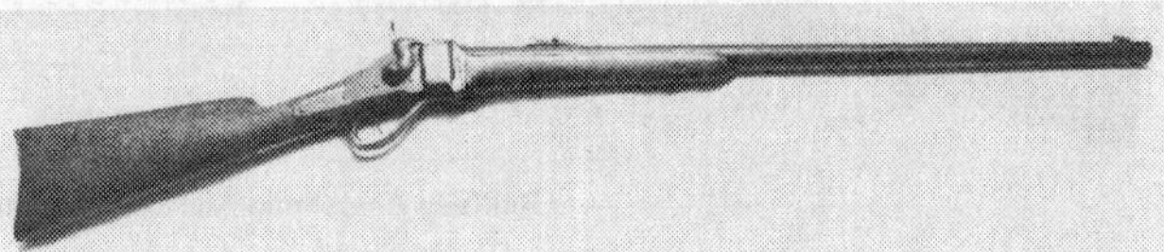

Courtesy Mike Stuckslager

Exc.	V.G.	Good	Fair	Poor
—	—	6000	3250	1000

Sporting Rifle

Offered in a variety of calibers, barrel lengths, barrel weights, barrel styles and stock styles. Approximately 6,000 were manufactured.

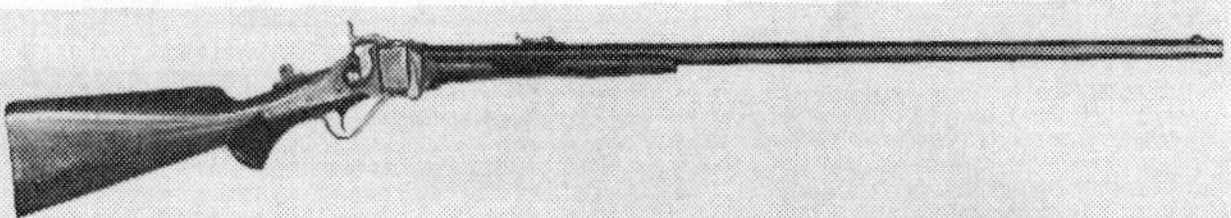

Courtesy Milwaukee Public Museum, Milwaukee, Wisconsin

Exc.	V.G.	Good	Fair	Poor
—	—	8500	4000	1500

Creedmoor Rifle

With a checkered pistol grip stock, vernier sights, combination wind gauge and spirit level front sight, set trigger and shotgun style butt. Approximately 150 were made.

Exc.	V.G.	Good	Fair	Poor
—	—	17500	8500	2000

Mid-Range Rifle

Similar to the above, with a crescent buttplate. Approximately 180 were made.

Courtesy Bonhams & Butterfields

Exc.	V.G.	Good	Fair	Poor
—	—	15000	6500	1500

Long-Range Rifle

As above with a 34" octagonal barrel. Approximately 425 were manufactured.

Exc.	V.G.	Good	Fair	Poor
—	—	16500	6000	1500

Schuetzen Rifle

Similar to the above, with a checkered pistol grip stock and forend, a large Schuetzen style buttplate, double-set triggers and a vernier tang sight. Approximately 70 were manufactured.

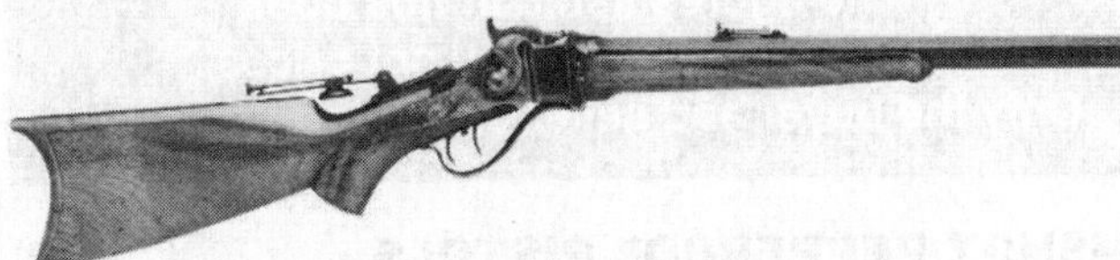

Courtesy Bonhams & Butterfields

Exc.	V.G.	Good	Fair	Poor
—	—	15000	6500	2000

A Sharps Model 1877 Long Range No. 2 Sporting Rifle sold at auction for $34,000. Chambered for the .44-100 cartridge and fitted with a 32" round barrel. With target sights. Condition is 75 percent case color and about 96 percent blue.
Little John's Auction Service, Inc.

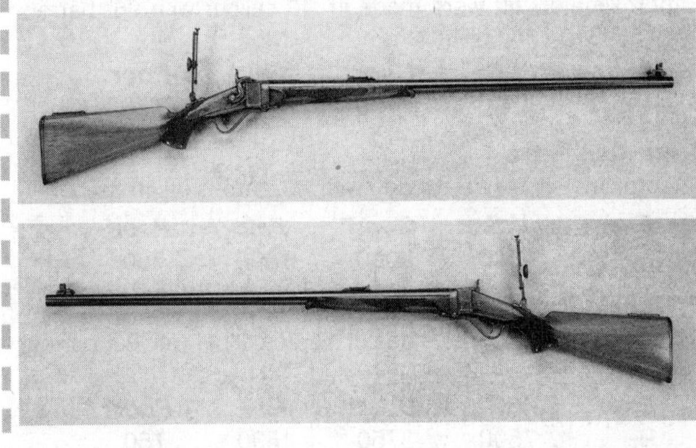

Model 1877

Similar to the Model 1874, and in .45-70 caliber with a 34" or 36" barrel which is marked "Sharps Rifle Co. Bridgeport, Conn. Old Reliable." Approximately 100 were manufactured in 1877 and 1878.

Exc.	V.G.	Good	Fair	Poor
—	30000	10000	5000	2000

MODEL 1878 SHARPS-BORCHARDT

An internal hammer breechloading rifle manufactured from 1878 to approximately 1880. The frame marked "Borchardt Patent Sharps Rifle Co. Bridgeport Conn. U.S.A."

NOTE: Be advised that the actions on Borchardt Sporting Rifles are worth a minimum of $750. Military actions are not as difficult to locate as Sporting actions. For the sake of continuity rifles in poor condition, but with usable actions, are priced at the minimum of $750.

Carbine

Approximately 385 were made in .45-70 caliber with a 24" barrel. The forend is secured by one barrel band.

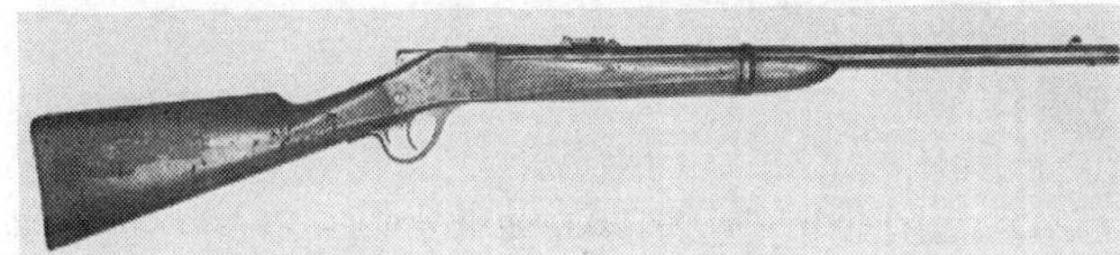

Courtesy Milwaukee Public Museum, Milwaukee, Wisconsin

Exc.	V.G.	Good	Fair	Poor
—	—	3750	1500	750

Military Rifle

Approximately 12,000 were made in .45-70 caliber with 32.25" barrels and full stocks secured by two barrel bands.

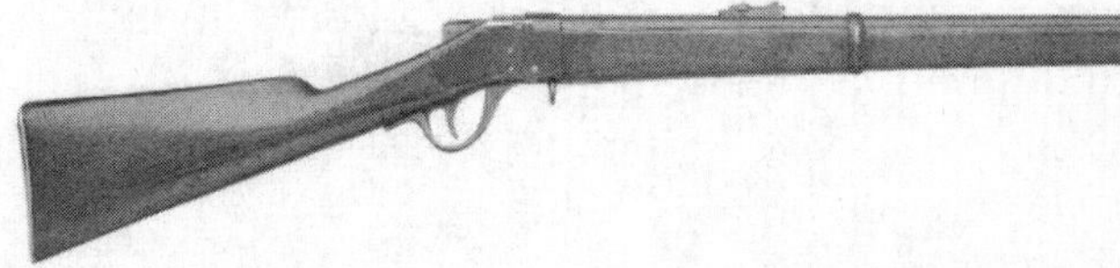

Courtesy Bonhams & Butterfields

Exc.	V.G.	Good	Fair	Poor
—	3000	1250	900	750

This symbol denotes "Sleepers" with rapidly-rising values and/or significant collector potential. 

Sporting Rifle

Approximately 1,600 were made in .45-70 caliber with 30" round or octagonal barrels.

Exc.	V.G.	Good	Fair	Poor
—	6000	2500	800	750

Hunter's Rifle

Approximately 60 were made in .40 caliber with 26" barrels and plain walnut stocks.

Exc.	V.G.	Good	Fair	Poor
—	4500	1750	1000	750

Business Rifle

Approximately 90 were made with 28" barrels in .40 caliber.

Exc.	V.G.	Good	Fair	Poor
—	4500	2000	1000	750

Officer's Rifle

Approximately 50 were made in .45-70 caliber with 32" barrels and checkered walnut stocks.

Exc.	V.G.	Good	Fair	Poor
—	7500	3750	1500	750

Express Rifle

Approximately 30 were made in .45-70 caliber with 26" barrels, set triggersand checkered walnut stocks.

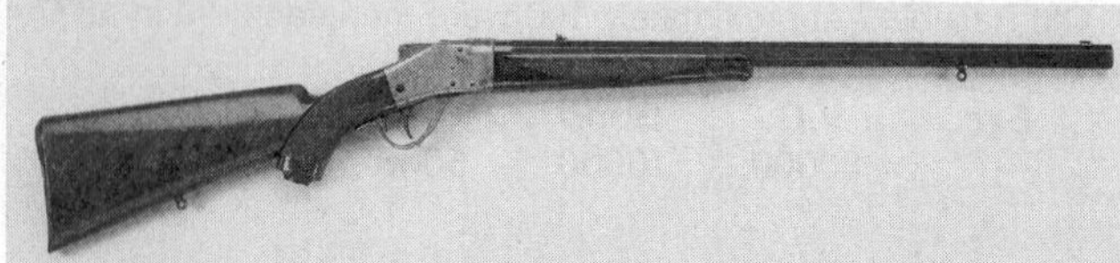

Courtesy Little John's Auction Service, Inc., Paul Goodwin photo

Exc.	V.G.	Good	Fair	Poor
—	12500	6000	2000	800

Short-Range Rifle

Approximately 155 were made in .40 caliber with 26" barrels, vernier rear sights, wind gauge front sight and a checkered walnut stock.

Courtesy Little John's Auction Service, Inc., Paul Goodwin photo

Exc.	V.G.	Good	Fair	Poor
—	7500	3750	1000	800

Mid-Range Rifle

Similar to the above, with a 30" barrel. Approximately 250 were manufactured.

Courtesy Little John's Auction Service, Inc., Paul Goodwin photo

Exc.	V.G.	Good	Fair	Poor
10000	7000	4000	2000	900

Long-Range Rifle

Similar to the above, with different sights. Approximately 230 were manufactured.

Courtesy Amoskeag Auction Company

Exc.	V.G.	Good	Fair	Poor
—	16000	6500	2500	900

C. Sharps & Company and Sharps & Hankins Company Breechloading, Single-Shot Pistol

A .31, .34, or .36 caliber breechloading percussion pistol with 5" or 6.5" round barrels. Blued, case hardened with walnut stock.

Courtesy Buffalo Bill Historical Center, Cody, Wyoming

Exc.	V.G.	Good	Fair	Poor
—	—	5000	2000	600

Pistol-Grip Rifle

A .31 or .38 caliber breechloading percussion rifle resembling the above. Manufactured in a variety of barrel lengths. Blued, case hardened with a walnut stock having German silver mounts.

Courtesy Bonhams & Butterfields

Exc.	V.G.	Good	Fair	Poor
—	—	4750	2500	750

Percussion Revolver

A .25 caliber percussion revolver with a 3" octagonal barrel and 6-shot cylinder. Blued with walnut grips. The barrel marked "C. Sharps & Co., Phila. Pa." Approximately 2,000 were manufactured between 1857 and 1858.

Exc.	V.G.	Good	Fair	Poor
—	—	3000	1250	500

REMINDER
The figures listed in this book reflect relative values, not prices. Only the buyer and seller can determine price.

4-SHOT PEPPERBOX PISTOLS

Between 1859 and 1874, these companies manufactured 4 barrel cartridge pocket pistols in a variety of calibers, barrel lengths and finishes. The barrels slide forward for loading. The major models are listed.

Courtesy Buffalo Bill Historical Center, Cody, Wyoming

Model 1

Manufactured by C. Sharps & Co. and in .22 rimfire caliber.

Exc.	V.G.	Good	Fair	Poor
—	—	600	250	100

Model 2

As above, in .30 rimfire caliber.

Exc.	V.G.	Good	Fair	Poor
—	—	600	250	100

Model 3

Manufactured by Sharps & Hankins and marked "Address Sharps & Hankins Philadelphia Penn." on the frame. Caliber. 32 short rimfire.

Exc.	V.G.	Good	Fair	Poor
—	—	750	300	150

Model 4

Similar to the above, in .32 Long rimfire and with a rounded bird's-head grip.

Courtesy John J. Stimson, Jr.

Exc.	V.G.	Good	Fair	Poor
—	—	750	300	150

Model 1861 Navy Rifle

A .54 Sharps & Hankins caliber breechloading single-shot rifle with a 32.75" barrel and full stock secured by three barrel bands. Blued, case hardened with a walnut stock. Approximately 700 were made in 1861 and 1862.

Courtesy Milwaukee Public Museum, Milwaukee, Wisconsin

Exc.	V.G.	Good	Fair	Poor
—	—	5000	2000	700

Model 1862 Navy Carbine

A .54 caliber breechloading carbine with a 24" leather covered barrel. Case hardened with a walnut stock. The frame marked "Sharps & Hankins Philada." Approximately 8,000 were manufactured between 1861 and 1862.

Courtesy Milwaukee Public Museum, Milwaukee, Wisconsin

Exc.	V.G.	Good	Fair	Poor
—	—	5000	2000	700

Short Cavalry Carbine

Similar to the above, with a 19" blued barrel. Approximately 500 were manufactured.

Exc.	V.G.	Good	Fair	Poor
—	—	5000	2000	700

Army Model

Similar to the above, with a 24" barrel that does not have a leather covering. Approximately 500 were purchased by the Army.

Exc.	V.G.	Good	Fair	Poor
—	—	4750	1750	700

SHATTUCK, C. S.

Hatfield, Massachusetts

Double-Barrel Shotguns

In addition to single-barrel shotguns, Shattuck made about 1,000 hammerless doubles.

Courtesy Nick Niles

Exc.	V.G.	Good	Fair	Poor
1000	500	400	300	200

Boom

A .22 caliber spur trigger revolver with a 2" octagonal barrel and 6-shot cylinder. Nickel-plated with rosewood or walnut grips. The barrel marked "Boom" and "Pat. Nov. 4. 1879." Manufactured during the 1880s.

Exc.	V.G.	Good	Fair	Poor
—	400	150	100	75

Pocket Revolver

A .32 caliber spur trigger revolver with a 3.5" octagonal barrel and 5-shot cylinder. Nickel-plated with hard rubber grips. The barrel marked "C. S. Shattuck Hatfield, Mass. Pat. Nov. 4, 1879." Manufactured during the 1880s.

Exc.	V.G.	Good	Fair	Poor
—	500	200	150	100

SHAW & LEDOYT
Stafford, Connecticut

Under Hammer Pistol
A .31 caliber under hammer percussion pistol with a 2.5" to 3.5" half-octagonal barrel. Blued with a brass mounted walnut grip. The frame marked "Shaw & LeDoyt/Stafford. Conn." Manufactured during the 1850s.

Exc.	V.G.	Good	Fair	Poor
—	—	1150	500	150

SHAWK & McLANAHAN
St. Louis, Missouri

Navy Revolver
A .36 caliber percussion revolver with an 8" round barrel and 6-shot cylinder. Blued with a brass frame and walnut grips. Marked "Shawk & McLanahan, St. Louis, Carondelet, Mo." Produced in limited quantities prior to 1860. Prospective purchasers are advised to secure a qualified appraisal prior to acquisition.

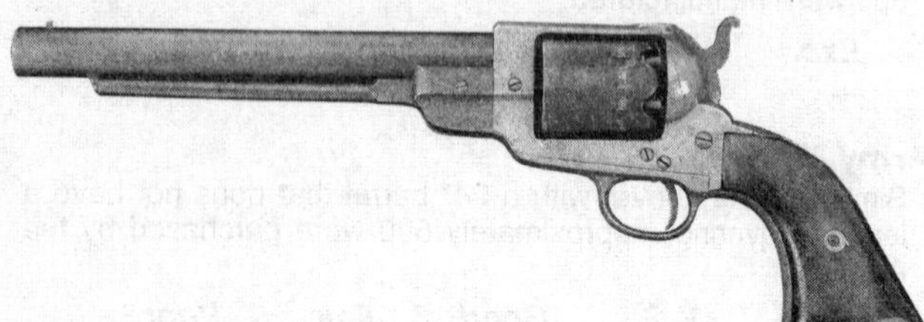

Courtesy Little John's Auction Service, Inc., Paul Goodwin photo

Exc.	V.G.	Good	Fair	Poor
—	—	10500	5000	2000

SHERIDEN PRODUCTS, INC.
Racine, Wisconsin

Knockabout
A .22 caliber single-shot pistol with a 5" barrel having fixed sights. Blued with plastic grips. Manufactured between 1953 and 1960.

Exc.	V.G.	Good	Fair	Poor
250	200	150	100	50

SHILEN RIFLES, INC.
Ennis, Texas

Model DGA Sporter
A .17 Remington to .258 Winchester caliber bolt-action sporting rifle with a 24" barrel furnished without sights. Blued with a walnut stock.

Exc.	V.G.	Good	Fair	Poor
650	550	450	400	350

Model DGA Varminter
As above, in varmint calibers with a 25" barrel.

Exc.	V.G.	Good	Fair	Poor
650	550	450	400	350

Model DGA Silhouette Rifle
As above, in .308 Winchester only.

Exc.	V.G.	Good	Fair	Poor
650	550	450	400	350

Model DGA Bench Rest Rifle
A centerfire single-shot bolt-action rifle with a 26" barrel and either fiberglass or walnut stock.

Exc.	V.G.	Good	Fair	Poor
750	650	550	500	450

SHILOH RIFLE MFG. CO., INC.
Big Timber, Montana

Established in Farmingdale, New York, in 1976, this company moved to Big Timber, Montana, in 1983 with the name Shiloh Products. It changed its name to Shiloh Rifle Manufacturing Co. in that same year. In 1985 the company began marketing its products factory direct. In 1991 Robert, Phyllis, and Kirk Bryan purchased the company. Those interested in the Sharps reproduction rifles manufactured by this company are advised to contact them in Big Timber.

NOTE: The company will build a rifle to customers' specifications. It is therefore possible that many of these rifles have special-order features that are not reflected in the base model price. Since Shiloh is in effect a custom (or at least semi-custom) manufacturer, the rifles listed here are representative but not inclusive.

Model 1863 Military Rifle
A .54 caliber percussion rifle with a 30" barrel, single- or double-set triggers and full-length walnut stock secured by three barrel bands.

NIB	Exc.	V.G.	Good	Fair	Poor
1750	1400	1000	—	—	—

Model 1863 Sporting Rifle
As above, with a 30" octagonal barrel, sporting sights and a half-length stock.

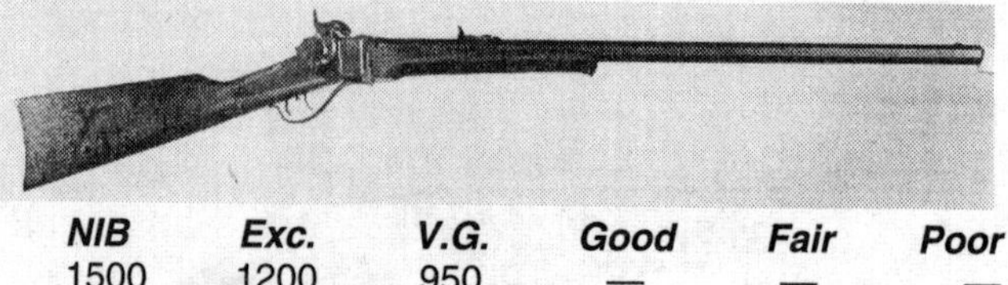

NIB	Exc.	V.G.	Good	Fair	Poor
1500	1200	950	—	—	—

Model 1863 Military Carbine
The Model 1863 with a 22" round barrel and carbine stock secured by one barrel band.

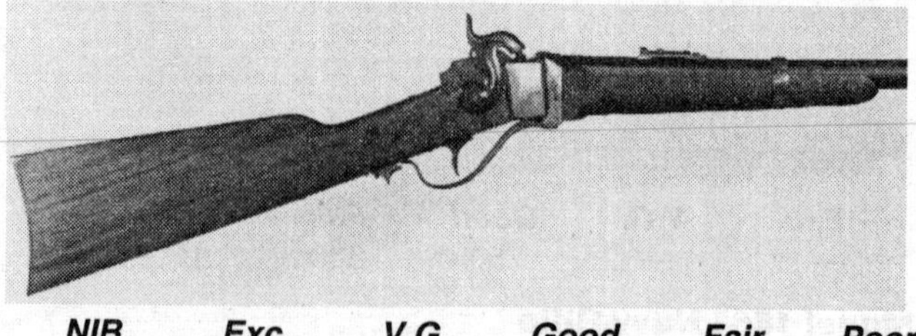

NIB	Exc.	V.G.	Good	Fair	Poor
1500	1200	950	—	—	—

Model 1862 Confederate Robinson
As above, with a 21.5" barrel, brass buttplate and barrel band.

NIB	Exc.	V.G.	Good	Fair	Poor
800	750	650	550	450	400

Model 1874 Creedmore Target Rifle
This model is furnished with a 32" 1/2 round, 1/2 octagon barrel. Extra-fancy wood stock with pistol grip, no cheek rest, and shotgun butt. Single trigger. No sights.

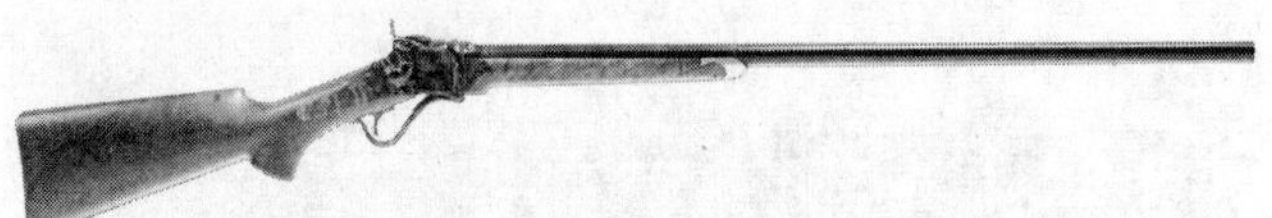

NIB	Exc.	V.G.	Good	Fair	Poor
2440	1950	1500	1000	—	—

Model 1874 Buffalo Rifle (Quigley)

Offered in .45-70 or .45-110 with 34" heavy octagon barrel. Mid-range tang sight with globe front sight. Semi buckhorn rear sight. Double-set triggers. Military buttstock with patch box. No cheek rest and straight-grip stock.

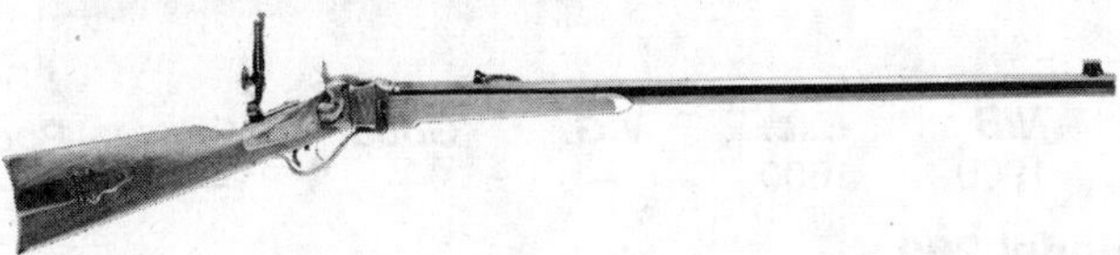

NIB	Exc.	V.G.	Good	Fair	Poor
2850	2300	1750	—	—	—

Model 1874 Long Range Express Rifle

Manufactured in a variety of calibers with a 34" octagonal barrel, double-set triggers, vernier rear sight and globe front sight.

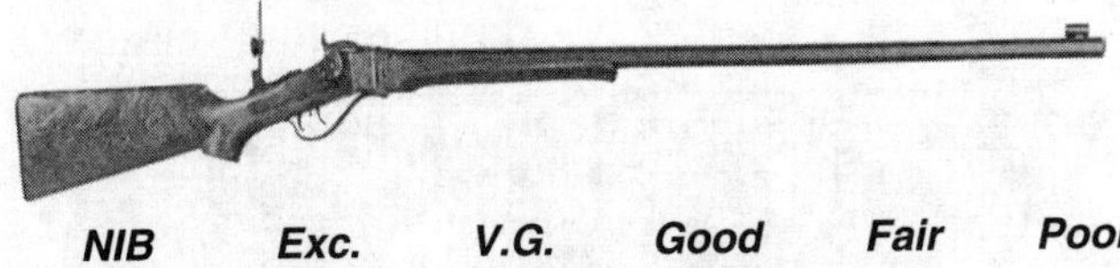

NIB	Exc.	V.G.	Good	Fair	Poor
1600	1300	950	600	—	—

Model 1874 Montana Roughrider Rifle

As above, with either octagonal or half-octagonal barrels ranging in lengths from 24" to 34".

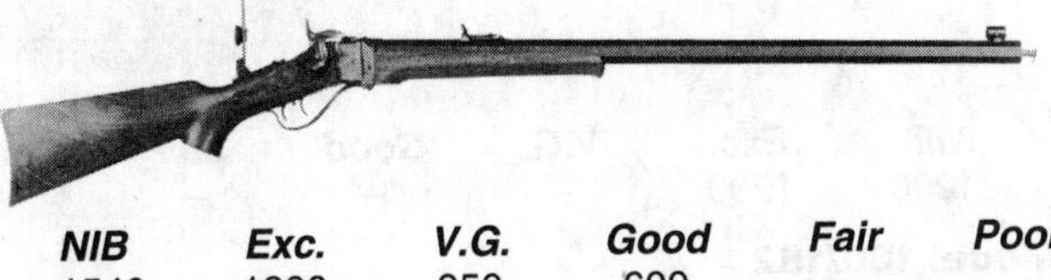

NIB	Exc.	V.G.	Good	Fair	Poor
1540	1200	950	600	—	—

Saddle Rifle

As above, with a 26" barrel and shotgun butt.

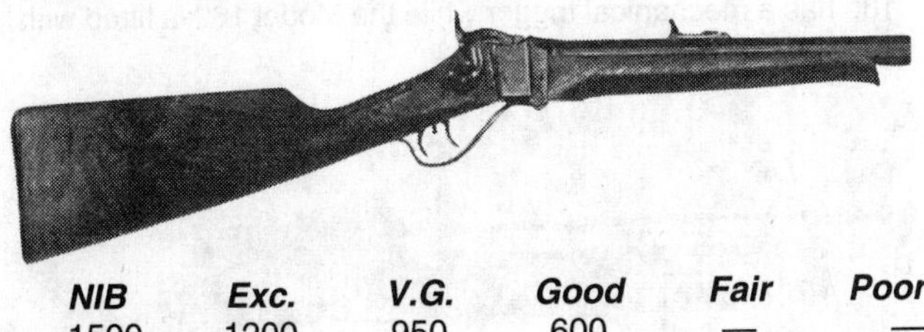

NIB	Exc.	V.G.	Good	Fair	Poor
1500	1200	950	600	—	—

No. 1 Sporter Deluxe Rifle

Similar to the above, with a 30" octagonal barrel.

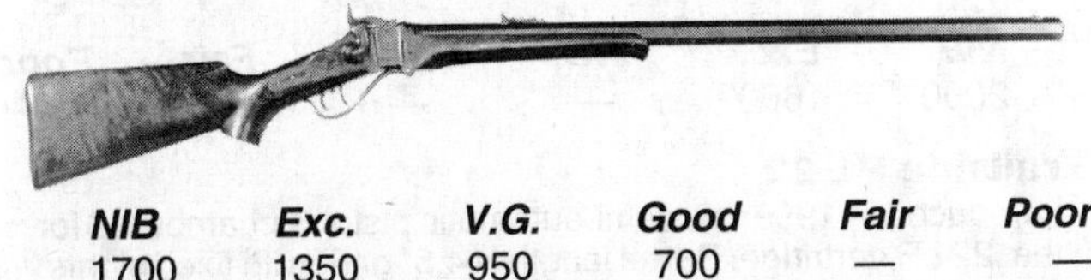

NIB	Exc.	V.G.	Good	Fair	Poor
1700	1350	950	700	—	—

No. 3 Standard Sporter

As above, with a military-style stock.

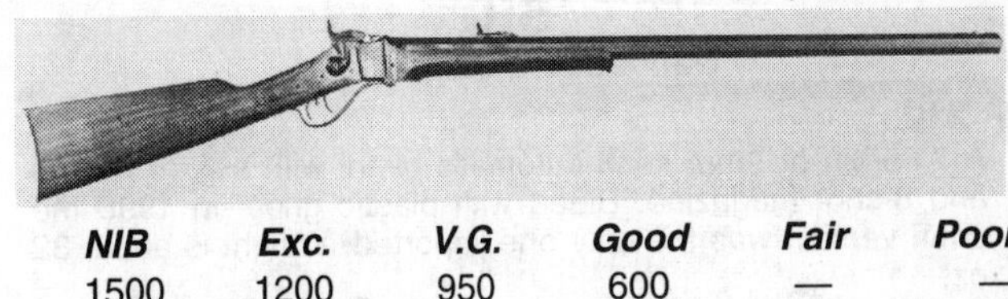

NIB	Exc.	V.G.	Good	Fair	Poor
1500	1200	950	600	—	—

The Business Rifle

As above, with a heavy 28" barrel.

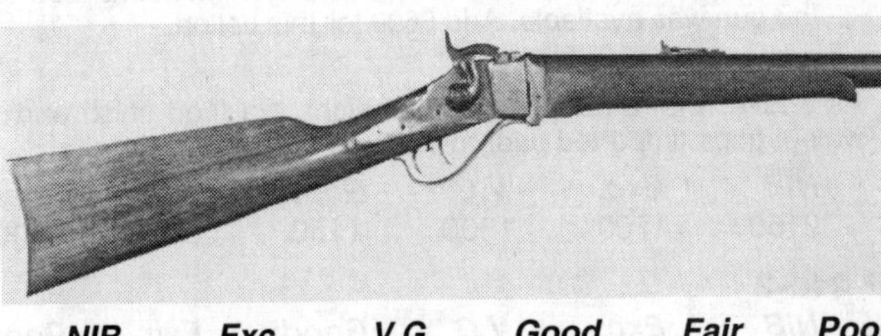

NIB	Exc.	V.G.	Good	Fair	Poor
1500	1200	950	600	—	—

Model 1874 Military Rifle

The Model 1874 with a 30" round barrel, military sights and full-length stocks secured by three barrel bands.

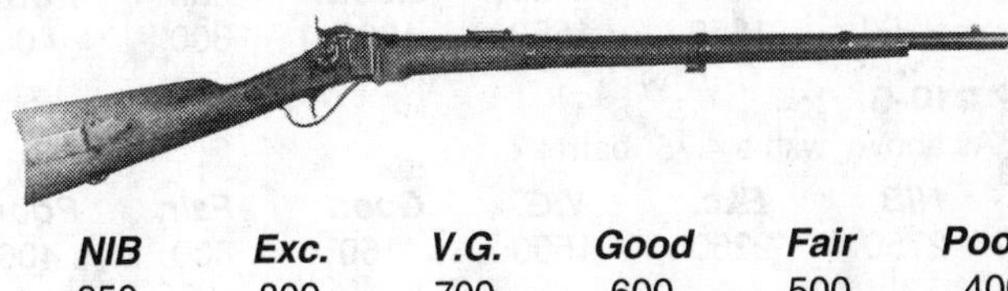

NIB	Exc.	V.G.	Good	Fair	Poor
850	800	700	600	500	400

Model 1874 Carbine

Similar to the above, with a 24" round barrel.

NIB	Exc.	V.G.	Good	Fair	Poor
1500	1200	950	600	—	—

The Jaeger

The Model 1874 with a 26" half-octagonal barrel, open sights and pistol-grip stock with a shotgun butt.

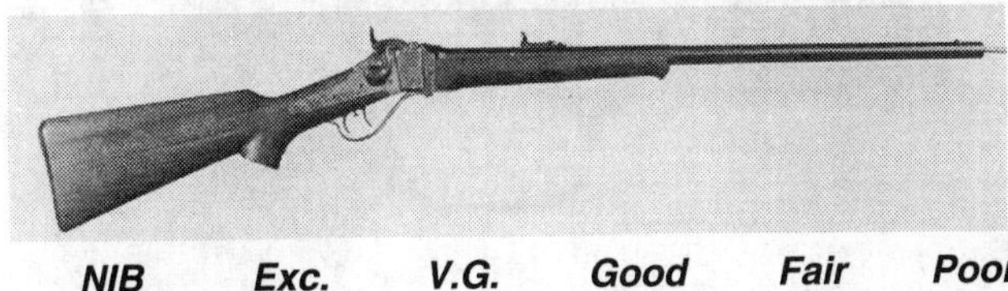

NIB	Exc.	V.G.	Good	Fair	Poor
800	750	650	550	450	400

Hartford Model

A reproduction of the Sharps Hartford Model.

NIB	Exc.	V.G.	Good	Fair	Poor
1700	1350	950	600	—	—

Model 1874 Military Carbine

Similar to the Military Rifle, but with a 22" round barrel.

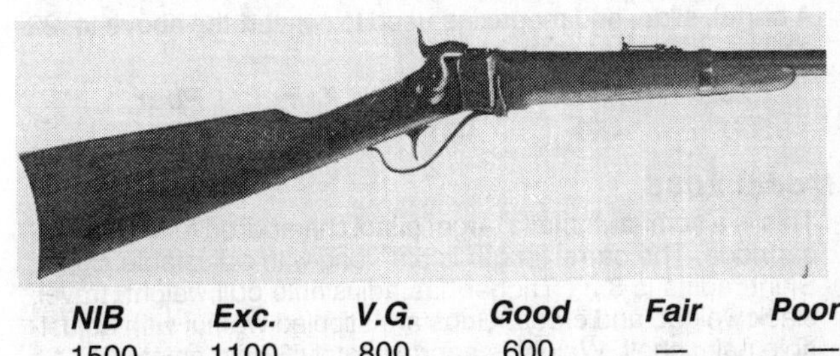

NIB	Exc.	V.G.	Good	Fair	Poor
1500	1100	800	600	—	—

SIG

Neuhausen, Switzerland

P 210

A 7.65mm or 9mm semi-automatic pistol with a 4.75" barrel and 8-shot magazine. Blued with plastic grips. In 1996 the 9mm version was the only one imported. Weight is about 32 oz.

NIB	Exc.	V.G.	Good	Fair	Poor
2300	1500	1300	1100	800	500

NOTE: For 1996 a .22 caliber conversion unit serialized to the gun was available. Add $600 for this option.

P 210-1

As above, with an adjustable rear sight, polished finish and walnut grips. Imported prior to 1987.

NIB	Exc.	V.G.	Good	Fair	Poor
2150	1700	1500	1150	800	400

P 210-2

NIB	Exc.	V.G.	Good	Fair	Poor
2000	1750	1350	1000	750	300

P 210-5

As above, with an extended length barrel, adjustable rear sight and walnut grips.

NIB	Exc.	V.G.	Good	Fair	Poor
2250	1850	1650	1000	800	400

P 210-6

As above, with a 4.75" barrel.

NIB	Exc.	V.G.	Good	Fair	Poor
2750	2250	1500	1150	800	400

SIG-HAMMERLI

Lenzburg, Switzerland

Model P240 Target Pistol

A .32 Smith & Wesson Long Wadcutter or .38 Midrange caliber semi-automatic pistol with a 5.9" barrel, adjustable rear sight, adjustable trigger and 5-shot magazine. Blued, with adjustable walnut grips. Imported prior 1987.

Courtesy John J. Stimson, Jr.

Exc.	V.G.	Good	Fair	Poor
1300	1150	950	750	600

.22 Conversion Unit

A barrel, slide, and magazine used to convert the above to .22 caliber.

Exc.	V.G.	Good	Fair	Poor
500	450	400	300	200

Model 208S

This is a semi-automatic target pistol chambered for the .22 LR cartridge. The barrel length is 5.9" long with adjustable sights. Sight radius is 8.2". Trigger has adjustable pull weight, travel, slack weight, and creep. Grips are stippled walnut with adjustable palm shelf. Weight is approximately 37 oz. empty.

NIB	Exc.	V.G.	Good	Fair	Poor
1900	1600	—	—	—	—

Model 280

This model is a semi-automatic pistol chambered for the .22 LR cartridge or the .32 S&W Long Wadcutter. Single-action-only. Barrel length is 4.6" with a sight radius of 8.7". Adjustable sights. Trigger is adjustable for pull weight, take-up, let-off, and creep. Stippled walnut grip with adjustable palm shelf. Weight is 35 oz. for the .22 caliber and 42 oz. for the .32 caliber. Magazine capacity is six .22 caliber rounds and five .32 caliber rounds.

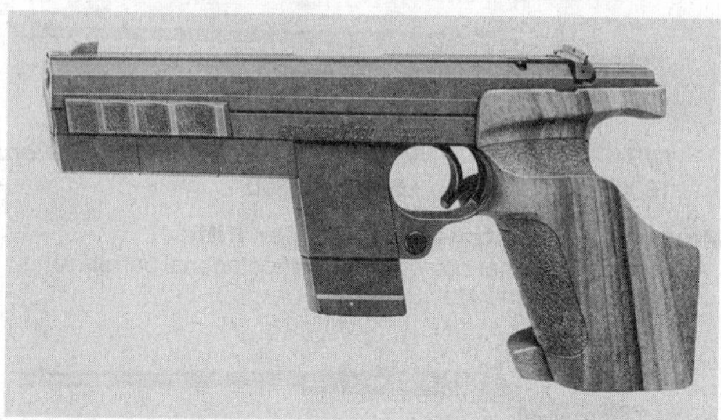

NIB	Exc.	V.G.	Good	Fair	Poor
1200	1200	—	—	—	—

Model 160/162

This .22 LR single-shot pistol is designed for international free pistol competition. Barrel length is 11.3" with a sight radius of 14.6". Trigger is fully adjustable as are the sights. Stippled walnut grips with adjustable palm shelf and rake angle. The Model 160 has a mechanical trigger while the Model 162 is fitted with an electric trigger.

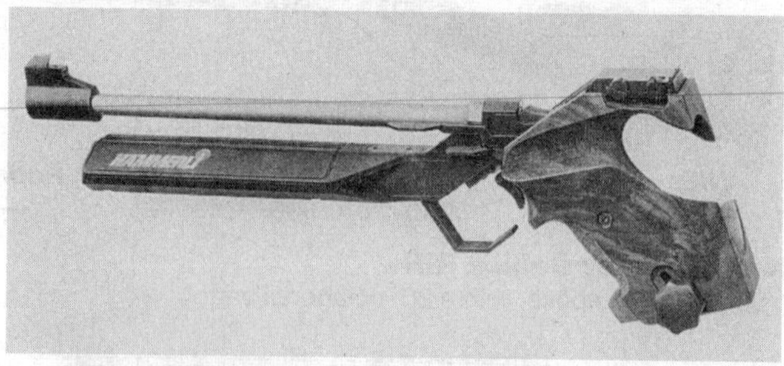

NIB	Exc.	V.G.	Good	Fair	Poor
2000	1600	—	—	—	—

Trailside PL 22

Introduced in 1999 this semi-automatic pistol is chambered for the .22 LR cartridge. Barrel length is 4.5" or 6" with fixed sights. Synthetic grips. Two-tone finish. Magazine capacity is 10 rounds. Weight is about 28 oz. with 4.5" barrel and 30 oz. with 6" barrel.

NIB	Exc.	V.G.	Good	Fair	Poor
455	350	—	—	—	—

NOTE: Add $90 for 6" barrel.

Trailside PL 22 Target

Similar to the PL 22 with the addition of adjustable sights and walnut grips. Introduced in 1999.

NIB	Exc.	V.G.	Good	Fair	Poor
535	400	—	—	—	—

NOTE: Add $25 for 6" barrel.

Trailside Competition

Introduced in 2004 this .22 caliber model features a 6" barrel with adjustable sights and adjustable competition grip, counterweights, and two-tone finish. Magazine capacity is 10 rounds. Weight is about 36 oz.

NIB	Exc.	V.G.	Good	Fair	Poor
710	525	—	—	—	—

SIGARMS

Eckernforde, West Germany

This old-line Swiss firm was established in 1853 and is now a broadly based engineering consortium. Its first successful commercial design was the SP 47/8 introduced in 1948. SIG, a Swiss company, associated itself with the German firm of Sauer in 1970. SIG-Sauer pistols are SIG designs assembled in Germany. At the present time the P239 and P229 SIG pistols are produced in New Hampshire.

Note: SIGARMS currently offers an almost innumerable variety of semi-auto pistols. The main models are listed here. Values for similar models (i.e., those with similar model numbers) are generally comparable to the values given here with a 5-10 percent premium for scarce or desirable options.

PISTOLS

CLASSIC SERIES

NOTE: Maximum magazine capacity for all currently manufactured SIG pistols is 10 rounds regardless of caliber and previous capacity.

NOTE: For pistols with factory installed night sights add $90. Add $45 for pistols with K-Kote finish. Add $35 for nickel slides.

P210

This model was reintroduced into the U.S. in 2001 and is based on the Swiss military version first built in 1949. It is designed primarily as a target pistol and is furnished in four different variations. All variations are chambered for the 9mm cartridge.

NOTE: Older P210 models imported before 1968 without importer stammps and pistols built during the late 1940s and early 1950s may bring a premium to the collector. Be aware that extra barrels, conversion kits, and other special order features will add additional value.

P210-8-9

This variation has adjustable target sights, select wood grips, lateral magazine catch, blued sandblasted finish, and adjustable trigger stop. Heavy frame. Barrel length is 4.8". Weight is about 37 oz.

NIB	Exc.	V.G.	Good	Fair	Poor
4275	3500	—	—	—	—

P210-6-9

This variation has adjustable target sights, wood grips, target grade trigger, and blued sandblasted finish. Barrel length is 4.8". Weight is about 32 oz.

NIB	Exc.	V.G.	Good	Fair	Poor
2695	2000	—	—	—	—

P210-5-9

This variation has extended 5.85" barrel with compensator, ribbed front frame grip, wood grip plates, adjustable target sights, and target trigger. Weight is about 34 oz.

NIB	Exc.	V.G.	Good	Fair	Poor
3000	2200	—	—	—	—

P210-2-9

This variation is similar to the Swiss Army service pistol and has wood grip plates and standard fixed sights. Barrel length is 4.8". Weight is about 32 oz.

NIB	Exc.	V.G.	Good	Fair	Poor
1675	1350	—	—	—	—

NOTE: A .22 LR conversion is available for the P210-2/5/6 series but not the P210-8. Retail price is $700.00.

P210-9-6S

This 9mm pistol is fitted with a heavy frame, target sights, wood grips, and U.S.-style magazine release. Introduced in 2004.

NIB	Exc.	V.G.	Good	Fair	Poor
3000	2200	—	—	—	—

P220

This is a high-quality, double-action semi-automatic pistol chambered for .38 Super, .45 ACP, and 9mm Parabellum. It has a 4.41" barrel and fixed sights and features the de-cocking lever that was found originally on the Sauer Model 38H. There are two versions of this pistol—one with a bottom magazine release (commonly referred to as the European model) and the other with the release on the side (commonly referred to as the American model) as on the Model 1911 Colt. The frame is a lightweight alloy that is matte-finished and is available in either blue, nickel, or K-Kote finish with black plastic grips. The .45 ACP magazine capacity is 7 rounds and the pistol weighs 25.7 oz.; the .38 Super magazine capacity is 9 rounds and the pistol weighs 26.5 oz.; the 9mm magazine holds 9 rounds and the overall weight is 26.5 oz. This model was manufactured from 1976 and is still in production. The 9mm version in this model is no longer in production. The prices listed are for guns with a standard blue finish.

NOTE #1: For the K-Kote finish add $40, for nickel slide add $40. Stainless steel add $100. In 2004 a blued version with tactical rail was offered.

NOTE #2: At the present the P220 pistol is offered only in .45 ACP.

P220 with tactical rail

NIB	Exc.	V.G.	Good	Fair	Poor
800	550	400	300	200	150

P220 ST

As above, chambered for the .45 ACP cartridge and features a stainless steel frame and slide with tactical rail. Also includes a SIGARMS tactical knife and aliminum carrying case. Weight is about 39 oz.

NIB	Exc.	V.G.	Good	Fair	Poor
875	700	550	—	—	—

P220 Sport

Introduced in 1999, this .45 ACP pistol is similar to the P220 with the addition of 5.5" barrel with stainless steel compensator. The frame and slide are stainless steel. Magazine capacity is 7 rounds. Weight is about 44 oz.

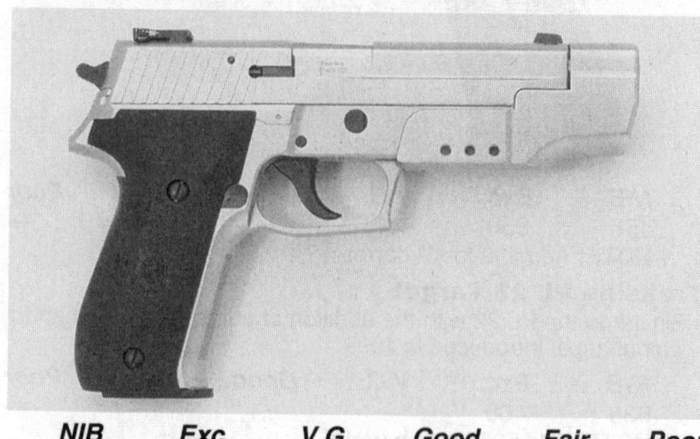

NIB	Exc.	V.G.	Good	Fair	Poor
1300	1000	700	—	—	—

P220R SAO

An 8+1 or 10+1 capacity single-action semi-auto chambered for .45 ACP. Polymer grip and Nitron finish, 4.4" barrel, 30.4 oz., 5-lb. trigger. Picatinny rail. Introduced 2006.

NIB	Exc.	V.G.	Good	Fair	Poor
650	—	—	—	—	—

P220R DAK

Semi-auto with 8+1 or 10+1 capacity chambered for .45 ACP. Polymer grip and Nitron finish, 4.4" barrel, 30.4 oz., 7.5-lb. trigger. Picatinny rail. Introduced 2006.

NIB	Exc.	V.G.	Good	Fair	Poor
650	—	—	—	—	—

P220 SAS

An 8+1 capacity double-action semi-auto chambered for .45 ACP. Fixed sights, wood grips, 4.4" barrel, 30.4 oz., 6.5-lb. trigger. Introduced 2006.

NIB	Exc.	V.G.	Good	Fair	Poor
750	—	—	—	—	—

P220 Carry SAS

An 8+1 capacity double-action semi-auto chambered for .45 ACP. Fixed sights, wood grips, 3.9" barrel, 30.4 oz., 6.5-lb. trigger. Introduced 2006.

NIB	Exc.	V.G.	Good	Fair	Poor
750	—	—	—	—	—

P220 Carry

An 8+1 or 10+1 capacity single/double-action semi-auto chambered for .45 ACP. Fixed sights, polymer grips, 3.9" barrel, 30.4 oz. Introduced 2006.

NIB	Exc.	V.G.	Good	Fair	Poor
800	—	—	—	—	—

P220R Equinox

An 8+1 or 10+1 capacity single/double-action semi-auto chambered for .45 ACP. Fixed sights, wood grips, 4.4" barrel, 30.4 oz. Introduced 2006.

NIB	Exc.	V.G.	Good	Fair	Poor
775	—	—	—	—	—

P220R Carry Equinox

An 8+1 or 10+1 capacity single/double-action semi-auto chambered for .45 ACP. Fixed sights, wood grips, 3.9" barrel, 30.4 oz. Introduced 2006.

NIB	Exc.	V.G.	Good	Fair	Poor
800	—	—	—	—	—

P220 Langdon Edition

This .45 ACP pistol, introduced in 2004, features a 4.4" barrel, Nill wood grips, fiber optic sight, competition rear sight, front serrations, short trigger and other special features. Two-tone finish. Magazine capacity is 8 rounds. Weight is about 41 oz.

NIB	Exc.	V.G.	Good	Fair	Poor
800	595	—	—	—	—

P220 Combat

Similar to P220 but with sand-colored alloy slide and steel frame. Threaded barrel for suppressor. Capacity 8+1 or 10+1. Designed for SOCOM sidearm trials. Introduced in 2007.

NIB	Exc	V.G.	Good	Fair	Poor
1000	—	—	—	—	—

P220 Match

Similar to P220 but with 5-inch barrel and adjustable sights. Introduced 2007.

NIB	Exc	V.G.	Good	Fair	Poor
900	—	—	—	—	—

P220 Super Match

Super-accurized version of P220 Match with single-action-only trigger, beavertail safety and custom wood grips. Limited edition.

NIB	Exc	V.G.	Good	Fair	Poor
1150	—	—	—	—	—

P220 Compact

Similar to P220 but with 3.9-inch barrel and 6+1 capacity. Single-action-only or single-/double-action. Various finish, grip and sight options.

NIB	Exc	V.G.	Good	Fair	Poor
700	—	—	—	—	—

P225

This is similar to the Model P220 except that it is chambered for 9mm cartridge. It is a more compact pistol, with a 3.86" barrel. It has an 8-shot detachable magazine and adjustable sights. The finish is matte blue. K-Kote, or electroless nickel plate with black plastic grips.The overall length is 7.1" with an overall height of 5.2". The pistol weighs 26.1 oz. No longer in production.

NIB	Exc.	V.G.	Good	Fair	Poor
625	575	500	400	200	150

NOTE: For K-Kote finish add $70. For nickel slide add $70.

P225 Limited

This 9mm 3.9" model features a Novak low-carry rear sight, three magazines, SIG-Sauer range bag. Introduced in 2004. Weight is about 26 oz.

NIB	Exc.	V.G.	Good	Fair	Poor
800	600	—	—	—	—

P226

This model is a full size, high-capacity pistol with a 4.41" barrel chambered for the 9mm or .40 S&W cartridge. In 1996 this model was also available chambered for the .357 SIG cartridge. It is available with a 15- or 20-round detachable magazine and high-contrast sights. It is either blued, electroless nickel plated, or has a polymer finish known as K-Kote. Overall length is 7.7" and overall height is 5.5". The pistol weighs 26.5 oz. This model was introduced in 1983. Add $50 for K-Kote finish and $50 for nickel slide. In 2003 this pistol was available with an integral rail system on the frame. In 2004 this pistol was offered with optional Crimson Trace laser grips.

NIB	Exc.	V.G.	Good	Fair	Poor
825	600	550	450	300	200

NOTE: Add $125 for Crimson Trace laser grips.

P226 Navy Seal

This special limited edition 9mm pistol is fitted with a 4.4" barrel and special serial numbers from "NSW0001" and above. Black finish.

NIB	Exc.	V.G.	Good	Fair	Poor
N/A	—	—	—	—	—

P226 ST

As above but with stainless steel frame and slide. Offered in 9mm, .40 S&W, and .357 SIG. Barrel length is 4.4". Magazine capacity is 10 rounds. Weight is about 39 oz. Introduced in 2002.

NIB	Exc.	V.G.	Good	Fair	Poor
1000	750	—	—	—	—

P226 Sport Stock

Introduced in 2002 this 9mm pistol features a heavy match barrel and adjustable rear sight. Hand tuned. Specifications are the same as the P226 ST. Available by special order only.

NIB	Exc.	V.G.	Good	Fair	Poor
1600	1200	—	—	—	—

P226 Sport

Introduced in 2001 this model is similar to the other SIG Sport models and is chambered for the 9mm Luger cartridge. Stainless steel slide and frame with adjustable target sights and competition barrel weight.

NIB	Exc.	V.G.	Good	Fair	Poor
1350	1000	—	—	—	—

JP226 Jubilee Pistol

This variation is a special limited edition of the P226. Each gun carries a special serial number prefixed JP. The grips are hand carved select European walnut. The slide and frame are covered with solid gold wire inlays, while the trigger, hammer, decocking lever, slide catch lever, and magazine catch are all gold plated. Each pistol comes in a custom fitted hard case of full leather. This pistol is no longer imported into the U.S. Fewer than 250 were imported between 1991 and 1992.

NIB	Exc.	V.G.	Good	Fair	Poor
1200	850	600	500	400	200

P226 ST

This .40 caliber model, introduced in 2004, features a reverse two-tone finish, 3-dot sights, and Hogue rubber grips. Weight is about 31 oz. Magazine capacity is 10 rounds.

NIB	Exc.	V.G.	Good	Fair	Poor
1085	800	—	—	—	—

P226R DAK

Introduced in 2005 this model features double action only DAK trigger system with double strike capability. Chambered for the 9mm, .357 SIG, or .40 S&W cartridge with a 4.4" barrel. Fixed sights. Magazine capacity is 10, 12, or 15 rounds depending on caliber. Weight is about 32 oz. for 9mm and 34 oz. for .357 SIG or .40 S&W models.

NIB	Exc.	V.G.	Good	Fair	Poor
840	625	—	—	—	—

P226 X-Five

This single action model is chambered for the 9mm or .40 S&W cartridge and fitted with a 5" barrel. Adjustable rear sight and adjustable trigger pull. Slide has front cocking serrations. Checkered wood Null grips. Magazine capacity is 19 rounds for the 9mm and 14 rounds for the .40 S&W. Stainless steel finish. Weight is about 47 oz.

NIB	Exc.	V.G.	Good	Fair	Poor
2100	—	—	—	—	—

P226 Tactical

This 9mm pistol has a 4.98" extended threaded barrel. Fixed sights. Alloy frame. Magazine capacity is 15 rounds. Weight is about 32 oz. Black finish. Ellett Brothers exclusive. Introduced in 2005.

NIB	Exc.	V.G.	Good	Fair	Poor
800	—	—	—	—	

P226 SAS

Double-action semi-auto with 12+1 capacity chambered for .40 S&W. Fixed sights, wood grips, 4.4" barrel, 34 oz., 6.5-lb. trigger. Introduced 2006.

NIB	Exc.	V.G.	Good	Fair	Poor
700	—	—	—	—	

P226R Equinox

An 10+1 or 12+1 capacity single/double-action semi-auto chambered for .40 S&W. Fixed sights, wood grips, 4.4" barrel, 34 oz. Introduced 2006.

NIB	Exc.	V.G.	Good	Fair	Poor
850	—	—	—	—	

Mosquito

This model is essentially a P226 reduced to 90 percent of its original size. Double action/single action trigger and fitted with a 3.98" barrel chambered for the .22 Long Rifle cartridge. Polymer frame with Picatinny rail. Fixed sights. Magazine capacity is 10 rounds. Weight is about 24.5 oz. Black finish. Introduced in 2005.

NIB	Exc.	V.G.	Good	Fair	Poor
360	275	—	—	—	—

P228

This model is a compact version of the P226 fitted with a 3.86" barrel and chambered for the 9mm cartridge. Like the P 226 it is available in blue, K-Kote, or nickel finish with black grips. Overall length is 7.1" and overall height is 5.4". Pistol weighs 26.1 oz. No longer in production.

NIB	Exc.	V.G.	Good	Fair	Poor
650	600	550	450	350	250

NOTE: For K-Kote finish add $50 and for nickel slide add $50.

P228 Limited (New Model)

Reintroduced in 2004 in a limited edition, this 9mm pistol features a Hi-Viz fiber optic front sight and 2-dot rear sight. One 15-round pre-ban magazine magazine included. Weight is aobut 26 oz.

NIB	Exc.	V.G.	Good	Fair	Poor
800	600	—	—	—	—

P229

This model is similar to the P228 except that it is chambered for the .40 S&W cartridge and has a blackened stainless steel slide and lightweight aluminum alloy frame. The slide is slightly larger to accommodate the more powerful cartridge. In 1996 the 9mm chamber was also offered in this model. Its overall length is 7.1" and overall height is 5.4". Introduced in 1992. The pistol weighs 27.54 oz. and has a magazine capacity of 12 rounds. In 1994 the company introduced a new caliber for this model; the .357 SIG developed by Federal. Magazine capacity is 12 rounds.

NIB	Exc.	V.G.	Good	Fair	Poor
700	600	500	375	300	200

P229 Nickel

Same as the standard P229 but with full nickel finish over a stainless steel slide and alloy frame. Weight is about 27.5 oz. Introduced in 1998.

NIB	Exc.	V.G.	Good	Fair	Poor
775	650	500	—	—	—

P229 Stainless

Introduced in 2005, has all the same features as the standard P229 except for the stainless steel slide and frame. Weight is about 41 oz. Magazine capacity is 12 rounds.

NIB	Exc.	V.G.	Good	Fair	Poor
775	—	—	—	—	—

P229 Sport

Chambered for the .357 SIG cartridge this model is fitted with a 4.8" barrel with a muzzle compensator. Adjustable target sights. Both frame and slide are stainless steel. Magazine capacity is 10 rounds. Weight is approximately 41 oz. Introduced in 1998.

NIB	Exc.	V.G.	Good	Fair	Poor
1150	800	—	—	—	—

P229 Limited

This .40 S&W pistol features a 3.9" barrel with fixed sights. Stainless steel slide with Nitron finish. Scroll engraving on top of slide, high polished 24 kt gold accents on trigger, hammer, magazine catch, and grip screws. Hardwood grips.

NIB	Exc.	V.G.	Good	Fair	Poor
915	675	—	—	—	—

P229 Combo

This pistol is chambered for the .40 S&W cartridge and fitted with a 3.9" barrel. Fixed sights. Black Nitron finish. A spare SIG barrel chambered for the .357 SIG is included. Magazine capacity is 10 rounds. Weight is about 30 oz. Introduced in 2004.

NIB	Exc.	V.G.	Good	Fair	Poor
845	625	—	—	—	—

P229R DAK

Introduced in 2005 this model features double action only DAK trigger system with double strike capability. Chambered for the 9mm, .357 SIG, or .40 S&W cartridge with a 4.4" barrel. Fixed sights. Magazine capacity is 10, 12, or 15 rounds depending on caliber. Weight is about 32 oz. for 9mm and 34 oz. for .357 SIG or .40 S&W models.

NIB	Exc.	V.G.	Good	Fair	Poor
840	625	—	—	—	—

P239

Introduced in 1996 this pistol is chambered for the 9mm, .40 S&W, or .357 SIG cartridge. It is double/single-action or double-action-only. The barrel is 3.6" long and the overall length is 6.6". Weight is 25 oz. It is fitted with a single column magazine with 7 rounds for the .357 SIG and 8 rounds for the 9mm.

NIB	Exc.	V.G.	Good	Fair	Poor
600	450	350	250	200	150

NOTE: All of the above SIG pistols from the P220 to the P239 are available with "SIGLITE" night sights. Add $80 for these optional sights.

P239 Limited

This .40 S&W model features a rainbow titanium slide. Trigger, hammer, grip screws, and control levers also rainbow titanuim. Magazine capacity is 7 rounds. Weight is about 27 oz. Introduced in 2004.

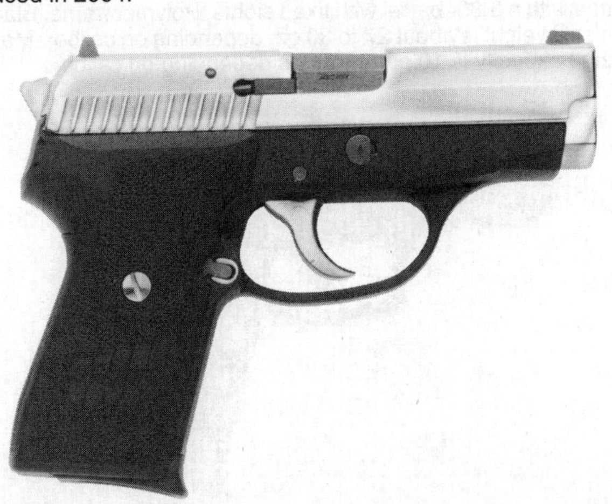

NIB	Exc.	V.G.	Good	Fair	Poor
670	500	—	—	—	—

P230

This is a semi-automatic, compact, pocket-type pistol chambered for .22 LR, .32 ACP, .380 ACP, and 9mm Ultra. It has a 3.62" barrel and either a 10-, 8-, or 7-round magazine, depending on the caliber chambered. The pistol weighs between 16.2 oz. and 20.8 oz. The finish is blued or stainless, with black plastic grips; and it was manufactured from 1976. In 1996 a two-tone finish was offered. No longer in production.

NIB	Exc.	V.G.	Good	Fair	Poor
450	375	300	250	200	150

NOTE: For stainless steel finish add $85 and for stainless steel slide add $35.

P232

An improved model of the P230. Incorporates numerous changes to improve function and reliability. Basic features, operation, and dimensions remain the same as the P230.

NIB	Exc.	V.G.	Good	Fair	Poor
450	375	300	250	200	150

P232 (1998 Model)

In 1998 this model has as standard features night sights and Hogue grips with an all stainless steel finish. Chambered for .380 ACP, the pistol has a 7-round magazine capacity. Weight is about 21 oz.

NIB	Exc.	V.G.	Good	Fair	Poor
500	375	300	—	—	—

P232 Limited

This .380 pistol features a black finish, night sights, and satin nickel accents. Hogue rubber grips with finger grooves. Magazine capacity is 7 rounds. Weight is about 28 oz. Introduced in 2004.

NIB	Exc.	V.G.	Good	Fair	Poor
585	425	—	—	—	—

P245 Compact

Introduced in 1999 this model is chambered for the .45 ACP cartridge. It is fitted with a 3.9" barrel. Magazine capacity is 6 rounds. Overall length is 7.3". Weight is about 28 oz. Available finishes are blue and K-Kote. SIGLITE night sights are also available.

NIB	Exc.	V.G.	Good	Fair	Poor
775	600	—	—	—	—

P245 Custom Shop

Introduced in 2004 this .45 ACP pistol is limited to 75 guns. It features a Teflon-impregnated nickel slide, frame, trigger, hammer, etc. Hand-tuned action. Target crowned barrel. Novak low-carry sights, limited edition markings. Weight is about 27 oz.

NIB	Exc.	V.G.	Good	Fair	Poor
2100	—	—	—	—	—

SIG PRO SERIES

SP2340

Introduced in 1998 this model is chambered for the .357 SIG or .40 S&W cartridge. It is built on a polymer frame with accessory rails on the dust cover. Barrel length is 3.9". Standard finish is blue. Weight is about 28 oz. Comes with two sets of interchangeable grips and two 10-round magazines. Available in single-action/double-action or double-action-only.

SP2340 with laser sights

NIB	Exc.	V.G.	Good	Fair	Poor
600	475	—	—	—	—

SP2009

Similar to the SP2340 but chambered for the 9mm cartridge. Weight is about 25 oz. Magazine capacity is 10 rounds.

NIB	Exc.	V.G.	Good	Fair	Poor
375	300	—	—	—	—

SP2022

Chambered for the 9mm, .357 SIG, or .40 S&W cartridges and fitted with a 3.85" barrel with fixed sights. Polymer frame. Black finish. Weight is about 27 to 30 oz. depending on caliber. Magazine capacity is 10 or 12 rounds depending on caliber.

NIB	Exc.	V.G.	Good	Fair	Poor
575	475	—	—	—	—

Model GSR

This .45 ACP pistol was introduced in 2004. Fitted with a 5" barrel. Single-action only. It is offered with white stainless steel frame and slide or blued frame and slide. Also offered with black Nitron finish. Tac rail standard. Hand fitted. Magazine capacity is 8 rounds. Weight is about 39 oz.

NIB	Exc.	V.G.	Good	Fair	Poor
775	650	—	—	—	—

REVOLUTION SERIES

Revolution

All-stainless frames and slides in four configurations. Novak Night Sights, Rose- or Diamond Wood custom grips. Stainless or Nitron finish. 8+1 capacity, 45 ACP, single-action, 5" barrel, 40.3 oz. Introduced 2006.

NIB	Exc.	V.G.	Good	Fair	Poor
675	—	—	—	—	—

Revolution Custom STX

Single-action .45 ACP stainless semi-auto with 8+1 capacity. Adjustable combat night sights and custom wood grip panels, 5" barrel, 40.6 oz. Introduced 2006.

NIB	Exc.	V.G.	Good	Fair	Poor
900	—	—	—	—	—

Revolution TTT

Stainless semi-auto with 8+1 capacity. Single-action .45 ACP. Adjustable combat night sights and custom wood grip panels, 5" barrel, 40.3 oz. Introduced 2006.

NIB	Exc.	V.G.	Good	Fair	Poor
950	—	—	—	—	—

Revolution XO

Single-action .45 ACP stainless semi-auto with 8+1 capacity. Polymer grip panels. 8.65" LOA, 5" barrel, 40.3 oz. Introduced 2006.

NIB	Exc.	V.G.	Good	Fair	Poor
859	—	—	—	—	—

Revolution Target

Single-action .45 ACP stainless semi-auto with 8+1 capacity. Adjustable target night sights. Custom wood grip panels, 5" barrel, 40.3 oz. Stainless or Nitron finish. Introduced 2006.

NIB	Exc.	V.G.	Good	Fair	Poor
725	—	—	—	—	—

Revolution Carry

Single-action .45 ACP stainless semi-auto with 8+1 capacity. Fixed sights. Custom wood grip panels, 4" barrel, 35.4 oz. Stainless or Nitron finish. Introduced 2006.

NIB	Exc.	V.G.	Good	Fair	Poor
600	—	—	—	—	—

Revolution Compact

Stainless semi-auto single-action .45 ACP with 6+1 capacity. Fixed sights. Custom wood grip panels, 4" barrel, 30.3 oz. Stainless or Nitron finish. Introduced 2006.

NIB	Exc.	V.G.	Good	Fair	Poor
600	—	—	—	—	—

Revolution Custom Compact RCS

Stainless semi-auto single-action .45 ACP with 6+1 capacity. Fixed sights. Custom wood grip panels, 4" barrel, 30.3 oz. Stainless or Nitron finish. Introduced 2006.

NIB	Exc.	V.G.	Good	Fair	Poor
700	—	—	—	—	—

Revolution Compact SAS

Dehorned version of Revolution Compact.

NIB	Exc.	V.G.	Good	Fair	Poor
750	—	—	—	—	—

Revolution Compact C3

Similar to Revolution Compact but with black anodized alloy frame and stainless or Nitron-finished slide.

NIB	Exc.	V.G.	Good	Fair	Poor
900	—	—	—	—	—

SHOTGUNS

Model SA3 Hunter

Introduced in 1997 this over-and-under shotgun is chambered for the 20 gauge shell and fitted with 26" or 28" barrels. It has single-selective trigger and automatic ejectors. The stock is figured walnut with pistol grip. The receiver is polished steel with engraved game scenes. Weight is approximately 6.8 lbs.

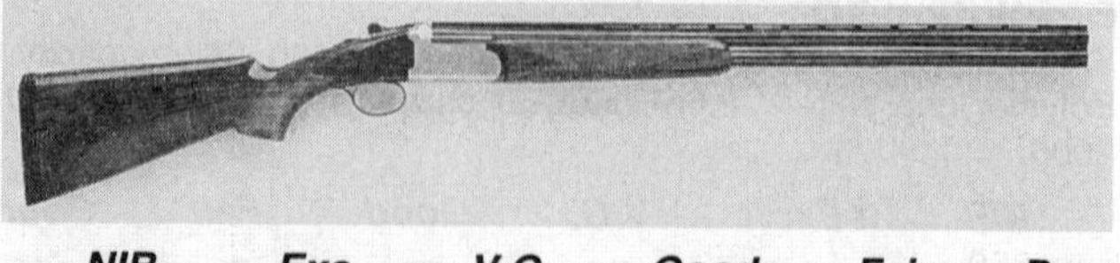

NIB	Exc.	V.G.	Good	Fair	Poor
1325	1050	750	—		

Model SA3 Sporting

This 12 gauge over-and-under gun was introduced in 1998 and features a 28" or 29.5" barrel with wide 11mm rib and front and mid-target sights. Both barrels and action are blued. Walnut stock with pistol grip and recoil pad. Weight is about 7.3 lbs.

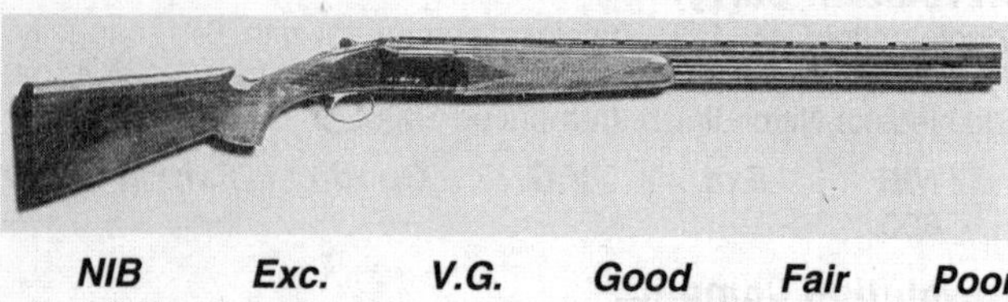

NIB	Exc.	V.G.	Good	Fair	Poor
1675	1250	—	—	—	—

Model SA5 Sporting

Introduced in 1998 this 12 gauge is fitted with a choice of 28" or 29.5" barrels. Single-selective trigger and automatic ejectors are standard. Barrels are fitted with a 10mm rib. Receiver is polished steel with engraved clay target on each side. Weight is about 7.6 lbs.

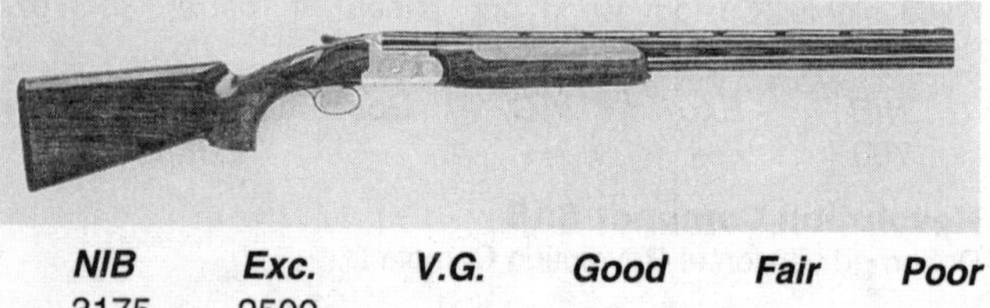

NIB	Exc.	V.G.	Good	Fair	Poor
3175	2500	—	—	—	—

AURORA SERIES

These shotguns were first imported and introduced into the SIG product line in 2000. They are made in Italy by B. Rizzini. All the guns in this series are over-and-under guns.

Aurora TR Field Shotguns

All of the TR field guns are offered in 12, 20, and 28 gauge as well as .410 bore. All have single triggers and ejectors. Barrel lengths are 26" or 28". Weights vary from 7 lbs. for the 12 gauge to 6 lbs. for the .410. Select walnut stock with oil finish. Cut checkering of 20 lpi. Choke tubes on the 12 and 20 gauge models and fixed chokes on the 28 and .410 models.

TR 20U

This model features a boxlock action with case hardened frame. No engraving. Straight-grip stock.

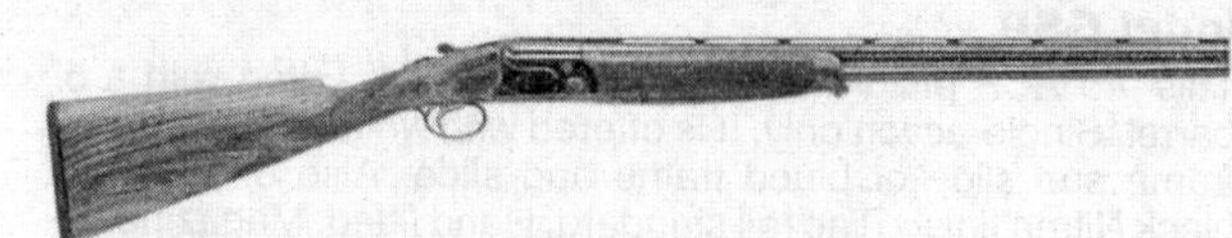

Aurora TR 20U 28 gauge

NIB	Exc.	V.G.	Good	Fair	Poor
1850	1400	—	—	—	—

TR 20

This model features a boxlock action with nickel finish and no engraving. Pistol grip.

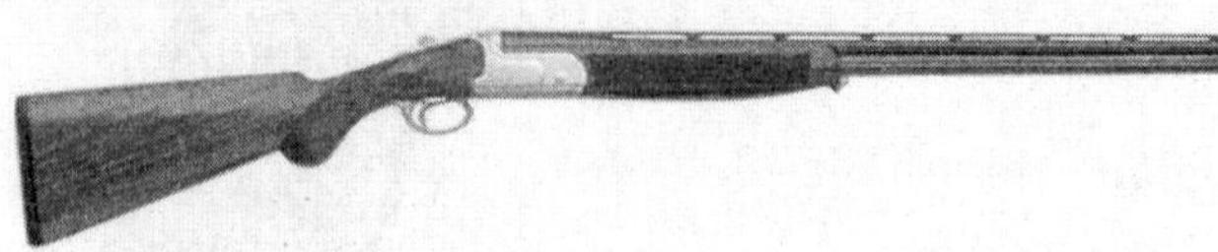

Aurora TR 20 .410 bore

NIB	Exc.	V.G.	Good	Fair	Poor
1850	1400	—	—	—	—

TR 30

This model features a case hardened action with side plates. No engraving. Pistol grip.

Aurora TR 30 12 gauge

NIB	Exc.	V.G.	Good	Fair	Poor
2225	1650	—	—	—	—

TR 40 Silver

This model features a silver action with side plates with gold inlaid game scenes. Pistol grip.

Aurora TR 40 Silver

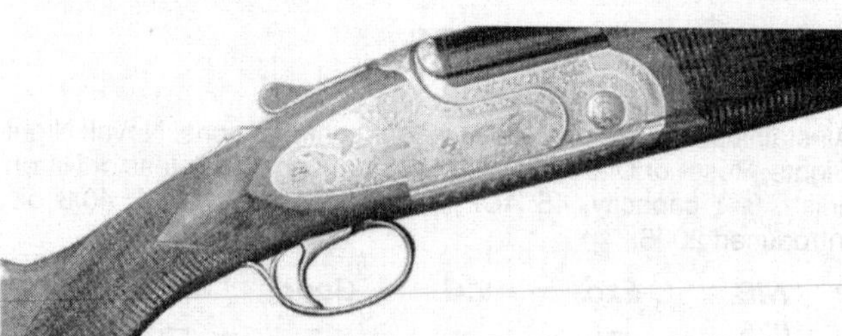

Aurora TR 40 Silver receiver

NIB	Exc.	V.G.	Good	Fair	Poor
2575	1950	—	—	—	—

TR 40 Gold

This features a case hardened action with side plates and gold inlaid game scenes. Pistol grip.

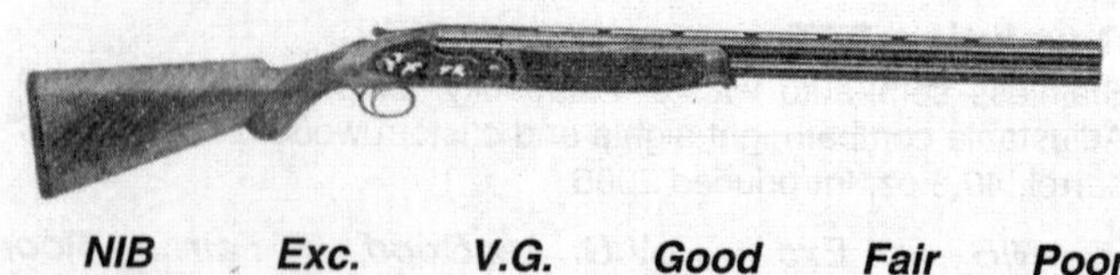

NIB	Exc.	V.G.	Good	Fair	Poor
2675	2000	—	—	—	—

New Englander

Introduced in 2000 jointly by SIG and L.L. Bean this over-and-under gun is chambered in 12 and 20 gauge with choice of 26" or 28" barrels. Single-selective trigger, auto ejectors, choke tubes all standard. L.L. Bean logo inlaid in gold on receiver. Select turkish walnut stock with oil finish. Prince of Wales-style pistol grip and rubber recoil pad.

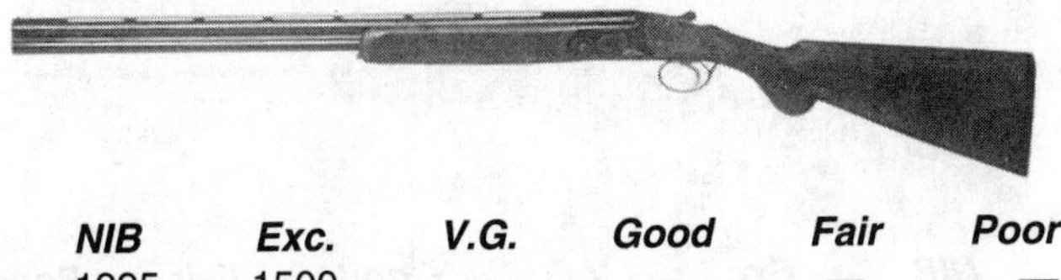

NIB	Exc.	V.G.	Good	Fair	Poor
1995	1500	—	—	—	—

AURORA TT 25 COMPETITION SHOTGUNS

TT25

This model is offered in both 12 and 20 gauge with a choice of 28" to 32" barrels for the 12 gauge and 28" or 30" barrels for the 20 gauge. Choke tubes. Single-selective auto ejectors are standard. Wide competition vent rib. Pistol grip on select walnut stock with 20 lpi checkering. Weight for 12 gauge is about 7.25 lbs. while the 20 gauge weighs about 6.75 lbs.

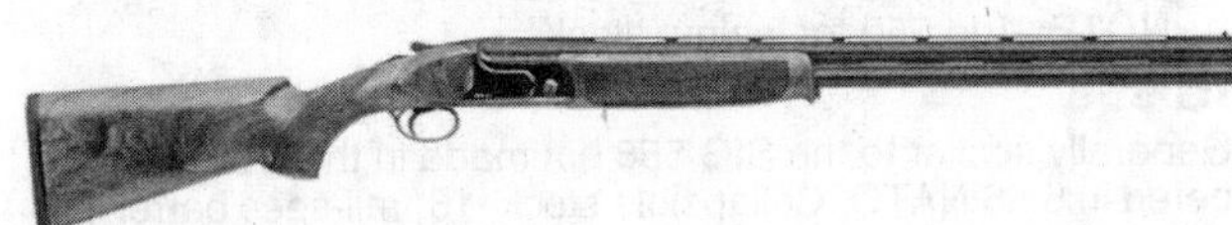

Aurora TT 25 12 gauge

NIB	Exc.	V.G.	Good	Fair	Poor
1995	1500	—	—	—	—

TT45

Similar to the TT25 but with the addition of a case hardened receiver and side plates with engraving and gold inlay game scenes.

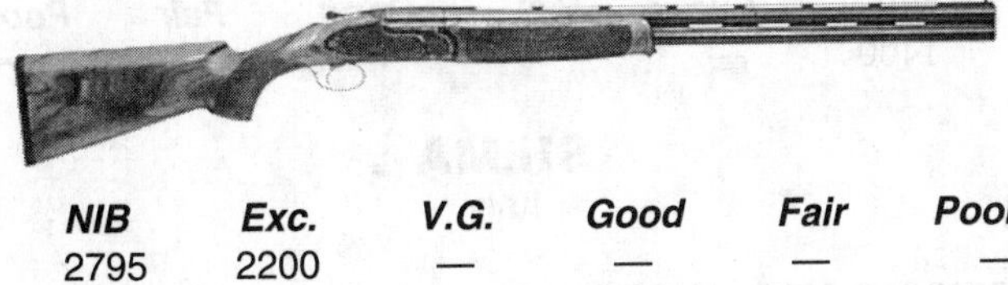

NIB	Exc.	V.G.	Good	Fair	Poor
2795	2200	—	—	—	—

RIFLES

SIG AMT

This is a semi-automatic rifle chambered for .308 cartridge. Fitted with a 19" barrel and wooden buttstock and forearm. Folding bipod standard. Box magazine capacity is 5, 10, or 20 rounds. Weight is about 10 lbs. Built from 1960 to 1974.

Courtesy Rock Island Auction Company

NIB	Exc.	V.G.	Good	Fair	Poor
4500	3800	3100	2500	1500	1000

SIG PE-57

Similar to the above but chambered for the 7.5x55 Swiss cartridge.

NIB	Exc.	V.G.	Good	Fair	Poor
4500	3800	3000	2500	1500	1000

SIG 550

This semi-automatic rifle is chambered for .223 cartridge and fitted with a 18" barrel.

NIB	Exc.	V.G.	Good	Fair	Poor
9000	7000	5500	3000	—	—

SIG 551

Same as above but fitted with a 16" barrel.

NIB	Exc.	V.G.	Good	Fair	Poor
10500	9500	7500	4000	—	—

SSG 2000

This is a high-grade, bolt-action, sniping-type rifle chambered for .223, 7.5mm Swiss, .300 Weatherby Magnum, and .308 Winchester. It has a 24" barrel and was furnished without sights. It has a 4-round box magazine. The finish is matte blue with a thumbhole-style stippled walnut stock with an adjustable cheekpiece. This model was discontinued in 1986.

NIB	Exc.	V.G.	Good	Fair	Poor
8000	6000	3500	1500	—	—

SSG 3000

Chambered for the .308 Win. cartridge this model is fitted with a 23.4" barrel and ambidextrous McMillian Tactical stock. Magazine capacity is 5 rounds. Overall length is 46.5", and approximate weight is 12 lbs. This model comes in three different packages.

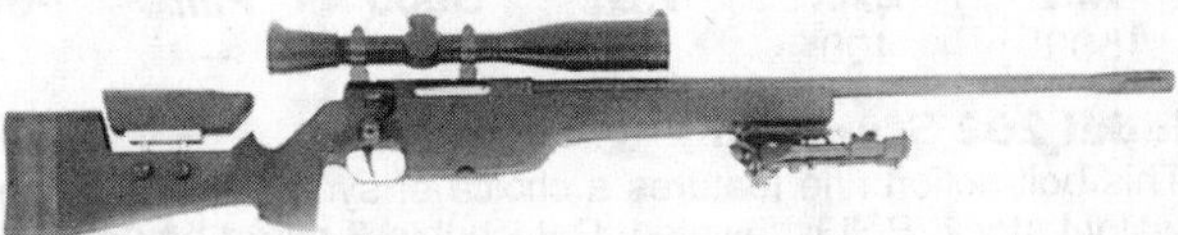

Level I

Base model with no bipod or scope, but with carrying case.

NIB	Exc.	V.G.	Good	Fair	Poor
2550	2000	—	—	—	—

Level II

At this level a Leupold Vari-X III 3.5-10x40mm Deplex scope and Harris bipod with carrying case.

NIB	Exc.	V.G.	Good	Fair	Poor
3500	2750	—	—	—	—

Level III

Rifle is supplied with a Leupold Mark 4 M1-10x40mm Mil-Dot Scope with Harris bipod and carrying case.

NIB	Exc.	V.G.	Good	Fair	Poor
4500	3500	—	—	—	—

Conversion Kit—.22 LR

In 2001 a .22 caliber conversion was offered for the SSG 3000 rifle. The kit includes a heavy contured barrel, bolt, and 5-round magazine.

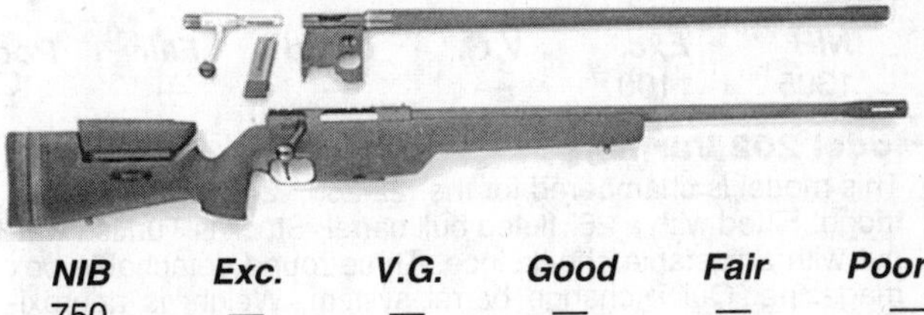

NIB	Exc.	V.G.	Good	Fair	Poor
750	—	—	—	—	—

Model SHR 970

Introduced in 1998 this bolt-action rifle is chambered for the .25-06 Rem., .270, .280 Rem., .30-06, or .308 cartridges. It has a 22" barrel and the receiver is drilled and tapped for scope mounts. Detachable box magazine. Stock is black synthetic or walnut. Barrels are interchangeable. Weight is about 7.2 lbs.

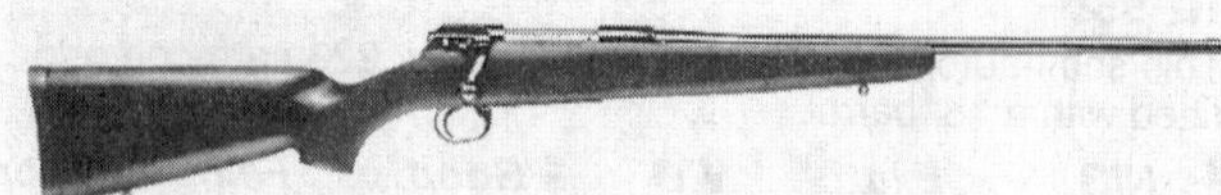

NIB	Exc.	V.G.	Good	Fair	Poor
500	400	—	—	—	—

NOTE: Add $30 for walnut stock.

Model SHR 970 Magnum

Same as above but chambered for 7mm Rem. Mag or .300 Win. Mag. Barrel length is 24". Weight is about 7.4 lbs.

NIB	Exc.	V.G.	Good	Fair	Poor
500	400	—	—	—	—

NOTE: Add $30 for walnut stock.

Model SHR 970 Tactical

This model was introduced in 2000 and features a McMillan stock, non-reflective metal coating, heavy fluted contoured barrel, integral muzzlebrake. The rifle is chambered for .308 Win. or .300 Win. Mag cartridges. Receiver is drilled and tapped for scope mount and the stock has a fitted rubber recoil pad.

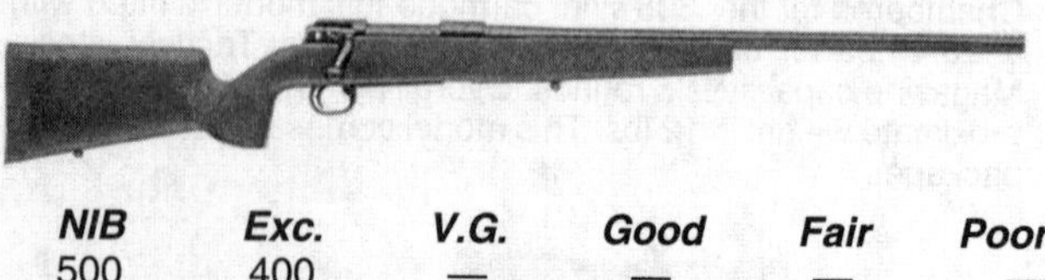

NIB	Exc.	V.G.	Good	Fair	Poor
500	400	—	—	—	—

Model 202 Standard

This bolt-action rifle features a choice of synthetic or Turkish walnut stock. Bolt is jeweled. Detachable 3-round box magazine. Offered in standard calibers from .22-250 to .30-06 and magnum calibers from 7mm Rem. Mag. to .375 H&H Mag. Barrel length is 24" for standard calibers and 26" for magnum calibers. Weight is about 7.5 lbs. depending on caliber.

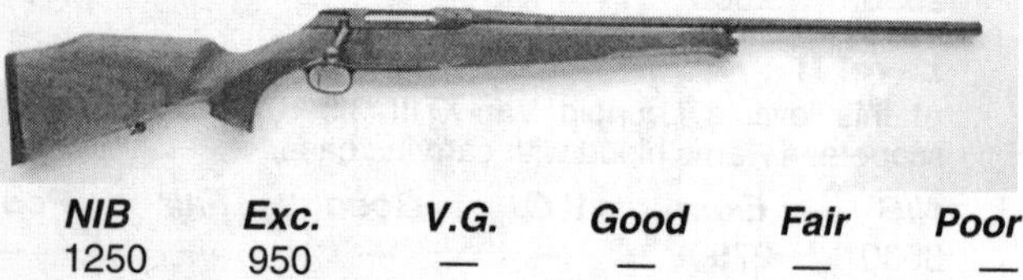

NIB	Exc.	V.G.	Good	Fair	Poor
1250	950	—	—	—	—

Model 202 Lightweight

This model features a black synthetic stock fluted barrel chambered for the .22-250, .243, .25-06, .270, or .30-05 calibers. Barrel length is 24". Magazine capacity is 3 rounds. Alloy receiver and quick change barrel system are standard. Weight is about 6.5 lbs. Introduced in 2001.

NIB	Exc.	V.G.	Good	Fair	Poor
1395	1100	—	—	—	—

Model 202 Varmint

This model is chambered for the .22-250, .243, or .25-06 cartridge. Fitted with a 26" fluted bull barrel. Stock is Turkish walnut with adjustable cheekpiece. Three-round detachable box magazine. Quick change barrel system. Weight is approximately 9.5 lbs.

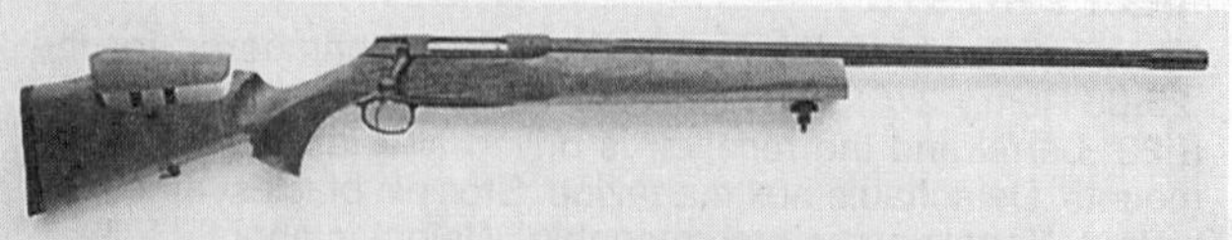

NIB	Exc.	V.G.	Good	Fair	Poor
1495	1200	—	—	—	—

Model 202 Supreme

This bolt-action model is chambered for .243, .25-06, 6.5x55 Swedish, .270 Win., .308 Win., or .30-06. It is fitted with a 24" barrel with choice of synthetic or walnut stock. Magazine capacity is 3 rounds. Weight is approximately 7.7 lbs. No sights.

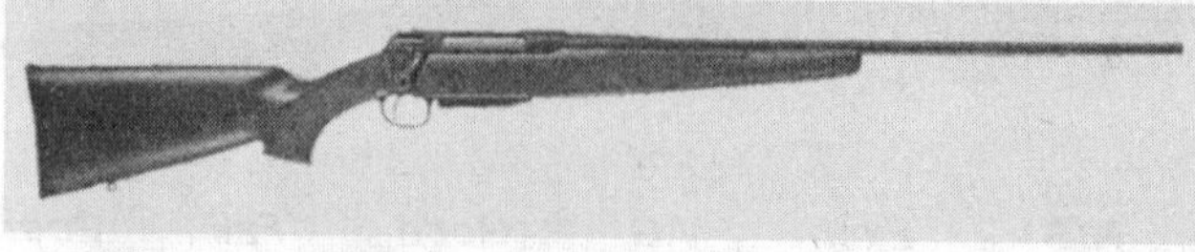

NIB	Exc.	V.G.	Good	Fair	Poor
1050	775	—	—	—	—

NOTE: Add $50 for walnut stock.

Model 202 Supreme Magnum

As above but chambered for 7mm Rem. Mag, .300 Win. Mag, .300 Wby Mag., or .375 H&H Mag. Magazine capacity is 3 rounds. Choice of synthetic or walnut stock. Weight is about 8.4 lbs.

NIB	Exc.	V.G.	Good	Fair	Poor
1250	850	—	—	—	—

NOTE: Add $50 for walnut stock.

SIG 556

Generally similar to the SIG 556 but made in the USA. Chambered in 5.56 NATO. Collapsible stock, 16" mil-spec barrel, picatinny rail and all the trendy tactical goodies. Introduced 2006.

NIB	Exc	V.G.	Good	Fair	Poor
1400	—	—	—	—	—

SILMA

Italy

STANDARD MODELS

Model 70 EJ

This over-and-under gun is chambered for the 12 or 20 gauge shell with 28" vent rib barrels with choke tubes. Single-selective trigger and auto ejectors. Checkered walnut stock. Weight for 12 gauge is about 7.6 lbs. and for the 20 gauge about 6.9 lbs. Silver engraved receiver.

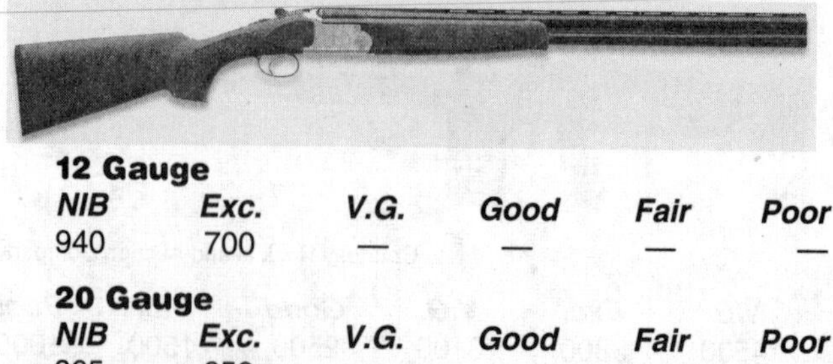

12 Gauge

NIB	Exc.	V.G.	Good	Fair	Poor
940	700	—	—	—	—

20 Gauge

NIB	Exc.	V.G.	Good	Fair	Poor
865	650	—	—	—	—

DELUXE MODELS

Model 70 EJ

This model is chambered for the 12, 20, 28, or .410 shell and fitted with 28" vent rib barrels. Checkered select walnut stock with deluxe engraved receiver. Weights are 7.6 lbs. for 12 gauge and 6.9 lbs. for smaller gauges.

12 Gauge

NIB	Exc.	V.G.	Good	Fair	Poor
1020	750	—	—	—	—

20 Gauge

NIB	Exc.	V.G.	Good	Fair	Poor
940	700	—	—	—	—

28 and .410 Gauge

NIB	Exc.	V.G.	Good	Fair	Poor
1060	800	—	—	—	—

Superlight

This model is offered in 12 or 20 gauge with 28" barrels with choke tubes. Checkered select wanut stock. Receiver is made from alloy steel. Weight for 12 gauge is about 6.7 lbs. and about 6.3 lbs. for the 20 gauge.

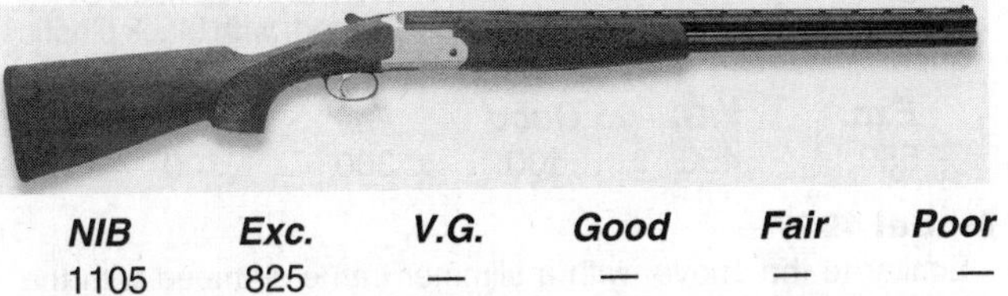

NIB	Exc.	V.G.	Good	Fair	Poor
1105	825	—	—	—	—

Clays Model

This model is designed for sporting clays and is chambered for the 12 gauge 3" shell. Fitted with a 28" barrel with choke tubes and wide ventilated rib. Checkered select walnut stock.

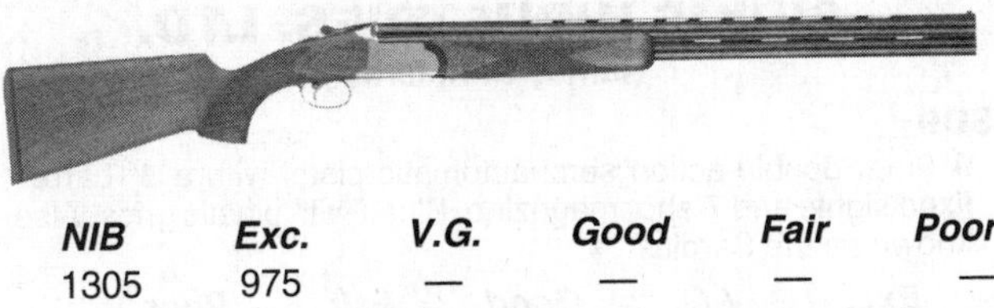

NIB	Exc.	V.G.	Good	Fair	Poor
1305	975	—	—	—	—

SIMPLEX

Unknown

Simplex

A German design based on the Bergmann-Mars pistol. An 8mm caliber semi-automatic pistol with a 2.6" barrel and a front mounted 5-round magazine. Blued with hard rubber grips having the trade name "Simplex" cast in them. Manufactured from approximately 1901 to around 1906. Early samples may have come from Germany and later pistols are thought to have been produced in Belgium.

Exc.	V.G.	Good	Fair	Poor
1500	950	500	400	200

SIMPSON, R. J.

New York, New York

Pocket Pistol

A .41 caliber single-shot percussion pocket pistol with a 2.5" barrel, German silver mounts and walnut stock. Manufactured during the 1850s and 1860s.

Exc.	V.G.	Good	Fair	Poor
—	—	1750	700	300

SIMSON & COMPANY

Suhl, Germany

SEE—Luger

NOTE: The models listed and pictured are taken from a mid-1930s Simson catalog. Because the company was Jewish-owned the Nazis took control in the mid-1930s changing the name to "Berlin Suhler Waffen." Prices are estimates.

SHOTGUNS

Model 235

Side-by-side shotgun chambered for 12 or 16 gauge with Anson & Deely action. Scalloped frame with scroll engraving. Walnut stock with pistol grip. Double triggers.

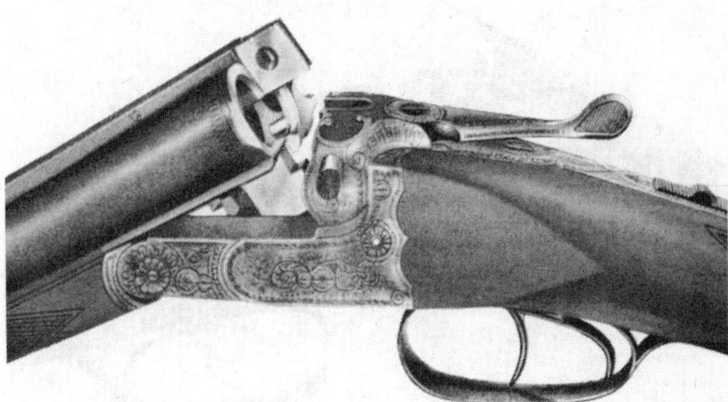

Courtesy Jim Cate

Exc.	V.G.	Good	Fair	Poor
900	700	550	400	350

Model 73

Similar to the above model but with more scroll engraving coverage.

Courtesy Jim Cate

Exc.	V.G.	Good	Fair	Poor
950	750	600	400	350

Model 74

This model features deep cut game scene engraving. Select walnut stock with fine-line checkering.

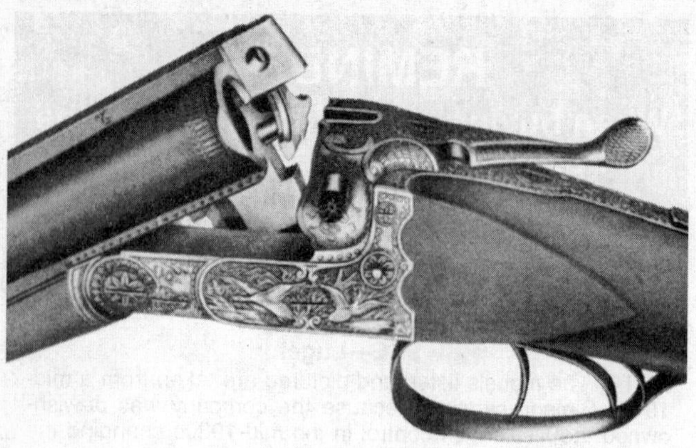

Courtesy Jim Cate

Exc.	V.G.	Good	Fair	Poor
1100	800	600	450	350

Model 74E

Same as above but with automatic ejectors.

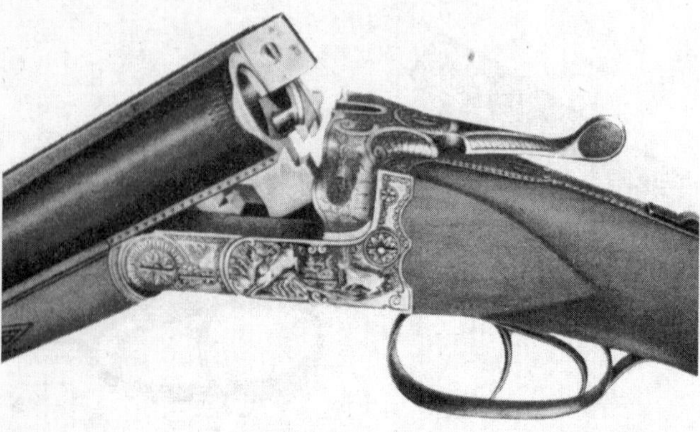

Courtesy Jim Cate

Exc.	V.G.	Good	Fair	Poor
1200	850	650	450	350

Model 76

This side-by-side model is fitted with game scene engraved side plates and offered in 12 or 16 gauge.

Courtesy Jim Cate

Exc.	V.G.	Good	Fair	Poor
1400	1100	800	550	400

Model 76E

As above but with automatic ejectors.

Courtesy Jim Cate

Exc.	V.G.	Good	Fair	Poor
1500	1200	850	550	400

PISTOLS

Model 1922

A 6.35mm semi-automatic pistol with a 2" barrel and 6-shot magazine. The slide marked "Selbstlade Pistole Simson DRP" and "Waffenfabrik Simson & Co Suhl." Blued, with black plastic grips.

Exc.	V.G.	Good	Fair	Poor
550	450	400	300	100

Model 1927

Similar to the above, with a slimmer frame stamped with the trademark of three overlapping triangles having the letter "S" enclosed.

Exc.	V.G.	Good	Fair	Poor
550	450	400	300	100

SIRKIS INDUSTRIES, LTD.

Ramat-Gan, Israel

SD9

A 9mm double-action semi-automatic pistol with a 3" barrel, fixed sights and 7-shot magazine. Blued with plastic grips. Also known as the Sardius.

Exc.	V.G.	Good	Fair	Poor
325	275	225	175	100

Model 35 Match Rifle

A .22 caliber single-shot bolt-action rifle with a 26" free floating barrel, adjustable rear sight and adjustable trigger. Blued with a walnut stock.

Exc.	V.G.	Good	Fair	Poor
600	550	500	400	200

Model 36 Sniper's Rifle

A 7.62x54mm caliber semi-automatic rifle with a 22" barrel. Matte blued with a composition stock.

Exc.	V.G.	Good	Fair	Poor
675	600	550	450	200

SKB ARMS COMPANY

Tokyo, Japan

SIDE-BY-SIDE GUNS

Model 100

A boxlock 12 or 20 gauge double-barrel shotgun with 25" to 30" barrels, single-selective trigger and automatic ejectors. Blued with a walnut stock. Imported prior to 1981. Discontinued.

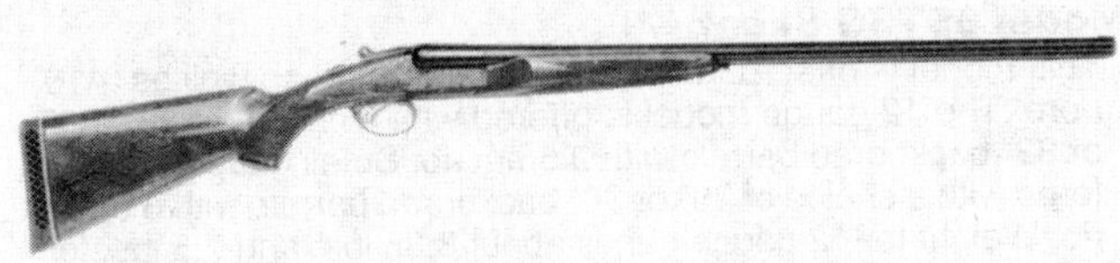

NIB	Exc.	V.G.	Good	Fair	Poor
550	425	375	300	200	100

Model 150

As above, with some engraving, a beavertail forearm and a figured walnut stock. Imported from 1972 to 1974.

NIB	Exc.	V.G.	Good	Fair	Poor
600	450	400	300	200	100

Model 200

As above, with a French case hardened and scalloped receiver. Discontinued.

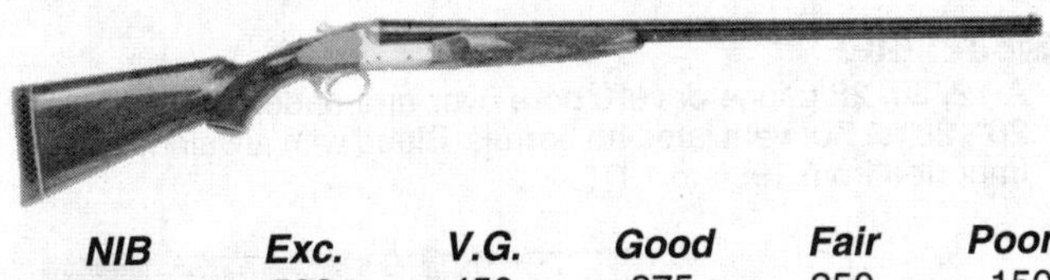

NIB	Exc.	V.G.	Good	Fair	Poor
600	500	450	375	250	150

Model 200E

As above, with an English-style stock. Imported prior to 1989.

NIB	Exc.	V.G.	Good	Fair	Poor
800	675	600	475	275	150

Model 280

Same as the Model 200 but fitted with a straight grip stock. Discontinued.

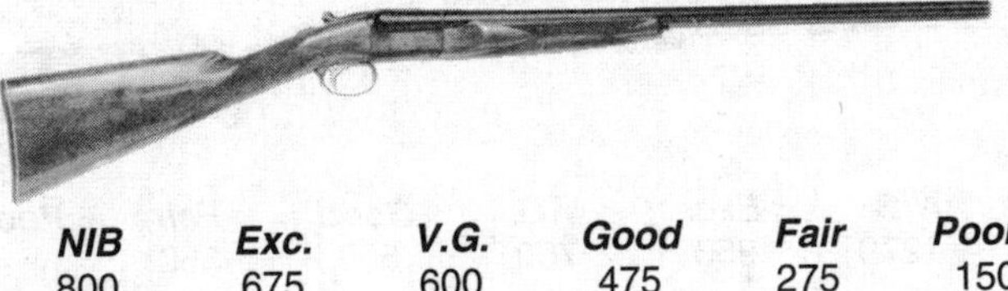

NIB	Exc.	V.G.	Good	Fair	Poor
800	675	600	475	275	150

Model 300

As above, with more engraving and a figured walnut stock. Discontinued.

NIB	Exc.	V.G.	Good	Fair	Poor
800	675	600	475	275	150

Model 385

Similar to the Model 300 but chambered for the 12, 20 or 28 gauge shell. Scroll engraved frame with semi-fancy walnut. Pistol-grip or straight-grip stock. Limited quantities imported. Weight is approximately 7 lbs. depending on barrel length and gauge. Discontinued.

NIB	Exc.	V.G.	Good	Fair	Poor
2000	1500	1000	700	450	200

Model 385 2 Barrel Set

Same as above but with a 20 and 28 gauge set of barrels in either 26" or 28". Discontinued.

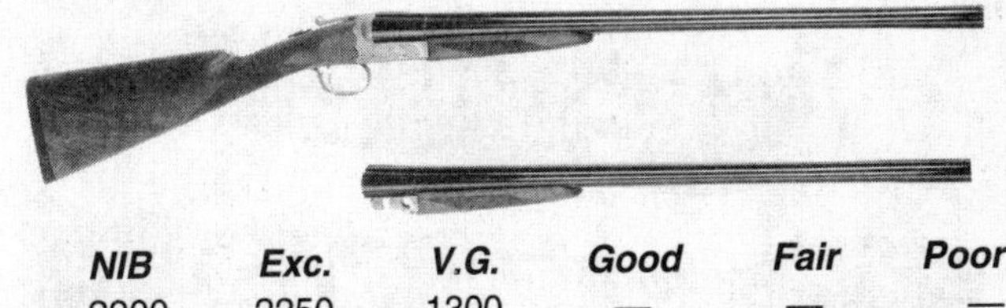

NIB	Exc.	V.G.	Good	Fair	Poor
2900	2250	1300	—	—	—

Model 385 Sporting Clays

This model is chambered for 12, 20, or 28 gauge and fitted with a 28" barrel. Pistol-grip stock. Weight is about 7 lbs. depending on gauge. Discontinued.

NIB	Exc.	V.G.	Good	Fair	Poor
2150	1700	1150	750	500	300

NOTE: For extra set of 20 or 28 gauge barrels add $900.

Model 400E

As above, with engraved false sideplates and an English-style stock. Imported prior to 1990.

NIB	Exc.	V.G.	Good	Fair	Poor
975	875	750	600	300	150

Model 480E

As above, with a French case hardened receiver and more finely figured walnut stocks. Discontinued.

NIB	Exc.	V.G.	Good	Fair	Poor
1200	1000	850	650	350	150

Model 485

This model features an engraved sideplate boxlock action chambered for 12, 20, or 28 gauge with 26" or 28" barrels. Choke tubes. Weight is approximately 7.7 lbs. Discontinued.

NIB	Exc.	V.G.	Good	Fair	Poor
2750	2100	1500	900	650	300

Model 485 2 barrel set

Same as above but with an extra set of barrels in 20/28 gauge combinations with 26" barrels. Choice of pistol-grip or straight-grip stock. Discontinued.

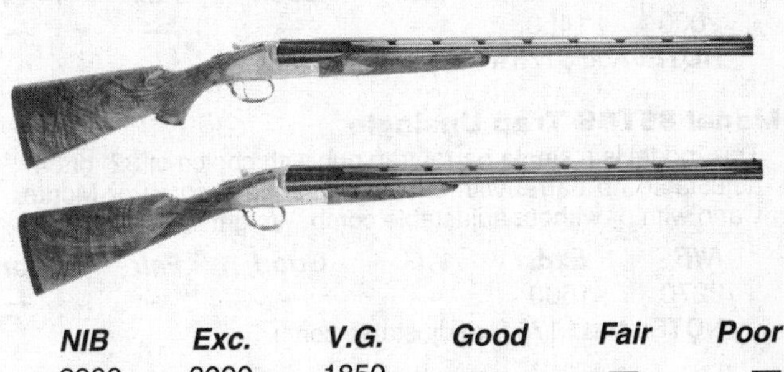

NIB	Exc.	V.G.	Good	Fair	Poor
3900	3000	1850	—	—	—

OVER-AND-UNDER GUNS

MODEL 85TSS SERIES

This series, introduced in 2004, features a low-profile boxlock action fitted with an inertia trigger (12 and 20 gauge), mechanical on 28 and .410 bore. Single-selective trigger with manual safety. Silver nitride finish. Barrels have automatic ejectors, ventilated rib and choke tubes. Pigeon porting is optional. Stocks are American walnut with matte finish and fitted with Pachmayr recoil pad. Adjustable comb stock is optional.

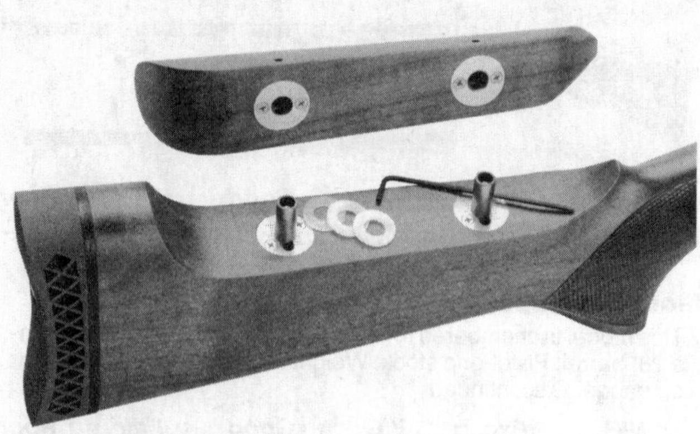

Close-up of adjustable comb

Model 85TSS Sporting Clays

Chambered for the 12, 20, 28 gauge, and .410 bore, this model features a choice of 28", 30", or 32" barrels on the 12 gauge guns and 28" or 30" barrels on the small bore guns. Choke tubes. Choice of fixed or adjustable comb. Choice of multiple barrel sets. Weight on 12 gauge guns is about 8.5 lbs. depending on barrel length and 7.5 lbs. on the smaller bore guns.

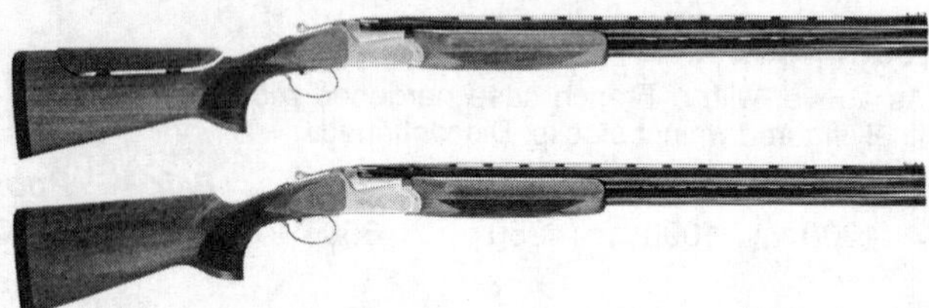

NIB	Exc.	V.G.	Good	Fair	Poor
2000	1450	—	—	—	—

NOTE: Add $175 for adjustable comb, $1,200 for two- barrel sets and $2,800 for three-barrel 20, 28 and .410 set.

Model 85TSS Trap

This 12 gauge 3" trap model is fitted with a choice of 30" or 32" backbored barrels with adjustable 12mm rib. Choice of fixed or adjustable comb with or without Monte Carlo. Weight is about 8.75 lbs.

NIB	Exc.	V.G.	Good	Fair	Poor
2000	1450	—	—	—	—

NOTE: Add $175 for adjustable comb.

Model 85TSS Trap Unsingle

This model is a single barrel trap gun with choice of 32" or 34" adjustable rib barrel with choice of standard comb or Monte Carlo with or without adjustable comb. Weight is about 9 lbs.

NIB	Exc.	V.G.	Good	Fair	Poor
2270	1600	—	—	—	—

NOTE: Add $175 for adjustable comb.

Model 85TSS Trap Unsingle Combo

This model features a 32" or 34" single barrel and 30" or 32" over/under barrels. Barrel rib is adjustable. Choice of Monte Carlo or standard stock with or without adjustable comb.

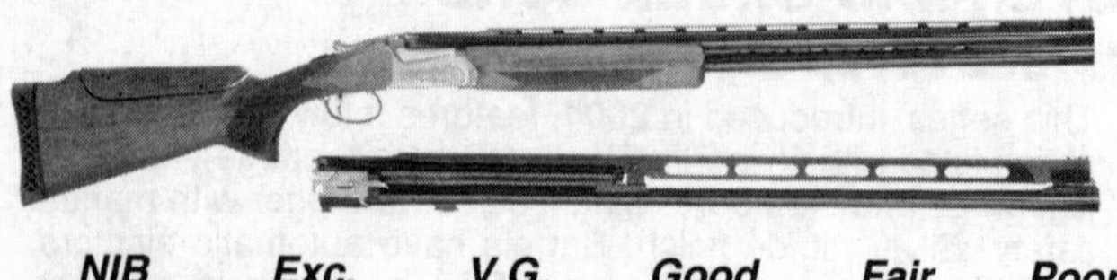

NIB	Exc.	V.G.	Good	Fair	Poor
3190	2250	—	—	—	—

NOTE: Add $175 for adjustable comb.

Model 85TSS Skeet

This model is offered in 12, 20, and 28 gauge as well as .410 bore. The 12 gauge model is offered with a choice of 28", 30" or 32" backbored barrels with 9.5mm rib. Small gauges are offered with a choice of 28" or 30" backbored barrels with 8.5mm rib. Weight for 12 gauge gun is about 8.35 lbs. and 7.5 lbs. for smaller gauges. Choice of fixed or adjustable comb.

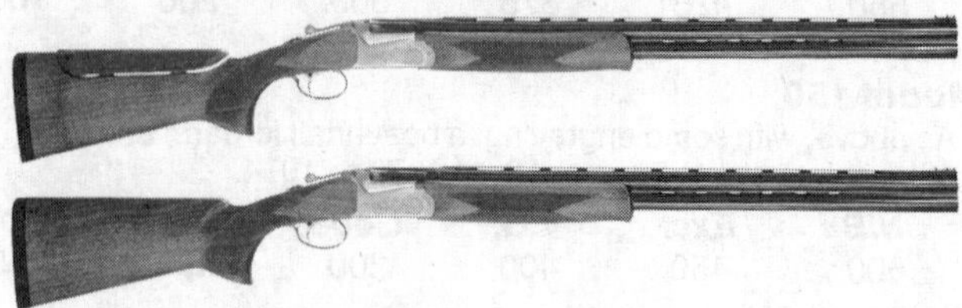

NIB	Exc.	V.G.	Good	Fair	Poor
2000	1450	—	—	—	—

NOTE: Add $175 for adjustable comb. Add $2,800 for three-barrel set.

Model 500

A 12, 20, 28 gauge or .410 bore over-and-under shotgun with 26", 28" or 30" ventilated rib barrels. Blued with a walnut stock. Imported from 1966 to 1979.

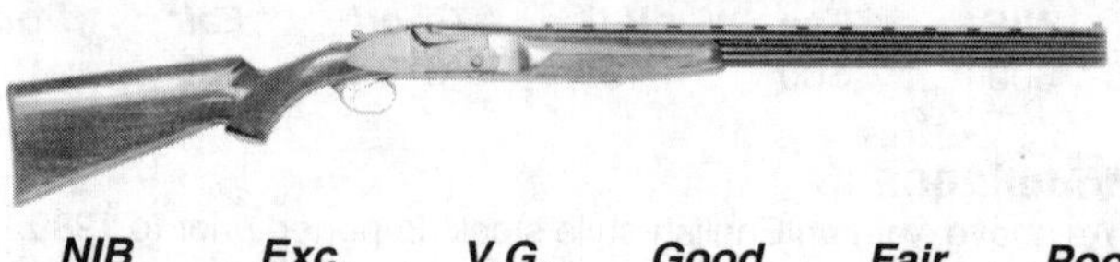

NIB	Exc.	V.G.	Good	Fair	Poor
600	450	375	300	150	100

Model 505 Field

A 12 or 20 gauge over-and-under shotgun with screw-in choke tubes, single-selective trigger and automatic ejectors. Blued, checkered walnut stock.

NIB	Exc.	V.G.	Good	Fair	Poor
1270	950	700	500	350	—

The 505 Series is also produced in sporting clays, trap and skeet configurations, which are valued at approximately 10 percent additional.

Model 505 3-Gauge Skeet Set

As above, with 3 sets of barrels.

NIB	Exc.	V.G.	Good	Fair	Poor
2500	1800	1400	975	650	650

Model 585

Similar to the Model 505 but offered in 12, 20, and 28 gauge and .410 bore as well. Barrel lengths are 26" or 28". Weight is about 7.25 lbs. for small bores and 8 lbs. for 12 gauge guns.

NIB	Exc.	V.G.	Good	Fair	Poor
1550	1150	850	600	400	300

Model 585 Gold Package

Has all of the features of the 585 series with the addition of a gold-plated trigger, gold-plated game scenes, and schnabel forend. Choice of blued or silver receiver.

NIB	Exc.	V.G.	Good	Fair	Poor
1740	1300	850	—	—	—

Model 585 Skeet

Offered in 12, 20, or 28 gauge as well as .410 bore with 28" barrels. Skeet stock and beavertail forearm. Black recoil pad. Weight in 12 gauge about 8 lbs.

NIB	Exc.	V.G.	Good	Fair	Poor
1500	1100	800	550	400	—

Model 585—3 Barrel Skeet Set

Fitted with 20, 28 gauge and .410 bore barrels. Skeet choked.

NIB	Exc.	V.G.	Good	Fair	Poor
2750	2250	1700	1200	850	400

Model 585—3 Barrel Skeet Set Gold Package

Same as above but with engraving and choice of silver or blued receiver.

NIB	Exc.	V.G.	Good	Fair	Poor
3250	2500	1850	—	—	—

Model 585 Youth/Ladies

This model is similar to the 585 but with a shortened length of pull to 13.5". Weight of 20 gauge model is approximately 6.6 lbs. Weight of 12 gauge is about 7.5 lbs.

NIB	Exc.	V.G.	Good	Fair	Poor
1550	1150	750	500	400	200

Model 585 Youth Gold Package

Same as above but with gold trigger, gold-plated game scenes, and schnabel forend. Choice of silver or blued receiver.

NIB	Exc.	V.G.	Good	Fair	Poor
1740	1300	850	—	—	—

Model 585 Upland

Similar to the 585 series except for straight-grip stock. Offered in 12, 20, and 28 gauge all with 26" barrels. Weight for 12 gauge is about 7.75 lbs. and for 20 and 28 gauge about 6.75 lbs.

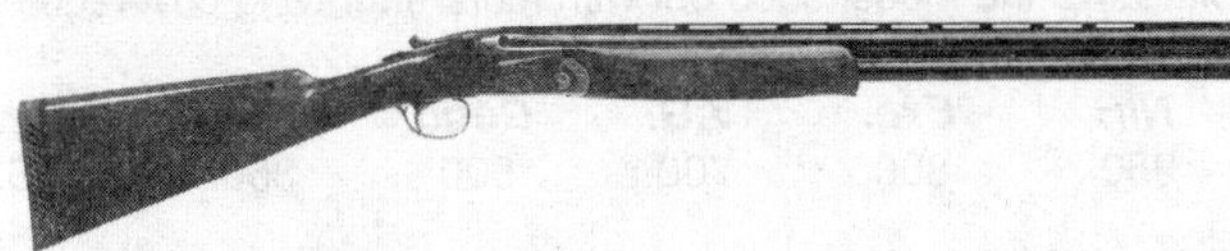

NIB	Exc.	V.G.	Good	Fair	Poor
1550	1150	750	500	400	200

Model 585 Upland Gold Package

This model has the additional gold package features of gold trigger, gold game scenes, and schnabel forend. Choice of silver or blued receiver.

NIB	Exc.	V.G.	Good	Fair	Poor
1740	1300	850	—	—	—

Model 600

As above, with a silver-plated receiver and better quality wood.

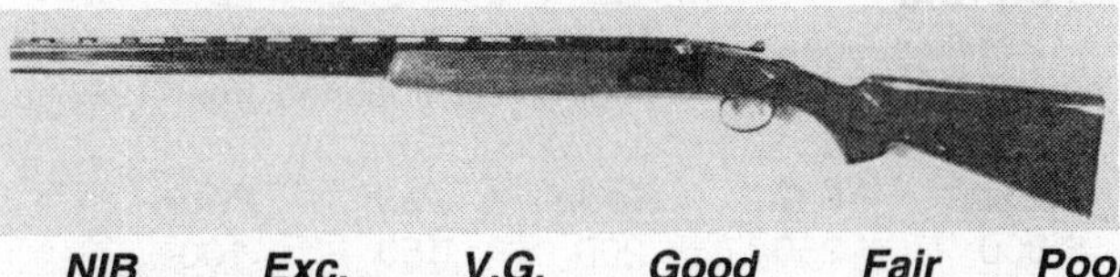

NIB	Exc.	V.G.	Good	Fair	Poor
750	625	550	450	325	150

Model 600 Magnum

As above, chambered for 3", 12 gauge cartridges. Imported from 1969 to 1972.

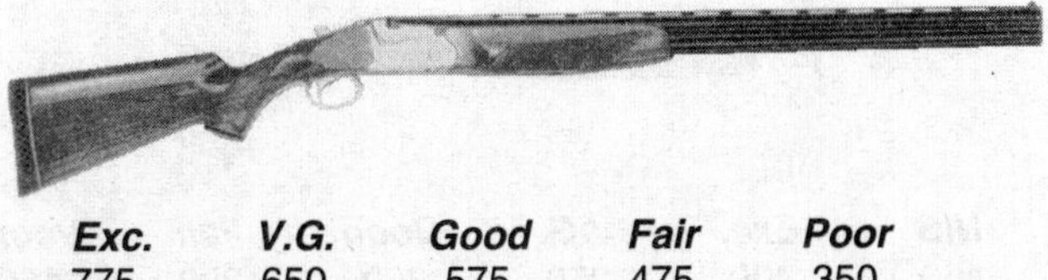

Exc.	V.G.	Good	Fair	Poor
775	650	575	475	350

Model 600 Trap Gun

As above, with 30" or 32" barrels trap choked, with a high comb walnut stock.

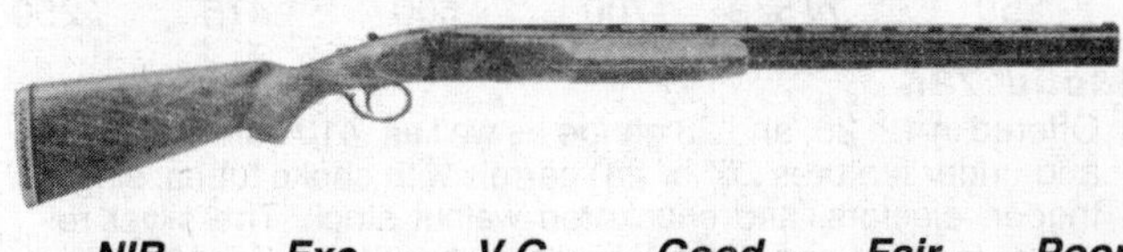

NIB	Exc.	V.G.	Good	Fair	Poor
700	600	525	425	300	150

Model 600 Skeet Gun

As above, chambered for 12, 20, 28 or .410 bore cartridges with 26" or 28" barrels that are skeet choked.

NIB	Exc.	V.G.	Good	Fair	Poor
750	625	550	450	325	150

Model 600 Skeet Combo Set

As above, with an extra set of interchangeable barrels. Furnished with a carrying case.

NIB	Exc.	V.G.	Good	Fair	Poor
1000	700	550	450	325	150

Model 605

As above, with an engraved and French case hardened receiver.

NIB	Exc.	V.G.	Good	Fair	Poor
1250	950	700	500	400	400

NOTE: The 605 Series is also available in trap or skeet configurations. The values are similar.

Model 605 3-Gauge Skeet Set

As above, with three extra sets of barrels.

NIB	Exc.	V.G.	Good	Fair	Poor
2000	1800	1550	1250	1000	850

Model 680E

Similar to the Model 600, with an engraved receiver and English-style stock. Imported from 1973 to 1976.

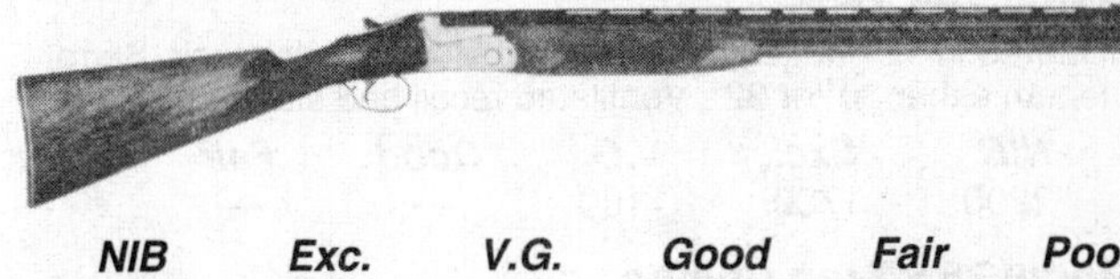

NIB	Exc.	V.G.	Good	Fair	Poor
725	650	575	475	350	200

Model 685

This over-and-under shotgun is offered in 12, 20, and 28 gauge as well as .410 bore. Barrel lengths are 26" or 28" with choke tubes. The engraved receiver has a silver finish with gold inlays. The walnut stock is semi-fancy.

NIB	Exc.	V.G.	Good	Fair	Poor
1400	1100	850	600	500	250

Model 700 Trap Gun

Similar to the Model 600 Trap, with a wider rib, additional engraving and a figured walnut stock. Imported from 1969 to 1975.

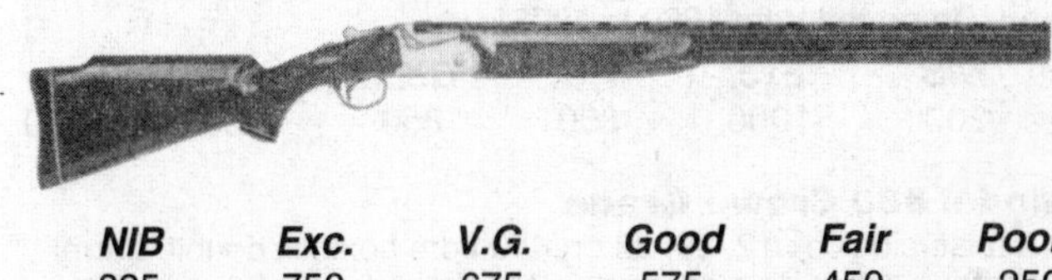

NIB	Exc.	V.G.	Good	Fair	Poor
825	750	675	575	450	250

Model 700 Skeet Gun

As above, with skeet chokes.

NIB	Exc.	V.G.	Good	Fair	Poor
850	775	700	600	475	250

Model 785

Offered in 12, 20, and 28 gauge as well as .410 bore this over-and-under features 26" or 28" barrels with choke tubes, single trigger, ejectors, and checkered walnut stock. The silver receiver is scroll engraved. Weight is about 8 lbs. for 12 gauge and 7.25 lbs. for small bores.

NIB	Exc.	V.G.	Good	Fair	Poor
2100	1500	900	750	500	300

Model 785—2 Barrel Set

These two barrel sets are in combination 12/20, 20/28, and 28/.410 bore with 26" and 28" barrels.

NIB	Exc.	V.G.	Good	Fair	Poor
2450	1900	1400	—	—	—

Model 785 Sporting Clays

Chambered for 12, 20, and 28 gauge with barrels lengths from 28" to 32" in 12 gauge and 28" in 20 and 28 gauge. Recoil pad standard.

NIB	Exc.	V.G.	Good	Fair	Poor
2250	1750	1150	—	—	—

NOTE: For Sporting Clays set add $900.

Model 785 Skeet

Offered in 12, 20, 28, and .410 bore with 28" barrels. Recoil pad standard.

NIB	Exc.	V.G.	Good	Fair	Poor
2200	1700	1150	—	—	—

Model 785 3-Gauge Skeet Set

This model furnished with 12, 20, and 28 gauge barrel all 28" in length. Weight is about 7.3 lbs. regardless of gauge.

NIB	Exc.	V.G.	Good	Fair	Poor
4400	3250	2500	—	—	—

Model 785 Trap

Offered in 12 gauge with or without Monte Carlo stock. Barrel length either 30" or 32". Ventilated recoil pad standard.

NIB	Exc.	V.G.	Good	Fair	Poor
2200	1700	1100	—	—	—

Model 785 Trap Combo

Features a 30" or 32" over-and-under barrels with a single 32" or 34" barrel. Choice of standard stock or Monte Carlo.

NIB	Exc.	V.G.	Good	Fair	Poor
3050	2250	1250	—	—	—

Model 800 Trap Gun

As above, but with trap chokes and more engraving. Imported from 1969 to 1975.

NIB	Exc.	V.G.	Good	Fair	Poor
2000	1000	850	650	550	250

Model 800 Skeet Gun

As above, in 12 or 20 gauge with 26" or 28" skeet choked barrels. Imported from 1969 to 1975.

NIB	Exc.	V.G.	Good	Fair	Poor
2000	1000	850	650	550	250

Model 880 Crown Grade

A false sidelock 12, 20, 28 or .410 bore boxlock double-barrel shotgun with a single-selective trigger and automatic ejectors. The engraved sideplates and receiver are French case hardened, and the figured walnut stock is checkered. Imported prior to 1981.

NIB	Exc.	V.G.	Good	Fair	Poor
1700	1500	1250	1100	900	450

Model 885

A false sidelock 12, 20, 28 or .410 bore boxlock shotgun. Similar to the model 800.

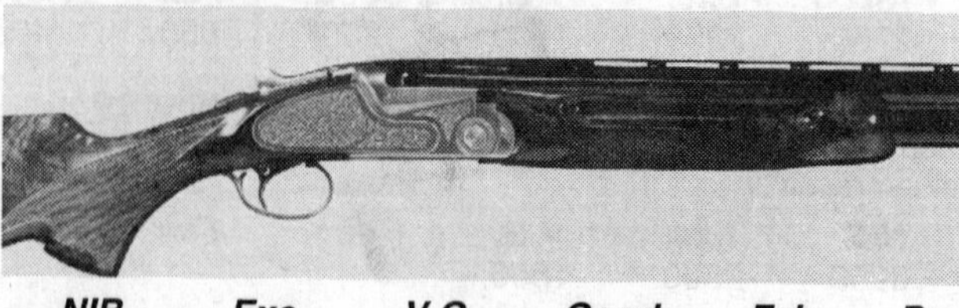

NIB	Exc.	V.G.	Good	Fair	Poor
1250	1050	900	700	600	300

Model 5600

This over-and-under gun is offered in 12 gauge only in either trap or skeet configurations.

NIB	Exc.	V.G.	Good	Fair	Poor
600	450	400	350	300	150

Model 5700

Similar to the above but with light scroll engraving on the receiver and figured walnut stock.

NIB	Exc.	V.G.	Good	Fair	Poor
750	575	500	400	300	150

Model 5800

Similar to the Model 5600 but with more engraving coverage on the receiver and fancy walnut stock.

NIB	Exc.	V.G.	Good	Fair	Poor
950	800	700	500	350	175

Model 7300

A 12 or 20 gauge slide-action shotgun. Blued with a walnut stock. Imported prior to 1981.

Exc.	V.G.	Good	Fair	Poor
300	250	200	150	100

Model 7900

As above, but skeet choked.

NIB	Exc.	V.G.	Good	Fair	Poor
400	300	250	200	150	100

Model 300

A 12 or 20 gauge semi-automatic shotgun with 26", 28", or 30" barrels. Blued with a walnut stock. Imported from 1968 to 1972.

Exc.	V.G.	Good	Fair	Poor
300	250	200	150	100

NOTE: Ventilated rib barrel add 20 percent.

Model 1300

A redesigned version of the Model 300 with a ventilated rib barrel and screw-in choke tubes. Imported since 1988.

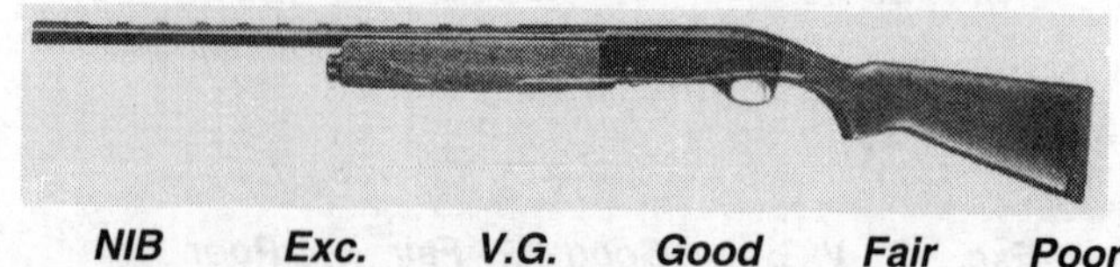

NIB	Exc.	V.G.	Good	Fair	Poor
450	400	350	300	200	150

Model XL 900 MR

A 12 gauge, semi-automatic shotgun with 26" to 30" ventilated-rib barrels, and etched alloy receiver and checkered walnut stock. Imported prior to 1981.

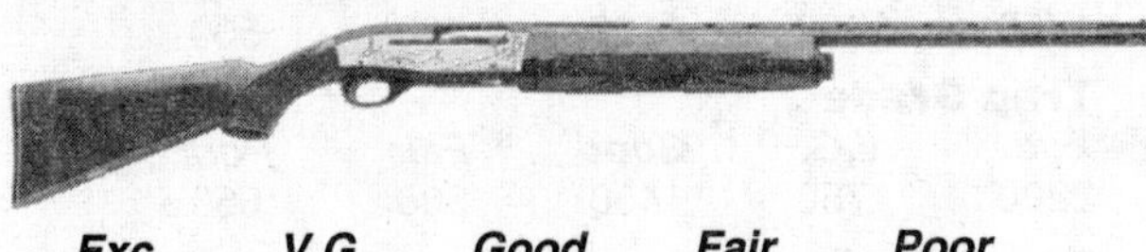

Exc.	V.G.	Good	Fair	Poor
325	275	225	175	125

Model 1900

As above, but also chambered for 20 gauge shells and available with 22", 26", or 28" ventilated rib barrels and screw-in choke tubes. Blued with a walnut stock.

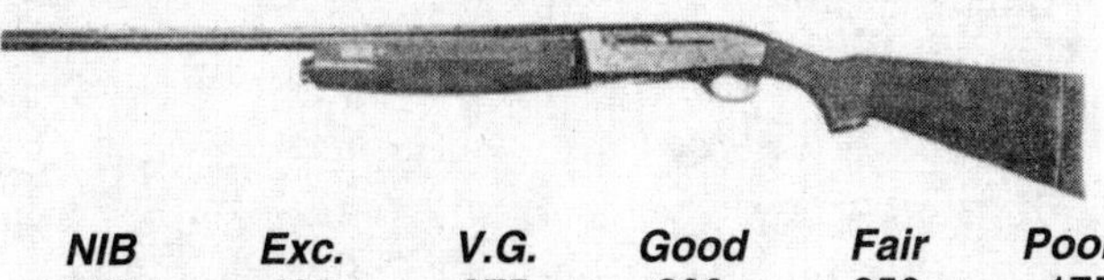

NIB	Exc.	V.G.	Good	Fair	Poor
500	425	375	300	250	175

Model 3000

Similar to the above, with a modified receiver design. Imported prior to 1990.

Exc.	V.G.	Good	Fair	Poor
475	400	350	250	150

SKS

Former Communist Bloc

NOTE: For history, technical data, descriptions, and prices see the *Standard Catalog of Military Firearms, 2nd Edition* under country of issue.

SLOTTER & CO.

Philadelphia, Pennsylvania

Pocket Pistol

A .41 caliber percussion pocket pistol with a 2.5" to 3.5" barrel, German silver mounts and walnut stock. Marked "Slotter & Co. Phila." Manufactured during 1860s.

Exc.	V.G.	Good	Fair	Poor
—	—	2000	900	250

SMITH AMERICAN ARMS COMPANY

Springfield, Massachusetts

Smith Carbine

A .50 caliber breechloading percussion carbine with a 21.75" round barrel having an octagonal breech. Blued, case hardened with a walnut stock. The barrel marked "Address/Poultney & Trimble/Baltimore, USA" and the frame "Smith's Patent/June 23, 1857" as well as "American Arms Co./Chicopee Falls." Approximately 30,000 were manufactured, most of which were purchased by the United States government. The sales agents were Poultney & Trimble of Baltimore, Maryland.

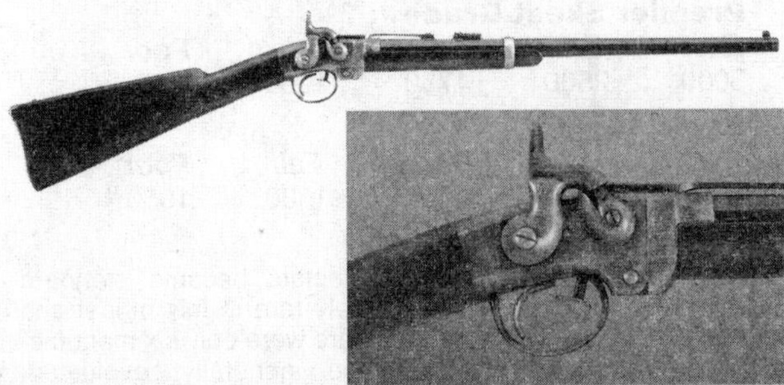

Exc.	V.G.	Good	Fair	Poor
—	3500	1600	500	200

SMITH, L. C.

Syracuse, New York
Hunter Arms Company
Fulton, New York

One of the finest American-made double-barrel shotguns and very collectible in today's market. It was manufactured between 1880 and 1888 in Syracuse, New York; and between 1890 and 1945, in Fulton, New York, by the Hunter Arms Company. In 1945 Marlin Firearms Company acquired Hunter Arms, and the L.C. Smith was made until 1951. In 1968 the L.C. Smith was resurrected for five years, and production ceased totally in 1973. The values given are approximate for standard production models; and we strongly feel that competent, individual appraisals should be secured, especially on the rarer and higher grade models, if a transaction is contemplated.

The values given are for fluid steel, hammerless guns only. Damascus-barreled guns have become collectible if they are in very good or better condition, and values are approximately the same as for the fluid steel models. Damascus guns in less than good condition are worth considerably less.

Early Hammerless Shotguns

The models listed were manufactured between 1890 and 1913. They are chambered for 10, 12, 16, and 20 gauge and were produced with various barrel lengths and choke combinations. They feature full sidelock actions. The difference in the models and their values is based on the degree of ornamentation and the quality of materials and workmanship utilized in their construction. The general values furnished are for 10, 12 or 16 gauge guns only.

NOTE: 20 gauge add 50 percent. A premium for 25 percent for 10 gauge and 16 gauge guns should be added. Single-selective trigger add $250. Automatic ejectors add 30 percent.

00 Grade

60,000 manufactured.

Exc.	V.G.	Good	Fair	Poor
1500	1250	1000	650	400

0 Grade

30,000 manufactured.

Exc.	V.G.	Good	Fair	Poor
1600	1350	1050	700	450

No. 1 Grade

10,000 manufactured.

Exc.	V.G.	Good	Fair	Poor
2500	2000	1500	800	550

No. 2 Grade

13,000 manufactured.

Exc.	V.G.	Good	Fair	Poor
3000	2250	1750	900	700

No. 3 Grade

4,000 manufactured.

Exc.	V.G.	Good	Fair	Poor
3500	2750	1800	1000	750

Pigeon Grade

1,200 manufactured.

Exc.	V.G.	Good	Fair	Poor
3500	2750	1800	1000	750

No. 4 Grade

500 manufactured.

Exc.	V.G.	Good	Fair	Poor
10000	7500	5000	3000	2000

A-1 Grade

700 manufactured, all damascus, No 20 gauge.

Exc.	V.G.	Good	Fair	Poor
5000	3500	2500	1750	1000

No. 5 Grade

500 manufactured.

Exc.	V.G.	Good	Fair	Poor
8500	7000	5000	2750	2000

Monogram Grade

100 manufactured.

Exc.	V.G.	Good	Fair	Poor
11000	8500	6000	3750	2500

A-2 Grade

200 manufactured.

Exc.	V.G.	Good	Fair	Poor
15000	10000	7500	4500	3750

A-3 Grade

20 manufactured.

This is too rare to generalize a value.

Later Production Hammerless Shotguns

These were manufactured at Fulton, New York, between 1914 and 1951. They are side-by-side double-barrel shotguns chambered for 12, 16, and 20 gauge, as well as the .410. They are offered with various barrel lengths and choke combinations. They feature a full sidelock action and are available with double or single triggers, extractors, and automatic ejectors. The finishes are blued and case colored, with checkered walnut stocks that are of either straight, semi-pistolgrip, or pistolgrip configurations. The various models differ as to the degree of ornamentation and the quality of materials and workmanship utilized in their construction. These are highly collectible American shotguns. Because these guns were manufactured as late as 1951, mint original specimens and even unfired new in the box guns will be offered for sale occasionally. These guns are worth considerably more than excellent condition guns and more than ever an individual, expert authentication and appraisal is recommended if a transaction is anticipated.

NOTE: The values supplied are for 12 gauge models only. For 16 gauge add 25 percent premium. For 20 gauge add 50 percent premium. For .410 bore add 200 percent premium (field grade), 300 percent to 400 percent for higher grades. Single-selective triggers add $250 premium. For automatic ejectors add 30 percent premium.

Courtesy Milwaukee Public Museum, Milwaukee, Wisconsin

Field Grade

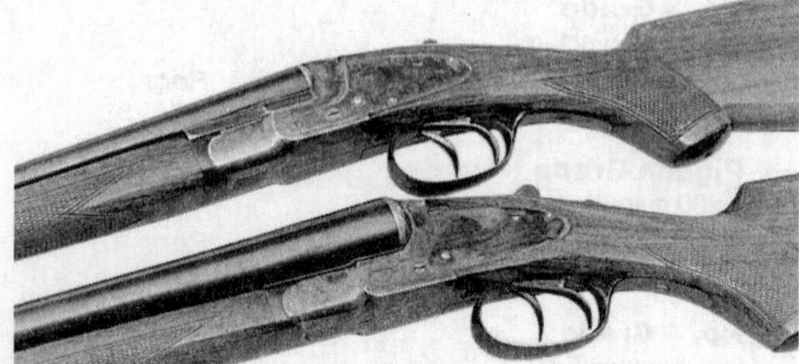

L.C. Smith 12 gauge and .410 bore Field Grade

Courtesy William Hammond

Exc.	V.G.	Good	Fair	Poor
1250	1000	750	500	350

Ideal Grade

Exc.	V.G.	Good	Fair	Poor
1750	1400	1150	700	500

Trap Grade

Exc.	V.G.	Good	Fair	Poor
2200	1750	1450	900	650

Specialty Grade

Courtesy William Hammond

Exc.	V.G.	Good	Fair	Poor
3000	2500	1750	1000	600

Skeet Special Grade

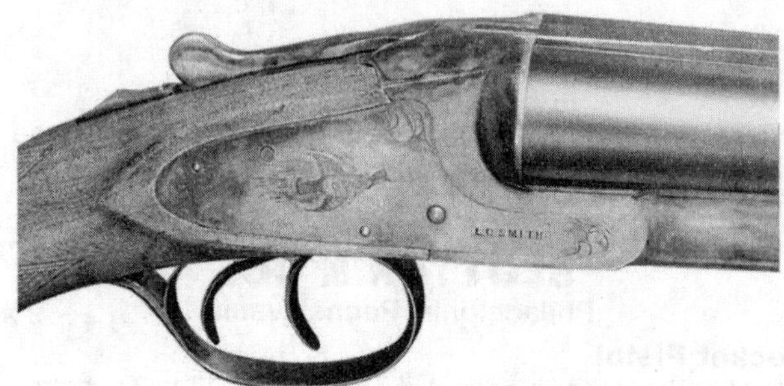

Courtesy William Hammond

Exc.	V.G.	Good	Fair	Poor
3000	2500	1750	1000	600

REMINDER

You don't have to specialize in Colts or Winchesters to have a nice collection. Collecting Marlin or Mossberg .22 semi-autos, for example, can be just as rewarding.

Premier Skeet Grade

Exc.	V.G.	Good	Fair	Poor
3000	2500	1750	1000	600

Eagle Grade

Exc.	V.G.	Good	Fair	Poor
4500	3600	2600	1500	1050

Crown Grade

With this grade, automatic ejectors became standard equipment. The .410 is extremely rare in this model and nonexistent in higher grades; there were only six manufactured, and they cannot be generally evaluated.

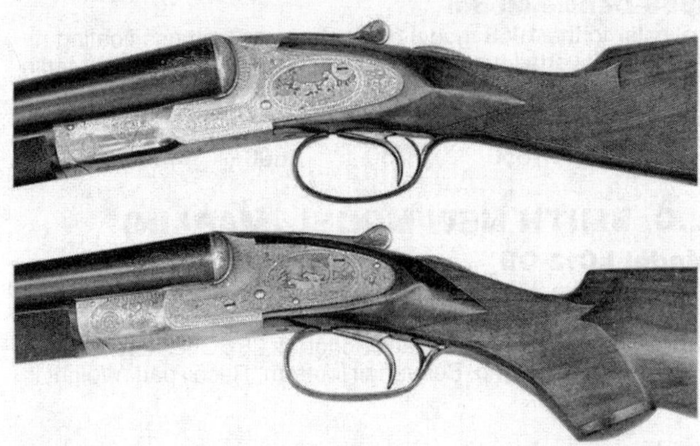

12 and 20 gauge Crown Grades Courtesy William Hammond

Exc.	V.G.	Good	Fair	Poor
6000	4500	3750	2750	2000

Monogram Grade

This version is offered standard with automatic ejectors and a single-selective trigger.

Exc.	V.G.	Good	Fair	Poor
12500	10000	7500	5000	3750

There were two higher grades offered: the Premier Grade and the Deluxe Grade. They are extremely rare, and there have not been enough transactions to generally evaluate them.

HUNTER ARMS BOXLOCKS

These shotguns have been maligned over the years being referred to as "cheap boxlocks not to be confused with the L.C. Smith." These guns, in fact, are inexpensive, high quality boxlocks built with quality equal to the Field Grade L.C. Smith. The receiver, forend iron, trigger guard and triggers are all machined from forgings. Durablity of these guns has proven to be excellent.

Fulton Model

A utility side-by-side boxlock shotgun chambered for 12, 16, 20 gauge and .410 bore. It was offered with various barrel length and choke combinations. It has double triggers and extractors with a non-selective single trigger option. Values given are for 12 gauge only.

Exc.	V.G.	Good	Fair	Poor
500	400	300	225	150

NOTE: For 20 gauge add 50 percent premium. For .410 bore add 250 percent premium. For 16 gauge add 25 percent. For single trigger add $150.

Fulton Special

A slightly higher grade version of the Fulton Model featuring modest engraving and pointed checkering.

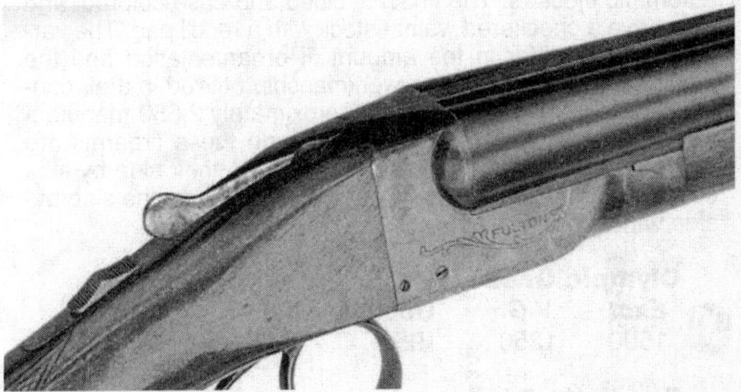

Courtesy William Hammond

Exc.	V.G.	Good	Fair	Poor
650	550	450	300	200

NOTE: For 20 gauge add 50 percent premium. For 16 gauge add 25 percent. For single trigger add $200.

Hunter Special

Similar to the Fulton Model but features the L.C. Smith rotary locking bolt.

A Hunter Arms L.C. Smith Crown Grade sold at auction for $5,175. Chambered for the 12 gauge shell and fitted with 30" vent rib barrels. Monte Carlo trap stock. Condition is 99 percent.
Amoskeag Auction Company

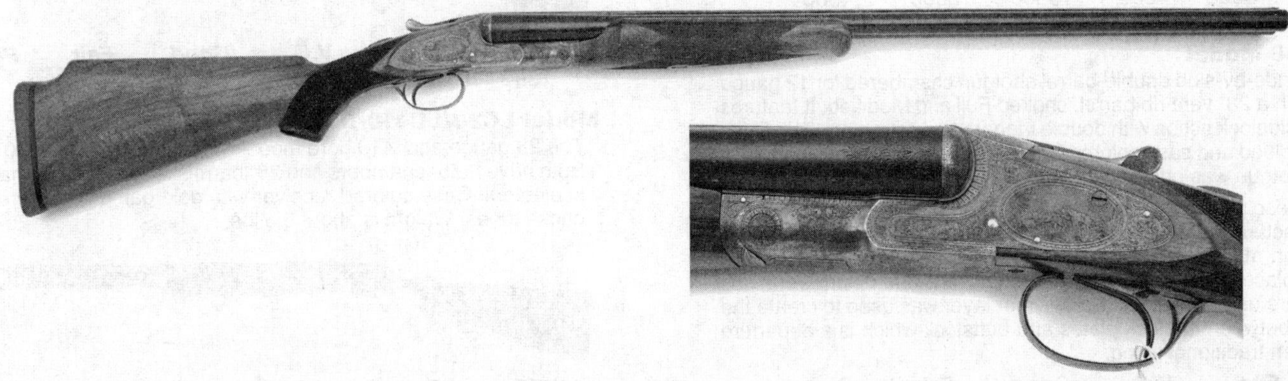

Courtesy William Hammond

Exc.	V.G.	Good	Fair	Poor
650	550	450	300	200

NOTE: For 20 gauge add 50 percent premium. For .410 bore add 300 percent premium. for 16 gauge add 25 percent.

Single Barrel Trap Guns

High quality, break-open, single-shot trap guns chambered for 12 gauge only. They feature 32" or 34" vent rib barrels that are full-choked. They have boxlock actions and are standard with automatic ejectors. The finish is blued and case colored, and they have a checkered walnut stock with a recoil pad. The various models differ in the amount of ornamentation and the quality of the materials and workmanship utilized in their construction. There was a total of approximately 2,650 manufactured between 1917 and 1951. Although these firearms are actually rarer and just as high in quality as their side-by-side counterparts, they are simply not as collectible as the side-by-side variations.

Olympic Grade

Exc.	V.G.	Good	Fair	Poor
1500	1250	950	700	600

Specialty Grade

Exc.	V.G.	Good	Fair	Poor
2000	1750	1300	1000	800

Crown Grade

Exc.	V.G.	Good	Fair	Poor
3500	3000	2250	1500	1250

Monogram Grade

Exc.	V.G.	Good	Fair	Poor
6500	5500	3800	2600	1750

Premier Grade

Exc.	V.G.	Good	Fair	Poor
12000	10000	7000	5000	3000

Deluxe Grade

Exc.	V.G.	Good	Fair	Poor
16000	14000	10500	8000	4500

1968 Model

A side-by-side double-barrel shotgun chambered for 12 gauge with a 28" vent rib barrel, choked Full and Modified. It features a sidelock action with double triggers and extractors. The finish is blued and case colored, with a checkered walnut stock. This shotgun was offered by Marlin between 1968 and 1973.

These are less desirable than earlier models because of manufacturing expedients used. Investment cast receiver rather than machined forgings were used. Cyanide case-hardening replaced bone charcoal hardening and aluminum vent ribs were used. A thin brown polymer layer was used to create the fit between the lock plates and buttstock which is a departure from traditional fitting.

Exc.	V.G.	Good	Fair	Poor
700	600	550	450	300

1968 Deluxe Model

Similar to the 1968 model but features a Simmons floating rib and a beavertail-type forearm. It was manufactured by Marlin between 1971 and 1973.

Exc.	V.G.	Good	Fair	Poor
1000	850	750	600	400

L.C. SMITH NEW MODEL (MARLIN)

Model LC12-DB

Introduced in 2005 this Italian-made side-by-side gun is chambered for the 12 gauge 3" shell. Single trigger, selective ejectors, and 3 choke tubes. Barrel length is 28". Checkered walnut stock with pistol grip. Beavertail forearm. Recoil pad. Weight is about 6.25 lbs.

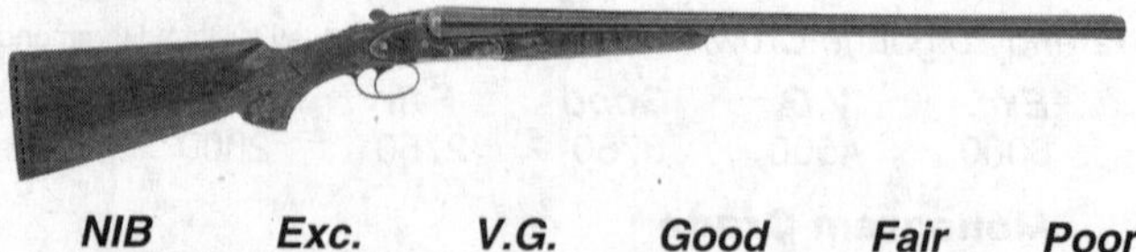

NIB	Exc.	V.G.	Good	Fair	Poor
1880	1400	—	—	—	—

Model LC20-DB

As above but chambered for the 20 gauge 3" shell and fitted with a 26" barrel. Weight is about 6 lbs. Introduced in 2005.

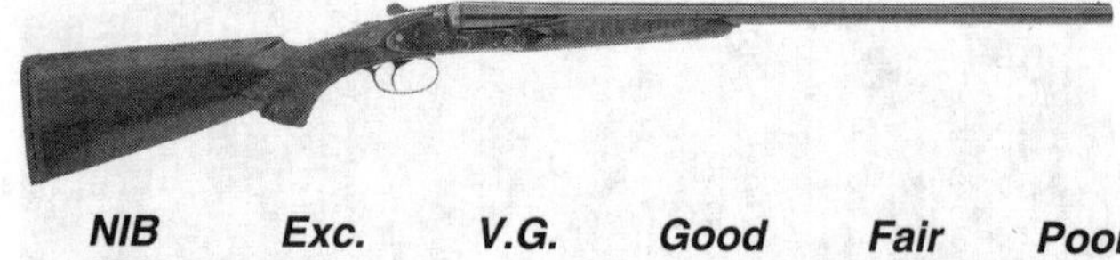

NIB	Exc.	V.G.	Good	Fair	Poor
1880	1400	—	—	—	—

Model LC12-OU

This is a 12 gauge 3" over-and-under gun with 28" vent rib barrels. Checkered walnut stock with pistol grip. Choke tubes. Weight is about 7.25 lbs. Introduced in 2005.

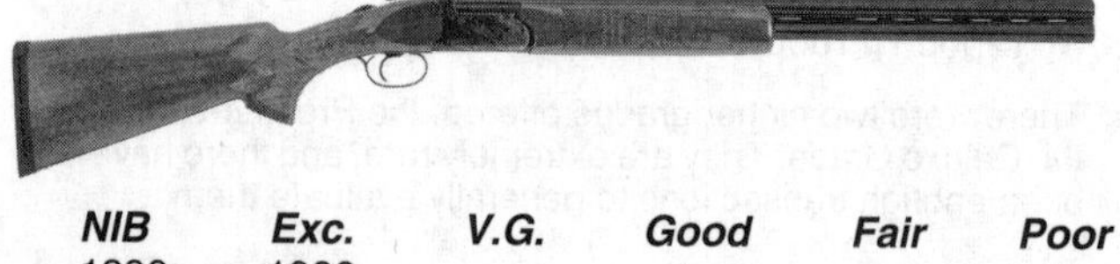

NIB	Exc.	V.G.	Good	Fair	Poor
1390	1000	—	—	—	—

Model LC20-OU

As above but in 20 gauge with 3" chamber. Barrel length is 26". Weight is about 6.75 lbs. Introduced in 2005.

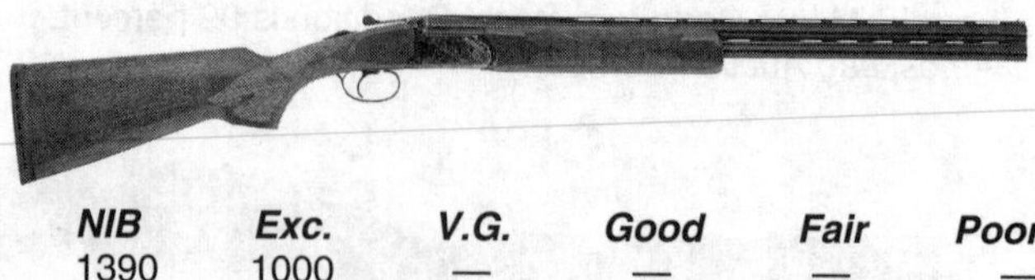

NIB	Exc.	V.G.	Good	Fair	Poor
1390	1000	—	—	—	—

Model LC28/LC410-DB

The 28 gauge and .410 bore models were introduced in 2007. Both have 2.75" chambers and 26" barrels. Selective automatic ejectors. Case-colored receiver with gold game bird. Three choke tubes. Weight is about 6.5 lbs.

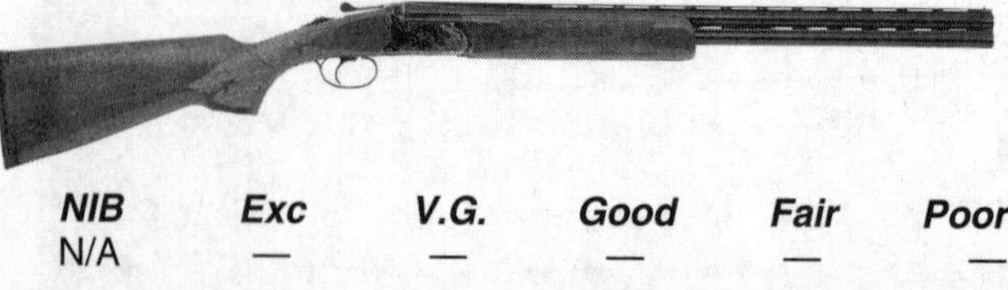

NIB	Exc	V.G.	Good	Fair	Poor
N/A	—	—	—	—	—

SMITH, OTIS
Rockfall, Connecticut

This company manufactured a line of single-action, spur-trigger revolvers that are chambered for .22, .32, .38, and .41 rimfire cartridges. The pistols have varying barrel lengths. The cylinder access pin is retained by a button on the left side of the frame. The cylinder usually holds five shots. The finishes are either blued or nickel-plated, with bird's-head grips. The quality was considered to be mediocre.

Model 1883 Shell-Ejector

A single-action, break-open, self ejecting revolver with a ribbed 3.5" barrel chambered for .32 centerfire. It has a 5-shot fluted cylinder and a spur trigger. It was quite well made. The finish is nickel-plated, with black plastic grips.

Exc.	V.G.	Good	Fair	Poor
—	400	200	100	75

Model 1892

A double-action, concealed-hammer revolver chambered for the .38 centerfire cartridge. It has a 4" barrel and, for the first time, a conventional trigger and trigger guard. It is gateloaded and has a solid frame. It is nickel-plated with black plastic grips and also appeared under the Maltby, Henley & Company banner marked "Spencer Safety Hammerless" or "Parker Safety Hammerless." The Otis Smith Company ceased operations in 1898.

Exc.	V.G.	Good	Fair	Poor
—	400	200	100	75

SMITH & WESSON
Springfield, Massachusetts

SMITH & WESSON ANTIQUE HANDGUNS

NOTE: A surprising number of pistols are still found in their original boxes, even for older models. This can add 100 percent to the value of the pistol.

Model 1, 1st Issue Revolver

This was the first metallic-cartridge arm produced by Smith & Wesson. It is a small revolver that weighs approximately 10 oz. and is chambered for the .22 Short rimfire cartridge. The octagonal barrel is 3.25" long. It holds 7 cartridges. The barrel and nonfluted cylinder pivot upward upon release of the under the frame. This model has a square butt with rosewood grips. The oval brass frame is silver-plated. The barrel and cylinder are blued. The barrel is stamped with the company name and address; the patent dates also appear. The sides of the frame are rounded on the 1st issue. Other characteristics which distinguish the more valuable 1st issue from later issues include a perfectly round side plate and a hinged hammer spur. Smith & Wesson manufactured approximately 11,000 of these revolvers between 1857 and 1860. Since this was the first of its kind, it is not difficult to understand the need for the number of variations within this model designation. Many small improvements were made on the way to the next model. These variations are as follows:

1st Type

Serial range 1 to low 200s, revolving recoil shield, bayonet type catch on frame.

Exc.	V.G.	Good	Fair	Poor
—	15000	10000	8000	—

NOTE: Rarity makes valuation speculative.

2nd Type

Serial range low 200s to 1130, improved recoil plate.

Exc.	V.G.	Good	Fair	Poor
—	9000	5000	2500	—

3rd Type

Serial range 1130 to low 3000s, bayonet catch dropped for spring-loaded side catch.

Exc.	V.G.	Good	Fair	Poor
—	3500	2500	1500	—

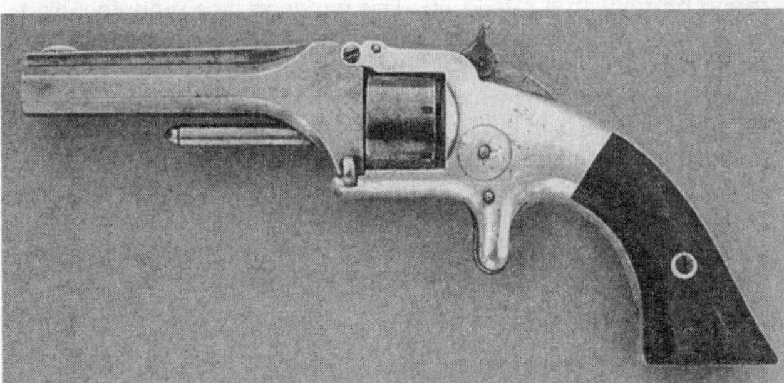

Typical configuration for 3rd-6th type, Model 1 1st Issue

Courtesy Jim Supica, Old Town Station

4th Type

Serial range low 3000s to low 4200s, recoil shield made much smaller.

Exc.	V.G.	Good	Fair	Poor
—	3250	2000	1250	—

5th Type

Serial range low 4200s to low 5500s, has 5-groove rifling instead of 3.

Exc.	V.G.	Good	Fair	Poor
—	3250	2000	1250	—

6th Type

Serial range low 5500s to end of production 11670. A cylinder ratchet replaced the revolving recoil shield.

Exc.	V.G.	Good	Fair	Poor
—	3000	1750	1000	—

Model 1 2nd Issue

Similar in appearance to the 1st Issue this 2nd Issue variation has several notable differences that make identification rather simple. The sides of the frame on the 2nd Issue are flat not rounded as on the 1st Issue. The sideplate is irregular in shape—not round like on the 1st Issue. The barrel was 3-3/16" in length. The barrel is stamped "Smith & Wesson" while the cylinder is marked with the three patent dates: April 3, 1858, July 5 1859, and December 18, 1860. There have been 2nd Issue noted with full silver or nickel-plating. Smith & Wesson manufactured approximately 115,000 of these revolvers between 1860 and 1868. The serial numbers started around 1100 where the 1st Issue left off and continued to 126400. There were approximately 4,400 revolvers marked "2D Quality" on the barrels. These revolvers were slightly defective and were sold at a lesser price. They will bring an approximate 100 percent premium on today's market.

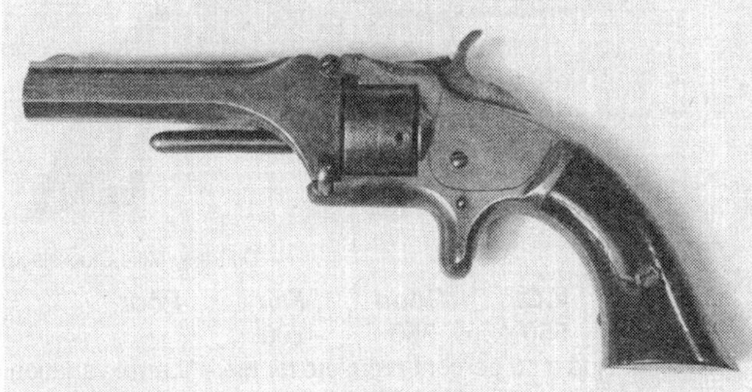

Courtesy Mike Stuckslager

Exc.	V.G.	Good	Fair	Poor
—	700	400	250	—

Model 1 3rd Issue

This is a redesigned version of its forerunners. Another .22 Short rimfire, 7-shot revolver, this model has a fluted cylinder and round barrel with a raised rib. This variation was manufactured totally from wrought iron. The three patent dates are stamped on top of the ribbed barrel as is "Smith & Wesson." It features bird's-head type grips of rosewood and is either fully blued nickel-plated, or two-toned with the frame nickel and the barrel and cylinder blued. There are two barrel lengths offered: 3.25" and 2-11/16". The shorter barrel was introduced in 1872. Serial numbering began with #1 and continued to 131163. They were manufactured between 1868 and 1882. The Model 1 3rd Issue was the last of the tip-up style produced by Smith & Wesson.

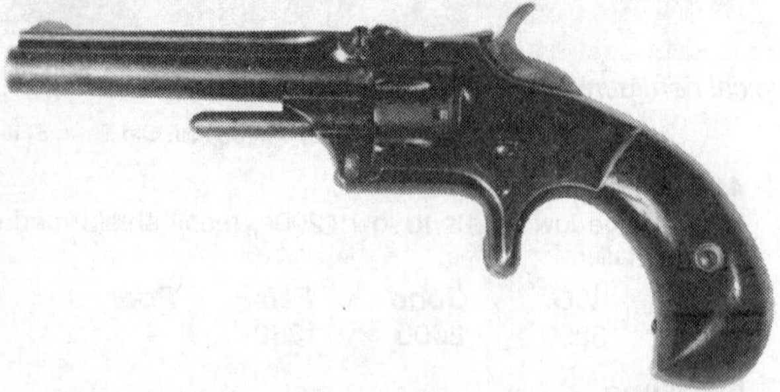

Courtesy Mike Stuckslager

Shorter Barreled Version

Rare.

Exc.	*V.G.*	*Good*	*Fair*	*Poor*
—	1350	800	400	—

Longer Barreled Version

Standard.

Exc.	*V.G.*	*Good*	*Fair*	*Poor*
—	500	275	200	—

Model 1-1/2 1st Issue (1-1/2 Old Model)

This model was the first of the .32-caliber Rimfire Short revolvers that S&W produced. It is a larger version of the Model 1 but is physically similar in appearance. The Model 1-1/2 was offered with a 3.5" octagonal barrel and has a 5-shot nonfluted cylinder and a square butt with rosewood grips. In 1866 a 4" barrel version was produced for a short time. It is estimated that about 200 were sold. The finish is blued or nickel-plated. The serial numbering on this model ran from serial number 1 to 26300; and, interestingly to note, S&W had most of the parts for this revolver manufactured on contract by King & Smith of Middletown, Connecticut. Smith & Wesson merely assembled and finished them. They were produced between 1865 and 1868.

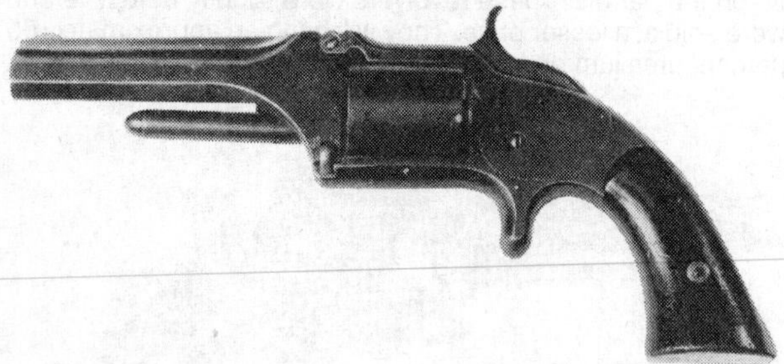

Courtesy Mike Stuckslager

Exc.	*V.G.*	*Good*	*Fair*	*Poor*
—	550	350	200	—

NOTE: Add a 50 percent premium for the 4" barrel variation.

Model 1-1/2 2nd Issue (1-1/2 New Model)

The factory referred to this model as the New Model 1-1/2 and it is an improved version of the 1st Issue. It is somewhat similar in appearance with a few notable exceptions. The barrel is 2.5" or 3.5" in length, round with a raised rib. The grip is of the bird's-head configuration, and the 5-shot cylinder is fluted and chambered for the .32 Long rimfire cartridge. The cylinder stop is located in the top frame instead of the bottom. The finish and grip material are the same as the 1st Issue. There were approximately 100,700 manufactured between 1868 and 1875.

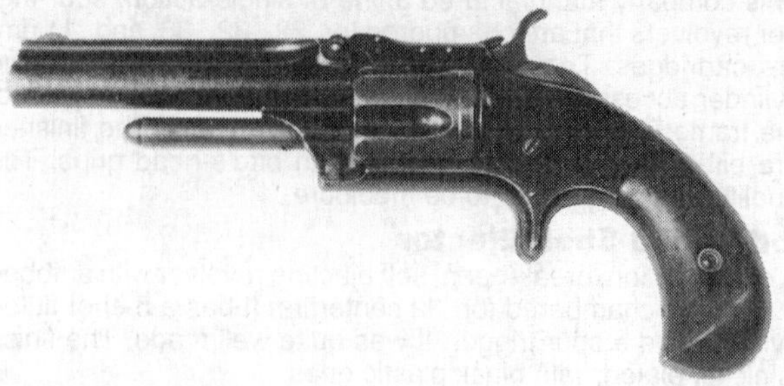

Courtesy Mike Stuckslager

3.5" Barrel

Standard.

Exc.	*V.G.*	*Good*	*Fair*	*Poor*
—	450	275	175	—

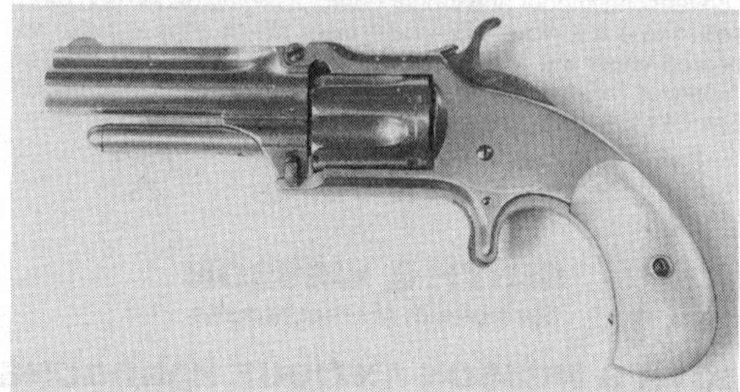

Courtesy Mike Stuckslager

2.5" Barrel

Rare.

Exc.	*V.G.*	*Good*	*Fair*	*Poor*
—	1100	600	350	—

Model 1-1/2 Transitional Model

Approximately 650 of these were produced by fitting 1st Issue cylinders and barrels to 2nd Issue frames. They also have 1st Model octagon barrels with 2nd Model bird's-head grips. These revolvers fall into the serial number range 27200-28800.

Exc.	*V.G.*	*Good*	*Fair*	*Poor*
—	3000	1500	800	—

Model 2 Army or Old Model

Similar in appearance to the Model 1 2nd Issue, this revolver was extremely successful from a commercial standpoint. It was released just in time for the commencement of hostilities in the Civil War. Smith & Wesson had, in this revolver, the only weapon able to fire self-contained cartridges and be easily carried as a backup by soldiers going off to war. This resulted in a backlog of more than three years before the company finally stopped taking orders. This model is chambered for .32 Long rimfire cartridge and has a 6-shot nonfluted cylinder and 4", 5", or 6" barrel lengths. It has a square butt with rosewood grips and is either blued or nickel-plated. There were approximately 77,155 manufactured between 1861 and 1874.

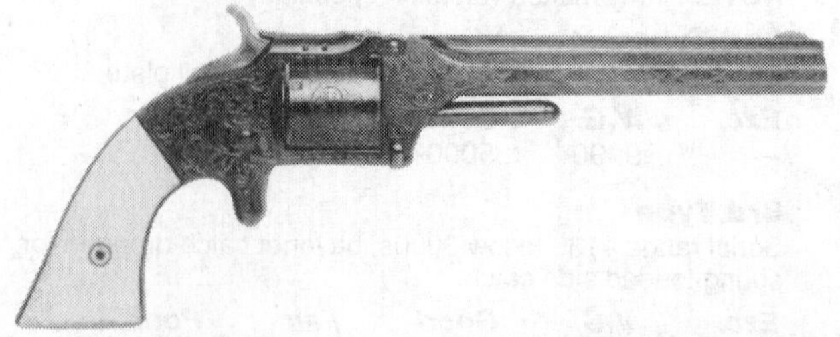

Courtesy Chester Krause

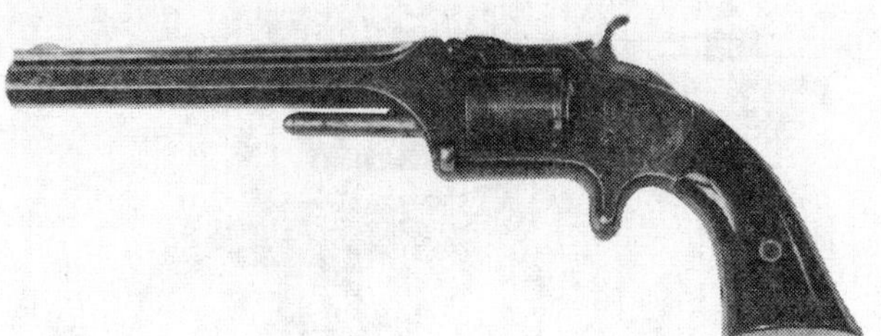

Courtesy Mike Stuckslager

5" or 6" Barrel

Standard barrel.

Exc.	V.G.	Good	Fair	Poor
—	1500	950	450	—

4" Barrel

Rare, use caution.

Exc.	V.G.	Good	Fair	Poor
—	5000	3000	1500	—

NOTE: A slight premium for early two-pin model.

.32 Single-Action (Model 1-1/2 Centerfire)

This model represented the first .32 S&W centerfire caliber top-break revolver that automatically ejected the spent cartridges upon opening. It is similar in appearance to the Model 1-1/2 2nd Issue. This model has a 5-shot fluted cylinder and a bird's-head grip of wood or checkered hard rubber and was offered with barrel lengths of 3", 3.5", 6", 8", and 10". The 8" and 10" barrel are rare and were not offered until 1887. This model pivots downward on opening and features a rebounding hammer that made the weapon much safer to fully load. There were approximately 97,599 manufactured between 1878 and 1892.

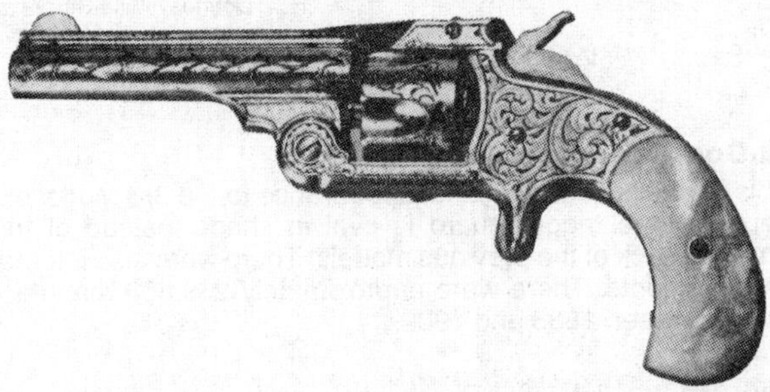

Courtesy W.P. Hallstein III and son Chip

Early Model w/o Strain Screw—Under #6500

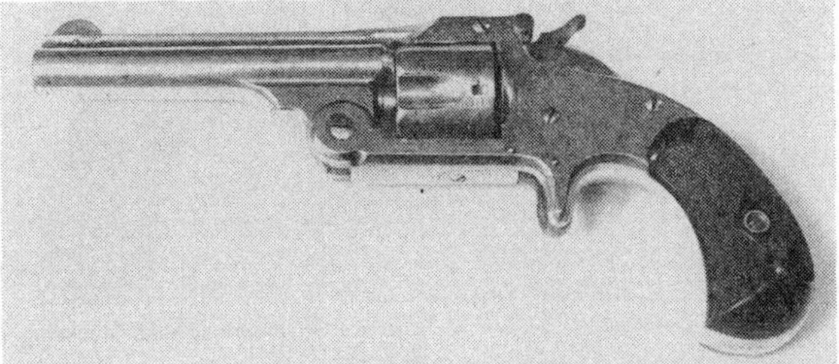

Courtesy Mike Stuckslager

Exc.	V.G.	Good	Fair	Poor
—	500	300	175	—

Later Model with Strain Screw

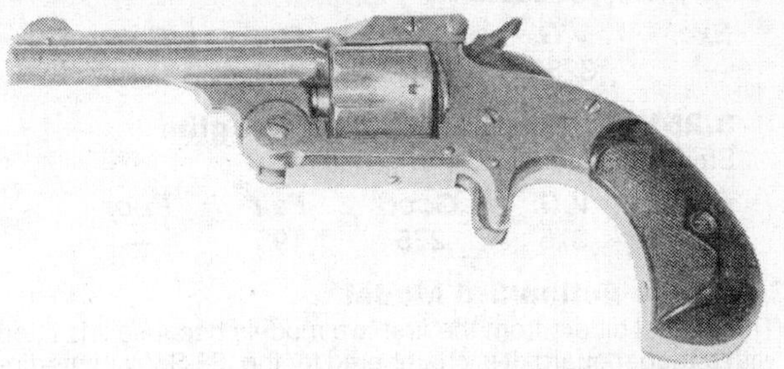

Courtesy Mike Stuckslager

Exc.	V.G.	Good	Fair	Poor
—	350	250	150	—

8" or 10" Barrel

Very rare, use caution.

Exc.	V.G.	Good	Fair	Poor
—	3000	2000	800	—

.38 Single-Action 1st Model (Baby Russian)

This model is sometimes called the "Baby Russian." It is a top break, automatic-ejecting revolver chambered for the .38 S&W centerfire cartridge. Offered with either a 3.25" or 4" round barrel with a raised rib, has a 5-shot fluted cylinder, and finished in blue or nickel plating. A 5" barrel was added as an option a short time later. The butt is rounded, with wood or checkered hard rubber grips inlaid with the S&W medallion. It has a spur trigger. Approximately 25,548 were manufactured in 1876 and 1877, of which 16,046 were nickel and 6,502 were blued.

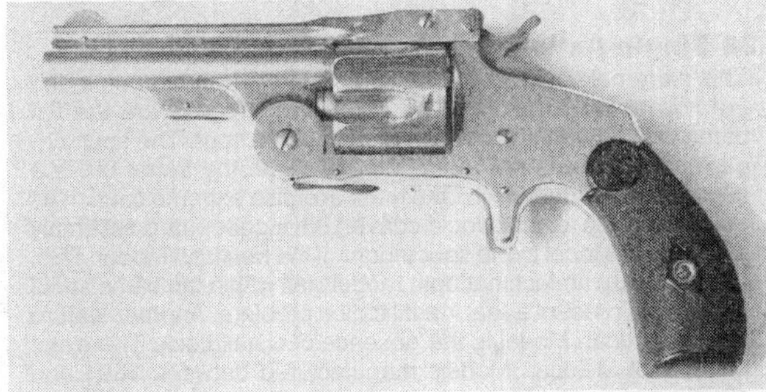

Courtesy Mike Stuckslager

Exc.	V.G.	Good	Fair	Poor
—	1500	900	350	—

.38 Single-Action 2nd Model

With the exception of an improved and shortened extractor assembly and the availability of additional barrel lengths of 3.25", 4", 5", 6", 8", and 10" with the 8" and 10" barrel lengths being the most rare, this model is quite similar in appearance to the 1st Model. There were approximately 108,225 manufactured between 1877 and 1891.

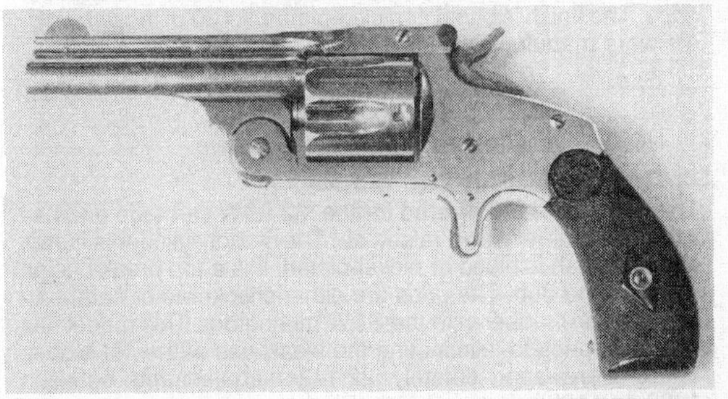

Courtesy Mike Stuckslager

8" and 10" Barrel

Very rare, use caution.

Exc.	V.G.	Good	Fair	Poor
—	3250	2250	950	—

3.25", 4", 5", and 6" Barrel Lengths

Small premium for 5" or 6" lengths.

Exc.	V.G.	Good	Fair	Poor
—	375	275	195	—

.38 Single-Action 3rd Model

This model differs from the first two models because it is fitted with a trigger guard. It is chambered for the .38 S&W centerfire cartridge, has a 5-shot fluted cylinder, and is a top break design with automatic ejection upon opening. The barrel lengths are 3.25", 4", and 6". The finish is blued or nickel-plated. The butt is rounded, with checkered hard rubber grips featuring S&W medallions. There were approximately 26,850 manufactured between 1891 and 1911.

Courtesy Mike Stuckslager

Exc.	V.G.	Good	Fair	Poor
—	1700	1000	600	—

.38 Single-Action Mexican Model

This extremely rare model is quite similar in appearance to the 3rd Model Single-Action. The notable differences are the flat hammer sides with no outward flaring of the spur. The spur trigger assembly was not made integrally with the frame but is a separate part added to it. One must exercise extreme caution as S&W offered a kit that would convert the trigger guard assembly of the Third Model to the spur trigger of the Mexican Model. This, coupled with the fact that both models fall within the same serial range, can present a real identification problem. Another feature of the Mexican Model is the absence of a half cock. The exact number of Mexican Models manufactured between 1891 and 1911 is unknown but it is estimated that the number is small.

Exc.	V.G.	Good	Fair	Poor
—	3650	1500	950	—

.32 Double-Action 1st Model

This is one of the rarest of all S&W revolvers. There were only 30 manufactured. It also has a straight-sided sideplate that weakened the revolver frame. Perhaps this was the reason that so few were made. This model was the first break-open, double-action, automatic-ejecting .32 that S&W produced. It features a 3" round barrel with raised rib, a 5-shot fluted cylinder, and round butt with plain, uncheckered, black hard rubber grips. The finish is blued or nickel-plated. All 30 of these revolvers were manufactured in 1880.

Exc.	V.G.	Good	Fair	Poor
—	12000	7500	4000	—

NOTE: Rarity makes valuation speculative.

.32 Double-Action 2nd Model

This revolver is chambered for the .32 S&W cartridge and has a 3" round barrel with a raised rib. The 5-shot cylinder is fluted, and the finish is blued or nickel-plated. It is a top break design with a round butt. The grips are either checkered or floral-embossed hard rubber with the S&W monogram. This model has an oval sideplate, eliminating the weakness of the 1st Model. There were approximately 22,142 manufactured between 1880 and 1882.

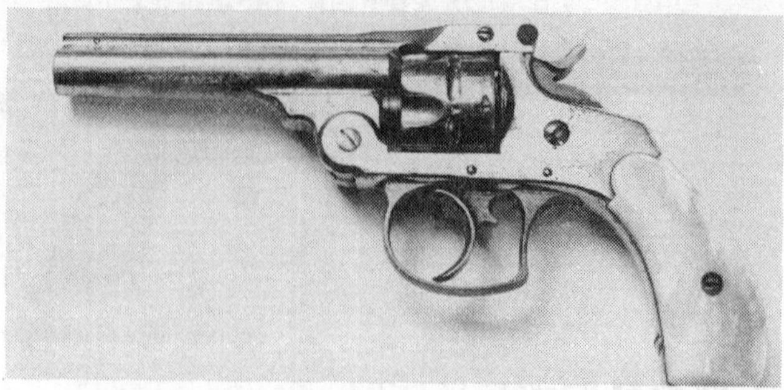

Courtesy Mike Stuckslager

Exc.	V.G.	Good	Fair	Poor
—	350	225	175	—

.32 Double-Action 3rd Model

This model incorporates internal improvements that are not evident in appearance. The most notable identifiable difference between this model and its predecessors is in the surface of the cylinder. The flutes are longer; there is only one set of stops instead of two; and the free groove is no longer present. There were approximately 21,232 manufactured in 1882 and 1883.

Courtesy Mike Stuckslager

Exc.	V.G.	Good	Fair	Poor
—	350	250	175	—

.32 Double-Action 4th Model

This model is quite similar in appearance to the 3rd Model except that the trigger guard is oval in shape instead of the squared back of the previous models. There were also internal improvements. There were approximately 239,600 manufactured between 1883 and 1909.

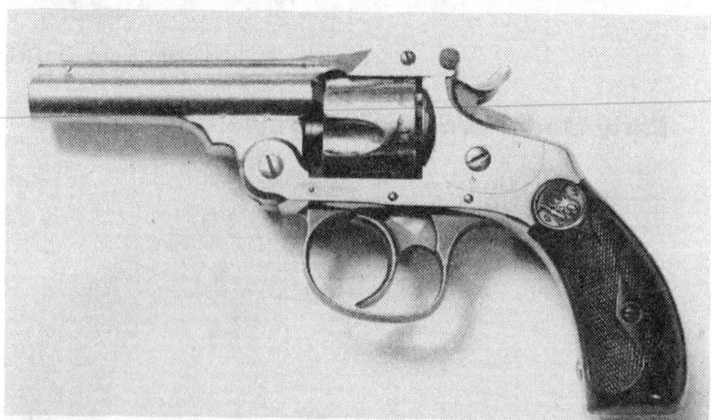

Courtesy Mike Stuckslager

Exc.	V.G.	Good	Fair	Poor
375	200	175	125	65

NOTE: Add a 50 percent premium for revolvers built before 1898.

.32 Double-Action 5th Model

The only difference between this model and its predecessors is that this model has the front sight machined as an integral part of the barrel rib. On the other models, the sight was pinned in place. There were approximately 44,641 manufactured between 1909 and 1919.

Courtesy Mike Stuckslager

Exc.	V.G.	Good	Fair	Poor
375	275	200	125	100

SAFETY HAMMERLESS

This model was a departure from what was commonly being produced at this time. Some attribute the Safety Hammerless design to D.B. Wesson's hearing that a child had been injured by cocking and firing one of the company's pistols. This story has never been proven. Nevertheless, the concealed hammer and grip safety make this an ideal pocket pistol for those needing concealability in a handgun. This is a small revolver chambered for .32 S&W and .38 S&W cartridges. It has a 5-shot fluted cylinder and is offered with a 2", 3", and 3.5" round barrel with a raised rib. The butt is rounded and has checkered hard rubber grips with the S&W logo. The finish is blue or nickel plated. The revolver is a top break, automatic-ejecting design; and the 1st Model has the latch for opening located in the rear center of the top strap instead of at the sides. The latch is checkered for a positive grip. This model is commonly referred to as the "Lemon Squeezer" because the grip safety must be squeezed as it is fired.

Courtesy Mike Stuckslager

.32 Safety Hammerless (aka .32 New Departure or .32 Lemon Squeezer)

1st Model

Push button latch serial number 1- 91417, built 1888-1902.

Exc.	V.G.	Good	Fair	Poor
375	225	165	100	50

NOTE: Add a 50 percent premium for revolvers built before 1898.

.32 Safety Hammerless 2nd Model

T-bar latch, pinned front sight, serial number 91418-169999, built 1902 to 1909.

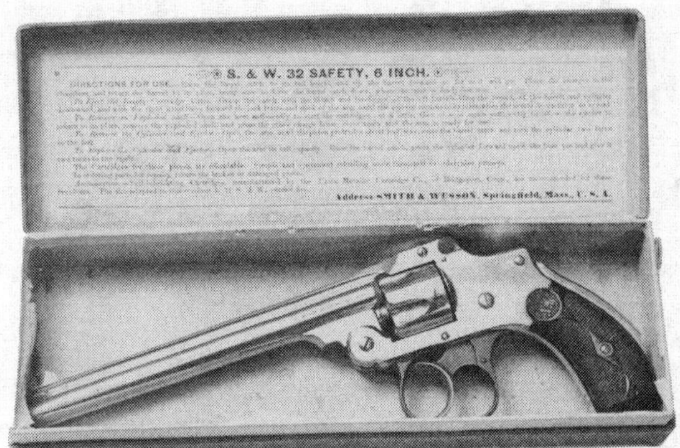

Courtesy Mike Stuckslager

Exc.	V.G.	Good	Fair	Poor
350	225	165	100	50

.32 Safety Hammerless 3rd Model

T-bar latch, integral forged front sight, serial number 170000-242981, built 1909 to 1937.

Exc.	V.G.	Good	Fair	Poor
400	225	165	100	50

NOTE: For 2" barrel, Bicycle Model add 100 percent.

.38 Double-Action 1st Model

This model is similar in appearance to the .32 1st Model, having a straight cut side-plate, but is chambered for the .38 S&W cartridge. The grips are checkered, and there were 4,000 manufactured in 1880.

Exc.	V.G.	Good	Fair	Poor
—	850	500	250	—

.38 Double-Action 2nd Model

This is similar in appearance to the .32 2nd Model but is chambered for the .38 S&W cartridge. There were approximately 115,000 manufactured between 1880 and 1884.

Courtesy Mike Stuckslager

Exc.	V.G.	Good	Fair	Poor
—	400	250	200	—

.38 Double-Action 3rd Model

Essentially the same in appearance as the .32 Model but chambered for the .38 S&W cartridge, it is also offered with a 3.25", 4", 5", 6", 8", and 10" barrel. There were numerous internal changes in this model similar to the .32 Double-Action 3rd Model. There were approximately 203,700 manufactured between 1884 and 1895.

8" and 10" Barrel

Rare, use caution.

Exc.	V.G.	Good	Fair	Poor
—	2500	1500	800	—

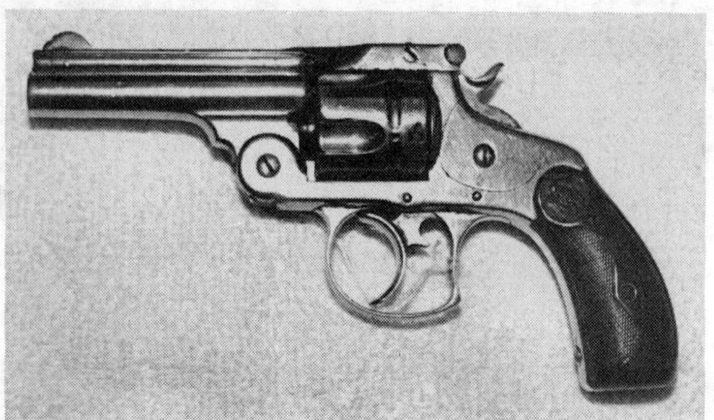
Courtesy Mike Stuckslager

Standard Barrel

Exc.	V.G.	Good	Fair	Poor
—	400	250	200	—

.38 Double-Action 4th Model

This is the .38 S&W version of the 4th Model and is identical in outward appearance to the 3rd Model. The relocation of the sear was the main design change in this model. There were approximately 216,300 manufactured between 1895 and 1909.

Exc.	V.G.	Good	Fair	Poor
385	250	195	150	75

NOTE: Add a 20 percent premium for revolvers built before 1898.

.38 Double-Action 5th Model

This model is the same as the .32 except that it is chambered for the .38 S&W cartridge. There were approximately 15,000 manufactured between 1909 and 1911.

Courtesy Mike Stuckslager

Exc.	V.G.	Good	Fair	Poor
425	285	195	150	75

.38 Double-Action Perfected

A unique top-break with both a barrel latch similar to the other top-breaks and a thumbpiece similar to the hand ejectors; also the only top-break where the trigger guard is integral to the frame rather than a separate piece. Produced from 1909 to 1911 in their own serial number range. About 59,400 were built.

Exc.	V.G.	Good	Fair	Poor
550	365	200	165	85

.38 Safety Hammerless 1st Model

Z-bar latch, serial number range 1 to 5250, made 1887 only.

Exc.	V.G.	Good	Fair	Poor
—	700	425	250	—

NOTE: Also offered with a 6" barrel. RARE! Add 50 percent.

.38 Safety Hammerless 2nd Model

Push button latch protrudes above frame, serial number 5251-42483, built 1887-1890.

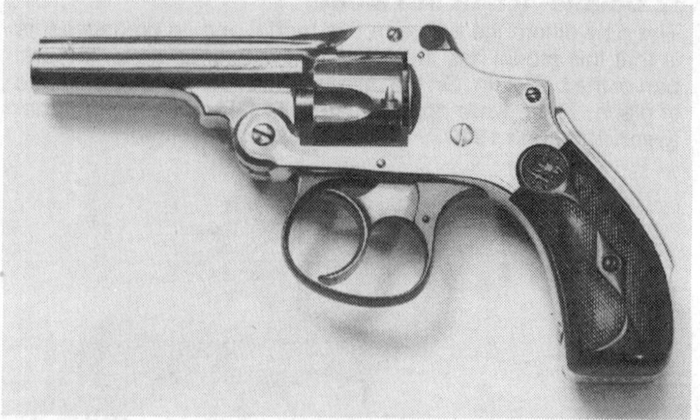
Courtesy Mike Stuckslager

Exc.	V.G.	Good	Fair	Poor
—	350	250	175	—

.38 Safety Hammerless 3rd Model

Push button latch flush with frame, serial number 42484-116002, 1890-1898.

Exc.	V.G.	Good	Fair	Poor
—	325	225	165	—

.38 Safety Hammerless Army Test Revolver

There were approximately 100 sold to U.S. government in 1890. They have 3rd Model features but are in the 2nd Model serial number range, 41333-41470. Fitted with 6" barrels and marked "US."

CAUTION: Be very wary of fakes. Seek an expert appraisal prior to a sale.

Exc.	V.G.	Good	Fair	Poor
—	8500	6500	4000	

NOTE: Rarity makes valuation speculative.

.38 Safety Hammerless 4th Model

This model was produced in .38 S&W only, and the only difference in the 4th Model and the 3rd Model is the adoption of the standard T-bar type of barrel latch as found on most of the top break revolvers. ".38 S&W Cartridge" was also added to the left side of the barrel. There were approximately 104,000 manufactured between 1898 and 1907; serial number range 116003 to 220000.

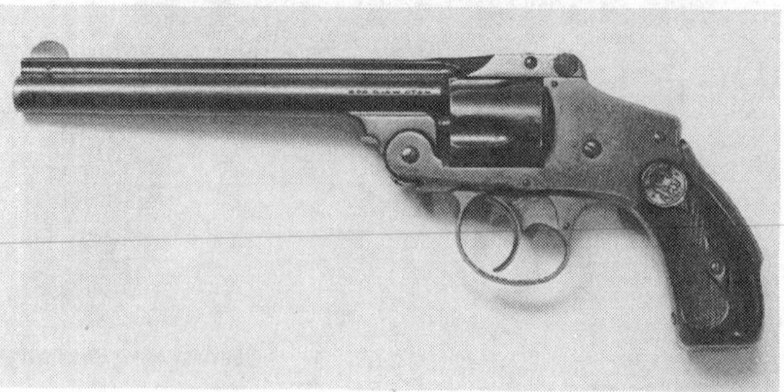
Courtesy Mike Stuckslager

Exc.	V.G.	Good	Fair	Poor
350	235	175	110	50

.38 Safety Hammerless 5th Model

This is the last of the "Lemon Squeezers," and the only appreciable difference between this model and the 4th Model is that the front sight blade on the 5th Model is an integral part of the barrel and not a separate blade pinned onto the barrel. There were approximately 41,500 manufactured between 1907 and 1940; serial number range 220001 to 261493.

 *This symbol denotes "Sleepers" with rapidly-rising values and/or significant collector potential.*

Courtesy Mike Stuckslager

Exc.	V.G.	Good	Fair	Poor
385	265	175	110	50

NOTE: 2" barrel version add 50 percent.

Model 3 American 1st Model

This model represented a number of firsts for the Smith & Wesson Company. It was the first of the top break, automatic ejection revolvers. It was also the first Smith & Wesson in a large caliber (it is chambered for the .44 S&W American cartridge as well as the .44 Henry rimfire on rare occasions). It was also known as the 1st Model American. This large revolver is offered with an 8" round barrel with a raised rib as standard. Barrel lengths of 6" and 7" were also available. It has a 6-shot fluted cylinder and a square butt with walnut grips. It is blued or nickel-plated. It is interesting to note that this model appeared three years before Colt's Single-Action Army and perhaps, more than any other model, was associated with the historic American West. There were only 8,000 manufactured between 1870 and 1872.

Standard Production Model

Exc.	V.G.	Good	Fair	Poor
—	7000	3500	1500	—

NOTE: Add 25 percent for "oil hole" variation found on approximately the first 1,500 guns. Add 50 percent for unusual barrel lengths other than standard 8". Original "Nashville Police" marked guns worth a substantial premium.

Transition Model

Serial number range 6466-6744. Shorter cylinder (1.423"), improved barrel catch.

Exc.	V.G.	Good	Fair	Poor
—	6000	3000	1500	—

U.S. Army Order

Serial number range 125-2199. One thousand (1,000) produced with "U.S." stamped on top of barrel; "OWA," on left grip.

Exc.	V.G.	Good	Fair	Poor
—	17500	7500	3000	—

.44 Rimfire Henry Model

Only 200 produced throughout serial range.

Exc.	V.G.	Good	Fair	Poor
—	12000	6000	3000	—

NOTE: Rarity makes valuation speculative.

Model 3 American 2nd Model

An improved version of the 1st Model. The most notable difference is the larger diameter trigger pivot pin and the frame protrusions above the trigger to accommodate it. The front sight blade on this model is made of steel instead of nickel silver. Several internal improvements were also incorporated into this model. This model is commonly known as the American 2nd Model. The 8" barrel length was standard on this model. There were approximately 20,735 manufactured, including 3,014 chambered for .44 rimfire Henry, between 1872 and 1874.

NOTE: There have been 5.5", 6", 6.5", and 7" barrels noted; but they are extremely scarce and would bring a 40 percent premium over the standard 8" model. Use caution when purchasing these short barrel revolvers.

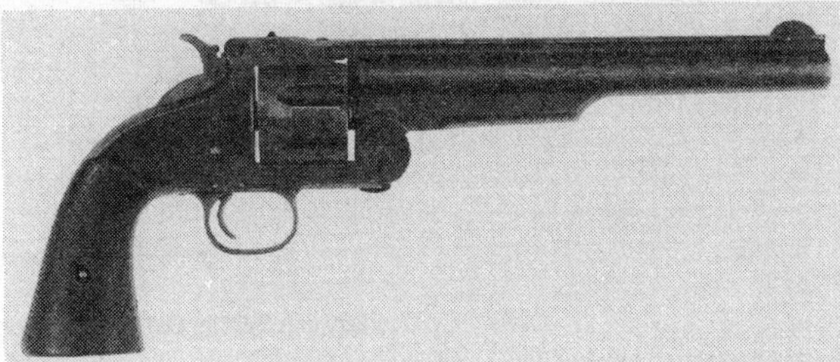

Courtesy Buffalo Bill Historical Center, Cody, Wyoming

.44 Henry Rimfire

Exc.	V.G.	Good	Fair	Poor
—	6500	3250	1500	—

Standard 8" Model, .44 American Centerfire

Exc.	V.G.	Good	Fair	Poor
—	5000	3000	1250	—

Model 3 Russian 1st Model

This model is quite similar in appearance to the American 1st and 2nd Model revolvers. S&W made several internal changes to this model to satisfy the Russian government. The markings on this revolver are distinct; and the caliber for which it is chambered, .44 S&W Russian, is different. There were approximately 20,000 Russian-Contract revolvers. The serial number range is 1-20000. They are marked in Russian Cyrillic letters. The Russian double-headed eagle is stamped on the rear portion of the barrel with inspector's marks underneath it. All of the contract guns have 8" barrels and lanyard swivels on the butt. These are rarely encountered, as most were shipped to Russia. The commercial run of this model numbered approximately 4,655. The barrels are stamped in English and include the words "Russian Model." Some are found with 6" and 7" barrels, as well as the standard 8". There were also 500 revolvers that were rejected from the Russian contract series and sold on the commercial market. Some of these are marked in English; some, Cyrillic. Some have the Cyrillic markings ground off and the English restamped. This model was manufactured from 1871 to 1874.

Russian Contract Model, Cyrillic Barrel Address

Exc.	V.G.	Good	Fair	Poor
—	7000	3500	2000	—

Commercial Model

Exc.	V.G.	Good	Fair	Poor
—	5000	2750	1250	—

Rejected Russian Contract Model

Exc.	V.G.	Good	Fair	Poor
—	5000	2750	1250	—

Model 3 Russian 2nd Model

This revolver was known as the "Old Model Russian." This is a complicated model to understand as there are many variations within the model designation. The serial numbering is quite complex as well, and values vary greatly due to relatively minor model differences. Before purchasing this model, it would be advisable to secure competent appraisal as well as to read reference materials solely devoted to this firearm. This model is chambered for the .44 S&W Russian, as well as the .44 Henry rimfire cartridge. It has a 7" barrel and a round butt featuring a projection on the frame that fits into the thumb web. The grips are walnut, and the finish is blue or nickel-plated. The trigger guard has a reverse curved spur on the bottom. There were approximately 85,200 manufactured between 1873 and 1878.

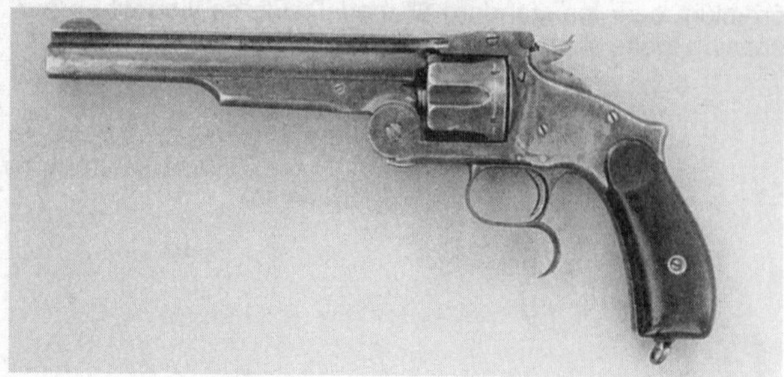

Courtesy Jim Supica, Old Town Station

Commercial Model

6,200 made, .44 S&W Russian, English markings.

Exc.	V.G.	Good	Fair	Poor
—	3250	1500	850	—

.44 Rimfire Henry Model

500 made.

Exc.	V.G.	Good	Fair	Poor
—	4750	2250	1000	—

Russian Contract Model

70,000 made; rare, as most were shipped to Russia. Cyrillic markings; lanyard swivel on butt.

Exc.	V.G.	Good	Fair	Poor
—	3500	1750	950	—

1st Model Turkish Contract

.44 rimfire Henry, special rimfire frames, serial-numbered in own serial number range 1-1000.

Exc.	V.G.	Good	Fair	Poor
—	6000	3750	1750	—

2nd Model Turkish Contract

Made from altered centerfire frames from the regular commercial serial number range. 1,000 made. Use caution with this model.

Exc.	V.G.	Good	Fair	Poor
—	4500	2250	1000	—

Japanese Govt. Contract

Five thousand made between the 1-9000 serial number range. The Japanese naval insignia, an anchor over two wavy lines, found on the butt. The barrel is Japanese proofed, and the words "Jan.19, 75 REISSUE July 25, 1871" are stamped on the barrel, as well.

Exc.	V.G.	Good	Fair	Poor
—	3500	1700	950	—

Model 3 Russian 3rd Model

This revolver is also known as the "New Model Russian." The factory referred to this model as the Model of 1874 or the Cavalry Model. It is chambered for the .44 S&W Russian and the .44 Henry rimfire cartridge. The barrel is 6.5", and the round butt is the same humped-back affair as the 2nd Model. The grips are walnut; and the finish, blue or nickel-plated. The most notable differences in appearance between this model and the 2nd Model are the shorter extractor housing under the barrel and the integral front sight blade instead of the pinned-on one found on the previous models. This is another model that bears careful research before attempting to evaluate. Minor variances can greatly affect values. Secure detailed reference materials and qualified appraisal. There were approximately 60,638 manufactured between 1874 and 1878.

Commercial Model

.44 S&W Russian, marked "Russian Model" in English, 13,500 made.

Exc.	V.G.	Good	Fair	Poor
—	9000	5000	2500	—

.44 Henry Rimfire Model

Exc.	V.G	Good	Fair	Poor
—	4500	2700	900	—

Turkish Model

Five thousand made from altered centerfire frames. Made to fire .44 Henry rimfire. "W" inspector's mark on butt. Fakes have been noted; be aware.

Exc.	V.G	Good	Fair	Poor
—	4500	2700	900	—

Japanese Contract Model

One thousand made; has the Japanese naval insignia, an anchor over two wavy lines, stamped on the butt.

Exc.	V.G	Good	Fair	Poor
—	3100	1950	850	—

Russian Contract Model

Barrel markings are in Russian Cyrillic. Approximately 41,100 were produced.

Exc.	V.G	Good	Fair	Poor
—	3100	1950	850	—

Model 3 Russian 3rd Model (Loewe & Tula Copies)

The German firm of Ludwig Loewe produced a copy of this model that is nearly identical to the S&W. This German revolver was made under Russian contract, as well as for commercial sales. The contract model has different Cyrillic markings than the S&W and the letters "HK" as inspector's marks. The commercial model has the markings in English. The Russian arsenal at Tula also produced a copy of this revolver with a different Cyrillic dated stamping on the barrel.

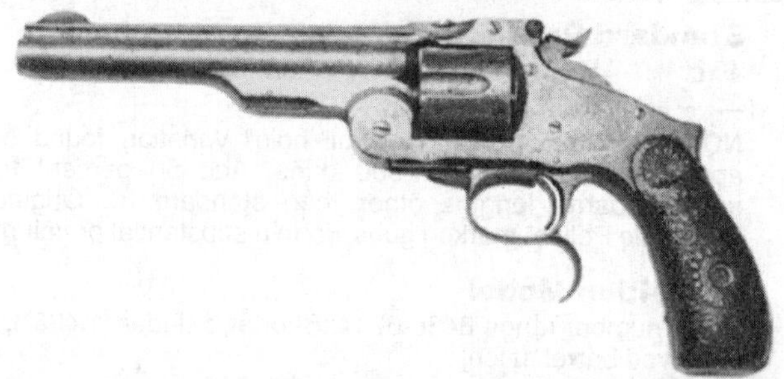

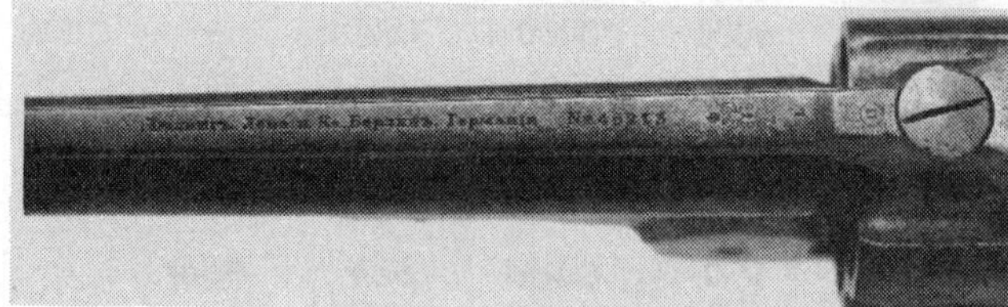

Courtesy Mike Stuckslager

Loewe

Exc.	V.G	Good	Fair	Poor
—	2900	1750	700	—

Tula

Exc.	V.G	Good	Fair	Poor
—	3350	2000	800	—

Model 3 Schofield 1st Model

"US" Contract

3,000 issued.

Exc.	V.G.	Good	Fair	Poor
—	8000	4250	2250	—

Civilian Model

No "US" markings, 35 made, Very Rare.

NOTE: Use caution. UNABLE TO PRICE. At least double the military model values. Expert appraisal needed.

Model 3 Schofield 2nd Model

"US" Contract

4,000 issued.

Exc.	V.G.	Good	Fair	Poor
—	7500	4000	2250	—

Civilian Model

646 made.

Exc.	V.G.	Good	Fair	Poor
—	7000	4000	2000	—

Model 3 Schofield—Surplus Models

After the government dropped the Schofield as an issue cavalry sidearm, the remaining U.S. inventory of these revolvers was sold off as military surplus. Many were sold to National Guard units; and the remainder were sold either to Bannerman's or to Schuyler, Hartley & Graham, two large gun dealers who then resold the guns to supply the growing need for guns on the Western frontier. Schuyler, Hartley & Graham sold a number of guns to the Wells Fargo Express Co. These weapons were nickel-plated and had the barrels shortened to 5", as were many others sold during this period. Beware of fakes when contemplating purchase of the Wells Fargo revolvers.

Wells Fargo & Co. Model

Exc.	V.G.	Good	Fair	Poor
—	8000	4000	2000	—

Surplus Cut Barrel—Not Wells Fargo

Exc.	V.G.	Good	Fair	Poor
—	3500	2000	1200	—

NEW MODEL NO. 3 SINGLE-ACTION

Always interested in perfecting the Model 3 revolver D.B. Wesson redesigned and improved the old Model 3 in the hopes of attracting more sales. The Russian contracts were almost filled so the company decided to devote the effort necessary to improve on this design. In 1877 this project was undertaken. The extractor housing was shortened; the cylinder retention system was improved; and the shape of the grip was changed to a more streamlined and attractive configuration. This New Model has a 3.5", 4", 5", 6", 6.5", 7", 7.5", or 8" barrel length with a 6-shot fluted cylinder. The 6.5" barrel and .44 S&W Russian chambering is the most often encountered variation of this model, but the factory considered the 3-1/2" and 8" barrels as standard and these were kept in stock as well. The New Model No. 3 was also chambered for .32 S&W, .32-44 S&W, .320 S&W Rev. Rifle, .38 S&W, .38-40, .38-44 S&W, .41 S&W, .44 Henry rimfire, .44 S&W American, .44-40, .45 S&W Schofield, .450 Rev., .45 Webley, .455 MkI and .455 MkII. They are either blued or nickel-plated and have checkered hard rubber grips with the S&W logo molded into them, or walnut grips. There are many sub-variations within this model designation, and the potential collector should secure detailed reference material that deals with this model. There were approximately 35,796 of these revolvers manufactured between 1878 and 1912. Nearly 40 percent were exported to fill contracts with Japan, Australia, Argentina, England, Spain, and Cuba. There were some sent to Asia, as well. The proofmarks of these countries will establish their provenance but will not add appreciably to standard values.

Standard Model

6.5" barrel, .44 S&W Russian.

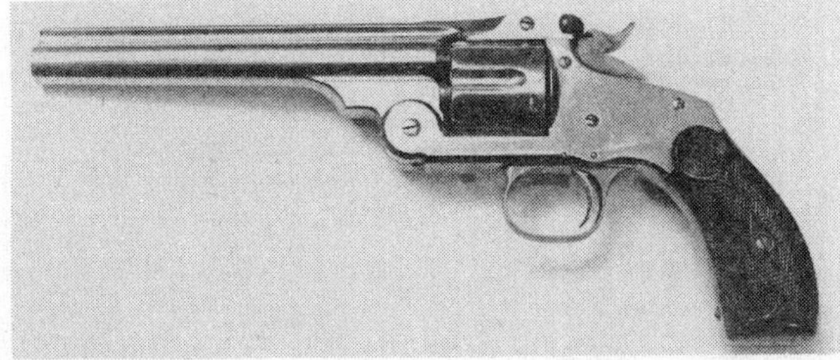

Courtesy Mike Stuckslager

Exc.	V.G.	Good	Fair	Poor
—	3700	2000	1000	—

Japanese Naval Contract

This was the largest foreign purchaser of this model. There were more than 1,500 produced with the anchor insignia stamped on the frame.

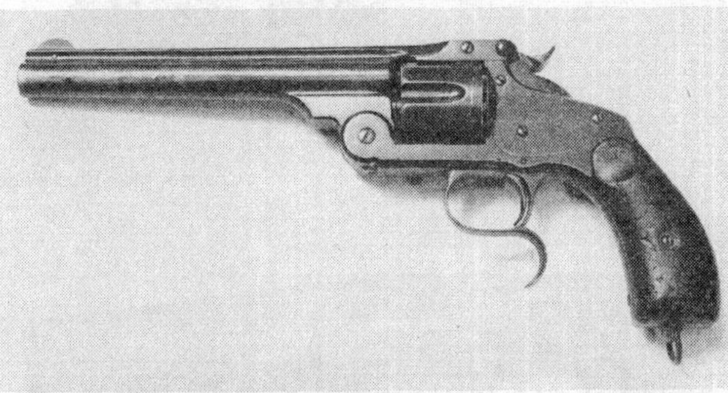

Courtesy Mike Stuckslager

Exc.	V.G.	Good	Fair	Poor
—	3700	2000	1000	—

Japanese Artillery Contract

This variation is numbered in the 25000 serial range. They are blued, with a 7" barrel and a lanyard swivel on the butt. Japanese characters are stamped on the extractor housing.

Exc.	V.G.	Good	Fair	Poor
—	5000	2500	1250	—

Maryland Militia Model

This variation is nickel-plated, has a 6.5" barrel, and is chambered for the .44 S&W Russian cartridge. The butt is stamped "U.S.," and the inspector's marks "HN" and "DAL" under the date 1878 appear on the revolver. There were 280 manufactured between serial-numbers 7126 and 7405.

Exc.	V.G.	Good	Fair	Poor
—	10000	6000	3000	—

NOTE: Rarity makes valuation speculative.

Argentine Model

This was essentially not a factory contract but a sale through Schuyler, Hartley and Graham. They are stamped "Ejercito/Argentino" in front of the trigger guard. The order amounted to some 2,000 revolvers between the serial numbers 50 and 3400.

Exc.	V.G.	Good	Fair	Poor
—	7000	3500	1750	—

Australian Contract

This variation is nickel-plated, is chambered for the .44 S&W Russian cartridge, and is marked with the Australian Colonial Police Broad Arrow on the buff. There were 250 manufactured with 7" barrels and detachable shoulder stocks. The stock has the Broad Arrow stamped on the lower tang. There were also

30 manufactured with 6.5" barrels without the stocks. They all are numbered in the 12000-13000 serial range.

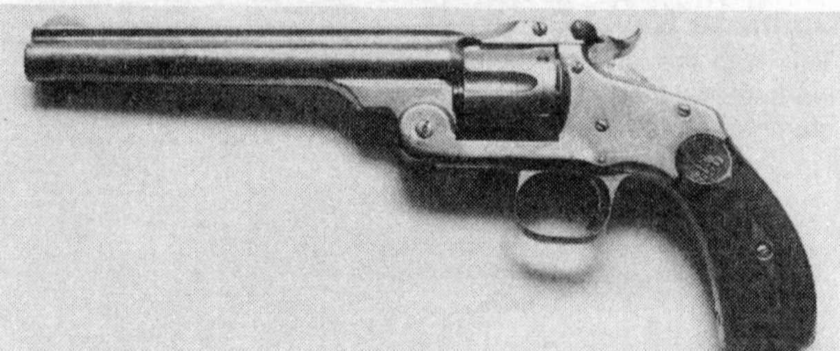

Courtesy Mike Stuckslager

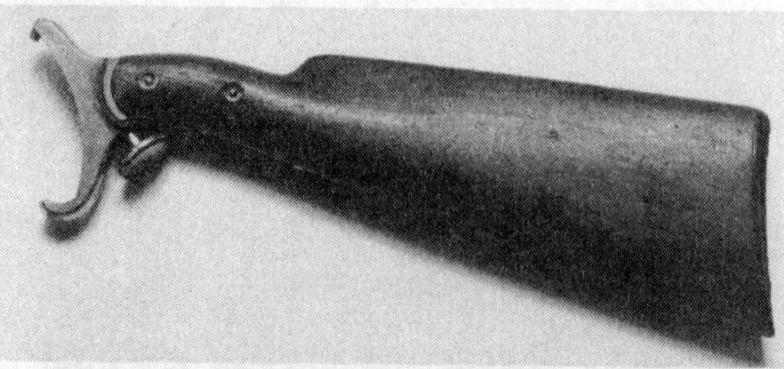

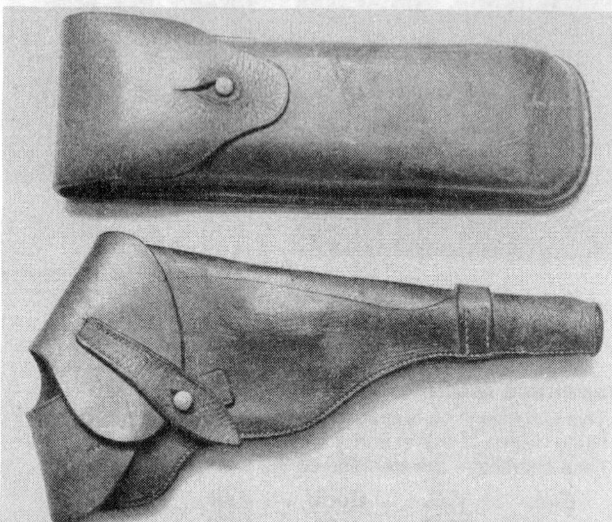

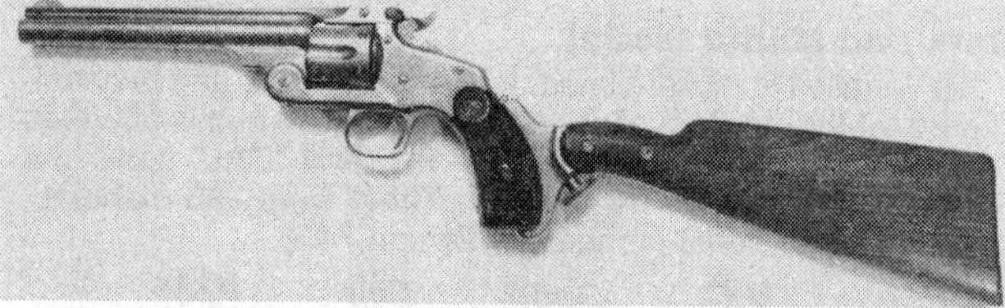

Courtesy Mike Stuckslager

Revolver with Stock and Holsters

Exc.	*V.G.*	*Good*	*Fair*	*Poor*
—	8000	4750	2750	—

NOTE: Deduct 40 percent for no stock.

Turkish Model

This is essentially the New Model No. 3 chambered for the .44 rimfire Henry cartridge. It is stamped with the letters "P," "U" and "AFC" on various parts of the revolver. The barrels are all 6.5"; the finish, blued with walnut grips. Lanyard swivels are found on the butt. There were 5,461 manufactured and serial numbered in their own range, starting at 1 through 5461 between 1879 and 1883.

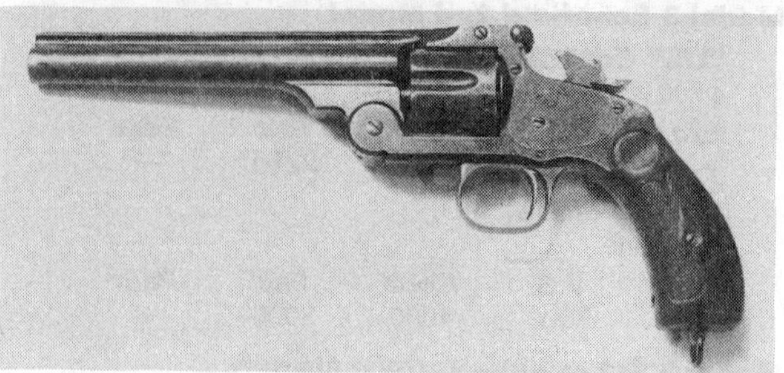

Courtesy Mike Stuckslager

Exc.	*V.G.*	*Good*	*Fair*	*Poor*
—	7000	3500	1750	—

New Model No. 3 Target Single-Action

This revolver is similar in appearance to the standard New Model No. 3, but was the company's first production target model. It has a 6.5" round barrel with a raised rib and 6-shot fluted cylinder and is finished in blue or nickel-plated. The grips are either walnut or checkered hard rubber with the S&W logo molded into them. This model is chambered in either .32 S&W or.38 S&W. The company referred to these models as either the .32-44 Target or the .38-44 Target depending on the caliber. The designation of .44 referred to the frame size, i.e. a .32 caliber built on a .44 caliber frame. This model was offered with a detachable shoulder stock as an option. These stocks are extremely scarce on today's market. There were approximately 4,333 manufactured between 1887 and 1910.

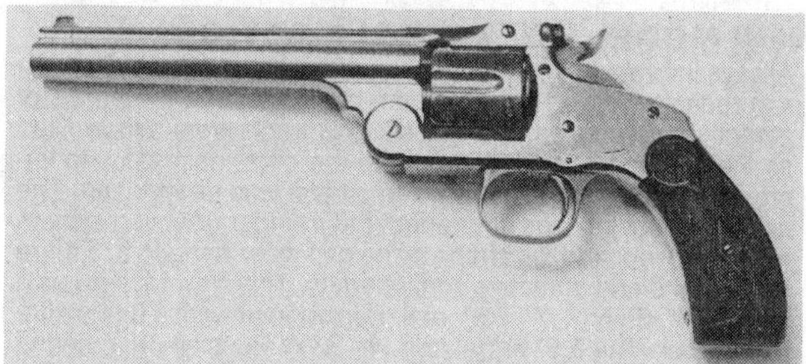

Courtesy Mike Stuckslager

Exc.	*V.G.*	*Good*	*Fair*	*Poor*
—	3100	1350	850	—

NOTE: Shoulder stock add 50 percent.

New Model No. 3 Frontier Single-Action

This is another model similar in appearance to the standard New Model No. 3. It has a 4", 5", or 6.5" barrel and is chambered for the .44-40 Winchester Centerfire cartridge. Because the original New Model No. 3 cylinder was 1-7/16" in length this would not accommodate the longer .44-40 cartridge. The cylinder on the No. 3 Frontier was changed to 1-9/16" in length. Later the company converted 786 revolvers to .44 S&W Russian and sold them to Japan. This model is either blued or nickel-plated and has checkered grips of walnut or hard rubber. They are serial numbered in their own range from 1 through 2072 and were manufactured from 1885 until 1908. This model was designed to compete with the Colt Single-Action Army but was not successful.

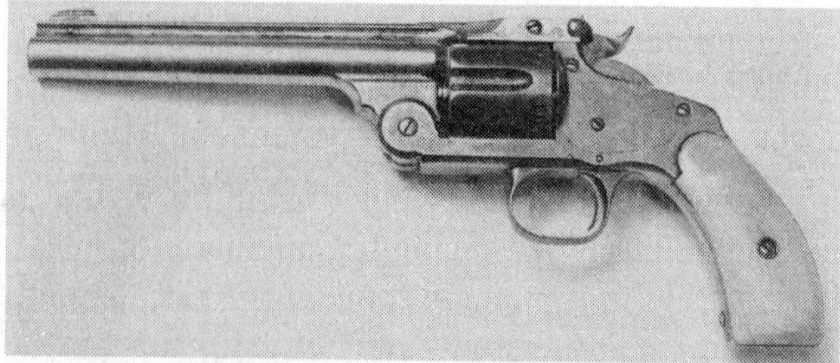

Courtesy Mike Stuckslager

.44-40—Commercial Model

Exc.	V.G.	Good	Fair	Poor
—	5000	2500	1250	—

Japanese Purchase Converted to .44 S&W Russian

Exc.	V.G.	Good	Fair	Poor
—	4000	2000	1000	—

New Model No. 3—.38 Winchester

This variation was the last of the New Model No. 3s to be introduced. It was offered in .38-40 Winchester as a separate model from 1900 until 1907. The finish is blue or nickel-plate, and the grips are checkered hard rubber or walnut. Barrel lengths of 4" or 6.5" were offered. This model was not at all popular, as only 74 were manufactured in their own serial range 1 through 74. Today's collectors are extremely interested in this extremely rare model.

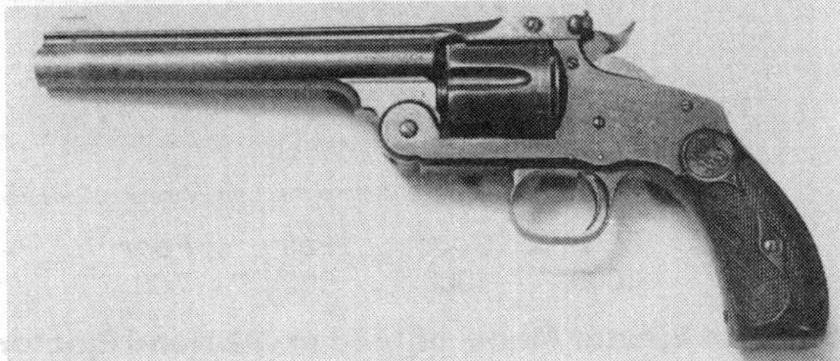

Courtesy Mike Stuckslager

Exc.	V.G.	Good	Fair	Poor
—	14000	8000	4000	—

NOTE: Rarity makes valuation speculative. A New Model #3 .38 Winchester in Good condition was offered in Old Town Station Dispatch for $6,850 in 1999.

A Smith & Wesson New Model No. 3 with detachable shoulder stock sold at auction for $10,125. Chambered for the .44 caliber and fitted with an 8" ribbed barrel. Condition is mint with 100 percent finish. Shoulder stock near mint.

Greg Martin Auctions, April 2005

.44 Double-Action 1st Model

This model is a top break revolver that automatically ejects the spent cartridge cases upon opening. The barrel latch is located at the top and rear of the cylinder; the pivot, in front and at the bottom. This model was also known as "The D.A. Frontier" or "The New Model Navy." The revolver is chambered for the .44 S&W Russian and was built on a modified Model 3 frame. It is also found on rare occasions chambered for the .38-40 and the .44-40 Winchester. The barrel lengths are 4", 5", 6", and 6.5", round with a raised rib. A 3-1/2" barrel was produced on this model by special request. Collectors should be aware that the barrel for this model and the New Model No. 3 were interchangeable and the factory did in fact use barrels from either model. The serial number on the rear of the barrel should match the number on the butt, cylinder and barrel latch. The cylinder holds 6 shots and is fluted. It has double sets of stop notches and long free grooves between the stops. It is serial numbered in its own range, beginning at 1. There were approximately 54,000 manufactured between 1881 and 1913.

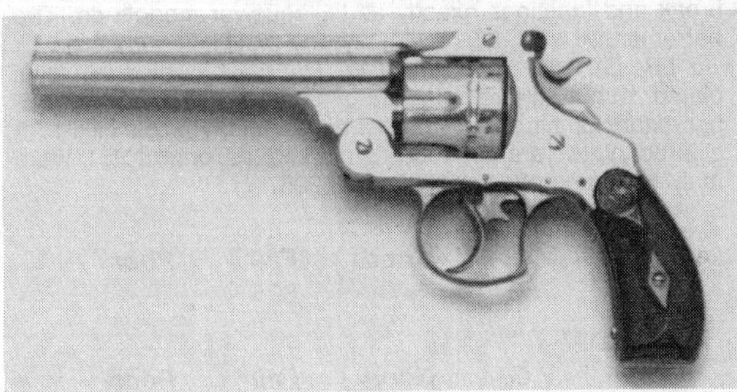

Courtesy Bonhams & Butterfields, San Francisco, California

Standard .44 S&W Russian

Exc.	V.G.	Good	Fair	Poor
—	1300	700	400	—

Model .44 Double-Action Wesson Favorite

The Favorite is basically a lightened version of the 1st Model D.A. .44. The barrel is thinner and is offered in 5" length only. There are lightening cuts in the frame between the trigger guard and the cylinder; the cylinder diameter was smaller, and there is a groove milled along the barrel rib. The Favorite is chambered for the .44 S&W Russian cartridge and has a 6-shot fluted cylinder with the same double-cylinder stop notches and free grooves as the 1st Model Double-Action .44. The company name and address, as well as the patent dates, are stamped into the edge of the cylinder instead of on the barrel rib. It is serial-numbered in the same range, between 9000 and 10100. The revolver was most often nickel-plated but was also offered blued. The grips are walnut or checkered hard rubber with the S&W logo molded in. There were approximately 1,000 manufactured in 1882 and 1883. Use caution when purchasing a blued model.

Exc.	V.G.	Good	Fair	Poor
—	9000	5000	2500	—

NOTE: Rarity makes valuation speculative. Blued finish add 25 percent.

Model .44 Double-Action Frontier

Chambered for the .44-40 cartridge. This is a separate model from the .44 Double-Action 1st Model. It has a longer 19/16" cylinder like the later .44 double-action 1st Model's. Produced from 1886 to 1916 with their own serial number range. Approximately 15,340 built.

Courtesy Mike Stuckslager

Exc.	V.G.	Good	Fair	Poor
—	1600	850	450	—

Model .38 Winchester Double-Action

Similar to the .44 Double-Action 1st Model except for the chamber. Fitted with long cylinder. Approximately 276 produced in their own serial number range from 1900 to 1910.

Exc.	V.G.	Good	Fair	Poor
—	5500	3000	1250	—

1st Model Single-Shot

This unusual pistol combines the frame of the .38 Single-Action 3rd Model with a single-shot barrel. This model is a top break and functions exactly as the revolver models do. The barrel length is 6", 8", or 10"; and the pistol is chambered for .22 LR, .32 S&W, and .38 S&W. The finish is blue or nickel plated, with a square butt. The grips are checkered hard rubber extension types for a proper target hold. This pistol is considered quite rare on today's market, as only 1,251 were manufactured between 1893 and 1905.

.22 L.R.

Exc.	*V.G.*	*Good*	*Fair*	*Poor*
—	750	500	325	—

.32 S&W

Exc.	*V.G.*	*Good*	*Fair*	*Poor*
—	950	550	400	—

.38 S&W

Exc.	*V.G.*	*Good*	*Fair*	*Poor*
—	1100	700	425	—

2nd Model Single-Shot

The 2nd Model single-shot has a frame with the recoil shield removed, is chambered for the .22 LR only, and is offered with the 10" barrel. The finish is blue or nickel plated, and the grips are checkered hard rubber extension types. There were approximately 4,617 manufactured between 1905 and 1909.

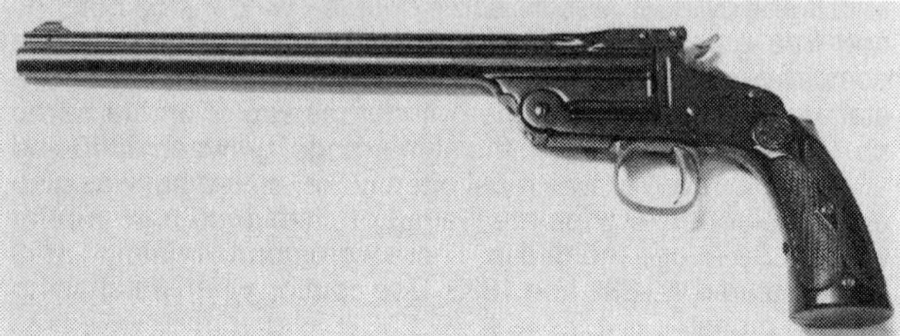

Courtesy Mike Stuckslager

Exc.	*V.G.*	*Good*	*Fair*	*Poor*
700	575	450	250	175

3rd Model Single-Shot

The basic difference between this model and the 2nd Model is that this pistol could be fired double-action as well as single-action, and the frame came from the double-action perfected model. There were 6,949 manufactured between 1909 and 1923.

Courtesy Mike Stuckslager

Exc.	*V.G.*	*Good*	*Fair*	*Poor*
700	575	450	250	175

Straight Line Single-Shot

This is a unique pistol that very much resembles a semi-automatic. The barrel is 10" in length and pivots to the left for loading. It is chambered for .22 LR cartridge and is finished in blue, with walnut grips inlaid with the S&W medallions. The hammer is straight-line in function and does not pivot. There were 1,870 manufactured between 1925 and 1936.

Courtesy Bonhams & Butterfields, San Francisco, California

Exc.	*V.G.*	*Good*	*Fair*	*Poor*
2250	1600	1000	500	300

.32 Hand Ejector Model of 1896 or .32 Hand Ejector 1st Model

This model was the first time S&W made a revolver with a swing-out cylinder. Interestingly, there is no cylinder latch; but the action opens by pulling forward on the exposed portion of the cylinder pin. This frees the spring tension and allows the cylinder to swing free. Another novel feature of this model is the cylinder stop location, which is located in the top of the frame over the cylinder. This model is chambered for the .32 S&W Long cartridge, has a 6-shot fluted cylinder, and is offered with 3.25", 4.25", and 6" long barrels. It is available with either a round or square butt, has checkered hard rubber grips, and is blued or nickel-plated. Factory installed target sights were available by special order. The company name, address, and patent dates are stamped on the cylinder instead of on the barrel. There were approximately 19,712 manufactured between 1896 and 1903.

Courtesy Mike Stuckslager

Exc.	*V.G.*	*Good*	*Fair*	*Poor*
1100	700	550	300	150

Hand Ejector Model of 1903

This model is quite different from its predecessor. The cylinder locks front and back; the cylinder stop is located in the bottom of the frame, and the familiar sliding cylinder latch is found on the left side of the frame. The barrel lengths are 3.25", 4.25", and 6". The 6-shot cylinder is fluted, and the revolver is chambered for .32 S&W Long. It is offered either blued or nickel-plated, and the round butt grips are checkered hard rubber. There were approximately 19,425 manufactured in 1903 and 1904; serial number range 1 to 19425.

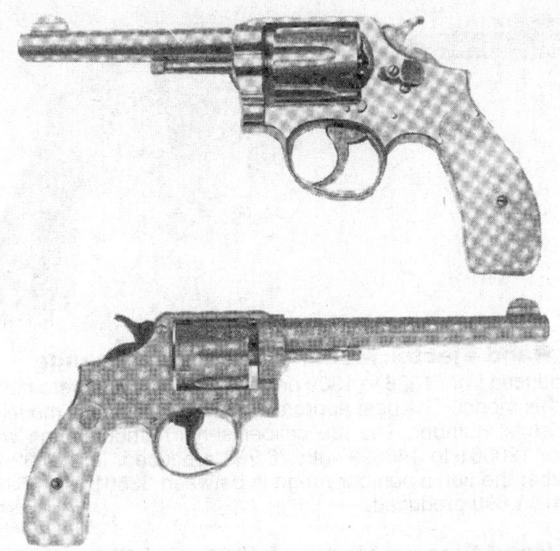

Courtesy Mike Stuckslager

Exc.	V.G.	Good	Fair	Poor
350	250	200	150	100

.32 Hand Ejector Model of 1903 1st Change

This model differs from the model of 1903 internally, and the serial number range 19426 to 51126 is really the only way to differentiate the two. There were approximately 31,700 manufactured between 1904 and 1906.

Exc.	V.G.	Good	Fair	Poor
350	250	200	150	100

.32 Hand Ejector Model of 1903 2nd Change

Produced from 1906 to 1909 in serial number range 51127 to 95500. A total of 44,373 manufactured.

.32 Hand Ejector Model of 1903 3rd Change

Produced from 1909 to 1910 in serial number range 95501 to 96125. A total of 624 manufactured.

.32 Hand Ejector Model of 1903 4th Change

Produced in 1910 in serial number range 96126 to 102500. A total of 6,374 manufactured.

.32 Hand Ejector Model of 1903 5th Change

Produced from 1910 to 1917 in serial number range 102500 to 263000. A total of 160,500 manufactured.

.32 Hand Ejector Third Model

Produced from 1911 to 1942 in serial number range 263001 to 536684. A total of 273,683 were manufactured.

Exc.	V.G.	Good	Fair	Poor
350	200	150	125	90

.22 Ladysmith 1st Model

This model was designed primarily as a defensive weapon for women. Its small size and caliber made it ideal for that purpose. The 1st Model Ladysmith is chambered for .22 Long cartridge and has a 7-shot fluted cylinder and 3" and 3.5" barrel lengths. This little revolver weighed 9-5/8 ounces. It is either blued or nickel-plated and has a round butt with checkered hard rubber grips. The 1st Model has a checkered cylinder-latch button on the left side of the frame. There were approximately 4,575 manufactured between 1902 and 1906.

Exc.	V.G.	Good	Fair	Poor
1900	1250	850	650	450

.22 Ladysmith 2nd Model

This is essentially quite similar in appearance to the 1st Model, the difference being in the pull-forward cylinder latch located under the barrel, replacing the button on the left side of the frame. The new method allowed lockup front and back for greater action strength. The 2.25" barrel length was dropped; caliber and finishes are the same. There were approximately 9,374 manufactured between 1906 and 1910; serial number range 4576 to 13950.

Courtesy Mike Stuckslager

Exc.	V.G.	Good	Fair	Poor
1650	950	800	600	400

.22 Ladysmith 3rd Model

This model is quite different in appearance to the 2nd Model, as it features a square butt and smooth walnut grips with inlaid S&W medallions. The barrel lengths remained the same, with the addition of a 2.25" and 6" variation. The under barrel cylinder lockup was not changed, nor were the caliber and finishes. There were approximately 12,200 manufactured between 1910 and 1921; serial number range 13951 to 26154.

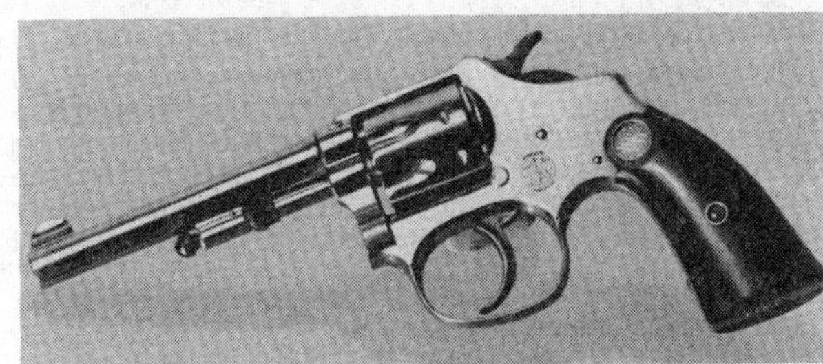

Courtesy W.P. Hallstein III and son Chip

Exc.	V.G.	Good	Fair	Poor
1500	1000	800	600	400

NOTE: Add a 50 percent premium for 2.25" and 6" barrel lengths.

.38 Hand Ejector Military & Police 1st Model or Model of 1899

This was an early swing-out cylinder revolver, and it has no front lockup for the action. The release is on the left side of the frame. This model is chambered for .38 S&W Special cartridge and the .32 Winchester centerfire cartridge (.32-20), has a 6-shot fluted cylinder, and was offered with a 4", 5", 6", 6.5", or 8" barrel in .38 caliber and 4", 5", and 6-1/2" in .32-20 caliber. The finish is blued or nickel-plated; the grips, checkered walnut or hard rubber. There were approximately 20,975 manufactured between 1899 and 1902 in .38 caliber; serial number range 1 to 20975. In the .32-20 caliber 5,311 were sold between 1899 and 1902; serial number range 1 to 5311.

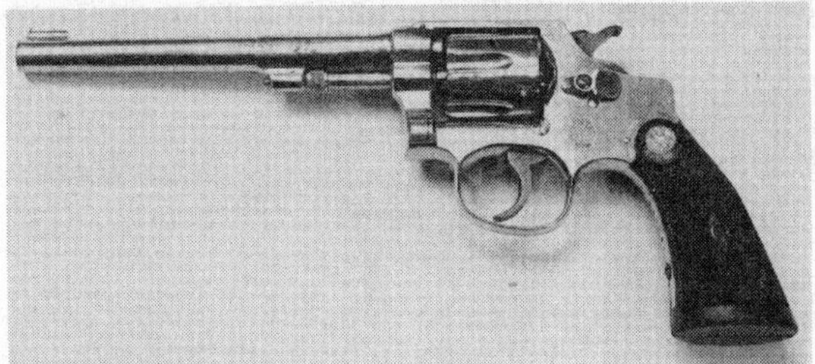

Courtesy Mike Stuckslager

Commercial Model

Exc.	V.G.	Good	Fair	Poor
800	650	600	450	350

U.S. Navy Model

One thousand produced in 1900, .38 S&W, 6" barrel, blued with checkered walnut grips, "U.S.N." stamped on butt, serial number range 5000 to 6000.

Exc.	V.G.	Good	Fair	Poor
1450	1000	700	500	300

U.S. Army Model

One thousand produced in 1901, same as Navy Model except that it is marked "U.S.Army/Model 1899" on butt, "K.S.M." and "J.T.T." on grips, serial number range 13001 to 14000.

Exc.	V.G.	Good	Fair	Poor
1450	1000	700	500	300

.38 Hand Ejector M&P 2nd Model or Model of 1902

The 2nd Model is similar in appearance to the 1st Model. The major difference is the addition of the front lockup under the barrel, and the ejector rod was increased in diameter. Barrel lengths for the .38 S&W were 4", 5", 6", or 6-1/2" while the .32-20 was available in 4", 5", or 6-1/2" barrel lengths. Both calibers were offered in round butt only configuration. There were approximately 12,827 manufactured in .38 S&W in 1902 and 1903; serial number range 20976 to 33803. In the .32-20 caliber 4,499 were produced; serial number range 5312 to 9811.

Exc.	V.G.	Good	Fair	Poor
550	350	300	250	100

.38 Hand Ejector M&P 2nd Model, 1st Change

Built between 1903 and 1905 this variation represents the change to the square butt, which made for better shooting control and standardized frame shape. Both the .38 S&W and the .32-20 were available in 4", 5", or 6-1/2" barrel lengths. The company manufactured 28,645 .38 calibers; serial number range 33804 to 62449 and produced 8,313 .32-20s; serial number 9812 to 18125.

Exc.	V.G.	Good	Fair	Poor
550	350	300	250	100

.38 Hand Ejector Model of 1905

This model was a continuation of the .38 M&P Hand Ejector series. Built from 1905 to 1906 it was available in 4", 5", 6", and 6-1/2" barrels for both the .38 and .32-20 calibers. Finished in either blue or nickel with round or square butt the .38 caliber model serial number range was from 62450 to 73250 or about 10,800 produced. The .32-20 caliber serial number range spans 18126 to 22426 or 4,300 produced.

Exc.	V.G.	Good	Fair	Poor
650	475	300	250	150

NOTE: Prices for the following four variations will be the same as those noted above.

.38 Hand Ejector Model of 1905, 1st Change

Produced from 1906 to 1908 this model is similar to the original model of 1905 with regard to barrel lengths, finish and butt styles. The 1st change in .38 caliber was produced in serial number range 73251 to 120000 with 46,749 sold. In .32-20 caliber the serial-number range was 22427 to 33500 with 11,073 sold.

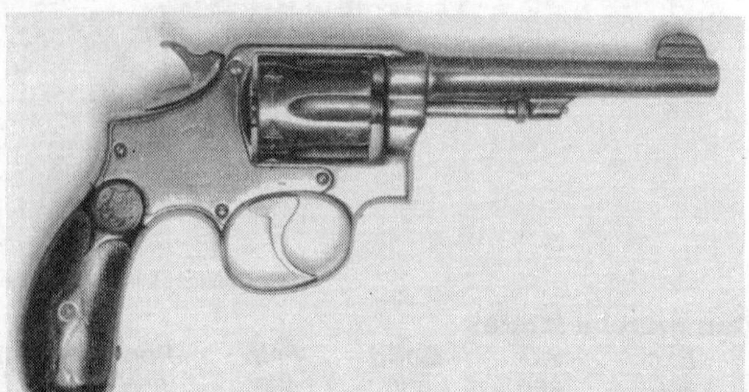

.38 Hand Ejector Model of 1905, 2nd Change

Produced from 1908 to 1909 only internal changes were made to this model. The best approach to differentiate this model is by serial number. The .38 caliber serial number range was from 120001 to 146899 with 26,898 produced. In the .32-20 caliber the serial number range is between 33501 and 45200 with 11,699 produced.

.38 Hand Ejector Model of 1905, 3rd Change

Produced from 1909 to 1915 the 3rd Change variation was available in only 4" or 6" barrel lengths for both the .38 and .32-20 models. The .38 caliber serial number range was between 146900 to 241703 with 94,803 sold.

Courtesy Mike Stuckslager

.38 Hand Ejector Model of 1905, 4th Change

This last variation was also the longest production run. Produced from 1915 to 1942 the .38 caliber model was available in 2", 4", 5", or 6", barrel lengths while the .32-20 caliber was offered in 4", 5", or 6" barrel lengths. The .38 caliber serial number range was from 241704 to 1000000. The .32-20 caliber model was produced from 1915 to 1940 in serial number range from 65701 to 144684.

Courtesy Mike Stuckslager

.22-32 Hand Ejector

This is a very interesting model from the collector's point of view. Phillip B. Bekeart, a San Francisco firearms dealer requested that S&W manufacture a .22 caliber target-grade revolver on the heavier .32 frame. He believed in his idea so passionately that he immediately ordered 1,000 of the guns for himself. This initial order is found within the serial number range 1 to 3000 and are known to collectors as the authentic Bekearts. The remainder of the extensive production run are simply .22-32 Hand Ejectors. This model is chambered for .22 LR cartridge and has a 6-shot fluted cylinder with 6" barrel. The finish is blue, with square butt and checkered extension-type walnut grips. There were only 292 revolvers of his initial order delivered to Mr. Bekeart, but the first 1,000 pistols are considered to be True Bekearts. The production number of each respective pistol is stamped into the base of the extended wooden grips. S&W went on to manufacture several hundred thousand of these revolvers between 1911 and 1953.

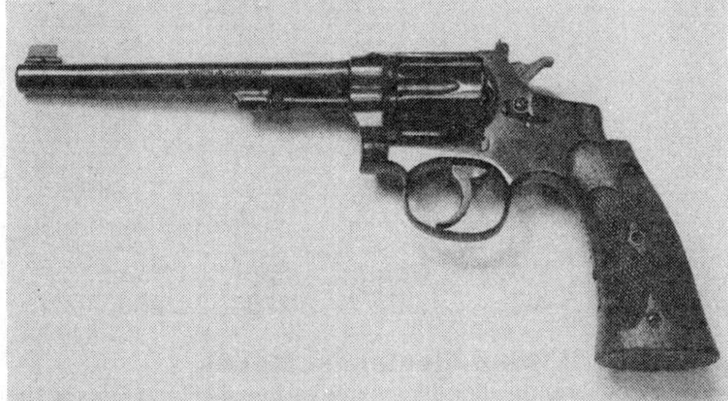

Courtesy Mike Stuckslager

"The True Bekeart"

Serial number range 138226 to 139275 in the .32 Hand Ejector series, production number stamped on butt. Professional appraisal should be secured.

Exc.	V.G.	Good	Fair	Poor
850	600	400	300	250

Standard Model

Exc.	V.G.	Good	Fair	Poor
600	400	250	200	125

REMINDER
The prices given in this book are RETAIL prices. They are a general guide as to what a willing buyer and willing seller might agree on.

.44 Hand Ejector 1st Model

This model is also known by collectors as the ".44 Triple Lock" or "The New Century." The Triple Lock nickname came from a separate locking device located on the extractor rod shroud that is used in addition to the usual two locks. This model is chambered for the .44 S&W Special cartridge or the .44 S&W Russian. On a limited basis it is also chambered in .44-40, .45 Colt, and .38-40. The fluted cylinder holds 6 shots, and the barrel was offered in standard lengths of 5" or 6.5". A limited quantity of 4" barrel was produced. The finish is blued or nickel-plated; and the grips are checkered walnut, with the gold S&W medallion on later models. There were approximately 15,375 manufactured between 1908 and 1915.

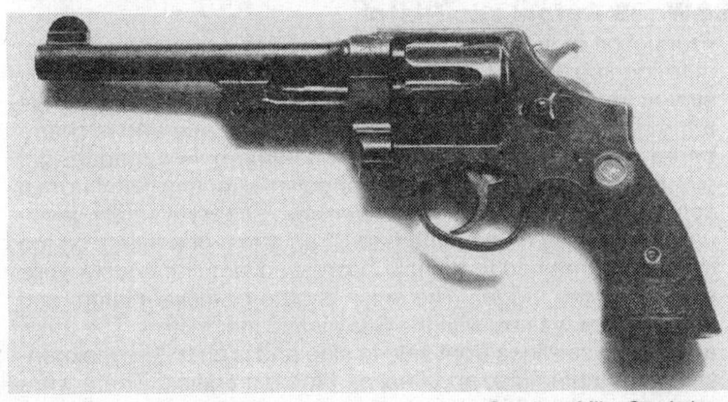

Courtesy Mike Stuckslager

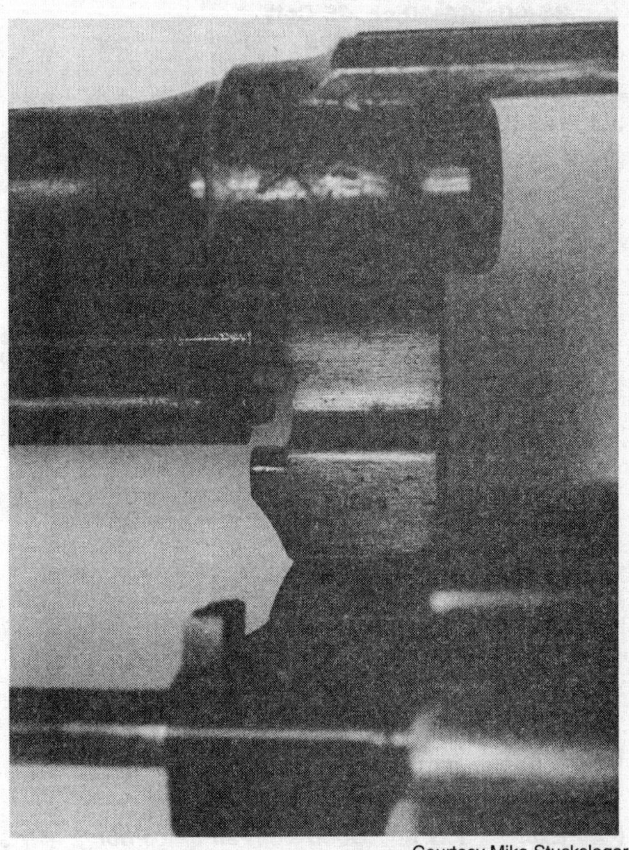

Courtesy Mike Stuckslager

.44 S&W Special and .44 S&W Russian

Exc.	V.G.	Good	Fair	Poor
1000	750	500	350	200

Other Calibers (Rare)

Exc.	V.G.	Good	Fair	Poor
1250	850	600	450	300

.44 Hand Ejector 2nd Model

This model is quite similar in appearance to the 1st Model. The major difference is the elimination of the third or triple lock device and the heavy ejector rod shroud. Other changes are internal and not readily apparent. This model is also standard in .44 S&W Special chambering but was offered rarely in .38-40, .44-40, and .45 Colt. Specimens have been noted with adjustable sights in 6-1/2" barrel lengths. Standard barrel lengths were 4", 5", and 6-1/2". There were approximately 17,510 manufactured between 1915 and 1937 in serial number range 15376 to 60000.

Courtesy Mike Stuckslager

.44 S & W Special

Exc.	V.G.	Good	Fair	Poor
700	600	500	350	200

.38-40, .44-40 or .45 Colt

Exc.	V.G.	Good	Fair	Poor
800	650	550	400	250

.44 Hand Ejector 3rd Model or Model of 1926

This model is similar in appearance to the 2nd Model but brought back the heavy ejector rod shroud of the 1st Model without the triple lock device. Barrel lengths were 4", 5", and 6-1/2". The .44 Hand Ejector Model was manufactured between 1926 and 1949.

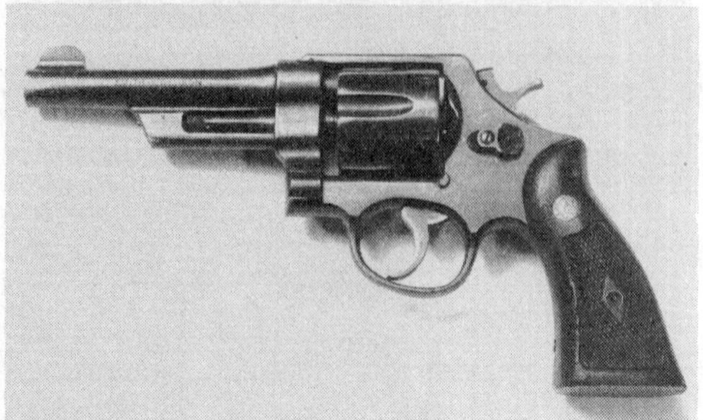

Courtesy Mike Stuckslager

.44 S & W Special

Exc.	V.G.	Good	Fair	Poor
700	450	350	275	150

.44-40 or .45 Colt

Exc.	V.G.	Good	Fair	Poor
850	550	400	300	150

.44 Hand Ejector 4th Model (Target Model)

The 4th Model featured a ribbed barrel, micrometer adjustable sight, and short throw hammer. Never a popular seller this model had only 5,050 pistol produced between 1950 and 1966.

Exc.	V.G.	Good	Fair	Poor
750	450	325	250	200

.45 Hand Ejector U.S. Service Model of 1917

WWI was on the horizon, and it seemed certain that the United States would become involved. The S&W people began to work with the Springfield Armory to develop a hand ejector model that would fire the .45-caliber Government cartridge. This was accomplished in 1916 by the use of half-moon clips. The new revolver is quite similar to the .44 Hand Ejector in appearance. It has a 5.5" barrel, blued finish with smooth walnut grips, and a lanyard ring on the butt. The designation "U.S.Army Model 1917" is stamped on the butt. After the war broke out, the government was not satisfied with S&W's production and actually took control of the company for the duration of the war. This was the first time that the company was not controlled by a Wesson. The factory records indicate that there were 163,476 Model 1917s manufactured between 1917 and 1919, the WWI years. After the war, the sale of these revolvers continued on a commercial and contract basis until 1949, when this model was finally dropped from the S&W product line.

Military Model

Exc.	V.G.	Good	Fair	Poor
550	350	300	200	150

Brazilian Contract

25,000 produced for the Brazilian government in 1938. The Brazilian crest is stamped on the sideplate.

Exc.	V.G.	Good	Fair	Poor
350	250	200	150	100

Commercial Model

High gloss blue and checkered walnut grips.

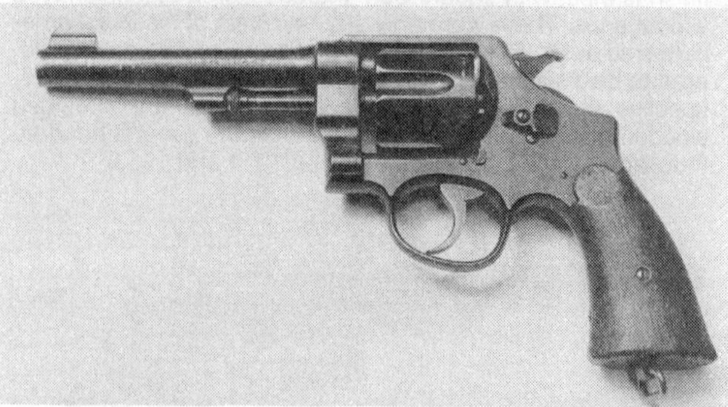

Courtesy Mike Stuckslager

Exc.	V.G.	Good	Fair	Poor
650	450	350	275	200

.455 Mark II Hand Ejector 1st Model

This model was designed the same as the .44 Hand Ejector 1st Model with no caliber stamping on the barrel. It has a barrel length of 6.4". Of the 5,000 revolvers produced and sold only 100 were commercial guns, the rest were military. Produced between 1914 and 1915. The commercial model is worth a premium.

Exc.	V.G.	Good	Fair	Poor
750	575	400	300	200

.455 Mark II Hand Ejector 2nd Model

Similar to the first model without an extractor shroud. Barrel length was also 6.5". Serial number range was 5000 to 74755. Manufactured from 1915 to 1917.

Exc.	V.G.	Good	Fair	Poor
500	300	250	225	175

Courtesy Smith & Wesson

S&W .35 Automatic Pistol

Production of the .35 Automatic was S&W's first attempt at an auto-loading pistol. As was always the case, the company strived for maximum safety and dependability. This model has a 3.5" barrel and a 7-shot detachable magazine and is chambered in .35 S&W Automatic, a one-time-only cartridge that eventually proved to be the major downfall of this pistol from a commercial standpoint. There were two separate safety devices—a revolving cam on the backstrap and a grip safety on the front strap that had to be fully depressed simultaneously while squeezing the trigger. The finish is blue or nickel-plated; and the grips are walnut, with the S&W inlaid medallions. The magazine release slides from side to side and is checkered, expensive to manufacture, and destined to be modified. There were approximately 8,350 manufactured.

Exc.	V.G.	Good	Fair	Poor
550	350	250	200	150

S&W .32 Automatic Pistol

In 1921 it became apparent to the powers that controlled S&W that the .35-caliber automatic was never going to be a commercial success. Harold Wesson, the new president, began to redesign the pistol to accept the .32 ACP, a commercially accepted cartridge, and to streamline the appearance to be more competitive with the other pistols on the market, notably Colt's. This new pistol used as many parts from the older model as possible for economy's sake. The pivoting barrel was discontinued, as was the cam-type safety in the rear grip strap. A magazine disconnector and a reduced-strength recoil spring to ease cocking were employed. The barrel length was kept at 3.5", and the 7-shot magazine was retained. The finish is blued only, and the grips are smooth walnut. There were only 957 of these manufactured between 1924 and 1936. They are eagerly sought by collectors.

Courtesy James Rankin

Exc.	V.G.	Good	Fair	Poor
2000	1500	1000	700	500

SMITH & WESSON MODERN HANDGUNS

NOTE: A surprising number of pistols are still found in their original boxes even for older models. This can add 100 percent to the value of the pistol.

With the development of the Hand Ejector Models and the swingout cylinders, Smith & Wesson opened the door to a number of new advancements in the revolver field. This new system allowed for a solid frame, making the weapon much stronger than the old top break design. The company also developed different basic frame sizes and gave them letter designations. The I frame, which later developed into the slightly larger J frame, was used for the .22-32 and the small, concealable .38 revolvers. The medium K frame was used for .38 duty- and target-type weapons. The N frame was the heavy-duty frame used for the larger .357 and .44 and .45 caliber revolvers. The hand ejector went through many evolutionary changes over the years. We strongly recommend that the collector secure a detailed volume that deals exclusively with Smith & Wesson (see the bibliography), and learn all that is available on this fascinating firearm. Models are catalogued the by their numerical designations, brief description are given, and current values offered. It is important to note that the S&W revolver that we see marketed by the company today has undergone many changes in reaching its present configuration. The early models featured five screws in their construction, not counting the grip screw. There were four screws fastening the sideplate and another through the front of the trigger guard that retained the cylinder stop plunger. The first change involved the elimination of the top sideplate screw, and the five-screw Smith & Wesson became the four-screw. Later the frame was changed to eliminate the cylinder stop plunger screw, and the three-screw was created. Some models were offered with a flat cylinder latch that was serrated instead of the familiar checkering. Recently in 1978, the method of attaching the barrel to the frame was changed; and the familiar pin was eliminated. At the same time, the recessed cylinder commonly found on magnum models was also eliminated. All of these factors have a definite affect on the value and collectibility of a particular S&W handgun.

NOTE: The pre-model number designations are listed in parentheses after the model number.

IMPORTANT PRICING INFORMATION

Values reflected will be affected by the following factors:

Five Screw Models add 40 to 50 percent.
Four Screw Models add 30 percent.
Models with flat latches add 20 percent.
Models not pinned or recessed deduct 10 percent.

Courtesy Smith & Wesson

Model 10 (.38 Military & Police)

This model has been in production in one configuration or another since 1899. It was always the mainstay of the S&W line and was originally known as the .38 Military and Police Model. The Model 10 is built on the K, or medium frame, and was always meant as a duty gun. It was offered with a 2", 3", 4", 5", or 6" barrel. Currently only the 4" and 6" are available. A round or square butt is offered. It is chambered for the .38 Special and is offered in blue or nickel-plate, with checkered walnut grips. The model designation is stamped on the yoke on all S&W revolvers. This model, with many other modern S&W pistols, underwent several engineering changes. These changes may affect the value of the pistol and an expert should be consulted. The dates of these changes are as follows:

10-None-1957	**10-1-1959**	**10-2-1961**
10-3-1961	**10-4-1962**	**10-5-1962**
10-6-1962		

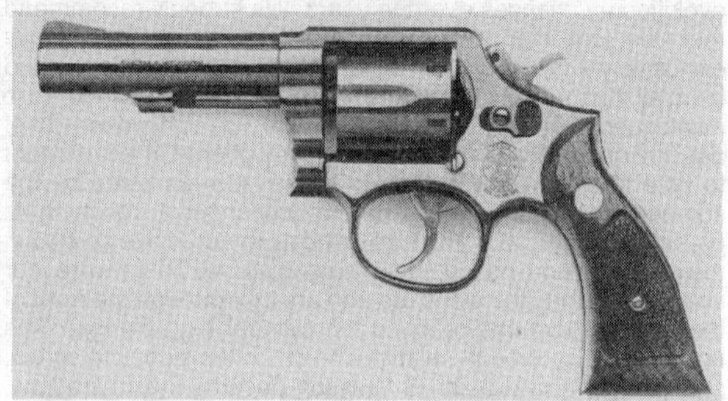

NIB	Exc.	V.G.	Good	Fair	Poor
350	250	200	150	125	90

Victory Model

Manufactured during WWII, this is a Model 10 with a sand-blasted and parkerized finish, a lanyard swivel, and smooth walnut grips. The serial number has a V prefix. This model was available in only 2" and 4" barrel lengths. The Victory Model was discontinued on April 27, 1945, with serial number VS811119.

Victory Model marked "N.Y.M.I." Courtesy Richard M. Kumor, Sr.

Exc.	V.G.	Good	Fair	Poor
350	200	150	100	75

NOTE: Top strap marked Navy will bring a 75 percent premium. Navy variation with both top strap and side plate marked will bring a 100 percent premium. Navy variation marked "N.Y.M.I." will bring a 125 percent premium. Revolvers marked "U.S.G.C." or "U.S.M.C." will bring a premium of unknown amount. Exercise caution.

Model 11 (.38/200 British)

First produced in 1947 S&W received many contracts for this service pistol. Nicknamed the .38/200 British Service Revolver, the company sold many of these models throughout the 1950s and 1960s. There are several rare variations of this model that will greatly affect its value. Consult an expert if special markings and barrel lengths are encountered.

Exc.	V.G.	Good	Fair	Poor
350	200	150	100	75

Model 12 (.38 Military & Police Airweight)

The Model 12 was introduced in 1952, starting serial number C223999, and is merely a Model 10 with a lightweight alloy frame and cylinder. In 1954 the alloy cylinder was replaced with one of steel that added an additional 4 ounces in weight. Discontinued in 1986.

Exc.	V.G.	Good	Fair	Poor
350	200	150	125	100

NOTE: Aluminum cylinder model add 40 percent.

USAF M-13 (Aircrewman)

In 1953 the Air Force purchased a large quantity of Model 12s with alloy frames and cylinders. They were intended for use by flight crews as survival weapons in emergencies. This model was not officially designated "13" by S&W, but the Air Force stamped "M13" on the top strap. This model was rejected by the Air Force in 1954 because of trouble with the alloy cylinder.

Exc.	V.G.	Good	Fair	Poor
900	750	600	450	250

Model 13 (.357 Military & Police)

This is simply the Model 10 M&P chambered for the .357 Magnum and fitted with a heavy barrel. It was introduced in 1974.

Exc.	V.G.	Good	Fair	Poor
325	250	200	175	125

Model 14 (K-38 Masterpiece)

This model is also known as the "K-38." In 1957 "Model 14" was stamped on the yoke. This model is offered in a 6" barrel with adjustable sights. In 1961 a single-action version with faster lock time was offered. This would be worth a small premium. This model was discontinued in 1981.

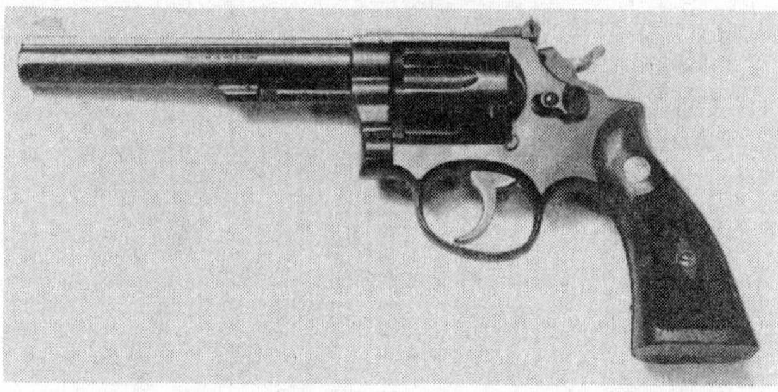

Courtesy Mike Stuckslager

Exc.	V.G.	Good	Fair	Poor
300	250	200	175	125

NOTE: Single-action model add 20 percent.

Model 15 (K-38 Combat Masterpiece)

Also known as the "Combat Masterpiece" this model was produced at the request of law enforcement officers who wanted the "K-38" fitted with a 4" barrel. The model went into production in 1950 and was discontinued in 1987.

Exc.	V.G.	Good	Fair	Poor
350	250	200	175	125

Model 16 (K-32 Masterpiece)

Also known as the "K-32" until 1957, this model is identical in appearance to the Model 14 except that it is chambered for .32 S&W. The Model 16 did not enjoy the commercial popularity of the Model 14 and was dropped from the line in 1973. Only 3,630 K-32s/Model 16s were sold between 1947 and 1973. Reintroduced in 1990 in .32 Magnum and discontinued in 1993.

Courtesy Mike Stuckslager

Post-War

Exc.	V.G.	Good	Fair	Poor
1000	700	450	300	250

Pre-War

Exc.	V.G.	Good	Fair	Poor
2000	1400	900	600	500

Model 16 (.32 Magnum)

Reintroduced in 1990 in .32 Magnum and discontinued in 1993.

NIB	Exc.	V.G.	Good	Fair	Poor
400	300	250	200	150	100

K-32 Combat Masterpiece

S&W produced a limited number of 4" barreled K-32 revolvers. They were never given a number designation, as they were discontinued before 1957 when the numbering system began.

Exc.	V.G.	Good	Fair	Poor
1200	800	500	350	300

Model 17 (K-22)

This is the numerical designation that S&W placed on the "K-22" in 1957. This target model .22 rimfire revolver has always been popular since its introduction in 1946. It is offered in 4", 6", and 8-3/8" barrel lengths, with all target options. The 8-3/8" barrel was dropped from the product line in 1993. The finish is blued, and it has checkered walnut grips.

Courtesy Mike Stuckslager

NIB	Exc.	V.G.	Good	Fair	Poor
350	275	225	175	125	100

Model 17 Plus

Introduced in 1996 this new version of the old Model 17 has a 10-round cylinder for its .22 LR cartridges. It features a 6" full lug barrel with Patridge front sight and adjustable rear sight. The hammer is semi-target style and the trigger is a smooth combat style. Finish is matte black and the grips are Hogue black rubber. Drilled and tapped for scope mounts. Weight is about 42 oz.

NIB	Exc.	V.G.	Good	Fair	Poor
350	300	250	200	150	100

REMINDER

An "N/A" or "—" instead of a price indicates that tpricing is not available for that gun in that condition, or that sales for that particular model are so few that a reliable price cannot be given.

Model 617 Plus

Identical to the Model 17 but furnished with stainless steel frame and cylinder.

NIB	Exc.	V.G.	Good	Fair	Poor
375	300	250	200	150	100

Model 647

Introduced in 2003 this revolver is chambered for the .17 HMR cartridge. Fitted with a 8.375" barrel with full lug. Six-round cylinder capacity. Stainless steel finish. Adjustable rear sight. Hogue rubber grips. Fitted with a target trigger and hammer. Drilled and tapped for scope. Weight is about 52.5 oz.

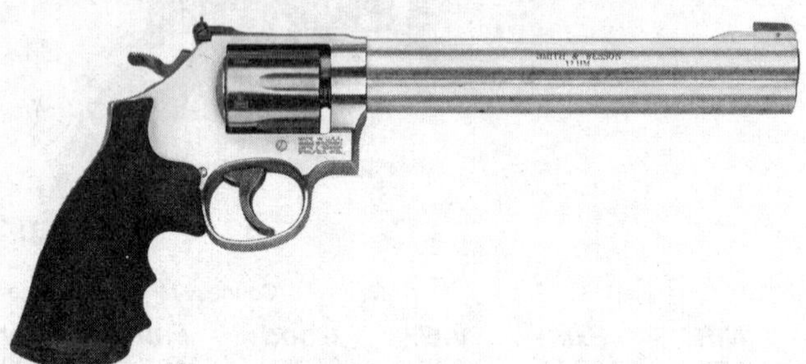

NIB	Exc.	V.G.	Good	Fair	Poor
675	525	—	—	—	—

Model 648

Identical to the Model 617 but chambered for the .22 Magnum rimfire cartridge.

NIB	Exc.	V.G.	Good	Fair	Poor
325	300	275	225	175	100

Model 648 (New Model)

Introduced in 2003 this medium frame revolver is chambered for the .22 WMR cartridge and fitted with a 6" full lug barrel. Pinned Patridge front sight and adjustable rear sight. New extractor system. Drilled and tapped for scope mount. Stainless steel finish. Weight is 45 oz.

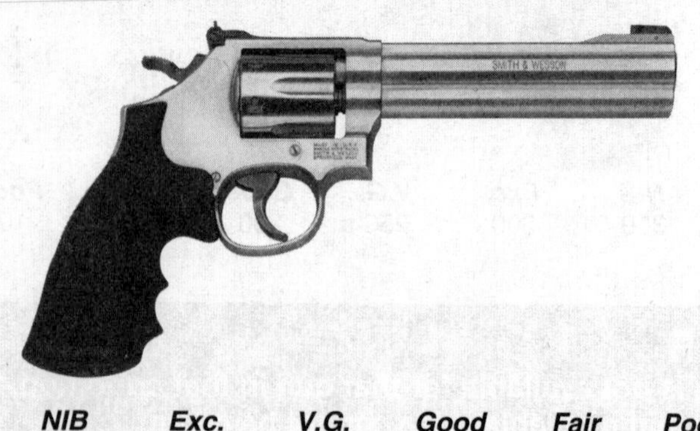

NIB	Exc.	V.G.	Good	Fair	Poor
660	525	—	—	—	—

Note On "K Frame" Target Models:

1. The factory eliminated the upper corner screw from the side plate in 1955. The 5-screw became a 4-screw. This change occurred around serial number K260000.
2. Model number designations were stamped on the yoke in 1957.

Model 18 (K-22 Combat Masterpiece)

This is the model designation for the 4"-barrel "Combat Masterpiece" chambered for the .22 rimfire.

Exc.	V.G.	Good	Fair	Poor
350	275	250	200	125

Model 19 (.357 Combat Magnum)

Introduced in 1954 at the urging of Bill Jordan, a competition shooter with the U.S. Border Patrol who went on to become a respected gun writer, this model is one of Smith and Wesson's most popular pistols. It was built on the "K-Frame" and was the first medium frame revolver chambered for the powerful .357 Magnum cartridge. Since its inception the Model 19 has been one of S&W's most popular revolvers. It was the first revolver to be introduced as a three-screw model. Originally it was offered with a 4" heavy barrel with extractor shroud; the 6" became available in 1963. The finish is blued or nickel plated, and the grips are checkered walnut. The Goncalo Alves target stocks first appeared in 1959. In 1968 a 2.5" round butt version was introduced. The Model 19 has been the basis for two commemoratives—the Texas Ranger/with Bowie Knife and the Oregon State Police/with Belt Buckle. This model is no longer in production.

NIB	Exc.	V.G.	Good	Fair	Poor
400	250	225	200	150	100

Texas Ranger Cased with Knife

NIB
700

Oregon State Police Cased with Buckle

NIB
900

Model 20 (.38/.44 Heavy Duty)

Known as the ".38/.44 Heavy Duty" before the change to numerical designations this model was brought out in 1930 in response to requests from law enforcement personnel for a more powerful sidearm. This model, along with the .38-44 S&W Special cartridge, was an attempt to solve the problem. The revolver was manufactured with a standard 5" long barrel but has been noted rarely as short as 3-1/2" and as long as 8-3/8". It was built on the large N-frame and is blued or nickel-plated, with checkered walnut grips. Eventually the popularity of the .357 Magnum made the Model 20 superfluous, and it was discontinued in 1966. Post-war production for this model was about 20,000 revolvers.

Courtesy Mike Stuckslager

Exc.	V.G.	Good	Fair	Poor
700	450	300	250	150

NOTE: Pre-war .44 Special add 50 percent.

Model 21 (1950 Military)

This model was known as the "1950 Military" and the "4th Model .44 Hand Ejector" before the Model 21 designation was applied in 1957. The Model 21 was chambered for the .44 Special cartridge and equipped with fixed sights. The Model 21 was built on the N frame and is quite rare, as only 1,200 were manufactured in 16 years of production. It was discontinued in 1966.

Exc.	V.G.	Good	Fair	Poor
1350	1300	950	650	500

Model 696

Introduced in 1997 this model features a 3" underlug barrel. chambered for the .44 Special and fitted on an L-frame, capacity is 5 rounds. Grips are Hogue black rubber. Finish is stainless steel. Weight is approximately 48 oz.

NIB	Exc	V.G.	Good	Fair	Poor
450	400	350	—	—	—

Model 22 (1950 .45 Military)

This model was known as the "1950 .45 Military" before 1957. It was actually introduced in 1951 and is similar in appearance to the Model 21 except that it is chambered for the .45 Auto Rim or .45 ACP cartridge. Half-moon clips are used with the latter. There were 3,976 manufactured between 1951 and 1966. Beginning serial number for this model was S85,000.

Exc.	V.G.	Good	Fair	Poor
800	650	550	300	200

Model 23 (.38-44 Outdoorsman)

The .38-44 Outdoorsman was the model name of this N-frame revolver before the 1957 designation change. This is simply the Model 20 with adjustable sights. It was introduced in 1931 as a heavy-duty sporting handgun with hunters in mind. S&W produced 4,761 of these pre-war revolvers. It features a 6.5" barrel and blued finish and was the first S&W to have the new checkered walnut "Magna" grips. After 1949 this revolver was thoroughly modernized and had the later ribbed barrel. There were a total of 8,365 manufactured before the model was discontinued in 1966. 6,039 were of the modernized configuration.

Courtesy Mike Stuckslager

Exc.	V.G.	Good	Fair	Poor
750	550	400	250	200

Model 22 - Thunder Ranch .45 ACP

Limited edition six-shot single/double-action chambered for .45 ACP. Blued with 4" tapered barrel, 37.5 oz. Cocobolo grips engraved with Thunder Ranch insignia. Fixed sights. SNs begin with TRR0000. MSRP: 750

Model 24 (.44 Target Model of 1950)

This model was introduced as the .44 Target Model of 1950. It is simply the N-frame Model 21 with adjustable target sights. This revolver was quite popular with the long-range handgunning devotees and their leader, Elmer Keith. The introduction of the .44 Magnum in 1956 began the death knell of the Model 24, and it was finally discontinued in 1966. S&W produced a total of 5,050 Model 24s. It was reintroduced in 1983 and 1984—and then was dropped again.

Exc.	V.G.	Good	Fair	Poor
750	550	400	300	250

Model 25 (.45 Target Model of 1950)

Prior to the model designation change in 1957 this model was also known as the .45 Target Model of 1955, this was an improved version of the 1950 Target .45. The Model 25 features a heavier barrel 4", 6.5", or 8" in length with blued or nickel-plated finish. All target options were offered. The Model 25 is chambered for the .45 ACP or .45 Auto-rim cartridges. This model is still available chambered for .45 Colt as the Model 25-5.

Exc.	V.G.	Good	Fair	Poor
650	450	350	250	200

Model 25-3 125th Anniversary with Case

NIB
450

Model 25-2

This is the discontinued modern version of the Model 25 chambered in .45 ACP. The 6.5" barrel is shortened to 6" and is available in a presentation case.

Exc.	V.G.	Good	Fair	Poor
550	450	300	200	—

Model 25 Mountain Gun

Introduced in 2004 this .45 Colt N-frame round butt model features a 4" tapered barrel with black blade front sight and adjustable rear sight. Cocobolo wood grips. Blued finish. Weight is about 40 oz.

NIB	Exc.	V.G.	Good	Fair	Poor
800	625	—	—	—	—

Model 625-2

This is the stainless steel version of the Model 25-2. It is fitted with a 5" barrel and has Pachmayr SK/GR gripper stocks as standard. Designed for pin shooting. Weight is about 45 oz.

NIB	Exc.	V.G.	Good	Fair	Poor
700	550	450	300	200	—

Notes on N Frame Revolvers:

1. N-frame models were changed from 5-screw to 4-screw between 1956 and 1958. Serial number SI75000.
2. Trigger guard screw was eliminated in 1961.
3. The pinned barrel and recessed cylinder were discontinued in 1978.

Model 625 IDPA

As above but fitted with a 4" barrel, adjustable rear sight, patridge front sight, and Hogue grips. Introduced in 2002. Weight is about 43 oz.

NIB	Exc.	V.G.	Good	Fair	Poor
700	550	—	—	—	—

Model 625 JM

Introduced in 2005 this model is chambered for the .45 ACP cartridge and fitted with a 4" full lug barrel with adjustable rear sight and Patridge front sight. Capacity is 6 rounds. Wood grips. Weight is about 43 oz.

NIB	Exc.	V.G.	Good	Fair	Poor
845	625	—	—	—	—

Model 625 Mountain Gun

Offered for the first time in 1996 this model is chambered for the .45 Colt cartridge. It is fitted with a 4" tapered barrel with ramp front sight and adjustable rear sight. The frame is drilled and tapped for a scope mount. In 2000 this model was offered in .45 ACP caliber.

NOTE: The Model 625 Mountain Gun is a limited production revolver limited to between 2,500 and 3,000 guns. When those units are sold the model is no longer in production until re-issued by S&W.

NIB	Exc.	V.G.	Good	Fair	Poor
650	500	400	350	—	—

Model 610

Introduced in 1998 this revolver is chambered for the 10mm cartridge. It is fitted with a 6.5" full-lug barrel and an unfluted cylinder. Hogue grips are standard. Adjustable rear sight. Interchangeable front sight. Weight is approximately 52 oz.

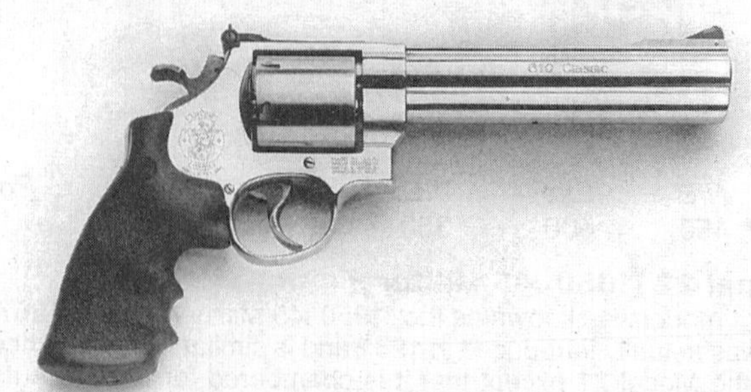

NIB	Exc.	V.G.	Good	Fair	Poor
750	525	—	—	—	—

Model 26 (1950 .45 Target)

This is the numerical designation of the 1950 .45 Target Model. This large N-frame revolver is basically the same as the Model 25 but has a lighter, thinner barrel. This caused its unpopularity among competitive shooters who wanted a heavier revolver. This brought about the Model 25 and the demise of the Model 26 in 1961 after only 2,768 were manufactured. The Model 26 also has two additional variations and are marked 26-1 and 26-2.

Exc.	V.G.	Good	Fair	Poor
850	700	500	400	250

Factory Registered .357 Magnum

In the early 1930s, a gun writer named Phillip B. Sharpe became interested in the development of high performance loads to be used in the then-popular .38-44 S&W revolvers. He repeatedly urged the company to produce a revolver especially made to handle these high pressure loads. In 1934 S&W asked Winchester to produce a new cartridge that would create the ballistics that Sharpe was seeking. This new cartridge was made longer than the standard .38 Special case so that it could not inadvertently be fired in an older gun. The company never felt that this would be a commercially popular venture and from the onset visualized the ".357 Magnum" as a strictly deluxe hand-built item. They were to be individually numbered, in addition to the serial number, and registered to the new owner. The new Magnum was to be the most expensive revolver in the line. The gun went on the market in 1935, and the first one was presented to FBI Director J. Edgar Hoover. The gun was to become a tremendous success. S&W could only produce 120 per month, and this did not come close to filling orders. In 1938 the practice of numbering and registering each revolver was discontinued after 5,500 were produced. The ".357 Magnum," as it was designated, continued as one of the company's most popular items.

The Factory Registered Model was built on the N-frame. It could be custom ordered with any barrel length from 3.5" up to 8-3/8". The finish is blue, and the grips are checkered walnut. This model was virtually hand-built and test targeted. A certificate of registration was furnished with each revolver. The registration number was stamped on the yoke of the revolver with the prefix "Reg." This practice ceased in 1938 after 5,500 were produced.

Courtesy Mike Stuckslager

Exc.	V.G.	Good	Fair	Poor
2000	1200	800	550	400

Pre-war .357 Magnum

This is the same as the Factory Registered Model without the certificate and the individual numbering. Approximately 1,150 were manufactured between 1938 and 1941. Production ceased for WWII weapons production.

Exc.	V.G.	Good	Fair	Poor
850	600	450	300	250

Model 27 (.357 Magnum)

In 1948 after the end of WWII, production of this revolver commenced. The new rebound slide operated hammer block and short throw hammer were utilized, and the barrel lengths offered were 3.5", 5", 6", 6-1/2", and 8-3/8". In 1957 the model designation was changed to Model 27; and in 1975 the target trigger, hammer and Goncalo Alves target grips were made standard. This revolver is still available from S&W and has been in production longer than any other N-frame pistol. Some additional variations may be of interest to the collector. Around serial number SI71584 the three-screw side plate model was first produced. In 1960 the model designation -1 was added to the model to indicate the change to a left-hand thread to the extractor rod. In 1962 the cylinder stop was changed, which disposed of the need for a plunger spring hole in front of the trigger guard. This change was indicated by a -2 behind the model number.

NIB	Exc.	V.G.	Good	Fair	Poor
625	325	300	250	200	150

Model 627

This is special edition stainless steel version of the Model 27 and is offered with a 5-1/2" barrel. Manufactured in 1989 only. Approximately 4,500 produced.

NIB	Exc.	V.G.	Good	Fair	Poor
600	400	350	300	200	150

Model 28 (Highway Patrolman)

The Model 27 revolver was extremely popular among law enforcement officers, and many police agencies were interested in purchasing such a weapon—except for the cost. In 1954 S&W produced a new model called, at the time, the "Highway Patrolman." This model had all the desirable performance features of the deluxe Model 27 but lacked the cosmetic features that drove up the price. The finish is a matte blue; the rib is sandblasted instead of checkered or serrated, and the grips are the standard checkered walnut. Barrel lengths are 4" and 6.5". On late models the 6.5" barrel was reduced to 6", as on all S&Ws. The model designation was changed to Model 28 in 1957. S&W discontinued the Model 28 in 1986.

Exc.	V.G.	Good	Fair	Poor
425	250	225	175	100

Model 29 (.44 Magnum)

In the early 1950s, handgun writers, under the leadership of Elmer Keith, were in the habit of loading the .44 Special cartridge to high performance levels and firing them in the existing .44 Hand Ejectors. They urged S&W to produce a revolver strong enough to consistently fire these heavy loads. In 1954 Remington, at the request of S&W produced the .44 Magnum cartridge. As was the case with the .357 Magnum, the cases were longer so that they would not fit in the chambers of the older guns. The first .44 Magnum became available for sale in early 1956. The first 500 were made with the 6.5" barrel; the 4" became available later that year. In 1957 the model designation was changed to 29, and the 8-3/8" barrel was introduced. The Model 29 is available in blue or nickel-plate. It came standard with all target options and was offered in a fitted wood case. The Model 29 is considered by many knowledgeable people to be the finest revolver S&W has ever produced. The older Model 29 revolvers are in a different collector category than most modern S&W revolvers. The early four-screw models can be worth a 50 percent premium in excellent condition. These early models were produced from 1956 to 1958 and approximately 6,500 were sold. One must regard these revolvers on a separate basis and have them individually appraised for proper valuation. In 1993 the 4" barrel was dropped from production. This model is no longer in production.

NIB	Exc.	V.G.	Good	Fair	Poor
775	525	300	250	200	150

Early 5-Inch Barrel Model 29

This is the rarest of the Model 29s. A total of 500 were manufactured in 1958. Collectors are cautioned to exercise care before purchasing one of these rare Model 29 variations.

NIB	Exc.	V.G.	Good	Fair	Poor
2250	1500	1200	800	500	300

Model 629

This revolver is simply a stainless steel version of the Model 29 chambered for the .44 Magnum. In 2002 this model was offered with HiViz sights.

NIB	Exc.	V.G.	Good	Fair	Poor
595	400	300	250	225	200

Model 629 Classic

This model has additional features that the standard Model 629 does not have such as: Chamfered cylinder, full lug barrel, interchangeable front sights, Hogue combat grips, and a drilled and tapped frame to accept scope mounts.

NIB	Exc.	V.G.	Good	Fair	Poor
575	375	325	250	225	200

Model 629 Classic DX

Has all of the features of the Model 629 Classic, introduced in 1991, plus two sets of grips and five interchangeable front sights. Available in 6.5" or 8-3/8" barrel. A 5" barrel option was offered in 1992 but dropped in 1993.

NIB	Exc.	V.G.	Good	Fair	Poor
695	500	450	350	300	150

Model 629 Classic Powerport

Introduced in 1996 this model offers a integral compensator with a 6.5" full lug barrel. The Patridge front sight is pinned and the rear sight is fully adjustable. The frame is drilled and tapped for scope mounts. Synthetic Hogue combat-style grips are standard. Weight is approximately 52 oz.

This symbol denotes "Sleepers" with rapidly-rising values and/or significant collector potential.

NIB	Exc.	V.G.	Good	Fair	Poor
675	550	—	—	—	—

Model 629 Backpacker

This 1994 variation of the Model 629 is built on the N-frame with round butt. Cylinders are fluted and chamfered. Barrel length is 3" with adjustable rear sight. The finish is stainless steel and Hogue rubber grips are standard. Weight is approximately 40 oz.

NIB	Exc.	V.G.	Good	Fair	Poor
700	600	500	400	300	200

Model 629 Mountain Gun

This limited edition 6-shot revolver, introduced in 1993, features a 4" barrel chambered for the .44 Magnum. Built on the large N frame this pistol is made from stainless steel and is drilled and tapped for scope mounts. It is equipped with a Hogue round butt rubber monogrip. Standard sights are a pinned black ramp front sight and an adjustable black rear blade. Weight is approximately 40 oz. Model was re-introduced in 1999.

NIB	Exc.	V.G.	Good	Fair	Poor
600	450	400	350	300	150

Fiftieth Anniversary Model 29

A commemorative edition of the classic .44 Magnum. Carbon steel with polished blue finish. Double-action 6-shot. LOA 12", 6.5" barrel, 48.5 oz. Cocobolo wood grips with 24kt gold anniversary logo.

NIB	Exc.	V.G.	Good	Fair	Poor
1100	—	—	—	—	—

Model 30 (The .32 Hand Ejector)

This model was built on the small I frame and based on the .32 Hand Ejector Model of 1903. This older model was dropped from production in 1942. It was re-introduced in 1949 in a more modern version but still referred to as the .32 Hand Ejector. In 1957 the model designation was changed to Model 30. In 1960 this frame size was dropped, and the J frame, which had been in use since 1950, became standard for the Model 30. S&W stamped -1 behind the model number to designate this important change in frame size. The Model 30 is chambered for the .32 S&W long cartridge. It has a 6-shot cylinder and 2", 3", 4", and 6" barrel lengths. It has fixed sights and is either blued or nickel-plated. The butt is round, with checkered walnut grips. It was discontinued in 1976.

Courtesy W.P. Hallstein III and son Chip

Exc.	V.G.	Good	Fair	Poor
350	250	200	150	100

Model 31 (.32 Regulation Police)

This model is the same as the Model 30 with a square butt. It was known as the .32 Regulation Police before 1957. It is now discontinued.

Exc.	V.G.	Good	Fair	Poor
375	300	250	150	100

Model 31 (.32 Regulation Police Target)

The Target model of the Regulation Police is rare. Only 196 of these special variations were produced in 1957. All specifications are the same as the Model 31 except for the addition of adjustable sights.

Exc.	V.G.	Good	Fair	Poor
750	625	450	325	200

Model 32 (.38/.32 Terrier)

This model, known as the Terrier prior to 1957, was introduced in 1936. It is essentially a .38 Regulation Police chambered for .38 S&W and with a 2" barrel and round butt. Like the Model 30 and 31 this revolver was originally built on the I-frame, which was changed to the J frame in 1960. The -1 behind the model number signifies this change. It is offered in blue or nickel-plate and has a 5-shot cylinder, fixed sights, and checkered walnut grips. This model was discontinued in 1974.

Exc.	V.G.	Good	Fair	Poor
350	250	200	150	100

NOTE: A limited production version with alloy frame and steel cylinder was produced as the Model 032. Add 30 percent for this model.

Model 33 (.38 Regulation Police)

This model is simply the .38 Regulation Police with a square butt and 4" barrel chambered for the .38 S&W. The factory referred to this model as the .38-.32 revolver. It, too, was built on the small I frame and later changed to the J frame in 1960. The Model 33 was discontinued in 1974.

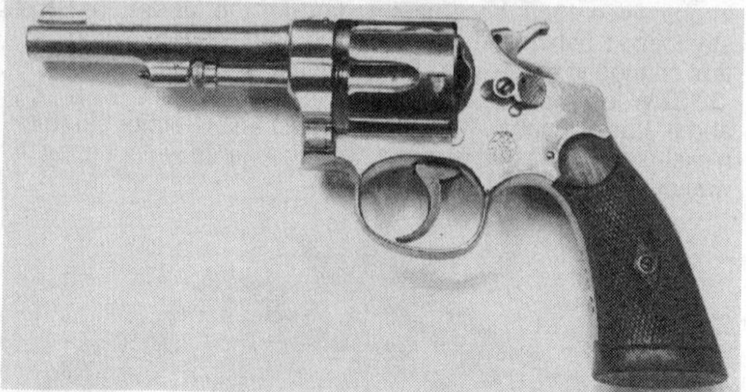

Courtesy Mike Stuckslager

Exc.	V.G.	Good	Fair	Poor
350	250	200	150	100

Model 34 (.22/.32 Kit Gun)

Introduced in 1936 as the .22-32 Kit Gun, it has a 2" or 4" barrel, either round or square butt, and adjustable sights. This model underwent several modifications before it reached its present form. S&W modernized this revolver in 1953 with the addition of a coil mainspring and micro-click sights. The Model 34 is built on this improved version. The revolver is a .32 Hand Ejector chambered for the .22 rimfire. It is built on the I frame until 1960 when the changeover to the improved J frame occurred. The -1 behind the model number indicates this variation. The Model 34 is offered blued or nickel-plate.

Courtesy Mike Stuckslager

NIB	Exc.	V.G.	Good	Fair	Poor
475	375	300	250	175	100

Model 35 (.22/.32 Target)

This is a square-butt, 6"-barreled version of the .22/32 Hand Ejector. It was known prior to 1957 as the .22/32 Target. It underwent the same changes as the Model 34 but was discontinued in 1973.

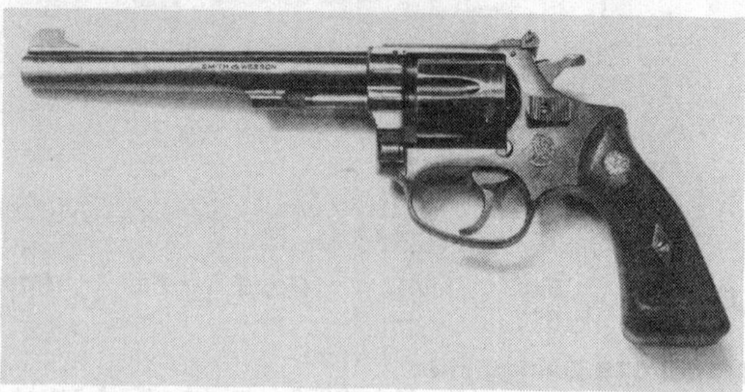

Courtesy Mike Stuckslager

Exc.	V.G.	Good	Fair	Poor
500	400	325	275	100

AIRLITE SERIES (TITANIUM CYLINDER—ALUMINUM ALLOY FRAME)

Model 317 AirLite

This 8-round revolver was introduced in 1997 and is chambered for the .22 LR cartridge. It is fitted with a 2" barrel, serrated ramp front sight, fixed rear sight, and Dymondwood boot grips. It is produced from carbon and stainless steel and also aluminum alloy on a J frame. Its weight is about 9.9 oz.

NIB	Exc.	V.G.	Good	Fair	Poor
425	375	325	—	—	—

Model 317 AirLite Kit Gun

This version of the Model 317 was introduced in 1998 and is fitted with a 3" barrel with adjustable rear sight. Choice of Dymondwood grips or Uncle Mike's Combat grips. Weight is about 12 oz. In 2001 this model was offered with HiViz green dot front sight.

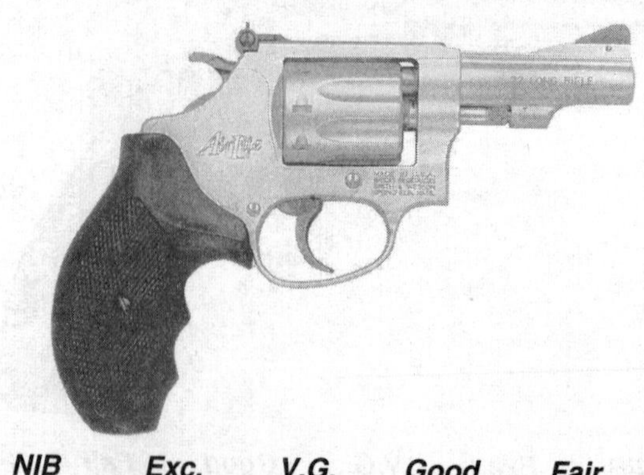

NIB	Exc.	V.G.	Good	Fair	Poor
500	400	325	—	—	—

This symbol denotes "Sleepers" with rapidly-rising values and/or significant collector potential.

Model 317 AirLite Ladysmith

This model features a 2" barrel and Dymondwood grips. Display case is standard. Weight is about 10 oz.

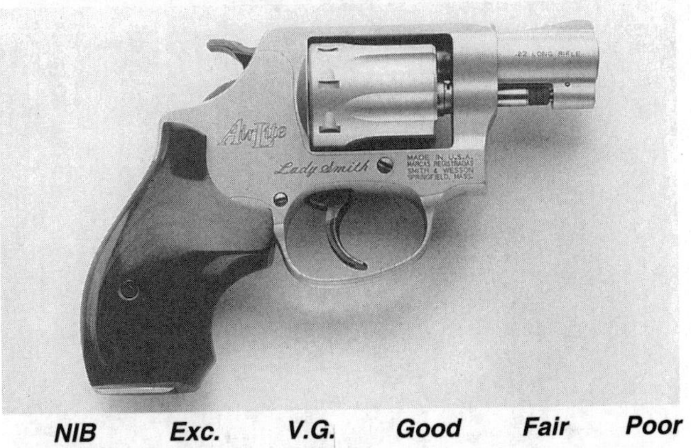

NIB	Exc.	V.G.	Good	Fair	Poor
500	400	325	—	—	—

Model 325PD

Introduced in 2004 this 6-round large frame revolver is chambered for the .45 ACP cartridge. Fitted with a 2.75" barrel. Wooden grips and HiViz sights. Black oxide finish. Weight is about 21.5 oz.

NIB	Exc.	V.G.	Good	Fair	Poor
900	700	—	—	—	—

Model 331 AirLite

This model is chambered for the .32 H&R Magnum cartridge on a J frame. Barrel length is 1-7/8". Exposed hammer offers single or double-action. The frame is aluminum, as is the barrel shroud and yoke. The cylinder is titanium. The barrel has a stainless steel liner. Matte finish. Because the revolver is made from aluminum and titanium it has a two-tone appearance because of the two different materials. Choice of wood or rubber boot grips. Capacity is 6 rounds. Weight is about 12 oz. with rubber grip and 11.2 oz. with wood grip. Introduced in 1999.

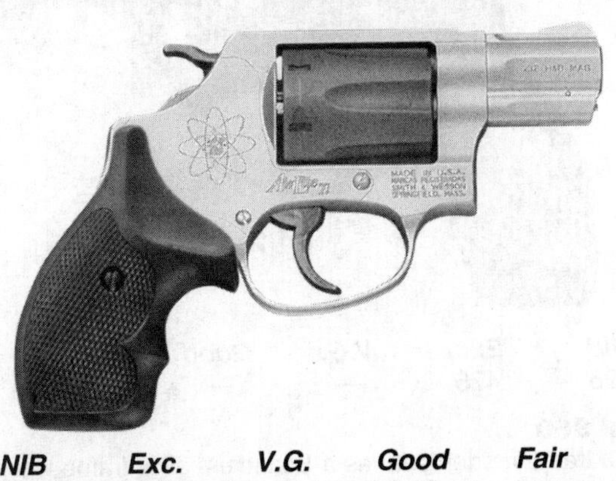

NIB	Exc.	V.G.	Good	Fair	Poor
550	450	—	—	—	—

Model 332 AirLite

This model is similar to the Model 331 above but with a concealed hammer, double-action configuration. Weight is 12 oz. with rubber grips and 11.3 oz. with wood grips.

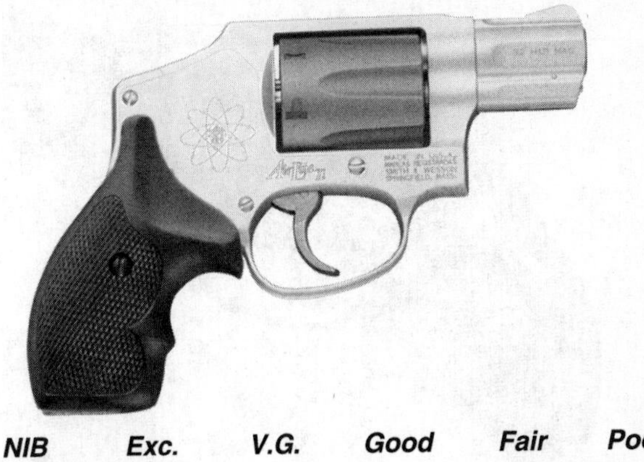

NIB	Exc.	V.G.	Good	Fair	Poor
550	450	—	—	—	—

Model 337 AirLite

This model has an aluminum frame, exposed hammer, titanium cylinder. Front sight is black and pinned. Smooth trigger. Cylinder capacity is five rounds. Chambered for .38 Special +P ammo. Barrel length is 1-7/8". Wood or rubber grips. Weight with wood groups is about 11.2 oz., with rubber grips about 12 oz. Introduced in 1999.

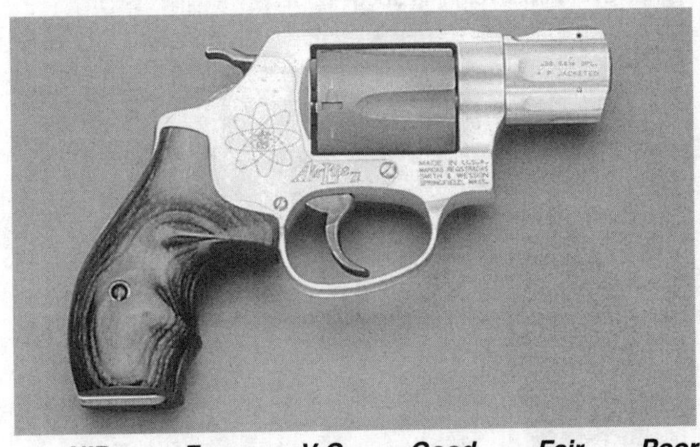

NIB	Exc.	V.G.	Good	Fair	Poor
575	450	—	—	—	—

Model 337 Kit Gun

Similar to the Model 337 but fitted with a 3" barrel. Adjustable rear sight. Weight is about 13.5 oz. In 2001 this model was offered with HiViz green dot front sight.

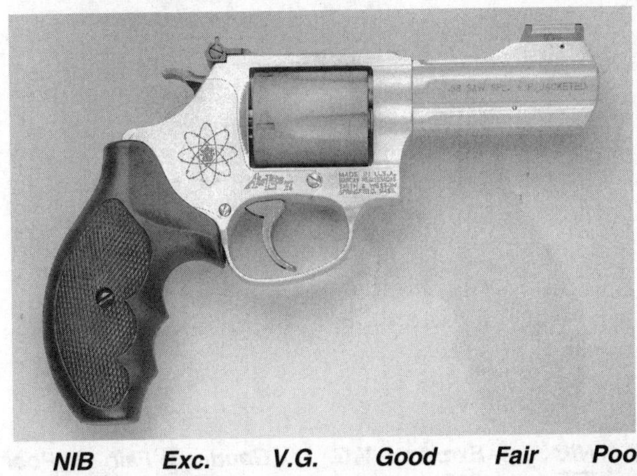

NIB	Exc.	V.G.	Good	Fair	Poor
650	475	—	—	—	—

Model 337 PD

Similar to the Model 337 but with a matte black finish over the aluminum frame and Hogue Bantam grips. Weight is 10.7 oz. Introduced in 2000.

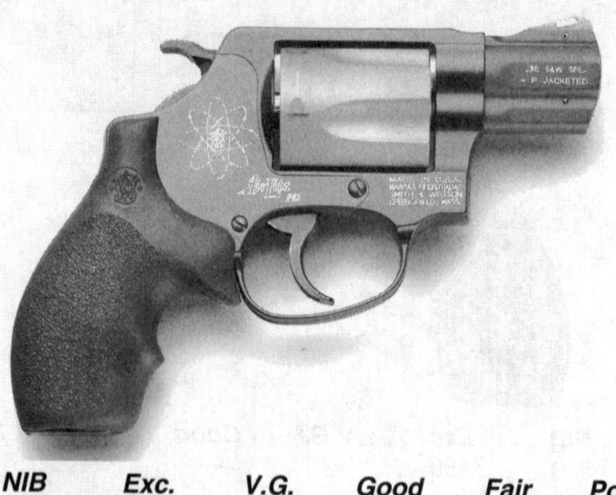

NIB	Exc.	V.G.	Good	Fair	Poor
600	450	—	—	—	—

Model 340

Introduced in 2001 this hammerless model features a Scandium alloy frame and is fitted with a 1.875" barrel. Chambered for the .357 Magnum cartridge with a 5-round cylinder. Matte stainless gray finish. Pinned black front sight. Hogue Bantam grips standard. Weight is about 12 oz.

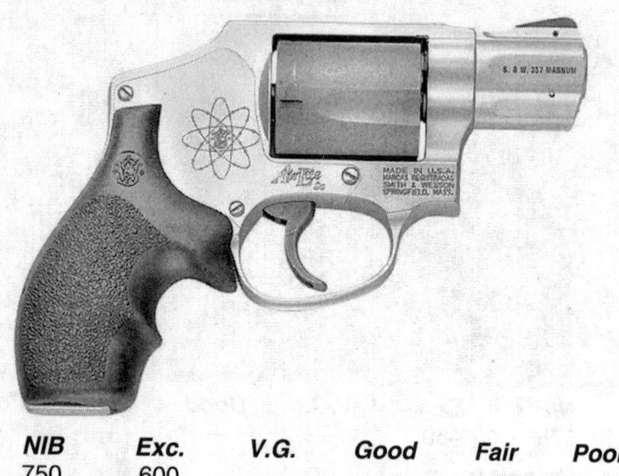

NIB	Exc.	V.G.	Good	Fair	Poor
750	600	—	—	—	—

Model 340 PD

Same as the Model 340 but with a gray/black finish. Also introduced in 2001.

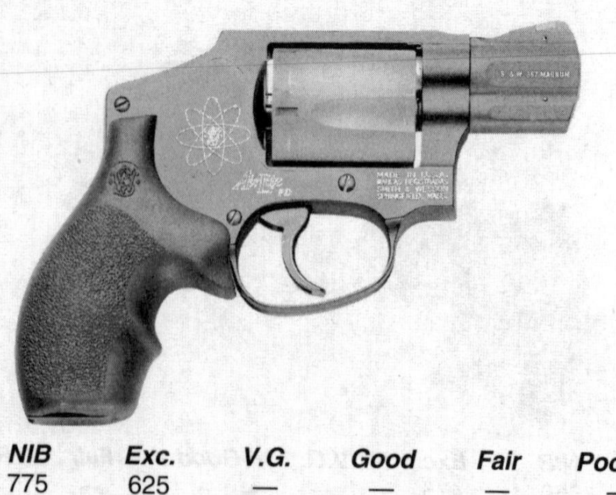

NIB	Exc.	V.G.	Good	Fair	Poor
775	625	—	—	—	—

Model 342 AirLite

This is similar to the above model but with double-action-only concealed hammer. Weight is 11.3 oz. with wood grips and 12 oz. with rubber grips. Introduced in 1999.

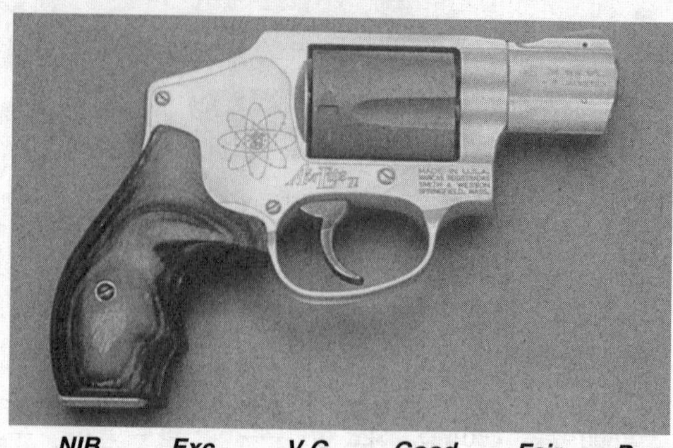

NIB	Exc.	V.G.	Good	Fair	Poor
575	450	—	—	—	—

Model 342 PD

Similar to the Model 337 but with matte black finish over the aluminum frame and Hogue Bantam grips. Weight is about 10.8 oz. Introduced in 2000.

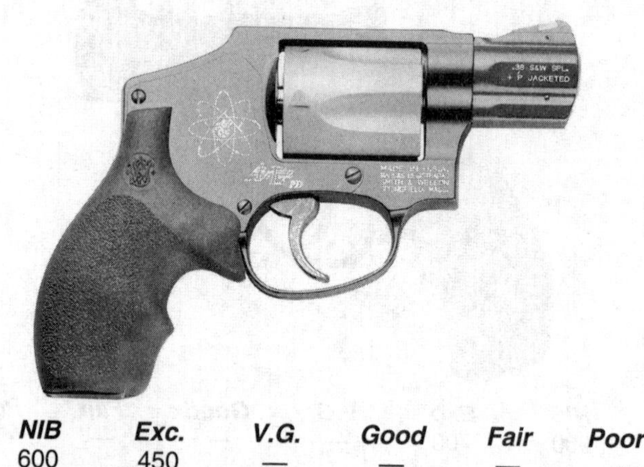

NIB	Exc.	V.G.	Good	Fair	Poor
600	450	—	—	—	—

Model 351PD

This 7-shot revolver is chambered for the .22 Magnum cartridge and fitted with a 1.875" barrel. Black oxide finish. Rubber grips. HiViz sights. Weight is about 10.6 oz.

NIB	Exc.	V.G.	Good	Fair	Poor
625	475	—	—	—	—

Model 360

This J frame model features a Scandium alloy frame with exposed hammer and 5-shot cylinder. Fixed sights on a 1.875" barrel. Matte stainless grey finish. Weight is about 12 oz. Introduced in 2001.

NIB	Exc.	V.G.	Good	Fair	Poor
750	600	—	—	—	—

Model 360 Kit Gun

This version of the M360 is fitted with a 3.125" barrel with HiViz green dot front sight and adjustable rear sight. Weight is about 14.5 oz. Introduced in 2001.

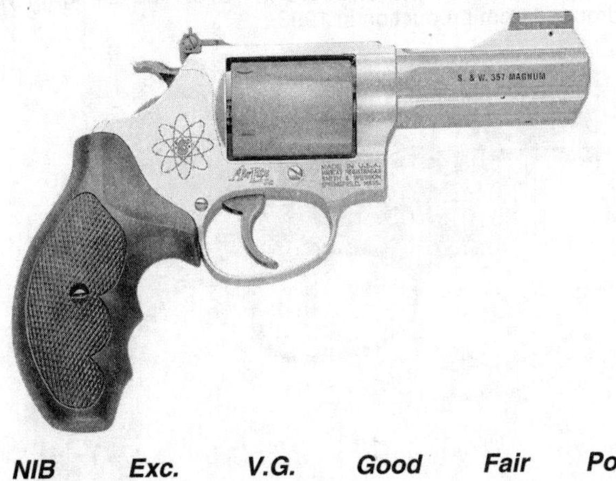

NIB	Exc.	V.G.	Good	Fair	Poor
875	700	—	—	—	—

Model 386

Introduced in 2001 this L frame model features a 6-shot cylinder chambered for the .357 Magnum cartridge. Fitted with a 3.125" barrel with HiViz green dot front sight and adjustable rear sight. Scandium alloy frame with matte stainless gray finish. Weight is about 18.5 oz. Hogue Batam grips.

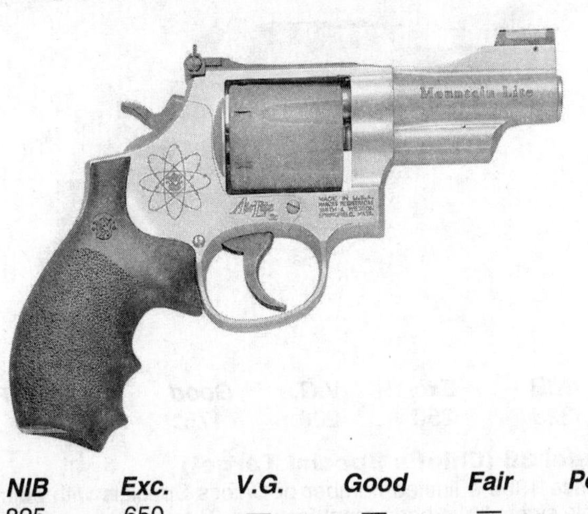

NIB	Exc.	V.G.	Good	Fair	Poor
825	650	—	—	—	—

Model 386 PD

Same as above but with gray/black finish and 2.5" barrel with red ramp front sight and adjustable rear sight. Weight is about 17.5 oz.

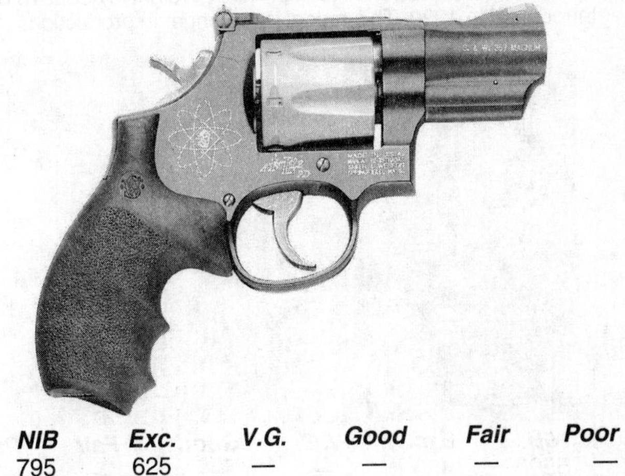

NIB	Exc.	V.G.	Good	Fair	Poor
795	625	—	—	—	—

Model 386 Sc/S

Single-/double-action L-frame revolver in .38/.357 Magnum. 7-shot cylinder, 2.5" barrel, Patridge front sight, adjustable rear, scandium/alloy frame, matte black finish, rubber grips. Introduced 2007.

NIB	Exc	V.G.	Good	Fair	Poor
869	—	—	—	—	—

Model 396 Mountain Lite

This L frame revolver is chambered for the .44 Special cartridge. It is fitted with a five round titanium cylinder and aluminum alloy frame. Barrel length is 3" and has a green HiViz front sight and an adjustable rear sight. Introduced in 2000. Weight is approximately 19 oz.

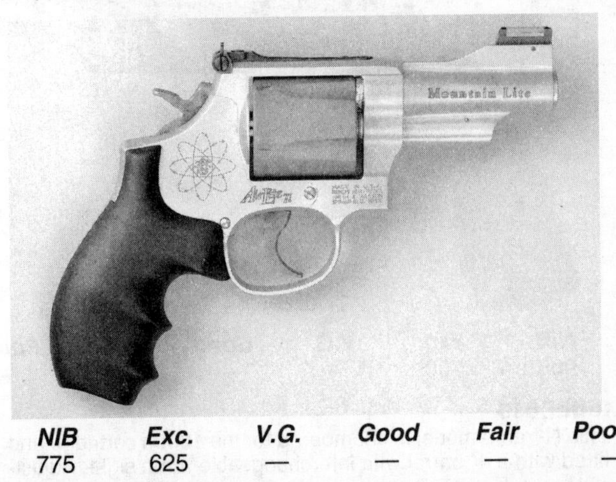

NIB	Exc.	V.G.	Good	Fair	Poor
775	625	—	—	—	—

Model 242

This medium frame revolver is chambered for the .38 Special +P cartridge. Semi-concealed hammer and 2.5" barrel. Pinned black ramp front sight. Black rubber boot grips. Seven-round cylinder. Matte alloy and titanium finish. Weight is about 19 oz. Introduced in 1999. This model is no longer in production.

NIB	Exc.	V.G.	Good	Fair	Poor
550	450	—	—	—	—

Model 296

Also a medium frame revolver chambered for the .44 Special cartridge. Fitted with a 2.5" barrel. Concealed hammer. Cylinder capacity is 5 rounds. Weight is about 19 oz. Introduced in 1999.

NIB	Exc.	V.G.	Good	Fair	Poor
550	450	—	—	—	—

Model 329PD

Chambered for the .44 magnum cartridge and fitted with a 4" barrel, this large frame revolver has a Scandium frame with matte black finish. Orange dot front sight and adjustable rear sight. Cylinder capacity is six rounds. Wood or rubber grips. Weight is approximately 26.5 oz. Introduced in 2003.

NIB	Exc.	V.G.	Good	Fair	Poor
900	700	—	—	—	—

Model 610

This N frame model is chambered for the 10mm cartridge and fitted with a 4" barrel with interchangeable ramp sight. Adjustable rear sight. Six-round non-fluted cylinder. Hogue rubber combat grips. Stainless steel finish. Weight is about 50 oz. Introduced in 2001.

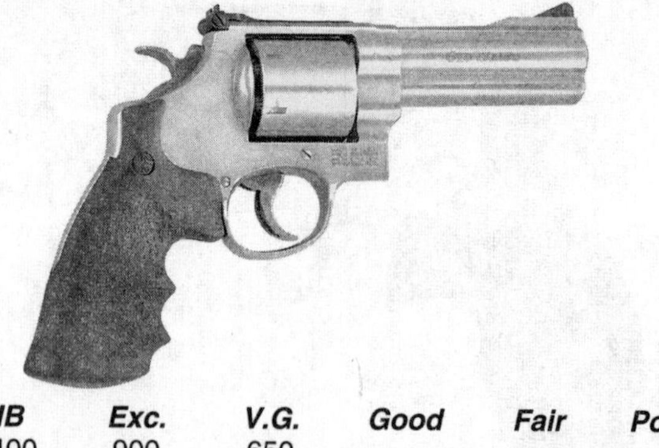

NIB	Exc.	V.G.	Good	Fair	Poor
1400	900	650	—	—	—

Model 36 (.38 Chief's Special)

This model, known as the Chief's Special, was introduced in 1950. It was built on the J frame and is chambered for the .38 Special cartridge. It holds 5 shots, has a 2" or 3" barrel, and was initially offered in a round butt. In 1952 a square-butt version was released. It is finished in blue or nickel-plate and has checkered walnut grips. A 3" heavy barrel was first produced in 1967 and became standard in 1975. The 2" barrel was dropped from production in 1993.

NIB	Exc.	V.G.	Good	Fair	Poor
375	325	275	200	150	100

Model 36LS (.38 Ladysmith)

This model is similar to the Model 36 with the exception that it is only offered with a 2" barrel, comes with rosewood grips and a soft carrying case. Weighs 20 oz.

NIB	Exc.	V.G.	Good	Fair	Poor
325	250	200	175	125	100

Model 36 (Chief's Special Target)

Since 1955 a limited number of Chief's Specials with adjustable sights have been manufactured. They have been offered with 2" or 3" barrels, round or square butts, and either blue or nickel-plated. Between 1957 and 1965, these target models were stamped Model 36 on the yoke. The revolvers manufactured between 1965 and the model discontinuance in 1975 were marked Model 50. This is a very collectible revolver. A total of 2,313 of these special target models were sold in various model designations. Some are more rare than others.

Courtesy W.P. Hallstein III and son Chip

Exc.	V.G.	Good	Fair	Poor
475	375	325	275	200

Model 37

Introduced in 1952 as the Chief's Special Airweight, this revolver initially had an alloy frame and cylinder. In 1954, following many complaints regarding damaged revolvers, the cylinders were made of steel. Barrel lengths, finishes, and grip options on the Airweight are the same as on the standard Chief Special. In 1957 the Model 37 designation was adopted. These early alloy frame and cylinder revolvers were designed to shoot only standard velocity .38 Special cartridges. The use of high velocity ammunition was not recommended by the factory.

NIB	Exc.	V.G.	Good	Fair	Poor
350	300	275	225	175	125

NOTE: All 1998 and later production models were rated for +P ammunition.

Model 637

Same as the model above but with aluminum frame and stainless steel finish.

NIB	Exc.	V.G.	Good	Fair	Poor
400	325	275	225	175	125

NOTE: Current production models are now rated for +P ammunition.

Model 637 Carry Combo

As above but supplied with Kydex carry holster. Introduced in 2004.

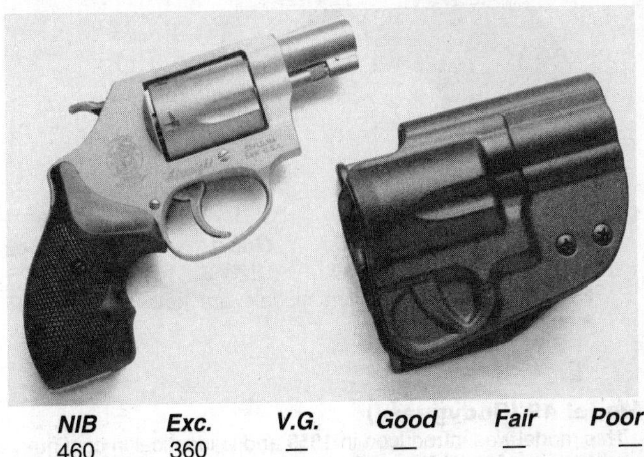

NIB	Exc.	V.G.	Good	Fair	Poor
460	360	—	—	—	—

REMINDER

The figures listed in this book reflect relative values, not prices. Only the buyer and seller can determine price.

Model 38 (Airweight Bodyguard)

This model was introduced in 1955 as the Airweight Bodyguard. This was a departure from S&W's usual procedure in that the alloy-framed version came first. The Model 38 is chambered for .38 Special and is available with a 2" barrel standard. Although a 3" barrel was offered, it is rarely encountered. The frame of the Bodyguard is extended to conceal and shroud the hammer but at the same time allow the hammer to be cocked by the thumb. This makes this model an ideal pocket revolver, as it can be drawn without catching on clothing. It is available either blue or nickel-plated, with checkered walnut grips.

NIB	Exc.	V.G.	Good	Fair	Poor
325	250	225	175	125	100

NOTE: All 1998 and later production models were rated for +P ammunition.

Model 638

Same as the model above but with aluminum frame and stainless steel finish.

NIB	Exc.	V.G.	Good	Fair	Poor
450	350	300	225	175	125

NOTE: Current production models are now rated for +P ammunition.

Model 49 (Bodyguard)

This model was introduced in 1959 and is identical in configuration to the Model 38 except that the frame is made of steel.

NIB	Exc.	V.G.	Good	Fair	Poor
400	350	300	225	150	100

Model 649 (Bodyguard Stainless)

This stainless steel version of the Model 49 was introduced in 1985. It is also available in .357 Magnum. As of 1998 this model was also offered in a .38 Special-only version.

NIB	Exc.	V.G.	Good	Fair	Poor
350	300	225	200	175	125

Model 40 (aka Model 42) Centennial

This model was introduced in 1952 as Smith & Wesson's 100th anniversary and appropriately called the "Centennial Model." It is of the Safety Hammerless design. This model was built on the J frame and features a fully concealed hammer and a grip safety. The Model 40 is chambered for the .38 Special cartridge. It is offered with a 2" barrel in either blue or nickel plate. The grips are checkered walnut. The Centennial was discontinued in 1974.

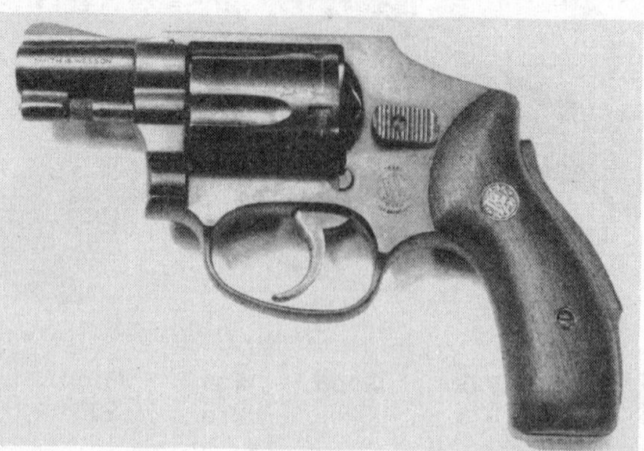

Courtesy Mike Stuckslager

Exc.	V.G.	Good	Fair	Poor
475	350	300	250	200

Model 42—Airweight Centennial

This model is identical in configuration to the Model 40 except that it was furnished with an aluminum alloy frame. It was also discontinued in 1974.

Editors Note: The first 37 Model 42s were manufactured with aluminum alloy cylinders. They weigh 11-1/4 ounces compared to 13 ounces for the standard model. The balance of Model 42 production was with steel cylinders. Add 300 percent for this extremely rare variation.

NIB	Exc.	V.G.	Good	Fair	Poor
450	400	325	200	150	100

Model 640 Centennial

A stainless steel version of the Model 40 furnished with a 2" or 3" barrel. Both the frame and cylinder are stainless steel. The 3" barrel was no longer offered as of 1993. As of 1998 this model was also offered in a .38 Special-only version.

NIB	Exc.	V.G.	Good	Fair	Poor
375	300	250	200	150	100

Model 640 Centennial .357 Magnum

Introduced in 1995 this version of the Model 640 is chambered for the .357 cartridge and fitted with a 2-1/8" barrel. The gun is stainless steel with a fixed notch rear sight and pinned black ramp front sight. It is 6-3/4" in length and weighs 25 oz.

This symbol denotes "Sleepers" with rapidly-rising values and/or significant collector potential.

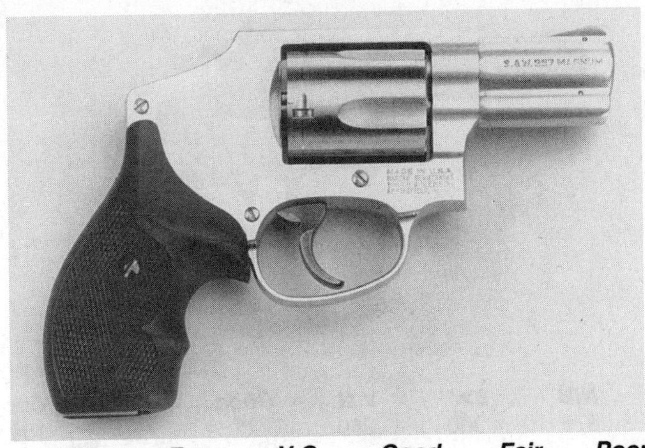

NIB	Exc.	V.G.	Good	Fair	Poor
375	300	250	200	150	100

Model 642 Centennial Airweight

Identical to the Model 640 with the exception of a stainless steel cylinder and aluminum alloy frame. Furnished with a 2" barrel. Discontinued in 1992. Replaced by the Model 442 which was introduced in 1993. This model was reintroduced in 1996.

NIB	Exc.	V.G.	Good	Fair	Poor
400	300	250	200	150	100

NOTE: Current production models are now rated for +P ammunition.

Model 642CT (Crimson Trace)

As above but fitted with Crimson Trace laser grips. Weight is about 15 oz. Introduced in 2004.

NIB	Exc.	V.G.	Good	Fair	Poor
695	550	—	—	—	—

Model 642LS

Same as above but fitted with smooth combat wood grips and a softside carry case.

NIB	Exc.	V.G.	Good	Fair	Poor
500	350	225	175	125	100

NOTE: Current production models are now rated for +P ammunition.

Model 940

Styled like the other Centennial models, this model is chambered for the 9mm Parabellum cartridge. It has a stainless steel cylinder and frame and is furnished with a 2" or 3" barrel. The 3" barrel version was dropped from production in 1993.

NIB	Exc.	V.G.	Good	Fair	Poor
600	400	225	175	125	100

Model 631

This revolver is chambered for the .32 Magnum cartridge and is fitted with a 2" (fixed sights) or 4" (adjustable sights) barrel. Stainless steel finish. Weight with 23" barrel is 22 oz. Produced in 1990.

NIB	Exc.	V.G.	Good	Fair	Poor
550	375	275	200	150	100

Model 631 Lady Smith

Similar to the above model but with rosewood grips and laser etched. Fitted with 2" barrel.

NIB	Exc.	V.G.	Good	Fair	Poor
525	350	275	200	150	100

Model 632 Centennial

This model is similar to the other Centennial models but is chambered for the .32 H&R Magnum cartridge. It comes standard with a 2" barrel, stainless steel cylinder and aluminum alloy frame. Dropped from the product line in 1993.

NIB	Exc.	V.G.	Good	Fair	Poor
700	475	225	175	125	100

Model 042 Centennial Airweight

This model was produced in 1992 but is not catalogued. It is chambered for .38 Special and fitted with a 2" barrel. The frame is alloy. Marked "MOD 042." No grip safety. Blued finish. Weight is about 16 oz.

NIB	Exc.	V.G.	Good	Fair	Poor
550	350	300	200	150	100

Model 442 Centennial Lightweight

This 5-shot revolver is chambered for the .38 Special and is equipped with a 2" barrel, aluminum alloy frame, and carbon steel cylinder. It has a fully concealed hammer and weighs 15.8 oz. The front ramp sight is serrated and the rear sight is a fixed square notch. Rubber combat grips from Michael's of Oregon are standard. Finish is either blue or satin nickel. Introduced in 1993.

NIB	Exc.	V.G.	Good	Fair	Poor
400	300	250	200	150	100

NOTE: Current production models are now rated for +P ammunition.

Model 43 (.22/.32 Kit Gun Airweight)

This model was built on the J frame, is chambered for .22 rimfire, has a 3.5" barrel, and is offered in a round or square butt, with checkered walnut grips. It has adjustable sights and is either blued or nickel-plated. The frame is made of aluminum alloy. Except for this, it is identical to the Model 34 or .22/.32 Kit Gun. This model has a rare 2" barrel configuration as well as a .22 MRF model. The Model 43 was introduced in 1954 and was discontinued in 1974.

Courtesy Mike Stuckslager

NIB	Exc.	V.G.	Good	Fair	Poor
375	300	250	200	150	100

Model 51 (.22/.32 Kit Gun Magnum)

This model is simply the Model 34 chambered for the .22 Winchester Magnum rimfire. It was first introduced in 1960 beginning with serial number 52637. Available in both round and square butt with the round butt variation having a total production of only 600. The Model 51 was discontinued in 1974.

NIB	Exc.	V.G.	Good	Fair	Poor
700	475	275	250	200	125

Model 651

This stainless steel version of the Model 51 .22 Magnum Kit Gun was manufactured between 1983 and 1987.

Exc.	V.G.	Good	Fair	Poor
675	400	250	200	125

Model 73

Produced in about 1973 this revolver was built on a special "C" size frame. Cylinder holds 6 rounds and is chambered for the .38 Special cartridge. Fitted with a 2" barrel. A total of 5,000 were built. All but 20 were destroyed. An extremely rare S&W revolver. Marked, "MOD 73" on yoke.

Courtesy Jim Supica, Old Town Station

NIB	Exc.	V.G.	Good	Fair	Poor
—	8500	—	—	—	—

Model 45 (Post Office)

This model is a special purpose K-frame Military & Police Model chambered for the .22 rimfire. It was designed as a training revolver for police departments and the U.S. Postal Service. This model was manufactured in limited quantities between 1948 and 1957. In 1963 production abruptly began and ended again. There were 500 of these revolvers released on a commercial basis, but they are rarely encountered.

NIB	Exc.	V.G.	Good	Fair	Poor
950	600	550	350	200	100

Model 48 (K-22 Masterpiece Magnum)

Introduced in 1959 and is identical to the Model 17 or K-22 except that it is chambered for the .22 WRM cartridge. Offered in 4", 6", and 8-3/8" barrel lengths, it has a blued finish. Discontinued in 1986.

NIB	Exc.	V.G.	Good	Fair	Poor
700	500	275	225	150	100

Model 53 (Magnum Jet)

Introduced in 1961 and chambered for the .22 Jet, a Remington cartridge. The barrel lengths were 4", 6", and 8-3/8" and the finish is blued. Sights were adjustable and the revolver was furnished with cylinder inserts that would allow .22 rimfire cartridges to be fired. The frame had two firing pins. Approximately 15,000 were produced before it was discontinued in 1974. Price includes guns with individual chambered inserts.

NIB	Exc.	V.G.	Good	Fair	Poor
1500	750	450	350	250	200

NOTE: Add $150 for auxiliary .22 LR cylinder.

Model 57

This revolver was introduced in 1964 and is chambered for the .41 Magnum cartridge. It is built on the N frame. Offered in 4", 6", and 8-3/8" barrel lengths, it has a blued frame and adjustable sights. Model designations are: 57-1 1982; 57-2 1988; 57-3 1990; 57-4 1993.

NIB	Exc.	V.G.	Good	Fair	Poor
600	400	275	225	200	150

Model 657

This is a stainless steel version of the Model 57 and was introduced in 1980. Still in production. In 2001 this model was reintroduced again with a 7.5" barrel with pinned front sight and adjustable rear sight. Hogue rubber combat grips. Weight is about 52 oz.

NIB	Exc.	V.G.	Good	Fair	Poor
670	525	425	295	—	—

Model 56 (KXT-38 USAF)

Introduced in 1962 this is a 2" heavy barrel built on the K frame. It is chambered for the .38 Special. There were approximately 15,000 of these revolvers built when it was discontinued in 1964. It was marked "US" on the backstrap. A total of 15,205 produced but most destroyed.

NIB	Exc.	V.G.	Good	Fair	Poor
4500	1750	1250	750	500	250

Model 58

This model is chambered for the .41 Magnum and is fitted with fixed sights. Offered in blued or nickel finish and with 4" barrel. Checkered walnut grips are standard. Introduced in 1964.

NIB	Exc.	V.G.	Good	Fair	Poor
1100	650	450	300	225	125

Model 547

Introduced in 1980 and chambered for the 9mm cartridge and offered with either 3" or 4" barrel. Finish is blued. Discontinued.

NIB	Exc.	V.G.	Good	Fair	Poor
650	475	375	275	200	125

Model 460 XVR

Introduced in 2005 this model is chambered for the .460 S&W magnum, which has the highest muzzle velocity of any production handgun. Fitted with a 8-3/8" barrel with interchangeable compensators. Frame size is extra large. Capacity is 5 rounds. Adjustable sights with Hi-Viz front sight. Finger groove grips. Satin stainless finish. Weight is about 72.5 oz.

NIB	Exc.	V.G.	Good	Fair	Poor
850	775	—	—	—	—

NOTE: Add $135 for 4" barrel model.

Model 460V

X-frame double-action trigger and 5" barrel in .460 S&W Magnum caliber. Also accepts .454 Casull and .45 Colt. Sorbothane recoil-reducing grip, interchangeable muzzle compensator. 5-shot, stainless with satin finish. 62.5 oz. Introduced 2006.

NIB	Exc.	V.G.	Good	Fair	Poor
850	775	—	—	—	—

Model 500

Introduced in 2003 this revolver is chambered for the .500 S&W Magnum cartridge. Fitted with a 8.375" barrel with compensator and built on the X frame. Cylinder holds five rounds. Stainless steel frame and barrel. Interchangeable front blade sight and adjustable rear sight. K-frame size Hogue grips. Weight is about 72.5 oz. In 2004 this model was offered with a 4" barrel with compensator. Weight is about 56 oz.

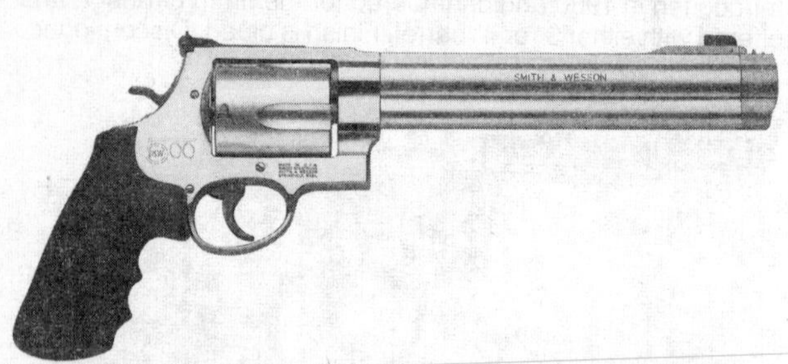

S&W Model 500 with 4" barrel

NIB	Exc.	V.G.	Good	Fair	Poor
875	695	—	—	—	—

NOTE: Add $135 for 4" barrel model.

Model 60

Introduced in 1965 this model is similar to the Model 36 but in stainless steel. Offered in 2" barrel with fixed sights, walnut grips, and smooth trigger. Some 2" Model 60s were produced with adjustable sights add 50 percent. The 3" barrel version comes with a full underlug, adjustable sights, serrated trigger, and rubber grips. The 2" version weighs about 20 oz. while the 3" version weighs approximately 25 oz. In 1996 this model was offered chambered for the .357 Magnum cartridge. This new version is fitted with a 2-1/8" barrel. The 2-1/8" barrel weighs about 23 oz. This model was also offered in a .38 Special-only version.

2" Barrel

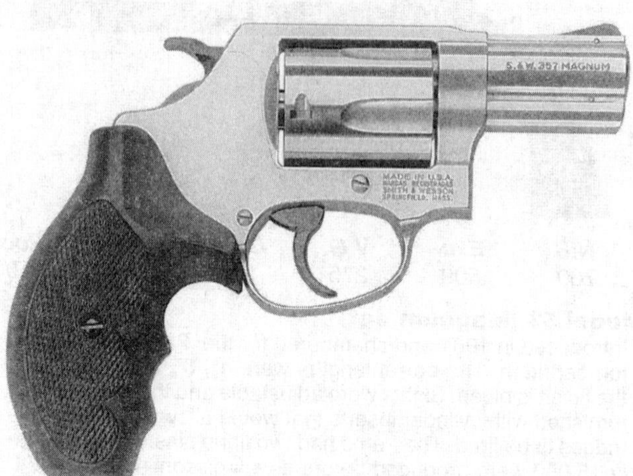

NIB	Exc.	V.G.	Good	Fair	Poor
450	350	300	200	125	100

3" Barrel

NIB	Exc.	V.G.	Good	Fair	Poor
475	375	350	250	150	100

5" Barrel

Introduced in 2005.

NIB	Exc.	V.G.	Good	Fair	Poor
550	475	—	—	—	—

Model 60LS (LadySmith)

Chambered for the .38 Special with 2" barrel and stainless steel frame and cylinder. This slightly smaller version of the Model 60 is made for small hands. A new version offered in 1996 is chambered for the .357 Magnum cartridge.

NIB	Exc.	V.G.	Good	Fair	Poor
375	305	250	200	150	100

Model 60 with Hi-Viz Sight

Similar to Model 60 but with light-gathering Hi-Viz red dot front sight and adjustable rear sight. Introduced 2007.

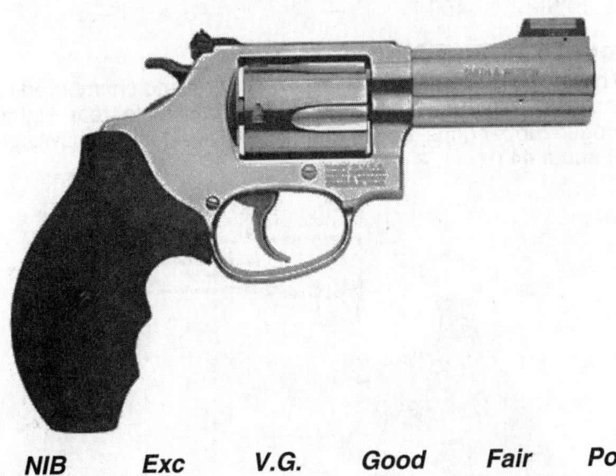

NIB	Exc	V.G.	Good	Fair	Poor
500	—	—	—	—	—

Model 63

This model, introduced in 1977, is simply the Model 34 made of stainless steel.

NIB	Exc.	V.G.	Good	Fair	Poor
350	275	250	225	200	150

Model 64 (Military & Police Stainless)

This model is the stainless steel version of the Model 10 M&P. It was introduced in 1970. The Model 64-1 variation was introduced in 1972 and is the heavy barrel version.

NIB	Exc.	V.G.	Good	Fair	Poor
380	300	275	225	175	125

Model 65 (.357 Military & Police Heavy Barrel Stainless)

This is the stainless steel version of the Model 13 M&P .357 Magnum. It was introduced in 1974.

NIB	Exc.	V.G.	Good	Fair	Poor
395	300	275	225	175	125

Model 66 (.357 Combat Magnum Stainless)

Released in 1970, this is the stainless steel version of the Model 19 or Combat Magnum. It is chambered for the .357 Magnum, has adjustable sights, a square butt with checkered walnut grips, and was initially offered with a 4" barrel. In 1974 a 2.5" barrel, round butt version was made available. It was available in a 6" barrel, as well as all target options until discontinued in 1993.

NIB	Exc.	V.G.	Good	Fair	Poor
500	310	250	200	150	125

Model 67 (.38 Combat Masterpiece Stainless)

Introduced in 1972 this is a stainless steel version of the Model 15 with a 4" barrel. It is chambered for the .38 Special cartridge. Model designation changes are as follows: {None} 1972 to 1977; {-1} 1977 to 1988; {-2} 1988 to 1993; {-3} 1993 to present.

NIB	Exc.	V.G.	Good	Fair	Poor
400	300	250	200	150	100

Model 650

Introduced in 1983 this stainless steel model is built on a J frame with a 3" heavy barrel chambered for the .22 WRM. It has a round butt and fixed sights. Discontinued in 1988.

NIB	Exc.	V.G.	Good	Fair	Poor
600	450	250	175	125	100

Model 651

This J-frame model was introduced in 1983 and chambered for the .22 WRM and fitted with a 4" barrel. Stainless steel finish and adjustable sights. Designation changes are: {None} 1983 to 1988; {-1} 1988 to 1990; {-2} 1988 to 1990.

NIB	Exc.	V.G.	Good	Fair	Poor
575	400	250	200	150	100

Model 686 Powerport

Introduced in 1995 this version of the Model 686 features a 6" full lug barrel with integral compensator. The frame is drilled and tapped for scope mounts. Hogue grips are furnished as standard.

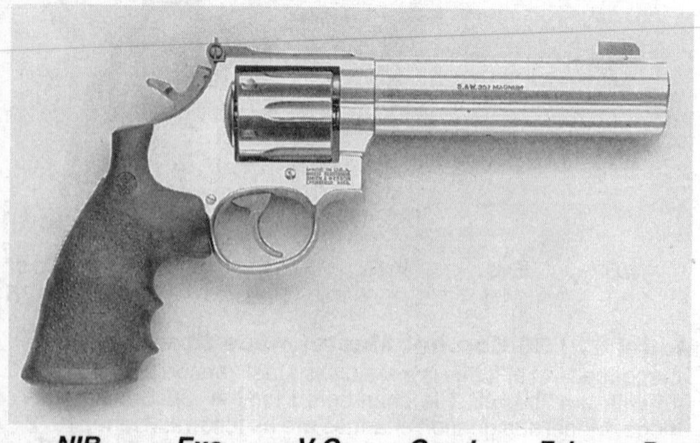

NIB	Exc.	V.G.	Good	Fair	Poor
600	550	450	400	300	200

Model 686 Magnum Plus

Offered for the first time in 1996 this model features a 7-shot cylinder. It is available with 2.5", 4", or 6" barrel lengths. It is fitted with a red ramp front sight and a fully adjustable rear sight. The frame is drilled and tapped for scope mounts. Hogue synthetic grips are standard. The stainless steel is satin finished. Weight is between 35 oz. and 45 oz. depending on barrel length.

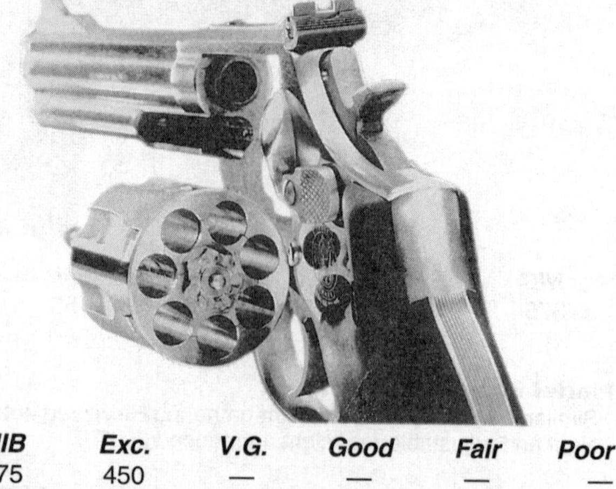

NIB	Exc.	V.G.	Good	Fair	Poor
575	450	—	—	—	—

Model 686 Plus Mountain Gun

This model is fitted with a 4" tapered barrel and chambered for the .357 Magnum cartridge. It has adjustable rear sights. Hogue rubber grips are standard. Stainless steel finish. Weight is about 44 oz.

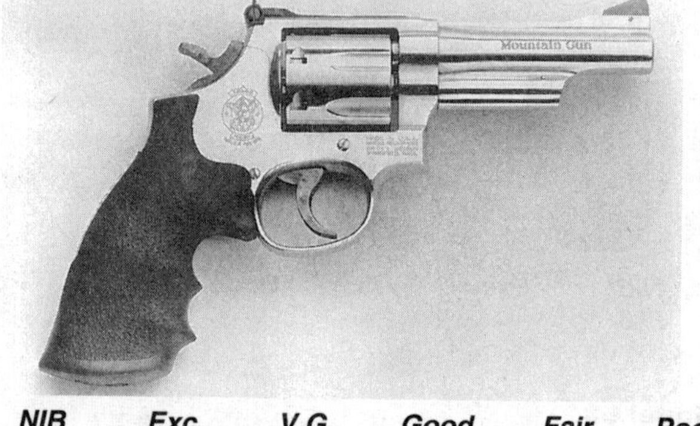

NIB	Exc.	V.G.	Good	Fair	Poor
650	475	—	—	—	—

Model 686—5" Barrel

This .357 Magnum stainless steel model is fitted with a 5" barrel with HiViz front sight and adjustable rear sight. Cylinder holds 7 rounds. Cocobolo wood grips. Weight is about 41 oz. Introduced in 2004.

NIB	Exc.	V.G.	Good	Fair	Poor
575	475	—	—	—	—

Model 686 Plus

Single-/double-action L-frame revolver in .38/.357 Magnum. 7-shot cylinder, 3" barrel, Patridge front sight, adjustable rear, stainless finish, rubber grips. Introduced 2007.

NIB	Exc	V.G.	Good	Fair	Poor
600	—	—	—	—	—

Model 619

This model is chambered for the .357 Magnum cartridge and fitted with a 4" two piece semi-lug barrel with fixed sights. Stainless steel frame and barrel. Capacity is 7 rounds. Medium frame. Weight is about 37.5 oz. Rubber grips. Introduced in 2005.

NIB	Exc.	V.G.	Good	Fair	Poor
550	475	—	—	—	—

Model 620

Similar to the model above but with a 4" barrel with adjustable rear sight and red ramp front sight. Weight is about 37.9 oz. Introduced in 2005.

NIB	Exc.	V.G.	Good	Fair	Poor
580	500	—	—	—	—

Model 3 Schofield

A reintroduction of the famous Schofield revolver. This is a single-action top-break model chambered for the .45 S&W cartridge. Barrel length is 7". Frame and barrel are blue while hammer and trigger are case hardened. Sights are a fixed rear notch and half moon post front. Walnut grips. Weight is 40 oz. Reintroduced in 2000. In 2002 this model was offered in a 7" nickel version as well as a 5" blue and 5" nickel configuration.

NIB	Exc.	V.G.	Good	Fair	Poor
1500	1200	—	—	—	—

HERITAGE SERIES REVOLVERS

These revolvers are built by the S&W Performance Center and produced for Lew Horton Distributing Co. Each model is similar in appearance to the original but has modern internal features. These handguns are produced in limited runs of from 100 units to 350 units.

Model 1917

Chambered for the .45 ACP cartridge and fitted with a 5.5" heavy tapered barrel. High-profile front blade sight with fixed rear sight. Checkered service grips with lanyard ring. Offered in blue, case-colored, or military finish. Shipped in a S&W collectible box.

NIB	Exc.	V.G.	Good	Fair	Poor
1050	—	—	—	—	—

NOTE: Add $60 for case color finish.

Model 15

This revolver is chambered for the .38 S&W Special. Fitted with a 4" barrel. Grips are S&W checkered target. Adjustable rear sight. Offered in nickel or color case hardnened.

NIB	Exc.	V.G.	Good	Fair	Poor
760	—	—	—	—	—

Model 15 McGivern

Similar to the above model but fitted with 5" barrel and checkered diamond grips. Engraved sideplate of McGivern's speed record. Blue finish.

NIB	Exc.	V.G.	Good	Fair	Poor
1040	—	—	—	—	—

Model 17

Chambered for the .22 caliber cartridge and fitted with a 6" barrel with patridge front sight and adjustable rear sight. Four screw sideplate. Diamond checkered S&W walnut grips. Blue or case colored finish.

NIB	Exc.	V.G.	Good	Fair	Poor
1040	—	—	—	—	—

NOTE: Add $30 for case colored finish.

Model 24

This model is chambered for the .44 Special cartridge and fitted with a 6.5" tapered barrel. McGivern gold-bead front sight with adjustable rear sight. Four-screw sideplate, chamfered charge holes, checkered diamond grips.

NIB	Exc.	V.G.	Good	Fair	Poor
1050	—	—	—	—	—

NOTE: Add $60 for case colored finish.

Model 25

Similar to the Model 24 but chambered for the .45 Colt cartridge. Blue or case colored finish.

NIB	Exc.	V.G.	Good	Fair	Poor
1040	—	—	—	—	—

NOTE: Add $30 for case colored finish.

Model 29

Similar to the Model 24 and Model 25 but chambered for the .44 Magnum cartridge. Oversized wood grips. Blue or nickel finish. Was to be produced in 2002 only. Serial numbers to begin with "DBW2005."

NIB	Exc.	V.G.	Good	Fair	Poor
1045	—	—	—	—	—

MILITARY & POLICE (M&P) SERIES

M&P340

Double-action-only revolver built on Centennial (hammerless J) frame. .357 Magnum/.38 Special; five-shot cylinder; 1.87" barrel with fixed night sights. Matte black finish on scandium/alloy frame. Introduced 2007.

NIB	Exc	V.G.	Good	Fair	Poor
725	—	—	—	—	—

M&P340CT

Similar to above but with Crimson Trace lasergrips. Introduced 2007.

NIB	Exc	V.G.	Good	Fair	Poor
825	—	—	—	—	—

M&P360

Double-action-only revolver built on Chief's Special (hammered J) frame. .357 Magnum/.38 Special; five-shot cylinder; 1.87" barrel with fixed night sights. Matte black finish on scandium/alloy frame. Introduced 2007.

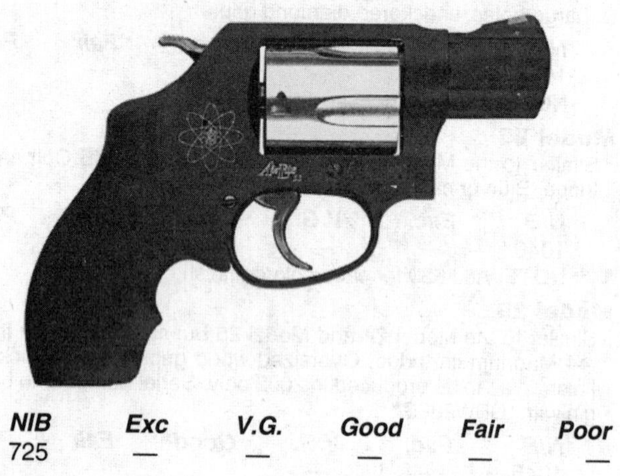

NIB	Exc	V.G.	Good	Fair	Poor
725	—	—	—	—	—

M&PR8

Double-action-only revolver built on large (N) frame. .357 Magnum/.38 Special; eight-shot cylinder; 5" barrel with adjustable Patridge sights with interchangeable inserts. Matte black finish on scandium/alloy frame. Introduced 2007.

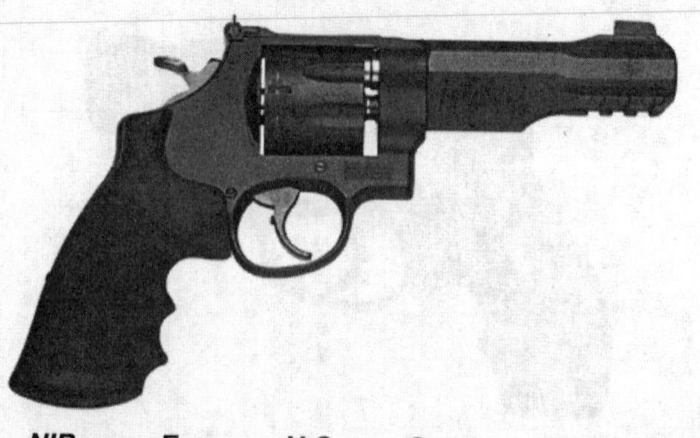

NIB	Exc	V.G.	Good	Fair	Poor
900	—	—	—	—	—

CLASSIC SERIES

Model 36 Classic

Replica of vintage Model 36 Chief's Special in .38 Special. Five-shot cylinder. Carbon steel frame, 1-7/8" or 3" barrel, fixed sights. Blued, case colored, or nickel finish with Altamont wood grips. Introduced 2007.

NIB	Exc	V.G.	Good	Fair	Poor
700	—	—	—	—	—

Model 21 Classic

Replica of vintage Model 21 N-frame revolver in .44 Special. Six-shot cylinder. Carbon steel frame, 4" barrel, fixed sights. Blued, case colored, or nickel finish with Altamont wood grips. Introduced 2007.

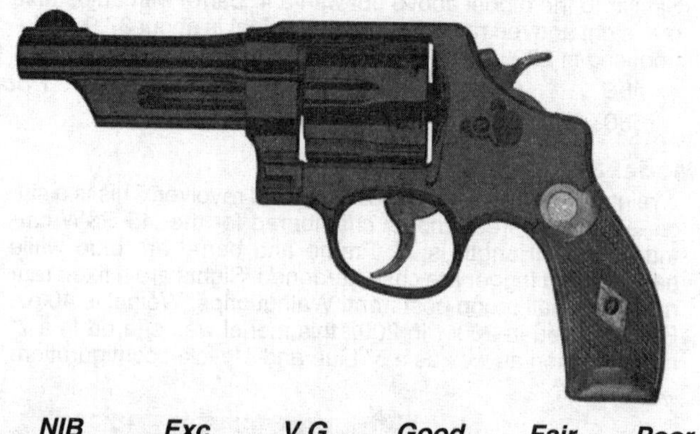

NIB	Exc	V.G.	Good	Fair	Poor
700	—	—	—	—	—

Model 22 Classic

Replica of vintage Model 22 N-frame revolver in .45 ACP. Six-shot cylinder. Carbon steel frame, 4" barrel, fixed sights. Blued, case colored, or nickel finish with Altamont wood grips. Introduced 2007.

NIB	Exc	V.G.	Good	Fair	Poor
700	—	—	—	—	—

Model 22 of 1917 Classic

Similar to Model 22 Classic but without ejector rod shroud and with lanyard ring on butt. Replica of U.S. Army WWI-era revolver. Introduced 2007.

NIB	Exc	V.G.	Good	Fair	Poor
700	—	—	—	—	—

Model 29 Classic

Replica of original (1956) Model 29 N-frame revolver in .44 Magnum. Six-shot cylinder. Carbon steel frame, 6.5" barrel, fixed sights. Blued or nickel finish with or without engraving. Altamont wood grips. Introduced 2007.

NIB	Exc	V.G.	Good	Fair	Poor
700	—	—	—	—	—

SEMI-AUTOMATIC PISTOLS

Courtesy Smith & Wesson

NOTE: For pistols with Smith and Wesson factory-installed night sights add $100 to NIB and Exc. prices. For S&W factory engraving add $1,000 for Class C (1/3 coverage), $1,250 for Class B (2/3 coverage), $1,500 for Class A (full coverage).

Model 39

This was the first double-action semi-automatic pistol produced in the United States. It was introduced in 1957. It had an alloy frame and was chambered for the 9mm Parabellum cartridge. The barrel was 4" and the finish was either blued or nickel with checkered walnut grips. The rear sight was adjustable. Magazine capacity is 8 rounds. Discontinued in 1982.

NIB	Exc.	V.G.	Good	Fair	Poor
400	350	250	200	150	100

Model 39 Steel Frame

A total of 927 steel frame Model 39s were produced. A rare pistol, use caution.

NIB	Exc.	V.G.	Good	Fair	Poor
1250	1000	700	550	400	250

Model 59

Introduced in 1971 this pistol is similar to the Model 39 but with a wide grip to hold a double column magazine of 14 rounds. Furnished with black checkered plastic grips. Discontinued in 1982.

NIB	Exc.	V.G.	Good	Fair	Poor
425	375	295	200	150	100

Model 439

Introduced in 1979 this is an improved version of the Model 39. Furnished with adjustable rear sight. Discontinued in 1988.

NIB	Exc.	V.G.	Good	Fair	Poor
450	400	350	325	250	100

Model 639

This is a stainless steel version of the Model 439. Introduced in 1984 and discontinued in 1988.

NIB	Exc.	V.G.	Good	Fair	Poor
400	325	300	250	200	100

Model 459

This improved-sight version of the 15-shot Model 59 9mm pistol was introduced in 1979 and discontinued in 1987.

NIB	Exc.	V.G.	Good	Fair	Poor
475	400	350	300	250	200

Model 659

This stainless steel version of the Model 459 9mm pistol features an ambidextrous safety and all other options of the Model 459. Introduced in 1982 and discontinued in 1988.

NIB	Exc.	V.G.	Good	Fair	Poor
475	425	350	300	250	150

Model 539

This is yet another version of the Model 439 9mm pistol. It incorporates all the features of the Model 439 with a steel frame instead of aluminum alloy. This model was introduced in 1980 and discontinued in 1983.

NIB	Exc.	V.G.	Good	Fair	Poor
450	400	350	300	250	200

Model 559

This variation of the Model 459 9mm pistol has a steel frame instead of aluminum alloy. It is identical in all other respects.

NIB	Exc.	V.G.	Good	Fair	Poor
450	400	350	300	250	200

Model 469

The Model 469 was brought out in answer to the need for a more concealable high-capacity pistol. It is essentially a "Mini" version of the Model 459. It is chambered for the 9mm Parabellum and has a 12-round detachable magazine with a finger-grip extension and a shortened frame. The barrel is 3.5" long; the hammer is bobbed and does not protrude; the safety is ambidextrous. The finish is matte blue, with black plastic grips. The Model 469 was introduced in 1983 and discontinued in 1988.

NIB	Exc.	V.G.	Good	Fair	Poor
450	375	325	275	200	150

Model 669

This is a stainless steel version of the Model 469 9mm pistol. All of the features of the 469 are incorporated. The Model 669 was manufactured from 1986 to 1988.

NIB	Exc.	V.G.	Good	Fair	Poor
475	425	350	300	250	200

Model 645

The Model 645 is a large-framed, stainless steel double-action pistol chambered for the .45 ACP cartridge. It has a 5" barrel, adjustable sights, and a detachable 8-shot magazine. It is offered with fixed or adjustable sights and an ambidextrous safety. The grips are molded black nylon. S&W manufactured this pistol between 1985 and 1988.

NIB	Exc.	V.G.	Good	Fair	Poor
500	425	375	325	250	150

Model 745—IPSC

This model is similar in outward appearance to the Model 645 but is quite a different pistol. The Model 745 is a single-action semi-automatic chambered for the .45 ACP cartridge. The frame is made of stainless steel, and the slide of blued carbon steel. The barrel is 5", and the detachable magazine holds eight rounds. The sights are fully adjustable target types. The grips are checkered walnut. Introduced in 1986 and discontinued in 1990.

NIB	Exc.	V.G.	Good	Fair	Poor
700	600	500	400	350	250

AIRLITE PISTOLS

Model 41

The Model 41 was introduced to the shooting public in 1957. It is a high quality .22 rimfire target pistol. It has a steel frame, steel slide, and either a 5.0", 5.5" or 7.375" barrel. It has a detachable 10-shot magazine, adjustable target sights, and checkered walnut target grips with thumb rest. The finish is blued. Weight with 5.5", barrel is about 41 oz. and for 7.375" barrel about 44 oz. Prices listed are for 5" lightweight barrel.

Other Barrel Options:

5.5" with extended sight add $100. 5.5" heavy with extended sight add $100. 7.375" with muzzlebrake add $75.

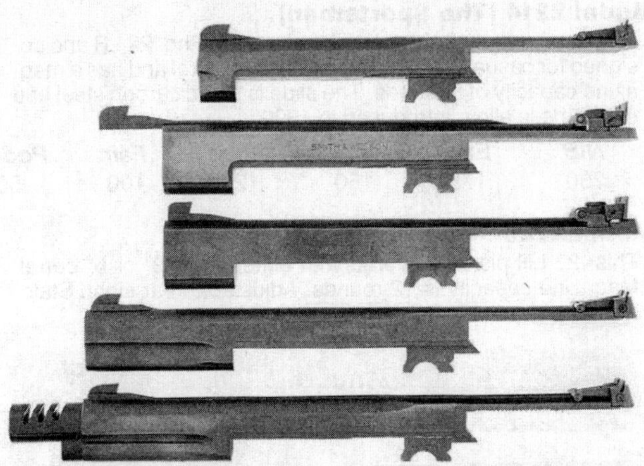

Model 41 barrel types Courtesy John J. Stimson, Jr.

NOTE: For full set of steel and aluminum barrel weights add up to $500 depending on condition. For .22 Short conversion kit add $750 depending on condition. For military marked pistols add 400 percent.

NIB	Exc.	V.G.	Good	Fair	Poor
850	600	400	300	225	150

REMINDER
Firearms are part of our nation's history and represent an opportunity to learn more about their role in that American experience. If done skillfully, firearms collecting can be a profitable hobby as well.

Model 41 (New Model)

This model was restyled in 1994 featuring recontoured hardwood stocks, a Millet adjustable rear sight, and a drilled and tapped barrel for scope mounting.

NIB	Exc.	V.G.	Good	Fair	Poor
650	575	500	400	300	150

Model 41-1

This model was introduced in 1960 and is chambered for the .22 Short rimfire only. It was developed for the International Rapid Fire competition. In appearance it is quite similar to the Model 41 except that the slide is made of aluminum alloy, as well as the frame, in order to lighten it to function with the .22 Short cartridge. This model was not a commercial success like the Model 41, so it was discontinued after fewer than 1,000 were manufactured.

Model 41-1 .22 Short with optional weights

Courtesy John J. Stimson, Jr.

NIB	Exc.	V.G.	Good	Fair	Poor
1200	900	725	500	375	225

Model 46

This was a lower-cost version of the Model 41. It was developed for the Air Force in 1959. Its appearance was essentially the same as the Model 41 with a 7" barrel. Later a 5" barrel was introduced, and finally in 1964 a heavy 5.5" barrel was produced. This economy target pistol never had the popularity that the more expensive Model 41 had, and it was discontinued in 1968 after approximately 4,000 pistols were manufactured.

Courtesy Mike Stuckslager

NIB	Exc.	V.G.	Good	Fair	Poor
700	600	450	350	250	200

Model 61 Escort

In 1970 the Model 61 was introduced as the only true pocket automatic that S&W produced. It was chambered for the .22 LR cartridge with a 2-1/2" barrel and 5-round magazine. It was offered in either blued or nickel finish with black checkered plastic grips. It was dropped from the product line in 1974.

NIB	Exc.	V.G.	Good	Fair	Poor
300	225	200	150	100	75

Model 52A

Introduced in 1961 in the .38 AMU caliber for the Army marksmanship training. Army rejected the pistol and the 87 units built were released to the public. The letter "A" is stamped behind the model designation. A rare find; only 87 were produced. Use caution.

NIB	Exc.	V.G.	Good	Fair	Poor
3000	2500	2000	1500	750	500

Model 52 (.38 Master)

Introduced in 1961 as a target pistol chambered for the .38 Special mid-range wad cutter cartridge. It is similar in appearance to the Model 39 but is single-action-only by virtue of a set screw. Fitted with a 5" barrel and a 5-round magazine. It has a blued finish with checkered walnut grips. About 3,500 of these pistols were produced in this configuration until discontinued in 1963.

NIB	Exc.	V.G.	Good	Fair	Poor
900	750	550	450	300	200

Model 52-1

In 1963 this variation featured a true single-action design and were produced until 1971.

NIB	Exc.	V.G.	Good	Fair	Poor
750	650	450	350	300	200

Model 52-2

Introduced in 1971 with a coil spring-style extractor. Model was discontinued in 1993.

NIB	Exc.	V.G.	Good	Fair	Poor
700	600	475	400	300	200

Model 2214 (The Sportsman)

This semi-automatic pistol is chambered for the .22 LR and designed for casual use. It is fitted with a 3" barrel and has a magazine capacity of 8 rounds. The slide is blued carbon steel and the frame is alloy. Introduced in 1990.

NIB	Exc.	V.G.	Good	Fair	Poor
200	175	150	125	100	50

Model 2206

This .22 LR pistol is offered with either a 4-1/2" or 6" barrel. Magazine capacity is 12 rounds. Adjustable rear sight. Stainless steel frame and slide.

NIB	Exc.	V.G.	Good	Fair	Poor
250	200	175	125	100	50

Model 2206 TGT (Target)

Introduced in 1995 this version of the Model 2206 features a selected 6" barrel, bead blasted sighting plane and polished flat side surfaces. A Patridge front sight and Millet adjustable rear sight are standard. In addition the model has a serrated trigger with adjustable trigger stop and a 10-round magazine.

NIB	Exc.	V.G.	Good	Fair	Poor
350	300	250	200	150	100

Model 422 Field

Introduced in 1987 this .22 LR pistol has a 4-1/2" barrel or 6" barrel with an alloy frame and steel slide. The magazine capacity is 10 rounds. This model has fixed sights and black plastic grips. Finish is matte blue.

NIB	Exc.	V.G.	Good	Fair	Poor
200	175	150	125	100	50

Model 422 Target

Same as the Field model but fitted with adjustable sights and checkered walnut grips.

This symbol denotes "Sleepers" with rapidly-rising values and/or significant collector potential.

NIB	Exc.	V.G.	Good	Fair	Poor
250	200	175	150	100	50

Model 622 Field

This is a stainless steel version of the Model 422 Field.

NIB	Exc.	V.G.	Good	Fair	Poor
225	200	175	150	125	75

Model 622 Target

This is the stainless steel version of the Model 422 Target.

NIB	Exc.	V.G.	Good	Fair	Poor
275	225	200	175	125	75

Model 622VR

Redesigned in 1996 this .22 caliber model features a 6" ventilated rib barrel. It is fitted with a matte black trigger and a new trigger guard. The front sight is a serrated ramp style with an adjustable rear sight. Weight is approximately 23 oz. Grips are black polymer.

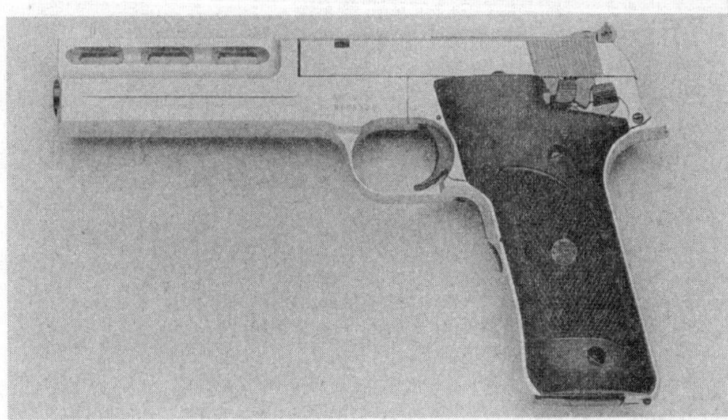

NIB	Exc.	V.G.	Good	Fair	Poor
300	250	200	150	100	75

Model 22A Sport

Introduced in 1997 this model features a choice of 4", 5.5", or 7" barrel. It is chambered for the .22 LR cartridge. Magazine capacity is 10 rounds. Rear sight is adjustable. Grips are either two-piece polymer or two-piece Soft Touch. Frame and slide are aluminum alloy and stainless steel. Finish is blue. Weight is approximately 28 oz. for 4" model and 32 oz. for 5.5" model. Weight of 7" model is about 33 oz. Prices quoted are for 4" model. In 2001 this model was furnished with a Hi-Viz green dot front sight.

NIB	Exc.	V.G.	Good	Fair	Poor
290	200	150	100	—	—

Model 22S Sport

This model, also introduced in 1997, is similar to the above model but with 5.5" and 7" barrel on stainless steel frames. Weight is about 41 oz. and 42 oz. respectively. In 2001 this model was fiurnished with a Hi-Viz green dot front sight.

NIB	Exc.	V.G.	Good	Fair	Poor
395	300	225	150	—	—

Model 22A Target

This .22 caliber target pistol has a 10-round magazine, adjustable rear sight, and target grips with thumb rest. The barrel is 5.5" bull barrel. Finish is blue. Weight is about 39 oz. Introduced in 1997.

NIB	Exc.	V.G.	Good	Fair	Poor
425	300	225	150	—	—

Model 22S Target

Same as above but with stainless steel frame and slide. Weight is approximately 48 oz.

NIB	Exc.	V.G.	Good	Fair	Poor
400	300	225	150	—	—

Model 22A Camo

Introduced in 2004 this .22 LR model features a Mossy Oak Break-Up finish. Weight is about 39 oz.

NIB	Exc.	V.G.	Good	Fair	Poor
365	275	—	—	—	—

Model 3904

In 1989 S&W redesigned the entire line of 9mm semi-automatic handguns. The 3904 is chambered for the 9mm Parabellum and has an 8-shot detachable magazine and 4" barrel with a fixed bushing. The frame is alloy, and the trigger guard is squared for two-hand hold. The magazine well is beveled, and the grips are one-piece wrap-around made of delrin. The three-dot sighting system is employed. This model has been discontinued.

NIB	Exc.	V.G.	Good	Fair	Poor
450	400	325	300	275	225

Model 3906

This is the stainless steel version of the Model 3904. The features are the same. It was introduced in 1989. This model has been discontinued.

NIB	Exc.	V.G.	Good	Fair	Poor
450	400	325	300	275	225

Model 3914

Offered as a slightly smaller alternative to the Model 3904, this 9mm pistol has a 3-1/2" barrel, 8-round magazine, and blued carbon steel slide and alloy frame.

NIB	Exc.	V.G.	Good	Fair	Poor
525	450	400	350	300	250

Model 3913

This version is similar to the Model 3914 but features a stainless steel slide and alloy frame.

NIB	Exc.	V.G.	Good	Fair	Poor
525	450	400	350	300	250

Model 3914LS

This is a redesigned Model 3914 that has a more modern appearance. The LS refers to LadySmith and is chambered for the 9mm cartridge. All other features are the same as the Model 3914 including the blued carbon slide and alloy frame.

NIB	Exc.	V.G.	Good	Fair	Poor
525	450	400	350	300	200

Model 3913LS

This model is identical to the Model 3914LS with the exception of the stainless steel slide.

NIB	Exc.	V.G.	Good	Fair	Poor
525	450	400	350	300	200

Model 3954

Similar to the Model 3914 but offered in double-action-only. Discontinued in 1993.

NIB	Exc.	V.G.	Good	Fair	Poor
525	450	400	350	300	200

Model 915

Introduced in 1993 this model is chambered for the 9mm cartridge and features a 4" barrel, matte blue finish, fixed rear sight, and wraparound rubber grips. Overall length is 7.5" and weight is about 28 oz.

NIB	Exc.	V.G.	Good	Fair	Poor
400	350	250	200	150	100

Model 5904

This is a full high capacity, 15-shot version of the Model 3904. It was introduced in 1989 and features a slide mounted decocking lever and 4" barrel. This version has a blued carbon steel slide and alloy frame. This model is no longer in production.

NIB	Exc.	V.G.	Good	Fair	Poor
525	450	375	325	275	200

Model 5906

This is a stainless steel version of the Model 5904. Both the slide and frame are stainless steel.

NIB	Exc.	V.G.	Good	Fair	Poor
525	450	375	275	200	—

Model 5906 Special Edition

A double-action semi-automatic pistol chambered for the 9mm with a 15-round magazine. The frame and slide have a special machine finish while the grips are one-piece wrap-around Xenoy. The front sight is a white dot post and the rear sight is a Novak L-Mount Carry with two white dots. This model has a manual safety/decocking lever and firing pin safety. Introduced in 1993.

NIB	Exc.	V.G.	Good	Fair	Poor
525	450	350	300	250	150

Model 5903

The same caliber and features as the Model 5904 and Model 5906, but furnished with a stainless steel slide and alloy frame.

NIB	Exc.	V.G.	Good	Fair	Poor
525	450	400	350	300	250

Model 5926

S&W offers a 9mm pistol similar to the 5906 but with a frame mounted decocking lever. Both the slide and frame are stainless steel. Discontinued in 1993.

NIB	Exc.	V.G.	Good	Fair	Poor
525	450	375	300	250	150

Model 5946

This 9mm pistol offers the same features as the Model 5926, but in a double-action-only mode. The hammer configuration on this model is semi-bobbed instead of serrated.

NIB	Exc.	V.G.	Good	Fair	Poor
525	450	400	350	300	250

Model 5967

This is a 9mm model with a M5906 frame and a 3914 slide. It has a stainless steel frame and blued slide. Novak Lo-Mount fixed sights. Introduced in 1990 and sold through Lew Horton.

NIB	Exc.	V.G.	Good	Fair	Poor
600	475	400	350	300	250

Model 6904

This is the concealable, shortened version of the Model 5904. It has a 12-shot magazine, fixed sights, bobbed hammer, and a 3.5" barrel.

NIB	Exc.	V.G.	Good	Fair	Poor
525	450	400	350	300	250

Model 6906

This version has a stainless steel slide and alloy frame but otherwise is similar to the Model 6904.

NIB	Exc.	V.G.	Good	Fair	Poor
525	450	400	350	300	200

Model 6946

This is a double-action version of the Model 6906.

NIB	Exc.	V.G.	Good	Fair	Poor
525	450	400	350	300	200

Model 4003

This pistol is chambered for the .40 S&W cartridge and is fitted with a 4" barrel, 11-round magazine, serrated hammer with a stainless steel slide and alloy frame.

NIB	Exc.	V.G.	Good	Fair	Poor
575	500	400	350	300	200

Model 4004

Identical to the Model 4003 except for a blue carbon steel slide and alloy frame. Discontinued in 1993.

NIB	Exc.	V.G.	Good	Fair	Poor
575	500	400	350	300	200

Model 4006

This model is identical to the Model 4003 except that both the slide and frame are made from stainless steel. This adds 8 oz. to the weight of the pistol.

NIB	Exc.	V.G.	Good	Fair	Poor
575	500	400	350	300	200

Model 4026

Similar to the Model 4006 this version has a frame-mounted decocking lever.

NIB	Exc.	V.G.	Good	Fair	Poor
575	500	400	350	300	200

Model 4046

Similar to the Model 4006 but with a double-action-only configuration.

NIB	Exc.	V.G.	Good	Fair	Poor
575	500	400	350	300	250

Model 4013

A compact version of the 4000 series, this .40 caliber model features a 3-1/2" barrel, eight-round magazine, and stainless steel slide and alloy frame.

NIB	Exc.	V.G.	Good	Fair	Poor
575	500	400	350	300	200

Model 4013 TSW

Similar to the Model 4013 but traditional double-action-only with some improvements. Magazine capacity is 9 rounds of .40 S&W cartridges. Finish is satin stainless. Weight is approximately 26 oz. Introduced in 1997.

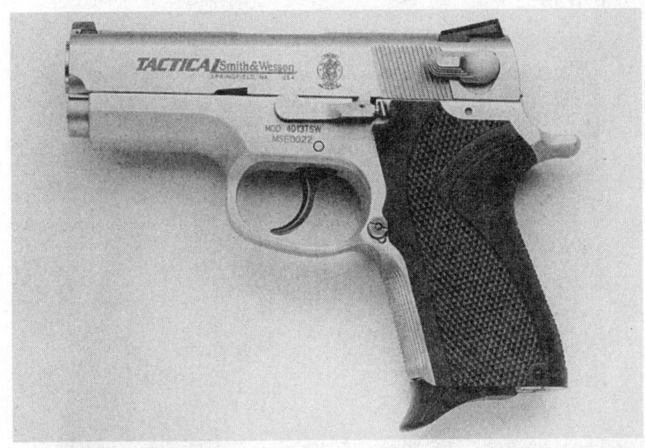

NIB	Exc.	V.G.	Good	Fair	Poor
700	625	—	—	—	—

Model 4014

Identical to the Model 4013 except for a blued carbon steel slide and alloy frame.

NIB	Exc.	V.G.	Good	Fair	Poor
575	500	400	350	300	200

Model 4053

Identical to the Model 4013, stainless steel slide and alloy frame, except offered in a double-action-only configuration.

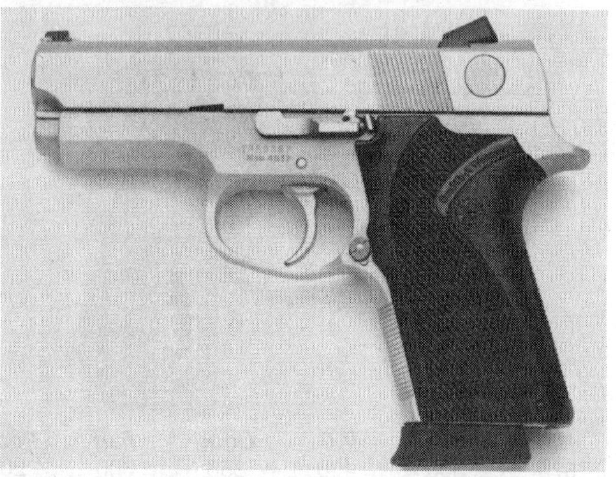

NIB	Exc.	V.G.	Good	Fair	Poor
575	500	400	350	300	200

Model 4054

This model is the same as the Model 4053 except for a blued carbon steel slide and alloy frame. Dropped from S&W product line in 1992.

NIB	Exc.	V.G.	Good	Fair	Poor
575	500	400	300	250	200

Model 4056 TSW

This is a double-action-only pistol chambered for the .40 S&W cartridge. Fitted with a 3.5" barrel with white dot sights. Curved backstrap. Stainless steel and alloy frame. Stainless steel finish. Magazine capacity is nine rounds. Introduced in 1997. Weight is approximately 36 oz.

NIB	Exc.	V.G.	Good	Fair	Poor
725	625	—	—	—	—

Model 411

This model was introduced in 1993 as a no frills model and features an alloy frame, 4" barrel, matte blue finish, fixed sights, and wrap-around rubber grips. Chambered for .40 S&W cartridge with 11-round magazine capacity. Overall length is 7.5" and weight is approximately 29 oz.

NIB	Exc.	V.G.	Good	Fair	Poor
400	350	300	250	200	150

Model 1006

This is a full-size 10mm pistol with a 5" barrel, nine-round magazine, and choice of fixed or adjustable sights. Both the slide and frame are stainless steel.

NIB	Exc.	V.G.	Good	Fair	Poor
675	550	400	350	300	200

Model 1066

This is a slightly smaller version of the Model 1006 and is furnished with a 4-1/4" barrel. Discontinued in 1993.

This symbol denotes "Sleepers" with rapidly-rising values and/or significant collector potential.

NIB	Exc.	V.G.	Good	Fair	Poor
675	550	400	350	300	200

Model 1076

Identical to the Model 1066 with the exception of the frame mounted decocking lever.

NIB	Exc.	V.G.	Good	Fair	Poor
675	550	400	350	300	200

Model 1086

Similar to the Model 1066 but offered in double-action-only. This model was discontinued in 1993.

NIB	Exc.	V.G.	Good	Fair	Poor
650	525	375	300	250	200

Model 1026

Similar to the Model 1006 with a 5" barrel this model has a frame mounted decocking lever.

NIB	Exc.	V.G.	Good	Fair	Poor
675	550	400	350	300	200

Model 4506

This is the newly designed double-action .45 ACP pistol. It is all stainless steel and has a 5" barrel, 8-shot detachable magazine, and wrap-around black Delrin grips. This model is no longer in production.

NIB	Exc.	V.G.	Good	Fair	Poor
550	475	400	350	300	250

Model 4505

This version is identical to the Model 4506 with the exception of a blued slide and frame.

NIB	Exc.	V.G.	Good	Fair	Poor
550	475	400	350	300	250

Model 4516

Offered in a .45 caliber this 4500 series is a compact version of the full size .45 caliber S&W autos. Furnished with a 3-3/4" barrel and a 7-round magazine this model has a stainless slide and frame. Discontinued in 1991. This model was reintroduced in 1994.

This symbol denotes "Sleepers" with rapidly-rising values and/or significant collector potential.

NIB	Exc.	V.G.	Good	Fair	Poor
550	475	425	375	300	250

Model 4536

A compact version and similar to the Model 4616 this pistol is offered with a decock lever on the frame.

NIB	Exc.	V.G.	Good	Fair	Poor
550	475	400	350	300	250

Model 4546

A full size version of the Model 4506 but offered in double-action-only.

NIB	Exc.	V.G.	Good	Fair	Poor
550	475	400	350	300	250

Model 4040PD

When introduced in 2003 this was the first Scandium frame S&W pistol. Chambered for the .40 S&W cartridge and fitted with a 3.5' barrel. White dot front sight with Novak Lo Mount rear sight. Matte black finish. Magazine capacity is seven rounds. Soft rubber grips. Weight is about 25.6 oz.

NIB	Exc.	V.G.	Good	Fair	Poor
785	625	—	—	—	—

Model SW1911

Introduced in 2003 this is a full size pistol chambered for the .45 ACP cartridge. Fitted with a 5" barrel with white dot front sight and Novak Lo-Mount rear sight. Stainless steel frame and slide. Checkered black rubber grips. Magazine capacity is 8 rounds. Weight is about 39 oz. In 2005 this model was also offered with wood grips and black oxide finish.

NIB	Exc.	V.G.	Good	Fair	Poor
750	625	—	—		

Model SW1911 Adjustable

As above but fitted with adjustable sights. Introduced in 2004.

NIB	Exc.	V.G.	Good	Fair	Poor
800	675	—	—	—	

Model SW1911Sc

This .45 ACP model is fitted with a Commander size slide and Scandium frame. Fixed sights. Checkered wood grips. Black oxide finish. Weight is about 28 oz. Introduced in 2004.

NIB	Exc.	V.G.	Good	Fair	Poor
1025	775	—	—	—	—

Model 1911 PD

This .45 ACP model is offered with either a 4.25" barrel or 5" barrel with Novak low mount sights. Wood grips. The frame is alloy with black finish. Magazine capacity is 8 rounds. Weight is about 28 oz. for 4.25" model and 29.5 oz. for the 5" model.

NIB	Exc.	V.G.	Good	Fair	Poor
775	600	—	—	—	

Model SW1911 DK (Doug Koenig)

Introduced in 2005 this .45 ACP model is fitted with a 5" stainless steel barrel. Adjustable rear sight with black blade front sight. Frame is stainless steel with black carbon steel slide. Wood grips. Magazine capacity is 8 rounds. Weight is about 41 oz.

NIB	Exc.	V.G.	Good	Fair	Poor
900	700	—	—	—	—

TSW SERIES (TACTICAL SMITH & WESSON)

This series is an upgrade of the older Smith & Wesson pistol series, many of which have been discontinued. These pistols come with either a traditional double-action trigger or a double-action-only trigger. All TSW pistols have an equipment rail for mounting lights or lasers. All are marked "TACTICAL S&W" on the slide.

3913/3953 TSW

Chambered for 9mm cartridge and fitted with a 3.5" barrel. White dot front sight and Novak Lo-Mount rear sight. Aluminum alloy frame. Magazine capacity is 7 rounds. Weight is about 25 oz. Stainless steel finish. The 3913 is traditional double-action while the 3953 is double-action-only.

NIB	Exc.	V.G.	Good	Fair	Poor
600	525	400	—	—	—

4013/4053 TSW

This pistol is chambered for the .40 S&W cartridge and fitted with a 3.5" barrel. White dot front sight and Novak Lo-Mount rear sight. Aluminum alloy frame and stainless steel slide. Magazine capacity is 9 rounds. Weight is about 27 oz. The 4013 is traditional double-action while the 4053 is double-action-only.

NIB	Exc.	V.G.	Good	Fair	Poor
595	400	350	—	—	—

4513/4553 TSW

This model is chambered for the .45 ACP cartridge and fitted with a 3.75" barrel. White dot front sight and Novak Lo-Mount rear sight. Aluminum alloy frame with stainless steel slide. Magazine capacity is 7 rounds. Weight is about 29 oz. The 4513 is traditional double-action while the 4553 is double-action-only.

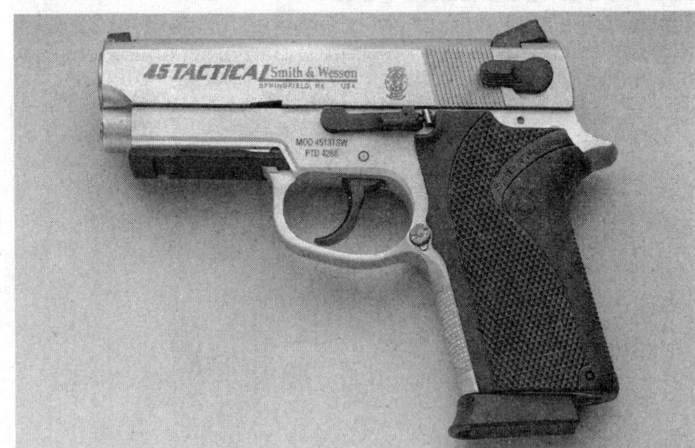

NIB	Exc.	V.G.	Good	Fair	Poor
650	525	475	—	—	—

NOTE: The double-action-only model 4553 is $50 less.

5903/5906/5943/5946 TSW

These pistols are chambered for the 9mm cartridge and fitted with a 4" barrel. Fixed sights standard (5903, 5906, 5943, 5946) adjustable sights (5906) optional as well as night sights (5906). Offered in traditional double-action (5903, 5906) as well as double-action-only (5943, 5946). Magazine capacity is 10 rounds and weight is about 38 oz. Stainless steel finish.

NIB	Exc.	V.G.	Good	Fair	Poor
650	495	400	—	—	—

NOTE: Add $100 for night sights, add $50 for adjustable sights.

4003/4006/4043/4046 TSW

This model comes in the same configurations as the 5903 group except these pistols are chambered for the .40 S&W cartridge. Magazine capacity is 10 rounds. Weight is about 28 oz.

NIB	Exc.	V.G.	Good	Fair	Poor
600	500	400	—	—	—

NOTE: Add $100 for night sights, add $50 for adjustable sights.

4563/4566/4583/4586 TSW

Similar to the above model but chambered for the .45 ACP cartridge and fitted with a 4.25" barrel. Same configurations as above. Weight is about 31 oz.

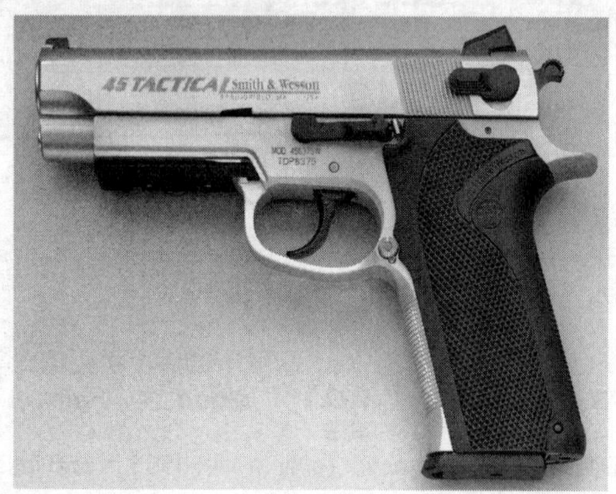

NIB	Exc.	V.G.	Good	Fair	Poor
600	500	450	—	—	—

NOTE: Add $100 for night sights, add $50 for adjustable sights.

CHIEF'S SPECIAL SERIES

CS9

Chambered for 9mm cartridge and fitted with a 3" barrel, this model has a stainless steel slide and aluminum alloy frame. Also available in blued finish. Hogue wraparound grips are standard. Fixed sights. Magazine capacity is 7 rounds. Weight is approximately 21 oz.

NIB	Exc.	V.G.	Good	Fair	Poor
550	395	315	—	—	—

CS45

Similar to the model above but chambered for the .45 ACP cartridge. Barrel length is 3.25". Magazine capacity is six rounds. Weight is about 24 oz.

NIB	Exc.	V.G.	Good	Fair	Poor
625	400	315	—	—	—

CS40

This Chief's Special model is chambered for the .40 S&W cartridge. Barrel length is 3.25". Magazine capacity is seven rounds. Weight is about 24 oz.

NIB	Exc.	V.G.	Good	Fair	Poor
550	395	315	—	—	—

CS40 Two-Tone

Same as above but with alloy frame and black slide. Limited edition. Introduced in 2000.

NIB	Exc.	V.G.	Good	Fair	Poor
575	425	340	—	—	—

SIGMA SERIES

SW40F

This new pistol was introduced in 1994 and was a departure from the traditional S&W pistol. The pistol features a stainless steel barrel, carbon steel slide, and polymer frame. Offered in .40 S&W and 9mm calibers with 15-round and 17-round capacities. Magazines built after 9/13/94 were limited to 10 rounds for all calibers per Federal law.

NIB	Exc.	V.G.	Good	Fair	Poor
450	400	350	300	250	200

Sigma Series Compact SW9C

Same as above but with barrel and slide 1/2" shorter than full size Sigma. Offered in both .40 S&W and 9mm.

NIB	Exc.	V.G.	Good	Fair	Poor
450	400	350	300	250	200

Sigma Series SW9M

Introduced in 1996 this pistol is chambered for the 9mm cartridge. It is fitted with a 3.25" barrel and has a magazine capacity of seven rounds. The frame is polymer and the slide carbon steel. Height is 4.5" and overall length is 6.25". Weight is 18 oz.

NIB	Exc.	V.G.	Good	Fair	Poor
450	400	350	300	250	200

Sigma SW9V

Chambered for the 9mm cartridge this model is fitted with a 4" barrel and 10-round magazine. It has a traditional double action. White dot sights are standard. Grips are integral to the frame. Stainless steel slide. Satin stainless finish with choice of gray or black frame. Weight is about 25 oz. Introduced in 1997.

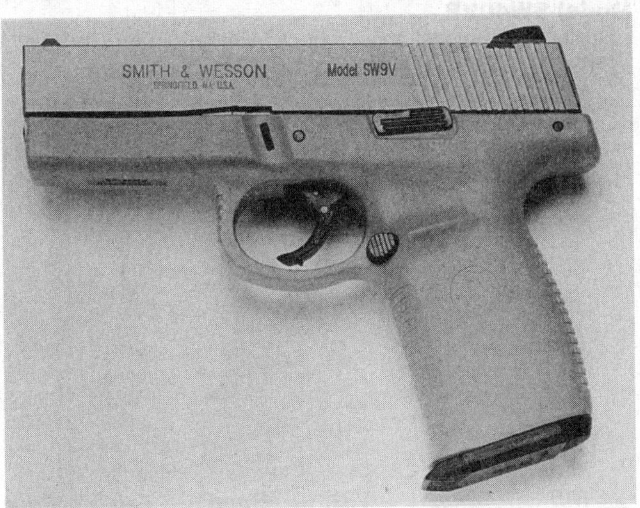

NIB	Exc.	V.G.	Good	Fair	Poor
425	325	295	—	—	—

Sigma SW9P

Same as the Model SW9V with the addition of a ported barrel. Introduced in 2001.

NIB	Exc.	V.G.	Good	Fair	Poor
430	330	—	—	—	—

Sigma SW9G

Same as the standard SW9 but with a black Melonite stainless steel slide and NATO green polymer frame. Introduced in 2001.

NIB	Exc.	V.G.	Good	Fair	Poor
350	325	—	—	—	—

Sigma SW40V

Same as above but chambered for .40 S&W cartridge. Weight is 25 oz. Introduced in 1997.

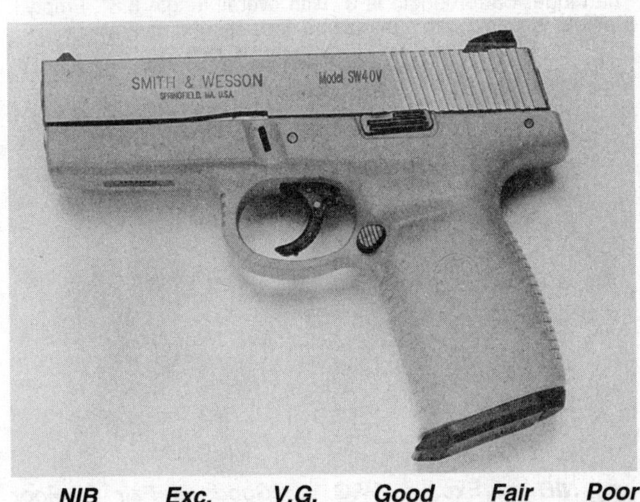

NIB	Exc.	V.G.	Good	Fair	Poor
325	275	—	—	—	—

Sigma SW40P

Same as the Model SW40V but with the addition of a ported barrel. Introduced in 2001.

NIB	Exc.	V.G.	Good	Fair	Poor
345	300	—	—	—	—

Sigma SW40G

Same as the standard SW40 pistol but with a black Melonite stainless steel slide and NATO green polymer frame. Introduced in 2001.

NIB	Exc.	V.G.	Good	Fair	Poor
350	325	—	—	—	—

Sigma SW380

Introduced in 1995 this model is chambered for the .380 ACP cartridge. Barrel length is 3" with overall length 5.8". Empty weight is 14 oz. with a magazine capacity of 6 rounds.

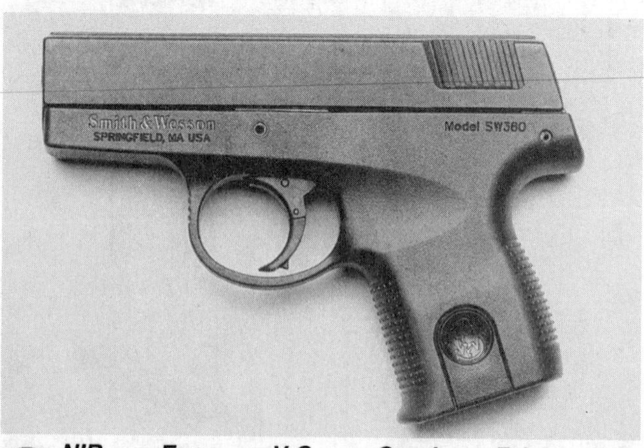

NIB	Exc.	V.G.	Good	Fair	Poor
295	275	200	150	100	75

ENHANCED SIGMA SERIES

Introduced in 1999 this series features a shorter trigger pull, slide stop guard, redesigned extractor and ejector. The ejection port is also lower. These pistols are also fitted with an accessory grove. Checkering pattern is more aggressive.

Model SW9E

Chambered for the 9mm cartridge this model has a 4" barrel with Tritium sights. Stainless steel slide with black Melonite finish. Magazine capacity is 10 rounds. Weight is about 25 oz.

NIB	Exc.	V.G.	Good	Fair	Poor
375	300	—	—	—	—

Model SW40E

Similar to the above model but chambered for the .40 S&W cartridge. Weight is about 24 oz.

NIB	Exc.	V.G.	Good	Fair	Poor
375	300	—	—	—	—

Model SW9VE

This model is chambered for the 9mm cartridge and fitted with a 4" barrel. Fixed sights and stainless steel slide. Weight is about 25 oz.

NIB	Exc.	V.G.	Good	Fair	Poor
375	300	—	—	—	—

Model SW40VE

Similar to the model above but chambered for the .40 S&W cartridge. Weight is about 24 oz.

NIB	Exc.	V.G.	Good	Fair	Poor
375	300	—	—	—	—

Model SW99

This model features a polymer frame designed and manufactured in Germany by Walther. The slide and barrel are manufactured by S&W in the U.S. Chambered for either the 9mm or .40 S&W cartridge this model is fitted with a 4" barrel on the 9mm model and a 4.125" barrel on the .40 S&W model. Adjust-

This symbol denotes "Sleepers" with rapidly-rising values and/or significant collector potential.

able rear sights. Decocking slide-mounted lever. Barrel and slide are stainless steel with black Melonite finish. Trigger is traditional double-action. Magazine capacity is 10 rounds. Weight is about 25 oz. Introduced in 1999.

NIB	Exc.	V.G.	Good	Fair	Poor
400	350	300	—	—	—

Model SW99 Compact

Introduced in 2003 this model is similar to the full size SW99 but with a 3.5" barrel and shorter grip frame. Chambered for both the 9mm or .40 S&W cartridge. Stainless steel barrel and slide with polymer frame. Magazine capacity is 10 rounds for 9mm and eight rounds for the .40 S&W. Weight is about 23 oz.

NIB	Exc.	V.G.	Good	Fair	Poor
400	350	300	—	—	—

Model SW99 .45 ACP

Same as the SW99 but chambered for the .45 ACP cartridge. Magazine is nine rounds. Weight is about 26 oz. Introduced in 2003.

NIB	Exc.	V.G.	Good	Fair	Poor
500	500	—	—	—	—

Model SW990L Compact

Introduced in 2005 this model is chambered for the 9mm or .40 S&W cartridge. Barrel length is 3.5". Adjustable rear sight with dot front sight. Polymer frame with stainless steel slide with Melonite finish. Plastic grips. Magazine capacity is 10 rounds for the 9mm and 8 rounds for the .40 S&W model. Weight is about 23 oz.

NIB	Exc.	V.G.	Good	Fair	Poor
475	400	—	—	—	

Model SW990L Full Size

Similar to the above model but chambered for the 9mm, .40 S&W and .45 ACP cartridges. Barrel lengths are 4" for the 9mm; 4.125" for the .40 S&W; and 4.25" for the .45 ACP. Magazine capacity is 16 rounds for the 9mm and 12 rounds for the .40 S&W model. Weight is about 25 oz. Introduced in 2005.

NIB	Exc.	V.G.	Good	Fair	Poor
495	425	—	—	—	—

NOTE: Add $40 for .45 ACP model.

Model 410

This model was first introduced in 1996. It features an alloy frame with carbon steel slide. It is chambered for the .40 S&W cartridge. Barrel length is 4". The magazine capacity is 10 rounds and the overall length is 7.5". Weight is approximately 29 oz.

NIB	Exc.	V.G.	Good	Fair	Poor
450	400	325	—	—	—

Model 410 Two-Tone

Same as the Model 410 but with alloy finish frame and black slide. Limited edition.

NIB	Exc.	V.G.	Good	Fair	Poor
475	400	325	—	—	—

Model 410S

Introduced in 2003 this is a stainless steel version of the Model 410. Weight is about 28 oz.

NIB	Exc.	V.G.	Good	Fair	Poor
475	400	—	—	—	—

Model 457

Introduced in 1996 this .45 ACP model features a 3.75" barrel with rounded trigger guard and double-action. It is fitted with a single side decocker. Magazine capacity is seven rounds. Overall length is 7.25" and weight is about 29 oz. The frame is alloy and the slide a carbon steel. Finish is matte black.

NIB	Exc.	V.G.	Good	Fair	Poor
450	400	300	—	—	—

Model 457S

Same as above but in stainless steel. Weight is about 29 oz. Introduced in 2003.

NIB	Exc.	V.G.	Good	Fair	Poor
475	425	—	—	—	—

Model 908

Introduced in 1996 this is an economy compact pistol. It is chambered for the 9mm cartridge and is fitted with a 3.5" barrel. The action is traditional double-action. Fixed rear sight. Magazine capacity is eight rounds. Overall length is 6-7/8" and weight is about 26 oz.

NIB	Exc.	V.G.	Good	Fair	Poor
450	400	—	—	—	—

Model 908S

Same as the Model 908 but in stainless steel. Weight is about 24 oz. Introduced in 2003.

NIB	Exc.	V.G.	Good	Fair	Poor
475	425	—	—	—	

Model 908S Carry Combo

Introduced in 2004 this model is the same as above with the addition of a Kydex carry holster.

NIB	Exc.	V.G.	Good	Fair	Poor
500	425	—	—	—	—

Model 909

Introduced in 1995 this pistol is chambered for the 9mm cartridge. It has a blue carbon steel slide, aluminum alloy frame,

This symbol denotes "Sleepers" with rapidly-rising values and/or significant collector potential.

and is double-action. It has a single column magazine and curved backstrap.

NIB	Exc.	V.G.	Good	Fair	Poor
350	300	200	150	100	—

Model 910

Also introduced in 1995. Same as above model but with double-column magazine and straight backstrap.

NIB	Exc.	V.G.	Good	Fair	Poor
350	300	200	150	100	—

Model 910S

Introduced in 2003 this is a stainless steel version of the Model 910. Weight is about 28 oz.

NIB	Exc.	V.G.	Good	Fair	Poor
450	395	—	—	—	—

MILITARY & POLICE (M&P) SERIES (2006)

M&P 9mm

Full-size Military and Police semi-auto chambered in 9mm. Capacity 17+1, 4.25" barrel, 6-1/2 lb. trigger, 24.25 oz. Picatinny rail and polymer frame. Optional tritium low-light sights. Introduced 2006.

NIB	Exc.	V.G.	Good	Fair	Poor
430	—	—	—	—	—

M&P 40

Full-size semi-auto chambered in .40 S&W; this is the first of the new Military and Police series. Capacity 15+1, 4.25" barrel, .5 lb. trigger, 24.25 oz. Polymer frame and Picatinny rail. Optional tritium low-light sights. Introduced 2006.

NIB	Exc.	V.G.	Good	Fair	Poor
550	—	—	—	—	—

M&P .357 SIG

Full-size Military and Police semi-auto chambered in .357 Magnum. Capacity 15+1, 4.25" barrel, 6.5 lb. trigger, 24.25 oz. Polymer frame and Picatinny rail. Optional tritium low-light sights. Introduced 2006.

NIB	Exc.	V.G.	Good	Fair	Poor
550	—	—	—	—	—

M&P45

Semi-auto; similar to M&P40 but in .45 ACP. Black or Dark Enarth Brown finish. Introduced 2007.

NIB	Exc.	V.G.	Good	Fair	Poor
550	—	—	—	—	—

M&P9c

Semi-auto; compact model; similar to M&P9 but with 3.5" barrel, short grip frame and 10+1 or 12+1 capacity. Black Melonite finish. Introduced 2007.

NIB	Exc.	V.G.	Good	Fair	Poor
475	—	—	—	—	—

M&P40c

Semi-auto; compact model; similar to M&P9c but in .40 S&W. Black Melonite finish. Introduced 2007.

NIB	Exc.	V.G.	Good	Fair	Poor
475	—	—	—	—	—

M&P357c

Semi-auto; compact model; similar to M&P40c but in .357 SIG. Black Melonite finish. Introduced 2007.

NIB	Exc.	V.G.	Good	Fair	Poor
475	—	—	—	—	—

SW9VE Allied Forces

Similar to SW9VE but with black Melonite slide. Adopted by Afghanistan internal security and border forces. Introduced 2007. Add 75 percent for "Disaster Ready Kit" (case and emergency supplies).

NIB	Exc	V.G.	Good	Fair	Poor
427	—	—	—	—	—

SW40VE Allied Forces

Similar to SW9VE Allied Forces but in .40 S&W. Introduced 2007. Add 75 percent for "Disaster Ready Kit" (case and emergency supplies).

NIB	Exc	V.G.	Good	Fair	Poor
427	—	—	—	—	—

SMITH & WESSON COMMEMORATIVES

Smith & Wesson has, over the years, built many special edition handguns. These guns have been to commemorate some important national or regional event or group. The company has also built a large number of special edition handguns for certain distributors such as Lew Horton which is listed. There are well over 200 special production guns not reflected in this pricing guide. Not even Smith & Wesson has all of the information on these guns and with many the number is so small that a market price would not be possible to establish. Listed are a number of Smith & Wesson Commemoratives that we do have information on. Due to the difficulty in determining value only the original retail price is listed. Remember to receive full value for these guns they must be NIB, unfired with unturned cylinders.

Model 14 Texas Ranger Comm.

Introduced in 1973. Supplied with 4" barrel and cased. Edition limited to 10,000. 8,000 of these had knives. Serial numbers TR 1 to TR 10000.

Original Retail Introductory Price: $250.00

Model 25-3 S&W 125th Anniversary Comm.

Introduced in 1977. Limited edition of 10,000. Serial numbers SW0000 to SW10000. Deluxe models marked 25-4.

Original Retail Introductory Price: $350.00

Model 26-4 Georgia State Police Comm.

Introduced in 1988/1989 and supplied with a 5" barrel. Total production of 802 guns. Known Serial numbers BBY00354 to BBY0434.

Original Retail Introductory Price: $405.00

 *This symbol denotes "Sleepers" with rapidly-rising values and/or significant collector potential.*

Model 27 .357 50th Anniversary Comm.

Introduced in 1985 and supplied with a 5" barrel and cased. Limited edition to 2,500 guns. Serial numbers REG0001 to REG2500.

Original Retail Introductory Price: N/A

Model 29-3 Elmer Keith Comm.

Introduced in 1986 and supplied with a 4" barrel. Gun etched in gold. Limited edition of 2,500 guns. Serial numbers EMK0000 to EMK0100 for Deluxe models and EMK 010 to EMK2500 for standard model.

Original Retail Introductory Price: $850.00

Model 544 Texas Wagon Train 150 Anniversary Comm.

Introduced in 1986 and limited to 7801 guns. Serial numbers TWT0000 to TWT7800.

Original Issue Introductory Price: N/A

Model 586 Mass. State Police Comm.

Introduced in 1986 and fitted with a 6" barrel. Limited to 631 guns. Serial numbers with ABT-AUC prefix.

Original Retail Introductory Price: N/A

Model 629-1 Alaska 1988 Iditarod Comm.

Introduced in 1987 and limited to 545 guns. Serial numbers from AKI0001 to AKI0545.

Original Retail Introductory Price: N/A

Model 745 IPSC Comm.

Introduced in 1986 and limited to 5362 guns. Serial numbers DVC0000 to DVC5362.

Original Retail Introductory Price: N/A

Model 4516-1 U.S. Marshall Comm.

Introduced in 1990 and limited to 500 guns. Serial numbers USM0000 to USM0499.

Original Retail Introductory Price: $599.95

Model SW1911 PD Gunsite Commemorative

Honors Lt. Col. Jeff Cooper's Gunsite Training Academy. Scandium alloy, single-action .45 ACP with 4.25" barrel and 8+1 capacity. Fixed sights. 28 oz. Introduced 2006.

NIB	*Exc.*	*V.G.*	*Good*	*Fair*	*Poor*
875	—	—	—	—	—

Model SW1911 – Rolling Thunder Commemorative

Limited edition commemorates American POW-MIAs. Rolling Thunder and POW-MIA logos in imitation bonded ivory grips. Chambered for .45 ACP. Blued, 8+1 capacity, 5" barrel, 38.5 oz. Introduced 2006.

NIB	*Exc*	*V.G.*	*Good*	*Fair*	*Poor*
850	—	—	—	—	—

SMITH & WESSON PERFORMANCE CENTER HANDGUNS

The role of Smith & Wesson's Performance Center has changed since it was established in 1990. What was once a specialized tune-up and competition one-off production department has now become a separate facility in providing specialized and limited handguns to the public often with distributors participation. This change came about around 1991, when the Performance Center initiated its own limited edition designs. These editions are generally limited to between 300 and 600 pistols for each model. The Performance Center, in fact, has its own distinct product line. Performance Center pistols are made in its own shop using its own designers. One of these distributors that has played a major role in offering these special guns to the public is the Lew Horton Distribution Company. The Center still continues to offer action jobs and accurate work but no longer executes one-of-a-kind customizing. The Performance Center has built about eight to twelve different models in the last two years. Plans call for more of these unique handguns to be built in the future. Pistols that are available from a certain distributor or the Performance Center will be noted in the description of each pistol.

Limited Edition Pistols and Revolvers of 1990

One of the first limited special series of Performance Center handguns was this offering, which consisted of custom engraved S&W handguns limited to 15 units on any current (1990) production pistol or revolver. This Limited Edition featured: 24 karat gold and sterling inlays, special bright mirror finish, decorated in light scroll pattern, specially assigned serial number beginning with the prefix "PEC," tuned action, solid walnut presentation case inlaid with blue or burgundy leather insert, embossed with gold with performance center logo. Interior of case is custom fitted with a matching colored velvet. Each handgun is hand numbered and has a signed certificate of authenticity. Because of the unique nature of the Limited Edition offering it is strongly recommended to secure a professional appraisal.

.40 S&W Tactical

A limited edition semi-automatic handgun offered exclusively by Lew Horton through the Performance Center. This special pistol is fitted with a 5" match-grade barrel, hand fit spherical barrel bushing, custom tuned action, special trigger job, oversized frame and slide rails, wrap-around straight backstrap grip. Replaceable front and Novak rear sights. Special serial numbers. Offered in 1992 and limited to 200 units.

Courtesy Smith & Wesson

Suggested Retail Introductory Price: $1,500

.40 S&W Compensated

Similar to the .40 S&W Tactical but furnished with a 4.625" barrel and single chamber compensator. This is also a Lew Horton/Performance pistol. A production of 250 units. Offered in 1992.

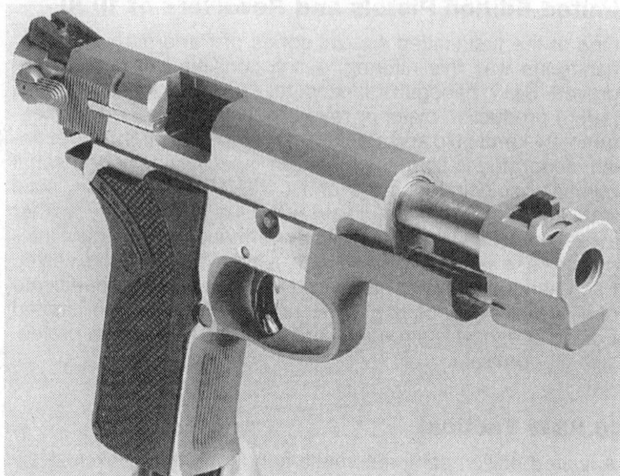

Suggested Retail Introductory Price: $1,700

.40 S&W Performance Action Pistol

Offered in limited quantities in 1990, this Performance Center .40 S&W semi-automatic pistol was used by the Smith & Wesson shooting team. The frame and barrel are stainless steel with blued carbon steel slide, two port compensator, two fitted and numbered 13-round magazines, 5.25" match grade barrel extended frame beavertail, square combat trigger guard, oversize magazine release button, spherical barrel bushing, wraparound straight backstrap grip, extended magazine funnel, and BoMar adjustable rear sight. The action is tuned for accuracy and precision.

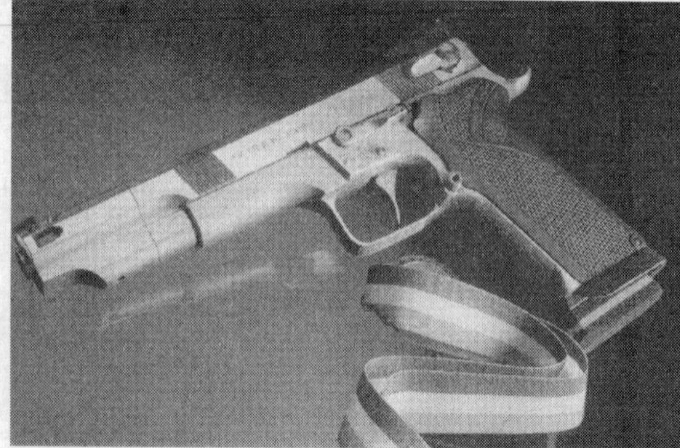

Suggested Retail Introductory Price: N/A

Model 681 Quadport

A Lew Horton revolver limited to 300 guns with special serial numbers. This 7-shot revolver has a 3" barrel underlug quadport barrel. The action is tuned, cylinders are chamfered and the trigger has an overtravel stop. Sights are fixed combat type.

Suggested Retail Introductory Price: $675

Model 686 Competitor

Introduced by Lew Horton and the Performance Center for 1993 this limited edition revolver features a match grade barrel and unique under barrel weight system. The action has been custom tuned and the receiver is drilled and tapped for scope mounts. Charge holes are chambered, ejector rod housing is enclosed, and the grip is an extended competition type. Special serial numbers.

Suggested Retail Introductory Price: $1,100

Model 686 Hunter

Similar to the Model 686 Competitor. This is also a limited edition Lew Horton revolver chambered for the .357 Magnum and features the under barrel weight system, internal scope mount, and custom tuned action. Special serial numbers.

Suggest Retail Introductory Price: $1,154

Model 686 Carry Comp 4"

Offered in limited quantities by Lew Horton and the Performance Center in 1992 this new design features the unique single chamber integral barrel compensator. Front is windage adjustable and the action is custom tuned. Chambered for the .357 Magnum cartridge. Special serial numbers.

Suggested Retail Introductory price: $1,000

Model 686 Carry Comp 3"

The 1993 Lew Horton limited edition version of the Model 686 Carry Comp 4" model with a 3" barrel. The same features apply to both models.

Suggested Retail Introductory Price: $1,000

Model 686 Plus

This Lew Horton model features a 7-round cylinder with chamfered charge holes for use with full moon clips for both .38 Special and .357 Magnum cartridges. Fitted with a tapered 6" barrel with countersunk muzzle. Gold bead front sight and adjustable rear sight. Altamont wood grips are standard. Stainless steel finish. Weight is approximately 44 oz.

Suggested Retail Introductory Price: $930

Model 686—.38 Super

Introduced in 2003 this six-round revolver is chambered for the .38 Super cartridge and fitted with a 4" barrel with tapered lug. Interchangeable red ramp front sight and adjustable rear sight. Stainless steel with glass bead finish. Cocobolo grips. Weight is about 37 oz. Distributed by Bangers.

Suggested Retail Introductory Price: N/A

Model 629 Hunter

Introduced in 1992 by Lew Horton and the Performance Center this limited edition revolver features a new design that utilizes a 6" under barrel weight system, special integral barrel compensator. The action has been custom tuned and the receiver has an integral scope mount. Chambered for the .44 Magnum. Special finger groove grips are standard. Special serial numbers.

Suggested Retail Introductory Price: $1,234

Model 629 Hunter II

Another Lew Horton/Performance Center limited edition revolver that features 2x Nikon scope with steel see-through rings. The barrel is Mag-Na-Ported and incorporates the Performance Center's under barrel weight arrangement. The action is custom tuned and the revolver is supplied with a ballistic nylon range carry bag. Special serial numbers.

Suggested Retail Introductory Price: $1,234

Model 629 Comped Hunter

Offered through RSR this model features a 6" barrel with 4-port detachable compensator. The cylinder is unfluted. Sights are adjustable, fitted with Altamount wood grips. Tuned action. Stainless steel. Weight is approximately 59 oz.

Suggested Retail Introductory Price: $1,100

Model 629 12" Hunter

Introduced in 2000 this Lou Horton revolver is fitted with a 12" barrel with Patridge front sight and Wilson silhouette adjustable rear sight. Hogue Combat grips. Finish is glassbead stainless steel. Comes with a Waller 21" gun rug. Weight is about 65 oz.

Suggested Retail Introductory Price: $1,025

Model 629 Magnum Hunter Trail Boss

Exclusive to RSR this limited edition model is chambered for the .44 Magnum cartridge and is fitted with a 3" barrel. Stainless steel finish.

Suggested Retail Introductory Price: $733

Model 629 Compensated Hunter

Chambered for the .44 Magnum cartridge and fitted with a 7.5" barrel with compensator. Barrel also has removable stainless steel scope mount. Open sights fitted with adjustable orange ramp front and adjustable rear sight. Rosewood grips. Six-round cylinder. Weight is 52 oz. Talo exclusive. Introduced in 2001.

Suggested Retail Introductory Price: $1190

Model 629 Stealth Hunter

Fitted with a 7.5" ported barrel and chambered for the .44 magnum cartridge. Six-round cylinder. The finish is black-T and NATO green. Red ramp Millett front sight and adjustable rear sight. Hogue rubber combat grips standard. Furnished with lockable aluminum case. Weight is about 56 oz. Introduced in 2001. Camfour Distributor exclusive.

Suggested Retail Introductory Price: $1,025

Model 629 Extreme

Chambered for the .44 Magnum cartridge and fitted with a 12" barrel with sling swivel. Bomar sights. Rubber grips.

Suggested Retail Introductory Price: $1,025

Model 629 Carry Comp

Introduced in 1992 by Lew Horton and the Performance Center this limited edition revolver is chambered for the .44 Magnum cartridge. It features an integral ported 3" barrel, fluted cylinder, radiused charge holes, dovetail front and fixed groove rear sight. Fitted with a rubber combat grip. The action is custom by the Performance Center. Special serial numbers.

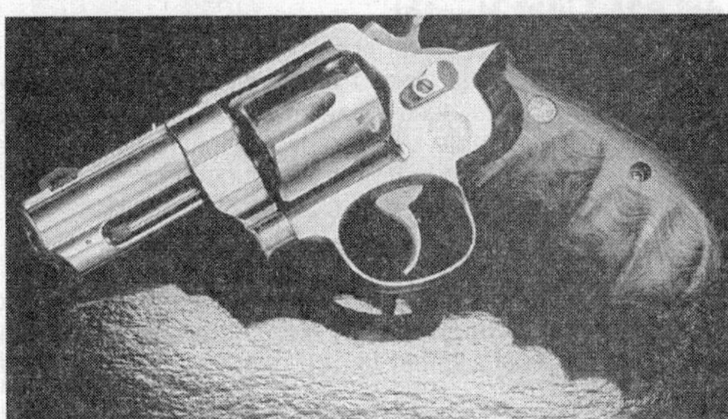

Suggested Retail Introductory Price: $1,000

Model 629 Carry Comp II

A limited edition 1993 offering by Lew Horton and the Performance Center similar to the 1992 Model 629 Carry Comp with the exception that this 1993 model has a special unfluted cylinder and fully adjustable rear sight. Special serial numbers.

Suggested Retail Introductory Price: $1,000

Model 629 Comped Hunter

Chambered for the .44 Magnum cartridge and built with a 7.5" barrel with a tapered full length lug and compensator. Front sight is drift adjustable orange ramp. Adjustable rear sight. Stainless steel with glass bead finish. Removable scope mount. Rosewood grips. Weight is about 52 oz. Introduced in 2003.

Suggested Retail Introductory Price: $1,100

Model 610

Introduced in 1998 by Lew Horton this model features a 3" full lug barrel chambered for the 10mm cartridge. Nonfluted cylinder, red ramp front sight and white outline rear sight. Rosewood grips. Limited to 300 revolvers.

Suggested Retail Introductory Price: $740

Model 640 Carry Comp

Introduced in 1991 by Lew Horton and the Performance Center this revolver is chambered for the .38 S&W Special, but with a strengthened action to handle +P loads. Fitted with a heavy 2.625" barrel with unique integral barrel compensator. The front sight is replaceable and adjustable for windage. The rear sight is a fixed groove. Custom trigger job and custom tuned action are also part of the package. Special serial numbers.

Suggested Retail Introductory Price: $750

Model 640 .357 Quadport

Introduced in 1996. Similar to the model above but chambered for the .357 Magnum cartridge and quadported. Limited to 190 revolvers. Special serial numbers.

Suggested Retail Introductory Price: $675

Model 460 Airweight

Chambered for the .38 Special cartridge, this model is fitted with a 2" Mag-Na-Ported barrel and a five-shot cylinder. Fixed sights. Eagle Secret Service grips. Weight is about 16 oz. Limited to 450 revolvers. Introduced in 1994.

Suggested Retail Introductory Price: $580

Model 625 Light Hunter

This is a large frame revolver chambered for the .45 Colt. It is fitted with a 6" Mag-Na-Ported barrel with integral Weaver-style base. It has a stainless steel finish and black Hogue rubber grips. Drift adjustable Millet front and fully adjustable rear sight. Offered in limited quantities. Introduced in 1997 by RSR.

Suggested Retail Introductory Price: $580

Model 625

Introduced in 1998 this model is chambered for the .45 ACP or .45 Colt cartridge. Fitted with a 3" full lug barrel, fluted cylinder, and rosewood grips. Limited to 150 revolvers in each chambering.

Suggested Retail Introductory Price: $755

Model 625 V-Comp

Chambered for the .44 Magnum cartridge this model is fitted with a 4" barrel and removable three-port compensator. Front sight is a red ramp with black adjustable rear sight. Hogue wood combat grips. Furnished with aluminum case. Weight is about 43 oz. Finish is stainless steel. Distributed by RSR. Introduced in 1999.

Suggested Retail Introductory Price: $1,000

Model 625—5.25"

Introduced in 2001 this model features a special Jerry Miculek Hogue laminated combat grip. Chambered for the .45 ACP cartridge and fitted with a 5.25" barrel. Stainless steel finish. Interchangeable gold bead front sight and adjustable rear sight. Weight is about 42 oz. Camfour exclusive.

Suggested Retail Introductory Price: N/A

Model 627—8 Shot

Chambered for the .357 Magnum cartridge this revolver has an 8-round capacity. Drilled and tapped with adjustable sights on a 5" tapered and contoured barrel. Tuned action. Hogue wood grips. Satin stainless steel finish. Weight is approximately 44 oz. A Lew Horton exclusive. Introduced in 1997.

Suggested Retail Introductory Price: $1,160

Model 627 Defensive—8 Shot

Chambered for the .357 Magnum this model is fitted with an eight-round unfluted cylinder recessed for full moon clips. Barrel length is 2-5/8". Adjustable rear sight and drift adjustable front sight. Wooden eagle boot grips. Weight is about 38 oz. Introduced in 1999. Furnished with aluminum case.

Suggested Retail Introductory Price: $1,025

Model 651

This is a limited edition revolver by RSR chambered for the .22 WMR cartridge. Fitted with a 2" barrel and boot grips. Stainless steel finish.

Suggested Retail Introductory Price: $492

"Shorty-Forty" .40 S&W

Introduced in 1992 and available exclusively from Lew Horton, this limited edition Performance Center pistol features a light alloy frame, oversize slide rails, and spherical barrel bushing. A match grade barrel is joined to a custom tuned action. Special serial numbers.

Suggested Retail Introductory Price: $950

Model 647 Varminter

Introduced in 2003 this model is chambered for the .17 HMR cartridge and fitted with a 12" fluted barrel with a removable black Patridge front sight. Adjustable rear sight. Integral scope mount on barrel. Six-round cylinder. Stainless steel finish. Weight is about 54 oz.

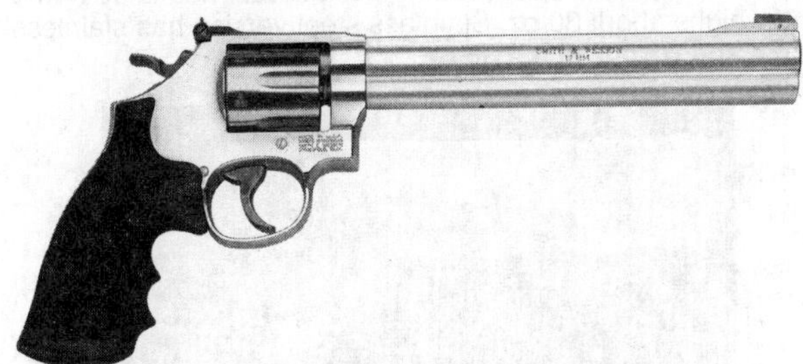

Suggested Retail Introductory Price: $1,100

Model 500 Magnum Hunter

Introduced in 2003 this revolver is chambered for the .500 S&W cartridge and fitted with a 10.5" barrel with compensator. Sling swivel studs and sling are standard. Orange dovetail ramp front sight and adjustable rear sight. Stainless steel with glass bead finish. Hogue rubber grips. Weight is approximately 82 oz.

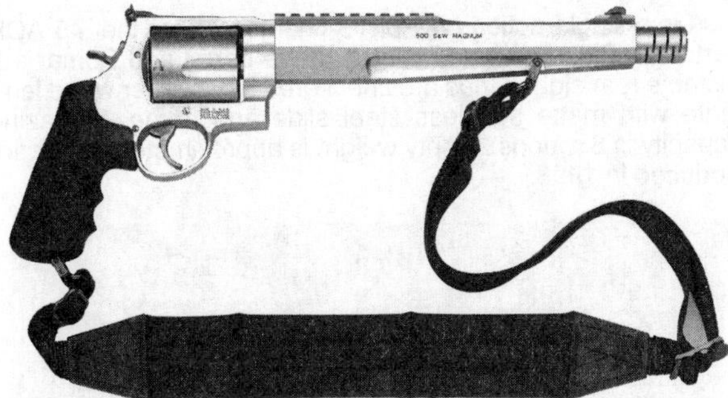

Suggested Retail Introductory Price: $1390

"Shorty Forty" Mark III

Offered in 1995 this Lew Horton exclusive features low-mount adjustable sights, hand-fitted titanium barrel bushing, checkered front strap. The action as been hand honed and the pistol is sold with two magazines; one 11 rounds and the other nine rounds.

Suggested Retail Introductory Price: $1,000

Shorty .45

Introduced by Lew Horton in 1996 this .45 ACP pistol has a hand-fitted titanium barrel bushing, oversize frame and slide rails, match grade barrel, checkered front strap, hand honed double-action, and special serial numbers.

Suggested Retail Introductory Price: $1,095

Shorty Nine

This Lew Horton exclusive is limited to 100 units. It features a hand-fitted titanium barrel bushing, oversize slide rails, action job, low mount adjustable sights, checkered front strap, match grade barrel, and two tone finish. Furnished with two 12-round magazines.

Suggested Retail Introductory Price: $1,000

9 Recon

This is an RSR exclusive and introduced in 1999. Chambered for the 9mm cartridge this model is fitted with a 3.5" barrel. Rear sight is Novak Lo-Mount. Hogue wraparound rubber grips. The slide is black carbon steel with an alloy frame. Magazine capacity is 12 rounds. Weight is about 27 oz.

Suggested Retail Introductory Price: $1,178

Performance Center .45 Limited

This Lew Horton model is a full-size single-action pistol. Hand-fitted titanium barrel bushing, fitted slide lock, match grade barrel, adjustable sights, oversize magazine well, tuned action, and checkered front strap.

Suggested Retail Introductory Price: $1,400

45 Recon

Another RSR pistol chambered for the .45 ACP cartridge, this model is an enhanced version of the "Shorty 45." The 4.25" barrel is ported with Novak Lo-Mount sights. Hogue wraparound rubber grips. Stainless steel slide and barrel with aluminum frame. Weight is about 28 oz. Magazine capacity is 7 rounds. Matte black finish. Furnished with aluminum case.

Suggested Retail Introductory Price: $1,221

Shorty .356 TSW

This new cartridge is also available in another Lew Horton/Performance Center limited edition pistol with a 4" barrel. It features a steel frame and hand-fitted slide, with spherical barrel bushing. The double-action is custom tuned by the Performance Center. Magazine holds 12 rounds. Similar in appearance to the "Shorty-Forty." Offered in 1993. Special serial numbers.

Suggested Retail Introductory Price: $1,000

Model .356 TSW "Limited" Series

This is a Lew Horton gun. This model is chambered for the new .356 TSW caliber (TSW stands for Team Smith & Wesson). This is a new caliber, actually a 9mm x 21.5mm cartridge, with ballistics of around 1,235 fps with a 147-grain bullet. Designed as a low-end .357 competition pistol. Built for the competitive shooter (IPSC) it features a 15-round magazine and distinctive profile and markings. The single-action trigger is adjustable for reach while the slide, frame, and barrel are custom fitted. The gun comes with a spherical barrel bushing and adjustable BoMar sights. The frame grip is checked 20 line to the inch, the magazine well is extended as is the magazine release. The magazine is fitted with a pad.

Suggested Retail Introductory Price: $1,350

Model 5906 Performance Center

Introduced in 1998 this 9mm pistol features front slide serrations, ambidextrous decocker, titanium coated barrel bushing, match grade barrel, and Novak Lo-Mount sights. Sold with one 15-round magazine and one 10-round magazine. Stainless steel finish.

Suggested Retail Introductory Price: $1,200

Model 845 of 1998

This .45 ACP caliber model has a 5" match grade barrel with hand lapped rails on frame and slide. Patridge front sight and adjustable Bomar rear sight. Single-action trigger is tuned and the slide has front serrations. Magazine capacity is 8 rounds. Stainless steel finish. Limited to 150 pistols.

Suggested Retail Introductory Price: $1,500

Model .45 CQB Combat

Introduced in 1998 this Lew Horton model features a 4" match grade barrel. Novak Lo-Mount sights. Double-action trigger with ambidextrous de-cocker. Available in both a matte black and stainless steel finish. Matte black model has alloy frame and weighs about 30 oz. Stainless steel version has stainless frame and weighs about 38 oz.

Suggested Retail Introductory Price: $1,200

Model 945

This is a single-action-only pistol chambered for the .45 ACP cartridge. Fitted with a 5" match grade barrel and Bomar adjustable rear sight. Grips are checkered black/silver wood laminate with matte stainless steel slide and frame. Magazine capacity is 8 rounds. Empty weight is approximately 44 oz. Introduced in 1998.

Suggested Retail Introductory Price: $1,600

Model 945 Black Model

This Performance Center Model features a 3.25" barrel with black stainless steel slide. Frame is aluminum. Novak Lo-Mount sights. Hogue checkered wood laminate grips. Furnished with two 6-round magazines and a locking aluminum gun case. Weight is about 24 oz. Exclusive with RSR.

Suggested Retail Introductory Price: $1,550

Model 945-40

This PC model is fitted with a 3.75" barrel chambered for the .40 S&W cartridge. Novak Lo-Mount sights and Hogue checkered wood laminate grips are standard. Furnished with two 7-round magazines and a locking aluminum case. Clear glass-bead finish. Exclusive with Sports South.

Suggested Retail Introductory Price: $1,275

Model 945 Micro

Similar to the Model 945 Black Model but with stainless steel finish. Exclusive with Camfour Distributor.

Suggested Retail Introductory Price: $1,300

Model SW945

This .45 ACP pistol is fitted with a 5" barrel with Wilson Combat adjustable rear sight. Scalloped slide serrations both front and rear. Checkered wood grips. Many special features. Weight is about 40.5 oz.

Suggested Retail Introductory Price: $2,085

Model SW1911

Chambered for the .45 ACP cartridge and fitted with a 5" barrel with adjustable rear sight. Checkered wood grips. Many special features. Scalloped slide serrations front and rear. Black Melonite finish. Magazine capacity is 8 rounds. Weight is about 41 oz. Also offered in a stainless steel version for $160 less.

Suggested Retail Price: $2270

Model SW1911 DK

This model is chambered for the .38 Super cartridge and fitted with a 5" barrel with adjustable rear sight. Smooth wood grips with DK logo. Stainless steel finish with scalloped serrations at rear of slide. Many special features. Magazine capacity is 10 rounds. Weight is about 41.5 oz. Introduced in 2005.

Suggested Retail Price : $2320

SW1911 Tactical Rail

One of Tactical Rail Series for SWAT Teams and tactical applications. Picatinny rail and fixed sights. Blued or stainless, single-action .45 ACP with 5" barrel and 8+1 capacity. 39 oz. Introduced 2006. MSRP: 1057

Model 66 .357 Magnum F-Comp

A Performance Center revolver designed as a carry gun. Furnished with a 3" ported barrel and full underlug. The thumbpiece has been cut down to accommodate all speed loaders and the charge holes are countersunk. The K-frame action has been custom tuned and the rear sight is a fully adjustable black blade while the front sight features a Tritium dot night sight. Furnished with a round butt combat-style rubber grip. This revolver has a stainless steel finish. Weight is about 35 oz. This is a Lew Horton special limited edition, 300 units.

NOTE: In 2003 this revolver was produced for all S&W stocking dealers.

Suggested Retail Introductory Price: $800

Model 66

An RSR exclusive this model is chambered for the .357 Magnum cartridge and fitted with a 3" barrel. Red ramp front sight. Stainless steel finish. Limited edition.

Suggested Retail Introductory Price: $490

Model 681 Quad Port

Chambered for the .357 Magnum cartridge and fitted with a 3" barrel with Quad porting. Fixed rear sight. Seven-round cylinder with moon clips. Two sets of grips are standard: Hogue Bantam and checkered wood laminate. Stainless steel finish. Weight is about 35 oz. Camfour exclusive. A 4" barrel version is also available.

This symbol denotes "Sleepers" with rapidly-rising values and/or significant collector potential. 

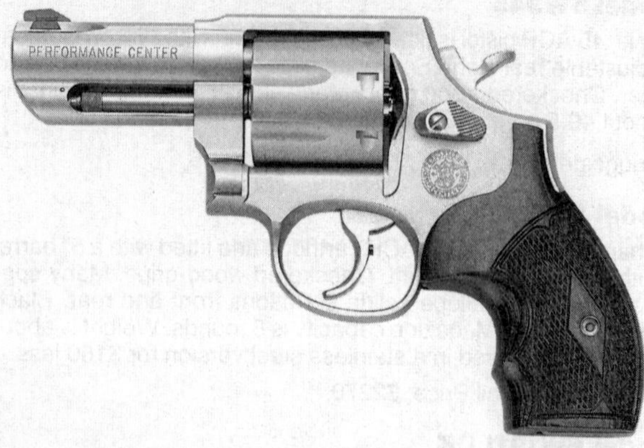

Suggested Retail Introductory Price: $850

Model 25

This PC model is a reintroduction of the original Model 25. Chambered for the .45 Colt cartridge and fitted with a tapered 6" barrel with pinned gold bead patridge front sight. Four screw frame. Furnished with locking aluminum case. Weight is about 42 oz. Sports South exclusive.

NIB	Exc.	V.G.	Good	Fair	Poor
900	750	650	550	375	—

Model 657

This Lew Horton/Performance Center revolver is fitted with a 3" full lug barrel chambered for the .41 Magnum cartridge. Fluted cylinder with red ramp front sight and white outline rear. Rosewood grips. Limited to 150 revolvers in 1998.

Suggested Retail Introductory Price: $720

Model 657 Classic

Offered in limited quantities of 350 units this Lew Horton/Performance Center revolver features an unfluted cylinder and 6.5" barrel on a drilled and tapped N frame. Chambered for the .41 Magnum cartridge this handgun is fitted with adjustable rear sight. Special serial numbers.

Suggested Retail Introductory Price: $550

Model 657 Defensive

Introduced in 1999 by Lou Horton, this .41 Magnum revolver is fitted with a 2-5/8" barrel with drift adjustable Millet front sight and fully adjustable rear sight. Stainless steel finish with 6-shot nonfluted cylinder. Hogue combat grips. Weight is about 40 oz. Furnished with aluminum case.

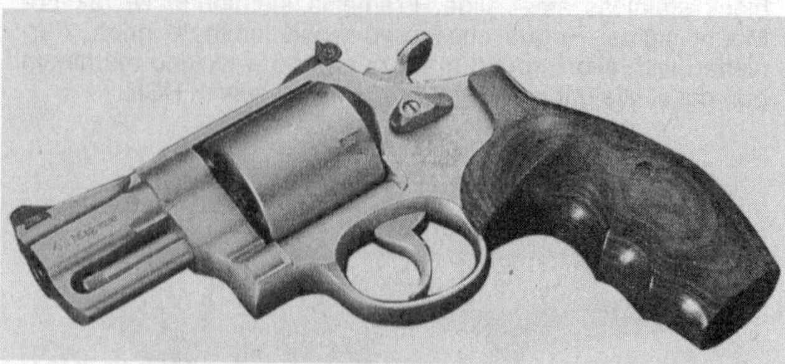

Suggested Retail Introductory Price: $1,025

Model 657 Hunter

Introduced in 1995 this is an RSR Wholesale Guns exclusive. Fitted with an integral weaver base, Mag-Na-Ported 6" barrel with Millet red ramp front sight and adjustable rear sight. This model has a stainless steel finish, special serial numbers, chamfered charge holes, and adjustable trigger stop. Limited to 500 guns.

Suggested Retail Introductory Price: $1,000

Model 19 .357 Magnum K-Comp

This is the same gun as the F-Comp but furnished with a black matte finish and is sold through stocking dealers on a unlimited basis.

Suggested Retail Introductory Price: $800

Model 60 Carry Comp

Introduced in the summer of 1993 this J-frame revolver is fitted with a 3" full underlug barrel with integral compensator. The charge holes are radiused for quick loading and the action is tuned by the Performance Center. The pistol is rated for +P ammunition. The grips are fancy wood contoured for speed loaders. This Lew Horton revolver is limited to 300 guns and has special serial numbers.

Suggested Retail Introductory Price: $795

Model 327 Carry

Introduced in 2004 this 8-shot model is chambered for the .357 Magnum cartridge. Barrel length is 2" with dovetail .260 orange ramp. Scandium alloy frame with stainless steel barrel, titanium cylinder and shroud. Black oxide finish except for gray cylinder. Cocobolo wood grips. Weight is about 21 oz.

Suggested Retail Price: $1,226

Paxton Quigley Model 640

This is a Performance Center offering restricted to 300 revolvers. Built around the Model 640 this limited edition handgun has a 2" compensated barrel, windage adjustable front sight, specially tuned action, and a tapestry soft gun case. Each gun has a distinct serial number range.

Suggested Retail Introductory Price: $720

Model 640 Centennial Powerport

Introduced in 1996 this model is a Lew Horton exclusive. It is fitted with a 2-1/8" barrel with integral compensator. The front sight is a black blade with Tritium insert and the rear is a fixed notch. The cylinder holds five .357 or .38 rounds. Stainless steel with Pachmayr decelerator compact grips. Overall length is 6.75" and weight is about 25 oz. Limited to 300 units.

Suggested Retail Introductory Price: $675

Model 940 Centennial .356

Offered exclusively from Lew Horton this J-frame revolver is chambered for the new .356 cartridge and has a 2" compensated barrel. It will also fire the 9mm cartridge. This gun features a tuned action, radius hammer and trigger and special serial numbers.

Suggested Retail Introductory Price: $760

Model 13 .357

This is a Lew Horton exclusive that features a 3" barrel with 4 Mag-Na-Ports, a bobbed hammer for double-action-only, chambered charge holes, beveled cylinder, contoured grip and thumb latch for speed loader clearance, overtravel trigger stop, and FBI grips. Limited to 300 guns.

Suggested Retail Introductory Price: $730

Model 845 Single-Action

Offered by Lew Horton this pistol is chambered for the .45 ACP and is designed for the competitive shooter. Adjustable reach trigger precision fitted slide, frame and barrel are some of the special features. The barrel bushing is spherical and the front sight is dovetailed. The magazine well is extended as is the magazine release and safety. Both front and rear sight are adjustable.

Suggested Retail Introductory Price: $1,470

Model 952

Chambered for the 9mm cartridge, this semi-automatic pistol has 5" barrel. Stainless steel frame and slide. Adjustable rear sight. Checkered wood grips. Magazine capacity is nine rounds. Weight is about 41 oz.

Suggested Retail Introductory Price: $2,030

Model 1911

This .45 ACP PC model features a 5" barrel, micro-click adjustable black rear sight and dovetail black front sight. Checkered wine laminate grips. Stainless steel frame and slide with black oxide finish. Magazine capacity is 8 rounds. Weight is about 41 oz. Introduced in 2004.

Suggested Retail Price: $2,270

SMITH & WESSON LONG ARMS

.320 Revolving Rifle Model

This model is rare and unique—a prize to a S&W collector. The Revolving Rifle is chambered for the .320 S&W Revolving Rifle cartridge, has a 6-shot fluted cylinder and is offered with a 16", 18", and 20" barrel. Only 76 of the rifles are nickel-plated, and the remainder of the production is blued. The butt is rounded, with red hard rubber checkered grips and a forearm of the same material. There is a detachable shoulder stock with a black hard rubber buttplate featuring the S&W logo. The rifle was furnished in a leather carrying case with accessories. As fine a firearm as this was, it was a commercial failure for S&W; and they finally came to the realization that the public did not want a revolving rifle. They manufactured only 977 of them between 1879 and 1887.

Exc.	*V.G.*	*Good*	*Fair*	*Poor*
8000	5500	3500	2000	1500

NOTE: Values are for complete unit. Deduct 40 percent without stock. Add 10 percent for 16" or 20" barrels.

Model A Rifle

A bolt-action with 23.75" barrel, chambered for .22-250, .243, .270, .308, .30-06, 7mm Magnum, and .300 Winchester Magnum. It has a folding rear sight and a checkered Monte Carlo stock with contrasting rosewood forend tip and pistol grip cap. It was manufactured for S&W by Husqvarna of Sweden.

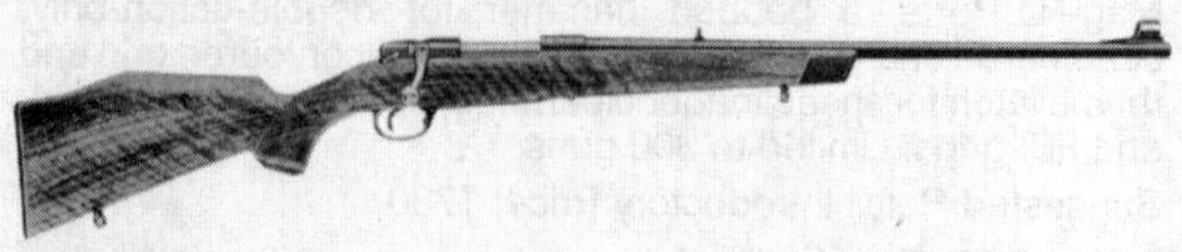

NIB	Exc.	V.G.	Good	Fair	Poor
400	325	275	200	150	100

Model B

As above, with a schnabel forend and 20.75" barrel.

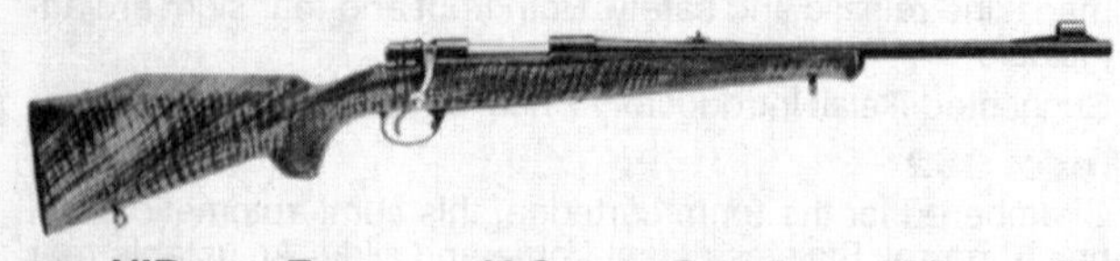

NIB	Exc.	V.G.	Good	Fair	Poor
400	325	275	200	150	100

Model C

As above, with a cheekpiece.

NIB	Exc.	V.G.	Good	Fair	Poor
425	350	300	225	175	125

Model D

As above, with a Mannlicher-style stock.

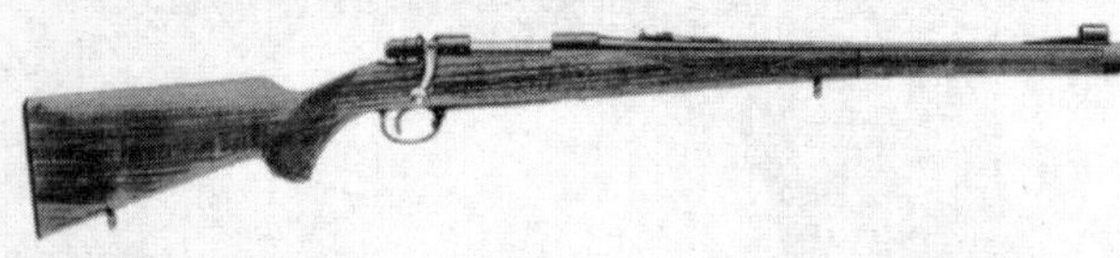

NIB	Exc.	V.G.	Good	Fair	Poor
600	500	400	350	250	150

M&P15 Military and Police Tactical Rifle

Gas-operated semi-auto built along lines of AR-15. Caliber: 5.56mm NATO. Magazine capacity: 30. Barrel: 16-inch 1:9. Stock: Six-position telescoping composite. Weight: 6.74 lbs. unloaded. Sights: Adjustable front and rear. Variants: M&P15A & M&P15T (no carry handle; folding battle sight). Introduced 2006. MSRP: 1200

M&P 15 PC

Generally similar to the M&P rifle but with accurized tubular floated barrel, 2-stage match trigger, 20" matte stainless barrel. No sights. Introduced 2007.

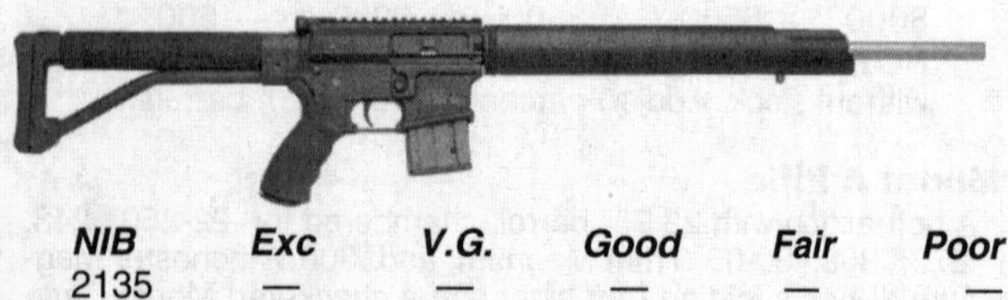

NIB	Exc	V.G.	Good	Fair	Poor
2135	—	—	—	—	—

SNAKE CHARMER

Little Field, Texas

Sporting Arms Manufacturing, Inc.

Snake Charmer

A .410 bore single-shot shotgun with an 18.5" barrel. Stainless steel with a composition stock.

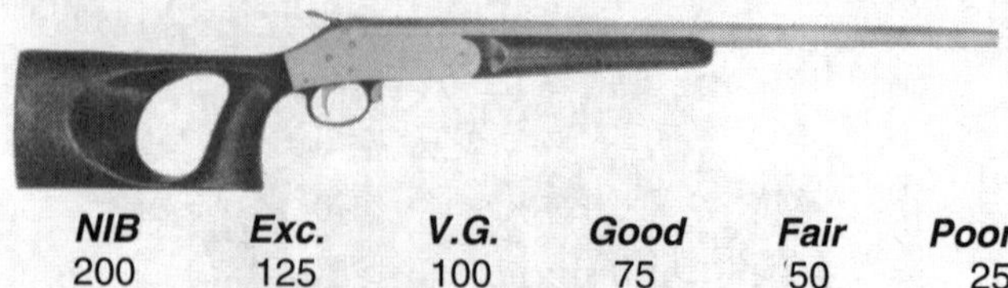

NIB	Exc.	V.G.	Good	Fair	Poor
200	125	100	75	50	25

SNEIDER, CHARLES E.

Baltimore, Maryland

Two-Cylinder Revolver

A .22 caliber spur trigger revolver with a 2.75" octagonal barrel and twin seven-shot cylinders that can be pivoted. The barrel marked "E. Sneider Pat. March 1862." Produced in limited quantities during the 1860s.

Exc.	V.G.	Good	Fair	Poor
—	—	10000	5000	1250

SODIA, FRANZ

Ferlach, Austria

A wide variety of double-barrel shotguns, drillings, and combination shotgun/rifles are made by this maker.

SOKOLOVSKY CORP. SPORT ARMS

Sunnyvale, California

.45 Automaster

A .45 caliber stainless steel semi-automatic pistol with a 6" barrel fitted with Millet adjustable sights and six-shot magazine. Approximately 50 of these pistols have been made since 1984.

NIB	Exc.	V.G.	Good	Fair	Poor
3250	2750	2250	1750	1250	800

SPALDING & FISHER

Worcester, Massachusetts

Double Barreled Pistol

A .36 caliber percussion double-barrel pocket pistol with 5.5" barrels, blued iron frame and walnut grips. The top of the barrels marked "Spalding & Fisher." Produced during the 1850s.

Exc.	V.G.	Good	Fair	Poor
—	—	850	350	100

SPANG & WALLACE

Philadelphia, Pennsylvania

Pocket Pistol

A .36 caliber percussion pocket pistol with a 2.5" to 6" barrel, German silver furniture and checkered walnut stock. The barrel marked "Spang & Wallace/Phila." Manufactured during late 1840s and early 1850s.

 *This symbol denotes "Sleepers" with rapidly-rising values and/or significant collector potential.*

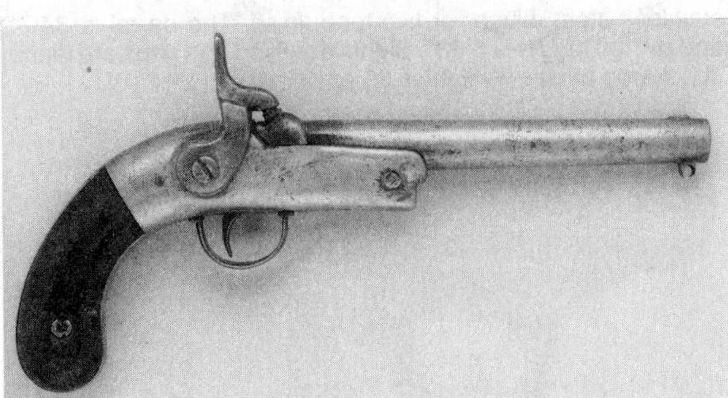

Courtesy Bonhams & Butterfields

Exc.	V.G.	Good	Fair	Poor
—	—	1250	650	200

SPENCER

Boston, Massachusetts

Spencer Carbine

This was one of the most popular firearms used by Union forces during the Civil War. It is chambered for a metallic rimfire cartridge known as the "No. 56." It is actually a .52 caliber and was made with a copper case. The barrel is 22" in length. The finish is blued, with a carbine-length walnut stock held on by one barrel band. There is a sling swivel at the butt. There were approximately 50,000 manufactured between 1863 and 1865.

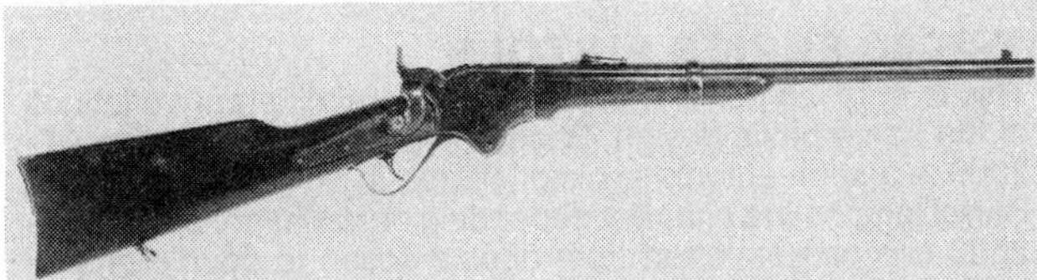

Courtesy Bonhams & Butterfields, San Francisco, California

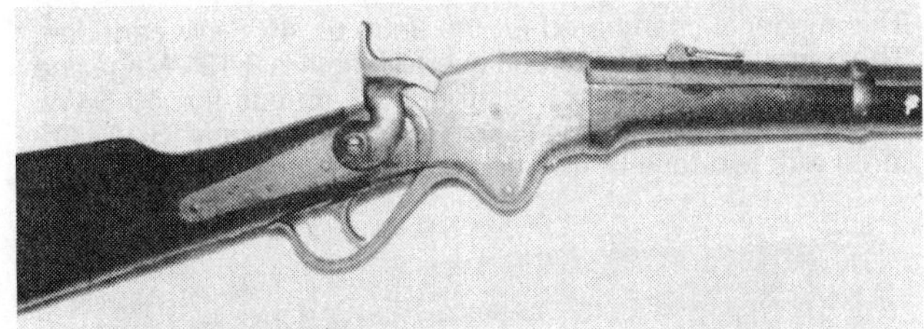

Exc.	V.G.	Good	Fair	Poor
—	—	4500	1750	500

Military Rifle—Navy Model

This model is similar to the carbine, with a 30" round barrel and a full-length walnut stock held on by three barrel bands. It features an iron forend tip and sling swivels. The Civil War production consisted of two models. A Navy model was manufactured between 1862 and 1864 (there were approximately 1,000 of these so marked).

Exc.	V.G.	Good	Fair	Poor
—	—	5000	2250	600

Military Rifle—Army Model

There were approximately 11,450 produced for the Army during the Civil War. They are similar to the Navy model except that the front sight doubles as a bayonet lug. They were manufactured in 1863 and 1864.

Courtesy Milwaukee Public Museum, Milwaukee, Wisconsin

Exc.	V.G.	Good	Fair	Poor
—	—	3750	1750	600

Springfield Armory Post-war Alteration

After the conclusion of the Civil War, approximately 11,000 carbines were refurbished and rechambered for .50 caliber rimfire. The barrels were sleeved, and a device known as the "Stabler cut-off" was added to convert the arm to single-shot function. Often they were refinished and restocked. The inspector's marks "ESA" will be found in an oval cartouche on the left side of the stock. These alterations took place in 1867 and 1868.

Exc.	V.G.	Good	Fair	Poor
—	—	3500	1500	500

Model 1865 Contract

This model was manufactured by the Burnside Rifle Company in 1865. They are similar to the Civil War-type carbine and are marked "By Burnside Rifle Co./Model 1865." There were approximately 34,000 manufactured. Old records show that 30,500 were purchased by the United States government, and 19,000 of these had the Stabler cut-off device.

A Spencer Rifle with 24 3/4" barrel sold at auction for $67,500. Inscribed on the receiver to "Lt. Philip Reade, 2nd Lieut. 3rd U.S. Infantry." Condition is 85 percent blue with 30 percent case colors. Fitted with a tang sight as well as rear ladder sight.
Greg Martin Auctions

Courtesy Wallis & Wallis, Lewes, Sussex, England

Exc.	V.G.	Good	Fair	Poor
—	—	3250	1250	500

SPENCER ARMS CO.

Windsor, Connecticut

Slide-Action Shotgun

From 1882 to 1889 they manufactured the first successful slide action repeating shotgun. Designed by Christopher M. Spencer who also designed the Civil War era Spencer military carbines. The shotgun came in both solid and takedown models in both 12 and 10 gauge. In 1890 Francis Bannerman & Sons of New York bought the patents and machinery and moved the operation to Brooklyn, New York. They produced what is known as the Spencer Bannerman models from 1890 to 1907. The later Bannerman models are worth 20 percent less than the Spencer models.

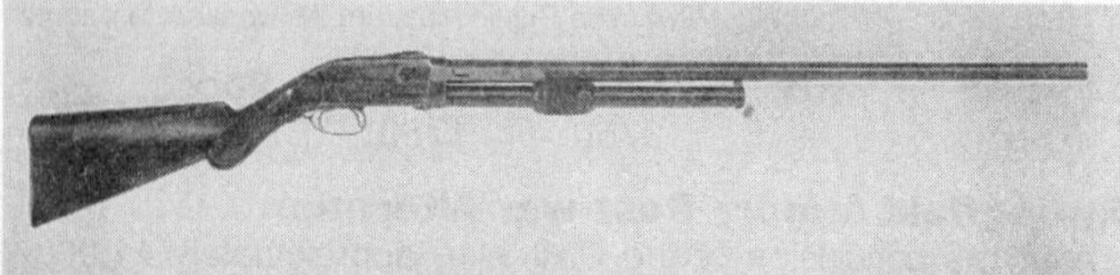

Exc.	V.G.	Good	Fair	Poor
—	1000	600	200	125

NOTE: The takedown model is worth 20 percent premium and 10 gauge models are worth a 10 percent premium.

SPENCER REVOLVER

Maltby, Henley & Company
New York, New York

Safety Hammerless Revolver

A .32 caliber hammerless double-action revolver with a 3" barrel. The frame and barrel made of brass, the cylinder of steel and the grips are of walnut. The barrel is marked "Spencer Safety Hammerless Pat. Jan. 24, 1888 & Oct. 29, 1889." Manufactured by the Norwich Pistol Company circa 1890.

Exc.	V.G.	Good	Fair	Poor
—	450	200	150	100

SPHINX

Sphinx Engineering SA
Porrentru, Switzerland
Imported by Sile Distributors Inc.

This Swiss-based company was founded in 1876 and produced the first automatic turning machine. The company made small drills, tungsten carbine tools, and tool coatings. After WWII Sphinx developed more exotic machines and drills. In 1990 Sphinx Engineering SA was established for the development and production of pistols. In 1991 the AT .380 was introduced to the market. The following year the AT 2000 was placed on the market. Sphinx purchased the rights to its current line of pistols from ITM AG, a Swiss firm that experienced financial problems with the development of its pistol line, in 1989. The AT series is essentially a copy of the famous Czech CZ 75 semi-automatic pistol.

AT-380

This semi-automatic pistol is a small .380 caliber in double-action-only. The magazine capacity is 11 rounds. It is offered in stainless steel, blued, or two-tone finish. The barrel is 3.27" and overall length is 6.03". Sights are fixed and grips are black checkered plastic. Weight is 25 oz.

NIB	Exc.	V.G.	Good	Fair	Poor
600	550	400	300	200	100

AT-2000 SERIES PISTOLS

This is a series number applied to several different variations of the same basic design. Based on the CZ 75 pistol the AT-2000 is a semi-automatic pistol offered in 9mm and .40 S&W. Barrel lengths are different depending on variation, but the AT-2000 can be converted from double-action to double only in just a matter of minutes.

AT-2000S/SDA

This model is chambered for the 9mm or .40 S&W cartridge. The barrel length is 4.53" and overall length is 8.12". Magazine capacity is 15 rounds for 9mm and 13 rounds for .40 S&W. Available in double-action (S) or double-action-only (SDA). Offered with two-tone or all blued finish. Weighs 35 oz.

NIB	Exc.	V.G.	Good	Fair	Poor
875	675	600	500	400	300

AT-2000P/PDA

This is a slightly smaller of the AT-2000S. Magazine capacity is 13 rounds for 9mm and 11 rounds for .40 S&W. The features are the same except that the barrel length is 3.66", overall length 7.25", and weight is 31 oz.

NIB	Exc.	V.G.	Good	Fair	Poor
650	600	500	400	300	200

AT-2000PS

This version, sometimes referred to as the Police Special, features the shorter barrel of the AT-2000P model on the larger AT-2000S frame. Barrel length is 3.66" and magazine capacity is 15 rounds for 9mm and 13 rounds for the .40 S&W.

NIB	Exc.	V.G.	Good	Fair	Poor
850	600	500	400	300	200

AT-2000H/HDA

This is the smallest version of the AT-2000 series. Magazine capacity is 10 rounds for 9mm and 8 rounds for .40 S&W. The barrel length is 3.34" and overall length is 6.78". Weight is 26 oz.

NIB	Exc.	V.G.	Good	Fair	Poor
850	600	500	400	300	200

AT-2000C

This is the competitor model. It features a competition slide, dual port compensator, match barrel, and Sphinx scope mount. Offered in double-action/single-action. Available in 9mm, 9x21, and .40 S&W.

NIB	Exc.	V.G.	Good	Fair	Poor
1600	1200	800	600	400	200

AT-2000CS

Same as above model but fitted with BoMar adjustable sights.

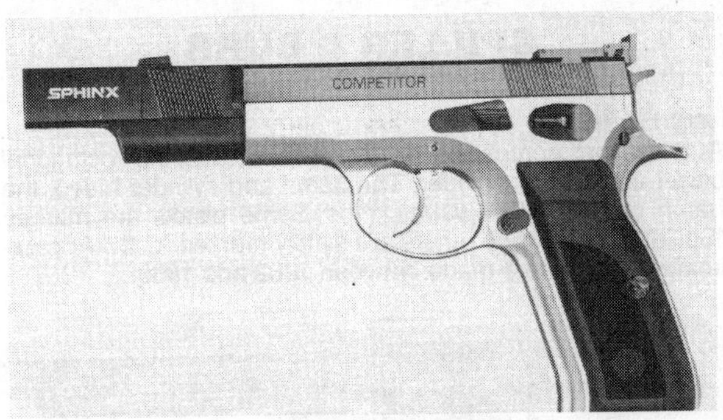

NIB	Exc.	V.G.	Good	Fair	Poor
1400	1000	600	400	300	200

AT-2000GM

The Grand Master model. Features are similar to the AT-2000C but offered in single-action-only.

NIB	Exc.	V.G.	Good	Fair	Poor
2100	1750	1250	600	300	200

AT-2000GMS

Same as above but fitted with BoMar adjustable sights.

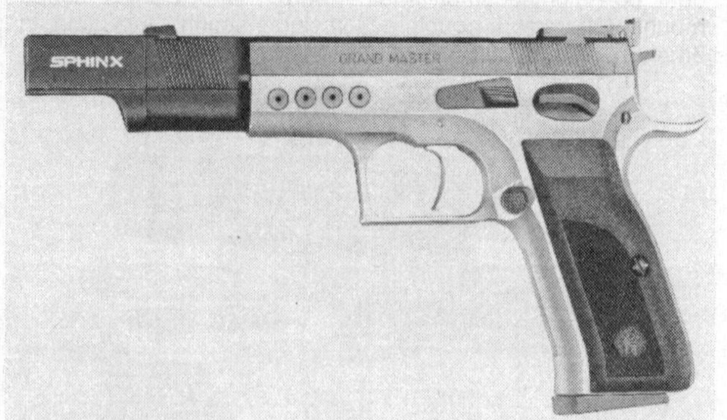

NIB	Exc.	V.G.	Good	Fair	Poor
2000	1650	1200	600	300	200

SPIES, A. W.

New York, New York

Pocket Pistol

A .41 caliber percussion pocket pistol with a 2.5" barrel, German silver furniture and a checkered walnut stock. Produced during the 1850s.

Exc.	V.G.	Good	Fair	Poor
—	—	1750	900	300

SPILLER & BURR

Atlanta, Georgia

Navy Revolver

A .36 caliber percussion revolver with a 6" or 6.5" octagonal barrel and 6-shot cylinder. The barrel and cylinder blued, the frame of brass with walnut grips. Some pistols are marked "Spiller & Burr" while others are simply marked "C.S." Approximately 1,450 were made between 1862 and 1865. .

Courtesy Milwaukee Public Museum, Milwaukee, Wisconsin

Exc.	V.G.	Good	Fair	Poor
—	—	40000	17500	—

REMINDER

"A well regulated militia being necessary to the security of a free State, the right of the People to keep and bear arms shall not be infringed."

SPITFIRE

JSL (Hereford) Ltd.
Hereford, England

This semi-automatic pistol is a design based on the CZ 75. This is a hand-built pistol designed by John Slough and built from a solid block of steel. The stainless steel frame and slide are cut with spark erosion and diamond grinding. Barrels are built and bored in the same factory. This is primarily a competition pistol.

Spitfire Standard Model (G1)

Chambered for the 9x21, 9mm Parabellum, or .40 S&W cartridges this pistol uses the locked breech concept. The trigger system is single and double-action and it is fitted with an ambidextrous safety. The barrel is 3.7" and the overall length is 7.1". Magazine capacity of the 9mm is 15 rounds. Sights are fixed. Empty weight is 35 oz. Finish is stainless steel. Comes supplied with presentation box, two magazines, and allen key.Discontinued.

NIB	Exc.	V.G.	Good	Fair	Poor
1300	900	700	500	300	200

Spitfire Master Model

This is similar to the Standard Model but without sights. It is fitted with a stainless steel bridge mount to take an Aimpoint sight. Also has a dual port compensator. Supplied with presentation box and two magazines. Discontinued.

NIB	Exc.	V.G.	Good	Fair	Poor
2100	1750	1250	800	400	200

Spitfire Squadron Model

This model has a Standard Model frame, adjustable rear sight slide, adjustable rear sight slide with compensator, Master Model slide and barrel with stainless steel bridge mount and Aimpoint sight, four magazines, screwdriver, allen key, oil bottle, spare springs, cleaning kit, and fitted leather case. Discontinued.

NIB	Exc.	V.G.	Good	Fair	Poor
6000	4800	2100	900	450	200

Spitfire Sterling Model (G2)

This model is chambered for the 9x21, 9mm Parabellum, or .40 S&W cartridges. Its features are the same as the Standard Model with the exception that it has adjustable sights. Discontinued.

NIB	Exc.	V.G.	Good	Fair	Poor
1400	1000	800	600	300	200

Spitfire Super Sterling (G7)

Also chambered for the 9x21, 9mm Parabellum, and .40 S&W this model features a single port compensator, 4.3" barrel, and overall length of 8.25". Weight is approximately 36 oz. Discontinued.

NIB	Exc.	V.G.	Good	Fair	Poor
1600	1200	900	700	350	200

Spitfire Competition Model (G3)

Chambered for 9x21, 9mm Parabellum, or .40 S&W cartridge this model features a tapered slide rib, adjustable rear sight, dual pod compensator, match hammer, adjustable trigger stop with presentation box. Barrel is 5.27" with compensator and weight is 40 oz. Discontinued.

NIB	Exc.	V.G.	Good	Fair	Poor
1800	1400	1000	800	400	200

Spitfire Battle of Britain Commemorative

This is a limited edition of 1,056 Spitfires in 9mm Parabellum. Each one represents one of the Spitfire aircraft. The stainless steel slide has the inscription "Battle of Britain-50th Anniversary," the grips are checkered walnut, log book of history of that particular aircraft, and a wooden presentation box with engraved plaque. Discontinued.

NIB	Exc.	V.G.	Good	Fair	Poor
1950	1400	1000	800	400	200

Westlake Britarms

This is a .22 LR Match pistol. Barrel length is 5.77", sight base is 8.42", magazine capacity is 5 rounds. Weight is approximately 47 oz. Trigger is adjustable for length, front and rear trigger stops, adjustable palm rest on contoured wood grips, take-down barrel design with removable weight. Limited importation.

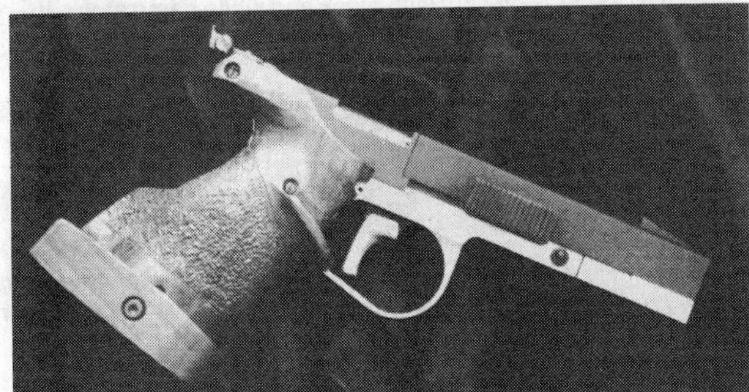

NIB	Exc.	V.G.	Good	Fair	Poor
1850	1400	1000	800	400	200

SPRINGFIELD ARMORY (MODERN)

SEE—Springfield Inc.

SPRINGFIELD ARMORY INC.

Geneseo, Illinois

NOTE: As of January 1993 Springfield Inc. purchased the inventory, name, patents, trademarks, and logo of the Springfield Armory Inc. and intends to carry on the tradition of quality products and service in the future. Products, services, and distribution patterns remain unchanged. The Springfield Custom Shop, producing "Raceguns," will continue as before.

RIFLES

M1 Garand Rifle

A .270 (discontinued), .308 or .30-06 caliber semi-automatic rifle with a 24" barrel and 8-shot magazine. Patterned directly after the U.S. M1 Rifle.

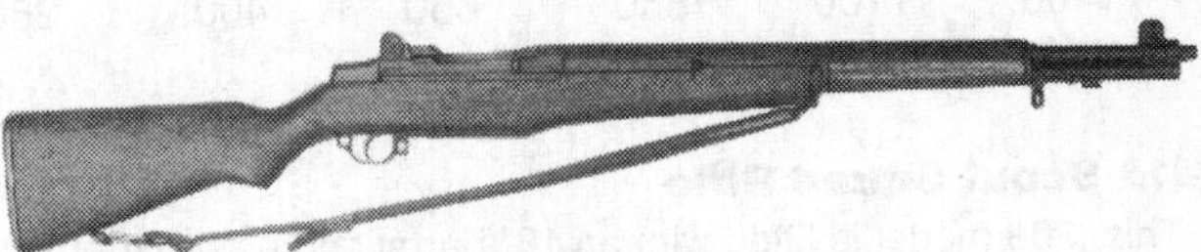

Courtesy Milwaukee Public Museum, Milwaukee, Wisconsin

Exc.	V.G.	Good	Fair	Poor
775	650	550	400	300

Iwo Jima M1 Garand

Similar to standard M1 Model but shipped in reproduction WWII-era crate with signed decorative lithograph. Introduced 2006.

NIB	Exc.	V.G.	Good	Fair	Poor
1550	1300	1000	800	400	200

M1A Basic Rifle

Chambered for .308 Win. and fitted with a painted black fiberglass stock. Barrel length is 22" without flash suppressor. Front sights are military square post and rear military aperture (battle sights). Magazine capacity is 5, 10, or 20 box. Rifle weighs 9 lbs.

NIB	Exc.	V.G.	Good	Fair	Poor
1250	1000	850	650	400	250

D-Day M1 Garand Limited Edition

Introduced in 2005 this model is chambered for the .30-06 cartridge and fitted with a 24" barrel. Military style sights. Two-stage military trigger. Limited to 1,944 rifles, each with a military-style wooden crate. Each side of the buttstock has stamped memorials to D-Day.

NIB	Exc.	V.G.	Good	Fair	Poor
1585	—	—	—	—	—

M1A Standard Rifle

This model is chambered for the .308 Win. or .243 cartridge. Also fitted with a 22" barrel but with adjustable rear sight. Fitted with a walnut stock with fiberglass hand guard, it comes equipped with a 20-round box magazine. Weighs 9 lbs.

NIB	Exc.	V.G.	Good	Fair	Poor
1500	1100	850	650	400	250

M1A-A1 Bush Rifle

Chambered for .308 or .243 cartridge with choice of walnut stock, black fiberglass, or folding stock (no longer produced). Fitted with 18.25" barrel. Rifle weighs 8.75 lbs.

NIB	Exc.	V.G.	Good	Fair	Poor
1400	1100	850	650	400	250

NOTE: Add $250 for folding stock.

M1A Scout Squad Rifle

This .308 model is fitted with an 18" barrel and a choice of fiberglass or walnut stock. Military sights. Supplied with 10-round magazine. Weight with fiberglass stock is about 9 lbs., with walnut stock about 9.3 pounds.

NIB	Exc.	V.G.	Good	Fair	Poor
1600	1100	750	550	—	—

M1A National Match

Chambered for .308 as standard or choice of .243 cartridge. Fitted with a medium weight National Match 22" glass bedded barrel and walnut stock. Special rear sight adjustable to half minute of angle clicks. Weighs 10.06 lbs.

NIB	Exc.	V.G.	Good	Fair	Poor
2050	1400	1000	700	500	250

M1A Super Match

This is Springfield's best match grade rifle. Chambered for .308 as standard and also .243 cartridge. Fitted with special oversize heavy walnut stock, heavy Douglas match glass bedded barrel, and special rear lugged receiver. Special rear adjustable sight. Weighs 10.125 lbs.

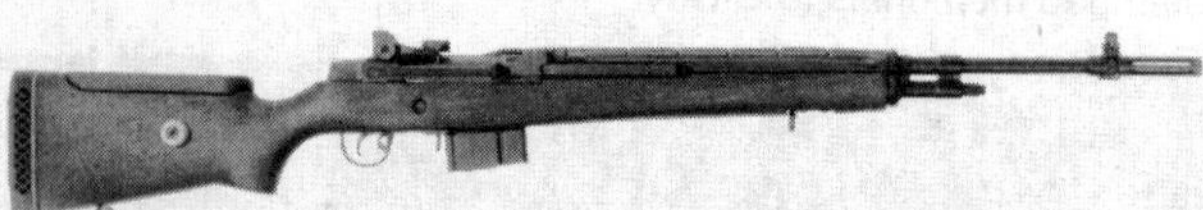

NIB	Exc.	V.G.	Good	Fair	Poor
2500	1850	1350	900	600	300

NOTE: For walnut stock and Douglas barrel add $165. For black McMillan stock and Douglas stainless steel barrel add $600. For Marine Corp. camo stock and Douglas stainless steel barrel add $600. For adjustable walnut stock and Douglas barrel add $535. For adjustable walnut stock and Krieger barrel add $900.

M1A Model 25 Carlos Hathcock

Introduced in 2001 this model features a match trigger, stainless steel heavy match barrel, McMillan synthetic stock with adjustable cheek pad, Harris Bi-pod, and other special featirtes. Chambered for the .308 cartridge. Weight is about 12.75 lbs. A special logo bears his signature.

NIB	Exc.	V.G.	Good	Fair	Poor
4650	3450	2500	—	—	—

M21 Law Enforcement/Tactical Rifle

Similar to the Super Match with the addition of a special stock with rubber recoil pad and height adjustable cheekpiece. Available as a special order only. Weighs 11.875 lbs.

NIB	Exc.	V.G.	Good	Fair	Poor
2400	1750	1350	900	650	350

M1A SOCOM 16

This M1A1 rifle features a 16.25" barrel with muzzlebrake. Black fiberglass stock with steel buttplate. Forward scout-style scope mount. Front sight post has tritium insert. Weight is about 9 lbs. Introduced in 2004.

NIB	Exc.	V.G.	Good	Fair	Poor
1525	1250	875	—	—	—

M1A SOCOM II

Introduced in 2005 this model features a full length top rail and short bottom rail for accessories. Weight is about 11 lbs.

NIB	Exc.	V.G.	Good	Fair	Poor
1700	1450	—	—	—	—

M1A SOCOM Urban Rifle

Similar to the SOCOM but with black and white camo stock. Introduced in 2005.

NIB	Exc.	V.G.	Good	Fair	Poor
1725	1475	—	—	—	—

M1 Garand

Chambered for the .30-06 or .308 cartridge this model features a new receiver, barrel, and walnut stock. All other parts are U.S. G.I. mil-spec. Barrel length is 24". Weight is about 9.5 lbs. Introduced in 2002 and limited to a total of 10,000 rifles.

NIB	Exc.	V.G.	Good	Fair	Poor
1100	895	600	475	—	—

IDF Mauser Rifle Model 66SP

This is a bolt-action rifle chambered for the .308 Win. cartridge. Adjustable trigger for pull and travel. Barrel length is 27". Specially designed stock has broad forend and a thumb hole pistol grip. Cheekpiece is adjustable as is the recoil pad. Supplied with case. This rifle is military issue. Less than 100 imported into the U.S.

NIB	Exc.	V.G.	Good	Fair	Poor
2200	1750	—	—	—	—

SAR-48

This is the pre-ban version of the SAR-4800.

NIB	Exc.	V.G.	Good	Fair	Poor
1400	1200	850	600	500	250

SAR-4800

This is a semi-automatic gas operated rifle, similar in appearance to the FN-FAL/LAR rifle, chambered for the .308 Win. cartridge. It is fitted with a 21" barrel and has a fully adjustable rear sight. Weight is approximately 9.5 lbs. No longer imported.

NIB	Exc.	V.G.	Good	Fair	Poor
1600	1200	800	600	400	250

SAR-8

This semi-automatic rifle is similar in appearance to the HK-91. It is chambered for the .308 Win. and is of the recoil operated delayed roller-lock design. Barrel length is 18" and the rear sight is fully adjustable. Weight is about 8.7 lbs. No longer imported.

NIB	Exc.	V.G.	Good	Fair	Poor
950	750	600	400	300	200

SAR-8 Tactical

Similar to the above model but fitted with a heavy barrel. Introduced in 1996. No longer imported. Less than 100 imported into U.S.

NIB	Exc.	V.G.	Good	Fair	Poor
1050	900	750	600	400	300

M6 Scout

A .22, .22 Magnum, or .22 Hornet and .410 bore over-and-under combination shotgun rifle with an 18" barrel. Black anodized finish with a synthetic stock. Discontinued.

NIB	Exc.	V.G.	Good	Fair	Poor
450	355	295	200	100	50

M6 Scout—Stainless Steel

Same as above but in stainless steel. First introduced in 1996. Discontinued.

NIB	Exc.	V.G.	Good	Fair	Poor
550	425	325	225	150	75

M6 Scout Pistol

As above but with 10" barrel and no folding stock. Parkerized or stainless steel finish. Weight is about 28 oz. Introduced in 2002. Discontinued.

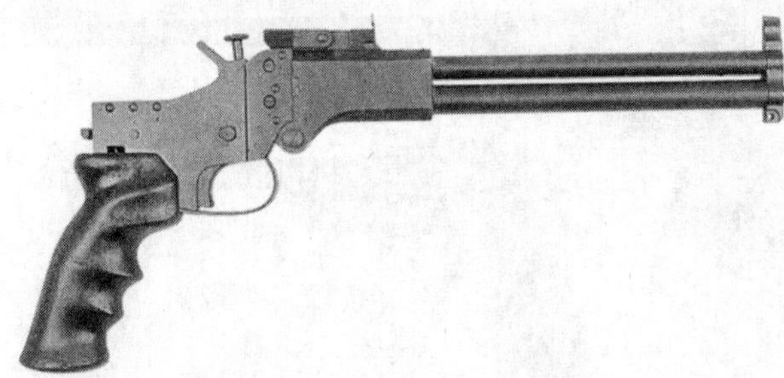

NIB	Exc.	V.G.	Good	Fair	Poor
450	355	295	200	100	50

NOTE: Add $30 for stainless steel.

PISTOLS

Model 1911-A1

A 9mm, .38 Super or .45 caliber copy of the Colt Model 1911-A1 semi-automatic pistol. Blued or Parkerized. Introduced in 1985.

NIB	Exc.	V.G.	Good	Fair	Poor
625	425	375	350	300	250

Model 1911-A1 Service Model

Introduced in 2003 this .45 ACP pistol has a 5" barrel with Bo-Mar adjustable three-dot rear sight. This model also has a number of special features such as extended mag well, titanium firing pin, and beavertail grip safety. Stainless steel magazine capacity is seven rounds. Black stainless steel finish. Weight is about 35 oz.

NIB	Exc.	V.G.	Good	Fair	Poor
925	750	—	—	—	—

Model 1911-A1 Service Mil-Spec

Chambered for the .45 ACP cartridge and fitted with a 5" barrel. Fixed sights. Matte stainless steel finish. Black plastic grips. Weight is about 36 oz. Introduced in 2003.

NIB	Exc.	V.G.	Good	Fair	Poor
610	475	—	—	—	—

Model 1911-A1 Service Model Lightweight

This .45 ACP pistol has a 5" barrel with lightweight alloy frame and bi-tone finish. Novak Lo-Mount sights. A large number of special features. Checkered cocobolo grips. Magazine capacity is seven rounds. Weight is about 30 oz. Introduced in 2003.

NIB	Exc.	V.G.	Good	Fair	Poor
875	700	—	—	—	—

This symbol denotes "Sleepers" with rapidly-rising values and/or significant collector potential. 

Model 1911-A2 S.A.S.S.

This is a single-shot pistol built on the Model 1911 frame. Available in two barrel lengths; 10.75" and 14.9". Offered in .22 LR, .223, 7mm-08, 7mmBR, .357 Magnum, .308, and .44 Magnum calibers. This conversion kit is available for those wishing to use it on their own Model 1911 pistol frames.

NIB	Exc.	V.G.	Good	Fair	Poor
225	200	175	150	100	50

Model 1911-A1 Stainless

Similar to the standard Model 1911 but chambered for the .45 ACP cartridge and offered in stainless steel. Equipped with three-dot sights, beveled magazine well, and checkered walnut grips. Weighs about 39.2 oz.

NIB	Exc.	V.G.	Good	Fair	Poor
750	625	400	350	300	200

NOTE: For Bomar sights add $50.

Model 1911-A1 Factory Comp

Chambered for the .45 ACP or the .38 Super this pistol is fitted with a three chamber compensator. The rear sight is adjustable, an extended thumb safety and Videcki speed trigger are standard features. Also checkered walnut grips, beveled magazine well and Commander hammer are standard. Weighs 40 oz.

NIB	Exc.	V.G.	Good	Fair	Poor
850	700	500	300	200	100

NOTE: Factory Comp pistols chambered for .38 Super may bring a small premium.

Model 1911-A1 Factory Comp High Capacity

Same as above but with 13-round magazine. New pistols sold in 1996 will be supplied with 10-round magazines except to law enforcement.

NIB	Exc.	V.G.	Good	Fair	Poor
975	850	700	600	400	200

Model 1911-A1 Defender

Chambered for the .45 ACP cartridge this pistol is fitted with a tapered cone dual port compensator. It also is fitted with reversed recoil plug, full length recoil spring guide, fully adjustable rear sight, serrated front strap, rubberized grips, and Commander-style hammer. Eight-round magazine capacity. The finish is bi-tone. Weighs 40.16 oz.

NIB	Exc.	V.G.	Good	Fair	Poor
650	500	400	300	200	100

Model 1911-A1 Loaded Defender Lightweight

As above but with loaded features: precision fit frames, slides and barrels, flat serrated mainspring housing, lowered and flared ejection port, Delta lightweight hammer, loaded chamber indicator, titanium firing pin, carry bevel treatment, ambidextrous thumb safety, high hand beavertail grip safety, dovetail front sight, Novak or adjustable rear sight, and adjustable speed trigger.

NIB	Exc.	V.G.	Good	Fair	Poor
900	775	—	—	—	

Model 1911-A1 Compact

Available in blue or bi-tone this .45 ACP is fitted with a 4.5" barvrel and compact compensator. It is equipped with Commander-style hammer and three-dot sights. Walnut grips are standard. Comes with 7-round magazine. Weighs 37.2 oz.

NIB	Exc.	V.G.	Good	Fair	Poor
500	400	300	250	200	100

NOTE: For stainless steel add $40.

Lightweight Compact Comp

Fitted with a 4-1/2" barrel and single port compensator. Magazine hold 8 rounds of .45 ACP. Frame is alloy and weight is 30 oz.

NIB	Exc.	V.G.	Good	Fair	Poor
500	400	300	250	200	100

Model 1911-A1 Compact Mil-Spec

This model is the same as the standard blued steel Compact model but with a Parkerized finish.

NIB	Exc.	V.G.	Good	Fair	Poor
500	400	300	250	200	100

Model 1911-A1 Long Slide

This model features a 6" barrel, 3-dot fixed sights, checkered wooden grips, and an 8-round magazine capacity. Finish is stainless steel. Weight is about 38 oz. Introduced in 1997.

NIB	Exc.	V.G.	Good	Fair	Poor
800	675	550	500	—	—

Model 1911-A1 Loaded Long Slide

As above but with loaded features: precision fit frames, slides and barrels, flat serrated mainspring housing, lowered and flared ejection port, Delta lightweight hammer, loaded chamber indicator, titanium firing pin, carry bevel treatment, ambidextrous thumb safety, high hand beavertail grip safety, dovetail front sight, Novak or adjustable rear sight, and adjustable speed trigger.

NIB	Exc.	V.G.	Good	Fair	Poor
950	800	—	—	—	—

Model 1911-A1 Champion

This .45 ACP pistol has a shortened slide, barrel, and reduced size frame. The Champion is fitted with 4" barrel, 8-round magazine, Commander hammer, checkered walnut grips, and special 3-dot sights. Weighs 33.4 oz.

NIB	Exc.	V.G.	Good	Fair	Poor
700	600	400	250	150	100

Model 1911-A1 Champion Mil-Spec

Same as above but with a Parkerized finish.

NIB	Exc.	V.G.	Good	Fair	Poor
525	375	300	200	150	100

Model 1911-A1 Stainless Champion

Same as above but offered in stainless steel. Weighs about 33.4 oz.

NIB	Exc.	V.G.	Good	Fair	Poor
595	435	375	275	200	150

Model 1911-A1 Loaded Champion Stainless

As above but with loaded features: precision fit frames, slides and barrels, flat serrated mainspring housing, lowered and flared ejection port, Delta lightweight hammer, loaded chamber indicator, titanium firing pin, carry bevel treatment, ambidextrous thumb safety, high hand beavertail grip safety, dovetail front sight, Novak or adjustable rear sight, and adjustable speed trigger.

NIB	Exc.	V.G.	Good	Fair	Poor
900	700	—	—	—	—

Champion Compact

Includes same features as Champion but with a shortened grip frame length and a 7-round magazine. Weighs 32 oz.

NIB	Exc.	V.G.	Good	Fair	Poor
500	350	250	200	150	100

Model 1911 Loaded Champion Lightweight

This model has a lightweight aluminum frame with Novak night sights. Checkered rubber grips. Finish is OD green and Black Armory Kote. Weight is about 28 oz. Introduced in 2004.

NIB	Exc.	V.G.	Good	Fair	Poor
700	550	—	—	—	—

Ultra Compact 1911-A1

This model features a 3-1/2" barrel with a 7-1/8" overall length. It has a stainless steel frame, beveled mag well, speed trigger, match grade barrel, and walnut grips. Weighs 31 oz.

NIB	Exc.	V.G.	Good	Fair	Poor
650	475	350	250	200	150

Ultra Compact Lightweight MD-1

Same as above but in .380 caliber with alloy frame. Weighs 24 oz.

NIB	Exc.	V.G.	Good	Fair	Poor
400	325	275	200	150	100

Ultra Compact 1911-A1 Mil-Spec

Same as the Ultra Compact Model but with a Parkerized or blued finish.

NIB	Exc.	V.G.	Good	Fair	Poor
650	475	350	350	200	150

V10 Ultra Compact 1911 A-1

Same as the Ultra Compact 1911 A-1 but fitted with a compensator built into the barrel and slide.

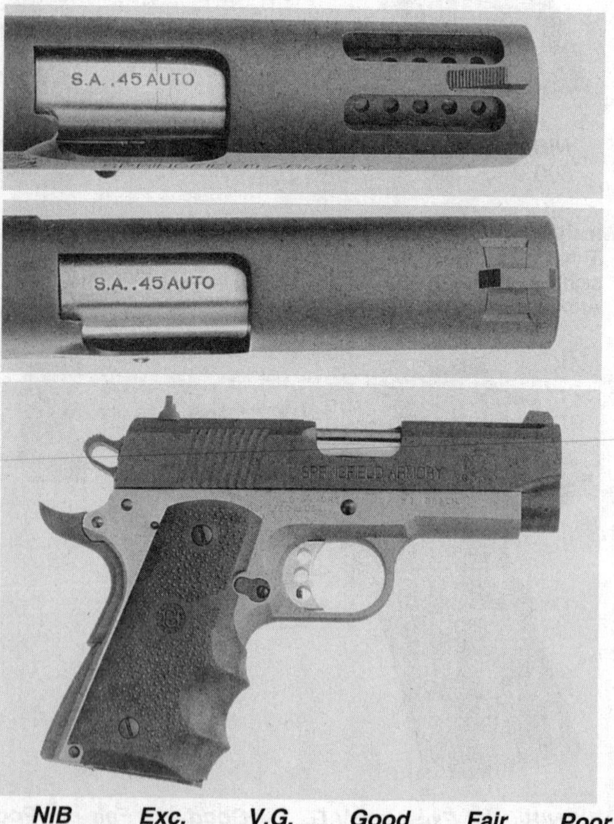

NIB	Exc.	V.G.	Good	Fair	Poor
600	525	400	300	200	150

V10 Ultra Compact 1911-A1 Mil-Spec

Same as above but with Parkerized finish.

NIB	Exc.	V.G.	Good	Fair	Poor
525	425	350	300	200	150

Model 1911-A1 High Capacity

This model is chambered in .45 ACP (10-round magazine) or 9mm caliber (16-round magazine). Standard features include Commander hammer, walnut grips, and beveled magazine well. Blued finish. Weighs 42 oz. In 1997 this model was offered in stainless steel and Parkerized finish.

NIB	Exc.	V.G.	Good	Fair	Poor
650	525	400	300	200	100

NOTE: For stainless steel add $40, for Parkerized finish deduct $25.

Compact High Capacity

Same as above but with an 11-round magazine. New pistols sold in 1996 will have 10-round magazine except to law enforcement.

NIB	Exc.	V.G.	Good	Fair	Poor
650	525	400	300	200	150

Ultra Compact High Capacity

This .45 ACP model is offered in three different 3.5" barrel variations: stainless steel, Parkerized, and ported. Standard magazine capacity is 10 rounds, 12 for law enforcement. Weight is about 31 oz.

NIB	Exc.	V.G.	Good	Fair	Poor
550	450	350	300	—	—

NOTE: Add $60 for stainless steel and $100 for ported models.

Micro Compact—Parkerized

Chambered for the .45 ACP cartridge and fitted with a 3" bull barrel. Aluminum frame with steel slide. Novak night sights. Cocobolo grips. Offered with Parkerized finish. Weight is about 24 oz. Magazine capacity is six rounds. Introduced in 2002.

NIB	Exc.	V.G.	Good	Fair	Poor
990	800	—	—	—	—

Micro Compact—Stainless

As above but with stainless steel frame and slide and Novak tritium night sights. Weight is about 24 oz. Introduced in 2003.

NIB	Exc.	V.G.	Good	Fair	Poor
990	800	—	—	—	—

Micro Compact—O.D. Green

As above but with Armory Kote green finish. Pearce grips. Introduced in 2003.

NIB	Exc.	V.G.	Good	Fair	Poor
990	800	—	—	—	—

Micro Compact—Black Stainless

As above but with black stainless steel finish and Slimline cocobolo grips. Weight is about 32 oz. Introduced in 2003.

NIB	Exc.	V.G.	Good	Fair	Poor
990	800	—	—	—	—

Micro Compact Lightweight

This model is similar to the other Micro models but is fitted with an aluminum frame and Novak night sights. Cocobolo wood grips. Bi-Tone finish. Equipped with XML Mini Light. Introduced in 2004. Weight is about 24 oz.

NIB	Exc.	V.G.	Good	Fair	Poor
925	750	—	—	—	

Loaded Micro Compact Lightweight

As above but with loaded features: precision fit frames, slides and barrels, flat serrated mainspring housing, lowered and flared ejection port, Delta lightweight hammer, loaded chamber indicator, titanium firing pin, carry bevel treatment, ambidextrous thumb safety, high hand beavertail grip safety, dovetail front sight, Novak or adjustable rear sight, and adjustable speed trigger. Introduced in 2005.

NIB	Exc.	V.G.	Good	Fair	Poor
1185	900	—	—	—	—

Model 1911-A1 Mil-Spec Operator

Chambered for the .45 ACP and fitted with a 5" barrel. This model features a Picatinny rail system on the frame. Fixed sights. Magazine capacity is 7 rounds. Parkerized finish.

NIB	Exc.	V.G.	Good	Fair	Poor
850	675	—	—	—	—

Model 1911-A1 Loaded Operator

Introduced in 2002 this model features a integral Picatinny rail on the frame. Chambered for the .45 ACP cartridge and fitted with a 5" barrel. Novak night sights. Parkerized finish. Magazine capacity is 7 rounds.

NIB	Exc.	V.G.	Good	Fair	Poor
1025	850	650	—	—	—

Combat Commander

A copy of the Colt Model 1911-A1 Combat Commander chambered for .45 ACP only. Introduced in 1988.

NIB	Exc.	V.G.	Good	Fair	Poor
475	425	400	350	300	250

Trophy Match

This model has special features such as fully adjustable target sights, match grade 5" barrel, and special wide trigger. Weight is approximately 36 oz. Available in blue, stainless steel, or bi-tone finish. In 1997 this model was offered chambered for the 9mm cartridge. Values would be the same for both .45 ACP and the 9mm models.

NIB	Exc.	V.G.	Good	Fair	Poor
850	750	650	500	400	300

NOTE: For stainless steel add $40.

Loaded Leatham Trophy Match

Introduced in 2005 this .40 S&W pistol is fitted with a 5" barrel with fully adjustable target sights. Black Polymer grips. Dawson magazine well, tuned trigger, match barrel and bushing, checkered front strap and other special features. Black finish. Weight is about 39 oz.

NIB	Exc.	V.G.	Good	Fair	Poor
1200	950	—	—	—	

1911 GI SERIES

GI Full Size

Chambered for the .45 ACP cartridge and fitted with a 5" barrel. Old style fixed sights. Standard checkered brown plastic grips. Lanyard loop on mainspring housing. Stainless steel frame and slide. Magazine capacity is 7 rounds. Weight is about 36 oz. Introduced in 2004. This model is also offered with Parkerized finish or OD green finish. Also offered in stainless steel.

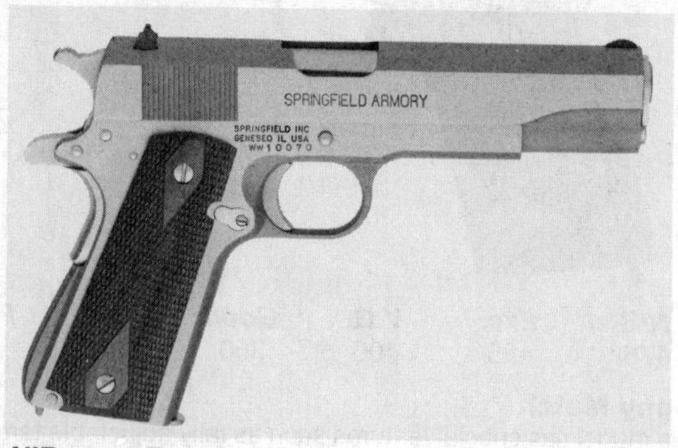

NIB	Exc.	V.G.	Good	Fair	Poor
475	395	—	—	—	—

NOTE: Deduct $45 for Parkerized or OD finish. Add $30 for stainless steel.

GI Full Size High-Capacity

As above but with 10-round magazine. Weight is about 38 oz. Introduced in 2005.

NIB	Exc.	V.G.	Good	Fair	Poor
500	425	—	—	—	—

GI Champion

This model is a scaled-down version of the full-size model above. Fitted with a 4" fully supported barrel and low-profile military sights. This model also has double diamond walnut grips. Black finish. Weight is about 34 oz. Introduced in 2004. Also offered with Parkerized finish.

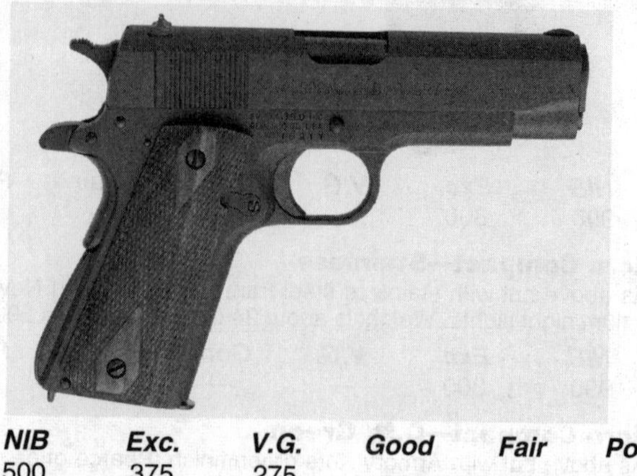

NIB	Exc.	V.G.	Good	Fair	Poor
500	375	275	—	—	—

GI Champion Lightweight

Introduced in 2005 this .45 ACP model is fitted with a 4" barrel with fully supported ramp. Low profile military sights. Checkered walnut grips. Weight is about 28 oz.

NIB	Exc.	V.G.	Good	Fair	Poor
500	375	—	—	—	—

GI Micro-Compact

As above but fitted with a 3" fully supported and ramped barrel. Magazine capacity is 6 rounds. Weight is about 32 oz. Introduced in 2004.

NIB	Exc.	V.G.	Good	Fair	Poor
575	425	300	—	—	—

The Springfield P9 Pistol

This is a double-action 9mm, .45 ACP, or .40 S&W pistol based on the Czech CZ 75 design. It incorporates several design features including: stainless steel trigger, sear safety mechanism, extended sear safety lever, redesigned back strap, lengthened beavertail grip area, and a new high strength slide stop. This model discontinued in 1993.

NIB	Exc.	V.G.	Good	Fair	Poor
450	375	300	250	200	100

Model P9 Standard

This is the standard pistol fitted with a 4.7" barrel, low profile target sights, and a ribbed slide. The 9mm has a 16-round magazine, the .45 ACP has a 10-round magazine, and the .40 S&W holds 12 rounds. Offered in either blue or stainless finish. Weighs about 35 oz.

NIB	Exc.	V.G.	Good	Fair	Poor
425	350	300	250	200	100

Model P9 Factory Comp.

This is a competition pistol fitted with triple port compensator, extended magazine release, adjustable rear sight, slim competition wood grips, and bi-tone finish. Weighs 34 oz. Dropped from the Springfield product line in 1993.

NIB	Exc.	V.G.	Good	Fair	Poor
500	450	400	300	200	100

Model P9 Ultra (IPSC Approved)

This competition pistol features a longer slide and barrel, 5". Special target sights, rubberized competition grips. Pistol is engraved with IPSC logo. Available in bi-tone finish only. Weighs 34.5 oz. Dropped from production in 1993.

NIB	Exc.	V.G.	Good	Fair	Poor
600	425	350	300	200	100

Super Tuned Champion

Introduced in 1997 this model features a 4" barrel chambered for the .45 ACP cartridge, Novak fixed Lo-Mount sights. Tuned and polished extractor and ejector. Polished feed ramp and barrel throat. Magazine capacity is 7 rounds. Choice of blued or Parkerized finish. Weight is approximately 36 oz.

NIB	Exc.	V.G.	Good	Fair	Poor
875	800	—	—	—	—

Super Tuned V10

Similar to the model above but with 3.5" barrel. Finish is bi-tone or stainless steel. Weight is about 33 oz. Introduced in 1997. Add $100 for stainless steel.

NIB	Exc.	V.G.	Good	Fair	Poor
950	825	650	—	—	—

Super Tuned Standard

This model features a 5" barrel with stainless steel finish. Weight is about 39 oz. Has all other super tune features. Introduced in 1997.

NIB	Exc.	V.G.	Good	Fair	Poor
900	775	600	—	—	—

Tactical Response Pistol (TRP)

This .45 ACP pistol is fitted with a 5" barrel and choice of stainless steel or black Armory Kote finish. Fully checkered front strap and mainspring housing. Novak Lo-Mount sights. Magazine capacity 8 rounds. Weight is about 37 oz.

NIB	Exc.	V.G.	Good	Fair	Poor
1360	1150	850	600	—	—

TRP Champion

Same as above but with a 3.9" barrel and black Armory Kote finish. Weight is about 33 oz.

NIB	Exc.	V.G.	Good	Fair	Poor
1175	950	800	600	—	—

TRP Pro

This model is fitted with a 5" barrel and many special features including Novak Lo-Mount tritium sights. Magazine capacity is 7 rounds. Meets specifications for FBI SWAT team. Weight is 36 oz.

NIB	Exc.	V.G.	Good	Fair	Poor
2000	1750	—	—	—	—

TRP Operator

This model has all the features of the TRP series with the addition of an integral light rail on the frame. Fitted with a 5" barrel. Adjustable night sights. Introduced in 2002.

NIB	Exc.	V.G.	Good	Fair	Poor
1350	1025	800	—	—	—

NOTE: Add $60 for night sights. Add $100 for OD green frame and slide.

Lightweight Operator

Blued, semi-auto .45 ACP with 5" bull barrel. Fixed sights, 5-6-lb. trigger pull, Cocobolo grips, 31 oz. Picatinny rail. Introduced 2006.

NIB	Exc.	V.G.	Good	Fair	Poor
1000	—	—	—	—	—

Lightweight Champion Operator

Similar to above but with 4" bull barrel. Introduced 2006.

NIB	Exc.	V.G.	Good	Fair	Poor
725	—	—	—	—	—

XD PISTOLS

These pistols are fitted with a polymer frame, grip safety, chamber indicator, and raised firing pin indicator. Offered in black finish as well as O.D. green.

XD 4"

Chambered for the 9mm, .40 S&W, .357 SIG, or .45 GAP cartridges. Barrel length is 4". Magazine capacity for 9mm is 15 rounds; for .40 S&W 12 rounds, for the .357 SIG 12 rounds, and for the .45 GAP 9 rounds. Weight is about 23 oz.

NIB	Exc.	V.G.	Good	Fair	Poor
425	375	—	—	—	—

NOTE: Add $60 for night sights. Add $100 for OD green frame and slide.

XD 4" Bi-Tone

Offered in 9mm or .40 S&W this 4" pistol has a black polymer frame and stainless steel slide. Magazine capacity is 10 rounds. Weight is about 26 oz. Introduced in 2003.

NIB	Exc.	V.G.	Good	Fair	Poor
475	400	300	200	—	—

XD V-10 Ported 4"

As above but with 4" ported barrel chambered for the 9mm, .40 S&W or .357 SIG. Black finish. Weight is about 26 oz.

NIB	Exc.	V.G.	Good	Fair	Poor
500	400	300	200	—	—

XD 5" Tactical

This model is fitted with a 5" barrel and chambered for the 9mm, .40 S&W or .357 SIG cartridges. Magazine capacity is 10 rounds. Weight is about 26 oz. Offered in black or O.D. green finish. In 2005 the .45 GAP cartridge was also offered for this model. Magazine capacity for 9mm is 15 rounds; for .40 S&W 12 rounds, for the .357 SIG 12 rounds, and for the .45 GAP 9 rounds. Weight is about 31 oz.

NIB	Exc.	V.G.	Good	Fair	Poor
600	450	300	200	—	—

XD 5" Tactical Pro

Introduced in 2003 this model features a Robar NP3 finish, fiber optic front sight and fixed rear sight. The frame is built with an oversized beavertail frame extension of a higher grip. Chambered for the 9mm, .357 SIG., 40 S&W, or the .45 GAP cartridge. Magazine capacity for 9mm is 15 rounds; for .40 S&W 12 rounds, for the .357 SIG 12 rounds, and for the .45 GAP 9 rounds. Weight is about 31 oz.

NIB	Exc.	V.G.	Good	Fair	Poor
1100	850	—	—	—	—

XD 5" Bi-Tone Tactical

Introduced in 2005 this model is chambered for the .45 GAP cartridge and fitted with a 5" barrel. Black polymer frame and stainless steel slide. Magazine capacity is 9 rounds. Weight is about 31 oz.

NIB	Exc.	V.G.	Good	Fair	Poor
570	425	—	—	—	—

XD Sub-Compact

Introduced in 2003 this polymer pistol is chambered for the 9mm or .40 S&W cartridge and fitted with a 3" barrel. Fitted with light rail on the dust cover. Grip safety and safe action trigger. Magazine capacity is 10 rounds. Weight is about 20 oz. Fixed sights.

NIB	Exc.	V.G.	Good	Fair	Poor
525	400	325	—	—	—

NOTE: For night sights add $60. Add $70 for XML Mini light.

XD 45 ACP

Polymer semi-auto in black, green or bi-tone holds 13+1 .45 ACP. Imported from Croatia. Fixed sights. Service model: 4" barrel, 30 oz. Tactical model: 5" barrel, 32 oz. Picatinny rail. Introduced 2006.

NIB	Exc.	V.G.	Good	Fair	Poor
525	—	—	—	—	—

LEATHAM LEGEND SERIES

This series was introduced in 2003 and will be identified with a unique series markings, serial number, and certificate of authenticity. Two sets of grips will come with each pistol: one cocobolo with lazer engraved signature of Rob Leatham and the other a black micarta double diamond slimline grips. A custom aluminum case is standard for this series.

TGO 1

This is a full custom pistol from the Springfield Custom Shop with Nowlin Match Grade throated barrel and bushing, Robar bi-tone finish, Bomar low-mount adjustable sights, and a number of other custom features. Chambered for the .45 ACP cartridge. Weight is about 38 oz. Four magazines are standard.

NIB	Exc.	V.G.	Good	Fair	Poor
3000	—	—	—	—	—

TGO 2

Similar to the TGO 1, but hand-built by the Springfield Armory.

NIB	Exc.	V.G.	Good	Fair	Poor
1900	1500	—	—	—	—

TGO 3

This model is an enhanced high-end production model with a lightweight aluminum slide. Bi-tone finish. Weight is about 30 oz.

NIB	Exc.	V.G.	Good	Fair	Poor
1295	1025	—	—	—	—

Enhanced Micro Pistol (EMP)

Tiny little 1911-style semi-auto chambered in 9mm Parabellum or .40 S&W. Short-action single-action design, 7-shot capacity, 3" bull barrel, fixed sights, stainless frame that is 1/8" shorter than the company's Compact models.

NIB	Exc	V.G.	Good	Fair	Poor
—	—	—	—	—	—

SPRINGFIELD CUSTOM SHOP

This specialty shop was formed to build custom pistols to the customer's own specifications. When these one-of-a-kind pistols are encountered it is advisable for the shooter or collector to get an independent appraisal. The Springfield Custom also offers standard custom and Racegun packages that are readily available and in stock. These pistols are commercially available.

Custom Carry

Chambered for the following cartridges: .45 ACP, 9mm Parabellum, .38 Super, 10mm, .40 S&W, 9mm x 21. Pistol is fitted with fixed 3-dot sights, speed trigger, Match barrel and bushing, extended thumb safety, beveled magazine well, Commander hammer, polished feed ramp and throated barrel, tuned extractor, lowered and flared ejection port, fitted slide to frame, full length spring guide rod, and walnut grips. Supplied with two magazines and plastic carrying case.

NIB	Exc.	V.G.	Good	Fair	Poor
1495	1100	—	—	—	—

Basic Competition Model

Chambered for the .45 ACP this model features a variety of special options for the competition shooter. Special BoMar sights, match trigger, custom slide to frame fit, polished feed-ramp and throated barrel are just some of the features of this pistol.

NIB	Exc.	V.G.	Good	Fair	Poor
1600	1200	—	—	—	—

N.R.A. PPC

Designed to comply with NRA rules for PPC competition this pistol is chambered for the .45 ACP cartridge with a match grade barrel and chamber. It has a polished feedramp, throated barrel, recoil buffer system, walnut grips, and fully adjustable sights. It is sold with a custom carrying case.

NIB	Exc.	V.G.	Good	Fair	Poor
1400	1150	850	—	—	—

Trophy Master Expert Limited Class

Chambered for .45 ACP Adjustable BoMar rear sight, match barrel, polished ramp and throated barrel, extended ambidextrous thumb safety, beveled and polished magazine well, full length recoil spring guide, match trigger, Commander hammer, lowered and flared ejection port, tuned extractor, fitted slide to frame, extended slide release, flat mainspring housing, Pachmayr wraparound grips, two magazines with slam pads and plastic carrying case.

NIB	Exc.	V.G.	Good	Fair	Poor
1800	1500	1000	750	500	300

Expert Pistol

Similar to the above model but progressive triple port compensator.

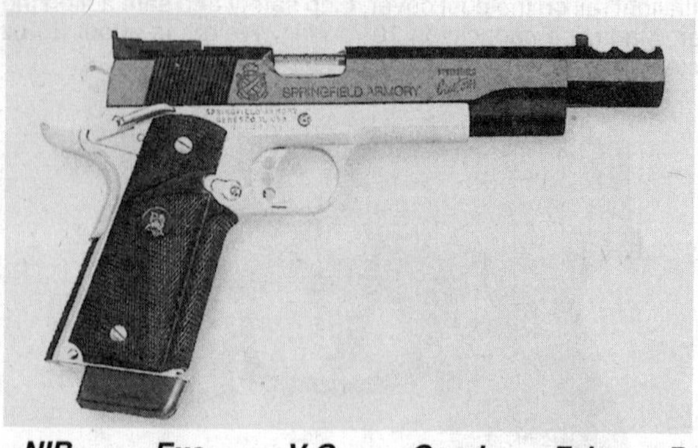

NIB	Exc.	V.G.	Good	Fair	Poor
1985	1475	1100	—	—	—

Bureau Model 1911-A1

Introduced in 1998 this model features a 5" match barrel, a speed trigger, lowered and flared ejection port, beavertail grip safety, Lo-Mount Novak night sights, front strap checkering, Black T finish and special serial numbers with FBI prefix. Bureau Model markings on slide.

NIB	Exc.	V.G.	Good	Fair	Poor
1895	1500	—	—	—	—

Bullseye Wadcutter

Chambered for .45 ACP, .38 Super, 10mm, and .40 S&W. Slide is fitted with BoMar rib. Standard features include full length recoil spring guide rod, speed trigger, Commander hammer, lowered and flared ejection port, tuned extractor, fitted slide to frame, beveled magazine well, checkered front strap, checkered main spring housing, removable grip cope mount, match barrel and bushing, polished feed ramp and throated barrel, walnut grips, and two magazines with slam pads.

NIB	Exc.	V.G.	Good	Fair	Poor
1725	1300	950	—	—	—

Springfield Formula "Squirtgun"

Chambered for .45 ACP, .38 Super, 9mmx19, 9mmx21, and 9mmx23. Fitted with a high capacity 20-round frame, customer specifications sights, hard chrome frame and slide, triple chambered tapered cone compensator, full recoil spring guide and reverse plug, shock butt, lowered and flared ejection port, fitted trigger, Commander hammer, polished feed ramp and throated barrel, flat checkered mainspring housing, extended ambidextrous thumb safety, tuned extractor, checkered front strap, bottom of trigger guard checkered, rear of slide serrated, cocking sensations on front of slide, built in beveled magazine well, and checkered wood grips.

NIB	Exc.	V.G.	Good	Fair	Poor
2900	2250	1250	—	—	—

Trophy Master Distinguished Pistol

This model is chambered for the following cartridges: .45 ACP, .38 Super, 10mm, .40 S&W, 9mmx21. Special BoMar adjustable rear sight with hidden rear leaf, triple port compensator on match barrel, full length recoil spring guide rod and recoil spring retainer, shock butt, lowered and flared ejection port, fitted speed trigger, Commander hammer, polished feed ramp and throated barrel, flat checkered magazine well and mainspring housing matched to beveled magazine well, extended ambidextrous thumb safety, tuned extractor, checkered front strap, flattened and checkered trigger guard, serrated slide top and compensator, cocking sensations on front of slide, checkered walnut grips, two magazines with slam pads, and carrying case.

NIB	Exc.	V.G.	Good	Fair	Poor
2450	1900	1350	—	—	—

Distinguished Limited Class

Similar to the above model but built to comply with USPSA "Limited Class" competition rules. This model has no compensator.

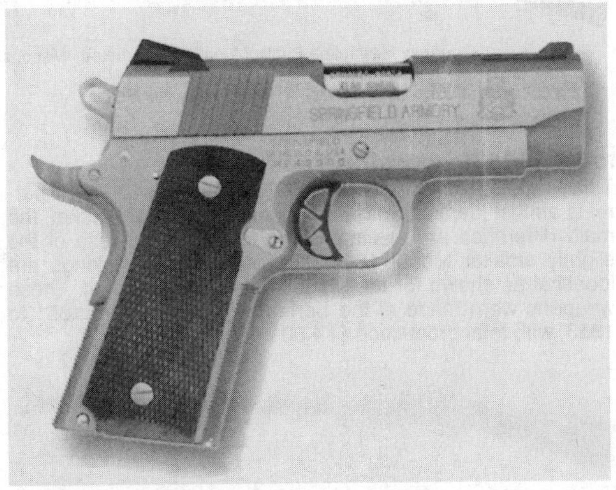

NIB	Exc.	V.G.	Good	Fair	Poor
2695	2000	1500	—	—	—

CMC Formula "Squirtgun"

Chambered for .45 ACP, .38 Super, 9mmx19, 9mmx21, 9mmx23. This pistol has a 20-round magazine and a modular frame. All other features the same as the Trophy Master.

NIB	Exc.	V.G.	Good	Fair	Poor
2750	2000	1200	800	400	200

National Match Model

As above, with a National Match barrel and bushing, adjustable sights and checkered walnut grips. Introduced in 1988.

NIB	Exc.	V.G.	Good	Fair	Poor
1535	1150	850	—	—	—

Competition Grade

As above, hand-tuned, Match Grade trigger, low-profile combat sights, an ambidextrous safety, and a Commander-type hammer. Furnished with Pachmayr grips. Introduced in 1988.

NIB	Exc.	V.G.	Good	Fair	Poor
1600	1200	900	—	—	—

A Model Master Grade Competition Pistol

Similar to the Custom Carry Gun, with a National Match barrel and bushing. Introduced in 1988.

NIB	Exc.	V.G.	Good	Fair	Poor
1700	1500	1250	850	400	250

Model B-1 Master Grade Competition Pistol

Specially designed for USPSA/IPSC competition. Introduced in 1988.

NIB	Exc.	V.G.	Good	Fair	Poor
2000	1750	1250	850	400	250

High Capacity Full-House Race Gun

Built with all available race gun options. Offered in .45 ACP, 9x25 Dillon, .38 Super, and custom calibers on request.

NIB	Exc.	V.G.	Good	Fair	Poor
3085	2300	1700	—	—	—

Night Light Standard

Introduced in 1996 as a limited edition from Springfield distributor Lew Horton this full size Model 1911A1 pistol is chambered for the .45 ACP. It has a lightweight frame and slide with Millett night sights with Hogue rubber wraparound grips. Fitted with extended beavertail safety. Weight 29 oz.

NIB	Exc.	V.G.	Good	Fair	Poor
620	500	400	300	—	—

Night Light Compact

This model was also introduced by Lew Horton in 1996 and is similar to the above model but fitted with a 4.25" barrel and lightweight frame and slide. Weight is 27 oz.

NIB	Exc.	V.G.	Good	Fair	Poor
620	500	400	300	—	—

Night Compact

Same as above but with a steel frame and slide.

NIB	Exc.	V.G.	Good	Fair	Poor
595	475	375	—	—	—

Omega

A .38 Super, 10mm Norma, or .45 caliber semi-automatic pistol with a 5" or 6" polygon rifled barrel, ported or unported, adjustable sights and Pachmayr grips. Patterned somewhat after the Colt Model 1911. Introduced in 1987.

NIB	Exc.	V.G.	Good	Fair	Poor
650	500	350	250	200	125

NOTE: Caliber Conversion Units add $400.

XD Custom Pro

This pistol is built in the Custom Shop and is available in service and tactical sizes. Tactical calibers offered are: 9mm, .40 S&W, and .45 GAP. In Tactical sizes the following calibers are offered: 9mm, .40 S&W, .357 SIG, and .45 GAP. Among some of the special features are: high hand frame relief, overtravel stop, low-mount Bomar sights. Extended magazine release. National Match barrel and special finish.

NIB	Exc.	V.G.	Good	Fair	Poor
1500	1100	—	—	—	—

XD Carry Pro

This model is offered in subcombact, service and tactical sizes. In subcompact size the following calibers are offered: 9mm and .40 S&W. Many special features as listed above.

NIB	Exc.	V.G.	Good	Fair	Poor
750	550	—	—	—	—

SPRINGFIELD ARMORY

Springfield, Massachusetts

This was America's first federal armory. It began producing military weapons in 1795. The armory has supplied military weapons to the United States throughout its history.

NOTE: For additional Springfield Armory military firearms history, technical data, descriptions, photos, and prices see the *Standard Catalog of Military Firearms* under United States, Rifles.

Model 1841 Cadet Musket

This is a single-shot, muzzle-loading rifle chambered for .57 caliber percussion. It has a 40" round barrel with a full-length stock held on by three barrel bands. This rifle features no rear sight. It is browned and case-colored, with iron mountings. There is a steel ramrod mounted under the barrel. The lockplate is marked "Springfield" with the date of manufacture and "US" over an eagle motif. There were approximately 450 produced between 1844 and 1845.

Exc.	V.G.	Good	Fair	Poor
—	—	20000	8000	3000

Model 1842 Musket

This is a single-shot muzzleloader chambered for .69 caliber percussion. It has a 42" round barrel and a full-length stock held on by three barrel bands. The finish is white with iron mountings and a steel ramrod mounted beneath the barrel. There were a total of approximately 275,000 manufactured between 1844 and 1855 by both the Springfield Armory and the Harper's Ferry Armory. They are so marked.

Courtesy Milwaukee Public Museum, Milwaukee, Wisconsin

Exc.	V.G.	Good	Fair	Poor
—	—	3500	1250	500

Model 1851 Percussion Cadet Musket

This single-shot muzzleloader in .57 caliber with 40" round barrel is almost identical with the Model 1841 Cadet Musket, the main difference and distinguishing feature is the use of the slightly smaller Model 1847 Musketoon lock. Markings are identical as shown for the Model 1841 Cadet Musket. These weapons were made at the Springfield Armory from 1851 to 1853, with total production of 4,000 guns.

Courtesy Little John's Auction Service, Inc., Paul Goodwin photo

Exc.	V.G.	Good	Fair	Poor
—	—	2500	1000	500

Model 1847 Artillery Musketoon

This is a single-shot muzzleloader chambered for .69 caliber percussion. It has a 26" round smooth bore barrel. The finish is white, with a full-length walnut stock held on by two barrel bands. The lock is marked "Springfield." There were approximately 3,350 manufactured between 1848 and 1859.

Paul Goodwin photo

Exc.	V.G.	Good	Fair	Poor
—	—	6000	2500	1000

Model 1847 U.S. Sappers Musketoon

Almost identical to the Model 1847 Artillery except for a lug for sword bayonet mounted on right side of upper barrel band with twin steel guides for bayonet mounted near muzzle. A total of about 830 produced. Be aware of altered Model 1847 Artillery Muskets passed as orginal Sappers Muskets.

Exc.	V.G.	Good	Fair	Poor
—	—	6500	2750	1000

Model 1847 U.S. Cavalry Musketoon

Similar to the Model 1847 Artillery except for a button head ramrod attached with iron swivels under the muzzle. No sling swivels. As many as 6,700 were manufactured.

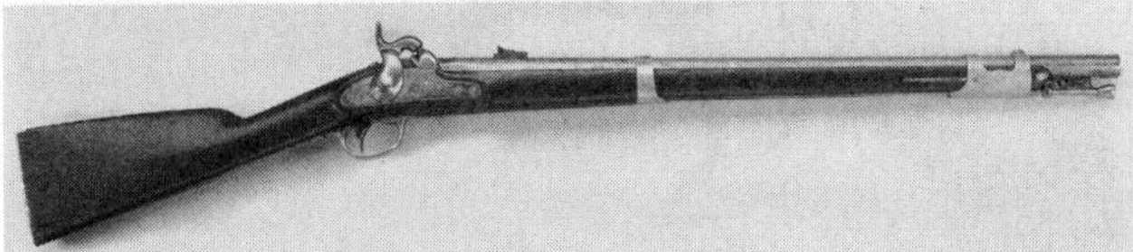

Courtesy Little John's Auction Service, Inc., Paul Goodwin photo

Exc.	V.G.	Good	Fair	Poor
—	—	7000	3000	1000

Model 1855 Rifle Musket

This is a single-shot muzzleloader chambered for .58 caliber percussion. It has a 40" round barrel with a full-length stock held on by three barrel bands. It has iron mountings and a ramrod mounted under the barrel. The front sight acts as a bayonet lug. The finish is white with a walnut stock. The lock is marked "U.S. Springfield." There was also a Harper's Ferry manufactured version that is so marked. There were approximately 59,000 manufactured between 1857 and 1861.

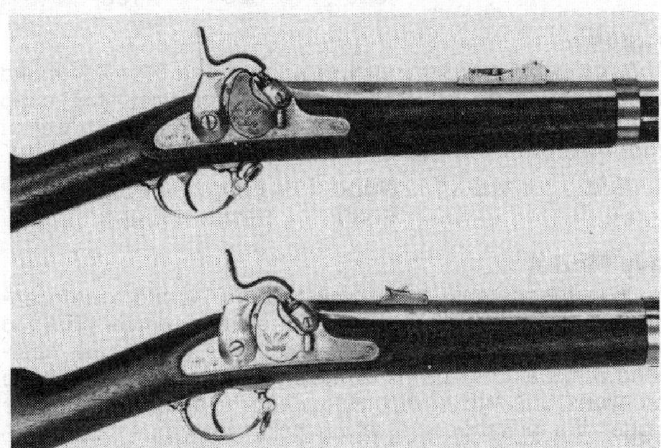

Courtesy Milwaukee Public Museum, Milwaukee, Wisconsin

Exc.	V.G.	Good	Fair	Poor
—	—	4500	1750	750

Model 1855 Rifled Carbine

This is a single-shot muzzleloader chambered for .54 caliber percussion. It has a 22" round barrel with a 3/4-length stock held on by one barrel band. The finish is white with iron mountings and a ramrod mounted under the barrel. The lock is marked "Springfield" and dated. There were approximately 1,000 manufactured between 1855 and 1856.

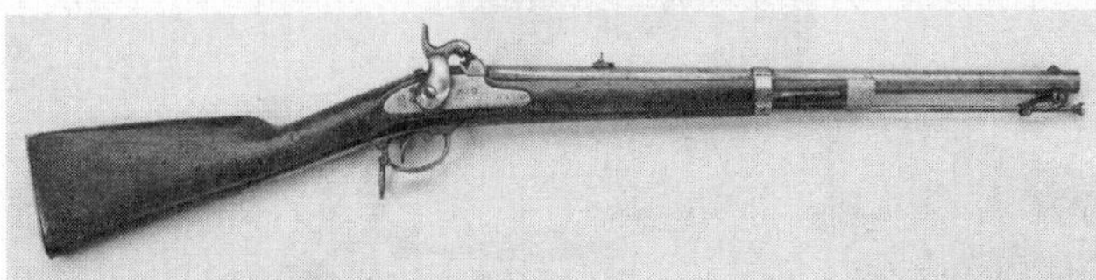

Courtesy Little John's Auction Service, Inc., Paul Goodwin photo

Exc.	V.G.	Good	Fair	Poor
—	—	25000	8500	2000

Model 1858 U.S. Cadet Rifle Musket

Similar to the Model 1855 Rifled Musket but with a 38" barrel and shorter stock. The buttstock is 1" shorter than the musket and the forearm is 2" shorter. About 2,500 were built.

Exc.	V.G.	Good	Fair	Poor
—	—	5000	2250	1000

Model 1861 Percussion Rifle Musket

The Model 1861 was the standard musket in use during the Civil War. This .58 caliber single-shot muzzleloader has a 40" barrel with three barrel bands and all iron mountings; all metal parts are finished bright (some rear sights are blued) and the stock is walnut. On the lock there is an eagle motif forward of the hammer, US/SPRINGFIELD, beneath the nipple bolster, and the date at the rear section of the lock. About 256,129 of these muskets were made at the Springfield Armory, while almost 750,000 more were made under contract.

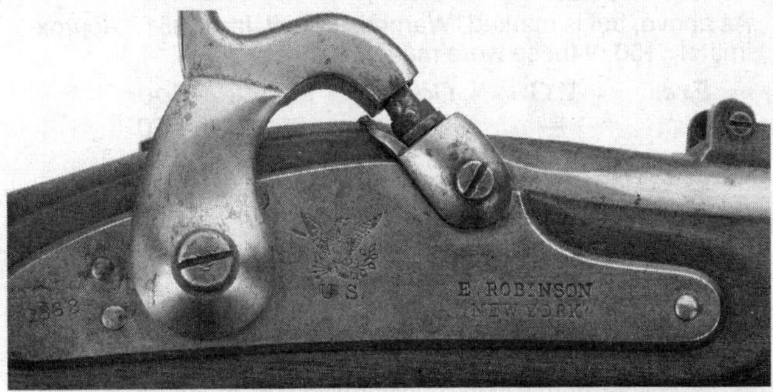

Paul Goodwin photo

Exc.	V.G.	Good	Fair	Poor
—	—	3500	1500	800

Model 1863 Rifle Musket, Type I

This is a single-shot muzzleloader chambered for .58 caliber percussion. It has a 40" round barrel and a full-length stock held on by three barrel bands. The finish is white with iron mountings, and the lock is marked "U.S. Springfield" and dated 1863. There were approximately 275,000 manufactured in 1863.

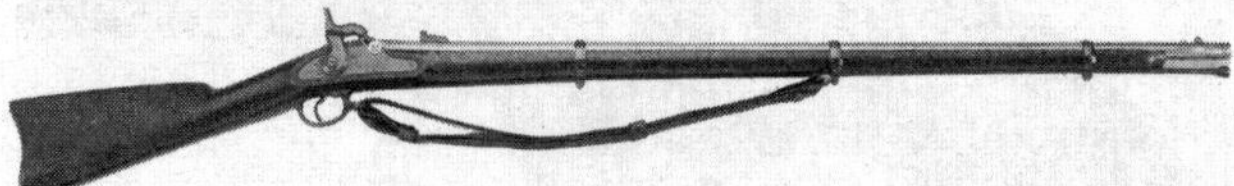

Courtesy Little John's Auction Service, Inc., Paul Goodwin photo

Exc.	V.G.	Good	Fair	Poor
—	—	3500	1500	800

Model 1863 Rifle Musket, Type II, aka Model 1864

This was the last U.S. martial regulation arm of muzzleloading design, and it was widely used during the latter part of the Civil War. Produced at the Springfield Armory between 1864 and

1865, with total production of 25,540 pieces. This weapon is identical to the Type I with the exception of the dating of the lock, which is either 1864 or 1865, a single leaf rear sight, and solid barrel bands secured by flat springs mounted in the stock. The ramrod was either the tulip head type, or the new knurled and slotted design.

Model 1863 Type II lock Paul Goodwin photo

Exc.	V.G.	Good	Fair	Poor
—	—	3500	1500	800

SPRINGFIELD ARMS COMPANY
Springfield, Massachusetts

Belt Model

A .31 caliber percussion revolver with 4", 5", or 6" round barrels, centrally mounted hammer, and an etched 6-shot cylinder. Made with or without a loading lever. Early production versions of this revolver are marked "Jaquith's Patent 1838" on the frame and later production were marked "Springfield Arms" on the top strap. Approximately 150 were made.

Exc.	V.G.	Good	Fair	Poor
—	—	1750	800	200

Warner Model

As above, but is marked "Warner's Patent Jan. 1851." Approximately 150 of these were made.

Exc.	V.G.	Good	Fair	Poor
—	—	2500	1200	250

Double Trigger Model

As above, with two triggers, one of which locks the cylinder. Approximately 100 were made in 1851.

Exc.	V.G.	Good	Fair	Poor
—	—	2000	800	200

Pocket Model Revolver

A .28 caliber percussion revolver with 2.5" round barrel, centrally mounted hammer, no loading lever and etched 6-shot cylinder. Marked "Warner's Patent Jan. 1851" and "Springfield Arms Company." Blued, case hardened with walnut grips. Early production examples of this revolver do not have a groove on the cylinder and have a rounded frame. Approximately 525 were made in 1851.

Courtesy Milwaukee Public Museum, Milwaukee, Wisconsin

Exc.	V.G.	Good	Fair	Poor
—	—	800	350	150

Ring Trigger Model

As above, but fitted with a ring trigger that revolved the cylinder. Approximately 150 were made in 1851.

Courtesy Milwaukee Public Museum, Milwaukee, Wisconsin

Exc.	V.G.	Good	Fair	Poor
—	—	1150	500	200

Double Trigger Model

As above, with two triggers set within a conventional trigger guard. The forward trigger revolves the cylinder. Approximately 350 were made in 1851.

Courtesy Milwaukee Public Museum, Milwaukee, Wisconsin

Exc.	V.G.	Good	Fair	Poor
—	—	1150	500	200

Late Model Revolver

As above, except that the cylinder is automatically turned when the hammer is cocked. The top strap marked "Warner's Patent/James Warner, Springfield, Mass." Approximately 500 were made in 1851.

Exc.	V.G.	Good	Fair	Poor
—	—	800	300	100

Dragoon

A .40 caliber percussion revolver with either a 6" or 7.5" round barrel, some fitted with loading levers, others without. The top strap marked "Springfield Arms Company." Blued with walnut grips. Approximately 110 revolvers were manufactured in 1851.

Exc.	V.G.	Good	Fair	Poor
—	—	8000	3500	950

Navy Model

A .36 caliber percussion revolver with a 6" round barrel, centrally mounted hammer, and 6-shot etched cylinder. The top strap marked "Springfield Arms Company." Blued, case hardened with walnut grips. This model was manufactured in two variations, one with a single trigger and the other with a double trigger, the forward one of which locks the cylinder. Both variations had loading levers. Approximately 250 of these pistols were made in 1851.

Exc.	V.G.	Good	Fair	Poor
—	—	3750	1500	500

Double-Barrel Shotguns

The Springfield Arms Co. was bought by Stevens who used the Springfield brand name on many good quality single and double-barrel shotguns. Values range from $100 to $1,600 depending on model, gauge, and condition. See also Stevens.

SQUIBBMAN

SEE—Squires, Bingham Mfg. Co., Inc.

SQUIRES BINGHAM MFG. CO., INC.

Rizal, Philippine Islands

Firearms produced by this company are marketed under the trademark Squibbman.

Model 100D

A .38 Special caliber double-action swingout cylinder revolver with a 3", 4", or 6" ventilated rib barrel, adjustable sights, matte black finish and walnut grips.

Exc.	V.G.	Good	Fair	Poor
175	100	80	60	40

Model 100DC

As above, without the ventilated rib.

Exc.	V.G.	Good	Fair	Poor
200	100	80	60	40

Model 100

As above, with a tapered barrel and uncheckered walnut grips.

Exc.	V.G.	Good	Fair	Poor
200	100	80	60	40

Thunder Chief

As above, but in .22 or .22 Magnum caliber with a heavier ventilated rib barrel, shrouded ejector, and ebony grips.

Exc.	V.G.	Good	Fair	Poor
225	125	100	80	60

SSK INDUSTRIES

Bloomingdale, Ohio

SSK-Contender

A custom-made pistol available in 74 different calibers from .178 Bee to .588 JDJ and built on a Thompson/Center action.

NIB	Exc.	V.G.	Good	Fair	Poor
575	500	475	425	350	275

SSK-XP100

A custom-made pistol utilizing a Remington XP100 action. Available in a variety of calibers and sight configurations.

NIB	Exc.	V.G.	Good	Fair	Poor
650	600	550	500	400	300

.50 Caliber XP100

As above, with an integral muzzlebrake and reinforced composition stock.

NIB	Exc.	V.G.	Good	Fair	Poor
1750	1500	1250	1000	750	500

STAFFORD, T. J.

New Haven, Connecticut

Pocket Pistol

A .22 caliber single-shot spur trigger pistol with a 3.5" octagonal barrel marked "T.J. Stafford New Haven Ct.," silver-plated brass frame and walnut or rosewood grips.

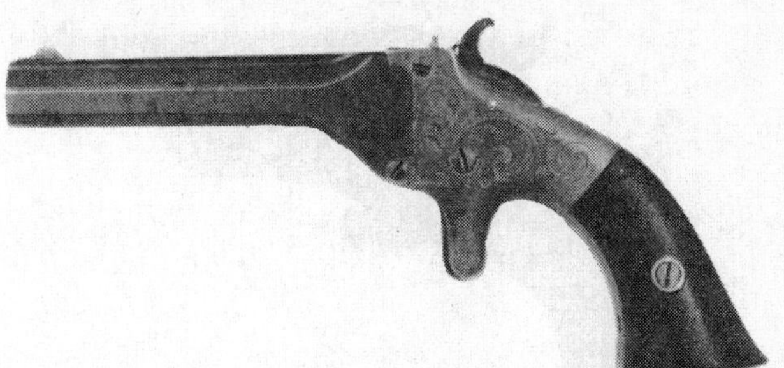

Courtesy W.P. Hallstein III and son Chip

Exc.	V.G.	Good	Fair	Poor
—	—	600	250	100

Large Frame Model

As above, but in .38 rimfire caliber with a 6" barrel.

Exc.	V.G.	Good	Fair	Poor
—	—	850	400	200

STALCAP, ALEXANDER T.F.M.

Nashville, Tennessee

First in business during the 1850s, Stalcap received a contract in 1862, to modify sporting arms for military use. Overall length 50-7/8" to 51-3/4"; octagonal barrels 35-1/4" - 36" turned round at muzzle for socket bayonets; .54 caliber. Rifles assembled with sporting locks, new stocks and brass furniture. At least 102 rifles were delivered in 1862. These arms are unmarked.

Exc.	V.G.	Good	Fair	Poor
—	—	4250	2000	1000

STANDARD ARMS CO.

Wilmington, Delaware

Model G

Chambered for .25 Remington, .30 Remington, and .35 Remington, with a 22" barrel, and open sights. Integral box magazine and closable gas port that allowed the rifle to be used as a slide action. Blued with a walnut stock. Produced in limited quantities, circa 1910. A notorious jamamatic.

Exc.	V.G.	Good	Fair	Poor
750	600	350	250	150

Model M

Manually-operated pump-only version of Model G. Add 20 percent to above values.

STAR, BONIFACIO ECHEVERRIA

Eibar, Spain

SEE—Echeverria

STARR, EBAN T.

New York, New York

Single-Shot Derringer

A .41 caliber single-shot pistol with a pivoted 2.75" round barrel. The hammer mounted on the right side of the frame and the trigger formed in the shape of a button located at the front of the frame. The frame marked "Starr's Pat's May 10, 1864." The brass frame silver-plated, the barrel blued or silver-plated with checkered walnut grips. Manufactured from 1864 to 1869.

Courtesy Milwaukee Public Museum, Milwaukee, Wisconsin

Exc.	V.G.	Good	Fair	Poor
—	—	1750	750	200

Four Barreled Pepperbox

A .32 caliber 4 barreled pocket pistol with 2.75" to 3.25" barrels. The frame marked "Starr's Pat's May 10, 1864." Brass frames, silver-plated. The barrel is blued with plain walnut grips. This pistol was produced in six variations.

Courtesy Milwaukee Public Museum, Milwaukee, Wisconsin

First Model

Fluted breech and a barrel release mounted on the right side of the frame.

Exc.	V.G.	Good	Fair	Poor
—	—	2500	800	200

Second Model

Flat breech.

Exc.	V.G.	Good	Fair	Poor
—	—	1750	600	200

Third Model

Rounded breech with a visible firing-pin retaining spring.

Exc.	V.G.	Good	Fair	Poor
—	—	1500	500	150

Fourth Model

Rounded breech without visible springs.

Exc.	V.G.	Good	Fair	Poor
—	—	1500	500	150

Fifth Model

A larger, more angular grip.

Exc.	V.G.	Good	Fair	Poor
—	—	1250	400	150

Sixth Model

The frame length of this variation is of increased size.

Exc.	V.G.	Good	Fair	Poor
—	—	1500	500	150

STARR ARMS COMPANY

New York, New York

1858 Navy Revolver

A .36 caliber double-action percussion revolver with a 6" barrel and 6-shot cylinder. Blued, case hardened with walnut grips. The frame marked "Starr Arms Co. New York." Approximately 3,000 were made between 1858 and 1860.

Courtesy Milwaukee Public Museum, Milwaukee, Wisconsin

Standard Model

Exc.	V.G.	Good	Fair	Poor
—	—	3250	1100	350

Martially Marked (JT)

Exc.	V.G.	Good	Fair	Poor
—	—	4250	1750	700

1858 Army Revolver

A .44 caliber double-action percussion revolver with a 6" barrel and 6-shot cylinder. Blued, case hardened with walnut grips. The frame marked "Starr Arms Co. New York." Approximately 23,000 were manufactured.

Exc.	V.G.	Good	Fair	Poor
—	—	2500	1100	300

1863 Army Revolver

Similar to the above, but single-action and with an 8" round barrel. Approximately 32,000 were manufactured between 1863 and 1865.

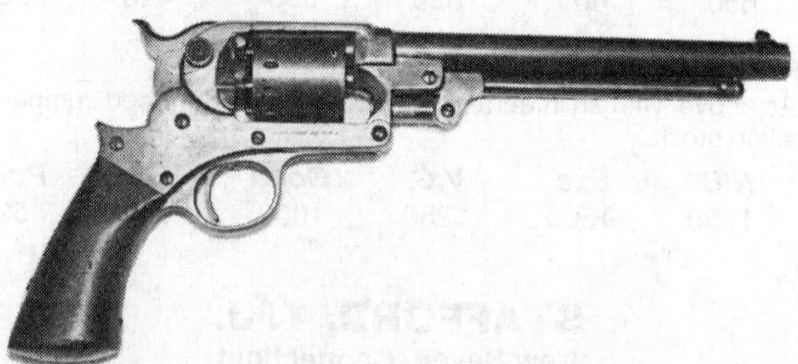

Courtesy Milwaukee Public Museum, Milwaukee, Wisconsin

Exc.	V.G.	Good	Fair	Poor
—	—	3250	1500	350

Percussion Carbine

A .54 caliber breechloading percussion carbine with a 21" round barrel secured by one barrel band. Blued, case hardened with a walnut stock. The lock marked "Starr Arms Co./Yonkers, N.Y."

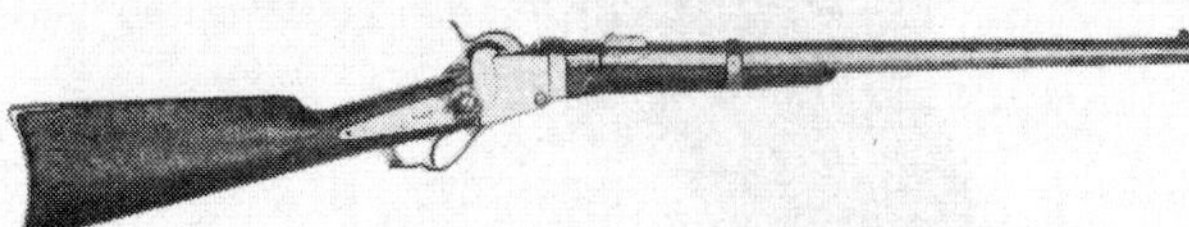

Courtesy Milwaukee Public Museum, Milwaukee, Wisconsin

Exc.	V.G.	Good	Fair	Poor
—	—	2750	1250	400

Cartridge Carbine

Similar to the above, but in .52 rimfire caliber. Approximately 5,000 were manufactured.

Courtesy Milwaukee Public Museum, Milwaukee, Wisconsin

Exc.	V.G.	Good	Fair	Poor
—	—	2500	1000	350

STEEL CITY ARMS, INC.

Pittsburgh, Pennsylvania

Double Deuce

A .22 caliber stainless steel double-action semi-automatic pistol with a 2.5" barrel, 7-shot magazine and plain rosewood grips. Introduced in 1984.

Courtesy J.B. Wood

Exc.	V.G.	Good	Fair	Poor
300	250	200	150	100

STENDA WAFFENFABRIK

Suhl, Germany

Pocket Pistol

A 7.65mm semi-automatic pistol similar to the "Beholla," the "Leonhardt," and the "Menta." Stenda took over the production of the Beholla pistol design at the close of WWI. The only major difference in the Stenda design was the elimination of the Beholla's worst feature, the pin that went through the slide and retained the barrel. It was replaced by a sliding catch that anchored it in place and unlocked the slide so that the barrel could be removed without the need of a vise and drift pin. The Stenda pistol can be identified by the fact that there are no holes through the slide and there is a catch on the frame above the trigger. The finish blued, with plastic grips; and the slide is marked "Waffenfabrik Stendawerke Suhl." Approximately 25,000 manufactured before production ceased in 1926.

Exc.	V.G.	Good	Fair	Poor
400	250	200	150	100

STERLING ARMAMENT LTD.

London, England

Parapistol MK 7 C4

A 9mm semi-automatic pistol with a 4" barrel, and detachable magazines of 10-round capacity. Black wrinkled paint finish with plastic grips.

NIB	Exc.	V.G.	Good	Fair	Poor
600	475	400	300	200	100

Parapistol MK 7 C8

As above, with a 7.8" barrel.

NIB	Exc.	V.G.	Good	Fair	Poor
625	500	400	300	200	100

Sterling MK 6

A semi-automatic copy of the Sterling submachine gun with a 16.1" barrel, folding metal stock and side mounted magazine. Finished as above.

NIB	Exc.	V.G.	Good	Fair	Poor
1500	950	750	500	300	200

Sterling AR 180

A copy of the Armalite Model AR18, 5.56mm rifle. Finished with either black wrinkled paint or, more rarely, blued.

NIB	Exc.	V.G.	Good	Fair	Poor
1100	750	600	500	350	200

STERLING ARMS CORPORATION

Gasport, New York

Model 283 Target 300

This pistol is similar in appearance to Hi-Standard semi-automatic pistols. Chambered for the .22 LR cartridge it was offered with 4", 4-1/2", or 8" barrels. Rear sight is adjustable and magazine holds 10 rounds. Grips are black plastic. Weight is approximately 36 oz.

NIB	Exc.	V.G.	Good	Fair	Poor
200	150	125	100	75	60

Model 284 Target 300L

Similar to the above model except for 4-1/2" or 6" tapered barrel with barrel band.

Courtesy John J. Stimson, Jr.

NIB	Exc.	V.G.	Good	Fair	Poor
225	175	125	100	75	60

Model 285 Husky

Similar to the Model 283 with the exception of fixed sights. Offered with 4-1/2" barrel only.

NIB	Exc.	V.G.	Good	Fair	Poor
200	150	125	100	75	60

Model 286 Trapper

Similar to the Model 284 except for fixed sights.

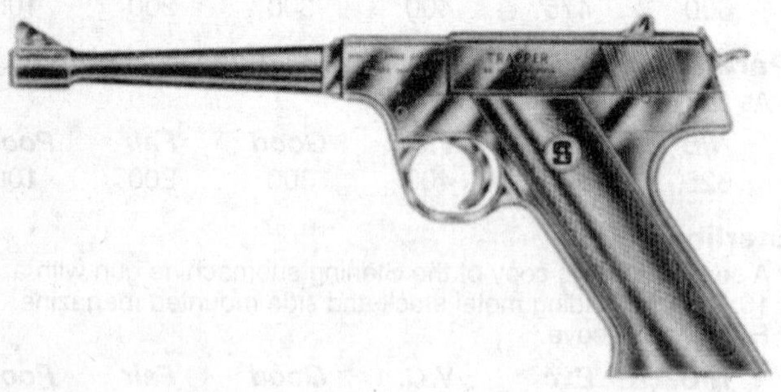

NIB	Exc.	V.G.	Good	Fair	Poor
200	150	125	100	75	60

Model 287 PPL .380

This is a pocket-size semi-automatic pistol chambered for the .380 ACP cartridge. Fitted with a 1" barrel it has a 5-1/4" length overall. Magazine holds 6 rounds. Weight is approximately 22 oz.

NIB	Exc.	V.G.	Good	Fair	Poor
125	75	60	50	40	30

Model PPL .22

This is a small pocket pistol similar to the Model 287 but chambered for the .22 LR cartridge. Barrel is 1" long. Pistol weighs about 24 oz.

NIB	Exc.	V.G.	Good	Fair	Poor
175	125	100	75	60	50

Model 300

Similar to the Model 287 but chambered for the .25 ACP cartridge. It has a 2-1/4" barrel with a 6-round magazine. Length is 5" overall and the weight is about 14 oz.

NIB	Exc.	V.G.	Good	Fair	Poor
150	125	100	75	50	40

Model 300S

This is the stainless steel version of the Model 300.

NIB	Exc.	V.G.	Good	Fair	Poor
165	135	115	75	50	40

Model 302

Identical to the Model 300 except that it is chambered for the .22 LR cartridge.

NIB	Exc.	V.G.	Good	Fair	Poor
150	125	100	75	50	40

Model 302S

Same as above but in stainless steel.

NIB	Exc.	V.G.	Good	Fair	Poor
165	135	115	75	60	50

Model 400

This is a double-action semi-automatic pistol chambered for the .380 ACP cartridge with a 3-1/2" barrel. Magazine holds 7 rounds. Pistol is 6-1/2" overall and the weight is approximately 24 oz.

NIB	Exc.	V.G.	Good	Fair	Poor
200	175	150	125	100	75

Model 400S

This is the stainless steel version of the Model 400.

NIB	Exc.	V.G.	Good	Fair	Poor
225	200	175	125	100	75

Model 402

Similar to the Model 400 except chambered for the .22 LR cartridge.

NIB	Exc.	V.G.	Good	Fair	Poor
150	125	100	75	60	40

Model X-Caliber

A single-shot .22 LR, .22 WMR, .357 Magnum, or .44 Magnum pistol with interchangeable barrels from 8" and 10". Adjustable rear sight. Finger groove grips. Deduct 50 percent for rimfire.

NIB	Exc.	V.G.	Good	Fair	Poor
350	300	250	225	150	100

STEVENS, J. ARMS CO.

Chicopee Falls, Massachusetts

In 1864 this firm began doing business as J. Stevens & Company. In 1888 it was incorporated as the J. Stevens Arms & Tool Company. It operated as such until 1920, when it was taken over by the Savage Arms Company. It has operated as an independent division in this organization since. This company produced a great many firearms—most that were of an affordable nature. They are widely collected, and one interested in them should take advantage of the literature available on the subject.

Vest Pocket Pistol

This is a single-shot pocket pistol chambered for the .22 and the .30 rimfire cartridges. The .22 caliber version is rarely encountered and would be worth approximately 25 percent more than the values illustrated. It has a 2.75" part-octagonal barrel that pivots upward for loading. It has an external hammer and a spur-type trigger. The frame is nickel-plated or blued, with a blued barrel. The odd shaped flared grips are made of rosewood. The first models were marked "Vest Pocket Pistol" only. Later models have the barrels marked "J. Stevens & Co. Chicopee Falls, Mass." There were approximately 1,000 manufactured between 1864 and 1876.

Courtesy Milwaukee Public Museum, Milwaukee, Wisconsin

Exc.	V.G.	Good	Fair	Poor
3300	2200	1650	1000	850

Pocket Pistol

This is a more conventional-appearing, single-shot pocket pistol chambered for either the .22 or the .30 rimfire cartridges. It has a 3.5" part-octagonal barrel that pivots upward for loading. It features a plated brass frame with either a blued or nickel-plated barrel and rosewood, two-piece grips. The barrel is marked "J. Stevens & Co. Chicopee Falls, Mass." There were approximately 15,000 manufactured between 1864 and 1886.

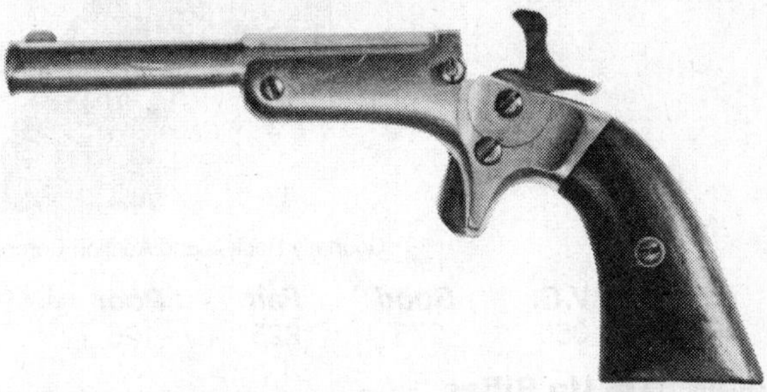

Courtesy Milwaukee Public Museum, Milwaukee, Wisconsin

Exc.	V.G.	Good	Fair	Poor
450	325	225	125	100

Gem Pocket Pistol

This is a single-shot, derringer-type pocket pistol chambered for either the .22 or .30 rimfire cartridges. It has a 3" part-octagonal barrel that pivots to the side for loading. It has a nickel-plated brass frame with either a blued or plated barrel. It has bird's-head grips made of walnut or rosewood. The barrel is marked "Gem." The Stevens name or address does not appear on this firearm. There were approximately 4,000 manufactured between 1872 and 1890.

Exc.	V.G.	Good	Fair	Poor
1000	800	550	425	300

.41 Caliber Derringer

This is a single-shot pocket pistol chambered for the .22 or .31 caliber rimfire cartridge. It has a 4" part-octagonal barrel that pivots upward for loading. It has a spur trigger and an external hammer. The frame is plated brass with a blued barrel. It has walnut bird's-head grips. This firearm is completely unmarked except for a serial number. There were approximately 100 manufactured in 1875.

.22 Caliber

Exc.	V.G.	Good	Fair	Poor
4500	4000	3000	2100	1200

.41 Caliber

Exc.	V.G.	Good	Fair	Poor
4200	3500	2700	1900	1200

Single-Shot Pistol

This is a single-shot pistol chambered for the .22 or .30 rimfire cartridges. It has a 3.5" part-octagonal barrel that pivots upward for loading. It is quite similar in appearance to the original pocket pistol. It has a plated brass frame and either a blued or nickel-plated barrel with walnut, square-butt grips. The barrel is marked "J. Stevens A&T Co." There were approximately 10,000 manufactured between 1886 and 1896.

Exc.	V.G.	Good	Fair	Poor
450	300	225	175	125

No. 41 Pistol

This is a single-shot pocket pistol chambered for the .22 and .30 Short cartridges. It has a 3.5" part-octagonal barrel that pivots upward for loading. It features an external hammer and a spur-type trigger. It has an iron frame with the firing pin mounted in the recoil shield. It is either blued or nickel-plated, with square-butt walnut grips. There were approximately 90,000 manufactured between 1896 and 1916.

REMINDER

You don't have to specialize in Colts and Winchesters to have a nice collection. Collecting Marlin or Mossberg .22 semi-autos, for example, can be just as rewarding.

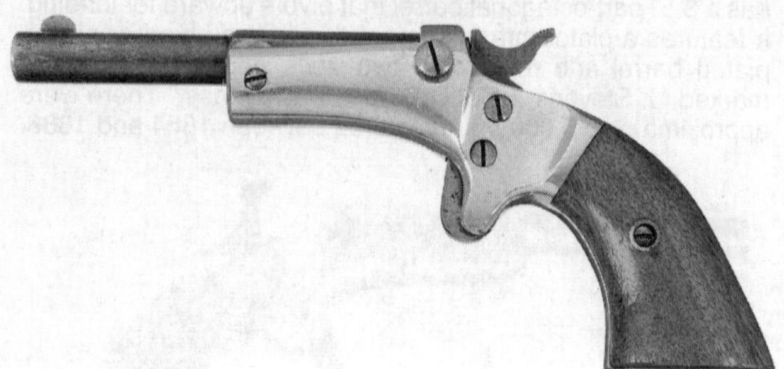

Courtesy Rock Island Auction Company

Exc.	V.G.	Good	Fair	Poor
400	350	275	225	125

Stevens Tip Up Rifles

This series of rifles was produced by Stevens beginning in the 1870s through 1895. There are a number of variations, but they are all quite similar in appearance. They feature a distinctive sloped frame made of iron and nickel-plated. Most frames are similar in size, but there is a slightly lighter frame used on the "Ladies Model" rifles. These Tip Up rifles are chambered for various calibers from the .22 rimfire to the .44 centerfire cartridges. They are offered with barrel lengths of 24", 26", 28", or 30". The actions are nickel-plated, as well as the trigger guards and the buttplates. The barrels are blued, and the two-piece stocks are of walnut. They are offered with various buttplates and sights. A shotgun version is also offered. There are a number of variations that differ only slightly, and the model numbers are not marked on the rifles. We suggest securing a qualified appraisal if in doubt. The major variations and their values are as follows:

Courtesy Milwaukee Public Museum, Milwaukee, Wisconsin

Ladies Model—.22 or .25 Rimfire Only, 24" or 26" Barrel

Exc.	V.G.	Good	Fair	Poor
3000	2500	1800	1200	600

Tip Up Rifle—Without Forend

Exc.	V.G.	Good	Fair	Poor
600	500	350	225	175

Tip Up Rifle—With Forend, Swiss-Type Buttplate

Exc.	V.G.	Good	Fair	Poor
950	750	450	325	200

Tip Up Shotgun—All Gauges, 30" or 32" Barrel

Exc.	V.G.	Good	Fair	Poor
350	300	200	150	100

Ideal Single-Shot Rifle

This excellent rifle was manufactured by Stevens between 1896 and 1933. It is a single-shot, falling-block type action that is activated by a trigger guard-action lever. It was produced in many popular calibers from .22 rimfire up to .30-40. It was also manufactured in a number of special Stevens calibers. It was offered with various length barrels in many different grades, from plain Spartan starter rifles up to some extremely high-grade Schuetzen-type target rifles with all available options. In 1901 Harry Pope of Hartford, Connecticut, went to work for Stevens and brought his highly respected barrel to the Stevens Company. He remained an employee for only two years, and the firearms produced during this period have the name "Stevens-Pope" stamped on the top of the barrel in addition to the other factory markings. Rifles marked in this manner and authenticated would be worth an approximate 50 percent premium if they are in very good to excellent condition. Due to numerous variations and options offered, we strongly recommend securing a qualified appraisal, especially on the higher-grade Ideal series rifles, if a transaction is contemplated.

No. 44

This version is chambered for various calibers and is offered with a 24" or 26" barrel. It has an open rear sight with a Rocky Mountain-type front sight. The finish is blued and case colored, with a walnut stock. There were approximately 100,000 manufactured between 1896 and 1933.

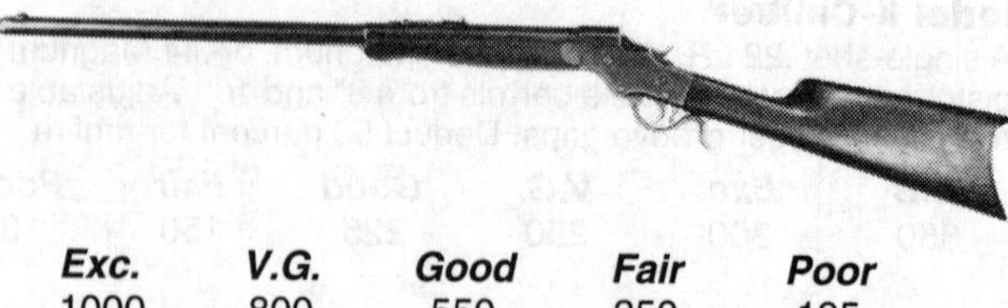

Exc.	V.G.	Good	Fair	Poor
1000	800	550	350	195

No. 44-1/2

This rifle is similar in appearance to the No. 44 but features an improved action. It has barrel lengths up to 34" and will be found with the Stevens-Pope barrel. It was manufactured between 1903 and 1916.

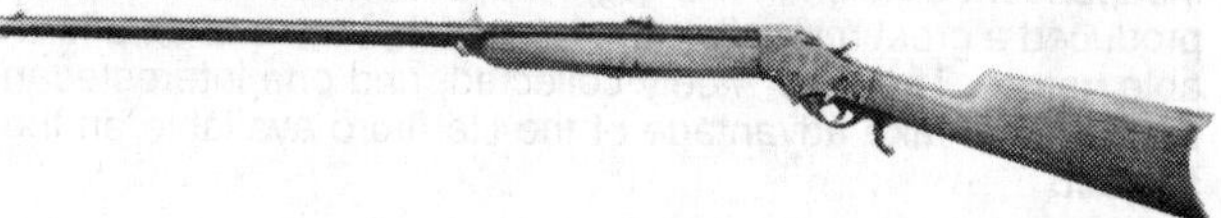

Courtesy J.B. Barnes

Exc.	V.G.	Good	Fair	Poor
1600	1400	1100	850	700

No. 044-1/2

This version is also known as the English Model rifle and is similar to the No. 44-1/2 except that it has a shotgun butt and a tapered barrel. There were a number of options offered that would affect the value. It was manufactured between 1903 and 1916.

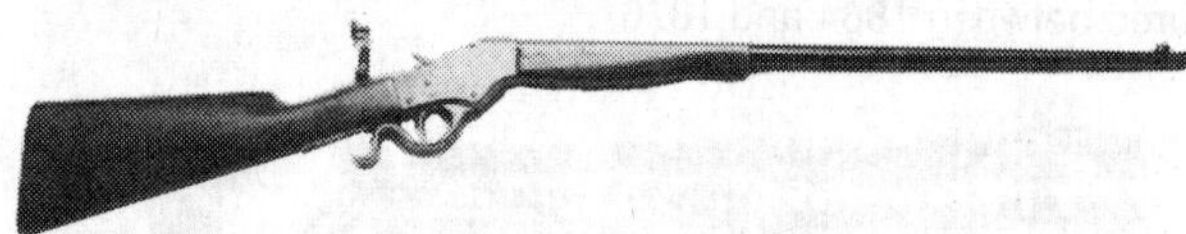

Courtesy Mike Stuckslager

Exc.	V.G.	Good	Fair	Poor
1600	1400	1100	850	700

No. 45

This version is also known as the Range Rifle, It is chambered for various calibers from the .22 rimfire to .44-40. Its identifying features are the Beach sights with an additional vernier tang sight and a Swiss-type buttstock. It is offered with a 26" or 28" part-octagonal barrel. It was manufactured between 1896 and 1916. Values listed are for the standard version.

Exc.	V.G.	Good	Fair	Poor
1800	1600	1200	950	725

NOTE: Deduct 25 percent for .44 action.

No. 46

Same as the No. 45 but with a fancy wood stock. Manufactured from 1896 to 1902. Built in No. 44 action-only.

Exc.	V.G.	Good	Fair	Poor
2200	1900	1550	1325	1000

No. 47

This version is similar to the No. 45, with a pistol grip buttstock.

Exc.	V.G.	Good	Fair	Poor
3500	3100	2300	1600	1000

NOTE: Deduct 25 percent for .44 action.

No. 48

Same as the No. 47 but with a fancy wood checkered stock. Manufactured from 1896 to 1902. Built in a No. 44 action-only. This is a very rare model.

Exc.	V.G.	Good	Fair	Poor
4250	3750	2750	1950	1250

No. 49

This model is also known as the "Walnut Hill Rifle." It is a high grade target rifle chambered for many calibers between the .22 rimfire and the .44-40. It is offered with a 28" or 30" part-octagonal barrel that is medium- or heavy-weight. It was furnished with a globe front sight and a vernier tang sight. It is blued with a case-colored frame and has a high-grade, checkered, varnished walnut stock that has a high comb and features a pistol grip, cheekpiece, Swiss-type buttplate, and a loop-type trigger guard lever that resembles that of a lever-action rifle. The receiver is engraved, and there were a number of options available that would increase the value when present. We recommend an appraisal when in doubt. This rifle was manufactured between 1896 and 1916.

Courtesy J.B. Barnes

Exc.	V.G.	Good	Fair	Poor
6000	5500	3300	2100	1600

Model 50

This version is identical to the Model 49 but was offered with a higher-grade walnut stock. This is a very rare model.

Courtesy J.B. Barnes

Exc.	V.G.	Good	Fair	Poor
7000	6500	3900	2500	1800

Model 51

This version is known as the "Schuetzen Rifle" and is quite similar to the No. 49 except that it features double-set triggers, a higher-grade walnut stock, a wooden insert in the trigger guard action lever, and a heavy, Schuetzen-type buttplate. There were many options available on this model, and we recommend securing an appraisal when in doubt. It was manufactured between 1896 and 1916.

Courtesy J.B. Barnes

Exc.	V.G.	Good	Fair	Poor
11000	9000	6300	3000	2100

No. 52

This version is also known as the "Schuetzen Junior." It is similar to the No. 51 except that it features more engraving and a higher-grade walnut stock. It was manufactured between 1897 and 1916.

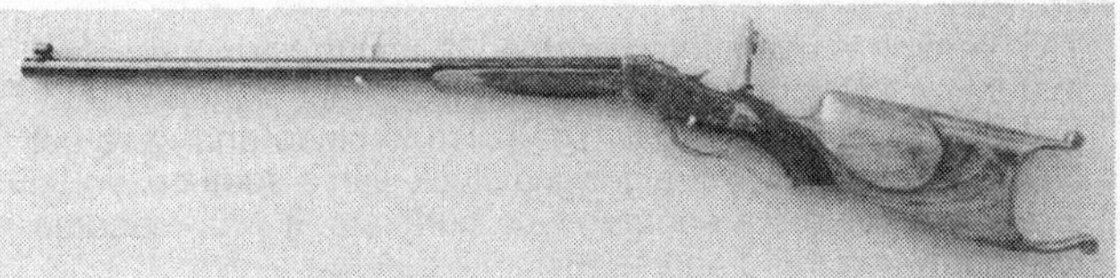

Courtesy J.B. Barnes

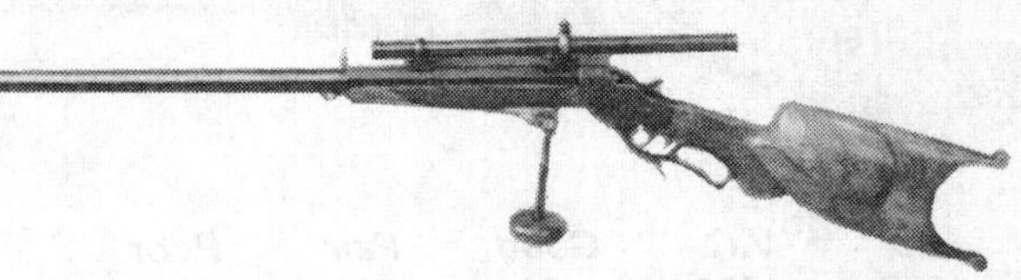

Courtesy J.B. Barnes

Exc.	V.G.	Good	Fair	Poor
11000	8500	5200	2900	1600

No. 53

This model is the same as the No. 51 except for the addition of a fancy wood stock and palm rest. Produced from 1896 to 1902 and offered only with a No. 44 action. This is a rare rifle.

Exc.	V.G.	Good	Fair	Poor
11500	8750	6000	3750	2500

No. 54

This is similar to the No. 52 except that it has double-set triggers and a palm rest, as well as a heavy, Swiss-style buttplate. It is offered with a 30" or 32" part-octagonal heavy barrel. This was Stevens' top-of-the-line rifle. It was offered with many options, and an appraisal should be secured if in doubt. It was manufactured between 1897 and 1916.

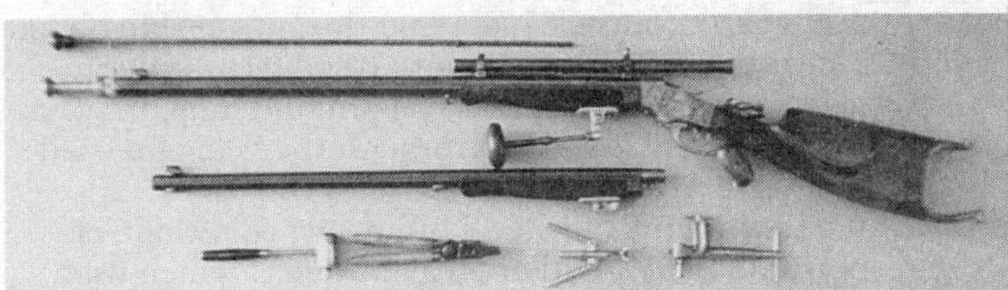

Courtesy J.B. Barnes

Exc.	V.G.	Good	Fair	Poor
15000	13000	9500	7000	5000

NOTE: The above prices are based on a No. 44-1/2 action. A No. 44 action will bring 20 percent less than the prices listed above.

No. 55

This version is one of the Stevens' Ideal Ladies Models. It is chambered for the smaller rimfire calibers between .22 Short and .32 Long rimfire. It features a 24" or 26" part-octagonal barrel with a vernier tang sight. The finish is blued and case-colored, with a checkered pistol grip walnut stock that features a Swiss-type buttplate. This is a lighter weight rifle that was manufactured between 1897 and 1916.

Exc.	V.G.	Good	Fair	Poor
4000	3500	2000	1150	800

No. 56

This Ladies' Model rifle is similar to the No. 55 except that it is chambered for centerfire cartridges and has a higher-grade walnut stock. It was made on the improved No. 44-1/2 action. It was manufactured between 1906 and 1916.

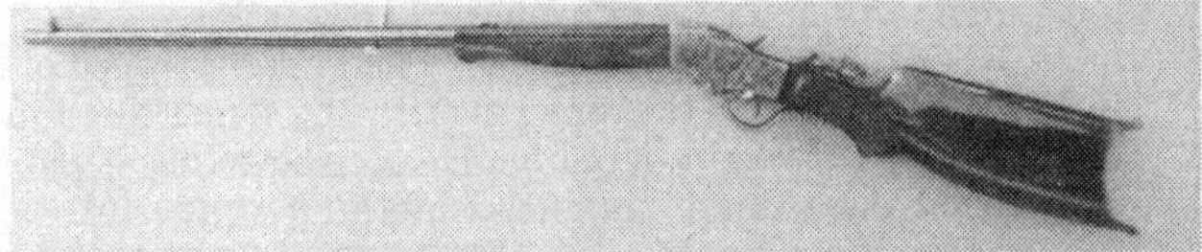

Courtesy J.B. Barnes

Exc.	V.G.	Good	Fair	Poor
4500	3800	2700	1600	900

No. 404

This version is chambered for the .22 rimfire cartridge only. It features a 28" round barrel with a globe front sight and a Lyman No. 42 receiver sight. The finish is blued and case-colored. It has a walnut straight-grip stock with a semi-beavertail forend. It features a shotgun-type buttplate. It was manufactured between 1910 and 1916.

Exc.	V.G.	Good	Fair	Poor
1200	1000	800	700	600

No. 414

This version is also known as the Armory Model and is chambered for the .22 LR cartridge only. It was built on a No. 44 action and features a 26" round barrel. It has a Rocky Mountain front sight with a Lyman receiver sight at the rear. The finish is blued and case-colored, with a straight-grip walnut stock and forend held on by a single barrel band. It was manufactured between 1912 and 1932.

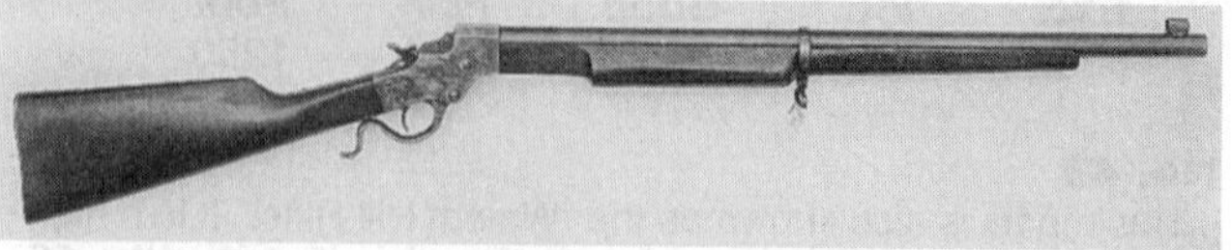

Courtesy Mike Stuckslager

Exc.	V.G.	Good	Fair	Poor
900	700	500	300	275

No. 417 Walnut Hill Model

This is a heavy single-shot, lever action target rifle chambered for the .22 LR, .22 Short, or .22 Hornet cartridges. Weight is approximately 10.5 lbs. Produced from 1932 to 1940.

Exc.	V.G.	Good	Fair	Poor
1500	1200	800	600	400

The Greatest Gunsmith You've Never Heard Of

Dan Shideler

The greatest custom gunsmith you've never heard of lives in Garrett, Indiana.

Richard Clauss, 67, entered the gunsmithing business in a strange way. Others might attend technical school or serve an apprenticeship in a tool-and-die shop, but Clauss became a custom gunsmith through the help of a fried chicken.

It's true. Clauss' father, Phillip, owned a chain of restaurants in nearby Fort Wayne, one of which was legendary throughout the Hoosier State during the baby boom years. In fact, if you lived within 300 miles of Fort Wayne and hadn't heard of the Hobby House, there was something wrong with you. One of the first restaurants in the country to offer Col. Harlan Sanders' Kentucky Fried Chicken, the Hobby House also earned a footnote in history as the training ground of a young busboy named Dave Thomas, who later founded Wendy's.

Thirty years later the Hobby House closed, much to the dismay of everyone who'd ever eaten there. But Clauss was sitting pretty. At last he could realize his ambition of being a full-time woodworker and gunsmith. It was the turning point of his life.

Clauss was then in his 40s. A late start, perhaps, but he quickly made up for lost time. He bought and installed a ton of new equipment – including a Bridgeport milling machine, a Harig surface grinder and a Logan metal lathe, all first-class stuff – and taught himself how to use it. Boy, did he ever.

Since I met Richard a decade ago, I've discovered he has a gift for fabricating parts—even entire guns. Working mostly with battered old single-shot actions (Stevens Favorites are his favorites), Clauss has designed and built some of the durndest things I've ever seen.

Let's imagine Clauss picks up a decrepit, stripped old receiver from an old Stevens Favorite .22, something I might use as a paperweight. Not him. He sees beyond the age, the wear, the abuse, and imagines something wonderful.

First, after consulting his voluminous Stevens reference material, he'll fabricate new innards from hardened tool steel: hammer, extractor, lever, breechblock, firing pin – whatever is needed. Then he'll find a barrel: maybe a .22, maybe not. He might go off the deep end and decide that old Favorite would make a nice single-shot .410 shotgun, so he'll have to thin the inner walls of the receiver to accommodate a wider breechblock. No matter. He has the tools and talent and all the time in the world.

After getting the metalwork squared away, Clauss might send the gun to Mike Sawmiller of Spencerville, Ohio, for engraving, or maybe to Don Menk of New Springfield, Ohio, for color case-hardening. Then he'll go to work on the wood.

I don't know where Clauss gets his magnificent wood. I once examined one of his customized Stevens Favorites that had a rich, deeply burled buttstock that started out as a walnut stairstep from the basement of the Hobby House. I wouldn't have looked twice at an old board in a basement, but then again I'm not Richard Clauss. He sees things.

Finally, when all the components are finished, Clauss builds his rifle. My favorite is his .22 Magnum survival gun. Built on a Favorite action, it has concealed within its lines a 7-inch filet knife, a 5-foot telescoping fishing rod with line, a compass, a lighter, a flashlight, several lures, a pliers/screwdriver combo and 20 rounds of ammunition. This is a hell of a survival gun for sure, but it has one flaw: It's much too pretty to use. In fact, if my float plane flamed out over the Kenai Peninsula and I had only one parachute, I think I'd put the chute on the survival gun and take my chances with the plane.

Clauss' idea of heaven is when someone sends him an old Stevens rifle with bad wood. His two passions converge like some mighty force of nature. He's restored hundreds of Stevens rifles, including an enormous batch from a California collector who sent them to him in groups of four and five. Clauss returned them in factory-new condition.

I asked Clauss how much he charges for such work.

"Gee, y'know," he said sheepishly, rubbing a hand over his close-cropped head, "I guess I get so excited about the work that I forget to charge what I probably should."

He actually said that. And I believe him.

Editor's Note: Richard Clauss can be reached at (260) 637-5401.

No. 417 1/2 Walnut Hill Model

This model is a sporting version of the Model 417. Weight is about 8.5 lbs. Manufactured from 1932 to 1940.

Exc.	V.G.	Good	Fair	Poor
1600	1300	900	700	450

No. 418 Walnut Hill Jr.

This is a light single-shot lever action target rifle chambered for .22 LR or .22 Short. Weight is about 6.5 lbs. Manufactured from 1932 to 1940.

Exc.	V.G.	Good	Fair	Poor
750	600	400	300	175

No. 418 1/2 Walnut Hill Jr.

Similar to the Model 418 but chambered for .25 rimfire or .22 WRF cartridges. It is also fitted with sporting sights. Manufactured from 1932 to 1940.

Exc.	V.G.	Good	Fair	Poor
750	600	400	300	175

BOY'S RIFLES

The Stevens Company produced an extensive line of smaller, single-shot rifles chambered for small calibers and intended primarily for use by young shooters. These firearms have become quite collectible and are considered a field of specialty by many modern collectors.

NOTE: There are many variations that were available with a number of options that would affect their value. We supply information and values for the major variations but would recommend securing a qualified appraisal if in doubt.

"FAVORITE" RIFLES

This series of rifles is chambered for the .22, .25, and .32 rimfire. It has a 22" part-octagonal barrel and is blued, with a case-colored frame. It has a takedown-type action with an interchangeable barrel feature. It was available with optional sights, as well as buttplates. There were approximately 1,000,000 manufactured between 1893 and 1939. The variations are listed.

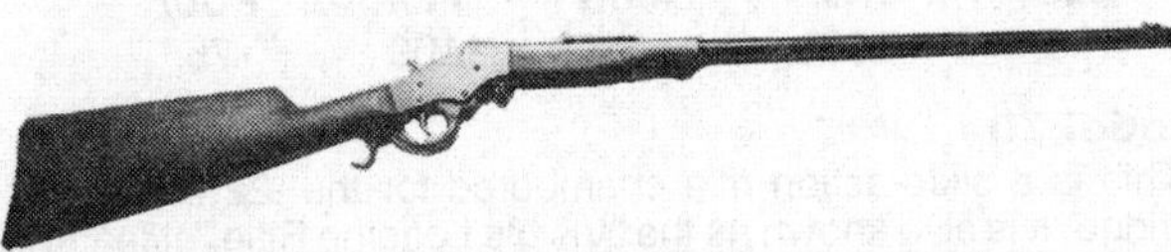

Courtesy Mike Stuckslager

Courtesy Buffalo Bill Historical Center, Cody, Wyoming

1st Model Favorite

This version is chambered for the .22 or .25 rimfire cartridge. It has a removable sideplate on the right side of the receiver not found on any other variation. There were approximately 1,000 manufactured between 1893 and 1894.

Exc.	V.G.	Good	Fair	Poor
1200	800	650	500	350

No. 17

This is the standard, plain version with open sights.

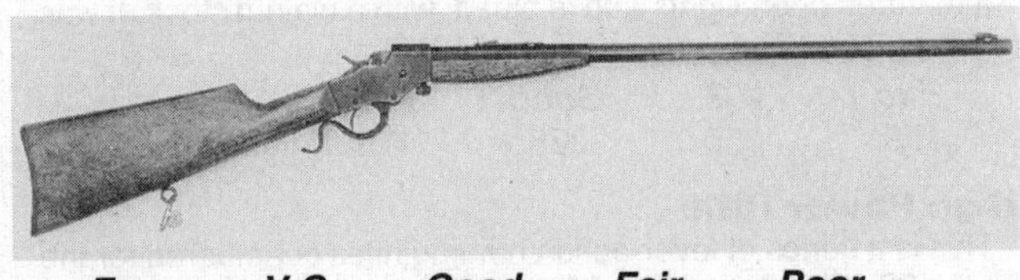

Exc.	V.G.	Good	Fair	Poor
450	300	250	175	125

No. 20

This version is chambered for the .22 or .32 rimfire shot cartridges and has a smoothbore barrel and no rear sight.

Exc.	V.G.	Good	Fair	Poor
500	350	250	175	125

No. 21

This version is known as the Bicycle rifle and features a 20" barrel with open sights standard. It was furnished with a canvas carrying case that would be worth approximately a 30 percent premium. It was manufactured between 1898 and 1903.

Exc.	V.G.	Good	Fair	Poor
550	375	250	150	100

No. 21 Ladies Model

This version bears the same model number as the Bicycle rifle but has a 24" barrel and a high grade, checkered walnut stock with a Swiss buttplate. It features a vernier tang sight. It was manufactured between 1910 and 1916.

Exc.	V.G.	Good	Fair	Poor
4100	3500	2100	1150	700

No. 16

This version is known as the "Crack Shot." It is chambered for .22 or .32 rimfire cartridges with a 20" round barrel. It has a rolling-block-type action with a thumb lever on the side. It is a utility-type rifle with open sights, a blued and case-colored finish, and a plain two-piece walnut stock with a rubber buttplate. The barrel is marked "Crack Shot" along with the standard Stevens' barrel address markings. It was manufactured between 1900 and 1913.

Exc.	V.G.	Good	Fair	Poor
350	250	125	100	75

No. 16-1/2

This version is similar to the No. 16 except that it is chambered for the .32 rimfire shot cartridge with a smoothbore barrel. It was manufactured between 1900 and 1913.

Exc.	V.G.	Good	Fair	Poor
400	300	175	125	100

No. 23—Sure Shot

This version is chambered for the .22 rimfire cartridge. It has a 20" round barrel that pivots to the right for loading. There is a barrel release on the frame. This version is blued and case-colored, with a plain walnut buttstock and no forend. It was manufactured between 1894 and 1897.

Exc.	V.G.	Good	Fair	Poor
2200	1800	1100	850	500

No. 15

This version is also known as the "Maynard Junior." It is chambered for the .22 rimfire cartridge and has an 18" part-octagonal barrel. The action is similar to the Civil War Maynard rifle with a trigger guard-activating lever. The finish is all blued, with a bored-type buttstock and no forearm. The barrel is marked "Stevens Maynard, J. R." in addition to the standard Stevens' barrel address. It was manufactured between 1902 and 1912.

Courtesy Mike Stuckslager

Exc.	V.G.	Good	Fair	Poor
450	350	200	150	100

No. 15-1/2

This is a smoothbore version of the No. 15.

Exc.	V.G.	Good	Fair	Poor
500	400	250	175	125

No. 14

This version is also known as the "Little Scout." It is a utility, takedown rifle that is blued, with a one-piece bored-type stock. It features a rolling-block-type action and was manufactured between 1906 and 1910.

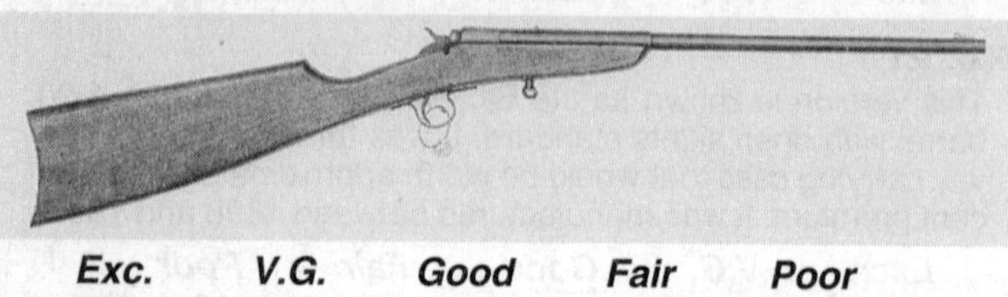

Exc.	V.G.	Good	Fair	Poor
450	350	200	150	100

No. 14-1/2

This version is similar to the No. 14 except that it has a two-piece stock. It is also marked "Little Scout." It was manufactured between 1911 and 1941.

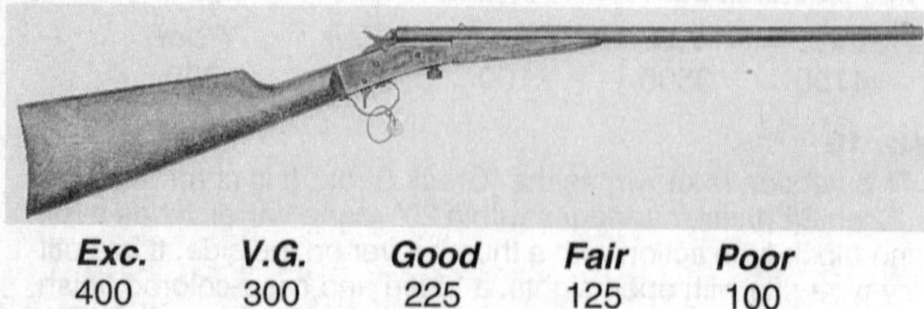

Exc.	V.G.	Good	Fair	Poor
400	300	225	125	100

No. 65

This version is known as the "Little Krag." It is a single-shot bolt-action rifle chambered for the .22 rimfire cartridge. It has a one-piece stock and a 20" round barrel that was marked "Little Krag." This version is quite scarce. It was manufactured between 1903 and 1910.

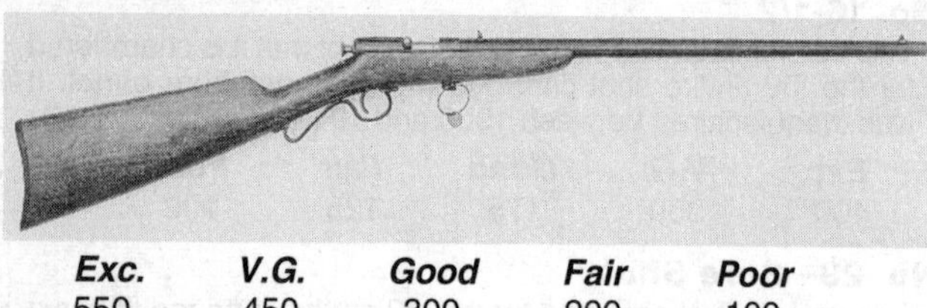

Exc.	V.G.	Good	Fair	Poor
550	450	300	200	100

No. 12

This version is also known as the "Marksman." It is chambered for the .22, .25, and the .32 rimfire cartridges. It has a 22" barrel that pivots upward for loading. It is activated by an S-shaped trigger guard lever. It was manufactured between 1911 and 1930.

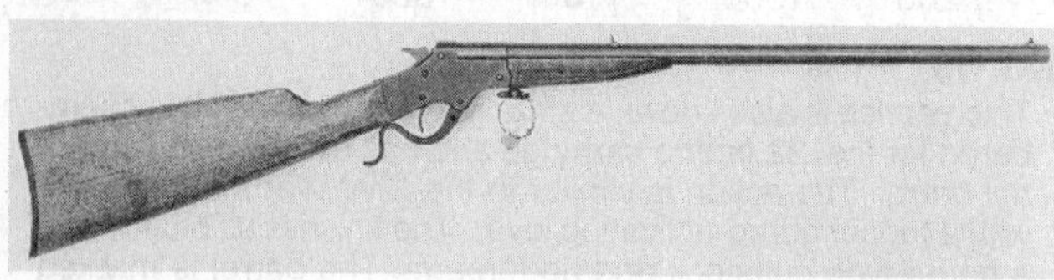

Courtesy Mike Stuckslager

Exc.	V.G.	Good	Fair	Poor
400	350	250	200	150

No. 26

This version is also known as the "Crack Shot." It has a rolling block-type action and is chambered for .22 or the .32 rimfire cartridges. It is offered with an 18" or 20" round barrel. It is blued and has a two-piece stock. It was manufactured between 1912 and 1939.

Courtesy Mike Stuckslager

Exc.	V.G.	Good	Fair	Poor
400	350	225	175	100

No. 26-1/2

This is the smoothbore version of the No. 26.

Exc.	V.G.	Good	Fair	Poor
425	375	250	175	100

No. 11—Junior

This is a single-shot, rolling block rifle chambered for the .22 rimfire cartridge. It has a 20" barrel, is blued, and has a bore-type stock without a buttplate. This was the last model offered in the Boy's Rifle series. It was manufactured between 1924 and 1931.

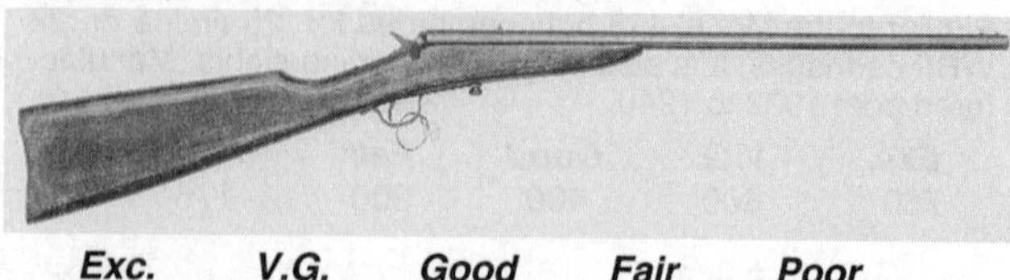

Exc.	V.G.	Good	Fair	Poor
350	300	175	100	75

Model 71

This was a reintroduced version of the "Stevens Favorite." It is chambered for the .22 LR cartridge and has a 22" octagonal barrel. The finish is blued and case-colored, with a plain walnut stock that has an inlaid medallion and a crescent buttplate. There were 10,000 manufactured in 1971.

Exc.	V.G.	Good	Fair	Poor
350	275	175	100	75

Model 72

This is a reintroduced version of the "Crack Shot" that features a single-shot, falling block action. It is chambered for the .22 rimfire cartridge and has a 22" octagon barrel with open sights. It is blued and case-colored, with a straight walnut stock. It was introduced in 1972.

Exc.	V.G.	Good	Fair	Poor
175	150	125	100	75

Model 70

This is a slide-action rifle chambered for the .22 rimfire cartridge. It is also known as the "Visible Loading Rifle." It features a 20" round barrel with a 3/4-length, tubular magazine. The finish is blued and case-colored, and it has a walnut stock. It features open sights but was available with other options. It was offered as the No. 70-1/2, 71, 71-1/2, 72, and 72-1/2. These different model numbers denote various sight combinations. Otherwise, they are identical. They were manufactured between 1907 and 1932.

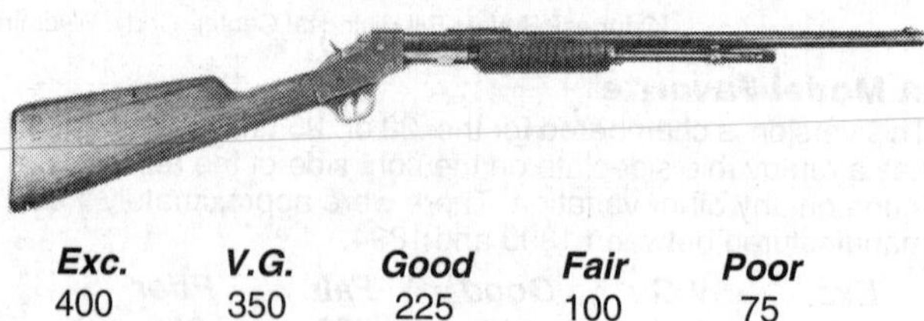

Exc.	V.G.	Good	Fair	Poor
400	350	225	100	75

No. 80

This is a slide-action repeating rifle chambered for the .22 rimfire cartridge. It has a 24" round barrel with a tubular magazine. It features open sights and is blued, with a walnut stock. It was manufactured between 1906 and 1910.

Exc.	V.G.	Good	Fair	Poor
450	350	225	175	100

High Power Rifle

This is a series of lever-action hunting rifles chambered for the .25, .30-30, .32, and the .35 centerfire cartridges. It features a 22" round barrel with a tubular magazine. The finish is blued, with a walnut stock. It is available in four variations: the No. 425, No. 430, No. 435, and the No. 440. These designations denote increased ornamentation and high quality materials and workmanship used in construction. There were approximately 26,000 manufactured between 1910 and 1917.

No. 425

Exc.	*V.G.*	*Good*	*Fair*	*Poor*
800	700	500	300	200

No. 430

Exc.	*V.G.*	*Good*	*Fair*	*Poor*
950	750	650	400	300

No. 435

Exc.	*V.G.*	*Good*	*Fair*	*Poor*
1600	1300	1000	600	400

No. 440

Exc.	*V.G.*	*Good*	*Fair*	*Poor*
3100	2800	2400	1600	850

Beginning in 1869 the Stevens Company produced a series of single-shot, break-open target and sporting pistols that pivot upward for loading. They are chambered for the .22 and the .25 rimfire cartridges, as well as various centerfire cartridges from the .32 Short Colt to the .44 Russian. These pistols were made with various barrel lengths and have either a spur trigger or conventional trigger with a guard. They are all single-actions with exposed hammers. The finishes are nickel-plated frames with blued barrels and walnut grips. These variations and their values are listed.

Six-inch Pocket Rifle

This version is chambered for the .22 rimfire cartridge and has a 6" part-octagonal barrel with open sights. The barrel is marked "J. Stevens & Co. Chicopee Falls, Mass." There were approximately 1,000 manufactured between 1869 and 1886.

Exc.	*V.G.*	*Good*	*Fair*	*Poor*
500	400	350	200	100

No. 36

This version is known as the Stevens-Lord pistol. It is chambered for various rimfire and centerfire calibers up to .44 Russian. It is offered with a 10" or 12" part-octagonal barrel and features a firing pin in the frame with a bushing. It has a conventional trigger with a spurred trigger guard. It features the standard Stevens barrel address. It was named after Frank Lord, a target shooter well-known at this time. There were approximately 3,500 manufactured from 1880 to 1911.

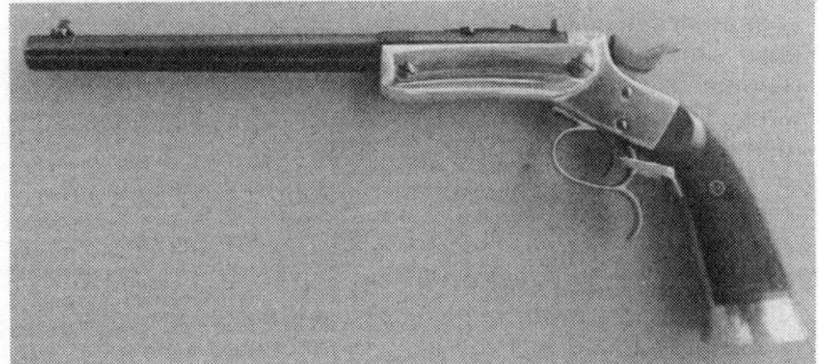

Courtesy J.B. Barnes

Exc.	*V.G.*	*Good*	*Fair*	*Poor*
1600	1300	950	650	400

First Issue Stevens-Conlin

This version is chambered for the .22 or.32 rimfire cartridges. It has a 10" or 12" part-octagonal barrel. It features a plated brass frame with a blued barrel and checkered walnut grips with a weighted buttcap. This version has a spur trigger either with or without a trigger guard. It was named after James Conlin, the owner of a shooting gallery located in New York City. There were approximately 500 manufactured between 1880 and 1884.

Courtesy J.B. Barnes

Exc.	*V.G.*	*Good*	*Fair*	*Poor*
2500	2100	1600	900	500

Second Issue Stevens-Conlin No. 38

This version is similar to the First Issue, with a conventional trigger and spurred trigger guard, as well as a fully adjustable rear sight. There were approximately 6,000 manufactured between 1884 and 1903.

Exc.	*V.G.*	*Good*	*Fair*	*Poor*
1700	1500	1200	800	450

No. 37

This version is also known as the Stevens-Gould and was named after a 19th century firearms writer. It resembles the No. 38 without the spur on the trigger guard. There were approximately 1,000 manufactured between 1889 and 1903.

Courtesy J.B. Barnes

Exc.	*V.G.*	*Good*	*Fair*	*Poor*
1900	1700	1300	850	450

No. 35

This version is chambered for the .22 rimfire, the .22 Stevens-Pope, and the .25 Stevens cartridges. It is offered with a 6", 8", 10", or 12.25" part-octagonal barrel. The firing pin has no bushing. It features an iron frame that is either blued or plated with a blued barrel. It has plain walnut grips with a weighted buttcap. It featured open sights. There were approximately 43,000 manufactured between 1923 and 1942.

Exc.	*V.G.*	*Good*	*Fair*	*Poor*
450	325	275	175	100

NOTE: Longer barrels worth a premium.

No. 35 Target

This version is similar to the No. 35 but has a better quality trigger guard and sights. There were approximately 35,000 manufactured between 1907 and 1916.

Exc.	*V.G.*	*Good*	*Fair*	*Poor*
500	400	325	200	100

STEVENS NO. 35 OFF-HAND SHOT GUN NFA, CURIO OR RELIC

Stevens No. 35 Auto-Shot

The Stevens No. 35 is a .410 bore pistol manufactured by the J. Stevens Arms Co., Chicopee Falls, Massachusetts. It was available with an 8" or 12.25" smoothbore barrel, for 2.5" shells only, in two variations: the **Off-Hand Shot Gun** (1923 to 1929) and the **Auto-Shot** (1929 to 1934). Total production is unknown because the .410 and .22 rimfire variations of the No. 35 share the same serial number range. Researcher Ken Cope estimates total Auto-Shot production was approximately 2,000, and Off-Hand production at 20,000 to 25,000. Production was halted after the government ruled the .410 Stevens to be a "firearm" in the "any other weapon" category under the NFA in 1934, when its retail price was about $12. The Stevens does not possess the same collector appeal as other .410 smoothbore pistols, because (1) its relatively light weight makes it an uncomfortable shooter, and (2) the gun is not well made.

Off-Hand Shot Gun

Serial range from 1 to 43357.

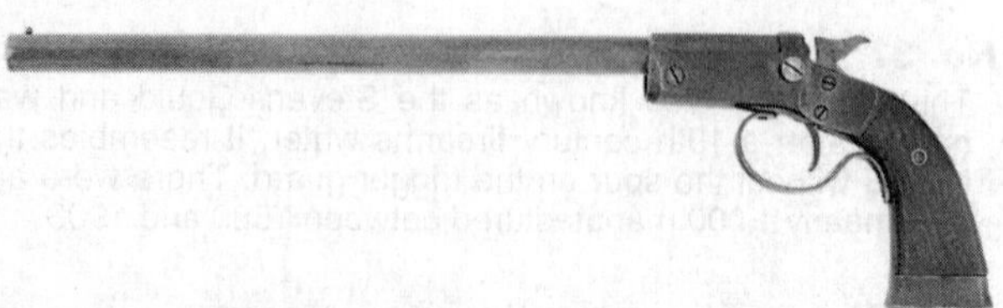

Courtesy John J. Stimson, Jr.

Exc.	V.G.	Good	Fair	Poor
400	250	200	100	75

Auto-Shot

Exc.	V.G.	Good	Fair	Poor
450	300	200	125	100

NOTE: 8" barrel commands a 25 to 50 percent premium.

No. 43

This version is also called the Diamond and was produced in two distinct variations called the First Issue and the Second Issue. The First Issue has a brass frame; and the Second Issue, an iron frame and no firing pin bushing. Otherwise they are quite similar and would be valued the same. They are chambered for the .22 rimfire cartridge and are offered with either a 6" or 10" part-octagonal barrel. The frames are either nickel-plated or blued with blued barrels and square-butt walnut grips. There were approximately 95,000 manufactured between 1886 and 1916.

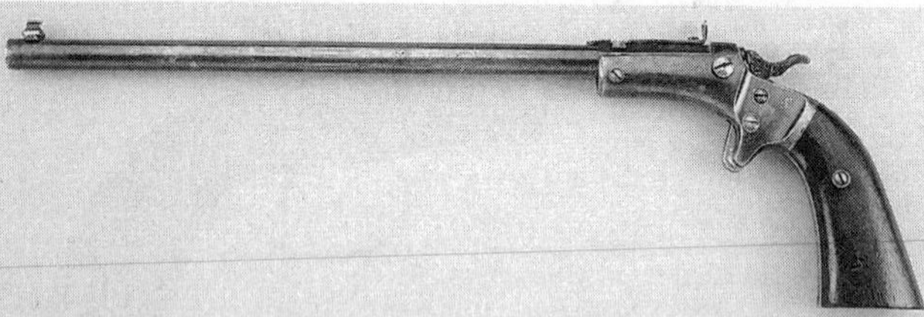

Paul Goodwin photo

Exc.	V.G.	Good	Fair	Poor
400	300	250	150	75

NOTE: Add a 25 percent premium for 10" barrels.

No. 10 Target Pistol

This version was a departure from its predecessors. It very much resembles a semi-automatic pistol but is, in reality, a single-shot. It is chambered for the .22 rimfire cartridge and has an 8" round barrel that pivots upward for loading. It has a steel frame and is blued, with checkered rubber grips. Instead of the usual exposed hammer, this version has a knurled cocking piece that extends through the rear of the frame. There were approximately 7,000 manufactured between 1919 and 1933.

Courtesy John J. Stimson, Jr.

Exc.	V.G.	Good	Fair	Poor
400	300	200	150	100

POCKET RIFLES

This series of pistols is similar to the target and sporting pistols except that these were produced with detachable shoulder stocks that bear the same serial number as the pistol with which they were sold. They are sometimes referred to as Bicycle rifles. The collector interest in these weapons is quite high; but it would behoove one to be familiar with the provisions of the Gun Control Act of 1968 when dealing in or collecting this variation—as when the stock is attached, they can fall into the category of a short-barreled rifle. Some are considered to be curios and relics, and others have been totally declassified; but some models may still be restricted. We strongly recommend securing a qualified, individual appraisal on these highly collectible firearms if a transaction is contemplated.

NOTE: The values supplied include the matching shoulder stock. If the stock number does not match the pistol, the values would be approximately 25 percent less; and with no stock at all, 50 percent should be deducted.

Old Model Pocket Rifle

This version is chambered for the .22 rimfire cartridge and has an 8" or 10" part-octagonal barrel. It has a spur trigger and an external hammer on which the firing pin is mounted. The extractor is spring-loaded. It has a plated brass frame, blued barrel, and either walnut or rosewood grips. The shoulder stock is either nickel-plated or black. The barrel is marked "J. Stevens & Co. Chicopee Falls, Mass." There were approximately 4,000 manufactured between 1869 and 1886.

Exc.	V.G.	Good	Fair	Poor
900	700	550	325	200

Reliable Pocket Rifle

This version is chambered for the .22 rimfire cartridge and in appearance is quite similar to the Old Model. The basic difference is that the extractor operates as a part of the pivoting barrel mechanism instead of being spring-loaded. The barrel is marked "J. Stevens A&T Co." There were approximately 4,000 manufactured between 1886 and 1896.

Exc.	V.G.	Good	Fair	Poor
800	625	500	400	300

No. 42 Reliable Pocket Rifle

This version is similar to the first issue Reliable except that it has an iron frame with the firing pin mounted in it without a bushing. The shoulder stock is shaped differently. There were approximately 8,000 manufactured between 1896 and 1916.

Exc.	V.G.	Good	Fair	Poor
700	575	475	350	250

First Issue New Model Pocket Rifle

This version is the first of the medium-frame models with a frame width of 1". All of its predecessors have a 5/8" wide frame. This model is chambered for the .22 and .32 rimfire cartridges and is offered with barrel lengths of 10", 12", 15", or 18" that are part-octagonal in configuration. The external hammer has the firing pin mounted on it. It has a plated brass frame, blued barrel, and either walnut or rosewood grips. The shoulder stock is nickel-plated and fitted differently than the small-frame models in that there is a dovetail in the butt and the top leg is secured by a knurled screw. The barrel is marked "J. Stevens & Co. Chicopee Falls, Mass." There were approximately 8,000 manufactured between 1872 and 1875.

Courtesy Mike Stuckslager

Exc.	V.G.	Good	Fair	Poor
1000	900	650	500	400

Second Issue New Model Pocket Rifle

This version is similar to the First Issue except that the firing pin is mounted in the frame with a bushing. There were approximately 15,000 manufactured between 1875 and 1896.

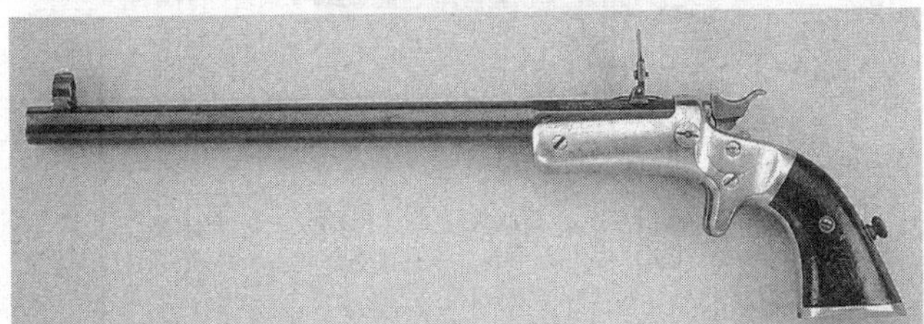

Paul Goodwin photo

Exc.	V.G.	Good	Fair	Poor
900	800	600	500	350

Vernier Model

This version is similar to the Second Issue except that it features a vernier tang sight located on the back strap. There were approximately 1,500 manufactured between 1884 and 1896.

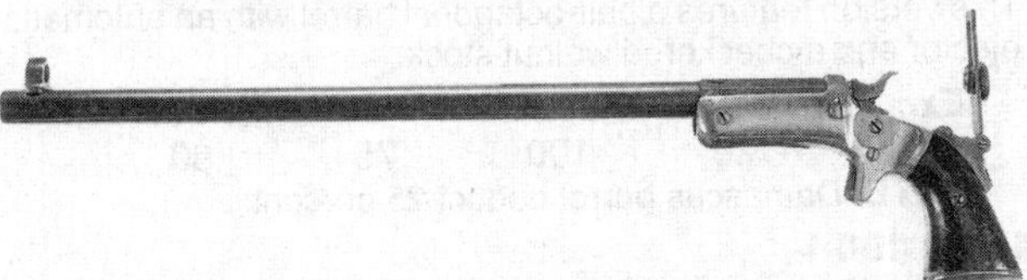

Courtesy Rock Island Auction Company

Exc.	V.G.	Good	Fair	Poor
1100	800	650	525	300

No. 40

This version is similar to its medium-frame predecessors except that it has a longer grip frame and a conventional trigger with trigger guard. There were approximately 15,000 manufactured between 1896 and 1916.

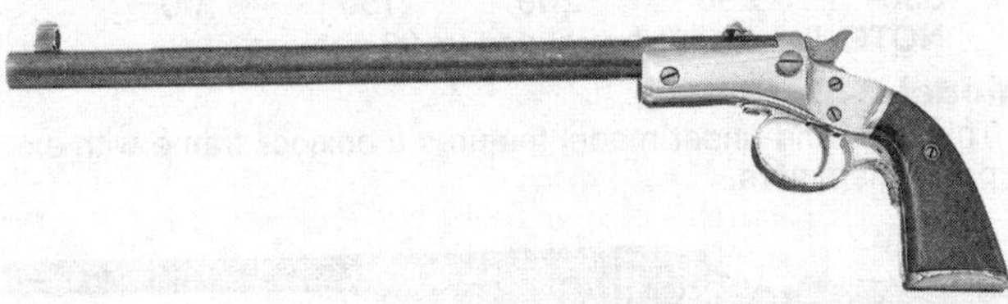

Courtesy Rock Island Auction Company

Exc.	V.G.	Good	Fair	Poor
900	800	650	400	300

No. 40-1/2

This version is similar to the No. 40, with a vernier tang sight mounted on the back strap. There were approximately 2,500 manufactured between 1896 and 1915.

Exc.	V.G.	Good	Fair	Poor
1000	900	700	550	400

No. 34 (Hunter's Pet)

This is the first of the heavy-frame pocket rifles that featured a 1.25" wide frame. This version is also known as the "Hunter's Pet." It is chambered for many popular cartridges from the .22 rimfire to the .44-40 centerfire. It is offered with a part-octagonal 18", 20", 22", or 24" barrel. It has a nickel-plated iron frame and blued barrel. The detachable stock is nickel-plated, and the grips are walnut. There were few produced with a brass frame; and if located, these would be worth twice the value indicated. The firing pin is mounted in the frame with the bushing, and it features a spur trigger. There were approximately 4,000 manufactured between 1872 and 1900.

Exc.	V.G.	Good	Fair	Poor
1150	1000	700	450	350

No. 34-1/2

This version is similar to the No. 34 except that it features a vernier tang sight mounted on the back strap. There were approximately 1,200 manufactured between 1884 and 1900.

Exc.	V.G.	Good	Fair	Poor
1300	1150	900	650	450

STEVENS BOLT-ACTION UTILITY RIFLES

The Stevens Company produced a number of inexpensive, utilitarian, bolt-action rifles. These were both single-shot and repeaters. They have been popular over the years as starter rifles for young shooters. Their values are quite similar, and they are listed for reference purposes only.

Model 053—Single-Shot
Model 066—Tube Magazine
Model 084—5-Shot Magazine
Model 15—Single-Shot
Model 419—Single-Shot
Model 49—Single-Shot
Model 51—Single-Shot
Model 53—Single-Shot
Model 66—Tube Magazine
Model 056—5-Shot Magazine
Model 083—Single-Shot
Model 086—Tube Magazine
Model 15Y—Single-Shot
Model 48—Single-Shot
Model 50—Single-Shot
Model 52—Single-Shot
Model 56—5-Shot Magazine

Exc.	V.G.	Good	Fair	Poor
—	200	100	70	50

Model 416

This is a target rifle chambered for the .22 LR cartridge. It has a 24" heavy barrel with aperture sights. It features a 5-round detachable magazine and is blued, with a target-type walnut stock.

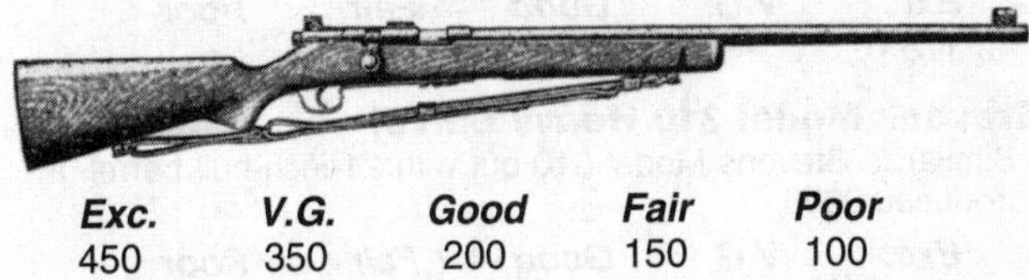

Exc.	V.G.	Good	Fair	Poor
450	350	200	150	100

Model 322

This is a bolt-action sporting rifle chambered for the .22 Hornet cartridge. It has a 20" barrel with open sights and a detachable box magazine. The finish is blued, with a plain walnut stock.

Exc.	V.G.	Good	Fair	Poor
175	125	100	75	50

Model 322-S

This version features an aperture rear sight.

Exc.	V.G.	Good	Fair	Poor
225	125	100	75	50

Model 89

This is a single-shot, Martini-type, falling-block rifle chambered for the .22 LR cartridge. It has an 18.5" barrel and a trigger guard loop-lever activator. The finish is blued, with a straight walnut stock. It was introduced in 1976 and is no longer manufactured.

Exc.	V.G.	Good	Fair	Poor
125	80	70	60	40

Model 87M

Designed to look like the M1 Garand this rifle was chambered for the .22 rimfire cartridge.

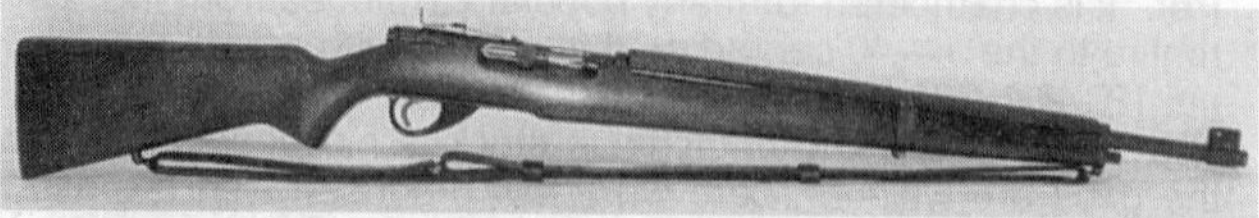

Courtesy Richard M. Kumor, Sr.

Exc.	V.G.	Good	Fair	Poor
600	500	375	—	—

Model 987

This is a blowback-operated semi-automatic rifle chambered for the .22 LR cartridge. It has a 20" barrel with a 15-round tubular magazine. The finish is blued, with a hardwood stock.

Exc.	V.G.	Good	Fair	Poor
150	100	75	50	25

STEVENS ECONOMY LINE (SAVAGE, 2006)

Stevens Model 200

Long- or short-action bolt rifle chambered in .223, .22-250, .243, 7MM-08, .308, .25-06, .270, .30-06, 7mm RM, or .300 WM. Gray checkered synthetic stock and 22-inch (short-action) or 24-inch (long-action) blued sightless barrel. Introduced 2006.

Exc.	V.G.	Good	Fair	Poor
285	—	—	—	—

Stevens Cadet Mini-Youth

Similar to Savage Cub .22 rimfire. Introduced 2006.

Exc.	V.G.	Good	Fair	Poor
150	—	—	—	—

Stevens Model 315 Youth

Similar to Cadet Mini-Youth but with sightless barrel. Introduced 2006.

Exc.	V.G.	Good	Fair	Poor
150	—	—	—	—

Stevens Model 310

Five-shot bolt-action repeater chambered for .17 HMR. Detachable box magazine, synthetic stock, blued 20.75-inch sightless barrel. Introduced 2006.

Exc.	V.G.	Good	Fair	Poor
175	—	—	—	—

Stevens Model 310 Heavy Barrel

Similar to Stevens Model 310 but with 21-inch bull barrel. Introduced 2006.

Exc.	V.G.	Good	Fair	Poor
195	—	—	—	—

Stevens Model 300

Clip-fed bolt-action repeater chambered for .22 rimfire. Gray synthetic stock and 20.75-inch blued barrel. Also available with scope package (add 10 percent). Introduced 2006.

Exc.	V.G.	Good	Fair	Poor
145	—	—	—	—

Stevens Model 305

Similar to Model 310 but chambered in .22 WMR. Introduced 2006.

Exc.	V.G.	Good	Fair	Poor
160	—	—	—	—

STEVENS SINGLE-SHOT SHOTGUNS

This company manufactured a number of single barrel, break-open, single-shot shotguns. They were produced chambered for various gauges with various-length barrels and chokes. They are quite similar in appearance and were designed as inexpensive, utility-grade weapons. There is little or no collector interest in them at this time, and their values are similar. They are listed for reference purposes only.

Model 100	Model 125	Model 94
Model 102	Model 140	Model 944
Model 104	Model 160	Model 94A
Model 105	Model 165	Model 94C
Model 106	Model 170	Model 95
Model 107	Model 180	Model 958
Model 108	Model 89	Model 97
Model 110	Model 90	Model 970
Model 120	Model 93	

Model 107

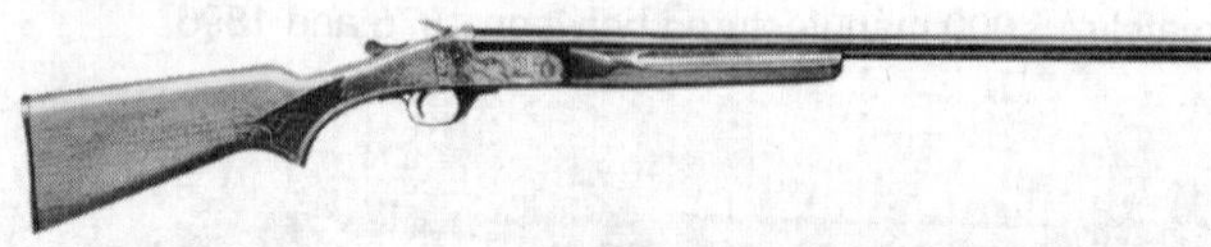

Model 94C

Exc.	V.G.	Good	Fair	Poor
150	100	75	50	25

Model 182

This is a single-shot, break-open shotgun chambered for 12 gauge. It is offered with a 30" or 32" trap choked barrels and features a hammerless action with an automatic ejector and a lightly engraved receiver. The finish is blued, with a checkered trap-grade stock.

Exc.	V.G.	Good	Fair	Poor
175	125	100	75	50

Model 185

This version features a half-octagonal barrel with an automatic ejector and a checkered walnut stock.

Exc.	V.G.	Good	Fair	Poor
175	125	100	75	50

NOTE: Damascus barrel deduct 25 percent.

Model 190

This is a 12-gauge hammerless gun with an automatic ejector. It is lightly engraved with a half-octagonal barrel.

Exc.	V.G.	Good	Fair	Poor
175	125	100	75	50

NOTE: Damascus barrel deduct 25 percent.

Model 195

This is another deluxe version that features engraving, a half-octagonal barrel, and a high-grade, checkered walnut stock.

Exc.	V.G.	Good	Fair	Poor
350	250	200	150	100

NOTE: Damascus barrel deduct 25 percent.

Model 240

This over-and-under model features a boxlock frame with exposed hammers.

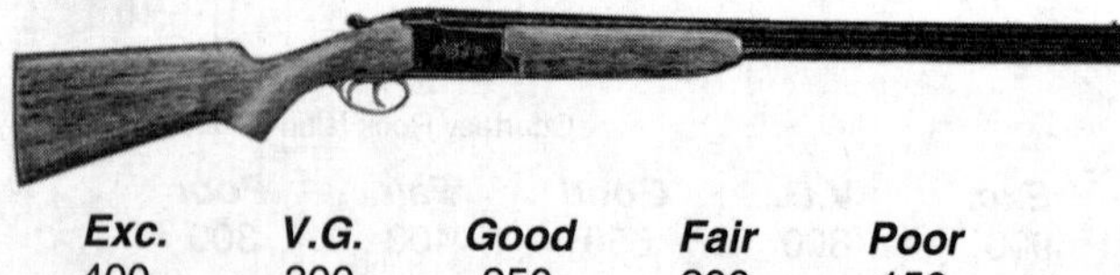

Exc.	V.G.	Good	Fair	Poor
400	300	250	200	150

Model .22/.410

Over/under .22/.410 combo gun with Tenite stock. Manufactured 1939-1950.

Exc.	V.G.	Good	Fair	Poor
350	300	250	175	100

STEVENS DOUBLE-BARREL SHOTGUNS

The firm of J. Stevens and its successors produced a number of utility-grade, side-by-side double-barrel shotguns between 1877 and 1988. They are chambered for 10, 12, 16, or 20 gauge as well as the .410 bore. Stevens shotguns in 10 gauge and .410 bore will normally bring a premium as do guns with single triggers and ejectors. They have various length barrels and choke combinations. They feature double triggers and extractors except where noted. A complete list of Stevens brand models including the three in-house brands: Riverside, Springfield, and Super Value, are listed.

STEVENS BRAND

Model 1877—Hammer Boxlock

NIB	Exc.	V.G.	Good	Fair	Poor
1200	575	450	350	250	200

Model 250—Hammer Sidelock

NIB	Exc.	V.G.	Good	Fair	Poor
1200	575	450	350	250	200

Model 225—Hammer Boxlock

Courtesy Nick Niles, Paul Goodwin photo

NIB	Exc.	V.G.	Good	Fair	Poor
1200	575	450	350	250	200

Model 260—Hammer Sidelock

NIB	Exc.	V.G.	Good	Fair	Poor
1200	575	450	350	250	200

Model 270—Hammer Sidelock

NIB	Exc.	V.G.	Good	Fair	Poor
1200	575	450	350	250	200

Model 280—Hammer Sidelock

NIB	Exc.	V.G.	Good	Fair	Poor
1200	575	450	350	250	200

Model 325—Hammerless Boxlock

NIB	Exc.	V.G.	Good	Fair	Poor
925	450	400	350	250	200

Model 350—Hammerless Boxlock

NIB	Exc.	V.G.	Good	Fair	Poor
925	450	400	350	250	200

Model 360—Hammerless Boxlock

NIB	Exc.	V.G.	Good	Fair	Poor
925	450	400	350	250	200

Model 370—Hammerless Boxlock

NIB	Exc.	V.G.	Good	Fair	Poor
925	450	400	350	250	200

Model 380—Hammerless Boxlock

NIB	Exc.	V.G.	Good	Fair	Poor
1200	575	450	350	250	200

Model 235—Hammer Boxlock

NIB	Exc.	V.G.	Good	Fair	Poor
925	450	400	350	250	200

Model 335 (Early)—Hammerless Boxlock

Courtesy Nick Niles, Paul Goodwin photo

NIB	Exc.	V.G.	Good	Fair	Poor
925	450	400	350	250	200

Model 335 (Late)—Hammerless Boxlock

NIB	Exc.	V.G.	Good	Fair	Poor
925	450	400	350	250	200

Model 255—Hammer Sidelock

NIB	Exc.	V.G.	Good	Fair	Poor
925	450	400	350	250	200

Model 265—Hammer Sidelock

Courtesy Nick Niles, Paul Goodwin photo

NIB	Exc.	V.G.	Good	Fair	Poor
925	450	400	350	250	200

Model 355—Hammerless Boxlock

NIB	Exc.	V.G.	Good	Fair	Poor
1600	800	575	450	350	250

Model 365—Hammerless Boxlock

Courtesy Nick Niles, Paul Goodwin photo

NIB	Exc.	V.G.	Good	Fair	Poor
1850	925	625	500	400	300

Model 375 (London Proofs)—Hammerless Boxlock

NIB	Exc.	V.G.	Good	Fair	Poor
2750	1500	950	700	450	350

Model 375 (U.S.)—Hammerless Boxlock

NIB	Exc.	V.G.	Good	Fair	Poor
2000	1100	700	575	400	300

Model 385 (London Proofs)—Hammerless Boxlock

NIB	Exc.	V.G.	Good	Fair	Poor
3250	1650	1050	700	450	350

Model 385 (U.S.)—Hammerless Boxlock

NIB	Exc.	V.G.	Good	Fair	Poor
2350	1200	850	575	450	300

Model 345—Hammerless Boxlock

Courtesy Nick Niles, Paul Goodwin photo

NIB	Exc.	V.G.	Good	Fair	Poor
1200	575	450	350	250	200

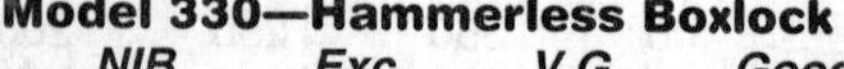

Model 330—Hammerless Boxlock

NIB	Exc.	V.G.	Good	Fair	Poor
925	450	400	350	250	200

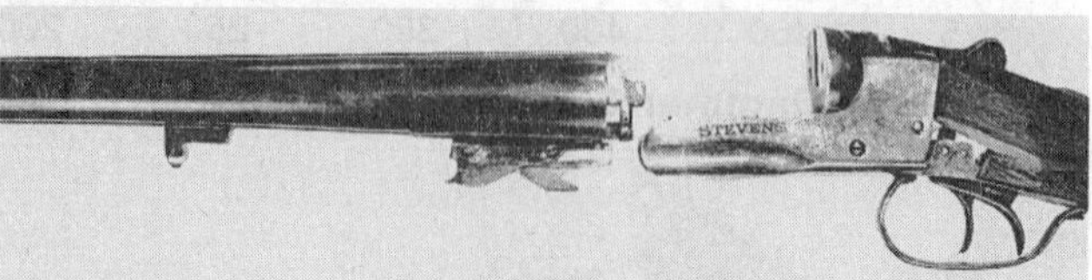

Stevens Model 330 early fork-type cocking lever

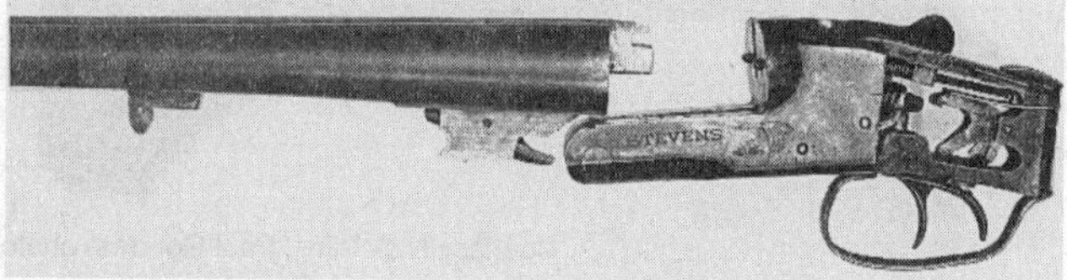

Stevens Model 330 late spade-type cocking lever

Model 515—Hammerless Boxlock

NIB	Exc.	V.G.	Good	Fair	Poor
1250	625	525	450	350	300

Model 515—Single Trigger Hammerless Boxlock

NIB	Exc.	V.G.	Good	Fair	Poor
1400	750	575	450	350	300

Model 500—Skeet Hammerless Boxlock

Courtesy Nick Niles, Paul Goodwin photo

NIB	Exc.	V.G.	Good	Fair	Poor
2300	1250	925	800	700	400

Model 530—Hammerless Boxlock

NIB	Exc.	V.G.	Good	Fair	Poor
925	450	400	350	250	200

Model 530M—Tenite Hammerless Boxlock

NIB	Exc.	V.G.	Good	Fair	Poor
925	450	400	350	250	200

Model 530M—Tenite Single Trigger Hammerless Boxlock

NIB	Exc.	V.G.	Good	Fair	Poor
1400	750	575	450	350	300

Model 530A—Hammerless Boxlock

Courtesy Nick Niles, Paul Goodwin photo

NIB	Exc.	V.G.	Good	Fair	Poor
925	450	400	350	250	200

Model 530A—Single Trigger Hammerless Boxlock

NIB	Exc.	V.G.	Good	Fair	Poor
1100	525	450	350	300	250

Model 311—Tenite Hammerless Boxlock

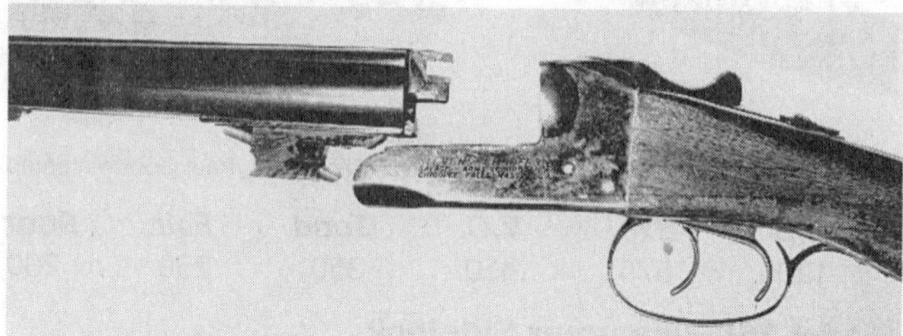

Stevens Model 311 Courtesy Nick Niles

NIB	Exc.	V.G.	Good	Fair	Poor
925	450	400	350	250	200

Model 331—Single Trigger Hammerless Boxlock

NIB	Exc.	V.G.	Good	Fair	Poor
1100	525	400	300	250	200

Model 311—Tenite Single Trigger Hammerless Boxlock

NIB	Exc.	V.G.	Good	Fair	Poor
1200	575	500	450	350	300

Model 311A—Hammerless Boxlock

NIB	Exc.	V.G.	Good	Fair	Poor
925	525	450	350	250	200

Model 311C—Hammerless Boxlock

Courtesy Nick Niles, Paul Goodwin photo

NIB	Exc.	V.G.	Good	Fair	Poor
800	400	350	250	200	150

Model 311D—Hammerless Boxlock

Courtesy Nick Niles, Paul Goodwin photo

NIB	Exc.	V.G.	Good	Fair	Poor
925	450	400	350	250	200

Model 311E—Hammerless Boxlock

NIB	Exc.	V.G.	Good	Fair	Poor
1250	600	450	400	300	250

Model 311F—Hammerless Boxlock

NIB	Exc.	V.G.	Good	Fair	Poor
925	450	400	350	250	200

Model 311H—Hammerless Boxlock

NIB	Exc.	V.G.	Good	Fair	Poor
925	450	400	350	250	200

Model 311H—Vent Rib Hammerless Boxlock

Courtesy Nick Niles, Paul Goodwin photo

NIB	Exc.	V.G.	Good	Fair	Poor
1050	500	450	350	300	250

Model 311J/R—Hammerless Boxlock

Courtesy Nick Niles, Paul Goodwin photo

NIB	Exc.	V.G.	Good	Fair	Poor
800	400	350	250	200	150

Model 311J/R—Solid Rib Hammerless Boxlock

NIB	Exc.	V.G.	Good	Fair	Poor
800	400	350	250	200	150

Model 311H—Waterfowler Hammerless Boxlock

NIB	Exc.	V.G.	Good	Fair	Poor
1400	700	575	450	350	250

Model 240—.410 Over-and-Under Hammer Tenite

NIB	Exc.	V.G.	Good	Fair	Poor
700	575	450	350	250	200

RIVERSIDE BRAND

Model 215—Hammer Boxlock

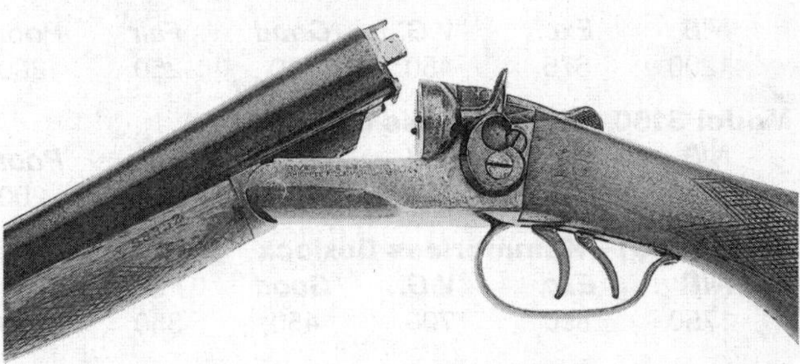

Courtesy Nick Niles, Paul Goodwin photo

NIB	Exc.	V.G.	Good	Fair	Poor
1500	750	525	400	250	200

Model 315 (Early)—Hammerless Boxlock

NIB	Exc.	V.G.	Good	Fair	Poor
1200	575	450	350	250	200

Model 315 (Late)—Hammerless Boxlock

NIB	Exc.	V.G.	Good	Fair	Poor
1200	575	450	350	250	200

SUPER VALUE BRAND

Model 511—Hammerless Boxlock

NIB	Exc.	V.G.	Good	Fair	Poor
1050	525	400	300	200	150

Model 511—Sunken Rib Hammerless Boxlock

NIB	Exc.	V.G.	Good	Fair	Poor
925	575	450	350	200	150

SPRINGFIELD BRAND

Model 215—Hammer Boxlock

NIB	Exc.	V.G.	Good	Fair	Poor
1200	575	450	350	250	150

Model 311—Hammerless Boxlock

Courtesy Nick Niles, Paul Goodwin photo

NIB	Exc.	V.G.	Good	Fair	Poor
925	575	450	350	250	150

Model 315—Hammerless Boxlock

Courtesy Nick Niles, Paul Goodwin photo

NIB	Exc.	V.G.	Good	Fair	Poor
1200	575	450	350	250	200

Model 3150—Hammerless Boxlock

NIB	Exc.	V.G.	Good	Fair	Poor
1400	700	575	400	250	200

Model 3151—Hammerless Boxlock

NIB	Exc.	V.G.	Good	Fair	Poor
1750	850	700	450	350	250

Model 3151—Single Trigger Hammerless Boxlock

NIB	Exc.	V.G.	Good	Fair	Poor
1850	950	800	575	450	300

Model 311—Single Trigger Hammerless Boxlock

NIB	Exc.	V.G.	Good	Fair	Poor
1600	800	700	575	450	300

Model 5151—Hammerless Boxlock

Courtesy Nick Niles, Paul Goodwin photo

NIB	Exc.	V.G.	Good	Fair	Poor
1200	575	450	350	250	200

Model 5151—Single Trigger Hammerless Boxlock

NIB	Exc.	V.G.	Good	Fair	Poor
1400	700	525	400	300	200

Model 311—New Style Hammerless Boxlock

Courtesy Nick Niles, Paul Goodwin photo

NIB	Exc.	V.G.	Good	Fair	Poor
925	575	450	350	250	150

Model 311—New Style Tenite Hammerless Boxlock

NIB	Exc.	V.G.	Good	Fair	Poor
925	575	450	350	250	150

Model 511—Sunken Rib Hammerless Boxlock

NIB	Exc.	V.G.	Good	Fair	Poor
925	575	450	350	250	150

Model 511—Hammerless Boxlock

NIB	Exc.	V.G.	Good	Fair	Poor
1050	525	400	300	200	150

Model 511A—Hammerless Boxlock

NIB	Exc.	V.G.	Good	Fair	Poor
1050	525	400	300	200	150

STEVENS/SAVAGE SHOTGUNS

Model 411 Upland Sporter

Introduced in 2003 this side-by-side shotgun is chambered for the 12 or 20 gauge, as well as the .410 bore. The 12 gauge is fitted with 28" barrels, while the 28 and .410 have 26" barrels. Single trigger with ejectors. False sideplates are laser engraved. European walnut stock with pistol grip and splinter forend. Weight is about 6.75 to 6.5 lbs. depending on gauge.

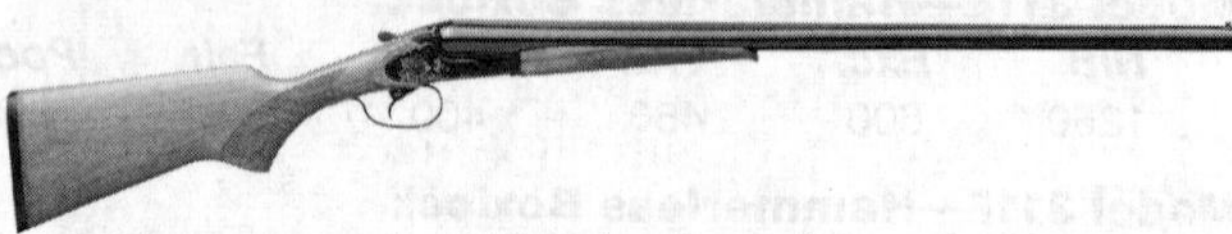

NIB	Exc.	V.G.	Good	Fair	Poor
395	325	—	—	—	—

NOTE: Add $35 for 20 and .410 models.

STEVENS DATE CODE

Collectors will find a date code stamped on every double-barrel shotgun in the Stevens brands produced between March 1949 and December 1968. Usually, it is behind the hinge pin or ahead of the trigger guard on the bottom of the frame. It will appear as a small circle containing a number and letter. The letters correspond to the years shown in the following table. Significance of the numbers is not known.

DATE CODES			
A-1949	B-1950	C-1951	D-1952
E-1953	F-1954	G-1955	H-1956
I-1957	J-1958	K-1959	L-1960
M-1961	N-1962	P-1963	R-1964
S-1965	T-1966	U-1967	V-1968
W-1969	X-1970		

STEVENS BOLT-ACTION SHOTGUNS

The Stevens Company produced a number of bolt-action shotguns that are either single-shot or repeaters. They are chambered for the 20 gauge or .410 and are blued, with walnut stocks. The values for these utility-grade shotguns are similar.

Model 237—Single-Shot
Model 258—Clip Fed
Model 37—Single-Shot
Model 38—Clip Fed
Model 39—Tube Magazine
Model 58—Clip Fed
Model 59—Tube Magazine

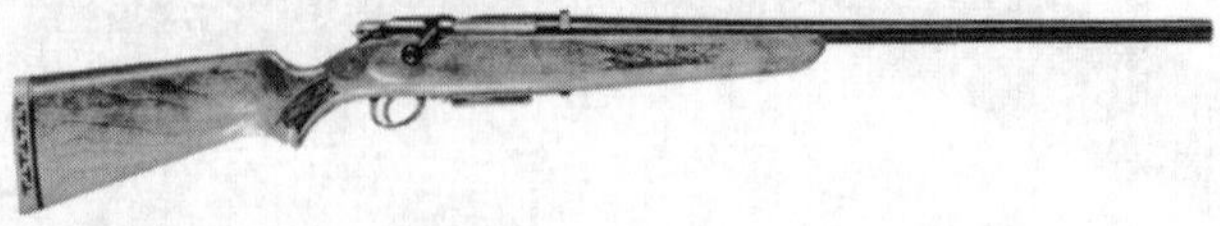

Model 58

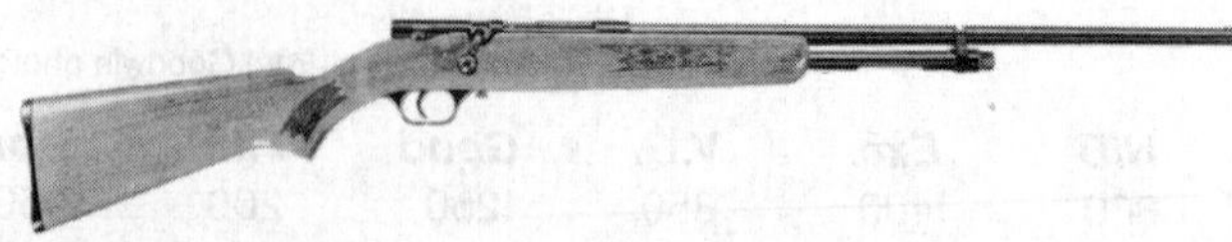

Model 59

Exc.	V.G.	Good	Fair	Poor
125	100	75	50	35

STEVENS SLIDE-ACTION UTILITY-GRADE SHOTGUNS

The J. Stevens Arms Company also produced a series of utility-grade slide-action shotguns. They are chambered for various gauges with various barrel lengths and chokes. The finishes are blued, with walnut stocks. The values are similar, and are listed for reference purposes are listed.

Model 520	**Model 67**	**Model 77-AC**
Model 522	**Model 67-VR**	**Model 77-M**
Model 620	**Model 77**	**Model 820**
Model 621	**Model 77-SC**	

Model 67

Exc.	*V.G.*	*Good*	*Fair*	*Poor*
200	150	125	100	75

Model 620 U.S. Marked Trench Gun

Courtesy Richard M. Kumor Sr.

Exc.	*V.G.*	*Good*	*Fair*	*Poor*
1200	975	600	—	—

NOTE: Add $150 for bayonet.

Model 124

This is a recoil-operated semi-automatic shotgun chambered for 12 gauge. It has a 28" barrel with various chokes, is blued, and has a brown plastic stock.

Exc.	*V.G.*	*Good*	*Fair*	*Poor*
150	100	75	65	50

Model 67

This is a slide-action shotgun chambered for 12 and 20 gauge, as well as .410. It has 3" chambers. It is offered with various length barrels and choke tubes with a 5-shot tube magazine. It features a steel receiver and is blued, with a walnut stock. It was discontinued in 1989.

Exc.	*V.G.*	*Good*	*Fair*	*Poor*
250	175	150	100	75

Model 675

This is a slide-action shotgun chambered for 12 gauge with a 24" vent rib barrel with iron sights. The finish is blued, with a hardwood stock and recoil pad. It was manufactured in 1987 and 1988.

Exc.	*V.G.*	*Good*	*Fair*	*Poor*
300	250	200	150	100

Model 69-RXL

This is a matte-finished riot version of the Model 67 series slide-action shotgun. It has an 18.25" cylinder-bore barrel and is furnished with a recoil pad. It was discontinued in 1989.

Exc.	*V.G.*	*Good*	*Fair*	*Poor*
250	175	150	100	75

STEYR

Steyr, Austria

STEYR & MANNLICHER PISTOLS

Text and prices by Joseph Schroeder

Not all Mannlicher pistols were made by Steyr, and many of the pistols made by Steyr were not designed by Mannlicher. However, since by far the greatest number of Mannlicher's pistols were made by Steyr we believe it will be appropriate to include all of Ferdinand Ritter von Mannlicher's pistols along with other Steyr designs under this heading.

Schoenberger

Considered by many to be the first "commercial" semi-automatic pistol even though apparently at the most only about two dozen were made in 1892. The Steyr-made 8mm Schoenberger was based on patents granted to Laumann in 1890-91 and had a magazine in front of the trigger guard.

Exc.	*V.G.*	*Good*	*Fair*	*Poor*

Too Rare to Price

Mannlicher Model 1894

Mannlicher's first "successful" self-loading pistol, the Model 1894 had a blow-forward action and double-action lockwork. Earliest examples were made in Austria, probably by Steyr, in 7.6mm but the greatest number were made by SIG in 1896-97 for Swiss army tests. These 100 pistols had a shorter barrel and smaller frame and were in 6.5mm. Prices are for Swiss examples.

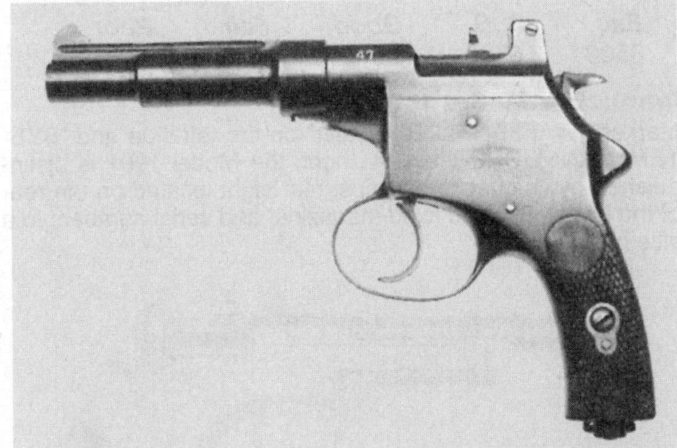

Courtesy Rock Island Auction Company

Exc.	*V.G.*	*Good*	*Fair*	*Poor*
12000	9000	6000	5000	3000

NOTE: Add 20 percent for 7.6mm pistols.

Mannlicher Model 1896/03

This is one of the most confusing of Mannlicher's pistols. Earliest examples, which have a fixed magazine and ribbed barrel, may have been made by Steyr and are very rare. Later versions, with a removable box magazine, have been called "Model 1896/03" and "Model 1901," and were made as both a pistol and pistol-carbine, possibly in Switzerland. Chambered for the 7.65mm Mannlicher cartridge, which is really a 7.65mm Borchardt. Prices listed are for the standard later model pistol or pistol-carbine (12" barrel, tangent sight); double prices for early pistol or late model pistol with detachable holster stock.

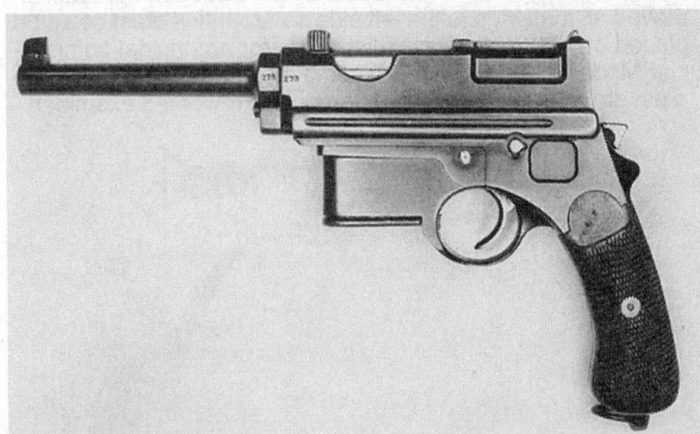

Courtesy Joseph Schroeder

Exc.	*V.G.*	*Good*	*Fair*	*Poor*
7500	5000	3500	2500	1500

Mannlicher Model 1899

Earliest version of Mannlicher's final semi-automatic pistol design, only about 250 were made by Dreyse in Soemmerda, Germany. Chambered for a tapered case 7.63mm Mannlicher cartridge. Distinguished by the large safety lever on the left side, takedown screw under the barrel, and the Dreyse markings.

Courtesy Joseph Schroeder

Exc.	V.G.	Good	Fair	Poor
8500	6500	4500	3500	2000

Mannlicher Model 1901

Marked "WAFFENFABRIK Steyr" on the left side and "SYSTEM MANNLICHER" on the right, the Model 1901 is distinguished by its checkered grips, rear sight located on the rear of the barrel, 8-round fixed magazine, and serial numbers to a little over 1000.

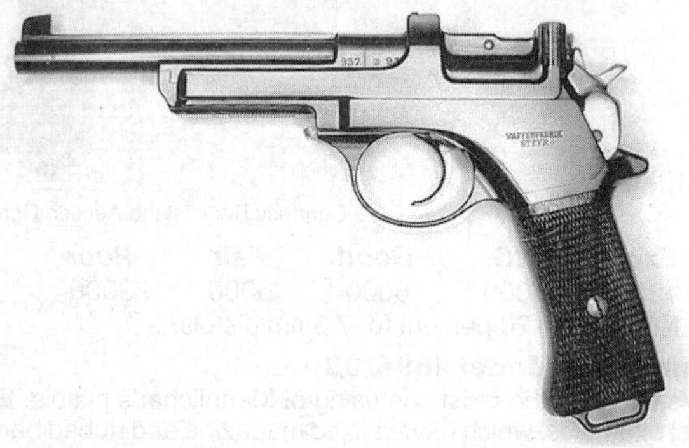

Courtesy Joseph Schroeder

Exc.	V.G.	Good	Fair	Poor
3000	2200	1600	900	700

Mannlicher Model 1905

Improved version of the Model 1901, with longer grip holding 10 rounds, grooved wooden grips, rear sight on rear of breechblock, and "MODEL 1905" added to right side. Later production moved all markings to the left side so Argentine crest could be placed on right side. Prices listed are for an original commercial Model 1905, NOT a reblued Argentine contract with the crest ground off. Subtract 60 percent for reworked examples.

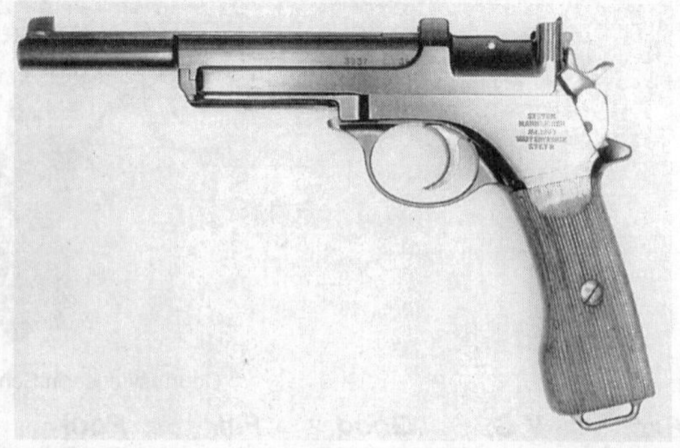

Courtesy Joseph Schroeder

Exc.	V.G.	Good	Fair	Poor
2200	1700	1400	800	400

Argentine Contract

Original crest on right side.

Exc.	V.G.	Good	Fair	Poor
2500	2000	1500	900	500

Roth Steyr Model 1907

Based on the patents granted to Karel Krnka and Georg Roth, the 8mm Model 1907 had a rotating barrel locking system and was the first self-loading pistol adopted by the Austro-Hungarian Army.

Courtesy Joseph Schroeder

Exc.	V.G.	Good	Fair	Poor
900	750	600	350	250

NOTE: Add 20 percent for early Steyr examples without a large pin visible on right side of frame, or for those made in Budapest instead of Steyr.

Steyr Model 1908 Pocket Pistol

Based on the Belgian patents of Nicholas Pieper, these .25 and .32 caliber pocket pistols featured tipping barrels were built by Steyr under license from Pieper in Liege. Production was suspended during WWI but may have resumed after the war ended. Prices are for either caliber.

Exc.	V.G.	Good	Fair	Poor
350	250	150	100	75

Steyr Hahn Model 1911

Commercially Marked

Exc.	V.G.	Good	Fair	Poor
2000	1500	1100	800	450

NOTE: For military versions of this model see the *Standard Catalog of Military Firearms.*

Steyr Model SP

Steyr's first post WWII pistol, the Model SP was a beautifully made .32 ACP which, being double-action-only and more ex-

This symbol denotes "Sleepers" with rapidly-rising values and/or significant collector potential.

pensive than most of its contemporaries, was not competitive and was discontinued in the early 1960s after fewer than 1,000 were made. Slide marked "STEYR-DAIMLER-PUCH A.G. MOD.SP KAL. 7.65mm."

Courtesy Joseph Schroeder

Exc.	V.G.	Good	Fair	Poor
850	750	500	350	200

Steyr Model GB

The GB was introduced in the mid-1970s as a 9mm Parabellum military pistol, large in size but with an 18-round magazine capacity. Other features included polygon rifling and a gas trap around the barrel to delay breech opening. Initially produced as the Rogak P-18 by L.E.S. of Morton Grove, Illinois, but discontinued due in part to quality control problems after just over 2,000 were made. Later production by Steyr as the GB was to much higher standards, but the GB never achieved much popularity and was discontinued in 1988.

Rogak P-18

Exc.	V.G.	Good	Fair	Poor
375	325	225	175	125

Steyr GB

Exc.	V.G.	Good	Fair	Poor
550	450	325	250	200

RIFLES

NOTE: *For earlier models see Mannlicher Schoenauer.*

Steyr Mannlicher Model 1950

A .257 Roberts, .270 Winchester, or .30-06 caliber bolt-action sporting rifle with a 24" barrel and 5-shot rotary magazine. Blued with a checkered walnut stock having an ebony pistol grip cap and forend tip. Manufactured from 1950 to 1952.

Exc.	V.G.	Good	Fair	Poor
1300	1150	900	700	450

Model 1950 Carbine

As above, with a 20" barrel and Mannlicher-style stock. Fitted with a steel forend cap. Manufactured in 1950 to 1952.

Exc.	V.G.	Good	Fair	Poor
1400	1200	1000	750	400

Model 1952

Similar to the above, with a swept back bolt handle. Manufactured from 1952 to 1956.

Exc.	V.G.	Good	Fair	Poor
1500	1200	1000	750	600

Model 1952 Carbine

As above, with a 20" barrel and Mannlicher-style stock.

Exc.	V.G.	Good	Fair	Poor
1500	1200	1000	750	600

Model 1956 Rifle

Similar to the above, in .243 and .30-06 caliber with a 22" barrel and high comb stock. Manufactured from 1956 to 1960.

Exc.	V.G.	Good	Fair	Poor
1350	1200	1000	800	650

Model 1956 Carbine

As above, with a 20" barrel and Mannlicher-style stock. Manufactured from 1956 to 1960.

Exc.	V.G.	Good	Fair	Poor
1450	1100	900	700	600

Model 1961 MCA Rifle

As above, with a Monte Carlo-style stock.

Exc.	V.G.	Good	Fair	Poor
1350	1200	1000	850	700

Model 1961 MCA Carbine

As above, with a Mannlicher-style Monte Carlo stock.

Exc.	V.G.	Good	Fair	Poor
1450	1250	1100	700	600

THE FOLLOWING STEYR/MANNLICHER GUNS WERE IMPORTED BY GSI INC. TRUSSVILLE, ALABAMA

NOTE: Currently GSI Inc. is no longer receiving shipments of Steyr/Mannlicher rifles or handguns, nor does GSI, Inc. anticipate futher deliveries. At the present time Steyr/Mannlicher rifles are imported by Dynamit Nobel. The present owner is Cura Investholding GmbH.

SPORTER SERIES

This series includes rifles that are lightweight and have a reduced overall length. All Sporter models have an interchangeable 5-round rotary magazine. The stock is oil-finished walnut in either the Mannlicher full stock design or the half stock version. In both stock configurations an oval European cheekpiece is standard. These rifles are offered in four different action lengths: **SL** (super light), **L** (light), **M** (medium), or **S** (magnum). They are also available with either single trigger or double set triggers.

Model M72 L/M

A .243, .270, 7x57mm, 7x64mm, .308 or .30-06 caliber bolt-action rifle with a 23" fluted barrel, and single or double set triggers. Blued, checkered walnut stock. Manufactured from 1972 to 1980.

Exc.	V.G.	Good	Fair	Poor
1200	950	750	550	450

Model SL

This model features the super light action and is offered with 20" barrel in full stock version or 23-1/6" barrel in half stock version. A rubber buttpad is standard. This model does not have a forend tip on its half stock variation. Offered in the following calibers: .222 Rem., .222 Rem. Mag., .223, and 5.6x50 Mag. Weighs approximately 6.2 lbs. with full stock and 6.3 lbs. with half stock.

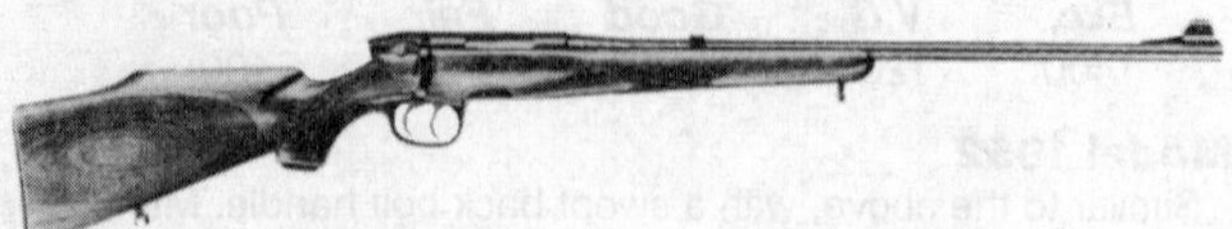

NIB	Exc.	V.G.	Good	Fair	Poor
1850	1650	1000	750	500	300

Model SL Carbine

As above, with a 20" fluted barrel and Mannlicher-style stock.

NIB	Exc.	V.G.	Good	Fair	Poor
1950	1750	1050	800	550	350

Varmint Model

This model features a heavy 26" barrel chambered for the .222 Rem., .223, 5.6x57, .243 Win., .308 Win., and .22-250. The forend of the stock is ventilated. The grip is enlarged and textured. Choice of single or double set triggers. Recoil pad is standard. Weighs about 8 lbs.

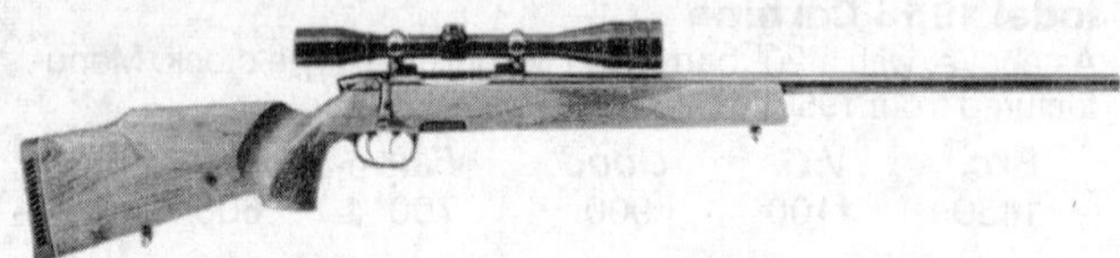

NIB	Exc.	V.G.	Good	Fair	Poor
1950	1750	1050	800	550	350

Model L

This rifle has the light action and is offered in the same stock configuration and barrel lengths as the Model SL. The calibers are: 5.6x57, .243 Win., .308, .22-250, and 6mm Rem. Weighs about 6.3 lbs. with full stock and 6.4 lbs. with half stock.

NIB	Exc.	V.G.	Good	Fair	Poor
1850	1650	1000	750	500	300

Luxus Series

This luxury model offers a choice of full or half stock variations in select walnut with fine line checkering. The pistol grip is steeply angled. The Luxus rifles are fitted with a swept back European cheekpiece. A single set trigger is standard. The box magazine holds 3 rounds. Optional engraving and stock carving may be encountered on these modes that will dramatically affect price. The Luxus rifles are available with light, medium, or magnum length actions.

Luxus Model L

Same dimensions and barrel lengths as the Sporter version. The calibers are: 5.6x57, .243 Win., .308, .22-250, and 6mm Rem.

NIB	Exc.	V.G.	Good	Fair	Poor
2400	2000	1100	800	600	350

Luxus Model M

Same dimensions and barrel lengths as the Sporter Model M. Available in these calibers: 6.5x57, .270 Win., 7x64, .30-06, 9.3x 626.5x55, 7.5 Swiss, 7x57, and 8x57JS.

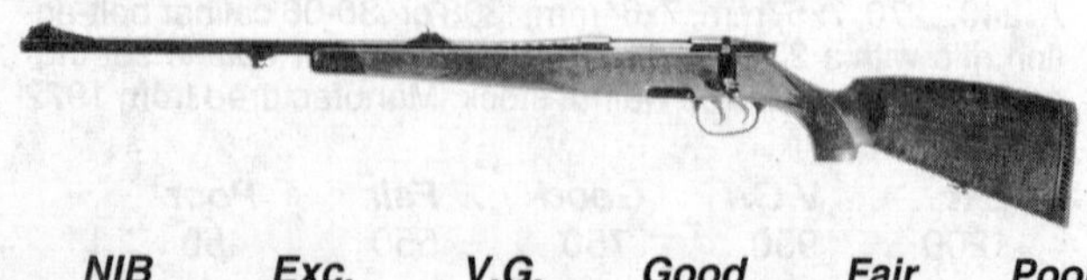

NIB	Exc.	V.G.	Good	Fair	Poor
2400	2000	1100	800	600	350

Luxus Model S

Same as the Sporter Model S. Offered in the following calibers: 6.5x68, 7mm Rem. Mag., .300 Win. Mag., and 8x68S.

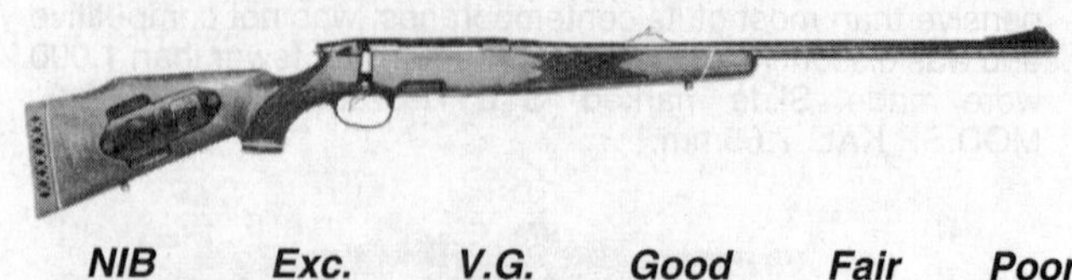

NIB	Exc.	V.G.	Good	Fair	Poor
2400	2000	1100	800	600	350

Model M

This model features the medium action and has the same barrel and stock configurations as the other two models listed above with the exception that it has no buttpad and it does have a forend tip on its half stock variation. Available in these calibers: 6.5x57, .270 Win., 7x64, .30-06, 9.3x62, 6.5x55, 7.5 Swiss, 7x57, and 8x57JS. Weighs approximately 6.8 lbs. with full stock and 7 lbs. with half stock.

NIB	Exc.	V.G.	Good	Fair	Poor
2500	2100	1200	900	600	300

Professional Model M

This model is fitted with a medium weight action and features a black synthetic checkered stock. Comes fitted with a ventilated rubber recoil pad. Offered with 20" or 23.6" barrel it is available with single or double set trigger. Available in these calibers: 6.5x57, .270 Win., 7x64, .30-06, 9.3x62, 6.5x55, 7.5 Swiss, 7x57, and 8x57JS. Weighs approximately 7.25 lbs.

NIB	Exc.	V.G.	Good	Fair	Poor
1500	1200	950	700	600	300

Model MIII Professional

Introduced in 1995 this is an economy version of the Model M Professional. It is fitted with a 23.5" barrel, black synthetic stock, and choice of single or double set triggers. Offered in .25-06, .270 Win., .30-06, and 7x64 calibers. Weight is approximately 7 lb. 5 oz.

NIB	Exc.	V.G.	Good	Fair	Poor
1000	800	600	400	300	200

NOTE: With checkered walnut stock add $100.

Model S

This rifle is offered with half stock only and is fitted with a 26" barrel. The action is magnum length and is offered in these calibers: 6.5x68, 7mm Rem. Mag., .300 Win. Mag., and 8x68S. Rifle weighs about 8.4 lbs.

NIB	Exc.	V.G.	Good	Fair	Poor
1950	1750	1150	900	700	300

Model S/T

Similar to the model above but in a heavy barreled version. Offered in these calibers: 9.3x64, .375 H&H, and .458 Win. Mag. An optional buttstock magazine is available. Weighs about 9 lbs.

NIB	Exc.	V.G.	Good	Fair	Poor
2100	1900	1400	1100	800	500

Tropical Rifle

As above, with a 26" heavy barrel chambered for .375 Holland & Holland and .458 Winchester Magnum. Not imported after 1985.

Exc.	V.G.	Good	Fair	Poor
2000	1750	1100	650	450

Steyr SBS (Safe Bolt System)

This series was introduced in 1997 and features a newly designed bolt. It is offered in two distinct models the SBS Forester and the SBS ProHunter.

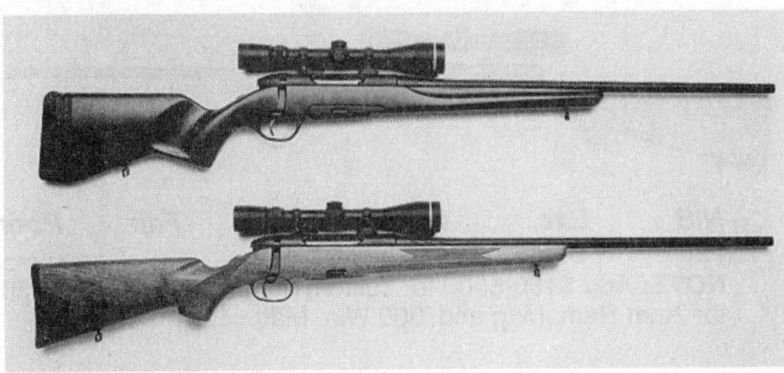

SBS ProHunter

This model has a 23.6" barrel with 4-round magazine and single adjustable trigger. Offered in .243 Win., .25-06, .270 Win., 7mm-08, .308 Win., .30-06, 7mm Rem. Mag., .300 Win. Mag., and several European calibers. Weight is approximately 7.5 lbs. This model is furnished with a black synthetic stock with recoil pad and buttspacers. Introduced in 1999.

NIB	Exc.	V.G.	Good	Fair	Poor
700	550	450	—	—	—

NOTE: Add $150-$300 for custom metric calibers. Add approximately $30 for 7mm mag and .300 Win. Mag calibers.

SBS ProHunter Stainless Steel

Same as the ProHunter model but with stainless steel action and barrel. Introduced in 2000.

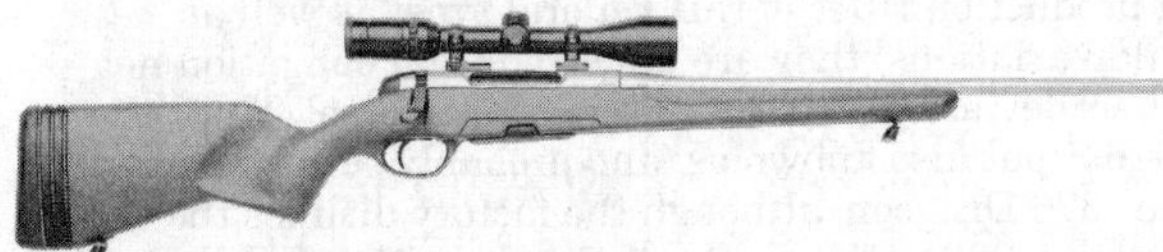

NIB	Exc.	V.G.	Good	Fair	Poor
800	600	—	—	—	—

NOTE: Add $150-$300 for custom metric calibers. Add approximately $30 for 7mm mag and .300 Win. Mag calibers.

SBS ProHunter Camo

Same as standard ProHunter but with camo synthetic stock.

NIB	Exc.	V.G.	Good	Fair	Poor
775	550	450	—	—	—

NOTE: Add $150-$300 for custom metric calibers. Add approximately $30 for 7mm mag and .300 Win. Mag calibers.

SBS ProHunter Camo Stainless Steel

Same as above but with stainless steel action and barrel.

NIB	Exc.	V.G.	Good	Fair	Poor
850	625	500	—	—	—

NOTE: Add $150-$300 for custom metric calibers. Add approximately $30 for 7mm mag and .300 Win. Mag calibers.

SBS ProHunter Mountain Rifle

Chambered for .243, .25-06, .270, and 7mm-08 calibers, this model is fitted with a 20" barrel with no sights. Receiver engraved "Mountain Rifle." Synthetic stock with recoil pad standard. Weight is 7.25 lbs. Introduced in 1999.

NIB	Exc.	V.G.	Good	Fair	Poor
725	550	400	—	—	—

SBS ProHunter Mountain Stainless Steel

Same as the ProHunter Mountain but with stainless steel action and barrel. Introduced in 2000.

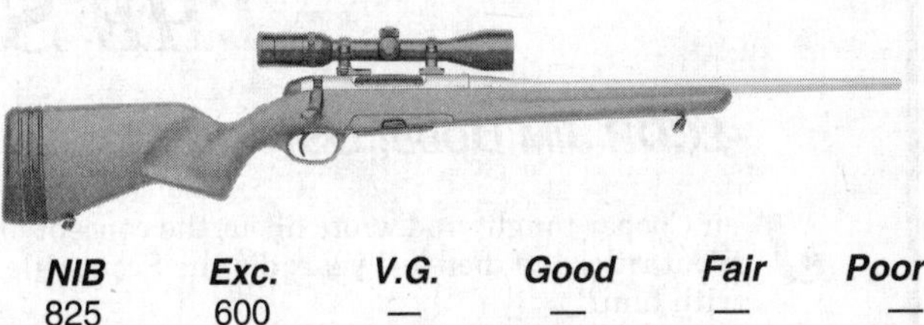

NIB	Exc.	V.G.	Good	Fair	Poor
825	600	—	—	—	—

SBS ProHunter Mountain Camo

Same as the ProHunter but with camo synthetic stock. Introduced in 2000.

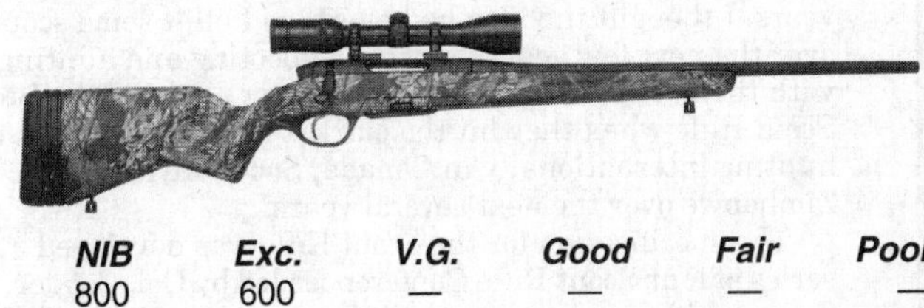

NIB	Exc.	V.G.	Good	Fair	Poor
800	600	—	—	—	—

SBS ProHunter Mountain Camo Stainless Steel

Same as above but with stainless steel action and barrel. Introduced in 2000.

NIB	Exc.	V.G.	Good	Fair	Poor
875	650	—	—	—	—

SBS ProHunter (Youth/Ladies)

This model is fitted with a walnut stock with buttspacers (to create a shorter length of pull) and extra thick recoil pad. Chambered for .243, 7mm-08, and .308. Weight is about 7.25 lbs. Introduced in 1999.

NIB	Exc.	V.G.	Good	Fair	Poor
800	650	550	—	—	—

SBS ProHunter Compact

Same as above but with black synthetic stock. Also offered with stainless steel action and barrel.

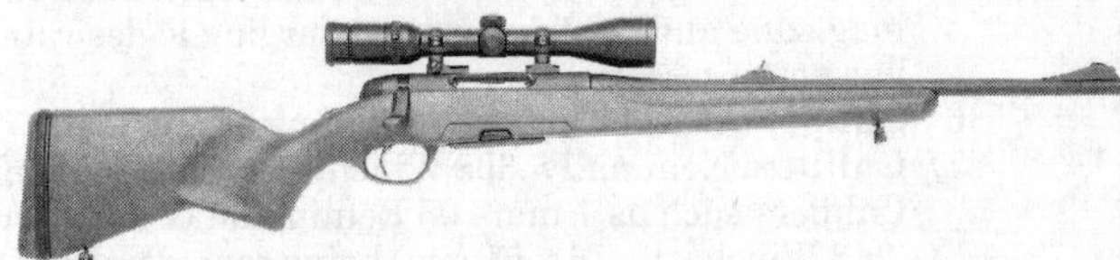

NIB	Exc.	V.G.	Good	Fair	Poor
800	650	550	—	—	—

NOTE: Add $80 for stainless steel model.

SBS ProHunter 376 Steyr

This model is chambered for the .376 Steyr cartridge. Fitted with a 20" barrel with iron sights. Synthetic stock with special thick pad. Weight is about 8 lbs. Introduced in 1999.

NIB	Exc.	V.G.	Good	Fair	Poor
800	650	550	—	—	—

SBS Forester

Same as above model but furnished with a walnut stock with recoil pad.

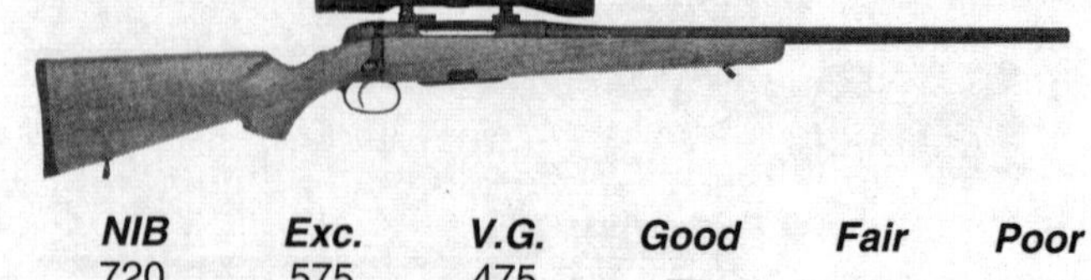

NIB	Exc.	V.G.	Good	Fair	Poor
720	575	475	—	—	—

NOTE: Add $150-$300 for custom metric calibers. Add $30 for 7mm Rem. Mag and .300 Win. Mag.

THE SCOUT RIFLE

–LCDR JIM DODD, USN (RET.)

Jeff Cooper taught and wrote about the concept of the scout rifle. Jeff died last year; did the Scout rifle die with him?

I first encountered the scout rifle concept reading retired US Marine LTC John Dean (Jeff) Cooper's writings, and then heard about it first hand when I went to his Paulden, Arizona, American Pistol Institute in the early 90s. I took the handgun, rifle and advanced rifle courses in different years. I thought the idea had merit, so I built some scouts over the next few years and began shooting and hunting with them. I also acquired a Jeff Cooper model of the Steyr Scout Rifle when they hit the market in 1998, and took it hunting internationally in Canada, South Africa and Zimbabwe over the next several years.

The specification for the Scout Rifle was developed at a series of four Scout Rifle Conferences led by Col. Cooper. The final specification and much discussion is available on the steyrscout.org website.

By the definition of the Scout Rifle Conferences held under the auspices of Jeff Cooper, the scout rifle has been defined as a *general purpose* rifle suitable for taking targets of up to 400 kg (880 pounds) at ranges to the limit of the shooters visibility (nominally 300 meters) that meets the following criteria:

1) **Weight-sighted and slung:** 3 kilograms (6.6 lb). This has been set as the ideal weight but the maximum has been stated as being 3.5 kg (7.7 pounds).
2) **Length:** 1 meter (39 inches)
3) **Nominal barrel length:** .48 meter (19 inches)
4) **Sighting system:** Typically a forward and low mounted (ahead of the action opening) long eye relief telescope of between 2x and 3x. Reserve iron sights desirable but not necessary. Iron sights of the ghost ring type, without a scope, also qualify, as does a low powered conventional position scope.
5) **Action:** Magazine fed bolt action. Detachable box magazine and/or stripper clip charging is desirable but not necessary.
6) **Sling:** Fast loop-up type, i.e. Ching or CW style.
7) **Caliber:** Nominally .308 Winchester (7.62 x 51 mm). Calibers such as 7 mm - 08 Remington (7 x 51 mm) or .243 Winchester (6 x 51 mm) being considered for frail individuals or where "military" calibers are proscribed.
8) **Built-in bipod:** Desirable but not mandatory.
9) **Accuracy:** Should be capable of shooting into 2 minutes of angle or less (4") at 200 yards/meters (3 shot groups).

Author and Scout Team member John Schaefer has also commented:

"Rifles that do not meet all of these specifications are technically not 'scout rifles.' Thus rifles of this general design in calibers other than those stated above are not true scout rifles but actually 'pseudo-scouts'. However, even though Steyr Mannlicher (and now Savage and Ruger) are making production rifles of this general type (as well as some wild variations) they are under no legal obligation not to call their deviations 'scouts' as a marketing tool. Thus, the Steyr .376 Scout also known as (and probably better referred to as the '.376 Dragoon' although the factory dislikes the term) nor the .223 variation are true scout rifles. For that matter neither are the custom made scout-like rifles made up in .30-06, .375 H&H, or what ever caliber. However, there are many parts of the scout design that can be handily used on non-scout rifles."

The problem I and others have found with the Scout Concept is target visibility. Although the rifle is advertised as general purpose, the sighting system of a low-power scope mounted forward (on the barrel) is not up to many scenarios hunters commonly encounter. A low-power variable scope of about 1.5-6X with about 36 mm objective mounted over the action is more general in application. The Concept does do well on square ranges, or otherwise when the light and contrast levels are high – for example from 8:00 am to 5:00 pm with light targets with dark bulls. The forward-mount scope is also vulnerable to glare flooding the scope from any light source behind the shooter (that is not shaded by the shooters head or hat). I discovered this last problem trying to deliver a cross-canyon shot on a trophy nyala at sunset with the South African setting sun behind me. Low light level shooting at shaded dark targets is also problematical.

Early Scouts were built using barrels with integral pillars machined as part of the barrel. This is expensive, and contributed to the high cost of the early Scouts. Unfortunately, it wasn't really necessary.

The Steyr-Mannlicher staff worked with Jeff Cooper before, during and after they developed their Safe Bolt System (SBS) rifle in the early to mid 90s. The SBS rifles entered the market in 1996, and the Scout version was ready for sale in 1998. The Steyr Scout captured most of the Scout specification, especially the short overall length, light weight, forward scope, detachable box magazine, bolt action, Ching Sling and integral bipod requirements. The styling and construction of the rifle are sufficient to startle most walnut and blue steel bolt-action rifle aficionados. It does grow on you with use.

SBS Forester Mountain Rifle

Walnut stock with 20" barrel and no sights. Chambered for a variety of calibers including .243, .25-06, .270, 7mm-08, .308, .30-06 and 6.5x55. Receiver engraved "Mountain Rifle." Introduced in 1999.

NIB	Exc.	V.G.	Good	Fair	Poor
750	600	500	—	—	—

SBS Classic American

This model features a 23.6" barrel with a single adjustable trigger and stain finish walnut stock with recoil pad. Offered in calibers from .243 to .300 Win. Mag. Weight is about 7.2 lbs. Introduced in 2000.

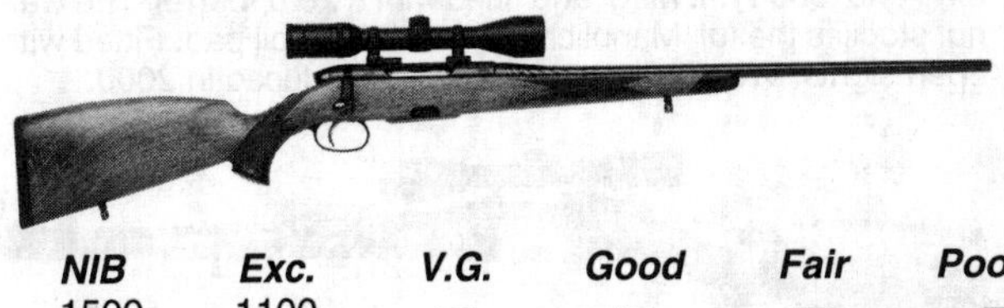

NIB	Exc.	V.G.	Good	Fair	Poor
1500	1100	—	—	—	—

NOTE: Add $150-$300 for custom metric calibers. Add approximately $30 for 7mm Mag and .300 Win. Mag calibers.

THE SCOUT RIFLE (CONT.)

The Steyr-Mannlicher staff worked with Jeff Cooper before, during and after they developed their Safe Bolt System (SBS) rifle in the early to mid 90s. The SBS rifles entered the market in 1996, and the Scout version was ready for sale in 1998. The Steyr Scout captured most of the Scout specification, especially the short overall length, light weight, forward scope, detachable box magazine, bolt action, Ching Sling and integral bipod requirements. The styling and construction of the rifle are sufficient to startle most walnut and blue steel bolt-action rifle aficionados. It does grow on you with use.

The Steyr Scout entered the market with a list price of over $2,500 for the Jeff Cooper package (with a Leupold 2.5X28 long-eye relief scope and a Ching Sling). This price level caused sticker shock for most American shooters, who could buy a custom rifle for this amount.

Early adopters of the Steyr Scout noted that the rifle had difficulty with light primer hits on military 7.62X51 ammunition (with mil spec thick primers). The cure is to replace the factory cocking cam with a redesigned unit, to reposition the firing pin spring and to remove some sharp production edges in the bolt interior.

Collecting Opportunities

Steyr: Look for the Jeff Cooper Version of the .308 Win rifle (with certificate of authenticity). All of the 7.5X55 Swiss chambered versions are rare. Some .308 Win models sold in Europe had barrels with 10" twist, while North American models were all 12". There were very many fewer 7-08, .243 Win and .223 Rem rifles sold. The Tactical models are rare too, and the .376 Steyr version of the Scout was abandoned by the factory early on.

Savage: The Savage Scout was developed from their M10 short action, and was designated M10FCM. It also captured much of the Scout specification, and at 30% of the list price of the Steyr Scout, it was a serious bargain if you want to try out the concept. Like the Steyr, the Savage is synthetic and black rifle in appearance. It is a heavier rifle than the Steyr, and is limited to .308 Win and 7-08 chamberings. The sling is pretty much only a carrying strap. The rifle comes from Savage with backup iron sights and an unattractive scope base. Users recommend ordering the rifle from the Custom Shop and having a third stud fitted for a Ching Sling and magazines matched to the rifle.

The Savage Scout is like many of the Savage rifles: ugly but very effective. The factory is very good at customer support, and should be applauded for this.

The Savage earned a really big positive for the left-hand version of their Scout. The factory has been very supportive of this rifle, and their Custom Shop is the recommended source because they ensure the magazines operate properly.

All of the Savage Scouts I have seen have been .308 Win, indicating that the 7-08 version is relatively scarce. The Savage Scout was discontinued but at this writing has returned to the Savage lineup.

Ruger Frontier: Ruger took its time introducing a rifle into the Scout sweepstakes, and did not choose to use the Scout name – instead their rifle is named the Frontier. The rifle uses a Ruger No. 1 style rib forward-mounted on the barrel to permit a forward scope mount with Ruger rings. This is by coincidence the same sight mount system I used on the first Scout rifle I built on a .308 Win Tikka Whitetail Battue carbine in 1993. It is sturdy, and much cheaper to build than an integral pillar barrel.

The Ruger Frontier has a slick barrel, no sights other than the scope are part of the package. The MKII action also retains the normal Ruger integral mounts, and the standard trigger, not the new LC06 (Light Crisp 2006) trigger. The test item trigger weighed 4 lbs. on a Lyman electronic gauge, and was heavy but crisp.

The only known issue with the Ruger Frontier is related to the sales so far: there just aren't that many of them being used in the field. In 2007 Ruger introduced Frontier versions in .338 Federal and .358 Win. Both of these rifles are likely to be low sellers.

Summary

Scout rifles are really excellent light, short rifles with a lot of power in a small package. They are good for hunting, especially with a low-power variable scope mounted over the action. They are not popular. I expect they will be even less so going forward as no gun writers are beating the drum for the concept now that Jeff Cooper is gone.

The process for developing the Scout Concept specification was well thought out and deliberate, but as we can see that does not guarantee success. I had the opportunity to discuss my observations on the Scouts with Jeff. I can't say he was happy to hear my points, but he — as he always was — was eager to talk guns, hunting, and improving the art of the rifle. May we remember his contributions as his legacy.

SBS Classic Mannlicher

Offered in the same calibers as above except for 7mm Rem. Mag and .300 Win. Mag. and fitted with a 25.6" barrel. The walnut stock is the full Mannlicher style with recoil pad. Fitted with open sights. Weight is about 7.2 lbs. Introduced in 2000.

NIB	Exc.	V.G.	Good	Fair	Poor
1700	1250	—	—	—	—

Mannlicher SBS European—Half Stock

Fitted with a 23.6" barrel with iron sights and chambered for a wide variety of American and European calibers from .243 to 9.3x62. European style figured walnut stock. Adjustable trigger. Recoil pad. Weight is about 7.5 lbs.

NIB	Exc.	V.G.	Good	Fair	Poor
2795	2200	1750	—	—	—

Mannlicher SBS European—Half Stock Carbine

Same as model above but with 20" barrel.

NIB	Exc.	V.G.	Good	Fair	Poor
2895	2300	1850	—	—	—

Mannlicher SBS European—Full Stock

Same as above but with full European stock covering a 20" barrel.

NIB	Exc.	V.G.	Good	Fair	Poor
3000	2400	1950	—	—	—

Mannlicher SBS Magnum European—Half Stock

This model is chambered for the 7mm Rem. Mag., .300 Win. Mag., and the 6.5x68 and 8x68S calibers. Fitted with a 25.6" barrel with iron sights. Walnut stock. Weight is about 7.75 lbs.

NIB	Exc.	V.G.	Good	Fair	Poor
3000	2400	1950	—	—	—

Steyr Scout—Jeff Cooper Package

Developed by Col. Jeff Cooper this model is chambered for the .308 Win. cartridge. It is fitted with a 19" fluted barrel. Stock is gray synthetic with removable buttspacers and folding bi-pod. Magazine capacity is 5 rounds with optional 10-round magazines available. Weight is approximately 7 lbs. with scope. Weight is 6.3 lbs. with no scope. Adjustable single trigger. Factory-installed Leupold M8 2.5x28mm scope. Introduced in 1998.

NIB	Exc.	V.G.	Good	Fair	Poor
2600	2000	1600	—	—	—

Steyr Scout Package

Similar to the Jeff Cooper Package but without the Jeff Cooper logo. Stock is black synthetic. Also offered in .223 Rem., .243 Win., 7mm-08 as well as .308 and .375 Steyr calibers.

NIB	Exc.	V.G.	Good	Fair	Poor
2600	2000	1600	—	—	—

Steyr Scout

Same as above but rifle only.

NIB	Exc.	V.G.	Good	Fair	Poor
1895	1500	1200	—	—	—

Steyr Scout Tactical

This model has a 19.25" fluted barrel and is chambered for the .223 or .308 Win. cartridge. Integral bipod. Emergency Ghost Ring sights.

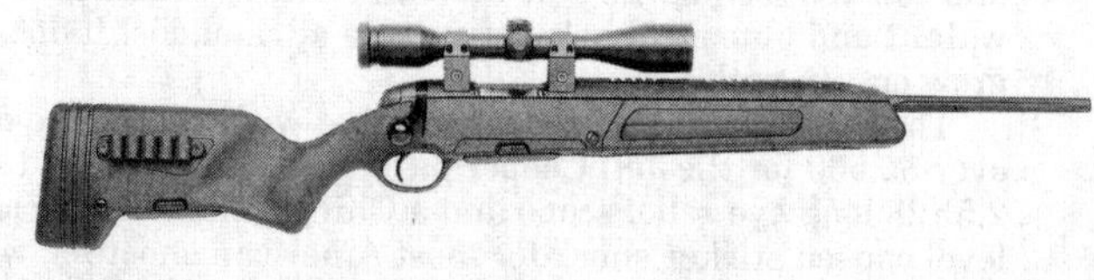

NIB	Exc.	V.G.	Good	Fair	Poor
2050	1500	1000	—	—	—

NOTE: Add $100 for stainless steel model.

PRECISION/TACTICAL RIFLES

Model SSG-PI

This model features a black synthetic stock originally designed as a military sniper rifle. Fitted with a cocking indicator, single or double set trigger, 5-round rotary magazine, or 10-round magazine. Receiver is milled to NATO specifications for Steyr ring mounts. Barrel length is 26". Rifle weighs about 9 lbs. Offered in .308 Win.

NOTE: This model was originally called the SSG 69.

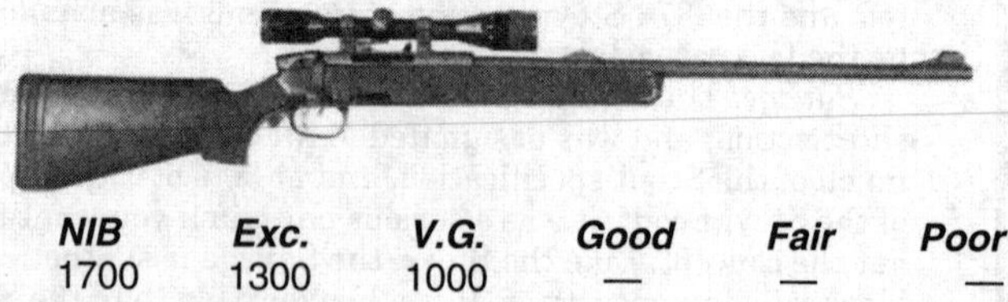

NIB	Exc.	V.G.	Good	Fair	Poor
1700	1300	1000	—	—	—

SSG-PII Police Rifle

This version of the SSG has a heavier 26" barrel and a larger knob-style bolt handle. Weighs about 10 lbs. 11 oz.

NIB	Exc.	V.G.	Good	Fair	Poor
1700	1300	1000	—	—	—

This symbol denotes "Sleepers" with rapidly-rising values and/or significant collector potential.

SSK-PIIK Police Kurz

Similar to the above model but with a 20" heavy barrel. Weight is about 10 lbs.

NIB	Exc.	V.G.	Good	Fair	Poor
1700	1300	1000	—	—	—

SSG-PII & PIIK McMillan

Fitted with a McMillan A-3 stock with adjustable cheekpiece and removable buttspacers. Special forearm rail.

NIB	Exc.	V.G.	Good	Fair	Poor
2300	1750	1350	—	—	—

SSG-PIV

Again similar to the above PIIK but with a 16.75" heavy barrel with a removable flash hider. Barrel is threaded. Weight is about 9 lbs. 11 oz.

NIB	Exc.	V.G.	Good	Fair	Poor
2500	2000	1500	1000	750	400

Match

NIB	Exc.	V.G.	Good	Fair	Poor
3000	2500	2000	1500	800	400

Match UIT

Designed as an international target rifle this model features special shaped pistol grip, an adjustable trigger for length of pull and pressure. Enlarged bolt handle and nonglare barrel. Chambered for .308 Win. cartridge.

NIB	Exc.	V.G.	Good	Fair	Poor
3900	3500	3000	2000	1500	1000

JAGD Match

Introduced in 1995 this model features a choice of 23.5" or 20" barrel with sights. The stock is laminated. A full stock version is offered on 20" barrel models and a half stock is offered on the 23.5" barrel models. Available in a variety of configurations with calibers from .222 Rem. to .458 Win. Mag.

NIB	Exc.	V.G.	Good	Fair	Poor
1750	1250	900	500	350	200

SBS TACTICAL SERIES

SBS Tactical

Fitted with a black synthetic stock and 20" barrel with no sights. This model is chambered for the .308 cartridge. Removable buttspacers. Black bolt body. Receiver engraved "SBS Tactical." Introduced in 1999. Weight is about 7.25 lbs.

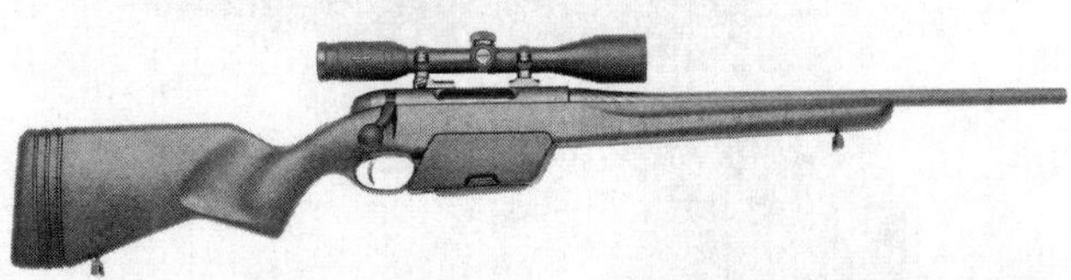

NIB	Exc.	V.G.	Good	Fair	Poor
950	750	600	—	—	—

NOTE: Add $100 for stainless steel model (introduced 2000).

SBS Tactical Heavy Barrel

This model also has a black synthetic stock but is fitted with a 26" heavy barrel and no sights. Black bolt body. Receiver engraved "SBS Tactical HB." Weight is about 8 lbs. Introduced in 1999. Also offered with 20" barrel called "HBC." Both barrel lengths chambered for .308 cartridge.

NIB	Exc.	V.G.	Good	Fair	Poor
950	750	600	—	—	—

SBS Tactical Heavy Barrel Carbine

This model features a 20" heavy barrel, no sights, matte blue finish. Chambered for .308 caliber. Introduced in 2000.

NIB	Exc.	V.G.	Good	Fair	Poor
1000	700	—	—	—	—

SBS Tactical McMillan

This model is fitted with a 26" barrel chambered for the .308 cartridge and has a McMillan A-3 stock. Oversize bolt handle. Weight is about 9.8 lbs. Introduced in 1999.

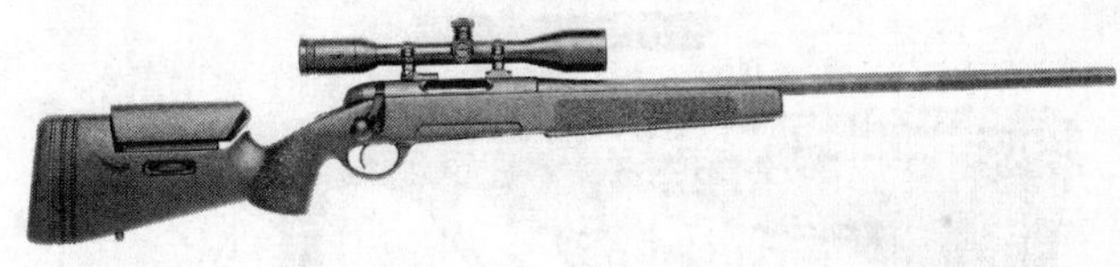

NIB	Exc.	V.G.	Good	Fair	Poor
1600	1250	950	—	—	—

SBS CISM Rifle

This model is chambered for the .308 cartridge and fitted with a 19.7" heavy barrel. The stock is laminated wood with black lacquer finish. The stock has a forearm rail with handstop, adjustable buttplate, and cheekpiece. The trigger is adjustable. Weight is approximately 10.25 lbs. Introduced in 1999.

NIB	Exc.	V.G.	Good	Fair	Poor
3295	2500	—	—	—	—

SBS Tactical Elite Heavy Barrel

This model, introduced in 2000, features a 26" heavy barrel, no sights, matte blue finish, Zytel stock with adjustable cheekpiece and adjustable buttplate. Full length Picatinny mounting rail. Magazine capacity is 5 or 10 rounds. Chambered for .308 cartridge.

NIB	Exc.	V.G.	Good	Fair	Poor
2400	1750	—	—	—	—

NOTE: Add $100 for stainless steel model. Add $1,000 for ZF optics.

SBS Tactical Elite Heavy Barrel Carbine

Same as the Tactical Elite Heavy Barrel model but fitted with a 20" heavy barrel. Introduced in 2000.

NIB	Exc.	V.G.	Good	Fair	Poor
2400	1750	—	—	—	—

Steyr AUG

A 5.56mm semi-automatic, Bullpup rifle with a 20" barrel incorporating a Swarovski 1.5x telescopic sight. Green carbon composite stock. Weight is about 8.5 lbs. Recommend independent, local appraisals.

NIB	Exc.	V.G.	Good	Fair	Poor
4200	3700	3100	2500	1600	1300

Steyr AUG—Police Model

Same as above but with black stock and 16" barrel.

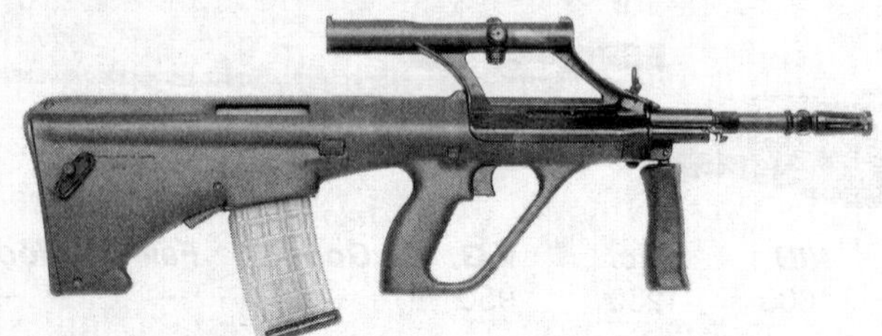

NIB	Exc.	V.G.	Good	Fair	Poor
4500	4000	3400	2800	1900	1500

Steyr AUG Special Receiver

Receiver only. Special flattop with Stanag mounting.

NIB	Exc.	V.G.	Good	Fair	Poor
2500	2000	1800	1200	800	600

Steyr USR

This model is the post-ban version of the AUG. Fitted with a Swarovski 1.5x scope and gray synthetic stock.

NIB	Exc.	V.G.	Good	Fair	Poor
2850	2600	2200	1500	800	600

Steyr Zepher

This model is a .22 caliber rimfire bolt-action carbine. It has a 5-round detachable magazine, dovetailed receiver for scope rings. It is fitted with a full stock. Made from 1953 to 1968.

Exc.	V.G.	Good	Fair	Poor
1200	1000	900	700	350

PISTOLS

Model SPP

Introduced in 1993 this is a 9mm semi-automatic pistol. It is made from synthetic materials and operates on a delayed blowback, rotating barrel system. The magazine capacity is either 15 or 30 rounds. The barrel is 5.9" in length overall length is 12.75" and weight is about 42 oz. Due to its appearance and design this pistol was banned for importation into the United States shortly after its introduction. Because of this circumstance the price of this pistol may fluctuate widely.

NIB	Exc.	V.G.	Good	Fair	Poor
900	750	600	500	400	300

Model M

Chambered for the .40 S&W, 9mm, or .357 SIG cartridge this semi-automatic pistol has a polymer frame and 3 user selectable safety systems. Loaded chambered indicator. Triangle/Trapezoid sights. Limited access lock with key. Weight is about 28 oz. Magazine capacity is 10 rounds. Introduced in 1999.

NIB	Exc.	V.G.	Good	Fair	Poor
600	450	—	—	—	—

Model S

This model is similar to the Model M but is fitted with a 3.58" barrel. Chambered for the .40 S&W, 9mm, or .357 SIG cartridges. Magazine capacity is 10 rounds. Weight is approximately 22 oz. Introduced in 2000.

NIB	Exc.	V.G.	Good	Fair	Poor
600	450	—	—	—	—

STEYR HAHN

SEE—Steyr

STEYR MANNLICHER

SEE—Steyr

STI INTERNATIONAL

Georgetown, Texas

LS9 & LS40

Single stack pistol chambered for the 9mm or .40 S&W cartridge. Fitted with a 3.4" barrel and short grip. Heine Low Mount sights. Rosewood grips. Matte blue finish. Magazine capacity is 7 rounds for 9mm and 6 rounds for .40 S&W. Weight is about 28 oz.

NIB	Exc.	V.G.	Good	Fair	Poor
850	600	—	—	—	—

BLS9 & BLS40

Same as above but with full length grip. Magazine capacity is 9 rounds for 9mm and 8 rounds for .40 S&W.

NIB	Exc.	V.G.	Good	Fair	Poor
840	675	—	—	—	—

Ranger

Chambered for the .45 ACP cartridge and fitted with a 3.9" barrel with short grip. Fixed STI sights. Blued frame with stainless steel slide. Weight is about 29 oz.

NIB	Exc.	V.G.	Good	Fair	Poor
950	775	—	—	—	—

Ranger II

Chambered for the .45 ACP cartridge and fitted with a 4.15" ramped bull barrel. Slide is flat top with rear serrations and chamfered fore end. Ambidextrous safety and high rise grip safety. Adjustable rear sight. Hard chrome upper with blued lower frame. Weight is about 39 oz.

NIB	Exc.	V.G.	Good	Fair	Poor
1000	825	—	—	—	—

Trojan

Chambered for the .45 ACP, .40 Super, .40 S&W, and 9mm cartridge. Fitted with a 5" barrel. Rosewood grips. Matte blue finish. Eight-round magazine capacity. Weight is about 36 oz.

NIB	Exc.	V.G.	Good	Fair	Poor
1025	800	600	—	—	—

NOTE: For .40 Super with .45 ACP conversion add $275. For Trojan with 6" slide add $250.

Tactical 4.15

Chambered for the 9mm, .40 S&W, or the 45 ACP cartridge. Fully supported ramped 4.15" bull barrel. Frame has tactical rail. Slide has rear serrations. Fixed rear sight. Aluminum magazine well. Black polycoat finish. Weight is about 34.5 oz.

NIB	Exc.	V.G.	Good	Fair	Poor
1720	1450	—	—	—	—

Tactical

As above but with 5" barrel. Flat blue finish. Weight is about 39 oz.

NIB	Exc.	V.G.	Good	Fair	Poor
1720	1450	—	—	—	—

Trubor

Chambered for the 9mm major, 9x23, or .38 Super cartridges. Steel frame. Fully supported and ramped one piece with bull barrel with integral compensator. Slide has front and rear serrations. Sights are C-More or OK Red Dot reflix. Blued finish. Weight is about 42.5 oz. with scope.

NIB	Exc.	V.G.	Good	Fair	Poor
2300	1875	—	—	—	—

Lawman

This .45 ACP pistol has a 5" ramped barrel with match grade bushing. Aluminum trigger. Series 70 grip safety. Novak 3 dot sights. Checkered walnut grips. Polymer finish with brown slide over tan frame. Weight is about 36 oz.

NIB	Exc.	V.G.	Good	Fair	Poor
1345	1000	—	—	—	—

Xcaliber Single Stack

Chambered for the .450 SMC cartridge and fitted with a 6" slide. Adjustable rear sight. Weight is about 38 oz. Blue finish. Single stack magazine. Discontinued.

NIB	Exc.	V.G.	Good	Fair	Poor
1465	1175	—	—	—	—

Xcaliber Double Stack

Same as the Xcaliber Single Stack except that this model has a double stack magazine. Discontinued.

NIB	Exc.	V.G.	Good	Fair	Poor
2125	1700	—	—	—	—

Executive

Chambered for the .40 S&W cartridge. Fitted with a 5" ramped bull barrel. Adjustable rear sight. Gray synthetic grip and hard chrome slide. Weight is about 39 oz. Double stack magazine.

NIB	Exc.	V.G.	Good	Fair	Poor
2390	1800	—	—	—	—

VIP

Chambered for the .45 ACP cartridge and fitted with a 3.9" ramped bull barrel. Stainless steel flat top slide. Fixed rear sight. Ten-round magazine capacity. Weight is about 25 oz.

NIB	Exc.	V.G.	Good	Fair	Poor
1650	1250	—	—	—	—

Edge

Chambered for the 9mm, 10mm, .40 S&W, and .45 ACP cartridge with 5" ramped bull barrel. Dual stack magazine. Bomar style sights. Blue finish. Weight is about 39 oz.

NIB	Exc.	V.G.	Good	Fair	Poor
1795	1400	—	—	—	—

Eagle

Chambered for customer's choice of caliber and fitted with 5" ramped bull barrel. Fixed sights. Blued frame and stainless steel slide. Weight is about 30 oz.

NIB	Exc.	V.G.	Good	Fair	Poor
1700	1400	—	—	—	—

Duty One

Chambered for the 9mm, .40 S&W, or .45 ACP cartridges. Five-inch bull barrel is fully supported and ramped. Steel frame with single stack magazine with front strap checkering and tactical rail. Grips are rosewood. Slide has front and rear serrations. Adjustable sights. Finish is flat blue. Weight is about 38 oz.

NIB	Exc.	V.G.	Good	Fair	Poor
1650	1225	—	—	—	—

Duty CT

1911-style steel frame single-stack with integral tactical rail and rosewood grips. 5" slide/barrel, fixed 2-dot tritium rear sight. 36.6 oz. Also available in 4.15" commander size. Blued. Introduced 2006. MSRP: 1648

Competitor

Chambered for the .38 Super cartridge and fitted with a 5.5" ramped bull barrel with compensator. Fitted with a C-More scope. Stainless steel slide. Weight is about 44 oz. with scope and mount. Discontinued.

NIB	Exc.	V.G.	Good	Fair	Poor
2500	1900	—	—	—	—

Grandmaster

Custom built to customer's specifications in 9mm major, 9x23, and .38 Super.

NIB	Exc.	V.G.	Good	Fair	Poor
2395	1800	—	—	—	—

Rangemaster

Fitted with a 5" fully supported and ramped bull barrel and chambered for the 9mm or .45 ACP cartridge, this pistol has a full length dust cover, checkered front strap and mainspring housing and square trigger guard. Front and rear slide serrations. Adjustable sights. Rose grips. Polished blue finish. Weight is about 38 oz.

NIB	Exc.	V.G.	Good	Fair	Poor
1440	1050	—	—	—	—

Rangemaster II

Single-stack blued variation of Rangemaster. Chambered for 9mm, .40 S&W, .45 ACP. 5" slide/barrel, 37 oz. Introduced 2006.

NIB	Exc.	V.G.	Good	Fair	Poor
1344	—	—	—	—	—

Targetmaster

As above but with 6" barrel.

NIB	Exc.	V.G.	Good	Fair	Poor
1440	1050	—	—	—	—

Stinger

Chambered for the 9mm or .38 Super cartridge. Fitted with a 3.9" barrel with compensator. Sights are OKO or C-More on STI mount. Blued finish. Weight is about 38 oz.

NIB	Exc.	V.G.	Good	Fair	Poor
2775	2100	—	—	—	—

Hawk 4.3

This pistol is modeled on the 1911 design and is equipped with a 4.3" barrel with steel slide. The frame of the pistol is made from polymer and features and increased magazine capacity while retaining the 1911 grip thickness. Chambered for .38 Super, .45 ACP, .40 S&W, 10mm, and 9x25 calibers. Built primarily for competition shooting. Discontinued.

NIB	Exc.	V.G.	Good	Fair	Poor
1775	1400	900	—	—	—

Night Hawk 4.3

Chambered for .45 ACP only with 4.3" bull barrel and a host of special features such a narrow tactical safety, front and rear slide serrations, and extended dust cover. Tritium sights optional. Blued finish. Weight is 33 oz. Discontinued.

NIB	Exc.	V.G.	Good	Fair	Poor
1925	1500	—	—	—	—

Falcon 3.9

Similar to the above model but fitted with a 3.9" barrel. Weight is approximately 30 oz. with steel frame and 25 oz. with Aluminum frame. Discontinued.

NIB	Exc.	V.G.	Good	Fair	Poor
1925	1500	—	—	—	—

Sparrow 5.0

Chambered for the .22 LR cartridge only and fitted with a 5" bull barrel with fixed sights. Weight is approximately 30 oz. Discontinued.

NIB	Exc.	V.G.	Good	Fair	Poor
990	800	600	—	—	—

Edge 5.1

Chambered for .40 S&W only with 5" bull barrel and many special features. BoMar front and rear sights. Weight is 39 oz.

NIB	Exc.	V.G.	Good	Fair	Poor
1875	1400	—	—	—	—

Eagle 5.1

Similar to the Model 2011 Hawk but furnished with a 5" barrel. Comes standard with BoMar adjustable sights.

NIB	Exc.	V.G.	Good	Fair	Poor
1975	1400	900	—	—	—

Eagle 5.5

Similar to above model but furnished with a 5-1/2" barrel with compensator.

NIB	Exc.	V.G.	Good	Fair	Poor
2475	1900	1250	—	—	—

Eagle 6.0

Chambered for 9mm, .38 Super, .40 S&W, or .45 ACP cartridges. Fitted with a 6" bull barrel. Many special features. BoMar front and rear sights. Blued finish. Weight is about 42 oz.

NIB	Exc.	V.G.	Good	Fair	Poor
1925	1500	—	—	—	—

Hunter 6.0

Chambered for the 10mm cartridge only and fitted with a 6" bull barrel. Heavy extended frame. Many special features. Leupold 2x scope. Blued finish. Weight with scope 51 oz.

NIB	Exc.	V.G.	Good	Fair	Poor
2350	1850	—	—	—	—

Special Edition

Chambered for the 9mm, .40 S&W or .45 ACP cartridge and fitted with a fully supported and ramped 5" bull barrel. Hi-Rise grip. Sights are Dawson fiber optic with adjustable rear. Slide has Saber Tooth serrations and custom engraving. Finish is 24 karat gold on all steel parts except barrel. Weight is about 38 oz.

NIB	Exc.	V.G.	Good	Fair	Poor
2930	—	—	—	—	—

I.P.S.C. 30th Anniversary

Similar to the Special Edition but with hard chrome upper with color inlays and blued lower.

NIB	Exc.	V.G.	Good	Fair	Poor
2775	2075	—	—	—	—

FPI 2260 Rifle

Chambered for the .22 Long Rifle cartridge. Aluminum receiver with adjustable trigger and quick magazine release. Integral scope mount.

NIB	Exc.	V.G.	Good	Fair	Poor
1100	825	—	—	—	—

TruSight

Semi-auto pistol chambered for 9mm, .40 S&W, .45 ACP; double-stack magazine. Steel frame, 4.15" slide/barrel. Dawson fiber optic front sight, adjustable rear sight. 36.1 oz. Blued with multiple options. IPSC, USPSA approved. Introduced 2006.

NIB	Exc.	V.G.	Good	Fair	Poor
1800	—	—	—	—	—

Legacy

Chambered for .45 ACP single-stack. 5" slide/barrel, LOA 8.5", 38 oz. with adjustable rear sight. Cocobola smooth grips. IDPA, USPSA approved. Introduced 2006.

NIB	Exc.	V.G.	Good	Fair	Poor
1500	—	—	—	—	—

STOCK, FRANZ

Berlin, Germany

Stock

A .22, 6.35mm or 7.65mm semi-automatic pistol with an open topped slide. The frame marked "Franz Stock Berlin." Blued with black composition grips impressed with the name "Stock" at the top. Manufactured from 1918 to the early 1930s.

Courtesy J.B. Wood

Exc.	V.G.	Good	Fair	Poor
450	300	250	150	100

STOCKING & CO.

Worcester, Massachusetts

Pepperbox

A .28 or .316 barreled percussion pepperbox revolver with barrel lengths from 4" to 6". The hammer is fitted with a long cocking piece at the rear and the trigger guard may or may not be made with a spur at the rear. Blued with walnut grips. The barrel group marked "Stocking & Co., Worcester." Manufactured between 1846 and 1854.

Courtesy Wallis & Wallis, Lewes, Sussex, England

Exc.	V.G.	Good	Fair	Poor
—	—	1500	600	200

Single-Shot Pistol

A .36 caliber single-shot percussion pistol of the same pattern as the pepperbox with a 4" half octagonal barrel. Marked as above. Manufactured from 1849 to 1852.

Exc.	V.G.	Good	Fair	Poor
—	—	850	350	100

STOEGER, A. F.

South Hackensack, New Jersey

.22 Luger

A .22 caliber simplified copy of the German Model P.08 semi-automatic pistol with a 4.5" or 5.5" barrel and an aluminum frame. The word "Luger" is roll engraved on the right side of the frame. Blued with checkered brown plastic grips.

Exc.	V.G.	Good	Fair	Poor
300	250	200	150	100

Target Luger

As above, with adjustable target sights.

Exc.	V.G.	Good	Fair	Poor
325	275	225	175	125

Luger Carbine

As above, with an 11" barrel, walnut forend and checkered walnut grips. Furnished with a red velvet lined black leatherette case. Manufactured during the 1970s.

Exc.	V.G.	Good	Fair	Poor
550	400	350	250	175

American Eagle Luger

This is identical to the German design. It is chambered for the 9mm with a 7-round magazine and fitted with a 4" barrel. Checkered walnut grips. Stainless steel. Weight is about 32 oz.

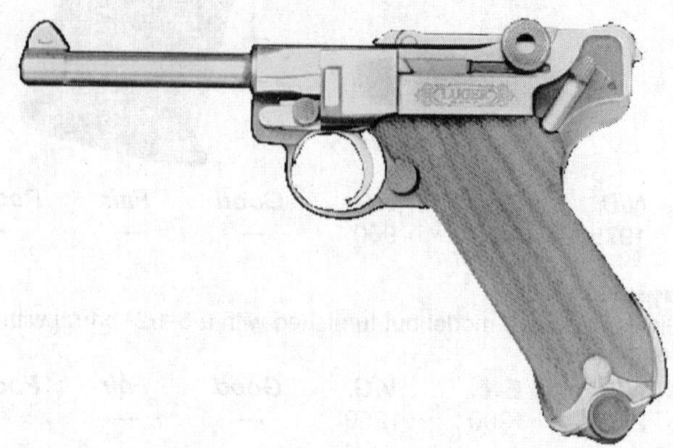

NIB	Exc.	V.G.	Good	Fair	Poor
850	650	400	250	200	100

American Eagle Navy Model

Same as above but with a 6" barrel.

NIB	Exc.	V.G.	Good	Fair	Poor
850	650	400	250	200	100

SHOTGUNS

Model 2000

This is a semi-automatic shotgun chambered for the 12 gauge shell. Fitted with 26", 28", or 30" vent rib barrel. Single trigger with screw-in chokes. Weight is about 7 lbs. Introduced in 2001.

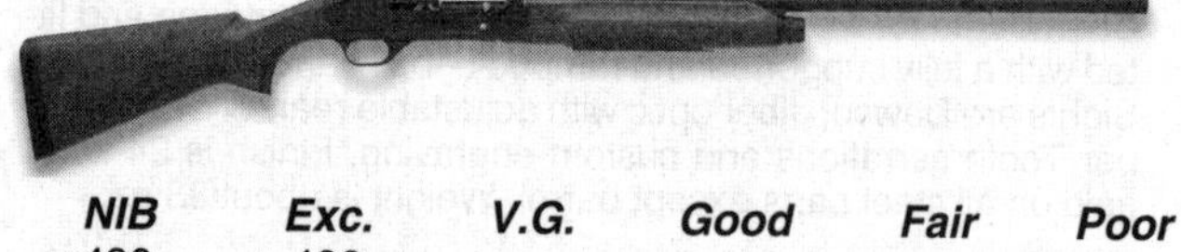

NIB	Exc.	V.G.	Good	Fair	Poor
490	400	—	—	—	—

Model 2000 Deluxe

Same as above but with high grade walnut stock and etched receiver with gold trigger.

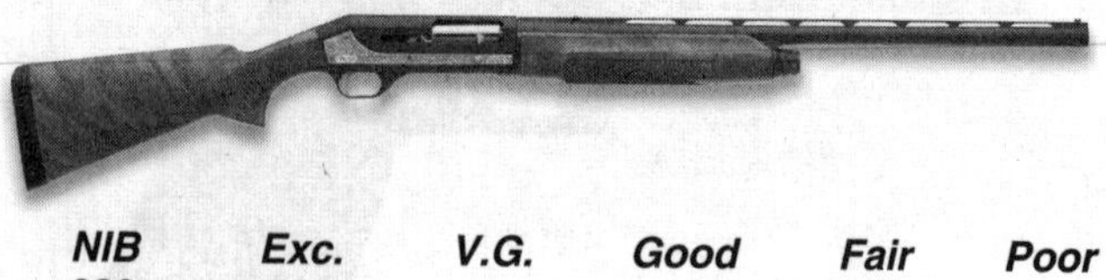

NIB	Exc.	V.G.	Good	Fair	Poor
620	500	—	—	—	—

Model 2000 Camo

As above but with Advantage Timber HD camo stock.

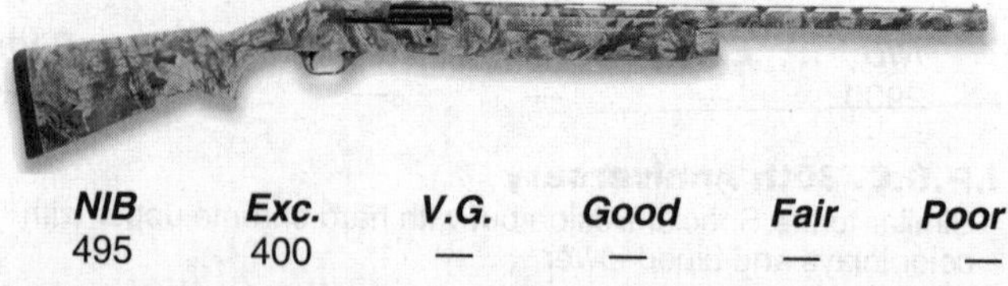

NIB	Exc.	V.G.	Good	Fair	Poor
495	400	—	—	—	—

Model 2000 Slug

This model is chambered for the 12 gauge shell with 3" chamber. Barrel length is 24". The gun is fitted with a black synthetic stock. Smooth bore barrel. Adjustable rifle-type sights. Optional field-style barrels in 24", 26", or 28". Weight is approximately 6.7 lbs. Introduced in 2003.

NIB	Exc.	V.G.	Good	Fair	Poor
430	325	—	—	—	—

Model 2000 Synthetic

As above but choice of 24", 26", or 28" vent rib barrel and black synthetic stock. Weight is about 6.8 lbs. Introduced in 2003.

NIB	Exc.	V.G.	Good	Fair	Poor
420	325	—	—	—	—

Coach Gun

This is a side-by-side gun chambered for the 12 or 20 gauge shell as well as the .410 shell. Fitted with 20" barrels with double triggers. Improved Cylinder and Modified fixed chokes. Weight is about 7 lbs.

NIB	Exc.	V.G.	Good	Fair	Poor
320	250	—	—	—	—

NOTE: Add $50 for nickel finish.

Silverado Coach Gun

Offered in 12 and 20 gauge as well as .410 bore with straight- or pistol-grip stock and matte nickel finish. Straight-stock version is offered in 12 and 20 gauge only. Weight is about 6.5 lbs.

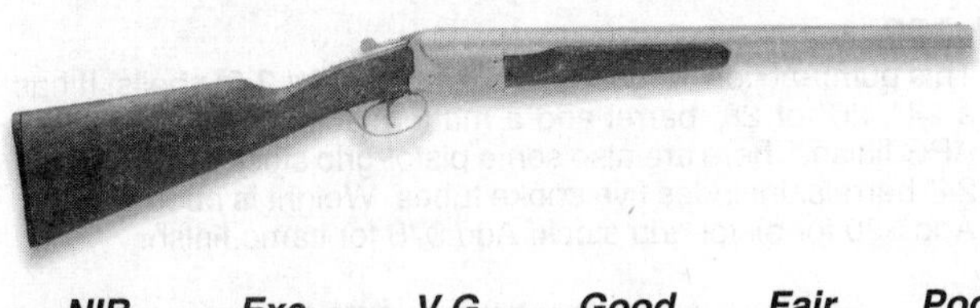

NIB	Exc.	V.G.	Good	Fair	Poor
375	300	—	—	—	—

Coach Gun Supreme

This model is similar to the above but offered with blue, stainless, or nickel receiver. Introduced in 2004.

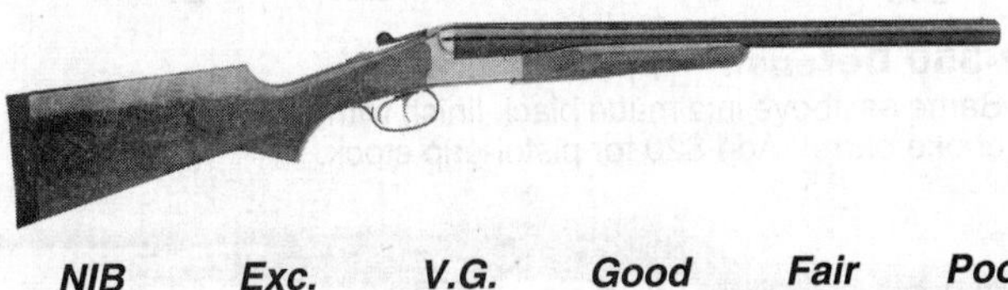

NIB	Exc.	V.G.	Good	Fair	Poor
380	300	—	—	—	—

NOTE: Add $10 for stainless and $30 for nickel.

Uplander

This side-by-side shotgun is chambered for the 12, 16, 20, 28, and .410 bores. with choice of 26" or 28" barrels. Fixed chokes. Double triggers. Weight is about 7.25 lbs.

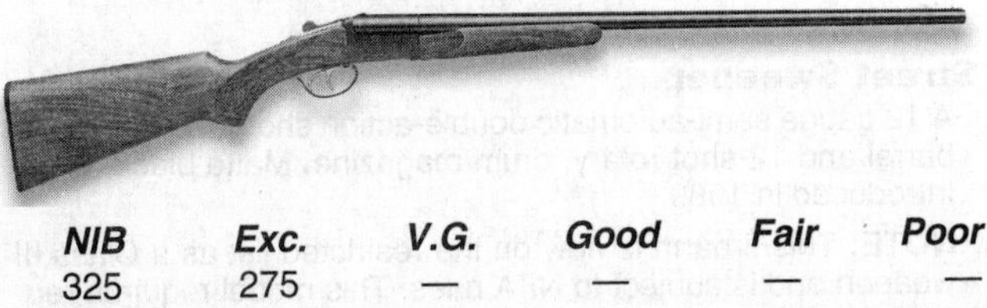

NIB	Exc.	V.G.	Good	Fair	Poor
325	275	—	—	—	—

Uplander Special

As above but with straight grip and oil finish stock. Offered in 12, 20, or 28 gauge. Weight is about 7.3 lbs.

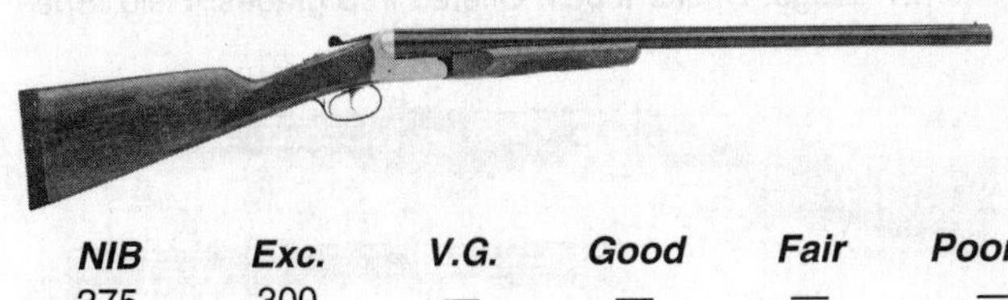

NIB	Exc.	V.G.	Good	Fair	Poor
375	300	—	—	—	—

Uplander Supreme

Same as above but with select wood and screw-in chokes.

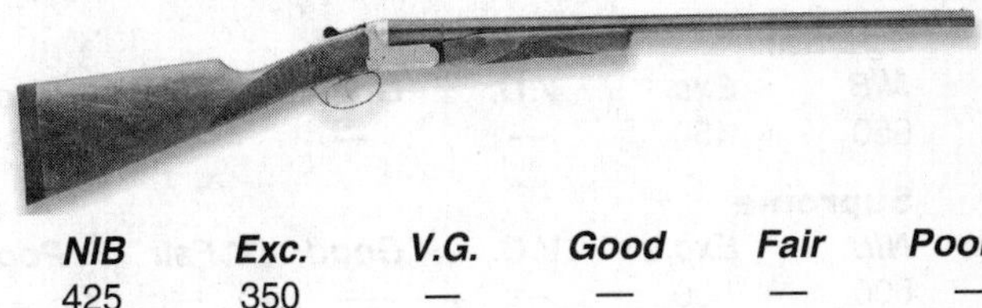

NIB	Exc.	V.G.	Good	Fair	Poor
425	350	—	—	—	—

Uplander English

This variation is fitted with a straight-grip stock and chambered for the 20 gauge or .410 bore. Fitted with 24" barrels. Weight is about 7 lbs. Also available with a short stock.

NIB	Exc.	V.G.	Good	Fair	Poor
340	275	—	—	—	—

Uplander Youth

Offered in 20 gauge or .410 bore this model features a 13" LOP with 22" barrels choked Improved Modified and Modified. Weight is about 6.75 lbs.

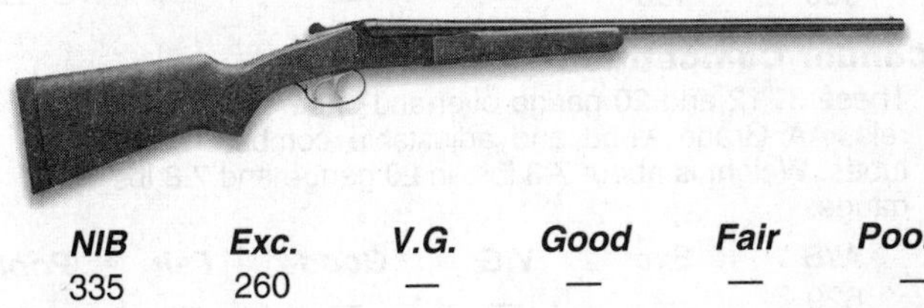

NIB	Exc.	V.G.	Good	Fair	Poor
335	260	—	—	—	—

Condor

This over-and-under shotgun is chambered 12, 16 and 20 gauges and .410 bore. Available with 26" and 28" barrels in all gauges and 26" barrel in .410 bore. Single trigger. Blued finish. The 16-gauge is chambered for 2.75" shells. All others have 3" chambers. Weights run from 6 lbs. to 7.4 lbs. depending on bore.

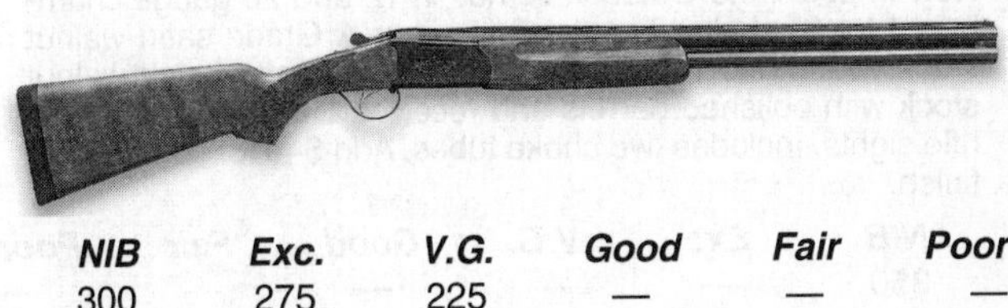

NIB	Exc.	V.G.	Good	Fair	Poor
300	275	225	—	—	—

Condor Special

Similar to the standard Condor model but with matte stainless receiver and rubbed oil finish stock. Introduced in 2003.

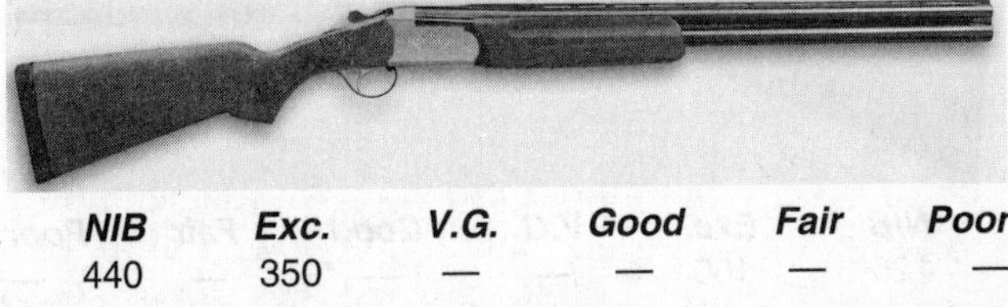

NIB	Exc.	V.G.	Good	Fair	Poor
440	350	—	—	—	—

Condor Combo

This model, introduced in 2004, features a two-barrel set of 12 and 20 gauge. Barrel length on the 12 gauge is 28" and 26" on the 20 gauge. Choke tubes. Offered in 3 grades: Field, Special, and Supreme. Introduced in 2004.

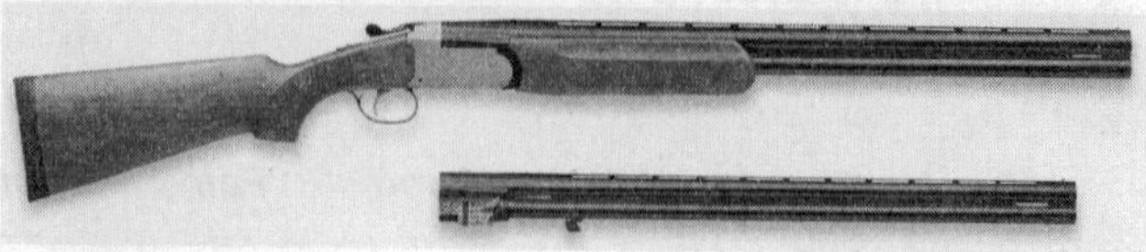

Field

NIB	Exc.	V.G.	Good	Fair	Poor
500	400	—	—	—	—

Special

NIB	Exc.	V.G.	Good	Fair	Poor
550	450	—	—	—	—

Supreme

NIB	Exc.	V.G.	Good	Fair	Poor
600	500	—	—	—	—

Condor Supreme Deluxe

Similar to the above model but with cut checkering and high polish blue. Offered in 12 and 20 gauge with 26" or 28" barrels as well as 24" barrels for the 20 gauge. Automatic ejectors.

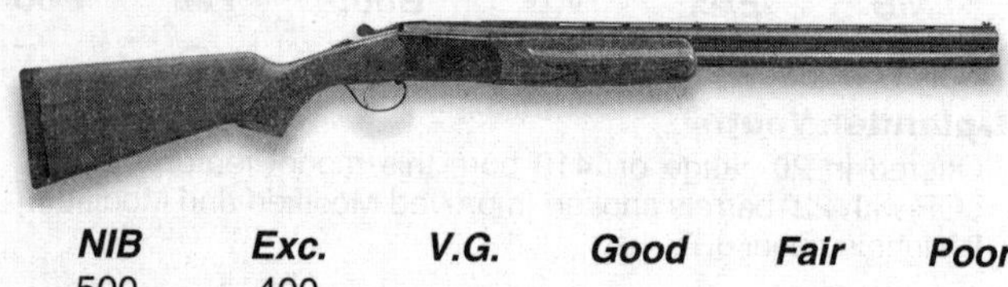

NIB	Exc.	V.G.	Good	Fair	Poor
500	400	—	—	—	—

Condor Competition

These 3" 12 and 20 gauge over-and-unders feature 30" barrels, AA Grade wood and adjustable combs. Three choke tubes. Weight is about 7.3 lbs. in 20 gauge and 7.8 lbs. in 12 gauge.

NIB	Exc	V.G.	Good	Fair	Poor
629	—	—	—	—	—

Condor Competition Combo

As above with 12 gauge and 20 gauge barrels.

NIB	Exc	V.G.	Good	Fair	Poor
749	—	—	—	—	—

Condor Outback

New in 2007, the Outback comes in 12 and 20 gauge chambered for 3" shells. The finish is either A Grade satin walnut stock with blued barrels and receiver or matte black walnut stock with polished barrels and receiver. Barrels are 20" with rifle sights. Includes two choke tubes. Add $40 for black/nickel finish.

NIB	Exc	V.G.	Good	Fair	Poor
350	—	—	—	—	—

Single Barrel Classic Youth

Available in 20 gauge or .410 bore with a 13" length of pull and 22" vent rib barrel. Straight-grip stock. Weight is about 5 lbs.

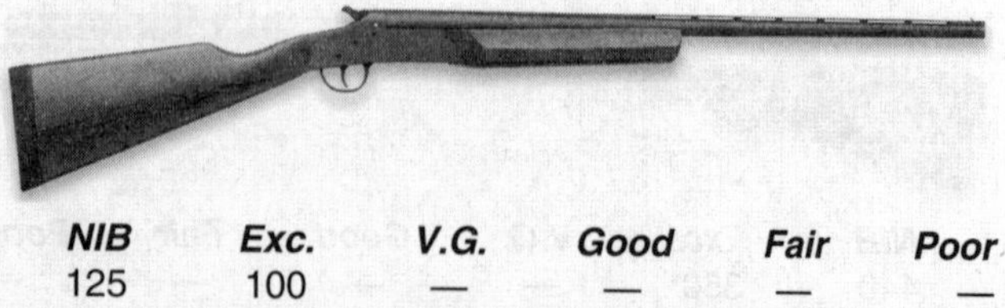

NIB	Exc.	V.G.	Good	Fair	Poor
125	100	—	—	—	—

Single Barrel Classic

As above but with standard length of pull and available in 12, 20 or .410 bore. Barrel length on 12 gauge is 26" or 28"; on 20 gauge length is 26". On .410 bore barrel length is 24". Open pistol grip. Weight is about 5.5 lbs.

NIB	Exc.	V.G.	Good	Fair	Poor
120	90	—	—	—	—

Single Barrel Special

As above but with stainless steel frame. Offered in 12, 20, or .410 bore. Weight is about 5.5 lbs.

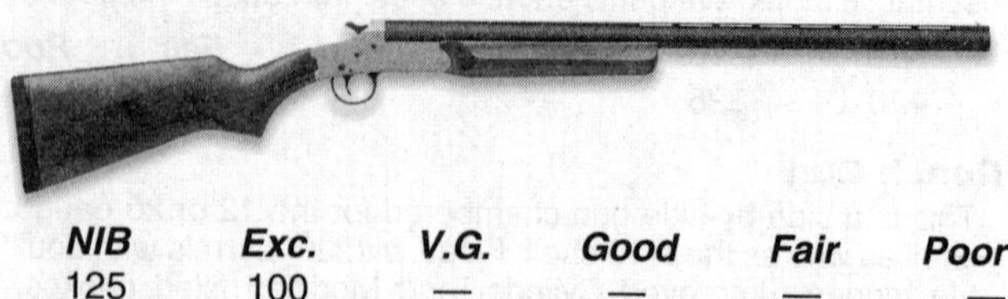

NIB	Exc.	V.G.	Good	Fair	Poor
125	100	—	—	—	—

P-350

This pump-action 12 gauge shotgun was introduced in 2005. All versions are chambered for 3.5" shells. Available with 24", 26" or 28" barrel in matte black synthetic or Advantage Timber camo finish; available with 26" or 28" barrel in Max-4 camo finish. Comes with 5 choke tubes. Weight is about 6.8 lbs. Also available is a Defense model with 18.5" barrel and fixed cylinder bore. Add 15 percent for camo models.

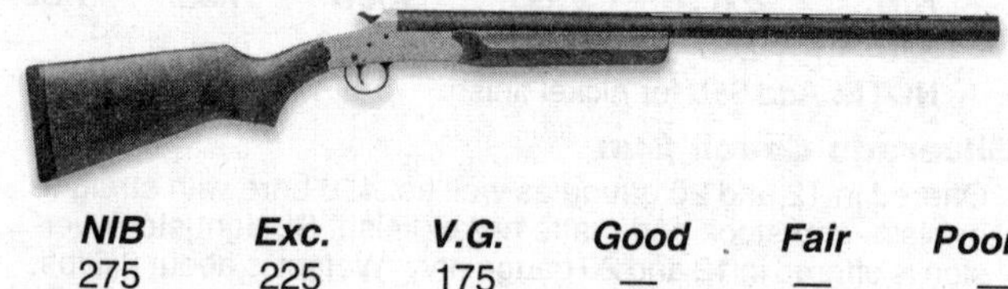

NIB	Exc.	V.G.	Good	Fair	Poor
275	225	175	—	—	—

P-350

This pump-action 12 gauge is chambered for 3.5" shells. It has a 24", 26" or 28" barrel and a matte black, Max-4, Timber or APG finish. There are also some pistol-grip stock offerings with 24" barrels. Includes five choke tubes. Weight is about 6.8 lbs. Add $20 for pistol-grip stock. Add $75 for camo finish.

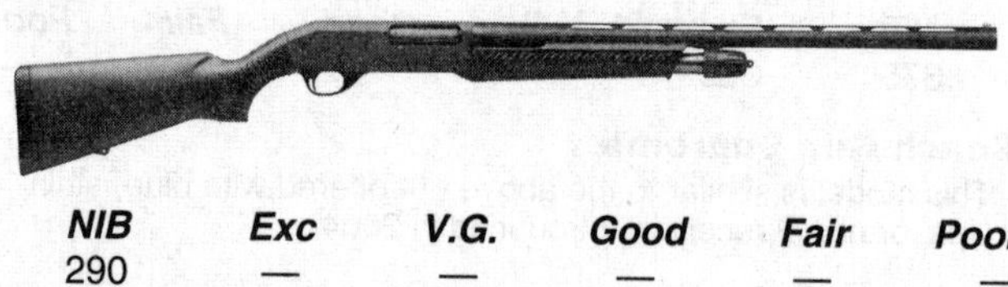

NIB	Exc	V.G.	Good	Fair	Poor
290	—	—	—	—	—

P-350 Defense

Same as above in a matte black finish with 18.5", fixed cylinder choke barrel. Add $20 for pistol-grip stock.

NIB	Exc	V.G.	Good	Fair	Poor
290	—	—	—	—	—

STREET SWEEPER
Atlanta, Georgia

Street Sweeper

A 12 gauge semi-automatic double-action shotgun with an 18" barrel and 12-shot rotary, drum magazine. Matte black finish. Introduced in 1989.

NOTE: This firearm is now on the restricted list as a Class III weapon and is subject to NFA rules. This model requires registration with the BATF to avoid federal penalties. Make sure that the shotgun is transferable prior to sale.

NIB	Exc.	V.G.	Good	Fair	Poor
1250	950	750	600	—	—

STURDIVANT, LEWIS G.

Talladega, Alabama

Received contract from the state of Alabama for 2,000 "Mississippi" or "Enfield" rifles. Two hundred and eighty were received on this contract. These arms resemble U.S. Model 1841 Rifles without patchboxes. Overall length 48-1/2"; barrel length 33"; .577 caliber. Unmarked.

STURM, RUGER & CO.

Southport, Connecticut

In 1946 William B. Ruger applied for his first patent on a blowback operated, semi-automatic, .22 caliber pistol. In 1949 Bill Ruger and Alexander Sturm released this pistol for sale, and the Ruger dynasty began. This pistol was as perfect for the American marketplace as could be. It was accurate, reliable, and inexpensive and ensured the new company's success. In 1951 Alexander Sturm passed away, but Mr. Ruger continued forward. At this time the fledgling television industry was popularizing the early American West, and Colt had not reintroduced the Single-Action Army after WWII. Ruger decided that a Western-style six shooter would be a successful venture, and the Single Six was born. This was not a Colt copy but a new design based on the Western look. Again Ruger scored in the marketplace, and this has been pretty much the rule ever since. With few exceptions this company has shown itself to be accurate in gauging what the gun-buying public wants. They have expanded their line to include double-action revolvers, single-shots, semi-auto and bolt-action rifles, percussion revolvers, and even a semi-automatic wonder nine. They have stayed ahead of the legal profession as much as possible by introducing safety devices and comprehensive instruction manuals and generally insured their future success. For such a relatively new company, collector interest in certain models is quite keen. There are a number of factors that govern Ruger collector values. All models made in 1976 were designated "200th Year of Liberty" models and if in NIB condition will bring up to a 25 percent premium if a market is found. The newer models that have a safety warning stamped on the barrel are generally purchased only by shooters and have no collector appeal whatsoever. The astute individual must be aware of these nuances when dealing in Rugers. There are some excellent works written on the Ruger (not as many as there are on the Colt or the Smith & Wesson), and the new collector can educate himself if he so desires. We list this company's models in chronological order.

NOTE: William B. Ruger died in 2002 at the age of 86.

SEMI-AUTOMATIC RIMFIRE PISTOLS

Standard Model "Red Eagle Grips"

This is a blowback semi-automatic with a fixed, exposed, 4.75" barrel. The receiver is tubular, with a round bolt. There is a 9-shot detachable magazine, and the sights are fixed. The finish is blued, and the black hard rubber grips on this first model feature a red Ruger eagle or hawk medallion on the left side. There were approximately 25,600 manufactured before Alexander Sturm's death in 1951, but this model may be seen as high as the 35000 serial number range. Because variations of this model exist an expert opinion should be sought before a final price is established.

NIB	Exc.	V.G.	Good	Fair	Poor
650	550	450	325	250	150

NOTE: Factory verified plated pistols will bring between $2,500 and $5,000 depending on condition. For pistols in factory original wood "cod box" shipping carton add $2,000.

Standard Model

This model is identical to the Red Eagle except that after Sturm's death the grip medallions were changed from red to black and have remained so ever since. This pistol was produced from 1952-1982 in 4-3/4" and 6" barrels. There are a great many variations of this pistol, but a book dealing with this pistol alone should be consulted as the differences in variations are subtle and valuation of these variations is definitely a matter for individual appraisal.

Exc.	V.G.	Good	Fair	Poor
275	200	125	100	85

Standard Model—Marked "Hecho en Mexico"

These pistols were assembled and sold in Mexico. Approximately 200 were built with 4-3/4" barrels and about 50 were produced with 6" barrels. Only a few of these pistols have been accounted for and for this reason an expert should be consulted.

Exc.	V.G.	Good	Fair	Poor
1500	1200	850	600	400

Mark I Target Model

The success of the Ruger Standard Model led quite naturally to a demand for a more accurate target model. In 1951 a pistol that utilized the same frame and receiver with a 6-7/8", target-type barrel and adjustable sights was introduced. Early target models number 15000 to 16999 and 25000 to 25300 have Red Eagle grips. In 1952 a 5-1/4" tapered barrel model was introduced, but was soon discontinued. In 1963 the popular 5-1/2" bull barrel model was introduced. These models enjoyed well deserved success and were manufactured from 1951-1982.

Red Eagle

6-7/8" barrel.

Exc.	V.G.	Good	Fair	Poor
595	450	250	200	150

Black or Silver Eagle

6-7/8" barrel.

Exc.	V.G.	Good	Fair	Poor
325	275	175	150	125

NOTE: For original hinged box add 35 percent. With factory supplied muzzlebrake add $75-100. For other Mark I Target models under serial number 72500 in original hinged box add 50 percent.

5-1/4" Tapered Barrel Model

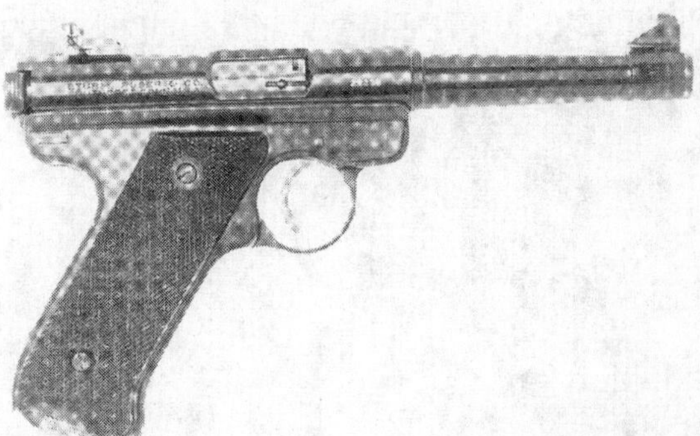

Exc.	V.G.	Good	Fair	Poor
700	600	400	250	125

NOTE: Add 50 percent if in original 5-1/4" marked hinged box.

5-1/2" Bull Barrel Model

Exc.	V.G.	Good	Fair	Poor
375	275	150	125	95

Mark I Target Model Rollmarked with U.S. on Top of Frame

These pistols will have either 1/16" or 1/8" high serial numbers.

Exc.	V.G.	Good	Fair	Poor
700	500	300	200	150

NOTE: Add 25 percent to price if pistol has 1/8" high serial numbers.

Stainless Steel 1 of 5,000

This model is a special commemorative version of the first standard with the "Red Eagle" grips. It is made of stainless steel and is rollmarked with Bill Ruger's signature on it. The pistol is encased in a wood "salt cod" case.

NIB	Exc.	V.G.	Good	Fair	Poor
395	350	300	225	175	125

MARK II .22 CALIBER PISTOL SPECIFICATIONS

Supplied in .22 LR with various barrel weights and lengths. Magazine capacity is 10 rounds. Trigger is grooved with curved finger surface. High speed hammer provides fast lock time. Grips are sharply checkered and made of black gloss delrin material. Stainless steel models have a brushed satin finish. Today, each model except the MK-10 and KMK-10, come from the factory with a lockable plastic case and Ruger lock.

NOTE: In 2004 all Ruger adjustable sight .22 pistols are drilled and tapped for an included Weaver-type scope base adapter.

Mark II Standard Model

This is a generally improved version of the first Ruger pistol. There is a hold-open device, and the magazine holds 10 rounds. This model was introduced in 1982.

Standard Mark II Model MK4

Blued finish with 4.75" barrel. Checkered composition grips. Weight about 35 oz.

NIB	Exc.	V.G.	Good	Fair	Poor
225	175	150	125	100	75

Standard Mark II Model MK450

Introduced in 1999 to commemorate the 50th anniversary of the first Ruger rimfire pistol. Fitted with a 4.75" barrel with fixed sights. Chambered for the .22 LR cartridge. The pistols grips have a red Ruger medallion and Ruger crest on the barrel. Furnished in a red case. Weight is about 35 oz. Production limited to one year.

NIB	Exc.	V.G.	Good	Fair	Poor
285	225	—	—	—	—

Standard Mark II Model MK6

Same as above but with 6" barrel. Weight 37 oz.

NIB	Exc.	V.G.	Good	Fair	Poor
225	175	150	125	100	75

Standard Mark II Model KMK4

This model is the same as the Mark II Standard except that it is made of stainless steel.

NIB	Exc.	V.G.	Good	Fair	Poor
330	295	200	150	125	100

Standard Mark II Model KMK6

Same as above but with 6" barrel. Weight is about 37 oz.

NOTE: In 1997, Ruger produced 650 of the Model MK6 with special features for the "Friends of the NRA" auction of the same year. These guns have high polish blueing, faux ivory grips panels, a gold inlaid National Rifle Association inscription and a gold inlaid number of "1 of 650" to "650 of 650". The NIB price for these pistols is $550.

NIB	Exc.	V.G.	Good	Fair	Poor
330	295	200	150	125	100

Mark II Target Model

This model incorporates the same improvements as the Mark II Standard but is offered with 5.5" bull, 6-7/8" tapered and 10" heavy barrel. A 5-1/4" tapered barrel was added in 1990 but discontinued in 1994. Blued finish. This model has adjustable target sights and was introduced in 1982.

NOTE: In 1989, approximately 2,000 5-1/2" bull barrel Mark II pistols with blue barreled receivers and stainless steel grip frames were produced by Ruger on order from a Ruger distributor. They exist in the 215-25xxx to 215-43xxx serial number range. The NIB price for these pistols is $375.

NIB	Exc.	V.G.	Good	Fair	Poor
315	275	200	150	125	100

Stainless Steel Mark II Target Model

This model is the same as the blued version but is made of stainless steel.

NIB	Exc.	V.G.	Good	Fair	Poor
360	285	250	200	175	125

Government Model

This model is similar to the blue Mark II Target, with a 6-7/8" bull barrel. It is the civilian version of a training pistol that the military is purchasing from Ruger. The only difference is that this model does not have the U.S. markings.

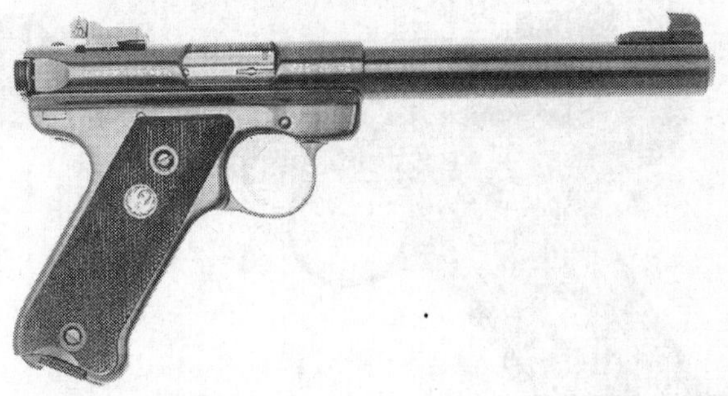

NIB	Exc.	V.G.	Good	Fair	Poor
357	285	225	200	150	100

Stainless Steel Government Model

Stainless steel version of the Government Model.

NOTE: Same with U.S. markings. These are found in the serial number range of 210-00001 to 210-18600. Only a couple dozen are in civilian hands. The NIB price for these pistols is $1,000.00.

NIB	Exc.	V.G.	Good	Fair	Poor
427	340	250	225	175	125

Mark II Competition Model KMK678GC

The Competition model features a stainless steel frame with checkered laminated hardwood thumb rest grips, heavy 6-7/8" bull barrel factory drilled and tapped for scope mount, Partridge type front sight undercut to prevent glare and an adjustable rear sight. Pistol weighs 45 oz.

NOTE: In 1997 Ruger produced 204 of these pistols in blue instead of stainless steel for one of their distributors. They are very scarce. The NIB for these pistols is $350.

In 1995 Ruger produced a similar blued pistol (1,000 total, 500 each with or without scope rings) with 5-1/2" slab side barrels. These are not marked "Competition Target Model" like the previously described variation. The NIB price for these pistols is $350 and with rings $375.

NIB	Exc.	V.G.	Good	Fair	Poor
427	350	275	200	125	100

Mark II Bull Barrel Model MK4B

Introduced in 1996 this bull barrel variation has a blued finish with a 4" barrel. Grips are checkered composition. Weight is about 38 oz.

NIB	Exc.	V.G.	Good	Fair	Poor
300	200	175	150	125	100

Ruger 22/45 Model

This .22 LR caliber pistol has the same grip angle and magazine latch as the Model 1911 .45 ACP. The semi-automatic action is stainless steel and the grip frame is made from Zytel, a fiberglass reinforced lightweight composite material. Front sight is Patridge-type. This model is available in several different configurations. A 4" tapered barrel and standard model sights, a 5.25" tapered barrel with target sights, or a 5.5" bull barrel with target sights. The 5.25" barrel was discontinued in 1994.

KP4

This model features a 4.75" standard weight barrel with fixed sights. Pistol weighs 28 oz.

NIB	Exc.	V.G.	Good	Fair	Poor
300	275	250	200	125	75

KP514

Furnished with a target tapered barrel 5.25" in length. Comes with adjustable sights. Pistol weighs 38 oz. Model now discontinued.

NIB	Exc.	V.G.	Good	Fair	Poor
300	200	175	150	100	75

KP512

This model is equipped with a 5.5" bull barrel with adjustable sights. Weighs 42 oz.

NOTE: In 1995 Ruger produced 500 22/45s with stainless steel 6-7/8" Government type barreled receivers for one of their distributors.They appear around the 220-59xxx serial number range. The NIB price for these pistols is $350.00.

In 1997 another Ruger distributor succeeded in contracting Ruger to make a similar 22/45 only in blue and with 6-7/8" slab side bull barrels. Approximately 1,000 were produced with serial numbers extending to the 220-87xxx serial number range. The NIB price is $300.00.

NIB	Exc.	V.G.	Good	Fair	Poor
300	200	175	150	100	75

P4

A limited number, about 1,000, of this variation were produced in 1995 with a 4" bull barrel on a P frame. It was introduced into the product line as a production pistol in 1997. Weight is approximately 31 oz.

NIB	Exc.	V.G.	Good	Fair	Poor
525	350	200	150	100	75

P512

This variation of the stainless steel version has a blued receiver with P-style frame.

NIB	Exc.	V.G.	Good	Fair	Poor
210	175	125	100	75	60

This symbol denotes "Sleepers" with rapidly-rising values and/or significant collector potential.

MARK III .22 CALIBER PISTOL SPECIFICATIONS

The Mark III series was introduced in 2004. This series features a newly designed magazine release button located on the left side of the frame. Mark III pistols also have a visible loaded chamber indicator, an internal lock, magazine disconnect, re-contontured sights and ejection port.

Mark III Standard Pistol

Introduced in 2005 this .22 caliber pistol is fitted with a 4.75" or 6" barrel. Fixed rear sight. Blued finish. Magazine capacity is 10 rounds. Black checkered grips. Weight is about 35 oz. depending on barrel length.

NIB	Exc.	V.G.	Good	Fair	Poor
320	250	—	—	—	—

Mark III Hunter

This .22 caliber pistol is fitted with a 6.88" target crowned fluted stainless steel barrel. Adjustable rear sight with Hi-Viz front sight. Checkered Cocobolo grips. Drilled and tapped for scope mount. Supplied with green case, scope base adapter, and 6 interchangeable LitePipes for front sight. Weight is about 41 oz. Introduced in 2005.

NIB	Exc.	V.G.	Good	Fair	Poor
425	365	—	—	—	—

Mark III Competition

This .22 caliber model features a 6.88" flat sided heavy barrel with adjustable rear sight and Patridge front sight. Stainless steel finish. Checkered wood grips. Weight is about 45 oz. Introduced in 2005.

NIB	Exc.	V.G.	Good	Fair	Poor
425	315	—	—	—	—

Mark III Pistol

This .22 caliber pistol has a grip frame similar to the Colt 1911 pistol. The 4" bull barrel is flat sided. Blued steel frame. Fixed sights. Magazine capacity is 10 rounds. Grips are checkered black polymer. Weight is about 29 oz.

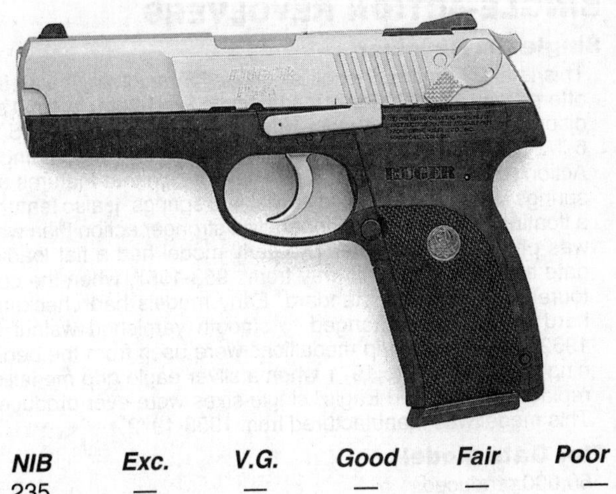

NIB	Exc.	V.G.	Good	Fair	Poor
235	—	—	—	—	—

Mark III 512 Pistol

This .22 LR pistol has a 5.5" barrel and adjustable rear sight. Steel frame is blued. Checkered black synthetic grips. Weaver-style scope base adapter included. Magazine capacity is 10 rounds. Weight is about 41 oz.

Ruger® Mark III Pistol
MKIII512

NIB	Exc.	V.G.	Good	Fair	Poor
380	300	—	—	—	—

22/45 Mark III Hunter

Similar to 22/45 .22 pistol but with Mark III-style improvements. 6-7/8" or 4-1/2" fluted barrel, HiViz front sight with six interchangeable inserts. Blued or stainless finish. Pricing is for stainless model. Introduced in 2007.

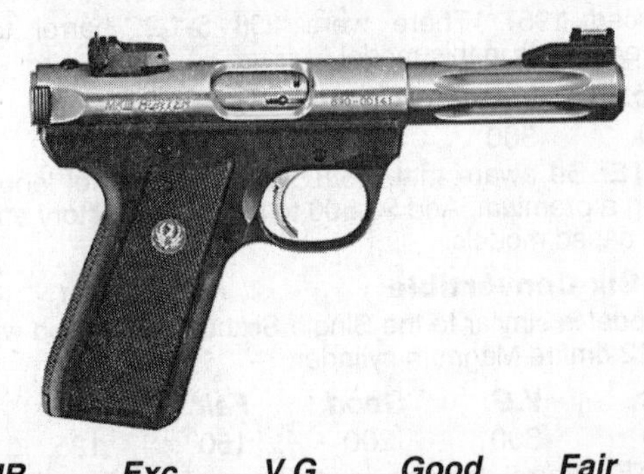

NIB	Exc	V.G.	Good	Fair	Poor
390	—	—	—	—	—

SINGLE-ACTION REVOLVERS

Single Six Revolver

This is a .22 rimfire, 6-shot, single-action revolver. It was first offered with a 5-1/2" barrel length and a fixed sight. In 1959 additional barrel lengths were offered for this model in 4-5/8", 6-1/2", and 9-1/2". It is based in appearance on the Colt Single-Action Army, but internally it is a new design that features coil springs instead of the old-style, flat leaf springs. It also features a floating firing pin and is generally a stronger action than what was previously available. The early model had a flat loading gate and was made this way from 1953-1957, when the contoured gate became standard. Early models had checkered hard rubber grips changed to smooth varnished walnut by 1962. Black eagle grip medallions were used from the beginning of production to 1971 when a silver eagle grip medallion replaced it. No "Red Eagle" single-sixes were ever produced. This model was manufactured from 1953-1972.

Flat Gate Model

60,000 produced.

NOTE: Be aware that revolvers serial numbered under 2000 will bring a premium of 25 percent to 125 percent depending on condition, low serial number, and color of cylinder frame—bright reddish purple the most desirable.

Courtesy John C. Dougan

Courtesy *Know Your Ruger Single-Action Revolvers 1953-63.* Blacksmith Corp.

NIB	*Exc.*	*V.G.*	*Good*	*Fair*	*Poor*
700	600	450	225	150	125

Contoured Gate Model

Introduced 1957. There were 258 5-1/2" barrel factory engraved pistols in this model.

Exc.	*V.G.*	*Good*	*Fair*	*Poor*
400	300	200	150	125

NOTE: Be aware that 4-5/8" and 9-1/2" barrel lengths will bring a premium. Add $3,500 to $6,000 for factory engraved and cased models.

Single Six Convertible

This model is similar to the Single Six but is furnished with an extra .22 rimfire Magnum cylinder.

Exc.	*V.G.*	*Good*	*Fair*	*Poor*
400	300	200	150	125

NOTE: Barrel lengths in 4-5/8" and 9-1/2" will bring a premium.

Single Six .22 Magnum Model

This model is similar to the Single Six except that it is chambered for the .22 rimfire Magnum and the frame was so marked. It was offered in the 6.5" barrel length only and was manufactured for three years. An extra long rifle cylinder was added later in production. The serial numbers are in the 300000-340000 range.

Exc.	*V.G.*	*Good*	*Fair*	*Poor*
400	300	250	200	175

Lightweight Single Six

This model is similar to the Single Six, with an aluminum alloy frame and 4-5/8" barrel. This variation was produced between 1956 and 1958 and was in the 200000-212000 serial number range. Approximately the first 6,500 were produced with alloy cylinders with steel chamber inserts.

NOTE: Stamped after the serial number or on the bottom of the frame. Varieties of "S" marked lightweights exist. Individual evaluation and appraisal is recommended. These are factory seconds and are verifiable.

Courtesy *Know Your Ruger Single-Action Revolvers 1953-63.* Blacksmith Corp.

Courtesy *Know Your Ruger Single-Action Revolvers 1953-63.* Blacksmith Corp.

Silver Anodized Frame with Aluminum Cylinder Model with Martin Hardcoat Finish

Exc.	*V.G.*	*Good*	*Fair*	*Poor*
775	550	400	225	195

Black Anodized Aluminum Frame and Cylinder Model

Exc.	*V.G.*	*Good*	*Fair*	*Poor*
850	600	500	300	250

Black Anodized Frame with Blue Steel Cylinder Model

Exc.	*V.G.*	*Good*	*Fair*	*Poor*
550	450	350	225	195

Silver Anodized with Blue Steel Cylinder Model

Only a few hundred pistols in this variation were produced by the factory with an "S" suffix.

Exc.	*V.G.*	*Good*	*Fair*	*Poor*
1100	850	600	400	200

NOTE: For original Lightweight Single-Six boxes add 25 percent to 40 percent.

Super Single Six

Introduced in 1964, this is the Single Six with adjustable sights. Prices listed are for pistols with 5-1/2" and 6-1/2" barrels.

NOTE: The listed models are factory verifiable.

Courtesy *Know Your Ruger Single-Actions: The Second Decade.* Blacksmith Corp.

Exc.	V.G.	Good	Fair	Poor
400	300	200	125	100

4-5/8" Barrel

200 built.

Exc.	V.G.	Good	Poor
1000	900	750	400

Nickel-Plated Model

Approximately 100 built.

Exc.	V.G.	Good	Poor
2250	1600	1200	—

Bearcat (Old Model)

This is a scaled-down version of the single-action. It is chambered for .22 rimfire and has a 4" barrel and an unfluted, roll engraved cylinder. The frame is alloy, and it has a brass colored anodized alloy trigger guard. The finish is blue, and the grips are plastic impregnated wood until 1963, thereafter walnut with eagle medallions were used. This model was manufactured from 1958-1970.

Courtesy *Know Your Ruger Single-Actions: The Second Decade.* Blacksmith Corp.

Serial Number under 30000

Exc.	V.G.	Good	Fair	Poor
400	300	225	150	125

Alphabet Model

Exc.	V.G.	Good	Fair	Poor
500	400	295	275	225

Black Anodized Trigger Guard Model

109 built.

Exc.	V.G.	Good	Fair	Poor
800	600	500	400	—

Serial Number over 30000 or with 90-prefix

Exc.	V.G.	Good	Fair	Poor
350	300	265	225	175

Super Bearcat (Old Model)

This model is similar to the with a steel frame and, on later models, a blued steel trigger guard and grip frame. The early examples still used brass. This model was manufactured from 1971 to 1974.

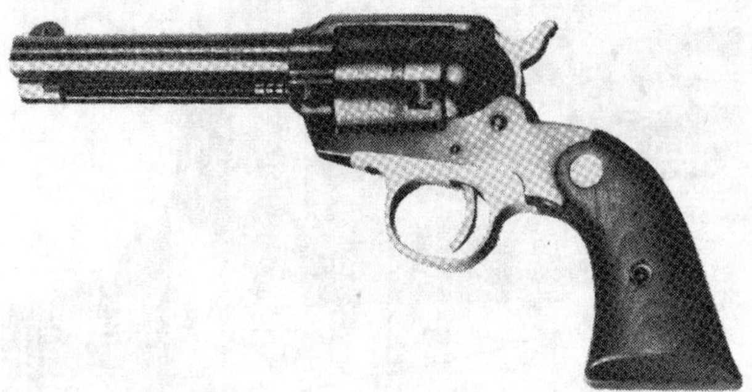

Courtesy W.P. Hallstein III and son Chip

Exc.	V.G.	Good	Fair	Poor
450	350	250	225	175

Flattop—.357 Magnum

The success of the Single Six led to the production of a larger version chambered for the .357 Magnum cartridge. This model is a single-action, with a 6-shot fluted cylinder and a flat top strap with adjustable "Micro sight." The barrel length is 4-5/8", 6.5", and 10". The finish is blue with checkered hard rubber grips on the early examples and smooth walnut on later ones. There were approximately 42,600 manufactured between 1955 and 1962.

Courtesy *Know Your Ruger Single-Action Revolvers 1953-63.* Blacksmith Corp.

Courtesy *Know Your Ruger Single-Action Revolvers 1953-63.* Blacksmith Corp.

4-5/8" Barrel

NIB	Exc.	V.G.	Good	Fair	Poor
900	700	500	350	250	200

6-1/2" Barrel

NIB	Exc.	V.G.	Good	Fair	Poor
1000	850	600	450	350	250

10" Barrel

NIB	Exc.	V.G.	Good	Fair	Poor
1650	1300	950	850	750	600

Blackhawk Flattop .44 Magnum

Courtesy *Know Your Ruger Single-Action Revolvers 1953-63*. Blacksmith Corp.

In 1956 the .44 Magnum was introduced, and Ruger jumped on the bandwagon. This is similar in appearance to the .357 but has a slightly heavier frame and a larger cylinder. It was available in a 6.5", 7.5", and 10" barrel. It was manufactured from 1956-1963. There were approximately 29,700 manufactured.

Courtesy *Know Your Ruger Single-Action Revolvers 1953-63*. Blacksmith Corp.

6-1/2" Barrel

NIB	Exc.	V.G.	Good	Fair	Poor
1100	800	600	450	350	250

7-1/2" Barrel

NIB	Exc.	V.G.	Good	Fair	Poor
1325	950	700	600	450	300

10" Barrel

NIB	Exc.	V.G.	Good	Fair	Poor
1750	1300	900	800	700	400

REMINDER
There's a big difference between value and price. Price is what the other guy pays.

Blackhawk

This model is similar to the "Flattop," but the rear sight is protected by two raised protrusions—one on each side. It was available chambered for the .30 Carbine, .357 Magnum, .41 Magnum, or the .45 Colt cartridge. Barrel lengths are 4-5/8" or 6.5" in .357 Magnum and .41 Magnum. .45 Colt version has 4-5/8" and 7.5" barrel lengths. The .30 Carbine is furnished with a 7.5" barrel only. The finish is blue, and the grips are walnut with Ruger medallions. This model was produced from 1962 to 1972. Note that the "Old Style" Blackhawk (i.e., pre-transfer bar) is a popular platform for custom revolvers, so prices may exceed those shown depending on circumstances.

Courtesy *Know Your Ruger Single-Action Revolvers 1953-63*. Blacksmith Corp.

NIB	Exc.	V.G.	Good	Fair	Poor
700	500	350	200	150	125

NOTE: Add 20 percent for .41 Mag. and 50 percent for .45 Colt and 35 percent for .30 Carbine. Original verified factory brass grip frame will add at least $200 to above prices. It was available chambered for the .357 Magnum or .41 Magnum (4-5/8" or 6-1/2" barrel), or .45 Long Colt (4-5/8" or 7-1/2" barrel). The .41 Magnum with factory installed brass frame will bring $800 to $1500 depending on condition.

Blackhawk Convertible

This model is the same as the Blackhawk with an extra cylinder to change or convert calibers. The .357 Magnum has a 9mm cylinder, and the .45 Colt has a .45 ACP cylinder.

.357/9mm

NIB	Exc.	V.G.	Good	Fair	Poor
550	450	400	300	200	—

.45 L.C./.45 ACP

NIB	Exc.	V.G.	Good	Fair	Poor
800	650	500	300	200	—

NOTE: The 4-5/8" barrel will bring a slight premium. Nonprefix serial numbered .357/9mm Blackhawks will bring a premium.

Super Blackhawk

The formidable recoil of the .44 Magnum cartridge was difficult to handle in a revolver with a small grip such as found on the Blackhawk, so it was decided to produce a larger-framed revolver with increased size in the grip. The rear of the trigger guard was squared off, and the cylinder was left unfluted to increase mass. This model was offered with a 7.5" barrel; 600 6.5" barrel Super Blackhawks were produced by factory error. This model is blued and has smooth walnut grips with medallions. The first of these revolvers were offered in a fitted wood case and are rare today. The Super Blackhawk was made from 1959-1972.

NOTE: For pistols with verified factory installed brass grip frame each example should be appraised.

NIB	Exc.	V.G.	Good	Fair	Poor
600	500	400	300	200	150

Early Model in Wood Presentation Case

NIB	Exc.	V.G.	Good	Fair	Poor
1000	850	650	475	400	300

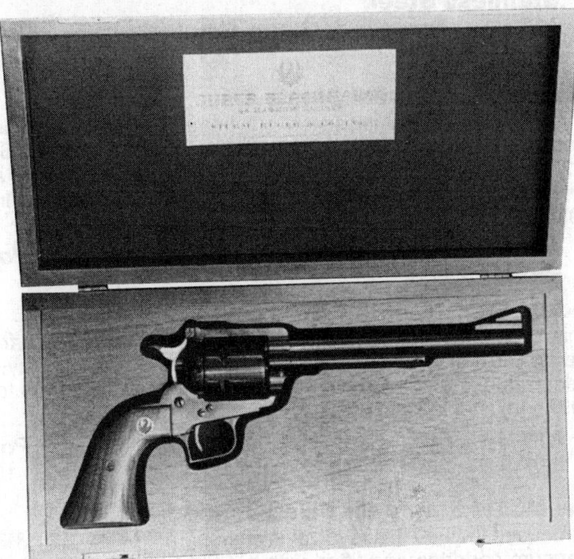

Super Blackhawk in scarce mahogany case, serial numbers 1-8500 Courtesy *Know Your Ruger Single-Action Revolvers 1953-63.* Blacksmith Corp.

In Fitted White Cardboard Case

NIB	Exc.	V.G.	Good	Fair	Poor
1200	1100	1000	950	875	675

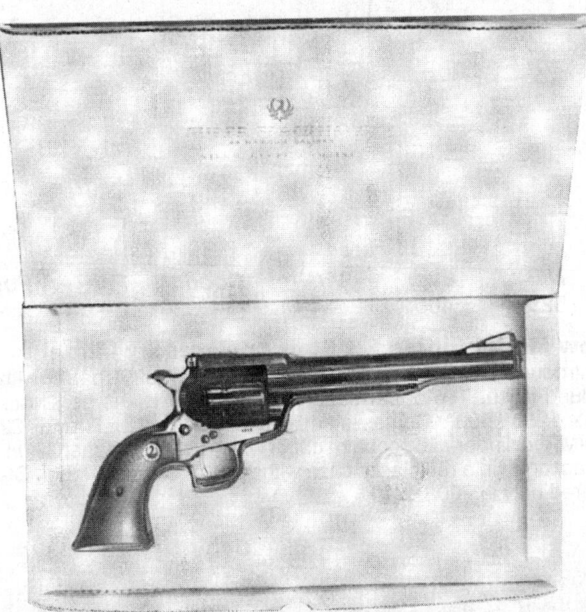

Super Blackhawk in rare white cardboard case, serial numbers 3500-10500 Courtesy *Know Your Ruger Single-Action Revolvers 1953-63.* Blacksmith Corp.

Long Grip Frame in Wood Case

300 guns built.

NIB	Exc.	V.G.	Good	Fair	Poor
1500	1250	1150	1050	800	675

Factory Verified 6-1/2" Barrel

Approximately 600 guns built in the 23000-25000 serial number range.

NIB	Exc.	V.G.	Good	Fair	Poor
950	850	650	550	450	375

NOTE: For pistols with brass grip frames add $250 to the prices listed.

Hawkeye Single-Shot

The shooting public wanted a small-caliber, high-velocity handgun. The Smith & Wesson Model 53, chambered for the .22 Jet, appeared in 1961; and the cartridge created extraction problems for a revolver. Ruger solved the problem with the introduction of the Hawkeye—a single-shot that looked like a six shooter. In place of the cylinder was a breech block that cammed to the side for loading. This pistol was excellent from an engineering and performance standpoint but was not a commercial success. The Hawkeye is chambered for the .256 Magnum, a bottleneck cartridge, and has an 8.5" barrel and adjustable sights. The finish is blued with walnut, medallion grips. The barrel is tapped at the factory for a 1" scope base. This pistol is quite rare as only 3,300 were produced in 1963 and 1964.

Courtesy John C. Dougan

NIB	Exc.	V.G.	Good	Fair	Poor
2000	1700	1400	850	600	500

Editor's Comment: All of the above single-action Ruger pistols fitted with factory optional grips will bring a premium regardless of model. This premium applies to pistols manufactured from 1954 to 1962 only. For the optional grips the premium is: Ivory $800, Stag $400.

NEW MODEL SERIES

The Ruger firm has always demonstrated keen perception and in 1973 completely modified their single-action lockwork to accommodate a hammer block or transfer bar. This hammer block or transfer bar prevented accidental discharge should a revolver be dropped. In doing so, the company circumvented a great deal of potential legal problems and made collectibles out of the previous models. There are many individuals who simply do not care for the "New Models," as they are called, and will not purchase them; but judging from the continued success and growth of the Ruger company, those individuals must be the exception, not the rule.

Super Single Six Convertible (New Model)

This model is similar in appearance to the old model but has the new hammer block safety system. The frame has two pins instead of three screws, and opening the loading gate frees the cylinder stop for loading. Barrel lengths are 4-5/8", 5.5", 6.5", and 9.5". The sights are adjustable; the finish is blued. The grips are walnut with a medallion, and an interchangeable .22 Magnum cylinder is supplied. This model was introduced in 1973 and is currently in production.

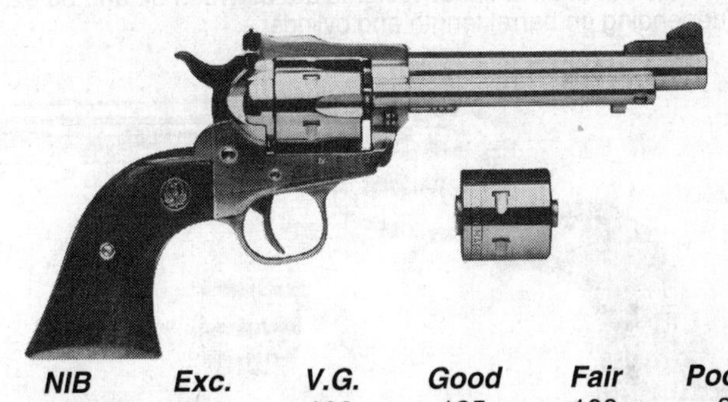

NIB	Exc.	V.G.	Good	Fair	Poor
315	275	200	125	100	80

Stainless Steel Single Six Convertible

The same as the standard blued model but made from stainless steel. Offered with a 4-5/8", 6-1/2", and 9-1/2" barrel.

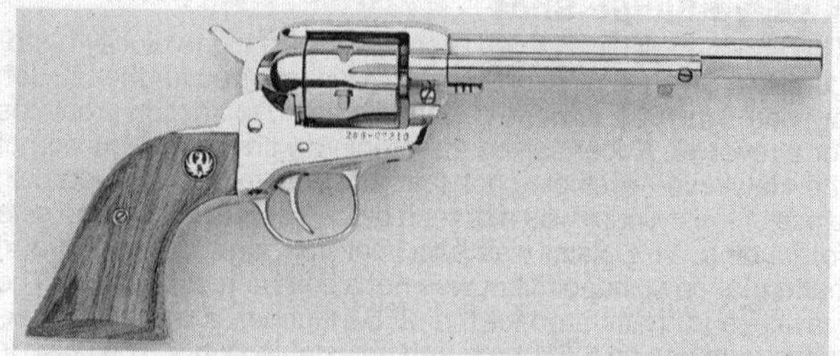

NIB	Exc.	V.G.	Good	Fair	Poor
395	300	200	175	125	100

NOTE: Pre-warning pistols (1973-1976) with 4-5/8" or 9-1/2" barrel will bring an additional 40 percent premium. Pistols with 4-5/8" barrels with "made in the 200th year of American Liberty" rollmark on the barrel will bring at least 100 percent premium to the NIB prices.

New Model Single-Six (.22 LR only) "Star" Model

This model was produced in blue and stainless for one year only in 4-5/8", 5-1/2", 6-1/2", and 9-1/2" barrel lengths. Very low production on this model.

Blue Variation

5.5" or 6.5" Barrel

NIB	Exc.	V.G.	Good	Fair	Poor
450	400	350	300	275	—

9.5" Barrel—Rare

NIB	Exc.	V.G.	Good	Fair	Poor
550	500	450	400	350	—

4.62" Barrel—Very Rare

NIB	Exc.	V.G.	Good	Fair	Poor
800	750	450	400	350	—

Stainless Variation

5.5" or 6.5" Barrel

NIB	Exc.	V.G.	Good	Fair	Poor
450	350	275	—	—	—

9.5" Barrel

NIB	Exc.	V.G.	Good	Fair	Poor
600	500	400	—	—	—

4.62" Barrel—Rare

NIB	Exc.	V.G.	Good	Fair	Poor
650	550	500	—	—	—

Fixed Sight New Model Single Six

First made as drift adjustable rear sight (500 each in 4-5/8", 5-1/2", and 6-1/2" blue) and now a catalogued item as a pinched frame style fixed rear sight. Barrel lengths are offered in 5-1/2" and 6-1/2" lengths. Finish is blued or glossy stainless steel. Rear sight is fixed. Weights are between 32 and 38 oz. depending on barrel length and cylinder.

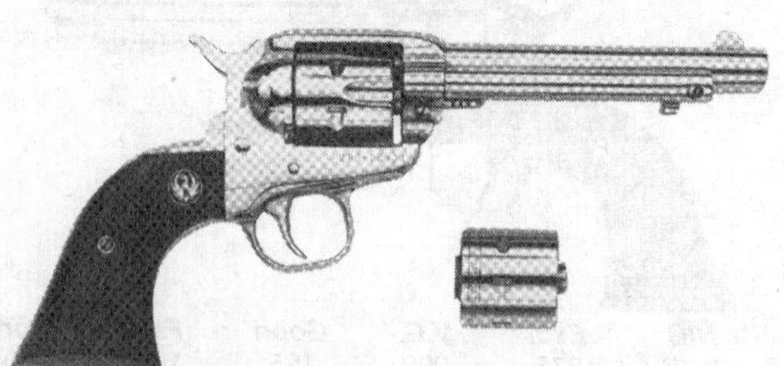

Blued Finish

NIB	Exc.	V.G.	Good	Fair	Poor
300	225	200	150	125	100

Stainless Steel

NIB	Exc.	V.G.	Good	Fair	Poor
395	300	250	200	150	125

Colorado Centennial Single Six

This model had a stainless steel grip frame, and the balance is blued. It has walnut grips with medallion insert. The barrel is 6-1/2", and the revolver is furnished with a walnut case with a centennial medal insert. There were 15,000 manufactured in 1975.

NIB	Exc.	V.G.	Good	Fair	Poor
500	400	—	—	—	—

Model "SSM" Single Six

This is the Single Six chambered for the .32 H&R Magnum cartridge. The first 800 pistols were marked with "SSM" on the cylinder frame and will bring a slight premium. Sold from 1984 to 1997. Adjustable sights.

NIB	Exc.	V.G.	Good	Fair	Poor
450	350	200	150	125	100

New Model Single Six Fixed Sight

Introduced in 2000 this revolver is chambered for the .32 H&R Magnum cartridge and fitted with a 4.625" barrel. Offered in blue or stainless steel. Short (1/4" shorter) simulated ivory grips. Vaquero-style frame with fixed sights.

NIB	Exc.	V.G.	Good	Fair	Poor
525	400	—	—	—	—

New Model Single Six 50th Anniversary Model

Introduced in 2003 this model features a 4.625" barrel with blued finish. Top of barrel is rollmarked "50 YEARS OF SINGLE SIX 1953-2003". Comes standard with both .22 LR and .22 WMR cylinders. Cocobolo grips with red Ruger medallion. Packaged in a red plastic case with special "50 Year" label. Offered only in 2003.

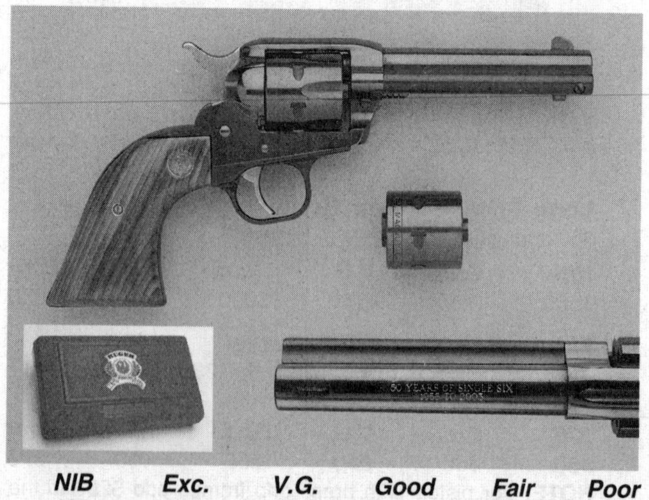

NIB	Exc.	V.G.	Good	Fair	Poor
425	350	—	—	—	—

New Model Super Single Six

Chambered for the .22 LR and a separate cylinder for the .22 WMR cartridge. Barrel lengths are 4.625", 5.5", 6.5", and 9.5". Rosewood grips and adjustable or fixed sights. Blued finish except for optional stainless steel on 5.5" or 6.5" revolvers. Weight is about 35 oz. depending on barrel length.

NIB	Exc.	V.G.	Good	Fair	Poor
410	325	—	—	—	—

NOTE: For stainless steel models add $80.

New Model Super Single Six, .17 HMR

As above but with 6.5" barrel and chambered for the .17 HMR cartridge. Weight is about 35 oz. Introduced in 2003.

NIB	Exc.	V.G.	Good	Fair	Poor
400	325	—	—	—	—

New Model Single Six Hunter Convertable

This model is chambered for the .17 HMR/.17 Mach 2. Fitted with a 7.5" barrel with adjustable rear sight. Stainless steel finish with black laminate grips. The integral barrel rib machined for scope rings. Weight is about 45 oz. Introduced in 2005.

NIB	Exc.	V.G.	Good	Fair	Poor
675	500	—	—	—	—

Buckeye Special

This model was built in 1989 and 1990. It is chambered for the .38-40 or 10mm and .32-20 or .32 H&R cartridges.

NIB	Exc.	V.G.	Good	Fair	Poor
650	500	300	250	125	—

New Model Blackhawk

This model is similar in appearance to the old model Blackhawk, offered in the same calibers and barrel lengths. It has the transfer bar safety device. It was introduced in 1973 and is currently in production.

NIB	Exc.	V.G.	Good	Fair	Poor
560	425	300	200	150	125

50th Anniversary New Model Blackhawk NVB34-50

Introduced in 2005 this model features a smaller, original size XR-3 grips frame with checkered hard rubber grips. Adjustable rear sight. Special commemorative golf roll mark on top of barrel. Chambered for the .357 Mag and fitted with a 4.625" barrel. Weight is about 45 oz.

NIB	Exc.	V.G.	Good	Fair	Poor
580	425	—	—	—	—

Stainless Steel Blackhawk (New Model)

This is simply the New Model Blackhawk made from stainless steel. To date it has been offered in .357, .44, and .45 L.C. calibers.

NIB	Exc.	V.G.	Good	Fair	Poor
400	325	275	225	175	150

Blackhawk Convertable (New Model)

This model is the same as the Blackhawk with interchangeable conversion cylinders—.357 Magnum/9mm and .45 Colt/.45 ACP. Prices listed are for blued model.

NIB	Exc.	V.G.	Good	Fair	Poor
465	350	250	175	150	125

.45 ACP & .45 Long Colt Convertable (1998)

NIB	Exc.	V.G.	Good	Fair	Poor
500	400	—	—	—	—

Stainless Model .357/9mm

300 guns built.

NIB	Exc.	V.G.	Good	Fair	Poor
—	700	600	500	375	250

Fiftieth Anniversary .44 Magnum Flattop New Model Blackhawk

Six-shot, single-action .44 Magnum (also accepts .44 Special) with 6.5" barrel and adjustable rear sight, 47 oz. Recreation of original .44 Falt-Top Blackhawk. Blued with checkered rubber grips. Gold, color-filled rollmark on top of barrel. Introduced 2006. MSRP: 605

Fiftieth Anniversary .44 Magnum New Model Ruger Blackhawk Flattop

Chambered for .44 Mag, blued single-action limited edition 6-shooter with gold-filled rollmark on barrel: "50 Years of .44 Magnum – 1956 to 2006." 6.5" barrel, hard rubber grips. Introduced 2006. MSRP: 605

Model SRM Blackhawk

This is the New Model Blackhawk with a 7.5" or 10.5" barrel. It was chambered for the .357 Maximum and was intended for silhouette shooting. This model experienced problems with gas erosion in the forcing cone and under the top strap and was removed from production in 1984 after approximately 9200 were manufactured.

Exc.	V.G.	Good	Fair	Poor
650	500	400	275	250

Super Blackhawk (New Model)

This model is similar in appearance to the old model but has the transfer bar safety device. It was manufactured from 1973 to the present and commenced at serial number 81-00001.

NIB	Exc.	V.G.	Good	Fair	Poor
500	400	275	225	175	125

Super Blackhawk Stainless Steel

This model is the same as the blued version but is made of stainless steel. In 1998 this model was offered in 4-5/8" or 7-1/2" barrels with hunter grip frame and laminated grip panels.

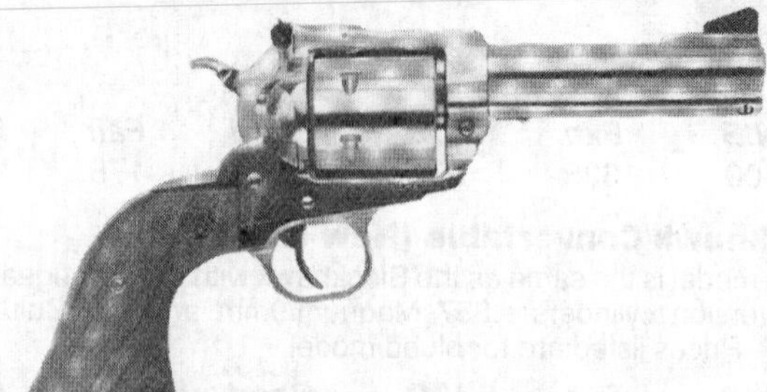

NIB	Exc.	V.G.	Good	Fair	Poor
550	450	300	250	200	150

NOTE: Add $50 to prices for hunter grip frame and laminated grip panels.

Super Blackhawk Hunter

Introduced in 2002 this .44 Magnum model features a 7.5" barrel with integral full-length solid rib for scope mounts. Stainless steel. Adjustable rear sight. Scope rings included. Weight is about 52 oz.

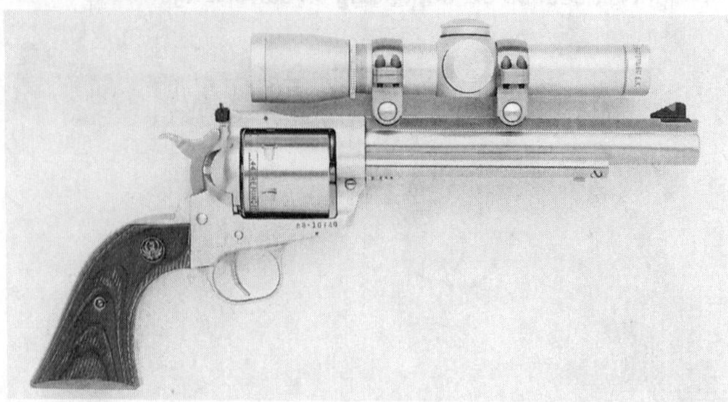

NIB	Exc.	V.G.	Good	Fair	Poor
640	500	400	—	—	—

"Cowboy Pair"

Matched pair of engraved and consecutively serial-numbered New Vaquero revolvers in .45 Colt. Includes lined wood collector case. Production limited to 500 sets. Introduced 2007.

NIB	Exc	V.G.	Good	Fair	Poor
3863	—	—	—	—	—

50th Anniversary Matched Set .357 and .44 Magnum

Matched pair of Ruger New Blackhawks, one in .44 and the other in .357, commemorating 50th anniversary of Ruger Blackhawk revolver. Gold-filled rollmarked 6-1/2" and 4-5/8" barrels, respectively. Includes presentation case. Production limited. Introduced 2007.

NIB	Exc	V.G.	Good	Fair	Poor
1350	—	—	—	—	—

Bisley Model

This model has the modified features found on the famous old Colt Bisley Target model—the flat top frame, fixed or adjustable sights, and the longer grip frame that has become the Bisley trademark. The Bisley is available chambered for .22 LR, .32 H&R Magnum, .357 Magnum, .41 Magnum, .44 Magnum, and .45 Long Colt. The barrel lengths are 6.5" and 7.5"; cylinders are either fluted or unfluted and roll engraved. The finish is a satin blue, and the grips are smooth Goncalo Alves with medallions. The Bisley was introduced in 1986.

.22 LR and .32 H&R Magnum

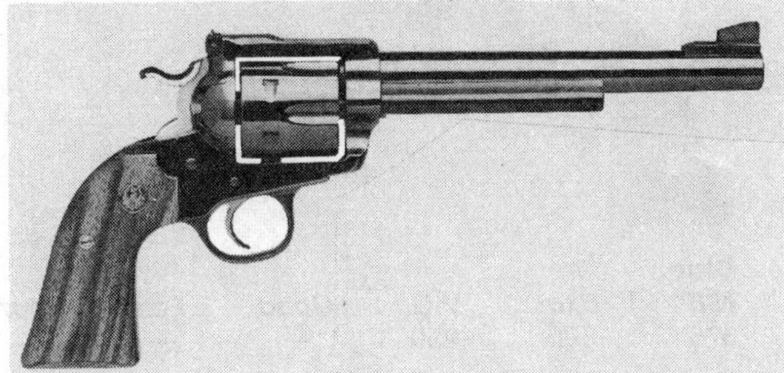

NIB	Exc.	V.G.	Good	Fair	Poor
380	305	225	200	150	125

NOTE: Add $100 for .32 Magnum Bisley.

.357 Magnum, .41 Magnum, .44 Magnum, and .45 Long Colt

NIB	Exc.	V.G.	Good	Fair	Poor
450	365	275	250	200	175

NOTE: Approximately 750 stainless grip frame .22 caliber Bisleys were made. These will demand a premium.

Shootists Bisley

Produced in 1994 for the Shootist organization in memory of Tom Ruger. Chambered for the .22 cartridge these revolvers were limited to 52 total produced. They were stainless steel and were fitted with 4-5/8" barrels. The barrels were marked, "IN MEMORY OF OUR FRIEND TOM RUGER THE SHOOTIST 1994". Some of these revolvers, but not all, have the name of the owner engraved on the backstrap.

Courtesy Jim Taylor

NIB	Exc.	V.G.	Good	Fair	Poor
1500	—	—	—	—	—

Old Army Percussion Revolver

This model is a .45 caliber percussion revolver with a 7-1/2" barrel. It has a 6-shot cylinder, with a blued finish and walnut grips. For 1994 this model is offered with fixed sights. Weight is about 46 oz.

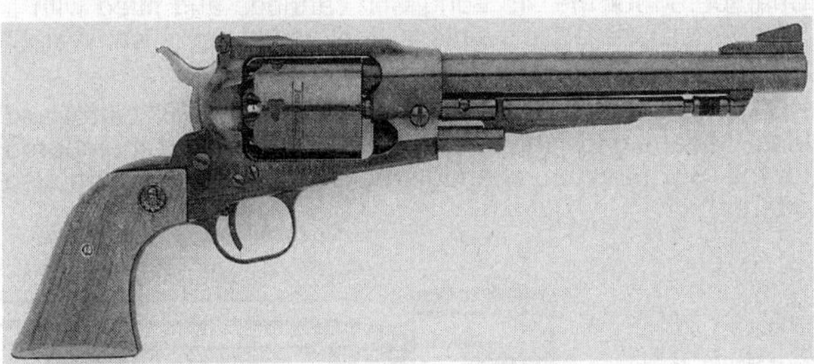

NIB	Exc.	V.G.	Good	Fair	Poor
400	325	250	100	100	100

NOTE: For pistols with original factory installed brass grip frame add $150 to prices listed.

Old Army Stainless Steel

This model is the same as the blued version except that it is made of stainless steel. Add 200 percent for stainless 200th Year model.

NIB	Exc.	V.G.	Good	Fair	Poor
465	400	275	100	100	100

Ruger Vaquero

This single-action pistol was introduced in 1993 and was voted handgun of the year by the shooting industry. It is a fixed sight version of the New Model Blackhawk. It is available in stainless steel or blued with case-colored frame. Offered in three different barrel lengths: 4.62", 5.5", and 7.5". Chambered for the .45 Long Colt. In 1994 the .44-40 and .44 Magnum calibers were added to the Vaquero line. Capacity is 6 rounds. Weighs between 39 and 41 oz. depending on barrel length. Discontinued.

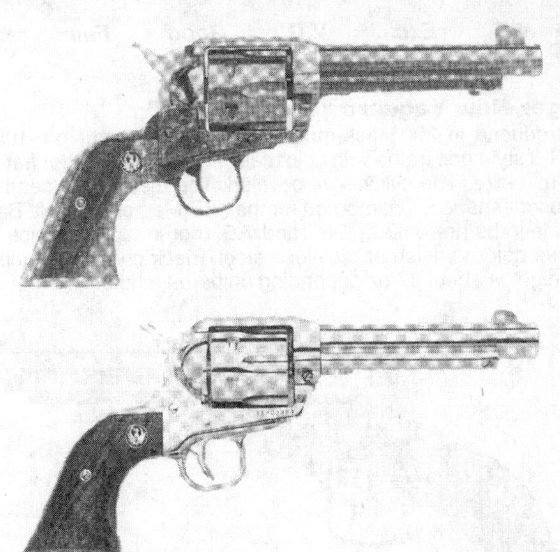

NIB	Exc.	V.G.	Good	Fair	Poor
495	400	300	200	150	100

NOTE: Vaqueros with 4-5/8" barrel chambered for .44 Magnum in both blue and stainless are uncatalogued, add 25 percent.

Ruger Vaquero Bird's-head

Introduced in 2001 this model features a bird's-head grip. Chambered for the .45 Long Colt cartridge and fitted with a 5.5" barrel. Offered in stainless steel and blued finish. Weight is about 40 oz. Discontinued.

NOTE: In 2002 this model was offered with 3.75" barrel and black Micarta grips. In 2003 this model was offered chambered for the .357 Magnum cartridge. Simulated ivory grips are also offered.

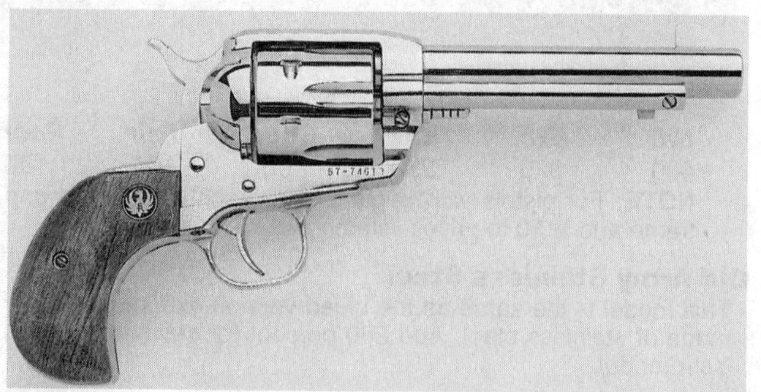

NIB	Exc.	V.G.	Good	Fair	Poor
575	450	—	—	—	—

Ruger Bisley Vaquero

Introduced in 1997 this model features a 5.5" barrel chambered for .44 Magnum or .45 Long Colt. Grips are smooth rosewood. Finish is blued with case colored frame. Blade front sight and notch rear. Weight is about 40 oz. Discontinued.

NIB	Exc.	V.G.	Good	Fair	Poor
425	350	—	—	—	—

Ruger New Vaquero "Small Frame"

Introduced in 2005 this model features a slimmer pre-1962 XR-3 style grip frame with color case finish. The cylinder frame is mid-size. The cylinder is beveled. The ejector rod head is cresent shaped. Chambered for the .357 Mag or .45 Colt. Barrel lengths are 4.625", 5.5", and 7.5" (not in .357). Choice of case colored finish or stainless steel. Black checkered grips. Weight is about 37 oz depending on barrel length.

NIB	Exc.	V.G.	Good	Fair	Poor
450	325	—	—	—	—

New Ruger Bearcat (Super Bearcat)

The return of an old favorite was made in 1994. This new version is furnished with a .22 LR cylinder and a .22 WMR cylinder. Barrel length is 4" with fixed sights. Grips are walnut. Offered with blued finish.

NOTE: There was a factory recall on the magnum cylinders. Bearcats with both cylinders are very rare.

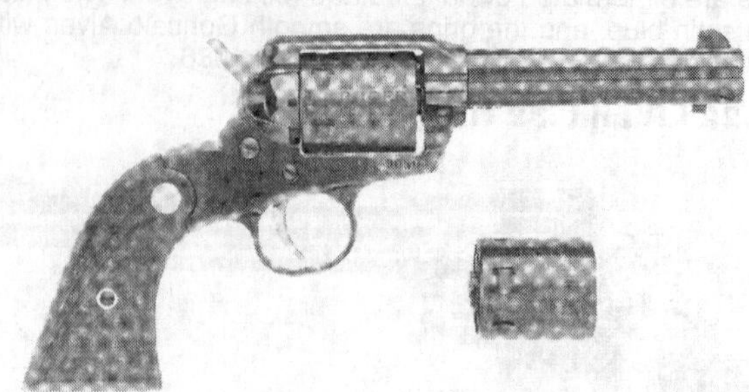

Blue

NIB	Exc.	V.G.	Good	Fair	Poor
375	300	250	—	—	—

Stainless Steel

NIB	Exc.	V.G.	Good	Fair	Poor
400	325	275	—	—	—

Convertible (Recalled)

NIB	Exc.	V.G.	Good	Fair	Poor
1100	1000	900	—	—	—

New Model Super Bearcat

Reintroduced in 2002 this .22 caliber model features a stainless steel or blued finish, 4" barrel with fixed sights and Rosewood grips. Weight is about 24 oz.

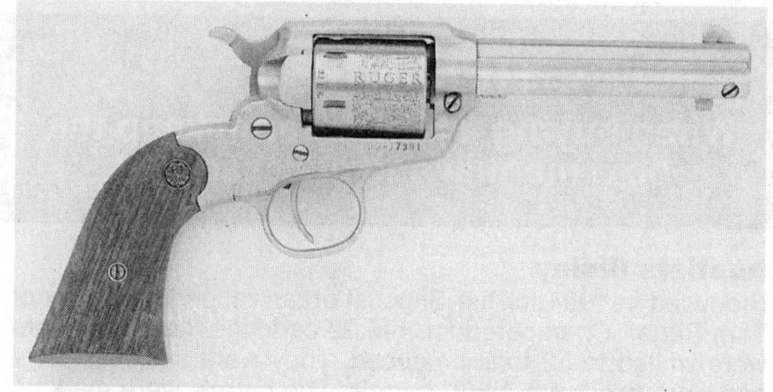

NIB	Exc.	V.G.	Good	Fair	Poor
450	365	295	200	—	—

NOTE: Add $50 for stainless steel version.

DOUBLE-ACTION REVOLVERS

Security Six

This revolver, also known as the Model 117, is chambered for the .357 Magnum cartridge and has a 2.75", 4", or 6" barrel. It features adjustable sights and a square butt, with checkered walnut grips. It was manufactured between 1970 and 1985. Early guns with fixed sights and square butt were also marked "Security-Six". The model was later termed "Service-Six" and was so marked. The prices listed are only for the adjustable sight and square butt "Security-Six" models. Round butt Security-Sixes with adjustable are worth a premium.

Exc.	V.G.	Good	Fair	Poor
350	275	200	150	100

NOTE: Fixed sight guns marked Security-Six and round butt Security-Sixes with adjustable sights are worth a premium.

Stainless Steel Model 717

This model is the Security-Six made from stainless steel.

Exc.	V.G.	Good	Fair	Poor
300	250	225	175	125

 *This symbol denotes "Sleepers" with rapidly-rising values and/or significant collector potential.*

Speed Six

This model is known as the Model 207, chambered for .357 Magnum; Model 208, chambered for .38 Special; and Model 209, chambered for 9mm. It has a 2.75" or 4" barrel, fixed sights, and a round butt with checkered walnut grips and was blued. There are some with factory bobbed hammers. This model was introduced in 1973.

Exc.	*V.G.*	*Good*	*Fair*	*Poor*
300	250	200	150	100

Models 737, 738, 739

These are the designations for the stainless steel versions of the Speed-Six. They are the same revolver except for the material used in the manufacture.

Exc.	*V.G.*	*Good*	*Fair*	*Poor*
300	250	225	175	125

GP-100

This model is chambered for the .357 Magnum/.38 Special. It is available with fixed or adjustable sights in barrel lengths of 3", 4", or 6" barrel and has a frame designed for constant use of heavy magnum loads. The rear sight has a white outline, and the front sight features interchangeable colored inserts. The finish is blued, and the grips are a new design made of rubber with smooth Goncalo Alves inserts. This model was introduced in 1986.

NIB	*Exc.*	*V.G.*	*Good*	*Fair*	*Poor*
400	300	200	150	125	—

GP-100 Stainless

This model is the same as the GP-100 except that the material used is stainless steel.

NIB	*Exc.*	*V.G.*	*Good*	*Fair*	*Poor*
425	325	225	150	150	—

SP-101

This model is similar in appearance to the GP-100 but has a smaller frame and is chambered for the .22 LR (6-shot), .38 Special (5-shot), .357 Magnum (5-shot), and 9mm (5-shot). The grips are all black synthetic, and the sights are adjustable for windage. Barrel lengths are 2" or 3", and construction is of stainless steel. This model was introduced in 1989. 6" barrel is available for .22 caliber.

NIB	*Exc.*	*V.G.*	*Good*	*Fair*	*Poor*
425	375	300	200	150	125

SP-101 Spurless-Hammer

This model was introduced in 1993 and features an SP-101 without an exposed hammer spur. Available in two calibers: .38 Special and .357 Magnum with 2-1/4" barrel. This double-action revolver has fixed sights, holds 5 rounds and weighs about 26 oz.

NIB	*Exc.*	*V.G.*	*Good*	*Fair*	*Poor*
515	375	300	250	200	150

Redhawk

This model is a large-frame, double-action revolver which was chambered for the .357 and .41 Magnums until 1992, and currently for the .44 Magnum cartridges. The barrel lengths are 5-1/2" and 7-1/2". The finish is blued, and the grips are smooth walnut. The Redhawk was introduced in 1979. Add 15 percent for .357 and .41.

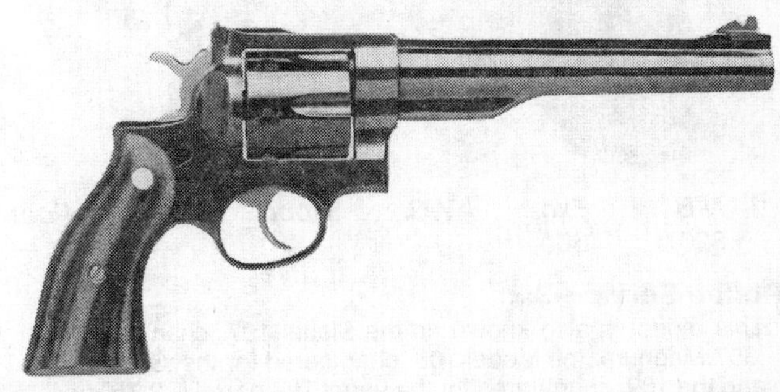

NIB	*Exc.*	*V.G.*	*Good*	*Fair*	*Poor*
630	475	350	250	200	150

Redhawk Stainless Steel

The same as the blued version except constructed of stainless steel. It was chambered for .357 Magnum until 1985, the .41 Magnum until 1992, and currently for the .44 Magnum. In 1998 this model was offered chambered for .45 Long Colt cartridge in barrel lengths of 4", 5.5" and 7.5". Add 15 percent for .357 and .41.

NIB	Exc.	V.G.	Good	Fair	Poor
695	525	400	275	200	150

Super Redhawk

This is a more massive version of the Redhawk. It weighs 53 oz. and is offered with a 7.5" or 9.5" barrel. It is made of stainless steel, and the barrel rib is milled to accept the Ruger scope-ring system. The grips are the combination rubber and Goncalo Alves-type found on the GP-100. This revolver was introduced in 1987. In 1999 this model was offered chambered for the .454 Casull cartridge with 7.5" or 9.5" barrel. In 2001 this model was offered in .480 Ruger caliber in 7.5" or 9.5" barrel.

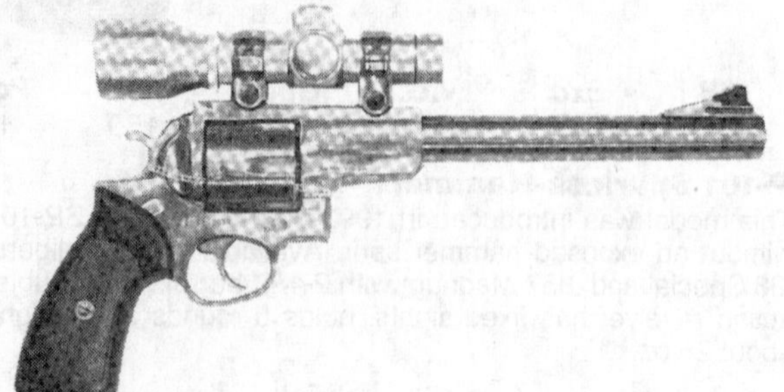

NIB	Exc.	V.G.	Good	Fair	Poor
740	550	400	275	200	150

NOTE: Add $200 for .454 Casull or .480 Ruger caliber. Revolvers chambered for the .454 Casull also accept .45 Long Colt cartridges.

Super Redhawk Alaskan

This revolver is chambered for the .454 Casull and the .45 Colt interchangeable or the .480 Ruger cartridge. Barrel length is 2.5" with adjustable rear sight. Cylinder capacity is 6 rounds. Stainless steel finish. Hogue Tamer rubber grips. Weight is about 42 oz. Introduced in 2005. .44 Magnum chambering added 2007.

NIB	Exc.	V.G.	Good	Fair	Poor
820	600	—	—	—	—

Police Service-Six

This model is also known as the Model 107, chambered for .357 Magnum; the Model 108, chambered for the .38 Special; and the 109, chambered for the 9mm. The barrel is 2.75" or 4". A few 6" barrel Service-Sixes were also produced and these are worth a premium. It has fixed sights and a square butt, with checkered walnut grips. The finish is blued. The 9mm was discontinued in 1984; the other two calibers, in 1988.

Exc.	V.G.	Good	Fair	Poor
300	250	200	150	100

Model 707 and 708

This is the designation for the stainless versions of the Police Service-Six. It was not produced in 9mm, and only the 4" barrel was offered. This model was discontinued in 1988.

Exc.	V.G.	Good	Fair	Poor
300	250	225	175	125

SEMI-AUTOMATIC HANDGUNS

P-85 or P-89

This model represents Ruger's entry into the wonder-nine market. The P-85 is a double-action, high-capacity (15-shot detachable magazine) semi-automatic, with an alloy frame and steel slide. It has a 4.5" barrel, ambidextrous safety, and three-dot sighting system. It has a matte black finish and black synthetic grips. The latest option for this model is a decocking device to replace the standard safety. There is also an optional molded locking case and extra magazine with loading tool available. It is more reasonably priced than many of its competitors. This pistol was introduced in 1987 and was sold at large premium for some time due to limited supply and great demand. As of this writing, Ruger is producing this pistol in a new plant in Prescott, Arizona; and the premium situation no longer exists. This model is also produced in a 9x21 cartridge for non-NATO countries. In 1991 the internal mechanism was changed slightly with the result that a name change occurred "P85 Mark II".

NIB	Exc.	V.G.	Good	Fair	Poor
360	300	275	250	200	150

P85 Stainless Steel

This model is the same as the matte black version except that the receiver assembly is made of stainless steel.

NIB	Exc.	V.G.	Good	Fair	Poor
400	335	300	200	200	150

REMINDER
You don't have to specialize in Colts or Winchesters to have a nice collection. Collecting Marlin or Mossberg .22 semi-autos, for example, can be just as rewarding.

KP89X
Introduced in 1993 this pistol features a stainless steel convertible safety model which comes with both 9mm and .30 Luger barrels. The barrels are interchangeable without the use of tools. Magazine capacity is 15 rounds. Less than 6,000 produced.

NIB	Exc.	V.G.	Good	Fair	Poor
420	380	345	245	200	150

P89
Introduced in 1991 this semi-automatic pistol is chambered for the 9mm cartridge. It has a blued finish and a 15-round magazine. The safety is a manual ambidextrous lever type. The barrel is 4.5" and the empty weight is approximately 36 oz.

NIB	Exc.	V.G.	Good	Fair	Poor
350	300	200	150	100	80

KP89
This model is the same configuration as the P89 but furnished with a stainless steel finish. Introduced in 1991.

NIB	Exc.	V.G.	Good	Fair	Poor
400	300	250	200	150	100

P89DC
This model features a blued finish and is chambered for the 9mm Parabellum cartridge but is fitted with a decock-only lever (no manual safety). After decocking the gun can be fired by a double-action pull of the trigger.

NIB	Exc.	V.G.	Good	Fair	Poor
375	350	250	200	150	100

KP89DC
This is the stainless steel version of the P89DC with decock only.

NIB	Exc.	V.G.	Good	Fair	Poor
375	350	250	200	150	100

KP89DAO
Chambered for the 9mm cartridge this model is the stainless steel double-action-only version of the above model.

NIB	Exc.	V.G.	Good	Fair	Poor
375	300	250	200	150	100

KP90
Chambered for the .45 ACP cartridge, this model is in stainless steel and holds 7 rounds in the magazine. It is fitted with a manual safety. Introduced in 1991.

NIB	Exc.	V.G.	Good	Fair	Poor
475	375	275	200	150	100

KP90DC
This stainless steel version of the KP90 has a decock-only system. Chambered for the .45 ACP cartridge.

NIB	Exc.	V.G.	Good	Fair	Poor
460	350	275	200	150	100

P90
Same as above model but with blued finish. Introduced in 1998.

NIB	Exc.	V.G.	Good	Fair	Poor
450	350	—	—	—	—

KP91DC
This model features a stainless steel finish and is chambered for the .40 S&W cartridge. Magazine capacity is 11 rounds. It has a decock-only system. Introduced in 1992. Discontinued.

NIB	Exc.	V.G.	Good	Fair	Poor
375	325	275	200	150	100

KP91DAO
Chambered for the .40 S&W with stainless steel finish it features a double-action-only system. Discontinued.

NIB	Exc.	V.G.	Good	Fair	Poor
375	325	275	200	150	100

P93D
This is a blued version with ambidextrous decocker and 3.9" barrel. Introduced in 1998.

NIB	Exc.	V.G.	Good	Fair	Poor
400	325	—	—	—	—

KP93DC
Introduced in 1993 this pistol is a new addition to the P series as a compact model. Stainless steel and chambered for the 9mm cartridge it has a magazine capacity of 15 rounds. Available in decock-only configuration. Barrel length is 3.9" and the weight is about 24 oz. empty.

NIB	Exc.	V.G.	Good	Fair	Poor
500	400	300	250	150	100

KP93DAO
The double-action-only version of the KP93 compact series.

NIB	Exc.	V.G.	Good	Fair	Poor
490	400	300	250	150	100

KP94

Introduced in 1994 this model is smaller than the full-size P series pistols and the compact P93 pistols. Offered in 9mm or .40 S&W calibers this pistol has an aluminum alloy frame and stainless steel slide. Barrel length is 4-1/4" and magazine capacity for the 9mm is 15 rounds and for the .40 11 rounds. Weight is approximately 33 oz. It is offered in double-action-only as well as traditional double-action. A decock-only model is available also.

NIB	Exc.	V.G.	Good	Fair	Poor
415	350	300	250	200	150

KP94DC

This is similar to the model above but in decock only.

NIB	Exc.	V.G.	Good	Fair	Poor
415	350	300	250	200	150

P94

This is a blued version of the KP94. Introduced in 1998.

NIB	Exc.	V.G.	Good	Fair	Poor
400	325	—	—	—	—

KP94DAO

Same as the KP94 model but in double-action-only.

NIB	Exc.	V.G.	Good	Fair	Poor
400	350	300	250	200	150

KP944

Chambered for the .40 S&W cartridge this model has a stainless steel tapered slide, an 11-round magazine, and a manual safety. Models made after September 1994 have a 10-round magazine.

NIB	Exc.	V.G.	Good	Fair	Poor
415	350	300	250	200	150

KP944DC

Same as a model above but fitted with a decock-only system.

NIB	Exc.	V.G.	Good	Fair	Poor
415	350	300	250	200	150

KP944DAO

Same as model above but with a double-action-only model of fire.

NIB	Exc.	V.G.	Good	Fair	Poor
415	350	300	250	200	150

P95

Introduced in 1996 this 9mm pistol features a 3.9" barrel, polymer frame and stainless steel slide. Decocker only. Fixed 3-dot sights are standard. Overall length is 7.3". Empty weight is about 29 oz. In 2001 this model was offered with a manual safety and blued finish.

NIB	Exc.	V.G.	Good	Fair	Poor
450	350	300	225	150	100

KP95DC

This model is the same as the matte black version of the P95, only this is in stainless steel. It has a decock only safety.

NIB	Exc.	V.G.	Good	Fair	Poor
450	350	300	225	150	100

P95DAO

Same as above but in double-action-only.

NIB	Exc.	V.G.	Good	Fair	Poor
450	350	300	225	150	100

KP95DAO

Same as the model above but in double-action-only. In 2001 this model was offered with a manual safety and blued finish.

NIB	Exc.	V.G.	Good	Fair	Poor
450	350	300	225	150	100

KP97D

Introduced in 1999 this decock-only model is chambered for the .45 ACP cartridge. It has a stainless steel slide. Magazine capacity is 7 rounds. Fixed sights. Weight is about 27 oz.

NIB	Exc.	V.G.	Good	Fair	Poor
450	350	—	—	—	—

KP97DAO

Same specifications as the model above but in double-action-only. Introduced in 1999.

NIB	Exc.	V.G.	Good	Fair	Poor
450	350	—	—	—	—

KP345

Introduced in 2004 this .45 ACP model features a 4.2" stainless steel barrel and stainless steel slide. Fixed sights. Internal lock, loaded chamber indicator, magazine disconnect, and a new cam block design to reduce recoil. Black polymer checkered grips. Magazine capacity is 8 rounds. Weight is about 29 oz.

NIB	Exc.	V.G.	Good	Fair	Poor
540	425	—	—	—	—

KP345PR

Similar to the model above but fitted with a Picatinny-style rail under the forward portion of the frame. Introduced in 2004.

NIB	Exc.	V.G.	Good	Fair	Poor
550	425	—	—	—	—

SEMI-AUTOMATIC RIFLES

10/22 Standard Carbine With Walnut Stock

This model has an 18.5" barrel and is chambered for the .22 LR. It has a 10-shot, detachable rotary magazine and a folding rear sight. The stock is smooth walnut, with a barrel band and carbine-style buttplate. This rifle enjoys a fine reputation for accuracy and dependability and is considered an excellent value. It was introduced in 1964.

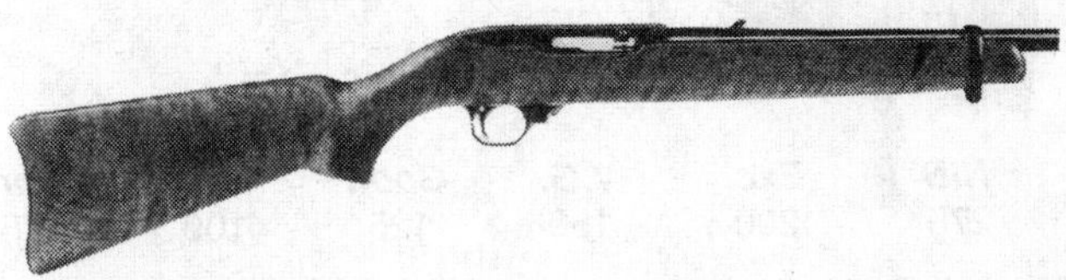

NIB	Exc.	V.G.	Good	Fair	Poor
300	250	125	100	75	50

NOTE: Birch stock deduct $20.

10/22 Standard Carbine Stainless Steel

Same as above but with stainless steel barrel and receiver.

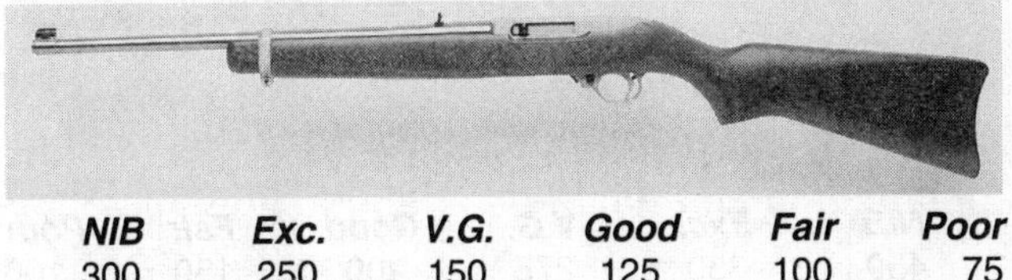

NIB	Exc.	V.G.	Good	Fair	Poor
300	250	150	125	100	75

10/22 Magnum

Introduced in 1999, this model is chambered for the .22 Magnum cartridge. Barrel length is 18.5". Folding rear sight and gold bead front sight. Hardwood stock. Weight is about 5.5 lbs.

NIB	Exc.	V.G.	Good	Fair	Poor
535	400	300	200	150	100

10/22 Sporter (Finger Groove Old Model)

This model is similar to the Standard Carbine except that it has a Monte Carlo stock, finger-groove forend, and no barrel band. It was manufactured between 1966 and 1971.

Exc.	V.G.	Good	Fair	Poor
500	400	300	175	125

NOTE: Factory hand checkering add 300 percent.

10/22 Deluxe Sporter

The same as the Sporter with a checkered stock and better buttplate. Introduced in 1971.

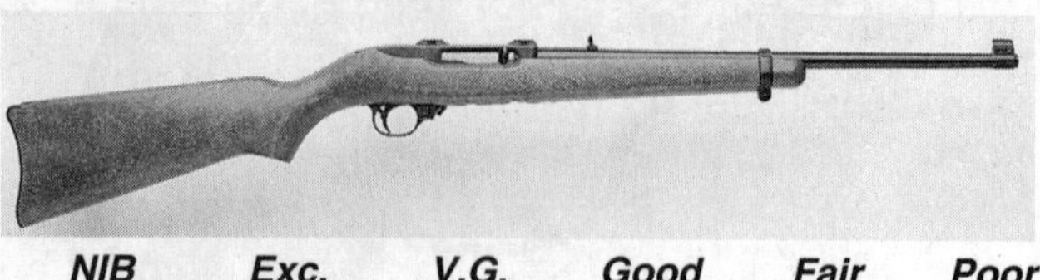

NIB	Exc.	V.G.	Good	Fair	Poor
325	250	150	125	100	75

10/22 International Carbine

This model is similar to the Standard Carbine, with a full-length, Mannlicher-style stock. It was manufactured between 1966 and 1971 and is fairly rare on today's market.

Exc.	V.G.	Good	Fair	Poor
550	425	350	300	250

NOTE: Factory hand checkering add 50 percent.

10/22 International Carbine (New Model)

This 1994 model is a reintroduction of the older version. It is offered in either a blued or stainless steel finish. Barrel length is 18-1/2". Magazine capacity is 10 rounds. The hardwood stock had no checkering when this model was first introduced. Shortly after introduced the factory began checkering these stocks. Weight is about 5.2 lbs.

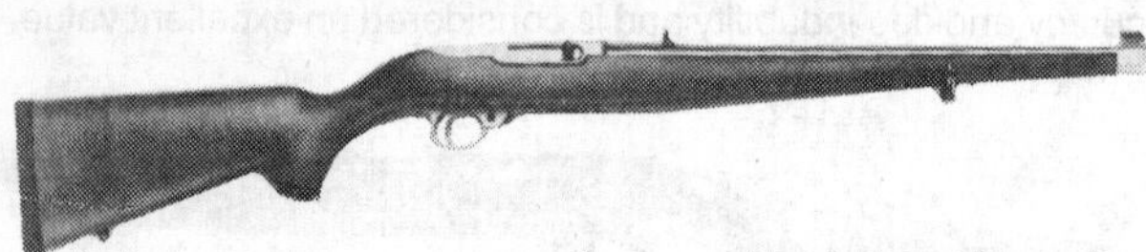

NIB	Exc.	V.G.	Good	Fair	Poor
275	200	150	125	100	75

Model 10/22T

Introduced in 1996 this model is a target version of the 10/22 line. It has a laminated American hardwood stock with blued heavy barrel with hammer-forged spiral finish. Rifle comes standard without sights. Barrel length is 20". Weight is approximately 7.25 lbs.

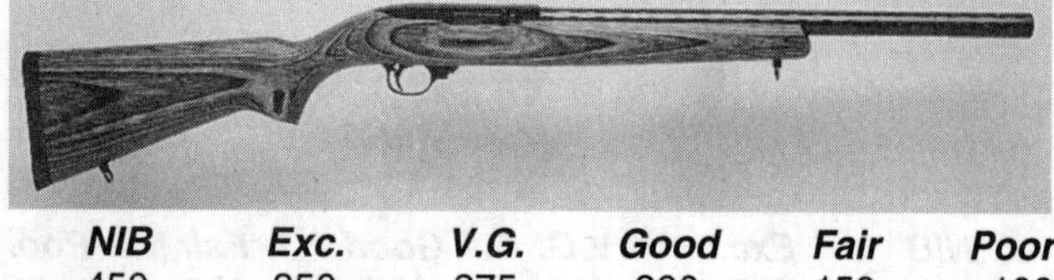

NIB	Exc.	V.G.	Good	Fair	Poor
450	350	275	200	150	100

Model 10/22TNZ

This target model features a 20" stainless steel barrel and receiver with laminated thumbhole stock. No sights. Weight is about 7 lbs. Introduced in 2001.

NIB	Exc.	V.G.	Good	Fair	Poor
500	375	275	200	150	100

Model 10/22 Canadian Centennial

In 1966 and 1967 approximately 4,500 10/22 Sporters were built for the Canadian Centennial. The first 2,000 were sold with a Remington Model 742 in .308 caliber with matching serial numbers. The Ruger Sporter may be checkered or unchecked. The two-gun set was either boxed separately or together.

Two Gun Set

NIB
700

10/22 Only

NIB
450

10/22 Laminated Stock Carbine

Produced in varying quantities since 1986 these models are becoming quite collectible. The stocks range in color from dark green to gray and various shades of brown. Because there are so many different variations each should be individually appraised. Prices listed are for blued carbine models.

NIB	Exc.	V.G.	Good	Fair	Poor
250	200	175	150	125	100

NOTE: In stainless steel add approximately $40 to NIB price.

10/22 Laminated Stock Sporter Model

This model has a tree bark laminated stock.

NIB	Exc.	V.G.	Good	Fair	Poor
325	275	225	175	150	100

10/22 Laminated Stock International

This stainless steel model was an exclusive Wal-Mart product. A few of these models in blue were also produced.

Blue

NIB	Exc.	V.G.	Good	Fair	Poor
400	325	250	200	150	100

Stainless Steel

NIB	Exc.	V.G.	Good	Fair	Poor
350	275	225	175	125	100

10/22 All Weather

This model is fitted with a stainless steel barrel and action and synthetic stock. Introduced in 1997. In 2001 this model was offered with blued finish.

NIB	Exc.	V.G.	Good	Fair	Poor
300	225	175	125	100	70

NOTE: Deduct $40 for blued model.

Model 10/22 Carbine 40th Anniversary

This model is blued with hardwood stock. It is equipped with a 40th anniversary clear magazine with red rotor and original scope base adapter. A nickel-silver medallion is inlaid on the right side of the buttstock.

NIB	Exc.	V.G.	Good	Fair	Poor
280	225	—	—	—	—

Ruger 10/22 Compact Rifle 10/22 CRR

Similar to 10/22 standard rifle but with 16.25-inch blued barrel, shorter hardwood stock, fiber optic sights and 34.5-inch overall length. Introduced 2006. MSRP: 275

K10/22T Ruger 10/22 Target Stainless

Similar to 10/22 Target but with stainless steel barrel and laminated stock.

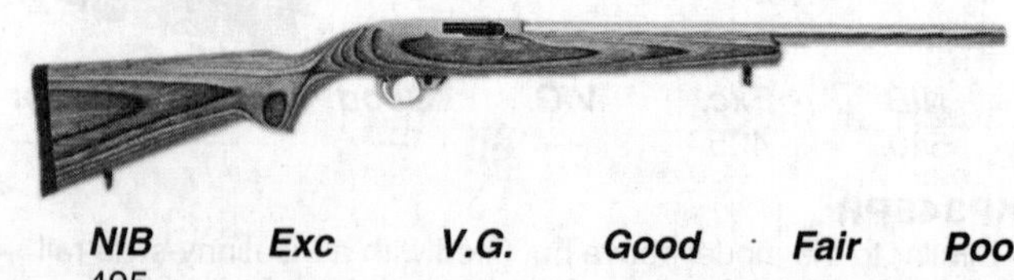

NIB	Exc	V.G.	Good	Fair	Poor
495	—	—	—	—	—

10/22-T

Similar to 100/22 Target Stainless but with blued steel barrel and blued receiver. Introduced in 2007.

NIB	Exc	V.G.	Good	Fair	Poor
450	—	—	—	—	—

Model 10/17

Introduced in 2004 this model is chambered for the .17 HMR cartridge. Fitted with a 20" barrel. Magazine capacity is 9 rounds. Weight is about 6.5 lbs.

NIB	Exc.	V.G.	Good	Fair	Poor
510	400	—	—	—	—

Model 44 Carbine

This model is a short, 18.5" barreled, gas-operated carbine chambered for the .44 Magnum cartridge. It has a 4-shot, non-detachable magazine, a folding rear sight, and a plain walnut stock. This is a handy deer hunting carbine manufactured between 1961 and 1985.

NIB	Exc.	V.G.	Good	Fair	Poor
550	450	350	300	200	150

Deerstalker Model

The same as the Model 44 Carbine with "Deerstalker" stamped on it. This model was manufactured in 1961 and 1962 only.

NIB	Exc.	V.G.	Good	Fair	Poor
950	800	600	400	300	200

Model 44RS

This is the Model 44 with sling swivels and an aperture sight.

Exc.	V.G.	Good	Fair	Poor
525	400	300	200	150

NOTE: "Liberty"-marked 44RS carbines are extremely rare and will bring a premium. An individual appraisal is recommended.

Model 44 Sporter (Finger Groove Old Model)

This version has a Monte Carlo stock, finger groove forend, and no barrel band. It was manufactured until 1971.

Exc.	V.G.	Good	Fair	Poor
750	600	400	250	200

NOTE: Factory hand checkered models will bring at least a 75 percent premium.

Model 44 International Carbine

This version features a full-length, Mannlicher-style stock. It was discontinued in 1971 and is quite collectible.

Exc.	V.G.	Good	Fair	Poor
800	600	425	350	275

NOTE: Factory hand checkered models will bring at least a 50 percent premium.

Model 44 25th Anniversary Model

This version is lightly engraved, has a medallion in the stock and was only made in 1985, the last year of production.

NIB	Exc.	V.G.	Good	Fair	Poor
550	400	350	300	250	200

Model 99/44 Deerfield Carbine

A new and improved version, introduced in 2000, of the original Model 44 Carbine. Fitted with a 18.5" barrel this gas operated rifle has a hardwood stock and 4-round magazine capacity. Adjustable rear sight. Blued finish. Weight is about 6.2 lbs. This rifle will not cycle .44 Special ammo. Discontinued.

NIB	Exc.	V.G.	Good	Fair	Poor
700	525	400	275	200	150

Mini-14

This is a paramilitary-style carbine chambered for the .223 Remington and on a limited basis for the .222 cartridge. It has an 18.5" barrel and is gas-operated. The detachable magazines originally offered held 5, 10, or 20 rounds. The high-capacity magazines are now discontinued, and prices of them are what the market will bear. The Mini-14 has a military-style stock and aperture sight. It was introduced in 1975.

NIB	Exc.	V.G.	Good	Fair	Poor
750	550	400	275	200	150

Mini-14 Stainless Steel

The same as the Mini-14 except constructed of stainless steel.

NIB	Exc.	V.G.	Good	Fair	Poor
810	600	450	300	200	150

Mini-14 Ranch Rifle

This model is similar to the standard Mini-14, with a folding rear sight and the receiver milled to accept the Ruger scope-ring system. The rings are supplied with the rifle.

NIB	Exc.	V.G.	Good	Fair	Poor
500	450	350	300	250	175

NOTE: Models chambered in .222 caliber will bring a premium.

Stainless Steel Mini-14 Ranch Rifle

This model is the same as the blued version except that it is made of stainless steel.

NIB	Exc.	V.G.	Good	Fair	Poor
810	600	450	300	200	150

Mini-14 All-Weather Ranch Rifle

Introduced in 1999 this model has all the features of the stainless steel Ranch Rifle with the addition of a black polymer stock. Weight is about 6.5 lbs.

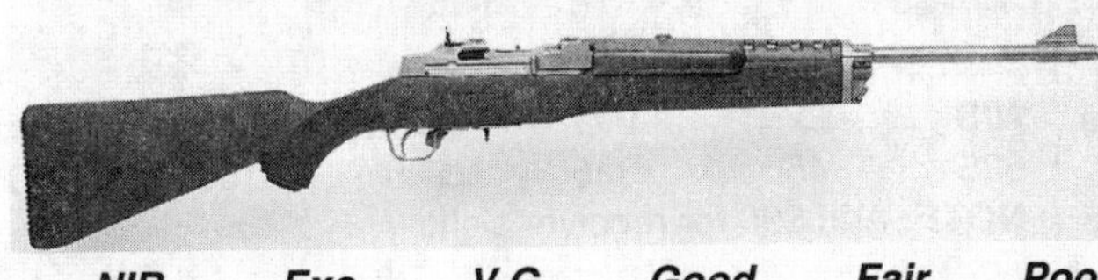

NIB	Exc.	V.G.	Good	Fair	Poor
810	600	450	300	200	150

Mini-14 Target Rifle

Accurized version of the Mini-14 but with matte stainless barrel and reciver, black laminated thumbhole stock, adjustable harmonic dampener. No sights. Introduced in 2007.

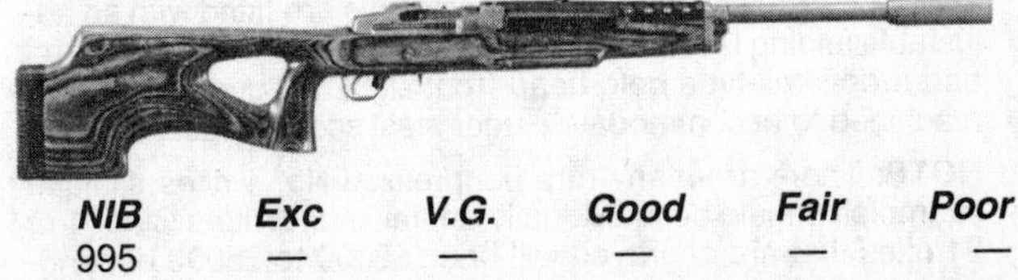

NIB	Exc	V.G.	Good	Fair	Poor
995	—	—	—	—	—

Mini-30

This model was brought out by Ruger in 1987 in answer to the influx of weapons imported from China that were chambered for this cartridge—the 7.62mmx39 Russian. This cartridge is touted as a fine hunting cartridge for deer-sized game; and by adding this chambering, the handy Mini-14 becomes a legitimate hunting gun—and a new market opened. This model is similar in appearance to the standard Mini-14 and is supplied with Ruger scope rings. 6.8mm chambering added 2007.

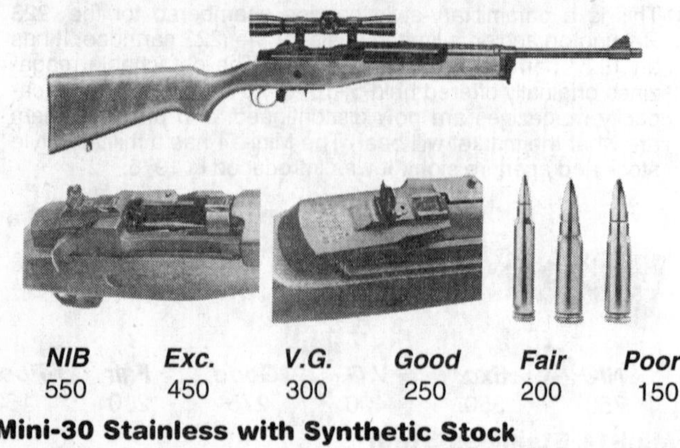

NIB	Exc.	V.G.	Good	Fair	Poor
550	450	300	250	200	150

Mini-30 Stainless with Synthetic Stock

NIB	Exc.	V.G.	Good	Fair	Poor
700	550	450	300	200	150

GB Model

This model has a factory-installed folding stock, flash suppressor, and bayonet lug. It was designed and sold by Ruger to law enforcement agencies. A number have come on the civilian market through surplus sales and police trade-ins. With the assault rifle hysteria, prices of this model have fluctuated wildly in some areas. Now that Ruger has discontinued the folding stock and the high-capacity magazines, this could become even less predictable. Note that this is a semi-automatic and totally different than the full-auto version of this weapon available only through Class 3 dealers.

Exc.	V.G.	Good	Fair	Poor
1100	800	650	400	300

Ruger PC4/PC9 Carbine

This is a semi-automatic carbine chambered for the 9mm (PC9) or .40 S&W (PC4) cartridges. It is fitted with a 16.25" barrel and black synthetic stock. Post front sight with adjustable rear sight. A receiver is also offered. Detachable magazine has 10-round capacity. Weight is approximately 6.4 lbs. Introduced in 1998.

NIB	Exc.	V.G.	Good	Fair	Poor
625	450	325	225	150	100

NOTE: Add $30 for receiver sight.

SINGLE-SHOT RIFLES

All Ruger single-shot rifles feature a sliding shotgun-type safety, that engage both the sear and the hammer, all metal parts are polished and blued, each receiver and stock is hand fitted, and the stock is American walnut with a satin finish. The pistol grip and forearm are hand checkered with 20 lines to the inch. Those No. 1 rifles offered with open sights are fitted with an adjustable folding leaf rear sight set into a quarter rib on the barrel and a dovetail-type gold bead front sight. All quarter ribs are machined to accommodate Ruger steel scope rings.

NOTE: There are many rare nonprefixed No. 1 rifles. Unique examples should be individually appraised. "Writers Club" 1 of 21 rifles that are engraved will bring $3000 to $5000 depending on the amount of engraving and gold inlay, caliber, and the person that it was presented to.

Ruger No. 1 Light Sporter (1-A)

This model features open sights, barrel band on lightweight barrel, and Alexander Henry-style forearm. Offered with a 22" barrel in four calibers. Rifle weighs 7.25 lbs.

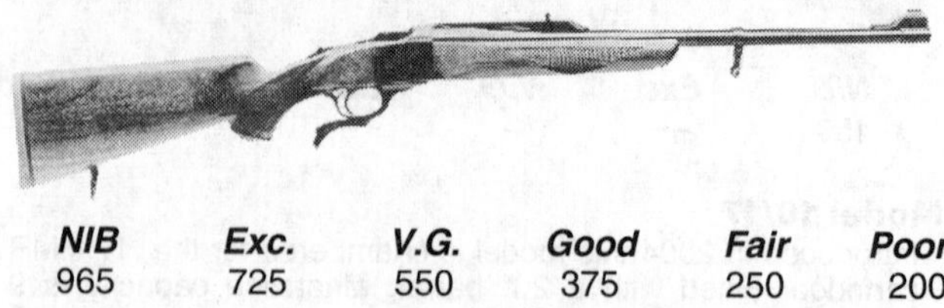

NIB	Exc.	V.G.	Good	Fair	Poor
965	725	550	375	250	200

Ruger Number 1 Light Standard (1-AB)

Similar to Light Sporter 1-A but with 22-inch sightless blued barrel. Cambered in .204 Ruger only; introduced 2006. MSRP: 1000

Ruger No. 1 Standard (1-B)

This model is furnished with no sights, medium barrel, semi-beavertail forearm, and quarter rib with 1" Ruger scope rings. Weighs 8 lbs.

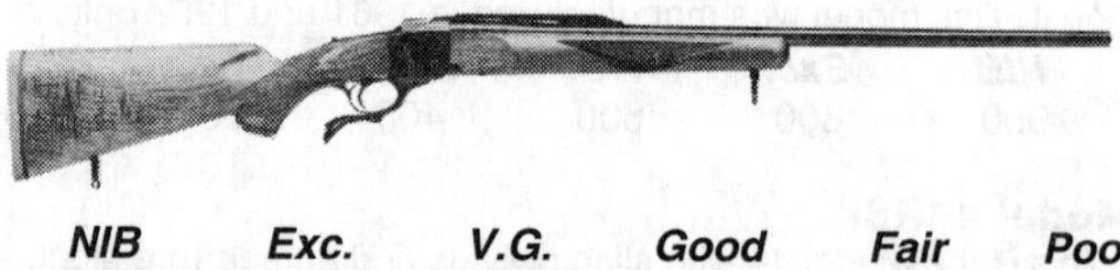

NIB	Exc.	V.G.	Good	Fair	Poor
965	725	550	375	250	200

Ruger No. 1 Standard Stainless (1-B-BBZ)

Introduced in 2000 this model features a laminated wood stock. It is chambered for the .243 Win., .25-06, 7mm Mag., 7mm STW, .30-06, .300 Win. Mag. Fitted with a 26" barrel. Weight is approximately 8 lbs.

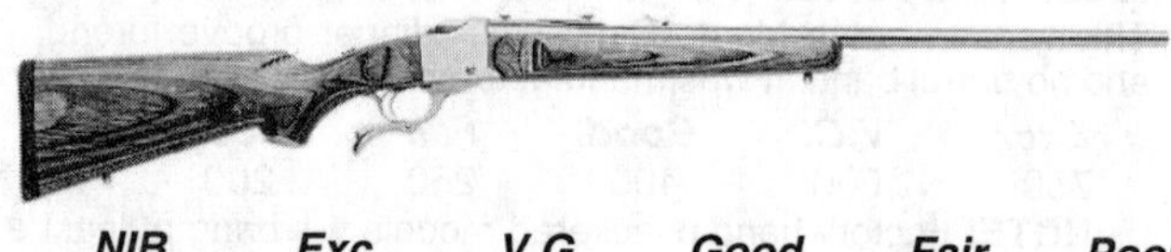

NIB	Exc.	V.G.	Good	Fair	Poor
995	750	550	375	250	200

Ruger No. 1 Tropical (1-H)

Fitted with open sights this model has a barrel band on a heavy barrel with Alexander Henry-style forearm. Rifle weighs 9 lbs.

NOTE: In 2001 this model was also offered with stainless steel finish and black laminated stock in .375 H&H. In 2003 the .458 Lott and .405 Win. cartridges were added to this model.

NIB	Exc.	V.G.	Good	Fair	Poor
965	725	550	375	250	200

NOTE: A few 24" heavy barrel 1-H rifles were chambered for the .45-70 Government cartridge up to 1976. These bring a substantial premium and should be appraised individually. The recently catalogued .404 Jeffery has been discontinued. Only a few of these rifles were produced. Add 100 percent for .404 Jeffery caliber.

Ruger No. 1 International (1-RSI)

This No. 1 rifle features a lightweight barrel with full length forearm, open sights. Rifle weighs 7.25 lbs.

NIB	Exc.	V.G.	Good	Fair	Poor
995	750	550	375	250	200

Ruger No. 1 Medium Sporter (1-S)

The Medium Sporter is equipped with open sights, a barrel band on a medium weight barrel, and Alexander Henry-style forearm. Rifle weighs 8 lbs. In 2001 this model was also offered in stainless steel and black laminated stock in .45-70 caliber.

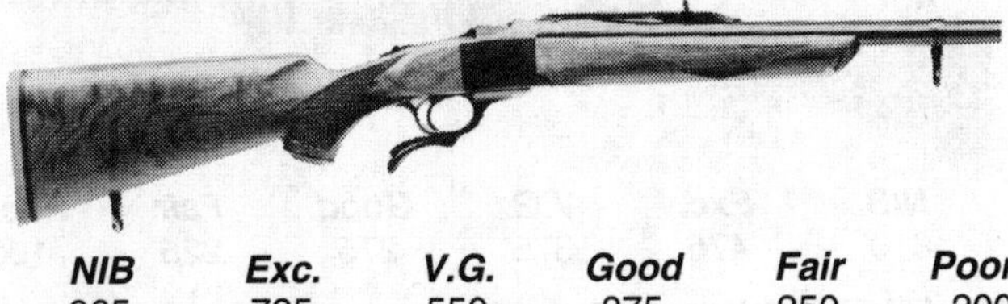

NIB	Exc.	V.G.	Good	Fair	Poor
965	725	550	375	250	200

Ruger No. 1 Special Varminter (1-V)

This model is furnished with no sights, a heavy barrel, target scope blocks with 1" Ruger scope rings, and semi-beavertail forearm. Rifle weighs about 9 lbs.

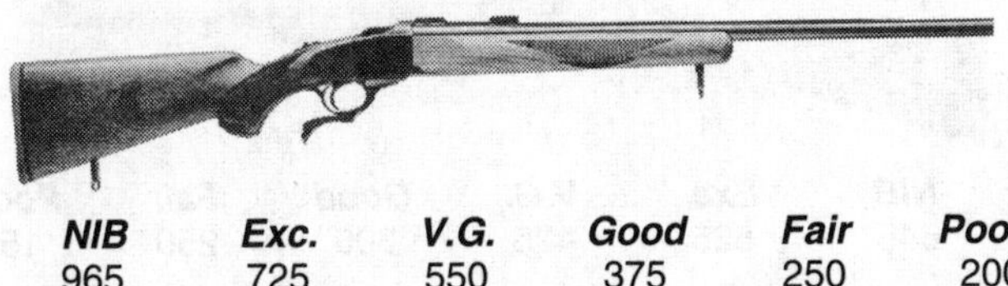

NIB	Exc.	V.G.	Good	Fair	Poor
965	725	550	375	250	200

Ruger No. 1 Stainless Varminter (1-V-BBZ)

Introduced in 2000 this model features a laminated wood stock and stainless steel finish. Chambered for .22-250 and fitted with a 24" barrel. Weight is approximately 9 lbs.

NIB	Exc.	V.G.	Good	Fair	Poor
995	750	550	375	250	200

Number 3 Carbine

This model is a less elaborate, inexpensive version of the Number 1. The action is the same except that the lever is less ornate in appearance and lacks the locking bar. The unchecked stock is of a military carbine style with a barrel band. It is similar in appearance to the Model 44 and the 10/22. This serviceable rifle was chambered for the .45-70 when it was released in 1972. Later chamberings added the .22 Hornet, .30-40 Krag, .223, .44 Magnum, and the .375 Winchester. The barrel is 22" long, and there is a folding rear sight. This model was discontinued in 1987. Add 10 percent for .30-40 Krag.

Exc.	V.G.	Good	Fair	Poor
625	500	300	200	125

BOLT-ACTION RIFLES

Ruger introduced the Model 77R in 1968. It filled the need for a good quality, reasonably priced, bolt-action hunting rifle. It has been a commercial success. There are certain variations of this rifle that collectors actively seek. One should avail oneself of the specialized literature on this model and secure individual appraisals on the rare variations as the differences are slight and beyond the scope of this book.

Model 77-R/RS

This model was introduced in 1968. It is offered with a 22", 24", or 26" barrel. The Model 77 is chambered for most calibers from .22-250 through .458 Win. Mag. The action is of a modified Mauser-type, finished in blue with a checkered walnut stock and red rubber buttplate. The rifle is available milled for Ruger scope rings or in the round-top style that allows the mounting of any popular scope ring system. This model is designated 77R when supplied with rings only; and 77RS, when supplied with rings and sights. This model was replaced by the Model 77 MK II.

NIB	Exc.	V.G.	Good	Fair	Poor
500	400	350	300	250	200

Model 77-RS

NIB	Exc.	V.G.	Good	Fair	Poor
550	450	400	300	250	200

Model 77 Flat Bolt

This is an example of the slight variations that make this model collectible. This is essentially the same rifle with the knob on the bolt handle flattened. They were only produced in the configuration until 1972. Watch for fakes, and read specialized material. Calibers such as the 6.5 Rem. Mag., .284, and .350 Rem. Mag. will bring a premium especially in the RS model.

NOTE: Nonprefixed rifles exists in calibers and configurations other than those advertised by Ruger. These should be individually appraised.

Exc.	V.G.	Good	Fair	Poor
650	500	400	350	275

Model 77 RL & RLS

This variation is similar to the standard model except that it features an ultralight 20" barrel and black forearm tip. This model was also available in an 18.5" carbine version with sights designated the RLS. This model was also in an 18.5" carbine version with sights designated the RLS. They were chambered for the .22-250, .243, .257, .270, .250-3000, .308, and .30-06. Weight is only 6 lbs.

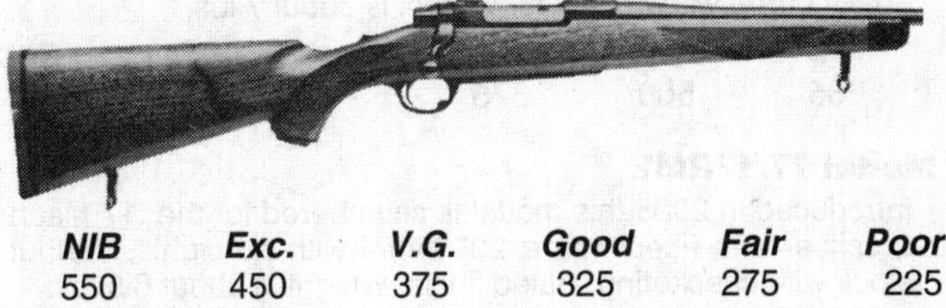

NIB	Exc.	V.G.	Good	Fair	Poor
550	450	375	325	275	225

Model 77V Varmint

This variation is similar to the standard Model 77 except that it has a 24" heavy barrel that is drilled and tapped for target-scope bases and has a wider beavertail forearm. It is chambered for the .22-250, .243, 6mm, .25-06, .280, and .308. This model was also chambered for the .220 Swift in a 26" heavy-weight barrel.

NIB	Exc.	V.G.	Good	Fair	Poor
500	400	350	300	250	200

Model 77 RSI

This version of the Model 77 has a full-length, Mannlicher-style stock and was chambered for the .22-250, .250-3000, .243, .270, 7mm-08, .308 and the .30-06.

NIB	Exc.	V.G.	Good	Fair	Poor
700	600	500	300	275	200

Model 77 RS African

This is a heavier-barreled version, with a steel trigger guard and floorplate. Earlier versions were stocked with fine-quality Circassian walnut. This rifle is chambered for the .458 Winchester Magnum.

NOTE: Fewer than 50 rifles chambered for the .416 Taylor cartridge were produced up to 1976. Selling prices range from $3,000 to $5,000 and should be individually appraised.

NIB	Exc.	V.G.	Good	Fair	Poor
700	550	400	350	300	250

NOTE: Add $100 for early models with Circassian walnut stocks.

Model 77/17

Introduced in 2003, this rifle is chambered for the .17 HMR cartridge and fitted with a 22" barrel with no sights. Walnut stock with blued finish. Magazine capacity is nine rounds. Weight is about 6 lbs.

NIB	Exc.	V.G.	Good	Fair	Poor
610	475	350	250	—	—

Model 77/17 Synthetic

As above but with black synthetic stock and blued finish.

NIB	Exc.	V.G.	Good	Fair	Poor
610	475	350	250	—	—

Model 77/17 Varmint

As above but with black laminate stock and 24" stainless steel heavy barrel with no sights. Weight is about 7 lbs.

NIB	Exc.	V.G.	Good	Fair	Poor
685	500	375	—	—	—

Model 77/17RM2

Introduced in 2005 this model is chambered for the .17 Mach 2 caliber and fitted with a 20" barrel with no sights. Walnut stock with checkering. Blued finish. Weight is about 6.5 lbs.

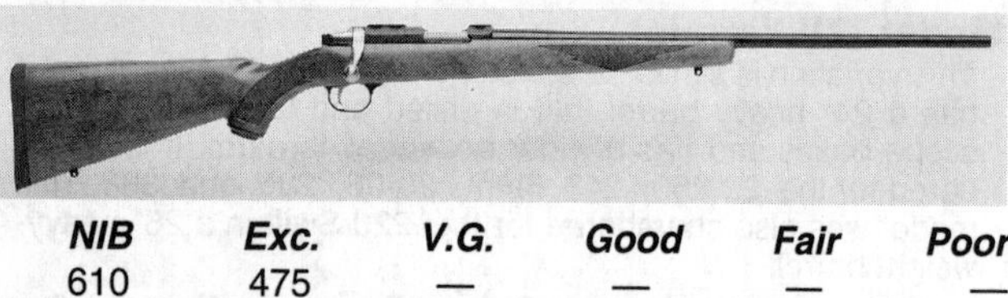

NIB	Exc.	V.G.	Good	Fair	Poor
610	475	—	—	—	—

Model 77/17RM2 Stainless Steel

As above but with stainless steel finish and black laminate stock. Weight is about 7.25 lbs. Introduced in 2005.

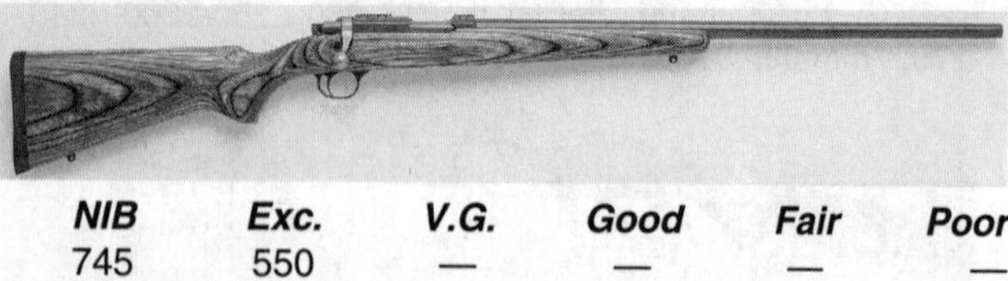

NIB	Exc.	V.G.	Good	Fair	Poor
745	550	—	—	—	—

Model 77/22

This is a high quality, .22 rimfire rifle designed for the serious shooter. This model has a 20" barrel and a 10-shot, detachable rotary magazine. It is made of steel and stocked with checkered walnut. It is available with sights, scope rings, or both as an extra-cost ($20) option. This model was introduced in 1984. Early guns without the 77/22 rollmark on the receiver will bring a premium.

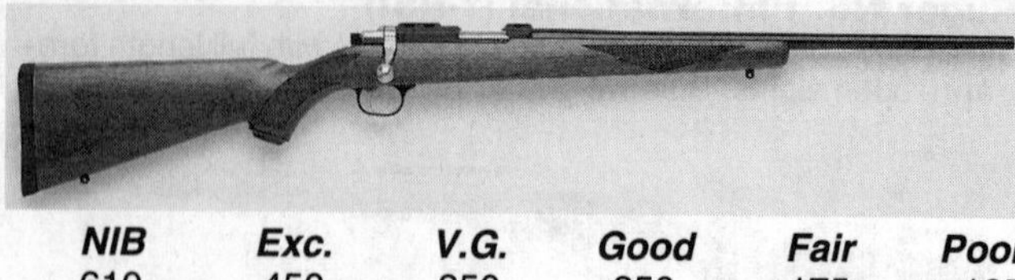

NIB	Exc.	V.G.	Good	Fair	Poor
610	450	350	250	175	125

Model 77/22 Synthetic Stock

This version is quite similar to the standard 77/22, with a black-matte-finished synthetic stock.

NIB	Exc.	V.G.	Good	Fair	Poor
610	450	350	250	200	150

Model 77/22 Stainless Steel/Synthetic Stock

This model is the same as the blued version except that it is made of stainless steel.

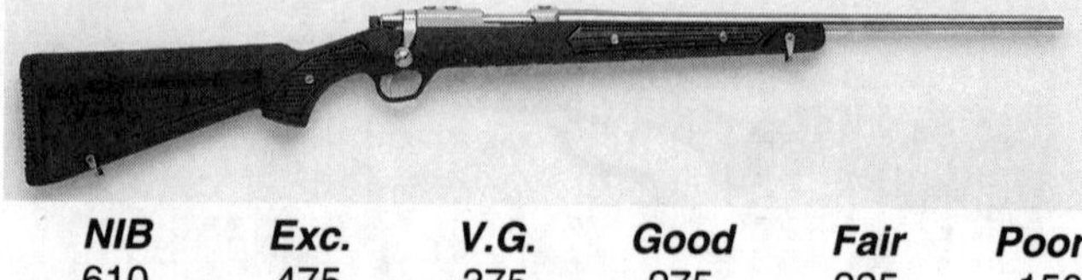

NIB	Exc.	V.G.	Good	Fair	Poor
610	475	375	275	225	150

Model 77/22 Varmint

Introduced in 1993 this model features a stainless steel finish, laminated wood stock, heavy 20" varmint barrel with no sights. Scope rings are included as standard. Chambered for the .22 LR or Win. Mag. Rimfire.

NIB	Exc.	V.G.	Good	Fair	Poor
645	525	425	300	250	150

Model 77/22M

This model is simply the 77/22 chambered for the .22 Magnum cartridge. The finish is blue, and the magazine capacity is 9 rounds.

NIB	Exc.	V.G.	Good	Fair	Poor
610	450	350	250	175	125

Model 77/22 Stainless Steel

This is the same as the blued 77/22M constructed of stainless steel.

NIB	Exc.	V.G.	Good	Fair	Poor
600	475	375	275	225	150

Model 77/22—.22 Hornet

Introduced in 1994 this version of the 77/22 series is chambered for the .22 Hornet cartridge. This model is furnished with or without sights. The barrel is 20" and it has a 6-round detachable rotary magazine. The stock is checkered walnut with sling swivels. Weight is approximately 6 lbs.

NOTE: This model is offered with (77/22RSH) or without (77/22RH) sights.

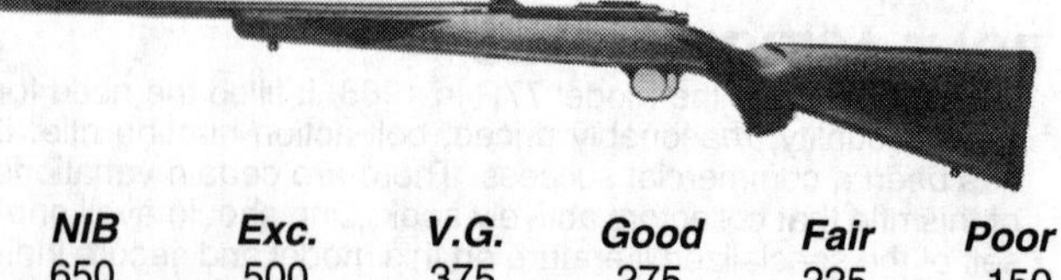

NIB	Exc.	V.G.	Good	Fair	Poor
650	500	375	275	225	150

Model K77/22VHZ

Introduced in 1995 this .22 Hornet variation features a stainless steel heavyweight barrel and laminated American hardwood stock. Offered without sights.

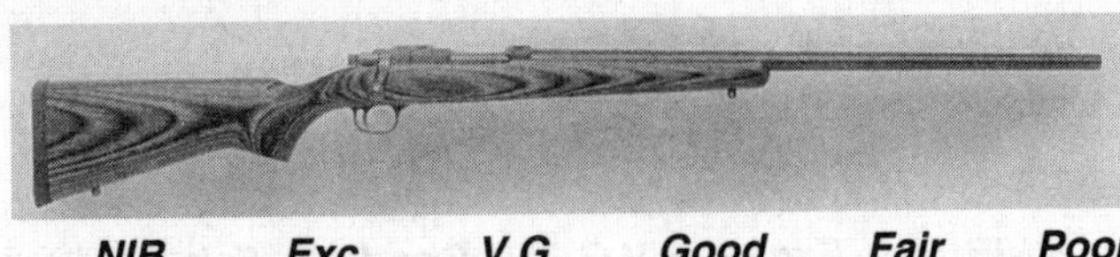

NIB	Exc.	V.G.	Good	Fair	Poor
685	525	425	300	250	150

Ruger Model 77: Mark I vs. Mark II

This Ruger bolt action was produced in the Mark I version until November 1991 when it was dropped from the product line. In December 1991 Ruger began producing a new bolt-action Model 77 design referred to as the Mark II. There are several noticeable and important differences between the two versions. The Model 77 Mark I features a sliding tang safety while the Mark II has a new three-position wing safety. The Mark I designed Model 77 holds 5 rounds while the newer Mark II holds 4 rounds. The Mark I incorporates and chrome moly bolt and the Mark II has a stainless steel bolt. The Mark I has a spring loaded ejector while the Mark II has a fixed pin design. The Mark I has an adjustable trigger as opposed to the newer Mark II's nonadjustable trigger. The Mark I bolt face does not incorporate a central feed system while the Mark II does have a central feed. The Mark II design also features a slimmer action that the older Mark I design.

Model 77R MKII

Introduced in 1992 this model is the basic Model 77 rifle. Features blued metal parts and no sights. Available in 15 different calibers from .223 to .338 Win. Mag. in barrel lengths from 22" to 24" depending on caliber. Comes from factory with scope bases and rings. Rifle weighs approximately 7 lbs.

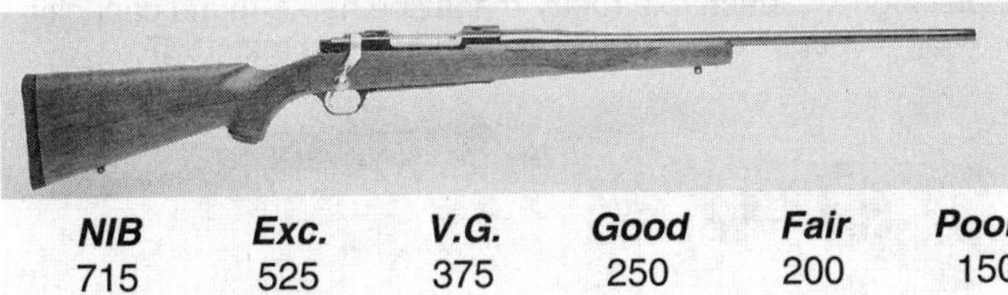

NIB	Exc.	V.G.	Good	Fair	Poor
715	525	375	250	200	150

Model 77RP MKII

This model was also introduced in 1992 and differs from the Model 77R with the addition of stainless steel barrel and receiver and synthetic stock. Available in 10 calibers. In 1998 the .25-06 caliber was added to this model.

NIB	Exc.	V.G.	Good	Fair	Poor
715	525	375	250	200	150

Model 77RS MKII

This is a blued version of the basic rifle with the addition of open sights. Available in 9 calibers from .243 Win. to .458 Win. Mag.

NIB	Exc.	V.G.	Good	Fair	Poor
760	600	450	350	250	175

Model 77RSP MKII

The stainless version of the basic rifle with the addition of a synthetic stock and open sights. Available in 6 calibers: .243, .270, 7MM Rem. Mag., .30-06, .330 Win. Mag., .338 Win. Mag. Introduced in 1993.

NIB	Exc.	V.G.	Good	Fair	Poor
500	400	350	300	250	175

Model 77RSI MKII

Also introduced in 1993 this model features a blued barrel and full-length walnut stock. Offered in four calibers, all with 18" barrel. The calibers are: .243, .270, .30-06, and .308.

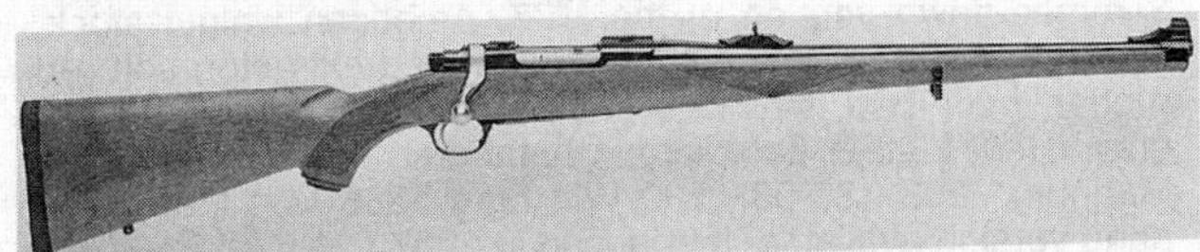

NIB	Exc.	V.G.	Good	Fair	Poor
820	600	450	350	250	175

Model 77RL MKII

This model features a short action in six calibers from .223 to .308, all with 20" barrel. Rifle weighs about 6 lbs. Introduced in 1992.

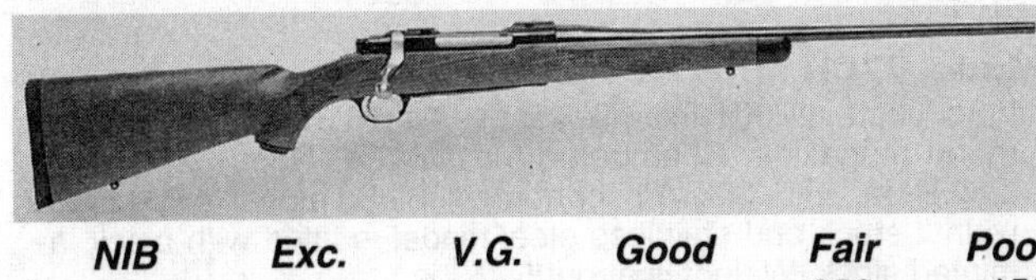

NIB	Exc.	V.G.	Good	Fair	Poor
770	575	425	300	200	150

Model 77LR MKII

This model is a left-handed rifle furnished in long action calibers: .270, 7mm Rem. Mag., .30-06, .300 Win. Mag. Introduced in 1992.

NIB	Exc.	V.G.	Good	Fair	Poor
770	575	425	300	200	150

Model 77RLP MKII

Introduced in 1999 this model is similar to the RL model above, but with an all-weather synthetic stock. Weight is about 6.5 lbs.

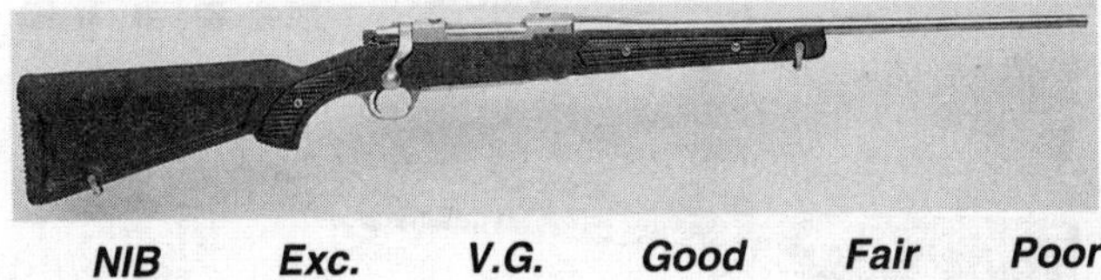

NIB	Exc.	V.G.	Good	Fair	Poor
715	525	400	275	200	150

Model 77VT MKII

This rifle was introduced in 1993 and is a target rifle. Furnished with no sights, heavy laminated wood stock with beavertail forend, and adjustable trigger. Barrel, bolt, and action are stainless steel. Weighs approximately 9.75 lbs. Furnished in eight calibers from .223 to .308.

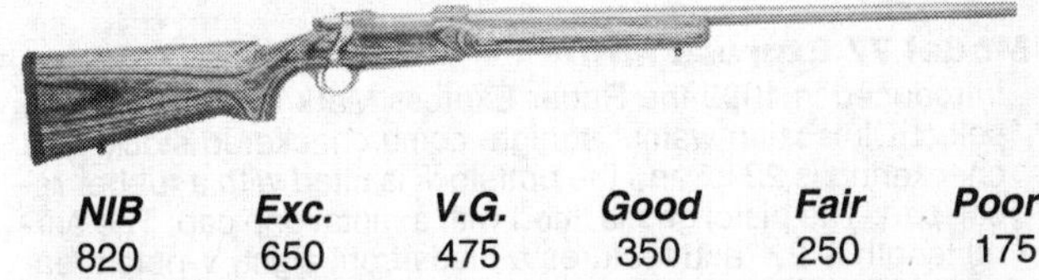

NIB	Exc.	V.G.	Good	Fair	Poor
820	650	475	350	250	175

Model 77RBZ MKII

This model features a stainless steel barrel and action fitted with laminated hardwood stock. No sights. Weight is approximately 7.25 lbs. Offered in a wide variety of calibers from .223 to .338 Win. Mag. Introduced in 1997.

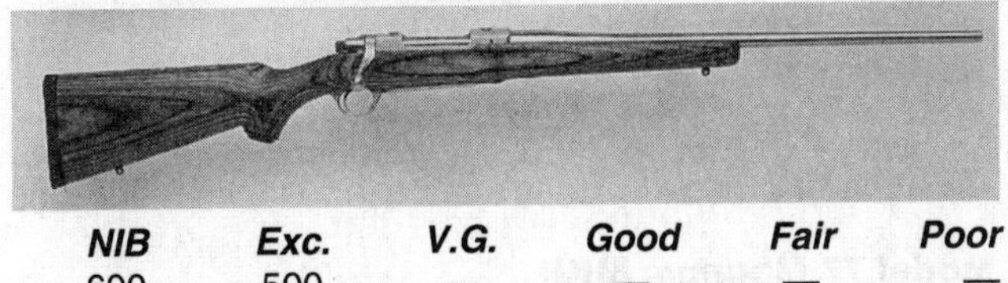

NIB	Exc.	V.G.	Good	Fair	Poor
600	500	—	—	—	—

Model 77RSBZ MKII

Same as above but fitted with open sights. Also introduced in 1997.

NIB	Exc.	V.G.	Good	Fair	Poor
800	650	475	350	—	—

Model 77CR MKII Compact Rifle

Introduced in 2001 this rifle features a 16.5" barrel with four-round magazine. Chambered for the .223 Rem., .243 Win., .260 Rem., and .308 Win. cartridges. Blued model is fitted with walnut stock and stainless steel model is fitted with black laminted stock. Weight is about 5.75 lbs.

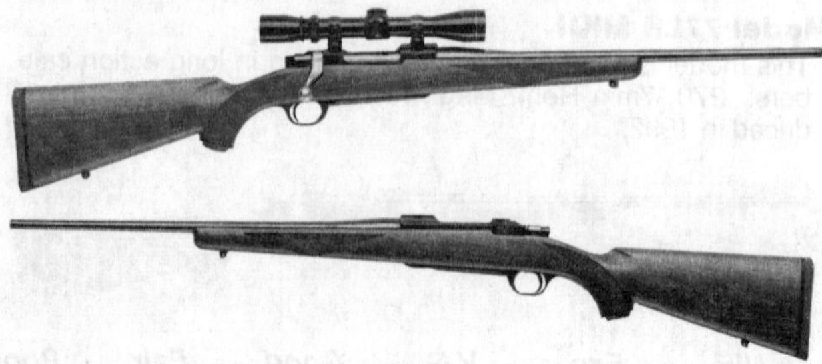

Ruger M-77 Mark II .223 Remington.

NIB	Exc.	V.G.	Good	Fair	Poor
715	525	400	275	200	150

NOTE: Add $50 for stainless steel model (M77CRBBZ).

Top to bottom: M77 MK II Magnum, M77 MK II Standard, M77 MK II Compact

Model 77 Express MKII

Introduced in 1992 the Ruger Express Mark II rifle features a select Circassian walnut straight comb checkered stock. The checkering is 22 lpi and the buttstock is fitted with a rubber recoil pad. The pistol grip is fitted with a metal grip cap. The barrel length is 22" and features a blade front sight, V-notch rear express sights, and the receiver is machined for scope mounts, which are included. Available in these calibers: .270, .30-06, 7mm Rem. Mag., .300 Win. Mag., .338 Win. Mag. Rifle weighs about 7.5 lbs.

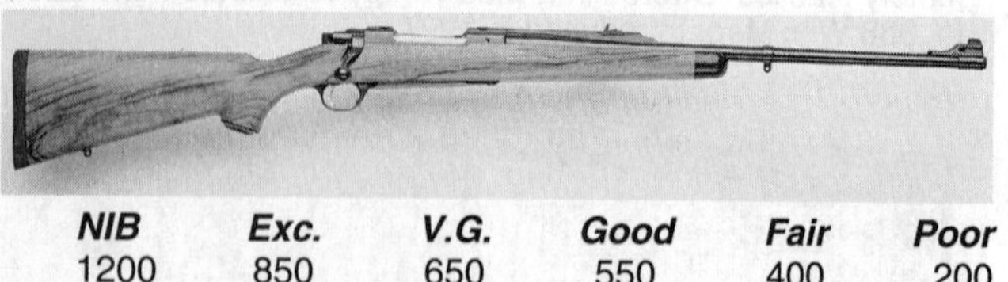

NIB	Exc.	V.G.	Good	Fair	Poor
1200	850	650	550	400	200

Model 77 Magnum MKII

Similar in all respects to the Model 77 Express MKII except offered in these calibers: .375 H&H and .416 Rigby. The .375 and weighs about 9.25 lbs. while the .416 weighs about 10.25 lbs.

NOTE: In 2003 the .458 Lott cartridge was added to this model.

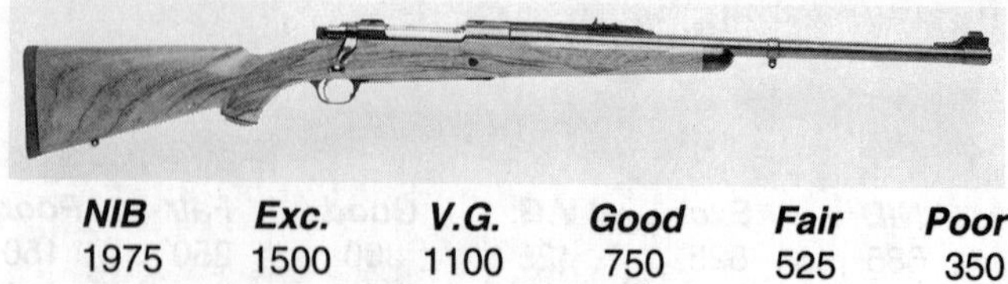

NIB	Exc.	V.G.	Good	Fair	Poor
1975	1500	1100	750	525	350

Ruger M77 MkII Frontier Rifle

Bolt-action rifle based on M77 MkII chassis but configured for "scout"-style scope mount system. Chambered in .243, .308, 7mm-08, .300 WSM, .325 WSM. 338 Federal. Gray laminated stock, 16.5-inch blued or stainless barrel (add 15 percent for stainless). Introduced 2005; stainless model introduced 2006 (add 10 percent).

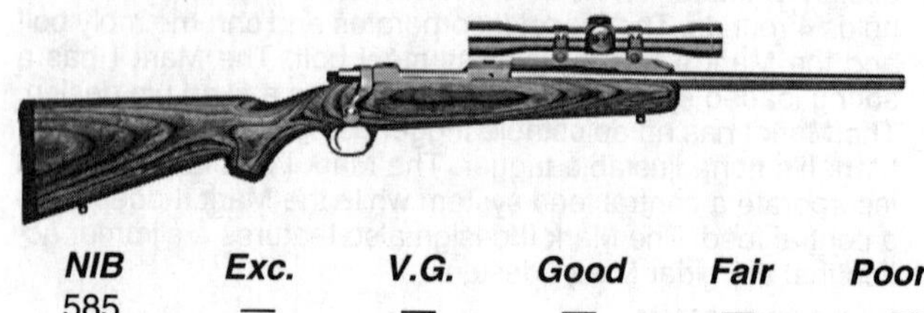

NIB	Exc.	V.G.	Good	Fair	Poor
585	—	—	—	—	—

Model 77/44RS

This bolt-action is chambered for the .44 Magnum cartridge. It features an 18.5" barrel with open sights. The stock is American walnut with rubber buttpad and checkering on forearm and pistol grip. Detachable rotary magazine has 4-round capacity. Weight is approximately 6 lbs. Introduced in mid-1997.

NIB	Exc.	V.G.	Good	Fair	Poor
575	450	—	—	—	—

Model 77/44RSP

Introduced in 1999 this model has a matte stainless steel barrel and action and a black synthetic stock. Chambered for .44 Magnum cartridge. Weight is about 6 lbs.

NIB	Exc.	V.G.	Good	Fair	Poor
575	450	—	—	—	—

Model 77/17RM

Similar in appearance to the .22 caliber Model 77 series this rifle is chambered for the .17 HMR cartridge. Fitted with a 22" barrel and walnut stock. Magazine capacity is nine rounds. Weight is about 6.25 lbs. Introduced in 2002.

NIB	Exc.	V.G.	Good	Fair	Poor
565	475	—	—	—	—

HM77R Hawkeye

Slimmed-down version of the M77. American walnut stock, blued barrel, Mauser-style controlled feed extractor, soft red rubber recoil pad, stainless steel bolt, new LC6 trigger, engraved solid steel floorplate. Chambered in 7mm-08, 7mm Magnum, .308, .30-06, .300 Win Mag, .338 Win Mag. Left-hand version available. Introduced in 2007.

 *This symbol denotes "Sleepers" with rapidly-rising values and/or significant collector potential.*

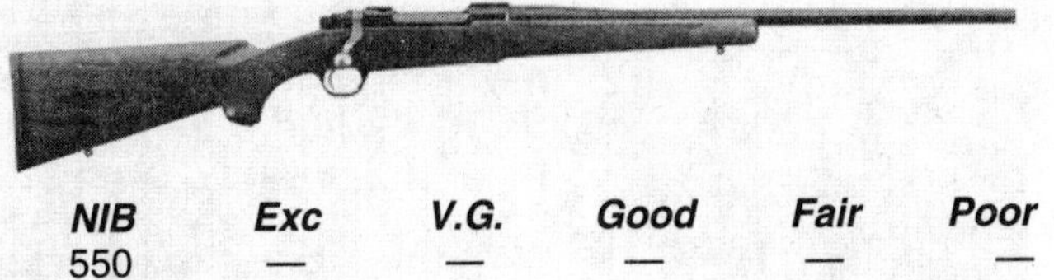

NIB	Exc	V.G.	Good	Fair	Poor
550	—	—	—	—	—

HK77RFP Hawkeye

All-weather version of the HM77R Hawkeye but with synthetic stock and stainless barrel. Same chamberings as HM77R but with .338 Federal and .358 Winchester as well. Introduced in 2007.

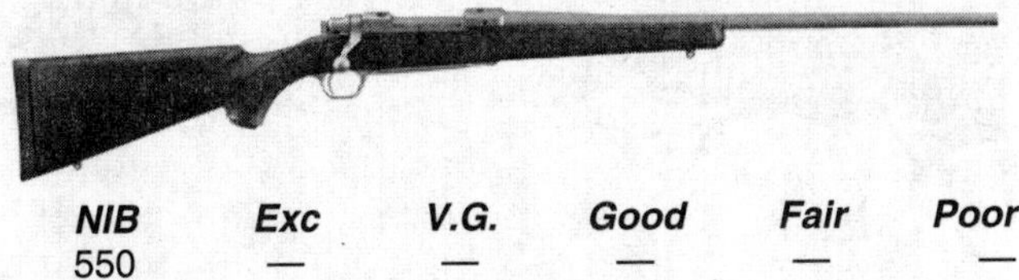

NIB	Exc	V.G.	Good	Fair	Poor
550	—	—	—	—	—

HM77RSPHAB Hawkeye Alaskan

Similar to HK77RFP but with iron sights, Diamondblack finish and Hogue stock. Chambered in .375 Ruger. Introduced in 2007.

NIB	Exc	V.G.	Good	Fair	Poor
850	—	—	—	—	—

Model 77/50RS

This model is an in-line percussion rifle chambered for .50 caliber. It is fitted with a 22" barrel with open sights. Stock is birch with rubber buttplate and no checkering. Blued finish. Weight is approximately 6.5 lbs. Introduced in mid-1997.

NIB	Exc.	V.G.	Good	Fair	Poor
425	325	225	175	—	—

Model 77/50RSO

Similar to the model above but with a straight-grip checkered walnut stock with curved buttplate. Introduced in 1998.

NIB	Exc.	V.G.	Good	Fair	Poor
475	350	250	200	—	—

Model 77/50RSBBZ

This model was introduced in 1998 and features all of the specifications of the Model 77/50RS with the addition of a black/gray laminated stock and a stainless steel finish.

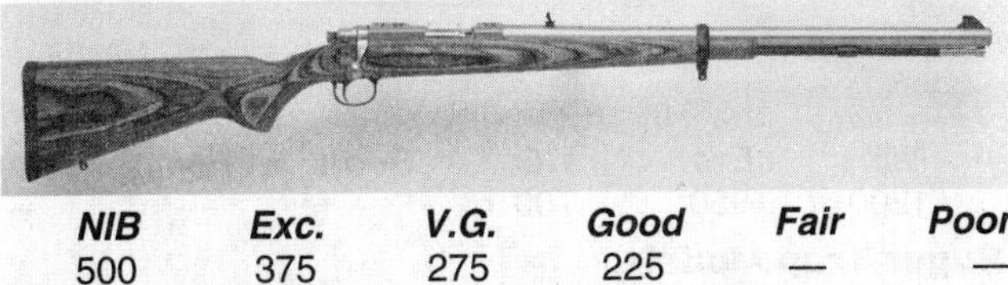

NIB	Exc.	V.G.	Good	Fair	Poor
500	375	275	225	—	—

Model 77/50RSP

This model is fitted with a stainless steel barrel and action and fitted with a black synthetic stock with pistol grip. Weight is about 6.5 lbs. Introduced in 1999.

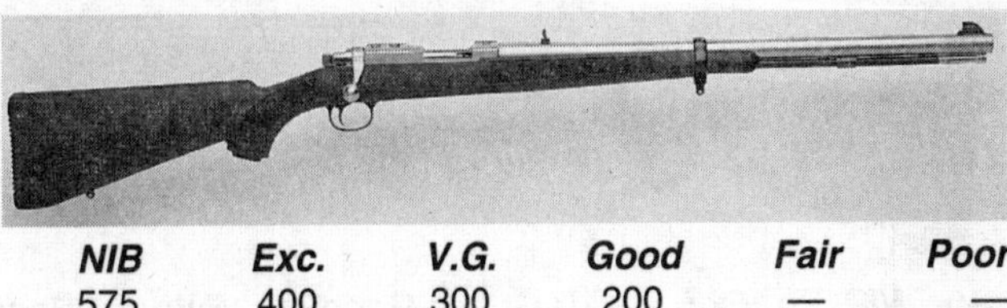

NIB	Exc.	V.G.	Good	Fair	Poor
575	400	300	200	—	—

LEVER-ACTION RIFLES

Model 96/17

Introduced in 2003 this model is chambered for the .17 HMR cartridge and fitted with an 18.5" barrel. Magazine capacity is nine rounds. Hardwood stock and open sights. Weight is about 5.25 lbs.

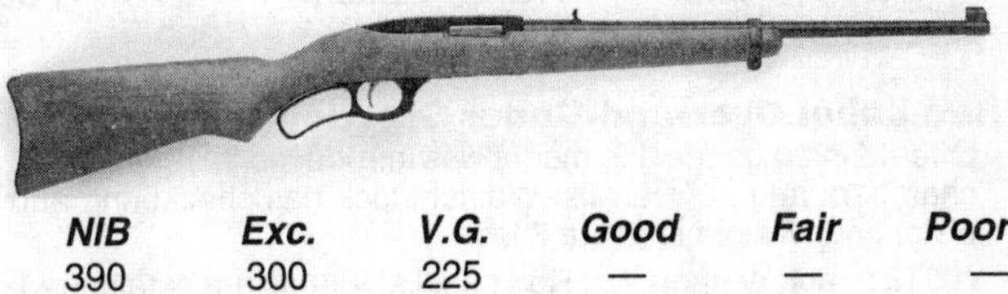

NIB	Exc.	V.G.	Good	Fair	Poor
390	300	225	—	—	—

Model 96/22

Introduced into the Ruger line in 1996 this lever action rifle is chambered for the .22 LR. The stock is American hardwood and the barrel length is 18.5". Magazine capacity is 10 rounds. Open sights are standard. Weight is approximately 5.25 lbs.

NIB	Exc.	V.G.	Good	Fair	Poor
350	275	200	175	150	100

Model 96/22M

Same as above but chambered for the .22 WMR cartridge. Magazine capacity is nine rounds.

NIB	Exc.	V.G.	Good	Fair	Poor
390	300	225	175	150	100

Model 96/44

Same as the .22 caliber except chambered for the .44 Magnum cartridge. Magazine capacity is four rounds and the weight is about 5-7/8 lbs.

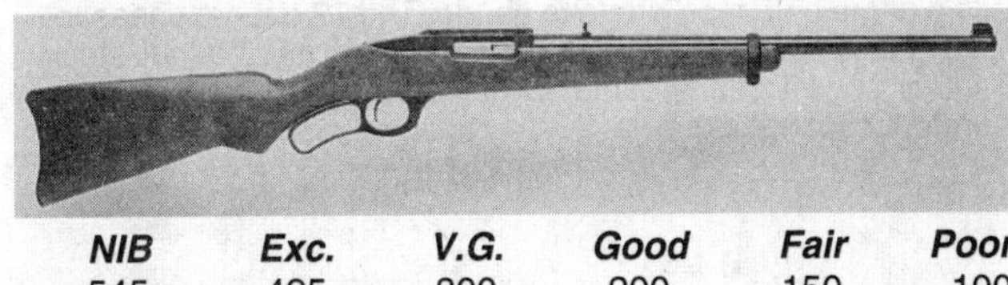

NIB	Exc.	V.G.	Good	Fair	Poor
545	425	300	200	150	100

SHOTGUNS

Red Label Over-and-Under Early Production

Ruger introduced the Red Label in 20 gauge in 1977; the 12 gauge followed five years later. This high quality shotgun is offered with 3" chambers in 26" or 28" barrel lengths. Various chokes are available. They are boxlocks with automatic ejectors. The stock is of checkered walnut. The finish is blue on the earlier guns.

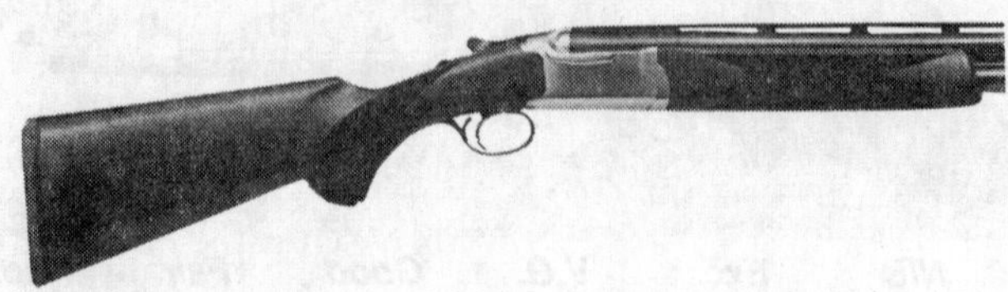

NIB	Exc.	V.G.	Good	Fair	Poor
800	650	550	400	300	250

Red Label Over-and-Under Current Production

The new 12 and 20 gauge Red Label shotgun has a stainless steel receiver and blued barrels. They are offered with screw-in choke tubes. Otherwise they are similar to the earlier models. In 1994 Ruger added the 28 gauge with 26" or 28" barrels to the Red Label line.

NIB	Exc.	V.G.	Good	Fair	Poor
1150	850	650	400	300	—

Red Label Over-and-Under Sporting Clays

Offered in 20 gauge this model was introduced in 1994 with 3" chambers and 30" barrels. Walnut stock has checkering and pistol grip. Weight is about 7 lbs.

NOTE: Factory engraved Red Label shotguns are catalogued, as of 1996, as available with three different engraving coverages. A total of 375 were produced. Prices for these engraved guns are:
Grade 1—EXC.—$2200
Grade 2 (1/3 coverage)—EXC.—$2400
Grade 3 (2/3 coverage)—EXC.—$2750

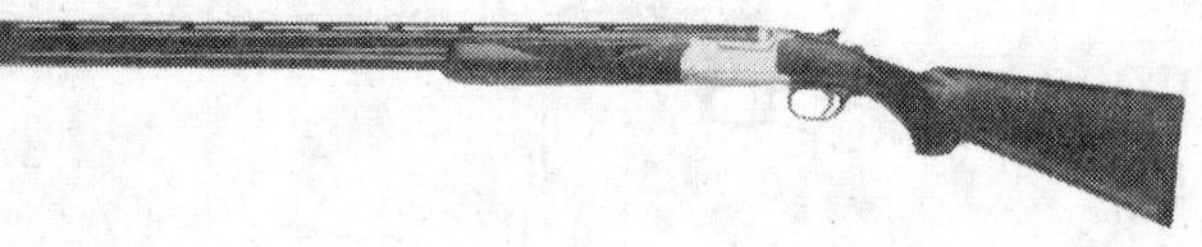

Courtesy compliments of Bill Ruger, John C. Dougan

NIB	Exc.	V.G.	Good	Fair	Poor
1050	950	750	500		—

Red Label All-Weather Over-and-Under

Offered in 12 gauge only with 26", 28", or 30" barrels this model is fitted with a black synthetic stock with pistol grip. Weight is about 7.5 lbs. Introduced in 1999.

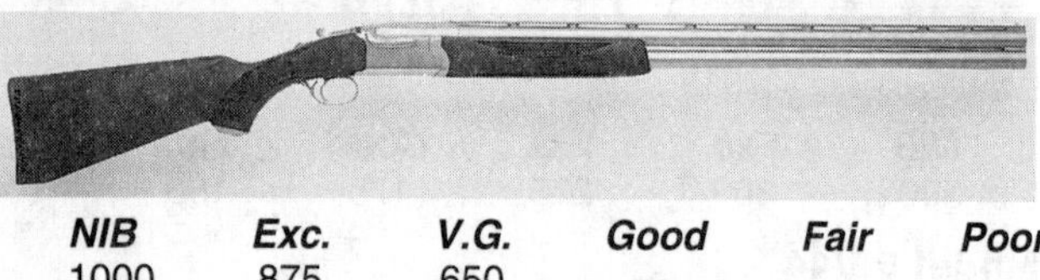

NIB	Exc.	V.G.	Good	Fair	Poor
1000	875	650	—	—	

Engraved Red Label Over-and-Under

This model features a scroll engraved receiver with a gold inlaid game bird appropriate to gauge. The 12 gauge: pheasant; 20 gauge: grouse; and 28 gauge: woodcock. Walnut stock. Other specifications same as standard Red Label shotguns. Introduced in 2000.

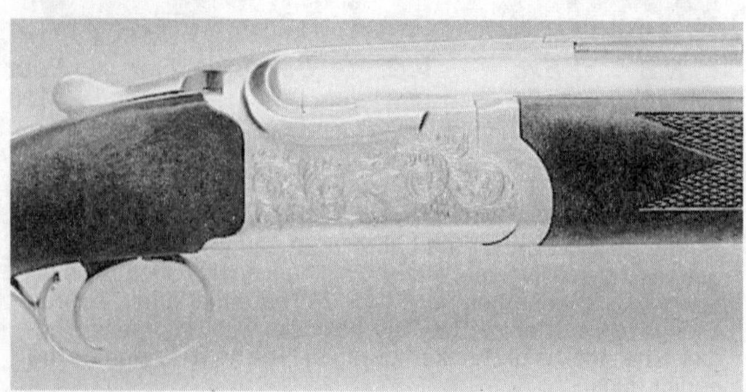

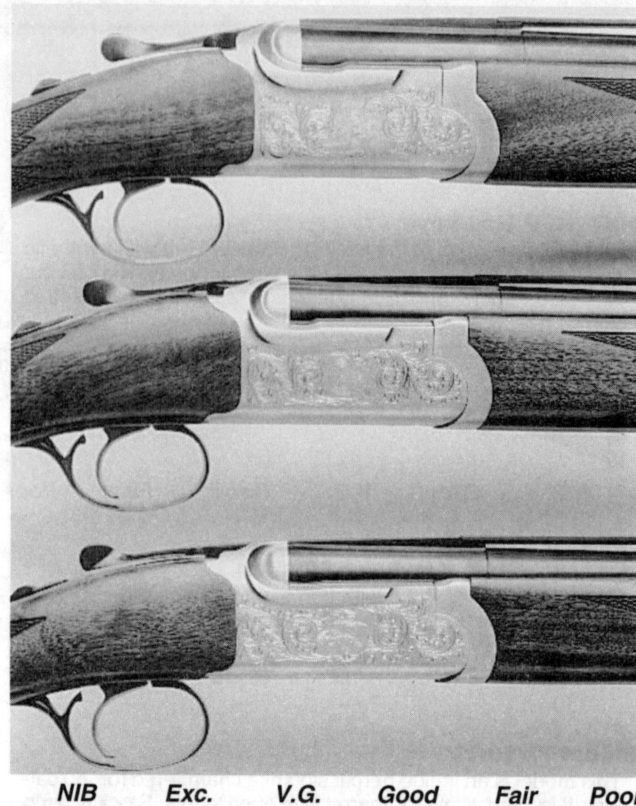

NIB	Exc.	V.G.	Good	Fair	Poor
1650	1300	—	—	—	—

Engraved Red Label All-Weather Over-and-Under

Introduced in 2000 this model features a scroll engraved receiver with gold inlaid duck. Offered in 12 gauge only with 26", 28", or 30" barrel.

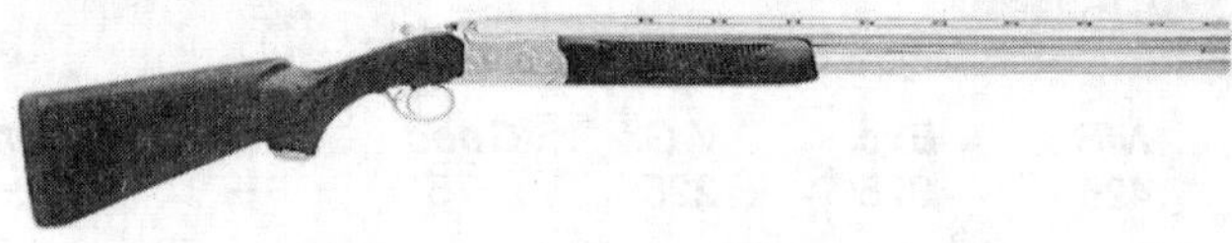

NIB	Exc.	V.G.	Good	Fair	Poor
1650	1300	975	—	—	—

Ruger Woodside Over-and-Under

Introduced in 1995 this new model features a Circassian walnut stock with either pistol grip or straight grip. Available in 12 or 20 gauge with barrel lengths of 26", 28", or 30". Screw-in chokes are standard.

NOTE: The Woodside shotgun is also available in three different engraving patterns.

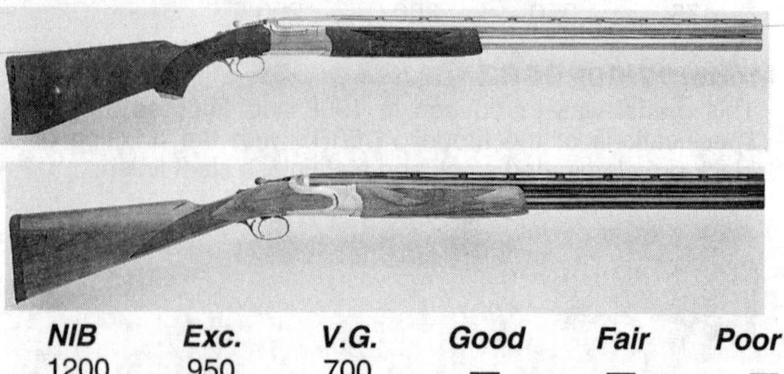

NIB	Exc.	V.G.	Good	Fair	Poor
1200	950	700	—	—	—

Ruger Trap Model

Introduced in 2000 this model is a 12 gauge single-barrel trap gun with a 34" barrel choked Full and Modified. It is fitted with a mechanical trigger and auto ejector. The stock is select walnut with adjustable cheekpiece and buttplate. Receiver is engraved. Weight is approximately 9 lbs.

NIB	Exc.	V.G.	Good	Fair	Poor
3000	2500	1750	—	—	—

Ruger Gold Label Side-by-Side

Introduced in 2002 this model is chambered for the 12 gauge 3" shell. Offered with 28" barrels with choke tubes. Choice of pistol or straight grip checkered walnut stock. Ejectors and single trigger. Weight is about 6.33 lbs.

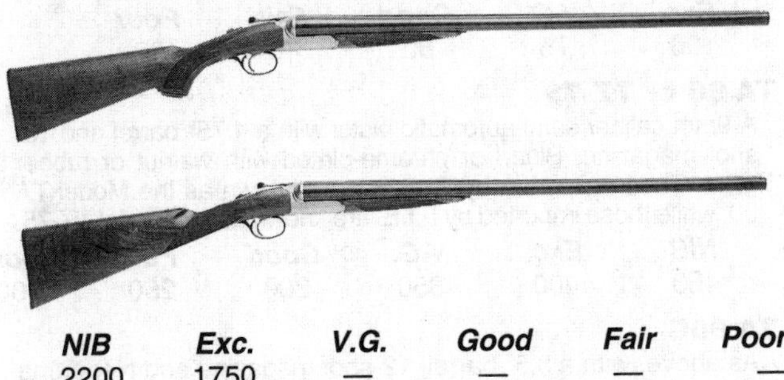

NIB	Exc.	V.G.	Good	Fair	Poor
2200	1750	—	—	—	—

SUNDANCE INDUSTRIES, INC.

North Hollywood, California

This company was in business from 1989 to 2002.

Model D-22M

A .22 or .22 Magnum caliber double-barrel over-and-under pocket pistol with 2.5" barrels and an aluminum alloy frame. Blackened finish or chrome-plated with either simulated pearl or black grips. Introduced in 1989.

Exc.	V.G.	Good	Fair	Poor
225	175	125	100	75

Model BOA

Introduced in 1991 this semi-automatic pistol is chambered for the .25 ACP cartridge. Fitted with a 2.5" barrel with fixed sights. Grip safety. Choice of black or chrome finish. Magazine capacity is 7 rounds. Weight is about 16 oz.

NIB	Exc.	V.G.	Good	Fair	Poor
95	80	70	50	—	—

Model A-25

Similar to the BOA but without grip safety.

NIB	Exc.	V.G.	Good	Fair	Poor
80	65	50	40	—	—

Model Laser 25

Similar to the Model BOA with grip safety but equipped with a laser sight. Laser activated by squeezing grip safety. Weight with laser 18 oz. Introduced in 1995.

NIB	Exc.	V.G.	Good	Fair	Poor
220	175	125	—	—	—

Sundance Point Blank

This is an over-and-under derringer chambered for the .22 LR cartridge. It is fitted with a 3" barrel and double-action trigger. Enclosed hammer. Matte black finish. Weight is about 8 oz. Introduced in 1994.

NIB	Exc.	V.G.	Good	Fair	Poor
95	80	70	50	—	—

REMINDER

"A well regulated militia being necessary to the security of a free State, the right of the People to keep and bear arms shall not be infringed."

SUPER SIX LTD.

Fort Atkinson, Wisconsin

Bison Bull

Massive single-action .45-70 revolver with blued carbon steel (Bison Bull) or engraved molybdenum bronze (Golden Bison Bull) frame. Adjustable sights, 10.5" barrel, 17.5" overall length, weight 6 lbs. Introduced 2006. Value shown is for blued version. Add 350 percent for engraved version.

NIB	Exc	V.G.	Good	Fair	Poor
995	—	—	—	—	—

SUTHERLAND, S.

Richmond, Virginia

Pocket Pistol

A .41 caliber percussion single-shot pistol with round barrels of 2.5" to 4" in length, German silver mounts and a walnut stock. The lock normally marked "S. Sutherland" or "S. Sutherland/Richmond". Manufactured during the 1850s.

Exc.	V.G.	Good	Fair	Poor
—	—	2000	800	300

SYMS, J. G.

New York, New York

Pocket Pistol

A .41 caliber single-shot percussion pistol with 1.5" to 3.5" barrels, German silver mounts and a walnut stock. The lock normally marked "Syms/New York". Manufactured during the 1850s.

Exc.	V.G.	Good	Fair	Poor
—	—	2000	800	300

T

TACONIC FIREARMS LTD.

Cambridge, New York

M98 Ultimate Hunter

This bolt-action rifle is based on the M98 Mauser action. It is available in calibers from .22-250 to .358 Win. Stainless steel barrel length is 22". Titanium grip cap. Stock is XXX English walnut with cheekpiece and oil finish. Ebony forend tip. Scope bases are integral to the receiver. The prices listed is for the standard rifle. There are an extensive list of options which will greatly affect price. For example an optional quarter rib will add $1000 to the base price of the gun.

NIB	Exc.	V.G.	Good	Fair	Poor
6000	4750	—	—	—	—

TALLASSEE

Tallassee, Alabama

Carbine

A .58 caliber single-shot percussion carbine with a 25" round barrel and full-length stock secured by two barrel bands. Fitted with sling swivels. Barrel and lock finished in the bright, brass furniture and walnut stock. The lock marked "C.S./Tallassee/Ala." Approximately 500 of these carbines were manufactured in 1864. Very Rare.

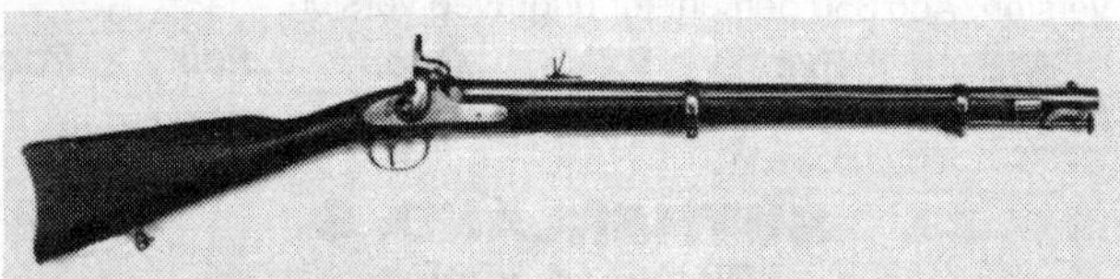

Courtesy Milwaukee Public Museum, Milwaukee, Wisconsin

Exc.	V.G.	Good	Fair	Poor
—	—	65000	30000	—

TANFOGLIO

Valtrompia, Italy

The products of this company, which was established in the late 1940s, have been imported into the United States by various companies including Eig Corporation, F.I.E. of Hialeah, Florida, and Excam.

Sata

A .22 or 6.35mm caliber semi-automatic pistol with a 3" barrel. The slide marked "Pistola SATA Made in Italy" and the grips "SATA." Blued with black plastic grips.

Exc.	V.G.	Good	Fair	Poor
175	150	125	90	75

Titan

A 6.35mm caliber semi-automatic pistol with a 2.5" barrel and external hammer. The slide marked "Titan 6.35" and on U.S. imported examples, "EIG." Blued with plastic grips.

Exc.	V.G.	Good	Fair	Poor
100	75	50	40	30

TA 90 or TZ-75

A 9mm caliber semi-automatic pistol with a 4.75" barrel and 15-shot magazine. Blued or chrome-plated with walnut or rubber grips. Those imported by Excam were known as the Model TA 90, while those imported by F.I.E. are known as the Model TZ-75.

NIB	Exc.	V.G.	Good	Fair	Poor
450	400	350	300	250	200

TA 90B

As above, with a 3.5" barrel, 12-shot magazine and Neoprene grips. Introduced in 1986.

NIB	Exc.	V.G.	Good	Fair	Poor
500	450	400	350	300	250

TA 90 SS

As above, with a ported 5" barrel, adjustable sights and two-tone finish. Introduced in 1989.

NIB	Exc.	V.G.	Good	Fair	Poor
650	600	500	450	400	300

TA 41

As above, in .41 Action Express caliber. Introduced in 1989.

NIB	Exc.	V.G.	Good	Fair	Poor
500	450	400	350	300	250

TA 41 SS

As above, with a ported 5" barrel, adjustable sights and two-tone finish. Introduced in 1989.

NIB	Exc.	V.G.	Good	Fair	Poor
650	600	500	450	400	300

TA 76

A .22 caliber single-action revolver with a 4.75" barrel and 6-shot cylinder. Blued or chrome-plated with a brass back strap and trigger guard. Walnut grips.

NIB	Exc.	V.G.	Good	Fair	Poor
100	90	80	65	50	25

TA 76M Combo

As above, with a 6" or 9" barrel and an interchangeable .22 Magnum caliber cylinder.

NIB	Exc.	V.G.	Good	Fair	Poor
110	100	90	75	60	35

TA 38SB

A .38 Special caliber over-and-under double-barrel pocket pistol with 3" barrels and a hammer block safety. Blued with checkered nylon grips. Discontinued in 1985.

Exc.	V.G.	Good	Fair	Poor
100	90	80	60	40

TANNER, ANDRE

Switzerland

Model 300 Free Rifle

A 7.5mm Swiss or .308 caliber single-shot rifle with varying length barrels having adjustable target sights, adjustable trigger, and a walnut stock fitted with a palm rest and adjustable cheekpiece. Blued.

NIB	Exc.	V.G.	Good	Fair	Poor
4750	3750	3000	2500	1500	750

Model 300S

As above, with a 10-shot magazine and not fitted with a palm rest. Discontinued in 1988.

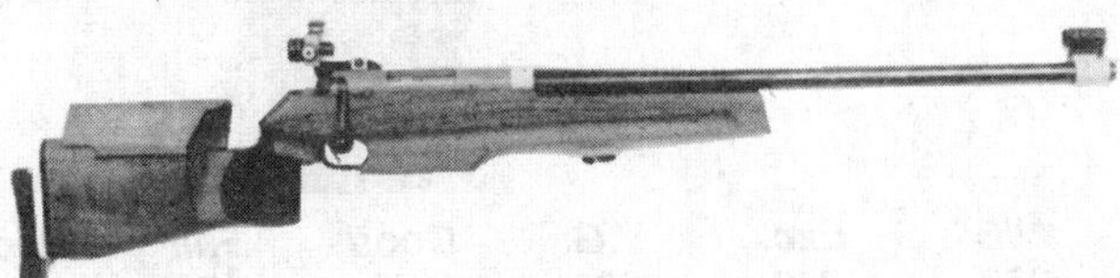

NIB	Exc.	V.G.	Good	Fair	Poor
4500	3500	2750	2250	1250	750

Model 50F

As above, in .22 caliber with a thumb hole stock. Discontinued in 1988.

NIB	Exc.	V.G.	Good	Fair	Poor
3750	3000	2500	1750	900	500

TARPLEY J. & F. AND E. T. GARRETT & CO.

Greensboro, North Carolina

Carbine

A .52 caliber breechloading single-shot percussion carbine with a 22" round barrel and a plain walnut buttstock. Blued with a case hardened frame. The tang marked "J H Tarpley's./Pat Feb 14./1863." Over 400 of these carbines were manufactured.

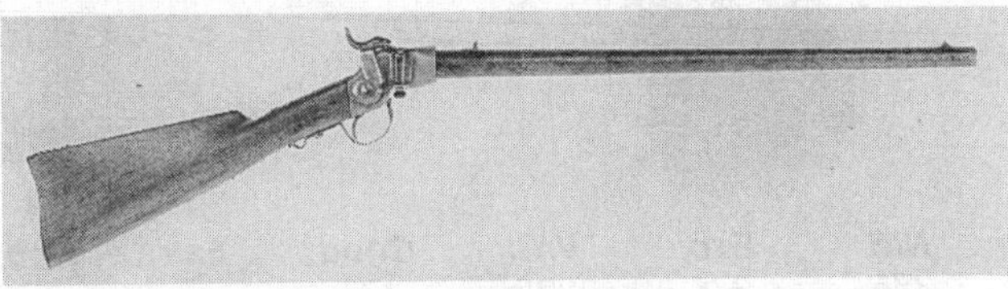

Exc.	V.G.	Good	Fair	Poor
—	—	65000	30000	—

TAURUS INTERNATIONAL MFG. CO.

Porto Alegre, Brazil

PISTOLS

PT-92C

This 9mm model is a large capacity semi-automatic pistol with a 4.25" barrel. Drift adjustable 3-dot combat rear sight. Magazine holds 13 rounds in a double column. Choice of blued, stain nickel, or stainless steel finish. Brazilian hardwood grips are standard. Weighs 31 oz.

NIB	Exc.	V.G.	Good	Fair	Poor
450	325	275	220	160	100

PT-92

A slightly larger and heavier version of the PT-92C. This model has a 5" barrel with drift adjustable 3-dot combat rear sight. Magazine capacity is 15 rounds. This model is 1" longer overall than the above model and weighs 34 oz. Also available in blued, nickel, and stainless steel.

NIB	Exc.	V.G.	Good	Fair	Poor
400	300	225	150	100	—

NOTE: Add $20 for stainless steel and $50 for blue with gold finish, $60 for stainless steel with gold accents. A blued or stainless steel .22 LR conversion kit will add $250.

PT-99

Similar in appearance and specifications to the PT-92, this version has the additional feature of fully adjustable 3-dot rear sight.

NIB	Exc.	V.G.	Good	Fair	Poor
425	325	250	150	100	—

NOTE: Add $20 for stainless steel finish.

PT-92AF

A 9mm caliber double-action semi-automatic pistol with a 4.92" barrel, exposed hammer, and 15-shot magazine. Blued or nickel-plated with plain walnut grips.

NIB	Exc.	V.G.	Good	Fair	Poor
400	350	300	250	200	150

PT-100

This model is similar to the other full-size Taurus semi-automatics except that it is chambered for the .40 S&W cartridge. Supplied with a 5" barrel, with drift adjustable rear sight, it has a magazine capacity of 11 rounds. Also available in blued, nickel, or stainless steel. Weighs 34 oz.

NIB	Exc.	V.G.	Good	Fair	Poor
500	400	300	200	150	100

NOTE: For Special Edition, blued steel with gold fixtures and rosewood grips add $50. For blued steel with gold fixtures and pearl grips add $110.

PT-101

Same as the model above but furnished with fully adjustable rear 3-dot combat sight.

NIB	Exc.	V.G.	Good	Fair	Poor
450	350	300	250	150	100

Deluxe Shooter's Pak

Offered by Taurus as a special package it consists of the pistol, with extra magazine, in a fitted custom hard case. Available for these models: PT-92, PT-99, PT-100, and PT-101.

NOTE: Add approximately 10 percent to the prices of these models for this special feature.

PT-111

This is a double-action-only pistol chambered for the 9mm cartridge. Fitted with a 3.3" barrel and polymer frame. Magazine capacity is 10 rounds. Weight is about 16 oz. Choice of blue or stainless steel. Introduced in 1997.

NIB	Exc.	V.G.	Good	Fair	Poor
350	250	200	175	150	100

NOTE: Add $20 for stainless steel finish.

PT-138

Introduced in 1998 this polymer frame pistol is chambered for the .380 cartridge. It is fitted with a 4" barrel in either blue or stainless steel. Weight is about 16 oz. Magazine capacity is 10 rounds.

Blue

NIB	Exc.	V.G.	Good	Fair	Poor
350	250	200	175	—	—

Stainless Steel

NIB	Exc.	V.G.	Good	Fair	Poor
375	275	225	175	—	—

PT-908

A semi-automatic double-action pistol chambered for the 9mm Parabellum cartridge. It is fitted with a 3.8" barrel, with drift adjustable rear 3-dot combat sight. Magazine capacity is 8 rounds in a single column. Available in blued, satin nickel, or stainless steel. Stocks are black rubber. Pistol weighs 30 oz. Introduced in 1993.

NIB	Exc.	V.G.	Good	Fair	Poor
375	325	275	225	150	100

PT-911

This model was introduced in 1997 and is chambered for the 9mm cartridge. It is fitted with a 4" barrel and has a magazine capacity of 10 rounds. Choice of blue or stainless steel. Weight is about 28 oz. Black rubber grips are standard.

NIB	Exc.	V.G.	Good	Fair	Poor
450	350	275	225	175	125

NOTE: Add $20 for stainless steel.

PT-111

Chambered for the 9mm cartridge and fitted with a 3.25" barrel. Magazine is 10 rounds. Weight is about 19 oz.

NIB	Exc.	V.G.	Good	Fair	Poor
375	300	250	—	—	—

NOTE: For matte stainless steel finish add $15. For night sights add $80.

PT-140

Chambered for the .40 S&W cartridge and fitted with a 3.25" barrel. Magazine capacity is 10 rounds. Weight is about 19 oz.

NIB	Exc.	V.G.	Good	Fair	Poor
390	315	265	—	—	—

NOTE: For matte stainless steel finish add $15. For night sights add $80.

PT-140 Millennium

Chambered for the .40 S&W cartridge and fitted with a 3.25" barrel, this model features a polymer frame and either a blue or stainless steel slide. Fixed sights. Magazine capacity is 10 rounds. Weight is about 19 oz.

Blue

NIB	Exc.	V.G.	Good	Fair	Poor
375	315	275	200	150	100

Stainless Steel

NIB	Exc.	V.G.	Good	Fair	Poor
425	325	250	175	100	—

NOTE: For night sights add $75.

PT-145 Millennium

Similar to the PT-140 but chambered for the .45 ACP cartridge. Barrel length is 3.27". Weight is about 23 oz.

Blue

NIB	Exc.	V.G.	Good	Fair	Poor
375	315	275	200	150	100

Stainless Steel

NIB	Exc.	V.G.	Good	Fair	Poor
425	325	250	175	100	—

NOTE: For night sights add $75.

Millennium Pro

Introduced in 2003 this pistol is a third generation series in the Millennium line. It features a captured dual spring and guide assembly, a reengineered magazine release, and an internal firing pin lock. A larger 3-dot sighting system, positive slide serrations, internal magazine base extension, and an enlarged external safety with positive click are other improvements.

NIB	Exc.	V.G.	Good	Fair	Poor
400	300	200	150	100	—

PT-400/400SS

Chambered for the .400 CorBon cartridge and fitted with a 4.25" ported barrel with fixed sights. Magazine capacity is 8 rounds. Offered in blue or stainless steel. Rubber grips. Weight is about 30 oz.

Blue

NIB	Exc.	V.G.	Good	Fair	Poor
400	300	200	150	100	—

Stainless Steel

NIB	Exc.	V.G.	Good	Fair	Poor
425	325	225	150	100	—

PT-132

Chambered for the .32 ACP cartridge and fitted with a 3.25" barrel. Magazine capacity is 10 rounds. Weight is about 20 oz.

NIB	Exc.	V.G.	Good	Fair	Poor
350	275	200	—	—	—

NOTE: For matte stainless steel finish add $15.

PT-58

This model was introduced in 1988. Chambered for the .380 ACP cartridge it is fitted with a 4" barrel with drift adjustable rear sight. It is a conventional double-action design. Available in blued, satin nickel, or stainless steel. It is fitted with Brazilian hardwood grips. Pistol weighs 30 oz.

NIB	Exc.	V.G.	Good	Fair	Poor
350	300	250	200	150	100

PT-138

Chambered for the .380 ACP cartridge and fitted with a 3.25" barrel. Magazine capacity is 10 rounds. Weight is about 19 oz.

NIB	Exc.	V.G.	Good	Fair	Poor
350	300	245	195	—	—

NOTE: For matte stainless steel finish add $15.

PT-145

Chambered for the .45 ACP cartridge and fitted with a 3.25" barrel. Magazine capacity is 10 rounds. Weight is about 23 oz.

NIB	Exc.	V.G.	Good	Fair	Poor
375	315	250	—	—	—

NOTE: For matte stainless steel finish add $15. For night sights add $80.

PT-45

Introduced in 1994 this semi-automatic double-action pistol is chambered for the .45 ACP cartridge. The barrel is 3-3/4" in length and the magazine capacity is 8 rounds. Offered in blued or stainless steel with grips of Brazilian hardwood. Fixed sights are standard. Overall length is 7.1" and weight is approximately 30 oz.

Blue

NIB	Exc.	V.G.	Good	Fair	Poor
395	350	275	200	150	100

Stainless Steel

NIB	Exc.	V.G.	Good	Fair	Poor
455	400	325	250	200	150

PT-745B/SS

Chambered for the .45 ACP cartridge and fitted with a 3.25" barrel. Fixed sights. Polymer grips. Blue or stainless steel. Magazine capacity is 6 rounds. Weight is about 21 oz. Introduced in 2004.

NIB	Exc.	V.G.	Good	Fair	Poor
375	315	280	—	—	—

NOTE: Add $15 for stainless steel.

PT-640B/SS

Similar to the above model but chambered for the .40 S&W cartridge. Magazine capacity is 10 rounds. Weight is about 24 oz. Introduced in in 2004.

NIB	Exc.	V.G.	Good	Fair	Poor
375	315	280	—	—	—

NOTE: Add $15 for stainless steel.

PT-24/7-45B

This .45 ACP pistol is fitted with a 4.25" barrel with fixed sights. Ribbed grips. Blued receiver. Magazine capacity is 12 rounds. Weight is about 27 oz. Introduced in 2004.

NIB	Exc.	V.G.	Good	Fair	Poor
450	400	285	—	—	—

NOTE: Add $15 for stainless steel slide.

PT-24/7-9B

As above but chambered for the 9mm cartridge. Magazine capacity is 17 rounds. Weight is about 27 oz. Introduced in 2005.

NIB	Exc.	V.G.	Good	Fair	Poor
450	400	285	—	—	—

NOTE: Add $15 for stainless steel slide.

PT-24/7-40B

As above but chambered for the .40 S&W cartridge. Magazine capacity is 15 rounds. Weight is about 27 oz. Introduced in 2005.

NIB	Exc.	V.G.	Good	Fair	Poor
450	400	285	—	—	—

NOTE: Add $15 for stainless steel slide.

PT24/7LS-9SS-17

Full-size stainless semi-auto chambered for 9mm. Long grip, long slide. Capacity 17+1. Single/double action. 5" barrel, 27.2

oz. Fixed, 2-dot rear sight. Also in short grip 10+1 capacity. Introduced 2006. Price is for stainless.

NIB	Exc.	V.G.	Good	Fair	Poor
515	—	—	—	—	—

PT24/79SSC-17

Compact stainless semi-auto chambered for 9mm, short grip, short slide. Capacity 15+1. Single/double action. 5" barrel, 27.2 oz. Fixed, 2-dot rear sight. Also in short grip 10+1 capacity. Introduced 2006. Price is for stainless.

NIB	Exc.	V.G.	Good	Fair	Poor
400	325	—	—	—	—

PT24/7PLS-9SSPTi-17

Full-size semi-auto chambered for 9mm. Capacity 17+1 or 10+1. Single/double action. Titanium slide, 4" barrel, 27.2 oz. Introduced 2006.

NIB	Exc.	V.G.	Good	Fair	Poor
445	370	—	—	—	—

24/7 OSS

Introduced in 2007. Available in .45 ACP, .40 S&W and 9mm Parabellum. 12+ 1 capacity (.45), single-/double-action. Ambidextrous decock and safety, match grade barrel, polymer frame with steel upper. Claimed to exceed all requirements set by United States Special Operations Command and developed to compete is SOCOM pistol trials. MSRP: TBA

PT24/7PLS-9SSCTi-17

Compact semi-auto chambered for 9mm. Capacity 17+1. Single/double action. Titanium slide, 3.3" barrel, 25.4 oz. Introduced 2006.

NIB	Exc.	V.G.	Good	Fair	Poor
445	370	—	—	—	—

PT191140B

1911-style .40 caliber semi-auto. Blued steel. 5" barrel, 8+1 capacity, 32 oz. Fixed Heinie two-dot straight-eight sight. Blue or stainless. Introduced 2006. Add 10 percent for stainless.

NIB	Exc.	V.G.	Good	Fair	Poor
475	—	—	—	—	—

PT1911SS

1911-style single action semi-auto in 9mm. Blued steel. 5" barrel, 8+1 capacity. LOA 8.5" and 32 oz. Fixed Heinie two-dot straight-eight sight. Blue or stainless. Numerous options. Add 10 percent for stainless. Introduced 2006.

NIB	Exc.	V.G.	Good	Fair	Poor
535	—	—	—	—	—

PT1911

Blued or stainless 1911-style single action in .45 ACP. 8+1 capacity. LOA 8.5", 32 oz., 5" barrel, fixed Heinie two-dot straight-eight sight. Numerous options. Add 10 percent for stainless. Introduced 2006. Add 10 percent for alloy frame and picatinny rail versions (added 2007).

NIB	Exc.	V.G.	Good	Fair	Poor
475	415	—	—	—	—

PT-745GB

Blued semi-auto in .45 GAP with 7+1 capacity. 3.25" barrel, fixed sights, 22 oz., polymer grip plates. Introduced 2006.

NIB	Exc.	V.G.	Good	Fair	Poor
360	—	—	—	—	—

PT745B/SS-LS

Blued or stainless semi-auto in .45 ACP. 4.25" barrel, 23.3 oz. 7+1 capacity, polymer grip plates. Introduced 2006.

NIB	Exc.	V.G.	Good	Fair	Poor
375	—	—	—	—	—

PT917B20

9mm blued or stainless semi-auto with 20+1 capacity. Fixed sights, 4" barrel, 31.8 oz. Introduced 2006.

NIB	Exc.	V.G.	Good	Fair	Poor
375	—	—	—	—	—

PT609Ti-13

This 9mm semi-auto has a titanium finish plus 13+1 capacity, 3.25" barrel. Fixed sights, 19.2 oz. Introduced 2006.

NIB	Exc.	V.G.	Good	Fair	Poor
400	—	—	—	—	—

PT59B/SS-15

Blued or stainless semi-auto in .380 ACP with 15+1 capacity. Fixed sights, 5" barrel, 32.8 oz. Introduced 2006.

NIB	Exc.	V.G.	Good	Fair	Poor
345	—	—	—	—	—

PT-38B/SS

Chambered for the .38 Super cartridge and fitted with a 4.25" barrel with fixed sights. Grips are checkered rubber. Blued or stainless steel. Magazine capacity is 10 rounds. Weight is about 30 oz. Introduced in 2004.

NIB	Exc.	V.G.	Good	Fair	Poor
500	400	295	—	—	—

NOTE: Add $15 for stainless steel.

PT-38SSSPRL

Introduced in 2005 this model is chambered for the .38 Super cartridge and fitted with a 4.25" barrel. Magazine capacity is 10 rounds. Finish is stainless steel and gold. Weight is about 30 oz.

NIB	Exc.	V.G.	Good	Fair	Poor
575	475	—	—	—	—

NOTE: Deduct $60 for stainless steel only.

Model 917

Lightweight, compact version of Model 92 chambered in 9mm Parabellum. Matte blue or stainless finish, 19+1 capacity. Introduced 2007.

NIB	Exc.	V.G.	Good	Fair	Poor
400	—	—	—	—	—

PT-945C

Introduced in 1995 this .45 ACP double-action pistol features a 4" barrel with an 8-round magazine. The grips are black rubber. The sights are drift adjustable 3-dot combat style. Approximate weight is 30 oz. Offered in blue or stainless steel with or without ported barrel.

Blue

NIB	Exc.	V.G.	Good	Fair	Poor
475	350	250	200	150	100

NOTE: Add $45 for blued finish with gold accents and ported barrel. Add $35 for ported barrel and blue finish. Add $40 for ported barrel.

Stainless Steel

NIB	Exc.	V.G.	Good	Fair	Poor
500	400	300	250	150	100

NOTE: Add $40 for ported barrel with stainless steel finish or Stainless steel finish with gold accents.

PT-945S

Same as the model above but chambered for the .45 Super cartridge. Introduced in 1998.

Blue

NIB	Exc.	V.G.	Good	Fair	Poor
450	350	250	200	150	100

Stainless Steel

NIB	Exc.	V.G.	Good	Fair	Poor
475	375	275	225	150	100

PT-940

Similar to the PT-945 except chambered for the .40 S&W cartridge. Fitted with a 4" barrel. Magazine capacity is 10 rounds. Choice of blue or stainless steel. Black rubber grips. Weight is approximately 28 oz. Introduced in 1997.

NIB	Exc.	V.G.	Good	Fair	Poor
425	315	265	200	125	75

NOTE: Add $20 for stainless steel.

PT-938

This model is chambered for the .380 ACP cartridge and fitted with a 3" barrel. Black rubber grips and choice of blue or stainless steel. Weight is about 27 oz. Introduced in 1997.

NIB	Exc.	V.G.	Good	Fair	Poor
365	300	245	175	80	50

Model 922 Sport

Introduced in 2003 this semi-automatic .22 caliber pistol features a lightweight polymer frame. Single- or double-action trigger. Barrel length is 6". Magazine capacity is 10 rounds. Adjustable sights. Weight is about 25 oz.

NIB	Exc.	V.G.	Good	Fair	Poor
310	250	—	—	—	—

NOTE: For matte stainless steel finish add $15.

PT-22

This is a semi-automatic double-action-only pistol that features a 2.75" barrel with fixed sights and a manual safety. It is chambered for the .22 LR cartridge and has a magazine capacity of 8 rounds. The stocks are Brazilian hardwood and the finish is available in either blue, blue with gold trim, nickel, or two-tone. Pistol weighs 12.3 oz.

NIB	Exc.	V.G.	Good	Fair	Poor
200	150	100	75	60	50

NOTE: For Special Edition, blued steel with gold fixtures and rosewood grips, add $50. For blued steel with gold fixtures and pearl grips add $110.

PT-922

This .22 caliber pistol has a 6" barrel with fiber optic adjustable sights. Polymer grips. Ten-round magazine. Blued finish. Weight is about 29 oz. Introduced in 2004.

NIB	Exc.	V.G.	Good	Fair	Poor
370	300	—	—	—	—

PT-25

Similar in appearance to the PT-22, this model is chambered for the .25 ACP cartridge and has a magazine capacity of 9 rounds. This model is also fitted with a 2.75" barrel. Offered in blue, blue with gold trim, two-tone finish, or nickel.

NIB	Exc.	V.G.	Good	Fair	Poor
200	150	100	75	60	50

NOTE: For Special Edition, blued steel with gold fixtures and rosewood grips, add $50. For blued steel with gold fixtures and pearl grips add $110.

REVOLVERS

Model 17MB2/MSS2

This 8-shot revolver is chambered for the .17 HMR cartridge and fitted with a 1.75" barrel with fixed sights. Blued or stainless steel. Hard rubber grips. Weight is about 22 oz. Introduced in 2004.

NIB	Exc.	V.G.	Good	Fair	Poor
360	280	—	—	—	—

NOTE: Add $45 for stainless steel.

Model 22H

This revolver is chambered for the .22 Hornet cartridge and fitted with a 10" vent rib barrel. Sights are fully adjustable. Cylinder holds 8 rounds. Finish is matte stainless steel. Rubber grips. Weight is about 50 oz. Stamped "RAGING HORNET" on the barrel.

NIB	Exc.	V.G.	Good	Fair	Poor
900	725	550	—	—	—

Model 73

A .32 Smith & Wesson Long double-action swing-out cylinder revolver, with a 3" barrel and 6-shot cylinder. Blued or nickel plated with walnut grips.

NIB	Exc.	V.G.	Good	Fair	Poor
200	175	150	125	100	75

Model 80

A full-size 6-round .38 Special with 3" or 4" heavy tapered barrel. Supplied with fixed sights and offered with blued or stainless steel (offered new in 1993) finish. Brazilian hardwood grips are standard. Weighs 30 oz.

NIB	Exc.	V.G.	Good	Fair	Poor
190	175	135	110	85	70

NOTE: Add $40 for stainless steel.

Model 82

Nearly identical to the Model 80, the Model 82 has a 3" or 4" heavy, solid rib barrel in place of the heavy tapered barrel. Pistol weighs 34 oz.

NIB	Exc.	V.G.	Good	Fair	Poor
285	195	135	110	85	70

NOTE: Add $40 for stainless steel.

Model 82B4

Chambered for the .38 Special +P cartridge and fitted with a 4" heavy solid rib barrel. Cylinder holds 6 rounds. Rubber grips. Fixed sights. Blue finish. Weight is about 37 oz.

NIB	Exc.	V.G.	Good	Fair	Poor
295	250	200	—	—	—

Model 82SS4

Same as above but with stainless steel finish. Weight is about 37 oz.

NIB	Exc.	V.G.	Good	Fair	Poor
315	265	185	—	—	—

Model 827B4

Chambered for the .38 Special +P cartridge and fitted with a 4" heavy barrel with solid rib. Cylinder is 7 shots. Rubber grips. Blued finish. Weight is about 37 oz. Fixed sights.

NIB	Exc.	V.G.	Good	Fair	Poor
300	250	200	—	—	—

Model 827SS4

Same as above but with stainless steel finish. Weight is about 35 oz.

NIB	Exc.	V.G.	Good	Fair	Poor
350	300	250	—	—	—

Model 83

Similar to the Model 82 except for a fully adjustable rear sight and Patridge-type front sight. Offered with 4" barrel only with blued or stainless steel (new for 1993) finish. Pistol weighs 34 oz.

NIB	Exc.	V.G.	Good	Fair	Poor
200	175	150	125	100	75

Model 85

A double-action revolver chambered for the .38 Special. This model is available in either a 2" or 3" heavy, solid rib barrel fitted with ejector shroud. Sights are fixed. Blued finish and stainless steel (new for 1993) are offered with Brazilian hardwood grips. Pistol weighs 21 oz. with 2" barrel. Beginning in 1996 this model was furnished with Uncle Mike's Boot Grips.

NIB	Exc.	V.G.	Good	Fair	Poor
200	175	150	125	100	75

NOTE: For Special Edition, blued steel with gold fixtures and rosewood grips, add $50. For blued steel with gold fixtures and pearl grips add $110.

Model 85 Stainless

As above, in stainless steel. Beginning in 1996 this model was furnished with Uncle Mike's Boot Grips.

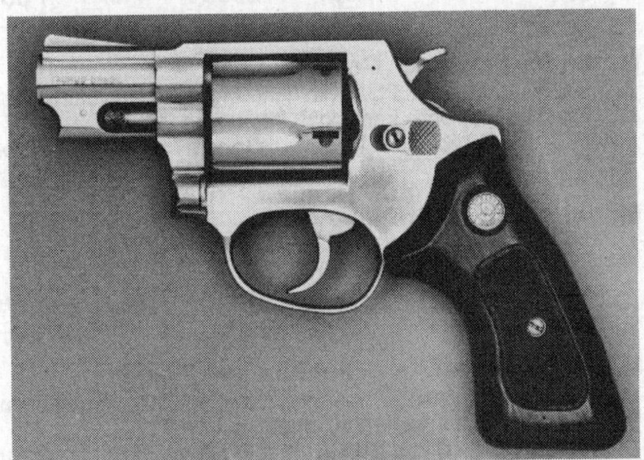

NIB	Exc.	V.G.	Good	Fair	Poor
220	190	175	150	125	100

Model 85CH

Same as above but offered in 2" or 3" barrel with shrouded hammer. Double-action-only.

NIB	Exc.	V.G.	Good	Fair	Poor
250	200	150	125	100	75

NOTE: Add $50 for stainless steel and $25 for ported barrel on 2" models.

Model 85 UL

This double-action revolver is built on a small aluminum frame and is chambered for the .38 Special cartridge. It is fitted with a 2" barrel. Choice of blue or stainless steel finish. Weight is approximately 17 oz. Introduced in 1997.

NIB	Exc.	V.G.	Good	Fair	Poor
300	250	—	—	—	—

NOTE: For Special Edition, blued steel with gold fixtures and rosewood grips add $50. For blued steel with gold fixtures and pearl grips add $110. Add $30.00 for stainless steel.

Model 85 Hy-Lite Magnesium

Similar to Model 85 but weighs only 13.8 oz. Gray alloy frame. Introduced 2007.

NIB	Exc.	V.G.	Good	Fair	Poor
N/A	—	—	—	—	—

Model 85 Ultra-Lite Gray

Similar to Model 85 but with lightweight magnesium frame. Fixed or fiber-optic front sight. Introduced 2007.

NIB	Exc.	V.G.	Good	Fair	Poor
N/A	—	—	—	—	—

Model 85 Ultra-Lite Scandium

Similar to Model 85 Magnesium but with scandium frame. Weighs 14.1 oz. Introduced 2007.

NIB	Exc.	V.G.	Good	Fair	Poor
N/A	—	—	—	—	—

Model 85 Ultra-Lite Scandium and Titanium

Similar to Model 85 Ultra-Lite Scandium but with titanium cylinder and barrel shroud. Introduced 2007.

NIB	Exc.	V.G.	Good	Fair	Poor
N/A	—	—	—	—	—

Model 850 Ultra-Lite Blue

Similar to Model 850 but with lightweight alloy frame. Introduced 2007.

NIB	Exc.	V.G.	Good	Fair	Poor
N/A	—	—	—	—	—

Model 850 Ultra-Lite Stainless Steel

Similar to Model 850 Ultra-Lite Blue but with stainless finish. Introduced 2007.

NIB	Exc.	V.G.	Good	Fair	Poor
N/A	—	—	—	—	—

Model 850 Ultra-Lite Scandium

Similar to Model 850 but with lightweight scandium frame. Introduced 2007.

NIB	Exc.	V.G.	Good	Fair	Poor
N/A	—	—	—	—	—

Model 605

Similar to Model 650 but with ultra-lightweight frame. Blue or stainless finish. Weight 23 oz. Introduced 2007.

NIB	Exc.	V.G.	Good	Fair	Poor
N/A	—	—	—	—	—

Model 850

Chambered for the .38 Special cartridge. Fitted with a 2" barrel with fixed sights. Hammerless with 5-round cylinder. Rubber grips. Weight is about 23 oz. Choice of blue or stainless steel.

NIB	Exc.	V.G.	Good	Fair	Poor
375	300	—	—	—	—

NOTE: Add $50 for stainless steel.

Model 650

As above but chambered for the .357 Magnum cartridge.

NIB	Exc.	V.G.	Good	Fair	Poor
375	300	—	—	—	—

NOTE: Add $50 for stainless steel.

Model 86

Similar to the Model 83 with the exception of a 6" barrel, target hammer, adjustable trigger, and blue-only finish. Weighs 34 oz.

NIB	Exc.	V.G.	Good	Fair	Poor
250	225	200	150	125	100

Model 94

This double-action revolver is chambered for the .22 LR cartridge. The swing-out cylinder holds 9 rounds. It is available with a heavy, solid rib, 3" or 4" barrel. In 1996 a 5" barrel option was added to this model in both blue and stainless steel. Ramp front sight with fully adjustable rear sight. Offered in blued or stainless steel with Brazilian hardwood grips. Pistol weighs 25 oz. with 4" barrel.

Blue

NIB	Exc.	V.G.	Good	Fair	Poor
225	175	150	125	100	75

Stainless Steel

NIB	Exc.	V.G.	Good	Fair	Poor
275	225	175	150	100	75

Model 94 UL

Introduced in 1997 this model is built on a small aluminum frame with 2" barrel and chambered for the .22 LR cartridge. choice of blue or stainless steel. Weight is approximately 14 oz.

NIB	Exc.	V.G.	Good	Fair	Poor
325	250	200	—	—	—

Model 941

Similar in appearance to the Model 94 this version is chambered for the .22 WMR. Available with a choice of 3" or 4" heavy, solid rib barrel. In 1996 a 5" barrel option was added to this model. This model holds 8 rounds. Ramp front sight with fully adjustable rear sight. Available in blued or stainless steel with Brazilian hardwood grips. Pistol weighs 27.5 oz.

Blue

NIB	Exc.	V.G.	Good	Fair	Poor
250	200	175	125	100	75

Stainless Steel

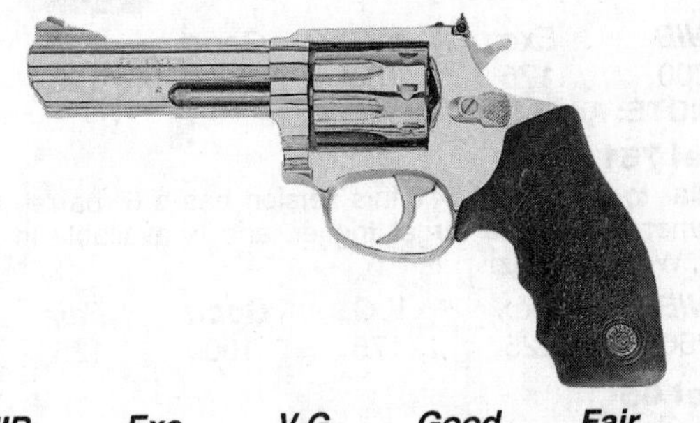

NIB	Exc.	V.G.	Good	Fair	Poor
300	250	200	150	100	75

Model 941 UL

Same as the standard Model 941 but with an aluminum frame and 2" barrel. Weight is about 18 oz. Introduced in 1997.

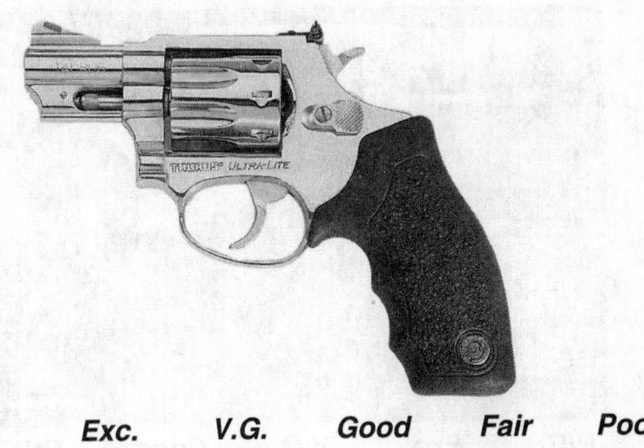

NIB	Exc.	V.G.	Good	Fair	Poor
350	275	225	—	—	—

Model 96

A full-size .22 LR revolver with 6" heavy, solid rib barrel. Fully adjustable rear sight with target hammer and adjustable target trigger. Cylinder holds 6 rounds. Available in blued only with Brazilian hardwood grips. Pistol weighs 34 oz.

NIB	Exc.	V.G.	Good	Fair	Poor
250	225	175	125	100	75

Model 741

This double-action revolver is chambered for the .32 H&R Mag. cartridge. It features a 3" or 4" heavy, solid rib barrel with fully adjustable rear sight. Swing-out cylinder holds 6 rounds. Available in either blued or stainless steel (stainless steel model introduced in 1993) with Brazilian hardwood grips. Pistol weighs 30 oz.

NIB	Exc.	V.G.	Good	Fair	Poor
200	175	150	125	100	75

NOTE: Add $40 for stainless steel.

Model 761

Similar to the Model 741 this version has a 6" barrel, target hammer, adjustable target trigger, and is available in blued only. Weighs 34 oz.

NIB	Exc.	V.G.	Good	Fair	Poor
250	225	175	150	125	100

Model 65

This double-action revolver is chambered for the .357 Magnum cartridge. It is offered with 2.5" or 4" heavy, solid rib barrel with ejector shroud. Fitted with fixed sights and Brazilian hardwood grips it is available in blued or stainless steel. The 2.5" barrel is a new addition to the Model 65 for 1993. Pistol weighs 34 oz. with 4" barrel.

NIB	Exc.	V.G.	Good	Fair	Poor
300	250	200	150	125	100

NOTE: Add $40 for stainless steel.

Model 605

Introduced in 1995 this revolver is chambered for the .357 Magnum cartridge. It is fitted with a 2-1/4" or 3" heavy barrel and is offered in blue or stainless steel. Weighs 25 oz.

Blue

NIB	Exc.	V.G.	Good	Fair	Poor
300	250	200	150	125	100

Stainless Steel

NIB	Exc.	V.G.	Good	Fair	Poor
340	275	225	175	125	100

Model 605 Custom (B2C)

Same as above but offered with a 2-1/4" compensated barrel.

Blue

NIB	Exc.	V.G.	Good	Fair	Poor
300	250	200	150	125	100

Stainless Steel

NIB	Exc.	V.G.	Good	Fair	Poor
340	275	225	175	125	100

Model 605CHB2/SS2

Chambered for the .357 Magnum cartridge and fitted with a 2.25" solid rib barrel and 5-shot cylinder. This model is also offered with a concealed hammer. Weight is about 24 oz.

Blue

NIB	Exc.	V.G.	Good	Fair	Poor
300	250	200	150	125	100

Stainless Steel

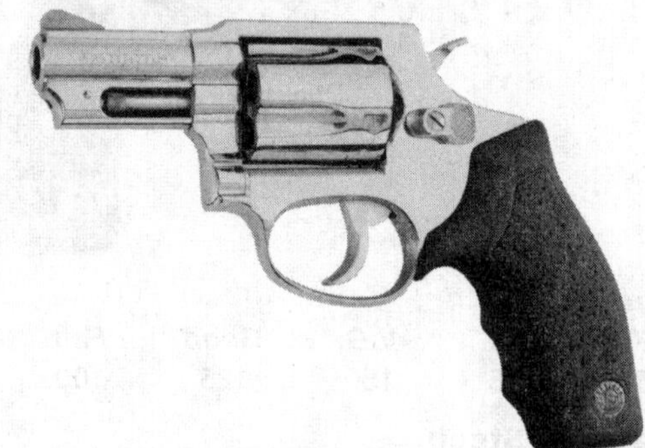

NIB	Exc.	V.G.	Good	Fair	Poor
340	275	225	175	125	100

Model 605CHB2C/SS2C

Same as above but with concealed hammer and ported barrels.

Blue

NIB	Exc.	V.G.	Good	Fair	Poor
320	250	200	150	125	100

Stainless Steel

NIB	Exc.	V.G.	Good	Fair	Poor
360	275	225	175	125	100

Model 66

Similar to the Model 65 but offered with a choice of 2.5", 4", or 6" barrel with fully adjustable rear sight. Offered with either blued or stainless steel. Weighs 35 oz. with 4" barrel. The 2.5" barrel was introduced in 1993.

NIB	Exc.	V.G.	Good	Fair	Poor
225	200	175	150	125	100

Model 66CP

This model is similar to the Model 66 but features a compensated heavy, solid rib 4" or 6" ejector shroud barrel. Introduced in 1993. Pistol weighs 35 oz.

NIB	Exc.	V.G.	Good	Fair	Poor
250	225	200	150	125	100

Model 66B4/SS4

Chambered for the .357 Magnum cartridge with 4" solid rib barrel and 7-shot cylinder. Adjustable sights. Rubber grips. Weight is about 38 oz.

Blue

NIB	Exc.	V.G.	Good	Fair	Poor
350	275	225	150	125	100

Stainless Steel

NIB	Exc.	V.G.	Good	Fair	Poor
400	325	275	225	150	100

Model 607

Introduced in 1995 this .357 Magnum model features a choice of 4" or 6-1/2" integral compensated barrel in either blue or stainless steel. The 6-1/2" barrel is fitted with a vent rib.

Blue

NIB	Exc.	V.G.	Good	Fair	Poor
325	275	225	200	150	100

Stainless Steel

NIB	Exc.	V.G.	Good	Fair	Poor
400	350	300	200	150	100

Model 606

Introduced in 1997 this 6-round model is chambered for the .357 Magnum cartridge. Fitted with a 2" solid rib barrel with ramp front sight and notched rear sight. Available in double-action, single or double-action-only. Offered in blue or stainless steel. Rubber grips are standard. Weight is approximately 29 oz. A number of variations are offered on this model.

NIB	Exc.	V.G.	Good	Fair	Poor
350	300	225	165	—	—

NOTE: For stainless steel models add $50.

Model 608

Introduced in 1996 this revolver is chambered for the .357 Magnum cartridge. The cylinder is bored for 8 rounds. Offered in 4" and 6.5" barrel lengths with integral compensator. The front sight is serrated ramp with red insert and the rear is adjustable. Offered in both blued and stainless steel versions. Weight is approximately 51.5 oz. with 6.5" barrel.

Blue

NIB	Exc.	V.G.	Good	Fair	Poor
425	325	250	200	150	100

Stainless Steel

NIB	Exc.	V.G.	Good	Fair	Poor
450	350	300	200	150	100

Model 689

This model is chambered for the .357 Magnum cartridge and features a heavy, vent rib barrel in either 4" or 6" lengths. Fully adjustable rear sight is standard. Offered in blued or stainless steel. Pistol weighs 37 oz. In 1998 this model was fitted with a 7-round cylinder.

NIB	Exc.	V.G.	Good	Fair	Poor
250	225	200	150	125	100

Model 617

Chambered for the .357 Magnum cartridge with 7-round cylinder. It is fitted with a 2" barrel. Choice of blue or stainless steel finish. Some variations offered a ported barrel. Introduced in 1998.

Blue

Stainless Steel

NIB	Exc.	V.G.	Good	Fair	Poor
400	325	275	225	—	—

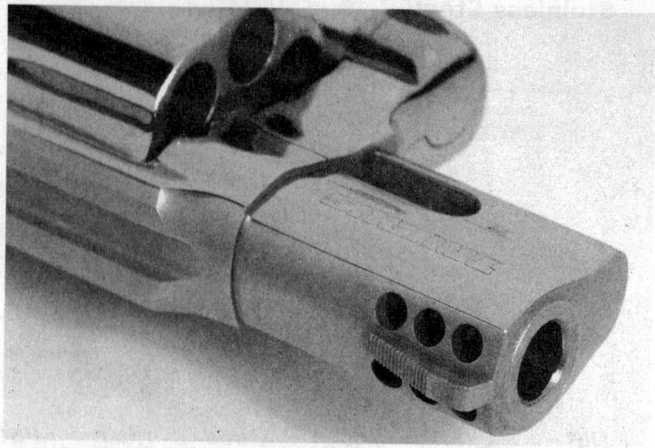

Model 617 with ported barrel

NIB	Exc.	V.G.	Good	Fair	Poor
350	275	225	175	—	—

NOTE: Add $20 for ported barrels.

Model 617 CHB2/SS2

Chambered for the .357 Magnum cartridge this model features a concealed hammer, 2" solid rib barrel, and fixed sights.

Blue

NIB	Exc.	V.G.	Good	Fair	Poor
350	275	225	175	—	—

Stainless Steel

NIB	Exc.	V.G.	Good	Fair	Poor
400	325	275	225	—	—

Model 627

This model is chambered for the .357 Magnum cartridge and has a 7-round cylinder. The 4" barrel is ported with a heavy underlug. Adjustable rear sight. Matte stainless steel finish. Introduced in 2000.

NIB	Exc.	V.G.	Good	Fair	Poor
425	325	275	225	—	—

Model 669

This model is chambered for the .357 Magnum cartridge and features a 4" or 6" heavy, solid rib barrel with full shroud. It has fully adjustable rear sight and is available with blued or stainless steel finish. Brazilian hardwood grips are standard. Pistol weighs 37 oz. with 4" barrel.

NIB	Exc.	V.G.	Good	Fair	Poor
275	225	200	150	125	100

NOTE: Add $60 for stainless steel.

Model 669CP

This variation of the Model 699 was introduced in 1993 and features a 4" or 6" compensated barrel. Fully adjustable rear sights are standard and it is offered with either blue or stainless steel finish. Weighs 37 oz. In 1998 this model was fitted with a 7-round cylinder.

NIB	Exc.	V.G.	Good	Fair	Poor
285	225	200	150	125	100

NOTE: Add $60 for stainless steel.

Model 415

Chambered for .41 Magnum cartridge and fitted with a 2.5" ported barrel. Fixed sights. Rubber grips. Matte stainless steel finish. Weight is about 30 oz.

NIB	Exc.	V.G.	Good	Fair	Poor
450	350	275	—	—	—

Model 431

Chambered for the .44 Special cartridge this double-action revolver is furnished with a 3" or 4" heavy, solid rib barrel with ejector shroud. Cylinder capacity is 5 rounds. Fixed sights are standard. Choice of blued or stainless steel finish. Pistol weighs 35 oz.

NIB	Exc.	V.G.	Good	Fair	Poor
395	300	240	150	125	100

NOTE: Add $60 for stainless steel.

Model 817 (Ultra-Lite)

Chambered for the .357 Magnum cartridge and fitted with a 7-shot cylinder and 2" solid rib barrel, this model features an alloy frame. Stainless steel or blued finish. Some models are ported. Weight is about 21 oz.

Blue

NIB	Exc.	V.G.	Good	Fair	Poor
350	275	225	175	125	100

Stainless Steel

NIB	Exc.	V.G.	Good	Fair	Poor
390	325	275	225	175	100

NOTE: Add $20 for ported barrels.

Model 441

Similar to the Model 431 but furnished with an additional choice of a 6" barrel as well as a 3" or 4". Comes standard with fully adjustable rear sight. Cylinder capacity is 5 rounds. Blued or stainless steel finish. Pistol weighs 40.25 oz. with 6" barrel.

NIB	Exc.	V.G.	Good	Fair	Poor
395	300	240	150	125	100

NOTE: Add $60 for stainless steel.

Model 444 Multi

This model features a 4" barrel with adjustable sights chambered for the .44 Magnum cartridge. Cylinder holds 6 rounds. Frame is alloy with titanium cylinder. Grips have cushion inset. Weight is about 28 oz. Introduced in 2004.

NIB	Exc.	V.G.	Good	Fair	Poor
575	475	—	—	—	—

Model 905I-B1/SS1

Introduced in 2003 this revolver is chambered for the 9mm pistol cartridge. Barrel length is 2". Cylinder capacity is 5 rounds. Weight is about 21 oz. Blue or stainless steel finish.

NIB	Exc.	V.G.	Good	Fair	Poor
385	300	—	—	—	—

NOTE: For matte stainless steel finish add $45.

Model 951SH2

Chambered for the 9mm cartridge and fitted with a 2" barrel with adjustable sights. Cylinder holds 5 rounds. Titanium frame and finish. Rubber grips. Weight is about 16 oz.

NIB	Exc.	V.G.	Good	Fair	Poor
475	350	265	—	—	—

Model 907SH2

This 9mm revolver has a 7-shot cylinder, 2" barrel with fixed sights and rubber grips. Titanium frame and finish. Weight is about 17 oz. Introduced in 2004.

NIB	Exc.	V.G.	Good	Fair	Poor
475	350	265	—	—	—

Model 907B2/SS2

Chambered for the 9mm cartridge and fitted with a 2" barrel with fixed sights. Rubber grips. Ultra light alloy frame in blue or stainless steel. Weight is about 18.5 oz. Introduced in 2004.

NIB	Exc.	V.G.	Good	Fair	Poor
390	300	—	—	—	—

NOTE: Add $45 for stainless steel.

800 Series

Double-action semi-auto chambered in 9mm Parabellum (17+1), .40 S&W (15+1) and .45 ACP (12+1). Four-inch barrel; blued or stainless frame slide on polymer frame with integral grips. External hammer with "Strike Two" (trigger reset) feature. Introduced 2007.

NIB	Exc.	V.G.	Good	Fair	Poor
TBA	—	—	—	—	—

RAGING BULL SERIES

Model 218 (Raging Bee)

Introduced in 2002 this model is chambered for the .218 Bee cartridge and fitted with a 10" vent rib barrel with adjustable sights. Cylinder holds 8 rounds. Matte stainless steel finish.

NIB	Exc.	V.G.	Good	Fair	Poor
580	485	395	—	—	—

Model 22H (Raging Hornet)

This model is chambered for the .22 Hornet cartridge and has a 10" barrel with base mount and adjustable sights. Matte stainless steel finish. Cylinder holds 8 rounds. Rubber grips.

NIB	Exc.	V.G.	Good	Fair	Poor
580	485	395	—	—	—

Model 30C (Raging Thirty)

Chambered for the .30 Carbine cartridge and fitted with a 10" vent rib barrel with adjustable sights. Cylinder holds 8 rounds. Supplied with full moon clips. Matte stainless steel finish. Introduced in 2002.

NIB	Exc.	V.G.	Good	Fair	Poor
580	485	395	—	—	—

Model 416 (Raging Bull)

This model has a 6.5" vent rib ported barrel with adjustable sights. Chambered for the .41 Magnum cartridge. Matte stainless steel finish. Introduced in 2002. Cylinder holds 6 rounds.

NIB	Exc.	V.G.	Good	Fair	Poor
625	500	—	—	—	—

This symbol denotes "Sleepers" with rapidly-rising values and/or significant collector potential.

Model 454 (Raging Bull)

This model is chambered for the .454 Casull. It is built on a large frame with a 5-round capacity. Barrel lengths are 5", 6.5" or 8.375". Barrels are fitted with a ventilated rib and integral compensator. Sights are adjustable. Finish is blue or stainless steel. Black rubber or walnut grips. Weight is 53 oz. with 6.5" barrel. Add $60 for stainless steel model. Introduced in 1997.

Blue

NIB	Exc.	V.G.	Good	Fair	Poor
625	550	475	375	—	—

Stainless Steel

NIB	Exc.	V.G.	Good	Fair	Poor
675	600	525	400	—	—

Black Stainless Steel

NIB	Exc.	V.G.	Good	Fair	Poor
700	650	525	425	—	—

Model 500 Magnum Raging Bull

Introduced in 2004 this revolver is chambered for the .500 Magnum cartridge. Ventilated barrel length is 10" with adjustable sights. Cushion inset grips. Stainless steel finish. Weight is about 72 oz.

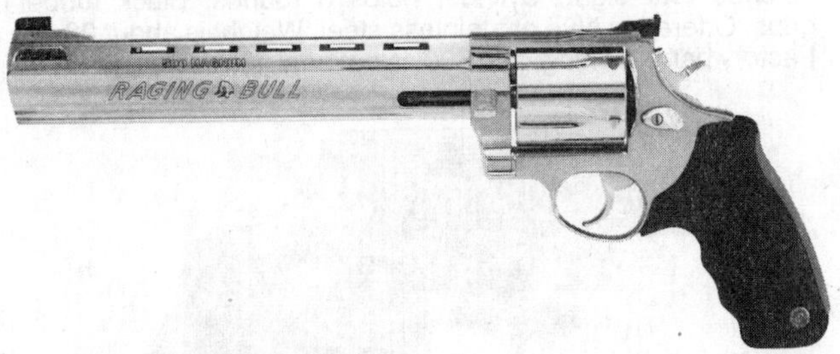

NIB	Exc.	V.G.	Good	Fair	Poor
775	650	375	—	—	—

Raging Bull Model 500, 500MSS2

Stainless .500 S&W Magnum with 5-shot capacity, 2.25" or 10" barrel, soft rubber grips. 68 oz. Adjustable rear sight, single/double action. Introduced 2006.

NIB	Exc.	V.G.	Good	Fair	Poor
775	650	375	—	—	—

Raging Bull .223

Similar to other Raging Bull models but chambered in .223 Remington with 7-shot cylinder. Ten-inch ventilated rib barrel. Introduced 2007.

NIB	Exc.	V.G.	Good	Fair	Poor
TBA	—	—	—	—	—

Model 44/444

Introduced in 1994 this heavy frame revolver is chambered for the .44 Magnum cartridge. Offered with choice of three barrel lengths: 4" with solid rib, 6-1/2" with vent rib, and 8-3/8" with vent rib. All Model 44s have a built in compensator. The front sight is a serrated ramp with adjustable rear sight. Offered in either blued or stainless finish. Weight of 6-1/2" barrel gun is 53 oz.

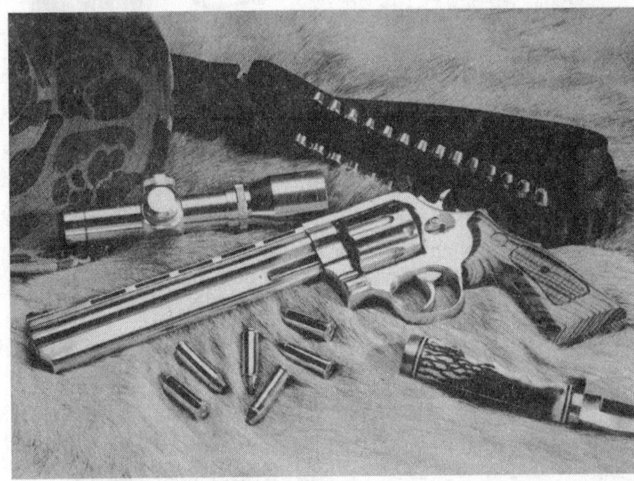

Blue

NIB	Exc.	V.G.	Good	Fair	Poor
545	425	300	200	150	100

Stainless Steel

NIB	Exc.	V.G.	Good	Fair	Poor
600	475	375	250	200	125

IMPORTANT PRICING INFORMATION

A collectible pistol MUST have ALL original parts and original finish to be considered NIB.

TRACKER SERIES

Model 17

Introduced in 2002 this model features a 6.5" or 12" vent rib barrel chambered for the .17 HMR cartridge. Adjustable sights. Matte stainless steel finish. Cylinder holds 7 rounds. Weight is about 41 oz. for 6.5" model and 50 oz. for the 12" model.

NIB	*Exc.*	*V.G.*	*Good*	*Fair*	*Poor*
300	200	165	110	—	—

Model 970

This model is chambered for the .22 LR cartridge and fitted with a 6.5" vent rib heavy barrel with adjustable sights. Matte stainless steel finish. Rubber grips. Cylinder holds 7 rounds. Introduced in 2002.

NIB	*Exc.*	*V.G.*	*Good*	*Fair*	*Poor*
300	200	165	110	—	—

Model 971

Same as the Model 970 but chambered for the .22 Magnum cartridge. Introduced in 2002.

NIB	*Exc.*	*V.G.*	*Good*	*Fair*	*Poor*
300	200	165	110	—	—

Model 425 Tracker

Chambered for the .41 Magnum cartridge this model features a 4" heavy underlug ported barrel. Adjustable rear sight. Cylinder is chambered for 5 rounds. Matte stainless steel finish. Introduced in 2000.

NIB	*Exc.*	*V.G.*	*Good*	*Fair*	*Poor*
395	325	265	—	—	—

Model 44 Tracker

This .44 Magnum revolver has a 4" barrel with adjustable sights and Ribber (ribbed) grips. Five-shot cylinder. Stainless steel finish. Weight is about 34 oz. Introduced in 2004.

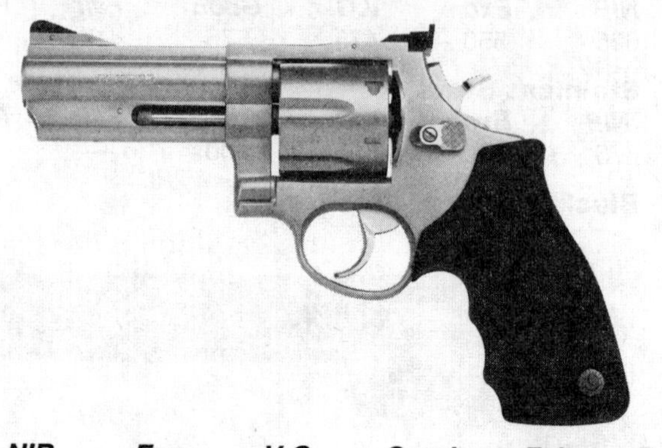

NIB	*Exc.*	*V.G.*	*Good*	*Fair*	*Poor*
395	325	265	—	—	—

Tracker .45

Similar to other Tracker models but chambered in .45 ACP (via full-moon clips) with 5-shot cylinder. Four-inch barrel with Picatinny rail. Stainless steel frame and cylinder. Introduced 2007.

NIB	*Exc.*	*V.G.*	*Good*	*Fair*	*Poor*
450	—	—	—	—	—

Model 445

This small frame revolver is chambered for the .44 Special cartridge. It is fitted with a 2" barrel with ramp front sight and notched rear sight. Cylinder holds 5 rounds. Black rubber grips. Offered in blue or stainless steel. Weight is about 28 oz. Factory barrel porting, add $20, is optional. Introduced in 1997.

NIB	*Exc.*	*V.G.*	*Good*	*Fair*	*Poor*
395	295	200	175	—	—

NOTE: Add $50 for stainless steel.

Model 450

Chambered for the .45 Long Colt cartridge this model features a 2" heavy solid rib barrel with 5-shot cylinder and fixed sights. Ported barrel. Rubber grips. Stainless steel finish. Weight is about 28 oz.

NIB	Exc.	V.G.	Good	Fair	Poor
425	350	275	225	175	125

NOTE: Add $30 for Ultra Lite model.

Model 455

This model, introduced in 2002, is chambered for the .45 ACP cartridge. Offered with a choice of 2", 4", or 6.5" barrel. Barrels of 4" and 6.5" have adjustable sights. Matte stainless steel finish. Rubber grips. Supplied with full moon clips.

NIB	Exc.	V.G.	Good	Fair	Poor
425	350	275	225	—	—

Model 460

Chambered for the .45 Long Colt cartridge and fitted with either a 4" or 6.5" vent rib barrel with adjustable sights. Matte stainless steel finish. Introduced in 2002.

NIB	Exc.	V.G.	Good	Fair	Poor
425	350	275	225	—	—

Model 45

Chambered for the .45 Long Colt and fitted with a choice of 6.5" or 8-3/8" heavy vent rib barrels. Cylinder holds 6 rounds. Rubber grips, ported barrels, and adjustable sights are standard. Weight with 6.5" barrel is about 53 oz.

Blue

NIB	Exc.	V.G.	Good	Fair	Poor
425	350	275	225	150	100

Stainless Steel

NIB	Exc.	V.G.	Good	Fair	Poor
425	350	275	225	200	125

Model 627

This model is chambered for the .357 magnum cartridge and fitted with a 4" ported or 6.5" vent rib ported barrel with adjustable sights. Rubber grips. Matte stainless steel finish. Introduced in 2002.

NIB	Exc.	V.G.	Good	Fair	Poor
425	350	275	225	—	—

NOTE: Add $200 for titanium model.

Tracker 10mm 10TSS4

Matte stainless 10mm with 4" barrel and fixed sights. 5-shot, 34.8 oz, rubber grip. Introduced 2006.

NIB	Exc.	V.G.	Good	Fair	Poor
465	—	—	—	—	—

Tracker 10SS8

10mm 6-shot matte stainless with either 6.5" (54.5 oz.) or 8.375" (59.5 oz.) barrel. Fixed sights and rubber grips. Introduced 2006.

NIB	Exc.	V.G.	Good	Fair	Poor
485	—	—	—	—	—

Tracker 4410 10TKR2SS

Shoots 2.5" .410 bore shells or .45 Colt. Holds 5 shots. Stainless or blued, 2.25" or 6.5" barrel, rubber grip. Single/double action, 32 oz., 9.1" LOA. Introduced 2006.

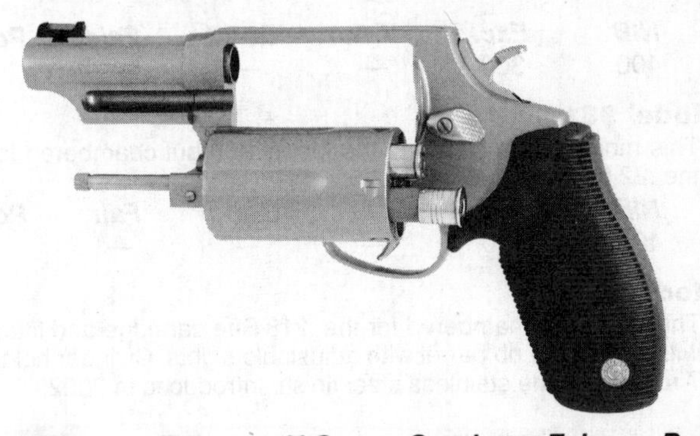

NIB	Exc.	V.G.	Good	Fair	Poor
469	365	—	—	—	—

Judge

Stainless steel- or lightweight alloy-frame version of Tracker Model 4410. Chambered in 3" .410/.45 Colt (4510TKR-3MAG) or 2.5" .410/.45 Colt (4510TKR-3UL) with 3" (3" Magnum) or 2.5" barrel (2.5"). Introduced 2007.

NIB	Exc.	V.G.	Good	Fair	Poor
480	—	—	—	—	—

SILHOUETTE SERIES

Model 17-12

Chambered for the .17 HMR cartridge and fitted with a 12" vent rib silhouette barrel. Adjustable sights. Cylinder holds 7 rounds. Matte stainless steel finish. Introduced in 2002.

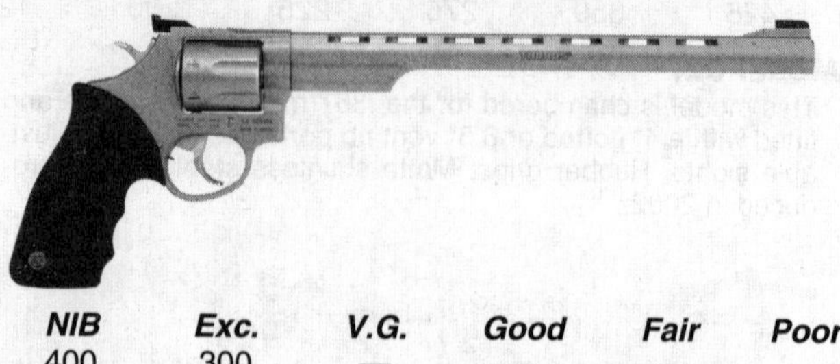

NIB	Exc.	V.G.	Good	Fair	Poor
400	300	—	—	—	—

Model 66

Chambered for the .357 Magnum cartridge and fitted with a 12" barrel with adjustable sights. Choice of blue or stainless steel finish. Rubber grips. Introduced in 2002.

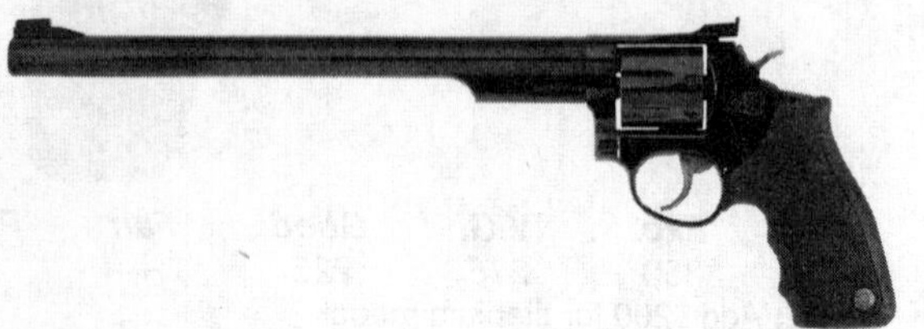

NIB	Exc.	V.G.	Good	Fair	Poor
400	300	—	—	—	—

NOTE: Add $60 for stainless steel.

Model 980

This model is chambered for the .22 LR cartridge. Fitted with a 12" target barrel with adjustable sights. Cylinder holds 7 rounds. Matted stainless steel finish. Rubber grips. Introduced in 2002.

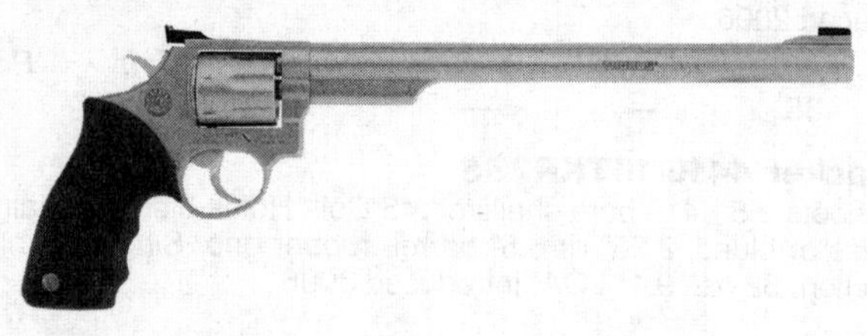

NIB	Exc.	V.G.	Good	Fair	Poor
400	300	—	—	—	—

Model 981

This model is the same as the Model 980 but chambered for the .22 Magnum cartridge.

NIB	Exc.	V.G.	Good	Fair	Poor
400	300	—	—	—	—

Model 217

This model is chambered for the .218 Bee cartridge and fitted with a 12" vent rib barrel with adjustable sights. Cylinder holds 7 rounds. Matte stainless steel finish. Introduced in 2002.

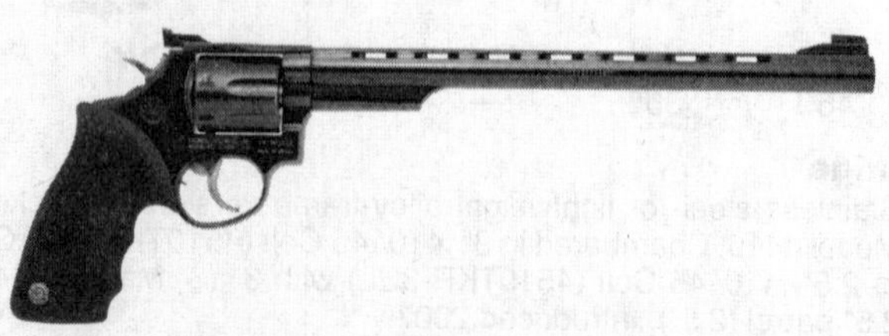

NIB	Exc.	V.G.	Good	Fair	Poor
460	350	—	—	—	—

TITANIUM SERIES REVOLVERS

Introduced in 1999 this series of revolvers feature titanium barrels with stainless steel bore liners, titanium frames and cylinders. Hammers, triggers, latches, ejector rod and other small parts are made from case hardened chrome moly steel. All Taurus Titanium revolvers have factory porting and are rated for +P ammunition. Rubber grips are standard. Three different finishes are offered: Bright Spectrum blue, Matte Spectrum blue, and Matte Spectrum gold.

Model 85Ti

Chambered for .38 Special and fitted with a 2" barrel with 5-shot cylinder. Fixed sights.

NIB	Exc.	V.G.	Good	Fair	Poor
525	425	—	—	—	—

Model 731Ti

Chambered for the .32 H&R Magnum and fitted with a 2" barrel with 6-shot cylinder. Fixed sights.

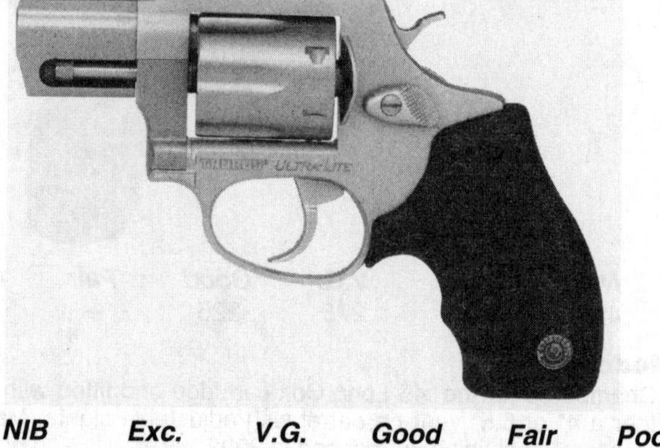

NIB	Exc.	V.G.	Good	Fair	Poor
525	425	—	—	—	—

Model 617Ti

Chambered for .357 Magnum and fitted with a 2" barrel and 7-shot cylinder. Fixed sights. Weight is about 20 oz.

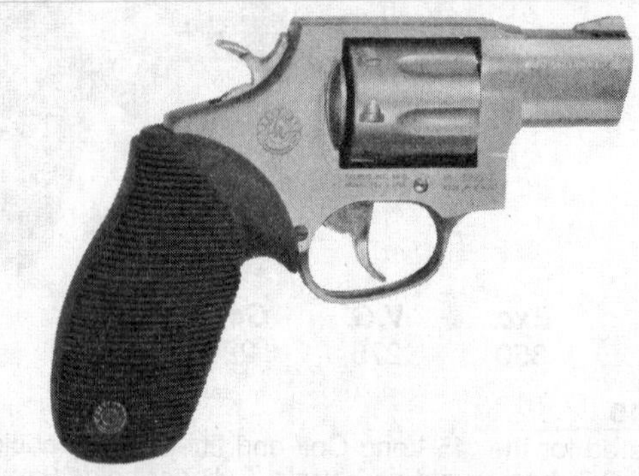

NIB	Exc.	V.G.	Good	Fair	Poor
600	475	—	—	—	—

Model 627Ti

This model features a 7-round cylinder chambered for the .357 Magnum cartridge. Fitted with a ported 4" barrel with adjustable sights. Gray finish. Weight is about 28 oz. depending on barrel length.

NIB	Exc.	V.G.	Good	Fair	Poor
675	500	—	—	—	—

Model 415Ti

Chambered for the .41 Magnum and fitted with a 2.5" barrel with 5-shot cylinder. Fixed sights. Weight is about 21 oz.

NIB	Exc.	V.G.	Good	Fair	Poor
600	475	—	—	—	—

Model 425Ti

This model is chambered for the .41 Magnum cartridge and has a 5-round cylinder. The barrel is ported and 4" with adjustable rear sight. Gray finish. Introduced in 2000.

NIB	Exc.	V.G.	Good	Fair	Poor
675	500	—	—	—	—

Model 450Ti

Chambered for the .45 Long Colt and fitted with a 2" barrel with 5-shot cylinder. Fixed sights. Weight is about 19 oz.

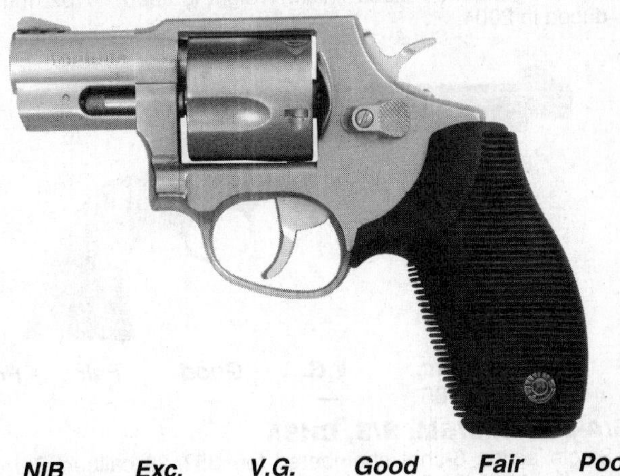

NIB	Exc.	V.G.	Good	Fair	Poor
600	475	—	—	—	—

Model 445Ti

Chambered for the .44 Special and fitted with a 2" barrel with 5-shot cylinder. Fixed sights. Weight is about 20 oz.

NIB	Exc.	V.G.	Good	Fair	Poor
600	475	—	—	—	—

Model UL/Ti

Chambered for the .38 Special this model has a Titanium cylinder and alloy frame. Fitted with a 2" unported barrel. Cylinder is 5 shot. Fixed sights.

NIB	Exc.	V.G.	Good	Fair	Poor
500	400	—	—	—	—

GAUCHO SERIES

S/A-45, B/S/SM

Chambered for the .45 Colt cartridge and fitted with a 5.5" barrel with fixed sights. Checkered wood grips. Blued or stainless steel finish. Weight is about 37 oz. Introduced in 2004.

NIB	Exc.	V.G.	Good	Fair	Poor
375	285	—	—	—	—

NOTE: Add $15 for stainless steel.

S/A-45, S/S/CH

Chambered for the .45 Colt cartridge and fitted with a 5.5" barrel with fixed sights. Choice of Sundance stainless steel finish or case hardened blued finish. Weight is about 37 oz. Introduced in 2004.

NIB	Exc.	V.G.	Good	Fair	Poor
375	285	—	—	—	—

S/A-357-B, S/SM, S/S, CHSA

Single action 6-shot chambered for .357/.38 caliber. Barrel lengths 4.75" (36.2 oz.), 5.5" (36.7 oz.), 7.5" (37.7 oz.). Fixed sights. Blued, matte stainless, polished stainless or blued/case hardened receiver. Introduced 2006. Pricing is for blued.

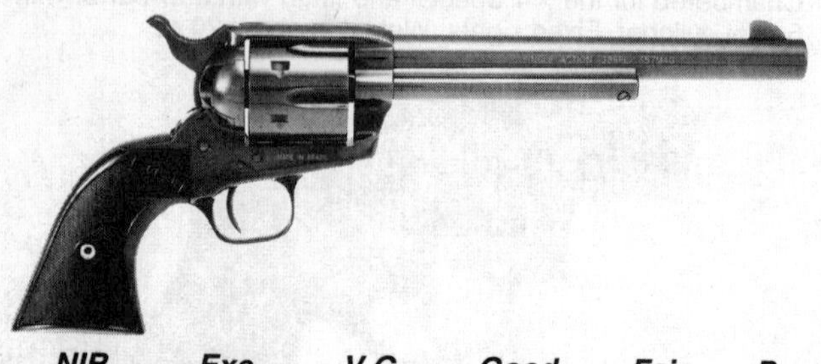

NIB	Exc.	V.G.	Good	Fair	Poor
375	285	—	—	—	—

S/A-44-40-B, S/SM, S/S, CHSA

Single action 6-shot chambered for .44-40 caliber. Barrel lengths 4.75" (36.2 oz.), 5.5" (36.7 oz.), 7.5" (37.7 oz.). Fixed sights. Blued, matte stainless, polished stainless or blued/case hardened receiver. Introduced 2006.

NIB	Exc.	V.G.	Good	Fair	Poor
375	285	—	—	—	—

S/A-45-B12, S/SM12, S/S12, CHSA12

Single action Buntline-style 6-shot revolver chambered for .45 Colt. Barrel length 12" (41.5 oz.). Fixed sights. Blued, matte stainless, polished stainless or blued/case hardened receiver. Introduced 2006. Pricing is for blued.

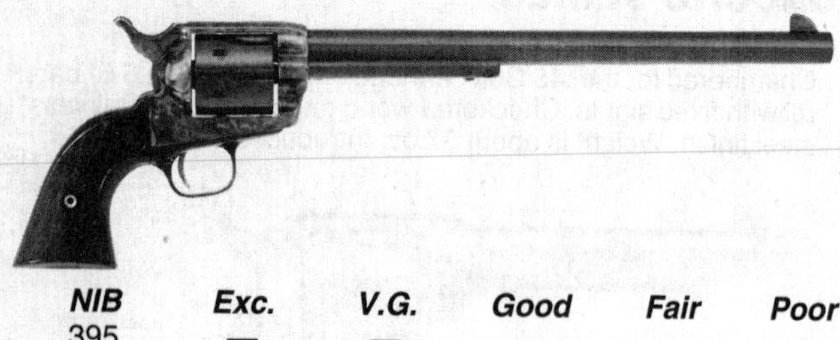

NIB	Exc.	V.G.	Good	Fair	Poor
395	—	—	—	—	—

RIFLES

Model 62

Introduced in 2000 this is a replica of the Winchester Model 62 .22 caliber rifle. Fitted with a 23" barrel and adjustable rear sight. Magazine capacity is 13 rounds. Weight is about 5 lbs. Hardwood stock.

NOTE: In 2003 this model was offered in both .22 WMR and .17 HMR calibers.

NIB	Exc.	V.G.	Good	Fair	Poor
285	200	150	—	—	—

NOTE: Add $15 for stainless steel.

Model 62 Carbine

Same as above but with a 16.5" barrel. Magazine capacity is 12 rounds. Weight is about 4.5 lbs. Introduced in 2000.

NIB	Exc.	V.G.	Good	Fair	Poor
285	200	150	—	—	—

NOTE: In 2003 this model was offered in .22 WMR and .17 HMR calibers. Add $15 for stainless steel.

Model 62 Upstart

This model is similar to the Model 62 above but with a shorter buttstock. Introduced in 2002.

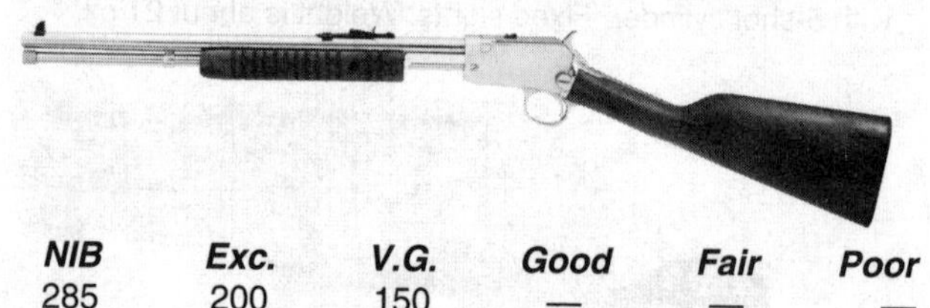

NIB	Exc.	V.G.	Good	Fair	Poor
285	200	150	—	—	—

Model 72

Same as the Model 62 but chambered for the .22 Magnum cartridge.

NIB	Exc.	V.G.	Good	Fair	Poor
295	225	—	—	—	—

NOTE: Add $15 for stainless steel.

Model 72 Carbine

Same as the Model 62 Carbine but chambered for the .22 Magnum cartridge.

NIB	Exc.	V.G.	Good	Fair	Poor
295	225	—	—	—	—

NOTE: Add $15 for stainless steel.

Model 174R-B

This lever action model resembles the Winchester Model 62 but without the slide action. Chambered for the .17 HMR and fitted with a 23" barrel. Checkered forearm but plain straight grip buttstock. Choice of blue of stainless steel finish. Weight is about 5 lbs. Introduced in 2005.

NIB	Exc.	V.G.	Good	Fair	Poor
325	250	—	—	—	—

NOTE: Add $15 for stainless steel.

Model 63

Copy of the Winchester Model 63 in takedown. Chambered for the .22 LR cartridge and fitted with a 23" round barrel with adjustable rear sight. Offered in blue or stainless steel. Introduced in 2002. In 2003 this model was also offered chambered for the .17 rimfire cartridge.

NIB	Exc.	V.G.	Good	Fair	Poor
275	200	—	—	—	—

NOTE: Add $50 for the .17 rimfire models.

Model 62LAR Lever Rifle

Lever-action rifle chambered in .22 LR. 23-inch blued barrel, walnut-finish hardwood stock. Introduced 2006.

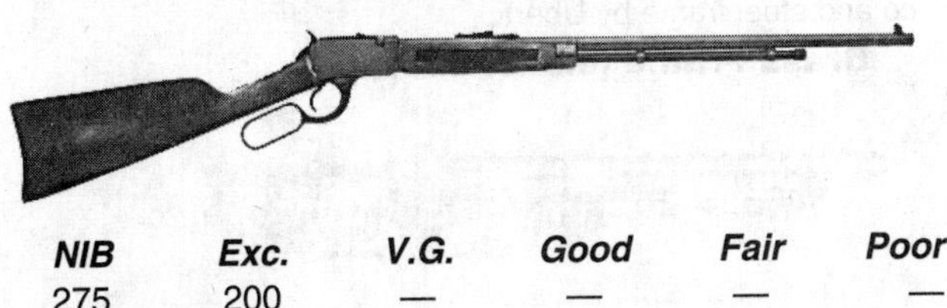

NIB	Exc.	V.G.	Good	Fair	Poor
275	200	—	—	—	—

Model 62LAR-SS

Similar to Model 62LAR but in stainless steel. Introduced 2006.

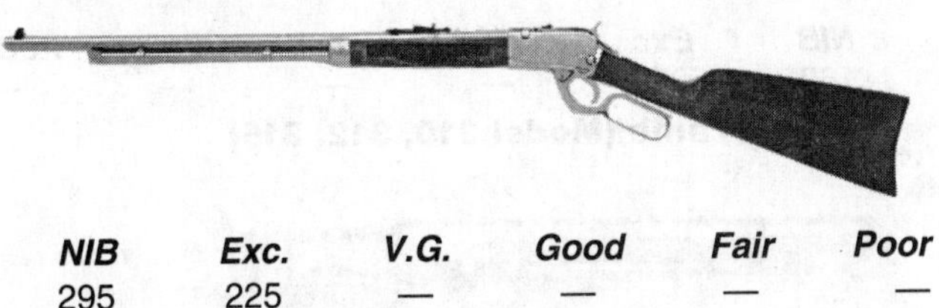

NIB	Exc.	V.G.	Good	Fair	Poor
295	225	—	—	—	—

Thunderbolt

This slide-action rifle is a copy of the Colt Lightning rifle and is chambered for the .45 Colt cartridge as well as the .38/.357 Magnum. Fitted with a 26" barrel with adjustable sights. Blued or stainless steel finish. Stocks are hardwood. Weight is about 8.125 lbs. Introduced in 2004.

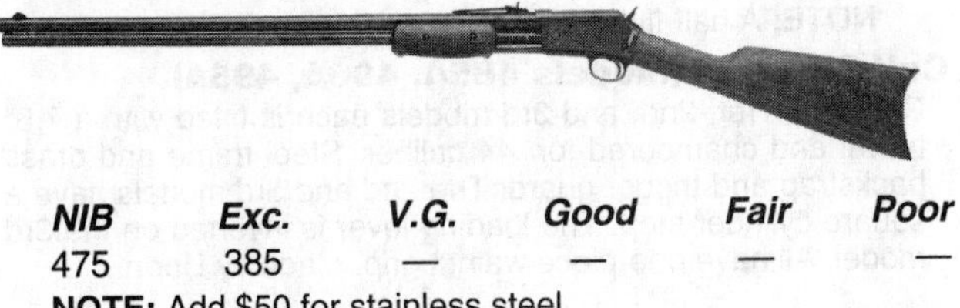

NIB	Exc.	V.G.	Good	Fair	Poor
475	385	—	—	—	—

NOTE: Add $50 for stainless steel.

TAYLOR'S & CO., INC.

Winchester, Virginia

PISTOLS

Napoleon Le Page Pistol (Model 551)

A percussion French-style duelling pistol. Chambered for .45 caliber and fitted with a 10" octagon barrel. Walnut stock silver plated buttcap and trigger guard. Double set triggers. Made by Uberti.

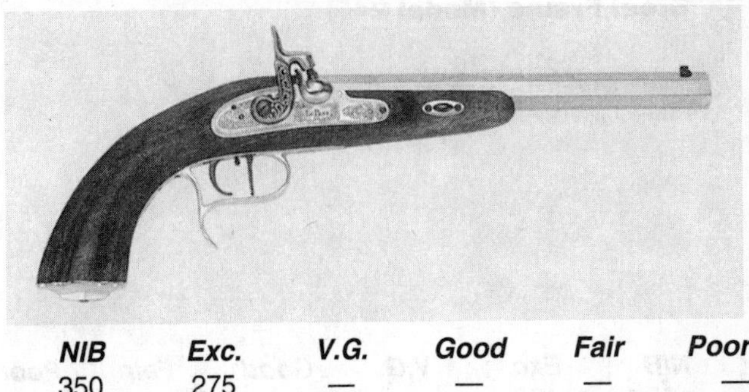

NIB	Exc.	V.G.	Good	Fair	Poor
350	275	—	—	—	—

Kentucky Pistol (Model 550)

Chambered for the .45 caliber ball and fitted with a 10" barrel. Bird's-head grip with brass ramrod thimbles and case hardened sidelock. Made by Uberti.

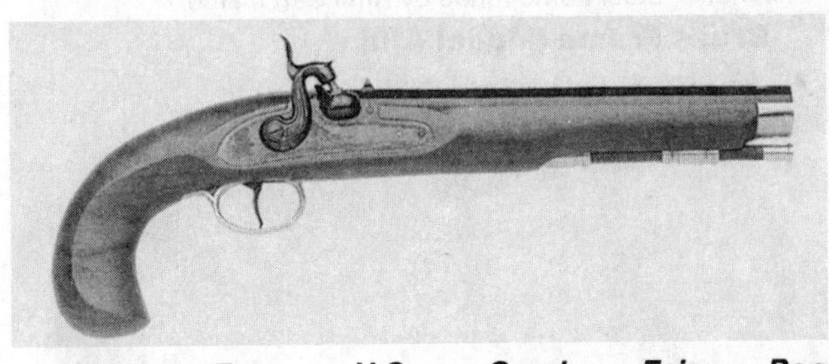

NIB	Exc.	V.G.	Good	Fair	Poor
185	150	—	—	—	—

Colt Model 1847 Walker (Model 500A)

Fitted with a 9" round barrel and chambered for .44 caliber. This model has a 6-round engraved cylinder. Steel frame and backstrap and brass trigger guard. One-piece walnut grips. Made by Uberti.

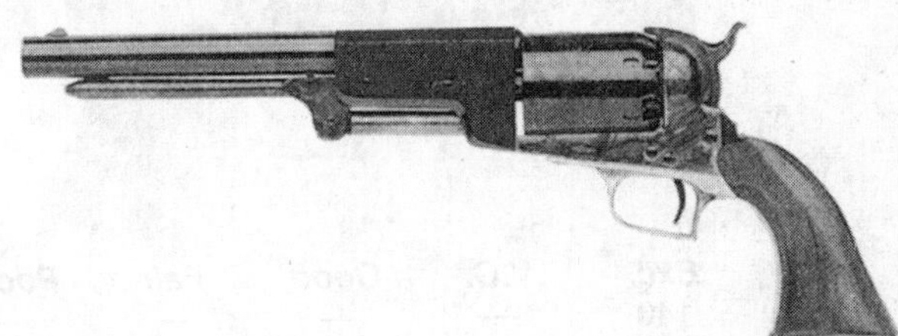

NIB	Exc.	V.G.	Good	Fair	Poor
370	300	—	—	—	—

Colt Model 1851 Navy

Offered with either brass or steel frame with brass backstrap and trigger guard. Chambered for .36 caliber and fitted with a 7.5" barrel. Cylinder holds 6 rounds. One-piece walnut grip. Brass frame model made by Armi San Marco. Steel frame model made by F.lli Pietta.

Brass Frame (Model 210)

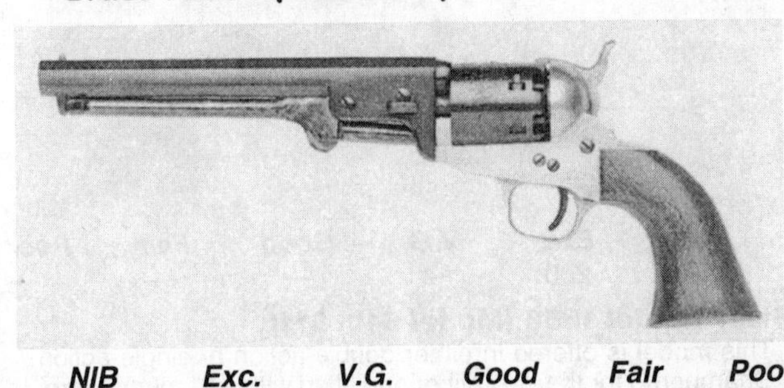

NIB	Exc.	V.G.	Good	Fair	Poor
135	100	—	—	—	—

Steel Frame (Model 245)

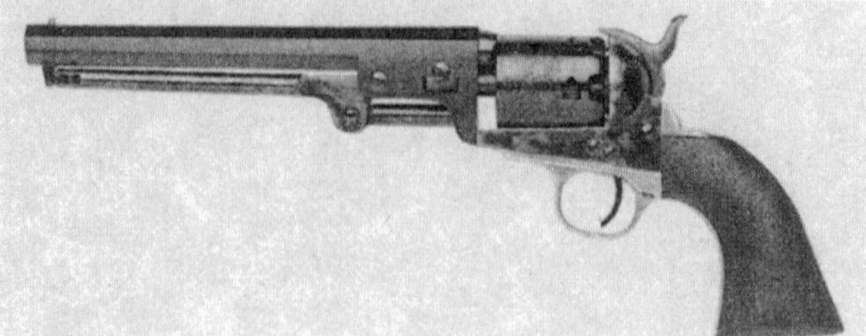

NIB	Exc.	V.G.	Good	Fair	Poor
165	125	—	—	—	—

Remington Model 1858

This is a .44 caliber either a brass frame or steel frame and brass trigger guard model with 8" octagon barrel. Cylinder holds 6 rounds. Two-piece walnut grips. Brass frame made by F.lli Pietta. Steel frame made by Armi San Marco.

Brass Frame (Model 410)

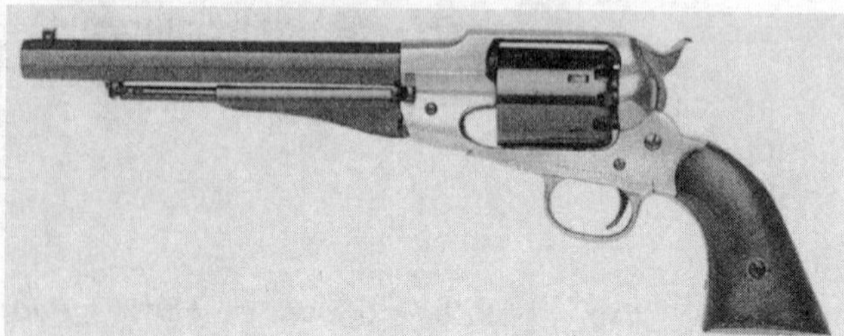

NIB	Exc.	V.G.	Good	Fair	Poor
150	120	—	—	—	—

Steel Frame (Model 430)

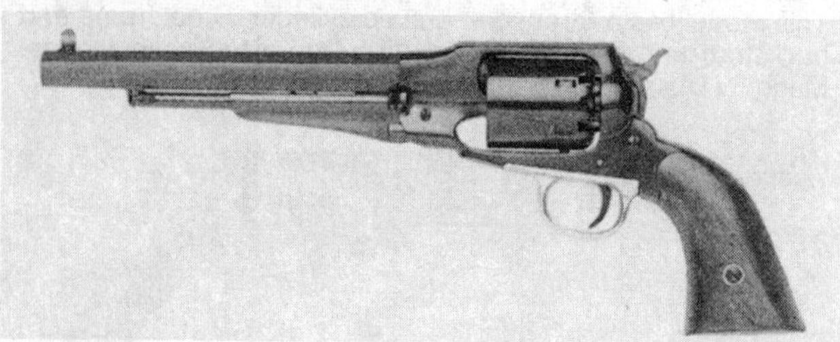

NIB	Exc.	V.G.	Good	Fair	Poor
185	140	—	—	—	—

Colt Model 1848 Baby Dragoon (Models 470, 471, 472)

Chambered for the .31 caliber and fitted with a 5-round cylinder. Barrel length is 4". Choice of blued or white steel frame. Brass backstrap and trigger guard. One-piece walnut grip. Made by Uberti.

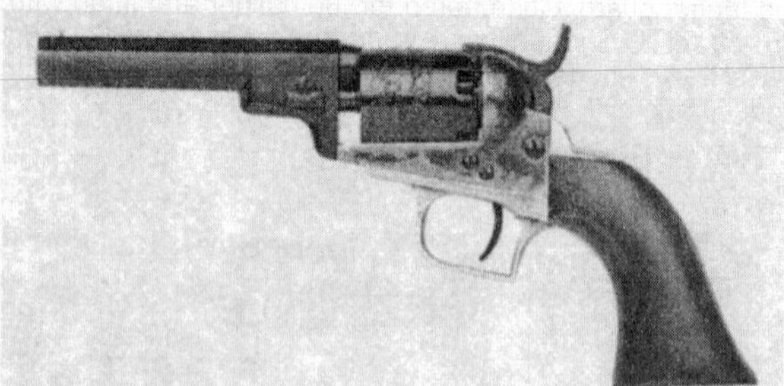

NIB	Exc.	V.G.	Good	Fair	Poor
250	200	—	—	—	—

Starr Model 1858 (Model 510, 511)

This model is offered in either double-action or single-action. Chambered for the .44 caliber and fitted with a 6" round barrel. Made by F.lli Pietta.

NIB	Exc.	V.G.	Good	Fair	Poor
370	300	—	—	—	—

Colt Model 1860 Army

This model features an 8" round barrel except for the Sheriff's model which is 5.5". Choice of brass or steel frame with brass backstrap and trigger guard. Chambered for .44 caliber. One-piece walnut grip. Brass frame model made by Armi San Marco and steel frame by Uberti.

Brass Frame (Model 300)

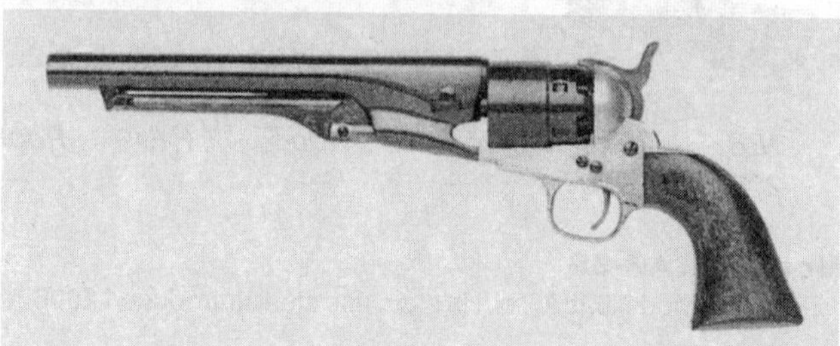

NIB	Exc.	V.G.	Good	Fair	Poor
160	250	—	—	—	—

Steel Frame (Model 310, 312, 315)

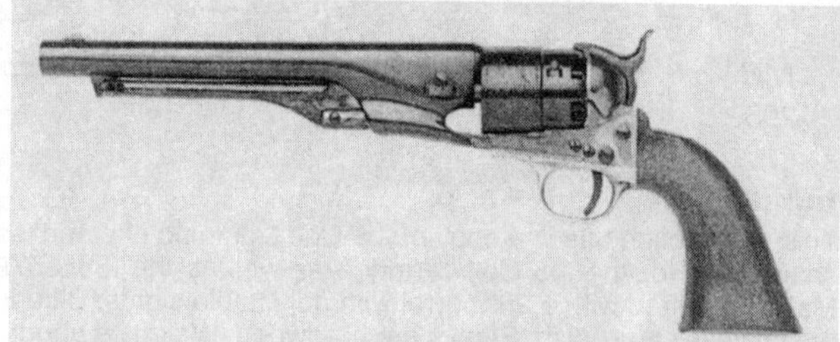

NIB	Exc.	V.G.	Good	Fair	Poor
250	200	—	—	—	—

NOTE: A half-fluted cylinder model is also offered.

Colt Dragoon (Models 485A, 490A, 495A)

Offered in 1st, 2nd, and 3rd models each is fitted with a 7.5" barrel and chambered for .44 caliber. Steel frame and brass backstrap and trigger guard. The 2nd and 3rd models have a square cylinder stop. The loading lever is inverted on the 3rd model. All have one-piece walnut grip. Made by Uberti.

NIB	Exc.	V.G.	Good	Fair	Poor
295	250	—	—	—	—

NOTE: Add $15 for 3rd model.

Colt Model 1861 Navy (Model 210)

This model is chambered for the .36 caliber and fitted with a 7.5" round barrel. Cylinder is 6 rounds. Brass frame and backstrap and trigger guard. One-piece walnut grip. Made by Uberti.

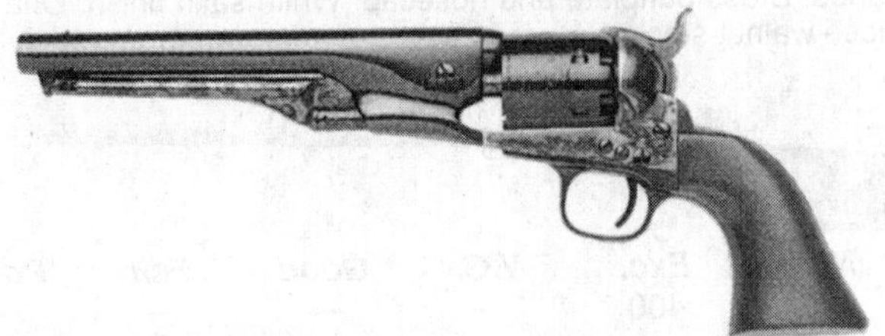

NIB	Exc.	V.G.	Good	Fair	Poor
250	200	—	—	—	—

Colt Model 1862 Police (Model 315B)

Fitted with a 6.5" round barrel and chambered for .36 caliber. Case hardened frame with brass backstrap and trigger guard. Made by Uberti.

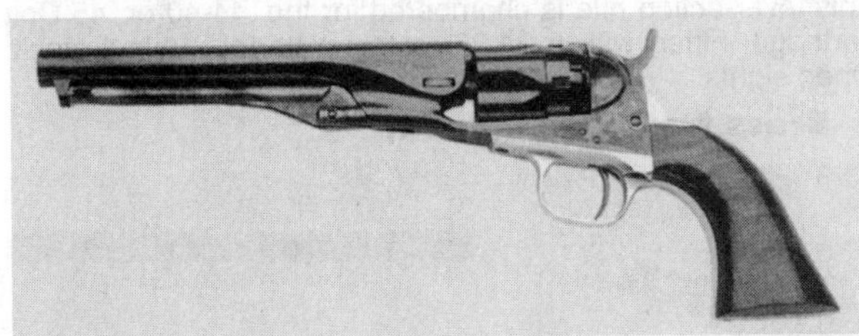

NIB	Exc.	V.G.	Good	Fair	Poor
265	200	—	—	—	—

Colt Model 1862 Pocket (Model 315C)

Similar to the above model but fitted with a 6.5" octagonal barrel. Made by Uberti.

NIB	Exc.	V.G.	Good	Fair	Poor
235	185	—	—	—	—

Remington Model 1863 Pocket (Model 435)

This revolver is chambered for the .31 caliber ball and fitted with a 3.5" barrel. Cylinder is 5 rounds. Frame, backstrap and trigger guard are brass. Walnut grip. Made by Armi San Marco.

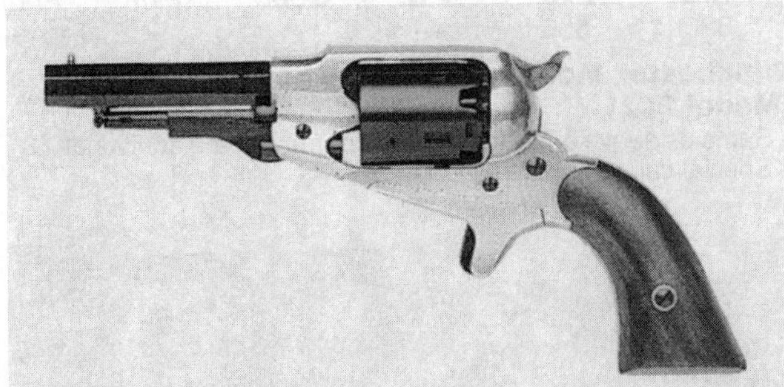

NIB	Exc.	V.G.	Good	Fair	Poor
150	100	—	—	—	—

Colt Model 1873 Cattleman (Models 700, 701, 702)

This famous replica is made in several different configurations. Offered in barrel lengths of 4.75", 5.5", and 7.5". Calibers are: .45 Colt, .44-40, .44 Special, .38-40, .357 Magnum, and .45 ACP. Frame is case hardened with steel backstrap. One-piece walnut grip. Made by Uberti.

NIB	Exc.	V.G.	Good	Fair	Poor
400	325	—	—	—	—

NOTE: Add $80 for dual cylinder and $80 for nickel finish.

Colt Model 1873 Bird's-head (Models 703A, 703B, 703C)

Same as above but offered with bird's-head grip.

NIB	Exc.	V.G.	Good	Fair	Poor
400	325	—	—	—	—

Colt Model 1873 "Outfitter"

Chambered for the .45 Colt or .357 Magnum cartridge and fitted with a 4.75", 5.5", or 7.5" barrel. Stainless steel finish and walnut grips.

NIB	Exc.	V.G.	Good	Fair	Poor
605	475	—	—	—	—

HARTFORD ARMORY MODELS

Introduced to the Taylor product line in 2004, this company produces revolvers made entirely in the U.S. Each gun comes with a lifetime warranty. All Hartford Armory revolvers come in a numbered wooden case with brass snap caps and brass plaque.

Remington Model 1875

This model is offered in these calibers: .38/.357, .44-40, .44 Special/Magnum, or .45 Colt. Barrel lengths are 5.75" or 7.5". Walnut grips. Armory dark blue finish.

NIB	Exc.	V.G.	Good	Fair	Poor
1495	1100	—	—	—	—

Remington Model 1890

This model is offered in .38/.357, .44-40, .44 Special/Magnum, or .45 Colt. Choice of 5.5" or 7.5" barrel. Armory dark blue finish. Walnut grips.

NIB	Exc.	V.G.	Good	Fair	Poor
1495	1100	—	—	—	—

RIFLES

Kentucky Rifle

Offered in either flintlock or percussion this rifle is .40 caliber and fitted with a 3.5" barrel. One-piece stock with brass fixtures.

Flintlock (Model 183)

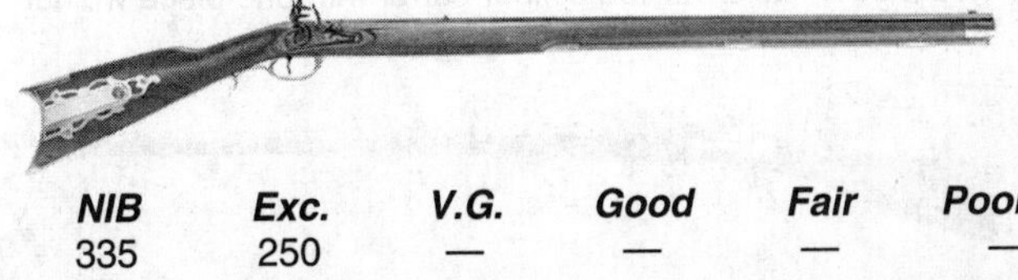

NIB	Exc.	V.G.	Good	Fair	Poor
335	250	—	—	—	—

Percussion (Model 182)

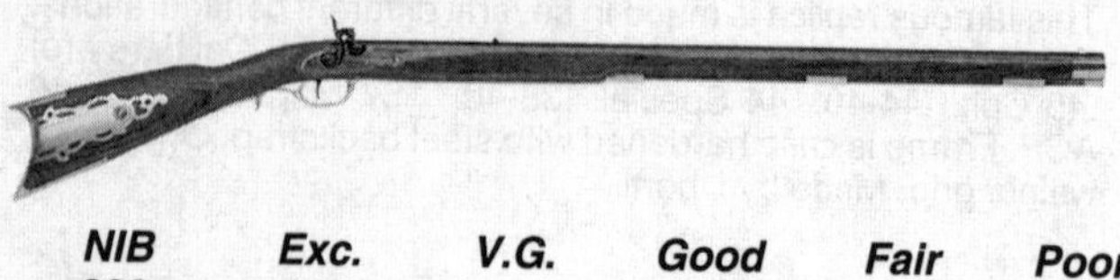

NIB	Exc.	V.G.	Good	Fair	Poor
300	240	—	—	—	—

Model 1842 U.S. Percussion Musket (Model 125)

This model is offered as a smoothbore or rifled musket with 42" .69 caliber barrel. Finish is in the white. One-piece walnut stock.

Smoothbore

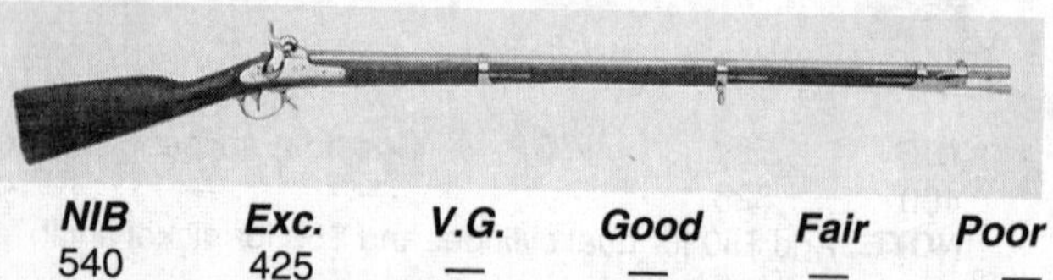

NIB	Exc.	V.G.	Good	Fair	Poor
540	425	—	—	—	—

Rifled Smoothbore with Rear Sight (Model 126)

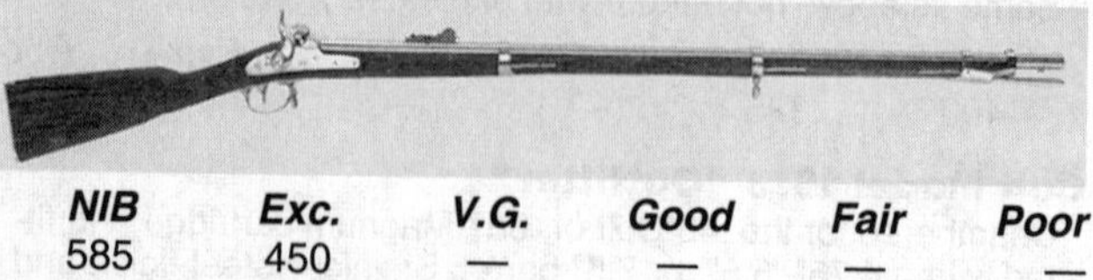

NIB	Exc.	V.G.	Good	Fair	Poor
585	450	—	—	—	—

Model 1855 U.S. Percussion Musket (Model 116)

This model has a .58 caliber 40" barrel with rear sight. One-piece walnut stock. White satin finish.

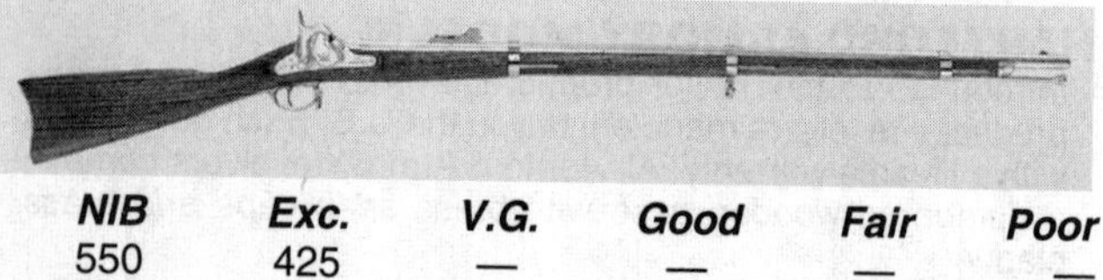

NIB	Exc.	V.G.	Good	Fair	Poor
550	425	—	—	—	—

Model 1853 3-Band Enfield Musket (Model 120)

This rifled musket has a 39" .58 caliber barrel. Blued finish. One-piece walnut stock. Brass buttplate, nosecap, and trigger guard.

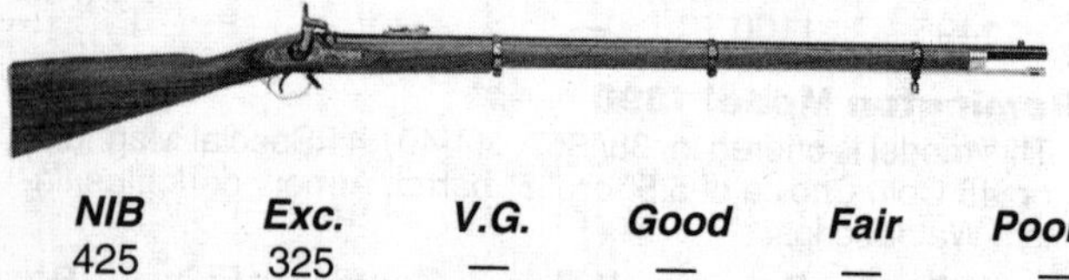

NIB	Exc.	V.G.	Good	Fair	Poor
425	325	—	—	—	—

Model 1858 2-Band Enfield Musket (Model 121)

Similar to the above model but fitted with a .58 caliber 33" barrel.

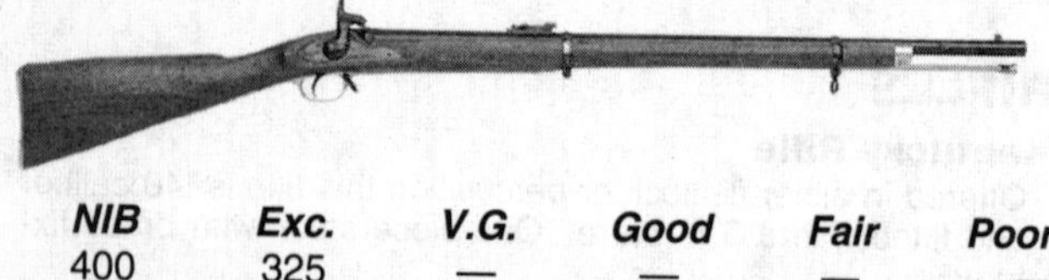

NIB	Exc.	V.G.	Good	Fair	Poor
400	325	—	—	—	—

Model 1861 Springfield Musket (Model 110)

This model has a 40" .58 caliber barrel with one-piece walnut stock. White satin finish.

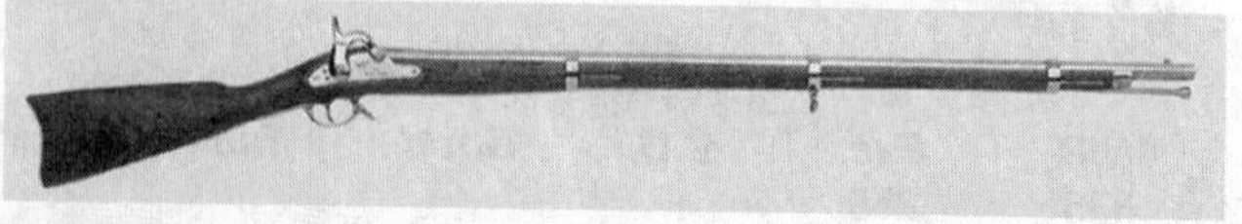

NIB	Exc.	V.G.	Good	Fair	Poor
475	375	—	—	—	—

Model 1862 C.S. Richmond Musket (Model 115)

This rifle is fitted with a 40" .58 caliber barrel with three barrel bands. Brass buttplate and nosecap. White satin finish. One-piece walnut stock.

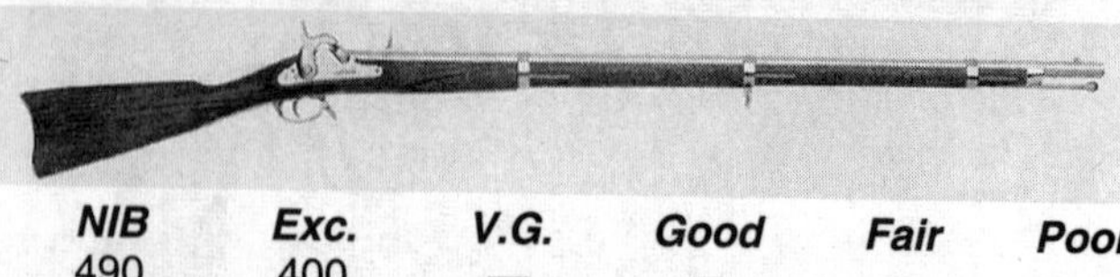

NIB	Exc.	V.G.	Good	Fair	Poor
490	400	—	—	—	—

Model 1863 Remington Zouave (Model 140)

Fitted with a 33" barrel chambered for the .58 caliber ball. One-piece walnut stock with blued finish, brass buttplate, nosecap, trigger guard, patchbox, and barrel bands.

NIB	Exc.	V.G.	Good	Fair	Poor
375	300	—	—	—	—

Henry Rifle

This lever-action rifle is chambered for the .44-40 or .45 Colt cartridge. Fitted with a 24.25" octagon barrel. Walnut stock. Open sights.

Brass frame (Model 198)

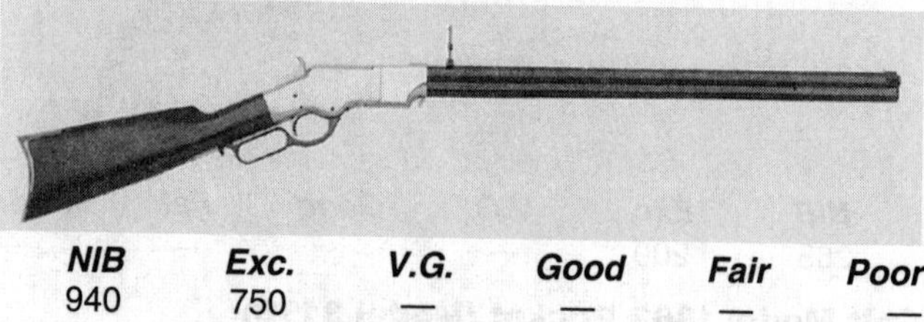

NIB	Exc.	V.G.	Good	Fair	Poor
940	750	—	—	—	—

Iron Frame (Model 199)

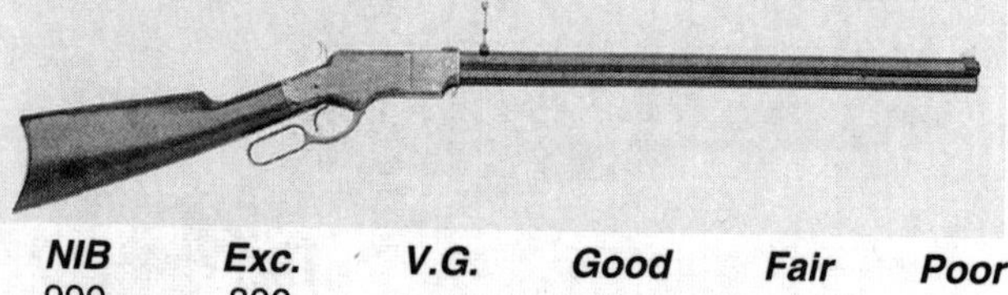

NIB	Exc.	V.G.	Good	Fair	Poor
990	800	—	—	—	—

Winchester Model 1866 (Model 201)

This model is chambered for the .44-40 or .45 Colt cartridge. Fitted with a 24.25" octagon barrel. Brass frame. Open sights. Made by Uberti.

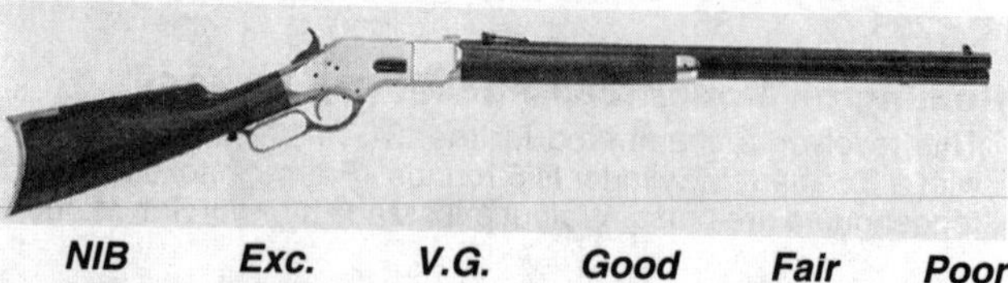

NIB	Exc.	V.G.	Good	Fair	Poor
830	650	—	—	—	—

Winchester Model 1866 Yellowboy Carbine (Model 202)

Same as above but with 19" round barrel and the additional .38 Special caliber. Made by Uberti.

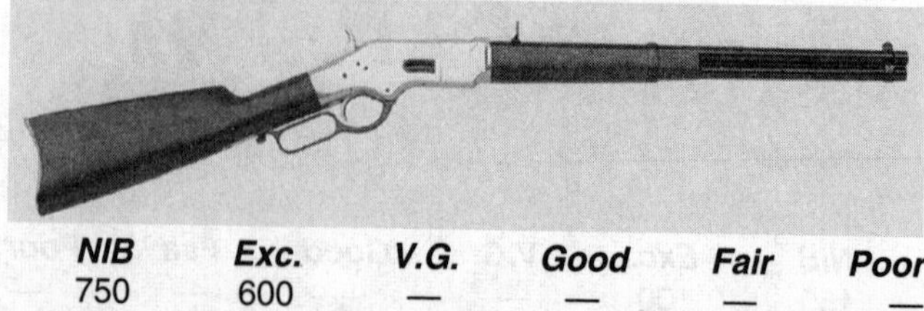

NIB	Exc.	V.G.	Good	Fair	Poor
750	600	—	—	—	—

Winchester Model 1873 (Model 200)

This lever action model is chambered for the .44-40 or .45 Colt cartridge and fitted with a 24.25" octagon barrel. Made by Uberti.

NIB	Exc.	V.G.	Good	Fair	Poor
750	600	—	—	—	—

Winchester Model 1873 Carbine (Model 200B)

Chambered for the .45 Long Colt cartridge and fitted with a 19" barrel. Magazine capacity is 10 rounds. Walnut stock and case colored frame.

NIB	Exc.	V.G.	Good	Fair	Poor
825	650	—	—	—	—

Winchester Model 1873 Sporting Rifle (Model 200C)

Chambered for the .45 Long Colt cartridge and fitted with a 30" octagon barrel. Checkered walnut stock with pistol grip. Case colored frame and blued barrel.

NIB	Exc.	V.G.	Good	Fair	Poor
925	750	—	—	—	—

Winchester Model 1885 High Wall (Model 203)

Offered with 30" or 32" barrels chambered for the .45-70 cartridge. Walnut stock.

NIB	Exc.	V.G.	Good	Fair	Poor
800	650	—	—	—	—

Winchester Model 1885 Low Wall Sporting Rifle (Model 204)

This single-shot rifle is chambered for the .22 LR, .32-20, or .38-40 cartridge. Checkered walnut stock.

NIB	Exc.	V.G.	Good	Fair	Poor
800	650	—	—	—	—

Winchester Model 92

Introduced in 2004 this lever-action rifle is chambered for the .32-20, .32 H&R Magnum, .357 Magnum, .38 Special, .38-40, .44-40, .44 S&W, or the .45 Colt. Barrel length is 20" or 24" octagon. Takedown feature. Hardwood stock with blued barrel finish and case colored frame.

NIB	Exc.	V.G.	Good	Fair	Poor
965	750	—	—	—	—

Sharps Model 1859 Infantry (Model 151)

This rifle is fitted with a 30" round barrel and is chambered for the .54 caliber cartridge. One-piece walnut with 3 barrel bands. Adjustable rear sight.

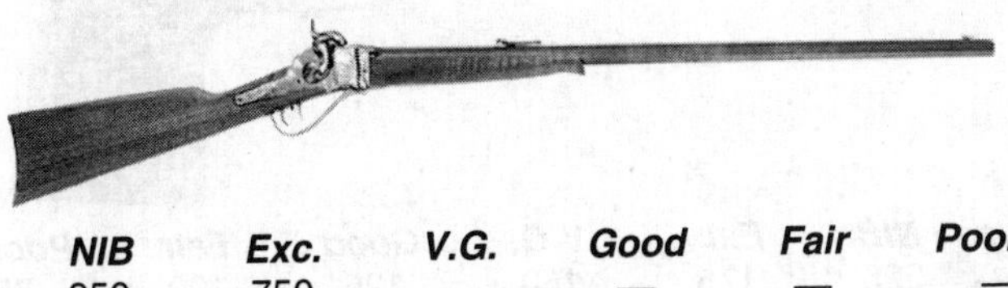

NIB	Exc.	V.G.	Good	Fair	Poor
950	750	—	—	—	—

Sharps Model 1859 Berdan Military (Model 152)

This .54 caliber rifle is fitted with a 30" round barrel. One-piece walnut stock with 3 barrel bands. Adjustable rear sight. This model is fitted with double set triggers.

NIB	Exc.	V.G.	Good	Fair	Poor
1000	800	—	—	—	—

Sharps Model 1859 Cavalry (Model 153)

This model has a 22" round barrel with adjustable rear sight. Chambered for .54 caliber. Walnut stock is fitted with patch box.

NIB	Exc.	V.G.	Good	Fair	Poor
825	650	—	—	—	—

Sharps Model 1863 Cavalry (Model 154)

Similar to the Model 1859 Cavalry but without the patch box.

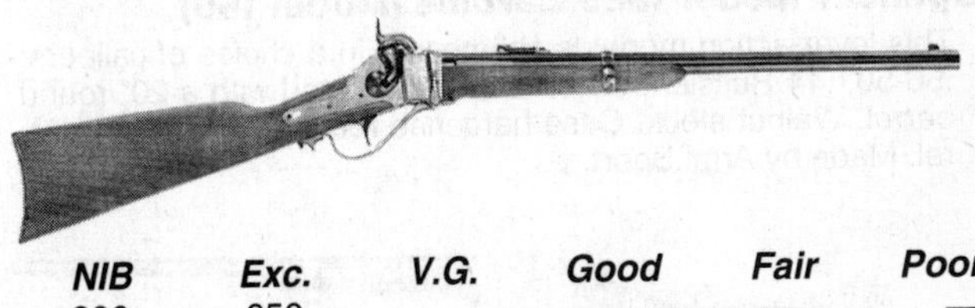

NIB	Exc.	V.G.	Good	Fair	Poor
800	650	—	—	—	—

Sharps Model 1863 Sporting Rifle (Model 131)

This .54 caliber model is offered with either 30" or 32" octagon barrel with single or double set triggers. Walnut stock.

NIB	Exc.	V.G.	Good	Fair	Poor
875	700	—	—	—	—

NOTE: Add $20 for double set trigger.

Sharps Model 1874 Sporting Rifle (Model 138)

This model is offered with a variety of features. Available in .45-70 with choice of 30" or 32" octagon barrel with a choice of single trigger or double set triggers. It is also available with Hartford-style pewter forend tip. In this configuration it is available in .45-70, .40-65, .45-90, or .45-120 calibers. Checkered stock with patch is optional.

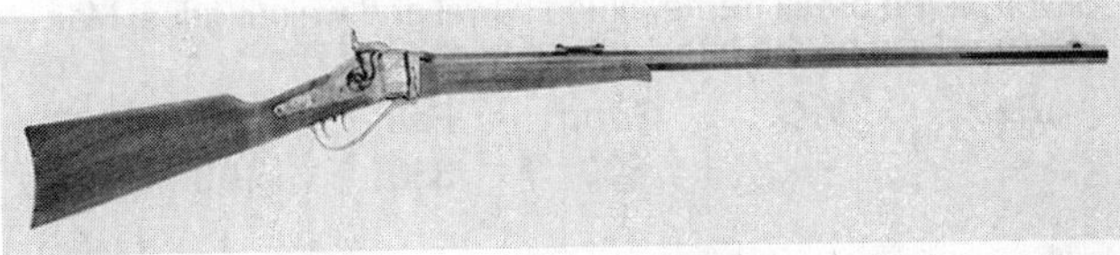

NIB	Exc.	V.G.	Good	Fair	Poor
895	700	—	—	—	—

NOTE: Add $125 for Hartford-style forend tip. Add $250 for checkered stock with patch box.

Sharps Model 1874 Deluxe Sporting Rifle (Model 155)

This .45-70 caliber model features a hand checkered walnut stock with oil finish. Receiver is in the white with standard scroll engraving.

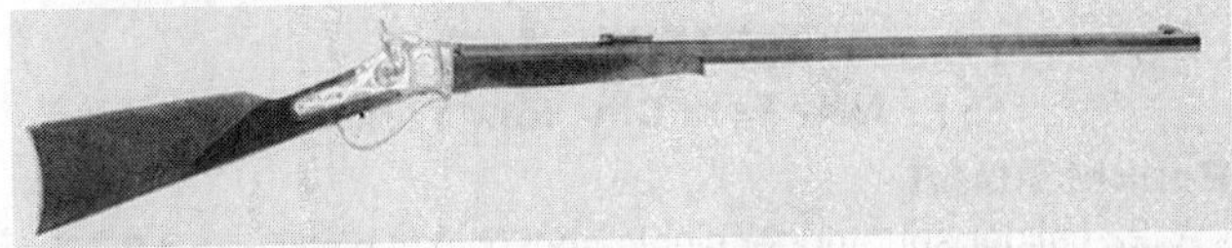

NIB	Exc.	V.G.	Good	Fair	Poor
1800	1350	—	—	—	—

NOTE: For Deluxe Model 1874 with gold inlay add $800.

Sharps Model 1874 Infantry Rifle (Model 157)

This .45-70 caliber model features a 30" round barrel with 3 barrel bands. One-piece walnut stock. Adjustable rear sight. Single trigger. Patch box in stock.

NIB	Exc.	V.G.	Good	Fair	Poor
1000	800	—	—	—	—

Sharps Model 1874 Berdan Rifle (Model 158)

Similar to the above model but with a double set trigger.

NIB	Exc.	V.G.	Good	Fair	Poor
1050	825	—	—	—	—

Sharps Model 1874 Cavalry (Model 159)

This .45-70 caliber model is fitted with a 22" round barrel. Adjustable rear sight.

NIB	Exc.	V.G.	Good	Fair	Poor
875	700	—	—	—	—

Spencer Model 1865 Carbine (Model 160)

This lever-action model is chambered in a choice of calibers: .56-50, .44 Russian, or .45 Schofield. Fitted with a 20" round barrel. Walnut stock. Case hardened receiver and blued barrel. Made by Armi Sport.

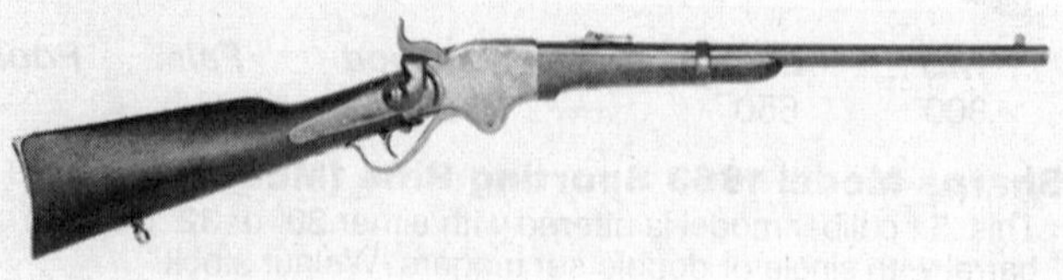

NIB	Exc.	V.G.	Good	Fair	Poor
1200	950	—	—	—	—

Spencer Model 1865 Rifle

As above but with 30" barrel with three barrel bands. Chambered for the .56-50 cartridge.

NIB	Exc.	V.G.	Good	Fair	Poor
1200	950	—	—	—	—

TAYLOR, L.B.

Chicopee, Massachusetts

Pocket Pistol

A .32 caliber spur trigger single-shot pocket pistol with a 3.5" octagonal barrel marked "L. B. Taylor & Co. Chicopee Mass." Silver-plated brass frame, blued barrel and walnut grips. Manufactured during the late 1860s and early 1870s.

Exc.	V.G.	Good	Fair	Poor
—	—	800	350	100

TERRIER ONE

Terrier One

A .32 caliber double-action swing-out cylinder revolver with a 2.25" barrel and 5-shot cylinder. Nickel-plated with checkered walnut grips. Manufactured from 1984 to 1987.

Exc.	V.G.	Good	Fair	Poor
100	75	50	30	25

TERRY, J. C.

New York City, New York

Pocket Pistol

A .22 caliber spur trigger single-shot pocket pistol with a 3.75" round barrel. The back strap marked "J.C. Terry/Patent Pending." Silver-plated brass frame, blued barrel and rosewood or walnut grips. Manufactured in the late 1860s.

Exc.	V.G.	Good	Fair	Poor
—	—	950	475	100

TEXAS CONTRACT RIFLES

Three contractors produced rifles for the State of Texas during 1862 and 1863. One of these patterns has a sporting back-action lock, Enfield barrel bands, an overall length of 47-3/8", heavy 32" long barrel of .58 caliber. Total deliveries by all contractors amounted to 1,464 rifles. Quality of these arms was decidedly inferior and often complained about.

TEXAS GUNFIGHTERS

Ponte Zanano, Italy

Shootist Single-Action

A .45 Long Colt caliber single-action revolver with a 4.75" barrel. Nickel-plated with one-piece walnut grips. This model is made by Aldo Uberti. Introduced in 1988.

NIB	Exc.	V.G.	Good	Fair	Poor
600	550	500	400	350	200

1-of-100 Edition

As above, with one-piece mother-of-pearl grips fitted in a case with an additional set of walnut grips. 100 were made in 1988.

NIB	Exc.	V.G.	Good	Fair	Poor
1250	1000	850	700	600	300

TEXAS LONGHORN ARMS, INC.

Richmond, Texas

Jezebel

A .22 or .22 Magnum single-shot pistol with a 6" barrel. Stainless steel with a walnut stock and forend. Introduced in 1987.

NIB	Exc.	V.G.	Good	Fair	Poor
225	175	150	125	100	75

Texas Border Special

A .44 Special or .45 Colt caliber single-action revolver with a 3.5" barrel and Pope-style rifling. Blued, case hardened with one-piece walnut grips.

REMINDER

You don't have to specialize in Colts and Winchesters to have a nice collection. Collecting Marlin or Mossberg .22 semi-autos, for example, can be just as rewarding.

This symbol denotes "Sleepers" with rapidly-rising values and/or significant collector potential.

NIB	Exc.	V.G.	Good	Fair	Poor
1500	1250	1000	800	600	300

Mason Commemorative

As above, in .45 Colt with a 4.75" barrel and the Mason's insignia. Gold inlaid. Introduced in 1987.

NIB	Exc.	V.G.	Good	Fair	Poor
1500	1250	1000	800	600	300

South Texas Army

As above, but with a 4.75" barrel also chambered for the .357 Magnum cartridge and fitted with conventional one-piece walnut grips.

NIB	Exc.	V.G.	Good	Fair	Poor
1500	1250	1000	800	600	300

West Texas Target

As above, with a 7.5" barrel, flat top frame and in .32-20 caliber in addition to the calibers noted above.

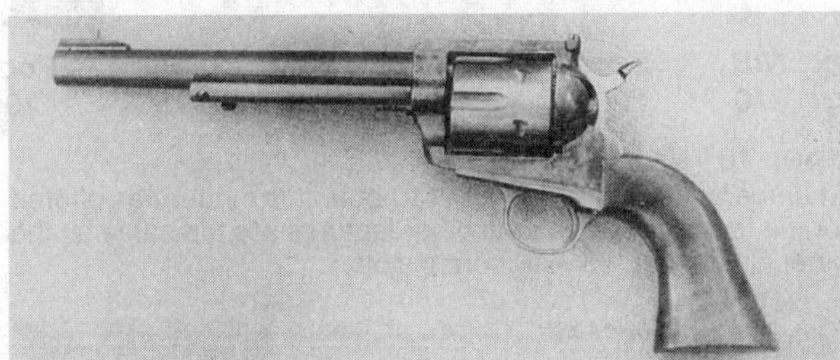

NIB	Exc.	V.G.	Good	Fair	Poor
1500	1250	1000	800	600	300

Grover's Improved Number Five

Similar to the above, in .44 Magnum with a 5.5" barrel. Serial Numbered K1 to K1200. Introduced in 1988.

NIB	Exc.	V.G.	Good	Fair	Poor
1300	950	700	600	500	250

Texas Sesquicentennial Commemorative

As above, engraved in the style of Louis D. Nimschke with one-piece ivory grips and a fitted case.

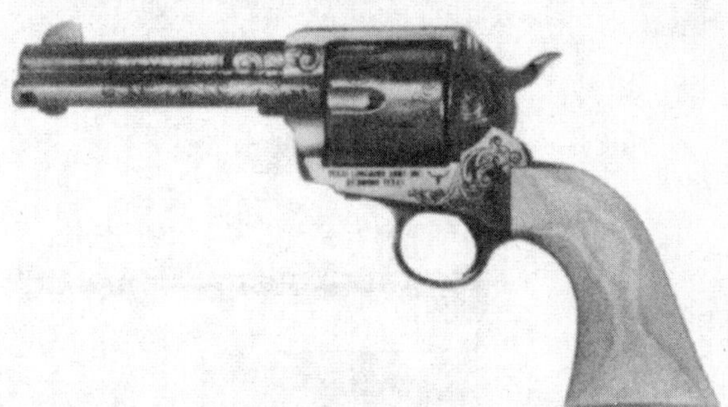

NIB	Exc.	V.G.	Good	Fair	Poor
2500	2000	1500	900	750	400

THAMES ARMS CO.

Norwich, Connecticut

A .22, .32, or .38 caliber double-action top break revolver with varying length barrels normally marked "Automatic Revolver," which refers to the cartridge ejector. Nickel-plated with walnut grips.

Exc.	V.G.	Good	Fair	Poor
500	200	100	75	50

THIEME & EDELER

Eibar, Spain

Pocket Pistol

A 7.65mm caliber semi-automatic pistol with a 3" barrel marked "T E." Blued with black plastic grips. Manufactured prior to 1936.

Exc.	V.G.	Good	Fair	Poor
250	150	100	75	50

THOMPSON

SEE—Auto Ordnance

THOMPSON/CENTER ARMS

Rochester, New Hampshire

NOTE: In late 2006 it was announced that Thompson/Center Arms had been acquired by Smith & Wesson.

Contender

Introduced in 1967 this model is the basis for all past and present variations. The standard version is offered with a 10" octagon barrel and is available in 10" Bull barrel, 10" vent rib barrel, 14" Super models, 14" Super with vent rib, 16" Super models, and 16" Super models with vent rib. A stainless steel finish is available on all models except the 10" octagon barrel. The action on these handguns is a single-shot, break open design. Unless otherwise stated the barrels are blued. The Competitor grip is walnut with rubber insert mounted on back of grip. A finger groove grip is also available made from walnut with finger notching and thumb rest. Forend is American black walnut in various length and designs depending on barrel size. Stainless steel models have rubber grips with finger grooves. Standard sights are standard Patridge rear with ramp front. An adjustable rear sight is offered as an option. Barrels with vent ribs are furnished with fixed rear sight and bead front sight. Due to the numerous variations of the Contender several breakdowns will be listed to help the reader find the closest possible handgun he may be looking for.

NOTE: Early frames with no engraving, called flatsides, and those with eagle engraving bring between $2,000 and $2,500 on the collector market.

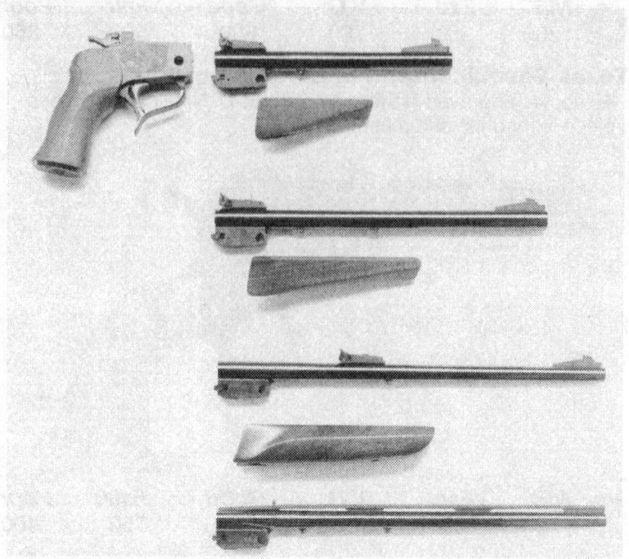

10" Octagon Barrel Model

This was the first Contender design and is offered in .22 LR only. It is supplied with adjustable rear sight and mounting holes for scope. Grips are Competitor or rubber. Weighs about 44 oz.

NIB	Exc.	V.G.	Good	Fair	Poor
360	300	250	200	150	100

10" Bull Barrel Model

Comes standard with adjustable rear sight, mounting holes for scope mounts, and Competitor grips for blued models and rubber grips on stainless models. Available in blued or stainless steel. Offered in these calibers as complete pistols: .22 LR, .22 LR Match, .22 Win. Mag. (blued only), .22 Hornet, .223, 7mm T.C.U. (blued only), .30-30, .32-20 (blued only), .357 Mag., .357 Rem. Max (blued only), .44 Mag., .45 Colt, .410 bore. In 1994 Thompson/Center introduced the .300 Whisper cartridge to its Contender product line. Weighs approximately 50 oz.

NIB	Exc.	V.G.	Good	Fair	Poor
350	300	250	200	150	100

10" Vent Rib Model

This features a raised vent rib and is chambered for the .45 Long Colt/.410 bore. The rear sight is fixed and the front sight is a bead. A detachable choke screws into the muzzle for use with the .410 shell. Furnished with Competitor grips or rubber grips.

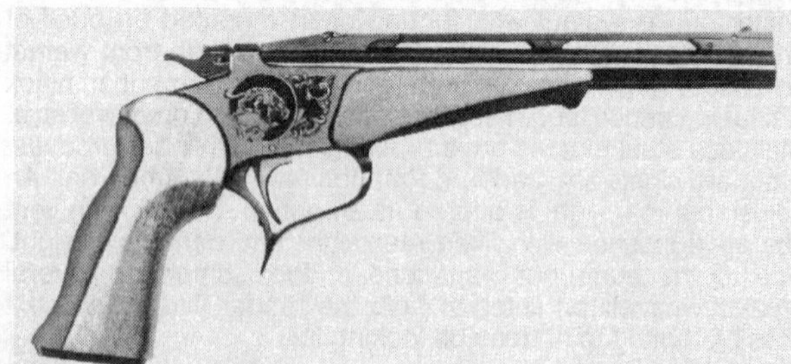

NIB	Exc.	V.G.	Good	Fair	Poor
370	320	270	220	150	100

Super 14" Model

This model features a 14" bull barrel. Furnished with adjustable rear sight and ramp front sight. Drilled and tapped for scope mounts. Competitor or rubber grips are offered. Available in blued or stainless steel finish. Furnished in these calibers in a complete pistol only: .22 LR, .22 LR Match, .17 Rem. (blued only), .22 Hornet, .222 Rem. (blued only), .223 Rem., 7mm T.C.U. (blued only), 7-30 Waters, .30-30, .357 Rem. Max (blued only), .35 Rem., .375 Win. (blued only), .44 Mag. (blued only). Weighs approximately 56 oz.

NIB	Exc.	V.G.	Good	Fair	Poor
360	300	250	200	150	100

Super 14" Vent Rib Model

Similar to the 10" vent rib model chambered for the .45 Long Colt/.410 bore but furnished with a 14" vent rib barrel.

NIB	Exc.	V.G.	Good	Fair	Poor
385	325	275	215	150	100

Super 16" Model

Fitted with a 16.25" tapered barrel, two position adjustable rear sight. Drilled and tapped for scope mount. Furnished with Competitor grips or rubber grips and choice of blued or stainless steel finish. Available in these calibers as complete pistols only: .22 LR, .22 Hornet, .223 Rem., 7-30 Waters, .30-30, .35 Rem., .45-70 Government. Weighs approximately 56 oz.

NIB	Exc.	V.G.	Good	Fair	Poor
370	320	275	215	150	100

Super 16" Vent Rib Model

Chambered for .45 Long Colt/.410 bore this model was offered for the first time in 1993. All other features are the same as the other Contender .45/.410 bore pistols.

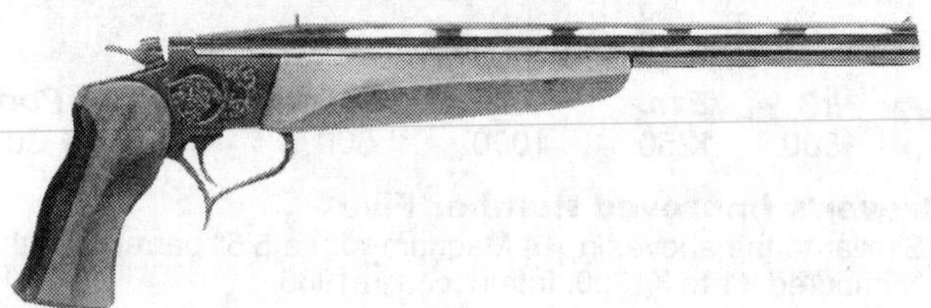

NIB	Exc.	V.G.	Good	Fair	Poor
390	350	300	250	175	125

Contender Hunter Model

This model is designed for handgun hunting and is offered in two barrel lengths: 12" and 14". The barrels are fitted with a compensator and a 2.5 power scope. There are no iron sights fitted. A nylon carrying sling and soft leather carrying case are standard. Offered in these calibers: 7-30 Waters, .30-30 Win., .35 Rem., .45-70 Government, .44 Mag., .223 Rem., and .375 Win. Fitted with Competitor grips and offered in blued or stainless steel finish. Weighs approximately 64 oz.

NIB	Exc.	V.G.	Good	Fair	Poor
575	500	400	300	200	100

NOTE: Barrel interchangeability is acceptable for blued barrels and frames with stainless steel barrels and frames. DO NOT interchange Alloy II barrels and frames with either blued or stainless steel components.

G2 CONTENDER SERIES

Introduced in 2003, this is a second generation Contender that features a slightly different look, a simplified internal design that allows re-cocking the hammer without having to break open the action, and differently shaped grips that give more clearance between the grip and the finger guard. These G2 firearms will accept previously manufactured Contender barrels and forends but not grips.

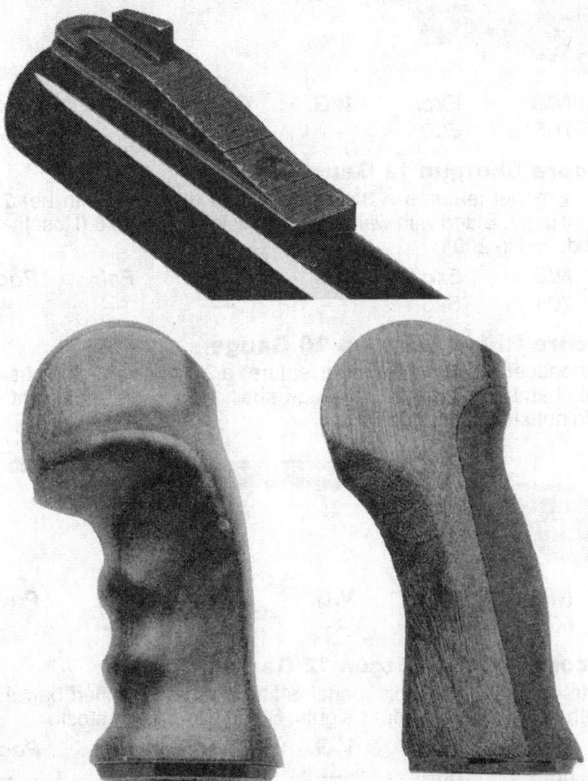

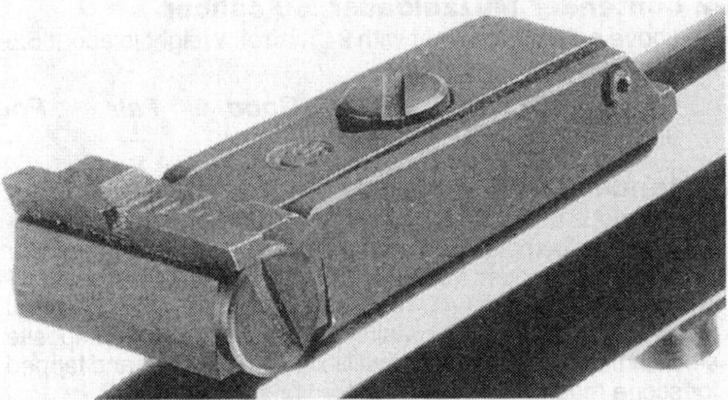

G2 Contender

Offered with both 12" and 14" barrels. Chambered for .22 Hornet, .357 Mag., .44 Mag., .45 Colt/.410 in 12" barrels. In 14" barrel chambered for the .17 HMR, .22 LR, .22 Hornet, .223 Rem., 7-30 Waters, .30-30, .44 Mag., .45 Colt/.410 and the .45-70. Adjustable sights and drilled and tapped for scope mounts. Walnut grips. Weight for 12" barreled guns is about 3.5 lbs., for 14" barreled guns about 3.75 lbs. In 2004 the .204 Ruger and .375 JDJ calibers were added.

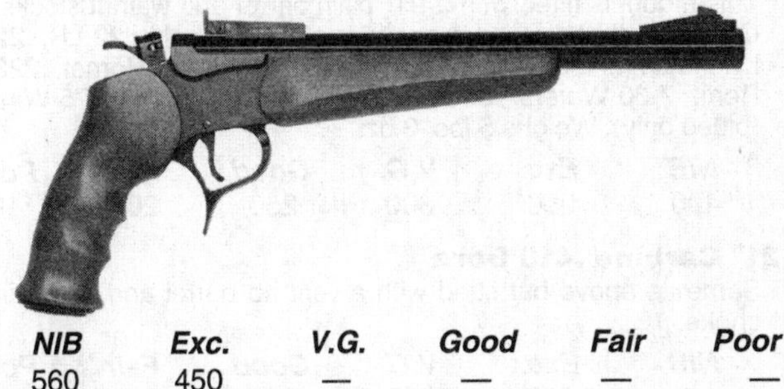

NIB	Exc.	V.G.	Good	Fair	Poor
560	450	—	—	—	—

G2 Contender Rifle

This rifle is fitted with a 23" barrel with no sights and is chambered for the .17 HMR, .22 LR, .223 Rem., .30-30, and the .45-70. Walnut stock with blued finish. Weight is about 5.4 lbs. In 2004 the .375 JDJ and .204 Ruger calibers were added.

NIB	Exc.	V.G.	Good	Fair	Poor
600	475	—	—	—	—

G2 Contender Shotgun

Chambered for the .410 bore shell and fitted with a 24" ventilated rib barrel. Walnut stock. Weight is about 5.4 lbs. Introduced in 2004.

NIB	Exc.	V.G.	Good	Fair	Poor
660	500	—	—	—	—

G2 Contender Muzzleloader

As above but a 209x45 24" muzzleloader barrel. Will interchange with G2 Contender rifle barrels. Weight is about 5.5 lbs.

NIB	Exc.	V.G.	Good	Fair	Poor
635	500	—	—	—	—

G2 Contender Muzzeloader .50 caliber

As above but in .50 caliber with 24" barrel. Weight is about 6.5 lbs. Introduced in 2005.

NIB	Exc.	V.G.	Good	Fair	Poor
650	500	—	—	—	—

Contender Carbine Model

This model is built from the same design as the Contender Model. It features completely interchangeable barrels chambered for 12 different cartridges from .22 LR to .35 Rem. A .410 bore shotgun barrel is also offered. The standard model has a 21" barrel stocked with walnut. For stainless steel models a composite stock in fitted walnut is also available. All are drilled and tapped for scope mounts. Available in blued or stainless steel.

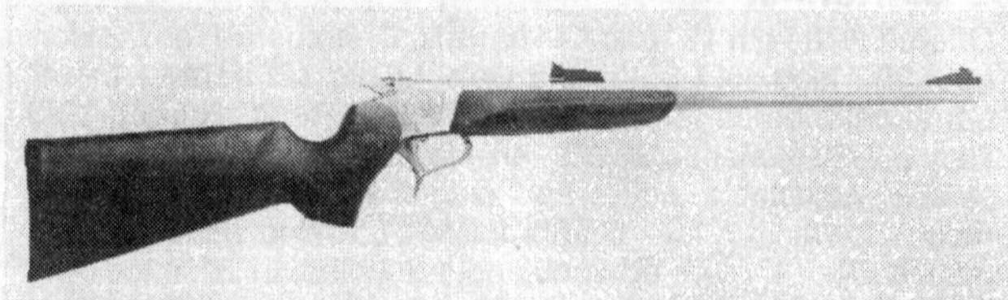

Standard 21" Carbine

This model is fitted with a 21" plain barrel and walnut stocks. Offered in these calibers as a complete gun only: .22 LR, .22 LR Match (blued only), .17 Rem. (blued only), .22 Hornet, .223 Rem., 7-30 Waters, .30-30, .35 Rem. (blued only), .375 Win. (blued only). Weighs 5 lbs. 3 oz.

NIB	Exc.	V.G.	Good	Fair	Poor
400	350	300	250	200	100

21" Carbine .410 Bore

Same as above but fitted with a vent rib barrel and screw-in choke.

NIB	Exc.	V.G.	Good	Fair	Poor
410	360	300	250	200	100

16" Youth Model Carbine

A special walnut buttstock with 12" length of pull and 16.25" barrel. Short buttstock can be replaced with standard buttstock. Blued or stainless steel finish. Complete guns are offered in the same calibers as the 21" Carbine with the exception of the .375 Win. and the addition of the .45 Long Colt/.410 bore with vent rib barrel.

NIB	Exc.	V.G.	Good	Fair	Poor
350	300	250	200	150	100

Encore Pistol

Introduced in 1996 this single-shot pistol will feature barrels chambered for the .30-06, .308 Win., 7mm-08 Rem., .223 Rem., .22-250 Rem., .44 Magnum, and 7mmBR. Offered with 10.625", 15", or 24" barrels this new handgun is designed for use with higher pressure cartridges. Barrels will not interchange with the Contender. Weight with 10.625" barrel is 56 oz., with 15" barrel about 4 lbs. and with 24" barrel about 6.75 lbs.

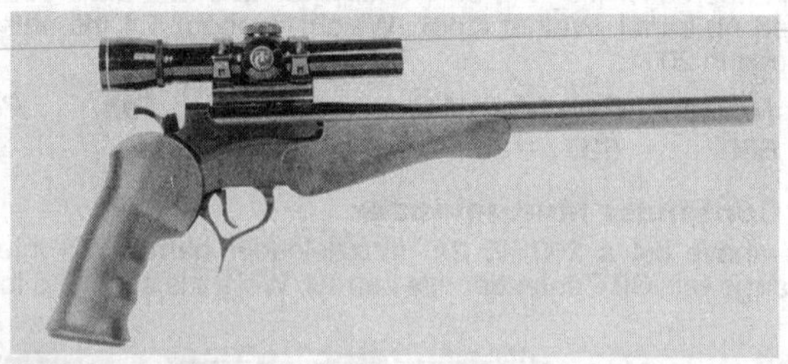

NIB	Exc.	V.G.	Good	Fair	Poor
500	450	—	—	—	—

NOTE: Add $60 for stainless steel frame and barrels.

Encore Rifle

Similar to the Encore pistol but with longer barrels and walnut stock and forearm. A wide variety of calibers are offered from .22-250 to .300 Win. Mag. in barrels lengths from 24" to 26". Heavy barrels are offered in 7mm Rem Mag., .300 Win. Mag., and .22-250. These are offered with no sights. Weight is about 6 lbs. 12 oz. for 7mm-08 with 24" barrel. Introduced in 1997. In 1998 the .260 Rem., .280 Rem., and .45-70 Government cartridges were added. In 1999 stainless steel frame and barrels were offered as well as blued. In 2003 the .375 H&H Magnum with a 26" barrel without sights was offered. In 2004 the .280 Rem., .204 Ruger, and the .405 Win. were added.

NIB	Exc.	V.G.	Good	Fair	Poor
650	525	—	—	—	—

NOTE: Add about $60 for stainless steel frame and barrels.

Encore Katahdin Carbine

This model is fitted with a heavy 18" barrel with integral muzzle-brake. Offered in .444 Marlin, .450 Marlin, and .45-70 Government calibers. Blued finish with composite stock and adjustable fiber optic sights. Weight is about 6.75 lbs. Introduced in 2002.

NIB	Exc.	V.G.	Good	Fair	Poor
290	225	—	—	—	—

Encore Katahdin Turkey Gun

This is a 12 gauge 3" chamber gun with 20" barrel and screw-in Turkey chokes. Open sights. Realtree Hardwoods HD camo composite stock. Weight is about 6 lbs. Introduced in 2005.

NIB	Exc.	V.G.	Good	Fair	Poor
750	575	—	—	—	—

Encore Shotgun 20 Gauge

Introduced in 1998 this model is fitted with a 26" 20 gauge vent rib barrel with walnut stock and forend. Choke tubes are standard.

NIB	Exc.	V.G.	Good	Fair	Poor
625	475	—	—	—	—

Encore Camo Shotgun 12 Gauge

This model features a 24" smoothbore barrel with screw-in turkey choke, camo stock and metal pattern. Blued frame with composite stock. Introduced in 2002.

NIB	Exc.	V.G.	Good	Fair	Poor
765	600	—	—	—	—

Encore Shotgun 12 Gauge

This model features a 3" 26" ventilated rib barrel with bead front sight. Blued with walnut stock. Weight is about 6.6 lbs. Introduced in 2004.

NIB	Exc.	V.G.	Good	Fair	Poor
705	525	—	—	—	—

Encore Rifled Shotgun 20 Gauge

Introduced in 2000 this model features a 26" rifled shotgun barrel chambered for the 20 gauge shell. Adjustable rear sight. Walnut stock and blued finish.

NIB	Exc.	V.G.	Good	Fair	Poor
600	450	—	—	—	—

Encore Rifled Shotgun 12 Gauge

Introduced in 2002 this model is fitted with a 24" rifled barrel with adjustable fiber optic sights. Blued with walnut stock.

NIB	Exc.	V.G.	Good	Fair	Poor
665	500	—	—	—	—

Encore Turkey Gun

Introduced in 2005 this model is chambered for the 20 gauge shell with 3" chamber, 26" barrel with open sights and screw-in Turkey chokes. Realtree Hardwoods HD camo composite stock.

NIB	Exc.	V.G.	Good	Fair	Poor
760	575	—	—	—	—

Encore 209x50 Mag Rifle

This muzzleloading rifle is chambered for .50 caliber and fitted with a 26" barrel. Designed to handle magnum loads of up to 150 grains of FFG black powder. Blued or stainless steel finish. Introduced in 1998.

NIB	Exc.	V.G.	Good	Fair	Poor
650	500	400	275	200	—

NOTE: Add $75 for stainless steel. Add $140 for Reattree camo stock.

Encore 209x50 Mag Carbine

Similar to the above model but fitted with a 20" ported barrel. Realtree camo stock. Weight is about 6.75 lbs. Introduced in 2004.

NIB	Exc.	V.G.	Good	Fair	Poor
700	525	—	—	—	—

Encore 209x50 Pistol

This model features a 15" barrel chambered for .50 caliber. Walnut stock and blued finish. Approximate weight is 16 oz. Introduced in 2000.

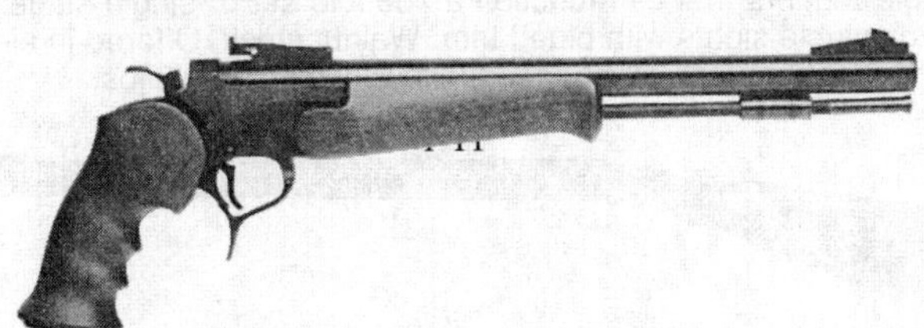

NIB	Exc.	V.G.	Good	Fair	Poor
550	425	—	—	—	—

Pro Hunter

Similar to Encore rifle but with plain or fluted barrel and various finish and stock options. Barrels interchange with standard Encore barrels. Muzzleloading and pistol versions available. Introduced 2007.

NIB	Exc.	V.G.	Good	Fair	Poor
1895	—	—	—	—	—

Icon

Bolt-action centerfire rifle chambered in .22-250, .243, .308 and .30 Thompson-Center. Barrel length 22" (iron sight) or 24" (sightless). Detachable box magazine, Introduced in 2007.

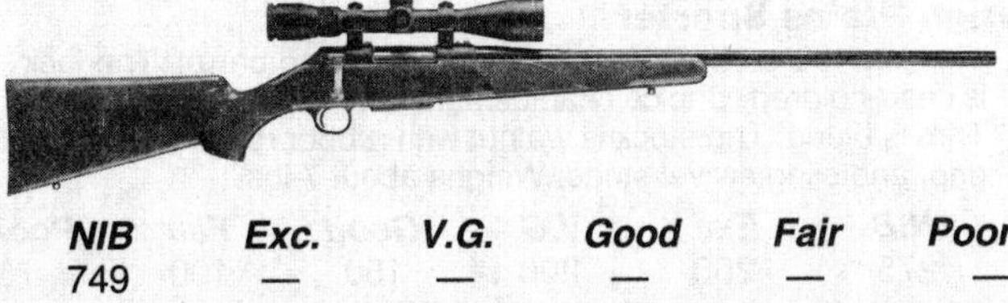

NIB	Exc.	V.G.	Good	Fair	Poor
749	—	—	—	—	—

Model R55

This semi-automatic rifle is chambered for the .17 Mach 2 cartridge and fitted with a 20" match grade barrel with adjustable sights. Black composite or laminated hardwood stock. Receiver is blued or stainless steel. Magazine capacity is 5 rounds. Weight is about 5.5 lbs. Introdoced in 2005.

NIB	Exc.	V.G.	Good	Fair	Poor
480	350	—	—	—	—

NOTE: Add $65 for black composite stock.

TCR Hunter Model

This single-shot top lever rifle is chambered for cartridges from .22 LR to .308 Win. Fitted with a 23" barrel. The finish is blue with walnut stock. Discontinued as a regular production rifle in 1993.

NIB	Exc.	V.G.	Good	Fair	Poor
425	375	300	250	200	100

T/C 22 LR Classic

Introduced in 2000 this model is a semi-automatic rifle chambered for the .22 LR cartridge. It is fitted with a 22" match grade barrel. Walnut stock with Monte Carlo comb. Adjustable rear sight. Magazine capacity is 8 rounds. Weight is about 5.5 lbs.

NIB	Exc.	V.G.	Good	Fair	Poor
325	250	—	—	—	—

.22 Classic Benchmark

An updated version of the Classic with an 18" heavy barrel and no sights. Wood laminated target stock. Magazine capacity is 10 rounds. Weight is about 6.8 lbs. Introduced in 2003.

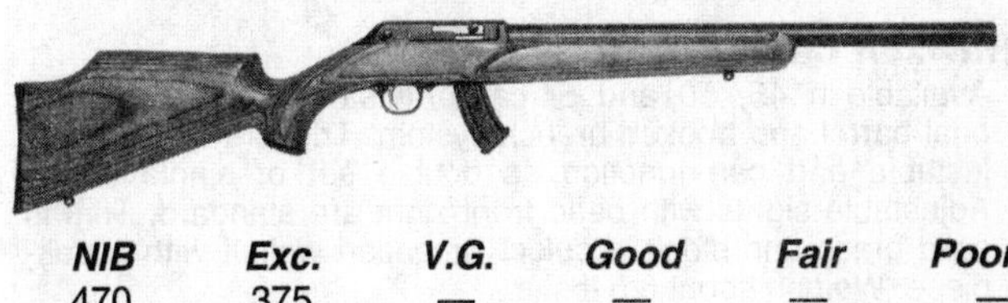

NIB	Exc.	V.G.	Good	Fair	Poor
470	375	—	—	—	—

Silver Lynx

This .22 caliber semi-automatic rifle, introduced in 2004, is fitted with a .20 stainless steel barrel. Black composite stock with Monte Carlo comb. Magazine capacity is 5 rounds. Weight is about 5.5 lbs.

NIB	Exc.	V.G.	Good	Fair	Poor
400	300	—	—	—	—

BLACKPOWDER FIREARMS

System 1

Introduced in 1997 this concept features a complete muzzleloading system with interchangeable barrels. Offered with .32, .50, .54, .58 caliber and 12 gauge shotgun barrels with walnut stock and blued finish. Or stainless steel with synthetic stock. Barrel lengths are 26". Approximate weight is 7.5 lbs. Sights are adjustable.

NIB	Exc.	V.G.	Good	Fair	Poor
350	300	—	—	—	—

NOTE: Add $30 for synthetic stock and stainless steel.

Thunder Hawk

Introduced in 1993, this rifle features a .50 caliber caplock inline ignition with 21" round barrel. Rear sight is adjustable with ramp front sight. The stock is a plain American black walnut with rubber recoil pad. Trigger is adjustable. In 1994 this model was available in stainless steel. Weighs 6.75 lbs.

NIB	Exc.	V.G.	Good	Fair	Poor
225	200	175	150	100	75

Thunder Hawk Shadow

Introduced in 1996, this model features an in-line ignition in .50 or .54 caliber with a 24" round barrel. It comes standard with a black checkered composite stock. Weight is approximately 7 lbs. In 1997 this model was offered with camouflage stock and blued finish.

NIB	Exc.	V.G.	Good	Fair	Poor
300	250	200	150	100	75

Grey Hawk

This stainless steel composite stock rifle is a .50 caliber caplock with 24" round barrel. It utilizes a hooked breech system. The lock is a heavy-duty coil spring with floral engraving pattern. Adjustable rear sight and bead front sight are standard. Weighs about 7 lbs.

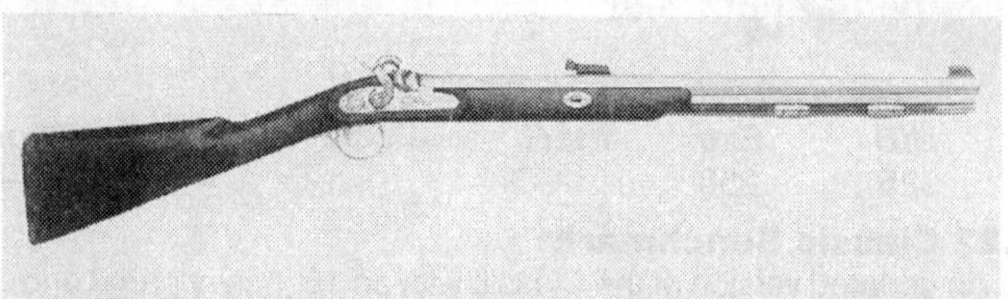

NIB	Exc.	V.G.	Good	Fair	Poor
225	200	175	150	100	75

Hawken Caplock Rifle

Available in .45, .50, and .54 caliber this rifle has a 28" octagonal barrel and hooked breech system. Triggers are fully adjustable and can function as double set or single stage. Adjustable sights with bead front sight are standard. Trim is solid brass and stock is select American walnut with cheekpiece. Weighs about 8.5 lbs.

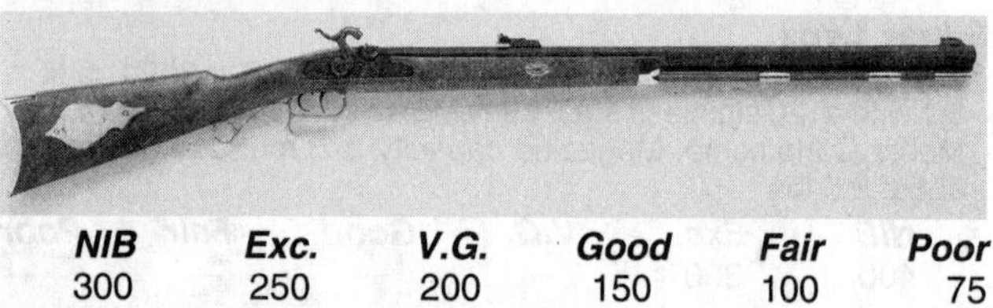

NIB	Exc.	V.G.	Good	Fair	Poor
300	250	200	150	100	75

Hawken Flintlock Rifle

Offered in .50 caliber with 28" octagonal barrel. All other features are the same as above.

NIB	Exc.	V.G.	Good	Fair	Poor
310	260	200	150	100	75

Hawken Custom/Elite

Introduced in 1994 this model is a .50 caliber traditional caplock rifle with double set triggers, crescent butt, and select American walnut stock with no patch box. The finish is a high luster blue.

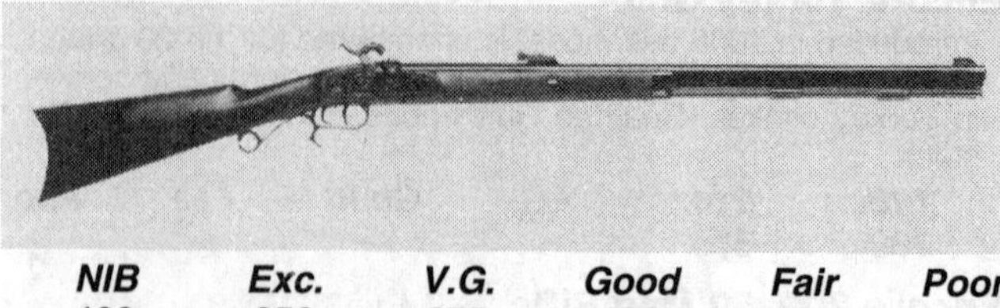

NIB	Exc.	V.G.	Good	Fair	Poor
400	350	275	175	100	75

Omega 45/Omega 50

This muzzleloader is chambered for .45 or .50 and fitted with a 28" round barrel. Adjustable sights. Composite or laminated stock. Weight is about 7 lbs. Introduced in 2002.

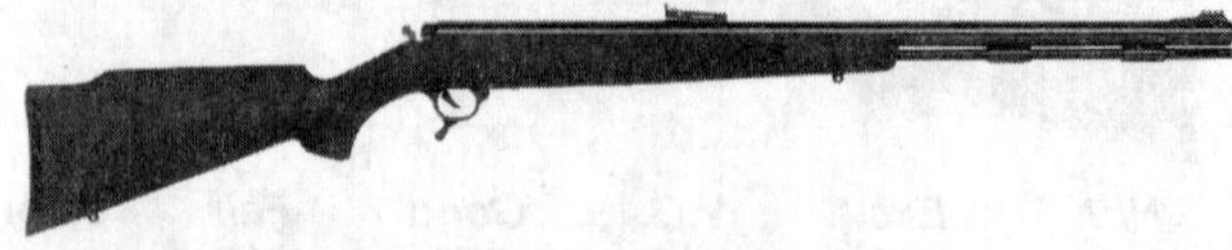

NIB	Exc.	V.G.	Good	Fair	Poor
535	400	—	—	—	—

NOTE: For stainless steel add $50. Add $60 for Realtree camo stock.

Omega Pivoting Breech Rifle

Introduced in 2004 this rifle has a 28" stainless steel fluted barrel bored for the .50 caliber slug. Laminated wood thumbhole stock. Fiber optic sights. Weight is about 7 lbs.

NIB	Exc.	V.G.	Good	Fair	Poor
635	475	—	—	—	—

Renegade Caplock Rifle

Offered in .50 or .54 caliber with 26" octagonal barrel. Adjustable triggers that can function as double set or single stage. Adjustable sights with blued trim. Walnut stock. Offered in either right hand or left hand models. Weighs about 8 lbs.

NIB	Exc.	V.G.	Good	Fair	Poor
460	350	250	150	100	75

Renegade Flintlock

Available in .50 caliber only and right hand only. Other features are the same as Caplock model.

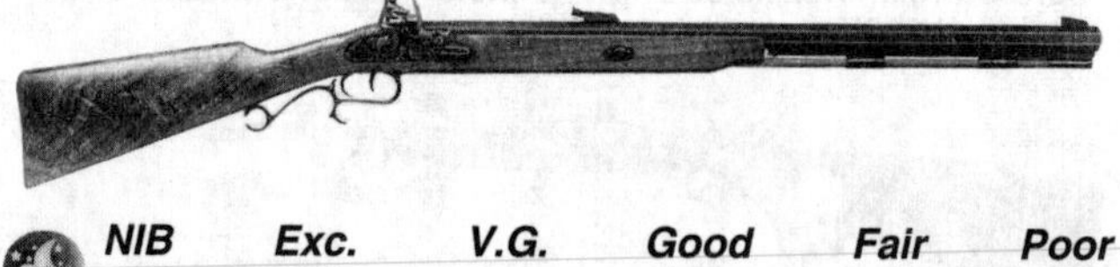

NIB	Exc.	V.G.	Good	Fair	Poor
275	250	200	150	100	75

Big Boar Rifle

This hooked breech model features the .58 caliber with 26" octagonal barrel. Single trigger and adjustable sights are standard. Trim is blued steel. American walnut stock with rubber pad. Weighs about 7.75 lbs.

NIB	Exc.	V.G.	Good	Fair	Poor
500	400	300	250	200	100

High Plains Sporter

This is a .50 caliber caplock with a 24" round barrel. The lock is case-colored. Choice of adjustable open sights or tang sight. Trim is blued. The stock is walnut with rubber recoil pad, pistol grip, and sling swivel studs. Weighs about 7 lbs.

NIB	Exc.	V.G.	Good	Fair	Poor
275	250	200	150	100	75

Tree Hawk

Available in either .50 caliber caplock or 12 gauge caplock. The .50 caliber carbine has a 21" barrel and is offered in camo colors. The 12 gauge shotgun is fitted with a 27" barrel and also comes in camo colors. Weight is about 6.75 lbs.

Rifle

NIB	Exc.	V.G.	Good	Fair	Poor
275	250	200	150	100	75

Shotgun

NIB	Exc.	V.G.	Good	Fair	Poor
275	250	200	150	100	75

White Mountain Carbine

Available in either .45, .50, or .54 caliber caplock or .50 flintlock. Fitted with a 20-1/2" octagon barrel. The lock is case-colored and trim is blued. Stock is walnut with rubber recoil pad. Weighs about 6.5 lbs. Discontinued.

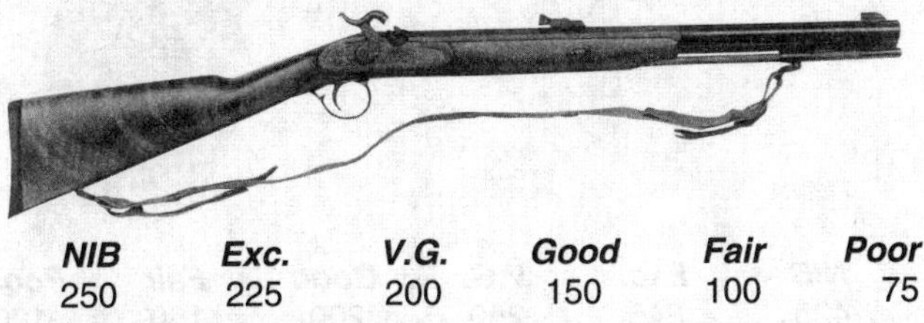

NIB	Exc.	V.G.	Good	Fair	Poor
250	225	200	150	100	75

Black Mountain Magnum

Introduced in 1999 this model features a 26" round barrel with choice of walnut or composite stock. Chambered for .50 or .54 caliber or 12 gauge with 27" round barrel. All models are caplock. Blued finish. Discontinued.

NIB	Exc.	V.G.	Good	Fair	Poor
350	275	—	—	—	—

Pennsylvania Hunter

Offered in .50 caliber caplock or flintlock and fitted with either a 31-1/2" octagon/round barrel or a 21-1/2" octagon/round barrel. Fully adjustable sights, walnut stock, and blued trim are standard. Rifle weighs about 7.5 lbs. while the carbine weighs about 6.5 lbs. Discontinued.

Rifle

NIB	Exc.	V.G.	Good	Fair	Poor
400	325	250	200	150	100

Carbine

NIB	Exc.	V.G.	Good	Fair	Poor
400	325	250	200	150	100

Pennsylvania Match Rifle

Similar to the Pennsylvania Hunter Rifle except equipped with a tang peep sight and a globe front sight. Discontinued.

NIB	Exc.	V.G.	Good	Fair	Poor
350	275	200	150	100	75

New Englander Rifle

Offered in either .50 or .54 caliber caplock with walnut stock and 26" round barrel. Adjustable sights. Weighs about 7 lbs. 15 oz. A 12" barrel is optional. Discontinued.

NIB	Exc.	V.G.	Good	Fair	Poor
200	175	150	125	90	75

NOTE: Add $150 for interchangeable shotgun barrel.

New Englander Shotgun

Same as above, but fitted with a 27" 12 gauge barrel with screw in full choke. Weighs about 6 lbs. 8 oz. Discontinued.

NIB	Exc.	V.G.	Good	Fair	Poor
230	200	175	150	100	75

New Englander Composite

Offered with composite stock. The .50 or .54 caliber rifle has a 24" barrel and the 12 gauge shotgun has a 27" barrel. Discontinued.

Rifle

NIB	Exc.	V.G.	Good	Fair	Poor
200	175	150	125	100	75

Shotgun

NIB	Exc.	V.G.	Good	Fair	Poor
225	200	175	150	100	75

Scout Carbine

This is a muzzleloading carbine of .50 or .54 caliber with an inline ignition system. Offered with either walnut stock or composite stock (first offered in 1993) it is fitted with a 21" round barrel. Adjustable rear sight and fixed blade front sight. Brass barrel band and trigger guard on walnut stock and blued barrel band and trigger guard on composite stock model. Weighs about 7 lbs. 4 oz. Discontinued.

Walnut stock

NIB	Exc.	V.G.	Good	Fair	Poor
325	275	200	150	100	75

Composite stock

NIB	Exc.	V.G.	Good	Fair	Poor
250	225	175	150	100	75

Scout Rifle

Similar to the Scout Carbine but fitted with a 24" stepped half-round, half-octagonal barrel. Weight is approximately 8 lbs. Discontinued.

Walnut Stock

NIB	Exc.	V.G.	Good	Fair	Poor
350	300	225	175	125	100

Composite Stock

NIB	Exc.	V.G.	Good	Fair	Poor
275	250	200	150	100	75

Scout Pistol

The same design as the Scout carbine this single-action pistol is available in .45, .50, or .54 caliber. Fitted with a 12" barrel, adjustable rear sight, and blued finish with brass trigger guard. Black walnut grips. Weighs 4 lbs. 6 oz. Discontinued.

NIB	Exc.	V.G.	Good	Fair	Poor
250	225	200	175	100	75

Fire Hawk Deluxe

Introduced in 1996 this is an in-line muzzleloader. Offered in either .50 or .54 caliber with blued or stainless steel. Semi-fancy checkered walnut stock has a cheekpiece. The round barrel is 24" long. Adjustable rear leaf sight with ramp style front bead. Weight is about 7 lbs.

NIB	Exc.	V.G.	Good	Fair	Poor
400	325	250	200		

Fire Hawk

Similar to the Deluxe Fire Hawk but with standard American walnut stock or composition stock.

NIB	Exc.	V.G.	Good	Fair	Poor
300	250	200	150		

Fire Hawk Thumbhole Stock

NIB	Exc.	V.G.	Good	Fair	Poor
325	275	225	175	—	—

Fire Hawk Camo Stock

NIB	Exc.	V.G.	Good	Fair	Poor
325	275	225	175	—	—

Fire Hawk Bantam

NIB	Exc.	V.G.	Good	Fair	Poor
275	225	175	125	—	—

Fire Hawk .32 & .58 caliber models

NIB	Exc.	V.G.	Good	Fair	Poor
300	250	200	150	—	—

Fire Storm

Offered as a percussion or flintlock and fitted with a 26" barrel chambered for .50 caliber. Black composite stock. Adjustable fiber optics rear sight. Weight is about 7 lbs. Introduced in 2000.

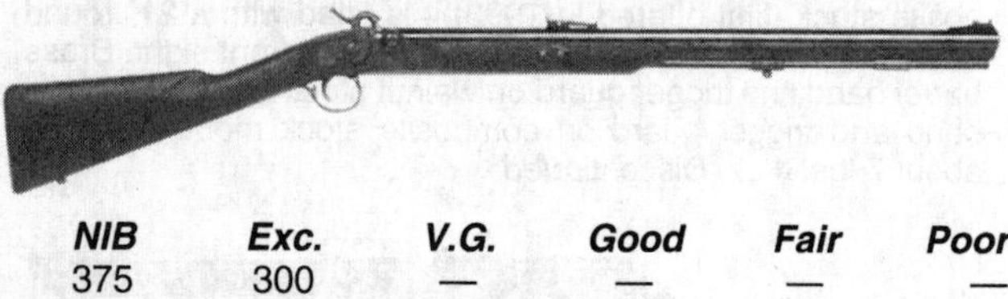

NIB	Exc.	V.G.	Good	Fair	Poor
375	300	—	—	—	—

Black Diamond

This is an in-line muzzleloading rifle with removable breech plug. Fitted with a 22.5" .50 caliber barrel. Stock is Rynite. Choice of blue or stainless steel. Introduced in 1998. Discontinued.

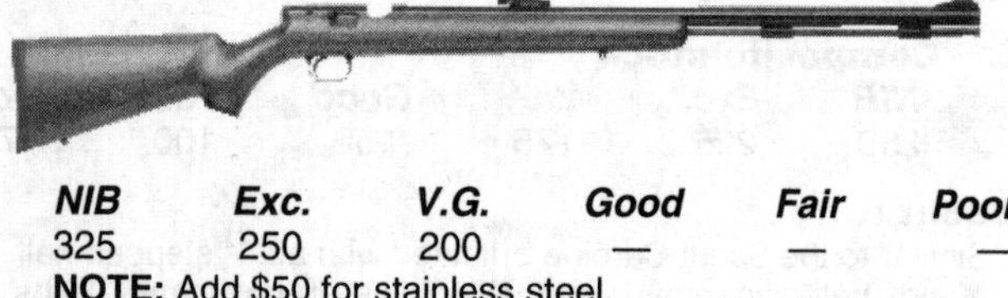

NIB	Exc.	V.G.	Good	Fair	Poor
325	250	200	—	—	—

NOTE: Add $50 for stainless steel.

Black Diamond XR

This .45 caliber or .50 caliber muzzleloader is fitted with a 26" round barrel. Offered with blued finish, camo, or stainless steel. Weight is about 6.75 lbs. Introduced in 2002. Discontinued.

NIB	Exc.	V.G.	Good	Fair	Poor
N/A	—	—	—	—	—

Triumph

Fifty-caliber toggle-breech inline muzzleloader with only four moving parts. Blued/synthetic, Weathershield/synthetic, or Weathershield/stainless finish. Introduced 2007.

NIB	Exc.	V.G.	Good	Fair	Poor
1895	—	—	—	—	—

THUNDER FIVE

MIL Inc.
Piney Flats, Tennessee

Five shot, double-action, 2" rifled barrel, matte finish, ambidextrous hammer block safety, Pachmayr grips, chambered in .45 Long Colt/.410 shotgun.

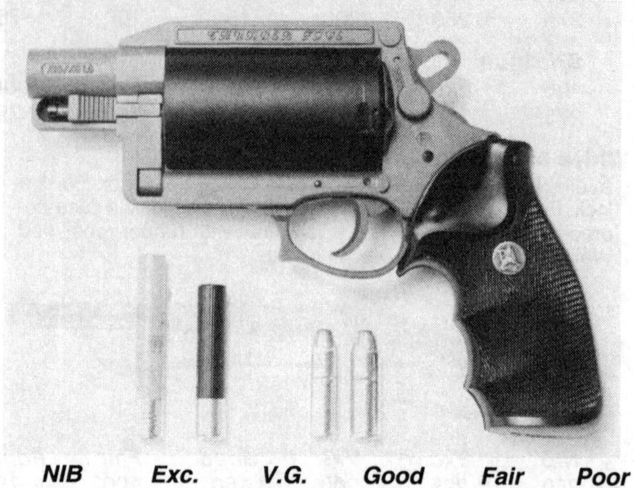

NIB	Exc.	V.G.	Good	Fair	Poor
425	345	250	200	150	100

TIKKA

Tikkakoski, Finland

RIFLES

Whitetail Hunter

This rifle features a hand checkered walnut stock with matte lacquer finish. These rifles are furnished without sights, but receiver is grooved. Magazine is detachable box type. Three action lengths are offered: short, medium, and long. In short action calibers the choices are: .17 Rem., .223, .22-250, .243, and .308 with 22.4" barrels and weight of 7 lbs. The medium action calibers are: .270 and .30-06 with 22.4" barrels and weight of 7.3 lbs. In long are the 7mm Rem. Mag., .300 and .338 Win. Mag. with 24.4" barrel and weight of 7.5 lbs.

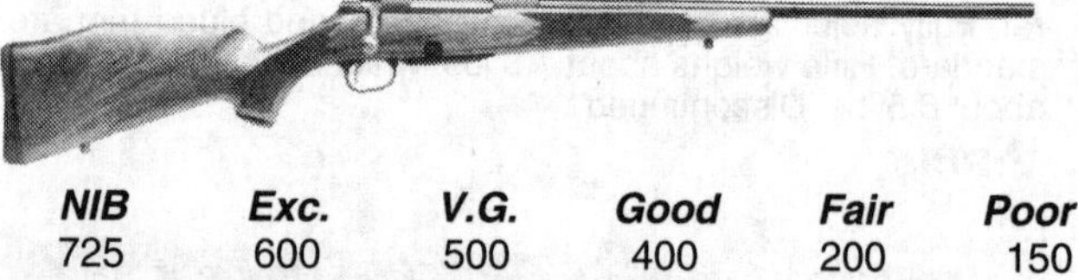

NIB	Exc.	V.G.	Good	Fair	Poor
725	600	500	400	200	150

Whitetail Hunter Deluxe

Similar to standard model above but furnished with cheekpiece, select walnut stock, rosewood pistol grip cap and forend tip. Metal surfaces are a highly polished blue. Same calibers as offered above.

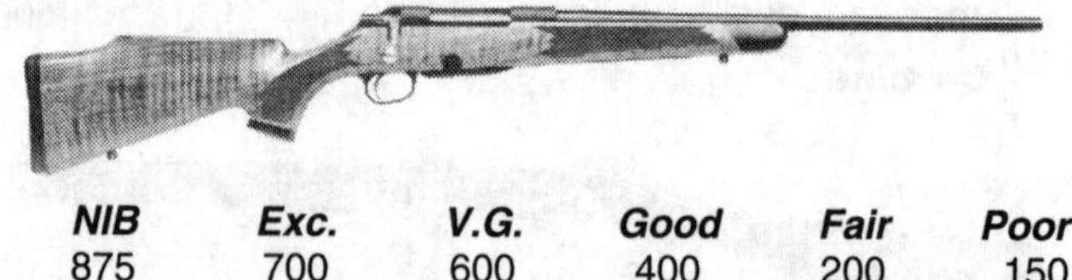

NIB	Exc.	V.G.	Good	Fair	Poor
875	700	600	400	200	150

Whitetail/Battue Rifle

This rifle was originally designed for the French market. The barrel is 20.5" long and is fitted with a raised quarter rib. The walnut is checkered with rubber recoil pad standard. A black fiberglass stock is offered as an option. In the medium action the only caliber is .308. In a long action the calibers are: .270, .30-06, 7mm Rem. Mag., .300 and .338 Win. Mag. All models weigh about 7 lbs. In 2000 this was offered in a left-hand model.

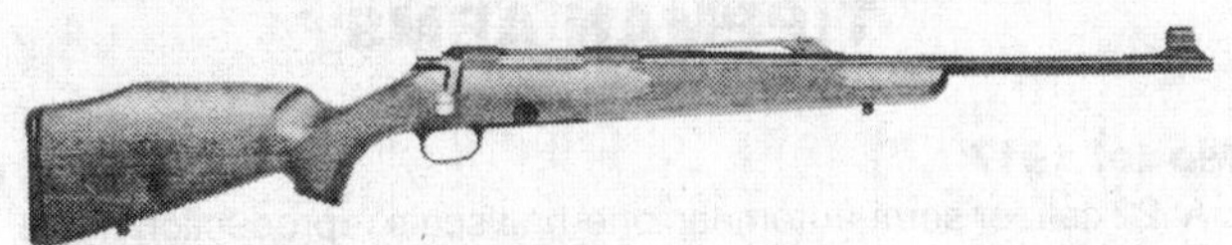

NIB	Exc.	V.G.	Good	Fair	Poor
600	475	375	—	—	—

NOTE: Add $50 for stainless steel finish. Add $20 for magnum calibers. Add $60 for left hand model.

Varmint/Continental Rifle

This model features a 23.5" heavy barrel without sights. The checkered walnut stock has a wide forend. Offered in .17 Rem., .223, .22-250, .243, and .308. Weighs approximately 8.5 lbs.

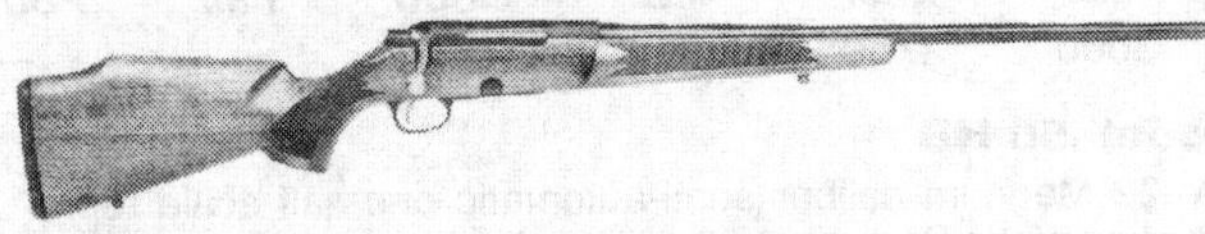

NIB	Exc.	V.G.	Good	Fair	Poor
700	550	—	—	—	—

Long Range Hunting

Same as above but in .25-06, .270, .7mm Mag., and .300 Win. Mag. Fitted with 26" heavy barrel.

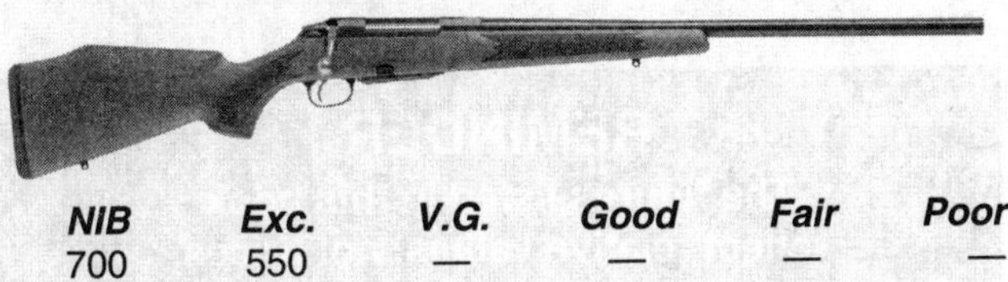

NIB	Exc.	V.G.	Good	Fair	Poor
700	550	—	—	—	—

Sporter

Introduced in 1998 this model features a select walnut stock, adjustable cheekpiece, adjustable buttplate, adjustable trigger. Comes without open sights. Detachable 5-round magazine. Chambered for .223, .22-250, and .308 calibers.

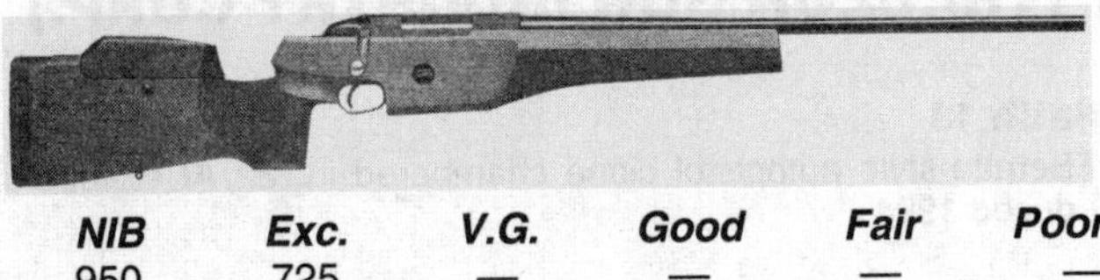

NIB	Exc.	V.G.	Good	Fair	Poor
950	725	—	—	—	—

T3 Hunter

Introduced in 2003 this bolt-action rifle features a hand-forged barrel and adjustable trigger. Offered in standard and magnum calibers from .223 to .338 Win. Mag. Walnut stock with recoil pad. Detachable magazine holds three rounds for all calibers except .223 (four). No sights. Barrel lengths are 22.5" and 24.25" for standard and magnum calibers respectively. Weight is about 6.75 lbs.

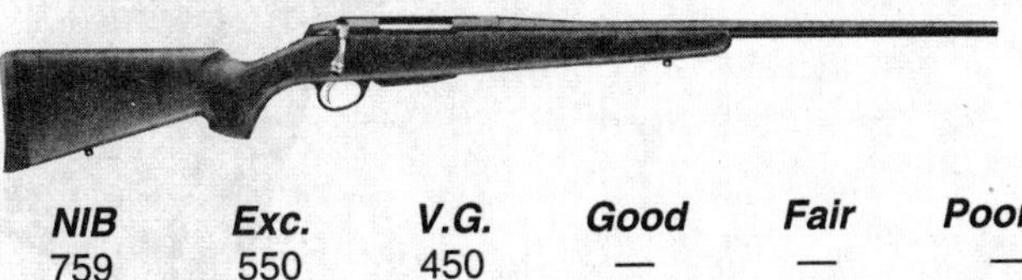

NIB	Exc.	V.G.	Good	Fair	Poor
759	550	450	—	—	—

T3 Lite

As above but fitted with a black synthetic stock with blued finish. Introduced in 2003.

NIB	Exc.	V.G.	Good	Fair	Poor
674	500	400	—	—	—

T3 Lite Stainless

As above but with stainless steel barrel and synthetic stock.

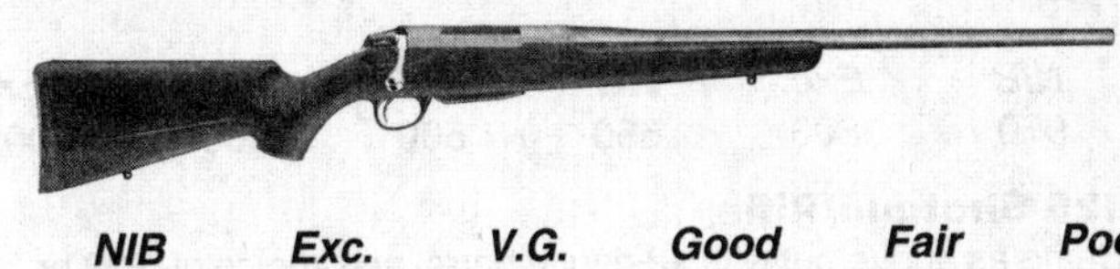

NIB	Exc.	V.G.	Good	Fair	Poor
690	500	—	—	—	—

T3 Big Boar

This bolt action rifle is chambered for the .308, .30-06, or .300 WSM cartridges. Fitted with a 19" barrel with no sights. Black synthetic stock with recoil pad. Blued finish. Magazine capacity is 3 rounds. Weight is about 6 lbs. Introduced in 2005.

NIB	Exc.	V.G.	Good	Fair	Poor
719	550	—	—	—	—

T3 Super Varmint

This bolt action model is chambered for the .223 Rem., .22-250 Rem., or the .308 cartridge. Stainless steel receiver and barrel with Picatinny rail on receiver. Barrel length is 23.3". Black synthetic stock has adjustable comb. Adjustable trigger. Detachable magazine. Introduced in 2005.

NIB	Exc.	V.G.	Good	Fair	Poor
1668	1250	—	—		

T3 Varmint

Chambered for the .223, .22-250, and .308 cartridges. Fitted with a 23.3" barrel with no sights. Synthetic stock with blued finish. Adjustable trigger. Rubber recoil pad.

NIB	Exc.	V.G.	Good	Fair	Poor
839	625	500	—	—	—

NOTE: Add $70 for stainless steel version.

T3 Tactical

Introduced in 2004 this rifle is chambered for the .223 or .308 cartridge. Fitted with a 20" barrel with muzzlebrake. Black synthetic varmint-style stock with adjustable cheekpiece. Detachable magazine capacity is 5 rounds. Picatinny rail on receiver top.

NIB	Exc.	V.G.	Good	Fair	Poor
1440	1050	700	—	—	—

Tikka Target

This bolt-action rifle is chambered for the .223, .22-250, 7mm-08 Rem., .308 Win., and the 6.5x55 Swedish Mauser cartridge. Fitted with a 23.25" barrel and adjustable walnut target stock, the trigger is adjustable for weight. No sights. Weight is about 9 lbs.

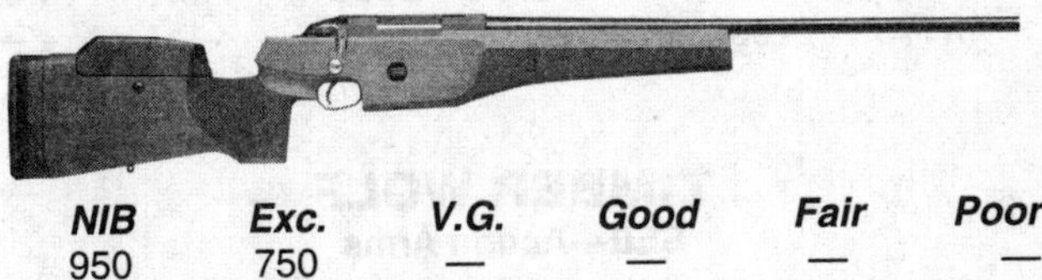

NIB	Exc.	V.G.	Good	Fair	Poor
950	750	—	—	—	—

SHOTGUNS/DOUBLE RIFLES (FORMERLY VALMET)

Tikka, Valmet and Sako have been merged into one company, SAKO Ltd. These firearms are now manufactured in Italy under the brand name Tikka. Parts are interchangeable between the Valmet guns, made in Finland, and the Tikka guns, made in Italy.

412S Shotgun

This over-and-under shotgun is available in 12 gauge only with 26" or 28" barrels. The stock is checkered European walnut. Weighs about 7.25 lbs.

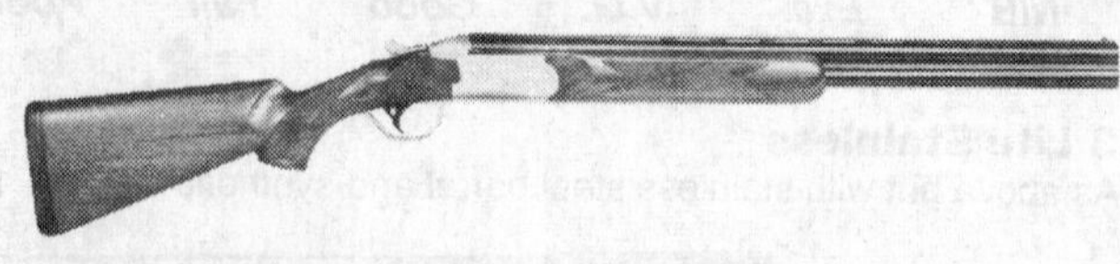

NIB	Exc.	V.G.	Good	Fair	Poor
950	800	650	500	300	200

412S Shotgun/Rifle

Same as above but with 12 gauge barrel and choice of .222 or .308 barrel. Barrel length is 24" and weighs 8 lbs.

NIB	Exc.	V.G.	Good	Fair	Poor
1000	850	700	500	300	200

412S Double Rifle

Same as above but fitted with a 24" over-and-under rifle barrel in 9.3x74R. Weighs about 8.5 lbs.

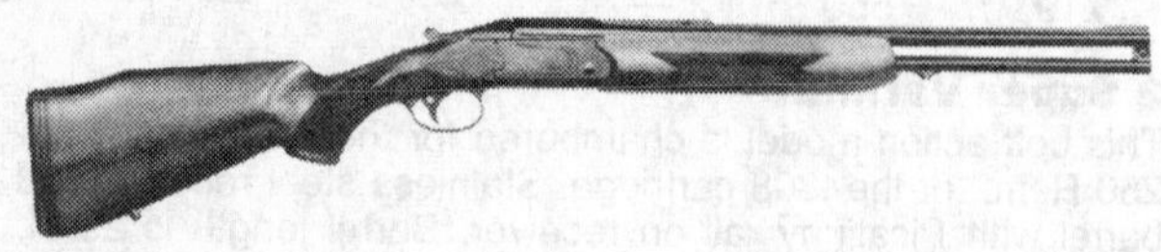

NIB	Exc.	V.G.	Good	Fair	Poor
1150	950	750	500	300	200

412S Sporting Clays

Introduced in 1993 this model is offered in 12 gauge with 28" barrels with choke tubes.

NIB	Exc.	V.G.	Good	Fair	Poor
1000	850	700	500	300	200

512S Field Grade

Introduced in 2000 this over-and-under gun is chambered for the 12 gauge 3" shell and fitted with either a 26" or 28" choke tube barrels.

NIB	Exc.	V.G.	Good	Fair	Poor
1125	850	—	—	—	—

NOTE: For shotgun/rifle barrel sets add $650 per set.

512S Sporting Clays

This 12 gauge 3" model is fitted with a 30" barrel with choke tubes.

NIB	Exc.	V.G.	Good	Fair	Poor
1175	900	—	—	—	—

TIMBER WOLF

SEE—Action Arms

TIPPING & LAWDEN

Birmingham, England

Thomas Revolver

A .320, .380, or .450 double-action revolver with a 4.5" barrel and 5-shot cylinder, utilizing a cartridge extraction system designed by J. Thomas of Birmingham in which the barrel and cylinder may be moved forward. Manufactured from 1870 to 1877.

Exc.	V.G.	Good	Fair	Poor
—	—	950	400	175

TIPPMAN ARMS

Fort Wayne, Indiana

Model 1917

A .22 caliber semi-automatic one-half scale reproduction of the Browning Model 1917 water-cooled machine gun. Barrel length 10". A tripod was sold with this model. Manufactured in 1986 and 1987.

NIB	Exc.	V.G.	Good	Fair	Poor
5750	5250	—	—	—	—

Model 1919 A-4

A .22 caliber semi-automatic one-half scale reproduction of the Browning Model 1919 A-4 machine gun. Barrel length 11" and furnished with a tripod. Manufactured in 1986 and 1987.

NIB	Exc.	V.G.	Good	Fair	Poor
3000	2750	—	—	—	—

Model .50 HB

A .22 Magnum caliber semi-automatic one-half scale reproduction of the Browning .50 caliber machine gun. Barrel length 18.25", furnished with a tripod. Manufactured in 1986 and 1987.

NIB	Exc.	V.G.	Good	Fair	Poor
6000	5500	—	—	—	—

REMINDER

The figures listed in this book reflect relative values, not prices. Only the buyer and seller can determine price.

TISAS (TRABZON GUN INDUSTRY CORP.)

Trabzon, Turkey

Fatih 13

Beretta-style autopistol clone chambered in .32 ACP. Introduced 1994.

NIB	Exc.	V.G.	Good	Fair	Poor
300	—	—	—	—	—

Kanuni 16

Single-/double-action autopistol chambered in 9mm Parabellum with 15- or 17-shot capacity. Black, chrome or chrome/gold finish. Introduced 1999.

NIB	Exc.	V.G.	Good	Fair	Poor
325	—	—	—	—	—

Kanuni s

Lightweight version of Kanuni 16. Black, chrome or chrome/black finish. Introduced 2000.

NIB	Exc.	V.G.	Good	Fair	Poor
325	—	—	—	—	—

Zigana M16

Single-/double-action autopistol chambered in 9mm Parabellum with 15- or 17-shot capacity and 5" barrel. Introduced 2000.

NIB	Exc.	V.G.	Good	Fair	Poor
395	—	—	—	—	—

Zigana K

Compact version of Zigana M16 with 4" barrel. Introduced 2002.

NIB	Exc.	V.G.	Good	Fair	Poor
395	—	—	—	—	—

Zigana T

Longer (5.5") barrel version of Zigana M16. Introduced 2002.

NIB	Exc.	V.G.	Good	Fair	Poor
395	—	—	—	—	—

Zigana Sport

Compensated version of Zigana K with 4.5" barrel. Introduced 2005.

NIB	Exc.	V.G.	Good	Fair	Poor
400	—	—	—	—	—

Zigana C45

Similar to Zigana M16 but chambered in .45 ACP with 4.75" barrel. Introduced 2005.

NIB	Exc.	V.G.	Good	Fair	Poor
400	—	—	—	—	—

Zigana F

"Meltdown" version of Zigana M16 with radiused edges and improved ergonomics. Introduced 2007.

NIB	Exc.	V.G.	Good	Fair	Poor
400	—	—	—	—	—

TOBIN ARMS MANUFACTURING CO.

Norwich, Connecticut and Windsor, Ontario, Canada

The Tobin Arms Manufacturing Co. operated from about 1905 to 1925 making an exposed hammer double and two hammerless models in four grades. The "Simplex" was cleverly designed (based on a patent by C.M. Wollam) side plated double-barrel internal hammer shotgun which resembled the Hopkins and Allen guns of that time. Some may have been private branded. Most of the Tobin doubles were made in Norwich, Conn., and are so marked. After 1909 operations were transferred to Windsor, Ont., Canada, and some guns will be found with that address. Tobin guns are not often seen by collectors and are highly prized because of their relative rarity and because they were considered good guns by top dealers such as C.J. Godfrey Co. of New York City and Iver Johnson Sporting Goods of Boston. Values depend on condition and range from $200 in poor condition to $1000 and up for engraved versions in good to very good condition.

TODD, GEORGE H.

Montgomery, Alabama

Rifled Musket

A .58 caliber single-shot percussion rifle with a 40" barrel and full length stock secured by three barrel bands. Barrel and lock finished in the bright, brass furniture and walnut stock. The lock marked "George H. Todd/ Montgomery, Ala." Very Rare.

Exc.	V.G.	Good	Fair	Poor
—	—	N/A	N/A	—

TOKAREV

Soviet State Arsenals

NOTE: For history, technical data, descriptions, photos, and prices see the *Standard Catalog of Military Firearms* under Russia.

TOMISKA, ALOIS

Pilsen, Czechoslovakia

Little Tom

A 6.35mm or 7.65mm caliber semi-automatic pistol with a 2.5" barrel. The slide marked "Alois Tomiska Plzen Patent Little Tom" and the grips inlaid with a medallion bearing the monogram "AT." Blued with checkered walnut grips. Manufactured from 1908 to 1918. Subsequently produced by the Wiener Waffenfabrik.

Exc.	V.G.	Good	Fair	Poor
550	425	350	250	125

TORKELSON ARMS CO.

Harfield, Warren, and Worcester, Massachusetts

Double-Barrel Shotguns

Reinhard T. Torkelson's company made double-barrel, boxlock, side-by-side, hammerless shotguns in four models at several locations between 1885 and 1910. He worked with Iver Johnson at Fitchburg, Mass., and also built guns carrying the Lovell (Boston) name. His "New Worcester" marked guns are quite common. they were sold by Sears and other large and well known houses.

Exc.	V.G.	Good	Fair	Poor
600	300	200	150	100

TRADEWINDS

Tacoma, Washington

Model H-170

A 12 gauge semi-automatic shotgun with a 26" or 28" ventilated rib barrel and 5-shot tubular magazine. Blued, anodized alloy receiver and walnut stock.

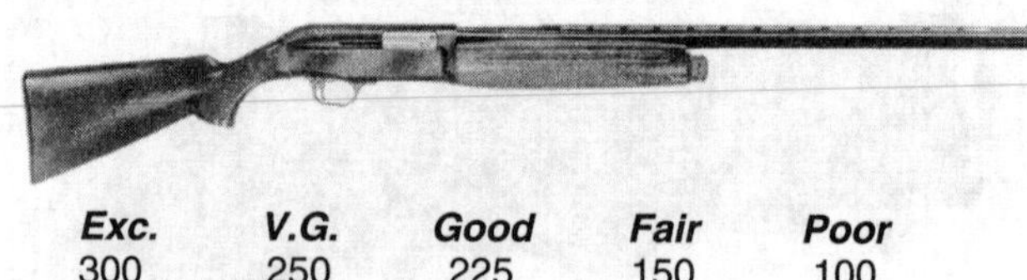

Exc.	V.G.	Good	Fair	Poor
300	250	225	150	100

Model 260-A

A .22 caliber semi-automatic rifle with a 22.5" barrel, open sights and 5-shot magazine. Blued with a walnut stock.

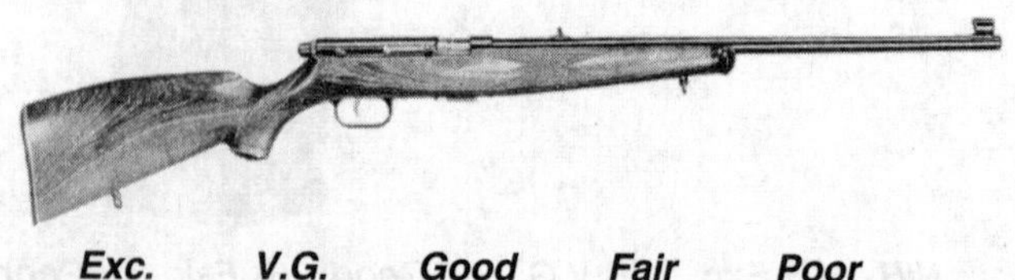

Exc.	V.G.	Good	Fair	Poor
200	175	125	100	75

Model 311-A

A .22 caliber bolt-action rifle with a 22.5" barrel, open sights and a 5-shot magazine. Blued with a walnut stock.

Exc.	V.G.	Good	Fair	Poor
175	150	100	75	50

Model 5000 "Husky"

A centerfire bolt-action rifle with a 24" barrel, adjustable sights and 4-shot magazine. Blued with a walnut stock.

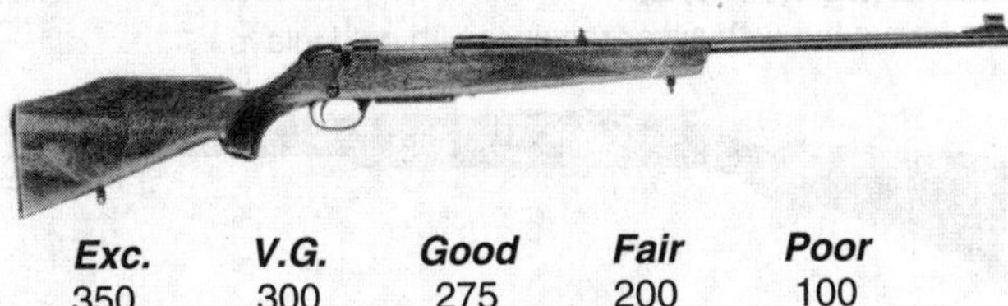

Exc.	V.G.	Good	Fair	Poor
350	300	275	200	100

TRADITIONS

Old Saybrook, Connecticut

OVER-AND-UNDER SHOTGUNS

NOTE: These shotguns are built by the Italian firm of Fausti Stefano and Emil Rizzini.

Hunter

Introduced in 2001 this model features a choice of 12 or 20 gauge chambers with 26" or 28" vent rib barrels with fixed chokes. Single-selective trigger. Extractors. Checkered walnut stock. Blued frame and barrels. Black rubber recoil pad. Weight is about 7.25 lbs. for 12 gauge and 6.75 lbs. for 20 gauge.

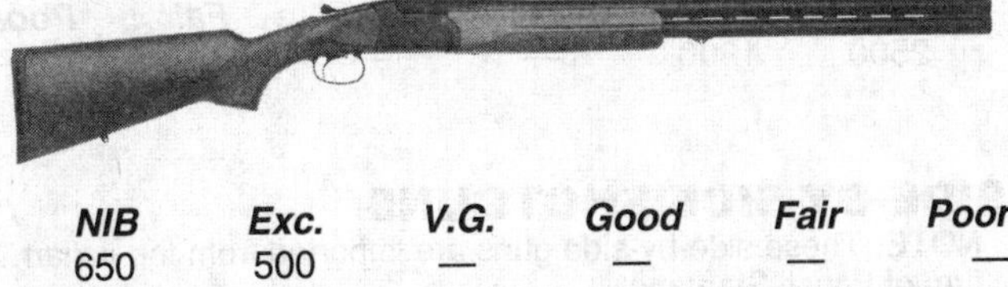

NIB	Exc.	V.G.	Good	Fair	Poor
650	500	—	—	—	—

Field I

This model is offered in 12, 20 and 28 gauge as well as .410 bore. Barrel lengths are 26". Fixed chokes. Single-selective trigger and extractors. Coin finish engraved receiver. Checkered walnut stock. Black rubber recoil pad. Weight is similar to the Hunter model with the .410 bore weighing about 6.5 lbs.

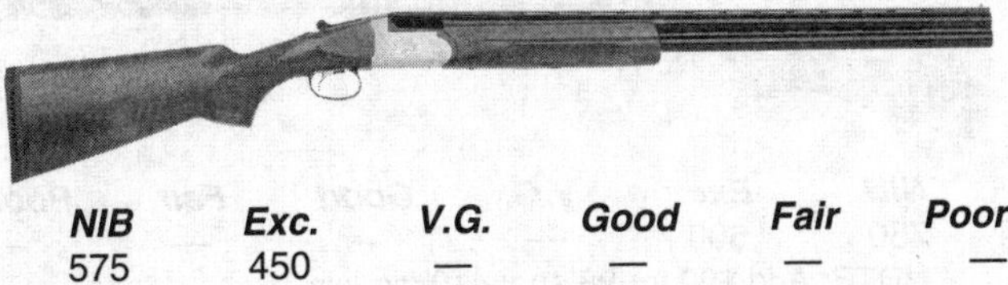

NIB	Exc.	V.G.	Good	Fair	Poor
575	450	—	—	—	—

Field II

Similar to the Field I but with the additional choice of a 16 gauge with 28" barrels. This model also features screw-in chokes and automatic ejectors.

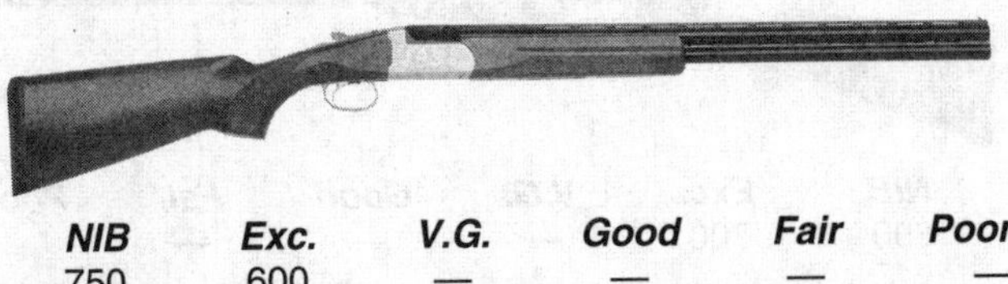

NIB	Exc.	V.G.	Good	Fair	Poor
750	600	—	—	—	—

Field II Combo

This model features a 20 gauge and .410 bore two barrel set. Both barrels are 26" with fixed chokes. Checkered walnut stock. Weight is about 6 lbs. Introduced in 2004.

NIB	Exc.	V.G.	Good	Fair	Poor
1600	1250	—	—	—	—

Field III Gold

Similar to the other Field series of guns but offered in 12 gauge only with 26" or 28" barrels. Select oil finish walnut stock. Engraved receiver with gold pheasants and woodcock.

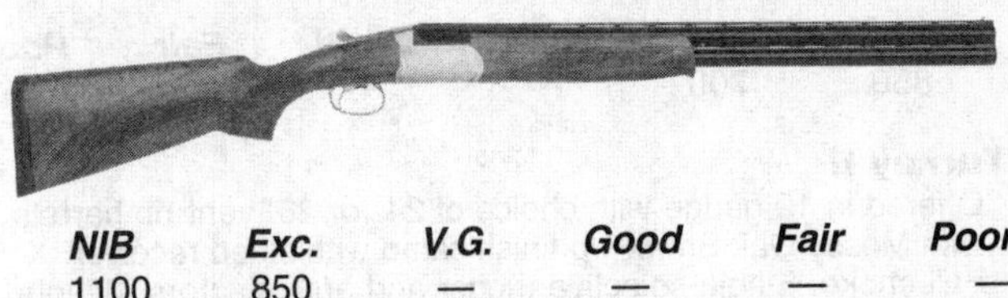

NIB	Exc.	V.G.	Good	Fair	Poor
1100	850	—	—	—	—

Upland II

Offered in both 12 and 20 gauge with 26" barrels in 12 gauge and 24" or 26" barrels in 20 gauge. Straight grip walnut stock. Engraved blued receiver. Schnabel forend. Choke tubes. Single-selective trigger and auto ejectors. Weight for 12 gauge gun is about 7.25 lbs. and for 20 gauge about 6.25 lbs.

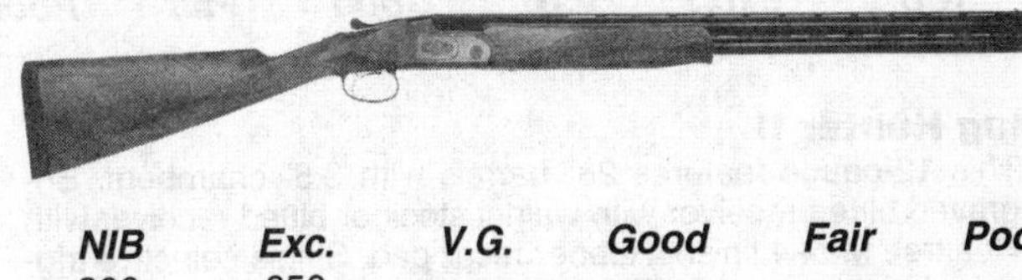

NIB	Exc.	V.G.	Good	Fair	Poor
800	650	—	—	—	—

Upland III

Introduced in 2001 this model features a 12 gauge gun with 26" vent rib barrels. High grade checkered walnut stock with hand engraved receiver with gold. Schnabel forend. Single-selective trigger and auto ejectors standard. Screw-in chokes. Black rubber recoil pad. Weight is about 7.25 lbs.

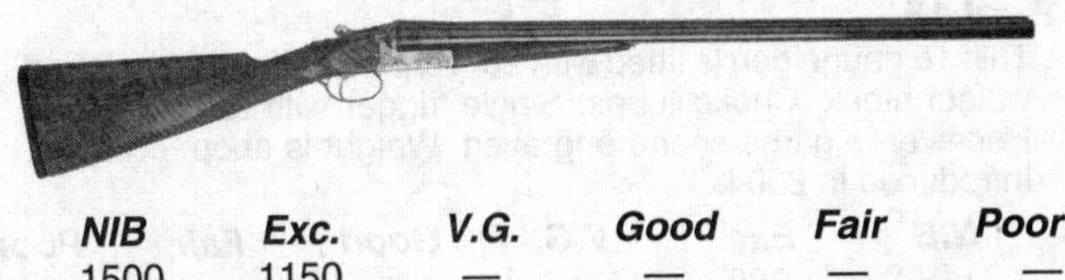

NIB	Exc.	V.G.	Good	Fair	Poor
1500	1150	—	—	—	—

Sporting Clay II

This 12 gauge gas operated model has either 28" or 30" vent rib ported barrels. Screw-in extended choke tubes. Checkered walnut stock with blued receiver and barrels. Weight is about 8 lbs.

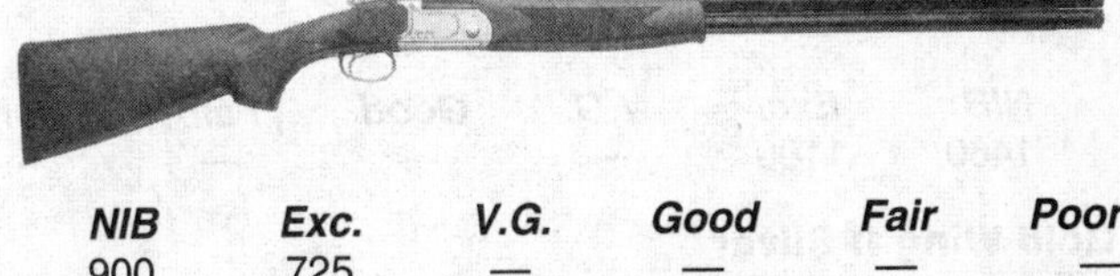

NIB	Exc.	V.G.	Good	Fair	Poor
900	725	—	—	—	—

Sporting Clay III

This model features a choice of 12 or 20 gauge with 28" or 30" vent rib barrels. High grade checkered walnut stock. Choke tubes. Weight is about 8.5 lbs. for 12 gauge and 8.25 lbs. for 20 gauge.

NIB	Exc.	V.G.	Good	Fair	Poor
1660	1250	—	—	—	—

NOTE: Add $200 for 20 gauge guns.

Waterfowl II

Introduced in 2001 this 12 gauge model is fitted with 28" vent rib barrels and 3.5" chambers. Finish on stock and barrels is Advantage Wetlands camo. Blued engraved receiver. Recoil pad. Single-selective trigger with auto ejectors. Weight is about 7.25 lbs.

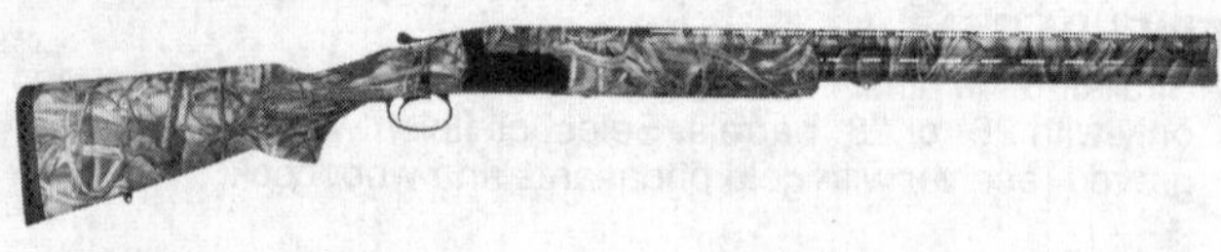

NIB	Exc.	V.G.	Good	Fair	Poor
850	700	—	—	—	—

Turkey II

Offered in 12 gauge with choice of 24" or 26" vent rib barrels with Mossy Oak Break-Up finish camo with blued receiver. X-Full choke. Single-selective trigger and auto ejectors. Weight is about 7 lbs.

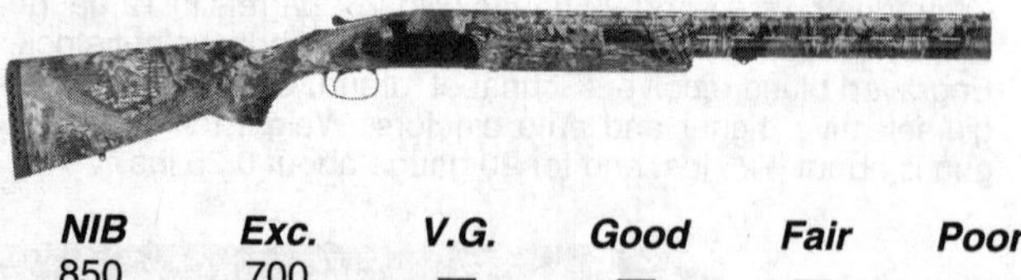

NIB	Exc.	V.G.	Good	Fair	Poor
850	700	—	—	—	—

Mag Hunter II

This 12-gauge features 28" barrels with 3.5" chambers. Engraved blued receiver with walnut stock or blued receiver with Realtree Max-4 finish. Rubber recoil pad. Single selective trigger with auto ejectors. Screw-in chokes. Weight is about 7 lbs. Add 10 percent for camo model. MSRP: 1169

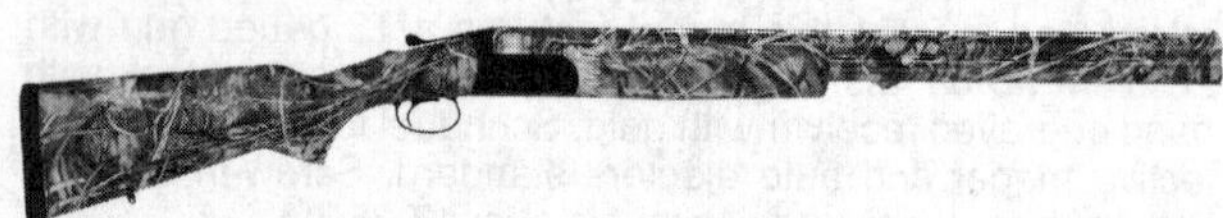

Real 16

This 16 gauge gun is fitted with 26" vent rib barrels. Checkered walnut stock. Choke tubes. Single trigger with auto ejectors. Receiver is game scene engraved. Weight is about 6.75 lbs. Introduced in 2004.

NIB	Exc.	V.G.	Good	Fair	Poor
1180	900	—	—	—	—

Real 16 Gold

As above but with gold-filled birds on receiver.

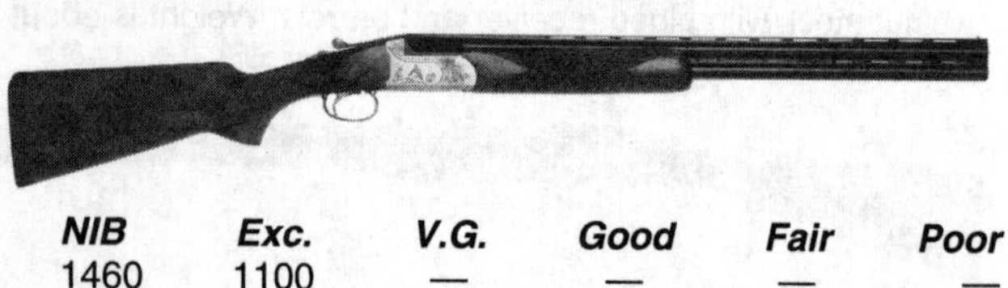

NIB	Exc.	V.G.	Good	Fair	Poor
1460	1100	—	—	—	—

Gold Wing II Silver

Chambered for the 12 gauge 3" shell and fitted with 28" vent rib barrels with choke tubes. Single trigger and auto ejectors. Receiver is engraved with game scenes. High grade walnut stock with oil finish. Weight is about 7.5 lbs.

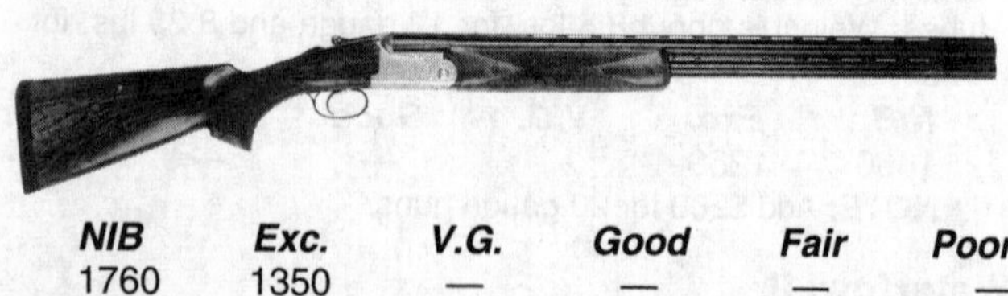

NIB	Exc.	V.G.	Good	Fair	Poor
1760	1350	—	—	—	—

Gold Wing III

As above but with case colored receiver with gold inlays.

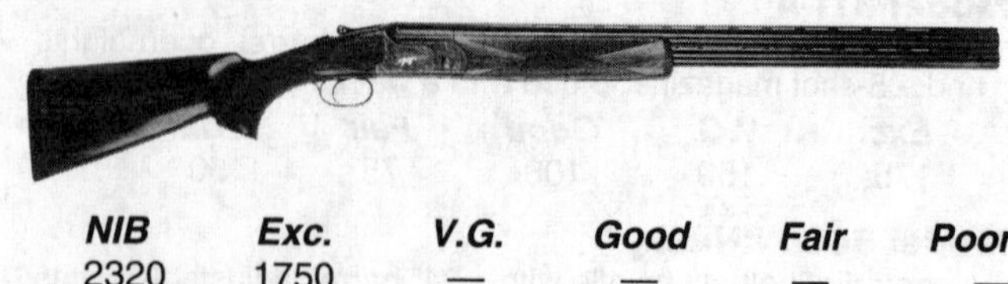

NIB	Exc.	V.G.	Good	Fair	Poor
2320	1750	—	—	—	—

Gold Wing III Silver

As above but with silver receiver with gold inlays.

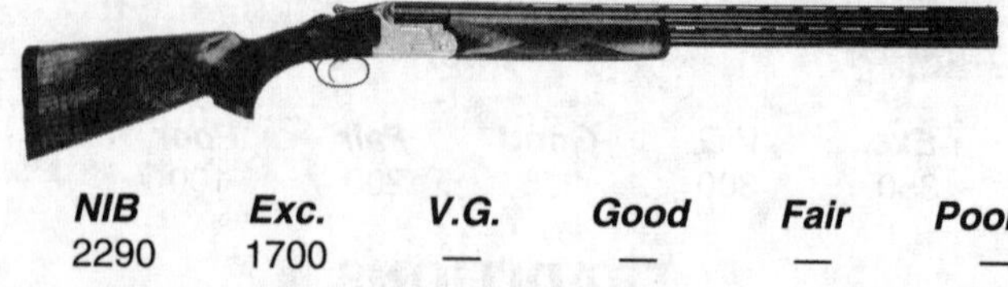

NIB	Exc.	V.G.	Good	Fair	Poor
2290	1700	—	—	—	—

Gold Wing SL III

As above but with case colored side plates and gold inlays.

NIB	Exc.	V.G.	Good	Fair	Poor
2540	1900	—	—	—	—

Gold Wing SL III Silver

As above but with silver side plates and gold inlays.

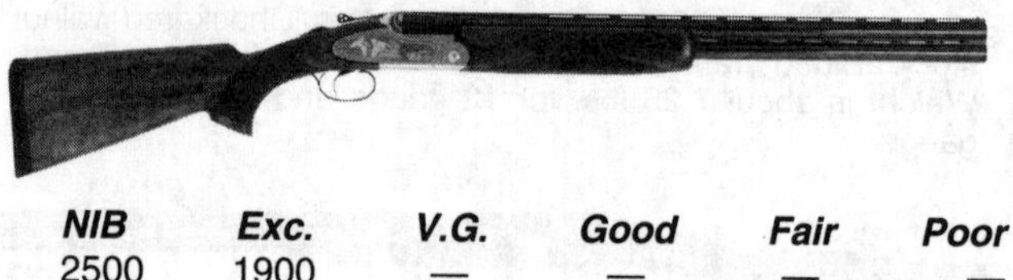

NIB	Exc.	V.G.	Good	Fair	Poor
2500	1900	—	—	—	—

SIDE-BY-SIDE SHOTGUNS

NOTE: These side-by-side guns are imported from the Italian firm of Fausti Stanfano.

Elite I DT

This model is offered in 12, 20, and 28 gauge as well as .410 bore. All gauges are fitted wtih 26" barrels with fixed chokes. Double triggers and extractors. Walnut stock. Weight about 6 lbs.

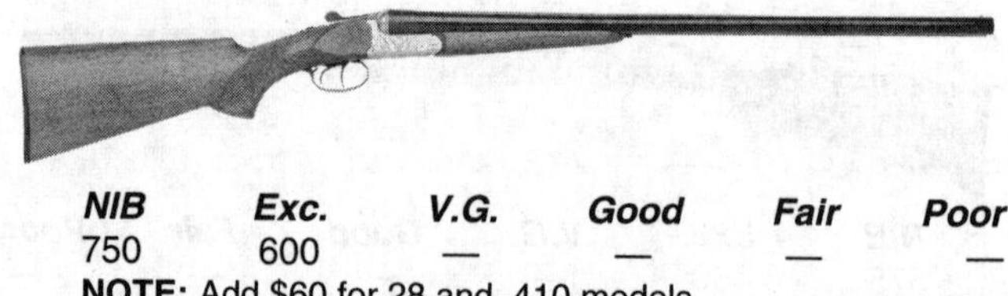

NIB	Exc.	V.G.	Good	Fair	Poor
750	600	—	—	—	—

NOTE: Add $60 for 28 and .410 models.

Elite I ST

Same as above but with single-selective trigger.

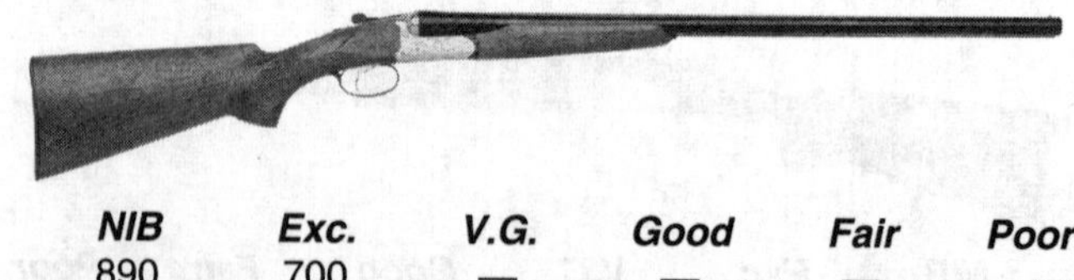

NIB	Exc.	V.G.	Good	Fair	Poor
890	700	—	—	—	—

Elite Hunter

Introduced in 2001 this model features either a 12 or 20 gauge gun with 26" barrels with screw-in chokes. Walnut stock with beavertail forend. Single non-selective trigger. Weight is about 6.5 lbs.

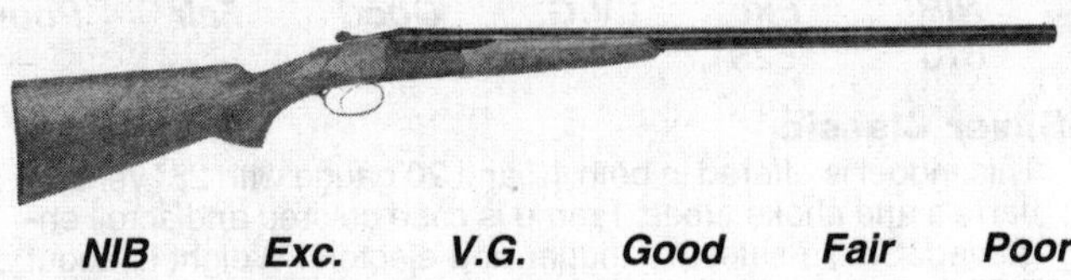

NIB	Exc.	V.G.	Good	Fair	Poor
950	750	—	—	—	—

Elite Field III ST

Introduced in 2001 this model is offered in either 28 or .410 bore with 26" barrels. High grade walnut stock with straight grip. Fixed chokes. Engraved receiver with gold. Weight is about 6.25 lbs.

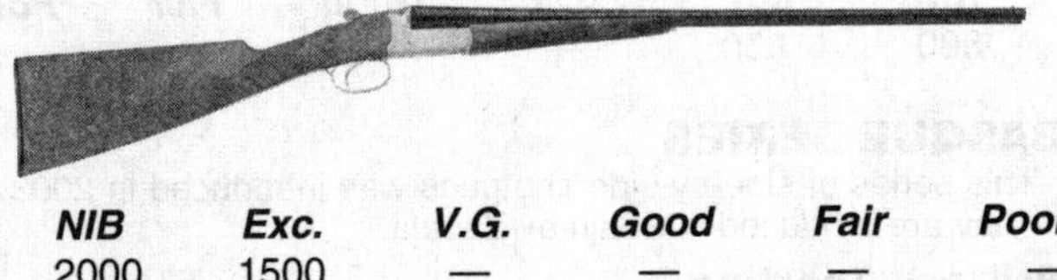

NIB	Exc.	V.G.	Good	Fair	Poor
2000	1500	—	—	—	—

Uplander II Silver

Chambererd for the 12 gauge with 28" barrels or 20 gauge with 26" barrels. Choke tubes. Silver receiver with light scroll engraving. Checkered stock with high grade walnut. Straight grip. Single trigger and auto ejectors. Weight is about 6.75 lbs.

NIB	Exc.	V.G.	Good	Fair	Poor
2130	1575	—	—	—	—

Uplander III Silver

As above but with more extensive engraving with gold inlays.

NIB	Exc.	V.G.	Good	Fair	Poor
2890	2150	—	—	—	—

Uplander V Silver

As above but with sideplates, extensive engraving and gold inlays.

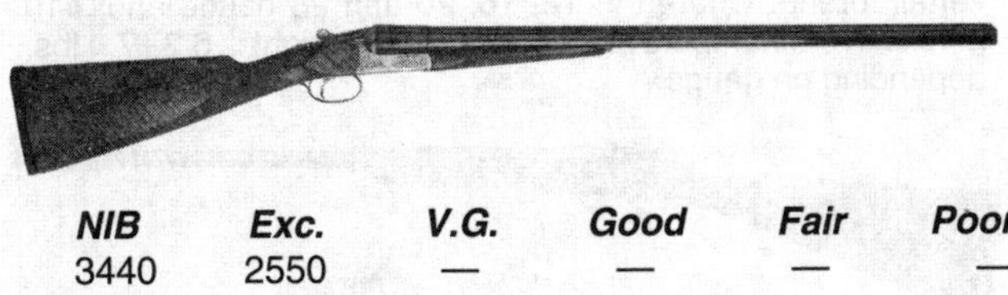

NIB	Exc.	V.G.	Good	Fair	Poor
3440	2550	—	—	—	—

SEMI-AUTOMATIC SHOTGUNS

ALS Field

Introduced in 2001 this model is offered in both 12 and 20 gauge with 24", 26", or 28" vent rib barrel. Walnut stock with black pad. Blued receiver and barrels. Screw-in chokes. Weight is about 6.25 lbs.

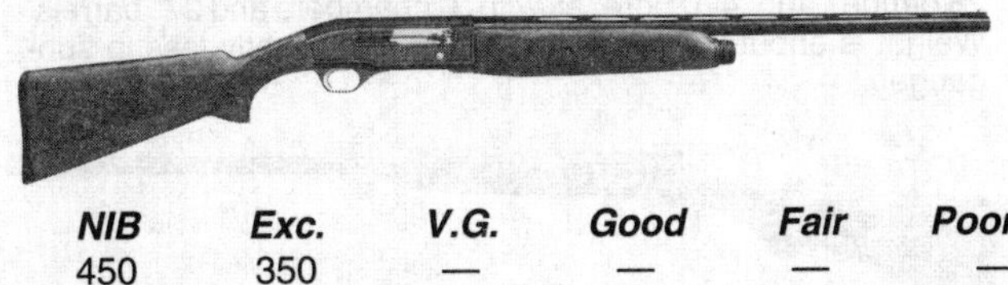

NIB	Exc.	V.G.	Good	Fair	Poor
450	350	—	—	—	—

ALS Hunter

Same as above but with synthetic stock with 26" or 28" barrels.

NIB	Exc.	V.G.	Good	Fair	Poor
425	325	—	—	—	—

ALS Waterfowl

This 12 gauge model has Advantage Wetlands camo and is fitted with a 28" barrel with screw-in chokes. Weight is about 6.5 lbs.

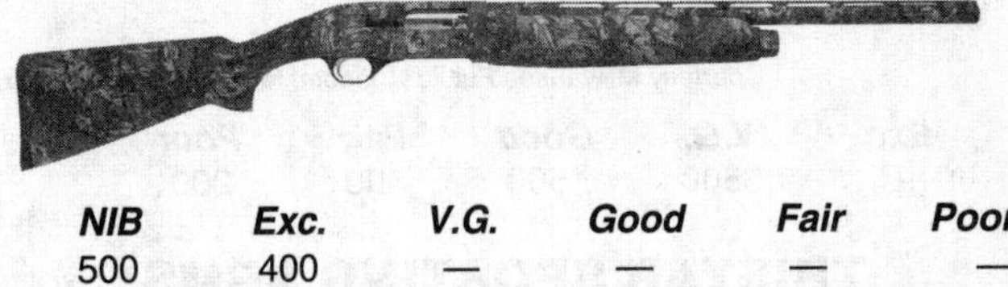

NIB	Exc.	V.G.	Good	Fair	Poor
500	400	—	—	—	—

ALS Turkey

Same as above but with 21" barrel and Mossy Oak Break-up camo. Weight is about 6 lbs.

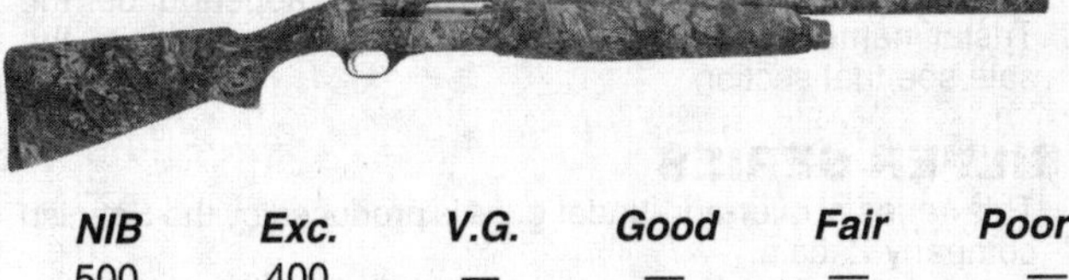

NIB	Exc.	V.G.	Good	Fair	Poor
500	400	—	—	—	—

TRANTER, WILLIAM

Birmingham, England

William Tranter produced a variety of revolvers on his own and a number of other makers produced revolvers based upon his designs. Consequently, "Tranter's Patent" is to be found on revolvers made by such firms as Deane, Adams and Deane, etc.

Courtesy Wallis & Wallis, Lewes, Sussex, England

Model 1872

A .38 caliber double-action revolver with a 6" octagonal barrel and 6-shot cylinder. Blued with walnut grips.

Exc.	V.G.	Good	Fair	Poor
—	2000	900	400	200

Model 1878

A .450 caliber double-action revolver with a 6" octagonal barrel. Blued with a walnut grip. Manufactured from 1878 to 1887.

Exc.	V.G.	Good	Fair	Poor
—	2500	1200	500	250

TRIPLETT & SCOTT/MERIDEN MANUFACTURING COMPANY

Meriden, Connecticut

Repeating Carbine

A .50 caliber carbine with either a 22" or 30" round barrel and a 7-shot magazine located in the butt. This model is loaded by turning the barrel until it comes in line with the magazine. Blued, case hardened with a walnut stock. Approximately 5,000 were made in 1864 and 1865.

Courtesy Milwaukee Public Museum, Milwaukee, Wisconsin

Exc.	V.G.	Good	Fair	Poor
—	3500	1500	500	200

TRISTAR SPORTING ARMS

N. Kansas City, Missouri

Tristar 300 series over-and-under guns are imported from Turkey. Tristar Nova series are imported from Italy.

NOTE: In 2000 Tristar bought American Arms. American Arms no longer exists but some of its models will appear under the Tristar name. For American Arms firearms built prior to the sale see that section.

SILVER SERIES

This series of over-and-under guns is produced by the Spanish company Zabala.

Silver Sporting

Offered in 12 gauge with 28" or 30" barrels with single-selective trigger, auto ejectors, choke tubes, ported barrels with target rib, checkered walnut stock with pistol grip and recoil pad.

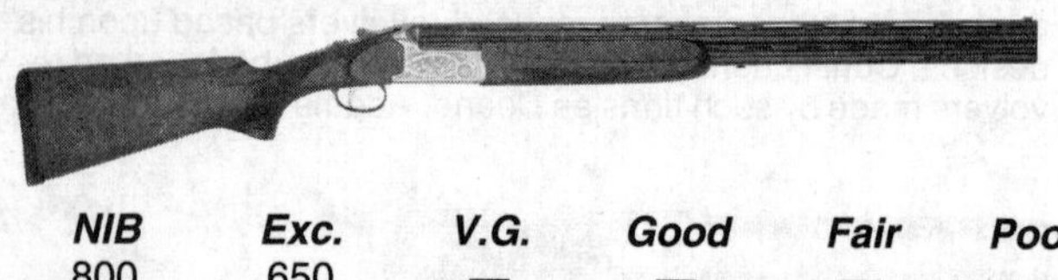

NIB	Exc.	V.G.	Good	Fair	Poor
800	650	—	—	—	—

Specialty Magnums

This is a 12 gauge magnum chambered for the 3.5" shell and fitted with a 28" barrel. Choke tubes. Checkered black walnut stock with pistol grip.

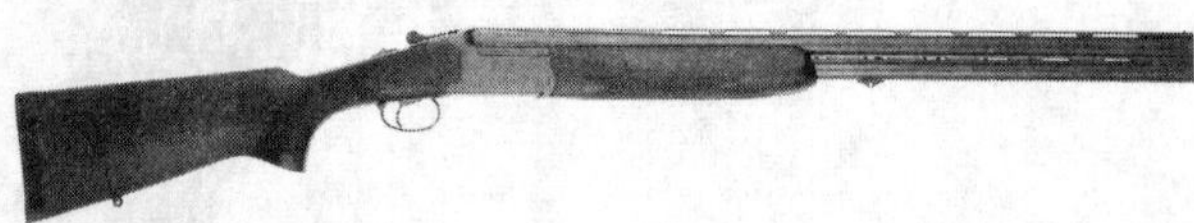

NIB	Exc.	V.G.	Good	Fair	Poor
645	500	—	—	—	—

NOTE: In 2003 a camo finish was offered for this model. Add $85 for camo.

Silver Hunter

Offered in both 12 and 20 gauge with 26" or 28" vent rib barrels with single-selective trigger, choke tubes, engraved receiver with silver finish. Checkered walnut stock with pistol grip.

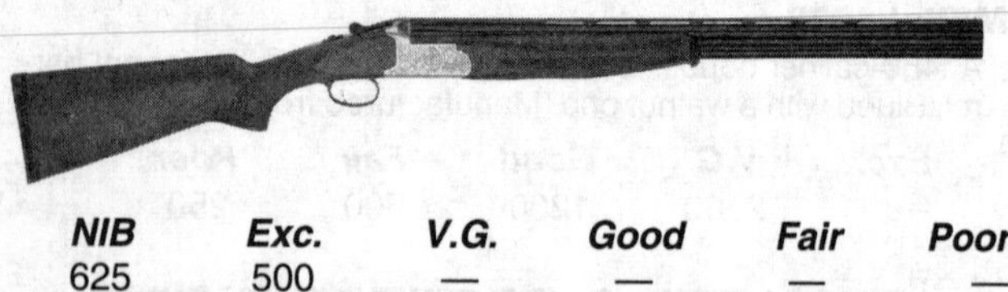

NIB	Exc.	V.G.	Good	Fair	Poor
625	500	—	—	—	—

Silver II

As above but also in 16 and 28 gauge as well as .410 bore. Fixed chokes for 16, 28, and .410 models.

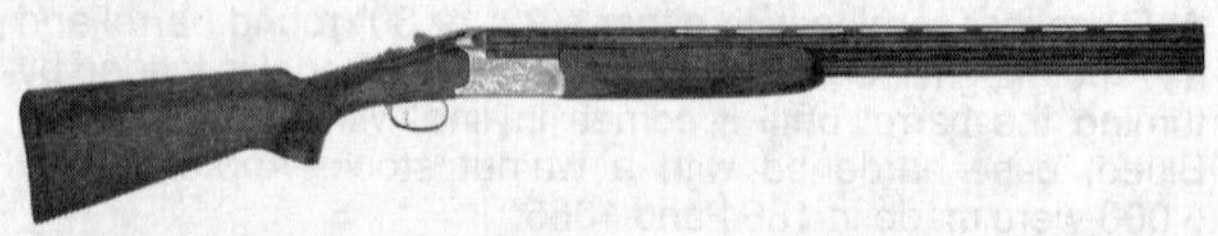

NIB	Exc.	V.G.	Good	Fair	Poor
670	525	—	—	—	—

Silver Classic

This model is offered in both 12 and 20 gauge with 28" vent rib barrels and choke tubes. Frame is case colored and scroll engraved. Single-selective trigger and ejectors. Weight is about 6.75 lbs.

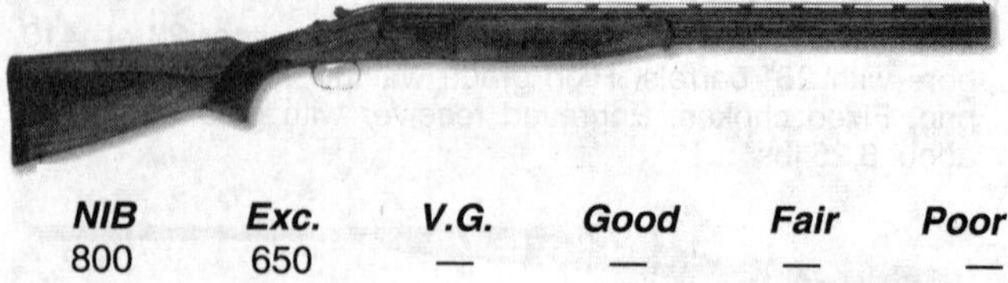

NIB	Exc.	V.G.	Good	Fair	Poor
800	650	—	—	—	—

BASQUE SERIES

This series of side-by-side shotguns was introduced in 2003. They are produced in Spain by Zabala.

Brittany Sporting

Offered in 12 and 20 gauge with 28" barrels with 3" chambers and choke tubes. The action is box lock with sideplates scroll engraved with case coloring. Semi-fancy checkered walnut stock with oil finish and pistol grip. Semi beavertail forend. Single-selective trigger and ejectors. Weight is around 6.75 lbs.

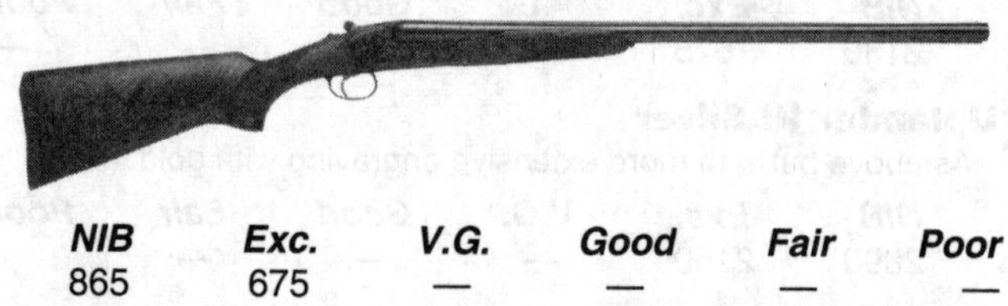

NIB	Exc.	V.G.	Good	Fair	Poor
865	675	—	—	—	—

Brittany

This model features a boxlock action with case-colored frame with scroll engraving. Straight grip walnut stock with semi-beavertail forend. Offered in 12, 16, 20 and 28 gauge and .410 bore with 3" chambers and choke tubes. Weight is 6.2 - 7.4 lbs. depending on gauge.

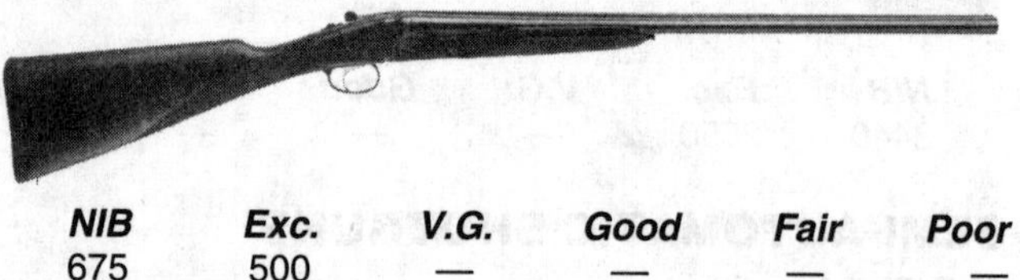

NIB	Exc.	V.G.	Good	Fair	Poor
675	500	—	—	—	—

Brittany Classic

Enhanced Brittany model features fancy walnut wood and rounded pistol grip, cut checkering, engraved case colored frame and auto selective ejectors. Available in 12, 16, 20 and 28 gauges and .410 bore, all with 3" chambers and 27" barrels. Weight is about 6.7 lbs. in 12 gauge and slightly less in subgauges.

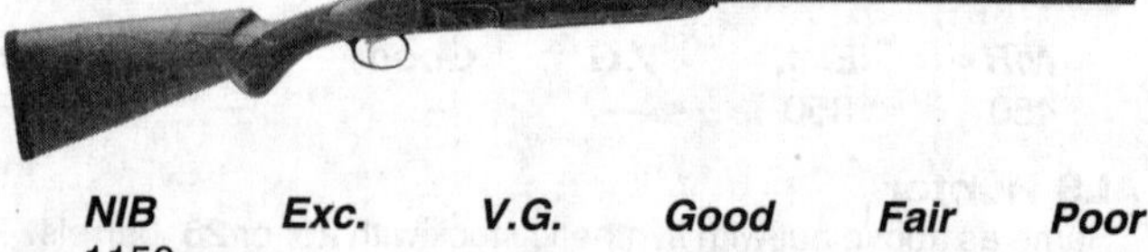

NIB	Exc.	V.G.	Good	Fair	Poor
1150	—	—	—	—	—

York

This side-by-side with blued engraved receiver and 3" chambers comes in 12 and 20 gauge with 26" or 28" barrels. Walnut, pistol grip stock and rubber recoil pad.

NIB	Exc.	V.G.	Good	Fair	Poor
515	—	—	—	—	—

Hunter Lite

Over-and-under with silver alloy engraved frame, 3" chambers, extractors, choke tubes and walnut pistol grip stock and forearm. 20-gauge with 26" barrels weighs 5.4 lbs.; 12 gauge with 28" barrels weighs 6 lbs.

NIB	Exc.	V.G.	Good	Fair	Poor
400	—	—	—	—	—

Hunter

Similar to Hunter Lite But with blued steel frame.

NIB	Exc.	V.G.	Good	Fair	Poor
375	—	—	—	—	—

Field Hunter

Based on the Hunter, this model includes selective auto ejectors and five choke tubes.

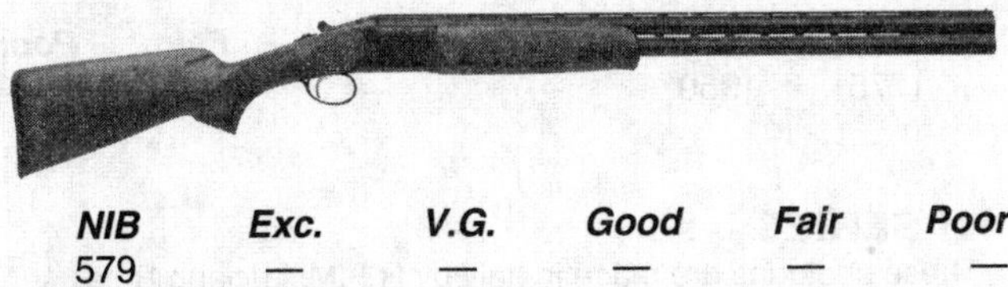

NIB	Exc.	V.G.	Good	Fair	Poor
579	—	—	—	—	—

Gentry/Gentry Coach

This model is offered in 12, 16, 20 or 28 gauge and .410 bore in the Gentry and 12 and 20 gauge in the Gentry Coach. Barrel length are 28" for the Gentry (26" for 28 and .410) and 20" for the Gentry Coach. Boxlock action with engraved antique silver finish. Walnut stock with pistol grip. Choke tubes. Single-selective trigger. Weight is about 6.5 lbs. for Gentry and Gentry Coach depending on gauge.

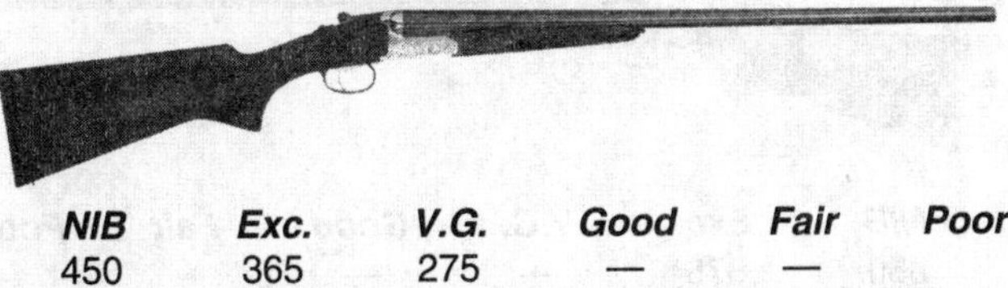

NIB	Exc.	V.G.	Good	Fair	Poor
450	365	275	—	—	

Derby Classic

This model features a sidelock frame and action that is engraved and case colored. Offered in 12 gauge with fixed chokes in modified and full. Fitted with 28" barrel. Double trigger and automatic ejectors. Weight is approximately 7.75 lbs.

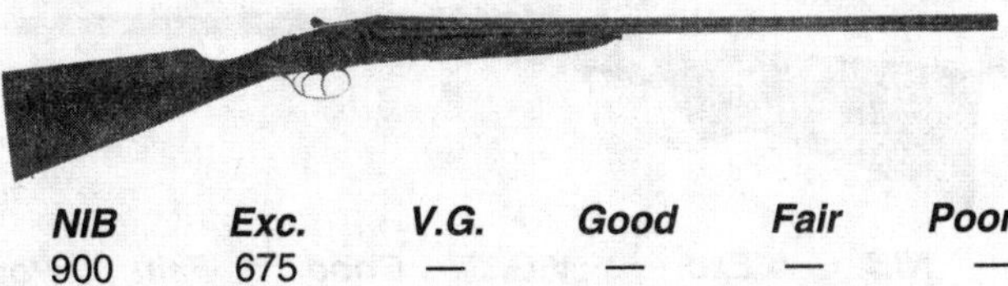

NIB	Exc.	V.G.	Good	Fair	Poor
900	675	—	—	—	—

TSA SERIES

Note: These gas-operated semi-automatics are available in 12 and 20 gauges with barrels from 24" to 26" depending on model.

TSA Field

Walnut forend and pistol grip stock, 3" chamber, 3 choke tubes and magazine-cut-off feature. Weight is around 5.7 lbs. in 20 gauge and 6.5 lbs. in 12 gauge depending on barrel length. 20 gauge available in youth model.

NIB	Exc.	V.G.	Good	Fair	Poor
375	325	275	—	—	

TSA Synthetic and Synthetic Mag

Same features as TSA Field Model but with non-glare black synthetic stock and forend. Also available with complete Realtree Max-4 coverage. Mag model has 3.5" chamber. MSRP: 380 (Synthetic); 475 (Mag). Add 15 percent for camo.

300 SERIES

NOTE: This series of over-and-under shotguns is no longer imported by Tristar.

Model 333

This over-and-under gun is available in 12 or 20 gauge with 26", 28", or 30" barrels in 12 gauge. Hand engraved frame. Fitted with 3" chambers and choke tubes. Single-selective triggers and auto ejectors. Fancy Turkish walnut stock. Weighs around 7.75 lbs. for 12 gauge and 7.5 lbs. for 20 gauge.

NIB	Exc.	V.G.	Good	Fair	Poor
650	600	425	—	—	—

Model 333SC

Similar to above model but with addition of 11mm sporting rib, recoil pad, forcing cones, and ported barrels. Extended choke tubes.

NIB	Exc.	V.G.	Good	Fair	Poor
700	650	475	—	—	

Model 333SCL

Same features as Model 333SC but with special stock.

NIB	Exc.	V.G.	Good	Fair	Poor
700	600	500	—	—	

Model 333L

This shotgun has the same features as the Model 333 but with a special stock designed for women. Length of pull is shorter with special Monte Carlo comb.

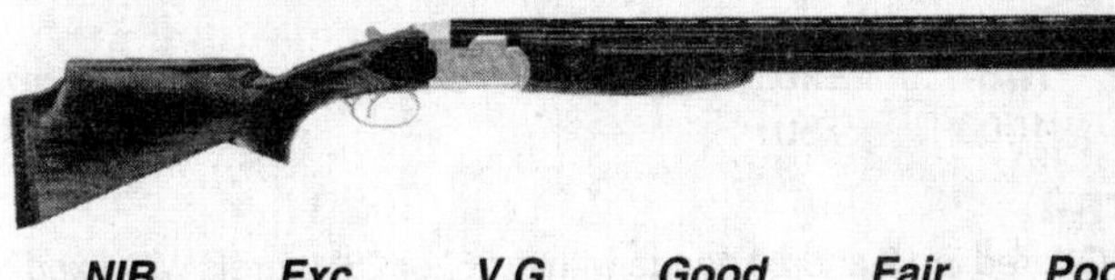

NIB	Exc.	V.G.	Good	Fair	Poor
650	550	400	—	—	

Model 330

This over-and-under model has a standard Turkish walnut stock with etched engraved frame. Offered in 12 and 20 gauge. Single trigger with extractors and fixed chokes.

NIB	Exc.	V.G.	Good	Fair	Poor
475	400	325	—	—	

Model 330D

This model is the same as the above but with the addition of selective auto ejectors.

NIB	Exc.	V.G.	Good	Fair	Poor
500	425	350	—	—	—

Model 300

This model features an underlug action lock with double triggers and extractors. Frame is etched. Offered in 12 gauge only with 26" or 28" barrels with fixed chokes.

NIB	Exc.	V.G.	Good	Fair	Poor
425	350	300	—	—	—

Model 311

This is a side-by-side gun in 12 or 20 gauge with 26" or 28" barrels with choke tubes. Standard Turkish walnut. Blued frame.

NIB	Exc.	V.G.	Good	Fair	Poor
500	450	300	—	—	

Model 311R

Same as above but with 20" barrel choked Cylinder and Cylinder.

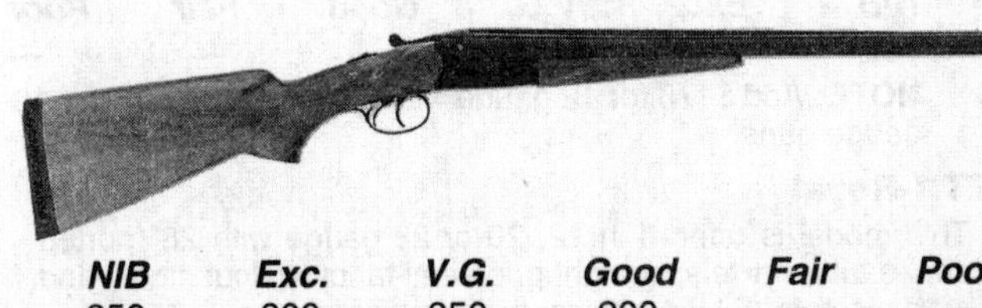

NIB	Exc.	V.G.	Good	Fair	Poor
350	300	250	200	—	—

EMILIO RIZZINI (OLD NOVA SERIES)

This gun line is no longer imported.

TR-L

Offered in 12 or 20 gauge with choice of 28" or 30" vent rib barrels. Choke tubes standard. Standard grade walnut with pistol grip. Action is silver finish boxlock with auto ejectors and single-selective trigger. Weight is approximately 7.5 lbs. Stock dimensions are made for a smaller shooter. Introduced in 1998.

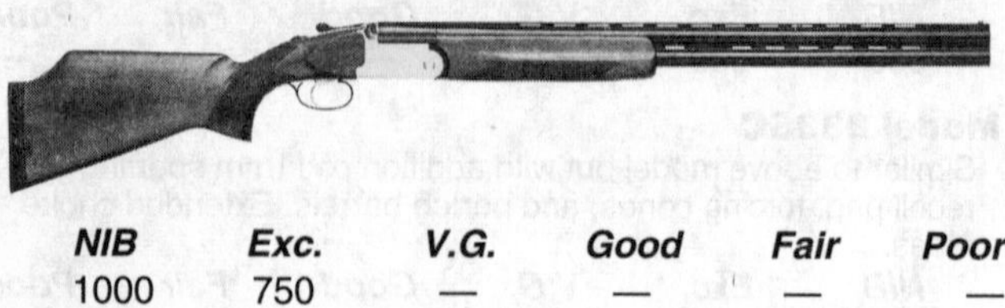

NIB	Exc.	V.G.	Good	Fair	Poor
1000	750	—	—	—	—

TR-SC

Similar to the Nova L but offered in 12 gauge only with standard stock dimensions and semi-fancy walnut stock with pistol grip. Black sporting clays-style recoil pad. Weight is between 7.5 and 8 lbs. depending on barrel length. Introduced in 1998.

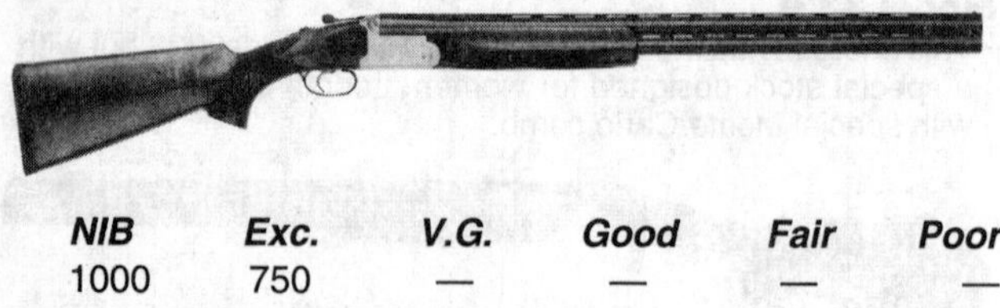

NIB	Exc.	V.G.	Good	Fair	Poor
1000	750	—	—	—	—

TR-I

Offered in 12 and 20 gauge with in 26" or 28" barrels with fixed chokes. Walnut stock with hand checkering and pistol grip. Beavertail forend. Boxlock action is blue with single-selective trigger and extractors. Weight is about 7.5 lbs. Introduced in 1998.

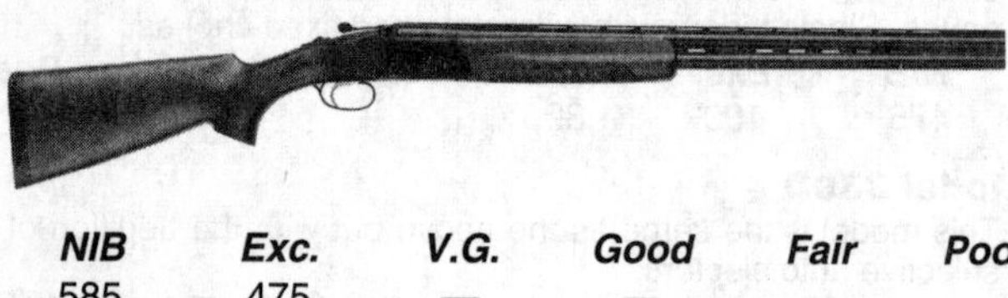

NIB	Exc.	V.G.	Good	Fair	Poor
585	475	—	—	—	—

TR-II (Nova II)

Same as above but fitted with automatic ejectors.

NIB	Exc.	V.G.	Good	Fair	Poor
875	700	—	—	—	—

TR-Mag

Similar to the Nova I but chambered for 10 and 12 gauge 3.5" shell. Choice of 24" or 28" vent rib barrels with choke tubes. Nonreflective, non-glare blue finish. Introduced in 1998.

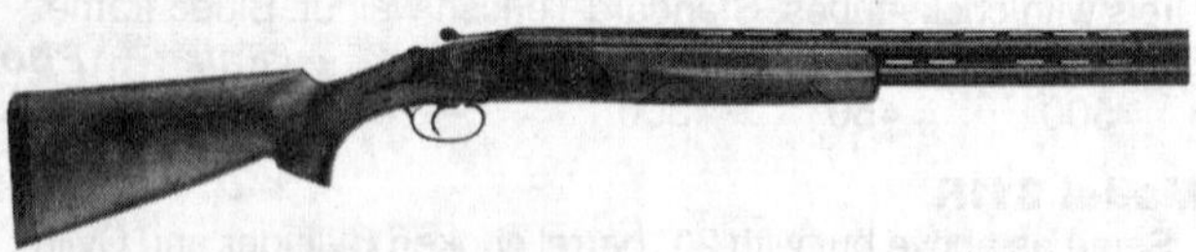

NIB	Exc.	V.G.	Good	Fair	Poor
750	600	—	—	—	—

NOTE: Add $175 for 12 gauge with ejectors and $350 for 10 gauge guns.

TTR-Royal

This model is offered in 12, 20 or 28 gauge with 28" ported choke tube barrels, straight grip semi-fancy walnut stock, and auto ejectors. Silver receiver with gold engraving.

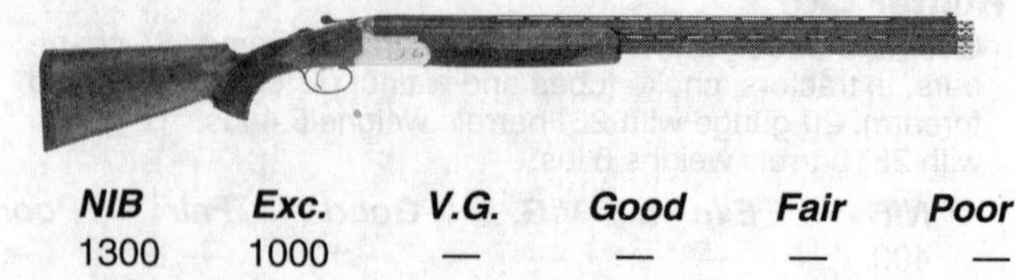

NIB	Exc.	V.G.	Good	Fair	Poor
1300	1000	—	—	—	—

TR-Class SL

Top-of-the-line model with sculptured frame and engraved side plates. Offered in 12 gauge only.

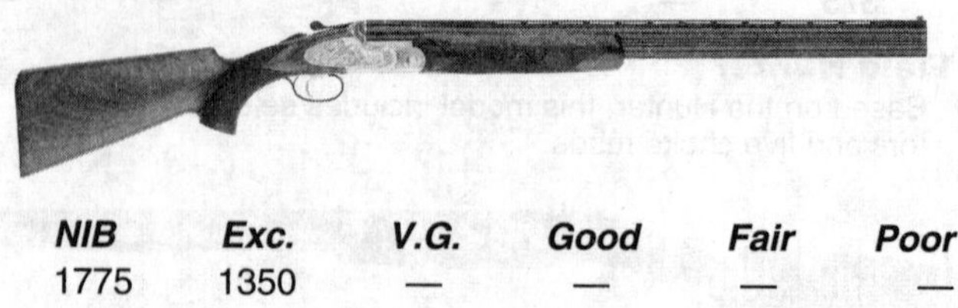

NIB	Exc.	V.G.	Good	Fair	Poor
1775	1350	—	—	—	—

411 SERIES

These shotguns are made in Italy by R.F.M. Luciano Rota.

Model 411

This side-by-side double is imported from Italy and introduced in 1998. Chambered for 12, 20, and .410 bore with choice of 26" or 28" barrels with choke tubes or fixed chokes. Boxlock action with engraving and case coloring. Double triggers and extractors. Standard walnut stock with pistol grip and splinter forearm. Weight is between 6 and 6.5 lbs.

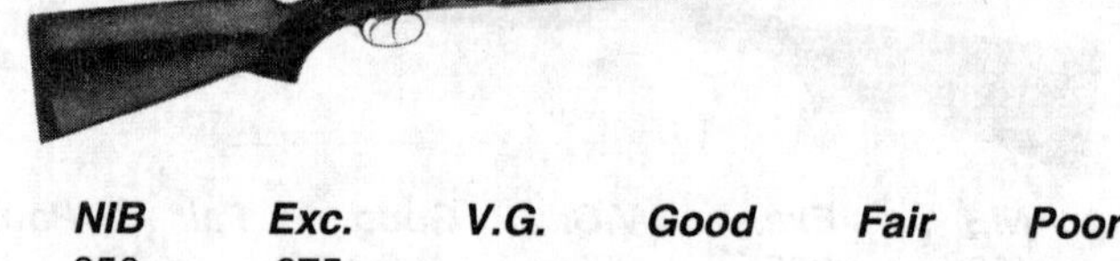

NIB	Exc.	V.G.	Good	Fair	Poor
850	675	—	—	—	—

Model 411R

Offered in 12 or 20 gauge with 20" barrel with fixed cylinder chokes. Extractors. Weight is about 6.5 lbs. for 12 gauge and 6 lbs. for 20 gauge.

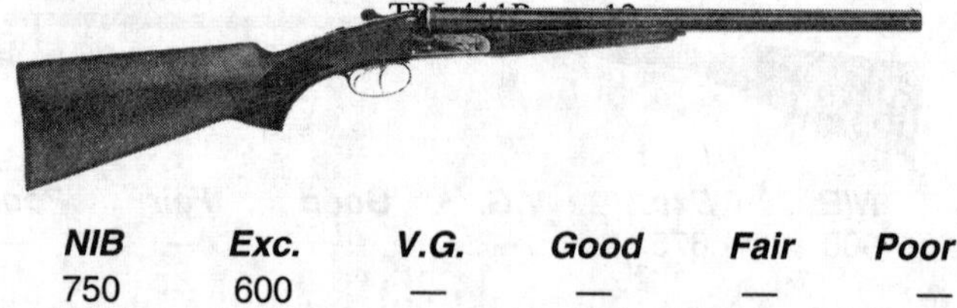

NIB	Exc.	V.G.	Good	Fair	Poor
750	600	—	—	—	—

Model 411D

This model is similar to the Model 411 but with engraved case, colored finish on the receiver, auto ejectors, single trigger, and straight grip stock. Weight for 28 gauge is about 6.25 lbs. and for the 12 gauge about 7 lbs.

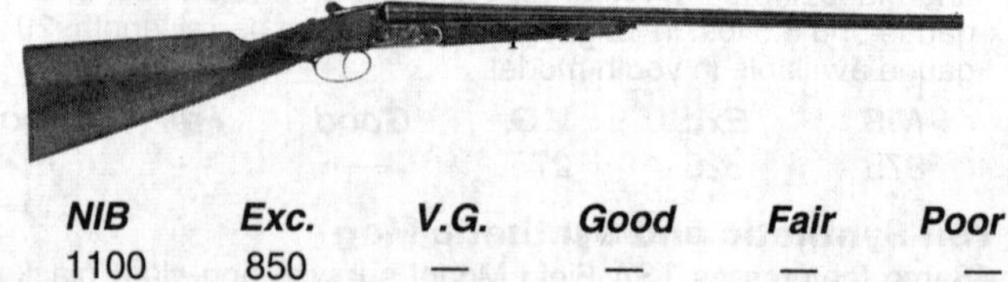

NIB	Exc.	V.G.	Good	Fair	Poor
1100	850	—	—	—	—

Model 411F

Same as the Model 411D but with silver engraved receiver.

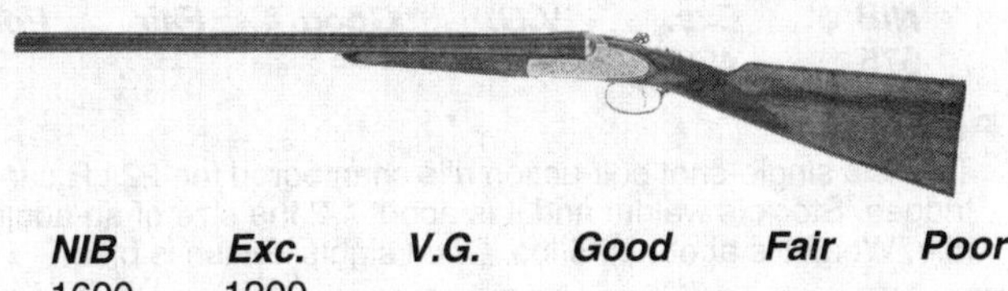

NIB	Exc.	V.G.	Good	Fair	Poor
1600	1200	—	—	—	—

PHANTOM SERIES

These shotguns are made in Turkey by Eqsilah and have been discontinued in favor of a new redesigned gun that is found under the Diana Series.

Phantom Field

This is a gas operated semi-automatic shotgun that is chambered for the 12 gauge 2.75" or 3" shell. Fitted with 24", 26", or 28" barrel. Checkered walnut stock with pistol grip. Screw-in chokes. Five-round magazine.

NIB	Exc.	V.G.	Good	Fair	Poor
425	325	—	—	—	—

NOTE: For magnum models add $75.

Phantom Synthetic

Same as above but with synthetic stock.

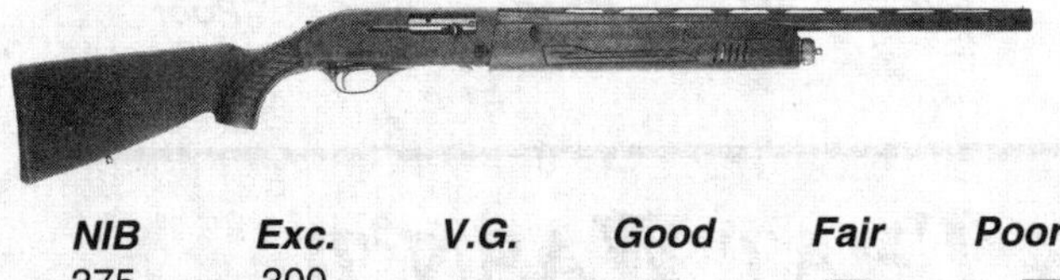

NIB	Exc.	V.G.	Good	Fair	Poor
375	300	—	—	—	—

NOTE: For magnum models add $75.

Phantom HP

Same features as the phantom field except with synthetic stock, 19" barrel, and swivel studs.

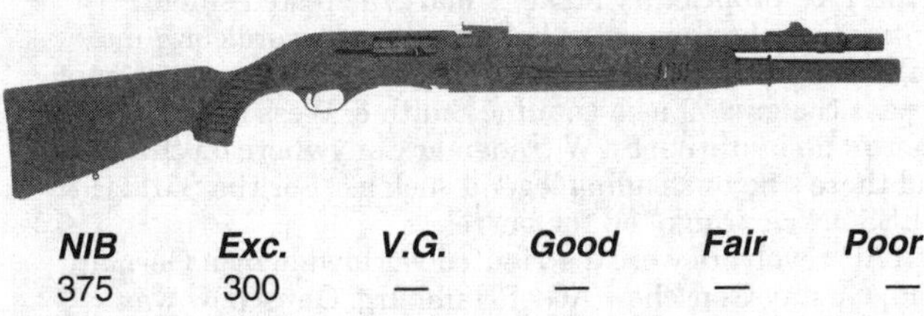

NIB	Exc.	V.G.	Good	Fair	Poor
375	300	—	—	—	—

BREDA SERIES

These semi-automatic shotguns are made in Italy by Breda. This series of guns was first imported by Tristar in 2003.

Ermes

Chambered for the 12 gauge 3" shell and fitted with either a 26" or 28" vent rib barrel. Inertia operated recoil system. Checkered walnut stock with pistol grip. Choice of black, nickel, gold, or silver alloy receiver finish. Receiver is engraved with hunting scenes. Adjustable stock spacers. Weight is about 7.75 lbs.

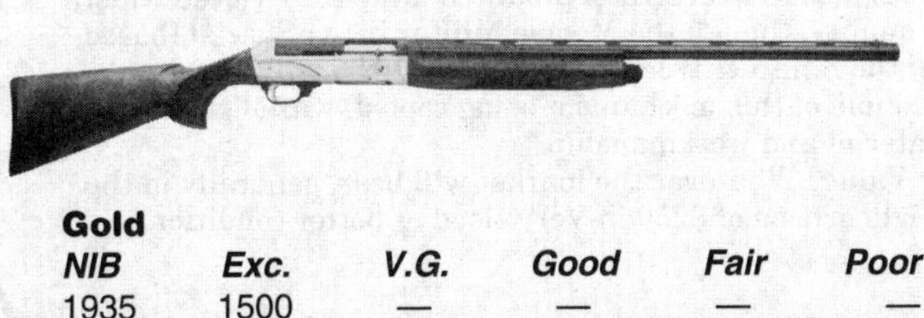

Gold

NIB	Exc.	V.G.	Good	Fair	Poor
1935	1500	—	—	—	—

Silver

NIB	Exc.	V.G.	Good	Fair	Poor
1725	1350	—	—	—	—

Nickel

NIB	Exc.	V.G.	Good	Fair	Poor
1650	1200	—	—	—	—

Black

NIB	Exc.	V.G.	Good	Fair	Poor
1260	975	—	—	—	—

Astra 20

This is a 20 gauge model with 26" vent rib barrel. Black receiver. Walnut with pistol grip and solid rubber recoil pad. Furnished with five choke tubes. Weight is about 6 lbs.

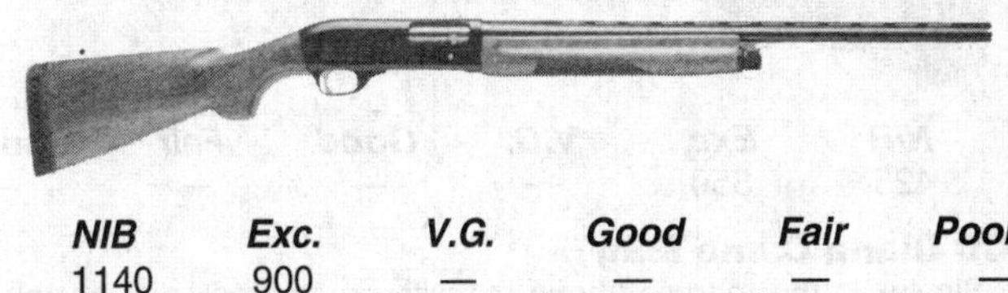

NIB	Exc.	V.G.	Good	Fair	Poor
1140	900	—	—	—	—

Mira Sporting

This semi-automatic shotgun is gas operated and chambered for the 12 gauge shell with 3" chamber. Fitted with a 30" vent rib barrel with 10mm wide rib. Checkered walnut stock with pistol grip. Weight is approximately 7 lbs.

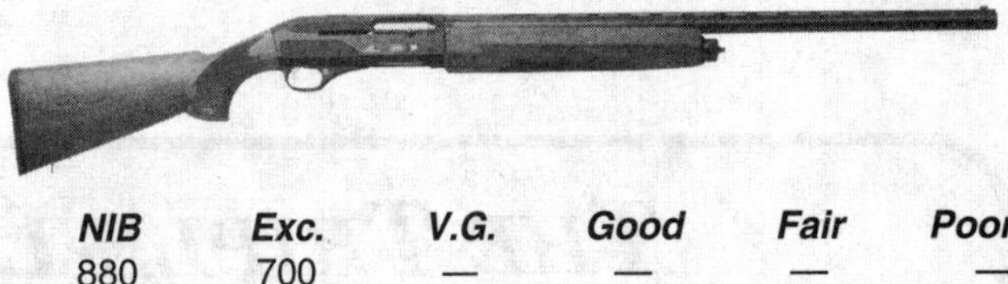

NIB	Exc.	V.G.	Good	Fair	Poor
880	700	—	—	—	—

Mira Camo

As above but with 28" barrel and camo finish.

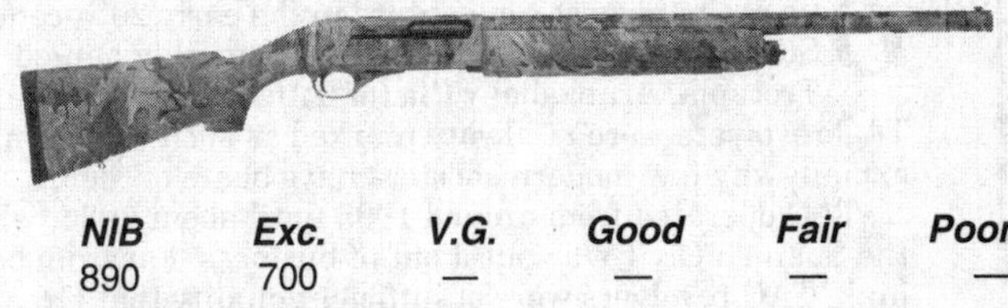

NIB	Exc.	V.G.	Good	Fair	Poor
890	700	—	—	—	—

CD DIANA SERIES

These shotguns are made in Turkey by Eqsilah. This line has replaced the Phantom Series and was first imported by Tristar in 2003.

CD Diana Field

This is a gas operated semi-automatic shotgun chambered for the 12 gauge 3" shell and fitted with a 26", 28", or 30" vent rib barrel. Checkered walnut stock with pistol grip. Choke tubes. Magazine cutoff. Weight is about 7 lbs. depending on barrel length.

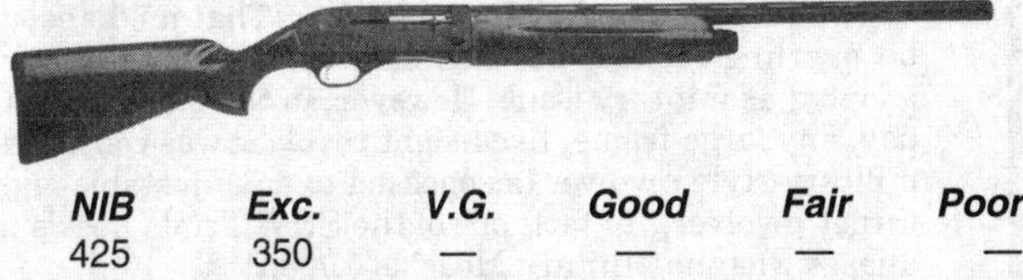

NIB	Exc.	V.G.	Good	Fair	Poor
425	350	—	—	—	—

CD Diana Synthetic

As above but with black synthetic stock. Also offered with 3.5" chamber. Weight is about 6.75 lbs.

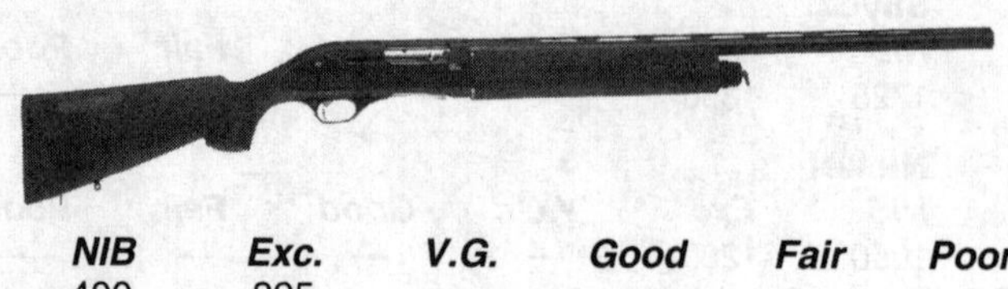

NIB	Exc.	V.G.	Good	Fair	Poor
400	325	—	—	—	—

NOTE: Add $90 for 3.5" Magnum model.

CD Diana Slug

This 12 gauge gun is fitted with a 24" rifled slug barrel with open adjustable sights. Black synthetic stock. Weight is about 6.75 lbs.

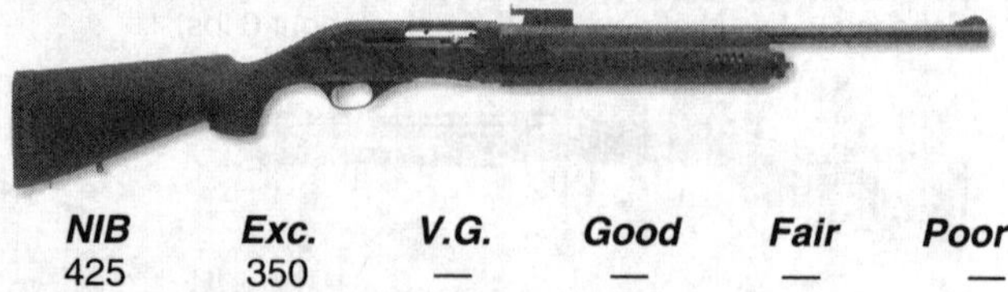

NIB	Exc.	V.G.	Good	Fair	Poor
425	350	—	—	—	—

CD Diana Camo Mag

Similar to the models above but with camo stock and barrel and choice of 24" or 28" barrel with 3.5" chamber. Weight is about 6.75 lbs.

NIB	Exc.	V.G.	Good	Fair	Poor
575	450	—	—	—	—

Pee Wee

This is a single-shot bolt-action rifle chambered for .22 LR cartridges. Stock is walnut and it is about 1/2 the size of an adult rifle. Weight is about 2.75 lbs. Open sights. Finish is blue.

NIB	Exc.	V.G.	Good	Fair	Poor
200	150	100	—	—	—

TROCAOLA
Eibar, Spain

This maker produced a variety of .32, .38, and .44 caliber top break revolvers between approximately 1900 and 1936. These pistols can be identified by the monogram "TAC" stamped on the left side of the frame. The value of all these revolvers is listed.

Exc.	V.G.	Good	Fair	Poor
200	125	100	75	50

TRYON, EDWARD K. & COMPANY
Philadelphia, Pennsylvania

Pocket Pistol

A .41 caliber single-shot percussion pocket pistol with a 2" or 4" barrel, German silver mounts and a walnut stock. The lock marked "Tryon/Philada." Manufactured during the 1860s and 1870s.

Exc.	V.G.	Good	Fair	Poor
—	—	1900	750	200

THE TRIPLE-LOCK THAT WASN'T

DAN SHIDELER

One of the biggest competitors in the early 20th-century S&W knockoff market was the memorably named Trocaola, Aranzabal y Cia (or TAC) of Eibar, Spain. TAC revolvers weren't always marked as such, which might explain why few modern shooters have hears of them.

TAC operated from around 1905 until about 1936, when the Spanish Civil War put it out of business. Far from being junk, TAC revolvers were of sufficient quality that Great Britain actually bought many of them as issue sidearms during World War I. Chambered in .455, these substitute British service revolvers were based on the Webley design and were known as the Pistol, Old Pattern with 5 Inch Barrel, No 2 Mark I.

At some time in the 1920s, TAC decided to knock off what was arguably the greatest revolver of all time: the Smith & Wesson Triple Lock, alias the New Century or .44 Hand Ejector, First Model. Talk about chutzpah! TAC's knocking off the Triple Lock was like Yugo knocking off a Rolls-Royce Silver Shadow.

TAC's Triple Lock clone, an extremely faithful copy, was known formally as the Modelo Militar. That might seem a bit puzzling because the original Triple Lock was never adopted as military issue. However, in the parlance of the day, any large-frame, fixed-sight revolver was considered a military-style revolver (as opposed to an adjustable-sighted target revolver). In fact, one of the S&W Triple Lock's many aliases was the Military Model of 1908.

The Model Militar is generously marked with Spanish proofs (an "R" encircled by the outline of a bomb, or maybe it's a turnip) on the barrel, frame and cylinder. Also present is the TAC proprietary maker's mark, a crested shield containing what appear to be two crossed swords or guns. Unlike other Spanish knockoffs, there is no obvious attempt to pass the gun off as a genuine Smith & Wesson product. There's no imitation S&W trademark anywhere on the gun, and there's no misleading legend such as "For the SMITH & WESSON cartridge" on the barrel.

TAC revolvers were distributed worldwide by a German firm, Gustav Genschow AG of Hamburg. Genschow was known by several names, the most commonly encountered of which is GECO. In fact, the GECO trademark (a large "G" encircling the letters "ECO") appears on the revolver's right front frame. Most TAC revolvers also had "TAC" in a circle stamped on their frames, but my Modelo Militar lacks this stamping.

Spanish gunmakers in those days rarely wrote anything down, so neither I nor anyone else has any idea how many .44 Modelo Militars were produced.

As Hogg and Walters say in the fourth edition of their indispensable *Pistols of the World* (Krause Publications, 2004), "[TAC's revolvers] produced after 1921 varied widely in quality, though the Modelo Militar in .44 Special [based on] the Smith & Wesson 'Triple Lock' (the only known example of this mechanism being copied) was of good material and workmanship."

Value? Whatever the market will bear, generally in the neighborhood of $250 in Very Good or better condition.

TUCKER SHERARD & COMPANY
Lancaster, Texas

Dragoon
A .44 caliber percussion revolver with a 7.75" round barrel fitted with a loading lever and a 6-shot cylinder. The barrel marked "Clark, Sherard & Co., Lancaster, Texas," and the cylinder etched in two panels with crossed cannons and the legend "Texas Arms." Approximately 400 revolvers of this type were made between 1862 and 1867. Prospective purchasers are advised to secure a qualified appraisal prior to acquisition.

Exc.	*V.G.*	*Good*	*Fair*	*Poor*
—	—	50000	20000	—

TUFTS & COLLEY
New York, New York

Pocket Pistol
A .44 caliber single-shot percussion pocket pistol with a 3.5" barrel, German silver mounts and walnut stock. The lock marked "Tufts & Colley" and the barrel "Deringer/Pattn." Manufactured during the 1860s.

Exc.	*V.G.*	*Good*	*Fair*	*Poor*
—	—	1750	750	200

TURBIAUX, JACQUES
Paris, France
SEE—Ames

TURNER, THOMAS
Redding, England

Pepperbox
A .476 double-action percussion pepperbox having 6 barrels. Blued, case hardened with walnut grips. The left side of the frame is engraved in an oval "Thomas Turner, Redding."

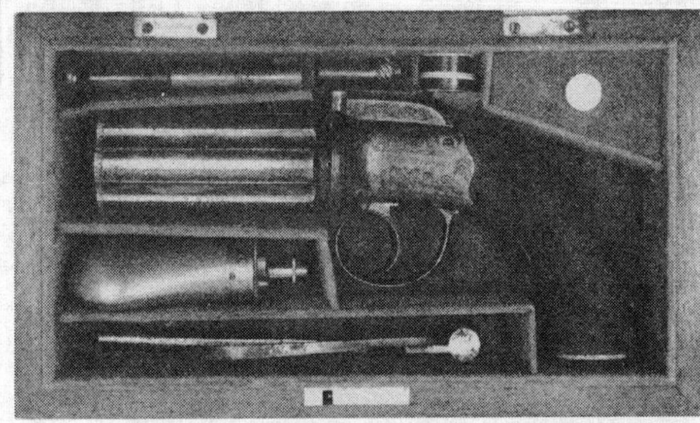

Courtesy Bonhams & Butterfields, San Francisco, California

Exc.	*V.G.*	*Good*	*Fair*	*Poor*
—	5000	1750	900	400

TYLER ORDNANCE WORKS
Tyler, Texas

This company produced 56 Austrian rifles, 508 Enfield rifles, 423 Hill rifles and 1,009 Texas rifles during the Civil War.

NOTE: Extreme caution is urged prior to purchasing any of these arms and a qualified appraisal should be sought. These rifles are very rare.

Tyler Texas Rifle
A .57 caliber single-shot rifle with a 27" barrel and a full stock secured by two barrel bands. The lock marked "Texas Rifle/Tyler/Cal. .57."

Exc.	*V.G.*	*Good*	*Fair*	*Poor*
—	—	40000	15000	—

Hill Rifle
A .54 caliber single-shot percussion rifle with a 27" barrel, full stock secured by two brass barrel bands and an iron trigger guard and buttplate. The lock marked "Hill Rifle/Tyler/Tex/ Cal. .54."

Exc.	*V.G.*	*Good*	*Fair*	*Poor*
—	—	40000	15000	—

U.S. ARMS CO.
Riverhead, New York
SEE—United Sporting Arms, Inc.

U.S. M1 CARBINE
Various Manufacturers

NOTE: For history, techinical data, descriptions, photos, and prices see the *Standard Catalog of Military Firearms* under United States, Rifles.

PRICING NOTE: The prices listed are for rifles in original, unaltered condition. For rifles that have been refinished or restored deduct about 50 percent.

Inland

Exc.	V.G.	Good	Fair	Poor
1500	1200	600	425	350

Underwood

Exc.	V.G.	Good	Fair	Poor
1600	1250	550	400	275

S.G. Saginaw

Exc.	V.G.	Good	Fair	Poor
2000	1400	700	450	375

IBM

Exc.	V.G.	Good	Fair	Poor
1800	1100	525	375	250

Quality Hardware

Exc.	V.G.	Good	Fair	Poor
1700	1100	525	375	250

National Postal Meter

Exc.	V.G.	Good	Fair	Poor
1800	1100	575	375	250

Standard Products

Exc.	V.G.	Good	Fair	Poor
1900	1200	600	425	250

Rockola

Exc.	V.G.	Good	Fair	Poor
2000	1400	750	475	350

SG Grand Rapids

Exc.	V.G.	Good	Fair	Poor
2000	1400	600	425	350

Winchester

Exc.	V.G.	Good	Fair	Poor
2000	1400	700	450	375

Irwin Pedersen

Exc.	V.G.	Good	Fair	Poor
4000	2200	950	650	500

M1 Carbine Cutaway

Exc.	V.G.	Good	Fair	Poor
2500	1500	900	600	500

M1 Carbine Sniper with infra red conversion

Exc.	V.G.	Good	Fair	Poor
1450	1000	800	400	300

U.S. M1 A1 Paratrooper Model

Exc.	V.G.	Good	Fair	Poor
4500	3500	2500	1250	750

U.S. ORDNANCE
Reno, Nevada

The models listed are machined to military specifications and are semi-automatic only.

M-60

This is a 7.62mm belt-fed semi-automatic weapon modeled after the famous machine gun used in Vietnam. Fitted with a 22" barrel, the weight of the gun is about 24 lbs.

NIB	Exc.	V.G.	Good	Fair	Poor
5995	—	—	—	—	—

M-60E3

A shorter, more lightweight version of the standard M-60 fitted with a 17" barrel. Weight reduced to about 18 lbs.

NIB	Exc.	V.G.	Good	Fair	Poor
6495	—	—	—	—	—

Browning Model 1919

This belt-fed model is chambered for the 7.62mm/.30-06 cartridges. Fitted with a 23" barrel. Weight is about 30 lbs. Prices listed are for gun only.

Model 1919 A6

Model 1919 with A4 tripod

NIB	Exc.	V.G.	Good	Fair	Poor
1995	—	—	—	—	—

NOTE: For A6 stock, bipod, and carry handle add $125. For A4 tripod add $450.

Vickers

This model is chambered for the .303 cartridge and is belt-fed. Weight is about 40 lbs. Prices listed are for gun only.

NIB	Exc.	V.G.	Good	Fair	Poor
4495	—	—	—	—	—

NOTE: For tripod add $500.

U.S. REPEATING ARMS CO.

SEE—Winchester

UBERTI, ALDO/UBERTI USA

Ponte Zanano, Italy

This company manufactures high-grade reproductions of famous Western-style American firearms. Their products have been imported over the years by a number of different companies. They produce both blackpowder guns and the cartridge firearms that are included in this section. This Italian manufacturer builds high quality firearms of the American West. Featured are Colt, Winchester, and Remington. Each importer stamps its name on the firearm in addition to the Uberti address.

NOTE: In 2000 Beretta Holding Company purchased Uberti.

Paterson Revolver

This is an exact copy of the famous and rare Colt pistol. Offered in .36 caliber with engraved 5-shot cylinder, the barrel is 7.5" long and octagonal forward of the lug. The frame is case hardened steel as is the backstrap. Grips are one-piece walnut. Overall length is 11.5" and weight is about 2.5 lbs.

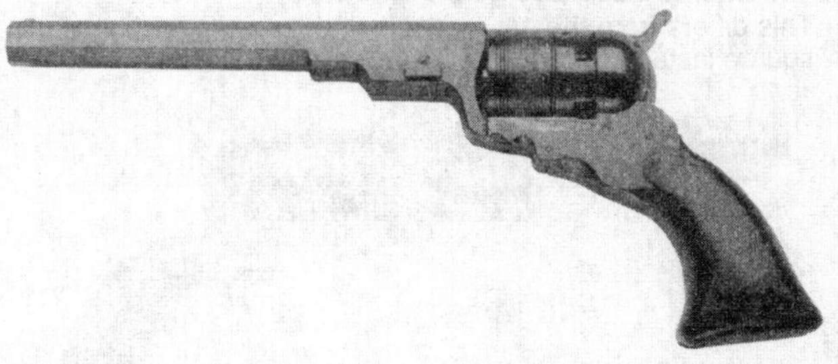

NIB	Exc.	V.G.	Good	Fair	Poor
400	300	200	125	100	75

Walker Colt Revolver

This is a faithful reproduction of the famous and highly sought-after Colts. Caliber is .44 and the round barrel is 9" in length. The frame is case hardened steel and the trigger guard is brass. The 6-shot cylinder is engraved with fighting dragoons scene. Grip is one-piece walnut. Overall length is 15.75" and weight is a hefty 70 oz.

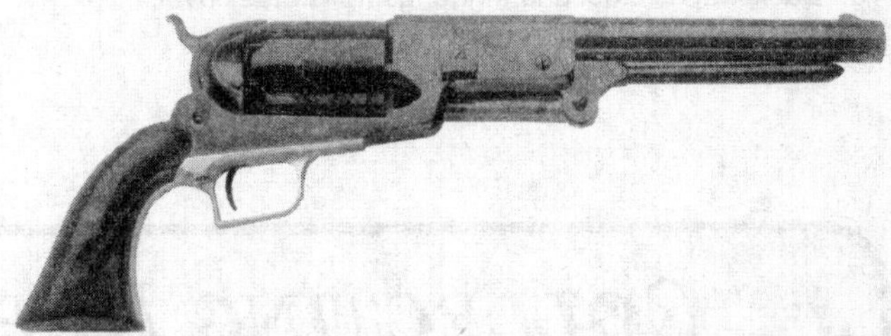

NIB	Exc.	V.G.	Good	Fair	Poor
400	300	200	125	100	75

Colt Whitneyville Dragoon

This was the transition Walker. A reduced version of the Model 1847 Walker. Fitted with a 7.5" barrel and chambered for the .44 caliber.

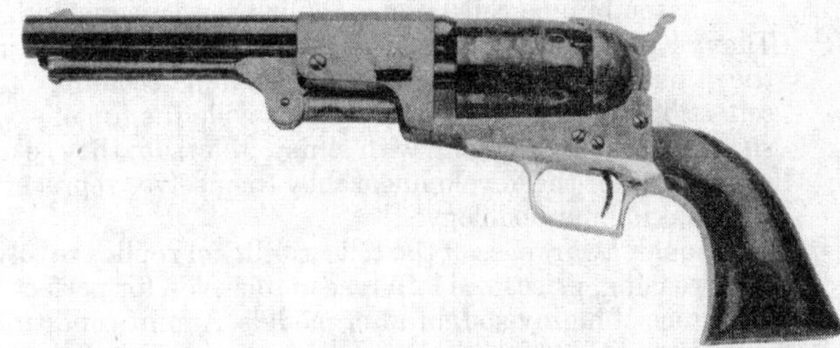

NIB	Exc.	V.G.	Good	Fair	Poor
375	275	200	125	100	75

Colt 1st Model Dragoon Revolver

This was a shorter version of the Walker and evolved directly from that original design. This model is a 6-shot .44 caliber with a 7.5" barrel. The frame is color case hardened steel while the backstrap and trigger guard are brass. Grips are one-piece walnut. Overall length is 13.5" and weight is about 63 oz.

NIB	Exc.	V.G.	Good	Fair	Poor
300	200	175	125	100	75

Colt 2nd Model Dragoon Revolver

This differs from the 1st model in that the cylinder bolt slot is square instead of oval.

NIB	Exc.	V.G.	Good	Fair	Poor
300	200	175	125	100	75

Colt 3rd Model Dragoon Revolver

This model varies from the 2nd model as follows:

a: Loading lever taper is inverted.
b: Loading lever latch hook is different shape.
c: Loading lever latch.
d: Backstrap is steel and trigger guard is brass oval.
e: Frame is cut for a shoulder stock.

NIB	Exc.	V.G.	Good	Fair	Poor
350	225	175	125	100	75

Colt Model 1849 Wells Fargo

This model has no loading lever. Chambered for .31 caliber cartridge. The barrel is octagonal. The frame is case colored and hardened steel while the backstrap and trigger guard are brass. Cylinder is engraved and holds 5 rounds. Grip is one-piece walnut. Overall length is 9.5" and weight is 34 oz.

NIB	Exc.	V.G.	Good	Fair	Poor
325	200	150	125	100	75

Colt Model 1849 Pocket Revolver

Same as the Wells Fargo with the addition of a loading lever.

NIB	Exc.	V.G.	Good	Fair	Poor
300	200	150	125	100	75

COLLECTING REPLICA BLACK POWDER REVOLVERS

TOM CACECI

Anyone interested in the technical and historic aspects of historical blackpowder revolvers should consider assembling a collection of replica versions instead. They're affordable, usable, as functional and attractive as the guns of yesteryear they duplicate—and becoming collectible in their own right. They provide the fun of shooting "old style" along with a history lesson; they're also significant for the development they themselves represent in gun-making methodology.

Though awareness of the collectibility of replica revolvers is increasing, prices are still reasonable even for perfect examples of highly-sought after models. A mint-condition cased set of Colt "Second Generation" guns will sell for far, far less than a pair of beaten-up originals. Kept in pristine condition the replica guns will likely appreciate in value as fast as the originals would, though would always sell for less. Even "shooters," when properly maintained, can appreciate significantly. In short, a collection of good quality replicas with appropriate accessories and accoutrements is an excellent investment that real people with real jobs can afford.

Several far-sighted individuals in the USA and in Europe are responsible for the happy fact that today we are blessed with any number of high-quality, accurate replica revolvers. They recognized the fascination of these guns held for American shooters and managed to resurrect them. In particular, during the 1950', as the originals were becoming very scarce and valuable, Val Forgett (founder of Navy Arms) and Turner Kirkland (founder of Dixie Gun Works) saw an opportunity. With the first year of the US Civil War Centennial (1960) looming, they recognized that the historic significance of that anniversary was creating a market for usable replica guns. Their companies and others entered into negotiations with a number of gunmakers in the Gardone region of northern Italy to make copies.

Gardone and the region around it is a historic center of arms manufacture, and has been for centuries (the very word "pistol" comes from Pistoia, an Italian city; and Pietro Beretta, also in Gardone, is the oldest industrial enterprise in the world.) By the mid 1960s several firms in Italy were making handguns for the US market. Even with the end of centennial celebrations the popularity of the replicas remained high, and it's safe to say that Italian gunmakers have made more percussion revolvers—*far* more—than were ever made in the nineteenth century, than all the original manufacturers combined ever did.

One reason replica black powder guns remain popular is because—like the originals—they are considered "antiques" under Federal and most state laws; hence there is no paperwork needed to buy one. They can be purchased directly from the seller (even by mail order) with no licensed dealer involvement and no Form 4473, because they're totally exempt from the provisions of the Gun Control Act of 1968 and its administrative regulations. Except in a few states, owning and shooting them is uncomplicated.

As with any other aspects of collecting, if you're contemplating getting into the field, there are many things to be considered besides the specific design being copied. The value of a replica revolver (to an even greater extent than is true of originals) depends in large measure on *who* made it, and less importantly, *when*. Current production guns are somewhat better made and more consistent than guns made 40 years ago, because manufacturing methods and quality control have improved and the manufacturers have gained much more experience since the 1960's.

Colt Model 1848 Baby Dragoon

Similar is appearance to the Model 1849 but with a 4" tapered octagonal barrel and a square back trigger guard. No loading lever. Weight is about 23 oz.

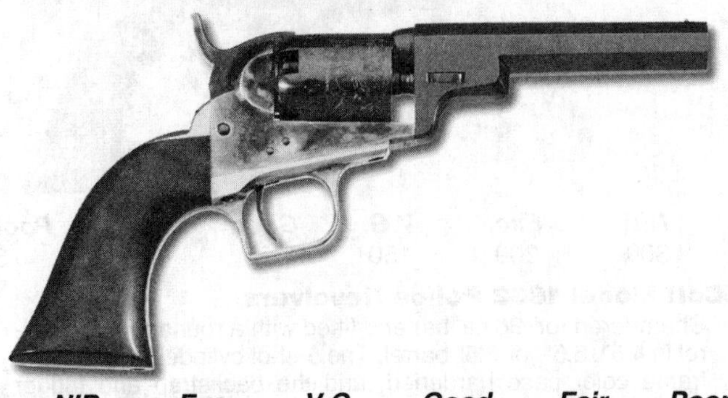

NIB	Exc.	V.G.	Good	Fair	Poor
300	200	150	125	100	75

Model 1851 Navy Colt

Chambered for .36 caliber with an engraved 6-shot cylinder. The tapered octagonal barrel is 7.5". The frame is case colored steel and the backstrap and oval trigger guard are brass. Grips are one-piece walnut. Overall length is 13" and weight is about 44 oz.

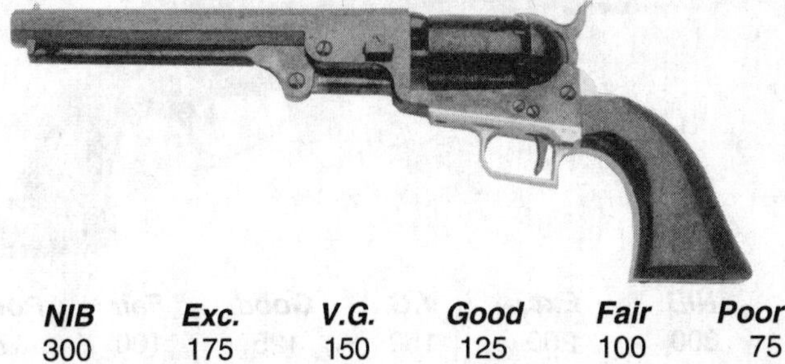

NIB	Exc.	V.G.	Good	Fair	Poor
300	175	150	125	100	75

Model 1861 Navy Colt

Sometimes referred to as the "New Navy" this model is similar in appearance to the Model 1851. Offered in two variations. The military version has a steel backstrap and trigger guard and is cut for a shoulder stock. The civilian version has a brass backstrap and trigger guard and is not cut for a shoulder stock.

COLLECTING REPLICA BLACK POWDER REVOLVERS (CONT.)

Some manufacturers have a "name" and their products command a higher price than those similar products by someone else. Nowadays *the* "name" in replicas is Uberti; for many years this company (which was one of Navy Arms' earliest suppliers: many older Navy Arms guns carry Uberti logos but not the name) has held a dominant position in the replica business. Identical guns by Uberti and one of its rivals will command different prices, with Uberti's invariably higher: fit-and-finish and overall craftsmanship of Uberti guns is pretty well regarded as the best of the various Italian producers. They were good enough to be the actual manufacturers of the "Second Generation" or "Signature Series" *Colt* replicas offered some years back. Colt's advertising implied (without actually saying so) that the guns were made in the USA. But in fact they were Uberti products. Ironically, an Uberti-made "Colt" will command twice the price an identical Uberti-marked gun will bring: "Colt" is still a valuable brand name. Guns made by Pietta (Fratelli Pietta, another firm in Gardone) are also of very high quality but typically sell for less than Uberti's products.

Many other Italian firms, some still in the business, some who have disappeared, have made percussion revolvers. Armi San Marco and Armi San Paolo are two more well-known brands, if less often seen and not so highly valued as the two big firms. The less-well-known manufacturers often make (or made) "private label" guns for large retailers or small runs of specialty products for importers who sell under their own brand name (Palmetto Arms, Dixie). There's nothing wrong with these guns, but they lack the name recognition of the two leading firms and will sell for lower prices.

Prices for current-production models of popular designs such as the 1860 Army or 1858 Remington are determined by what retailers charge for them new in box. There's not much point in paying more for such a gun than you could buy it for brand new from Cabela's or Dixie Gun Works. They're valuable to a collection as representative types but will not appreciate if shot.

Nevertheless, because the replica revolver business has now been up and running for almost half a century some of the small early importers no longer exist and guns with their names are part of the history of the replica industry. A lot of small firms got out of the game if their sales began to slack off after the Civil War centennial ended, or if they couldn't compete with the bigger players, so guns with names of defunct companies are relatively scarce. The "SPESCO" company of Atlanta, for example, was active in the early 1970's, importing guns made by Armi San Paolo: SPESCO-marked guns aren't common because very few were imported, so they may bring a premium from a collector who's looking for odd or unusual brands. "Centennial Arms" is another uncommon private label from a smaller importer.

Original percussion revolvers were often sold cased with accessories: a powder flask, nipple wrench, cap tins, bullets, oil bottle, etc. Relatively few such cased sets are sold today, but some, especially commemoratives, are on the market. These are of significant interest to collectors, and considered as a whole, make very desirable additions to a collection. An original cased Colt Walker with accessories could sell for upwards of half a million dollars on today's market, but an Armi San Marco-made example with all the goodies recently sold for less than $300 on Auction Arms! The catalog prices of the accessories and the case, leaving the gun out of the equation, make this a very good buy – and one not likely to make your theft insurance rates go through the roof!

Military Model

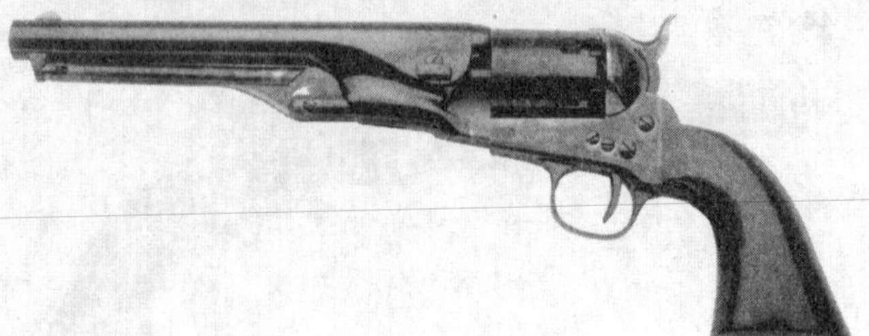

NIB	Exc.	V.G.	Good	Fair	Poor
300	200	150	125	100	75

Civilian Model

NIB	Exc.	V.G.	Good	Fair	Poor
300	200	150	125	100	75

Colt Model 1860 Army

Chambered for the .44 caliber ball and fitted with a round tapered 8" barrel, this revolver has a 6-shot engraved cylinder. Grips are one-piece walnut. Overall length is 13.75" and weight is approximately 42 oz.

Military

Steel backstrap and brass trigger guard and is cut for a shoulder stock.

NIB	Exc.	V.G.	Good	Fair	Poor
300	200	150	125	100	75

Civilian

Brass backstrap and trigger guard and is not cut for a shoulder stock.

NIB	Exc.	V.G.	Good	Fair	Poor
300	200	150	125	100	75

Fluted Cylinder

Military

NIB	Exc.	V.G.	Good	Fair	Poor
300	200	160	125	100	75

Civilian

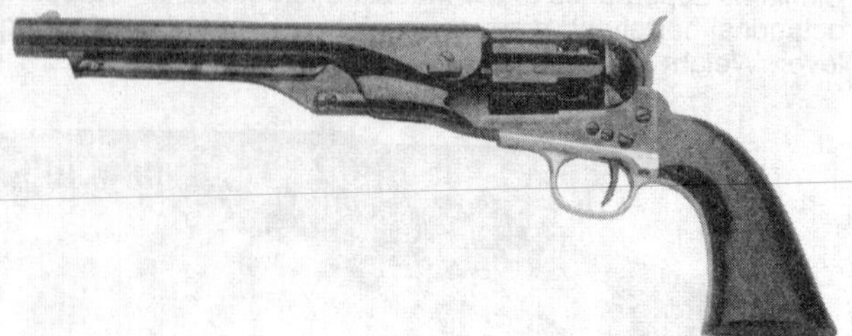

NIB	Exc.	V.G.	Good	Fair	Poor
300	200	150	125	100	75

Colt Model 1862 Police Revolvers

Chambered for .36 caliber and fitted with a round tapered barrel in 4.5", 5.5", or 6.5" barrel. The 5-shot cylinder is fluted, the frame color case hardened, and the backstrap and trigger guard are brass. Grips are one-piece walnut. Weight is about 25 oz.

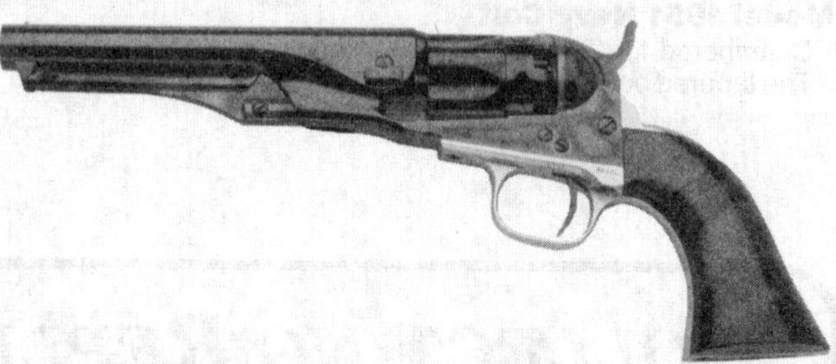

NIB	Exc.	V.G.	Good	Fair	Poor
300	200	175	150	125	100

Colt Model 1862 Pocket Navy Revolver

Similar to the Model 1862 Police model but fitted with a 5-shot engraved nonfluted cylinder. Barrel lengths are 4.5", 5.5", and 6.5". Weight is about 27 oz.

NIB	Exc.	V.G.	Good	Fair	Poor
300	200	175	150	125	100

Colt Model 1868 Army Thuer Conversion

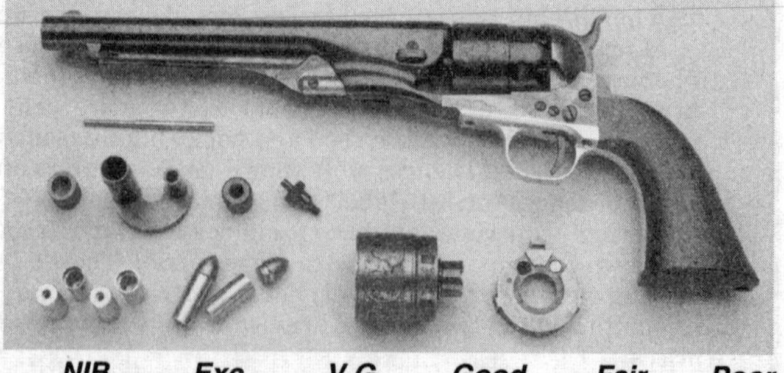

NIB	Exc.	V.G.	Good	Fair	Poor
450	325	225	175	150	100

Remington Model 1858 New Army .44 Caliber

Chambered for .44 caliber and fitted with a tapered octagonal 8" barrel. Cylinder holds 6 shots and the frame is blued steel.

trigger guard is brass. Grips are two-piece walnut. Overall length is 13.75" and weight is about 42 oz.

NIB	Exc.	V.G.	Good	Fair	Poor
300	200	150	125	100	75

Remington Model 1858 New Army .36 Caliber

Similar to above model but fitted with a 7-3/8" tapered octagonal barrel. Weight is approximately 40 oz.

NIB	Exc.	V.G.	Good	Fair	Poor
300	200	150	125	100	75

Remington Model 1858 New Army .44 Caliber Target

This version is fitted with a fully adjustable rear sight and ramp front sight.

NIB	Exc.	V.G.	Good	Fair	Poor
350	225	175	150	100	75

Remington Model 1858 New Army .44 Caliber Stainless Steel

All parts are stainless steel.

NIB	Exc.	V.G.	Good	Fair	Poor
400	275	225	150	100	75

Remington Model 1858 New Army .44 Cal. SS Target

Same as Target Model but all parts are stainless steel.

NIB	Exc.	V.G.	Good	Fair	Poor
425	300	225	175	100	75

Remington Model 1858 Target Revolving Carbine

Chambered for .44 caliber and fitted with an 18" octagon barrel. The frame is blued steel and the trigger guard is brass. Stock is select walnut. Overall length is 35" and weight is about 4.4 lbs.

NIB	Exc.	V.G.	Good	Fair	Poor
425	300	200	150	100	75

1875 Remington "Outlaw"

This is a replica of the original Remington cartridge pistol chambered for .357 Magnum, .44-40, .45 ACP, .45 ACP/.45 L.C. conversion, and .45 Colt. The frame is case colored steel and the trigger guard is brass. It is offered with a 7.5" round barrel and is either blued or nickel-plated, with two-piece walnut grips. Overall length is 13.75" and weight is about 44 oz.

NIB	Exc.	V.G.	Good	Fair	Poor
415	300	225	150	125	125

Remington Model 1875 Frontier

Introduced in 2005 this model features a 5.5" barrel chambered for the .45 Colt cartridge. Case colored frame with blued barrel, backstrap, and trigger guard. Two-piece walnut grips. Weight is about 40 oz.

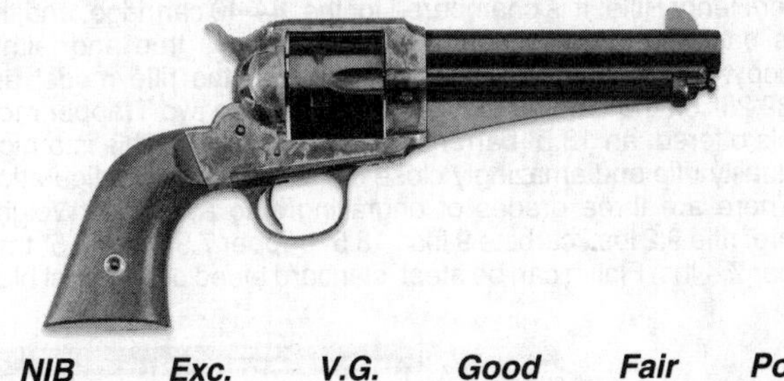

NIB	Exc.	V.G.	Good	Fair	Poor
415	300	—	—	—	—

Remington Model 1890 Police

This is a 5.5"-barreled replica of the original Remington Pistol. It is chambered for .357 Magnum, .44-40, .45 ACP, .45 ACP/.45 L.C. conversion, and .45 Colt. The frame is case colored steel and the trigger guard is brass. It was available in either blued or nickel-plate. Grips are two-piece walnut and are fitted with a grip ring. Overall length is 11.75" and weight is about 41 oz.

NIB	Exc.	V.G.	Good	Fair	Poor
440	325	250	175	125	125

Model 1871 Rolling Block Pistol

This is a single-shot target pistol chambered for .22 LR, .22 Magnum, .22 Hornet, .222 Rem., 223 Rem., .45 Long Colt, or .357 Magnum. It has a 9.5" half-octagonal, half-round barrel and is blued, with a case colored receiver and walnut grip and forearm. The trigger guard is brass. Overall length is 14" and weight is about 44 oz.

NIB	Exc.	V.G.	Good	Fair	Poor
400	300	225	200	150	100

Model 1871 Rolling Block Carbine

This model is similar to the pistol, with a 22.5" half-octagonal, half-round barrel and a full-length walnut stock. trigger guard and buttplate are brass. Overall length is 35.5" and weight is approximately 4.8 lbs.

NIB	Exc.	V.G.	Good	Fair	Poor
475	350	275	225	175	125

Henry Rifle

This is a brass-framed reproduction of the famous Winchester/Henry Rifle. It is chambered for the .44-40 cartridge, and this is basically the only departure from being a true and faithful copy. The octagonal barrel is 24.25" on the rifle model and 22.25" on the carbine model. There are also two Trapper models offered: an 18.5" barrel and a 16.5" version. This is a high-quality rifle and amazingly close to the original in configuration. There are three grades of engraving also available. Weights are: rifle 9.2 lbs., carbine 9 lbs., 18.5" trapper 7.9 lbs., 16.5" trapper 7.4 lbs. Finish can be steel, standard blued or charcoal blue.

NIB	Exc.	V.G.	Good	Fair	Poor
900	700	550	450	350	200

NOTE: Grade A add $350. Grade B add $450. Grade C add $600.

Winchester Model 1866

This is a faithful replica of the Winchester 1866. It is chambered for .22 LR, .22 Magnum, .38 Special, and .44-40, and .45 Long Colt. The rifle version has a brass frame and a 24.25" tapered octagon barrel. The frame finish is brass, with a walnut stock. Weight is about 8 lbs.

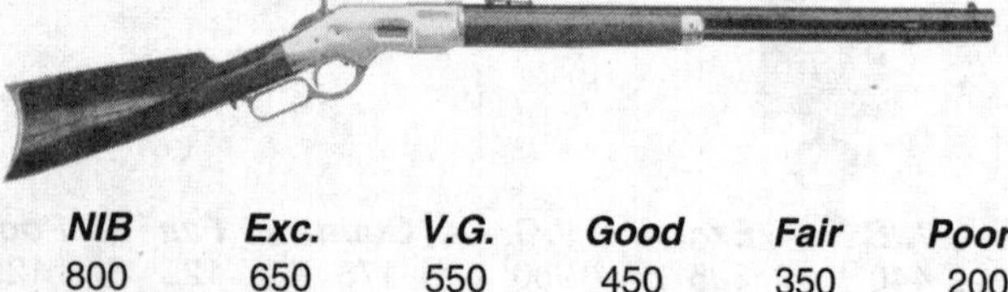

NIB	Exc.	V.G.	Good	Fair	Poor
800	650	550	450	350	200

1866 Yellowboy Carbine

This model is similar to the standard rifle, but is offered with a 19" round tapered barrel.

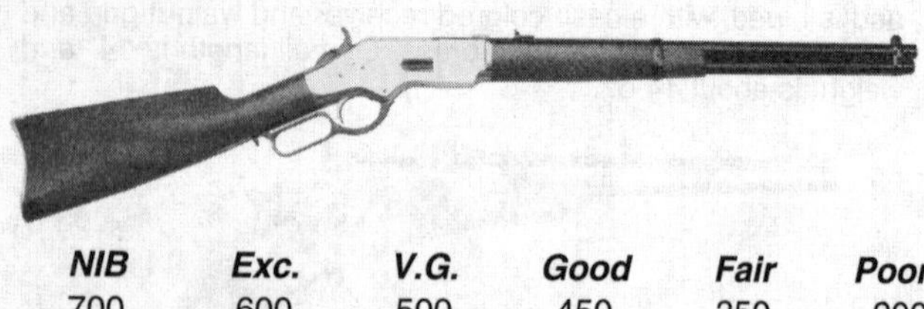

NIB	Exc.	V.G.	Good	Fair	Poor
700	600	500	450	350	200

Winchester Model 1873 Carbine

This is a reproduction of the Winchester 1873 chambered for .357 Magnum, .45 Long Colt, and .44-40. It has a case colored steel receiver and a 19" round tapered barrel. The lever is also case colored. The stock and forearm are walnut. Overall length is 38.25" and weight is about 7.4 lbs.

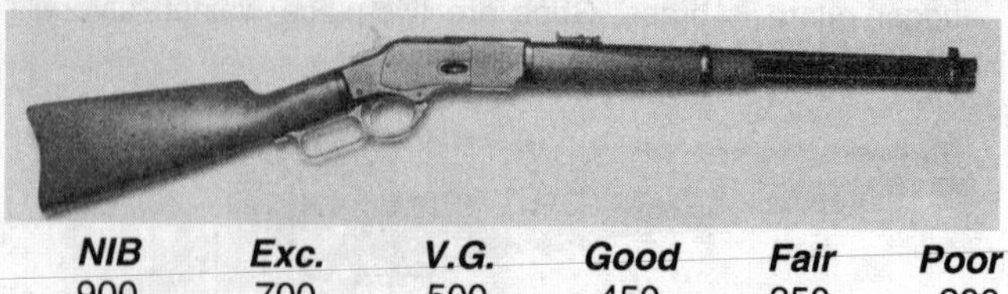

NIB	Exc.	V.G.	Good	Fair	Poor
900	700	500	450	350	200

Winchester Model 1873 Rifle

This model is similar to the Carbine, with a 24.25" octagonal barrel. Overall length is 43.25" and weight is approximately 8.2 lbs.

NIB	Exc.	V.G.	Good	Fair	Poor
950	750	600	450	350	200

NOTE: Extra barrel lengths from 30" to 20" in .45 L.C. and .44-40 are also offered at extra cost.

Winchester 1873 Short Sporting Rifle

As above but fitted with a 20" octagon barrel.

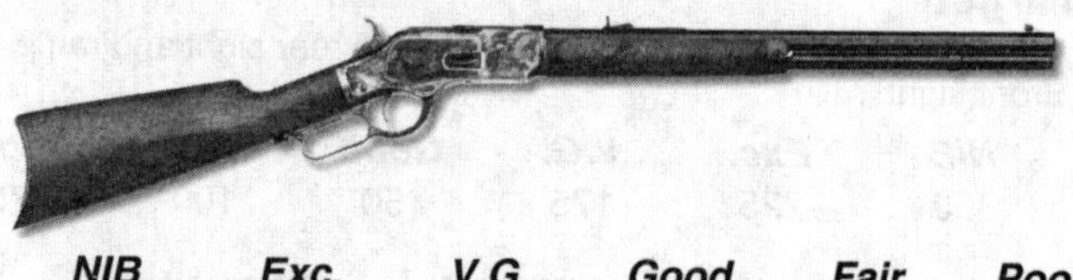

NIB	Exc.	V.G.	Good	Fair	Poor
950	750	—	—	—	—

Winchester 1873 Half-Octagon Rifle

Same as above but with 24.25" half octagon barrel. Stock has a checkered pistol grip.

NIB	Exc.	V.G.	Good	Fair	Poor
1000	800	600	450	350	200

Winchester 1873 Musket

Chambered for the .44-40 or .45 Long Colt cartridge and fitted with a 30" barrel with full stock and three barrel bands. Magazine capacity is 14 rounds. Weight is about 9 lbs.

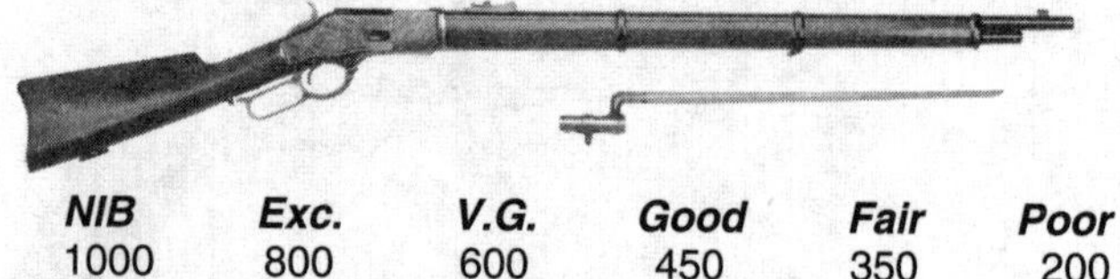

NIB	Exc.	V.G.	Good	Fair	Poor
1000	800	600	450	350	200

Model 1885 High Wall Single-Shot Carbine

Chambered for .38-55, .30-30, .44-40, .45 Colt, .40-65, or .45-70 with 28" barrel. Walnut stock.

NIB	Exc.	V.G.	Good	Fair	Poor
825	600	450	350	250	—

Model 1885 High Wall Single-Shot Rifle

Same as above but with 30" barrel.

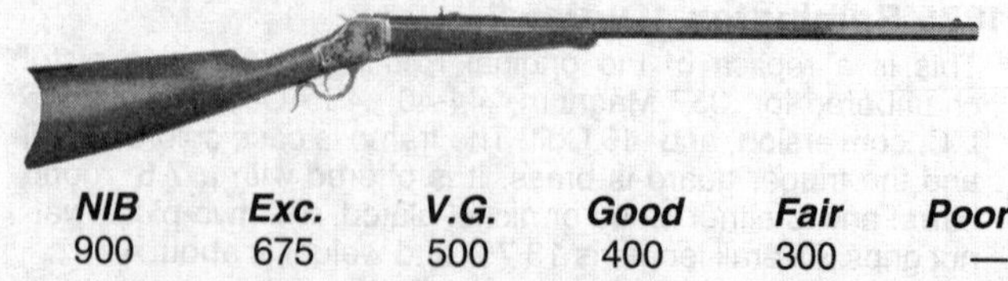

NIB	Exc.	V.G.	Good	Fair	Poor
900	675	500	400	300	—

Model 1885 High Wall Single-Shot Rifle Pistol Grip

Fitted with a 30" or 32" barrel and checkered pistol-grip stock. Same calibers as above.

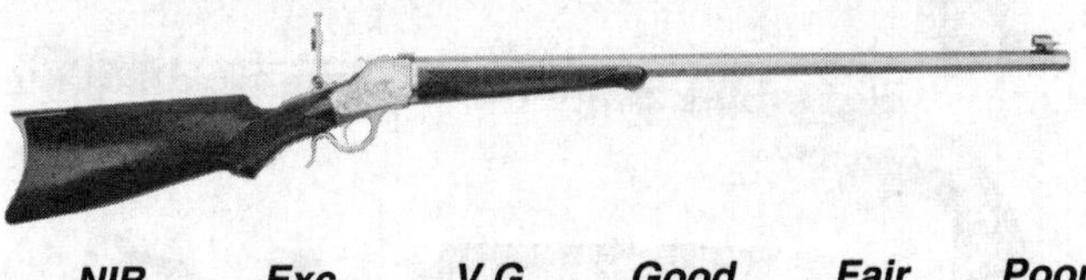

NIB	Exc.	V.G.	Good	Fair	Poor
1000	800	600	450	350	—

Winchester 1885 Low Wall Sporting Rifle

This version of the Low Wall Winchester is chambered for the .22 Hornet, .30-30, .44 Mag, or .45 Colt cartridges. Fitted with a 30" octagon barrel. Walnut stock with pistol grip. Weight is about 7.5 lbs. Introduced in 2004.

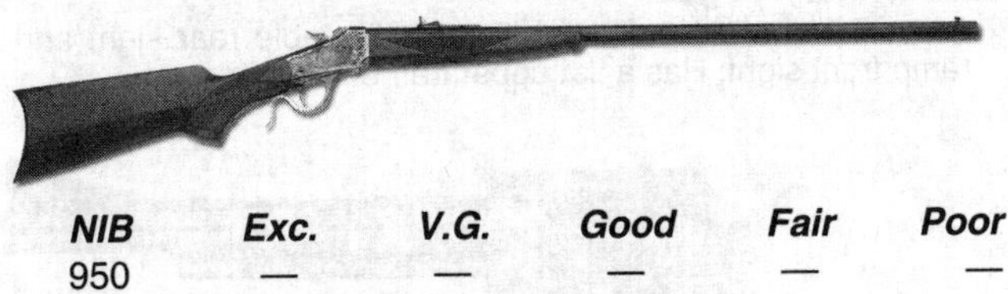

NIB	Exc.	V.G.	Good	Fair	Poor
950	—	—	—	—	—

Winchester 1885 Low Wall Schuetzen

As above but chambered for the .45 Colt cartridge and fitted with a palm rest and Swiss butt. Weight is about 7.75 lbs. Introduced in 2004.

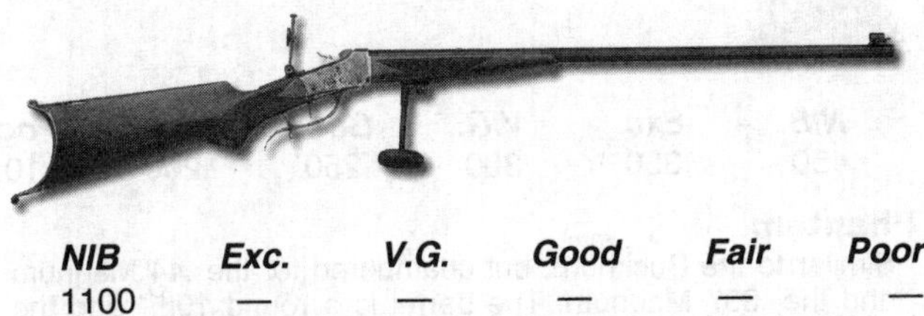

NIB	Exc.	V.G.	Good	Fair	Poor
1100	—	—	—	—	—

Hawken Santa Fe

Based on the famous original rifle this reproduction is bored for .54 caliber and fitted with a 32" octagon barrel. A double set trigger and case hardened lock plate are standard. The stock ferrule and wedge plates are German silver. The stock is walnut with cheekpiece. Overall length is 50" and weight is about 9.5 lbs. Also available in kit form.

NIB	Exc.	V.G.	Good	Fair	Poor
350	300	250	200	150	100

Cattleman

This is a single-action revolver patterned closely after the Colt Single-Action Army. It is chambered in various popular calibers: .357 Magnum, .44-40, .44 Special, .45 ACP, .45 L.C./.45 ACP convertible, and .45 Colt. It is offered with barrel lengths of 4.75", 5.5", and 7.5". It is offered with either a modern or black powder-type frame and brass or steel backstraps. The finish is blued, with walnut grips. A Sheriff's Model with a 3" barrel and no ejector rod chambered for .44-40 and .45 Colt is also available and is valued the same. Weight is approximately 38 oz. for 5.5" barrel gun.

NIB	Exc.	V.G.	Good	Fair	Poor
325	275	250	200	150	100

Cattleman Flattop Target Model

This model is similar to the standard Cattleman, with an adjustable rear sight.

NIB	Exc.	V.G.	Good	Fair	Poor
435	350	275	225	175	125

Cattleman Gunfighter NM

Chambered for the .45 Colt cartridge and fitted with a 4.75", 5.5", or 7.5" barrel. Black checkered grip with matte blued finish. Weight is around 37 oz. Introduced in 2005.

NIB	Exc.	V.G.	Good	Fair	Poor
360	275	—	—	—	—

Cattleman Cody NM

As above but with nickel finish and ivory-style grips.

NIB	Exc.	V.G.	Good	Fair	Poor
610	575	—	—	—	—

Cattleman Frisco NM

As above but with charcoal blued barrel and case colored frame. Pearl grips.

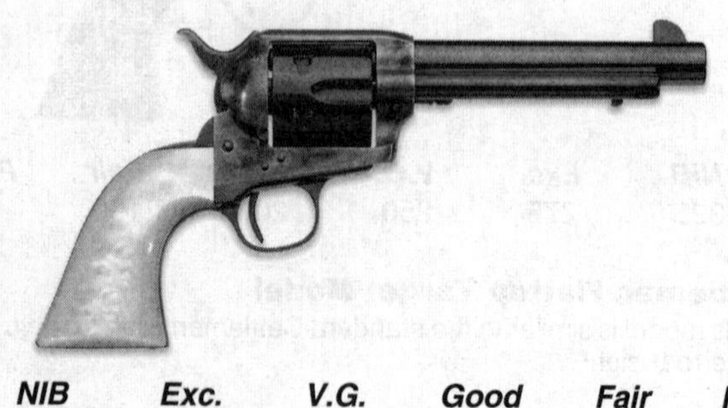

NIB	Exc.	V.G.	Good	Fair	Poor
595	575	—	—	—	—

Bisley

Chambered for the .32-20, .38 Special, .357 Mag, .38-40, .44-40, and .44 Special and fitted with either 4.75", 5.5", or 7.5" barrel. Case hardened frame with two-piece walnut grips.

NIB	Exc.	V.G.	Good	Fair	Poor
435	350	275	225	175	125

Bisley Flattop

As above but with adjustable rear sight.

NIB	Exc.	V.G.	Good	Fair	Poor
435	350	275	225	175	125

Buckhorn Buntline

This version is chambered for the .44 Magnum. It has an 18" round barrel, and it is cut for attaching a shoulder stock. Steel backstrap and trigger guard. Overall length is 23" and weight is about 57 oz.

NIB	Exc.	V.G.	Good	Fair	Poor
400	325	300	250	200	100

NOTE: Detachable shoulder stock add 25 percent.

Buckhorn Target

Same as above but fitted with an adjustable rear sight and ramp front sight. Has a flat upper frame.

NIB	Exc.	V.G.	Good	Fair	Poor
450	350	300	250	200	100

Phantom

Similar to the Buckhorn, but chambered for the .44 Magnum and the .357 Magnum. The barrel is a round 10.5" and the frame is blued with blued steel backstrap. One-piece walnut grips with anatomic profile. Adjustable sight. Weight is approximately 53 oz.

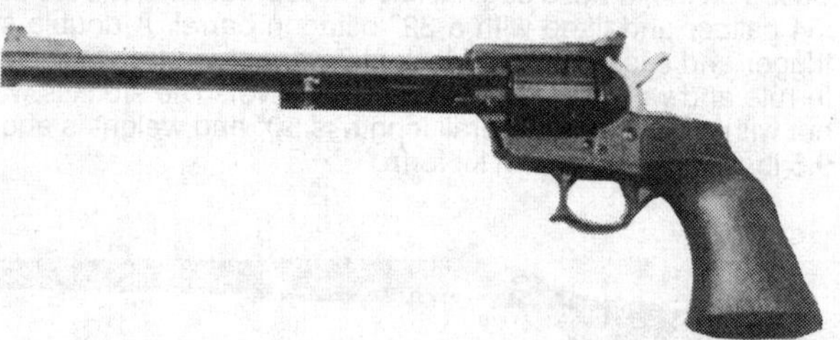

NIB	Exc.	V.G.	Good	Fair	Poor
350	325	300	250	200	100

Buntline Carbine

This version has the 18" barrel but is fitted with a permanently mounted shoulder stock with a brass buttplate and sling swivel. Chambered for .44-40, .45 Long Colt, .357 Magnum, and .44 Magnum. Offered with fixed or adjustable sights.

NIB	Exc.	V.G.	Good	Fair	Poor
450	400	350	300	250	200

New Thunderer Model

Designed and imported exclusively by Cimarron Arms for single-action shooting competition. Fitted with bird's-head grip with hard rubber, this model is chambered for the .357 Magnum, .44 Special, .44 WCF, and .45 Colt. Offered in barrel lengths of 3.5" and 4.75". Finish in nickel or blued with case colored frame.

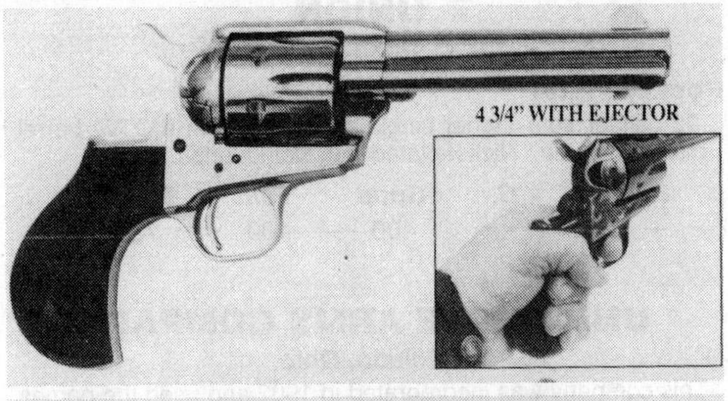

NIB	Exc.	V.G.	Good	Fair	Poor
450	350	300	250	200	100

Tornado

This 6-shot revolver is chambered for the .454 Casull and fitted with a 4.75", 5.5" or 7.5" with ported barrel. Sandblasted nickel finish. Weight is about 47 oz.

NIB	Exc.	V.G.	Good	Fair	Poor
750	600	500	—	—	—

1873 Stallion

This is a scaled-down version, chambered for .22 LR/.22 Magnum. It is blued with a case colored frame and features one-piece walnut grips.

NIB	Exc.	V.G.	Good	Fair	Poor
325	275	250	200	150	100

No. 3 Schofield Revolver

Patterned after the original S&W revolver this model is chambered for the .44-40 or .45 Colt cartridge. It is fitted with a 7", 5", or 3.5" barrel. Weight with 7" barrel is approximately 40 oz.

NIB	Exc.	V.G.	Good	Fair	Poor
775	550	400	300	—	—

No. 3 New Model Russian

Chambered for the .44 Russian cartridge and fitted with a 6" or 7" barrel.

NIB	Exc.	V.G.	Good	Fair	Poor
825	650	450	350	—	—

Inspector Model

This is a double-action revolver built on the same general lines as the Colt Detective model. Cylinder holds six cartridges and is chambered for the .38 Special. Offered in these barrel lengths with fixed sights: 2", 2.125", 2.5", 3", 4", 6" and also offered in 4" and 6" barrel lengths with adjustable sights. Grips are walnut and finish is blued or chrome. With the 3" barrel the weight is about 24 oz.

NIB	Exc.	V.G.	Good	Fair	Poor
275	200	150	125	100	75

UHLINGER, WILLIAM P.

Philadelphia, Pennsylvania

Pocket Revolver

A .32 caliber spur trigger revolver with a 2.75" or 3" octagonal barrel and an unfluted 6-shot cylinder. Blued with rosewood or walnut grips. Manufactured during the late 1860s and early 1870s.

NOTE: Uhlinger-manufactured pistols will often be found with retailer's names on them, such as D.D. Cone, Washington, D.C.; J.P. Lower; and W.L. Grant.

Long Cylinder (1-3/16")

Exc.	V.G.	Good	Fair	Poor
—	—	600	250	100

Short Cylinder (1")

Exc.	V.G.	Good	Fair	Poor
—	—	425	175	75

.32 Rimfire Model (5", 6", or 7" Barrel)

Exc.	V.G.	Good	Fair	Poor
—	—	600	250	100

ULTIMATE

SEE—Camex-Blaser

ULTRA LIGHT ARMS, INC.

Granville, West Virginia

This maker manufactures a variety of bolt-action rifles fitted with Douglas barrels of varying lengths, custom triggers, and reinforced graphite stocks. The values for standard production models are listed.

Model 20 (Short Action)

Weight is 4.5 lbs. with 22" barrel. Composte stock with choice of colors or camo finish. Adjustable trigger. No sights. Offered in left- or right-hand.

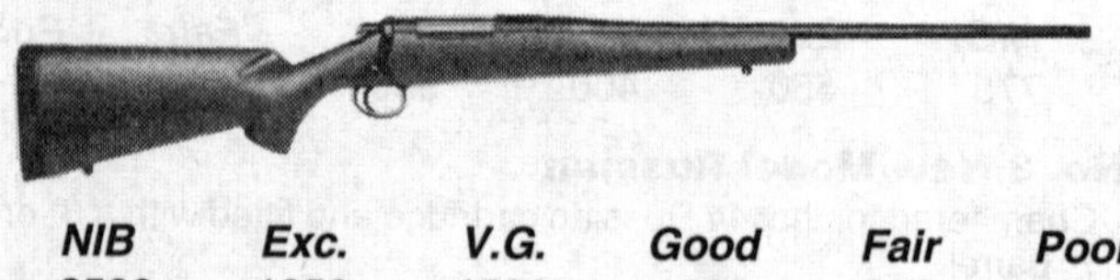

NIB	Exc.	V.G.	Good	Fair	Poor
2500	1850	1500	1250	900	700

Model 20 RF Rimfire

Weight is about 4.5 lbs. with 22" barrel. Stock is synthetic with choice of colors or camo finish. No sights. Adjustable trigger. Available as a single-shot or repeater.

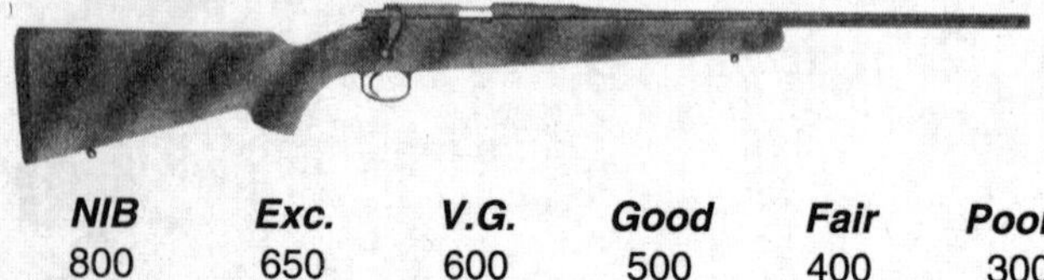

NIB	Exc.	V.G.	Good	Fair	Poor
800	650	600	500	400	300

Model 20 Hunter's Pistol

A bolt-action repeating pistol designed with the serious hunter in mind. It is offered in various popular calibers with a 14", high-quality Douglas heavy barrel. It has a 5-shot magazine and is matte blued, with a reinforced graphite Kevlar stock. It was introduced in 1987.

NIB	Exc.	V.G.	Good	Fair	Poor
1250	1000	850	750	600	500

Model 24 (Long Action)

Weight is approximately 5.25 lbs. with 22" barrel.

NIB	Exc.	V.G.	Good	Fair	Poor
2600	1850	1500	1250	900	700

Model 28 Magnum

Weight is about 5.75 lbs. with 24" barrel.

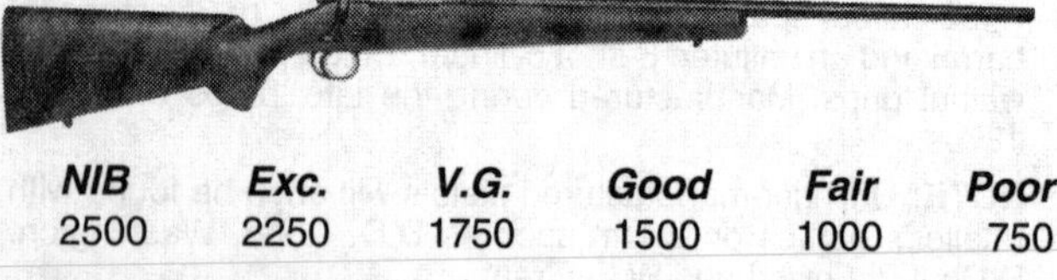

NIB	Exc.	V.G.	Good	Fair	Poor
2500	2250	1750	1500	1000	750

Model 40 Magnum

Weight is about 7.5 lbs. with 26" barrel.

NIB	Exc.	V.G.	Good	Fair	Poor
2900	2250	1750	1500	1000	700

Model 90

This is a muzzle-loading rifle built with either a .45 or .50 caliber barrel. Graphite stock. Williams sights. Barrel length is 28". Adjustable trigger. Weight is about 6 lbs.

NIB	Exc.	V.G.	Good	Fair	Poor
950	750	600	—	—	—

UNCETA

SEE—Astra-Unceta SA

UNION

Unknown

Pocket Pistol

.22 caliber spur trigger single-shot pistol with a 2.75" barrel marked "Union." Nickel-plated with walnut grips.

Exc.	V.G.	Good	Fair	Poor
—	—	400	100	75

UNION FIRE ARMS COMPANY

Toledo, Ohio

This company was incorporated in 1902 and used the names of Union Fire Arms, Union Arms Company, Illinois Arms Company (made for Sears) and Bee Be Arms Company. In 1917 the company was either bought up or absorbed by Ithaca Gun Company.

Double Barrel Shotguns

Union's predecessor, Colton Manufacturing Co. (1894-1902) made a double for Sears. It was cleverly designed with coil mainspring striker locks set into sideplates. The Union double in 12 and 16 gauge with steel or Damascus barrels derived from it, but was a traditional hammerless sidelock side-by-side well-made gun (1902-1913) and also sold by Sears. Values depend on grade and condition.

Union also offered, about 1905, an unusual boxlock hammer gun, the Model 25 in 12 gauge only. It employs external hammers but they are mounted within the frame and the spurs protrude in front of the topsnap opener. These guns are hard to find and values range from $300 to $1,200 depending on condition. They are produced with steel, twist, or Damascus barrels but only in a plain grade.

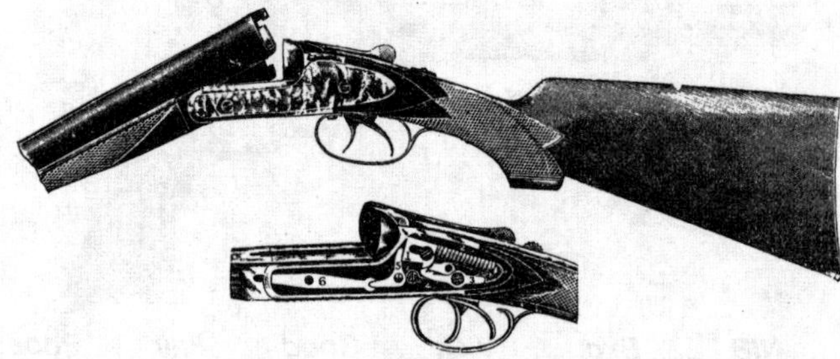

Courtesy Nick Niles

Exc.	V.G.	Good	Fair	Poor
1250	500	400	300	200

Model 24

Slide action, Model 25 Peerless that was a fancy version of the Model 24 and the Model 25A, which was a trap model, were manufactured from 1902 to 1913 in 12 or 16 gauge with 24", 26", 28", or 32" steel or Damascus barrels. This gun had a unique double trigger. The front trigger cocked and decocked an internal firing pin and the back trigger fired the gun. The gun is marked on the left side of the frame and the pump release is on the right side. This model had one serious drawback, in that the slide that extracted a spent shell extended back over the comb of the stock. This often hit the shooter's thumb knuckle and caused injury. In 1907 Union redesigned their slide by reducing its length and shielding it behind a steel plate that covered the rear half of the opening. These are the Model 24, 25, and 25A improved versions. Approximately 17,000 of all models combined were made.

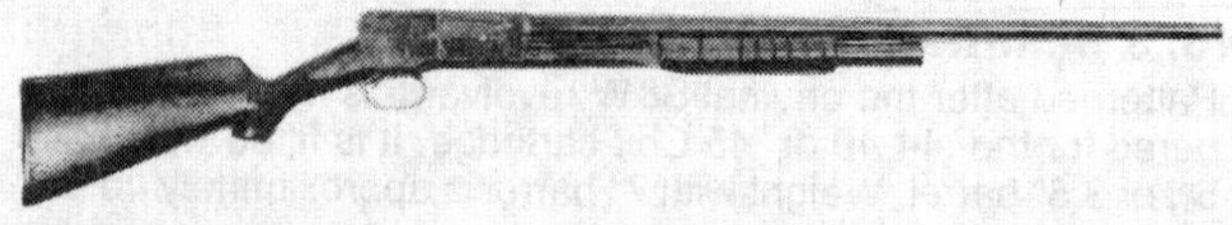

Exc.	V.G.	Good	Fair	Poor
—	750	300	200	100

Model 50

Manufactured 1911 to 1913. This was basically a redesign of the Model 24. The main distinguishing feature of the Model 50 was that the frame sloped down to meet the comb of the stock and the double trigger system was replaced by a single trigger. It came in 12 or 16 gauge with a 26", 28", 30", or 32" Krupp steel barrel. Fewer than 3,000 were made.

Exc.	V.G.	Good	Fair	Poor
—	850	400	300	200

Model 22

This was essentially a no frills Model 23. It had the same barrel length and steel options, but it had a plain walnut stock and no engraving. There were fewer than 10,000 Model 22 and 23s made.

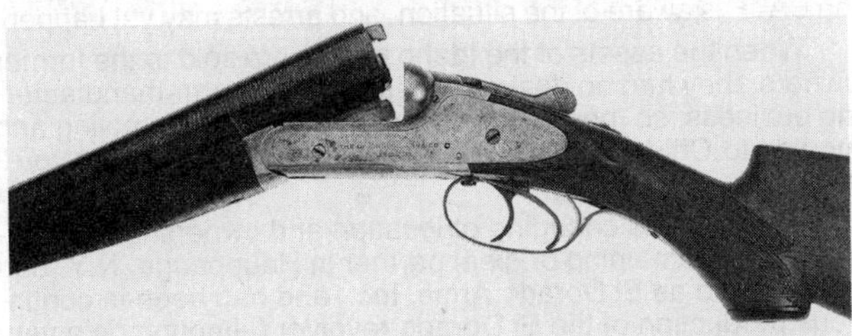

Courtesy Nick Niles, Paul Goodwin photo

Exc.	V.G.	Good	Fair	Poor
—	300	100	75	50

Model 23

Hammerless double, manufactured between 1902 and 1913 with or without automatic ejectors. With some engraving, it came in both single and double trigger models; this was their top grade gun. Came in 12 and 16 gauge with 28", 30", or 32" steel, twist, or Damascus barrels.

Exc.	V.G.	Good	Fair	Poor
—	450	150	125	100

Diamond Grade

Single-shot, manufactured between 1905 and 1910. It had a unique octagonal breech in 12 gauge only with 30" steel, laminated, or Damascus barrel. This was their premium grade single-shot. Few of these were made.

Exc.	V.G.	Good	Fair	Poor
—	450	200	100	50

Model 18

Single-shot, manufactured 1906 to 1913 came in 12 or 16 gauge. 30", 32", 34", or 36" steel barrel. A plain single-shot. Very few made.

Exc.	V.G.	Good	Fair	Poor
—	200	75	50	25

Reifngraber

A .32 or .38 S&W caliber gas operated semi-automatic pistol, with a 3" barrel. Blued with walnut grips, approximately 100 of these pistols were manufactured.

Exc.	V.G.	Good	Fair	Poor
—	2250	1100	500	350

Automatic Revolver

.32 S&W caliber, similar to the Webley Fosbery semi-automatic revolver with a 3" barrel. Blued with either walnut or hard rubber grips. The cylinder has zigzag grooves.

Exc.	V.G.	Good	Fair	Poor
—	3250	1250	500	250

UNIQUE

Hendaye, France

SEE—Pyrenees

UNITED SPORTING ARMS, INC.

Tucson, Arizona

THE HISTORY OF SEVILLE AND EL DORADO REVOLVERS

by J.C. Munnell

The history of United Sporting Arms, its related companies, and the Seville and El Dorado line of single-action revolvers is a long and tortuous one. It actually begins in 1973 or 1974, with the formation of United States Arms in Riverhead, New York, by three individuals. Before any but a few prototype guns were made, the partners split up, with one remaining as United States Arms, and the other two forming United Sporting Arms in nearby Hauppauge, New York.

United States Arms produced the Abilene revolver, intended to compete head-on price-wise with the Ruger Blackhawk, while United Sporting Arms, intending to make a superior (and higher-priced) product, initially produced the Seville in chrome moly steel, and slightly later, the El Dorado revolver out of stainless steel.

The Abilene was manufactured in Riverhead until 1979 or 1980 in calibers .357 and .44 magnum, and possibly the .45 Colt, all in blued steel. The assets of this company were eventually sold to A.I.G., Inc., which was a division of Mossberg. A.I.G. assembled guns from existing parts until 1983, at which time the Abilene production ended. These guns bore a North Haven, CT address, and utilized a distinctive hammer-nose safety device instead of the former transfer bar system. Calibers were the same, and all guns were made from carbon steel. Some guns had a Magnaloy finish, thereby giving rise to the misconception that some Abilenes were made from stainless steel, none were.

Meanwhile, the two remaining original partners began production of the United Sporting Arms Seville revolver in 1977. By late in that year, this company had accomplished several firearms "firsts" with production of the stainless steel El Dorado revolver. This was the first use of 17-4 pH stainless for a revolver frame, far pre-dating Freedom Arms, and was made at a time when Sturm Ruger's engineering department was sending lengthy letters explaining why stainless steel was totally unsuitable for guns chambered for the .44 magnum cartridge. It would be years until the rest of the firearms industry caught up to this fledgling company.

In 1979, one of the remaining partners established a second production facility in Tombstone, Arizona, under the name of United Sporting Arms of Arizona, Inc. Guns made in this plant still utilized frames made in New York, and therefore bore the Hauppauge, N.Y., frame inscription. However, Tombstone-built guns will contain the letter "T" as a suffix to the serial number. In Tombstone, the Silver Seville was born, having a highly-polished stainless grip frame on an otherwise blued gun. This is a striking combination, and has become quite popular on custom guns as well as some limited production runs from other makers. (Neither the guns themselves, nor the official company records reflect this designation, only the boxes for the guns do.) Here, to the .41 magnum and .45 Colt calibers were added to the Seville line. No stainless steel guns were made in Tombstone, Arizona.

Later in 1979, the Arizona facility was relocated to the town of Bisbee, Arizona. Less than 200 guns were made with the Bisbee address. These were all made from blued steel, and were all in .45 Colt or.44 Magnum, except as noted. Oddly enough, in the short time the company was at this location, three very distinct models were produced.

First was the Tombstone Commemorative. Although 200 were commissioned by the city of Tombstone, only about 60 were ever completed. These guns had blued frames, and stainless steel cylinders, barrels and grip frames. Some engraving was present on the cylinder and barrel, and the legend "Tombstone, Arizona 100 years of history 1879-1979" appears in three lines on the barrel. The guns came in a wooden case, and serial numbers began with TC-1. All were in .44-40 WCF caliber.

The second Bisbee gun was the Helldorado. Originally designed for the Old Tucson stunt man group "The Fall Guys," the gun had a flat-top frame with no sights, and was intended for blanks only. Only 4 were made. The final Bisbee introduction, and the only one to survive the next location change, was the Quik Kit. This was an ingenious multi-caliber system of interchangeable barrels and cylinders; invented by Ray Herriott of Centaur Systems. Only about 30 such guns were produced in Bisbee, some in blue and some in stainless. All bore the Centaur logo on the frame and all had the serial number prefix of "QK."

In late 1979, the company moved once again, this time to Tucson, Arizona. By now, the split from the New York concern was completed legally as well as physically, new guns were in blue and stainless, but all were called Sevilles. (The New York operation retained exclusive rights to the El Dorado name.) Also at this time, the frame marking on the guns simply read "Sporting Arms, Inc."

Between late 1979 and the end of 1981, several new variations of the Seville revolver were introduced. Shortly after Ruger announced the Blackhawk SRM in .357 Maximum caliber, United Sporting Arms offered a lengthened-frame stainless steel gun in this caliber. This gun did not suffer from the various maladies which eventually doomed the Ruger version, and was winning silhouette matches long after the demise of the Blackhawk SRM. This model also spawned the awesome .375 USA Seville—the same caliber later renamed the .375 Super Magnum by Dan Wesson. Although only two prototypes of this caliber were made before the next company change, several hundred guns were made in .357 Maximum.

Also during this period the Sheriffs' Model with 3-1/2" barrel was introduced. Most of these guns were produced in chrome moly steel, and most were shipped with a distinctive round-butt "bird's-head" grip frame. This proved very popular, and these guns became a mainstay of the company's line right until the end. Most of these Sheriffs' Models had fully adjustable sights, but at least three were made with Colt-like fixed sights, all of which, oddly, were convertibles in.45 Colt and .45 ACP.

Guns were produced in calibers 9mm Winchester Magnum, and .45 Winchester Magnum, primarily for export to Europe. A few guns were made in .44-40 and .44 Special. Also introduced was the Hunter Finish, a bead-blasted stainless steel, and the Rawhide finish, with the same treatment to a blued gun. A very few blued guns were made with a brass grip frame, as well as the "Silver Seville" configuration.

In early February of 1982, the company again changed ownership. The company name, and the frame marking on the guns, returned to United Sporting Arms, Inc. About half of the production was devoted to the so-called long-frame guns—.357 Maximum and .375 USA—and about half of these were silhouette guns with 10-1/2" barrels. The .454 magnum (.454 Casull) was added to the line. However, only 30 of these guns were ever made. (Note: perhaps as many as 50 guns in this chambering were made and marked "Sporting Arms, Inc." These guns were NOT made in any United Sporting Arms factory, and are very definitely of sub-standard quality.) These guns were made on a special frame, different from all other caliber guns.

Prototype guns were made—usually two in each caliber. Produced were .41 Super Magnum and .44 Super Magnum (long before Dan Wesson made guns available in .445 and .414 Super Magnums), as well as .375 Special, and, oddly enough, .218 Mashburn Bee. None of these went into regular; production.

Normal production guns were, as to be expected, with blued, stainless steel, "silver" and brass grip-frame guns were all produced. Quite a few bird's-head grip guns were made, not only in the Sherrif's Model configuration. Guns in heavy-recoiling calibers are particularly comfortable to shoot two-handed with this grip configuration. The author has a .454 Magnum Seville with a 6-1/2" barrel and the bird's-head grip frame, and it is by far the most comfortable gun I've ever shot, even with 325 grain bullets at over 1700 fps!

In November of 1985, the company was again sold, and this time it was moved to Post Fails, Idaho. Problems developed almost immediately, and even though it would be three years until the assets were sold (to the previous owners from Tucson), very few guns were ever made; less than 200. The only new product introduced in Idaho was the .32 H&R magnum chambering.

Caution: Several hundred frames "disappeared" from the Idaho plant right before the bankruptcy sale, and several bootleg guns have turned up. These guns are of distinctly dubious quality, as are many of the Idaho-marked guns. Supposedly, the BATF is aware of the situation, and arrests may yet happen.

When the assets of the Idaho plant were sold to the former owners, they had no desire to resume the firearm-manufacturing business, so they shipped the remaining parts, tooling and moulds to Chimney Rock, North Carolina. In a moment you'll see why.

While all this changing of location and ownership was going on, the remaining original partner in Hauppauge, N.Y. had reorganized as El Dorado Arms, Inc., and had been in continuous production of the El Dorado revolver (although on a very limited basis) since 1979. Until the mid-1980s, all El Dorados were made from 17-4 pH stainless steel, and nearly all were chambered for the .44 magnum cartridge.

In 1985, El Dorado Arms relocated to Chimney Rock, N.C., where production continued, and the model line was expanded to include the Laredo in blued steel, and the fixed-sight Rebel in both blued and stainless steel. Also introduced at this time (although at least two prototype guns so chambered had been made in New York) was the .22 long rifle chambering, complete with match chambers, specifically for the silhouette market. Eventually .22 rimfire magnum guns were added.

The only thing lacking from the North Carolina lineup was a long-frame revolver for the Super Magnum calibers. When the remaining Idaho assets were received in North Carolina, not only were there parts for the long-frame gun, but also the molds to produce more parts for these guns. In fact quite a few El Dorado .357 and .375 Super Magnum-chambered guns found their way into the silhouette winner's circle, alongside their smaller brothers.

Ironically, it had taken nine years, but all the components of United Sporting Arms had came full circle, and were reunited under one roof. And this was under the ownership of one of the founders of the original United States Arms!

Production of El Dorado revolvers always was very limited, and it finally ceased for good in 1997 or 1998.

Altogether, only about 6,000 or 7,000 guns were produced by all of the United Sporting Arms/El Dorado Arms companies. (Total production of the Abilene revolver by either United States Arms or A.I.G. is not available). However, even forgetting the eight different frame inscriptions, barrel lengths between 3-1/2" and 10-1/2" were made; there were all-blue, all stainless, blue and stainless, and blue and brass guns, standard finish, "hunter" and "rawhide" finishes as well as high-polish stainless; standard and bird's-head grip-frame guns; Quik-Kits, convertibles and Tombstone Commemoratives; long-frame, short-frame and

.454-frame guns. There were also at least 21 different chamberings. Thus, the variations are practically endless.

Quality, except for the very few noted instances, was always very high. An informal United Sporting Arms slogan was that a Seville was what a Super Blackhawk could be if Ruger had a custom shop. Given the truth of this statement, it must be admitted that an El Dorado Arms gun was what a custom Seville could have been.

Advertised prices for Sevilles and El Dorados run the full gamut from bargain "orphaned" gun prices to those reflecting the semi-custom nature of these guns. For the most part, what price stability does exist is on the higher end, and this is as it should be.

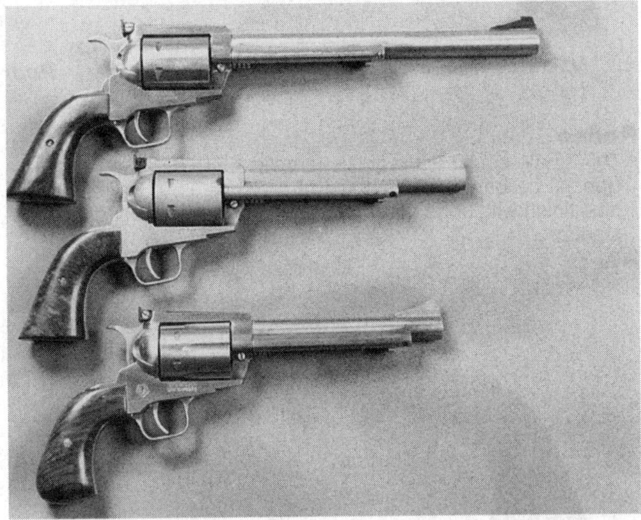

Three different barrel lengths of the long frame Seville. From top to bottom; 10-1/2", 7-1/2", and 6-1/2". All of these revolvers were made by United Sporting Arms, Inc. of Tucson, Arizona.

For most of the production of United Sporting Arms guns, and some of the El Dorado Arms guns, copies of original factory records are available. For a letter of verification for any particular gun (refunded if no records are available), send $20 to J.C. Munnell, 633 Long Run Rd., McKeesport, PA 15132.

These two United Sporting Arms, Inc. of Bisbee, Arizona, revolvers are the sightless Heldorados.

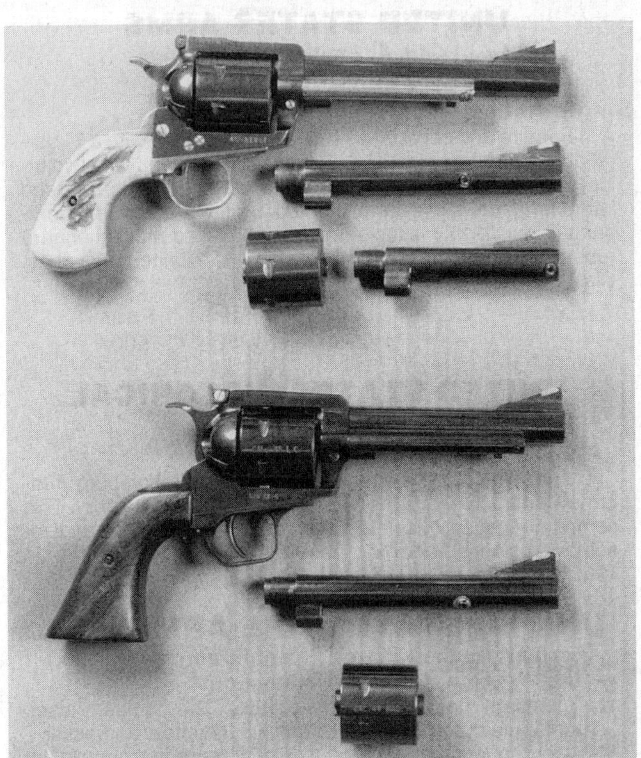

Two examples of Quik-Kit revolvers. At the top is a Ruger reworked by United Sporting Arms, Inc. of Tucson and at the bottom is a standard production revolver from the same company.

Blued Guns

NIB	Exc.	V.G.	Good	Fair	Poor
N/A	500	450	350	N/A	N/A

Blue Silhouette (10.5" barrels)

NIB	Exc.	V.G.	Good	Fair	Poor
N/A	600	550	500	N/A	N/A

NOTE: Add $100 for stainless, $250 for stainless long-frame models (calibers .357 Maximum/Super Mag. and .357 USA/Super Mag).

Silver Sevilles

NIB	Exc.	V.G.	Good	Fair	Poor
N/A	550	475	400	N/A	N/A

Stainless Steel Guns

NIB	Exc.	V.G.	Good	Fair	Poor
N/A	600	525	450	N/A	N/A

Tombstone Commemorative

NIB	Exc.	V.G.	Good	Fair	Poor
1000	750	N/A	N/A	N/A	N/A

Quik-Kit Stainless Steel

NIB	Exc.	V.G.	Good	Fair	Poor
1500	1250	N/A	N/A	N/A	N/A

Quik-Kit Blued

NIB	Exc.	V.G.	Good	Fair	Poor
1200	1000	N/A	N/A	N/A	N/A

NOTE: For Quik-Kit guns with extra barrel and cylinder add $200 for each barrel and cylinder. Deduct 10 percent if United Sporting Arms, Hauppauge, N.Y. Deduct 20 percent if United Sporting Arms, Post Falls, ID. Add 20 percent if El Dorado Arms (either N.Y. or N.C.). Add 10 percent for 1-1/2" barrel Sheriff's Model. Add 20 percent for 10-1/2" barrel. Add 20 percent for bird's-head grip frame. Add 20 percent if brass grip frame.

UNITED STATES ARMS

Otis A. Smith Company
Rockfall, Connecticut

Single-Action Revolver

A .44 rimfire and centerfire single-action revolver with a 7" barrel and integral ejector. The hammer nose is fitted with two firing pins so that rimfire or centerfire cartridges can be used interchangeably. The barrel marked "United States Arms Company - New York," the top strap "No. 44." Blued with either hard rubber or rosewood grips. Manufactured in limited quantities. Circa 1870 to 1875.

Exc.	V.G.	Good	Fair	Poor
—	—	3250	1250	500

UNITED STATES HISTORICAL SOCIETY

Richmond, Virginia

The arms listed are manufactured by the Williamsburg Firearms Manufactory and the Virginia Firearms Manufactory. This company ceased business under this name in 1994 and resumed business under the name of America Remembers in Mechanicsville, Va.

UNITED STATES FIRE ARMS MFG.

(Formerly United States Patent Firearms Mfg. Co.)
Hartford, Connecticut

This company began business in 1992. The company uses parts manufactured in the U.S. and fits, finishes, and assembles the gun in Hartford. Produces only reproductions of Colt revolvers and rifles.

NOTE: This company offers a wide variety of special order options on its revolvers, from special bluing to grips to engraving. These special order options will affect price to a significant degree.

Single-Action Army Revolver

Offered in a wide variety of calibers including .22 rimfire, .32 WCF, .38 S&W, .357 Magnum, .38-40, .41 Colt, .44 Russian, .44-40, .45 Colt, and .45 ACP. Barrel lengths are 4.75", 5.5", and 7.5" with or without ejector. A modern cross pin frame is available for an additional $10. Prices listed are for standard grips and finish, Armory bone case finish, and Dome blue finish.

NIB	Exc.	V.G.	Good	Fair	Poor
1250	975	—	—	—	—

Single-Action Army Revolver Pre-War

As above but with pre-war "P" frame.

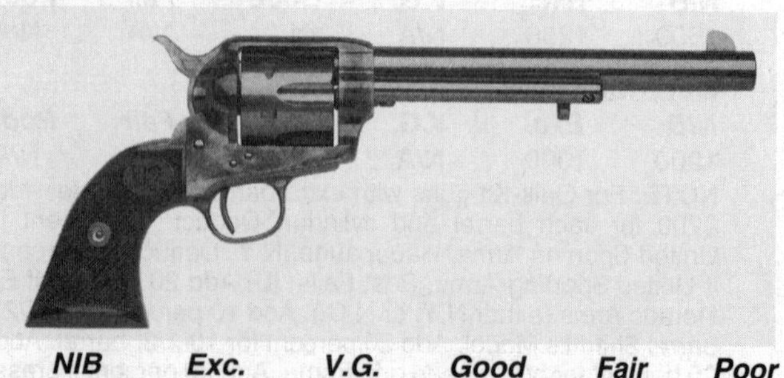

NIB	Exc.	V.G.	Good	Fair	Poor
1525	1100	—	—	—	—

Flattop Target Model

This model is offered with the same calibers as the Single-Action Army above. Barrel lengths are 4.75", 5.5", and 7.5". Grips are two-piece hard rubber. Prices listed are given for standard finish. Introduced in 1997.

NIB	Exc.	V.G.	Good	Fair	Poor
1000	725	575	—	—	—

Rodeo

This single-action revolver is offered in .45 Colt, .44-40 and .38 Special calibers with a choice of 4.75" or 5.50" barrel. Satin blue finish with bone case hammer. "US" hard rubber grips are standard.

NIB	Exc.	V.G.	Good	Fair	Poor
550	450	—	—	—	—

Buntline

This model features an all blued finish with 16" barrel. Chambered for the .45 Colt cartridge.

NIB	Exc.	V.G.	Good	Fair	Poor
2300	1750	—	—	—	—

Buntline Special

Fitted with a 16" barrel and chambered for the .45 Colt cartridge. Supplied with nickel stock. Limited edition. Cased.

NIB	Exc.	V.G.	Good	Fair	Poor
2895	2250	—	—	—	—

China Camp Cowboy Action Gun

Chambered for .45 Colt cartridge but other calibers also available from .32 WCF to .44 WCF. Barrel lengths are 4.75", 5.5", and 7.5". Special action job. Two-piece hard rubber grips standard. Finish is silver steel.

NIB	Exc.	V.G.	Good	Fair	Poor
1200	950	750	—	—	—

Model 1873 Cut Away

Chambered for the .45 Colt cartridge ***but not to be fired***. Fitted with a 7.5" barrel and brushed steel finish. Parts cut away for display. Discontinued.

NIB	Exc.	V.G.	Good	Fair	Poor
N/A	—	—	—	—	—

Henry Nettleton Revolver

This is an exact reproduction of the U.S. Government inspector model produced in the Springfield Armory. Offered in 7.5" and 5.5" models. Introduced in 1997. Discontinued.

NIB	Exc.	V.G.	Good	Fair	Poor
1100	800	600	—	—	—

The Plinker

Chambered for the .22 cartridge and fitted with a choice of barrel lengths of 4.75", 5.5", or 7.5". An extra .22 WMR cylinder is included.

NIB	Exc.	V.G.	Good	Fair	Poor
950	700	—	—	—	—

The .22 Target

As above but with adjustable rear sight and replaceable front sight blade.

NIB	Exc.	V.G.	Good	Fair	Poor
990	750	—	—	—	—

Gunslinger

Offered in .45 Colt, .44 Special, .44 WCF, .38 Special, .38 WCF, or .32 WCF and choice of 4.75", .5.5",or 7.5" barrel. Cross pin frame. Hard rubber grips. Aged bluing finish. Black style frame optional.

NIB	Exc.	V.G.	Good	Fair	Poor
910	700	—	—	—	—

NOTE: Add $135 for black powder frame.

Custom Custer Battlefield Gun

Replica of 1873 revolver used during height of Indian Wars, including Custer's Last Stand. Limited edition with cartouche of Ordnance Sub-inspector Orville W. Ainsworth; serial range 200-14,343. 7.5" barrel, six shot. Antique Patina aged blue. One-piece walnut stock.

NIB	Exc.	V.G.	Good	Fair	Poor
1275	850	600	—	—	—

The Hunter

This revolver is chambered for the .17 HMR cartridge and fitted with a 7.5" barrel with adjustable rear sight and replaceable front sight blade. Finish is matte blue.

NIB	Exc.	V.G.	Good	Fair	Poor
840	600	—	—	—	—

Sheriff's Model

Chambered for a wide variety of calibers from the .45 Colt to the .32 WCF. Choice of 2.5", 3", 3.5", or 4" barrel. No ejector.

NIB	Exc.	V.G.	Good	Fair	Poor
950	700	—	—	—	—

NOTE: Add $250 for nickel finish.

Omni-Potent Bird's-Head Model

Chambered for the .45 Colt, .45 ACP, .44 Special, .44 WCF, .38 Special, .38 WCF, or the .32 WCF cartridges. Offered with bird's-head grips and available with 3.5", 4", or 4.75" barrel lengths.

NIB	Exc.	V.G.	Good	Fair	Poor
1250	925	700	—	—	—

Omni-Potent Subnose

As above but with 2", 3", or 4" barrel without ejector.

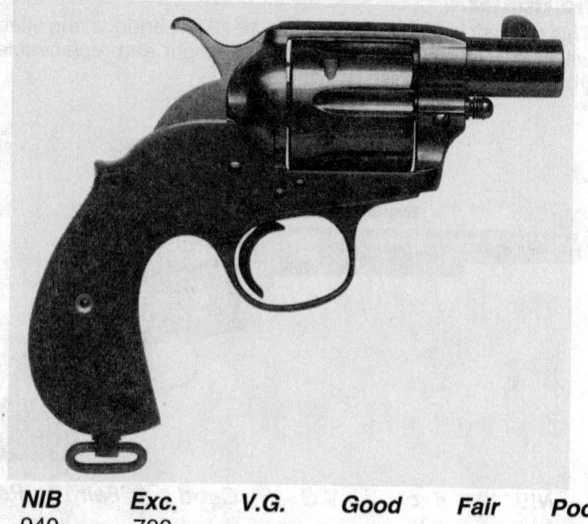

NIB	Exc.	V.G.	Good	Fair	Poor
940	700	—	—	—	—

Omni-Potent Target

Choice of 4.75", 5.5", or 7.5" barrel with adjustable rear sight and replaceable front blade sight.

NIB	Exc.	V.G.	Good	Fair	Poor
1195	900	—	—	—	—

Bisley Model

Based on the famous Bisley model this reproduction features barrel lengths of 4.75", 5.5", 7.5", and 10". The .45 Colt caliber is standard but .32 WCF, .38 S&W, .44 S&W, .41 Colt, .38 WCF, .44 WCF are optional. Introduced in 1997.

NIB	Exc.	V.G.	Good	Fair	Poor
1100	800	600	—	—	—

NOTE: Add $60 for 10" models.

Bisley Target

As above but with adjustable rear sight and replaceable blade front sight.

NIB	Exc.	V.G.	Good	Fair	Poor
1225	900	—	—	—	—

Pony Express

This model features a 5.50" barrel with special finish and engraved frame and barrel. Ivory grips are etched with pony express rider. Custom gun.

NIB	Exc.	V.G.	Good	Fair	Poor
3895	—	—	—	—	—

Sears 1902 Colt

This model is a replica of the Sears 1902 Colt SAA. Fitted with a 5.50" barrel, pearl grips, and full coverage engraving with gold line work on the cylinder and barrel. Custom gun.

NIB	Exc.	V.G.	Good	Fair	Poor
8995	—	—	—	—	—

Model 1910

This model, scheduled for production in 2006, is a stylized version of the early Colt Model 1910 .45 ACP pistol.

NIB	Exc.	V.G.	Good	Fair	Poor
1600	—	—	—	—	—

Model 1911

This model, scheduled for production in 2006, is a stylized version of the early Colt Model 1911 military model.

NIB	Exc.	V.G.	Good	Fair	Poor
1500	—	—	—	—	—

Ace .22 LR

Recreation of 1911-style Colt Ace. .22 LR with 10+1 capacity. Walnut grips. Introduced 2006. MSRP: 1995

Super .38

1911-style semi-auto. Blued finish; chambered for .38 Super Auto with 9+1 capacity. Walnut grips. Introduced 2006. MSRP: 1995

RIFLES

Cowboy Action Lightning

This is a copy of the Colt Lightning rifle chambered for the .44-40, .45 Colt, or the .38 WCF cartridge. Fitted with a 26" round barrel and walnut stock with crescent butt. Magazine capacity is 15 rounds. Introduced in the fall of 2003.

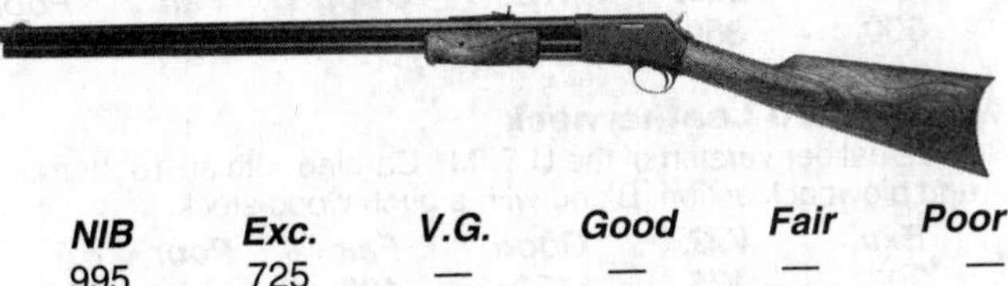

NIB	Exc.	V.G.	Good	Fair	Poor
995	725	—	—	—	—

Cowboy Action Carbine

As above but with 20" round barrel. Magazine capacity is 12 rounds.

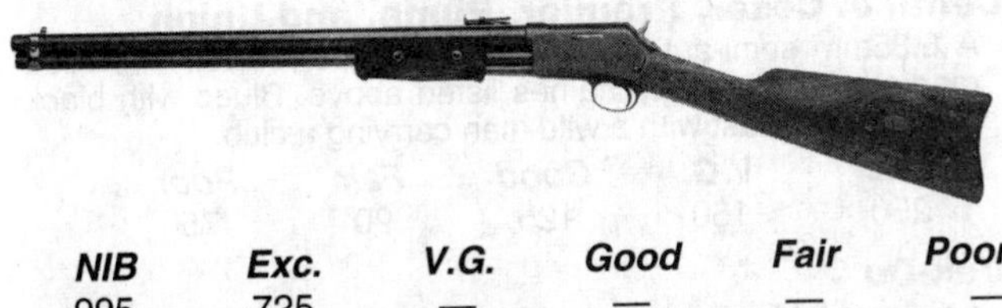

NIB	Exc.	V.G.	Good	Fair	Poor
995	725	—	—	—	—

Lightning Magazine Rifle

This model is a premium version of the Cowboy Action Lightning and features a choice of 26" round, half round, or octagon barrel. Checkered American walnut forearm with non-checkered stock with oil finish. Many extra cost options are offered for this model.

NIB	Exc.	V.G.	Good	Fair	Poor
1295	950	—	—	—	—

NOTE: Add $200 for half round barrel. Fancy wood, pistol grip, finish and engraving offered for this rifle.

Lightning Magazine Carbine

As above but with 20" round barrel.

NIB	Exc.	V.G.	Good	Fair	Poor
1295	950	—	—	—	—

Lightning Baby Carbine

This model is fitted with a 20" special round tapered barrel. Lightweight carbine forearm with border line.

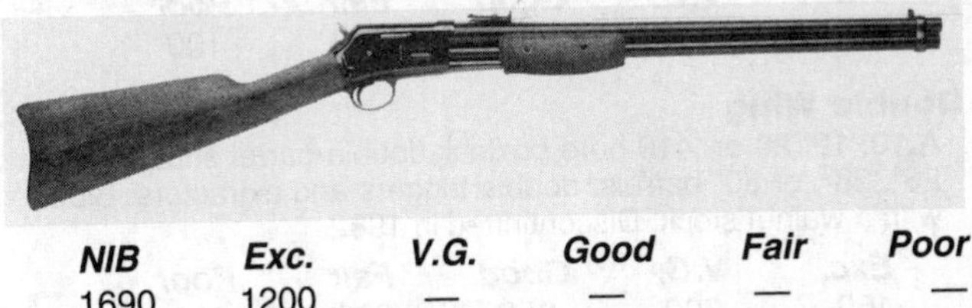

NIB	Exc.	V.G.	Good	Fair	Poor
1690	1200	—	—	—	—

UNITED STATES REVOLVER ASSOCIATION

SEE—Harrington & Richardson Arms Co.

UNITED STATES SMALL ARMS CO.

Chicago, Illinois

Huntsman Model Knife Pistol

Made from approximately 1918-1930.

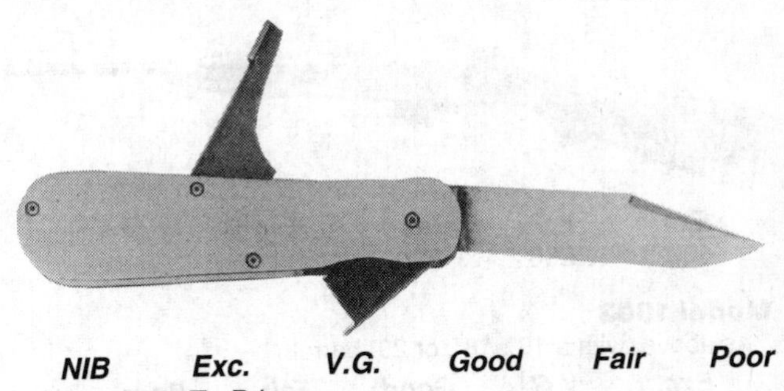

NIB	Exc.	V.G.	Good	Fair	Poor
Too Rare To Price					

UNIVERSAL FIREARMS

Sacksonville, Arkansas

Model 7312

A 12 gauge Over/Under shotgun with separated 30" ventilated rib barrels, single-selective trigger and automatic ejectors. The case hardened receiver engraved. Blued with a walnut stock. Discontinued in 1982.

Exc.	V.G.	Good	Fair	Poor
2000	1500	1250	900	450

Model 7412

As above, with extractors. Discontinued in 1982.

Exc.	V.G.	Good	Fair	Poor
1700	1250	1000	750	400

Model 7712

As above, with 26" or 28" barrels, nonselective single trigger and extractors. Discontinued in 1982.

Exc.	V.G.	Good	Fair	Poor
550	400	350	250	100

Model 7812

As above, with more detailed engraving and automatic ejectors. Discontinued in 1982.

Exc.	V.G.	Good	Fair	Poor
700	550	450	350	150

Model 7912

As above, with a gold wash frame and single-selective trigger. Discontinued in 1982.

Exc.	V.G.	Good	Fair	Poor
1350	1000	750	600	300

Model 7112

A 12 gauge double-barrel boxlock shotgun with 26" or 28" barrels, double triggers and extractors. Blued, case hardened with a walnut stock. Discontinued in 1982.

Exc.	V.G.	Good	Fair	Poor
450	300	250	200	100

Double Wing

A 10, 12, 20 or .410 bore boxlock double-barrel shotgun with 26", 28", or 30" barrels, double triggers and extractors. Blued with a walnut stock. Discontinued in 1982.

Exc.	V.G.	Good	Fair	Poor
450	300	250	200	100

Model 7212

A 12 gauge single-barrel trap shotgun with a 30" ventilated-rib ported barrel, and automatic ejector. Engraved, case hardened receiver and walnut stock. Discontinued in 1982.

Exc.	V.G.	Good	Fair	Poor
1200	850	650	450	300

Model 1000 Military Carbine

A copy of the U.S. M1 Carbine with an 18" barrel. Blued with a birch wood stock.

Exc.	V.G.	Good	Fair	Poor
400	250	200	100	75

Model 1003

As above, with a 16", 18", or 20" barrel.

Exc.	V.G.	Good	Fair	Poor
350	200	150	100	75

Model 1010

As above, but nickel-plated.

Exc.	V.G.	Good	Fair	Poor
375	225	175	125	100

Model 1015

As above, but gold-plated.

Exc.	V.G.	Good	Fair	Poor
400	250	200	150	125

Model 1005 Deluxe

As above, with a polished blue finish and Monte Carlo-style stock.

Exc.	V.G.	Good	Fair	Poor
375	225	150	100	75

Model 1006 Stainless

As the Model 1000, but in stainless steel.

Exc.	V.G.	Good	Fair	Poor
450	300	225	125	100

Model 1020 Teflon

As above, with a black or gray Dupont Teflon-S finish.

Exc.	V.G.	Good	Fair	Poor
375	225	175	125	100

Model 1256 Ferret

The Model 1000 in .256 Winchester Magnum caliber.

Exc.	V.G.	Good	Fair	Poor
350	200	175	125	100

Model 3000 Enforcer

A pistol version of the Model 1000 with an 11.25" barrel and 15- or 30-shot magazines.

Blued

Exc.	V.G.	Good	Fair	Poor
375	225	200	150	100

NOTE: Nickel finish add 20 percent. Gold-plated add 40 percent. Stainless steel add 30 percent. Teflon-S add 20 percent.

Model 5000 Paratrooper

The Model 1000, with a 16" or 18" barrel and folding stock. This model, in stainless steel, is known as the Model 5006.

Exc.	V.G.	Good	Fair	Poor
400	250	200	125	100

1981 Commemorative Carbine

A limited production version of the Model 1000 cased with accessories. Produced in 1981.

NIB	Exc.	V.G.	Good	Fair	Poor
500	350	250	200	100	75

Model 2200 Leatherneck

A .22 caliber version of the U.S. M1 Carbine with an 18" barrel and blowback action. Blued with a birch wood stock.

Exc.	V.G.	Good	Fair	Poor
300	175	150	100	75

URIZAR, TOMAS

Eibar, Spain

Celta, J. Cesar, Premier, Puma, and Union

A 6.35mm semi-automatic pistol with a 3" barrel. The slide marked with the trade names listed above. Blued with black plastic grips, cast with a wild man carrying a club.

Exc.	V.G.	Good	Fair	Poor
250	150	125	90	75

Dek-Du

A 5.5mm folding trigger double-action revolver with a 12-shot cylinder. Later versions were made in 6.35mm. Manufactured from 1905 to 1912.

Exc.	V.G.	Good	Fair	Poor
225	125	100	75	50

Express

A 6.35mm semi-automatic pistol with a 2" barrel. The slide marked "The Best Automatic Pistol Express." Blued with walnut grips. A 7.65mm variety exists with a 4" barrel.

Exc.	V.G.	Good	Fair	Poor
225	125	100	75	50

Imperial

A 6.35mm caliber semi-automatic pistol with a 2.5" barrel. This model was actually made by Aldazabal. Manufactured circa 1914.

Exc.	V.G.	Good	Fair	Poor
225	125	100	75	50

Le Secours or Phoenix

A 7.65mm semi-automatic pistol marked with either of the trade names listed above.

Exc.	V.G.	Good	Fair	Poor
225	125	100	75	50

Princeps

A 6.35mm or 7.65mm semi-automatic pistol marked on the slide "Made in Spain Princeps Patent."

Exc.	V.G.	Good	Fair	Poor
225	125	100	75	50

Venus

A 7.65mm semi-automatic pistol with the grips having the trade name "Venus" cast in them.

Exc.	V.G.	Good	Fair	Poor
225	125	100	75	50

USAS 12
DAEWOO PRECISION IND., LTD.
South Korea

USAS 12

A 12 gauge semi-automatic shotgun with a 18.25" cylinder-bored barrel, and either a 10-shot box magazine or 20-shot drum magazine. Parkerized, with a composition stock. This model is no longer imported.

NOTE: A local appraisal of this model is strongly recommended.

WARNING: As of May 1, 2001 this firearm must be registered with the ATF and a transfer tax of $200 paid. This firearm is classified as a destructive device. Unregistered guns will be considered contraband after this date, and persons in possession will be in violation of federal law.

USELTON ARMS INC.
Goodlettsville, Tennessee

Compact Classic Companion

Chambered for the .357 Sig or .40 S&W cartridge and fitted with a 5" barrel. Low-profile sights. Black or polymer ivory grips. Stainless or gray finish. Magazine capacity is 7 rounds. Weight is about 32 oz.

NIB	Exc.	V.G.	Good	Fair	Poor
2250	1600	—	—	—	—

Compact Classic

This model is chambered for the .45 ACP cartridge and has a 5" barrel. Checkered rosewood grips. Low-profile sights. Back and gray finish. Magazine capacity is 7 rounds. Weight is about 32 oz.

NIB	Exc.	V.G.	Good	Fair	Poor
1880	1350	—	—	—	—

Ultra Compact Classic

1911-style semi-auto .45 with fixed sights. 4.25" barrel, 34 oz. 3-4 lb. trigger pull, 7+1 capacity. Rosewood or imitation ivory grips. Introduced 2006. MSRP: 3250 (Titanium and Damascus); 2349 (Titanium and Stainless); 1949 (Stainless and Black)

Carry Classic

Chambered for the .45 ACP cartridge and fitted with a 4.25" barrel with low-profile sights. Rosewood or polymer ivory grips, gray and black finish. Magazine capacity is 7 rounds. Weight is about 34 oz.

NIB	Exc.	V.G.	Good	Fair	Poor
1900	1350	—	—	—	—

Ultra Carry

This .45 ACP model features a Damascus slide and titanium frame. Fitted with a 3" barrel with low-profile sights. Magazine capacity is 7 rounds. Weight is about 27 oz.

NIB	Exc.	V.G.	Good	Fair	Poor
3250	2400	—	—	—	—

NOTE: This model is also offered in titanium and stainless for $2350 and stainless and black for $1850.

Tactical 1911

Chambered for the .45 ACP cartridge and fitted with as 5" barrel with Caspian adjustable sights. Rubber grips and moly coat finish. Magazine capacity is 8 rounds. Weight is about 40 oz.

NIB	Exc.	V.G.	Good	Fair	Poor
1925	1400	—	—	—	—

Classic National Match

This .45 ACP pistol has a 5" barrel with Caspian adjustable sights. Black aluma grips and black finish. Magazine capacity is 8 rounds. Weight is about 40 oz.

NIB	Exc.	V.G.	Good	Fair	Poor
1650	1200	—	—	—	—

NOTE: Add $300 for compensator.

UZI ISRAELI MILITARY INDUSTRIES
SEE—Vector Arms, Inc.

Uzi Carbine Model A

Chambered for 9mm cartridge and fitted with a 16" barrel with 25-round magazine. Gray Parkerized finish. Built from 1980 to 1983.

NIB	Exc.	V.G.	Good	Fair	Poor
1600	1450	1200	800	600	450

Uzi Carbine Model B

A 9mm, .41 Action Express or .45 caliber semi-automatic carbine with a 16.1" barrel and 20-, 25-, or 32-shot box magazines. A 50-shot drum magazine is available in 9mm caliber. Black Parkerized finish, plastic grips and a folding stock. It is strongly suggested that a buyer or seller seek a qualified local appraisal. First produced in 1983. This model was no longer imported as of 1989.

NIB	Exc.	V.G.	Good	Fair	Poor
1500	1350	1100	750	550	400

Uzi Mini-Carbine

As above, in 9mm or .45 caliber with a 19.75" barrel. This model is no longer imported.

NIB	Exc.	V.G.	Good	Fair	Poor
2250	1600	1150	800	600	400

Uzi Pistol

As above in 9mm or .45 ACP, with a 4.5" barrel, pistol grip, no rear stock and a 20-shot magazine. This model is no longer imported.

NIB	Exc.	V.G.	Good	Fair	Poor
850	700	550	450	350	250

UZI EAGLE PISTOLS

NOTE: As of 1999 these pistols were no longer imported into the U.S.

Full Size Model

Introduced in 1997 this is a double-action pistol chambered for the 9mm and .40 S&W cartridge. Barrel length is 4.4". Overall length is 8.1". Tritium night sights are standard.

NIB	Exc.	V.G.	Good	Fair	Poor
550	375	—	—	—	—

Short Slide Model

Introduced in 1997 this is a double-action pistol chambered for the 9mm, .40 S&W and .45 ACP cartridge. Barrel length is 3.7". Overall length is 7.5". Tritium night sights are standard.

NIB	Exc.	V.G.	Good	Fair	Poor
600	400	—	—	—	—

Compact Model

Introduced in 1997 this is a double-action pistol chambered for the 9mm, .40 S&W and .45 ACP cartridge. Barrel length is 3.5". Overall length is 7.2". Tritium night sights are standard. Magazine capacity is 8 rounds for the .45 ACP and 10 rounds for the other calibers. Double-action-only is an option for this model.

NIB	Exc.	V.G.	Good	Fair	Poor
600	400	—	—	—	—

Polymer Compact Model

Introduced in 1997 this is a double-action pistol chambered for the 9mm and .40 S&W cartridge. Barrel length is 3.5". Overall length is 7.2". Tritium night sights are standard.

NIB	Exc.	V.G.	Good	Fair	Poor
550	375	—	—	—	—

VALKYRIE ARMS, LTD.
Olympia, Washington

Browning 1919 A4 .30 Caliber
This is a semi-automatic version of the famous Browning machine gun. It is chambered for the .30-06 or the .308 cartridge. It come equipped with a tripod, pintle, T&E, belly linker and 200 links. An A6 configuration is available. Introduced in1996.

NIB	Exc.	V.G.	Good	Fair	Poor
2850	2000	1500	—	—	—

U.S. M3-A1
A re-creation of the famous "grease gun" but in semi-auto. Barrel length is 16.5". Supplied with three 30-round magazines.

NIB	Exc.	V.G.	Good	Fair	Poor
695	550	—	—	—	—

NOTE: For dummy suppressor add $50. For real suppressor add $300 plus transfer tax of $200. All NFA rules and state laws must be followed for suppressors.

DeLisle Carbine
A copy of the famous World War II commando carbine used by British forces. Chambered for .45 ACP. Integral suppressor. All NFA rules must be followed. Only 167 original WWII carbines were produced.

NIB	Exc.	V.G.	Good	Fair	Poor
1595	1250	—	—	—	—

NOTE: For dummy suppressor deduct $300.

VALMET, INC.
Jyvaskyla, Finland

M-62S
A semi-automatic copy of the Finnish M-62 service rifle in 7.62x39 caliber that is patterned after the Russian AK47. Fitted with a walnut or tubular steel stock. Manufactured after 1962.

NIB	Exc.	V.G.	Good	Fair	Poor
3000	2800	2300	900	750	300

M-71S
As above, in 5.56mm caliber and available with a composition stock.

NIB	Exc.	V.G.	Good	Fair	Poor
1350	1000	850	650	450	300

Model 76S
As above, in 5.56mm, 7.62x39mm, or 7.62x51mm with either a 16.75" or 20.5" barrel.

5.56mm

NIB	Exc.	V.G.	Good	Fair	Poor
1750	1500	1250	750	600	500

7.62x39mm

NIB	Exc.	V.G.	Good	Fair	Poor
3000	2750	2500	2000	1250	—

Model 78
As above, in 7.62x51mm, 7.62x39, or .223 with a 24.5" barrel, wood stock, and integral bipod.

NIB	Exc.	V.G.	Good	Fair	Poor
2150	1700	1300	850	600	300

Lion
A 12 gauge Over/Under shotgun with 26", 28", or 30" barrels, single-selective trigger and extractors. Blued with a walnut stock. Manufactured from 1947 to 1968.

Exc.	V.G.	Good	Fair	Poor
450	375	300	250	100

VALTION (LAHTI)
SEE—Lahti

VALTRO
Italy

1998 A1
A Model 1911 clone chambered for .45 ACP and fitted with a match grade 5" barrel. Many special features include a checkered front strap, beavertail grip safety, deluxe wood grips, serrated slide front and back, beveled magazine well. Weight is approximately 40 oz. Introduced in 1998.

NIB	Exc.	V.G.	Good	Fair	Poor
1200	950	—	—	—	—

Tactical 98 Shotgun
Chambered for 12 gauge and fitted with a 18.5" or 20" ported barrel. Choice of pistol grip or standard stock. Extended magazine with 5 or 7 rounds. Ghost ring sights.

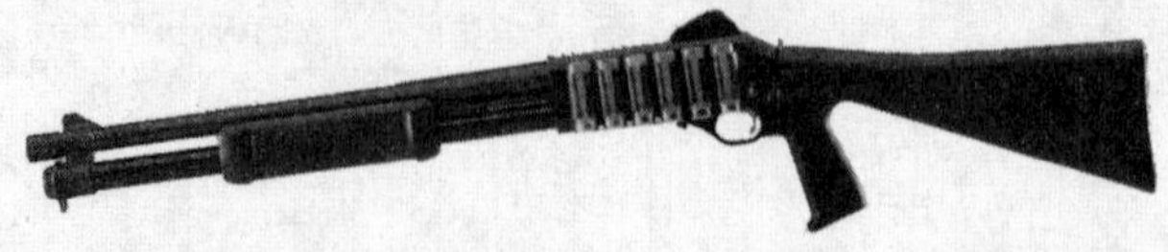

NIB	Exc.	V.G.	Good	Fair	Poor
850	675	—	—	—	—

PM5

This is a slide-action shotgun chambered for the 12 gauge 3" shell. Barrel length is 20" choked Cylinder. Box-fed magazine.

NIB	Exc.	V.G.	Good	Fair	Poor
400	300	—	—	—	—

VARNER SPORTING ARMS, INC.

Marietta, Georgia

NOTE: This company made several over-and-under shotguns and rifle/shotgun combination guns for the Savage Company. These are no longer being imported into this country.

The rifles listed are all patterned after the Stevens Favorite model.

Hunter

.22 caliber single-shot rifle with a 21.5" half-octagonal, takedown barrel fitted with an aperture rear sight. Blued with well-figured walnut stocks. Introduced in 1988.

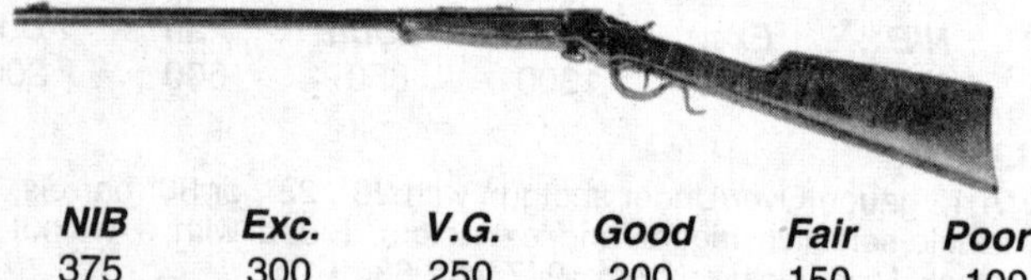

NIB	Exc.	V.G.	Good	Fair	Poor
375	300	250	200	150	100

Hunter Deluxe

As above, with a case hardened receiver and a more finely figured stock.

NIB	Exc.	V.G.	Good	Fair	Poor
500	400	350	250	175	125

Presentation Grade

As above, with a target hammer and trigger, and a hand checkered stock.

NIB	Exc.	V.G.	Good	Fair	Poor
575	475	425	350	250	200

No. 1 Grade

Engraved.

NIB	Exc.	V.G.	Good	Fair	Poor
650	550	500	450	350	200

No. 2 Grade

NIB	Exc.	V.G.	Good	Fair	Poor
775	650	600	500	400	200

No. 3 Grade

NIB	Exc.	V.G.	Good	Fair	Poor
1100	850	700	550	350	200

VECTOR ARMS, INC

North Salt Lake, Utah

Mini Uzi

A smaller version of the full size Uzi chambered for the 9mm cartridge only. Fitted with 18" barrel.

Pre-Ban

NIB	Exc.	V.G.	Good	Fair	Poor
2000	1700	—	—	—	—

Post-Ban

NIB	Exc.	V.G.	Good	Fair	Poor
1500	1250	—	—	—	—

UZI

This is a semi-automatic, pre-ban Uzi carbine with 18" barrel chambered for the 9mm cartridge. Receiver built by Group Industries of Louisville, Ky., prior to May 1986. Receiver fixed parts manufacturing and receiver assembly by Vector Arms. Only 97 of these semi-automatic receivers were manufactured.

Pre-Ban

NIB	Exc.	V.G.	Good	Fair	Poor
1300	1000	—	—	—	—

Post-Ban

NIB	Exc.	V.G.	Good	Fair	Poor
1100	900	—	—	—	—

NOTE: For .45 ACP or .22 caliber conversion kit, add $200.

VEKTOR

South Africa

No longer in business.

Model Z88

This is a semi-automatic pistol chambered for the 9mm cartridge. It has a 5" barrel and fixed sights. Weight is about 35 oz. Blue finish. Magazine capacity is 15 rounds or 10 in U.S.

NIB	Exc.	V.G.	Good	Fair	Poor
600	475	—	—	—	—

Model SP1 Service Pistol

This model is chambered for the 9mm cartridge and is fitted with a 4-5/8" barrel. Fixed sights. Weight is 35 oz. Blue finish. Magazine capacity is 15 rounds or 10 in U.S.

NIB	Exc.	V.G.	Good	Fair	Poor
600	475	—	—	—	—

NOTE: Add $30 for anodized or nickel finish.

Model SP1 Sport

Similar to the SP1 this model features a 5" barrel with 3 chamber compensator. Blue finish. Weight is about 38 oz.

NIB	Exc.	V.G.	Good	Fair	Poor
725	575	—	—	—	—

Model SP1 Tuned Sport

This model also has a three-chamber compensator on a 5" barrel but it has an adjustable straight trigger and LPA 3-dot sighting system. Nickel finish. Weight is about 38 oz.

NIB	Exc.	V.G.	Good	Fair	Poor
1200	950	—	—	—	—

Model SP1 Target

This 9mm model is fitted with a 6" barrel with adjustable straight trigger. LPA 3 dot sighting system. Weight is about 40.5 oz. Two-tone finish.

NIB	Exc.	V.G.	Good	Fair	Poor
1225	975	—	—	—	—

Model SP1 Compact (General's Model)

A compact version of the 9mm pistol fitted with a 4" barrel. Fixed sights. Blue finish. Magazine capacity is 15 rounds or 10 for U.S. Weight is about 31.5 oz.

NIB	Exc.	V.G.	Good	Fair	Poor
650	525	—	—	—	—

Model SP2

A full size service pistol chambered for the .40 S&W cartridge. fitted with a 4-5/8" barrel. Fixed sights. Magazine capacity is 11 rounds or 10 for U.S. Blued finish. Weight is about 35 oz.

NIB	Exc.	V.G.	Good	Fair	Poor
600	475	—	—	—	—

Model SP2 Compact (General's Model)

A compact .40 S&W pistol with 4" barrel. Magazine capacity is 11 rounds or 10 for U.S. Weight is about 31.5 oz. Blue finish. Fixed sights.

NIB	Exc.	V.G.	Good	Fair	Poor
650	525	—	—	—	—

Model SP2 Competition

This model is chambered for the .40 S&W cartridge and fitted with a 5.88" barrel. It features enlarged safety levers and magazine catch. The frame has been thickened for scope mount. Beavertail grip and straight trigger. Weight is about 42 oz.

NIB	Exc.	V.G.	Good	Fair	Poor
1000	750	—	—	—	—

Model SP1 Ultra Sport

This model is designed for IPSC open-class competition. Barrel length is 6" with 3 chamber compensator. Chambered for 9mm cartridge. Optical scope mount with Weaver rails. Magazine capacity is 19 rounds or 10 for U.S. Weight is about 41.5 oz. Priced with Lynx scope.

NIB	Exc.	V.G.	Good	Fair	Poor
2150	1700	—	—	—	—

Model SP2 Ultra Sport

Same as model above but chambered for .40 S&W cartridge. Magazine capacity is 14 rounds or 10 for U.S.

NIB	Exc.	V.G.	Good	Fair	Poor
2150	1700	—	—	—	—

Model SP2 Conversion Kit

Made for the SP2 this is a 9mm conversion kit that consists of a 9mm barrel, recoil spring, and 9mm magazine.

NIB	Exc.	V.G.	Good	Fair	Poor
190	150	—	—	—	—

Model CP-1 Compact

Chambered for the 9mm cartridge and fitted with a 4" barrel this model has a polymer frame. Fixed sights. Weight is about 25 oz. Magazine capacity is 13 rounds standard, 12 rounds compact or 10 rounds for U.S. Offered with black or nickel slide.

NIB	Exc.	V.G.	Good	Fair	Poor
475	375	—	—	—	—

NOTE: Add $20 for nickel slide.

RIFLES

Vektor H5 Pump-Action Rifle

This pump-action rifle is chambered for the .233 cartridge. It is fitted with a thumbhole stock and a 22" barrel. Magazine capacity is 5 rounds.

NIB	Exc.	V.G.	Good	Fair	Poor
850	625	—	—	—	—

Vektor 98

Built on a Mauser action, this rifle is chambered for a variety of calibers from .243 to .375 H&H. Fitted with a one-piece walnut stock with hand checkering. Magazine capacity is five rounds. Open sights on magnum calibers only.

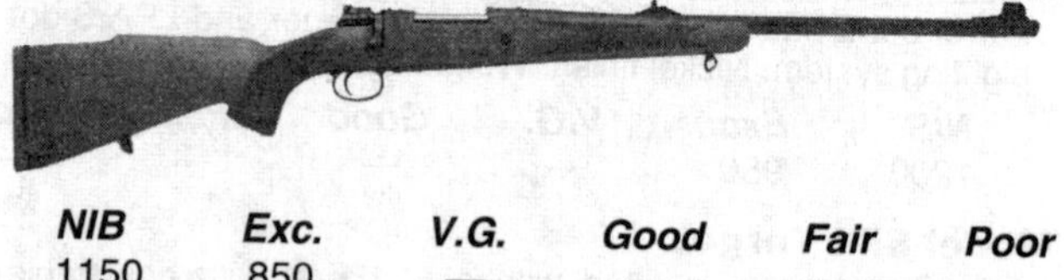

NIB	Exc.	V.G.	Good	Fair	Poor
1150	850	—	—	—	—

Vektor Lyttelton

This rifle features numerous special features and is fitted with a classic walnut stock with wraparound checkering. Fixed sights. Calibers offered are from .243 to .375 H&H.

NIB	Exc.	V.G.	Good	Fair	Poor
1595	1100	—	—	—	—

VENUS WAFFENWERKE

Zella Mehlis, Germany

Venus

A 6.35mm, 7.65mm, or 9mm semi-automatic pistol with a 3.5" barrel. Slide is marked "Original Venus Patent" and the grips bear the monogram "OW." Designed by Oskar Will. Blued, plastic grips. Manufactured from 1912 to 1914.

Exc.	V.G.	Good	Fair	Poor
700	550	400	250	100

VERNEY-CARRON

St. Etienne, France

Concours

A 12 gauge Over/Under boxlock shotgun with 26" or 28" ventilated rib barrels, single-selective triggers, automatic ejectors and profuse engraving. Blued, French case hardened with checkered walnut stock. First imported in 1978.

Exc.	V.G.	Good	Fair	Poor
1250	800	700	600	300

Skeet Model

As above, with a 28" Skeet-choked barrel and a pistol-grip stock.

Exc.	V.G.	Good	Fair	Poor
1400	950	700	600	300

VERONA
Italy

HUNTING SHOTGUNS

Model SX401/S

This 12 gauge 3" semi-automatic model is offered with either a 26" or 28" vent rib barrel with choke tubes. Checkered Turkish walnut stock. Weight is about 6.75 lbs.

NIB	Exc.	V.G.	Good	Fair	Poor
425	325	—	—	—	—

Model SX405/S/L

As above but with black composite stock. Weight is about 6.5 lbs.

NIB	Exc.	V.G.	Good	Fair	Poor
350	275	—	—	—	—

Model SX405W/H/SW/SH

This 12 gauge 3" Magnum semi-automatic gun is offered with a choice of 26" or 28" vent-rib barrel with wetland or hardwood camo patten. Weight is about 6.5 lbs.

NIB	Exc.	V.G.	Good	Fair	Poor
440	340	—	—	—	—

Model SX405T

This 12 gauge 3" semi-auto model features a 24" vent-rib barrel with hardwood camo pattern. Weight is about 6.5 lbs.

NIB	Exc.	V.G.	Good	Fair	Poor
440	340	—	—	—	—

Model SX405 Combo

This model features a 12 gauge 22" slug barrel and a 12 gauge 3" 26" vent-rib smoothbore barrel. Weight is about 6.5 lbs.

NIB	Exc.	V.G.	Good	Fair	Poor
500	400	—	—	—	—

Model SX405 Slug

This model features a hardwood camo stock with 22" slug barrel. Weight is about 6.5 lbs.

NIB	Exc.	V.G.	Good	Fair	Poor
490	390	—	—	—	—

LX501

This over-and-under shotgun is chambered for the 12, 20, 28, and .410 bore. Single-selective trigger. Ejectors. Blued steel receiver. Walnut stock with machine checkering. It is offered with 28" vent-rib barrels. Screw-in chokes for 12 and 20 gauges models. Fixed chokes for 28 and .410 bore. Chambers are 3" for all gauges except 28 gauge. Weight is between 6.25 lbs. and 6.75 lbs. depending on gauge.

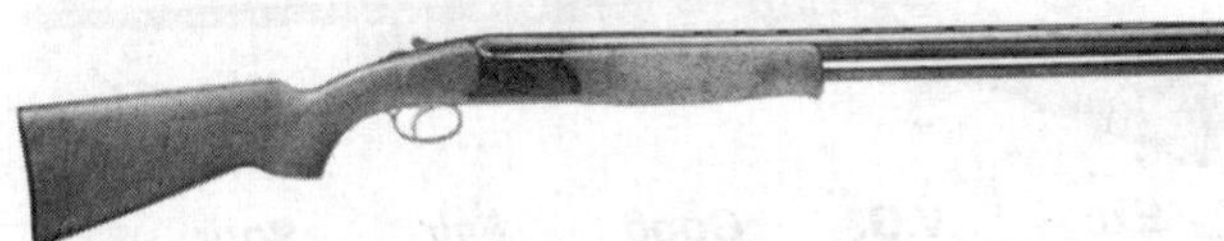

NIB	Exc.	V.G.	Good	Fair	Poor
800	600	—	—	—	—

NOTE: For 28 gauge and .410 bore add $30.

LX692G

This model is also offered in 12, 20, 28, and .410 bore with 28" vent-rib barrels. Receiver is fitted with sideplates with gold inlaid hunting scenes on three sides. Matte finish walnut stock with schnabel forearm, hand-cut checkering. Weight is between 7.25 lbs. and 7.75 lbs. depending on gauge.

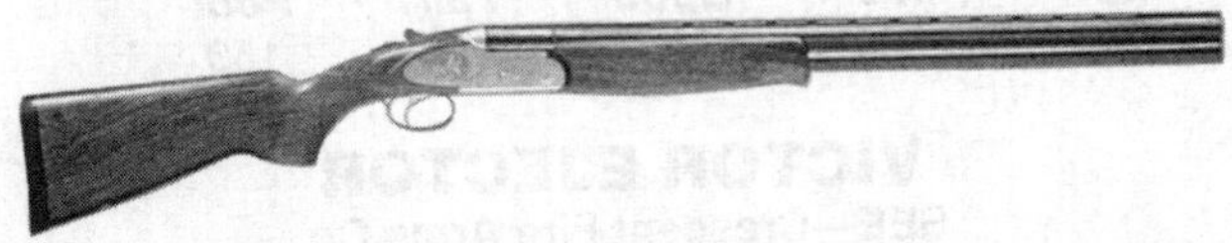

NIB	Exc.	V.G.	Good	Fair	Poor
1390	1050	—	—	—	—

NOTE: For 28 gauge add $40; for .410 bore add $25.

LX692G-20/28

This model has the features as above but features a 20 gauge gun with extra set of 28 gauge barrels. Choke tubes standard. Weight is about 7.5 lbs. with 20 gauge barrels.

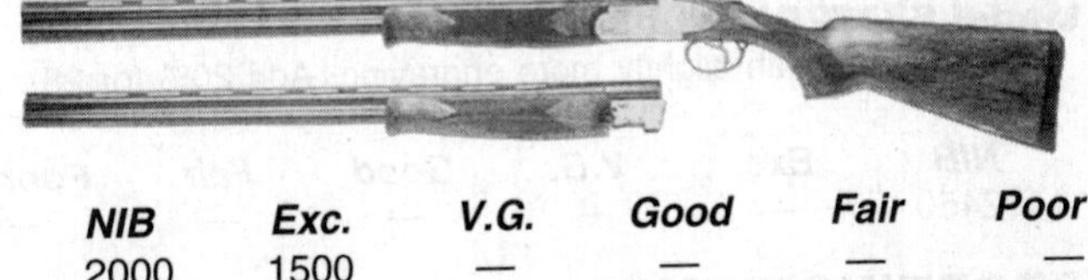

NIB	Exc.	V.G.	Good	Fair	Poor
2000	1500	—	—	—	—

LX702G

This model is offered in both 12 and 20 gauge with 28" barrel chambered for 3" shells. This model features a case colored receiver with side plates. The reciever is engraved on three sides with gold inlaid upland bird hunting scenes. Full-figured Turkish walnut with hand checkering and oil finish. Single-selective trigger, black recoil pad, ejectors and schnabel forearm. Weight for 12 gauge is about 7 lbs. For the 20 gauge about 6 lbs.

NIB	Exc.	V.G.	Good	Fair	Poor
1550	1150	—	—	—	—

Model LX1001 Express Combo

This over-and-under gun features two sets of barrels; one for 20 gauge 2.75" and the other for either .223, .243, .270, .308, or .30-06. The 20 gauge barrels are 28" vent rib and the rifle barrels are 22". Checkered walnut stock with oil finish. Engraved receiver.

NIB	Exc.	V.G.	Good	Fair	Poor
2580	1900	—	—	—	—

SIDE-BY-SIDE SHOTGUNS

Model SS662GL

This side-by-side gun is offered in 20 or 28 gauge with 28" barrels choked Modified and Full. Double triggers. Engraved receiver. Checkered walnut stock with straight grip. Weight is about 6 lbs. Made by Bernardelli. Add 20% for 28-gauge.

NIB	Exc.	V.G.	Good	Fair	Poor
2200	—	—	—	—	—

Model SS772GL

As above but with slightly more engraving. Add 20% for 28-gauge.

NIB	Exc.	V.G.	Good	Fair	Poor
2450	—	—	—	—	—

SPORTING/COMPETITION SHOTGUNS

LX680

Chambered for 12 or 20 gauge shells with 2.75" chambers. Single-selective trigger, ejectors, lightly engraved steel receiver. Walnut stock with beavertail firearm and hand-cut checkering. Ventilated recoil pad standard. Fitted with 28" barrels with ventilated rib between barrels. Choke tubes. Weight is about 6.5 lbs. depending on gauge.

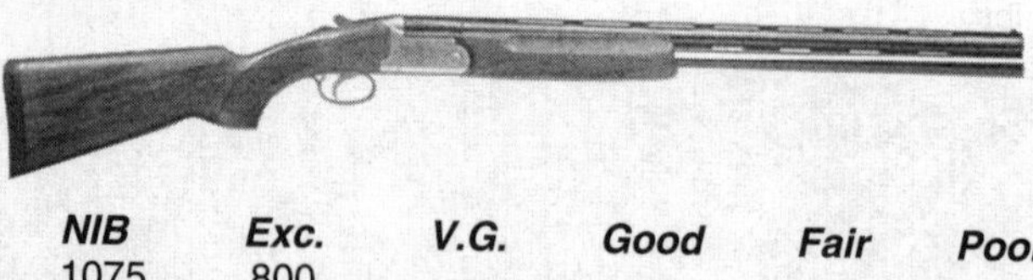

NIB	Exc.	V.G.	Good	Fair	Poor
1075	800	—	—	—	—

LX692GS

Similar to the above model but fitted with sideplates with gold inlaid hunting scenes.

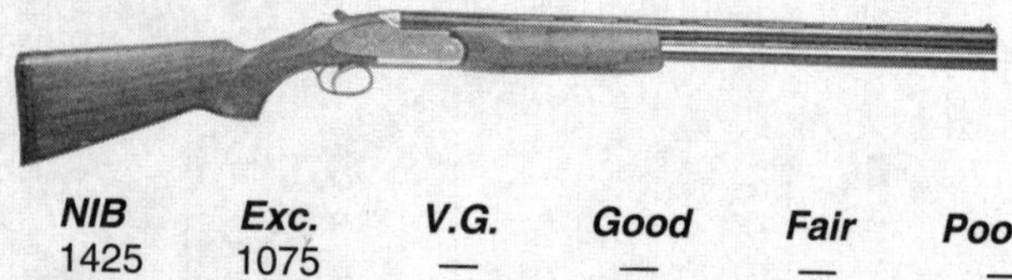

NIB	Exc.	V.G.	Good	Fair	Poor
1425	1075	—	—	—	—

LX680C S&T

This over-and-under model features a choice of 28" or 30" 11mm vent-rib barrels on a 12 gauge frame. Single-selective trigger, ejectors. Matte finish Turkish walnut stock with hand-cut checkering, beavertail forearm, wider comb. Lightly engraved steel receiver. Ventilated rib between barrels. Choke tubes. Weight is approximately 7.75 lbs. depending on barrel length. The 28" barrel model is designated as Skeet/Sporting and the 30" model is designated Trap.

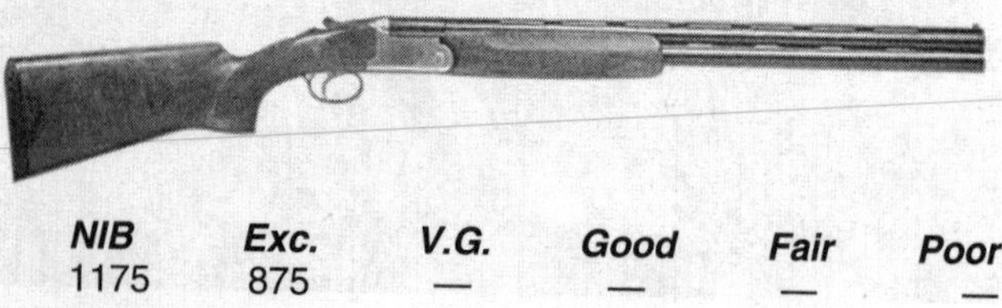

NIB	Exc.	V.G.	Good	Fair	Poor
1175	875	—	—	—	—

LX692GC S&T

Same as above but with sideplates with gold inlaid game scenes.

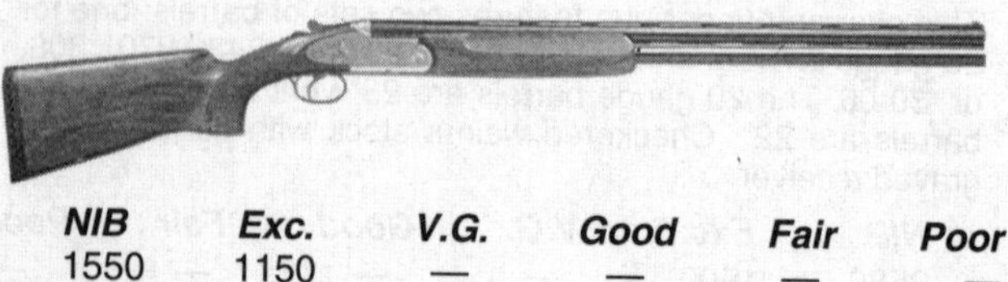

NIB	Exc.	V.G.	Good	Fair	Poor
1550	1150	—	—	—	—

LX702GC S&T

This model features a case colored receiver and sideplates with gold inlaid birds. Offered in 12 gauge only with choice of 28" or 30" barrels. Weight is about 7.5 lbs.

NIB	Exc.	V.G.	Good	Fair	Poor
1625	1225	—	—	—	—

Model SX801/L

This semi-automatic 12 gauge 2.75" shotgun is fitted with a choice of 28" or 30" vent-rib ported barrels with choke tubes and Hi-Viz sights. Walnut stock with choice of Monte Carlo comb or adjustable comb. Weight is about 6.75 lbs.

NIB	Exc.	V.G.	Good	Fair	Poor
865	650	—	—	—	—

Model SX801G/GL

As above but with higher grade walnut stock.

NIB	Exc.	V.G.	Good	Fair	Poor
1060	775	—	—	—	—

Model LX980CS

This 12 gauge 2.75" over-and-under gun is fitted with 30" ported barrels with extended choke tubes. Removable trigger assembly. Black receiver. Checkered select walnut stock. Weight is about 7.5 lbs.

NIB	Exc.	V.G.	Good	Fair	Poor
3525	2600	—	—	—	—

Model LX980GCS/GCT

As above but with choice of 30" ported barrels or 32" ported barrels. Select walnut stock has adjustable comb. Weight is about 7.5 lbs.

NIB	Exc.	V.G.	Good	Fair	Poor
3775	2800	—	—	—	—

VETTERLI

Switzerland

Various Manufacturers

NOTE: For techinical data, history, description, photos and prices see the *Standard Catalog of Military Firearms* under Switzerland, Rifles.

VICKERS, LTD.

Crayford/Kent, England

Jubilee

A .22 caliber single-shot Martini-action rifle with a 28" barrel, adjustable sights and pistol grip walnut stock. Blued. Manufactured prior to WWII.

Exc.	V.G.	Good	Fair	Poor
600	400	350	275	200

Empire

As above, with a 27" or 30" barrel and a straight stock.

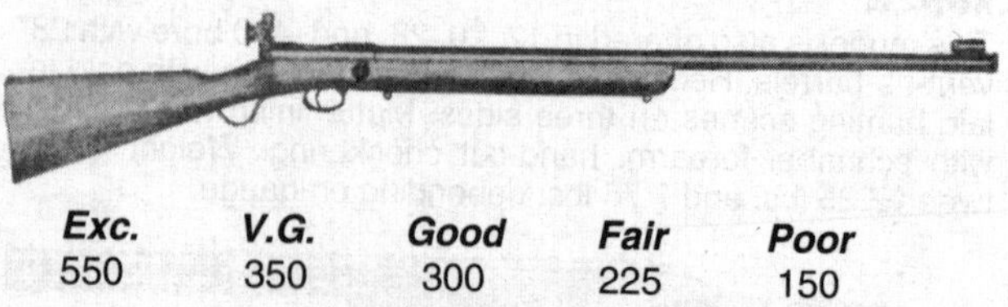

Exc.	V.G.	Good	Fair	Poor
550	350	300	225	150

VICTOR EJECTOR

SEE—Crescent Fire Arms Co.

VICTORY ARMS COT., LTD.

Northhampton, England

Model MC5

A 9mm, .38 Super, .41 Action Express, 10mm, or .45 caliber semi-automatic pistol with a 4.25", 5.75", or 7.5" barrel, 10-, 12-, or 17-shot magazine, decocking lever and Millett sights. Interchangeable barrels were available. Introduced in 1989.

NIB	Exc.	V.G.	Good	Fair	Poor
500	400	300	250	200	150

VIRGINIAN

SEE—Interarms

VOERE

Kufstein, Austria

In 1987 this company was purchased by Mauser-Werke. Voere actions are used in rifles made and sold by KDF, Inc., of Seguin, Texas. Values for older-production rifles are listed.

Model 1007

Bolt-action rifle chambered for .22 LR cartridge and fitted with an 18" barrel. Open sights. Beech stock. Introduced in 1984. Discontinued in 1991.

NIB	Exc.	V.G.	Good	Fair	Poor
225	175	150	125	100	75

Model 1013

This bolt-action rifle is chambered for the .22 WMR cartridge and fitted with an 18" barrel. Magazine capacity is 8 rounds. Open sight with adjustable rear. Military-style stock is oil finished. Double set triggers.

NIB	Exc.	V.G.	Good	Fair	Poor
275	225	200	150	125	100

Model 2107

This .22 LR bolt-action rifle has a 19.5" barrel with Monte Carlo stock. Eight-round magazine. Weight is about 6 lbs.

NIB	Exc.	V.G.	Good	Fair	Poor
325	250	225	200	150	125

Model 2107 Deluxe

Bolt-action rifle chambered for .22 LR cartridge has checkered stock with raised cheekpiece. Discontinued in 1988.

NIB	Exc.	V.G.	Good	Fair	Poor
350	275	225	200	150	125

Model 2114S

This is a semi-automatic rifle chambered for .22 LR cartridge and fitted with a 18" barrel. Magazine capacity is 15 rounds. Open sight. Stock is beechwood. Single-stage trigger. No longer in production.

NIB	Exc.	V.G.	Good	Fair	Poor
275	225	200	150	125	100

Model 2115

Similar to the model above but with checkered stock. Weight is about 5.75 lbs. Discontinued in 1995.

NIB	Exc.	V.G.	Good	Fair	Poor
300	250	225	175	150	100

Model 2150

This is a bolt-action centerfire rifle chambered for calibers from .22-250 to .338 Win. Mag. Fitted with 22" barrels (24" on magnums). Open sights with adjustable rear sight. Checkered walnut stock with oil finish. Built on M98 Mauser action. Weight is about 8 lbs. depending on caliber. Discontinued in 1995.

NIB	Exc.	V.G.	Good	Fair	Poor
800	650	550	450	300	200

Model 2155

Similar to the Model 2150 but with no sights and double set triggers. Discontinued in 1995.

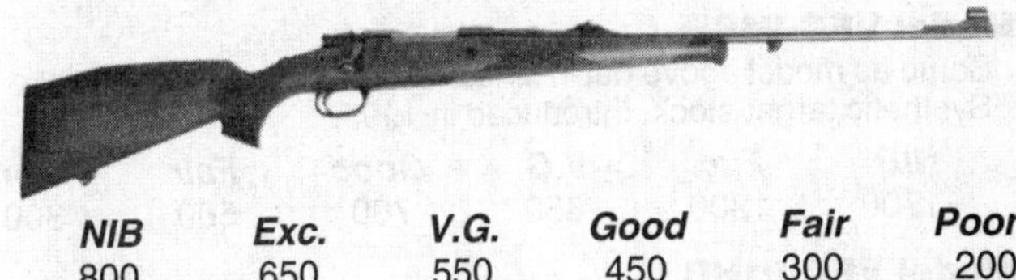

NIB	Exc.	V.G.	Good	Fair	Poor
800	650	550	450	300	200

Model 2165

Similar to the above model but with open sights, walnut stock with Bavarian cheekpiece and schnabel forearm. Rosewood grip cap. Discontinued.

NIB	Exc.	V.G.	Good	Fair	Poor
850	675	550	450	300	200

Model 2185

This is a semi-automatic centerfire rifle chambered for 7x64, .308, and .30-06 cartridges. Fitted with a 20" barrel and open sights with adjustable rear sight. Checkered walnut stock. Available with full stock as well.

NIB	Exc.	V.G.	Good	Fair	Poor
1700	1300	850	700	500	300

NOTE: Add $100 for Mannlicher stock.

Model 2185 Match

Same as the Model 2185 except for a 5-round magazine, hooded front sight, laminated stock with adjustable cheekpiece. Discontinued in 1994.

NIB	Exc.	V.G.	Good	Fair	Poor
3000	2400	1750	1150	650	400

Model Titan

This is a centerfire bolt-action rifle chambered in calibers from .243 to .375 H&H. Fitted with 24" or 26" barrels depending on caliber. No sights. Checkered Monte Carlo walnut stock with oil finish. Discontinued in 1988.

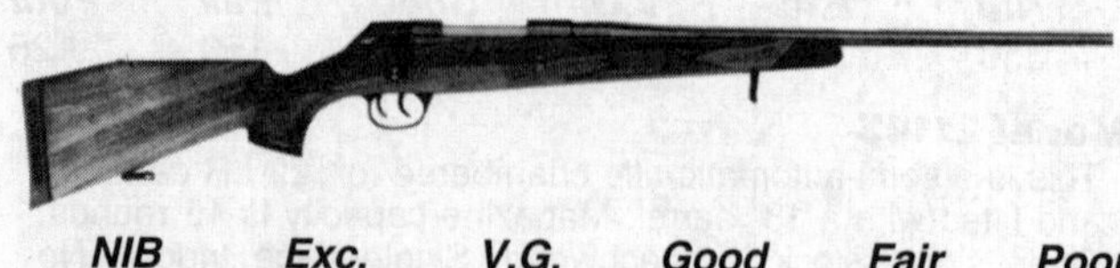

NIB	Exc.	V.G.	Good	Fair	Poor
800	650	550	450	300	200

Model Titan Menor

Bolt-action rifle chambered for .222 Rem, .223 Rem. Fitted with a 23.5" barrel and 3-round magazine. No sights. Checkered Monte Carlo walnut stock with rosewood grip cap. Introduced in 1986 and dropped in 1988.

NIB	Exc.	V.G.	Good	Fair	Poor
600	475	375	250	200	150

Model VEC-91 Lightning

Bolt-action rifle that fires caseless 6mm ammo. Adjustable rear sight on a 20" barrel. Checkered walnut stock with cheekpiece. Electronic trigger. Introduced in 1991.

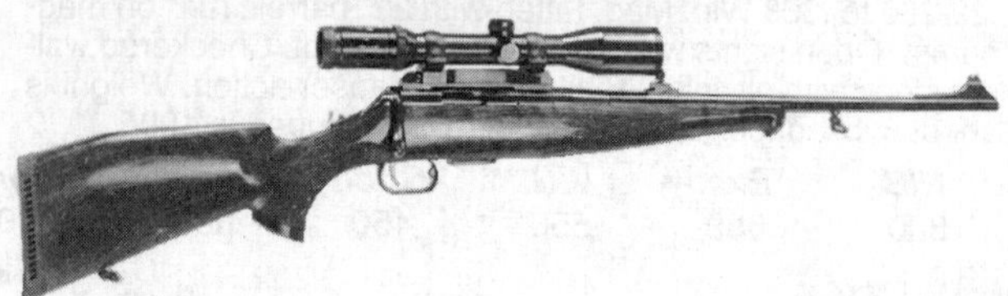

NIB	Exc.	V.G.	Good	Fair	Poor
1700	1300	850	700	500	300

Model VEC-91BR

Same as model above but in single-shot with heavy 20" barrel. Synthetic target stock. Introduced in 1995.

NIB	Exc.	V.G.	Good	Fair	Poor
1700	1300	850	700	500	300

Model VEC-91HB

Same as the VEC-91 except single-shot with heavy 22" barrel. Choice of synthetic stock or laminated wood stock. Introduced in 1995.

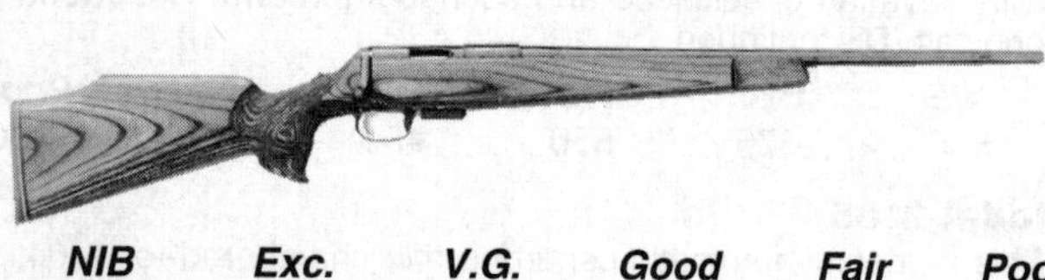

NIB	Exc.	V.G.	Good	Fair	Poor
1400	1100	750	600	450	200

Model VEC-91SS

This version has no sights and a synthetic stock. Introduced in 1995.

NIB	Exc.	V.G.	Good	Fair	Poor
1200	900	650	550	400	200

VOLCANIC ARMS COMPANY

New Haven, Connecticut

SEE—Winchester Repeating Arms Co.

VOLKSPISTOLE

Various Makers
Germany

Volkspistole

Quite mysterious, a few have ever been noted. It was designed as a cheaply manufactured, last-ditch weapon that was supposed to be used to flood the German countryside and cause casualties among the invaders at the close of WWII. It is chambered for the 9mm Parabellum cartridge and features a gas-operated, delayed blowback action. It has a 5.1" barrel with an 8-round, detachable box magazine. The construction is of steel stampings. It has no safety devices and no markings whatsoever. Examples noted are in the white, and there are no sights affixed to them. It appears that this weapon never actually went into production, and it would be impossible to estimate a value.

VOLQUARTSEN CUSTOM

Carroll, Iowa

This company was started in 1973, and began specializing in Ruger 10/22 aftermarket conversions. In 1997 the company began producing its own receivers.

SEMI-AUTO RIFLES

These rifles are based on the Ruger 10/22 design. They are chambered for the .22 LR or .22 WMR cartridge.

Standard

Fitted with an 18.5" stainless steel barrel and either a Hogue rubber stock or brown laminated stock. No sights. Integral Weaver rail.

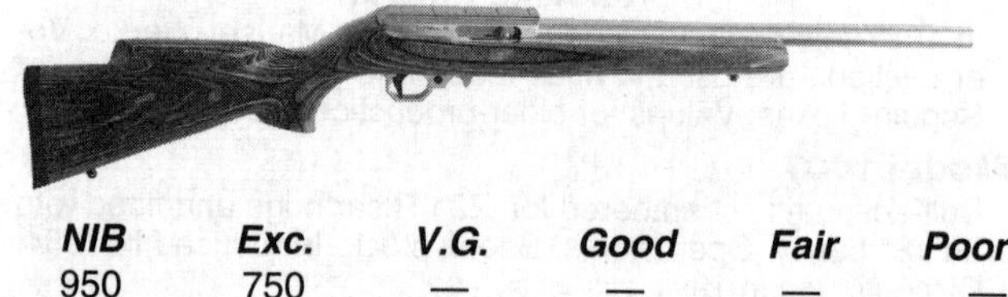

NIB	Exc.	V.G.	Good	Fair	Poor
950	750	—	—	—	—

Lightweight

This model has a 16.5" carbon-fiber barrel. Choice of rubber or laminated stock. Integral Weaver rail.

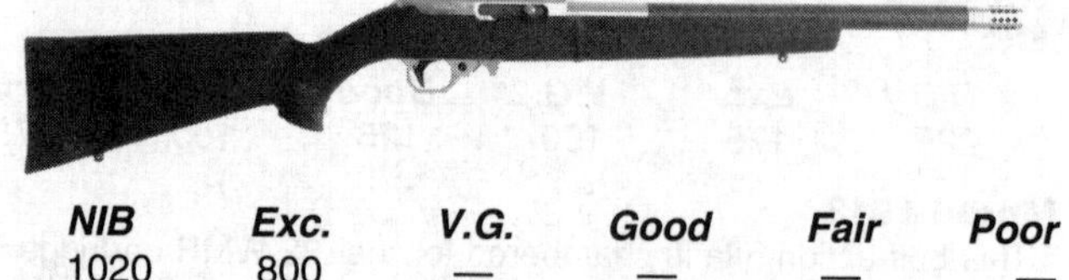

NIB	Exc.	V.G.	Good	Fair	Poor
1020	800	—	—	—	—

Deluxe

This model has a 20" stainless steel fluted and compensated barrel. Choice of laminated or rubber stock.

NIB	Exc.	V.G.	Good	Fair	Poor
1020	800	—	—	—	—

Signature Series

Fitted with a 20" stainless steel fluted and compensated barrel. Engraved receiver, trigger guard and rings. Comes with a Nikon 3.3x10 Titanium scope. Fancy walnut stock.

NIB	Exc.	V.G.	Good	Fair	Poor
2000	1500	—	—	—	—

VG-1

This model has a 20" stainless steel fluted and compensated barrel. Fitted with a green McMillan fiberglass stock. Finish is black epoxy powder coating. Offered in .22 WMR only.

NIB	Exc.	V.G.	Good	Fair	Poor
1475	1100	—	—	—	—

VX-2500

This model features a 20" stainless steel fluted and compensated barrel. Fitted with a VX-2500 stock with aluminum forearm. Designed for benchrest shooting.

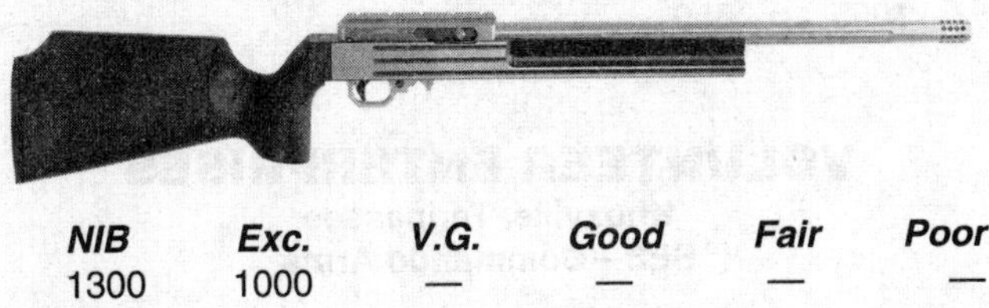

NIB	Exc.	V.G.	Good	Fair	Poor
1300	1000	—	—	—	—

VX-5000

Fitted with an 18" carbon-fiber lightweight barrel with compensator. Comes standard with VX-5000 stock with aluminum forend.

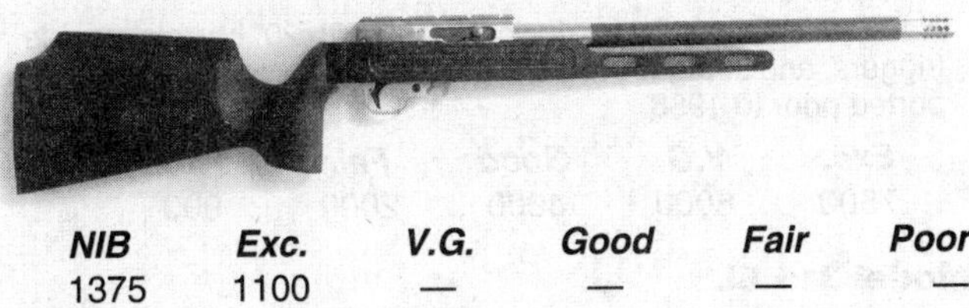

NIB	Exc.	V.G.	Good	Fair	Poor
1375	1100	—	—	—	—

PISTOLS

These pistols are based on the Ruger MK II design.

Black Cheetah Pistol

Special order only.

NIB	Exc.	V.G.	Good	Fair	Poor
N/A	—	—	—	—	—

Compact

Fitted with a 3.5" bull barrel and Hogue Monogrip. Adjustable rear sight and target front sight. Stainless steel finish. Weight is about 42 oz.

NIB	Exc.	V.G.	Good	Fair	Poor
640	500	—	—	—	—

Deluxe

This model is fitted with a 5" to 10" special heavy barrel depending on the customer's requirements. Adjustable rear sight and target front sight. Target grips. Stainless steel finish.

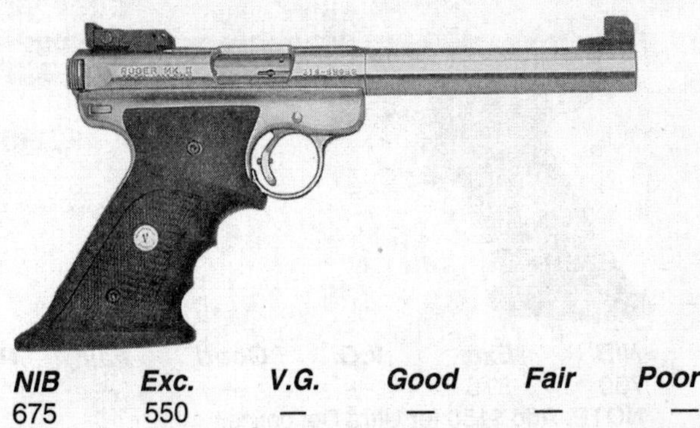

NIB	Exc.	V.G.	Good	Fair	Poor
675	550	—	—	—	—

Masters

The Masters features a 6.5" barrel with aluminum alloy-finned underlug. The top rib has a front blade sight with an adjustable rear sight. Rib is cut to accommodate optics. Integral compensator. Weight is about 56 oz.

NIB	Exc.	V.G.	Good	Fair	Poor
950	800	—	—	—	—

Olympic

The Olympic is designed for NRA or UIT competitive shooting. It has a 7.5" match barrel with a unique gas chamber for recoil-free shooting. Target front sight and adjustable rear sight. Weight is about 36 oz.

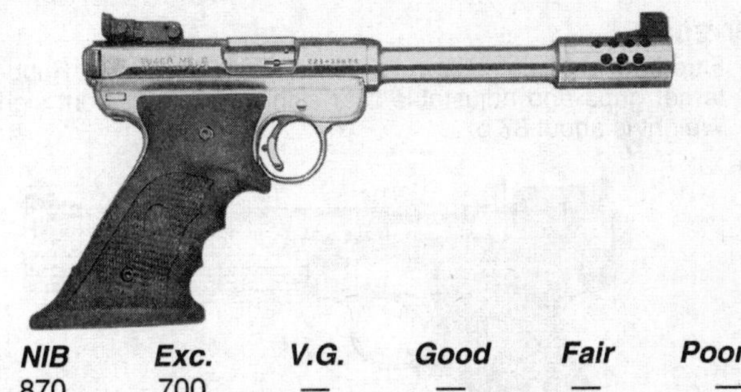

NIB	Exc.	V.G.	Good	Fair	Poor
870	700	—	—	—	—

Stingray

Fitted with a 7.5" match-grade barrel with radial flutes. Compensator standard. Supplied with either a Ultra Dot red dot optic or TL rear optic. Weight is about 56 oz.

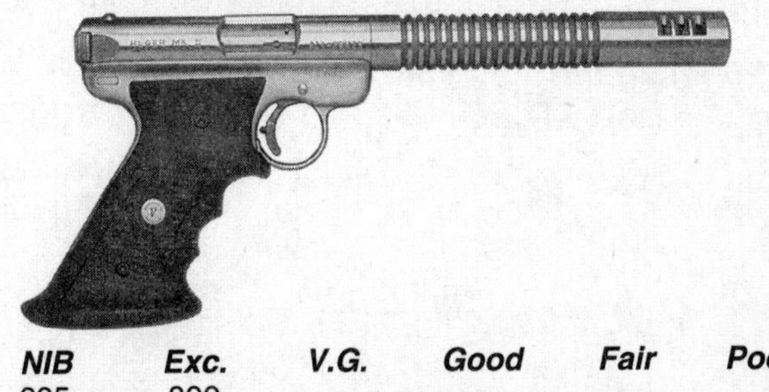

NIB	Exc.	V.G.	Good	Fair	Poor
995	800	—	—	—	—

Terminator

This model is fitted with a 7.5" match barrel with integral compensator. Choice of Weaver-style or 3/8" tip-off scope mounting system.

NIB	Exc.	V.G.	Good	Fair	Poor
730	575	—	—	—	—

NOTE: Add $150 for Ultra Dot optics.

Ultra-Lite Match

NIB	Exc.	V.G.	Good	Fair	Poor
820	650	—	—	—	—

V-6

The V-6 has a 6" vent-rib triangular-shaped match barrel with full-length underlug. Adjustable rear sight and target front sight. Rubber target grips. Weight is about 36 oz.

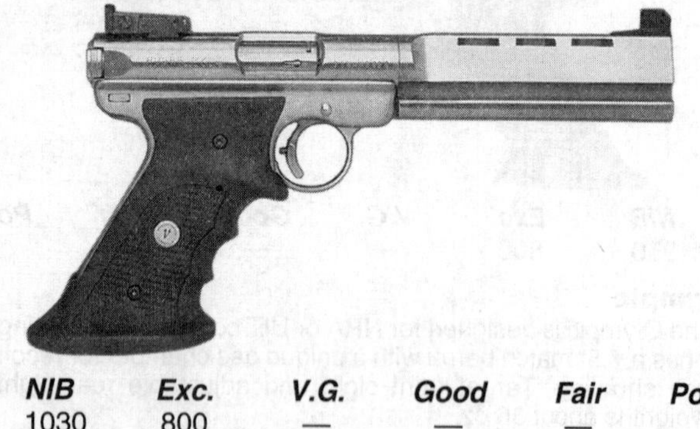

NIB	Exc.	V.G.	Good	Fair	Poor
1030	800	—	—	—	—

V-2000

Fitted with a 6" match barrel with alloy-finned underlug. Rubber target grips and adjustable rear sight with target front sight. Weight is about 37 oz.

NIB	Exc.	V.G.	Good	Fair	Poor
1085	875	—	—	—	—

V-Magic II

This model has an 8" fluted match barrel with integral compensator. Rubber target grips and Ultra Dot red dot optic. No open sights. Weight is about 46 oz.

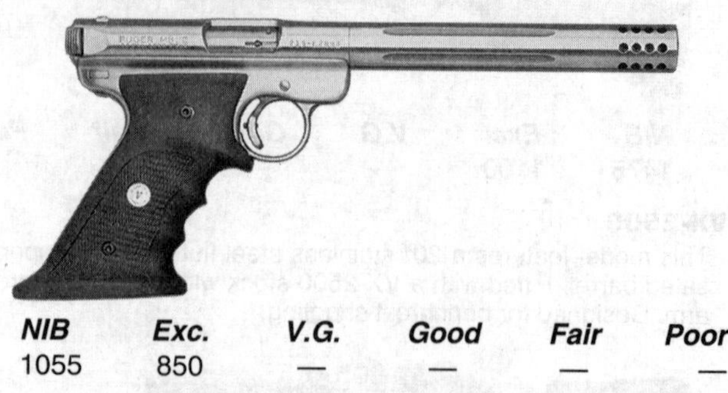

NIB	Exc.	V.G.	Good	Fair	Poor
1055	850	—	—	—	—

VOLUNTEER ENTERPRISES

Knoxville, Tennessee

SEE—Commando Arms

VOUZLAUD

Paris, France

Model 315 E

A 12, 16, or 20 gauge boxlock shotgun with 20" barrels, double triggers, and straight-gripped stock. Blued, case hardened. Imported prior to 1988.

Exc.	V.G.	Good	Fair	Poor
7500	6000	4000	2000	900

Model 315 EL

As above, with more engraving and also available in .28 or .410 bore, which are worth approximately $1,000 more than the values listed.

Exc.	V.G.	Good	Fair	Poor
10000	8000	5000	2500	1100

Model 315 EGL

As above, with a French case hardened receiver. Discontinued in 1987.

Exc.	V.G.	Good	Fair	Poor
15000	12000	8500	4000	1500

Model 315 EGL-S

As above, with engraved hunting scenes. Discontinued in 1987.

Exc.	V.G.	Good	Fair	Poor
5500	4500	3500	2000	1000

WALCH, JOHN

New York, New York

Navy Revolver

A .36 caliber superimposed load percussion revolver with a 6" octagonal barrel and a 6-shot cylinder fitted with 12 nipples, two hammers, and two triggers. The barrel marked "Walch Firearms Co. NY." and "Patented Feb. 8, 1859." Blued with walnut grips.

Exc.	*V.G.*	*Good*	*Fair*	*Poor*
—	—	9000	4000	950

Pocket Revolver

A spur trigger .31 caliber 10-shot percussion revolver with either a brass or iron frame and walnut grips. The iron frame version is worth approximately 50 percent more than the brass variety.

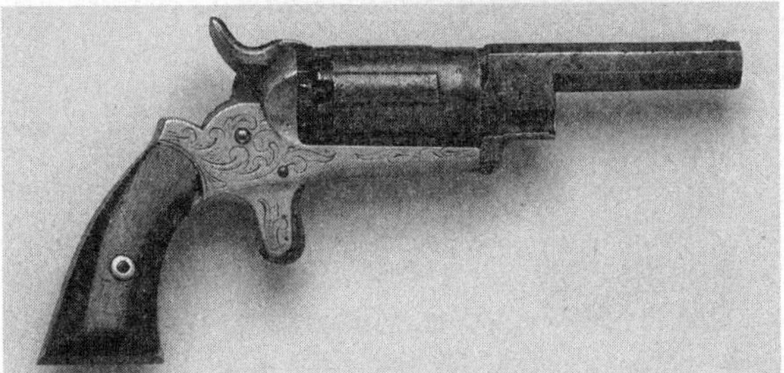

Courtesy Greg Martin Auctions

Exc.	*V.G.*	*Good*	*Fair*	*Poor*
—	—	2750	1000	300

WALDMAN

Germany

Waldman

A 7.65mm semi-automatic pistol with a 3.5" barrel and 8-shot magazine. The slide marked "1913 Model Automatic Pistol" and some examples are marked "American Automatic Pistol." Blued with checkered walnut grips inlaid with a brass insert marked "Waldman."

Exc.	*V.G.*	*Good*	*Fair*	*Poor*
300	225	200	150	100

WALLIS & BIRCH

Philadelphia, Pennsylvania

Pocket Pistol

A .41 caliber single-shot percussion pocket pistol with a 2.5" or 3" barrel, German silver furniture and walnut stock. The barrels marked "Wallis & Birch Phila." Produced during the 1850s.

Exc.	*V.G.*	*Good*	*Fair*	*Poor*
—	—	2250	800	250

WALTHER, CARL

Zella Mehilis and Ulm/Donau, Germany

In 1886 Carl Walther set up a workshop to make sporting arms. Until 1900 his operation remained small. In 1907 he designed the 6.35mm blowback pistol. This design was offered for sale in 1908. In less than a year after the introduction of the first pistol the second model was introduced. Called the Model 2, this pistol was more advanced than the first design and became a popular handgun in Germany prior to WWI. Two years later the Model 3 was introduced and successive models were designed and produced through 1921 when the Model 9 was announced. In 1929 Walther built the now famous Model PP, Polizei Pistole, which became synonymous with quality and advanced design. The Walther legend was born and has been maintained up to this date as a fine high-quality German-built pistol. After WWII the Walther company relocated in Ulm/Donau, Germany.

Editor's Comment: There are a large number of Walther variations, especially during the WWII era, and it requires years of experience to learn the subtleties of these variations. When dealing with expensive Walther pistols it is suggested that an expert appraisal be obtained before buying or selling these highly collectible handguns.

Model 1

A 6.35mm semi-automatic pistol barrel lengths of 2"-6". Blued with checkered hard rubber grips with the Walther logo on each grip. Introduced in 1908.

Courtesy James Rankin

Exc.	*V.G.*	*Good*	*Fair*	*Poor*
900	700	400	200	200

Model 2

A 6.35mm semi-automatic pistol with a knurled bushing at the muzzle that retains the mainspring. There are two variations: one with a fixed rear sight, and one with a pop-up rear sight. Blued with checkered hard rubber grips with the Walther logo on each grip. Introduced in 1909.

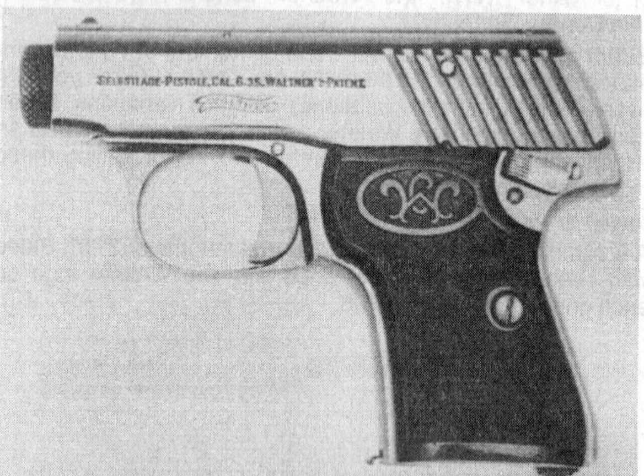

Courtesy James Rankin

Fixed Sights

Exc.	*V.G.*	*Good*	*Fair*	*Poor*
800	600	300	200	150

Pop Up Sights

Exc.	*V.G.*	*Good*	*Fair*	*Poor*
1500	800	600	400	300

Model 3

A 7.65mm semi-automatic pistol having a smooth barrel bushing. Blued with checkered hard rubber grips with the Walther logo on each. Introduced in 1910.

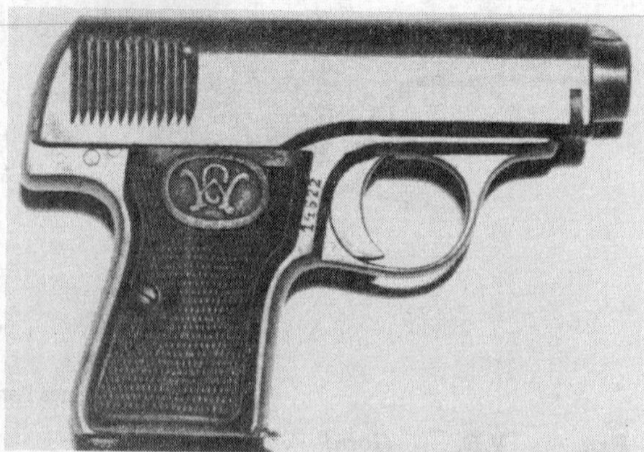

Courtesy James Rankin

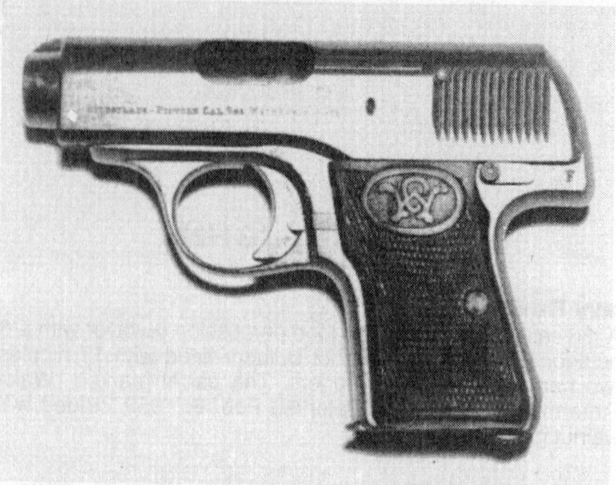

Courtesy James Rankin

Exc.	*V.G.*	*Good*	*Fair*	*Poor*
1500	1000	600	350	200

Model 4

A 7.65mm semi-automatic pistol larger than the preceding models. There were many variations of this model produced. Blued with checkered hard rubber grips with the Walther logo on each grip. Introduced 1910.

Courtesy James Rankin

Exc.	*V.G.*	*Good*	*Fair*	*Poor*
450	375	300	200	150

Model 5

A 6.35mm semi-automatic pistol that is almost identical to the Model 2. Fixed sights. Blued with checkered hard rubber grips with the Walther logo on each grip.

Courtesy James Rankin

Exc.	V.G.	Good	Fair	Poor
500	400	300	200	150

REMINDER
Practice your poker face. Use a mirror if necessary. Be inscrutable.

Model 6

A 9mm semi-automatic pistol. The largest of the Walther numbered pistols. Approximately 1,500 manufactured. Blued with checkered hard rubber grips with the Walther logo on each grip. Sometimes seen with plain checkered wood grips. Introduced 1915.

Courtesy James Rankin

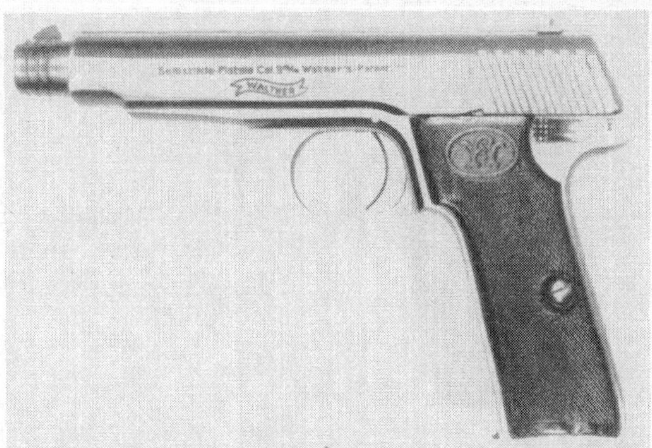

Courtesy James Rankin

Exc.	V.G.	Good	Fair	Poor
7000	5000	3000	1500	700

Model 7

A 6.35mm semi-automatic pistol in the same style as the Model 4. Blued with checkered hard rubber grips with the Walther logo on each side. Introduced in 1917.

Courtesy James Rankin

Exc.	V.G.	Good	Fair	Poor
550	400	300	200	150

Model 8

A 6.35mm semi-automatic pistol. Finishes in blue, silver, and gold. Three types of engraving coverage: slide only, slide and frame and complete coverage overall. The grips are checkered hard rubber with the WC logo on one grip, and 6.35mm on the opposite side. Ivory grips are seen with many of the engraved models. Introduced in 1920 and produced until 1944.

Courtesy James Rankin

Blue, Silver, and Gold Finish

Exc.	V.G.	Good	Fair	Poor
575	375	300	200	150

Engraved Slide

Exc.	V.G.	Good	Fair	Poor
1000	700	500	300	200

Engraved Slide and Frame

Exc.	V.G.	Good	Fair	Poor
2000	1400	850	450	300

Engraved, Complete Coverage

Exc.	V.G.	Good	Fair	Poor
2500	1750	900	500	300

Model 9

A 6.35mm semi-automatic pistol. Smaller than the Model 8, but built as the Model 1 with exposed barrel. Same finishes and engraving as the Model 8. Introduced 1921 and produced until 1944.

All values the same as the Model 8.

Courtesy James Rankin

Sport Model 1926
Walther Standard Sport
Sport Model Target
Walther Hammerless Target 22
Walther 1932 Olympia
Special Stoeger Model

All of these .22 LR caliber semi-automatic pistols are the same target pistol introduced by Walther in 1926. A well-made pistol with a barrel length of between 6"-16". It has one-piece checkered wrap-around wood grips. There was also a .22 Short version of the Olympia model produced for rapid fire Olympic shooting. There was also a torpedo-shape target weight available for shooters.

Courtesy Orvel Reichert

Courtesy James Rankin

Exc.	V.G.	Good	Fair	Poor
850	650	450	350	250

NOTE: Add $200 for target weight. Add $500 for case.

Walther 1936 Olympia

This semi-automatic target pistol in .22 caliber resembled the earlier 1932 Olympia, but with many improvements. There were four standard models produced with many variations of each one. These variations included many barrel lengths, and both round and octagon barrels. There were duraluminum slides, frames and triggers. Various weight configurations to as many as four separate weights to one gun. One-piece wrap-around checkered wood grips in different configurations for the individual shooter. Produced until 1944. The four models were:

Funfklamph Pentathlon
Jagerschafts—Hunter
Sport or Standard Model
Schnellfeuer—Rapid Fire

Olympia without weights

Courtesy John J. Stimson, Jr.

Olympia with weights Courtesy James Rankin

Exc.	V.G.	Good	Fair	Poor
1200	800	600	475	250

NOTE: Add $250 for weights.

Model MP

A 9mm semi-automatic pistol that was the forerunner of the Model AP and P.38 series. Found in variations that resemble a large Model PP or the P.38. Blued finish with one-piece wrap-around checkered wood grips.

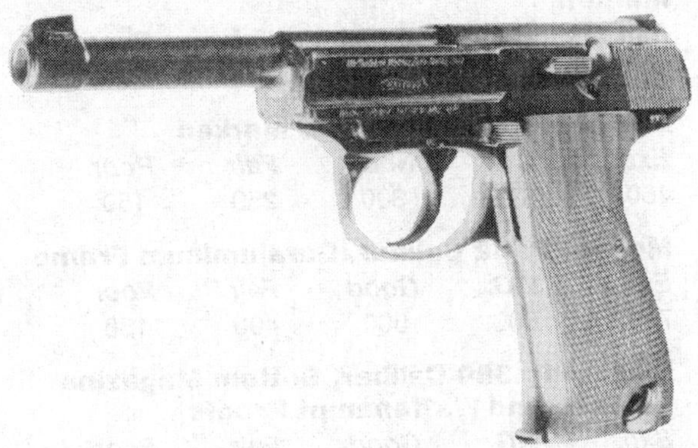

Courtesy James Rankin

Exc.	V.G.	Good	Fair	Poor
35000	30000	25000	20000	15000

Model AP

A 9mm semi-automatic pistol that was the forerunner of the Model P.38. A hammerless pistol in various barrel lengths. Sometimes with duraluminum frames, and some with stocks. Blued finish with one-piece wraparound checkered wood grips.

Exc.	V.G.	Good	Fair	Poor
28000	25000	20000	15000	10000

NOTE: With stock add $4000.

Model PP

A semi-automatic pistol in .22, .25, .32 and .380 caliber. Introduced in 1928. It was the first successful commercial double-action pistol. It was manufactured in finishes of blue, silver, and gold, and with three different types of engraving. Grips were generally two-piece black or white plastic with the Walther banner on each grip. Grips in wood or ivory are seen, but usually on engraved guns. There are many variations of the Model PP and numerous NSDAP markings seen on the pre-1946 models that were produced during the Nazi regime. All reflect various prices.

Model PP .22 Caliber

Exc.	V.G.	Good	Fair	Poor
800	600	350	250	150

Model PP .25 Caliber

Exc.	V.G.	Good	Fair	Poor
5800	4000	2500	1500	600

Model PP .32 Caliber High Polished Finish

Exc.	V.G.	Good	Fair	Poor
450	325	275	225	175

Courtesy James Rankin

Model PP .32 Caliber Milled Finish

Exc.	V.G.	Good	Fair	Poor
425	325	250	200	125

Model PP .380 Caliber

Exc.	V.G.	Good	Fair	Poor
950	750	550	475	350

Model PP .32 Caliber with Duraluminum Frame

Exc.	V.G.	Good	Fair	Poor
800	675	550	400	200

Model PP .32 Caliber with Bottom Magazine Release

Exc.	V.G.	Good	Fair	Poor
1100	800	600	400	200

Model PP .32 Caliber with Verchromt Finish

Exc.	V.G.	Good	Fair	Poor
2000	1450	1000	700	400

Model PP .32 Caliber, Allemagne Marked

Exc.	V.G.	Good	Fair	Poor
850	700	550	325	250

Model PP .32 Caliber, A. F. Stoeger Contract

Exc.	V.G.	Good	Fair	Poor
2500	1750	1050	700	400

Model PP .32 Caliber with Waffenampt Proofs, High Polished Finish

Exc.	V.G.	Good	Fair	Poor
1200	800	375	275	150

Model PP .32 Caliber with Waffenampt Proofs, Milled Finish

Exc.	V.G.	Good	Fair	Poor
450	375	325	250	150

Model PP .32 Caliber in Blue, Silver or Gold Finish and Full Coverage Engraving

Courtesy James Rankin

Courtesy Orvel Reichert

Blue

Exc.	V.G.	Good	Fair	Poor
5000	3500	3000	1200	700

Silver

Exc.	V.G.	Good	Fair	Poor
6000	4000	3000	1200	700

Gold

Exc.	V.G.	Good	Fair	Poor
6500	4500	3500	1500	700

NOTE: Add $250 for ivory grips with any of the three above. Add $700 for leather presentation cases. Add $500 for .22 caliber. Add $1000 for .380 caliber.

Model PP .32 Caliber, Police Eagle/C Proofed, High Polished Finish

Exc.	V.G.	Good	Fair	Poor
1200	800	375	250	150

Model PP .32 Caliber, Police Eagle/C and Police Eagle/F Proofed, Milled Finish

Exc.	V.G.	Good	Fair	Poor
900	600	375	275	150

Model PP .32 Caliber, NSKK Marked on the Slide

Exc.	V.G.	Good	Fair	Poor
2500	2000	850	550	300

NOTE: Add $700 with proper NSKK DRGM AKAH holster.

Model PP .32 Caliber, NSDAP Gruppe Markings

Exc.	V.G.	Good	Fair	Poor
2000	1500	1000	500	300

NOTE: Add $600 with proper SA DRGM AKAH holster.

Model PP .32 Caliber, PDM Marked with Bottom Magazine Release

Exc.	V.G.	Good	Fair	Poor
850	700	550	475	300

Model PP .32 Caliber, RJ Marked

Exc.	V.G.	Good	Fair	Poor
750	600	475	400	150

Model PP .32 Caliber, RFV Marked, High Polished or Milled Finish

Exc.	V.G.	Good	Fair	Poor
700	600	475	400	150

Model PP .32 Caliber, RBD Munster Marked

Exc.	V.G.	Good	Fair	Poor
2200	1750	1200	650	400

Model PP .32 Caliber, RpLt Marked

Exc.	V.G.	Good	Fair	Poor
950	750	475	375	200

Model PP .32 Caliber, Statens Vattenfallsverk Marked

Exc.	V.G.	Good	Fair	Poor
1000	800	550	375	200

Model PP .32 Caliber, AC Marked

Exc.	V.G.	Good	Fair	Poor
450	375	300	250	150

Model PP .32 Caliber, Duraluminum Frame

Exc.	V.G.	Good	Fair	Poor
750	600	500	400	150

Model PP .380 Caliber, Bottom Magazine Release and Waffenampt Proofs

Exc.	V.G.	Good	Fair	Poor
2000	1500	700	500	300

Model PPK

A semi-automatic pistol in .22, .25, .32 and .380 caliber. Introduced six months after the Model PP in 1929. A more compact version of the Model PP with one less round in the magazine and one-piece wraparound checkered plastic grips in brown, black, and white with the Walther banner on each side of the grips. The Model PPK will be found with the same types of finishes as the Model PP as well as the same styles of engraving. Grips in wood or ivory are seen with some of the engraved models. As with the Model PP there are many variations of the Model PPK and numerous NSDAP markings seen on the pre-1946 models that were produced during the Nazi regime. All reflect various prices.

Courtesy James Rankin

Courtesy Orvel Reichert

Model PPK .22 Caliber

Exc.	*V.G.*	*Good*	*Fair*	*Poor*
1200	700	475	325	175

Model PPK .25 Caliber

Exc.	*V.G.*	*Good*	*Fair*	*Poor*
6000	4000	1850	1000	500

Model PPK .32 Caliber, High Polished Finish

Exc.	*V.G.*	*Good*	*Fair*	*Poor*
550	450	325	250	150

Model PPK .32 Caliber, Milled Finish

Exc.	*V.G.*	*Good*	*Fair*	*Poor*
500	400	325	250	150

Model PPK .380 Caliber

Courtesy Orvel Reichert

Exc.	*V.G.*	*Good*	*Fair*	*Poor*
2200	1750	1300	750	375

Model PPK .32 Caliber with Duraluminum Frame

Exc.	*V.G.*	*Good*	*Fair*	*Poor*
950	800	600	400	200

Model PPK .32 Caliber Marked Mod. PP on Slide

Exc.	*V.G.*	*Good*	*Fair*	*Poor*
5000	4000	2500	1500	1000

Model PPK .32 Caliber with Panagraphed Slide

Exc.	*V.G.*	*Good*	*Fair*	*Poor*
750	550	450	300	200

Model PPK .32 Caliber with Verchromt Finish

Exc.	*V.G.*	*Good*	*Fair*	*Poor*
2500	1800	1200	700	350

Model PPK .32 Caliber in Blue, Silver or Gold Finish and Full Coverage Engraving

Blue

Exc.	*V.G.*	*Good*	*Fair*	*Poor*
5000	3500	2500	1200	700

Silver

Exc.	*V.G.*	*Good*	*Fair*	*Poor*
6000	4000	3000	1500	700

Gold

Exc.	*V.G.*	*Good*	*Fair*	*Poor*
6500	4500	3500	1500	700

NOTE: Add $750 for ivory grips with any of the three above. Add $700 for leather presentation cases. Add $500 for .22 caliber. Add $1000 for .380 caliber.

Model PPK .32 Caliber, Czechoslovakian Contract

Exc.	*V.G.*	*Good*	*Fair*	*Poor*
1850	1500	1000	550	300

Model PPK .32 Caliber, Allemagne Marked

Exc.	*V.G.*	*Good*	*Fair*	*Poor*
800	700	600	400	250

Model PPK .32 Caliber with Waffenampt Proofs and a High Polished Finish

Exc.	*V.G.*	*Good*	*Fair*	*Poor*
1800	1200	700	400	250

Model PPK .32 Caliber with Waffenampt Proofs and a Milled Finish

Exc.	*V.G.*	*Good*	*Fair*	*Poor*
1100	800	500	300	175

Model PPK .32 Caliber, Police Eagle/C Proofed, High Polished Finish

Exc.	*V.G.*	*Good*	*Fair*	*Poor*
1000	800	500	300	175

Model PPK .32 Caliber, Police Eagle/C Proofed. Milled Finish

Exc.	*V.G.*	*Good*	*Fair*	*Poor*
650	500	375	275	175

Model PPK .32 Caliber, Police Eagle/F Proofed, Duraluminum Frame, Milled Finish

Exc.	V.G.	Good	Fair	Poor
1100	800	550	350	225

Model PPK .22 Caliber, Late War, Black Grips

Exc.	V.G.	Good	Fair	Poor
1500	800	600	450	300

Model PPK .32 Caliber, Party Leader Grips, Brown

Exc.	V.G.	Good	Fair	Poor
4000	3000	2350	2250	2000

Model PPK .32 Caliber, Party Leader Grips, Black

Exc.	V.G.	Good	Fair	Poor
4000	3000	2750	2550	2500

NOTE: If grips are badly cracked or damaged on the two Party Leaders above, reduce $2000 each valuation. Add $500 with proper Party Leader DRGM AKAH holster.

Model PPK .32 Caliber, RZM Marked

Exc.	V.G.	Good	Fair	Poor
1200	900	500	400	300

Model PPK .32 Caliber, PDM Marked with Duraluminum Frame and Bottom Magazine Release

Exc.	V.G.	Good	Fair	Poor
2500	1800	1150	750	450

Model PPK .32 Caliber, RFV Marked

Exc.	V.G.	Good	Fair	Poor
2000	1750	1150	650	400

Model PPK .32 Caliber, DRP Marked

Exc.	V.G.	Good	Fair	Poor
800	650	550	450	275

Model PPK .32 Caliber, Statens Vattenfallsverk

Exc.	V.G.	Good	Fair	Poor
1400	1200	700	450	300

WALTHER POST-WORLD WAR II

Models PP and PPK

Manufactured by the firm of Manufacture de Machines du Haut Rhin at Mulhouse, France under license by Walther.

Model PP Some with Duraluminum Frames, Model PP .22 Caliber

Exc.	V.G.	Good	Fair	Poor
750	600	400	275	175

Model PP .32 Caliber

Exc.	V.G.	Good	Fair	Poor
500	375	350	275	175

Model PP .380Caliber

Exc.	V.G.	Good	Fair	Poor
750	600	400	275	175

Model PP, All Three Calibers Finished In Blue, Silver and Gold with Full Coverage Engraving

Blue

Exc.	V.G.	Good	Fair	Poor
1900	1500	900	600	300

Silver

Exc.	V.G.	Good	Fair	Poor
1900	1500	900	600	300

Gold

Exc.	V.G.	Good	Fair	Poor
1900	1500	900	600	300

Model PP Mark II

These Walthers were manufactured under license by Walther and produced by the Manurhin Company. They were sold exclusively by Interarms, Alexandria, Virginia. The Mark IIs were the same pistols as those above and have the same types of finish and engraving as well as the same value.

Model PP Manurhin

Manurhin Company manufactured with Manurhin logo and inscription. Usually "licensed by Walther" somewhere on the pistol. The same pistols as those above, bearing the same types of finish and engraving, and having the same values.

Model PP Sport, Manurhin

.22 caliber. This is the same gun as the Model PP with different barrel lengths running from 5-3/4" to 7-3/4". It is basically a target .22 with adjustable rear sights for elevation and windage. The front sight is also adjustable. There is a barrel bushing at the muzzle that attaches the front sight to the barrel. The grips are contoured checkered plastic and are either squared at the bottom of the grips or are in the shape of an inverted bird's-head.

Exc.	V.G.	Good	Fair	Poor
900	600	450	375	275

Model PP Sport C, Manurhin

.22 caliber. This is the same gun as the Model PP Sport but in single-action with a spur hammer. It has front and rear adjustable sights and squared target grips in checkered black, brown and plastic. Blued and silver finish.

Exc.	V.G.	Good	Fair	Poor
900	600	450	375	275

Model PP Sport, Walther

A .22 caliber Sport was manufactured by Manurhin, but sold by Walther with the Walther logo and inscription. This is the same gun as the Model PP Sport, Manurhin. Only sold for a period of two years.

Walther PP Sport Courtesy John J. Stimson, Jr.

Exc.	V.G.	Good	Fair	Poor
900	600	450	375	275

Model PP 50th Anniversary Commemorative Model

In .22 or .380 caliber. Blued with gold inlays and hand-carved grips with oak leaves and acorns. Walther banner carved into each side of the grips. Wood presentation case.

Exc.	V.G.	Good	Fair	Poor
1500	1000	750	500	300

Model PPK, Some with Duraluminum Frames

Model PPK .22 Caliber

Exc.	V.G.	Good	Fair	Poor
750	600	400	275	175

Model PPK .32 Caliber

Exc.	V.G.	Good	Fair	Poor
550	400	350	275	175

Model PPK .380 Caliber

Exc.	V.G.	Good	Fair	Poor
750	600	400	275	175

Model PPK, All Three Calibers Finished In Blue, Silver and Gold With Full Coverage Engraving

Blue

Exc.	V.G.	Good	Fair	Poor
1900	1500	750	450	300

Silver

Exc.	V.G.	Good	Fair	Poor
1900	1500	750	450	300

Gold

Exc.	V.G.	Good	Fair	Poor
1900	1500	750	450	300

Model PPK Mark II

These Walthers were manufactured under license by Walther and produced by the Manurhin Company. They were sold exclusively by Interarms, Alexandria, Virginia. The Mark IIs were the same pistols as those above and have the same types of finish and engraving as well as the same value.

Model PPK Manurhin

Manurhin Company manufactured with Manurhin logo and inscription. Usually "Licensed by Walther" somewhere on the pistol. The same pistols as above, bearing the same types of finish and engraving, and having the same value.

Courtesy James Rankin

Model PPK 50th Anniversary Commemorative Model

In .22 or .380 caliber. Blued with gold inlays and hand-carved grips with oak leaves and acorns. Walther banner carved into each side of the grips. Wood presentation case.

Exc.	V.G.	Good	Fair	Poor
2100	1800	1250	1000	500

Model PPK American

In 1986 the Model PPK was licensed by the Walther Company to be manufactured in the United States. The finish is stainless steel. Caliber is .380.

Exc.	V.G.	Good	Fair	Poor
500	375	300	200	150

Model PPK/S

This Walther was manufactured in .22, .32 and .380 caliber for sale in the United States market after the introduction of the United States Gun Control Act of 1968. It is basically a Model PP with a cut-off muzzle and slide. It has two-piece black checkered plastic grips as seen on the Model PP. It was finished in blue, nickel, dull gold and verchromt.

Exc.	V.G.	Good	Fair	Poor
550	475	375	300	200

Model PPK/S American

Manufactured in the United States. The same as the German Model PPK/S. This pistol is finished in blue and stainless steel. Caliber is .380.

Exc.	V.G.	Good	Fair	Poor
500	375	300	200	150

Model TP

A Walther-manufactured semi-automatic pistol in .22 and .25 calibers patterned after the earlier Model 9. Finish is blue and silver black plastic checkered grips with Walther banner medallions in each grip.

Exc.	V.G.	Good	Fair	Poor
900	700	500	375	250

Model TPH

A Walther-manufactured semi-automatic pistol in .22 and .25 calibers. This is a double-action pistol with a duraluminum frame. Finished in blue or silver. Two-piece black checkered plastic grips. Full coverage engraving available.

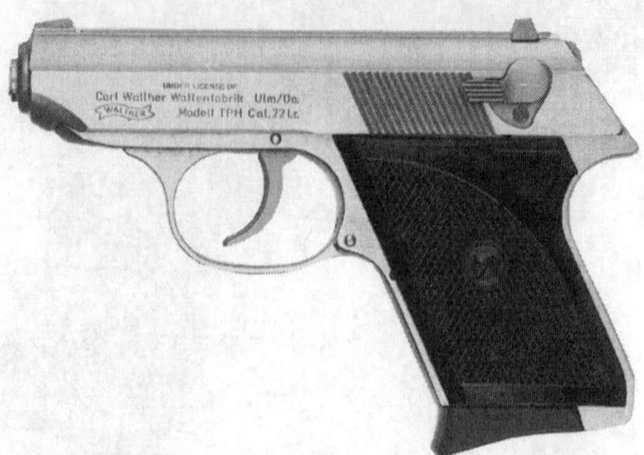

Exc.	V.G.	Good	Fair	Poor
650	500	450	350	250

NOTE: Add $300 for the engraved model.

Model TPH American

This semi-automatic is produced in both .22 and .25 calibers. It is licensed by Walther and manufactured in the United States. It is produced in stainless steel and has two-piece black plastic checkered grips. It is a double-action pistol.

Exc.	V.G.	Good	Fair	Poor
400	300	200	150	100

Model PP Super

This is a .380 and 9x18 caliber, double-action semi-automatic manufactured by Walther. It is similar in design to the Model PP, but with a P.38 type of mechanism. Finish is blue and the grips are wraparound black checkered plastic or a type of molded wood colored plastic.

Courtesy Orvel Reichert

Exc.	V.G.	Good	Fair	Poor
750	500	350	250	150

Model P.38

Following WWII, the P.38 was reintroduced in variety of calibers with a 5" barrel and alloy or steel frame.

.22 Caliber

NIB	Exc.	V.G.	Good	Fair	Poor
1200	850	650	500	350	200

Other Calibers

NIB	Exc.	V.G.	Good	Fair	Poor
750	600	500	400	300	200

Steel-Framed (Introduced 1987)

NIB	Exc.	V.G.	Good	Fair	Poor
1400	1250	1000	750	500	400

Factory-engraved versions of the P.38 pistol were blued, chrome, or silver or gold-plated. We suggest that a qualified appraisal be secured when contemplating purchase.

Model P.38K

As above, with a 2.8" barrel and front sight is mounted on the slide. Imported between 1974 and 1980.

Exc.	V.G.	Good	Fair	Poor
900	650	450	300	200

Model P.38 II

Exc.	V.G.	Good	Fair	Poor
800	550	350	250	200

Model P.38 IV

A redesigned version of the above, with a 4.5" barrel and 8-shot magazine. Fitted with a decocking lever and adjustable sights. Imported prior to 1983.

Exc.	V.G.	Good	Fair	Poor
900	650	450	300	200

CURRENTLY IMPORTED WALTHER PISTOLS—WALTHER USA

In 1999 Carl Walther Gmbh of Germany and Smith & Wesson entered into a joint agreement to import and distribute Walther-branded firearms and accessories into the U.S. beginning August 1, 1999.

Model PP Limited Edition

This model was introduced in 2000 and is a limited edition of 100 pistols chambered in .380 ACP and 50 pistols chambered in .32 ACP. The finish is a high-polish blue with the slide marked "LAST EDITION 1929-1999." Supplied with a special case with certificate and video of history of Walther.

NIB	Exc.	V.G.	Good	Fair	Poor
1100	—	—	—	—	—

Model PPK/E—Walther USA

Introduced in 2000 this pistol is chambered for the .380 or .32 ACP cartridges and later in that year the .22 LR. It has a double-action trigger. Produced in Hungary by Walther. Barrel length is 3.4". Magazine capacity is seven rounds for the .380 and eight rounds for the .32 ACP and .22 LR. Blued finish and plastic grips.

NIB	Exc.	V.G.	Good	Fair	Poor
275	225	—	—	—	—

Model PPK

Chambered for the .380 ACP or .32 ACP cartridge and fitted with a 3.35" barrel. Offered in blue or stainless steel. Black plastic grips. Fixed red-dot sights. Magazine capacity is six for the .380 ACP and seven for the .32 ACP. Weight is about 21 oz.

NIB	Exc.	V.G.	Good	Fair	Poor
525	425	—	—	—	—

Model PPK/S

Same as the PPK but with .25" longer grip. Magazine capacity is seven rounds for the .380 ACP and eight rounds for the .32 ACP. Weight is about 23 oz. Offered in blue, stainless steel and two-tone finish.

NIB	Exc.	V.G.	Good	Fair	Poor
525	425	—	—	—	—

Seventy-fifth Anniversary PPK

Blued with wood grips, machine engraving and available in .380 ACP with 6+1 capacity. Special SN beginning with 0000PPK, shipped with glass-top display case. Single/double-action, 3.3" barrel, 20.8 oz. Windage-adjustable rear sight. Introduced 2006.

NIB	Exc.	V.G.	Good	Fair	Poor
543	—	—	—	—	—

Model P5

A 9mm semi-automatic pistol with a double-action firing mechanism. One of the first Walthers to have a decocker lever. Finish is a combination of black matte and high polish. It has black plastic checkered grips.

NIB	Exc.	V.G.	Good	Fair	Poor
875	650	500	400	300	—

Model P5, Compact

A shorter version of the standard Model P5.

NIB	Exc.	V.G.	Good	Fair	Poor
850	700	600	375	250	—

Model P5 One Hundred Year Commemorative

Blued with gold inlays and hand-carved grips with oak leaves and acorns. Walther banner carved into each side of the grips.

Wood presentation case

NIB	Exc.	V.G.	Good	Fair	Poor
2000	1500	—	—	—	—

Model P88

A 9mm semi-automatic in double-action with ambidextrous decocking lever. Fifteen-shot magazine and two-piece black checkered plastic grips. Combination of high polish and black matte finish.

NIB	Exc.	V.G.	Good	Fair	Poor
875	700	600	500	300	—

Model P88 Compact

A shorter version of the standard Model P88.

NIB	Exc.	V.G.	Good	Fair	Poor
850	700	600	500	300	—

Model P99

Introduced in 1997, this is a single- and double-action design with a 4" barrel and polymer frame. Chambered for 9mm or .40 S&W cartridge it has a magazine capacity of 10 rounds (16 rounds in 9mm and 12 rounds in .40 S&W for law enforcement). Front sight is interchangeable and rear sight is windage adjustable. Total length of pistol is 7" and weight is approximately 25 oz. Finish is blue tenifer.

NIB	Exc.	V.G.	Good	Fair	Poor
700	550	450	—	—	—

Model P99 Compact AS/QA

This model is chambered for the 9mm cartridge with a double action trigger and 9mm or .40 S&W cartridges. Quick action, striker fired. Barrel length is 3.5" with fixed sights. Magazine capacity is 10 rounds for 9mm and 8 rounds for .40 S&W models. Weight is about 19 oz.

NIB	Exc.	V.G.	Good	Fair	Poor
670	525	—	—	—	—

Model P990

A double-action-only version of the P99.

NIB	Exc.	V.G.	Good	Fair	Poor
700	550	450	—	—	—

Model P99 QPQ

Similar to the P99 but with silver tenifer finish.

NIB	Exc.	V.G.	Good	Fair	Poor
700	550	450	—	—	—

Model P990 QPQ

A double-action-only version of the P99 QPQ.

NIB	Exc.	V.G.	Good	Fair	Poor
700	550	450	—	—	—

Model P99 QA

Similar to the P99 pistol but with a constant short trigger pull. Trigger pull is approximately 6.5 lbs. Offered in both 9mm and .40 S&W calibers. Introduced in 2000.

NIB	Exc.	V.G.	Good	Fair	Poor
700	550	450	—	—	—

Model P99 Military

Similar to the P99 but with military finish.

NIB	Exc.	V.G.	Good	Fair	Poor
700	550	450	—	—	—

Model P99 La Chasse DU

This model features laser engraving on the blue tenifer slide.

NIB	Exc.	V.G.	Good	Fair	Poor
750	600	—	—	—	—

Model P99 La Chasse

This model features hand engraving on a gray tenifer slide.

NIB	Exc.	V.G.	Good	Fair	Poor
1675	1250	—	—	—	—

Model P99 Commemorative

This is a limited edition P99 that features a high polish blue slide with a special serial number and the marking" COMMEMORATIVE FOR THE YEAR 2000." Offered in both 9mm and .40 S&W calibers. Each handgun comes with a special certificate and video of the history of Walther.

NIB	Exc.	V.G.	Good	Fair	Poor
720	—	—	—	—	—

Model P22 Standard

Introduced in 2002 this .22 caliber pistol is chambered for the LR cartridge. Barrel length is 3.4". Polymer frame with double-action trigger. Adjustable rear sight. Magazine capacity is 10 rounds. Weight is about 20 oz.

NOTE: In 2003 this model was offered with a military black slide and green frame or a silver slide with black frame. A carbon fiber-framed model is also available at about the same price as standard models.

P22 with laser, laser optional

NIB	Exc.	V.G.	Good	Fair	Poor
295	—	—	—	—	—

Model P22 Target

Similar to the standard P22 model but with a 5" barrel with barrel weight. Weight is about 21 oz.

NIB	Exc.	V.G.	Good	Fair	Poor
365	—	—	—	—	—

NOTE: Barrels are interchangeable on both P22 pistols.

Model FP

A .22 LR caliber, single-shot target pistol that fires electrically. It has micro-adjustable electric firing system along with micrometer sights and contoured wooden grips that are adjustable. The barrel is 11.7" and the finish is blued.

Exc.	V.G.	Good	Fair	Poor
2000	1600	1000	500	400

Model GSP

A semi-automatic target pistol in .22 LR and .32 calibers. This target pistol has a 4-1/2" barrel, 5-shot magazine and contoured wood target grips. Blued finish and sold with attache extra barrel, case and accessories.

Courtesy John J. Stimson, Jr.

Exc.	V.G.	Good	Fair	Poor
1600	1200	750	650	300

Model GSP-C

Almost the same pistol as the Model GSP, but in .32 caliber S&W wadcutter.

Exc.	V.G.	Good	Fair	Poor
1500	1100	750	650	300

Model OSP

A .22 Short semi-automatic target pistol that is similar to the Model GSP. This pistol is made for rapid fire target shooting. Blued finish with contoured wood grips.

Exc.	V.G.	Good	Fair	Poor
1800	1200	750	650	300

Free Pistol

A .22 caliber single-shot target pistol with an 11.7" barrel, micrometer sights, adjustable grips and an electronic trigger. Blued.

NIB	Exc.	V.G.	Good	Fair	Poor
1900	1600	1200	900	700	550

Model R99

This 6-shot revolver is chambered for the .357 Magnum cartridge. Barrel length is 3". Weight is about 28 oz. Offered in blue or stainless steel. Introduced in 1999.

NIB	Exc.	V.G.	Good	Fair	Poor
N/A	—	—	—	—	—

RIFLES

Model B

A .30-06 caliber bolt-action rifle with a 22" barrel, 4-shot magazine and single or double set triggers. Double set triggers are worth approximately 20 percent more than the values listed. Blued with a walnut stock.

Exc.	V.G.	Good	Fair	Poor
575	500	350	250	175

Olympic Single-Shot

A .22 caliber bolt-action rifle with a 26" barrel, adjustable target sights and a walnut stock fitted with a palm rest and adjustable buttplate. Blued.

Exc.	V.G.	Good	Fair	Poor
950	850	700	500	400

Model V

A .22 caliber single-shot bolt-action rifle with a 26" barrel and adjustable sights. Blued with a plain walnut stock. Manufactured before WWII.

Exc.	V.G.	Good	Fair	Poor
450	400	300	200	150

Model V Champion

As above, with a checkered walnut stock.

Exc.	V.G.	Good	Fair	Poor
500	400	350	250	200

Model KKM International Match

A .22 caliber single-shot bolt-action rifle with a 28" barrel and adjustable sights. Blued with a walnut stock fitted for a palm rest and with an adjustable buttplate. Manufactured after WWII.

Exc.	V.G.	Good	Fair	Poor
1400	1100	850	450	350

Model KKM-S

As above, with an adjustable cheekpiece.

Exc.	V.G.	Good	Fair	Poor
1400	1100	850	500	400

Model KKW

As above, with a military-style stock.

Exc.	V.G.	Good	Fair	Poor
900	700	500	350	300

Model KKJ Sporter

A .22 caliber bolt action rifle with a 22.5" barrel and 5-shot magazine. Blued with a checkered walnut stock. This model was available with double set triggers and their presence would add approximately 20 percent to the values listed. Manufactured after WWII.

Exc.	V.G.	Good	Fair	Poor
700	600	450	350	300

Model KKJ-MA

As above, in .22 Magnum rimfire.

Exc.	V.G.	Good	Fair	Poor
650	550	450	350	300

Model KKJ-HO

As above, in .22 Hornet.

Exc.	V.G.	Good	Fair	Poor
750	700	600	450	350

Model SSV Varmint

A .22 caliber bolt action single-shot rifle with a 25.5" barrel not fitted with sights and Monte Carlo-style stock. Blued. Manufactured after WWII.

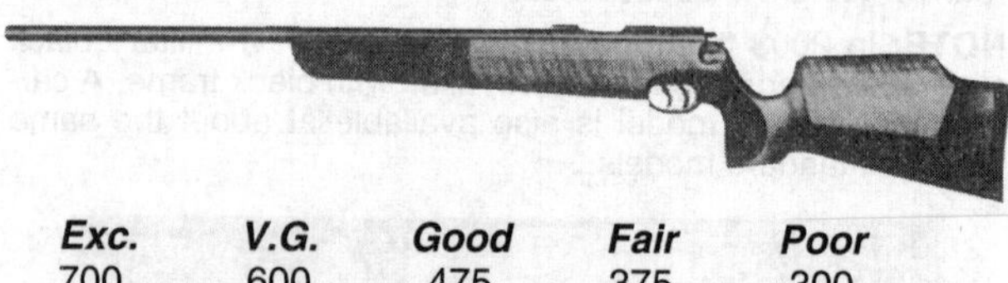

Exc.	V.G.	Good	Fair	Poor
700	600	475	375	300

Model UIT BV Universal

As above, with adjustable target sights and a walnut stock fitted with a palm rest and adjustable buttplate.

NIB	Exc.	V.G.	Good	Fair	Poor
1750	1500	1250	900	650	500

Model UIT Match

As above, with a stippled pistol grip and forend. Also available with an electronic trigger that would add approximately $50 to the values listed.

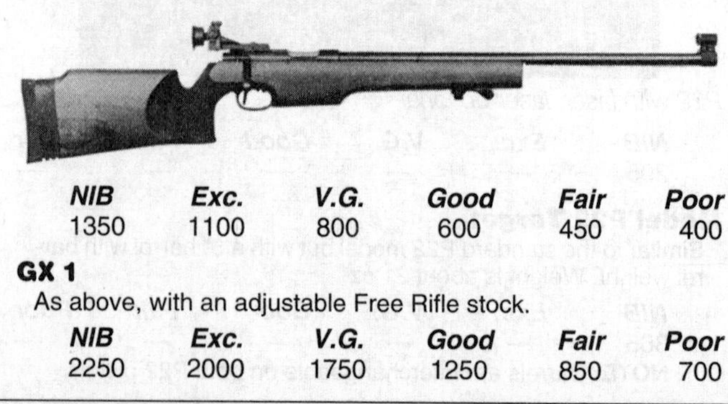

NIB	Exc.	V.G.	Good	Fair	Poor
1350	1100	800	600	450	400

GX 1

As above, with an adjustable Free Rifle stock.

NIB	Exc.	V.G.	Good	Fair	Poor
2250	2000	1750	1250	850	700

Prone Model 400

Target rifle in .22 caliber with a prone position stock.

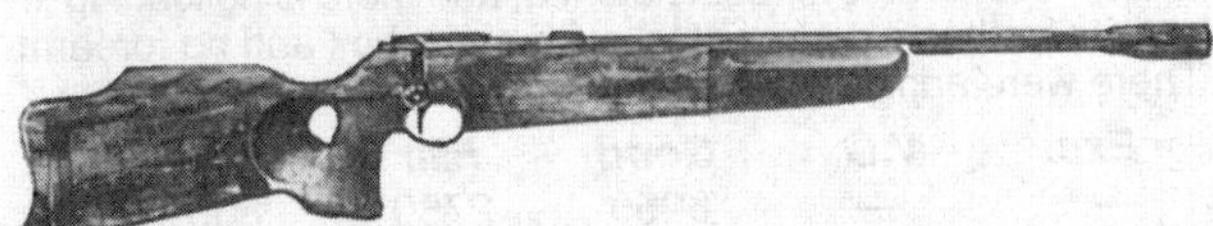

NIB	Exc.	V.G.	Good	Fair	Poor
800	700	600	450	350	300

Model KK/MS Silhouette

A .22 caliber bolt-action rifle with a 25.5" front-weighted barrel furnished without sights and a thumbhole stock with an adjustable buttplate. Introduced in 1984.

NIB	Exc.	V.G.	Good	Fair	Poor
1300	1100	850	700	550	400

Running Boar Model 500

As above, with a 23.5" barrel.

NIB	Exc.	V.G.	Good	Fair	Poor
1550	1350	950	750	600	450

Model WA-2000

A .300 Winchester Magnum or .308 caliber bolt-action sporting rifle produced on custom order. Prospective purchasers are advised to secure an appraisal prior to acquisition. Imported prior to 1989.

Exc.	V.G.	Good	Fair	Poor
6500	4750	3500	3000	2000

REMINDER

An "N/A" or "—" instead of a price indicates that pricing for that gun in that condition is not available, or that sales for that particular model are so few that a reliable price cannot be given.

Model SF

A 12 or 16 gauge boxlock double-barrel shotgun fitted with double triggers and extractors. Blued with a checkered walnut stock fitted with sling swivels.

Exc.	V.G.	Good	Fair	Poor
900	600	500	250	100

Model SFD

As above, with the stock having a cheekpiece.

Exc.	V.G.	Good	Fair	Poor
1000	750	650	425	250

Model G22

This is a .22 caliber rifle with a 20" barrel with adjustable sights. This model feastures a cocking indicator, intergrated lock, slide safety, and multi function rail. Black or green finish. Weight is about 6 lbs. This model is also sold in packages.

NIB	Exc.	V.G.	Good	Fair	Poor
400	300	—	—	—	—

Package A1 with Walther rifle scope

NIB	Exc.	V.G.	Good	Fair	Poor
440	325	—	—	—	—

Package A2 with laser

NIB	Exc.	V.G.	Good	Fair	Poor
470	350	—	—	—	—

Package A3 with Walther rifle scope & laser

NIB	Exc.	V.G.	Good	Fair	Poor
500	375	—	—	—	—

Package A4 with Walther PS22 red-dot sight

NIB	Exc.	V.G.	Good	Fair	Poor
470	350	—	—	—	—

WALTHER MANURHIN

Mulhouse, France

The Manurhin-manufactured Walther pistols are listed in the Walther section under their respective model headings.

WARNANT, L. AND J.

Ognee, Belgium

Revolver

Modeled after pistols manufactured by Smith & Wesson, the Warnants produced a variety of revolvers in .32, .38, or .45 caliber, between 1870 and 1890.

Exc.	V.G.	Good	Fair	Poor
—	200	75	60	50

Semi-Automatic Pistol

A 6.35mm semi-automatic pistol with a 2.5" barrel and 5-shot magazine. The slide marked "L&J Warnant Bte 6.35mm." Blued with black plastic grips bearing the monogram "L&JW." Manufactured after 1908.

Exc.	V.G.	Good	Fair	Poor
350	200	150	100	75

1912 Model

A 7.65mm caliber semi-automatic pistol with a 3" barrel and 7-shot magazine. The slide marked "L&J Warnant Brevetes Pist Auto 7.65mm." Manufactured prior to 1915.

Exc.	V.G.	Good	Fair	Poor
350	200	150	100	75

WARNER ARMS CORPORATION

Brooklyn, New York and Norwich, Connecticut

Established in 1912, this firm marketed revolvers, rifles, semi-automatic pistols and shotguns made for them by other companies (including N.R. Davis & Sons, Ithaca Gun Company and so forth). In 1917, the company was purchased by N.R. Davis & Company. *See also Davis-Warner.*

The arms marketed by Warner Prior to 1917 are listed.

SHOTGUNS

Single Trigger Hammerless Utica Special Double-Barrel

In 12 gauge with 28", 30", or 32" barrels.

Double Trigger Hammerless Double-Barrel

In 12 or 16 gauge with 28", 30", or 32" barrels.

Grade X, SF, XT, SFT, XD and XDF Hammer Guns

In 12, 16 or 20 gauge with 28", 30", or 32" barrels.

Field Grade Hammer Gun

In 12 or 16 gauge with 28" or 30" barrels.

Boxlock Hammerless

In 12 or 16 gauge with 28", 30", or 32" barrels.

RIFLES

Number 522

A .22 caliber single-shot rifle with an 18" barrel.

Number 532

A .32 caliber single-shot rifle with an 18" barrel.

REVOLVERS

Double-Action

.32 and .38 caliber with 4" or 5" barrels.

Double-Action Hammerless

.32 and .38 caliber with 4" or 5" barrels.

SEMI-AUTOMATIC PISTOLS

"Faultless": Warner-Schwarzlose Model C, .32 ACP

Exc.	V.G.	Good	Fair	Poor
—	500	300	200	100

WARNER, CHAS.

Windsor Locks, Connecticut

Pocket Revolver

A .31 caliber percussion revolver with a 3" round barrel and 6-shot unfluted cylinder. The cylinder marked "Charles Warner. Windsor Locks, Conn." Blued with walnut grips. Approximately 600 were made between 1857 and 1860.

Exc.	V.G.	Good	Fair	Poor
—	—	1150	450	100

WARNER, JAMES

Springfield, Massachusetts

Revolving Carbines

A variety of revolving carbines were made by this maker, nearly all of which are of .40 caliber, with octagonal barrels measuring 20" to 24" in length. The most commonly encountered variations are listed.

Manually Revolved Grooved Cylinder

This model is fitted with two triggers, one of which is a release so that the cylinder can be manually turned. Not fitted with a loading lever. The top strap marked "James Warner/Springfield, Mass." Approximately 75 were made in 1849.

Courtesy Milwaukee Public Museum, Milwaukee, Wisconsin

Exc.	V.G.	Good	Fair	Poor
—	—	4250	2000	500

Retractable Cylinder Model

This version has a cylinder that fits over the breech, and it must be retracted before it can be manually rotated. The cylinder release is a button located in front of the trigger. It is marked "James Warner/Springfield Mass" and with an eagle over the letters "U.S." The cylinder is etched, and there is no loading lever. It also has a walnut stock with patch box and no forearm. There were approximately 25 manufactured in 1849.

Exc.	V.G.	Good	Fair	Poor
—	—	6250	2750	800

Automatic Revolving Cylinder

The cylinder is automatically turned when the hammer is cocked. This model is fitted with a loading lever and is marked "Warner's Patent/Jan. 1851" and "Springfield Arms Co." Approximately 200 were made during the 1850s.

Courtesy Milwaukee Public Museum, Milwaukee, Wisconsin

Exc.	V.G.	Good	Fair	Poor
—	—	4250	1750	500

Belt Revolver

A .31 caliber double-action percussion revolver with a 4" or 5" round barrel and 6-shot etched cylinder. Blued with walnut grips. No markings appear on this model except for the serial number. Manufactured in 1851.

Courtesy Milwaukee Public Museum, Milwaukee, Wisconsin

Exc.	V.G.	Good	Fair	Poor
—	—	1500	600	100

Pocket Revolver

A .28 caliber percussion revolver with a 3" octagonal barrel marked "James Warner, Springfield, Mass., USA" and a 6-shot cylinder. Blued with walnut grips. Approximately 500 were made.

Exc.	V.G.	Good	Fair	Poor
—	—	650	250	100

Second Model

As above, with either a 3" or 4" barrel and marked "Warner's Patent 1857."

Courtesy Wallis & Wallis, Lewes, Sussex, England

Exc.	V.G.	Good	Fair	Poor
—	—	650	300	100

Third Model

As above, but in .31 caliber.

Exc.	V.G.	Good	Fair	Poor
—	—	600	275	100

Single-Shot Derringer

A .41 caliber rimfire single-shot pocket pistol with a 2.75" round barrel, brass frame and walnut grips. As this model is unmarked, it can only be identified by the large breechblock which lifts upward and to the left for loading.

Exc.	V.G.	Good	Fair	Poor
—	—	17500	6500	1000

Pocket Revolver

A .30 caliber rimfire revolver with a 3" barrel marked "Warner's Patent 1857" and 5-shot cylinder. Blued or nickel-plated with walnut grips. Approximately 1,000 were made during the late 1860s.

Exc.	V.G.	Good	Fair	Poor
—	—	550	150	75

WATSON BROTHERS

London, England

SEE—British Double Guns

WEATHERBY

Atascadero, California

This corporation was founded in 1945 by Roy Weatherby. He pioneered the high-velocity hunting rifle. His rifles were designed to fire cartridges that he also produced. They are examples of fine craftsmanship and have been used to take some of the top trophy animals from all around the world. Formerly these rifles were manufactured in West Germany. They are currently produced in Japan. Although the Japanese rifles are, in the opinion of the editors, every bit as fine a firearm as the German versions, collectors have given an approximate 15 percent premium to the German-manufactured versions. The values given are for the current-production Japanese weapons. Simply add the premium for a German-manufactured rifle. There are other premiums that collectors are paying in 1994 and these are listed.

NOTE: For German calibers .224 through .300 add 25 percent for 24" barrels and 35 percent for 26" barrels.

Mark V

This is a deluxe, bolt-action repeating rifle chambered for various popular standard calibers, as well as the full line of Weatherby cartridges from .240 Weatherby Magnum to .300 Weatherby Magnum. It is furnished with either a 24" or 26" barrel without sights. It has either a 3- or 5-round magazine, depending on the caliber. It has a deluxe, high-polish blued finish with a select, skip-line checkered walnut stock with a rosewood forearm tip and pistol grip cap. This rifle is available with a left-hand action.

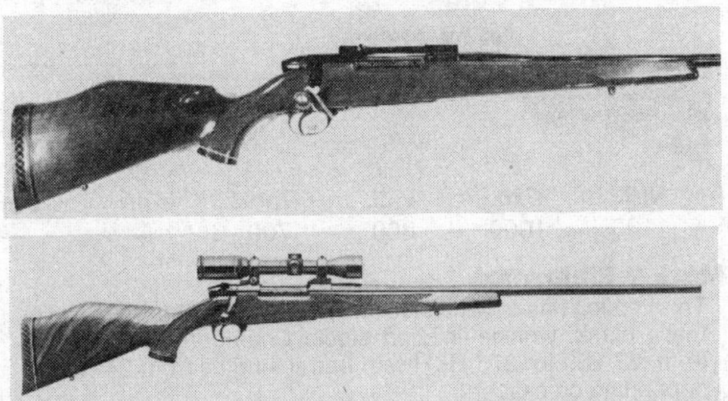

NIB	Exc.	V.G.	Good	Fair	Poor
1000	850	700	600	500	400

Weatherby Mark V Deluxe

Step-up version of classic Mark V. Features include deluxe Claro walnut Monte Carlo stock with rosewood forend, 26-inch or 28-inch high-polish blued sightless barrel. Chambered in .257, .270, 7mm, .300, .340, .378, .416, and .460 Weatherby Magnum. MSRP: 2500

Mark V Sporter

Introduced in 1993 this model is identical to the Mark V Deluxe without the custom features. The metal is a low luster finish, the stock is Claro walnut with high gloss finish. A Monte Carlo comb with raised cheekpiece and black 1" recoil pad are standard features on this model. Available in Weatherby calibers from .257 through .340 plus .270 Win., .30-06, 7mm Rem. Mag., .300 Win Mag., .338 Win. Mag. Weighs 8 to 8.5 lbs. depending on caliber.

NIB	Exc.	V.G.	Good	Fair	Poor
660	600	500	400	350	300

Mark V .375 Weatherby Magnum

This version was manufactured in Germany only and is chambered for the currently obsolete .375 Weatherby Magnum cartridge. This version has become very collectible.

NIB	Exc.	V.G.	Good	Fair	Poor
5000	3500	3000	2500	2000	1500

Mark V .378 Weatherby Magnum

This version is chambered for the .378 Weatherby Magnum cartridge and is considered to be one of the most powerful rifles currently available in the world. It is furnished with a 26" barrel only.

NIB	Exc.	V.G.	Good	Fair	Poor
1100	900	700	500	450	400

NOTE: For German guns in this caliber add 50 percent.

Mark V .416 Weatherby Magnum

This is an extremely powerful rifle suitable for hunting the biggest game. It is the first new caliber to be released by Weatherby since 1965. It was introduced in 1989.

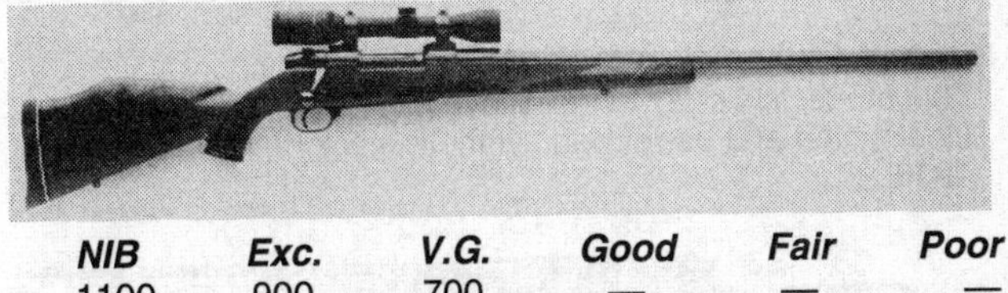

NIB	Exc.	V.G.	Good	Fair	Poor
1100	900	700	—	—	—

Mark V .460 Weatherby Magnum

This is the most powerful commercial rifle available in the world. It is considered to be overkill for any game except the largest and most dangerous creatures that roam the African continent. It is available with a 24" or 26" heavy barrel with an integral, recoil-reducing muzzlebrake. It has a custom reinforced stock.

NIB	Exc.	V.G.	Good	Fair	Poor
1350	1200	1000	800	—	—

NOTE: For German guns in this caliber add 100 percent.

Mark V .340 Weatherby Magnum

This version is chambered for a larger magnum cartridge and is offered with the 26" barrel only.

NIB	Exc.	V.G.	Good	Fair	Poor
1050	900	750	650	550	400

NOTE: For German guns in this caliber add 70 percent.

Mark V Dangerous Game Rifle

This model was introduced in 2001 and features a synthetic stock with Monte Carlo and 24" or 26" barrel with barrel band and hooded front sight depending on caliber. Chambered for the .378 Weatherby Mag., .416 Weatherby Mag., and the .460 Weatherby Mag. Adjustable trigger. Weight is between 8.74 and 9.5 lbs. depending on caliber. In 2003 the .458 Lott was offered for this model.

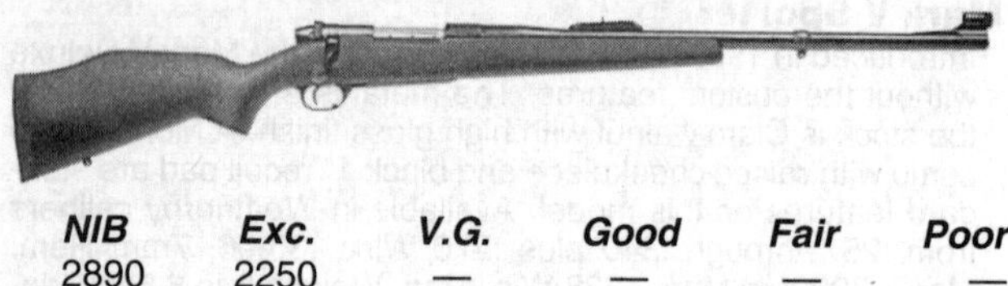

NIB	Exc.	V.G.	Good	Fair	Poor
2890	2250	—	—	—	—

Mark V Euromark

This model features a hand-checkered, oil-finished, Claro walnut stock with an ebony forend tip and pistol grip cap. It has a satin blued finish. It was introduced in 1986.

NIB	Exc.	V.G.	Good	Fair	Poor
1050	900	750	650	—	—

Mark V Fluted Stainless

Introduced late in 1996 this model features a fluted stainless steel barrel chambered for the .257 Weatherby Magnum to the .300 Weatherby Magnum calibers as well as the 7mm Rem. Mag. and the .300 Win. Mag. The stock is synthetic with raised comb and checkered stock. Weight varies depending on caliber.

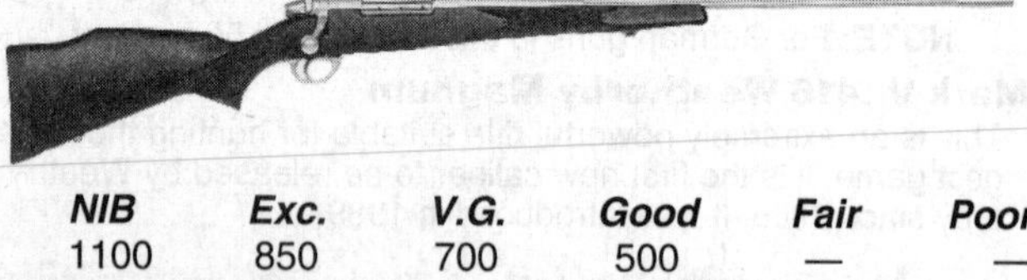

NIB	Exc.	V.G.	Good	Fair	Poor
1100	850	700	500	—	—

Mark V Fluted Synthetic

This model is similar to the above model with a blued carbon steel action and barrel with synthetic stock. Introduced late in 1996.

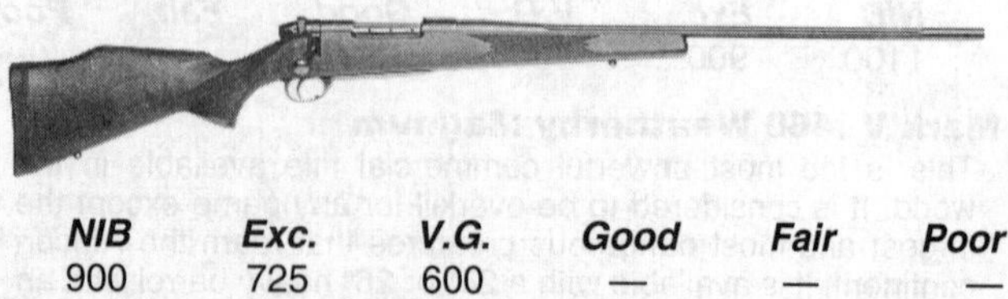

NIB	Exc.	V.G.	Good	Fair	Poor
900	725	600	—	—	—

Mark V SLS

This model features a stainless steel barreled action with laminated wood stock fitted with a 1" black recoil pad. Rifle is chambered for .257 through .340 Weatherby Magnum calibers as well as 7mm Rem. Mag., .300 and .338 Win. Mag., and the .375 H&H Mag. Weight is about 8.25 lbs. depending on caliber. Introduced in late 1996.

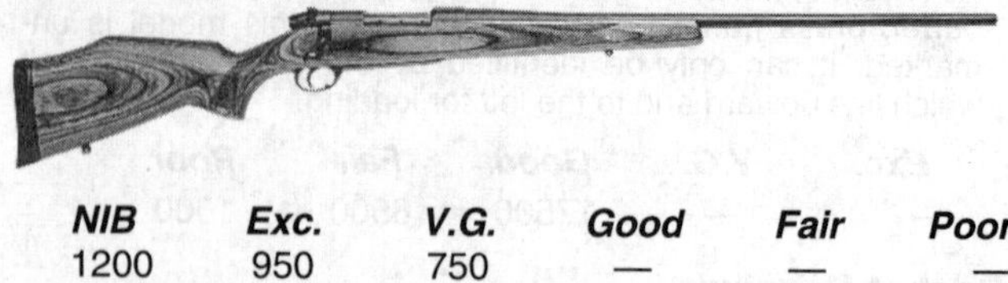

NIB	Exc.	V.G.	Good	Fair	Poor
1200	950	750	—	—	—

Mark V Varmint

This version is chambered for the .22-250 and the .224 Weatherby cartridge. It is offered with a 24" or 26" heavy barrel.

NIB	Exc.	V.G.	Good	Fair	Poor
975	800	750	550	450	400

NOTE: For German built add 50 percent.

Mark V Lazermark

This version had a laser-carved pattern on the stock and forearm in place of the usual checkering. It was introduced in 1985.

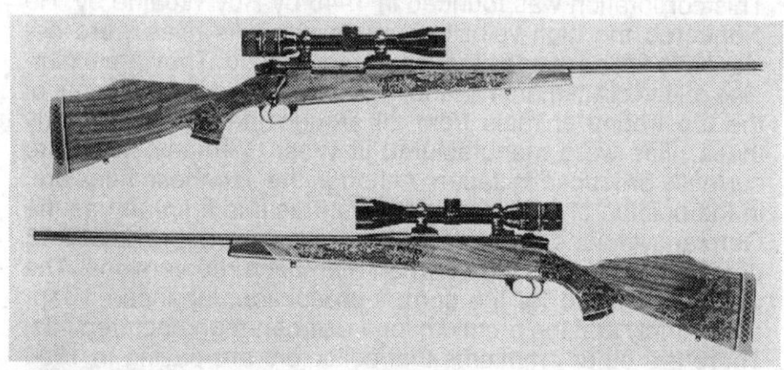

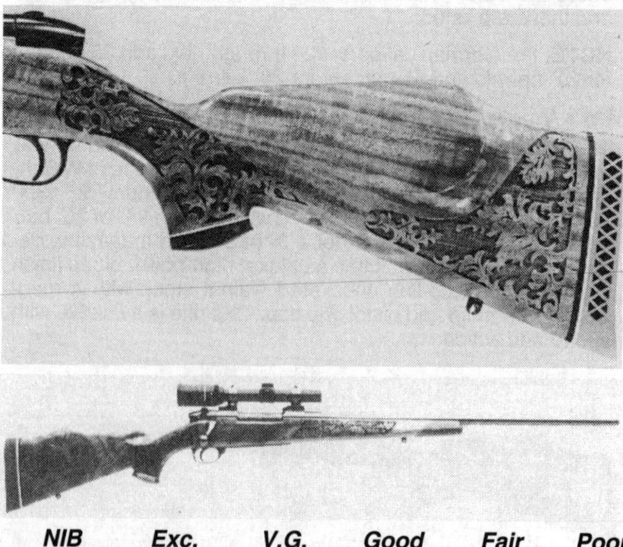

NIB	Exc.	V.G.	Good	Fair	Poor
1100	1000	800	700	—	—

Mark V Fibermark

This version has a matte blue finish and is furnished with a synthetic black, wrinkle-finished stock. Chambered for calibers from .22-250 to .375 H&H with barrel lengths from 24" to 26" depending on caliber.

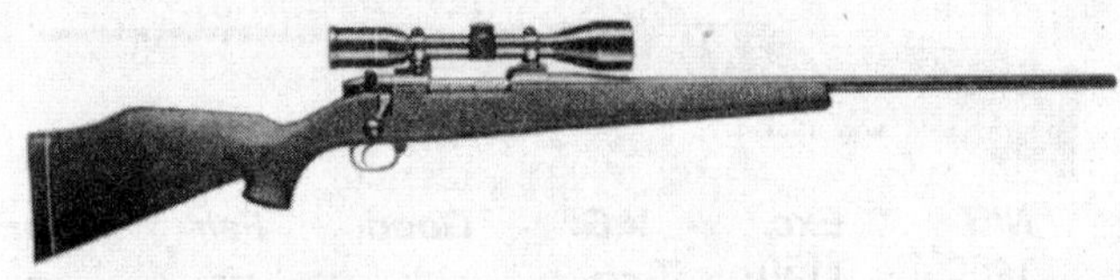

NIB	Exc.	V.G.	Good	Fair	Poor
900	700	—	—	—	—

NOTE: Add $200 for stainless steel models.

Mark V Ultramark

This is a custom-finished version with a glass-bedded action and a special, high-polish blue. The action is hand-honed, and the walnut stock features basket weave checkering. It was introduced in 1989.

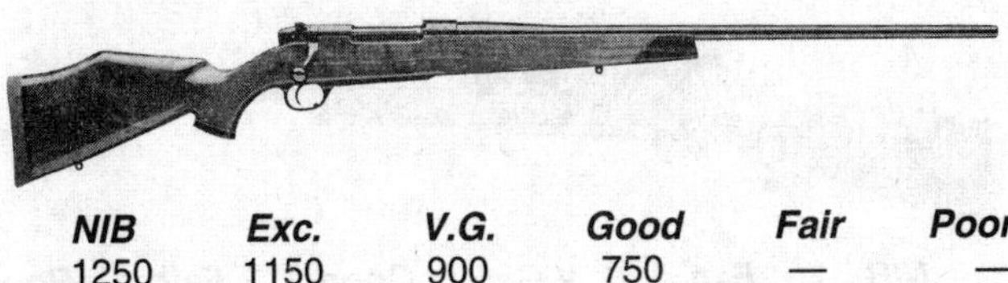

NIB	Exc.	V.G.	Good	Fair	Poor
1250	1150	900	750	—	—

Mark V Accumark

Introduced in 1995 this rifle features a Mark V Magnum action. The trigger is preset at the factory for 3.5 lbs. of pull. It is fully adjustable for sear engagement at let-off weight. The action metal is black oxide coated with a bead blast matte finish. The stainless steel barrel is 26" in length with a low luster brushed finish. Weight is approximately 8 lbs. and is offered in caliber from .257 to .340 Weatherby Magnum, 7mm Rem. Magnum, and .300 Win. Magnum. In August the company announced that this model would also be offered in the .30-.378 Weatherby caliber. In 1997 this model was offered chambered for the 7mm STW cartridge. Available in right-hand only.

Mark V Accumark

Mark V Accumark for .30-.378 Weatherby Magnum

NIB	Exc.	V.G.	Good	Fair	Poor
1250	1000	850	—	—	—

Mark V Accumark Left-Hand

This is a left-hand version of the Accumark. Introduced in 1999.

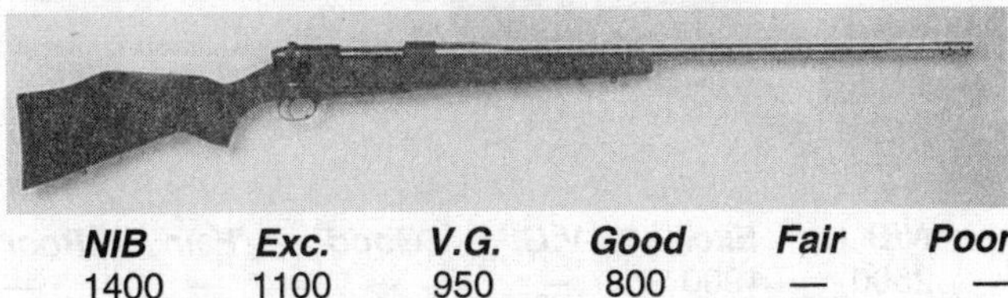

NIB	Exc.	V.G.	Good	Fair	Poor
1400	1100	950	800	—	—

35th Anniversary Commemorative Mark V

This specially embellished rifle commemorated the 35th anniversary of the company. There were 1,000 produced in 1980. As with all commemoratives, it must be NIB with all furnished materials to be worth top dollar.

NIB	Exc.	V.G.	Good	Fair	Poor
1500	1150	900	750	—	—

1984 Olympic Commemorative Mark V

This is a specially embellished Mark V rifle that has gold-plated accents and an exhibition-grade walnut stock with a star inlay. There were 1,000 manufactured in 1984. This is a commemorative rifle and must be NIB to bring premium value.

NIB	Exc.	V.G.	Good	Fair	Poor
1500	900	750	600	—	—

Safari Grade Mark V

This is a custom-order version that is available chambered from the .300 Weatherby Magnum through the .460 Weatherby Magnum. It is available with a number of custom options and can be ordered with an 8- to 10-month delivery delay.

NIB	Exc.	V.G.	Good	Fair	Poor
3000	2750	2000	1200	—	—

Crown Grade Mark V

This is Weatherby's best-grade rifle and is available on a custom-order basis only. It features an engraved receiver and barrel with an exhibition-grade, hand-checkered walnut stock. It is also furnished with an engraved scope mount.

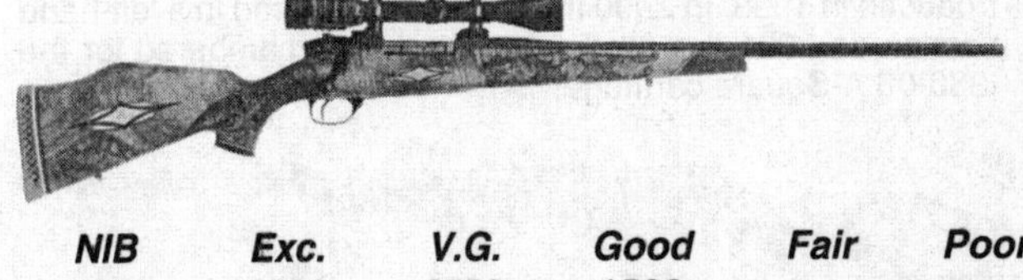

NIB	Exc.	V.G.	Good	Fair	Poor
4500	3500	2750	1500	—	—

Mark V Super Varmint Master (SVM)

Introduced in 2000 this model features a 26" stainless steel barrel. The stock is laminated with Monte Carlo comb. Fully adjustable trigger. Chambered for .220 Swift, .223 Rem., .22-250, .243 Win., 7mm-08, and .308 Win. Also offered in a single-shot configuration. Weight is about 8.5 lbs.

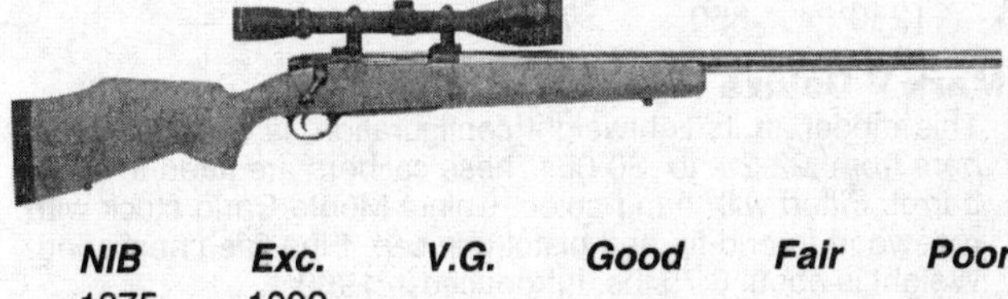

NIB	Exc.	V.G.	Good	Fair	Poor
1375	1000	—	—	—	—

Mark V Special Varmint Rifle (SVR)

Introduced in 2003 this model features a 22" Krieger heavy barrel, a Monte Carlo composite stock, a black recoil pad and matte black finish. Adjustable trigger is standard. Available in .223 Rem. and .22-250. Weight is approximately 7.25 lbs.

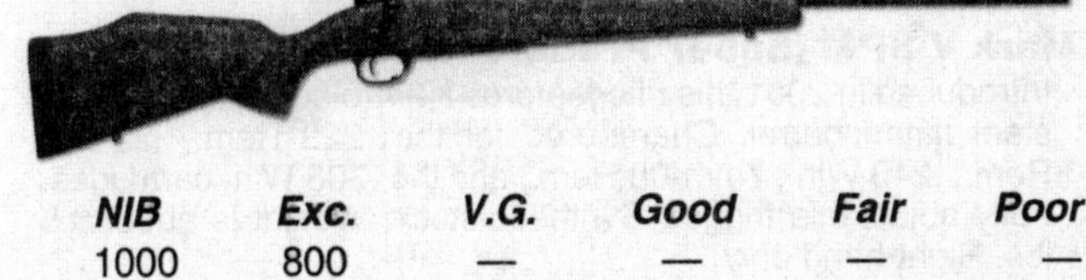

NIB	Exc.	V.G.	Good	Fair	Poor
1000	800	—	—	—	—

MARK V LIGHTWEIGHT RIFLES

Mark V Synthetic Lightweight

Chambered in calibers from .22-250 to .308 Win. fitted with a 24" barrel. Synthetic stock with Monte Carlo comb. Magazine capacity is 5 rounds. Weight is approximately 6.5 lbs. A carbine version is offered with 20" barrel in .243, 7mm-08, and .308. Weight is about 6 lbs.

NIB	Exc.	V.G.	Good	Fair	Poor
700	550	—	—	—	—

Mark V Stainless Lightweight

Similar to the model above but with stainless steel barrel and action. Weight is about 6.5 lbs. Carbine version also available.

NIB	Exc.	V.G.	Good	Fair	Poor
900	725	600	500	—	—

Mark V Sporter Lightweight

Chambered for calibers ranging from .22-250 to .308 Win. and fitted with a 24" barrel. Stock is Claro walnut with Monte Carlo comb. Weight is approximately 6.75 lbs.

NIB	Exc.	V.G.	Good	Fair	Poor
850	675	500	—	—	—

Mark V Accumark Lightweight

Chambered for calibers from .22-250 to .300 Wby. and fitted with a 24" barrel. Magazine capacity is 5 rounds. Special laminated synthetic stock. Weight is approximately 7 lbs. Introduced in 1998.

NIB	Exc.	V.G.	Good	Fair	Poor
1100	850	750	600	—	—

Mark V Ultra Lightweight

Similar to the above model but with lightened components. Calibers begin with .243 and go to .300 Wby. Fitted with a 24" or 26" barrel depending on caliber. Weight is about 5.75 lbs. Introduced in 1998. In 2000 this model was offered in a left-hand version. In 2001 this model was available chambered for the .338-06 A-Square cartridge.

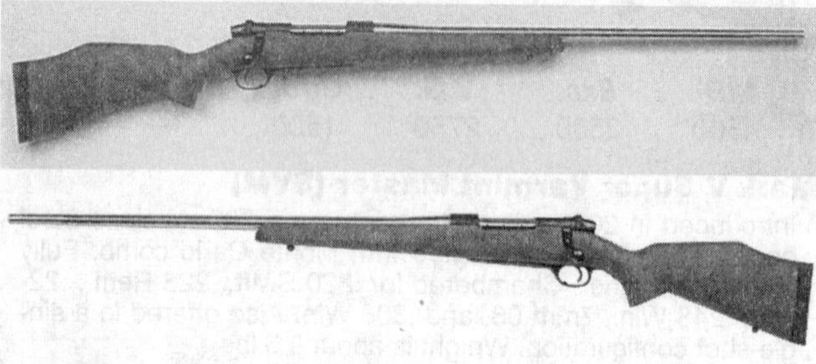

NIB	Exc.	V.G.	Good	Fair	Poor
1250	850	700	—	—	—

Mark V Deluxe Lightweight

This model, in its lightweight configuration, is offered in calibers from .22-25- to .30-06. These calibers are fitted to a 24" barrel. Fitted with hand select walnut Monte Carlo stock with rosewood forend tip and pistol grip cap. Fine line checkering. Weight is about 6.75 lbs. Introduced in 1999.

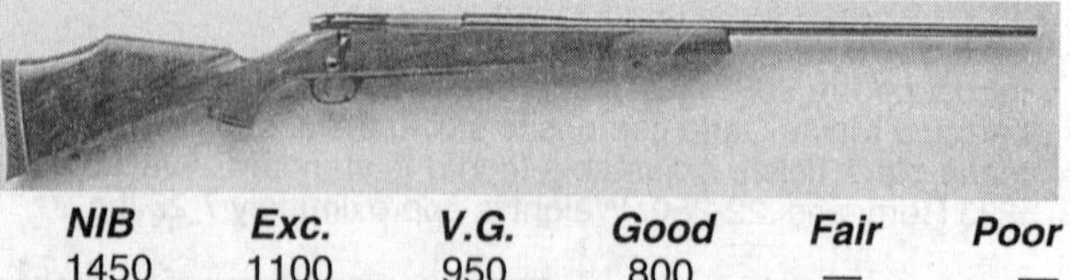

NIB	Exc.	V.G.	Good	Fair	Poor
1450	1100	950	800	—	—

Mark V SPM (Super Predator Master)

Introduced in 2001 this rifle features a 24" blackened stainless steel fluted barrel. Chambered for the .223 Rem., .22-250 Rem., .243 Win., 7mm-08 Rem., and the .308 Win. cartridges. Fully adjustable trigger. Synthetic stock. Weight is about 6.5 lbs. Right-hand only.

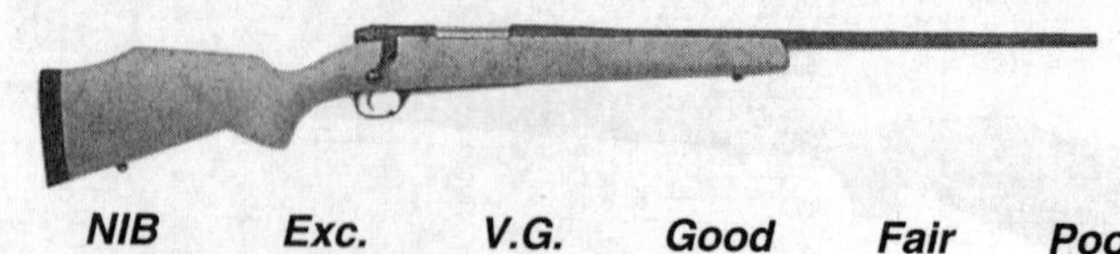

NIB	Exc.	V.G.	Good	Fair	Poor
1450	1150	—	—	—	—

Mark V SBGM (Super Big Game Master)

This model features a 24" blackened stainless steel barrel Krieger fluted barrel (26" for magnum calibers). Fully adjustable trigger. Tan composite stock with raised comb Monte Carlo. Pachmayr Decelerator recoil pad. Offered in a wide variety of caliber from .240 Weatherby Mag. to .300 Weatherby Mag. Weight is about 5.75 lbs. and 6.75 lbs. for magnum rifles. Introduced in 2002.

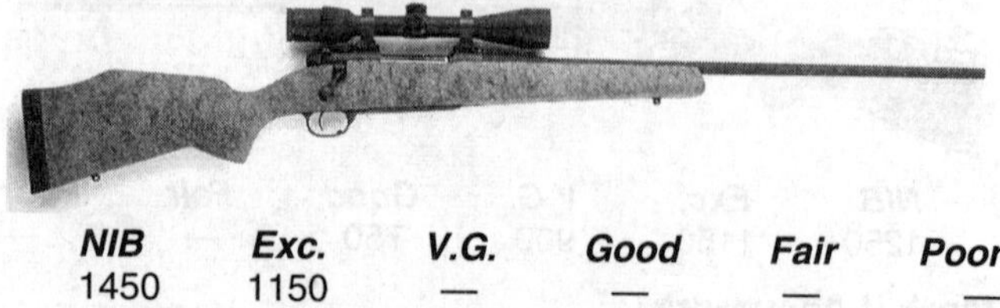

NIB	Exc.	V.G.	Good	Fair	Poor
1450	1150	—	—	—	—

NOTE: Add $60 for magnum calibers.

THREAT RESPONSE RIFLE SERIES

These rifles are based on the Mark V action.

TRR

Chambered for the .223 or .308 Win. cartridge and fitted with a 22" heavy-contour black Krieger barrel. Black composite stock with raised comb Monte Carlo. Flat-bottom forearm. Fully adjustable trigger. Recoil pad. Introduced in 2002.

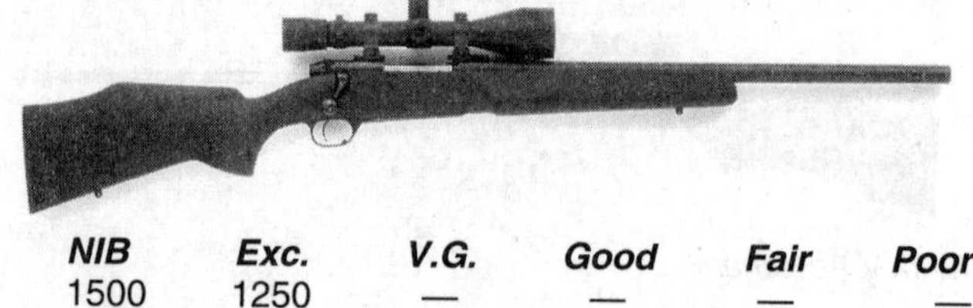

NIB	Exc.	V.G.	Good	Fair	Poor
1500	1250	—	—	—	—

TRR Magnum

As above but chambered for the .300 Win. Mag., .300 Wby. Mag., .30-378 Wby. Mag., or the .338-378 Wby. Mag. Barrel length is 26".

NIB	Exc.	V.G.	Good	Fair	Poor
1560	1300	—	—	—	—

NOTE: Add $150 for .30-378 and .338-378 calibers.

TRR Magnum Custom

This model has all the features of the TRR Magnum with the addition of a fully adjustable stock.

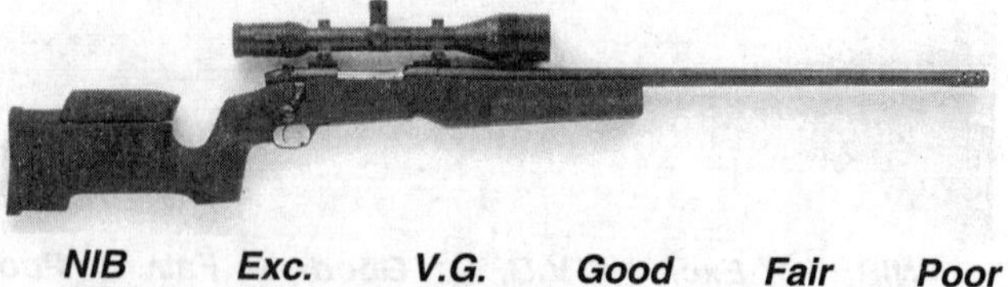

NIB	Exc.	V.G.	Good	Fair	Poor
2500	1900	—	—	—	—

NOTE: Add $150 for .30-378 or .338-378 calibers.

WARNING: WEATHERBY VANGUARD

DO NOT use this model until the company performs a safety upgrade to the bolt. The rifle can accidentally discharge without the bolt being fully engaged. The affected rifles bear serial numbers from one of these series on the receiver: 00001 through 03810; V00001 through V80966; VX00001 through VX44065; VS00001 through VS23699; VL00001 through VL46984; W00001 through W0099; NV0001 through NV0099.

Vanguard VGX

This was Weatherby's Japanese-manufactured economy rifle. It is chambered for various popular standard American cartridges from .22-50 to the .300 Winchester Magnum cartridge. It is a bolt-action repeater with a 24" barrel furnished without sights. It has either a 3-shot or 5-shot magazine; and the finish is polished blue, with a select, checkered walnut stock with a rosewood forend tip and pistol-grip cap. This model was discontinued in 1988.

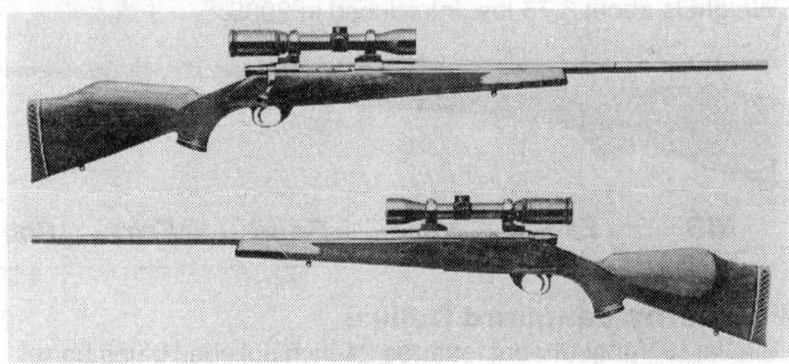

Exc.	V.G.	Good	Fair	Poor
500	400	350	300	250

Vanguard VGS

This satin-finish version was also discontinued in 1988.

Exc.	V.G.	Good	Fair	Poor
450	350	300	250	200

Vanguard VGL

This is a lightweight carbine version that has a 20" barrel. It was discontinued in 1988.

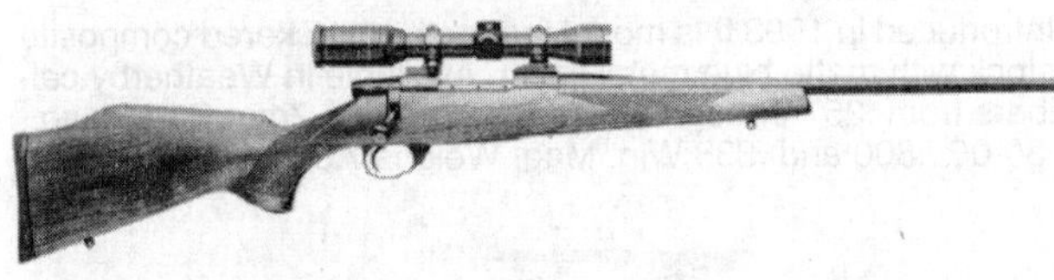

Exc.	V.G.	Good	Fair	Poor
450	350	300	250	200

Fiberguard

This version has a matte-blued finish with a green fiberglass stock. It was discontinued in 1988.

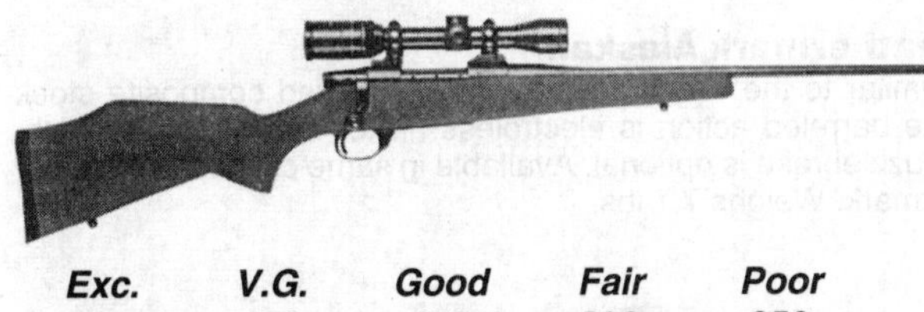

Exc.	V.G.	Good	Fair	Poor
500	400	350	300	250

Vanguard Classic I

This version is chambered for various popular standard calibers and has a 24" barrel and either a 3- or 5-shot magazine. It has a satin blue finish and a select checkered, oil-finished walnut stock. It was introduced in 1989.

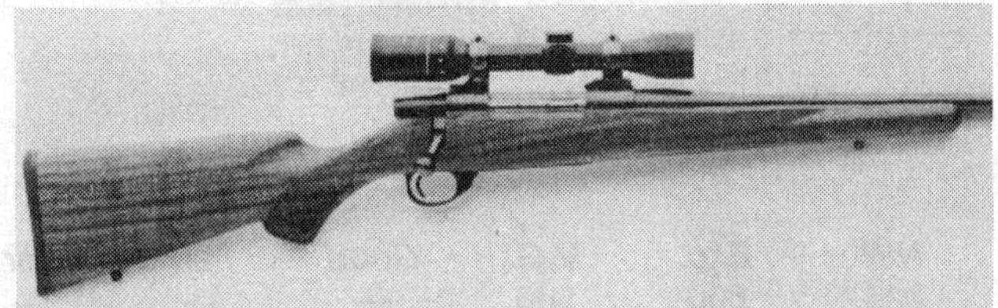

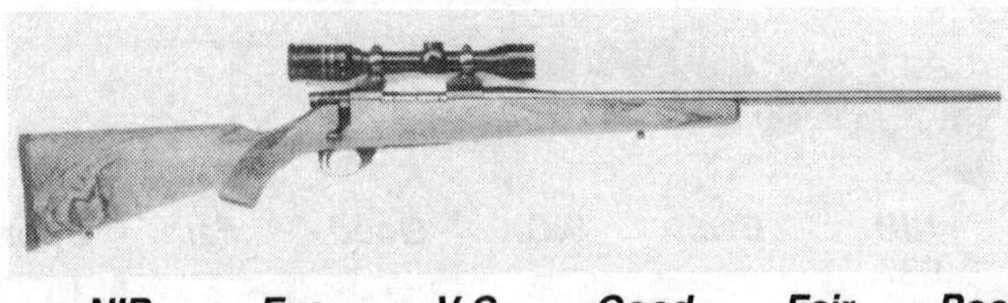

NIB	Exc.	V.G.	Good	Fair	Poor
475	400	375	300	250	200

Vanguard Classic II

This is a more deluxe version with a higher-grade walnut stock.

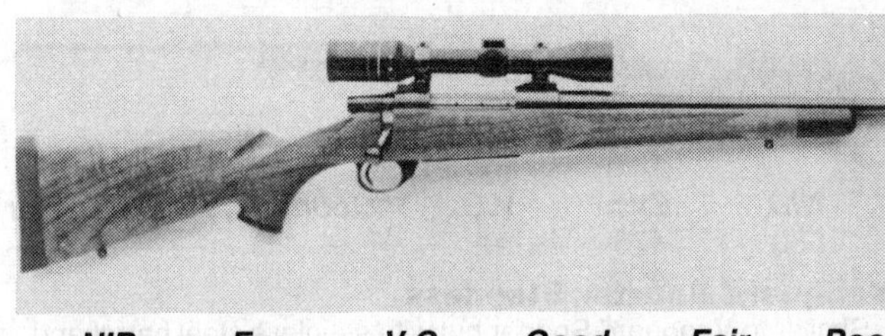

NIB	Exc.	V.G.	Good	Fair	Poor
600	550	475	400	300	250

Vanguard VGX Deluxe

This version has a high-gloss, Monte Carlo-type stock and a high-polished blued finish. It was introduced in 1989.

NIB	Exc.	V.G.	Good	Fair	Poor
600	550	475	400	300	250

Vanguard Weatherguard

This version has a wrinkle-finished, black synthetic stock. It was introduced in 1989. In 2003 this model was offered in stainless steel.

NIB	Exc.	V.G.	Good	Fair	Poor
475	375	250	—	—	—

NOTE: Add $120 for stainless steel.

Vanguard

This model features an upgraded composite stock with Monte Carlo comb, a ring/base scope mounting system, a 24" barrel, and calibers from .223 Rem. to .338 Win. Mag., including the .257 Weatherby. Weight is about 7.75 lbs. Introduced in 2004.

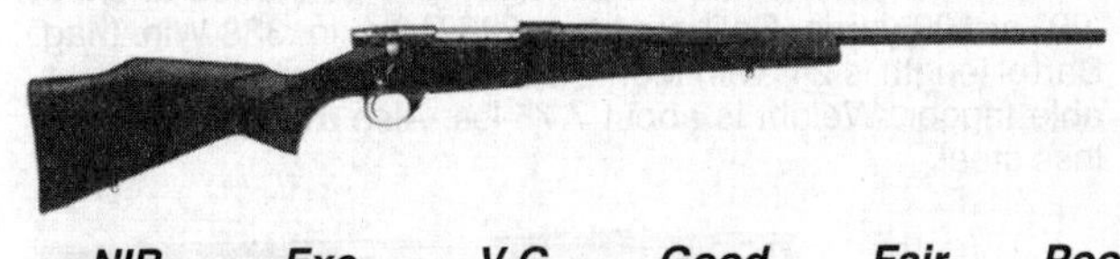

NIB	Exc.	V.G.	Good	Fair	Poor
475	375	—	—	—	—

NOTE: Add $120 for stainless steel.

Vanguard Stainless

Similar to Vanguard Synthetic but with stainless steel barrel and receiver.

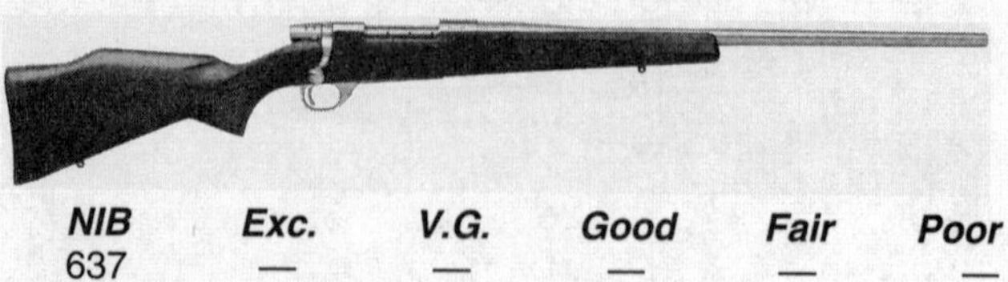

NIB	Exc.	V.G.	Good	Fair	Poor
637	—	—	—	—	—

Vanguard Sporter

Similar to the model above but with a figured walnut stock, rosewood forend tip and fine line checkering. Chambered for calibers from .270 to .338 Win. Mag. Barrel length is 24". Weight is about 8 lbs. Introduced in 2004.

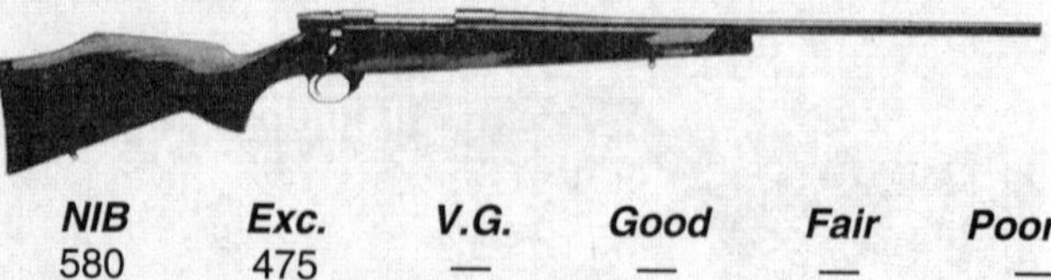

NIB	Exc.	V.G.	Good	Fair	Poor
580	475	—	—	—	—

Vanguard Sporter Stainless

Similar to Vanguard Sporter but with stainless steel barrel and receiver. MSRP: 785

Vanguard Varmint Special

Chambered in .223, .22-250, or .308. 22-inch blued #3 contour heavy crowned barrel, adjustable trigger, synthetic tan composite stock with black spiderweb pattern. Introduced 2006.

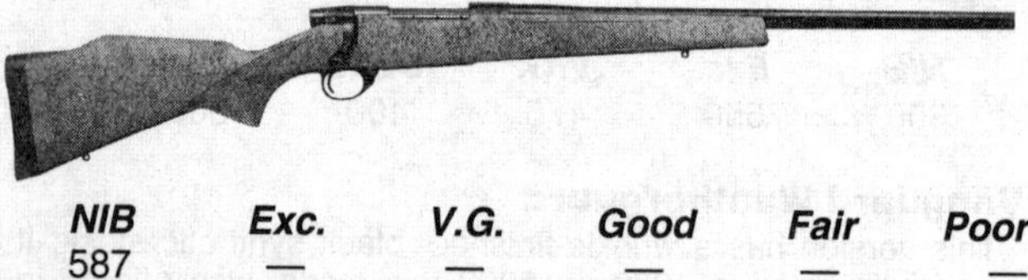

NIB	Exc.	V.G.	Good	Fair	Poor
587	—	—	—	—	—

Vanguard Synthetic Package

Introduced in 2004 this model features a 24" barrel with adjustable trigger. Chambered for a variety of calibers from the .223 Rem. to the .338 Win. Mag. Supplied with a Bushnell Banner 3-9x40 scope, sling, and hard case. Weight is about 7.75 lbs.

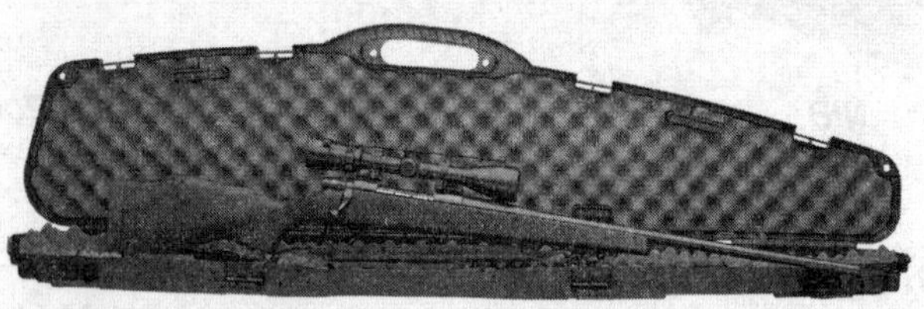

NIB	Exc.	V.G.	Good	Fair	Poor
595	500	—	—	—	—

Vanguard Sub-MOA

Introduced in 2005 this model features a guarantee to shoot .99" at 100 yards. Calibers from .223 Rem. to .338 Win. Mag. Barrel length is 24" with Monte Carlo Fiberguard stock. Adjustable trigger. Weight is about 7.75 lbs. Also available in stainless steel.

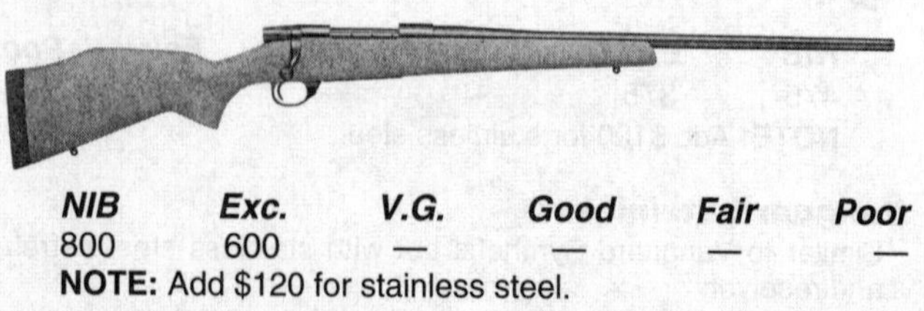

NIB	Exc.	V.G.	Good	Fair	Poor
800	600	—	—	—	—

NOTE: Add $120 for stainless steel.

Vanguard Sub-MOA Varmint Special

Similar to Vanguard Varmint Special but with ventilated beavertail forend. Introduced 2006. MSRP: 885

Vanguard Compact

This model, chambered for the .22-250, .243, or .308, is fitted with a 20" barrel and scaled-down hardwood stock with shorter length of pull. Also included is a full size composite stock. Weight is about 6.75 lbs. Introduced in 2005.

NIB	Exc.	V.G.	Good	Fair	Poor
550	425	—	—	—	—

Weatherby Vanguard Deluxe

Similar to Vanguard but features 24-inch polished blued barrel, glossy select Monte Carlo walnut stock with rosewood forend, adjustable trigger. Chambered in .270, .30-06, .257 Weatherby Mag., and .300 Weatherby Mag. Introduced 2006.

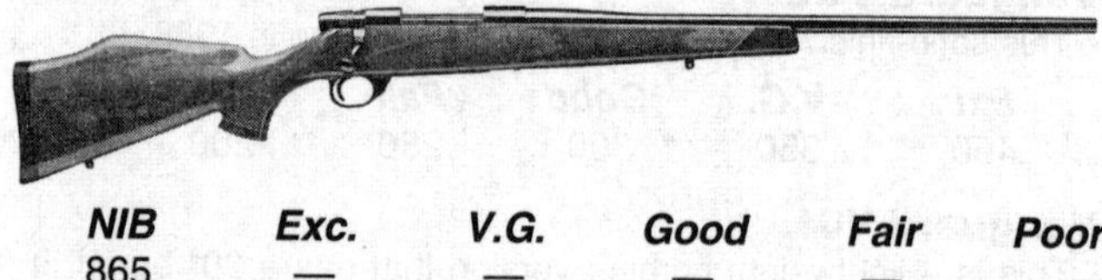

NIB	Exc.	V.G.	Good	Fair	Poor
865	—	—	—	—	—

Weathermark

Introduced in 1993 this model features a checkered composite stock with matte blue metal finish. Available in Weatherby calibers from .257 through .340 and .270 Win., 7mm Rem. Mag., .30-06, .300 and .338 Win. Mag. Weighs 7.5 lbs.

NIB	Exc.	V.G.	Good	Fair	Poor
550	450	—	—	—	—

Weathermark Alaskan

Similar to the Weathermark with checkered composite stock the barreled action is electroless nickel with nonglare finish. Muzzlebrake is optional. Available in same calibers as Weathermark. Weighs 7.7 lbs.

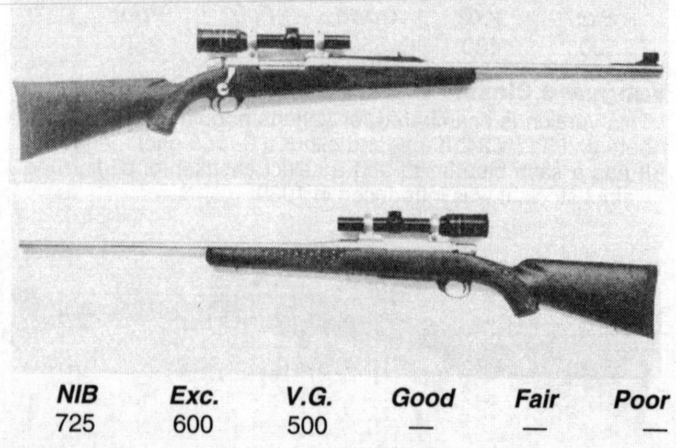

NIB	Exc.	V.G.	Good	Fair	Poor
725	600	500	—	—	—

Mark XXII

This is a semi-automatic rifle chambered for the .22 LR cartridge. There are two versions—one with a detachable magazine and the other with a tubular magazine. It has a 24" barrel with adjustable sights and a select checkered walnut stock with a rosewood forearm tip and pistol-grip cap. This model was originally produced in Italy and was later manufactured in Japan. It is now discontinued.

Mark XXII

Mark XXII Tube Model

NIB	Exc.	V.G.	Good	Fair	Poor
550	350	300	250	200	150

NOTE: For Italian guns add 35 percent.

CUSTOM RIFLES

NOTE: Weatherby custom rifles are offered with many different options that will affect price. Consult an expert prior to a sale.

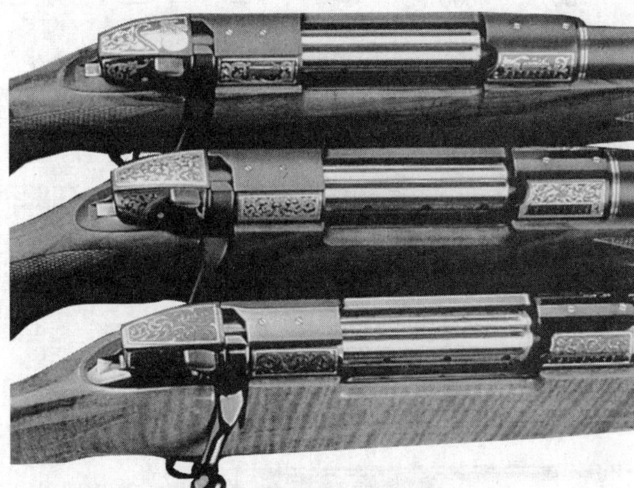

Weatherby Custom Grade engraving patterns

Classic Custom

This model features an oil-finished French walnut stock with 20 lpi checkering, ebony forend tip, metal grip cap, and skeltonized steel buttplate. All metal work is matte blue. Calibers are all Weatherby from .257 Wby. Mag to .340 Wby. Mag.

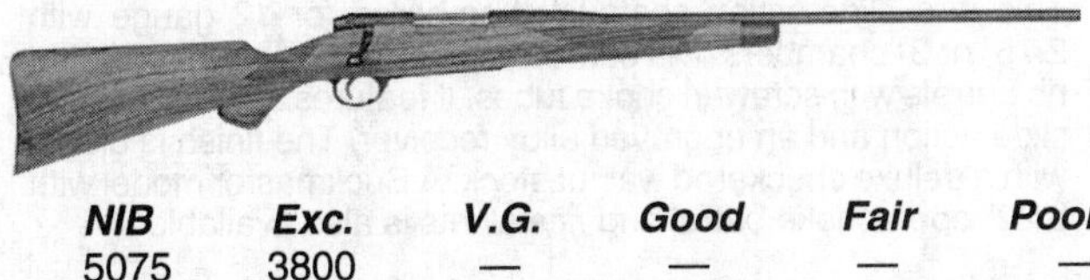

NIB	Exc.	V.G.	Good	Fair	Poor
5075	3800	—	—	—	—

Safari Grade Custom

This model features an oil-finish French walnut stock with Monte Carlo comb with fleur-de-lis checkering. Ebony forend tip and pistol-grip cap. Damascened bolt and follower with checkered bolt handle. Quarter rib. Engraved floorplate "Safari Custom." Calibers from .257 Wby. Mag. to .460 Wby. Mag.

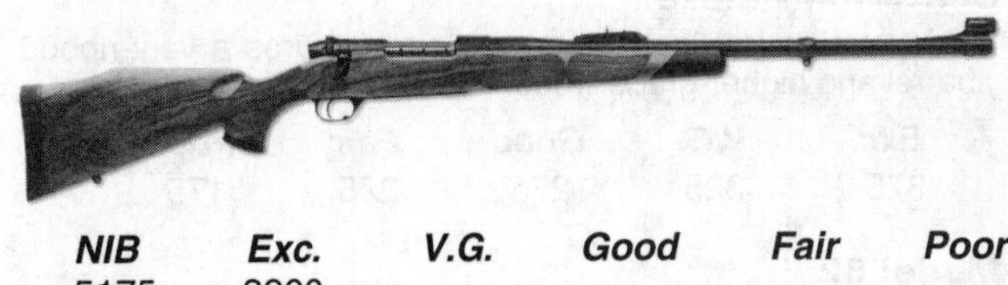

NIB	Exc.	V.G.	Good	Fair	Poor
5175	3900	—	—	—	—

Crown Custom

This model features a hand-carved walnut stock with buttstock inlay, damascened bolt and follower with checkered bolt handle. Engraved barrel, receiver and trigger guard. Floorplate engraved with gold inlays.

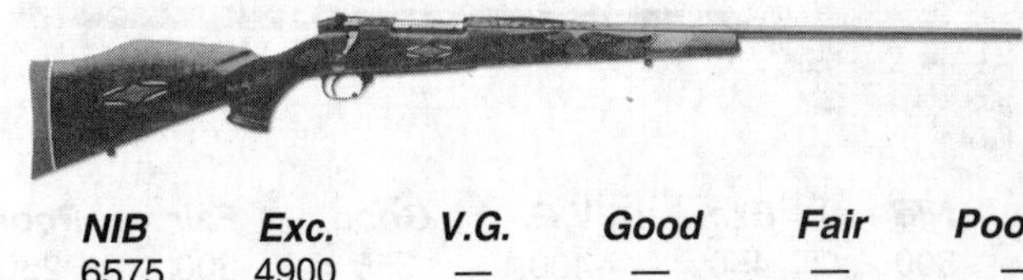

NIB	Exc.	V.G.	Good	Fair	Poor
6575	4900	—	—	—	—

Royal Custom

Introduced in 2002 this model features a Monte Carlo hand-checkered stock of fancy Claro walnut with high-gloss finish. Engraved receiver, bolt sleeve, and floorplate. Barrel length is 26". Available in a wide variety of calibers.

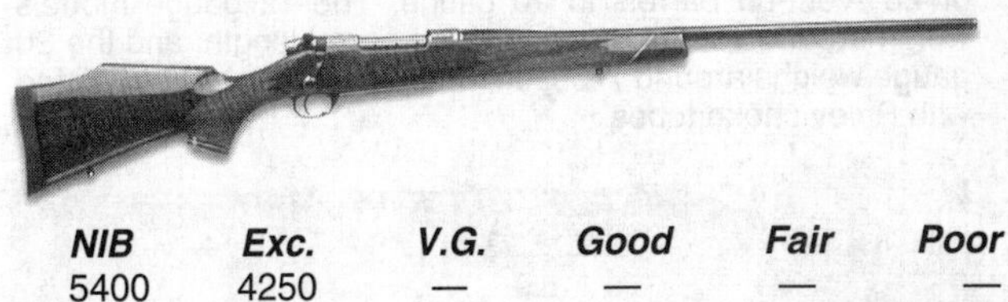

NIB	Exc.	V.G.	Good	Fair	Poor
5400	4250	—	—	—	—

Outfitter Custom

This model features a Bell & Carlson synthetic stock with custom camo and Pachmayr pad. Lightweight stainless steel fluted barrel. Titanium nitride finish on all metalwork.

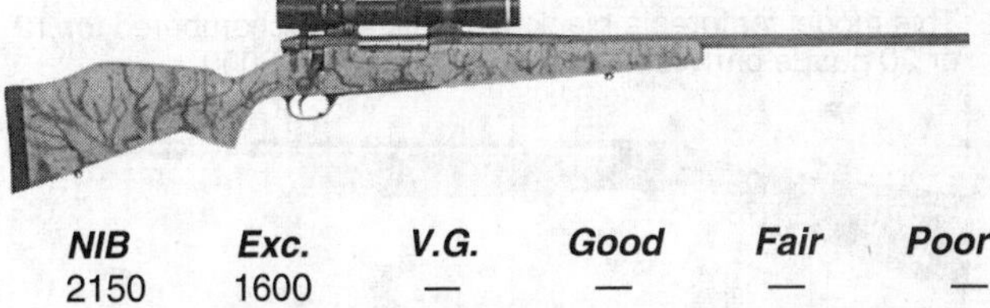

NIB	Exc.	V.G.	Good	Fair	Poor
2150	1600	—	—	—	—

Outfitter Krieger Custom

This model features a Bell & Carlson synthetic stock with custom camo and Pachmayr pad. Custom Krieger stainless steel fluted barrel. Titanium nitride finish on all metalwork.

NIB	Exc.	V.G.	Good	Fair	Poor
3500	2500	—	—	—	—

SHOTGUNS

Centurion

This is a gas-operated semi-automatic shotgun chambered for 12 gauge. It is offered with various barrel lengths and chokes. It has a checkered walnut stock. It was manufactured between 1972 and 1981.

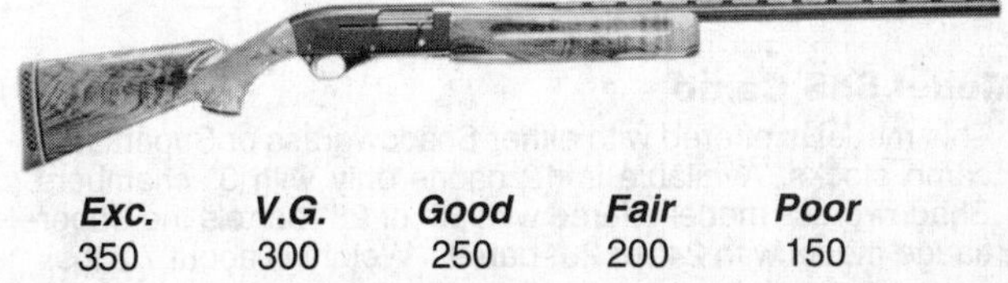

Exc.	V.G.	Good	Fair	Poor
350	300	250	200	150

Centurion Deluxe

This version is slightly engraved and features a vent-ribbed barrel and higher-grade wood.

Exc.	V.G.	Good	Fair	Poor
375	325	275	225	175

Model 82

This is a gas-operated semi-automatic shotgun chambered for 12 gauge with 2.75" or 3" chambers. It has various barrel lengths with vent-ribs and screw-in choke tubes. It features an alloy receiver and a deluxe, checkered walnut stock. It is also available as the Buckmaster with a 22" open-choked barrel. This model was introduced in 1983.

NIB	Exc.	V.G.	Good	Fair	Poor
500	450	400	350	300	250

Model SAS Field

Introduced in 1999 this gas-operated semi-automatic model features a high-grade Claro walnut stock with black pistol-grip cap. Fine-line checkering. Chambered for 12 or 20 gauge and fitted with 26", 28", or 30" vent-rib barrels in 12 gauge and 26" or 28" vent-rib barrels in 20 gauge. The 12 gauge models weigh around 7.5 lbs. depending on barrel length, and the 20 gauge weighs around 7 lbs. depending on barrel length. Fitted with Briley choke tubes.

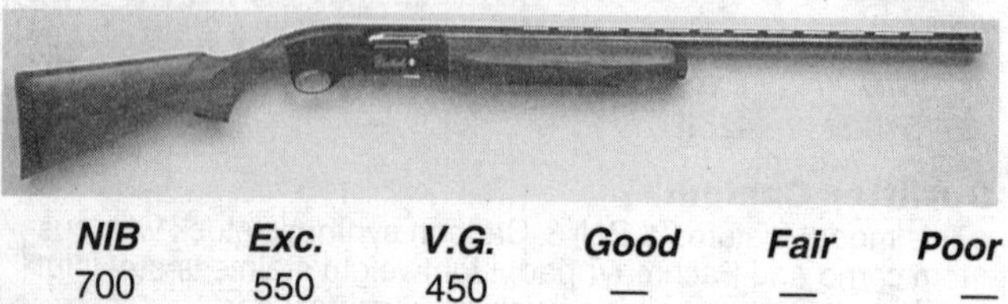

NIB	Exc.	V.G.	Good	Fair	Poor
700	550	450	—	—	—

Model SAS Synthetic

This model features a black synthetic stock chambered for 12 or 20 gauge barrels as above. Introduced in 2000.

NIB	Exc.	V.G.	Good	Fair	Poor
650	525	—	—	—	—

Model SAS Sporting Clays

This 12 gauge gun is fitted with a 28" or 30" vent-rib ported barrel. Walnut stock with pistol grip. Choke tubes standard. Weight is about 7.5 lbs. Introduced in 2002.

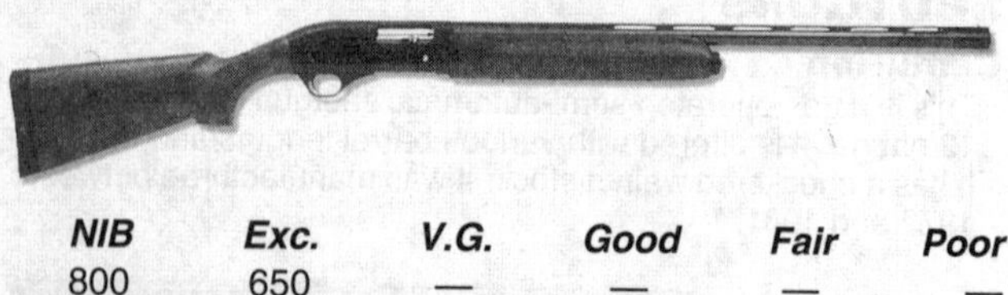

NIB	Exc.	V.G.	Good	Fair	Poor
800	650	—	—	—	—

Model SAS Camo

This model is offered with either Shadowgrass or Superflauge camo stocks. Available in 12 gauge only with 3" chambers. Shadowgrass model offered with 26" or 28" barrels the Superflauge model with 24" or 26" barrels. Weight is about 7.5 lbs.

Shadow Grass

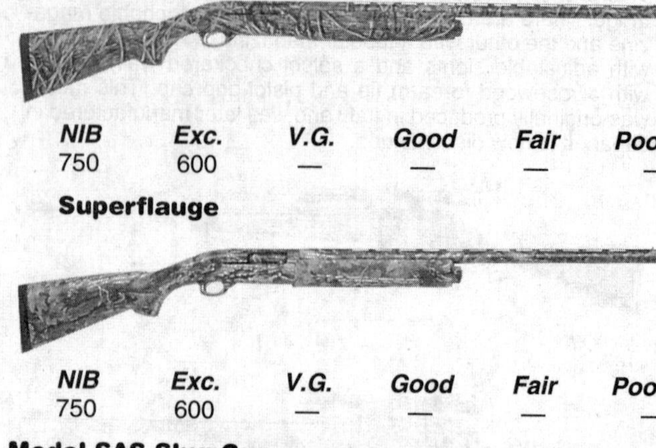

NIB	Exc.	V.G.	Good	Fair	Poor
750	600	—	—	—	—

Superflauge

NIB	Exc.	V.G.	Good	Fair	Poor
750	600	—	—	—	—

Model SAS Slug Gun

This model features a 22" rifled barrel chambered for the 3" 12 gauge shell. The barrel has a cantilever base for scope mounts. Walnut stock has a raised Monte Carlo comb. Sling swivel studs. Weight is about 7.25 lbs. Introduced in 2003.

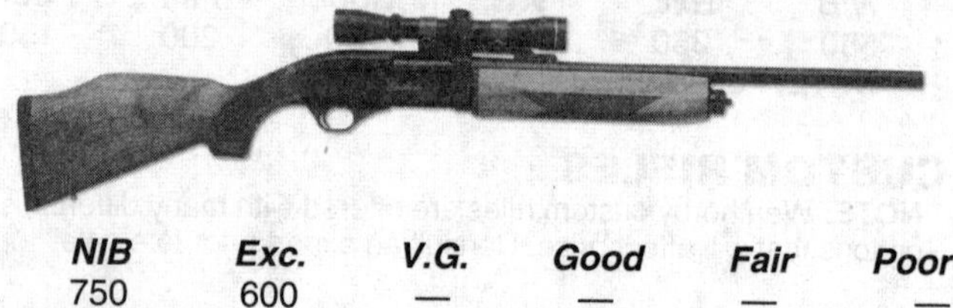

NIB	Exc.	V.G.	Good	Fair	Poor
750	600	—	—	—	—

Patrician

This is a slide-action shotgun chambered for 12 gauge. It is offered with various barrel lengths and choke combinations. It has a vent-rib barrel, a blued finish, and a checkered walnut stock. It was manufactured between 1972 and 1981.

Exc.	V.G.	Good	Fair	Poor
300	250	225	175	125

Patrician Deluxe

This is a slightly engraved version with fancier-grade walnut.

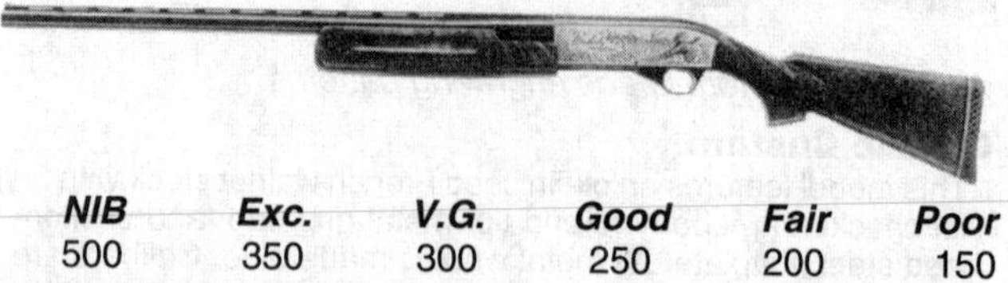

NIB	Exc.	V.G.	Good	Fair	Poor
500	350	300	250	200	150

Model 92

This is a slide-action shotgun chambered for 12 gauge with 2.75" or 3" chambers. It is offered with 26", 28", or 30" ventilated rib barrels with screw-in choke tubes. It features a short, twin-rail slide action and an engraved alloy receiver. The finish is blued, with a deluxe checkered walnut stock. A Buckmaster model with a 22" open-choke barrel and rifle sights is also available.

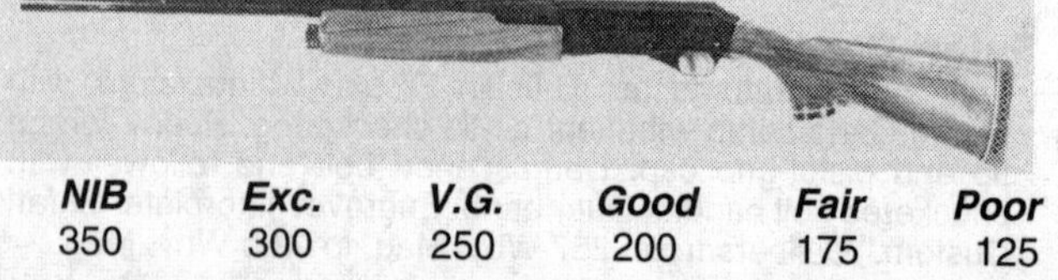

NIB	Exc.	V.G.	Good	Fair	Poor
350	300	250	200	175	125

SIDE-BY-SIDE GUNS

These shotgun are built in Spain.

Athena SBS

Introduced in 2002 this model features a case colored boxlock receiver with false sideplates with scroll engraving. Offered in 12 or 20 gauge with 26" or 28" barrels. Choke tubes. Turkish walnut stock with straight grip and recoil pad. Checkering is 22 lpi. Single trigger and ejectors. Weight is about 7 lbs.

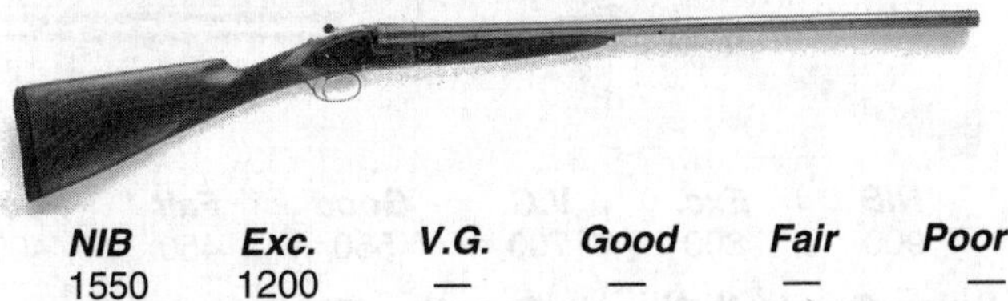

NIB	Exc.	V.G.	Good	Fair	Poor
1550	1200	—	—	—	—

Athena D'Italia

Introduced in 2005 this gun is chambered for the 12, 20, or 28 gauge and fitted with 28" barrels for the 12 gauge and 26" barrels for the 20 and 28 gauge guns. Receiver has silver sideplates with scroll engraving. Checkered walnut stock with straight grip. Weight is about 7 lbs.

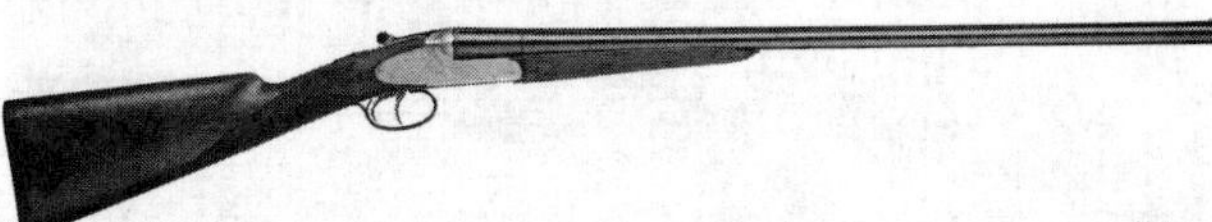

NIB	Exc.	V.G.	Good	Fair	Poor
2840	2100	—	—	—	—

NOTE: Add $135 for 28 gauge.

Athena D'Italia PG

Introduced in 2006, this model is offered in the same configurations as the D'Italia. It is identical in action and frame to the D'Italia but with a rounded pistol grip stock and single gold trigger. Laser-cut checkering at 20 lpi. Introduced 2006. Pricing is for 12 and 20 gauges. Add $200 for 28 ga.

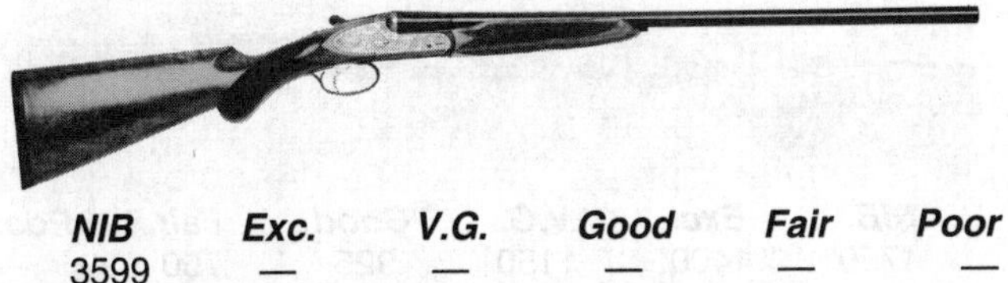

NIB	Exc.	V.G.	Good	Fair	Poor
3599	—	—	—	—	—

Athena D'Italia Deluxe

Renaissance floral engraving with Bolino style game scene and AAA Fancy Turkish walnut with 24 lpi hand checkering adorn this straight grip stocked model. Available in 12, 20 and 28 gauges with 26" or 28" barrels with fixed IC and Mod. chokes. Single trigger. Introduced 2006.

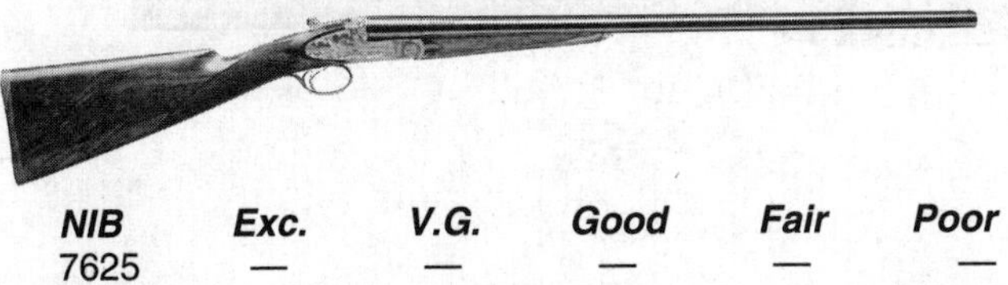

NIB	Exc.	V.G.	Good	Fair	Poor
7625	—	—	—	—	—

Orion SBS

This model is a lower cost alternative to the Athena. Turkish walnut stock with pistol grips and 18 lpi checkering. Case colored boxlock receiver. Offered in 12, 20, and 28 gauge as well as .410 bore. Choke tubes except for .410. Choice of 26" or 28" barrels. Weight is about 7 lbs. Introduced in 2002.

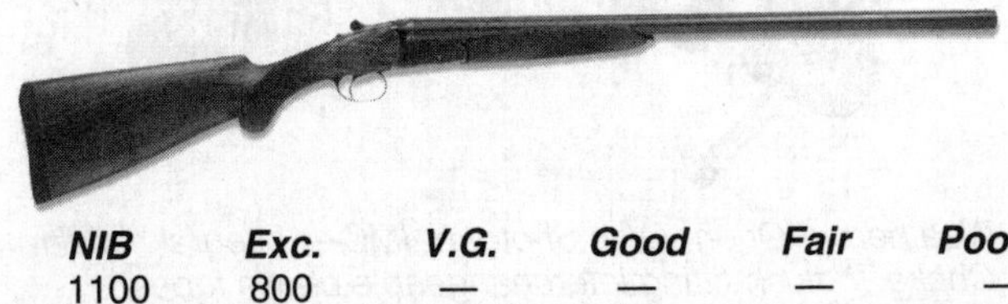

NIB	Exc.	V.G.	Good	Fair	Poor
1100	800	—	—	—	—

OVER-AND-UNDER GUNS

Regency Field Grade

This is an over-and-under double-barrel shotgun chambered for 12 or 20 gauge. It has various length vent-ribbed barrels and a boxlock action with engraved false sideplates. It features a single-selective trigger and automatic ejectors. The finish is blued, with a checkered walnut stock. This model was imported from Italy between 1972 and 1980. It is also offered as a trap grade with the same value.

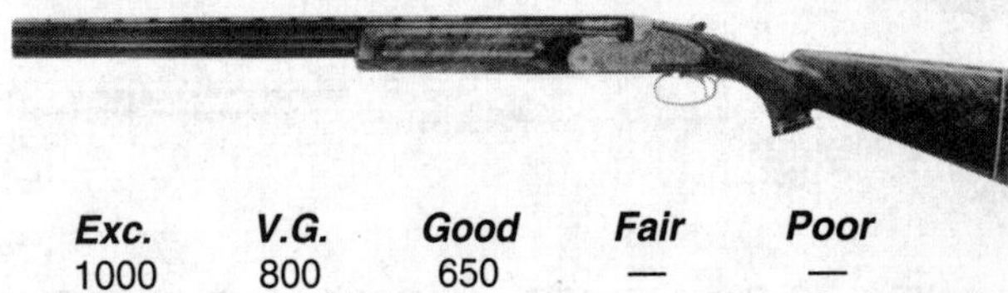

Exc.	V.G.	Good	Fair	Poor
1000	800	650	—	—

Olympian

This model is similar to the Regency, with less engraving. It was not imported after 1980. A skeet and a trap model, as well as a field-grade model, were available. The values were similar.

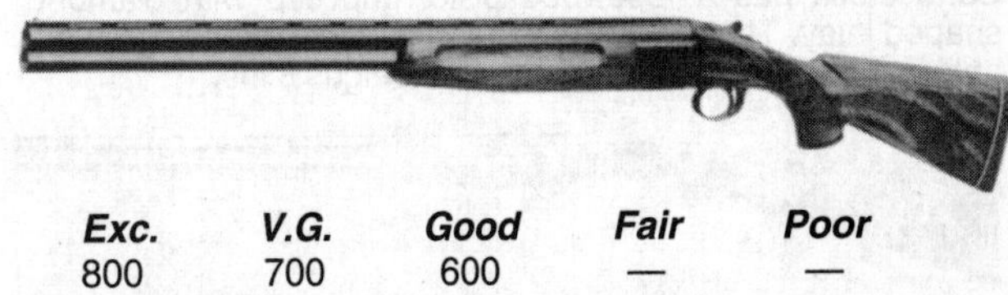

Exc.	V.G.	Good	Fair	Poor
800	700	600	—	—

Orion Upland

This 12 or 20 gauge model features a Claro walnut stock with rounded pistol grip and slim forearm. Plain blued receiver. Choice of 26" or 28" vent-rib barrel with 3" chambers. Multichoke system. Introduced in 1999.

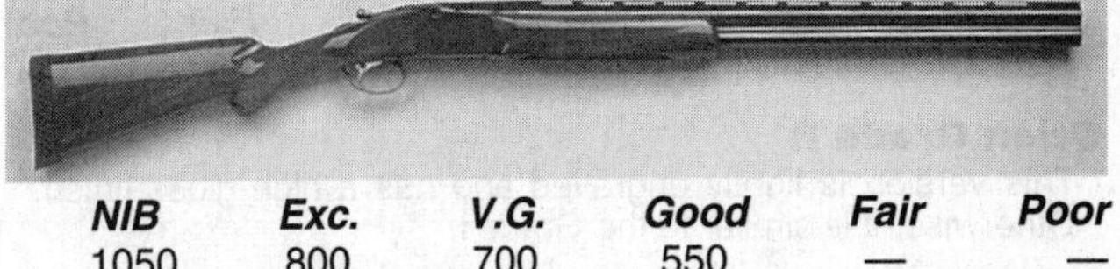

NIB	Exc.	V.G.	Good	Fair	Poor
1050	800	700	550	—	—

Orion Grade I

This is an over-and-under double-barrel shotgun chambered for 12 or 20 gauge with 3" chambers. It is offered with 26" or 28" vent-rib barrels with screw-in chokes. It has a single-selective trigger and automatic ejectors. The boxlock action features no engraving. The finish is blued, with a checkered walnut stock. It was introduced in 1989.

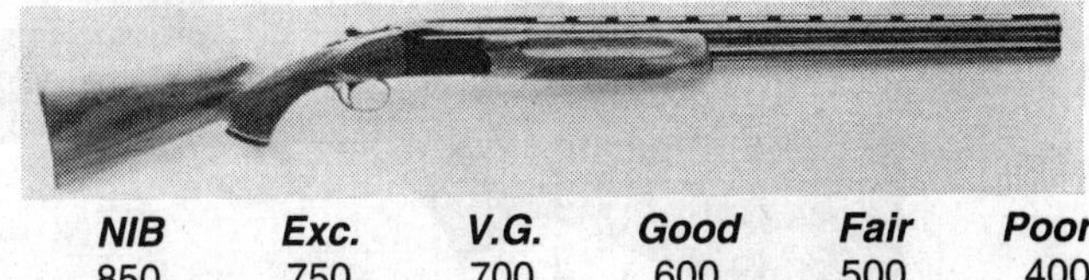

NIB	Exc.	V.G.	Good	Fair	Poor
850	750	700	600	500	400

Orion Grade II Skeet

This model is supplied with a Claro walnut checkered stock with full pistol grip with rosewood grip cap. The receiver is matte blue with scroll engraving. The barrel has a matte ventrib with side vents and mid-point head with white bead front sight. Special ventilated recoil pad. Offered in 12 gauge and 20 gauge with 26" barrels. Fixed Skeet chokes are standard. The 12 gauge weighs 7.5 lbs. while the 20 gauge weighs 7.25 lbs.

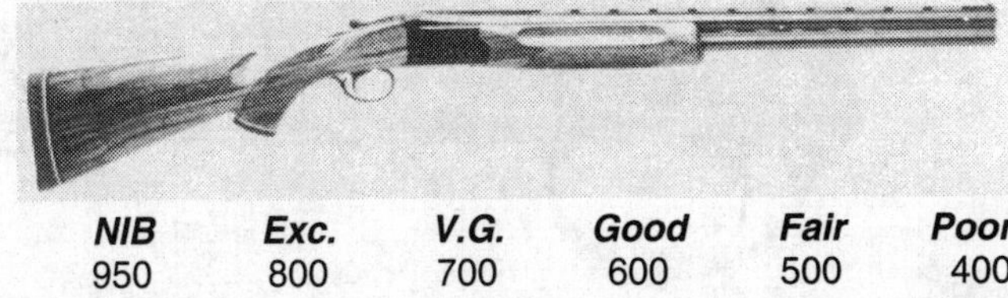

NIB	Exc.	V.G.	Good	Fair	Poor
950	800	700	600	500	400

Orion Grade II Sporting Clays

Similar to the Classic model but with a full pistol grip with rosewood grip cap. The receiver is silver gray with scroll engraving. The Claro walnut stock is checkered with a high-gloss finish. Offered in 12 gauge with 28" to 30" vent-rib barrels. Supplied with five screw-in choke tubes.

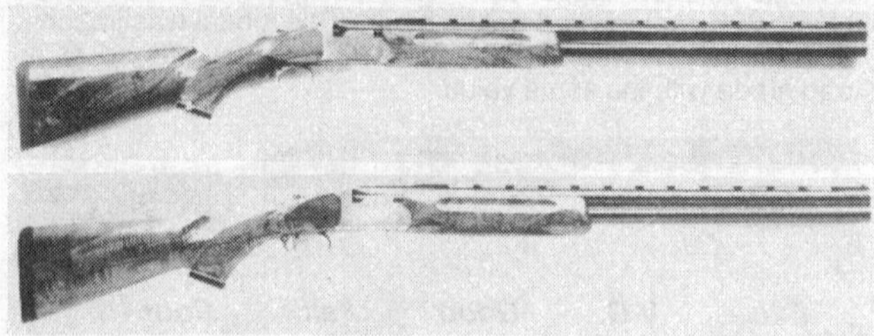

NIB	Exc.	V.G.	Good	Fair	Poor
1000	850	750	600	450	400

Orion Grade II Double Trap

This model features an integral multi-choke tube. The Monte Carlo stock has a rosewood pistol grip cap with diamond shaped inlay. The receiver is blue with scroll engraving. Available with 30" or 32" vent-rib barrels. Weighs 8 lbs.

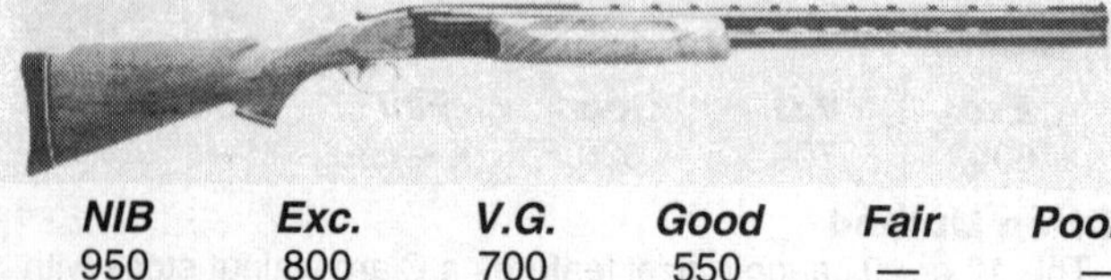

NIB	Exc.	V.G.	Good	Fair	Poor
950	800	700	550	—	—

Orion Grade II Single Trap

Similar to the Double Trap but furnished with a single 32" barrel. Weighs 8 lbs.

NIB	Exc.	V.G.	Good	Fair	Poor
950	800	700	550	450	400

Orion Grade II

This version is lightly engraved and has a high-gloss finish. Otherwise, it is similar to the Grade I.

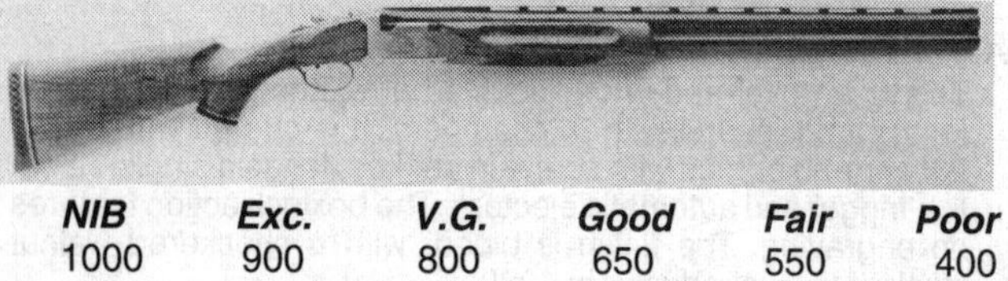

NIB	Exc.	V.G.	Good	Fair	Poor
1000	900	800	650	550	400

Orion Grade II Classic Field

Introduced in 1993 this model features a rounded pistol grip and slim forearm design. The walnut stock is oil finished. The receiver is blued with game scene engraving. A solid recoil pad is standard. Available in 12 gauge, 20 gauge, and 28 gauge with vent-rib barrel lengths from 26" to 30" depending on gauge. Screw-in choke tubes standard. Weighs 6.5 lbs. to 8 lbs. depending on gauge.

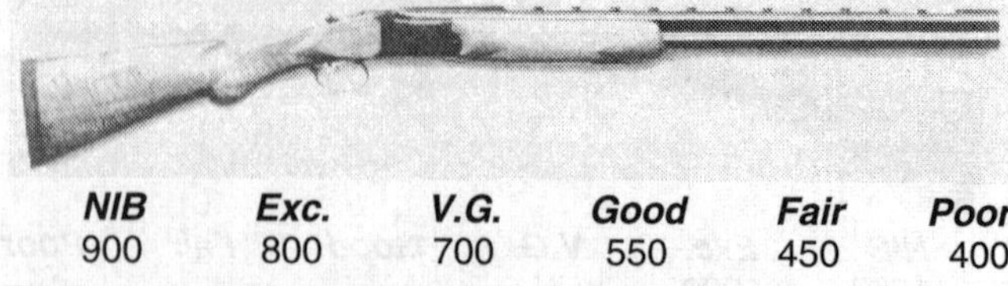

NIB	Exc.	V.G.	Good	Fair	Poor
900	800	700	550	450	400

Orion Grade II Classic Sporting Clays

Introduced in 1993 this model has a rounded pistol grip with slender forearm with an oil-finished stock. The receiver is blued with scroll engraving. A stepped competition matte vent-rib with additional side vents is supplied. The recoil pad has a special radius heel. Offered in 12 gauge with 28" barrel. Furnished with five screw-in choke tubes. Weighs 7.5 lbs.

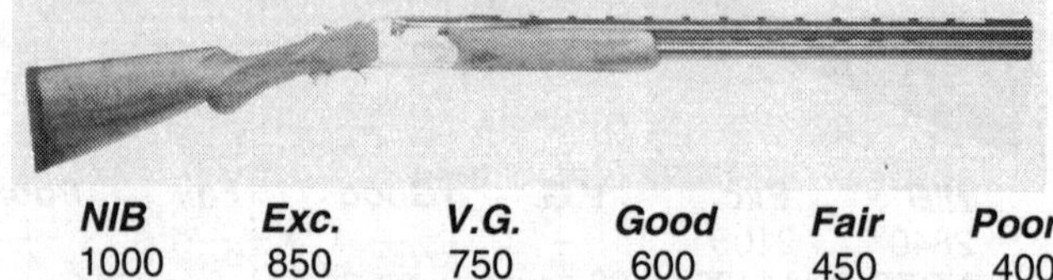

NIB	Exc.	V.G.	Good	Fair	Poor
1000	850	750	600	450	400

Orion Super Sporting Clays (SSC)

Introduced in 1999 this 12 gauge model features a walnut stock with sporter-style pistol grip and cast off. Barrel lengths are 28", 30" or 32" with 3" chambers and 12mm grooved rib. Barrels are also ported and backbored. Comes with five choke tubes. Weight is approximately 8 lbs.

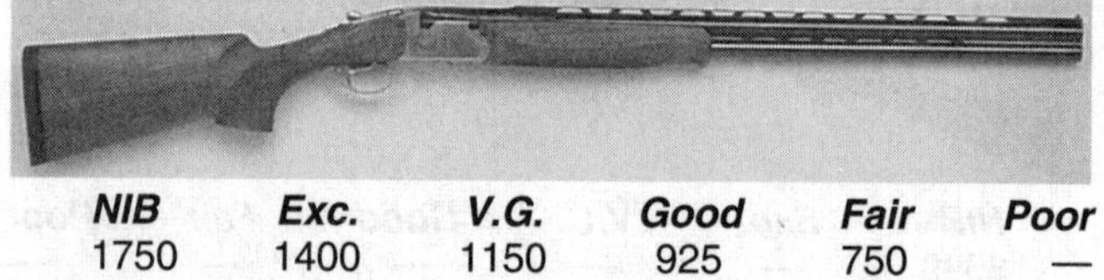

NIB	Exc.	V.G.	Good	Fair	Poor
1750	1400	1150	925	750	—

Orion Grade III

This version has a game scene-engraved, coin-finished receiver and higher-grade walnut. It was introduced in 1989.

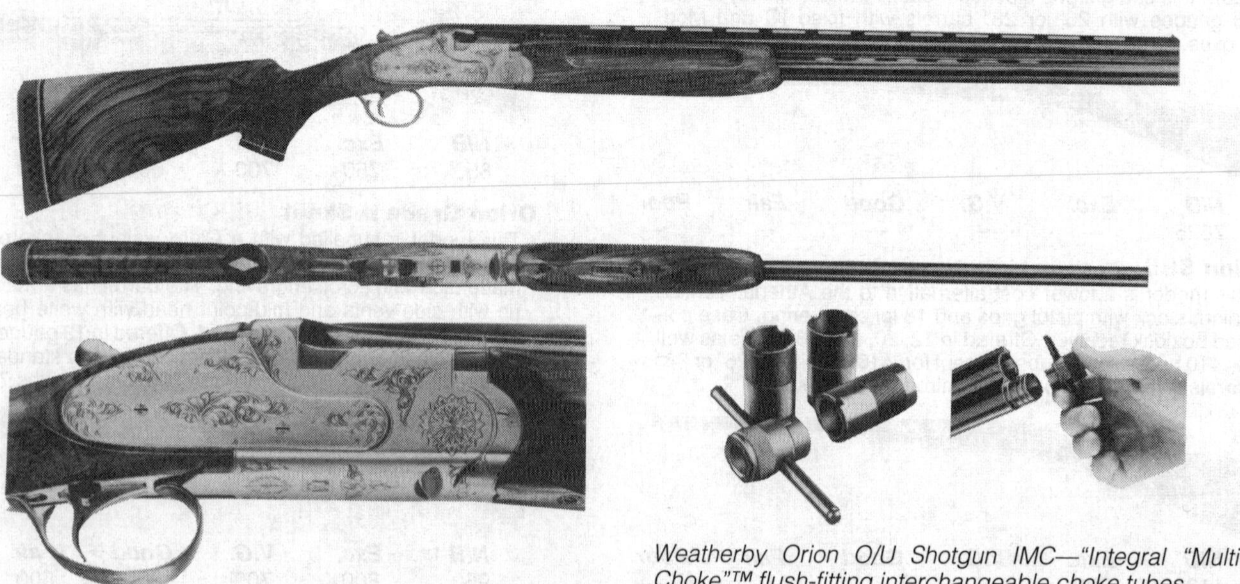

Weatherby Orion O/U Shotgun IMC—"Integral "Multi-Choke"™ flush-fitting interchangeable choke tubes

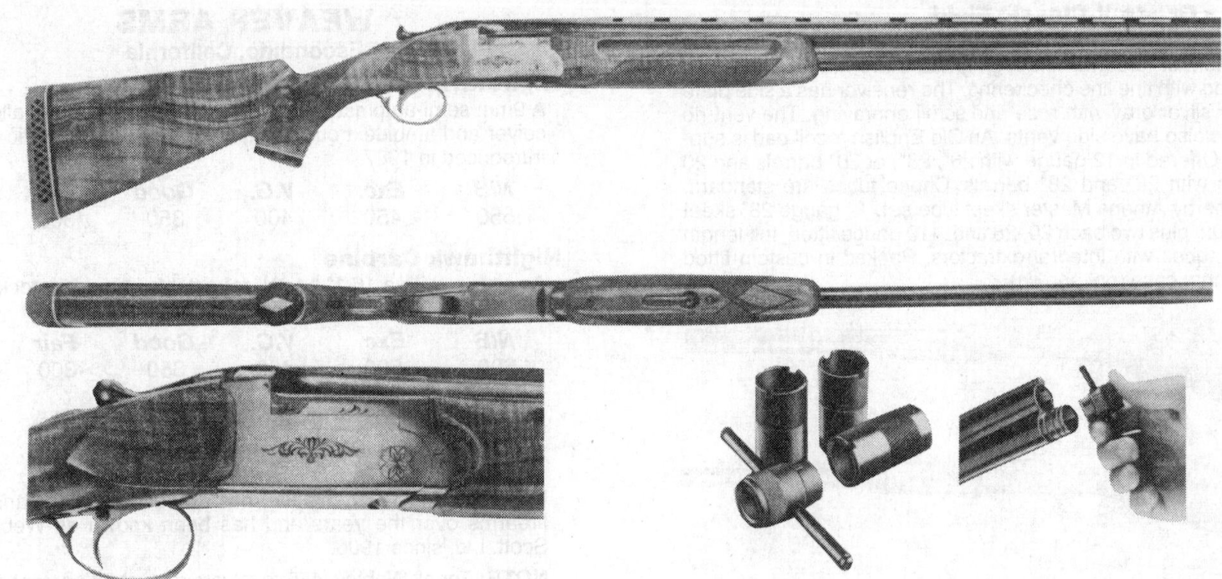

Weatherby Athena O/U Shotgun IMC—"Integral "Multi-Choke"™ flush-fitting interchangeable choke tubes

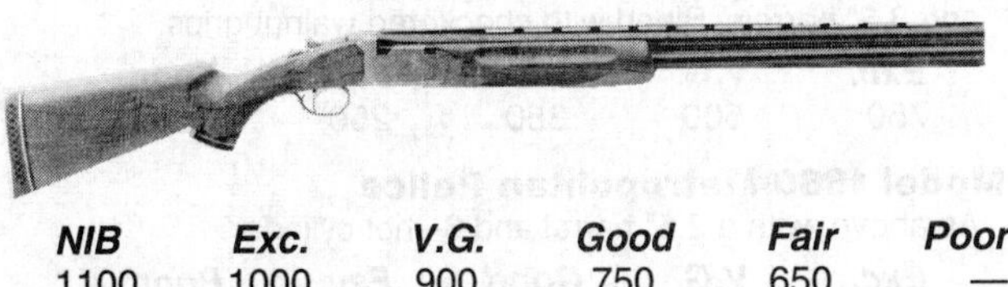

NIB	Exc.	V.G.	Good	Fair	Poor
1100	1000	900	750	650	—

Orion Grade III Classic Field

New for 1993 this model features a rounded pistol grip and slim forearm with oil finish Claro walnut with fine line checkering. The receiver is silver gray with scroll engraving and gold game bird overlays. Available in 12 gauge with 28" vent-rib barrels and 20 gauge with 26" vent-rib barrels. Screw-in choke tubes standard.

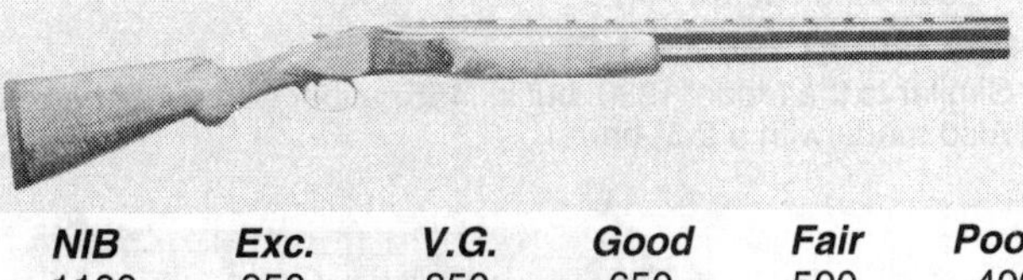

NIB	Exc.	V.G.	Good	Fair	Poor
1100	950	850	650	500	400

Orion Grade III Classic English Field

This model features an English-style straight-grip stock with a choice of 12 gauge with 28" barrel or 20 gauge with 26" or 28" barrels. The receiver is engraved and the stock is oil-finished hand-checkered. Weight of 12 gauge gun is about 7 lbs. and 20 gauge gun is about 6.5 lbs. Introduced in 1996.

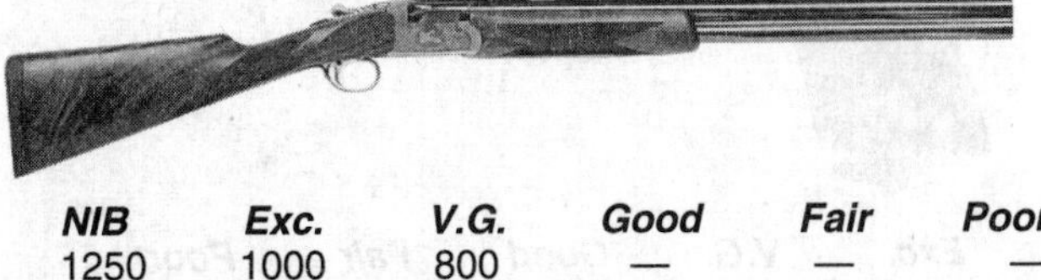

NIB	Exc.	V.G.	Good	Fair	Poor
1250	1000	800	—	—	—

Athena Grade III Classic Field

Offered in 12 or 20 gauge this model features a hand select Claro walnut stock with oil finish. The pistol grip is rounded. The silver-gray sideplates feature a rose and scroll engraving pattern with gold overlaid hunting scenes. Available with 26" or 28" vent-rib barrels with multi-choke system. Weight is around 7.5 lbs. for 12 gauge and 7 lbs. for 20 gauge. Introduced in 1999. In 2001 a 28 gauge version was offered with 26" or 28" barrels.

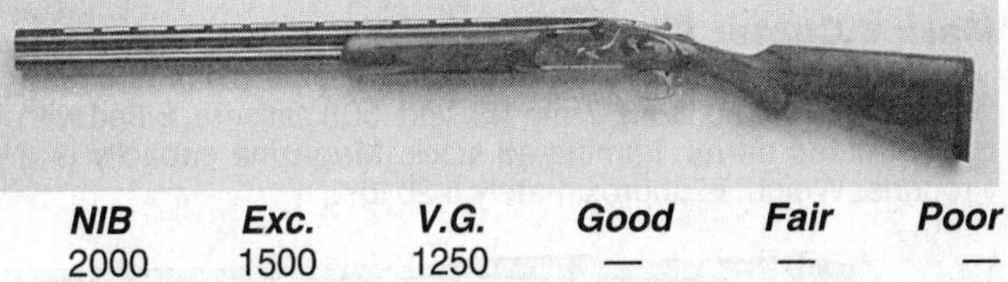

NIB	Exc.	V.G.	Good	Fair	Poor
2000	1500	1250	—	—	—

Athena Grade IV

This is an over/under double-barrel shotgun chambered for 12, 20, and 28 gauge, as well as .410. It has 3" chambers. It is offered with various barrel lengths with vent-ribs and screw-in choke tubes. It has a boxlock action with Greener crossbolt, single-selective trigger, and automatic ejectors. It has engraved false sideplates and a satin nickel-plated action. The barrels are blued, with a select checkered walnut stock. This model was introduced in 1989.

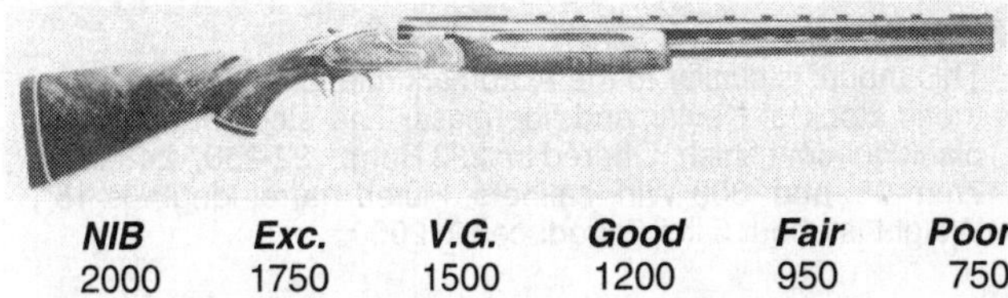

NIB	Exc.	V.G.	Good	Fair	Poor
2000	1750	1500	1200	950	750

Competition Model Athena

This is either a trap or skeet version with stock dimensions designed for either skeet or trap and competition-type ribs.

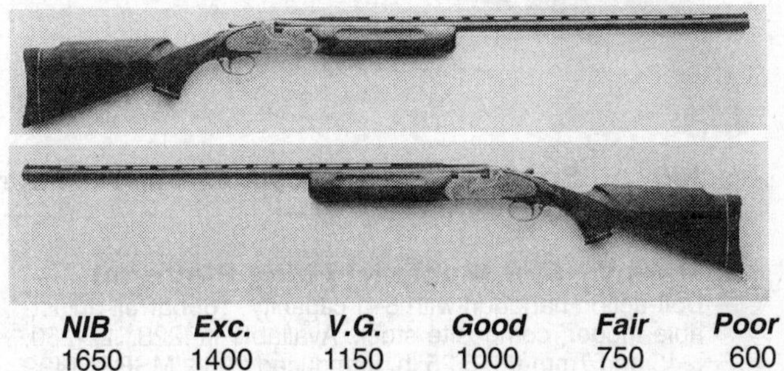

NIB	Exc.	V.G.	Good	Fair	Poor
1650	1400	1150	1000	750	600

Athena Grade V Classic Field

Introduced in 1993 this model features a rounded pistol grip with slender forearm. The high-grade Claro walnut stock is oil finished with fine line checkering. The receiver has a side plate that is silver gray with rose and scroll engraving. The vent-rib barrels also have side vents. An Old English recoil pad is supplied. Offered in 12 gauge with 26", 28", or 30" barrels and 20 gauge with 26" and 28" barrels. Choke tubes are standard. Weatherby Athena Master skeet tube set, 12 gauge 28" skeet shotgun, plus two each 20, 28 and .410 gauge fitted, full-length Briley tubes with integral extractors. Packed in custom fitted aluminum case (not shown).

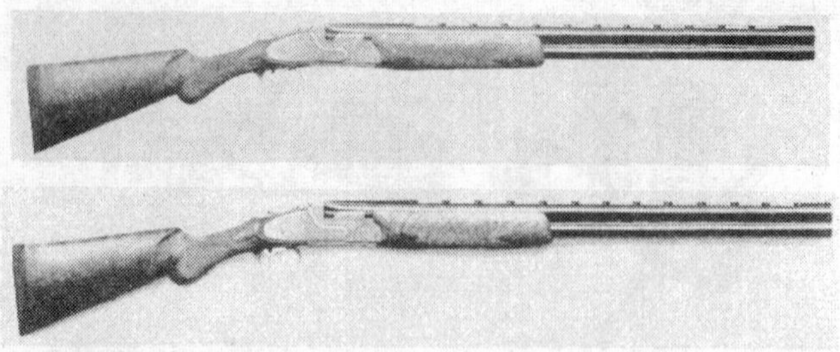

NIB	Exc.	V.G.	Good	Fair	Poor
1950	1750	1100	700	600	—

NOTE: Add 50 percent for Master Skeet Set.

HANDGUNS

Mark V Center Fire Pistol (CFP)

Introduced in 1998 this bolt action centerfire pistol is chambered for .22-250, .243, 7mm-08, and .308 calibers. Fitted with a 15" fluted barrel. Laminated stock. Magazine capacity is 3 rounds. Weight is approximately 5.25 lbs.

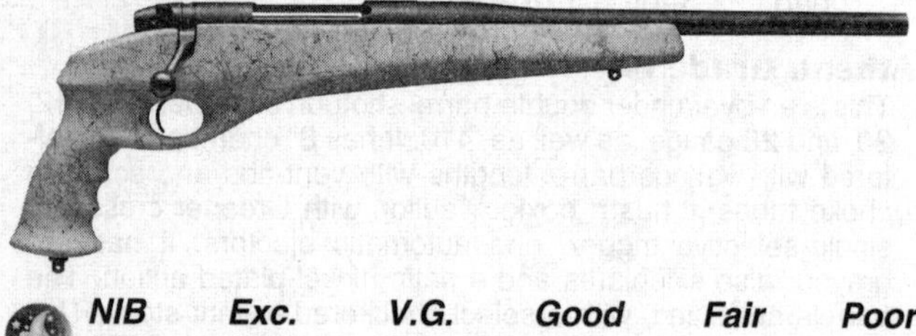

NIB	Exc.	V.G.	Good	Fair	Poor
1050	800	725	—	—	—

Mark V Accumark CFP

This model is similar to the Accumark rifle and features a synthetic stock of Kevlar and fiberglass. The stock has a matte black gel-coat finish. Offered in .223 Rem., .22-250, .243 Win., 7mm-08, and .308 Win. calibers. Fluted barrel length is 15". Weight is about 5 lbs. Introduced in 2000.

NIB	Exc.	V.G.	Good	Fair	Poor
1050	800	—	—	—	—

Mark V - CFP (Compact Firing Platform)

Bolt-action handgun with 5+1 capacity. 16" barrel, adjustable trigger, composite stock. Available in .223, .22-250, .243 and 7mm-08. 5.25 lb. Introduced 2006. MSRP: 1499

WEAVER ARMS

Escondido, California

Nighthawk Assault Pistol

A 9mm semi-automatic pistol with a 10" or 12" barrel, alloy receiver and ambidextrous safety. Blackened with plastic grips. Introduced in 1987.

NIB	Exc.	V.G.	Good	Fair	Poor
550	450	400	350	300	150

Nighthawk Carbine

As above, with a 16.1" barrel, retractable shoulder stock, 25-, 32-, 40-, or 50-shot magazine. Introduced in 1984.

NIB	Exc.	V.G.	Good	Fair	Poor
600	500	450	350	300	150

WEBLEY & SCOTT, LTD.

Birmingham, England

SEE ALSO—British Double Guns

Established in 1860, this firm has produced a wide variety of firearms over the years and has been known as Webley & Scott, Ltd. since 1906.

NOTE: For all Webley .455 revolvers deduct 35 percent if converted to .45 ACP/.45 Auto Rim.

Model 1872 Royal Irish Constabulary

A .450 double-action revolver with a 3.25" barrel, 5-shot cylinder and rotating ejector. This model was also offered with 2.5" and 3.5" barrels. Blued with checkered walnut grips.

Exc.	V.G.	Good	Fair	Poor
750	500	350	250	150

Model 1880 Metropolitan Police

As above, with a 2.5" barrel and 6-shot cylinder.

Exc.	V.G.	Good	Fair	Poor
650	475	325	200	150

Model 1878 Webley-Pryse

Chambered for the .455 and .476 Eley cartridge.

Exc.	V.G.	Good	Fair	Poor
1100	900	750	550	300

NOTE: Add 200 percent premium for revolvers chambered for .577. Deduct 50 percent for revolvers chambered for cartridges below .442.

New Model 1883 R.I.C.

Similar to the Model 1880, but in .455 caliber with a 4.5" barrel. Also made with a 2.5" barrel.

Exc.	V.G.	Good	Fair	Poor
700	550	425	250	100

Model 1884 R.I.C. Naval

As above, with a brass frame and oxidized finish. Barrel length 2.75" and of octagonal form.

Exc.	V.G.	Good	Fair	Poor
1000	800	700	600	500

British Bulldog

Similar to the new Model 1883 R.I.C. blued, checkered walnut grips. Those engraved on the back strap "W.R.A. Co." were sold through the Winchester Repeating Arms Company's New York sales agency and are worth a considerable premium over the values listed. Manufactured from 1878 to 1914.

Exc.	*V.G.*	*Good*	*Fair*	*Poor*
550	450	325	200	150

NOTE: Add a premium for U.S. dealer markings, see model description.

Model 1878 Army Express Revolver

A .455 caliber double-action revolver with a 6" barrel and integral ejector. Blued with one-piece walnut grips.

Exc.	*V.G.*	*Good*	*Fair*	*Poor*
1300	1000	750	500	350

NOTE: Add 100 percent premium for single-action version. Add 25 percent for .450 Long (.45 Colt) markings.

Webley Kaufmann Model 1880

A top break, hinged-frame double-action revolver chambered for the .450 centerfire cartridge, with a 5.75" barrel and a curved bird's-head butt. Blued, with walnut grips.

Exc.	*V.G.*	*Good*	*Fair*	*Poor*
1200	1000	800	—	—

Webley-Green Model

A double-action, top break revolver chambered for the .455 cartridge, with a 6" ribbed barrel and a 6-shot cylinder. The cylinder flutes on this model are angular and not rounded in shape. Blued, with checkered walnut, squared butt grips with a lanyard ring on the butt. Introduced in 1882 and manufactured until 1896.

Exc.	*V.G.*	*Good*	*Fair*	*Poor*
1000	800	600	—	—

Mark I

A .442, .455, or .476 double-action top break revolver with a 4" barrel and 6-shot cylinder. Blued with checkered walnut grips. Manufactured from 1887 to 1894.

Courtesy Faintich Auction Services, Inc., Paul Goodwin photo

Exc.	*V.G.*	*Good*	*Fair*	*Poor*
650	550	375	250	150

Mark II

As above, with a larger hammer spur and improved barrel catch. Manufactured from 1894 to 1897.

Exc.	*V.G.*	*Good*	*Fair*	*Poor*
625	525	350	225	100

Mark III

As above, with internal improvements. Introduced in 1897.

Exc.	*V.G.*	*Good*	*Fair*	*Poor*
575	500	325	200	75

Mark IV

As above, with a .455 caliber 3", 4", 5", or 6" barrel. This model was also available in .22 caliber with 6" barrel, .32 caliber with 3" barrel, and .38 caliber with 3", 4", or 5" barrel.

Courtesy Faintich Auction Services, Inc., Paul Goodwin photo

Exc.	*V.G.*	*Good*	*Fair*	*Poor*
700	575	375	200	75

Mark IV Target

Chambered for the .22 caliber cartridge and fitted with a 6" barrel with target sights.

Courtesy Rock Island Auction Company

Exc.	*V.G.*	*Good*	*Fair*	*Poor*
1250	1000	800	500	300

Mark V

Similar to Mark IV, with a 4" or 6" barrel. Manufactured from 1913 to 1915.

Courtesy Faintich Auction Services, Inc., Paul Goodwin photo

Exc.	*V.G.*	*Good*	*Fair*	*Poor*
750	595	395	250	150

Mark VI

Similar to Mark V in design but with a smaller frame, 4" or 6" barrel and modified grip. Chambered for .38/200 (.38 S&W). Pricing is for commercial version. Subtract 30 percent for WAR FINISH-marked examples.

Value Tracker: Webley Revolvers

Fifteen years or so ago, a craze for British guns began that has continued unabated. Webleys of all sorts have proved very popular with American collectors and shooters, perhaps none moreso than Webley's large-frame revolvers. Even Webley pocket models command good prices on today's market, a trend that hasn't yet fully extended to the Mk IV chambered in .38/200. The table below contains a potpourri of collectible Webleys.

*Legend: **RIA** = Rock Island Auctions; **B&B** = Butterfield & Butterfield; **AMOS** = Amoskeag; **JCD** = J. C. Devine; **JDJ** + James D. Julia; **GMA** = Greg Martin. Contact information for these fine auction houses can be found in the front pages of this book.*

Auction House/Date/Lot No.	Item Description	Estimated Value	Actually Sold For
JCD 08/14/05 Lot 767	Webley Mark I revolver #2624 (mfg 1894-97), .455, 4" flat-sided bbl. w/good bore, nickel finish w/checkered wood grips, British proof marks. About Fine, 95 percent+ nickel w/light wear on cylinder.	E: $300-$500	$402.50
B&B 04/05/05 Lot 1279	Webley Mark IV revolver #71718, .38, frame w/"WD" marks and stamped "WAR FINISH," checkered hard rubber grips. "Fine."	E:150-$250	$173
RIA 09/16-18/06 Lot 1858	Webley No. 1 Royal Irish Constabulary revolver #83919, .476 CF, 4.5" irregular bbl., walnut grips, "NEW MODEL" on frame, first refinish worn. Partially refinished, 50 percent blue remains w/touch up on left side of frame, mostly gray patina, excellent grips, mechanically fine.	E: $900-$1,200	$1,495
RIA 09/16-18/06 Lot 3569	Webley-Greene M. 1889 revolver #3665, .450, 6" slab-side bbl. marked "HOLLAND & HOLLAND," walnut grips, Webley logo on left frame and "'WG' MODEL 1889" on topstrap, w/military brown leather flap holster. "Very Good," 75 percent blue w/scattered flaking, grips and holster very good, mechanics fine.	E: $900-$1,200	$1,495
RIA 4/30-5/2/05 Lot 2690	Webley Mark IV revolver #B36039, .38 S&W, 5" flat bbl., hard rubber grips, post-WWII commercial proof marks and importer stamp. "Excellent," 95 percent-97 percent of brush finish, grip dull but have only light handling marks, action fine.	E: $250-$450	$546.25
RIA 4/30-5/2/05 Lot 2691	Webley Mark IV revolver #66794, .38 5" flat-sided bbl., plastic grips, "WAR FINISH" marking, "ENGLAND" canvas holster w/lanyard attached, Canadian and commercial markings. "Excellent," 85 percent wartime brush blue finish, grips, action and holster are fine.	E: $300-$450	$632.50
RIA 4/30-5/2/05 Lot 3740	P. Webley British Bulldog revolver #51415, .442, 2.5" round bbl., checkered birdshead walnut grips, made 1878-1914, 5-round unfluted cylinder, checkered hammer. "Fair," as the revolver was cleaned. Traces of finish and old patina, remainder polished to metal, grips and action in good working order.	E: $300-$600	$1,035
RIA 12/03-05/05 Lot 2052	Webley Mark VI revolver #184250 (mfg 1915), .45 ACP, 6" solid-rib bbl., hard rubber grips, cylinder faced for half-moon clips, both commercial and military proof marks. "Good as rechambered," 20 percent fading blue, surface rust and pitting, large chip from left grip and crack on right. Needs mechanical adjustment.	E: $250-$325	$316.25

Auction House/Date/Lot No.	Item Description	Estimated Value	Actually Sold For
RIA 12/03-05/05 Lot 2064	Webley Mark II revolver #55077, .455, 4" solid-rib bbl., hard rubber grips, large broad arrow filed across top strap. "Fine," 50 percent orig. blue, surface rust and pitting, battering on left side of bbl., sun-faded grips w/dents and scratches, mechanically fine.	E: $375-$550	$690
RIA 12/03-05/05 Lot 2066	Webley Mark IV revolver #93377, .45 ACP, 4" solid-rib bbl., hard rubber birdhead grips, commercial and military proof marks, w/tan canvas holster. "Fine" as rechambered, 80 percent thinning blue, grips w/minor scrapes and dents, action fine, holster faded.	E: $325-$475	$575
RIA 12/03-05/05 Lot 2067	Webley Mark IV revolver #61649, .38 Short, 5" solid-rib bbl., hard rubber grips, Parkerized finish with "WAR FINISH" mark, correct canvas holster and belt, cleaning rod and 1943 lanyard. About Very Good to Fine, refinished, large chip from left grip, action fine.	E: $300-$450	$258.75
RIA 12/03-05/05 Lot 2069	Webley Mark VI revolver #172569 (mfg 1915), .45 ACP, 6" solid-rib bbl., hard rubber grips, cylinder faced for half-moon clips, commercial and military proof marks. "Very Good" as rechambered, traces of blue amid patina w/ rust and pitting, grip scratches and gouges, front sight lowered, action fine.	E: $225-$325	$345
RIA 12/03-05/05 Lot 2072	Webley Mark VI revolver #253006 (mfg 1915), .45 ACP, 6" solid-rib bbl., hard rubber grips, cylinder faced for half-moon clips, military and postwar proof marks. "Fair refinish," some loss of original markings, grips good w/moderate wear, extractor does not work, w/heavily stained orig. holster.	E: $150-$275	$316.25
JCD 04/23/06 Lot 822	Webley Mark VI revolver #N798, altered to .45 ACP, 6" bbl., cylinder faced for half-moon clips. "Very Good condition overall."	E: $175-$275	$402.50
AMOS 03/25/06 Lot 779	Webley Mark VI revolver #343133, .45 ACP, 6v bbl. w/very good, bright bore, marked "NZ" (New Zealand). About Good to Very Good, 80 percent graying orig. blue, very good rubber grips, works double but not single action, w/an orig. canvas military holster w/moderate wear at tip.	E: $250-$350	$373.75
AMOS 01/14/06 Lot 395	Webley Mark IV revolver #54367, .380-200, 4" bbl. w/very good bore, w/import and Israeli property markings and plastic Webley grips. About Fine, 85 percent orig. blue with silvering.	E: $200-$300	$287.50
AMOS 01/14/06 Lot 396	Webley Mark IV revolver #49655, .380-200, 4" bbl. w/very good bore, recent Israeli import w/very good plastic Webley grips. About Fine, 85 percent orig. blue, minor handling marks and bruising on grips.	E: $200-$300	$258.75
B&B 06/20/06 Lot 5435	Webley Fosbery Model 1901 Zig-Zag Revolver #93, .455, 6" bbl, blued w/ checkered walnut grips and lanyard ring. "Very good," 50 percent-60 percent thinning blue, clean bore, grips w/scattered light marks.	E: $2,000-$3,000	$5,558
B&B 06/20/06 Lot 5436	Webley Mark VI service revolver #444277 (mfg 1919), .455, black plastic grips, "numerous War Department markings," with gray web service holster stamped "1941." "Very Good," 90-95 percent old reblued finish.	E: $250-$350	$644

Auction House/Date/Lot No.	Item Description	Estimated Value	Actually Sold For
B&B 06/20/06 Lot 5437	Webley Mark VI service revolver #264969 (mfg 1917), .455, black plastic grips, "numerous War Department markings," with gray web service holster stamped "1941." "Very Good," 99 percent old reblued finish.	E: $250-$350	$644
AMOS 01/15/05 Lot 532	"WG" Army Model Revolver #10875, 6" bbl w/fine bore, reblued and rechambered from .455/.476 to .45 Colt, replacement bird's head grips, "mechanism needed attention," fair condition.	E: $100-$200	$258.75
JCD 03/13/05 Lot 386	Webley & Scott Mark VI #208631 ("1916") .455, 6" bbl w/fine bore, plum patina w very fine light pitting, good rubber grips.	E: $250-$300	$402.50
JCD 03/13/05 Lot 387	Webley & Scott Mark VI #303729 ("1917") altered to .45 ACP, 6" bbl w/excellent bore, 90 percent dull orig. blue, v.g. rubber grips.	E: $300-$400	$488.75
JCD 03/13/05 Lot 388	Webley & Scott Mark VI #169979 ("1915") .455, 6" bbl w/excellent bore, no lanyard ring, 90 percent dull reblue over scattered pitting, v.g. rubber grips.	E: $250-$300	$460
JCD 03/13/05 Lot 389	Webley & Scott Mark VI #163398 ("1915") altered to .45 ACP, 6" bbl w/excellent bore, 90 percent dull reblue, v.g. rubber grips, frame stamped "128 RE" & "GREENFIELD."	E: $300-$350	$345
JCD 03/13/05 Lot 390	Webley & Scott Mark IV #65414, .38 S&W, 5" bbl w/excellent bore, marked "WAR FINISH" w/black paint traces over 95 percent dull orig. blue, good rubber grips.		E: $200-$300 $373.75
GMA 11/06-07/06 Lot 1477	Webley Mark VI #349296, .455 Eley, 6" bbl., checkered hard rubber grips, lanyard ring, in unmarked brown leather flap holster. "Good," with gray patina, scattered light pitting and traces of blue, grip worn, holster with light wear and scuffs.	E: $250-$350	$397.25
GMA 11/06-07/06 Lot 1791	Webley Mark II #55541, .45 ACP, 4v bbl, lightly worn checkered hard rubber grips. Very Good as refinished, with 90 percent-95 percent reblued finish, lanyard ring removed and hole filled. Action very good.	E: $100-$150	$340.50
GMA 11/06-07/06 Lot 1793	Webley & Scott Mark VI #316168, altered to .45 ACP, 6" bbl., worn checkered hard rubber grips and lanyard ring. Very Good as refinished and reconfigured, 85 percent-90 percent reblued finish, scattered wear and patina. Action good.	E: $300-$500	$312.13
JDJ 03/13-14/06 Lot 1112	Engraved Webley Model WC #6539, .455/.476, 6" bbl., nickel finish, "WC MODEL" on side of top strap, fine English scroll engraving over 50 percent, black birdshead composition checkered grips, lanyard loop. Good, w/65 percent-75 percent orig. nickel finish, large chip missing from bottom of left grip, fine mechanics and bore.	E: $1,500-$2,500	$6,900
JDJ 03/13-14/06 Lot 1113	Webley Mark I #36878, 455., 4" bbl., blued w/ checkered composition grips w/ lanyard loop. British military proofs. "Fine +," 85 percent orig. blue, lightly pitted cylinder, grips w/ wear, a few light dings. Mechanics crisp, bright shiny bore.	E: $1,250-$1,750	$747.50

Courtesy Faintich Auction Services, Inc., Paul Goodwin photo

Exc.	V.G.	Good	Fair	Poor
650	525	375	225	150

Mark VI .22 Rimfire

A standard-size Mark V chambered for the .22 rimfire cartridge used as a training pistol. Manufactured in 1918 and quite scarce.

Courtesy Faintich Auction Services, Inc., Paul Goodwin photo

Exc.	V.G.	Good	Fair	Poor
750	600	500	350	200

WEBLEY SEMI-AUTOMATIC PISTOLS

Text and prices by Joseph Schroeder

Webley's first attempt to enter the new self-loading pistol field occurred in the 1890s, when they actually made a few prototype Gabbet-Fairfax "Mars" pistols (see under Gabbet-Fairfax) before deciding that the design was hopelessly complicated and impractical. They then enjoyed some success with the Webley-Fosbery automatic Revolver, a natural for England's premier revolver maker, while experimenting with semi-automatic pistol designs in the 1903-1905 period. Their first commercial pistol, the .32 caliber 1905, was quickly followed by a variety of related designs in various calibers. An interesting sidebar on Webley commercial self-loading pistols is that they were all numbered in the same series, so serial numbers bear no relation to the quantity of a given model actually produced, but do indicate when they were made.

A Webley Fosbery Model 1902 semi-automatic revolver in .38 caliber sold at auction for $14,950. Fitted with a 6" barrel. Condition is 95 percent blue.
Bonham & Butterfield

Webley-Fosbery Automatic Revolver

Recoil forces the top half of this unusual pistol back to cock the hammer, while a stud in the frame cams the cylinder around to bring a fresh chamber into position. Early examples under serial number 75 or so appear to be hand-made as no two seem to be identical; these bring a 100 percent premium over late-model pistols. Other low-number guns, under serial number 300 or so, also differ in appearance from the later production and bring a 25 percent premium. Early production was all in .455 Webley with a 6-round cylinder; a .38 ACP version with an 8-round cylinder was introduced about 1903 but is much scarcer than the .455.

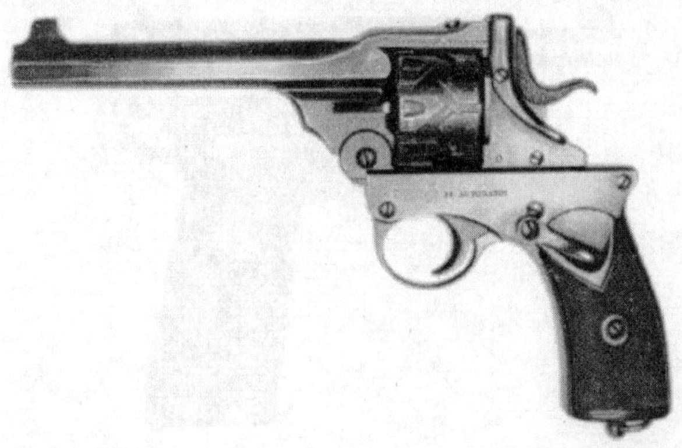

Courtesy Joseph Schroeder

.455 Caliber

Exc.	V.G.	Good	Fair	Poor
5500	4500	3000	2000	1250

.38 Caliber

Exc.	V.G.	Good	Fair	Poor
7500	6000	4500	3000	2000

Model 1904

Made experimentally in both .38 ACP and .455 calibers, the highest serial numbered 1904 known is in the 30s and very few seem to have survived. A later Webley experimental, the Model 1906, made in .45 for the U.S. Army trial but apparently never submitted. Either model is too rare to price.

Model 1904 Courtesy Joseph Schroeder

Model 1906 Courtesy Joseph Schroeder

Model 1905

Webley's first commercial semi-automatic pistol was this compact .32 caliber. The earliest Model 1905s have a diagonal flat machined on the slide and a hammer-mounted safety; these bring about a 50 percent premium. The Model 1905 was replaced by the Model 1908 after about perhaps 20,000 were made.

Courtesy Joseph Schroeder

Exc.	V.G.	Good	Fair	Poor
750	600	400	250	150

NOTE: Prices listed apply only to the Model 1905.

Model 1907

The 1907 is a .25 caliber pistol with an outside hammer and was one of Webley's most popular handguns; it remained in production until WWII and over 50,000 were made.

Courtesy Joseph Schroeder

Exc.	V.G.	Good	Fair	Poor
500	375	275	175	100

Model 1908

The Model 1908 is a slight redesign of the Model 1905. Webley's most popular self-loading pistol, it remained in production until WWII. Examples bearing a crown and the letters "MP" were made for the Metropolitan Police and bring a slight premium.

Exc.	V.G.	Good	Fair	Poor
450	350	250	175	125

Model 1909

The Model 1909 is a modified and enlarged version of the Model 1908, chambered for the 9mm Browning Long cartridge. It was never popular, and manufacture ended in 1914 with just under 1,700 made. Its most unusual feature was the slide release on top of the slide.

Courtesy Joseph Schroeder

Courtesy J.B. Wood

Exc.	V.G.	Good	Fair	Poor
1100	850	500	300	200

Model 1910 .380

The Model 1910 .380 was simply a Model 1908 modified to accept the .380 cartridge. Never very popular, under 2,000 were sold.

Courtesy Joseph Schroeder

Exc.	V.G.	Good	Fair	Poor
750	500	300	200	150

Model 1910 .38 ACP

This was Webley's first locked-breech pistol, based closely on the experimental Model 1906 design and chambered for the .38 ACP cartridge. There are two models, both with internal hammers, but one with a grip safety and the later without. Total production for both was under 1,000, so both are rare.

Courtesy Joseph Schroeder

Exc.	V.G.	Good	Fair	Poor
1800	1400	900	500	350

Model 1911

The Model 1911 is a single-shot .22 caliber training version of the Model 1908, and developed specifically for the Metropolitan Police. It features a "blow open" action that ejects the fired cartridge but remains open for reloading, and the bottom of the frame is slotted for attaching a shoulder stock. Stocks are quite rare, and will probably add more than 100 percent to the value of the pistol.

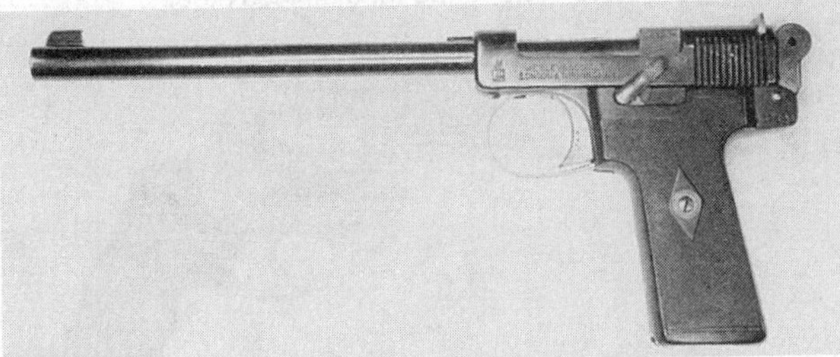

Courtesy Joseph Schroeder

Exc.	V.G.	Good	Fair	Poor
750	600	450	300	200

Model 1912

A perceived need for a hammerless version of the Model 1907 .25 caliber led to the introduction of the Model 1912. It actually does have an internal hammer, but the recoil spring is two coils in the slide instead of the large V-spring under the right grip frame found in all other Webley semi-automatic pistols. Not as popular as the Model 1907, production totaled almost 15,000 vs. over 50,000 for the hammer model.

Exc.	V.G.	Good	Fair	Poor
450	350	250	175	125

Model 1913

The Model 1913 was the result of years of development in conjunction with the British government and was finally adopted in 1913 as the Model 1913 MK1N for Royal Navy issue. It has the same breech-locking system as the Model 1910, but has an external hammer and is chambered for the .455 Webley Self-Loading cartridge. About 1,000 Model 1913s were sold commercially and serial-numbered along with the smaller-caliber pistols. In 1915 a variation of the Model 1913 with butt slotted for a shoulder stock, an adjustable rear sight, and a hammer safety adopted for use by the Royal Horse Artillery. Shoulder stocks are very rare, and will double values listed for the RHA model. All militaries were numbered in their own series; about 10,000 made in both variations.

Model 1913

Exc.	V.G.	Good	Fair	Poor
1500	1200	800	500	300

Model 1913 (RHA model)

Courtesy Joseph Schroeder

Exc.	V.G.	Good	Fair	Poor
2500	2000	1500	850	600

Model 1922

The Model 1922 was a redesign of the Model 1909 in hopes of military adoption. The grip safety was replaced by a manual safety mounted on the slide, the grip angle was changed, and a lanyard ring added to the butt. Unfortunately for Webley its only official use was by the Union Defence Force of South Africa (1,000 pistols). South African guns are marked with a large "U" with an arrow in it and bring a 20 percent premium.

Exc.	V.G.	Good	Fair	Poor
1350	900	600	350	200

WEIHRAUCH, HANS HERMANN

Melrichstadt, West Germany

Model HW 60M

A .22 caliber single-shot bolt action rifle with a 26.75" barrel and adjustable sights. Blued with a walnut stock.

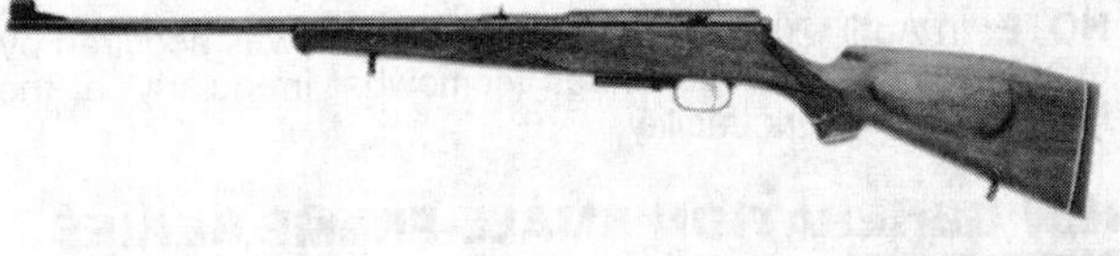

NIB	Exc.	V.G.	Good	Fair	Poor
800	650	550	400	350	250

Model HW 66

A .22 Hornet or .222 Remington bolt action rifle with a stainless steel 26" barrel and single- or double-set triggers. Blued with a walnut stock.

NIB	Exc.	V.G.	Good	Fair	Poor
700	550	500	350	300	200

Model HW-3

A double-action, solid-frame, swing-out cylinder revolver chambered for .22 LR or .32 Smith & Wesson long cartridges with a barrel length of 2.75", and a cylinder holding either seven or eight cartridges. Blued, with walnut grips. In America, this revolver was known as the Dickson Bulldog. In Europe it was known as the Gecado.

Exc.	V.G.	Good	Fair	Poor
100	75	50	35	25

Model HW-5

As above, with a 4" barrel. Sold in the United States under the trade name "Omega."

Exc.	V.G.	Good	Fair	Poor
100	75	50	35	25

Model HW-7

As above, in .22 caliber with a 6" barrel and 8-shot cylinder. Sold in the United States as the "Herter's Guide Model." Also available with target sights and thumbrest grips as the Model HW-7S.

Exc.	V.G.	Good	Fair	Poor
100	75	50	35	25

Model HW-9

Similar to the HW-7, with a 6-shot cylinder and 6" ventilated rib barrel fitted with target sights and target grips.

Exc.	V.G.	Good	Fair	Poor
100	75	50	35	25

These pistols all carry the Arminius trademark, a bearded head wearing a winged helmet. The model number will be found on the cylinder crane; the caliber, on the barrel; and the words "Made in Germany" on the frame.

WEISBURGER, A.

Memphis, Tennessee

Pocket Pistol

A .41 caliber percussion single-shot pocket pistol with 2.5" barrel, German silver furniture and a walnut stock. Manufactured during the 1850s.

Exc.	V.G.	Good	Fair	Poor
—	—	4750	3250	—

WESSON, DAN FIREARMS

Norwich, New York

In 1996 the assets of the Wesson Firearms Co. were purchased by the New York International Corp. All interchangeable barrel models were produced. There are no plans at this time to build fixed barrel models. At the present time, parts and service for original Dan Wesson revolvers are available from the new company. Full production of new models occurred in 1997. These firearms are laser marked on the barrel or frame with: "NYI" in an oval and below "DAN WESSON FIREARMS" on the next line "NORWICH, NEW YORK USA."

NOTE: In April, 2005 Dan Wesson Firearms was acquired by CZ-USA. Production continues (somewhat irregularly) at the Norwich, New York, facility.

NEW GENERATION SMALL-FRAME SERIES

NOTE: The "7" prefix denotes stainless steel frame and barrel. For models listed add between 4 percent and 9 percent depending on barrel length and for stainless steel.

Model 22/722

This is a 6-shot revolver chambered for .22 caliber cartridge. Interchangeable barrel lengths are 2.5", 4", 5.6", 8", and 10". Adjustable rear sight and interchangeable front sight. Hogue finger groove rubber grips. Weight is 36 oz. for 2.5" barrel and 58 oz. for 10" barrel.

NIB	Exc.	V.G.	Good	Fair	Poor
485	375	—	—	—	—

Model 22M/722M

Same as above but chambered for .22 Win. Mag. cartridge.

NIB	Exc.	V.G.	Good	Fair	Poor
520	400	—	—	—	—

Model 32/732

Same as above. Chambered for .32 H&R cartridge.

NIB	Exc.	V.G.	Good	Fair	Poor
550	425	—	—	—	—

Model 3220/73220

Same as above but chambered for the .32-20 cartridge.

NIB	Exc.	V.G.	Good	Fair	Poor
550	425	—	—	—	—

Model 15/715

Same as above but chambered for the .38 Special and .357 Magnum cartridges.

NIB	Exc.	V.G.	Good	Fair	Poor
485	375	—	—	—	—

NEW GENERATION LARGE-FRAME SERIES

NOTE: The "7" prefix denotes stainless steel frame and barrel. For models listed add between 4 percent and 9 percent depending on barrel length and for stainless steel.

Model 41/741

This is a large-frame revolver with 6-shot cylinder. Interchangeable barrels in 4", 6", 8", and 10". Adjustable rear sight with interchangeable front sight. Hogue finger grip rubber grips standard. Weight is from 49 oz. for 4" barrel to 69 oz. for 10" barrels.

NIB	Exc.	V.G.	Good	Fair	Poor
575	450	—	—	—	—

Model 44/744

Same as above but chambered for .44 Magnum cartridge.

NIB	Exc.	V.G.	Good	Fair	Poor
575	450	—	—	—	—

Model 45/745

Same as above but chambered for .45 Colt cartridge.

NIB	Exc.	V.G.	Good	Fair	Poor
600	475	—	—	—	—

Model 360/7360

Same as above but chambered for .357 Magnum cartridge.

NIB	Exc.	V.G.	Good	Fair	Poor
640	500	—	—	—	—

Model 460/7460

Same as above but chambered for the .45 ACP, .45 Auto Rim, .45 Super, .45 Win. Mag, or .460 Rowland.

NIB	Exc.	V.G.	Good	Fair	Poor
650	525	—	—	—	—

NEW GENERATION SUPERMAG-FRAME SERIES

NOTE: The "7" prefix denotes stainless steel frame and barrel. For models listed add between 4 percent and 9 percent depending on barrel length and for stainless steel.

Model 40/740

This is a 6-shot revolver chambered for .the .357 Magnum, .357 Super Magnum/Maximum cartridges with interchangeable barrels in 4", 6", 8", or 10" lengths. Adjustable rear sight and interchangeable front sights. Hogue finger groove rubber grips standard. Weight range from 51 oz. for 4" barrel to 76 oz. for 10" barrel.

NIB	Exc.	V.G.	Good	Fair	Poor
795	650	—	—	—	—

Model 414/7414

Same as above but chambered for .414 Super Magnum cartridge.

NIB	Exc.	V.G.	Good	Fair	Poor
795	650	—	—	—	—

Model 445/7445

Same as above but chambered for .445 Super Mag. cartridge.

NIB	Exc.	V.G.	Good	Fair	Poor
795	650	—	—	—	—

NEW GENERATION COMPENSATED SERIES

NOTE: The "7" prefix denotes stainless steel frame and barrel. For models listed add between 4 percent and 9 percent depending on barrel length and for stainless steel.

Model 15/715

This is a 6-shot revolver that is chambered for the .357 Magnum cartridge and offered with interchangeable barrels in 4", 6", or 10" lengths. Barrels have an integral compensator. Adjustable rear sight and interchangeable front sight. Hogue finger groove rubber grips.

NIB	Exc.	V.G.	Good	Fair	Poor
575	450	—	—	—	—

Model 41/741

Same as above but chambered for .41 Magnum cartridge.

NIB	Exc.	V.G.	Good	Fair	Poor
675	550	—	—	—	—

Model 44/744

Same as above but chambered for .44 Magnum cartridge.

NIB	Exc.	V.G.	Good	Fair	Poor
675	550	—	—	—	—

Model 45/745

Same as above but chambered for .45 Colt cartridge.

NIB	Exc.	V.G.	Good	Fair	Poor
675	550	—	—	—	—

Model 360/7360

Same as above but chambered for .357 Magnum on large frame.

NIB	Exc.	V.G.	Good	Fair	Poor
765	600	—	—	—	—

Model 445/7445 (Alaskan Guide)

Chambered for the .445 SuperMag cartridge. Fitted with a 4" heavy ported barrel. Special matte black coating over stainless steel. Introduced in 2002.

NIB	Exc.	V.G.	Good	Fair	Poor
995	800	—	—	—	—

Model 460/7460

Same as above but chambered for the .45 ACP, .45 Auto Rim, .45 Super, .45 Win. Mag., or the .460 Rowland cartridges.

NIB	Exc.	V.G.	Good	Fair	Poor
825	650	—	—	—	—

STANDARD SILHOUETTE SERIES

NOTE: All Standard Silhouette series revolvers are stainless steel.

Model 722 VH10

This is a 6-shot revolver chambered for the .22 caliber cartridge. Interchangeable barrel system. Choice of fluted or non-fluted cylinders. Patridge front sight and adjustable rear sight. Hogue finger groove rubber grips standard. Lightweight slotted 8" shroud.

NIB	Exc.	V.G.	Good	Fair	Poor
800	650	—	—	—	—

Model 7360 V8S

Same as above but chambered for the .357 Magnum cartridge.

NIB	Exc.	V.G.	Good	Fair	Poor
820	670	—	—	—	—

Model 741 V8S

Same as above but chambered for the .41 Magnum cartridge with 8" slotted shroud.

NIB	Exc.	V.G.	Good	Fair	Poor
800	650	—	—	—	—

Model 741 V10S

Same as above but with 10" slotted shroud.

NIB	Exc.	V.G.	Good	Fair	Poor
925	750	—	—	—	—

Model 744 V8S

Chambered for .44 Magnum cartridge and fitted with an 8" slotted shroud.

NIB	Exc.	V.G.	Good	Fair	Poor
825	675	—	—	—	—

Model 744 V10S

Same as above but fitted with a 10" slotted shroud.

NIB	Exc.	V.G.	Good	Fair	Poor
925	750	—	—	—	—

Model 740 V8S

Chambered for the .357 Super Mag. and fitted with an 8" slotted shroud.

NIB	Exc.	V.G.	Good	Fair	Poor
950	800	—	—	—	—

Model 7414 V8S

Chambered for the .414 Super Mag and fitted with an 8" slotted shroud.

NIB	Exc.	V.G.	Good	Fair	Poor
950	800	—	—	—	—

Model 7445 V8S

Chambered for the .445 Super Mag. and fitted with an 8" slotted shroud.

NIB	Exc.	V.G.	Good	Fair	Poor
950	800	—	—	—	—

Dan Wesson VH8

.445 SuperMag revolver designed for barrel interchangeability. Also fires standard .44-caliber rounds. Stainless, 6-shot; 8" barrel, 4.1 lb. Single/double action. Introduced 2006. MSRP: 1070

SUPER RAM SILHOUETTE SERIES

NOTE: All Super Ram Silhouette series revolvers are stainless steel.

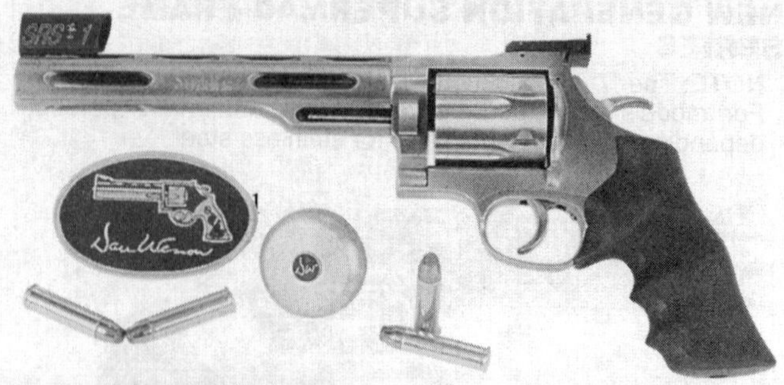

Model 722 VH10 SRS1

This model is chambered for the .22 caliber cartridge and is fitted with a 10" slotted shroud barrel. Interchangeable barrel system. Adjustable Bomar rear sight. Bomar SRS-1 hood front sight. Fluted or non-fluted cylinders. Hogue finger groove rubber grips.

NIB	Exc.	V.G.	Good	Fair	Poor
950	800	—	—	—	—

Model 7360 V8S SRS1

Same as above but chambered for .357 Magnum cartridge. Fitted with an 8" slotted shroud.

NIB	Exc.	V.G.	Good	Fair	Poor
1100	875	—	—	—	—

Model 741 V8S SRS1

Same as above but chambered for .41 Magnum cartridge and fitted with an 8" slotted shroud.

NIB	Exc.	V.G.	Good	Fair	Poor
1100	875	—	—	—	—

Model 741 V10S SRS1

Same as above but fitted with a 10" slotted shroud.

NIB	Exc.	V.G.	Good	Fair	Poor
1125	900	—	—	—	—

Model 744 V8S SRS1

Same as above but chambered for the .44 Magnum cartridge and fitted with an 8" slotted shroud.

NIB	Exc.	V.G.	Good	Fair	Poor
1100	875	—	—	—	—

Model 744 V10S SRS1

Same as above but fitted with a 10" slotted shroud.

NIB	Exc.	V.G.	Good	Fair	Poor
1125	900	—	—	—	—

Model 740 V8S SRS1

Same as above but chambered for .357 Super Mag. and fitted with an 8" slotted shroud.

NIB	Exc.	V.G.	Good	Fair	Poor
1200	950	—	—	—	—

Model 7414 V8S SRS1

Same as above but chambered for .414 Super Mag. and fitted with an 8" slotted shroud.

NIB	Exc.	V.G.	Good	Fair	Poor
1200	950	—	—	—	—

Model 7445 V8S SS1

Same as above but chambered for .445 Super Mag. and fitted with an 8" slotted shroud.

NIB	Exc.	V.G.	Good	Fair	Poor
1200	950	—	—	—	—

PISTOL PACK SERIES

This series consists of a Dan Wesson revolver of the customer's choice with adjustable rear sight and four barrel assemblies in the small-frame calibers (2.5", 4", 6", and 8"); the large frame and supermag frame have three barrel assemblies (4", 6", and 8"). Also included is a cleaning kit, wrench kit, extra exotic wood grips, instruction manual and fitted hard case. Choice of blue or stainless steel finish ("7" prefix).

Model 22/722
Chambered for .22 LR.

NIB	Exc.	V.G.	Good	Fair	Poor
1200	950	—	—	—	—

Model 32/732
Chambered for .32 H&R Magnum.

NIB	Exc.	V.G.	Good	Fair	Poor
1200	950	—	—	—	—

Model 3220/73220
Chambered for the .32-20.

NIB	Exc.	V.G.	Good	Fair	Poor
1200	950	—	—	—	—

Model 15/715
Cumbered for the .357 Magnum.

NIB	Exc.	V.G.	Good	Fair	Poor
1200	950	—	—	—	—

Model 41/741
Chambered for the .41 Magnum.

NIB	Exc.	V.G.	Good	Fair	Poor
1450	1150	—	—	—	—

Model 44/744
Chambered for the .44 Magnum.

NIB	Exc.	V.G.	Good	Fair	Poor
1450	1150	—	—	—	—

Model 45/745
Chamberedfor the .45 Colt.

NIB	Exc.	V.G.	Good	Fair	Poor
1450	1150	—	—	—	—

Model 460/7460
Chambered for the .45 ACP, .45 Auto Rim, .45 Super, .45 Win. Mag, .460 Rowland.

NIB	Exc.	V.G.	Good	Fair	Poor
1450	1150	—	—	—	—

Model 40/740
Chambered for the .357 Maximum.

NIB	Exc.	V.G.	Good	Fair	Poor
1650	1300	—	—	—	—

Model 414/7414
Chambered for the .414 Super Mag.

NIB	Exc.	V.G.	Good	Fair	Poor
1650	1300	—	—	—	—

Model 445/7445
Chambered for the .445 Super Mag.

NIB	Exc.	V.G.	Good	Fair	Poor
1650	1300	—	—	—	—

HUNTER PACK SERIES

The Hunter Pack comes with a Dan Wesson revolver of the customer's choice with adjustable rear sight and two 8" barrel assemblies, one with open sights and one drilled and tapped with Burris or Weaver mount installed. Extra set of exotic wood grips, wrench kit, cleaning kit, and manual. Offered in blue or stainless steel ("7" prefix).

Model 22/722
Chambered for .22 LR.

NIB	Exc.	V.G.	Good	Fair	Poor
1200	950	—	—	—	—

Model 32/732
Chambered for .32 H&R Magnum.

NIB	Exc.	V.G.	Good	Fair	Poor
1200	950	—	—	—	—

Model 3220/73220
Chambered for .32-20.

NIB	Exc.	V.G.	Good	Fair	Poor
1200	950	—	—	—	—

Model 15/715
Chambered for .357 Mag.

NIB	Exc.	V.G.	Good	Fair	Poor
1200	950	—	—	—	—

Model 41/741
Chambered for the .41 Mag.

NIB	Exc.	V.G.	Good	Fair	Poor
1450	1150	—	—	—	—

Model 44/744

Chambered for the .44 Mag.

NIB	Exc.	V.G.	Good	Fair	Poor
1450	1150	—	—	—	—

Model 45/745

Chambered for the .45 Colt.

NIB	Exc.	V.G.	Good	Fair	Poor
1450	1150	—	—	—	—

Model 460/7460

Chambered for the .45 ACP, .45 Auto Rim, .45 Super, .45 Win. Mag., .460 Rowland.

NIB	Exc.	V.G.	Good	Fair	Poor
1450	1150	—	—	—	—

Model 40/740

Chambered for the .357 Maximum.

NIB	Exc.	V.G.	Good	Fair	Poor
1650	1300	—	—	—	—

Model 414/7414

Chambered for the .414 Super Mag.

NIB	Exc.	V.G.	Good	Fair	Poor
1650	1300	—	—	—	—

Model 445/7445

Chambered for the .445 Super Mag.

NIB	Exc.	V.G.	Good	Fair	Poor
1650	1300	—	—	—	—

REMINDER

An "N/A" or "—" instead of a price indicates that pricing is not available for that gun in that condition, or that sales for that particular model are so few that a reliable price cannot be given.

PISTOLS

Pointman Major

This is a semi-auto pistol chambered for the .45 ACP cartridge. Many special features including interchangeable front sight, Jarvis match barrel, adjustable rear sight, beveled magazine well, and others. Stainless steel slide and frame. Rosewood checkered grips. Slide serrations both front and rear. A high sighting rib with interchangeable sights. Introduced in 2000.

NIB	Exc.	V.G.	Good	Fair	Poor
775	625	—	—	—	—

Pointman Minor

Same as above except blued slide and frame and no match barrel.

NIB	Exc.	V.G.	Good	Fair	Poor
600	450	—	—	—	—

Pointman Seven

Has many of the same features as the Pointman Major with blued slide and frame and no sighting rib.

NIB	Exc.	V.G.	Good	Fair	Poor
1000	750	—	—	—	—

Pointman Seven Stainless

Same as above with stainless steel frame and slide.

NIB	Exc.	V.G.	Good	Fair	Poor
1100	800	—	—	—	—

Pointman Guardian

This model is fitted with a 4.25" barrel and match trigger group. Adjustable rear sight, plus many other special features. Blued frame and slide with sighting rib.

NIB	Exc.	V.G.	Good	Fair	Poor
775	575	—	—	—	—

Pointman Guardian Duce

Same as above but with blued steel slide and stainless steel frame.

NIB	Exc.	V.G.	Good	Fair	Poor
825	600	—	—	—	—

Pointman Major Australian

Introduced in 2002 this model features a fully adjustable Bomar-style target sight. Unique slide top configuration that features a rounded radius with lengthwise sight serrations. Slide has Southern Cross engraved on right side. Chambered for the .45 ACP cartridge only.

NIB	Exc.	V.G.	Good	Fair	Poor
N/A	—	—	—	—	—

Pointman Hi-Cap

This .45 ACP pistol is fitted with a 5" barrel and blued carbon alloy wide-body frame with a 10-round magazine. Fixed rear target sight. Extended thumb safety as well as other special features.

NIB	Exc.	V.G.	Good	Fair	Poor
690	550	—	—	—	—

Pointman Dave Pruitt Signature Series

This pistol is fitted with a 5" match-grade barrel with a rounded top slide with bead blast matte finish. Chevron-style cocking serrations. Fixed rear sight with tactical/target ramp front sight. Many special features.

NIB	Exc.	V.G.	Good	Fair	Poor
900	600	—	—	—	—

Dan Wesson RZ-10

10mm single-action semi-auto with 8+1 capacity. 5" barrel, 2.4 lb. Fixed sights. Introduced 2006. MSRP: 1089

PATRIOT SERIES

Patriot Marksman

Introduced in 2002 this .45 ACP pistol has a 5" match grade barrel. Fixed sights. Many special features such as a beveled mag well, lowered and flared ejection port. Checkered wood grips. Magazine capacity is 8 rounds. Weight is about 38 oz.

NIB	Exc.	V.G.	Good	Fair	Poor
875	675	—	—	—	—

Patriot Expert

As above but fitted with a Bomar target-style adjustable rear sight.

NIB	Exc.	V.G.	Good	Fair	Poor
1295	975	—	—	—	—

RIFLES

Coyote Target

Chambered for the.22 LR or .22 Magnum cartridge and fitted with an 18.375" heavy bull barrel. Receiver is drilled and tapped for scope mount. Hardwood stock with high comb and flat-bottom forend. Magazine capacity is 6 or 10 rounds.

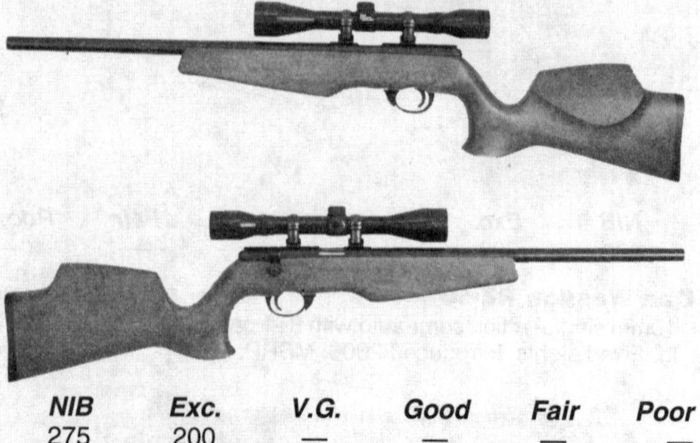

NIB	Exc.	V.G.	Good	Fair	Poor
275	200	—	—	—	—

Coyote Classic

This model is also chambered for the .22 LR or .22 Magnum cartridge. Fitted with a 22.75" barrel with open sights. Drilled and tapped for scope mount. Checkered hardwood stock. Magazine capacity is 6 or 10 rounds. Introduced in 2002.

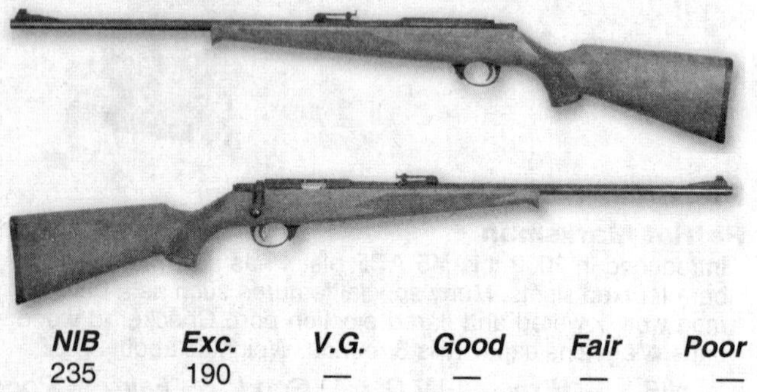

NIB	Exc.	V.G.	Good	Fair	Poor
235	190	—	—	—	—

WESSON FIREARMS CO., INC.

Palmer, Massachusetts

The company was founded in 1968 by Daniel B. Wesson, the great-grandson of D.B. Wesson, co-founder of Smith & Wesson. This line of handguns is unique for its barrel/shroud interchangeability. Dan Wesson revolvers have established themselves as champion metallic silhouette competition guns. The company offers a comprehensive line of handguns for almost every use. The company will also custom build a handgun to customer specifications. Dan Wesson Arms was restructured on January 4, 1991, and identified as Wesson Firearms Company, Inc. Wesson handguns made after this date will be stamped with this new corporate name. In 1995 the company declared bankruptcy. (See WESSON, DAN FIREARMS above.)

Model 11

A .357 Magnum caliber double-action swing-out cylinder revolver with interchangeable 2.5", 4", or 6" barrels and a 6-shot cylinder. Blued with walnut grips. Manufactured in 1970 and 1971.

NIB	Exc.	V.G.	Good	Fair	Poor
200	175	150	125	100	75

NOTE: Extra barrels add 25 percent per barrel.

Model 12

As above, with adjustable target sights.

NIB	Exc.	V.G.	Good	Fair	Poor
250	225	200	175	125	100

Model 14

As above, with a recessed barrel locking nut and furnished with a spanner wrench. Manufactured from 1971 to 1975.

NIB	Exc.	V.G.	Good	Fair	Poor
250	200	175	150	100	75

Model 15

As above, with adjustable target sights.

NIB	Exc.	V.G.	Good	Fair	Poor
275	225	200	175	125	100

Model 8

As above, in .38 Special caliber.

NIB	Exc.	V.G.	Good	Fair	Poor
225	175	150	125	100	75

Model 9

As the Model 15, with adjustable sights and in .38 Special caliber. Manufactured from 1971 to 1975.

NIB	Exc.	V.G.	Good	Fair	Poor
250	225	200	175	125	100

.22 CALIBER REVOLVERS

Model 22

This is a double-action target revolver chambered for the .22 LR cartridge. It is available in 2", 4", 6", and 8" barrel length with a choice of standard rib shroud, ventilated rib shroud, or ventilated heavy rib shroud. All variations feature an adjustable rear sight, red ramp interchangeable front sight and target grips. Offered in bright blue or stainless steel finish. For revolvers with standard barrel assembly weights are: 2"—36 oz., 4"—40 oz., 6"—44 oz., and 8"—49 oz.

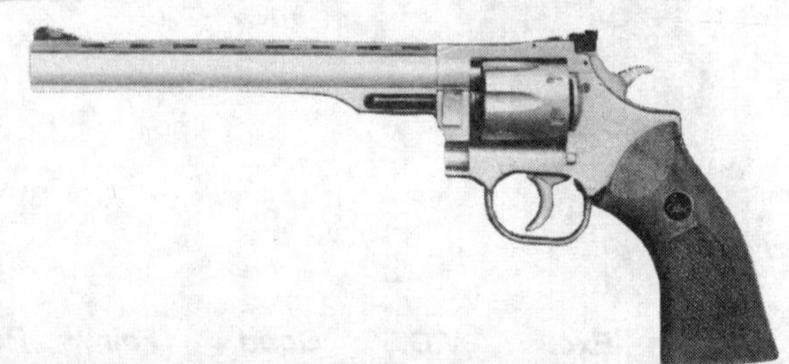

REMINDER

Firearms are part of our nation's history and represent an opportunity to learn more about their role in that American experience. If done skillfully, firearms collecting can be a profitable hobby as well.

Model 722

Same as above but with stainless steel finish.

Model 22M

Same as above but chambered for .22 Magnum with blued finish.

Model 722M

Same as above but chambered for .22 Magnum with stainless steel finish.

Standard Rib Shroud

NIB	Exc.	V.G.	Good	Fair	Poor
280	250	200	150	100	75

Ventilated Rib Shroud

NIB	Exc.	V.G.	Good	Fair	Poor
300	275	225	150	100	75

Ventilated Heavy Rib Shroud

NIB	Exc.	V.G.	Good	Fair	Poor
330	280	240	200	125	100

NOTE: Add 10 percent to prices for stainless steel finish.

P22 Pistol Pac

This model is also a target revolver similar to the Model 22 and its variations. Chambered for the .22 LR or .22 Magnum, it is also offered with three types of barrel shrouds: standard, ventilated, or ventilated heavy. It is available in blued or stainless steel finish. The principal feature of the Pistol Pac is the three barrel assemblies in 2.5", 4", 6", and 8" with extra grips, four additional front sights, and a fitted carrying case.

Standard Rib Shroud

NIB	Exc.	V.G.	Good	Fair	Poor
500	450	400	350	300	150

Ventilated Rib Shroud

NIB	Exc.	V.G.	Good	Fair	Poor
600	550	500	450	350	150

Ventilated Heavy Rib Shroud

NIB	Exc.	V.G.	Good	Fair	Poor
650	600	550	475	350	150

NOTE: Add 10 percent to prices for stainless steel finish.

HP22 Hunter Pac

This model is chambered for the .22 Magnum cartridge. The set includes a ventilated heavy 8" shroud, a ventilated 8" shroud only with Burris scope mounts and Burris scope in either 1.5x4X variable or fixed 2X, a barrel changing tool, and fitted carrying case. Finish is blued or stainless steel.

NOTE: Hunter Pacs are a special order item and should be evaluated at the time of sale.

.32 CALIBER REVOLVERS

Model 32

This model is a target revolver chambered for the .32 H&R Magnum cartridge. It is offered in 2", 4", 6", or 8" barrel lengths with choice of rib shrouds. All variations are fitted with adjustable rear sight, red ramp interchangeable front sight, and target grips. Available in blued or stainless steel finish. Weights depend on barrel length and shroud type but are between 35 oz. and 53 oz.

Model 732

Same as above but with stainless steel finish.

Model 322

Same as above but chambered for .32-20 cartridge with blued finish.

Model 7322

Same as above but chambered for .32-20 cartridge with stainless steel finish.

Standard Rib Shroud

NIB	Exc.	V.G.	Good	Fair	Poor
275	225	200	150	100	75

Ventilated Rib Shroud

NIB	Exc.	V.G.	Good	Fair	Poor
300	250	225	150	100	75

Ventilated Heavy Rib Shroud

NIB	Exc.	V.G.	Good	Fair	Poor
325	275	250	150	100	75

NOTE: Add 10 percent to prices for stainless steel finish.

P32 Pistol Pac

This set offers the same calibers, barrel shrouds, and finishes as the above models but in a set consisting of 2", 4", 6", and 8" barrels with extra grips, four additional sights, and fitted case.

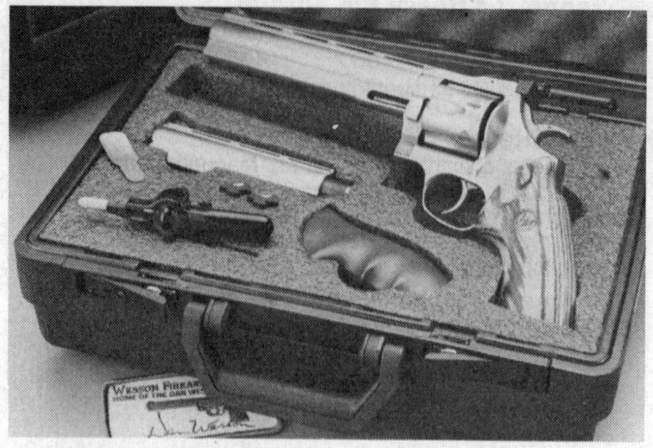

Standard Rib Shroud

NIB	Exc.	V.G.	Good	Fair	Poor
500	450	400	300	150	100

Ventilated Rib Shroud

NIB	Exc.	V.G.	Good	Fair	Poor
575	500	450	325	150	100

Ventilated Heavy Rib Shroud

NIB	Exc.	V.G.	Good	Fair	Poor
650	600	500	400	200	125

NOTE: Add 10 percent to prices for stainless steel finish.

HP32 Hunter Pac

This model is chambered for the .32 H&R Magnum or .32-20 cartridge. The set includes a ventilated heavy 8" shroud, a ventilated 8" shroud only with Burris scope mounts and Burris scope in either 1.5x4X variable or fixed 2X, a barrel-changing tool, and fitted carrying case. Finish is blued or stainless steel.

NOTE: Hunter Pacs are a special order item and should be evaluated at the time of sale.

.357 MAGNUM AND .38 CALIBER REVOLVERS

Model 14

This is a double-action service revolver chambered for the .357 Magnum cartridge. Available with 2", 4", or 6" barrel with service shroud. It has fixed sights, service grip, and is offered in blued or stainless steel finish.

Model 714

Same as above but with stainless steel finish.

Model 8

Same as above but chambered for .38 Special cartridge with blued finish.

Model 708

Same as above but chambered for .38 Special with stainless steel finish.

NIB	Exc.	V.G.	Good	Fair	Poor
225	175	150	125	100	75

NOTE: Add 10 percent to prices for stainless steel finish.

P14/8 Pistol Pac

This set consists of a 2", 4", and 6" barrel with service shroud and fixed sights. It has an extra grip and fitted carrying case. The P14 is chambered for the .357 Mag. and the P8 is chambered for the .38 Special.

NIB	Exc.	V.G.	Good	Fair	Poor
375	300	250	200	150	100

NOTE: Add 10 percent to prices for stainless steel finish.

Model 15

This model is designed as a double-action target revolver chambered for the .357 Magnum cartridge. It is available with 2", 4", 6", 8", and 10" barrel lengths with standard rib shroud. It features adjustable rear sight, red ramp interchangeable front sight, and target grips. Offered with blued finish. Weights according to barrel length are: 2"-32 oz., 4"-36 oz., 6"-40 oz., 8"-44 oz., 10"-50 oz.

Model 715

Same as above but with stainless steel finish.

Model 9

Same as above but chambered for .38 Special cartridge with blued finish.

Model 709

Same as above but with stainless steel finish.

Standard Rib Shroud

NIB	Exc.	V.G.	Good	Fair	Poor
275	225	200	150	100	75

Ventilated Rib Shroud

NIB	Exc.	V.G.	Good	Fair	Poor
300	250	225	150	100	75

Ventilated Heavy Rib Shroud

NIB	Exc.	V.G.	Good	Fair	Poor
325	275	250	150	100	75

NOTE: Add 10 percent to prices for stainless steel finish.

HP15 Hunter Pac

This model is chambered for the .357 Magnum cartridge. The set includes a ventilated heavy 8" shroud, a ventilated 8" shroud only with Burris scope mounts and Burris scope in either 1.5x4X variable or fixed 2X, a barrel changing tool, and fitted carrying case. Finish is blued or stainless steel.

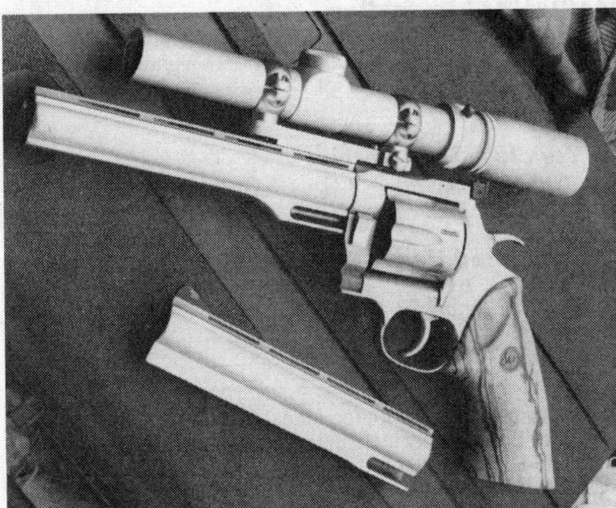

NOTE: Hunter Pacs are a special order item and should be evaluated at the time of sale.

Model 40/Supermag

This model is a target revolver chambered for the .357 Maximum cartridge. It has an adjustable rear sight, red ramp interchangeable front sight, ventilated rib shroud, and target grip. Barrel lengths are 4", 6", 8", or 10". A ventilated slotted shroud is available in 8" only. For 1993 a compensated barrel assembly, "CBA," was added to the product line as a complete gun. Finish is blued. Weighs approximately 64 oz. with ventilated rib shroud barrel.

Model 740

Same as above but with stainless steel finish.

Ventilated Rib Shroud

NIB	Exc.	V.G.	Good	Fair	Poor
400	350	300	250	200	100

Ventilated Slotted Shroud—8" barrel only

NIB	Exc.	V.G.	Good	Fair	Poor
450	400	350	300	200	100

Ventilated Heavy Rib Shroud

NIB	Exc.	V.G.	Good	Fair	Poor
475	425	375	300	200	100

NOTE: Add 10 percent to prices for stainless steel finish. For .357 Supermag with compensated barrel assembly add $30.

HP40 Hunter Pac

This model is chambered for the .357 Supermag cartridge. The set includes a ventilated heavy 8" shroud, a ventilated 8" shroud only with Burris scope mounts and Burris scope in either 1.5x4X variable or fixed 2X, a barrel changing tool, and fitted carrying case. Finish is blued or stainless steel.

NOTE: Hunter Pacs are a special order item and should be evaluated at the time of sale.

Model 375

This model, also known as the .375 Supermag, is chambered for the .357 Maximum cartridge, based on the .375 Winchester cartridge. Offered in 6", 8", 10" barrels in ventilated, ventilated heavy, or ventilated slotted rib barrels. Sights are interchangeable and adjustable. Available in bright blue finish only. Weighs approximately 64 oz. with ventilated rib shroud barrel.

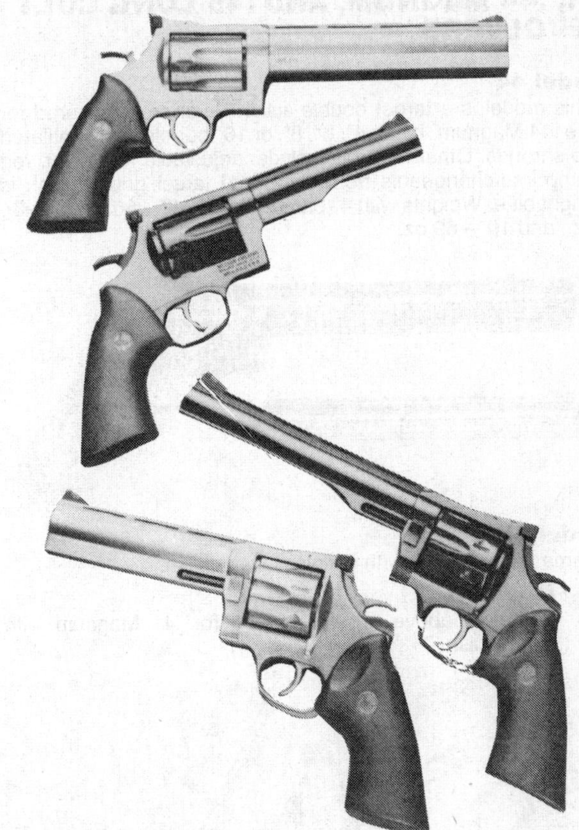

Ventilated Rib Shroud

NIB	Exc.	V.G.	Good	Fair	Poor
400	350	300	250	200	100

Ventilated Heavy Rib Shroud

NIB	Exc.	V.G.	Good	Fair	Poor
450	400	350	300	200	100

Ventilated Slotted Shroud—8" barrel only

NIB	Exc.	V.G.	Good	Fair	Poor
475	425	375	300	200	100

P15/9 Pistol Pac

This model is a set with 2", 4", 6", and 8" barrels with standard rib shroud. Chambered for the .357 or .38 Special with standard rib shroud, four additional sights, and extra grip, and carrying case. The P15 is chambered for the .357 Mag. while the P9 is chambered for the .38 Special.

Standard Rib Shroud

NIB	Exc.	V.G.	Good	Fair	Poor
500	450	400	350	150	100

Ventilated Rib Shroud

NIB	Exc.	V.G.	Good	Fair	Poor
575	500	450	350	150	100

Ventilated Heavy Rib Shroud

NIB	Exc.	V.G.	Good	Fair	Poor
650	575	500	400	200	100

NOTE: Add 10 percent to prices for stainless steel finish.

HP375 Hunter Pac

This model is chambered for the .375 Supermag cartridge. The set includes a ventilated heavy 8" shroud, a ventilated 8" shroud only with Burris scope mounts and Burris scope in either 1.5x4X variable or fixed 2X, a barrel changing tool, and fitted carrying case. Finish is blued or stainless steel.

NOTE: Hunter Pacs are a special order item and should be evaluated at the time of sale.

.41, .44 MAGNUM, AND .45 LONG COLT REVOLVERS

Model 44

This model is a target double-action revolver chambered for the .44 Magnum. It has 4", 6", 8", or 10" barrels with ventilated rib shrouds. Other features include: adjustable rear sight, red ramp interchangeable front sight, and target grips. Finish is bright blue. Weights with 4" barrel—40 oz., 6"—56 oz., 8"—64 oz., and 10"—69 oz.

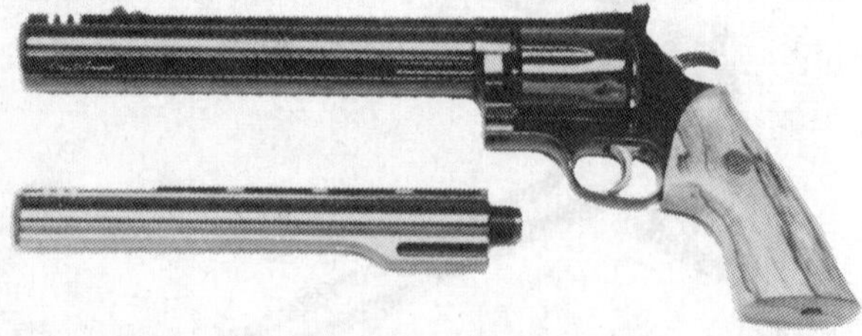

Model 744

Same as above but with stainless steel finish.

Model 41

Same as above but chambered for .41 Magnum with blued finish.

Model 741

Same as above but with stainless steel finish.

Model 45

Same as above but chambered for .45 Long Colt with bright blue finish.

Model 745

Same as above but with stainless steel finish.

Ventilated Rib Shroud

NIB	Exc.	V.G.	Good	Fair	Poor
350	300	250	200	100	75

Ventilated Heavy Rib Shroud

NIB	Exc.	V.G.	Good	Fair	Poor
375	325	275	200	100	75

NOTE: Add 10 percent to prices for stainless steel finish.

P44/P41/P45 Pistol Pac

This set features a 6" and 8" barrel assembly with ventilated rib shroud, an extra grip, two additional front sights, and a fitted carrying case. Chambered for .41 Magnum, .44 Magnum, or .45 Long Colt.

Ventilated Rib Shroud

NIB	Exc.	V.G.	Good	Fair	Poor
525	475	400	300	200	100

Ventilated Heavy Rib Shroud

NIB	Exc.	V.G.	Good	Fair	Poor
575	525	425	300	200	100

NOTE: Add 10 percent to prices for stainless steel finish.

HP41/44 Hunter Pac

This model is chambered for either the .41 or .44 Magnum cartridge. The set includes a ventilated heavy 8" shroud, a ventilated 8" shroud only with Burris scope mounts and Burris scope in either 1.5x4X variable or fixed 2X, a barrel changing tool, and fitted carrying case. Finish is blued or stainless steel.

NOTE: Hunter Pacs are a special order item and should be evaluated at the time of sale.

Model 445

This double-action target revolver is chambered for the .445 Supermag cartridge. Barrel lengths offered are 8" with ventilated slotted rib shroud, 8" ventilated heavy slotted rib shroud, or 10" ventilated slotted rib shroud. Barrel lengths are also available in 4", 6", 8", and 10" with choice of ventilated rib or ventilated heavy rib shrouds. Introduced in 1993 is a compensated barrel assembly available as a complete gun. This is designated the "CBA." Fitted with adjustable rear sights, red ramp interchangeable front sight, and target grips. Finish is bright blue. Typical weight with 8" ventilated rib shroud barrel is about 62 oz.

Model 7445

Same as above but with stainless steel finish.

Ventilated Rib Shroud

NIB	Exc.	V.G.	Good	Fair	Poor
400	350	300	250	200	100

This symbol denotes "Sleepers" with rapidly-rising values and/or significant collector potential.

Ventilated Heavy Rib Shroud

NIB	Exc.	V.G.	Good	Fair	Poor
430	380	330	250	200	100

NOTE: Add 10 percent to prices for stainless steel finish. For .44 Magnum and .445 Supermag with compensated barrel assembly add $30.

Model 7445 Alaskan Guide Special

This limited edition model (only 500 were produced) is chambered for the .445 Supermag cartridge. It features a 4" ventilated heavy compensated shroud barrel assembly, synthetic grips, and a matte black titanium nitride finish. Overall barrel length is 5.5" and the revolver weighs 56 oz.

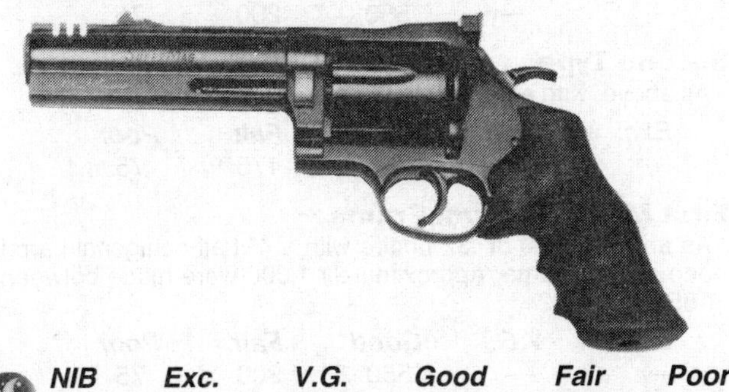

NIB	Exc.	V.G.	Good	Fair	Poor
900	700	600	350	200	100

REMINDER
Perhaps the best advice is for the collector to take his time. Do not be in a hurry, and do not allow yourself to be rushed into making a decision. Learn as much as possible about the firearm you are interested in collecting.

HP455 Hunter Pac

This model is chambered for the .445 Supermag cartridge. The set includes a ventilated heavy 8" shroud, a ventilated 8" shroud only with Burris scope mounts and Burris scope in either 1.5x4X variable or fixed 2X, a barrel changing tool, and fitted carrying case. Finish is blued or stainless steel.

NOTE: Hunter Pacs are a special order item and should be evaluated at the time of sale.

FIXED BARREL HANDGUNS

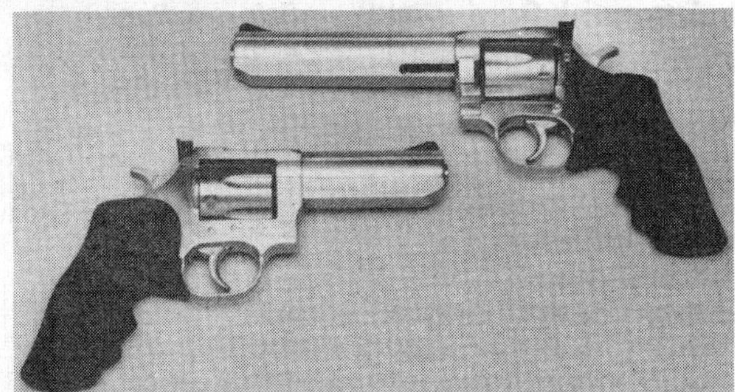

Model 38P

This model is a 5-shot double-action revolver designed for the .38 Special cartridge. Barrel is 2.5" with fixed sights. Choice of wood or rubber grips. Finish is blued. Weighs 24.6 oz.

NIB	Exc.	V.G.	Good	Fair	Poor
200	175	150	125	100	75

Wesson Firearms Silhouette .22

This model is a 6-shot .22 LR single-action-only revolver with a 10" barrel. Fitted with compact-style grips, narrow notch rear sight with choice of ventilated or ventilated heavy rib shroud. Finish is blued or stainless steel. Weighs 55 oz. with ventilated rib shroud and 62 oz. with ventilated heavy rib shroud.

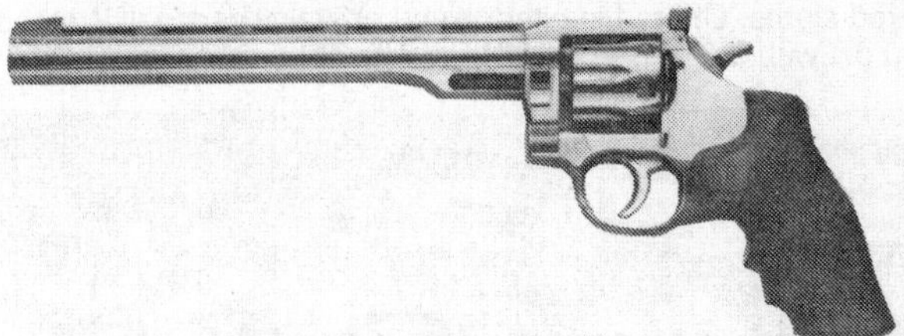

Ventilated Rib Shroud

NIB	Exc.	V.G.	Good	Fair	Poor
375	325	275	225	150	100

Ventilated Heavy Rib Shroud

NIB	Exc.	V.G.	Good	Fair	Poor
390	350	290	225	150	100

NOTE: Add 10 percent to prices for stainless steel finish.

Model 738P

Same as above but with stainless steel finish.

NIB	Exc.	V.G.	Good	Fair	Poor
220	190	160	135	100	75

Model 45/745 Pin Gun

This model uses a .44 Magnum frame with 5" barrel with two-stage compensator. Choice of ventilated or ventilated heavy rib shroud configuration. Chambered for .45 ACP with or without half moon clips. Finish is blued or stainless steel. Weighs 54 oz.

Ventilated Rib Shroud

NIB	Exc.	V.G.	Good	Fair	Poor
550	500	450	400	200	100

Ventilated Heavy Rib Shroud

NIB	Exc.	V.G.	Good	Fair	Poor
600	550	500	400	200	100

NOTE: Add 10 percent to prices for stainless steel finish.

Model 14/714 Fixed Barrel Service

Same features as the .357 Magnum Model 14 without the interchangeable barrels. Barrel length are either 2.5" or 4" with fixed sights. Offered in either blued or stainless steel. Weighs 30 oz. with 2.5" barrel and 34 oz. with 4" barrel.

NIB	Exc.	V.G.	Good	Fair	Poor
200	175	150	125	100	75

NOTE: Add 10 percent to prices for stainless steel finish.

Model 15/715 Fixed Barrel Target

Same as the .357 Magnum Model 15 with target sights and grips. Fixed barrel lengths are either 3" or 5". Available in blued or stainless steel. Weighs 37 oz. with 3" barrel and 42 oz. with 5" barrel.

NIB	Exc.	V.G.	Good	Fair	Poor
220	195	160	125	100	75

NOTE: Add 10 percent to prices for stainless steel finish.

WESSON, EDWIN

Hartford, Connecticut

Dragoon

A .45 caliber percussion revolver with a 7" round barrel and 6-shot unfluted cylinder. The barrel blued, the frame case hardened and the walnut grips fitted with a brass buttcap. Manufactured in 1848 and 1849.

Exc.	V.G.	Good	Fair	Poor
—	—	9000	5000	—

WESSON, FRANK

Worcester, Massachusetts
Springfield, Massachusetts

Manual Extractor Model

A .22 caliber spur trigger single-shot pistol with a 4" octagonal barrel and thin brass frame. The barrel release is located in the front of the trigger. No markings. Approximately 200 were made in 1856 and 1857.

Exc.	V.G.	Good	Fair	Poor
—	—	900	400	100

First Model Small Frame

As above, with a 3", 3.5", or 6" half-octagonal barrel. Blued with rosewood or walnut grips. The barrel marked "Frank Wesson Worcester Mass/Pat'd Oct. 25, 1859 & Nov. 11, 1862." Serial numbered from 1 to 2500.

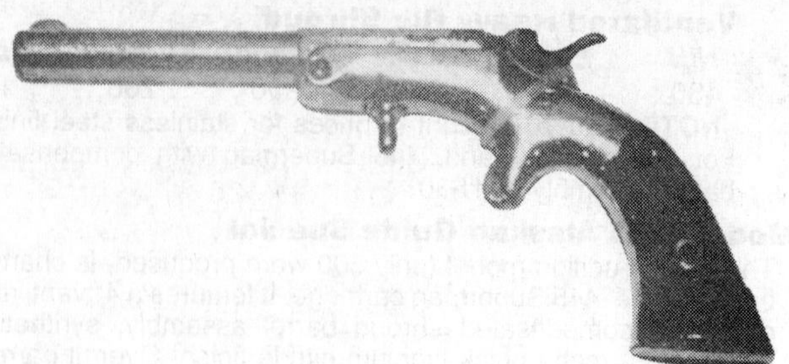

Exc.	V.G.	Good	Fair	Poor
—	—	550	200	75

Second Type

As above, with a flat sighted frame and a circular sideplate.

Exc.	V.G.	Good	Fair	Poor
—	—	500	175	75

First Model Medium Frame

As above, in .30 or .32 rimfire with a 4" half-octagonal barrel and an iron frame. Approximately 1,000 were made between 1859 and 1862.

Exc.	V.G.	Good	Fair	Poor
—	—	550	200	75

Medium Frame Second Model

As above, with a longer spur trigger and a slightly wider frame at the barrel hinge. Manufactured from 1862 to 1870.

Exc.	V.G.	Good	Fair	Poor
—	—	550	200	75

Small Frame Pocket Rifle

A .22 caliber spur trigger single-shot pistol with a 6" half octagonal barrel and narrow brass frame. This model is adopted for use with a detachable skeleton shoulder stock. The barrel marked "Frank Wesson Worcester, Mass." Manufactured from 1865 to 1875 with approximately 5,000 made.

Pistol Only

Exc.	V.G.	Good	Fair	Poor
—	—	850	300	100

NOTE: Matching shoulder stock add 100 percent.

Medium Frame Pocket Rifle

As above, in .22, .30, or .32 rimfire with a 10" or 12" half octagonal barrel. Approximately 1,000 were made from 1862 to 1870.

Pistol Only

Exc.	V.G.	Good	Fair	Poor
—	—	500	200	75

NOTE: Matching shoulder stock add 100 percent.

Model 1870 Small Frame Pocket Rifle

As above, in .22 caliber with a 10", 12", 15", or 18" or 20" half octagonal barrel that rotates to the side for loading. This model was made with either a brass or iron frame. It has a half cocked notch on the hammer.

Pistol Only

Exc.	V.G.	Good	Fair	Poor
—	—	550	200	75

NOTE: Matching shoulder stock add 100 percent.

1870 Medium Frame Pocket Rifle First Type

As above, but with a slightly larger frame chambered for .32 rimfire. Approximately 5,000 were made from 1870 to 1893.

Pistol Only

Exc.	V.G.	Good	Fair	Poor
—	—	500	175	75

NOTE: Match shoulder stock add 100 percent.

1870 Medium Frame Pocket Rifle Second Type

As above, with an iron frame and a push-button half cocked safety.

Pistol Only

Exc.	V.G.	Good	Fair	Poor
—	—	475	175	75

NOTE: Match shoulder stock add 100 percent.

1870 Medium Frame Pocket Rifle Third Type

As above, with three screws on the left side of the frame.

Pistol Only

Exc.	V.G.	Good	Fair	Poor
—	—	475	175	75

NOTE: Matching shoulder stock add 100 percent.

1870 Large Frame Pocket Rifle First Type

As above, in .32, .38, .42, or .44 rimfire with an octagonal barrel from 15" to 24" in length. The barrel marked "Frank Wesson Worcester, Mass Patented May 31, 1870." Fewer than 250 of these rifles were made between 1870 and 1880.

Pistol Only

Exc.	V.G.	Good	Fair	Poor
—	—	1500	550	200

NOTE: Matching shoulder stock add 100 percent.

1870 Large Frame Pocket Rifle Second Type

As above, with a sliding extractor.

Pistol Only

Exc.	V.G.	Good	Fair	Poor
—	—	1500	550	200

NOTE: Matching shoulder stock add 100 percent.

Small Frame Superposed Pistol

A .22 caliber spur trigger over/under pocket pistol with 2" or 2.5" octagonal barrels that revolve. Approximately 3,500 were made between 1868 and 1880. On occasion. this pistol is found with a sliding knife blade mounted on the side of the barrels. The presence of this feature would add approximately 25 percent to the values listed.

Exc.	V.G.	Good	Fair	Poor
—	—	1750	850	250

Medium Frame Superposed Pistol

As above, in .32 rimfire with 2.5" or 3.5" barrels. As with the smaller version, this pistol is occasionally found with a sliding knife blade mounted on the barrels that would add 25 percent to the values listed. Manufactured from 1868 to 1880.

First Type Marked "Patent Applied For"

Exc.	V.G.	Good	Fair	Poor
—	—	1250	400	100

Second Type Marked "Patent December 15, 1868"

Exc.	V.G.	Good	Fair	Poor
—	—	1200	400	100

Third Type Full-Length Fluted Barrels

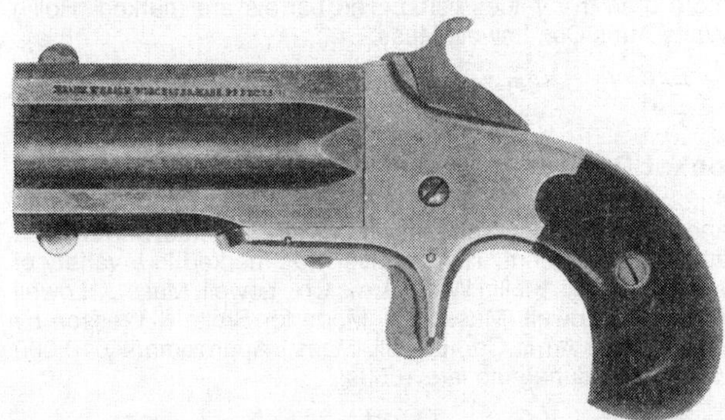

Courtesy W.P. Hallstein III and son Chip

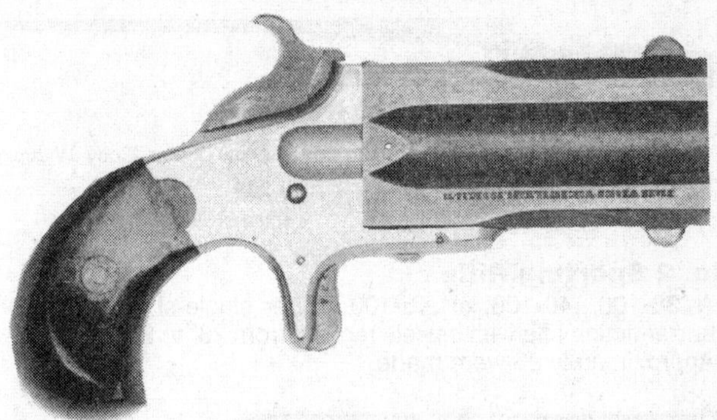

Courtesy W.P. Hallstein III and son Chip

Exc.	V.G.	Good	Fair	Poor
—	—	1500	450	150

Large Frame Superposed Pistol

As above, in .41 rimfire with a 3" octagonal barrel fitted with a sliding knife blade. Approximately 2,000 were made from 1868 to 1880.

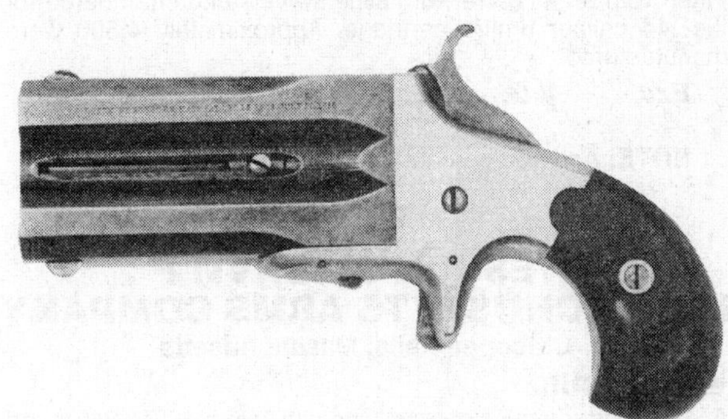

Courtesy W.P. Hallstein III and son Chip

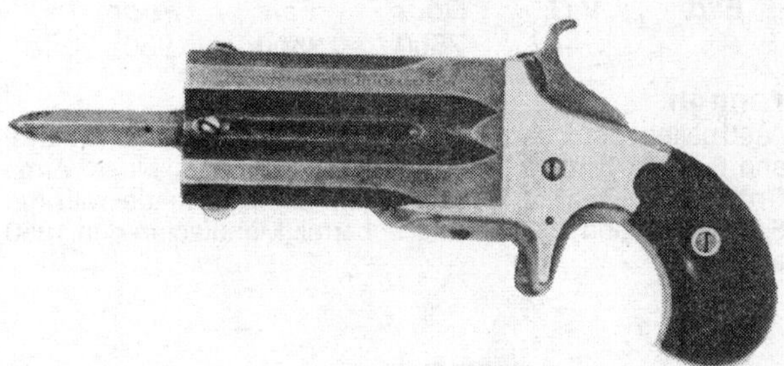

Courtesy W.P. Hallstein III and son Chip

Exc.	V.G.	Good	Fair	Poor
—	—	2750	1250	400

No. 1 Long Range Rifle

A .44-100 or .45-100 caliber single-shot dropping block rifle with a 34" octagonal barrel. Blued with a checkered walnut stock. The barrel marked "F. Wesson Mfr. Worcester, Mass. Long Range Rifle Creedmoor." Manufactured in 1876.

Exc.	V.G.	Good	Fair	Poor
—	12500	4500	2000	500

No. 2 Mid-Range or Hunting Rifle

Similar to the above, with the firing pin located in a bolster on the right side of the receiver. The trigger guard has a rear finger loop. Standard barrel length 28", 32", and 34" and marked "F. Wesson Maker Worcester, Mass." The 32" and 34" barrels are occasionally marked "Long Range Rifle Creedmoor." Approximately 100 were made.

Courtesy Buffalo Bill Historical Center, Cody, Wyoming

Exc.	V.G.	Good	Fair	Poor
—	7250	3750	1750	500

No. 2 Sporting Rifle

A .38-100, .40-100, or .45-100 caliber single-shot dropping-barrel-action rifle with barrels ranging from 28" to 34" in length. Approximately 25 were made.

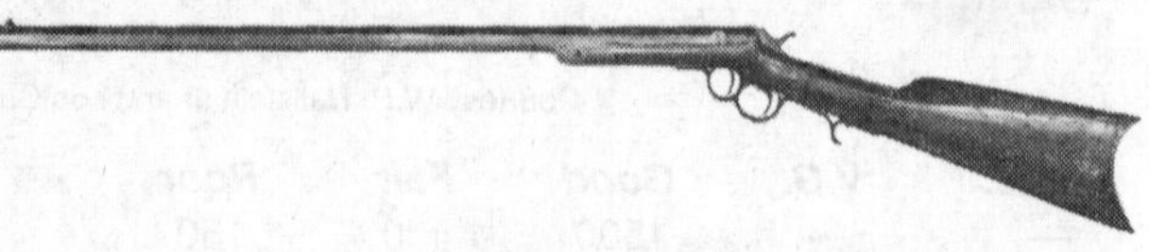

Courtesy Buffalo Bill Historical Center, Cody, Wyoming

Exc.	V.G.	Good	Fair	Poor
—	8250	3750	1750	500

Military Carbine

Fitted with a 24" barrel with sling swivels and chambered for the .44 caliber rimfire cartridge. Approximately 4,500 were manufactured.

Exc.	V.G.	Good	Fair	Poor
—	—	2500	1100	500

NOTE: Add 100 percent for martially marked examples.

WESSON & LEAVITT MASSACHUSETTS ARMS COMPANY

Chicopee Falls, Massachusetts

Revolving Rifle

A .40 caliber percussion revolving rifle with a 16" to 24" round barrel and 6-shot cylinder. Blued with a walnut stock. Approximately 25 were made in 1849.

Exc.	V.G.	Good	Fair	Poor
—	—	7500	3500	950

Dragoon

A .40 caliber percussion revolver with a 6.25" or 7" round barrel and 6-shot cylinder. These pistols are marked "Mass. Arms Co./Chicopee Falls." Approximately 30 were made with the 6.25" barrel and 750 with the 7" barrel. Manufactured in 1850 and 1851.

Courtesy Milwaukee Public Museum, Milwaukee, Wisconsin

Exc.	V.G.	Good	Fair	Poor
—	—	4750	2000	500

WESTERN ARMS

SEE—Bacon

WESTERN ARMS CORPORATION

SEE—Ithaca

WESTERN FIELD

Montgomery Ward

"Western Field" is the trade name used by Montgomery Ward & Company on arms that they retail. See Firearms Trade Names List at the end of this book.

WESTLEY RICHARDS & CO., LTD.

Birmingham, England

SEE—British Double Guns

A wide variety of firearms have been produced by this company since its founding. Presently, it produces boxlock and sidelock double-barrel shotguns of both side-by-side and over/under form, bolt-action rifles and double-barrel rifles. Prospective purchasers are advised to secure individual appraisals prior to acquisition.

Westley Richards Deluxe Sidelock

Westley Richards Magazine Rifle

WHEELER, ROBERT

SEE—English Military Firearms

WHITE, ROLLIN

Lowell, Massachusetts

Pocket Pistol

A .32 or .38 rimfire spur trigger single-shot pistol with a 3" or 5" octagonal barrel. Brass or iron frames with walnut grips. The .38 caliber version with the 5" barrel was not produced in large quantities and therefore is worth approximately 25 percent more than the values listed. The barrels are marked "Rollin White Arms Co., Lowell, Mass."

Exc.	V.G.	Good	Fair	Poor
—	—	750	350	150

Pocket Revolver

A .22 caliber spur trigger revolver with a 3.25" octagonal barrel and 7-shot cylinder. The brass frame silver-plated, barrel blued and grips of walnut. This revolver was marked in a variety of ways including "Rollin White Arms Co., Lowell, Mass.," "Lowell Arms Co., Lowell, Mass.," or "Made for Smith & Wesson by Rollin White Arms Co., Lowell, Mass." Approximately 10,000 were made during the late 1860s.

Exc.	V.G.	Good	Fair	Poor
—	—	600	250	75

WHITNEY ARMS COMPANY

INCLUDING
ELI WHITNEY, SR. / P. & E.W. BLAKE / ELI WHITNEY, JR.

As the United States' first major commercial arms maker, Eli Whitney's New Haven plant, which began production in 1798 and continued under family control for the next 90 years, was one of the more important American arms manufactories of the 19th century. Its products, accordingly, are eminently collectible. Moreover, during its 90 years of operation, the Whitney clan produced a number of unusual arms, some exact copies of regulation U.S. martial longarms, others variations and derivatives of U.S. and foreign longarms, a variety of percussion revolvers, and finally a variety of single-shot and repeating breechloading rifles in an attempt to capture a portion of the burgeoning market in these cartridge arms during the post-Civil War period. Contrary to the prevailing myth, Eli Whitney, Sr., who also invented the cotton gin, did NOT perfect a system of interchangeability of parts in the arms industry. His contributions in this line were more as a propagandist for the concept that was brought to fruition by others, notably Simeon North and John Hall.

Eli Whitney, Sr. Armory Muskets, 1798-1824.
1798 U.S. Contract Muskets, Types I-IV

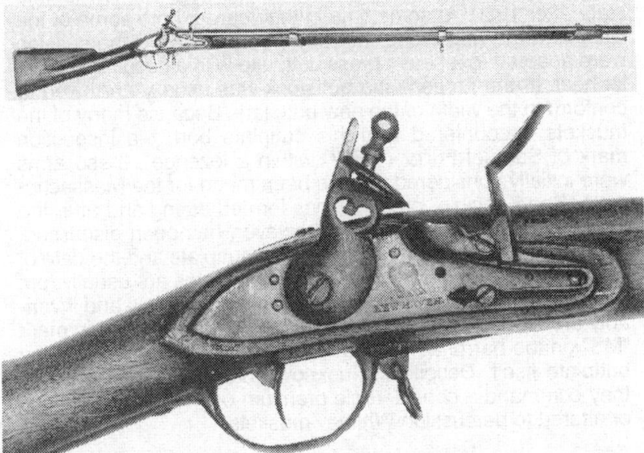

On 14 January 1798, Eli Whitney, Sr., having convinced the U.S. War Department that he could mass-produce interchangeable parts muskets, was awarded a contract for 10,000 muskets following the "Charlesville" (French M1766) pattern, then also being copied at the newly opened Springfield Armory and most of the U.S. musket contractors. Whitney's 1798 contract muskets measure between 58-7/8" and 57-3/4" in overall length, with the longer arms delivered earlier. The .69-caliber smoothbore barrels measure approximately 44", though most are shy of that length by anywhere from 1/16" to a maximum of 1-1/4". Lockplates are flat with a beveled edge and are marked "U.STATES" in a curve on the pointed tail and with a perched eagle with down folded wings over "NEW HAVEN" forward of the cock. Four differences in the material and manner of attachment of the pan distinguish the subtypes. The first deliver of 500 muskets in September of 1801 had an integral, faceted iron pan (Type I); the second delivery of 500 muskets in June of 1802 also had faceted iron pans, but were detachable (Type II). The 1,000 muskets delivered in September of 1802 and March of 1803 had faceted, detachable pans, but these were made of brass instead of iron (Type III). The final 8,000 muskets, delivered between 1803 and 1809, had detachable brass pans with a rounded bottom that Whitney copied from the French M1777 musket (Type IV) and a rounded cock, also copied from the French M1777 musket. Generally speaking, due to the limited production of Types I - III, they should command a higher price; prices are given for the more common Type IV 1798 contract musket. It should be noted however, that about 1804 Whitney delivered 112 Type IV muskets to Connecticut's "1st Company of Governor's Foot Guards." Although similar to the Type IV musket, these 112 arms are distinguished by the absence of the "U.STATES" on the tail of the lock and the addition of the name "CONNECTICUT" to the left side plate. Such an arm should demand a considerable premium over the usual Type IV musket.

Exc.	V.G.	Good	Fair	Poor
—	—	4500	2000	500

Whitney Connecticut, New York, and U.S. 1812 Contract Muskets

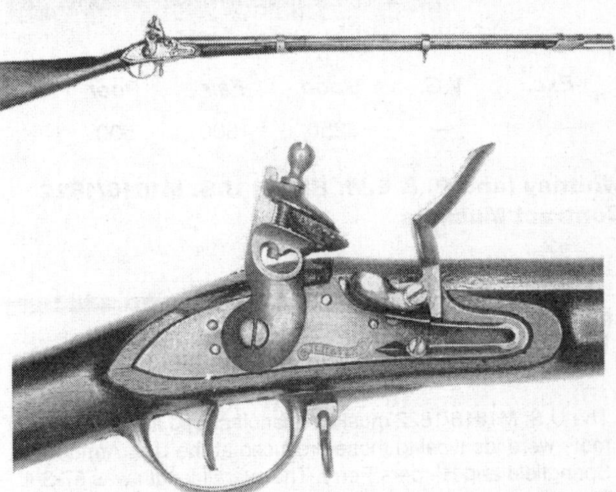

In 1808, Whitney received a contract from the state of New York for 2,000 muskets. In 1810, he received a second contract from the same source for an additional 2,000 muskets, all of which were eventually delivered by mid-1813. In the interim, in 1809, the state of Connecticut contracted with Whitney to deliver 700 muskets per year over the next three years. With the outbreak of the War of 1812, in July of 1812, a contract was let to Eli Whitney for 15,000 muskets (later extended by another 3,000 muskets), conforming to the pattern he had made for the state of New York, but with 42"-long barrels. All of these contract muskets shared most of the same features. Overall length was 58". The .69-caliber smoothbore barrel was nominally 42", though the two state contracts did not rigidly enforce that dimension. The lockplate of these muskets bore the inscription "NEW HAVEN" within a curving scroll forward of the cock. Like the Type III 1798 U.S. contract muskets, the lockplates incorporated a detachable round-bottomed brass pan and a round faced cock. The stock was distinguished by having a low, virtually nonexistent comb similar to that of the 1816 musket pattern. The New York state contract muskets are distinguished by having the state ownership mark "SNY" on the axis of the barrel near the breech. (It should be noted that the first 1,000 muskets delivered under the U.S. 1812 contract were also delivered to New York, but these have the mark across the breech at right angles to the axis of the barrel.) The Connecticut contract muskets are distinguishable by having the state-ownership mark "S.C." (for "state of Connecticut" on the barrel and the top of the comb of the stock. On Connecticut muskets in better condition, the Connecticut coat of arms (a shield with three clusters of grape vines) should also be visible struck into the wood on the left side of the musket opposite the lock. Verifiable Connecticut and New York contract muskets should bring a premium over the U.S. contract muskets.

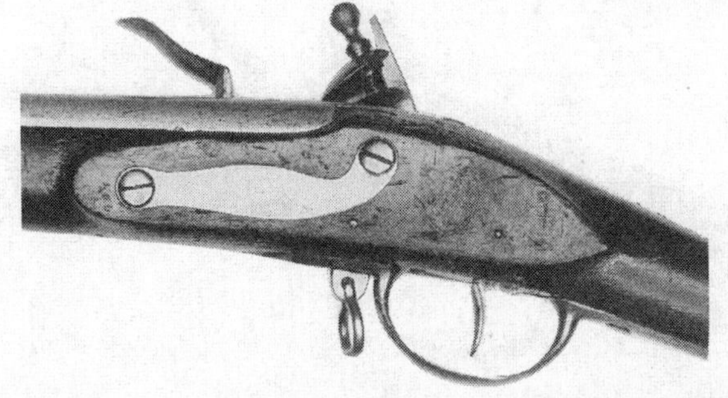

Exc.	V.G.	Good	Fair	Poor
—	—	3250	1500	500

Whitney (and P. & E.W. Blake) U.S. M1816/1822 Contract Muskets

The U.S. M1816/1822 muskets manufactured at Whitney's Armory were identical to those produced at the U.S. Armories at Springfield and Harpers Ferry. The overall length was 57-3/4". The 42"-long, .69-caliber smoothbore barrels were finished with a browning solution until 1831; after that date the metal was left in the polished "bright." The stock and the lock reflect Whitney's earlier attempts impart his design elements into the U.S. patterns. The stock had the low comb of his M1812 musket and the lock incorporated the rounded cock and round bottomed brass pan that he had championed from the French M1777 musket. The lock markings varied during the period that the arm was produced, though all were marked on the pointed tail with the vertical stamp: "NEW HAVEN" arced around the date (1825-1830), or in three vertical lines: "NEW / HAVEN / (date: 1831-1842)." Those made between 1825 and 1830 under the direct supervision of Whitney's nephews bore the two line mark "U.S. / P. & E.W. BLAKE" forward of the cock; those made from 1830 to 1837 bear the "U.S" over "E. WHITNEY" with a crossed arrow and olive branch between; after 1837 the crossed arrow and olive branch motif was eliminated in favor of the simple two lines. In addition to the Whitney Armory's federal contracts, Whitney executed at least one contract with the state of South Carolina in the mid-1830s for an estimated 800 to 2,000 muskets. Basically identical in configuration to the federal contract muskets, the South Carolina muskets were distinguished by the substitution of "S.C." for "U.S." over the "E. WHITNEY" stamp of the lockplate. They also bear the state ownership mark "So. CAROLINA" on the top of the barrel. Due to their relative rarity and Confederate usage (especially if altered to percussion by means of a brazed bolster), the South Carolina contract arms should bring a considerable premium.

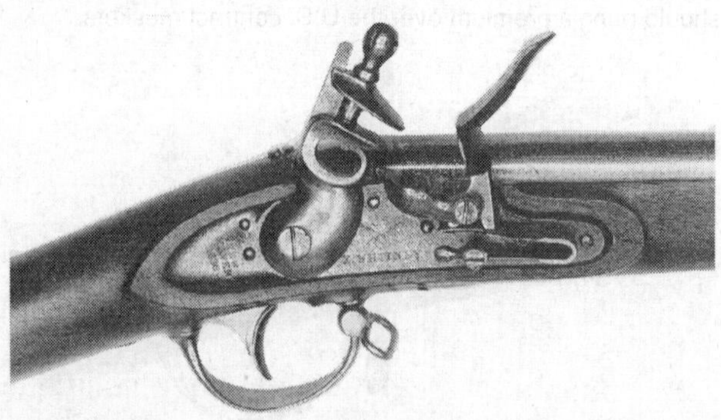

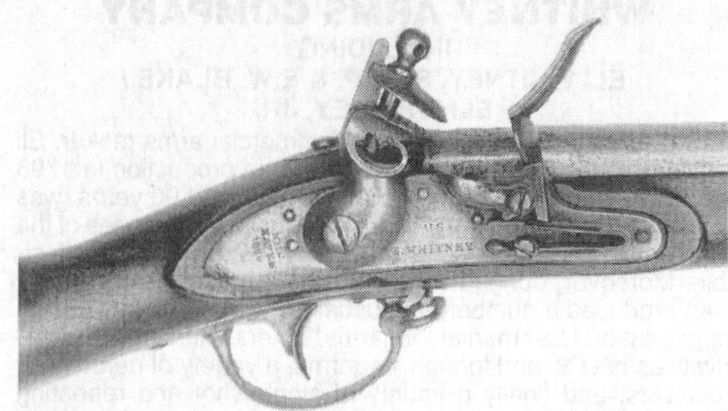

Exc.	V.G.	Good	Fair	Poor
—	—	3500	1500	500

Whitney Armory U.S. M1816/M1822 Muskets, Flintlock or Altered to Percussion and Adapted with "Sea Fencible" Heavy Buttplates

A number of the Whitney U.S. M1816/M1822 muskets were delivered to the Commonwealth of Massachusetts under the terms of the 1808 Militia Act. Many of these were subsequently altered to percussion at the Watertown Arsenal near Boston for the state after 1850. At some time in their career both some of the flintlock arms and those that had been altered to percussion were adapted to a heavy brass buttplate with a peculiar knob at its heel. In the process the buttstock was usually narrowed to conform to the width of the new buttplate. Because many of the muskets encountered with this buttplate bore the inspection mark of Samuel Fuller ("SF/V" within a lozenge), these arms were initially considered to have been made for the Massachusetts "Sea Fencible" organizations formed during and after the War of 1812. That appellation, however, has been dismissed, although the exact purpose of the new buttplate and the date of its application are not known. These butt-plates are usually (but not necessarily) found on Whitney contract muskets and invariably are marked with the Massachusetts state ownership mark "MS" on the barrel as well as rack numbers on the tang of the buttplate itself. Despite the unknown purpose of these arms, they command a considerable premium over standard flintlock or altered to percussion Whitney muskets.

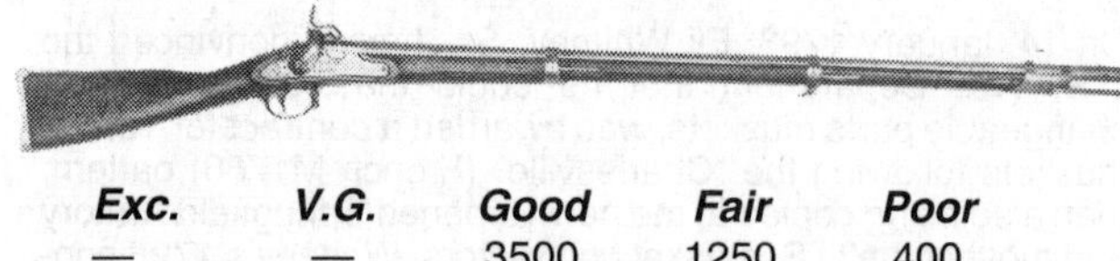

Exc.	V.G.	Good	Fair	Poor
—	—	3500	1250	400

Whitney Armory U.S. M1816/M1822 Muskets, Altered to Percussion

From 1850 through 1856, many of the contract muskets in store at the U.S. arsenals were altered from flintlock to percussion by means of the "Belgian" or "cone-in barrel" method. The system of alteration involved the removal of the flintlock battery from the lock, filing in the screw holes from those parts, substituting a percussion hammer for the cock, plugging the vent, removing the breech plug so as to "upset" the upper, right-hand side top of the barrel, drilling and threading the "upset" section for a cone, reinserting the breech plug, and screwing in a new percussion cone. The percussioned musket was effective but the barrel was considerably weakened by the process, and while some were rifled during the American Civil War, most saw service in that conflict as smoothbores. As a general rule, the muskets so altered generally command about one-third the price of the arm in original flintlock. Exceptions are those with state ownership marks (eg. "OHIO" in the stock), with regimental marks, or with the so-called "Sea Fencible" buttplate.

Whitney Armory Muskets, 1825-1842

Eli Whitney died in 1825. Although he had a son destined to take over the family business, Eli Whitney, Jr. was only 5 years old when his father passed away and could not assume legal possession until he turned 21 in 1842. In the interim, the company was administered by the senior Whitney's trustees, Henry Edwards and James Goodrich, while the plant itself was run by Whitney's nephews, Philo and Eli Whitney Blake. During their control of the factory, three contracts were fulfilled for the U.S. government, one awarded in August of 1822 for 15,000 muskets (delivered between 1826 and 1830), a second awarded in March of 1830 for 8,750 muskets (delivered between 1831 and 1836) and a final contract in January of 1840 for 3,000 muskets (delivered between 1840 and 1842). An additional 6,750 were delivered under annual allotments granted by the War Department between 1835 and 1839 over and above the contracts for distribution to the states under the 1808 Militia Act. Although the 1840 contract had originally called for U.S. M1840 muskets, in April of that year, the contract was altered so that Whitney's plant could continue to deliver what it had delivered consistently from 1824, the U.S. M1816/1822 flintlock musket.

Eli Whitney Jr. Armory Rifles and Rifle-Muskets, 1842-1865

Upon reaching the age of 21 in 1842, Eli Whitney, Jr. assumed command of his late father's gun making empire. Although he realized that the armory required updating to meet the improved tolerances adopted by the U.S. War Department, he also realized that a profit might be made in turning out arms of lesser standards for independent sale to the militia or the states. As a result, the younger Whitney's product line included not only several of the regulation U.S. longarms, but also a number of "good and serviceable" militia arms, including:

Whitney U.S. M1841 Contract Rifle (unaltered)

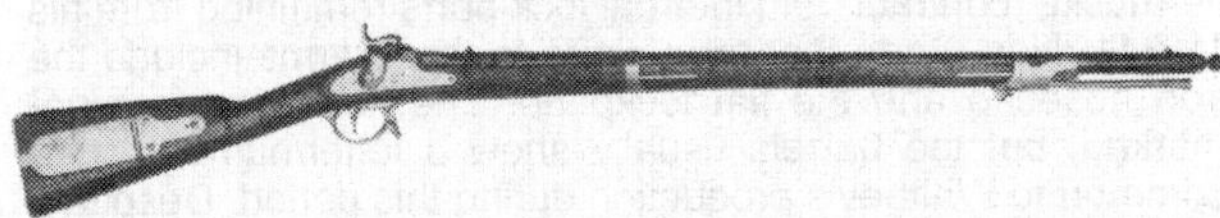

Between 1842 and 1855 Eli Whitney, Jr. received five contracts from the U.S. War Department to manufacture the newly adopted U.S. M1841 percussion rifle: 7,500 on October of 1842 (delivered between 1844 and 1847), 7,500 in March of 1848, subsequently extended to 10,000 in January of 1849 (delivered between 1849 and 1853) 5,000 (previously contracted for by Edward K. Tryon) in October of 1848 (delivered contiguous with the 1848 contract for 10,000), 5,000 in 1853 (delivered between 1853 and 1855), and 100 in 1855 (delivered that year). All except the final 1,100 delivered in 1855 conformed to the model made at Harpers Ferry, and of those 1,100, the only difference of 500 of them was the ramrod. This rifle was 49" in length, overall, having a 33" long browned barrel with .54 caliber rifled (7 groove) bore. The barrel bears the stamp of inspection at the breech, usually "U S /(inspectors' initials) / P," while the left flat (after mid-1848 for Whitney rifles) should also bear the stamping "STEEL" to indicate that the barrel had been rolled from "cast steel." Furniture is brass, the buttplate bearing the stamped letters, "U S." The lockplate is flat with a beveled edge and bears the horizontal two line inscription "E. WHITNEY" / "U S" forward of the hammer and the vertical, two line inscription "N. HAVEN" / (date) on the tail. (The date also appears on the breech plug tang). As originally made, the M1841 rifle was not adapted for a bayonet, though several modifications were made to the rifle between 1855 and 1862 to affect that adaptation.

Exc.	V.G.	Good	Fair	Poor
—	—	4750	1750	500

Whitney U.S. M1841/1855 Contract Rifle, Adapted to Saber Bayonet and Long Range Sights

Before the final 600 rifles (of the 2,600 made in 1855) left the factory, the U.S. War Department contracted with Whitney to bring them up to the standards of the modified U.S. M1841 rifle then being produced or adapted at the Harpers Ferry Armory. The adaptation was two fold. First, a long range rear "ladder" style rear sight, having a 2-1/4" base was soldered to the top of the barrel; then a 1/2" long bayonet lug with 1" guide was brazed to the right side of the barrel, 2-1/2" from the muzzle. To permit disassembly, the old front band was removed and replaced with a shortened version. A new ramrod (also applied to 500 rifles without this adaptation), having an integral iron head cupped for the newly adopted "Minie ball" replaced the flat brass headed ramrod to complete the process; the rifle remained in .54 caliber with 7 grooves. Neither was the front sight modified. Bayonets were furnished by the Ames Manufacturing Company on a separate contract. Rifles so adapted at the Whitney Armory are among the rarer variants of the U.S. M1841 line and prices reflect that rarity.

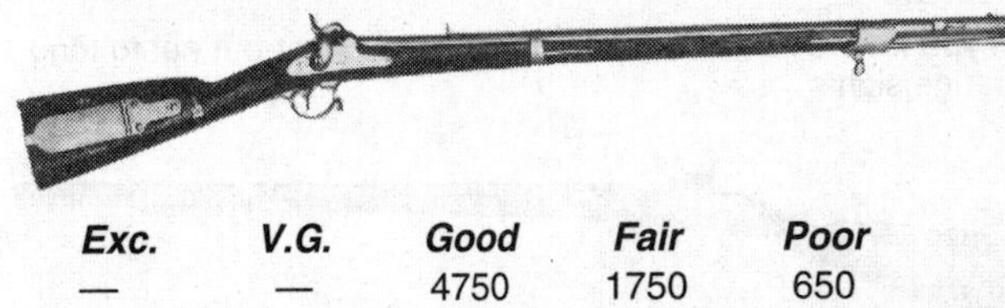

Exc.	V.G.	Good	Fair	Poor
—	—	4750	1750	650

Whitney U.S. M1841 Contract Rifles, Adapted to Saber Bayonets and Long Range Rear Sights (Colt 1862 Adaptation)

A large number of unaltered U.S. M1841 rifles remained on hand in U.S. Arsenals when the Civil War broke out, primarily those of Whitney's and Robbins & Lawrence's manufacture. To upgrade these rifles, revolver maker, Samuel Colt arranged to purchase 10,500 and adapt them to bayonets and long-range sights. The sight that he affixed consisted of the two leaf rear sight he had been using on his revolving rifles, with one leaf flopping forward and one flopping backward from the 100 yard block. The saber bayonet lug he attached consisted of a blued clamping ring with integral 1/2"-long lug attached that could fastened to the barrel so that the lug projected from the right side. These lugs were numbered both to the bayonet and the rifle's barrel, the number appearing on the lower surface of the barrel just behind the location of the clamping ring. Colt also bored the rifles up to .58 caliber, leaving some with 7 grooves but rerifling others with 3 wide grooves. An estimated half of the 10,200 rifles so modified by Colt were of Whitney's earlier production. Due to the Colt association, rifles so modified usually command slightly higher prices than other Civil War adaptations for saber or socket bayonets.

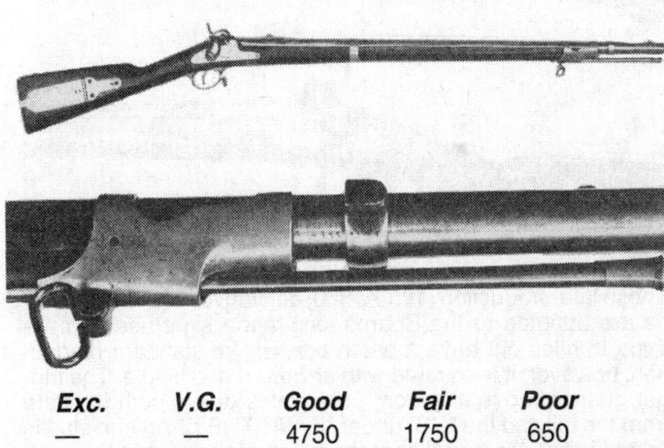

Exc.	V.G.	Good	Fair	Poor
—	—	4750	1750	650

Whitney South Carolina Contract M1841 Rifle

To meet the perceived needs of South Carolina during the anti-slavery debates following the Mexican War Annexation, Whitney produced a variant of the U.S. M1841 rifle for that state, delivering only 274 in 1849. The marking of this rifle differed only in having the letters "S C" on the plate beneath the "E. WHITNEY" stamp. Because South Carolina had previously contracted for 1,000 variant M1841 rifles from William Glaze & Co. in 1853 which accepted a socket bayonet, Whitney provided the 274 1849 dated rifles with that provision also, although the lug was located under the barrel instead of atop it. Because the socket bayonet dominated the forward 3" of the barrel, the front sight was relocated to the top of the upper strap of the front band. Rifles from this contract are exceedingly rare.

Exc.	V.G.	Good	Fair	Poor
—	—	6500	3250	950

Whitney "Good & Serviceable" M1841 Derivatives

From parts or entire rifles rejected for his federal contracts for U.S. M1841 rifles, between 1848 and 1860, Eli Whitney, Jr. assembled a number of rifles similar in overall characteristics to the federal contract rifles but differing both in quality and in a number of minor details. At least four variants were produced between 1855 and 1862 and sold to various states or independent militia companies. Distinguishing characteristics of these four are:

Type I. M1841 rifle adapted to saber bayonet but not to long range sights.

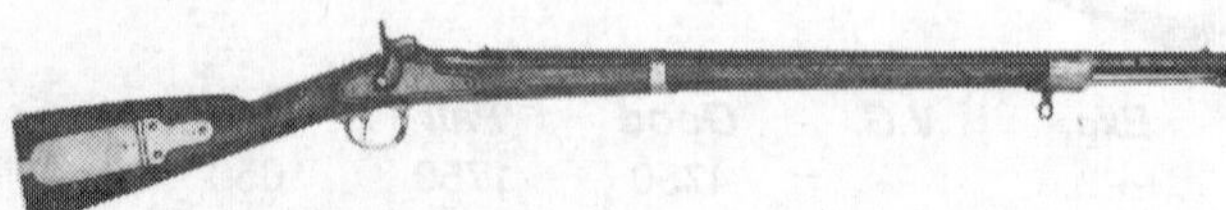

A 1/2"-long saber bayonet lug (either with or without the 1" guide) brazed to the right side of the barrel; long front band replaced with short double strapped band left over from 1855 contract. Some of this type (without 1" guide) are known with "OHIO" state ownership marks and are thought to be from among the 420 purchased by the state in 1861 from Schuyler, Hartley & Graham. Examples are known with the lockplate dated 1855 and without any date or "US" stamp below "E. WHITNEY."

Type II. M1841 rifle adapted to saber bayonet and Sharps long range sight.

These rifles also bear the 1/2" brazed saber bayonet lug (with the 1" guide) and the short front band, but they also have a Sharps M1853 "ladder" rear sight added in lieu of the standard notched iron block. Moreover, rifles in this configuration lack the brass patchbox lid and its underlying cavity for implements and greased patches.

Type III. M1841 rifle adapted to socket bayonet and Sharps long-range sight.

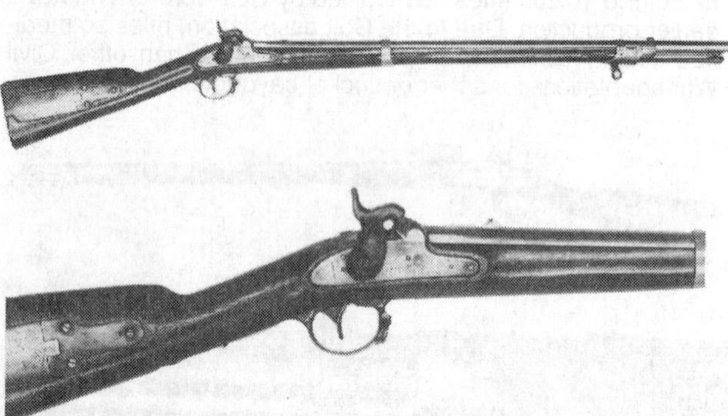

These late-production (1859-1860) derivatives of the M1841 rifle are adapted to the Sharps long-range sight used on the Type II. rifles but have a patch box. Unlike standard production, however, it is covered with an iron lid and hingle. The trigger guard strap is also iron. Lock plates delete both the date from the tail and the "US" under "E. WHITNEY." An iron stud is added below the barrel near the muzzle for a socket bayonet, necessitating the relocation of the brass blade front sight to the upper strap of the forward band. Probably fewer than 100 of this configuration were made, making it the most desirable of the derivative M1841 rifles.

Type IV. M1841 rifle unadapted using modified parts.

Rifles of this configuration use the same markings as the type III rifles but delete entirely the patch box and its lid (like the type II rifles). The trigger guard strap is iron and the lock screws seem to be the same as Whitney used for his Whitney short Enfield derivative rifles. It is suspected that these rifles were purchased from New York dealers and sold to Georgia during the secession crisis of 1860-1861, thereby enhancing their collector's value, though in general Whitney M1841 derivative rifles are equal in pricing:

Exc.	V.G.	Good	Fair	Poor
—	—	3250	1250	500

Whitney M1842 Rifled Musket Derivative

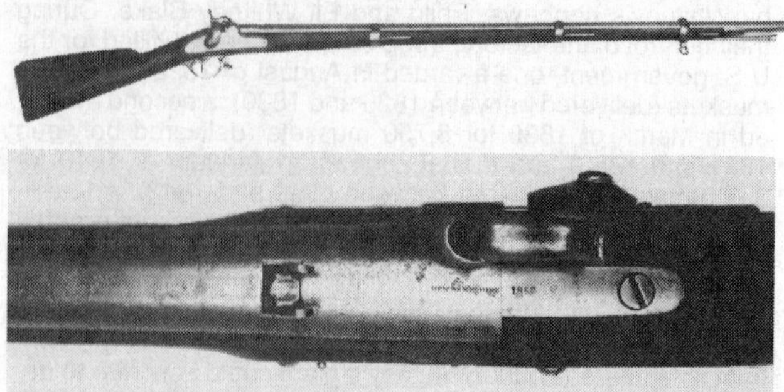

Using rejected U.S. M1842 barrels sold at auction by the Springfield Armory, Whitney assembled approximately 2,000 .69 caliber rifled muskets that he exchanged with the state of New Hampshire in 1858 for a number of old flintlock muskets owned by that state. These rifled muskets exhibit a number of anomalies from the U.S. M1842 musket, although overall length (57-3/4") and the barrel length (42") remain the same as that musket, the bores are rifles with 7 narrow grooves, and in addition to the dates and inspection marks placed at Springfield usually bear the state ownership mark "NEW HAMPSHIRE" on the top of the barrel. In finishing these rifled muskets, Whitney utilized a number of parts from other gun makers, including Sharps M1853 "ladder" style carbine rear sights, bands from the Robbins & Lawrence P1853 Enfield rifle-musket contract, and internal lock parts remaining from his M1841 rifles. Parts that are unique to these arms include the iron nosecap and the flat lockplate. The lockplates are unmarked, but the barrels usually show a letter/number code common to Whitney's production during this period. Despite a production of approximately 2,000 muskets, the survival rate for this type of arm is quite low.

Exc.	V.G.	Good	Fair	Poor
—	—	3250	1250	400

Whitney P1853 "Long Enfield" Rifle-Musket Derivative

Having secured a number of bands and other furniture from the Robbins & Lawrence contract for P1853 Enfield rifle-muskets, about 1859 Whitney developed a derivative of that arm that combined those bands with a 40"-barrel .58 caliber, rifled with 7 grooves that basically resembled the configuration of the U.S. M1855 rifle-musket, a copy of which Whitney was also making. The 56"-long rifle-musket that resulted was sold to state militia companies and two states, Maryland purchasing 2,000 and Georgia contracting for 1,700 (of which 1,225 were delivered). Although several of the components of the furniture were from the Robbins & Lawrence contract, the nosecap was pewter (Enfield style), and the iron buttplate and brass trigger guard bow/iron strap were of a style peculiar to Whitney' Enfield series. The rear sight resembled the ladder pattern of the U.S. M1855 rifle musket. The unique flat, unbeveled lockplate simply bears the one line stamp, "E. WHITNEY" forward of the hammer.

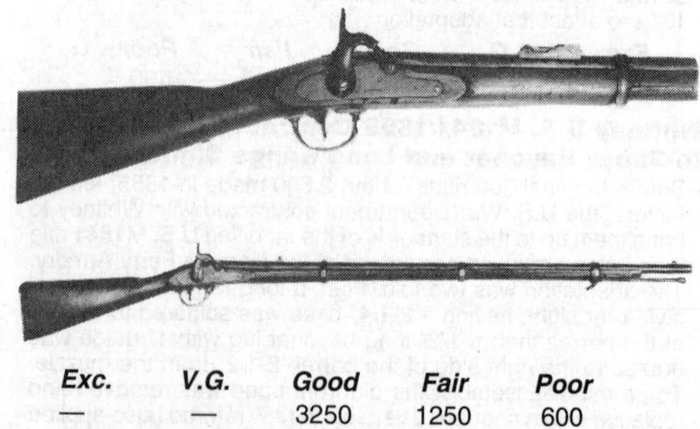

Exc.	V.G.	Good	Fair	Poor
—	—	3250	1250	600

Whitney P1853 "Short Enfield" Rifle Derivative

At the same time that Whitney developed his "Long Enfield" Derivative Rifle-Musket, he also prepared a short version of it similar to the British P1856 sergeant's rifle. Having an overall length of 49", the rifle version had a 33"-long barrel in .58 caliber and rifled with 7 grooves like the rifle-musket. The furniture was basically the same as the rifle-musket as well, with a pewter nosecap, iron buttplate, and combination brass bow and iron strap trigger guard (although some variants are known with all brass P1853 trigger guards). The two iron bands were from the Robbins & Lawrence contract salvage, as were the brass lock screw washers. The flat, unbeveled lockplate is the same style as used in the Long Enfield derivative rifle-muskets and is similarly marked "E. WHITNEY" forward of the hammer. In the manufacture of the rifle, four variants evolved.

Type I. Buttstock incorporated an oval iron patch box; front and rear sights were of standard U.S. M1841 configuration and no provision was made for a saber bayonet.

Type II. Buttstock continued to incorporate an oval iron patch box; rear sight was now the long range "ladder" type on a 2-5/16" base as used on the long Enfield rifle-musket derivative. Front sight was an iron block with integral blade. A 1/2" long saber bayonet lug was added to the right side of the barrel.

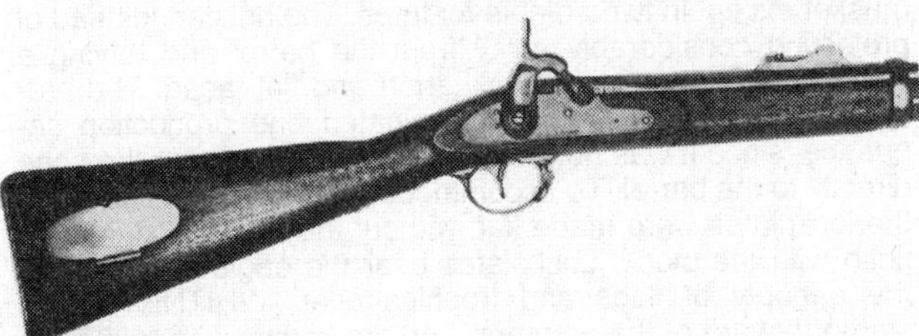

Type III. The oval iron patchbox was deleted from the buttstock. Front and rear sights remain as in Type II, as does bayonet lug.

Type IV. Identical to Type III but with a new single leaf rear sight on a 1-1/4" long base.

Total production of these rifles is estimated to have been between 800 and 1,000, with approximately half of the number going to southern states. Prices should not vary between the four types; however, confirmed Confederate usage will increase the value significantly.

Exc.	V.G.	Good	Fair	Poor
—	—	4250	2000	600

Whitney M1855 Rifle Derivative

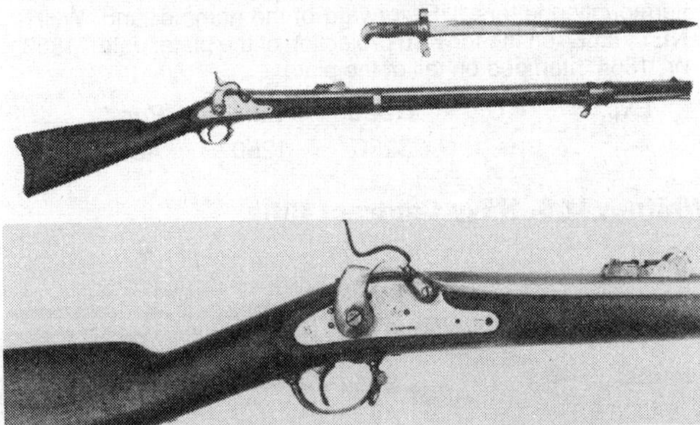

At the same time that Whitney advertised his Enfield derivative series of rifle-muskets and rifles, he also indicated the availability of a short rifle with saber bayonet. This rifle combined rejected barrels made at Harpers Ferry in 1858 for the U.S. M1855 rifles with rejected, unmilled Maynard tape primer lockplates that had been shaved of their top "hump," marked forward of the hammer with the single line stamp, "E. WHITNEY." The buttplate and the trigger guard also conform to that of the U.S. M1855 rifle, but the bands are brass, remaining from Whitney's M1841/1855 rifle contract. Early in production these rifles used round brass lock screw washers following the M1855 pattern; later production used the winged brass lock screw washers that Whitney inherited from the Robbins & Lawrence P1853 rifle-musket contract and which he used on his Enfield series derivatives. At least two patterns of saber bayonet were used on this rifle.

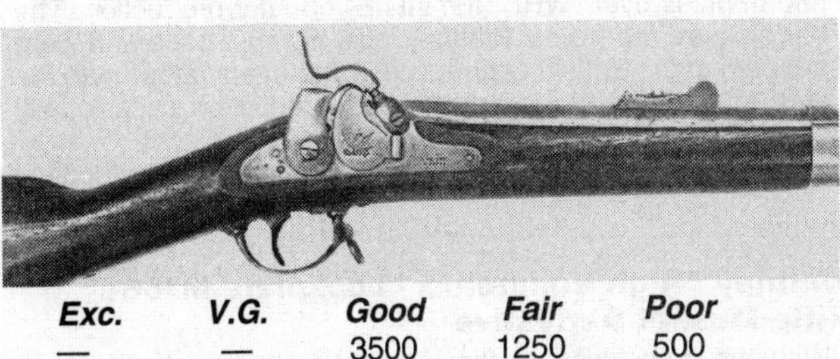

Exc.	V.G.	Good	Fair	Poor
—	—	3500	1250	500

Whitney M1855 Rifle-Musket Derivative

In 1861, Whitney accepted a U.S. contract to produce 40,000 U.S. "M1855" rifle-muskets. What Whitney had in mind under this contract and what the War Department demanded were two different arms. Whitney's product was similar to the U.S. M1855 rifle-musket but differed in a number of respects. The 40" barrel was .58 caliber but was rifled with 7 rather than 3 grooves and was adapted to the English P1853 socket bayonet he had been using on his Enfield derivative rifle-muskets. The initial rear sight, while similar to the U.S. M1855 type, was slightly shorter, having a 2-5/16" base. (On later production, Whitney substituted a shorter, 1-1/4"-long base with a single, pierced leaf sight.) The nosecap, moreover, was made of pewter and followed the Enfield pattern rather than being malleable iron of the U.S. M1855 pattern. On later production, Whitney also substituted brass winged lock screw washers from his Enfield derivative series. The lockplates for these arms were drawn from complete Maynard locks made at the federal armories in 1858 and 1859 but later rejected for flaws. Upon these plates Whitney stamped "E. WHITNEY / N. HAVEN," as on his early Connecticut contract M1861 derivative rifle-muskets. Except for the letter/number code, the barrels are unmarked. Examples are known whose stocks bear indications of issue to the 8th Connecticut Infantry during the Civil War, suggesting Whitney may have sold the few made to Connecticut under his first state contract. Arms with these regimental marks should command a premium over unmarked arms.

Exc.	V.G.	Good	Fair	Poor
—	—	3500	1250	500

Whitney M1861 Connecticut Contract Rifle-Musket Derivative

In 1861 and 1862, Eli Whitney, Jr. entered into two contracts with his home state of Connecticut for respectively 6,000 and 8,000 rifle-muskets generally conforming to the U.S. M1861 rifle musket. A number of exceptions to the U.S. model, however, were permitted. On the first contract, the 40" barrels were in .58 caliber but were made with 7 groove rifling instead of 3 groove; on the second contract, the arms were made with 3-groove rifling. Nosecaps for both contracts were of the U.S. M1855/1861 pattern but were cast in pewter instead of malleable iron. An exception was also permitted in the rear sights, which initially were the same 1-1/4" long base with pierced single leaf that Whitney had used on his Type IV short Enfield derivative rifles, though later the base was changed to conform to the pattern adopted for the U.S. M1861 rifle-musket but still retaining the single leaf. Lockplates were M1861-style, marked forward of the hammer "E. WHITNEY / N. HAVEN" on early production and with an eagle surmounting a panoply of flags and trophies over "WHITNEYVILLE" on later production. The barrels bore the typical Whitney letter/number code and were adapted to the Enfield pattern socket bayonets rather than the U.S. M1855 socket bayonets. Later production occasionally bears the inspection letters "G.W.Q."

Exc.	V.G.	Good	Fair	Poor
—	—	2750	1150	400

Whitney "High Humpback" Lockplate M1861 Rifle-Musket Derivative

With the completion of his Connecticut contracts, Whitney combined the excess parts from its production with some of the unmilled and unshaved lockplates that he still had on hand from his M1855 Rifle Derivatives. The 56"-long rifle-muskets that resulted have 40" barrels in .58 caliber with 3-groove rifling and a rear sight that conforms to the U.S. M1861 pattern that Whitney began making in 1863. The flat, beveled unmilled lockplates bear the two line stamp "E. WHITNEY / N. HAVEN" that Whitney had used on his M1855 rifle-musket derivative and on the early M1861 Connecticut contract rifle-muskets, but showing considerable wear, to the extent that the second line is often incomplete or missing entirely. Photograph evidence indicates that the 21st Connecticut Infantry received some of these rifle-muskets. They are often mistaken as a southern purchase, which artificially raises the asking prices.

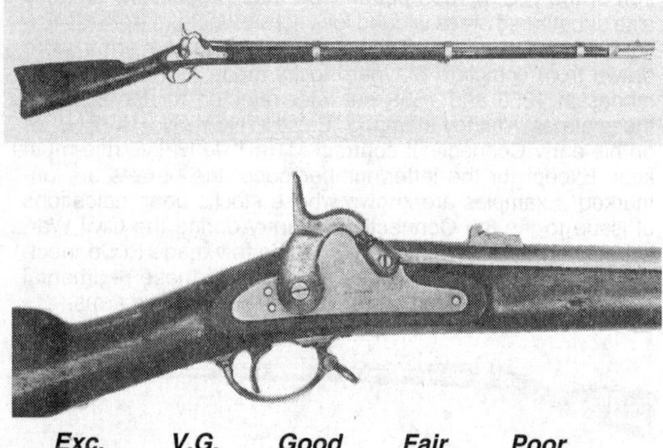

Exc.	V.G.	Good	Fair	Poor
—	—	3250	1250	500

Whitney "Manton" M1861 Rifle-Musket Derivative

In order to dispose of some of his inferior arms from the second Connecticut state contract, Whitney assembled at least 1,300 bearing a fictitious Old English lock stamp "Manton" forward of the hammer and the date "1862" on its tail. In most respects this arm resembled the U.S. M1861 rifle musket, complete with 3-groove rifling in its .58-caliber, 40" barrel with typical Whitney letter/number code near the muzzle (and often also marked "G.W.Q. on its left flat). Nosecaps, in typical Whitney style, were case from pewter instead of being formed from malleable iron. The rear sight closely follows the M1861 pattern but lacks the step on its side walls since it utilized a simple pierced leaf instead of the compound double leaf of the M1861 rifle-musket. These arms were disposed of in the New York City market after the 1863 Draft Riot and issued to the New York National Guard.

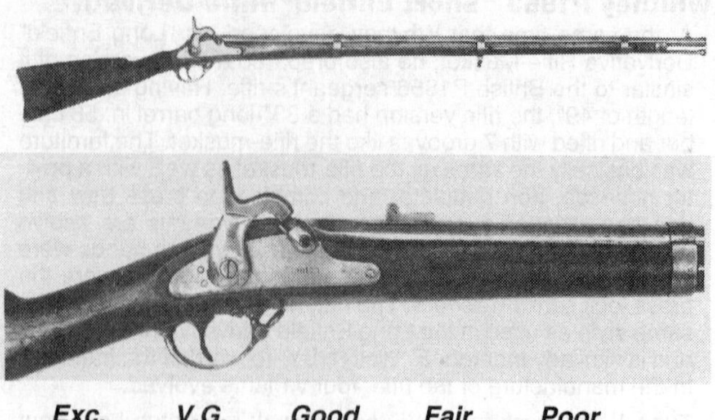

Exc.	V.G.	Good	Fair	Poor
—	—	4250	2000	600

Whitney "Direct Vent" M1861 Rifle-Musket Derivatives

In his continued efforts to dispose of surplus and rejected parts from his Connecticut and federal contracts, Whitney devised in 1863 a rifle-musket generally conforming to the M1861 rifle-musket except in two notable features. The bolster, instead of projecting considerably away from the barrel and having a clean-out screw was relatively short and flat faced. The process of making this bolster eliminated one production sequence, since it was not possible to drill the hole for the cone directly to the barrel. To accommodate the new cone position, the lockplates were made flat, without the bevel, and inletted flush with the stock. Lockplates bear the eagle surmounting the panoply of flags and trophies over "WHITNEYVILLE" stamp forward of the hammer, and are known with "1863" on the tail or without any date. The rear sight is the same as used on the "Manton" rifle-musket derivative. Arms with barrels than 40", 39", and 30" exist, all in .58 caliber with 3-groove rifling; however, the shortest of these may be post-war modifications for cadet use. Quantities made are not known, but surviving examples suggest limited production, probably to use faulty parts from the 1863 federal contract.

Exc.	V.G.	Good	Fair	Poor
—	—	3250	1250	400

Whitney U.S. M1861 Contract Rifle-Musket

In October of 1863, Whitney secured a contract with the U.S. War Department to produce 15,000 U.S. M1861 rifle-muskets. The arms manufactured under this contract conform in all respects to the Springfield Model adopted in 1861. The 40" barrel is in .58 caliber and rifled with 3 grooves; its rear sight conforms to the two-leaf model with stepped side walls. Nosecap is M1861 style and made of malleable iron. Socket bayonets furnished with them conform to the U.S. M1855/M1861 pattern. Marks include "US" on buttplate and standard inspection marks on barrel and stock. Lockplate marked with eagle surmounting letters "US" forward of the hammer and "WHITNEYVILLE" on the forward projection of the plate; date, "1863" or "1864" stamped on tail of the plate.

Exc.	V.G.	Good	Fair	Poor
—	—	3250	1250	400

Whitney U.S. Navy Contract Rifle

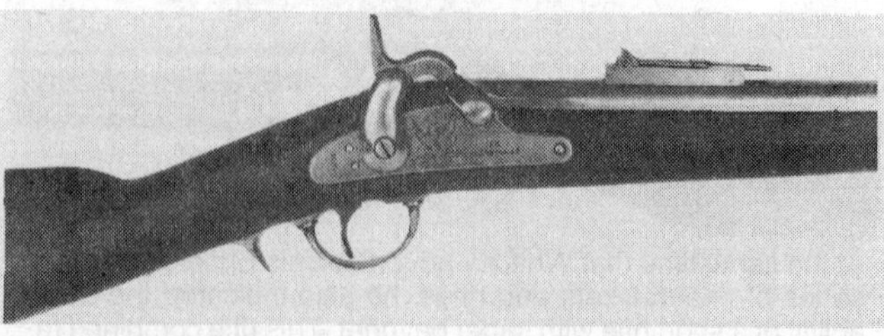

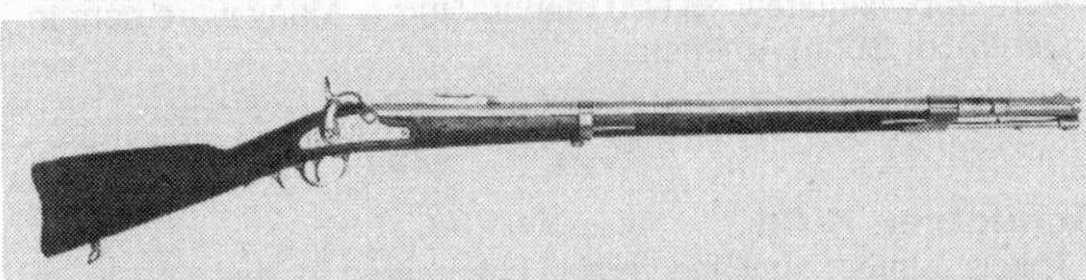

In July of 1861, Whitney entered a contact with the U.S. Navy to produce 10,000 rifles of the "Plymouth Pattern." So called after the U.S. Navy warship whereupon the first Harpers Ferry trial rifles had been developed, the new Navy rifle borrowed many of its characteristics from the French M1846 "carbine a tige." Overall length was 50" with a 34"-long barrel bearing a saber bayonet lug with guide extending nearly to the muzzle on its right side. The bore was .69 caliber, rifled with three broad lands and grooves. The rear sight copied the French M1846 and M1859 styles, i.e. it has an elevating ladder but no sidewalls. On early production the sights are serially numbered to the rifle's serial number (appearing on the breech plug tang). Barrels bear the standard U.S. inspection marks on the left quarter flat and the production date ("1863" or "1864") on the top of the barrel near the breech. Two lock markings have been encountered. The earlier production uses flat beveled plate marked with the date "1863" on its tail and an eagle surmounting a panoply of flags and trophies over the name "WHITNEYVILLE." In later (after serial no. 3,000) the lock's tail is marked "1864" and the stamping forward of the hammer matches that on the U.S. M1861 Whitney contract rifle-muskets, i.e. a small eagle over "U S" and "WHITNEYVILLE" in the forward projection of the plate. Inspector's initials (F.C.W.) appear on the barrel and in a cartouche on the stock.

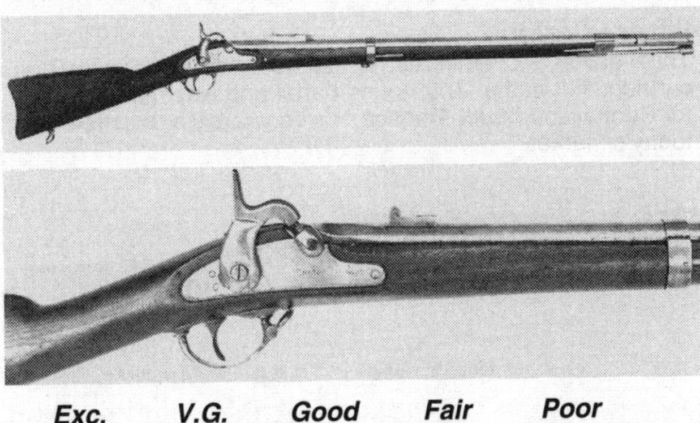

Exc.	V.G.	Good	Fair	Poor
—	—	4250	1750	600

The Whitney Arms Company, 1865-1888

With the close of the American Civil War, Eli Whitney, Jr. again turned his eyes to the manufacture of inexpensive arms from parts remaining on hand from his Civil War contracts. Extra barrels were turned into inexpensive muzzleloading shotguns, and a few breechloading designs were toyed with. Following Remington's example, Whitney soon realized that a substantial profit could be made in the production of single-shot martial arms for foreign governments. The result was a series of breechloading arms that copied many salient features of the Remington line, including a direct copy after the expiration of the Remington patent for the "rolling block" mechanism. Not until the late 1870s did Whitney acquire the rights to several patents that led to the production of a lever-action repeating rifle. During the post-war period, revolver production, which had begun with evasions of Colt's patents in the decade prior to the Civil War, mushroomed with the production of small spur-trigger rimfire cartridge revolvers. Despite the variety of arms produced, by 1883 Whitney was considering the sale of his company. Business reverses over the next five years necessitated the sale of the firm to Winchester in 1888. Primarily interested securing in the patent rights for Whitney's lever-action series of rifles, Winchester closed the plant and moved its machinery to New Haven. After 90 years of production, the Whitneyville Armory ceased to exist.

Single Barreled Percussion Shotgun

This firearm was manufactured by Whitney out of surplus .58 caliber rifle barrels that were opened up and converted to smoothbore .60-caliber shotgun barrels. They are offered in lengths of 28" to 36" and are marked "Whitney Arms Co., Whitneyville, Conn. Homogeneous Wrought Steel." The finish is blued, with varnished walnut stocks that are crudely checkered. There were approximately 2,000 manufactured between 1866 and 1869. These guns are rarely encountered on today's market.

Exc.	V.G.	Good	Fair	Poor
—	—	950	400	150

Double-Barreled Percussion Shotgun

The specifications for this version are similar to that of the single barrel except that there are two side-by-side barrels with double locks and hammers and double triggers. They are slightly more common than the single barreled version.

Exc.	V.G.	Good	Fair	Poor
—	—	950	400	150

Swing-Breech Carbine

This is a single-shot breechloading carbine chambered for the .46-caliber rimfire cartridge. It has a 22" round barrel with a button-released breechblock that swings to the side for loading. The finish is blued, with a walnut stock. There were fewer than 50 manufactured in 1866.

Exc.	V.G.	Good	Fair	Poor
—	—	3250	1750	600

Whitney-Cochran Carbine

This is a single-shot breechloading carbine chambered for the .44 rimfire cartridge. It has a 28" round barrel with a lever-activated breechblock that raises upward for loading. It was manufactured under license from J.W. Cochran. The finish is blued, with a walnut stock. There is a saddle ring on the left side of the frame. It is marked "Whitney Arms Co. - Whitneyville, Conn." This gun was produced for the 1867 Government Carbine Trials. There were fewer than 50 manufactured in 1866 and 1867.

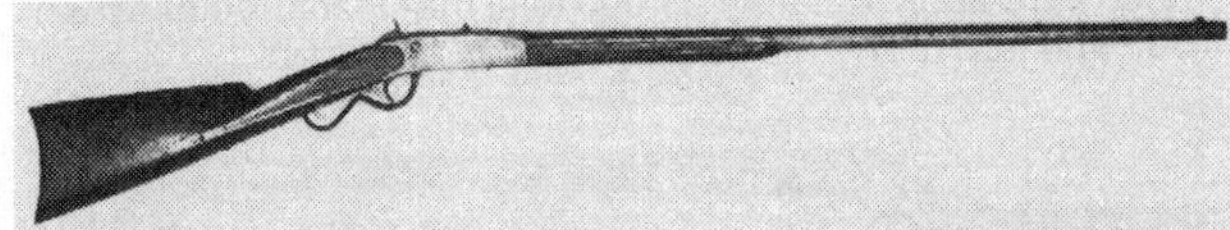

Courtesy Milwaukee Public Museum, Milwaukee, Wisconsin

Exc.	V.G.	Good	Fair	Poor
—	—	3500	1500	600

Excelsior

This is a single-shot rifle chambered for the .38, .44, or .50 rimfire cartridges. It is found with various-length octagonal or round barrels. The finish is blued, with a walnut stock and forearm held on by one barrel band. The breechblock pivots downward for loading. There is a center-mounted hammer. It is marked "Whitney Arms Co. Whitneyville Conn." The shorter barreled carbine versions have a saddle ring on the frame. There were approximately 200 manufactured between 1866 and 1870.

Exc.	V.G.	Good	Fair	Poor
—	—	2750	1150	400

Whitney-Howard Lever Action

This is a single-shot breechloader that is chambered for the .44 rimfire cartridge. It has also been noted as a shotgun chambered for 20 gauge smoothbore with barrels from 30" to 40" in length. The rifle version has barrel lengths from 22" to 28". The breechblock is opened by means of a combination lever and trigger guard. There is also a carbine version with barrel lengths of 18.5" or 19". There were approximately 2,000 manufactured totally between 1866 and 1870.

Shotgun

Courtesy Buffalo Bill Historical Center, Cody, Wyoming

Exc.	V.G.	Good	Fair	Poor
—	—	650	300	100

Rifle

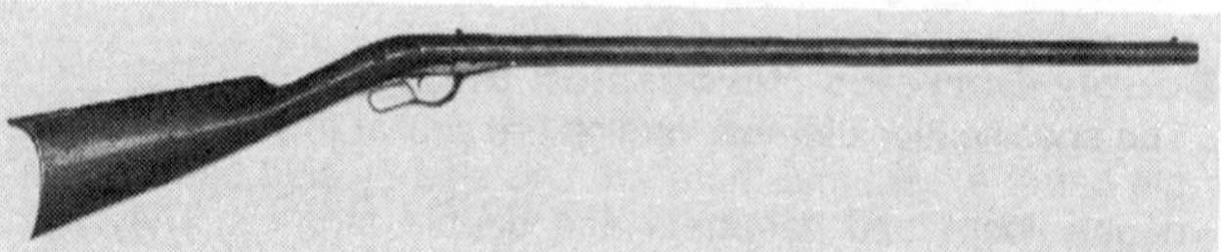

Courtesy Milwaukee Public Museum, Milwaukee, Wisconsin

Exc.	V.G.	Good	Fair	Poor
—	—	900	450	150

Carbine

Courtesy Milwaukee Public Museum, Milwaukee, Wisconsin

Exc.	V.G.	Good	Fair	Poor
—	—	1250	500	200

Whitney Phoenix

There is little known about the origin of this model. It is built on a patent issued to Whitney in 1874. There are a number of variations that are all marked "Phoenix, Patent May 24, 74." The Whitney name is not marked on any of the versions. They are all single-shot breechloaders with a breechblock that lifts to the right side and upward for loading. The barrels are all blued, with either case colored or blued receivers and walnut stocks. There were approximately 25,000 total manufactured between 1867 and 1881. The models and values are listed.

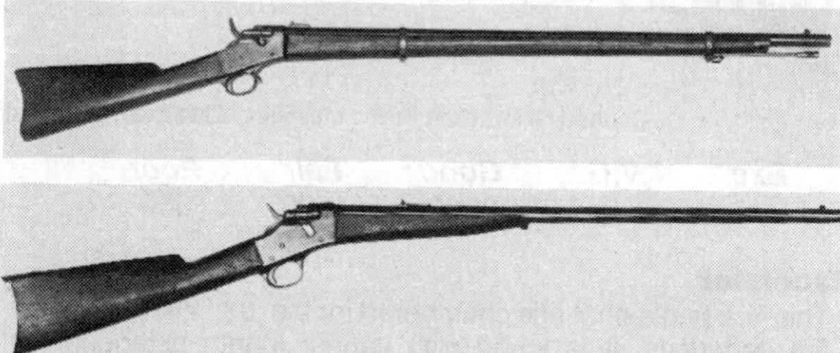

Courtesy Milwaukee Public Museum, Milwaukee, Wisconsin

Gallery Rifle

This version is chambered for the .22 rimfire caliber and has a 24" half-octagonal barrel. Its production was quite limited.

Exc.	V.G.	Good	Fair	Poor
—	—	1500	600	200

Shotgun

This is a smoothbore version chambered for 10, 12, 14, 16, or 22 gauge. It has smoothbore barrels between 26" and 32" in length. There were approximately 5,000 manufactured.

Exc.	V.G.	Good	Fair	Poor
—	—	600	250	100

Military Rifle

This version is chambered for the .433, .45, or .50 caliber centerfire cartridges. It has a 35" round barrel with a full-length, two-piece walnut stock held on by three barrel bands. There were approximately 15,000 manufactured. Many were sent to Central or South America.

Exc.	V.G.	Good	Fair	Poor
—	—	3000	1250	400

Schuetzen Rifle

This is a target-shooting version chambered for the .38, .40, or .44 centerfire cartridges. It has either a 30" or 32" octagonal barrel with a Schuetzen-type walnut stock and forearm that features hand checkering. It has a nickel-plated, Swiss-style buttplate and adjustable sights with a spirit level. This model has been noted with double-set triggers. There were few manufactured.

Exc.	V.G.	Good	Fair	Poor
—	—	3250	1250	400

Civilian Carbine

This version is chambered for the .44 caliber centerfire and has a 24" round barrel. The finish is blued, with a case colored frame and a walnut stock and forearm held on by one barrel band. It has military-type sights, buttplate, and a saddle ring mounted on the frame. There were approximately 500 manufactured.

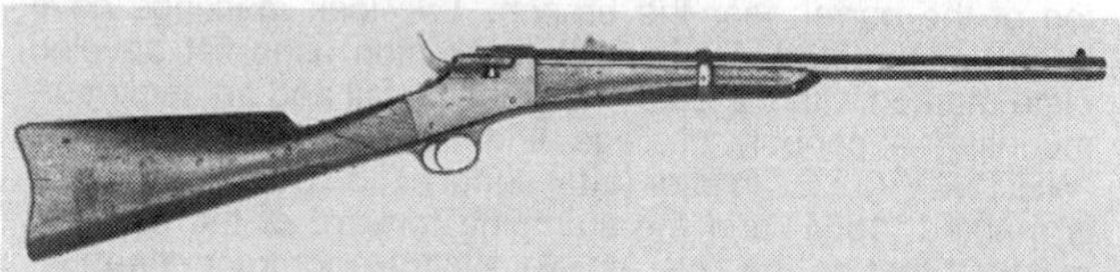

Courtesy Milwaukee Public Museum, Milwaukee, Wisconsin

Exc.	V.G.	Good	Fair	Poor
—	—	2500	850	400

Military Carbine

This version is chambered for the .433, .45, or .50 centerfire cartridges. It has a 20.5" round barrel and was manufactured for Central and South America. It is very rarely encountered on today's market.

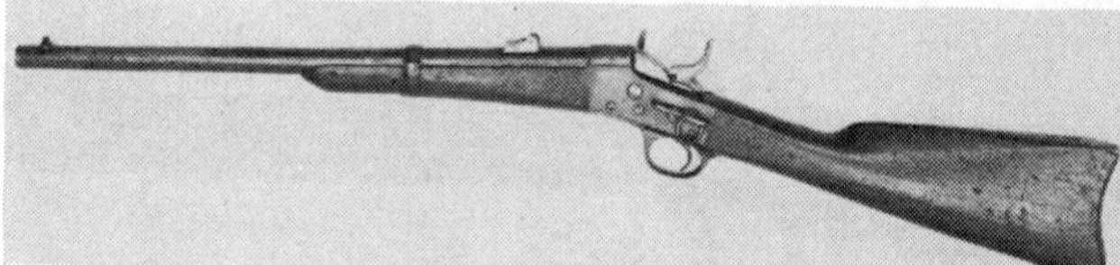

Courtesy Milwaukee Public Museum, Milwaukee, Wisconsin

Courtesy Milwaukee Public Museum, Milwaukee, Wisconsin

Exc.	V.G.	Good	Fair	Poor
—	—	2750	1000	400

Whitney-Laidley Model I Rolling Block

Whitney acquired manufacturing rights for this model from the inventors T. Laidley and C.A. Emery, who had received the patent in 1866. Whitney immediately started to modify the action to become competitive with the Remington Rolling Block. There were approximately 50,000 manufactured total between 1871 and 1881. There are a number of variations of this model.

Military Carbine

There were approximately 5,000 manufactured chambered for the .433, .45, or .50 centerfire cartridges. It has a 20.5" round barrel with military-type sights and a saddle ring on the receiver. The finish is blued, with a case colored frame and a walnut stock. Most of them were shipped to Central or South America.

Exc.	V.G.	Good	Fair	Poor
—	—	1750	700	250

Civilian Carbine

This version is chambered for .44 rimfire or centerfire and .46 rimfire. It has either an 18.5" or 19.5" barrel. It is blued, with a case colored frame. The stock is walnut. A nickel-plated version is also available. There were approximately 1,000 of this version manufactured.

Exc.	V.G.	Good	Fair	Poor
—	—	1750	700	250

Military Rifle

This version is chambered the same as the Military Carbine but has either a 32.5" or 35" round barrel with a full-length two-piece stock held on by three barrel bands. The finish is blued, with a case colored receiver and a walnut stock. There were approximately 30,000 manufactured. Most were shipped to Central or South America.

Courtesy Milwaukee Public Museum, Milwaukee, Wisconsin

Exc.	V.G.	Good	Fair	Poor
—	—	2000	800	300

Gallery Rifle

This is a .22 caliber sporting-rifle version with a 24" octagonal barrel. The finish is similar to the Military Rifle. There were approximately 500 manufactured.

Exc.	V.G.	Good	Fair	Poor
—	—	1750	700	250

Sporting Rifle

This version is chambered for .38, .40, .44, .45, or .50 centerfire, as well as .32, .38, or .44 rimfire. It features barrel lengths from 24" to 30" in either round or octagonal configurations. The finish is similar to the Military Rifle, and there were approximately 5,000 manufactured.

Exc.	V.G.	Good	Fair	Poor
—	—	2000	750	300

Creedmoor No. 1 Rifle

This version is chambered for the .44 caliber cartridge and has a 32" or 34" barrel that is either round or octagonal in configuration. It has a blued finish with case colored frame and a hand checkered, select walnut stock and forearm. It features vernier adjustable sights with a spirit level. It is marked "Whitney Creedmoor." There were fewer than 100 manufactured.

Exc.	V.G.	Good	Fair	Poor
—	—	6250	2750	850

Creedmoor No. 2 Rifle

This version is similar to the No. 1 Rifle except that it is chambered for the .40 caliber cartridge with either a 30" or 32" barrel.

Exc.	V.G.	Good	Fair	Poor
—	—	4250	1750	500

Whitney-Remington Model 2 Rolling Block

When Remington's patent for the Rolling Block action expired, Whitney was quick to reproduce the action, labeling it his "New Improved System." It is essentially quite similar to Remington's Rolling Block and is easily recognized when compared with the Model 1 because it has only two parts — the hammer and the breechblock. The frame is also rounded. The tang on this model is marked "Whitney Arms Company, New Haven Ct USA." There were approximately 50,000 total manufactured between 1881 and 1888. There are a number of variations are listed.

Shotgun

This is a smoothbore version chambered for 12, 14, 16, or 20 gauge. It is offered with barrel lengths between 26" and 30". Twenty inch barrels have also been noted.

Exc.	V.G.	Good	Fair	Poor
—	—	650	250	100

Military Carbine

This version is chambered for the .433 and .45 centerfire cartridges. It has a 20.5" barrel and is blued, with a case colored receiver and walnut stock. There were approximately 5,000 manufactured. Most were sent to South or Central America.

Exc.	V.G.	Good	Fair	Poor
—	—	1750	700	300

Civilian Carbine

This version is chambered for the .44 rimfire or centerfire cartridge with an 18.5" round barrel. The finish is similar to the Military Carbine. There were approximately 2,000 manufactured.

Exc.	V.G.	Good	Fair	Poor
—	—	1600	600	250

Military Rifle

This version is chambered for the .433, .45, or .50 centerfire cartridge. It has a 32.5" or 35" barrel. It is finished similarly to the Military Carbine. There were approximately 39,000 manufactured.

Courtesy Buffalo Bill Historical Center, Cody, Wyoming

Exc.	V.G.	Good	Fair	Poor
—	—	2000	750	300

No. 1 Sporting Rifle

This version is chambered for various popular sporting cartridges and is offered with barrel lengths from 26" to 30", either round or octagonal in configuration. The finish is blued, with a case colored receiver and a varnished walnut stock. There were many options available that could radically affect the value, and a qualified appraisal would be advisable. There were approximately 3,000 manufactured.

Exc.	V.G.	Good	Fair	Poor
—	—	2500	1000	400

No. 2 Sporting Rifle

This is a smaller version of the No. 1 Rifle, chambered for the .22 rimfire, .32, .38, and .44-40 centerfire cartridges. Again, a qualified appraisal would be helpful, as many options can affect the value.

Exc.	V.G.	Good	Fair	Poor
—	—	1750	700	250

Whitney-Burgess-Morse Rifle

This is a lever action repeating rifle chambered for the .45-70 Government cartridge. There are three variations. All have a magazine tube mounted beneath the barrel with blued finishes and walnut stocks. The barrels are marked "G. W. Morse Patented Oct. 28th 1856." The tang is marked "A. Burgess Patented Jan. 7th, 1873, Patented Oct 19th 1873." There were approximately 3,000 total manufactured between 1878 and 1882. The variations are listed.

Sporting Rifle

This version has a 28" octagonal or round barrel. The magazine tube holds 9 rounds. There are a number of options available that can increase the value drastically; and we recommend competent, individual appraisal. Value given is for a standard model.

Exc.	V.G.	Good	Fair	Poor
—	—	3250	1250	400

Military Rifle

This version has a 33" round barrel with a full-length forearm held on by two barrel bands. It features military sights and has an 11-round tubular magazine. It has a bayonet lug and sling swivels. This variation is also found chambered for the .43 Spanish and .42 Russian cartridges. There were approximately 1,000 manufactured.

Exc.	V.G.	Good	Fair	Poor
—	—	4250	2000	700

Carbine

This version has a 22" round barrel with a full-length forearm held on by one barrel band. It has a 7-round tubular magazine and a saddle ring attached to the frame. There were approximately 500 manufactured.

Exc.	V.G.	Good	Fair	Poor
—	—	4750	2250	750

Whitney-Kennedy Rifle

This is a lever action repeating rifle that was manufactured in two sizes. It has a magazine tube mounted under the barrel and a blued finish with a case colored lever. The stock is walnut. The barrel is marked "Whitney Arms Co New Haven, Conn. U.S.A." Occasionally, the word "Kennedy" is marked after the Whitney name. There are two major variations. One features a standard-type action lever; and the other, the same "S"-shaped lever that is found on the Burgess model. This version would be worth approximately 10 percent additional. As with many of the rifles of this era, there were many options available that will affect the values. We strongly recommend securing a qualified appraisal for all but the standard models if a transaction is contemplated. There were approximately 15,000 manufactured between 1879 and 1886. The variations of the Whitney-Kennedy and their values are listed.

Courtesy Buffalo Bill Historical Center, Cody, Wyoming

Small Frame Sporting Rifle

This version is chambered for the .32-20, .38-40, and the .40-40 cartridges. It has a 24" barrel that is either round or octagonal in configuration. Examples will be noted with either a full-length or half-length tubular magazine.

Exc.	V.G.	Good	Fair	Poor
—	—	2750	1200	500

Large Frame Sporting Rifle

This version is chambered for the .40-60, .45-60, .45-75, and the .50-90 cartridges. The .50-caliber version is uncommon and will bring a 20 percent premium. The barrel lengths offered are 26" or 28".

Exc.	V.G.	Good	Fair	Poor
—	—	3000	1350	500

Military Rifle

This is a large-frame model, chambered for the .40-.60, .44-.40, and the .45-60 cartridges. It has a 32.25" round barrel and either an 11- or 16-round tubular magazine. It has a full-length walnut forend held on by two barrel bands and features a bayonet lug and sling swivels. There were approximately 1,000 manufactured. Most were shipped to Central or South America.

Exc.	V.G.	Good	Fair	Poor
—	—	3750	1750	550

Military Carbine

This is built on either the small-frame or large-frame action and is chambered for the .38-40, .44-40, .40-60, or .45-60 cartridges. It has either a 20" or 22" round barrel and a 9- or 12-round tubular magazine, depending on the caliber. It has a short forend held on by a single barrel band. There were approximately 1,000 manufactured. Most were sent to Central or South America.

Courtesy Buffalo Bill Historical Center, Cody, Wyoming

Exc.	V.G.	Good	Fair	Poor
—	—	3750	1750	550

Hooded Cylinder Pocket Revolver

This is an unusual revolver that is chambered for .28 caliber percussion. It has a manually rotated, 6-shot hooded cylinder that has etched decorations. The octagonal barrel is offered in lengths of 3" to 6". There is a button at the back of the frame that unlocks the cylinder so that it can be rotated. The finish is blued, with a brass frame and two-piece rounded walnut grips. It is marked "E. Whitney N. Haven Ct." There were approximately 200 manufactured between 1850 and 1853.

Exc.	V.G.	Good	Fair	Poor
—	—	3250	1500	600

Two Trigger Pocket Revolver

This is a conventional-appearing pocket revolver with a manually rotated cylinder. There is a second trigger located in front of the conventional trigger guard that releases the cylinder so that it can be turned. It is chambered for .32 caliber percussion and has an octagonal barrel from 3" to 6" in length. It has a 5-shot unfluted cylinder that is etched and a brass frame. The remainder is blued, with squared walnut two-piece grips. An iron-frame version is also available, but only 50 were produced. It would bring approximately 60 percent additional. There were approximately 650 total manufactured between 1852 and 1854.

Courtesy Milwaukee Public Museum, Milwaukee, Wisconsin

Exc.	V.G.	Good	Fair	Poor
—	—	2000	850	300

Whitney-Beals Patent Revolver

This was an unusual, ring-trigger pocket pistol that was made in three basic variations.

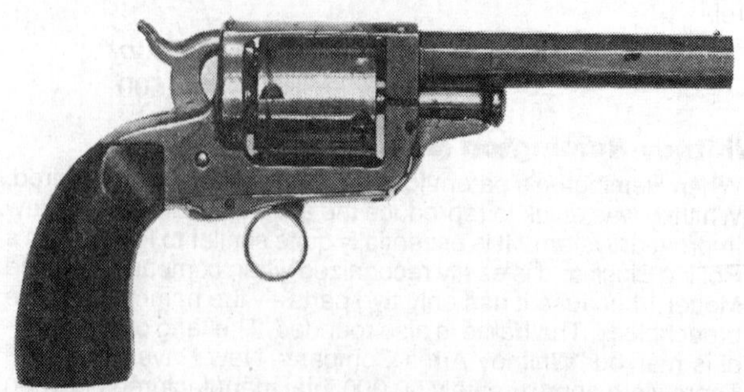

Courtesy Milwaukee Public Museum, Milwaukee, Wisconsin

First Model

This version is chambered for .31-caliber percussion and has barrels of octagonal configuration from 2" to 6" in length. It has a brass frame and a 6-shot cylinder. It is marked "F. Beals/New Haven, Ct." There were only 50 manufactured.

Exc.	V.G.	Good	Fair	Poor
—	—	3500	1500	450

.31 Caliber Model

This version has an iron frame and a 7-shot cylinder. The octagonal barrels are from 2" to 6" in length. It is marked "Address E. Whitney/Whitneyville, Ct." There were approximately 2,300 manufactured.

Exc.	V.G.	Good	Fair	Poor
—	—	1500	600	200

.28 Caliber Model

Except for the caliber, this model is similar to the .31 Caliber Model. There were approximately 850 manufactured.

Exc.	V.G.	Good	Fair	Poor
—	—	1750	700	300

Whitney 1851 Navy

This is a faithful copy of the 1851 Colt Revolver. It is virtually identical. There is a possibility that surplus Colt parts were utilized in the construction of this revolver. There were approximately 400 manufactured in 1857 and 1858.

Exc.	V.G.	Good	Fair	Poor
—	—	4250	1750	650

Whitney Navy Revolver

This is a single-action revolver chambered for .36 caliber percussion. It has a standard octagonal barrel length of 7.5". It has an iron frame and a 6-shot unfluted cylinder that is roll engraved. The finish is blued, with a case colored loading lever and two-piece walnut grips. The barrel is marked either "E. Whitney/N. Haven" or "Eagle Co." There are a number of minor variations on this revolver, and we strongly urge competent appraisal if contemplating a transaction. There were 33,000 total manufactured between 1858 and 1862.

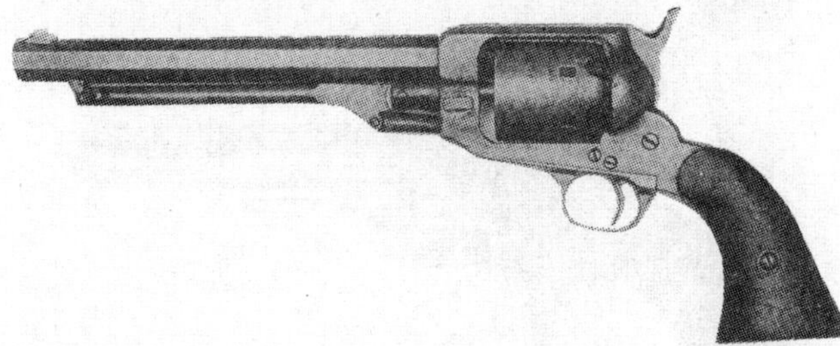

Courtesy Wallis & Wallis, Lewes, Sussex, England

First Model

Nearly the entire production of the First Model is marked "Eagle Co." The reason for this marking is unknown. There are four distinct variations of this model.

First Variation

This model has no integral loading-lever assembly and has a thin top strap. There were only 100 manufactured.

Exc.	V.G.	Good	Fair	Poor
—	—	3750	1500	550

Second Variation

This version is similar to the First Variation, with an integral loading lever. There were approximately 200 manufactured.

Exc.	V.G.	Good	Fair	Poor
—	—	3000	1200	400

Third Variation

This is similar to the Second, with a three-screw frame instead of four screws. The loading lever is also modified. There were approximately 500 manufactured.

Exc.	V.G.	Good	Fair	Poor
—	—	2500	1000	300

Fourth Variation

This version has a rounded frame and a safety notch between the nipples on the rear of the cylinder. There have been examples noted marked "E. Whitney/N. Haven." There were approximately 700 manufactured.

Exc.	V.G.	Good	Fair	Poor
—	—	2500	1000	300

Second Model

First Variation

This version features a more robust frame with a brass trigger guard. The barrel is marked "E. Whitney/N. Haven." The cylinder pin is secured by a wing nut, and there is an integral loading lever. There were approximately 1,200 manufactured.

Exc.	V.G.	Good	Fair	Poor
—	—	2000	900	300

Second Variation

This version has six improved safety notches on the rear of the cylinder. There were approximately 10,000 manufactured.

Exc.	V.G.	Good	Fair	Poor
—	—	1750	750	250

Third Variation

This version has an improved, Colt-type loading-lever latch. There were approximately 2,000 manufactured.

Exc.	V.G.	Good	Fair	Poor
—	—	1750	750	250

Fourth Variation

This is similar to the Third except the cylinder is marked "Whitneyville." There were approximately 10,000 manufactured.

Exc.	V.G.	Good	Fair	Poor
—	—	1750	750	250

Fifth Variation

This version has a larger trigger guard. There were approximately 4,000 manufactured.

Exc.	V.G.	Good	Fair	Poor
—	—	1750	750	250

Sixth Variation

This version has the larger trigger guard and five-groove rifling instead of the usual seven-groove. There were approximately 2,500 manufactured.

Exc.	V.G.	Good	Fair	Poor
—	—	1750	750	250

Whitney Pocket Revolver

This is a single-action revolver chambered for .31 caliber percussion. It has octagonal barrels between 3" and 6" in length. It has a 5-shot unfluted cylinder that is roll engraved and marked "Whitneyville." The frame is iron with a blued finish and a case colored integral loading lever. The grips are two-piece walnut. The development of this model, as far as models and variations go, is identical to that which we described in the Navy Model designation. The values are different, and we list them for reference. Again, we recommend securing qualified appraisal if a transaction is contemplated. There were approximately 32,500 manufactured from 1858 to 1862.

First Model

First Variation

Exc.	V.G.	Good	Fair	Poor
—		2000	900	300

Second Variation

Exc.	V.G.	Good	Fair	Poor
—	—	1250	500	200

Third Variation

Exc.	V.G.	Good	Fair	Poor
—	—	1000	400	150

Fourth Variation

Exc.	V.G.	Good	Fair	Poor
—	—	1000	400	150

Fifth Variation

Exc.	V.G.	Good	Fair	Poor
—	—	1000	400	150

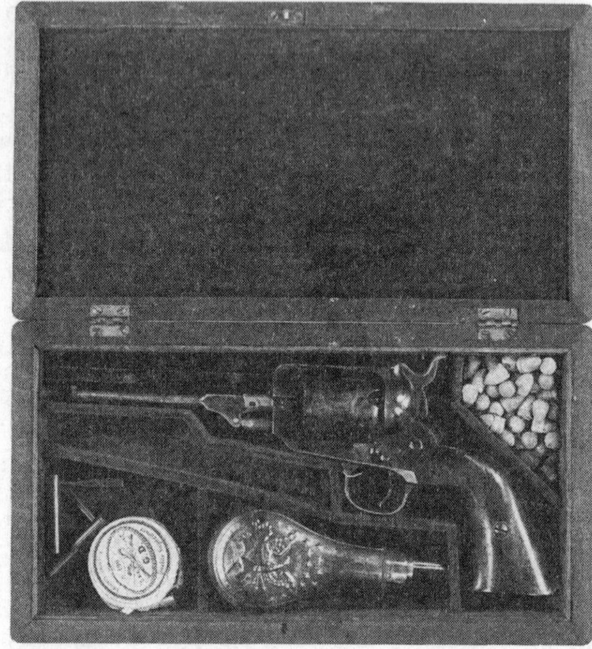

Courtesy Buffalo Bill Historical Center, Cody, Wyoming

Second Model

First Variation

Exc.	V.G.	Good	Fair	Poor
—	—	900	400	100

Second Variation

Exc.	V.G.	Good	Fair	Poor
—	—	900	400	100

Third Variation

Exc.	V.G.	Good	Fair	Poor
—	—	900	400	100

Fourth Variation

Exc.	V.G.	Good	Fair	Poor
—	—	1000	425	125

New Model Pocket Revolver

This is a single-action, spur-triggered pocket revolver chambered for .28-caliber percussion. It has a 3.5" octagonal barrel and a 6-shot roll engraved cylinder. It features an iron frame with a blued finish and two-piece walnut grips. The barrel is marked "E. Whitney/N. Haven." There were approximately 2,000 manufactured between 1860 and 1867.

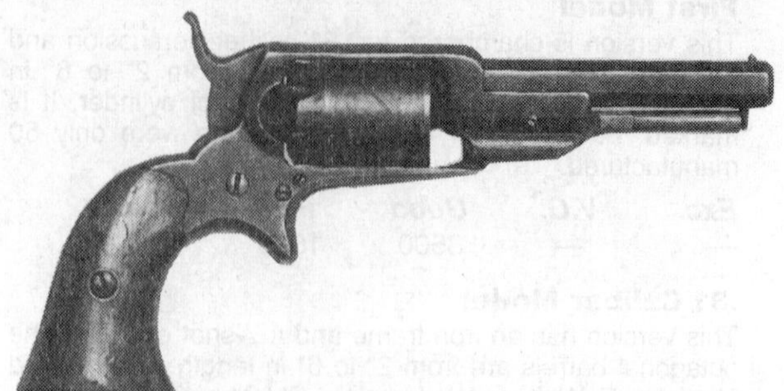

Courtesy Milwaukee Public Museum, Milwaukee, Wisconsin

Exc.	V.G.	Good	Fair	Poor
—	—	1250	500	200

Rimfire Pocket Revolver

This is a spur-trigger, single-action, solid-frame pocket revolver that was produced in three frame sizes, depending on the caliber. It is chambered for the .22, .32, and .38 rimfire cartridges. The frame is brass, and it is found in a variety of finishes-nickel-plated or blued, or a combination thereof. The bird's-head grips are rosewood or hard rubber; ivory or pearl grips are sometimes encountered and will bring a slight premium in value. The barrels are octagonal and from 1.5" to 5" in length. The barrels are marked "Whitneyville Armory Ct. USA." They have also been noted with the trade names "Monitor," "Defender," or "Eagle." They were commonly referred to as the Model No. 1, No. 1.5, Model 2, or Model 2.5. The values for all are quite similar. There were approximately 30,000 manufactured of all types between 1871 and 1879.

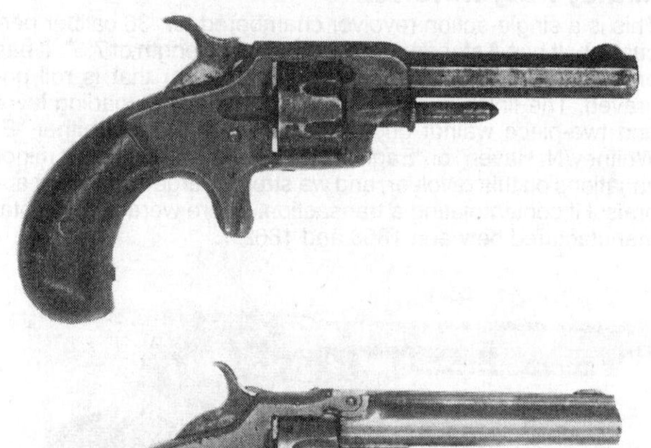

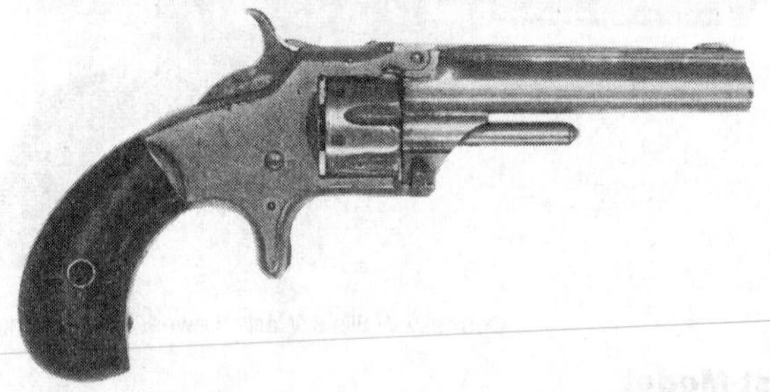

Courtesy Milwaukee Public Museum, Milwaukee, Wisconsin

Exc.	V.G.	Good	Fair	Poor
—	—	500	200	75

WHITNEY FIREARMS COMPANY

Hartford, Connecticut

Wolverine

A .22 caliber semi-automatic pistol with a 4.75" barrel. Blued or nickel-plated with plastic grips and an aluminum alloy frame. This pistol is readily distinguishable by its streamlined form. Approximately 13,000 examples were made with the blue finish and 900 with a nickel-plated finish. Some slides are marked "Wolverine Whitney Firearms Inc., New Haven, Conn USA." Others are marked "Whitney" only. The Wolverine-marked pistols are considered more rare. Pistol were produced in two locations: New Haven, Connecticut and Hartford, Connecticut. Manufactured from 1955 to 1962. Now being reproduced by Olympic Arms. Pricing is for original version.

Blue Finish

Blued pistols most often have brown or black grips.

Exc.	V.G.	Good	Fair	Poor
650	400	350	250	200

Nickel-Plated

Nickeled pistols most often have white plastic grips.

Exc.	V.G.	Good	Fair	Poor
895	650	475	300	250

WHITWORTH

SEE—Interarms

WICHITA ARMS, INC.

Wichita, Kansas

Classic Rifle

A single-shot bolt-action rifle produced in a variety of calibers with a 21" octagonal barrel. Offered with Canjar adjustable triggers. Blued with a checkered walnut stock.

NIB	Exc.	V.G.	Good	Fair	Poor
3000	2500	2250	1850	1250	1000

Varmint Rifle

As above, with a round barrel.

NIB	Exc.	V.G.	Good	Fair	Poor
2000	1750	1500	1250	1000	800

Silhouette Rifle

As above, with a 24" heavy barrel, gray composition stock and 2-oz. Canjar trigger.

NIB	Exc.	V.G.	Good	Fair	Poor
2200	1900	1700	1000	850	650

Wichita International Pistol

A single-shot pivoted barrel target pistol produced in a variety of calibers from .22 to .357 Magnum with a 10.5" or 14" barrel fitted with either adjustable sights or telescopic sight mounts. Stainless steel with walnut forestock and grips.

NIB	Exc.	V.G.	Good	Fair	Poor
500	450	400	350	300	200

Wichita Classic Pistol

A bolt action single-shot pistol chambered for a variety of calibers up to .308, with a left-hand action and 11.25" barrel. Blued with a walnut stock.

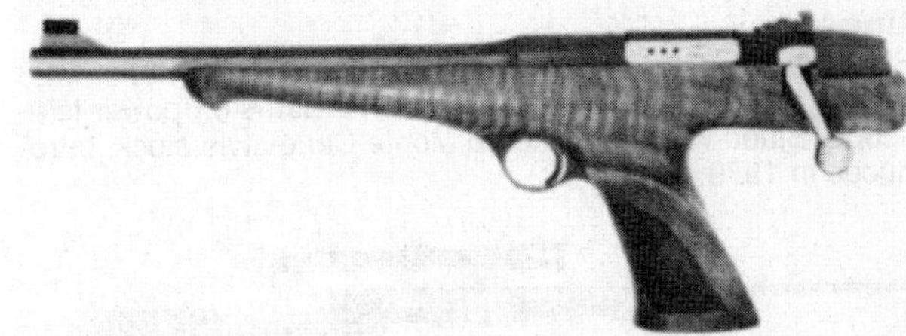

NIB	Exc.	V.G.	Good	Fair	Poor
3000	2500	2250	1850	1250	1000

Wichita Classic Engraved

As above, but embellished.

NIB	Exc.	V.G.	Good	Fair	Poor
5000	4250	3500	2500	2000	1500

Wichita Silhouette Pistol

As above, in 7mm HMSA or .308 with a 15" barrel. The walnut stock is made so that the pistol grip is located beneath the forward end of the bolt.

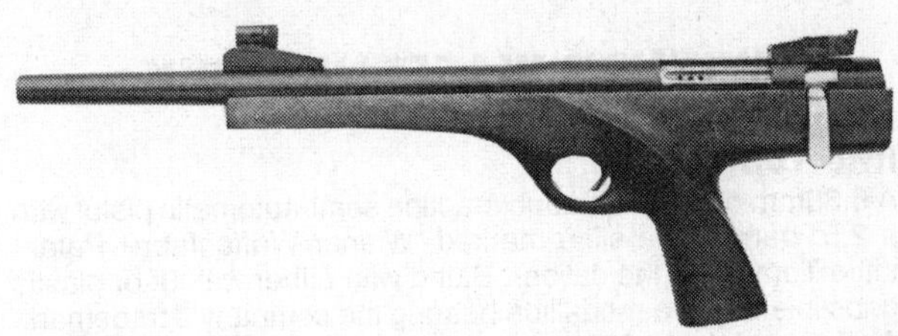

NIB	Exc.	V.G.	Good	Fair	Poor
1100	950	750	600	500	400

Wichita MK40

As above, with a 13" barrel, multi-range sights and either a composition or walnut stock. Standard finish is blued, however, this model was also made in stainless steel.

NIB	Exc.	V.G.	Good	Fair	Poor
1100	950	750	600	500	400

WICKLIFFE RIFLES

Triple S Development
Wickliffe, Ohio

Model 76

A single-shot falling-block rifle produced in a variety of calibers from .22 Hornet to .45-70 with a 22" lightweight or 26" heavyweight barrel. Blued with a walnut stock. Introduced in 1976. Discontinued.

Exc.	V.G.	Good	Fair	Poor
550	350	300	250	175

Model 76 Deluxe

As above, with a nickel-silver pistol grip cap, machine jeweled breechblock and more finely figured walnut stock. Introduced in 1976.

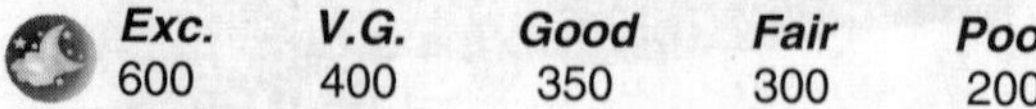

Exc.	V.G.	Good	Fair	Poor
600	400	350	300	200

Traditionalist

The Model 76 in .30-06 or .45-70 caliber with a 24" barrel having open sights and a checkered walnut buttstock. Introduced in 1979.

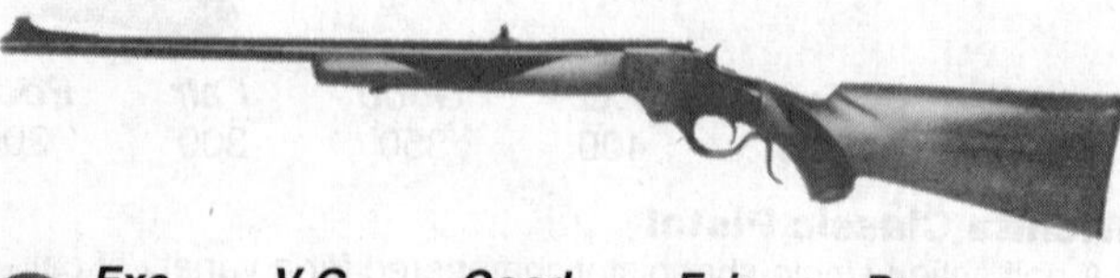

Exc.	V.G.	Good	Fair	Poor
550	350	300	250	175

Stinger

Similar to the Model 76, but chambered for .22 Hornet or .223 Remington with a 22" barrel fitted with a Burris 6X power telescope. Blued with a checkered Monte Carlo-style stock. Introduced in 1979.

Exc.	V.G.	Good	Fair	Poor
550	350	300	250	175

Stinger Deluxe

As above, with a superior grade of finish and more finely figured walnut stock.

Exc.	V.G.	Good	Fair	Poor
600	400	350	300	200

WIENER WAFFENFABRIK

Vienna, Austria

Little Tom

A 6.35mm or 7.65mm double-action semi-automatic pistol with a 2.5" barrel. The slide marked "Wiener Waffenfabrik Patent Little Tom," and the caliber. Blued with either walnut or plastic grips inlaid with a medallion bearing the company's trademark. Approximately 10,000 were made from 1919 to 1925.

Little Tom—6.35mm

Courtesy J.B. Wood

Little Tom—7.65mm

Paul Goodwin photo

Exc.	V.G.	Good	Fair	Poor
500	450	400	250	175

WILDEY FIREARMS CO., INC.

Cheshire, Connecticut
Newburg, New York
Warren, Connecticut

Wildey Auto Pistol

A gas-operated, rotary-bolt, double-action semi-automatic pistol chambered for the .357 Peterbuilt, the .45 Winchester Magnum, or the .475 Wildey Magnum cartridges. with 5", 6", 7", 8", or 10" ventilated rib barrels. The gas-operated action is adjustable and features a single-shot cutoff. The rotary bolt has three heavy locking lugs. Constructed of stainless steel with adjustable sights and wood grips. The values of this rarely encountered pistol are based on not only the condition, but the caliber—as well the serial-number range, with earlier-numbered guns being worth a good deal more than the later or current production models.

Cheshire, Conn., Address

Produced in .45 Winchester Magnum only and is serial numbered from No. 1 through 2489.

This symbol denotes "Sleepers" with rapidly-rising values and/or significant collector potential.

Serial No. 1 through 200

NIB	Exc.	V.G.	Good	Fair	Poor
2000	1500	1200	—	—	—

NOTE: Serial numbers above 200 would be worth approximately $200 less respectively in each category of condition.

Survivor Model

This pistol is presently manufactured in Brookfield, Connecticut.

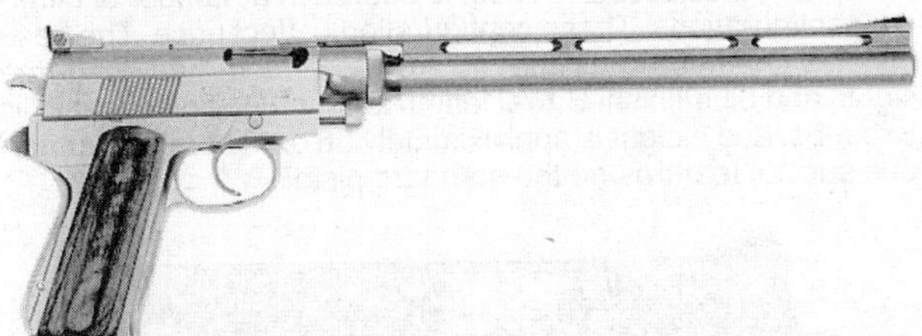

NIB	Exc.	V.G.	Good	Fair	Poor
1500	1000	750	550	450	300

NOTE: Add $100 for 12" barrel, $500 for 14" barrel, and $1,100 for 18" Silhouette model.

Hunter Model

As above but with matte stainless steel finish.

NIB	Exc.	V.G.	Good	Fair	Poor
1775	1250	900	—	—	—

Pin Gun

Gas-operated auto-loading pistol in polished or matte stainless for competition shooting. With muzzle brake; variety of calibers and barrel lengths (7", 8", 10", 12", 14"). 4.09 lb. (8" barrel). MSRP: 1650 – 2311

Wildey Carbine

This model features an 18" barrel with forearm in calibers from .44 Auto Mag to .475 Wildey Mag. Choice of polished or matte stainless steel.

NIB	Exc.	V.G.	Good	Fair	Poor
3020	2250	—	—	—	—

NOTE: Add $ 225 for matte stainless finish.

Presentation Model

As above, but engraved and fitted with hand-checkered walnut grips.

NIB	Exc.	V.G.	Good	Fair	Poor
2500	2000	1500	—	—	—

JAWS Viper

Jordanian Arms & Weapons System manufactured in Jordan. Semi-auto chambered for 9mm, .40 S&W, 45 ACP. Barrels: 4.4" and 5". 10-round magazine. Stainless finish with rubberized grip. MSRP: 793

WILKES, JOHN

London, England

SEE—British Double Guns

WILKINSON ARMS CO.

Covina, California

Diane

A .25 caliber semi-automatic pistol with a 2.25" barrel and 6-shot magazine. Blued with plastic grips.

Exc.	V.G.	Good	Fair	Poor
300	225	200	150	100

Terry Carbine

A 9mm caliber semi-automatic carbine with a 16.25" barrel, adjustable sights, and 30-shot magazine. Matte blued with either a black composition or maple stock.

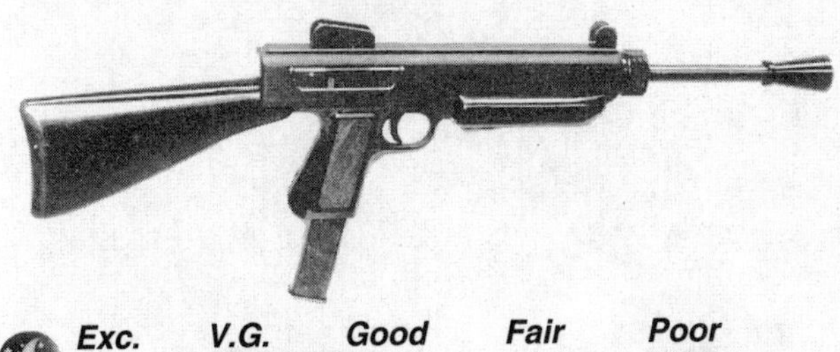

Exc.	V.G.	Good	Fair	Poor
675	450	325	200	125

WILLIAMSON MOORE FIREARMS COMPANY

New York, New York

Derringer

A .41 caliber single-shot pocket pistol with a 2.5" sliding barrel. Blued, with a silver-plated furniture and a checkered walnut grip. Barrel marked "Williamson's Pat. Oct. 2, 1866 New York."

This pistol was fitted with an auxiliary percussion cap chamber adaptor. Manufactured from 1866 to approximately 1870.

Exc.	V.G.	Good	Fair	Poor
—	—	1250	500	100

WILSON & CO.

SEE—English Military Firearms

WILSON, J. P.

Ilion, New York

Percussion Alarm Gun

This unusual little device is chambered for .22 caliber percussion. It consists of approximately a 1" rectangular brass block with a chamber bored into it that accepts a blackpowder charge. There is no provision for a projectile. There is a spring retained arm on top, which works as a hammer. As the device is activated by a door or a window, the hammer snaps closed, striking a percussion cap that causes the charge to fire, thereby creating an alarm notifying that the perimeter has been breached. It is marked "J. P. Wilson/Patented Feb. 8, 1859/Ilion, NY."

Exc.	V.G.	Good	Fair	Poor
—	—	850	350	100

WILSON COMBAT

Berryville, Arkansas

Wilson's began making custom 1911-style pistols using Colt slides and frames in 1977. This company produces a wide range of quality components for the 1911 pistol, such as slides, triggers, safeties, barrels, etc. The models listed are for complete factory-built-and-assembled guns. These factory-built pistols are sold with a lifetime warranty, even to subsequent buyers. The pistols listed are divided into two categories. Semi-custom pistols are off-the-shelf guns available through participating dealers. Custom pistols are special order guns. The models listed below are representative, not inclusive.

POLYMER FRAME PISTOLS

Tactical Carry (KZ-45)

Chambered for .45 ACP cartridge and fitted with a 5" stainless steel match barrel, this model has numerous special features such as night sights and front and rear slide serrations. Frame is stainless steel and reinforced polymer. Magazine capacity is 10 rounds. Finish is black polymer. Weight is approximately 31 oz. Introduced in 1999.

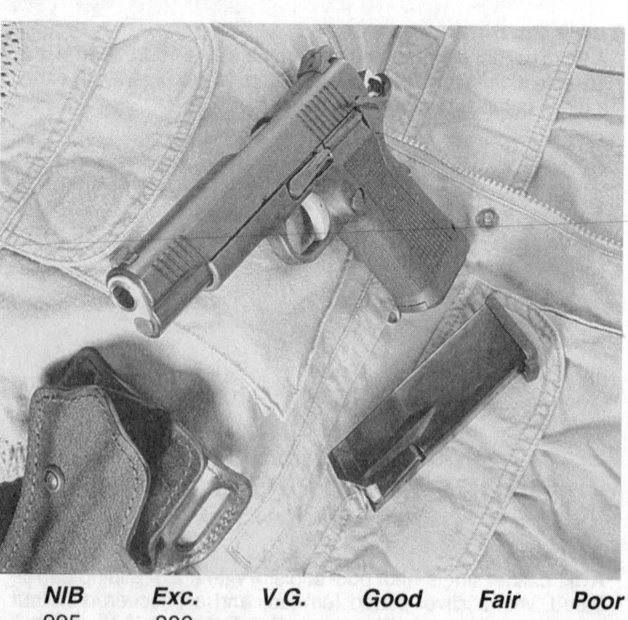

NIB	Exc.	V.G.	Good	Fair	Poor
995	800	—	—	—	—

KZ 9mm

Polymer-frame 1911 chambered for 9mm. Full size is 16+1 capacity with 5" barrel at 33 oz. Compact size is 14+1 capacity with 4.1" barrel at 31 oz. LOA Introduced 2006. MSRP: 1510 full size/1550 compact

ADP 9mm

Wilson's first production pistol. 11-round capacity, polymer frame. 19.5 oz. 6.3" overall length, 3.75" barrel. Introduced 2006. MSRP: 579

SEMI-CUSTOM PISTOLS

These pistols were first built in 1996 using Springfield Armory pistols as the base gun. The Protector Compact was built on the Springfield Compact pistol. In 1997 all Service Grade pistols are built on the new Wilson Combat slide and frame with the exception of the Protector compact which is built on a Colt commander slide and a Colt Officer Model frame. The semi-custom pistols are all marked with 1996A2 on the left-hand side of the slide. Service Grade pistols bear the name Protector, Protector Compact, or Classic on the rights side of the frame's dust cover.

Wilson Model 1996A2

This pistol, introduced in 1996, is offered in a number of different configurations. These configurations affect price. The base pistol is chambered for the .45 ACP cartridge, has snag-free sights and blue finish. Barrel length is 5", magazine capacity is 8 rounds, and weight is approximately 38 oz. There are numerous special features on the standard pistol.

NIB	Exc.	V.G.	Good	Fair	Poor
1350	1050	—	—	—	—

NOTE: Add $70 for tritium night sights, $125 for Wilson adjustable sights, $275 for nights sights, ambi safety, hard chrome frame, $325 for Wilson adjustable sights, ambi safety, hard chrome frame.

Service Grade Protector

This model is fitted to a 5" slide with match barrel adjustable sights, and numerous other special features. Weight is about 38 oz. Black polymer finish on slide and frame. Introduced in 1996.

NIB	Exc.	V.G.	Good	Fair	Poor
1695	1350	—	—	—	—

NOTE: Add $100 for stainless steel.

Service Grade Protector Compact

Same as above but fitted with a 4.25" match-grade barrel. Weight is about 34 oz. Introduced in 1996.

NIB	Exc.	V.G.	Good	Fair	Poor
1695	1350	—	—	—	—

Service Grade Sentinel Ultra Compact

This .45 ACP pistol is fitted with a 3.6" heavy tapered cone handfitted barrel, night sights, high-ride beavertail and numerous special features. Magazine capacity is 6 rounds. Weight is about 29 oz. Finish is a black polymer.

NIB	Exc.	V.G.	Good	Fair	Poor
1995	1550	—	—	—	—

Service Grade Tactical

This .45 ACP pistol is fitted with a 5" tapered cone handfitted barrel. Cocking serrations on front and rear of slide. High-ride beavertail safety and other special features. Night sights are standard. Cocobolo grips. Weight is about 38 oz. finish is black polymer. Magazine capacity is 8 rounds. Introduced in 1999.

NIB	Exc.	V.G.	Good	Fair	Poor
1725	1350	—	—	—	—

Service Grade Classic

This model has a 5" barrel, adjustable sights, hard chrome finish on frame, and other special features. Weight is about 38 oz. Introduced in 1996.

NIB	Exc.	V.G.	Good	Fair	Poor
1795	1400	—	—	—	—

NOTE: Add $100 for stainless steel.

Service Grade Target

Chambered for the .45 ACP cartridge, this model features a 5" stainless steel match handfitted barrel with full length guide rod. Front and rear cocking serrations. Magazine well is beveled and grips are cocobolo. Numerous other special features. Weight is about 38 oz. Finish is black polymer. Magazine capacity is 8 rounds.

NIB	Exc.	V.G.	Good	Fair	Poor
1725	1350	—	—	—	—

Custom Carry Revolver

Built on a Smith & Wesson .357 Magnum Model 66, this model features a 2.5" barrel with adjustable night sights. Cylinder is chambered and grip is black nylon with smooth finish. Stainless steel finish. Weight is about 30 oz.

NIB	Exc.	V.G.	Good	Fair	Poor
1075	850	—	—	—	—

.22 Classic Rimfire Pistol

Chambered for the .22 caliber rimfire cartridge and fitted with a 5" barrel. Hard chrome frame and black anodized slide. Weight is less than standard .45 caliber pistol. Introduced in 1996.

NIB	Exc.	V.G.	Good	Fair	Poor
1145	875	—	—	—	—

CUSTOM-BUILT PISTOLS

Wilson Custom pistols bear the Wilson Combat or Wilson Custom label on the right side of the frame on the dust cover. Full custom guns are typically built on a Colt, Springfield Armory, Norinco, STI, Strayer Voight or Wilson Combat gun.

Combat Classic Super Grade (Tactical Super Grade)

Fitted with a 5" match-grade handfit stainless steel barrel. Adjustable sights, high ride beavertail safety, contoured magazine well and polymer slide with hard chrome frame. Weight is approximately 45 oz.

NIB	Exc.	V.G.	Good	Fair	Poor
3495	2750	—	—	—	—

Tactical Super Grade Compact

Similar to the above model but with a 4.1" match grade barrel. Magazine capacity is 7 rounds. Weight is about 40 oz. Introduced in 2003.

NIB	Exc.	V.G.	Good	Fair	Poor
3495	2750	—	—	—	—

Stealth Defense System

Built with a 4.25" slide with match-grade stainless steel barrel. This model features night sights, checkered front strap and mainspring spring housing with numerous special features. Black polymer finish. Weight is approximately 34 oz.

NIB	Exc.	V.G.	Good	Fair	Poor
2895	2250	1500	—	—	—

Defensive Combat Pistol

This .45 ACP pistol is built with a 5" match-grade stainless steel barrel, night sights, and numerous special features. Finish is black polymer. Weight 38 oz.

NIB	Exc.	V.G.	Good	Fair	Poor
2395	1850	1250	—	—	—

Classic Master Grade

This .45 ACP pistol is fitted with a 5" stainless steel handfitted match-grade barrel. Numerous special features such as ultralight hammer, ambidextrous safety, etc. Finish is stainless steel frame and black polymer slide. Weight is about 38 oz. and magazine capacity is 8 rounds.

NIB	Exc.	V.G.	Good	Fair	Poor
2895	2250	—	—	—	—

Tactical Elite

This is similar to other Wilson pistols with the addition of the special tactical heavy tapered cone barrel.

NIB	Exc.	V.G.	Good	Fair	Poor
2950	2250	1500	—	—	—

Defensive Combat Pistol Deluxe

This model has a 5" match-grade stainless steel barrel and numerous special features. Fitted with adjustable sights. Weight is about 38 oz. Finish is black polymer.

NIB	Exc.	V.G.	Good	Fair	Poor
2595	2000	1350	—	—	—

Professional Model Pistol

Introduced in 2004 this .45 ACP pistol features a 4.1" stainless steel match barrel, tactical combat sights with tritium inserts. Many custom features. Magazine capacity is 8 rounds. Offered in gray/black, green/black, or all-black finish. Weight is about 35 oz.

NIB	Exc.	V.G.	Good	Fair	Poor
1975	1450	—	—	—	—

Competition Pistols

Wilson Combat offers a custom-built pistol to the customer's specifications. An expert appraisal is recommended prior to sale.

TACTICAL RIFLES

UT-15 Urban Tactical

This semi-auto rifle is fitted with a 16.25" fluted barrel with tactical muzzlebrake. Flattop receiver. Aluminum handguard. Chambered for the .223 cartridge. Parkerized finish. Accepts all M-16/AR-15 magazines. Weight is about 6.5 lbs.

NIB	Exc.	V.G.	Good	Fair	Poor
1600	1200	—	—	—	—

NOTE: Add $100 for Armor-Tuff finish.

TPR-15 Tactical Precision Rifle

This model is fitted with a match-grade 18" fluted barrel. Free-floating aluminum handguard. Chambered for .223 cartridge. Weight is about 6.5 lbs. Parkerized finish.

NIB	Exc.	V.G.	Good	Fair	Poor
1600	1200	—	—	—	—

NOTE: Add $100 for Armor-Tuff finish.

M-4T Tactical Carbine

This model features a 16.25" M-4 style heavy barrel with muzzlebrake. Flattop receiver. Chambered for .223 cartridge. Parkerized finish. Weight is about 6.5 lbs.

NIB	Exc.	V.G.	Good	Fair	Poor
1575	1150	—	—	—	—

NOTE: Add $100 for Armor-Tuff finish.

TL-15 Tactical Lightweight

Introduced in 2002, this flattop model features a match-grade 16.25" lightweight barrel with muzzlebrake. Aluminum handguard and fixed buttstock. Chambered for the .223 cartridge. Black Mil-Spec finish.

NIB	Exc.	V.G.	Good	Fair	Poor
1600	1200	—	—	—	—

NOTE: Add $100 for Armor-Tuff finish.

Super Sniper

Fitted with a 20" stainless steel match grade barrel with a 1 in 8 twist. Flat top receiver. Offered in Parkerized or Armor-Tuff finish.

NIB	Exc.	V.G.	Good	Fair	Poor
1800	1450	—	—	—	—

NOTE: Add $100 for Armor-Tuff finish.

WINCHESTER REPEATING ARMS COMPANY

New Haven, Connecticut

The prices given here are for the most part standard guns without optional features that were so often furnished by the factory. These optional or extra-cost features are too numerous to list and can affect the price of a shotgun or rifle to an enormous degree. In some cases these options are one of a kind. Collectors and those interested in Winchester firearms have the benefit of some of the original factory records. These records are now stored in the Cody Firearms Museum, Buffalo Bill Historical Center, P.O. Box 1000, Cody, Wyoming (307) 587-4771. For a $25 fee the museum will provide factory letters containing the original specifications of certain Winchester models using the original factory records.

CAUTION: Buyers should confirm by Cody letter any special-order feature on any Winchester within the Cody record range before paying a premium for a scarce feature.

Hunt Repeating Rifle

Walter Hunt described his repeating rifle as the Volition Repeater. Hunt was granted U.S. patent number 6663 in August 1849 for his repeating rifle that was to pave the way for future generations of Winchester repeating rifles. Hunt's rifle design was unique and innovative as was his patent number 5701 for a conical lead bullet that was to be fired in his rifle. This ingenious bullet had a hole in its base filled with powder and closed by a disc with an opening in the middle to expel the ignition from an independent priming source that used priming pellets made of fulminate of mercury. The rifle actually worked but only the patent model was built; it is now in the Cody Firearms Museum.

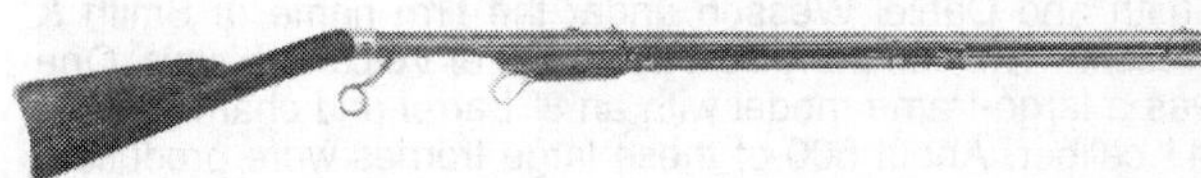

Jennings

Second in the evolutionary line of Winchester rifles is the Jennings. Made by Robbins & Lawrence of Windsor, Vermont, this rifle incorporated the original concept of the Hunt design with the additional improvements utilized by Lewis Jennings. The Jennings rifle is important not only as a link in the chain of repeating-rifle development but also because it introduced Benjamin Henry Tyler to the concept of the tubular magazine lever-action repeating rifle. The Jennings rifle was built in three separate and distinct models. While total production of the three types was contracted for 5,000 guns, it is probable that only about 1,000 were actually produced.

First Model

The First Model Jennings was built in a .54 caliber, breech-loading, single-shot configuration with a ring trigger, oval trigger guard, and 26" barrel. A ramrod was fixed to the underside of the barrel as well. This variation was made from 1850 to 1851.

Courtesy Milwaukee Public Museum, Milwaukee, Wisconsin

Exc.	V.G.	Good	Fair	Poor
—	—	4000	1750	700

Second Model

The Second Model Jennings was produced adopting the improvements made by Horace Smith. This Second Model is a breech-loading repeating rifle with an under barrel magazine tube and a 26" barrel. The frame is sculptured, unlike the First Model. The ring trigger is still present, but the trigger guard was removed as part of the design change. The caliber remained a .54, and the rifle was fitted with a 25" barrel. The Second Model was produced in 1851 and 1852.

Courtesy Milwaukee Public Museum, Milwaukee, Wisconsin

Exc.	V.G.	Good	Fair	Poor
—	—	8000	4000	1500

Third Model

The Third Model represents an attempt by investors to use the remaining parts and close out production. The .54 caliber Third Model was a muzzleloading rifle with a ramrod mounted under the barrel and a 26-1/2" barrel. The frame was the same as that used on the First Model, but the trigger was more of the conventional type. The trigger guard had a bow in the middle giving this model a distinctive appearance. This variation was produced in 1852 and marks the end of the early conceptual period in repeating rifle development.

Exc.	V.G.	Good	Fair	Poor
—	—	9500	4500	1500

Smith & Wesson Volcanic Firearms

An interesting connection in the evolution of the lever-action repeating firearm is found in the production of a small group of pistols and rifles built in Norwich, Connecticut, by Horace Smith and Daniel Wesson under the firm name of Smith & Wesson. The company built two types of Volcanic pistols. One was a large-frame model with an 8" barrel and chambered in .41 caliber. About 500 of these large frames were produced. The other pistol was a small-frame version with a 4" barrel chambered in .31 caliber. Slightly more of these small-frame pistols were built, about 700, than the large-frame version. In both variations the barrel, magazine, and frame were blued. Smith & Wesson also produced a lever-action repeating rifle. These rifles are exceedingly rare with fewer than 10 having been built. They were chambered for the .528 caliber and were fitted with 23" barrels. Because of the small number of rifles built, no value is offered.

Courtesy Buffalo Bill Historical Center, Cody, Wyoming

Courtesy Buffalo Bill Historical Center, Cody, Wyoming

4" Pistol

Exc.	V.G.	Good	Fair	Poor
—	—	11000	4000	1000

8" Pistol

Exc.	V.G.	Good	Fair	Poor
—	—	13000	6000	1500

Courtesy Buffalo Bill Historical Center, Cody, Wyoming

Volcanic Firearms (Volcanic Repeating Arms Company)

With the incorporation of the Volcanic Repeating Arms Company, a new and important individual was introduced who would have an impact on the American arms industry for the next 100 years: Oliver F. Winchester. This new company introduced the Volcanic pistol using the improvements made by Horace Smith and Daniel Wesson. Volcanic firearms are marked on the barrel, "THE VOLCANIC REPEATING ARMS CO. PATENT NEW HAVEN, CONN. FEB. 14, 1854." The Volcanic was offered as a .38 caliber breechloading tubular magazine repeater with blued barrel and bronze frame. These pistols were available in three barrel lengths.

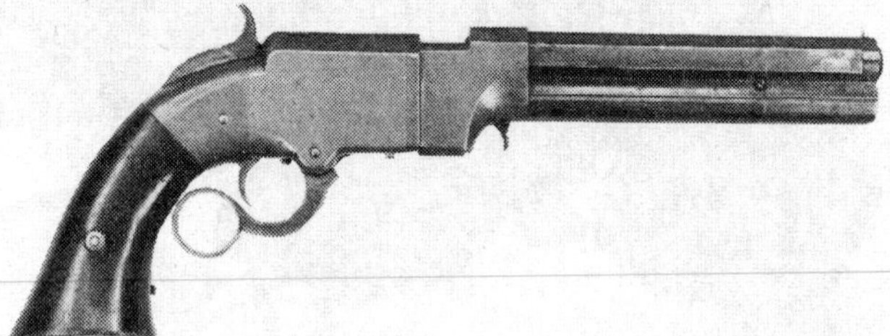

Courtesy Milwaukee Public Museum, Milwaukee, Wisconsin

6" Barrel

Exc.	V.G.	Good	Fair	Poor
—	—	7000	3500	1500

8" Barrel

Exc.	V.G.	Good	Fair	Poor
—	—	7000	3500	1500

16" Barrel

Exc.	V.G.	Good	Fair	Poor
—	—	14000	5500	2500

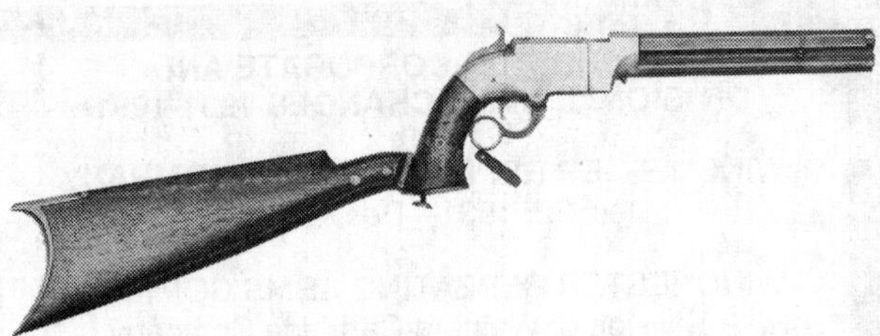

Courtesy Buffalo Bill Historical Center, Cody, Wyoming

NOTE: A few Volcanic pistols were produced with detachable shoulder stocks. These are considered quite rare. For original guns with this option, the prices listed should be increased by 25 percent.

Volcanic Firearms (New Haven Arms Company)

In 1857 the New Haven Arms Company was formed to continue the production of the former Volcanic Repeating Arms Company. Volcanic firearms continued to be built but were now marked on the barrel, "NEW HAVEN, CONN. PATENT FEB. 14, 1854." The Volcanic pistols produced by the New Haven Arms Company were built in .30 caliber and used the same basic frame as the original Volcanic. These pistols were produced in 3-1/2" and 6" barrel lengths.

3-1/2" Barrel

Exc.	*V.G.*	*Good*	*Fair*	*Poor*
—	—	5000	2500	1500

6" Barrel

Exc.	*V.G.*	*Good*	*Fair*	*Poor*
—	—	5750	3000	1500

Lever Action Carbine

New Haven Arms introduced, for the first time, a Volcanic rifle that featured a full-length slotted magazine tube with a spring-activated thumbpiece follower that moved along the entire length of the magazine tube. These rifles were chambered for .38 caliber cartridge and were offered in three barrel lengths: 16", 20", and 24".

Courtesy Buffalo Bill Historical Center, Cody, Wyoming

16" Barrel

Exc.	*V.G.*	*Good*	*Fair*	*Poor*
40000	26000	16000	6000	2000

20" Barrel

Exc.	*V.G.*	*Good*	*Fair*	*Poor*
45000	23000	19000	8000	3000

24" Barrel

Courtesy Little John's Auction Service, Inc., Paul Goodwin photo

Exc.	*V.G.*	*Good*	*Fair*	*Poor*
55000	37000	22500	10000	3000

Henry Rifle

With the development of B. Tyler Henry's improvements in the metallic rimfire cartridge and his additional improvements in the Volcanic frame, the direct predecessor to the Winchester lever-action repeater was born. The new cartridge was the .44 caliber rimfire, and the Henry rifle featured a 24" octagon barrel with a tubular magazine holding 15 shells. The rifle had no forearm, but was furnished with a walnut buttstock with two styles of buttplates: an early rounded heel crescent shape seen on guns produced from 1860 to 1862 and the later sharper heel crescent butt found on guns built from 1863 to 1866. The early models, produced from 1860 to 1861, were fitted with an iron frame, and the later models, built from 1861 to 1866, were fitted with brass frames. About 14,000 Henry rifles were made during the entire production period; only about 300 were iron frame rifles.

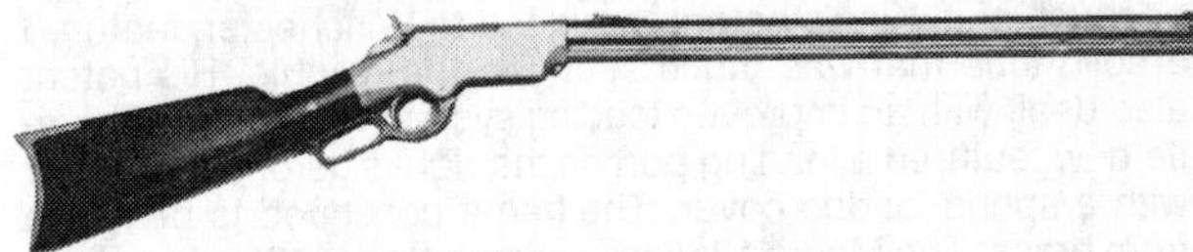

Courtesy Bonhams & Butterfields, San Francisco, California

Iron Frame Rifle

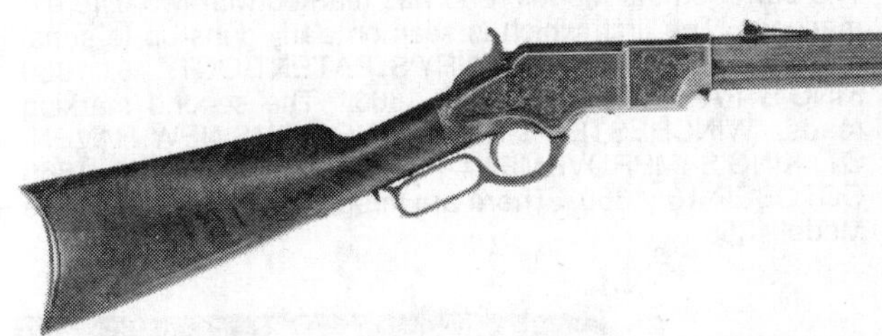

Courtesy Bonhams & Butterfields, San Francisco, California

Exc.	*V.G.*	*Good*	*Fair*	*Poor*
—	85000	65000	30000	—

Brass Frame Rifle

Exc.	*V.G.*	*Good*	*Fair*	*Poor*
—	—	37500	17500	9000

Martially Inspected Henry Rifles

Beginning in 1863 the Federal Government ordered 1,730 Henry Rifles for use in the Civil War. Most of these government-inspected rifles fall into serial number range 3000 to 4000 while the balance are close to this serial-number range. They are marked "C.G.C." for Charles G. Chapman, the government inspector. These Henry rifles were used under actual combat conditions and for that reason it is doubtful that there are any rifles that would fall into the excellent condition category. Therefore no price is given.

NOTE: There are many counterfeit examples of these rifles. It is strongly advised that an expert in this field be consulted prior to a sale.

Exc.	*V.G.*	*Good*	*Fair*	*Poor*
—	40000	32000	16000	12000

Winchester's Improvement Carbine

Overall length 43-1/2"; barrel length 24"; caliber .44 rimfire. Walnut stock with a brass buttplate; the receiver and magazine cover/forend of brass; the barrel and magazine tube blued. The magazine loading port is exposed by sliding the forend forward. This design was protected by O.F. Winchester's British Patent Number 3285 issued December 19, 1865. Unmarked except for internally located serial numbers. Approximately 700 manufactured in December of 1865 and early 1866, the majority of which were sold to Maximilian of Mexico. Prospective purchasers are strongly advised to secure an expert appraisal prior to acquisition.

Exc.	*V.G.*	*Good*	*Fair*	*Poor*
33000	26000	18500	12500	9000

Model 1866

In 1866 the New Haven Arms Company changed its name to the Winchester Repeating Arms Company. The first firearm to be built under the Winchester name was the Model 1866. This first Winchester was a much-improved version of the Henry. A new magazine tube developed by Nelson King, Winchester's plant superintendent, was a vast improvement over the slotted magazine tube used on the Henry and its predecessor. The old tube allowed dirt to enter through the slots and was weakened because of it. King's patent, assigned to Winchester, featured a solid tube that was much stronger and reliable. His patent also dealt with an improved loading system for the rifle. The rifle now featured a loading port on the right side of the receiver with a spring-loaded cover. The frame continued to be made from brass. The Model 1866 was chambered for the .44 caliber Flat Rimfire or the .44 caliber Pointed Rimfire. Both cartridges could be used interchangeably.

The barrel on the Model 1866 was marked with two different markings. The first, which is seen on early guns up to serial number 23000, reads "HENRY'S PATENT-OCT. 16, 1860 KING'S PATENT-MARCH 29, 1866." The second marking reads, "WINCHESTER'S-REPEATING-ARMS.NEW HAVEN, CT. KING'S-IMPROVEMENT-PATENTED MARCH 29, 1866 OCTOBER 16, 1860." There are three basic variations of the Model 1866:

Courtesy Milwaukee Public Museum, Milwaukee, Wisconsin

1. Sporting Rifle round or octagon barrel. Approximately 28,000 were produced.
2. Carbine round barrel. Approximately 127,000 were produced.
3. Musket round barrel. Approximately 14,000 were produced.

The rifle and musket held 17 cartridges, and the carbine had a capacity of 13 cartridges. Unlike the Henry, Model 1866s were fitted with a walnut forearm. The Model 1866 was discontinued in 1898 with approximately 170,000 guns produced. The Model 1866 was sold in various special order configurations, such as barrels longer or shorter than standard, including engraved guns. The prices listed represent only standard-model 1866s. For guns with special-order features, an independent appraisal from an expert is highly recommended.

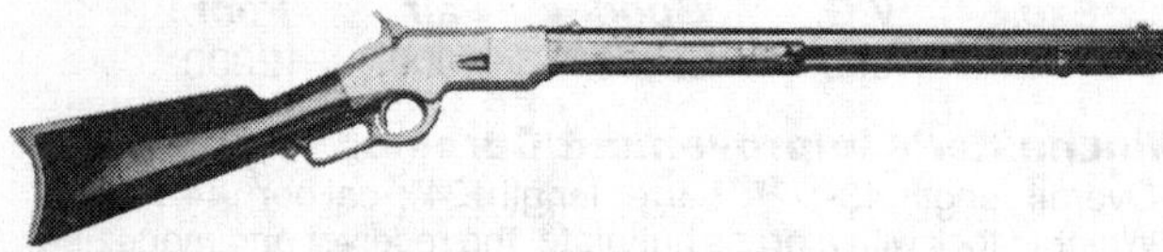

Courtesy Bonhams & Butterfields, San Francisco, California

First Model

This first style has both the Henry and King patent dates stamped on the barrel, a flat-loading port cover, and a two-screw upper tang. Perhaps the most distinctive feature of the First Model is the rapid drop at the top rear of the receiver near the hammer. This is often referred to as the "Henry Drop," a reference to the same receiver drop found on the Henry rifle. First Models will be seen up through the 15000 serial number range.

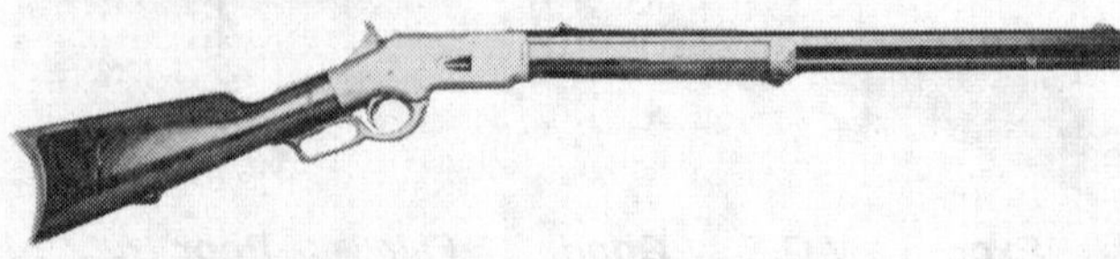

Courtesy Bonhams & Butterfields, San Francisco, California

WINCHESTER CORPORATE AND DIVISIONAL NAME CHANGES 1931-1991

WINCHESTER REPEATING ARMS COMPANY
Dec. 22, 1931—Dec. 31, 1938

WINCHESTER REPEATING ARMS COMPANY
A Division of Western Cartridge Company
Dec. 31, 1938—Dec. 30, 1944

WINCHESTER REPEATING ARMS COMPANY
A Division of Olin Industries, Inc.
Dec. 30, 1944—January 1952

WINCHESTER-WESTERN DIVISION
Olin Industries, Inc.
January 1952—Aug. 31, 1954

WINCHESTER-WESTERN DIVISION
Olin Mathieson Chemical Corporation
Aug. 31, 1954—Sept. 1, 1969

WINCHESTER-WESTERN DIVISION
OLIN CORPORATION
Sept. 1, 1969—July 21, 1981

U.S REPEATING ARMS COMPANY
July 21, 1981—Present

Rifle

Exc.	*V.G.*	*Good*	*Fair*	*Poor*
30000	19000	13000	8500	4000

Carbine

Exc.	*V.G.*	*Good*	*Fair*	*Poor*
26000	19000	13000	7500	5000

Second Model

The second style differs from the first most noticeably in its single screw upper tang and a flare at the front of the receiver to meet the forearm. The Second Model also has a more gradual drop at the rear of the receiver than the First Model. The Second Style Model 1866 appears through serial number 25000.

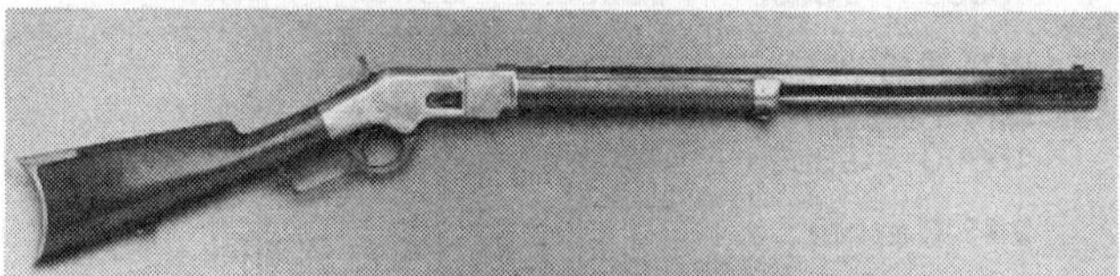

Courtesy Bonhams & Butterfields, San Francisco, California

Rifle

Exc.	*V.G.*	*Good*	*Fair*	*Poor*
22000	16000	9000	6000	4000

Courtesy Bonhams & Butterfields, San Francisco, California

Carbine

Exc.	*V.G.*	*Good*	*Fair*	*Poor*
15000	10000	8000	6000	3500

MODEL	SERIAL NUMBER
1866	124995 to 170101
1873	1 to 720496 (N/A 497-610 and 199551-199598)
1876	1 to 63871
Hotchkiss	1 to 84555
1885*	1 to 109999 (N/A 74459-75556)
1886	1 to 156599 (N/A 146000-150799)
1887 & 1901	1 to 72999
1890	1 to 329999 (N/A 20000-29999)
1906	1 to 79999
1892	1 to 379999
1893	1 to 34050
1897	1 to 377999
1894	1 to 353999
1895	1 to 59999
Lee	1 to 19999
1903	1 to 39999
1905	1 to 29078
1906	1 to 79999
1907	1 to 9999
21	1 to 35000

* Single-Shot

Third Model

The third style's most noticeable characteristic is the more moderately curved receiver shape at the rear of the frame. The serial number is now stamped in block numerals behind the trigger, thus allowing the numbers to be seen for the first time without removing the stock. The barrel marking is stamped with the Winchester address. The Third Model is found between serial numbers 25000 and 149000. For the first time, a musket version was produced in this serial-number range.

Rifle

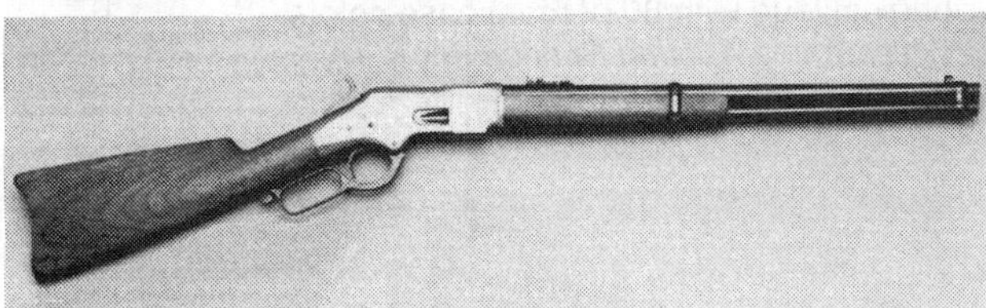

Courtesy Bonhams & Butterfields, San Francisco, California

Exc.	V.G.	Good	Fair	Poor
14000	9000	6500	4000	3000

Carbine

Exc.	V.G.	Good	Fair	Poor
—	12000	9500	5500	3500

Musket

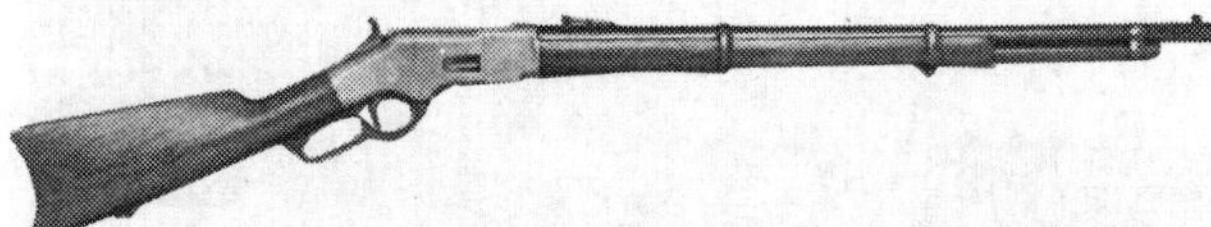

Courtesy Bonhams & Butterfields, San Francisco, California

Exc.	V.G.	Good	Fair	Poor
10000	8500	6500	3500	2500

Fourth Model

The fourth style has an even less pronounced drop at the top rear of the frame, and the serial number is stamped in script on the lower tang under the lever. The Fourth Model is seen between serial number 149000 and 170100 with the late guns having an iron buttplate instead of brass.

Rifle

Exc.	V.G.	Good	Fair	Poor
10000	8000	6500	4000	3000

Carbine

Exc.	V.G.	Good	Fair	Poor
16000	11000	9000	3500	2500

Musket

Exc.	V.G.	Good	Fair	Poor
12500	9000	6000	3500	2500

Model 1866 Iron Frame Rifle Musket

Overall length 54-1/2"; barrel length 33-1/4"; caliber .45 centerfire. Walnut stock with case hardened furniture, barrel burnished bright, the receiver case hardened. The finger lever catch mounted within a large bolster at the rear of the lever. Unmarked except for serial numbers that appear externally on the receiver and often the buttplate tang. Approximately 25 made during the early autumn of 1866. Prospective purchasers are strongly advised to secure an expert appraisal prior to acquisition. Due to the recent identification of this model pricing schedules have yet to be established.

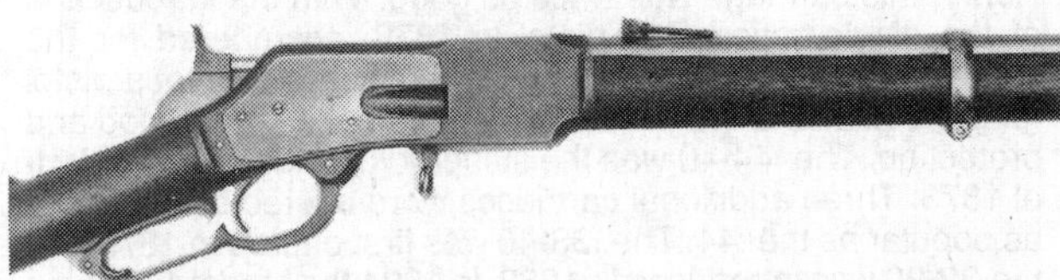

Model 1866 Iron Frame Swiss Sharpshooters Rifle

As above, but in .41 Swiss caliber and fitted with a Scheutzen style stock supplied by the firm of Weber Ruesch in Zurich. Marked Weber Ruesch, Zurich on the barrel and serial numbered externally. Approximately 400 to 450 manufactured in 1866 and 1867. Prospective purchasers are strongly advised to secure an expert appraisal prior to acquisition. Due to the recent identification of this model pricing schedules have yet to be established.

Model 1867 Iron Frame Carbine

Overall length 39-1/4"; barrel length 20"; caliber .44 rimfire. Walnut stock with case hardened furniture; the barrel and magazine tube blued; the receiver case hardened. The finger lever catch mounted within the rear curl of the lever. Unmarked except for serial numbers that appear externally on the receiver and often the buttplate tang. Approximately 20 manufactured. Prospective purchasers are strongly advised to secure an expert appraisal prior to acquisition. Due to the recent identification of this model pricing schedules have yet to be established.

Model 1868 Iron Frame Rifle Musket

Overall length 49-1/2" (.455 cal.), 50-1/2" or 53" (.45 and .47 cal.); barrel length 29-1/2" (.455 cal.) and 30-1/4" or 33" (.45 and .47 cal.); calibers .45, .455, and .47 centerfire. Walnut stock with case hardened or burnished bright (.45 and .47 cal.) furniture; the barrel burnished bright; the receiver case hardened or burnished bright (.45 and .47 cal.). The finger lever catch mounted on the lower receiver tang. The rear of the finger lever machined with a long flat extension on its upper surface. Unmarked except for serial number. Approximately 30 examples made in .45 and .455 caliber and 250 in .47 caliber. Prospective purchasers are strongly advised to secure an expert appraisal prior to acquisition. Due to the recent identification of this model pricing schedules have yet to be established.

Model 1868 Iron Frame Carbine

Overall length 40"; barrel length 20"; caliber .44 centerfire. Walnut stock with case hardened furniture; barrel and magazine tube blued; the receiver case hardened. The finger lever catch as above. Unmarked except for serial numbers (receiver and buttplate tang). Approximately 25 manufactured. Prospective purchasers are strongly advised to secure an expert appraisal prior to acquisition. Due to the recent identification of this model pricing schedules have yet to be established.

Model 1873

This Winchester rifle was one of the most popular lever-actions the company ever produced. This is the "gun that won the West" and with good reason. It was chambered for the more powerful centerfire cartridge, the .44-40. Compared to the .44 Henry, this cartridge was twice as good. With the introduction of the single-action Colt pistol in 1878, chambered for the same cartridge, the individual had the convenience of a pistol for protection and the accuracy of the Winchester for food and protection. The .44-40 was the standard cartridge for the Model 1873. Three additional cartridges were offered but were not as popular as the .44. The .38-40 was first offered in 1879 and the.32-20 was introduced in 1882. In 1884 the Model 1873 was offered in .22 caliber rimfire, with a few special order guns built in .22 extra long rimfire. Approximately 19,552 .22 caliber Model 1873s were produced.

Early Model 1873s were fitted with an iron receiver until 1884, when a steel receiver was introduced. The Model 1873 was offered in three styles:

1. Sporting Rifle, 24" round, octagon, or half-octagon barrel. Equipped standard with a crescent iron buttplate, straight-grip stock and capped forearm.
2. Carbine, 20" round barrel. Furnished standard with a rounded iron buttplate, straight-grip stock, and carbine style forend fastened to the barrel with a single barrel band.
3. Musket, 30" round barrel. Standard musket is furnished with a nearly full-length forearm fastened to the barrel with three barrel bands. The buttstock has a rounded buttplate.

The upper tang was marked with the model designation and the serial number was stamped on the lower tang. Caliber stampings on the Model 1873 are found on the bottom of the frame and on the breech end of the barrel. Winchester discontinued the Model 1873 in 1919, after producing about 720,000 guns.

The Winchester Model 1873 was offered with a large number of extra-cost options that greatly affect the value of the gun. For example, Winchester built two sets of special Model 1873s: the 1-of-100 and the 1-of-1000. Winchester sold only eight 1-of-100 Model 1873s, and 136 of the 1-of-1000 guns that were built. In 1991 a few of these special guns were sold at auction and brought prices exceeding $75,000. The prices listed here are for standard guns only. For Model 1873 with special features, it is best to secure an expert appraisal. Model 1873s with case colored receivers will bring a premium.

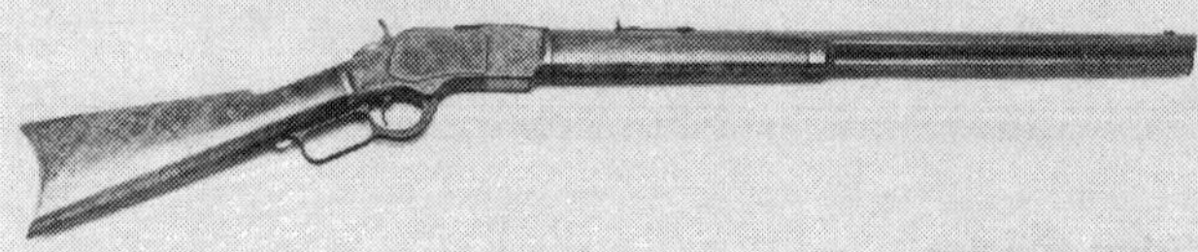

Courtesy Bonhams & Butterfields, San Francisco, California

A Winchester Model 1873 rifle, serial number 27, sold at auction for $55,000. Fitted with a 24" round barrel with experimental button magazine. Set trigger and blued finish. Condition is 90 percent original blue on action and 70 percent on barrel. Stock is very good.
Little John's Auction Service, Inc.

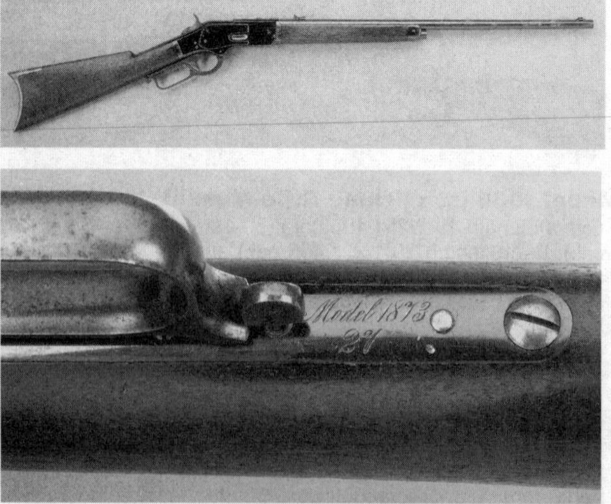

A First Model 1873 rifle sold at auction for $60,000. Factory engraved. Chambered for the .44-40 and fitted with a 24" octagon heavy barrel. Checkered fancy walnut stock. Set trigger. Tang sight. Condition is 96 percent original blue with 80 percent case colors.
Little John's Auction Service, Inc.

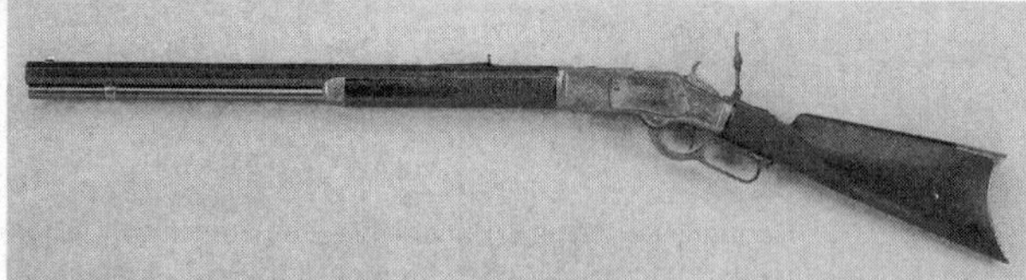

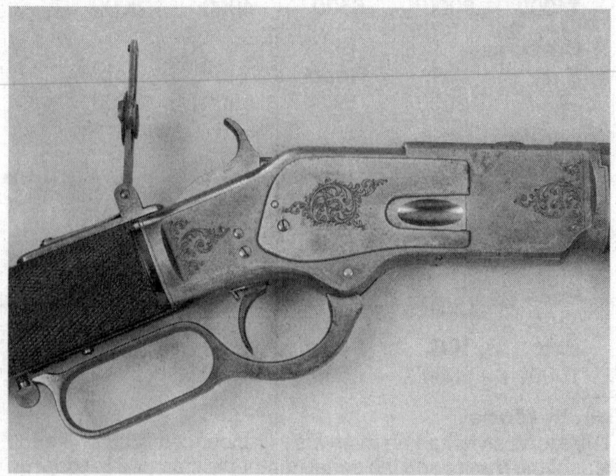

This symbol denotes "Sleepers" with rapidly-rising values and/or significant collector potential.

First Model

The primary difference between the various styles of the Model 1873 is found in the appearance and construction of the dust cover. The First Model has a dust cover held in place with grooved guides on either side. A checkered oval finger grip is found on top of the dust cover. The latch that holds the lever firmly in place is anchored into the lower tang with visible threads. On later First Models, these threads are not visible. First Models appear from serial number 1 to about 31000.

Courtesy Milwaukee Public Museum, Milwaukee, Wisconsin

Rifle

Exc.	V.G.	Good	Fair	Poor
14000	9000	4750	3000	1400

Carbine

Exc.	V.G.	Good	Fair	Poor
16000	10000	6000	4000	2500

Musket

Exc.	V.G.	Good	Fair	Poor
8000	6000	3000	1800	1000

Second Model

The dust cover on the Second Model operates on one central guide secured to the receiver with two screws. The checkered oval finger grip is still used, but on later Second Models this is changed to a serrated finger grip on the rear of the dust cover. Second Models are found in the 31000 to 90000 serial number range.

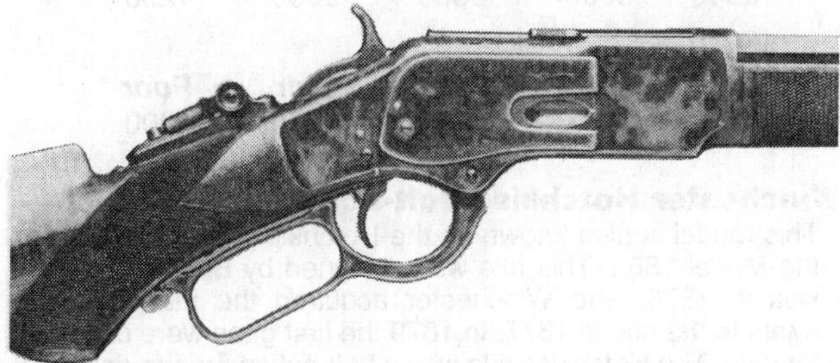

Courtesy Bonhams & Butterfields, San Francisco, California

Rifle

Exc.	V.G.	Good	Fair	Poor
6000	4000	2500	2000	1250

Carbine

Exc.	V.G.	Good	Fair	Poor
10000	6000	4500	3000	1000

Musket

Exc.	V.G.	Good	Fair	Poor
4500	2900	2000	1250	900

Third Model

The central guide rail is still present on the Third Model, but it is now integrally machined as part of the receiver. The serrated rear edges of the dust cover are still present on the Third Model.

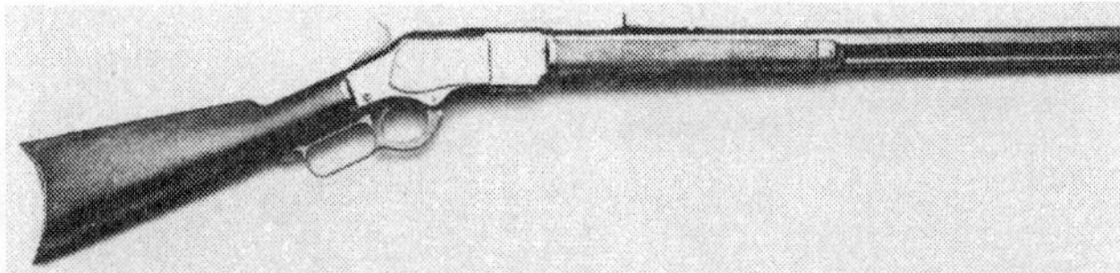

Courtesy Bonhams & Butterfields, San Francisco, California

A Third Model 1873 saddle ring carbine sold at auction for $19,500. Chambered for the .44-40. Condition is 98 percent original blue with 90 percent case colors.
Little John's Auction Service, Inc.

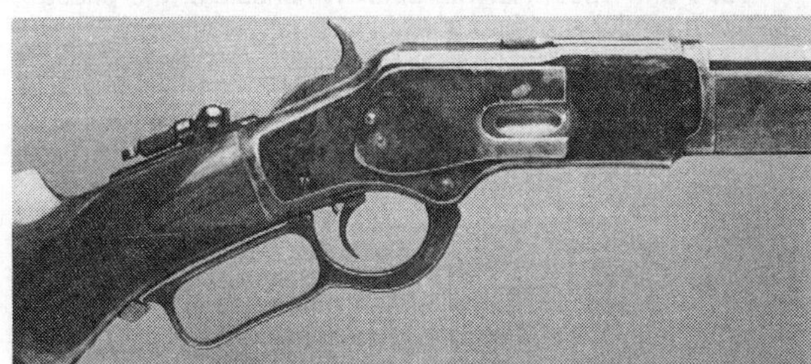

Courtesy Bonhams & Butterfields, San Francisco, California

Rifle

Exc.	V.G.	Good	Fair	Poor
5000	4000	2000	1000	750

Carbine

Exc.	V.G.	Good	Fair	Poor
10000	8000	5000	2000	800

Musket

Exc.	V.G.	Good	Fair	Poor
7000	2700	1500	850	500

Model 1873 .22 Rimfire Rifle

Winchester's first .22 caliber rifle and the first .22 caliber repeating rifle made in America was introduced in 1884 and discontinued in 1904. Its drawback was the small caliber. The general preference during this period of time was for the larger-caliber rifles. Winchester sold a little more than 19,000 .22 caliber Model 1873s.

Exc.	V.G.	Good	Fair	Poor
8000	6500	3000	1700	750

Model 1876

Winchester's Model 1876, sometimes referred to as the Centennial Model, was the company's response to the public's demand for a repeater rifle capable of handling larger and more potent calibers. Many single-shot rifles were available at this time to shoot more powerful cartridges, and Winchester redesigned the earlier Model 1873 to answer this need. The principal changes made to the Model 1873 were a larger and stronger receiver to handle more powerful cartridges. Both the carbine and the musket had their forearms extended to cover the full length of the magazine tube. The carbine barrel was increased in length from 20" to 22", and the musket barrel length was increased from 30 to 32". The Model 1876 was the first Winchester to be offered with a pistol-grip stock on its special Sporting Rifle. The Model 1876 was available in these calibers: .45-77 W.C.F., .50-95 Express, .45-60 W.C.F., .40-60 W.C.F. The Model 1876 was offered in four different styles:

1. Sporting Rifle, 28" round, octagon, or half-octagon barrel. This rifle was fitted with a straight-grip stock with crescent iron buttplate. A special sporting rifle was offered with a pistol-grip stock.
2. Express Rifle, 26" round, octagon, or half-octagon barrel. The same sporting rifle stock was used.
3. Carbine, 22" round barrel with full length forearm secured by one barrel band and straight-grip stock.
4. Musket, 32" round barrel with full-length forearm secured by one barrel band and straight-grip stock. Stamped on the barrel is the Winchester address with King's patent date. The caliber marking is stamped on the bottom of the receiver near the magazine tube and the breech end of the barrel. Winchester also furnished the Model 1876 in 1-of-100 and 1-of-1000 special guns. Only 8 1-of-100 Model 1876s were built and 54 1-of-1000 76s were built. As with their Model 1873 counterparts, these rare guns often sell in the $75,000 range or more. Approximately 64,000 Model 1876s were built by Winchester between 1876 and 1897. As with other Winchesters, the prices given are for standard guns.

First Model

As with the Model 1873, the primary difference in model types lies in the dust cover. The First Model has no dust cover and is seen between serial number 1 and 3000.

Rifle

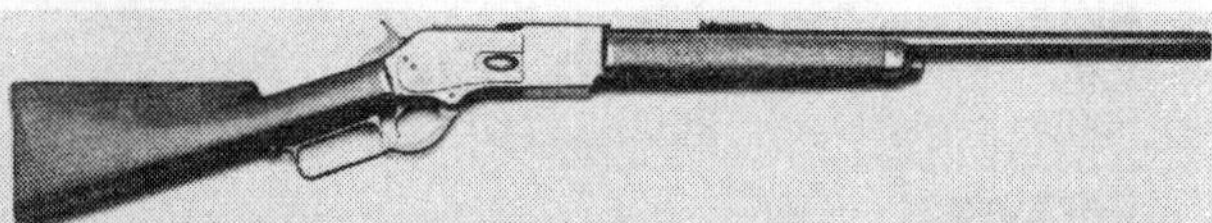

Courtesy Bonhams & Butterfields, San Francisco, California

Exc.	V.G.	Good	Fair	Poor
15000	10500	6000	2750	1000

Carbine

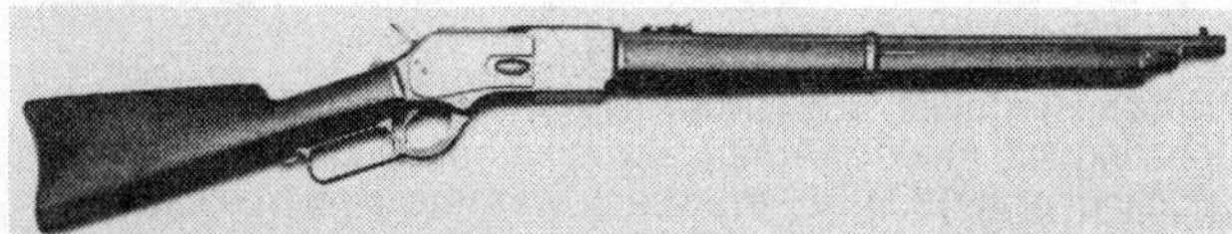

Courtesy Bonhams & Butterfields, San Francisco, California

Exc.	V.G.	Good	Fair	Poor
12000	9500	6500	2500	1000

Musket

Exc.	V.G.	Good	Fair	Poor
15000	12000	6500	3000	1500

Second Model

The Second Model has a dust cover with guide rail attached to the receiver with two screws. On the early Second Model an oval finger guide is stamped on top of the dust cover while later models have a serrated finger guide along the rear edge of the dust cover. Second Models range from serial numbers 3000 to 30000.

Rifle

Exc.	V.G.	Good	Fair	Poor
11000	7500	4000	2000	1000

Carbine

Exc.	V.G.	Good	Fair	Poor
11000	7500	4000	2000	1000

Musket

Exc.	V.G.	Good	Fair	Poor
20000	15000	8000	1750	1000

Northwest Mounted Police Carbine

The folding rear sight is graduated in meters instead of yards.

Courtesy Little John's Auction Service, Inc., Paul Goodwin photo

Exc.	V.G.	Good	Fair	Poor
15000	9000	4500	2000	1250

NOTE: Deduct 50 percent from prices if factory records do not confirm NPW use. A Model 1876 NWP in excellent condition is very rare. Proceed with caution.

Third Model

The dust cover guide rail on Third Model 76s is integrally machined as part of the receiver with a serrated rear edge on the dust cover. Third Model will be seen from serial numbers 30000 to 64000.

Rifle

Exc.	V.G.	Good	Fair	Poor
9000	5500	3250	1500	750

Carbine

Exc.	V.G.	Good	Fair	Poor
12500	8000	3000	2000	1250

Musket

Exc.	V.G.	Good	Fair	Poor
14000	10000	7500	4000	1000

Winchester Hotchkiss Bolt-Action Rifle

This model is also known as the Hotchkiss Magazine Gun or the Model 1883. This rifle was designed by Benjamin Hotchkiss in 1876, and Winchester acquired the manufacturing rights to the rifle in 1877. In 1879 the first guns were delivered for sale. The Hotchkiss rifle was a bolt-action firearm designed for military and sporting use. It was the first bolt-action rifle made by Winchester. The rifle was furnished in .45-70 Government, and although the 1884 Winchester catalog lists a .40-65 Hotchkiss as being available, no evidence exists that such a chamber was ever actually furnished. The Model 1883 was available in three different styles:

1. Sporting Rifle, 26" round, octagon, or half-octagon barrel fitted with a rifle-type stock that included a modified pistol grip or straight-grip stock.

A Third Model 1876 Deluxe rifle sold at auction for $24,000. Chambered for the .50-95 cartridge and fitted with a 22" round barrel. Checkered pistol grip stock with fancy wood. Condition is 90 percent case colors and 93 percent original blue. Stock in very good condition.
Little John's Auction Service, Inc.

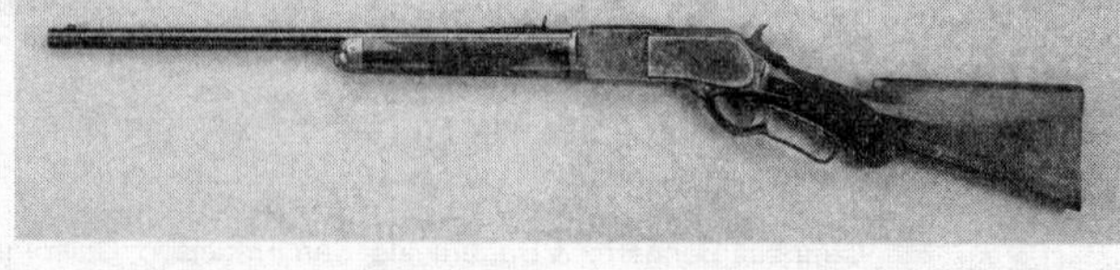

This symbol denotes "Sleepers" with rapidly-rising values and/or significant collector potential.

2. Carbine, 24" round or 22-1/2" round barrel with military-style straight-grip stock.
3. Musket, 32" or 28" round barrel with almost full-length military-style straight-grip stock. Winchester produced the Model 1883 until 1899, having built about 85,000 guns.

First Model

This model has the safety and a turn button magazine cut-off located above the trigger guard on the right side. The Sporting Rifle is furnished with a 26" round or octagon barrel while the carbine has a 24" round barrel with a saddle ring on the left side of the stock. The musket has a 32" round barrel with two barrel bands, a steel forearm tip, and bayonet attachment under the barrel. The serial number range for the First Model is between 1 and about 6419.

Sporting Rifle

Courtesy Bonhams & Butterfields, San Francisco, California

Courtesy George Hoyem

Exc.	V.G.	Good	Fair	Poor
2000	1650	1250	800	400

Carbine

Exc.	V.G.	Good	Fair	Poor
5500	2500	1500	900	500

Musket

Exc.	V.G.	Good	Fair	Poor
2000	1650	1250	800	400

Second Model

On this model the safety is located on the top left side of the receiver, and the magazine cutoff is located on the top right side of the receiver to the rear of the bolt handle. The sporting rifle remains unchanged from the First Model with the above exceptions. The carbine has a 22-1/2" round barrel with a nickeled forearm cap. The musket now has a 28" barrel. Serial number range for the Second Model runs from 6420 to 22521.

Sporting Rifle

Courtesy Milwaukee Public Museum, Milwaukee, Wisconsin

Courtesy George Hoyem

Exc.	V.G.	Good	Fair	Poor
1750	1400	900	600	300

Carbine

Exc.	V.G.	Good	Fair	Poor
1750	1400	900	600	300

Musket

Exc.	V.G.	Good	Fair	Poor
4500	2250	1000	750	500

Third Model

The Third Model is easily identified by the two-piece stock separated by the receiver. The specifications for the sporting rifle remain the same as before, while the carbine is now fitted with a 20" barrel with saddle ring and bar on the left side of the frame. The musket remains unchanged from the Second Model with the exception of the two-piece stock. Serial numbers of the Third Model range from 22552 to 84555.

Sporting Rifle

Exc.	V.G.	Good	Fair	Poor
1650	1250	800	500	300

Carbine

Exc.	V.G.	Good	Fair	Poor
1650	1250	800	500	300

Musket

Courtesy Bonhams & Butterfields, San Francisco, California

Exc.	V.G.	Good	Fair	Poor
1650	1250	800	500	300

Model 1885 (Single-Shot)

The Model 1885 marks an important development between Winchester and John M. Browning. The Single-Shot rifle was the first of many Browning patents that Winchester would purchase and provided the company with the opportunity to diversify its firearms line. The Model 1885 was the first single-shot rifle built by Winchester. The company offered more calibers in this model than any other. A total of 45 centerfire calibers were offered from the .22 extra long to the 50-110 Express, as well as 14 rimfire caliber from .22 B.B. cap to the .44 Flat Henry. Numerous barrel lengths, shapes, and weights were available as were stock configurations, sights, and finishes. These rifles were also available in solid frame and takedown styles. One could almost argue that each of the 139,725 Model 1885s built are unique. Many collectors of the Winchester Single-Shot specialize in nothing else. For this reason it is difficult to provide pricing that will cover most of the Model 1885s that the collector will encounter. However the prices given here are for standard guns in standard configurations.

The Model 1885 was offered in two basic frame types:

A. The High Wall was the first frame type produced and is so called because the frame covers the breech and hammer except for the hammer spur.

B. The breech and hammer are visible on the Low Wall frame with its low sides. This frame type was first introduced around the 5000 serial number range.

Both the High Wall and the Low Wall were available in two type frame profiles; the Thickside and the Thinside. The Thickside frame has flat sides that do not widen out to meet the stock. The Thickside is more common on the low wall rifle and rare on the High Walls.

The Thinside frame has shallow milled sides that widen out to meet the stock. Thinside frames are common on High Wall guns and rare on Low Wall rifles.

1. The standard High Wall rifle was available with octagon or round barrel with length determined by caliber. The butt stock and forearm were plain walnut with crescent buttplate and blued frame.
2. The standard Low Wall featured a round or octagon barrel with length determined by caliber and a plain walnut stock and forearm with crescent buttplate.
3. The High Wall musket most often had a 26" round barrel chambered for the .22 caliber cartridge. Larger calibers were available as were different barrel lengths. The High Wall Musket featured an almost full length forearm fastened to the barrel with a single barrel band and rounded buttplate.
4. The Low Wall musket is most often referred to as the Winder Musket named after the distinguished marksman, Colonel C.B. Winder. This model features a Lyman receiver sight and was made in .22 caliber.
5. The High Wall Schuetzen rifle was designed for serious target shooting and was available with numerous extras including a 30" octagon barrel medium weight without rear sight seat; fancy walnut checkered pistol grip Schuetzen-style cheekpiece; Schuetzen-style buttplate; checkered forearm; double set triggers; spur finger lever, and adjustable palm rest.
6. The Low Wall carbine was available in 15", 16", 18", and 20" round barrels. The carbine featured a saddle ring on the left side of the frame and a rounded buttplate.
7. The Model 1885 was also available in a High Wall shotgun in 20 gauge with 26" round barrel and straight-grip stock with shotgun style rubber buttplate. The Model 1885 was manufactured between 1885 and 1920 with a total production of about 140,000 guns.

CALIBER NOTE: As stated above it is difficult to provide pricing on specific rifles, especially calibers, because of the wide range of variables. However, the collector may find it useful to know that the most common rimfire calibers were the .22 Short, .22 WCF, and .22 Long, in that order, with the .22 Long Rifle a distant fourth. The most common centerfire chambers were the .32 WCF and the .32-40. Other popular centerfire calibers were the .38-55, .25-20, .44 WCF, .32 Long WCF, and the .45-70. There were a number of chamberings that are extremely rare (one of each built). It is strongly recommended that research is done prior to a sale.

Courtesy Bonhams & Butterfields, San Francisco, California

Standard High Wall Rifle

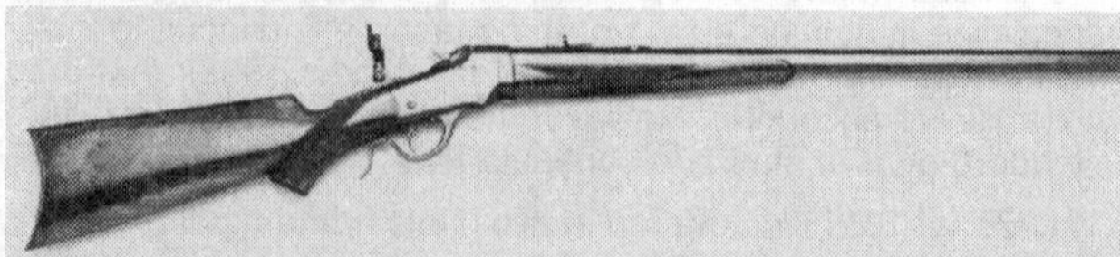

Deluxe High Wall

Courtesy Bonhams & Butterfields, San Francisco, California

Exc.	*V.G.*	*Good*	*Fair*	*Poor*
5000	3500	2200	1500	950

Standard Low Wall Rifle

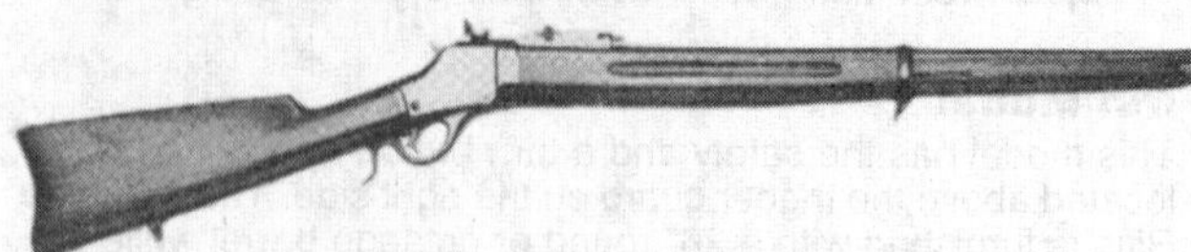

Courtesy Bonhams & Butterfields, San Francisco, California

Exc.	*V.G.*	*Good*	*Fair*	*Poor*
2500	1800	1200	1400	900

High Wall Musket

Exc.	*V.G.*	*Good*	*Fair*	*Poor*
2200	1500	1000	700	425

Low Wall Musket (Winder Musket)

Courtesy Buffalo Bill Historical Center, Cody, Wyoming

Exc.	*V.G.*	*Good*	*Fair*	*Poor*
1700	1200	800	500	300

High Wall Schuetzen Rifle

Exc.	*V.G.*	*Good*	*Fair*	*Poor*
14000	7000	3000	1850	1000

Low Wall Carbine

Exc.	*V.G.*	*Good*	*Fair*	*Poor*
7500	5000	3500	2750	1500

High Wall Shotgun

Courtesy Buffalo Bill Historical Center, Cody, Wyoming

Exc.	*V.G.*	*Good*	*Fair*	*Poor*
4500	3000	2250	1250	850

NOTE: Model 1885s with case colored frames bring a premium of 25 percent over guns with blued frames. Model 1885s in calibers .50-110 and .50-100 will bring a premium depending on style and configuration.

Model 1886

Based on a John Browning patent, the Model 1886 was one of the finest and strongest lever-actions ever utilized in a Winchester rifle. Winchester introduced the Model 1886 in order to take advantage of the more powerful centerfire cartridges of the time.

Model 1886 rifles and carbines were furnished with walnut stocks, case hardened frames, and blued barrels and magazine tubes. In 1901 Winchester discontinued the use of case hardened frames on all its rifles and used blued frames instead. For this reason, case hardened Model 1886 rifles will bring a premium. Winchester provided a large selection of extra cost options on the Model 1886, and for rifles with these options, a separate valuation should be made by a reliable source. The Model 1886 was produced from 1886 to 1935 with about 160,000 in production.

The rifle was available in 10 different chambers:

.45-70 U.S. Government	.50-110 Express
.45-90 W.C.F.	.40-70 W.C. F.
.40-82 W.C.F.	.38-70 W.C. F.
.40-65 W.C.F.	.50-100-450
.38-56 W.C.F.	.33 W.C. F.

The most popular caliber was the .45-70 Government. Prices of the Model 1886 are influenced by caliber, with the larger calibers bringing a premium. The 1886 was available in several different configurations.

1. Sporting Rifle, 26", round, octagon, or half-octagon barrel, full or half magazine and straight-grip stock with plain forearm.
2. Fancy Sporting Rifle, 26", round or octagon barrel, full or half magazine and fancy checkered walnut pistol-grip stock with checkered forearm.
3. Takedown Rifle, 24" round barrel, full or half magazine with straight-grip stock fitted with shotgun rubber buttplate and plain forearm.
4. Extra Lightweight Takedown Rifle, 22" round barrel, full or half magazine with straight-grip stock fitted with shotgun rubber buttplate and plain forearm.
5. Extra Lightweight Rifle, 22" round barrel, full or half magazine with straight-grip stock fitted with a shotgun rubber butt-plate and plain forearm.
6. Carbine, 22" round barrel, full or half magazine, with straight-grip stock and plain forearm.
7. Musket, 30" round barrel, musket-style forearm with one barrel band. Military-style sights. About 350 Model 1886 Muskets were produced.

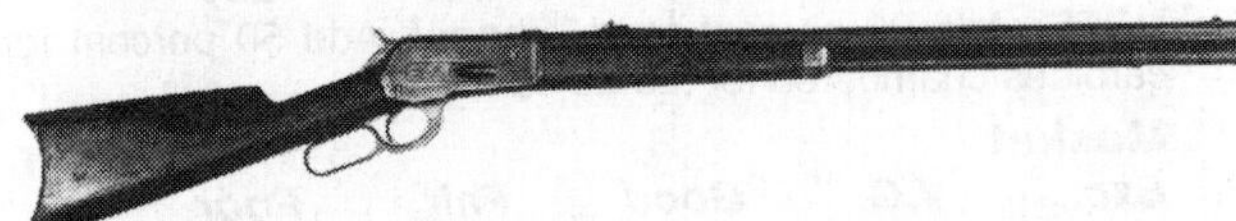

Courtesy Milwaukee Public Museum, Milwaukee, Wisconsin

Sporting Rifle

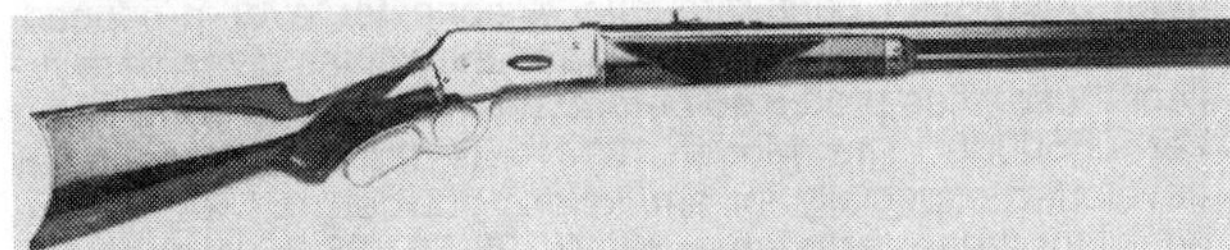

Courtesy Bonhams & Butterfields, San Francisco, California

Exc.	*V.G.*	*Good*	*Fair*	*Poor*
15000	10000	7500	5000	2500

Fancy Sporting Rifle

Exc.	*V.G.*	*Good*	*Fair*	*Poor*
25000	14000	8000	6000	3000

Takedown Rifle—Standard

Exc.	*V.G.*	*Good*	*Fair*	*Poor*
12500	8500	4200	2000	700

Extra Lightweight Takedown Rifle—.33 caliber

Exc.	*V.G.*	*Good*	*Fair*	*Poor*
8000	4000	2000	750	400

Extra Lightweight Takedown Rifle—Other Calibers

Exc.	*V.G.*	*Good*	*Fair*	*Poor*
7750	5500	1800	1250	500

Extra Lightweight Rifle—.33 caliber

Exc.	*V.G.*	*Good*	*Fair*	*Poor*
5000	3500	1800	1000	500

Extra Lightweight Rifle—Other Calibers

Exc.	*V.G.*	*Good*	*Fair*	*Poor*
7000	5000	3000	950	500

Carbine

Model 1886 carbine barrels are 22". A few were Trappers with 20" barrels. Add 50 percent if Trapper.

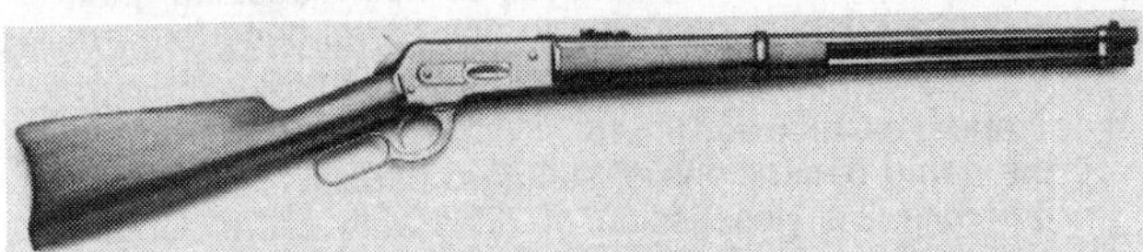

Courtesy Bonhams & Butterfields, San Francisco, California

Exc.	*V.G.*	*Good*	*Fair*	*Poor*
18000	10500	7500	4500	2000

Musket

Exc.	*V.G.*	*Good*	*Fair*	*Poor*
18000	14500	9000	3500	1500

NOTE: For .50 Express add a premium of 20 percent. Case colored Model 1886s will bring a premium of 20 percent.

Model 71

When Winchester dropped the Model 1886 from its line in 1935, the company replaced its large-bore lever-action rifle with the Model 71 chambered for the .348 caliber. The Model 71 is similar in appearance to the Model 1886 with some internal parts strengthened to handle the powerful .348 cartridge. The rifle was available in three basic configurations:

1. Standard Rifle, 24" round barrel, 3/4 magazine, plain walnut pistol-grip stock and semi-beavertail forearm.
2. Standard Rifle (Carbine), 20" round barrel, 3/4 magazine, plain walnut pistol-grip stock and semi-beavertail forearm.
3. Deluxe Rifle, 24" round barrel, 3/4 magazine, checkered walnut pistol-grip stock and checkered semi-beavertail forearm. The frames and barrels were blued on all models of this rifle.
4. Deluxe Rifle (Carbine), 20" round barrel, 3/4 magazine, checkered walnut pistol-grip stock and checkered semi-beavertail forearm. The frames and barrels were blued on all models of this rifle.

The Model 71 was produced from 1935 to 1957 with about 47,000 built.

Standard Rifle

Exc.	*V.G.*	*Good*	*Fair*	*Poor*
1400	1000	800	400	300

Standard Rifle (Carbine)

Exc.	*V.G.*	*Good*	*Fair*	*Poor*
3250	2000	1600	1200	650

Deluxe Rifle

Exc.	*V.G.*	*Good*	*Fair*	*Poor*
2500	1800	800	525	425

Deluxe Rifle (Carbine)

Exc.	*V.G.*	*Good*	*Fair*	*Poor*
3750	3000	2000	1250	700

NOTE: For pre-war Model 71s add a premium of 20 percent. The pre-war Model 71 has a longer tang than its post-war equivalent. For a bolt peep sight add 10 percent.

Model 1892

The Model 1892 was an updated successor to the Model 1873 using a scaled down version of the Model 1886 action. The rifle was chambered for the popular smaller cartridges of the day, namely the .25-20, .32-20, .38-40, .44-40, and the rare .218 Bee. The rifle was available in several different configurations:

1. Sporting Rifle, solid frame or takedown (worth an extra premium of about 20 percent), 24" round, octagon, or

half-octagon barrel with 1/2, 2/3, or full magazines. Plain straight-grip walnut stock with capped forearm.

2. Fancy Sporting Rifle, solid frame or takedown (worth 20 percent premium), 24" round, octagon, or half-octagon barrel with 1/2, 2/3, or full magazine. Checkered walnut pistol-grip stock with checkered capped forearm.
3. Carbine, 20" round barrel, full or half magazine, plain walnut straight-grip stock with one barrel band forearm. Carbines were offered only with solid frames.
4. Trapper's Carbine, 18", 16", 15", or 14" round barrel with the same dimensions of standard carbine. Federal law prohibits the possession of rifles with barrel lengths shorter than 16". The Model 1892 Trapper's Carbine can be exempted from this law as a curio and relic with a federal permit providing the trapper is an original trapper and left the factory with the short trapper barrel.
5. Musket, 30" round barrel with full magazine. Almost full-length forearm held by two barrel bands. Buttstock is plain walnut with straight grip.

The Model 1892 was built between 1892 and 1932 with slightly more than 1 million sold. The Model 1892 carbine continued to be offered for sale until 1941.

NOTE: Antique Winchester Model 1892s (pre-1898 manufacture) will bring a premium of 10 percent.

Sporting Rifle

Courtesy Bonhams & Butterfields, San Francisco, California

Exc.	*V.G.*	*Good*	*Fair*	*Poor*
5000	3500	1250	700	350

An engraved Model 1892 Saddle Ring carbine sold at auction for $84,375. Engraved by John Ulrich. Chambered for the .44-40 cartridge and fitted with a 20-inch barrel. Engraved in Style No. 6 with gold plated frame. Fancy walnut stock with checkering. Gold plated barrel band. Condition is 98 percent nickel barrel with 99 percent gold plating on frame. Stock varnish is 98 percent. *Greg Martin Auctions*

Fancy Sporting Rifle

Courtesy Bonhams & Butterfields, San Francisco, California

Exc.	*V.G.*	*Good*	*Fair*	*Poor*
12000	7500	4000	2500	1000

Carbine

Courtesy Bonhams & Butterfields, San Francisco, California

Exc.	*V.G.*	*Good*	*Fair*	*Poor*
3500	2500	1700	1200	600

Trapper's Carbine

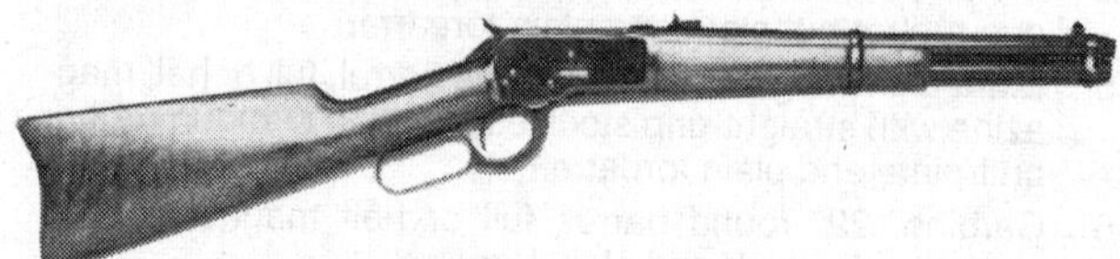

Courtesy Bonhams & Butterfields, San Francisco, California

Exc.	*V.G.*	*Good*	*Fair*	*Poor*
12000	8500	4000	2500	1250

NOTE: Add 20 percent for 15" barrel. Add 50 percent for carbines chambered for .25-20 cartridge.

Musket

Exc.	*V.G.*	*Good*	*Fair*	*Poor*
—	9500	4500	2500	1500

Model 1894

Based on a John M. Browning patent, the Model 1894 was the most successful centerfire rifle Winchester ever produced. This model is still in production, and the values given here reflect those rifles produced before 1964, or around serial number 2550000. The Model 1894 was the first Winchester developed especially for smokeless powder and was chambered for these cartridges: .32-40, .38-55, .25-35 Winchester, .30-30 Winchester, and the .32 Winchester Special. The rifle was available in several different configurations:

1. Sporting Rifle, 26" round, octagon, or half-octagon barrel, in solid frame or takedown. Full, 2/3 or 1/2 magazines were available. Plain walnut straight or pistol-grip stock with crescent buttplate and plain capped forearm.
2. Fancy Sporting Rifle, 26" round, octagon, or half-octagon barrel, in solid frame or takedown. Full, 2/3, or 1/2 magazines were available. Fancy walnut checkered straight or pistol-grip stock with crescent buttplate and checkered fancy capped forearm.
3. Extra lightweight Rifle, 22" or 26" round barrel with half magazine. Plain walnut straight-grip stock with shotgun buttplate and plain capped forearm.
4. Carbine, 20" round barrel, plain walnut straight-grip stock with carbine style buttplate. Forearm was plain walnut uncapped with one barrel band. Carbines were available with solid frame only. Carbines made prior to 1925 were fitted with a saddle ring on the left side of receiver and worth a premium over carbines without saddle ring.
5. Trapper's Carbine, 18", 16", 15", or 14". Buttstock, forearm, and saddle ring specifications same as standard carbine. All Model 1894s were furnished with blued frames and barrels, although case hardened frames

were available as an extra-cost option. Case colored Model 1894s are rare and worth a considerable premium, perhaps as much as 1,000 percent. Guns with extra-cost options should be evaluated by an expert to determine proper value. Between 1894 and 1963, approximately 2,550,000 Model 1894s were sold.

NOTE: Antique Winchester Model 1894s (pre-1898 manufacture) will bring a premium of 10 percent. First year production guns, October 1894 to December 1894, documented by the Cody Museum will command a 100 percent premium.

First Model Sporting Rifle

Very early model that incorporates a screw entering the receiver over the loading port from the outside. Rare.

Exc.	V.G.	Good	Fair	Poor
7000	4000	2000	1250	500

Sporting Rifle

Courtesy Bonhams & Butterfields, San Francisco, California

Exc.	V.G.	Good	Fair	Poor
4000	3000	1500	850	450

NOTE: Takedown versions are worth approximately 20 percent more.

Fancy Sporting Rifle

Courtesy Bonhams & Butterfields, San Francisco, California

Exc.	V.G.	Good	Fair	Poor
12000	7500	3500	2000	900

NOTE: Takedown versions are worth approximately 20 percent more. Fancy Sporting Rifles were also engraved at the customer's request. Check factory where possible and proceed with caution. Factory engraved Model 1894s are extremely valuable.

Extra Lightweight Rifle

Courtesy Bonhams & Butterfields, San Francisco, California

Exc.	V.G.	Good	Fair	Poor
5000	3500	1500	1000	450

Carbine

Exc.	V.G.	Good	Fair	Poor
3000	2000	600	400	200

NOTE: Above values are for guns with saddle rings. For carbines without saddle rings deduct 35 percent. Add 25 percent for carbines chambered for .25-35 or .38-55 cartridge.

Trapper's Carbine

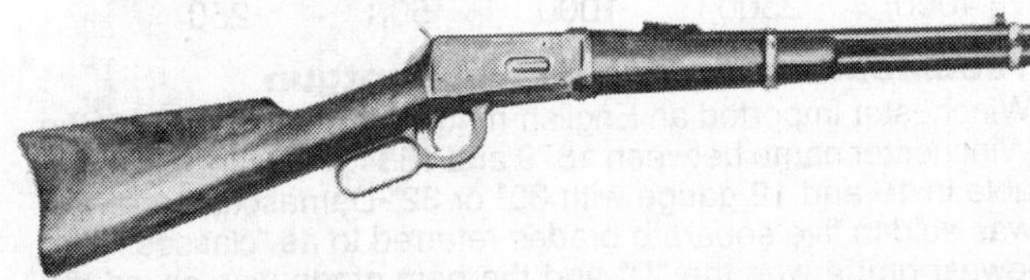

Courtesy Bonhams & Butterfields, San Francisco, California

Exc.	V.G.	Good	Fair	Poor
6500	4250	2500	1500	700

NOTE: Add 30 percent for carbines chambered for .25-35 or .38-55 calibers.

Model 53

This model was in fact a slightly more modern version of the Model 1892 offered in these calibers: .25-20, .32-20, and the .44-40. It was available in only one style: the Sporting Rifle, 22" round barrel, half magazine, straight- or pistol-grip plain walnut stock with shotgun butt. It was available in solid frame or takedown with blued frame and barrel. The Model 53 was produced from 1924 to 1932 with about 25,000 built.

Sporting Rifle

Exc.	V.G.	Good	Fair	Poor
3000	2000	1000	500	300

NOTE: Add 10 percent for takedown model. Add 40 percent for rifles chambered for .44-40 cartridge. A few of these rifles were fitted with stainless steel barrel in the early 1930s. If the black paint on these barrels is in good condition, they will bring a substantial premium.

Model 55

This model was a continuation of the Model 1894 except in a simplified version. Available in the same calibers as the Model 1894, this rifle could be ordered only with a 24" round barrel, plain walnut straight-grip stock with plain forend and shotgun butt. Frame and barrel were blued with solid or takedown features. This model was produced between 1924 and 1932 with about 21,000 sold. Serial numbers for the Model 55 were numbered separately until about serial number 4500; then the guns were numbered in the Model 1894 sequence.

Standard Rifle

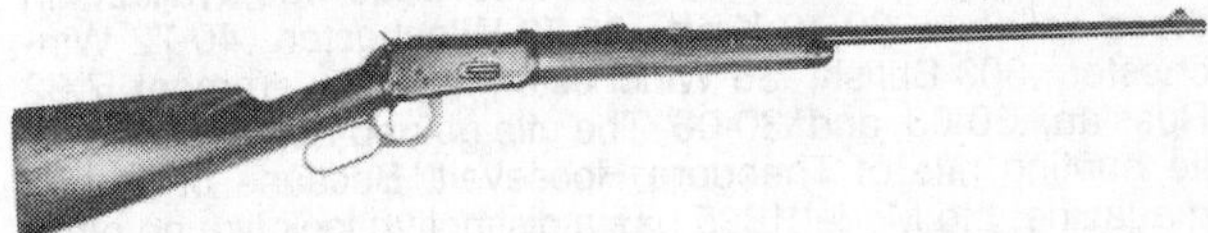

Exc.	V.G.	Good	Fair	Poor
1500	1000	650	450	200

NOTE: .25-35 caliber will bring about a 60 percent premium. Add 10 percent for models with solid frame.

Model 64

An improved version of the Model 55, this gun featured a larger magazine, pistol-grip stock, and forged front sight ramp. The trigger pull was also improved. Frame and barrel were blued. Chambered for the .25-35 Win., .30-30 Win., .32 Win. Special, and the .219 zipper added in 1938 (and discontinued in the Model 64 in 1941). Serial number of the Model 64 was concurrent with the Model 1894. Built between 1933 and 1957, approximately 67,000 were sold. This model was reintroduced in 1972 and discontinued in 1973. The values listed are for the early version only.

Standard Rifle

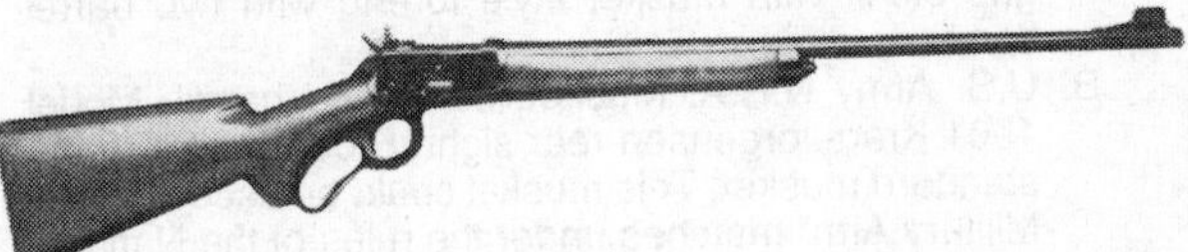

Courtesy Bonhams & Butterfields, San Francisco, California

Exc.	V.G.	Good	Fair	Poor
1200	900	500	300	200

Carbine

20" barrel.

Exc.	V.G.	Good	Fair	Poor
1550	1000	650	500	250

NOTE: For Deluxe model add 50 percent to above prices. For Carbine model add 50 percent to above prices. For rifles chambered for the .219 Zipper and .25-35 cartridges add 50 percent. Add 10 percent for bolt peep sight. Model 64s in .219 Zipper left the factory with bolt peep sights as original equipment.

Model 65

This model was a continuation of the Model 53 and was offered in three calibers: .25-20, .32-20, and .218 Bee. It had several improvements over the Model 53, namely the magazine capacity was increased to seven cartridges, forged ramp for front sight, and a lighter trigger pull. The Model 65 was available only in solid blued frame with blued barrel and pistol grip with plain walnut stock. Only about 5,700 of these rifles were built between 1933 and 1947.

Model 65 in .218 Bee Courtesy Rock Island Auction Company

Standard Rifle

Exc.	V.G.	Good	Fair	Poor
3500	2500	1000	550	250

NOTE: Add 10 percent for bolt peep sight. Model 65s in .218 Bee left the factory with bolt peep sights as original equipment.

Model 1895

The Model 1895 was the first nondetachable box magazine rifle offered by Winchester. Built on a John M. Browning patent, this rifle was introduced by Winchester to meet the demand for a rifle that could handle the new high-power, smokeless hunting cartridges of the period. The Model 1895 was available in these calibers: .30-40 Krag, .38-72 Winchester, .40-72 Winchester, .303 British, .35 Winchester, .405 Government, 7.62 Russian, .30-03, and .30-06. The rifle gained fame as a favorite hunting rifle of Theodore Roosevelt. Because of its box magazine, the Model 1895 has a distinctive look like no other Winchester lever-action rifle. The rifle was available in several different configurations:

1. Sporting Rifle, 28" or 24" (depending on caliber) round barrel, plain walnut straight-grip stock with plain forend. The first 5,000 rifles were manufactured with flat-sided receivers, and the balance of production were built with the receiver sides contoured. After serial-number 60000, a takedown version was available.
2. Fancy Sporting Rifle, 28" round barrel, fancy walnut checkered straight-grip stock and fancy walnut checkered forearm. Rifles with serial numbers below 5000 had flat sided frames.
3. Carbine, 22" round barrel, plain walnut straight-grip stock with military-style hand guard forend. Some carbines are furnished with saddle rings on left side of receiver.
4. Musket:
   A. Standard Musket, 28" round, plain walnut straight-grip stock with musket style forend with two barrel bands.
   B. U.S. Army N.R.A. Musket, 30" round barrel, Model 1901 Krag-Jorgensen rear sight. Stock similar to the standard musket. This musket could be used for "Any Military Arm" matches under the rules of the National Rifle Association.
   C. N.R.A. Musket, Models 1903 and 1906, 24" round barrel with special buttplate. Also eligible for all matches under "Any Military Arm" sponsored by the NRA. This musket was fitted with the same stock as listed above.
   D. U.S. Army Musket, 28" round barrel chambered for the .30-40 Krag. Came equipped with or without knife bayonet. These muskets were furnished to the U.S. Army for use during the Spanish-American War and are "US" marked on the receiver.
   E. Russian Musket, similar to standard musket but fitted with clip guides in the top of the receiver and with bayonet. Approximately 294,000 Model 1895 Muskets were sold to the Imperial Russian Government between 1915 and 1916. The first 15,000 Russian Muskets had 8" knife bayonets, and the rest were fitted with 16" bayonets.

The Model 1895 was produced from 1895 to 1931 with about 426,000 sold.

NOTE: Add a 10 percent premium for rifles built before 1898.

Sporting Rifle

Flat-side rifle Courtesy Bonhams & Butterfields, San Francisco, California

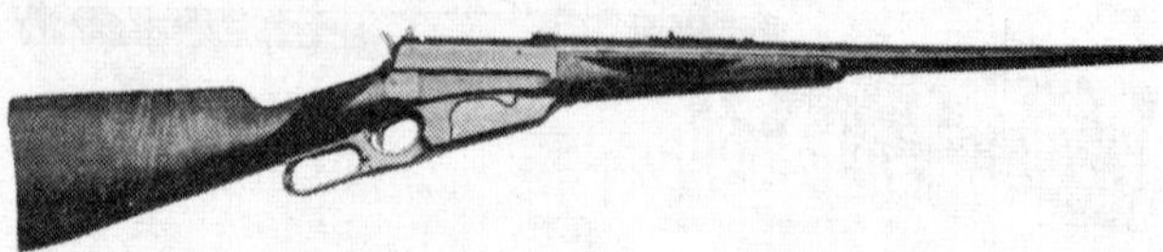

Courtesy Bonhams & Butterfields, San Francisco, California

Exc.	V.G.	Good	Fair	Poor
5000	3000	1200	700	300

NOTE: Flat-side rifles will bring a premium of 100 percent. Takedown rifles will add an additional 15 percent.

Fancy Sporting Rifles

Exc.	V.G.	Good	Fair	Poor
7000	5000	1500	1100	500

NOTE: Flat-side rifles will bring a premium of 100 percent. Takedown rifles will add an additional 15 percent.

Carbine

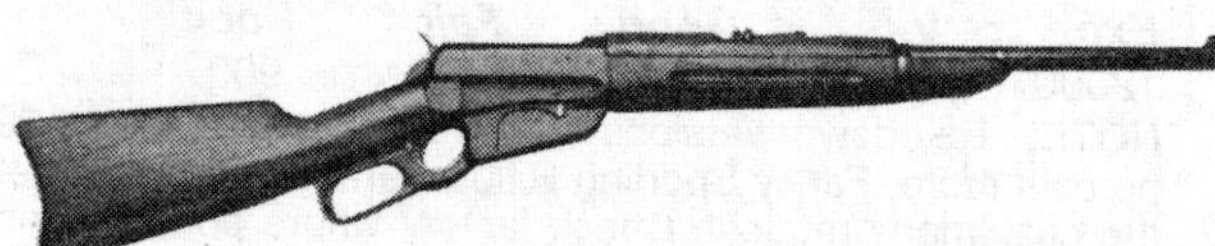

Courtesy Bonhams & Butterfields, San Francisco, California

Exc.	V.G.	Good	Fair	Poor
3000	1750	1050	600	300

Standard Musket

Exc.	V.G.	Good	Fair	Poor
3000	1750	1050	600	300

U.S. Army N.R.A. Musket

Exc.	V.G.	Good	Fair	Poor
4500	2000	1200	800	400

N.R.A. Musket, Model 1903 and 1906

Exc.	V.G.	Good	Fair	Poor
5500	2500	1200	800	400

U.S. Army Musket

Exc.	V.G.	Good	Fair	Poor
5000	3000	1500	850	450

Russian Musket

Exc.	V.G.	Good	Fair	Poor
4000	2500	1000	500	250

Breechloading Double-Barrel Shotgun

Winchester imported an English-made shotgun sold under the Winchester name between 1879 and 1884. The gun was available in 10 and 12 gauge with 30" or 32" Damascus barrels. It was sold in five separate grades referred to as "classes." The lowest grade was the "D" and the best grade was called the "Match Grade." These were marked on the sidelocks. The center rib was stamped "Winchester Repeating Arms Co., New Haven, Connecticut, U.S.A." Prices shown for "D" grade. Add 10 percent for "C" grade; 20 percent for "B" grade; and 30 percent for "A" grade. About 10,000 of these guns were imported by Winchester.

Class A, B, C, and D

Exc.	V.G.	Good	Fair	Poor
2500	2250	1250	850	500

Match Gun

Exc.	V.G.	Good	Fair	Poor
5000	4000	1800	850	500

Model 1887 Shotgun

Winchester enjoyed a great deal of success with its imported English shotgun, and the company decided to manufacture a shotgun of its own. In 1885 it purchased the patent for a lever-action shotgun designed by John M. Browning. By 1887 Winchester had delivered the first model 1887 in 12 gauge and shortly after offered the gun in 10 gauge. Both gauges were offered with 30" or 32" Full choked barrels, with the 30" standard on the 12 gauge and 32" standard on the 10 gauge. A Riot Gun was offered in 1898 both in 10, and 12 gauge with 20" barrels choked cylinder. Both variations of the Model 1887 were offered with plain walnut pistol-grip stocks with plain forend. The frame was case hardened and the barrel blued. Between 1887 and 1901 Winchester sold approximately 65,000 Model 1887 shotguns.

Standard Shotgun

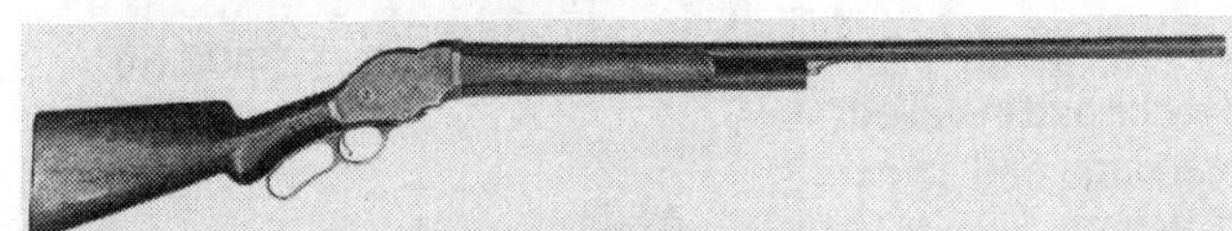

Courtesy Milwaukee Public Museum, Milwaukee, Wisconsin

Exc.	V.G.	Good	Fair	Poor
2500	1500	850	500	300

Riot Shotgun

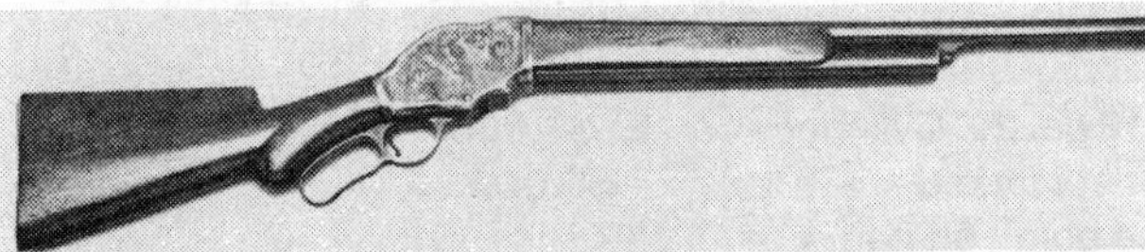

Courtesy Bonhams & Butterfields, San Francisco, California

Exc.	V.G.	Good	Fair	Poor
3000	2000	950	600	400

Model 1901 Shotgun

This model is a redesign of the Model 1887 shotgun and was offered in 10 gauge only with a 32" barrel choked Full, Modified, or Cylinder. The barrel was reinforced to withstand the new smokeless powder loads and the frame was blued instead of case hardened. The stock was of plain walnut with a modified pistol and plain forearm. The Model 1901 was built between 1901 and 1920 with about 65,000 guns sold.

Standard Shotgun

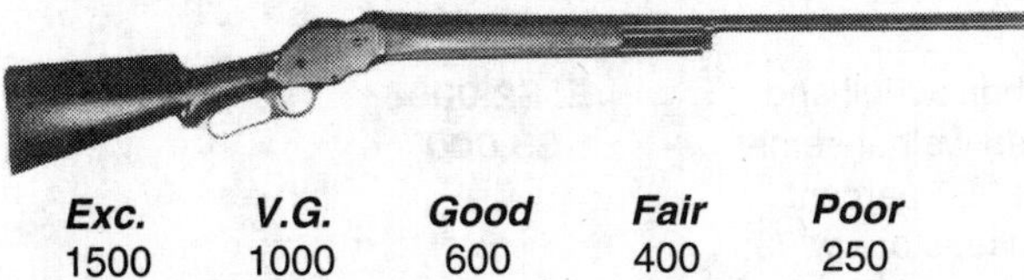

Exc.	V.G.	Good	Fair	Poor
1500	1000	600	400	250

Model 1893

This was the first slide-action repeating shotgun built by Winchester. It featured an exposed hammer and side ejection. Based on a John M. Browning patent, this model was not altogether satisfactory. The action proved to be too weak to handle smokeless loads, even though the gun was designed for black powder. The gun was offered in 12 gauge with 30" or 32" barrels choked Full. Other chokes were available on special order and will command a premium. The stock was plain walnut with a modified pistol grip, grooved slide handle, and hard rubber buttplate. The receiver and barrel were blued. Winchester produced the Model 1893 between 1893 and 1897, selling about 31000 guns.

Standard Shotgun

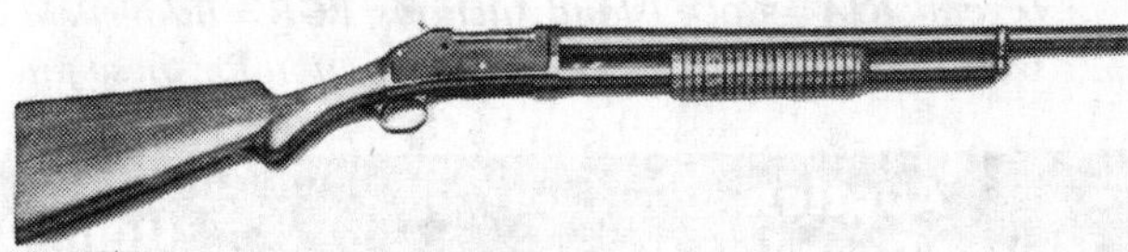

Courtesy Bonhams & Butterfields, San Francisco, California

Exc.	V.G.	Good	Fair	Poor
1000	700	600	325	250

Model 1897

The Model 1897 replaced the Model 1893, and while similar to the Model 1893, the new model had several improvements such as a stronger frame, chamber made longer to handle 2-3/4" shells, frame top was covered to force complete side ejection, the stock was made longer and with less drop. The Model 1897 was available in 12 or 16 gauge with the 12 gauge offered either in solid or takedown styles and the 16 gauge available in takedown only. The Model 1897 was available with barrel lengths of 20", 26", 28", 30", and 32" and in practically all choke options from full to cylinder. The shotgun could be ordered in several different configurations:

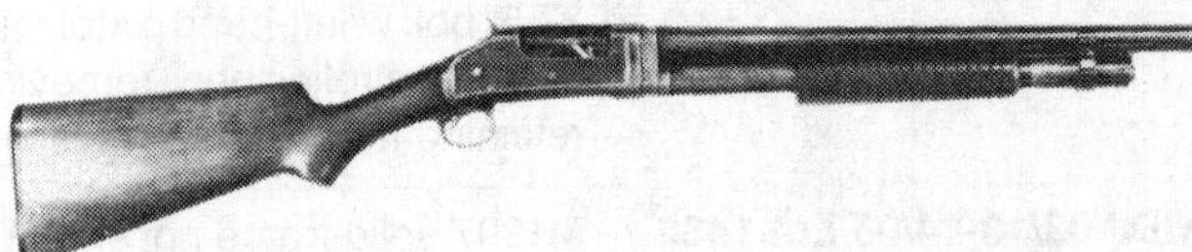

1. Standard Gun, 12 or 16 gauge, 30" barrel in 12 gauge and 28" barrel in 16 gauge, with plain walnut modified pistol-grip stock and grooved slide handle. Steel buttplate standard.
2. Trap Gun 12 or 16 gauge, 30" barrel in 12 gauge and 28" barrel in 16 gauge, fancy walnut stock with oil finish checkered pistol-grip or straight-grip stock with checkered slide handle. Marked "TRAP" on bottom of frame.
3. Pigeon Gun, 12 or 16 gauge, 28" barrel on both 12 and 16 gauge, straight- or pistol-grip stock same as Trap gun, receiver hand engraved.
4. Tournament Gun, 12 gauge only with 30" barrel, select walnut checkered straight-grip stock and checkered slide handle, top of receiver is matted to reduce glare.
5. Brush Gun, 12 or 16 gauge, 26" barrel, Cylinder choke, has a slightly shorter magazine tube than standard gun, plain walnut modified pistol-grip stock with grooved slide handle.
6. Brush Gun, Takedown, same as above with takedown feature and standard length magazine tube.
7. Riot Gun, 12 gauge, 20" barrel bored to shoot buckshot, plain walnut modified pistol-grip stock with grooved slide handle. Solid frame or takedown.
8. Trench Gun, same as Riot Gun but fitted with barrel hand guard and bayonet.

The Winchester Model 1897 was a great seller for Winchester. During its 60-year production span, 1,025,000 guns were sold.

Standard Gun

Exc.	V.G.	Good	Fair	Poor
800	650	450	300	200

Trap Gun

Exc.	V.G.	Good	Fair	Poor
1200	1000	600	500	400

Value Tracker: Winchester Model 1897

A refinement of the blackpowder-only Model 1893, the Browning-designed Winchester Model 1897 became the most popular pump shotgun of all time. It was in production for over 60 years, a record that has never been equaled by any other American shotgun. Though the M1897 was discontinued almost half a century ago, Chinese replicas of the gun are imported even today, a testimonial to its enduring popularity.

*Legend: **RIA** = Rock Island Auctions; **B&B** = Butterfield & Butterfield; **AMOS** = Amoskeag; **JCD** = J. C. Devine; **JDJ** + James D. Julia; **GMA** = Greg Martin. Contact information for these fine auction houses can be found in the front pages of this book.*

Auction House/Date/Lot No.	Item Description	Estimated Value	Actually Sold For
AMOS 03/24/07 Lot 125	M1897 solid-frame trench shotgun, #(E)711669 (mfg 1922) 12 ga., 20" plain bbl. marked "CYL," excellent bore, bayonet lug and ventilated handguard. About Very Good, with 94 percent original blue, moderate pitting and minor scratches on frame at right, cracks on buttstock and minor dings on forend. Includes military-style sling.	**E: $1,500-$2,000**	**$1,840**
AMOS 03/24/07 Lot 126	M1897 solid-frame riot shotgun, #588247 (mfg 1916) 12 ga., 20" plain bbl. marked "CYL," excellent bore, plain pistol grip stock and 18-groove forend. Very Good + with 97 percent-98 percent original blue, wood near excellent with minor dings and handling marks.	**E: $1,000-$2,000**	**$1,380**
JDJ 10/09-11/06 Lot 1883	Custom M. 1897 shotgun, #298812 (mfg 1906), 12 ga. plain 27.5" bbl. w/left-hand pistol grip stock and recoil pad installed. "Good" as refinished, removing various markings and retaining most reblued finish, w/functional action.	**E: $200-$300)**	**$402.50**
JDJ 03/13-14/06 Lot 1432	M1897 solid-frame riot shotgun, #688521, 12 ga. plain 20" Cylinder barrel with semi-pistol grip stock and small ribbed forearm. "Good," with 40 percent-85 percent orig. blue turning plum, bright bore, buttstock with hairline wrist crack at receiver and most of an old refinish. Broken buttplate.	**E: $1,250-$1,750**	**$747.50**
GMA 11/06-07/06 Lot 455	Composite M1897 trench gun, #6867766, 12 ga. 20" Cylinder vent-rib bbl., with leather sling, 1917 bayonet marked "REMINGTON 1917," "U.S." and Ordnance bomb on frame. "Very Good" w/75 percent blue, wear; buttstock cleaned and a possible replacement. Vent rib may be later replacement.	**E: $2,000-$3,000**	**$2,043**
GMA 11/06-07/06 Lot 45	M1897 trench shotgun #354224, 12 ga. 20" bbl. w/ventilated handguard, "U.S." and Ordnance bomb on frame, sling-mount stock with "G.H.D." cartouche. "Very Good" as partially refinished, w/70 percent-75 percent blued finish, remainder with wear and patina. Wood excellent, front sling ring missing.	**E: $3,000-$5,000**	**$3,405**
GMA 11/14-16/05 Lot 1908	Deluxe M1897 sporting shotgun #561106, 16 ga., 28" Full bbl., oil-finished checkered semi-pistol grip stock w/composition buttplate. "Very Good;" brown patina; pitting; stock with wear.	**E: $500-$700**	**$737.75**
GMA 04/24/06 Lot 528	M1897 riot shotgun #C 94072, 12 ga., 20" bbl. w/Full and Cylinder choke marked on breech, varnished walnut semi-pistol grip stocks, steel buttplate. "Excellent," 97 percent finish, few light marks and scratches, little use, stock w/99 percent varnish. Factory letter suggests this may be one of the earliest M1897 riot guns.	**E: $2,000-$3,000**	**$2,270**

Auction House/Date/Lot No.	Item Description	Estimated Value	Actually Sold For
GMA 06/26-27/06 Lot 870	M1897 #383388 (mfg 1908), 12 ga., 30" bbl., walnut stock. "Excellent as partially refinished," 90 percent-95 percent reblued finish w/light pitting visible beneath finish on left frame. Barrel assembly excellent, wood w/light wear and marks.	E: $400-$600	$255.38
GMA 11/14-16/05 Lot 1237	M97 #1008537, 12 ga., 20" Full bbl., walnut stock w/ribbed forend, Pachmayr recoil pad. "Very Good," 90 percent-95 percent finish w/scattered wear to relief edges and slide. Wood w/minor wear and light marks.	E: $600-$800	$681
GMA 11/14-16/05 Lot 3244	M97 #838737, 12 ga., 30" Full bbl., checkered semi-pistol grip stock, composition buttplate. "Fine," 95 percent blue with light wear; stock possibly cleaned.	E: $1,000-$1,500	$1,248.50
GMA 04/25-27/05 Lot 637	M97 #728566, 12 ga., 30" Full bbl., with varnished walnut stocks; composition buttplate. "Poor to Fair," brown and rust patina; extensive pitting; scratches and mars to stocks. Mechanism malfunctioning.	E: $400-$600	$225
GMA 04/25-27/05 Lot 766	Wells Fargo-marked M1897 #623827, 12 ga., 18" bbl., frame and walnut pistol grip stock stamped "W.F. & Co." "Good," gray-brown patina w/scattered light pitting overall, traces of blue on magazine, wood worn w/many dents and blemishes.	E: $2,500-$3,500	$2,137.50
GMA 04/25-27/05 Lot 931	M1897 riot gun #E644378, 12 ga., 19.5" Full bbl., oil-finished walnut stock. "Good to Very Good," 15 percent-20 percent blue, balance brown and gray; pitting, wear and nicks; missing bead front sight and buttplate, worn and with blemishes; cracked at wrist. Bore fine.	E: $500-$700	$393.75
GMA 04/25-27/05 Lot 1328	M1897 #447163, 12 ga., 30" Full bbl., varnished semi-pistol grip stock; composition buttplate. "Very Good to Fine," 60 percent-65 percent blue and varnish, fading and with wear, stock worn w/light nicks.	E: $250-$350	$393.75
GMA 04/25-27/05 Lot 2258	M1897 trench gun #840100, 12 ga., 20.375" Cyl. bbl., "US 60" on rear frame and breech mount; "WP" monogram, varnished walnut stock, cast checkered brass buttplate; sling swivels. "Excellent," 95 percent blue, light marks and patina; small dent in handguard over barrel, excellent bore, stock with 100 percent varnish; few storage marks.	E: $1,500-$2,500	$3,093.75
LJA 01/10/05 Lot 512	M1897 riot gun #739213, 12 ga., 20" Cyl. bbl., "Original Very Good Condition," 90 percent-95 percent orig. blue thinning at edges, "Very Good +" stock w/even use, ex-Pasadena P.D.	E: $750-$1,500	$1,120
LJA 01/10/05 Lot 880	M1897 riot gun #751072, 12 ga., 20" Cyl. bbl., saddle ring added to frame. "Good to Very Good Condition," 70 percent-80 percent thinning and toning blue, loss of finish at muzzle, stock Excellent as lightly refinished.	E: $500-$1,000	$840
AMOS 08/05/06 Lot 207	M1897 solid-frame trench gun #695148, 12 ga., 20.5" plain bbl. w/ventilated handguard. About Good to Very Good, 98 percent hot immersion blued, buffed finish, stock w/cracks on both sides of tang, receiver electric-pencil marked "DTPD."	E: $700-$900.	$1, 035
AMOS 01/15/05 Lot 152	M1897 #100220, 12 ga., period-shortened 19.5" "FULL/CYL" bbl marked "AD. EX. CO." (Adams Express) used 1910-33, metal mostly brown, wood "about good"	E: $600-$800.	$517.50

Auction House/Date/Lot No.	Item Description	Estimated Value	Actually Sold For
B&B 06/20/06 Lot 5275	M1897 trench gun #952661, 12 ga., 20.75" bbl. w/ventilated handguard, U.S. Ordnance markings, walnut pistol grip stock without markings. "Excellent," 98 percent blue finish, fine wood w/one deep scratch to left above butt, replacement buttplate.	**E: $1,400-$1,800.**	**$2,925**
AMOS 05/20/06 Lot 25	M1897 WWII takedown trench gun #940423, 12 ga., 20" plain Cyl. bbl. w/ventilated handguard, U.S. Ordnance markings. About Fine, 60 percent-95 percent orig. blue, wood excellent plus with 95 percent orig. finish and crisp cartouches.	**E: $3,000-$4,000.**	**$4,600**
AMOS 05/20/06 Lot 518	M1897 riot gun #649391 (mfg 1918), 12 ga., 20" plain Cyl. bbl. w/large brass front bead, walnut pistol grip stock and grooved forend. About Very Good to Fine, 35 percent-93 percent orig. blue, 3" crack in forend.	**E: $650-$850.**	**$747.50**
AMOS 08/05/06 Lot 29	M1897 #918875, 12 ga., 30" plain Full bbl., plain pistol grip stock and grooved forend. About Very Fine, 90 percent-97 percent evenly thinning orig. blue, wood "rates Excellent +," "bright, excellent bore."	**E: $500-$700.**	**$805**
JCD 04/23/06 Lot 200	M1897 trench shotgun #E945683 (mfg 1942), 12 ga., 21" Cyl. bbl. w/excellent bore, ventilated handguard and takedown frame w/U.S. Ordnance markings, plus reproduction sling and "Vietnam era" M. 1917 Winchester bayonet without scabbard. About Very Fine, 90 percent orig. blue w/light pitting, wood without ordinance markings, forend w/some finish added.	**E: $2,250-$2,750**	**$5,635**
AMOS 03/25/06 Lot 792	M1897 #316541, 12 ga., 20" bbl. w/good bore, modified to trench gun configuration w/addition of ventilated handguard bayonet lug. About Very Good as reconfigured, metal has gray plum patina w/ some blue, wood w/orig. oil finish, blemishes and two cracks at wrist.	**E: $200-$300**	**$287.50**
RIA 12/03-05/05 Lot 4	M97 #860287, 12 ga., 30" round Full bbl., takedown frame w/sighting groove from factory. "Very Good," 70 percent blue, wood w/comparable wear, action tight.	**E: $350-$600**	**$460**
RIA 12/03-05/05 Lot 5	M97 #999404, 12 ga., 30" round Full bbl., short 11-groove forearm. "Fine," 80 percent blue w/most wear on tube, possibly some touch-up blue on receiver, wood fine, action tight.	**E: $400-$700**	**$747.50**
RIA 12/03-05/05 Lot 13	M97 riot shotgun #E929836 (mfg 1946), 12 ga., 21" round Cyl. bbl., takedown frame w/top dished out for sighting at factory. "Very Good," 90 percent finish w/wear on muzzle, tube and edges, spotting at muzzle, wood excellent w/scratches, buttplate cracked and broken.	**E: $800-$1,000**	**$1,035**
RIA 12/03-05/05 Lot 15	M97 #749259, 12 ga., 30" round Full bbl., long 18-groove forearm. "Fair," 30 percent heavily worn blue, butt broken and repaired with tape residue, forearm worn and chipped, mechanically fine.	**E: $250-$350**	**$373.75**
RIA 12/03-05/05 Lot 56	M97 riot shotgun #E718940, 12 ga., 20" round Cyl. bbl., oil-finished walnut stock and forearm. "Excellent as professionally refinished," stock w/orig. finish intact, buttplate fine w/moderate wear, forearm fine w/30 percent orig. finish.	**E: $1,400-$2,000**	**$1,610**

This symbol denotes "Sleepers" with rapidly-rising values and/or significant collector potential.

Pigeon Gun

Exc.	V.G.	Good	Fair	Poor
2500	1800	1400	1250	1000

Tournament Gun

Exc.	V.G.	Good	Fair	Poor
1500	1200	700	500	400

Brush Gun

Exc.	V.G	Good	Fair	Poor
950	750	600	500	400

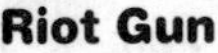

Riot Gun

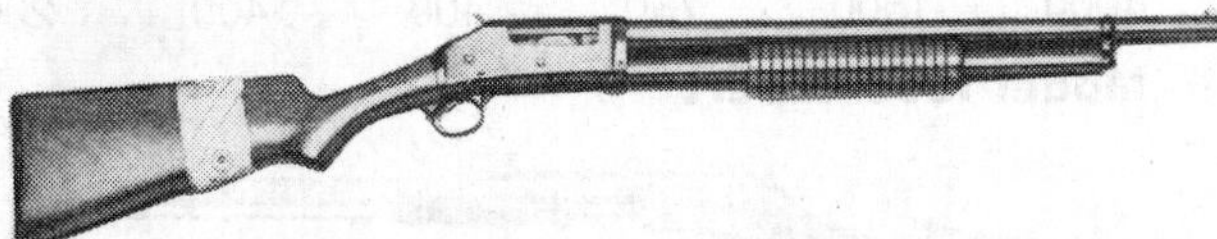

Courtesy Bonhams & Butterfields, San Francisco, California

Exc.	V.G.	Good	Fair	Poor
850	600	500	350	200

Trench Gun

Courtesy Bonhams & Butterfields, San Francisco, California

Exc.	V.G.	Good	Fair	Poor
2750	2000	1000	500	300

NOTE: Add 100 percent for 16 gauge guns in excellent, very good, and good condition.

Winchester-Lee Straight Pull Rifle

U.S. Navy Musket

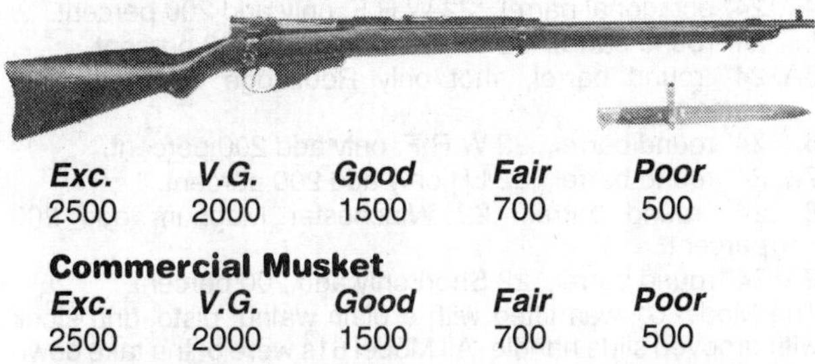

Exc.	V.G.	Good	Fair	Poor
2500	2000	1500	700	500

Commercial Musket

Exc.	V.G.	Good	Fair	Poor
2500	2000	1500	700	500

Sporting Rifle

Courtesy Amoskeag Auction Company

Exc.	V.G.	Good	Fair	Poor
2500	2000	1500	700	500

Model 1890

The Model 1890 was the first slide-action rifle ever produced by Winchester. Designed by John and Matthew Browning, this rifle was chambered for the .22 Short, Long, and Winchester Rimfire cartridges (the WRF cartridge was developed by Winchester specifically for the Model 1890) not on an interchangeable basis. In 1919 the .22 LR cartridge was offered as well. The rifle was a slide-action top ejecting rifle with an 18" under barrel magazine tube. All Model 1890s were furnished standard with plain walnut straight stocks with crescent buttplate and 12 groove slide handle. This rifle was one of the company's best selling small caliber firearms and was in worldwide use. The Model 1890 came in three separate and distinct variations that greatly affect its value:

1. First Model, solid frame, 24" octagon barrel, case hardened frame, and fixed rear sight. Approximately 15,552 of these First Model guns were produced, and their distinctive feature is concealed locking lugs and solid frame. Serial numbered on the lower tang only. Built from 1890 to 1892.
2. Second Model, takedown, 24" octagon barrel, case hardened frame, and adjustable rear sight. Serial numbered from 15553 to 112970 (on lower tang only) these Second Model guns feature the same concealed locking lugs but with the added takedown feature. A Deluxe version was offered with fancy walnut checkered straight- or pistol-grip stock and grooved slide handle.

2A. Second Model (blued frame variation), same as above but with blued frame. Serial numbered from 112971 to 325250 (on lower tang until 232328, then also on bottom front end of receiver) these blued frame Second Models are much more numerous than the case hardened variety. A Deluxe version was offered with fancy walnut checkered straight- or pistol-grip stock and grooved slide handle.

3. Third Model, takedown, 24" octagon barrel, blued frame, adjustable rear sight. Serial numbered from 325251 to as high as 853000 (numbered on both the lower tang and bottom front of receiver) the distinctive feature of the Third Model is the locking cut made on the front top of the receiver to allow the breech bolt to lock externally. A Deluxe version was offered with fancy walnut checkered stock, straight or pistol grip with grooved slide handle. Winchester offered many extra-cost options for this rifle that will greatly affect the value. Secure an expert appraisal before proceeding. The Model 1890 was produced from 1890 to 1932 with approximately 775,000 guns sold.

First Model—Standard Grade

Exc.	V.G.	Good	Fair	Poor
9000	5000	2500	1250	750

Second Model—Case Hardened Frame

Standard

Courtesy Bonhams & Butterfields, San Francisco, California

Exc.	V.G.	Good	Fair	Poor
6000	3500	2000	1000	500

Deluxe

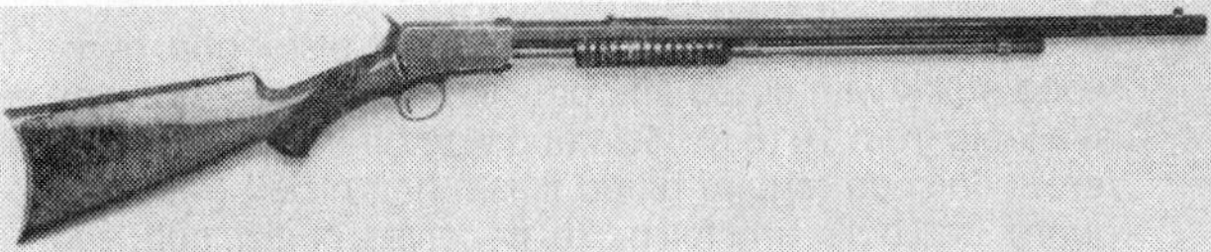

Courtesy Bonhams & Butterfields, San Francisco, California

Exc.	V.G.	Good	Fair	Poor
10000	7000	3500	2000	1000

Second Model—Blued Frame

Standard

Exc.	V.G.	Good	Fair	Poor
2500	1700	1500	750	250

A Model 1890 Second Model with case colored frame sold at auction for $4,312.50. Chambered for the .22 WRF cartridge. Condition is 95 percent overall. Lyman tang sight.
Amoskeag Auction Company

Deluxe

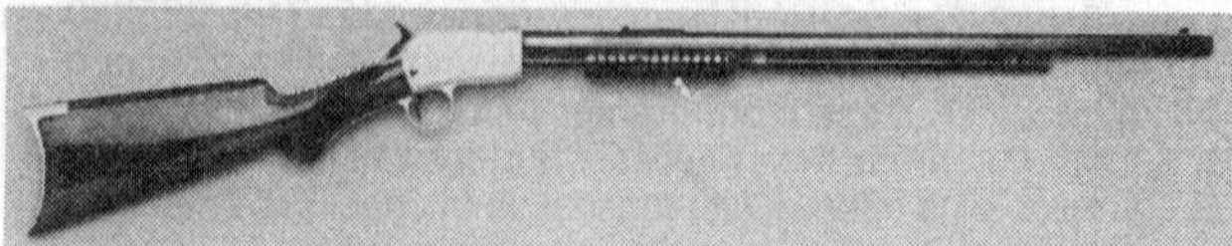

Courtesy Bonhams & Butterfields, San Francisco, California

Exc.	V.G.	Good	Fair	Poor
7500	5500	3000	1500	750

Third Model

Standard

Exc.	V.G.	Good	Fair	Poor
2000	1400	900	450	250

Deluxe

Exc.	V.G.	Good	Fair	Poor
6500	4000	2000	1000	750

NOTE: For Third Models chambered for .22 LR add 25 percent premium.

Model 1906

In 1906 Winchester decided to offer a lower-cost version of the Model 1890. The Model 1906 used the same receiver but was fitted with a 20" round barrel and plain gumwood straight-grip stock. When the Model 1906 was first introduced, it sold for two-thirds of the price of the Model 1890. For the first two years the gun was chambered for the .22 Short cartridge only. In 1908 the rifle was modified to shoot .22 Short, Long, and LR cartridges interchangeably. This modification ensured the Model 1906's success, and between 1906 and 1932 about 800,000 were sold. All Model 1906s were of the takedown variety. The Model 1906 is available in three important variations:

1. 22 Short Only, 20" round barrel, straight-grip gumwood stock and smooth slide handle. These were built from serial number 1 to around 113000.
2. Standard Model 1906, 20" round barrel, straight-grip gumwood stock with 12 groove slide handle. Serial numbered from 113000 to 852000.
3. Model 1906 Expert, 20" round barrel, pistol-grip gumwood stock with fluted smooth slide handle. Expert was available from 1918 to 1924 and was offered in three different finishes regular blued finish, half nickel (receiver, guard, and bolt), and full nickel (receiver, guard, bolt, and barrel nickeled).

Model 1906 .22 Short Only

Courtesy Bonhams & Butterfields, San Francisco, California

Exc.	V.G.	Good	Fair	Poor
2500	1750	750	500	200

Standard Model 1906

Courtesy Bonhams & Butterfields, San Francisco, California

NIB	Exc.	V.G.	Good	Fair	Poor
4000	1500	750	400	400	200

Model 1906 Expert

Courtesy Bonhams & Butterfields, San Francisco, California

Exc.	V.G.	Good	Fair	Poor
3500	1850	950	500	300

NOTE: Prices are for half-nickel Experts. Add 10 percent for blued guns and 100 percent for full nickel.

Model 61

Winchester developed the Model 61 in an attempt to keep pace with its competitors' hammerless .22 rifles. The Model 61 featured a 24" round or octagonal barrel and could be ordered by the customer in a variety of configurations. Collector interest in this rifle is high because of the fairly large number of variations. The Model 61 is often considered a companion to the Winchester Model 12 and Model 42 shotguns.The following is a list of chamber and barrel variations found in this model:

1. 24" round barrel, .22 Short, Long, LR
2. 24" octagonal barrel, .22 Short only add 200 percent.
3. 24" octagonal barrel, .22 LR only add 200 percent.
4. 24" octagonal barrel, .22 W.R.F. only add 200 percent.
5. 24" round barrel, .22 LR Shot only add 300 percent.

5A. 24" round barrel, shot only Routledge bore add 300 percent.

6. 24" round barrel, .22 W.R.F. only add 200 percent.
7. 24" round barrel, .22 LR only add 200 percent.
8. 24" round barrel, .22 Winchester Magnum add 200 percent.
9. 24" round barrel, .22 Short only add 200 percent.

The Model 61 was fitted with a plain walnut pistol-grip stock with grooved slide handle. All Model 61s were of the take down variety. Pre-war models will have a short slide handle. Manufactured between 1932 and 1963, approximately 342,000 guns were sold.

Pre-war Model 61

NIB	Exc.	V.G.	Good	Fair	Poor
3000	1500	800	600	325	200

NOTE: Single caliber models will command a premium of 50 percent depending on caliber. Octagon barrel models will command a premium of 75 percent. .22 LR shot only models will bring a premium of 250 percent.

Post-war Model 61

Courtesy Bonhams & Butterfields, San Francisco, California

NIB	Exc.	V.G.	Good	Fair	Poor
1750	800	550	450	250	150

Model 61 Magnum

NIB	Exc.	V.G.	Good	Fair	Poor
1950	950	775	600	400	250

NOTE: This variation (Model 61 Magnum) was produced from 1960 to 1963.

Model 62 and 62A

When the Model 1890 and Model 1906 were dropped from the Winchester product line in 1932, the company introduced the Model 62 to take their place. An updated version of the earlier slide-action .22 rifles, the Model 62 was fitted with a 23" round barrel and was capable of shooting .22 Short, Long, and LR cartridges interchangeably. Winchester offered a Gallery version of the Model 62 that was chambered for .22 Short only. Some of these Gallery guns have "Winchester" stamped on the left side of the receiver. Winchester Model 62 Gallery rifles have a triangular loading port on the loading tube that the standard models did not have. A change in the breech bolt mechanism brought about a change in the name designation from Model 62 to Model 62A. This occurred around serial number 98000. The letter "A" now appears behind the serial number. This model stayed in production until 1958, and collectors will concede a premium for guns built prior to WWII with small slide handles. The stock was of plain walnut with straight grip and grooved slide handle. Both the receiver and barrel were blued. All Model 62 and 62As were takedown. Approximately 409,000 guns were sold.

Pre-war Model 62

NIB	Exc.	V.G.	Good	Fair	Poor
3000	1750	850	400	250	150

NOTE: Barrels marked with Model 62 are worth more than barrels marked with Model 62A by approximately 15 percent. Gallery models will bring a premium of 300 percent.

Post-war Model 62

Courtesy Bonhams & Butterfields, San Francisco, California

NIB	Exc.	V.G.	Good	Fair	Poor
1300	600	450	325	225	125

Model 62 Gallery

.22 Short only with triangular loading port & "*WINCHESTER*" stamped on side of receiver.

NIB	Exc.	V.G.	Good	Fair	Poor
3200	2000	1000	650	400	200

NOTE: A Model 62 with "*WINCHESTER*" stamped on the side of the receiver is more desirable than one without the stamping. Deduct 10 percent for Gallery rifles without this stamping.

Model 1903

The first semi-automatic rifle produced by Winchester was designed by T.C. Johnson. This rifle was offered in a takedown version only and was available in a 20" round barrel chambered for the .22 Winchester Automatic Rimfire. This ammunition is no longer produced and when found is very expensive. The tubular magazine is located in the buttstock and holds 10 cartridges. The rifle was available in two different configurations:

1. Standard Rifle, 20" round barrel, plain walnut straight-grip stock with plain forend. Steel crescent butt was standard.
2. Deluxe Rifle, 20" round barrel, fancy checkered walnut pistol-grip stock with checkered forearm. Manufactured from 1903 to 1932, about 126,000 were sold.

Standard Rifle

Exc.	V.G.	Good	Fair	Poor
850	550	325	200	100

Deluxe Rifle

Courtesy Bonhams & Butterfields, San Francisco, California

Exc.	V.G.	Good	Fair	Poor
1800	1100	700	500	250

NOTE: The first 5,000 guns were built without safeties, and the first 15,000 guns were furnished with bronze firing pins instead of steel. These early Model 1903s will bring a premium of 30 percent.

Model 63

The Model 63 took the place of the Model 1903 in 1933 in an attempt by Winchester to solve the problem of having to use a special .22 caliber cartridge in the gun to operate the blowback system. It is a very high quality semi-automatic rifle. Many collectors and shooters considered it the best rimfire semi-automatic rifle ever produced.The Model 63 was chambered for the .22 LR cartridge and was available in a 20" barrel for the first four years or until about serial number 9800. Thereafter, the model was offered with a 23" round barrel for the remainder of the production period. The gun was fitted with a plain walnut pistol-grip stock and forearm. The tubular magazine was located in the buttstock that came with a steel buttplate. The last 10,000 Model 63s were sold with a grooved receiver top to make the addition of a scope easier. Manufactured between 1933 and 1958, about 175,000 guns were sold.

20" Barrel

Courtesy Bonhams & Butterfields, San Francisco, California

NIB	Exc.	V.G.	Good	Fair	Poor
2750	1400	800	500	400	250

23" Barrel

Courtesy Bonhams & Butterfields, San Francisco, California

NIB	Exc.	V.G.	Good	Fair	Poor
1600	1000	700	600	400	200

NOTE: Grooved top receivers command a premium of 20 percent.

Model 1905

The Model 1905 was a larger version of the Model 1903, developed by T.C. Johnson to handle the more powerful centerfire cartridges. It was chambered for the .32 Winchester Self-Loading and .35 Self-Loading cartridges, loading by means of a detachable box magazine. Available in takedown only, this model was offered in two different styles:

1. Sporting Rifle, 22" round barrel, plain walnut straight grip (changed to pistol grip in 1908) stock with plain forend.
2. Fancy Sporting Rifle, 22" round barrel, fancy walnut checkered pistol-grip stock with checkered forend. This model was the first Winchester semi-automatic rifle to fire centerfire cartridges. Produced from 1905 to 1920 with about 30,000 rifles sold.

Sporting Rifle

Exc.	V.G.	Good	Fair	Poor
500	350	250	175	125

Fancy Sporting Rifle

Exc.	V.G.	Good	Fair	Poor
600	400	300	200	150

Model 1907

The Model 1907 was an improved version of the Model 1905 and chambered for the new .351 Winchester Self-Loading cartridge. Outward appearance was the same as Model 1905 except for 20" round barrel. This rifle was available in three different styles:

1. Sporting Rifle, 20" round barrel, plain walnut pistol-grip stock with plain forend. Discontinued in 1937.
2. Fancy Sporting Rifle, 20" round barrel, fancy walnut checkered pistol-grip stock and checkered forend.
3. Police Rifle, 20" round barrel, plain walnut pistol-grip stock and beavertail forend. This version was fitted with a leather sling and with or without knife bayonet. First introduced in 1937. Winchester discontinued this model in 1957 after having sold about 59,000 guns.

Sporting Rifle

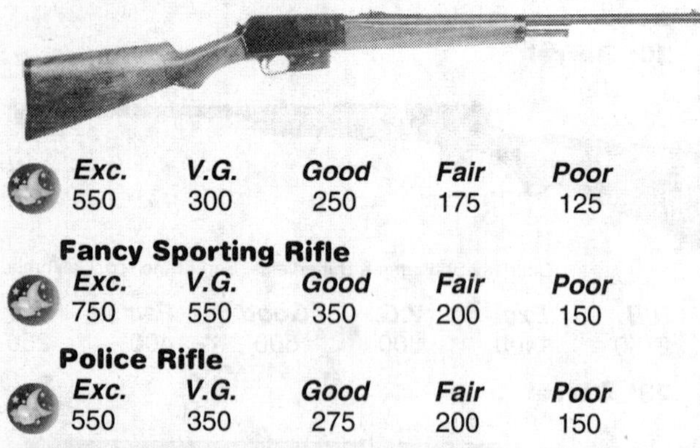

Exc.	V.G.	Good	Fair	Poor
550	300	250	175	125

Fancy Sporting Rifle

Exc.	V.G.	Good	Fair	Poor
750	550	350	200	150

Police Rifle

Exc.	V.G.	Good	Fair	Poor
550	350	275	200	150

Model 1910

This model was similar to the Model 1907 but the action was made stronger to handle the new Winchester .401 Self-Loading cartridge. The specifications for this model are the same as the Model 1907. Built between 1907 and 1936, only about 21,000 of these guns were sold.

Sporting Rifle

Courtesy Bonhams & Butterfields, San Francisco, California

Exc.	V.G.	Good	Fair	Poor
700	550	400	300	200

Fancy Sporting Rifle

Exc.	V.G.	Good	Fair	Poor
550	400	300	200	150

Model 55 (Rimfire Rifle)

Not to be confused with the lever-action model, this .22 caliber rifle was a semi-automatic single-shot with a 22" round barrel. Fitted with a plain walnut pistol-grip one-piece stock and forend. The safety goes on when each cartridge is inserted into the chamber. This model was not serial numbered and was produced from 1957 to 1961 with about 45,000 guns sold.

Standard Rifle

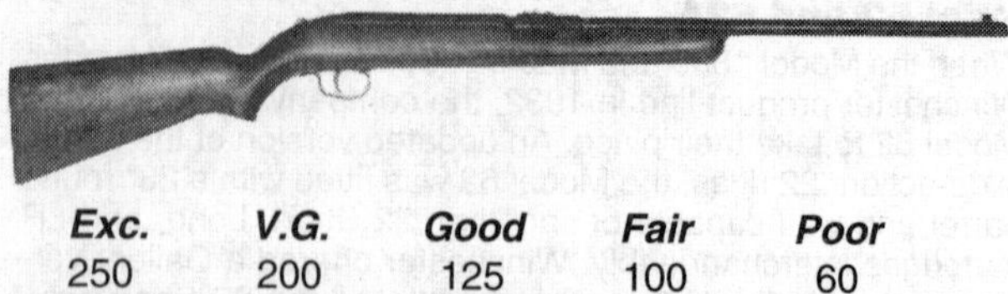

Exc.	V.G.	Good	Fair	Poor
250	200	125	100	60

Model 74

This was a semi-automatic chambered for either the .22 Short or the .22 LR. The rifle has a tubular magazine in the buttstock and a 24" round barrel. The bolt on this rifle was designed to be easily removed for cleaning or repair. The stock was plain walnut pistol-grip with semi-beavertail forend. A Gallery Special was offered that was chambered for the .22 Short and fitted with a steel shell deflector. This gallery model was also available with chrome trimmings at extra cost.

Sporting Rifle

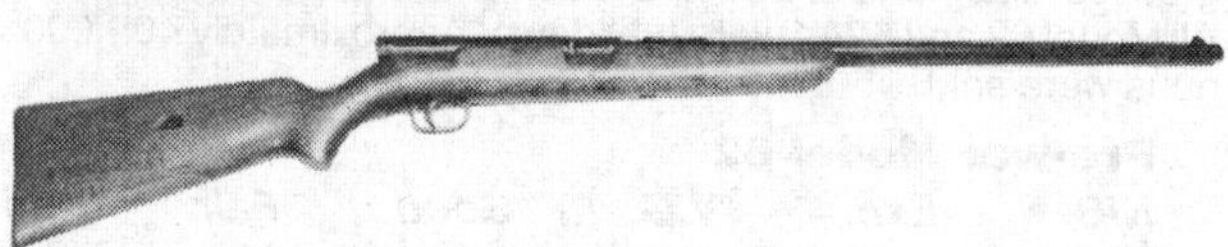

Courtesy C.H. Wolfersberger

Exc.	V.G.	Good	Fair	Poor
400	300	225	150	100

Gallery Special—.22 Short Only

Exc.	V.G.	Good	Fair	Poor
800	600	325	225	150

NOTE: For Gallery models with chrome trimmings, add a premium of 50 percent.

Model 77

This rifle was built on the blow-back design for semi-automatic rifles and is chambered for the .22 LR. It features a 22" round barrel and either a detachable box magazine or under barrel tubular magazine. The rifle has a trigger guard made of nylon. It has a plain walnut pistol-grip stock with semi-beavertail forend and composition buttplate. Built between 1955 and 1963, Winchester sold about 217,000 of these rifles.

Standard Rifle

Exc.	V.G.	Good	Fair	Poor
300	200	150	100	50

NOTE: Models with tubular magazines will bring a premium of 10 percent to 20 percent.

Model 100

This rifle is a gas operated semi-automatic and chambered for the .243, .308, and .284 caliber cartridges. The Model 100 was the first commercial Winchester self-loading, centerfire rifle made since the Winchester Model 1905, the Model 1907, and the Model 1910. These models were produced until 1936/37. Winchester did produce the M1 Carbine during WWII. It was available in a rifle version with a 22" round barrel and a carbine version with a 19" barrel. Both were furnished with a detachable box magazine. The stock was a one-piece design with pistol grip and was offered in either hand-cut checkering or pressed basket weave checkering. Rifles were introduced in 1960 and the carbine in 1967. The Model 100 was last produced in 1973 with about 263,000 guns sold.

WARNING: THE MODEL 100 WAS RECALLED IN 1990. DO NOT PURCHASE THIS MODEL WITHOUT FIRST DETERMINING IF THE PROBLEM HAS BEEN REPAIRED. CALL WINCHESTER PRODUCT SERVICE FOR INFORMATION.

Value Tracker: Winchester Model 1907

The Winchester M1907 was the most successful of the "Auto Loading" rifles designed by Thomas C. Johnson. These guns are not at all scarce, but many of them show signs of heavy use. Forearms are typically cracked, a result of the rifle's blowback action and heavy recoiling breechblock. A really cherry example is a rarity. Several custom reloaders are now offering .351 Winchester Self Loading ammunition, which is a good thing, since these charming old rifles, produced for half a century, richly deserve to be taken afield.

*Legend: **RIA** = Rock Island Auctions; **B&B** = Butterfield & Butterfield; **AMOS** = Amoskeag; **JCD** = J. C. Devine; **JDJ** + James D. Julia; **GMA** = Greg Martin. Contact information for these fine auction houses can be found in the front pages of this book.*

Auction House/Date/Lot No.	Item Description	Estimated Value	Actually Sold For
AMOS 09/24/05 Lot 647	M1907 #55055, .351 S.L., 20" round bbl., walnut stock. About Very Fine rifle in minty condition w/99 percent orig. blue, bright, excellent bore, plain walnut stock near excellent but for minor forend crack and pistol grip ding. Front sling swivel missing.	**E: $400- $600**	**$517.50**
RIA 08/27-29/05 Lot 606	M1907 #56163, .351 S.L., 20" round bbl., walnut stock. "Excellent," 98 percent finish thinning at muzzle and sharp edges of receiver w/ very minor pitting, wood very good to excellent overall w/90 percent-95 percent varnish, brown Chace sling excellent.	**E: $800- $1,200**	**$1,035**
RIA 4/30-5/2/05 Lot 254	M1907 #55403, .351 S.L., 20" round bbl., late production, wood appears lighter and fancier than usual. "Excellent," 97 percent blue, minor marks on wood.	**E: $1,200-$1,800**	**$546.25**
RIA 4/30-5/2/05 Lot 1091	M1907 #50581, .351 S.L., 20" round bbl., walnut pistol grip stock and forearm, checkered metal buttplate and scarce 10-round magazine. "Excellent," 98 percent finish intact, some bbl. spotting, stock excellent.	**E: $700-$1,100**	**$4,025**
RIA 12/03-05/05 Lot 70	M1907 #544781, .351 S.L., 20" round bbl., w/standard markings and features, 1" leather sling unmarked. "Fine," 90 percent+ blue, minor handling marks, wood w/light dents and scratches, action excellent.	**E: $450-$800**	**$632.50**
AMOS 03/25/06 Lot 679	M1907 #57333 (mfg 1955), .351 S.L., 20" round bbl. w/excellent bore, factory sling swivels and bulkier stock seen on later versions sold to law enforcement. About Excellent, 98 percent-99 percent orig. blue, wood rates excellent w/thin coat of linseed oil added.	**E: $350-$550**	**$1,207.50**
AMOS 08/05/06 Lot 365	M1907 #29827 (mfg 1914), .351 S.L., 20" round bbl., plain pistol grip stock and forend. About Fine to Very Fine, 97 percent-98 percent orig. blue except forend cap w/gray patina, 95 percent orig. varnish on wood, lengthy grain cracks to forend, sling swivel added to buttstock.	**E: $600-$800**	**$517.50**
AMOS 03/25/06 Lot 680	M1907 #12819 (mfg 1908), .351 S.L., 20" nickel steel bbl. w/excellent bore, period Marbles Sheard replacement front sight. About Very Good to Fine, 88 percent-90 percent orig. thinning blue, very good buttstock and forend w/ ∫" crack behind receiver, scratches and dings.	**E: $300-$400**	**$431.25**
JCD 09/19/04 Lot 710	M1907 #29374 (mfg 1913), .351 S.L., 20" round bbl., good bore. "Grades Good condition with a stock through bolt repair at the wrist."	**E: $150-$250**	**$166.75**

Auction House/Date/Lot No.	Item Description	Estimated Value	Actually Sold For
JCD 06/25/06 Lot 250	M1907 #56705, .351 S.L., 20" round bbl. w/Lyman ivory bead front sight. About Very Fine late production rifle, both wood and metal rate 97 percent, w/sling swivels and sling, semi-buckhorn rear sight, two 5-round magazines.	E: $500-$600	$718.75
JCD 06/25/06 Lot 604	M1907 #14892, .351 S.L., 20" round bbl. w/excellent bore. About Very Good to Fine, 93 percent blue w scratches and thinning at high points, wood w/50 percent finish and cracks at receiver.	E: $375-$450	$546.25
JDJ 10/04-07/04 Lot 804	Deluxe M1907 #3635, .351 S.L., 20" round bbl. w/Lyman ivory bead front sight, figure walnut semi-pistol grip stock and forearm with "H"-style checkering. "Very Fine +," 95 percent orig. blue w/some flaking, wood w/factory finish, hairline cracks.	E: $2,000-$3,500	$1,725
RIA 08/27-29/04 Lot 1969	M1907 #15671, .351 S.L., 20" round bbl., plain pistol grip stock and forend. "Near new, no loss of finish; very light handling marks overall."	E: $1,100-$1,400	$1,495
RIA 08/27-29/04 Lot 1970	M1907 #54945, .351 S.L., 20" round bbl., plain pistol grip stock and forend, replacement front sight, leather sling. "New without box."	E: $1,000-$1,400	$1,610
JCD 01/23/05 Lot 351	M1907 #54118 (mfg 1952) .351 S.L., 20" round bbl. w/"excellent bore," finish 40 percent blue with balance gray brown, "wood shows no varnish."	E: $175-$275.	$230
RIA 12/4-6/04 Lot 1911	M1907 #39394 (mfg 1919) .22 S.L.L.R. 22" round bbl. "About good" half of thinning blue mixed w/light pitting, cracked forearm, "fine" action.	E: $175-$325.	$195.50
RIA 12/4-6/04 Lot 1916	M1907 #23935 .351 S.L. 20" round bbl, replacement sights. Fair, scattered traces of blue mixed w/light pitting, dents, repaired buttstock, "fine" action.	E: $175-$325.	$195.50
RIA 12/4-6/04 Lot 1943	M1907 Police #50903 (mfg 1950) .351 S.L. 20" round bbl. w/beavertail forearm, leather sling. "Excellent," 95 percent blue, tight action.	E: $550-$900.	$632.50
RIA 12/4-6/04 Lot 2265	M1907 S.L. #55697 .351 S.L. 20" round bbl. w/sling swivels, steel buttplate, one 10-round and three 5-round magazines. New in Box with Winchester hang tag.	E: $1,000-$2,000.	$3,737.50
RIA 12/4-6/04 Lot 2418	M1907 #14626 .351 S.L. 20" round bbl. w/added swivel studs. "Good," 50 percent blue, revarnished wood with some forend cracks, replacement buttplate.	E: $250-$400.	$345
RIA 12/4-6/04 Lot 2427	M1907 Police #51187 (mfg 1950) .351 S.L. 20" round bbl. w/beavertail forearm, no sling. Excellent to new, trivial handling marks.	E: $450-$700.	$431.25
RIA 12/4-6/04 Lot 2428	M1907 #47686 .22 S.L.L.R. 20" round bbl., standard sporting sights, steel buttplate sling swivel, uncheckered forearm. "Excellent" w/98 percent blue, no stock wear or marks.	E: $1,000-$1,500.	$977.50

Auction House/Date/Lot No.	Item Description	Estimated Value	Actually Sold For
GMA 02/05-06/05 Lot 877	Cased M1907 Police Carbine #46971, .351 S.L., 20" bbl, standard sights and bayonet fixture at muzzle, w/one 10-round and one 5-round magazine velour-lined French-style metal travel case with bayonet and scabbard, military-style sling and two boxes of ammunition. "Excellent," 80 percent-85 percent finish with scattered light wear, wood "near mint," case with wear and patina.	E: $3,000-$4,000	$5,391.25
GMA 11/14-16/05 Lot 195	M1907 #15882, .351 S.L., open and adjustable sporting sights, varnished, checkered select pistol grip walnut stock and composition buttplate. "Very good," 65 percent blue with wear, stocks worn with nicks and mars. Lacks magazine. Fine bore.	E: $500-$800	$737.75
GMA 06/26-27/06 Lot 654	M1907 #53421, .351 S.L., 20" bbl. with elevation sights, frame drilled for telescopic sight. Checkered walnut pistol grip stock, sling mounts and steel buttplate. "Good to Very Good," 90 percent-95 percent finish w/scattered edge wear, wood refinished w/scattered light wear and blemishes.	E: $250-$350	$737.75
GMA 06/26-27/06 Lot 808	M1907 #27990, .351 S.L., 19.5" bbl., walnut pistol grip stock w/tiny inlaid compass, sling mounts. "Fair to Good," 70 percent-75 percent finish w/scattered wear and pitting, rear sight wedge missing. Buttstock w/crack repairs and splits.	E: $200-$300	$255.38
GMA 11/14-16/05 Lot 1914	M1907 #54290, .351 S.L., 20" bbl. w/open sporting sights, varnished walnut stock w/sling swivels. "Fine," 95 percent blue and varnish, light nicks and minor wear on wood. Rear sling swivel bent.	E: $500-$700	$567.50
GMA 11/14-16/05 Lot 1996	M1907 #31573, .351 S.L., 20" bbl., varnished walnut stock. Replacement folding tang peep sight. "Good to Very Good," blue turning brown, stock with old revarnish, wear and nicks.	E: $400-$500	$312.13
GMA 04/25-27/05 Lot 356	M1907 #45655, .351 S.L., 20" bbl., oil-finished walnut stock with composition buttplate. "Very Good," traces of blue w/pitting and gray and brown patina, stocks worn. Lacks magazine.	E: $300-$500	$196.88
GMA 04/25-27/05 Lot 816	M1907 #26514, .351 S.L., 20" bbl., standard finish, markings and walnut stocks. "Very Good," gray patina to frame with light pitting, barrel 75 percent fading blue, stocks worn. Sold with extra magazine.	E: $300-$500	$393.75

Rifle

Exc.	V.G.	Good	Fair	Poor
475	400	300	250	200

NOTE: Pre-1964 models 15 percent premium. Prices given are for .308 caliber; for .243 add 15 percent, for .284 add 20 percent.

Carbine

Only about 53,000 carbines were made, about one for every five rifles.

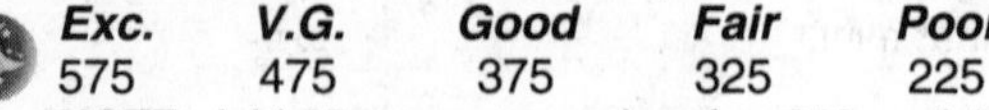

Exc.	V.G.	Good	Fair	Poor
575	475	375	325	225

NOTE: Add 25 percent premium for .243, and 100 percent for .284.

Model SXR Super X Rifle

Gas-operated semi-automatic patterned after Browning BAR ShortTrac and LongTrac. Calibers: .30-06 (4), .300WM (3), .270 WSM (3), .300 WSM (3). Barrel: 22-inch (.30-06), 24-inch. Weight: 7-1/4 lbs. Stock: Two-piece checkered walnut. Introduced 2006. MSRP: 839.

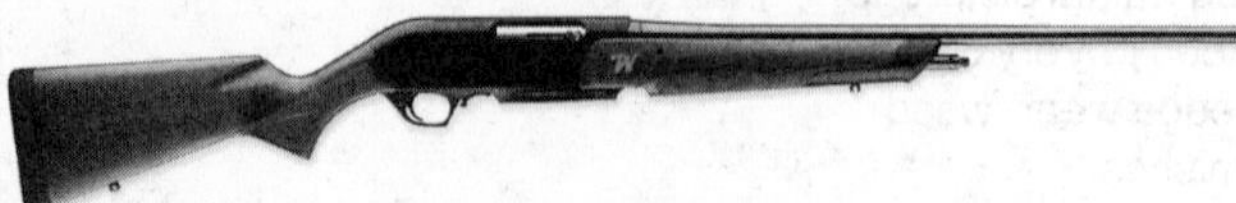

Model 88 "Centennial Model" (1855/1955)

The Model 88 was a modern short-stroke lever-action chambered for the .243, .308, 284, and .358 calibers. It was available in a rifle version with 22" round barrel and a carbine version with 19" round barrel. The carbine model was not chambered for the .358 cartridge. Both were furnished with a detachable box magazine. The stock was a one-piece design with pistol grip and was offered with hand-cut checkering or pressed basket weave checkering after 1964. The rifle was introduced in 1955 and the carbine was first offered in 1968. Both versions were discontinued in 1973 with about 283,000 sold.

Rifle

Exc.	V.G.	Good	Fair	Poor
750	500	300	250	150

NOTE: Pre-1964 models add 25 percent premium. Prices above are for .308 caliber; for .243 add 15 percent, .284 add 75 percent, and for 358 add 100 percent.

This model was offered with no front or rear sights (Gopher Special) for a few years prior to 1962. Add 100 percent for this variant. Beware of fakes.

Carbine

Only 28,000 carbines were built, about 1 for every 10 rifles. Rarely encountered.

Exc.	V.G.	Good	Fair	Poor
1200	1050	900	650	300

NOTE: Add 25 percent for .243, add 100 percent for .284 calibers. The carbine was not offered in .358 caliber.

Model 99 or Thumb Trigger

This rifle was a modification of the Model 1902 without a traditional trigger. The rifle was fired by depressing the trigger with the thumb, which was part of the sear and extractor located behind the bolt. The rifle was chambered for the .22 Short and Long until 1914 when it was also chambered for the .22 Extra Long. All cartridges could be shot interchangeably. The stock was the same as the Model 1902, Gumwood stained walnut, without the trigger or trigger guard. This model was not serial numbered. Built between 1904 and 1923. Winchester sold about 76,000 rifles.

Courtesy Bonhams & Butterfields, San Francisco, California

Exc.	V.G.	Good	Fair	Poor
2200	1000	600	300	200

Model 1900

This single-shot bolt-action .22 caliber rifle was based on a John M. Browning design. The rifle was furnished with an 18" round barrel and chambered for the .22 Short and Long interchangeably. The stock was a one-piece plain gumwood straight grip without a buttplate. The rifle was not serial numbered. It was produced from 1899 to 1902 with about 105,000 sold.

Courtesy Buffalo Bill Historical Center, Cody, Wyoming

Exc.	V.G.	Good	Fair	Poor
2000	1000	450	300	200

Model 1902

Also a single-shot, this model was of the same general design as the Model 1900 with several improvements: a special shaped metal trigger guard was added, a shorter trigger pull, a steel buttplate, a rear peep sight, and the barrel was made heavier at the muzzle. The rifle was chambered for the .22 Short and Long cartridges until 1914 when the .22 Extra Long was added. In 1927 the .22 Extra Long was dropped in favor of the more popular .22 LR. All of these cartridges were interchangeable. The stock was a one-piece plain gumwood with straight grip (the metal trigger guard added a pistol grip feel) and steel buttplate, which was changed to composition in 1907. This model was not serial numbered. About 640,000 Model 1902s were sold between 1902 and 1931 when it was discontinued.

Exc.	V.G.	Good	Fair	Poor
1000	750	400	225	125

Model 1904

This model was a slightly more expensive version of the Model 1902. It featured a 21" round barrel, a one-piece plain gumwood straight-grip stock (the metal trigger guard gave the rifle a pistol grip feel) with a small lip on the forend. Rifle was chambered for the .22 Short and Long until 1914 when the .22 Extra Long was added. The .22 LR cartridge was added in place of the Extra Long in 1927. This model was not serial numbered. Produced between 1904 and 1931, about 303,000 rifles were sold.

Exc.	V.G.	Good	Fair	Poor
850	600	350	200	100

Model D Military Rifle

Overall length 46-3/8"; barrel length 26"; caliber 7.62mm. Walnut stock with blued barrel, receiver, magazine housing and furniture. Receiver ring over barrel breech stamped with serial number and Winchester proofmark. A total of 500 Model D Rifles were shipped to Russia for trial in March of 1917.

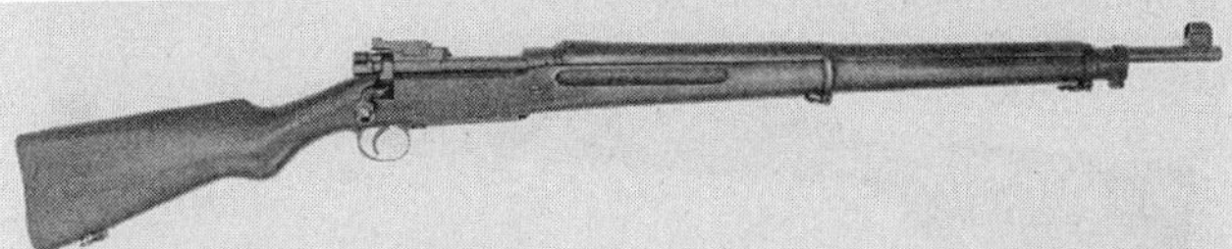

Prospective purchasers are strongly advised to secure an expert appraisal prior to acquisition. Due to the recent identification of this model pricing schedules have yet to be established.

Imperial Bolt-Action Magazine Rifle (Model 51)

Designed by T.C. Johnson, approximately 25 of these rifles were made during 1919 and 1920 in two different styles and three calibers. The takedown variation has an overall length of 42-1/4", barrel length 22" and was made in .27, .30-06 and .35 Newton calibers. The solid frame version is identical in form, dimensions and calibers. Sight configurations and markings vary.

Winchester Imperial Takedown

Winchester Imperial Solid Frame

Model 43

Introduced in 1949, this rifle was chambered for the .218 Bee, .22 Hornet, .25-20 Winchester, and the .32-20 Winchester. The rifle was a bolt-action with detachable box magazine, fitted with a 24" round barrel and front sight ramp forged integrally with barrel. **This model was not drilled and tapped for scope blocks except for a few late rifles.** This model was available in two styles:

1. Standard Rifle, 24" round barrel, plain walnut pistol-grip stock and forend. One inch sling swivels are standard.
2. Special Rifle, 24" round barrel, select walnut checkered pistol-grip stock and checkered forend. Furnished with either open sporting rear sight or Lyman 57A micrometer receiver sight.

The Model 43 was produced from 1949 to 1957 with about 63,000 sold.

Standard Rifle

Exc.	*V.G.*	*Good*	*Fair*	*Poor*
650	550	400	300	200

Special Rifle or Deluxe

Exc.	*V.G.*	*Good*	*Fair*	*Poor*
750	650	550	250	175

NOTE: For rifles chambered for .25-20 and .32-20 add a 50 percent premium. For rifles with non-factory drilled and tapped scope holes deduct 40 percent.

Model 47

This model was a single-shot bolt-action rifle chambered for the .22 Short, Long, and LR interchangeably. The rifle was furnished with a 25" round barrel, plain walnut pistol-grip stock and forend. The bolt, bolt handle, and trigger are chrome plated. This model has a special bolt with a post on the underside. This moves into the safety position when the bolt is closed.This model was not serial numbered. Produced between 1948 and 1954, Winchester sold about 43,000 guns.

Courtesy Buffalo Bill Historical Center, Cody, Wyoming

Exc.	*V.G.*	*Good*	*Fair*	*Poor*
450	350	250	200	150

Model 47 Target Rifle

Fitted with a 28" round standard weight or heavyweight barrel, plain walnut modified pistol-grip stock with correct bolt.

Exc.	*V.G.*	*Good*	*Fair*	*Poor*
650	500	350	250	150

NOTE: Add 10 percent premium for Model 47 with factory peep sight.

Model 52

Editor's Comment: According to Winchester factory records, Model 52 barrels were, "originally drilled and tapped for Winchester telescope bases designed for use with the Winchester 3A, 5A, and Lyman telescopes." These bases had a 6.2" center-to-center spacing ... a change in the bases and the spacing to be used was authorized on January 11, 1933. These new bases had a specially shaped Fecker-type notch added on the right-hand side of both bases. They are known as Winchester Combination Telescope Sight Bases and are satisfactory for use with Winchester, Lyman, Fecker, and Unertl telescopes. Bases are spaced 7.2" center to center ... All Model 52 targets were factory drilled for scope mounting but only the "C" series Sporters were factory drilled for scopes.

One of the finest small-caliber bolt-action rifles ever built, the Model 52 was Winchester's answer to the increased demand for a military-style target rifle following WWI. The Model 52 was a well-made quality-built bolt-action rifle. The rifle was chambered for the .22 LR cartridge. Designed by T.C. Johnson, this rifle was built in several different configurations over its production life:

1. Model 52 with finger groove in forend and one barrel band. Produced from 1920 to 1929.
2. Model 52 Target Rifle, same as above but without finger groove in forend and has first speed lock. Made from 1929 to 1932.
3. Model 52A Target Rifle, same as above with addition of reinforced receiver and locking lug. Made from 1932 to 1935.
4. Model 52B Target Rifle, same as above with addition of adjustable sling swivel and single-shot adaptor. Made from 1935 to 1947.
5. Model 52C Target Rifle, same as above with addition of an easily adjustable vibration-free trigger mechanism. Made from 1947 to 1961.
6. Model 52D Target Rifle, this is a single-shot rifle with free-floating barrel and new design stock with adjustable hand-stop channel.
7. Model 52 Bull Gun, same as target rifle but fitted with extra heavyweight barrel. Made from 1939 to 1960. The Bull Barrel measures 1.125" at the receiver juncture while the heavyweight measures 1". Both barrels measure .875" at the muzzle.
8. Model 52 International Match, a free-style stock with thumb hole and adjustable buttstock and forend intro-

duced in 1969. International Prone model with no thumb hole or adjustable buttplate and forend was introduced in 1975. Both discontinued in 1980.

9. Model 52 Sporter, 24" round barrel, select walnut checkered pistol-grip stock with cheekpiece and forend with black plastic tip. Pistol grip was furnished with hard-rubber grip cap. The Model 52 Sporter was introduced in 1934 and discontinued in 1958. It went through the same improvements as the Target Rifle, thus the designation Model 52A Sporter, etc.

Model 52 Standard

Exc.	V.G.	Good	Fair	Poor
750	600	450	350	200

Model 52 Target

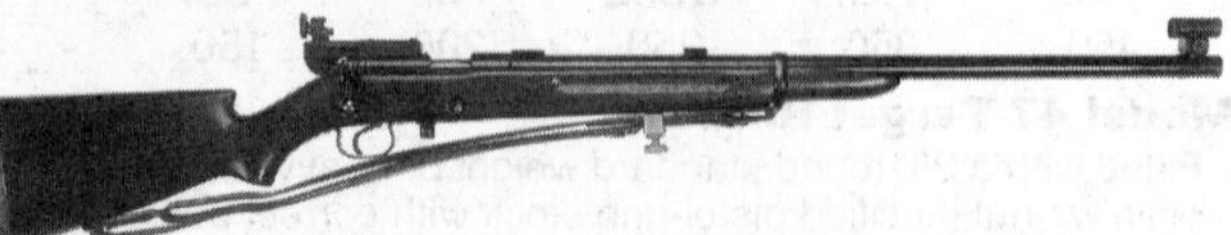

Courtesy Rock Island Auction Company

Exc.	V.G.	Good	Fair	Poor
1250	1100	850	700	350

Model 52 Target—Speed Lock

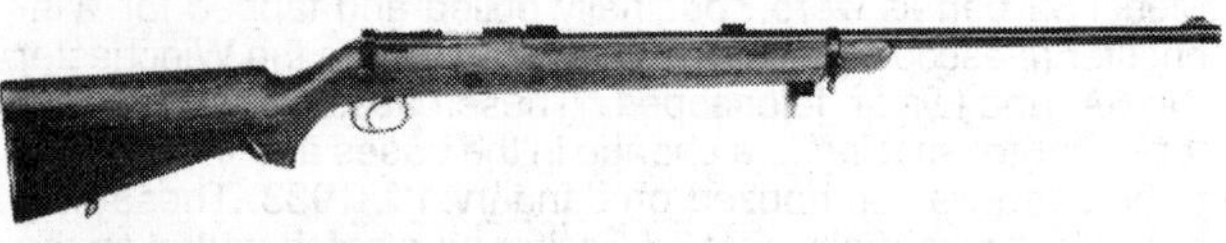

Exc.	V.G.	Good	Fair	Poor
1200	1000	750	600	350

Model 52A Target Heavy Barrel—Rare

Exc.	V.G.	Good	Fair	Poor
1200	1000	750	600	350

Model 52B Target Heavy & Standard Barrel

Exc.	V.G.	Good	Fair	Poor
1000	900	650	500	300

Model 52B Target Bull Barrel

Exc.	V.G.	Good	Fair	Poor
1200	1000	900	700	500

Model 52C Target

Courtesy Amoskeag Auction Company

Exc.	V.G.	Good	Fair	Poor
1200	1000	750	600	400

Model 52D Target

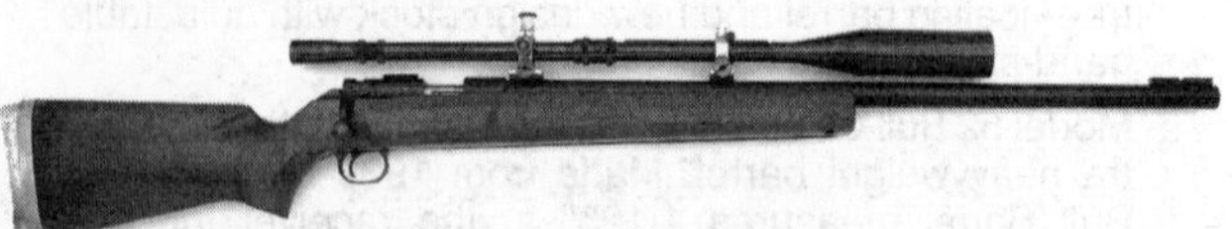

Courtesy Amoskeag Auction Company

Exc.	V.G.	Good	Fair	Poor
1300	1100	1000	850	400

A Model 52 Sporter prototype, built in 1932, sold at auction for $17,250. Originally owned by Major John Hession, world renowned target shooter. Condition is 98 percent original finish. Dockendorf front sight and Lyman receiver sight.

Amoskeag Auction Company

Model 52B Bull Gun

Exc.	V.G.	Good	Fair	Poor
1300	1100	1000	850	400

Model 52C Bull Gun

Exc.	V.G.	Good	Fair	Poor
1300	1100	1000	850	500

Model 52 International Match

Approximately 300 manufactured.

Free Style

Exc.	V.G.	Good	Fair	Poor
3250	2500	1750	1000	500

Prone

Exc.	V.G.	Good	Fair	Poor
1100	950	850	600	500

Model 52 Sporter—B & C Models

Exc.	V.G.	Good	Fair	Poor
3600	3000	2000	1600	900

NOTE: Add 50 percent to above prices for "A" or pre-"A" series sporters. These are very rare early models in the Sporter Series.

Model 54

The Model 54 was to centerfire cartridges what the Model 52 was to rimfire cartridges. The Model 54 was also a quality-made bolt-action rifle with a nondetachable box magazine and was chambered for a variety of calibers: .270, .30-06, .30-30, 7mm, 7.65, 9.mm, .250-3000, .22 Hornet, .220 Swift, and .257 Roberts. This was Winchester's first bolt-action rifle built for heavy, high velocity ammunition. The rifle was available in several different styles:

1. Standard Rifle, 24" or 20" round barrel (except .220 Swift which was 26"), plain walnut checkered pistol-grip stock and forend.
2. Carbine, 20" round barrel, plain walnut pistol-grip stock with finger groove on each side of forend.
3. Sniper's Rifle, 26" round heavyweight barrel, plain walnut pistol-grip stock and forend.
4. N.R.A. Rifle, 24" round barrel, select walnut checkered pistol-grip stock and forend.

5. Super Grade Rifle, 24" round barrel, select walnut checkered pistol-grip stock with cheekpiece and checkered forend with black plastic tip. Pistol grip was capped with hard rubber cap. Super Grade was equipped with 1" detachable sling swivels.
6. Target Rifle, 24" round heavyweight barrel, plain walnut checkered pistol-grip stock and forend.
7. National Match Rifle, 24" round barrel, plain walnut special target stock and forend.

The Model 54 was introduced in 1925 and was discontinued in 1936 with about 50,000 guns sold.

Standard Rifle

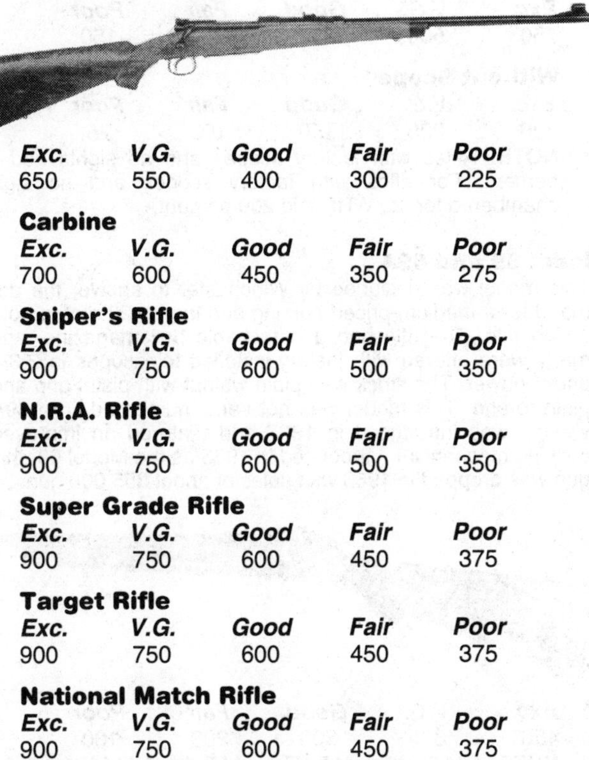

Exc.	*V.G.*	*Good*	*Fair*	*Poor*
650	550	400	300	225

Carbine

Exc.	*V.G.*	*Good*	*Fair*	*Poor*
700	600	450	350	275

Sniper's Rifle

Exc.	*V.G.*	*Good*	*Fair*	*Poor*
900	750	600	500	350

N.R.A. Rifle

Exc.	*V.G.*	*Good*	*Fair*	*Poor*
900	750	600	500	350

Super Grade Rifle

Exc.	*V.G.*	*Good*	*Fair*	*Poor*
900	750	600	450	375

Target Rifle

Exc.	*V.G.*	*Good*	*Fair*	*Poor*
900	750	600	450	375

National Match Rifle

Exc.	*V.G.*	*Good*	*Fair*	*Poor*
900	750	600	450	375

NOTE: The rare calibers are the 7mm, 7.65mm and the 9mm, which bring considerable premiums (in some cases as much as 250 percent) over standard calibers. Popular calibers such as .22 Hornet, .220 Swift, .30-30, and .257 Roberts will also bring a premium. Proceed with caution on Model 54s with rare caliber markings.

Model 56

This model was designed to be a medium-priced bolt-action rimfire rifle. It featured a detachable box magazine and was chambered for the .22 Short or .22 LR cartridges. The rifle was offered in two styles:

1. Sporting Rifle, 22" round barrel, plain walnut pistol-grip stock and forend.
2. Fancy Sporting Rifle, 22" round barrel, fancy walnut checkered pistol-grip stock and forend.

Both styles had a forend with a distinctive lip on the forend tip. The rifle was introduced in 1926 and was discontinued in 1929 with about 8,500 rifles sold.

Sporting Rifle

Exc.	*V.G.*	*Good*	*Fair*	*Poor*
1500	1000	750	525	400

Fancy Sporting Rifle

Very rare, use caution.

Exc.	*V.G.*	*Good*	*Fair*	*Poor*
3000	2000	1500	900	750

NOTE: Add a 50 percent premium for rifles chambered for .22 Short only.

Model 57

The Model 57 was close in appearance to the Model 56 with the addition of a heavier stock, target sights, and swivel bows attached to the stock. The rifle was chambered for the .22 Short or .22 LR and featured a 22" round barrel with detachable box magazine. The stock was plain walnut with pistol grip and plain forend. The rifle was introduced in 1927 and dropped from the Winchester line in 1936 having sold only about 19,000 guns.

Exc.	*V.G.*	*Good*	*Fair*	*Poor*
750	600	450	325	250

NOTE: Add 20 percent premium for web sling.

Model 58

This model was an attempt by the company to market a low-priced .22 caliber rimfire rifle in place of its Models 1902 and 1904. This was a single-shot bolt-action, cocked by pulling the firing pin head to the rear. It had an 18" round barrel and was chambered for the .22 Short, Long, and LR interchangeably. The stock was a one-piece plain wood with straight grip. This model was not serial-numbered. The Model 58 was introduced in 1928 and discontinued in 1931. About 39,000 were sold.

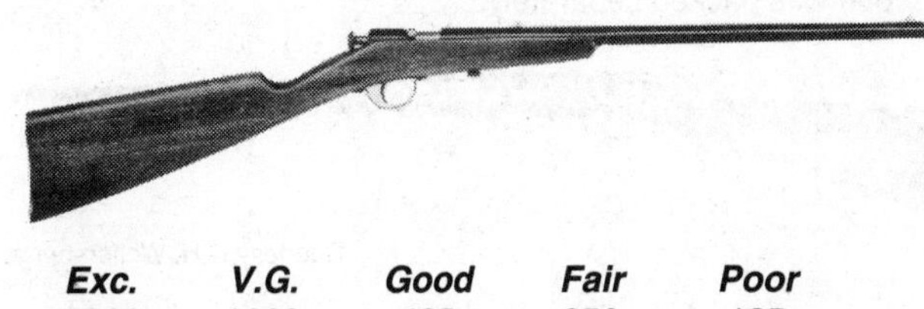

Exc.	*V.G.*	*Good*	*Fair*	*Poor*
2000	1000	425	250	125

Model 59

The Model 59 was essentially a Model 58 with the addition of a pistol-grip stock and a 23" round barrel. Introduced in 1930, it was dropped from the product line in the same year with a total sales of about 9,000 guns.

Courtesy Olin Corporation

Exc.	*V.G.*	*Good*	*Fair*	*Poor*
2000	1000	400	200	125

Model 60 and 60A

This rifle used the same action as that of the Model 59. When the rifle was first introduced in 1931, it was furnished with a 23" round barrel which was changed to 27" in 1933. Several other mechanical improvements were included with this model; perhaps the most noticeable were the chrome-plated bolt, bolt handle, and trigger. The stock was plain wood with pistol grip. In 1933 the Model 60A was added, which was the same rifle but in a target configuration. The front sight was a square top military blade with a Lyman 55W receiver sight. The Model 60 was discontinued in 1934 with about 166,000 rifles sold. The Model 60A was dropped in 1939 with only about 6,100 rifles sold.

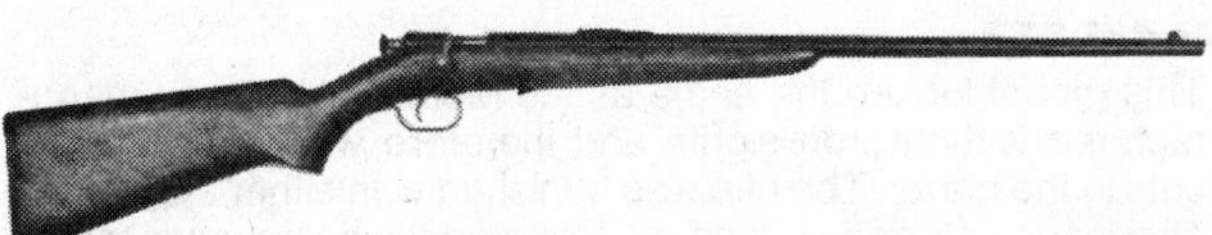

Courtesy Buffalo Bill Historical Center, Cody, Wyoming

Model 60

Exc.	*V.G.*	*Good*	*Fair*	*Poor*
400	250	200	150	100

Model 60A

Exc.	V.G.	Good	Fair	Poor
400	300	250	150	100

Model 67

Winchester again upgraded and improved the Model 60 with an expansion of the styles offered to the shooting public. The standard chamber for the rifle was .22 Short, Long, and LR interchangeably with the W.R.F. only added in 1935:

1. Sporting Rifle, 27" round barrel, stock similar to the Model 60.
2. Smoothbore Rifle, 27" barrel, chambered for the .22 long shot or .22 LR shot.
3. Junior Rifle, 20" round barrel and shorter stock.
4. Rifle with miniature target boring, 24" round barrel, chambered for .22 LR shot.

Model 67s were not serial numbered for domestic sales but were numbered for foreign sales. Introduced in 1934 the gun was dropped from the line in 1963 having sold about 384,000. Many of these models were fitted at the factory with telescopes, and the bases were mounted on the rifle and the scope was packed separately.

Courtesy C.H. Wolfersberger

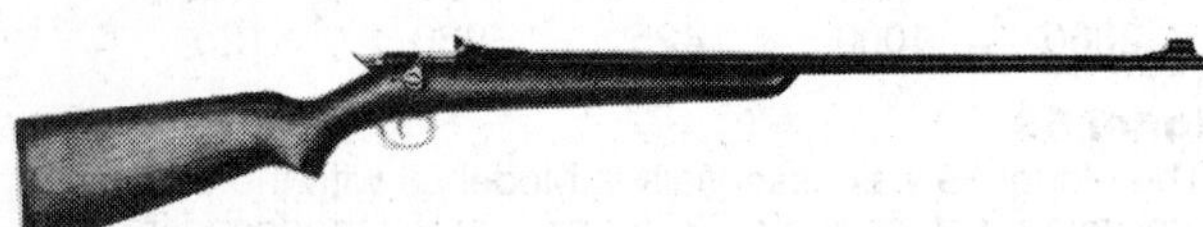

Courtesy Buffalo Bill Historical Center, Cody, Wyoming

Sporting Rifle

Exc.	V.G.	Good	Fair	Poor
200	150	125	100	75

Smoothbore Rifle

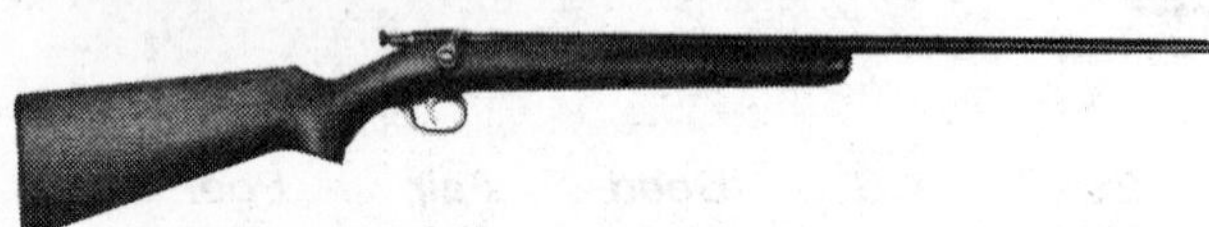

Courtesy Buffalo Bill Historical Center, Cody, Wyoming

Exc.	V.G.	Good	Fair	Poor
800	600	400	250	200

Junior Rifle

Exc.	V.G.	Good	Fair	Poor
250	200	175	150	125

Miniature Target Rifle

This model is marked "FOR SHOT ONLY" and has beads instead of standard iron rifle sights.

Exc.	V.G.	Good	Fair	Poor
1200	900	700	400	300

Model 677

This model looked the same as the Model 67 but was manufactured without iron sights and therefore will have no sight cuts in the barrel. The rifle was furnished with either 2-3/4 power scopes or 5 power scopes. This model was not serial numbered. Introduced in 1937 and discontinued in 1939.

Exc.	V.G.	Good	Fair	Poor
2250	1350	900	600	300

NOTE: Add 100 percent premium for rifles chambered for .22 WRF.

Model 68

Another takeoff on the Model 67, this model differed only in the sight equipment offered. Winchester fitted this rifle with its own 5-power telescopes. First sold in 1934 the Model 68 was dropped in 1946 with sales of about 101,000.

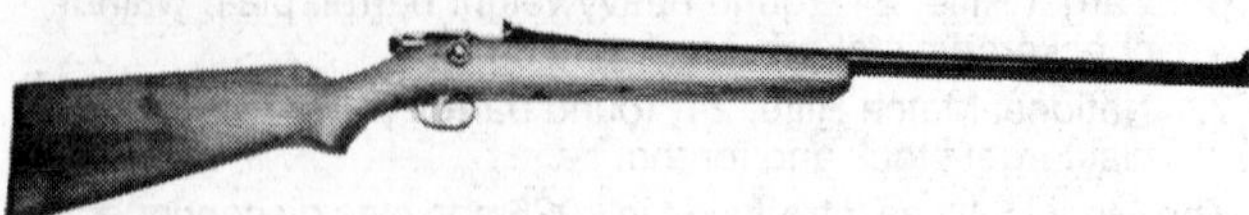

Courtesy C.H. Wolfersberger

With Scope

Exc.	V.G.	Good	Fair	Poor
750	500	300	200	150

Without Scope

Exc.	V.G.	Good	Fair	Poor
300	225	150	100	75

NOTE: Rifles with factory scopes and no sights add 50 percent. For rifles with factory scopes and no sights chambered for .22 WRF add 200 percent.

Model 69 and 69A

This model was designed by Winchester to answer the demand for a medium-priced hunting and target .22 rimfire bolt-action rifle. The rifle had a detachable box magazine, and many were offered with factory-installed telescopes in 2-3/4 and 5 power. The stock was plain walnut with pistol grip and plain forend. This model was not serial numbered. The 69A version was introduced in 1937 and featured an improved cocking mechanism. Introduced in 1935 as the Model 69, this gun was dropped in 1963 with sales of about 355,000 guns.

Exc.	V.G.	Good	Fair	Poor
450	375	300	200	100

NOTE: Add 25 percent for Target Model. Add 20 percent for grooved receiver.

Model 697

The Model 697 was similar in appearance to the Model 69 except it was equipped exclusively for a telescope. Winchester offered either a 2-3/4 or 5-power scope with the bases attached at the factory and the scope packed separately. Built between 1937 and 1941 with small sales, this model was not serial numbered.

Exc.	V.G.	Good	Fair	Poor
2000	1200	800	600	400

NOTE: For factory scopes with no sights add 50 percent.

Model 70

Considered by many as the finest bolt-action rifle ever built in the United States, the pre-1964 Model 70 is highly sought after by shooters and collectors alike. Its smooth, strong action has no peer. It is often referred to as "The Riflemen's Rifle." The Model 70 is an updated and improved version of the Model 54 and features a hinged floorplate, new speed locks, new safety design that does not interfere with telescope, manually releasable bolt stop, more attractive buttstock and forend, and forged steel trigger guard. Like many Winchesters, the Model 70 was available with several extra-cost options that should be evaluated by an expert. The values listed are given for pre-1964 Model 70s with serial numbers from 1 to 581471. This rifle was available in several different styles:

1. Standard Grade, 24" round barrel (except 26" barrel for .220 Swift and .300 H&H Magnum—25" round barrel for .375 H&H Magnum after 1937), plain walnut

checkered pistol stock and forend. Built from 1936 to 1963.

2. Standard Grade Carbine, 20" round barrel, chambered for .22 Hornet, .250-3000, .257 Roberts, .270, 7mm, and .30-06, same stock as Standard Grade. Built from 1936 to 1946.
3. Super Grade Rifle, same barrel and calibers as Standard Grade, select walnut checkered and capped pistol-grip stock with cheekpiece and checkered forend with plastic tip. Built from 1936 to 1960.
4. Featherweight, 22" round barrel chambered for .243, .264, .270, .308, .30-06, and .358. Fitted with aluminum trigger guard, aluminum buttplate, and aluminum floor plate. Later versions with plastic buttplate. Built from 1952 to 1963.
5. Featherweight Super Grade, same as above except not chambered for the .358 cartridge, but fitted with Super Grade stock. Built from 1952 to 1963.
6 National Match, same as Standard Grade but fitted with target type stock and telescope bases. Chambered for .30-06 only. Discontinued in 1960.
7. Target, 24" round medium-weight barrel with same stock as National Match in .243 and .30-06 calibers. Discontinued in 1963.
8. Varmint, 26" round heavy barrel, with heavier varmint stock, chambered for .243 and the rare .220 Swift. Built from 1956 to 1963.
9. Westerner, 26" round barrel with Standard Grade stock, chambered for .264 Winchester Magnum. Built from 1960 to 1963. Fitted with a solid rubber pad for early production guns and a vented pad for later guns.
10. Alaskan, 25" round barrel, with Standard Grade stock, chambered for .338 Winchester Magnum and .375 H&H Magnum. Built from 1960 to 1963. Fitted with a solid rubber pad marked Winchester for early production guns and a vented pad both marked Winchester for later guns.
11. Bull Gun, 28" round barrel, same stock as National Match, chambered for .30-06 and .300 H&H Magnum. Built from 1936 to 1963.

The standard calibers offered for the Model 70 are these, in order of rarity: .300 Savage, .35 Rem., .458 Win Magnum, 7mm, .358 Win., .250-3000 Savage, .300 Win Magnum, .338 Win. Magnum, .375 H&H Magnum, .257 Roberts, .220 Swift, .22 Hornet, .264 Win. Magnum, .300 H&H Magnum, .308 Win., .243 Win., .270 W.C.F., .30-06.

NOTE: Prices for the Model 70 are, in many cases, based on the caliber of the rifle; the more rare the caliber, the more premium the gun will command. Many pre-1964 Model 70s are still available in new condition in the original box with all papers. Add 100 percent if the box is serial numbered to the gun. **Use caution** prior to purchase of NIB guns due to fake boxes and papers.

PRICING NOTE: The asterisk **(*)** signifies the value of the rifle with respect to a usable action. Model 70 unaltered receivers

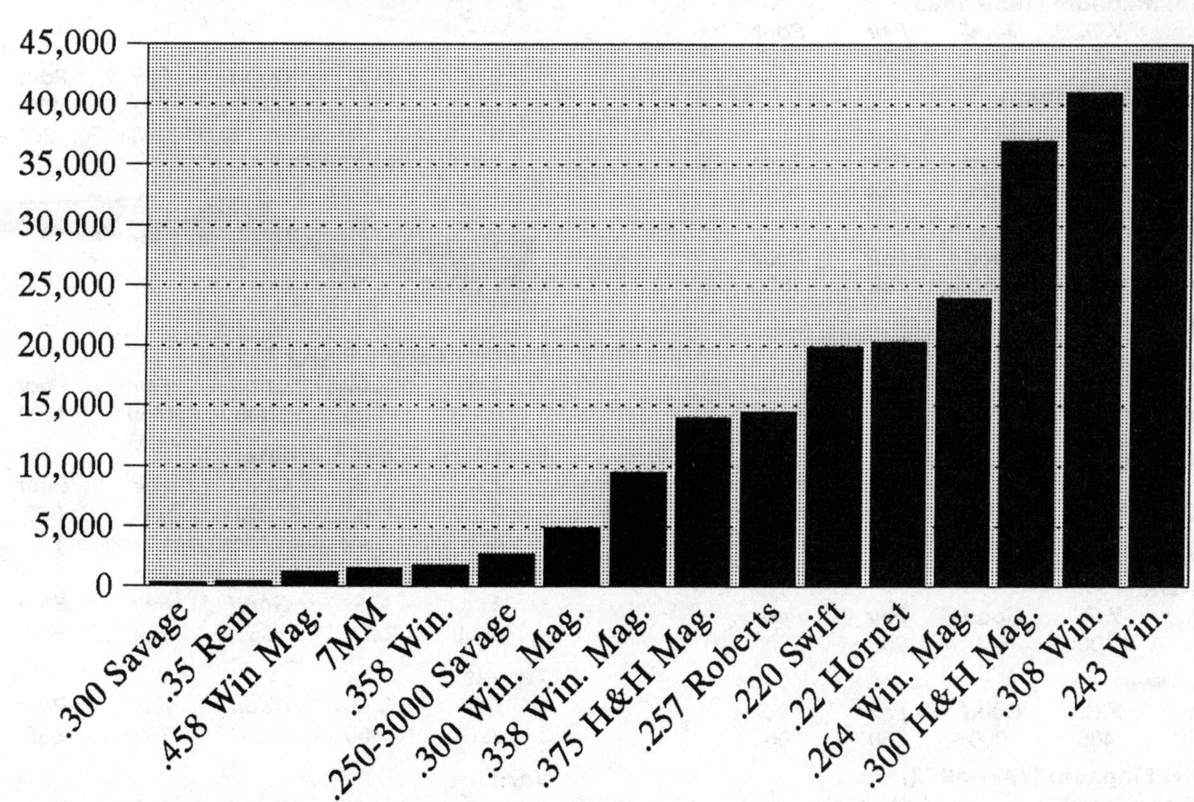

bring $500 regardless of the condition of the barrel and stock. If the receiver is unusable then the rifle is worth the value of its usable parts, i.e. less than $500.

For Model 70s with "X" or "D" prefix add a collector premium of 10 percent. These letters indicate that there were two rifles mistakenly stamped with the same serial number.

Standard Rifle

.30-06 Springfield (1937-1963)

Pre-War

Exc.	V.G.	Good	Fair	Poor
1600	1000	800	500*	500*

Post-War

Exc.	V.G.	Good	Fair	Poor
1150	925	600	500*	500*

.270 Win. (1937-1963)

Pre-War

Exc.	V.G.	Good	Fair	Poor
1800	1650	800	500*	500*

Post-War

Exc.	V.G.	Good	Fair	Poor
1150	950	600	500*	500*

.243. Win. (1955-1963)

Exc.	V.G.	Good	Fair	Poor
2750	2000	1000	500*	500*

.300 H&H Magnum (1937-1963)

Pre-War

Exc.	V.G.	Good	Fair	Poor
2200	1600	1300	800	500*

Post-War

Exc.	V.G.	Good	Fair	Poor
1650	1250	900	750	500*

.264 Win. Magnum (1959-1963)

Exc.	V.G.	Good	Fair	Poor
1800	1450	900	750	500*

.22 Hornet (1937-1958)

Pre-War

Exc.	V.G.	Good	Fair	Poor
300	2100	1400	1000	500*

Post-War

Exc.	V.G.	Good	Fair	Poor
2000	1600	1150	750	500*

.220 Swift (1937-1963)

Pre-War

Exc.	V.G.	Good	Fair	Poor
2750	2000	1250	900	500*

Post-War

Exc.	V.G.	Good	Fair	Poor
1700	1150	900	650	500*

.257 Roberts (1937-1959)

Pre-War

Exc.	V.G.	Good	Fair	Poor
2500	2100	1650	950	500*

Post-War

Exc.	V.G.	Good	Fair	Poor
1700	1400	1000	750	500*

.375 H&H Magnum (1937-1963)

Pre-War

Exc.	V.G.	Good	Fair	Poor
3900	3400	2000	1350	500*

Post-War

Exc.	V.G.	Good	Fair	Poor
2500	2000	1350	900	500*

.338 Win. Magnum (1959-1963)

Exc.	V.G.	Good	Fair	Poor
2750	2250	1350	900	500*

.300 Win. Magnum (1962-1963)

Exc.	V.G.	Good	Fair	Poor
2250	1950	1000	750	500*

.250-3000 Savage (1937-1949)

Exc.	V.G.	Good	Fair	Poor
4000	3000	1650	950	500*

7mm (1937-1949)

Exc.	V.G.	Good	Fair	Poor
5500	4500	2500	1700	700

.35 Rem. (1944-1947)

Exc.	V.G.	Good	Fair	Poor
8500	5750	3500	2000	950

.300 Savage (1944-1950s?)

Exc.	V.G.	Good	Fair	Poor
9000	8000	3600	2000	950

.458 African

Built in Supergrade only, 1956-1963.

Exc.	V.G.	Good	Fair	Poor
7000	5250	4000	2750	1350

Featherweight

Exc.	V.G.	Good	Fair	Poor
1800	1150	875	700	450

NOTE: Add 100 percent for .358 Win. For .264 and .270 calibers add 25 percent.

Featherweight Super Grade

Exc.	V.G.	Good	Fair	Poor
5000	4000	3000	1650	1000

Standard Grade Carbine

Exc.	V.G.	Good	Fair	Poor
2500	1700	1200	950	650

NOTE: For Supergrade rifles add 100 percent.

National Match

Exc.	V.G.	Good	Fair	Poor
3000	2250	1650	950	600

Target

Exc.	V.G.	Good	Fair	Poor
2250	1800	950	750	550

Varmint

Exc.	V.G.	Good	Fair	Poor
1950	1650	750	600	375*

NOTE: Add 40 percent premium for .220 Swift.

Bull Gun

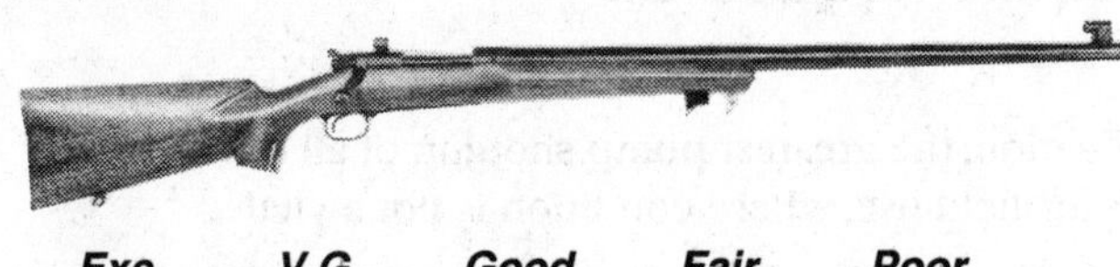

Exc.	V.G.	Good	Fair	Poor
3500	2900	2250	850	600

Model 72

This model is a bolt-action rifle with tubular magazine. It is chambered for the .22 Short, Long, and LR cartridges interchangeably. Early rifles were available with 2-3/4 or 5 power telescopes, but the majority were furnished with either open sights or peep sights. This rifle was available in two different configurations:

1. Sporting Rifle, 25" round barrel, chambered for the .22 Short, Long, and LR cartridges, one-piece plain walnut pistol-grip stock and forend.
2. Gallery Special, 25" round barrel, chambered for .22 Short only, stock same as Sporting Rifle.

This model was not serial numbered. It was built between 1938 and 1959 with about 161,000 rifles sold.

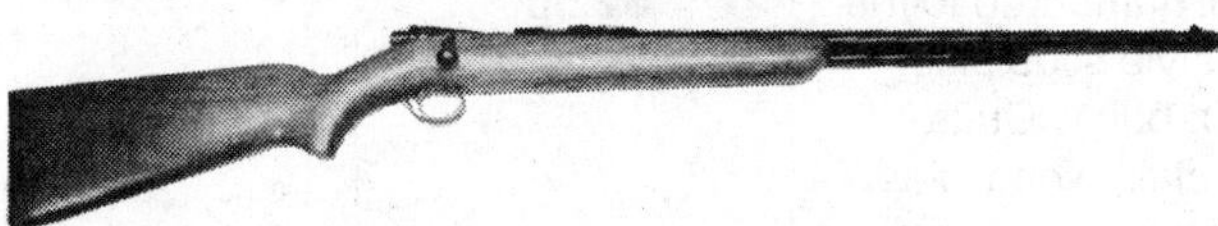

Courtesy C.H. Wolfersberger

Exc.	V.G.	Good	Fair	Poor
425	350	275	200	125

NOTE: Gallery Special will command a premium of 100 percent. For rifles with factory scopes and no sights add 200 percent depending on condition. Add 25 percent premium for peep sights. Add 20 percent for Model 72A with grooved receiver.

Model 75

Available in two styles:

1. Sporting Rifle, 24" round barrel, chambered for .22 LR, select walnut checkered pistol-grip stock and forend. This rifle was furnished with either open rear sights or a Lyman 57 E receiver sight.
2. Target Rifle, 28" round barrel, chambered for .22 LR, plain walnut pistol-grip stock and forend. The Target Rifle was furnished with either a Winchester 8-power telescope or a variety of target sights.

This model was discontinued in 1958 with about 89,000 sold.

Model 75 Sporter

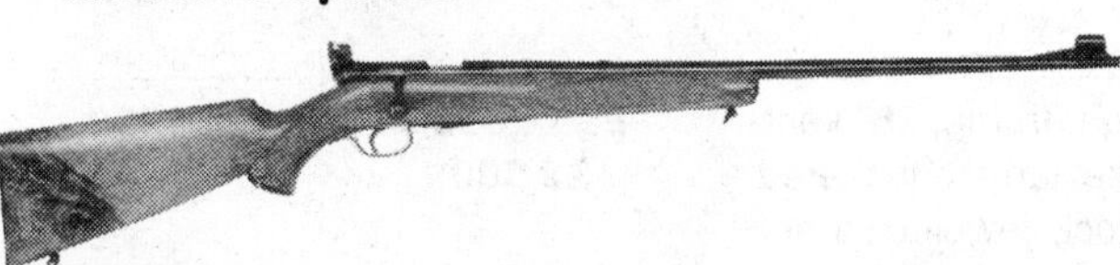

NIB	Exc.	V.G.	Good	Fair	Poor
2000	900	700	500	350	200

Model 75 Target

Exc.	V.G.	Good	Fair	Poor
700	600	500	350	200

Model 12

This model was designed by T.C. Johnson and was the first slide-action hammerless shotgun built by Winchester. The Model 12 has enjoyed great success in its 51-year history, and over 1,900,000 were sold. This was a high quality, well-made shotgun that is still in use in the hunting and shooting fields across the country. All Model 12s were of the takedown variety. The Model 12 was dropped from regular product line in 1963, but a special model was produced in the Custom Shop until 1979. In 1972 Winchester resurrected the Model 12 in its regular production line in 12 gauge only and ventilated rib. This reintroduced Model 12 was dropped in 1980. The prices listed are for guns made prior to 1964 or for guns with serial numbers below 1968307. This shotgun was offered in several different styles:

1. Standard Grade, 12, 16, 20, and 28 gauge, with plain, solid rib, or vent rib round barrels of standard lengths (26", 28", 30", 32"), plain walnut pistol-grip stock with grooved slide handle. Built from 1912 to 1963.
2. Featherweight, same as above with lightweight alloy trigger guard. Built between 1959 and 1962.
3. Riot Gun, in 12 gauge only with 20" round choked cylinder, stock same as Standard Grade. Built between 1918 and 1963.
4. Trench Gun, chambered for 12 gauge only with 20" round barrel with ventilated hand guard over barrel, fitted with bayonet lug. All metal surfaces are "Parkerized," and these shotguns should be U.S. marked as a military firearm. Introduced in 1918 and built for U.S. Armed Forces on special order.
5. Skeet Grade, chambered for 12, 16, 20, and 28 gauge with 26" round barrel with solid or ventilated rib, select walnut checkered pistol stock and special checkered extension slide handle (longer than standard). Built from 1933 to 1963.
6. Trap Grade, chambered for 12 gauge only with 30" round barrel with solid rib or ventilated rib, select walnut pistol or straight-grip stock, checkered extension slide handle. Built from 1914 to 1963.
7. Heavy Duck Gun, chambered in 12 gauge only with 30" or 32" round barrel with plain, solid, or ventilated rib, plain walnut pistol-grip stock fitted with Winchester solid red rubber recoil pad, plain grooved slide handle. Built from 1935 to 1963.
8. Pigeon Grade, chambered for 12, 16, 20, and 28 gauges with standard barrel lengths and choice of ribs. This was a special order shotgun and will be seen in many different variations, most of these guns were factory engraved. Built 1914 to 1963.

The Model 12 shotgun will be seen in many different combinations of gauges, barrel lengths, ribs, and stocks, all of which determine value. The more rare a particular combination, the higher the price. The buyer is urged to be extremely cautious before purchasing the more rare combinations, such as a 28 gauge. The best advice is to seek assistance from an expert and get as many opinions as possible. The prices listed are for guns in standard configurations.

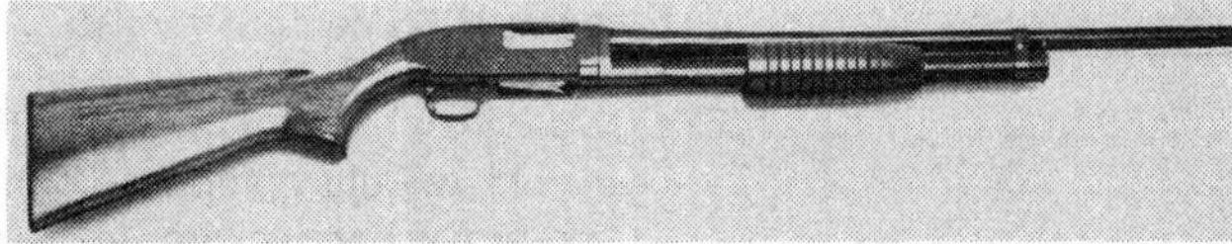

Courtesy Bonhams & Butterfields, San Francisco, California

Standard Grade—12 gauge

Exc.	V.G.	Good	Fair	Poor
700	400	300	300	200

Featherweight

Exc.	V.G.	Good	Fair	Poor
600	450	350	275	200

Riot Gun

Exc.	V.G.	Good	Fair	Poor
900	650	550	400	250

Trench Gun

Exc.	V.G.	Good	Fair	Poor
2750	1750	1100	600	400

Value Tracker: Winchester Model 12

The Winchester Model 12 has been called, with considerable justification, the greatest pump shotgun of all time. Model 12s have always been collectible, and even today many are bought for field use, where condition is not a vital consideration.

*Legend: **RIA** = Rock Island Auctions; **B&B** = Butterfield & Butterfield; **AMOS** = Amoskeag; **JCD** = J. C. Devine; **JDJ** + James D. Julia; **GMA** = Greg Martin. Contact information for these fine auction houses can be found in the front pages of this book.*

Auction House/Date/Lot No.	Item Description	Estimated Value	Actually Sold For
JCD 04/15/07 Lot 23	Winchester M12 Pigeon Grade # 968143 (mfg 1963), 20 ga. 26" vent-rib bbl., excellent bore, highly figured deluxe walnut pistol grip buttstock and forearm with old tight wood checks. Near Excellent w/95 percent blue, some stock finish loss where fabric cheekpiece was removed.	E: $4,000-$5,000	$3,335
JCD (2702) 04/15/07 Lot 30	Winchester Deluxe M12 with Extra Barrel set #749381 (mfg 1937), 28 ga. 28" solid rib bbl. choked Full numbered to the gun w/fancy checkered walnut extension-style slide plus second unnumbered 26" Simmons vent-rib bbl. w/Cutts compensator marked Skeet w/checkered plain wood slide, both w/excellent bores. Very Fine w/95 percent of a good looking reblue with finish loss on tubes, wood w/95 percent finish with light scratches.	E: $2,000-$2,500	$7,360
JCD (2702) 04/15/07 Lot 164	M12 #1541040 (mfg 1955), 20 ga. 28" solid matte rib Modified barrel w/excellent bore. About Fine with 90 percent blue, plain pistol grip buttstock and checkered forearm with field use handling marks.	E: $550-$650	$1,610
JCD (2702) 04/15/07 Lot 207	M12 #1769643 (mfg 1959), 20 ga. 28" plain Full bbl. w/excellent bore. About Excellent, retaining 98 percent+ blue, pistol grip buttstock and pump handle with few handling marks. Winchester buttplate needs cleaning.	E: $700-$900	$1,035
JDJ 03/12-13/07 Lot 1465	Martially marked M12 riot gun, #1012664, 12 ga., 20.5" Full bbl., U.S. Ordnance proofs and markings, built as a takedown model made non-takedown with addition of a fixed magazine tube, likely as an aerial gunnery training gun. Receiver w/plugged holes top left, probably from scope mount. "Very fine," w/most orig. factory blue, bright bore, wood sound w/60 percent-95 percent varnish.	E: $800.00-$1,200.00	$575
JDJ 03/12-13/07 Lot 1467	M12 Skeet Gun. #1350940, 28 ga. w/20 ga. frame, 25" vent-rib bbl. w/Cutts compensator missing choke, large checkered forearm w/unchecked semi-pistol grip stock, jeweled carrier and bolt. "Good to Very Good," bbl. and tube w/old refinish, bright bore, wood w/60 percent-75 percent orig. finish, tip crack in forearm. 28 ga shell will not hold in magazine tube.	E: $2,000-$2,500	$1,150
JDJ 03/12-13/07 Lot 1468	Deluxe M12 Skeet Gun #1582410, 12 ga., 26" Simmons vent-rib bbl. choked WS-1 w/two ivory beads, large flame-grain checkered walnut forearm and pistol grip stock w/ ivory grip cap, receiver coin finished and engraved with large marsh scene vignettes signed "E.B."and full foliate arabesques. "Very fine," w/ virtually all custom finish to metal and wood, mechanics crisp, bore bright.	E: $4,000-$6,000	$4,140

Auction House/Date/Lot No.	Item Description	Estimated Value	Actually Sold For
JDJ 03/12-13/07 Lot 1470	Pigeon-Grade M12 #1534483, 28 ga., 25.625" vent-rib Imp. Cyl. bbl w/ivory and silver beads, flame-grain checkered walnut forearm and pistol grip stock, pigeon engraved above serial number. 28 ga. snap caps did not function; magazine tube appears oversized and action jams. "Extremely fine, as new." Appears to be unfired, w/ canvas and leather trunk case.	**E: $3,000-$5,000**	**$5,175**
JDJ 03/12-13/07 Lot 1472	M12 #1902945, 12 ga., 26.125" vent-rib bbl. w/choke marked "WS-1" Muzzle has been trimmed and been taper honed. "Fine," 90 percent blue worn on sharp edges and around takedown point, wood w/minor dents, scratches. Mechanically fine.	**E: $1,000-$1,500**	**$575**
JDJ 03/12-13/07 Lot 1473	M12 #1904569, 12 ga., 28" round bbl., Modified choke. Excellent to new, with only minor handling marks on operator rod.	**E: $750-$1,250**	**$575**
JDJ 10/09-11/06 Lot 1882	Deluxe M12 skeet gun #1614208, 28 ga., 26" vent-rib Skeet bbl w/ivory and silver beads, premium checkered walnut forearm and pistol grip stock. "Very fine, as completely and professionally restored;" crack in wrist, scrape on forearm, replacement buttplate. Mechanics fine.	**E: $2,500-$4,000**	**$4,025**
JDJ 10/09-11/06 Lot 1884	Field Grade M12 #800826, 16 ga., 27.75" plain Modified bbl, flat-bottom grooved forearm with semi-pistol grip stock. "Fine, as restored," w/most professional restored metal and wood finish, crisp mechanics.	**E: $400-$700**	**$460**
JDJ 03/13-14/06 Lot 1422	M12 Heavy Duck #1873951, 3" 12 ga, 30" plain Full bbl., walnut pistol grip stock and large ribbed forend, w/orig. box, hang tag and instructions. As new in box; probably unfired.	**E: $1,000-$1,500**	**$1,610**
JDJ 03/13-14/06 Lot 1423	Field Grade M12 #1943485, 12 ga., 30" plain Full bbl., walnut pistol grip stock and large ribbed forend w/orig. box, hang tag and instructions. As new in box; probably unfired.	**E: $750-$1,250**	**$1,380**
JDJ 03/13-14/06 Lot 1424	Deluxe Field Grade M12 #1613737X, 28 ga., 25.75v solid rib Skeet bbl. w/silver beads, shell grain walnut checkered large replacement forearm with pistol grip stock. "Extremely fine," 97 percent-98 percent bright orig. blue, receiver w/small scratches, sound wood with most finish, crisp mechanics.	**E: $3,000-$5,000**	**$6,037.50**
JDJ 03/13-14/06 Lot 1426	Standard M12 #1357782, 16 ga., 27.75" plain Modified bbl. w/bore apparently honed to more open choke, short, flat bottomed, ribbed forearm and semi-pistol grip stock. "Fine as completely professionally restored, possibly factory," with small pinned repair at bottom of wrist. Bright bore.	**E: $300-$500**	**$632.50**
JDJ 03/13-14/06 Lot 1427	Trap Grade Black Diamond M12 #488449, 12 ga., 29.75" vent-rib Full bbl. marked "Trap" on bottom of receiver, highly figured small round checkered forearm and straight grip stock with a black diamond. "Extremely fine," 98 percent-99 percent orig. blue, wood sound w/most orig. oil finish.	**E: $1,000-$1,500**	**$2,300**
JDJ 03/13-14/06 Lot 1428	Deluxe Skeet Grade M12 #1870241, 12 ga., 26v vent-rib bbl. choked WS-1 w/ivory and silver beads, colorful deluxe walnut large round forearm w/checkered side panels and pistol grip stock, orig. hang tag. "Very fine," metal and wood w/ most of a very professionally restored finish, probably factory.	**E: $1,000-$1,500**	**$920**

Auction House/Date/Lot No.	Item Description	Estimated Value	Actually Sold For
JDJ 03/13-14/06 Lot 1429	M12 Heavy Duck #1631348, 3" 12 ga., 30" vent-rib Full bbl. w/ silver beads, checkered large round forearm and semi-pistol grip stock of slab-sawn walnut. "Exceptionally fine," as new, possibly unfired, w/virtually orig. finish.	E: $750-$1,250	$3,450
JDJ 03/13-14/06 Lot 1430	Field Grade M12 #1850288, 20 ga., 28" plain Modified bbl., round ribbed forearm and unchecked semi-pistol grip stock. "Very fine +," 95 percent-98 percent bright orig. blue, stock w/hairline crack by left wrist, minor nicks, but most orig. finish.	E: $500-$800	$747.50
JDJ 03/13-14/06 Lot 1431	Field Grade M12 #1956985, 12 ga., 28" plain Modified bbl, unchecked large ribbed walnut forearm and semi-pistol grip stock. "Exceptionally fine," appears unfired. Stock has one or two minor nicks.	E: $500-$800	$690
GMA 11/06-07/06 Lot 457	Custom Black Diamond M12 Trap Two-Barrel Set. #398057, 12 ga., 29.75" bbls with solid ribs and reblued slide action; action and bbls. engraved in Winchester No. 6 pattern w/foliate scroll and game scenes: Checkered straight grip stock of well figured crotch-grained walnut w/ebony diamond inserts at grip, checkered forends for each barrel. "Excellent, as upgraded and partially redone;" 95 percent- 97 percent reblued finish with losses to magazine tube, bright bores.	E: $2,000-$3,000	$2,270
GMA 11/06-07/06 Lot 547	M12 Skeet Gun #1968117, 20 ga., 26" vent-rib bbl., finely checkered pistol grip stock of highly figured walnut. "Excellent, showing little use;" 94 percent-99 percent bluing, bright bore, one-inch scratch at toe of stock.	E: $2,000-$3,000	$2,270
GMA 11/06-07/06 Lot 718	Martially marked M12 #963452, 12 ga., 20" bbl., frame and stock w/U.S. Ordnance proofs and markings, walnut stock and forend. "Excellent as arsenal refinished," 95 percent-98 percent reblued finish with light slide wear, wood with minor wear and marks. "Mechanically excellent."	E: $1,000-$1,500	$1,135
GMA 11/06-07/06 Lot 1079	M12 #1370555, 12 ga., 30" plain Full bbl., walnut forend and pistol grip stock. "Fair," 30 percent-40 percent finish with wear and gray age patina. Wood with wear and numerous dents and bruises.	E: $200-$300	$141.88
GMA 11/06-07/06 Lot 1093	Customized M12 #864087, 12 ga., 28" Simmons vent-rib bbl., highly figured custom walnut checkered forend and stock w/roll-over cheekpiece. "Excellent, as partially redone;" barrel assembly w/98 percent reblued finish, balance 70 percent-98 percent bluing, stock w/shrinkage cracks, light marks.	E: $400-$600	$482.38
GMA 11/06-07/06 Lot 1094	Customized M12 #526710, 12 ga., 30" reblued Simmons vent-rib bbl., custom pistol grip stock of semi-figured walnut with cheekpiece, oversized custom forend of highly figured walnut. Extra choke tubes. "Excellent, as partially redone." Barrel 98 percent reblued finish, balance 80 percent-95 percent bluing.	E: $400-$600	$567.50
GMA 11/06-07/06 Lot 1095	Custom-Engraved M12 riot shotgun #1740600, 12 ga., 20" bbl. Frame custom engraved with floral scrolls and game scenes "engraved by Rachel Wells for Bill Atkinson, '78." Ribbed walnut forend and checkered pistol grip stock. "Good, as configured;" 85 percent-90 percent finish w/slide wear, missing stock bolt and screw. Frame with age patina.	E: $400-$600	$539.13

Auction House/Date/Lot No.	Item Description	Estimated Value	Actually Sold For
GMA 11/06-07/06 Lot 1096	M12 riot shotgun #1740762, 12 ga., 20" bbl. Checkered simulated wood forend and walnut pistol grip stock. "Good," 75 percent-80 percent finish, scattered small patches of pitting on barrel and magazine. Wood with light wear.	E: $300-$500	$397.25
GMA 11/06-07/06 Lot 1260	M12 #450756, 12 ga., 32" solid rib bbl., half pistol grip stock of straight-grain walnut, grooved forend. "Fine;" 50 percent-95 percent bluing, stock w/nicks and a few scratches. Period recoil pad has hardened.	E: $300-$400	$425.63
GMA 06/26-27/06 Lot 618	M12 #329098, 20 ga., 28" Full bbl., walnut stock. "Good," 60 percent-65 percent finish w/wear to frame and relief edges, wood w/minor wear and marks.	E: $600-$900	$368.88

Skeet Grade

Exc.	*V.G.*	*Good*	*Fair*	*Poor*
1500	850	700	400	350

Trap Grade

Exc.	*V.G.*	*Good*	*Fair*	*Poor*
1000	700	600	450	400

Heavy Duck Gun

Exc.	*V.G.*	*Good*	*Fair*	*Poor*
750	600	450	325	300

NOTE: For Heavy Duck Guns with solid ribs add 25 percent premium.

Pigeon Grade

Exc.	*V.G.*	*Good*	*Fair*	*Poor*
3000	2000	1400	650	500

NOTE: For 16 gauge deduct 10 percent. For 20 gauge add 20 percent. For 28 gauge add 600 percent. For guns with solid rib add 20 percent. For guns with Winchester Special ventilated rib add 30 percent. For guns with milled rib add 40 percent. Add 20 percent for 32" barrels on any Model 12 model. Add 30 percent premium for original box and papers.

Model 25

This model is similar in appearance to the Model 12 but does not have the takedown feature. All guns were solid frame. The Model 25 was furnished in 12 gauge with 26" or 28" plain round barrel, plain walnut pistol-grip stock with grooved slide handle. This was an attempt by Winchester to introduce a less expensive version of the Model 12. Introduced in 1949 it was dropped from the product line in 1954 having sold about 88,000 guns.

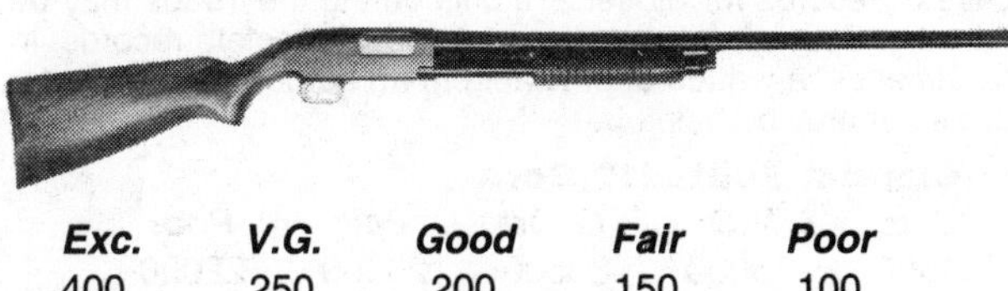

Exc.	*V.G.*	*Good*	*Fair*	*Poor*
400	250	200	150	100

Model 20

In order to utilize the expanded production facilities left over from WWI, Winchester introduced a series of three different models of single-shot shotguns; the Model 20 was the first of the three. This model has a visible hammer and a top lever frame. It was the first Winchester to have this type of breakdown action. It was chambered for the .410, 2-1/2" shell. The barrel is 26" round choked full, plain walnut pistol-grip stock with hard rubber buttplate. The forend has a small lip on the front end. The Model 20 was dropped from the product line in 1924 having sold about 24,000 guns.

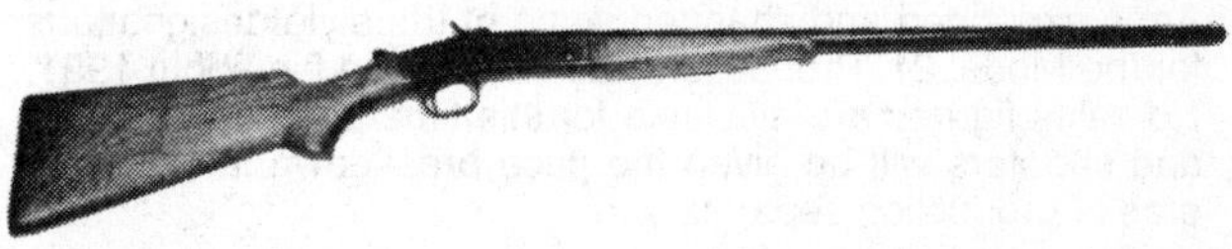

Courtesy C.H. Wolfersberger

Exc.	*V.G.*	*Good*	*Fair*	*Poor*
700	500	350	200	150

Model 36

The Model 36 was the second of the single-shot shotguns to be introduced in 1920. This model features a bolt-action that is cocked by pulling the firing pin head to the rear. It is fitted with an 18" round barrel, chambered for the 9mm Long Shot, 9mm Short Shot, and 9mm Ball interchangeably, plain gumwood straight-grip stock with special metal pistol grip trigger guard. Winchester referred to this model as the "Garden Gun" for use against birds and pests around the house and barn. This model was not serial numbered. It was dropped from the product line in 1927 having sold about 20,000 guns.

Exc.	*V.G.*	*Good*	*Fair*	*Poor*
750	475	375	300	225

Model 41

This was the third of the low-priced single-shot shotguns to be announced in 1920. Like the Model 36, the Model 41 was a bolt-action arrangement but of much stronger construction and design. It features a 24" round barrel, chambered for the .410 2-1/2" shell, plain walnut pistol-grip stock and forend. Straight-grip stock was furnished at no extra charge. This model was not serial numbered. It was discontinued in 1934 having sold about 22,000 guns.

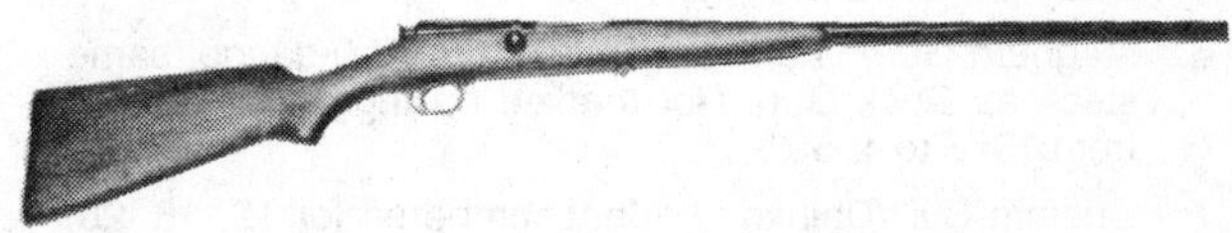

Courtesy C.H. Wolfersberger

Exc.	*V.G.*	*Good*	*Fair*	*Poor*
600	500	350	300	200

Model 21

The Model 21 was Winchester's finest effort with regard to quality, reliability, and strength. Developed in the late 1920s the introduction of this fine side-by-side shotgun was delayed by the company's financial troubles. When Winchester was purchased by the Olin family, the Model 21 was assured the attention it richly deserved due to John M. Olin's love for the gun. Despite the Model 21 being offered as a production gun it was, in fact, a hand-built custom-made shotgun. Almost each Model 21 built has a personality of its own because each shotgun is slightly different with regard to chokes, barrel lengths, stock dimensions, and embellishments. The gun was introduced in 1931. From 1931 to 1959 the Model 21 was considered a production line gun and about 30,000 were sold. In 1960, when the Custom Shop was opened, the Model 21 was built there using the same procedures. Sales during the Custom Shop era were about 1,000 guns. Winchester changed the name of some of the Model 21 styles but the production methods stayed the same. In 1981 Winchester sold its firearms division to U.S. Repeating Arms Company including the right to build the Model 21. Again the production procedures stayed the same as did many of the former employees. U.S. Repeating Arms expanded and changed some of the style designations for the Model 21. Production was discontinued in about 1991. No sales figures are available for this time period. Collectors and shooters will be given the price breakdown for all three eras of production separately.

NOTE: Fewer than 50 .410 Model 21s were built between 1931 and 1959 in all grades. The number of 28 gauge Model 21s built is unknown but the number is probably no greater than the .410 bore.

Editor's Comment: There were eight 28 gauge Model 21s built during this period and five .410 bores built. These guns obviously command a large premium. Factory letters are available on these guns.

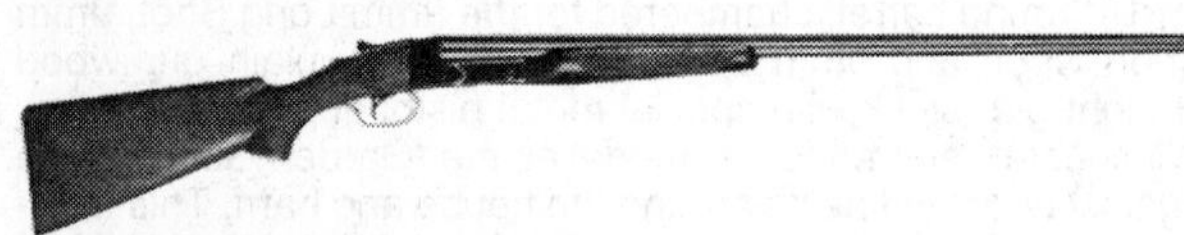

Model 21—1931 to 1959

The Model 21 was available in several different styles and configurations:

1. Standard Grade, chambered in 12, 16, and 20 gauge with barrel length from 26", 28", 30", and 32" with matted rib or ventilated rib, select walnut checkered pistol- or straight-grip stock with checkered beavertail forend. Built from 1931 to 1959.
2. Tournament Grade, same as above with special dimension stock. Marked "TOURNAMENT" on bottom of trigger plate. Built from 1933 to 1934.
3. Trap Grade, same as above with slightly better-grade wood and stock made to customers' dimensions. Marked "TRAP" on trigger plate. Built from 1932 to 1959.
4. Skeet Grade, same as above with the addition of the 28 gauge, stock furnished with checkered butt. Marked "SKEET" on trigger plate. Built from 1936 to 1959.
5. Duck Gun, chambered for 12 gauge 3" magnum shells, 30" or 32" barrels, Standard Grade stock except for shorter length of pull. Marked "DUCK" on trigger plate. Built from 1940 to 1952.
6. Magnum Gun, chambered for 3" 12 or 20 gauge, same stock as Duck Gun. Not marked on trigger plate. Built from 1953 to 1959.
7. Custom Built/Deluxe Grade, chambered for 12, 16, 20, 28, and .410, barrel lengths from 26" to 32", stock built to customer's specifications using fancy walnut. Marked "CUSTOM BUILT" on top of rib or "DELUXE" on trigger plate. These grades are frequently but not always engraved. Built from 1933 to 1959.

NOTE: Some early Model 21s were furnished with double triggers, extractors, and splinter forends. This combination reduces the price of the gun regardless of grade. Deduct about 25 percent.

Standard Grade

	Exc.	V.G.	Good	Fair	Poor
12 gauge	4000	3000	2000	1500	1000
16 gauge	6900	6200	5400	4700	4200
20 gauge	7000	6500	5700	5100	4700

Tournament Grade

	Exc.	V.G.	Good	Fair	Poor
12 gauge	5500	4700	3900	3500	3300
16 gauge	7500	6700	5800	5000	4500
20 gauge	7700	6900	6000	5400	4800

Trap Grade

	Exc.	V.G.	Good	Fair	Poor
12 gauge	5800	4800	4000	3800	3600
16 gauge	7500	6800	5900	5300	4900
20 gauge	7700	7000	6300	5800	5300

Skeet Grade

	Exc.	V.G.	Good	Fair	Poor
12 gauge	5500	4500	3700	3400	3200
16 gauge	6900	5800	5200	4900	4400
20 gauge	6900	5900	5200	4800	4200

Duck/Magnum Gun

Exc.	V.G.	Good	Fair	Poor
5600	4600	4200	4000	3800

NOTE: Add 30 percent for 20 gauge Magnum. Factory ventilated ribs command a premium of about $1,800 on 12 gauge guns and $2,500 on 20 and 16 gauge guns. Models 21s with factory furnished extra barrels will bring an additional premium of about $2,500. Refinished and restored Model 21s are in a somewhat unique category of American-made collectible shotguns. A gun that has been professionally refinished by a master craftsman will approximate 90 percent of the value of factory original guns.

Custom Built/Deluxe Grade

The prices paid for guns of this grade are determined by gauge, barrel and choke combinations, rib type, stock specifications, and engraving. Expert appraisal is recommended.

	Exc.	V.G.	Good	Fair	Poor
12 gauge	7000	6500	5500	4500	4000
16 gauge	8000	7500	6500	5500	4500
20 gauge	8500	8000	7000	6000	5000

It is best to secure a factory letter from the Cody Firearms Museum. With respect to such letter, it is important to note that these records are incomplete and may be inaccurate in a few cases. Records for Model 21s built during the 1930s may be missing. Special-order guns may have incomplete records. In such cases, a written appraisal from an authoritative collector or dealer may be helpful.

Custom Built .410 Bore

Exc.	V.G.	Good	Fair	Poor
45000	35000	30000	26000	22000

Custom Shop Model 21s—1960 to 1981

When Winchester moved the production of the Model 21 into the Custom Shop, the number of styles was greatly reduced. There were now three distinct styles:

1. Custom Grade, chambered in 12, 16, 20, 28 gauge, and .410 bore in barrel lengths from 26" to 32". Matted rib, fancy walnut checkered pistol- or straight-grip stock with checkered forend. Guns with pistol grips furnished with steel grip cap. A small amount of scroll engraving was provided on the frame of this grade.

2. Pigeon Grade, same chambers and barrel lengths as above with the addition of choice of matted or ventilated rib, leather-covered recoil pad, style "A" carving on stock and forend, and gold engraved pistol grip cap. The frame was engraved with the 21-6 engraving pattern.
3. Grand American Grade, same chambers and barrel lengths as Pigeon Grade with the addition of "B" carving on the stock and forend, 21-6 engraving with gold inlays, extra set of interchangeable barrels with extra forend. All of this was enclosed in a leather trunk case.

Custom Grade—12 Gauge

Exc.	*V.G.*	*Good*	*Fair*	*Poor*
9800	7500	6800	6000	5200

NOTE: Add $4,000 for 16 gauge. Add $5,000 for 20 gauge.

Pigeon Grade—12 Gauge

Exc.	*V.G.*	*Good*	*Fair*	*Poor*
18000	15000	12000	10000	8000

NOTE: Add $6,000 for 16 gauge. Add $5,000 for 20 gauge.

Grand American—12 Gauge

Exc.	*V.G.*	*Good*	*Fair*	*Poor*
26000	20000	16000	14000	13000

NOTE: Add $15,000 for 16 gauge (extremely rare). Add $5,000 for 20 gauge.

ENGRAVED MODEL 21S

Winchester catalogued a number of special-order engraving patterns which ranged from a small amount of scroll (#1) to full-coverage game scene and scroll (#6). In addition, there were a few guns engraved on special order to the customer's request. Engraved guns are extremely rare, and the value added will vary with the rarity of the gauge and the date of manufacture. The following table represents the value added for various standard engraving patterns on 12 gauge guns for the "Custom Shop" (1960-1982) and "Pre-Custom Shop" (1932-1959) periods. However, it is advisable to seek the opinion of an authorative collector or dealer prior to a sale.

Engraving Pattern	*Pre-Custom Shop*	*Custom Shop*
#1	30 percent	20 percent
#2	40 percent	30 percent
#3	60 percent	45 percent
#4	70 percent	50 percent
#5	90 percent	70 percent
#6	100 percent	80 percent

Custom Shop Model 21s—1982 to Present

When U.S. Repeating Arms Company took over the production of the Model 21, the Pigeon Grade was dropped from the line. The Grand American Grade was retained with all the features of its predecessor but with the addition of a small-bore set featuring a 28 gauge and .410 bore set of barrels. Two new grades were introduced in 1983: the Standard Custom Grade and the Special Custom Built. In addition to these grades, the factory would undertake to build for its customers whatever was desired. Due to the unique nature of these guns, it is advised that an expert appraisal be sought to establish a value. While the changeover from Winchester to U.S. Repeating Arms was a transfer of business assets and the craftsmen and personnel remained the same, collectors are reluctant to assign the same values to U.S. Repeating Arms Model 21s as those produced by Winchester. No official production figures are available for U.S.R.A. Model 21s, but the number is most likely small; perhaps around 200 guns.

Standard Custom Built

NIB	*Exc.*	*V.G*	*Good*	*Fair*	*Poor*
8000	6500	5500	5000	4500	4000

Grand American

NIB	*Exc.*	*V.G.*	*Good*	*Fair*	*Poor*
18000	13000	10000	8500	6000	5000

Grand American Small Gauge Set—28 or .410 bore

NIB	*Exc.*	*V.G.*	*Good*	*Fair*	*Poor*
60000	45000	35000	27000	22000	20000

Model 24

The Model 24 was Winchester's attempt to develop a medium-priced double-barrel shotgun. Like the Model 21, it was a top lever breakdown model that was available in 12, 16, and 20 gauge in various barrel lengths from 26" to 30". Offered in a Standard model only with double triggers, raised matted rib, plain walnut pistol- or straight-grip stock with semi-beavertail forend, the Model 24 was introduced in 1939 and was discontinued in 1957 with about 116,000 guns sold.

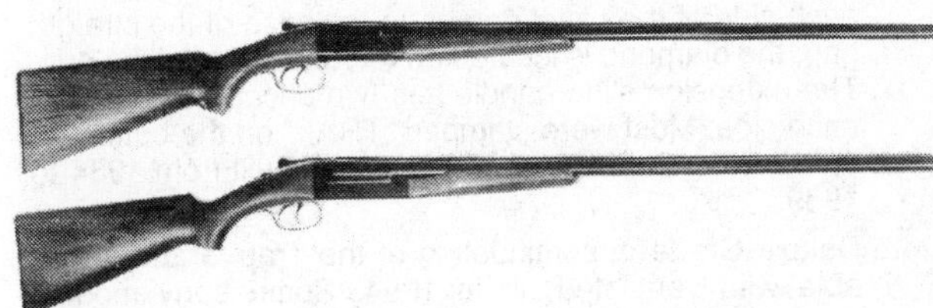

Top: Model 24 Standard; bottom: Model 24 Improved

Exc.	*V.G.*	*Good*	*Fair*	*Poor*
650	500	400	250	200

NOTE: Add 10 percent for 16 gauge. Add 25 percent for 20 gauge.

Model 37

This model was developed to keep pace with Winchester's competitors in the low-price single-barrel exposed-hammer shotgun market. The shotgun was available in 12, 16, 20, 28 gauge, and .410 bore with barrel lengths from 26" to 30". The stock was plain walnut with pistol grip and semi-beavertail forend. This model was not serial numbered. Introduced in 1936 it stayed in the company line until 1963, having sold slightly over 1,000,000 guns.

NOTE: Do not confuse this model with the Model 37A.

Courtesy C.H. Wolfersberger

	Exc.	*V.G.*	*Good*	*Fair*	*Poor*
12 gauge	350	300	250	150	50
16 gauge	450	400	350	300	75
20 gauge	600	525	500	425	100
28 gauge	2000	1600	1150	850	450
.410 bore	1000	850	500	300	100

Youth Model

26" Modified choke barrel, Win. red factory pad.

	Exc.	*V.G.*	*Good*	*Fair*	*Poor*
20 gauge	550	450	350	250	125

NOTE: For 12 and 16 gauge guns add a 50 percent premium for 32" barrels. Use caution for 28 gauge guns. Many fakes are seen for sale.

Model 42

This was the first slide-action shotgun ever developed exclusively for the .410 bore. Invented by William Roemer, the Model 42 was in effect, at least in outward appearance, a miniature Model 12. This shotgun was a quality-built, fast-handling, racy looking shotgun that many refer to as "Everybody's Sweetheart." The Model 42 was the first American .410 bore chambered for the new 3" shell as well as the 2.5" shell. The Model 42 was offered in several different configurations throughout its production. These configurations will greatly influence value:

1. Standard Grade, 26" or 28" plain or solid rib barrel, plain walnut pistol-grip stock with grooved slide handle, fitted with composition buttplate. A straight grip was offered on the Standard Grade on a special order basis, but it is extremely rare. Built from 1933 to 1963.
2. Skeet Grade, 26" or 28" plain, solid rib, or ventilated rib barrel, select walnut checkered pistol or straight-grip stock with checkered extension slide handle. The Skeet Grade was offered in Full, Modified, Improved Cylinder, Cylinder as well as Skeet chokes. Built from 1933 to 1963.
3. Trap Grade, 26" or 28" plain or solid rib barrel, fancy walnut special checkered pistol or straight-grip stock with special checkered extension slide handle. The Trap Grade checkering pattern has one closed diamond on each side of the pistol grip or, in the case of the straight grip, the diamond is located on the underside of the grip. The extension slide handle has two uncut diamonds on each side. Most were stamped "TRAP" on the bottom of the receiver under the serial number. Built from 1934 to 1939.
4. Deluxe Grade, a continuation of the Trap Grade, available with ventilated rib in 1954. Some early models stamped "DELUXE" on bottom of receiver. This stamping is seldom seen and was probably discontinued around 1949. Built from 1940 to 1963.
5. Pigeon Grade, same as above Deluxe Grade but engraved with a pigeon on the lower magazine tube. Very few of this grade were built by Winchester, and the majority were done in the late 1940s. Authentic Pigeon Grade 42s appear to have been built between 1945 and 1949. Some estimate that less than 50 were produced. this is a rare Model 42. Seek an expert opinion before a sale.

NOTE: Engraved Model 42s will occasionally be seen. Collectors are urged to seek expert advice on these rare and expensive guns. The Model 42 was produced from 1933 to 1963. About 164,000 were sold. Factory service and repair for this model were discontinued in February of 1972.

Extra Barrels: Winchester offered extra interchangeable barrels for its Model 42s at the customer's request beginning in 1934. These extra sets of barrels are a rare option. Both barrels should have the same barrel markings and matching serial numbers before originality can be considered. Values are difficult to determine, but as a general rule add 60 percent to the price of a Model 42 if it has a factory-original extra barrel.

Editor's Comment: Contrary to traditional views, Winchester did install factory ventilated ribs on its Model 42. Former employees and factory drawings substantiate this fact. However, the subject of what is a factory rib and what is not has been covered in great detail in an excellent book on the Model 42. Seek expert advice before selling or purchasing any Model 42 with a ventilated rib.

Standard Grade

NIB	*Exc.*	*V.G.*	*Good*	*Fair*	*Poor*
2000	1200	950	700	500	250

NOTE: For Standard Grade guns with solid ribs add 50 percent. For pre-war guns add 30 percent.

Skeet Grade—Solid Rib

NIB	*Exc.*	*V.G.*	*Good*	*Fair*	*Poor*
4000	3000	2500	1650	850	500

NOTE: Add 25 percent guns chambered for 2-1/2" shells. For pre-war guns add 30 percent. For Skeet Grade guns with no rib deduct 25 percent.

Skeet Grade—Ventilated Rib

NIB	*Exc.*	*V.G.*	*Good*	*Fair*	*Poor*
5000	4000	3250	1500	900	650

NOTE: Add 25 percent of guns chambered for 2-1/2" shells.

Trap Grade

Exc.	*V.G.*	*Good*	*Fair*	*Poor*
8500	6000	4250	2500	900

Deluxe Grade—Solid Rib

Exc.	*V.G.*	*Good*	*Fair*	*Poor*
6000	4000	2750	950	600

Deluxe Grade—Ventilated Rib

Exc.	*V.G.*	*Good*	*Fair*	*Poor*
7500	5000	2500	950	600

NOTE: For Pigeon Grade Model 42s with documentation on expert authentication add 100 percent.

Cutts Compensator Guns: Approximately 66 original Cutts Compensator guns were produced in the factory, making this one of the rarest options on the Model 42. These original guns will have ***no choke markings***, and were only offered with a vent rib. Add 25 percent for original Cutts guns, deduct 50 percent for non-original Cutts guns.

Model 1911

This was Winchester's first self-loading shotgun and was developed by T.C. Johnson in order to keep pace with the Remington Auto-Loading Shotgun Model 11, which was developed by John M. Browning with help from T.C. Johnson. Because of the delays involved in developing a brand new design, the Model 1911 was introduced on October 7, 1911. The shotgun was a recoil operated mechanism, had a tubular magazine and had the takedown feature. The shotgun was available in two styles:

1. Plain Model 1911, 26" or 28" barrel, 12 gauge, choked full, modified, or cylinder, plain birch laminated pistol-grip stock and forend with hard rubber buttplate.
2. Fancy Model 1911, same as above with fancy birch laminated stock.

Because of the hurry in getting the model ready for production, the shotgun demonstrated design weakness and never proved satisfactory. It was discontinued in 1925 with about 83,000 guns sold.

Model 1911—Plain

Exc.	*V.G.*	*Good*	*Fair*	*Poor*
550	375	300	250	200

Model 1911—Fancy

Exc.	*V.G.*	*Good*	*Fair*	*Poor*
800	500	400	300	250

Model 40

This model represents Winchester's second attempt to build a self-loading long recoil-operated repeating shotgun. This shotgun was a hammerless tubular magazine gun without the hump at the rear of the receiver. Available in 12 gauge only with barrel lengths from 28" to 30". The Standard Grade had plain walnut pistol-grip stock and forend. The Skeet Grade was fitted with select walnut checkered pistol-grip stock and checkered forend. The Model 40 suffered from the same design problems as the Model 11, and sales were small. Introduced in 1940 and discontinued in 1941, Winchester sold about 12,000 guns.

Standard Grade

Exc.	*V.G.*	*Good*	*Fair*	*Poor*
600	500	400	275	200

Skeet Grade

Exc.	*V.G.*	*Good*	*Fair*	*Poor*
800	600	500	300	250

Model 50

The Model 50 was the company's third attempt to produce a satisfactory self-loading repeating shotgun. Winchester went to the short recoil system, utilizing a floating chamber design. This model was available in several different styles:

1. Standard Grade, 12 or 20 gauge with plain or ventilated rib in lengths from 26" to 30", plain walnut checkered pistol-grip stock and forend.
2. Skeet Grade, 12 or 20 gauge with 26" ventilated rib barrel. Walnut checkered pistol-grip stock and forend.

3. Trap Grade, 12 gauge with 30" ventilated rib barrel, walnut checkered Monte Carlo stock and forend.
4. Pigeon Grade, 12 or 20 gauge with barrel lengths to customers' specifications. Fancy walnut checkered stock and forend. Made on special orders only.
5. Featherweight, a lighter version of all the above except Trap Grade.

This model begins with serial number 1000. This model was successful and was built between 1954 and 1961. Winchester sold about 200,000 guns.

Standard Grade

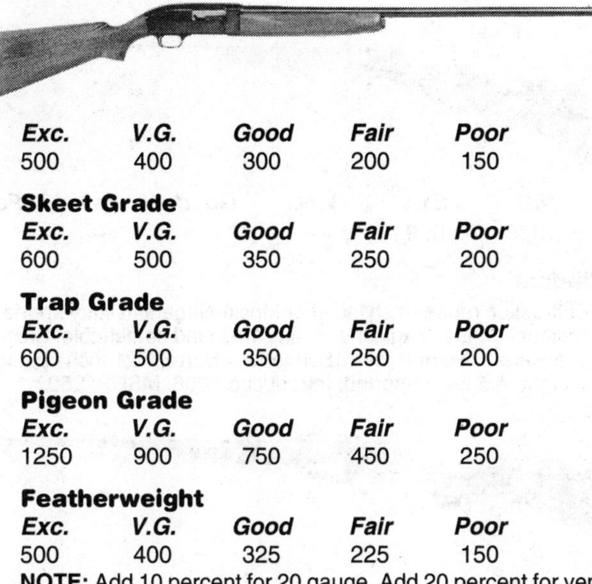

Exc.	V.G.	Good	Fair	Poor
500	400	300	200	150

Skeet Grade

Exc.	V.G.	Good	Fair	Poor
600	500	350	250	200

Trap Grade

Exc.	V.G.	Good	Fair	Poor
600	500	350	250	200

Pigeon Grade

Exc.	V.G.	Good	Fair	Poor
1250	900	750	450	250

Featherweight

Exc.	V.G.	Good	Fair	Poor
500	400	325	225	150

NOTE: Add 10 percent for 20 gauge. Add 20 percent for vent rib on standard grade guns.

Model 59

The fourth and final pre-1964 Winchester self-loading shotgun featured a steel and fiberglass barrel with aluminum alloy receiver. The gun was available in 12 gauge only with barrel lengths from 26" to 30" with a variety of chokes. In 1961 Winchester introduced the "Versalite" choke tube, which gave the shooter a choice of Full, Modified, or Improved Cylinder chokes in the same barrel. This model was available in two different styles:

1. Standard Grade, plain walnut checkered pistol-grip stock and forend.
2. Pigeon Grade, select walnut checkered pistol-grip and forend.

Winchester sold about 82,000 of these guns between 1960 and 1965.

NOTE: This shotgun was also made in 10 gauge (very rare), 20 gauge, and 14 gauge. If any of these very low production or prototype guns are encountered, use extreme caution and seek an expert appraisal.

Standard Grade

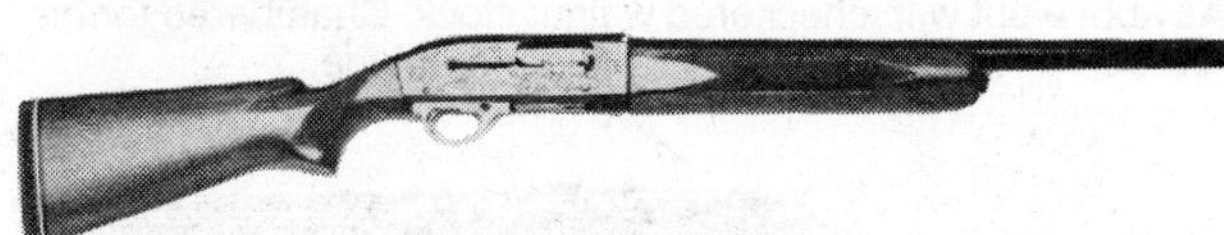

Courtesy Bonhams & Butterfields, San Francisco, California

Exc.	V.G.	Good	Fair	Poor
650	550	450	350	250

Pigeon Grade

Exc.	V.G.	Good	Fair	Poor
1500	1100	850	600	300

NOTE: Add 40 percent premium for barrels with three Versalite chokes and wrench. Add 20 percent premium for original box and papers.

POST-1963 RIFLES AND SHOTGUNS

RIFLES

Model 121

This is a single-shot, bolt-action rifle chambered for the .22 rimfire cartridge. It has a 20.75" barrel with open sights. The finish is blued, with a plain walnut stock. It was manufactured between 1967 and 1973. A youth model with a shorter stock was designated the 121Y and is valued the same.

Courtesy Buffalo Bill Historical Center, Cody, Wyoming

Exc.	V.G.	Good	Fair	Poor
175	100	80	60	40

Model 131

This is a bolt-action repeater chambered for the .22 rimfire cartridge. It has a 20.75" barrel with open sights and a 7-round, detachable magazine. The finish is blued, with a plain walnut stock. It was manufactured between 1967 and 1973. A tubular magazine version was designated the Model 141 and is valued the same.

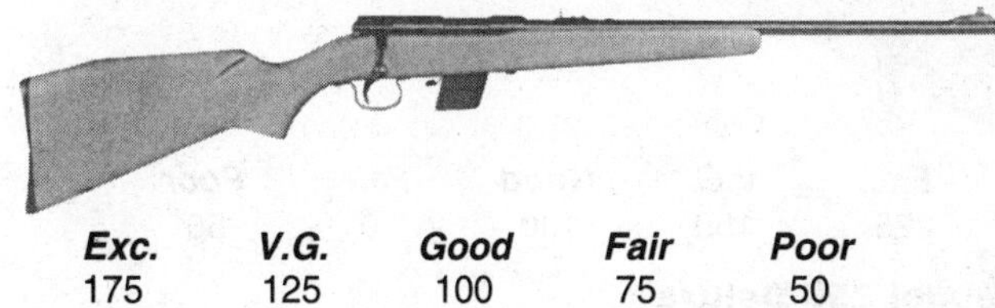

Exc.	V.G.	Good	Fair	Poor
175	125	100	75	50

Model 310

This is a single-shot, bolt-action rifle chambered for the .22 rimfire cartridge. It features a 22" barrel with open sights. The finish is blued, with a checkered walnut stock. It was manufactured between 1972 and 1975.

Courtesy Buffalo Bill Historical Center, Cody, Wyoming

Exc.	V.G.	Good	Fair	Poor
250	150	125	100	75

Model 320

This is a bolt-action repeating rifle that is similar in configuration to the Model 310 single-shot. It has a 5-round, detachable box magazine. It was manufactured between 1972 and 1974.

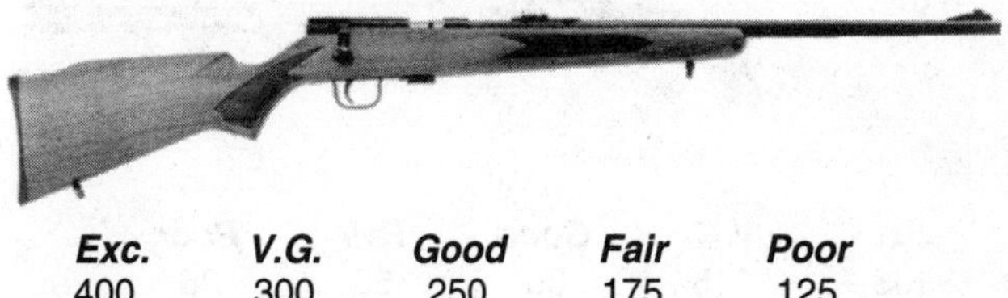

Exc.	V.G.	Good	Fair	Poor
400	300	250	175	125

Model 250

This is a lever-action repeating rifle with a hammerless action. It is chambered for the .22 rimfire cartridge and has a 20.5" barrel with open sights and a tubular magazine. The finish is blued, with a checkered pistol-grip stock. It was manufactured between 1963 and 1973.

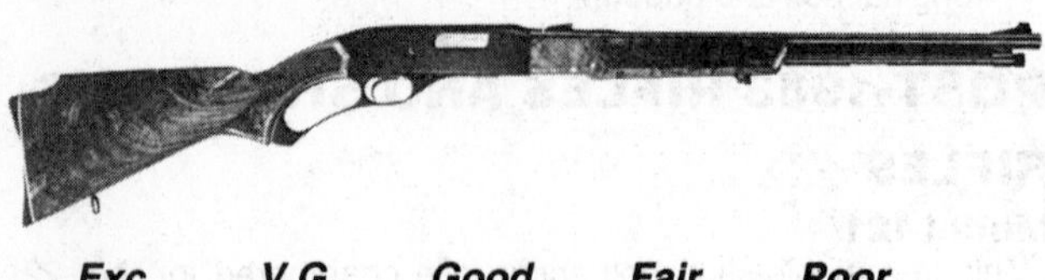

Exc.	V.G.	Good	Fair	Poor
200	125	80	60	40

Model 250 Deluxe

This version is similar to the Model 250 and is furnished with select walnut and sling swivels. It was manufactured between 1965 and 1971.

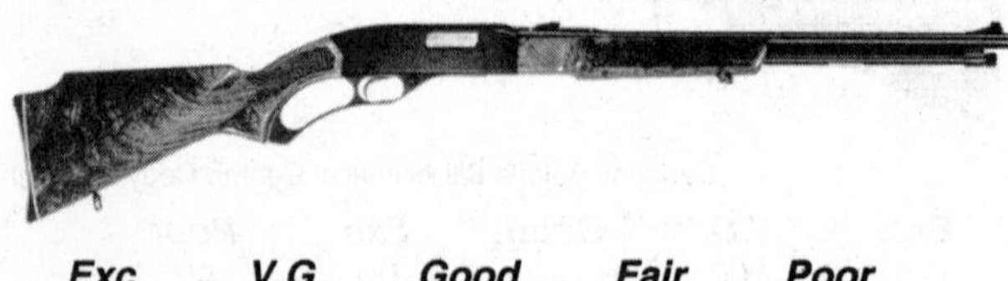

Exc.	V.G.	Good	Fair	Poor
250	175	125	100	75

Model 255

This version is simply the Model 250 chambered for the .22 WMR cartridge. It was manufactured between 1964 and 1970.

Exc.	V.G.	Good	Fair	Poor
225	150	100	70	50

Model 255 Deluxe

This version was offered with select walnut and sling swivels. It was manufactured between 1965 and 1973.

Exc.	V.G.	Good	Fair	Poor
250	175	125	100	75

Model 490

This is a blowback-operated, semi-automatic rifle chambered for the .22 LR cartridge. It has a 22" barrel with open sights and a 5-round, detachable magazine. The finish is blued, with a checkered stock. It was manufactured between 1975 and 1980.

Exc.	V.G.	Good	Fair	Poor
325	225	165	100	75

Model 270

This is a slide-action rifle chambered for the .22 rimfire cartridge. It has a 20.5" barrel and a tubular magazine. The finish is blued, with a checkered walnut stock. It was manufactured between 1963 and 1973.

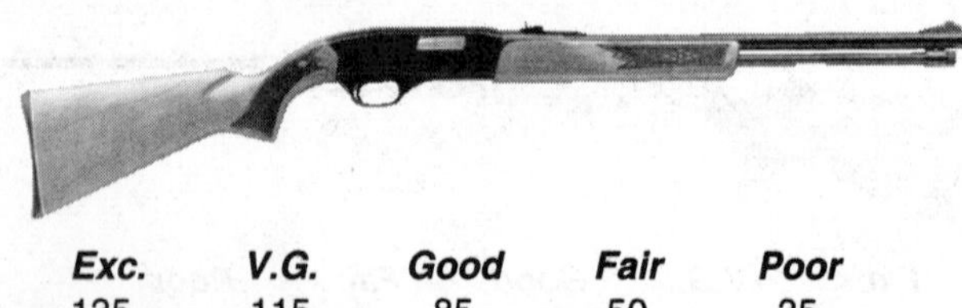

Exc.	V.G.	Good	Fair	Poor
135	115	85	50	35

Model 63

Introduced in 1997 this is a re-creation of the famous Model 63 .22 caliber auto. Fitted with a 23" barrel and 10-round tubular magazine. the receiver top is grooved for scope mounting.

Grade I

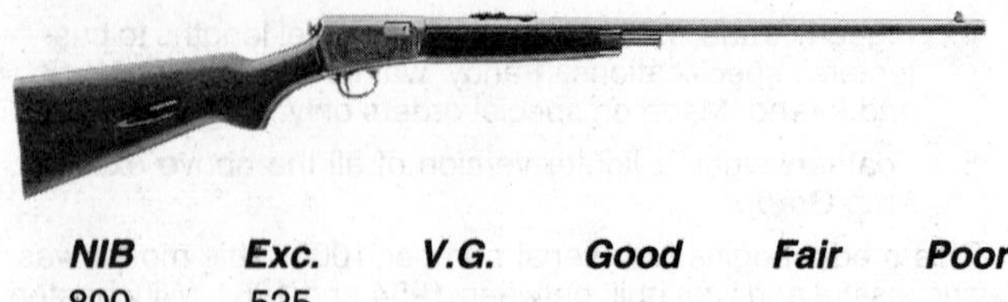

NIB	Exc.	V.G.	Good	Fair	Poor
800	525	—	—	—	—

High Grade

Engraved receiver with gold accents and select walnut stock.

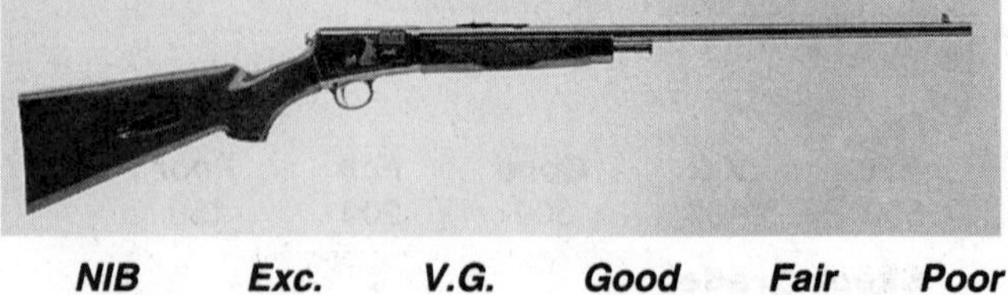

NIB	Exc.	V.G.	Good	Fair	Poor
1075	850	—	—	—	—

Wildcat

Bolt-action repeater styled after Mosin-Nagant military sporter. Caliber: .22 LR. Magazine: 5- and 10-round detachable. Stock: checkered walnut with Schnabel. Barrel: 21-inch blued. Weight: 4.5 lbs. Imported. Introduced 2006. MSRP: 250

Model 94

This is the post-1964 lever-action carbine chambered for the .30-30, 7-30 Waters, and the .44 Magnum cartridges. It is offered with a 20" or 24" barrel and has a 6- or 7-round, tubular magazine depending on barrel length. The round barrel is offered with open sights. The forearm is held on by a single barrel band. The finish is blued, with a straight-grip walnut stock. In 1982 it was modified to angle ejection to simplify scope mounting. It was introduced as a continuation of the Model 94 line in 1964. In 2003 a top-tang safety was installed and the .480 Ruger caliber was added. The Model 94 series was discontinued in 2006.

NIB	Exc.	V.G.	Good	Fair	Poor
450	325	225	150	100	75

Model 94 Traditional—CW

As above but with checkered walnut stock. Chambered for the .30-30, .44 Mag., and the .480 Ruger cartridge.

NIB	Exc.	V.G.	Good	Fair	Poor
460	350	—	—	—	—

NOTE: For .44 Mag. add $20. For the .480 Ruger add $70.

Model 94 Ranger

Chambered for .30-30 cartridge and fitted with a 20" barrel. Weight is about 6.25 lbs. In 2003 a top-tang safety was installed.

NIB	Exc.	V.G.	Good	Fair	Poor
400	300	225	150	100	75

Model 94 Ranger Compact

Introduced in 1998 this model features a 16" barrel with 12.5" lop. Chambered for .30-30 or .357 Magnum. Furnished with black recoil pad. Post-style front sight with adjustable rear sight. Hardwood stock. Weight is approximately 5.87 lbs

NIB	Exc.	V.G.	Good	Fair	Poor
350	250	225	200	—	—

Model 94 Black Shadow

This model features a black synthetic stock with nonglare finish and black recoil pad. Offered in .30-30, .44 Magnum, or .444 Marlin. Fitted with a 20" barrel. Weight is about 6.5 lbs. Introduced in 1998.

NIB	Exc.	V.G.	Good	Fair	Poor
375	275	250	225	—	—

Model 94 Deluxe

Checkered stock.

NIB	Exc.	V.G.	Good	Fair	Poor
400	300	250	200	175	150

Model 94 Win-Tuff

Laminated stock.

NIB	Exc.	V.G.	Good	Fair	Poor
375	275	225	165	125	100

Model 94 XTR

Select, checkered walnut stock, discontinued 1988.

Exc.	V.G.	Good	Fair	Poor
450	350	250	175	125

Model 94 XTR Deluxe

Fancy checkering.

Exc.	V.G.	Good	Fair	Poor
475	375	275	200	150

Model 94 Trapper

16" barrel. Chambered for the .30-30, .357 Mag., .44 Mag, or .45 Colt cartridge. In 2003 a top-tang safety was installed.

NIB	Exc.	V.G.	Good	Fair	Poor
450	350	250	150	100	75

Model 94 Antique Carbine

Gold-plated saddle ring.

Exc.	V.G.	Good	Fair	Poor
400	275	240	150	125

Model 94 Wrangler

.32 Win. Special.

Exc.	V.G.	Good	Fair	Poor
400	300	190	125	100

Model 94 Wrangler II

Loop lever.

NIB	Exc.	V.G.	Good	Fair	Poor
375	300	250	200	150	100

Model 94 Legacy 20-inch

This Model 94 is fitted with a 20" barrel and chambered for the .30-30 Win. but it is fitted with a half pistol-grip stock. Both walnut buttstock and forearm are cut checkered. Weight is 6.5 lbs. In 2003 a top-tang safety was installed.

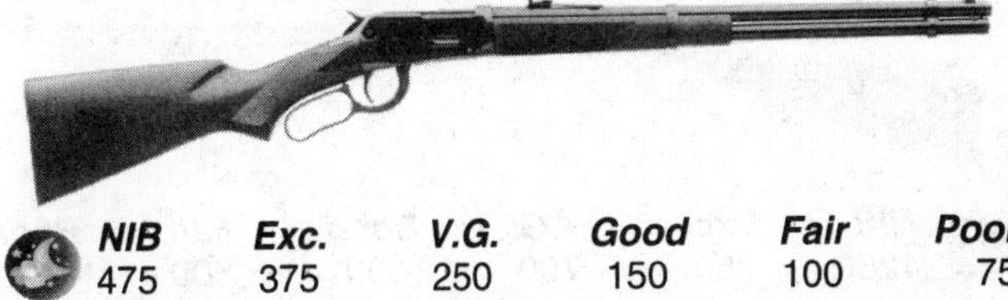

NIB	Exc.	V.G.	Good	Fair	Poor
475	375	250	150	100	75

Model 94 Legacy 24-inch

Introduced in 2005 this model features a 24" round barrel with full length magazine. Checkered walnut stock with semi-pistol grip. Chambered for the .30-30, .357 Mag., .44 Rem. Mag. or the .45 Colt cartridge. Drilled and tapped for scope mount. Blued finish. Weight is about 6.75 lbs.

NIB	Exc.	V.G.	Good	Fair	Poor
485	375	—	—	—	—

Model 94 Legacy 26-inch

Similar to the model above but offered in both round and octagon barrel and blue or case colored receiver. Marbles' tang sight. Chambered for the .30-30 or .38-55 calibers. Weight is about 7 lbs. Introduced in 2005.

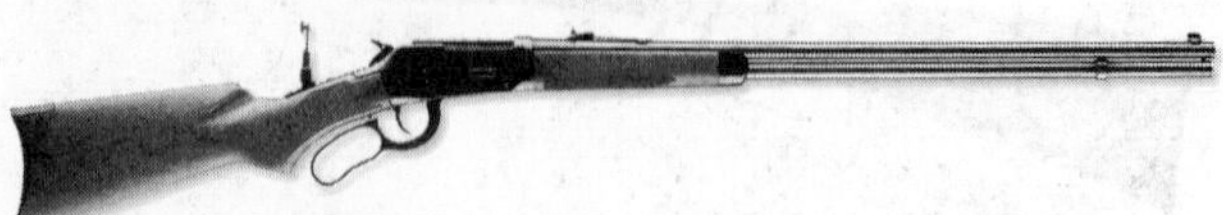

NIB	Exc.	V.G.	Good	Fair	Poor
780	575	—	—	—	—

NOTE: Add $55 for case colored receiver. Add $100 for octagon barrel.

Model 94 XTR Big Bore

This version is chambered for the .307, .356, or the .375 Win. cartridges. It features the angle-ejection and is blued with a walnut, Monte Carlo-type stock and recoil pad. The round barrel is 20" in length. It has a 6-round, tubular magazine. It was introduced in 1978.

NIB	Exc.	V.G.	Good	Fair	Poor
475	375	300	250	200	150

Model 94 Centennial Limited Editions

Introduced in 1994 these models celebrate the 100-year anniversary of the Winchester Model 1894. Offered in three grades, these models are of limited production. The Grade I is limited to 12,000 rifles while the High Grade is limited to 3,000 rifles. Only 94 of the Custom Limited model were produced. Each Limited model has different grades of select walnut and engraving coverage. All are chambered for the .30-30 Winchester cartridge.

Grade I

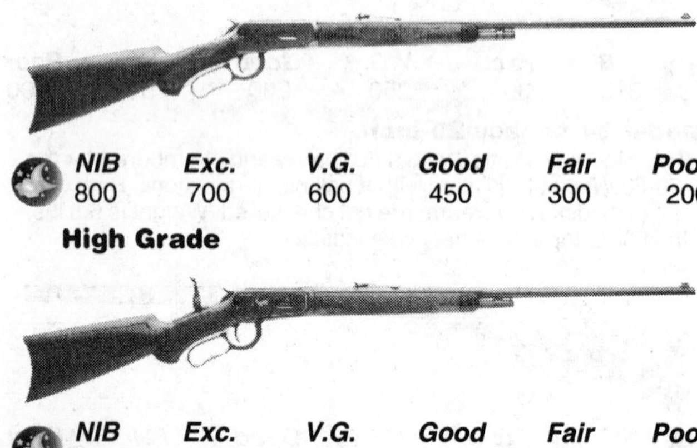

NIB	Exc.	V.G.	Good	Fair	Poor
800	700	600	450	300	200

High Grade

NIB	Exc.	V.G.	Good	Fair	Poor
1200	950	700	500	300	200

Custom High Grade

NIB	Exc.	V.G.	Good	Fair	Poor
4750	3900	2500	1000	750	450

Model 94 Heritage—Limited 1 of 1000

Introduced in 2002 and limited to 1,000 rifles. Fitted with half round/half octagon 26" barrel. Engraved with #3 pattern with gold plate. Fancy walnut stock. Chambered for the .38-55 cartridge.

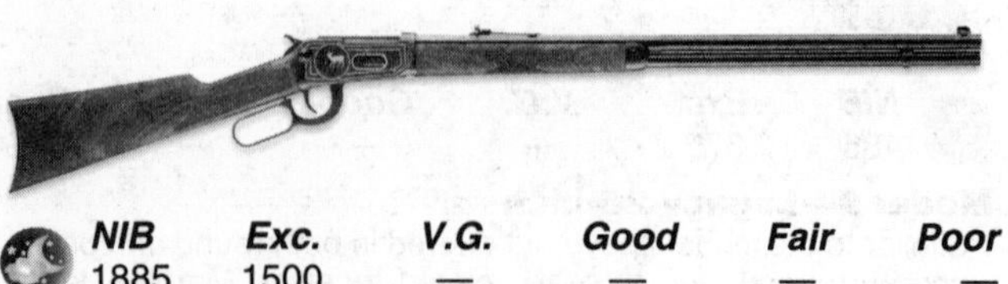

NIB	Exc.	V.G.	Good	Fair	Poor
1885	1500	—	—	—	—

Model 94 Heritage—Custom 1 of 100

Similar to the above model but with finer wood and engraved with #2 pattern with gold. Limited to 100 rifles. Introduced in 2002.

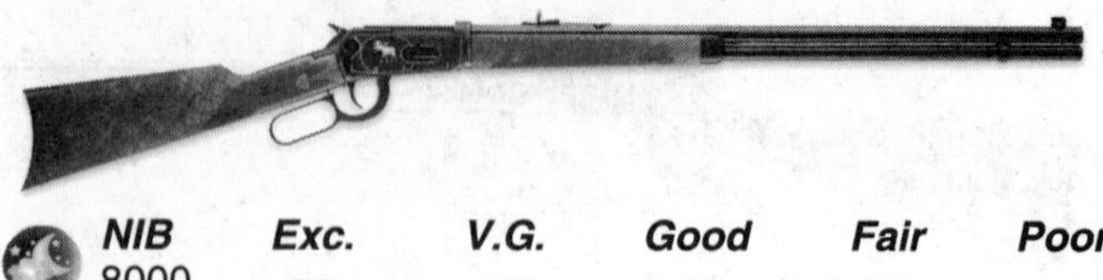

NIB	Exc.	V.G.	Good	Fair	Poor
8000	—	—	—	—	—

Model 94 Trails End

This model is chambered for the .357 Mag., .44 Mag., and .45 Colt. Offered with standard-size loop lever or Wrangler-style loop. Introduced in 1997.

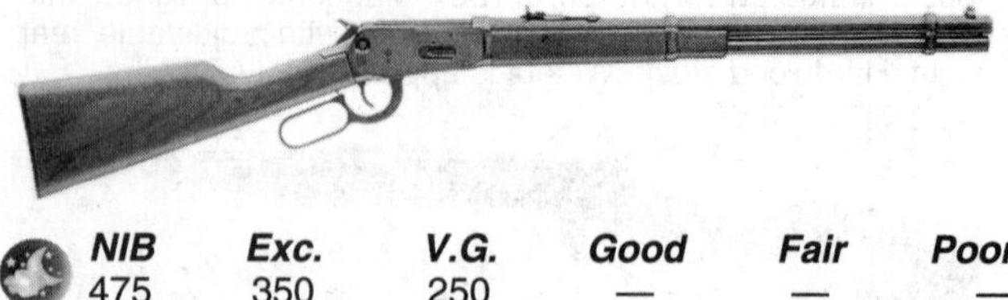

NIB	Exc.	V.G.	Good	Fair	Poor
475	350	250	—	—	—

Model 94 Trails End Octagon

As above but with 20" octagon barrel and choice of blued or case colored receiver. Crescent butt. Weight is about 6.75 lbs. Introduced in 2004.

NIB	Exc.	V.G.	Good	Fair	Poor
755	550	—	—	—	—

NOTE: Add $60 for case colored receiver.

Model 94 Trails End Hunter

Offered in .25-35 Win, .30-30 Win, or .38-55 Win and fitted with a 20" round or octagon barrel. Plain walnut stock. Blued finish on round barrel model and case colored finish on octagon model. Weight is about 6.5 lbs. Introduced in 2005.

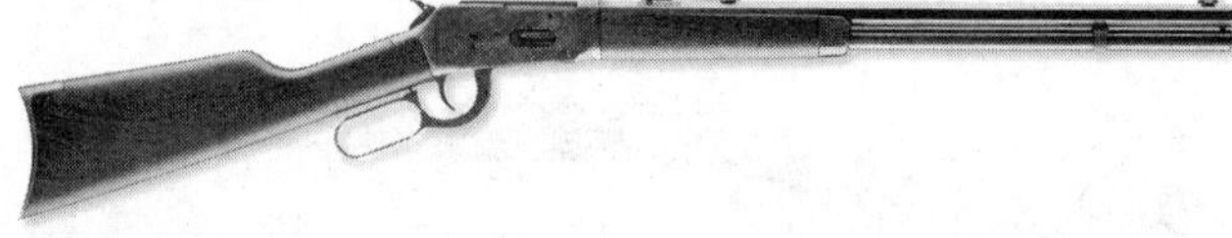

NIB	Exc.	V.G.	Good	Fair	Poor
465	350	—	—	—	—

NOTE: Add $290 for octagon barrel model.

Model 94 Timber Carbine

Introduced in 1999 this model is chambered for the .444 Marlin cartridge. Barrel is 17.75" long and ported. Hooded front sight. Magazine capacity is 5 rounds. Weight is about 6 lbs. Finish is blue. Walnut stock. In 2004 this rifle was chambered for the .450 Marlin cartridge.

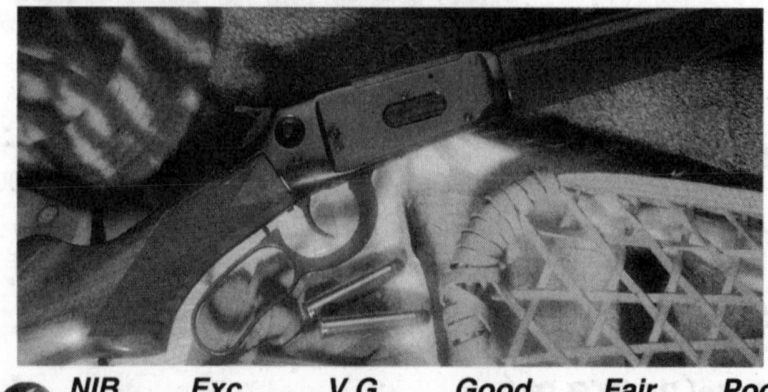

NIB	Exc.	V.G.	Good	Fair	Poor
600	450	350	—	—	—

Model 94 Timber Scout

This model, introduced in 2005, features an 18" barrel chambered for the .30-30 Win. or .44 Rem. Mag. cartridges with a quick detachable scope mount attached to the barrel for long eye relief. Plain walnut stock with pistol grip. Blued finish. Weight is about 6 lbs. Scope not included.

NIB	Exc.	V.G.	Good	Fair	Poor
595	450	—	—	—	—

Model 94 Pack Rifle

This lever-action model features an 18" barrel chambered for the .30-30 or .44 Magnum. It has a walnut stock with pistol grip and no checkering. Magazine is 3/4-style and has a 4-round capacity for the .30-30, and five rounds for the .44 Mag. Open sights. Weight is about 6.25 lbs. Introduced in 2000.

NIB	Exc.	V.G.	Good	Fair	Poor
475	350	—	—	—	—

MODEL 9400 SERIES

Model 9410

Introduced in 2001 this model features a .410 shotgun in a lever-action configuration. Barrel length is 24" and is smoothbore with Cylinder choke. Chambered is 2.5". Magazine capacity is nine rounds. Tru-glo front sight. Weight is about 6.75 lbs. In 2003 a top-tang safety was installed.

NIB	Exc.	V.G.	Good	Fair	Poor
550	400	—	—	—	—

Model 9410 Semi-Fancy

As above but with semi-fancy walnut stock with checkering. Introduced in 2004.

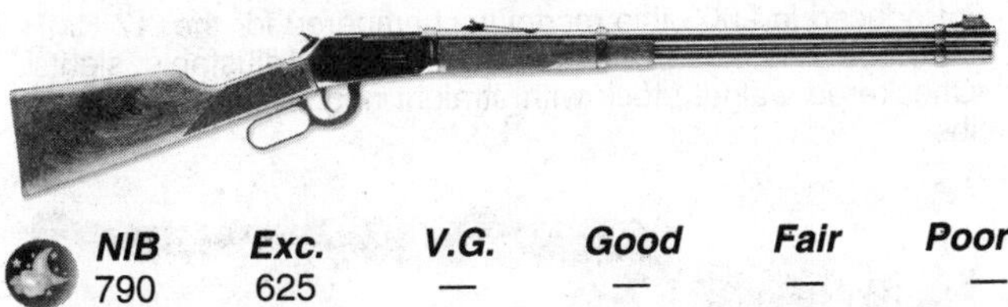

NIB	Exc.	V.G.	Good	Fair	Poor
790	625	—	—	—	—

Model 9410 Packer

Introduced in 2002 this model features a 20" barrel with 3/4 magazine and pistol-grip stock. Weight is about 6.5 lbs.

NIB	Exc.	V.G.	Good	Fair	Poor
575	425	—	—	—	—

Model 9410 Packer Compact

Introduced in 2003 this model features a reduced length of pull to 12-1/2". Fitted with Invector chokes. Weight is about 6.25 lbs.

NIB	Exc.	V.G.	Good	Fair	Poor
655	525	—	—	—	—

Model 9410 Ranger

This version is the same as the standard or traditional Model 9410 but hardwood stock without checkering. Weight is about 6.75 lbs. Fitted with top-tang safety. Introduced in 2003.

NIB	Exc.	V.G.	Good	Fair	Poor
540	425	—	—	—	—

Model 9422

Introduced in 1972 this model is chambered for the .22 rimfire and .22 Magnum rimfire cartridges. It was fitted with a 20.5" barrel, front ramp sight with hood, and adjustable semi-buckhorn rear sight. Tubular magazine holds 21 Shorts, 17 Longs, and 15 LR cartridges. The Magnum version holds 11 cartridges. Weight is about 6.25 lbs. Two-piece American walnut stock with no checkering. Between 1972 and 1992 approximately 750,000 Model 9422s were produced.

NIB	Exc.	V.G.	Good	Fair	Poor
500	400	275	225	175	125

Model 9422 XTR

This is a deluxe lever-action rifle chambered for the .22 rimfire cartridge. It is a takedown rifle with a 20.5", round barrel and a tubular magazine. The finish is blued with a checkered, high-gloss, straight-grip walnut stock. It was introduced in 1978. A .22 Magnum version is also available and would be worth approximately $10 additional.

NIB	Exc.	V.G.	Good	Fair	Poor
425	350	300	250	175	135

Model 9422 XTR Classic

This version is similar to the standard Model 9422 XTR except that it features a 22.5" barrel and a satin-finished, plain, pistol-grip walnut stock. It was manufactured between 1985 and 1987.

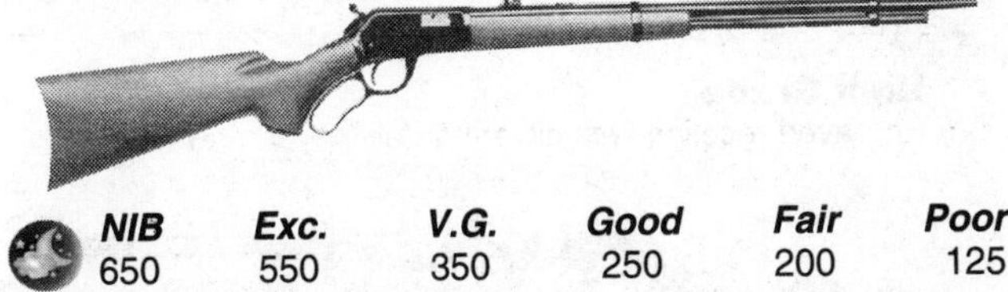

NIB	Exc.	V.G.	Good	Fair	Poor
650	550	350	250	200	125

Model 9422 WinTuff

This model features an uncheckered laminated wood stock that is brown in color. Chambered for both the .22 Rimfire and the .22 Winchester Magnum Rimfire. Weighs 6.25 lbs. Other features are the same as the standard Model 9422.

NIB	Exc.	V.G.	Good	Fair	Poor
400	325	250	200	150	125

Model 9422 WinCam

This model is chambered only for the .22 Winchester Magnum Rimfire. The laminated stock is a green color. Weighs 6.25 lbs.

NIB	Exc.	V.G.	Good	Fair	Poor
425	325	250	200	125	100

Model 9422 Trapper

Introduced in 1996 this model features a 16.5" barrel. It has an overall length of 33". Weight is 5.5 lbs.

NIB	Exc.	V.G.	Good	Fair	Poor
425	325	250	200	150	100

Model 9422 High Grade

This variation of the Model 9422 series features a specially engraved receiver and fancy wood stock. Barrel length is 20.5". Weight is about 6 lbs.

NIB	Exc.	V.G.	Good	Fair	Poor
575	475	375	325	250	200

Model 9422 25th Anniversary Rifle

Introduced in 1997 this model features 20.5" barrel. Limited quantities.

Grade I

Engraved receiver.

NIB	Exc.	V.G.	Good	Fair	Poor
700	575	425	—	—	—

High Grade

Engraved receiver with silver border.

NIB	Exc.	V.G.	Good	Fair	Poor
1350	1100	—	—	—	—

Model 9422 Legacy

This model has a semi-pistol-grip stock of checkered walnut. Will shoot .22 caliber LR, L, or S cartridges. Fitted with a 16" barrel. Weight is about 6 lbs. Introduced in 1998.

NIB	Exc.	V.G.	Good	Fair	Poor
550	450	350	275	200	150

Model 9422 Large Loop & Walnut

Introduced in 1998 this model features a walnut stock with large loop lever. Large loop offered on .22 LR, L, or S model. Standard lever on .22 WMR version. Fitted with 16" barrel. Weight is about 6 lbs.

NIB	Exc.	V.G.	Good	Fair	Poor
500	400	325	275	—	—

Model 9422 High Grade Series II

This model features a high-grade walnut stock with cut checkering. Receiver engraved with dogs and squirrels. Fitted with 16" barrel. Weight is about 6 lbs. Introduced in 1998.

NIB	Exc.	V.G.	Good	Fair	Poor
650	550	400	325	200	125

Model 9417 Traditional

Introduced in 2003 this model is chambered for the .17 HMR cartridge and fitted with a 20.5" barrel. Adjustable sights. Checkered walnut stock with straight grip. Weight is about 6 lbs.

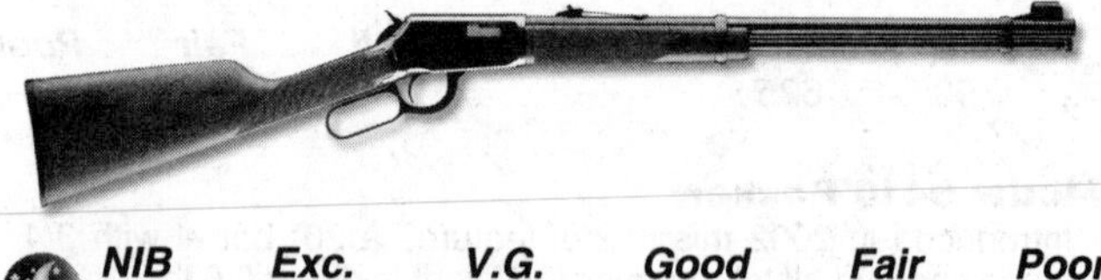

NIB	Exc.	V.G.	Good	Fair	Poor
550	450	375	—	—	—

Model 9417 Legacy

Similar to the model above but fitted with a 22.5" barrel and checkered walnut with pistol grip. Weight is about 6 lbs. Introduced in 2003.

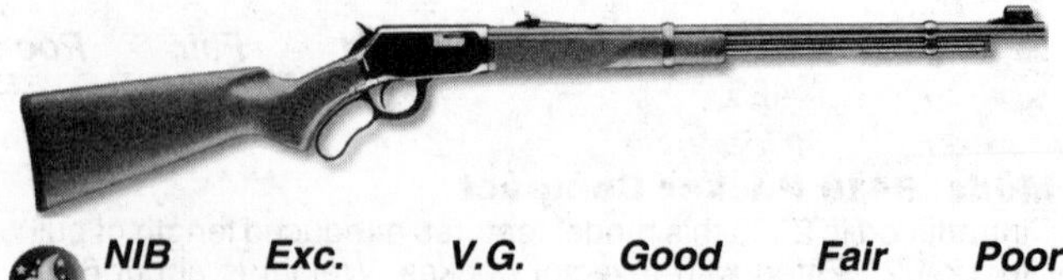

NIB	Exc.	V.G.	Good	Fair	Poor
575	475	400	—	—	—

This symbol denotes "Sleepers" with rapidly-rising values and/or significant collector potential.

MODEL 9422 TRIBUTE SERIES

As of 2005 the Model 9422 production will end. These final production Model 9422s will be limited to a total production of 9,422 rifles. Each rifle will have the Winchester Horse and Rider on one side and the Model 9422 tribute logo on the other side.

Model 9422 High Grade Traditional Tribute

This model features a 20.5" barrel with high grade checkered walnuty stock. Blued receiver with high-relief silver inlay on both sides of the receiver.

NIB	Exc.	V.G.	Good	Fair	Poor
1200	950	700	—	—	—

Model 9422 High Grade Legacy Tribute

Similar to the model above but with semi-pistol grip and 22.5" barrel.

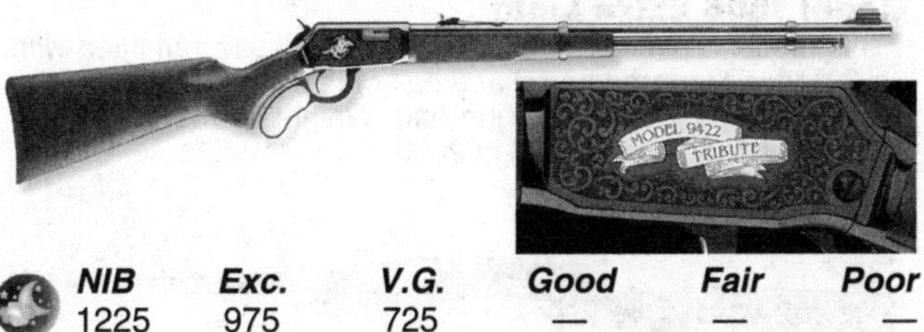

NIB	Exc.	V.G.	Good	Fair	Poor
1225	975	725	—	—	—

Model 9422 Custom Traditional Tribute

This model is fitted with a 20.5" barrel, high grade checkereed walnut stock. High-relief scroll engraved receiver with gold logos on both sides. Limited to 222 rifles.

NIB	Exc.	V.G.	Good	Fair	Poor
2500	1950	1500	—	—	—

Model 9422 Special Edition Traditional Tribute

This model has a 20.5" barrel with checkered walnut straight grip stock and engraved blued receiver. Engraved logos on both sides of receiver.

NIB	Exc.	V.G.	Good	Fair	Poor
580	475	375	—	—	—

Model 9422 Special Edition Legacy Tribute

This 22.5" barrel model has a checkered semi-pistol grip stock Blued receiver with engraved logos on both sides.

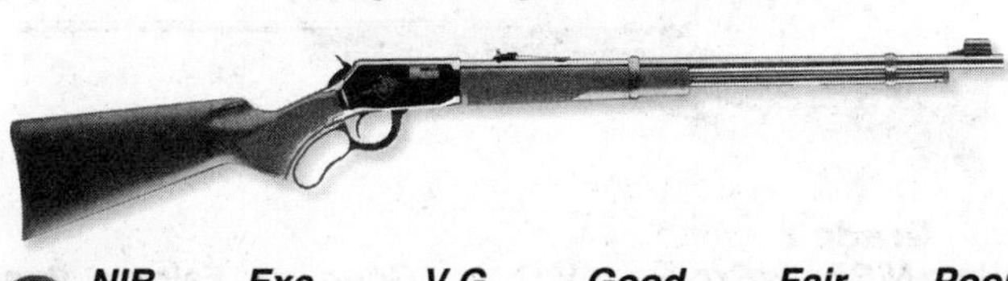

NIB	Exc.	V.G.	Good	Fair	Poor
650	475	375	—	—	—

Model 64

This is a post-1964 version of the lever-action Model 64. It is chambered for the .30-30 cartridge and has a 24" round barrel with open sights and a 5-round, 2/3-length tubular magazine. The finish is blued with a plain walnut pistol-grip stock. It was manufactured between 1972 and 1974.

Exc.	V.G.	Good	Fair	Poor
300	250	190	125	100

Model 1885 Low Wall

Introduced in fall of 1999 this single-shot model is chambered for the .22 LR cartridge. It is fitted with a 24.5" half octagon barrel with leaf rear sight. Drilled and tapped for a tang sight. Crescent steel buttplate. Walnut stock. Weight is about 8 lbs. Limited to 2,400 rifles.

Grade I

NIB	Exc.	V.G.	Good	Fair	Poor
875	725	600	500	—	—

High Grade

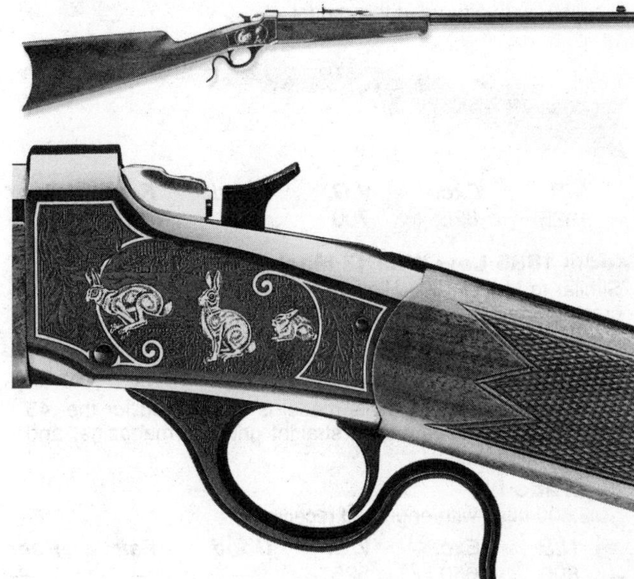

Left side detail of High Grade 1885 Low Wall

Right side detail of High Grade 1885 Low Wall

NIB	Exc.	V.G.	Good	Fair	Poor
1225	925	—	—	—	—

Model 1885 High Wall Hunter

Single-shot; patterned after original Model 1885 designed by John Browning. Calibers: .223, .22-250, .270 WSM, 7mm WSM, .300 WSM, .325 WSM. Stock: Checkered walnut. Barrel: 28-inch blued, sightless octagon with Pachmayr pad. Weight: 8-1/2 lbs. MSRP: 875

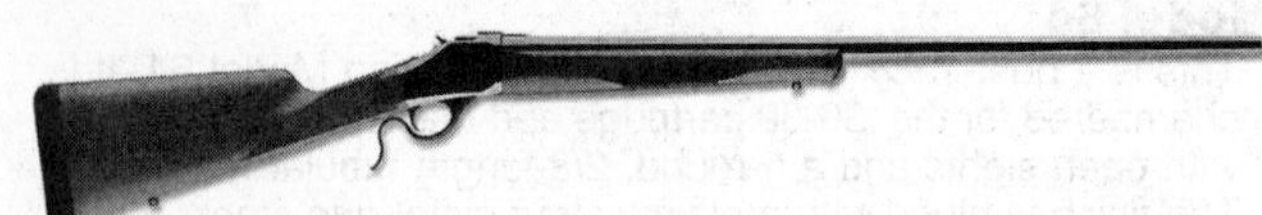

Model 1885 .30-06 Centennial High Wall Hunter

Similar to Model 1885 High Wall Hunter but with premium wood and gold inlay on receiver. Commemorates centennial of .30-06 cartridge. Introduced 2006. MSRP: 1617

Model 1885 Low Wall Classic

This single-shot rifle is chambered for the .17 HMR cartridge and fitted with a 24" octagon barrel. Checkered walnut stock with straight grip and schnabel forend. Adjustable sights. Weight is about 8 lbs. Introduced in 2003. In 2005 the .17 Mach 2 caliber was offered in this model.

NIB	Exc.	V.G.	Good	Fair	Poor
1025	825	700	—	—	—

Model 1885 Low Wall 17 Mach 2

Similar to Model 1885 High Wall but with low-profile receiver, crescent buttplate, and 24-inch barrel. Chambered for 17 Mach 2 rimfire cartridge. Introduced 2006. MSRP: 1014

Model 1892

Introduced in mid-1997 this model is chambered for the .45 Colt cartridge. It features a straight grip, full magazine, and crescent buttplate.

Grade I

2,500 rifles with engraved receiver.

NIB	Exc.	V.G.	Good	Fair	Poor
800	650	525	—	—	—

High Grade

1,000 rifle with gold accents.

NIB	Exc.	V.G.	Good	Fair	Poor
1400	1175	925	—	—	—

Model 1892 Short Rifle

This model is fitted with a 20" barrel and chambered for the .45 Colt, .357 Magnum, .44 Magnum, and .44-40 cartridges. Walnut stock and blued barrel and receiver. Weight is about 6.25 lbs. Introduced in 1999.

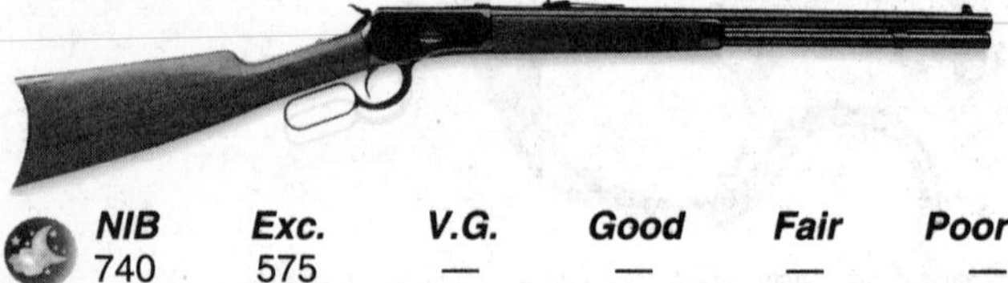

NIB	Exc.	V.G.	Good	Fair	Poor
740	575	—	—	—	—

Model 1886

Introduced to the Winchester line in 1997 this was a noncatalogued item. This model features a 26" octagon barrel, semi-pistol grip, and crescent buttplate.

Grade I

2,500 rifles blued receiver.

NIB	Exc.	V.G.	Good	Fair	Poor
1000	800	—	—	—	—

High Grade

1,000 rifles with gold accents on receiver.

NIB	Exc.	V.G.	Good	Fair	Poor
1575	1300	—	—	—	—

Model 1886 Take Down Classic

Introduced in 1999 this model is chambered for the .45-70 cartridge and features a 26" barrel with takedown feature. Walnut stock with pistol grip and crescent butt. Magazine capacity is 8 rounds. Weight is about 9.25 lbs.

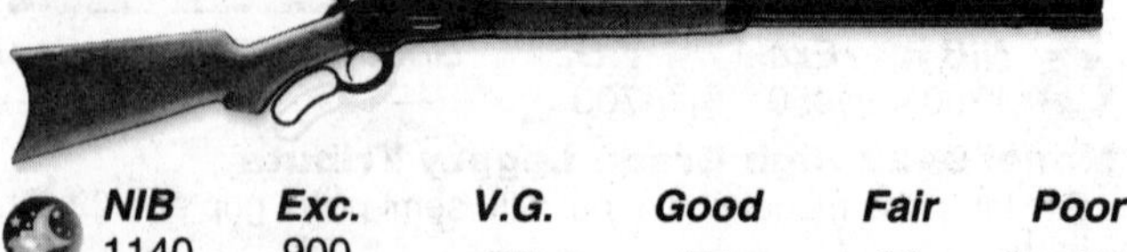

NIB	Exc.	V.G.	Good	Fair	Poor
1140	900	—	—	—	—

Model 1886 Extra Light

This model is similar to the Model 1886 Classic but fitted with a 22" round tapered barrel and half magazine. Chambered for the .45-70 cartridge. Shotgun butt. Weight is about 7.25 lbs. Limited edition. Introduced in 2000.

Grade I (3,500)

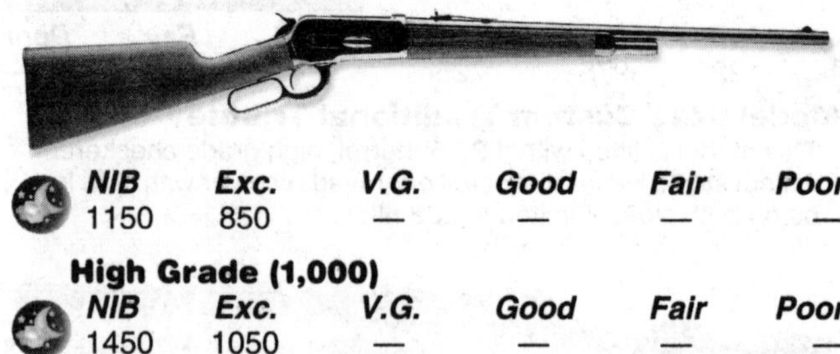

NIB	Exc.	V.G.	Good	Fair	Poor
1150	850	—	—	—	—

High Grade (1,000)

NIB	Exc.	V.G.	Good	Fair	Poor
1450	1050	—	—	—	—

Model 1895 Limited Edition

Introduced in 1995 this reproduction of the famous Model 1895 is offered in .30-06 caliber with 24" barrel. Magazine capacity is 4 rounds. Weight is approximately 8 lbs. Available in two grades, each limited to 4,000 rifles.

Grade I

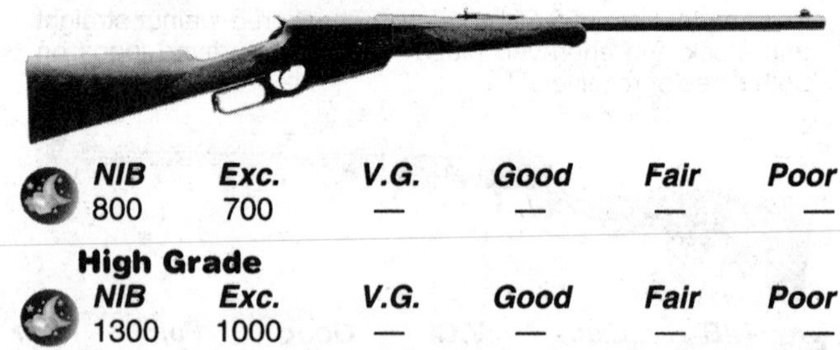

NIB	Exc.	V.G.	Good	Fair	Poor
800	700	—	—	—	—

High Grade

NIB	Exc.	V.G.	Good	Fair	Poor
1300	1000	—	—	—	—

Model 1895—Limited Edition for the year 2000

Same as above but chambered for the .405 Win. cartridge. Introduced in 2000.

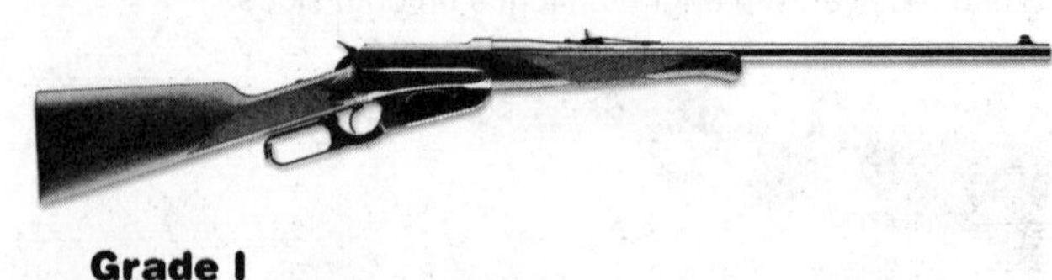

Grade I

NIB	Exc.	V.G.	Good	Fair	Poor
1150	800	—	—	—	—

High Grade

NIB	Exc.	V.G.	Good	Fair	Poor
1550	1150	—	—	—	—

Model 1895 Saddle Ring Carbine

Patterned after original Model 1895 carbine. Features include blued 22-inch barrel, ladder style rear sight; D&T for Lyman side mount; saddle ring on left side of receiver; rollmarked -inch.30 Gov't '06.-inch Chambered in .30-06 only; commemorates centennial of .30-06 cartridge. Introduced 2006. MSRP: 1399

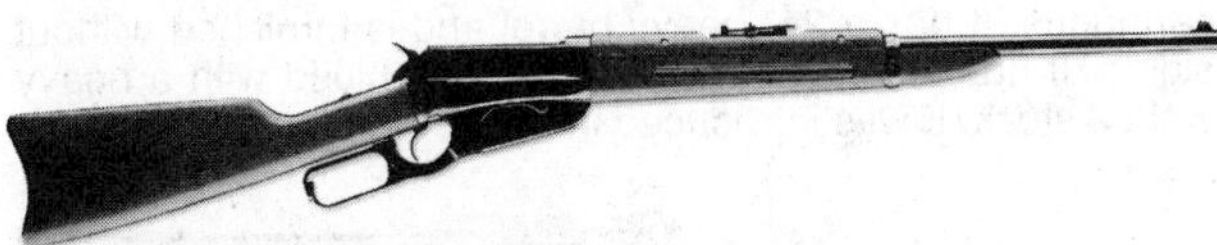

Model 52B Sporting Rifle

A 1993 limited-edition rifle (6,000 guns) that is a faithful reproduction of the famous Winchester Model 52 Sporter. Equipped with a 24" barrel, adjustable trigger, and "B" style cheekpiece. This model was reissued in 1997 and limited to 3,000 rifles.

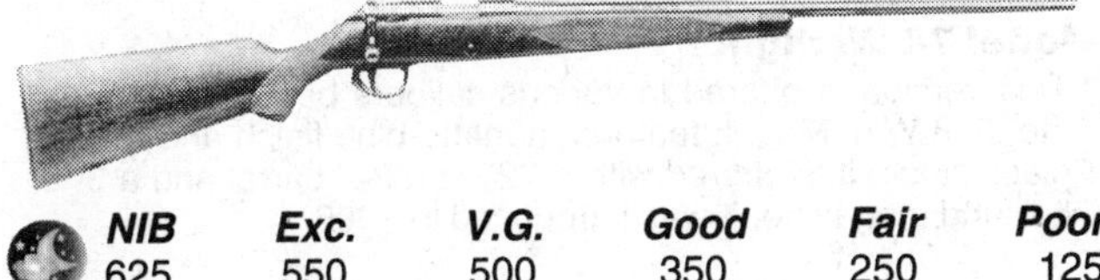

NIB	Exc.	V.G.	Good	Fair	Poor
625	550	500	350	250	125

POST-1964 MODEL 70S

These post-Model 70 rifles were fitted with redesigned actions and bolt with free-floating barrels, and new style stock with impressed checkering.

NOTE: In 1994, U.S. Repeating Arms reintroduced the pre-1964 Model 70 action on many of its Model 70 rifles. At the present time this new action does not affect values but may do so in the future depending on shooter reaction.

In 2006, the Model 70 was discontinued by US Repeating Arms. It is uncertain whether the bulk of post-'64 Model 70s will become truly collectible, although the potential is there.

In the editor's opinion, there was never anything really wrong with the post-'64 Model 70. It might even be argued that in "dumbing down" the M70, Winchester was simply ahead of its time, as many of the manufacturing "shortcuts" that characterized the post-'64 M70 have come to be accepted as commonplace.

Nevertheless, as the M70 reached the end of its seven-decade run, it had lost much of its premium status. The Ruger M77, the Remington M700 and Model Seven, the Browning A-Bolt and other high-end bolt rifles gave it a serious run for its money.

In October of 2007, just as this edition was going to press, Winchester Repeating Arms announced that the pre-'64-style Model 70 would once again be produced – this time at the FN plant in Columbia, SC. We wish it well!

Model 70—Standard Grade

This is a bolt-action sporting rifle chambered for various popular calibers such as the .22-250, .222 Rem., .243 Win., .270 Win., .30-06, and .308 Win. It features a 22" barrel with open sights and a 5-round, integral box magazine. The finish is blued with a Monte Carlo-type stock furnished with sling swivels. It was manufactured between 1964 and 1971.

Exc.	V.G.	Good	Fair	Poor
400	275	225	175	110

Model 70 Varmint

Chambered for the .22-25, .222 Rem., and .243 Win. cartridges this rifle is fitted with a 24" heavyweight barrel with no sights. Magazine capacity is 5 rounds. Weight is about 9.75 lbs. Built from 1964 to 1971.

Exc.	V.G.	Good	Fair	Poor
400	250	200	150	100

Model 70 Westerner

This model is chambered for the .264 Win. Magnum and .300 Win. Magnum cartridges. Open sights, 24" barrel. Ventilated recoil pad. Weight is about 7.25 lbs. Built from 1964 to 1971.

Exc.	V.G.	Good	Fair	Poor
450	275	225	175	110

Model 70 African

Chambered for the .458 Win. Magnum cartridge this rifle is fitted with a 22" barrel with open sights. Magazine capacity is 3 rounds. Weight is about 8.5 lbs. Built from 1964 to 1971.

Exc.	V.G.	Good	Fair	Poor
725	550	385	275	175

Model 70 Magnum

Chambered for the 7mm Rem. Mag., .300 Win. Mag., and .375 H&H cartridges. Barrel length is 24". Weight is about 7.75 lbs. Built from 1964 to 1971.

Exc.	V.G.	Good	Fair	Poor
550	385	275	225	175

Model 70 Deluxe

Built from 1964 to 1971, this rifle features a Monte Carlo stock with hand checkering and ebony forend tip. Offered in .243, .270, .30-06, .300 Win. Mag. Fitted with 22" barrel except magnums, which have 24" barrel. Weight is about 7.5 lbs.

Exc.	V.G.	Good	Fair	Poor
550	375	250	175	125

Model 70 Mannlicher

This is a full-length, Mannlicher-type stocked version of the Model 70 bolt-action rifle that is chambered for the .243, .270, .308, and the .30-06 cartridges. It was introduced in 1969. It features a 19" barrel with open sights. The finish is blued. It was discontinued in 1972. Only 2,401 were produced. Excellent quality.

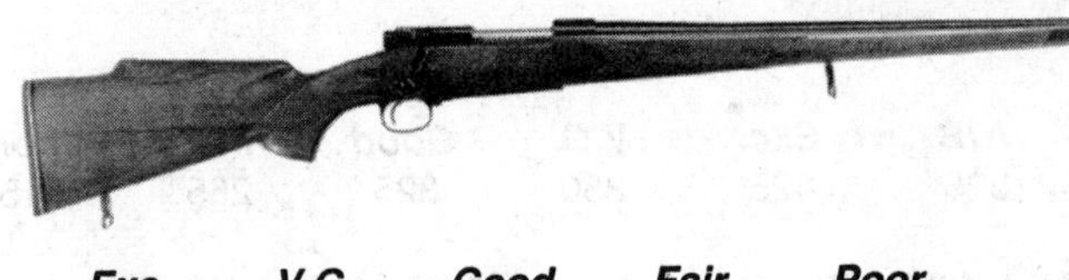

Exc.	V.G.	Good	Fair	Poor
775	625	525	425	310

Model 70 Target Rifle

This version is chambered for the .308 or the .30-06 cartridges. It was offered with a 24" heavy barrel without sights. It is furnished with bases for a target scope. The finish is blued with a heavy walnut target stock with a palm rest. Weight is approximately 10.25 lbs.

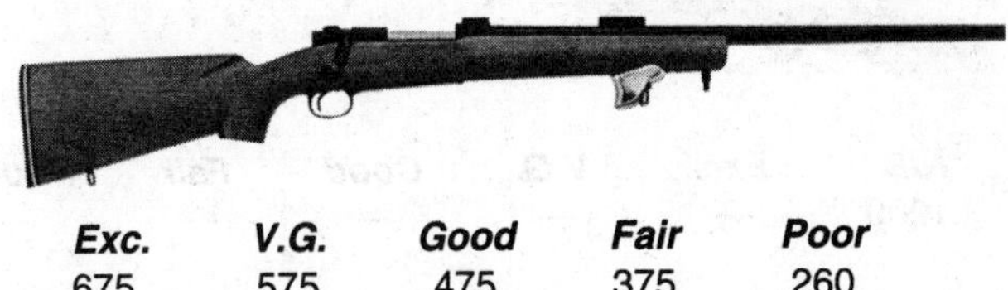

Exc.	V.G.	Good	Fair	Poor
675	575	475	375	260

Model 70 International Match Army

This version is chambered for the .308 cartridge and has a 24" heavy barrel furnished without sights. It has an adjustable trigger and is blued, with a target-type heavy stock that had an accessory rail and an adjustable butt.

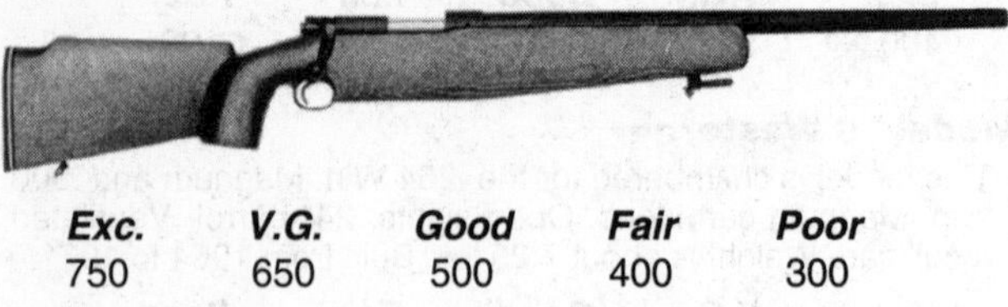

Exc.	V.G.	Good	Fair	Poor
750	650	500	400	300

Model 70A

This is a utility version of the bolt-action post-1964 Model 70. It was furnished without a hinged floorplate. The finish is blued, with a walnut stock. It was manufactured between 1972 and 1978.

Exc.	V.G.	Good	Fair	Poor
375	300	250	200	125

Model 670

Economy-grade version of the Model 70. Hardwood stock, iron sights, non-hinged floorplate, 22" blued barrel. Manufactured from 1967 to 1973.

NIB	Exc.	V.G.	Good	Fair	Poor
749	—	—	—	—	—

Model 70 XTR Featherweight

This gun was built after the takeover by the U.S.R.A. Company. It is a bolt-action sporting rifle chambered for various calibers from .22-250 up to the .30-06 cartridges. It has a 22" barrel that is furnished without sights and features either a short- or medium-length action. It has a 5-round, integral magazine. The finish is blued, with a checkered walnut stock. It was introduced in 1981.

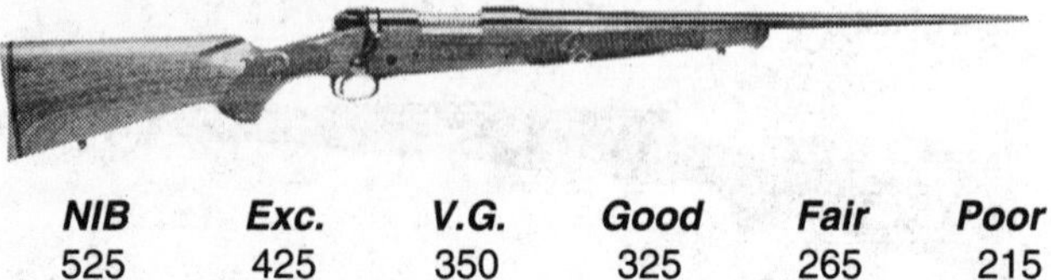

NIB	Exc.	V.G.	Good	Fair	Poor
525	425	350	325	265	215

Model 70 Fiftieth Anniversary Model

This is a commemorative version of the post-1964 Model 70 bolt-action rifle. It is chambered for the .300 Win. Mag. and is offered with a 24" barrel. It is engraved and high-gloss blued with a deluxe, checkered walnut stock. There were 500 manufactured in 1987. In order to realize collector potential, it must be NIB with all supplied materials.

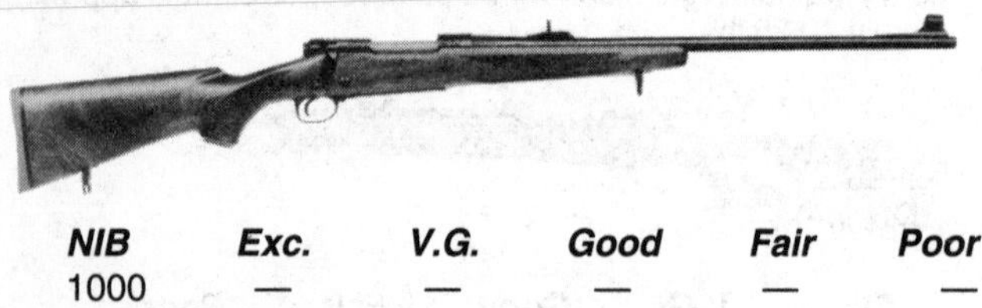

NIB	Exc.	V.G.	Good	Fair	Poor
1000	—	—	—	—	—

Model 70 XTR Super Express

This is a heavy-duty version of the post-1964 Model 70 chambered for the .375 H&H and the .458 Win. Mag. cartridges. It is offered with a 22" or 24" heavy barrel and a 3-round, integral box magazine. This version has extra recoil lugs mounted in the stock and is blued with a select, straight-grain walnut stock and a recoil pad standard.

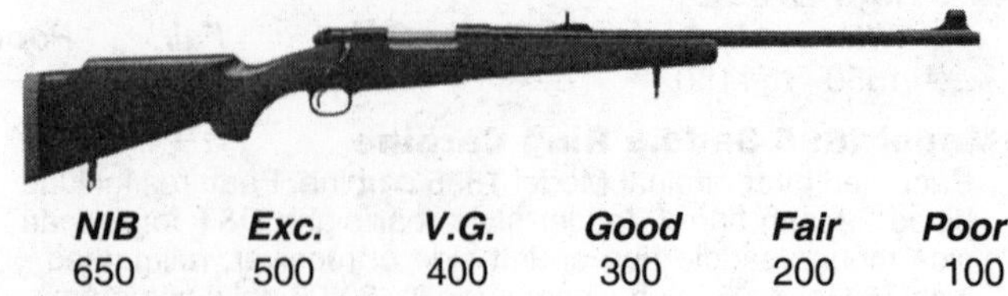

NIB	Exc.	V.G.	Good	Fair	Poor
650	500	400	300	200	100

Model 70 XTR Varmint

This version is chambered for the .22-250, .223, and the .243 cartridges. It has a 24" heavy barrel and is furnished without sights. It has a 5-round magazine and is blued with a heavy walnut stock. It was introduced in 1972.

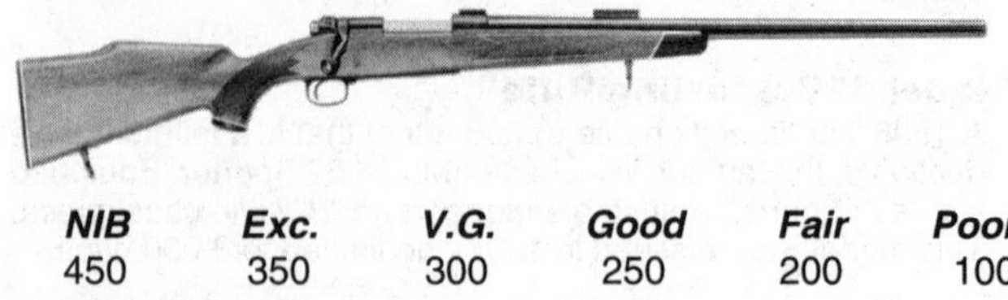

NIB	Exc.	V.G.	Good	Fair	Poor
450	350	300	250	200	100

Model 70 Winlight

This version is offered in various calibers between .270 and the .338 Win. Mag. It features a matte-blue finish and a fiberglass stock. It is offered with a 22" or a 24" barrel and a 3- or 4-round magazine. It was introduced in 1986.

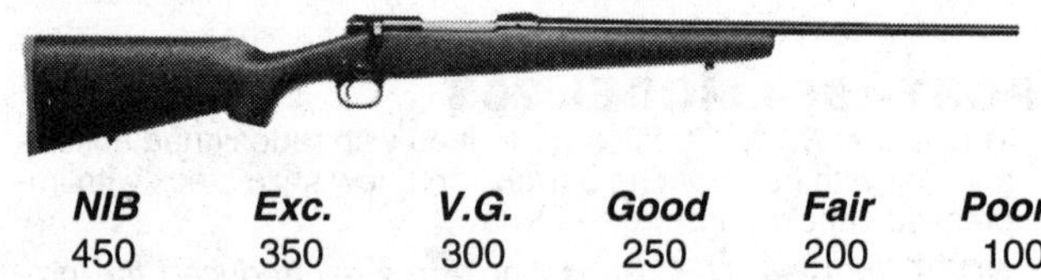

NIB	Exc.	V.G.	Good	Fair	Poor
450	350	300	250	200	100

Ranger (Model 70)

This is a utility-grade, bolt-action rifle chambered for the .270 Win., .30-06, and the 7mm Rem. Mag. cartridges. It is offered with a 22" or a 24" barrel with open sights and has a 3- or 4-round box magazine. The finish is blued with a plain hardwood stock.

NIB	Exc.	V.G.	Good	Fair	Poor
400	300	275	225	150	100

Model 70 Featherweight Classic

A U.S.R.A. model with 22" barrel, walnut stock, and claw controlled round feeding. The bolt is jeweled and the bolt handle knurled. Comb is straight. Available in .270, .280, and .30-06 calibers. In 1997 this model was offered in the 6.5x55mm Swedish caliber. Rifle weighs about 7.25 lbs. In 2001 this model was offered chambered for the .300 Winchester Short Magnum (WSM) cartridge. In 2005 this model was offered in stainless steel.

NIB	Exc.	V.G.	Good	Fair	Poor
850	650	450	375	225	125

NOTE: In 2003 a left-hand model was offered. Add $35. For stainless steel model add $60.

Model 70 Featherweight Classic All-Terrain

Introduced in 1996, this model features a weather-resistant stainless steel barrel and action with fiberglass/graphite black synthetic stock. Offered in .270 Win., .30-06, 7mm Rem. Mag., .330 Win. Mag. Weight is about 7.25 lbs. Also offered with the BOSS system.

NIB	Exc.	V.G.	Good	Fair	Poor
850	650	450	325	225	125

NOTE: Add $100 for BOSS.

Model 70 Featherweight Super Short

Introduced in 2003 this rifle features a shorter receiver to handle the .223 WSSM and .243 WSSM cartridges. Fitted with a 22" barrel and a checkered walnut stock with solid recoil pad. Weight is about 6 lbs.

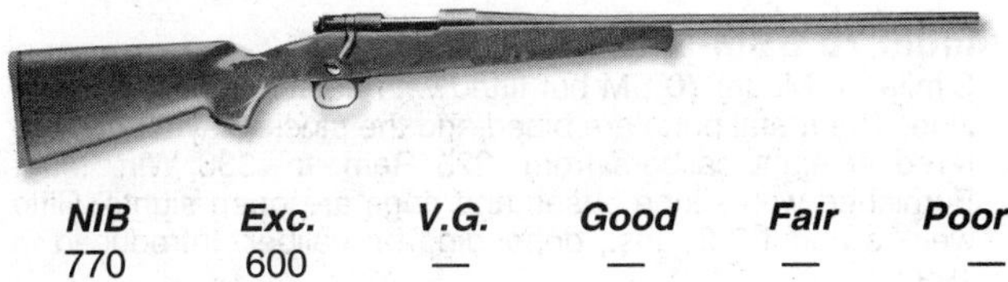

NIB	Exc.	V.G.	Good	Fair	Poor
770	600	—	—	—	—

Model 70 Classic Laredo

First offered in 1996, this model features a heavy 26" barrel with pre-1964 action on a gray synthetic stock. Chambered for the 7mm Rem. Mag and the .300 Win. Mag. The forearm is a beavertail. Finish is matte blue. In 1997 this model was offered chambered for the 7mm STW cartridge. In 1998 this model was offered with fluted barrel.

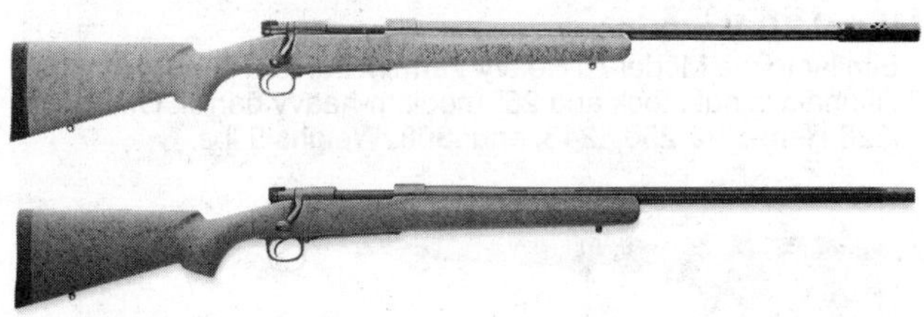

NIB	Exc.	V.G.	Good	Fair	Poor
750	650	550	500	400	300

NOTE: Add $100 for BOSS. Add $125 for fluted barrel.

Model 70 Classic Compact

Introduced in 1998, this model is a scaled-down version of the Featherweight. It has a length of pull of 12.5" and a 20" barrel. Chambered for .243, .308, and 7mm-08 calibers. Checkered walnut stock. Weight is about 6.5 lbs.

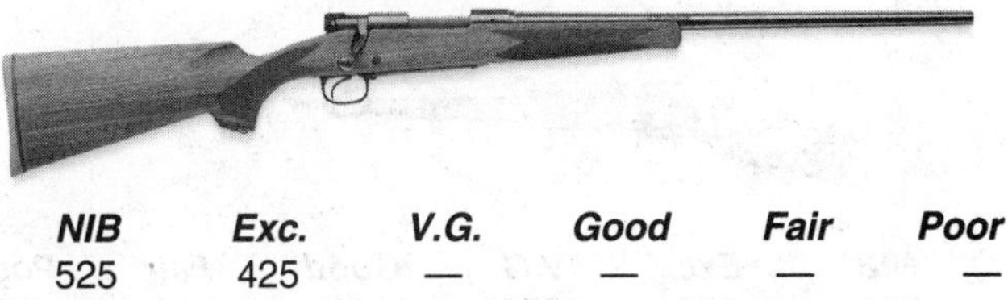

NIB	Exc.	V.G.	Good	Fair	Poor
525	425	—	—	—	—

Model 70 Classic Sporter LT

Introduced in 1999, this model is chambered for a wide variety of calibers from .25-06 to .338 Win. Mag. Fitted with a 24" or 26" barrel depending on caliber and no sights. Walnut stock with butt pad. Blued finish. Also offered in left-hand models from .270 to .338 Win. Mag. Weight is about 8 lbs.

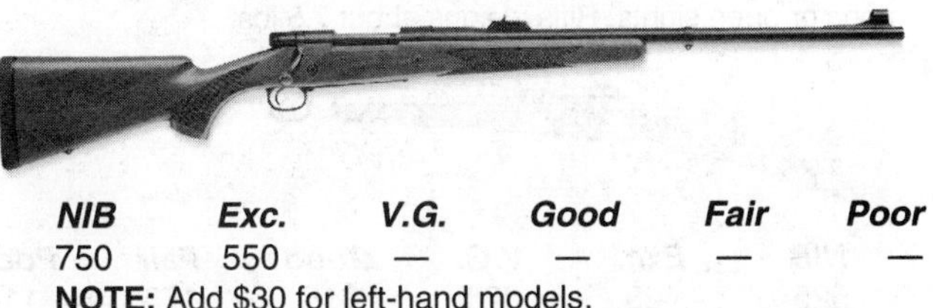

NIB	Exc.	V.G.	Good	Fair	Poor
750	550	—	—	—	—

NOTE: Add $30 for left-hand models.

Model 70 Classic Safari Express

This model is chambered for the .375 H&H Mag, .416 Rem. Mag, and .458 Win. Mag. fitted with a 24" barrel magazine capacity is 4 rounds. Walnut stock with open sights. Left-hand model offered in .375 H&H. Weight is about 8.5 lbs. Introduced in 1999.

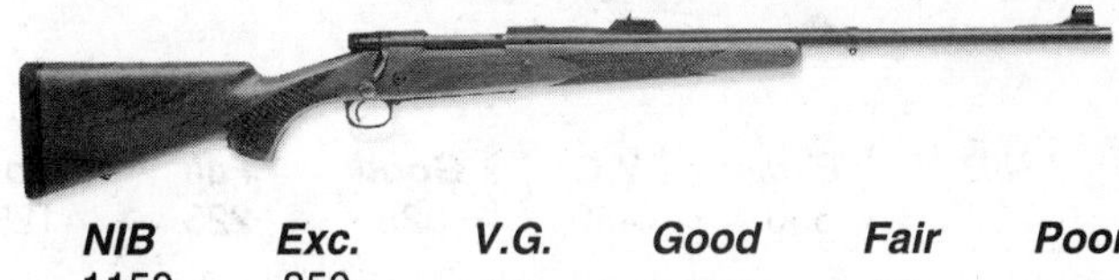

NIB	Exc.	V.G.	Good	Fair	Poor
1150	850	—	—	—	—

NOTE: Add $30 for .375 H&H left-hand model.

Model 70 Super Grade

Another U.S.R.A. rifle that features a select walnut stock, claw-controlled round feed, a single reinforced cross bolt, 24" barrel shipped with bases and rings. The buttstock has a straight comb with classic cheekpiece and deep-cut checkering. Available in .270, .30-06, 7mm Rem. Mag., .300 Win. Mag., .338 Win. Mag. Rifle weighs approximately 7.75 lbs. Currently in production.

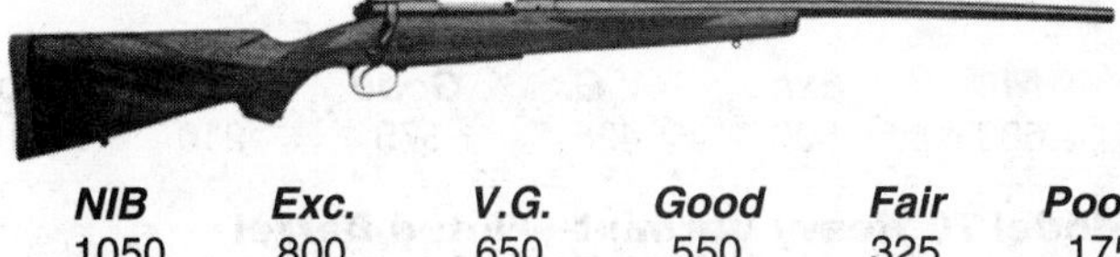

NIB	Exc.	V.G.	Good	Fair	Poor
1050	800	650	550	325	175

Model 70 RMEF Super Grade

As above but with stainless steel action and barrel. Chambered for the .300 Win. Mag. cartridge. Fitted with a 26" barrel. Checkered walnut stock with solid recoil pad. Weight is about 8 lbs. Introduced in 2003. Special RMEF (Rock Mountain Elk Foundation) emblem on grip cap. Limited production.

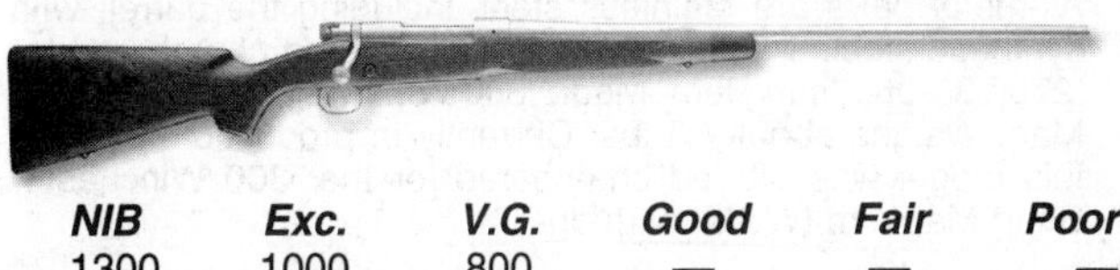

NIB	Exc.	V.G.	Good	Fair	Poor
1300	1000	800	—	—	—

Model 70 RMEF Super Grade III

This model is chambered for the .325 WSM or .300 WSM calibers and fitted with a 24" stainless steel barrel without sights. Super Grade walnut checkered stock with shadow line cheek piece. Weight is about 7.75 lbs. RMEF grip cap medallion. Introduced in 2005.

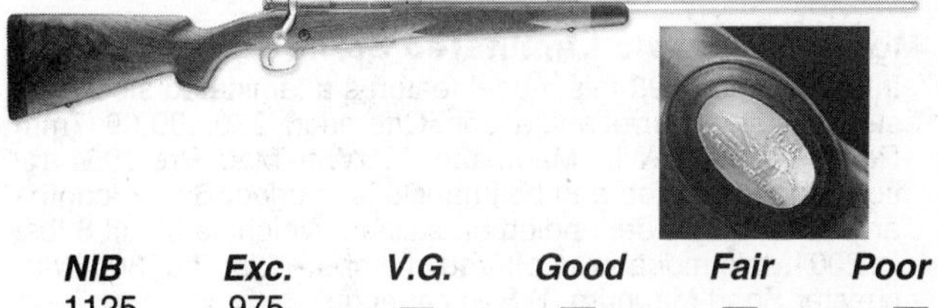

NIB	Exc.	V.G.	Good	Fair	Poor
1125	975	—	—	—	—

Model 70 Classic Super Grade III

Similar to the model above but chambered for a variety of short action calibers including WSM calibers. Fitted with a 24" barrel with no sights except for .300 Win. Mag. and .338 Win. Mag. which have 26" barrels. Weight is about 7.75 to 8 lbs. depending on caliber. Introduced in 2005.

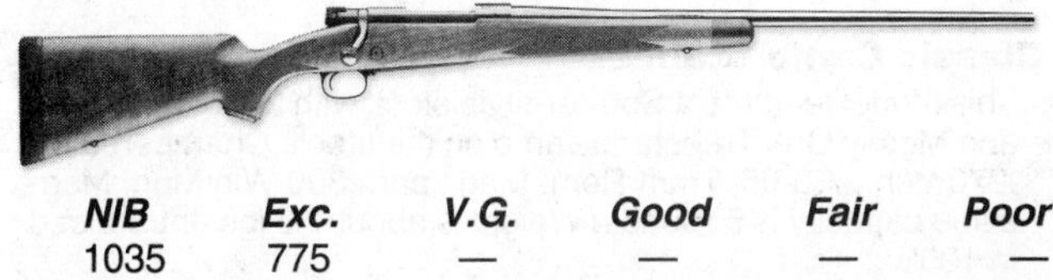

NIB	Exc.	V.G.	Good	Fair	Poor
1035	775	—	—	—	—

Model 70 Super Express

A U.S.R.A. version of the post-1964 XTR Super Express. Specifications are the same as the earlier model. Rifle weighs 8.5 lbs. Introduced in 1993.

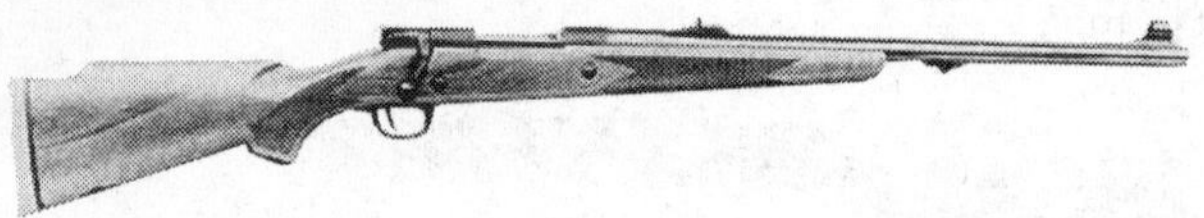

NIB	Exc.	V.G.	Good	Fair	Poor
725	550	450	325	225	125

Model 70 Heavy Varmint

Introduced by U.S.R.A. in 1993, this rifle features a fiberglass/graphite stock with heavy 26" stainless steel barrel. Offered in .223, .22-250, .243, and .308. In 1997, this model was offered chambered for the .222 Rem. cartridge. Rifle weighs about 10.75 lbs.

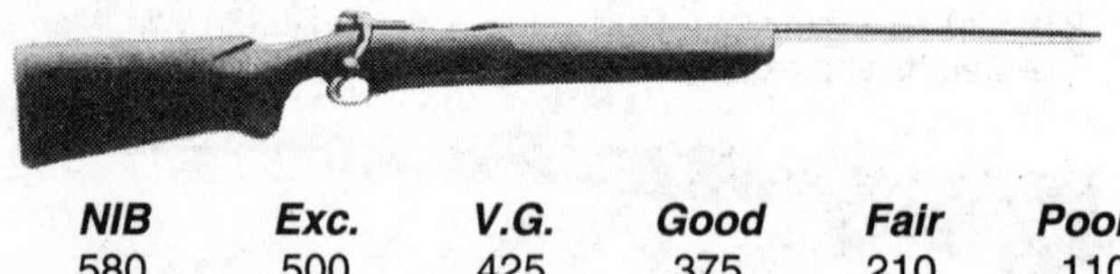

NIB	Exc.	V.G.	Good	Fair	Poor
580	500	425	375	210	110

Model 70 Heavy Varmint—Fluted Barrel

Introduced in 1997, this model is similar to the above Varmint with the addition of a fluted barrel. Calibers are also the same as the above model.

NIB	Exc.	V.G.	Good	Fair	Poor
625	500	475	350	275	175

Model 70 Stainless

All-metal parts are stainless steel, including the barrel, with synthetic stock. Available with 24" barrel and chambered for .270, .30-06, 7mm Rem. Mag., .300 Win. Mag., and .338 Win. Mag. Weighs about 7.5 lbs. Currently in production. In 2001 this model was offered chambered for the .300 Winchester Short Magnum (WSM) cartridge.

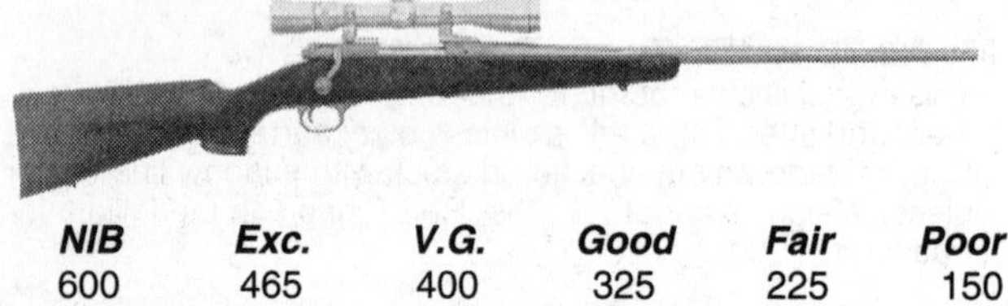

NIB	Exc.	V.G.	Good	Fair	Poor
600	465	400	325	225	150

Model 70 Classic Laminated Stainless

Introduced in 1998 this model features a laminated stock and stainless steel barrel and action. Offered in .270, .30-06, 7mm Rem. Mag., .300 Win. Mag., and .338 Win. Mag. Pre-1964 action. Bolt is jeweled and bolt handle is knurled. Barrel lengths are 24" and 26", depending on caliber. Weight is about 8 lbs. In 2001, this model was offered chambered for the .300 Winchester Short Magnum (WSM) cartridge.

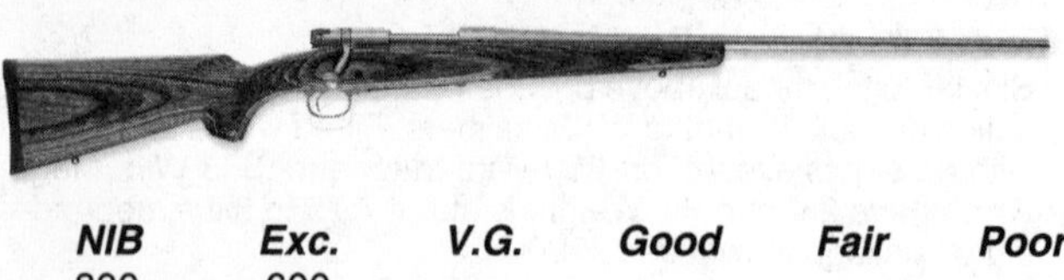

NIB	Exc.	V.G.	Good	Fair	Poor
800	600	—	—	—	—

Classic Camo Stainless

This model features a Sporter-style stock with 24" or 26" barrel and Mossy Oak Treestand camo on the stock. Chambered for .270 Win., .30-06, 7mm Rem. Mag., and .300 Win Mag. Magazine capacity is 5 rounds. Weight is about 7.5 lbs. Introduced in 1998.

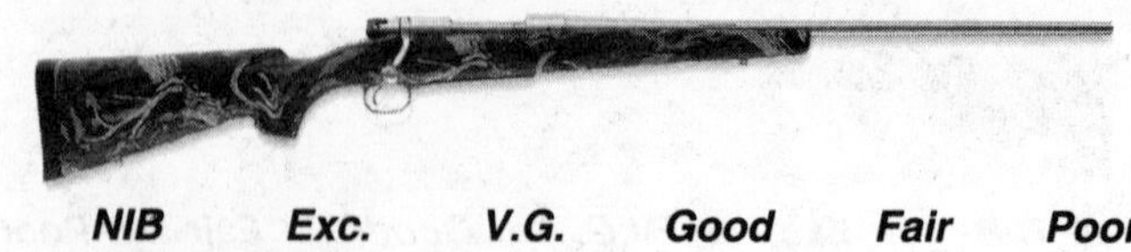

NIB	Exc.	V.G.	Good	Fair	Poor
725	550	—	—	—	—

Model 70 SM

This rifle features a synthetic stock with black matte finish. Barrel length is 24". Available in 10 calibers from .223 Rem. to .375 H&H Mag. Depending on caliber, rifle weighs between 7 and 8 lbs. Currently in production.

NIB	Exc.	V.G.	Good	Fair	Poor
525	400	300	200	150	100

Model 70 DBM-S

Similar to Model 70 SM but fitted with detachable box magazine. The metal parts are blued and the stock is synthetic. Offered in eight calibers from .223 Rem. to .338 Win. Mag. Furnished with scope bases and rings are open sights. Rifle weighs about 7.25 lbs., depending on caliber. Introduced in 1993.

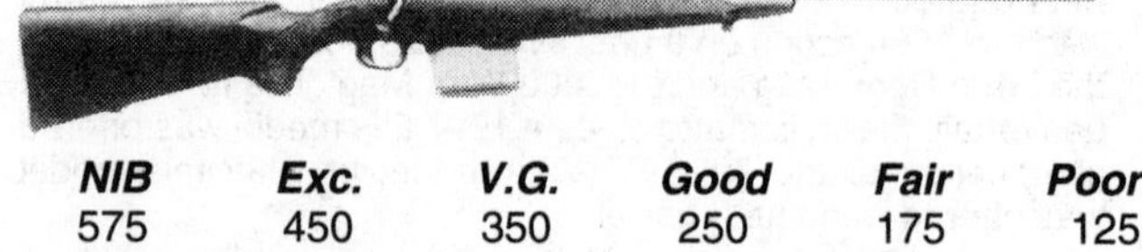

NIB	Exc.	V.G.	Good	Fair	Poor
575	450	350	250	175	125

Model 70 Varmint

Similar to the Model 70 Heavy Varmint but furnished with a traditional walnut stock and 26" medium-heavy barrel. Offered in .223 Rem., .22-250, .243, and .308. Weighs 9 lbs.

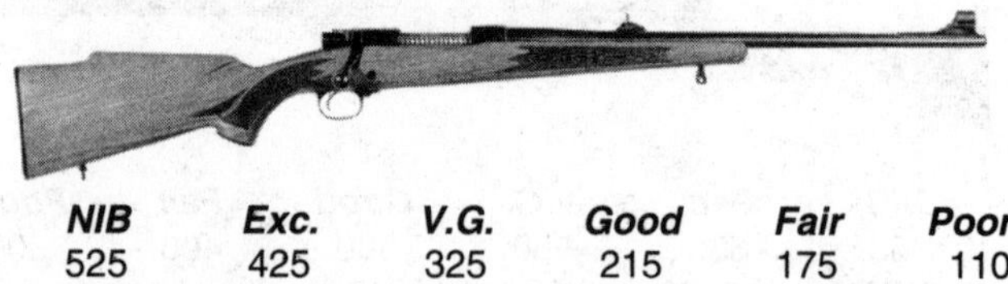

NIB	Exc.	V.G.	Good	Fair	Poor
525	425	325	215	175	110

Model 70 DBM

DBM stands for detachable box magazine. Fitted with a straight-comb walnut stock. Jeweled bolt with blued receiver. Shipped with scope bases and rings or open sights. Rifle offered in eight calibers from .223 Rem. to .300 Win. Mag. Rifle weighs about 7.35 lbs., depending on caliber. Introduced in 1993.

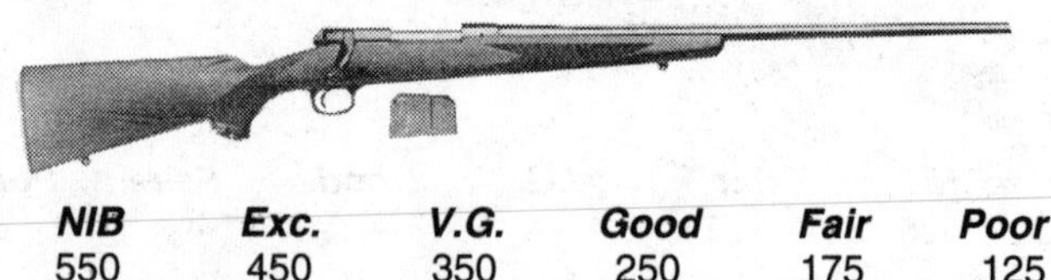

NIB	Exc.	V.G.	Good	Fair	Poor
550	450	350	250	175	125

Model 70 Sporter

U.S.R.A.'s basic Model 70 offering. Straight-comb walnut stock with checkering, jeweled bolt and blued receiver and barrel are standard. Available in 12 calibers from .223 Rem. to .338 Win. Mag. including .270 Weatherby Mag. and .300 Weatherby Mag. Barrel length is 24" and is available with either scope bases and rings or open sights. Rifle weighs about 7.5 lbs.

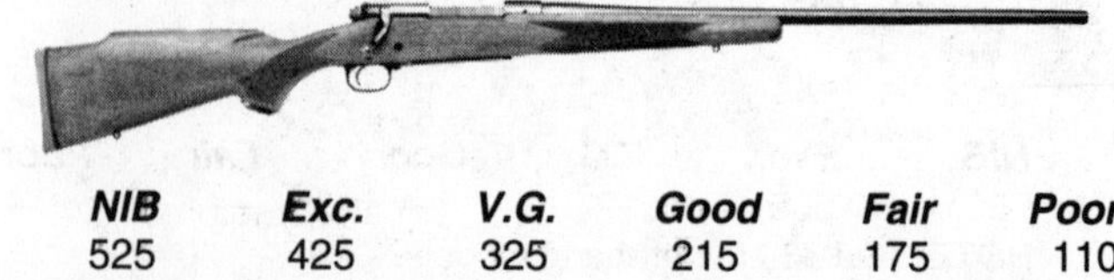

NIB	Exc.	V.G.	Good	Fair	Poor
525	425	325	215	175	110

Model 70 WinTuff

Similar to the Sporter except fitted with a laminated hardwood straight-comb stock with cheekpiece. Offered in 24" barrel lengths with a choice of 6 calibers from .270 Win. to .338 Win. Mag. Furnished with scope bases and rings. Rifle weighs about 7.65 lbs., depending on caliber.

NIB	Exc.	V.G.	Good	Fair	Poor
525	425	325	215	175	110

Model 70 Lightweight

Similar to the Model 70 Winlight. Offered with straight-comb checkered walnut stock with knurled bolt and blued receiver and barrel. The barrel is 22" without sights. Offered in 5 calibers: .223, .243, .270, .308, and .30-06. Rifle weighs about 7 lbs., depending on caliber.

NIB	Exc.	V.G.	Good	Fair	Poor
475	375	325	215	165	110

Model 70 Black Shadow

Chambered for the .270, .30-06, 7mm Rem. Mag., and .300 Win. Mag. and fitted with a 22" or 24" barrel, depending on caliber. Finish is matte black with composite stock. Push-feed action. Weight is 7.25 lbs. Introduced in 1998.

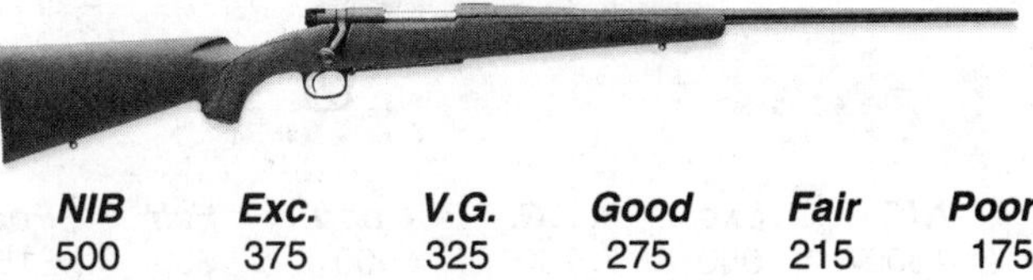

NIB	Exc.	V.G.	Good	Fair	Poor
500	375	325	275	215	175

Model 70 Ultimate Shadow

Introduced in 2003 this bolt-action model features a new black synthetic stock design with improved gripping surfaces and soft recoil pad. This model has a blued action and barrel. Chambered for the .300 WSM, .270 WSM, or the 7mm WSM cartridges. Fitted with a 24" barrel. Weight is about 6.75 lbs. Also offered with stainless action and barrel.

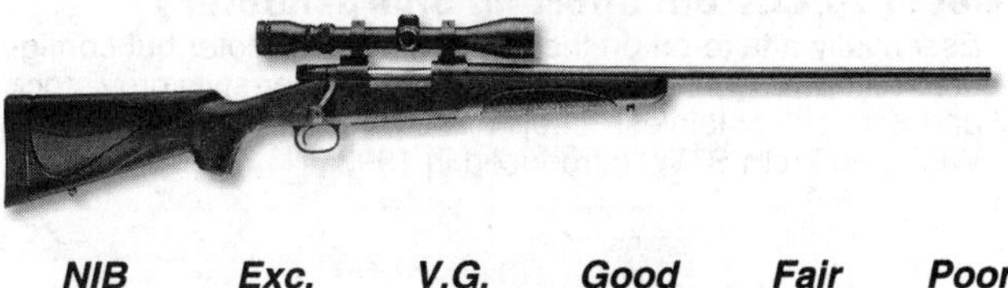

NIB	Exc.	V.G.	Good	Fair	Poor
850	675	525	—	—	—

NOTE: For stainless steel model add $45.

Model 70 Ultimate Shadow Camo

As above but with Mossy Oak New Break-Up camo. Introduced in 2004.

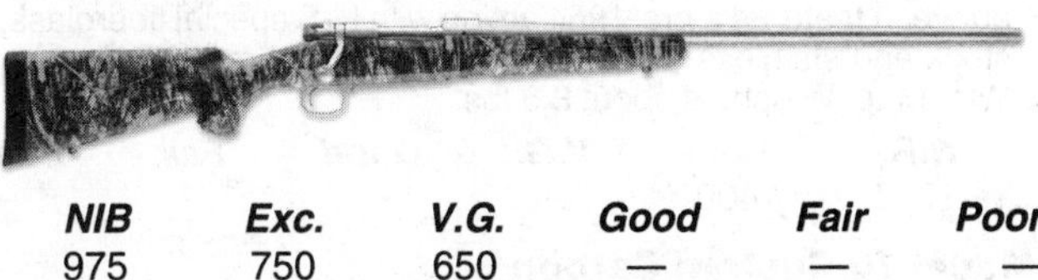

NIB	Exc.	V.G.	Good	Fair	Poor
975	750	650	—	—	—

Model 70 Super Shadow Super Short

Similar to the above model but chambered for the .223 WSM or .243 WSM cartridge. Fitted with a 22" barrel and blind magazine. Weight is about 6 lbs. Introduced in 2003.

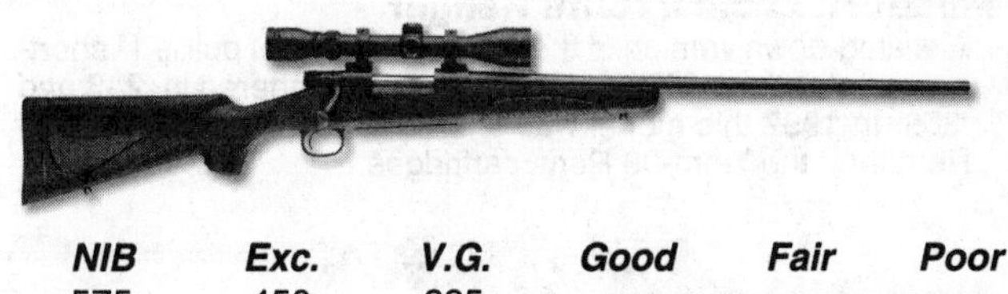

NIB	Exc.	V.G.	Good	Fair	Poor
575	450	335	—	—	—

Model 70 Super Shadow

Similar to the Ultimate Shadow but fitted with a controlled round push feed bolt. Chambered for the .300 WSM, .270 WSM, or the 7mm WSM cartridge. Fitted with a 22" barrel, composite stock and blind magaziine. Weight is about 6.75 lbs. Introduced in 2003. New calibers: .243, .308, .270, .30-06, .300WM.

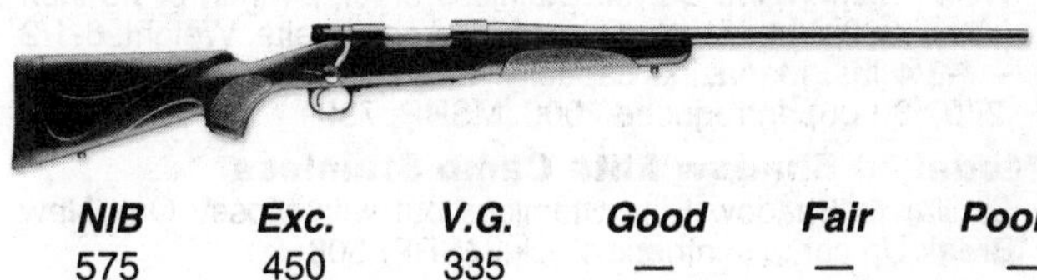

NIB	Exc.	V.G.	Good	Fair	Poor
575	450	335	—	—	—

Model 70 Stealth

This is a varmint model with 26" heavy barrel chambered for .223 Rem., .22-250, or .308 Win. It has a push-feed bolt-action. Black synthetic stock. Matte black finish. Weight is approximately 10.85 lbs. In 2004 the .223 WSSM, .243 WSSM and the .25 WSSM calibers were added.

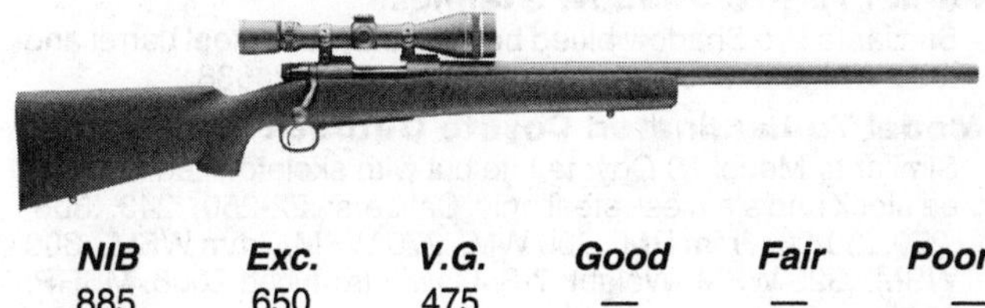

NIB	Exc.	V.G.	Good	Fair	Poor
885	650	475	—	—	—

Model 70 Coyote

This model, introduced in 2000, has a push-feed bolt-action and is chambered for the .223 Rem, .22-250, and .243 Win. calibers. Fitted with a medium-heavy 24" stainless steel barrel with laminated stock and large forend. Weight is about 9 lbs. In 2002 the rifle was offered in .270 WSM, 7mm WSM, and .300 WSM. In 2005 the .325 WSM was added to this model. Discontinued 2006.

NIB	Exc.	V.G.	Good	Fair	Poor
725	500	—	—	—	—

Model 70 Coyote Lite

Introduced in 2005 this model features a lightweight composite stock with skeletonized aluminum block bedding. Recoil pad. Fluted 24" medium-heavy barrel with no sights. Offered in .223 Rem and all WSSM and WSM calibers. New calibers: .22-250, .243, .308.

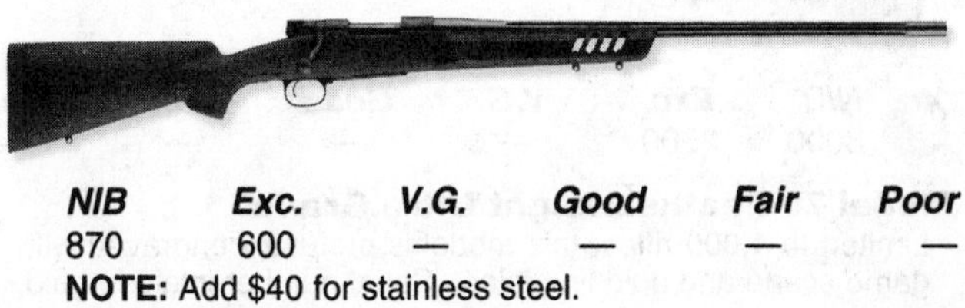

NIB	Exc.	V.G.	Good	Fair	Poor
870	600	—	—	—	—

NOTE: Add $40 for stainless steel.

Model 70 Ladies/Youth Ranger

A scaled-down version of the Ranger. Length of pull is 1" shorter than standard. Rifle weighs 6.5 lbs. Chambered in .243 and .308. In 1997 this model was offered chambered for the .223 Rem. and the 7mm-08 Rem. cartridges.

NIB	Exc.	V.G.	Good	Fair	Poor
450	350	300	200	150	100

Model 70 Shadow Elite Stainless

Bolt-action rifle. Calibers: .22-250, .243, .308, .270, .30-06, .300 WM, .338 WM, .375 H&H, .270 WSM, 7mm WSM, .300 WSM, .325 WSM. Barrel: Stainless steel, 24-inch or 26-inch (.300, .338 WM). Stock: Overmolded composite. Weight: 6-1/2 – 7-3/4 lbs. Magazine capacity: 3 or 5 (.22-250, .243, .308, .270, .30-06). Introduced 2006. MSRP: 739

Model 70 Shadow Elite Camo Stainless

Similar to Shadow Elite Stainless but with Mossy Oak New Break Up camo synthetic stock. MSRP: 808

Model 70 Pro Shadow Blued

Bolt-action rifle. Calibers: .22-250, .243, .308, .270, .30-06, 7mm RM, .300 WM, .270 WSM, 7mm WSM, .300 WSM, .325 WSM. Barrel: Blued steel, 22-inch (standard) or 24-inch (magnum). Stock: Overmolded composite. Weight: 6-1/2 – 7 lbs. Magazine capacity: 3 (magnum) or 5 (standard). Introduced 2006. MSRP: 594

Model 70 Pro Shadow Stainless

Similar to Pro Shadow blued but with stainless steel barrel and .338 WM and .375 H&H chamberings. MSRP: 638

Model 70 Laminated Coyote Outback Stainless

Similar to Model 70 Coyote Lite but with skeletonized laminated stock and stainless steel only. Calibers: .22-250, .243, .308, .270, .30-06, 7mm RM, .300 WM, .270 WSM, 7mm WSM, .300 WSM, .325 WSM. Weight: 7-3/4 lbs. Introduced 2006. MSRP: 1016

Model 70 Laminated Coyote Gray or Brown Stainless

Similar to Model 70 Laminated Coyote Outback but with non-fluted barrel and choice of brown or gray laminated stock. MSRP: 689

WINCHESTER CUSTOM GUN SHOP

NOTE: There a number of special order options offered by the Custom shop that will greatly affect price, such as special-order engraving, stock carving, wood, sights, etc. It is strongly suggested that an independent appraisial be secured prior to a sale.

Model 94 Custom Limited Edition New Generation

This lever-action rifle is stocked with fancy checkered walnut with pistol grip and long nose forend. Custom engraved with gold inlaid moose on right side and gold inlaid buck and doe on the left side. Fitted with tang safety. Barrel is 20" and chambered for the .30-30 cartridge. Introduced in 2003. Weight is about 6.25 lbs.

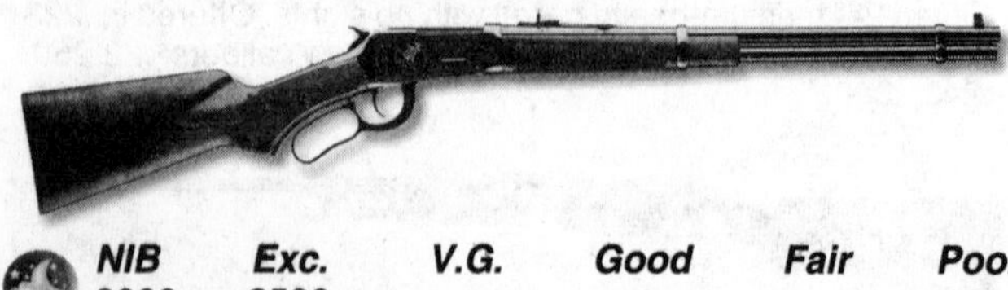

NIB	Exc.	V.G.	Good	Fair	Poor
3000	2500	—	—	—	—

Model 70 Featherweight Ultra Grade

Limited to 1,000 rifles, this model is profusely engraved with game scene and gold line inlaid. Serial number inlaid in gold. Offered in .270 caliber with very fine-figured walnut stock with fine line checkering. Mahogany fitted case. Strongly suggest a qualified appraisal before sale.

NIB	Exc.	V.G.	Good	Fair	Poor
5000	—	—	—	—	—

Model 70 Custom Featherweight

Introduced in 2003 this rifle is chambered for the .270, 7mm Win. Mag., or the .30-06. Fitted with a 22" barrel. Semi-fancy walnut stock with schnabel forend. Offered in blued or stainless steel finish in either right- or left-hand models. Weight is about 7.25 lbs.

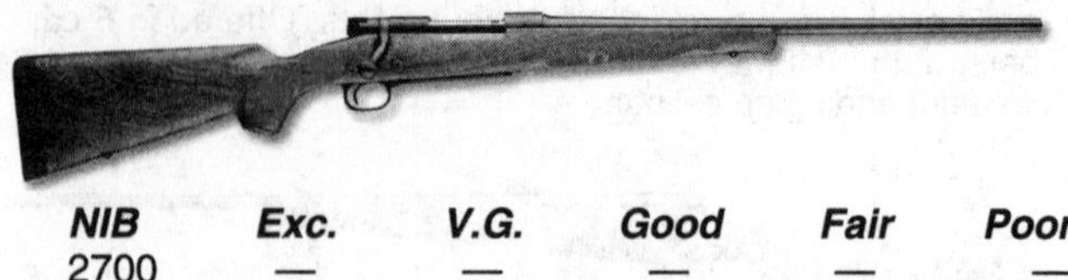

NIB	Exc.	V.G.	Good	Fair	Poor
2700	—	—	—	—	—

Model 70 Custom Sharpshooter

A U.S.R.A. Custom Shop gun. This model is fitted with a stainless steel Schneider barrel with hand-honed action and hand fitted. The stock is a custom McMillan A-2 glass bedded stock. Offered in .223 Rem., .22-250 Rem., .308 Win. and .300 Win. Mag. Comes from the factory with a hard case. Currently in production.

NIB	Exc.	V.G.	Good	Fair	Poor
1300	950	750	500	300	150

Model 70 Custom Classic Sharpshooter II

Same as above but introduced in 1996 with an H-S heavy target stock, a pre-1964 action stainless steel H-S barrel. Weight is about 11 lbs. Offered in .22-250, .308, .30-06, and .300 Win. Mag.

NIB	Exc.	V.G.	Good	Fair	Poor
1800	1400	—	—	—	—

Model 70 Custom Sporting Sharpshooter

Essentially a take-off on the Custom Sharpshooter but configured for hunting. Fitted with a McMillan sporter-style gray stock and Schneider stainless steel barrel. Offered in .270 Win., .300 Win., and 7mm STW. Introduced in 1993.

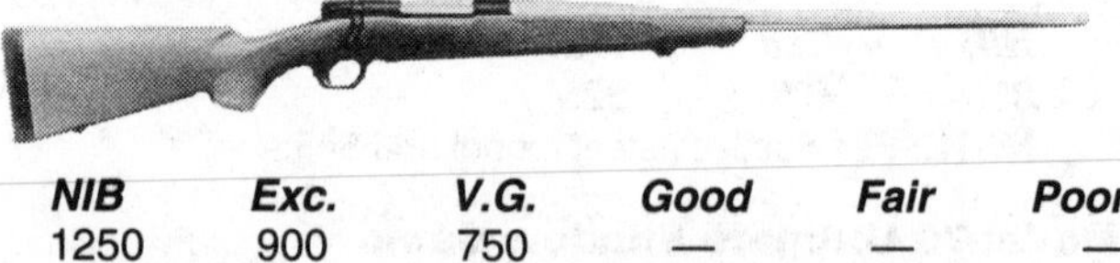

NIB	Exc.	V.G.	Good	Fair	Poor
1250	900	750	—	—	—

Model 70 Custom Classic Sporting Sharpshooter II

Introduced in 1996 this is an updated version of the model above. It features a pre-1964 action with H-S special fiberglass stock and stainless steel barrel. Available in 7mm STW, .300 Win. Mag. Weight is about 8.5 lbs.

NIB	Exc.	V.G.	Good	Fair	Poor
1700	1400	—	—	—	—

Model 70 Custom Carbon

This rifle features a stainless steel action with Shilen barrel wrapped in graphite epoxy. Fitted with a black composite stock. Chambered for the .270 WSM, 7mm WSM, .300 WSM, .25-06 Rem., or the .338 Win. Mag. cartridge. Fitted with a 24" barrel on all calibers but the .338 (26"). Weight is about 6.5 lbs.

This symbol denotes "Sleepers" with rapidly-rising values and/or significant collector potential.

on the WSM calibers and 7 lbs. of the others. Magazine capacity is three rounds. Introduced in 2003.

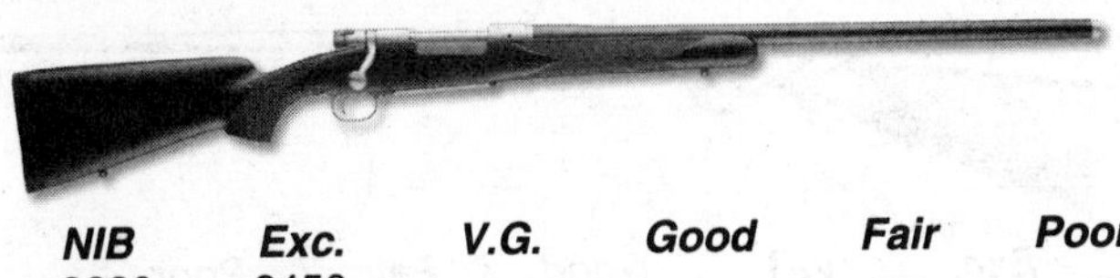

NIB	Exc.	V.G.	Good	Fair	Poor
3230	2450	—	—	—	—

Model 70 Custom Grade

This custom built Model 70 is hand finished, polished, and fitted in the Custom Shop. Internal parts are hand honed while the barrel is lead lapped. The customer can order individual items to his or her own taste, including engraving, special stock dimensions and carvings, etc. Each Custom Grade Model 70 should be priced on an individual basis.

Model 70 Custom Express

Also built in the Custom Shop this model features figured walnut, hand-honed internal parts, bolt and follower are engine turned. A special 3-leaf rear sight is furnished also. Offered in .375 H&H Mag., .375 JRS, .416 Rem. Mag., .458 Win. Mag., and .470 Capstick.

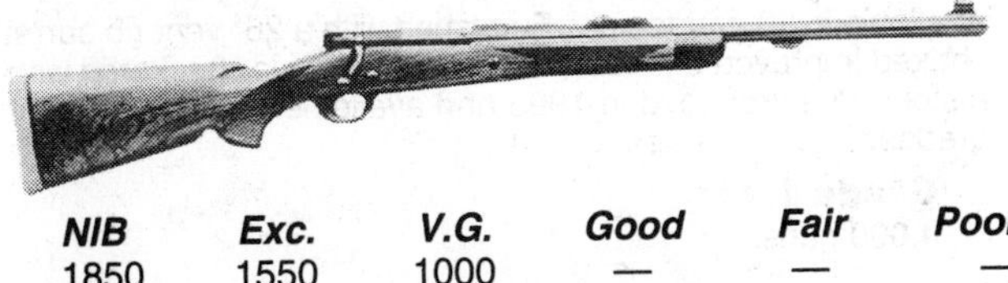

NIB	Exc.	V.G.	Good	Fair	Poor
1850	1550	1000	—	—	—

Model 70 Custom African Express

Introduced in 1999 this model is chambered for the .340 Wby., .358 STA, .375 H&H, .416 Rem. Mag., and the .458 Win. Mag. Fitted with a 24" barrel and a magazine capacity of 4 rounds. Express sights. Weight is about 9.75 lbs. Ebony pistol grip cap, and select walnut stock.

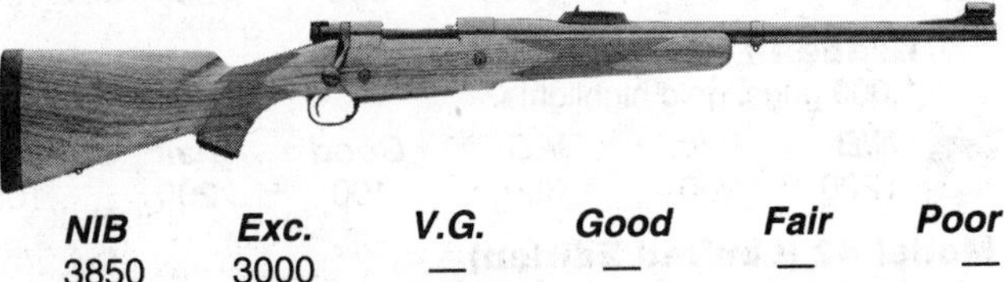

NIB	Exc.	V.G.	Good	Fair	Poor
3850	3000	—	—	—	—

Model 70 Custom Safari Express

This model has a figured walnut stock with the bolt and follower engine turned. Express sights. Chambered in .340 Wby., .358 STA, .375 H&H, .416 Rem. Mag., and .458 Win. Mag. Barrel length is 24". Weight is about 9.5 lbs. Introduced in 1999.

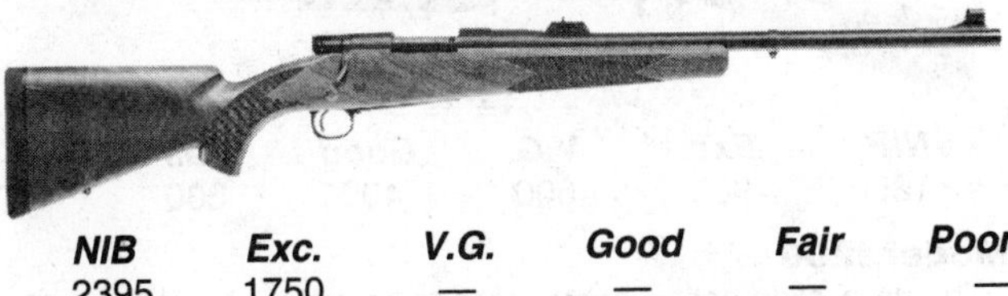

NIB	Exc.	V.G.	Good	Fair	Poor
2395	1750	—	—	—	—

Model 70 Custom "Ultra Light" Mannlicher

This model features a full-length stock of figured walnut with smooth tapered barrel and blued action. Chambered for .260 Rem., .308 Win., and 7mm-08. Fitted with a 19" barrel with optional open sights. Weight is about 6.75 lbs. Introduced in 1999.

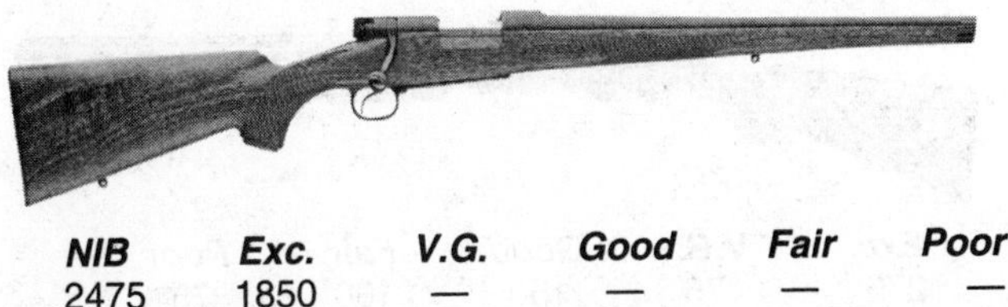

NIB	Exc.	V.G.	Good	Fair	Poor
2475	1850	—	—	—	—

Model 70 Ultimate Classic

This model features a number of special options as standard. Included is a pre-1964 action, choice of round, round fluted, 1/2 octagon 1/2 round barrel, full tapered octagon barrel, blued or stainless steel barrel actions, fancy American walnut stock, special Custom Shop serial numbers and proof stamp, inletted swivel bases, red recoil pad, fine cut checkering, and a hard case. Offered in a wide variety of calibers from .25-06 to .338 Win. Mag. Weight is about 7.5 to 7.75 lbs. depending on caliber. Also available in stainless steel.

NIB	Exc.	V.G.	Good	Fair	Poor
2450	1950	1500	—	—	—

NOTE: In 1997 this model was introduced in a left-hand version.

Model 70 Custom Take Down

Introduced in 1998 this composite stock rifle has a special take down feature. Chambered for .375 H&H, .416 Rem. Mag., .300 Win Mag., 7mm STW. Magazine capacity is 3 rounds. Barrel length is 26". Weight is between 8.5 and 9 lbs. Offered in fluted barrel in .300 Win. Mag. and 7mm STW.

NIB	Exc.	V.G.	Good	Fair	Poor
3300	2500	—	—	—	—

Model 70 Custom Short Action

This custom shop model is fitted with a 22" match-grade barrel Controlled feed. Chambered for short-action calibers from .243 to .358. Semi-fancy walnut stock. Hand-cut checkering. Supplied with hard case. Weight is about 7.5 lbs. Introduced in 2000. In 2003 this model was offered in a left-hand version.

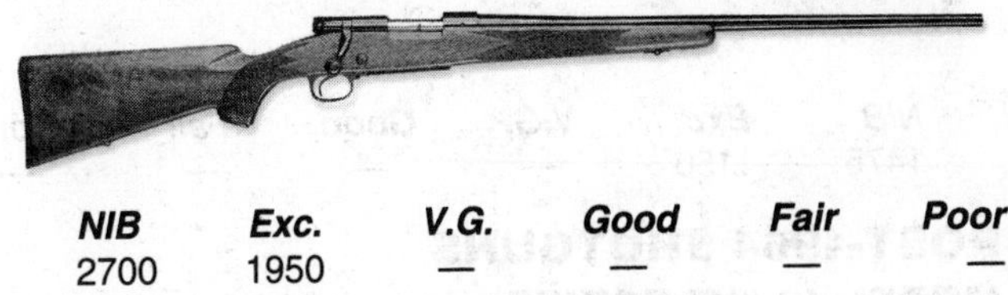

NIB	Exc.	V.G.	Good	Fair	Poor
2700	1950	—	—	—	—

Model 70 Custom Extreme Weather

This custom shop model is fitted with a round or fluted 24" match-grade barrel. Both barrel and action are stainless steel. McMillan fiberglass stock with cheekpiece. Chambered in calibers from .25-06 to .338 Win. Mag. Weight is about 7.5 lbs. Introduced in 2000. Lightweight Extreme Weather II model introduced 2006 (6-1/4 – 7 lbs.). MSRP: 2800.

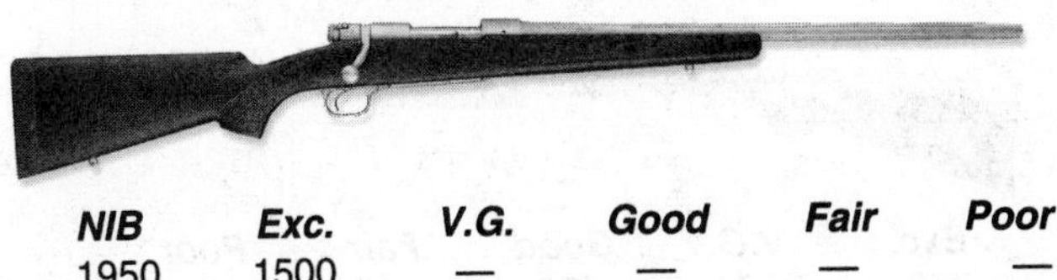

NIB	Exc.	V.G.	Good	Fair	Poor
1950	1500	—	—	—	—

Model 70 Custom 100th Anniversary .30-06

Semi-fancy walnut Featherweight stock with single steel cross-bolt, one-piece engraved floorplate, high-lustre blued and engraved 22-inch barrel. Commemorates centennial of .30-06 cartridge. Introduced 2006; only 100 manufactured. MSRP: 2660

Model 70 Custom Special "70 Years of the Model 70"

Calibers: .270, .30-06 Springfield, .300 WM. Barrel: 24-inch or 26-inch (.300 WM) blued sightless. Engraved floorplate and barrel. Stock: semi-fancy checkered walnut. Introduced 2006, only 70 manufactured per caliber. MSRP: 2800

Model 70 Custom Maple

Calibers: .284, .270, .308, .30-06. Barrel: 24-inch blued. Weight: 7-3/4 lbs. Stocked in fiddleback maple with pre-'64 pattern checkering. Quantities "very limited." Introduced 2006. MSRP: 4355

Model 70 Custom Continental Hunter

Calibers: .284, .270, .308, .30-06. Barrel: 22-inch blued or stainless Krieger. Stock: glossy claro walnut, round knob pistol grip, schnabel forend. MSRP: 5226

Model 70 Custom Stainless Laminate

Calibers: .270 WSM, 7mm WSM, .300 WSM, .325 WSM. Barrel: 24-inch stainless sporter. Stock: black/gray or brown Featherweight laminated with Schnabel and Pachmayr pad. MSRP: 2332

Model 94 Custom Limited Edition

This is essentially a special order Model 94 with choice of engraving and stock carving. Chambered for the .44-40 and fitted with a 24" octagonal barrel. Fancy walnut stock. Limited to 75 rifles. Weight is about 7.75 lbs. Suggest an appraisal prior to a sale.

NIB	Exc.	V.G.	Good	Fair	Poor
2250	1750	—	—	—	—

Model 9410 Custom

Introduced in 2005 this .410 shotgun is fitted with a 24" round barrel and full length magazine. Case colored receiver with semi-fancy checkered walnut stock. Weight is about 7 lbs.

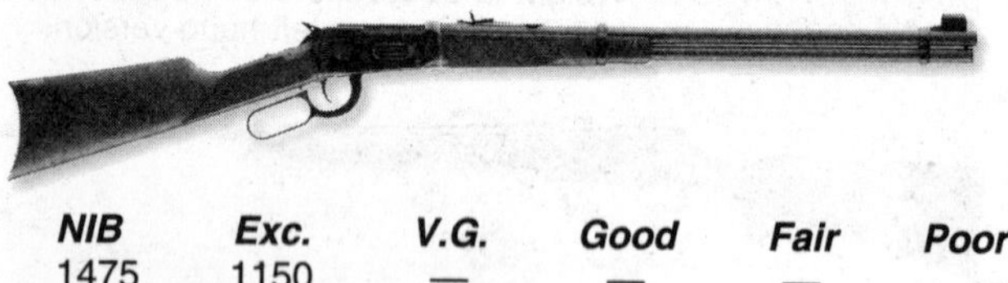

NIB	Exc.	V.G.	Good	Fair	Poor
1475	1150	—	—	—	—

POST-1964 SHOTGUNS

MODEL 12 "Y" SERIES

Model 12 Field Grade

This is a later version of the slide-action Model 12, chambered for 12 gauge only. It was offered with a 26", 28", or 30" vent rib barrel with various chokes. The finish is blued with a jeweled bolt and a hand-checkered, select walnut stock. This version is easily recognizable as it has the letter Y serial number prefix. It was manufactured between 1972 and 1976.

Exc.	V.G.	Good	Fair	Poor
710	600	450	385	300

Model 12 Super Pigeon Grade

This is a deluxe version that features extensive engraving and fancy checkering. It was offered with a turned action and select, fancy-grade walnut. It was a limited-production item produced between 1964 and 1972. It was briefly reintroduced in 1984 and discontinued again in 1985.

Exc.	V.G.	Good	Fair	Poor
2500	2000	1850	1400	950

Model 12 Skeet

This version is similar to the Field Grade but is offered with a 26", vent rib, skeet-bored barrel. The finish is blued, with a skeet-type stock and recoil pad. It was manufactured between 1972 and 1975.

Exc.	V.G.	Good	Fair	Poor
750	650	550	350	300

Model 12 Trap Grade

This version features a 30" vent rib barrel with a Full choke. It is blued with a trap-type, standard, or Monte Carlo stock with a recoil pad. It was manufactured between 1972 and 1980.

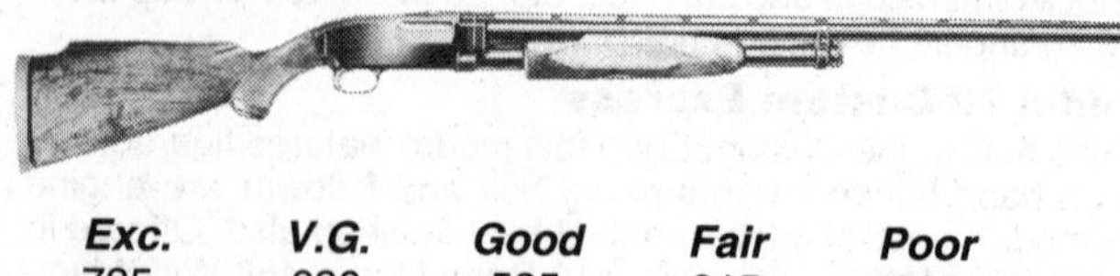

Exc.	V.G.	Good	Fair	Poor
735	630	525	315	215

Model 12 (Limited Edition)

Available in 20 gauge only. Furnished with a 26" vent rib barrel choked Improved Cylinder. The walnut stock is checkered with pistol grip. Introduced in 1993 and available in three different grades.

Grade 1

4,000 guns.

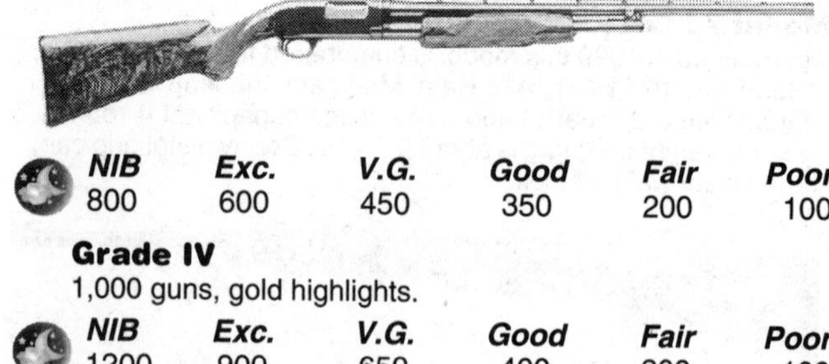

NIB	Exc.	V.G.	Good	Fair	Poor
800	600	450	350	200	100

Grade IV

1,000 guns, gold highlights.

NIB	Exc.	V.G.	Good	Fair	Poor
1200	900	650	400	200	100

Model 42 (Limited Edition)

A reproduction of the famous Winchester Model 42 .410 bore slide-action shotgun. Furnished with a 26" ventilated rib barrel choked Full. The receiver is engraved with gold border. Introduced in 1993 and limited to 850 guns.

NIB	Exc.	V.G.	Good	Fair	Poor
1250	900	600	400	300	150

Model 1200

This is a slide-action shotgun chambered for 12, 16, or 20 gauge. It was offered with a 26", 28", or 30", vent rib barrel with various chokes. It has an alloy receiver and is blued, with a checkered walnut stock and recoil pad. It was manufactured between 1964 and 1981. This model was offered with the plastic Hydrocoil stock, and this would add approximately 35 percent to the values given.

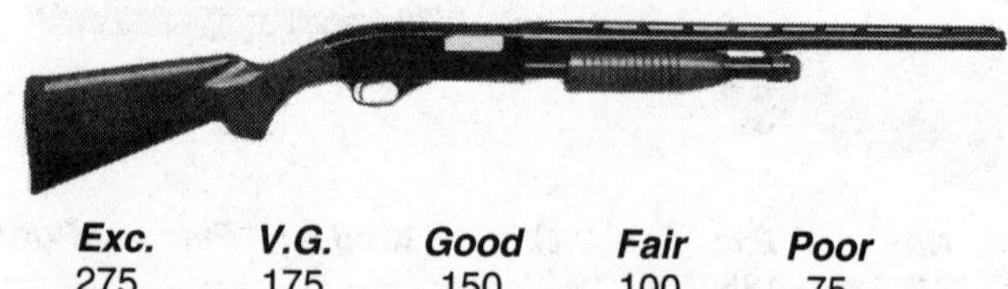

Exc.	V.G.	Good	Fair	Poor
275	175	150	100	75

 *This symbol denotes "Sleepers" with rapidly-rising values and/or significant collector potential.*

Ducks Unlimited Model

Available through Ducks Unlimited chapters. An independent appraisal is suggested.

MODEL 1300 SERIES

Discontinued in 2006.

Model 1300 XTR

This is the current slide-action shotgun offered by Winchester. It is chambered for 12 and 20 gauge with 3" chambers. It is a takedown gun that is offered with various-length vent rib barrels with screw-in choke tubes. It has an alloy frame and is blued with a walnut stock. It was introduced in 1978.

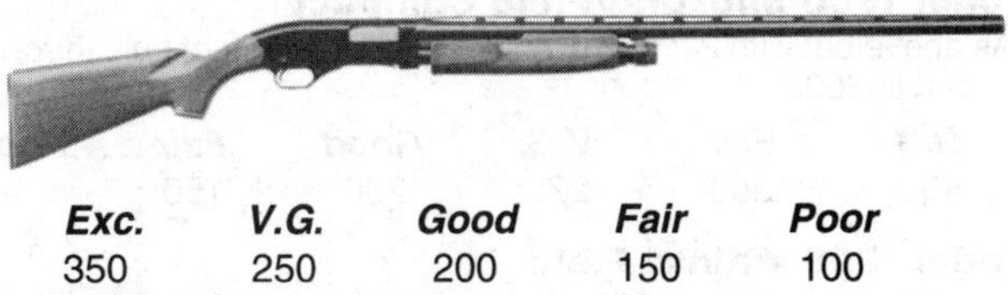

Exc.	V.G.	Good	Fair	Poor
350	250	200	150	100

Model 1300 Waterfowl

This version is chambered for 12 gauge, 3" only. It has a 30" vent rib barrel with screw-in choke tubes. It is matte-blued, with a satin-finished walnut stock and a recoil pad. It was introduced in 1984. A laminated WinTuff stock was made available in 1988 and would add $10 to the value.

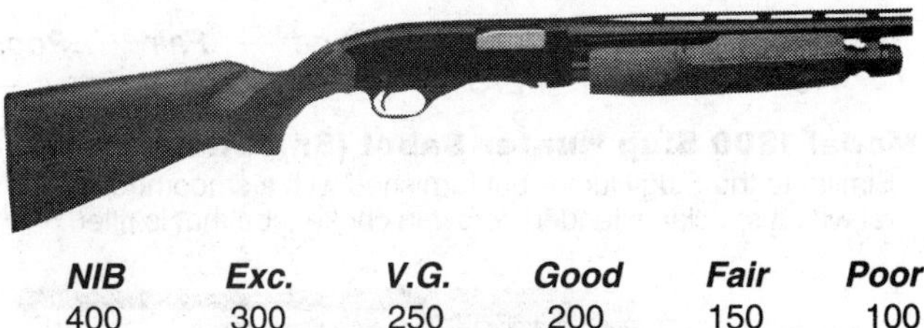

NIB	Exc.	V.G.	Good	Fair	Poor
400	300	250	200	150	100

Model 1300 New Shadow Grass

Introduced in 2004 this 12 gauge 3" gun is fitted with either a 26" or 28" vent rib barrel with choke tubes. Composite stock has New Shadow Grass camo pattern. Weight is about 7 lbs.

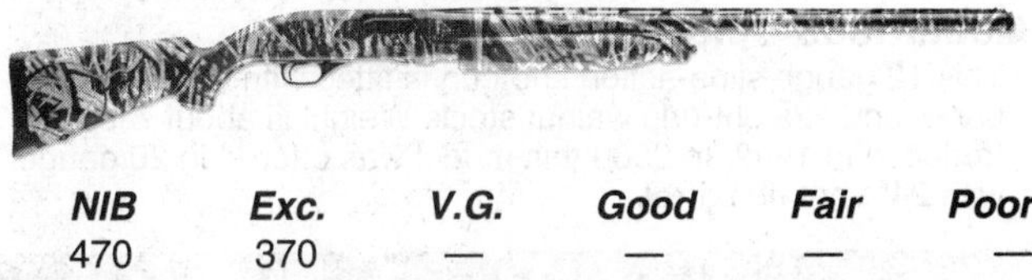

NIB	Exc.	V.G.	Good	Fair	Poor
470	370	—	—	—	—

Model 1300 WinCam Turkey Gun

This version is similar to the Model 1300 Turkey Gun, with a green, laminated hardwood stock. It was introduced in 1987. A WinTuff version is also available and would add $20 to the values given.

NIB	Exc.	V.G.	Good	Fair	Poor
425	325	250	200	150	125

Model 1300 Stainless Security

This version is chambered for 12 or 20 gauge and is constructed of stainless steel. It has an 18" cylinder-bore barrel and a 7- or 8-shot tubular magazine. It is available with a pistol-grip stock, which would add approximately 50 percent to the values given.

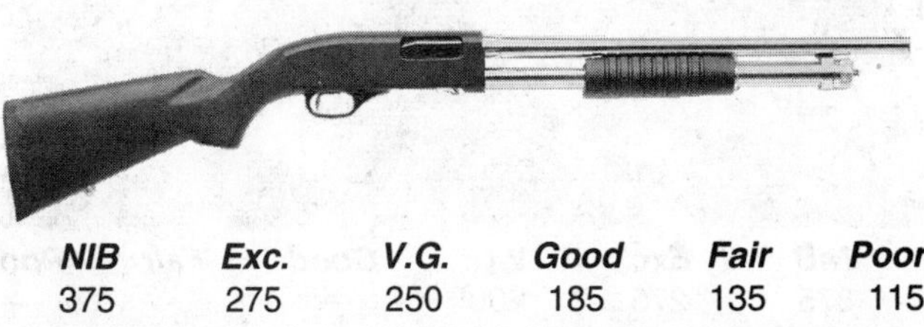

NIB	Exc.	V.G.	Good	Fair	Poor
375	275	250	185	135	115

Model 1300 Turkey

This slide-action model features a 22" vent rib barrel chambered for 3" 12 gauge shells. Supplied with choke tubes. Gun weighs 7.25 lbs.

NIB	Exc.	V.G.	Good	Fair	Poor
400	300	250	200	150	100

Model 1300 Realtree Turkey

Introduced in 1994, this model features a synthetic stock camouflaged with Realtree. The receiver and 22" barrel are matte finish.

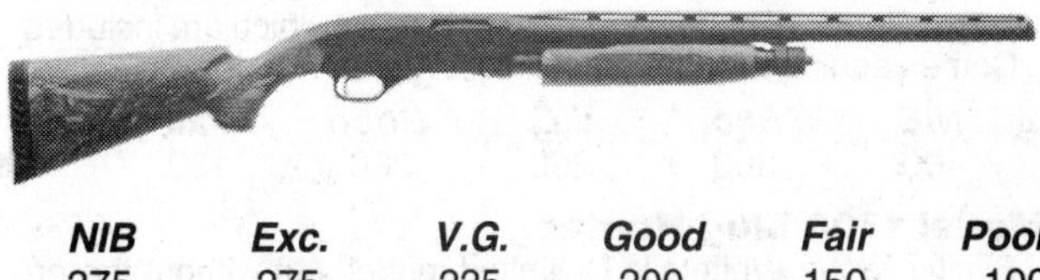

NIB	Exc.	V.G.	Good	Fair	Poor
375	275	225	200	150	100

Model 1300 Mossy Oak Break-Up Turkey

Same as above but with Mossy Oak Break-Up camo stock and gun. Introduced in 2000.

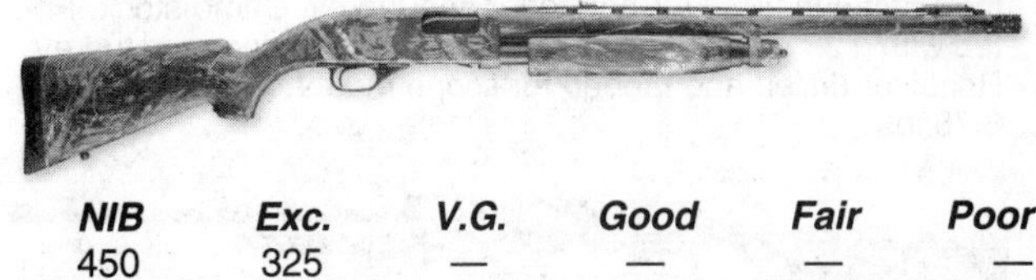

NIB	Exc.	V.G.	Good	Fair	Poor
450	325	—	—	—	—

Model 1300 Black Shadow Turkey

This model was also introduced in 1994 and features a black composite stock with a nonglare finish on the barrel, receiver, bolt, and magazine. Barrel has vent rib and is 22" in length.

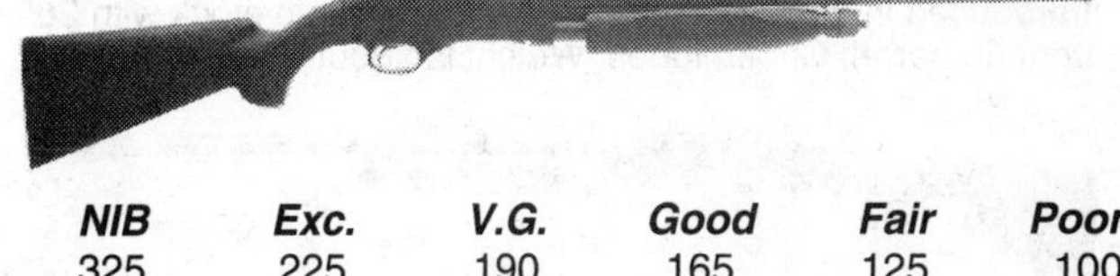

NIB	Exc.	V.G.	Good	Fair	Poor
325	225	190	165	125	100

Model 1300 National Wild Turkey Federation Series III

Engraved receiver, camo stock, open sights on a 22" plain barrel, and all metal and wood parts are nonglare. Comes with a quick detachable sling. Offered in 12 gauge only. Gun weighs 7.25 lbs.

NIB	Exc.	V.G.	Good	Fair	Poor
425	320	250	200	150	100

Model 1300 National Wild Turkey Federation Series IV

Introduced in 1993, this model is similar to the Series II with the addition of a 22" vent rib barrel. Stock is black laminated. Comes with quick detachable sling. Gun weight 7 lbs.

NIB	Exc.	V.G.	Good	Fair	Poor
400	320	250	200	150	100

Model 1300 NWTF Short Turkey

This 12 gauge gun is fitted with an 18" barrel with extended choke tubes. Fiber Optic sights. Mossy Oak camo stock. NWTF medallion on pistol grip cap. Weight is about 6.5 lbs. Introduced in 2005.

NIB	Exc.	V.G.	Good	Fair	Poor
505	375	—	—	—	—

Model 1300 Whitetails Unlimited Slug Hunter

This slide-action model features a full-length rifle barrel chambered for 3" 12 gauge shells. Barrel is choked Cylinder. Fitted with a checkered walnut stock with engraved receiver. Receiver is drilled and tapped for bases and rings, which are included. Comes equipped with camo sling. Weighs 7.25 lbs.

NIB	Exc.	V.G.	Good	Fair	Poor
400	300	250	200	150	100

Model 1300 Slug Hunter

Similar to the Whitetails Unlimited model, but without the engraved receiver.

NIB	Exc.	V.G.	Good	Fair	Poor
400	300	250	200	150	100

Model 1300 Buck and Tom

Introduced in 2002 for both deer and turkey. Camo stock. Fitted with a 22" barrel with choke tubes for both deer and turkey. Receiver drilled and tapped for scope mount. Weight is about 6.75 lbs.

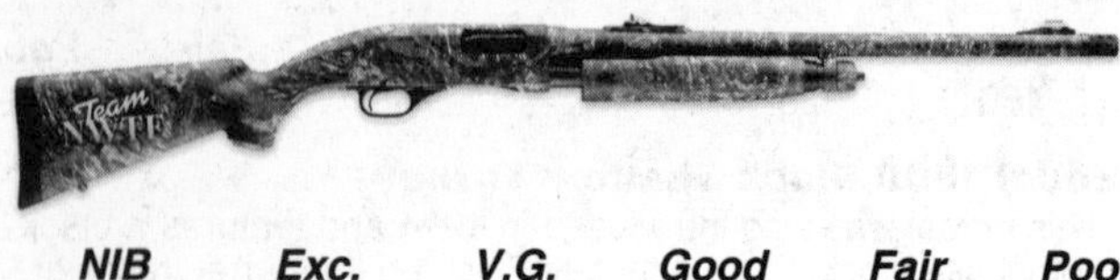

NIB	Exc.	V.G.	Good	Fair	Poor
525	400	—	—	—	—

Model 1300 Universal Hunter

Introduced in 2002, this model features a camo stock with 26" vent rib barrel. Choke tubes. Weight is about 7 lbs.

NIB	Exc.	V.G.	Good	Fair	Poor
550	425	—	—	—	—

Model 1300 Black Shadow Deer

Introduced in 1994, this 12 gauge Model 1300 features a black composite stock with nonglare finish on the bolt, barrel, receiver, and magazine. Barrel is 22" with ramp front sight and adjustable rear sight. In 2000 this model was offered with a rifled barrel for shooting sabot slugs.

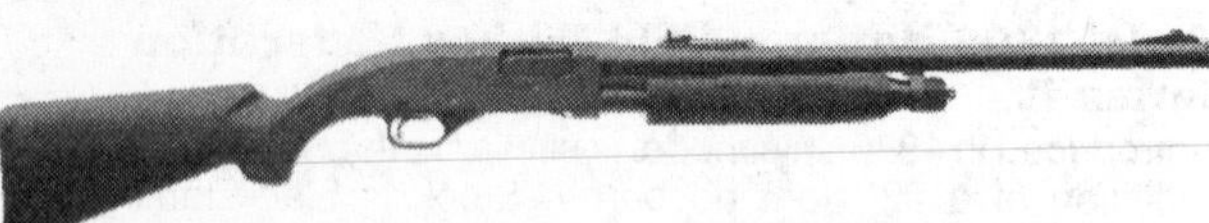

NIB	Exc.	V.G.	Good	Fair	Poor
350	250	175	150	125	100

NOTE: Add $25 for rifled barrel.

Model 1300 Black Shadow Field

Same as above but fitted with a 26" or 28" vent rib barrel chambered for 3" Mag. shells. Weight is about 7 lbs.

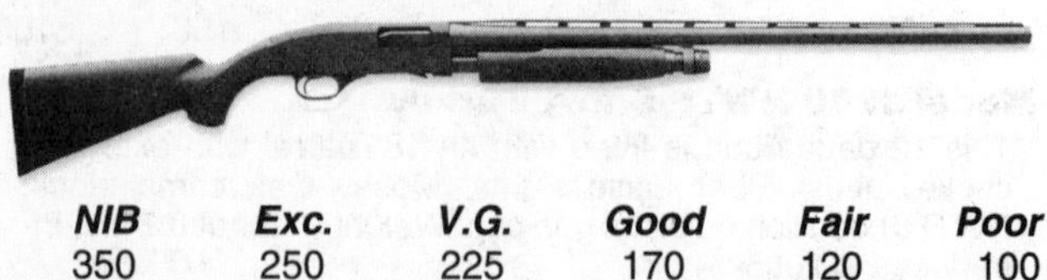

NIB	Exc.	V.G.	Good	Fair	Poor
350	250	225	170	120	100

Model 1300 Sporting/Field

This 12 gauge gun has a 28" vent rib barrel with five choke tubes. Checkered walnut stock. Black recoil pad. Weight is about 7.5 lbs. Introduced in 2002.

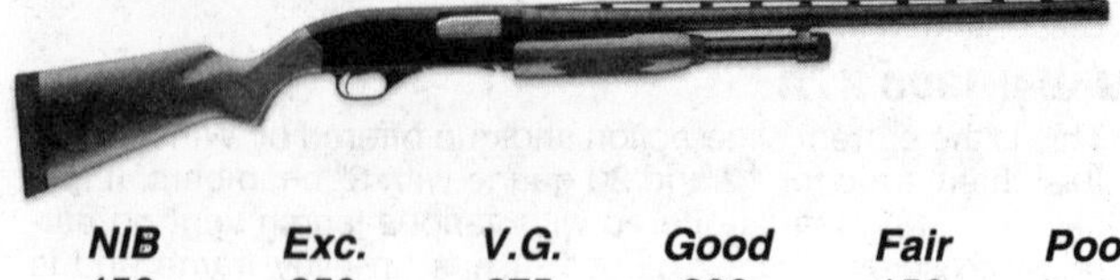

NIB	Exc.	V.G.	Good	Fair	Poor
450	350	275	200	150	—

Model 1300 Sporting/Field Compact

As above but with 24" barrel and 1" shorter length of pull. Introduced in 2002.

NIB	Exc.	V.G.	Good	Fair	Poor
450	350	275	200	150	—

Model 1300 Walnut Field

This 12 gauge 3" gun is fitted with either 26" or 28" vent rib barrels with choke tubes. Checkered walnut stock with recoil pad. Weight is about 7.25 lbs. Introduced in 2004.

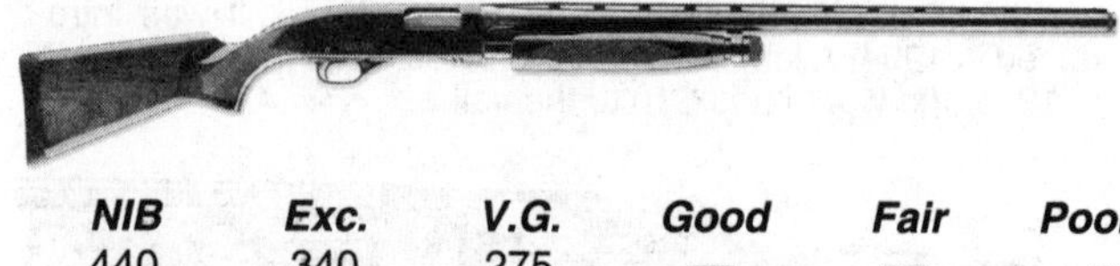

NIB	Exc.	V.G.	Good	Fair	Poor
440	340	275	—	—	—

Model 1300 Slug Hunter Sabot (Smoothbore)

Similar to the Slug Hunter but furnished with a smoothbore barrel with a special extended screw-in choke tube that is rifled.

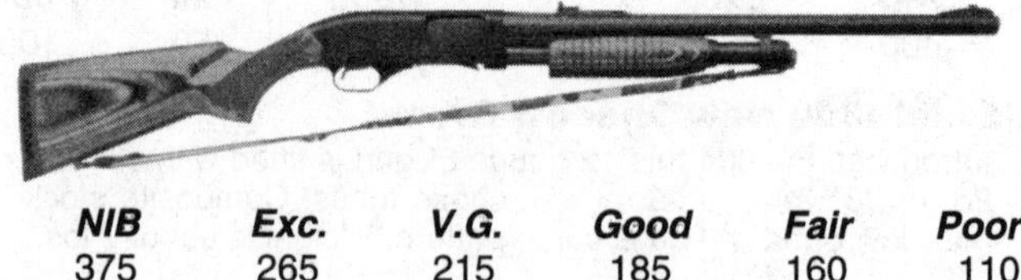

NIB	Exc.	V.G.	Good	Fair	Poor
375	265	215	185	160	110

Model 1300 Upland Special

This 12 gauge slide-action shotgun is fitted with a 24" vent rib barrel and straight-grip walnut stock. Weight is about 7 lbs. Introduced in 1999. In 2000 this model was offered in 20 gauge with 24" vent rib barrel.

NIB	Exc.	V.G.	Good	Fair	Poor
375	275	200	—	—	—

Model 1300 Upland Special Field

This model, introduced in 2004, features a choice of 12 or 20 gauge 3" guns with 24" vent rib barrel with choke tube. Checkered walnut stock with straight grip. Weight is about 6.75 lbs.

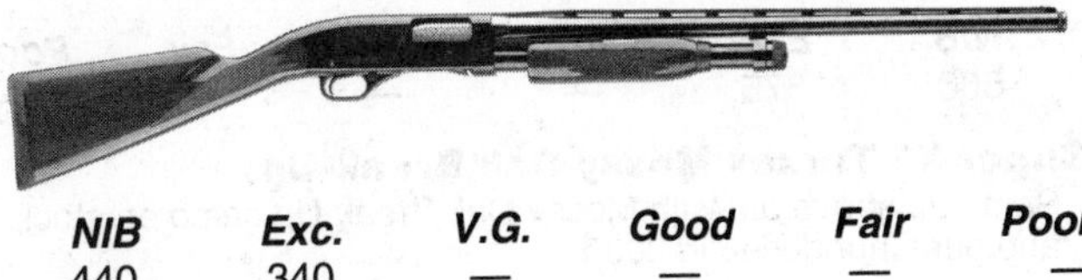

NIB	Exc.	V.G.	Good	Fair	Poor
440	340	—	—	—	—

Model 1300 Ranger

This slide-action shotgun is a lower-cost version of the Model 1300. Furnished with a hardwood stock and available in 12 or 20 gauge with 26" or 28" vent rib barrel. WinChokes are included.

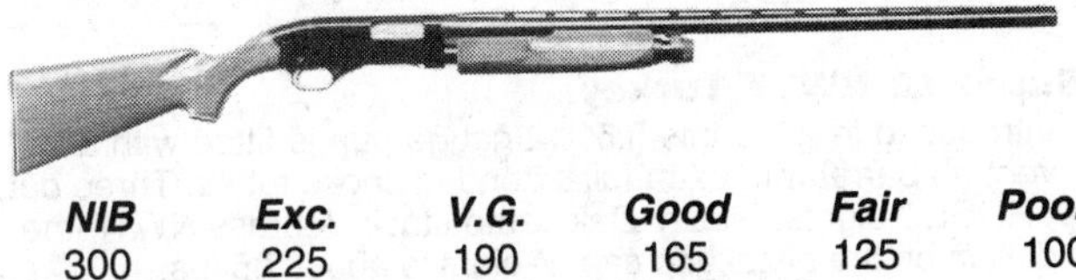

NIB	Exc.	V.G.	Good	Fair	Poor
300	225	190	165	125	100

Model 1300 Ranger Ladies/Youth-Compact

Available in 20 gauge only this model has a 1" shorter than standard length of pull and a 22" vent rib barrel. Choke tubes are included. Gun weighs 6.75 lbs.

NIB	Exc.	V.G.	Good	Fair	Poor
300	225	190	165	125	100

Model 1300 Ranger Deer Slug

Comes in two principal configurations: a 12 gauge 22" smooth barrel with Cylinder choke; and a 12 gauge 22" rifled barrel. Both are chambered for 3" shells and weigh 6.75 lbs.

NIB	Exc.	V.G.	Good	Fair	Poor
300	200	175	150	125	100

Model 1300 Ranger Deer Combo

The Model 1300 Ranger Deer Combos are available in three different configurations. One: 12 gauge 22" smooth barrel and 28" vent rib barrel with WinChokes. Two: 12 gauge 22" rifled barrel with 28" vent rib barrel with WinChokes. Three: 20 gauge 22" smooth barrel with 28" vent rib barrel with WinChokes.

12 Gauge Combo

NIB	Exc.	V.G.	Good	Fair	Poor
375	275	225	190	165	100

20 Gauge Combo

NIB	Exc.	V.G.	Good	Fair	Poor
375	275	225	190	165	100

Model 1300 Defender Combo

This personal defense slide-action shotgun features an 18" Cylinder choked barrel and a 28" vent rib barrel with modified WinChoke and an accessory pistol grip. A hardwood stock comes fitted to the gun.

NIB	Exc.	V.G.	Good	Fair	Poor
350	250	200	175	150	100

Model 1300 Defender 5-Shot

Same as above but furnished with a hardwood stock only and 18" barrel.

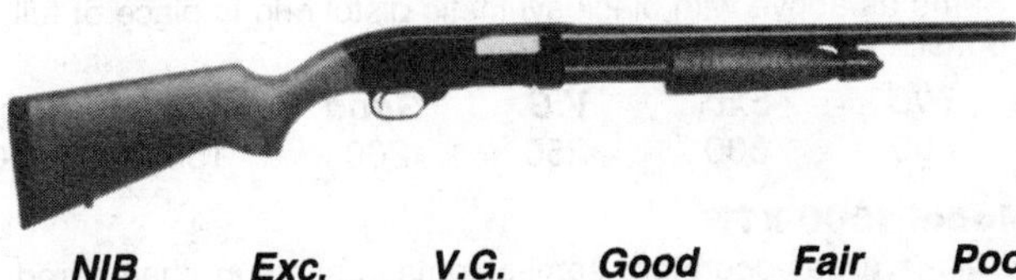

NIB	Exc.	V.G.	Good	Fair	Poor
300	200	175	150	125	100

Model 1300 Camp Defender

Introduced in 1999 this 12 gauge model features a 22" barrel and walnut stock. Magazine capacity is five rounds. Barrel fitted with rifle sights. Weight is about 7 lbs. Comes with Cylinder choke tube.

NIB	Exc.	V.G.	Good	Fair	Poor
350	275	—	—	—	—

Model 1300 Defender 8-Shot

Same as above but furnished with an 18" barrel with extended magazine tube.

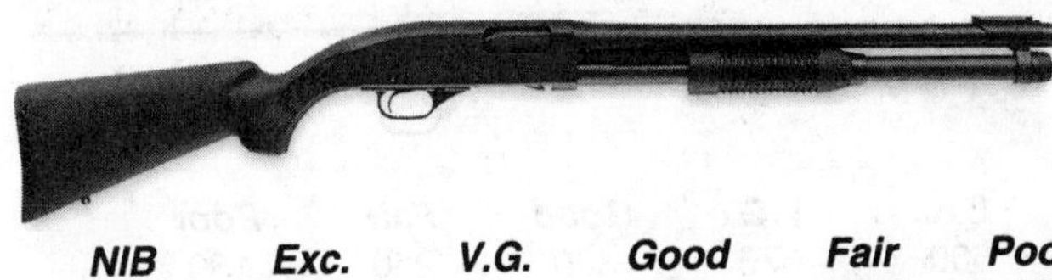

NIB	Exc.	V.G.	Good	Fair	Poor
300	200	175	150	125	100

Model 1300 Defender Synthetic Stock

Same as above but fitted with a black synthetic full stock. Available in either 12 or 20 gauge.

NIB	Exc.	V.G.	Good	Fair	Poor
300	200	175	150	125	100

Model 1300 Defender Pistol Grip

Same as above but fitted with a black synthetic pistol grip and extended magazine tube.

NIB	Exc.	V.G.	Good	Fair	Poor
300	200	175	150	125	100

Model 1300 Lady Defender

Chambered for the 20 gauge shell, this model features an 18" barrel with 8-round capacity. Pistol-grip stock. Introduced in 1997.

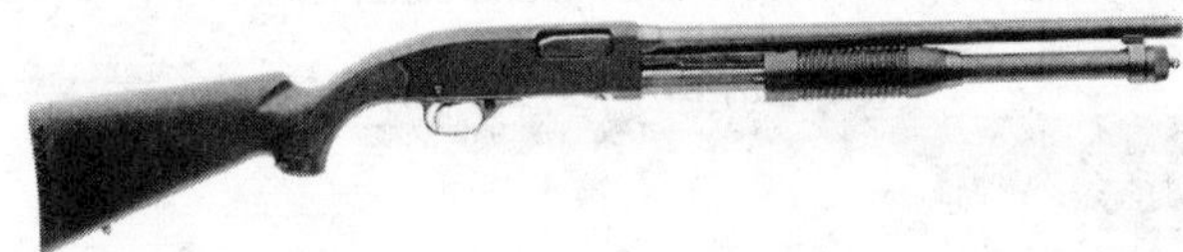

NIB	Exc.	V.G.	Good	Fair	Poor
340	250	185	140	110	95

Model 1300 Stainless Marine

This 12 gauge slide-action shotgun comes with a black synthetic full stock with all metal parts chrome plated. Barrel is 18" and magazine tube holds 7 rounds. Gun weighs 6.75 lbs.

NIB	Exc.	V.G.	Good	Fair	Poor
450	350	300	240	175	110

Model 1300 Stainless Marine with Pistol Grip

Same as above with black synthetic pistol grip in place of full buttstock. Gun weighs 5.75 lbs.

NIB	Exc.	V.G.	Good	Fair	Poor
400	300	250	200	150	100

Model 1500 XTR

This is a gas-operated, semi-automatic shotgun chambered for 12 or 20 gauge, with a 28" vent rib barrel with screw-in chokes. The finish is blued, with a walnut stock. It was manufactured between 1978 and 1982.

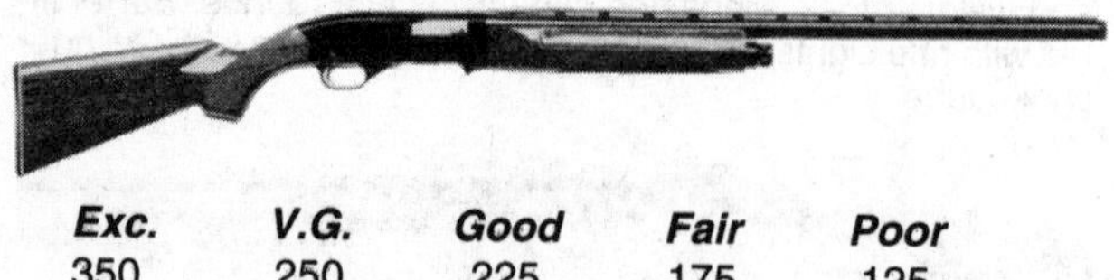

Exc.	V.G.	Good	Fair	Poor
350	250	225	175	125

Super X Model I

This is a self-compensating, gas-operated, semi-automatic shotgun chambered for 12 gauge. It was offered with a 26", 28", or 30" vent rib barrel with various chokes. It features all-steel construction and is blued, with a checkered walnut stock. It was manufactured between 1974 and 1981.

Exc.	V.G.	Good	Fair	Poor
500	375	300	250	150

Super X Model 1 Custom Competition

This is a custom-order trap or skeet gun that features the self compensating, gas-operated action. It is available in 12 gauge only from the Custom Shop. It is offered with a heavy degree of engraving on the receiver and a fancy, checkered walnut stock. Gold inlays are available and would add approximately 50 percent to the values given. This model was introduced in 1987.

NIB	Exc.	V.G.	Good	Fair	Poor
1450	1100	925	775	650	500

Super X2 3.5" Magnum

Introduced in 1999, this model is a gas-operated design chambered for 3.5" 12 gauge shells. Fitted with a black synthetic stock and choice of 24", 26", or 28" vent rib barrels. Invector chokes. Magazine capacity is five rounds. Weight is about 7.5 lbs. depending on barrel length. Matte black finish.

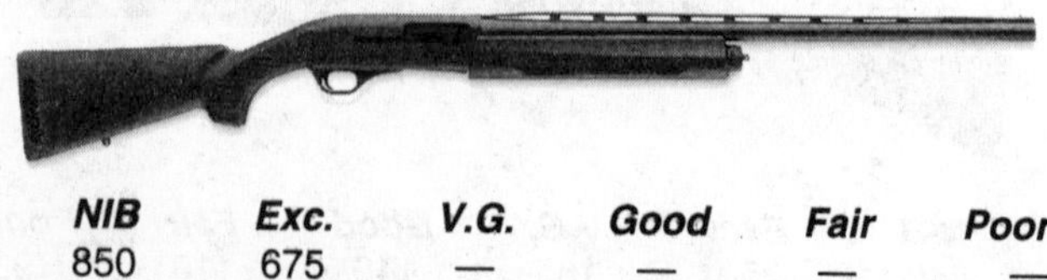

NIB	Exc.	V.G.	Good	Fair	Poor
850	675	—	—	—	—

Super X2 Turkey

Similar to the X2 Magnum but with 24" vent rib barrel with truglo sights. Extra-Full choke. Weight is about 7.25 lbs. Black synthetic stock. Introduced in 1999.

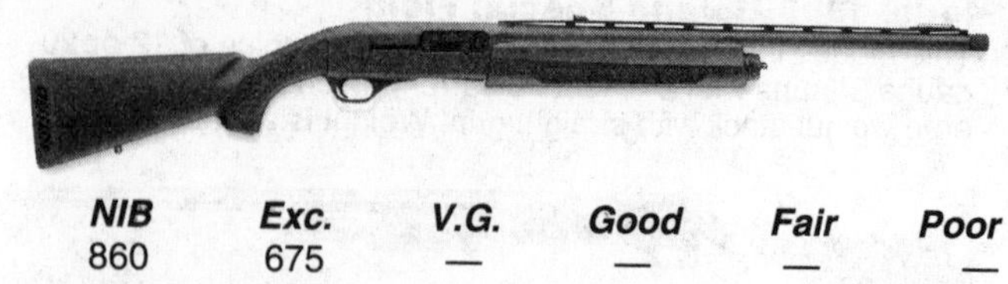

NIB	Exc.	V.G.	Good	Fair	Poor
860	675	—	—	—	—

Super X2 Turkey Mossy Oak Break-Up

Same as above but with Mossy Oak Break-Up camo on stock and gun. Introduced in 2000.

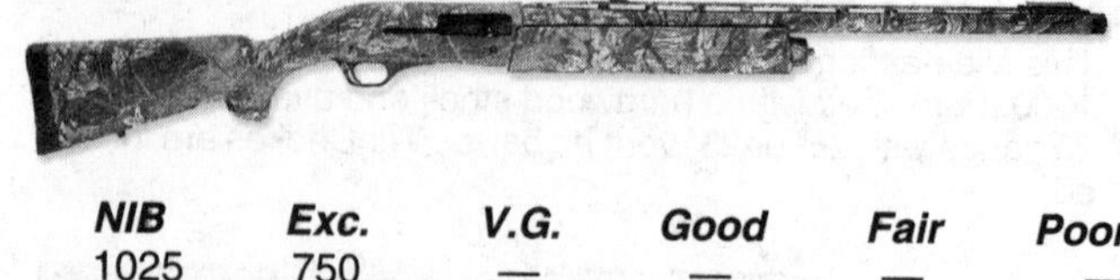

NIB	Exc.	V.G.	Good	Fair	Poor
1025	750	—	—	—	—

Super X2 NWTF Turkey

Introduced in 2005 this 3.5" 12 gauge gun is fitted with a 24" vent rib barrel with extra full extended choke tubes. Three dot TRUGLO sights. Mossy Oak camo stock. A brass NWTF medallion on the pistol grip cap. Weight is about 7.5 lbs.

NIB	Exc.	V.G.	Good	Fair	Poor
1235	950	—	—	—	—

Super X2 Universal Hunter

Similar to the Super X2 Turkey but with a 26" barrel with Extra-Full choke tube. Weight is about 7.75 lbs. Introduced in 2002.

NIB	Exc.	V.G.	Good	Fair	Poor
1100	850	—	—	—	—

Super X2 Camo Waterfowl

Chambered for 12 gauge 3.5" shells and fitted with a 28" vent rib barrel, this model features a Mossy Oak camo finish. Weight is about 8 lbs. Introduced in 1999. In 2004 a New Shadow Grass camo pattern was added.

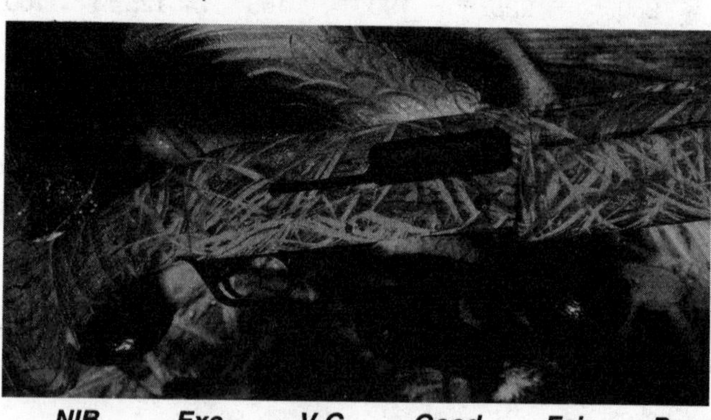

NIB	Exc.	V.G.	Good	Fair	Poor
1140	850	650	—	—	—

Super X2 Magnum Greenhead

Introduced in 2002, this model is chambered for the 12 gauge 3.5" shell and has a composite stock that is green in color. Fitted with 28" barrel. Weight is about 8 lbs.

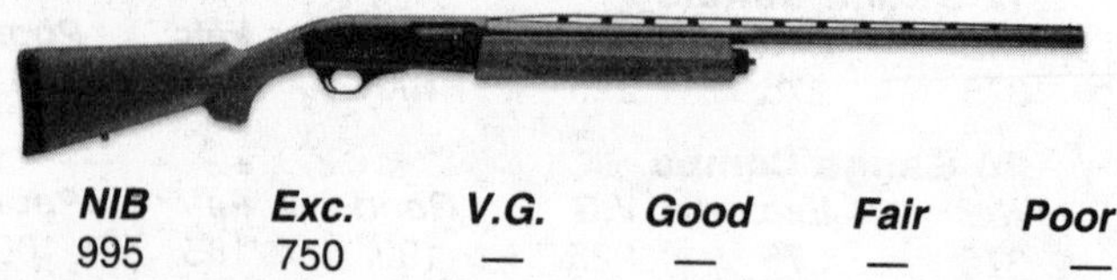

NIB	Exc.	V.G.	Good	Fair	Poor
995	750	—	—	—	—

Super X2 Magnum Field

This model is chambered for the 12 gauge 3" shell and is offered with either a walnut stock or black synthetic stock. Choice of 26" or 28" vent rib barrel with invector chokes. Weight is about 7.25 lbs. Introduced in 1999.

NIB	Exc.	V.G.	Good	Fair	Poor
800	625	—	—	—	—

Super X2 Light Field

Checkered walnut stock with choice of 26" or 28" vent rib barrel with choke tubes are featured on this 12 gauge gun. Weight is about 6.5 lbs. Introduced in 2005.

NIB	Exc.	V.G.	Good	Fair	Poor
945	700	—	—	—	—

Super X2 Cantilever Deer

This 12 gauge model has a 22" fully rifled barrel with fold-down rear sight and scope mount. Black composite stock. Weight is about 7.25 lbs. Introduced in 2002.

NIB	Exc.	V.G.	Good	Fair	Poor
860	650	—	—	—	—

Super X2 Practical

Introduced in 2002, this model is designed for competition shooting. Fitted with a 22" barrel with ghost ring sight and 8-round magazine. Black composite stock. Weight is about 8 lbs.

NIB	Exc.	V.G.	Good	Fair	Poor
1065	800	—	—	—	—

Super X2 Sporting Clays

Introduced in 2001, this model features a 12 gauge gun with choice of 28" or 30" barrels with high post rib. Barrels are back bore with Invector chokes. Adjustable comb. Weight is about 8 lbs.

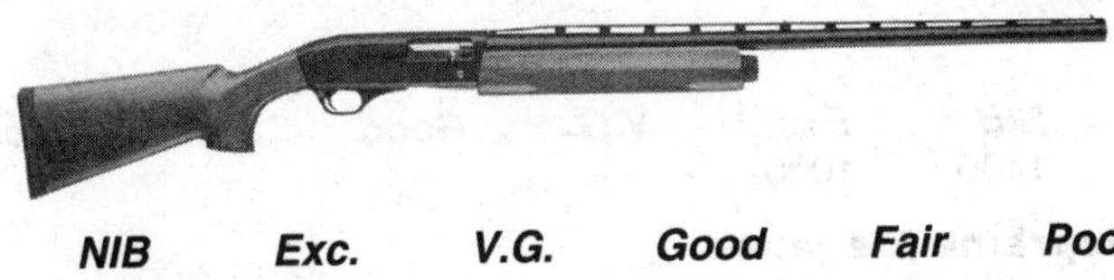

NIB	Exc.	V.G.	Good	Fair	Poor
1200	950	—	—	—	—

Super X2 Sporting Clays Signature II

This 3" 12 gauge gun is fitted with a 30" barrel with choke tubes. The hardwood stock is painted black metallic. The receiver is a red anodized alloy. Weight is about 8.25 lbs. Introduced in 2005.

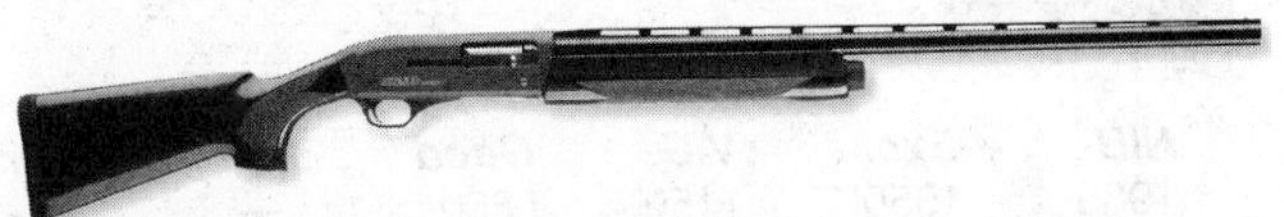

NIB	Exc.	V.G.	Good	Fair	Poor
1015	800	—	—	—	—

Super X2 Signature Red Sporting

This 12 gauge 3" shell model features a hardwood stock with red Dura-Touch coating. Fitted with a 30" vent rib barrel with five choke tubes. Weight is about 8 lbs. Introduced in 2003.

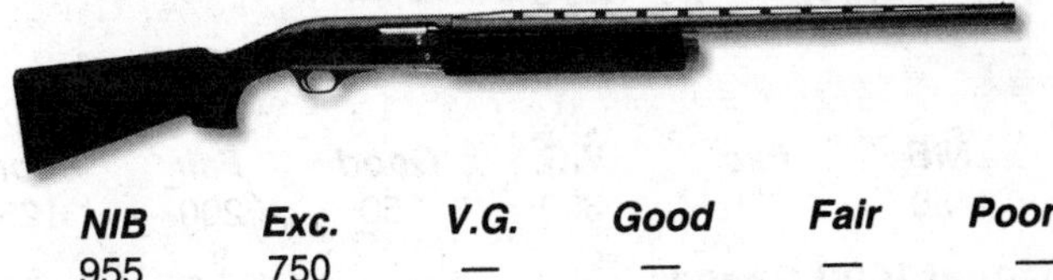

NIB	Exc.	V.G.	Good	Fair	Poor
955	750	—	—	—	—

SUPER X3 SERIES

Introduced in 2006, The Super X3 12 gauge features weight and recoil reducing features and a .742" back-bored barrel. It is available in a variety of configurations weighing under 7 lbs. in the 3" Field model and about 7.5 lbs. in composite, camo and 3.5" models. All models except Cantilever Deer included three choke tubes.

Super X3 Field

Walnut stock and 26" or 28" barrel. MSRP: 979

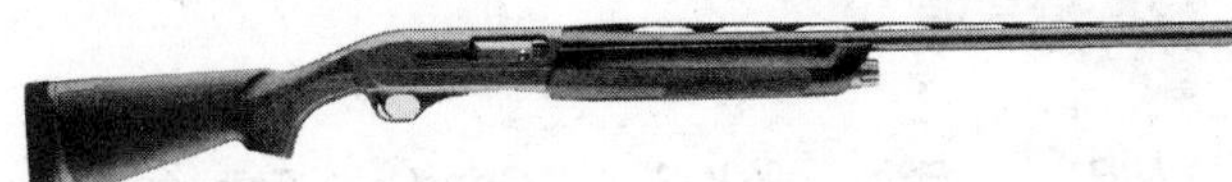

Super X3 Composite

Matte black stock and forend. Available in 26" or 28" barrel and 3" or 3.5" chamber. Add 100 for 3.5" model. MSRP: 945

Super X3 Camo

Composite camo stock with 3.5" chamber. Available in various camo patterns with 26" and 28" barrel. MSRP: 1217

Super X3 Cantilever Deer

Slug gun with 22" barrel with cantilever scope mount and 3" chamber. MSRP: 994

Model 1400

This is a gas-operated, semi-automatic shotgun chambered for 12, 16, or 20 gauge. It was offered with a 26", 28", or 30" vent rib barrel with various chokes. The finish is blued, with a checkered walnut stock. It was manufactured between 1964 and 1981. The Hydrocoil plastic stock was available on this model and would add approximately 35 percent to the values given.

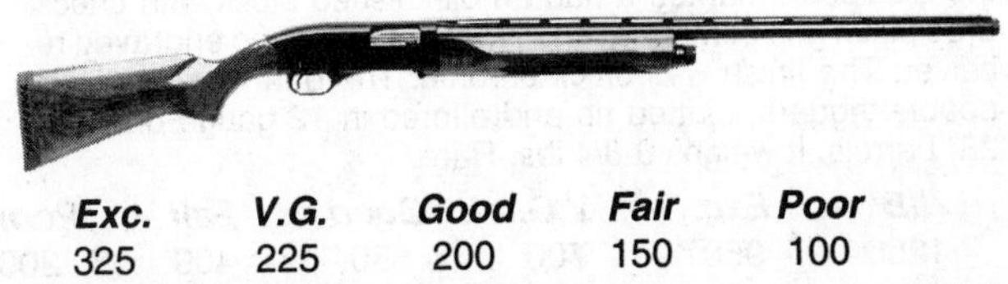

Exc.	V.G.	Good	Fair	Poor
325	225	200	150	100

New Model 1400

This is a gas-operated, semi-automatic shotgun chambered for 12 or 20 gauge. It is offered with a 22" or 28" vent rib barrel with screw-in chokes. The finish is blued, with a checkered walnut stock. It was introduced in 1989.

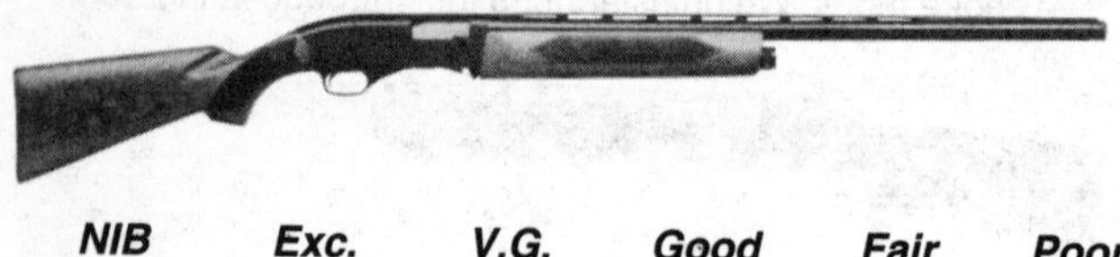

NIB	Exc.	V.G.	Good	Fair	Poor
450	350	300	250	200	125

Model 1400 Ranger

This is a utility-grade, gas-operated, semi-automatic shotgun chambered for 12 or 20 gauge. It is offered with a 28" vent rib barrel with screw-in chokes, as well as a 24" slug barrel with rifle sights. The finish is blued, with a checkered stock. A combination two-barrel set that includes the deer barrel would be worth approximately 20 percent additional. This model was introduced in 1983.

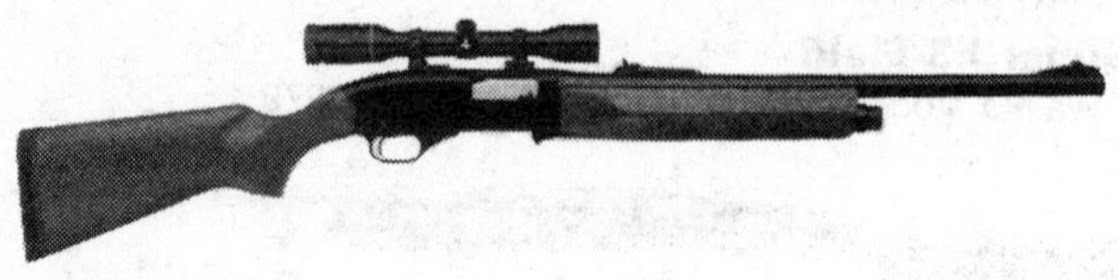

NIB	Exc.	V.G.	Good	Fair	Poor
400	300	250	200	150	100

Model 1400 Quail Unlimited

This 12 gauge semi-automatic shotgun model was introduced in 1993. It features compact engraved receiver with 26" vent rib barrel supplied with WinChoke tubes. Stock is checkered walnut. Gun weighs 7.25 lbs.

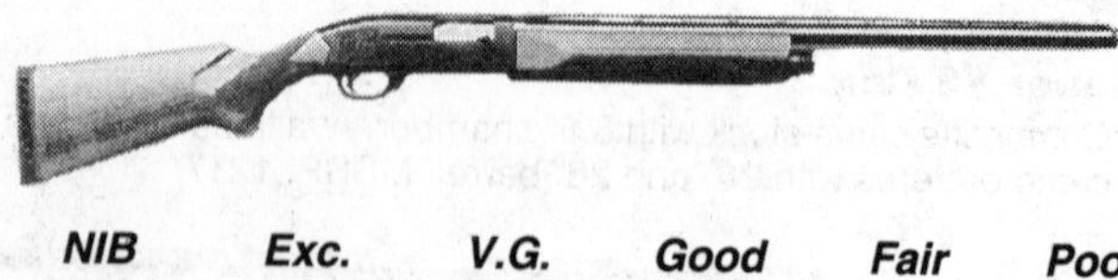

NIB	Exc.	V.G.	Good	Fair	Poor
400	300	250	200	150	100

Model 1400 Ranger Deer Combo

This model features a 12 gauge 22" smooth barrel and a 28" vent rib barrel with three WinChokes.

NIB	Exc.	V.G.	Good	Fair	Poor
400	300	250	200	150	100

Model 37A

Introduced in 1973. It is single-shot shotgun with exposed hammer. Offered in 12, 16, 20, and 28 gauge as well as .410 bore. All guns choked Full except youth model choked Modified. Walnut finish on wardwood stock. Pistol-grip cap with white spacer. Weight is about 6 lbs. About 395,000 were produced until 1980.

Exc.	V.G.	Good	Fair	Poor
350	250	225	175	115

Model 22

Introduced in 1975 this side-by-side shotgun was manufactured by Laurona in Spain to Winchester's specifications for the European market. It had an oil-finished stock with checkered pistol grip semi-beavertail forearm and hand engraved receiver. The finish was black chrome. The gun was fitted with double triggers, matted rib and offered in 12 gauge only with 28" barrels. It weighs 6-3/4 lbs. Rare.

NIB	Exc.	V.G.	Good	Fair	Poor
1250	950	700	550	400	200

Model 91

This over-and-under shotgun was built for Winchester by Laurona for its European markets. Offered in 12 gauge only with 28" barrels the barrels were fitted with a ventilated rib. The gun was offered with single or double triggers with hand-checkered walnut stock with oil finish and hand-engraved receiver. The finish was black chrome. Gun weighs 7-1/2 lbs. Rare.

NIB	Exc.	V.G.	Good	Fair	Poor
1100	800	600	500	400	200

Supreme Field

Introduced in 2000, this over-and-under gun is chambered for the 12 gauge 3" shell and fitted with 28" vent rib barrels with Invector chokes. Walnut stock with pistol grip and blued engraved receiver. Weight is about 7.5 lbs.

NIB	Exc.	V.G.	Good	Fair	Poor
1240	975	—	—	—	—

Supreme Sporting

Similar to the above model but fitted with a choice of 28" or 30" barrels chambered for 12 gauge 2.75" shells. Barrels are ported. Adjustable trigger. Polished silver receiver with blued barrels. Weight is about 7.5 lbs. Introduced in 2000.

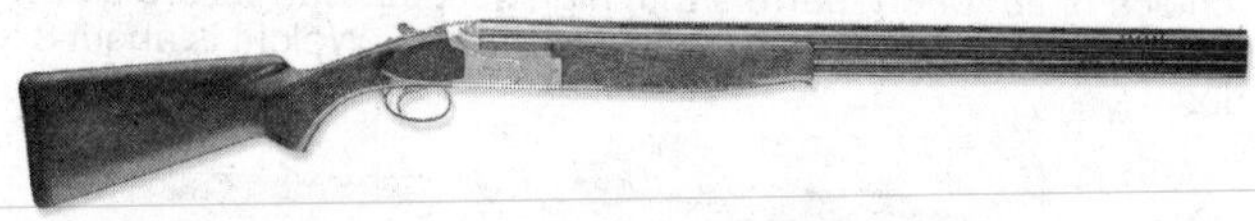

NIB	Exc.	V.G.	Good	Fair	Poor
1400	1000	—	—	—	—

Supreme Elegance

Introduced in 2003 this over-and-under model is chambered for the 12 gauge 3" shell. Choice of 26" or 28" vent rib barrels with three choke tubes. Grayed receiver with scroll and bird scenes. Weight is about 7 lbs. depending on barrel length.

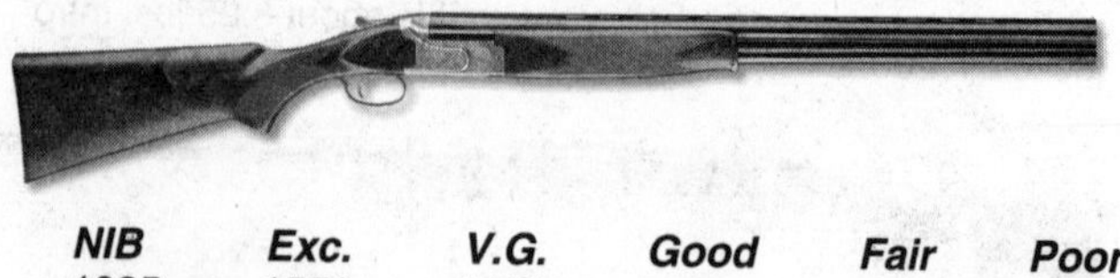

NIB	Exc.	V.G.	Good	Fair	Poor
1985	1550	1150	850	—	—

MODEL 23 SERIES

Model 23 XTR

This is a side-by-side, double-barrel shotgun chambered for 12 or 20 gauge. It is offered with 25.5", 26", 28", or 30" vent rib barrels with 3" chambers and various choke combinations. It is a boxlock gun that features a single trigger and automatic ejectors. It is scroll-engraved with a coin-finished receiver, blued barrels, and a checkered, select walnut stock. It was introduced in 1978. This model is available in a number of configurations that differ in the amount of ornamentation and the quality of materials and workmanship utilized in their construction. These models and their values are listed.

Grade I

Discontinued.

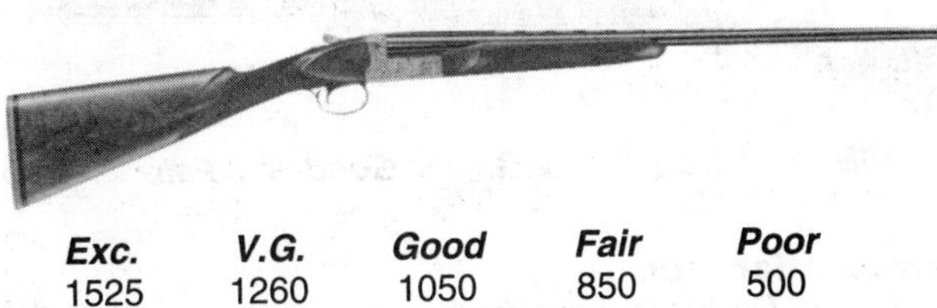

Exc.	V.G.	Good	Fair	Poor
1525	1260	1050	850	500

Pigeon Grade

With WinChokes.

Exc.	V.G.	Good	Fair	Poor
1650	1375	1150	925	600

Pigeon Grade Lightweight

Straight stock.

Exc.	V.G.	Good	Fair	Poor
2100	1725	1400	1175	735

Golden Quail

This series was available in 28 gauge and .410, as well as 12 or 20 gauge. It features 25.5" barrels that are choked improved cylinder/modified. It features a straight-grip, English-style stock with a recoil pad. The .410 version would be worth approximately 10 percent more than the values given. This series was discontinued in 1987.

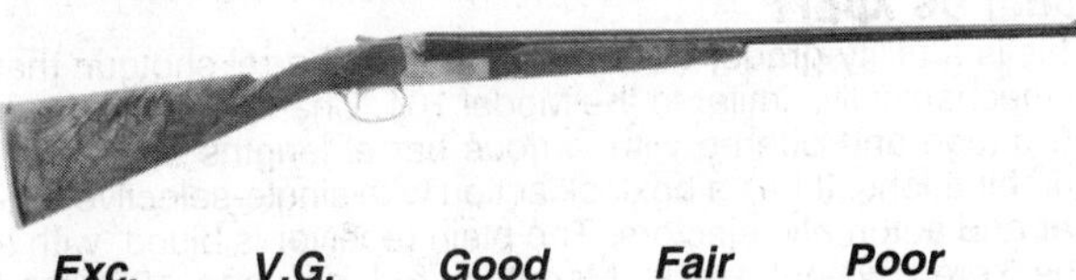

Exc.	V.G.	Good	Fair	Poor
2350	1975	1650	1225	925

Model 23 Light Duck

This version is chambered for 20 gauge and was offered with a 28" Full and Full-choked barrel. There were 500 manufactured in 1985.

Exc.	V.G.	Good	Fair	Poor
1650	1475	1225	925	825

Model 23 Heavy Duck

This version is chambered for 12 gauge with 30" Full and Full-choked barrels. There were 500 manufactured in 1984.

Exc.	V.G.	Good	Fair	Poor
1650	1475	1225	925	825

Model 21

This is a high-quality, side-by-side, double-barrel shotgun that features a boxlock action and is chambered for 12, 16, 20, and 28 gauges, as well as .410. It is featured with various barrel lengths and choke combinations. Since 1960, the Model 21 has been available on a custom-order basis only. It is available in five basic configurations that differ in the options offered, the amount of ornamentation, and the quality of materials and workmanship utilized in their construction. See previous Model 21 entry.

MODEL 101 SERIES

Model 101 Field Grade

This is an Over/Under, double-barrel shotgun chambered for 12, 20, and 28 gauge, as well as .410. It was offered with 26", 28", or 30" vent rib barrels with various choke combinations. Since 1983 screw-in chokes have been standard, and models so furnished would be worth approximately $50 additional. This is a boxlock gun with a single-selective trigger and automatic ejectors. The receiver is engraved; the finish, blued with a checkered walnut stock. It was manufactured between 1963 and 1987.

Exc.	V.G.	Good	Fair	Poor
875	700	550	425	300

NOTE: 28 gauge add 40 percent; .410 add 50 percent.

Waterfowl Model

This version of the Model 101 is chambered for 12 gauge with 3" chambers. It has 30" or 32" vent rib barrels and a matte finish.

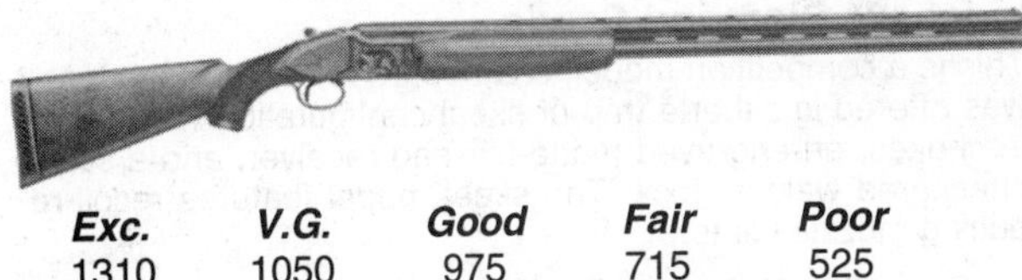

Exc.	V.G.	Good	Fair	Poor
1310	1050	975	715	525

Model 101 Magnum

This version is similar to the Field Grade, chambered for 12 or 20 gauge with 3" Magnum chambers. It was offered with 30" barrels with various chokes. The stock is furnished with a recoil pad. It was manufactured between 1966 and 1981.

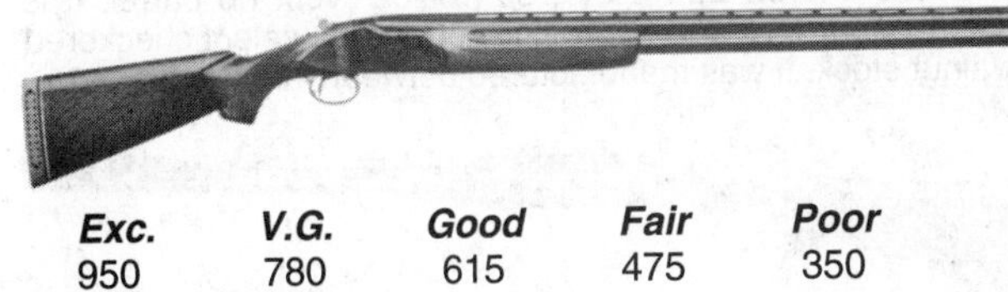

Exc.	V.G.	Good	Fair	Poor
950	780	615	475	350

Model 101 Skeet Grade

This version was offered with 26" skeet-bored barrels with a competition rib and a skeet-type walnut stock. It was manufactured between 1966 and 1984.

Exc.	V.G.	Good	Fair	Poor
1200	925	825	550	400

Model 101 Three-Gauge Skeet Set

This combination set was offered with three barrels, chambered for 20 and 28 gauge, as well as .410. It was furnished with a fitted case and manufactured between 1974 and 1984.

Exc.	V.G.	Good	Fair	Poor
3000	2100	1400	—	—

Model 101 Trap Grade

This version is chambered for 12 gauge only and was offered with 30" or 32" competition ribbed barrels, choked for trap shooting. It is furnished with a competition-type stock. It was manufactured between 1966 and 1984.

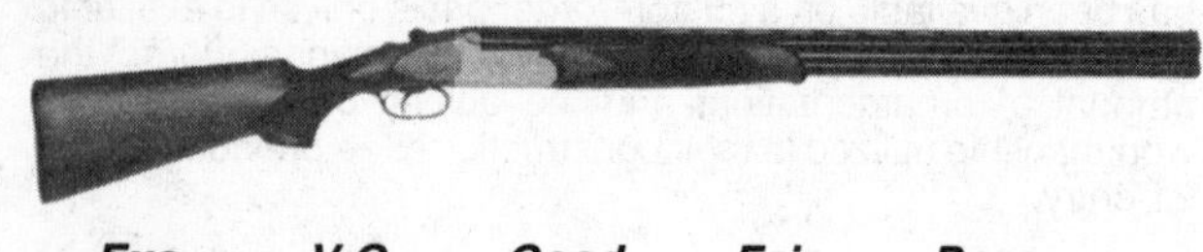

Exc.	V.G.	Good	Fair	Poor
1400	1100	925	700	500

Model 101 Pigeon Grade

This is a more deluxe-engraved version of the Model 101, chambered for 12, 20, or 28 gauge, as well as .410. It features a coin-finished receiver with a fancy checkered walnut stock. It was introduced in 1974.

Exc.	V.G.	Good	Fair	Poor
2000	1600	1300	975	750

Super Pigeon Grade

This is a deluxe version of the Model 101, chambered for 12 gauge. It is heavily engraved with several gold inlays. The receiver is blued, and it features a high-grade walnut stock with fleur-de-lis checkering. It was imported between 1985 and 1987.

Exc.	V.G.	Good	Fair	Poor
4000	3500	2500	—	—

Model 101 Diamond Grade

This is a competition model, chambered for all four gauges. It was offered in either a trap or skeet configuration with screw-in chokes, an engraved matte-finished receiver, and a select checkered walnut stock. The skeet model features recoil-reducing muzzle vents.

Exc.	V.G.	Good	Fair	Poor
2000	1625	1250	900	680

Model 501 Grand European

This is an Over/Under, double-barrel shotgun chambered for 12 or 20 gauge. It was available in trap or skeet configurations and was offered with a 27", 30", or 32" vent rib barrel. It is heavily engraved and matte-finished, with a select checkered walnut stock. It was manufactured between 1981 and 1986.

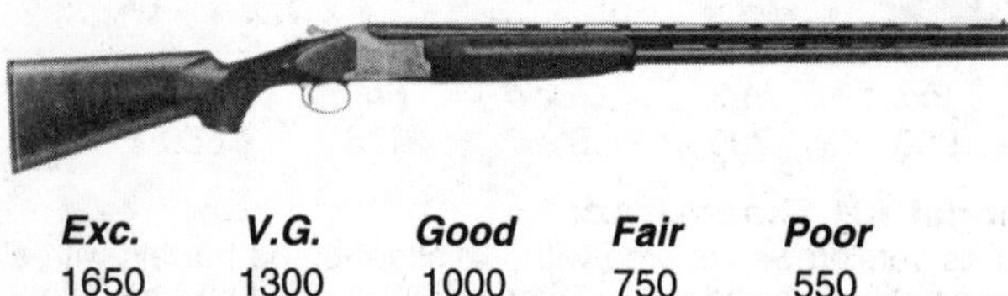

Exc.	V.G.	Good	Fair	Poor
1650	1300	1000	750	550

Model 501 Presentation Grade

This is a deluxe version chambered in 12 gauge only. It is ornately engraved and gold-inlaid. The stock is made out of presentation-grade walnut. It was furnished with a fitted case. It was manufactured between 1984 and 1987.

Exc.	V.G.	Good	Fair	Poor
3400	2750	2200	1600	1250

Select Model 101 Field

This Belgian-made version of Winchester's popular Model 101 was introduced in 2007. It features Grade II/III walnut, 26" or 28" barrels and deep-relief engraving on the blued receiver that mimics the original 101. Classic white line spacer and vented recoil pad. Three choke tubes. Weight is about 7.2 lbs. Introduced in 2007.

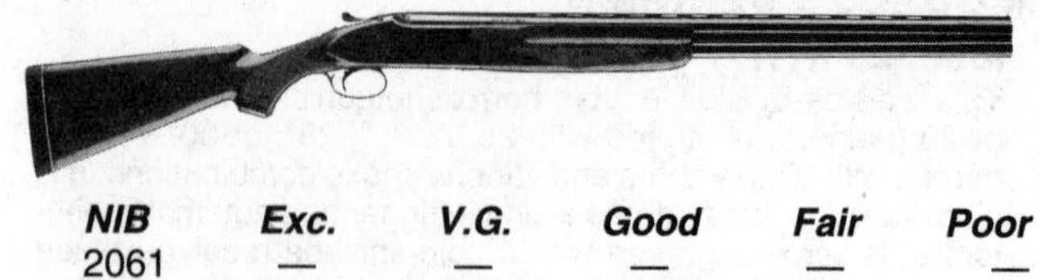

NIB	Exc.	V.G.	Good	Fair	Poor
2061	—	—	—	—	—

Select Model 101 Sporting

Similar to Field model plus competition features such as a wider rib, adjustable trigger, white mid-bead and five extended Signature choke tubes. Ported barrels are 28", 30" or 32".

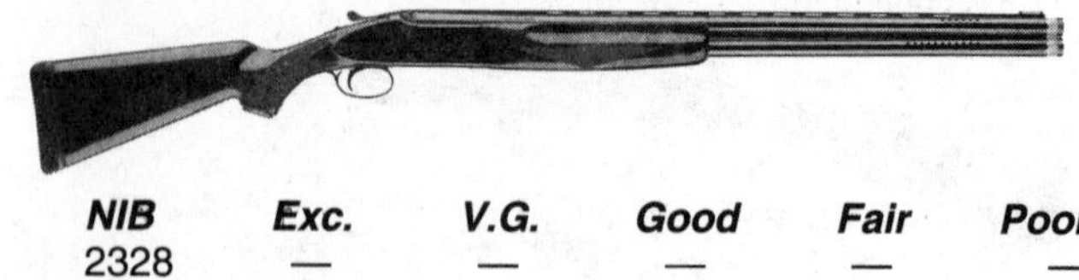

NIB	Exc.	V.G.	Good	Fair	Poor
2328	—	—	—	—	—

Combination Gun

This is an Over/Under rifle/shotgun combination chambered for 12 gauge over .222, .223, .30-06, and the 9.3x74R cartridges. It features 25" barrels. The shotgun tube has a screw-in choke. It is engraved in the fashion of the Model 501 Grand European and features a select checkered walnut stock. It was manufactured between 1983 and 1985.

Exc.	V.G.	Good	Fair	Poor
3000	2500	1600	—	—

Express Rifle

This is an Over/Under, double-barreled rifle chambered for the .257 Roberts, .270, 7.7x65R, .30-06, and the 9.3x74R cartridges. It features 23.5" barrels with a solid rib and express sights. It is engraved with game scenes and has a satin-finished receiver. The stock is checkered select walnut. It was manufactured in 1984 and 1985.

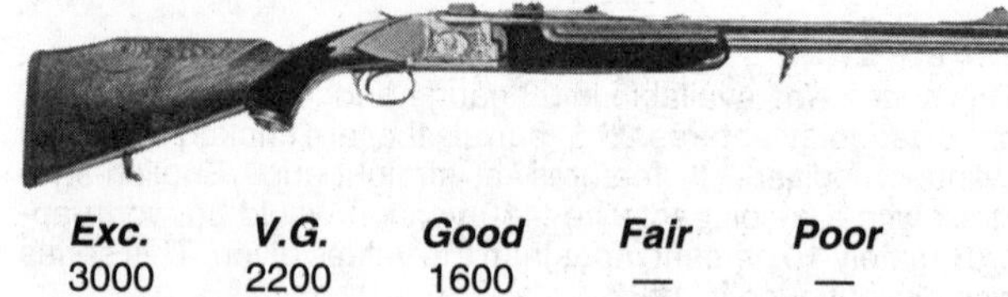

Exc.	V.G.	Good	Fair	Poor
3000	2200	1600	—	—

Model 96 Xpert

This is a utility-grade, Over/Under, double-barrel shotgun that is mechanically similar to the Model 101. Chambered for 12 or 20 gauge and offered with various barrel lengths and choke combinations. It has a boxlock action with single-selective trigger and automatic ejectors. The plain receiver is blued, with a checkered walnut stock. Manufactured between 1976 and 1982. A competition-grade model for trap or skeet was also available and would be worth approximately the same amount.

Exc.	V.G.	Good	Fair	Poor
650	550	450	350	275

Model 1001 Field

A new addition to the U.S.R.A. product line for 1993. This Over/Under shotgun is available in 12 gauge only, with a 28" ventilated rib barrel furnished with WinPlus choke tubes. A walnut checkered pistol stock is standard. The finish is blued with scroll engraving on the receiver. The receiver top has a matte finish. The gun weighs 7 lbs.

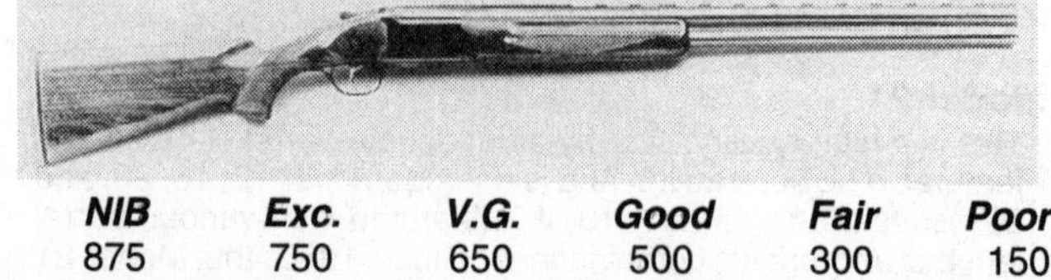

NIB	Exc.	V.G.	Good	Fair	Poor
875	750	650	500	300	150

Model 1001 Sporting Clays I & II

This model features different stock dimensions, a fuller pistol grip, a radiused recoil pad, and a wider vent rib fitted on a 28" barrel (Sporting Clays I model, the Sporting Clays II features a 30" barrel). Comes complete with choke tubes. The frame has a silver nitrate finish and special engraving featuring a flying clay target. Introduced in 1993. Gun weighs 7.75 lbs.

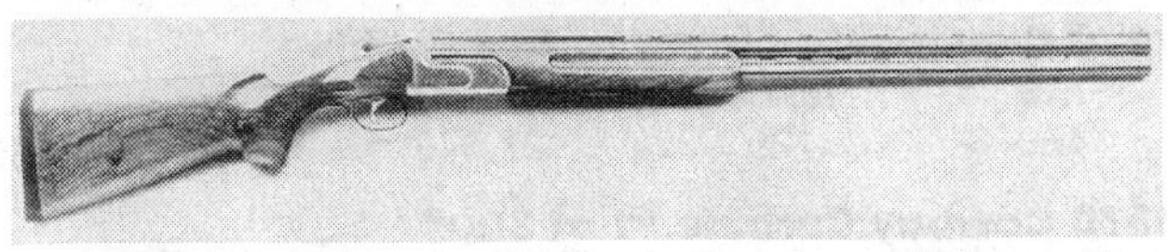

NIB	Exc.	V.G.	Good	Fair	Poor
1000	800	700	550	300	150

Select Midnight

High-gloss bluing on receiver and barrels with gold accent game bird pattern on both sides and bottom of the receiver. Satin finished Grade II/III walnut. Oval checkering pattern. Choke tubes. Introduced 2006. Available in 26" and 28" barrels. MSRP: 2380

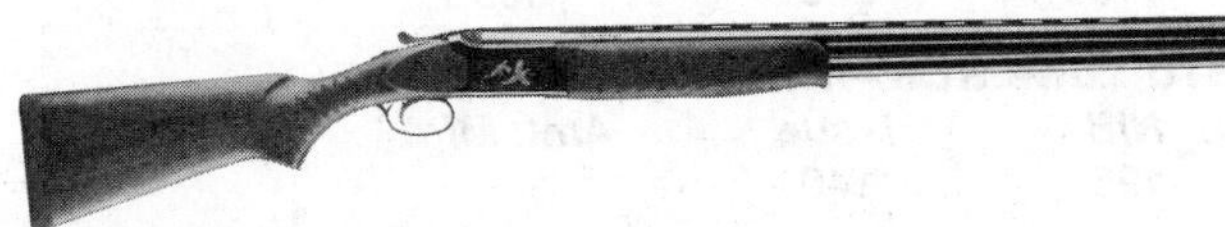

Select White Field

An engraved silver nitride receiver is featured on both versions of the White Field. The Traditional model has traditional checkering and the Extreme model features the Select Series' unique oval checkering pattern. Both versions have choke tubes and are available in 26" and 28" barrels. Introduced 2006. MSRP: 1533

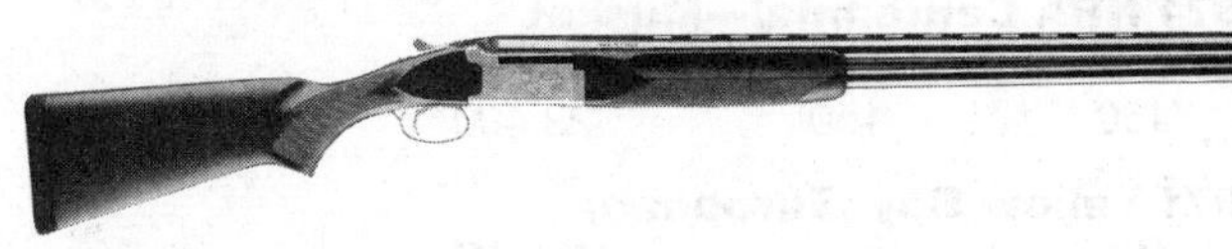

SELECT OVER/UNDER SERIES

This series of over-and-under shotguns was introduced into the Winchester line in 2004. The series features a low-profile receiver with unique engraving, lightweight barrels, and contoured walnut stocks with distinctive checkering patterns.

Select Energy Sporting

Chambered for the 12 gauge 2.75" shell and offered with a choice of 28", 30", or 32" vent rib barrels with choke tubes and porting. Truglo front sight. Adjustable trigger shoe. Walnut stock with recoil pad. Weight is about 7.62 lbs. Adjustable comb available.

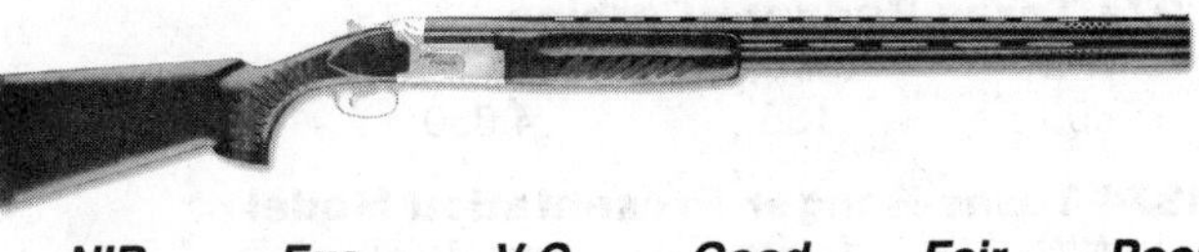

NIB	Exc.	V.G.	Good	Fair	Poor
1200	900	—	—	—	—

NOTE: Add $150 for adjustable comb.

Select Energy Trap

This 12 gauge model is fitted with a choice of 30" or 32" back-bored ported barrels. Wide vent rib. Choke tubes. Walnut stock with Monte Carlo comb. Weight is about 7.8 lbs. Adjustable comb available.

NIB	Exc.	V.G.	Good	Fair	Poor
1300	925	—	—	—	—

NOTE: Add $150 for adjustable comb.

Select Extreme Elegance

This 12 gauge gun features full coverage engraving with game scenes. Choice of 26" or 28" vent rib barrels with choke tubes. Walnut stock with unique checkering pattern. Weight is about 7 lbs.

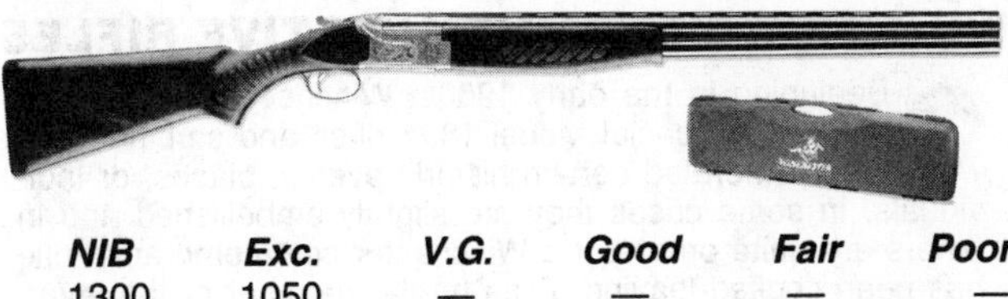

NIB	Exc.	V.G.	Good	Fair	Poor
1300	1050	—	—	—	—

Select Field

This 12 gauge 3" gun is fitted with a choice of 26" or 28" vent ribs barrels with choke tubes. Engraved receiver with oval checkering pattern. Weight is about 7 lbs.

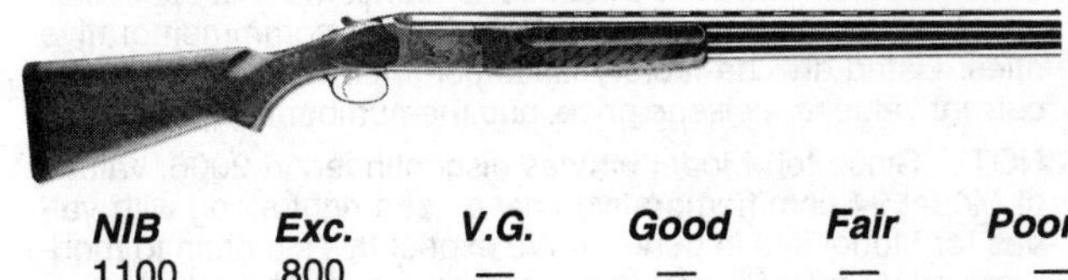

NIB	Exc.	V.G.	Good	Fair	Poor
1100	800	—	—	—	—

Select Traditional Elegance

Similar to the Extreme Elegance but with traditional checkering pattern.

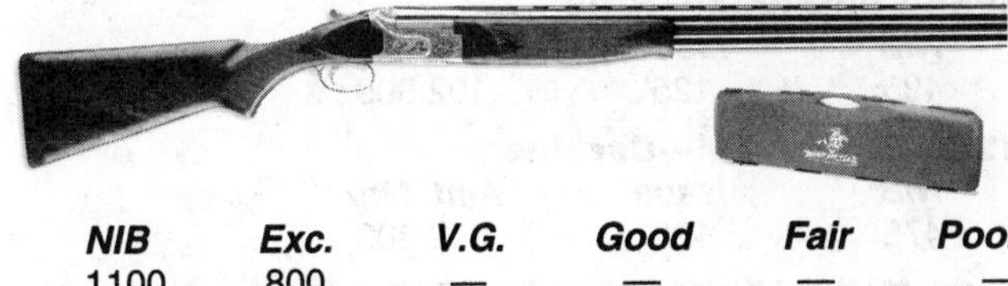

NIB	Exc.	V.G.	Good	Fair	Poor
1100	800	—	—	—	—

Select Deluxe Field

New in 2007, this Belgian-made 3" 12 gauge features an engraved steel receiver with silver nitride finish and Grade II walnut. Barrels are 26", 28" or 30". Three chokes included. Weight is about 7.25 lbs.

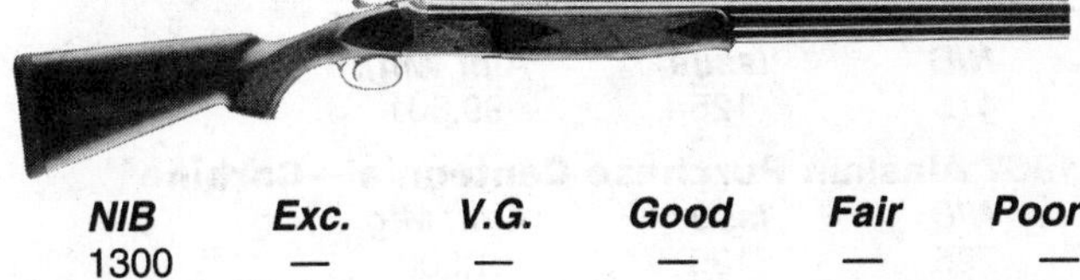

NIB	Exc.	V.G.	Good	Fair	Poor
1300	—	—	—	—	—

Select Platinum Field

This 3" 12 gauge was introduced in 2007. It is Belgian-made and comes with 28" or 30" barrels, Grade II/III walnut and deep relief engraving. Includes three Signature extended choke tubes and hard case.

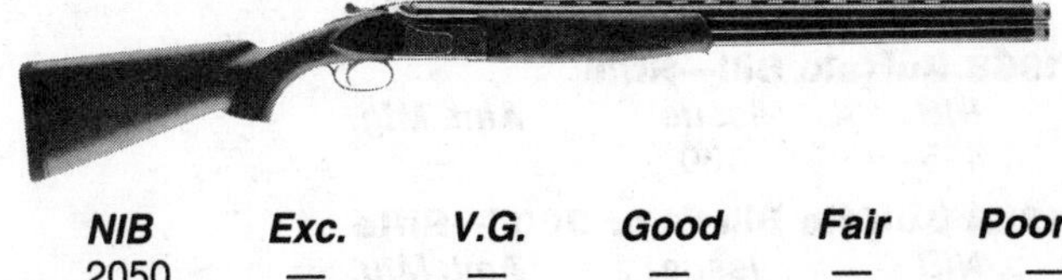

NIB	Exc.	V.G.	Good	Fair	Poor
2050	—	—	—	—	—

Select Platinum Sporting

Similar to the Platinum Field with 28", 30" or 32" ported barrels, wide rib, adjustable trigger shoe and five Signature extended choke tubes and hard case.

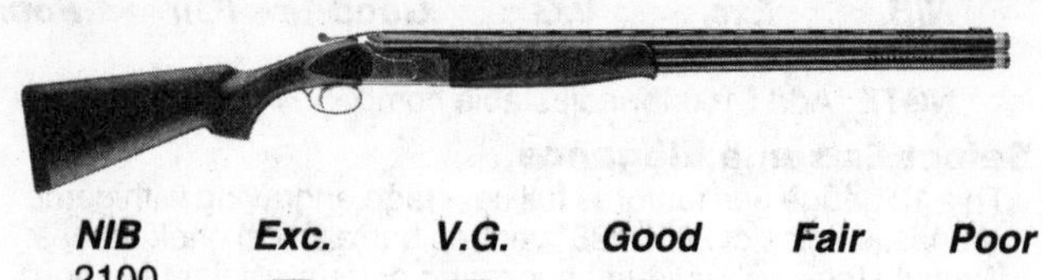

NIB	Exc.	V.G.	Good	Fair	Poor
2100	—	—	—	—	—

WINCHESTER COMMEMORATIVE RIFLES

Beginning in the early 1960s, Winchester produced a number of special Model 1894 rifles and carbines that commemorated certain historic events, places, or individuals. In some cases they are slightly embellished and in others are quite ornate. If a Winchester commemorative rifle has been cocked leaving a line on the hammer or the lever, many collectors will show little or no interest in its acquisition. If they have been fired, they will realize little premium over a standard, Post-1964 Model 94. A number of commemoratives have been ordered by outside concerns and are technically not factory issues. Most have less collectibility than the factory-issued models. There are a number of concerns that specialize in marketing the total range of Winchester commmemorative rifles. Listed are the factory-issue commemoratives with their current value, their issue price, and the number manufactured.

NOTE: Since teh Model 94 was discontinued in 2006, values of Model 94 commemoratives have risen right along with values for Model 94s in general. We expect this situation to moderate over time but for the present, it's a seller's market.

1964 Wyoming Diamond Jubilee—Carbine

NIB	Issue	Amt. Mfg.
795	100	1,500

1966 Centennial—Rifle

NIB	Issue	Amt. Mfg.
495	125	102,309

1966 Centennial—Carbine

NIB	Issue	Amt. Mfg.
475	125	102,309

1966 Nebraska Centennial—Rifle

NIB	Issue	Amt. Mfg.
795	100	2,500

1967 Canadian Centennial—Rifle

NIB	Issue	Amt. Mfg.
495	125	—

1967 Canadian Centennial—Carbine

NIB	Issue	Amt. Mfg.
475	125	90,301

1967 Alaskan Purchase Centennial—Carbine

NIB	Issue	Amt. Mfg.
795	125	1,500

1968 Illinois Sesquicentennial—Carbine

NIB	Issue	Amt. Mfg.
395	110	37,648

1968 Buffalo Bill—Carbine

NIB	Issue	Amt. Mfg.
475	130	112,923

1968 Buffalo Bill—Rifle

NIB	Issue	Amt. Mfg.
495	130	—

1968 Buffalo Bill "1 or 300"—Rifle

NIB	Issue	Amt. Mfg.
2750	1000	300

1969 Theodore Roosevelt—Rifle

NIB	Issue	Amt. Mfg.
495	135	—

1969 Theodore Roosevelt—Carbine

NIB	Issue	Amt. Mfg.
475	135	52,386

1969 Golden Spike Carbine

NIB	Issue	Amt. Mfg.
495	120	69,996

1970 Cowboy Commemorative Carbine

NIB	Issue	Amt. Mfg.
450	125	27,549

1970 Cowboy Carbine "1 of 300"

NIB	Issue	Amt. Mfg.
2750	1000	300

1970 Northwest Territories (Canadian)

NIB	Issue	Amt. Mfg.
850	150	2,500

1970 Northwest Territories Deluxe (Canadian)

NIB	Issue	Amt. Mfg.
1100	250	500

1970 Lone Star—Rifle

NIB	Issue	Amt. Mfg.
495	140	—

1970 Lone Star—Carbine

NIB	Issue	Amt. Mfg.
475	140	38,385

1971 NRA Centennial—Rifle

NIB	Issue	Amt. Mfg.
450	150	21,000

1971 NRA Centennial—Musket

NIB	Issue	Amt. Mfg.
450	150	23,400

1971 Yellow Boy (European)

NIB	Issue	Amt. Mfg.
1150	250	500

1971 Royal Canadian Mounted Police (Canadian)

NIB	Issue	Amt. Mfg.
795	190	9,500

1971 Mounted Police (Canadian)

NIB	Issue	Amt. Mfg.
795	190	5,100

1971 Mounted Police, Presentation

NIB	Issue	Amt. Mfg.
9995	—	10

1974 Texas Ranger—Carbine

NIB	Issue	Amt. Mfg.
695	135	4,850

1974 Texas Ranger Presentation Model

NIB	Issue	Amt. Mfg.
2750	1000	150

1974 Apache (Canadian)

NIB	Issue	Amt. Mfg.
795	150	8,600

1974 Commanche (Canadian)

NIB	Issue	Amt. Mfg.
795	230	11,500

1974 Klondike Gold Rush (Canadian)

NIB	Issue	Amt. Mfg.
795	240	10,500

This symbol denotes "Sleepers" with rapidly-rising values and/or significant collector potential.

1975 Klondike Gold Rush—Dawson City Issue (Canadian)

NIB	Issue	Amt. Mfg.
8500	—	25

1976 Sioux (Canadian)

NIB	Issue	Amt. Mfg.
795	280	10,000

1976 Little Bighorn (Canadian)

NIB	Issue	Amt. Mfg.
795	300	11,000

1976 U.S. Bicentennial Carbine

NIB	Issue	Amt. Mfg.
595	325	19,999

1977 Wells Fargo

NIB	Issue	Amt. Mfg.
495	350	19,999

1977 Legendary Lawman

NIB	Issue	Amt. Mfg.
495	375	19,999

1977 Limited Edition I

NIB	Issue	Amt. Mfg.
1395	1500	1,500

1977 Cheyenne—.22 Cal. (Canadian)

NIB	Issue	Amt. Mfg.
750	320	5,000

1977 Cheyenne—.44-40 Cal. (Canadian)

NIB	Issue	Amt. Mfg.
795	300	11,225

1977 Cherokee—.22 Cal. (Canadian)

NIB	Issue	Amt. Mfg.
750	385	3,950

1977 Cherokee—.30-30 Cal. (Canadian)

NIB	Issue	Amt. Mfg.
795	385	9,000

1978 "One of One Thousand" (European)

NIB	Issue	Amt. Mfg.
7500	5000	250

1978 Antler Game Carbine

NIB	Issue	Amt. Mfg.
550	375	19,999

1979 Limited Edition II

NIB	Issue	Amt. Mfg.
1395	1500	1,500

1979 Legendary Frontiersman Rifle

NIB	Issue	Amt. Mfg.
550	425	19,999

1979 Matched Set of 1,000

NIB	Issue	Amt. Mfg.
2250	3000	1,000

1979 Bat Masterson (Canadian)

NIB	Issue	Amt. Mfg.
795	650	8,000

1980 Alberta Diamond Jubilee (Canadian)

NIB	Issue	Amt. Mfg.
795	650	2,700

1980 Alberta Diamond Jubilee Deluxe (Canadian)

NIB	Issue	Amt. Mfg.
1495	1900	300

1980 Saskatchewan Diamond Jubilee (Canadian)

NIB	Issue	Amt. Mfg.
795	695	2,700

1980 Saskatchewan Diamond Jubilee Deluxe (Canadian)

NIB	Issue	Amt. Mfg.
1495	1995	300

1980 Oliver Winchester

NIB	Issue	Amt. Mfg.
695	375	19,999

1981 U.S. Border Patrol

NIB	Issue	Amt. Mfg.
595	1195	1,000

1981 U.S. Border Patrol—Member's Model

NIB	Issue	Amt. Mfg.
595	695	800

1981 Calgary Stampede (Canadian)

NIB	Issue	Amt. Mfg.
1250	2200	1,000

1981 Canadian Pacific Centennial (Canadian)

NIB	Issue	Amt. Mfg.
550	800	2,000

1981 Canadian Pacific Centennial Presentation (Canadian)

NIB	Issue	Amt. Mfg.
1100	2200	300

1981 Canadian Pacific Employee's Model (Canadian)

NIB	Issue	Amt. Mfg.
550	800	2,000

1981 John Wayne (Canadian)

NIB	Issue	Amt. Mfg.
1495	995	1,000

1981 John Wayne

NIB	Issue	Amt. Mfg.
1395	600	49,000

1981 Duke

NIB	Issue	Amt. Mfg.
3500	2250	1,000

1981 John Wayne "1 of 300" Set

NIB	Issue	Amt. Mfg.
6500	10000	300

1982 Great Western Artist I

NIB	Issue	Amt. Mfg.
1295	2200	999

1982 Great Western Artist II

NIB	Issue	Amt. Mfg.
1295	2200	999

1982 Annie Oakley

NIB	Issue	Amt. Mfg.
795	699	6,000

1983 Chief Crazy Horse

NIB	Issue	Amt. Mfg.
695	600	19,999

1983 American Bald Eagle

NIB	Issue	Amt. Mfg.
595	895	2,800

1983 American Bald Eagle—Deluxe

NIB	Issue	Amt. Mfg.
4000	2995	200

1983 Oklahoma Diamond Jubilee

NIB	Issue	Amt. Mfg.
1395	2250	1,001

1984 Winchester—Colt Commemorative Set

NIB	Issue	Amt. Mfg.
2250	3995	2,300

1985 Boy Scout 75th Anniversary .22 Cal.

NIB	Issue	Amt. Mfg.
750	615	15,000

1985 Boy Scout 75th Anniversary—Eagle Scout

NIB	Issue	Amt. Mfg.
4500	2140	1,000

Texas Sesquicentennial Model—Rifle .38-55 Cal.

NIB	Issue	Amt. Mfg.
2400	2995	1,500

Texas Sesquicentennial Model—Carbine .38-55 Cal.

NIB	Issue	Amt. Mfg.
695	695	15,000

Texas Sesquicentennial Model Set with Bowie Knife

NIB	Issue	Amt. Mfg.
6250	7995	150

1986 Model 94 Ducks Unlimited

NIB	Issue	Amt. Mfg.
650	—	2,800

1986 Statue of Liberty

NIB	Issue	Amt. Mfg.
7500	6500	100

1986 120th Anniversary Model—Carbine .44-40 Cal.

NIB	Issue	Amt. Mfg.
895	995	1,000

1986 European 1 of 1,000 Second Series (European)

NIB	Issue	Amt. Mfg.
7000	6000	150

1987 U.S. Constitution 200th Anniversary 44-40

NIB	Issue	Amt. Mfg.
14000	12000	17

1990 Wyoming Centennial-30-30

NIB	Issue	Amt. Mfg.
1495	895	500

1991 Winchester 125th Anniversary

NIB	Issue	Amt. Mfg.
5750	4995	61

1992 Arapaho—30-30

NIB	Issue	Amt. Mfg.
1495	895	500

1992 Ontario Conservation-30-30

NIB	Issue	Amt. Mfg.
1495	1195	400

1992 Kentucky Bicentennial-30-30

NIB	Issue	Amt. Mfg.
1495	995	500

1993 Nez Perce—30-30

NIB	Issue	Amt. Mfg.
1495	995	600

1995 Florida Sesquicentennial Carbine

NIB	Issue	Amt. Mfg.
1495	1195	360

1996 Wild Bill Hickok Carbine

NIB	Issue	Amt. Mfg.
1495	1195	350

WINDSOR

Windsor, Vermont
Robbins & Lawrence
Hartford, Connecticut

Windsor Rifle-Musket

A .577 caliber single-shot percussion rifle with a 39" round barrel secured by three barrel bands. The lock marked "Windsor." Rifles of this pattern were contracted for by the British Government. The lock and barrel finished in the white, brass furniture, and a walnut stock. Approximately 16,000 were made from 1855 to 1858.

Exc.	V.G.	Good	Fair	Poor
—	—	3000	950	300

WINSLOW ARMS CO.

Camden, South Carolina

Bolt Action Rifle

A high-grade, semi-custom sporting rifle built upon a number of actions and offered in all popular calibers from .17 Remington to the .458 Winchester Magnum with a 24" barrel and a 3-shot magazine. The larger Magnum models have a 26" barrel and a 2-shot magazine. Two basic stocks are offered—the Conventional Bushmaster, which features a standard pistol grip and a beavertail forearm; and also the Plainsmaster, which has a full curled, hooked pistol grip and a wide, flat beavertail forearm. Both have Monte Carlo-style stocks with recoil pads and sling swivels. Offered in a choice of popular woods with rosewood forend tips and pistol gripcaps. Eight different grades of this rifle are available and the following lists the values applicable for each.

Commander Grade

Figured walnut stock. Rosewood forearm tip and grip cap. White line recoil pad. FN Supreme action.

Exc.	V.G.	Good	Fair	Poor
550	450	400	350	300

Regal Grade

All features of Commander Grade plus ivory and ebony inlay on stock, French-style checkering, jeweled bolt.

Exc.	V.G.	Good	Fair	Poor
650	550	450	375	200

Regent Grade

As above with addition of hand-carved checkering.

Exc.	V.G.	Good	Fair	Poor
800	700	500	450	200

Regimental Grade

As above but with addition of basket weave carving, two ivory stock inlays and large ivory and ebony inlay on both side of butt stock with animal silhouette.

Exc.	V.G.	Good	Fair	Poor
950	850	650	550	250

Crown Grade

As above but with more elaborate ivory inlays on stock.

Exc.	V.G.	Good	Fair	Poor
1500	1250	1000	750	350

Royal Grade

As above but with addition even more elaborate stock carving and ivory and ebony inlay.

Exc.	V.G.	Good	Fair	Poor
1750	1400	1150	850	400

Imperial Grade

As above but with addition of engraved barrel from receiver to 11" forward. Engraved receiver ring, bolt handle and trigger guard. Engraved scope mounts and rings.

Exc.	V.G.	Good	Fair	Poor
4000	3000	2500	2000	1000

Emperor Grade

As above but with addition of gold raised relief animals engraved receiver and forward part of barrel with muzzle tip engraved engraved as well. Highest Winslow grade.

Exc.	V.G.	Good	Fair	Poor
6250	5000	4000	3000	1500

WISEMAN, BILL & CO.

Bryan, Texas

A custom order bolt-action rifle utilizing a Sako action, McMillan stainless steel barrel and laminated stock. The action components Teflon coated. It is made in four styles: the Hunter, Hunter Deluxe, Maverick, and the Varminter.

Exc.	V.G.	Good	Fair	Poor
1500	1250	950	—	—

Silhouette Pistol

A custom made single-shot pistol produced in a variety of calibers with a 14" fluted stainless steel barrel and laminated pistol-grip stock. Furnished without sights. Introduced in 1989.

Exc.	V.G.	Good	Fair	Poor
1300	1000	800	—	—

WITNESS

SEE—European American Armory

WOLF SPORTING PISTOLS

Importer—Handgunner Gunshop
Topton, Pennsylvania

Wolf SV Target

Chambered for 9x19, 9x21, 9x23, .38 Super, .40 S&W, or .45 ACP. Barrel is 4.5" long. Weight is 44 oz. Many special features. Built in Austria. Price listed is for basic pistol. A number of special order items are offered. Check with importer before a sale. First imported in 1998.

NIB	Exc.	V.G.	Good	Fair	Poor
2000	1600	—	—	—	—

Wolf SV Match

Chambered for 9x19, 9x21, 9x23, .38 Super, .40 S&W, or .45 ACP. Barrel is 5.5" long. Weight is 44 oz. Many special features. Built in Austria. Price listed is for basic pistol. A number of special order items are offered. Check with importer before a sale. First imported in 1998.

NIB	Exc.	V.G.	Good	Fair	Poor
2000	1600	—	—	—	—

WOODWARD, JAMES & SONS

London, England

SEE—British Double Guns

Prior to WWII, this company produced a variety of boxlock and sidelock shotguns that are regarded as some of the best made. Prospective purchasers should secure a qualified appraisal prior to acquisition.

WURFFLEIN, ANDREW & WILLIAM

Philadelphia, Pennsylvania

Pocket Pistol

A .41 caliber percussion single-shot pocket pistol with either a 2.5" or 3" barrel, German silver furniture and checkered walnut stock. The lock marked "A. Wurfflein / Phila." Manufactured during the 1850s and 1860s.

Exc.	V.G.	Good	Fair	Poor
—	—	1750	700	200

Single-Shot Target Pistol

A .22 caliber single-shot pistol with half-octagonal barrels measuring from 8" to 16" in length. The barrel pivots downward for loading and is marked "W. Wurfflein Philad'a Pa. U.S.A. Patented June 24th, 1884." Blued with walnut grips. This model is also available with a detachable shoulder stock, which if present, would add approximately 35 percent to the values listed. Manufactured from 1884 to 1890.

Exc.	V.G.	Good	Fair	Poor
—	—	1750	700	200

Single-Shot Rifle

A single-shot rifle produced in a variety of calibers with octagonal barrels of 24" to 28" length. This rifle was available with a wide variety of optional features.

Exc.	V.G.	Good	Fair	Poor
—	—	1250	350	150

Mid-range Model

As above, with a 28" or 30" half-octagonal barrel.

Exc.	V.G.	Good	Fair	Poor
—	—	3000	950	400

Model No. 25

The highest grade rifle manufactured by Wurfflein.

Exc.	V.G.	Good	Fair	Poor
—	—	3500	1250	600

XL
HOPKINS & ALLEN
Norwich, Connecticut

Derringer
A .41 caliber spur trigger single-shot pistol with a 2.75" octagonal barrel and either iron or brass frame. Blued, nickel-plated with rosewood grips. The barrel marked "XL Derringer." Manufactured during the 1870s.

Exc.	V.G.	Good	Fair	Poor
—	—	850	500	150

Vest Pocket Derringer
As above, in .22 caliber with a 2.25" round barrel and normally full nickel-plated. The barrel marked "XL Vest Pocket." Manufactured from 1870s to 1890s.

Exc.	V.G.	Good	Fair	Poor
—	—	750	325	125

XPERT
HOPKINS & ALLEN
Norwich, Connecticut

Xpert Derringer
A .22 or .30 caliber spur trigger single-shot pistol with round barrels, 2.25" to 6" in length and a nickel-plated finish with rosewood grips. The breechblock pivots to the left side for loading. The barrel marked "Xpert-Pat. Sep. 23. 1878." Manufactured during the 1870s.

Exc.	V.G.	Good	Fair	Poor
—	—	900	400	125

Xpert Pocket Rifle
Similar to the derringer with the same size frame but fitted with a 7.5" barrel and chambered for the .22 cartridge, as well as the .30 caliber rimfire. Supplied with wire stock. Values are for gun with stock. Produced from about 1870 to 1890s.

Exc.	V.G.	Good	Fair	Poor
—	—	1150	500	150

Z-B RIFLE CO.
Brno, Czechoslovakia

Model ZKW-465 Varmint Rifle
A Mauser bolt-action rifle chambered for the .22 Hornet cartridge. It has a 23" barrel with a three-leaf, folding rear sight. It is offered standard with double-set triggers. The finish is blued, with a select walnut checkered stock.

Exc.	V.G.	Good	Fair	Poor
1500	1100	950	800	500

ZANOTTI, FABIO
Brescia, Italy
Importer—New England Arms Co.
Kittery Point, Massachusetts

Model 625
A 12 to .410 bore boxlock double-barrel shotgun with automatic ejectors and single-selective trigger. Blued with checkered walnut stock.

NIB	Exc.	V.G.	Good	Fair	Poor
4500	3500	2500	2000	1500	750

Model 626
As above, engraved with either scroll work or hunting scenes.

NIB	Exc.	V.G.	Good	Fair	Poor
5000	4500	3000	2500	1500	750

Giacinto
An external hammer boxlock shotgun produced in a variety of gauges with double triggers.

NIB	Exc.	V.G.	Good	Fair	Poor
4750	3500	2750	2000	1200	750

Maxim
Similar to the Model 625, but fitted with detachable sidelocks.

NIB	Exc.	V.G.	Good	Fair	Poor
7500	6500	5000	3500	2250	1200

Edward
As above, but more intricately engraved.

NIB	Exc.	V.G.	Good	Fair	Poor
10000	8000	6500	4500	3000	1500

Cassiano I
As above, with exhibition grade engraving.

NIB	Exc.	V.G.	Good	Fair	Poor
11000	9000	7000	6000	4000	2000

Cassiano II
As above, with gold inlays.

NIB	Exc.	V.G.	Good	Fair	Poor
12500	10000	8500	7000	5000	2500

Cassiano Executive
A strictly custom-made shotgun produced to the client's specifications. Prospective purchasers should secure a qualified appraisal prior to acquisition. Prices listed are for base model only.

NIB	Exc.	V.G.	Good	Fair	Poor
15000	12500	—	—	—	—

ZEHNER, E. WAFFENFABRIK
Suhl, Germany

Zehna
A 6.35mm semi-automatic pistol with a 2.5" barrel and 5-shot magazine. The slide marked "Zehna DRPA," and the caliber on later production models. Blued with a black plastic grips bearing the monogram "EZ." Approximately 20,000 were made from 1921 to 1927.

Exc.	V.G.	Good	Fair	Poor
450	300	250	175	100

ZEILINGER
SEE—Austrian Military Firearms

ZEPHYR
Eibar, Spain
Importer—Stoegers

Woodlander II
A 12 or 20 gauge boxlock shotgun with varying length barrels, double triggers and extractors. Blued with a walnut stock.

NIB	Exc.	V.G.	Good	Fair	Poor
600	450	400	300	200	100

Uplander
A 12, 16, 20, 28 or .410 bore sidelock double-barrel shotgun with varying length barrels, double triggers, and automatic ejectors. Blued with a walnut stock.

NIB	Exc.	V.G.	Good	Fair	Poor
850	700	500	400	300	150

Upland King
As above, in 12 or 16 gauge with ventilated-rib barrels.

NIB	Exc.	V.G.	Good	Fair	Poor
1150	800	700	600	400	250

Vandalia
A 12 gauge single-barrel trap gun with a 32" Full choked barrel. Blued with a walnut stock.

NIB	Exc.	V.G.	Good	Fair	Poor
750	600	550	450	300	150

Sterlingworth II
Identical to the Woodlander, but with sidelocks.

NIB	Exc.	V.G.	Good	Fair	Poor
850	700	550	450	300	150

Victor Special
A 12 gauge boxlock double-barrel shotgun with 25", 28", or 30" barrels, double triggers and extractors. Blued with a walnut stock.

NIB	Exc.	V.G.	Good	Fair	Poor
525	400	300	250	175	100

Thunderbird
A 10 gauge Magnum boxlock double-barrel shotgun with 32" full choked barrels, double triggers, and automatic ejectors. Blued with a walnut stock.

NIB	Exc.	V.G.	Good	Fair	Poor
950	700	600	500	400	200

Honker

A 10 gauge Magnum single-barrel shotgun with a 36" fuçll choked and ventilated-rib barrel. Blued with a walnut stock.

NIB	Exc.	V.G.	Good	Fair	Poor
600	450	400	300	200	100

ZM WEAPONS

Bernardton, Massachusetts

LR-300 Sport Rifle

This is a highly modified AR-15 chambered for the .223 cartridge. It is fitted with a 16.25" barrel and a true folding stock. A Ghost Ring rear sight and an adjustable post front sight with tritium insert is standard. Weight is approximately 7.2 pounds. Introduced in 1997.

NIB	Exc.	V.G.	Good	Fair	Poor
1995	1600	1200	—	—	—

ZOLI USA, ANGELO

Brescia, Italy

Slide-Action Shotgun

A 12 gauge Magnum slide-action shotgun produced with a variety of barrel lengths with detachable choke tubes. Blued with a walnut stock.

NIB	Exc.	V.G.	Good	Fair	Poor
400	300	250	200	150	100

Diano I

A 12, 20 or .410 bore single-shot folding barrel shotgun. Produced in a variety of barrel lengths. Blued with a walnut stock.

NIB	Exc.	V.G.	Good	Fair	Poor
175	100	90	80	60	40

Diano II

As above, but with a bottom lever instead of a top release lever.

NIB	Exc.	V.G.	Good	Fair	Poor
175	100	90	80	60	40

Apache

A 12 gauge Magnum lever-action shotgun with a 20" barrel fitted with detachable choke tubes. Blued with a walnut stock.

NIB	Exc.	V.G.	Good	Fair	Poor
500	400	350	300	250	150

Quail Special

A .410 Magnum bore double-barrel shotgun with 28" barrels and a single trigger. Blued with a walnut stock.

NIB	Exc.	V.G.	Good	Fair	Poor
325	200	150	125	100	75

Falcon II

As above with 26" or 28" barrels and double triggers.

NIB	Exc.	V.G.	Good	Fair	Poor
325	200	150	125	100	75

Pheasant

A 12 gauge Magnum double-barrel shotgun with 28" barrels, single trigger, and automatic ejectors. Blued with a walnut stock.

NIB	Exc.	V.G.	Good	Fair	Poor
450	350	300	250	200	150

Classic

As above, with 26" to 30" barrels fitted with detachable choke tubes, single-selective trigger, and automatic ejectors. Blued with a walnut stock.

NIB	Exc.	V.G.	Good	Fair	Poor
850	700	600	500	300	200

Snipe

A .410 bore over-and-under shotgun with 26" or 28" barrels and a single trigger.

NIB	Exc.	V.G.	Good	Fair	Poor
400	300	200	175	150	100

Dove

Similar to the above.

NIB	Exc.	V.G.	Good	Fair	Poor
400	300	200	175	150	100

Texas

A 12, 20 or .410 bore over-and-under shotgun with 26" or 28" barrels, double triggers, and a bottom barrel release lever.

NIB	Exc.	V.G.	Good	Fair	Poor
350	250	200	150	100	75

Field Special

A 12 or 20 gauge Magnum double-barrel shotgun produced in a variety of barrel lengths with a single trigger and extractors. Blued with a walnut stock.

NIB	Exc.	V.G.	Good	Fair	Poor
550	400	300	250	200	100

Pigeon Model

As above, but more finely finished.

NIB	Exc.	V.G.	Good	Fair	Poor
550	400	300	250	200	100

Standard Model

Similar to the above but in 12 and 20 gauge only.

NIB	Exc.	V.G.	Good	Fair	Poor
500	400	300	250	200	100

Special Model

As above, with detachable choke tubes and a single-selective trigger.

NIB	Exc.	V.G.	Good	Fair	Poor
600	450	300	250	200	100

Deluxe Model

As above, but engraved and with better quality walnut.

NIB	Exc.	V.G.	Good	Fair	Poor
800	600	500	400	300	150

Presentation Model

As above, with false sidelocks and finely figured walnut stock.

NIB	Exc.	V.G.	Good	Fair	Poor
950	700	600	450	350	200

St. George's Target

A 12 gauge over-and-under shotgun trap or skeet bore with various length barrels, single-selective trigger, and automatic ejectors. Blued with a walnut stock.

NIB	Exc.	V.G.	Good	Fair	Poor
1200	900	700	600	550	250

St. George Competition

A 12 gauge single-barrel gun with an extra set of over and under barrels.

NIB	Exc.	V.G.	Good	Fair	Poor
1950	1600	1200	950	500	300

Express Rifle

A .30-06, 7x65Rmm or 9.3x74Rmm over-and-under double-barrel rifle with single triggers and automatic ejectors. Blued with a walnut stock.

NIB	Exc.	V.G.	Good	Fair	Poor
4250	3500	2500	1750	1200	600

Express EM

As above, but more finely finished.

NIB	Exc.	V.G.	Good	Fair	Poor
5500	4000	3000	1500	1000	750

Savana E

As above, with double triggers.

NIB	Exc.	V.G.	Good	Fair	Poor
6500	5250	4500	3500	2750	1500

Savana Deluxe

As above, but engraved with hunting scenes.

NIB	Exc.	V.G.	Good	Fair	Poor
8000	7000	6000	4750	3500	2000

AZ 1900C

A .243, .270, 6.5x55mm, .308, or .30-06 bolt-action rifle with a 24" barrel having open sights. Blued with a walnut stock.

NIB	Exc.	V.G.	Good	Fair	Poor
850	700	500	400	300	150

AZ 1900M

Same as above but fitted with a Bell & Carlson composite stock.

NIB	Exc.	V.G.	Good	Fair	Poor
750	600	450	350	275	200

AZ 1900 Deluxe

As above, but more finely finished.

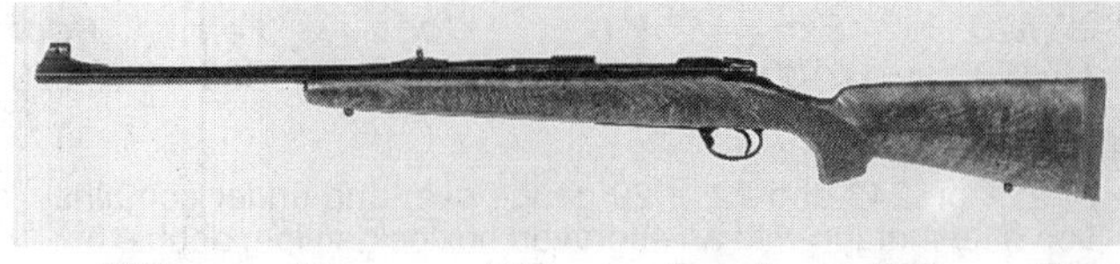

NIB	Exc.	V.G.	Good	Fair	Poor
1100	800	650	500	400	200

AZ 1900 Super Deluxe

As above, but engraved with a finely figured walnut stock.

NIB	Exc.	V.G.	Good	Fair	Poor
1500	1000	800	600	450	250

Patricia Model

As above, in .410 Magnum bore with 28" ventilated rib barrels, various chokes, single-selective trigger, and automatic ejectors. Engraved, blued with finely figured walnut stock.

NIB	Exc.	V.G.	Good	Fair	Poor
1500	1100	950	750	650	400

Condor

A .30-06 or .308 and 12 gauge over-and-under combination shotgun rifle with double triggers, extractors and sling swivels. Blued with a walnut stock.

NIB	Exc.	V.G.	Good	Fair	Poor
1500	1050	850	700	500	300

Airone

As above, with false sidelocks.

NIB	Exc.	V.G.	Good	Fair	Poor
1650	1250	1000	800	600	300

Leopard Express

A .30-06, .308, 7x65Rmm, or .375 Holland & Holland over-and-under double-barrel rifle with 24" barrels having express sights, double triggers and extractors. Blued with a walnut stock.

NIB	Exc.	V.G.	Good	Fair	Poor
1750	1400	1000	800	600	300

ZOLI, ANTONIO

Brescia, Italy

Silver Hawk

A 12 or 20 gauge boxlock double-barrel shotgun produced in a variety of barrel lengths and chokes with a double trigger. Engraved, blued with walnut stock.

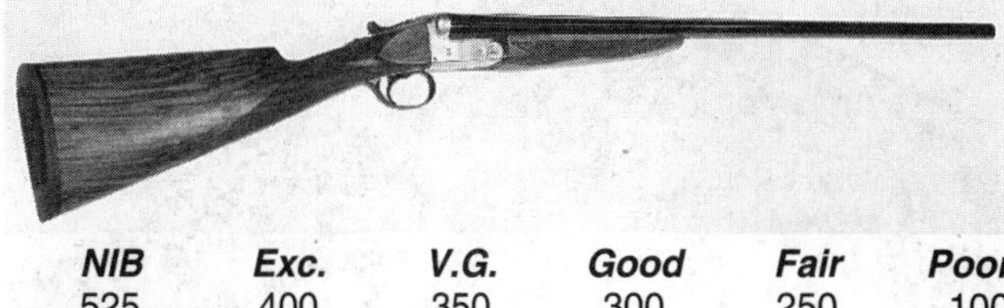

NIB	Exc.	V.G.	Good	Fair	Poor
525	400	350	300	250	100

Ariete M2

A 12 gauge boxlock double-barrel shotgun with 26" or 28" barrels, non-selective single trigger and automatic ejectors. Engraved, blued with a walnut stock.

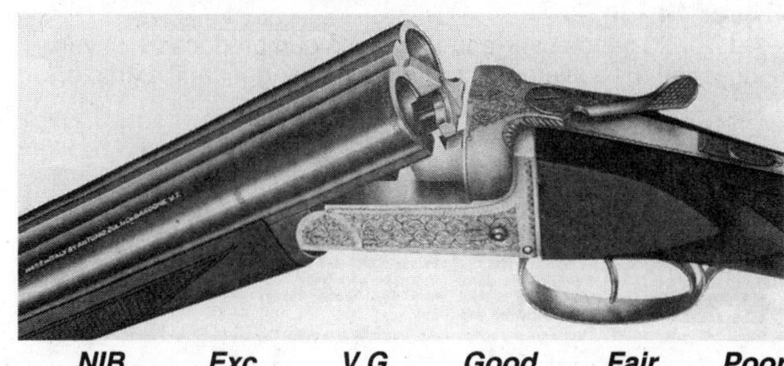

NIB	Exc.	V.G.	Good	Fair	Poor
650	500	450	400	350	200

Empire

As above, in 12 or 20 gauge with 27" or 28" barrels. Engraved, French case hardened, blued with a walnut stock.

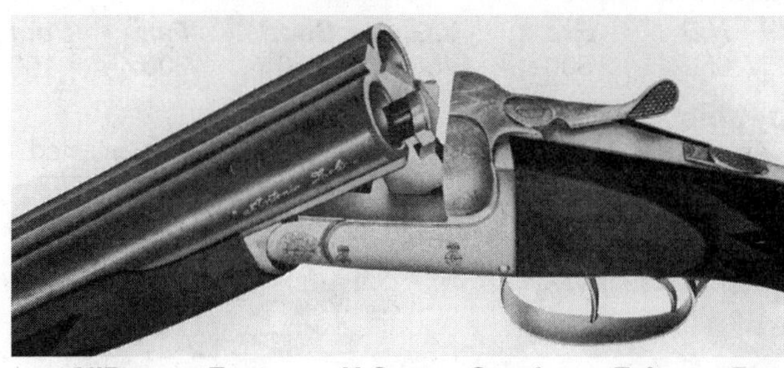

NIB	Exc.	V.G.	Good	Fair	Poor
1800	1450	1200	950	750	400

Volcano Record

A 12 gauge sidelock double-barrel shotgun with 28" barrels available in a variety of chokes, single-selective trigger and automatic ejectors. Engraved, French case hardened, blued with a walnut stock.

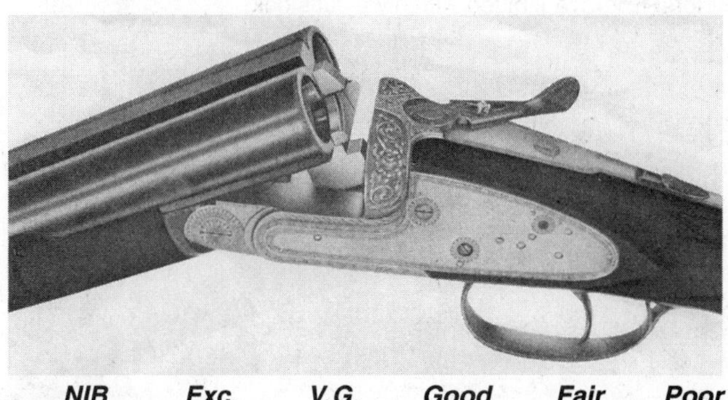

NIB	Exc.	V.G.	Good	Fair	Poor
6000	5000	4000	3000	2000	1000

Volcano Record ELM

This model is strictly a custom-ordered shotgun produced to the purchaser's specifications. A qualified appraisal is suggested prior to acquisition.

NIB	Exc.	V.G.	Good	Fair	Poor
14000	11500	8500	6500	3500	1500

Silver Snipe

A 12 or 20 gauge over-and-under shotgun produced with varying lengths, ventilated rib barrels, single trigger and extractors. Engraved, blued with a walnut stock.

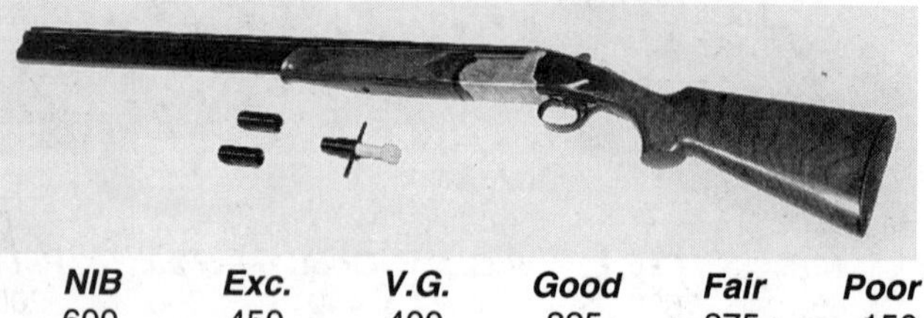

NIB	Exc.	V.G.	Good	Fair	Poor
600	450	400	325	275	150

Golden Snipe

As above, but more finely finished and fitted with automatic ejectors.

NIB	Exc.	V.G.	Good	Fair	Poor
650	500	450	350	300	150

Delfino

As above, in 12 or 20 gauge Magnum with 26" or 28" ventilated rib barrels, non-selective single trigger and automatic ejectors. Engraved, blued with walnut stock.

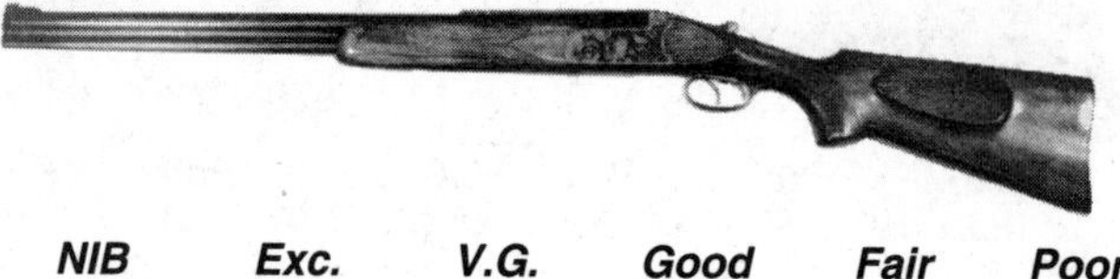

NIB	Exc.	V.G.	Good	Fair	Poor
575	425	325	275	250	150

Ritmo Hunting Gun

As above, in 12 gauge Magnum with 26" or 28" separated ventilated rib barrels, single-selective trigger and automatic ejectors. Engraved, blued with a walnut stock.

NIB	Exc.	V.G.	Good	Fair	Poor
650	500	450	400	350	200

Condor Model

As above, in 12 gauge with 28" skeet bored barrels having a wide competition rib, single-selective trigger and automatic ejectors. Engraved, French case hardened, blued with a walnut stock.

NIB	Exc.	V.G.	Good	Fair	Poor
1100	800	650	500	400	200

Angel Model

As above, in a field grade version.

NIB	Exc.	V.G.	Good	Fair	Poor
1100	800	600	500	400	200

Ritmo Pigeon Grade IV

As above, with 28" separated ventilated rib barrels, single-selective trigger, automatic ejectors and extensively engraved. French case hardened, blued with a finely figured walnut stock.

NIB	Exc.	V.G.	Good	Fair	Poor
2250	1600	1200	800	600	300

Model 208 Target

As above, with 28" or 30" trap or skeet bored barrels fitted with a wide ventilated rib.

NIB	Exc.	V.G.	Good	Fair	Poor
1200	850	700	600	500	250

Model 308 Target

As above, but more finely finished.

NIB	Exc.	V.G.	Good	Fair	Poor
1500	1100	850	700	500	250

Combinato

A .222 or .243 and 12 or 20 gauge over-and-under combination rifle/shotgun with an engraved boxlock-action, double triggers, and a folding rear sight. French case hardened, blued with a walnut stock.

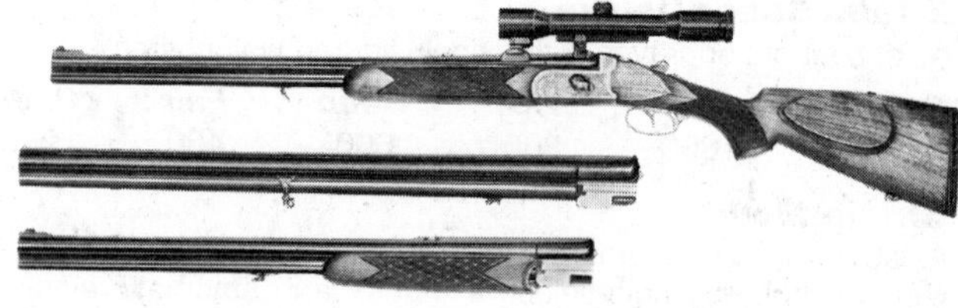

NIB	Exc.	V.G.	Good	Fair	Poor
1700	1250	950	850	600	300

Safari Deluxe

As above, but with false sidelocks that are engraved with scrolls or hunting scenes.

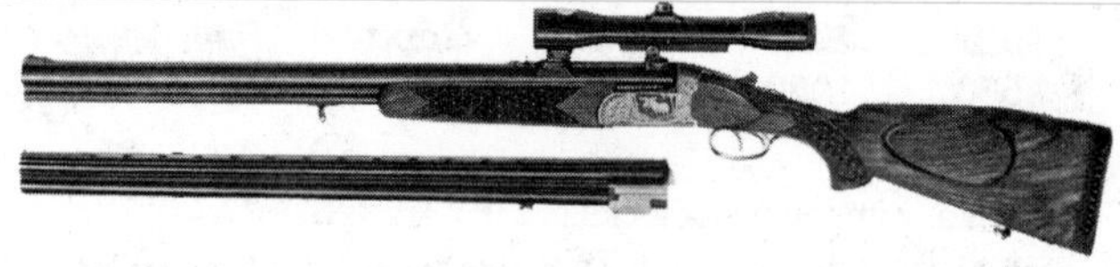

NIB	Exc.	V.G.	Good	Fair	Poor
5000	4000	2850	1500	1200	650

ZULAICA, M.

Eibar, Spain

Zulaica

A solid-frame .22 caliber revolver with a 6-shot cylinder that has zigzag grooves on its exterior surface. It is fired by an external hammer and the frame is hollow with a rod inside of it that connects to the breechblock. There is a serrated cocking piece connected to this rod that is found at the top rear of the frame. When fired, the cartridge case blows from the cylinder and activates the breechblock similar to a semi-automatic pistol.

Exc.	*V.G.*	*Good*	*Fair*	*Poor*
850	600	500	350	250

ROYAL

The name Royal was applied to a number of pistols produced by this company, as listed.

Royal

A 6.35mm or 7.65mm semi-automatic pistol that is normally marked on the slide "Automatic Pistol 6.35 Royal" or "Automatic Pistol 7.65 Royal."

Exc.	*V.G.*	*Good*	*Fair*	*Poor*
250	125	100	75	50

Royal

As above, in 7.65mm caliber with a 5.5" barrel and 12-shot magazine.

Exc.	*V.G.*	*Good*	*Fair*	*Poor*
275	150	125	100	75

Royal

A rather poor copy of the Mauser Model C/96 semi-automatic pistol with fixed lockwork.

Exc.	*V.G.*	*Good*	*Fair*	*Poor*
700	500	400	300	150

Vincitor

A 6.35mm or 7.65mm caliber semi-automatic pistol patterned after the Model 1906 Browning. The slide marked "SA Royal Vincitor." Blued with plastic grips.

Exc.	*V.G.*	*Good*	*Fair*	*Poor*
250	150	125	100	75

FIREARMS TRADE NAMES

A.A. Co.: Inexpensive pocket revolvers of unknown manufacture.

Acme:
a) Trade name used by the W.H. Davenport Firearms Company on shotguns.
b) Trade name used by the Hopkins and Allen Company on revolvers produced for the Merwin, Hulbert and Company and the Herman Boker Company of New York.
c) Trade name used by the Maltby, Henley and Company of New York on inexpensive pocket revolvers.

Acme Arms Company: Trade name used by the J. Stevens Arms and Tool Company on pistols and shotguns produced for the Cornwall Hardware Company of New York.

Aetna: Trade name used by the firm of Harrington and Richardson on inexpensive pocket revolvers.

Alamo Ranger: The name found on inexpensive Spanish revolvers.

Alaska: Trade name used by the Hood Firearms Company on inexpensive pocket revolvers.

Alert: Trade name used by the Hood Firearms Company on inexpensive pocket revolvers.

Alexander Gun Company: Trade name believed to have been used by E.K. Tryon of Philadelphia on imported shotguns.

Alexis: Trade name used by the Hood Firearms Company on inexpensive pocket revolvers.

Allen 22: Trade name used by the Hopkins and Allen Company on inexpensive pocket revolvers.

America: Trade name used by the Crescent Firearms Company on inexpensive pocket revolvers.

American: Trade name used by the Ely and Wray on inexpensive pocket revolvers.

American Barlock Wonder: Trade name used by the H. & D. Folsom Arms Company on Shotguns made for the Sears, Roebuck Company of Chicago.

American Boy: Trade name used on firearms retailed by the Townley Metal and Hardware Company of Kansas City, Missouri.

American Bulldog: Trade name used by the Iver Johnson Arms and Cycle Works on inexpensive pocket revolvers.

American Bulldog Revolver: Trade name used by Harrington and Richardson Arms Company on an inexpensive pocket revolver.

American Eagle: Trade name used by the Hopkins and Allen Company on inexpensive pocket revolvers.

American Gun Company: Trade name used by H. & D. Folsom Arms Company on pistols and shotguns that firm retailed.

American Gun Barrel Company: Trade name used by R. Avis of West Haven, Connecticut, between 1916 and 1920.

American Nitro: Trade name used by H. & D. Folsom Arms Co. on shotguns.

Americus: Trade name used by the Hopkins and Allen Company on inexpensive pocket revolvers.

Angel: Trade name found on inexpensive pocket revolvers of unknown manufacture.

Arab, The: Trade name used by the Harrington and Richardson Arms Company on shotguns.

Aristocrat:
a) Trade name used by the Hopkins and Allen Company on inexpensive pocket revolvers.
b) Trade name used by the Supplee-Biddle Hardware Company of Philadelphia on firearms they retailed.

Armory Gun Company: Trade name used by H. & D. Folsom Arms Co. on shotguns.

Aubrey Shotgun: Trade name found on shotguns made for the Sears, Roebuck and Company of Chicago by Albert Aubrey of Meriden, Connecticut.

Audax: Trade name used by the Manufacture d'Armes Pyrenees on semiautomatic pistols.

Aurora: Trade name found on inexpensive Spanish semiautomatic pistols.

Autogarde: Trade name used by the Societe Francaise des Munitions on semiautomatic pistols.

Automatic:
a) Trade name used by the Forehand and Wadsworth Company on inexpensive pocket revolvers.
b) Trade name used by the Harrington and Richardson Arms Company on inexpensive pocket revolvers.
c) Trade name used by the Iver Johnson Arms and Cycle Works on inexpensive pocket revolvers.

Auto Stand: Trade name used by the Manufacture Francaise d'Armes et Cycles, St. Etiene on semiautomatic pistols.

Avenger: Trade name found on inexpensive pocket revolvers of unknown manufacture.

Baby Hammerless: Trade mark used successively by Henry Kolb and R.F. Sedgley on pocket revolvers they manufactured.

Baby Russian: Trade name used by the American Arms Company on revolvers they manufactured.

Baker Gun Company: Trade name used by the H. & D. Folsom Arms Company on shotguns they retailed.

Baker Gun and Forging Company: Trade name used by the H. & D. Folsom Arms Company on shotguns they retailed.

Bang: Trade name found on inexpensive pocket revolvers of unknown manufacture.

Bang Up: Trade name used on inexpensive pocket revolvers retailed by the Graham and Haines Company of New York.

Bartlett Field: Trade name used on shotguns retailed by Hibbard, Spencer, Bartlett and Company of Chicago.

Batavia: Trade name used on shotguns produced by the Baker Gun Company.

Batavia Leader: Trade name used on shotguns produced by the Baker Gun Company.

Bay State: Trade name used by the Harrington and Richardson Arms Company on both inexpensive pocket revolvers and shotguns.

Belknap: Trade name used by the Belknap Hardware Company of Louisville, Kentucky, on shotguns made by the Crescent Fire Arms Company, which they retailed.

Bellmore Gun Company: Trade name used by the H. & D. Folsom Arms Company on shotguns made for them by the Crescent Fire Arms Company.

Berkshire: Trade name used by the H. & D. Folsom Arms Company on shotguns made for the Shapleigh Hardware Company of St. Louis, Missouri.

Bicycle: Trade name used on firearms made by the Harrington and Richardson Arms Company.

Big All Right: Trade name used on shotguns manufactured by the Wright Arms Company.

Big Bonanza: Trade name found on inexpensive pocket revolvers of unknown manufacture.

Bismarck: Trade name found on inexpensive pocket revolvers of unknown manufacture.

Black Beauty: Trade name used by the Sears, Roebuck and Company on imported shotguns they retailed.

Black Diamond: Trade name found on Belgian made shotguns retailed by an unknown American wholesale house.

Black Diana: Trade name used by the Baker Gun Company on shotguns.

Blackfield: Trade name used by the Hibbard, Spencer, Bartlett and Company of Chicago on shotguns they retailed.

Blackhawk: Trade name found on inexpensive pocket revolvers of unknown manufacture.

Black Prince: Trade name used by the Hopkins and Allen Company on inexpensive pocket revolvers.

Bliss: Trade name believed to have been used by the Norwich Arms Company.

Blood Hound: Trade name found on inexpensive pocket revolvers of unknown manufacture.

Bluefield: Trade name used by the W.H. Davenport Firearms Company on shotguns.

Bluegrass: Trade name used by the Belknap Hardware Company of Louisville, Kentucky, on shotguns they retailed.

Bluegrass Arms Company: Trade name of shotguns made by H. & D. Folsom Arms Co. for Belknap Hardware of Louisville, Kentucky.

Blue Jacket: Trade name used by the Hopkins and Allen Company on inexpensive pocket revolvers they made for the Merwin, Hulbert and Company of New York.

Blue Leader: Trade name found on inexpensive pocket revolvers of unknown manufacture.

Blue Whistler: Trade name used by the Hopkins and Allen Company on inexpensive pocket revolvers they made for the Merwin, Hulbert and Company of New York.

Bogardus Club Gun: Trade name found on Belgian made shotguns retailed by an unknown American wholesaler (possibly B. Kittredge and Company of Cincinnati, Ohio).

Boltun: Trade name used by F. Arizmendi on semiautomatic pistols.

Bonanza: Trade name used by the Bacon Arms Company on inexpensive pocket revolvers.

Boom: Trade name used by the Shattuck Arms Company on inexpensive pocket revolvers.

Boone Gun Company: Trade name used by the Belknap Hardware Company of Louisville, Kentucky, on firearms they retailed.

Boss:
a) Trade name used by E.H. and A.A. Buckland of Springfield, Massachusetts, on single-shot derringers designed by Holt & Marshall.
b) Trade name used on inexpensive pocket revolvers of unknown American manufacture.

Boys Choice: Trade name used by the Hood Firearms Company on inexpensive pocket revolvers.

Bride Black Prince: Trade name used by H. & D. Folsom Arms Co. on shotguns.

Bridge Gun Company: Registered trade name of the Shapleigh Hardware Company, St. Louis, Missouri.

Bridgeport Arms Company: Trade name used by H. & D. Folsom Arms Co. on shotguns.

Bright Arms Company: Trade name used by H. & D. Folsom Arms Company

British Bulldog: Trade name found on inexpensive pocket revolvers of unknown American and English manufacture.

Brownie:
a) Trade name used by the W.H. Davenport Firearms Company on shotguns.
b) Trade name used by the O.F. Mossberg Firearms Company on a four-shot pocket pistol.

Brutus: Trade name used by the Hood Firearms Company on inexpensive pocket revolvers.

Buckeye: Trade name used by the Hopkins and Allen Company on inexpensive pocket revolvers.

Buffalo: Trade name used by Gabilongo y Urresti on semiautomatic pistols.

Buffalo: Trade name found on bolt action rifles made in France.

Buffalo: Trade name used by the Western Arms Company on an inexpensive pocket revolver.

Buffalo Bill: Trade name used by the Iver Johnson Arms and Cycle Works on an inexpensive pocket revolver.

Buffalo Stand: Trade name used by the Manufacture Francaise d'Armes et Cycles on target pistols.

Bull Dog: Trade name used by the Forehand and Wadsworth Company on inexpensive pocket revolvers.

Bull Dozer:
a) Trade name used by the Norwich Pistol Company on inexpensive pocket revolvers.
b) Trade name used by the Forehand and Wadsworth Company on inexpensive pocket revolvers.
c) Trade name on Hammond Patent pistols made by the Connecticut Arms and Manufacturing Company.

Bull Frog: Trade name used by the Hopkins and Allen Company on rifles.

Bulls Eye: Trade name used by the Norwich Falls Pistol Company (O.A. Smith) on inexpensive pocket revolvers.

Burdick: Trade name used by the H. & D. Folsom Arms Company on shotguns made for the Sears, Roebuck and Company of Chicago.

Cadet: Trade name used by the Crescent Firearms Company on rifles.

Canadian Belle: Trade name used by H. & D. Folsom Arms Co. on shotguns.

Cannon Breech: Trade name used by the Hopkins and Allen Company on shotguns.

Captain: Trade name used by Manufacture d'Armes de Pyrenees on semiautomatic pistols.

Captain Jack: Trade name used by Hopkins & Allen on inexpensive pocket revolvers.

Carolina Arms Company: Trade name used by the H. & D. Folsom Arms Company on shotguns produced for the Smith, Wadsworth Hardware Company of Charlotte, North Carolina.

Caroline Arms: Trade name used by the H. & D. Folsom Arms Co.

Caruso: Trade name used by the Crescent Firearms Company on shotguns made for the Hibbard, Spencer, Bartlett and Company of Chicago.

Centennial 1876:
a) Trade name used by the Deringer Pistol Company on inexpensive pocket revolvers.
b) Trade name used by the Hood Firearms Company on inexpensive pocket revolvers.

Central Arms Company: Trade name used by the W. H. Davenport Firearms Company on shotguns made for the Shapleigh Hardware Company of St. Louis, Missouri.

Century Arms Company: Trade name used by the W. H. Davenport Firearms Company on shotguns made for the Shapleigh Hardware Company of St. Louis, Missouri.

Challenge:
a) Trade name found on inexpensive pocket revolvers of unknown manufacture.
b) Trade name used by the Sears, Roebuck and Company of Chicago on shotguns made by Albert Aubrey of Meriden, Connecticut.

Challenge Ejector: Trade name used by the Sears, Roebuck and Company of Chicago on shotguns made by Albert Aubrey of Meriden, Connecticut.

Champion:
a) Trade name used by H.C. Squires on shotguns.
b) Trade name used by J.P. Lovell on shotguns.
c) Trade name used by the Iver Johnson Arms and Cycle Works on shotguns and inexpensive pocket revolvers.
d) Trade name used by the Norwich Arms Company on inexpensive pocket revolvers.

Chantecler: Trade name used by Manufacture d'Armes de Pyrenees on semiautomatic pistols.

Charles Richter Company: Trade name used by the H. & D. Folsom Arms Company on firearms made for the New York Sporting Goods Company of New York.

Chatham Arms Company: Trade name used by H. & D. Folsom Arms Company used on shotguns.

Cherokee Arms Company: Trade name used by the H. & D. Folsom Arms Company on shotguns made for C.M. McLung and Company of Knoxville, Tennessee.

Chesapeake Gun Company: Trade name used by the H. & D. Folsom Arms Company of New York.

Chicago: Trade name found on shotguns retailed by the Hibbard, Spencer, Bartlett and Company of Chicago.

Chicago Ledger: Trade name used by the Chicago Firearms Company on inexpensive pocket revolvers.

Chicago Long Range Wonder: Trade name used by the H. & D. Folsom Arms Company on shotguns made for the Sears, Roebuck and Company of Chicago.

Chichester: Trade name used by Hopkins & Allen on inexpensive pocket revolvers.

Chicopee Arms Company: Trade name used by the H. & D. Folsom Arms Company of New York.

Chieftan: Trade name found on inexpensive pocket revolvers of unknown manufacture.

Christian Protector: Trade name found on inexpensive pocket revolvers of unknown manufacture.

Climax XL: Trade name used by Herman Boker and Company of New York on revolvers, rifles and shotguns.

Club Gun: Trade name used by B. Kittredge and Company of Cincinnati, Ohio, on shotguns they retailed.

Cock Robin: Trade name used by the Hood Firearms Company on inexpensive pocket revolvers.

Colonial: Trade name used by Manufacture d'Armes de Pyrenees on semiautomatic pistols.

Colonial: Trade name used by H. & D. Folsom Company on shotguns.

Columbian Automatic: Trade name used by Foehl & Weeks on inexpensive pocket revolvers.

Colton Arms Company: Trade name used by the Shapleigh Hardware Company of St. Louis, Missouri, on imported shotguns they retailed.

Colton Firearms Company: Trade name used by the Sears, Roebuck and Company of Chicago on shotguns they retailed.

Columbia:
a) Trade name found on inexpensive pocket revolvers of unknown manufacture.
b) Trade name used by H.C. Squires on shotguns.

Columbia Arms Company: Registered trade name of Henry Keidel, Baltimore, Maryland.

Columbian: Trade name found on inexpensive pocket revolvers of unknown manufacture.

Columbian Firearms Company:
a) Trade name used by the Maltby, Henly and Company on inexpensive pocket revolvers.
b) Trade name used by the Crescent Firearms Company on shotguns.

Combat: Trade name used by Randall Firearms Co. for its service model with a flat rib top and fixed sights.

Comet: Trade name used by the Prescott Pistol Company on inexpensive pocket revolvers.

Commander: Trade name used by the Norwich Arms Company on inexpensive pocket revolvers.

Commercial: Trade name used by the Norwich Falls Pistol Company (O.A. Smith) on inexpensive pocket revolvers.

Compeer: Trade name used by the H. & D. Folsom Arms Company on firearms made for the Van Camp Hardware and Iron Company of Indianapolis, Indiana.

Competition: Trade name used by John Meunier of Milwaukee, Wisconsin, on rifles.

Conestoga Rifle Works: Trade name of Henry Leman, Philadelphia, Pennsylvania.

Connecticut Arms Company: Trade name used by H. & D. Folsom Arms Company on shotguns.

Constable: Trade name used by Astra on semiautomatic pistols.

Constabulary: Trade name used by L. Ancion-Marx of Liege on revolvers.

Continental: Trade name used by the Great Western Gun Works of Pittsburgh, Pennsylvania, on firearms they retailed.

Continental Arms Company: Trade name used by the Marshall Wells Company of Duluth, Minnesota, on firearms they retailed.

Cotton King: Trade name found on inexpensive pocket revolvers of unknown manufacture.

Cowboy: Trade name used by the Hibbard, Spencer, Bartlett and Company of Chicago on imported, inexpensive pocket revolvers they retailed.

Cowboy Ranger: Trade name used by the Rohde Spencer Company of Chicago on inexpensive pocket revolvers.

Crack Shot: Trade name used by the J. Stevens Arms and Tool Company on rifles.

Cracker Jack: Trade name used by the J. Stevens Arms and Tool Company on pistols.

Creedmoore:
a) Trade name used by the Hopkins and Allen Company on inexpensive pocket revolvers.
b) Trade name used by the Chicago Firearms Company on inexpensive pocket revolvers.
c) Trade name used by William Wurflein on rifles.

Creedmoore Armory: Trade name used by A.D. McAusland of Omaha, Nebraska on rifles.

Creedmoore Arms Company: Trade name found on imported shotguns retailed by an unknown American wholesaler.

Crescent: Trade name used by the Crescent Arms Company on inexpensive pocket revolvers.

Crescent International 1XL: Trade name used by Herman Boker and Company of New York on shotguns.

Creve Coeur: Trade name used by the Isaac Walker Hardware Company of Peoria, Illinois, on imported shotguns they retailed.

Crown: Trade name used by the Harrington and Richardson Arms Company on inexpensive pocket revolvers.

Crown Jewel: Trade name used by the Norwich Arms Company on inexpensive pocket revolvers.

Cruso: Trade name used by the H. & D. Folsom Arms Company on shotguns made for Hibbard, Spencer, Bartlett and Company of Chicago.

Cumberland Arms Company: Trade name used by the H. & D. Folsom Arms Company on shotguns made for the Gray and Dudley Hardware Company of Nashville, Tennessee.

Czar:
a) Trade name used by the Hopkins and Allen Company on inexpensive pocket revolvers.
b) Trade name used by the Hood Firearms Company on inexpensive pocket revolvers.

Daisy:
a) Trade name used by the Bacon Arms Company on inexpensive pocket revolvers.
b) Registered proprietary trade name engraved on firearms made by the Winchester Repeating Arms Company for the F. Lassetter and Company, Limited of Sydney, Australia.

Daniel Boone Gun Company: Trade name used by H. & D. Folsom Arms Company on shotguns made for Belknap Hardware Company of Louisville, Kentucky.

Daredevel: Trade name used by Lou J. Eppinger of Detroit, Michigan, on pistols.

Dash: Trade name found on inexpensive pocket revolvers of unknown manufacture.

Davis Guns: Trade names used successively by N.R. Davis, Davis Warner, and the Crescent-Davis Arms Company on various firearms.

Dead Shot:
a) Trade name found on inexpensive pocket revolvers of unknown manufacture.
b) Trade name used by the Meriden Firearms Company on rifles.

Deer Slayer: Trade name used by J. Henry and Son of Boulton, Pennsylvania on rifles.

Defender:
a) Trade name used by the Iver Johnson Arms and Cycle Works on inexpensive pocket revolvers.
b) Trade name used by the U.S. Small Arms Company on knife pistols.

Defiance: Trade name used by the Norwich Arms Company on inexpensive pocket revolvers.

Delphian Arms Company:
a) Trade name used by the Supplee-Biddle Hardware Company of Philadelphia, Pennsylvania, on shotguns they retailed that were supplied by the H. & D. Folsom Company of New York.
b) Trade name used by the H. & D. Folsom Arms Company of New York on shotguns.

Delphian Manufacturing Company: Trade name used by the H. & D. Folsom Arms Company of New York on shotguns.

Demon: Trade name used by Manufacture d'Armes de Pyrenees on semiautomatic pistols.

Demon Marine: As above.

Dexter: Trade name found on inexpensive pocket revolvers of unknown manufacture.

Diamond Arms Company: Trade name used by the Shapleigh Hardware Company of St. Louis, Missouri, on imported shotguns they retailed.

Dictator: Trade name used by the Hopkins and Allen Company on inexpensive pocket revolvers.

Dominion Pistol: Trade name found on inexpensive pocket revolvers of unknown manufacture.

Double Header: Trade name used by E.S. Renwick on Perry and Goddard Patent derringers.

Douglas Arms Company: Trade name used by the Hopkins and Allen Company on shotguns.

Dreadnought: Trade name used by the Hopkins and Allen Company on shotguns and inexpensive pocket revolvers.

Duchess: Trade name used by the Hopkins and Allen Company on inexpensive pocket revolvers.

Duke: Trade name found on inexpensive pocket revolvers which may have been made by the Hopkins and Allen Company.

Dunlop Special: Trade name used by the Davis Warner Arms Company on shotguns made for the Dunlop Hardware Company of Macon, Georgia.

Duplex: Trade name used by the Osgood Gun Works of Norwich, Connecticut.

E.B.A.C.: Trade name used by Manufacture d'Armes de Pyrenees on semiautomatic pistols.

Eagle: Trade name used by the Iver Johnson Arms and Cycle Works on inexpensive pocket revolvers.

Eagle Arms Company: Trade name used by the Iver Johnson Arms and Cycle Works on inexpensive pocket revolvers.

Earlhood: Trade name used by E.L. Dickinson on inexpensive pocket revolvers.

Earnest Companion: Trade name found on inexpensive pocket revolvers of unknown manufacture.

Earthquake: Trade name used by E.L. Dickinson on inexpensive pocket revolvers.

Eastern Arms Company: Trade name used by the Sears, Roebuck and Company of Chicago on both shotguns and inexpensive revolvers made by the Iver Johnson Arms and Cycle Works.

Eclipse:
a) Trade name found on single-shot derringers of unknown manufacture.
b) Trade name used by E.C. Meacham on imported shotguns.

Electric: Trade name found on inexpensive pocket revolvers of unknown manufacture.

Electric City Single Hammer: Trade name found on single-shot shotguns retailed by the Wyeth Hardware and Manufacturing Company of St. Joseph, Missouri.

Elector: Trade name found on inexpensive pocket revolvers of unknown manufacture.

Elgin Arms Company: Trade name used by the H. & D. Folsom Arms Company on shotguns made for the Strauss and Schram Company of Chicago.

Elita: Trade name used by the W.H. Davenport Fire Arms Company on shotguns.

Empire:
a) Trade name used by the Rupertus Patented Pistol Manufacturing Company on inexpensive pocket revolvers.
b) Trade name used by the Crescent Firearms Company on shotguns.

Empire Arms Company: Trade name used by the H. & D. Folsom Arms Company on firearms made for the Sears, Roebuck and Company of Chicago.

Enders Royal Shotgun: Trade name used by the Crescent Davis Firearms Company on shotguns made for the Simmons Hardware Company of St. Louis, Missouri.

Enders Special Service: Trade name used by the Crescent Davis Firearms Company on shotguns made for the Simmons Hardware Company of St. Louis, Missouri.

Enterprise: Trade name used by the Enterprise Gun Works on inexpensive pocket revolvers.

Essex Gun Works: Trade name used by the Crescent - Davis Firearms Company on shotguns made for the Belknap Hardware Company of Louisville, Kentucky.

Eureka: Trade name used by the Iver Johnson Arms and Cycle Works on inexpensive pocket revolvers.

Excel: Trade name used by both the H. & D. Folsom Arms Company and the Iver Johnson Arms and Cycle Works on shotguns made for the Montgomery Ward and Company of Chicago.

Excelsior:
a) Trade name found on inexpensive pocket revolvers of unknown manufacture.
b) Trade name used by the Iver Johnson Arms and Cycle Works on shotguns.

Expert:
a) Trade name found on single-shot derringers of unknown manufacture.
b) Trade name used by the W.J. Davenport Firearms Company on shotguns made for the Witte Hardware Company of St. Louis, Missouri.

Express: Trade name used by the Bacon Arms Company on inexpensive pocket revolvers.

Express: Trade name used by Tomas de Urizar on a variety of semiautomatic pistols.

Farwell Arms Company: Trade name used by the Farwell, Ozmun, Kirk and Company of St. Paul, Minnesota, on shotguns.

Fashion: Trade name found on inexpensive pocket revolvers of unknown manufacture.

Faultless: Trade name used by the H. & D. Folsom Arms Company on shotguns made for the John M. Smythe Merchandise Company of Chicago.

Faultless Goose Gun: Trade name used by the H. & D. Folsom Arms Company on shotguns made for the John M. Smythe Merchandise Company of Chicago.

Favorite:
a) Trade name used by the J. Stevens Arms and Tool Company on rifles.
b) Trade name used by the Iver Johnson Arms and Cycle Works on inexpensive pocket revolvers.

Favorite Navy: Trade name used by the Iver Johnson Arms and Cycle Works on inexpensive pocket revolvers.

Featherlight: Trade name used by the Sears, Roebuck and Company of Chicago on firearms they retailed.

Federal Arms Company: Trade name used by Meriden Firearms Company.

Folks Gun Works: Trade name of William and Samuel Folk of Bryan, Ohio on rifles and shotguns.

Frank Harrison Arms Company: Trade name used by the Sickles and Preston Company of Davenport, Iowa, on firearms they retailed.

Freemont Arms Company: Trade name found on shotguns distributed by an unknown retailer.

Frontier: Trade name used by the Norwich Falls Pistol Company (O.A. Smith) on inexpensive pocket revolvers made for the firm of Maltby, Curtis and Company of New York.

Fulton: Trade name used by the Hunter Arms Company on shotguns.

Fulton Arms Company: Trade name used by the W.H. Davenport Firearms Company on shotguns.

Furor: Trade name used by Manufacture d'Armes de Pyrenees on semiautomatic pistols.

Gallia: Trade name used by Manufacture d'Armes de Pyrenees on semiautomatic pistols.

Game Getter: Registered trade mark of the Marble Arms and Manufacturing Company on combination rifle-shotguns.

Gaulois: Trade name used by Manufacture d'Armes et Cycles on squeezer type pistols (see also Mitrailleuse).

Gem:
a) Trade name used by the J. Stevens Arms and Tool Company on single-shot pocket pistols.
b) Trade name used by the Bacon Arms Company on inexpensive pocket revolvers.

Gen Curtis E. LeMay: Trade name used for Randall Firearms Co. for its small compact pistol made from the General's own gun.

General: Trade name used by the Rupertus Patented Pistol Manufacturing Company on inexpensive pocket revolvers.

General Butler: Trade name found on inexpensive pocket revolvers of unknown manufacture.

Gerrish: Trade name of G.W. Gerrish of Twin Falls, Idaho, used on shotguns.

Gibralter: Trade name of Albert Aubrey on shotguns made for the Sears, Roebuck and Company of Chicago.

Gladiator: Trade name of Albert Aubrey on shotguns made for the Sears, Roebuck and Company of Chicago.

Gold Field: Trade name found on inexpensive pocket revolvers of unknown manufacture.

Gold Hibbard: Trade name used by Hibbard, Spencer, Bartlett and Company of Chicago on firearms they retailed.

Gold Medal Wonder: Trade name used by H. & D. Folsom Arms Co. on shotguns.

Governor: Trade name used by the Bacon Arms Company on inexpensive pocket revolvers.

Guardian: Trade name used by the Bacon Arms Company on inexpensive pocket revolvers.

Gut Buster: Trade name found on inexpensive pocket revolvers of unknown manufacture.

Gypsy: Trade name found on inexpensive pocket revolvers of unknown manufacture.

Half Breed: Trade name found on inexpensive pocket revolvers of unknown manufacture.

Hamilton Arms: Registered trade name of the Wiebusch and Hilger Company, New York.

Hammerless Auto Ejecting Revolver: Trade name of the Meriden Firearms Company used on revolvers made for the Sears, Roebuck and Company of New York.

Hanover Arms Co.: If no foreign proofmarks then trade name used by H. & D. Folsom Arms Company.

Hardpan: Trade name found on inexpensive American pocket revolver.

Hard Pan: Trade name used by Hood Arms Company on inexpensive pocket revolvers.

Hart Arms Company: Trade name used by a Cleveland, Ohio, wholesaler (possibly the George Worthington Company).

Hartford Arms Company: Trade name used by the H. & D. Folsom Arms on shotguns made for the Simmons Hardware Company of St. Louis, Missouri.

Harvard: Trade name used by the H. & D. Folsom Arms Company on shotguns made for the George Worthington Company of Cleveland, Ohio.

Hercules: Trade name used by the Iver Johnson Arms and Cycle Works on shotguns made for the Montgomery Ward and Company of Chicago.

Hermitage Arms Company: Trade name used by the H. & D. Folsom Arms Company on shotguns made for the Gray and Dudley Hardware Company of Nashville, Tennessee.

Hero:
a) Trade name used by the American Standard Tool Company on percussion pistols.
b) Trade name used by the Manhattan Firearms Manufacturing Company on percussion pistols.

Hexagon: Trade name used by the Sears, Roebuck and Company of Chicago on shotguns they retailed.

Hinsdale: Trade name used by the Hopkins and Allen Company on inexpensive pocket revolvers.

Hornet: Trade name used by the Prescott Pistol Company on inexpensive pocket revolvers.

Howard Arms Company: Trade name used by the H. & D. Folsom Arms Company on shotguns they distributed.

Hudson: Trade name used by the Hibbard, Spencer, Bartlett and Company of Chicago on shotguns they retailed.

Hunter: Trade name used by the H. & D. Folsom Arms Company on shotguns made for the Belknap Hardware Company of Louisville, Kentucky.

Hunter, The: Trade name used by the Hunter Arms Company on shotguns.

Hurricane: Trade name found on inexpensive pocket revolvers of unknown manufacture.

I.O.A.: Trade name used by the Brown, Camp Hardware Company of Des Moines, Iowa on firearms they retailed.

I.X.L.:
a) Trade name used by B.J. Hart on percussion revolvers.
b) Trade name used by the W.H. Davenport Firearms Company on shotguns made for the Witte Hardware Company of St. Louis, Missouri.

Illinois Arms Company: Trade name used by the Rohde, Spencer Company of Chicago on firearms they retailed.

Imperial: Trade name used by the Lee Arms Company on inexpensive pocket revolvers.

Imperial Arms Company: Trade name used by the Hopkins and Allen Company on inexpensive pocket revolvers.

Infallible: Trade name used by the Lancaster Arms Company of Lancaster, Pennsylvania on shotguns they retailed.

Infallible Automatic Pistol: Trade name used by the Kirtland Brothers Company of New York on inexpensive pistols they retailed.

International:
a) Trade name found on inexpensive pocket revolvers of unknown manufacture.
b) Trade name used by E.C. Meacham on shotguns.

Interstate Arms Company: Trade name used by the H. & D. Folsom Arms Company on shotguns made for the Townley Metal and Hardware Company of Kansas City, Missouri.

Invincible: Trade name used by the Iver Johnson Arms and Cycle Works on both shotguns and inexpensive pocket revolvers.

Ixor: Trade name used by Manufacture d'Armes de Pyrenees on semiautomatic pistols.

J.J. Weston: Trade name used by the H. & D. Folsom Arms Company on shotguns.

J.S.T. & Company: Trade name used by the Iver Johnson Arms and Cycle Works on inexpensive pocket revolvers.

Jackson Arms Company: Trade name used by the H. & D. Folsom Arms Company on shotguns made for C.M. McLung and Company of Knoxville, Tennessee.

Jewel: Trade name used by the Hood Fire Arms Company on inexpensive pocket revolvers.

John M. Smythe & Company: Trade name used by H. & D. Folsom Arms Company for shotguns made for John M. Smythe Hardware Company of Chicago.

John W. Price: Trade name used by the Belknap Hardware Company of Louisville, Kentucky, on firearms they retailed.

Joker: Trade name used by the Marlin Firearms Company on inexpensive pocket revolvers.

Joseph Arms Company (Norwich, Connecticut): Trade name used by H. & D. Folsom Arms Company.

Judge: Trade name found on inexpensive pocket revolvers of unknown manufacture.

Jupitor: Trade name used by Fabrique d'Armes de Grand Precision, Eibar, Spain, on semiautomatic pistols.

K.K.: Trade name used by the Hopkins and Allen Company on shotguns made for the Shapleigh Hardware Company of St. Louis, Missouri.

Keno: Trade name found on inexpensive pocket revolvers of unknown manufacture.

Kentucky: Trade name used by the Iver Johnson Arms and Cycle Works on inexpensive pocket revolvers.

Keystone Arms Company: Trade name used by the W.H. Davenport Firearms Company on shotguns made for the E.K. Tryon Company of Philadelphia, Pennsylvania.

Kill Buck: Trade name of the Enterprise Gun Works (James Bown), Pittsburgh, Pennsylvania.

Killdeer: Trade name used by the Sears, Roebuck and Company of Chicago on firearms bearing their trade name Western Arms Company.

King Nitro: Trade name used by the W.H. Davenport Firearms Company on shotguns made for the Shapleigh Hardware Company of St. Louis, Missouri.

King Pin: Trade name found on inexpensive single-shot and revolving pocket pistols.

Kingsland Gun Company: Trade name used by the H. & D. Folsom Arms Company on shotguns made for the Geller, Ward and Hasner Company of St. Louis, Missouri.

Kirk Gun Company: Trade name used by Farwell, Ozmun, and Kirk Company of St. Paul, Minnesota.

Knickerbocker: Trade name used by the Crescent-Davis Firearms Company on shotguns.

Knickerbocker Club Gun: Trade name used by Charles Godfrey of New York on imported shotguns he retailed.

Knockabout: Trade name used by the Montgomery Ward and Company of Chicago on shotguns they retailed.

Knox-All: Trade name used by the Iver Johnson Arms and Cycle Works on firearms they made for the H. & D. Folsom Arms Company of New York.

L'Agent: Trade name used by Manufacture Francaises d'Armes et Cycles on revolvers.

Lakeside: Trade name used by the H. & D. Folsom Arms Company on firearms they made for the Montgomery Ward and Company of Chicago.

Le Colonial: Trade name used by Manufacture Francaises d'Armes et Cycles on revolvers.

Le Colonial: As above.

Le Francais: Trade name used by Manufacture Francaises d'Armes et Cycles on semiautomatic pistols.

Le Francais: As above on semiautomatic pistols.

Le Petit Forminable: Trade name used by Manufacture Francaises d'Armes et Cycles on revolvers.

Le Petit Forminable: As above on revolvers.

Le Protecteur: Trade name used by J.E. Turbiaux of Paris on squeezer pistols of the type later made by the Ames Sword Company.

Le Terrible: Trade name used by Manufacture Francaises d'Armes et Cycles on revolvers.

Leader:
a) Trade name used by the Shattuck Arms Company on inexpensive pocket revolvers.
b) Trade name used by the Harrington and Richardson Arms Company on inexpensive pocket revolvers.

Leader Gun Company: Trade name used by the H. & D. Folsom Arms Company on shotguns they made for the Charles Williams Stores, Inc. of New York.

Lee's Hummer: Trade name used by the H. & D. Folsom Arms Company on firearms they made for the Lee Hardware Company of Salina, Kansas.

Lee's Special: Trade name used by the H. & D. Folsom Arms Company on firearms they made for the Lee Hardware Company of Salina, Kansas.

Liberty: Trade name used by the Norwich Falls Pistol Company (O.A. Smith) on inexpensive pocket revolvers.

Liege Gun Company: Trade name used by the Hibbard, Spencer, Bartlett and Company of Chicago on imported shotguns they retailed.

Lion: Trade name used by the Iver Johnson Arms and Cycle Works on inexpensive pocket revolvers.

Little Giant: Trade name used by the Bacon Arms Company on inexpensive pocket revolvers.

Little John: Trade name used by the Hood Firearms Company on inexpensive pocket revolvers.

Little Joker: Trade name found on inexpensive pocket revolvers of unknown manufacture.

Little Pal: Registered trade name for knife pistols made by L.E. Pulhemus.

Little Pet: Trade name used by the Sears, Roebuck and Company of Chicago on inexpensive pocket revolvers they retailed.

London Revolver: Trade name found on inexpensive pocket revolvers of unknown manufacture.

Lone Star: Trade name found on inexpensive pocket revolvers of unknown manufacture.

Long Range Winner: Trade name used by the Sears, Roebuck and Company of Chicago on shotguns they retailed.

Long Range Wonder: Trade name used by the Sears, Roebuck and Company of Chicago on shotguns they retailed.

Long Tom: Trade name used by the Sears, Roebuck and Company of Chicago on shotguns they retailed.

Looking Glass: Trade name used on semiautomatic pistols of unknown Spanish manufacture.

Marquis of Horne: Trade name used by Hood Arms Company on inexpensive pocket revolvers.

Mars: Trade name used by Manufacture d'Armes de Pyrenees on semiautomatic pistols.

Marshwood: Trade name used by the H. & D. Folsom Arms Company on shotguns they made for the Charles Williams Stores Inc. of New York.

Marvel: Trade name used by the J. Stevens Arms and Tool Company on various firearms.

Massachusetts Arms Company: Trade name used by both the J. Stevens Arms and Tool Company and the H. & D. Folsom Arms Company on firearms made for the Blish, Mizet and Silliman Hardware Company of Atchinson, Kansas.

Maximum: Trade name found on inexpensive pocket revolvers of unknown manufacture.

Metropolitan: Trade name used by the H. & D. Folsom Arms Company on firearms they made for the Siegal-Cooper Company of New York.

Metropolitan Police:
a) Trade name used by the Maltby, Curtiss and Company on inexpensive pocket revolvers.
b) Trade name used by the Rohde-Spencer Company of Chicago on inexpensive pocket revolvers.

Midget Hammerless: Trade name used by the Rohde-Spencer Company of Chicago on inexpensive pocket revolvers.

Mikros: Trade name used by Manufacture d'Armes de Pyrenees on semiautomatic pistols.

Minnesota Arms Company: Trade name used by the H. & D. Folsom Arms Company on shotguns they made for the Farwell, Ozmun, Kirk and Company of St. Paul, Minnesota.

Missaubi Arms Company: Trade name used by the Hunter Arms Company, possibly for the Farwell, Ozmun, Kirk and Company of St. Paul, Minnesota.

Mississippi Arms Company: Trade name used by the H. & D. Folsom Arms Company on firearms made for the Shapleigh Hardware Company of St. Louis, Missouri.

Mississippi Valley Arms Company: Trade name used by the H. & D. Folsom Arms Company on firearms made for the Shapleigh Hardware Company of St. Louis, Missouri.

Mitrailleuse: Alternate trade name of the Gauluis squeezer pistol.

Mohawk: Trade name used by the H. & D. Folsom Arms Company on firearms made for the Blish, Mizet and Silliman Hardware Company of Atchinson, Kansas.

Mohegan: Trade name used by the Hood Firearms Company on inexpensive pocket revolvers.

Monarch:
a) Trade name used by the Hopkins and Allen Company on inexpensive pocket revolvers.
b) Trade name used by the Osgood Gun Works on Duplex revolvers.

Monitor:
a) Trade name used by the Whitneyville Armory on inexpensive pocket revolvers.
b) Trade name used by the H. & D. Folsom Arms Company on firearms made for the Paxton and Gallagher Company of Omaha, Nebraska.

Montgomery Arms Company: Trade name used by the H. & D. Folsom Arms Company on a variety of firearms.

Mountain Eagle: Trade name used by the Hopkins and Allen Company on inexpensive pocket revolvers.

Mount Vernon Arms Company: Trade name used by the H. & D. Folsom Arms Company on firearms made for the Carlin, Hullfish Company of Alexandria, Virginia.

My Companion: Trade name found on inexpensive pocket revolvers of unknown manufacture.

My Friend: Trade name used by James Reid of New York.

N.R. Adams: Trade name used by the N.R. Davis and Company on shotguns.

Napoleon: Trade name used by the Thomas J. Ryan Pistol Manufacturing Company of Norwich, Connecticut, on inexpensive pocket revolvers.

National Arms Company: Trade name used by the H. & D. Folsom Arms Company on firearms made both for the May Hardware Company of Washington, D.C., and the Moskowitz and Herbach Company of Philadelphia, Pennsylvania.

Nevermiss: Trade name used by the Marlin Firearms Company on single-shot pocket pistols.

New Aubrey: Trade name used by Albert Aubrey of Meriden, Connecticut, on both revolvers and shotguns made for the Sears, Roebuck and Company of Chicago.

New Britain Arms Company: Trade name used by H. & D. Folsom Arms Company.

New Defender: Trade name used by Harrington & Richardson on revolvers.

New Elgin Arms Company: Trade name used by H. & D. Folsom Arms Company.

New Empire: Trade name used by H. & D. Folsom Arms Company.

New England Arms Company: Trade name believed to have been used by Charles Godfrey on shotguns made for the Rohde-Spencer Company of Chicago.

New Era Gun Works: Trade name used by the Baker Gun Company on firearms made for an unknown retailer.

New Haven Arms Company: Trade name found on Belgian shotguns imported by either E.K. Tryon of Philadelphia or the Great Western Gun Works of Pittsburgh, Pennsylvania.

New Liberty: Trade name used by the Sears, Roebuck and Company of Chicago on inexpensive pocket revolvers they retailed.

New Rival: Trade name used by the H. & D. Folsom Arms Company on firearms made for the Van Camp Hardware and Iron Company of Indianapolis, Indiana.

New Worcester: Trade name used by the Torkalson Manufacturing Company of Worcester, Massachusetts.

New York Arms Company: Trade name used by the H. & D. Folsom Arms Company on firearms made for the Garnet Carter Company of Chattanooga, Tennessee.

New York Gun Company: Trade name used by the H. & D. Folsom Arms Company on firearms made for the Garnet Carter Company of Chattanooga, Tennessee.

New York Club: Trade name used by the H. & D. Folsom Arms Company on rifles.

New York Machine Made: Trade name used by the H. & D. Folsom Arms Company.

New York Pistol Company: Trade name used by the Norwich Falls Pistol Company (O.A. Smith) on inexpensive pocket revolvers.

Newport:
a) Trade name found on inexpensive pocket revolvers of unknown manufacture.
b) Trade name used by the H. & D. Folsom Arms Company on shotguns made for Hibbard, Spencer, Bartlett and Company of Chicago.

Nightingale: Trade name found on inexpensive pocket revolvers of unknown manufacture.

Nitro Bird: Trade name used by the Richards and Conover Hardware Company of Kansas City, Missouri.

Nitro Hunter: Trade name used by the H. & D. Folsom Arms Company on shotguns made for the Belknap Hardware Company of Louisville, Kentucky.

Nitro King: Trade name used by the Sears, Roebuck and Company of Chicago on shotguns of unknown manufacture.

Nitro Special: Trade name used by the J. Stevens Arms and Tool Company on shotguns.

Northfield Knife Company: Trade name used by the Rome Revolver and Novelty Works of Rome, New York, on inexpensive pocket revolvers.

Norwich Arms Company:
a) Trade name used by the Hood Firearms Company on inexpensive pocket revolvers.
b) Trade name found on shotguns retailed by the Marshall, Wells Company of Duluth, Minnesota, and Winnipeg, Manitoba, Canada.

Norwich Falls Pistol Company: Trade name used by the O.A. Smith Company on inexpensive pocket revolvers made for Maltby, Curtis and Company of New York.

Norwich Lock Manufacturing Company: Trade name used by F.W. Hood Firearms Company on inexpensive pocket revolvers.

Not-Nac Manufacturing Company: Trade name used by the H. & D. Folsom Arms Company on firearms made for the Canton Hardware Company of Canton, Ohio.

Novelty: Trade name used by D.F. Mossberg & Sons on Shattuck Unique pistols.

OK:
a) Trade name used by the Marlin Firearms Company on single-shot pocket pistols.
b) Trade name used by Cowles and Son of Chicopee Falls, Massachusetts, on single-shot pocket pistols.
c) Trade name found on inexpensive pocket revolvers of unknown manufacture.

Old Hickory:
a) Trade name found on inexpensive pocket revolvers of unknown manufacture.
b) Trade name used by the Hibbard, Spencer, Bartlett and Company of Chicago on shotguns they retailed.

Old Reliable: Trade name used by the Sharps Rifle Company.

Olympic:
a) Trade name used by the J. Stevens Arms and Tool Company on rifles and pistols.
b) Trade name used by the Morley and Murphy Hardware Company of Green Bay, Wisconsin, on firearms they retailed (possibly made by the J. Stevens Arms and Tool Company).

Osprey: Trade name used by Lou J. Eppinger of Detroit, Michigan, on firearms he made.

Our Jake: Trade name used by E.L. and J. Dickinson of Springfield, Massachusetts, on inexpensive pocket revolvers.

Oxford Arms Company: Trade name used by the H. & D. Folsom Arms Company on firearms made for the Belknap Hardware Company of Louisville, Kentucky.

Pagoma: Trade name used by the H. & D. Folsom Arms Company on firearms made for the Paxton and Gallagher Company of Omaha, Nebraska.

Peoria Chief: Trade name found on inexpensive pocket revolvers.

Perfect: Trade name used by the Foehl and Weeks Firearms Manufacturing Company of Philadelphia, Pennsylvania, on inexpensive pocket revolvers.

Perfect: Trade name used by Manufacture d'Armes de Pyrenees on semiautomatic pistols.

Perfection:
a) Trade name used by the H. & D. Folsom Arms Company on firearms made for the H.G. Lipscomb and Company of Nashville, Tennessee.
b) Trade name used by the John M. Smythe Merchandise Company of Chicago on firearms they retailed.

Pet: Trade name found on inexpensive pocket revolvers of unknown manufacture.

Petrel: Trade name found on inexpensive pocket revolvers of unknown manufacture.

Phenix: Trade name used by J. Reid of New York on revolvers.

Phoenix:
a) Trade name used by J. Reid of New York on revolvers.
b) Trade name used by the Whitneyville Armory on percussion revolvers.

Piedmont: Trade name used by the H. & D. Folsom Arms Company on firearms made for the Piedmont Hardware Company of Danville, Pennsylvania.

Pinafore: Trade name used by the Norwich Falls Pistol Company (O.A. Smith) on inexpensive pocket revolvers.

Pioneer: Trade name found on inexpensive pocket revolvers of unknown manufacture.

Pioneer Arms Company: Trade name used by the H. & D. Folsom Arms Company on firearms made for the Kruse and Baklmann Hardware Company of Cincinnati, Ohio.

Pittsfield: Trade name used by the Hibbard, Spencer, Bartlett and Company of Chicago on firearms probably made by the H. & D. Folsom Arms Company.

Plug Ugly: Trade name found on inexpensive pocket revolvers of unknown manufacture.

Plymouth: Trade name used by Spear and Company of Pittsburgh, Pennsylvania, on firearms they retailed.

Pocahontas: Trade name found on inexpensive pocket revolvers of unknown manufacture.

Pointer: Trade name found on single-shot pocket pistols of unknown manufacture.

Prairie Fire: Trade name found on inexpensive pocket revolvers of unknown manufacture.

Prairie King:
a) Trade name used by the Bacon Arms Company on inexpensive pocket revolvers.
b) Trade name used by the H. & D. Folsom Arms Company on inexpensive pocket revolvers.

Premier:
a) Trade name used by the Thomas E. Ryan Company on inexpensive pocket revolvers.
b) Trade name used by the Harrington and Richardson Arms Company on revolvers.
c) Trade name used by the Montgomery Ward and Company of Chicago on firearms they retailed.
d) Registered trade name of Edward K. Tryon and Company of Philadelphia, Pennsylvania.

Premium: Trade name used by the Iver Johnson Arms and Cycle Works on inexpensive pocket revolvers.

Princess: Trade name found on inexpensive pocket revolvers of unknown American manufacture.

Progress: Trade name used by Charles J. Godfrey of New York on shotguns.

Protection: Trade name used by the Whitneyville Armory on revolvers.

Protector:
a) Trade name found on inexpensive pocket revolvers of unknown manufacture.
b) Trade name used by the Chicago Firearms Company on inexpensive pocket revolvers.

Protector Arms Company: Trade name used by the Rupertus Patented Pistol Manufacturing Company on inexpensive pocket revolvers.

Providence: Trade name found on inexpensive pocket revolvers of unknown manufacture.

Puppy: Trade name found on inexpensive pocket revolvers made by several European makers.

Quail: Trade name used by the Crescent-Davis Arms Company on shotguns.

Queen:
a) Trade name used by the Hood Firearms Company on inexpensive pocket revolvers.
b) Trade name used by the Hyde and Shattuck Company on inexpensive single-shot pocket pistols.

Queen City: Trade name used by the H. & D. Folsom Arms Company on firearms made for the Elmira Arms Company of Elmira, New York.

Raider: Randall Firearms Co. Commander size pistol named after Gen Randall's flight squadron; "Randall's Raiders".

Ranger:
a) Trade name found on inexpensive pocket revolvers of unknown manufacture.
b) Trade name used by the Eastern Arms Company on various firearms made for the Sears, Roebuck and Company of Chicago.
c) Trade name of the Sears, Roebuck and Company of Chicago on a wide variety of firearms marketed by that firm.

Rapid-Maxim: Trade name used by Manufacture d'Armes de Pyrenees on semiautomatic pistols.

Reassurance: Trade name found on inexpensive pocket revolvers of unknown manufacture.

Red Chieftan: Trade name used by the Supplee Biddle Hardware Company of Philadelphia, Pennsylvania, on inexpensive pocket pistols they retailed.

Red Cloud: Trade name used by the Ryan Pistol Manufacturing Company on inexpensive pocket revolvers.

Red Hot: Trade name found on inexpensive pocket revolvers of unknown manufacture.

Red Jacket:
a) Trade name used by the Lee Arms Company on inexpensive pocket revolvers.
b) Trade name used by the Hopkins and Allen Company on inexpensive pocket revolvers.

Reliable: Trade name found on inexpensive pocket revolvers of unknown manufacture.

Reliance: Trade name used by John Meunier of Milwaukee, Wisconsin, on rifles.

Rev-O-Noc: Trade name used by the H. & D. Folsom Arms Company on firearms made for the Hibbard, Spencer, Bartlett and Company of Chicago.

Rich-Con: Trade name used by the H. & D. Folsom Arms Company for shotguns made for Richardson & Conover Hardware Company.

Richmond Arms Company: Trade name used by the H. & D. Folsom Arms Company on firearms made for an unknown retailer.

Rickard Arms Company: Trade name used by the H. & D. Folsom Arms Company on firearms made for the J.A. Rickard Company of Schenectady, New York.

Rip Rap: Trade name used by the Bacon Arms Company on inexpensive pocket revolvers.

Rival: Trade name used by the H. & D. Folsom Arms Company on firearms made for the Van Camp Hardware and Iron Company of Indianapolis, Indiana.

Riverside Arms Company: Trade name used by the J. Stevens Arms and Tool Company on various types of firearms.

Robin Hood: Trade name used by the Hood Firearms Company on inexpensive pocket revolvers.

Rocky Hill: Trade name found on inexpensive cast iron percussion pocket pistols made in Rocky Hill, Connecticut.

Rodgers Arms Company: Trade name used by the Hood Firearms Company on firearms made for an unknown retailer.

Royal Gun Company: Trade name used by the Three Barrel Gun Company.

Royal Service: Trade name used by the Shapleigh Hardware Company of St. Louis, Missouri, on firearms they retailed.

Rummel Arms Company: Trade name used by the H. & D. Folsom Arms Company on firearms made for the A.J. Rummel Arms Company of Toledo, Ohio.

Russel Arms Company: Registered trade name of the Wiebusch and Hilger Company of New York.

Russian Model: Trade name used by the Forehand and Wadsworth Company on inexpensive pocket revolvers.

S. Holt Arms Company: Trade name used by the Sears, Roebuck and Company of Chicago on shotguns they retailed.

S.A.: Trade mark of the Societe d'Armes Francaises.

S.H. Harrington: If no foreign proofmarks then trade name used by H. & D. Folsom Arms Company.

Safe Guard: Trade name found on inexpensive pocket revolvers of unknown manufacture.

Safety Police: Trade name used by the Hopkins and Allen Company on inexpensive pocket revolvers.

Scott: Trade name used by the Hopkins and Allen Company on inexpensive pocket revolvers.

Secret Service Special: Trade name used by the Rohde-Spencer Company of Chicago on inexpensive pocket revolvers.

Selecta: Trade name used by Manufacture d'Armes de Pyrenees on semiautomatic pistols.

Senator: Trade name found on inexpensive pocket revolvers of unknown manufacture.

Sentinal: Trade name found on inexpensive pocket revolvers of unknown manufacture.

Service Model C: The predecessor to the "Raider" pistol.

Sheffield, The: Trade name used by the A. Baldwin and Company, Limited of New Orleans, Louisiana, on shotguns they retailed.

Sickels-Arms Company: Trade name used by the Sickels and Preston Company of Davenport, Iowa, on firearms they retailed.

Simson: Trade name used by the Iver Johnson Arms and Cycle Works on firearms made for the Iver Johnson Sporting Goods Company of Boston, Massachusetts.

Sitting Bull: Trade name found on inexpensive pocket revolvers of unknown manufacture.

Skue's Special: Trade name used by Ira M. Skue of Hanover, Pennsylvania, on shotguns.

Smoker: Trade name used by the Iver Johnson Arms and Cycle Works on inexpensive pocket revolvers.

Southern Arms Company: Trade name used by the H. & D. Folsom Arms Company on firearms made for an unknown retailer.

Southerner:
a) Trade name used by the Brown Manufacturing Company and the Merrimac Arms Manufacturing Company on single-shot pocket pistols.
b) Registered trade name of Asa Farr of New York on pistols.

Southron: Trade name found on inexpensive pocket pistols of unknown manufacture.

Special Service: Trade name used by the Shapleigh Hardware Company of St. Louis, Missouri, on inexpensive pocket revolvers.

Spencer Gun Company: Trade name used by the H. & D. Folsom Arms Company.

Splendor: Trade name found on inexpensive pocket revolvers of unknown manufacture.

Sportsman, The: Trade name used by the H. & D. Folsom Arms Company on firearms made for the W. Bingham Company of Cleveland, Ohio.

Springfield Arms Company: Trade name used by the J. Stevens Arms and Tool Company.

Spy: Trade name found on inexpensive pocket revolvers of unknown manufacture.

Square Deal: Trade name used by the H. & D. Folsom Arms Company on firearms made for the Stratton, Warren Hardware Company of Memphis, Tennessee.

St. Louis Arms Company: Trade name used by the H. & D. Folsom Arms Company on firearms made for the Shapleigh Hardware Company of St. Louis, Missouri.

Standard: Trade name used by the Marlin Firearms Company on revolvers.

Stanley Arms: Registered trade name of the Wiebusch and Hilger Company of New York on firearms they retailed.

Stanley Double Gun: Trade name used by the H. & D. Folsom Arms Company on shotguns they retailed.

Star:
a) Trade name found on inexpensive single-shot pocket pistols of unknown manufacture.
b) Trade name used by the Prescott Pistol Company on inexpensive pocket revolvers.
c) Trade name used by Johnson & Bye on single-shot cartridge derringers.

State Arms Company: Trade name used by the H. & D. Folsom Arms Company on firearms made for the J.H. Lau and Company of New York.

Sterling:
a) Trade name used by E.L. and J. Dickinson of Springfield, Massachusetts, on single-shot pistols.
b) Trade name used by the H. & D. Folsom Arms Company on shotguns they retailed.

Stinger: Registered proprietary trade name engraved on firearms made by the Winchester Repeating Arms Company for the Perry Brothers Limited of Brisbane, Australia.

Stonewall:
a) Trade name used by the Marlin Firearms Company on single-shot derringers.
b) Trade name used by T.F. Guion of Lycoming, Pennsylvania, on single-shot percussion pistols he retailed.

Striker: Trade name found on inexpensive pocket revolvers of unknown manufacture.

Sullivan Arms Company: Trade name used by the H. & D. Folsom Arms Company on firearms made for the Sullivan Hardware Company of Anderson, South Carolina.

Superior: Trade name of the Paxton and Gallagher Company of Omaha, Nebraska, on revolvers and shotguns.

Super Range: Trade name of the Sears, Roebuck and Company of Chicago on shotguns.

Sure Fire: Trade name found on inexpensive pocket revolvers of unknown manufacture.

Swamp Angel: Trade name used by the Forehand and Wadsworth Company on inexpensive pocket revolvers.

Swift: Trade name used by the Iver Johnson Arms and Cycle Works on firearms made for the John P. Lovell & Sons, Boston, Massachusetts.

Syco: Trade name used by the Wyeth Hardware Company of St. Joseph, Missouri, on firearms they retailed.

Sympathique: Trade name used by Manufacture d'Armes de Pyrenees on semiautomatic pistols.

T. Barker: Trade name used by the H. & D. Folsom Arms Company of New York on shotguns they retailed.

Ten Star: Trade name used by the H. & D. Folsom Arms Company on firearms made for the Geller, Ward and Hasner Company of St. Louis, Missouri.

Terrier: Trade name used by the Rupertus Patented Pistol Manufacturing Company on inexpensive pocket revolvers.

Terror: Trade name used by the Forehand and Wadsworth Company on inexpensive pocket revolvers.

Texas Ranger: Trade name used by the Montgomery Ward and Company of Chicago on inexpensive pocket revolvers they retailed.

Thames Arms Company: Trade name used by the Harrington and Richardson Arms Company on firearms they made for an unknown wholesaler.

Tiger:
a) Trade name used by the Iver Johnson Arms and Cycle Works on inexpensive pocket revolvers.
b) Trade name used by the J.H. Hall and Company of Nashville, Tennessee, on shotguns they retailed.

Tobin Simplex: Trade name used on shotguns of unknown manufacture that were retailed by the G.B. Crandall Company, Limited of Woodstock, Ontario, Canada.

Toledo Firearms Company:
a) Trade name used by the Hopkins and Allen Company on inexpensive pocket revolvers.
b) Trade name used by E.L. and J. Dickinson on inexpensive pocket revolvers.

Toronto Belle: Trade name found on inexpensive pocket revolvers of unknown manufacture.

Touriste: Trade name used by Manufacture d'Armes de Pyrenees on semiautomatic pistols.

Tower's Police Safety: Trade name used by Hopkins & Allen on inexpensive pocket revolvers.

Townley's Pal and Townley's American Boy: Trade name used by H. & D. Folsom Arms Company for shotguns made for Townley Metal and Hardware Company of Kansas City, Missouri.

Tramps Terror: Trade name used by the Forehand and Wadsworth Company on inexpensive pocket revolvers.

Traps Best: Trade name believed to have been used by the H. & D. Folsom Arms Company on firearms made for the Watkins, Cottrell Company of Richmond, Virginia.

Triumph: Trade name used by the H. & D. Folsom Arms Company on shotguns.

Trojan: Trade name found on inexpensive pocket revolvers of unknown manufacture.

True Blue: Trade name found on inexpensive pocket revolvers of unknown manufacture.

Tryon Special: Trade name used by the Edward K. Tryon Company of Philadelphia, Pennsylvania, on shotguns they retailed.

Tycoon: Trade name used by the Iver Johnson Arms and Cycle Works on inexpensive pocket revolvers.

U.S. Arms Company: Trade name used successively by the Alexander Waller and Company (1877), the Barton and Company (1878) and the H. & D. Folsom Arms Company (1879 forward) on a variety of firearms.

U.S. Revolver: Trade name used by the Iver Johnson Arms and Cycle Works on inexpensive pocket revolvers.

U.S. Single Gun: Trade name used by the Iver Johnson Arms and Cycle Works on single barrel shotguns.

Uncle Sam: Trade name used by Johnson & Bye on percussion pocket pistols.

Union:
a) Trade name found on inexpensive single-shot pocket pistols of unknown manufacture.
b) Trade name used by the Hood Firearms Company on inexpensive pocket revolvers.
c) Trade name used by the Prescott Pistol Company on inexpensive pocket revolvers.

Union Arms Company: Trade name used by the H. & D. Folsom Arms Company on firearms made for the Bostwick, Braun Company of Toledo, Ohio.

Union Jack: Trade name found on inexpensive pocket revolvers of unknown manufacture.

Union N.Y.: Trade name used by the Whitneyville Armory on inexpensive pocket revolvers.

Unique: Trade name used by the C.S. Shattuck Arms Company on revolvers and four barrel pocket pistols.

United States Arms Company: Trade name used by Norwich Falls Pistol Company (O.A. Smith) on inexpensive pocket revolvers.

Universal: Trade name used by the Hopkins and Allen Company on inexpensive pocket revolvers.

Utica Firearms Company: Trade name used by the Simmons Hardware Company of St. Louis, Missouri, on firearms they retailed.

Valient: Trade name used by the Spear and Company of Pittsburgh, Pennsylvania, on firearms they retailed.

Veiled Prophet: Trade name used by the T.E. Ryan Pistol Manufacturing Company on inexpensive pocket revolvers.

Venus: Trade name used by the American Novelty Company of Chicago on inexpensive pocket revolvers.

Veteran: Trade name found on inexpensive pocket revolvers of unknown manufacture.

Veto: Trade name found on inexpensive pocket revolvers of unknown manufacture.

Victor:
a) Trade name used by the Marlin Firearms Company on single-shot pocket pistols.
b) Trade name used by the Harrington and Richardson Arms Company on inexpensive pocket revolvers.
c) Trade name used by the H. & D. Folsom Arms Company on inexpensive pocket pistols and revolvers.

Victor Arms Company: Trade name used by the H. & D. Folsom Arms Company on firearms made for the Hibbard, Spencer, Bartlett and Company of Chicago.

Victor Special: Trade name used by the H. & D. Folsom Arms Company on firearms made for the Hibbard, Spencer, Bartlett and Company of Chicago.

Victoria: Trade name used by the Hood Firearms Company on inexpensive pocket revolvers.

Vindix: Trade name used by Manufacture d'Armes de Pyrenees on semiautomatic pistols.

Viper: Trade name used on inexpensive pocket revolvers of unknown American manufacture.

Virginia Arms Company: Trade name used by the H. & D. Folsom Arms Company and later the Davis-Warner Arms Company on firearms made for the Virginia-Carolina Company of Richmond, Virginia.

Volunteer: Trade name used by the H. & D. Folsom Arms Company on inexpensive pocket revolvers made for the Belknap Hardware Company of Louisville, Kentucky.

Vulcan: Trade name used by the H. & D. Folsom Arms Company on firearms made for the Edward K. Tryon Company of Philadelphia, Pennsylvania.

Walnut Hill: Trade name used by the J. Stevens Arms and Tool Company on rifles.

Warner Arms Corporation: Trade name used by the H. & D. Folsom Arms Company on firearms made for the Kirtland Brothers, Inc. of New York.

Wasp: Trade name found on inexpensive pocket revolvers of unknown manufacture.

Wautauga: Trade name used by the Whitaker, Holtsinger Hardware Company of Morristown, Tennessee on firearms they retailed.

Western: Trade name used by the H. & D. Folsom Arms Company on firearms made for the Paxton and Gallagher Company of Omaha, Nebraska.

Western Arms Company:
a) Trade name used by the Bacon Arms on various types of firearms.
b) Trade name used by W.W. Marston on revolvers.
c) Trade name used by Henry Kolb and later R.F. Sedgly of Philadelphia, Pennsylvania, on Baby Hammerless revolvers.
d) Trade name used by the Ithaca Gun Company on shotguns believed to have been made for the Montgomery Ward and Company of Chicago.

Western Field: Trade name used by Montgomery Ward and Company of Chicago on shotguns of various makes that they retailed.

Western Field: Trade name used by Manufacture d'Armes de Pyrenees on revolvers.

Whippet: Trade name used by the H. & D. Folsom Arms Company on firearms made for the Hibbard, Spencer, Bartlett and Company of Chicago.

Whistler: Trade name used by the Hood Firearms Company on inexpensive pocket revolvers.

White Powder Wonder: Trade name used by Albert Aubrey of Meriden, Connecticut on shotguns made for the Sears, Roebuck and Company of Chicago.

Wildwood: Trade name used by the H. & D. Folsom Arms Company for shotguns made for Sears, Roebuck & Company.

Wilkinson Arms Company: Trade name used by the H. & D. Folsom Arms Company on firearms made for the Richmond Hardware Company of Richmond, Virginia.

Wiltshire Arms Company: Trade name used by the H. & D. Folsom Arms Company on firearms made for the Stauffer, Eshleman and Company of New Orleans, Louisiana.

Winfield Arms Company: Trade name used by the H. & D. Folsom Arms Company on various types of firearms.

Winner: Trade name found on inexpensive pocket revolvers of unknown manufacture.

Winoca Arms Company: Trade name used by the H. & D. Folsom Arms Company on firearms made for the N. Jacobi Hardware Company of Wilmington, North Carolina.

Witte's Expert: Trade name used by the Witte Hardware Company of St. Louis, Missouri, on shotguns they retailed.

Witte's IXL: Trade name used by the Witte Hardware Company of St. Louis, Missouri, on shotguns they retailed.

Wolverine Arms Company: Trade name used by the H. & D. Folsom Arms Company on firearms made for the Fletcher Hardware Company of Wilmington, North Carolina.

Woodmaster: Trade name found on Belgian shotguns imported by an unknown wholesaler.

Worlds Fair: Trade name used by the Hopkins and Allen Company on shotguns.

Worthington Arms Company: Trade name used by the H. & D. Folsom Arms Company on various types of firearms.

Wyco: Trade name used by the Wyeth Hardware and Manufacturing Company of St. Joseph, Missouri, on firearms they retailed.

XL:
a) Trade name used by the Hopkins and Allen Company on inexpensive pocket revolvers.
b) Trade name used by the Marlin Firearms Company on single-shot pocket pistols.

Xpert:
a) Trade name used by the Hopkins and Allen Company on inexpensive pocket revolvers.
b) Trade name used by the Iver Johnson Arms and Cycle Works on inexpensive single-shot pocket pistols.

XXX Standard: Trade name used by the Marlin Firearms Company on revolvers.

You Bet: Trade name used on inexpensive pocket revolvers of unknown American manufacture.

Young America: Trade name used by J.P. Lindsay of New York on superimposed - load percussion pistols.

Young American: Trade name used by the Harrington and Richardson Arms Company on revolvers.

FIREARMS MANUFACTURERS AND IMPORTERS

Accu-Tek
4510 Carter Ct.
Chino, CA 91710
909-627-2404
FAX: 909-627-7817
www.accu-tekfirearms.com

AcuSport Corporation
One Hunter Place
Bellefontaine, OH 43311
513-593-7010
FAX: 513-592-5625
www.acusport.com

American Derringer Corp.
127 N. Lacy Drive
Waco, TX 76715
254-799-9111
FAX: 254-799-7935
www.amderringer.com

American Frontier Firearms
40725 Brook Trails Way
Aguanga, CA 92536
909-763-0014
FAX: 909-763-0014

AR-7 Industries
998 N. Colony Rd.
Meriden, CT 06450
203-630-3536
FAX: 203-630-3637
www.ar-7.com

ArmaLite, Inc.
P.O. Box 299
Geneseo, IL 61254
309-944-6939
FAX: 309-944-6949
www.armalite.com

Armscorp USA Inc.
4424 John Avenue
Baltimore, MA 21227
410-247-6200
FAX: 410-247-6205

A-Square Co. Inc.
205 Fairfield Avenue
Jeffersonville, IN 47130
812-283-0577
FAX: 812-283-0375

Austin & Halleck
2150 South 950 East
Provo, UT 84606
877-543-3256
FAX: 801-374-9998
www.austinhalleck.com

Autauga Arms
Pratt Plaza Mall No. 13
Pratville, AL 36067
800-262-9563
FAX: 334-361-2961

Auto-Ordnance Corp.
P.O. Box 220
Blauvelt, NY 10913
845-735-4500
FAX: 845-735-4610
www.auto-ordnance.com

Axtell Rifle Company
Riflesmith, Inc.
353 Mill Creek Road
Sheridan, MT 59749
406-842-5814
www.riflesmith.com

Aya-Agiurre Y Aranzabal, S.A.L.
P.O. Box 45
Eibar (Guipuzcoa), Spain
+34 943 82 04 37
FAX: +34 943 20 01 33

B.C. Outdoors
P.O. Box 61497
Boulder City, NV 89005
702-294-3056
FAX: 702-294-0413

Ballard Rifle and Cartridge Co.
113 W. Yellowstone Ave.
Cody, WY 82414
307-587-4914
FAX: 307-527-6097
www.ballardrifles.com

Barrett Firearms Mfg.
P.O.Box 1077
Murfreesboro, TN 37133
615-896-2938
FAX: 615-896-7313

Benelli U.S.A.
17603 Indian Head Highway
Accokeek, MD 20607
301-283-6981
FAX: 301-283-6988
www.benelliusa.com

Beretta U.S.A. Corp.
17601 Beretta Drive
Accokeek, MD 20607
301-283-2191
FAX: 301-283-0435
www.berettausa.com

Bernardelli Vincenzo, S.P.A.
Via Grande, 10
Sede Legale Torbole Casaglia
Brescia, Italy
+39 30 8912851-2-3
FAX: +39 030 215 0963

Bond Arms
P.O. Box 1296
Grandbury, TX 76048
817-573-4445
FAX: 817-573-5636
www.bondarms.com

Briley Mfg. Company
1230 Lumpkin Road
Houston, TX 77043
800-331-5718
FAX: 713-932-1043

Brown, E. Arthur Co.
4353 State Highway 27 East
Alexandria, MN 56308
320-762-8847
FAX: 320-763-4310
www.eabco.com

Brown Precision Inc.
7786 Molinos Ave.
P.O. Box 270 W.
Los Molinos, CA 96055
530-384-2506
FAX: 530-384-1638
www.brownprecision.com

Brown, Ed Products
P.O. Box 492
Perry, MO 63462
573-565-3261
FAX: 573-565-2791
www.edbrown.com

Browning
One Browning Place
Morgan, UT 84050
801-876-2711
Parts & Service
800-322-4626
www.browning.com

Bushmaster Firearms
999 Roosevelt Trail
Windham, ME 04062
800-998-7928
FAX: 207-892-8068
www.bushmaster.com

Caspian Arms, Ltd.
14 N. Main St.
Hardwick, VT 05843
802-472-6454
FAX: 802-472-6709

Casull Arms Company, Inc.
P.O. Box 1629
Afton, WY 83110
307-886-0200
www.casullarms.com

Century International Arms
430 S. Congress Ave., Suite 1.
Delray Beach, FL 33445-4701
800-527-1252
FAX: 561-265-4520
www.centuryarms.com

Champlin Firearms
P.O. Box 3191/Woodring Airport
Enid, OK 73702
580-237-7388
FAX: 580-242-6922

Charter 2000, Inc.
273 Canal Street
Shelton, CT 06484
203-922-1652
FAX: 203-922-1469

Cimarron Arms
P.O. Box 906
105 Winding Oak Road
Fredericksburg, TX 78624
830-997-9090
FAX: 830-997-0802
www.cimarron-firearms.com

Cobra Enterprises
1960 S. Milestone Dr., Suite F
Salt Lake City, UT 84104
801-908-8300
FAX: 801-908-8301
www.cobrapistols.com

Colt Firearms
P.O. Box 1868
Hartford, CT 06144
800-962-COLT
FAX: 860-244-1449
www.colt.com

Colt Blackpowder Arms Co.
110 8th Street
Brooklyn, NY 11215
212-925-2159
FAX: 212-966-4986

Competitor Corporation Inc.
26 Knight Street, Unit 3
Jaffrey, NH 03452
603-532-9483
FAX: 603-532-8209
www.competitor-pistol.com

Connecticut Shotgun Manufacturing Co.
A. H. Fox Shotguns
35 Woodland Street
Box 1692
New Britain, CT 06051
860-225-6581
FAX: 860-832-8708

Connecticut Valley Arms, Inc. (CVA)
5988 Peachtree Corners East
Norcross, GA 30071
770-449-4687
FAX: 770-242-8546
www.cva.com

Cooper Arms
P.O. Box 114
Stevensville, MT 59870
406-777-0373
FAX: 406-777-5228

CZ-U.S.A.
P.O. Box 171073
Kansas City, KS 66117- 0073
913-321-1811
FAX: 913-321-2251
www.cz-usa.com

Dakota Arms, Inc.
130 Industry Rd.
Sturgis, SD 57785
605-347-4686
FAX: 605-347-4459
www.dakotaarms.com

Daly, Charles Inc.
P.O. Box 6625
Harrisburg, PA 17112
866-325-9486
FAX: 717-540-8567
www.charlesdaly.com

Dixie Gun Works
P.O. Box 130
Union City, TN 38281
731-885-0700
FAX: 731-885-0440

Downsizer Corp.
P.O. Box 710316
Santee, CA 92072
619-448-5510
www.downsizer.com

DSA, Inc.
P.O. Box 370
27 West 990 Industrial Ave.
Barrington, IL 600110
847-277-7258
FAX: 847-277-7259
www.dsarms.com

Dumoulin, Ernst
Rue Florent Boclinville 8-10
13-4041 Votten, Beligium
41 27 78 78 92

Eagle Imports
1750 Brielle Ave., Unit B1
Wanamassa, NJ 07712
908-493-0333

Ellett Bros.
P.O. Box 128
Chapin, SC 29036
803-345-3751
FAX: 803-345-1820

EMF Co., Inc.
1900 E. Warner Ave. Suite 1-D
Santa Ana, CA 92705
949-261-6611
FAX: 949-756-0133

Entreprise Arms Inc.
5321 Irwindale Ave.
Irwindale, CA 91706
626-962-8712
FAX: 626-962-4692
www.entreprise.com

Euro-Imports
412 Slayden St.
Yoakum, TX 77995
361-293-9353
FAX: 361-293-9353

European American Armory
P.O. Box 1299
Sharpes, FL 32959
321-639-4842
FAX: 321-639-7006
www.eacorp.com

F.N. Manufacturing, Inc.
P.O. Box 24257
Columbia, SC 29224
803-736-0522

Fieldsport
3313 W. South Airport Road
Traverse City, MI 49684
616-933-0767

Fiocchi Of America
5030 Fremont Road
Ozark, MO 65721
417-725-4118
FAX: 417-725-1039

Fletcher-Bidwell
305 E. Terhune Street
Viroqua, WI 54665
866-637-1860
FAX: 608-637-6922

Francotte, Aug.
Rue du 3 Juin, 109
4400 Herstal-Liege, Belgium
32-4-948-11-79

Freedom Arms
P.O. Box 150
Freedom, WY 83120
307-883-2468
FAX: 307-883-2005
www.freedomarms.com

Furr Arms
91 North 970 West
Orem, UT 84057
801-226-3877
FAX: 801-226-3877

Galaxy Imports
P.O. Box 3361
Victoria, TX 77903
361-573-4867
FAX: 361-576-9622

Gamba, Renato
Via Artigiana 93
25063 Gardone Val Trompia
Brescia, Italy
+39 30 8911640
FAX: +39 30 8912180

Gamba, U.S.A.
P.O. Box 60452
Colorado Springs, CO 80960
719-578-1145
FAX: 719-444-0731

Glock, Inc.
6000 Highlands Parkway
Smyrna, GA 30082
770-432-1202
FAX: 770-433-8719
www.glock.com

Griffin & Howe, Inc.
33 Claremont Road
Bernardsville, NJ 07924
908-766-2287
FAX: 908-766-1068
www.griffinhowe.com

GSI, Inc. (Merkel)
7661 Commerce Lane
P.O. Box 129
Trussville, AL 35173
205-655-8299
FAX: 205-655-7078
www.gsifirearms.com

H-S Precision, Inc.
1301 Turbine Drive
Rapid City, SD 57703
605-341-3006
FAX: 605-342-8964
www.hsprecision.com

Hammerli USA
19296 Oak Grove Circle
Groveland, CA 95321
209-962-5311
FAX: 209-962-5931
www.hammerliusa.com

Hanus, Bill Birdguns
P.O. Box 533
Newport, OR 97365
541-265-7433
FAX: 541-265-7400

Harrington & Richardson (H&R 1871)
60 Industrial Rowe
Gardner, MA 01440
508-632-9393
FAX: 508-632-2300
www.hr1871.com

Heckler & Koch, Inc.
21480 Pacific Boulevard
Sterling, VA 20166
703-450-1900
FAX: 703-450-8160
www.hecklerkoch-usa.com

Henry Repeating Arms Co
110 8th Street
Brooklyn, NY 11215
718-499-5600
FAX: 718-768-8056

Heritage Manufacturing, Inc.
4600 NW 135th St.
Opa Locka, FL 30054
305-685-5966
FAX: 305-687-6721

High Standard Mfg. Co.
5200 Mitchelldale, Suite E-17
Houston, TX 77092
713-462-4200
FAX: 713-681-5665
www.highstandard.com

Horton, Lew, Distributing Co., Inc.
15 Walkup Drive
Westboro, MA 01581
508-366-7400
FAX: 508-366-5332

Ithaca Classic Doubles
No. 5 Railroad Street
Victor, NY 14564
716-924-2710
FAX: 716-924-2737

Ithaca Gun/Ithaca Acq. Corp.
901 Route 34B
King Ferry, NY 13081
315-364-7171
FAX: 315-364-5134
www.ithacagun.com

KDF
2485 Highway 46 North
Seguin, TX 78155
830-379-8141
FAX: 830-379-5420

Kahr Arms
P.O. Box 220
Blauvelt, NY 10913
845-735-4500
FAX: 845-735-4610
www.kahr.com

Kel-Tec CNC, Inc.
1475 Cox Rd.
Cocoa, FL 32926
321-631-0068
FAX: 321-631-1169
www.kel-tec.com

Kimber
1 Lawton Street
Yonkers, NY 10705
800-880-2418
www.kimberamerica.com

Knight Rifles/Modern Muzzleloading, Inc.
21852 Hwy. J46
P.O. Box 130
Centerville, IA 52544
641-856-2626
www.knightrifles.com

Knight's Manufacturing Co.
701 Columbia Blvd.
Titusville, FL 32780
321-607-9900
FAX: 321-268-1498

Krieghoff International
P.O. Box 549
7528 Easton Rd.
Ottsville, PA 18942
610-847-5173
FAX: 610-847-8691
www.krieghoff.com

L.A.R. Manufacturing
4133 West Farm Road
West Jordan, UT 84088
801-280-3505
FAX: 801-280-1972

Laurona
P.O. Box 260
20600 Eibar (Guipuzcoa), Spain
34-43-700600
FAX: 34-43-700616

Lazzeroni Arms Co.
P.O. Box 26696
Tucson, AZ 85726
888-492-7247
FAX: 520-624-4250
www.lazzeroni.com

Legacy Sports International
206 South Union Street
Alexandria, VA 22314
703-548-4837
FAX: 549-7826
www.legacysports.com

Les Baer Custom Inc.
29601 34th Ave.
Hillsdale, IL 61257
309-658-2716
FAX: 309-658-2610
www.lesbaer.com

Ljutic Industries
732 N. 16th Ave. Suite 22
Yakima, WA 98902
509-248-0476
FAX: 509-576-8233
www.ljuticgun.com

Lone Star Rifle Company
11231 Rose Road
Conroe, TX 77303
936-856-3363
FAX: 936-856-3363

Lyman
475 Smith Street
Middletown, CT 06457
860-632-2020
FAX: 860-632-1699

Magnum Research, Inc.
7110 University Avenue N.E.
Minneapolis, MN 55432
763-574-1868
FAX: 763-574-0109
www.magnumresearch.com

Marlin Firearms
P.O. Box 248
North Haven, CT 06473
800-544-8892
www.marlinfirearms.com

Maverick Arms Inc.
7 Grasso Ave.
P.O. Box 497
North Haven, CT 06473
203-230-5300
FAX: 203-230-5420

McMillan (McBros Rifles)
1638 W. Knudsen No. 102
Phoenix, AZ 85027
623-582-3713
FAX: 623-582-3930
www.mcmfamily.com

M.O.A. Corp.
285 Government Valley Rd.
Sundance, WY 82729
307-283-3030
www.moaguns.com

Moore, William Larkin & Co.
8340 E. Raintree Dr., Suite B-7
Scottsdale, AZ 85260
480-951-8913
FAX: 480-951-3677

Mossberg, O. F., & Sons, Inc.
7 Grasso Avenue
North Haven, CT 06473
203-230-5300
FAX: 203-230-5420
www.mossberg.com

Navy Arms Co.
219 Lawn St.
Martinsburg, WV 25401
304-262-9870
FAX: 304-262-1658
www.navyarms.com

New England Arms Co.
Lawrence Lane
Box 278
Kittery Point, ME 03905
207-439-0593
FAX: 207-439-6726
www.newenglandarms.com

New England Custom Gun Service
438 Willow Brook Road
Plainfield, NH 03781
603-469-3450
FAX: 603-469-3471

New England Firearms
60 Industrial Rowe
Gardner, MA 01440
978-632-9393
FAX: 978-632-2300

North American Arms
2150 South 950 East
Provo, UT 84606
801-374-9990
FAX: 801-374-9998
www.naaminis.com

Northwest Arms
26884 Pearl Road
Parma, ID 83660
208-722-6771
FAX: 208-722-1062
www.northwest-arms.com

Nowlin Manufacturing Co.
20622 South 4092 Road
Claremore, OK 74019
918-342-0689
FAX: 918-342-0624
www.nowlinguns.com

Ohio Ordnance Works
P.O. Box 687
310 Park Drive
Chardon, Ohio 44024
440-285-3481
FAX: 286-8571

Olympic Arms, Inc.
624 Old Pacific Highway SE
Olympia, WA 98513
360-459-7940
FAX: 360-491-3447
www.olyarms.com

Para-Ordnance
980 Tapscott Rd.
Toronto, Ontario M1X 1C3
416-297-7855
FAX: 416-297-1289
www.paraord.com

Pedersoli Davide & Co.
Via Artigiani, 57-25063
Gardone Val Trompia, Brescia
Italy 25063

Perazzi U.S.A. Inc.
1010 West Tenth
Azusa, CA 91702
626-334-1234
FAX: 626-334-0344

Phoenix Arms
4231 Brickell St.
Ontario, CA 91761
909-937-6900
FAX: 909-937-0060

Prairie Gun Works
1-761 Marion Street
Winnipeg, Manitoba
Canada R2J OK6
204-231-2976
FAX: 204-231-8566

Reeder, Gary Custom Guns
2601 7th Avenue East
Flagstaff, AZ 86004
928-526-3313
FAX: 928-526-1287
www.reedercustomguns.com

Remington Arms Co., Inc.
P.O. Box 700
870 Remington Drive
Madison, NC 27025-0700
800-243-9700
FAX: 336-548-7801
www.remington.com

Rock River Arms Inc.
1042 Cleveland Rd.
Colona, IL 61241
866-980-7625
FAX: 309-792-5781
www.rockriverarms.com

Rogue Rifle Co.
1140 36th Street N, Suite B
Lewiston, ID 83501
208-743-4355
FAX: 208-743-4163
www.roguerifle.com

Rogue River Rifleworks
500 Linne Rd., Suite D
Paso Robles, CA 93446
805-227-4706
FAX: 805-227-4723

Savage Arms
100 Springdale Road
Westfield, MA 01085
413-568-7001
FAX: 413-568-8386
www.savagearms.com

Seecamp, L.W.C.
301 Brewster Rd.
Milford, CT 06460
203-877-3429

Shiloh Rifle Mfg. Co., Inc.
P.O. Box 279
201 Centennial Drive
Big Timber, MT 59011
406-932-4454
FAX: 406-932-5627
www.shilohrifle.com

SIGARMS, Inc.
18 Industrial Drive
Exeter, NH 03833
603-772-2302
FAX: 603-772-9082
www.sigarms.com

SKB Shotguns
4325 South 120th St.
Omaha, NE 68137
800-752-2767
FAX: 402-330-8029
www.skbshotguns.com

Smith & Wesson
2100 Roosevelt Road
Springfield, MA 01104
800-331-0852
FAX: 413-747-3317
www.smith-wesson.com

Springfield Armory, Inc.
420 West Main Street
Geneseo, IL 61254
309-944-5631
FAX: 309-944-3676
www.springfield-armory.com

SSK Industries
590 Woodvue Lane
Wintersville, OH 43953
740-264-0176
FAX: 740-264-2257
www.sskindustries.com

S.T.I. International, Inc.
114 Halmar Cove
Georgetown, TX 78628
800-959-8201
FAX: 512-819-0465
www.stiguns.com

Stoeger Industries
17603 Indian Head Highway
Accokeek, MD 20607
301-283-6300
FAX: 301-283-6986

Sturm Ruger & Co., Inc
Lacey Place
Southport, CT 06890
203-259-7843
FAX: 203-256-3367
www.ruger-firearms.com

Taconic Firearms Ltd.
P.O. Box 553
Perry Lane
Cambridge, NY 12816
518-677-2704
FAX: 518-677-5974

Taurus International
16175 NW 49th Av.
Miami, FL 33014
305-624-1115
FAX: 305-623-1126
www.taurususa.com

Thompson/Center Arms Co.
Farmington Road
P.O. Box 5002
Rochester, NH 03867
603-332-2394
FAX: 603-332-5133
www.tcarms.com

Traditions Performance Firearms
1375 Boston Post Road
P.O. Box 776
Old Saybrook, CT 06475
860-388-4656
FAX: 860-388-4657

Tristar Sporting Arms
P.O. Box 7496
18116 Linn St.
North Kansas City, MO 64116
816-421-1400
FAX: 816-421-4182
www.tristarsportingarms.com

Turnbull, Doug Restoration, Inc.
6680 Route 5 & 20
P.O. Box 471
Bloomfield, NY 14469
585-657-6338
FAX: 585-657-6338
www.turnbullrestoration.com

U.S. Repeating Arms/Winchester
275 Winchester Ave.
New Haven, CT 06511
800-333-3288
www.winchester-guns.com

United States Fire Arms Manufacturing Co.
55 Van Dyke Av.
Hartford, CT 06106
877-277-6901
FAX: 860-724-6809
www.usfirearms.com

Valtro U.S.A.
24800 Mission Blvd.
Hayward, CA 94544
510-489-8477
FAX: 510-489-8477

Vector Arms, Inc.
270 W. 500 N.
North Salt Lake, UT 84054
801-295-1917
FAX: 801-295-9316
www.vectorarms.com

Volquartsen Custom
24276 240th Street
Carroll, IA 51401
712-792-4238
FAX: 712-792-2542
www.volquartsen.com

Weatherby, Inc.
3100 El Comino Real
Atascadero, CA 93422
805-466-1767
FAX: 805-466-2527
www.weatherby.com

Wesson, Dan Firearms
5169 Highway 12 South
Norwich, NY 13815
607-336-1174
FAX: 607-336-2730
www.danwessonfirearms.com

Westley Richards & Co. Ltd.
40 Grange Road, Bournbrook
Birmingham, England B29 5A
44 121 472 2953
FAX: 44 121 414 1138

Wichita Arms
923 E. Gilbert
Wichita, KS 67211
316-265-0061
FAX: 316-265-0760
www.wichitaarms.com

Wildey, Inc.
45 Angevine Rd.
Warren, CT 06754
860-355-9000
FAX: 860-354-7759
www.wildeyguns.com

Wilson Combat
2234 CR 719
P.O. Box 578
Berryville, AR 72616
870-545-3635
FAX: 870-545-3310
www.wilsoncombat.com

ZM Weapons
203 South Street
Bernardston, MA 01337
413-648-9501
FAX: 413-648-0219

Zoli, Antonio
Via Zanardelli, 39
I-25063 Gardone V.T. (BS) Italy

GUN COLLECTORS ASSOCIATIONS

Alabama Gun Collectors
P.O. Box 70965
Tuscalossa, AL 35407

Alaska Gun Collectors Association
5240 Litte Tree
Anchorage, AK 99507

American Society of Arms Collectors
P.O. Box 2567
Waxahachie, TX 75165

Arizona Arms Association
4837 Bryce Ave.
Glendale, AZ 85301

Ark-La-Tex Gun Collectors Association
919 Hamilton Road
Bossier City, LA 71111

Bay Colony Weapons Collectors, Inc.
Box 111
Hingham, MA 02043

Boardman Valley Collectors Guild
County Road 600
Manton, MI 49663

Browning Collectors Association
2749 Keith Dr.
Villa Ridge, MO 63089

California Arms and Collectors Assoc.
8290 Carburton St.
Long Beach, CA 90808

Colorado Gun Collectors
2553 South Quitman Street
Denver, CO 80219

Colt Collectors Association
25000 Highland Way
Los Gatos, CA 95030

Derringer Collectors Association
500 E. Old 66
Shamrock, TX 79079

Florida Gun Collectors Association
P.O. Box 43
Branford, FL 32008

Freedom Arms Collectors Association
P.O. Box 160302
Miami, FL 33116

High Standard Collectors Association
540 W 92nd Street
Indianapolis, In 46260

Houston Gun Collectors Association
P.O. Box 741429
Houston, TX 77274

Indianhead Firearms Association
Route 9, Box 186
Chippewa Falls, WI 54729

Indian Territory Gun Collectors Association
Box 4491
Tulsa, OK 74159

International Society of Mauser Arms Collectors
P.O. Box 277
Alpharetta, GA 30239

Iroquois Arms Collectors Association
P.O.Box 142
Ransomville, NY 14131

Jefferson State Arms Collectors
521 South Grape
Medford, OR 97501

Jersey Shore Antique Arms Collectors
P.O. Box 100
Bayville, NJ 08721

Kentuckiana Arms Collectors Association
P.O. Box 1776
Louisville, KY 40201

Kentucky Gun Collectors Association
P.O. Box 64
Owensboro, KY 42376

Lehigh Valley Military Collectors Association
P.O. Box 72
Whitehall, PA 18052

Long Island Antique Gun Collectors Association
35 Beach Street
Farmingdale, L.I., NY 11735

Marlin Firearms Collectors Association
44 Main Street
Champaign, IL 61820

Maryland Arms Collectors Association
P.O. Box 20388
Baltimore, MD 21284-0388

Memphis Antique Weapons Association
4672 Barfield Road
Memphis, TN 38117

Minnesota Weapons Collectors Association
P.O. Box 662
Hopkins, MN 55343

Missouri Valley Arms Collectors Association
P.O. Box 33033
Kansas City, MO 64114

Montana Arms Collectors Association
308 Riverview Drive
East Great Falls, MT 59404

National Automatic Pistol Collectors Association
Box 15738-TOGS
St. Louis, MO 63163

National Rifle Association
11250 Waples Mill Rd.
Fairfax, VA 22030

New Hampshire Arms Collectors, Inc.
P.O. Box 5
Cambridge, MA 02139

Northeastern Arms Collectors Association, Inc.
P.O. Box 185
Amityville, NY 11701

Ohio Gun Collectors Association
P.O. Box 9007
Maumee, OH 43537

Oregon Arms Collectors
P.O. Box 13000-A
Portland, OR 97213

Pelican Arms Collectors Association
P.O. Box 747
Clinton, LA 70722

Pennsylvania Antique Gun Collectors Association
28 Fulmer Avenue
Havertown, PA 19083

Pikes Peak Gun Collectors Guild
406 E. Uintah
Colorado Springs, CO 80903

Potomac Arms Collectors Association
P.O. Box 1812
Wheaton, MD 20915

Randall Collectors Club
228 Columbine Dr.
Casper WY 82609-3948

Remington Society of America
8267 Lone Feather
Las Vegas, NV 89123

Ruger Collectors Association, Inc.
P.O. Box 240
Greens Farms, CT 06436

Sako Collectors Association, Inc.
202 N. Locust
Whitewater, KS 67154

Santa Barbara Antique Arms Collectors Association
P.O. Box 6291
Santa Barbara, CA 93160-6291

San Bernardino Valley Arms Collectors
1970 Mesa Street
San Bernardino, CA 92405

Santa Fe Gun Collectors Association
1085 Nugget
Los Alamos, NM 87544

San Fernando Valley Arms Collectors Association
P.O. Box 65
North Hollywood, CA 91603

Shasta Arms Collectors Association
P.O. Box 3292
Redding, CA 96049

Smith & Wesson Collectors Association
2711 Miami St.
St. Louis, MO 63118

Tampa Bay Arms Collectors Association
2461 67th Avenue South
St. Petersburg, FL 33712

Texas Gun Collectors Association
P.O. Box 12067
El Paso, TX 79913

Washington Arms Collectors, Inc.
P.O. Box 7335
Tacoma, WA 98407

Weapons Collectors Society of Montana
3100 Bancroft
Missoula, MT 59801

Weatherby Collectors Association, Inc.
21569 448th Avenue
Oldham, SD 57051

Willamette Valley Arms Collectors Association, Inc.
P.O. Box 5191
Eugene, OR 97405

Winchester Arms Collectors Association
P.O. Box 6754
Great Falls, MT 59406.

Ye Connecticut Gun Guild
U.S. Route 7
Kent Road
Cornwall Bridge, CT 06754

Zumbro Valley Arms Collectors, Inc.
Box 6621
Rochester, MN 55901

BIBLIOGRAPHY

Bady, Donald *Colt Automatic Pistols.* Alhambra, California: Borden Publishing Company, 1973.

Baer, Larry L. *The Parker Gun.* Los Angeles, California: Beinfeld Publications, 1980.

Bailey, D. and Nie, D. *English Gunmakers.* London: Arms and Armour Press, 1978.

Ball, W.D., *Remington Firearms: The Golden Age of Collecting*, Iola, WI: Krause Publications, 1995.

Ball, W.D., *Mauser Military Rifles of the World.* Iola, WI: Krause Publications, 1996.

Belford, James & Dunlap, Jack *The Mauser Self-Loading Pistol.* Alhambra, California: Borden Publishing, 1969.

Bishop, Chris and Drury, Ian *Combat Guns.* Secaucus, New Jersey: Chartwell Books, 1987.

Blackmore, H. *Gunmakers of London.* York, Pennsylvania: Geo. Shumway, 1986.

Blackmore, H. *Guns and Rifles of the World.* New York, New York: Viking Press, 1965.

Blair, C. *Pistols of the World.* London: B.T. Batsford, Ltd., 1968.

Bogdanovic & Valencak *The Great Century of Guns.* New York, New York: Gallery Books, 1986.

Bowen, T.G. *James Reid and his Catskill Knuckledusters.* Lincoln, Rhode Island: Andrew Mowbray, Inc., 1989.

Breathed, J. and Schroeder, J. *System Mauser.* Glenview, Illinois: Handgun Press, 1967.

Brophy, Lt. Col. William S., USAR, Ret. *The Krag Rifle.* Los Angeles, California: Beinfeld Publications, 1980.

Brophy, Lt. Col. William S., USAR, Ret. *L.C. Smith Shotguns.* Los Angeles, California: Beinfeld Publications, 1977.

Brophy, W. *Marlin Firearms.* Harrisburg, Pennsylvania: Stackpole Books, 1989.

Browning, J. and Gentry, C. *John M. Browning; American Gunmaker.* Ogden, Utah: Browning, 1989.

Butler, David F. *The American Shotgun.* New York, New York: Winchester Press, 1973.

Buxton, Warren *The P 38 Pistol.* Dallas, Texas: Taylor Publishing Company, 1978.

Carr, J. *Savage Automatic Pistols.*

Chant, Christopher *The New Encyclopedia of Handguns.* New York, New York: Gallery Books.

Conley, F.F. *The American Single Barrel Trap Gun.* Carmel Valley, California: F.F. Conley, 1989.

Cope, K.L. *Stevens Pistols and Pocket Rifles.* Ottawa, Ontario: Museum Restoration Service.

Cormack, A.J.R. *Small Arms, a Concise History of Their Development.* Profile Publications, Ltd.

Cormack, A.J.R. *Small Arms in Profile, Volume I.* Garden City, New York: Doubleday & Company, Inc.,1973.

deHass, Frank *Bolt Action Rifles.* Northfield, Illinois: Digest Books, Inc., 1971.

deHass, Frank *Single-shot Rifles and Actions.* Northfield, Illinois: Digest Books, Inc., 1969.

Eastman, Matt, *Browning Sporting Arms of Distinction*; 1903-1992. Fitzgerald, Georgia, 1994.

Eberhart, L. D. & Wilson, R. L. *The Deringer in America: Volume Two - The Cartridge Era.* Lincoln, RI: Andrew Mowbray Inc., 1993.

Dance, T. *High Standard: A Collector's Guide to the Hamden & Hartford Target Pistols.* Lincoln, RI: Andrew Mowbray Inc., 1991

Dunlap, J. *Pepperbox Firearms.* Palo Alto, California: Pacific Books, 1964.

Ezell, Edward C. *Small Arms Today.* Harrisburg, Pennsylvania: Stackpole Books.

Frasca & Hill *The 45-70 Springfield.* Northridge, California: Springfield Publishing Company, 1980.

Fuller, C. *The Whitney Firearms.* Huntington, West Virginia: Standard Pub., Inc., 1946.

Gaier & Francotte, *FN 100 Years; The Story of a Great Liege Company, 1889-1989.* Brussels, Belgium, 1989.

Gander, Terry, editor, *Janes Infantry Weapons*, 23rd edition, Surry, England, 1997.

Goddard, W. H. D. *The Government Models.* The Development of the Colt Model of 1911. Lincoln, RI: Andrew Mowbray Inc., 1988.

Graham, R., Kopec, J., Moore, C. *A Study of the Colt Single Action Army Revolver.* Dallas, Texas: Taylor Publishing Co., 1978.

Greener, W. *The Gun and Its Development.* Secaucus, New Jersey: Chartwell Books, 1988.

Gun Digest 1967 through 1989 Editions. Northfield, Illinois: DBI Books.

Guns of the World Los Angeles, California: Petersen Publishing Company, 1972.

Hayward, J.F. *Art of the Gunmaker, Vol.* 1. London: Barrie & Rockliff, 1962; Vol. 2. London: Barrie & Rockliff, 1963.

Henshaw, Thomas, et. al., *The History of Winchester Firearms 1866-1992, 6th Ed.* Winchester Press, 1993.

Hiddleson, C. *Encyclopedia of Ruger Semi-Automatic Pistols: 1949-1992.* Iola, WI: Krause Publications, 1993.

Hinman, Bob *The Golden Age of Shotgunning,* New York, N.Y., Winchester Press, 1975.

Hoff, A. *Airguns and Other Pneumatic Arms.* London: Barrie & Jenkins, 1972.

Hoffschmidt, E.J. *Know Your. 45 Auto Pistols Models 1911 &* Al. Southport, Connecticut: Blacksmith Corporation, 1974.

Hoffschmidt, E.J. *Know Your Walther PP & PPK Pistols.* Southport, Connecticut: Blacksmith Corporation, 1975.

Hogg, Ian V. *German Pistols and Revolvers 1871-1945.* Harrisburg, Pennsylvania: Stackpole Books, 1971.

Hogg, Ian V. and Weeks, John *Military Small Arms of the 20th Century.* Fifth Edition. Northfield, Illinois: DBI Books, 1985.

Hogg, Ian V. and Weeks, John *Pistols of the World. Revised Edition.* Northfield, Illinois: DBI Books, 1982.

Honeycutt, Fred L., Jr. *Military Pistols of Japan.* Lake Park, Florida: Julin Books, 1982.

Houze, H. *The Winchester Model 52: Perfection in Design,* Iola, WI: Krause Publications, 1997.

Houze, H. *To The Dreams Of Youth: Winchester .22 Caliber Single-shot Rifle.* Iola, WI: Krause Publications, 1993.

Houze, H. *Winchester Repeating Arms Company Its History and Development 1865 to 1981.* Iola, WI: Krause Publications, 1994.

Houze, H. *Colt Rifles & Muskets: 1847-1870.* Iola, WI: Krause Publications, 1996.

Jamieson, G. Scott *Bullard Arms.* Erin, Ontario: Boston Mills Press, 1988.

Jinks, R.G. *History of Smith A. Wesson.* Beinfeld Pub., Inc., 1977.

Karr, C.L. and C.R. *Remington Handguns.* Harrisburg, Pennsylvania: Stackpole Co., 1956.

Kenyon, C. *Lugers at Random.* Glenview, Illinois: Handgun Press, 1990.

Kindig, J., Jr. *Thoughts on the Kentucky Rifle in its Golden Age.* New York, New York: Bonanza Books, 1964.

Laidacker, John S. *Collected Notes Concerning Developmental Cartridge Handguns In .22 Calibre As Produced in the United States and Abroad From 1855 to 1875.* Bloomsburg, PA: J.S. Laidacker, 1994.

Larson, Eric *Variations of the Smooth Bore H&R Handy-Gun.* Takoma Park, Maryland: 1993.

Leithe, Frederick E. *Japanese Handguns.* Alhambra, California: Borden Publishing Company, 1968.

Lenk, T. *The Flintlock, Its Origins and Development.* New York, New York: Bramhall House, 1965.

Lewis, Jack, editor, *Gun Digest Book of Assault Weapons*, 4th edition, Krause Publications, Iola, WI, 1996.

Lippard, K. *Fabbri Shotguns*, Colorado Springs, Colorado, VM Publications, 1998.

Lippard, K, *Perazzi Shotguns*, Colorado Springs, Colorado, VM Publications, 1996.

Lugs, J. *Firearms Past and Present.* London: Grenville, 1975.

Madis, George *The Winchester Model 12.* Brownsboro, Texas: Art & Reference House, 1982.

Madis, George *The Winchester Book.* Brownsboro, Texas: Art & Reference House, 1977.

Marcot, R. *Spencer Repeating Firearms.* Irvine, California: Northwood Heritage Press, 1990.

Markham, George *Japanese Infantry Weapons of World War Two.* New York, New York: Hippocrene Books, Inc., 1976.

McDowell, R. *Evolution of the Winchester.* Tacoma, Washington: Armory Pub., 1985.

McDowell, R. *A Study of Colt Conversions and Other Percussion Revolvers*, Iola, WI; Krause Publications, 1997.

McIntosh, Michael *A.H. Fox; The Finest Gun in the World.* Countrysport Press, 1992.

Moller, G. D. *American Military Shoulder Arms, Volume 1, Colonial and Revolutionary War Arms.* Niwot, CO: University Press of Colorado, 1993.

Murphy, J. M.D. *Confederate Carbines & Musketoons.* J. Murphy, M.D., n.p.: 1986.

Murray, Douglas P. *The 99: A History of the Savage Model 99 Rifle.* Murray, 1976.

Myatt, Major Frederick, M.D. *Pistols and Revolvers.* New York, New York: Crescent Books, 1980.

Nutter, W.E. *Manhattan Firearms.* Harrisburg, Pennsylvania: Stackpole Co., 1958.

Olson, Ludwig *Mauser Bolt Rifles.* Third Edition. Montezuma, Iowa: Brownell & Sons, 1976.

Parsons, J. E. *Henry Deringer's Pocket Pistol.* New York, New York: Wm. Morrow & Co., 1952.

Pender, Roy G. *III Mauser Pocket Pistols 1910-1946.* Houston, Texas: Collectors Press, 1971.

Peterson, H.L. *Arms and Armor in Colonial America.* New York, New York: Brandhall House, 1956.

Petty, Charles E. *High Standard Automatic Pistols 1932-1950.* Highland Park, NJ: The Gun Room Press, 1989.

Rankin, J. *Walther Models PP and PPK.* Coral Gables, Florida: Rankin, 1989.

Rankin, J. *Walther Volume III,* 1908-1980. Coral Gables, Florida: Rankin, 1981.

Reese, Michael *11 Luger Tips.* Union City, Tennessee: Pioneer Press, 1976.

Reilly, R. *United States Martial Flintlocks.* Lincoln, Rhode Island: Andrew Mowbray, Inc., 1986.

Reilly, R. *United States Military Small Arms 1816-1865.* Baton Rouge, Louisiana: Eagle Press, Inc., 1970.

Renneberg, R.C. *The Winchester Model 94: The First 100 Years.* Iola, WI: Krause Publications, 1992.

Riling, R. *The Powder Flask Book.* New York, New York: Bonanza Books, 1953.

Rosenberger, R.F.& Kaufmann, C. *The Long Rifles of Westem Pennsylvania-Allegheny and Westmoreland Counties.* Pittsburgh, PA: University of Pittsburgh Press, 1993.

Rule, R. *The Rifleman's Rifle: Winchester's Model 70, 1936-1963.* Northridge, California: Alliance Books, 1982.

Ruth, L. *War Baby! Comes Home-The U.S. Caliber .30 Caliber Carbine Volume II.* Toronto, Ontario: Collector Grade Publications, Inc., 1993.

Ruth, L. *War Baby! The U.S. Caliber .30 Carbine.* Toronto, Ontario: Collector Grade Publications, Inc., 1992.

Schroeder, Joseph J. *Gun Collector's Digest, Volume II* Northfield, Illinois: Digest Books, Inc., 1977.

Schwing, N. *Winchester's Finest, The Model 21.* Iola, WI: Krause Pub., 1990.

Schwing, N. *The Winchester Model 42.* Iola, WI: Krause Pub., 1990.

Schwing, N. *Winchester Slide Action Rifles, Vol. Model 1890 and Model 1906.* Iola, WI: Krause Publications, 1992.

Schwing, N. *Winchester Slide Action Rifles, Vol. Model 61 and Model 62.* Iola, WI: Krause Publications, 1993.

Schwing, N. *The Browning Superposed: John Browning's Last Legacy.* Iola, WI: Krause Publications, 1996.

Sellers, F. *Sharps Firearms.* North Hollywood, California: Beinfeld Pub., Inc., 1978.

Sellers, F. *American Gunsmiths.* Highland Park, New Jersey: Gun Room Press, 1983.

Sellers, F. and Smith, S. *American Percussion Revolvers.* Ottawa, Ontario: Museum Restoration Service, 1971.

Serven, James E. *200 Years of American Firearms.* Chicago, Illinois: Follett Publishing Company, 1975.

Serven, J. *Collecting of Guns.*

Sharpe, P. *The Rifle in America.* Funk and Wagnalls Co., 1953.

Sheldon, Douglas G. *A Collector's Guide to Colt's. 38 Automatic Pistols.* Sheldon, 1987.

Smith, W. *The Book of Pistols and Revolvers.* Harrisburg, Pennsylvania: Stackpole Co., 1962.

Stadt, R.W. *Winchester Shotguns and Shotshells.* Tacoma, Washington: Armory Publications, 1984.

Stevens, R. *The Browning High Power Automatic Pistol.* Toronto, Canada: Collector Grade Publications, 1990.

Stoeger's Catalog & Handbook. 1939 Issue. Hackensack, New Jersey: Stoeger Arms Corporation.

Supica J. & Nahas R., *Standard Catalog of Smith & Wesson.* Iola, WI: Krause Publications, 1996.

Sutherland, R.Q. & Wilson, R. L. *The Book of Colt Firearms.* Kansas City, Missouri: R.Q. Sutherland,1971.

Tivey, T. *The Colt Rifle, 1884-1902.* N.S.W. Australia: Couston & Hall, 1984.

Vorisek, Joleph T *Shotgun Markings:* 1865 to 1940, Canton, CT: Armsco Press 1990.

Wahl, Paul *Wahl's Big Gun Catalog II.* Cut And Shoot, Texas: Paul Wahl Corporation, 1988.

Walter, John *The German Rifle.* Ontario, Canada: Fortress Publishing, Inc., 1979.

Whitaker, Dean H. *The Winchester Model 70 1937-1964.* Dallas, Texas: Taylor Publishing Company, 1978.

Wilkerson, Don *The Post War Colt Single Action Army Revolver.* Dallas, Texas: Taylor Publishing Company, 1978.

Wilson, R.L. *Colt An American Legend.* New York, New York: Abbeville Press, 1985.

Wilson, R.L. *Colt Engraving.* Beinfeld Publishing, Inc., n.p., 1982.

Wilson, R.L. *Winchester Engraving.* Palm Springs, California: Beinfeld Books, 1989.

Wilson, R.L. *The Colt Heritage.* New York, New York: Simon & Schuster, 1979.

Wilson, R.L. *Winchester An American Legend.* New York, New York: 1991.

Winant, L. *Early Percussion Firearms.* New York, New York: Wm. Morrow & Co., 1959.

Winant, L. *Firearms Curiosa.* New York, New York: Greenburg Pub., 1955.

Workman, W.E. *The Ruger 10/22*, Iola, WI: Krause Publications, 1994.

Zhuk, A.B. *The Illustrated Encyclopedia of Handguns.* London, England, Greenhill Books, 1995.

MANUFACTURER & MODEL INDEX

A

A.A. 23
A.A. 23
Reims 23

A.A.A. 23
Modelo 1919 23

A. J. ORDNANCE 23

A-SQUARE 23
Caesar Grade 23
Genghis Khan Model 24
Hamilcar Grade 24
Hannibal Grade 23

A & R SALES SOUTH 24
45 Auto 24
Mark IV Sporter 24

ABADIE 24
System Abadie Model 1878 24
System Abadie Model 1886 24

ABBEY, F.J. & CO. 24
Rifle 24
Shotgun 24

ABBEY, GEORGE T. 24
Over-and-Under Double-Barrel .44 Cal. 24
Side-by-Side Double-Barrel .44 Cal. . . 24
Single-Barrel .44 Cal. 24

ABESSER & MERKEL 24
Crown Grade 24
Diamond Grade 24
Diana Grade 25
Empire Grade 24
Excelsior Grade 25
Magazine Rifle 25
Nimrod 25
Vandalia Grade 25

ACCU-MATCH 25
Accu-Match Custom Pistol 25

ACCU-TEK 25
AT-32SS 26
AT-380SS 25
AT-380 II 26
BL-9 26
BL-380 26
CP-9SS 26
CP-40SS 26
CP-45SS 26
HC-380SS 26

ACHA 27
Atlas 27
Looking Glass (Ruby-Style) 27
Looking Glass 27

ACME 27

ACME ARMS 27
.32 Revolver 27
.22 Revolver 27
Shotgun 27

ACME HAMMERLESS 27
Acme Hammerless 27

ACTION 27
Action 27

ACTION ARMS LTD. 28
Action Arms/IMI Uzi Carbine Models A and B 28
AT-84, AT-88 28
AT-84H, AT-88H 28
AT-84P, AT-88P 28
Timber Wolf Carbine 28

ADAMS 28
Adams Model 1851 Self-Cocking Revolver 28
Adams Pocket Revolver 28
Beaumont-Adams Revolver 28

ADAMY GEBRUDER 28
Over-and-Under Shotgun 28

ADIRONDACK ARMS CO. or A.S. BABBITT CO. 29
First Model 29
Orvil M. Robinson Patent Rifle 29
Second Model 29

ADLER 29

ADVANCED SMALL ARMS INDUSTRIES 29
one Pro .45 29

ADVANTAGE ARMS U.S.A., INC. 29
Model 422 29

AERO 30
Model 1914 (Aero) 30

AETNA ARMS CO. 30

AFC 30
Model 1895 30
Semi-Auto 31
Trainer 30

AFFERBACH, W. A. 31

AGNER (SAXHOJ PRODUCTS INC.) . . 31
Model M 80 31

AGUIRRE 31
Basculant 31
LeDragon 31

AGUIRRE Y ARANZABAL (AyA) 31
SIDE-BY-SIDE 31
Bolero Side-by-Side 31
Iberia II Side-by-Side 31
Iberia Side-by-Side 31
Matador II Side-by-Side 31
Matador III Side-by-Side 31
Matador Side-by-Side 31
Model 106 Side-by-Side 32
Model 107-LI Side-by-Side 32
Model 116 Side-by-Side 32
Model 117 "Quail Unlimited" Side-by-Side 32
Model 117 Side-by-Side 32
Model 210 Side-by-Side 32
Model 711 Boxlock Side-by-Side 32
Model 711 Sidelock Side-by-Side 32
Senior Side-by-Side 32
OVER-AND-UNDERS 32
Model 77 Over-and-Under 32
Model 79 "A" Over-and-Under 32
Model 79 "B" Over-and-Under 32
Model 79 "C" Over-and-Under 32
Coral "A" Over-and-Under 32
Coral "B" Over-and-Under 33
SIDELOCK/SIDE-BY-SIDE 33
Model No. 1 33
Model No. 1 Deluxe 33
Model No. 1 Round Body 33
Model No. 2 33
Model No. 2 Round Body 34
Model No. 53 34
Model No. 56 34
Model XXV—Sidelock 34
BOXLOCK SIDE-BY-SIDE 34
Model XXV—Boxlock 34
Model No. 4 34
Model No. 4 Deluxe 34
OVER-AND-UNDER 34
Model Augusta 35
Model No. 37 Super 34

AIR MATCH 35
Air Match 500 35

AJAX ARMY 35
Single-Action 35

ALAMO RANGER 35

ALASKA 35

ALDAZABAL 35
Aldazabal 36
Military Model 35
Model 1919 35

ALERT 36

ALEXIA 36

ALFA 36

ALKARTASUNA FABRICA DE ARMAS 36
Alkar 36
Alkar (Ruby-Style) 36

ALL RIGHT FIREARMS CO. 36
Little All Right Palm Pistol 36

ALLEN, ETHAN 36
.41 Derringer 40
.32 Derringer 40
.32 Side Hammer Rimfire Revolver . . . 39
First Model 39
Second Model 39
Third Model 39
.32 Single-Shot Center Hammer 39
.22 Side Hammer Rimfire Revolver . . . 39
Early Model First Issue 39
Second Issue 39
Third Issue 39
Fourth to Eighth Issue 39
Allen & Wheelock Center Hammer Pistol 37
Allen Thurber & Company Target Pistol 37
Bar Hammer Pistol 37
Center Hammer Army Revolver 38
Center Hammer Muzzleloading Rifle . . 40
Center Hammer Navy Revolver 39
Center Hammer Percussion Revolver . 39
Center Hammer Pistol 37
Combination Gun 40
Double-Barrel Pistol 37
Double-Barrel Shotgun 40
Drop Breech Rifle 40
Ethan Allen Pepperboxes 37
First Model Pocket Rifle 37
Large Frame Pocket Revolver 37
Lipfire Army Revolver 39
Early Model 39
Late Model 39
Lipfire Navy Revolver 39
Lipfire Pocket Revolver 39
Lipfire Revolving Rifle 40
Second Model Pocket Rifle 37

Side Hammer Pistol . . . 37
Small Frame Pocket Revolver . . . 38
Side Hammer Belt Revolver . . . 38
Side Hammer Breech-loading Rifle . . . 40
Side Hammer Muzzleloading Rifle . . . 40
Side Hammer Navy Revolver . . . 38
Standard Model . . . 38
Side Hammer Pocket Revolver . . . 38
Early Production . . . 38
Standard Production . . . 38
Single-Shot Center Hammer . . . 39
Early Issue . . . 39
Standard Issue . . . 39
Standard Model . . . 38
Tube Hammer Pistol . . . 37
Vest Pocket Derringer . . . 40

ALLEN & THURBER . . . 41

ALLEN & WHEELOCK . . . 41

ALLEN FIREARMS . . . 41

ALPHA ARMS CO. . . . 41
Alpha Alaskan . . . 41
Alpha Big - Five . . . 41
Alpha Custom . . . 41
Alpha Grand Slam . . . 41
Alpha Jaguar Grade I . . . 41
Jaguar Grade II . . . 41
Jaguar Grade III . . . 41
Jaguar Grade IV . . . 41

ALSOP, C.R. . . . 41
First Model Navy Revolver . . . 41
Pocket Model Revolver . . . 41
Standard Model Navy Revolver . . . 41

AMAC . . . 41
AMAC 22 Compact or 25 Compact . . . 42
Enforcer .30 Carbine . . . 42
Li'L Champ Bolt-Action Rifle . . . 42
Long Range Rifle System . . . 42
M .30 Cal. Carbine . . . 42
Paratrooper .30 Carbine . . . 42
Targetmaster Pump-Action Rifle . . . 42
TP-22 and TP-25 . . . 42
U.S. Carbine .22 . . . 42
Wagonmaster Lever Action Rifle . . . 42
Wagonmaster .22 Magnum . . . 42

AMERICAN ARMS . . . 42
Eagle .380 . . . 42

AMERICAN ARMS CO. . . . 42
Double-Barrel Derringers . . . 43
.41 caliber R.F., Both Barrels . . . 43
.38 caliber R.F., Both Barrels . . . 43
.32 cal. R.F., Both Barrels . . . 43
.32 caliber R.F., Both Barrels . . . 43
Combination .22 caliber R.F. and .32 caliber R.F. . . . 43
Fox Model "Swing Out" Hammer Double . . . 42
Hammerless Model 1890 Double-Action . . . 43
Semi-Hammerless Double . . . 43
Semi-Hammerless Single-Barrel . . . 43
Spur Trigger—Single-Action Five-Shot Revolver . . . 43
Standard Trigger Double-Action Model 1886 Revolver . . . 43
Whitmore Model Hammerless Double . . . 43

AMERICAN ARMS, INC. . . . 44
10 Gauge Magnum Shotgun . . . 44
12 Gauge Magnum Shotgun . . . 44
10 Gauge Model . . . 46
1860 Henry . . . 47
1866 Winchester . . . 47
1873 Winchester . . . 47
1885 Single-Shot High Wall . . . 47
AASB . . . 46
AKC47 . . . 46
AKF39 . . . 46
AKF47 . . . 46
AKY39 . . . 46
Aussie Model . . . 48
Brittany . . . 44
Bristol (Sterling) . . . 45
Campers Special . . . 46
Combo Model . . . 46
Derby . . . 44
Excelsior . . . 46
EXP-64 Survival Rifle . . . 46
F.S. 200 . . . 44
F.S. 300 . . . 44
F.S. 400 . . . 44
F.S. 500 . . . 45
Gentry-York . . . 44
Grulla #2 . . . 44
Lince . . . 45
Model CX-22 . . . 47
Model EP-.380 . . . 47
Model PK-22 . . . 47
Model TT Tokarev . . . 48
Model ZC-.380 . . . 48
Model ZCY.308 . . . 46
Phantom Field . . . 46
Phantom HP . . . 46
Phantom Synthetic . . . 46
Regulator . . . 48
Regulator Deluxe . . . 48
Royal . . . 45
Sharps 1874 Deluxe Sporting Rifle . . . 47
Sharps Cavalry Carbine . . . 47
Sharps Frontier Carbine . . . 47
Sharps Sporting Rifle . . . 47
Silver Competition/Sporting . . . 45
Silver Hunter . . . 45
Silver I . . . 45
Silver II . . . 45
Silver II Lite . . . 45
Silver Model . . . 45
Single-Barrel Shotguns Youth Model . . . 46
Sir . . . 45
Slugger . . . 46
SM-64 TD Sporter . . . 46
Specialty Model . . . 44
Turkey Special . . . 44
Turkey Special . . . 45
Waterfowl 10 Gauge . . . 45
Waterfowl Special . . . 44, 45

AMERICAN BARLOCK WONDER . . . 48

AMERICAN DERRINGER CORP. . . . 48
Cop 4-Shot . . . 50
Cowboy Series 2000 . . . 51
DA 38 Double-Action Derringer . . . 50
Double-Action Derringer . . . 50
Gambler Millennium 2000 . . . 51
LM-5 . . . 51
Millennium Series 2000 . . . 51
Mini Cop 4-Shot . . . 50
Model 1 125th Anniversary Commemorative . . . 49
Deluxe Engraved . . . 49
Model 1 Derringer . . . 48
Caliber: .22 Long Rifle through .357 Mag. and .45 ACP . . . 48
Calibers: .41 Mag., .44-40, .44 Special, .44 Mag., .45 Long Colt, .410 Bore, .22 Hornet, .223 Rem., 30-30, and .45-70 Gov't. . . . 48
Model 1 Lady Derringer . . . 48
Deluxe Engraved Grade . . . 48
Deluxe Grade . . . 48
Model 1 NRA 500 Series . . . 49
Model 1 Texas Commemorative . . . 49
Caliber: .38 Special . . . 49
Calibers: .45 Colt and .44-40 . . . 49
Deluxe Engraved . . . 49
Model 2—Pen Pistol . . . 49
Model 3 . . . 49
Model 4 . . . 49
Model 4—Engraved . . . 49
Model 4—Alaskan Survival Model . . . 49
Model 6 . . . 49
Model 6—Engraved . . . 50
Model 7 Derringer—Lightweight . . . 50
.32 S&W Long/.32 Magnum . . . 50
.38 S&W and .380 ACP . . . 50
.22 LR and .38 Special . . . 50
.44 Special . . . 50
Model 8 . . . 50
Model 8—Engraved . . . 51
Model 10 Derringer . . . 51
Model 11 Derringer . . . 51
Semmerling LM-4 . . . 51
Women of Texas Series . . . 51

AMERICAN FIRE ARMS MFG. CO., INC. . . . 51
American .25 Automatic . . . 52
American .38 Special Derringer . . . 51
American .380 Automatic . . . 52

AMERICAN FRONTIER FIREARMS . . . 52
1860 Richards Army Model . . . 52
1871-72 Open Top Standard Model . . . 52
Richards & Mason Conversion 1851 Navy Standard Model . . . 52

AMERICAN GUN CO., NEW YORK . . . 52
Knickerbocker Pistol . . . 52
Side-by-Side Shotgun . . . 52

AMERICAN HISTORICAL FOUNDATION . . . 52

AMERICAN INDUSTRIES . . . 53
Calico M-100 . . . 53
Calico M-100P/M-110 . . . 53
Calico M-100S Sporter/M-105 . . . 53
Calico M-101 Solid Stock Carbine . . . 53
Calico M-900 . . . 53
Calico M-950 Pistol . . . 53
Calico M-951 . . . 53
Calico M-951S . . . 53

AMERICAN INTERNATIONAL . 53
American 180 Carbine (SAM-180) . . . 53

AMERICAN WESTERN ARMS INC. (AWA) . . . 53
AWA Lightning Rifle . . . 53
AWA Lightning Rifle LE . . . 53
AWA Lightning Carbine . . . 53

AMES, N.P. PISTOLS . . . 53

AMES SWORD CO. . . . 54
(See Chicago Firearms Co. and Minneapolis Firearms Co.) . . . 54
Turbiaux Le Protector . . . 54

AMT . . . 54
.380 Back Up II . . . 56
.400 Accelerator . . . 57
Automag II . . . 55
Automag III . . . 55
Automag IV . . . 55
Automag V . . . 55
Baby Automag . . . 54
Back Up Pistol . . . 56
Back Up .38 Super, .357 Sig, .400 CorBon . . . 56
Back Up .45 ACP, .40 S&W, 9mm . 56

Bolt-Action Repeating Rifle—Deluxe . . 58
Bolt-Action Repeating Rifle—Standard 58
Bull's Eye Regulation Target 54
Challenge Edition 58
Combat Skipper 58
Commando 57
Government Model 57
Hardballer 57
Hardballer/Government Model 57
Hardballer Longslide 57
Hunter Rifle 58
Javelina 56
Lightning 54
Lightning Rifle 58
Magnum Hunter 58
On Duty 57
Single-Shot Deluxe Rifle 58
Single-Shot Standard Rifle 58
Skipper 57
Small Game Hunter 58
Small Game Hunter II 58
Target Model 58

ANCION & CIE 58

ANCION MARX 58

ANDERSON 59
Anderson Under Hammer Pistol 59

ANDRUS & OSBORN 59
Andrus & Osborn Under Hammer Pistol 59

ANSCHUTZ 59
Achiever 63
Achiever Super Target 63
Anschutz Model 1907 Club 64
Bavarian 1700 63
Classic 1700 63
Custom 1700 63
Exemplar 65
Exemplar Hornet 65
Exemplar XIV 65
Mark 10 Target Rifle 59
Model 54 Sporter 61
Model 54.18MS 61
Model 54.MS REP 62
Model 54M 61
Model 64 61
Model 64MS 61
Model 64 MPR 61
Model 64P 61
Model 64P Mag 61
Model 141 61
Model 141M 61
Model 153 61
Model 153-S 61
Model 164 61
Model 164M 61
Model 184 61
Model 520/61 64
Model 525 Sporter 65
Model 1403D 59
Model 1407 59
Model 1408 59
Model 1411 59
Model 1413 Match 59
Model 1416D Custom 59
Model 1416D HB Classic 59
Model 1416D KL Classic 59
Model 1418D KL Mannlicher 59
Model 1418/19 60
Model 1433D 60
Model 1449D Youth 60
Model 1451E Target 60
Model 1451R Sporter Target 60
Model 1451D Custom 60
Model 1451D Classic 60
Model 1502 D HB Classic 64
Model 1516D KL Classic 60
Model 1516D KL Custom 60
Model 1517D Classic 60
Model 1517D HB Classic 60
Model 1517D Monte Carlo 60
Model 1517MPR Multi Purpose Rifle . . 60
Model 1518D Mannlicher 61
Model 1700 FWT 63
Model 1700 FWT Deluxe 63
Model 1700 Mannlicher 63
Model 1702 D HB Classic 64
Model 1710 D Classic 63
Model 1710 D HB Classic 63
Model 1710 D HB Classic 150 Years Anniversary Version 63
Model 1710 D KL Monte Carlo 63
Model 1712 Silhouette Sporter 63
Model 1717 D Classic 64
Model 1717 D HB Classic 64
Model 1730 D Classic 64
Model 1730 D HB Classic 64
Model 1730 D KL Monte Carlo 64
Model 1733D KL Mannlicher 64
Model 1740 D Classic 64
Model 1740 D HB Classic 64
Model 1740 D KL Monte Carlo 64
Model 1803D 62
Model 1808D RT Super 62
Model 1827B Biathlon 62
Model 1827BT Biathlon 62
Model 1903D 62
Model 1907ISU Standard Match 62
Model 1910 Super Match II 62
Model 1911 Prone Match 62
Model 1913 Super Match 62
Model 2000 MK 62
Model 2007 Supermatch 62
Model 2013 Supermatch 62
Model Woodchucker 60

ANTI GARROTTER 65

APACHE 65

APALOZO HERMANOS 65
Apaloza 65
Paramount 65
Triomphe 65

AR-7 INDUSTRIES 66
AR-7 Bolt-Action 66
AR-7 Explorer 66
AR-7 Sporter 66
AR-7 Target 66
AR-7C Explorer 66

ARCUS 66
Arcus-94 66

ARIZAGA, G. 66
Arizaga (Model 1915) 66
Mondial 66
Pinkerton 66
Warwick 66

ARIZMENDI ZULAICA 66
Cebra 66
Cebra Revolver 66

ARIZMENDI, FRANCISCO 66
Arizmendi 67
Boltun—1st Variation 67
6.35mm 68
7.65mm 68
Boltun—2nd Variation 68
Kaba Spezial 68
Pistolet Automatique 68
Puppy 68
Roland 68
6.35mm 68
7.65mm 68
Singer 66
6.35mm 66
7.65mm 67
Teuf Teuf 67
6.35mm 67
7.65mm 67
Walman 67
.380 67
6.35mm 67
7.65mm 67
Ydeal 68
.380 68
6.35mm 68
7.65mm 68

ARMALITE, INC. 69
AR-7 Custom 69
AR-7 Explorer Rifle 69
AR-10A2 Carbine 69
AR-10A2 Rifle 69
AR-10A4 Carbine 69
AR-10A4 Rifle 69
AR-10B 70
AR-10(T) Carbine 70
AR-10(T) Rifle 70
AR-10(T) Ultra 70
AR-10 SOF 70
AR-17 Shotgun 69
AR-24 Pistol 69
AR-30M 71
AR-50 71
AR-180 69
Howa 69
Sterling 69
AR-180B 69
M15 SOF 70
M15A2 HBAR 70
M15A2 National Match 70
M15A2-M4A1C Carbine 70
M15A2-M4C Carbine 70
M15A4(T) Eagle Eye 70
M15A4 Action Master 71
M15A4 Eagle Spirit 71
M15A4 Special Purpose Rifle (SPR) . . 71
Golden Eagle 71
HBAR 71
M4C Carbine 71

ARMAS DE FUEGO 71

ARMERO ESPECIALISTAS 71
Alfa 71
Omega 72

ARMES DE CHASSE 72
Balmoral 72
Chesapeake 72
Highlander 72
Model 70E 72
Model 74E 72
Model 76E 72
Model EJ 72
Model EU 72

ARMINEX LTD. 72
Target Model 72
Tri-Fire 72

ARMINUS 72

ARMITAGE INTERNATIONAL, LTD. 72
Scarab Skorpion 72

ARMS CORPORATION OF THE PHILIPPINES 73
MAP1 FS 73
MAPP1 FS 73
Model 12Y 73
Model 14Y 73
Model 20C 74

Model 30D 73
Model 30DG 73
Model 30R 73
Model 30RP 73
Model 30 SAS1 73
Model 200DC 74
Model 200P 74
Model 200TC 74
Model 201S 74
Model 202 74
Model 206 74
Model 210 74
Model 1400 73
Model 1911-A1 75
Model 1911-A2 75
Model AK22F 74
Model AK22S 74
Model M14D 73
Model M14P 73
Model M20P 74
Model M100 74
Model M1500 73
Model M1600 73
Model M1600C 74
Model M1600R 73
Model M1600W 74
Model M1800 74
Model M2000 74

ARMSCO FIREARMS CORP. . . . 75
Model 101BE 75
Model 101SE 75
Model 103C 75
Model 103CE 75
Model 103D 75
Model 103DE 75
Model 103F 75
Model 103FE 75
Model 104A 75
Model 200A 75
Model 201A 75
Model 202A 75
Model 202B 75
Model 205A 75
Model 210AE 75
Model 210BE 75
Model 301A 75
Model 401A 76
Model 401B 76
Model 501GA 76
Model 501GB 76
Model 601GA 76
Model 601GB 76
Model 701GA 76
Model 701GB 76
Model 801A 76
Model 801B 76

ARMSCORP OF AMERICA 76
Detective HP—Compact 76
Expert Model 76
FAL 76
Hi-Power 76
M14R 76
M14 National Match 76
M36 Israeli Sniper Rifle 76
P22 76
SD9 76

ARMY & NAVY CO-OPERATIVE SOCIETY 77

ARNOLD ARMS 77
1,000 Yard Match Rifles 78
African Synthetic Rifle 78
African Trophy Rifle 78
Alaskan Rifle 77
Alaskan Trophy Rifle 77
Alaskan Guide Rifle 77
Synthetic Stock 77
Walnut Stock 77
Benchrest Rifles 78
Fully Accurized Production Rifles 78
Grand African Rifle 78
Grand Alaskan Rifle 77
"AAA" English Walnut 77
"Exhibition" Grade Walnut 77
Neutralizer Rifle Mark I 78
Neutralizer Rifle Mark II 78
Prone Rifles 78
Safari Rifle 77
"A" Fancy English Walnut 78
"AA" Fancy English Walnut 78
Serengeti Synthetic Rifle 78
Varminter I 77
Varminter II 77
X-Course Rifles 78

AROSTEGUI, EULOGIO 78
Azul 6.35mm 79
Azul 7.65mm 79
Azul Royal (Model 31) 78
Super Azul (M-34) 79
Velo-Dog 79

ARRIETA S.L. 79
490 Eder 79
500 Titan 79
501 Palomara 79
505 Alaska 79
510 Montana 79
550 Field 79
557 Standard 79
558 Patria 79
560 Cumbre 79
570 Lieja 79
575 Sport 79
578 Victoria 79
585 Liria 80
588 Cima 80
590 Regina 80
595 Principe 80
600 Imperial 80
601 Imperial Tiro 80
801 80
802 80
803 80
871 80
872 80
873 81
874 81
875 81
R-1 Double Rifle 81
R-2 Double Rifle 81

ARRIZABALAGA, HIJOS de C. . 81
Arrizabalaga 81
Campeon 81
Jo Lo Ar 81
Sharpshooter 82

ARSENAL, INC. 82
SA M-7 82
SA M-7 Classic 82
SA M-7S 82
SA RPK-7 82

ASCASO 82
Spanish Rebublican Government 82

ASHEVILLE ARMORY 82
Enfield Type Rifle 82

ASHTON, PETER & WILLIAM . . 82
Ashton Under Hammer Pistol 82

ASTON, H./H. ASTON & CO. PISTOLS 82

ASTRA-UNCETA SA 83
.357 Double-Action Revolver 86
.44/.45 Double-Action Revolver 86
Astra 100 83
Astra 200 83
Astra 400 or Model 1921 83
Astra 300 84
Astra 600 84
Astra 700 84
Astra 800 84
Astra 900 84
Astra 1000 84
Astra 1911 83
Astra 1924 83
Astra 2000 85
Astra 3000 85
Astra 4000 85
Astra 5000 85
Astra 7000 85
Astra A-80 85
Astra A-90 85
Astra Cadix 86
Constable A-60 86
Convertible Revolver 86
Model A-70 87
Model A-75 87
Model A-100 86
Model A-100 Carry Comp 86
Terminator 86
Victoria 83

ATCSA 87
Colt Police Positive Copy 87
Target Pistol 87

ATKIN, HENRY 87

AUBREY, A.J. 87
Double-Barrel Shotguns 87

AUER, B. 87
Auer Pocket Pistol 87

AUGUSTA MACHINE WORKS . 87
1851 Colt Navy Copy 87

AUSTIN & HALLECK, INC. 87
Model 320 LR BLU 87
Model 320 S/S 87
Model 420 LR Classic 87
Model 420 LR Monte Carlo 87
Mountain Rifle 88

AUSTRALIAN AUTOMATIC ARMS LTD. 88
SAP 88
SAR 88
SP 88

AUSTRIAN MILITARY FIREARMS 88
Austrian M1842 Yager Rifle 89
Austrian M1844 "Extra Corps" Musketoon 89
Altered to percussion and rifled (Boker) 89
Austrian M1849 Yager Rifle 89
Austrian M1850 Carbine 90
Austrian M1850 Horse Pistol 89
Austrian M1854/67 "Wanzel" Alteration to Breechloader 90
Austrian M1859 Horse Pistol 90
Austrian M1867 "Werndl" Breechloading Rifle 90
Austrian Musket, M1828 88
Austrian Musket, M1835 88
Austrian Musket, M1840 88

Austrian Musket, M1842 88
Altered to percussion (Cincinnati contractors) 89
Altered to percussion (Leman) 89
Altered to percussion and rifled (Boker) 89
In original tubelock 89
M1854 Rifle-Musket (The "Lorenz") . . . 90
M1854 Yager Rifle 90

AUTAUGA ARMS INC. 90
Autauga MK II 90

AUTO MAG 90
.44 AMP 91
.357 AMP 91

AUTO ORDNANCE CORP. 91
1927 A1 Commando 93
1927 A1 Deluxe 93
1927 A1C 93
1927 A3 93
1927 A5 93
Auto-Ordnance M1 Carbine 94
M1 Carbine 94
M1SB 94
Model 1911CAF 91
Model 1911TC 91
T1SB 94
Thompson 1911 A—Satin Nickel 92
Thompson 1911 A1 Custom High Polish 92
Thompson 1911 A1—10mm 92
Thompson 1911 A1—Competition 92
Thompson 1911 A1—Deluxe 92
Thompson 1911 A1—Duo Tone 92
Thompson 1911 A1—General 92
Thompson 1911 A1—Parkerized 92
Thompson 1911 A1—Pit Bull 92
Thompson 1911 A1—Standard 92
Thompson 1927 A1 Standard 92
ZG-51 "Pit Bull" 92

AUTO POINTER 94
Auto Pointer Shotgun 94

AXTELL RIFLE CO. 94
#1 Long Range Creedmore 94
#2 Long Range 94
Business Rifle 94
Lower Sporting Rifle 94
New Model Sharps 1877 94
Overbaugh Schuetzen 94

AZPIRI 94
Avion 94
Colon 94

B

B.R.F. 95
B.R.F. 95

BABBIT, A. S. 95

BABCOCK, MOSES 95
Babcock Under Hammer Cane Gun . . 95

BACON ARMS CO. 95

BAER CUSTOM, LES 95
AR .223 IPSC Action Model 102
AR .223 M4-A2 Flattop 102
AR .223 Ultimate NRA Match 102
AR .223 Ultimate Super Match 102
AR .223 Ultimate Super Varmint 102
Baer 1911 Bullseye Wadcutter Pistol . . 96
Baer 1911 Concept I 100
Baer 1911 Concept II 100
Baer 1911 Concept III 100
Baer 1911 Concept IV 100
Baer 1911 Concept IX 101
Baer 1911 Concept V 100
Baer 1911 Concept V 6" 100
Baer 1911 Concept VI 101
Baer 1911 Concept VI L.W. 101
Baer 1911 Concept VII 101
Baer 1911 Concept VIII 101
Baer 1911 Concept X 101
Baer 1911 Custom Carry—Commanche Length 98
Baer 1911 IPSC Action Pistol 96
Baer 1911 Monolith 98
Baer 1911 Monolith Commanche 99
Baer 1911 Monolith Commanche Heavyweight 99
Baer 1911 Monolith Heavyweight 99
Baer 1911 Monolith Tactical Illuminator 99
Baer 1911 National Match Hardball Pistol 96
Baer 1911 P.P.C. Distinguished Match 96
Baer 1911 P.P.C. Open Class 97
Baer 1911 Premier II 97
Baer 1911 Premier II Super-Tac 98
Baer 1911 Premier II—6" barrel 97
Baer 1911 Premier II—Light Weight (LW1) 97
Baer 1911 Premier II—Light Weight (LW2) 97
Baer 1911 Prowler III 98
Baer 1911 Prowler IV 98
Baer 1911 Stinger 99
Baer 1911 Stinger Stainless 99
Baer 1911 Target Master 96
Baer 1911 Thunder Ranch Special . . . 98
Baer 1911 Thunder Ranch Special Engraved Model 98
Baer 1911 Ultimate Master Combat Pistol 95
5" Model 96
6" Model 96
Baer 1911 Ultimate Master Combat Pistol-Compensated 95
Baer 1911 Ultimate Master Steel Special 95
Baer 1911 Ultimate Master Para 96
Baer Custom Carry—5" 98
Baer Lightweight .22 caliber 1911 Models 102
4-1/2" Model with fixed sights 102
5" Model with fixed sights 102
5" Model with Bo-Mar sights 102
Baer Limited Edition Presentation Grade 1911 102
Baer S.R.P. (Swift Response Pistol) . . 98
Bullpup Muzzleloader 102
Limited Model 96
Model 1911 Twenty-Fifth Anniversary 102
Thunder Ranch Rifle 102
Ultimate Recon 102
Unlimited Model 96

BAFORD, ARMS, INC. 103
Fire Power Model 35 103
Thunder Derringer 103

BAIKAL 103
Baikal IJ-27E1C 103
Baikal TOZ - 34 103
IZH18 103
IZK18MAX 103
IZH27 104
IZH35 104
IZH43 103
IZH43K 103
IZH81 104
IZH94 104
Model MC-5-105 103
Model MC-7 103
Model MC-8-0 103
Model MC-109 103
MP131K 104
MP133 104
MP153 104
MP213 Coach Gun 103
MP233 104

BAILONS GUNMAKERS, LTD. . 104
Hunting Rifle 104

BAKER GAS SEAL 104

BAKER GUN & FORGING CO. . 104
Baker Hammer Gun 106
Baker Trap Gun 105
Batavia Automatic Rifle 106
Batavia Brush Gun 106
Batavia Damascus 106
Batavia Leader 106
Batavia Special 106
Black Beauty Double Shotgun 105
Deluxe Grade Double Shotgun 105
Elite Grade 105
Expert Grade Double Shotgun 105
Grade R Double Shotgun 105
Grade S Double Shotgun 105
Paragon Grade Shotgun 105
Paragon Grade—Model NN 105
Superba 105

BAKER, M.A. 106

BAKER, THOMAS 106

BAKER, WILLIAM 106

BALL REPEATING CARBINE . 106
Ball Repeating Carbine 106

BALLARD PATENT ARMS 107
Ballard (Ball & Williams) "Kentucky" Full-Stock Rifles 108
Ballard (Ball & Williams) "Kentucky" Half-Stock Rifles 107
Ballard (Ball & Williams) Military Carbines (Serial numbers 1500-7500, and 8500-10,500) 107
Ballard (Ball & Williams) Sporting Rifles, First Type (Serial numbers 1-100) 107
Ballard (Ball & Williams) Sporting Rifles, Second Type (Serial numbers 200-1600, and 1600-14,000, interspersed with martial production) 107
Ballard (Ball & Williams) Sporting Rifles, Third Type (Serial numbers 14,000-15,000) 107
Ballard (Brown Mfg. Co.) Full-Stock Military Rifles 109
Ballard (Dwight, Chapin & Co.) Carbines 108
Ballard (Dwight, Chapin & Co.) Full-Stock Rifles 108
Ballard (R. Ball) & Co. Carbines 108
Ballard (R. Ball) & Co. Sporting Rifles 108
Ballard (Merrimack Arms & Manufacturing Co.) Carbines 109
Ballard (Brown Manufacturing Co.) Sporting Rifles 109
Ballard (Merrimack Arms & Manufacturing Co.) Sporting Rifles . 108

BALLARD RIFLE AND CARTRIDGE CO. 109
Model 1885 High Wall 110
No. 1-1/2 Hunter's Rifle 110
No. 1-3/4 Far West Rifle 109
No. 2 Sporting Model 110
No. 3 Gallery Rifle 110
No. 3F Fine Gallery Rifle 110

No. 4 Perfection Model 110
No. 4-1/2 Mid Range Model 109
No. 5 Pacific Model 109
No. 5-1/2 Montana Model 110
No. 6 Off-Hand Rifle Model (Schuetzen) 110
No. 7 Long Range Model 109
No. 8 Union Hill Model 110

BALLESTER—MOLINA 110

BALLARD, C. H. 110
Single-Shot Derringer 110

BARNETT 110

BARRETT F.A. MFG. CO. 110
Model 82 Rifle 110
Model 82A1 111
Model 95M 111
Model 99 111
Model 99-1 111
Model 107 111
Model 468 111

BARRETT, J. B. and A.B. & CO. 111
Barrett Muskets and Rifled Muskets . . 111

BAR-STO PRECISION MACHINE 111
Bar-Sto 25 111

BASCARAN, MARTIN A. 111
Martian 6.35mm 111
Martian 7.65mm 111
Thunder 112

BAUER F. A. CORP. 112
Bauer 25 Automatic 112
The Rabbit 112

BAYARD 112

BAYONNE, MANUFACTURE D'ARMES 112
MAB Model A 112
MAB Model B 113
MAB Model C 113
MAB Model D 113
MAB Model E 113
MAB Model F 113
MAB Model G 113
MAB Model GZ 114
MAB Model P-8 & P-15 114
MAB Model R 114
.22 Long Rifle 114
7.65mm & 7.65mm Long & .380 . . 114
9mm Parabellum 114
MAB Model R PARA Experimential . . 114
Model "Le Chasseur" 114
Model P-15 M1 Target 114

BEATTIE, J. 115
Beattie Gas Seal Revolver 115

BEAUMONT 115
1873 Dutch Service Revolver, New Model 115
1873 Dutch Service Revolver, Old Model 115
1873 KIM, Small Model 115

BEAUMONT, ADAMS 115

BEAUMONT-VITALI 115

BECKER AND HOLLANDER . . 115
Beholla 115

BEEMAN PRECISION ARMS, INC. 115
MP-08 115
P-08 115
SP Deluxe 115
SP Standard 115

BEERSTECHER, FREDERICK . 116
Superposed Load Pocket Pistol 116

BEESLEY, FREDERICK 116

BEHOLLA 116

BEISTEGUI, HERMANOS 116

BENELLI 116
Black Eagle 120
Black Eagle Competition Gun 119
Black Eagle Executive Series 120
Cordoba 120
Grade I 120
Grade II 120
Grade III 120
Legacy 120
Legacy (2005) 120
Legacy Limited Edition 120
Legacy—20 Gauge 120
M1 Field Steady Grip 117
M1 Practical 117
M1 Super 90 Camo Field 117
M1 Super 90 Defense Gun 117
M1 Super 90 Entry Gun 117
M1 Super 90 Field 117
M1 Super 90 Slug Gun 117
M1 Super 90 Sporting Special 118
M1 Super 90 Tactical 117
M2 Field with ComforTech 118
M2 Field without ComforTech 118
M2 Practical with ComforTech 118
M2 Tactical 118
M3 Super 90 116
M3 Super 90 Folding Stock 116
M4 116
M1014 Limited Edition 117
Model B-76 122
Model B-76S 122
Model B-77 122
Model B-80 122
Model B-80S 122
Model MP90S Match (World Cup) . . . 123
Model MP95E Match (Atlanta) 123
Model R 1 Carbine 122
Model R 1 Rifle 122
Model SL 121 Slug 116
Model SL 201 116
Model SL-121 V 116
Model SL-123 V 116
Montefeltro (2005) 118
Montefeltro 20 Gauge 118
Montefeltro 20 Gauge Camo 118
Montefeltro 20 Gauge Limited 118
Montefeltro Super 90 118
Nova 121
Nova Field Slug Combo 121
Nova H2O Pump 121
Nova Rifled Slug 121
Nova Slug 121
R1 ComforTech Rifle 122
Sport II Model 122
Sport Model 121
Super Black Eagle 119
Super Black Eagle Camo Gun 119
Super Black Eagle Custom Slug Gun . 119
Super Black Eagle II Rifled Slug with ComforTech 119
Super Black Eagle II Steady Grip 119
Super Black Eagle II Turkey Gun 119
Super Black Eagle II with ComforTech 119
Super Black Eagle II without ComforTech 119
Super Black Eagle Left-Hand 119
Super Black Eagle Limited Edition . . . 119
Super Black Eagle Steady Grip 119
Supernova 121
Supernova SteadyGrip 121
Supernova Tactical 121
SuperSport with ComforTech 122
Ultra Light 122

BENTLEY, DAVID 123

BENTLEY, JOSEPH 123
Bentley Revolver 123

BENTZ 123

BERETTA, DR. FRANCO 123
Alpha Three 124
America Deluxe 123
America Standard 123
Beta Three 124
Black Diamond Field Grade 123
Grade Four 123
Grade One 123
Grade Three 123
Grade Two 123
Europa 123
Europa Deluxe 124
Francia Standard 124
Gamma Deluxe 123
Gamma Standard 123
Gamma Target 123

BERETTA, PIETRO 124
12 Gauge 155
20 Gauge 155
20 gauge 156
90-Two 138
92 Steel-I 134
471 Silver Hawk 142
626 Onyx 152
627 EELL 152
627 EL 152
682 4 BBL Set 146
682 Gold "Live Bird" 147
682 Gold Skeet with Adjustable Stock 147
682 Gold Trap with Adjustable Stock . 147
682 Mono Combo Trap 147
682 Skeet 146
682 Sporting Combo 146
682 Sporting/682 Gold Sporting 146
682 Super Skeet 146
682 Super Sporting/682 Gold Sporting Ported 146
682 Super Trap 146
682 Top Combo 147
682 Top Combo Super Trap 147
682 Top Single Super Trap 147
682 Top Single Trap 147
682 Trap 147
686 Blackwing 149
686 Collection Sport 149
686 Collection Trap 149
686 EL/Gold Perdiz 149
686 Hunter Sport 149
686 L/686 Silver Perdiz 148
686 Onyx 148
686 Onyx 2 BBL Set 148
686 Onyx Hunter Sport 149
686 Quail Unlimited 2002 Covey Limited Edition 150
686 Ringneck Pheasants Forever . . . 150
686 Silver Pigeon 149
686 Silver Pigeon S 149
686 Silver Pigeon Sporting 149
686 Silver Pigeon Trap (30") 149
686 Silver Pigeon Trap Top Mono (32" or 34") 149
686 Silver Receiver 148
686 Sporting Combo 149
686 Ultra Light Onyx 148
686 Whitewing 149

686E Sporting . . . 149
687 EELL 12 and 20 gauge . . . 151
687 EELL 12 gauge . . . 151
687 EELL 28 gauge and .410 bore . . 151
687 EELL 4 BBL Set . . . 151
687 EELL Combo . . . 151
687 EELL Diamond Pigeon Skeet . . . 151
687 EELL Diamond Pigeon Skeet with Adjustable Stock . . . 151
687 EELL Diamond Pigeon Sporting . 152
687 EELL Top Combo . . . 152
687 EELL Trap . . . 152
687 EELL/Diamond Pigeon . . . 151
687 EL 12 and 20 gauge . . . 151
687 EL 28/.410 . . . 151
687 EL Gold Pigeon Sporting . . . 151
687 EL/687 Gold Pigeon . . . 151
687 L/Silver Pigeon . . . 150
687 Silver Pigeon II . . . 150
687 Silver Pigeon II Sporting . . . 150
687 Silver Pigeon IV . . . 151
687 Silver Pigeon Sporting . . . 150
687 Silver Pigeon V . . . 151
687 Sporting Combo . . . 151
3901 Ambassador . . . 157
3901 Citizen . . . 157
3901 Statesman . . . 157
3901 Target RL . . . 157
A391 Teknys Gold Target . . . 159
A391 Xtrema2 . . . 159
A391 Xtrema2 Slug Gun . . . 159
Air Force "RA" marked . . . 125
AL-1 . . . 153
AL-2 . . . 153
AL-2 Competition . . . 154
AL-2 Magnum . . . 154
AL-3 . . . 154
AL-3 Deluxe Trap . . . 154
AL390 Camo . . . 156
AL390 NWTF Special Youth . . . 156
AL390 Skeet . . . 156
AL390 Sport Diamond Sporting . . . 156
AL390 Sport Gold Sporting . . . 156
AL390 Sport Sporting Youth . . . 156
AL390 Sport Sporting Youth Collection . . . 156
AL390 Sporting . . . 156
AL390 Super Skeet . . . 156
AL390 Super Trap . . . 156
AL390 Trap . . . 156
AL391 Covey . . . 159
AL391 Ringneck . . . 159
AL391 Teknys . . . 159
AL391 Teknys Gold . . . 159
AL391 Teknys King Ranch . . . 159
AL391 Urika 2 Gold . . . 158
AL391 Urika 2 Gold Parallel Target . . 159
AL391 Urika 2 Gold Sporting . . . 159
AL391 Urika 2 Kick-Off . . . 158
AL391 Urika 2 Parallel Target X-Tra Grain . . . 159
AL391 Urika 2 Sporting X-Tra Grain . 159
AL391 Urika2 X-Tra Grain . . . 158
Alley Cat . . . 129
AR-70 . . . 138
ASE 90 Gold X Trap Combo . . . 152
ASE 90 Pigeon . . . 152
ASE 90 Skeet . . . 152
ASE 90 Sporting Clay . . . 153
ASE 90 Trap . . . 152
ASE Deluxe Sporting . . . 144
ASEL Model . . . 141
BL-1 . . . 140
BL-2 . . . 140
BL-2 Stakeout . . . 140
BL-2/S (Speed Trigger) . . . 140
BL-3 . . . 140
BL-3 Competition . . . 140
BL-4 . . . 140
BL-4 Competition . . . 140
BL-5 . . . 140
BL-5 Competition . . . 140
BL-6 . . . 140
BL-6 Competition . . . 140
BM-59 Standard Grade . . . 138
Camouflage . . . 156
Cx4 Storm . . . 138
Deluxe Grade/Gold Mallard . . . 156
Deluxe Model . . . 133
Diamond Sable . . . 139
Diana . . . 145
DT 10 Trident Skeet . . . 153
DT 10 Trident Sporting . . . 153
DT 10 Trident Trap . . . 153
DT 10 Trident Trap Bottom Single . . . 153
DT 10 Trident Trap Combo Top . . . 153
ES100 NWTF Special Camo . . . 155
ES100 Pintail Rifled Slug . . . 155
ES100 Pintail Synthetic . . . 154
ES100 Rifled Slug . . . 155
ES100 Rifled Slug Combo . . . 155
Field Grade . . . 154
Field Grade . . . 155
Gold Pigeon . . . 153
Gold Sable . . . 139
Golden Snipe . . . 141
Imperiale Montecarlo . . . 145
Jubilee Field Grade (Giubileo) . . . 144
Jubilee II (Giublio) . . . 144
Jubilee Sporting Grade . . . 144
Kit Price Only . . . 133
Laramie . . . 138
M9A1 . . . 134
Mark II Trap . . . 152
Matched Pair . . . 144
Matched Pair . . . 144
Matched Pair . . . 145
Mato Deluxe . . . 139
Mato Standard . . . 139
Model 20 . . . 129
Model 21 Inox . . . 129
Model 21/21 Bobcat . . . 129
Model 21EL . . . 129
Model 57 E . . . 141
Model 70 (Model 100) . . . 127
Model 70S . . . 127
Model 71/Jaguar (Model 101) . . . 127
Model 72 . . . 127
Model 76 (102) . . . 127
Model 84/Cheetah . . . 136
Model 84BB . . . 136
Model 85/Cheetah . . . 136
Model 86/Cheetah . . . 137
Model 87 Target . . . 137
Model 87/Cheetah . . . 137
Model 89/Gold Standard . . . 137
Model 90 . . . 129
Model 92 . . . 130
Model 92 Billennium . . . 133
Model 92 Competition Conversion Kit 133
Model 92/96 Border Marshall . . . 134
Model 92/96 Combo . . . 133
Model 92/96 Compact "Type M" . . . 132
Model 92/96 Custom Carry . . . 135
Model 92/96 Vertec . . . 133
Model 92/96D . . . 132
Model 92/96DS . . . 133
Model 92/96FS Centurion . . . 131
Model 92/96FS Inox . . . 131
Model 92/96M Compact Inox . . . 132
Model 92D Compact Type M . . . 132
Model 92F . . . 131
Model 92F Compact . . . 132
Model 92FS . . . 130
Model 92FS "470th Anniversary" Limited Edition . . . 132
Model 92FS Deluxe . . . 132
Model 92FS Inox . . . 130
Model 92FS INOX Tactical . . . 135
Model 92FS/96 Brigadier . . . 131
Model 92FS/96 Brigadier Inox . . . 131
Model 92G Elite II . . . 134
Model 92G/96G . . . 133
Model 92G/96G Elite . . . 134
Model 92G-SD/96G-SD . . . 131
Model 92SB Compact . . . 130
Model 92SB-P . . . 130
Model 96 . . . 130
Model 96 Combat . . . 130
Model 96 Stock . . . 131
Model 301 . . . 154
Model 302 . . . 154
Model 302 Super Lusso . . . 154
Model 303 Youth Gun . . . 155
Model 318 . . . 126
Model 409 PB . . . 141
Model 410 . . . 141
Model 410 E . . . 141
Model 411 E . . . 141
Model 418 . . . 126
Model 420 . . . 126
Model 421 . . . 126
Model 424 . . . 141
Model 426 E . . . 141
Model 450 Series . . . 145
Model 451 Series . . . 145
Model 452 . . . 145
Model 452 EELL . . . 145
Model 455 . . . 139
Model 455 EELL . . . 140
Model 470 Silver Hawk . . . 141
Model 470 Silver Hawk EL . . . 142
Model 500 Custom . . . 138
Model 500DEELL . . . 138
Model 500DEELLS . . . 138
Model 500DL . . . 138
Model 500S . . . 138
Model 501 . . . 139
Model 502 . . . 139
Model 625 . . . 141
Model 626 Field Grade . . . 152
Model 682/682 Gold . . . 145
Model 685 . . . 148
Model 686 Essential/Silver Essential . 148
Model 686/686 Silver Perdiz Sporting 148
Model 687 EELL Gallery Special . . . 145
Model 687 EELL King Ranch . . . 152
Model 687/687 Silver Pigeon Sporting 150
Model 948 . . . 126
Model 949 Olympic Target . . . 126
Model 950 Jetfire Inox . . . 128
Model 950/Jetfire . . . 127
Model 950B/Jetfire . . . 128
Model 951 . . . 129
Model 1200 Field Grade . . . 154
Model 1200 Magnum . . . 154
Model 1200 Riot . . . 154
Model 1201 . . . 154
Model 1915 . . . 124
Model 1915/1919 . . . 124
Model 1919 . . . 125
Model 1923 . . . 125
Model 1931 . . . 125
Model 1934 . . . 125
Model 1934 Rumanian Contract . . . 125
Model 1935 . . . 125
Model 3032 Tomcat . . . 128
Model 3032 Tomcat Inox . . . 128
Model 3032 Tomcat Titanium . . . 128
Model 3901 . . . 157
Model 3901 Camo . . . 157
Model 3901 RL . . . 157
Model 8000/8040/8045 Cougar . . . 135
Model 8000/8040/8045 Mini Cougar . 135

Model 8000F—Cougar L 135
Model 9000D 136
Model 9000F 135
Model 9000S 136
Model A-303 155
Model A-303 Competition (Trap or Skeet) 155
Model A-303 Ducks Unlimited 155
Model A-303 Slug Gun 155
Model A-303 Sporting Clay 155
Model A-303 Upland 155
Model ASE 90/Gold Series 152
Model FS-1 152
Model M9 Limited Edition 133
Model S55 B 140
Model S56 E 141
Model S58 Competition 141
Model S689 Sable 139
Model SL-2 153
Model SO-1 142
Model SO-2 142
Model SO-3 142
Model SO-4 (Garcia SO3EL) 142
Model SO-5 (Garcia SO-3 EELL) 142
Model SO-6 (450 or 451 EL) Side-by-Side 142
Model SO-7 (451 EELL) Side-by-Side 142
Model Vittoria/Pintail 154
Navy "RM" marked 125
NWTF Special Camo 156
NWTF Special Synthetic 156
Onyx 145
Onyx Pro 145
Onyx Pro 3.5 145
Onyx Waterfowler 3.5 145
Pigeon Series 153
Ported 156
Px4 Storm Pistol, Type F 137
Riot Model 154
Ruby Pigeon 153
S682 Gold E Skeet 147
S682 Gold E Sporting 148
S682 Gold E Trap 147
S682 Gold E Trap Combo 147
Silver Hawk 141
Silver Pigeon 153
Silver Pigeon S 150
Silver Pigeon S Combo 150
Silver Sable 139
Silver Snipe 141
Single Gun 144
Single Gun 144
Single Gun 145
Slug Gun 155
SO-5 Skeet 143
SO-5 Sporting Clays 142
SO-5 Trap 142
SO-5 Trap 2 BBL Set 142
SO-6 EELL 143
SO-6 EESS 143
SO-6 EL 143
SO-6 Skeet 143
SO-6 Sporting Clays 143
SO-6 Trap 143
SO-7 143
SO-9 143
Special Combo—20/28 Gauge 145
SSO Express 139
SSO5 Express 139
SSO6 139
SSO6 EELL 139
Stampede Bisley 138
Stampede Blue 138
Stampede Deluxe 138
Stampede Nickel 138
Standard Model 129
Standard Model 133
Super Skeet 157
Super Trap 156
Synthetic Stock 156
TR-1 Trap 152
TR-2 Trap 152
U22 Neos 4.5 Inox/6.0 Inox 126
U22 Neos 4.5/6.0 126
U22 Neos 6.0/7.5 DLX 126
U22 Neos 6.0/7.5 Inox DLX 126
UGB25 XCEL 159
Ultralight 150
Ultralight Deluxe 150
Urika 157
Urika Camo 157
Urika Gold 157
Urika Gold Sporting 158
Urika Gold Trap 158
Urika Optima 158
Urika Optima Camo 158
Urika Parallel Target RL/SL 158
Urika Sporting 158
Urika Synthetic 157
Urika Synthetic Optima 158
Urika Trap 158
Urika Youth 158
Waterfowl/Turkey Model 156
White Onyx 145
Xtrema 3.5 159

BERGER, JEAN MARIUS 160
Berger 160

BERGMANN, THEODOR 160
Bergmann Bayard Model 1908 162
Bergmann Einhand 163
Bergmann Erben Model II Pistol 163
Bergmann Erben Pistols 162
Bergmann Erben Spezial 162
Bergmann "Mars" 161
Bergmann Post War Pistols 162
Bergmann Simplex 161
Model 2 and 3 162
Model 2a and 3a 162
Model 1894 Bergmann Schmeisser . . 160
Model 1896, Number 2 160
  Folding Trigger Number 2 160
  Conventional Number 2 160
Model 1896 Number 3 160
  First Variation 160
  Second Variation 161
  Third Variation 161
  Holster and Stock Model 161
Model 1896 Number 4 161
Model 1897 Number 5 161
Model 1897 Number 5a Carbine 161

BERN, WAFFENFABRIK 163

BERNARDELLI, VINCENZO . . .163
Baby Model 163
Brescia 166
Carbina VB Target 167
Comb 2000 168
Elio 167
Elio E 167
Express 2000 168
Express VB 168
Express VB Deluxe 168
Giardino 167
Hemingway 167
Hemingway Deluxe 167
Holland V.B. Extra 167
Holland V.B. Gold 167
Holland V.B. Inciso 167
Holland V.B. Liscio 167
Holland V.B. Lusso 167
Italia 166
Italia Extra 166
Las Palomas Pigeon Model 167
Luck 167
Minerva 168
Model 115 165
Model 115 Trap 165
Model 115E 165
Model 115E Trap 165
Model 115L 165
Model 115S 165
Model 115S Trap 165
Model 190 165
Model 190 Combo Gun 165
Model 190 Special 165
Model 190MC 165
Model 60 163
Model 68 163
Model 69 164
Model 80 163
Model AMR 164
Model P. One 164
Model P. One-Compact 165
Model PO10 164
Model PO18 164
Model PO18 Compact 164
Model USA 165
Orione 165
Orione E 166
Orione L 166
Orione S 165
Pocket Model 163
Practical VB Custom 165
Practical VB Target 165
Revolvers 163
Roma 3 166
Roma 3E 166
Roma 4 167
Roma 4E 167
Roma 6 167
Roma 6E 167
Roma 7 167
Roma 8 167
Roma 9 167
S. Uberto 1E 166
S. Uberto 2 166
S. Uberto 2E 166
S. Uberto F.S. 166
S. Uberto F.S.E. 166
S. Uberto I 166
S. Uberto I Gamecock 166
Sporter Model 163
Vest Pocket Model 163

BERNARDON MARTIN 168
1907/8 Model 168
1908/9 Model 168

BERNEDO, VINCENZO 168
B C 168
Bernado 168

BERSA 169
Model 23 169
Model 83 170
Model 85 170
Model 86 170
Model 97 169
Model 223 169
Model 224 169
Model 225 169
Model 226 169
Model 323 169
Model 383 169
Model 383A 170
Model 622 169
Model 644 169
Series 95/Thunder 380 170
Thunder 9 170
Thunder 9 Ultra Compact 170
Thunder 9/40 High Capacity Series . . 170
Thunder 380 Matte Plus 170
Thunder Deluxe 170

BERTHIER 170

BERTRAND, JULES 171
Le Novo 171
Le Rapide 171
Lincoln 171

BERTUZZI 171
Ariete 171
Ariete Extra Lusso 171
Gull Wing 171
Orione 171
Venere 171
Zeus 171
Zeus Extra Lusso 171
Zeus Boss System 171

BIGHORN ARMS CO. 171
Shotgun 171
Target Pistol 171

BIGHORN RIFLE CO. 171
Bighorn Rifle 171

BILHARZ, HALL & CO. 172
Bilharz, Hall & Co. Breechloading ("Rising Breech") Carbine 172
Bilharz, Hall & Co. Muzzleloading Carbine 172

BILLINGHURST, WILLIAM . . . 172
Revolving Rifle 172
W. Billinghurst Under Hammer Pistol . 172

BILLINGS 172
Billings Pocket Pistol 172

BINGHAM LTD. 172
AK-22 172
Bantam 172
PPS 50 172

BISMARCK 172
Bismarck Pocket Revolver 172

BITTERLICH, FRANK J. 172

BITTNER, GUSTAV 173
Bittner 173

BLAKE, J. H. 173
Blake Bolt-Action Rifle 173

BLANCH, JOHN 173
Blanch Percussion Pistol 173
Double Barrel Shotguns 173

BLAND, THOMAS & SONS . . . 173
Double Barrel Shotguns 173

BLASER JAGDWAFFEN 173
Blaser F3 173
Blaser HHS 175
Blaser S2 Double Rifle 175
Model K77 173
Model R-84 173
Model R-93 (LRS2) 174
Model R-93 Attache 174
Model R-93 Classic 174
Model R-93 Grand Luxe 174
Model R-93 Long Range Sporter 174
Model R-93 Luxus 174
Model R-93 LX 173
Model R-93 Prestige 174
Model R-93 Synthetic 174
Model R-93 Safari Attache 174
Model R-93 Safari Classic 174
Model R-93 Safari LX 174
Model R-93 Safari Synthetic 174
Model K-95 Luxus 175
Model K-95 Standard 174
Model K-95 Stutzen 175

Special Order Ultimate 175
Ultimate Deluxe 175
Ultimate Exclusive 175
Ultimate Royal 175
Ultimate Super Deluxe 175
Ultimate Super Exclusive 175
Ultimate Bolt-Action 175

BLISS, F. D. 175
Bliss Pocket Revolver 175

BLISS & GOODYEAR 175
Pocket Model Revolver 175

BLISSETT 175

BLUNT & SYMS 175
Derringer Style Pistol 176
Double Barrel Pistol 176
Double Barrel Under Hammer Pistol . 176
Dueling Pistol 176
Ring Trigger Pistol 176
Single-Shot Bar Hammer 176
Side Hammer Belt Pistol 176
Side Hammer Pocket Pistol 176
Under Hammer Pepperbox 175
Medium Frame Round Handle .31 Caliber 176
Medium Frame Saw Handle .31 Caliber 176
Round Handle Dragoon .36 Caliber 176
Saw Handle Dragoon .36 Caliber . 176
Small Frame Round Handle .25-.28 Caliber 176

BODEO 176
Italian Service Revolver 176
Modello 1889 (Officer's Model) . . . 176
System Bodeo Modello 1889 (Enlisted Model) 176

BOLUMBURO, G. 176
Bristol 176
Marina 6.35mm 176
Marina 7.65mm 177
Rex 177

BOND 177

BOND ARMS INC. 177
Century 2000 178
Cowboy Defender 177
Snake Slayer 177
Snake Slayer IV 177
Texas Defender 177

BOOM 178

BORCHARDT 178
Borchardt 178
Pistol Only 178
Pistol with Case and Accessories . 178

BORSIG 178

BOSIS, LUCIANO 178
Over-and-Under 178
Side-by-Side 178

BOSS & CO. 178

BOSWELL, CHARLES 178
Double Barrel Shotguns 178
Double Rifle, Boxlock 178
Double Rifle, Sidelock 178

BOSWORTH, B. M. 178
Bosworth Under Hammer Pistol 178

BOWEN CLASSIC ARMS CORP. 178
Alpine (RD02) 179
Colt SAA Lightweight (CS02) 179
Nimrod (RS09/RS09S & RS10/RS10S) 179

BRAENDLIN ARMOURY 179

BRAND 179
Brand Breech Loading Carbine 179

BREDA, ERNESTO 179
Andromeda Special 179
Gold Series Antares Standard 179
Gold Series Argus 179
Gold Series Aries 179
Magnum Model 179
Sirio Standard 179
Standard Semi-Automatic 179
Grade I 179
Grade II 179
Grade III 179
Vega Special 179
Vega Special Trap 179

BREN 10 180
Dual-Master Presentation Model 180
Initial Commemorative 180
M & P Model 180
Marksman Model 180
Pocket Model 180
Special Forces Model 180
Standard Bren 10 180

BRETTON 180
Baby Standard 180
Deluxe Grade 180

BRIGGS, H. A. 180
Briggs Single-Shot Pistol 180

BRILEY MANUFACTURING INC. 180
Carry Comp Model—Defense 181
El Presidente Model—Unlimited 180
Lightning Model—Action Pistol 181
Versatility Model—Limited 181
Versatility Plus Model—Limited 180

BRITISH DOUBLES 181
ENGLISH GUNMAKERS IN NORTH AMERICA 181

BRIXIA 185
Model 12 185

BRNO ARMS 185
Model 21H 186
Model 22F 187
Model 98 Standard 187
Model 98 Full Stock 187
Model 300 Combo 186
Model 500 186
Model I 187
Model II 187
Super Express Rifle 187
Grade I 187
Grade II 187
Grade III 187
Grade IV 187
Grade V 187
Grade VI 187
Standard Model 187
ZBK-100 186
ZBK 110 187
ZBK 110 LUX 187
ZBK 110 Super Lux 187
ZBK 680 187
ZG-47 185
Deluxe 185
Standard 185
ZH-300 186
ZH-301 186
ZH-302 186
ZH-304 186
ZH-305 186
ZH-306 186
ZH-308 186

ZH-309 . . . 186
ZH-321 . . . 186
ZH-324 . . . 186
ZH-328 . . . 186
ZH-344/348/349 . . . 187
ZH-30312 . . . 186
ZK 99 . . . 187
ZKM 451 . . . 187
ZKM 451 LUX . . . 187
ZKM 611 . . . 187
ZKR 551 . . . 187
ZKW-465 (Hornet Sporter) . . . 186
ZP-49 . . . 186
ZP-149 . . . 186
ZP-349 . . . 186

BROLIN ARMS . . . 187
BL-12 Field . . . 190
BL-12 Security . . . 190
Formula One RS . . . 191
Formula One RZ . . . 191
Formula Z . . . 191
Lawman Series—Personal Security Shotgun . . . 189
Legacy . . . 190
Lightning Hunter All Weather Model . . 190
Lightning Hunter Model . . . 190
Lightning Model . . . 190
Lightning Professional . . . 191
Lightning Sniper . . . 191
Lightning Varmint Model . . . 191
M40 . . . 188
M45 . . . 188
M90 . . . 188
MB40 . . . 189
MB90 . . . 189
MC40 . . . 189
MC90 . . . 189
Mitchell PPS-50 . . . 190
Model 20/22 . . . 191
Model 98 . . . 191
Model 1898 Commemorative . . . 191
Model 2000 Classic . . . 191
Model 2000 Professional . . . 191
Model 2000 Sniper . . . 191
Model 2000 Varmint . . . 191
Model HC28SB . . . 190
Model HC28SR . . . 190
Model HC28WB . . . 190
Model HC28WR . . . 190
Model HF24SB . . . 189
Model HF24WB . . . 190
Model HF28SB . . . 189
Model HF28WB . . . 190
Model HL18SB . . . 189
Model HL18SBN . . . 189
Model HL18SR . . . 189
Model HL18WB . . . 189
Model HL18WR . . . 189
Model L45—Standard Auto Pistol . . . 187
Model L45C—Compact Auto Pistol . . 188
Model L45T . . . 188
Model P45 Comp—Standard Carry Comp . . . 188
Model P45C Comp—Compact Carry Comp . . . 188
Model P45T . . . 188
Model Pro-Comp-Competition Pistol . 189
Model Pro-Stock—Competition Pistol 189
Model TAC-11 . . . 188
MS45 . . . 188
SAS-12 Security . . . 190
Single-Action Army Model . . . 191
Slug Special . . . 190
Turkey Special . . . 190

BRONCO . . . 191

BROOKLYN F. A. CO. . . . 191
Slocum Pocket Revolver . . . 191
Slocum Unfluted Cylinder Pocket Revolver . . . 191

BROWN CUSTOM, ED . . . 192
Model 76, Bushveld . . . 192
Model 702, Denali . . . 192
Model 702, Light Tactical . . . 192
Model 702, Marine Sniper . . . 192
Model 702, Ozark . . . 192
Model 702, Peacekeeper . . . 192
Model 702, Savanna . . . 192
Model 702, Tactical . . . 192
Model 702, Varmint . . . 192

BROWN PRODUCTS, INC., ED . . . 192
A3 Tactical . . . 194
Bushveld . . . 194
Class A Limited . . . 193
Classic Custom . . . 193
Commander Bobtail . . . 192
Compact Varmint . . . 193
Damara . . . 193
Executive Carry . . . 193
Executive Elite . . . 193
Executive Target . . . 193
Kobra Carry .45 . . . 193
Kobra Custom .45 . . . 193
M-704 Express . . . 194
Marine Sniper . . . 194
Savanna . . . 193
Special Forces . . . 193

BROWN MANUFACTURING CO. . . . 194
Brown Mfg. Co./Merrill Patent Breechloading Rifles . . . 194
Southerner Derringer . . . 194
Brass Frame 4" Barrel . . . 194
Brass Framed . . . 194
Iron Frame . . . 194

BROWN PRECISION, INC. . . . 194
Blaser Rifle . . . 194
Brown Precision Rifle . . . 194
High Country Standard . . . 194
Law Enforcement Model . . . 194
Open Country Varmint Rifle . . . 194
Pro-Hunter . . . 194

BROWN, A.A. . . . 195

BROWN, DAVID MCKAY . . . 195

BROWN, E.A. MANUFACTURING CO. . . . 195
Brown Classic Single-Shot Pistol . . . 195
Brown Model 97D Single-Shot Rifle . . 195

BROWNING ARMS CO. . . . 195
.22 Semi-Auto/Model SA-22 (Miroku Mfg.) . . . 232
Grade I . . . 232
Grade II . . . 232
Grade III . . . 232
Grade VI . . . 232
.22 Caliber Semi-Auto . . . 232
Grade I . . . 232
Grade II—French Grayed Receiver . . . 232
Grade III . . . 232
2000 Series . . . 220
A-5 DU 50th Anniversary . . . 219
A-5 DU Sweet Sixteen . . . 219
A-500G/A-500R . . . 224
A-500G Sporting Clays . . . 224
A-500R Hunting Model . . . 224
A-500R Buck Special . . . 224
A-Bolt Big Horn Sheep Issue . . . 230
A-Bolt Carbon Fiber Stainless Stalker . . . 229
A-Bolt Classic Hunter WSSM . . . 228
A-Bolt Composite Stalker . . . 228
A-Bolt Composite Stalker WSSM . . . 228
A-Bolt Custom Trophy . . . 230
A-Bolt Eclipse M-1000 . . . 229
A-Bolt Eclipse M-1000 WSM & Stainless . . . 229
A-Bolt Eclipse Varmint . . . 229
A-Bolt Hunter . . . 227
A-Bolt Medallion Model . . . 229
A-Bolt Mountain, Ti . . . 228
A-Bolt Pronghorn Issue . . . 230
A-Bolt Shotgun . . . 226
Hunter Version . . . 227
Stalker Version . . . 227
A-Bolt Special Hunter RMEF . . . 230
A-Bolt Stainless Stalker . . . 228
A-Bolt Stainless Stalker, WSSM . . . 228
A-Bolt Varmint Stalker . . . 229
A-Bolt Varmint Stalker WSSM . . . 229
A-Bolt White Gold Medallion, RMEF . . 230
A-Bolt White Gold RMEF . . . 231
A-Bolt II Classic Hunter . . . 228
A-Bolt II Composite Stalker . . . 228
A-Bolt II Composite Stainless Stalker . 228
A-Bolt II Euro Bolt . . . 229
A-Bolt II Gold Medallion . . . 230
A-Bolt II Heavy Barrel Varmint . . . 229
A-Bolt II Hunter . . . 227
A-Bolt II Hunter WSSM . . . 227
A-Bolt II Medallion . . . 229
A-Bolt II Medallion WSSM . . . 229
A-Bolt II Micro Hunter . . . 228
A-Bolt II Micro-Medallion . . . 230
A-Bolt II White Gold Medallion . . . 230
Acera Straight Pull Rifle . . . 231
American Browning Auto-5 . . . 218
Auto-5 Buck Special . . . 219
Auto-5 Classic . . . 219
Classic . . . 219
Gold Classic . . . 219
Auto-5 Final Tribute Limited Edition . . 220
Auto-5 Light 12 . . . 219
Auto-5 Light 20 . . . 219
Auto-5 Light Buck Special . . . 219
Auto-5 Lightweight . . . 218
Auto-5 Magnum . . . 218, 219
Auto-5 Skeet . . . 218, 219
Auto-5 Stalker . . . 219
Light Stalker . . . 220
Magnum Stalker . . . 220
Auto-5 Trap Model . . . 218
B27 . . . 208
City of Liege Commemorative . . . 208
Deluxe . . . 208
Deluxe Skeet . . . 208
Deluxe Trap . . . 208
Grand Deluxe . . . 208
Standard . . . 208
B-92 Carbine . . . 238
B-2000 . . . 220
B-2000 Buck Special . . . 220
B-2000 Magnum . . . 220
B-2000 Skeet . . . 220
B-2000 Trap . . . 220
BAR-22 . . . 233
BAR-22 Grade II . . . 233
BAR Composite Stalker . . . 234
BAR High Grade Models . . . 234
BAR HIGH POWER RIFLE . . . 233
Grade I . . . 233
Grade I Magnum . . . 233
Grade II Deluxe . . . 233
Grade II Deluxe Magnum . . . 233
Grade III . . . 233
Grade III Magnum . . . 234

Grade IV ... 234
Grade IV Magnum ... 234
Grade V ... 234
Grade V Magnum ... 234
BAR Long Trac ... 235
BAR LongTrac Left-Hand ... 235
BAR LongTrac Stalker ... 235
BAR Mark II Lightweight ... 234
BAR Mark II Safari Rifle ... 234
BAR Short Trac ... 235
BAR ShortTrac Left-Hand ... 235
BAR ShortTrac Stalker ... 235
BDA-380 ... 197
BDM Pistol ... 198
Bicentennial Model ... 207
BL-17 Field Series Grade I ... 235
BL-17 Field Series Grade II ... 235
BL-17 Grade II Octagon ... 236
BL-22 Classic ... 236
BL-22 Field Series Grade I ... 235
BL-22 Field Series Grade II ... 235
BL-22 Grade I ... 235
BL-22 Grade II ... 235
BL-22 Grade II Octagon ... 236
BL-22 Gray Laminate Stainless ... 236
BL-22 NRA Grade 1 ... 236
BLR Lightweight Takedown ... 236
BOSS™ SYSTEM ... 227
BPR-22 ... 232
BPR-22 Grade II ... 232
BPS 10 Gauge ... 225
Mossy Oak Shadow Grass Camo (1999) ... 225
BPS 10 Gauge Turkey ... 225
BPS 12 Gauge ... 225
Waterfowl Camo (1999) ... 225
Waterfowl Mossy Oak Break-Up ... 225
BPS Field Grade ... 224
28 Gauge ... 224
BPS Game Gun ... 225
BPS Magnum Model ... 224
BPS Micro 20 Gauge ... 225
BPS NWTF Series ... 225
BPS 10 Gauge ... 225
BPS 12 Gauge ... 225
3.5" Chamber ... 225
3" Chamber ... 225
BPS Pigeon Grade ... 225
BPS Small Gauge ... 225
BPS Stalker ... 225
BPS Stalker—Combo ... 225
BPS Upland Special ... 225
22" Barrel, Straight Stock ... 225
Browning Collector's Association Edition ... 199
BSS ... 216
BSS Grade II ... 216
BSS Sidelock ... 216
BSS Sporter ... 216
BT-99 ... 215
BT-99 Golden Clays ... 215
BT-99 Pigeon Grade ... 215
BT-99 Plus ... 215
BT-99 Plus Micro ... 215
BT-99 Plus Stainless—Grade I ... 215
BT-99 Plus—Golden Clays ... 215
BT-99 Plus—Pigeon Grade ... 215
BT-99 Plus—Signature Grade ... 215
BT-99 Signature Grade I ... 215
BT-99 Stainless ... 215
Buck Field Plus ... 201
Buck Mark ... 200
Buck Mark 5.5 ... 201
5.5 Blued Target ... 201
5.5 Blued Target (2005) ... 201
5.5 Field ... 201
5.5 Field (2005) ... 201
5.5 Gold Target ... 201
Buck Mark 22 Micro ... 200
Buck Mark Bullseye ... 201
Buck Mark Bullseye Target Stainless ... 202
Buck Mark Bullseye Target URX ... 202
Buck Mark Camper ... 202
Buck Mark Contour 5.5 URX ... 203
Buck Mark Contour Lite 5.5 URX ... 203
Buck Mark Field Target Gray Laminate Rifle ... 233
Buck Mark FLD Plus Rosewood UDX 203
Buck Mark Hunter ... 202
Buck Mark Limited Edition 25th Anniversary ... 202
Buck Mark Lite Splash 5.5 URX ... 203
Buck Mark Micro Bull ... 203
Buck Mark Micro Standard Stainless URX ... 203
Buck Mark Plus ... 200
Buck Mark Plus Nickel ... 200
Buck Mark Plus Stainless Black Laminated UDX ... 203
Buck Mark Plus UDX ... 203
Buck Mark Plus Stainless UDX ... 203
Buck Mark Rifle ... 233
Sporter Model ... 233
Target Model ... 233
Buck Mark Silhouette ... 200
Micro Plus ... 201
Micro Plus Nickel ... 201
Buck Mark Standard Stainless URX ... 204
Buck Mark Unlimited Match ... 202
Buck Mark Varmint ... 200
Buck Special ... 218, 226
Challenger ... 198
Challenger II ... 199
Challenger III ... 199
Citori 525 Field ... 210
Citori 525 Golden Clays Sporting ... 210
Citori 525 Sporting ... 210
Citori Classic Lightning Feather Grade I ... 210
Citori Classic Lightning Grade I ... 210
Citori Esprit ... 210
Citori Feather XS ... 210
Citori Hunter ... 209
Citori Lightning ... 209
Grade I ... 209
Grade III ... 209
Grade IV ... 209
Grade VI ... 209
Grade VII ... 209
Citori Lightning Feather ... 209
Citori Lightning Feather Combo ... 210
Citori Plus ... 212
Golden Clays ... 212
Grade I ... 212
Pigeon Grade ... 212
Signature Grade ... 212
Citori Plus Combo ... 215
Citori Privilege ... 211
Citori Satin Hunter ... 209
Citori Series ... 208
Grade I ... 208
Grade II—1978 to 1983 ... 208
Grade II—Choke Tubes ... 208
Grade V—1978 to 1984 ... 208
Grade V with sideplates—1981 to 1984 ... 208
Grade VI—Choke Tubes ... 208
Upland Special—Grade I ... 208
Citori Skeet ... 213
Golden Clays ... 213
Grade I ... 213
Grade II ... 213
Grade III ... 213
Grade V ... 213
Grade VI ... 213
3 Gauge Set ... 213
Grade I ... 213
Grade III ... 213
Grade VI ... 213
4 Gauge Set ... 213
Grade I ... 214
Grade III ... 214
Grade VI ... 214
Citori Sporting Hunter ... 209
Citori Superlight Feather ... 210
Citori Super Lightning Grade I ... 210
Citori Sporting Clays ... 211
Citori Superlight ... 212
Citori Superlight Feather ... 212
Citori Trap ... 214
Grade I ... 214
Grade II ... 214
Grade III ... 214
Grade V ... 214
Grade VI ... 214
Plus Trap ... 214
Citori Ultra XS Skeet ... 211
Citori XS Special ... 212
Citori XS Sporting Clays ... 211
Citori White Lightning ... 213
Citori White Upland Special ... 213
Citori XT Trap ... 214
Golden Clays ... 214
Signature Grade ... 214
Citori XT Trap Gold ... 214
Classic ... 207
Continental Set ... 239
Custom Shop B25 & B125 Superposed ... 207
12 Gauge Sporting ... 207
12 & 20 Gauge Hunting and Superlight ... 207
B-25 ... 207
B-125 ... 207
Custom Shop BSL ... 207
Case Colored Receiver (BSL Grade LC1) ... 207
Engraved Gray Receiver (BSL Grade LC2) ... 207
Custom Shop Express Rifles ... 239
Cynergy Classic Field ... 216
Cynergy Classic Sporting ... 217
Cynergy Field ... 216
Cynergy Field Small Gauge ... 217
Cynergy Sporting ... 217
Cynergy Sporting Small Gauge ... 217
Cynergy Sporting, Adjustable Comb . 217
Double Automatic Shotgun ... 220
Ducks Unlimited Versions ... 226
Early Production Auto-5 ... 217
Grade I—Matte Rib ... 217
Grade I—Plain Barrel ... 217
Grade I—Vent Rib ... 217
Grade II—Matte Rib ... 218
Grade II—Plain Barrel ... 218
Grade II—Vent Rib ... 218
Grade III—Matte Rib ... 218
Grade III—Plain Barrel ... 218
Grade III—Vent Rib ... 218
Grade IV—Matte Rib ... 218
Grade IV—Plain Barrel ... 218
Grade IV—Vent Rib ... 218
Early Semi-Automatic Pistols ... 195
Euro-Bolt ... 229
Express Rifle ... 238
FN/Browning Superposed ... 207
Full Line Dealer Buck Mark Plus Rosewood UDX ... 203
Game Gun ... 226
Gold 3-1/2" 12 Gauge ... 221
Gold 10 Gauge Combo ... 221
Gold 12 Gauge ... 223
3" Chamber ... 223
3.5" Chamber Ultimate Turkey Gun ... 223
3.5" Chamber, Shadow Grass ... 223
Gold 12 Gauge Hunter ... 221
Gold 20 Gauge Hunter ... 223
Gold Classic ... 207
Gold Classic 20 Gauge ... 222

Gold Classic High Grade 222
Gold Classic Hunter 221
Gold Classic Stalker 221
Gold Deer Hunter 222
Gold Deer Hunter—20 gauge 222
Gold Deer Stalker 222
Gold Deer—Mossy Oak 222
Gold Evolve 221
Gold Fusion 223
Gold Fusion High Grade 223
Gold "Golden Clays" Ladies
Sporting Clays 223
Gold "Golden Clays" Sporting Clays . 223
Gold Ladies/Youth Sporting Clays ... 223
Gold Light 10 Gauge 222
Gold Light 10 Gauge Camo 221
Gold Line Challenger 199
Gold Line Medalist 200
Gold Medallion 230
Gold Medallion A-Bolt .22 231
Gold Micro 223
Gold NWTF Series 222
Gold Sporting Clays 223
Gold Stalker 221
Gold Superlite FLD Hunter 224
Gold Superlite Hunter 224
Gold Superlite Micro 224
Gold Turkey/Waterfowl Hunter 222
Gold Turkey/Waterfowl Stalker 222
Gold Turkey/Waterfowl—Mossy Oak . 222
Gold Upland 223
Gold Waterfowl—Mossy Oak
Shadow Grass 222
Gold Waterfowl—Mossy Oak
Breakup 222
Golden Clays 224
Grade I A—Bolt .22 231
Gran Lightning 213
Grade I 213
Grade III 213
Grade V 213
Grade VI 213
GTI Model 212
Golden Clays 212
Grade I 212
Signature Grade 212
Hi-Power .40 S&W 197
Hi-Power Capitan 196
Hi-Power Centennial Model 196
Hi-Power Mark III 197
Hi-Power Modern Production 195
Spur Hammer Version 195
Round Hammer Version 195
Hi-Power Practical 197
Hi-Power Silver Chrome Model 197
Hi-Power—.30 Luger 196
High-Power Bolt-Action Rifle 227
Medallion Grade 227
Olympian Grade 227
Safari Grade 227
International Medalist 199
Jonathan Browning Centennial
Mountain Rifle 237
Jonathan Browning Mountain Rifle ... 237
Late Production Auto-5—B.C. Miroku
Manufacture 219
Liege 207
Light Sporting 802ES
(Extended Swing) 215
Lightning Sporting Model 211
Golden Clays 211
Pigeon Grade 211
Limited Edition Model 42 226
Grade I 226
Grade V 226
Louis XVI Model 196
Diamond Grip Model 196
Medallion Grip Model 196
Medalist 199
Micro Lightning 212
Micro-Medallion Model 230
Mid-Production Auto-5—FN Manufacture
Standard Weight 218
Matte Rib 218
Plain Barrel 218
Vent Rib 218
Model 12 226
Grade I 226
Grade IV 226
Model 52 Limited Edition 231
Model 53 236
Model 65 Grade I 236
Model 65 High Grade 236
Model 71 Grade I 237
Model 71 High Grade 237
Model 81 BLR 237
Model 325 Sporting Clays 214
Model 425 Sporting Clays 214
Model 425 Golden Clays 214
Model 1878 237
Model 1885 BPCR (Black Powder
Cartridge Rifle) 237
Model 1885 BPCR Creedmore Type . 238
Model 1885 High Wall 237
Model 1885 Low Wall 237
Model 1885 Low Wall Traditional
Hunter 237
Model 1885 High Wall Traditional
Hunter 238
Model 1886 Grade I 238
Model 1886 Grade I Carbine 238
Model 1886 High Grade 238
Model 1886 High Grade Carbine 238
Model 1886 Montana Centennial 238
Model 1895 Grade I 238
Model 1895 High Grade 238
Model B-78 236
Model B-80 220
Model B-80 Buck Special 220
Model B-80 DU Commemorative 220
Model BBR 227
Model BDA 197
Model BDM Silver Chrome 198
Model BDM Practical 198
Model BLR Lightning (Lightweight) ... 236
Model BLR Lightweight '81 236
Model BPM-D 198
Model BRM-DAO 198
Model BPR 235
Model BT-100 215
Model BT-100 Satin 216
Model BT-100 Thumbhole 216
Model Gold 10 221
Nomad 198
North American Deer Rifle Issue 234
NRA A-Bolt Wildlife Conservation
Collection 230
Patent 1900 High Power 233
Pre-War Superposed,
1930-1940 204
Grade I 204
Pigeon 204
Diana 204
Midas 204
Pro-9/Pro-40 197
Recoilless Trap 216
Renaissance Challenger 198
Renaissance Hi-Power 196
Adjustable Sight Spur Hammer
Model 196
Cased Renaissance Set 196
Renaissance .25 Caliber 196
Renaissance .380 Caliber 196
Renaissance .380 Caliber
(Model 1971) 196
Ring Hammer Model 196
Spur Hammer Model 196
Renaissance Medalist 200
Second Model International Medalist . 199
Silver Hunter 224
Silver Series 224
Silver Stalker 224
Silver–Mossy Oak 224
Special Sporting 214
Golden Clays 214
Grade I 214
Signature Grade 214
Pigeon Grade 214
ST-100 208
Superposed From 1947-1959 204
Grade I 204
Grade II 204
Grade III 204
Grade IV 204
Grade V 204
Grade VI 204
Superposed From 1960-1976 204
1981 Mallard Issue 206
1982 Pintail Issue 206
1983 Black Duck Issue 207
Diana Grade 205
Grade I 204, 205
Midas Grade 205
Pigeon Grade 205
Pointer Grade—Rare 205
Presentation I (without gold inlays) 206
Presentation 1 Gold-inlaid 206
Presentation 2 Gold-inlaid 206
Presentation 2
(without gold inlays) 206
Presentation 3 Gold-inlaid 206
Presentation 4 Gold-inlaid 206
Sweet Sixteen 218, 219
T-Bolt (2006) 231
T-Bolt Model T-1 231
T-Bolt Model T-2 231
T-Bolt Target/Varmint 231
Tangent Sight Model 196
Trap Combination Set 212
Trap Model 226
Trombone Model 231
Twelvette Double Auto 220
Twentyweight Double Auto 220
Two Millionth Commemorative 218
Ultra Sporter—Sporting Clays 212
Ultra Sporter Sporting
Clays—Golden Clays 212
Waterfowl Deluxe 226
Youth Model 226

BRUCE & DAVIS 239
Double-Barreled Pistol 239

BRUCHET 239
Model A Shotgun 239
Model B 239

BRUFF, R.P. 239
Bruff Pocket Pistol 239

BRYCO ARMS 239

BSA GUNS LTD. 239
200 Series 241
300 SM Series 241
Centurian Match Rifle 239
CFT Target Rifle 240
Classic 240
Falcon 240
Falcon Sporting 240
Herters U9 240
Majestic Deluxe 240
Majestic Deluxe Featherweight 240
Martini International Match 239
Martini International Light 239
Martini International ISU 239
Model 13 Sporter 239
Monarch Deluxe 240
No. 12 Cadet Martini 239
Regal Custom 240

Royal 239, 240
Silver Eagle 240
Silver Eagle II 241
Sporter/Classic 240
Stutzen Rifle 240
Varminter 240

BUCO 241
Buco Gas Pistol 241

BUDISCHOWSKY 241
.22 Rimfire Caliber 241
.25 ACP Caliber 241
TP-70 241

BUL TRANSMARK LTD. 241
Model M5 241

BULLARD REPEATING ARMS CO. 241
Carbine 241
Large Frame 241
Musket 241
Small Frame 241

BULLDOG SINGLE-SHOT PISTOL 242
Bulldog 242

BURGESS GUN CO. 242
12 Gauge Slide Action Shotgun 242
Burgess engraving grades (1-4) . . 242
Folding Shotgun 242
Slide Action Rifle 242

BURGSMULLER, K. 242
Burgo 242
Regent 242

BURNSIDE RIFLE CO. 242
2nd Model 242
3rd Model 242
4th Model 242
Bristol, Rhode Island 242
Burnside Carbine 1st Model 242

BUSHMASTER FIREARMS INC. 243
Bushmaster DCM Competition Rifle . 243
Bushmaster M4 Post-Ban Carbine . . . 243
Bushmaster M4A3 Post-Ban Carbine 243
Bushmaster M17S Bullpup 243
Bushmaster XM15-E2S Dissipator . . . 243
Bushmaster XM15-E2S Shorty Carbine 243
Bushmaster XM15-E2S Target Model 243
Bushmaster XM15-E2S V-Match Carbine 243
Bushmaster XM15-E2S V-Match Competition Rifle 243
Carbon 15 .22 Rimfire Rifle 244
Carbon 15 9mm Carbine 244
Carbon 15 Top Loading Rifle 244
Predator 244

BUTLER, WM. S. 244
Butler Single-Shot Pistol 244

BUTTERFIELD, JESSE 244
Butterfield Army Revolver 244
Butterfield Pocket Pistol 244

C

CABANAS, INDUSTRIAS S.A. 245
Espronceda IV 245
Leyre 245
Master 245
Mini-82 Youth 245
R-83 Larger Youth 245
Safari A 245
Varmint 245

CABELAS, INC. 245
AYA Grade II Custom 245
Hemingway Model 245

CALICO 245

CAMEX-BLASER USA, INC. . . 245

CAMPO GIRO 245
Esperanza y Unceta Model 1904 245
Model 1910 245
Model 1913 245
Model 1913/16 246

CARCANO 246

CARD, S. W. 246
Under Hammer Pistol 246

CARLTON, M. 246
Under Hammer Pistol 246

CASARTELLI, CARLO 246
Africa Model 246
Kenya Double Rifle 246
Safari Model 246
Sidelock Shotgun 246

CASE WILLARD & CO. 246
Under Hammer Pistol 246

CASPIAN ARMS, LTD. 246
Viet Nam Commemorative 246

CASULL ARMS, INC. 247
CA 2000 247
CA 3800 247

CENTURY GUN COMPANY/NEW CENTURY MANFACTURING 247

CENTURY INTERNATIONAL ARMS CO. 247
Centurion 98 Sporter 247
Century Centurion 14 248
Centurion Shotgun 247
Enfield Sporter No. I Mark III 248
Enfield Sporter No. 4 Mark I 248
FAL Sporter 248
M-14 Rifle 248
Mexican Mauser Model 1910 Sporter 248
Tiger Dragunov Rifle 248
TOZ-17 248
TOZ-17-1 248

CETME 248
Cetme Autoloading Rifle 248

CHAMELOT-DELVIGNE 248

CHAMPLIN FIREARMS 249
Bolt-Action Rifle 249

CHAPMAN C. 249
Chapman Rifle 249

CHAPMAN CHARLES 249

CHAPMAN, G. & J. 249
Chapman Pocket Revolver 249

CHAPUIS ARMES 249
African PH Model Grade I 249
.470 Nitro & .416 Rigby 249
.300 Win. Mag. 249
.30-06, 9.3x74 R 249
375 H&H 249
African PH Model Grade II 249
RG Progress 249
RG Express Model 89 249
St. Bonnet Model 249
Utility Grade Express Model 249

CHARLEVILLE 249

CHARTER 2000, INC. 249
Bulldog 249
Dixie Derringer 250
Field King Carbine 250
Field King Rifle 250
Mag Pug 250
Off Duty 250
Pathfinder 250
Police Bulldog 249
Undercover 250

CHARTER ARMS CORP. 250
AR-7 Explorer Rifle 252
Bulldog 250
Bulldog Pug 251
Bulldog Tracker 251
Dixie Derringer 252
Explorer II Pistol 252
Mag Pug 252
Model 40 252
Model 42T 252
Model 79K 252
Off Duty 251
Pathfinder 250
Pathfinder Stainless Steel 250
Pit Bull 251
Police Bulldog 251
Police Undercover 250
Stainless Steel Bulldog 250, 251
Stainless Steel Police Bulldog 251
Target Bulldog 250
Undercover Stainless Steel 250
Undercoverette 250

CHASSEPOT 252
MLE 1866 252

CHEYTAC 252
M-200 252
M-310 252

CHICAGO F. A. CO. 253
Protector Palm Pistol 253
Standard Model Nickel-Plated/Black Grips 253

CHIPMUNK RIFLES/ROGUE RIFLE CO. 253
Chipmunk .17 HMR 253
Chipmunk Single-Shot Standard Rifle 253
Chipmunk TM 253
Deluxe Chipmunk 253
Silhouette Pistol 253

CHRISTENSEN ARMS 253
Carbon Cannon 253
Carbon Challenge I 254
Carbon Challenge II 254
Carbon Conquest 254
Carbon King 253
Carbon Lite 253
Carbon One 253
Carbon One Hunter 254
Carbon Ranger Repeater 254
Carbon Ranger Single Shot 254
Carbon Tactical 254

CHURCHILL 254
Highlander 255
Monarch 254
Regent 255
Regent Grade Semi-Automatic 255
Regent II 255
Regent Shotgun/Rifle Combination . . 255
Royal 254
Windsor Grade Semi-Automatic 255
Windsor Grade Slide-Action 255
Windsor I 254
Windsor II 254

Windsor III 254
Windsor IV 255
Windsor VI 254

CHURCHILL, E. J. LTD. 255
Baronet Magazine Rifle 255
Double Barrel Shotguns 255
One of One Thousand Rifle 255
Premier Double Rifle 255
Premier Over-and-Under 255
Premier Side-by-Side 255

CHYLEWSKI, WITOLD 255

CIMARRON F. A. CO. 256
A.P. Casey Model P U.S. Cavalry . . . 258
Adobe Walls Rolling Block 260
Big Fifty Model 261
Billy Dixon 1874 Sharps (Armi-Sport) . 260
Billy Dixon Model 1874 Sharps (Pedersoli) 260
Cimarron 1880 Frontier Flat Top 258
Cimarron Bisley 258
Cimarron Bisley Flat Top 258
Colt Single-Action Army Configurations 256
El Pistolero 259
Evil Roy Model 258
Frontier Six Shooter 256
General Custer 7th Cavalry Model . . . 256
Henry Civil War Model 259
Henry Civilian Model 259
Lightning 257
Lightning .32s 257
Model 1851 259
Model 1855 Spencer 259
Model 1860 259
Model 1861 259
Model 1866 Yellowboy Carbine 259
Model 1866 Yellowboy Rifle 259
Model 1866 Yellowboy Trapper 259
Model 1872 Open Top 256
Model 1873 Carbine 259
Model 1873 Deluxe Sporting Rifle . . . 260
Model 1873 Evil Roy Rifle 260
Model 1873 Larry Crow Signature Series Rifle 260
Model 1873 Long Range Rifle 259
Model 1873 Short Rifle 259
Model 1873 Trapper 260
Model 1873 Winchester Rifle 259
Model 1885 Deluxe High Wall 260
Model 1885 High Wall 260
Model 1885 Low Wall 260
Model 1892 Solid Frame Rifle 260
Model 1892 Takedown Rifle 260
Model No. 3 Schofield 256
Schofield Civilian Model 256
Schofield Military Model 256
Schofield Wells Fargo 256
Model P Jr. 258
Model P Jr. .32s 258
New Model P 257
New Sheriff's Model w/ejector 257
New Thunderer 257
Pride of the Plains Model 261
Professional Hunter Model 261
Quigley Sharps Sporting Rifle 260
Relic Finish 259
Remington Rolling Block 260
Rinaldo A. Carr Model P U.S. Artillery 258
Rough Rider U.S. Artillery Model 256
Sharp's No. 1 Sporting Rifle 261
Sharps Silhoutte 260
Sheriff's Model w/no ejector 256
Springfield Trapdoor Carbine 261
Springfield Trapdoor Officer's Model . 261
Stainless Frontier Model P 258
Texas Ranger Carbine 260
Thunderer Long Tom 257
Wyatt Earp Buntline 257

CLAPP, HOFFMAN & CO. CLAPP, GATES & CO. RIFLES 261

CLARK, F. H. 261
Pocket Pistol 261

CLASSIC DOUBLES 261
Classic Field Grade II 262
Classic Skeet 262
Classic Skeet 4 Gauge Set 262
Classic Sporter 262
Classic Trap Combo 262
Classic Trap Over-and-Under 262
Classic Trap Single 262
Model 101 Classic Field Grade I 261
Model 201 Classic 261
Model 201 Small Bore Set 261
Waterfowl Model 262

CLEMENT, CHAS. 262
American Model 263
Model 1903 262
Model 1907 262
Model 1908 263
Model 1909 263
Model 1910 263
Model 1912 263

CLERKE PRODUCTS 263
Deluxe Hi-Wall 264
Hi-Wall 263

COBRA ENTERPRISES, INC. . . 264
Big Bore Series 264
C-9mm 264
C-32/C-380 264
Long Bore Series 264
Patriot .45 264
Standard Series 264

COBRAY INDUSTRIES 265
M-11 Pistol 265
M-12 265
Terminator Shotgun 265
TM-11 Carbine 265
TM-12 Carbine 265

COCHRAN TURRET 265
Pistol 265
Under Hammer Turret Rifle 265
1st Type 265
2nd Type 265
3rd Type 265

CODY, MICHAEL & SONS 265

COFER, T. W. 265
Cofer Navy Revolver 265

COGSWELL 265
Cogswell Pepperbox Pistol 265

COGSWELL & HARRISON, LTD. 266

COLT'S PATENT FIRE ARMS MANUFACTURING COMPANY 266
Belt Model Paterson No. 2 266
Belt Model Paterson No. 3 266
Colt Paterson Models 266
Ehlers Belt Model Paterson 266
Ehlers Model Pocket Paterson 266
Pocket or Baby Paterson Model No. 1 266
Texas Paterson Model No. 5 266

COLT .22 RIMFIRE SEMI-AUTOMATIC PISTOLS 320

COLT 1911/1911A1 303
Colt "1911 Commercial Government Model" Argentine Contracts 304
Colt "1911 Commercial Government Model" British Contract 304
Colt "1911 Commercial Government Model" Canadian Contract 304
Colt "1911 Commercial Government Model" Russian Order 304
Early Colt "1911 Commercial Government Model" 303
FOREIGN CONTRACTS 304
Norwegian Kongsberg Vapenfabrikk Pistol Model 1912 (Extremely Rare) 305
Norwegian Kongsberg Vapenfabrikk Pistol Model 1914 305
Kongsberg Vapenfabrikk Model 1914 (Norwegian) Copy 305
Standard Colt "1911 Commercial Government Model" with Numbered Slide 304
Standard Colt "1911 Commercial Model" with Un-numbered Slide 304
Colt 1911A1 Commercial Government Model 305
Model 1911 Automatic Pistol, Military Series 305
Pre-WWII Colt "1911A1 Commercial Government Model" 305
Argentine Colt-made 1911A1 model pistols without Swartz safeties 305
Argentine Contract Pistols "Modelo Argentino 1927, Calibre .45" 307
Brazilian, Mexican, and other South American (except Argentina) 305
Colt National Match Caliber Pre-WWII, .45. Pre-WWII (with "Swartz Safeties") 307
Fixed Sights 307
Stevens Adjustable Sights 307
Colt National Match Caliber .45, Pre-WWII, .45 (without Swartz safeties) 305
With Adjustable Sights 305
Fixed Sights 306
Reworks of Colt 1911 and 1911A1 Commercial "GOVERNMENT MODEL" Pistols 307
Standard 1911A1 Pre-WWII, "GOVERNMENT MODEL" Export Sales 307
Standard Colt "1911A1 Commercial Government Model" Domestic Sales 305
Standard Colt "1911A1 Commercial Government Model" Export Sales . . 305
Standard Colt 1911A1 Commercial "GOVERNMENT MODEL" Marked Pistol with Numbered Slide 307
SWARTZ SAFETIES, PRE-WWII, FIRING PIN AND HAMMER/SEAR . 306
Normal Brazilian and Mexican Pistols (w/Swartz Safeties) 307
"Military to Commercial Conversions" . 307
Post WWII Commercial Produced, Domestic Sales, 1946-1969 307
SN C220,000 to about C220,500 . 307
SN C220,500 to about C249,000 verified proof and "GOVERNMENT MODEL" marking 308
SN 249,500-C to about 335,000-C, verified proof and "GOVERNMENT MODEL" marking 308

SN 255,000-C to about 258,000-C Slide Factory Roll Marked "PROPERTY OF THE STATE OF NEW YORK," verified proof, and "GOVERNMENT MODEL" marking (250 pistols total) 308
SN 334,500-C to about 336,169-C, BB (Barrel Bushing) marked .. 308
Super .38 1929 Model, Pre-WWII ... 308
Super Match .38 1935 Model, Pre-WWII 308
Adjustable Sights 308
Fixed Sights 308

COLT 1991 SERIES MODEL O PISTOLS 317
.38 Super (2006) 318
.380 Series 80 Government Model .. 320
1911 – WWI Replica 317
Colt CZ40 320
Colt Defender 317
Colt Defender Model O (07000D) ... 317
Colt Concealed Carry 318
Colt Model 2000 320
Colt O-Model Commander (04691) .. 317
Colt O-Model Commander Stainless (04091U) 317
Colt O-Model Gold Cup 317
Colt O-Model Commander (04691) .. 317
Colt O-Model Commander Stainless (04091U) 317
Colt O-Model Gold Cup 317
Colt O-Model Government Matte (01991) 317
Colt O-Model Government Stainless (01091) 317
Colt Pony 319
Colt Pony PocketLite 319
Double Eagle 318
Double Eagle Combat Commander .. 318
Double Eagle First Edition 318
Double Eagle Officer's Model 318
Government Pocketlite LW 319
Mustang 319
Mustang Plus II 319
Mustang PocketLite 319
Pocket Nine 318
Tac Nine 318

COLT ACE and SERVICE MODEL ACE 309
Ace Model .22 Pistol 309
Colt 1911A1 AMU (Army Marksmanship Unit) 311
Conversion Units .22-.45, .45-.22 ... 309
Post-war Conversion Units 309
Post-war .22 Conversion Unit Unnumbered 310
Pre-war and Post-war "U" numbered Service Model Ace Conversion Unit, .22-.45 (to convert .45 cal. to .22 cal.) 309
Pre-war Service Model Ace (Re-) Conversion Unit, .45-22 309
Gold Cup MKIII National Match 311
Gold Cup National Match (pre-series 70) 310
Military National Match .45 pistols ... 310
Military National Match Pistols (Drake Slide) 310
Pre-1945 Service Model Ace .22 R. F. Pistol 309
Blued pistols (before about SN SM 3840) 309
Parkerized pistols (after about SN SM 3840) 309
Service Model Ace-Post-War 309

COLT ANTIQUE LONG ARMS . 286
Berdan Single-Shot Rifle 286
Carbine Russian Order 286
Carbine U.S. Sales 286
Rifle Russian Order 286
Rifle U.S. Sales 286
Colt-Franklin Military Rifle 286
Colt-Burgess Lever-Action Rifle 286
Baby Carbine 286
Carbine 286
Rifle 286
Baby Carbine 287
Double-Barrel Rifle 287
Lightning Slide-Action, Medium-Frame 286
Baby Carbine 287
Carbine 287
Military Rifle or Carbine 287
Rifle 287
San Francisco Police Rifle 287
Lightning Slide-Action Small-Frame .. 287
Lightning Slide-Action, Large-Frame . 287
Carbine 287
Rifle 287
Model 1878 Double-Barrel Shotgun .. 287
Model 1883 Double-Barrel Shotgun .. 287

COLT ANTIQUE SINGLE-ACTION ARMY REVOLVER 280
.44 Rimfire Model 1875-1880 280
1st Year Production "Pinched Frame" 1873 Only 280
Artillery Model 1895-1903 280
Bisley Model 1894-1915 281
Bisley Model Flattop Target 1894-1913 281
Early Military Model 1873-1877 280
Early Civilian Model 1873-1877 280
Flattop Target Model 1888-1896 281
Frontier Six-Shooter 1878-1882 281
Late Military Model 1878-1891 280
London Model 281
Sheriff's or Storekeeper's Model 1882-1898 281
Standard Civilian Production Models 1876-1898 281

COLT AR-15 & SPORTER RIFLES 327
AR-15 9mm Carbine (Model #6450) . 327
AR-15 Carbine (Model #6420) 327
AR-15 Carbine Flat-top Heavyweight/Match Target Competition (Model #6731) 329
AR-15 Sporter (Model #6000) 327
AR-15 Sporter w/Collapsible Stock (Model #6001) 327
AR-15 Tactical Carbine (Model #6721) 329
AR-15A2 Delta H-Bar (Model #6600DH) 328
AR-15A2 Government Model (Model #6550) 327
AR-15A2 Government Model Carbine (Model #6520) 327
AR-15A2 H-Bar (Model #6600) 328
AR-15A2 Sporter II (Model #6500) ... 327
Colt AR-15 (XM16E1) 328
Match Target Competition H-BAR Compensated (Model #6700C) 329
Match Target H-BAR Compensated (Model #6601C) 328
Sporter Competition H-Bar (Model #6700) 328
Sporter Competition H-Bar Select w/scope (Model #6700CH) 328
Sporter H-Bar Elite/Accurized Rifle (Model #6724) 329
Sporter Lightweight Rifle 328
Sporter Match Delta H-Bar (Model #6601 DH) 328
Sporter Match H-Bar (Model #6601) . 328
Sporter Target Model Rifle (Model #6551) 328

COLT BLACKPOWDER ARMS 335
3rd Model Dragoon 336
Fluted Cylinder 336
Steel Backstrap 336
1842 Paterson Colt No. 5 Holster Model 335
Cochise Dragoon 336
Colt 1849 Model Pocket 336
Colt 1851 Model Navy 336
Dual Cylinder 336
Colt 1860 Officer's Model 336
Colt 1860 Heirloom Edition 337
Colt 1861 Musket 337
Colt 1861 Musket—Artillery Model ... 337
Colt 1861 Musket Presentation 1 of 1000 337
Colt Model 1860 Army Gold U.S. Cavalry 336
Stainless Steel 336
Colt 1861 Musket Presentation 1 of 1000—Artillery Model 337
Colt Gamemaster .50 337
Colt Model 1860 Army 336
Dual Cylinder 336
Fluted Cylinder 336
Colt Model 1861 Navy 337
Colt Model 1861 Navy General Custer 337
Colt Model 1862 Pocket Navy 337
Colt Model 1862 Trapper-Pocket Police 337
Marine Dragoon 336
Walker 335
Walker 150th Anniversary Model 335
Whitneyville Hartford Dragoon 335

COLT COMMEMORATIVES . . . 331

COLT CURRENT PRODUCTION SINGLE-ACTION ARMY 1982-PRESENT 284
Colt Cowboy (CB1850) 284
Colt Single-Action Army "The Legend" 284
Optional Features: 284
Standard Single-Action Army 284

COLT CUSTOM SHOP 329
125th Anniversary Edition Peacemaker 330
Anaconda Hunter 330
Bobbed Detective Special 330
Colt Classic .45 Special Edition 329
Compensated .45 ACP Commander . 330
Compensated Model .45 ACP 330
Custom Anaconda 330
Deluxe Tactical Model 330
Gold Cup Commander 329
Gold Cup Trophy 329
Limited Class .45 ACP 330
McCormick Commander 329
McCormick Factory Racer 329
McCormick Officer 329
Nite Lite .380 330
Python Elite 330
Special Combat Government Model (Competition) 329
Special Combat Government Model (Carry) 329
Standard Tactical Model 330
Superior Tactical Model 330

U.S. Shooting Team Gold Cup 329
Ultimate Python 330

COLT DERRINGERS AND POCKET REVOLVERS 276
First Model Derringer 276
House Model Revolver 277
Cloverleaf with 1.5" Round Barrel . 277
Cloverleaf with 3" Barrel 277
House Pistol with 5-Shot Round Cylinder 277
New Line Revolver .22 278
1st Model 278
2nd Model 278
New Line Revolver .30 278
New Line Revolver .32 278
New Line Revolver .38 278
New Line Revolver .41 279
New House Model Revolver 279
New Police Revolver 279
Long Barrel Model with Ejector . . . 279
Open Top Pocket Revolver 277
Early Model with Ejector Rod 278
Production Model without Ejector Rod 278
Second Model Derringer 277
Third Model Derringer 277
First Variation, Early Production . . 277
First Variation, Late Production . . . 277
Production Model 277

COLT DOUBLE-ACTION REVOLVERS 291
Agent 1st Issue 297
Agent L.W. 2nd Issue 297
Aircrewman Special 298
Anaconda 300
.45 Colt 300
.44 Magnum 300
Realtree Camo Model—Adjustable Sights 300
Realtree Camo Model—Scope Mounts 300
Army Special Model 294
Banker's Special 297
Boa 299
Border Patrol 297
Camp Perry Single-Shot 295
Cobra 1st Issue 297
Cobra 2nd Issue 297
Colt .357 Magnum 298
Colt .38 SF-VI 296
Colt .38 SF-VI Special Lady 296
Colt Magnum Carry 297
Commando Model 296
Courier 298
Detective Special 1st Issue 296
Detective Special 2nd Issue 296
Detective Special II (DS-II) 297
Diamondback 298
King Cobra 300
Blued 300
High Polish Stainless Steel 300
Stainless Steel 300
Lawman MK III 299
Lawman MK V 299
Marshall Model 296
Metropolitan MK III 299
Model 1877 "Lightning" and "Thunderer" 291
Without Ejector, 2.5" and 3.5" Barrel 291
With Ejector, 4.5" and 6" Barrel . . 291
Model 1878 "Frontier" 291
Model 1878 "Frontier" Omnipotent . . . 291
Model 1878 "Frontier" Standard 291
Model 1889 Navy—Civilian Model . . . 291
Model 1889 U.S. Navy—Martial Model 292
Model 1892 "New Army and Navy"—Civilian Model 292
Model 1892 U.S. Army—Martial Model 292
Model 1892 U.S. Navy—Martial Model 292
Model 1896/1896 Army 292
Model 1902 (Philippine or Alaskan Model) 291
Model 1905 Marine Corps 292
New Pocket Model 294
New Service Model 293
Early Model, #1-21000 293
Early Model Target, #6000-15000 . 293
Improved Model, #21000-325000 . 293
Improved Target Model, #21000-325000 293
Late Model New Service, #325000-356000 294
Model 1917 Civilian, #335000-336000 293
U.S. Army Model 1909, #30000-50000 293
U.S. Army Model 1917, #150000-301000 293
U.S. Marine Corps Model 1909, #21000-23000 293
U.S. Navy Model 1909, #50000-52000 293
New Police Model 294
Officer's Model Match 295
.22 Caliber in Short Action—Single-Action-Only . . . 295
Officer's Model Target 1st Issue 295
Officer's Model Target 2nd Issue 295
Official Police 295
Peacekeeper 299
Pocket Positive 294
Police Positive 294
Police Positive Target 294
Police Positive Special 295
Police Positive Special Mark V 295
Python .38 Special 299
Python 298
Matte Stainless Steel 298
"The Ultimate" Bright Stainless . . . 299
Python Elite 299
Python Hunter 299
Sheriff's Model 291
Shooting Master, #333000-350000 . . 294
Magnum Model New Service, Over #340000 294
Trooper 298
Trooper MK III 299
Trooper MK V 299
Viper 298

COLT ENHANCED GOVERNMENT MODELS . . . 312
Colt 1991A1 313
Combat Commander 313
Combat Elite 316
Combat Target Model 316
Combat Target Combat Commander 316
Combat Target Officer's ACP 316
Commander 312
Concealed Carry Officer's Model 315
Delta Elite 316
Blued 316
Polished Stainless Steel 316
Stainless Steel 316
Delta Gold Cup 315
Lightweight Officer's ACP 315
MK IV Series 80 Government Model . 313
Blued 313
Nickel Plated 313
Polished Stainless Steel 313
Stainless Steel 313
M1991A1 Commander 314
M1991A1 Compact 314
MK IV Series 80 Gold Cup National Match 315
Blued 315
Polished Stainless Steel 315
Stainless Steel 315
Officer's ACP 315
Blued 315
Matte Blued 315
Satin Nickel 315
Stainless Steel 315
Special Combat Government 316
Colt O-Model Commander (04012XS) 317
Colt O-Model Concealed Carry Officer's (09850XS) 317
Colt O-Model Government (01070XS) 316
Colt O-Model Lightweight Commander (04860XS) 317

COLT LICENSED AND UNLICENSED FOREIGN-MADE 1911A1 AND VARIATIONS . 311
Argentine D.G.F.M. 311
Argentine-Made Ballester Molina 311
Brazilian Models 1911A1 312
Model 1911A1 Automatic Pistol
Military Model 312

COLT METALLIC CARTRIDGE CONVERSIONS 274
Model 1862 Police and Pocket Navy Conversions 275
3.5" Round Barrel Without Ejector 276
4.5" Octagonal Barrel Without Ejector 276
Model 1862 Pocket Navy Octagon Barrel with Ejector 276
Model 1862 Police Round Barrel with Ejector 276
Round Barrel Pocket Navy with Ejector 276
Model 1871-1872 Open Top Revolver 276
1860 Army Grip Frame 276
Richards Conversion, 1860 Army Revolver 274
Civilian Model 274
Martially Marked Variation 274
Transition Richards Model 275
Richards-Mason Conversions 1851 Navy Revolver 275
Production Model Serial #1-3800 . 275
U.S. Navy Model Serial #41000-91000 275
Richards-Mason Conversion, 1860 Army Revolver 275
Richards-Mason Conversion 1861 Navy Revolver 275
Standard Production Model Serial #100-3300 275
U.S. Navy Model Serial #1000-9999 275
Thuer Conversion Revolver 274
Model 1849 Pocket Conversion . . 274
Model 1851 Navy Conversion 274
Model 1860 Army Conversion 274
Model 1861 Navy Conversion 274
Model 1862 Pocket Navy Conversion 274
Models 1862 Police Conversion . . 274

COLT MODEL 1911A1 SEMI-AUTOMATIC PISTOL . 312
MKIV Series 70 Gold Cup National Match 312
MKIV Series 70 Government Model . . 312
Series 70 1911 Service Model WWI . . 312
Series 70 Gunsite Pistol 312
Series 70 Gunsite Pistol Commander . 312

COLT MODERN LONG ARMS 325
Colt "57" Bolt-Action Rifle 326
Colt Light Rifle 326

Colt Sauer Bolt-Action Rifle 326
Colt Sauer Drilling 327
Colt Sauer Short Action 326
Colt-Sharps Rifle 327
Colteer 326
Colteer I-22 325
Coltsman Bolt-Action Rifle 326
Coltsman Pump Shotgun 326
Courier 326
Double-Barrel Shotgun 326
Semi-Auto Shotgun 326
Stagecoach 326

COLT PERCUSSION REVOLVERS 272
Civilian Model 273
Full Fluted Cylinder Model 273
Shoulder Stock 2nd Type (Fluted Cylinder Model) 273
Model 1860 Army Revolver 272
Martial Marked Model 273
Model 1861 Navy Revolver 273
Civilian Model 273
Fluted Cylinder Model 273
Military Model 273
Revolver 273
Shoulder Stock Model 273
Stock 273
Model 1862 Pocket Navy Revolver .. 273
Standard Production Model 274
Model 1862 Police Revolver 274
Standard Production Model 274

COLT POST-WAR SINGLE-ACTION ARMY REVOLVER 283
.38 Special 283
.44 Special 283
.45 Colt 283
.357 Magnum 283
7.5" Barrel Model 283
Buntline Special 1957-1975 283
New Frontier 1961-1975 283
New Frontier Buntline Special 1962-1967 283
Sheriff's Model 1960-1975 283
Standard Post-war Model 1956-1975 283

COLT PRE-WAR SINGLE-ACTION ARMY REVOLVER 1899-1940 282
Long Fluted Cylinder Model 1913-1915 283
Standard Production Pre-war Models 282

COLT REPRODUCTION PERCUSSION REVOLVERS 334
First Model Dragoon 334
Model 1848 Pocket Pistol 335
Model 1851 Navy Revolver 335
Model 1860 Army Revolver 335
Model 1861 Navy Revolver 335
Model 1862 Pocket Pistol 335
Model 1862 Police Revolver 335
Second Model Dragoon 334
Third Model Dragoon 334
Walker 334
Walker Heritage Model 334

COLT REVOLVING LONG GUNS 1837-1847 267
First Model Ring Lever Rifle 267
Model 1839 Shotgun 267
Model 1839 Carbine 267
Model 1839/1850 Carbine 267
Model 1854 Russian Contract Musket 267
Second Model Ring Lever Rifle 267

COLT SCOUT MODEL SINGLE-ACTION ARMY 285
Frontier Scout 1957-1971 285
Peacemaker Scout & New Frontier .. 286
Scout Model SAA 1962-1971 286

COLT SEMI-AUTOMATIC PISTOLS 301
Model 1900 301
Standard Civilian Production 301
U.S. Navy Military Model 301
U.S. Army Military Model—1st Contract 301
U.S. Army Military Model—2nd Contract 301
Model 1902 Sporting Pistol 301
Model 1902 Military Pistol 301
Early Model with Front of Slide Serrated 301
Standard Model with Rear of Slide Serrated 301
U.S. Army Marked, #15001-15200 with Front Serrations 301
Model 1903 Pocket Pistol 301
Model 1903 Hammerless, .32 Pocket Pistol 302
U.S. Military Model 302
Model 1905 .45 Automatic Pistol 303
Civilian Model 303
Military Model, Serial #1-201 303
Model 1908 Hammerless .380 Pocket Pistol 302
Military Model 302
Standard Civilian Model 302
Model 1908 Hammerless .25 Pocket Pistol 302
Civilian Model 303
Military Model 303

COLT SIDE HAMMER MODELS 270
Model 1855 Side Hammer "Root" Pocket Revolver 270
Model 2 Serial #476-25000 271
Model 3 Serial #25001-30000 271
Model 3A and 4 Serial #1-2400 .. 271
Model 5 Serial #2401-8000 271
Model 5A Serial #2401-8000 271
Models 1 and 1A Serial #1-384 ... 271
Models 6 and 6A Serial #8001-11074 271
Models 7 and 7A Serial #11075-14000 271

COLT SIDE HAMMER LONG GUNS 271
1855 1st Model Carbine 271
1855 Full Stock Military Rifle 271
Martially Marked Models 272
Without Martial Markings 272
1855 Full Stock Sporting Rifle 272
1855 Half Stock Sporting Rifle 271
1855 Sporting Rifle, 1st Model 271
Early Model 271
Production Model 271
Model 1855 Artillery Carbine 272
Model 1855 British Carbine 272
Model 1855 Revolving Carbine 272
Model 1855 Revolving Shotgun 272
.60 Caliber (20 gauge) 272
.75 Caliber (10 gauge) 272
Model 1861 Single-Shot Rifled Musket 272
Production Model 272

COLT'S SINGLE-ACTION ARMY REVOLVER 279

COLT THIRD GENERATION SINGLE-ACTION ARMY 1976-1981 283
.357 Magnum 284
.44 Special 284
.44-40 284
.44-40 Black Powder Frame (Screw Retaining Cylinder Pin) 284
.45 Colt 284
7.5" Barrel 284
Buntline Special 3rd Generation 284
New Frontier 3rd Generation 284
Sheriff's Model 3rd Generation 284

COLT WALKER-DRAGOON MODELS 267
Civilian Walker Revolver 268
First Model Dragoon 268
Civilian Model 268
Military Model 268
Hartford English Dragoon 269
London Model 1849 Pocket Revolver . 269
London Model 1851 Navy Revolver .. 270
1st Model 270
2nd Model 270
Hartford Manufactured Variation .. 270
Martial Model 270
Model 1848 Baby Dragoon 269
Stagecoach Holdup Scene 269
Texas Ranger/Indian Scene 269
Model 1849 Pocket Revolver 269
Model 1851 Navy Revolver 270
Large Round Trigger Guard, Serial #85001-215000 270
Square Back Trigger Guard, 1st Model, Serial #1-1000 270
Square Back Trigger Guard, 2nd Model, Serial #1001-4200 270
Small Round Trigger Guard, Serial #4201-85000 270
Second Model Dragoon 268
Civilian Model 268
Military Model 268
Militia Model 268
Shoulder Stock Variations 270
Stock Only 270
3rd Model Cut For Stock 270
Stock 270
Third Model Dragoon 268
Civilian Model 269
Military Model 269
Shoulder Stock Cut Revolvers ... 269
Shoulder Stocks 269
C.L. Dragoon 269
8" Barrel Late Issue 269
Walker Model Revolver 267
Walker Replacement Dragoon 268
Whitneyville Hartford Dragoon 268

COLT WOODSMAN 320
Cadet / Colt .22 325
Challenger 323
4-1/2 inch barrel 323
6 inch barrel 323
Colt .22 Target 325
Colt Junior Pocket Model 325
Huntsman 325
4-1/2 or 6 inch barrel 325
Military Woodsman Match Target 322
Pre-Woodsman 321
Targetsman 325
6 inch barrel, 4-1/2 inch (rare) 325
Woodsman Match Target .. 322, 323-324
4-1/2 inch barrel 323-324
6 inch barrel 323-324
Woodsman Sport 321, 323-324
4-1/2 inch barrel 323-324
Woodsman Target 321, 323-324
6 inch barrel 323, 324

COLTON MANUFACTURING CO. 337

COLUMBIA ARMORY 337

COLUMBUS F. A. MFG. CO. . . 338
Columbus Revolver 338

COMANCHE (also see FIRESTORM) 338
Comanche I 338
Comanche II 338
Comanche III 338
Super Comanche 338

COMBLAIN 338
Single-Shot Rifle 338

COMMANDO ARMS 338
Mark .45 338
Mark 9 Carbine 338
Mark III Carbine 338

COMPETITOR CORP. 338
Competitor Single-Shot 338

CONNECTICUT ARMS CO. . . . 339
Pocket Revolver 339

CONNECTICUT VALLEY ARMS CO. 339
3rd Model Dragoon 341
1851 Navy 342
1858 Remington 342
1858 Remington Target 342
1860 Army 342
1861 Navy 342
Apollo Brown Bear 339
Apollo Carbelite 339
Apollo Classic 339
Apollo Eclipse Rifle 339
Apollo Dominator 339
Apollo Shadow SS 339
Apollo Starfire 339
Bison 342
Blazer Rifle 339
Brittany 11 Shotgun 341
Bushwacker Rifle 340
Classic Turkey Double-Barrel Shotgun 341
Colt Walker Replica 341
Electra 341
Express Rifle 339
Frontier Carbine 340
Frontier Hunter Carbine 340
Grey Wolf Rifle 340
Hawken Pistol 342
Hawken Rifle 339
Kentucky 341
Kentucky Rifle 339
Lone Grey Wolf Rifle 340
Mountain Rifle 339
Over-and-Under Rifle 339
Panther Carbine 340
Pennsylvania Long Rifle 339
Philadelphia Derringer 341
Plainsman Rifle 340
Pocket Police 341
Pocket Revolver 342
Presentation Grade Hawken 339
Remington Bison 341
Sheriff's Model 341
Siber 341
Stag Horn 341
Timber Wolf Rifle 340
Tracker Carbine LS 341
Trapper Shotgun 341
Trophy Carbine 340
Varmint Rifle 340
Wells Fargo 342
Woodsman Rifle LS 340

CONSTABLE, R. 342
Pocket Pistol 342

CONTENTO/VENTUR 342
Mark 2 342
Mark 3 342
Mark 3 Combo 342
Model 51 342
Model 52 342
Model 53 342
Model 62 342
Model 64 342

CONTINENTAL 343
Continental Pocket Pistol (6.35mm) . . 343
Continental Pocket Pistol (7.65mm) . . 343

CONTINENTAL ARMS CO. 343
Double Rifle 343

CONTINENTAL ARMS CO. 343
Pepperbox 343

COOK & BROTHER RIFLES AND CARBINES 343
Cook & Brother Carbines (New Orleans production) 343
Cook & Brother Carbines (Athens production) 344
Cook & Brother Rifles (New Orleans & Selma production) 343
Cook & Brother Rifles (Athens production) 343

COONAN ARMS CO. 344
.41 Magnum Model 345
Cadet 344
Cadet II 344
Comp I 344
Comp I Deluxe 344
Classic 344
Model A 344
Model B 344

COOPER ARMS 345
Model 21 345
Benchrest w/Jewell Trigger 345
Classic 345
Custom Classic 345
Varmint Extreme 345
Western Classic 345
Model 22 345
Benchrest w/Jewell Trigger 345
Pro Varmint Extreme 345
Model 22 Repeater 345
Classic 345
Custom Classic 345
Western Classic 345
Model 36 Marksman 345
BR-50 w/Jewell Trigger 345
Classic 345
Custom Classic 345
Featherweight w/Jewell Trigger . . 345
IR-50-50 w/Jewell Trigger 345
Standard 345
Western Classic 345
Model 38/40 345
Classic 345
Custom Classic 345
Western Classic 345
Model 72/Montana Plainsman 345

COOPER, J. M. & CO. 346
Pocket Revolver 346

COOPERATIVA OBRERA 346
Longines 346

COPELAND, FRANK 346
Copeland .32 Revolver 346
Copeland Pocket Revolver .22 346

COSMI, A. & F. 346
Semi-Automatic 346
Deluxe Model 346
Standard Model 346

COSMOPOLITAN ARMS CO. . 346
Breech Loading Rifle 346

COWLES & SON 346
Single-Shot 346

CPA RIFLES 346
Schuetzen Rifle 346
Silhouette Rifle 347
Sporting Rifle 347
Varmint Rifle 347

CRAUSE, CARL PHILLIP MUSKETS AND RIFLES . . . 347
Hanseatic League M1840 Rifled Musket 347
Oldenberg M1849 Rifled Musket 347

CRESCENT F. A. CO. 347
American Gun Co. Midget Field No. 28—Hammer Sidelock 348
American Gun Co. Midget Field No. 44—Hammer Sidelock 349
American Gun Co. No. 0—Armory Straight Stock—Hammer Sidelock . . 348
American Gun Co. No. 3—Damascus Barrels Hammer Sidelock 348
American Gun Co. No. 4—Hammer Sidelock 348
American Gun Co. No. 5—Damascus Barrels Hammer Sidelock 348
American Gun Co. No. 28—Nitro Straight Stock—Hammer Sidelock . . 348
American Gun Co. No. 44—Nitro Straight Stock—Hammer Sidelock . . 348
American Gun Co. NY No. 1 Armory—Hammerless Sidelock 348
American Gun Co. NY No. 2—Hammerless Sidelock 348
American Gun Co. Small Bore No. 28—Straight Stock Hammer Sidelock . . . 348
American Gun Co. Small Bore No. 44—Straight Stock Hammer Sidelock . . . 348
American Machine Made 2641—Hammer Sidelock 348
American Machine Made 2650—Hammer Sidelock 348
American Machine Made 2660—Damascus Barrels Hammer Sidelock 348
Brand Names Used by Crescent Arms 350
Crescent 1922 Model No. 66—Quail—Hammerless Sidelock 349
Crescent American Hammer Gun No. 0—Hammer Sidelock 347
Crescent Firearms Co. No. 0—Hammer Sidelock 349
Crescent Firearms Co. No. 0—Nickel—Hammer Sidelock 349
Crescent Firearms Co. No. 6—Peerless—Hammerless Sidelock . . . 349
Crescent Certified Empire No. 9—Hammerless Sidelock 349
Crescent Certified Empire No. 60—Hammerless Sidelock 349
Crescent Certified Empire No. 88—Hammerless Sidelock 350
Crescent Certified Shotgun nfa, curio or relic 350

Crescent Davis No. 600—Hammerless Boxlock 350
Crescent Davis No. 900—Hammerless Boxlock 350
Crescent Empire No. 60—Hammerless Sidelock 349
Crescent Firearms Co. No. 6—Peerless—Hammerless Sidelock . . 349
Crescent Firearms Co. No. 6E—Peerless Engraved—Hammerless Sidelock . . 349
Crescent Firearms Co. No. 44—Improved—Hammer Sidelock 349
Crescent Firearms Co. No. 60—Empire—Hammerless Sidelock 349
Crescent Firearms Co. No. 66—Quail—Hammerless Sidelock 349
Crescent New Empire No. 88—Hammerless Sidelock 349
Crescent New Empire No. 9—Hammerless Sidelock 349
Folsom Arms Co. No. 0 Armory—Hammer Sidelock 348
Folsom Arms Co. No. 2—Hammer Sidelock 348
Folsom Arms Co. No. 3—Damascus Barrel 348
Knickerbocker No. 6 Armory—Hammerless Sidelock 348
Knickerbocker No. 7—Hammerless Sidelock 348
Knickerbocker No. 8—Damascus Barrels Hammerless Sidelock 348
Model 2655—Laminated Barrels Hammer Sidelock 347
Model 2665—Damascus Barrels Hammer Sidelock 347
New Crescent Empire Red Butt—Hammerless Sidelock 349
New Knickerbocker Armory—Hammerless Sidelock 348
New Knickerbocker Damascus Barrels—Hammerless Sidelock 348
New Knickerbocker WT—Hammerless Sidelock 348
Revolver 350
Single-Shot 350
Triumph—Hammerless Boxlock 347

CRISPIN, SILAS 352
Crispin Revolver 352

CROSSFIRE 353
MK-1 353

CRUCELEGUI, HERMANOS . . 353

CUMMINGS, O. S. 353
Cummings Pocket Revolver 353

CUMMINGS & WHEELER 353
Pocket Revolver 353

CUSTOM GUN GUILD 353
Wood Model IV 353

CZ 353
Amarillo 360
Army Pistol 1922 (Nickl-Pistole) 353
Bobwhite 360
Canvasback 360
CZ 100 366
CZ 1921 Praga 353
CZ 1922 354
CZ 1924 354
CZ 1927 354
CZ 1936 354
CZ 1938 354
CZ 1945 355
CZ 1950 355
CZ 1952 355
CZ 2075 RAMI 365
CZ 40B 364
CZ 452 American Classic 356
CZ 452 FS 356
CZ 452 Scout 356
CZ 452 Silhouette 356
CZ 452 Style 356
CZ 452 Varmint 356
CZ 452-2E LUX 355
CZ 452-2E ZKM Style 356
CZ 511 356
CZ 513 Basic 356
CZ 527 American Classic 357
CZ 527 Carbine 357
CZ 527 FS 357
CZ 527 Lux 357
CZ 527 Premium (Lux) 357
CZ 527 Prestige 357
CZ 527 Varmint 357
CZ 527 Varmint 357
CZ 527 Varmint Laminate 357
CZ 550 American Classic 358
CZ 550 American Safari Magnum . . . 359
CZ 550 Lux 358
CZ 550 Medium Magnum 359
CZ 550 Premium 359
CZ 550 Prestige 358
CZ 550 Safari Classic Custom 359
CZ 550 Safari Magnum 359
CZ 550 Ultimate Hunting Rifle 359
CZ 550 Varmint 358
CZ 550 Varmint Laminate 358
CZ 700 Sniper M1 359
CZ 712 360
CZ 720 360
CZ 74 30th Anniversary 361
CZ 75 361
CZ 75 B 361
CZ 75 B SA 362
CZ 75 B Tactical 362
CZ 75 BD 362
CZ 75 Champion 363
CZ 75 Compact 361
CZ 75 Compact D 361
CZ 75 D PCR Compact 363
CZ 75 DAO 363
CZ 75 Kadet Conversion 365
CZ 75 M IPSC 363
CZ 75 Semi-Compact 362
CZ 75 Silver Anniversary Model 364
CZ 75 SP-01 Shadow 364
CZ 75 Stainless 364
CZ 75 Standard IPSC (ST) 363
CZ 75 Tactical Sport 364
CZ 750 Sniper 360
CZ 83 365
CZ 85 B 364
CZ 85 Combat 364
CZ 97 B 366
CZ BD Compact 362
CZ BD Compact Carry 362
CZ Engraved Model 75 and Model 83 Pistols 365
CZ Kadet 365
CZ Model 3 355
CZ Model 527 357
CZ Model 537 358
CZ Model 550 358
CZ Model 550 Battue Lux 358
CZ Model 550 FS Battue 358
CZ Model 550 Minnesota 358
CZ Model 550 Minnesota DM 358
CZ P-01 363
CZ ZKK 600 359
CZ ZKK 601 359
CZ ZKK 602 359
CZ ZKM-452D 356
CZ452 Training Rifle 356
CZ-581 359
CZ-584 359
Durango 360
Fox 353
Hammer Coach 361
Mallard 360
Model 1970 355
Model 52 (7.62 x 45) 355
Model 52/57 (7.62 x 39) 355
Redhead 360
Ringneck 360
Ringneck Custom Grade 360
Woodcock 360
Woodcock Custom Grade 360

CZ 366
Model TT 40/45/9 366

D

D (anchor) C 367

D. W. M. 367
Model 22 367

DAEWOO 367
DH380 368
DH-40 367
DP-51B 367
DP-51CB 367
DP-51SB 367
DP-52 367
DR200 368
K1A1 (Max II) 368
K-2/AR-100 (Max I) 368

DAISY 368
Model 2201/2211 368
Model 2202/2212 368
Model 2203/2213 368
VL Cased Presentation Model 368
VL Presentation Model 368
VL Rifle 368

DAKIN GUN CO. 368
Model 100 368
Model 147 368
Model 160 369
Model 170 369
Model 215 369

DAKOTA ARMS, INC. 369
African Grade 369
All-Weather Predator 370
Alpine Grade 369
Classic Grade 371
Classic Predator 370
Dakota .22 Long Rifle Sporter 370
Dakota .22 Long Rifle Sporter (New Model) 370
Dakota 76 Classic 369
Dakota 76 Varmint 369
Dakota American Legend 371
Dakota Shotgun 371
Double Rifle 370
Field 372
  Grade II 372
  Grade III 372
Little Sharps Rifle 371
Limited Edition .30-06 Model 76 371
Limited Edition .30-06 Model 10 371
Model 7 371
  Boss—no engraving 372
  Esposizione 372
  H.H. Model—no engraving 372
  Hammer Gun 372
  L'Inglesina 372
  Model E "Fantasy" 372
  Prince Model 371
  Prince Model Side Lever 371

Rex . . . 372
Premier . . . 372
Sideplate Model . . . 372
Sideplate Model with Gold . . . 372
Sideplate with Scroll . . . 372
Model 10 Single-Shot . . . 369
Model 10 Single-Shot Magnum . . . 370
Model 76 Traveler . . . 370
Traveler African . . . 370
Traveler Classic . . . 370
Traveler Safari . . . 370
Model 97 Lightweight Hunter . . . 370
Model 97 Long Range Hunter . . . 370
Model T-76 Longbow Tactical Rifle . . 370
Premier Grade . . . 371
Safari Grade . . . 369
Serious Predator . . . 370
Varmint Grade . . . 369
Varmint Hunter . . . 369

DALY, CHARLES . . . 373
.22 Caliber Conversion Kit . . . 379
Charles Daly Automatic . . . 374
Charles Daly Empire Over-and-Under 376
Charles Daly Field Grade Over-and-Under . . . 376
Charles Daly Field Ultra Light . . . 376
Commanidor Over-and-Under Model 100 . . . 373
Commanidor Over-and-Under Model 200 . . . 373
Country Squire Over-and-Under Folding . . . 378
Country Squire Side-by-Side Folding . 378
Daly Classic 1873 Single Action . . . 381
Daly HP . . . 380
Daly M-5 Commander . . . 380
Daly M-5 Government . . . 380
Daly M-5 IPCS . . . 381
Daly M-5 Ultra-X . . . 380
Daly ZDA . . . 379
Diamond Grade . . . 374
Diamond Grade Drilling . . . 373
Diamond Grade Mono . . . 377
Diamond Grade Over-and-Under 373, 377
Diamond Grade Side-by-Side . . . 373
Diamond Grade Sporting . . . 377
Diamond Grade Trap Combo . . . 377
Diamond Grade Trap or Skeet . . . 374
Diamond Grade Trap or Skeet . . . 377
Diamond Side-by-Side . . . 378
Empire 1911 Target EFST . . . 380
Empire 1911-A1 EFS . . . 379
Empire Custom Match Target . . . 380
Empire Express . . . 376
Empire Grade . . . 373
Empire Grade Combination . . . 376
Empire Grade Rimfire . . . 378
Empire Grade Side-by-Side . . . 373
Empire Grade Trap Combo . . . 377
Empire II EDL Hunter . . . 376
Empire Over-and-Under . . . 373
Empire Side-by-Side . . . 373
Empire Side-by-Side . . . 378
Empire Sporting . . . 376
Empire Trap . . . 376
Empire Trap Mono . . . 376
Field 1911 Target EFST . . . 379
Field 1911-A1 FS/MS/CS . . . 379
Field 1911-A1 PC . . . 379
Field 1911-A2P . . . 379
Field Grade . . . 374
Field Grade . . . 374
Field Grade . . . 375
Field Grade Mauser 98 . . . 378
Field Grade Mini-Mauser 98 . . . 378
Field Grade Rimfires . . . 378
Field Hunter . . . 377
Field Hunter Maxi-Mag VR-MC Pump . . . 376
Field Hunter Maxi-Mag VR-MC Semi-Auto . . . 375
Field Hunter MM (Maxi-Mag) . . . 376
Field Hunter VR-MC . . . 375
Field Hunter VR-MC Youth . . . 375
Field Tactical . . . 375
Model 105 . . . 375
Model 106 . . . 375
Model 306 . . . 375
Novamatic Lightweight . . . 374
Novamatic Trap . . . 374
Over-and-Unders . . . 374
Presentation Grade Over-and-Under . 377
Regent Diamond Grade . . . 373
Regent Diamond Grade Drilling . . . 373
Regent Diamond Grade Side-by-Side 373
Superior 1911-A1 EFS/EMS/ECS . . . 379
Superior 1911-A1 PC . . . 379
Superior Grade . . . 374
Superior Grade Combination . . . 377
Superior Grade Drilling . . . 373
Superior Grade Express . . . 377
Superior Grade Hunter . . . 374
Superior Grade Mauser 98 . . . 378
Superior Grade Mini-Mauser 98 . . . 378
Superior Grade Rimfire . . . 378
Superior Grade Single Barrel Trap . . . 374
Superior Grade Sporting . . . 374
Superior Grade Sporting . . . 377
Superior Grade Trap . . . 374
Superior Grade Trap . . . 375
Superior Grade Trap . . . 377
Superior Hunter . . . 377
Superior II . . . 375
Superior II Grade Rimfire . . . 378
Superior II Hunter . . . 375
Superior II Sport . . . 375
Superior II Trap . . . 375
Superior Over-and-Under . . . 377
Superior Side-by-Side . . . 373
Venture Grade . . . 374
Venture Grade Skeet or Trap . . . 374

DAN ARMS OF AMERICA . . . 381
Deluxe Field Grade . . . 381
Field Grade . . . 381
Lux Grade I . . . 381
Lux Grade II . . . 381
Lux Grade III . . . 381
Lux Grade IV . . . 381
Silver Snipe . . . 381

DANCE & BROTHERS CONFEDERATE REVOLVERS . . . 381
.36 Caliber . . . 381
.44 Caliber . . . 381

DANDOY, C/A LIEGE . . . 381

DANSK REKYLRIFFEL SYNDIKAT . . . 381
Model 1907 . . . 382
Schouboe 1902 . . . 381
Schouboe 1904 . . . 382
Schouboe Model 1907 9mm . . . 382
Schouboe Model 1910/12 . . . 382
Schouboe Model 1916 . . . 382

DARDICK CORP. . . . 383
Series 1100 . . . 383
Series 1500 . . . 383

DARLING, B. & B. M. . . . 383
Darling Pepperbox Pistol . . . 383

DARNE, S. A. . . . 383
Darne Side-by-Side Shotguns . . . 383
Model R11 . . . 383
Model R15 . . . 383
Model V19 . . . 383
Model V22 . . . 383
Model V Hors Series No. I . . . 383

DAUDETEAU . . . 383
Model 1896 . . . 383

DAVENPORT FIREARMS CO. 383
8 Gauge Goose Gun . . . 384
Double-Barrel Shotguns . . . 383
1st Model . . . 383
2nd Model . . . 383
3rd Model . . . 384
4th Model . . . 384
Falling Block Single-Shot Rifle . . . 384
Single Barrel Shotgun . . . 384

DAVIDSON F. A. . . . 384
Model 63B . . . 384
Model 69 SL . . . 384
Stagecoach Model 73 . . . 384

DAVIS, A. JR. . . . 384
Under Hammer Pistol . . . 384

DAVIS, N.R. & CO. DAVIS, N.R. & SONS . . . 384
Grade A and B Hammerless Shotguns . . . 384
Grade C Hammerless Shotgun . . . 384
Grade D and DS Hammer Shotguns . 384
Grade E and F Single-Barrel Shotguns . . . 384
N.R. Davis Brands . . . 385
1st Button Opener—Hammer Boxlock . . . 385
1st Sidelever—Hammer Boxlock . . 385
1st Toplever—Hammer Boxlock . . 385
2nd Sidelever—Hammer Boxlock . 385
2nd Toplever—Hammer Boxlock . 385
3rd Toplever—Hammer Boxlock . . 385
1879 1st Model—Hammer Boxlock 385
1879 2nd Model—Damascus Barrels—Hammer Boxlock . . . 385
1885 "Hammerless"—Hammerless Boxlock . . . 385
1886 Rival—Hammerless Boxlock 385
1886 Rival Improved—Hammerless Boxlock . . . 385
1897 "G"—Hammer Sidelock . . . 385
"D.S." Straight Stock—Engraved—Hammerless Boxlock . . . 385
Davis "B" Manga Steel—Hammerless Boxlock . . . 385
Davis Special—Hammerless Boxlock . . . 385
Hammerless 1900—Hammerless Boxlock . . . 385
Hammerless A—Damascus Barrels—Hammerless Boxlock . . . 385
Hammerless B—Hammerless Boxlock . . . 385
Hammerless C—Engraved Damascus Barrel—Hammerless Boxlock . 385
Hammerless D—Engraved—Hammerless Boxlock . . . 385
Model No. 600—Hammerless Boxlock . . . 385
Model No. 900—Hammerless Boxlock . . . 385
New Model—Hammerless Boxlock 385

DAVIS & BOZEMAN . . . 385
Pattern 1841 Rifle . . . 385

DAVIS INDUSTRIES . . . 385
Big Bore D-Series . . . 386
D-Series Deringer . . . 386
Long Bore D-Series . . . 386
P-380 . . . 386
P-32 . . . 386

DAVIS-WARNER ARMS CORPORATION 387
"BS"—Hammerless Boxlock 387
"DS"—Hammerless Boxlock 387
"Maximin"—Hammerless Boxlock . . . 387
Ajax (Model 800) 388
Ajax—Hammerless Boxlock 387
Certified (Savage) 387
Davis Grade B.S. Hammerless Shotgun 387
Davis-Warner Expert Hammerless . . . 387
Davis-Warner Semi-Automatic Pistols 388
Davis-Warner Swing Out Revolver . . 388
Deluxe Special (Model 805) 387
Deluxe—Hammerless Boxlock 387
Hypower—Hammerless Boxlock 387
Peerless Ejector—Hammerless Boxlock 387
Premier (Model 801) 388
Premier Special (Model 802) 388
Premier—Hammerless Boxlock 387
Warner Infallible Semi-Automatic Pistol 388

DAW, G. H. 388
Daw Revolver 388

DEANE, ADAMS & DEANE . . . 388

DEANE-HARDING 388
Deane-Harding Revolver 388

DECKER, WILHELM 388

DEFIANCE ANTI-BANDIT GUN 388
Defiance Anti-Bandit Gun curio or relic, nfa 388

DEMIRETT, J. 389
Under Hammer Pistol 389

DEMRO 389
T.A.C. Model 1 389
XF-7 Wasp Carbine 389

DERINGER REVOLVER AND PISTOL CO. 389
Deringer Model I 389
Deringer Model II 389

DERINGER, HENRY RIFLES AND PISTOLS 389
Centennial 1876 389
Deringer U.S. M1814 Military Rifle . . . 389
Deringer U.S. M1817 Military Rifle (Types I & II) 389
(altered to percussion) 389
(in flintlock) 389
Deringer Original Percussion Martial Rifles (Types I & II) 389
Deringer Original Percussion Rifle-Muskets 389
Deringer Percussion Pocket Pistols . . 390
Agent Names Found On Deringer Pocket Pistols 390
Principal Makers of Deringer-Style Pocket Pistols 390
Deringer U.S. Navy Contract "Boxlock" Pistols 390

DESENZANI, LABORATORIES ARMI 391
Over-and-Under 391
Side-by-Side 391

DESERT EAGLE/ISRAELI MILITARY INDUSTRIES 391
Baby Eagle 392
Baby Eagle .40 S&W (Standard) 392
Baby Eagle .41 Action Express 392
Baby Eagle 9mm (Standard) 392
Baby Eagle Compact Polymer 393
Baby Eagle Semi-Compact Polymer . 393
Baby Eagle Short Barrel (Semi-Compact) 392
Baby Eagle Short Barrel/Short Grip (Compact) 393
Desert Eagle .357 Magnum 391
Desert Eagle .41 Magnum/.44 Magnum 391
Desert Eagle .50 Action Express 391
Desert Eagle Mark XIX 392
.357 Mag. w/6" Barrel 392
.357 Mag. w/10" Barrel 392
.440 Cor-Bon w/6" Barrel (1999) . . 392
.440 Cor-Bon w/10" Barrel (1999) . 392
.44 Mag. w/6" Barrel 392
.44 Mag. w/10" Barrel 392
.50A.E. w/6" Barrel 392
.50A.E. w/10" Barrel 392
Bolt Assembly—.44/.50 or .357 . . 392
Lone Eagle 394
Lone Eagle (New Model) 394
Magnum Lite Centerfire Rifles 394
Heavy Barrel 394
Sport Taper Barrel 394
Magnum Lite Rimfire Rifles 394
Fajen Thumbhole Silhouette 394
Fajen Thumbhole Sporter 394
Hogue and Fajen Scope-Hi Stock . 394
Turner Barracuda 394
Mark XIX Component System 392
6" & 10" Component System 392
6" Component System 392
10" Component System 392
Mountain Eagle 393
Mountain Eagle Compact Edition 393
Mountain Eagle Rifle 394
Mountain Eagle Target Edition 393
Mountain Eagle Varmint Edition 394
Tactical Rifle 394

DESERT INDUSTRIES 395

DESTROYER CARBINE 395
Destroyer Carbine 395

DETONICS MANUFACTURING CORP. 395
Combat Master 395
Combat Master Mark V 395
Combat Master Mark VI 395
Combat Master Mark VII 395
Janus Competition Scoremaster 395
Mark I 395
Mark II 395
Mark III 395
Mark IV 395
Military Combat MC2 395
Pocket 9 396
Scoremaster 395
Servicemaster 396

DETONICS USA, LLC 396
Combat Master 396
Model 9-11-01 396
Street Master 396

DEUTSCHE WERKE 396
Ortgies 396
Ortgies 9mmk 396

DEVISME, F. P. 397

DIAMOND 397
Gold Series Auto 397
Gold Series Pump 397
Silver Series Mariner Pump 397
Silver Series Mariner Semi-Auto 397
Diamond Elite Pump 397
Diamond Elite Semi-Auto 397
Diamond Panther Semi-Auto 397

DICKINSON 397

DICKINSON, E. L. & J. 397
Ranger 397
Single-Shot 397

DICKSON, JOHN 397

DICKSON, NELSON & CO. 397
Dickson, Nelson Rifle 397

DIMICK, H.E. 397

DOMINGO ACHA 397

DOMINO 397
Model OP 601 Match Pistol 397
Model SP 602 Match Pistol 398

DORMUS 398
8MM Special 398

DORNHAUS & DIXON 398

DORNHEIM, G.C. 398
Gecado 7.65mm 398
Gecado Model 11 398

DOUBLESTAR, CORP. 398
DSC Expedition Rifle 399
DSC Star 15 9mm Rifle 399
DSC Star 15 Lightweight Tactical 399
DSC Star CMP Improved Service Rifle 399
DSC Star Dissipator 399
DSC Star-15 CMP Service Rifle 399
Star Carbine 398
Star Critterslayer 399
Star DS-4 Carbine 398
Star EM-4 398
Star Lightweight Tactical Rifle 398
Star Super Match Rifle 399
Star-15 398

DOUG TURNBULL RESTORATION, INC. 399
Classic Cowboy 400
Colt/Winchester Cased Set 399
DT Colt 399
Year Offered—1998 399
Year Offered—1999 399
Year Offered—2000 399
EHBM Colt 399
General Patton Colt 400
Smith & Wesson No. 3 Schofield 399
Theodore Roosevelt Colt 400
Theodore Roosevelt Winchester Model 1876 400

DOWNSIZER CORPORATION . 400
Model WSP 400

DPMS 400
LR-204 403
LR-243 403
LR-260 403
LRT-SASS 403
Panther 20th Anniversary Rifle 403
Panther 6.8 Rifle 403
Panther A-15 Pump Pistol 404
Panther A-15 Pump Rifle 403
Panther Arctic 402
Panther Bull 24 400
Panther Bull A-15 400
Panther Bull Classic 401
Panther Bull SST 16 401
Panther Bull Sweet 16 401
Panther Bulldog 401
Panther Classic 402
Panther Classic 16 Post Ban 402
Panther DCM 402
Panther Deluxe Bull 24 Special 401
Panther Extreme Super Bull 24 401
Panther Free Float 16 Post Ban 402
Panther Mark 12 403

Panther Race Gun ... 402
Panther SDM-R ... 403
Panther Southpaw Post Ban ... 402
Panther Tuber ... 403
Panthera Pardus ... 403
Single Shot Rifle ... 403

DREYSE ... 404

DRISCOLL, J.B. ... 404
Single-Shot Pocket Pistol ... 404

DSA, INC. ... 404
B&T TP9 Tactical Pistol ... 406
CVI Carbine ... 405
DSA Z4 Gas Trap Carbine (GTC) ... 406
DS-AR Carbine ... 406
DS-AR CQB MRP ... 406
DS-AR DCM Rifle ... 406
DS-AR Rifle ... 406
DS-AR S Series Rifle ... 406
DS-MP1 ... 406
DS-MP1 .308 Custom Bolt Action ... 405
LE4 Carbine ... 405
S1 Rifle ... 405
SA58 21" Bull ... 404
SA58 24" Bull ... 404
SA58 Carbine ... 404
SA58 Congo ... 405
SA58 Graywolf ... 405
SA58 Medium Contour ... 404
SA58 Para Congo ... 405
SA58 Predator ... 405
SA58 Stainless Steel Carbine ... 405
SA58 Standard ... 404
SA58 T48 Replica ... 405
SA58 Tactical ... 404
SR58 Medium Contour Stainless Steel ... 405

DUBIEL ARMS CO. ... 406

DUMOULIN ... 406
African Pro ... 408
Amazone ... 407
Aristocrat Model ... 407
Bavaria Deluxe ... 407
Boss Royal Model ... 407
Centurion Classic ... 407
Centurion Model ... 407
Continental I Model ... 407
Continental Model ... 407
Diane ... 407
Eagle Model Combination Gun ... 407
Etendart Model ... 407
Europa I ... 407
Europa Model ... 407
Leige Model ... 407
Pionier Express Rifle ... 407
Safari Model ... 407
Safari Sportsman ... 408
Superposed Express International ... 407

DURLOV ... 408
Durlov Model 70 Standard ... 408
Durlov Model 70 Special ... 408
Durlov Model 75 ... 408
Pav ... 408

DUSEK, F. ... 408
Duo ... 408
Perla ... 408

E

E.M.F. CO., INC. ... 409
Hartford Bisley ... 409
Hartford Express ... 409
Hartford Pinkerton ... 409

EAGLE ARMS CO. ... 409

EAGLE ARMS ... 409
Golden Eagle ... 409
Golden Eagle ... 410
HBAR ... 409
M4C Carbine ... 409
M4A1C Carbine ... 409
SPR ... 409

ECHAVE & ARIZMENDI ... 410
Basque, Echasa, Dickson, or Dickson Special Agent ... 410
Bronco Model 1913 ... 410
Bronco Model 1918 ... 410
Echasa ... 410
Lightning ... 410
Lur Panzer ... 410
Pathfinder ... 410
Protector Model 1915 and 1918 ... 410
Selecta Model 1918 ... 411

ECHEVERRIA, STAR-BONIFACIO SA ... 411
Modelo Militar ... 412
Star Model 1908 ... 411
Star Model 1914 ... 411
Star Model 1919 ... 411
Star Model 1919 New Variation ... 411
Star Model 1941 S ... 414
Star Model 28 ... 414
Star Model 30/PK ... 415
Star Model 30M ... 415
Star Model A ... 412
Star Model B ... 412
Star Model BKM ... 414
Star Model BKS "Starlight" ... 414
Star Model BM ... 414
Star Model C ... 412
Star Model CO ... 412
Star Model CU "Starlet" ... 413
Star Model D ... 412
Star Model E ... 412
Star Model F ... 412
Star Model F Olympic ... 413
Star Model F Olympic Rapid Fire ... 413
Star Model F Sport ... 413
Star Model F Target ... 413
Star Model FM ... 413
Star Model FR ... 413
Star Model FRS ... 413
Star Model H ... 413
Star Model HK ... 413
Star Model HN ... 413
Star Model I ... 413
Star Model M ... 413
Star Model P ... 413
Star Model PD ... 414

ECHEVERRIA ... 415
Megastar ... 415
Firestar-M/43, M/40, and M45 ... 415
Firestar Plus ... 415
Starfire Model 31P ... 415
Starfire Model 31PK ... 415
Ultrastar ... 415

ECLIPSE ... 416
Single-Shot Derringer ... 416

84 GUN CO. ... 416
Classic Rifle ... 416
Lobo Rifle ... 416
Pennsylvania Rifle ... 416

EL DORADO ARMS ... 416

ELGIN CUTLASS ... 416
C. B. Allen-Made Pistols ... 416
Civilian Model ... 416
U.S. Navy Elgin Cutlass Pistol ... 416
Morill, Mosman and Blair-Made Pistols ... 416
Large Model ... 416
Small Model ... 416

ELLS, JOSIAH ... 417
Model 1 ... 417
Model 2 ... 417
Model 3 ... 417
Pocket Revolver ... 417

ENDERS, CARL ... 417
Side-by-Side Shotgun ... 417

ENFIELD ROYAL SMALL ARMS FACTORY ... 417

ENFIELD AMERICAN, INC. ... 417
MP-45 ... 417

ENGLISH MILITARY FIREARMS ... 417
American-Made Copies of the English P1853 Rifle Musket ... 418
"Brazilian Naval Rifle" ... 419
"Brunswick" Rifles (first model or P1837) and (second model or P1845) ... 418
John P. Moore P1853 Rifle Muskets ... 419
New Land Pattern Musket ... 418
Orison Blunt P1853 Rifle Muskets ... 419
Pattern of 1839 (P1839) Musket ... 418
Pattern of 1842 (P1842) Musket (and Rifled Musket) ... 418
Pattern of 1851 (P1851) Rifle Musket ... 418
Pattern of 1853 (P1853) Artillery Carbine (First, Second, and Third Models) ... 419
Pattern of 1853 (P1853) Rifle Musket (first through fourth types) ... 418
Patterns of 1856, 1858, 1860, and 1861 (P1856, P1858, P1860, P1861) Sergeant's Rifles ... 419
Patterns of 1856 (P1856) and Pattern of 1861 (P1861) Cavalry Carbines ... 419
Robbins & Lawrence P1853 Rifle Muskets ... 418

ENTREPRISE ARMS, INC. ... 420
Boxer Model ... 420
Elite 325 ... 420
Elite P425 ... 420
Elite P500 ... 420
Tactical P325 ... 420
Tactical P325 Plus ... 420
Tactical P425 ... 420
Tactical P500 ... 420
Titleist P500 ... 420
TSM I ... 421
TSM II ... 421
TSM III ... 421

ERA ... 421
Era Double Barrel Shotgun ... 421
Era Over-and-Under Shotgun ... 421

ERICHSON, G. ... 421
Erichson Pocket Pistol ... 421

ERMA WERKE WAFFENFABRIK ... 421
.22 Target Pistol (Old Model) ... 421
.22 Target Pistol (New Model) Master Model ... 421
EG-72, EG-722 ... 423
EG-712, EG-73 ... 423
EM1.22 ... 423
EP-25 ... 422
ER-772 Match ... 423
ER-773 Match ... 423
ER-777 ... 423
Erma .22 Luger Conversion Unit ... 421
ESP 85A ... 422

ET-22 Luger Carbine 422
KGP-22 422
KGP-32 & KGP-38 422
KGP-68 422
KGP-69 422
KGP-Series 422
RX-22 and PX-22 422
SR-100 423

ERQUIAGA 423
Fiel 423
Fiel 6.35 424
Marte 424

ERRASTI, A. 424
Dreadnaught, Goliath and Smith Americano 424
Errasti 424
Errasti Oscillante 424
M1889 424
Velo-Dog 424

ESCODIN, M. 424

ESPIRIN, HERMANOS 424
Euskaro 424

ESCORT 424
AimGuard 425
Combo Model 425
Field Hunter 425
Model AS 424
Model PS 424
Model PS AimGuard 424

EUROARMS OF AMERICA 425
1803 Harper's Ferry 425
1841 Mississippi Rifle 426
1851 "Griswold & Gunnison" Navy 425
1851 "Schneider & Glassick" Navy 425
1851 Navy 425
1851 Navy Police Model 425
1851 Navy Sheriff's Model 425
1853 Enfield Rifled Musket 425
1858 Enfield Rifled Musket 425
1858 Remington Army or Navy 425
1860 Army 425
1861 Enfield Musketoon 425
1861 Navy 425
1862 Police 425
1862 Remington Rifle 426
1863 J.P. Murray 425
Buffalo Carbine 426
Cape Gun 426
Cook & Brother Carbine 425
Duck Gun 426
Hawken Rifle 426
Pennsylvania Rifle 426
Standard Side-by-Side 426
Zouave Rifle 426

EUROPEAN AMERICAN ARMORY CORP. 426
BUL Commander 429
BUL Government 429
BUL Stinger 430
EAA Astra Pistol 432
EAA Benelli Silhouette Pistol 432
EAA Big Bore Bounty Hunter 430
EAA Bounty Hunter Shotgun—External Hammers 430
EAA Bounty Hunter Shotgun—Traditional 430
EAA European Standard Pistol 430
EAA European Target Pistol 430
EAA F.A.B. 92 Pistol 430
EAA HW 60 Rifle 431
Match Grade 431
Target Grade 431
EAA PM2 Shotgun 431
EAA Rover 870 432
EAA Saba 432
EAA Sabatti 431
EAA Sabatti Falcon 431
28/.410 431
EAA Small Bore Bounty Hunter 430
EAA SP 1822 432
EAA SP 1822H 432
EAA SP 1822TH 432
EAA Sporting Clay Basic 431
EAA Sporting Clay Pro 431
EAA Sporting Clay Pro Gold 432
EAA Stock 429
EAA Windicator Basic Grade 431
EAA Windicator Standard Grade 431
EAA Windicator Tactical Grade 431
2" Barrel 431
4" Barrel 431
EAA Windicator Target Grade 431
EAA Witness Limited Class Pistol 429
EAA Witness P-Series Full Size 426
EAA Witness P-Series Carry-Comp 426
EAA Witness P-Series Compact 426
EAA Witness P-S Series 426
EAA Witness Carry Comp 427
New Configuration 427
Old Configuration 427
EAA Witness Combo 9/40 428
EAA Witness Gold Team Match 428
EAA Witness Hunter 428
EAA Witness Multi Class Pistol Package 429
EAA Witness Silver Team Match 428
EAA Witness Sport 428
New Configuration 428
Old Configuration 428
EAA Witness Sport L/S 427
New Configuration 427
Old Configuration 427
EAA Witness Standard 427
New Configuration 427
Old Configuration 427
EAA Witness Subcompact 427
New Configuration 427
Old Configuration 427
EAA/Baikal Shotguns 432
EAA/Saiga Shotgun 432
EAA/Saiga Rifle 432
Thor 429
Witness Elite Match 429
Witness FCP 429
Witness Pistols 426
Zastava EZ Pistol 429

EVANS REPEATING RIFLE CO. 432
"Montreal Carbine" 433
Carbine 433
Lever-Action Rifle 432
Military Musket 433
New Model 433
Old Model 432
Sporting Rifle 433
Transitional Model 433

EVANS, J. E. 433
Evans Pocket Pistol 433

EVANS, WILLIAM 433

EXCAM 433
BTA-90B 434
GT 22 434
GT 22T 434
GT 32 434
GT 380 434
GT 380XE 434
TA 38 Over-and-Under Derringer 433
TA 41, 41C, and 41 SS 434
TA 76 433
TA 90 434
TA 90 SS 434
Model W357 434
Model W384 434
Targa GT 26 434
Alloy Frame Version 434
Steel Frame Version 434
Warrior Model W 722 434

EXEL ARMS OF AMERICA 434

EXCEL INDUSTRIES 434
Accelerator Pistol 434
Accelerator Rifle 434

F

F&T 435

F.A.S. 435
Model 601 435
Model 602 435
Model 603 435

F.I.E. 435
222, 232, and 382TB 437
532TB 437
722 437
732B 437
Brute 437
Buffalo Scout 436
Cowboy 436
D38 Derringer 436
D86 Derringer 436
Gold Rush 436
Hombre 436
KG-99 435
Law-12 438
Legend S.A.A. 436
Model 122 437
Model 3572 437
Model 357TB 437
Model 522TB 437
Models 384TB and 386TB 437
S.O.B. 437
SAS-12 438
Single-Shot 437
SPAS-12 437
Spectre Assault Pistol 435
Standard Revolver 437
Sturdy Over-and-Under 437
Super Titan 11 435
Texas Ranger 436
Titan 25 436
Titan E32 435
Titan II .22 435
Titan Tigress 436
TZ 75 435
TZ 75 Series 88 435

F.L. SELBSTLADER 438

FABARM 438
Beta Europe 438
Beta Model 438
Black Lion Competition 441
Camo Lion 439
Camo Turkey Mag. 442
Classic Lion Elite 442
Classic Lion Grade I 442
Classic Lion Grade II 442
Ellegi Standard 438
Ellegi Innerchoke 438
Ellegi Magnum 438
Ellegi Multichoke 438
Ellegi Police 438
Ellegi Slug 438
Ellegi Super Goose 438
Field Model 438
FP6 440

FP6 Field Pump ... 440
FP6 Field Pump Camo ... 440
FP6 with Rail ... 440
Gamma Field ... 439
Gamma Paradox Gun ... 439
Gamma Sporting Competition Model . 439
Gamma Trap or Skeet ... 439
Gold Lion ... 439
Gold Lion Mark III ... 439
H368 ... 440
Home Security HD ... 440
Max Lion ... 441
Max Lion Light ... 441
Max Lion Paradox ... 441
Model S.D.A.S.S. ... 438
Martial Model ... 438
Special Police ... 438
Monotrap ... 441
Omega Goose Gun ... 438
Omega Standard ... 438
Red Lion ... 439
Red Lion Ducks Unlimited 2001 ... 439
Rex Lion ... 439
Silver Lion ... 441
Silver Lion Youth ... 441
Sporting Clays Competition Extra ... 441
Sporting Clays Competition Lion ... 441
Sporting Clays Extra ... 440
Sporting Clays Lion ... 439
Sporting Clays Max Lion ... 441
Super Light Lion ... 442
Super Light Lion Youth ... 442
Tactical Semi-Auto ... 440
Ultra Camo Mag. Lion ... 442
Ultra Mag Lion ... 442

FABBRI, ARMI ... 442
Over-and-Under Shotgun ... 442
Side-by-Side Shotgun ... 442

FABRIQUE NATIONALE ... 442
"Baby" Model ... 444
Captured Pre-war Commercial Model 445
Deluxe Sporter ... 446
FN FAL "G" Series (Type I Receiver) . 446
FN CAL ... 446
Lightweight ... 446
Standard ... 446
FN Supreme ... 446
FNC ... 446
Paratrooper Model ... 446
Standard ... 446
FN-FAL ... 446
50.00—21" Rifle Model ... 446
50.63—18" Paratrooper Model ... 446
50.64—21" Paratrooper Model ... 446
50.41—Synthetic Butt H-Bar ... 446
50.42—Wood Butt H-Bar ... 446
Model 30-11 Sniper Rifle ... 445
Model 1889 ... 445
Model 1900 ... 443
Model 1903 ... 443
Model 1906 ... 443
1st Variation, Under Serial Number 100000 ... 444
2nd Variation, Over Serial Number 100000 ... 444
Model 1910 "New Model" ... 444
Model 1922 ... 444
Model 1935 ... 444
Model 1949 or SAFN 49 ... 445
Musketeer Sporting Rifles ... 446
Post-war Commercial Model ... 445
Fixed Sight ... 445
Slotted and Tangent Sight ... 445
Tangent Sight ... 445
Post-war Military Contract ... 445
Fixed Sight ... 445
Slotted and Tangent Sight ... 445
Tangent Sight ... 445
Pre-war Commercial Model ... 444
Fixed Sight Version ... 444
Tangent Sight Version ... 444
Pre-war Military Contract ... 444
Belgium ... 444
Canada and China (See John Inglis & Company) ... 444
Denmark ... 444
German Military Pistole Modell 640(b) ... 445
Great Britain ... 444
Estonia ... 445
Holland ... 445
Latvia ... 445
Lithuania ... 445
Romania ... 445
Fixed Sight Model ... 445
Tangent Sight Model ... 445
Supreme Magnum Model ... 446

FAIRBANKS, A. B. ... 446
Fairbanks All Metal Pistol ... 446

FALCON FIREARMS ... 446
Gold Falcon ... 446
Portsider ... 446
Portsider Set ... 446

FAMARS, A. & S. ... 446
African Express ... 448
Engraving Pattern Descriptions (Older Discontinued Patterns) ... 446
Jorema Royal ... 447
In the white ... 447
S2 pattern ... 447
S3 pattern ... 447
S4 pattern ... 447
S5 pattern ... 447
S4E pattern ... 447
S5E pattern ... 447
SXO pattern ... 448
Excaliber BL ... 448
Excalibur BL Extra ... 448
Excalibur BL Prestige ... 448
Excalibur BLX ... 448
Excalibur BLX Extra ... 448
Excalibur BLX Prestige ... 448
Excalibur Express ... 448
Excalibur Express Extra ... 448
Excalibur Express Prestige ... 448
Excalibur SL ... 448
Excalibur SL Extra ... 448
Excalibur SL Prestige ... 448
Tribute ... 447
D2 pattern ... 447
In the white ... 447
S3 pattern ... 447
Veneri ... 447
D2 pattern ... 447
Venus ... 447
D2 pattern ... 447
D3 pattern ... 447
D4 pattern ... 447
D5 pattern ... 447
D4E pattern ... 447
D5E pattern ... 447
DXO pattern ... 447
In the white ... 447
Venus Express Extra ... 448
Venus Express Professional ... 448
Zeus ... 447
D2 pattern ... 447
In the white ... 447
S3 pattern ... 447

FARROW ARMS CO. ... 448
Farrow Falling Block Rifle ... 448
No. 1 Model ... 448
No. 2 Model ... 448

FAYETTEVILLE ARMORY PISTOLS AND RIFLES ... 449
Fayetteville Armory Percussion Pistols (U.S. M1836 Pistols, Altered) ... 449
Fayetteville Armory Rifles (Types I through IV) ... 449

FEATHER INDUSTRIES, INC. . 449
AT-22 ... 449
AT-9 ... 449
Guardian Angel ... 450
KG-9 ... 449
KG-22 ... 450
Mini-AT ... 450
SAR-180 ... 450

FEDERAL ENGINEERING CORP. ... 450
XC-220 ... 450
XC-450 ... 450
XC-900 ... 450

FEDERAL ORDNANCE, INC. . 450
M-14 Semi-Automatic ... 450
Model 713 Deluxe ... 450
Model 713 Mauser Carbine ... 450
Model 714 Broomhandle Mauser ... 450
Ranger 1911A1 ... 450
Standard Broomhandle ... 450

FEG (FEGYVER ES GAZKESZULEKGYAR) ... 451
Frommer Baby Model ... 451
Frommer Lilliput ... 451
Frommer Stop Model 1912 ... 451
Model 1901 ... 451
Model 1906 ... 451
Model 1910 ... 451
Model 1929 ... 452
.22 Caliber ... 452
Model 1937 ... 452
9mm Short Hungarian Military Version ... 452
Nazi Proofed 7.65mm Version ... 452
Model AP-9 ... 452
Model B9R ... 452
Model FP-9 ... 453
Model PA-63 ... 452
Model P9R ... 453
Blue ... 453
Chrome ... 453
Model P9RK ... 453
Model PPH ... 452
Model R-9 ... 452
SA-2000-M ... 453

FEINWERKBAU ... 453
Match Rifle ... 454
Mini 2000 ... 453
Model 2000 Universal ... 453
Model 2600 Ultra Match Free Rifle ... 454
Running Boar Rifle ... 453

FEMARU ... 454
Hege ... 454
Model 37 ... 454
Tokagypt ... 454
Walam ... 454

FERLACH ... 454

FERLIB ... 455
Hammer Gun ... 455
Model F.VI ... 455
Model F.VII ... 455
Model F.VII Sideplate ... 455
Model F.VII/SC ... 455
Model F.VII/SC Sideplate ... 455

FERRY, ANDREWS & CO. ... 455
Under Hammer Pistol ... 455

FIALA ARMS COMPANY 455
Fiala Repeating Target Pistol 455
Complete, Three Barrels, Stock, Tools, and Case 455
Gun Only 456

FINNISH LION 456
Champion Free Rifle 456
ISU Target Rifle 456
Match Rifle 456

FIOCCHI OF AMERICA, INC. . . 456

FIREARMS INTERNATIONAL . 456

FIRESTORM 456
1911 Mil-Spec Standard Government 457
Compact Firestorm .45 Government . 457
Firestorm .22 LR 456
Firestorm .32 456
Firestorm .380 456
Firestorm .45 Government 457
Mini Firestorm .40 S&W 457
Mini Firestorm .45 Government 457
Mini Firestorm 9mm 457

FLETCHER BIDWELL, LLC . . . 457
Spencer 1860 Military Carbine 457

FLORENCE ARMORY 457

FNH USA, INC. 457
.338 Lapua 460
FN A1 SPR 459
FN A1a SPR 459
FN A2 SPR 459
FN A3 SPR 459
FN A4 SPR 459
FN A5 SPR 459
FN A5a SPR 459
FN PBR (Patrol Bolt Rifle) 459
FN Police Shotgun 460
FN Self-Loading Police 460
FN Tactical Police 460
FN-Mini-Hecate 460
Hecate II 460
Model BDA/BDAO Compact 458
Model FNP-9 458
Model Forty-Nine 457
Model HP-DA/HP-DAO 458
Model HP-DA/HP-DAO Compact 458
Model HP-SA 458
Model HP-SA-SFS 458
OM .50 Nemesis 460
Ultima Ratio Commando I 459
Ultima Ratio Intervention 459
Ultima Ration Commando II 460

FOEHL & WEEKS 460
Columbian 460
Columbian Automatic 460
Perfect 461

FOEHL, C. 461
Foehl Derringer 461

FOGARTY 461
Fogarty Repeating Rifle and Carbine . 461
Rifle 461
Carbine 461

FOLSOM, H. 461
Derringer 461

FOLSOM, H&D ARMS CO. . . . 461
Double-Barrel Shotguns 461

FOREHAND & WADSWORTH . 461
British Bulldog 462
British Bulldog .44 462
Center Hammer 461
Double-Action Revolver 462
Double-Barrel Shotguns 462
Forehand Arms Co. 1898-1902
New Model Army Single-Action Revolver 462
Old Model Army Single-Action Revolver 461
Perfection Automatic 462
Side Hammer .22 461
Single-Shot .41 Derringer 461
Single-Shot Derringer 461
Swamp Angel 462

FOWLER, B. JR. 462
Percussion Pistol 462

FOX, A. H. 462
CE Grade 464
DE Grade 464
Exhibition Grade 464
FE Grade 464
HE Grade 462
High Grade Guns A-FE 462
A Grade 462
AE Grade (Automatic Ejectors) . . . 462
B Grade 463
BE Grade 463
C Grade 463
CE Grade 463
D Grade 463
DE Grade 463
F Grade 463
FE Grade 463
XE Grade 463
Single Barrel Trap Guns 463
J Grade 463
K Grade 464
L Grade 464
M Grade 464
SP Grade 462
Sterlingworth 462
Sterlingworth Deluxe 462
XE Grade 464

FRANCHI, L. 464
Airone 464
AL 48 Deluxe (Modern) 470
AL 48 Deluxe English Stock (Modern) 470
AL 48 (Modern) 470
AL 48 Short Stock (Modern) 470
Alcione Classic 466
Alcione Classic SX 467
Alcione Field Model 466
Alcione Field SX 467
Alcione LF 466
Alcione SL Sport 466
Alcione SP 467
Alcione Sporting 466
Alcione T (Titanium) 466
Alcione T Two Barrel Set 466
Aristocrat 465
Aristocrat Deluxe 466
Aristocrat Imperial 466
Aristocrat Magnum 465
Aristocrat Monte Carlo 466
Aristocrat Silver King 465
Aristocrat Supreme 466
Astore 464
Astore II 464
Astore 5 464
Black Magic Game Model 469
Black Magic Hunter 469
Black Magic Lightweight Hunter 469
Centennial Semi-Automatic 471
Crown Grade, Diamond Grade, Imperial Grade 468
Crown Grade 468
Diamond Grade 468
Imperial Grade 468
Eldorado AL48 (1954-1975) 468
Elite Model 469
Falconet 465
Falconet International Skeet 465
Falconet International Trap 465
Falconet Skeet 465
Falconet Trap 465
Highlander 465
Hunter Model AL48 (1950-1970) 468
I-12 471
I-12 White Gold 471
Model 500 469
Model 520 "Eldorado Gold" 469
Model 530 Trap 469
Model 712 470
Camo 470
Synthetic 470
Weathercoat 470
Model 720 470
Camo 470
Walnut Short Stock 470
WeatherCoat 471
Model 2003 Trap 466
Model 2004 Trap 466
Model 2005 Combination Trap 466
Model 3000 "Undergun" 466
Peregrine Model 400 465
Peregrine Model 451 465
Prestige Model 469
Priti Deluxe Model 465
Renaissance Classic 468
Renaissance Elite 468
Renaissance Field 468
Renaissance Sporting 468
Sidelock Double-Barrel Shotguns 464
Condor 464
Imperial 465
Imperial Monte Carlo Extra 465
Imperiales 465
No. 5 Imperial Monte Carlo 465
No. 11 Imperial Monte Carlo 465
SPAS12 469
Standard Model AL48 (1950-1970) . . 468
Variomax 912 469
Variomax 912 Camo 469
Variomax 912 SteadyGrip 469
Variopress 612 Defense 470
Variopress 612 Field 469
Variopress 612 Sporting 469
Variopress 620 Field 470
Variopress 620 Short Stock 470
Veloce 467
Veloce English Stock 467
Veloce Grade II 467
Veloce Squire Set 468

FRANCOTTE, A. 471
Custom Bolt-Action Rifles 473
Custom Double Rifles 473
Custom Single-Shot Mountain Rifles . 473
Custom Side-by-Side Shotguns 473
Deluxe Sidelock Side-by-Side 473
Jubilee 471
Eagle Grade No. 45 473
No. 14 471
No. 18 471
No. 20 471
No. 25 471
No. 30 473
Knockabout 473
Sidelock Side-by-Side 473

FRANKLIN, C. W. 473
Damascus Barrel Double 474
Single-Barrel 473
Steel Barrel Double 474

FRANKONIAJAGD 474
Favorit Deluxe 474
Favorit Standard 474
Heeren Rifle 474
Safari Model 474

FRASER, DANIEL & SON 474

FRASER F. A. CORP. 474
Fraser .25 cal. 474

FREEDOM ARMS 474
Bostonian (aka Boot Gun) 474
Casull Field Grade Model 83 474
Casull Premier Grade Model 83 475
Celebrity 474
Ironsides 474
Minuteman 474
Model 83 .500 Wyoming Express 476
Model 97 475
Model 252 475
Silhouette Class 475
Varmint Class 475
Model 353 475
Field Grade 475
Premier Grade 475
Signature Edition 475
Model 757 475
Field Grade 475
Premier Grade 475
Model 654 475
Field Grade 475
Premier Grade 475
Patriot (aka Boot Gun) 474
"Percussion" Mini-Revolver 474

FREEMAN, AUSTIN T. 476
Freeman Army Model Revolver 476

FRENCH MILITARY FIREARMS 476
French M1816 Flintlock Musket (for Infantry/Light Infantry) 476
Altered to percussion, rifled and sighted 476
In flintlock 476
French M1822 Cavalry and Lancer Flintlock Musketoons (and "T") 477
In flintlock 477
In percussion and rifled 477
French M1822 Cavalry Flintlock Pistol (and "T bis") 477
In flintlock 477
In percussion and rifled 477
French M1822 Flintlock Musket (for Infantry/Light Infantry) 476
Altered to percussion, and rifled . . 477
In flintlock 477
French M1829 Artillery Flintlock Carbine (and "T bis") 477
In percussion and rifled 477
French M1837 Rifle 4" Carbine a la Poncharra") 477
French M1840 and M1842 Percussion Muskets (Infantry/Light Infantry) . . . 477
French M1840 Rifle ("Carbine de Munition") 477
French M1846 and M1853 Rifles ("Carbine a tige") 478
French M1853 Musket, M1853 "T" and M1857 Rifle-Muskets 477
French M1853 "T" and M1859 Rifles ("Carbine de Vincennes") 478

FRENCH STATE 478

FRIGON 478
FS-4 478
FT I 478
FTC 478

FROMMER 478

FRUHWIRTH 478
M1872 Fruhwirth System Rifle 478

FUNK, CHRISTOPH 478

FURR ARMS 479

FYRBERG, ANDREW 479
Double-Barrel Shotguns 479
Revolvers 479

G

G M 480

GABBET-FAIRFAX, H. 480
Mars 480

GABILONDO Y CIA 480

GABILONDO Y URRESTI 480
Bufalo 6.35mm 480
Bufalo 7.65mm 481
Bufalo 9mmK 481
Danton 6.35mm 481
Danton War Model 481
Nine-Round Magazine 481
Twenty-Round Magazine 481
Perfect 481
Plus Ultra 481
Radium 480
Ruby 480
Velo-Dog Revolver 480

GALAND, C.F. 482
Galand, Galand & Sommerville, Galand Perrin 482
Le Novo 482
Tue-Tue 482
Velo-Dog 482

GALAND & SOMMERVILLE . . . 482

GALEF 482
Companion 482
Monte Carlo Trap 482
Silver Snipe, Golden Snipe, and Silver Hawk 482
Zabala Double 482

GALENA INDUSTRIES INC. . . . 482
AMT Backups 482
Automag .440 CorBon 483
Automag II 483
Automag III 483
Automag IV 483
Galena Accelerator 483
Galena Commando 484
Galena Hardballer 483
Galena Longslide 483

GALESI, INDUSTRIA ARMI . . . 484
Model 6 484
Model 9 484
Model 1923 484
Model 1930 484
9mm Parabellum 484

GALIL 485
Hadar II 485
Model AR 485
Model ARM 485
Sniper Rifle 485

GALLAGER 485
Gallager Carbine 485
Percussion Model 485
Spencer Cartridge Model 485

GAMBA, RENATO 485
Ambassador Executive 485
Ambassador Gold and Black 485
Boyern 88 Combination Gun 486
Concorde 2nd Generation 487
Concorde Game Grade 7 Engraving . 487
Concorde Game Grade 8 Engraving . 487
Concorde Game Shotguns 487
Concorde Skeet 487
Concorde Sporting 487
Concorde Trap 487
Country Model 485
Daytona America Trap 486
Daytona Game 486
Daytona Grade 6 Engraving 486
Daytona Sporting Model 486
Daytona Trap and Skeet Models . . 486
Daytona Grade 5 Engraving 486
Daytona Sporting Model 486
Daytona Trap and Skeet Models . . 486
Daytona Grade 4 Engraving 486
Daytona Sporting Model 486
Daytona Trap and Skeet Models . . 486
Daytona SL Grade 3 Engraving 487
Daytona Game 487
Daytona Sporting Model 487
Daytona Trap and Skeet Models . . 487
Daytona Skeet 486
Daytona SLHH Grade 2 Engraving . . . 487
Daytona SLHH Grade 1 Gold Engraving 487
Daytona SLHH "One of Thousand" . . . 487
Daytona Sporting 486
Daytona Trap 486
Edinburg Match 486
Europa 2000 486
Gamba 624 Extra 485
Gamba 624 Prince 485
Grifone Model 485
Grinta Trap and Skeet 486
Hunter II 487
Hunter Super 485
Le Mans 487
London 485
London Royal 485
Mustang 487
Oxford 90 485
Oxford Extra 485
Principessa 485
RGZ 1000 488
RGX 1000 Express 488
SAB G90 488
SAB G91 Compact 488
Safari Express 487
Trident Fast Action 488
Trident Match 900 488
Trident Super 488
Victory Trap and Skeet 486

GARAND 488
AMF Rebuild 488
British Garands (Lend Lease) 489
DCM Rifles 488
Gas tap/modified to gas port 488
H&R Rebuild 488
Harrington & Richardson Production 489
International Harvester Production 489
International Harvester/with Harrington & Richardson Receiver 489
International Harvester/with Springfield Receiver (postage stamp) 489
International Harvester/with Springfield Receiver (arrow head) 489
International Harvester/with Springfield Receiver (Gap letter) 489
M1 Garand Cutaway 489
M1C 489
MC 1952 (USMC Issue) M1D 489
Navy Trophy Rifles U.S.N. Crane Depot Rebuild 488
Post-WWII Production sn: ca 4,200,000-6,099,361 489

Pre-Dec. 7, 1941 gas port production pn sn: ca 410,000 488
Rebuilt Rifle, any manufacture . . . 488
Springfield Armory Production Gas trap sn: ca 81-52,000 488
Winchester Educational Contract sn: 100,000-100,500 489
Winchester sn: 100,501-165,000 . 489
Winchester sn: 1,200,00-1,380,000 489
Winchester sn: 2,305,850-2,536,493 489
Winchester sn: 1,601,150-1,640,000 "win-13" 489
WWII Production sn: ca 410,000-3,880,000 489
National Match 489
Type I 489
Type II 489

GARATE, ANITUA 489
British Service Old Pattern No.2 Mk. I Trocaola Aranzabal Military Revolver 490
Charola 489
Cosmopolite 489
El Lunar 489
Express or Danton 489
G.A.C. 489
L'Eclair 490
La Lira 490
"Modelo Militar" 489
Sprinter 490
Triumph 490

GARATE, HERMANOS 490
Cantabria 490
Velo-Stark 490

GARBI 490
Express Rifle 491
Model 51-B 490
Model 62-B 490
Model 71 490
Model 100 490
Model 101 490
Model 102 490
Model 103A 491
Model 103A Royal 491
Model 103B 491
Model 103B Royal 491
Model 120 491
Model 200 491
Model Special 491

GARCIA 491
Garcia Bronco 491
Garcia Bronco .22/.410 491
Garcia Musketeer 491

GARRET, J. & F. CO. 491
Garrett Single-Shot Pistol 491

GASSER, LEOPOLD 492
Gasser-Kropatschek M1876 492
M1870 492
M1870/74 492
Montenegrin Gasser 492
Rast & Gasser M1898 492

GATLING ARMS CO. 492
Kynoch-Dimancea 492

GAUCHER 492
GN 1 492

GAULOIS 492

GAVAGE, A. 492

GAZANAGA, ISIDRO 493
Destroyer M1913 493
Destroyer M1916 493
Destroyer Revolver 493
Super Destroyer 493
Surete 493

GECO 493

GEHA 493

GEM 493
Gem Pocket Revolver 493

GENEZ, A. G. 493
Double-Barrel Shotgun 493
Pocket Pistol 493

GENSCHOW, G. 493
Geco 493
German Bulldog 493

GEORGIA ARMORY 493

GERING, H. M. & CO. 494
Leonhardt 494

GERMAN WWII MILITARY RIFLES 494

GERSTENBERGER & EBERWEIN 494
Em-Ge, G.& E., Omega & Pic 494

GEVARM 494
E-1 Autoloading Rifle 494
Model A-6 494

GIB 494
10 Gauge Shotgun 494

GIBBS 494
Gibbs Carbine 494
Gibbs Pistol 494

GIBBS, J. & G. LATER GIBBS, GEORGE 494

GIBBS GUNS, INC. 495
Mark 45 Carbine 495

GIBBS RIFLE COMPANY 495
Enfield No. 5 Jungle Carbine 495
Enfield No.7 Jungle Carbine 495
Mauser M71/84 495
Mauser M88 Commission Rifle 495
Quest Extreme Carbine 495
Quest II Extreme Carbine 495
Quest III Extreme Carbine 495
Summit 45-70 Carbine 495

GIBBS TIFFANY & CO. 495
Under Hammer Pistol 495

GILLAM & MILLER 495

GILLESPIE 495
Derringer Type Pocket Pistol 495

GLAZE, W. & CO. 495

GLISENTI 495
Glisenti Model 1906-1910 495

GLOCK 496
Glock 17 496
Glock 17C 496
Glock 17CC 496
Glock 17L Competition Model 496
Glock 19 497
Glock 19C 497
Glock 19CC 497
Glock 20 and Glock 21 497
Glock 20C and 21C 498
Glock 20CC/21CC 498
Glock 21 SF 498
Glock 22 496
Glock 22C 496
Glock 22CC 496
Glock 23C 497
Glock 23CC 497
Glock 24 497
Glock 24C 497
Glock 24CC 497
Glock 26 and Model 27 498
Glock 29 and Glock 30 498
Glock 31 499
Glock 31C 499
Glock 31CC 499
Glock 32 499
Glock 32C 500
Glock 32CC 500
Glock 33 500
Glock 34 500
Glock 35 500
Glock 36 499
Model 23 497
Model 37 500
Model 38 500
Model 39 500

GODDARD 500

GOLDEN EAGLE 501
Golden Eagle Model 5000 Grade I . . . 501
Grade I Skeet 501
Grade I Trap 501
Grandee Grade III 501
Model 5000 Grade II 501
Model 7000 African 501
Model 7000 Grade I 501
Model 7000 Grade II 501

GONCZ CO. 501
GA Collectors Edition 501
GA Pistol 501
GAT-9 Pistol 501
GC Carbine 501
GC Collector's Edition 501
GC Stainless 501
GS Collectors Edition 501
GS Pistol 501
Halogen Carbine 501
Laser Carbine 501

GOUDRY, J.F. 502

GOVERNOR 502
Governor Pocket Revolver 502

GRABNER G. 502

GRAND PRECISION, FABRIQUE D'ARMES DE . . . 502
Bulwark 6.35mm 502
Bulwark Model 1913 502
Bulwark Model 1914 502
Libia 6.35mm 502
Libia 7.65mm 503

GRANGER, G. 503
Side-by-Side Shotgun 503

GRANT, STEPHEN 503

GRAS 503
Model 1874 503

GREAT WESTERN ARMS COMPANY 503
.22 Long Rifle Single-Action 503
Centerfire Single-Action 503
Deputy Model 503
Derringer Model .38 Special & .38 S&W 504
Derringer Model—.22 Magnum RF . . 503
Fast Draw Model 503
Target Model 504
Unassembled Kit Gun—In the White . 504

GREEN, E. 504
Green 504

GREENE 504
Greene Breechloading Rifle 504

GREENER, W. W. LTD. 504

GREIFELT & CO. 504
Combination Gun 504
Drilling 505
Grade No. 1 504
Grade No. 3 504
Model 143E 504
Model 22 504
Model 22E 504
Model 103 504
Model 103E 505

GRENDEL, INC. 505
P-10 Pistol 505
P-12 505
P-30 505
P-30L 505
P-30M 505
P-31 505
R-31 Carbine 505
SRT-20F Compact Rifle 505
SRT-24 505

GRIFFIN & HOWE 506

GRIFFON 506
Griffon 1911 A1 Combat 506

GRISWOLD & GRIER 506

GRISWOLD & GUNNISON 506
1851 Navy Type 506

GROSS ARMS CO. 506
Pocket Revolver 506

GRUBB, J. C. & CO. 506
Pocket Pistol 506

GRULLA 506
Model 216RL 506
Royal 506

GUEDES-CASTRO 506
Model 1885 506

GUERINI, CAESAR 507
Essex 508
Flyway 507
Forum/Forum Sporting 507
Magnus 507
Magnus Light 507
Magnus Sporting 507
Summit Sporting/Summit Limited 507
Tempio 507
Woodlander 507

GUIDE LAMP 508
Liberator 508

GUION, T. F. 508
Pocket Pistol 508

GULIKERS, V./A LIEGE 508

GUNWORKS LTD. 508
Model 9 Derringer 508

GUSTAF, CARL 508
Bolt-Action Rifle 508
Grade II 508
Grade III 508
Deluxe Bolt-Action 508
Grand Prix Target 508
Model 2000 508
Varmint Model 508

GWYN & CAMPBELL 508
Union Carbine 508

H

H.J.S. INDUSTRIES, INC. 509
Frontier Four Derringer 509
Lone Star Derringer 509

H-S PRECISION, INC. 509
BHR Big Game Professional Hunter Rifle 509
HTR Heavy Tactical Rifle 510
PHR Professional Hunter Rifle 509
PHL Professional Hunter Lightweight Rifle 509
Professional Hunter Take-Down Rifle 509
RDR Rapid Deployment Rifle 510
Short Tactical 510
Silhouette Pistol 510
SPL Lightweight Sporter 509
SPR Sporter Rifle 509
TTD Tactical Take-Down System 510
VAR Varmint Rifle 509
Varmint Take-Down Rifle 509
Varmint Pistol 509

HAENEL, C. G. 510
Model 1 510
Model 2 510

HAFDASA 510
Ballester-Molina 510
Campeon 511
Criolla 510
Hafdasa 511
Rigaud 511
Zonda 511

HAKIM 511

HAHN, WILLIAM 511
Pocket Pistol 511

HALE, H. J. 511
Under Hammer Pistol 511

HALE & TULLER 511
Under Hammer Pistol 511

HALL, ALEXANDER 511
Revolving Rifle 511

HALL-NORTH 511
Model 1840 Carbine 511
Type 1 Carbine 511
Type 2 Carbine 511

HAMBUSH, JOSEPH 512
Boxlock Side-by-Side Shotgun 512
Sidelock Side-by-Side Shotgun 512

HAMILTON RIFLE COMPANY .512
Model 027 513
Model 7 512
Model 11 513
Model 15 513
Model 19 513
Model 23 513
Model 27 513
Model 31 513
Model 35 or Boys' Military Rifle 513
Model 39 513
Model 43 513
Model 47 513
Model 51 513
Model 55 513

HAMMERLI, SA 514
Dakota 516
Large Calibers 516
International Model 206 515
International Model 207 515
International Model 208 515
International Model 208 Deluxe 515
International Model 209 515
International Model 210 515
International Model 211 515
Model 45 Smallbore Rifle 514
Model 54 Smallbore Rifle 514
Model 100 Free Pistol 514
Model 101 514
Model 102 514
Model 103 514
Model 104 514
Model 105 514
Model 106 514
Model 107 514
Model 107 Deluxe 515
Model 120 Heavy Barrel 515
Model 120-1 Free Pistol 515
Model 120-2 515
Model 150 515
Model 152 515
Model 212 516
Model 230 516
Model 232 516
Model 280 516
Model 503 Smallbore Free Rifle 514
Model 506 Smallbore Match Rifle 514
Model SP 20 516
Olympic 300 Meter 514
Sporting Rifle 514
Super Dakota 516
Virginian 516

HAMMERLI-WALTHER 516
Model 200 Type 1958 517
Model 201 517
Model 202 517
Model 203 517
Model 204 517
Model 205 517
Olympia Model 200 Type 1952 516

HAMMOND BULLDOG 517
Hammond Bulldog 517

HAMMOND, GRANT MFG. CO. 517
Grant Hammond 7.65mm Pistol 517
Military Automatic Pistol 517

H&R 1871, LLC 517

HANKINS, WILLIAM 517
Pocket Revolver 517

HANUS, BILL 518
Bill Hanus Classic 518

HARPERS FERRY ARMORY MUSKETS AND CARBINES 518
Harpers Ferry U.S. M1816 Muskets (Types I to III) 518
Altered to percussion 518
In flintlock 518
Harpers Ferry U.S. M 1841 Muzzleloading Rifle—The "Mississippi Rifle" 519
Harpers Ferry U.S. M1819 Hall Rifle (Types I and II) 518
Altered to percussion 519
In flintlock 518
Harpers Ferry U.S. M1836 Hall Carbine (Types I & II) 519
Harpers Ferry U.S. M1841 Hall Rifle . 519
Harpers Ferry U.S. M1842 Musket ... 518
Harpers Ferry U.S. M1842 Hall Carbine 519
Harpers Ferry U.S. M1842 Musket ... 519
Harpers Ferry U.S. M1855 Rifle-Musket (Type I & II) 519
Harpers Ferry U.S. M1855 Rifles (Type I & II) 519
Type I 520
Type II 520

HARRINGTON & RICHARDSON, INC. 520
.22 Special 522
.22 U.S.R.A./Model 195 Single-Shot Match Target Pistol 522
.22 U.S.R.A./Model 195 Pistol, Variations 1 to 3 522
.22 U.S.R.A./Model 195 Pistol, Variation 4 522
100th Anniversary Officer's Model ... 533
Amtec 2000 526
Buffalo Classic 532
Camo Laminate Turkey NWTF Edition 527
Camo Laminate Turkey Youth NWTF Edition 527
CR Carbine 532
Custer Memorial Issue 533
Enlisted Men's Model 533
Officer's Model 533
Defender 522
Engraved Model 999 526
Excell Auto 5 529
Excell Auto 5 Combo 529
Excell Auto 5 Turkey 529
Excell Auto 5 Waterfowl 529
Expert 522
First Model Hand Ejector 521
H&R Handy-Gun (rifled barrel) curio or relic 527
.22 rimfire serial range from 1 (?) to 223 (?) 527
.32-20 W.C.F. serial range mostly from 43851 (?) to 43937 (?) .. 527
H&R Handy-Gun (smooth bore) nfa, curio or relic 527
.410 bore, Model 2, Types II and III 528
28 gauge, Model 2, Type I 528
Hammerless Double 526
A Grade 526
B Grade 526
C Grade 526
D Grade 526
Handi-Rifle 531
Harrich No. 1 526
Hunter 521
Knife Model 522
Long Tom Classic 530
Model 058 530
Model 088 528
Model 099 529
Model 1 Double-Action Revolver 521
Model 1-1/2 520
Model 2 522
Model 2-1/2 520
Model 3-1/2 520
Model 4-1/2 520
Model 65 Military 530
Model 150 530
Model 155 (Shikari) 530
Model 157 530
Model 158 530
Model 162 529
Model 171 530
Model 171-DL 530
Model 174 533
Model 176 529
Model 178 533
Model 258 530
Model 300 Ultra 531
Model 301 Carbine 531
Model 317 Ultra Wildcat 531
Model 317P 531
Model 333 532
Model 340 532
Model 360 Ultra Automatic 532
Model 400 529
Model 401 529
Model 402 529
Model 440 529
Model 442 529
Model 403 529
Model 404 529
Model 451 Medalist 532
Model 504 522
Model 532 523
Model 586 523
Model 603 523
Model 604 523
Model 622 523
Model 623 523
Model 632 523
Model 642 523
Model 649 523
Model 650 523
Model 660 524
Model 666 524
Model 676 524
Model 686 524
Model 700 532
Model 700 DL 532
Model 732 524
Model 733 524
Model 750 532
Model 865 532
Model 900 524
Model 901 524
Model 903 524
Model 904 524
Model 905 524
Model 922 First Issue 522
Model 922 Second Issue 524
Model 923 524
Model 925 524
Model 935 525
Model 929 525
Model 929 Sidekick—New Model 525
Model 929 Sidekick Trapper Edition .. 525
Model 930 525
Model 939 Ultra Sidekick 525
Model 939 Premier 525
Model 940 525
Model 949 525
Model 949 Western 525
Model 950 525
Model 976 525
Model 999 Sportsman 525
Model 1212 530
Model 1880 520
Model 5200 532
Model 5200 Sporter 533
Model No. 1 520
New Defender 522
No. 199 Sportsman 522
Pinnacle 529
Reising Model 60 530
Self-Loader 521
Single-Barrel Shotguns 526
Tamer 527
Target Model 522
The American Double-Action 520
The Young America Double-Action .. 520
Topper (New Production) 526
Topper (Old Production) 528
Topper Deluxe 526
Topper Deluxe Classic 526
Topper Deluxe Slug 526
Topper Jr. Classic 526
Topper Jr. in 20 Gauge and .410 Bore Only 526
Trapper 521
Turkey Mag 526
Ultra .22 Magnum Rifle 531
Ultra Rifle—Hunting 531
Ultra Rifle—Varmint 531
Ultra Rifle—Comp 531
Ultra Rifle Rocky Mountain Elk Foundation Commemorative 531
Ultra Rifle Whitetails Unlimited 1997 Commemorative Edition 532
Ultra Slug Hunter 527
Ultra Slug Hunter Bull Barrel 527
Ultra Slug Hunter Deluxe 527
12 Gauge 527
20 Gauge 527
Ultra Slug Youth Model 527
Ultra Slug Youth Bull Barrel 527
Ultra Sportsman 522
Ultra Varmint Fluted 531
Ultra Varmint Rifle 531
Wesson & Harrington Brand 125th Anniversary Rifle 532
Youth Turkey Gun 526

HARRIS GUNWORKS 533
Antietam Sharps Rifle 534
Double Rifle/Shotgun 535
Boxlock 535
Side Lock 535
Long Range Rifle 534
Model 86 Sniper Rifle 533
Model 87 Series 533
Model 88 533
Model 89 Sniper Rifle 533
Model 93 533
Model 95 534
Model 96 534
National Match Rifle 533
Signature Classic Sporter 534
Signature Classic Stainless Sporter .. 534
Signature Super Varminter 535
Signature Alaskan 535
Signature Titanium Mountain Rifle ... 535
Sportsman 97 535
Talon Safari Rifle 535
Talon Sporter Rifle 535
Target/Benchrest Rifle 534

HARTFORD ARMS & EQUIPMENT CO. 535
Model 1925 536
Single-Shot Target 535

HATFIELD RIFLE COMPANY .. 536
Squirrel Rifle 536
Uplander Golden Quail Grade IV 536
Uplander Grade I 536
Uplander Pigeon Grade II 536
Uplander Super Pigeon Grade III 536
Uplander Woodcock Grade V 536

HAVILAND & GUNN 536
Gallery Pistol 536

HAWES 536
Chief Marshal 537
Courier 536
Deputy Marshal 537
Diplomat 537
Federal Marshal 537
Medalion 537
Montana Marshal 537
Silver City Marshal 537
Texas Marshal 537
Tip-Up Target Pistol 537
Trophy 537
Western Marshal 537

HAWES & WAGGONER 538
Pocket Pistol 538

HAWKEN 538

HDH, SA. 538
Cobold 538
Left Wheeler 538
Lincoln 538

Lincoln-Bossu . . . 538
Puppy . . . 538

HEAVY EXPRESS INC. . . . 538
Heavy Express Monarch—Winchester M70 Classic . . . 538
Heavy Express Monarch—Ruger 77 MK II . . . 539
Heavy Express Premier—Ruger M77 Mk II . . . 538
Heavy Express Premier—Winchester M70 Classic . . . 539
Heavy Express Single-Shot—Ruger #1 . . . 539

HECKLER & KOCH . . . 539
BASR Model . . . 541
HK4 . . . 541
.22 Caliber or .380 Caliber . . . 541
.25 Caliber or .32 Caliber . . . 541
Conversion Units . . . 541
Mark 23 . . . 547
Mark II UTL (Universal Tactical Light) 547
Mk 23 Suppressor . . . 547
Model 91 A2 . . . 539
Model 91 A3 . . . 539
Model 93 A2 . . . 539
Model 93 A3 . . . 539
Model 94 A2 . . . 539
Model 94 A3 . . . 540
Model 270 . . . 540
Model 300 . . . 540
Model 630 . . . 540
Model 770 . . . 540
Model 820 . . . 540
Model 877 . . . 540
Model 940 . . . 540
Model SL6 . . . 540
Model SL7 . . . 540
Model SR9 . . . 540
Model SR9 (T) Target . . . 540
Model SR9 (TC) Target Competition . 541
Model SL8-1 . . . 541
Model USC . . . 541
Optical Sight/Scope Mount . . . 547
P7 K3 . . . 542
.22 Caliber Conversion Kit . . . 543
.32 ACP Caliber Conversion Kit . . 543
P7 M8 . . . 543
P7 M10 . . . 543
P7 M13 . . . 543
P7 PSP . . . 542
P9 . . . 541
P9S . . . 541
P9S Competition . . . 542
P9S Target Model . . . 542
P2000 GPM . . . 547
P2000 SK . . . 547
PSG-1 . . . 541
Quik-Comp . . . 547
SLB 2000 . . . 541
SP89 . . . 543
Tritium Sights . . . 547
USP .357 Compact . . . 546
USP 40 . . . 544
USP 9 . . . 544
USP 9 Compact . . . 545
USP 9SD . . . 544
USP 40 Compact . . . 545
USP 45 . . . 544
USP 45 50th Anniversary Commemorative . . . 547
USP 45 Match . . . 545
USP 45 Compact . . . 546
USP 45 Compact Tactical . . . 546
USP 45 Tactical . . . 546
USP 45 Expert . . . 546
USP Compact LEM (Law Enforcement Modification) . . . 545
USP Elite . . . 546
VP 70Z . . . 542

HEINZELMANN, C.E. . . . 548
Heim . . . 548

HEISER, CARL . . . 548

HELFRICHT . . . 548
Model 3 Pocket Pistol . . . 548
Model 4 Pocket Pistol . . . 548

HELLIS, CHARLES . . . 548

HENRION & DASSY . . . 548
Semi-Automatic . . . 548

HENRY . . . 548

HENRY, ALEXANDER . . . 548
Double Rifle . . . 548
Single-Shot Rifle . . . 548

HENRY REPEATING ARMS COMPANY . . . 549
Big Boy .44 Magnum "Wildlife Edition" . . . 549
Big Boy .45 Colt "Cowboy Edition" . . . 549
Henry Acu-Bolt . . . 550
Henry Big Boy . . . 549
Henry Big Boy Deluxe Engraved .44 Magnum . . . 549
Henry Carbine . . . 549
Henry Deluxe Engraved Golden Boy Magnum . . . 549
Henry Golden Boy . . . 549
Henry Golden Boy Deluxe . . . 549
Henry Lever Action Frontier Model . . . 549
Henry Lever-Action . . . 549
Henry Lever-Action .22 Magnum . . . 549
Henry Mini Bolt . . . 550
Henry Pump Action .22 Octagon Rifle 550
Henry Pump-Action Rifle . . . 549
Henry U.S. Survival Rifle . . . 550
Henry Varmint Express . . . 549
Henry Youth Model . . . 549

HERITAGE MANUFACTURING, INC. . . . 550
Model H25S . . . 550
Rough Rider . . . 550
Rough Rider .17 HMR . . . 551
With Bird's-Head Grip & Combo Cylinder . . . 551
With Combination Cylinder—.22 Mag. . . . 551
Rough Rider .32 . . . 551
Rough Rider Big-Bore Series . . . 551
Sentry . . . 550
Stealth . . . 550

HEROLD . . . 551
Bolt-Action Rifle . . . 551

HERTER'S . . . 551
Guide . . . 551
J-9 or U-9 Hunter . . . 551
J-9 or U-9 Presentation or Supreme . . 551
Power-Mag Revolver . . . 551
Western . . . 551

HESSE ARMS . . . 551
FAL-H Congo Rifle . . . 552
FAL-H High Grade . . . 552
FAL-H Standard Grade . . . 552
FALO Congo Rifle . . . 552
FALO Heavy Barrel . . . 552
FALO Tactical Rifle . . . 552
H-22 Competition Rifle . . . 553
H-22 Standard Rifle . . . 553
H-22 Tigershark . . . 553
H-22 Wildcat . . . 553
HAR-15A2 Bull Gun . . . 552
HAR-15A2 Carbine . . . 553
HAR-15A2 Dispatcher . . . 553
HAR-15A2 National Match . . . 552
HAR-15A2 Standard Rifle . . . 552
Hesse Model 47 Rifle . . . 553
M14-H Brush Rifle . . . 553
M14-H Standard Rifle . . . 553
Omega Match . . . 552

HEYM, F. W. . . . 553
Heym Magnum Express . . . 555
Model 22 Safety . . . 554
Model 33 . . . 554
Model 33 Deluxe . . . 554
Model 37 . . . 555
Model 37 Deluxe . . . 555
Model 55BF/77BF . . . 554
Model 55BFSS . . . 554
Model 55BSS . . . 554
Model 77B/55B Over-and-Under Rifle 554
Model 88 B . . . 554
Model 88 BSS . . . 554
Model 88 Safari . . . 554
Model HR-30 . . . 554
Model HR-38 . . . 554
Model SR-20 . . . 555
Model SR-20 Alpine . . . 555
SR-20 Classic Safari . . . 555
SR-20 Classic Sportsman . . . 555
SR-20 Trophy . . . 555

HI-POINT FIREARMS . . . 555
.380 ACP Compensated . . . 556
.40 S&W Carbine . . . 556
Model .40 Polymer . . . 556
Model .45 Polymer . . . 556
Model 40SW . . . 556
Model 995 Carbine . . . 556
Model C . . . 555
Model C Comp . . . 556
Model C Polymer . . . 556
Model CF . . . 556
Model JH . . . 556

HIGGINS, J. C. . . . 556

HIGH STANDARD MANUFACTURING CORPORATION . . . 557
100 Series Models . . . 561
Dura-Matic M-100 . . . 562
Field King FK-100 . . . 561
Flite King LW-100 . . . 561
Olympic O-100 . . . 561
Sport King Lightweight SK-100 . . . 561
Sport King SK-100 . . . 561
Supermatic S-100 . . . 561
101 Series Models . . . 562
Conversion Kits . . . 562
Dura-Matic M-101 . . . 562
Field King FK-101 . . . 562
Olympic O-101 . . . 562
Supermatic S-101 . . . 562
102 & 103 Series Models . . . 563
Conversion Kits . . . 564
Flite King . . . 564
Olympic . . . 563
Olympic ISU . . . 563
Olympic Trophy ISU . . . 563
Sharpshooter . . . 563
Sport King . . . 564
Supermatic Citation . . . 563
Supermatic Tournament . . . 563
Supermatic Trophy . . . 563
104 Series Models . . . 564
Olympic . . . 564
Olympic ISU . . . 564
Supermatic Citation . . . 564

Supermatic Trophy 564
Victor 564
106 Series Models 564
Olympic 565
Olympic ISU 565
Supermatic Citation 565
Supermatic Tournament 565
Supermatic Trophy 565
107 Series Models 564
10-X 567
Olympic ISU 566
Olympic ISU 1980 Commemorative .. 566
Sharpshooter 567
Sport King 566
Supermatic Citation 565
Supermatic Tournament 566
Supermatic Trophy 565
Supermatic Trophy 1972 Commemorative 565
Survival Kit 567
Victor 566
Currently Manufactured Houston Models 568
10-X 569
10-X—Shea model 569
Olympic ISU 569
Olympic Model 569
Olympic Rapid Fire 569
Sport King 569
Supermatic Citation 568
Supermatic Citation MS 569
Supermatic Tournament 569
Supermatic Trophy 569
Victor 569
Gold-Plated Derringers 570
High Standard Derringers 570
Blued finish, white or Black Grips, 1962-1984 570
High Standard Revolvers 570
Bicentennial 1776-1976 574
Camp Gun 571
Crusader 572
Double Nine with Aluminum Frame .. 572
Double Nines with Steel Frame 572
Durango 574
Flite King Brush 575
Flite King Citation 576
Flite King Deluxe 576
Flite King Field 575
Flite King Skeet 576
Flite King Special 576
Flite King Trap 576
Flite King Trophy 576
Griswold & Gunnison 574
Gun/High Sierra, The 574
Hi-Power Deluxe 577
Hi-Power Field Grade 577
Hombre 574
Kit Gun 571
Leech & Rigdon 574
Longhorn 572
Longhorns with Steel Frame 572
Marshall 572
Model 10-A 576
Model 10-B 576
Model 200 576
Model 514 576
Natchez 572
Police-Style Revolvers 570
Posse 572
Power Plus 572
Pump 576
Schneider & Glassick 574
Semi-Automatic 576
Sentinel aluminum frames 570
Gold 570
Pink 570
Turquoise 570
Sentinel Deluxe 570
Sentinel Imperial 570
Sentinel Mark I 571
Sentinel Mark II 571
Sentinel Mark III 571
Sentinel Mark IV 571
Sentinel Snub 570
Sentinel Steel Frames 571
Special Presentation Bicentennial ... 574
Sport King Carbine 577
Sport King Deluxe/Sport King 577
Sport King Field 577
Sport King Special 577
Sport King/Flite King 577
Supermatic Citation 575
Supermatic Deer Gun 575
Supermatic Deluxe 575
Supermatic Duck 575
Supermatic Field 575
Supermatic Skeet 575
Supermatic Special 575
Supermatic Trap 575
Supermatic Trophy 575
Supermatic Shadow Automatic 576
Supermatic Shadow Indy Over-and-Under 577
Supermatic Shadow Seven Over-and-Under 577
Letter Models 557
G-.380 559
G-B 559
G-D 559
G-E 560
Hammer Letter Models 558
Lever Letter Models 559
Model A 557
Model B 557
Model B-US 557
Model C 557
Model D 557
Model E 557
Model H-A 558
Model H-B, Type 1 Pre-War 558
Model H-B, Type 2 Post-War 558
Model H-D 558
Model H-D Military 559
Model H-E 558
Model S 558
Model USA—Model HD 559
Model USA—Model HD-MS 559
Olympic (commonly called “G-O”) 560
Lever Name Models 560
Field King 560
Olympic 560
Sport King 560
Supermatic 560
SH Series Models 567
10-X 568
Citation II 567
Conversion Kits for Military Frame Guns 568
Sharpshooter 568
Sport King 567
Supermatic Citation 567
Supermatic Trophy 567
Survival Kit 568
Victor 568
Silver-Plated Derringer 570

HILL, W.J. 577
Hill's Self-Extracting Revolver 577

HILLIARD, D. H. 577
Under Hammer Pistol 577

HINO-KOMURA 577

HODGKINS, D. C. & SONS 577

HOFER, P. 578

HOFFMAN, LOUIS 578
Pocket Pistol 578

HOLDEN, C. B. 578
Open Frame Rifle 578

HOLECK, EMANUEL 578
Holeck Rifle 578

HOLLAND & HOLLAND, LTD. .578
Best Quality Rifle 578
H&H .700 Bore Side-by-Side Rifle 578
No. 2 Grade Double Rifle 578
Royal Side-by-Side Rifle 578

HOLLIS & SONS 578

HOLLOWAY ARMS CO. 578
HAC Model 7 578
HAC Model 7C 578
HAC Model 7S 578

HOLMES FIREARMS 578
MP-22 578
MP-83 579

HOOD F. A. CO. 579

HOPKINS & ALLEN 579
Army Revolver 579
Derringer 579
Dictator 579
Double-Barrel Shotguns 579
Falling Block Rifle 579
Navy Revolver 579
Schuetzen Rifle 579

HORSLEY, THOMAS 579

HOTCHKISS 579

HOWA MACHINE COMPANY . .579
Model 1500 Custom 580
Model 1500 Hunter 580
Model 1500 JRS Classic 580
Model 1500 Lightning Rifle 580
Model 1500 Mountain 580
Model 1500 PCS (Police Counter Sniper) 581
Model 1500 Thumbhole Sporter 580
Model 1500 Trophy 580
Model 1500 Varmint 580
Model 1500 Varmint Supreme 580
Model 1500 Youth 580
Realtree Camo Rifle 581
Texas Safari Rifle 581

HOWARD-WHITNEY 581

HUGLU 581
Amarillo 582
Bobwhite 581
Canadian 582
Canvasback 582
Canvasback Deluxe 582
Cottontail 582
Custom Grade II 582
Custom Grade IV 583
Custom Grade IV with Upgrade 583
Custom Grade VI 583
Durango 582
English Sporter 582
Mallard 581
Redhead 581
Redhead Deluxe 581
Ringneck 581
Sharptail 582
Teal 582

Vandalia Trap 582
Woodcock 581
Woodcock Deluxe 581

HUNGARY 583
SA-85M 583

HUNT 583

HUNTER ARMS CO. 583

HUSQVARNA 583
Hi-Power 583
Lahti 583
Model 456 584
Model 1100 Deluxe 583
Model 1000 Super Grade 583
Model 1907 583
Model 3100 Crown Grade 583
Model 4100 Lightweight 583
Model 6000 584
Model 9000 Crown Grade 584
Model 8000 Imperial Grade 584

HY-HUNTER, INC. 584
Accurate Ace 584
Automatic Derringer 584
Chicago Cub 584
Detective 584
Favorite 584
Frontier Six Shooter 584
Frontier Six Shooter 584
Gold Rush Derringer 584
Maxim 584
Military 584
Panzer 584
Stingray 584
Stuka 584
Target Model 584

HYDE & SHATTUCK 584
Queen Derringer 584

HYPER 584
Single-Shot Rifle 584

I

I.G.I. 585
Domino OP601 585
Domino SP602 585

IAB 585
C-300 Combo 585
C-300 Super Combo 585
S-300 585

IAI-AMERICAN LEGENDS 585
M-333 M1 Garand 585
M-777 585
M-888 M1 Carbine 585
M-999 585
M-2000 585
M-6000 585
M-5000 585

IAR 585

IGA 585
Coach Gun 586
Condor II 586
Condor Supreme Deluxe 586
Deluxe Over-and-Under ERA 2000 . . 586
Single-Barrel Shotgun 585
Single-Barrel Shotgun Youth Model . . 585
Standard Over-and-Under Condor I . . 586
Standard Side-by-Side Uplander Model 586
Uplander Supreme 586
Uplander Youth Model 586

INDIAN ARMS CORP. 586
Indian Arms .380 586

INDUSTRIA ARMI GALESI 586

INGLIS, JOHN & COMPANY . . 586

INGRAM 587
MAC 10 587
MAC 10AI 587
MAC 11 587

INTERARMS 587
22-ATD 588
Alaskan Model 587
Cavalier 587
Continental Carbine 587
FEG PPH 588
FEG R-9 588
Helwan Brigadier 588
Mannlicher Carbine 587
Mark II AP 588
Mark II APK 588
Mark X American Field 587
Mark X Lightweight 587
Mark X Viscount 587
Mauser Parabellum Cartridge Counter 588
Mauser Parabellum Karabiner 588
Mini Mark X 587
Stainless Dragoon 588
Virginian .22 Convertible 588
Virginian Dragoon 588
Virginian Stainless .22 Convertible . . 588
Whitworth Express Rifle 587
Whitworth Mannlicher Carbine 587

INTERDYNAMICS OF AMERICA 588
KG-9 588
KG-99 588
KG-99 Stainless 588
KG-99M 588

INTRATEC USA, INC. 589
TEC-9 589
TEC-9C 589
TEC-9M 589
TEC-22 "Scorpion" 589
TEC-38 589

IRVING, W. 589
1st Model 589
2nd Model 589
Single-Shot Derringer 589

IRWINDALE ARMS, INC. 589

ISRAELI MILITARY INDUSTRIES 589

ITHACA GUN CO. 589
Century Grade Trap (SKB) 596
Century II (SKB) 596
Crass Model 590
Quality 1 590
Quality 1-1/2 590
Quality 1P 590
Quality 2 591
Quality 3 591
Quality 4 591
Flues Model 592
Field Grade 592
Grade 1 592
Grade 1 Special 592
Grade 1-1/2 592
Grade 2 592
Grade 3 592
Grade 4 592
Grade 5 592
Grade 6 592
Grade 7 592
Sousa 592
Flues Model Single-Barrel Trap Gun (1914 to 1922) 594
Grade 4E 595
Grade 5E 595
Grade 6E 595
Grade 7E 595
Sousa Grade 595
Victory Grade 595
Hi-Grade Ithaca Model 37 Guns 598
$1,000 Grade 598
$2,000 Grade 598
$3,000 Grade 598
Ithaca Auto & Burglar Gun NFA, Curio or Relic 596
Ithaca Baker Model 590
Quality A 590
Quality B 590
Ithaca Model 37 Repeater 596
Knick Model Single-Barrel Trap 595
$1,000 to $2,500 Grades 595
$3,000 through the Dollar Grade . . 596
Grade 4E 595
Grade 5E 595
Grade 7E 595
Sousa Grade 595
Victory Grade 595
Lewis Model 591
Quality 1 591
Quality 1 Special 591
Quality 1-1/2 591
Quality 2 591
Quality 3 591
Quality 4 591
Quality 5 591
Quality 6 591
Quality 7 591
Long Range Double 594
Long Range Double Deluxe 594
LSA-55 or 65 Series 602
LSA-55 Deluxe 602
LSA-55 Standard 602
LSA-55 Varmint Heavy Barrel 602
LSA-65 Long Action 602
LSA-65 Deluxe 602
LSA-55 Turkey Gun 602
Mag-10 Series 601
Deluxe Vent Rib Grade 601
National Wild Turkey Federation . . 601
Presentation Grade 601
Roadblocker—Military and Police Model 601
Standard Grade 601
Standard Vent Rib Grade 601
Supreme Grade 601
Minier Model 591
Field Grade 591
Quality 1 591
Quality 1 Special 591
Quality 1-1/2 591
Quality 2 591
Quality 3 592
Quality 4 592
Quality 5 592
Quality 6 592
Quality 7 592
Model 37 2500 Series Centennial 598
Model 37 Basic Featherlight—1979-1983 597
Model 37 Bicentennial 598
Model 37 Camo 598
Model 37 Deerslayer II 600
Model 37 Deerslayer—1959-1987 . . . 597
Model 37 Deluxe Deerslayer—1959-1971 597
Model 37 Deluxe Field 600
Model 37 Deluxe Field English Style . 600
Model 37 DS Police Special—1962-1986 599
Model 37 Ducks Unlimited Commemorative, Auction Grade . . 598
Model 37 Ducks Unlimited Commemorative, Trade Grade 598

Model 37 English UltraLight—1982-1987 . . . 598
Model 37 Field Grade Magnum—1984-1987 . . . 598
Model 37 Field Grade Standard—1983-1985 . . . 597
Model 37 Field Grade Vent—1983-1986 . . . 597
Model 37 Law Enforcement Weapons 598
Model 37 Magnum 3" Chamber—1978-1987 . . . 598
Model 37 Military and Police (M&P)—1962-1986 . . . 598
Model 37 Military Marked (WWII) . . . 597
Model 37 New Classic . . . 601
Model 37 Presentation Series Centennial . . . 598
Model 37 Sporting Clays . . . 600
Model 37 Super Deluxe Deerslayer—1959-1987 . . . 597
Model 37 Supreme Grade—1967-1987 . . . 597
Model 37 Trap . . . 600
Model 37 Turkeyslayer . . . 601
Model 37 UltraLight—1978 to 1987 . . 598
Model 37 Ultra Featherlight Grouse Special . . . 600
Model 37 Ultra Featherlight Youth . . . 600
Model 37 Waterfowler . . . 601
Model 37 Women's Endowment Shotgun . . . 600
Model 37/Standard Grade—1937-1983 . . . 596
Model 37D/Deluxe—1955-1977 . . . 597
Model 37DV/Deluxe Vent Rib—1961-1987 . . . 597
Model 37R/Solid Rib—1940-1967 . . . 597
Model 37RD/Deluxe Solid Rib—1954-1962 . . . 597
Model 37RV/Deluxe Vent Rib—1961-1966 . . . 597
Model 37S/Skeet Grade—1937-1953 596
Model 37T/Trap—1937-1953 . . . 597
Model 37T/Target—1954-1961 . . . 597
Model 37V/Vent Rib—1961-1983 . . . 597
Model 49 Saddlegun—1961-1979 . . . 602
Model 49 Saddlegun Deluxe Grade . . 602
Model 49 Saddlegun Presentation Grade . . . 602
Model 49R—1968-1971 . . . 602
Model 51 Ducks Unlimited Commemorative . . . 601
Model 51 Presentation . . . 601
Model 51 Supreme Skeet . . . 601
Model 51 Supreme Trap . . . 601
Model 51A Deerslayer . . . 601
Model 51A Magnum . . . 601
Model 51A Standard . . . 601
Model 51A Turkey Gun . . . 601
Model 51A Waterfowler . . . 601
Model 66 Buck Buster (RS Barrel) . . . 596
Model 66 Vent Rib . . . 596
Model 66 Youth Grade . . . 596
Model 66—1963-1978 . . . 596
Model 87 Basic—1989-1994 . . . 599
Model 87 Camo—1987-1994 . . . 599
Model 87 Deerslayer Basic—1989-1996 . . . 599
Model 87 Deerslayer—1989-1996 . . . 599
Model 87 Deerslayer II—1988-1996 . 599
Model 87 Deluxe Deerslayer—1989-1996 . . . 599
Model 87 Deluxe—1987-1996 . . . 599
Model 87 DS Police Special—1987-1996 . . . 600
Model 87 English—1993-1996 . . . 599
Model 87 Field Grade—1987-1990 . . 599
Model 87 Home Protection and Law Enforcement Models . . . 600
Model 87 Magnum . . . 599
Model 87 Military & Police—1987-1996 . . . 600
Model 87 Supreme Grade—1987-1996 . . . 599
Model 87 Turkey Gun—1987-1996 . . . 599
Model 87 Ultralite Deluxe . . . 599
Model 87 Ultralite—1987-1990 . . . 599
Model A . . . 596
Serial numbered from 343336 to 398365 . . . 596
Model B . . . 596
Serial numbered from 425000 to 464699 . . . 596
Model X5-C . . . 601
Model X5T Lightning . . . 602
Model X-15 Lightning . . . 602
Model 72 Saddlegun—1973-1979 . . . 602
"New Double Bolted Hammer Gun" . . 590
Quality A . . . 590
Quality AA . . . 590
Quality B . . . 590
Quality X . . . 590
New Ithaca Double . . . 593
Field Grade . . . 593
Grade 1 . . . 593
Grade 2 . . . 593
Grade 3 . . . 593
Grade 4 . . . 593
Grade 5 . . . 593
Grade 7 . . . 593
Sousa Grade . . . 593
New Ithaca Gun . . . 590
Quality A . . . 590
Quality AA . . . 590
Quality B . . . 590
Quality X . . . 590
New Model 37 . . . 600
Rifled Deluxe . . . 600
Smooth Bore Deluxe . . . 600
Special Field Grade . . . 593
Grade 4E . . . 594
Grade 7E . . . 594
Sousa Grade . . . 594
X-Caliber . . . 602

IVER JOHNSON ARMS, INC. . . 602
.22 Target Single-Action . . . 603
1911 .45 . . . 606
1911 .22 LR . . . 606
American Bulldog . . . 604
Carbine .30 Caliber . . . 605
Cattleman Series . . . 604
Champion . . . 605
Delta-786 Carbine . . . 605
Frontier Four Derringer . . . 606
Hercules Grade . . . 605
JJ 9mm Carbine . . . 605
Li'L Champ . . . 605
Long Range Rifle . . . 605
Matted Rib Grade . . . 605
Model 2X . . . 605
Model 50 . . . 604
Model 55A Sportsmen Target . . . 603
Model 55S-A Cadet . . . 604
Model 57A Target . . . 604
Model 66 Trailsman . . . 604
Model 67 Viking . . . 604
Model 67S Viking Snub . . . 604
Model 844 . . . 603
Model 855 . . . 603
Model 1900 . . . 603
Model IJ .22 HB Semi-Automatic (Trail Blazer) . . . 605
Model X . . . 605
Model X300 Pony . . . 604
Model XA . . . 605
Petite . . . 603
Protector Sealed 8 . . . 603
Rookie . . . 604
Safety Automatic Double-Action . . . 602
Safety Cycle Automatic . . . 603
Silver Shadow . . . 606
Skeeter Model . . . 606
Slide Action Targetmaster . . . 605
Super Trap . . . 606
Supershot 9 . . . 603
Supershot Sealed 8 . . . 603
TP22/TP25 Pistol . . . 605
Trade Name Revolvers . . . 602
Trailsman . . . 604
Trap Grade . . . 605
Trigger Cocker Single-Action . . . 603
U.S. Carbine .22 Caliber . . . 605
Wagonmaster Model EW .22 HBL Lever Action . . . 605

IXL . . . 606
Navy Revolver . . . 606
Pocket Revolver . . . 606

J

JACQUESMART, JULES . . . 607
Le Monobloc . . . 607

JACQUITH, ELIJAH . . . 607
Revolving Under Hammer Rifle . . . 607

JAGER WAFFENFABIK . . . 607
Jager Semi-Automatic Pistol . . . 607

JAPANESE STATE MILITARY WEAPONS . . . 607

JEFFERY, W. J. & CO. LTD. . . . 607
Boxlock Double Rifle . . . 608
Sidelock Double Rifle . . . 608
Single-Shot . . . 607

JENISON, J. & CO. . . . 608
Under Hammer Pistol . . . 608

JENKS CARBINE . . . 608
Jenks "Mule Ear Carbine" . . . 608
Jenks Navy Rifle . . . 608

JENKS-HERKIMER . . . 608
Jenks Carbine . . . 608

JENKS-MERRILL . . . 608

JENNINGS . . . 608

JENNINGS F. A., INC. . . . 608
Bryco Model 25 . . . 608
Bryco Model 38 . . . 608
Bryco Model 48 . . . 609
J-22 . . . 608

JERICHO . . . 609
Jericho . . . 609

JIEFFCO . . . 609

JOHNSON AUTOMATIC RIFLE . . . 609

JOHNSON, STAN, BYE & CO. . 609
American Bulldog . . . 609
Defender, Eagle, Encore, Eureka, Favorite, Lion, Smoker, and Tycoon 609
Eclipse . . . 609

JOSEF JESCHER . . . 609

JOSLYN . . . 609
Model 1855 Carbine . . . 609
Model 1855 Rifle . . . 609

JOSLYN . . . 609
.50-70 Alteration . . . 610
Joslyn Breechloading Rifle . . . 609

JOSLYN FIREARMS COMPANY . . . 610
Army Model Revolver . . . 610

First Model . . . 610
Model 1862 Carbine . . . 610
Model 1864 Carbine . . . 610
Second Model . . . 610

JURRAS, LEE . . . 610
Howdah Pistol . . . 610

JUSTICE, P. S. . . . 610
Percussion Rifle . . . 610

K

K.F.C. . . . 611
E-1 Trap or Skeet Over-and-Under . . . 611
E-2 Trap or Skeet Over-and-Under . . . 611
Field Grade Over-and-Under . . . 611
Model 250 . . . 611

KAHR ARMS . . . 611
CW40 . . . 613
Kahr CW9 . . . 613
Kahr K9 . . . 611
Kahr K9 Compact Polymer Covert . . . 611
Kahr K9 Elite . . . 611
Kahr K40 . . . 612
Kahr K40 Covert . . . 612
Kahr K40 Elite . . . 612
Kahr Lady K9 . . . 611
Kahr MK9 . . . 613
Kahr MK9 Elite . . . 611
Kahr MK40 . . . 613
Kahr MK40 Elite . . . 613
Kahr P9 Compact Polymer . . . 611
Kahr P40 . . . 613
Kahr P45 . . . 613
Kahr PM9 . . . 612
Kahr PM9 Micro . . . 612
Kahr TP9 . . . 611
Model 1911 Standard . . . 614
Model 1911C . . . 614
Model 1911PKZ . . . 614
Model 1911WGS Deluxe . . . 614
TP40 . . . 612
Wilson Combat Kahr Pistols . . . 614

KASSNAR IMPORTS, INC. . . . 614
Deluxe Over-and-Under . . . 614
Deluxe Side-by-Side . . . 614
Standard Over-and-Under . . . 614
Standard Side-by-Side . . . 614

KBI, INC. . . . 614
PSP-25 . . . 614

KDF, INC. . . . 614
Brescia . . . 615
Condor . . . 614
K-14 Insta Fire Rifle . . . 615
K-15 . . . 615
K-15 Dangerous Game . . . 615
K-15 Pro-Hunter . . . 615
K-15 Swat Rifle . . . 615
K-16 . . . 615
K-22 . . . 615
K-22 Deluxe . . . 615
K-22 Deluxe Custom . . . 615
K-22 Deluxe Special Select . . . 615
Model 2005 . . . 615
Model 2107 . . . 615
Model 2112 . . . 615
Titan .411 KDF Mag. . . . 615
Titan II Magnum . . . 615
Titan II Standard . . . 615
Titan Menor . . . 615

KEBERST INTERNATIONAL . . . 615
Keberst Model 1A . . . 615

KEL-TEC CNC INDUSTRIES . . . 615
P-3AT . . . 616
P-11 . . . 615
P-32 . . . 616
P-40 . . . 616
PLR-16 . . . 616
RFB Rifle . . . 616
SU-16 . . . 616
SUB-2000 Rifle . . . 616

KEMPER, SHRIVER & COMPANY . . . 616

KENDALL, INTERNATIONAL . . . 616

KENDALL, NICANOR . . . 617
Under Hammer Pistol . . . 617

KENO . . . 617
Derringer . . . 617

KERR . . . 617
Kerr Revolver . . . 617

KERR . . . 617

KESSLER ARMS CORPORATION . . . 617
Bolt-Action Shotgun . . . 617
Levermatic Shotgun . . . 617

KETTNER, EDWARD . . . 617
Drilling . . . 617

KIMBALL ARMS COMPANY . . . 617
Semi-Automatic Pistol . . . 617

KIMBER MFG., INC. . . . 617
.22 LR Conversion Kit . . . 637
8400 Classic Select Grade . . . 622
Anniversary Custom . . . 626
Anniversary Gold Match . . . 626
Anniversary Match Pair Custom . . . 626
Augusta Field . . . 623
Augusta Skeet . . . 623
Grade I . . . 623
Grade II . . . 623
Augusta Sporting . . . 623
Augusta Trap . . . 623
BP Ten II . . . 628, 635
Brownell . . . 618
Cascade Model . . . 618
Centennial . . . 618
Classic . . . 620
Classic Varmint . . . 620
Combat Carry . . . 631
Compact . . . 629
Compact Aluminum . . . 629
Compact Stainless . . . 629
Compact Stainless II . . . 629
Compact Stainless Aluminum . . . 629
Continental . . . 618
Custom . . . 624
Custom Aegis II . . . 637
Custom CDP . . . 633
Custom CDP II . . . 633
Custom Classic . . . 620
Custom Classic Model . . . 618
Custom Covert II . . . 636
Custom Heritage Edition . . . 624
Custom II . . . 624
Custom Match Limited Edition . . . 621
Custom Royal . . . 625
Custom Royal II . . . 625
Custom Stainless . . . 624
Custom Target . . . 624
Custom TLE II (Tactical Law Enforcement) . . . 624
Custom TLE/RL II . . . 625
Custom TLE/RL II Special Edition . . . 625
Deluxe Grade . . . 618
Desert Warrior . . . 626
Eclipse Custom II . . . 634
Eclipse Pro II . . . 634
Eclipse Pro Target II . . . 634
Eclipse Target II . . . 634
Eclipse Ultra II . . . 634
Elite Carry . . . 630
Gold Combat . . . 631
Gold Combat II . . . 631
Gold Combat RL II . . . 632
Gold Combat Stainless . . . 631
Gold Guardian . . . 631
Gold Match . . . 626
Gold Match II . . . 626
Gold Match Ten II . . . 628, 635
Gold Team Match II . . . 626
Grand Raptor . . . 632
HS (Hunter Silhouette) . . . 621
Hunter . . . 620, 621
KPD 40 . . . 636
LTP II . . . 631, 632
Marias Grade I . . . 623
Marias Grade II . . . 623
Mini Classic . . . 618
Model 82 Classic . . . 617
Model 82A Government . . . 618
Model 82C Classic . . . 619
Model 82C Custom Match . . . 619
Model 82C Custom Shop SuperAmerica (Basic) . . . 619
Model 82C HS (Hunter Silhouette) . . . 619
Model 84C Single-Shot Varmint . . . 619
Model 82C Stainless Classic Limited Edition . . . 619
Model 82C Super America . . . 619
Model 82C SVT (Short Varmint/Target) . . . 619
Model 84 Series—Discontinued Models . . . 618
Classic Model . . . 618
Continental . . . 618
Custom Classic Model . . . 618
Deluxe Grade Sporter . . . 618
Super America . . . 618
Super Continental . . . 618
Super Grade . . . 618
Model 84M Classic . . . 621
Model 84M LongMaster Classic . . . 622
Model 84M LongMaster Pro . . . 622
Model 84M LongMaster VT . . . 622
Model 84M Montana . . . 621
Model 84M Pro Varmint . . . 621
Model 84M SuperAmerica . . . 621
Model 84M SVT . . . 622
Model 84M Tactical . . . 622
Model 84M Varmint . . . 621
Model 89 Series/BGR (Big Game Rifles) . . . 619
Classic Model . . . 619
Custom Classic Model . . . 619
Deluxe Grade . . . 619
Super America . . . 619
Super Grade . . . 619
Model 8400 Advanced Tactical . . . 622
Model 8400 Classic . . . 622
Model 8400 Montana . . . 622
Model 8400 SuperAmerica . . . 622
Model 8400 Tactical . . . 622
Polymer . . . 627
Polymer Pro Carry Stainless . . . 627
Polymer Stainless . . . 627
Polymer Stainless Gold Match . . . 627
Polymer Stainless Target . . . 627
Polymer Target . . . 627
Predator . . . 618
Hunter Grade . . . 618
Super Grade . . . 618
Pro Aegis II . . . 636
Pro BP Ten II . . . 628, 635
Pro Carry II . . . 629
Pro Carry II Night Sights . . . 629
Pro Carry Stainless . . . 629

Pro Carry Stainless Night Sights 630
Pro Carry Ten II 628, 635
Pro CDP 633
Pro CDP II 633
Pro Covert II 636
Pro Raptor II 632
Pro TLE/RL II 630
Pro Varmint 620, 621
Raptor II 632
Rimfire Custom 637
Rimfire Super 637
Rimfire Target 637
Royal Carry 630
Sporterized Model 98 Swedish
Mausers 619-620
Stainless Gold Match 626
Stainless II 625
Stainless II (polished) 625
Stainless Limited Edition 624
Stainless Pro TLE/RL II 630
Stainless Target II 625
Stainless Target II 9mm/10mm 625
Stainless Target II (polished) ... 625
Stainless Target Limited Edition . 625
Stainless Ten II 635
Super America 618
Super Continental 618
Super Grade 618
Super Match 631
Super Match II 631
Super Varmint 618
SuperAmerica 620, 633
SVT (Short Varmint/Target) 620
Tactical Custom II 635
Tactical Pro II 636
Tactical Ultra II 636
Target Match 632
Team Match II .38 Super 627
Ultra Aegis II 637
Ultra Carry 630
Ultra Carry II 630
Ultra Carry Stainless 630
Ultra Carry Stainless II 630
Ultra CDP 633
Ultra CDP II 633
Ultra Covert II 636
Ultra Raptor II 632
Ultra RCP II 632
Ultra Ten II 628, 634
Ultra Ten CDP II 628
Ultra Varmint 618
Warrior 625
Youth 621

KIMBER OF AMERICA 638

KIMBER OF OREGON, INC. .. 638

KING PIN 638
Derringer 638

KIRRIKALE, ENDUSTRISI 638
Kirrikale Pistol 638

KLIPZIG & COMPANY 638
Pocket Pistol 638

KNICKERBOCKER 638
Double-Barrel Shotgun 638
Knickerbocker Pistol nfa 638

KNIGHT RIFLES 638
American Knight 639
Bighorn Magnum 638
Disc Magnum 638
HK-94 Hawkeye Pistol 639
Knight Long Range Hunter 639
Knight Rolling Block Rifle 639
LK-93 Wolverine 639
LK-93 Wolverine Youth 639
MK-85 Hunter 639
MK-85 Knight Hawk 639
MK-85 Predator 639
MK-86 Shotgun 639
MK-85 Stalker 639
T-Bolt Magnum 639

KNIGHT'S MANUFACTURING CO. 639
SR-15 E3 URX Carbine 640
SR-15 M-4 Carbine 640
SR-15 M-5 Rifle 639
SR-15 Match 639
SR-25 Competition Match 640
SR-25 Lightweight Match 640
SR-25 Match 640
SR-25 Mk11 Mod 0 Match Rifle 640
SR-25 Stoner Carbine 640
SR-50 Rifle 640

KOHOUT & SPOLECNOST ... 640
Mars 640
Niva, PZK 640

KOLB, HENRY M. 641
Baby Hammerless 641
New Baby Hammerless 641

KOLIBRI 641
2.7mm 641
3mm 641

KOMMER, THEODOR WAFFENFABRIK 641
Model 1 641
Model 2 641
Model 3 642
Model 4 642

KONGSBERG 642
Classic Rifle 642
Thumbhole Sporter 642

KORRIPHILIA 642
HSP 642
HSP—Single-Action Only 642
Odin's Eye 642

KORTH 642
Combat Revolver 643
Match Revolver 643
Semi-Automatic Pistol 642

KRAG JORGENSEN 643

KRAUSER, ALFRED 643
Helfricht or Helkra 643

KRICO 643
Model 300 643
Model 302 and 304 643
Model 311 Smallbore 643
Model 320 643
Model 340 643
Model 340 Kricotronic 643
Model 340 Mini-Sniper 643
Model 360S Biathlon Rifle 644
Model 360S2 Biathlon Rifle 644
Model 400 Match 644
Model 400 Sporter 644
Model 420 644
Model 440 644
Model 500 Kricotronic Match Rifle . 644
Model 600 Match Rifle 644
Model 600 Sniper Rifle 644
Model 600 Sporter 644
Model 620 644
Model 640 Deluxe Sniper Rifle 644
Model 640 Sniper Rifle 644
Model 640 Varmint Rifle 644
Model 700 Sporter 644
Model 720 644
Model 720 Limited Edition 645
Sporting Carbine 643
Sporting Rifle 643
Varmint Special Rifle 643

KRIDER, J. H. 645
Militia Rifle 645
Pocket Pistol 645

KRIEGHOFF, HEINRICH, GUN CO. 645
Classic 646
Classic Big Five 646
KS-5 Single Barrel Trap 647
KS-5 Special 647
KS-80 Trap 647
Over-and-Under Trap 647
Top Single Trap 647
Trap Combos 647
Unsingle Trap 647
K-80 Sporting Clays 647
K-80 Skeet 647
4 Barrel Set 647
International Skeet 647
Lightweight Skeet 647
Standard Weight Skeet 647
Model 32 Standard 646
Crown Grade 646
Monte Carlo Grade 646
San Remo Grade 646
Single Barrel Trap Gun 646
Super Crown Grade 646
Neptun Dural 645
Neptun Model 645
Neptun Primus Dural 645
Neptun Primus Model 645
Plus Model 645
Teck 646
Teck Dural 646
Teck Over-and-Under 645
Trumpf Dural 645
Trumpf Model 645
Ulm 646
Ulm Dural 646
Ulm Model 645
Ulm Primus 645-646
Ulm Primus Dural 646
Ultra 646-647

KRNKA, KAREL 648
Model 1892 648

KROPATSCHEK 648
Model 1878 648

KSN INDUSTRIES 648
GAL 649
Golan 648
Kareen MK II 648
Kareen MK II-Compact 649

KUFAHL, G. L. 649
Kufahl Needle-Fire Revolver 649

KYNOCH GUN FACTORY 649
Early Double Trigger Revolver 649
Late Double Trigger Revolver 649

L

LAGRESE 650
Lagrese Revolver 650

LAHTI 650
Lahti 650

LAKELANDER 650
Model 389 Classic 650
Model 389 Match-Maker 650
Model 389 Premium 650

LAMB, H. C. & CO. 650
Muzzle Loading Rifle 650

LAMES 650
California Trap Grade 651
Field Grade 651
Skeet or Trap Grade 650

LANBER ARMAS S.A. 651
Model 844 EST 651
Model 844 EST CHR 651
Model 844 MST 651
Model 844 ST 651
Model 2004 LCH 651
Model 2008 LCH and Model 2009 LCH 651

LANCASTER, CHARLES 651
2 Barreled Pistol 651
4 Barreled Pistol 651
4 Barreled Shotgun 652
Bolt Action Rifle 652

LANG, J. 652
Gas Seal Revolver 652
Percussion Pistol 652

LANGENHAN, FRIEDRICH . . . 652
Langenhan Army Model 652
Langenhan Closed Model 652
Langenhan Open Model 652
Model 2 652
Model 3 653

LAR MFG. CO. 653
Grizzly 50 Big Boar 653
Grizzly Mark I 653
Grizzly Mark II 653
Grizzly Mark IV 653
Grizzly Mark V 653
Grizzly State Pistol 653

LASALLE 654
Semi-Automatic Shotgun 654
Slide-Action Shotgun 654

LASERAIM ARMS 654
Series I 654
Series II 654
Series III 654

LAURONA 654
Model 11 656
Model 13 656
Model 13E 656
Model 13X 656
Model 13XE 656
Model 15 Economic Pluma 656
Model 15E Economic Pluma 656
Model 15X 656
Model 15XE 656
Model 52 Pluma 656
Model 52E Pluma 656
Model 67 654
Model 71 654
Model 82 Game 654
Model 82 Pigeon Competition 655
Model 82 Super Game 654
Model 82 Super Pigeon 655
Model 82 Super Skeet 655
Model 82 Super Trap (U only) 655
Model 82 Trap Combi 654
Model 82 Trap Competition 655
Model 84S Super Game 655
Model 83MG Super Game 655
Model 84S Super Trap 655
Model 85MS Special Sporting 655
Model 85MS Super Game 655
Model 85MS Super Pigeon 655
Model 85MS Super Trap 655
Model 84S SuperSkeet 655
Silhouette 300 Trap 655
Silhouette 300 Sporting Clays 656
Silhouette 300 Ultra Magnum 656
Laurona Side-by-Side Sidelocks 656
Model 103 656
Model 103E 656
Model 104X 656
Model 104XE 656
Model 105X Feather 656
Model 105XE Feather 656
Model 502 Feather 657
Model 801 Deluxe 657
Model 802 Eagle 657

LAW ENFORCEMENT ORDNANCE CORP. 657
Striker 12 657

LAZZERONI ARMS COMPANY 657
Model 700ST 658
Model 2000 ST-F 657
Model 2000 ST-W 657
Model 2000DG 657
Model 2000SA 657
Model 2000ST-28 657
Model 2000ST-FW 657
Model 2000SLR 657
Model 2000SP-F 657
Model 2000SP-FW 657
Model 2000SP-W 657
Sako TRG-S 658
Savage 16 LZ 658
Swarovski P.H. 3-12x50 Rifle 658

LE FORGERON 658
Boxlock Shotgun 658
Model 6020 Double Rifle 658
Model 6030 658
Model 6040 658
Sidelock Shotgun 658

LE FRANCAIS 658
Gaulois 658
Le Francais Model 28 (Type Armee) . 658
Officer's Model (Pocket Model) . . . 659
Police Model (Type Policeman) 658
Target Model (Type Champion) 659

LE MAT 659
Baby LeMat 659
LeMat 659
LeMat Revolving Carbine 660

LE PAGE SA. 660
Pinfire Revolver 660
Pocket Pistol 660
Semi-Automatic Pistol 660

LEBEAU COURALLY 660
Boxlock Side-by-Side 660
Express Rifle 660
Over-and-Under Boss-Verees 660
Sidelock Side-by-Side 660

LEBEL 660

LEE FIREARMS CO. 660
Lee Single-Shot Carbine 660
Lee Sporting Rifle 661

LEE-ENFIELD 661

LEE-METFORD 661

LEECH & RIGDON 661
Leech & Rigdon Revolver 661

LEFAUCHAUX, CASIMER & EUGENE 661
Pinfire Revolver 661

LEFEVER ARMS CO. 661
A Grade (Model 5) 663
Double-Barrel Ventilated Rib Trap (Model 4) 662
Long Range Single-Barrel Trap and Field (Model 2) 662
Nitro Special 662
Sideplated Shotgun 661
A Grade 662
AA Grade 662
B Grade 662
BE Grade 662
C Grade 662
CE Grade 662
D Grade 662
DE Grade 662
DS Grade 662
DSE Grade 662
E Grade 662
EE Grade 662
F Grade 662
FE Grade 662
G Grade 662
GE Grade 662
H Grade 661
HE Grade 661
Single-Barrel Trap Ventilated Rib (Model 3) 662
Skeet Special (Model 6) 663

LEFEVER, D. M., SONS & COMPANY 663
Lefever Double-Barrel Shotgun 663
AA Grade, No. 4 663
B Grade, No. 5 663
C Grade, No. 6 663
D Grade, No. 7 663
E Grade, No. 8 663
Excelsior Grade—Auto Ejectors . . 663
F Grade, No. 9 663
O Excelsior Grade—Extractors . . . 663

LEMAN, H. E. 663
Leman Militia Rifle 663

LEONARD, G. 663
Pepperbox 663

LES, INC. 664
Rogak P-18 664

LEWIS, G.E. 664

LIDDLE & KAEDING 664
Pocket Revolver 664

LIEGEOISE D ARMES 664
Liegeoise Pistol 664
Side-by-Side Boxlock Shotgun 664

LIGNOSE 664
Einhand Model 2A 664
Einhand Model 3A 665
Lignose Model 2 664
Lignose Model 3 664
Liliput Model I 664

LILLIPUT 665

LINDE A. 665
Pocket Pistol 665

LINDSAY, JOHN P. 665
2 Shot Belt Pistol 665
2 Shot Martial Pistol 665
2 Shot Pocket Pistol 665

LINS, A. F. 666
Pocket Pistol 666
Rifled Musket 666

LITTLE SHARPS RIFLE MFG. CO. 666
Little Sharps Rifle 666

LJUNGMAN 666

LJUTIC INDUSTRIES 666
Bi-Gun Combo 667
Bi-Gun Over-and-Under 666

Bi-Matic Semi-Automatic 666
Dynatrap Single-Barrel 666
LM-6 Super Deluxe 667
LTX Model 666
Model X-73 Single-Barrel 666
Mono Gun Single-Barrel 666
Space Gun 666

LLAMA 667
Llama Comanche I 671
Llama Comanche II 671
Llama Comanche III 671
Llama Compact Frame Semi-Automatic 670
Llama Large Frame Semi-Automatic . 670
Llama Martial 671
Llama Small Frame Semi-Automatic . 670
Llama Super Comanche 671
Micro-Max 669
Mini-Max Sub Compact 669
Mini-Max Sub Compact 669
Model 82 670
Model 87 Competition 670
Model I-A 667
Model II 667
Model III 667
Model III-A 667
Model IV 667
Model IX 667
Model IX-A 668
Model IX-B 668
Model IX-C 668
Model IX-D 668
Model Max-I 669
Model Max-I with Compensator 669
Model Mini-Max 669
Model Omni 668
Model V 667
Model VI 667
Model VII 667
Model VIII 667
Model X 668
Model X-A 668
Model XI 668
Model XI-B 668
Model XII 670
Model XII-B 668
Model XIII 671
Model XIV 671
Model XV 668
Model XVI 668
Model XVII 668
Model XVIII 668
Model XXII Olimpico 671
Model XXIX Olimpico 671
Model XXVI 671
Model XXVII 671
Model XXVIII 671
Model XXXII Olimpico 671
Mugica 670
Ruby Extra Models 670
Tauler 670

LOEWE, LUDWIG & CO. 671
Loewe Smith & Wesson Russian Revolver 671

LOHNER, C. 672
Pocket Pistol 672

LOMBARD, H. C. & CO. 672
Pocket Pistol 672

LONDON ARMOURY COMPANY 672

LONE STAR RIFLE COMPANY 672
Sporting Rifle 672
Target Rifle 672

LORCIN ENGINEERING CO., INC. 672
Derringer 673
Model I-380 10th Anniversary 672
Model L-9mm 673
Model L-22 672
Model L-25 672
Model L-32 673
Model L-380 672
Model LH-380 673
Model LT-25 672

LOWELL ARMS CO. 673

LOWER, J. P. 673

LUGERS 673
.45 ACP 684
2nd Series Krieghoff Commercial 683
4 Digit Dated Krieghoff 683
36 Date Krieghoff 683
41/42 Code 681
1899/1900 Swiss Test Model 673
1900 American Eagle 674
1900 Bulgarian Contract 674
1900 Carbine 674
1900 Commercial 673
1900 Swiss Contract 673
1902 American Eagle 674
1902 American Eagle Cartridge Counter 674
1902 Carbine 674
1902 Commercial—"Fat Barrel" 674
1902 Presentation Carbine 674
1902 Prototype 674
1902/06 Carbine (Transitional) 674
1903 Commercial 674
1904 Navy 674
1906 American Eagle 675
1906 American Eagle (Marked Safety) 675
1906 American Eagle 4.75" Barrel . . . 675
1906 Brazilian Contract 676
1906 Bulgarian Contract 676
1906 Commercial 675
1906 Commercial (Marked Safety) . . . 675
1906 Dutch Contract 676
1906 Navy 1st Issue 677
1906 Navy 2nd Issue 677
1906 Navy Commercial 675
1906 Republic of Portugal Navy 676
1906 Royal Portuguese Army (M2) . . . 676
1906 Royal Portuguese Navy 676
1906 Russian Contract 676
1906 Swiss Commercial 675
1906 Swiss Military 675
1906 Swiss Police Cross in Shield . . . 675
1906 U.S. Army Test Luger .45 Caliber 675
1906 Vickers Dutch 680
1908 Commercial 677
1908 Erfurt 680
1908 Military 1st Issue 677
1908 Military Dated Chamber (1910-1913) 677
1908 Navy 677
1908 Navy Commercial 677
1913 Commercial 678
1914 Artillery 678
1914 Erfurt Artillery 680
1914 Erfurt Military 680
1914 Military 678
1914 Navy 677
1920 Carbine 678
1920 Commercial 678
1920 Commercial Artillery 678
1920 Commercial Navy 678
1920 Long Barrel Commercial 678
1920 Navy Carbine 678
1920 Police Rework 678
1920 Swiss Commercial 679
1923 Commercial 679
1923 Commercial Safe & Loaded 679
1923 Dutch Commercial & Military . . . 679
1923 DWM/Krieghoff Commercial . . . 682
1923 Stoeger Commercial 679
1934 Mauser Commercial 681
1934 Mauser Dutch Contract 682
1934 Mauser German Contract 682
1934 Mauser Swedish Commercial . . 682
1934 Mauser Swedish Contract 682
1934/06 Dated Commercial 681
1934/06 Swiss Commercial Mauser . . 681
1935/06 Portuguese "GNR" 681
Abercrombie & Fitch Commercial 100 679
Artillery Stock with Holster 683
Austrian Bundes Heer (Federal Army) 682
Baby Luger .380 ACP 684
Baby Luger 9mm & 7.65mm 684
byf Code 681
Cartridge Counter 684
Code 42 Dated Chamber 681
Commemorative Bulgarian 684
Commemorative Russian 684
Dated Chamber S/42 681
Deaths Head Rework 680
Detachable Carbine Stocks 683
Double Date Erfurt 680
Drum Carrying Case 684
Drum Magazine 1st Issue 683
Drum Magazine 2nd Issue 684
Drum Magazine Loading Tool 684
Drum Magazine Unloading Tool 684
DWM Double Dated 678
DWM/Krieghoff Commercial 682
Grip Safety Krieghoff 683
Holsters 684
Ideal Stock/Holster with Grips 683
Kadetten Institute Rework 680
Krieghoff Commercial Inscribed Side Frame 682
Krieghoff Post-war Commercial 683
Ku Luger (Prefix or suffix) 682
Martz Luger Carbine 684
Mauser 2 Digit Date 682
Mauser Oberndorf 680
Mauser Unmarked Rework 680
Modern Production Carbine 684
Navy Stock without Holster 683
P.08 Interarms 684
Persian Contract 4" 681
Persian Contract Artillery 681
Post-war Krieghoff 683
Royal Dutch Air Force 679
S Code Krieghoff 682
S/42 Commercial Contract 681
S/42 G Date 681
S/42 K Date 681
Simson & Co. Rework 680
Simson Dated Military 680
Simson Grip Safety Rework 680
Simson S Code 680
Swiss Eagle Interarms 684

LUNA 684
Model 200 Free Pistol 684
Model 300 Free Pistol 684
Target Rifle 685

LYMAN 685
Deerstalker Rifle 685
Deerstalker Carbine 685
Great Plains Rifle 685
Lyman In-Line 685
Plains Pistol 685
Trade Rifle 685

M

M.O.A. CORP. 686
Carbine 686
Maximum 686
MAB 686
MAC 686
MAS 686
MACNAUGHTON & SON 686
MADSEN 686
Model 47 686
MAGNUM RESEARCH, INC. . . 686
BFR (Long Cylinder) 686
BFR Little Max (Short Cylinder) 686
IMI SP-21 686
MAKAROV 686
MALIN, F. E. 687
Boxlock 687
Basic Model 687
Sidelock 687
Basic Model 687
MALTBY, HENLEY AND CO. . . 687
Spencer Safety Hammerless Revolver 687
MANHATTAN FIREARMS COMPANY 687
.22 Caliber Pocket Revolver 688
.36 Caliber Percussion Revolver 688
Model I 688
Model II 688
Model III 688
Model IV 688
Model V 688
American Standard Manufactured 688
Bar Hammer Pistol 687
London Pistol Company 688
Manhattan Manufactured 688
Manhattan-American Standard Hero 688
Pepperbox 687
Five-shot with 3", 4", 5" Barrel 687
Six-shot with 3" or 4" Barrel 687
Six-shot with 5" Barrel 687
Three-shot with 3" Barrel 687
Pocket Revolver 687
First Model—Five-Shot 687
Second Model—Six-Shot 687
Shotgun Hammer Pistol 687
MANN, FRITZ 688
6.35mm Pocket Pistol 688
7.65mm Pocket Pistol 688
MANNLICHER PISTOL 688
MANNLICHER SCHOENAUER 688
High Velocity Rifle 689
Model 1903 Carbine 688
Model 1905 Carbine 689
Model 1908 Carbine 689
Model 1910 Carbine 689
Model 1924 Carbine 689
Model 1950 689
Model 1950 Carbine 689
Model 1950 6.5 Carbine 689
Model 1952 689
Model 1952 Carbine 689
Model 1952 6.5mm Carbine 689
Model 1956 Carbine 689
Model 1956 Rifle 689
Model 1961 MCA Rifle 689
Model 1961 MCA Carbine 689
Model M72 LM Rifle 689
MANUFRANCE 689
Auto Stand 689
Buffalo Stand 690
Le Agent 690
Le Colonial 690
LeFrancais 690
MANURHIN 690
Model 73 Convertible 690
Model 73 Defense Revolver 690
Model 73 Gendarmerie 690
Model 73 Sport 690
Model 73 Silhouette 690
Model PP 690
Model PP Sports 691
Model PPK/S 690
MARATHON PRODUCTS, INC. 691
.22 First Shot 691
.22 Super Shot 691
.22 Hot Shot Pistol 691
Centerfire Rifle 691
MARBLE'S ARMS & MFG. CO. 691
Marble's Game Getter Gun nfa, curio or relic 691
Marble's Game Getter Pistol and other special-order or experimental Game Getters nfa, curio or relic 692
Model 1908 691
Model 1921 691
MARGOLIN 692
Model MT Sports 692
Model MTS-1 693
Model MTS-2 693
MARIETTE BREVETTE 693
4 Barrel Pepperbox 693
6 Barrel Pepperbox 693
MARLIN FIREARMS CO. 693
1st Model Derringer 698
1970 100th Year Commemorative Matched Pair 706
Ballard Rifles 693
Lightweight Model 701
Little Joker Revolver 700
Marlin 38 Standard 1878 Pocket Revolver 701
Marlin 1887 Double-Action Revolver 701
Marlin Glenfield Lever-Action Rifles 711
Marlin No. 32 Standard 1875 Pocket Revolver 701
Marlin "Trap Gun" 722
Marlin XX Standard 1873 Pocket Revolver 700
Early Octagon Barrel Model 700
Round Barrel—Fluted Cylinder 700
Round Barrel—Non-Fluted Cylinder 701
Marlin XXX Standard 1872 Pocket Revolver 700
Octagon Barrel—Early Variation 700
Round Barrel—Long Fluted Cylinder 700
Round Barrel—Non-Fluted Cylinder 700
Round Barrel—Short Fluted Cylinder 700
Model .410 Deluxe 724
Model .410 Lever-Action Shotgun (Old) 724
Model .410 (New) 724
Model 9 Camp Carbine 715
Model 9N 715
Model 15N 718
Model 15YN 718
Model 15YS (Youth) 718
Model 16 Slide-Action Shotgun 721
Grade A 721
Grade B 721
Grade C 721
Grade D 721
Model 17 Brush Gun 721
Model 17 Riot Gun 721
Model 17 Slide-Action Shotgun 721
Model 17V 718
Model 17VS 718
Model 18 Slide-Action Rifle 704
Model 19 Slide-Action Shotgun 721
Grade A 722
Grade B 722
Grade C 722
Grade D 722
Model 20 Slide-Action Rifle 704
Model 21 "Trap" Slide-Action Shotgun 722
Grade A 722
Grade B 722
Grade C 722
Grade D 722
Model 24 Slide-Action Shotgun 722
Grade A 722
Grade B 722
Grade C 722
Grade D 722
Model 25 Slide-Action Rifle 704
Model 25MG 726
Model 25MN 718
Model 25MNC 718
Model 25N 717
Model 25NC 718
Model 26 Brush Gun 722
Model 26 Riot Gun 722
Model 26 Slide-Action Shotgun 722
Model 27 Slide-Action Rifle 704
Model 27S Slide-Action Rifle 704
Model 28 Hammerless Slide-Action Shotgun 722
Grade A 722
Grade B 722
Grade C 722
Grade D 722
Model 28T Trap Gun 723
Model 28TS Trap Gun 722
Model 29 Slide-Action Rifle 705
Model 30 Field Grade 723
Model 30 Slide-Action Shotgun 723
Grade A 723
Grade B 723
Grade C 723
Grade D 723
Model 30AS 708
Model 30AW 712
Model 31 Slide-Action Shotgun 723
Grade A 723
Grade B 723
Grade C 723
Grade D 723
Model 32 Slide-Action Rifle 705
Model 36 Lever-Action Rifle or Carbine (1937-1948) 705
Third Variation—Blued Receiver 705
Model 36 Sporting Carbine 706
Model 36A-DL Lever-Action Rifle 706
Model 37 Slide-Action Rifle 705
Model 38 Slide-Action Rifle 705
Model 39 712
Deluxe Rifle 712
Standard Rifle 712
Model 39 Lever-Action Rifle 712
Model 39A 1960 Presentation Model 712
Model 39A Lever-Action Rifle 712
"Golden 39A's" 712
Post-war Variations 712
Pre-war Variations 712
Model 39A Mountie 712
1st Variation 712
Standard 712
Model 39 Carbine 713

Model 39 Century Limited 713
Model 39A Article II 713
Model 39A Octagon 713
Model 39ADL Lever-Action Rifle 713
Model 39AS Lever-Action Rifle 713
Model 39AWL 714
Model 39D Lever-Action Rifle 713
Model 39M Article II 713
Model 39M Mountie 1960
Presentation Model 713
Model 39M Octagon 713
Model 39TDS Lever-Action Rifle 713
Model 40 Slide-Action Rifle 705
Model 42/42A Slide-Action Shotgun . 723
Model 43A Slide-Action Shotgun 723
Model 43T Slide-Action Shotgun 723
Model 43TS Slide-Action Shotgun . . . 723
Model 44A Slide-Action Shotgun 723
Model 44S Slide-Action Shotgun 723
Model 45 Camp Carbine 715
Model 47 Slide-Action Rifle 705
Model 49 Slide-Action Shotgun 723
Model 50DL 725
Model 53 Slide-Action Shotgun 724
Model 55 Bolt-Action Shotgun 725
Model 55 Goose Gun 725
Model 55 Swamp Gun 725
Model 55GDL 726
Model 55S Slug Gun 725
Model 56 "Clipper King" Levermatic . . 714
Model 56 Levermatic Rifle 714
Model 57 Levermatic Rifle 714
Model 57M Levermatic Rifle 714
Model 60 716
Model 60 Single-Barrel Shotgun 724
Model 60C 716
Model 60DL 716
Model 60SB 716
Model 60SN 716
Model 60SS 716
Model 60SSK 716
Model 62 Levermatic Rifle 714
Model 63 Slide-Action Shotgun 724
Model 63T Slide-Action Shotgun 724
Model 63TS Slide-Action Shotgun . . . 724
Model 70HC 714
Model 70P "Papoose" 714
Model 70PSS 715
Model 81TS 718
Model 83TS 719
Model 90 Over-and-Under Shotgun . . 724
Model 120 Slide-Action Shotgun 725
Model 308MX 711
Model 308MXLR 711
Model 322 Bolt-Action Rifle 716
Model 336 706
Model 336 .44 Magnum 706
Model 336 Carbine
(R.C. Regular Carbine) 706
Model 336 "Centennial" 706
Model 336 Cowboy 707
Model 336 "Marauder" 706
Model 336 MicroGroove Zipper 706
Model 336 Octagon 707
Model 336 "Zane Grey Century" 707
Model 336A 706
Model 336ADL 706
Model 336C 706
Model 336CC 707
Model 336CS 707
Model 336DT 706
Model 336ER (Extra Range) 707
Model 336LTS 707
Model 336M 707
Model 336SC (Sporting Carbine) 706
Model 336SD
(Sporting Deluxe Carbine) 706
Model 336T (Texan) 706
Model 336XLR 707
Model 336Y "Spike Horn" 707
Model 375 Lever-Action 708
Model 422 Bolt-Action Rifle 716
Model 444 Lever-Action 708
Model 444S 708
Model 444SS 708
Model 444P Outfitter 708
Model 444XLR 708
Model 455 Bolt-Action Rifle 717
Model 512 Slugmaster 726
Model 512DL Slugmaster 726
Model 512P 726
Model 717M2 719
Model 778 Slide-Action Shotgun
(Glenfield) 725
Model 795 716
Model 795SS 716
Model 880 717
Model 880SQ 717
Model 880SS 717
Model 881 717
Model 882 719
Model 882L 719
Model 882SS 717, 719
Model 882SSV 719
Model 883 719
Model 883N 719
Model 883SS 719
Model 917 720
Model 917M2 720
Model 917M2S 720
Model 917V 720
Model 917VR 720
Model 917VS 720
Model 917VSF 720
Model 922M 715
Model 925 721
Model 925C 721
Model 925M 721
Model 925MC 721
Model 980S 721
Model 980S-CF 721
Model 980V 721
Model 981T 721
Model 982 720
Model 982L 720
Model 982S 720
Model 982VS 720
Model 983 720
Model 983S 720
Model 983T 720
Model 995 715
Model 995SS 715
Model 990L 715
Model 1881 Lever-Action Rifle 701
Model 1888 Lever-Action Rifle 702
Model 1889 Lever-Action Rifle 702
Carbine 20" Barrel and Saddle
Ring on Left Side of Receiver . 702
Musket 702
Production Model 702
Short Carbine 702
Model 1891 Lever-Action Rifle 702
1st Variation 702
2nd Variation 702
Model 1892 Lever-Action Rifle 702
.32 Rimfire and Centerfire 703
Model 1893 Lever-Action Rifle 703
Antique Production (Pre-1898) . . . 703
Modern Production 1899-1935 . . . 703
Model 1894 Century Limited 709
Model 1894 Century Limited
Employee Edition 709
Model 1894 Cowboy 709
Model 1894 Cowboy 32 709
Model 1894 Cowboy Competition . . . 710
Model 1894 Cowboy II 709
Model 1894 Lever-Action 708
Model 1894 Lever-Action Rifle 703
Antique Production (Pre-1898) . . . 703
Modern Production (1899-1935) . . 703
Model 1894 Octagon Barrel 708
Model 1894 Sporter 708
Model 1894CL (Classic) Lever-Action
Rifle 709
Model 1894CL (Classic) New 709
Model 1894CP 709
Model 1894CS Lever-Action 709
Model 1894FG 710
Model 1894M Lever-Action Rifle 709
Model 1894P 708
Model 1894PG 710
Model 1894S Lever-Action Rifle 709
Model 1894SS 710
Model 1895 and 1895SS Lever-Action 710
Model 1895 Century Limited 704, 710
Model 1895 Century Limited
Employee Edition 710
Model 1895 Cowboy 710
Model 1895 Lever-Action Rifle 703
Antique Production (Pre-1898) . . . 703
Modern Production (1899-1917) . . 703
Model 1895G 710
Model 1895GS 710
Model 1895M Guide Gun 703
Model 1895MR 703
Model 1895MXLR 711
Model 1895RL 711
Model 1895XLR 711
Model 1897 Annie Oakley 711
Model 1897 Century Limited 711
Model 1897 Century Limited
Employee Edition 711
Model 1897 Cowboy 711
Model 1897 Lever-Action Rifle 704
Deluxe Rifle 704
Standard Production Rifle 704
Model 1897 Texan 711
Model 1898 Slide-Action Shotgun . . . 721
Grade A 721
Grade A Brush or Riot 721
Grade B 721
Grade C 721
Grade D 721
Model 1936 Lever-Action Rifle or
Carbine 705
1st Variation (early 1936) 705
2nd Variation (late 1936-1947) . . . 705
Model 2000 717
Model 2000A 717
Model 2000L 717
Model 5510 Bolt-Action Shotgun 725
Model 7000 715
Model 7000T 716
Model Golden 39A Lever-Action Rifle 713
Model MLS-50/54 726
Model MR-7 719
Model MR-7B 719
Nevermiss Model Derringer 699
.22 Caliber Model 699
.32 Caliber Model 699
.41 Caliber Model 699
O.K. Model Derringer 698
O.K. Pocket Revolver 699
Premier Mark I Slide-Action Shotgun . 724
Premier Mark II 725
Premier Mark IV 725
Stonewall Model Derringer 699
Victor Model Derringer 698
Ball & Williams Ballards 694
Civil War Military Carbine 694
Dual Ignition System 694
First Model 694
Military Rifle 694
Sporting Carbine 694
Sporting Rifle 694
Marlin-Ballard Rifles 695

Ballard Hunters Rifle ... 695
Ballard No. 1 Hunters Rifle ... 695
Ballard No. 1-1/2 Hunters Rifle ... 695
Ballard No. 1-3/4 "Far West" Hunters Rifle ... 695
Ballard No. 2 Sporting Rifle ... 695
Ballard No. 3 Gallery Rifle ... 695
Ballard No. 3-1/2 Target Rifle ... 696
Ballard No. 3F Gallery Rifle ... 695
Ballard No. 4 Perfection Rifle ... 695
Ballard No. 4-1/2 A-1 Mid Range Target Rifle ... 696
Ballard No. 4-1/2 Mid Range Rifle ... 696
Ballard No. 5 Pacific Rifle ... 696
Ballard No. 5-1/2 Montana Rifle ... 696
Ballard No. 6 Schuetzen Off Hand Rifle ... 696
Ballard No. 6 Schuetzen Rifle ... 696
Ballard No. 6-1/2 Off Hand Mid Range Rifle ... 696
Ballard No. 6-1/2 Off Hand Rifle ... 696
Ballard No. 6-1/2 Rigby Off Hand Mid Range Rifle ... 696
Ballard No. 7 "Creedmore A-1" Long Range Rifle ... 697
Ballard No. 7 Long Range Rifle ... 697
Ballard No. 7A-1 Extra Grade Long Range Rifle ... 697
Ballard No. 7A-1 Long Range Rifle ... 697
Ballard No. 8 Union Hill Rifle ... 698
Ballard No. 9 Union Hill Rifle ... 698
Ballard No. 10 Schuetzen Junior Rifle ... 698
Merrimack Arms Co. and Brown Manufacturing Co. ... 694
Military Rifle ... 694
Shotgun ... 694
Sporting Carbine ... 694
Sporting Rifle ... 694

MAROCCHI ARMI ... 726
Classic Doubles Model 92 ... 727
Field Master I ... 726
Field Master II ... 726
Lady Sport Left-Handed ... 727
Grade I ... 727
Spectrum Left-Handed ... 727
Lady Sport Model ... 727
Grade I ... 727
Spectrum Grade—Colored Frame 727
Model 99 Grade I ... 727
Model 99 Grade III ... 727
Model 2000 ... 726
Skeet Model ... 727
Grade I ... 727
Grade II ... 727
Grade III ... 727
Sporting Clays Left-Hand Model ... 727
Grade I ... 727
Sporting Clays Model ... 726
Grade I ... 726
Grade II ... 727
Grade III ... 727
Sporting Light ... 727
Grade I ... 727
Trap Model ... 727
Grade I ... 727
Grade II ... 727
Grade III ... 727

MARS ... 727

MARSTON, S.W. ... 727
2 Barrel Pistol ... 727
Double-Action Pepperbox ... 727

MARSTON, W. W. & CO. ... 727
.32 Caliber 3 Barrel Derringer ... 728
3 Barreled Derringer ... 728
Knife Bladed Model ... 728
Model Without Knife ... 728
Breech Loading Pistol ... 728
Brass Frame ... 728
Iron Frame ... 728
Double-Action Pepperbox ... 728
Double-Action Single-Shot Pistol ... 728
Navy Revolver ... 727
Pocket Revolver ... 727
Single-Action Pistol ... 728

MASQUELIER S. A. ... 728
Ardennes ... 729
Boxlock Side-by-Side Shotgun ... 729
Carpathe ... 728
Express ... 728
Sidelock Side-by-Side Shotgun ... 729

MASSACHUSETTS ARMS CO. 729
1st Model ... 730
Commercial Model ... 730
U.S. Martially Marked and AUTHENTICATED ... 730
2nd Model ... 730
Adams Patent Navy Revolver ... 729
Early Model with 6" Barrel ... 729
Fully Marked 7" Barrel Standard Model ... 729
Maynard Carbine ... 730
Maynard Patent Sporting Rifles ... 730
Maynard Primed Belt Revolver ... 729
Maynard Primed Pocket Revolver ... 729
Single-Shot Pocket Pistol ... 729
Wesson & Leavitt Belt Revolver ... 729
Wesson & Leavitt Dragoon ... 729

MATEBA ARMS ... 730
AutoRevolver ... 730
AutoRevolver Carbine ... 730

MATRA MANURHIN DEFENSE ... 730

MAUSER WERKE ... 730
IDF Mauser Rifle Model 66SP ... 740
Model 66 Magnum ... 740
Model 66 Safari ... 740
Model 66 Standard ... 740
Model 66 Stuzen ... 740
Model 77 ... 740
Model 77 Big Game ... 741
Model 77 Mannlicher ... 741
Model 77 Ultra ... 740
Model 80 SA ... 741
Model 86 SR ... 741
Model 90 DA ... 741
Model 93 SR ... 741
Model 96 ... 741
Model 98 (SIG Arms) ... 741
Model 99 Magnum ... 741
Model 99 Standard ... 741
Model 107 ... 740
Model 201 Standard ... 740
Model 201 Luxus ... 740
Model 225 ... 739
Model 2000 ... 739
Model 3000 ... 739
Model 3000 Magnum ... 739
Model 4000 ... 739
Model DSM34 ... 739
Model EL320 ... 739
Model EN310 ... 739
Model ES340 ... 739
Model ES340B ... 740
Model ES350 ... 739
Model KKW ... 739
Model M410 ... 739
Model M420 ... 739
Model MS350B ... 740
Model MS420B ... 739-740
Model MM41OBN ... 740
Early Sporting Rifles ... 730
Type A—Long Action ... 730
Type A—Medium Action ... 730
Type A—Short Action ... 730
Type B ... 730
Type K ... 731
Type M ... 731
Type S ... 731
Model 1896 "Broomhandle Mauser Pistol" ... 731
9mm Export Model ... 733
9mm Parabellum Military Contract ... 734
1920 Rework ... 734
Chinese Marked, Handmade Copies . 736
Cone Hammer Flat Side Carbine ... 735
Deep-Milled Panel Model ... 732
Early Flat Side ... 732
Early Large Ring Hammer Bolo ... 732
Early Model 1930 ... 735
Early Post-war Bolo Model ... 734
Early Small Ring Hammer Bolo Model 733
Early Small Ring Hammer Model, Transitional ... 733
Early Transitional Large Ring Hammer 732
Fixed Sight Cone Hammer ... 732
Flat Side Bolo ... 732
French Gendarme Model ... 735
Large Ring Hammer Flatside Carbine 735
Large Ring Hammer Transitional Carbine ... 735
Late Flat Side ... 732
Late Large Ring Hammer Bolo ... 733
Late Model 1930 ... 735
Late Post-war Bolo Model ... 734
Luger Barreled 1920 Rework ... 734
Mauser Banner Model ... 733
Model 1899 Flat Side—Italian Contract ... 732
Model 1910 ... 736
Later Production (Model 1910/14) . 736
Sidelatch Model ... 736
Model 1912/14 ... 737
Model 1914 ... 736
Model 1914 "Humpback" ... 736
Model 1914 (later) ... 737
Model 1930 Removable Magazine ... 735
Model 1934 ... 737
6.35mm ... 738
7.65mm Commercial ... 738
7.65mm Eagle L proofed ... 738
7.56mm Large Eagle over M (Navy) ... 738
Model Compact DA ... 741
Model M2 (Imported by SIGARMS) ... 741
Model WTP I ... 737
Model WTP II ... 737
Persian Contract ... 733
Shallow-Milled Panel Model ... 732
Shansei Arsenal Model ... 736
Six-Shot Large Ring Bolo ... 733
Six-Shot Small Ring Hammer Model . 733
Six-Shot Standard Cone Hammer ... 731
Six-Shot Step-Barrel Cone Hammer . . 731
Small Ring Hammer Carbine ... 736
Standard Cone Hammer ... 731
Standard Pre-war Commercial ... 733
Standard Wartime Commercial ... 733
System Mauser 10-Shot Cone Hammer ... 731
Taku-Naval Dockyard Model ... 736
Twenty-Shot Step-Barrel Cone Hammer ... 731
Twenty-Shot Cone Hammer ... 731
Turkish Contract Cone Hammer ... 732
Model HSc ... 738
Early Commercial Model ... 738
Early Nazi Army Model ... 738
Early Nazi Navy Model ... 738
Early Nazi Police Model ... 738

French Manufactured Model 738
Late Nazi Army Model 738
Low Grip Screw Model 738
Model HSc Post-war Production 738
Gamba Production 739
Mauser Production (.32) 738
Transition Model 738
Wartime Commercial Model 738
Wartime Nazi Navy Model 738
Wartime Nazi Police Model 738

MAVERICK ARMS, INC. 742
Model 88 742
Model 88 Six-Shot Security Model . . . 742
Model 88 Slug Pump Shotgun 742

MAYNARD/PERRY 742
Brass Framed Carbine 742

M. B. ASSOCIATES-GYROJET 742
Mark I Model A 742
Mark I Model A Carbine 742
Mark I Model B 742
Mark I Model B Carbine 742
Mark II Model C 742

McMILLAN, G. & CO. INC. 742
Competition Model 742
Model 300 Phoenix Long Range Rifle 743
Model 40 Sniper 744
Model 86 Sniper's Rifle 742
Model 86 System 743
Model 87 Long Range Snipers Rifle . 743
Model 87 System 743
Model 92 Bullpup 744
Model 93 SN 744
Signature Alaskan 743
Signature Model 743
Signature Stainless 743
Signature Titanium Mountain 743
Signature Varminter 743
Talon Safari 743
Talon Sporter 743

MEAD & ADRIANCE 744

MEIJA 744

MENDENHALL, JONES & GARDNER 744
Muzzle Loading Rifle 744

MENZ, AUGUST 744
Liliput 744
Menta 744
Menz Model II 744
Menz VP Model 744
Model III 744

MERCURY 744
Model 622 VP 744

MERCURY 744
Double-Barreled Shotgun 744

MERIDEN FIREARMS CO. 744
Double-Barrel Shotguns 745
Pocket Pistol 744
Single-Barrel Shotguns and Rifles . . . 745

MERKEL, GEBRUDER 745
KR-1 Premium 754
KR-1 Weimar 755
Model 8 745
Model 47E 746
Model 47SL 746
Model 95K Drilling 754
Model 96K 754
Model 96K—Engraved 754
Model 102E 748
Model 103E 748
Model 117/117E 745
Model 118/118E 745
Model 122 746
Model 124 746
Model 124/125 746
Model 125 746
Model 126 746
Model 127 746
Model 130 746
Model 132E 753
Model 140-1 753
Model 140-1.1 753
Model 140-2 753
Model 140-2.1 753
Model 147 746
Model 147E 746
Model 147EL 746
Model 147SL 747
Model 147SSL 747
Model 150-1 753
Model 150-1.1 753
Model 160S Luxus Double Rifle 753
Model 160S-2.1 753
Model 170 746
Model 180 752
Model 183 752
Model 190 752
Model 200E 749
Model 200ES 750
Model 200ET 750
Model 200SC (Sporting Clays) 750
Model 201E 749
Model 201ES 750
Model 201ET 750
Model 202E 750
Model 203E 750
Model 204E 749
Model 210E Rifle/Shotgun Combination 753
Model 211E Rifle/Shotgun Combination 753
Model 213E Rifle/Shotgun Combination 754
Model 220E Over-and-Under Double Rifle 754
Model 221E Over-and-Under Double Rifle 754
Model 223E Over-and-Under Double Rifle 754
Model 240-1 754
Model 240-1.1 754
Model 247S 747
Model 280 747
Model 280EL 747
Model 280SL 747
Model 280/360 Two Barrel Set 748
Model 280/360EL Two Barrel Set . . . 748
Model 280/360SL Two Barrel Set . . . 748
Model 300 752
Model 301E 749
Model 302E 749
Model 303 Luxus 749
Model 303E 750
Model 303EL 750
Model 304E 749
Model 311E 752
Model 312E 752
Model 313E 752
Model 313E Rifle/Shotgun Combination 754
Model 314E 752
Model 323E Over-and-Under Double Rifle 754
Model 347S 747
Model 360 747
Model 360EL 747
Model 360SL 748
Model 400E 749
Model 401E 749
Model 410E 752
Model 411 E 752
Model 447SL 747
Model 1620 748
Model 1620E 748
Model 1620EL 748
Model 1620SL 748
Model 1622 748
Model 1622E 748
Model 1622EL 748
Model 2000CL 751
Model 2000CL Sporter 751
Model 2000EL 750
Model 2000EL Sporter 751
Model 2001EL 751
Model 2001EL Sporter 751
Model 2002EL 751
Model 2016EL 751
Model 2016EL Two Barrel Set 751
Model 2116EL 751
Model 2116EL Two Barrel Set 752
Model K-1 Jagd 754
Models 247S/347S 747
Side-by-Side Double Rifles
Model 128E 752

MERRILL 755
Sportsman 755

MERRILL, JAMES H. 755
Merrill Carbine 755
1st Type 755
2nd Type 755
Merrill Rifle 755

MERRILL, LATROBE & THOMAS 756
Carbine 756

MERRIMACK ARMS 756

MERWIN & BRAY 756
Merwin & Bray Pocket Pistol 756

MERWIN HULBERT & CO. 756
First Model Frontier Army, .44 open top 756
Fourth Model Frontier Army, Double-Action, .44, topstrap 757
Fourth Model Frontier Army, Single-Action, .44, topstrap 757
Large-Frame Merwin Hulbert Sixguns 756
Second Model Frontier Army, .44 open top 756
Second Model Pocket Army, .44 open top 756
Third Model Frontier Army, Double-Action, .44, topstrap 757
Third Model Frontier Army, Single-Action, .44, topstrap 757
Third Model Pocket Army, Double-Action, .44, topstrap 757
Third Model Pocket Army, Single-Action, .44 topstrap 757
Small Frame Merwin Hulbert Pocket Revolvers 757
Double-Action Pocket Model, medium frame 758
Double-Action Pocket Model, small frame 758
First Pocket Model Single-Action 757
Merwin Hulbert Rifles 758
Second Pocket Model Single-Action . 757
Third Pocket Model Single-Action Spur-Trigger 757
Third Pocket Model Single-Action w/Trigger Guard 758
Tip-up .22 Spur-Trigger 758

METROPOLITAN ARMS CO. . . 758
1851 Navy Revolver . . . 758
H.E. Dimick Navy Model . . . 758
Standard Navy Model . . . 758
1861 Navy Revolver . . . 758
Police Revolver . . . 758

MIIDA . . . 758
Model 612 . . . 758
Model 612 Skeet . . . 758
Model 2100 Skeet . . . 758
Model 2200 Trap or Skeet . . . 758
Model 2300 Trap or Skeet . . . 758
Model GRT Trap or GRS Skeet . . . 758

MILLER ARMS . . . 758
Low Boy . . . 759
Model F . . . 759
Standard Rifle . . . 759

MILTECH . . . 759
German Mauser Model 98k . . . 759
M1 Carbine . . . 759
M1 Garand . . . 759
M1D Garand . . . 759
Model 1903 Mark I Springfield . . . 759
Model 1903 Springfield . . . 759
Model 1903A3 Springfield . . . 759
Model 1917 U.S. Enfield . . . 759
Model 1941 Johnson . . . 759

MINNEAPOLIS F. A. CO. . . . 759
Palm Pistol . . . 759

MIROKU B. C. . . . 759

MITCHELL ARMS, INC. . . . 759
AK-22 . . . 760
Citation II . . . 760-761
Galil . . . 760
High Standard Collectors' Association Special Editions . . . 761
M-16 . . . 759
MAS . . . 759
Olympic I.S.U. . . . 760
PPSH-30/50 . . . 760
Sharpshooter II . . . 760
Six Gun Set . . . 761
Skorpion . . . 761
Spectre . . . 761
Three Gun Set . . . 761
Trophy II . . . 760-761
Victor II . . . 760-761
Victor II with Weaver Rib . . . 761

MITCHELL'S MAUSERS . . . 761
Black Arrow . . . 761
Centurion Revolver . . . 761
Escalade . . . 761
Gold Series '03 Pistol . . . 761
Mauser M98 African/Alaskan . . . 761
Mauser M98 Basic . . . 761
Mauser M98 Varmint . . . 761
Sabre . . . 761
Valkyrie Revolver . . . 761

MK ARMS, INC. . . . 762
K 760 . . . 762

MKE . . . 762
Kirrikale . . . 762

MODESTO SANTOS CIA. . . . 762
Action, Corrientes, and M.S. . . . 762

MONDRAGON . . . 762

MONTENEGRAN-GASSER . . . 762

MOORE-ENFIELD . . . 762

MOORES PATENT FIREARMS CO. . . . 762
Belt Revolver . . . 762
No. 1 Derringer . . . 762
1st Variation Marked "Patent Applied For" . . . 762
2nd Variation Marked "D. Moore Patented Feb. 19 1861" . . . 762
Iron Model . . . 762
National Arms Co. Production . . . 762
Standard Model Marked "Moore's Pat F.A. Co." . . . 762
Pocket Revolver . . . 762

MORGAN & CLAPP . . . 763
Single-Shot Pocket Pistol . . . 763

MORINI . . . 763
C-80 Standard . . . 763
CM-80 Super Competition . . . 763
Model 84E Free Pistol . . . 763

MORRONE . . . 763

MORSE . . . 763
Morse Carbine . . . 763

MOSIN-NAGANT . . . 763

MOSSBERG, O. F. & SONS, INC. . . . 763
4x4 Rifle . . . 766
100 ATR Super Bantam . . . 765
817 Plinkster Rifle . . . 765
Bolt-Action Rifles . . . 764
Bolt-Action Shotguns . . . 766
Brownie . . . 763
Model 100 ATR (All-Terrain Rifle) . . . 765
Model 200K . . . 766
Model 400 Palomino . . . 764
Model 472 One in Five Thousand . . . 765
Model 472C . . . 765
Model 472P . . . 765
Model 479 PCA . . . 765
Model 479 RR . . . 765
Model 500 Bantam . . . 767
Model 500 Bullpup . . . 767
Model 500 Camper . . . 767
Model 500 Combo . . . 768
Model 500 Cruiser . . . 767
Model 500 Field Grade . . . 767
Model 500 Flyway Series . . . 768
Model 500 Grand Slam Turkey . . . 768
Model 500 Hi-Rib Trap . . . 767
Model 500 HS (Home Security) . . . 768
Model 500 Mariner . . . 767
Model 500 Muzzleloader Combo . . . 767
Model 500 Persuader . . . 767
Model 500 Pigeon Grade . . . 767
Model 500 Pigeon Grade Trap . . . 767
Model 500 Regal . . . 767
Model 500 Slug Gun Viking Grade . . . 768
Model 500 Slugster . . . 767
Model 500 Steel Shot . . . 767
Model 500 Super Bantam Combo . . . 767
Model 500 Super Bantam Field . . . 767
Model 500 Super Bantam Slug . . . 767
Model 500 Super Bantam Turkey . . . 767
Model 500 Super Grade . . . 767
Model 500 USA . . . 768
Model 505 Youth . . . 768
Model 535 ATS (All Terrain Shotgun) Field . . . 768
Model 535 ATS Combos . . . 785
Model 535 ATS Slugster . . . 785
Model 535 ATS Turkey . . . 768
Model 535 ATS Waterfowl . . . 768
Model 590 Bullpup . . . 785
Model 590 Mariner . . . 785
Model 590 Special Purpose . . . 785
Model 590DA . . . 785
Model 695 . . . 766
Model 695 Camo . . . 766
Model 702 Plinkster . . . 764
Model 702 International Plinkster . . . 764
Model 800 . . . 765
Model 800D . . . 765
Model 800M . . . 765
Model 800SM . . . 765
Model 800V . . . 765
Model 802 Plinkster Bolt Action . . . 765
Model 810 . . . 765
Model 835 Ulti-Mag . . . 785
Model 835 Ulti-Mag Crown Grade . . . 785
Model 835 Ulti-Mag Crown Grade Combo Model . . . 785
Model 835 Ulti-Mag Grand Slam Turkey . . . 785
Model 835 Ulti-Mag Thumbhole Turkey . . . 785
Model 1500 Varmint . . . 766
Model 1550 . . . 766
Model 1700 LS . . . 766
Model K Rifle . . . 764
Model L Rifle . . . 764
Model M Rifle . . . 764
Semi-Automatic Rifles . . . 764
SSi-One Slug . . . 766
SSi-One Sporter . . . 765
SSi-One Turkey . . . 766
Model 1500 Mountaineer Grade I . . . 766
Model 1500 Mountaineer Grade II . . . 766
SSi-One Varmint . . . 766

MOSSBERG, O. F. & SONS, INC. . . . 785
Model 835 American Field . . . 786
Model 835 Ulti-Mag Tactical Turkey . . . 786
Model 835 Ulti-Mag Viking Grade . . . 786
Model 835 Wild Turkey Federation . . . 786
Model 930 Field . . . 786
Model 930 Slugster . . . 787
Model 930 Turkey . . . 786
Model 930 Waterfowl . . . 787
Model 935 Grand Slam Turkey . . . 786
Model 935 Magnum Turkey Camo . . . 786
Model 935 Magnum Turkey Synthetic . . . 786
Model 935 Magnum Waterfowl Camo . . . 786
Model 935 Magnum Waterfowl Synthetic . . . 786
Model 1000 . . . 787
Model 1000 Slug . . . 787
Model 1000 Super Skeet . . . 787
Model 1000 Super Slug . . . 787
Model 1000 Super Trap . . . 787
Model 1000 Super Waterfowler . . . 787
Model 3000 . . . 787
Model 3000 Law Enforcement . . . 787
Model 3000 Waterfowler . . . 787
Model 5500 MKI I . . . 787
Model 9200 Combos . . . 788
Model 9200 Crown Grade Bantam . . . 788
Model 9200 Deer Combo . . . 788
Model 9200 Jungle Gun . . . 788
Model 9200 Special Hunter . . . 788
Model 9200 Turkey Camos . . . 788
Model 9200 USST Crown Grade . . . 788
Model 9200 Viking Grade . . . 787
Onyx Reserve Sporting . . . 788
Silver Reserve Field . . . 788
Silver Reserve Sporting . . . 788

MOUNTAIN ARMS . . . 788
Wildcat . . . 788

MOUNTAIN RIFLES, INC. . . . 788
Mountaineer . . . 788
Pro Mountaineer . . . 788
Pro Safari . . . 789

Super Mountaineer 788
Ultra Mountaineer 789

MUGICA, JOSE 789

MURATA 789

MURFEESBORO ARMORY . . . 789

MURRAY, J. P. 789
Percussion Rifle 789

MURPHY & O'CONNEL 789
Pocket Pistol 789

MUSGRAVE 789
Premier NR5 789
RSA NR I Single-Shot Target Rifle . . 789
Valiant NR6 789

MUSKETEER RIFLES 789
Carbine 789
Deluxe Sporter 789
Sporter 789

N

NAGANT, EMILE & LEON 790

NAMBU 790

NATIONAL ARMS CO. 790
Large Frame Teat-Fire Revolver 790
No. 2 Derringer 790

NAVY ARMS COMPANY 790
2A Tanker Carbine 804
18th Georgia Le Mat Pistol 798
1777 Charleville Musket 791
1777 Standard Charleville Musket . . . 791
1808 Springfield Musket 791
1816 M.T. Wickham Musket 791
1841 Mississippi Rifle 792
1847 Walker Dragoon 799
Single Cased Set 799
Single Deluxe Cased Set 799
1851 Navy 798
Double Cased Set 798
Single Cased Set 798
1851 Navy Conversion 799
1858 New Model Remington-Style Pistol 799
Double Cased Set 799
Single Cased Set 799
1858 Target Model 800
1859 Berdan Sharps Rifle 793
1859 Sharps Infantry Rifle 793
1860 Army Conversion 799
1860 Army Pistol 799
Double Cased Set 799
Single Cased Set 799
1861 Navy Conversion 800
1861 Springfield Rifle 792
1862 C.S. Richmond Rifle 792
1862 New Model Book-Style Cased Set 798
1862 New Model Police 798
1863 Springfield Rifle 792
1866 "Yellowboy" Carbine 794
1866 "Yellowboy" Rifle 794
1866 "Yellowboy" Short Rifle 794
1872 Colt Open Top 800
1873 Border Model 794
1873 Colt-Style Single-Action Army . . 800
1873 Flat Top Target 801
1873 Pinched Frame Model 801
1873 Sharps No. 2 Creedmore 793
1873 Sharps Quigley 793
1873 Sporting Long Range Rifle 794
1873 Springfield Cavalry Carbine 796
1873 Springfield Infantry Rifle 796
1873 U.S. Cavalry Model 801
1873 Winchester Carbine 794
1873 Winchester Rifle 794
1873 Winchester Sporting Rifle 794
1874 Sharps Buffalo Rifle 794
1874 Sharps Infantry Rifle 793
1874 Sharps No. 3 Long Range Rifle . 794
1874 Sharps Plains Rifle 794
1874 Sharps Sniper Rifle 793
1874 Sharps Sporting Rifle 794
1875 Remington-Style Revolver 802
1885 High Wall 796
1890 Remington-Style Revolver 802
1892 Brass Frame Carbine 795
1892 Brass Frame Rifle 795
1892 Carbine 795
1892 Rifle 795
1892 Short Rifle 795
1895 U.S. Artillery Model 802
Army Le Mat 798
Augusta 1851 Navy Pistol 799
Beauregard Le Mat Pistol 798
Bisley Flat Top Target 802
Bisley Model 801
Blued Iron Frame Henry 795
Brass Framed 1858 New Model Army 800
Double Cased Set 800
Single Cased Set 800
Brown Bess Carbine 791
Brown Bess Musket 791
Cavalry Le Mat 798
Deluxe 1858 New Model Army 800
Deluxe 1873 Colt Revolver 801
Deluxe Tryon Rifle 792
Deputy Single-Action Army 801
Engraved Paterson Revolver 798
Fowler Shotgun 796
Grand Prix Silhouette Pistol 805
Harpers Ferry Flint Rifle 791
Harpers Ferry "Journey of Discovery" Rifle 791
Harpers Ferry Pistol 797
Single Cased Set 797
Hawken Hunter Carbine 796
Hawken Hunter Rifle 796
Hawken Rifle 796
Henry Carbine 795
Henry Trapper 795
Iron Frame Henry 795
Ishapore 2A No. 1 MK III Rifle 804
Ithaca/Navy Hawken Rifle 796
J.P. Murray Carbine 792
Japanese Matchlock 797
"John Bodine" Rolling Block Rifle 795
JW-15 Rifle 804
Kentucky Flintlock Pistol 797
Double Cased Set 797
Single Cased Set 797
Kentucky Pistol 797
Double Cased Set 797
Single Cased Set 797
Kentucky Rifle 791
Flintlock 791
Percussion 791
Kodiak MKIV Double Rifle 796
Le Page Flintlock 797
Le Page Pistol 797
Double Cased Set 797
Single Cased Set 797
Le Page Smoothbore Flintlock Pistol . 797
Single Cased Set 797
Double Cased Set 797
Lithgow No. 1 MK III Rifle 804
"London Gray" Rogers and Spencer Pistol 800
Luger 805
Martini Target Rifle 804
Military Henry 795
MK III Tanker Carbine 804
Model 83 790
Model 93 790
Model 95 790
Model 96 Sportsman 790
Model 100 790
Model 100 Side-by-Side 790
Model 105 791
Model 105 Deluxe 791
Model 150 790
Model 1851 Navy Frontiersman 799
Model 1873 SAA Stainless Gunfighter 801
Economy Model 1873 S.A.A. 801
Nickel 1873 S.A.A. 801
Model 1873 Springfield Officer's Trapdoor 792
Model 1875 Schofield Founder's Model 802
Model 1875 Schofield—B Engraved . 802
Model 1875 Schofield—C Engraved . 802
Model 1875 Schofield—Cavalry 7" barrel 802
Model 1875 Schofield—Deluxe 802
Model 1875 Schofield—Hideout 803
Model 1875 Schofield—Wells Fargo 5" barrel 802
Mortimer Flintlock Rifle 791
Mortimer Flintlock Shotgun 796
Navy Arms 1858 Two Band Musket . . 793
Navy Arms Musketoon 793
Navy Arms Revolving Carbine 793
Navy Arms Steel Shot Magnum 796
Navy Arms Three Band Musket 793
Navy Le Mat 798
New Model Russian 803
No. 1 MK III Enfield Rifle 804
No. 2 Creedmoor Target Rifle 795
No. 4 MK I Enfield Rifle 804
No. 4 Tanker Carbine 804
No. 5 Enfield Jungle Carbine 804
No. 6 Enfield Jungle Carbine 804
Parker-Hale 3 Band Volunteer Rifle . . 792
Parker-Hale 1858 Two Band Musket . 793
Parker-Hale 1861 Musketoon 793
Parker-Hale Sniper Rifle 804
Parker-Hale Three Band Musket 793
Parker-Hale Volunteer Rifle 792
Parker-Hale Whitworth Rifle 792
Paterson Revolver 798
Pennsylvania Long Rifle 791
Flintlock 791
Percussion 791
Reb 1860 Sheriff's Model 799
Reb Model 1860 Pistol 799
Rigby Target Rifle 792
Rogers and Spencer 800
Rogers and Spencer Target Model . . 800
Rolling Block Buffalo Rifle 795
Half Octagon Barrel Model 795
RPKS-74 804
Savage No. 4 MK I Rifle 804
Scout Small Frame Revolver 801
Sharps #2 Silhouette Rifle 793
Sharps #2 Sporting Rifle 793
Sharps Cavalry Carbine 794
Sharps Cavalry Carbine Cartridge Model 794
Shootist Model S.A.A. 801
SKS "Cowboy's Companion" Carbine 803
Military Version 803
SKS "Hunter" Carbine 803
SKS Type 56 w/Scope Rail 803
Spiller and Burr Pistol 800
Double Cased Set 800
Single Cased Set 800
Stainless Steel 1858 New Model Army 799
Double Cased Set 800
Single Cased Set 800

Standard SKS Type 56 803
With Scope and Bipod 803
Standard Tryon Rifle 792
Starr Double-Action Model 1858 Army 798
Starr Single-Action Model 1863 Army . 798
T&T Shotgun 797
Tryon Creedmoor Rifle 792
TT-Olympia Pistol 803
TU-33/40 Carbine 804
TU-90 Pistol 803
TU-KKW Sniper Trainer 804
TU-KKW Training Rifle 803
Zouave Rifle 792

NEAL, W. 805
Under Hammer Pistol 805

NEPPERHAN FIREARMS CO. . 805
Pocket Revolver 805

NESIKA BAY PRECISION, INC. 805
Heavy Tactical Rifle 805
Hunting Rifles 805
Urban Tactical Rifle 805
Varmint Rifles 805

NEW ENGLAND FIREARMS CO. 805
Handi-Rifle (aka Handi-Gun) 806
Handi-Rifle Combo 806
Huntsman 806
Model R22 805
Pardner 805
Pardner Pump 805
Pardner Pump Turkey 805
Pardner Pump Combo 806
Pardner Youth 805
Sidekick Muzzleloader 807
Special Purpose 806
Sportster 806
Sportster .17 HMR 807
Sportster .17 M2 807
Sportster SL 807
Sportster Versa-Pack 807
Sportster Youth 807
Super Light Rifles 806
Survivor 806
Tracker 806
Tracker II 806

NEWBURY ARMS CO. 807
Pocket Pistol 807
Pocket Revolver 807

NEWCOMB, H. G. 807
Pocket Pistol 807

NEWTON ARMS CO. 807
Buffalo Newton Rifle 808
Newton-Mauser Rifle 807
Standard Rifle First Type 807
Standard Rifle Second Model 808

NICHOLS & CHILDS 808
Percussion Belt Revolver 808
Revolving Percussion Rifle 808

NIGHTHAWK CUSTOM 808
Custom Predator 808
Custom Talon 808
GRP 808

NOBLE 808
Model 10 808
Model 20 808
Model 33 809
Model 33A 809
Model 40 809
Model 50 809
Model 60 809
Model 65 809
Model 66 RLP 809
Model 66CLP 809
Model 66RCLP 809
Model 66XL 809
Model 70CLP 809
Model 70RCLP 809
Model 70RLP 809
Model 70XL 809
Model 80 810
Model 166L 810
Model 222 809
Model 236 809
Model 275 809
Model 420 810
Model 450E 810
Model 602CLP 810
Model 602RCLP 810
Model 602RLP 810
Model 602XL 810
Model 662 810

NORINCO 810
1911 A1 811
ATD .22 810
EM-321 810
Model 97 Hammer Pump 811
Model 213 Pistol 811
Model HL-12-102 Shotgun 810
Model HL-12-203 Shotgun 810
SKS Rifle 811
Type 54-1 Tokarev 811
Type 59 Makarov 811
Type 81S 811
Type 81S-1 811
Type 84S AK 811
Type 84S-1 811
Type 84S-3 811
Type 84S-5 811

NORTH AMERICAN ARMS 811
Black Widow 812
Companion 812
Guardian 813
Guardian .380 813
Mini-Master 812
Mini-Revolver 811
2 Cylinder Magnum Convertible Version 811
Cased .22 Magnum 812
Deluxe 3 Gun Set 812
Magnum Version 812
Standard 3 Gun Set 812
Standard Rimfire Version 811
Viper Belt Buckle Version 811
Single-Action Revolver 812
Super Companion 812

NORTH AMERICAN ARMS CORP. 813
Brigadier 813

NORTH AMERICAN SAFARI EXPRESS 813

NORTH & COUCH 813
Animal Trap Gun 813
Disk Hammer Model 813
Spur Hammer Model 813

NORTON ARMS CO. 813

NOSLER CUSTOM 813
NoslerCustom Model 48 Sporter 813

NORWICH PISTOL CO. 813

NOWLIN MANUFACTURING COMPANY 813
Compact Carry 813
Match Classic 813
Match Master 813

O

O.D.I. 814
Viking 814
Viking Combat 814

O.K. 814

O'CONNELL, DAVID 814
Pocket Pistol 814

O'DELL, STEPHEN 814
Pocket Pistol 814

OBREGON 814

OHIO ORDNANCE INC. 814
1919A4 814
Colt Browning Water Cooled Gun . . . 814
Model 1918A3 Self-Loading Rifle 814

OJANGUREN Y VIDOSA 814
Apache (Model 1920) 815
Apache (Model 1920) 815
Ojanguren 815
Tanque 815

OLD WEST GUN CO. 815

OLYMPIC ARMS, INC. 815
Black Widow 815
Black-Tac 816
Cohort 815
Constable 816
Custom Journeyman 816
Custom Street Deuce 816
Enforcer 815
GI-16 818
K3B 817
K3B-CAR 818
K3B-FAR 818
K3B-M4 817
K4B 818
K4B-A4 818
K7 Eliminator 818
K9/K10/K40/K45 818
K9-GL/K40-GL 818
K16 818
K30 818
LTF 818
LT-M4 818
Match Master 815
Match Master 6" 815
ML-1 817
ML-2 817
Model CAR-97 817
Model K8 817
Model K8-MAG 817
Model OA-93 TG 817
Model OA-93-PT 816
Model OA-93-PT 818
Model OA-96 817
Model OA-98 817
Model PCR-2 816
Model PCR-3 816
Model PCR-4 816
Model PCR-5 816
Model PCR-6 817
Model PCR-7 "Eliminator" 817
Model PCR-Service Match 817
OA-93-CAR 818
Plinker Plus 818
Plinker Plus 20 818
Safari G.I. 815
Schuetzen Pistol Works Big Deuce . . 815
Schuetzen Pistol Works Carrier 816
Schuetzen Pistol Works Crest 816
Schuetzen Pistol Works Griffon 816
SGW Ultra Match (PCR-1) 816
SM-1 817

SM-1P ... 817
Trail Boss ... 816
Ultra CSR Tactical Rifle ... 817
UM-1 ... 817
UM-1P ... 817
Westerner ... 816
Wolverine ... 816

OMEGA ... 818
Over-and-Under Shotgun ... 818
Side-by-Side Double Barreled Shotgun ... 818
Single Barreled Shotgun ... 818

OMEGA ... 818

OMEGA ... 818
Omega Pistol ... 818

OMEGA FIREARMS CO. ... 819
Bolt-Action Rifle ... 819

OPUS SPORTING ARMS, INC. 819
Opus One ... 819
Opus Three ... 819
Opus Two ... 819

ORBEA & CIA ... 819
Pocket Pistol ... 819

ORTGIES, HEINRICH & CO. ... 819
Ortgies Pistol ... 819

ORVIS ... 819

OSBORN, S. ... 819
Under Hammer Pistol ... 819

OSGOOD GUN WORKS ... 819
Duplex Revolver ... 819

OVERTON, JOHN ... 819

OWA ... 820
OWA Pocket Pistol ... 820

P

P.38 ... 821
480 Code ... 821
"AC" Codes ... 821
"ac" (no date) ... 821
"AC40" ... 821
Added ... 821
Standard ... 821
"AC41" ... 821
1st Variation ... 821
2nd Variation ... 821
3rd Variation ... 821
"AC42" ... 821
1st Variation ... 821
2nd Variation ... 821
"AC43" ... 821
1st Variation ... 821
2nd Variation ... 821
Single Line Slide ... 821
AC43/44—FN slide ... 822
"AC44" ... 822
"AC45" ... 822
1st Variation ... 822
2nd Variation ... 822
3rd Variation ... 822
"byf42" ... 822
"byf43" ... 822
"byf44" ... 822
"SVW45" ... 822
French Proofed ... 822
German Proofed ... 822
"svw46"—French Proofed ... 822
German WWII Service Pistol ... 821
Mauser "Police" P.38 ... 822
"ac/43" ... 822
"ac/44" ... 822
"byf/43" ... 822
"byf/44" ... 822
"svw/45" ... 822
Post-war Pistols ... 822
Manurhin ... 822
Single Line Code (Rare) ... 822
Standard Slides ... 822
Spreewerke Military ... 822
"cyq" ... 822
1st Variation ... 822
Eagle /211 on frame ... 822
Standard Variation ... 822
Zero Series ... 822
Walther Commercial ... 821
"ac45" Zero Series ... 821
MOD HP ... 821
.30 caliber, extremely rare ... 821
Croatian contract, 100 built, 6 known ... 821
Early w/High Gloss Blue ... 821
Early w/High Gloss Blue & Alloy Frame ... 821
H Prefix w/rectangular firing pin ... 821
Late w/Military Blue Finish ... 821
MOD P38—Late with Military Blue 821
Walther Military ... 821
Zero Series ... 821
First Issue ... 821
Second Issue ... 821
Third Issue ... 821

P.A.F. ... 822
P.A.F. Junior ... 822

P.S.M.G. GUN CO. ... 822
Six-In-One Supreme ... 822

PAGE-LEWIS ARMS CO. ... 822
Challenge Model 49 ... 823
Model A Target ... 822
Model B Sharpshooter ... 822
Model C Olympic ... 823

PALMER ... 823
Palmer Bolt-Action Carbine ... 823

PANTHER ARMS ... 823

PAPE, W.R. ... 823

PARA-ORDNANCE MFG. INC. 823
1911 SSP ... 827
Black Watch Companion ... 831
Black Watch SSP ... 831
Carry 12 ... 831
Carry Model ... 830
CCO (Companion Carry Option) ... 830
CCW ... 831
Colonel ... 832
Covert Black Nite-Tac ... 832
Hi-Cap .40 ... 832
Hi-Cap .45 ... 832
Hi-Cap 9 ... 832
Hi-Cap Limited .40 ... 833
Hi-Cap Limited .45 ... 833
Hi-Cap Limited 9 ... 833
Hi-Cap LTC ... 829
Limited ... 831
Lite Hawg 9 ... 828
Midnight Blue P14-45 ... 829
Model 13.45/P12.45 Limited ... 824
Model 1911 ... 827
Model C6.45 LDA (Para Carry) ... 825
Model C7.45 LDA (Para Companion) ... 825
Model Hawg 9 ... 827
Model LTC ... 826
Model LTC Alloy ... 827
Model LTC Stainless ... 827
Model OPS ... 826, 827
Model P10.45 Limited ... 825
Model P10.45/P10.40/P10.9 ... 825
Model P12.45 LDA/P12.45 LDA ... 824
Model P12.45/P12.40 ... 824
Model P13.45 ... 824
Model P14.45 ... 823
Model P14.45 LDA/P14.45 LDA Stainless ... 823
Model P14.45 Limited ... 823
Model P16.40 ... 823
Model P16.40 LDA ... 824
Model P16.40 Limited ... 823
Model P18.9 ... 825
Model P18.9 LDA ... 825
Model Para CCW ... 826
Model Para Companion Carry Option 826
Model Stealth Carry ... 826
Model Tac-Four ... 826
Model Tac-Four LE ... 826
Nite-Tac .40 ... 832
Nite-Tac 9 ... 832
Nite-Tac ... 832
P12.45 ... 828
P13.45 ... 829
P14.45 ... 829
P18.45 ... 829
S12.45 Limited ... 829
S13.45 Limited ... 829
S14.45 Limited ... 830
S16.40 Limited ... 830
Slim Hawg ... 828
SSP ... 831
Stainless Warthog ... 828
Stealth Carry ... 830
Stealth S14.45 Limited ... 830
Stealth S16.40 Limited ... 830
Stealth Hi-Cap .45 ... 832
Stealth Hi-Cap 9 ... 832
Stealth Hi-Cap Ltd .45 ... 833
Stealth Hi-Cap Limited 9 ... 833
Stealth Limited ... 831
Stealth P14.45 ... 829
Stealth Warthog ... 828
Tac-Five ... 832
Tac-Four ... 831
TAC-S ... 831
Todd Jarrett .40 USPSA ... 830
Todd Jarrett .45 USPSA ... 830
Warthog ... 828

PARDINI ... 833
Centerfire Pistol ... 833
Free Pistol ... 833
Rapidfire Pistol ... 833
Standard Target Pistol ... 833

PARKER ... 833
4-Shot Pistol ... 833

PARKER BROS. ... 833
A-1 Special ... 836
AAH ... 835
AH ... 835
BH ... 835
CH ... 834
DH ... 834
GH ... 834
PH ... 834
Single-Barrel Trap ... 836
S.A. Grade ... 836
S.A.A. Grade ... 836
S.A-1 Special Grade ... 836
S.B. Grade ... 836
S.C. Grade ... 836
Trojan ... 836
Under Lifter Hammer Gun ... 836
VH ... 834

PARKER FIELD & SONS ... 836
Gas Seal Revolver ... 836

PARKER-HALE LTD. 836
1853 Enfield Rifle Musket 837
1858 Enfield Naval Pattern Rifle 837
1861 Enfield Artillery Carbine
Musketoon 837
Model 81 African 837
Model 81 Classic 837
Model 84 Target 837
Model 85 Sniper 837
Model 640A 837
Model 640E Shotgun 837
Model 645E 837
Model 670E 837
Model 680E—XXV 837
Model 1100 Lightweight 837
Model 1200 836
S&W Victory Conversion 836
Volunteer Percussion Target Rifle ... 838
Whitworth Military Target Rifle 837
Whitworth Sniping Rifle 837

PARKER REPRODUCTIONS . . 838
16/20 Combination 838
28 Gauge 838
28 Gauge/.410 Bore Combination 838
A-1 Special 838
12 or 20 Gauge 838
28 Gauge 838
A-1 Special Custom Engraved 838
B-Grade Limited Edition 838
28 Gauge/.410 Bore Combination 838
D-Grade 838
12 or 20 Gauge 838
DHE Grade Steel-Shot Special 838

PEABODY 838
Creedmoor 839
Creedmoor Mid-Range 839
Kill Deer 839
Peabody Rifle and Carbine 838
Peabody-Martini Sporting Rifles 839
Sporting Rifle 839
What Cheer 839
What Cheer Mid-Range 839

PEAVY, A. J. 839
Knife-Pistol 839

PECARE & SMITH 839
Pepperbox 839
Ten-Shot Pepperbox (rare) 839

PEDERSEN, JOHN D. 839
Pedersen Carbine 839
Pedersen Rifle 839

PEDERSEN CUSTOM GUNS . . 839
Model 1000 840
Grade I 840
Grade II 840
Model 1000 Magnum 840
Grade I 840
Grade II 840
Model 1000 Skeet 840
Grade I 840
Grade II 840
Model 1000 Trap 840
Grade I 840
Grade II 840
Model 1500 840
Model 1500 Skeet 840
Model 1500 Trap 840
Model 2000 840
Grade I 840
Grade II 840
Model 2500 840
Model 3000 840
Grade III—Plain 840
Grade II 840
Grade I 840
Model 4000 Shotgun 839
Model 4000 Trap 839
Model 4500 839
Model 4500 Trap 839
Model 4700 840

PEDERSOLI, DAVIDE 840
1859 Sharps Cavalry Carbine 845
1862 Robinson Confederate Sharps . 845
1873 Trapdoor Springfield 845
1874 Sharps 845
Alamo Rifle 844
An IX Dragoon Musket 844
An IX Pistol 842
An XIII Pistol 842
Austrian 1798 Flintlock Musket 844
Bounty Pistol 842
Bristlen A. Morges Target Rifle 843
Brown Bess Flintlock Musket 844
Carleton Underhammer Pistol 841
Charles Moore Duelling Pistol 841
Coach Shotgun 846
Corrige An IX 844
Country Hunter 844
Cub Dixie 844
Derringer Liegi 842
Double Percussion Shotgun 846
Frontier Rifle 843
Gibbs Rifle 843
Harper's Ferry 1816 Musket 845
Harper's Ferry Pistol 842
Indian Trade Musket 843
Jager Rifle 844
Kentucky Pistol 841
Kentucky Rifle 844
Kodiak Combination Gun 845
Kodiak Double Rifle 845
Kodiak Mark IV Express Rifle 845
Kuchenreuter Pistol 841
Leger 1763 Charleville Musket 844
LePage Dueller 841
Mang In Graz Pistol 841
Mortimer Pistol 841
Mortimer Rifle 843
Mortimer Shotgun 846
Navy Moll Pistol 842
Pedersoli Lightning Rifle 846
Prussian 1809 Flintlock Musket 844
Queen Anne Pistol 842
Remington Pattern Target Revolver . . 841
Remington Rider Derringer 842
Revolutionnaire 1777 Musket 844
Rocky Mountain Hawken 845
Rogers & Spencer Target
Percussion Target Revolver 841
Rolling Block Rifle 845
Saloon Pistol 843
Sharps 1863 Sporting Rifle 845
Springfield 1795 Musket 844
Springfield 1861 Rifle 845
Swiss Rifle 843
Swivel-Breech Rifle 843
Tryon Rifle 843
Waadtlander Target Rifle 843
Wurttemberg Mauser 843
Zimmer Pistol 843
Modern Muzzleloaders 846
Brutus 94 846
Brutus Ovation 846
Denali 846
Rolling Block Percussion Rifle 846

PERAZZI 846
COMP1-SB TRAP 846
Standard Grade 847
COMP1-TRAP 847
Standard Grade 847
DB81 Special 849
SC3 Grade 849
SCO Grade 849
Standard Grade 849
DHO Extra Gold 847
DHO Model 847
Grand American Special 847
Extra Grade 847
Extra Gold Grade 847
Gold Grade 847
Gold Grade w/Sideplates 847
SC3 Grade 847
SCO Grade 847
SCO Grade w/Sideplates 847
Standard Grade 847
Light Game Model 847
Standard Grade 847
Mirage Special 849
Standard Grade 849
Mirage Special 4-Gauge Set 850
SC3 Grade 850
SCO Grade 850
Standard Grade 850
Mirage Special Sporting 849
Standard Grade 849
Mirage Special Sporting Classic 849
Standard Grade 849
Mirage MX8 850
Standard Grade 850
MT-6 Model 847
Standard Grade 847
MX3 847
Gold Grade 847
SC3 Grade 847
SCO Grade 847
Standard Grade 847
MX7 849
Standard Grade 849
MX7C 849
Standard Grade 849
MX8 Special 848
SC3 Grade 848
SCO Grade 848
Standard Grade 848
Standard Grade MX 8 Trap
Combo 848
MX8/20 848
SC3 Grade 848
SCO Grade 849
Standard Grade 848
MX8/20-8/20C 849
SC3 Grade 849
SCO Grade 849
Standard Grade 849
MX9 847
SC3 Grade 848
SCO Grade 848
Standard Grade 848
Standard Grade Trap Combo
MX 9 848
MX10 848
SC3 Grade 848
SCO Grade 848
Standard Grade 848
Standard Grade Combo Model 848
MX12/12C 850
SC3 Grade 850
SCO Grade 850
Standard Grade 850
MX20/20C 850
SC3 Grade 850
SCO Grade 850
Standard Grade 850
MX28 and MX410 850
SC3 Grade 850
SCO Grade 850
Standard Grade 850
SCO Model 850
SCO Grade 850
SHO Model 847
TM I Special 848
SC3 Grade 848
Standard Grade 848
TMX Special 848
SC3 Grade 848
SCO Grade 848
Standard Grade 848

PERRY & GODDARD 850
Derringer 850

PERRY PATENT FIREARMS CO. 851
Perry Carbine 851
Perry Single-Shot Pistol 851
1st Type 851
2nd Type 851

PERUGINI & VISINI 851
Bolt-Action Rifle 851
Boxlock Express Rifle 851
Classic Model 851
Deluxe Bolt-Action Rifle 851
Eagle Single-Shot 851
Liberty Model 851
Magnum Over-and-Under 851
Selous Side-by-Side Rifle 851
Super Express Rifle 851
Victoria Side-by-Side Rifle 851

PETTINGILL C. S. 851
Army Model Revolver 852
Navy Revolver 852
Pocket Revolver 851
1st Model 851
2nd Model 852
3rd Model 852

PFANNL, FRANCOIS 852
Erika 852

PGM PRECISION 852
Model PGM 852

PHILLIPS & RODGERS INC. . . 852
Medusa Model 47 852
Ruger 50 Conversion 852
Wilderness Explorer 852

PHOENIX 852
Pocket Pistol 852

PHOENIX ARMS 852
HP22 852
HP22/HP25 Target 853
HP25 853
Raven 853

PHOENIX ARMS CO. 853

PICKERT, FRIEDRICH 853
Arminius 7.65mm 853
Arminius Single-Shot Target Pistol . . 853
Pickert Revolver 854

PIEPER, HENRI & NICOLAS . . 854
Bayard 854
Legia 854
Model 1908/Basculant 854
Pieper Bayard Revolver 854
Pieper Model 1907 854

PILSEN, ZBROVKA 855
Pocket Pistol 855

PIOTTI 855
Model King Extra 855
Model King No. I 855
Model Lunik 855
Model Monaco 855
Monaco No. 1 or No. 2 856
Monaco No. 3 856
Monaco No. 4 856
Model Piuma (BSEE) 855
Monte Carlo Model 855
Over-and-Under Gun 855
Westlake Model 855

PIRKO 856

PLAINFIELD MACHINE CO. . . 856
M1 Carbine 856
MI Paratrooper Carbine 856
Super Enforcer 856

PLAINFIELD ORDNANCE CO. 856
Model 71 856
.22 or .25 Caliber Pistol 856
Conversion Kit 856
Model 72 856

PLANT'S MANUFACTURING CO. 856
Army Model Revolver 856
1st Model Brass Frame 856
1st Model Iron Frame 856
2nd Model Iron Frame 856
2nd Model Rounded Brass Frame 856
3rd Model 856
Pocket Revolver 856

POINTER 857
Single-Shot Derringer 857

POLY-TECHNOLOGIES, INC. . 857
AK-47/S 857
AKS-762 857
M-14/S 857
SKS 857

POND, LUCIUS, W. 857
Pocket Revolver 857
Brass Framed Revolver 857
Iron Framed Revolver 857
Separate Chamber Revolver 857
.22 Caliber Version 857
.32 Caliber Version 857

PORTER, P. W. 858
1st Model with Canister Magazine . . . 858
2nd Model (New York) 858
3rd Model (New York) 858
4th Model (New York) 858
Turret Revolver 858
Turret Rifle 858

POWELL, W. & SON LTD. . . . 858

PRAGA, ZBROVKA 858
Praga 1921 858
VZ2L 858

PRAIRIE GUN WORKS 858
M-15 858
M-18 858

PRANDELLI & GASPARINI . . . 858
Boxlock Over-and-Under Shotgun . . . 858
Boxlock Side-by-Side Shotgun . . . 858
Sidelock Over-and-Under Shotgun . . . 858
Sidelock Side-by-Side Shotgun . . . 858

PRATT, GEORGE 858
Trap Gun 858

PRATT, H. 859
Under Hammer Pistol 859

PRECISION SMALL ARMS . . . 859
Diplomat Model 859
Featherweight Model 859
Imperiale 859
Montreaux Model 859
PSA-25 859
Renaissance Model 859

PREMIER 859
Ambassador Model 860
Brush King 859
Presentation Custom Grade 860
Regent Magnum 859
Regent Side-by-Side Shotgun 859

PRESCOTT, E. A. 860
Army Revolver 860
Belt Revolver 860
Navy Revolver 860
Percussion Pocket Revolver 860
Pocket Revolver 860

PRETORIA 860

PRINZ 860
Grade 1 Bolt-Action Rifle 860
Grade 2 Bolt-Action Rifle 860
Model 85 "Princess" 860
Tip Up Rifle 860

PRITCHETT, POTTS & HUNT . . 860

PROFESSIONAL ORDNANCE, INC. 860
Carbon-15 Pistol—Type 21 861
Carbon-15 Pistol—Type 97 860
Carbon-15 Rifle—Type 21 861
Carbon-15 Rifle—Type 97 861
Carbon-15 Rifle—Type 97S 861

PROTECTION 861
1st Model 861
2nd Model 861
Protection Pocket Revolver 861

PTK INTERNATIONAL, INC. . . . 861

PULASKI ARMORY 861

PUMA (Rossi) 861
Model 92 Carbine 861
Model 92 Rifle 861
Model 92 Trapper 861

PURDEY, J. & SONS LTD. . . . 862
Double-Barreled Rifle 862
Hammerless Ejector Over-and-Under Gun 862
Hammerless Ejector Side-by-Side Game Gun 862

PYRENEES 862
Model 10 Unique 862
Model 11 862
Model 12 862
Model 13 862
Model 14 862
Model 15 862
Model 16 862
Model 17 862
Model 18 863
Model 19 863
Model 20 863
Model 21 863
Model 2000 863
Model BCF66 863
Model C 863
Model D 863
Model Des 69 863
Model DES/VO 863
Model F 863
Model L 863

Q

QUACKENBUSH 864
Bicycle Rifle 864
Junior Safety Rifle 864
Quackenbush Safety Cartridge Rifle . 864

QUINABAUG MFG. CO. 864
Under Hammer Pistol 864

R

R. G. INDUSTRIES 865
RG-14 865
RG-16 865

RG-17 . . . 865
RG-25 . . . 865
RG-30 . . . 865
RG-40 . . . 865
RG-57 . . . 865
RG-63 . . . 865
RG-66 . . . 865
RG-66T . . . 865
RG-74 . . . 866
RG-88 . . . 866

R.E. . . . 866

RADOM . . . 866
VIS-35 Reissue . . . 866

RANDALL FIREARMS CO. . . . 866
Austrian Randall . . . 869
Model A111 . . . 866
Model A111/111 Matched Set . . . 868
Model A112 . . . 866
Model A121 . . . 866
Model A122 . . . 866
Model A131 . . . 866
Model A211 . . . 866
Model A212 . . . 867
Model A231 . . . 866
Model A232 . . . 867
Model A311 . . . 867
Model A312 . . . 867
Model A331 Curtis LeMay . . . 867
Model A332 . . . 867
Model B111 . . . 867
Model B121 . . . 867
Model B122 . . . 867
Model B123 . . . 867
Model B131 . . . 867
Model B311 . . . 867
Model B312 . . . 868
Model B321 SET . . . 868
Model B331 . . . 868
Model C311 . . . 868
Model C332 . . . 868
Randall Magazines . . . 869
.45 LeMay—Dogleg Left-Hand . . . 869
.45 LeMay—Dogleg Right-Hand . . . 869
.45 LeMay—Left-Hand . . . 869
.45 LeMay—Right-Hand . . . 869
.45 Service—Left-Hand . . . 869
.45 Service—Right-Hand . . . 869
9mm Service—Left-Hand . . . 869
9mm Service—Right-Hand . . . 869

RANGER ARMS, INC. . . . 869
Governor . . . 869
Governor Magnum . . . 869
Senator . . . 869
Senator Magnum . . . 869
Statesman . . . 869
Statesman Magnum . . . 869

RAPTOR ARMS CO. . . . 869
Raptor Bolt-Action Rifle . . . 869

RASHID . . . 869
Rashid Carbine . . . 869

RAST & GASSER . . . 870

RAU ARMS CORP. . . . 870
Wildcat . . . 870
Wildcat Model 500 . . . 870
Wildcat Model 600 Deluxe . . . 870

RAVELL . . . 870
Maxim Double Rifle . . . 870

RAVEN ARMS . . . 870
MP-25 . . . 871
P-25 . . . 870

READ & WATSON . . . 871

RECORD-MATCH ANSCHUTZ . 871
Model 200 Free Pistol . . . 871
Model 210 Free Pistol . . . 871
Model 210A . . . 871

REEDER, GARY CUSTOM GUNS . . . 871
African Hunter . . . 873
Alaskan Classic . . . 874
Alaskan Grizzly . . . 873
Alaskan Survivalist . . . 874
American Hunter . . . 874
Arizona Ranger Classic . . . 871
Badlands Classic . . . 872
Big 5 Classic . . . 875
Black Widow . . . 871
Black Widow II . . . 871
Buffalo Hunter . . . 874
Classic 45 . . . 875
Classic Hunter . . . 873
Cowboy Classic . . . 872
Cowtown Classic . . . 872
Coyote Classic . . . 873
Doc Holliday Classic . . . 872
Double Duce . . . 875
Gamblers Classic . . . 872
Kodiak Hunter . . . 874
Lone Star Classic . . . 872
Long Colt Hunter . . . 873
Long Colt Hunter II . . . 873
Long Rider Classic . . . 872
Montana Hunter . . . 874
Night Rider . . . 873
Professional Hunter . . . 874
Southern Comfort . . . 874
Texas Ranger Classic . . . 872
The BMF . . . 875
Tombstone Classic . . . 872
Trail Rider Classic . . . 872
Ultimate 41 . . . 873
Ultimate 44 . . . 874
Ultimate 480 . . . 875
Ultimate 500 . . . 875
Ultimate Back Up 2 . . . 874
Ultimate Bisley . . . 873
Ultimate Black Widow . . . 875
Ultimate Encore . . . 874
Ultimate Vaquero . . . 873

REFORM . . . 875
Reform Pistol . . . 875

REICHS REVOLVER . . . 875
Model 1879 . . . 875
Model 1883 . . . 875

REID, JAMES . . . 875
.41 Caliber Knuckle Duster . . . 876
.32 Caliber Knuckle Duster . . . 876
Brass Frame . . . 876
Iron Frame . . . 876
Model 1 Revolver . . . 875
Model 2 Revolver . . . 876
Model 3 Revolver . . . 876
Model 4 Revolver . . . 876
Model No. 1 Knuckle Duster . . . 876
Model No. 2 Knuckle Duster . . . 877
Model No. 3 Derringer . . . 877
Model No. 4 Derringer . . . 877
"My Friend" Knuckle Duster . . . 876
Brass Frame . . . 876
Iron Frame . . . 876
New Model Knuckle Duster . . . 877

REISING ARMS CO. . . . 877
Standard Model . . . 877
Hartford Manufacture . . . 877
New York Manufacture . . . 877

REMINGTON ARMS COMPANY, INC. . . . 877
1st Model Remington-Beals Revolver 877
2nd Model Remington-Beals Revolver 877
3rd Model Remington-Beals Revolver 878
1861 Army Revolver . . . 878
1861 Navy Revolver . . . 878
Army Rifle . . . 888
Baby Carbine . . . 886
Black Hills Rifle . . . 886
Shotgun . . . 886
Breech-Loading Carbine . . . 884
Frontier Model . . . 888
Genesis Muzzleloaders . . . 909
Hammerless Shotgun Model 1894 . . . 890
Large-Bore Vest Pocket Pistol . . . 881
Long-Range Creedmoor Rifle . . . 885
Mark III Signal Pistol . . . 883
Mid-Range Target Rifle . . . 885
Model 1-1/2 Sporting Rifle . . . 886
Model 2 Sporting Rifle . . . 886
Model 5 . . . 901
Model 8 . . . 890
Standard Grade . . . 890
Model 8A . . . 890
Model 8C . . . 890
Model 8D Peerless . . . 890
Model 8E Expert . . . 890
Model 8F Premier . . . 890
Model 10 . . . 898
10 (SB) . . . 898
Model 10A . . . 911
Model 10C . . . 899
Model 11 . . . 898
Model 11 . . . 912
Model 11B Special . . . 912
Model 11D Tournament . . . 912
Model 11E Expert . . . 912
Model 11F Premier . . . 912
Model 11R . . . 912
Model 11-48 . . . 918
Model 11-87 Custom Grade . . . 922
D Grade . . . 922
F Grade . . . 922
F Grade with Gold Inlay . . . 922
Model 11-87 Dale Earnhardt Tribute . 920
Model 11-87 Police . . . 922
Model 11-87 Premier . . . 920
Model 11-87 Premier 20 Gauge . . . 920
Model 11-87 Premier Cantilever Scope Mount Deer Gun . . . 921
Model 11-87 Premier SC (Sporting Clays) . . . 921
Model 11-87 Premier Trap . . . 921
Model 11-87 SC NP (Sporting Clays Nickel-Plated) . . . 921
Model 11-87 SP Super Magnum . . . 922
Model 11-87 SP Thumbhole . . . 923
Model 11-87 SP-T Thumbhole . . . 923
Model 11-87 Sportsman Camo . . . 923
Model 11-87 Sportsman Camo Rifled . 923
Model 11-87 Sportsman Camo Youth 923
Model 11-87 Sportsman NRA Edition . 922
Model 11-87 Sportsman Rifled . . . 922
Model 11-87 Sportsman Synthetic . . . 922
Model 11-87 Sportsman Youth . . . 922
Model 11-87 SPS . . . 921
Model 11-87 SPS Super Magnum . . . 922
Model 11-87 SPS Super Magnum Waterfowl . . . 923
Model 11-87 SPS-BG Camo . . . 921
Model 11-87 SPS-Deer . . . 921
Model 11-87 SPS-T . . . 921
Model 11-87 SPS-T Camo . . . 921
Model 11-87 SPS-T Camo NWTF 25th Anniversary . . . 922
Model 11-87 SPS-T Super Magnum . . 923

Model 11-87 SPS-T Super Magnum (NWTF Edition) . . . 922
Model 11-87 Upland Special . . . 920
Model 11-87 Waterfowl . . . 921
Model 11-96 Euro Lightweight . . . 923
Model 12 . . . 898
Model 12 or 12 A . . . 890
Model 12A . . . 890
Model 12B . . . 890
Model 12C . . . 890
Model 12C N.R.A. Target . . . 891
Model 12CS . . . 891
Model 12D Peerless . . . 891
Model 12E Expert . . . 891
Model 12F Premier . . . 891
Model 14 or 14A . . . 891
Model 14-1/2 . . . 891
Model 14R . . . 891
Model 16 . . . 891
Model 17 . . . 912
Model 24 . . . 892
Model 25 . . . 891
Model 29 . . . 912
Model 30A . . . 892
Model 30S . . . 892
Model 31 . . . 912
Model 32 . . . 924
Standard Grade . . . 924
Model 32 Skeet . . . 924
Model 32 TC . . . 924
Model 32D . . . 924
Model 32E Expert . . . 924
Model 32F Premier . . . 924
Model 37 . . . 893
Model 37-1940 . . . 893
Model 40X Centerfire . . . 901
Model 40X Sporter . . . 901
Model 40XB BR . . . 901
Model 40XB Stainless . . . 901
Model 40XB Tactical Rifle . . . 901
Model 40XR KS Sporter . . . 902
Model 40X-BR . . . 901
Model 41A "Targetmaster" . . . 892
Model 41AS . . . 892
Model 41P . . . 892
Model 41SB . . . 893
Model 48 Sportsman . . . 917
Model 51 . . . 884
Model 53 . . . 884
Model 55-2G . . . 892
Model 58 Sportsman . . . 918
Model 66 . . . 899
66 (AB) . . . 899
66 (AB) "Apache" Black . . . 899
66 (AN) . . . 899
66 (AN) "150th Anniversary Rifle" . . . 899
66 (BD) . . . 899
66 (BD) "Black Diamond" . . . 899
66 (BI) . . . 899
66 (BI) "Bicentennial Rifle" . . . 899
66 (GS) . . . 899
66 (GS) "Gallery Special" . . . 899
66 (MB) . . . 899
66 (MB) "Mohawk" Brown . . . 899
66 (SG) . . . 899
66 (SG) "Seneca" Green . . . 899
Model 66 Bicentennial Commemorative . . . 899
Model 74 Sportsman . . . 897
Model 76 . . . 899
76 (AB) . . . 899
76 (AB) "Trailrider" . . . 899
76 (MB) . . . 899
76 (MB) "Trailrider" . . . 899
76 (not cataloged) . . . 899
Model 76 Sportsman . . . 896
Model 77 . . . 899
Model 77 Apache . . . 899
Model 78 Sportsman . . . 902
Model 81 Woodsmaster . . . 890
Standard Grade . . . 890
Model 81A . . . 890
Model 81D Peerless . . . 890
Model 81F Premier . . . 890
Model 90-T Single-Barrel Trap . . . 925
Model 90-T Single-Barrel Trap (High Rib) . . . 925
Model 105CTi . . . 924
Model 121 and/or 121A . . . 891
Standard Grade . . . 891
Model 121D Peerless . . . 891
Model 121F Premier . . . 891
Model 121S . . . 891
Model 121SB—Smoothbore . . . 891
Model 141 . . . 891
Model 241 Speedmaster . . . 892
Model 241 . . . 892
Model 241D Peerless . . . 892
Model 241E Expert . . . 892
Model 241F Premier . . . 892
Model 300 Ideal . . . 924
Model 332 . . . 925
Model 396 Custom Grade . . . 925
Model 396 Skeet . . . 925
Model 396 Sporting . . . 925
Model 412 . . . 911
Model 504 . . . 893
Model 504 Custom . . . 893
Model 504-T LS HB . . . 893
Model 511 Scoremaster . . . 893
Model 513 TR Matchmaster . . . 893
Model 513 S . . . 894
Model 521 TL Jr. . . . 894
Model 522 Viper . . . 899
Model 541 S Custom . . . 900
Model 541T . . . 900
Model 541T Heavy Barrel . . . 900
Model 547 . . . 893
Model 550A . . . 892
Model 550P . . . 892
Model 552 BDL . . . 894
Model 552 BDL Deluxe Speedmaster NRA Edition . . . 894
Model 552 NRA Edition Speedmaster 894
Model 552A Speedmaster . . . 894
Model 572 BDL . . . 894
Model 572 BDL Smoothbore . . . 895
Model 572 Fieldmaster . . . 894
Model 572SB . . . 894
Model 580 . . . 895
Model 580 BR . . . 895
Model 580SB . . . 895
Model 581 . . . 895
Model 581 Left-Hand . . . 895
Model 581-S . . . 895
Model 582 . . . 895
Model 591 . . . 895
Model 592 . . . 895
Model 597 . . . 900
Model 597 Custom Target . . . 901
Model 597 Custom Target Magnum . . 901
Model 597 HB . . . 900
Model 597 HB Magnum . . . 900
Model 597 LSS . . . 900
Model 597 LSS . . . 901
Model 597 Magnum . . . 900
Model 597 Magnum LS . . . 901
Model 597 Sporter . . . 900
Model 597 SS . . . 900
Model 597 Stainless Sporter . . . 900
Model 597 Synthetic Scope Combo . . 901
Model 600 . . . 902
Model 600 Magnum . . . 903
Model 600 Mohawk . . . 903
Model 660 . . . 903
Model 660 Magnum . . . 903
Model 673 Guide Rifle . . . 902
Model 700 ABG (African Big Game) . . 907
Model 700 ADL . . . 903
Model 700 ADL Synthetic . . . 903
Model 700 ADL Synthetic Youth . . . 903
Model 700 Alaskan Ti . . . 908
Model 700 APR (African Plains Rifle) . 907
Model 700 AWR (Alaskan Wilderness Rifle) . . . 907
Model 700 BDL . . . 903
Model 700 BDL (DM) . . . 903
Model 700 BDL European . . . 905
Model 700 BDL LH (Left-Hand) . . . 903
Model 700 BDL LSS . . . 903
Model 700 BDL SS Camo Special Edition (RMEF) . . . 904
Model 700 BDL SS DM—Magnum Rifle . . . 903
Model 700 BDL SS Short Action . . . 904
Model 700 BDL Stainless Synthetic . . 905
Model 700 BDL Stainless Synthetic (DM) . . . 905
Model 700 CDL . . . 905
Model 700 CDL Boone and Crockett 908
Model 700 CDL SF LTD. . . . 905
Model 700 Classic . . . 907
Model 700 Custom . . . 907
Model 700 Custom "C" Grade . . . 907
Model 700 EtronX . . . 904
Model 700 FS . . . 905
Model 700 LSS 50th Anniversary of the .280 Remington . . . 908
Model 700 LSS LH (Laminated Stock SS Left-Hand) . . . 906
Model 700 LSS Mountain Rifle . . . 905
Model 700 LV SF (Light Varmint) . . . 906
Model 700 ML . . . 908
Model 700 ML Custom . . . 909
Model 700 ML Youth . . . 909
Model 700 MLS . . . 909
Model 700 MLS Custom . . . 909
Model 700 Mountain Rifle . . . 904
Model 700 Mountain Rifle (DM) . . . 905
Model 700 Mountain Rifle Stainless Synthetic . . . 905
Model 700 Police . . . 908
Model 700 Police DM . . . 908
Model 700 Police Lightweight Tactical 908
Model 700 RS . . . 905
Model 700 Safari Grade . . . 905
Model 700 Safari KS Stainless . . . 908
Model 700 Sendero . . . 904
Model 700 Sendero Composite . . . 904
Model 700 Sendero SF . . . 904
Model 700 Sendero SF-II . . . 904
Model 700 SPS . . . 906
Model 700 SPS Buckmasters Edition . 908
Model 700 SPS DM . . . 907
Model 700 SPS Stainless . . . 907
Model 700 SPS Tactical . . . 908
Model 700 SPS Varmint . . . 908
Model 700 SPS Youth . . . 907
Model 700 Tactical Weapons System 909
Model 700 Titanium . . . 905
Model 700 Varmint Laminated Stock (VLS) . . . 906
Model 700 Varmint Special Synthetic . 906
Model 700 Varmint Special Wood . . . 906
Model 700 VL SS Thumbhole . . . 908
Model 700 VS Composite (Varmint Synthetic Composite) . . . 906
Model 700 VS SF (Varmint Synthetic Stainless Fluted) . . . 906
Model 700 VS SF II . . . 906
Model 700 VSF . . . 906
Model 700 XCR . . . 907
Model 700 XCR (Rocky Mountain Elk Foundation) . . . 907

Model 700 XCR Tactical
Long Range Rifle 908
Model 700KS Mountain Rifle 904
Model 710 909
Model 710 Youth 909
Model 715 Sportsman 910
Model 720A 902
Model 721 902
Model 721 ADL 902
Model 721 BDL 902
Model 721A Magnum 902
Model 722 BDL 902
Model 725 ADL 902
Model 725 Kodiak 902
Model 740 895
Model 740 ADL 895
Model 740 BDL 895
Model 742 895
Model 742 BDL 895
Standard Grade 895
Model 742D Peerless 896
Model 742F Premier (Game Scene) . 896
Model 742F Premier (Gold Inlaid) . . . 896
Model 742 Bicentennial 896
Model 750 Woodsmaster 898
Model 750 Synthetic 898
Model 760 Carbine 894
Model 760 894
Standard Model 894
Model 760 ADL 894
Model 760 BDL 894
Model 760 Bicentennial 894
Model 760D Peerless 894
Model 760F Premier 894
Model 760F Gold Inlaid 894
Model 770 910
Model 770 Youth 910
Model 788 909
Model 798 910
Model 798 Stainless Laminate 911
Model 799 911
Model 870 20 Gauge Express Youth
Camo Turkey 914
Model 870 Brushmaster Deer Gun . . . 915
Model 870 Classic Trap 915
Model 870 Custom Grade 917
D Grade 917
F Grade 917
F Grade with Gold Inlay 917
Model 870 Dale Earnhardt Limited
Edition 916
Model 870 Express 913
Model 870 Express Camo Turkey . . . 914
Model 870 Express Combos 914
Model 870 Express Deer Gun 914
Model 870 Express Deer/Turkey
Combo 914
Model 870 Express HD
(Home Defense) 914
Model 870 Express Jr. NWTF Edition 913
Model 870 Express Left-Hand 914
Model 870 Express Small Game 914
Model 870 Express Super Magnum . . 913
Model 870 Express Super Magnum
Fall Flight 913
Model 870 Express Super Magnum
Turkey 914
Model 870 Express Synthetic 913
Model 870 Express Synthetic Deer . . . 914
Model 870 Express Synthetic Youth . 913
Model 870 Express Turkey 914
Model 870 Express Youth Gun 915
Model 870 Express Youth Turkey
Camo 915
Model 870 Field Wingmaster 912
Model 870 Field Wingmaster
16 Gauge 913
Model 870 Field Wingmaster
Small Bores 913
Model 870 Magnum 913
Model 870 Marine Magnum 916
Model 870 Police 916
Model 870 Rifle Deer Gun 915
Model 870 Security 915
Model 870 Special Field 915
Model 870 Special Purpose
Thumbhole 917
Model 870 SPS 916
Model 870 SPS Fully Rifled
Deer Gun 916
Model 870 SPS MAX Gobbler 917
Model 870 SPS Super Magnum
Camo 915
Model 870 SPS Super Slug Deer Gun 916
Model 870 SPS-BG Camo 915
Model 870 SPS-Camo 915
Model 870 SPS-Deer 916
Model 870 SPS-T 916
Model 870 SPS-T Camo 916
Model 870 SPS-T Camo 916
Model 870 SPS-T Camo NWTF
25th Anniversary 916
Model 870 SPS-T Super Mag 917
Model 870 SPS-T Super Magnum
Camo 916
Model 870 SPS-T Youth Turkey
Camo 915
Model 870 SPS-T/20 917
Model 870 SP-T Super Magnum
Thumbhole 916
Model 870 SP-T Thumbhole 917
Model 870 Tac-2 SpecOps Stock 917
Model 870 Tac-3 Folder 917
Model 870 Tac-3 Speedfeed IV 917
Model 870 Wingmaster 912
Model 870 Wingmaster Jr. 913
Model 870 Wingmaster NRA Edition . 913
Model 870 XCS Marine Magnum 917
Model 870 Youth Deer Gun 915
Model 870TA Trap 913
Model 870TB Trap 914
Model 870TC Trap 914
Model 878 Automaster 918
Model 1100 Classic Field 918
Model 1100 Classic Trap 919
Model 1100 Competition 919
Model 1100 Competition Master 919
Model 1100 Custom Grade 920
D Grade 920
F Grade 920
F Grade with Gold Inlay 920
Model 1100 G3 920
Model 1100 LT-20 919
Model 1100 LT-20 Deer Gun 919
Model 1100 LT-20 Magnum 919
Model 1100 LT-20 Synthetic 919
Model 1100 LT-20 Synthetic Camo
NWTF 25th Anniversary 920
Model 1100 Small Game 918
Model 1100 Sporting 12 919
Model 1100 Sporting 20 919
Model 1100 Sporting 28 919
Model 1100 Synthetic 920
Model 1100 Synthetic Deer Gun 920
Model 1100 Tactical Speedfeed IV . . . 920
Model 1100 Tactical Standard Stock . 920
Model 1100 Tournament Skeet 918
Model 1100 Tournament Skeet,
12 Gauge 918
Model 1100 Youth Gun 918
Model 1100 Youth Synthetic 918
Model 1100 Youth Synthetic Camo . . 918
Model 1816 Commemorative
Flint Lock Rifle 911
Model 1841 "Mississippi Rifle" 884
Model 1861 U.S. Rifle Musket 884
Model 1863 Zouave Rifle 884
Model 1865 Navy Rolling Block
Pistol 881
Model 1867 Navy Cadet Rifle 885
Model 1867 Navy Rolling Block Pistol 882
Model 1871 Army Rolling Block Pistol 882
Model 1875 Single-Action Army 883
Model 1879 Military Rifle 889
Model 1879 Sharps Mfg. 888
Model 1879 Sporting Rifle 888
Model 1879 U.S. Navy Model 888
Model 1882 Army Contract 889
Model 1882 Shotgun 889
Model 1882 & 1885 Carbine 889
Model 1882 & 1885 Military Rifles . . . 889
Model 1882 & 1885 Sporting Rifle . . . 889
Model 1883 through 1889 Shotgun . . . 889
Model 1885 Navy Contract 889
Model 1890 Single-Action Army 883
Model 1891 Target Rolling Block
Pistol 883
Model 1893 (No. 9) 890
Model 1897 886
Carbine 886
Model 1899 889
Military Carbine 889
Military Rifle 889
Model 1900 Shotgun 890
Model 1901 Target Rolling Block 883
Model 3200 924
Field Grade 924
Model 3200 4-Gauge Set 924
Model 3200 Competition Trap 924
Model 3200 Magnum 924
Model 3200 "One of One Thousand" 924
Model 3200 Premier 924
Model 3200 Skeet 924
Model 3200 Special Trap 924
Model 3200 Trap 924
Model 7400 897
Model 7400 Buckmasters ADF
(American Deer Foundation) 898
Model 7400 Carbine 898
Model 7400 Custom Grade 898
D Grade 898
F Grade 898
F Grade with Gold Inlay 898
Model 7400 Special Purpose 898
Model 7400 Synthetic 897
Model 7400 Weathermaster 897
Model 7600 896
Standard Grade 896
Model 7600 Buckmasters ADF
(American Deer Foundation) 896
Model 7600 Custom Grade 897
D Grade 897
F Grade 897
F Grade with Gold Inlay 897
Model 7600 Premier 896
Model 7600 Synthetic 896
Model 7600 Special Purpose 896
Model 7600D Peerless 896
Model 7600F Premier 896
Model 7600P Patrol Rifle 896
Model 7615 Camo Hunter 897
Model 7615 Ranch Carbine 897
Model 7615 Special Purpose
Synthetic 897
Model 7615 Tactical Pump Carbine . . 897
Model Four 897
Model No. 4 S Military Rifle 886
Model Seven 909
Model Seven FS 909
Model Seven SS (Stainless Synthetic) 910
Model Seven LSS 910
Model Seven LS 910
Model Seven MS 910
Model Seven AWR 910

Model Seven Youth . . . 910
Model Seven CDL . . . 910
Model Seven XCR Camo . . . 910
Model Six . . . 897
Model SP-10 . . . 923
Model SP-10 Custom Grade . . . 924
Model SP-10 Magnum Camo . . . 923
Model SP-10 Magnum Camo NWTF 25th Anniversary . . . 923
Model SP-10 Magnum Thumbhole Camo . . . 924
Model SP-10 Magnum Waterfowl . . . 924
Model SP-10 RC/VT . . . 923
Model SP-10 Synthetic . . . 923
Model SPR 18 . . . 927
Model SPR 22 . . . 927
Model SPR 94 . . . 927
Model SPR 100/Sporting . . . 927
Model SPR 210 . . . 927
Model SPR 220 . . . 927
Model SPR 310 . . . 927
Model SPR 310S . . . 927
Model SPR18 Single Shot Rifle . . . 911
Model SPR22 Double Rifle . . . 911
Model SPR94 Combo Gun . . . 911
Model XC . . . 902
Model XP-100 . . . 926
Model XP-100 Custom . . . 926
Model XP-100 Hunter . . . 926
Model XP-100 Silhouette . . . 926
Model XP-100R Repeater . . . 927
Model XR-100 Rangemaster . . . 902
Navy Rifle . . . 888
Carbine . . . 888
New Model Army Revolver . . . 879
.44 or .46 Cartridge Conversion . . 879
Civilian Model—No Government Inspector's Markings . . . 879
Standard Model—Military Version 879
New Model Navy Revolver . . . 879
.38 Cartridge Conversion—1873 to 1888 . . . 879
Civilian Version . . . 879
Military Version . . . 879
New Model Pocket Revolver . . . 880
.32 Cartridge Conversion . . . 880
1st Version . . . 880
2nd Version . . . 880
3rd Version . . . 880
New Model Police Revolver . . . 879
New Model Single-Action Belt Revolver . . . 879
No. 1 Rolling Block Sporting Rifle . . . 885
No. 3 High-Power Rifle . . . 888
No. 3 Long-Range Creedmoor Rifle . . . 887
No. 3 Long-Range Military Rifle . . . 887
Fancy Grade . . . 887
Plain Grade . . . 887
No. 3 Match Rifle . . . 887
A Quality . . . 887
B Quality . . . 887
No. 3 Mid-Range Creedmoor Rifle . . . 887
No. 3 Schuetzen Match Rifle . . . 887
Breechloading Version . . . 888
Muzzleloading Version . . . 888
No. 4 Revolver . . . 882
No. 4 Rolling Block Rifle . . . 886
No. 5 Rolling Block Rifle . . . 886
No. 5 Sporting or Target Rifle . . . 886
No. 6 Rolling Block Rifle . . . 886
No. 7 Rolling Block Rifle . . . 887
Premier Field Grade . . . 925
Premier RGS . . . 926
Premier STS Competition . . . 925
Premier Upland Grade . . . 925
Remington 180th Anniversary Limited Edition Rifles and Shotguns . . . 928
Remington 1911 and 1911A1 . . . 884
Remington Custom Shop . . . 928
Remington Iroquois Revolver . . . 883
Remington Lebel Bolt-Action Rifle . . . 889
Remington Mid-Range Sporter Rolling Block . . . 911
Remington Mosin-Nagant Bolt-Action Rifle . . . 889
Remington No. 1 Rolling Block Mid-Range . . . 911
Remington Over-and-Under Derringer . . . 881
Early Type I . . . 881
Type I Mid-Production . . . 881
Type I Late Production . . . 881
Type II . . . 881
Type III . . . 881
Remington Peerless . . . 925
Remington-Beals Army Revolver . . . 878
Remington-Beals Navy Revolver . . . 878
Remington-Beals Rifle . . . 885
Remington-Elliot Derringer . . . 880
4-shot .32 caliber . . . 880
5-shot .22 caliber . . . 880
Remington-Elliot Single-Shot Derringer . . . 881
Remington-Hepburn No. 3 Rifle . . . 887
Remington-Keene Magazine Rifle . . . 888
Remington-Lee Magazine Rifle . . . 888
Remington-Rider Derringer . . . 880
Remington-Rider Double-Action Belt Revolver . . . 879
Remington-Rider Magazine Pistol . . . 881
Remington-Rider Revolver . . . 878
Remington-Smoot No. 1 Revolver . . . 882
Remington-Smoot No. 2 Revolver . . . 882
Remington-Smoot No. 3 Revolver . . . 882
Remington-Whitmore Model 1874 . . . 889
Combination Gun (Rare) . . . 889
Double Rifle . . . 889
Shotgun . . . 889
Revolving Rifle . . . 885
Rolling Block Military Rifles . . . 885
Short-Range Rifle . . . 885
Sporting Rifle . . . 888-889
Standard No. 1 Sporting Rifle . . . 885
Standard Version . . . 902
U.S. Model 1917 Magazine Rifle . . . 889
U.S. Navy Rolling Block Carbine . . . 885
Vest Pocket Pistol . . . 880
Zig-Zag Derringer . . . 880

RENETTE, GASTINNE . . . 929
Deluxe Mauser Bolt-Action . . . 929
Mauser Bolt-Action . . . 929
Model 98 . . . 929
Model 105 . . . 929
Model 202 . . . 929
Model 353 . . . 929
Type G Rifle . . . 929
Type R Deluxe . . . 929
Type PT President . . . 929

RENWICK ARMS CO. . . . 929

REPUBLIC ARMS, INC. . . . 929
RAP 440 . . . 929
Republic Patriot . . . 929

RETOLAZA HERMANOS . . . 929
Brompetier . . . 929
Gallus or Titan . . . 930
Liberty, Military, Retolaza, or Paramount . . . 930
Puppy . . . 930
Stosel . . . 930
Titanic . . . 930

REUNIES . . . 930
Dictator . . . 930
Texas Ranger or Cowboy Ranger . . . 930

REUTH, F. . . . 930
Animal Trap Gun . . . 930

REXIODE ARMAS . . . 930
Outfitter Single-Shot . . . 930
Outfitter Single-Shot Compact . . . 931
RJ 22 . . . 930
RJ 38 . . . 930
RS 22 . . . 930
RS 22M . . . 930
RS 357 . . . 930

RHEINMETALL . . . 931
Dreyse 6.35mm Model 1907 . . . 931
Dreyse 7.65mm Model 1907 . . . 931
Dreyse 9mm . . . 931
Dreyse Light Rifle or Carbine . . . 932
Rheinmetall 9mm . . . 931
Rheinmetall 32 . . . 931

RHODE ISLAND ARMS CO. . . . 932
Morrone . . . 932

RICHLAND ARMS CO. . . . 932
Model 41 Ultra Over-and-Under . . . 932
Model 80 LS . . . 932
Model 200 . . . 932
Model 202 . . . 932
Model 707 Deluxe . . . 932
Model 711 Magnum . . . 932
Model 747 Over-and-Under . . . 932
Model 757 Over-and-Under . . . 932
Model 787 Over-and-Under . . . 932
Model 808 Over-and-Under . . . 932

RICHMOND ARMORY . . . 932
Carbine . . . 932
Musketoon . . . 933
Rifled Musket . . . 933

RIEDL RIFLE CO. . . . 933
Single-Shot Rifle . . . 933

RIFLESMITH INC. . . . 933

RIGBY, JOHN & CO., LTD. . . . 933
Best Quality Sidelock Double Rifle . . . 933
Large Bore Magazine Rifle . . . 933
Magazine Rifle . . . 933
Second Quality Boxlock Double Rifle . 933
Single-Shot Rifle . . . 933
Third Quality Boxlock Double Rifle . . . 933

RIGDON, ANSLEY & CO. . . . 933
1851 Colt Navy Type . . . 933
Early Production Model . . . 933
Standard Production Model . . . 933

RIPOMANTI, GUY . . . 934
Over-and-Under Double Rifle . . . 934
Side-by-Side Shotgun . . . 934
Side-by-Side Double Rifles . . . 934

RIVERSIDE ARMS CO. . . . 934
Double-Barrel Shotguns . . . 934

RIZZINI, BATTISTA . . . 934
Artemis . . . 934
Artemis Deluxe . . . 934
Artemis EL . . . 934
Aurum Light . . . 934
Express 90 L . . . 936
Express 92 EL . . . 936
Premier Sporting . . . 935
Upland EL . . . 935
S780 Emel . . . 935
S782 Emel . . . 935
S790 EL Sporting . . . 936
S790 Emel . . . 935
S792 Emel . . . 935
Sporting EL . . . 935

RIZZINI, FRATELLI 936
Extra Lusso Grade—Scalloped receiver 936
.410 bore 936
12 gauge 936
20 gauge 936
28 gauge 936
Lusso Grade 936
12 gauge 936
20 gauge 936
28 gauge and .410 bore 936
Model R-1 936
12, 16, or 20 gauge 936
28 gauge or .410 bore 936
Model R-2 936

ROBAR AND de KIRKHAVE .. 937
Melior Model .22 Long Rifle 938
Melior Model .22 Target 938
Melior Model 1907 937
Melior Model 1913-1914 938
Melior Pocket Model 938
Melior Vest Pocket Model 938
Mercury 939
Model 1909-1910 937
Model 1911 937
Model 1912 937
New Model Jieffeco (6.35mm) 938
New Model Jieffeco (7.65mm) 938

ROBAR COMPANIES 939
Robar Elite Tactical Shotgun 939
Robar MK I Tactical Rifle 939
Robar MK II Tactical Rifle 939
Robar Patriot Tactical Shotgun 939
Robar Spec Ops Tactical Shotgun 939
Robar SR60 Precision Rifle 939

ROBBINS & LAWRENCE 939
Pepperbox 939

ROBERTSON 939
Pocket Pistol 939

ROBINSON ARMAMENT CO. . 939
M-96 Carbine 939
M-96 Expeditonary Rifle 939
M-96 Top Fed 939
Super VEPR 939

ROBINSON, ORVIL 940

ROBINSON, S.C. 940
Confederate Sharps 940
Robinson Sharps 940

ROCK ISLAND ARMORY (TRADE NAME OF ARMSCOR) 940

ROCK RIVER ARMS, INC. 940
Basic Carry 942
Basic Limited Match 941
Bullseye Wadcutter 941
CAR A2 942
CAR A2M 942
CAR A4 943
CAR A4M 943
Elite CAR A4 943
Elite CAR UTE 2 944
Elite Commando 940
Entry Tactical 944
Government Model 943
Hi-Cap Basic Limited 941
Limited Match 941
Limited Police Competition 9mm 942
Match Master Steel 941
National Match A2 943
National Match Hardball 940
NM A2-DCM Legal 943
Pro Carry 942
Standard A2 943
Standard A4 Flattop 943
Standard Match 940
Tactical CAR A4 943
Tactical CAR UTE (Universal Tactical Entry) 2 944
Tactical Pistol 942
TASC Rifle 944
Ultimate Match Achiever 941
Unlimited Police Competition 9mm 942
Varmint EOP (Elevated Optical Platform) 943
Varmint Rifle 943

ROGERS & SPENCER 944
Army Revolver 944

ROGUE RIFLE COMPANY 944

ROGUE RIVER RIFLEWORKS . 944
Boxlock Double Rifle 944
Sidelock Double Rifle 944

ROHM GMBH 944

ROHRBAUGH 944
R9/R9S 944

ROMERWERKE 945
Romer 945

RONGE, J. B. 945
Bulldog 945

ROSS RIFLE CO. 945
Mark I 945
Mark I Carbine 945
Mark 2 945
Mark 3 945
Mark 3B 945
Sporting Rifle 945

ROSSI, AMADEO 945
Field Grade Shotgun 945
Match Pair Combo Guns 946
Model 31 948
Model 51 947
Model 59 946
Model 62 946
Model 65 946
Model 68 948
Model 68S 947
Model 69 947
Model 70 947
Model 84 947
Model 88S 948
Model 89 949
Model 92 946
Model 92 Large Loop 946
Model 92 Rifle 946
Model 351 948
Model 352 948
Model 461 947
Model 462 947
Model 511 Sportsman 947
Model 677 948
Model 720 950
Model 851 948
Model 877 949
Model 951 948
Model 971 949
Model 971 Comp 949
Model 971 Stainless 949
Model 971 VRC (vented rib compensator) 949
Model 972 949
Model 988 Cyclops 949
Muzzleloader Matched Pair 946
Muzzleloading Rifle 946
Overland Shotgun 945
Rossi Blued Synthetic Matched Pair 947
Rossi Stainless Synthetic Matched Pair 947
Single Shot Rifle—Heavy Barrel 946
Single-Shot Rifle 946
Squire Shotgun 945
Youth Model Shotgun 946

ROTH-SAUER 950

ROTH-STEYR 950

ROTTME, TH. 950

ROTTWEIL 950
Model 72 950
Model 72 American Skeet 950
Model 72 Adjustable American Trap 950
Model 72 American Trap 950
Model 72 International Skeet 950
Model 72 International Trap 950
Model 650 950

ROYAL AMERICAN SHOTGUNS 950
Model 100 950
Model 100AE 950
Model 600 950
Model 800 950

RUBY ARMS COMPANY 951
Ruby 951

RUGER 951

RUPERTUS, JACOB 951
Army Revolver 951
Double-Barrel Pocket Pistol 951
Navy Revolver 951
Pocket Model Revolver 951
Single-Shot Pocket Pistol 951
Spur Trigger Revolver 951

RWS 951
Model 820 K 951
Model 820 S 951
Model 820 SF 951

S

S.A.C.M. 952

S.A.E. 952
Model 66C 952
Model 70 952
Model 210S 952
Model 340X 952
Model 209E 952

S.E.A.M. 952
Praga 952
S.E.A.M. 952
Silesia 952

S.W.D., INC. 952
Cobray M-11 952
M-11 Carbine 952
Terminator 952

SABATTI 952

SACKET, D. D. 952
Under Hammer Pistol 952

SAFARI ARMS 952
Black Widow 953
Counter Sniper Rifle 953
Enforcer 952
Match Master 953
Model 81 953
Model 81L 953
Survivor I Conversion Unit 953
Ultimate Unlimited 953

SAKO 953
Anniversary Model 954

Carbine . . . 955
Long Action . . . 955
Medium Action . . . 955
Classic Grade . . . 955
Deluxe Grade . . . 955
Long Action . . . 956
Medium Action . . . 955
Short Action . . . 956
Deluxe Model . . . 953
FiberClass . . . 955
FiberClass Carbine . . . 955
Finnbear . . . 953
Finnfire . . . 954
Finnfire Heavy Barrel . . . 954
Finnfire Hunter . . . 954
Finnfire Sporter . . . 954
Finnwolf . . . 954
FN Action . . . 954
FN Magnum Action . . . 954
Forester . . . 953
Hunter . . . 954
Carbine . . . 954
Long Action . . . 954
Medium Action . . . 954
Short Action . . . 954
Laminated Model . . . 955
Long Action . . . 955
Medium Action . . . 955
Long Range Hunting Rifle . . . 955
Model 75 Big Game Deluxe . . . 956
Model 75 Custom Deluxe . . . 957
Model 75 Custom Single Shot . . . 957
Model 75 Deluxe . . . 956
Model 75 Finnlight . . . 957
Model 75 Grey Wolf . . . 957
Model 75 Hunter . . . 956
Model 75 Stainless Synthetic . . . 956
Model 75 Super Deluxe . . . 957
Model 75 Varmint . . . 956
Model 75 Varmint Set Trigger . . . 956
Model 75 Varmint Stainless . . . 957
Model 75 Varmint Stainless Set Trigger . . . 957
Model 78 . . . 957
Model 2700 Finnsport . . . 957
PPC Bench Rest/Varmint . . . 955
Safari 80th Anniversary Model . . . 957
Safari Grade . . . 956
Sako 85 Finnlight . . . 959
Sako 85 Hunter . . . 957
Sako 85 Laminated SS Varmint . . . 959
Sako 85 Stainless Synthetic . . . 957
Sako 85 Varmint . . . 959
Sako Quad Combo . . . 954
Standard Sporter . . . 953
Super Grade/Super Deluxe . . . 956
Long Action . . . 956
Medium Action . . . 956
Short Action . . . 956
TRG-21 . . . 959
TRG-22 . . . 959
TRG-41 . . . 959
TRG-42 . . . 959
TRG-S . . . 959
Varmint-Heavy Barrel . . . 955
Medium Action . . . 955
Short Action . . . 955
Vixen . . . 953

SAM, INC. . . . 959
Model 88 Crossfire . . . 959

SAMCO GLOBAL ARMS, INC. 959

SARASQUETA, FELIX . . . 959
Merke . . . 959

SARASQUETA, J. J. . . . 960
Model 107E . . . 960
Model 119E . . . 960
Model 130E . . . 960
Model 131E . . . 960
Model 1882 E LUXE . . . 960

SARASQUETA, VICTOR . . . 960
Model 3 . . . 960
Model 4 . . . 960
Model 4E (Auto-ejectors) . . . 960
Model 6E . . . 960
Model 7E . . . 960
Model 10E . . . 960
Model 11E . . . 960
Model 12E . . . 960
Model 203 . . . 960
Model 203E . . . 960

SARDIUS . . . 960
SD-9 . . . 960

SARSILMAZ . . . 961
Bernardelli . . . 961
Hancer 2000/2000 Light . . . 961
K2 . . . 961
Kama . . . 961
Kama Sport . . . 961
Kilinc 2000 Light . . . 961
Kilinc 2000 Mega . . . 961
Professional . . . 961

SAUER, J. P. & SON . . . 961
1926 Export Model . . . 965
1930 Commercial Model . . . 966
Duralumin (rural) Variation, 7.65mm . . . 966
Standard Commercial . . . 966
Standard Commercial in .22 LR (.22 Long) . . . 966
Standard Commercial with NIROSTA marked barrel, 7.65mm . . . 966
Amsterdam Police . . . 966
Behorden Commercial . . . 966
Bolt-Action Rifle . . . 961
Commercial variation . . . 964
Caliber 7.65mm variation . . . 964
Caliber 7.65 variation with all words in English (i.e Son, Prussia, etc.) . . . 964
Department of Finance . . . 966
Duralumin Model (Dural) . . . 966
Blue Anodized Variation . . . 966
Nonanodized Variation . . . 966
Presentation Examples of Anodized and Nonanodized Variations . . . 967
Dutch models . . . 966
Dutch Police . . . 966
Grade I Artemis . . . 963
Grade II Artemis . . . 963
Imperial Military variations . . . 964
Caliber 7.65mm Imperial Military accepted pistols . . . 964
Late Behorden Commercial . . . 966
Luftwaffe Survival Drilling . . . 963
Model 36/37 . . . 967
Model 38 . . . 967
One Line Slide Legend Variation (inned magazine release button - no screw) . . . 967
SA der NSDAP Gruppe Thuringen Marked Variation . . . 968
Two Line Slide Legend Variation (magazine release button) . . . 967
Two Line Slide Legend Variation (pinned magazine release button - no screw) . . . 967
Model 38 and 38-H (H Model) Variations . . . 967
Model 38 pistols converted to H Models by Sauer factory. . . . 968
Model 38-H or H Model . . . 968
Flash Light Model . . . 968
L.M. Model . . . 968
Police Accepted Variation . . . 968
SA der NSDAP Gruppe Thuringia Variation . . . 968
Standard Commercial Variation . . . 968
Model 54 Combo . . . 963
Model 60 . . . 963
Model 66 . . . 963
Grade I . . . 963
Grade II . . . 963
Grade III . . . 963
Model 90 . . . 962
Model 90 Safari . . . 962
Model 90 Stutzen . . . 962
Model 90 Supreme . . . 962
Model 200 . . . 961
Model 200 Carbon Fiber . . . 961
Model 200 Lightweight . . . 961
Model 200 Lux . . . 961
Model 202 Supreme . . . 961
Model 202 Takedown . . . 962
Model 1913/19 in 6.35mm . . . 965
Caliber 6.35mm first subvariation . 965
Caliber 6.35mm second subvariation . . . 965
Caliber 6.35mm third subvariation 965
Caliber 6.35mm English export variation . . . 965
Model 1920 . . . 966
Model 1928 . . . 966
Model 1930 variations . . . 966
Model 1933 . . . 966
Model 3000 Drilling . . . 963
Model S202 Forest . . . 962
Model S202 Hardwood . . . 962
Model S202 Highland . . . 962
Model S202 Match . . . 962
Model S202 Outback . . . 962
Model S202 Team Sauer . . . 962
Model S202 Wolverine . . . 962
Navy . . . 966
Norwegian police usage, post World War II . . . 964
Paramilitary marked Sauer pistols of the 1925-35 period . . . 964
Police Models . . . 967
Diamond in Sunburst Police Acceptance . . . 967
Grip Strap Marked Variations . . . 967
Sunburst K Police Acceptance . . . 967
Police variations . . . 964
Caliber 6.35mm police marked but without Zusatzsicherung . . 964
Caliber 6.35mm police marked with Zusatzsicherung . . . 964
Caliber 7.65mm police marked without Zusatzsicherung . . . 964
Caliber 7.65mm police marked with Zusatzsicherung . . . 964
R.F.V. (Reich Finanz Verwaltung) . . . 964
Caliber 6.35mm R.F.V. marked pistols . . . 964
Caliber 7.65mm R.F.V. marked pistols . . . 964
Roth-Sauer Model . . . 963
Royal Model . . . 963
Sauer Model 1913 . . . 963
A. European variation: . . . 963
B. English Export variation: . . . 964
SG 550 Sniper . . . 962
S.M.N. . . . 966
SSG-3000 . . . 962
W.T.M.-Westentaschen Model—Vest Pocket Model . . . 965
Type Five Model 38 & H Model Pistols . . . 970
First Variation . . . 970
Second Variation . . . 970
Type Four 38-H Model (H Model) . . . 969

A. H Model . . . 969
Commercial . . . 969
Eigentum NSDAP SA Gruppe Alpenland Slide Marked Pistols . . . 969
Himmler Presentation Pistols . . . 970
Military Accepted . . . 969
NSDAP SA Gruppe Alpenland Slide Marked Pistols . . . 970
Police Accepted with the Police Eagle C Acceptance . . . 969
Model 38 . . . 970
Commercial . . . 970
Military Accepted . . . 970
Police Accepted with the Police Eagle C Acceptance . . . 970
Police Accepted with the Police Eagle F Acceptance . . . 970
Type Three 38-H Model (H Model) . . . 969
A. H Model . . . 969
Commercial . . . 969
Military Accepted . . . 969
Police Accepted with the Police Eagle C Acceptance . . . 969
Type Two Model 38-H (H Model) . . . 968
A. H Model . . . 968
.22 Caliber Variation . . . 968
German Military Variation . . . 968
Jager Model . . . 968
Police Eagle C Acceptance . . . 969
Police Eagle C and Eagle F Acceptance Variations . . . 968
Second Military Variation . . . 968
Standard Commercial . . . 968

SAVAGE ARMS CORPORATION . . . 971

Combination Cased Set .300 Savage/.410 Barrel . . . 972
Fox Model B—Chicopee Falls, Mass. (later Westfield, Mass.) . . . 993
Fox Model B—Single Trigger . . . 993
Fox Model B—Utica, NY . . . 993
Fox Model BDE . . . 993
Fox Model BDL . . . 993
Fox Model BE . . . 994
Fox Model BSE . . . 994
Fox Model BST . . . 993
Long Range Precision Varminter . . . 985
Mark I-G . . . 988
Mark I-GSB . . . 988
Mark I-GY (Youth Model) . . . 988
Mark II-F . . . 989
Mark II-FSS . . . 989
Mark II-FV . . . 989
Mark II-FXP . . . 989
Mark II-G . . . 989
Mark II-GXP . . . 989
Mark II-GY (Youth Model) . . . 989
Mark II-LV . . . 989
Milano . . . 994
Model 3 . . . 976
Model 4 . . . 976
Model 4M . . . 976
Model 5 . . . 976
Model 6 . . . 975
Model 6.35mm . . . 995
Model 7 . . . 975
Model 10 Predator Hunter . . . 983
Model 10FCM—Scout Rifle . . . 982
Model 10FCM—Sierra . . . 982
Model 10FCP Choate . . . 983
Model 10FCP McMillan . . . 983
Model 10FCP-HS Precision . . . 983
Model 10FLP . . . 982
Model 10FM—Sierra . . . 982
Model 10FP-HS . . . 983
Model 10FP-LE1 . . . 983
Model 10FP-LE1A . . . 983
Model 10FP-LE2B . . . 983
Model 10FP-LE2 . . . 983
Model 10FP-LE2A . . . 983
Model 10FP—Tactical (Short Action) . 982
Model 10FPXP-HS Precision . . . 983
Model 10FPXP-LE . . . 983
Model 10FPXP-LEA . . . 983
Model 10GY Youth . . . 983
Model 10ML-II . . . 984
Model 10ML-II Camo . . . 984
Model 10ML-IIXP . . . 984
Model 10MLBSS-II . . . 984
Model 10MLSS-II . . . 984
Model 10MLSS-II Camo . . . 984
Model 10MLSS-IIXP . . . 984
Model 11F . . . 984
Model 11FCNS . . . 984
Model 11FCXP3 . . . 986
Model 11FHNS . . . 986
Model 11FL . . . 984
Model 11FLHSS Weather Warrior . . . 985
Model 11FNS . . . 984
Model 11FYCAK . . . 985
Model 11FYCXP3 . . . 986
Model 11G . . . 984
Model 11GL . . . 984
Model 11GNS . . . 984
Model 11GCNS . . . 984
Model 12 F-Class Target Rifle . . . 982
Model 12 LRPV Long Range Precision Varminter . . . 982
Model 12 Varminter Low Profile . . . 982
Model 12BVSS . . . 981
Model 12BVSS-S . . . 981
Model 12BVSS-SXP . . . 981
Model 12FLV . . . 981
Model 12FV (Short Action) . . . 981
Model 12FVSS . . . 981
Model 12FVSS-S . . . 981
Model 12VSS—Varminter (Short Action) . . . 982
Model 14 Classic . . . 985
Model 14 Euro Classic . . . 985
Model 16BSS . . . 985
Model 16FCSAK . . . 985
Model 16FCSS . . . 985
Model 16FHSAK . . . 985
Model 16FHSS . . . 985
Model 16FLSS . . . 985
Model 16FSS . . . 985
Model 19 NRA . . . 976
Model 19H . . . 976
Model 19L . . . 976
Model 19M . . . 976
Model 21 . . . 992
Model 23A . . . 977
Model 23AA . . . 977
Model 23B . . . 977
Model 23C . . . 977
Model 23D . . . 977
Model 24 . . . 990
Model 24 Field—Lightweight Version . . . 990
Model 24C . . . 990
Model 24DL . . . 990
Model 24F . . . 990
Model 24MS . . . 990
Model 24S . . . 990
Model 24VS . . . 990
Model 25 . . . 975
Model 28 . . . 992
Model 29 . . . 975
Model 30 . . . 992
Model 30G "Favorite" Takedown . . . 988
Model 30G "Stevens Favorite" . . . 988
Model 35 . . . 977
Model 40 . . . 977, 982
Model 40 Varmint Hunter . . . 977
Model 45 Super . . . 977
Model 46 . . . 977
Model 60 . . . 986
Model 64F . . . 986
Model 64FSS . . . 986
Model 64FV . . . 986
Model 64FVSS . . . 986
Model 64FVXP . . . 986
Model 64FXP . . . 986
Model 64G . . . 986
Model 64GXP . . . 986
Model 88 . . . 986
Model 90 Carbine . . . 986
Model 93BTVS . . . 987
Model 93F . . . 987
Model 93FV . . . 988
Model 93FVSS . . . 987
Model 93FVSS-XP . . . 988
Model 93FSS . . . 988
Model 93G . . . 987
Model 93-FS . . . 987
Model 93R17 Classic . . . 988
Model 93R17-BTVS . . . 988
Model 93R17-BV . . . 988
Model 93R17-BVSS . . . 987
Model 93R17-Camo . . . 987
Model 93R17-F . . . 987
Model 93R17-FSS . . . 987
Model 93R17-FVSS . . . 987
Model 93R17-FXP . . . 988
Model 93R17-GV . . . 987
Model 93R17-GVXP . . . 987
Model 99A Saddle Gun . . . 974
Model 99CE (Centennial Edition) . . . 974
Model 99-.358 and 99-.375 Brush Guns . . . 974
Model 99-A 24" Featherweight Rifle . . . 973
Model 99-B 26"/24" Standard Weight Takedown . . . 972
Model 99-C 22" Standard Weight Short Rifle . . . 972
Model 99-C Clip Magazine Rifle . . . 974
Model 99-CD Deluxe Clip Model . . . 974
Model 99-D 22" Standard Weight Takedown Rifle . . . 972
Model 99-DE Citation Grade Rifle . . . 974
Model 99-DL Deluxe Monte Carlo Rifle . . . 974
Model 99-E Economy Rifle . . . 974
Model 99-E Lightweight Rifle . . . 972
Model 99-EG Standard Weight Rifle . . 973
Model 99-F Featherweight Rifle . . . 973
Model 99-F Lightweight Takedown Rifle . . . 972
Model 99-G Deluxe Takedown Pistol Grip Rifle . . . 972
Model 99-H Carbine/Barrel Band Carbine . . . 972
Model 99-K Deluxe Engraved Rifle . . . 973
Model 99-PE Presentation Grade Rifle . . . 974
Model 99-R Heavy Stocked Rifle . . . 973
Model 99-RS Special Sights . . . 973
Model 99-T Deluxe Featherweight Rifle . . . 973
Model 101 . . . 996
Model 110 Sporter . . . 977
Model 110-CY . . . 978
Model 110-D . . . 978
Model 110-F . . . 978
Model 110-FP . . . 978
Model 110-FX . . . 978
Model 110-G . . . 978
Model 110-GX . . . 978
Model 110-M . . . 977
Model 110-P Premier Grade . . . 978
Model 110-PE . . . 978

Model 110FP Duty 978
Model 110FP Tactical 978
Model 110FP-LE1 978
Model 110FP-LE2 978
Model 111 Classic Hunter Series 978
Model 111F 979
Model 111FAK 979
Model 111FC 979
Model 111FCNS 979
Model 111FCXP3 979
Model 111FL 979
Model 111FHNS 985
Model 111FXP3 979
Model 111FYCAK 985
Model 111G 978
Model 111GC 979
Model 111GCNS 979
Model 111GL 979
Model 112 Series Varmint Rifles 979
Model 112 Varmint, Low Profile 985
Model 112BT / 112BT-S (Long Action) 979
Model 112BT—Competition Grade 980
Model 112BVSS (Long Action) 979
Model 112BVSS-S 980
Model 112FV 980
Model 112FVSS 980
Model 112FVSS-S 980
Model 114 Classic 985
Model 114 Euro Classic 985
Model 114C—Classic 980
Model 114CE—Classic European 980
Model 114CU 980
Model 114U—Ultra 980
Model 116BSS 980
Model 116FCS 981
Model 116FCSAK (Long Action) 980
Model 116FHSAK 985
Model 116FHSS 985
Model 116FSAK (Long Action) 980
Model 116FSK—Kodiak (Long Action) 981
Model 116FSS (Long Action) 981
Model 116SE—Safari Express 981
Model 116US 981
Model 170 975
Model 210F 990
Model 210F Slug Warrior 991
Model 210F Slug Warrior Camo 991
Model 210FT 991
Model 220 991
Model 242 992
Model 312 Field Over-and-Under 993
Model 312 Sporting Clay 993
Model 312 Trap 993
Model 320 991
Model 320 Field 993
Model 330 993
Model 333 993
Model 333T 993
Model 340 977
Model 342 977
Model 411 Upland Sporter 990
Model 412 991
Model 412F 991
Model 420 990
Model 420 with Single Trigger 991
Model 430 991
Model 430 with Single Trigger 991
Model 440 992
Model 440A 992
Model 440B-T 992
Model 440T 993
Model 444 993
Model 444 Deluxe 992
Model 444B 993
Model 501FXP 996
Model 501F—Sport Striker 996
Model 502F—Sport Striker 996
Model 503F—Sport Striker 996
Model 503FSS—Sport Striker 996
Model 510F Striker 996
Model 516BSAK 997
Model 516BSS 997
Model 516FSAK 997
Model 516FSAK Camo 997
Model 516FSS 996
Model 550 992
Model 720 991
Model 726 Upland Sporter 991
Model 740C Skeet 991
Model 745 991
Model 755 991
Model 775 991
Model 750 992
Model 900 TR—Target 990
Model 900B—Biathlon 990
Model 900S—Silhouette 990
Model 1895 971
Model 1899-A 22" Barrel Short Rifle 971
Model 1899-A 26" Round Barrel Rifle 971
Model 1899-B 26" Octagon Barrel Rifle 971
Model 1899-C 26" Half Octagon Barrel Rifle 971
Model 1899-D Military Musket 971
Model 1899-F Saddle Ring Carbine 971
Model 1899-CD Deluxe Rifle 971
Model 1899-H Featherweight Rifle 972
Model 1899 .250-3000 Savage Rifle 972
Model 1895 Anniversary Edition 974
Model 1903 974
Model 1903 Gallery Model 975
Model 1903 Factory Engraved Models 975
Expert Grade 975
Gold Medal Grade 975
Grade EF 975
Grade GH 975
Model 1904 976
Model 1905 976
Model 1905 Style "B" 976
Model 1905 Special Target Rifle 976
Model 1907 994
Model 1907 Portugese Contract 994
Model 1907 Test Pistol 995
Model 1909 975
Model 1910 Test Pistol 995
Model 1911 975
Model 1911 Test Pistol 995
Model 1912 975
Model 1914 975
Model 1915 994
.380 Caliber 994
.32 Caliber 994
Model 1917 994
Model 1920 976
Model 1922 977
Model 2400 990
Model CUB-G (Mini-Youth) 988
Model CUB-T 988
Model FA-1 992
Model FP-1 992
Model Mark I-FVT 988
Model Mark II-BV 989
Model Mark II-FVT 989
Model Mark II-FVXP 989
Model Mark II BTVS 989
Model Mark II Camo 989
Model Mark II Classic 989

SAVAGE & NORTH 997
Figure 8 Revolver 997
First Model 997
Fourth Model 997
Second Model 997
Third Model 997

SAVAGE REVOLVING FIREARMS CO. 997
Navy Revolver 997

SCATTERGUN TECHNOLOGIES 998
TR-870 998
Wilson Combat Current Production Models 998
Border Patrol Model 998
Entry Model 998
K-9 Model 998
Professional Model 998
Standard Model 998
SWAT Model 998

SCHALK, G. S. 998
Rifle Musket 998

SCHALL & CO. 999
Repeating Pistol 999

SCHMIDT, HERBERT 999
Frontier Model or Texas Scout 999
Model 11 Target 999
Model 11, Liberty 11, and Eig Model E-8 999

SCHMIDT, E. & COMPANY 999
Pocket Pistol 999

SCHMIDT-RUBIN 999

SCHNEIDER & CO. 999
Pocket Pistol 999

SCHNEIDER & GLASSICK 999
Pocket Pistols 999

SCHOUBOE 999

SCHUERMAN ARMS, LTD. 999
Model SA40 999

SCHULER, AUGUST 999
Reform 999

SCHULTZ & LARSEN 1000
Model 47 Match Rifle 1000
Model 54 Free Rifle 1000
Model 61 Match Rifle 1000
Model 62 Match Rifle 1000
Model 68 DL 1000

SCHWARZLOSE, ANDREAS .1000
Military Model 1898 (Standart) 1000

SEARS, ROEBUCK & CO. BRAND 1000
Double-Barrel Shotguns 1000

SEAVER, E.R. 1000
Pocket Pistol 1000

SECURITY INDUSTRIES 1000
Model PM357 1001
Model PPM357 1001
Model PSS 1000

SEDCO INDUSTRIES, INC. 1001
Model SP22 1001

SEDERE, TH. 1001

SEDGELY, R. F., INC. 1001

SEECAMP, L. W. CO., INC. 1001
LWS .380 Model 1001
LWS .25 ACP Model 1001
LWS .32 ACP Model 1001
Matched Pair 1001

SEMMERLING 1001

SERBU FIREARMS 1001
BFG-50A 1001

BFG-50 Carbine 1001
BFG-50 Rifle 1001

SHARPS, C. ARMS CO. 1001
Model 1874 Boss Gun 1002
Model 1874 Bridgeport Sporting Rifle 1002
Model 1874 Sharps Hartford Sporting Rifle 1001
Model 1875 Carbine—Hunters Rifle . 1002
Model 1875 Classic Rifle 1002
Model 1875 Target & Sporting Rifle . 1002
Model 1885 High Wall Classic Rifle . 1002
Model 1885 High Wall Sporting Rifle 1002

SHARPS RIFLE MANUFACTURING COMPANY 1002
Army Model 1007
Business Rifle 1005
C. Sharps & Company and Sharps & Hankins Company Breechloading, Single-Shot Pistol 1006
Coffee-Mill Model 1004
Creedmoor Rifle 1005
Hunter's Rifle 1004
Long-Range Rifle 1005
Metallic Cartridge Conversions 1004
Mid-Range Rifle 1005
Military Carbine 1004
Military Rifle 1004
Model 1 1007
Model 2 1007
Model 3 1007
Model 4 1007
Model 1849 1002
Model 1850 1002
Model 1851 Carbine 1002
Model 1852 1002
Military Carbine 1002
Military Rifle 1002
Shotgun 1003
Sporting Rifle 1003
Model 1853 1003
Military Carbine 1003
Military Rifle 1003
Shotgun 1003
Sporting Rifle 1003
Model 1855 1003
Model 1855 British Carbine 1003
Model 1855 U.S. Navy Rifle 1003
Model 1859 Carbine 1003
22" Barrel, Brass Mountings 1003
Iron Mountings 1003
Model 1859 Rifle 1004
30" Barrel 1004
36" Barrel 1004
Model 1861 Navy Rifle 1007
Model 1862 Navy Carbine 1007
Model 1863 Carbine 1003
Model 1863 Rifle 1004
Model 1865 Carbine 1003
Model 1865 Rifle 1004
Model 1869 1004
Carbine 1004
Military Rifle 1004
Sporting Rifle 1004
Model 1870 Springfield Altered 1004
Carbine 1004
First Type 1004
Second Type 1004
Model 1874 1004
Model 1877 1005
Model 1878 Sharps-Borchardt 1005
Business Rifle 1006
Carbine 1005
Express Rifle 1006
Hunter's Rifle 1006
Long-Range Rifle 1006
Mid-Range Rifle 1006
Military Rifle 1005
Officer's Rifle 1006
Short-Range Rifle 1006
Sporting Rifle 1006
Percussion Revolver 1006
Pistol-Grip Rifle 1006
Schuetzen Rifle 1005
Sharps Straight Breech Models 1003
Short Cavalry Carbine 1007
Sporting Rifle 1004-1005

SHATTUCK, C. S. 1007
Boom 1007
Double-Barrel Shotguns 1007
Pocket Revolver 1007

SHAW & LEDOYT 1008
Under Hammer Pistol 1008

SHAWK & McLANAHAN 1008
Navy Revolver 1008

SHERIDEN PRODUCTS, INC. 1008
Knockabout 1008

SHILEN RIFLES, INC. 1008
Model DGA Bench Rest Rifle 1008
Model DGA Silhouette Rifle 1008
Model DGA Sporter 1008
Model DGA Varminter 1008

SHILOH RIFLE MFG. CO., INC. 1008
Business Rifle 1009
Hartford Model 1009
Jaeger 1009
Model 1862 Confederate Robinson . 1008
Model 1863 Military Carbine 1008
Model 1863 Military Rifle 1008
Model 1863 Sporting Rifle 1008
Model 1874 Buffalo Rifle (Quigley) . . 1009
Model 1874 Carbine 1009
Model 1874 Creedmore Target Rifle 1008
Model 1874 Long Range Express Rifle 1009
Model 1874 Military Carbine 1009
Model 1874 Military Rifle 1009
Model 1874 Montana Roughrider Rifle 1009
No. 1 Sporter Deluxe Rifle 1009
No. 3 Standard Sporter 1009
Saddle Rifle 1009

SIG 1010
P 210 1010
P 210-1 1010
P 210-2 1010
P 210-5 1010
P 210-6 1010

SIG-HAMMERLI 1010
.22 Conversion Unit 1010
Model 160/162 1010
Model 208S 1010
Model 280 1010
Model P240 Target Pistol 1010
Trailside Competition 1011
Trailside PL 22 1010
Trailside PL 22 Target 1011

SIGARMS 1011
Aurora TR Field Shotguns 1020
Aurora TT 25 Competition Shotguns 1021
JP226 Jubilee Pistol 1014
Model 202 Lightweight 1022
Model 202 Standard 1022
Model 202 Supreme 1022
Model 202 Supreme Magnum 1022
Model 202 Varmint 1022
Model GSR 1019
Model SA3 Hunter 1020
Model SA3 Sporting 1020
Model SA5 Sporting 1020
Model SHR 970 1021
Model SHR 970 Magnum 1022
Model SHR 970 Tactical 1022
Mosquito 1015
New Englander 1021
P210 1011
P210-2-9 1011
P210-5-9 1011
P210-6-9 1011
P210-8-9 1011
P210-9-6S 1011
P220 1011
P220 Carry 1012
P220 Carry SAS 1012
P220 Combat 1013
P220 Compact 1013
P220 Langdon Edition 1013
P220 Match 1013
P220 SAS 1012
P220 Sport 1012
P220 ST 1012
P220 Super Match 1013
P220R Carry Equinox 1013
P220R DAK 1012
P220R Equinox 1013
P220R SAO 1012
P225 1013
P225 Limited 1014
P226 1014
P226 Navy Seal 1014
P226 SAS 1015
P226 Sport 1014
P226 Sport Stock 1014
P226 ST 1014
P226 ST 1014
P226 Tactical 1015
P226 X-Five 1015
P226R DAK 1015
P226R Equinox 1015
P228 1015
P228 Limited (New Model) 1016
P229 1016
P229 Combo 1017
P229 Limited 1016
P229 Nickel 1016
P229 Sport 1016
P229 Stainless 1016
P229R DAK 1017
P230 1017
P232 1017
P232 (1998 Model) 1017
P232 Limited 1017
P239 1017
P239 Limited 1017
P245 Compact 1018
P245 Custom Shop 1018
Revolution 1019
Revolution Carry 1019
Revolution Compact 1019
Revolution Compact C3 1020
Revolution Compact SAS 1019
Revolution Custom Compact RCS . . 1019
Revolution Custom STX 1019
Revolution Target 1019
Revolution TTT 1019
Revolution XO 1019
SIG 550 1021
SIG 551 1021
SIG 556 1022
SIG AMT 1021
SIG PE-57 1021
SP2009 1018
SP2022 1018
SP2340 1018
SSG 2000 1021

SSG 3000 1021
Conversion Kit—.22 LR 1021
Level I 1021
Level II 1021
Level III 1021
TR 20 1020
TR 20U 1020
TR 30 1020
TR 40 Gold 1020
TR 40 Silver 1020
TT25 1021
TT45 1021

SILMA 1022
Clays Model 1023
Deluxe Models 1022
Model 70 EJ 1022
12 Gauge 1023
20 Gauge 1023
28 and .410 Gauge 1023
Superlight 1023
Standard Models 1022
Model 70 EJ 1022
12 Gauge 1022
20 Gauge 1022

SIMPLEX 1023
Simplex 1023

SIMPSON, R. J. 1023
Pocket Pistol 1023

SIMSON & COMPANY 1023
Model 73 1023
Model 74 1023
Model 74E 1024
Model 76 1024
Model 76E 1024
Model 235 1023
Model 1922 1024
Model 1927 1024

SIRKIS INDUSTRIES, LTD. . . 1024
Model 35 Match Rifle 1024
Model 36 Sniper's Rifle 1024
SD9 1024

SKB ARMS COMPANY 1024
Model 85TSS Skeet 1026
Model 85TSS Sporting Clays 1026
Model 85TSS Trap 1026
Model 85TSS Trap Unsingle 1026
Model 85TSS Trap Unsingle Combo 1026
Model 100 1024
Model 150 1025
Model 200 1025
Model 200E 1025
Model 280 1025
Model 300 . . . . . 1025, 1028
Model 385 1025
Model 385 2 Barrel Set 1025
Model 385 Sporting Clays 1025
Model 400E 1025
Model 480E 1025
Model 485 1025
Model 485 2 barrel set 1025
Model 500 1026
Model 505 Field 1026
Model 505 3-Gauge Skeet Set 1026
Model 585 1026
Model 585 Gold Package 1026
Model 585 Skeet 1027
Model 585—3 Barrel Skeet Set 1027
Model 585—3 Barrel Skeet Set
Gold Package 1027
Model 585 Youth Gold Package . . . 1027
Model 585 Youth/Ladies 1027
Model 585 Upland 1027
Model 585 Upland Gold Package . . . 1027
Model 600 1027
Model 600 Magnum 1027
Model 600 Skeet Combo Set 1027
Model 600 Skeet Gun 1027
Model 600 Trap Gun 1027
Model 605 1027
Model 605 3-Gauge Skeet Set 1027
Model 680E 1027
Model 685 1027
Model 700 Skeet Gun 1028
Model 700 Trap Gun 1027
Model 785 1028
Model 785—2 Barrel Set 1028
Model 785 3-Gauge Skeet Set 1028
Model 785 Skeet 1028
Model 785 Sporting Clays 1028
Model 785 Trap 1028
Model 785 Trap Combo 1028
Model 880 Crown Grade 1028
Model 800 Skeet Gun 1028
Model 800 Trap Gun 1028
Model 885 1028
Model 1300 1028
Model 1900 1029
Model 3000 1029
Model 5600 1028
Model 5700 1028
Model 5800 1028
Model 7300 1028
Model 7900 1028
Model XL 900 MR 1029

SKS 1029

SLOTTER & CO. 1029
Pocket Pistol 1029

SMITH AMERICAN ARMS COMPANY 1029
Smith Carbine 1029

SMITH, L. C. 1029
Early Hammerless Shotguns 1029
00 Grade 1029
0 Grade 1029
A-1 Grade 1030
A-2 Grade 1030
A-3 Grade 1030
Monogram Grade 1030
No. 1 Grade 1029
No. 2 Grade 1029
No. 3 Grade 1029
No. 4 Grade 1029
No. 5 Grade 1030
Pigeon Grade 1029
Later Production Hammerless
Shotguns 1030
Crown Grade 1030
Eagle Grade 1030
Field Grade 1030
Ideal Grade 1030
Premier Skeet Grade 1030
Specialty Grade 1030
Skeet Special Grade 1030
Trap Grade 1030

SMITH, L. C. 1030
1968 Deluxe Model 1032
1968 Model 1032
Fulton Model 1031
Fulton Special 1031
Hunter Special 1031
Model LC12-DB 1032
Model LC12-OU 1032
Model LC20-DB 1032
Model LC20-OU 1032
Model LC28/LC410-DB 1032
Single Barrel Trap Guns 1032
Crown Grade 1032
Deluxe Grade 1032
Monogram Grade 1032
Premier Grade 1032
Olympic Grade 1032
Specialty Grade 1032

SMITH, OTIS 1033
Model 1883 Shell-Ejector 1033
Model 1892 1033

SMITH & WESSON 1033
.455 Mark II Hand Ejector 1st Model 1048
.455 Mark II Hand Ejector 2nd Model 1048
.320 Revolving Rifle Model 1101
.45 Hand Ejector U.S. Service
Model of 1917 1048
Brazilian Contract 1048
Commercial Model 1048
Military Model 1048
.44 Double-Action 1st Model 1043
.44 Hand Ejector 1st Model 1047
.44 S&W Special and .44 S&W
Russian 1047
Other Calibers (Rare) 1047
.44 Hand Ejector 2nd Model 1047
.44 S & W Special 1047
.38-40, .44-40 or .45 Colt 1048
.44 Hand Ejector 3rd Model or
Model of 1926 1048
.44 S & W Special 1048
.44-40 or .45 Colt 1048
.44 Hand Ejector 4th Model
(Target Model) 1048
.40 S&W Tactical 1093
.40 S&W Compensated 1094
.40 S&W Performance Action Pistol . 1094
.38 Double-Action 1st Model 1037
.38 Double-Action 2nd Model 1037
.38 Double-Action 3rd Model 1037
8" and 10" Barrel 1037
Standard Barrel 1038
.38 Double-Action 4th Model 1038
.38 Double-Action 5th Model 1038
.38 Double-Action Perfected 1038
.38 Hand Ejector Military & Police
1st Model or Model of 1899 1045
Commercial Model 1045
U.S. Army Model 1046
U.S. Navy Model 1046
.38 Hand Ejector M&P 2nd Model
or Model of 1902 1046
.38 Hand Ejector M&P 2nd Model,
1st Change 1046
.38 Hand Ejector Model of 1905 1046
.38 Hand Ejector Model of 1905,
1st Change 1046
.38 Hand Ejector Model of 1905,
2nd Change 1046
.38 Hand Ejector Model of 1905,
3rd Change 1046
.38 Hand Ejector Model of 1905,
4th Change 1046
.38 Safety Hammerless 1st Model . . 1038
.38 Safety Hammerless 2nd Model . 1038
.38 Safety Hammerless 3rd Model . . 1038
.38 Safety Hammerless Army Test
Revolver 1038
.38 Safety Hammerless 4th Model . . 1038
.38 Safety Hammerless 5th Model . . 1038
.38 Single-Action 1st Model
(Baby Russian) 1035
.38 Single-Action 2nd Model 1035
8" and 10" Barrel 1036
3.25", 4", 5", and 6" Barrel
Lengths 1036
.38 Single-Action 3rd Model 1036
.38 Single-Action Mexican Model . . . 1036
.32 Double-Action 1st Model 1036
.32 Double-Action 2nd Model 1036
.32 Double-Action 3rd Model 1036
.32 Double-Action 4th Model 1036
.32 Double-Action 5th Model 1037
.32 Hand Ejector Model of 1896
or .32 Hand Ejector 1st Model 1044
.32 Hand Ejector Model of 1903
1st Change 1045

.32 Hand Ejector Model of 1903
2nd Change ... 1045
.32 Hand Ejector Model of 1903
3rd Change ... 1045
.32 Hand Ejector Model of 1903
4th Change ... 1045
.32 Hand Ejector Model of 1903
5th Change ... 1045
.32 Hand Ejector Third Model ... 1045
.32 Safety Hammerless (aka .32 New Departure or .32 Lemon Squeezer) 1037
1st Model ... 1037
.32 Safety Hammerless 2nd Model ... 1037
.32 Safety Hammerless 3rd Model ... 1037
.32 Single-Action
(Model 1-1/2 Centerfire) ... 1035
Early Model w/o Strain Screw—Under #6500 ... 1035
Later Model with Strain Screw ... 1035
8" or 10" Barrel ... 1035
.22 Ladysmith 1st Model ... 1045
.22 Ladysmith 2nd Model ... 1045
.22 Ladysmith 3rd Model ... 1045
.22-32 Hand Ejector ... 1046
9 Recon ... 1097
45 Recon ... 1097
3913/3953 TSW ... 1085
4003/4006/4043/4046 TSW ... 1086
4013/4053 TSW ... 1085
4513/4553 TSW ... 1085
4563/4566/4583/4586 TSW ... 1086
5903/5906/5943/5946 TSW ... 1085
CS9 ... 1086
CS40 ... 1086
CS40 Two-Tone ... 1086
CS45 ... 1086
Fiftieth Anniversary Model 29 ... 1057
Hand Ejector Model of 1903 ... 1044
K-32 Combat Masterpiece ... 1051
Limited Edition Pistols and Revolvers of 1990 ... 1093
Military & Police (M&P) Series (2006) ... 1091
Model .356 TSW "Limited" Series ... 1098
Model .45 CQB Combat ... 1098
Model .44 Double-Action Wesson Favorite ... 1043
Model .44 Double-Action Frontier ... 1043
Model .38 Winchester Double-Action 1043
1st Model Single-Shot ... 1043
.38 S&W ... 1044
.32 S&W ... 1044
.22 L.R. ... 1044
2nd Model Single-Shot ... 1044
3rd Model Single-Shot ... 1044
Model 042 Centennial Airweight ... 1066
Model 1, 1st Issue Revolver ... 1033
1st Type ... 1033
2nd Type ... 1033
3rd Type ... 1033
4th Type ... 1033
5th Type ... 1033
6th Type ... 1033
Model 1 2nd Issue ... 1033
Model 1 3rd Issue ... 1033
Longer Barreled Version ... 1034
Shorter Barreled Version ... 1034
Model 1-1/2 1st Issue
(1-1/2 Old Model) ... 1034
Model 1-1/2 2nd Issue
(1-1/2 New Model) ... 1034
2.5" Barrel ... 1034
3.5" Barrel ... 1034
Model 1-1/2 Transitional Model ... 1034
Model 2 Army or Old Model ... 1034
4" Barrel ... 1035
5" or 6" Barrel ... 1035
Model 3 American 1st Model ... 1039
.44 Rimfire Henry Model ... 1039
Standard Production Model ... 1039
Transition Model ... 1039
U.S. Army Order ... 1039
Model 3 American 2nd Model ... 1039
.44 Henry Rimfire ... 1039
Standard 8" Model, .44 American Centerfire ... 1039
Model 3 Russian 1st Model ... 1039
Commercial Model ... 1039
Rejected Russian Contract Model ... 1039
Russian Contract Model, Cyrillic Barrel Address ... 1039
Model 3 Russian 2nd Model ... 1039
.44 Rimfire Henry Model ... 1040
1st Model Turkish Contract ... 1040
2nd Model Turkish Contract ... 1040
Commercial Model ... 1040
Japanese Govt. Contract ... 1040
Russian Contract Model ... 1040
Model 3 Russian 3rd Model ... 1040
.44 Henry Rimfire Model ... 1040
Commercial Model ... 1040
Turkish Model ... 1040
Japanese Contract Model ... 1040
Russian Contract Model ... 1040
Model 3 Russian 3rd Model
(Loewe & Tula Copies) ... 1040
Loewe ... 1040
Tula ... 1040
Model 3 Schofield ... 1071
Model 3 Schofield 1st Model ... 1040
Civilian Model ... 1040
"US" Contract ... 1040
Model 3 Schofield 2nd Model ... 1041
Civilian Model ... 1041
"US" Contract ... 1041
Model 3 Schofield—Surplus Models . 1041
Surplus Cut Barrel—Not Wells Fargo ... 1041
Wells Fargo & Co. Model ... 1041
Model 10 (.38 Military & Police) ... 1049
Model 11 (.38/200 British) ... 1050
Model 12 (.38 Military & Police Airweight) ... 1050
Model 13 .357 ... 1101
Model 13 (.357 Military & Police) ... 1050
Model 14 Texas Ranger Comm. ... 1092
Model 14 (K-38 Masterpiece) ... 1050
Model 15 ... 1071
Model 15 McGivern ... 1071
Model 15
(K-38 Combat Masterpiece) ... 1050
Model 16 (.32 Magnum) ... 1051
Model 16 (K-32 Masterpiece) ... 1051
Post-War ... 1051
Pre-War ... 1051
Model 17 ... 1071
Model 17 (K-22) ... 1051
Model 17 Plus ... 1051
Model 18
(K-22 Combat Masterpiece) ... 1052
Model 19 .357 Magnum K-Comp ... 1100
Model 19 (.357 Combat Magnum) ... 1052
Oregon State Police Cased with Buckle ... 1052
Texas Ranger Cased with Knife ... 1052
Model 20 (.38/.44 Heavy Duty) ... 1053
Model 21 Classic ... 1072
Model 21 (1950 Military) ... 1053
Model 22 Classic ... 1072
Model 22 of 1917 Classic ... 1073
Model 22 (1950 .45 Military) ... 1053
Model 22A Camo ... 1078
Model 22A Sport ... 1077
Model 22A Target ... 1077
Model 22S Sport ... 1077
Model 22S Target ... 1078
Model 22 – Thunder Ranch .45 ACP 1053
Model 23 (.38-44 Outdoorsman) ... 1053
Model 24 ... 1071
Model 24 (.44 Target Model of 1950) 1053
Model 25 ... 1071, 1100
Model 25 (.45 Target Model of 1950) 1053
Model 25 Mountain Gun ... 1054
Model 25-2 ... 1054
Model 25-3 125th Anniversary with Case ... 1054
Model 25-3 S&W 125th Anniversary Comm. ... 1092
Model 26 (1950 .45 Target) ... 1055
Factory Registered .357 Magnum 1055
Pre-war .357 Magnum ... 1055
Model 26-4 Georgia State Police Comm. ... 1092
Model 27 .357 50th Anniversary Comm. ... 1093
Model 27 (.357 Magnum) ... 1055
Model 28 (Highway Patrolman) ... 1056
Model 29 ... 1071
Model 29 Classic ... 1073
Model 29 (.44 Magnum) ... 1056
Early 5-Inch Barrel Model 29 ... 1056
Model 29-3 Elmer Keith Comm. ... 1093
Model 30 (The .32 Hand Ejector) ... 1057
Model 31 (.32 Regulation Police) ... 1057
Model 31
(.32 Regulation Police Target) ... 1057
Model 32 (.38/.32 Terrier) ... 1057
Model 33 (.38 Regulation Police) ... 1058
Model 34 (.22/.32 Kit Gun) ... 1058
Model 35 (.22/.32 Target) ... 1058
Model 36 Classic ... 1072
Model 36 (.38 Chief's Special) ... 1062
Model 36 (Chief's Special Target) ... 1062
Model 36LS (.38 Ladysmith) ... 1062
Model 37 ... 1063
Model 38 (Airweight Bodyguard) ... 1063
Model 39 ... 1073
Model 39 Steel Frame ... 1073
Model 40 (aka Model 42) Centennial 1064
Model 41 ... 1074
Model 41 (New Model) ... 1075
Model 41-1 ... 1075
Model 42—Airweight Centennial ... 1064
Model 43 (.22/.32 Kit Gun Airweight) 1066
Model 45 (Post Office) ... 1067
Model 46 ... 1075
Model 48
(K-22 Masterpiece Magnum) ... 1067
Model 49 (Bodyguard) ... 1064
Model 51 (.22/.32 Kit Gun Magnum) . 1066
Model 52 (.38 Master) ... 1076
Model 52-1 ... 1076
Model 52-2 ... 1076
Model 52A ... 1076
Model 53 (Magnum Jet) ... 1067
Model 56 (KXT-38 USAF) ... 1067
Model 57 ... 1067
Model 58 ... 1067
Model 59 ... 1073
Model 60 ... 1068
2" Barrel ... 1068
3" Barrel ... 1068
5" Barrel ... 1068
Model 60 Carry Comp ... 1100
Model 60 with HI-VIZ Sight ... 1069
Model 60LS (LadySmith) ... 1068
Model 61 Escort ... 1076
Model 63 ... 1069
Model 64
(Military & Police Stainless) ... 1069
Model 65 (.357 Military & Police Heavy Barrel Stainless) ... 1069
Model 66 ... 1099
Model 66 .357 Magnum F-Comp ... 1099

Model 66 (.357 Combat Magnum Stainless) . 1069
Model 67 (.38 Combat Masterpiece Stainless) 1069
Model 73 1066
Model 242 1062
Model 296 1062
Model 317 AirLite 1058
Model 317 AirLite Kit Gun 1058
Model 317 AirLite Ladysmith 1059
Model 325PD 1059
Model 327 Carry 1101
Model 329PD 1062
Model 331 AirLite 1059
Model 332 AirLite 1059
Model 337 AirLite 1059
Model 337 Kit Gun 1059
Model 337 PD 1060
Model 340 1060
Model 340 PD 1060
Model 342 AirLite 1060
Model 342 PD 1060
Model 351PD 1060
Model 360 1060
Model 360 Kit Gun 1061
Model 386 1061
Model 386 PD 1061
Model 386 Sc/S 1061
Model 396 Mountain Lite 1061
Model 410 1089
Model 410 Two-Tone 1089
Model 410S 1089
Model 411 1082
Model 422 Field 1076
Model 422 Target 1076
Model 439 1073
Model 442 Centennial Lightweight . . 1066
Model 457 1090
Model 457S 1090
Model 459 1074
Model 460 Airweight 1096
Model 460 XVR 1067
Model 460V 1068
Model 469 1074
Model 500 1068
Model 500 Magnum Hunter 1097
Model 539 1074
Model 544 Texas Wagon Train 150 Anniversary Comm. 1093
Model 547 1067
Model 559 1074
Model 586 Mass. State Police Comm. 1093
Model 610 . . . . 1054, 1062, 1096
Model 617 Plus 1052
Model 619 1071
Model 620 1071
Model 622 Field 1077
Model 622 Target 1077
Model 622VR 1077
Model 625 1096
Model 625 IDPA 1054
Model 625 JM 1054
Model 625 Light Hunter 1096
Model 625 Mountain Gun 1054
Model 625 V-Comp 1096
Model 625-2 1054
Model 625—5.25" 1096
Model 627 1055
Model 627 Defensive—8 Shot 1096
Model 627—8 Shot 1096
Model 629 1056
Model 629 12" Hunter 1095
Model 629 Carry Comp 1095
Model 629 Carry Comp II 1095
Model 629 Classic 1056
Model 629 Classic DX 1056
Model 629 Classic Powerport 1056
Model 629 Comped Hunter . . 1095, 1096
Model 629 Compensated Hunter . . . 1095
Model 629 Backpacker 1057
Model 629 Extreme 1095
Model 629 Hunter 1095
Model 629 Hunter II 1095
Model 629 Magnum Hunter Trail Boss 1095
Model 629 Mountain Gun 1057
Model 629 Stealth Hunter 1095
Model 629-1 Alaska 1988 Iditarod Comm. 1093
Model 631 1065
Model 631 Lady Smith 1065
Model 632 Centennial 1065
Model 637 1063
Model 637 Carry Combo 1063
Model 638 1063
Model 639 1073
Model 640 .357 Quadport 1096
Model 640 Carry Comp 1096
Model 640 Centennial 1064
Model 640 Centennial .357 Magnum 1064
Model 642 Centennial Airweight . . . 1065
Model 640 Centennial Powerport . . . 1101
Model 642CT (Crimson Trace) 1065
Model 642LS 1065
Model 645 1074
Model 647 1052
Model 647 Varminter 1097
Model 648 1052
Model 648 (New Model) 1052
Model 649 (Bodyguard Stainless) . . 1064
Model 650 1070
Model 651 . . . . 1066, 1070, 1096
Model 657 1067
Model 657 1100
Model 657 Classic 1100
Model 657 Defensive 1100
Model 657 Hunter 1100
Model 659 1074
Model 669 1074
Model 681 Quad Port 1099
Model 681 Quadport 1094
Model 686 Carry Comp 3" 1094
Model 686 Carry Comp 4" 1094
Model 686 Competitor 1094
Model 686 Hunter 1094
Model 686 Magnum Plus 1070
Model 686 Plus 1071, 1094
Model 686 Plus Mountain Gun 1070
Model 686 Powerport 1070
Model 686—.38 Super 1094
Model 686—5" Barrel 1070
Model 696 1053
Model 745 IPSC Comm. 1093
Model 745—IPSC 1074
Model 845 of 1998 1098
Model 845 Single-Action 1101
Model 908 1090
Model 908S 1090
Model 908S Carry Combo 1090
Model 909 1090
Model 910 1091
Model 910S 1091
Model 915 1079
Model 940 1065
Model 940 Centennial .356 1101
Model 945 1098
Model 945 Black Model 1099
Model 945 Micro 1099
Model 945-40 1099
Model 952 1101
Model 1006 1082
Model 1026 1083
Model 1066 1082
Model 1076 1083
Model 1086 1083
Model 1911 1101
Model 1911 PD 1085
Model 1917 1071
Model 2206 1076
Model 2206 TGT (Target) 1076
Model 2214 (The Sportsman) 1076
Model 3904 1078
Model 3906 1078
Model 3913 1078
Model 3914 1078
Model 3914LS 1079
Model 3913LS 1079
Model 3954 1079
Model 4003 1080
Model 4004 1081
Model 4006 1081
Model 4026 1081
Model 4046 1081
Model 4013 1081
Model 4013 TSW 1081
Model 4014 1082
Model 4040PD 1084
Model 4053 1082
Model 4054 1082
Model 4056 TSW 1082
Model 4505 1083
Model 4506 1083
Model 4516 1083
Model 4516-1 U.S. Marshall Comm. 1093
Model 4536 1084
Model 4546 1084
Model 5903 1079
Model 5904 1079
Model 5906 1079
Model 5906 Performance Center . . . 1098
Model 5906 Special Edition 1079
Model 5926 1080
Model 5946 1080
Model 5967 1080
Model 6904 1080
Model 6906 1080
Model 6946 1080
Model A Rifle 1101
Model B 1102
Model C 1102
Model D 1102
Model SW9E 1088
Model SW40E 1088
Model SW9VE 1088
Model SW40VE 1088
Model SW99 1088
Model SW99 Compact 1089
Model SW99 .45 ACP 1089
Model SW945 1099
Model SW990L Compact 1089
Model SW990L Full Size 1089
Model SW1911 . . . . 1084, 1099
Model SW1911 Adjustable 1084
Model SW1911 DK 1099
Model SW1911 DK (Doug Koenig) . . 1085
Model SW1911 PD Gunsite Commemorative 1093
Model SW1911 – Rolling Thunder Commemorative 1093
Model SW1911Sc 1084
M&P .357 SIG 1091
M&P 9mm 1091
M&P 15 PC 1102
M&P 40 1091
M&P9c 1091
M&P15 Military and Police Tactical Rifle 1102
M&P40c 1092
M&P45 1091
M&P340 1071
M&P340CT 1072
M&P357c 1092
M&P360 1072

M&PR8 . . . 1072
New Model No. 3 Frontier Single-Action . . . 1042
.44-40—Commercial Model . . . 1043
Japanese Purchase Converted to .44 S&W Russian . . . 1043
New Model No. 3 Single-Action . . . 1041
Argentine Model . . . 1041
Australian Contract . . . 1041
Revolver with Stock and Holsters . . . 1042
Japanese Artillery Contract . . . 1041
Japanese Naval Contract . . . 1041
Maryland Militia Model . . . 1041
Standard Model . . . 1041
Turkish Model . . . 1042
New Model No. 3 Target Single-Action . . . 1042
New Model No. 3—.38 Winchester . 1043
Paxton Quigley Model 640 . . . 1101
Performance Center .45 Limited . . . 1097
Shorty .356 TSW . . . 1097
Shorty .45 . . . 1097
"Shorty-Forty" .40 S&W . . . 1097
"Shorty Forty" Mark III . . . 1097
Shorty Nine . . . 1097
Sigma Series Compact SW9C . . . 1087
Sigma Series SW9M . . . 1087
Sigma SW9G . . . 1087
Sigma SW9P . . . 1087
Sigma SW9V . . . 1087
Sigma SW40G . . . 1088
Sigma SW40P . . . 1088
Sigma SW40V . . . 1087
Sigma SW380 . . . 1088
Standard .44 S&W Russian . . . 1043
Straight Line Single-Shot . . . 1044
SW9VE Allied Forces . . . 1092
SW40F . . . 1086
SW40VE Allied Forces . . . 1092
SW1911 Tactical Rail . . . 1099
S&W .32 Automatic Pistol . . . 1049
S&W .35 Automatic Pistol . . . 1048
"The True Bekeart" . . . 1047
Standard Model . . . 1047
USAF M-13 (Aircrewman) . . . 1050
Victory Model . . . 1050

SNAKE CHARMER . . . 1102
Snake Charmer . . . 1102

SNEIDER, CHARLES E. . . . 1102
Two-Cylinder Revolver . . . 1102

SODIA, FRANZ . . . 1102

SOKOLOVSKY CORP. SPORT ARMS . . . 1102
.45 Automaster . . . 1102

SPALDING & FISHER . . . 1102
Double Barreled Pistol . . . 1102

SPANG & WALLACE . . . 1102
Pocket Pistol . . . 1102

SPENCER . . . 1103
Military Rifle—Army Model . . . 1103
Military Rifle—Navy Model . . . 1103
Model 1865 Contract . . . 1103
Spencer Carbine . . . 1103
Springfield Armory Post-war Alteration . . . 1103

SPENCER ARMS CO. . . . 1104
Sllide-Action Shotgun . . . 1104

SPENCER REVOLVER . . . 1104
Safety Hammerless Revolver . . . 1104

SPHINX . . . 1104
AT-380 . . . 1104
AT-2000C . . . 1105
AT-2000CS . . . 1105
AT-2000GM . . . 1105
AT-2000GMS . . . 1106
AT-2000H/HDA . . . 1105
AT-2000PS . . . 1105
AT-2000P/PDA . . . 1104
AT-2000S/SDA . . . 1104

SPIES, A. W. . . . 1106
Pocket Pistol . . . 1106

SPILLER & BURR . . . 1106
Navy Revolver . . . 1106

SPITFIRE . . . 1106
Spitfire Battle of Britain Commemorative . . . 1107
Spitfire Competition Model (G3) . . . 1106
Spitfire Master Model . . . 1106
Spitfire Squadron Model . . . 1106
Spitfire Standard Model (G1) . . . 1106
Spitfire Sterling Model (G2) . . . 1106
Spitfire Super Sterling (G7) . . . 1106
Westlake Britarms . . . 1107

SPRINGFIELD ARMORY (MODERN) . . . 1107

SPRINGFIELD ARMORY INC. 1107
A Model Master Grade Competition Pistol . . . 1119
Basic Competition Model . . . 1117
Bullseye Wadcutter . . . 1118
Bureau Model 1911-A1 . . . 1118
Champion Compact . . . 1111
CMC Formula "Squirtgun" . . . 1119
Combat Commander . . . 1113
Compact High Capacity . . . 1112
Competition Grade . . . 1119
Custom Carry . . . 1117
D-Day M1 Garand Limited Edition . . . 1107
Distinguished Limited Class . . . 1119
Enhanced Micro Pistol (EMP) . . . 1117
Expert Pistol . . . 1118
GI Champion . . . 1114
GI Champion Lightweight . . . 1114
GI Full Size . . . 1114
GI Full Size High-Capacity . . . 1114
GI Micro-Compact . . . 1114
High Capacity Full-House Race Gun . . . 1120
IDF Mauser Rifle Model 66SP . . . 1108
Iwo Jima M1 Garand . . . 1107
Lightweight Champion Operator . . . 1116
Lightweight Compact Comp . . . 1111
Lightweight Operator . . . 1116
Loaded Leatham Trophy Match . . . 1114
Loaded Micro Compact Lightweight . 1113
M1 Garand . . . 1108
M1 Garand Rifle . . . 1107
M1A Basic Rifle . . . 1107
M1A Model 25 Carlos Hathcock . . . 1108
M1A National Match . . . 1108
M1A Scout Squad Rifle . . . 1108
M1A SOCOM 16 . . . 1108
M1A SOCOM II . . . 1108
M1A SOCOM Urban Rifle . . . 1108
M1A Standard Rifle . . . 1107
M1A Super Match . . . 1108
M1A-A1 Bush Rifle . . . 1108
M6 Scout . . . 1109
M6 Scout Pistol . . . 1109
M6 Scout—Stainless Steel . . . 1109
M21 Law Enforcement/Tactical Rifle . . . 1108
Micro Compact Lightweight . . . 1113
Micro Compact—Black Stainless . . . 1113
Micro Compact—O.D. Green . . . 1113
Micro Compact—Parkerized . . . 1112
Micro Compact—Stainless . . . 1113
Model 1911 Loaded Champion Lightweight . . . 1111
Model 1911-A1 . . . 1109
Model 1911-A1 Champion . . . 1111
Model 1911-A1 Champion Mil-Spec . 1111
Model 1911-A1 Compact . . . 1110
Model 1911-A1 Compact Mil-Spec . . 1111
Model 1911-A1 Defender . . . 1110
Model 1911-A1 Factory Comp . . . 1110
Model 1911-A1 Factory Comp High Capacity . . . 1110
Model 1911-A1 High Capacity . . . 1112
Model 1911-A1 Loaded Champion Stainless . . . 1111
Model 1911-A1 Loaded Defender Lightweight . . . 1110
Model 1911-A1 Loaded Long Slide . 1111
Model 1911-A1 Loaded Operator . . . 1113
Model 1911-A1 Long Slide . . . 1111
Model 1911-A1 Mil-Spec Operator . . 1113
Model 1911-A1 Service Mil-Spec . . . 1109
Model 1911-A1 Service Model . . . 1109
Model 1911-A1 Service Model Lightweight . . . 1109
Model 1911-A1 Stainless . . . 1110
Model 1911-A1 Stainless Champion 1111
Model 1911-A2 S.A.S.S. . . . 1110
Model B-1 Master Grade Competition Pistol . . . 1119
Model P9 Factory Comp. . . . 1115
Model P9 Standard . . . 1115
Model P9 Ultra (IPSC Approved) . . . 1115
N.R.A. PPC . . . 1118
National Match Model . . . 1119
Night Compact . . . 1120
Night Light Compact . . . 1120
Night Light Standard . . . 1120
Omega . . . 1120
SAR-48 . . . 1109
SAR-4800 . . . 1109
SAR-8 . . . 1109
SAR-8 Tactical . . . 1109
Springfield Formula "Squirtgun" . . . 1118
Springfield P9 Pistol . . . 1115
Super Tuned Champion . . . 1115
Super Tuned Standard . . . 1115
Super Tuned V10 . . . 1115
Tactical Response Pistol (TRP) . . . 1115
TGO 1 . . . 1117
TGO 2 . . . 1117
TGO 3 . . . 1117
Trophy Master Distinguished Pistol . 1119
Trophy Master Expert Limited Class . 1118
Trophy Match . . . 1113
TRP Champion . . . 1116
TRP Operator . . . 1116
TRP Pro . . . 1116
Ultra Compact 1911-A1 . . . 1112
Ultra Compact 1911-A1 Mil-Spec . . . 1112
Ultra Compact High Capacity . . . 1112
Ultra Compact Lightweight MD-1 . . . 1112
V10 Ultra Compact 1911 A-1 . . . 1112
V10 Ultra Compact 1911-A1 Mil-Spec . . . 1112
XD 4" . . . 1116
XD 4" Bi-Tone . . . 1116
XD 45 ACP . . . 1117
XD 5" Bi-Tone Tactical . . . 1116
XD 5" Tactical . . . 1116
XD 5" Tactical Pro . . . 1116
XD Carry Pro . . . 1120
XD Custom Pro . . . 1120
XD Sub-Compact . . . 1117
XD V-10 Ported 4" . . . 1116

SPRINGFIELD ARMORY . . . 1120
Model 1841 Cadet Musket . . . 1120
Model 1842 Musket . . . 1120

Model 1847 Artillery Musketoon 1120
Model 1847 U.S. Cavalry Musketoon 1121
Model 1847 U.S. Sappers Musketoon 1121
Model 1851 Percussion Cadet Musket 1120
Model 1855 Rifle Musket 1121
Model 1855 Rifled Carbine 1121
Model 1858 U.S. Cadet Rifle Musket 1121
Model 1861 Percussion Rifle Musket 1121
Model 1863 Rifle Musket, Type I 1121
Model 1863 Rifle Musket, Type II, aka Model 1864 1121

SPRINGFIELD ARMS COMPANY 1122
Belt Model 1122
Double Trigger Model 1122
Double Trigger Model 1122
Double-Barrel Shotguns 1123
Dragoon 1122
Late Model Revolver 1122
Navy Model 1122
Pocket Model Revolver 1122
Ring Trigger Model 1122
Warner Model 1122

SQUIBBMAN 1123

SQUIRES BINGHAM MFG. CO., INC. 1123
Model 100 1123
Model 100D 1123
Model 100DC 1123
Thunder Chief 1123

SSK INDUSTRIES 1123
.50 Caliber XP100 1123
SSK-Contender 1123
SSK-XP100 1123

STAFFORD, T. J. 1123
Large Frame Model 1123
Pocket Pistol 1123

STALCAP, ALEXANDER T.F.M. 1123

STANDARD ARMS CO. 1123
Model G 1123
Model M 1123

STAR, BONIFACIO ECHEVERRIA 1123

STARR, EBAN T. 1123
Four Barreled Pepperbox 1124
Fifth Model 1124
First Model 1124
Fourth Model 1124
Second Model 1124
Sixth Model 1124
Third Model 1124
Single-Shot Derringer 1123

STARR ARMS COMPANY ... 1124
1858 Army Revolver 1124
1858 Navy Revolver 1124
Martially Marked (JT) 1124
Standard Model 1124
1863 Army Revolver 1124
Cartridge Carbine 1125
Percussion Carbine 1125

STEEL CITY ARMS, INC. 1125
Double Deuce 1125

STENDA WAFFENFABRIK .. 1125
Pocket Pistol 1125

STERLING ARMAMENT LTD. 1125
Parapistol MK 7 C4 1125
Parapistol MK 7 C8 1125
Sterling AR 180 1125
Sterling MK 6 1125

STERLING ARMS CORPORATION 1125
Model 283 Target 300 1125
Model 284 Target 300L 1125
Model 285 Husky 1126
Model 286 Trapper 1126
Model 287 PPL .380 1126
Model 300 1126
Model 300S 1126
Model 302 1126
Model 302S 1126
Model 400 1126
Model 400S 1127
Model 402 1127
Model PPL .22 1126
Model X-Caliber 1127

STEVENS, J. ARMS CO. 1127
.22 Caliber 1127
.41 Caliber 1127
.41 Caliber Derringer 1127
"Favorite" Rifles 1131
1st Model Favorite 1131
Auto-Shot 1134
First Issue New Model Pocket Rifle . 1134
First Issue Stevens-Conlin 1133
Gem Pocket Pistol 1127
High Power Rifle 1132
Ideal Single-Shot Rifle 1128
Ladies Model—.22 or .25 Rimfire Only, 24" or 26" Barrel 1128
Model .22/.410 1136
Model 50 1129
Model 51 1129
Model 67 1141
Model 69-RXL 1141
Model 70 1132
Model 71 1132
Model 72 1132
Model 87M 1136
Model 89 1135
Model 124 1141
Model 182 1136
Model 185 1136
Model 1877—Hammer Boxlock 1137
Model 190 1136
Model 195 1136
Model 215—Hammer Boxlock 1139
Model 215—Hammer Boxlock 1139
Model 225—Hammer Boxlock 1137
Model 235—Hammer Boxlock 1137
Model 240 1136
Model 240—.410 Over-and-Under Hammer Tenite 1139
Model 250—Hammer Sidelock 1137
Model 255—Hammer Sidelock 1137
Model 260—Hammer Sidelock 1137
Model 265—Hammer Sidelock 1137
Model 270—Hammer Sidelock 1137
Model 280—Hammer Sidelock 1137
Model 311—Hammerless Boxlock .. 1139
Model 311—New Style Hammerless Boxlock 1140
Model 311—New Style Tenite Hammerless Boxlock 1140
Model 311—Single Trigger Hammerless Boxlock 1140
Model 311—Tenite Hammerless Boxlock 1138
Model 311—Tenite Single Trigger Hammerless Boxlock 1138
Model 311A—Hammerless Boxlock . 1138
Model 311C—Hammerless Boxlock . 1138
Model 311D—Hammerless Boxlock . 1139
Model 311E—Hammerless Boxlock . 1139
Model 311F—Hammerless Boxlock . 1139
Model 311H—Hammerless Boxlock . 1139
Model 311H—Vent Rib Hammerless Boxlock 1139
Model 311H—Waterfowler Hammerless Boxlock 1139
Model 311J/R—Hammerless Boxlock 1139
Model 311J/R—Solid Rib Hammerless Boxlock 1139
Model 315 (Early)—Hammerless Boxlock 1139
Model 315 (Late)—Hammerless Boxlock 1139
Model 315—Hammerless Boxlock .. 1140
Model 322 1135
Model 322-S 1135
Model 325—Hammerless Boxlock .. 1137
Model 330—Hammerless Boxlock .. 1138
Model 331—Single Trigger Hammerless Boxlock 1138
Model 335 (Early)—Hammerless Boxlock 1137
Model 335 (Late)—Hammerless Boxlock 1137
Model 345—Hammerless Boxlock .. 1138
Model 350—Hammerless Boxlock .. 1137
Model 355—Hammerless Boxlock .. 1137
Model 360—Hammerless Boxlock .. 1137
Model 365—Hammerless Boxlock .. 1137
Model 370—Hammerless Boxlock .. 1137
Model 375 (London Proofs)—Hammerless Boxlock 1137
Model 375 (U.S.)—Hammerless Boxlock 1137
Model 380—Hammerless Boxlock .. 1137
Model 385 (London Proofs)—Hammerless Boxlock 1138
Model 385 (U.S.)—Hammerless Boxlock 1138
Model 411 Upland Sporter 1140
Model 416 1135
Model 500—Skeet Hammerless Boxlock 1138
Model 511A—Hammerless Boxlock . 1140
Model 511—Hammerless Boxlock .. 1139
Model 511—Hammerless Boxlock .. 1140
Model 511—Sunken Rib Hammerless Boxlock 1139
Model 511—Sunken Rib Hammerless Boxlock 1140
Model 515—Hammerless Boxlock .. 1138
Model 515—Single Trigger Hammerless Boxlock 1138
Model 530A—Hammerless Boxlock . 1138
Model 530A—Single Trigger Hammerless Boxlock 1138
Model 530—Hammerless Boxlock .. 1138
Model 530M—Tenite Hammerless Boxlock 1138
Model 530M—Tenite Single Trigger Hammerless Boxlock 1138
Model 620 U.S. Marked Trench Gun 1141
Model 675 1141
Model 987 1136
Model 3150—Hammerless Boxlock . 1140
Model 3151—Hammerless Boxlock . 1140
Model 3151—Single Trigger Hammerless Boxlock 1140
Model 5151—Hammerless Boxlock . 1140
Model 5151—Single Trigger Hammerless Boxlock 1140
No. 044-1/2 1128
No. 10 Target Pistol 1134
No. 11—Junior 1132
No. 12 1132
No. 14 1132
No. 14-1/2 1132

No. 15 1131
No. 15-1/2 1131
No. 16 1131
No. 16-1/2 1131
No. 17 1131
No. 20 1131
No. 21 1131
No. 21 Ladies Model 1131
No. 23—Sure Shot 1131
No. 26 1132
No. 26-1/2 1132
No. 34 (Hunter's Pet) 1135
No. 34-1/2 1135
No. 35 1133
No. 35 Target 1133
No. 36 1133
No. 37 1133
No. 40 1135
No. 40-1/2 1135
No. 404 1130
No. 41 Pistol 1127
No. 42 Reliable Pocket Rifle 1134
No. 43 1134
No. 44 1128
No. 44-1/2 1128
No. 45 1128
No. 46 1128
No. 47 1128
No. 48 1129
No. 49 1129
No. 52 1129
No. 53 1129
No. 54 1129
No. 55 1129
No. 56 1129
No. 65 1132
No. 80 1132
No. 414 1130
No. 417 1/2 Walnut Hill Model 1131
No. 417 Walnut Hill Model 1130
No. 418 1/2 Walnut Hill Jr. 1131
No. 418 Walnut Hill Jr. 1131
No. 425 1133
No. 430 1133
No. 435 1133
No. 440 1133
Off-Hand Shot Gun 1134
Old Model Pocket Rifle 1134
Pocket Pistol 1127
Reliable Pocket Rifle 1134
Second Issue New Model Pocket Rifle 1135
Second Issue Stevens-Conlin No. 38 1133
Single-Shot Pistol 1127
Six-inch Pocket Rifle 1133
Stevens Cadet Mini-Youth 1136
Stevens Model 200 1136
Stevens Model 300 1136
Stevens Model 305 1136
Stevens Model 310 1136
Stevens Model 310 Heavy Barrel 1136
Stevens Model 315 Youth 1136
Stevens No. 35 Auto-Shot 1134
Stevens Tip Up Rifles 1128
Tip Up Rifle—With Forend, Swiss-Type Buttplate 1128
Tip Up Rifle—Without Forend 1128
Tip Up Shotgun—All Gauges, 30" or 32" Barrel 1128
Vernier Model 1135
Vest Pocket Pistol 1127

STEYR 1141

Argentine Contract 1142
Commercially Marked 1142
JAGD Match 1149
Luxus Model L 1144
Luxus Model M 1144
Luxus Model S 1144
Luxus Series 1144
Mannlicher Model 1894 1141
Mannlicher Model 1896/03 1141
Mannlicher Model 1899 1142
Mannlicher Model 1901 1142
Mannlicher Model 1905 1142
Mannlicher SBS European—Full Stock 1148
Mannlicher SBS European—Half Stock 1148
Mannlicher SBS European—Half Stock Carbine 1148
Mannlicher SBS Magnum European—Half Stock 1148
Match 1149
Match UIT 1149
Model 1950 Carbine 1143
Model 1952 1143
Model 1952 Carbine 1143
Model 1956 Carbine 1143
Model 1956 Rifle 1143
Model 1961 MCA Carbine 1143
Model 1961 MCA Rifle 1143
Model L 1144
Model M 1144
Model M 1150
Model M72 L/M 1143
Model MIII Professional 1144
Model S 1144
Model S 1150
Model S/T 1144
Model SL 1143
Model SL Carbine 1144
Model SPP 1150
Model SSG-PI 1148
Professional Model M 1144
Rogak P-18 1143
Roth Steyr Model 1907 1142
SBS CISM Rifle 1149
SBS Classic American 1147
SBS Classic Mannlicher 1148
SBS Forester 1146
SBS Forester Mountain Rifle 1147
SBS ProHunter 1145
SBS ProHunter (Youth/Ladies) 1145
SBS ProHunter 376 Steyr 1145
SBS ProHunter Camo 1145
SBS ProHunter Camo Stainless Steel 1145
SBS ProHunter Compact 1145
SBS ProHunter Mountain Camo 1145
SBS ProHunter Mountain Camo Stainless Steel 1145
SBS ProHunter Mountain Rifle 1145
SBS ProHunter Mountain Stainless Steel 1145
SBS ProHunter Stainless Steel 1145
SBS Tactical 1149
SBS Tactical Elite Heavy Barrel 1149
SBS Tactical Elite Heavy Barrel Carbine 1150
SBS Tactical Heavy Barrel 1149
SBS Tactical Heavy Barrel Carbine 1149
SBS Tactical McMillan 1149
Schoenberger 1141
SSG-PII & PIIK McMillan 1149
SSG-PII Police Rifle 1148
SSG-PIV 1149
SSK-PIIK Police Kurz 1149
Steyr AUG 1150
Steyr AUG Special Receiver 1150
Steyr AUG—Police Model 1150
Steyr GB 1143
Steyr Hahn Model 1911 1142
Steyr Mannlicher Model 1950 1143
Steyr Model 1908 Pocket Pistol 1142
Steyr Model GB 1143
Steyr Model SP 1142
Steyr SBS (Safe Bolt System) 1144
Steyr Scout 1148
Steyr Scout Package 1148
Steyr Scout Tactical 1148
Steyr Scout—Jeff Cooper Package 1148
Steyr USR 1150
Steyr Zepher 1150
Tropical Rifle 1144
Varmint Model 1144

STEYR HAHN 1151

STEYR MANNLICHER 1151

STI INTERNATIONAL 1151

BLS9 & BLS40 1151
Competitor 1153
Duty CT 1153
Duty One 1153
Eagle 1153
Eagle 5.1 1154
Eagle 5.5 1155
Eagle 6.0 1155
Edge 1153
Edge 5.1 1154
Executive 1152
Falcon 3.9 1154
FPI 2260 Rifle 1155
Grandmaster 1153
Hawk 4.3 1154
Hunter 6.0 1155
I.P.S.C. 30th Anniversary 1155
Lawman 1152
Legacy 1155
LS9 & LS40 1151
Night Hawk 4.3 1154
Rangemaster 1154
Rangemaster II 1154
Ranger 1151
Ranger II 1151
Sparrow 5.0 1154
Special Edition 1155
Stinger 1154
Tactical 1152
Tactical 4.15 1152
Targetmaster 1154
Trojan 1151
Trubor 1152
TruSight 1155
VIP 1153
Xcaliber Double Stack 1152
Xcaliber Single Stack 1152

STOCK, FRANZ 1155

Stock 1155

STOCKING & CO. 1156

Pepperbox 1156
Single-Shot Pistol 1156

STOEGER, A. F. 1156

.22 Luger 1156
American Eagle Luger 1156
American Eagle Navy Model 1156
Coach Gun 1157
Coach Gun Supreme 1157
Condor 1157
Condor Combo 1158
Field 1158
Special 1158
Supreme 1158
Condor Competition 1158
Condor Competition Combo 1158
Condor Outback 1158
Condor Special 1157
Condor Supreme Deluxe 1158
Luger Carbine 1156
Model 2000 1156

Model 2000 Deluxe 1156
Model 2000 Camo 1156
Model 2000 Slug 1157
Model 2000 Synthetic 1157
P-350 1158
P-350 1158
P-350 Defense 1158
Silverado Coach Gun 1157
Single Barrel Classic 1158
Single Barrel Classic Youth 1158
Single Barrel Special 1158
Target Luger 1156
Uplander 1157
Uplander English 1157
Uplander Special 1157
Uplander Supreme 1157
Uplander Youth 1157

STREET SWEEPER 1158
Street Sweeper 1158

STURDIVANT, LEWIS G. 1159

STURM, RUGER & CO. 1159
10/22 All Weather 1178
10/22 Deluxe Sporter 1178
10/22 International Carbine 1178
10/22 International Carbine
(New Model) 1178
10/22 Laminated Stock Carbine 1178
10/22 Laminated Stock International 1178
Blue 1178
Stainless Steel 1178
10/22 Laminated Stock Sporter
Model 1178
10/22 Magnum 1177
10/22 Sporter
(Finger Groove Old Model) 1177
10/22 Standard Carbine
Stainless Steel 1177
10/22 Standard Carbine with
Walnut Stock 1177
10/22-T 1179
22/45 Mark III Hunter 1163
50th Anniversary Matched Set
.357 and .44 Magnum 1170
50th Anniversary New Model
Blackhawk NVB34-50 1169
Bearcat (Old Model) 1165
Alphabet Model 1165
Black Anodized Trigger Guard
Model 1165
Serial Number under 30000 1165
Serial Number over 30000 or
with 90-prefix 1165
Bisley Model 1171
.357 Magnum, .41 Magnum,
.44 Magnum, and .45
Long Colt 1171
.22 LR and .32 H&R Magnum . . . 1171
Blackhawk 1166
Blackhawk Convertible 1166
.357/9mm 1166
.45 L.C./.45 ACP 1166
Blackhawk Convertable
(New Model) 1169
.45 ACP & .45 Long Colt
Convertable (1998) 1169
Stainless Model .357/9mm 1170
Blackhawk Flattop .44 Magnum 1166
6-1/2" Barrel 1166
7-1/2" Barrel 1166
10" Barrel 1166
Buckeye Special 1169
Colorado Centennial Single Six 1168
Contoured Gate Model 1164
"Cowboy Pair" 1170
Deerstalker Model 1179
Engraved Red Label All-Weather
Over-and-Under 1186
Engraved Red Label
Over-and-Under 1186
Fiftieth Anniversary .44 Magnum
Flattop New Model Blackhawk 1170
Fiftieth Anniversary .44 Magnum New
Model Ruger Blackhawk Flattop . . 1170
Fixed Sight New Model Single Six . . 1168
Blued Finish 1168
Stainless Steel 1168
Flat Gate Model 1164
Flattop—.357 Magnum 1165
4-5/8" Barrel 1165
6-1/2" Barrel 1165
10" Barrel 1165
GB Model 1180
Government Model 1161
GP-100 1173
GP-100 Stainless 1173
Hawkeye Single-Shot 1167
HK77RFP Hawkeye 1185
HM77R Hawkeye 1184
HM77RSPHAB Hawkeye Alaskan . . 1185
K10/22T Ruger 10/22 Target
Stainless 1178
KP4 1162
KP89 1175
KP89DAO 1175
KP89DC 1175
KP89X 1175
KP90 1175
KP90DC 1175
KP91DC 1175
KP91DAO 1175
KP93DC 1175
KP93DAO 1175
KP94 1176
KP94DAO 1176
KP94DC 1176
KP95DC 1176
KP95DAO 1177
KP97D 1177
KP97DAO 1177
KP345 1177
KP345PR 1177
KP512 1162
KP514 1162
KP944 1176
KP944DC 1176
KP944DAO 1176
Lightweight Single Six 1164
Black Anodized Aluminum Frame
and Cylinder Model 1164
Black Anodized Frame with Blue
Steel Cylinder Model 1164
Silver Anodized with Blue Steel
Cylinder Model 1164
Silver Anodized Frame with
Aluminum Cylinder Model
with Martin Hardcoat Finish . . 1164
Mark I Target Model 1159
5-1/4" Tapered Barrel Model 1159
5-1/2" Bull Barrel Model 1160
Black or Silver Eagle 1159
Red Eagle 1159
Mark I Target Model Rollmarked
with U.S. on Top of Frame 1160
Mark II Bull Barrel Model MK4B . . . 1161
Mark II Competition Model
KMK678GC 1161
Mark II Standard Model 1160
Mark II Target Model 1161
Mark III 512 Pistol 1163
Mark III Competition 1163
Mark III Hunter 1163
Mark III Pistol 1163
Mark III Standard Pistol 1163
Mini-14 1179
Mini-14 Stainless Steel 1179
Mini-14 Ranch Rifle 1179
Mini-14 All-Weather Ranch Rifle . . . 1179
Mini-14 Target Rifle 1179
Mini-30 1180
Mini-30 Stainless with
Synthetic Stock 1180
Model 10/17 1179
Model 10/22 Canadian Centennial . . 1178
10/22 Only 1178
Two Gun Set 1178
Model 10/22 Carbine
40th Anniversary 1178
Model 10/22T 1178
Model 10/22TNZ 1178
Model 44 25th Anniversary Model . . 1179
Model 44 Carbine 1179
Model 44 International Carbine 1179
Model 44 Sporter (Finger Groove
Old Model) 1179
Model 44RS 1179
Model 77 Express MKII 1184
Model 77 Flat Bolt 1181
Model 77 Magnum MKII 1184
Model 77 RL & RLS 1181
Model 77 RS African 1181
Model 77 RSI 1181
Model 77/17 1182
Model 77/17 Synthetic 1182
Model 77/17 Varmint 1182
Model 77/17RM 1184
Model 77/17RM2 1182
Model 77/17RM2 Stainless Steel . . . 1182
Model 77/22 1182
Model 77/22 Stainless Steel 1182
Model 77/22 Stainless
Steel/Synthetic Stock 1182
Model 77/22 Synthetic Stock 1182
Model 77/22 Varmint 1182
Model 77/22—.22 Hornet 1182
Model 77/22M 1182
Model 77/44RS 1184
Model 77/44RSP 1184
Model 77/50RS 1185
Model 77/50RSBBZ 1185
Model 77/50RSO 1185
Model 77/50RSP 1185
Model 77CR MKII Compact Rifle . . . 1184
Model 77LR MKII 1183
Model 77R MKII 1183
Model 77-R/RS 1181
Model 77RBZ MKII 1183
Model 77RL MKII 1183
Model 77RLP MKII 1183
Model 77RP MKII 1183
Model 77-RS 1181
Model 77RS MKII 1183
Model 77RSBZ MKII 1183
Model 77RSI MKII 1183
Model 77RSP MKII 1183
Model 77V Varmint 1181
Model 77VT MKII 1183
Model 96/17 1185
Model 96/22 1185
Model 96/22M 1185
Model 96/44 1185
Model 99/44 Deerfield Carbine 1179
Model 707 and 708 1174
Model K77/22VHZ 1182
Model SRM Blackhawk 1170
Model "SSM" Single Six 1168
Models 737, 738, 739 1173
New Model Blackhawk 1169
New Model Single Six
50th Anniversary Model 1168
New Model Single Six Fixed Sight . 1168
New Model Single Six Hunter
Convertable 1169

New Model Single-Six (.22 LR only)
"Star" Model ... 1168
Blue Variation ... 1168
4.62" Barrel—Very Rare ... 1168
5.5" or 6.5" Barrel ... 1168
9.5" Barrel—Rare ... 1168
Stainless Variation ... 1168
4.62" Barrel—Rare ... 1168
5.5" or 6.5" Barrel ... 1168
9.5" Barrel ... 1168
New Model Super Bearcat ... 1172
New Model Super Single Six ... 1169
New Model Super Single Six, .17 HMR ... 1169
New Ruger Bearcat (Super Bearcat) 1172
Blue ... 1172
Convertible (Recalled) ... 1172
Stainless Steel ... 1172
Number 3 Carbine ... 1181
Old Army Percussion Revolver ... 1171
Old Army Stainless Steel ... 1171
P4 ... 1162
P85 Stainless Steel ... 1174
P89 ... 1175
P89DC ... 1175
P90 ... 1175
P93D ... 1175
P94 ... 1176
P95 ... 1176
P95DAO ... 1176
P512 ... 1162
Police Service-Six ... 1174
P-85 or P-89 ... 1174
Red Label All-Weather Over-and-Under ... 1186
Red Label Over-and-Under Current Production ... 1186
Red Label Over-and-Under Early Production ... 1185
Red Label Over-and-Under Sporting Clays ... 1186
Redhawk ... 1173
Redhawk Stainless Steel ... 1173
Ruger 10/22 Compact Rifle 10/22 CRR ... 1178
Ruger 22/45 Model ... 1162
Ruger Bisley Vaquero ... 1172
Ruger Gold Label Side-by-Side ... 1187
Ruger M77 MkII Frontier Rifle ... 1184
Ruger Model 77: Mark I vs. Mark II 1183
Ruger New Vaquero "Small Frame" 1172
Ruger No. 1 International (1-RSI) ... 1181
Ruger No. 1 Light Sporter (1-A) ... 1180
Ruger No. 1 Medium Sporter (1-S) . 1181
Ruger No. 1 Special Varminter (1-V) 1181
Ruger No. 1 Stainless Varminter (1-V-BBZ) ... 1181
Ruger No. 1 Standard (1-B) ... 1180
Ruger No. 1 Standard Stainless (1-B-BBZ) ... 1180
Ruger No. 1 Tropical (1-H) ... 1180
Ruger Number 1 Light Standard (1-AB) ... 1180
Ruger PC4/PC9 Carbine ... 1180
Ruger Trap Model ... 1186
Ruger Vaquero ... 1171
Ruger Vaquero Bird's-head ... 1172
Ruger Woodside Over-and-Under .. 1186
Security Six ... 1172
Shootists Bisley ... 1171
Single Six .22 Magnum Model ... 1164
Single Six Convertible ... 1164
Single Six Revolver ... 1164
SP-101 ... 1173
SP-101 Spurless-Hammer ... 1173
Speed Six ... 1173
Stainless Steel 1 of 5,000 ... 1160
Stainless Steel Blackhawk (New Model) ... 1169
Stainless Steel Government Model . 1161
Stainless Steel Mark II Target Model 1161
Stainless Steel Mini-14 Ranch Rifle 1179
Stainless Steel Model 717 ... 1172
Stainless Steel Single Six Convertible ... 1167
Standard Mark II Model KMK4 ... 1160
Standard Mark II Model KMK6 ... 1160
Standard Mark II Model MK4 ... 1160
Standard Mark II Model MK6 ... 1160
Standard Mark II Model MK450 ... 1160
Standard Model ... 1159
Standard Model "Red Eagle Grips" . 1159
Standard Model—Marked "Hecho en Mexico" ... 1159
Super Bearcat (Old Model) ... 1165
Super Blackhawk ... 1166
Early Model in Wood Presentation Case ... 1166
In Fitted White Cardboard Case . 1167
Long Grip Frame in Wood Case . 1167
Factory Verified 6-1/2" Barrel ... 1167
Super Blackhawk Hunter ... 1170
Super Blackhawk Stainless Steel ... 1170
Super Blackhawk (New Model) ... 1170
Super Redhawk ... 1174
Super Redhawk Alaskan ... 1174
Super Single Six ... 1165
4-5/8" Barrel ... 1165
Nickel-Plated Model ... 1165
Super Single Six Convertible (New Model) ... 1167

SUNDANCE INDUSTRIES, INC. ... 1187
Model A-25 ... 1187
Model BOA ... 1187
Model D-22M ... 1187
Model Laser 25 ... 1187
Sundance Point Blank ... 1187

SUPER SIX LTD. ... 1187
Bison Bull ... 1187

SUTHERLAND, S. ... 1187
Pocket Pistol ... 1187

SYMS, J. G. ... 1187
Pocket Pistol ... 1187

T

TACONIC FIREARMS LTD. .. 1188
M98 Ultimate Hunter ... 1188

TALLASSEE ... 1188
Carbine ... 1188

TANFOGLIO ... 1188
Sata ... 1188
TA 38SB ... 1188
TA 41 ... 1188
TA 41 SS ... 1188
TA 76 ... 1188
TA 76M Combo ... 1188
TA 90 or TZ-75 ... 1188
TA 90B ... 1188
TA 90 SS ... 1188
Titan ... 1188

TANNER, ANDRE ... 1188
Model 50F ... 1189
Model 300 Free Rifle ... 1188
Model 300S ... 1189

TARPLEY J. & F. AND E. T. GARRETT & CO. ... 1189
Carbine ... 1189

TAURUS INTERNATIONAL MFG. CO. ... 1189
24/7 OSS ... 1193
800 Series ... 1204
Deluxe Shooter's Pak ... 1190
Judge ... 1207
Millennium Pro ... 1191
Model 17 ... 1206
Model 17MB2/MSS2 ... 1195
Model 17-12 ... 1208
Model 22H ... 1195
Model 22H (Raging Hornet) ... 1204
Model 30C (Raging Thirty) ... 1204
Model 44/444 ... 1205
Blue ... 1205
Stainless Steel ... 1205
Model 44 Tracker ... 1206
Model 45 ... 1207
Blue ... 1207
Stainless Steel ... 1207
Model 62 ... 1210
Model 62 Carbine ... 1210
Model 62 Upstart ... 1210
Model 62LAR Lever Rifle ... 1211
Model 62LAR-SS ... 1211
Model 63 ... 1211
Model 65 ... 1200
Model 66 ... 1201, 1208
Model 66CP ... 1201
Model 66B4/SS4 ... 1201
Blue ... 1201
Stainless Steel ... 1201
Model 72 ... 1210
Model 72 Carbine ... 1210
Model 73 ... 1196
Model 80 ... 1196
Model 82 ... 1196
Model 82B4 ... 1196
Model 82SS4 ... 1196
Model 83 ... 1197
Model 85 ... 1197
Model 85 Stainless ... 1197
Model 85 UL ... 1198
Model 85 Hy-Lite Magnesium ... 1198
Model 85 Ultra-Lite Gray ... 1198
Model 85 Ultra-Lite Scandium ... 1198
Model 85 Ultra-Lite Scandium and Titanium ... 1198
Model 85CH ... 1197
Model 85Ti ... 1208
Model 86 ... 1198
Model 94 ... 1199
Blue ... 1199
Stainless Steel ... 1199
Model 94 UL ... 1199
Model 96 ... 1199
Model 174R-B ... 1210
Model 217 ... 1208
Model 218 (Raging Bee) ... 1204
Model 431 ... 1203
Model 441 ... 1203
Model 415 ... 1203
Model 415Ti ... 1209
Model 416 (Raging Bull) ... 1204
Model 425 Tracker ... 1206
Model 425Ti ... 1209
Model 444 Multi ... 1203
Model 445 ... 1206
Model 445Ti ... 1209
Model 450 ... 1207
Model 450Ti ... 1209
Model 454 (Raging Bull) ... 1205
Black Stainless Steel ... 1205
Blue ... 1205
Stainless Steel ... 1205
Model 455 ... 1207
Model 460 ... 1207
Model 500 Magnum Raging Bull ... 1205

Model 605 .... 1198, 1200
Blue 1200
Stainless Steel 1200
Model 605 Custom (B2C) 1200
Blue 1200
Stainless Steel 1200
Model 605CHB2/SS2 1200
Blue 1200
Stainless Steel 1200
Model 605CHB2C/SS2C 1200
Blue 1200
Stainless Steel 1201
Model 606 1201
Model 607 1201
Blue 1201
Stainless Steel 1201
Model 608 1201
Blue 1201
Stainless Steel 1202
Model 617 1202
Blue 1202
Stainless Steel 1202
Model 617 CHB2/SS2 1202
Blue 1202
Stainless Steel 1202
Model 617Ti 1208
Model 627 .... 1202, 1207
Model 627Ti 1209
Model 650 1198
Model 669 1203
Model 669CP 1203
Model 689 1202
Model 731Ti 1208
Model 741 1199
Model 761 1200
Model 817 (Ultra-Lite) 1203
Blue 1203
Stainless Steel 1203
Model 827B4 1196
Model 827SS4 1197
Model 850 1198
Model 850 Ultra-Lite Blue 1198
Model 850 Ultra-Lite Stainless Steel 1198
Model 850 Ultra-Lite Scandium 1198
Model 905I-B1/SS1 1204
Model 907B2/SS2 1204
Model 907SH2 1204
Model 917 1194
Model 922 Sport 1195
Model 941 1199
Blue 1199
Stainless Steel 1199
Model 941 UL 1199
Model 951SH2 1204
Model 970 1206
Model 971 1206
Model 980 1208
Model 981 1208
Model UL/Ti 1209
PT24/7LS-9SS-17 1192
PT24/7PLS-9SSPTi-17 1193
PT24/79SSC-17 1193
PT24/7PLS-9SSCTi-17 1193
PT59B/SS-15 1193
PT609Ti-13 1193
PT745B/SS-LS 1193
PT917B20 1193
PT1911 1193
PT191140B 1193
PT1911SS 1193
PT-22 1195
PT-24/7-9B 1192
PT-24/7-40B 1192
PT-24/7-45B 1192
PT-25 1195
PT-38B/SS 1193
PT-38SSSPRL 1194
PT-45 1192
Blue 1192
Stainless Steel 1192
PT-58 1191
PT-92 1189
PT-92AF 1190
PT-92C 1189
PT-99 1189
PT-100 1190
PT-101 1190
PT-111 .... 1190, 1191
PT-132 1191
PT-138 .... 1190, 1192
Blue 1190
Stainless Steel 1190
PT-140 1191
PT-140 Millennium 1191
Blue 1191
Stainless Steel 1191
PT-145 1192
PT-145 Millennium 1191
Blue 1191
Stainless Steel 1191
PT-400/400SS 1191
Blue 1191
Stainless Steel 1191
PT-640B/SS 1192
PT-745B/SS 1192
PT-745GB 1193
PT-908 1190
PT-911 1191
PT-922 1195
PT-938 1194
PT-940 1194
PT-945C 1194
Blue 1194
Stainless Steel 1194
PT-945S 1194
Blue 1194
Stainless Steel 1194
Raging Bull .223 1205
Raging Bull Model 500, 500MSS2 1205
S/A-44-40-B, S/SM, S/S, CHSA 1210
S/A-45-B12, S/SM12, S/S12, CHSA12 1210
S/A-45, B/S/SM 1209
S/A-45, S/S/CH 1210
S/A-357-B, S/SM, S/S, CHSA 1210
Thunderbolt 1211
Tracker .45 1206
Tracker 10mm 10TSS4 1207
Tracker 10SS8 1207
Tracker 4410 10TKR2SS 1207

TAYLOR'S & CO., INC. 1211

Colt Dragoon (Models 485A, 490A, 495A) 1212
Colt Model 1847 Walker (Model 500A) 1211
Colt Model 1848 Baby Dragoon (Models 470, 471, 472) 1212
Colt Model 1851 Navy 1211
Brass Frame (Model 210) 1211
Steel Frame (Model 245) 1212
Colt Model 1860 Army 1212
Brass Frame (Model 300) 1212
Steel Frame (Model 310, 312, 315) 1212
Colt Model 1861 Navy (Model 210) 1213
Colt Model 1862 Police (Model 315B) 1213
Colt Model 1862 Pocket (Model 315C) 1213
Colt Model 1873 Cattleman (Models 700, 701, 702) 1213
Colt Model 1873 Bird's-head (Models 703A, 703B, 703C) 1213
Colt Model 1873 "Outfitter" 1213
Henry Rifle 1214
Brass frame (Model 198) 1214
Iron Frame (Model 199) 1214
Kentucky Pistol (Model 550) 1211
Kentucky Rifle 1213
Flintlock (Model 183) 1213
Percussion (Model 182) 1214
Model 1842 U.S. Percussion Musket (Model 125) 1214
Rifled Smoothbore with Rear Sight (Model 126) 1214
Smoothbore 1214
Model 1853 3-Band Enfield Musket (Model 120) 1214
Model 1855 U.S. Percussion Musket (Model 116) 1214
Model 1858 2-Band Enfield Musket (Model 121) 1214
Model 1861 Springfield Musket (Model 110) 1214
Model 1862 C.S. Richmond Musket (Model 115) 1214
Model 1863 Remington Zouave (Model 140) 1214
Napoleon Le Page Pistol (Model 551) 1211
Remington Model 1858 1212
Brass Frame (Model 410) 1212
Steel Frame (Model 430) 1212
Remington Model 1863 Pocket (Model 435) 1213
Remington Model 1875 1213
Remington Model 1890 1213
Sharps Model 1859 Berdan Military (Model 152) 1215
Sharps Model 1859 Cavalry (Model 153) 1215
Sharps Model 1859 Infantry (Model 151) 1215
Sharps Model 1863 Cavalry (Model 154) 1215
Sharps Model 1863 Sporting Rifle (Model 131) 1215
Sharps Model 1874 Berdan Rifle (Model 158) 1216
Sharps Model 1874 Cavalry (Model 159) 1216
Sharps Model 1874 Deluxe Sporting Rifle (Model 155) 1215
Sharps Model 1874 Infantry Rifle (Model 157) 1215
Sharps Model 1874 Sporting Rifle (Model 138) 1215
Spencer Model 1865 Carbine (Model 160) 1216
Spencer Model 1865 Rifle 1216
Starr Model 1858 (Model 510, 511) 1212
Winchester Model 92 1215
Winchester Model 1866 (Model 201) 1214
Winchester Model 1866 Yellowboy Carbine (Model 202) 1214
Winchester Model 1873 (Model 200) 1215
Winchester Model 1873 Carbine (Model 200B) 1215
Winchester Model 1873 Sporting Rifle (Model 200C) 1215
Winchester Model 1885 High Wall (Model 203) 1215
Winchester Model 1885 Low Wall Sporting Rifle (Model 204) 1215

TAYLOR, L.B. 1216

Pocket Pistol 1216

TERRIER ONE 1216

Terrier One 1216

TERRY, J. C. 1216

Pocket Pistol 1216

TEXAS CONTRACT RIFLES 1216

TEXAS GUNFIGHTERS 1216

1-of-100 Edition 1216
Shootist Single-Action 1216

TEXAS LONGHORN ARMS, INC. 1216
Grover's Improved Number Five ... 1217
Jezebel 1216
Mason Commemorative 1217
South Texas Army 1217
Texas Border Special 1216
Texas Sesquicentennial Commemorative 1217
West Texas Target 1217

THAMES ARMS CO. 1217

THIEME & EDELER 1217
Pocket Pistol 1217

THOMPSON 1217

THOMPSON/CENTER ARMS . 1217
.22 Classic Benchmark 1221
10" Bull Barrel Model 1218
10" Octagon Barrel Model 1218
10" Vent Rib Model 1218
16" Youth Model Carbine 1220
21" Carbine .410 Bore 1220
Big Boar Rifle 1222
Black Diamond 1224
Black Diamond XR 1224
Black Mountain Magnum 1223
Contender 1217
Contender Carbine Model 1220
Contender Hunter Model 1218
G2 Contender 1219
G2 Contender Muzzleloader 1219
G2 Contender Muzzleloader .50 caliber 1220
G2 Contender Rifle 1219
G2 Contender Shotgun 1219
Encore 209x50 Mag Carbine 1221
Encore 209x50 Mag Rifle 1221
Encore 209x50 Pistol 1221
Encore Camo Shotgun 12 Gauge .. 1220
Encore Katahdin Carbine 1220
Encore Katahdin Turkey Gun 1220
Encore Pistol 1220
Encore Rifle 1220
Encore Rifled Shotgun 12 Gauge ... 1220
Encore Rifled Shotgun 20 Gauge ... 1220
Encore Shotgun 12 Gauge 1220
Encore Shotgun 20 Gauge 1220
Encore Turkey Gun 1221
Fire Hawk 1224
Fire Hawk .32 & .58 caliber models 1224
Fire Hawk Bantam 1224
Fire Hawk Camo Stock 1224
Fire Hawk Thumbhole Stock 1224
Fire Hawk Deluxe 1223
Fire Storm 1224
Grey Hawk 1222
Hawken Caplock Rifle 1222
Hawken Custom/Elite 1222
Hawken Flintlock Rifle 1222
High Plains Sporter 1222
Icon 1221
Model R55 1221
New Englander Composite 1223
Rifle 1223
Shotgun 1223
New Englander Rifle 1223
New Englander Shotgun 1223
Omega 45/Omega 50 1222
Omega Pivoting Breech Rifle 1222
Pennsylvania Hunter 1223
Carbine 1223
Rifle 1223
Pennsylvania Match Rifle 1223
Pro Hunter 1221
Renegade Caplock Rifle 1222
Renegade Flintlock 1222
Scout Carbine 1223
Composite stock 1223
Walnut stock 1223
Scout Pistol 1223
Scout Rifle 1223
Composite Stock 1223
Walnut Stock 1223
Silver Lynx 1221
Standard 21" Carbine 1220
Super 14" Model 1218
Super 14" Vent Rib Model 1218
Super 16" Model 1218
Super 16" Vent Rib Model 1218
System 1 1221
TCR Hunter Model 1221
T/C 22 LR Classic 1221
Thunder Hawk 1221
Thunder Hawk Shadow 1222
Tree Hawk 1223
Rifle 1223
Shotgun 1223
Triumph 1224
White Mountain Carbine 1223

THUNDER FIVE 1224

TIKKA 1224
412S Double Rifle 1226
412S Shotgun 1225
412S Shotgun/Rifle 1226
412S Sporting Clays 1226
512S Field Grade 1226
512S Sporting Clays 1226
Long Range Hunting 1225
Sporter 1225
T3 Big Boar 1225
T3 Hunter 1225
T3 Lite 1225
T3 Lite Stainless 1225
T3 Super Varmint 1225
T3 Tactical 1225
T3 Varmint 1225
Tikka Target 1225
Varmint/Continental Rifle 1225
Whitetail Hunter 1224
Whitetail Hunter Deluxe 1224
Whitetail/Battue Rifle 1224

TIMBER WOLF 1226

TIPPING & LAWDEN 1226
Thomas Revolver 1226

TIPPMAN ARMS 1226
Model .50 HB 1226
Model 1917 1226
Model 1919 A-4 1226

TISAS (TRABZON GUN INDUSTRY CORP.) 1226
Fatih 13 1226
Kanuni 16 1226
Kanuni s 1227
Zigana C45 1228
Zigana F 1228
Zigana K 1227
Zigana M16 1227
Zigana Sport 1227
Zigana T 1227

TOBIN ARMS MANUFACTURING CO. 1228

TODD, GEORGE H. 1228
Rifled Musket 1228

TOKAREV 1228

TOMISKA, ALOIS 1228
Little Tom 1228

TORKELSON ARMS CO. ... 1228
Double-Barrel Shotguns 1228

TRADEWINDS 1228
Model H-170 1228
Model 260-A 1228
Model 311-A 1229
Model 5000 "Husky" 1229

TRADITIONS 1229
ALS Field 1231
ALS Hunter 1231
ALS Turkey 1231
ALS Waterfowl 1231
Elite Field III ST 1231
Elite Hunter 1230
Elite I DT 1230
Elite I ST 1230
Field I 1229
Field II 1229
Field II Combo 1229
Field III Gold 1229
Gold Wing II Silver 1230
Gold Wing III 1230
Gold Wing III Silver 1230
Gold Wing SL III 1230
Gold Wing SL III Silver 1230
Hunter 1229
Mag Hunter II 1230
Real 16 1230
Real 16 Gold 1230
Sporting Clay II 1229
Sporting Clay III 1229
Turkey II 1230
Upland II 1229
Upland III 1229
Uplander II Silver 1231
Uplander III Silver 1231
Uplander V Silver 1231
Waterfowl II 1229

TRANTER, WILLIAM 1231
Model 1872 1231
Model 1878 1231

TRIPLETT & SCOTT/MERIDEN MANUFACTURING COMPANY 1231
Repeating Carbine 1231

TRISTAR SPORTING ARMS . 1232
Astra 20 1235
Brittany 1232
Brittany Classic 1232
Brittany Sporting 1232
CD Diana Camo Mag 1236
CD Diana Field 1235
CD Diana Slug 1236
CD Diana Synthetic 1235
Derby Classic 1233
Ermes 1235
Black 1235
Gold 1235
Nickel 1235
Silver 1235
Field Hunter 1233
Gentry/Gentry Coach 1233
Hunter 1233
Hunter Lite 1233
Mira Camo 1235
Mira Sporting 1235
Model 300 1233
Model 311 1233
Model 311R 1233
Model 330 1233
Model 330D 1233
Model 333 1233
Model 333L 1233
Model 333SC 1233
Model 333SCL 1233

Model 411 1234
Model 411D 1234
Model 411F 1234
Model 411R 1234
Pee Wee 1236
Phantom Field 1235
Phantom HP 1235
Phantom Synthetic 1235
Silver Classic 1232
Silver Hunter 1232
Silver II 1232
Silver Sporting 1232
Specialty Magnums 1232
TR-Class SL 1234
TR-I 1234
TR-II (Nova II) 1234
TR-L 1234
TR-Mag 1234
TR-SC 1234
TSA Field 1233
TSA Synthetic and Synthetic Mag . . 1233
TTR-Royal 1234
York 1232

TROCAOLA 1236

TRYON, EDWARD K. & COMPANY 1236
Pocket Pistol 1236

TUCKER SHERARD & COMPANY 1237
Dragoon 1237

TUFTS & COLLEY 1237
Pocket Pistol 1237

TURBIAUX, JACQUES 1237

TURNER, THOMAS 1237
Pepperbox 1237

TYLER ORDNANCE WORKS 1237
Tyler Texas Rifle 1237
Hill Rifle 1237

U

U.S. ARMS CO. 1238

U.S. M1 CARBINE 1238
IBM 1238
Inland 1238
Irwin Pedersen 1238
M1 Carbine Cutaway 1238
M1 Carbine Sniper with infra red conversion 1238
National Postal Meter 1238
Quality Hardware 1238
Rockola 1238
SG Grand Rapids 1238
S.G. Saginaw 1238
Underwood 1238
U.S. M1 A1 Paratrooper Model 1238
Winchester 1238

U.S. ORDNANCE 1238
Browning Model 1919 1238
M-60 1238
M-60E3 1238
Vickers 1239

U.S. REPEATING ARMS CO. 1239

UBERTI, ALDO/UBERTI USA 1239
1866 Yellowboy Carbine 1244
1873 Stallion 1247
1875 Remington "Outlaw" 1243
Bisley 1246
Bisley Flattop 1246
Buckhorn Buntline 1246
Buckhorn Target 1246
Buntline Carbine 1246
Cattleman 1245
Cattleman Cody NM 1245
Cattleman Flattop Target Model 1245
Cattleman Frisco NM 1246
Cattleman Gunfighter NM 1245
Colt Whitneyville Dragoon 1239
Colt 1st Model Dragoon Revolver . . 1239
Colt 2nd Model Dragoon Revolver . . 1240
Colt 3rd Model Dragoon Revolver . . 1240
Colt Model 1848 Baby Dragoon 1241
Colt Model 1849 Pocket Revolver . . 1240
Colt Model 1849 Wells Fargo 1240
Colt Model 1860 Army 1242
Civilian 1242
Military 1242
Colt Model 1862 Pocket Navy Revolver 1242
Colt Model 1862 Police Revolvers . . 1242
Colt Model 1868 Army Thuer Conversion 1242
Fluted Cylinder 1242
Civilian 1242
Military 1242
Hawken Santa Fe 1245
Henry Rifle 1244
Inspector Model 1247
Model 1851 Navy Colt 1241
Model 1861 Navy Colt 1241
Civilian Model 1242
Military Model 1242
Model 1871 Rolling Block Carbine . . 1244
Model 1871 Rolling Block Pistol 1243
Model 1885 High Wall Single-Shot Carbine 1244
Model 1885 High Wall Single-Shot Rifle 1244
Model 1885 High Wall Single-Shot Rifle Pistol Grip 1245
New Thunderer Model 1246
No. 3 New Model Russian 1247
No. 3 Schofield Revolver 1247
Paterson Revolver 1239
Phantom 1246
Remington Model 1858 New Army .36 Caliber 1243
Remington Model 1858 New Army .44 Caliber 1242
Remington Model 1858 New Army .44 Caliber Stainless Steel 1243
Remington Model 1858 New Army .44 Cal. SS Target 1243
Remington Model 1858 New Army .44 Caliber Target 1243
Remington Model 1858 Target Revolving Carbine 1243
Remington Model 1875 Frontier 1243
Remington Model 1890 Police 1243
Tornado 1247
Walker Colt Revolver 1239
Winchester Model 1866 1244
Winchester Model 1873 Carbine . . . 1244
Winchester Model 1873 Rifle 1244
Winchester 1873 Short Sporting Rifle 1244
Winchester 1873 Half-Octagon Rifle 1244
Winchester 1873 Musket 1244
Winchester 1885 Low Wall Sporting Rifle 1245
Winchester 1885 Low Wall Schuetzen 1245

UHLINGER, WILLIAM P. 1247
Pocket Revolver 1247
.32 Rimfire Model
(5", 6", or 7" Barrel) 1247
Long Cylinder (1-3/16") 1247
Short Cylinder (1") 1247

ULTIMATE 1247

ULTRA LIGHT ARMS, INC. . . . 1248
Model 20 (Short Action) 1248
Model 20 Hunter's Pistol 1248
Model 20 RF Rimfire 1248
Model 24 (Long Action) 1248
Model 28 Magnum 1248
Model 40 Magnum 1248
Model 90 1248

UNCETA 1248

UNION 1248
Pocket Pistol 1248

UNION FIRE ARMS COMPANY 1248
Automatic Revolver 1249
Diamond Grade 1249
Double Barrel Shotguns 1248
Model 18 1249
Model 22 1249
Model 23 1249
Model 24 1248
Model 50 1249
Reifngraber 1249

UNIQUE 1249

UNITED SPORTING ARMS, INC. 1249
Blue Silhouette (10.5" barrels) 1251
Blued Guns 1251
Quik-Kit Blued 1251
Quik-Kit Stainless Steel 1251
Silver Sevilles 1251
Stainless Steel Guns 1251
Tombstone Commemorative 1251

UNITED STATES ARMS 1252
Single-Action Revolver 1252

UNITED STATES HISTORICAL SOCIETY 1252

UNITED STATES FIRE ARMS MFG. 1252
.22 Target 1253
Ace .22 LR 1255
Bisley Model 1254
Bisley Target 1254
Buntline 1252
Buntline Special 1252
China Camp Cowboy Action Gun . . . 1252
Cowboy Action Carbine 1255
Cowboy Action Lightning 1255
Custom Custer Battlefield Gun 1253
Flattop Target Model 1252
Gunslinger 1253
Henry Nettleton Revolver 1252
Hunter 1253
Lightning Baby Carbine 1255
Lightning Magazine Carbine 1255
Lightning Magazine Rifle 1255
Model 1873 Cut Away 1252
Model 1910 1254
Model 1911 1254
Omni-Potent Bird's-Head Model 1253
Omni-Potent Subnose 1253
Omni-Potent Target 1254
Plinker 1253
Pony Express 1254
Rodeo 1252
Sears 1902 Colt 1254
Sheriff's Model 1253
Single-Action Army Revolver 1252
Single-Action Army Revolver Pre-War 1252
Super .38 1255

UNITED STATES REVOLVER ASSOCIATION **1255**

UNITED STATES SMALL ARMS CO. **1255**
Huntsman Model Knife Pistol 1255

UNIVERSAL FIREARMS **1255**
1981 Commemorative Carbine 1256
Double Wing 1256
Model 1000 Military Carbine 1256
Model 1003 1256
Model 1010 1256
Model 1015 1256
Model 1005 Deluxe 1256
Model 1006 Stainless 1256
Model 1020 Teflon 1256
Model 1256 Ferret 1256
Model 2200 Leatherneck 1256
Model 3000 Enforcer 1256
Blued 1256
Model 5000 Paratrooper 1256
Model 7112 1256
Model 7212 1256
Model 7312 1255
Model 7412 1256
Model 7712 1256
Model 7812 1256
Model 7912 1256

URIZAR, TOMAS **1256**
Celta, J. Cesar, Premier, Puma, and Union 1256
Dek-Du 1256
Express 1257
Imperial 1257
Le Secours or Phoenix 1257
Princeps 1257
Venus 1257

USAS 12 DAEWOO PRECISION IND., LTD. **1257**
USAS 12 1257

USELTON ARMS INC. **1257**
Carry Classic 1257
Classic National Match 1257
Compact Classic 1257
Compact Classic Companion 1257
Tactical 1911 1257
Ultra Carry 1257
Ultra Compact Classic 1257

UZI ISRAELI MILITARY INDUSTRIES **1257**
Compact Model 1258
Full Size Model 1258
Polymer Compact Model 1258
Short Slide Model 1258
Uzi Carbine Model A 1257
Uzi Carbine Model B 1257
Uzi Mini-Carbine 1258
Uzi Pistol 1258

V

VALKYRIE ARMS, LTD. **1259**
Browning 1919 A4 .30 Caliber 1259
DeLisle Carbine 1259
U.S. M3-A1 1259

VALMET, INC. **1259**
Lion 1259
M-62S 1259
M-71S 1259
Model 76S 1259
5.56mm 1259
7.62x39mm 1259
Model 78 1259

VALTION (LAHTI) **1259**

VALTRO **1259**
1998 A1 1259
PM5 1260
Tactical 98 Shotgun 1259

VARNER SPORTING ARMS, INC. **1260**
Hunter 1260
Hunter Deluxe 1260
Presentation Grade 1260
No. 1 Grade 1260
No. 2 Grade 1260
No. 3 Grade 1260

VECTOR ARMS, INC **1260**
Mini Uzi 1260
Post-Ban 1260
Pre-Ban 1260
UZI 1260
Post-Ban 1260
Pre-Ban 1260

VEKTOR **1260**
Model CP-1 Compact 1262
Model SP1 Compact (General's Model) 1261
Model SP1 Target 1261
Model SP1 Service Pistol 1260
Model SP1 Sport 1261
Model SP1 Tuned Sport 1261
Model SP1 Ultra Sport 1261
Model SP2 1261
Model SP2 Compact (General's Model) 1261
Model SP2 Competition 1261
Model SP2 Conversion Kit 1262
Model SP2 Ultra Sport 1262
Model Z88 1260
Vektor 98 1262
Vektor H5 Pump-Action Rifle 1262
Vektor Lyttelton 1262

VENUS WAFFENWERKE **1262**
Venus 1262

VERNEY-CARRON **1262**
Concours 1262
Skeet Model 1262

VERONA **1263**
LX501 1263
LX680 1264
LX680C S&T 1264
LX692G 1263
LX692G-20/28 1263
LX692GC S&T 1264
LX692GS 1264
LX702G 1263
LX702GC S&T 1264
Model LX1001 Express Combo 1263
Model LX980CS 1264
Model LX980GCS/GCT 1264
Model SS662GL 1264
Model SS772GL 1264
Model SX401/S 1263
Model SX405 Combo 1263
Model SX405 Slug 1263
Model SX405/S/L 1263
Model SX405T 1263
Model SX405W/H/SW/SH 1263
Model SX801/L 1264
Model SX801G/GL 1264

VETTERLI **1264**

VICKERS, LTD. **1264**
Empire 1264
Jubilee 1264

VICTOR EJECTOR **1264**

VICTORY ARMS COT., LTD. . . **1265**
Model MC5 1265

VIRGINIAN **1265**

VOERE **1265**
Model 1007 1265
Model 1013 1265
Model 2107 1265
Model 2107 Deluxe 1265
Model 2114S 1265
Model 2115 1265
Model 2150 1265
Model 2155 1265
Model 2165 1265
Model 2185 1265
Model 2185 Match 1265
Model Titan 1265
Model Titan Menor 1266
Model VEC-91 Lightning 1266
Model VEC-91BR 1266
Model VEC-91HB 1266
Model VEC-91SS 1266

VOLCANIC ARMS COMPANY 1266

VOLKSPISTOLE **1266**
Volkspistole 1266

VOLQUARTSEN CUSTOM . . **1266**
Black Cheetah Pistol 1267
Compact 1267
Deluxe 1266
Deluxe 1267
Lightweight 1266
Masters 1267
Olympic 1267
Signature Series 1266
Standard 1266
Stingray 1267
Terminator 1267
Ultra-Lite Match 1268
V-2000 1268
V-6 1268
VG-1 1266
VX-2500 1266
VX-5000 1267
V-Magic II 1268

VOLUNTEER ENTERPRISES 1268

VOUZLAUD **1268**
Model 315 E 1268
Model 315 EGL 1268
Model 315 EGL-S 1268
Model 315 EL 1268

W

WALCH, JOHN **1269**
Navy Revolver 1269
Pocket Revolver 1269

WALDMAN **1269**
Waldman 1269

WALLIS & BIRCH **1269**
Pocket Pistol 1269

WALTHER, CARL **1269**
Free Pistol 1281
Funfklamph Pentathlon Jagerschafts—Hunter Sport or Standard Model Schnellfeur—Rapid Fire 1272
GX 1 1282
Model 1 1269
Model 2 1270
Fixed Sights 1270
Pop Up Sights 1270
Model 3 1270
Model 4 1270

Model 5 1270
Model 6 1271
Model 7 1271
Model 8 1271
Blue, Silver, and Gold Finish 1272
Engraved Slide 1272
Engraved Slide and Frame 1272
Engraved, Complete Coverage 1272
Model 9 1272
Model AP 1273
Model B 1282
Model G22 1283
Package A1 with Walther rifle scope 1283
Package A2 with laser 1283
Package A3 with Walther rifle scope & laser 1283
Package A4 with Walther PS22 red-dot sight 1283
Model KK/MS Silhouette 1283
Model KKJ Sporter 1282
Model KKJ-HO 1282
Model KKJ-MA 1282
Model KKM International Match 1282
Model KKM-S 1282
Model KKW 1282
Model MP 1273
Model FP 1281
Model GSP 1281
Model GSP-C 1281
Model OSP 1281
Model P.38 1278
.22 Caliber 1278
Other Calibers 1278
Steel-Framed (Introduced 1987) 1278
Model P.38 II 1278
Model P.38 IV 1278
Model P.38K 1278
Model P5 1279
Model P5 One Hundred Year Commemorative 1279
Wood presentation case 1279
Model P5, Compact 1279
Model P22 Standard 1281
Model P22 Target 1281
Model P88 1279
Model P88 Compact 1279
Model P99 1280
Model P99 Commemorative 1281
Model P99 Compact AS/QA 1280
Model P99 La Chasse 1281
Model P99 La Chasse DU 1280
Model P99 Military 1280
Model P99 QA 1280
Model P99 QPQ 1280
Model P990 1280
Model P990 QPQ 1280
Model PP 1273
Blue 1274
Gold 1274
Model PP .22 Caliber 1273
Model PP .25 Caliber 1273
Model PP .32 Caliber High Polished Finish 1273
Model PP .32 Caliber in Blue, Silver or Gold Finish and Full Coverage Engraving 1274
Model PP .32 Caliber Milled Finish 1273
Model PP .32 Caliber with Bottom Magazine Release 1273
Model PP .32 Caliber with Duraluminum Frame 1273
Model PP .32 Caliber with Verchromt Finish 1273
Model PP .32 Caliber with Waffenampt Proofs, High Polished Finish 1273
Model PP .32 Caliber with Waffenampt Proofs, Milled Finish 1273
Model PP .32 Caliber, A. F. Stoeger Contract 1273
Model PP .32 Caliber, AC Marked 1274
Model PP .32 Caliber, Allemagne Marked 1273
Model PP .32 Caliber, Duraluminum Frame 1274
Model PP .32 Caliber, NSDAP Gruppe Markings 1274
Model PP .32 Caliber, NSKK Marked on the Slide 1274
Model PP .32 Caliber, PDM Marked with Bottom Magazine Release 1274
Model PP .32 Caliber, Police Eagle/C and Police Eagle/F Proofed, Milled Finish 1274
Model PP .32 Caliber, Police Eagle/C Proofed, High Polished Finish 1274
Model PP .32 Caliber, RBD Munster Marked 1274
Model PP .32 Caliber, RFV Marked, High Polished or Milled Finish 1274
Model PP .32 Caliber, RJ Marked 1274
Model PP .32 Caliber, RpLt Marked 1274
Model PP .32 Caliber, Statens Vattenfallsverk Marked 1274
Model PP .380 Caliber 1273
Model PP .380 Caliber, Bottom Magazine Release and Waffenampt Proofs 1274
Silver 1274
Model PP 50th Anniversary Commemorative Model 1276
Models PP and PPK 1276
Blue 1276
Gold 1276
Model PP .32 Caliber 1276
Model PP .380 Caliber 1276
Model PP Some with Duraluminum Frames, Model PP .22 Caliber 1276
Model PP, All Three Calibers Finished In Blue, Silver and Gold with Full Coverage Engraving 1276
Silver 1276
Model PP Limited Edition 1278
Model PP Mark II 1276
Model PP Manurhin 1276
Model PP Sport C, Manurhin 1276
Model PP Sport, Manurhin 1276
Model PP Sport, Walther 1276
Model PP Super 1278
Model PPK 1274, 1278
Blue 1275
Gold 1275
Model PPK .22 Caliber 1275
Model PPK .22 Caliber, Late War, Black Grips 1276
Model PPK .25 Caliber 1275
Model PPK .32 Caliber in Blue, Silver or Gold Finish and Full Coverage Engraving 1275
Model PPK .32 Caliber Marked Mod. PP on Slide 1275
Model PPK .32 Caliber with Duraluminum Frame 1275
Model PPK .32 Caliber with Panagraphed Slide 1275
Model PPK .32 Caliber with Verchromt Finish 1275
Model PPK .32 Caliber with Waffenampt Proofs and a High Polished Finish 1275
Model PPK .32 Caliber with Waffenampt Proofs and a Milled Finish 1275
Model PPK .32 Caliber, Allemagne Marked 1275
Model PPK .32 Caliber, Czechoslovakian Contract 1275
Model PPK .32 Caliber, DRP Marked 1276
Model PPK .32 Caliber, High Polished Finish 1275
Model PPK .32 Caliber, Milled Finish 1275
Model PPK .32 Caliber, Party Leader Grips, Black 1276
Model PPK .32 Caliber, Party Leader Grips, Brown 1276
Model PPK .32 Caliber, PDM Marked with Duraluminum Frame and Bottom Magazine Release 1276
Model PPK .32 Caliber, Police Eagle/C Proofed, High Polished Finish 1275
Model PPK .32 Caliber, Police Eagle/C Proofed. Milled Finish 1275
Model PPK .32 Caliber, Police Eagle/F Proofed, Duraluminum Frame, Milled Finish 1276
Model PPK .32 Caliber, RFV Marked 1276
Model PPK .32 Caliber, RZM Marked 1276
Model PPK .32 Caliber, Statens Vattenfallsverk 1276
Model PPK .380 Caliber 1275
Silver 1275
Model PPK 50th Anniversary Commemorative Model 1277
Model PPK American 1277
Model PPK Manurhin 1277
Model PPK Mark II 1277
Model PPK, All Three Calibers Finished In Blue, Silver and Gold with Full Coverage Engraving 1277
Blue 1277
Gold 1277
Silver 1277
Model PPK, Some with Duraluminum Frames 1276
Model PPK .380 Caliber 1277
Model PPK .22 Caliber 1276
Model PPK .32 Caliber 1276
Model PPK/E—Walther USA 1278
Model PPK/S 1277, 1278
Model PPK/S American 1277
Model R99 1282
Model SF 1283
Model SFD 1283
Model SSV Varmint 1282
Model TP 1277
Model TPH 1277
Model TPH American 1278
Model UIT BV Universal 1282
Model UIT Match 1282
Model V 1282
Model V Champion 1282
Model WA-2000 1283
Olympic Single-Shot 1282
Prone Model 400 1283
Running Boar Model 500 1283
Seventy-fifth Anniversary PPK 1279
Walther 1936 Olympia 1272

WALTHER MANURHIN 1283

WARNANT, L. AND J. 1283
1912 Model 1283
Revolver 1283
Semi-Automatic Pistol 1283

WARNER ARMS CORPORATION 1283
Boxlock Hammerless 1284
Double-Action 1284

Double-Action Hammerless 1284
Double Trigger Hammerless
Double-Barrel 1284
"Faultless": Warner-Schwarzlose
Model C, .32 ACP 1284
Field Grade Hammer Gun 1284
Grade X, SF, XT, SFT, XD and XDF
Hammer Guns 1284
Number 522 1284
Number 532 1284
Single Trigger Hammerless Utica
Special Double-Barrel 1284

WARNER, CHAS. 1284
Pocket Revolver 1284

WARNER, JAMES 1284
Automatic Revolving Cylinder 1284
Belt Revolver 1284
Manually Revolved Grooved
Cylinder 1284
Pocket Revolver 1284
Pocket Revolver 1285
Retractable Cylinder Model 1284
Revolving Carbines 1284
Second Model 1284
Single-Shot Derringer 1285
Third Model 1285

WATSON BROTHERS 1285

WEATHERBY 1285
35th Anniversary Commemorative
Mark V 1287
1984 Olympic Commemorative
Mark V 1287
Athena D'Italia 1293
Athena D'Italia Deluxe 1293
Athena D'Italia PG 1293
Athena Grade III Classic Field 1295
Athena Grade IV 1295
Athena Grade V Classic Field 1296
Athena SBS 1293
Centurion 1291
Centurion Deluxe 1292
Classic Custom 1291
Competition Model Athena 1295
Crown Custom 1291
Crown Grade Mark V 1287
Fiberguard 1289
Mark V 1285
Mark V .340 Weatherby Magnum . . . 1286
Mark V .375 Weatherby Magnum . . . 1285
Mark V .378 Weatherby Magnum . . . 1285
Mark V .416 Weatherby Magnum . . . 1285
Mark V .460 Weatherby Magnum . . . 1285
Mark V Accumark 1287
Mark V Accumark CFP 1296
Mark V Accumark Left-Hand 1287
Mark V Accumark Lightweight 1288
Mark V Center Fire Pistol (CFP) . . . 1296
Mark V Dangerous Game Rifle . . . 1286
Mark V Deluxe Lightweight 1288
Mark V Euromark 1286
Mark V Fibermark 1286
Mark V Fluted Stainless 1286
Mark V Fluted Synthetic 1286
Mark V Lazermark 1286
Mark V SBGM
(Super Big Game Master) 1288
Mark V SLS 1286
Mark V Special Varmint Rifle (SVR) . 1287
Mark V SPM
(Super Predator Master) 1288
Mark V Sporter 1285
Mark V Sporter Lightweight 1288
Mark V Stainless Lightweight 1288
Mark V Super Varmint Master (SVM) 1287
Mark V Synthetic Lightweight 1288
Mark V Ultra Lightweight 1288
Mark V Ultramark 1287
Mark V Varmint 1286
Mark V – CFP
(Compact Firing Platform) 1296
Mark XXII 1291
Model 82 1292
Model 92 1292
Model SAS Camo 1292
Shadow Grass 1292
Superflauge 1292
Model SAS Field 1292
Model SAS Slug Gun 1292
Model SAS Sporting Clays 1292
Model SAS Synthetic 1292
Olympian 1293
Orion Grade I 1293
Orion Grade II 1294
Orion Grade II Classic Field 1294
Orion Grade II Classic
Sporting Clays 1294
Orion Grade II Double Trap 1294
Orion Grade II Single Trap 1294
Orion Grade II Skeet 1293
Orion Grade II Sporting Clays 1294
Orion Grade III 1294
Orion Grade III Classic English Field 1295
Orion Grade III Classic Field 1295
Orion SBS 1293
Orion Super Sporting Clays (SSC) . . 1294
Orion Upland 1293
Outfitter Custom 1291
Outfitter Krieger Custom 1291
Patrician 1292
Patrician Deluxe 1292
Regency Field Grade 1293
Royal Custom 1291
Safari Grade Custom 1291
Safari Grade Mark V 1287
TRR 1288
TRR Magnum 1288
TRR Magnum Custom 1288
Vanguard 1289
Vanguard Classic I 1289
Vanguard Classic II 1289
Vanguard Compact 1290
Vanguard Sporter 1290
Vanguard Sporter Stainless 1290
Vanguard Stainless 1289
Vanguard Sub-MOA 1290
Vanguard Sub-MOA Varmint Special 1290
Vanguard Synthetic Package 1290
Vanguard Varmint Special 1290
Vanguard VGL 1289
Vanguard VGS 1289
Vanguard VGX 1289
Vanguard VGX Deluxe 1289
Vanguard Weatherguard 1289
Weatherby Mark V Deluxe 1285
Weatherby Vanguard Deluxe 1290
Weathermark 1290
Weathermark Alaskan 1290

WEAVER ARMS 1296
Nighthawk Assault Pistol 1296
Nighthawk Carbine 1296

WEBLEY & SCOTT, LTD. 1296
British Bulldog 1297
Mark I 1297
Mark II 1297
Mark III 1297
Mark IV 1297
Mark IV Target 1297
Mark V 1297
Mark VI 1297
Mark VI .22 Rimfire 1301
Model 1872 Royal Irish Constabulary 1296
Model 1878 Army Express Revolver 1297
Model 1878 Webley-Pryse 1296
Model 1880 Metropolitan Police 1296
Model 1884 R.I.C. Naval 1296
Model 1904 1301
Model 1905 1302
Model 1907 1302
Model 1908 1302
Model 1909 1302
Model 1910 .380 1302
Model 1910 .38 ACP 1302
Model 1911 1303
Model 1912 1303
Model 1913 1303
Model 1913 1303
Model 1913 (RHA model) 1303
Model 1922 1303
New Model 1883 R.I.C. 1296
Webley Kaufmann Model 1880 1297
Webley-Fosbery Automatic Revolver 1301
.455 Caliber 1301
.38 Caliber 1301
Webley-Green Model 1297

WEIHRAUCH, HANS HERMANN 1303
Model HW 60M 1303
Model HW 66 1303
Model HW-3 1303
Model HW-5 1303
Model HW-7 1304
Model HW-9 1304

WEISBURGER, A. 1304
Pocket Pistol 1304

WESSON, DAN FIREARMS . 1304
Coyote Classic 1310
Coyote Target 1310
Dan Wesson RZ-10 1309
Dan Wesson VH8 1306
Model 15/715 1304
Model 15/715 1305
Model 15/715 1307
Model 15/715 1307
Model 22/722 1304
Model 22/722 1307
Model 22/722 1307
Model 22M/722M 1304
Model 32/732 1304
Model 32/732 1307
Model 32/732 1307
Model 3220/73220 1304
Model 3220/73220 1307
Model 3220/73220 1307
Model 360/7360 1304
Model 360/7360 1305
Model 40/740 1305
Model 40/740 1307
Model 40/740 1308
Model 41/741 1304
Model 41/741 1305
Model 41/741 1307
Model 41/741 1307
Model 414/7414 1305
Model 414/7414 1307
Model 414/7414 1308
Model 44/744 1304
Model 44/744 1305
Model 44/744 1307
Model 44/744 1308
Model 445/7445 1305
Model 445/7445 1307
Model 445/7445 1308
Model 445/7445 (Alaskan Guide) . . . 1305
Model 45/745 1304
Model 45/745 1305
Model 45/745 1307
Model 45/745 1308
Model 460/7460 1304

Model 460/7460 . . . 1305
Model 460/7460 . . . 1307
Model 460/7460 . . . 1308
Model 722 VH10 . . . 1305
Model 722 VH10 SRS1 . . . 1306
Model 7360 V8S . . . 1306
Model 7360 V8S SRS1 . . . 1306
Model 740 V8S . . . 1306
Model 740 V8S SRS1 . . . 1306
Model 741 V10S . . . 1306
Model 741 V10S SRS1 . . . 1306
Model 741 V8S . . . 1306
Model 741 V8S SRS1 . . . 1306
Model 7414 V8S . . . 1306
Model 7414 V8S SRS1 . . . 1306
Model 744 V10S . . . 1306
Model 744 V10S SRS1 . . . 1306
Model 744 V8S . . . 1306
Model 744 V8S SRS1 . . . 1306
Model 7445 V8S . . . 1306
Model 7445 V8S SS1 . . . 1306
Patriot Expert . . . 1309
Patriot Marksman . . . 1309
Pointman Dave Pruitt Signature Series . . . 1309
Pointman Guardian . . . 1308
Pointman Guardian Duce . . . 1308
Pointman Hi-Cap . . . 1309
Pointman Major . . . 1308
Pointman Major Australian . . . 1309
Pointman Minor . . . 1308
Pointman Seven . . . 1308
Pointman Seven Stainless . . . 1308

WESSON FIREARMS CO., INC. . . . 1310
HP15 Hunter Pac . . . 1312
HP22 Hunter Pac . . . 1311
HP32 Hunter Pac . . . 1312
HP40 Hunter Pac . . . 1313
HP41/44 Hunter Pac . . . 1314
HP375 Hunter Pac . . . 1313
HP455 Hunter Pac . . . 1315
Model 8 . . . 1310, 1312
Model 9 . . . 1310, 1312
Model 11 . . . 1310
Model 12 . . . 1310
Model 14 . . . 1310, 1312
Model 14/714 Fixed Barrel Service . 1316
Model 15 . . . 1310, 1312
Model 15/715 Fixed Barrel Target . . 1316
Model 22 . . . 1310
Model 22M . . . 1311
Model 32 . . . 1311
Model 38P . . . 1315
Model 40/Supermag . . . 1313
Model 41 . . . 1314
Model 44 . . . 1314
Model 45 . . . 1314
Model 45/745 Pin Gun . . . 1315
Ventilated Heavy Rib Shroud . . . 1315
Ventilated Rib Shroud . . . 1315
Model 322 . . . 1311
Model 375 . . . 1313
Ventilated Heavy Rib Shroud . . . 1313
Ventilated Rib Shroud . . . 1313
Ventilated Slotted Shroud—8" barrel only . . . 1313
Model 445 . . . 1314
Model 708 . . . 1312
Model 709 . . . 1312
Standard Rib Shroud . . . 1312
Ventilated Heavy Rib Shroud . . . 1312
Ventilated Rib Shroud . . . 1312
Model 714 . . . 1312
Model 715 . . . 1312
Model 722 . . . 1311
Model 722M . . . 1311
Standard Rib Shroud . . . 1311
Ventilated Heavy Rib Shroud . . . 1311
Ventilated Rib Shroud . . . 1311
Model 732 . . . 1311
Model 738P . . . 1315
Model 740 . . . 1313
Ventilated Heavy Rib Shroud . . . 1313
Ventilated Rib Shroud . . . 1313
Ventilated Slotted Shroud—8" barrel only . . . 1313
Model 741 . . . 1314
Model 744 . . . 1314
Model 745 . . . 1314
Ventilated Heavy Rib Shroud . . . 1314
Ventilated Rib Shroud . . . 1314
Model 7322 . . . 1311
Standard Rib Shroud . . . 1311
Ventilated Heavy Rib Shroud . . . 1311
Ventilated Rib Shroud . . . 1311
Model 7445 . . . 1314
Ventilated Heavy Rib Shroud . . . 1315
Ventilated Rib Shroud . . . 1314
Model 7445 Alaskan Guide Special . 1315
P14/8 Pistol Pac . . . 1312
P15/9 Pistol Pac . . . 1313
Standard Rib Shroud . . . 1313
Ventilated Heavy Rib Shroud . . . 1313
Ventilated Rib Shroud . . . 1313
P22 Pistol Pac . . . 1311
Standard Rib Shroud . . . 1311
Ventilated Heavy Rib Shroud . . . 1311
Ventilated Rib Shroud . . . 1311
P32 Pistol Pac . . . 1311
Standard Rib Shroud . . . 1312
Ventilated Heavy Rib Shroud . . . 1312
Ventilated Rib Shroud . . . 1312
P44/P41/P45 Pistol Pac . . . 1314
Ventilated Heavy Rib Shroud . . . 1314
Ventilated Rib Shroud . . . 1314
Wesson Firearms Silhouette .22 . . . 1315
Ventilated Heavy Rib Shroud . . . 1315
Ventilated Rib Shroud . . . 1315

WESSON, EDWIN . . . 1316
Dragoon . . . 1316

WESSON, FRANK . . . 1316
1870 Large Frame Pocket Rifle First Type . . . 1317
Pistol Only . . . 1317
1870 Large Frame Pocket Rifle Second Type . . . 1317
Pistol Only . . . 1317
1870 Medium Frame Pocket Rifle First Type . . . 1316
Pistol Only . . . 1316
1870 Medium Frame Pocket Rifle Second Type . . . 1316
Pistol Only . . . 1317
1870 Medium Frame Pocket Rifle Third Type . . . 1317
Pistol Only . . . 1317
First Model Medium Frame . . . 1316
First Model Small Frame . . . 1316
Large Frame Superposed Pistol . . . 1317
Manual Extractor Model . . . 1316
Medium Frame Pocket Rifle . . . 1316
Pistol Only . . . 1316
Medium Frame Second Model . . . 1316
Medium Frame Superposed Pistol . . 1317
First Type Marked "Patent Applied For" . . . 1317
Second Type Marked "Patent December 15, 1868" . 1317
Third Type Full-Length Fluted Barrels . . . 1317
Military Carbine . . . 1318
Model 1870 Small Frame Pocket Rifle . . . 1316
Pistol Only . . . 1316
No. 1 Long Range Rifle . . . 1317
No. 2 Mid-Range or Hunting Rifle . . . 1317
No. 2 Sporting Rifle . . . 1318
Second Type . . . 1316
Small Frame Pocket Rifle . . . 1316
Pistol Only . . . 1316
Small Frame Superposed Pistol . . . 1317

WESSON & LEAVITT MASSACHUSETTS ARMS COMPANY . . . 1318
Dragoon . . . 1318
Revolving Rifle . . . 1318

WESTERN ARMS . . . 1318

WESTERN ARMS CORPORATION . . . 1318

WESTERN FIELD . . . 1318

WESTLEY RICHARDS & CO., LTD. . . . 1318

WHEELER, ROBERT . . . 1318

WHITE, ROLLIN . . . 1318
Pocket Pistol . . . 1318
Pocket Revolver . . . 1318

WHITNEY ARMS COMPANY . 1319
Double-Barreled Percussion Shotgun . . . 1325
Eli Whitney Jr. Armory Rifles and Rifle-Muskets, 1842-1865 . . . 1321
Eli Whitney, Sr. Armory Muskets, 1798-1824. 1798 U.S. Contract Muskets, Types I-IV . . . 1319
Excelsior . . . 1325
New Model Pocket Revolver . . . 1330
Rimfire Pocket Revolver . . . 1330
Single Barreled Percussion Shotgun 1325
Swing-Breech Carbine . . . 1325
Whitney 1851 Navy . . . 1329
Whitney (and P. & E.W. Blake) U.S. M1816/1822 Contract Muskets . . . 1320
Whitney Armory Muskets, 1825-1842 1320
Whitney Armory U.S. M1816/M1822 Muskets, Altered to Percussion . . 1320
Whitney Armory U.S. M1816/M1822 Muskets, Flintlock or Altered to Percussion and Adapted with "Sea Fencible" Heavy Buttplates . . . 1320
Whitney Arms Company, 1865-1888 1325
Whitney Connecticut, New York, and U.S. 1812 Contract Muskets . . . 1319
Whitney "Direct Vent" M1861 Rifle-Musket Derivatives . . . 1324
Whitney "Good & Serviceable" M1841 Derivatives . . . 1322
Whitney "High Humpback" Lockplate M1861 Rifle-Musket Derivative . . . 1324
Whitney M1842 Rifled Musket Derivative . . . 1322
Whitney M1855 Rifle Derivative . . . 1323
Whitney M1855 Rifle-Musket Derivative . . . 1323
Whitney M1861 Connecticut Contract Rifle-Musket Derivative . . 1323
Whitney "Manton" M1861 Rifle-Musket Derivative . . . 1324
Whitney Navy Revolver . . . 1329
First Model . . . 1329
First Variation . . . 1329
Fourth Variation . . . 1329
Second Variation . . . 1329
Third Variation . . . 1329
Second Model . . . 1329
Fifth Variation . . . 1329
First Variation . . . 1329
Fourth Variation . . . 1329
Second Variation . . . 1329

    - Sixth Variation ... 1329
    - Third Variation ... 1329
- Whitney Phoenix ... 1326
  - Civilian Carbine ... 1326
  - Gallery Rifle ... 1326
  - Military Carbine ... 1326
  - Military Rifle ... 1326
  - Schuetzen Rifle ... 1326
  - Shotgun ... 1326
- Whitney Pocket Revolver ... 1329
  - First Model ... 1330
    - Fifth Variation ... 1330
    - First Variation ... 1330
    - Fourth Variation ... 1330
    - Second Variation ... 1330
    - Third Variation ... 1330
  - Second Model ... 1330
    - First Variation ... 1330
    - Fourth Variation ... 1330
    - Second Variation ... 1330
    - Third Variation ... 1330
- Whitney U.S. M1841 Contract Rifle (unaltered) ... 1321
- Whitney U.S. M1841/1855 Contract Rifle, Adapted to Saber Bayonet and Long Range Sights ... 1321
- Whitney U.S. M1841 Contract Rifles, Adapted to Saber Bayonets and Long Range Rear Sights (Colt 1862 Adaptation) ... 1321
- Whitney U.S. M1861 Contract Rifle-Musket ... 1324
- Whitney South Carolina Contract M1841 Rifle ... 1321
- Whitney P1853 "Long Enfield" Rifle-Musket Derivative ... 1322
- Whitney P1853 "Short Enfield" Rifle Derivative ... 1323
- Whitney U.S. Navy Contract Rifle ... 1324
- Whitney-Beals Patent Revolver ... 1328
  - .28 Caliber Model ... 1329
  - .31 Caliber Model ... 1329
  - First Model ... 1329
- Whitney-Burgess-Morse Rifle ... 1327
  - Carbine ... 1328
  - Military Rifle ... 1328
  - Sporting Rifle ... 1327
- Whitney-Cochran Carbine ... 1325
- Whitney-Howard Lever Action ... 1325
  - Carbine ... 1326
  - Rifle ... 1326
  - Shotgun ... 1326
- Whitney-Kennedy Rifle ... 1328
  - Hooded Cylinder Pocket Revolver ... 1328
  - Large Frame Sporting Rifle ... 1328
  - Military Carbine ... 1328
  - Military Rifle ... 1328
  - Small Frame Sporting Rifle ... 1328
  - Two Trigger Pocket Revolver ... 1328
- Whitney-Laidley Model I Rolling Block ... 1326
  - Civilian Carbine ... 1327
  - Creedmoor No. 1 Rifle ... 1327
  - Creedmoor No. 2 Rifle ... 1327
  - Gallery Rifle ... 1327
  - Military Carbine ... 1326
  - Military Rifle ... 1327
  - Sporting Rifle ... 1327
- Whitney-Remington Model 2 Rolling Block ... 1327
  - Civilian Carbine ... 1327
  - Military Carbine ... 1327
  - Military Rifle ... 1327
  - No. 1 Sporting Rifle ... 1327
  - No. 2 Sporting Rifle ... 1327
  - Shotgun ... 1327

WHITNEY FIREARMS COMPANY ... 1330
- Wolverine ... 1330
  - Blue Finish ... 1331
  - Nickel-Plated ... 1331

WHITWORTH ... 1331

WICHITA ARMS, INC. ... 1331
- Classic Rifle ... 1331
- Silhouette Rifle ... 1331
- Varmint Rifle ... 1331
- Wichita Classic Engraved ... 1331
- Wichita Classic Pistol ... 1331
- Wichita International Pistol ... 1331
- Wichita MK40 ... 1331
- Wichita Silhouette Pistol ... 1331

WICKLIFFE RIFLES ... 1331
- Model 76 ... 1331
- Model 76 Deluxe ... 1332
- Stinger ... 1332
- Stinger Deluxe ... 1332
- Traditionalist ... 1332

WIENER WAFFENFABRIK ... 1332
- Little Tom ... 1332

WILDEY FIREARMS CO., INC. ... 1332
- Cheshire, Conn., Address ... 1332
  - Serial No. 1 through 200 ... 1333
- Hunter Model ... 1333
- JAWS Viper ... 1333
- Pin Gun ... 1333
- Presentation Model ... 1333
- Survivor Model ... 1333
- Wildey Auto Pistol ... 1332
- Wildey Carbine ... 1333

WILKES, JOHN ... 1333

WILKINSON ARMS CO. ... 1333
- Diane ... 1333
- Terry Carbine ... 1333

WILLIAMSON MOORE FIREARMS COMPANY ... 1333
- Derringer ... 1333

WILSON & CO. ... 1334

WILSON, J. P. ... 1334
- Percussion Alarm Gun ... 1334

WILSON COMBAT ... 1334
- .22 Classic Rimfire Pistol ... 1336
- ADP 9mm ... 1334
- Classic Master Grade ... 1336
- Combat Classic Super Grade (Tactical Super Grade) ... 1336
- Competition Pistols ... 1337
- Custom Carry Revolver ... 1335
- Defensive Combat Pistol ... 1336
- Defensive Combat Pistol Deluxe ... 1336
- KZ 9mm ... 1334
- M-4T Tactical Carbine ... 1337
- Professional Model Pistol ... 1337
- Service Grade Classic ... 1335
- Service Grade Protector ... 1334
- Service Grade Protector Compact ... 1335
- Service Grade Sentinel Ultra Compact ... 1335
- Service Grade Tactical ... 1335
- Service Grade Target ... 1335
- Stealth Defense System ... 1336
- Super Sniper ... 1337
- Tactical Carry (KZ-45) ... 1334
- Tactical Elite ... 1336
- Tactical Super Grade Compact ... 1336
- TL-15 Tactical Lightweight ... 1337
- TPR-15 Tactical Precision Rifle ... 1337
- UT-15 Urban Tactical ... 1337
- Wilson Model 1996A2 ... 1334

WINCHESTER REPEATING ARMS COMPANY ... 1337
- 1964 Wyoming Diamond Jubilee—Carbine ... 1402
- 1966 Centennial—Carbine ... 1402
- 1966 Centennial—Rifle ... 1402
- 1966 Nebraska Centennial—Rifle ... 1402
- 1967 Alaskan Purchase Centennial—Carbine ... 1402
- 1967 Canadian Centennial—Carbine ... 1402
- 1967 Canadian Centennial—Rifle ... 1402
- 1968 Buffalo Bill "1 or 300"—Rifle ... 1402
- 1968 Buffalo Bill—Carbine ... 1402
- 1968 Buffalo Bill—Rifle ... 1402
- 1968 Illinois Sesquicentennial—Carbine ... 1402
- 1969 Golden Spike Carbine ... 1402
- 1969 Theodore Roosevelt—Carbine ... 1402
- 1969 Theodore Roosevelt—Rifle ... 1402
- 1970 Cowboy Carbine "1 of 300" ... 1402
- 1970 Cowboy Commemorative Carbine ... 1402
- 1970 Lone Star—Carbine ... 1402
- 1970 Lone Star—Rifle ... 1402
- 1970 Northwest Territories (Canadian) ... 1402
- 1970 Northwest Territories Deluxe (Canadian) ... 1402
- 1971 Mounted Police (Canadian) ... 1402
- 1971 Mounted Police, Presentation ... 1402
- 1971 NRA Centennial—Musket ... 1402
- 1971 NRA Centennial—Rifle ... 1402
- 1971 Royal Canadian Mounted Police (Canadian) ... 1402
- 1971 Yellow Boy (European) ... 1402
- 1974 Apache (Canadian) ... 1402
- 1974 Commanche (Canadian) ... 1402
- 1974 Klondike Gold Rush (Canadian) ... 1402
- 1974 Texas Ranger Presentation Model ... 1402
- 1974 Texas Ranger—Carbine ... 1402
- 1975 Klondike Gold Rush—Dawson City Issue (Canadian) ... 1403
- 1976 Little Bighorn (Canadian) ... 1403
- 1976 Sioux (Canadian) ... 1403
- 1976 U.S. Bicentennial Carbine ... 1403
- 1977 Cherokee—.22 Cal. (Canadian) ... 1403
- 1977 Cherokee—.30-30 Cal. (Canadian) ... 1403
- 1977 Cheyenne—.22 Cal. (Canadian) ... 1403
- 1977 Cheyenne—.44-40 Cal. (Canadian) ... 1403
- 1977 Legendary Lawman ... 1403
- 1977 Limited Edition I ... 1403
- 1977 Wells Fargo ... 1403
- 1978 "One of One Thousand" (European) ... 1403
- 1978 Antler Game Carbine ... 1403
- 1979 Bat Masterson (Canadian) ... 1403
- 1979 Legendary Frontiersman Rifle ... 1403
- 1979 Limited Edition II ... 1403
- 1979 Matched Set of 1,000 ... 1403
- 1980 Alberta Diamond Jubilee (Canadian) ... 1403
- 1980 Alberta Diamond Jubilee Deluxe (Canadian) ... 1403
- 1980 Oliver Winchester ... 1403
- 1980 Saskatchewan Diamond Jubilee (Canadian) ... 1403
- 1980 Saskatchewan Diamond Jubilee Deluxe (Canadian) ... 1403
- 1981 Calgary Stampede (Canadian) ... 1403

1981 Canadian Pacific Centennial (Canadian) 1403
1981 Canadian Pacific Centennial Presentation (Canadian) 1403
1981 Canadian Pacific Employee's Model (Canadian) 1403
1981 Duke 1403
1981 John Wayne 1403
1981 John Wayne (Canadian) 1403
1981 John Wayne "1 of 300" Set . . . 1403
1981 U.S. Border Patrol 1403
1981 U.S. Border Patrol—Member's Model 1403
1982 Annie Oakley 1403
1982 Great Western Artist I 1403
1982 Great Western Artist II 1403
1983 American Bald Eagle 1403
1983 American Bald Eagle—Deluxe 1403
1983 Chief Crazy Horse 1403
1983 Oklahoma Diamond Jubilee . . . 1404
1984 Winchester—Colt Commemorative Set 1404
1985 Boy Scout 75th Anniversary .22 Cal. 1404
1985 Boy Scout 75th Anniversary—Eagle Scout 1404
1986 120th Anniversary Model—Carbine .44-40 Cal. 1404
1986 European 1 of 1,000 Second Series (European) 1404
1986 Model 94 Ducks Unlimited . . . 1404
1986 Statue of Liberty 1404
1987 U.S. Constitution 200th Anniversary 44-40 1404
1990 Wyoming Centennial-30-30 . . . 1404
1991 Winchester 125th Anniversary 1404
1992 Arapaho—30-30 1404
1992 Kentucky Bicentennial-30-30 . 1404
1992 Ontario Conservation-30-30 . . 1404
1993 Nez Perce—30-30 1404
1995 Florida Sesquicentennial Carbine 1404
1996 Wild Bill Hickok Carbine 1404
Breechloading Double-Barrel Shotgun 1350
Class A, B, C, and D 1351
Match Gun 1351
Combination Gun 1400
Custom Shop Model 21s—1960 to 1981 1374
Custom Grade—12 Gauge 1375
Grand American—12 Gauge . . . 1375
Pigeon Grade—12 Gauge 1375
Custom Shop Model 21s—1982 to Present 1375
Grand American 1375
Grand American Small Gauge Set—28 or .410 bore 1375
Standard Custom Built 1375
Ducks Unlimited Model 1393
Express Rifle 1400
Golden Quail 1399
Henry Rifle 1339
Brass Frame Rifle 1339
Iron Frame Rifle 1339
Hunt Repeating Rifle 1337
Imperial Bolt-Action Magazine Rifle (Model 51) 1363
Jennings 1337
First Model 1337
Second Model 1338
Third Model 1338
Lever Action Carbine 1339
16" Barrel 1339
20" Barrel 1339
24" Barrel 1339
Martially Inspected Henry Rifles 1339
Miniature Target Rifle 1366
Model 12 1369
Featherweight 1369
Heavy Duck Gun 1373
Pigeon Grade 1373
Riot Gun 1369
Skeet Grade 1373
Standard Grade—12 gauge 1369
Trap Grade 1373
Trench Gun 1369
Model 12 Field Grade 1392
Model 12 Skeet 1392
Model 12 Super Pigeon Grade 1392
Model 12 Trap Grade 1392
Model 12 (Limited Edition) 1392
Grade 1 1392
Grade IV 1392
Model 20 1373
Model 21 . . . . 1374, 1399
Model 21—1931 to 1959 1374
Custom Built .410 Bore 1374
Custom Built/Deluxe Grade 1374
Duck/Magnum Gun 1374
Skeet Grade 1374
Standard Grade 1374
Tournament Grade 1374
Trap Grade 1374
Model 22 1398
Model 23 Heavy Duck 1399
Model 23 Light Duck 1399
Model 23 XTR 1399
Grade I 1399
Pigeon Grade 1399
Pigeon Grade Lightweight 1399
Model 24 1375
Model 25 1373
Model 36 1373
Model 37 1375
Youth Model 1375
Model 37A 1398
Model 40 1376
Skeet Grade 1376
Standard Grade 1376
Model 41 1373
Model 42 1375
Deluxe Grade—Solid Rib 1376
Deluxe Grade—Ventilated Rib 1376
Skeet Grade—Solid Rib 1376
Skeet Grade—Ventilated Rib . . . 1376
Standard Grade 1376
Trap Grade 1376
Model 42 (Limited Edition) 1392
Model 43 1363
Special Rifle or Deluxe 1363
Standard Rifle 1363
Model 47 1363
Model 47 Target Rifle 1363
Model 50 1376
Featherweight 1377
Pigeon Grade 1377
Skeet Grade 1377
Standard Grade 1377
Trap Grade 1377
Model 52 1363
Free Style 1364
Model 52 International Match . . . 1364
Model 52 Standard 1364
Model 52 Target 1364
Model 52 Target—Speed Lock . . 1364
Model 52A Target Heavy Barrel—Rare 1364
Model 52B Bull Gun 1364
Model 52B Target Bull Barrel . . . 1364
Model 52B Target Heavy & Standard Barrel 1364
Model 52C Bull Gun 1364
Model 52C Target 1364
Model 52D Target 1364
Prone 1364
Model 52 Sporter—B & C Models . . 1364
Model 52B Sporting Rifle 1385
Model 53 1349
Sporting Rifle 1349
Model 54 1364
Carbine 1365
N.R.A. Rifle 1365
National Match Rifle 1365
Sniper's Rifle 1365
Standard Rifle 1365
Super Grade Rifle 1365
Target Rifle 1365
Model 55 1349
Standard Rifle 1349
Model 55 (Rimfire Rifle) 1358
Standard Rifle 1358
Model 56 1365
Fancy Sporting Rifle 1365
Sporting Rifle 1365
Model 57 1365
Model 58 1365
Model 59 . . . . 1365, 1377
Pigeon Grade 1377
Standard Grade 1377
Model 60 and 60A 1365
Model 60 1365
Model 60A 1366
Model 61 1356
Pre-war Model 61 1356
Post-war Model 61 1356
Model 61 Magnum 1357
Model 62 and 62A 1357
Model 62 Gallery 1357
Post-war Model 62 1357
Pre-war Model 62 1357
Model 63 . . . . 1357, 1378
20" Barrel 1357
23" Barrel 1357
Grade I 1378
High Grade 1378
Model 64 . . . . 1349, 1383
Carbine 1349
Standard Rifle 1349
Model 65 1350
Standard Rifle 1350
Model 67 1366
Junior Rifle 1366
Smoothbore Rifle 1366
Sporting Rifle 1366
Model 68 1366
With Scope 1366
Without Scope 1366
Model 69 and 69A 1366
Model 70 1366
Model 70 African 1385
Model 70 Black Shadow 1389
Model 70 Classic Compact 1387
Model 70 Classic Laminated Stainless 1388
Classic Camo Stainless 1388
Model 70 Classic Laredo 1387
Model 70 Classic Safari Express . . . 1387
Model 70 Classic Sporter LT 1387
Model 70 Classic Super Grade III . . . 1387
Model 70 Coyote 1389
Model 70 Coyote Lite 1389
Model 70 Custom "Ultra Light" Mannlicher 1391
Model 70 Custom 100th Anniversary .30-06 1391
Model 70 Custom African Express . . 1391
Model 70 Custom Carbon 1390
Model 70 Custom Classic Sharpshooter II 1390
Model 70 Custom Classic Sporting Sharpshooter II 1390
Model 70 Custom Continental Hunter 1392
Model 70 Custom Express 1391
Model 70 Custom Extreme Weather 1391
Model 70 Custom Featherweight . . . 1390
Model 70 Custom Grade 1391
Model 70 Custom Maple 1392
Model 70 Custom Safari Express . . . 1391
Model 70 Custom Sharpshooter 1390
Model 70 Custom Short Action 1391

Model 70 Custom Special "70 Years of the Model 70" 1391
Model 70 Custom Sporting Sharpshooter 1390
Model 70 Custom Stainless Laminate 1392
Model 70 Custom Take Down 1391
Model 70 DBM 1388
Model 70 DBM-S 1388
Model 70 Deluxe 1385
Model 70 Featherweight Classic . . . 1386
Model 70 Featherweight Classic All-Terrain 1386
Model 70 Featherweight Super Short 1387
Model 70 Featherweight Ultra Grade 1390
Model 70 Fiftieth Anniversary Model 1386
Model 70 Heavy Varmint 1388
Model 70 Heavy Varmint—Fluted Barrel 1388
Model 70 International Match Army . 1385
Model 70 Ladies/Youth Ranger 1390
Model 70 Laminated Coyote Gray or Brown Stainless 1390
Model 70 Laminated Coyote Outback Stainless 1390
Model 70 Lightweight 1389
Model 70 Magnum 1385
Model 70 Mannlicher 1385
Model 70 Pro Shadow Blued 1390
Model 70 Pro Shadow Stainless . . . 1390
Model 70 RMEF Super Grade 1387
Model 70 RMEF Super Grade III . . . 1387
Model 70 Shadow Elite Camo Stainless 1390
Model 70 Shadow Elite Stainless . . . 1390
Model 70 SM 1388
Model 70 Sporter 1388
Model 70 Stainless 1388
Model 70 Stealth 1389
Model 70 Super Express 1388
Model 70 Super Grade 1387
Model 70 Super Shadow 1389
Model 70 Super Shadow Super Short 1389
Model 70 Target Rifle 1385
Model 70 Ultimate Classic 1391
Model 70 Ultimate Shadow 1389
Model 70 Ultimate Shadow Camo . . 1389
Model 70 Varmint 1385
Model 70 Varmint 1388
Model 70 Westerner 1385
Model 70 Winlight 1386
Model 70 WinTuff 1389
Model 70 XTR Featherweight 1386
Model 70 XTR Super Express 1386
Model 70 XTR Varmint 1386
Model 70A 1386
Model 70—Standard Grade 1385
Model 71 1347
Deluxe Rifle 1347
Deluxe Rifle (Carbine) 1347
Standard Rifle 1347
Standard Rifle (Carbine) 1347
Model 72 1369
Model 74 1358
Gallery Special—.22 Short Only . 1358
Sporting Rifle 1358
Model 75 1369
Model 75 Sporter 1369
Model 75 Target 1369
Model 77 1358
Standard Rifle 1358
Model 88 "Centennial Model" (1855/1955) 1362
Carbine 1362
Rifle 1362
Model 91 1398
Model 94 1378
Model 94 Antique Carbine 1379
Model 94 Black Shadow 1379
Model 94 Centennial Limited Editions 1380
Custom High Grade 1380
Grade I 1380
High Grade 1380
Model 94 Custom Limited Edition . . . 1392
Model 94 Custom Limited Edition New Generation 1390
Model 94 Deluxe 1379
Model 94 Heritage—Custom 1 of 100 1380
Model 94 Heritage—Limited 1 of 1000 1380
Model 94 Legacy 20-inch 1379
Model 94 Legacy 24-inch 1379
Model 94 Legacy 26-inch 1379
Model 94 Pack Rifle 1381
Model 94 Ranger 1379
Model 94 Ranger Compact 1379
Model 94 Timber Carbine 1380
Model 94 Timber Scout 1381
Model 94 Traditional—CW 1378
Model 94 Trails End 1380
Model 94 Trails End Hunter 1380
Model 94 Trails End Octagon 1380
Model 94 Trapper 1379
Model 94 Win-Tuff 1379
Model 94 Wrangler 1379
Model 94 Wrangler II 1379
Model 94 XTR 1379
Model 94 XTR Big Bore 1380
Model 94 XTR Deluxe 1379
Model 96 Xpert 1400
Model 99 or Thumb Trigger 1362
Model 100 1358
Carbine 1362
Rifle 1362
Model 101 Diamond Grade 1400
Model 101 Field Grade 1399
Model 101 Magnum 1399
Model 101 Pigeon Grade 1400
Model 101 Skeet Grade 1399
Model 101 Three-Gauge Skeet Set . 1399
Model 101 Trap Grade 1399
Model 121 1377
Model 131 1377
Model 250 1377
Model 250 Deluxe 1378
Model 255 1378
Model 255 Deluxe 1378
Model 270 1378
Model 310 1377
Model 320 1377
Model 490 1378
Model 501 Grand European 1400
Model 501 Presentation Grade 1400
Model 670 1386
Model 677 1366
Model 697 1366
Model 1001 Field 1400
Model 1001 Sporting Clays I & II . . . 1401
Model 1200 1392
Model 1300 Black Shadow Deer . . . 1394
Model 1300 Black Shadow Field . . . 1394
Model 1300 Black Shadow Turkey . . 1393
Model 1300 Buck and Tom 1394
Model 1300 Camp Defender 1395
Model 1300 Defender 5-Shot 1395
Model 1300 Defender 8-Shot 1395
Model 1300 Defender Combo 1395
Model 1300 Defender Pistol Grip . . . 1395
Model 1300 Defender Synthetic Stock 1395
Model 1300 Lady Defender 1395
Model 1300 Mossy Oak Break-Up Turkey 1393
Model 1300 National Wild Turkey Federation Series III 1393
Model 1300 National Wild Turkey Federation Series IV 1393
Model 1300 New Shadow Grass . . . 1393
Model 1300 NWTF Short Turkey . . . 1393
Model 1300 Ranger 1395
Model 1300 Ranger Deer Slug 1395
Model 1300 Ranger Deer Combo . . . 1395
12 Gauge Combo 1395
20 Gauge Combo 1395
Model 1300 Ranger Ladies/Youth-Compact 1395
Model 1300 Realtree Turkey 1393
Model 1300 Slug Hunter 1394
Model 1300 Slug Hunter Sabot (Smoothbore) 1394
Model 1300 Sporting/Field 1394
Model 1300 Sporting/Field Compact 1394
Model 1300 Stainless Marine 1395
Model 1300 Stainless Marine with Pistol Grip 1396
Model 1300 Stainless Security 1393
Model 1300 Turkey 1393
Model 1300 Universal Hunter 1394
Model 1300 Upland Special 1394
Model 1300 Upland Special Field . . . 1395
Model 1300 Walnut Field 1394
Model 1300 Waterfowl 1393
Model 1300 Whitetails Unlimited Slug Hunter 1394
Model 1300 WinCam Turkey Gun . . 1393
Model 1300 XTR 1393
Model 1400 1397
Model 1400 Quail Unlimited 1398
Model 1400 Ranger 1398
Model 1400 Ranger Deer Combo . . . 1398
Model 1500 XTR 1396
Model 1866 1340
First Model 1340
Carbine 1340
Rifle 1340
Second Model 1340
Carbine 1340
Rifle 1340
Third Model 1341
Carbine 1341
Musket 1341
Rifle 1341
Fourth Model 1341
Carbine 1341
Musket 1341
Rifle 1341
Model 1866 Iron Frame Rifle Musket 1341
Model 1866 Iron Frame Swiss Sharpshooters Rifle 1341
Model 1867 Iron Frame Carbine 1341
Model 1868 Iron Frame Rifle Musket 1341
Model 1868 Iron Frame Carbine 1342
Model 1873 1342
First Model 1343
Carbine 1343
Musket 1343
Rifle 1343
Second Model 1343
Carbine 1343
Musket 1343
Rifle 1343
Third Model 1343
Carbine 1343
Musket 1343
Rifle 1343
Model 1873 .22 Rimfire Rifle 1343
Model 1876 1343
First Model 1344
Carbine 1344
Musket 1344
Rifle 1344

Second Model 1344
Carbine 1344
Musket 1344
Rifle 1344
Model 1885 .30-06 Centennial High Wall Hunter 1384
Model 1885 High Wall Hunter 1383
Model 1885 Low Wall 17 Mach 2 1384
Model 1885 Low Wall 1383
Grade I 1383
High Grade 1383
Model 1885 Low Wall Classic 1384
Model 1885 (Single-Shot) 1345
High Wall Musket 1346
High Wall Schuetzen Rifle 1346
High Wall Shotgun 1346
Low Wall Carbine 1346
Low Wall Musket (Winder Musket) 1346
Standard High Wall Rifle 1346
Standard Low Wall Rifle 1346
Model 1886 . . . . 1346, 1384
Carbine 1347
Extra Lightweight Rifle—.33 caliber 1347
Extra Lightweight Rifle—Other Calibers 1347
Extra Lightweight Takedown Rifle—.33 caliber 1347
Extra Lightweight Takedown Rifle—Other Calibers 1347
Fancy Sporting Rifle 1347
Grade I 1384
High Grade 1384
Musket 1347
Sporting Rifle 1347
Takedown Rifle—Standard 1347
Model 1886 Extra Light 1384
Grade I (3,500) 1384
High Grade (1,000) 1384
Model 1886 Take Down Classic 1384
Model 1887 Shotgun 1351
Riot Shotgun 1351
Standard Shotgun 1351
Model 1890 1355
First Model—Standard Grade 1355
Second Model—Case Hardened Frame 1355
Deluxe 1355
Standard 1355
Second Model—Blued Frame 1355
Deluxe 1356
Standard 1355
Third Model 1356
Deluxe 1356
Standard 1356
Model 1892 . . . . 1347, 1384
Carbine 1348
Fancy Sporting Rifle 1348
Grade I 1384
High Grade 1384
Musket 1348
Sporting Rifle 1348
Trapper's Carbine 1348
Model 1892 Short Rifle 1384
Model 1893 1351
Standard Shotgun 1351
Model 1894 1348
Carbine 1349
Fancy Sporting Rifle 1349
Extra Lightweight Rifle 1349
First Model Sporting Rifle 1349
Sporting Rifle 1349
Trapper's Carbine 1349
Model 1895 1350
Carbine 1350
Fancy Sporting Rifles 1350
N.R.A. Musket, Model 1903 and 1906 1350
Sporting Rifle 1350
Standard Musket 1350
Russian Musket 1350
U.S. Army N.R.A. Musket 1350
U.S. Army Musket 1350
Model 1895 Limited Edition 1384
Grade I 1384
High Grade 1384
Model 1895—Limited Edition for the year 2000 1384
Grade I 1384
High Grade 1385
Model 1895 Saddle Ring Carbine 1385
Model 1897 1351
Brush Gun 1355
Pigeon Gun 1355
Riot Gun 1355
Standard Gun 1351
Tournament Gun 1355
Trap Gun 1351
Trench Gun 1355
Model 1900 1362
Model 1901 Shotgun 1351
Standard Shotgun 1351
Model 1902 1362
Model 1903 1357
Deluxe Rifle 1357
Standard Rifle 1357
Model 1904 1362
Model 1905 1357
Fancy Sporting Rifle 1358
Sporting Rifle 1358
Model 1906 1356
Model 1906 .22 Short Only 1356
Model 1906 Expert 1356
Standard Model 1906 1356
Model 1907 1358
Fancy Sporting Rifle 1358
Police Rifle 1358
Sporting Rifle 1358
Model 1910 1358
Fancy Sporting Rifle 1358
Sporting Rifle 1358
Model 1911 1376
Model 1911—Fancy 1376
Model 1911—Plain 1376
Model 9410 1381
Model 9410 Custom 1392
Model 9410 Packer 1381
Model 9410 Packer Compact 1381
Model 9410 Ranger 1381
Model 9410 Semi-Fancy 1381
Model 9417 Legacy 1382
Model 9417 Traditional 1382
Model 9422 1381
Model 9422 25th Anniversary Rifle 1382
Grade I 1382
High Grade 1382
Model 9422 Custom Traditional Tribute 1383
Model 9422 High Grade 1382
Model 9422 High Grade Legacy Tribute 1383
Model 9422 High Grade Series II 1382
Model 9422 High Grade Traditional Tribute 1383
Model 9422 Large Loop & Walnut 1382
Model 9422 Legacy 1382
Model 9422 Special Edition Legacy Tribute 1383
Model 9422 Special Edition Traditional Tribute 1383
Model 9422 Trapper 1382
Model 9422 WinCam 1382
Model 9422 WinTuff 1381
Model 9422 XTR 1381
Model 9422 XTR Classic 1381
Model D Military Rifle 1363
Model SXR Super X Rifle 1362
New Model 1400 1398
Northwest Mounted Police Carbine 1344
Third Model 1344
Carbine 1344
Musket 1344
Rifle 1344
Ranger (Model 70) 1386
Select Deluxe Field 1401
Select Energy Sporting 1401
Select Energy Trap 1401
Select Extreme Elegance 1401
Select Field 1401
Select Midnight 1401
Select Model 101 Field 1400
Select Model 101 Sporting 1400
Select Platinum Field 1401
Select Platinum Sporting 1401
Select Traditional Elegance 1401
Select White Field 1401
Smith & Wesson Volcanic Firearms 1338
4" Pistol 1338
8" Pistol 1338
Standard Rifle 1368
.458 African 1368
Featherweight 1368
Featherweight Super Grade 1368
.375 H&H Magnum (1937-1963) 1368
Post-War 1368
Pre-War 1368
.338 Win. Magnum (1959-1963) 1368
.300 H&H Magnum (1937-1963) 1368
Post-War 1368
Pre-War 1368
.300 Savage (1944-1950s?) 1368
.300 Win. Magnum (1962-1963) 1368
.270 Win. (1937-1963) 1368
Post-War 1368
Pre-War 1368
.264 Win. Magnum (1959-1963) 1368
.257 Roberts (1937-1959) 1368
Post-War 1368
Pre-War 1368
.250-3000 Savage (1937-1949) 1368
.243. Win. (1955-1963) 1368
.220 Swift (1937-1963) 1368
Post-War 1368
Pre-War 1368
.35 Rem. (1944-1947) 1368
.30-06 Springfield (1937-1963) 1368
Post-War 1368
Pre-War 1368
.22 Hornet (1937-1958) 1368
Post-War 1368
Pre-War 1368
7mm (1937-1949) 1368
Bull Gun 1369
National Match 1368
Standard Grade Carbine 1368
Target 1368
Varmint 1368
Super Pigeon Grade 1400
Super X Model 1 Custom Competition 1396
Super X Model I 1396
Super X2 3.5" Magnum 1396
Super X2 Camo Waterfowl 1396
Super X2 Cantilever Deer 1397
Super X2 Light Field 1397
Super X2 Magnum Field 1397
Super X2 Magnum Greenhead 1396
Super X2 NWTF Turkey 1396
Super X2 Practical 1397
Super X2 Signature Red Sporting 1397
Super X2 Sporting Clays 1397
Super X2 Sporting Clays Signature II 1397
Super X2 Turkey 1396
Super X2 Turkey Mossy Oak Break-Up 1396
Super X2 Universal Hunter 1396
Super X3 Camo 1397
Super X3 Cantilever Deer 1397
Super X3 Composite 1397
Super X3 Field 1397
Supreme Elegance 1398
Supreme Field 1398
Supreme Sporting 1398

Texas Sesquicentennial Model Set with Bowie Knife 1404
Texas Sesquicentennial Model—Rifle .38-55 Cal. 1404
Texas Sesquicentennial Model—Carbine .38-55 Cal. 1404
Volcanic Firearms (New Haven Arms Company) 1339
3-1/2" Barrel 1339
6" Barrel 1339
Volcanic Firearms (Volcanic Repeating Arms Company) 1338
6" Barrel 1338
8" Barrel 1338
16" Barrel 1338
Waterfowl Model 1399
Wildcat 1378
Winchester Hotchkiss
Bolt-Action Rifle 1344
First Model 1345
Carbine 1345
Musket 1345
Sporting Rifle 1345
Second Model 1345
Carbine 1345
Musket 1345
Sporting Rifle 1345
Third Model 1345
Carbine 1345
Musket 1345
Sporting Rifle 1345
Winchester's Improvement Carbine . 1339
Winchester-Lee Straight Pull Rifle . . 1355
Commercial Musket 1355
Sporting Rifle 1355
U.S. Navy Musket 1355

WINDSOR 1404
Windsor Rifle-Musket 1404

WINSLOW ARMS CO. 1404
Bolt Action Rifle 1404
Commander Grade 1404
Crown Grade 1404
Emperor Grade 1405
Imperial Grade 1405
Regal Grade 1404
Regent Grade 1404
Regimental Grade 1404
Royal Grade 1405

WISEMAN, BILL & CO. 1405
Silhouette Pistol 1405

WITNESS 1405

WOLF SPORTING PISTOLS . 1405
Wolf SV Match 1405
Wolf SV Target 1405

WOODWARD, JAMES & SONS 1405

WURFFLEIN, ANDREW & WILLIAM 1405
Mid-range Model 1405
Model No. 25 1405
Pocket Pistol 1405
Single-Shot Rifle 1405
Single-Shot Target Pistol 1405

X

XL HOPKINS & ALLEN 1406
Derringer 1406
Vest Pocket Derringer 1406

XPERT HOPKINS & ALLEN . . 1406
Xpert Derringer 1406
Xpert Pocket Rifle 1406

Z

Z-B RIFLE CO. 1407
Model ZKW-465 Varmint Rifle 1407

ZANOTTI, FABIO 1407
Cassiano Executive 1407
Cassiano I 1407
Cassiano II 1407
Edward 1407
Giacinto 1407
Maxim 1407
Model 625 1407
Model 626 1407

ZEHNER, E. WAFFENFABRIK 1407
Zehna 1407

ZEILINGER 1407

ZEPHYR 1407
Honker 1408
Sterlingworth II 1407
Thunderbird 1407
Upland King 1407
Uplander 1407
Vandalia 1407
Victor Special 1407
Woodlander II 1407

ZM WEAPONS 1408
LR-300 Sport Rifle 1408

ZOLI USA, ANGELO 1408
Airone 1409
Apache 1408
AZ 1900 Deluxe 1409
AZ 1900 Super Deluxe 1409
AZ 1900C 1409
AZ 1900M 1409
Classic 1408
Condor 1409
Deluxe Model 1408
Diano I 1408
Diano II 1408
Dove 1408
Express EM 1408
Express Rifle 1408
Falcon II 1408
Field Special 1408
Leopard Express 1409
Patricia Model 1409
Pheasant 1408
Pigeon Model 1408
Presentation Model 1408
Quail Special 1408
Savana Deluxe 1409
Savana E 1409
Slide-Action Shotgun 1408
Snipe 1408
Special Model 1408
St. George Competition 1408
St. George's Target 1408
Standard Model 1408
Texas 1408

ZOLI, ANTONIO 1409
Angel Model 1410
Ariete M2 1409
Combinato 1410
Condor Model 1410
Delfino 1410
Empire 1409
Golden Snipe 1410
Model 208 Target 1410
Model 308 Target 1410
Ritmo Hunting Gun 1410
Ritmo Pigeon Grade IV 1410
Safari Deluxe 1410
Silver Hawk 1409
Silver Snipe 1410
Volcano Record 1409
Volcano Record ELM 1410
Ritmo Hunting Gun 1410
Ritmo Pigeon Grade IV 1410

ZULAICA, M. 1410
Royal 1411
Vincitor 1411
Zulaica 1410